RIA Federal Tax Regulations

For customer service or to obtain the name and telephone number of your local account representative, please call 1-800-431-9025. Additional copies of this product are available, at a fee. Please call 1-800-950-1216 or visit our Product Store at http://ria.thomson.com to order.

"This publication is designed to provide accurate and authoritative information in regard to the subject matter covered. It is sold with the understanding that the publisher is not engaged in rendering legal, accounting or other professional service. If legal advice or other expert assistance is required, the services of a competent professional person should be sought." — from a Declaration of Principles jointly adopted by a Committee of The American Bar Association and a Committee of Publishers and Associations

By

Thomson/RIA

395 Hudson Street

New York, N.Y. 10014

 Any gaps in the numbering of pages are intentional and are intended to allow for editorial growth and expansion.

RIA FEDERAL TAX REGULATIONS

Including Proposed Regulations

Current through December 31, 2007

VOLUME 3

---

§ 1.501(a)-1 Exemption from taxation.

Caution: The Treasury has not yet amended Reg § 1.501(a)-1 to reflect changes made by P.L. 101-73, P.L. 100-647, P.L. 100-203, P.L. 99-514.

(a) In general; proof of exemption. *(1)* Section 501(a) provides an exemption from income taxes for organizations which are described in section 501(c) or (d) and section 401(a), unless such organization is a "feeder organization" (see section 502), or unless it engages in a transaction described in section 503. However, the exemption does not extend to "unrelated business taxable income" of such an organization (see part III (Section 511 and following), subchapter F, chapter 1 of the Code).

(2) An organization, other than an employees' trust described in section 401(a), is not exempt from tax merely because it is not organized and operated for profit. In order to establish its exemption, it is necessary that every such organization claiming exemption file an application form as set forth below with the district director for the internal revenue district in which is located the principal place of business or principal office of the organization. Subject only to the Commissioner's inherent power to revoke rulings because of a change in the law or regulations or for other good cause, an organization that has been determined by the Commissioner or the district director to be exempt under section 501(a) or the corresponding provision of prior law may rely upon such determination so long as there are no substantial changes in the organization's character, purposes, or methods of operation. An organization which has been determined to be exempt under the provisions of the Internal Revenue Code of 1939 or prior law is not required to secure a new determination of exemption merely because of the enactment of the Internal Revenue Code of 1954 unless affected by substantive changes in law made by such Code.

(3) An organization claiming exemption under section 501(a) and described in any paragraph of section 501(c) (other than section 501(c)(1)) shall file the form of application prescribed by the Commissioner and shall include thereon such information as required by such form and the instructions issued with respect thereto. For rules relating to the obtaining of a determination of exempt status by an employees' trust described in section 401(a), see the regulations under section 401.

(b) Additional proof by particular classes of organizations. *(1)* Organizations mentioned below shall submit with and as a part of their applications the following information:

(i) Mutual insurance companies shall submit copies of the policies or certificates of membership issued by them.

(ii) In the case of title holding companies described in section 501(c)(2), if the organization for which title is held has not been specifically notified in writing by the Internal Revenue Service that it is held to be exempt under section 501(a), the title holding company shall submit the information indicated herein as necessary for a determination of the status of the organization for which title is held.

(iii) An organization described in section 501(c)(3) shall submit with, and as a part of, an application filed after July 26, 1959, a detailed statement of its proposed activities.

(2) In addition to the information specifically called for by this section, the Commissioner may require any additional information deemed necessary for a proper determination of whether a particular organization is exempt under section 501(a), and when deemed advisable in the interest of an efficient administration of the internal revenue laws, he may in the cases of particular types of organizations prescribe the form in which the proof of exemption shall be furnished.

(3) An organization claiming to be specifically exempted by section 6033(a) from filing annual returns shall submit with and as a part of its application a statement of all the facts on which it bases its claim.

(c) "Private shareholder or individual" defined. The words "private shareholder or individual" in section 501 refer to persons having a personal and private interest in the activities of the organization.

(d) Requirement of annual returns. For the annual return requirements of organizations exempt under section 501(a), see section 6033 and § 1.6033-1.

(e) Certain Puerto Rican pension, etc., trusts. Effective for taxable years beginning after December 31, 1973, section 1022(i)(1) of the Employee Retirement Income Security Act of 1974 (ERISA) (88 Stat. 942) provides that trusts under certain Puerto Rican pension, etc., plans (as defined under P.R. Laws Ann. tit. 13, section 3165, and the articles thereunder), all of the participants of which are residents of the Commonwealth of Puerto Rico, are to be treated only for purposes of section 501(a) as trusts described in section 401(a). The practical effect of section 1022(i)(1) is to exempt these trusts from U.S. income tax on income from their U.S. investments. For purposes of section 1022(i)(1), the term "residents of the Commonwealth of Puerto Rico" means bona fide residents of Puerto Rico, and persons who perform labor or services primarily within the Commonwealth of Puerto Rico, regardless of residence for other purposes, and the term "participants" is restricted to current employees who are not excluded under the eligibility provisions of the plan.

T.D. 6301, 7/8/58, amend T.D. 6391, 6/25/59, T.D. 7428, 8/13/76, T.D. 7859, 12/1/82.

---

§ 1.501(c)(2)-1 Corporations organized to hold title to property for exempt organizations.

Caution: The Treasury has not yet amended Reg § 1.501(c)(2)-1 to reflect changes made by P.L. 103-66.

(a) A corporation described in section 501(c)(2) and otherwise exempt from tax under section 501(a) is taxable upon its unrelated business taxable income. For taxable years beginning before January 1, 1970, see § 1.511-2(c)(4). Since a corporation described in section 501(c)(2) cannot be exempt under section 501(a) if it engages in any business other than that of holding title to property and collecting income therefrom, it cannot have unrelated business taxable income as defined in section 512 other than income which is treated as unrelated business taxable income solely because of the applicability of section 512(a)(3)(C); or debt financed income which is treated as unrelated business taxable income solely because of section 514; or certain interest, annuities, royalties, or rents which are treated as unrelated business taxable income solely because of section 512(b)(3)(B)(ii) or (13). Similarly, exempt status under section 501(c)(2) shall not be affected where certain rents from personal property leased with real property are treated as unrelated business taxable income under section 512(b)(3)(A)(ii) solely because such rents attributable to such personal property are more than incidental when compared to the total rents received or accrued under the lease, or under section 512(b)(3)(B)(i) solely because such rents attributable to such personal property exceed 50 percent of the total rents received or accrued under the lease.

(b) A corporation described in section 501(c)(2) cannot accumulate income and retain its exemption, but it must turn over the entire amount of such income, less expenses, to an organization which is itself exempt from tax under section 501(a).

T.D. 6301, 7/8/58, amend T.D. 7698, 5/20/80.

§ 1.501(c)(3)-1 Organizations organized and operated for religious, charitable, scientific, testing for public safety, literary, or educational purposes, or for the prevention of cruelty to children or animals.

Caution: The Treasury has not yet amended Reg § 1.501(c)(3)-1 to reflect changes made by P.L. 105-33.

(a) Organizational and operational tests. *(1)* In order to be exempt as an organization described in section 501(c)(3), an organization must be both organized and operated exclusively for one or more of the purposes specified in such section. If an organization fails to meet either the organizational test or the operational test, it is not exempt.

(2) The term "exempt purpose or purposes", as used in this section, means any purpose or purposes specified in section 501(c)(3), as defined and elaborated in paragraph (d) of this section.

(b) Organizational test. *(1) In general.* (i) An organization is organized exclusively for one or more exempt purposes only if its articles of organization (referred to in this section as its "articles") as defined in subparagraph (2) of this paragraph:

(a) Limit the purposes of such organization to one or more exempt purposes; and

(b) Do not expressly empower the organization to engage, otherwise than as an insubstantial part of its activities, in activities which in themselves are not in furtherance of one or more exempt purposes.

(ii) In meeting the organizational test, the organization's purposes, as stated in its articles, may be as broad as, or more specific than, the purposes stated in section 501(c)(3). Therefore, an organization which, by the terms of its articles, is formed "for literary and scientific purposes within the meaning of section 501(c)(3) of the Code" shall, if it otherwise meets the requirements in this paragraph, be considered to have met the organizational test. Similarly, articles stating that the organization is created solely "to receive contributions and pay them over to organizations which are described in section 501(c)(3) and exempt from taxation under section 501(a)" are sufficient for purposes of the organizational test. Moreover, it is sufficient if the articles set forth the purpose of the organization to be the operation of a school for adult education and describe in detail the manner of the operation of such school. In addition, if the articles state that the organization is formed for "charitable purposes", such articles ordinarily shall be sufficient for purposes of the organizational test (see subparagraph (5) of this paragraph for rules relating to construction of terms).

(iii) An organization is not organized exclusively for one or more exempt purposes if its articles expressly empower it to carry on, otherwise than as an insubstantial part of its activities, activities which are not in furtherance of one or more exempt purposes, even though such organization is, by the terms of such articles, created for a purpose that is no broader than the purposes specified in section 501(c)(3). Thus, an organization that is empowered by its articles "to engage in a manufacturing business", or "to engage in the operation of a social club" does not meet the organizational test regardless of the fact that its articles may state that such organization is created "for charitable purposes within the meaning of section 501(c)(3) of the Code."

(iv) In no case shall an organization be considered to be organized exclusively for one or more exempt purposes, if, by the terms of its articles, the purposes for which such organization is created are broader than the purposes specified in section 501(c)(3). The fact that the actual operations of such an organization have been exclusively in furtherance of one or more exempt purposes shall not be sufficient to permit the organization to meet the organizational test. Similarly, such an organization will not meet the organizational test as a result of statements or other evidence that the members thereof intend to operate only in furtherance of one or more exempt purposes.

(v) An organization must, in order to establish its exemption, submit a detailed statement of its proposed activities with and as a part of its application for exemption (see paragraph (b) of § 1.501(a)-1.

(2) Articles of organization. For purposes of this section, the term "articles of organization" or "articles" includes the trust instrument, the corporate charter, the articles of association, or any other written instrument by which an organization is created.

(3) Authorization of legislative or political activities. An organization is not organized exclusively for one or more exempt purposes if its articles expressly empower it:

(i) To devote more than an insubstantial part of its activities to attempting to influence legislation by propaganda or otherwise; or

(ii) Directly or indirectly to participate in, or intervene in (including the publishing or distributing of statements), any political campaign on behalf of or in opposition to any candidate for public office; or

(iii) To have objectives and to engage in activities which characterize it as an "action" organization as defined in paragraph (c)(3) of this section.

The terms used in subdivisions (i), (ii), and (iii) of this subparagraph shall have the meanings provided in paragraph (c)(3) of this section. An organization's articles will not violate the provisions of paragraph (b)(3)(i) of this section even though the organization's articles expressly empower it to make the election provided for in section 501(h) with respect to influencing legislation and, only if it so elects, to make lobbying or grass roots expenditures that do not normally exceed the ceiling amounts prescribed by section 501(h)(2)(B) and (D).

(4) Distribution of assets on dissolution. An organization is not organized exclusively for one or more exempt purposes unless its assets are dedicated to an exempt purpose. An organization's assets will be considered dedicated to an exempt purpose, for example, if, upon dissolution, such assets would, by reason of a provision in the organization's articles or by operation of law, be distributed for one or more exempt purposes, or to the Federal government, or to a State or local government, for a public purpose, or would be distributed by a court to another organization to be used in such manner as in the judgment of the court will best accomplish the general purposes for which the dissolved organization was organized. However, an organization does not meet the organizational test if its articles or the law of the State in which it was created provide that its assets would, upon dissolution, be distributed to its members or shareholders.

(5) Construction of terms. The law of the State in which an organization is created shall be controlling in construing the terms of its articles. However, any organization which contends that such terms have under State law a different meaning from their generally accepted meaning must establish such special meaning by clear and convincing reference to relevant court decisions, opinions of the State attorney-general, or other evidence of applicable State law.

(6) Applicability of the organizational test. A determination by the Commissioner or a district director that an organization is described in section 501(c)(3) and exempt under section 501(a) will not be granted after July 26, 1959 (regardless of when the application is filed), unless such organization meets the organizational test prescribed by this paragraph. If, before July 27, 1959, an organization has been determined by the Commissioner or district director to be exempt as an organization described in section 501(c)(3) or in a corresponding provision of prior law and such determination has not been revoked before such date, the fact that such organization does not meet the organizational test prescribed by this paragraph shall not be a basis for revoking such determination. Accordingly, an organization which has been determined to be exempt before July 27, 1959, and which does not seek a new determination of exemption is not required to amend its articles of organization to conform to the rules of this paragraph, but any organization which seeks a determination of exemption after July 26, 1959, must have articles of organization which meet the rules of this paragraph. For the rules relating to whether an organization determined to be exempt before July 27, 1959, is organized exclusively for one or more exempt purposes, see 26 CFR (1939) 39.101(6)-1 (Regulations 118) as made applicable to the Code by Treasury Decision 6091, approved August 16, 1954 (19 FR 5167; C.B. 1954-2, 47).

(c) Operational test. *(1) Primary activities.* An organization will be regarded as "operated exclusively" for one or more exempt purposes only if it engages primarily in activities which accomplish one or more of such exempt purposes specified in section 501(c)(3). An organization will not be so regarded if more than an insubstantial part of its activities is not in furtherance of an exempt purpose.

(2) Distribution of earnings. An organization is not operated exclusively for one or more exempt purposes if its net earnings inure in whole or in part to the benefit of private shareholders or individuals. For the definition of the words "private shareholder or individual", see paragraph (c) of § 1.501(a)-1.

(3) "Action" organizations. (i) An organization is not operated exclusively for one or more exempt purposes if it is an "action" organization as defined in subdivisions (ii), (iii), or (iv) of this subparagraph.

(ii) An organization is an "action" organization if a substantial part of its activities is attempting to influence legislation by propaganda or otherwise. For this purpose, an organization will be regarded as attempting to influence legislation if the organization:

(a) Contacts, or urges the public to contact, members of a legislative body for the purpose of proposing, supporting, or opposing legislation; or

(b) Advocates the adoption or rejection of legislation.

The term "legislation", as used in this subdivision, includes action by the Congress, by any State legislature, by any local council or similar governing body, or by the public in a referendum, initiative, constitutional amendment, or similar procedure. An organization will not fail to meet the operational test merely because it advocates, as an insubstantial part of its activities, the adoption or rejection of legislation. An organization for which the expenditure test election of section 501(h) is in effect for a taxable year will not be considered an "action" organization by reason of this paragraph (c)(3)(ii) for that year if it is not denied exemption from taxation under section 501(a) by reason of section 501(h).

(iii) An organization is an "action" organization if it participates or intervenes, directly or indirectly, in any political campaign on behalf of or in opposition to any candidate for public office. The term "candidate for public office" means an individual who offers himself, or is proposed by others, as a contestant for an elective public office, whether such office be national, State, or local. Activities which constitute participation or intervention in a political campaign on behalf of or in opposition to a candidate include, but are not limited to, the publication or distribution of written or printed statements or the making of oral statements on behalf of or in opposition to such a candidate.

(iv) An organization is an "action" organization if it has the following two characteristics: (a) Its main or primary objective or objectives (as distinguished from its incidental or secondary objectives) may be attained only by legislation or a defeat of proposed legislation; and (b) it advocates, or campaigns for, the attainment of such main or primary objective or objectives as distinguished from engaging in nonpartisan analysis, study, or research and making the results thereof available to the public. In determining whether an organization has such characteristics, all the surrounding facts and circumstances, including the articles and all activities of the organization, are to be considered.

(v) An "action" organization, described in subdivisions (ii) or (iv) of this subparagraph, though it cannot qualify under section 501(c)(3), may nevertheless qualify as a social welfare organization under section 501(c)(4) if it meets the requirements set out in paragraph (a) of § 1.501(c)(4)-1.

(d) Exempt purposes. *(1) In general.* (i) An organization may be exempt as an organization described in section 501(c)(3) if it is organized and operated exclusively for one or more of the following purposes:

(a) Religious,

(b) Charitable,

(c) Scientific,

(d) Testing for public safety,

(e) Literary,

(f) Educational, or

(g) Prevention of cruelty to children or animals.

(ii) An organization is not organized or operated exclusively for one or more of the purposes specified in subdivision (i) of this subparagraph unless it serves a public rather than a private interest. Thus, to meet the requirement of this subdivision, it is necessary for an organization to establish that it is not organized or operated for the benefit of private interests such as designated individuals, the creator or his family, shareholders of the organization, or persons controlled, directly or indirectly, by such private interests.

(iii) Since each of the purposes specified in subdivision (i) of this subparagraph is an exempt purpose in itself, an organization may be exempt if it is organized and operated exclusively for any one or more of such purposes. If, in fact, an organization is organized and operated exclusively for an exempt purpose or purposes, exemption will be granted to such an organization regardless of the purpose or purposes specified in its application for exemption. For example, if an organization claims exemption on the ground that it is "educational", exemption will not be denied if, in fact, it is "charitable".

(2) Charitable defined. The term "charitable" is used in section 501(c)(3) in its generally accepted legal sense and is, therefore, not to be construed as limited by the separate enumeration in section 501(c)(3) of other tax-exempt purposes which may fall within the broad outlines of "charity" as developed by judicial decisions. Such term includes: Relief of the poor and distressed or of the underprivileged; advancement of religion; advancement of education or science; erection or maintenance of public buildings, monuments, or works; lessening of the burdens of Government; and promotion of social welfare by organizations designed to accomplish any of the above purposes, or (i) to lessen neighborhood tensions; (ii) to eliminate prejudice and discrimination; (iii) to defend human and civil rights secured by law; or (iv) to combat community deterioration and juvenile delinquency. The fact that an organization which is organized and operated for the relief of indigent persons may receive voluntary contributions from the persons intended to be relieved will not necessarily prevent such organization from being exempt as an organization organized and operated exclusively for charitable purposes. The fact that an organization, in carrying out its primary purpose, advocates social or civic changes or presents opinion on controversial issues with the intention of molding public opinion or creating public sentiment to an acceptance of its views does not preclude such organization from qualifying under section 501(c)(3) so long as it is not an "action" organization of any one of the types described in paragraph (c)(3) of this section.

(3) Educational defined. (i) In general. The term "educational", as used in section 501(c)(3), relates to:

(a) The instruction or training of the individual for the purpose of improving or developing his capabilities; or

(b) The instruction of the public on subjects useful to the individual and beneficial to the community.

An organization may be educational even though it advocates a particular position or viewpoint so long as it presents a sufficiently full and fair exposition of the pertinent facts as to permit an individual or the public to form an independent opinion or conclusion. On the other hand, an organization is not educational if its principal function is the mere presentation of unsupported opinion.

(ii) Examples of educational organizations. The following are examples of organizations which, if they otherwise meet the requirements of this section, are educational:

Example (1). An organization, such as a primary or secondary school, a college, or a professional or trade school, which has a regularly scheduled curriculum, a regular faculty, and a regularly enrolled body of students in attendance at a place where the educational activities are regularly carried on.

Example (2). An organization whose activities consist of presenting public discussion groups, forums, panels, lectures, or other similar programs. Such programs may be on radio or television.

Example (3). An organization which presents a course of instruction by means of correspondence or through the utilization of television or radio.

Example (4). Museums, zoos, planetariums, symphony orchestras, and other similar organizations.

(4) Testing for public safety defined. The term "testing for public safety", as used in section 501(c)(3), includes the testing of consumer products, such as electrical products, to determine whether they are safe for use by the general public.

(5) Scientific defined. (i) Since an organization may meet the requirements of section 501(c)(3) only if it serves a public rather than a private interest, a "scientific" organization must be organized and operated in the public interest (see subparagraph (1)(ii) of this paragraph). Therefore, the term "scientific", as used in section 501(c)(3), includes the carrying on of scientific research in the public interest. Research when taken alone is a word with various meanings; it is not synonymous with "scientific"; and the nature of particular research depends upon the purpose which it serves. For research to be "scientific", within the meaning of section 501(c)(3), it must be carried on in furtherance of a "scientific" purpose. The determination as to whether research is "scientific" does not depend on whether such research is classified as "fundamental" or "basic" as contrasted with "applied" or "practical". On the other hand, for purposes of the exclusion from unrelated business taxable income provided by section 512(b)(9), it is necessary to determine whether the organization is operated primarily for purposes of carrying on "fundamental", as contrasted with "applied", research.

(ii) Scientific research does not include activities of a type ordinarily carried on as an incident to commercial or industrial operations, as, for example, the ordinary testing or inspection of materials or products or the designing or construction of equipment, buildings, etc.

(iii) Scientific research will be regarded as carried on in the public interest:

(a) If the results of such research (including any patents, copyrights, processes, or formulae resulting from such research) are made available to the public on a nondiscriminatory basis;

(b) If such research is performed for the United States, or any of its agencies or instrumentalities, or for a State or political subdivision thereof; or

(c) If such research is directed toward benefiting the public. The following are examples of scientific research which will be considered as directed toward benefiting the public, and, therefore, which will be regarded as carried on in the public interest: (1) Scientific research carried on for the purpose of aiding in the scientific education of college or university students; (2) scientific research carried on for the purpose of obtaining scientific information, which is published in a treatise, thesis, trade publication, or in any other form that is available to the interested public; (3) scientific research carried on for the purpose of discovering a cure for a disease; or (4) scientific research carried on for the purpose of aiding a community or geographical area by attracting new industry to the community or area or by encouraging the development of, or retention of, an industry in the community or area. Scientific research described in this subdivision will be regarded as carried on in the public interest even though such research is performed pursuant to a contract or agreement under which the sponsor or sponsors of the research have the right to obtain ownership or control of any patents, copyrights, processes, or formulae resulting from such research.

(iv) An organization will not be regarded as organized and operated for the purpose of carrying on scientific research in the public interest and, consequently, will not qualify under section 501(c)(3) as a "scientific" organization, if:

(a) Such organization will perform research only for persons which are (directly or indirectly) its creators and which are not described in section 501(c)(3), or

(b) Such organization retains (directly or indirectly) the ownership or control of more than an insubstantial portion of the patents, copyrights, processes, or formulae resulting from its research and does not make such patents, copyrights, processes, or formulae available to the public. For purposes of this subdivision, a patent, copyright, process, or formula shall be considered as made available to the public if such patent, copyright, process, or formula is made available to the public on a nondiscriminatory basis. In addition, although one person is granted the exclusive right to the use of a patent, copyright, process, or formula, such patent, copyright, process, or formula shall be considered as made available to the public if the granting of such exclusive right is the only practicable manner in which the patent, copyright, process, or formula can be utilized to benefit the public. In such a case, however, the research from which the patent, copyright, process, or formula resulted will be regarded as carried on in the public interest (within the meaning of subdivision (iii) of this subparagraph) only if it is carried on for a person described in subdivision (iii)(b) of this subparagraph or if it is scientific research described in subdivision (iii)(c) of this subparagraph.

(v) The fact that any organization (including a college, university, or hospital) carries on research which is not in furtherance of an exempt purpose described in section 501(c)(3) will not preclude such organization from meeting the requirements of section 501(c)(3) so long as the organization meets the organizational test and is not operated for the primary purpose of carrying on such research (see paragraph (e) of this section, relating to organizations carrying on a trade or business). See paragraph (a)(5) of § 1.513-2, with respect to research which constitutes an unrelated trade or business, and section 512(b)(7), (8), and (9), with respect to income derived from research which is excludable from the tax on unrelated business income.

(vi) The regulations in this subparagraph are applicable with respect to taxable years beginning after December 31, 1960.

(e) Organizations carrying on trade or business. *(1) In general.* An organization may meet the requirements of section 501(c)(3) although it operates a trade or business as a substantial part of its activities, if the operation of such trade or business is in furtherance of the organization's exempt purpose or purposes and if the organization is not organized or operated for the primary purpose of carrying on an unrelated trade or business, as defined in section 513. In determining the existence or nonexistence of such primary purpose, all the circumstances must be considered, including the size and extent of the trade or business and the size and extent of the activities which are in furtherance of one or more exempt purposes. An organization which is organized and operated for the primary purpose of carrying on an unrelated trade or business is not exempt under section 501(c)(3) even though it has certain religious purposes, its property is held in common, and its profits do not inure to the benefit of individual members of the organization. See, however, section 501(d) and § 1.501(d)-1, relating to religious and apostolic organizations.

(2) Taxation of unrelated business income. For provisions relating to the taxation of unrelated business income of certain organizations described in section 501(c)(3), see section 511 to 515, inclusive, and the regulations thereunder.

(f) Applicability of regulations in this section. The regulations in this section are, except as otherwise expressly provided, applicable with respect to taxable years beginning after July 26, 1959. For the rules applicable with respect to taxable years beginning before July 27, 1959, see 26 CFR (1939) 39.101(6)-1 (Regulations 118) as made applicable to the Code by Treasury Decision 6091, approved August 16, 1954 (19 F.R. 5167; C.B. 1954-2, 47).

T.D. 6391, 6/25/59, amend T.D. 6525, 1/10/61, T.D. 6939, 12/11/67, T.D. 7428, 8/13/76, T.D. 8308, 8/30/90.

PAR. 3. The authority citation for part 53 continues to read, in part, as follows:

Authority: 26 U.S.C. 7805.

PAR. 3. In § 1.501(c)(3)-1, paragraphs (d)(1)(iii) and (g) are added to read as follows:

Proposed § 1.501(c)(3)-1 Organizations organized and operated for religious, charitable, scientific, testing for public safety, literary, or educational purposes, or for the prevention of cruelty to children or animals. *[For Preamble, see ¶ 152,699]*

* * * * *

(d) * * *

(1) * * *

(iii) Examples. The following examples illustrate the requirement of paragraph (d)(1)(ii) of this section that an organization serve a public rather than a private interest:

Example (1). (i) O is an educational organization the purpose of which is to study history and immigration. The focus of O's historical studies is the genealogy of one family, tracing the descent of its present members. O actively solicits for membership only individuals who are members of that one family. O's research is directed toward publishing a history of that family that will document the pedigrees of family members. A major objective of O's research is to identify and locate living descendants of that family to enable those descendants to become acquainted with each other.

(ii) O's educational activities primarily serve the private interests of members of a single family rather than a public interest. Therefore, O is operated for the benefit of private interests in violation of the restriction on private benefit in § 1.501(c)(3)-1(d)(1)(ii). Based on these facts and circumstances, O is not operated exclusively for exempt purposes and, therefore, is not described in section 501(c)(3).

Example (2). (i) O is an art museum. O's sole activity is exhibiting art created by a group of unknown but promising local artists. O is governed by a board of trustees unrelated to the artists whose work O exhibits. All of the art exhibited is offered for sale at prices set by the artist. Each artist whose work is exhibited has a consignment arrangement with O. Under this arrangement, when art is sold, the museum retains 10 percent of the selling price to cover the costs of operating the museum and gives the artist 90 percent.

(ii) The artists in this situation directly benefit from the exhibition and sale of their art. As a result, the sole activity of O serves the private interests of these artists. Because O gives 90 percent of the proceeds from its sole activity to the individual artists, the direct benefits to the artists are substantial and O's provision of these benefits to the artists is more than incidental to its other purposes and activities. This arrangement causes O to be operated for the benefit of private interests in violation of the restriction on private benefit in § 1.501(c)(3)-1(d)(1)(ii). Based on these facts and circumstances, O is not operated exclusively for exempt purposes and, therefore, is not described in section 501(c)(3).

Example (3). (i) O is an educational organization the purpose of which is to train individuals in a program developed by P, O's president. All of the rights to the program are owned by Company K, a for-profit corporation owned by P. Prior to the existence of O, the teaching of the program was conducted by Company K. O licenses, from Company K, the right to use a reference to the program in O's name and the right to teach the program, in exchange for specified royalty payments. Under the license agreement, Company K provides O with the services of trainers and with course materials on the program. O may develop and copyright new course materials on the program but all such materials must be assigned to Company K without consideration if the license agreement is terminated. Company K sets the tuition for the seminars and lectures on the program conducted by O. O has agreed not to become involved in any activity resembling the program or its implementation for 2 years after the termination of O's license agreement.

(ii) O's sole activity is conducting seminars and lectures on the program. This arrangement causes O to be operated for the benefit of P and Company K in violation of the restriction on private benefit in § 1.501(c)(3)-1(d)(1)(ii), regardless of whether the royalty payments from O to Company K for the right to teach the program are reasonable. Based on these facts and circumstances, O is not operated exclusively for exempt purposes and, therefore, is not described in section 501(c)(3).

* * * * *

(g) Interaction with section 4958. *(1) Application process.* An organization that applies for recognition of exemption under section 501(a) as an organization described in section 501(c)(3) must establish its eligibility under this section. The Commissioner may deny an application for exemption for failure to establish any of this section's requirements for exemption. Section 4958 does not apply to transactions with an organization that has failed to establish that it satisfies all of the requirements for exemption under section 501(c)(3). See § 53.4958-2 of this chapter.

(2) Substantive requirements for exemption still apply to applicable tax-exempt organizations described in section 501(c)(3). (i) In general. Regardless of whether a particular transaction is subject to excise taxes under section 4958, the substantive requirements for tax exemption under section 501(c)(3) still apply to an applicable tax-exempt organization (as defined in section 4958(e) and § 53.4958-2 of this chapter) described in section 501(c)(3) whose disqualified persons or organization managers are subject to excise taxes under section 4958. Accordingly, an organization may no longer meet the requirements for tax-exempt status under section 501(c)(3) because the organization fails to satisfy the requirements of paragraph (b), (c) or (d) of this section. See § 53.4958-8(a) of this chapter.

(ii) Determining whether revocation of tax-exempt status is appropriate when section 4958 excise taxes also apply. In determining whether to continue to recognize the tax-exempt status of an applicable tax-exempt organization (as defined in section 4958(e) and § 53.4958-2 of this chapter) described in section 501(c)(3) that engages in one or more excess benefit transactions (as defined in section 4958(c) and § 53.4958-4 of this chapter) that violate the prohibition on inurement under this section, the Commissioner will consider all relevant facts and circumstances, including, but not limited to, the following—

(A) The size and scope of the organization's regular and ongoing activities that further exempt purposes before and after the excess benefit transaction or transactions occurred;

(B) The size and scope of the excess benefit transaction or transactions (collectively, if more than one) in relation to the size and scope of the organization's regular and ongoing activities that further exempt purposes;

(C) Whether the organization has been involved in repeated excess benefit transactions;

(D) Whether the organization has implemented safeguards that are reasonably calculated to prevent future violations; and

(E) Whether the excess benefit transaction has been corrected (within the meaning of section 4958(f)(6) and § 53.4958-7 of this chapter), or the organization has made good faith efforts to seek correction from the disqualified persons who benefited from the excess benefit transaction.

(iii) All factors will be considered in combination with each other. Depending on the particular situation, the Commissioner may assign greater or lesser weight to some factors than to others. The factors listed in paragraphs (g)(2)(ii)(D) and (E) of this section will weigh more strongly in favor of continuing to recognize exemption where the organization discovers the excess benefit transaction or transactions and takes action before the Commissioner discovers the excess benefit transaction or transactions. Further, with respect to the factor listed in paragraph (g)(2)(ii)(E) of this section, correction after the excess benefit transaction or transactions are discovered by the Commissioner, by itself, is never a sufficient basis for continuing to recognize exemption.

(iv) Examples. The following examples illustrate the principles of paragraph (g)(2)(ii) of this section. For purposes of each example, assume that O is an applicable tax-exempt organization (as defined in section 4958(e) and § 53.4958-2 of this chapter) described in section 501(c)(3) for all relevant periods. The examples are as follows:

Example (1). (i) O was created as a museum for the purpose of exhibiting art to the general public. In Years 1 and 2, O engages in fundraising and in selecting, leasing, and preparing an appropriate facility for a museum. In Year 3, a new board of trustees is elected. All of the new trustees are local art dealers. Beginning in Year 3 and continuing to the present, O uses almost all of its revenues to purchase art solely from its trustees at prices that exceed fair market value. O exhibits and offers for sale all of the art it purchases. O's Form 1023, "Application for Recognition of Exemption," did not disclose the possibility that O's trustees would be selling art to O.

(ii) O's purchases of art from its trustees at more than fair market value constitute excess benefit transactions between an applicable tax-exempt organization and disqualified persons under section 4958. Therefore, these transactions are subject to the appropriate excise taxes provided in that section. In addition, O's purchases of art from its trustees at more than fair market value violate the proscription against inurement under section 501(c)(3) and § 1.501(c)(3)-1(c)(2).

(iii) The application of the factors in § 1.501(c)(3)-1(g)(2)(ii) to these facts is as follows. Beginning in Year 3, O does not engage in any regular and ongoing activities that further exempt purposes because almost all of O's activities consist of purchasing art from its trustees and exhibiting and offering for sale all of the art it purchases. The size and scope of the excess benefit transactions collectively are significant in relation to the size and scope of any of O's ongoing activities that further exempt purposes. O has been involved in repeated excess benefit transactions, namely, purchases of art from its trustees at more than fair market value. O has not implemented safeguards that are reasonably calculated to prevent such improper purchases in the future. The excess benefit transactions have not been corrected, nor has O made good faith efforts to seek correction from the disqualified persons who benefited from the excess benefit transactions (the trustees). The trustees continue to control O's Board. Based on the application of the factors to these facts, O is no longer described in section 501(c)(3) effective in Year 3.

Example (2). (i) The facts are the same as in Example 1, except that in Year 4, O's entire board of trustees resigns, and O no longer offers all exhibited art for sale. The former board is replaced with members of the community who are not in the business of buying or selling art and who have skills and experience running educational programs and institutions. O promptly discontinues the practice of purchasing art from current or former trustees, adopts a written conflicts of interest policy, adopts written art valuation guidelines, hires legal counsel to recover the excess amounts O had paid its former trustees, and implements a new program of educational activities.

(ii) O's purchases of art from its former trustees at more than fair market value constitute excess benefit transactions between an applicable tax-exempt organization and disqualified persons under section 4958. Therefore, these transactions are subject to the appropriate excise taxes provided in that section. In addition, O's purchases of art from its trustees at more than fair market value violate the proscription against inurement under section 501(c)(3) and § 1.501(c)(3)-1(c)(2).

(iii) The application of the factors in § 1.501(c)(3)-1(g)(2)(ii) to these facts is as follows. In Year 3, O does not engage in any regular and ongoing activities that further exempt purposes. However, in Year 4, O elects a new board of trustees comprised of individuals who have skills and experience running educational programs and implements a new program of educational activities. As a result of these actions, beginning in Year 4, O engages in regular and ongoing activities that further exempt purposes. The size and scope of the excess benefit transactions that occurred in Year 3, taken collectively, are significant in relation to the size and scope of O's regular and ongoing exempt function activities that were conducted in Year 3. Beginning in Year 4, however, as O's exempt function activities are established and grow, the size and scope of the excess benefit transactions that occurred in Year 3 become less and less significant as compared to the size and extent of O's regular and ongoing exempt function activities that began in Year 4 and continued thereafter. O was involved in repeated excess benefit transactions in Year 3. However, by discontinuing its practice of purchasing art from its current and former trustees, by replacing its former board with independent members of the community, and by adopting a conflicts of interest policy and art valuation guidelines, O has implemented safeguards that are reasonably calculated to prevent future violations. In addition, O has made a good faith effort to seek correction from the disqualified persons who benefited from the excess benefit transactions (its former trustees). Based on the application of the factors to these facts, O continues to meet the requirements for tax exemption under section 501(c)(3).

Example (3). (i) O conducts educational programs for the benefit of the general public. Since its formation, O has employed its founder, C, as its Chief Executive Officer. Beginning in Year 5 of O's operations and continuing to the present, C caused O to divert significant portions of O's funds to pay C's personal expenses. The diversions by C significantly reduced the funds available to conduct O's ongoing educational programs. The board of trustees never authorized C to cause O to pay C's personal expenses from O's funds. Certain members of the board were aware that O was paying C's personal expenses. However, the board did not terminate C's employment and did not take any action to seek repayment from C or to prevent C from continuing to divert O's funds to pay C's personal expenses. C claimed that O's payments of C's personal expenses represented loans from O to C. However, no contemporaneous loan documentation exists, and C never made any payments of principal or interest.

(ii) The diversions of O's funds to pay C's personal expenses constituted excess benefit transactions between an applicable tax-exempt organization and a disqualified person under section 4958. Therefore, these transactions are subject to the appropriate excise taxes provided in that section. In addition, these transactions violate the proscription against inurement under section 501(c)(3) and § 1.501(c)(3)-1(c)(2).

(iii) The application of the factors in § 1.501(c)(3)-1(g)(2)(ii) to these facts is as follows. O has engaged in regular and ongoing activities that further exempt purposes both before and after the excess benefit transactions occurred. However, the size and scope of the excess benefit transactions engaged in by O beginning in Year 5, collectively, are significant in relation to the size and scope of O's activities that further exempt purposes. Moreover, O has been involved in repeated excess benefit transactions. O has not implemented any safeguards that are reasonably calculated to prevent future diversions. The excess benefit transactions have not been corrected, nor has O made good faith efforts to seek correction from C, the disqualified person who benefited from the excess benefit transactions. Based on the application of the factors to these facts, O is no longer described in section 501(c)(3) effective in Year 5.

Example (4). (i) O conducts activities that further exempt purposes. O employs C as its Chief Executive Officer. C, on behalf of O, entered into a contract with Company K to construct an addition to O's existing building. The addition to O's building is a significant undertaking in relation to O's other activities. C owns all of the voting stock of Company K. Under the contract, O paid Company K an amount that substantially exceeded the fair market value of the services Company K provided. When O's board of trustees approved the contract with Company K, the board did not perform due diligence that could have made it aware that the contract price for Company K's services was excessive. Subsequently, but before the IRS commences an examination of O, O's board of trustees determines that the contract price was excessive. Thus, O concludes that an excess benefit transaction has occurred. After the board makes this determination, it promptly removes C as Chief Executive Officer, terminates C's employment with O, and hires legal counsel to recover the excess payments to Company K. In addition, O promptly adopts a conflicts of interest policy and significant new contract review procedures designed to prevent future recurrences of this problem.

(ii) The purchase of services by O from Company K at more than fair market value constitutes an excess benefit transaction between an applicable tax-exempt organization and disqualified persons under section 4958. Therefore, this transaction is subject to the appropriate excise taxes provided in that section. In addition, this transaction violates the proscription against inurement under section 501(c)(3) and § 1.501(c)(3)-1(c)(2).

(iii) The application of the factors in § 1.501(c)(3)-1(g)(2)(ii) to these facts is as follows. O has engaged in regular and ongoing activities that further exempt purposes both before and after the excess benefit transaction occurred. Although the size and scope of the excess benefit transaction were significant in relation to the size and scope of O's activities that further exempt purposes, the transaction with Company K was a one-time occurrence. By adopting a conflicts of interest policy and significant new contract review procedures and by terminating C, O has implemented safeguards that are reasonably calculated to prevent future violations. Moreover, O took corrective actions before the IRS commenced an examination of O. In addition, O has made a good faith effort to seek correction from Company K, the disqualified person who benefited from the excess benefit transaction. Based on the application of the factors to these facts, O continues to be described in section 501(c)(3).

Example (5). (i) O is a large organization with substantial assets and revenues. O conducts activities that further exempt purposes. O employs C as its Chief Financial Officer. During Year 1, O pays $2,500 of C's personal expenses. O does not make these payments under an accountable plan under § 53.4958-4(a)(4) of this chapter. In addition, O does not report any of these payments on C's Form W-2, "Wage and Tax Statement," or on a Form 1099-MISC, "Miscellaneous Income," for C for Year 1, and O does not report these payments as compensation on its Form 990, "Return of Organization Exempt From Income Tax," for Year 1. Moreover, none of these payments can be disregarded under section 4958 as nontaxable fringe benefits and none consisted of fixed payments under an initial contract under § 53.4958-4(a)(3) of this chapter. C does not report the $2,500 of payments as income on his individual federal income tax return for Year 1. O does not repeat this reporting omission in subsequent years and, instead, reports all payments of C's personal expenses not made under an accountable plan as income to C.

(ii) O's payment in Year 1 of $2,500 of C's personal expenses constitutes an excess benefit transaction between an applicable tax-exempt organization and a disqualified person under section 4958. Therefore, this transaction is subject to the appropriate excise taxes provided in that section. In addition, this transaction violates the proscription against inurement in section 501(c)(3) and § 1.501(c)(3)-1(c)(2).

(iii) The application of the factors in § 1.501(c)(3)-1(g)(2)(ii) to these facts is as follows. O engages in regular and ongoing activities that further exempt purposes. The payment of $2,500 of C's personal expenses represented only a de minimis portion of O's assets and revenues; thus, the size and scope of the excess benefit transaction were not significant in relation to the size and scope of O's activities that further exempt purposes. The reporting omission that resulted in the excess benefit transaction in Year 1 is not repeated in subsequent years. Based on the application of the factors to these facts, O continues to be described in section 501(c)(3).

(3) Effective date. The rules in paragraph (g) of this section will apply with respect to excess benefit transactions occurring after the date of publication in the Federal Register of a Treasury Decision adopting these rules as final regulations.

§ 1.501(c)(4)-1 Civic organizations and local associations of employees.

Caution: The Treasury has not yet amended Reg § 1.501(c)(4)-1 to reflect changes made by P.L. 104-168.

(a) Civic organizations. *(1) In general.* A civic league or organization may be exempt as an organization described in section 501(c)(4) if—

(i) It is not organized or operated for profit; and

(ii) It is operated exclusively for the promotion of social welfare.

(2) Promotion of social welfare. (i) In general. An organization is operated exclusively for the promotion of social welfare if it is primarily engaged in promoting in some way the common good and general welfare of the people of the community. An organization embraced within this section is one which is operated primarily for the purpose of bringing about civic betterments and social improvements. A "social welfare" organization will qualify for exemption as a charitable organization if it falls within the definition of "charitable" set forth in paragraph (d)(2) of § 1.501(c)(3)-1 and is not an "action" organization as set forth in paragraph (c)(3) of § 1.501(c)(3)-1.

(ii) Political or social activities. The promotion of social welfare does not include direct or indirect participation or intervention in political campaigns on behalf of or in opposition to any candidate for public office. Nor is an organization operated primarily for the promotion of social welfare if its primary activity is operating a social club for the benefit, pleasure, or recreation of its members, or is carrying on a business with the general public in a manner similar to organizations which are operated for profit. See, however, section 501(c)(6) and § 1.501(c)(6)-1, relating to business leagues and similar organizations. A social welfare organization that is not, at any time after October 4, 1976, exempt from taxation as an organization described in section 501(c)(3) may qualify under section 501(c)(4) even though it is an "action" organization described in § 1.501(c)(3)-1(c)(3)(ii) or (iv), if it otherwise qualifies under this section. For rules relating to an organization that is, after October 4, 1976, exempt from taxation as an organization described in section 501(c)(3), see section 504 and § 1.504-1.

(b) Local associations of employees. Local associations of employees described in section 501(c)(4) are expressly entitled to exemption under section 501(a). As conditions to exemption, it is required (1) that the membership of such an association be limited to the employees of a designated person or persons in a particular municipality, and (2) that the net earnings of the association be devoted exclusively to charitable, educational, or recreational purposes. The word "local" is defined in paragraph (b) of § 1.501(c)(12)-1. See paragraph (d)(2) and (3) of § 1.501(c)(3)-1 with reference to the meaning of "charitable" and "educational" as used in this section.

T.D. 6391, 6/25/59, amend T.D. 8308, 8/30/90.

§ 1.501(c)(5)-1 Labor, agricultural, and horticultural organizations.

Caution: The Treasury has not yet amended Reg § 1.501(c)(5)-1 to reflect changes made by P.L. 101-73, P.L. 100-647, P.L. 100-203, P.L. 99-514.

(a) The organizations contemplated by section 501(c)(5) as entitled to exemption from income taxation are those which:

(1) Have no net earnings inuring to the benefit of any member, and

(2) Have as their objects the betterment of the conditions of those engaged in such pursuits, the improvement of the grade of their products, and the development of a higher degree of efficiency in their respective occupations.

(b) *(1)* An organization is not an organization described in section 501(c)(5) if the principal activity of the organization is to receive, hold, invest, disburse or otherwise manage funds associated with savings or investment plans or programs, including pension or other retirement savings plans or programs.

(2) Exception. Paragraph (b)(1) of this section shall not apply to an organization which—

(i) Is established and maintained by another labor organization described in section 501(c)(5), (determined without regard to this paragraph (b)(2));

(ii) Is not directly or indirectly established or maintained in whole or in part by one or more—

(A) Employers;

(B) Governments or agencies or instrumentalities thereof; or

(C) Government controlled entities;

(iii) Is funded by membership dues from members of the labor organization described in this paragraph (b)(2) and earnings thereon; and

(iv) Has not at any time after September 2, 1974 (the date of enactment of the Employee Retirement Income Security Act of 1974, Pub. L. 93-406, 88 Stat. 829) provided for, permitted or accepted employer contributions.

(3) Example. The principles of this paragraph (b) are illustrated by the following example;

Example. Trust A is organized in accordance with a collective bargaining agreement between labor union K and multiple employers. Trust A forms part of a plan that is established and maintained pursuant to the agreement and which covers employees of the signatory employers who are members of K. Representatives of both the employers and K serve as trustees. A receives contributions from the employers who are subject to the agreement. Retirement benefits paid to K's members as specified in the agreement are funded exclusively by the employers' contributions and accumulated earnings. A also provides information to union members about their retirement benefits and assists them with administrative tasks associated with the benefits. Most of A's activities are devoted to these functions. From time to time, A also participates in the renegotiation of the collective bargaining agreement. A's principal activity is to receive, hold, invest, disburse, or otherwise manage funds associated with a retirement savings plan. In addition, A does not satisfy all the requirements of the exception described in paragraph (b)(2) of this section. (For example, A accepts contributions from employers). Therefore, A is not a labor organization described in section 501(c)(5).

(c) Organizations described in section 501(c)(5) and otherwise exempt from tax under section 501(a) are taxable upon their unrelated business taxable income. See part II (section 511 and following), subchapter F, chapter 1 of the Code, and the regulations thereunder.

T.D. 6301, 7/8/58, amend T.D. 8726, 7/28/97.

---

§ 1.501(c)(6)-1 Business leagues, chambers of commerce, real estate boards, and boards of trade.

Caution: The Treasury has not yet amended Reg § 1.501(c)(6)-1 to reflect changes made by P.L. 101-73, P.L. 100-647, P.L. 100-203, P.L. 99-514.

A business league is an association of persons having some common business interest, the purpose of which is to promote such common interest and not to engage in a regular business of a kind ordinarily carried on for profit. It is an organization of the same general class as a chamber of commerce or board of trade. Thus, its activities should be directed to the improvement of business conditions of one or more lines of business as distinguished from the performance of particular services for individual persons. An organization whose purpose is to engage in a regular business of a kind ordinarily carried on for profit, even though the business is conducted on a cooperative basis or produces only sufficient income to be self-sustaining, is not a business league. An association engaged in furnishing information to prospective investors, to enable them to make sound investments, is not a business league, since its activities do not further any common business interest, even though all of its income is devoted to the purpose stated. A stock or commodity exchange is not a business league, a chamber of commerce, or a board of trade within the meaning of section 501(c)(6) and is not exempt from tax. Organizations otherwise exempt from tax under this section are taxable upon their unrelated business taxable income. See part II (section 511 and following), subchapter F, chapter 1 of the Code, and the regulations thereunder.

T.D. 6301, 7/8/58.

---

§ 1.501(c)(7)-1 Social clubs.

Caution: The Treasury has not yet amended Reg § 1.501(c)(7)-1 to reflect changes made by P.L. 100-647, P.L. 100-203, P.L. 99-514, P.L. 96-601, P.L. 94-568.

(a) The exemption provided by section 501(a) for organizations described in section 501(c)(7) applies only to clubs which are organized and operated exclusively for pleasure, recreation, and other nonprofitable purposes, but does not apply to any club if any part of its net earnings inures to the benefit of any private shareholder. In general, this exemption extends to social and recreation clubs which are supported solely by membership fees, dues, and assessments. However, a club otherwise entitled to exemption will not be disqualified because it raises revenue from members through the use of club facilities or in connection with club activities.

(b) A club which engages in business, such as making its social and recreational facilities available to the general public or by selling real estate, timber, or other products, is not organized and operated exclusively for pleasure, recreation, and other nonprofitable purposes, and is not exempt under section 501(a). Solicitation by advertisement or otherwise for public patronage of its facilities is prima facie evidence that the club is engaging in business and is not being operated exclusively for pleasure, recreation, or social purposes. However, an incidental sale of property will not deprive a club of its exemption.

T.D. 6301, 7/8/58.

---

§ 1.501(c)(8)-1 Fraternal beneficiary societies.

Caution: The Treasury has not yet amended Reg § 1.501(c)(8)-1 to reflect changes made by P.L. 100-647, P.L. 100-203, P.L. 99-514, P.L. 96-601, P.L. 94-568.

(a) A fraternal beneficiary society is exempt from tax only if operated under the "lodge system" or for the exclusive benefit of the members so operating. "Operating under the lodge system" means carrying on its activities under a form of organization that comprises local branches, chartered by a parent organization and largely self-governing, called lodges, chapters, or the like. In order to be exempt it is also necessary that the society have an established system for the payment to its members or their dependents of life, sick, accident, or other benefits.

(b) [Deleted]

T.D. 6301, 7/8/58, amend T.D. 7061, 9/22/70.

§ 1.501(c)(9)-1 Voluntary employees' beneficiary associations, in general.

To be described in section 501(c)(9) an organization must meet all of the following requirements:

(a) The organization is an employees' association,

(b) Membership in the association is voluntary,

(c) The organization provides for the payment of life, sick, accident, or other benefits to its members or their dependents or designated beneficiaries, and substantially all of its operations are in furtherance of providing such benefits, and

(d) No part of the net earnings of the organization inures, other than by payment of the benefits referred to in paragraph (c) of this section, to the benefit of any private shareholder or individual.

T.D. 7750, 12/30/80.

§ 1.501(c)(9)-2 Membership in a voluntary employees' beneficiary association; employees; voluntary association of employees.

(a) Membership. *(1) In general.* The membership of an organization described in section 501(c)(9) must consist of individuals who become entitled to participate by reason of their being employees and whose eligibility for membership is defined by reference to objective standards that constitute an employment-related common bond among such individuals. Typically, those eligible for membership in an organization described in section 501(c)(9) are defined by reference to a common employer (or affiliated employers), to coverage under one or more collective bargaining agreements (with respect to benefits provided by reason of such agreement(s)), to membership in a labor union, or to membership in one or more locals of a national or international labor union. For example, membership in an association might be open to all employees of a particular employer, or to employees in specified job classifications working for certain employers at specified locations and who are entitled to benefits by reason of one or more collective bargaining agreements. In addition, employees of one or more employers engaged in the same line of business in the same geographic locale will be considered to share an employment-related bond for purposes of an organization through which their employers provide benefits. Employees of a labor union also will be considered to share an employment-related common bond with members of the union, and employees of an association will be considered to share an employment-related common bond with members of the association. Whether a group of individuals is defined by reference to a permissible standard or standards is a question to be determined with regard to all the facts and circumstances, taking into account the guidelines set forth in this paragraph. Exemption will not be denied merely because the membership of an association includes some individuals who are not employees (within the meaning of paragraph (b) of this section), provided that such individuals share an employment-related bond with the employee-members. Such individuals may include, for example, the proprietor of a business whose employees are members of the association. For purposes of the preceding two sentences, an association will be considered to be composed of employees if 90 percent of the total membership of the association on one day of each quarter of the association's taxable year consists of employees (within the meaning of paragraph (b) of this section).

(2) Restrictions. (i) In general. Eligibility for membership may be restricted by geographic proximity, or by objective conditions or limitations reasonably related to employment, such as a limitation to a reasonable classification of workers, a limitation based on a reasonable minimum period of service, a limitation based on maximum compensation, or a requirement that a member be employed on a full-time basis. Similarly, eligibility for benefits may be restricted by objective conditions relating to the type or amount of benefits offered. Any objective criteria used to restrict eligibility for membership or benefits may not, however, be selected or administered in a manner that limits membership or benefits to officers, shareholders, or highly compensated employees of an employer contributing to or otherwise funding the employees' association. Similarly, eligibility for benefits may not be subject to conditions or limitations that have the effect of entitling officers, shareholders, or highly compensated employees of an employer contributing to or otherwise funding the employees' association to benefits that are disproportionate in relation to benefits to which other members of the association are entitled. See § 1.501(c)(9)-4(b). Whether the selection or administration of objective conditions has the effect of providing disproportionate benefits to officers, shareholders, or highly compensated employees generally is to be determined on the basis of all the facts and circumstances.

(ii) Generally permissible restrictions or conditions. In general the following restrictions will not be considered to be inconsistent with § 1.501(c)(9)-2(a)(2)(i) or § 1.501(c)(9)-4(b):

(A) In the case of an employer-funded organization, a provision that excludes or has the effect of excluding from membership in the organization or participation in a particular benefit plan employees who are members of another organization or covered by a different plan, funded or contributed to by the employer, to the extent that such other organization or plan offers similar benefits on comparable terms to the excluded employees.

(B) In the case of an employer funded-organization, a provision that excludes from membership, or limits the type or amount of benefits provided to, individuals who are included in a unit of employees covered by an agreement which the Secretary of Labor finds to be a collective bargaining agreement between employee representatives and one or more employers, if there is evidence that the benefit or benefits provided by the organization were the subject of good faith bargaining between such employee representatives and such employer or employers.

(C) Restrictions or conditions on eligibility for membership or benefits that are determined through collective bargaining, by trustees designated pursuant to a collective bargaining agreement, or by the collective bargaining agents of the members of an association or trustees named by such agent or agents.

(D) The allowance of benefits only on condition that a member or recipient contribute to the cost of such benefits, or the allowance of different benefits based solely on differences in contributions, provided that those making equal contributions are entitled to comparable benefits.

(E) A requirement that a member (or a member's dependents) meet a reasonable health standard related to eligibility for a particular benefit.

(F) The provision of life benefits in amounts that are a uniform percentage of the compensation received by the individual whose life is covered.

(G) The provision of benefits in the nature of wage replacement in the event of disability in amounts that are a uniform percentage of the compensation of the covered individuals (either before or after taking into account any disability benefits provided through social security or any similar plan providing for wage replacement in the event of disability).

(3) Examples. The provisions of this section may be illustrated by the following examples:

Example (1). Pursuant to a collective bargaining agreement entered into by X Corporation and W, a labor union which represents all of X Corporation's hourly-paid employees, the X Corporation Union Benefit Plan is established to provide life insurance benefits to employees of X represented by W. The Plan is funded by contributions from X, and is jointly administered by X and W. In order to provide its non-unionized employees with comparable life insurance benefits, X also establishes and funds the X Corporation Life Insurance Trust. The Trust will not be ineligible for exemption as an organization described in section 501(c)(9) solely because membership is restricted to those employees of X who are not members of W.

Example (2). The facts are the same as in Example (1) except that the life insurance benefit provided to the non-unionized employees of X differs from the life insurance benefit provided to the unionized employees of X pursuant to the collective bargaining agreement. The trust will not be ineligible for exemption as an organization described in section 501(c)(9) solely because the life insurance benefit provided to X's nonunionized employees is not same as the life insurance benefit provided to X's unionized employees.

Example (3). S corporation established a plan to provide health benefits to all its employees. In accordance with the provisions of the plan each employee may secure insurance coverage by making an election under which the employee agrees to contribute periodically to the plan an amount which is determined solely by whether the employee elects a high option coverage or a low option coverage and on whether the employee is unmarried or has a family. As an alternative, the employee may elect high or low options, self only or self and family, coverage through a local prepaid group medical plan. The contributions required of those electing the prepaid group medical plan also vary with the type of coverage selected, and differ from those required of employees electing insurance. The difference between the amount contributed by employees electing the various coverages and the actual cost of purchasing the coverage is made up through contributions by S to the plan, and under the plan, S provides approximately the same proportion of the cost for each coverage. To fund the plan, S established an arrangement in the nature of a trust under applicable local law and contributes all employee contributions, and all amounts which by the terms of the plan it is required to contribute, to the trust. The terms of the plan do not provide for disproportionate benefits to the employees of S and will not be considered inconsistent with § 1.501(c)(9)-2(a)(2)(i).

Example (4). The facts are the same as in Example (3) except that, for those employees or former employees covered by Medicare, the plan provides a distinct coverage which supplements Medicare benefits. Eligibility for Medicare is an objective condition relating to a type of benefit offered, and the provision of separate coverage for those eligible for Medicare will not be considered inconsistent with § 1.501(c)(9)-2(a)(2)(i).

(b) Meaning of "employee". Whether an individual is an "employee" is determined by reference to the legal and bona fide relationship of employer and employee. The term "employee" includes the following:

(1) An individual who is considered an employee:

(i) For employment tax purposes under Subtitle C of the Internal Revenue Code and the regulations thereunder, or

(ii) For purposes of a collective bargaining agreement,

whether or not the individual could qualify as an employee under applicable common law rules. This would include any person who is considered an employee for purposes of the Labor Management Relations Act of 1947, 61 Stat. 136, *as amended,* 29 U.S.C. 141 (1979).

(2) An individual who became entitled to membership in the association by reason of being or having been an employee. Thus, an individual who would otherwise qualify under this paragraph will continue to qualify as an employee even though such individual is on leave of absence, works temporarily for another employer or as an independent contractor, or has been terminated by reason of retirement, disability or layoff. For example, an individual who in the normal course of employment is employed intermittently by more than one employer in an industry characterized by short-term employment by several different employers will not, by reason of temporary unemployment, cease to be an employee within the meaning of this paragraph.

(3) The surviving spouse and dependents of an employee (if, for purposes of the 90-percent test of § 1.501(c)(9)-2(a)(1) they are considered to be members of the association).

(c) Description of voluntary association of employees. *(1) Association.* To be described in section 501(c)(9) and this section there must be an entity, such as a corporation or trust established under applicable local law, having an existence independent of the member-employees or their employer.

(2) Voluntary. Generally, membership in an association is voluntary if an affirmative act is required on the part of an employee to become a member rather than the designation as a member due to employee status. However, an association shall be considered voluntary although membership is required to all employees, provided that the employees do not incur a detriment (for example, in the form of deductions from pay) as the result of membership in the association. An employer is not deemed to have imposed involuntary membership on the employee if membership is required as the result of a collective bargaining agreement or as an incident of membership in a labor organization.

(3) Of employees. To be described in this section, an organization must be controlled—

(i) By its membership,

(ii) By independent trustee(s) (such as a bank), or

(iii) By trustees or other fiduciaries at least some of whom are designated by, or on behalf of, the membership. Whether control by or on behalf of the membership exists is a question to be determined with regard to all of the facts and circumstances, but generally such control will be deemed to be present when the membership (either directly or through its representative) elects, appoints or otherwise designates a person or persons to serve as chief operating officer(s), administrator(s), or trustee(s) of the organization. For purposes of this paragraph an organization will be considered to be controlled by independent trustees if it is an "employee welfare benefit plan", as defined in section 3(1) of the Employee Retirement Income Security Act of 1974 (ERISA), and, as such, is subject to the requirements of Parts 1 and 4 of Subtitle B, Title I of ERISA. Similarly, a plan will be considered to be controlled by its membership if it is controlled by one or more trustees designated pursuant to a collective bargaining agreement (whether or not the bargaining agent of the represented employees bargained for and obtained the right to participate in selecting the trustees).

(4) Examples. The provisions of this section may be illustrated by the following examples:

Example (1). X, a labor union, represents all the hourly-paid employees of Y Corporation. A health insurance benefit plan was established by X and Y as the result of a collective bargaining agreement entered into by them. The plan established the terms and conditions of membership in, and the benefits to be provided by, the plan. In accordance with the terms of the agreement, Y Corporation is obligated to establish a trust fund and make contributions thereto at specified rates. The trustees, some of whom are designated by X and some by Y, are authorized to hold and invest the assets of the trust and to make payments on instructions issued by Y Corporation in accordance with the conditions contained in the plan. The interdependent benefit plan agreement and trust indenture together create a voluntary employees' beneficiary association over which the employees posses the requisite control through the trustees designated by their representative, X.

Example (2). Z Corporation unilaterally established an educational benefit plan for its employees. The purpose of the plan is to provide payments for job-related educational or training courses, such as apprenticeship training programs, for Z Corporation employees, according to objective criteria set forth in the plan. Z establishes a separate bank account which it uses to fund payments to the plan. Contributions to the account are to be made at the discretion of and solely by Z Corporation, which also administers the plan and retains control over the assets in the fund. Z Corporation's educational benefit plan and the related account do not constitute an association having an existence independent of Z Corporation and therefore do not constitute a voluntary employees' beneficiary association.

Example (3). A, an individual, is the incorporator and chief operating officer of Lawyers' Beneficiary Association (LBA). LBA is engaged in the business of providing medical benefits to members of the Association and their families. Membership is open only to practicing lawyers located in a particular metropolitan area who are neither self-employed nor partners in a law firm. Membership in LBA is solicited by insurance agents under the control of X Corporation (owned by A) which, by contract with LBA, is the exclusive sales agent. Medical benefits are paid from a trust account containing periodic "contributions" paid by the members, together with proceeds from the investment of those contributions. Contribution and benefit levels are set by LBA. The "members" of LBA do not hold meetings, have no right to elect officers or directors of the Association, and no right to replace trustees. Collectively, the subscribers for medical benefits from LBA cannot be said to control the association and membership is neither more than nor different from the purchase of an insurance policy from a stock insurance company. LBA is not a voluntary employees' beneficiary association.

Example (4). U corporation unilaterally established a plan to provide benefits to its employees. In accordance with the provisions of the plan, each employee may secure insurance or benefit coverage by making an election under which the employee agrees to contribute to the plan an amount which is determined solely by whether the employee elects a high option coverage or a low option coverage and on whether the employee elects self only or self and family coverage. The difference between the amount contributed by employees electing the various coverages and the actual cost of the coverage is made up through contributions by U to the plan. To fund the plan, U established an arrangement in the nature of a trust under applicable local law and contributed all employee contributions, and all amounts which by the term of the plan it was required to provide to the plan, to the trust. The trust constitutes an "employee welfare benefit plan" within the meaning of, and subject to relevant requirements of, ERISA. It will be considered to meet the requirements of § 1.501(c)(9)-2(c)(3).

T.D. 7750, 12/30/80.

PAR. 2. In § 1.501(c)(9)-2, paragraph (a)(1) is amended by adding a sentence between the fourth and fifth sentences, and a new paragraph (d) is added, to read as follows:

Proposed § 1.501(c)(9)-2 Membership in a voluntary employees' beneficiary association; employees; voluntary association of employees. [*For Preamble, see ¶ 151,401*]

(a) * * *

(1) In general. * * * (See paragraph (d) of this section for the meaning of geographic locale.)

* * * * *

(d) Meaning of geographic locale. *(1) Three-state safe harbor.* An area is a single geographic locale for purposes of paragraph (a)(1) of this section if it does not exceed the boundaries of three contiguous states, i.e., three states each of which shares a land or river border with at least one of the others. For this purpose, Alaska and Hawaii are deemed to be contiguous with each other and with each of the following states: Washington, Oregon, and California.

(2) Discretionary authority to recognize larger areas as geographic locales. In determining whether an organization covering employees of employers engaged in the same line of business is a voluntary employees beneficiary association (VEBA) described in section 501(c)(9), the Commissioner may recognize an area that does not satisfy the three-state safe harbor in paragraph (d)(1) of this section as a single geographic locale if—

(i) It would not be economically feasible to cover employees of employers engaged in that line of business in that area under two or more separate VEBAs each extending over fewer states; and

(ii) Employment characteristics in that line of business, population characteristics, or other regional factors support the particular states included. This paragraph (d)(2)(ii) is deemed satisfied if the states included are contiguous.

(3) Examples. The following examples illustrate this paragraph (d).

Example (1). The membership of the W Association is made up of employers whose business consists of the distribution of produce in Virginia, North Carolina, and South Carolina. Because Virginia and South Carolina each share a land border with North Carolina, the three states are contiguous states and form a single geographic locale.

Example (2). The membership of the X Association is made up of employers whose business consists of the retail sale of computer software in Montana, Wyoming, North Dakota, South Dakota, and Nebraska, which are contiguous states. X establishes the X Trust to provide life, sick, accident, or other benefits for the employees of its members. The X Trust applies for recognition of exemption as a VEBA, stating that it intends to permit employees of any employer that is a member of X to join the proposed VEBA. In its application, the X Trust provides summaries of employer data and economic analyses showing that no division of the region into smaller groups of states would enable X to establish two or more separate VEBAs each with enough members to make the formation of those separate VEBAs economically feasible. Furthermore, although some possible divisions of the region into three-state or four-state areas could form an economically feasible VEBA, any such division of the five-state region covered by X would leave employees of X's employer-members located in at least one state without a VEBA. The Commissioner may as a matter of administrative discretion, recognize the X Trust as a VEBA described in section 501(c)(9) based on its showing that the limited number of employees in each state would make any division of the region into two or more VEBAs economically infeasible.

Example (3). The membership of the Y Association is made up of employers whose business consists of shipping freight by barge on the Mississippi and Ohio Rivers. Some of the members of Y conduct their business out of ports in Louisiana, while others operate out of ports in Arkansas, Missouri, and Ohio. Y establishes the Y Trust to provide life, sick, accident, or other benefits to the employees of its members. The Y Trust applies for recognition of exemption as a VEBA, stating that it intends to permit the employees of any employer that is a member of Y to join the proposed VEBA. In its application, the Y Trust sets forth facts tending to show that there are so few members of Y in each of the four states that any division of those states into two or more separate regions would result in creating VEBAs that would be too small to be economically feasible, that all of the members of Y are engaged in river shipping between inland and Gulf ports that are united by the existence of a natural waterway, and that the labor force engaged in providing transportation by river barge is distinct from that engaged in providing other means of transportation. Even though Ohio, Louisiana, Arkansas, and Missouri are not contiguous because Ohio does not share a land or river border with any of the other three states, the Commissioner may as a matter of administrative discretion, recognize the Y Trust as a VEBA described in section 501(c)(9) based on its showing that the establishment of separate VEBAs would not be economically feasible and that the characteristics of the river shipping business justify permitting a VEBA to cover the scattered concentrations of employees in that business located in Louisiana, Arkansas, Missouri, and Ohio.

Example (4). The membership of the Z Association is made up of employers whose business consists of the retail sale of agricultural implements in the states west of the Mississippi River except California, Alaska, and Hawaii. There are 21 states in the region covered by Z. Z establishes the Z1 Trust, the Z2 Trust, and the Z3 Trust to provide life, sick, accident or other benefits to in the employees of its members. The trusts cover different subregions which were formed by dividing the Z region into three areas each consisting of seven contiguous states. Each trust applies for recognition of exemption as a VEBA, stating that it intends to permit the employees of any employer that is a member of Z located within its subregion to join its proposed VEBA. Each trust sets forth facts in its application tending to show that four states within its particular subregion would be needed to create a VEBA large enough to be economically feasible, so that any further division of its seven-state subregion would leave employees of at least some of Z's employer-members located in the subregion in an area too small to support an economically feasible VEBA. The applications contain no justification for the choice of three seven-state subregions. Since the applicants have not shown that it would not be economically feasible to divide the Z region into smaller subregions (e.g., four containing four states and one containing five states), the applicants have not satisfied paragraph (d)(2)(i) of this section, and the Commissioner does not have the discretion to recognize the Z1, Z2, and Z3 Trusts as VEBAs in described in section 501(c)(9).

§ 1.501(c)(9)-3 Voluntary employees' beneficiary associations; life, sick, accident, or other benefits.

(a) In general. The life, sick, accident, or other benefits provided by a voluntary employees' beneficiary association must be payable to its members, their dependents, or their designated beneficiaries. For purposes of section 501(c)(9), "dependent" means the member's spouse; any child of the member or the member's spouse who is a minor or a student (within the meaning of section 151(e)(4)); any other minor child residing with the member; and any other individual who an association, relying on information furnished to it by a member, in good faith believes is a person described in section 152(a). Life, sick, accident, or other benefits may take the form of cash or noncash benefits. A voluntary employees' beneficiary association is not operated for the purpose of providing life, sick, accident, or other benefits unless substantially all of its operations are in furtherance of the provision of such benefits. Further, an organization is not described in this section if it systematically and knowingly provides benefits (of more than a de minimis amount) that are not permitted by paragraphs (b), (c), (d), or (e) of this section.

(b) Life benefits. The term "life benefits" means a benefit (including a burial benefit or a wreath) payable by reason of the death of a member or dependent. A "life benefit" may be provided directly or through insurance. It generally must consist of current protection, but also may include a right to convert to individual coverage on termination of eligibility for coverage through the association, or a permanent benefit as defined in, and subject to the conditions in, the regulations under section 79. A "life benefit" also includes the benefit provided under any life insurance contract purchased directly from an employee-funded association by a member or provided by such an association to a member. The term "life benefit" does not include a pension, annuity or similar benefit, except that a benefit payable by reason of the death of an insured may be settled in the form of an annuity to the beneficiary in lieu of a lump-sum death benefit (whether or not the contract provides for settlement in a lump sum).

(c) Sick and accident benefits. The term "sick and accident benefits" means amounts furnished to or on behalf of a member or a member's dependents in the event of illness or personal injury to a member or dependent. Such benefits may be provided through reimbursement to a member or a member's dependents for amounts expended because of illness or personal injury, or through the payment of premiums to a medical benefit or health insurance program. Similarly, a sick and accident benefit includes an amount paid to a member in lieu of income during a period in which the member is unable to work due to sickness or injury. Sick benefits also include benefits designed to safeguard or improve the health of members and their dependents. Sick and accident benefits may be provided directly by an association to or on behalf of members and their dependents, or may be provided indirectly by an association through the payment of premiums or fees to an insurance company, medical clinic, or other program under which members and their dependents are entitled to medical services or to other sick and accident benefits. Sick and accident benefits may also be furnished in noncash form, such as, for example, benefits in the nature of clinical care services by visiting nurses, and transportation furnished for medical care.

(d) Other benefits. The term "other benefits" includes only benefits that are similar to life, sick, or accident benefits. A benefit is similar to a life, sick, or accident benefit if:

(1) It is intended to safeguard or improve the health of a member or a member's dependents, or

(2) It protects against a contingency that interrupts or impairs a member's earning power.

(e) Examples of "other benefits". Paying vacation benefits, providing vacation facilities, reimbursing vacation expenses, and subsidizing recreational activities such as athletic leagues are considered "other benefits". The provision of child-care facilities for preschool and school-age dependents are also considered "other benefits". The provision of job readjustment allowances, income maintenance payments in the event of economic dislocation, temporary living expense loans and grants at times of disaster (such as fire or flood), supplemental unemployment compensation benefits (as defined in section 501(c)(17)(D)(i) of the Code), severance benefits (under a severance pay plan within the meaning of 29 CFR § 2510.3-2(b)) and education or training benefits or courses (such as apprentice training programs) for members, are considered "other benefits" because they protect against a contingency that interrupts earning power. Personal legal service benefits which consist of payments or credits to one or more organizations or trusts described in section 501(c)(20) are considered "other benefits". Except to the extent otherwise provided in these regulations, as amended from time to time, "other benefits" also include any benefit provided in the manner permitted by paragraphs (5) *et seq.* of section 302(c) of the Labor Management Relations Act of 1947, 61 Stat. 136, as amended, 29 U.S.C. 186(c) (1979).

(f) Examples of nonqualifying benefits. Benefits that are not described in paragraphs (d) or (e) of this section are not "other benefits". Thus, "other benefits" do not include the payment of commuting expenses, such as bridge tolls or train fares, the provision of accident or homeowner's insurance benefits for damage to property, the provision of malpractice insurance, or the provision of loans to members except in times of distress (as permitted by § 1.501(c)(9)-3(e)). "Other benefits" also do not include the provision of savings facilities for members. The term "other benefits" does not include any benefit that is similar to a pension or annuity payable at the time of mandatory or voluntary retirement, or a benefit that is similar to the benefit provided under a stock bonus or profit-sharing plan. For purposes of section 501(c)(9) and these regulations, a benefit will be considered similar to that provided under a pension, annuity, stock bonus or profit-sharing plan if it provides for deferred compensation that becomes payable by reason of the passage of time, rather than as the result of an unanticipated event. Thus, for example, supplemental unemployment benefits, which generally become payable by reason of unanticipated layoff, are not, for purposes of these regulations, considered similar to the benefit provided under a pension, annuity, stock bonus or profit-sharing plan.

(g) Examples. The provisions of this section may be further illustrated by the following examples:

Example (1). V was organized in connection with a vacation plan created pursuant to a collective bargaining agreement between M, a labor union, which represents certain hourly paid employees of T corporation, and T. The agreement calls for the payment by T to V of a specified sum per hour worked by T employees who are covered by the collective bargaining agreement. T includes the amounts in the covered employees' wages and withholds income and FICA taxes. The amounts are paid by T to V to provide vacation benefits provided under the collective bargaining agreement. Generally, each covered employee receives a check in payment of his or her vacation benefit during the year following the year in which contributions were made by T to V. The amount of the vacation benefit is determined by reference to the contributions during the prior year to V by T on behalf of each employee, and is distributed in cash to each such employee. If the earnings on investments by V during the year preceding distribution are sufficient after deducting the expenses of administering the plan, each recipient of a vacation benefit is paid an amount, in addition to the contributions on his or her behalf, equal to his/her ratable share of the net earnings of V during such year. The plan provides a vacation benefit that constitutes an eligible "other benefit" described in section 501(c)(9) and § 1.501(c)(9)-3(e).

Example (2). The facts are the same as in Example 1, except that each covered employee of T is entitled, at his or her discretion, to contribute up to an additional $1,000 each year to V, which agrees in respect of such sum to pay interest at a stated rate from the time of contribution until the time at which the contributing employee's vacation benefit is distributed. In addition, each employee may elect to leave all or a portion of his/her distributable benefit on deposit past the time of distribution, in which case interest will continue to accrue. Because the plan more closely resembles a savings arrangement than a vacation plan, the benefit payable to the covered employees of T is not a "vacation benefit" and is not an eligible "other benefit" described in section 501(c)(9) and § 1.501(c)(9)-3(d) or (e).

T.D. 7750, 12/30/80.

---

§ 1.501(c)(9)-4 Voluntary employees' beneficiary associations; inurement.

(a) General rule. No part of the net earnings of an employees' association may inure to the benefit of any private shareholder or individual other than through the payment of benefits permitted by § 1.501(c)(9)-3. The disposition of property to, or the performance of services for, a person for less than the greater of fair market value or cost (including indirect costs) to the association, other than as a life, sick, accident or other permissible benefit, constitutes prohibited inurement. Generally, the payment of unreasonable compensation to the trustees or employees of the association, or the purchase of insurance or services for amounts in excess of their fair market value from a company in which one or more of the association's trustees, officers or fiduciaries has an interest, will constitute prohibited inurement. Whether prohibited inurement has occurred is a question to be determined with regard to all of the facts and circumstances, taking into account the guidelines set forth in this section. The guidelines and examples contained in this section are not an exhaustive list of the activities that may constitute prohibited inurement, or the persons to whom the association's earnings could impermissibly inure. See § 1.501(a)-1(c).

(b) Disproportionate benefits. For purposes of subsection (a), the payment to any member of disproportionate benefits, where such payment is not pursuant to objective and nondiscriminatory standards, will not be considered a benefit within the meaning of § 1.501(c)(9)-3 even though the benefit otherwise is one of the type permitted by that section. For example, the payment to highly compensated personnel of benefits that are disproportionate in relation to benefits received by other members of the association will constitute prohibited inurement. Also, the payment to similarly situated employees of benefits that differ in kind or amount will constitute prohibited inurement unless the difference can be justified on the basis of objective and reasonable standards adopted by the association or on the basis of standards adopted pursuant to the terms of a collective bargaining agreement. In general, benefits paid pursuant to standards or subject to conditions that do not provide for disproportionate benefits to officers, shareholders, or highly compensated employees will not be considered disproportionate. See § 1.501(c)(9)-2(a)(2) and (3).

(c) Rebates. The rebate of excess insurance premiums, based on the mortality or morbidity experience of the insurer to which the premiums were paid, to the person or persons whose contributions were applied to such premiums, does not constitute prohibited inurement. A voluntary employees' beneficiary association may also make administrative adjustments strictly incidental to the provision of benefits to its members.

(d) Termination of plan or dissolution of association. It will not constitute prohibited inurement if, on termination of a plan established by an employer and funded through an association described in section 501(c)(9), any assets remaining in the association, after satisfaction of all liabilities to existing beneficiaries of the plan, are applied to provide, either directly or through the purchase of insurance, life, sick, accident or other benefits within the meaning of § 1.501(c)(9)-3 pursuant to criteria that do not provide for disproportionate benefits to officers, shareholders, or highly compensated employees of the employer. See § 1.501(c)(9)-2(a)(2). Similarly, a distribution to members upon the dissolution of the association will not constitute prohibited inurement if the amount distributed to members are determined pursuant to to the terms of a collective bargaining agreement or on the basis of objective and reasonable standards which do not result in either unequal payments to similarly situated members or in disproportionate payments to officers, shareholders, or highly compensated employees of an employer contributing to or otherwise funding the employees' association. Except as otherwise provided in the first sentence of this paragraph, if the association's corporate charter, articles of association, trust instrument, or other written instrument by which the association was created, as amended from time to time, provides that on dissolution its assets will be distributed to its members' contributing employers, or if in the absence of such provision the law of the state in which the association was created provides for such distribution to the contributing employers, the association is not described in section 501(c)(9).

(e) Example. The provisions of this section may be illustrated by the following example:

Example. Employees A, B and C, members of the X voluntary employees' beneficiary association, are unemployed. They receive unemployment benefits from X. Those to A include an amount in addition to those provided to B and C, to provide for A's retraining. B has been found pursuant to objective and reasonable standards not to qualify for the retraining program. C, although eligible for retraining benefits has declined. X's additional payment to A for retraining does not constitute prohibited inurement.

T.D. 7750, 12/30/80.

§ 1.501(c)(9)-5 Voluntary employees' beneficiary associations; recordkeeping requirements.

(a) Records. In addition to such other records which may be required (for example, by section 512(a)(3) and the regulations thereunder), every organization described in section 501(c)(9) must maintain records indicating the amount contributed by each member and contributing employer, and the amount and type of benefits paid by the organization to or on behalf of each member.

(b) Cross reference. For provisions relating to annual information returns with respect to payments, see section 6041 and the regulations thereunder.

T.D. 7750, 12/30/80.

§ 1.501(c)(9)-6 Voluntary employees' beneficiary associations; benefits includible in gross income.

(a) In general. Cash and noncash benefits realized by a person on account of the activities of an organization described in section 501(c)(9) shall be included in gross income to the extent provided in the Internal Revenue Code of 1954, including, but not limited to, sections 61, 72, 101, 104 and 105 of the Code and regulations thereunder.

(b) Availability of statutory exclusions from gross income. The availability of any statutory exclusion from gross income with respect to contributions to, or the payment of benefits from, an organization described in section 501(c)(9) is determined by the statutory provision conferring the exclusion, and the regulations and rulings thereunder, not by whether an an individual is eligible for membership in the organization or by the permissibility of the benefit paid. Thus, for example, if a benefit is paid by an employer-funded organization described in section 501(c)(9) to a member who is not an "employee", a statutory exclusion from gross income that is available only for "employees" would be unavailable in the case of a benefit paid to such individual. Similarly, the fact that, for example, under some circumstances educational benefits constitute "other benefits" does not of itself mean that such benefits are eligible for the exclusion of either section 117 or section 127 of the Code.

T.D. 7750, 12/30/80.

§ 1.501(c)(9)-7 Voluntary employees' beneficiary associations; section 3(4) of ERISA.

The term "voluntary employees' beneficiary association" in section 501(c)(9) of the Internal Revenue Code is not necessarily coextensive with the term "employees' beneficiary association" as used in section 3(4) of the Employee Retirement Income Security Act of 1974 (ERISA), 29 U.S.C. 1002(4), and the requirements which an organization must meet to be an "employees' beneficiary association" within the meaning of section 3(4) of ERISA are not necessarily identical to the requirements that an organization must meet in order to be a "voluntary employees' beneficiary association" within the meaning of section 501(c)(9) of the Code.

T.D. 7750, 12/30/80.

§ 1.501(c)(9)-8 Voluntary employees' beneficiary associations; effective date.

(a) General rule. Except as otherwise provided in this section, the provisions of §§ 1.501(c)(9)-1 through 1.501(c)(9)-7 shall apply with respect to taxable years beginning after December 31, 1954.

(b) Pre-1970 taxable years. For taxable years beginning before January 1, 1970, section 501(c)(9)(B) (relating to the requirement that 85 percent or more of the association's income consist of amount collected from members and contributed by employers), as in effect for such years, shall apply.

(c) Existing associations. Except as otherwise provided in paragraph (d), the provisions of §§ 1.501(c)(9)-2(a)(1) and (c)(3) shall apply with respect to taxable years beginning after December 31, 1980.

(d) Collectively-bargained plans. In the case of a voluntary employees' beneficiary association which receives contributions from one or more employers pursuant to one or more collective bargaining agreements in effect on December 31, 1980, the provisions of §§ 1.501(c)(9)-1 through 1.501(c)(9)-5 shall apply with respect to taxable years beginning after the date on which the agreement terminates (determined without regard to any extension thereof agreed to after December 31, 1980).

(e) Election. Notwithstanding paragraphs (c) and (d) of this section, an organization may choose to be subject to all or a portion of one or more of the provisions of these regulations for any taxable year beginning after December 31, 1954.

T.D. 7750, 12/30/80.

§ 1.501(c)(10)-1 Certain fraternal beneficiary societies.

(a) For taxable years beginning after December 31, 1969, an organization will qualify for exemption under section 501(c)(10) if it:

(1) Is a domestic fraternal beneficiary society order, or association, described in section 501(c)(8) and the regulations thereunder except that it does not provide for the payment of life, sick, accident, or other benefits to its members, and

(2) Devotes its net earnings exclusively to religious, charitable, scientific, literary, educational, and fraternal purposes.

Any organization described in section 501(c)(7), such as, for example, a national college fraternity, is not described in section 501(c)(10) and this section.

T.D. 7172, 3/16/72.

§ 1.501(c)(12)-1 Local benevolent life insurance associations, mutual irrigation and telephone companies, and like organizations.

Caution: The Treasury has not yet amended Reg § 1.501(c)(12)-1 to reflect changes made by P.L. 100-647, P.L. 100-203, P.L. 99-514, P.L. 96-605.

(a) An organization described in section 501(c)(12) must receive at least 85 percent of its income from amounts collected from members for the sole purposes of meeting losses and expenses. If an organization issues policies for stipulated cash premiums, or if it requires advance deposits to cover the cost of the insurance and maintains investments from which more than 15 percent of its income is derived, it is not entitled to exemption. On the other hand, an organization may be entitled to exemption, although it makes advance assessments for the sole purpose of meeting future losses and expenses, provided that the balance of such assessments remaining on hand at the end of the year is retained to meet losses and expenses or is returned to members.

(b) The phrase "of a purely local character" applies to benevolent life insurance associations, and not to the other organizations specified in section 501(c)(12). It also applies to any organization seeking exemption on the ground that it is an organization similar to a benevolent life insurance association. An organization of a purely local character is one whose business activities are confined to a particular community, place, or district, irrespective, however, of political subdivisions. If the activities of an organization are limited only by the borders of a State it cannot be considered to be purely local in character.

(c) For taxable years of a mutual or cooperative telephone company beginning after December 31, 1974, the 85 percent member-income test described in paragraph (a) of this section is applied without taking into account income received or accrued from another telephone company for the performance of communication services involving the completion of long distance calls to, from, or between members of the mutual or cooperative telephone company. For example, if, in one year, a cooperative telephone company receives $85x from its members for telephone calls, $15x as interest income, and $20x as credits under long distance interconnection agreements with other telephone companies for the performance of communication services involving the completion of long distance calls to, from, or between members of the mutual or cooperative telephone company. For example, if, in one year, a cooperative telephone company receives $85x from its members for telephone calls, $15x as interest income, and $20x as credits under long distance interconnection agreements with other telephone companies for the performance of communication services involving the completion of long distance calls to, from, or between the cooperative's members (whether or not the credits may be offset, in whole or in part, by amounts due the other companies under the interconnection agreements), the member-income fraction is calculated without taking into account, either in the numerator or denominator, the $20x credits received from the other telephone companies.

In this example, the 85 percent member-income test is satisfied because at least 85 percent

$$\frac{\text{(member income}}{\text{(total income}} = \frac{85x}{85x + 15x} = \frac{85)}{100)} = 85\%$$

of the cooperative's total income is derived from member income.

T.D. 6301, 7/8/58, amend T.D. 7648, 10/15/79.

§ 1.501(c)(13)-1 Cemetery companies and crematoria.

(a) Nonprofit mutual cemetery companies. A nonprofit cemetery company may be entitled to exemption if it is owned by and operated exclusively for the benefit of its lot owners who hold such lots for bona fide burial purposes and not for the purpose of resale. A mutual cemetery company which also engages in charitable activities, such as the burial of paupers, will be regarded as operating in conformity with this standard. Further, the fact that a mutual cemetery company limits its membership to a particular class of individuals, such as members of a family, will not affect its status as mutual so long as all the other requirements of section 501(c)(13) are met.

(b) Nonprofit cemetery companies and crematoria. Any nonprofit corporation, chartered solely for the purpose of the burial, or (for taxable years beginning after December 31, 1970) the cremation of bodies, and not permitted by its charter to engage in any business not necessarily incident to that purpose, is exempt from income tax, provided that no part of its net earnings inures to the benefit of any private shareholder or individual.

(c) Preferred stock. *(1) In general.* Except as provided in subparagraph (3) of this paragraph, a cemetery company or crematorium is not described in section 501(c)(13) if it issues preferred stock on or after November 28, 1978.

(2) Transitional rule for preferred stock issued prior to November 28, 1978. In the case of preferred stock issued prior to November 28, 1978, a cemetery company or crematorium which issued such stock shall not fail to be exempt from income tax solely because it issued preferred stock which entitled the holders to dividends at a fixed rate, not exceeding the legal rate of interest in the State of incorporation or 8 percent per annum, whichever is greater, on the value of the consideration for which the stock was issued, if its articles of incorporation require:

(i) That the preferred stock be retired at par as rapidly as funds therefore become available from operations, and

(ii) That all funds not required for the payment of dividends upon or for the retirement of preferred stock be used by the company for the care and improvement of the cemetery property.

The term "legal rate of interest" shall mean the rate of interest prescribed by law in the State of incorporation which prevails in the absence of an agreement between contracting parties fixing a rate.

(3) Transitional rule for preferred stock issued on or after November 28, 1978. In the case of preferred stock issued on or after November 28, 1978, a cemetery company or crematorium shall not fail to be exempt from income tax if its articles of incorporation and the preferred stock meet the requirements of paragraph (c)(2) and if such stock is issued pursuant to a plan which has been reduced to writing and adopted prior to November 28, 1978. The adoption of the plan must be shown by the acts of the duly constituted responsible officers and appear upon the official records of the cemetery company or crematorium.

(d) Sales to exempt cemetery companies and crematoria. Except as provided in paragraph (c)(2) or (c)(3) of this section (relating to transitional rules for preferred stock), no person may have any interest in the net earnings of a tax-exempt cemetery company or crematorium. Thus, a cemetery company or crematorium is not exempt from tax if property is transferred to such organization in exchange for an interest in the net earnings of the organization so long as such interest remains outstanding. An interest in a cemetery company or crematorium that constitutes an equity interest within the meaning of section 385 will be considered an interest in the net earnings of the cemetery. However, an interest in a cemetery company or crematorium that does not constitute an equity interest within the meaning of section 385 may nevertheless constitute an interest in the net earnings of the organization. Thus, for example, a bond or other evidence of indebtedness issued by a cemetery company or crematorium which provides for a fixed rate of interest but which, in addition, provides for additional interest payments contingent upon the revenues or income of the organization is considered an interest in the net earnings of the organization. Similarly, a convertible debt obligation issued by a cemetery company or crematorium after July 7, 1975, is considered an interest in the net earnings of the organization.

T.D. 6301, 7/8/58, amend T.D. 7698, 5/20/80.

PAR. 2. Paragraph (a) of proposed § 1.501(c)(13)-1, as published in the FEDERAL REGISTER on July 8, 1975 (40 FR 28613), is amended by adding at the end thereof a new sentence to read as follows:

Proposed § 1.501(c)(13)-1 Cemetery companies and crematoria. [*For Preamble, see ¶ 150,405*]

* * * * *

(a) Nonprofit mutual cemetery companies. * * * Further, the fact that a mutual cemetery company limits its membership to a particular class of individuals, such as members of a family, will not affect its status as mutual so long as all the other requirements of section 501(c)(13) are met.

PAR. 3. Paragraph (c) of proposed § 1.501(c)(13)-1, as published in the FEDERAL REGISTER on July 8, 1975 (40 FR 28613), is amended to read as follows:

Proposed § 1.501(c)(13)-1 Cemetery companies and crematoria. [*For Preamble, see ¶ 150,405*]

* * * * *

(c) Preferred stock. *(1) In general.* A cemetery company or crematorium is not exempt from income tax under section 501(c)(13) if it issues preferred stock on or after November 28, 1978.

(2) Transitional rule. In the case of preferred stock issued prior to November 28, 1978, a cemetery company or crematorium which issued such stock shall not fail to be exempt under section 501(c)(13) solely because it issued preferred stock which entitled the holders to dividends at a fixed rate, not exceeding the legal rate of interest in the State of incorporation or 8 percent per annum, whichever is greater, on the value of the consideration for which the stock was issued, if its articles of incorporation require:

(1) That the preferred stock be retired at par as soon as sufficient funds available therefor are realized from sales, and

(2) That all funds not required for the payment of dividends upon or for the retirement of preferred stock be used

by the company for the care and improvement of the cemetery property.

For purposes of this subparagraph, the term "legal rate of interest" shall mean the rate of interest prescribed by law in the State of incorporation which prevails in the absence of an agreement between contracting parties fixing a rate.

PAR. 4. Paragraph (d) of proposed § 1.501(c)(13)-1, as published in the FEDERAL REGISTER on July 8, 1975 (40 FR 28613), is amended by revising the first sentence to read as follows:

Proposed § 1.501(c)(13)-1 Cemetery companies and crematoria. [*For Preamble, see ¶ 150,405*]

* * * * *

(d) Sales to exempt cemetery companies and crematoria. Except as provided in paragraph (c)(2) of this section (relating to transitional rule for preferred stock), a cemetery company or crematorium is not exempt from income tax if property is transferred to such organization in exchange for an equity interest so long as such equity interest remains outstanding and retains its character as an equity interest. * * *

§ 1.501(c)(14)-1 Credit unions and mutual insurance funds.

Caution: The Treasury has not yet amended Reg § 1.501(c)(14)-1 to reflect changes made by P.L. 99-514, P.L. 89-352.

Credit unions (other than Federal credit unions described in section 501(c)(1)) without capital stock, organized and operated for mutual purposes and without profit, are exempt from tax under section 501(a). Corporations or associations without capital stock organized before September 1, 1951, and operated for mutual purposes and without profit for the purpose of providing reserve funds for, and insurance of, shares or deposits in:

(a) Domestic building and loan associations as defined in section 7701(a)(19),

(b) Cooperative banks without capital stock organized and operated for mutual purposes and without profit, or

(c) Mutual savings banks not having capital stock represented by shares, are also exempt from tax under section 501(a). In addition, corporations or associations of the type described in the preceding sentence which were organized on or after September 1, 1951, but before September 1, 1957, are exempt from tax under section 501(a) for taxable years beginning after December 31, 1959.

T.D. 6301, 7/8/58, amend T.D. 6493, 9/26/60.

§ 1.501(c)(15)-1 Mutual insurance companies or associations.

Caution: The Treasury has not yet amended Reg § 1.501(c)(15)-1 to reflect changes made by P.L. 108-218, P.L. 99-514.

(a) Taxable years beginning after December 31, 1962. An insurance company or association described in section 501(c)(15) is exempt under section 501(a) if it is a mutual company or association (other than life or marine) or if it is a mutual interinsurer or reciprocal underwriter (other than life or marine) and if the gross amount received during the taxable year from the sum of the following items does not exceed $150,000:

(1) The gross amount of income during the taxable year from:

(i) Interest (including tax-exempt interest and partially tax-exempt interest), as described in § 1.61-7. Interest shall be adjusted for amortization of premium and accrual of discount in accordance with the rules prescribed in section 822(d)(2) and the regulations thereunder.

(ii) Dividends, as described in § 1.61-9.

(iii) Rents and royalties, as described in § 1.61-8.

(iv) The entering into of any lease, mortgage, or other instrument or agreement from which the company may derive interest, rents, or royalties.

(v) The alteration or termination of any instrument or agreement described in subdivision (iv) of this subparagraph.

(2) The gross income from any trade or business (other than an insurance business) carried on by the company or association, or by a partnership of which the company or association is a partner.

(3) Premiums (including deposits and assessments).

(b) Taxable years beginning after December 31, 1954, and before January 1, 1963. An insurance company or association described in section 501(c)(15) and paragraph (a) of this section is exempt under section 501(a) if the gross amount received during the taxable year from the sum of the items described in paragraph (a)(1), (2), and (3) of this section does not exceed $75,000.

(c) No double inclusion of income. In computing the gross income from any trade or business (other than an insurance business) carried on by the company or association, or by a partnership of which the company or association is a partner, any item described in section 822(b)(1)(A), (B), or (C) and paragraph (a)(1) of this section shall not be considered as gross income arising from the conduct of such trade or business, but shall be taken into account under section 822(b)(1)(A), (B), or (C) and paragraph (a)(1) of this section.

(d) Taxable years beginning after December 31, 1953, and before January 1, 1955. An insurance company or association described in section 501(c)(15) is exempt under section 501(a) if it is a mutual company or association (other than life or marine) or if it is a mutual interinsurer or reciprocal underwriter (other than life or marine) and if the gross amount received during the taxable year from the sum of the following items does not exceed $75,000:

(1) The gross amount of income during the taxable year from—

(i) Interest (including tax-exempt interest and partially tax-exempt interest), as described in § 1.61-7. Interest shall be adjusted for amortization of premium and accrual of discount in accordance with the rules prescribed in section 822(d)(2) and § 1.822-3.

(ii) Dividends, as described in § 1.61-9.

(iii) Rents (but excluding royalties), as described in § 1.61-8.

(2) Premiums (including deposits and assessments).

(e) Exclusion of capital gains. Gains from sales or exchanges of capital assets to the extent provided in subchapter P (section 1201 and following, relating to capital gains and losses), chapter 1 of the Code, shall be excluded from the amounts described in this section.

T.D. 6301, 7/8/58, amend T.D. 6662, 7/8/63.

§ 1.501(c)(16)-1 Corporations organized to finance crop operations.

A corporation organized by a farmers' cooperative marketing or purchasing association, or the members thereof, for the purpose of financing the ordinary crop operations of such members or other producers is exempt, provided the marketing or purchasing association is exempt under section 521 and the financing corporation is operated in conjunction with the marketing or purchasing association. The provisions of § 1.521-1 relating to a reserve or surplus and to capital stock shall also apply to corporations coming under this section.

T.D. 6301, 7/8/58.

§ 1.501(c)(17)-1 Supplemental unemployment benefit trusts.

Caution: The Treasury has not yet amended Reg § 1.501(c)(17)-1 to reflect changes made by P.L. 99-514.

(a) Requirements for qualification. *(1)* A supplemental unemployment benefit trust may be exempt as an organization described in section 501(c)(17) if the requirements of subparagraphs (2) through (6) of this paragraph are satisfied.

(2) The trust is a valid, existing trust under local law and is evidenced by an executed written document.

(3) The trust is part of a written plan established and maintained by an employer, his employees, or both the employer and his employees, solely for the purpose of providing supplemental unemployment compensation benefits (as defined in section 501(c)(17)(D) and paragraph (b)(1) of § 1.501(c)(17)-1).

(4) The trust is part of a plan which provides that the corpus and income of the trust cannot (in the taxable year, and at any time thereafter, before the satisfaction of all liabilities to employees covered by the plan) be used for, or diverted to, any purpose other than the providing of supplemental unemployment compensation benefits. Thus, if the plan provides for the payment of any benefits other than supplemental unemployment compensation benefits as defined in paragraph (b) of this section, the trust will not be entitled to exemption as an organization described in section 501(c)(17). However, the payment of any necessary or appropriate expenses in connection with the administration of a plan providing supplemental unemployment compensation benefits shall be considered a payment to provide such benefits and shall not affect the qualification of the trust.

(5) The trust is part of a plan whose eligibility conditions and benefits do not discriminate in favor of employees who are officers, shareholders, persons whose principal duties consist of supervising the work of other employees, or highly compensated employees. See sections 401(a)(3)(B) and 401(a)(4) and §§ 1.401-3 and 1.401-4. However, a plan is not discriminatory within the meaning of section 501(c)(17)(A)(iii), relating to the requirement that the benefits paid under the plan be nondiscriminatory, merely because the benefits received under the plan bear a uniform relationship to the total compensation, or the basic or regular rate of compensation, of the employees covered by the plan. Accordingly, the benefits provided for highly paid employees may be greater than the benefits provided for lower paid employees if the benefits are determined by reference to their compensation; but, in such a case, the plan will not qualify if the benefits paid to the higher paid employees bear a larger ratio to their compensation than the benefits paid to the lower paid employees bear to their compensation. In addition, section 501(c)(17)(B) sets forth certain other instances in which a plan will not be considered discriminatory (see paragraph (c) of § 1.501(c)(17)-2).

(6) The trust is part of a plan which requires that benefits are to be determined according to objective standards. Thus, a plan may provide similarly situated employees with benefits which differ in kind and amount, but may not permit such benefits to be determined solely in the discretion of the trustees.

(b) Meaning of terms. The following terms are defined for purposes of section 501(c)(17):

(1) Supplemental unemployment compensation benefits. The term "supplemental unemployment compensation benefits" means only:

(i) Benefits paid to an employee because of his involuntary separation from the employment of the employer, whether or not such separation is temporary, but only when such separation is one resulting directly from a reduction in force, the discontinuance of a plant or operation, or other similar conditions; and

(ii) Sick and accident benefits subordinate to the benefits described in subdivision (i) of this subparagraph.

(2) Employee. The term "employee" means an individual whose status is that of an employee under the usual common-law rules applicable in determining the employer-employee relationship. The term "employee" also includes an individual who qualifies as an "employee" under the State or Federal unemployment compensation law covering his employment, whether or not such an individual could qualify as an employee under such common-law rules.

(3) Involuntary separation from the employment of the employer. Whether a "separation" from the employment of the employer" occurs is a question to be decided with regard to all the facts and circumstances. However, for purposes of section 501(c)(17), the term "separation" includes both a temporary separation and a permanent severance of the employment relationship. Thus, for example, an employee may be separated from the employment of his employer even though at the time of separation it is believed that he will be reemployed by the same employer. Whether or not an employee is "involuntarily" separated from the employment of the employer is a question of fact. However, normally, an employee will not be deemed to have separated himself voluntarily from the employment of his employer merely because his collective bargaining agreement provides for the termination of his services upon the happening of a condition subsequent and that condition does in fact occur. For example, if the collective bargaining agreement provides that the employer may automate a given department and thereby dislocate several employees, the fact that the employees' collective bargaining agent has consented to such a condition will not render any employee's subsequent unemployment for such cause voluntary.

(4) Other similar conditions. Involuntary separation directly resulting from "other similar conditions" includes, for example, involuntary separation from the employment of the employer resulting from cyclical, seasonal, or technological causes. Some causes of involuntary separation from the employment of the employer which are not similar to those enumerated in section 501(c)(17)(D)(i) are separation for disciplinary reasons or separation because of age.

(5) Subordinate sick and accident benefits. In general, a sick and accident benefit payment is an amount paid to an employee in the event of his illness or personal injury (whether or not such illness or injury results in the employee's separation from the service of his employer). In ad-

dition, the phrase "sick and accident benefits" includes amounts provided under the plan to reimburse an employee for amounts he expends because of the illness or injury of his spouse or a dependent (as defined in section 152). Sick and accident benefits may be paid by a trust described in section 501(c)(17) only if such benefits are subordinate to the separation payments provided under the plan of which the trust forms a part. Whether the sick and accident benefits provided under a supplemental unemployment compensation benefit plan are subordinate to the separation benefits provided under such plan is a question to be decided with regard to all the facts and circumstances.

T.D. 6972, 9/11/68.

§ 1.501(c)(17)-2 General rules.

(a) Supplemental unemployment compensation benefits. Supplemental unemployment compensation benefits as defined in section 501(c)(17)(D) and paragraph (b)(1) of § 1.501(c)(17)-1 may be paid in a lump sum or installments. Such benefits may be paid to an employee who has, subsequent to his separation from the employment of the employer, obtained other part-time, temporary, or permanent employment. Furthermore, such payments may be made in cash, services, or property. Thus, supplemental unemployment compensation benefits provided to involuntarily separated employees may include, for example, the following: Furnishing of medical care at an established clinic, furnishing of food, job training and schooling, and job counseling. If such benefits are furnished in services or property, the fair market value of the benefits must satisfy the requirements of section 501(c)(17)(A)(iii), relating to nondiscrimination as to benefits. However, supplemental unemployment compensation benefits may be provided only to an employee and only under circumstances described in paragraph (b)(1) of § 1.501(c)(17)-1. Thus, a trust described in section 501(c)(17) may not provide, for example, for the payment of a death, vacation, or retirement benefit.

(b) Sick and accident benefits. If a trust described in section 501(c)(17) provides for the payment of sick and accident benefits, such benefits may only be provided for employees who are eligible for receipt of separation benefits under the plan of which the trust is a part. However, the sick and accident benefits need not be provided for all the employees who are eligible for receipt of separation benefits, so long as the plan does not discriminate in favor of persons with respect to whom discrimination is proscribed in section 501(c)(17)(A)(ii) and (iii). Furthermore, the portion of the plan which provides for the payment of sick and accident benefits must satisfy the nondiscrimination requirements of section 501(c)(17)(A)(ii) and (iii) without regard to the portion of the plan which provides for the payment of benefits because of involuntary separation.

(c) Correlation with other plans. *(1)* In determining whether a plan meets the requirements of section 501(c)(17)(A)(ii) and (iii), any benefits provided under any other plan shall not be taken into consideration except in the particular instances enumerated in section 501(c)(17)(B)(i), (ii), and (iii). In general, these three exceptions permit a plan providing for the payment of supplemental unemployment compensation benefits to satisfy the nondiscrimination requirements in section 501(c)(17)(A)(ii) and (iii) if the plan is able to satisfy such requirements when it is correlated with one or more of the plans described in section 501(c)(17)(B).

(2) Under section 501(c)(17)(B)(i), a plan will not be considered discriminatory merely because the benefits under the plan which are first determined in a nondiscriminatory manner (within the meaning of section 501(c)(17)(A)) are then reduced by any sick accident, or unemployment compensation benefits received under State or Federal law, or are reduced by a portion of these benefits if determined in a nondiscriminatory manner. Under this exception, a plan may, for example, satisfy the requirements of section 501(c)(17)(A)(iii) if it provides for the payment of an unemployment benefit and the amount of such benefit is determined as a percentage of the employee's compensation which is then reduced by any unemployment benefit which the employee receives under a State plan. In addition, a plan could provide for the reduction of such a plan benefit by a percentage of the State benefit. Furthermore, a plan may also satisfy the requirements of section 501(c)(17)(A) if it provides for the payment to an employee of an amount which when added to any State unemployment benefit equals a percentage of the employee's compensation.

(3) Under section 501(c)(17)(B)(ii), a plan will not be considered discriminatory merely because the plan provides benefits only for employees who are not eligible to receive sick, accident, or unemployment compensation benefits under State or Federal law. In such a case, however, the benefits provided under the plan seeking to satisfy the requirements of section 501(c)(17) must be the same benefits, or a portion of the same benefits if determined in a non-discriminatory manner, which such ineligible employees would receive under State or Federal law if they were eligible for such benefits. Under this exception, for example, an employer may establish a plan only for employees who have exhausted their benefits under the State law, and, if the plan provides for such employees the same benefits which they would receive under the State plan, the State plan and the plan of the employer will be considered as one plan in determining whether the requirements relating to nondiscrimination in section 501(c)(17)(A) are satisfied. Furthermore, such a plan could also qualify even though it does not provide all of the benefits provided under the State plan. Thus, a plan could provide for the payment of a reduced amount of the benefits, or for the payment of only certain of the types of benefits, provided by the State plan. For example, if the State plan provides for the payment of sick, accident, and separation benefits, the plan of the employer may provide for the payment of only separation benefits, or for the payment of an amount equal to only one-half of the State provided benefit. However, if a plan provides benefits for employees who are not eligible to receive the benefits provided under a State plan and such benefits are greater or of a different type than those under the State plan, the plan of the employer must satisfy the requirements of section 501(c)(17)(A) without regard to the benefits and coverage provided by the State plan.

(4) Under section 501(c)(17)(B)(iii), a plan is not considered discriminatory merely because the plan provides benefits only for employees who are not eligible to receive benefits under another plan which satisfies the requirements of section 501(c)(17)(A) and which is funded solely by contributions of the employer. In such a case, the plan seeking to qualify under section 501(c)(17) must provide the same benefits, or a portion of such benefits if determined in a nondiscriminatory manner, as are provided for the employees under the plan funded solely by employer contributions. Furthermore, this exception only applies if the employees eligible to receive benefits under both plans would satisfy the requirements in section 501(c)(17)(A)(ii), relating to nondiscrimination as to coverage. The plan of the employer which is being correlated with the plan seeking to satisfy the

requirements of section 501(c)(17) may be a plan which forms part of a voluntary employees' beneficiary association described in section 501(c)(9), if such plan satisfies all the requirements of section 501(c)(17)(A). Under this exception, for example, if an employer has established a plan providing for the payment of supplemental unemployment compensation benefits for his hourly wage employees and such plan satisfies the requirements of section 501(c)(17)(A) (even though the plan forms part of a voluntary employees' beneficiary association described in section 501(c)(9)), the salaried employees of such employer may establish a plan for themselves, and, if such plan provides for the same benefits as the plan covering hourly-wage employees, both plans may be considered as one plan in determining whether the plan covering the salaried employees satisfies the requirement that it be nondiscriminatory as to coverage. The foregoing example would also be applicable if the benefits provided for the salaried employees were funded solely or in part by employer contributions.

(d) Permanency of the plan. A plan providing for the payment of supplemental unemployment compensation benefits contemplates a permanent as distinguished from a temporary program. Thus, although there may be reserved the right to change or terminate the plan, and to discontinue contributions thereunder, the abandonment of the plan for any reason other than business necessity within a few years after it has taken effect will be evidence that the plan from its inception was not a bona fide program for the purpose of providing supplemental unemployment compensation benefits to employees. Whether or not a particular plan constitutes a permanent arrangement will be determined by all of the surrounding facts and circumstances. However, merely because a collective bargaining agreement provides that a plan may be modified at the termination of such agreement, or that particular provisions of the plan are subject to renegotiation during the duration of such agreement, does not necessarily imply that the plan is not a permanent arrangement. Moreover, the fact that the plan provides that the assets remaining in the trust after the satisfaction of all liabilities (including contingent liabilities) under the plan may be returned to the employer does not imply that the plan is not a permanent arrangement nor preclude the trust from qualifying under section 501(c)(17).

(e) Portions of years. A plan must satisfy the requirements of section 501(c)(17) throughout the entire taxable year of the trust in order for the trust to be exempt for such year. However, section 501(c)(17)(C) provides that a plan will satisfy the nondiscrimination as to classification requirements of section 501(c)(17)(A) if on at least one day in each quarter of the taxable year of the trust it satisfies such requirements.

(f) Several trusts constituting one plan. Several trusts may be designated as constituting part of one plan which is intended to satisfy the requirements of section 501(c)(17), in which case all of such trusts taken as a whole must meet the requirements of such section. The fact that a combination of trusts fails to satisfy the requirements of section 501(c)(17) as one plan does not prevent such of the trusts as satisfy the requirements of section 501(c)(17) from qualifying for exemption under that section.

(g) Plan of several employers. A trust forming part of a plan of several employers, or the employees of several employers, will be a supplemental unemployment benefit trust described in section 501(c)(17) if all the requirements of that section are otherwise satisfied.

(h) Investment of trust funds. No specific limitations are provided in section 501(c)(17) with respect to investments which may be made by the trustees of a trust qualifying under that section. Generally, the contributions may be used by the trustees to purchase any investments permitted by the trust agreement to the extent allowed by local law. However, the tax-exempt status of the trust will be forfeited if the investments made by the trustees constitute "prohibited transactions" within the meaning of section 503. See section 503 and the regulations thereunder. In addition, such a trust will be subject to tax under section 511 with respect to any "unrelated business taxable income" (as defined in section 512) realized by it from its investments. See sections 511 to 515, inclusive, and the regulations thereunder.

(i) Allocations. If a plan which provides sick and accident benefits is financed solely by employer contributions to the trust, and such sick and accident benefits are funded by payment of premiums on an accident or health insurance policy (whether on a group or individual basis) or by contributions to a separate fund which pays such sick and accident benefits, the plan must specify that portion of the contributions to be used to fund such benefits. If a plan which is financed in whole or in part by employee contributions provides sick and accident benefits, the plan must specify the portion, if any, of employee contributions allocated to the cost of funding such benefits, and must allocate the cost of funding such benefits between employer contributions and employee contributions.

(j) Required records and returns. Every trust described in section 501(c)(17) must maintain records indicating the amount of separation benefits and sick and accident benefits which have been provided to each employee. If a plan is financed, in whole or in part, by employee contributions to the trust, the trust must maintain records indicating the amount of each employee's total contributions allocable to separation benefits. In addition, every trust described in section 501(c)(17) which makes one or more payments totaling $600 or more in 1 year to an individual must file an annual information return in the manner described in paragraph (b)(1) of § 1.6041-2. However, if the payments from such trust are subject to income tax withholding under section 3402(o) and the regulations thereunder, the trust must file, in lieu of such annual information return, the returns of income tax withheld from wages required by section 6011 and the regulations thereunder. In such circumstances, the trust must also furnish the statements to the recipients of trust distributions required by section 6051 and the regulations thereunder.

T.D. 6972, 9/11/68, amend T.D. 7068, 11/10/70.

§ 1.501(c)(17)-3 Relation to other sections of the Code.

(a) Taxability of benefit distributions. *(1) Separation benefits.* If the separation benefits described in section 501(c)(17)(D)(i) are funded entirely by employer contributions, then the full amount of any separation benefit payment received by an employee is includible in his gross income under section 61(a). If any such separation benefit is funded by both employer and employee contributions, or solely by employee contributions, the amount of any separation benefit payment which is includible in the gross income of the employee is the amount by which such distribution and any prior distributions of such separation payments exceeds the employee's total contributions to fund such separation benefits.

(2) Sick and accident benefits. Any benefit payment received from the trust under the part of the plan, if any,

which provides for the payment of sick and accident benefits must be included in gross income under section 61(a), unless specifically excluded under section 104 or 105 and the regulations thereunder. See section 105(b) and § 1.105-2 for benefit payments expended for medical care, benefit payments in excess of actual medical expenses, and benefit payments which an employee is entitled to receive irrespective of whether or not he incurs expenses for medical care. See section 213 and § 1.213-1(g) for benefit payments representing reimbursement for medical expenses paid in prior years. See § 1.501(c)(17)-2(i) for the requirement that a trust described in section 501(c)(17) which receives employee contributions must be part of a written plan which provides for the allocation of the cost of funding sick and accident benefits.

(b) Exemption as a voluntary employees' beneficiary association. Section 501(c)(17)(E) contemplates that a trust forming part of a plan providing for the payment of supplemental unemployment compensation benefits may, if it qualifies, apply for exemption from income tax under section 501(a) either as a voluntary employees' beneficiary association described in section 501(c)(9) or as a trust described in section 501(c)(17).

(c) Returns. A trust which is described in section 501(c)(17) and which is exempt from tax under section 501(a) must file a return in accordance with section 6033 and the regulations thereunder. If such a trust realizes any unrelated business taxable income, as defined in section 512, the trust is also required to file a return with respect to such income.

(d) Effective date. Section 501(c)(17) shall apply to taxable years beginning after December 31, 1959, and shall apply to supplemental unemployment benefit trusts regardless of when created or organized.

T.D. 6972, 9/11/68.

§ 1.501(c)(18)-1 Certain funded pension trusts.

Caution: The Treasury has not yet amended Reg § 1.501(c)(18)-1 to reflect changes made by P.L. 100-647, P.L. 99-514.

(a) In general. Organizations described in section 501(c)(18) are trusts created before June 25, 1959, forming part of a plan for the payment of benefits under a pension plan funded only by contributions of employees. In order to be exempt, such trusts must also meet the requirements set forth in section 501(c)(18)(A), (B), and (C), and in paragraph (b) of this section.

(b) Requirements for qualification. A trust described in section 501(c)(18) must meet the following requirements—

(1) Local law. The trust must be a valid, existing trust under local law, and must be evidenced by an executed written document.

(2) Funding. The trust must be funded solely from contributions of employees who are members of the plan. For purposes of this section, the term "contributions of employees" shall include earnings on, and gains derived from, the assets of the trust which were contributed by employees.

(3) Creation before June 25, 1959. (i) In general. The trust must have been created before June 25, 1959. A trust created before June 25, 1959 is described in section 501(c)(18) and this section even though changes in the makeup of the trust have occurred since that time so long as these are not fundamental changes in the character of the trust or in the character of the beneficiaries of the trust. Increases in the beneficiaries of the trust by the addition of employees in the same or related industries, whether such additions are of individuals or of units (such as local units of a union) will generally not be considered a fundamental change in the character of the trust. A merger of a trust created after June 25, 1959 into a trust created before such date is not in itself a fundamental change in the character of the latter trust if the two trusts are for the benefit of employees of the same or related industries.

(ii) Examples. The provisions of this subparagraph may be illustrated by the following examples:

Example (1). Assume that trust C, for the benefit of members of participating locals of National Union X, was established in 1950 and adopted by 29 locals before June 25, 1959. The subsequent adoption of trust C by additional locals of National Union X in 1962 will not constitute a fundamental change in the character of trust C, since such subsequent adoption is by employees in a related industry.

Example (2). Assume the facts as stated in example (1), except that in 1965 National Union X merged with National Union Y, whose members are engaged in trades related to these engaged in by X's members. Assume further that trust D, the employee funded pension plan and fund for employees of Y, was subsequently merged into trust C. The merger of trust D into trust C would not in itself constitute a fundamental change in the character of trust C, since both C and D are for the benefit of employees of related industries.

(4) Payment of benefits. The trust must provide solely for the payment of pension or retirement benefits to its beneficiaries. For purposes of this section, the term "retirement benefits" is intended to include customary and incidental benefits, such as death benefits within the limits permissible under section 401.

(5) Diversion. The trust must be part of a plan which provides that, before the satisfaction of all liabilities to employees covered by the plan, the corpus and income of the trust cannot (within the taxable year and at any time thereafter) be used for, or diverted to, any purpose other than the providing of pension or retirement benefits. Payment of expenses in connection with the administration of a plan providing pension or retirement benefits shall be considered a payment to provide such benefits and shall not affect the qualification of the trust.

(6) Discrimination. The trust must be part of a plan whose eligibility conditions and benefits do not discriminate in favor of employees who are officers, shareholders, persons whose principal duties consist of supervising the work of other employees, or highly compensated employees. See sections 401(a)(3)(B) and 401(a)(4) and §§ 1.401-3 and 1.401-4. However, a plan is not discriminatory within the meaning of section 501(c)(18) merely because the benefits received under the plan bear a uniform relationship to the total compensation, or the basic or regular rate of compensation, of the employees covered by the plan. Accordingly, the benefits provided for highly paid employees may be greater than the benefits provided for lower paid employees if the benefits are determined by reference to their compensation; but, in such a case, the plan will not qualify if the benefits paid to the higher paid employees are a larger portion of compensation than the benefits paid to lower paid employees.

(7) Objective standards. The trust must be part of a plan which requires that benefits be determined according to objective standards. Thus, while a plan may provide similarly situated employees with benefits which differ in kind and amount, these benefits may not be determined solely in the discretion of the trustees.

(c) Effective date. The provisions of section 501(c)(18) and this section shall apply with respect to taxable years beginning after December 31, 1969.

T.D. 7172, 3/16/72.

§ 1.501(c)(19)-1 War veterans organizations.

(a) In general. *(1)* For taxable years beginning after December 31, 1969, a veterans post or organization which is organized in the United States or any of its possessions may be exempt as an organization described in section 501(c)(19) if the requirements of paragraphs (b) and (c) of this section are met and if no part of its net earnings inures to the benefit of any private shareholder or individual. Paragraph (b) of this section contains the membership requirements such a post or organization must meet in order to qualify under section 501(c)(19). Paragraph (c) of this section outlines the purposes, at least one of which such a post or organization must have in order to so qualify.

(2) In addition, an auxiliary unit or society described in paragraph (d) of this section of such a veterans post or organization and a trust or foundation described in paragraph (e) of this section for such post or organization may be exempt as an organization described in section 501(c)(19).

(b) Membership requirements. *(1)* In order to be described in section 501(c)(19) under paragraph (a)(1) of this section, an organization must meet the membership requirements of section 501(c)(19)(B) and this paragraph. There are two requirements that must be met under this paragraph. The first requirement is that at least 75 percent of the members of the organization must be war veterans. For purposes of this section the term "war veterans" means persons, whether or not present members of the United States Armed Forces, who have served in the Armed Forces of the United States during a period of war (including the Korean and Vietnam conflicts).

(2) The second requirement of this paragraph is that at least 97.5 percent of all members of the organization must be described in one or more of the following categories:

(i) War veterans,

(ii) Present or former members of the United States Armed Forces,

(iii) Cadets (including only students in college or university ROTC programs or at Armed Services academies), or

(iv) Spouses, widows, or widowers of individuals referred to in paragraph (b)(2)(i), (ii) or (iii) of this section.

(c) Exempt purposes. In addition to the requirements of paragraphs (a)(1) and (b) of this section, in order to be described in section 501(c)(19) under paragraph (a)(1) of this section an organization must be operated exclusively for one or more of the following purposes:

(1) To promote the social welfare of the community as defined in § 1.501(c)(4)-1(a)(2),

(2) To assist disabled and needy war veterans and members of the United States Armed Forces and their dependents, and the widows and orphans of deceased veterans,

(3) To provide entertainment, care, and assistance to hospitalized veterans or members of the Armed Forces of the United States,

(4) To carry on programs to perpetuate the memory of deceased veterans and members of the Armed Forces and to comfort their survivors,

(5) To conduct programs for religious, charitable, scientific, literary, or educational purposes,

(6) To sponsor or participate in activities of a patriotic nature,

(7) To provide insurance benefits for their members or dependents of their members or both, or

(8) To provide social and recreational activities for their members.

(d) Auxiliary units or societies for war veterans organizations. A unit or society may be exempt as an organization described in section 501(c)(19) and paragraph (a)(2) of this section if it is an auxiliary unit or society of a post or organization of war veterans described in paragraph (a)(1) of this section. A unit or society is an auxiliary unit or society of such a post or organization if it meets the following requirements:

(1) It is affiliated with, and organized in accordance with, the bylaws and regulations formulated by an organization described in paragraph (a)(1) of this section,

(2) At least 75 percent of its members are either war veterans, or spouses of war veterans, or are related to a war veteran within two degrees of consanguinity (i.e., grandparent, brother, sister, grandchild, represent the most distant allowable relationships),

(3) All of its members are either members of an organization described in paragraph (a)(1) of this section, or spouses of a member of such an organization or are related to a member of such an organization, within two degrees of consanguinity, and

(4) No part of its net earnings inures to the benefit of any private shareholder or individual.

(e) Trusts or foundations. A trust or foundation may be exempt as an organization described in section 501(c)(19) and paragraph (a)(2) of this section if it is a trust or foundation for a post or organization of war veterans described in paragraph (a)(1) of this section. A trust or foundation is a trust or foundation for such a post or organization if it meets the following requirements:

(1) The trust or foundation is in existence under local law and, if organized for charitable purposes, has a dissolution provision described in § 1.501(c)(3)-1(b)(4).

(2) The corpus or income cannot be diverted or used other than for the funding of a post or organization of war veterans described in paragraph (a)(1) of this section, for section 170(c)(4) purposes, or as an insurance set aside (as defined in § 1.512(a)-4(b).

(3) The trust income is not unreasonably accumulated and, if the trust or foundation is not an insurance set aside, a substantial portion of the income is in fact distributed to such post or organization or for section 170(c)(4) charitable purposes, and

(4) It is organized exclusively for one or more of those purposes enumerated in paragraph (c) of this section.

T.D. 7438, 10/7/76.

Proposed § 1.501(c)(20)-1 Qualified group legal services plan trust. [*For Preamble, see ¶ 150,581*]

(a) Qualified group legal services plan. For purposes of this section, a "qualified group legal services plan" is a plan that satisfies the requirements of section 120(b) and § 1.120-2.

(b) General requirements for exemption. Under section 501(c)(20), an organization or trust created or organized in the United States is exempt as provided in section 501(a) if the exclusive function of the organization or trust is to form part of a qualified group legal services plan or plans.

(c) Exception for trust associated with section 501(c) organization. As described in section 120(c)(5)(C), employer contributions under a qualified group legal services plan may be paid to an organization described in section 501(c) if that organization is permitted by section 501(c) to receive payments from an employer for support of a qualified group legal services plan. However, that organization must, in turn, pay or credit the contributions to an organization or trust described in section 501(c)(20). In such a case, the organization or trust to which the contributions are finally paid or credited is considered to satisfy the requirement that the *exclusive* function of the organization or trust be to form part of a qualified group legal services plan or plans, notwithstanding that the organization or trust provides legal services or indemnification against the cost of legal services unassociated with such a qualified plan. This exception applies, however, only if any such legal service or indemnification is provided under a program established and maintained by the organization described in section 501(c) to which the employer contributions under a qualified group legal services plan are first paid under section 120(c)(5)(C). Whether providing legal services or indemnification against the cost of legal services unassociated with a qualified group legal services plan is a permissible activity of an organization described in section 501(c) is determined under the rules under that paragraph of section 501(c) in which the organization is described.

§ 1.501(c)(21)-1 Black lung trusts—certain terms.

(a) Created or organized in the United States. A trust is not "created or organized in the United States" unless it is maintained at all times as a domestic trust in the United States. For this purpose, section 7701(a)(9) limits the term "United States" to the District of Columbia and States of the United States.

(b) Insurance company. The term "insurance company" means an insurance, surety, bonding or other company whose liability for the kinds of claims to which section 501(c)(21)(A)(i) applies is as an insurer or guarantor of the liabilities of another.

(c) Black Lung Acts. The term "Black Lung Acts" includes any State law providing compensation for disability or death due to pneumoconiosis even though the State law compensates for other kinds of injuries. In such a case, section 501(c)(21) applies only to the extent that the liability is attributable to disability or death due to pneumoconiosis. For this purpose, the term "pneumoconiosis" has the same meaning as it has under federal law. See 30 U.S.C. 902.

(d) Insurance exclusively covering such liability. The term "insurance exclusively covering such liability" includes insurance that covers risk for liabilities in addition to the liabilities to which section 501(c)(21)(A)(i) applies. In such a case, payment for premiums may be made from the trust only to the extent of that portion of the premiums that has been separately allocated and stated by the insurer as attributable solely to coverage of the liabilities to which section 501(c)(21)(A)(i) applies.

(e) Administrative and other incidental expenses. The term "administrative and other incidental expenses" means expenditures that are appropriate and helpful to the trust making them in carrying out the purposes for which its assets may be used under section 501(c)(21)(B). The term includes any excise tax imposed on the trust under section 4952 (relating to taxes on taxable expenditures) and reasonable expenses, such as legal expenses, incurred by the trust in connection with an assertion against the trust of liability for a taxable expenditure. The term does not include an excise tax imposed on the trustee or on other disqualified persons under section 4951 (relating to taxes on self-dealing) or under section 4953 (relating to tax on excess contributions to black lung benefit trusts) or any expenses incurred in connection with the assertion of these taxes other than expenses that are treated as part of reasonable compensation under section 4951(d)(2)(C). See §§ 53.4941(d)-2(f)(3) and (d)-3(c) for interpretations of similar provisions under section 4941(d)(2)(E), relating to reasonable compensation for private foundation disqualified persons.

(f) Public debt securities of the United States. The term "public debt securities of the United States" means obligations that are taken into consideration for purposes of the public debt limit. See, for example, 31 U.S.C. 757b.

(g) Obligations of a State or local government. The term "obligations of a State or local government" means the obligations of a State or local governmental unit the interest on which is exempt from tax under section 103(a). See § 1.103-1(a).

(h) Time or demand deposits. The term "time or demand deposits" includes checking accounts, savings accounts, certificates of deposit or other time or demand deposits. The term does not include common or collective trust funds such as a common trust fund as defined in section 584.

T.D. 7644, 9/6/79.

§ 1.501(c)(21)-2 Same—trust instrument.

A trust does not meet the requirements of section 501(c)(21) if it is not established and maintained pursuant to a written instrument. The trust instrument must definitely and affirmatively prohibit a diversion or use of trust assets that is not permitted under section 501(c)(21)(B) or section 4953(c), whether by operation or natural termination of the trust, by power of revocation or amendment, by the happening of a contingency, by collateral arrangement, or by any other means. No particular form for the trust instrument is required. A trust may meet the requirements of section 501(c)(21) although the trust instrument fails to contain provisions the effects of which are to prohibit acts that are subject to section 4951 (relating to taxes on self-dealing), section 4952 (relating to taxes on taxable expenditures) or the retention of contributions subject to section 4953 (relating to tax on excess contributions to black lung benefit trusts).

T.D. 7644, 9/6/79.

§ 1.501(d)-1 Religious and apostolic associations or corporations.

(a) Religious or apostolic associations or corporations are described in section 501(d) and are exempt from taxation under section 501(a) if they have a common treasury or community treasury, even though they engage in business for the common benefit of the members, provided each of the members includes (at the time of filing his return) in his gross income his entire pro rata share, whether distributed or not, of the net income of the association or corporation for the taxable year of the association or corporation ending with or during his taxable year. Any amount so included in the gross income of a member shall be treated as a dividend received.

(b) For annual return requirements of organizations described in section 501(d), see section 6033 and paragraph (a)(5) of § 1.6033-1.

T.D. 6301, 7/8/58.

---

§ 1.501(e)-1 Cooperative hospital service organizations.

Caution: The Treasury has not yet amended Reg § 1.501(e)-1 to reflect changes made by P.L. 100-647.

(a) General rule. Section 501(e) is the exclusive and controlling section under which a cooperative hospital service organization can qualify as a charitable organization. A cooperative hospital service organization which meets the requirements of section 501(e) and this section shall be treated as an organization described in section 501(c)(3), exempt from taxation under section 501(a), and referred to in section 170(b)(1)(A)(iii) (relating to percentage limitations on charitable contributions). In order to qualify for tax exempt status, a cooperative hospital service organization must—

(1) Be organized and operated on a cooperative basis,

(2) Perform, on a centralized basis, only one or more specifically enumerated services which, if performed directly by a tax exempt hospital, would constitute activities in the exercise or performance of the purpose or function constituting the basis for its exemption, and

(3) Perform such service or services solely for two or more patron-hospitals as described in paragraph (d) of this section.

(b) Organized and operated on a cooperative basis. *(1) In general.* In order to meet the requirements of section 501(e), the organization must be organized and operated on a cooperative basis (whether or not under a specific statute on cooperatives) and must allocate or pay all of its net earnings within 8½ months after the close of the taxable year to its patron-hospitals on the basis of the percentage of its services performed for each patron. To "allocate" its net earnings to its patron-hospitals, the organization must make appropriate bookkeeping entries and provide timely written notice to each patron-hospital disclosing to the patron-hospital the amount allocated to it on the books of the organization. For the recordkeeping requirements of a section 501(e) organization, see § 1.521-1(a)(1).

(2) Percentage of services defined. The percentage of services performed for each patron-hospital may be determined on the basis of either the value or the quantity of the services provided by the organization to the patron-hospital, provided such basis is realistic in terms of the actual cost of the services to the organization.

(3) Retention of net earnings. Exemption will not be denied a cooperative hospital service organization solely because the organization, instead of paying all net earnings to its patron-hospitals, retains an amount for such purposes as retiring indebtedness, expanding the services of the organization, or for any other necessary purpose and allocates such amounts to its patrons. However, such funds may not be accumulated beyond the reasonably anticipated needs of the organization. See, § 1.537-1(b). Whether there is an improper accumulation of funds depends upon the particular circumstances of each case. Moreover, where an organization retains net earnings for necessary purposes, the organization's records must show each patron's rights and interests in the funds retained. For purposes of this paragraph, the term "net earnings" does not include capital contributions to the organization and such contributions need not satisfy the allocation or payment requirements.

(4) Nonpatronage and other income. An organization described in section 501(e) may, in addition to net earnings, receive membership dues and related membership assessment fees, gifts, grants and income from nonpatronage sources such as investment of retained earnings. However, such an organization cannot be exempt if it engages in any business other than that of providing the specified services, described in paragraph (c), for the specified patron-hospitals, described in paragraph (d). Thus, an organization described in section 501(e) generally cannot have unrelated business taxable income as defined in section 512, although it may earn certain interest, annuities, royalties, and rents which are excluded from unrelated business taxable income because of the modifications contained in section 512(b)(1), (2) or (3). An organization described in section 501(e) may, however, have debt-financed income which is treated as unrelated business taxable income solely because of the applicability of section 514. In addition, exempt status under section 501(e) will not be affected where rent from personal property leased with real property is treated as unrelated business taxable income under section 512(b)(3)(A)(ii) solely because the rent attributable to the personal property is more than incidental or under section 512(b)(3)(B)(i) solely because the rent attributable to the personal property exceeds 50 percent of the total rent received or accrued under the lease. Exemption will not be affected solely because the determination of the amount of rent depends in whole or in part on the income or profits derived from the property leased. See section 512(b)(3)(B)(ii). An organization described in section 501(e) may also derive nonpatronage income from sources that are incidental to the conduct of its exempt purposes or functions. For example, income derived from the operation of a cafeteria or vending machines primarily for the convenience of its employees or the disposition of by-products in substantially the same state they were in on completion of the exempt function (e.g., the sale of silver waste produced in the processing of x-ray film) will not be considered unrelated business taxable income. See, section 513(a)(2) and § 1.513-1(d)(4)(ii). The nonpatronage and other income permitted under this subparagraph (4) must be allocated or paid as provided in subparagraph (1) or retained as provided in subparagraph (3).

(5) Stock ownership. (i) Capital stock of organization. An organization does not meet the requirements of section 501(e) unless all of the organization's outstanding capital stock, if there is such stock, is held solely by its patron-hospitals. However, no amount may be paid as dividends on the capital stock of the organization. For purposes of the preceding sentence, the term "capital stock" includes common stock (whether voting or nonvoting), preferred stock, or any other form evidencing a proprietary interest in the organization.

(ii) Stock ownership as a condition for obtaining credit. If by statutory requirement a cooperative hospital service organization must be a shareholder in a United States or state chartered corporation as a condition for obtaining credit from that corporate-lender, the ownership of shares and the payment of dividends thereon will not for such reason be a basis for the denial of exemption to the organization. See, e.g., National Consumer Cooperative Bank, 12 U.S.C. 3001 *et seq.*

(c) Scope of services. *(1) Permissible services.* An organization meets the requirements of section 501(e) only if the organization performs, on a centralized basis, one or more of the following services and only such services: data processing, purchasing (including the purchasing and dispensing of drugs and pharmaceuticals to patron-hospitals), warehousing, billing and collection, food, clinical (including radiology), industrial engineering (including the installation, maintenance and repair of biomedical and similar equipment), laboratory, printing, communications, record center, and personnel (including recruitment, selection, testing, training, education and placement of personnel) services. An organization is not described in section 501(e) if, in addition to or instead of one or more of these specified services, the organization performs any other service (other than services referred to under paragraph (b)(4) that are incidental to the conduct of exempt purposes or functions).

(2) Illustration. The provisions of this subparagraph may be illustrated by the following example.

Example. An organization performs industrial engineering services on a cooperative basis solely for patron-hospitals each of which is an organization described in section 501(c)(3) and exempt from taxation under section 501(a). However, in addition to this service, the organization operates laundry services for its patron-hospitals. This cooperative organization does not meet the requirements of this paragraph because it performs laundry services not specified in this paragraph.

(d) Patron-hospitals. *(1) Defined.* Section 501(e) only applies if the organization performs its services solely for two or more patron-hospitals each of which is—

(i) An organization described in section 501(c)(3) which is exempt from taxation under section 501(a),

(ii) A constituent part of an organization described in section 501(c)(3) which is exempt from taxation under section 501(a) and which, if organized and operated as a separate entity, would constitute an organization described in section 501(c)(3), or

(iii) Owned and operated by the United States, a State, the District of Columbia, or a possession of the United States, or a political subdivision or an agency or instrumentality of any of the agency or instrumentality of any of the foregoing.

(2) Business with nonvoting patron-hospitals. Exemption will not be denied a cooperative hospital service organization solely because the organization (whether organized on a stock or membership basis) transacts business with patron-hospitals which do not have voting rights in the organization and therefore do not participate in the decisions affecting the operation of the organization. Where the organization has both patron-hospitals with voting rights and patron-hospitals without such rights, the organization must provide at least 50 percent of its services to patron-hospitals with voting rights in the organization. Thus, the percentage of services provided to nonvoting patrons may not exceed the percentage of such services provided to voting patrons. A patron-hospital will be deemed to have voting rights in the cooperative hospital service organization if the patron-hospital may vote directly on matters affecting the operation of the organization or if the patron-hospital may vote in the election of cooperative board members. Notwithstanding that an organization may have both voting and nonvoting patron-hospitals, patronage refunds must nevertheless be allocated or paid to all patron-hospitals solely on the basis specified in paragraph (b) of this section.

(3) Services to other organizations. An organization does not meet the requirements of section 501(e), if, in addition to performing services for patron-hospitals (entities described in subdivisions (i), (ii) or (iii) of subparagraph (1)), the organization performs any service for any other organization. For example, a cooperative hospital service organization is not exempt if it performs services for convalescent homes for children or the aged, vocational training facilities for the handicapped, educational institutions which do not provide hospital care in their facilities, and proprietary hospitals. However, the provision of the specified services between or among cooperative hospital service organizations meeting the requirements of section 501(e) and this section is permissible. Also permissible is the provision of the specified services to entities which are not patron-hospitals, but only if such services are de minimis and are mandated by a governmental unit as, for example, a condition for licensing.

(e) Effective dates. An organization, other than an organization performing clinical services, may meet the requirements of section 501(e) and be a tax exempt organization for taxable years ending after June 28, 1968. An organization performing clinical services may meet the requirements of section 501(e) and be a tax exempt organization for taxable years ending after December 31, 1976. However, pursuant to the authority contained in section 7805(b) of the Internal Revenue Code, these regulations shall not become effective with respect to an organization which has received a ruling or determination letter from the Internal Revenue Service recognizing its exemption under section 501(e) until January 2, 1987.

T.D. 8100, 9/3/86.

---

§ 1.501(h)-1 Application of the "expenditure test" to expenditures to influence legislation; introduction.

(a) Scope. *(1)* There are certain requirements an organization must meet in order to be a "charity" described in section 501(c)(3). Among other things, section 501(c)(3) states that "no substantial part of the activities of [a charity may consist of] carrying on propaganda, or otherwise attempting to influence legislation, (except as otherwise provided in subsection (h))." This requirement is called the "substantial part test."

(2) Under section 501(h), many public charities may elect the "expenditure test" as a substitute for the substantial part test. The expenditure test is described in section 501(h) and this § 1.501(h). A public charity is any charity that is not a private foundation under section 509(a). (Unlike a public charity, a private foundation may not make any lobbying expenditures: if a private foundation does make a lobbying expenditure, it is subject to an excise tax under section 4945). Section 1.501(h)-2 lists which public charities are eligible to make the expenditure test election. Section 1.501(h)-2 also provides information about how a public charity makes and revokes the election to be covered by the expenditure test.

(3) A public charity that makes the election may make lobbying expenditures within specified dollar limits. If an electing public charity's lobbying expenditures are within the dollar limits determined under section 4911(c), the electing public charity will not owe tax under section 4911 nor will it lose its tax exempt status as a charity by virtue of section 501(h). If, however, that electing public charity's lobbying expenditures exceed its section 4911 lobbying limit, the organization is subject to an excise tax on the excess lobbying expenditures. Further, under section 501(h), if an electing public charity's lobbying expenditures normally are more than 150 percent of its section 4911 lobbying limit, the organization will cease to be a charity described in section 501(c)(3).

(4) A public charity that elects the expenditure test may nevertheless lose its tax exempt status if it is an action organization under § 1.501(c)(3)-1(c)(3)(iii) or (iv). A public charity that does not elect the expenditure test remains subject to the substantial part test. The substantial part test is applied without regard to the provisions of section 501(h) and 4911 and the related regulations.

(b) Effective date. The provisions of § 1.501(h)-1 through § 1.501(h)-3, are effective for taxable years beginning after August 31, 1990. An election made before August 31, 1990, under the provisions of § 7.0(c)(4) or the instructions to Form 5768, will be effective under these regulations without again filing Form 5768.

T.D. 8308, 8/30/90.

§ 1.501(h)-2 Electing the expenditure test.

(a) In general. The election to be governed by section 501(h) may be made by an eligible organization (as described in paragraph (b) of this section) for any taxable year of the organization beginning after December 31, 1976, other than the first taxable year for which a voluntary revocation of the election is effective (see paragraph (d) of this section). The election is made by filing a completed Form 5768, Election/Revocation of Election by an Eligible Section 501(c)(3) Organization to Make Expenditures to Influence Legislation, with the appropriate Internal Revenue Service Center listed on that form. Under section 501(h)(6), the election is effective with the beginning of the taxable year in which the form is filed. For example, if an eligible organization whose taxable year is the calendar year files Form 5768 on December 31, 1979, the organization is governed by section 501(h) for its taxable year beginning January 1, 1979. Once made, the expenditure test election is effective (without again filing Form 5768) for each succeeding taxable year for which the organization is an eligible organization and which begins before a notice of revocation is filed under paragraph (d) of this section.

(b) Organizations eligible to elect the expenditure test. *(1) In general.* For purposes of section 501(h) and the regulations thereunder, an organization is an eligible organization for a taxable year if, for that taxable year, it is—

(i) Described in section 501(c)(3) (determined, in any year for which an election is in effect, without regard to the substantial part test of section 501(c)(3)),

(ii) Described in section 501(h)(4) and paragraph (b)(2) of this section, and

(iii) Not a disqualified organization described in section 501(h)(5) and paragraph (b)(3) of this section.

(2) Certain organizations listed. An organization is described in section 501(h)(4) and this paragraph (b)(2) if it is an organization described in—

(i) Section 170(b)(1)(A)(ii) (relating to educational institutions),

(ii) Section 170(b)(1)(A)(iii) (relating to hospitals and medical research organizations),

(iii) Section 170(b)(1)(A)(iv) (relating to organizations supporting government schools),

(iv) Section 170(b)(1)(A)(vi) (relating to organizations publicly supported by charitable contributions),

(v) Section 509(a)(2) (relating to organizations publicly supported by admissions, sales, etc.), or

(vi) Section 509(a)(3) (relating to organizations supporting public charities), except that for purposes of this paragraph (b)(2), section 509(a)(3) shall be applied without regard to the last sentence of section 509(a).

(3) Disqualified organizations. An organization is a disqualified organization described in section 501(h)(5) and this paragraph (b)(3) if the organization is—

(i) Described in section 170(b)(1)(A)(i) (relating to churches),

(ii) An integrated auxiliary of a church or of a convention or association of churches (see § 1.6033-2(g)(5)), or

(iii) Described in section 501(c)(3) and affiliated (within the meaning of § 56.4911-7) with one or more organizations described in paragraph (b)(3)(i) or (ii) of this section.

(4) Other organizations ineligible to elect. Under section 501(h)(4), certain organizations, although not disqualified organizations, are not eligible to elect the expenditure test. For example, organizations described in section 509(a)(4) are not listed in section 501(h)(4) and therefore are not eligible to elect. Similarly, private foundations (within the meaning of section 509(a)) are not eligible to elect. For the treatment of expenditures by a private foundation for the purpose of carrying on propaganda, or otherwise attempting, to influence legislation, see § 53.4945-2.

(c) New organizations. A newly created organization may submit Form 5768 to elect the expenditure test under section 501(h) before it is determined to be an eligible organization and may submit Form 5768 at the time it submits its application for recognition of exemption (Form 1023). If the newly created organization is determined to be an eligible organization, the election will be effective under the provisions of paragraph (a) of this section, that is, with the beginning of the taxable year in which the Form 5768 is filed by the eligible organization. However, if a newly created organization is determined by the Service not to be an eligible organization, the organization's election will not be effective and the substantial part test will apply from the effective date of its section 501(c)(3) classification.

(d) Voluntary revocation of expenditure test election. *(1) Revocation effective.* An organization may voluntarily revoke an expenditure test election by filing a notice of voluntary revocation with the appropriate Internal Revenue Service Center listed on Form 5768. Under section 501(h)(6)(B), a voluntary revocation is effective with the beginning of the first taxable year after the taxable year in which the notice is filed. If an organization voluntarily revokes its election, the substantial part test of section 501(c)(3) will apply with respect to the organization's activities in attempting to influence legislation beginning with the taxable year for which the voluntary revocation is effective.

(2) Re-election of expenditure test. If an organization's expenditure test election is voluntarily revoked, the organization may again make the expenditure test election, effective no earlier than for the taxable year following the first taxable year for which the revocation is effective.

(3) Example. X, an organization whose taxable year is the calendar year, plans to voluntarily revoke its expenditure test election effective beginning with its taxable year 1985. X must file its notice of voluntary revocation on Form 5768 after December 31, 1983, and before January 1, 1985. If X files a notice of voluntary revocation on December 31, 1984, the revocation is effective beginning with its taxable year 1985. The organization may again elect the expenditure test by filing Form 5768. Under paragraph (d)(2) of this section, the election may not be made for taxable year 1985. Under paragraph (a) of this section, a new expenditure test election will be effective for taxable years beginning with taxable

year 1986, if the Form 5768 is filed after December 31, 1985, and before January 1, 1987.

(e) Involuntary revocation of expenditure test election. If, while an election by an eligible organization is in effect, the organization ceases to be an eligible organization, its election is automatically revoked. The revocation is effective with the beginning of the first full taxable year for which it is determined that the organization is not an eligible organization. If an organization's expenditure test election is involuntarily revoked under this paragraph (e) but the organization continues to be described in section 501(c)(3), the substantial part test of section 501(c)(3) will apply with respect to the organization's activities in attempting to influence legislation beginning with the first taxable year for which the involuntary revocation is effective.

(f) Supersession. This section supersedes § 7.0(c)(4) of the Temporary Income Tax Regulations under the Tax Reform Act of 1976, effective August 31, 1990.

T.D. 8308, 8/30/90.

---

§ 1.501(h)-3 Lobbying or grass roots expenditures normally in excess of ceiling amount.

(a) Scope. This section provides rules under section 501(h) for determining whether an organization that has elected the expenditure test and that is not a member of an affiliated group of organizations (as defined in § 56.4911-7(e)) either normally makes lobbying expenditures in excess of its lobbying ceiling amount or normally makes grass roots expenditures in excess of its grass roots ceiling amount. Under section 501(h) and this section, an organization that has elected the expenditure test and that normally makes expenditures in excess of the corresponding ceiling amount will cease to be exempt from tax under section 501(a) as an organization described in section 501(c)(3). For similar rules relating to members of an affiliated group of organizations, see § 56.4911-9.

(b) Loss of exemption. *(1) In general.* Under section 501(h)(1), an organization that has elected the expenditure test shall be denied exemption from taxation under section 501(a) as an organization described in section 501(c)(3) for the taxable year following a determination year if—

(i) The sum of the organization's lobbying expenditures for the base years exceeds 150 percent of the sum of its lobbying nontaxable amounts for the base years, or

(ii) The sum of the organization's grass roots expenditures for its base years exceeds 150 percent of the sum of its grass roots nontaxable amounts for the base years.

The organization thereafter shall not be exempt from tax under section 501(a) as an organization described in section 501(c)(3) unless, pursuant to paragraph (d) of this section, the organization reapplies for recognition of exemption and is recognized as exempt.

(2) Special exception for organization's first election. For the first, second, or third consecutive determination year for which an organization's first expenditure test election is in effect, no determination is required under paragraph (b)(1) of this section, and the organization will not be denied exemption from tax by reason of section 501(h) and this section if, taking into account as base years only those years for which the expenditure test election is in effect—

(i) The sum of the organization's lobbying expenditures for such base years does not exceed 150 percent of the sum of its lobbying nontaxable amounts for the same base years, and

(ii) The sum of the organization's grass roots expenditure for those base years does not exceed 150 percent of the sum of its grass roots nontaxable amounts for such base years. If an organization does not satisfy the requirements of this paragraph (b)(2), paragraph (b)(1) of this section will apply.

(c) Definitions. For purposes of this section—

(1) The term "lobbying expenditures" means lobbying expenditures as defined in section 4911(c)(1) or section 4911(f)(4)(A) and § 56.4911-2(a).

(2) The term "lobbying nontaxable amount" is defined in § 56.4911-1(c)(1).

(3) An organization's "lobbying ceiling amount" is 150 percent of the organization's lobbying nontaxable amount for a taxable year.

(4) The term "grass roots expenditures" means expenditures for grass roots lobbying communications as defined in section 4911(c)(3) or section 4911(f)(4)(A) and §§ 56.4911-2 and 3.

(5) The term "grass roots nontaxable amount" is defined in § 56.4911-1(c)(2).

(6) An organization's "grass roots ceiling amount" is 150 percent of the organization's grass roots nontaxable amount for a taxable year.

(7) In general, the term "base years" means the determination year and the three taxable years immediately preceding the determination year. The base years, however, do not include any taxable year preceding the taxable year for which the organization is first treated as described in section 501(c)(3).

(8) A taxable year is a "determination year" if it is a year for which the expenditure test election is in effect, other than the taxable year for which the organization is first treated as described in section 501(c)(3).

(d) Reapplication for recognition of exemption. *(1) Time of application.* An organization that is denied exemption from taxation under section 501(a) by reason of section 501(h) and this section may apply on Form 1023 for recognition of exemption as an organization described in section 501(c)(3) for any taxable year following the first taxable year for which exemption is so denied. See paragraphs (d)(2) and (d)(3) of this section for material to be included with an application described in the preceding sentence.

(2) Section 501(h) calculation. An application described in paragraph (d)(1) of this section must demonstrate that the organization would not be denied exemption from taxation under section 501(a) by reason of section 501(h) if the expenditure test election had been in effect for all of its last taxable year ending before the application is made by providing the calculations, described either in paragraph (b)(1)(i) and (ii) of this section or in § 56.4911-9(b), that would have applied to the organization for that year.

(3) Operations not disqualifying. An application described in paragraph (d)(1) of this section must include information that demonstrates to the satisfaction of the Commissioner that the organization will not knowingly operate in a manner that would disqualify the organization for tax exemption under section 501(c)(3) by reason of attempting to influence legislation.

(4) Reelection of expenditure test. If an organization is denied exemption from tax for a taxable year by reason of section 501(h) and this section, and thereafter is again recognized as an organization described in section 501(c)(3) pursuant to this paragraph (d), it may again elect the expen-

diture test under section 501(h) in accordance with § 1.501(h)-2(a).

(e) Examples. The provisions of this section are illustrated by the following examples, which also illustrate the operation of the tax imposed by section 4911.

Example (1). (1) The following table contains information used in this example concerning organization X.

Year	Exempt Purpose Expenditures (EPE)	Calculation	Lobbying Nontaxable Amount (LNTA)	Lobbying Expenditures (LE)
1979	$ 400,000	(20% of $400,000 =)	$ 80,000	$100,000
1980	300,000	(20% of $300,000 =)	60,000	100,000
1981	600,000	(20% of $500,000 + 15% of $100,000 =)	115,000	120,000
1982	500,000	(20% of $500,000 =)	100,000	100,000
Totals:	$1,800,000		$355,000	$420,000

(2) Organization X, whose taxable year is the calendar year, was organized in 1971. X first made the expenditure test election under section 501(h) effective for taxable years beginning with 1979 and has not revoked the election. None of X's lobbying expenditures for its taxable years 1979 through 1982 are grass roots expenditures. Under section 4911(a) and § 56.4911-1(a), X must determine for each year for which the expenditure test election is effective whether it is liable for the 25 percent excise tax imposed by section 4911(a) on excess lobbying expenditures. X is liable for this tax for each of its taxable years 1979, 1980, and 1981, because in each year its lobbying expenditures exceeded its lobbying nontaxable amount for the year. For 1979, the tax imposed by section 4911(a) is $5,000 (25% × ($100,000 − $80,000) = $5,000). For 1980, the tax is $10,000. For 1981, the tax is $1,250.

(3) The taxable years 1979 through 1981 are all determination years under paragraph (c)(8) of this section. On its annual return for determination year 1979, the first year of its first election, X can demonstrate, under paragraph (b)(2) of this section, that its lobbying expenditures during 1979 ($100,000) do not exceed 150 percent of its lobbying nontaxable amount for 1979 ($120,000). For determination year 1980, under paragraph (b)(2), X can demonstrate that the sum of its lobbying expenditures for 1979 and 1980 ($200,000) does not exceed 150 percent of the sum of its lobbying nontaxable amounts for 1979 and 1980 ($210,000. For 1981, under paragraph (b)(2), X can demonstrate that the sum of its lobbying expenditures for 1979, 1980, and 1981 ($320,000) does not exceed 150 percent of the sum of its lobbying nontaxable amounts for 1979, 1980, and 1981 ($382,500). For each of the determination years 1979, 1980, and 1981, the first three years of its first election, X satisfies the requirements of paragraph (b)(2). Accordingly, no determination under paragraph (b)(1) of this section is required for those years, and X is not denied tax exemption by reason of section 501(h).

(4) Under paragraph (b)(1) of this section, X must determine for its determination year 1982 whether it has normally made lobbying expenditures in excess of the lobbying ceiling amount. This determination takes into account expenditures in base years 1979 through 1982. The sum of X's lobbying expenditures for the base years ($420,000) does not exceed 150% of the sum of the lobbying nontaxable amounts for the base years (150% × $355,000 = $532,500). Accordingly, X is not denied tax exemption by reason of section 501(h).

Example (2). (1) The following table contains information used in this example concerning W.

Year	Exempt Purpose Expenditures (EPE)	Calculation	Lobbying Nontaxable Amount (LNTA)	Lobbying Expenditures (LE)	Grass Roots Nontaxable Amount (25% of LNTA)	Grass Roots Expenditures
1979	$ 700,000	(20% of $500,000 + 15% of $200,000 =)	$130,000	$120,000	$ 32,500	$ 30,000
1980	$ 800,000	(20% of $500,000 + 15% of $300,000 =)	145,000	100,000	36,250	50,000
1981	$ 800,000	(20% of $500,000 + 15% of $300,000 =)	145,000	100,000	36,250	65,000
1982	$ 900,000	(20% of $500,000 + 15% of $400,000 =)	160,000	150,000	40,000	65,000
Totals:	$3,200,000		$580,000	$470,000	$145,000	$220,000

(2) Organization W, whose taxable year is the calendar year, made the expenditure test election under section 501(h) effective for taxable years beginning with 1979 and has not revoked the election. W has been treated as an organization described in section 501(c)(3) for each of its taxable years beginning with its taxable year 1974.

(3) Under section 4911(a) and § 56.4911-1(a), W must determine for each year for which the expenditure test election is effective whether it is liable for the 25 percent excise tax imposed by section 4911(a) on excess lobbying expenditures. In 1980, 1981, and 1982, W has excess lobbying expenditures because its grass roots expenditures in each of those years exceeded its grass roots nontaxable amount for the

year. Therefore, W is liable for the excise tax under section 4911(a) for those years. The tax imposed by section 4911(a) for 1980 is $5,937.50 (25% × ($60,000 − $36,250) = $5,937.50). For 1981, the tax is $7,187.50. For 1982, the tax is $6,250.

(4) On its annual return for its determination years 1979, 1980, and 1981, the first three years of its first election, W demonstrates that it satisfies the requirements of paragraph (b)(2) of this section. Accordingly, no determination under paragraph (b)(1) of this section is required for those years, and W is not denied tax exemption by reason of section 501(h).

(5) On its annual return for its determination year 1982, W must determine under paragraph (b)(1) whether it has normally made lobbying expenditures or grass roots expenditures in excess of the corresponding ceiling amount. This determination takes into account expenditures in base years 1979 through 1982. The sum of W's lobbying expenditures for the base years ($470,000) does not exceed 150% of the sum of W's lobbying nontaxable amounts for those years (150% × $580,000 = $870,000). However, the sum of W's grass roots expenditures for the base years ($220,000) does exceed 150% of the sum of W's grass roots nontaxable amounts for those years (150% × $145,000 = $217,500). Under section 501(h), W is denied tax exemption under section 501(a) as an organization described in section 501(c)(3) for its taxable year 1983. For its taxable year 1984 and any taxable year thereafter, W is exempt from tax as an organization described in section 501(c)(3) only if W applies for recognition of its exempt status under paragraph (d) of this section and is recognized as exempt from tax.

Example (3). (1) The following table contains information used in this example concerning organization Y.

Taxable Year	Exempt Purpose Expenditures (EPE)	Calculation	Lobbying Nontaxable Amount (LNTA)	Lobbying Expenditures (LE)	Grass roots Nontaxable Amount (25% of LNTA)	Grass roots Expenditures
1977	$ 700,000	(20% of $500,000 + 15% of $200,000 =)	$130,000	$182,000	$ 32,500	$ 30,000
1978	$ 800,000	(20% of $500,000 + 15% of $300,000 =)	$145,000	$224,750	$ 36,250	$ 35,000
Subtotal	$1,500,000		$275,000	$406,750	$ 68,750	$ 65,000
1979	900,000	(20% of $500,000 + 15% of $400,000 =)	$160,000	$264,000		
	$ 40,000	$50,000				
Totals:	$2,400,000		$435,000	$670,750	$108,750	$115,000

(2) Organization Y, whose taxable year is the calendar year, was first treated as an organization described in section 501(c)(3) on February 1, 1977. Y made the expenditure test election under section 501(h) effective for taxable years beginning with 1977 and has not revoked the election.

(3) For 1977, Y has excess lobbying expenditures of $52,000 because its lobbying expenditures ($182,000) exceed its lobbying nontaxable amount ($130,000) for the taxable year. Accordingly, Y is liable for the 25 percent excise tax imposed by section 4911(a). The amount of the tax is $13,000 (25% × ($182,000 − $130,000) = $13,000).

(4) For 1978, Y again has excess lobbying expenditures and is again liable for the 25 percent excise tax imposed by section 4911(a). The amount of the tax is $19,937.50 (25% × ($224,750 − $145,000) = $19,937.50).

(5) For 1979, Y's lobbying expenditures ($264,000) exceed its lobbying nontaxable amount ($160,000) by $104,000, and its grass roots expenditures ($50,000) exceed its grass roots nontaxable amount ($40,000) by $10,000. Under § 56.4911-1(b), Y's excess lobbying expenditures are the greater of $104,000 or $10,000. The amount of the tax, therefore, is $26,000 (25% × $104,000 = $26,000).

(6) Under paragraph (c)(8) of this section, 1977 is not a determination year because it is the first year for which the organization is treated as described in section 501(c)(3). For 1977, Y need not determine whether it has normally made lobbying expenditures or grass roots expenditures in excess of the corresponding ceiling amount for purposes of determining whether it is denied exemption under section 501(h) for its taxable year 1978.

(7) For determination year 1978, Y must determine whether it has normally made lobbying or grass roots expenditures in excess of the corresponding ceiling amount, taking into account expenditures for the base years 1977 and 1978. For Y, the determination under paragraph (b)(2) of this section considers the same base years as the determination under paragraph (b)(1) of this section and is, therefore, redundant. Accordingly, Y proceeds to determine, under (b)(1), whether it is denied exemption. Y's grass roots expenditures for 1977 and 1978 ($65,000) did not exceed 150 percent of the sum of its grass roots nontaxable amounts for those years ($103,125). Y's lobbying expenditures for 1977 and 1978 ($406,750) did not exceed 150% of its lobbying nontaxable amount for those years (150% × $275,000 = $412,500). Therefore, Y is not denied tax exemption under section 501(h) for its taxable year 1979.

(8) For determination year 1979, the sum of Y's grass roots expenditures in base years 1977, 1978, and 1979 does not exceed 150 percent of its grass roots nontaxable amount (calculation omitted). However, the sum of Y's lobbying expenditures for the base years ($670,750) does exceed 150% of the sum of the lobbying nontaxable amounts for those years (150% × $435,000 = $652,500). Since Y was not described in section 501(c)(3) prior to 1977, only the years 1977, 1978, and 1979 may be considered in determining whether Y has normally made lobbying expenditures in excess of its lobbying ceiling. Therefore, Y determines that it has normally made lobbying expenditures in excess of its lobbying ceiling. Under section 501(h), Y is denied tax exemption under section 501(a) as an organization described in section 501(c)(3) for its taxable year 1980. For its taxable year 1981, and any taxable year thereafter, Y is exempt from tax as an organization described in section 501(c)(3) only if Y applies for recognition of its exempt status under para-

graph (d) of this section and is recognized as exempt from tax.

Example (4). Organization M made the expenditure test election under section 501(h) effective for taxable years beginning with 1977 and has not revoked the election. M has $500,000 of exempt purpose expenditures during each of the years 1981 through 1984. In addition, during each of those years, M spends $75,000 for direct lobbying and $25,000 for grass roots lobbying. Since the amount expended for M's lobbying (both total lobbying and grass roots lobbying) is within the respective nontaxable expenditure limitations, M is not liable for the 25 percent excise tax imposed under section 4911(a) upon excess lobbying expenditures, nor is M denied tax-exempt status by reason of section 501(h).

Example (5). Assume the same facts as in Example (4), except that, on behalf of M, numerous unpaid volunteers conduct substantial lobbying activities with no reimbursement. Since the substantial lobbying activities of the unpaid volunteers are not counted towards the expenditure limitations and the amount expended for M's lobbying is within the respective nontaxable expenditure limitations, M is not liable for the 25 percent excise tax under section 4911, nor is M denied tax-exempt status by reason of section 501(h).

T.D. 8308, 8/30/90.

---

§ 1.501(k)-1 Communist-controlled organizations.

Under section 11(b) of the Internal Security Act of 1950 (50 U.S.C. 790(b)), as amended, which is made applicable to the Code by section 7852(b) of that Code, no organization is entitled to exemption under sections 501(a) or 521(a) for any taxable year if at any time during such year such organization is registered under section 7 of such Act or if there is in effect a final order of the Subversive Activities Control Board established by section 12 of such Act requiring such organization to register under section 7 of such Act, or determining that it is a Communist-infiltrated organization.

T.D. 6301, 7/8/58, amend T.D. 8100, 9/3/86.

---

§ 1.502-1 Feeder organizations.

(a) In the case of an organization operated for the primary purpose of carrying on a trade or business for profit, exemption is not allowed under section 501 on the ground that all the profits of such organization are payable to one or more organizations exempt from taxation under section 501. In determining the primary purpose of an organization, all the circumstances must be considered, including the size and extent of the trade or business and the size and extent of those activities of such organization which are specified in the applicable paragraph of section 501.

(b) If a subsidiary organization of a tax-exempt organization would itself be exempt on the ground that its activities are an integral part of the exempt activities of the parent organization, its exemption will not be lost because, as a matter of accounting between the two organizations, the subsidiary derives a profit from its dealings with its parent organization, for example, a subsidiary organization which is operated for the sole purpose of furnishing electric power used by its parent organization, a tax-exempt educational organization, in carrying on its educational activities. However, the subsidiary organization is not exempt from tax if it is operated for the primary purpose of carrying on a trade or business which would be an unrelated trade or business (that is, unrelated to exempt activities) if regularly carried on by the parent organization. For example, if a subsidiary organization is operated primarily for the purpose of furnishing electric power to consumers other than its parent organization (and the parent's tax-exempt subsidiary organizations), it is not exempt since such business would be an unrelated trade or business if regularly carried on by the parent organization. Similarly, if the organization is owned by several unrelated exempt organizations, and is operated for the purpose of furnishing electric power to each of them, it is not exempt since such business would be an unrelated trade or business if regularly carried on by any one of the tax-exempt organizations. For purposes of this paragraph, organizations are related only if they consist of:

(1) A parent organization and one or more of its subsidiary organizations; or

(2) Subsidiary organizations having a common parent organization.

An exempt organization is not related to another exempt organization merely because they both engage in the same type of exempt activities.

(c) In certain cases an organization which carries on a trade or business for profit but is not operated for the primary purpose of carrying on such trade or business is subject to the tax imposed under section 511 on its unrelated business taxable income.

(d) Exception. *(1) Taxable years beginning before January 1, 1970.* For purposes of section 502 and this section, for taxable years beginning before January 1, 1970, the term "trade or business" does not include the rental by an organization of its real property (including personal property leased with the real property).

(2) Taxable years beginning after December 31, 1969. For purposes of section 502 and this section, for taxable years beginning after December 31, 1969, the term "trade or business" does not include:

(i) The deriving of rents described in section 512(b)(3)(A),

(ii) Any trade or business in which substantially all the work in carrying on such trade or business is performed for the organization without compensation, or

(iii) Any trade or business (such as a "thrift shop") which consists of the selling of merchandise, substantially all of which has been received by the organization as gifts or contributions.

For purposes of the exception described in subdivision (i) of this subparagraph, if the rents derived by an organization would not be excluded from unrelated business income pursuant to section 512(b)(3) and the regulations thereunder, the deriving of such rents shall be considered a "trade or business".

(3) Cross references and special rules. (i) For determination of when rents are excluded from the tax on unrelated business income see section 512(b)(3) and the regulations thereunder.

(ii) The rules contained in § 1.513-1(e)(1) shall apply in determining whether a trade or business is described in section 502(b)(2) and subparagraph (2)(ii) of this paragraph.

(iii) The rules contained in § 1.513-1(e)(3) shall apply in determining whether a trade or business is described in section 502(b)(3) and subparagraph (2)(iii) of this paragraph.

T.D. 6560, 11/26/60, amend T.D. 6662, 7/8/63, T.D. 7083, 12/30/70.

---

§ 1.503(a)-1 Denial of exemption to organizations engaged in prohibited transactions.

(a) *(1)* Prior to January 1, 1970, section 503 applies to those organizations described in sections 501(c)(3), 501(c)(17), and section 401(a) except:

(i) A religious organization (other than a trust);

(ii) An educational organization which normally maintains a regular faculty and curriculum and normally has a regularly enrolled body of pupils or students in attendance at the place where its educational activities are regularly carried on;

(iii) An organization which normally receives a substantial part of its support (exclusive of income received in the exercise or performance by such organizations of its charitable, educational, or other purpose or function constituting the basis for its exemption under section 501(a)) from the United States or any State or political subdivision thereof or from direct or indirect contributions from the general public;

(iv) An organization which is operated, supervised, controlled or principally supported by a religious organization (other than a trust) which in itself not subject to the provisions of this section; and

(v) An organization the principal purposes or functions of which are the providing of medical or hospital care or medical education or medical research or agricultural research.

(2) Effective January 1, 1970, and prior to January 1, 1975, section 503 shall apply only to organizations described in section 501(c)(17) or (18) or section 401(a).

(3) Effective January 1, 1975, section 503 shall apply only to organizations described in section 501(c)(17) or (18) or described in section 401(a) and referred to in section 4975(g)(2) or (3).

(b) The prohibited transactions enumerated in section 503(b) are in addition to and not in limitation of the restrictions contained in section 501(c)(3), (17), or (18) or section 401(a). Even though an organization has not engaged in any of the prohibited transactions referred to in section 503(b), it still may not qualify for tax exemptions in view of the general provisions of section 501(c) (3), (17), or (18) or section 401(a). Thus, if a trustee or other fiduciary of the organization (whether or not he is also a creator or such organization) enters into a transaction with the organization, such transaction will be closely scrutinized in the light of the fiduciary principle requiring undivided loyalty to ascertain whether the organization is in fact being operated for the stated exempt purpose.

(c) An organization. *(1)* Described in section 501(c)(3) which after July 1, 1950, has engaged in any prohibited transaction as defined in section 503(b), unless it is excepted by the provisions of paragraph (a)(1) of this section;

(2) Described in section 401(a) and referred to in section 4975(g)(2) or (3) which after March 1, 1954, has engaged in any prohibited transactions as defined in section 503(d);

(3) Described in section 401(a) and not referred to in section 4975(g)(2) or (3) which after March 1, 1954, but before January 1, 1975, has engaged in any prohibited transaction as defined in section 503(b) or which after December 31, 1962, but before January 1, 1975, has engaged in any prohibited transaction as defined in section 503(g) prior to its repeal by section 2003(b)(5) of the Employee Retirement Income Security Act of 1974 (88 Stat. 978);

(4) Described in section 501(c)(17) which after December 31, 1959, has engaged in any prohibited transaction as defined in section 503(b); or

(5) Described in section 501(c)(18) which after December 31, 1969, has engaged in any prohibited transaction described in section 503(b);

shall not be exempt from taxation under section 501(a) for any taxable year subsequent to the taxable year in which there is mailed to it a notice in writing by the Commissioner that it has engaged in such prohibited transaction. Such notification by the Commissioner shall be by registered or certified mail to the last known address of the organization. However, notwithstanding the requirement of notification by the Commissioner, the exemption shall be denied with respect to any taxable year if such organization during or prior to such taxable year commenced the prohibited transaction with the purpose of diverting income or corpus from its exempt purposes and such transaction involved a substantial part of the income or corpus of such organization. For the purpose of this section, the term "taxable year" means the established annual accounting period of the organization; or, if the organization has no such established annual accounting period, the "taxable year" of the organization means the calendar year. See 26 CFR § 1.503(j)-1 (rev. as of Apr. 1, 1974) for provisions relating to the definition of prohibited transactions in the case of trusts benefitting certain owner-employees after December 31, 1962, but prior to January 1, 1975. See also section 2003(c)(1)(B) of the Employee Retirement Income Security Act of 1974 (88 Stat. 978) in the case of an organization described in section 401(a) with respect to which a disqualified person elects to pay a tax in the amount and manner provided with respect to the tax imposed by section 4975 of the Code so that the organization may avoid denial of exemption under section 503. For further guidance regarding the definition of last known address, see § 301.6212-2 of this chapter.

(d) The application of section 503(b) may be illustrated by the following examples:

Example (1). A creates a foundation in 1954 ostensibly for educational purposes. B, a trustee, accumulates the foundation's income from 1957 until 1959 and then uses a substantial part of this accumulated income to send A's children to college. The foundation would lose its exemption for the taxable years 1957 through 1959 and for subsequent taxable years until it regains its exempt status.

Example (2). If under the facts in example (1) such private benefit was the purpose of the foundation from its inception, such foundation is not exempt by reason of the general provisions of section 501(c)(3), without regard to the provisions of section 503, for all years since its inception, that is, for the taxable years 1954 through 1959 and subsequent taxable years, since under section 501(c)(3) the organization must be organized and operated exclusively for exempt purposes. See § 1.501(c)(3)-1.

T.D. 6301, 7/8/58, amend T.D. 6722, 4/13/64, T.D. 6972, 9/11/68, T.D. 7428, 8/13/76, T.D. 8939, 1/11/2001.

§ 1.503(b)-1 Prohibited transactions.

(a) In general. The term "prohibited transaction" means any transaction set forth in section 503(b) engaged in by any organization described in paragraph (a) of § 1.503(a)-1. Whether a transaction is a prohibited transaction depends on the facts and circumstances of the particular case. This section is intended to deny tax-exempt status to such organizations which engage in certain transactions which inure to the private advantage of (1) the creator of such organization (if it is a trust); (2) any substantial contributor to such organization; (3) a member of the family (as defined in section

267(c)(4)) of an individual who is such creator of or such substantial contributor to such organization; or (4) a corporation controlled, as set forth in section 503(b), by such creator or substantial contributor.

(b) Loans as prohibited transactions under section 503(b)(1). *(1) Adequate security.* For the purposes of section 503(b)(1), which treats as prohibited transactions certain loans by an organization without receipt of adequate security and a reasonable rate of interest, the term "adequate security" means something in addition to and supporting a promise to pay, which is so pledged to the organization that it may be sold, foreclosed upon, or otherwise disposed of in default of repayment of the loan, the value and liquidity of which security is such that it may reasonably be anticipated that loss of principal or interest will not result from the loan. Mortgages or liens on property, accommodation endorsements of those financially capable of meeting the indebtedness, and stock or securities issued by corporations other than the borrower may constitute security for a loan to the persons or organizations described in section 503(b). Stock of a borrowing corporation does not constitute adequate security. A borrower's evidence of indebtedness, irrespective of its name, is itself not security for a loan, whether or not it was issued directly to the exempt organization. However, if any such evidence of indebtedness provides for security that may be sold, foreclosed upon, or otherwise disposed of in default of repayment of the loan, there may be adequate security for such loan. If an organization subject to section 503(b) purchases debentures issued by a person specified in section 503(b), the purchase is considered, for purposes of section 503(b)(1), as a loan made by the purchaser to the issuer on the date of such purchase. For example, if an exempt organization subject to section 503(b) makes a purchase through a registered security exchange of debentures issued by a person described in section 503(b), and owned by an unknown third party, the purchase will be considered as a loan to the issuer by the purchaser. For rules relating to loan of funds to, or investment of funds in stock or securities of, persons described in section 503(b) by an organization described in section 401(a), see paragraph (b)(5) of § 1.401-1.

(2) Effective dates. The effective dates for the application of the definition of adequate security in paragraph (b)(1) of this paragraph are:

(i) March 15, 1956, for loans (other than debentures) made after March 15, 1956;

(ii) January 31, 1957, for loans (other than debentures) made before March 16, 1956, and continued after January 31, 1957;

(iii) November 8, 1956, for debentures which were purchased after November 8, 1956;

(iv) December 1, 1958, for debentures which were purchased before November 9, 1956, and held after December 1, 1958;

(v) If an employees' pension, stock bonus, or profit-sharing trust described in section 401(a) made a loan before March 1, 1954, repayable by its terms after December 31, 1955, and which would constitute a prohibited transaction if made on or after March 1, 1954, the loan shall not constitute a prohibited transaction if held until maturity (determined without regard to any extension or renewal thereof);

(vi) January 1, 1960, for loans (including the purchase of debentures) made by supplemental unemployment benefit trusts, described in section 501(c)(17);

(vii) January 1, 1970, for loans (including the purchase of debentures) made by employees' contribution pension plan trusts described in section 501(c)(18).

(3) Certain exceptions to section 503(b)(1). See section 503(e) and §§ 1.503(e)-1, 1.503(e)-2, and 1.503(e)-3 for special rules providing that certain obligations acquired by trusts described in section 401(a) or section 501(c)(17) or (18) shall not be treated as loans made without the receipt of adequate security for purposes of section 503(b)(1). See section 503(f) and § 1.503(f)-1 for an exception to the application of section 503(b)(1) for certain loans made by employees' trusts described in section 401(a).

(c) Examples. The principles of this section are illustrated by the following examples: (Assume that section 503(e) and (f) are not applicable.)

Example (1). A, creator of an exempt trust subject to section 503, borrows $100,000 from such trust in 1960, giving his unsecured promissory note. The net worth of A is $1,000,000. The net worth of A is not "security" for such loan and the transaction is a prohibited transaction. If, however, the note is secured by a mortgage on property of sufficient value, or is accompanied by acceptable collateral of sufficient value, or carries with it the secondary promise of repayment by an accommodation endorser financially capable of meeting the indebtedness, it may be adequately secured. However, subordinated debenture bonds of a partnership which are guaranteed by the general partners are not adequately secured since the general partners are liable for the firm's debt and their guaranty adds no additional security.

Example (2). Assume the same facts as in example (1) except that A's promissory note in the amount of $100,000 to the trust is secured by property which has a fair market value of $75,000. A's promissory note secured to the extent of $75,000 is not adequately secured within the meaning of section 503(b)(1) since the security at the time of the transaction must be sufficient to repay the indebtedness, interest, and charges which may pertain thereto.

Example (3). Corporation M, a substantial contributor to an exempt organization subject to section 503, borrows $150,000 from such organization in 1960, giving its promissory note accompanied by stock of the borrowing corporation with a fair market value of $200,000. Since promissory notes and debentures have priority over stock in the event of liquidation of the corporation, stock of a borrowing corporation is not adequate security. Likewise, debenture bonds which are convertible on default into voting stock of the issuing corporation do not constitute "adequate security" under section 503(b)(1).

Example (4). B, creator of an exempt trust subject to section 503, borrows $100,000 from such trust in 1960, giving his secured promissory note at the rate of 3 percent interest. The prevailing rate of interest charged by financial institutions in the community where the transaction takes place is 5 percent for a loan of the same duration and similarly secured. The loan by the trust to the grantor is a prohibited transaction since section 503(b)(1) requires both adequate security and a reasonable rate of interest. Further, a promise to repay the loan plus a percentage of future profits which may be greater than the prevailing rate of interests does not meet the reasonable rate of interest requirement.

Example (5). N Corporation, a substantial contributor to an exempt organization subject to section 503 borrows $50,000 on or after March 16, 1956, from the organization. If the loan is not adequately secured, the organization has committed a prohibited transaction at the time the loan was made. If the loan had been made on or before March 15, 1956, and is continued after January 31, 1957, it must be adequately secured on February 1, 1957, or it will be considered a prohibited transaction on that date. However, if the exempt organization were an employees' trust, described in section 401(a), and the loan were made before March 1, 1954, repayable by its terms after December 31, 1955, it would not have to be adequately secured on February 1, 1957. Moreover, if the exempt organization were a supplemental unemployment benefit trust, described in section 501(c)(17), and the loan were made before January 1, 1960, repayable by its terms after December 31, 1959, it would not have to be adequately secured on January 1, 1960.

Example (6). An exempt organization subject to section 503 purchases a debenture issued by O Corporation, which is a substantial contributor to the organization. The organization purchases the debenture in an arm's length transaction from a third person on or after November 9, 1956. The purchase is considered as a loan by the organization to O Corporation. The loan must be adequately secured when it is made, or it is considered as a prohibited transaction at that time. If the organization purchased the debenture before November 9, 1956, and holds it after December 1, 1958, the debenture must be adequately secured on December 2, 1958, or it will then be considered as a prohibited transaction. However, if the organization were an employees' trust described in section 401(a), and if the debenture were purchased before March 1, 1954, and its maturity date is after December 31, 1955, the debenture does not have to be adequately secured. Moreover, if the organization were an employees' contribution pension plan trust described in section 501(c)(18), and if the debenture were purchased before January 1, 1970, and its maturity date is after December 31, 1969, the debenture does not have to be adequately secured.

T.D. 7428, 8/13/76.

§ 1.503(c)-1 Future status of organizations denied exemption.

(a) Any organization described in section 501(c)(3), (17), or (18), or an employees' trust described in section 401(a), which is denied exemption under section 501(a) by reason of the provisions of section 503(a), may file, in any taxable year following the taxable year in which notice of denial was issued, a claim for exemption. In the case of organizations described in section 501(c)(3), (17), or (18), the appropriate exemption application shall be used for this purpose, and shall be filed with the district director. In the case of an employees' trust described in section 401(a), the information described in § 1.404(a)-2 shall be submitted with a letter claiming exemption. An employees' trust described in section 401(a) shall submit this information to the district director with whom a request for a determination as to its qualification under section 401 and exemption under section 501 may be submitted under paragraph (s) of § 601.201 of this chapter (Statement of Procedural Rules). A claim for exemption must contain or have attached to it, in addition to the information generally required of such an organization claiming exemption as an organization described in section 501(c)(17), or (18), or section 401(a) (or section 501(c)(3) prior to January 1, 1970), a written declaration made under the penalties of perjury by a principal officer of such organization authorized to make such declaration that the organization will not knowingly again engage in a prohibited transaction, (as defined in section 503(b) (or 4975(c) if such section applies to such organization)). In the case of section 501(c)(3) organizations which have lost their exemption after December 31, 1969, pursuant to section 503, a claim for exemption must contain or have attached to it a written agreement made under penalties of perjury by a principal officer of such organization authorized to make such agreement that the organization will not violate the provisions of chapter 42. In addition, such organization must comply with the rules for governing instruments as prescribed in § 1.508-3. See § 1.501(a)-1 for proof of exemption requirements in general.

(b) If the Commissioner is satisfied that such organization will not knowingly again engage in a prohibited transaction (as defined under section 503(b) or 4975(c), as applicable to such organization) or in the case of a section 501(c)(3) organization, will not violate the provisions of chapter 42, and the organization also satisfied all the other requirements under section 501(c)(3), (17), or (18), or section 401(a), the organization will be so notified in writing. In such case the organization will be exempt (subject to the provisions of section 501(c)(3), or sections 501(c)(17), (18) or 401(a), and 503, and 504 when applicable) with respect to the taxable years subsequent to the taxable year in which the claim described in section 503(c) is filed. Section 503 contemplates that an organization denied exemption because of the terms of such section will be subject to taxation for at least one full taxable year. For the purpose of this section, the term "taxable year" means the established annual accounting period of the organization; or, if the organization has no such established annual accounting period, the "taxable year" of the organization means the calendar year.

(c) For taxable years beginning after December 31, 1969, the denial of an exemption pursuant to this section, for a taxable year prior to January 1, 1970, of an organization described in section 501(c)(3) shall not cause such organization to cease to be described in section 501(c)(3) for purposes of part II of subchapter F, chapter 1 and for purposes of the application of chapter 42 taxes.

(d) In the case of an organization described in section 501(c)(3), which has lost its exemption pursuant to section 503, and which has not notified the Commissioner that it is applying for recognition of its exempt status under section 508(a) and this section, no gift or contribution made after December 31, 1969, which would otherwise be deductible under sections 170, 642(c), or 545(b)(2) shall be allowed as a deduction. For rules relating to the denial of deductions with respect to gifts or contributions made before January 1, 1970, see, § 1.503(e)-4.

T.D. 6301, 7/8/58, amend T.D. 6493, 9/26/60, T.D. 6722, 4/16/64, T.D. 6972, 9/11/68, T.D. 7428, 8/13/76, T.D. 7896, 5/26/83.

§ 1.503(d)-1 Cross references.

For provisions relating to loans described in section 503(b)(1) by a trust described in section 401(a), see § 1.503(b)-1 and section 503(e) and (f) and the regulations thereunder.

T.D. 6301, 7/8/58, amend T.D. 6972, 9/11/68, T.D. 7428, 8/13/76.

§ 1.503(e)-1 Special rules.

(a) In general. *(1)* Section 503(e) provides that for purposes of section 503(b)(1) (relating to loans made without the receipt of adequate security and a reasonable rate of interest) the acquisition of a bond, debenture, note, or certificate or other evidence of indebtedness shall not be treated as a loan made without the receipt of adequate security if certain requirements are met. Those requirements are described in § 1.503(e)-2.

(2) Section 503(e) does not affect the requirement in section 503(b)(1) of a reasonable rate of interest. Thus, although the acquisition of a certificate of indebtedness which meets all of the requirements of section 503(e) and of § 1.503(e)-2 will not be considered as a loan made without the receipt of adequate security, the acquisition of such an indebtedness does constitute a prohibited transaction if the indebtedness does not bear a reasonable rate of interest.

(3) The provisions of section 503(e) do not limit the effect of section 401(a) and § 1.401-2, section 501(c)(17)(A)(i), or section 501(c)(18)(A), all relating to the use of diversion of corpus or income of the respective employee trusts. Furthermore, the provisions of section 503(e) do not limit the effect of any of the provisions of section 503 other than section 503(b)(1). Thus, for example, although a loan made by employees' trust described in section 503(a)(1)(B) meets all the requirements of section 503(e) and therefore is not treated as a loan made without the receipt of adequate security, such an employees' trust making such a loan will lose its exempt status if the loan is not considered as made for the exclusive benefit of the employees or their beneficiaries. Similarly, a loan which meets the requirements of section 503(e) will constitute a prohibited transaction within the meaning of section 503(b)(6) if it results in a substantial diversion of the trust's income or corpus to a person described in section 503(b).

(b) Definitions. For purposes of section 503(e):

(1) The term "obligation" means bond, debenture, note, or certificate or other evidence of indebtedness.

(2) The term "issuer" includes any person described in section 503(b) who issues an obligation.

(3) (i) The term "person independent of the issuer" means a person who is not related to the issuer by blood, by marriage, or by reason of any substantial business interests. Persons who will be considered not to be independent of the issuer include but are not limited to:

(a) The spouse, ancestor, lineal descendant, or brother or sister (whether by whole or half blood) of an individual who is the issuer of an obligation;

(b) A corporation controlled directly or indirectly by an individual who is the issuer, or directly or indirectly by the spouse, ancestor, lineal descendant, or brother or sister (whether by whole or half blood) of an individual who is the issuer;

(c) A corporation which directly or indirectly controls, or is controlled by, a corporate issuer;

(d) A controlling shareholder of a corporation which is the issuer, or which controls the issuer;

(e) An officer, director, or other employee of the issuer, of a corporation controlled by the issuer, or of a corporation which controls the issuer;

(f) A fiduciary of any trust created by the issuer, by a corporation which controls the issuer, or by a corporation which is controlled by the issuer; or

(g) A corporation controlled by a person who controls a corporate issuer.

(ii) For purposes of paragraph (b)(3)(i) of this section, the term "control" means, with respect to a corporation, direct or indirect ownership of 50 percent or more of the total combined voting power of all voting stock or 50 percent or more of the total value of shares of all classes of stock. If the aggregate amount of stock in a corporation owned by an individual and by the spouse, ancestors, lineal descendants, brothers and sisters (whether by whole or half blood) of the individual is 50 percent or more of the total combined voting power of all voting stock or is 50 percent or more of the total value of all classes of stock, then each of these persons shall be considered as the controlling shareholder of the corporation.

(iii) In determining family relationships for purposes of paragraph (b)(3)(i) of this section, a legally adopted child of an individual shall be treated as a child of such individual by blood.

(4) The term "issue" means all the obligations of a issuer which are offered for sale on substantially the same terms. Obligations shall be considered offered for sale on substantially the same terms if such obligation would, at the same time and under the same circumstances, be traded on the market at the same price. On the other hand, if the terms on which obligations are offered for sale differ in such manner as would cause such obligations to be traded on the market at different prices, then such obligations are not part of the same issue. The following are examples of terms which, if different, would cause obligations to be traded on the market at different prices: (i) Interest rate; (ii) Maturity date; (iii) Collateral; and (iv) Conversion provisions.

The fact that obligations are offered for sale on different dates will not preclude such obligations from being part of the same issue if they all mature on the same date and if the terms on which they are offered for sale are otherwise the same, since such obligations would, at the same time and under the same conditions, be traded on the market at the same price. Obligations shall not be considered part of the same issue merely because they are part of the same authorization or because they are registered as part of the same issue with the Securities and Exchange Commission.

T.D. 7428, 8/13/76.

§ 1.503(e)-2 Requirements.

(a) In general. The requirements which must be met under section 503(e) for an obligation not to be treated as a loan made without the receipt of adequate security for purposes of section 503(b)(1) are described in paragraphs (b), (c), and (d) of this section. For purposes of this section, the term "employee trust" shall mean any of the three kinds of organizations described in section 503(a)(1).

(b) Methods of acquisition. *(1) In general.* The employee trust must acquire the obligation of the market, by purchase from an underwriter, or by purchase from the issuer, in the manner described in subparagraph (2), (3), or (4) of this paragraph.

(2) On the market. (i) An obligation is acquired on the market when it is purchased through a national securities exchange which is registered with the Securities and Exchange Commission, or when it is purchased in an over-the-counter transaction. For purposes of the preceding sentence, securities purchased through an exchange which is not a national securities exchange registered with the Securities and Exchange Commission shall be treated as securities purchased in an over-the-counter transaction.

(ii) (a) If the obligation is listed on a national securities exchange registered with the Securities and Exchange Commission, it must be purchased through such an exchange or in an over-the-counter transaction at a price not greater than the price of the obligation prevailing on such an exchange at the time of the purchase by the employee trust.

(b) For purposes of section 503(e), the price of the obligation prevailing at the time of the purchase means the price which accurately reflects the market value of the obligation. In the case of an obligation purchased through a national securities exchange which is registered with the Securities and Exchange Commission, the price paid for the obligation will be considered the prevailing price of the obligation. In the case of an obligation purchased in an over-the-counter transaction, the prevailing price may be the price at which the last sale of the obligation was affected on such national securities exchange immediately before the employee trust's purchase of such obligation on the same day or may be the mean between the highest and lowest prices at which sales were effected on such exchange on the same day or on the immediately preceding day or on the last day during which there were sales of such obligation or may be a price determined by any other method which accurately reflects the market value of the obligation.

(iii) (a) If the obligation is not listed on a national securities exchange which is registered with the Securities and Exchange Commission, it must be purchased in an over-the-counter transaction at a price not greater than the offering price for the obligation as established by current bid and asked prices quoted by persons independent of the issuer.

(b) For purposes of section 503(e) the offering price for the obligation at the time of the purchase means the price which accurately reflects the market value of the obligation. The offering price may be the price at which the last sale of the obligation to a person independent of the issuer was effected immediately before the employee trust's purchase of such obligation on the same day or may be the mean between the highest and lowest prices at which sales to persons independent of the issuer were effected on the same day or on the last day during which they were sales of such obligation or may be a price determined by any other method which accurately reflects the market value of the obligation. The offering price for an obligation must be a valid price for the amount of the obligations which the trust is purchasing. For example, if an employees' trust described in section 503(a)(1)(B) purchases 1,000 bonds of the employer corporation at the offering price established by current prices for a lot of 10 such bonds, such offering price may not be a valid price for 1,000 bonds and the purchase may therefore not meet the requirements of this subdivision. For a purchase of an obligation to qualify under this subdivision, there must be sufficient current prices quoted by persons independent of the issuer to establish accurately the current value of the obligation. Thus, if there are no current prices quoted by persons independent of the issuer, an over-the-counter transaction will not qualify under this subparagraph even though the obligation was purchased in an arms length transaction from a person independent of the issuer.

(iv) For purposes of this section, an over-the-counter transaction is one not executed on a national securities exchange which is registered with the Securities and Exchange Commission. An over-the-counter transaction may be made through a dealer or an exchange which is not such a national securities exchange or may be made directly from the seller to the purchaser.

(3) From an underwriter. An obligation may be purchased from an underwriter if it is purchased at a price not greater than:

(i) The public offering price for the obligation as set forth in a prospectus or offering circular filed with the Securities and Exchange Commission, or

(ii) The price at which a substantial portion of the issue including such obligation is acquired by persons independent of the issuer, whichever is the lesser price. For purposes of this subparagraph, a portion of the issue will be considered substantial if the purchasers of such portion by persons independent of the issuer are sufficient to establish that fair market value of the obligations included in such issue. In determining whether the purchases are sufficient to establish the fair market value, all the surrounding facts and circumstances will be considered, including the number of independent purchasers, the aggregate amount purchased by each such independent purchaser, and the number of transactions. In the case of a large issue, purchases of a small percentage of the outstanding obligations may be considered purchases of a substantial portion of the issue; whereas, in the case of a small issue, purchases of a larger percentage of the outstanding obligations will ordinarily be required. The requirement in paragraph (b)(3)(ii) of this section contemplates purchase of the obligations by persons independent of the issuer contemporaneously with the purchase by the employee trust. If a substantial portion has been purchased at different prices, the price of the portion may be based on the average of such prices, and if several substantial portions have been sold to persons independent of the issuer, the price of any of the substantial portions may be used for purposes of this subparagraph

(4) From the issuer. An obligation may be purchased directly from the issuer at a price not greater than the price paid currently for a substantial portion of the same issue by persons independent of the issuer. This requirement contemplates purchase of a substantial portion of the same issue by persons independent of the issuer contemporaneously with the purchase by the employee trust. For purposes of this subparagraph, a portion of the issue will be considered substantial if the purchases of such portion by persons independent of the issuer are sufficient to establish the fair market value of the obligations included in such issue. In determining whether the purchases are sufficient to establish the fair market value, all the surrounding facts and circumstances will be considered, including the number of independent purchasers, the aggregate amount purchased by each such independent purchaser, and the number of transactions. In the case of a large issue, purchases of a small percentage of the outstanding obligations may be considered purchases of a substantial portion of the issue; whereas, in the case of a small issue, purchases of a larger percentage of the outstanding obligations will ordinarily be required. The price paid for a substantial portion of the issue may be determined in the manner provided in paragraph (b)(3) of this section.

(c) Limitations on holdings of obligations. *(1)* Immediately following acquisition of the obligation by the employee trust:

(i) Not more than 25 percent of the aggregate amount of the obligations issued in such issue and outstanding immediately after acquisition by the trust may be held by the trust, and

(ii) At least 50 percent of such aggregate amount must be held by persons independent of the issuer.

(2) (i) For purposes of paragraph (c)(1) of this section, an obligation is not considered as outstanding if it is held by the issuer. For example, if an obligation which has been issued and outstanding is repurchased and held by the issuer, without cancellation or retirement, such an obligation is not considered outstanding.

(ii) For purposes of paragraph (c)(1) of this section, the amounts of the obligations held by the trust and by persons independent of the issuer shall be computed on the basis of the face amount of the obligations.

(d) Limitation on amount invested in obligations. *(1)* (i) Immediately following acquisition of the obligation, not more 25 percent of the assets of the employee trust may be invested in all obligations of all persons described in section 503(b). For purposes of determining the amount of the trust's assets which are invested in obligations of persons described in section 503(b) immediately following acquisition of the obligation, those obligations shall be valued as follows:

(a) Those obligations included in the acquisition in respect of which the percentage test in the first sentence of this subdivision is being applied shall be valued at their adjusted basis, as provided in section 1011, relating to adjusted basis for determining gain or loss; and

(b) All other obligations of persons described in section 503(b) which were part of the trust's assets immediately before the acquisition of the obligations described in (d)(1)(i)(a) of this section shall be valued at their fair market value on the day that the obligations described in (d)(1)(i)(a) of this section were acquired. For purposes of determining the total amount of the assets of the trust(including obligations of persons described in section 503(b)), there shall be used the fair market value of those assets on the day the obligation is acquired.

(ii) The application of the rules in paragraph (d)(1)(i) of this section may be illustrated by the following example:

Example. On February 1, 1960, an exempt employees' trust described in section 401(a) purchases unsecured debentures issued by the employer corporation for $1,000. At the time of this purchase, such debentures have a fair market value of $1,200. Immediately after the purchase of such unsecured debentures, the assets of the trust consist of the following:

	Cost	Fair market value on Feb. 1, 1960
(a) Assets other than obligations of persons described in sec. 503(b)	$5,000	$7,800
(b) Obligations of persons described in sec. 503(b) acquired before Feb. 1, 1960	500	1,000
(c) Unsecured debentures of employer purchased on Feb. 1, 1960	1,000	1,200

Immediately following acquisition of the unsecured debentures by the trust, the percent of the assets of the trust that are invested in all obligations of all persons described in section 503(b) is computed as follows:

(1) Obligations of persons described in section 503(b) acquired before Feb. 1, 1960 (valued at fair market value)	$1,000
(2) Unsecured debentures of employer purchased on Feb. 1, 1960 (valued at cost)	1,000
(3) Total amount of trust's assets invested in obligations of persons described in section 503(b)((1) plus (2))	2,000
(4) Assets of the trust other than obligations of persons described in section 503(b) (valued at fair market value on Feb. 1, 1960)	7,800
(5) Obligations of persons described in section 503(b) acquired before Feb. 1, 1960 (valued at fair market value on Feb. 1, 1960)	1,000
(6) Unsecured debentures of employer purchased on Feb. 1, 1960 (valued at fair market value on Feb. 1, 1960)	$1,200
(7) Total assets of the trust valued at fair market value on Feb. 1, 1960 (sum of (4), (5), and (6))	10,000
(8) Percent of assets of the trust invested in all obligations of all persons described in section 503(b) immediately following purchase of unsecured debentures on Feb. 1, 1960 ((3) ÷ (7), that is, $2,000 ÷ $10,000)	20%

(2) In determining for purposes of subparagraph (1) of this paragraph the amount invested in obligations of persons described in section 503(b), there shall be included amounts invested in any obligations issued by any such person, irrespective of whether the obligation is secured, and irrespective of whether the obligation meets the conditions of section 503(e) or section 503(f). Obligations of persons described in section 503(b) other than the issuer of the obligation to which section 503(e) applies are also included within the 25 percent limitation. For example, if on February 19, 1959, an exempt employees' trust described in section 401(a) purchases unsecured debentures issued by the employer corporation in a transaction effected on the New York Stock Exchange, and if immediately after the purchase 10 percent of the trust's assets is invested in such debentures and 20 percent of its assets is invested in a loan made with adequate security on January 12, 1959, to the wholly-owned subsidiary of the employer corporation, then the purchase of the employer's debentures will not qualify under section 503(e), since 30 percent of the trust's assets are then invested in obligations of persons described in section 503(b).

(e) Change of terms of an obligation. A change in terms of an obligation is considered as the acquisition of a new obligation. If such new obligation is not adequately secured, the requirements of section 503(e) must be met at the time the terms of the obligation are changed for such section to be applicable to such new loan.

T.D. 7428, 8/13/76.

§ 1.503(e)-3 Effective dates.

(a) Section 503(e) and §§ 1.503(e)-1 and 1.503(e)-3 are effective in the case of an employees' trust described in section 401(a) for taxable years ending after March 15, 1956. Thus, if during a taxable year ending before March 16, 1956, an employees' trust made a loan which meets the requirements of section 503(e), such loan will not be treated as made without the receipt of adequate security and will not cause the loss of exemption for taxable years ending after March 15, 1956, although such loan was not considered adequately secured when made. (However, section 503 does not apply to organizations described in section 401(a) not referred to in section 4975(g) (2) or (3) for transactions occurring after December 31, 1974.)

(b) *(1)* In the case of obligations acquired by an employees' trust described in section 401(a) before September 2, 1958, which were held on that date, the requirements described in paragraphs (c) and (d) of § 1.503(e)-2 which were not satisfied immediately following the acquisition shall be treated as satisfied at that time if those requirements would have been satisfied had the obligations been acquired on September 2, 1958. For example, on January 3, 1955, an employees' trust described in section 401(a) purchased through the New York Stock Exchange unsecured debentures issued by the employer corporation. Under section 503(e) the acquisition of such debentures by the trust will not be treated for taxable years ending after March 15, 1956, as a loan made without the receipt of adequate security if the debentures were held by the employees' trust on September 2, 1958, and if the requirements of paragraphs (c) and (d) of § 1.503(e)-2 which were not met on January 3, 1955, were met on September 2, 1958, as if that date were the date of acquisition.

(2) In the case of obligations acquired before September 2, 1958, which were not held by the employees' trust described in section 401(a) on that date, only the requirements described in paragraph (b) of § 1.503(e)-2 must be satisfied for section 503(e) to be applicable to such acquisition. For example, if on December 5, 1956, an employees' trust lent money to the employer corporation by purchasing a debenture issued by the employer and if the trust sold the debenture on August 1, 1958, such loan would not be treated as made without the receipt of adequate security if the requirement described in paragraph (b) of § 1.503(e)-2 was met on December 5, 1956.

(c) Section 503(e) and §§ 1.503(e)-1 and 1.503(e)-2 are effective in the case of trusts described in section 501(c)(17) with respect to loans made, renewed, or, in the case of demand loans, continued after December 31, 1959, and in the case of trust described in section 501(c)(18) with respect to loans made, renewed or, in the case of demand loans, continued after December 31, 1969.

(d) See paragraph (b)(2) of § 1.503(b)-1 for the effective dates for the application of the definition of adequate security.

T.D. 7428, 8/13/76.

§ 1.503(e)-4 Disallowance of charitable deductions for certain gifts made before January 1, 1970.

Paragraphs (a), (b), and (c) of this section shall apply only to gifts or contributions made before January 1, 1970, to an organization described in section 501(c)(3). For rules relating to the denial of deductions with respect to gifts or contributions made after December 31, 1969, see § 1.503(c)-1(d).

(a) No gift or contribution which would otherwise be allowable as a charitable or other deductions under section 170, 642(c), or 545(b)(2) shall be allowed as a deduction if made to an organization described in section 501(c)(3) which at the time the gift or contribution is made is not exempt under section 501(a) by reason of the provisions of section 503.

(b) If an organization which is described in section 501(c)(3) is not exempt because it engaged in a prohibited transaction involving a substantial part of its income of corpus with the purpose of diverting its income or corpus from its exempt purposes, and if the organization receives a gift or contribution during, or prior to, its taxable year in which such prohibited transaction occurred, then a deduction by the donor with respect to the gift or contribution shall not be disallowed under section 503(b) unless the donor (or any member of his family if the donor is an individual) is a party to such prohibited transaction. For the purpose of the preceding sentence family is defined in section 267(c)(4) and includes brothers and sisters, whether by whole or half blood, spouse, ancestors, and lineal descendants. See the regulations under section 267(c).

(c) The application of § 1.503(e)-4 may be illustrated by the following example:

Example. In 1954, Corporation M, which files its income tax returns on the calendar year basis, creates a foundation purportedly for charitable purposes and deducts from its gross income for that year the amount of the gift to the foundation. Corporation M makes additional gifts to this foundation in 1955, 1956, and 1957, and takes charitable deductions for such years. B, an individual, also contributes to the foundation in 1955, 1956, and 1957, and takes charitable deductions for such years. In 1955, the foundation commences purposely to divert its corpus to the benefit of Corporation M, and a substantial amount of such corpus is so diverted by the close of the taxable year 1956. For 1955 and subsequent taxable years, the exemption allowed the foundation as an organization described in section 501(c)(3) is denied by reason of the provisions of section 503(a). Both Corporation M and individual B would be disallowed any deduction for the contributions made during 1957 to the foundation. Moreover, the charitable deductions taken by Corporation M for contributions to the foundation in the years 1955 and 1956 would also be disallowed since Corporation M was a party to the prohibited transactions. If the facts and surrounding circumstances indicate that the contribution in 1954 by Corporation M was for the purpose of the prohibited transaction, then the charitable deduction for the year 1954 shall also be disallowed with respect to Corporation M, since the prohibited transaction would then have commenced with the making of such contribution and the exemption allowed the foundation would then be denied for 1954 by reason of the provisions of § 1.503(e)-4. B's deductions for his contributions for the years 1955 and 1956 will not be disallowed since he was not a party to the prohibited transaction.

T.D. 7428, 8/16/76.

§ 1.503(f)-1 Loans by employers who are prohibited from pledging assets.

(a) In general. *(1)* Section 503(f) provides that section 503(b)(1) shall not apply to a loan made to the employer by an employees' trust described in section 401(a) if the loan bears a reasonable rate of interest and certain conditions are met. Section 503(f) also applies to the renewal of loans to the employer and, in the case of demand loans, to the continuation of such loans.

(2) The provisions of section 503(f) do not limit the effect of section 401(a) and § 1.401-2, relating to use or diversion of corpus or income of an employees' trust, or the effect of any of the provisions of section 503 other than section 503(b)(1). Consequently, although a loan made by an employees' trust described in section 503(a)(1)(B) meets all the requirements of section 503(f) and therefore is not treated as a loan made without the receipt of adequate security, an employees' trust making such a loan will lose its exemption status if the loan is not considered as made for the exclusive benefit of the employees or their beneficiaries. Similarly, a loan which meets the requirements of section 503(f) will constitute a prohibited transaction within the meaning of section 503(b)(6) if it results in a substantial diversion of the trust's income or corpus to a person described in section 503(b).

(b) Conditions. *(1)* Section 503(f) applies to a loan only if, with respect to the making or renewal of the loan, the conditions described in paragraphs (b)(2), (3), and (4) of this section are met. For purpose of this paragraph, the mere continuance of a demand loan is not considered as the making or renewal of such a loan.

(2) The employer must be prohibited (at the time of the making or renewal of the loan) by any law of the United States or regulations thereunder from directly or indirectly pledging, as security for such a loan, a particular class or classes of his assets the value of which (at such time) represents more than one-half of the value of all his assets. If a loan is made or renewed when the employer is prohibited by a law of the United States (or the regulations thereunder) from pledging a class of his assets, the qualification of such a loan under section 503(f) will not be affected by a subsequent change in such law or regulations permitting the employer to pledge such assets, unless such loan is renewed after such change. See section 8(a) of the Securities Exchange Act of 1934, as amended (15 U.S.C. 78h(a)), which prohibits certain persons from pledging a class of assets as security for loans, and 12 CFR 220.5(a) (credit by brokers, dealers, and members of national securities exchanges).

(3) The making or renewal, as the case may be, must be approved in writing as an investment which is consistent with the exempt purposes of the trust by a trustee who is independent of the employer, and such written approval must not have been previously refused by any other such trustee. A trustee is independent of the employer, for purposes of this subparagraph, if he is entirely free of influence or controlled by the employer. For example, if the employer is a partnership then a partner in such partnership, or a member of a partner's family would not be considered independent of the employer. Similarly, an employee of the employer would not be considered independent of the employer. For purposes of this subparagraph, the term "trustee" means, with respect to any trust for which there are two trustees who are independent of the employer, both of such trustees and, with respect to any trust for which there are more than two such independent trustees, a majority of the trustees independent of the employer.

(4) (i) Immediately following the making or renewal, as the case may be, the aggregate amount lent by the trust to the employer, without the receipt of adequate security must not exceed 25 percent of the value of all the assets of the trust.

(ii) For purposes of paragraph (b)(4)(i) of this section, the determination as to whether any amount lent by the trust to the employer is a loan made without the receipt of adequate security shall be made without regard to section 503(e). Thus, if an employees' trust makes a loan on January 2, 1959, to the employer without adequate security (but which loan is not considered as made without adequate security under section 503(e)), and if immediately after making such loan 10 percent of the value of all its assets is invested in such loan, then the trust may on that day invest not more than an additional 15 percent of its assets in a loan which would be considered made without adequate security if it were not for the provisions of section 503(f).

(iii) For purposes of paragraph (b)(4)(i) of this section, in determining the value of all the assets of the trust, there shall be used the fair market value of those assets on the day of the making or renewal.

(c) Reasonable rate of interest. Section 503(f) only applies if, in addition to meeting the conditions described in paragraph (b) of this section, the loan bears a reasonable rate of interest when it is made, renewed, or, in the case of demand loans, during the period of its existence.

(d) Change of terms of loan. A change in the terms of a loan (including a reduction in the security for a loan) is considered as the making of a new loan. If such a new loan is not adequately secured, the requirements of section 503(f) must be met at the time the terms of the loan are changed for such section to be applicable to such new loan.

(e) Effective date. *(1)* This section and section 503(f) are effective for taxable years ending after September 2, 1958, but only with respect to periods after such date. Thus, if a loan was made on or before September 2, 1958, without the receipt of adequate security and if, when such loan was made, it met all of the requirements of section 503(f) and this section, then the loan is not subject to section 503(b)(1) after September 2, 1958, and would not constitute a prohibited transaction after that date because of a lack of adequate security.

(2) See paragraph (b)(2) of § 1.503(b)-1 for the effective dates for application of the definition of adequate security.

T.D. 7428, 8/13/76.

§ 1.504-1 Attempts to influence legislation; certain organizations formerly described in section 501(c)(3) denied exemption.

Section 504(a) and this section apply to an organization that is exempt from taxation at any time after October 4, 1976, as an organization described in section 501(c)(3), and that ceases to be described in that section because it—

(a) Is an "action" organization within the meaning of § 1.501(c)(3)-1(c)(3)(ii) or (iv), on account of activities occurring after October 4, 1976, or

(b) Is denied exemption under the provisions of section 501(h) (see § 1.501(h)-3 or § 56.4911-9).

This section does not apply, however, to an organization that was described in section 501(h)(5) and § 1.501(h)-2(b)(3) (relating generally to churches) for its taxable year immediately preceding the first taxable year for which it is no longer an organization described in section 501(c)(3). An organization to which section 504(a) and this section apply shall not be treated as described in section 501(c)(4) at any time after the organization ceases to be described in section 501(c)(3). Further, an organization denied treatment as an organization described in section 501(c)(4) under this section may not be treated as an organization described in section 501(c) other than as an organization described in section 501(c)(3). For rules relating to recognition of exemption after exemption is denied under section 501(h), see § 1.501(h)-3(d).

T.D. 6301, 7/8/58, amend T.D. 7428, 8/13/76, T.D. 8308, 8/30/90.

§ 1.504-2 Certain transfers made to avoid section 504(a).

(a) Scope. Under section 504(b), a transfer described in paragraph (b) or (c) of this section to an organization exempt from tax under section 501(a) may result in loss of exemption by the transferee unless the Commissioner determines, under paragraph (e) of this section, that the original transfer did not effect an avoidance of section 504(a). For purposes of this section, the term "transfer" includes any use by, or for the benefit of, the recipient of the transfer, but does not include any transfer made for adequate and full consideration.

(b) Transferor and transferee commonly controlled. *(1) Loss of exemption.* A transfer is described in this paragraph (b) if it is described in paragraphs (b)(2) through (b)(6). The transferee of a transfer described in this paragraph will cease to be exempt from tax under section 501(a), unless the provisions of paragraph (e) of this section apply.

(2) Transferor organization. A transfer is described in this paragraph (b)(2) only if it is from an organization that—

(i) Is or was described in section 501(c)(3), but not in section 501(h)(5), and

(ii) Is determined to be an "action" organization (as defined in § 1.501(c)(3)-1(c)(3)(ii) or (iv)), or is denied exemption from tax by reason of section 501(h) and either § 1.501(h)-3 or § 56.4911-9.

(3) Transferor and transferee commonly controlled. A transfer is described in this paragraph (b)(3) only if, at the time of the transfer or at any time during the transferee's ten taxable years following the year in which the transfer was made, the transferee is controlled (directly or indirectly), as defined in paragraph (f) of this section, by the same person or persons who control the transferor.

(4) Time of transfer. A transfer is described in this paragraph (b)(4) only if the transfer is made—

(i) After the date that is 24 months before the earliest of the effective date of the determination under section 501(h) that the transferor is not exempt, the effective date of the Commissioner's determination that the transferor is an "action" organization (as defined in § 1.501(c)(3)(ii) or (iv)), or the date on which the Commissioner proposes to treat it as no longer described in section 501(c)(3), and

(ii) Before the transferor again is recognized as an organization described in section 501(c)(3).

(5) Transferee. A transfer is described in this paragraph (b)(5) only if the transferee is exempt from tax under section 501(a) but the transferee is neither—

(i) An organization described in section 501(c)(3), nor

(ii) An organization described in section 401(a) to which the transferor contributes as an employer.

(6) Amount of transfer. A transfer is described in this paragraph (b)(6) only if the amount of the transfer exceeds the lesser of 30 percent of the net fair market value of the transferor's assets or 50 percent of the net fair market value of the transferee's assets, computed immediately before the transfer. For purposes of this paragraph (b)(6)—

(i) The amount of a transfer by a transferor is the sum of the amounts transferred to any number of transferees in any number of transfers, all of which are described in paragraphs (b)(2) through (b)(5) of this section, and the time of the transfer is the time of the first transfer so taken into account; and

(ii) The amount of a transfer to a transferee is the sum of the amounts transferred by a transferor to the transferee in any number of transfers, all of which are described in paragraphs (b)(2) through (b)(5) of this section, and the time of the transfer is the time of the first transfer so taken into account.

(c) Other transfers. *(1) Transfers included.* A transfer is described in this paragraph (c) if it would be described in paragraph (b) of this section except that either—

(i) The amount of the transfer is less than the amount determined in paragraph (b)(6) of this section, or

(ii) The transferor and transferee are not commonly controlled as described in paragraph (b)(3) of this section, or

(iii) The transferee is an organization described in sections 501(c)(3) and 501(h)(4).

(2) Loss of exemption. The transferee of a transfer described in this paragraph (c) will cease to be exempt under section 501(a) if the commissioner determines on all the facts and circumstances that the transfer effected an avoidance of section 501(a). In determining whether a transfer effected an avoidance of section 501(a), the Commissioner may consider whether the transferee engages, or has engaged, in attempts to influence legislation and may also consider any factors enumerated in paragraph (e) of this section.

(d) Date of loss of exempt status. A transferee of a transfer described in paragraph (b), (c)(1)(ii), or (c)(1)(iii) of this section will cease to be exempt from tax under section 501(a) on the date that all requirements of paragraph (b), (c)(1)(ii), or (c)(1)(iii) (other than the determination by the Commissioner) are satisfied. A transferee of a transfer described in paragraph (c)(1)(i) of this section will cease to be exempt from tax under section 501(a) on the date of the last transfer preceding notification of the transferee that the Commissioner proposes to treat the transferee as other than an exempt organization.

(e) Transfers not in avoidance of section 504(a). Notwithstanding paragraph (b) of this section, if, based on all the facts and circumstances, the Commissioner determines that a transfer described in paragraph (b) did not effect an avoidance of section 504(a), the transferee will not be denied exemption from tax by reason of section 504(b) and this section. In making the determination called for in the preceding sentence, the Commissioner may consider all relevant factors including:

(1) Whether enforceable and effective conditions on the transfer preclude use of any of the transferred assets for any purpose that, if it were a substantial part of an organization's activities, would be inconsistent with exemption as an organization described in section 501(c)(3);

(2) In the absence of conditions described in paragraph (e)(1) of this section, whether the transferred assets are used exclusively for purposes that are consistent with the transferor's exemption as an organization described in section 501(c)(3);

(3) Whether the assets transferred would be described in § 53.4942(a)-2(c)(3) before, as well as after, the transfer if both the transferor and transferee were private foundations;

(4) Whether and to what extent the transfer would satisfy the provisions of § 1.507-2(a)(7) and (8) if the transferor were a private foundation;

(5) Whether all of the transferred assets have been expended during a period when the transferee was not controlled (directly or indirectly) by the same person or persons who controlled the transferor; and

(6) Whether the entire amount of the transferred assets were in turn transferred, before the close of the transferee's taxable year following the taxable year in which the transferred assets were received, to one or more organizations described in section 507(b)(1)(A) none of which are controlled (directly or indirectly) by the same persons who control either the original transferor or transferee.

(f) Control. For purposes of section 504 and the regulations thereunder—

(1) The transferor will be presumed to control any organization with which it is affiliated within the meaning of § 56.4911-7(a), or would be if both organizations were described in section 501(c)(3), and

(2) The transferee will be treated as controlled (directly of indirectly) by the same person or persons who control the

transferor if the transferee would be treated as controlled under § 53.4942(a)-3(a)(3), for which purpose the transferor shall be treated as a private foundation.

T.D. 8308, 8/30/90.

§ 1.505(c)-1T Questions and answers relating to the notification requirement for recognition of exemption under paragraphs (9), (17) and (20) of section 501(c) (temporary).

Caution: The Treasury has not yet amended Reg § 1.505(c)-1T to reflect changes made by P.L. 99-514.

Q-1. What does section 505(c) of the Internal Revenue Code provide?

A-1. Section 505(c) provides that an organization will not be recognized as exempt under section 501(c)(9) as a voluntary employees' beneficiary association, under section 501(c)(17) as a trust forming part of a plan providing for the payment of supplemental unemployment compensation benefits, or under section 501(c)(20) as a trust forming part of a qualified group legal services plan unless notification is given to the Internal Revenue Service. The notification required of a trust created pursuant to section 501(c)(20) and forming part of a qualified group legal services plan is set forth in Q&A-2. The notification required of an organization organized after July 18, 1984, and applying for exempt status as an organization described in section 501(c)(9) or (17) is set forth in Q&A-3 through Q&A-8. The notification required of an organization organized on or before July 18, 1984, and claiming exemption as an organization described in section 501(c)(9) or (17) is set forth in Q&A-9 through Q& A-11. However, an organization that has previously notified the Internal Revenue Service of its claim to exemption under section 501(c)(9), (17), or (20) or its claim to exemption under those sections pursuant to another provision of the Code, is not required, under section 505(c), to submit a renotification (See Q&A-2 and Q&A-12).

Section 501(c)(20) Trusts

Q-2. What is the notice required of a trust created pursuant to section 501(c)(20) and forming part of a qualified group legal services plan under section 120?

A-2. (a) A trust claiming exemption as an organization described in section 501(c)(20) will be recognized as exempt if the exclusive function of the trust is to form part of a qualified group legal services plan or plans. Exemption of the trust under section 501(c)(20) will generally be dependent upon and coextensive with recognition of the plan as a qualified group legal services plan. Therefore, a trust organized pursuant to section 501(c)(20) after July 18, 1984, need not file a separate notice with the Internal Revenue Service of its claim to exemption because the notice required by section 120(c)(4) will suffice for purposes of section 505(c), provided a copy of the trust instrument is filed with the Form 1024 submitted by the group legal services plan. If the trust instrument has not been filed with the Form 1024 submitted by the group legal services plan, the trust must comply with (and exemption will be dependent upon) the filing applicable to a trust organized on or before July 18, 1984. For the notice required and effective dates of exemption of a qualified group legal services plan under section 120, see § 1.120-3.

(b) A trust organized on or before July 18, 1984, that claims exempt status as a trust described in section 501(c)(20) and that forms part of a qualified group legal services plan which has been recognized as exempt under section 120, must file a copy of its trust instrument with the Internal Revenue Service before February 4, 1987. If a copy of the trust instrument is filed within the time provided, the trust's exemption will be recognized retroactively to the date the qualified group legal services plan was recognized as exempt under section 120. However, if a copy of the trust instrument is filed after the time provided, exemption will be recognized only for the period after the copy of the trust instrument is filed with the Internal Revenue Service. See Q&A-7 for a further discussion of "date of filing." A trust that has previously filed a copy of its trust instrument with the Service need not refile that document.

Section 501(c)(9) and (17) Organizations Organized After July 18, 1984

Q-3. What is the notice required of an organization or trust, organized after July 18, 1984, that is applying for recognition of tax exempt status under section 501(c)(9) or (17)?

A-3. An organization or trust that is organized after July 18, 1984, will not be treated as described in paragraphs (9) or (17) of section 501(c), unless the organization notifies the Internal Revenue Service that it is applying for recognition of exemption. In addition, unless the required notice is given in the manner and within the time prescribed by these regulations, an organization will not be treated as exempt for any period before the giving of the required notice. The notice is filed by submitting a properly completed and executed Form 1024, "Application for Recognition of Exemption Under Section 501(a) or for Determination Under Section 120" together with the additional information required under Q&A-4 and Q&A-5. The notice is filed with the district director for the key district in which the organization's principal place of business or principal office is located.

The notice may be filed by either the plan administrator (as defined in section 414(g)) or the trustee. The Internal Revenue Service will not accept a Form 1024 for any organization or trust before such entity has been organized.

Q-4. What information, in addition to the information required by Form 1024, must be submitted by an organization or trust seeking recognition of exemption under section 501(c)(9) or (17)?

A-4. A notice will not be considered complete unless, in addition to a properly completed and executed Form 1024, the organization or trust submits a full description of the benefits available to participants under section 501(c)(9) or (17). Moreover, both the terms and conditions of eligibility for membership and the terms and conditions of eligibility for benefits must be set forth. This information may be contained in a separate document, such as a "plan document," or it may be contained in the creating document of the entity (e.g., the articles of incorporation or association, or a trust indenture). For benefits provided through a policy or policies of insurance, all such policies must be included with the notice. Where individual policies of insurance are provided to the participants, single exemplar copies, typical of policies generally issued to participants, are acceptable, provided they adequately describe all forms of insurance available to participants. In providing a full description of the benefits available, the benefits provided must be sufficiently described so that each benefit is definitely determinable. A benefit is definitely determinable if the amount of the benefit, its duration, and the persons eligible to receive it are ascertainable from the plan document or other instrument. Thus, a benefit is not definitely determinable if the rules governing either its amount, its duration, or its recipients are not ascertainable from the plan document or other instrument but are instead subject to the discretion of a person or committee. Likewise, a benefit is not definitely determinable if the amount for any individual is based upon a percentage share of any item that is within the discretion of the employer. However, a disability benefit will not fail to be considered definitely determinable merely because the determination of whether an individual is disabled is made under established guidelines by an authorized person or committee.

Q-5. What is the notice required of collectively bargained plans?

A-5. If an organization or trust claiming exemption under section 501(c)(9) or (17) is organized and maintained pursuant to a collective bargaining agreement between employee representatives and one or more employer, only one Form 1024 is required to be filed for the organization or trust, regardless of the number of employers originally participating in the agreement. Moreover, once a Form 1024 is filed pursuant to a collective bargaining agreement, an additional Form 1024 is not required to be filed by an employer who thereafter participates in that agreement. When benefits are provided pursuant to a collective bargaining agreement, the notice will not be considered complete unless, in addition to a properly completed and executed Form 1024, a copy of the collective bargaining agreement is also submitted together with the additional information delineated in Q&A-4.

Q-6. When must the required notice be filed by an organization or trust, organized after July 18, 1984, that seeks recognition of exemption under section 501(c)(9) or (17)?

A-6. An organization or trust applying for exemption must file the required notice by the later of February 4, 1987 or 15 months from the end of the month in which the organization or trust was organized. An extension of time for filing the required notice may be granted by the district director if the request is submitted before the end of the applicable period and it is demonstrated that additional time is needed.

Q-7. What is the effective date of exemption for a new organization or trust, organized after July 18, 1984, that has submitted the required notice?

A-7. If the required notice is filed within the time provided by these regulations, the organization's exemption will be recognized retroactively to the date the organization was organized, provided its purpose, organization and operation (including compliance with the applicable nondiscrimination requirements) during the period prior to the date of the determination letter are in accordance with the applicable law. However, if the required notice is filed after the time provided by these regulations, exemption will be recognized only for the period after the application is filed with the Internal Revenue Service. The date of filing is the date of the United States postmark on the cover in which an exemption application is mailed or, if no postmark appears on the cover, the date the application is stamped as received by the Service. If an extension for filing the required notice has been granted to the organization, a notice filed on or before the last day specified in the extension will be considered timely and not the otherwise applicable date under Q&A-6.

Q-8. What is the effect on exemption of the filing of an incomplete notice?

A-8. Although a properly completed and executed form 1024 together with the required additional information (See Q&A-4 and Q&A-5) must be submitted to satisfy the notice required by section 505(c), the failure to file, within the time specified, all of the information necessary to complete such notice will not alone be sufficient to deny recognition of exemption from the date of organization to the date the completed information is submitted to the Service. If the notice which is filed with the Service within the required time is substantially complete, and the organization supplies the necessary additional information requested by the Service within the additional time allowed, the original notice will be considered timely. However, if the notice is not substantially complete or the additional information is not provided within the additional time allowed, exemption will be recognized only from the date of filing of the additional information.

Section 501(c)(9) and (17) Organizations Organized on or Before July 18, 1984

Q-9. What is the notice required of an organization or trust organized on or before July 18, 1984, that claims exempt status as an organization described in section 501(c)(9) or (17)?

A-9. Section 505(c) provides a special rule for existing organizations and trusts organized on or before July 18, 1984. Such an organization or trust will not be treated as described in paragraphs (9) or (17) of section 501(c) unless the organization or trust notifies the Internal Revenue Service in the manner and within the time prescribed in these regulations that it is claiming exemption under the particular section. The type of notice, the manner for filing that notice, and the additional information required is the same as that set forth in Q& A-3 through Q&A-5 for new organizations.

Q-10. When must the required notice be filed by an organization or trust organized on or before July 18, 1984?

A-10. An organization or trust organized on or before July 18, 1984, that claims exempt status as an organization described in section 501(c)(9) or (17), must file the required notice before February 4, 1987. An extension of time for filing the required notice may be granted by the district director if the request is submitted before the due date of the notice and it is demonstrated that additional time is needed.

Q-11. What is the effective date of exemption for an organization or trust organized on or before July 18, 1984, that has submitted the required notice?

A-11. If the required notice is filed within the time provided by these regulations, the organization's exemption will be recognized retroactively to the date the organization was organized, provided its purpose, organization and operation (including compliance with the applicable nondiscrimination requirements) during the period prior to the date of the determination letter are in accordance with the applicable law. If, on the other hand, the required notice is filed after the time provided by these regulations, exemption will be recognized only for the period after the notice is received by the Internal Revenue Service. See Q&A-7 for a further discussion of "date of filing." See also Q&A-8 for the effect on exemption of a notice that has been timely filed but is incomplete.

Exceptions to Notice Requirement

Q-12. Are any organizations or trusts claiming recognition of exemption as an organization described in section 501(c)(9) or (17) excepted from the notice requirement of section 505(c)?

A-12. An organization or trust that has previously notified the Internal Revenue Service of its claim to exemption by filing Form 1024 is not required, under section 505(c), to renotify the Service. Thus, an organization that has filed a Form 1024 that is pending with the Service need not refile that form. Also, an organization that has received a ruling or determination letter from the Service recognizing its exemption from taxation need not submit the notification required by section 505(c).

T.D. 8073, 1/29/86.

§ 1.507-1 General rule.

(a) In general. Except as provided in § 1.507-2, the status of any organization as a private foundation shall be terminated only if—

(1) Such organization notifies the district director of its intent to accomplish such termination, or

(2) (i) With respect to such organization, there have been either willful repeated acts (or failures to act), or a willful and flagrant act (or failure to act), giving rise to liability for tax under chapter 42, and

(ii) The Commissioner notifies such organization that, by reason of subdivision (i) of this subparagraph, such organization is liable for the tax imposed by section 507(c), and either such organization pays the tax imposed by section 507(c) (or any portion not abated under section 507(g)) or the entire amount of such tax is abated under section 507(g).

(b) Termination under section 507(a)(1). *(1)* In order to terminate its private foundation status under paragraph (a)(1) of this section, an organization must submit a statement to the district director of its intent to terminate its private foundation status under section 507(a)(1). Such statement must set forth in detail the computation and amount of tax imposed under section 507(c). Unless the organization requests abatement of such tax pursuant to section 507(g), full payment of such tax must be made at the time the statement is filed under section 507(a)(1). An organization may request the abatement of all of the tax imposed under section 507(c), or may pay any part thereof and request abatement of the unpaid portion of the amount of tax assessed. If the organization requests abatement of the tax imposed under section 507(c) and such request is denied, the organization must pay such tax in full upon notification by the Internal Revenue Service that such tax will not be abated. For purposes of subtitle F of the Code, the statement described in this subparagraph, once filed shall be treated as a return.

(2) Termination of private foundation status under section 507(a)(1) does not relieve a private foundation, or any disqualified person with respect thereto, of liability for tax under chapter 42 with respect to acts or failures to act prior to termination or for any additional taxes imposed for failure to correct such acts or failures to act. See subparagraph (8) of this paragraph as to the possible imposition of transferee liability in cases not involving termination of private foundation status.

(3) In the case of an organization which has terminated its private foundation status under section 507(a) and continues in operation thereafter, if such organization wishes to be treated as described in section 501(c)(3), then pursuant to section 509(c) and § 1.509(c)-1 such organization must apply for recognition of exemption as an organization described in section 501(c)(3) in accordance with the provisions of section 508(a).

(4) See § 53.4947-1(c)(7) of this chapter as to the application of section 507(a) to certain split-interest trusts.

(5) For purposes of section 508(d)(1), the Internal Revenue Service shall make notice to the public (such as by publication in the Internal Revenue Bulletin) of any notice received from a private foundation pursuant to section 507(a)(1) or of any notice given to a private foundation pursuant to section 507(a)(2).

(6) If a private foundation transfers all or part of its assets to one or more other private foundations (or one or more private foundations and one or more section 509(a)(1), (2), (3), or (4) organizations) pursuant to a transfer described in section 507(b)(2) and § 1.507-3(c), such transferor foundation will not have terminated its private foundation status under section 507(a)(1). See § 1.507-3, however, for the special rules applicable to private foundations participating in section 507(b)(2) transfers.

(7) Neither a transfer of all of the assets of a private foundation nor a significant disposition of assets (as defined in § 1.507-3(c)(2)) by a private foundation (whether or not any portion of such significant disposition of assets is made to another private foundation) shall be deemed to result in a termination of the transferor private foundation under section 507(a) unless the transferor private foundation elects to terminate pursuant to section 507(a)(1) or section 507(a)(2) is applicable. Thus, if a private foundation transfers all of its assets to one or more persons, but less than all of its net assets to one or more organizations described in section 509(a)(1) which have been in existence and so described for a continuous period of 60 calendar months, for purposes of this paragraph such transferor foundation will not be deemed by reason of such transfer to have terminated its private foundation status under section 507(a) or (b) unless section 507(a)(2) is applicable. Such foundation will continue to be treated as a private foundation for all purposes. For example, if a private foundation transfers all of its net assets to a section 509(a)(2) organization in 1971 and receives a bequest in 1973, the bequest will be regarded as having been made to a private foundation and the foundation will be subject to the provisions of chapter 42 with respect to such funds. If a private foundation makes a transfer of all of its net assets to a section 509(a)(2) or (3) organization, for example, it must retain sufficient income or assets to pay the tax imposed under section 4940 for that portion of its taxable year prior to such transfer. For additional rules applicable to a transfer by a private foundation of all of its net assets to a section 509(a)(1) organization which has not been in existence and so described for a continuous period of 60 calendar months, see § 1.507-3(e).

(8) If a private foundation makes a transfer described in subparagraph (7) of this paragraph and prior to, or in connection with, such transfer, liability for any tax under chapter 42 is incurred by the transferor foundation, transferee liability may be applied against the transferee organization for payment of such taxes. For purposes of this subparagraph, liability for any tax imposed under chapter 42 for failure to correct any act or failure to act shall be deemed incurred on the date on which the act or failure to act giving rise to the initial tax liability occurred.

(9) A private foundation which transfers all of its net assets is required to file the annual information return required by section 6033, and the foundation managers are required to file the annual report of a private foundation required by section 6056, for the taxable year in which such transfer occurs. However, neither such foundation nor its foundation managers will be required to file such returns for any taxable year following the taxable year in which the last of any such transfers occurred, if at no time during the subsequent taxable years in question the foundation has either legal or equitable title to any assets or engages in any activity.

(c) Involuntary termination under section 507(a)(2). *(1)* For purposes of section 507(a)(2)(A), the term "willful repeated acts (or failures to act)" means at least two acts or failures to act both of which are voluntary, conscious, and intentional.

(2) For purposes of section 507(a)(2)(A), a "willful and flagrant act (or failure to act)" is one which is voluntarily, consciously, and knowingly committed in violation of any provision of chapter 42 (other than section 4940 or 4948(a)) and which appears to a reasonable man to be a gross violation of any such provision.

(3) An act (or failure to act) may be treated as an act (or failure to act) by the private foundation for purposes of section 507(a)(2) even though tax is imposed upon one or more foundation managers rather than upon the foundation itself.

(4) For purposes of section 507(a)(2), the failure to correct the act or acts (or failure or failures to act) which gave rise to liability for tax under any section of chapter 42 by the close of the correction period for such section may be a willful and flagrant act (or failure to act).

(5) No motive to avoid the restrictions of the law or the incurrence of any tax is necessary to make an act (or failure to act) willful. However, a foundation's act (or failure to act) is not willful if the foundation (or a foundation manager, if applicable) does not know that it is an act of self-dealing, a taxable expenditure, or other act (or failure to act) to which chapter 42 applies. Rules similar to the regulations under chapter 42 (see, for example, § 53.4945-1(a)(2)(iii) of this chapter) shall apply in determining whether a foundation or a foundation manager "knows" that an act (or failure to act) is an act of self-dealing a taxable expenditure or other such act (or failure to act).

T.D. 7233, 12/20/72, amend T.D. 7290, 11/16/73.

§ 1.507-2 Special rules; transfer to, or operation as, public charity.

(a) Transfer to public charities. *(1) General rule.* Under section 507(b)(1)(A) a private foundation, with respect to which there have not been either willful repeated acts (or failures to act) or a willful and flagrant act (or failure to act) giving rise to liability for tax under chapter 42, may terminate its private foundation status by distributing all of its net assets to one or more organizations described in section 170(b)(1)(A) (other than in clauses (vii) and (viii)) each of which has been in existence and so described for a continuous period of at least 60 calendar months immediately preceding such distribution. Since section 507(a) does not apply to such a termination, a private foundation which makes such a termination is not required to give the notification described in section 507(a)(1). A private foundation which terminates its private foundation status under section 507(b)(1)(A) does not incur tax under section 507(c) and, therefore, no abatement of such tax under section 507(g) is required.

(2) Effect of current ruling. (i) Distributions before final regulations. With respect to distributions made before (insert day after the date these regulations are filed by the Office of the Federal Register), an organization to which a distribution of net assets is made will qualify as an organization "described in section 170(b)(1)(A) (other than clauses (vii) and (viii))" for purposes of meeting the requirements of section 507(b)(1)(A) without a further showing if such distributee organization:

(A) Has been in existence for a continuous period of at least 60 calendar months preceding the distribution described in subparagraph (1) of this paragraph;

(B) Has received a ruling or determination letter that it is an organization described in clause (i), (ii), (iii), (iv), (v), or (vi) of section 170(b)(1)(A);

(C) The facts and circumstances forming the basis for the issuance of the ruling have not substantially changed during the 60-month period referred to in (A) of this subdivision; and

(D) The ruling or determination letter referred to in (B) of this subdivision has not been revoked expressly or by a subsequent change of the law or regulations under which the ruling was issued.

(ii) Distributions after final regulations. With respect to distributions made after December 29, 1972, a private foundation seeking to terminate its private foundation status pursuant to section 507(b)(1)(A) may rely on a ruling or determination letter issued to a potential distributee organization that such distributee organization is an organization described in clause (i), (ii), (iii), (iv), (v), or (vi) of section 170(b)(1)(A) in accordance with the provisions of § 1.509(a)-7.

(3) Organizations described in more than one clause of section 170(b)(1)(A). For purposes of this paragraph and section 507(b)(1)(A), the parenthetical term "other than in clauses (vii) and (viii)" shall refer only to an organization which is described only in section 170(b)(1)(A)(vii) or (viii). Thus, an organization described in clause (i), (ii), (iii), (iv), (v), or (vi) of section 170(b)(1)(A) will not be precluded from being a distributee described in section 507(b)(1)(A) merely because it also appears to meet the description of an organization described in section 170(b)(1)(A)(vii) or (viii).

(4) Applicability of chapter 42 to foundations terminating under section 507(b)(1)(A). Except as provided in subparagraph (5) of this paragraph, an organization which terminates its private foundation status pursuant to section 507(b)(1)(A) will remain subject to the provisions of chapter 42 until the distribution of all of its net assets to distributee organizations described in section 507(b)(1)(A) has been completed.

(5) Special transitional rule. (i) Section 4940(a) imposes a tax upon private foundations with respect to the carrying on of activities for each taxable year. For purposes of section 4940, an organization which terminates its private foundation status under section 507(b)(1)(A) by the end of the period described in subdivision (ii) of this subparagraph will not be considered as carrying on activities within the meaning of section 4940 during such period. Such organization will therefore not be subject to the tax imposed under section 4940(a) for such period.

(ii) The period referred to in subdivision (i) of this subparagraph is the 12-month period beginning with the first day of the organization's first taxable year which begins after December 31, 1969, but such period shall not be treated as ending before February 20, 1973. In the case of a private foundation distributing assets pursuant to section 507(b)(1)(A) to a medical research organization or a community trust (or in the case of a private foundation seeking to terminate into such an organization or trust pursuant to section 507(b)(1)(B)), the period described in this subdivision shall not be treated as ending before:

(A) In the case of a distribution to a medical research organization, March 29, 1976; or

(B) In the case of a community trust, May 11, 1977.

(iii) If the period described in subdivision (ii) of this subparagraph has not expired prior to the due date for the organization's annual return required to be filed by section 6033 or 6012 (determined with regard to any extension of time for filing the return) for its first taxable year which begins after December 31, 1969 (or for any other taxable year ending before the expiration of the period referred to in subdivision (ii) of this subparagraph), and if the organization has not terminated its private foundation status under section 507(b)(1)(A), by such date, then notwithstanding the provisions of subdivision (ii) of this subparagraph, the organization must take either of the following courses of action:

(A) Complete and file its annual return, including the line relating to excise taxes on investment income, by such date, and pay the tax on investment income imposed under section 4940 at the time it files its annual return. If such organization subsequently terminates its private foundation status under section 507(b)(1)(A) within the period specified in subdivision (ii) of this subparagraph, it may file a claim for refund of the tax paid under section 4940; or

(B) Complete and file its annual return, except for the line relating to excise taxes on investment income, by such date, and, in lieu of paying the tax on investment income imposed under section 4940, file a statement with its annual return which establishes that the organization has taken affirmative action by such date to terminate its private foundation status under section 507(b)(1)(A). Such statement must indicate the type of affirmative action taken and explain how such action will result in the termination of its private foundation status under section 507(b)(1)(A). Such affirmative action may include making application to the appropriate State court for approval of the distribution of all net assets pursuant to section 507(b)(1)(A) in the case of a charitable trust, or the passage of a resolution by the organization's governing body directing the distribution of all net assets pursuant to section 507(b)(1)(A) in the case of a not-for-profit corporation. A written commitment or letter of agreement by the trustee or governing body to one or more section 509(a)(1) distributees indicating an intent to distribute all of the organization's net assets to such distributees will also constitute appropriate affirmative action for purposes of this subdivision. An organization may take such affirmative action and may terminate its private foundation status under section 507(b)(1)(A) in reliance upon 26 CFR 13.12 (rev. as of Jan. 1, 1972) and upon the provisions of the notices of proposed rule making under sections 170(b)(1)(A), 507(b)(1), and 509. Thus, if a distributee organization meets the requirements of the provisions of the notices of proposed rule making under sections 170(b)(1)(A), 507, or 509 as a distributee under section 507(b)(1)(A), the distributor organization may terminate its private foundation status under section 507(b)(1)(A) in reliance upon such provisions prior to the expiration of the period described in subdivision (ii) of this subparagraph. If such organization, however, fails to terminate its private foundation status under section 507(b)(1)(A) within the period specified in subdivision (ii) of this subparagraph by failing to meet the requirements of either the notices of proposed rulemaking under section 170(b)(1)(A), 507(b)(1), or 509 or the final regulations published under these Code sections, the tax imposed under section 4940 shall be treated as if due from the due date for its annual return (determined without regard to any extension of time for filing its return).

(6) Return required from organizations terminating private foundation status under section 507(b)(1)(A). (i) An organization which terminates its private foundation status under section 507(b)(1)(A) is required to file a return under the provisions of section 6043(b), rather than under the provisions of section 6050.

(ii) An organization which terminates its private foundation status under section 507(b)(1)(A) is not required to comply with section 6104(d) for the taxable year in which such termination occurs. For purposes of this subdivision, the term "taxable year" shall include the period described in subparagraph (5)(ii) of this paragraph.

(7) Distribution of net assets. A private foundation will meet the requirement that it "distribute all of its net assets" within the meaning of section 507(b)(1)(A) only if it transfers all of its right, title, and interest in and to all of its net assets to one or more organizations referred to in section 507(b)(1)(A).

(8) Effect of restrictions and conditions upon distributions of net assets. (i) In general. In order to effectuate a transfer of "all of its right, title, and interest in and to all of its net assets" within the meaning of paragraph (a)(7) of this section, a transferor private foundation may not impose any material restriction or condition that prevents the transferee organization referred to in section 507(b)(1)(A) (herein sometimes referred to as the "public charity") from freely and effectively employing the transferred assets, or the income derived therefrom, in furtherance of its exempt purposes. Whether or not a particular condition or restriction imposed upon a transfer of assets is "material" (within the meaning of paragraph (a)(8) of this section) must be determined from all of the facts and circumstances of the transfer. Some of the more significant facts and circumstances to be considered in making such a determination are:

(A) Whether the public charity (including a participating trustee, custodian, or agent in the case of a community trust) is the owner in fee of the assets it receives from the private foundation;

(B) Whether such assets are to be held and administered by the public charity in a manner consistent with one or more of its exempt purposes;

(C) Whether the governing body of the public charity has the ultimate authority and control over such assets, and the income derived therefrom; and

(D) Whether, and to what extent, the governing body of the public charity is organized and operated so as to be independent from the transferor.

(ii) Independent governing body. As provided in paragraph (a)(8)(i)(D) of this section, one of the more significant facts and circumstances to be considered in making the determination whether a particular condition or restriction imposed upon a transfer of assets is "material" within the meaning of paragraph (a)(8) of this section is whether, and the extent to which, the governing body is organized and operated so as to be independent from the transferor. In turn, the determination as to such factor must be determined from all of the facts and circumstances. Some of the more significant facts and circumstances to be considered in making such a determination are:

(A) Whether, and to what extent, members of the governing body are comprised of persons selected by the transferor private foundation or disqualified persons with respect thereto, or are themselves such disqualified persons;

(B) Whether, and to what extent, members of the governing body are selected by public officials acting in their capacities as such; and

(C) How long a period of time each member of the governing body may serve as such. In the case of a transfer that is a community trust, the community trust shall meet paragraph (a)(8)(ii)(C) of this section if it meets the requirements of § 1.170A-9(e)(13)(iv) (other than § 1.170A-9(e)(13)(iv)(C) or (D)), relating to rules for governing body.

(iii) Factors not adversely affecting determination. The presence of some or all of the following factors will not be considered as preventing the transferee "from freely and effectively employing the transferred assets, or the income derived therefrom, in furtherance of its exempt purposes" (within the meaning of paragraph (a)(8)(i) of this section):

(A) Name. The fund is given a name or other designation which is the same as or similar to that of the transferor private foundation or otherwise memorializes the creator of the foundation or his family.

(B) Purpose. The income and assets of the fund are to be used for a designated purpose or for one or more particular section 509(a)(1), (2), or (3) organizations, and such use is consistent with the charitable, educational, or other basis for the exempt status of the public charity under section 501(c)(3).

(C) Administration. The transferred assets are administered in an identifiable or separate fund, some or all of the principal of which is not to be distributed for a specified period, if the public charity (including a participating trustee, custodian, or agent in the case of a community trust) is the legal and equitable owner of the fund and the governing body exercises ultimate and direct authority and control over such fund, as, for example, a fund to endow a chair at a university or a medical research fund at a hospital. In the case of a community trust, the transferred assets must be administered in or as a component part of the community trust within the meaning of § 1.170A-9(e)(11).

(D) Restrictions on disposition. The transferor private foundation transfers property the continued retention of which by the transferee is required by the transferor if such retention is important to the achievement of charitable or other similar purposes in the community because of the peculiar features of such property, as, for example, where a private foundation transfers a woodland preserve which is to be maintained by the public charity as an arboretum for the benefit of the community. Such a restriction does not include a restriction on the disposition of an investment asset or the distribution of income.

(iv) Adverse factors. The presence of any of the following factors will be considered as preventing the transferee "from freely and effectively employing the transferred assets, or the income derived therefrom, in furtherance of its exempt purposes" (within the meaning of paragraph (a)(8)(i) of this section):

(A) Distributions. (1) With respect to distributions made after April 19, 1977, the transferor private foundation, a disqualified person with respect thereto, or any person or committee designated by, or pursuant to the terms of an agreement with, such a person (hereinafter referred to as "donor"), reserves the right, directly or indirectly, to name (other than by designation in the instrument of transfer of particular section 509(a)(1), (2), or (3) organizations) the persons to which the transferee public charity must distribute, or to direct the timing of such distributions (other than by direction in the instrument of transfer that some or all of the principal, as opposed to specific assets, not be distributed for a specified period) as, for example, by a power of appointment. The Internal Revenue Service will examine carefully whether the seeking of advice by the transferee from, or the giving of advice by, any donor after the assets have been transferred to the transferee constitutes an indirect reservation of a right to direct such distributions. In any such case, the reservation of such a right will be considered to exist where the only criterion considered by the public charity in making a distribution of income or principal from a donor's fund is advice offered by the donor. Whether there is a reservation of such a right will be determined from all of the facts and circumstances, including, but not limited to, the facts contained in paragraph (a)(8)(iv)(A)(2) and (3) of this section.

(2) The presence of some or all of the following factors will indicate that the reservation of such a right does not exist:

(i) There has been an independent investigation by the staff of the public charity evaluating whether the donor's advice is consistent with specific charitable needs most deserving of support by the public charity (as determined by the public charity);

(ii) The public charity has promulgated guidelines enumerating specific charitable needs consistent with the charitable purposes of the public charity and the donor's advice is consistent with such guidelines;

(iii) The public charity has instituted an educational program publicizing to donors and other persons the guidelines enumerating specific charitable needs consistent with the charitable purposes of the public charity;

(iv) The public charity distributes funds in excess of amounts distributed from the donor's fund to the same or similar types of organizations or charitable needs as those recommended by the donor; and

(v) The public charity's solicitations (written or oral) for funds specifically state that such public charity will not be bound by advice offered by the donor.

(3) The presence of some or all of the following factors will indicate the reservation of such a right does exist:

(i) The solicitations (written or oral) or funds by the public charity state or imply, or a pattern of conduct on the part of the public charity creates an expectation, that the donor's advice will be followed;

(ii) The advice of a donor (whether or not restricted to a distribution of income or principal from the donor's trust or fund) is limited to distributions of amounts from the donor's fund, and the factors described in paragraph (a)(8)(iv)(A)(2)(i) or (ii) of this section are not present;

(iii) Only the advice of the donor as to distributions of such donor's fund is solicited by the public charity and no procedure is provided for considering advice from persons other than the donor with respect to such fund; and

(iv) For the taxable year and all prior taxable years the public charity follows the advice of all donors with respect to their funds substantially all of the time.

(B) Other action or withholding of action. The terms of the transfer agreement, or any expressed or implied understanding, required the public charity to take or withhold action with respect to the transferred assets which is not designed to further one or more of the exempt purposes of the public charity, and such action or withholding of action would, if performed by the transferor private foundation with respect to such assets, have subjected the transferor to tax under chapter 42 (other than with respect to minimum investment return requirement of section 4942(e)).

(C) Assumption of leases, etc. The public charity assumes leases, contractual obligations, or liabilities of the transferor private foundation, or takes the assets thereof subject to such liabilities (including obligations under commitments or pledges to donees of the transferor private foundation), for purposes inconsistent with the purposes or best interests of the public charity, other than the payment of the transferor's chapter 42 taxes incurred prior to the transfer to the public charity to the extent of the value of the assets transferred.

(D) Retention of investment assets. The transferee public charity is required by any restriction or agreement (other than a restriction or agreement imposed or required by law or regulatory authority), express or implied, to retain any securities or other investment assets transferred to it by the private foundation. In a case where such transferred assets consistently produce a low annual return of income, the Internal Revenue Service will examine carefully whether the transferee is required by any such restriction or agreement to retain such assets.

(E) Right of first refusal. An agreement is entered into in connection with the transfer of securities or other property which grants directly or indirectly to the transferor private foundation or any disqualified person with respect thereto a right of first refusal with respect to the transferred securities or other property when and if disposed of by the public charity, unless such securities or other property was acquired by the transferor private foundation subject to such right of first refusal prior to October 9, 1969.

(F) Relationships. An agreement is entered into between the transferor private foundation and the transferee public charity which establishes irrevocable relationships with respect to the maintenance or management of assets transferred to the public charity, such as continuing relationships with banks, brokerage firms, investment counselors, or other advisors with regard to the investments or other property transferred to the public charity (other than a relationship with a trustee, custodian, or agent for a community trust acting as such). The transfer of property to a public charity subject to contractual obligations which were established prior to November 11, 1976 between the transferor private foundation and persons other than disqualified persons with respect to such foundation will not be treated as prohibited under the preceding sentence, but only if such contractual obligations were not entered into pursuant to a plan to terminate the private foundation status of the transferor under section 507(b)(1)(A) and if the continuation of such contractual obligations is in the best interests of the public charity.

(G) Other conditions. Any other condition is imposed on action by the public charity which prevents it from exercising ultimate control over the assets received from the transferor private foundation for purposes consistent with its exempt purposes.

(v) Examples. The provisions of paragraph (a)(8) of this section may be illustrated by the following examples:

Example (1). The M Private Foundation transferred all of its net assets to the V Cancer Institute, a public charity described in section 170(b)(1)(A)(iii). Prior to the transfer, M's activities consisted of making grants to hospitals and universities to further research into the causes of cancer. Under the terms of the transfer, V is required to keep M's assets in a separate fund and use the income and principal to further cancer research. Although the assets may be used only for a limited purpose, this purpose is consistent with and in furtherance of V's exempt purposes, and does not prevent the transfer from being a distribution for purposes of section 507(b)(1)(A).

Example (2). The N Private Foundation transferred all of its net assets to W University, a public charity described in section 170(b)(1)(A)(ii). Under the terms of the transfer, W is required to use the income and principal to endow a chair at the university to be known as the "John J. Doe Memorial Professorship", named after N's creator. Although the transferred assets are to be used for a specified purpose by W, this purpose is in furtherance of W's exempt educational purposes, and there are no conditions on investment or reinvestment of the principal or income. The use of the name of the foundation's creator for the chair is not a restriction which would prevent the transfer from being a distribution for purposes of section 507(b)(1)(A).

Example (3). The O Private Foundation transferred all of its net assets to X Bank as trustee for the P Community Trust, a community trust which is a public charity described in section 170(b)(1)(A)(vi). Under the terms of the transfer, X is to hold the assets in trust for P and is directed to distribute the income annually to the Y Church, a public charity described in Section 170(b)(1)(A)(i). The distribution of income to Y Church is consistent with P's exempt purposes. If the trust created by this transfer otherwise meets the requirements of § 1.170A-9(e)(11) as a component part of P Community Trust, the assets transferred by O to X will be treated as distributed to one or more public charities within the meaning of section 507(b)(1)(A). The direction to distribute the income to Y Church meets the conditions of paragraph (a)(8)(iii)(B) of this section and will therefore not disqualify the transfer under section 507(b)(1)(A).

Example (4). The U Private Foundation transferred all of its net assets to Z Bank as trustee for the R Community Trust, a community trust which is a public charity described in section 170(b)(1)(A)(vi). Under the terms of the transfer, Z is to hold the assets in trust for R and distribute the income to those public charities described in section 170(b)(1)(A)(i) through (vi) that are designated by B, the creator of U. R's governing body has no authority during B's lifetime to vary B's direction. Under the terms of the transfer, it is intended that Z retain the transferred assets in their present form for a period of 20 years, or until the date of B's death if it occurs before the expiration of such period. Upon the death of B, R will have the power to distribute the income to such public charities as it selects and may dispose of the corpus as it sees fit.

Under paragraph (a)(8)(iv)(A) or (D) of this section, as a result of the restrictions imposed with respect to the transferred assets, there has been no distribution of all U's net assets within the meaning of section 507(b)(1)(A) at the time of the transfer. In addition, U has not transferred its net assets to a component part of R Community Trust, but rather to a separate trust described in § 1.170A-9(e)(14).

(vi) Transitional rule. If the governing instrument of the public charity (or an instrument of transfer) lacks the factors described in paragraph (a)(8)(i)(D) or (ii) of this section, but with respect to gifts or bequests acquired before January 1, 1982, the public charity changes its governing instrument (or instrument of transfer) by the later of November 11, 1977, or one year after the gift or bequest is acquired, in order to conform such instrument to such provisions, then such an instrument shall be treated as consistent with such provisions for taxable years beginning prior to the date of change. In addition, if prior to the later of such dates, the organization has instituted court proceedings in order to conform such an instrument, then it may apply (prior to the later of such dates) for an extension of the period to conform such instrument to such provisions. Such application shall be made to the Commissioner of Internal Revenue, Attention E:EO, Washington, D.C. 20224. The Commissioner, at the Commissioner's discretion, may grant such an extension, if in the Commissioner's opinion such a change will conform the instrument to such provisions, and the change will be made within a reasonable time.

(b) Operation as a public charity. *(1) In general.* Under section 507(b)(1)(B) an organization can terminate its private foundation status if the organization:

(i) Meets the requirements of section 509(a)(1), (2), or (3) by the end of the 12-month period (as extended by paragraph (c)(3)(i) of this section) beginning with its first taxable year which begins after December 31, 1969, or for a continuous period of 60 calendar months beginning with the first day of any taxable year which begins after December 31, 1969;

(ii) In compliance with section 507(b)(1)(B)(ii) and subparagraph (3) of this paragraph, properly notifies the district director before the commencement of such 12-month or 60-month period or before March 29, 1973 that it is terminating its private foundation status; and

(iii) Properly establishes immediately after the expiration of such 12-month or 60-month period that such organization has complied with the requirements of section 509(a)(1), (2), or (3) by the end of the 12-month period or during the 60-month period, as the case may be, in the manner described in subparagraph (4) of this paragraph.

(2) Relationship of section 507(b)(1)(L) to section 507(a), (c), and (g). Since section 507(a) does not apply to a termination described in section 507(b)(1)(B), a private foundation's notification that it is commencing a termination pursuant to section 507(b)(1)(B) will not be treated as a notification described in section 507(a) even if the private foundation does not successfully terminate its private foundation status pursuant to section 507(b)(1)(B). A private foundation which terminates its private foundation status under section 507(b)(1)(B) does not incur tax under section 507(c) and, therefore, no abatement of such tax under section 507(g) is required.

(3) Notification of termination. In order to comply with the requirements under section 507(b)(1)(B)(ii), an organization shall before the commencement of the 12-month or 60-month period under section 507(b)(1)(B)(i) (or before March 29, 1973) or, in the case of the 12-month period for a community trust, before May 11, 1977, notify the district director of its intention to terminate its private foundation status. Such notification shall contain the following information:

(i) The name and address of the private foundation;

(ii) Its intention to terminate its private foundation status;

(iii) Whether the 12-month or 60-month period shall apply;

(iv) The Code section under which it seeks classification (section 509(a)(1), (2), or (3));

(v) If section 509(a)(1) is applicable, the clause of section 170(b)(1)(A) involved;

(vi) The date its regular taxable year begins; and

(vii) The date of commencement of the 12-month or 60-month period.

(4) Establishment of termination. In order to comply with the requirements under section 507(b)(1)(B)(iii), an organization shall within 90 days after the expiration of the 12-month or 60-month period, file such information with the district director as is necessary to make a determination as to the organization's status as an organization described under section 509(a)(1), (2), or (3) and the regulations thereunder. See paragraphs (c) and (d) of this section as to the information required to be submitted under this subparagraph.

(5) Incomplete information: 12- and 60-month terminations. The failure to supply, within the required time, all of the information required by subparagraph (3) or (4) of this paragraph is not alone sufficient to constitute a failure to satisfy the requirements of section 507(b)(1)(B). If the information which is submitted within the required time is incomplete and the organization supplies the necessary additional information at the request of the Commissioner within the additional time period allowed by him, the original submission will be considered timely.

(6) Application of special rules and filing requirements. An organization which has terminated its private foundation status under section 507(b)(1)(B) is not required to comply with the special rules set forth in section 508 (a) and (b). Such organization is also not required to file a return under the provisions of section 6043(b) or 6050 by reason of termination of its private foundation status under the provisions of section 507(b)(1)(B).

(7) Extension of time to assess deficiencies. If a private foundation files a notification (described in subparagraph (3) of this paragraph) that it intends to begin a 60-month termination pursuant to section 507(b)(1)(B) and does not file a request for an advance ruling pursuant to paragraph (e) of this section, such private foundation may file with the notification described in subparagraph (3) of this paragraph a consent under section 6501(c)(4) to the effect that the period of limitation upon assessment under section 4940 for any taxable year within the 60-month termination period shall not expire prior to 1 year after the date of the expiration of the time prescribed by law for the assessment of a deficiency for the last taxable year within the 60-month period. Such consents, if filed, will ordinarily be accepted by the Commissioner. See paragraph (f)(3) of this section for an illustration of the procedure required to obtain a refund of the tax imposed by section 4940 in a case where such a consent is not in effect.

(c) Twelve-month terminations. *(1) Method of determining normal sources of support.* (i) In general. The 12-month termination provisions of section 507(b)(1)(B) permit a private foundation to terminate its private foundation status by changing its organizational structure, its operations, the sources of its support, or any combination thereof, in order to conform to the requirements of section 509(a)(1), (2), or (3) by the end of the 12-month period.

(ii) Support requirements for 12-month termination under section 170(b)(1)(A)(vi). A private foundation attempting to meet the requirements of section 509(a)(1) as an organization described in section 170(b)(1)(A)(vi) will be considered "normally" to receive a substantial part of its support from governmental units or direct or indirect contributions from the general public if it can establish that it has changed the sources of its support before the close of the 12-month period to those of an organization described in section 170(b)(1)(A)(vi) and it can reasonably be expected to maintain its publicly supported status for subsequent years. In order to establish these facts, an organization shall submit all information sufficient to make a determination under § 1.170A-9(e) as if such provisions applied, including a description of all organizational and operational changes which have occurred during the 12-month period. It shall also submit detailed information with respect to its sources of support for the 12-month period, as well as for the four taxable years immediately preceding the 12-month period. In applying the tests contained in § 1.170A-9(e), however, data from periods preceding the 12-month period shall be disregarded except for purposes of determining whether the organization has effectively changed its sources of support and whether it can reasonably be expected to maintain such publicly supported status for subsequent years. Thus, for example, in applying the mathematical tests of § 1.170A-9(e) only data for the 12-month period may enter into the computation.

(iii) Support requirements for 12-month terminations under section 170(b)(1)(A)(iv). Section 170(b)(1)(A)(iv) describes an organization which "normally" receives a substantial part of its support (exclusive of income from related activities) from the United States or any State or political subdivision thereof, or from the general public, and which is organized and operated exclusively to receive, hold, invest, and administer property and to make expenditures to or for the benefit of certain colleges or universities. For purposes of the 12-month termination period, the rule set forth in subdivision (ii) of this subparagraph with respect to section 170(b)(1)(A)(vi) organizations shall be applicable in determining whether an organization "normally" receives a substantial part of its support from the sources required under section 170(b)(1)(A)(iv).

(iv) Support requirements for 12-month terminations under section 509(a)(2). An organization attempting to terminate its private foundation status under section 507(b)(1)(B) by meeting the requirements of section 509(a)(2) by the end of the 12-month period will be considered as "normally" receiving its support in compliance with the one-third support requirements of section 509(a)(2) if:

(A) For the 12-month period under section 507(b)(1)(B), the organization receives more than one-third of its support from gifts, grants, contributions, membership fees, and gross receipts from related activities (as limited by section 509(a)(2)(A)(ii)) and not more than one-third of its support from items described in section 509(a)(2)(B), and

(B) The organization can establish that it can reasonably be expected to maintain its continued public support for subsequent years. In order to establish a reasonable expectation of continued public support, an organization shall submit a detailed statement describing its past and current operations, any organizational or operational changes and when such changes have occurred, and any changes in its foundation managers (as defined in section 4946(b)(1)). Duplicate copies of its governing instrument and bylaws, with an indication of any amendments made, and detailed information with respect to its sources of support for the 4 taxable years immediately preceding the 12-month period shall also be submitted as part of the evidence that the organization can reasonably be expected to maintain its publicly supported status.

(2) Organizational and operational tests. (i) Section 509(a)(3) organizations. (A) In general. An organization attempting to terminate its private foundation status under section 507(b)(1)(B) by meeting the requirements of section 509(a)(3) by the end of the 12-month period is required to meet the organizational and operational test of section 509(a)(3)(A), in addition to the requirements of section 509(a)(3)(B) and (C), by the end of the 12-month period beginning with its first taxable year which begins after December 31, 1969. An organization may qualify under section 509(a)(3)(A) even though its original governing instrument did not limit its purposes to those set forth in section 509(a)(3)(A) and even though it operated for some other purpose before the end of the 12-month period, if it has amended its governing instrument and changed its operations to conform to the requirements of section 509(a)(3) by the end of the 12-month period.

(B) Proof of changed status. In order to establish that an organization described in (A) of this subdivision will continue to be operated exclusively for the required purposes in years subsequent to the end of the 12-month period, such organization shall submit a detailed statement describing its past and current operations, any organizational or operational changes and when such changes have occurred, any changes in foundation managers (as defined in section 4946(b)(1)), and duplicate copies of its governing instrument and bylaws, with an indication of any amendments made. A detailed statement of the relationship between such organization and the specified organizations described in section 509(a)(1) or (2) (as required by section 509(a)(3)(A) and (B)) and all pertinent information to establish that the organization does not violate the control requirements of section 509(a)(3)(C) shall also be submitted.

(ii) Section 509(a)(1) organizations other than those described in section 170(b)(1)(A)(vi)—

(A) In general. An organization attempting to terminate its private foundation status under section 507(b)(1)(B) by meeting the requirements of section 170(b)(1)(A)(i), (ii), (iii), (iv), or (v) by the end of the 12-month period is required to be operated as an organization described in clauses (i), (ii), (iii), (iv), or (v) of section 170(b)(1)(A) by the end of the 12-month period beginning with its first taxable year which begins after December 31, 1969.

(B) Proof of changed status. In order to establish that it will continue to be operated as an organization described in section 509(a)(1) in years subsequent to the end of the 12-month period, the organization shall submit a detailed statement describing its past and current operations, any organizational or operational changes and when such changes have occurred, and any changes in its foundation managers (as defined in section 4946(b)(1)). Duplicate copies of its governing instrument and bylaws, with an indication of any amendments made, and its financial statements for the 4-taxable years immediately preceding the 12-month period shall also be submitted as evidence that the organization can reasonably be expected to maintain its status as an organization described in section 170(b)(1)(A)(i), (ii), (iii), (iv), or (v).

(3) Extensions of the 12-month period. (i) For purposes of this section, an organization may accomplish a 12-month termination if it meets the requirements of section 507(b)(1)(B) and this paragraph for such a termination with respect to any of the following periods:

(A) The 12-month period beginning with the organization's first taxable year which begins after December 31, 1969;

(B) The period described in paragraph (a)(5)(ii) of this section; or

(C) Any period consisting of two or more taxable years beginning with the organization's first taxable year beginning after December 31, 1969, and ending with any taxable year ending before the end of the period described in paragraph (a)(5)(ii) of this section.

(ii) An organization will be considered as "normally" meeting the requirements of section 170(b)(1)(A)(iv) or (vi) or 509(a)(2), as the case may be, if it meets the requirements of such provision with respect to any period described in subdivision (i)(A), (B), or (C) of this subparagraph. Thus, for example, an organization on a calendar year basis which seeks to convert to a section 509(a)(2) organization under section 507(b)(1)(B) may meet the one-third support requirement on the aggregate support received during a period described in subdivision (i)(A), (B), or (C) of this subparagraph, for purposes of subparagraph (1)(iv) of this paragraph.

(4) Status of organization subsequent to the 12-month period. For purposes of section 507 through 509, an organization, the status of which as a private foundation is terminated under section 507(b)(1), shall (except as provided in

paragraph (b)(6) of this section) be treated as an organization created on the day after the date of such termination. However, termination of private foundation status under the provisions of section 507(b)(1)(B) is based upon an organization's submission of information establishing compliance by the end of the 12-month period with the requirements of subparagraph (1) or (2) of this paragraph. Therefore, if in the 4 taxable years immediately following the end of the 12-month period, the sources of support or the methods of operation of the organization are materially different from the facts and circumstances presented during the 12-month period upon which the determination under section 507(b)(1)(B)(iii) was made (and such material difference adversely affects such determination), the organization will be deemed not to have satisfied the requirements of section 507(b)(1)(B). Under such circumstances, section 509(c) will not apply and the organization will continue to remain subject to the provisions of section 507. However, the status of grants and contributions under sections 170, 4942, and 4945 will not be affected until the Internal Revenue Service makes notice to the public (such as by publication in the Internal Revenue Bulletin) that the organization has been deleted from classification as an organization described in section 509(a)(1), (2), or (3) unless the donor (1) was in part responsible for or was aware of, the act or failure to act that resulted in the organization's inability to satisfy the requirements of section 507(b)(1)(B), or (2) had knowledge that such organization would be deleted from classification as an organization described in section 509(a)(1), (2), or (3). Prior to the making of any grant or contribution which allegedly will not result in the grantee's loss of classification under section 509(a)(1), (2), or (3), a potential grantee organization may request a ruling whether such grant or contribution may be made without such loss of classification. A request for such ruling may be filed by the grantee organization with the district director. The issuance of such ruling will be at the sole discretion of the Commissioner.

(d) Sixty-month terminations. *(1) Method of determining normal sources of support.* (i) In order to meet the requirement of section 507(b)(1)(B) for the 60-month termination period as a section 509(a)(1) or (2) organization, an organization must meet the requirements of section 509(a)(1) or (2), as the case may be, for a continuous period of at least 60 calendar months. In determining whether an organization seeking status under section 509(a)(1) as an organization described in section 170(b)(1)(A)(iv) or (vi) or under section 509(a)(2) "normally" meets the requirements set forth under such sections, support received in taxable years prior to the commencement of the 60-month period shall not be taken into consideration, except as otherwise provided in this section. Therefore, in such cases rules similar to the rules applicable to new organizations would apply.

(ii) For purposes of section 507(b)(1)(B), an organization will be considered to be a section 509(a)(1) organization described in section 170(b)(1)(A)(vi) for a continuous period of 60 calendar months only if the organization satisfies the provisions of § 1.170A-9(e) based upon aggregate data for such entire period, rather than for any shorter period set forth in § 1.170A-9(e). Except for the substitution of such 60-month period for the periods described in § 1.170A-9(e), all other provisions of such regulations pertinent to determining an organization's normal sources of support shall remain applicable.

(iii) For purposes of section 507(b)(1)(B), an organization will be considered to be a section 509(a)(2) organization only if such organization meets the support requirements set forth in section 509(a)(2)(A) and (B) for the continuous period of 60 calendar months prescribed under section 507(b)(1)(B), rather than for any shorter period set forth in the regulations under section 509(a)(2). Except for the substitution of such 60-month period for the periods described in the regulations under section 509(a)(2), all other provisions of such regulations pertinent to determining an organization's normal sources of support shall remain applicable.

(2) Organizational and operational tests. In order to meet the requirements of section 507(b)(1)(B) for the 60-month termination period as an organization described in section 170(b)(1)(A)(i), (ii), (iii), (iv), or (v) or section 509(a)(3), as the case may be, an organization must meet the requirements of the applicable provision for a continuous period of at least 60 calendar months. For purposes of section 507(b)(1)(B), an organization will be considered to be such an organization only if it satisfies the requirements of the applicable provision (including with respect to section 509(a)(3), the organizational and operational test set forth in subparagraph (A) thereof) at the commencement of such 60-month period and continuously thereafter during such period.

(e) Advance rulings for 60-month terminations. *(1) In general.* An organization which files the notification required by section 507(b)(1)(B)(ii) that it is commencing a 60-month termination may obtain an advance ruling from the Commissioner that it can be expected to satisfy the requirements of section 507(b)(1)(B)(i) during the 60-month period. Such an advance ruling may be issued if the organization can reasonably be expected to meet the requirements of section 507(b)(1)(B)(i) during the 60-month period. The issuance of a ruling will be discretionary with the Commissioner.

(2) Basic consideration. In determining whether an organization can reasonably be expected (within the meaning of subparagraph (1) of this paragraph) to meet the requirements of section 507(b)(1)(B)(i) for the 60-month period, the basic consideration is whether its organizational structure (taking into account any revisions made prior to the beginning of the 60-month period), proposed programs or activities, intended method of operation, and projected sources of support are such as to indicate that the organization is likely to satisfy the requirements of section 509(a)(1), (2), or (3) and paragraph (d) of this section during the 60-month period. In making such a determination, all pertinent facts and circumstances shall be considered.

(3) Reliance by grantors and contributors. For purposes of sections 170, 545(b)(2), 556(b)(2), 642(c), 4942, 4945, 2055, 2106(a)(2), and 2522, grants or contributions to an organization which has obtained a ruling referred to in this paragraph will be treated as made to an organization described in section 509(a)(1), (2), or (3), as the case may be, until notice that such advance ruling is being revoked is made to the public (such as by publication in the Internal Revenue Bulletin). The preceding sentence shall not apply, however, if the grantor or contributor was responsible for, or aware of, the act or failure to act that resulted in the organization's failure to meet the requirements of section 509(a)(1), (2), or (3), of acquired knowledge that the Internal Revenue Service had given notice to such organization that its advance ruling would be revoked. Prior to the making of any grant or contribution which allegedly will not result in the grantee's failure to meet the requirements of section 509(a)(1), (2), or (3), a potential grantee organization may request a ruling whether such grant or contribution may be made without such failure. A request for such ruling may be filed by the grantee organization with the district director. The issuance of such ruling will be at the sole discretion of the Commis-

sioner. The organization must submit all information necessary to make a determination on the factors referred to in subparagraph (2) of this paragraph. If a favorable ruling is issued, such ruling may be relied upon by the grantor or contributor of the particular contribution in question for purposes of sections 170, 507, 545(b)(2), 556(b)(2), 642(c), 4942, 4945, 2055, 2106(a)(2), and 2522.

(4) Reliance by organization. An organization obtaining an advance ruling pursuant to this paragraph cannot rely on such a ruling. Consequently, if the organization does not pay the tax imposed by section 4940 for any taxable year or years during the 60-month period, and it is subsequently determined that such tax is due for such year or years (because the organization did not in fact complete a successful termination pursuant to section 507(b)(1)(B) and was not treated as an organization described in section 509(a)(1), (2), or (3) for such year or years), the organization is liable for interest in accordance with section 6601 if any amount of tax under section 4940 has not been paid on or before the last date prescribed for payment. However, since any failure to pay such tax during the 60-month period (or prior to the revocation of such ruling) is due to reasonable cause, the penalty under section 6651 with respect to the tax imposed by section 4940 shall not apply.

(5) Extension of time to assess deficiencies. The advance ruling described in subparagraph (1) of this paragraph shall be issued only if such organization's request for an advance ruling is filed with a consent under section 6501(c)(4) to the effect that the period of limitation upon assessment under section 4940 for any taxable year within the advance ruling period shall not expire prior to 1 year after the date of the expiration of the time prescribed by law for the assessment of a deficiency for the last taxable year within the 60-month period.

(f) Effect on grantors or contributors and on the organization itself. *(1) Effect of satisfaction of requirements for terminations.* (i) Treatment during the termination period. In the event that an organization satisfies the requirements of section 507(b)(1)(B) for termination of its private foundation status by the end of the 12-month period or during the continuous 60-month period, such organization shall be treated for such entire 12-month or 60-month period in the same manner as an organization described in section 509(a)(1), (2), or (3).

(ii) Twelve-month terminations by fiscal year organizations. In the case of an organization which operates on a fiscal year basis and terminates its private foundation status by the end of the 12-month period beginning with its first taxable year which begins after December 31, 1969, such 12-month period shall, for purposes of this paragraph, be treated as including the period between January 1, 1970, and the last day of the taxable year immediately preceding its first taxable year which begins after December 31, 1969, so long as the requirements of section 507(b)(1)(B) and paragraph (c) of this section are met by the end of the 12-month period (including such additional period).

(2) Failure to meet termination requirements. (i) In general. Except as otherwise provided in subdivision (ii) of this subparagraph and paragraph (e) of this section, any organization which fails to satisfy the requirements of section 507(b)(1)(B) for termination of its private foundation status by the end of the 12-month period or during the continuous 60-month period shall be treated as a private foundation for the entire 12-month or 60-month period, for purposes of sections 507 through 509 and chapter 42, and grants or contributions to such an organization shall be treated as made to a private foundation for purposes of sections 170, 507(b)(1)(A), 4942, and 4945.

(ii) Certain 60-month terminations. Notwithstanding subdivision (i) of this subparagraph, if an organization fails to satisfy the requirements of section 509(a)(1), (2), or (3) for the continuous 60-month period but does satisfy the requirements of section 509(a)(1), (2), or (3), as the case may be, for any taxable year or years during such 60-month period, the organization shall be treated as a section 509(a)(1), (2), or (3) organization for such taxable year or years and grants or contributions made during such taxable year or years shall be treated as made to an organization described in section 509(a)(1), (2), or (3). In addition, sections 507 through 509 and chapter 42 shall not apply to such organization for any taxable year within such 60-month period for which it does meet such requirements. For purposes of determining whether an organization satisfies the requirements of section 509(a)(1), (2), or (3) for any taxable year in the 60-month period, the organization shall be treated as if it were a new organization with its first taxable year beginning on the date of the commencement of the 60-month period. Thus, for example, if an organization were attempting to terminate its private foundation status under section 507(b)(1)(B) by meeting the requirements of section 170(b)(1)(A)(vi), the rules under § 1.170A-9(e) relating to the initial determination of status of a new organization would apply.

(iii) Aggregate tax benefit. For purposes of section 507(d), the organization's aggregate tax benefit resulting from the organization's section 501(c)(3) status shall continue to be computed from the date from which such computation would have been made, but for the notice filed under section 507(b)(1)(B)(ii), except that any taxable year within such 60-month period for which such organization meets the requirements of section 509(a)(1), (2), or (3) shall be excluded from such computations.

(iv) Excess business holdings. See section 4943 and the regulations thereunder for rules relating to decreases in a private foundation's holdings in a business enterprise which are caused by the foundation's failure to terminate its private foundation status after giving the notification for termination under section 507(b)(1)(B)(ii).

(3) Example. The provisions of this paragraph may be illustrated by the following example:

Example. Y, a calendar year private foundation, notifies the district director that it intends to terminate its private foundation status by converting into a publicly supported organization described in section 170(b)(1)(A)(vi) and that its 60-month termination period will commence on January 1, 1974. Y does not obtain a ruling described in paragraph (e) of this section. Based upon its support for 1974 Y does not qualify as a publicly supported organization within the meaning of § 1.170A-9(e) and this paragraph. Consequently, in order to avoid the risks of penalties and interest if Y fails to terminate within the 60-month period, Y files its return as a private foundation and pays the tax imposed by section 4940. Similarly, based upon its support for the period 1974 through 1975, Y fails to qualify as such a publicly supported organization and files its return and pays the tax imposed by section 4940 for both 1975 and 1976. Since a consent (described in paragraph (b)(7) of this section) which would prevent the period of limitation from expiring is not in effect, in order to be able to file a claim for refund, Y and the district director agree to extend the period of limitation for all taxes imposed under chapter 42. However, based upon its support for the period 1974 through 1976 Y does qualify as a publicly supported organization, and therefore shall not be treated as a private foundation for either 1977 or 1978 even if it fails to terminate within the 60-month period. However, based upon the aggregate data for the entire 60-month period (1974 through 1978), Y does qualify as an organization described in section 170(b)(1)(A)(vi). Consequently, pursuant to this paragraph, Y is treated as if it had been a publicly supported organization for the entire 60-month period. Y files claim for refund for the taxes paid under section 4940 for the years 1974, 1975, and 1976, and such taxes are refunded.

(g) Special transitional rules for organizations operating as public charities. Section 4940 imposes a tax upon private foundations with respect to the carrying on of activities for each taxable year. For purposes of section 4940, an organization which terminates its private foundation status under section 507(b)(1)(B) by the end of the period described in paragraph (a)(5)(ii) of this section will not be considered as carrying on activities within the meaning of section 4940 during such period. Such organization will therefore not be subject to the tax imposed under section 4940 for such period. Consequently, in the case of an organization seeking to terminate its private foundation status under section 507(b)(1)(B) if the period described in paragraph (a)(5)(ii) of this section has not expired prior to the due date for the organization's annual return required to be filed under section 6033 or 6012 (determined with regard to any extension of time for filing the return) for its first taxable year which begins after December 31, 1969 (or any other taxable year ending before the expiration of the period described in paragraph (a)(5)(ii) of this paragraph) and if the organization has not terminated its private foundation status under section 507(b)(1)(B) by such date, then notwithstanding the provisions of paragraph (f) of this section, the organization must take either of the following courses of action:

(1) Complete and file its annual return including the line relating to excise taxes on investment income, by such date, and pay the tax on investment income under section 4940 at the time it files its annual return. If such organization subsequently terminates its private foundation status under section 507(b)(1)(B) within a period specified in paragraph (c)(3)(i) of this section, it may file a claim for refund of the tax paid under section 4940; or

(2) Complete and file its annual return, except for the line relating to excise taxes on investment income, by such date, and in lieu of paying the tax on investment income imposed under section 4940, file a statement with its annual return which establishes that the organization has taken affirmative action by such date to terminate its private foundation status under section 507(b)(1)(B). Such statement must indicate the type of affirmative action taken and explain how such action will result in the termination of its private foundation status under section 507(b)(1)(B). Such affirmative action may include making application to the appropriate State court for approval to amend the provisions of the organization's trust instrument to limit payments to specified section 509(a)(1) or (2) beneficiaries pursuant to section 509(a)(3) in the case of a charitable trust; commencing a fund-raising drive among the general public in the case of an organization seeking to become a section 170(b)(1)(A)(vi) or 509(a)(2) organization; or the passage of a resolution by the organization's governing body or the filing of an amendment to the organization's articles of incorporation permitting a change in the operations of the organization to enable it to conform to the provisions of section 509(a)(1), (2), or (3) in the case of a not-for-profit corporation. An organization may take such affirmative action and may terminate its private foundation status under section 507(b)(1)(B) in reliance upon 26 CFR 13.12 (rev. as of Jan. 1, 1972) and upon the provisions of the notices of proposed rulemaking under sections 170(b)(1)(A), 507(b)(1), and 509. Thus, if an organization meets the requirement of the provisions of the notice of proposed rulemaking as a section 509(a)(3) organization, such organization may terminate its private foundation status under section 507(b)(1)(B) in reliance upon such provisions prior to the expiration of the period described in paragraph (a)(5)(ii) of this section. If such organization, however, fails to terminate its private foundation status under section 507(b)(1)(B) within the period specified in paragraph (a)(5)(ii) of this section by failing to meet the requirements of either the notices of proposed rulemaking under section 170(b)(1)(A), 507(b)(1), or 509 or the final regulations published under these Code sections, the tax imposed under section 4940 shall be treated as if due from the due date for its annual return (determined without regard to any extension of time for filing its return).

T.D. 7248, 12/29/72, amend T.D. 7290, 11/16/73, T.D. 7440, 11/11/76, T.D. 7465, 1/19/77, T.D. 7784, 7/22/81.

§ 1.507-3 Special rules; transferee foundations.

(a) General rule. *(1)* For purposes of Part II, Subchapter F, Chapter 1 of the Code, in the case of a transfer of assets of any private foundation to another private foundation pursuant to any liquidation, merger, redemption, recapitalization, or other adjustment, organization, or reorganization, the transferee organization shall not be treated as a newly created organization. Thus, in the case of a significant disposition of assets to one or more private foundations within the meaning of paragraph (c) of this section, the transferee organization shall not be treated as a newly created organization. A transferee organization to which this paragraph applies shall be treated as possessing those attributes and characteristics of the transferor organization which are described in subparagraphs (2), (3), and (4) of this paragraph.

(2) (i) A transferee organization to which this paragraph applies shall succeed to the aggregate tax benefit of the transferor organization in an amount determined as follows: Such amount shall be an amount equal to the amount of such aggregate tax benefit multiplied by a fraction the numerator of which is the fair market value of the assets (less encumbrances) transferred to such transferee and the denominator of which is the fair market value of the assets of the transferor (less encumbrances) immediately before the transfer. Fair market value shall be determined as of the time of the transfer.

(ii) Notwithstanding subdivision (i) of this subparagraph, a transferee organization which is not effectively controlled (within the meaning of § 1.482-1(a)(3)), directly or indirectly, by the same person or persons who effectively control the transferor organization shall not succeed to an aggregate tax benefit in excess of the fair market value of the assets transferred at the time of the transfer.

(iii) This subparagraph may be illustrated by the following examples:

Example (1). Pursuant to a transfer described in section 507(b)(2), F, a private foundation, transfers to G, a private foundation, all of its assets, which have a fair market value of $400,000. Immediately before the transfer F's aggregate tax benefit was $200,000, and G's aggregate tax benefit was $300,000. After the transfer G's aggregate tax benefit is $500,000 ($200,000 + $300,000).

Example (2). Pursuant to a transfer described in section 507(b)(2), M, a private foundation, transfers all of its assets, which immediately prior to the transfers have a fair market value of $100,000. The assets were transferred to the following organizations at the following fair market values (determined at the time of transfer) $40,000 to N, a private foundation, $30,000 to O, a private foundation, and $30,000 to P, an organization described in section 170(b)(1)(A)(vi). Immediately before the transfer M's aggregate tax benefit was $50,000. Therefore, N succeeds to M's aggregate tax benefit to the extent of $20,000 ($50,000 × $40,000/$100,000) and O succeeds to M's aggregate tax benefit to the extent of $15,000 ($50,000 + $30,000/$100,000). The remaining $15,000 of M's aggregate tax benefit is retained by M as M has not terminated under section 507.

Example (3). Assume the same facts as in Example (2) except that the transfers were made as follows: M transferred $30,000 to N on January 1, 1972, $40,000 to P on July 1, 1972, and $30,000 to O on December 31, 1972. Further, assume that the fair market value of the assets and the aggregate tax benefit do not change during 1972 and that O is not effectively controlled (directly or indirectly) by the same person or persons who effectively control M. N succeeds to M's aggregate tax benefit to the extent of $15,000 ($50,000 × $30,000/$100,000). However, since $40,000 of the remaining $70,000 ($100,000 – $30,000) of assets of M was transferred to P on July 1, 1972, immediately before the transfer to O, the fair market value of the assets held by M is $30,000 ($70,000 – $40,000). On the other hand, because P is not a private foundation, M's aggregate tax benefit immediately before the transfer to O remains $35,000 ($50,000 – $15,000). Therefore, before applying subdivision (ii) of this subparagraph, O would succeed to $35,000 ($35,000 × $30,000/$30,000) of M's aggregate tax benefit. However, applying subdivision (ii) of this subparagraph since M transferred only $30,000 to O, O shall succeed to only $30,000 of M's aggregate tax benefit. The remaining $5,000 ($35,000 – $30,000) of M's aggregate tax benefit is retained by M as M has not terminated under section 507.

(3) For purposes of section 507(d)(2), in the event of a transfer of assets described in section 507(b)(2), any person who is a "substantial contributor" (within the meaning of section 507(d)(2)) with respect to the transferor foundation shall be treated as a "substantial contributor" with respect to the transferee foundation, regardless of whether such person meets the $5,000-two percent test with respect to the transferee organization at any time. If a private foundation makes a transfer described in section 507(b)(2) to two or more transferee private foundations, any person who is a "substantial contributor" with respect to the transferor foundation prior to such transfer shall be considered a "substantial contributor" with respect to each transferee private foundation.

(4) If a private foundation incurs liability for one or more of the taxes imposed under chapter 42 (or any penalty resulting therefrom) prior to, or as a result of, making a transfer of assets described in section 507(b)(2) to one or more private foundations, in any case where transferee liability applies each transferee foundation shall be treated as receiving the transferred assets subject to such liability to the extent that the transferor foundation does not satisfy such liability.

(5) Except as provided in subparagraph (9) of this paragraph, a private foundation is required to meet the distribution requirements of section 4942 for any taxable year in which it makes a section 507(b)(2) transfer of all or part of its net assets to another private foundation. Such transfer shall itself be counted toward satisfaction of such requirements to the extent the amount transferred meets the requirements of section 4942(g). However, where the transferor has disposed of all of its assets, the recordkeeping requirements of section 4942(g)(3)(B) shall not apply during any period in which it has no assets. Such requirements are applicable for any taxable year other than a taxable year during which the transferor has no assets.

(6) For purposes of section 4943(c)(4), (5), and (6), whenever a private foundation makes a section 507(b)(2) transfer of all or part of its net assets to another private foundation, the applicable period of time described in section 4943(c)(4), (5), or (6) shall include both the period during which the transferor foundation held such assets and the period during which the transferee foundation holds such assets.

(7) Except as provided in subparagraph (9) of this paragraph, where the transferor has disposed of all of its assets, during any period in which the transferor has no assets, section 4945(d)(4) and (h) shall not apply to the transferee or the transferor with respect to any "expenditure responsibility" grants made by the transferor. However, the exception contained in this subparagraph shall not apply with respect to any information reporting requirements imposed by section 4945 and the regulations thereunder for any year in which any such transfer is made.

(8) (i) Except as provided in subdivision (ii) of this subparagraph or subparagraph (6) or (9) of this paragraph, or whenever a private foundation makes a transfer of assets described in section 507(b)(2) to one or more private foundations, the transferee foundation:

(a) Will not be treated as being in existence prior to January 1, 1970, with respect to any transferred assets;

(b) Will not be treated as holding the transferred assets prior to January 1, 1970; and

(c) Will not be treated as having engaged in, or become subject to, any transaction, lease, contract, or other obligation with respect to the transferred assets prior to January 1, 1970.

(ii) Notwithstanding subdivision (i) of this subparagraph, the provisions enumerated in (a) through (g) of this subdivision shall apply to the transferee foundation with respect to the assets transferred to the same extent and in the same manner that they would have applied to the transferor foundation had the transfer described in section 507(b)(2) not been effected:

(a) Section 4940(c)(4)(B) and the regulations thereunder with respect to basis of property,

(b) Section 4942(f)(4) and the regulations thereunder with respect to distributions of income,

(c) Section 101(l)(2) of the Tax Reform Act of 1969 (83 Stat. 533), as amended by sections 1301 and 1309 of the Tax Reform Act of 1976 (90 Stat. 1713, 1729), with respect to the provisions of section 4941.

(d) Section 101(l)(3)(A) of the Tax Reform Act of 1969 (83 Stat. 534) with respect to the provisions of section 4942, but only if the transferor qualified for the application of such section immediately before the transfer, and at least 85 percent of the fair market value of the net assets of the transferee immediately after the transfer was received pursuant to the transfer,

(e) Section 101(l)(3)(B) through (E) of the Tax Reform Act of 1969 (83 Stat. 534) with respect to the provisions of section 4942,

(f) Section 101(l)(5) of the Tax Reform Act of 1969 (83 Stat. 535) with respect to the provisions of section 4945, and

(g) Section 101(l)(6) of the Tax Reform Act of 1969 (83 Stat. 535) with respect to the provisions of section 508(e).

(9) (i) If a private foundation transfers all of its net assets to one or more private foundations which are effectively controlled (within the meaning of § 1.482-1(a)(3)), directly or indirectly, by the same person or persons which effectively controlled the transferor private foundation, for purposes of chapter 42 (section 4940 *et seq.*) and part II of subchapter F of chapter 1 of the Code (sections 507 through 509) such a transferee private foundation shall be treated as if it were the transferor. However, where proportionality is appropriate, such a transferee private foundation shall be treated as if it were the transferor in the proportion which the fair market value of the assets (less encumbrances) transferred to such transferee bears to the fair market value of the assets (less encumbrances) of the transferor immediately before the transfer.

(ii) Subdivision (i) of this subparagraph shall not apply to the requirements under sections 6033, 6056, and 6104 which must be complied with by the transferor private foundation, nor to the requirement under section 6043 that the transferor file a return with respect to its liquidation, dissolution, or termination.

(iii) This subparagraph may be illustrated by the following examples:

Example (1). The trustees of X charitable trust, a private foundation, form the Y charitable corporation, also a private foundation, in order to facilitate the conduct of their activities. The trustees of X are also the directors of Y. Y has the same charitable purposes as X. All of the assets of X are transferred to Y, and Y continues to carry on X's charitable activities. Under such circumstances, Y shall be treated as if it were X for purposes of subdivision (i) of this subparagraph. Thus, for example, Y will be permitted to take advantage of any special rules or savings provisions with respect to chapter 42 to the same extent as X could have if X had continued in existence.

Example (2). A and B are the trustees of the P charitable trust, a private foundation, and are the only substantial contributors to P. On July 1, 1973, in order to facilitate accomplishments of diverse charitable purposes, A and B create and control the R Foundation, the S Foundation and the T Foundation and transfer the net assets of P to R, S, and T. As of the end of 1973, P has an outstanding grant to Foundation W and has been required to exercise expenditure responsibility with respect to this grant under sections 4945(d)(4) and (h). Under these circumstances, R, S, and T shall each be treated as if they are P in the proportion the fair market value of the assets transferred to each bears to the fair market value of the assets of P immediately before the transfer. Since R, S, and T are treated as P, absent a specific provision for exercising expenditure responsibility with respect to the grant to W, each of them is required to exercise expenditure responsibility with respect to such grant. If, as a part of the transfer to R, P assigned, and R assumed, P's duties with respect to the expenditure responsibility grant to W, only R would be required to exercise expenditure responsibility with respect to the grant to W. Since R, S, and T are treated as P rather than as recipients of "expenditure responsibility" grants, there are no expenditure responsibility requirements which must be exercised under sections 4945(d)(4) and (h) with respect to the transfers of assets to R, S, and T.

(10) For certain rules relating to filing requirements where a private foundation has transferred all its net assets, see § 1.507-1(b)(9).

(b) Status of transferee organization under section 507(b)(2). Since a transfer of assets pursuant to any liquidation, merger, redemption, recapitalization, or other adjustment, organization or reorganization to an organization not described in section 501(c)(3) (other than an organization described in section 509(a)(4)) or 4947 is a taxable expenditure under section 4945(d)(5), in order for such a transfer of assets not to be a taxable expenditure, it must be to an organization described in section 501(c)(3) (other than an organization described in section 509(a)(4)) or treated as described in section 501(c)(3) under section 4947. See § 53.4945-6(c)(3) of this chapter. Consequently, unless such a transferee is an organization described in section 509(a)(1), (2), or (3), the transferee is a private foundation and the rules of section 507(b)(2) and paragraph (a) of this section apply. On the other hand, if such a transfer of assets is made to a transferee organization which is not described in either section 501(c)(3) (other than an organization described in section 509(a)(4) or 4947, and in order to correct the making of a taxable expenditure, such assets are transferred to a private foundation, section 507(b)(2) and paragraph (a) of this section shall apply as if the transfer of assets had been made directly to such private foundation.

(c) Section 507(b)(2) transfers. *(1)* A transfer of assets is described in section 507(b)(2) if it is made by a private foundation to another private foundation pursuant to any liquidation, merger, redemption, recapitalization, or other adjustment, organization, or reorganization. This shall include any organization or reorganization described in subchapter C of chapter 1. For purposes of section 507(b)(2), the terms "other adjustment, organization, or reorganization" shall include any partial liquidation or any other significant disposition of assets to one or more private foundations, other than transfers for full and adequate consideration or distributions out of current income. For purposes of this paragraph, a distribution out of current income shall include any distribution described in section 4942(h)(1)(A) and (B).

(2) The term "significant disposition of assets to one or more private foundations" shall include any disposition for a taxable year where the aggregate of:

(i) The dispositions to one or more private foundations for the taxable year, and

(ii) Where any disposition to one or more private foundations for the taxable year is part of a series of related dispositions made during prior taxable years, the total of the related dispositions made during such prior taxable years, is 25 percent or more of the fair market value of the net assets of the foundation at the beginning of the taxable year (in the case of subdivision (i) of this subparagraph) or at the beginning of the first taxable year in which any of the series of related dispositions was made (in the case of subdivision (ii) of this subparagraph). A "significant disposition of assets" may occur in a single taxable year (as in subdivision (i) of this subparagraph) or over the course of two or more taxable years (as in subdivision (ii) of this subparagraph). The determination whether a significant disposition has occurred through a series of related distributions (within the meaning of subdivision (ii) of this subparagraph) will be made on the basis of all the facts and circumstances of the particular case. However, if one or more persons who are disqualified persons (within the meaning of section 4946) with respect to the transferor private foundation are also disqualified persons with respect to any of the transferee private foundations, such fact shall be evidence that the transfer is part of a series of related dispositions (within the meaning of subdivision (ii) of this subparagraph). In the case of a series of related dispositions described in subdivision (ii) of this subparagraph, each transferee private foundation shall (on any date) be subject to the provisions of section 507(b)(2) (with respect to all such dispositions made to it on or before such date) to the extent described in paragraphs (a) and (b) of this section.

(3) A private foundation which fails to meet the requirements of section 507(b)(1)(A) for a taxable year may be required to file a return under section 6043(b) by reason of a transfer of assets to one or more section 509(a)(1), (2), or (3) organizations. Hence, such filing does not necessarily mean that a section 507(b)(2) transfer has occurred. See § 1.6043-3(f)(1).

(4) This paragraph applies to any section 507(b)(2) transfer made by a private foundation referred to in section 170(b)(1)(E)(i), (ii), or (iii).

(5) The provisions of this paragraph may be illustrated by the following examples:

Example (1). M is a private foundation on the calendar year basis. It has net assets worth $100,000 as of January 1, 1971. In 1971, in addition to distributions out of current income, M transfers $10,000 to N, $10,000 to O, and $10,000 to P. N, O, and P are all private foundations. Under subparagraph (2)(i) of this paragraph, M has made a significant disposition of its assets in 1971 since M has disposed of more than 25 percent of its net assets (with respect to the fair market value of such assets as of January 1, 1971). M has therefore made section 507(b)(2) transfers within the meaning of this paragraph, and section 507(b)(2) applies to the transfers made to N, O, and P.

Example (2). U, a tax-exempt private foundation on the calendar year basis, has net assets worth $100,000 as of January 1, 1971. As part of a series of related dispositions in 1971 and 1972, U transfers in 1971, in addition to distributions out of current income, $10,000 to private foundation X and $10,000 to private foundation Y, and in 1972, in addition to distributions out of current income, U transfers $10,000 to private foundation Z. Under subparagraph (2)(ii) of this paragraph, U is treated as having made a series of related dispositions in 1971 and 1972. The aggregate of the 1972 disposition (under subparagraph (2)(i) of this paragraph) and the series of related dispositions (under subparagraph (2)(ii) of this paragraph) is $30,000, which is more than 25 percent of the fair market value of U's net assets as of the beginning of 1971 ($100,000), the first year in which any such disposition was made. Thus, U has made a significant disposition of its assets and has made transfers described in section 507(b)(2). The provisions of paragraphs (a) and (b) of this section apply to each of the transferees as of the date on which it received assets from U.

(d) Inapplicability of section 507(a) to section 507(b)(2) transfers. Unless a private foundation voluntarily gives notice pursuant to section 507(a)(1), a transfer of assets described in section 507(b)(2) will not constitute a termination of the transferor's private foundation status under section 507(a)(1). Such transfer must, nevertheless, satisfy the requirements of any pertinent provisions of chapter 42. See subparagraphs (5) through (7) of paragraph (a) of this section. However, if such transfer constitutes an act or failure to act which is described in section 507(a)(2)(A), then such transfer will be subject to the provisions of section 507(a)(2) rather than section 507(b)(2). For example, X, a private nonoperating foundation, transfers all of its net assets to Y, a private operating foundation, in 1971. X does not file the notice referred to in section 507(a)(1) and the transfer does not constitute either a willful and flagrant act (or failure to act), or one of a series of willful repeated acts (or failures to act), giving rise to liability for tax under chapter 42. Under these circumstances the transfer is described in section 507(b)(2) and the provisions of paragraph (a) of this section apply with respect to Y. The private foundation status of X has not been terminated under section 507(a).

(e) Transfers to certain section 509(a)(1), (2), or (3) organizations. If a private foundation transfers all or part of its assets to one or more organizations described in section 509(a)(1), (2), or (3) and, within a period of 3 years from the date of such transfers, one or more of the transferee organizations lose their section 509(a)(1), (2), or (3) status and become private foundations, then for purposes of this section, a transfer of assets within the meaning of paragraph (c) of this section to such an organization which becomes a private foundation will be treated as a transfer described in section 507(b)(2), and the provisions of paragraph (a) of this section shall be treated as applying to such a transferee organization from the date on which any such transfer was made to it.

(f) Certain transfers made during section 507(b)(1)(B) terminations. If;

(1) During the course of the 12-month or 60-month period described in section 507(b)(1)(B), a private foundation makes one or more transfers to one or more private foundations;

(2) Such transfers are described in § 1.507-3(c)(1); and

(3) Even though the transferor foundation thereafter meets the requirements of section 507(b)(1)(B),

then for purposes of this section, the provisions of § 1.507-2(e) shall not apply with respect to such transfers, and such transfers will be treated as transfers described in section 507(b)(2) and § 1.507-3 rather than as transfers from an organization described in section 509(a)(1), (2), or (3).

T.D. 7233, 12/20/72, amend T.D. 7678, 2/25/80.

§ 1.507-4 Imposition of tax.

(a) General rule. Section 507(c) imposes on each organization the private foundation status of which is terminated under section 507(a) a tax equal to the lower of:

(1) The amount which such organization substantiates by adequate records (or other corroborating evidence which may be required by the Commissioner) as the aggregate tax benefit (as defined in section 507(d)) resulting from the section 501(c)(3) status of such organization, or

(2) The value of the net assets of such organization.

(b) Transfers not subject to section 507(c). Private foundations which make transfers described in section 507(b)(1)(A) or (2) are not subject to the tax imposed under section 507(c) with respect to such transfers unless the provisions of section 507(a) become applicable. See §§ 1.507-1(b), 1.507-2(a)(6) and 1.507-3(d).

T.D. 7233, 12/20/72.

§ 1.507-5 Aggregate tax benefit; in general.

(a) General rule. For purposes of section 507(c)(1), the aggregate tax benefit resulting from the section 501(c)(3) status of any private foundation is the sum of:

(1) The aggregate increases in tax under chapters 1, 11, and 12 (or the corresponding provisions of prior law) which would have been imposed with respect to all substantial contributors to the foundation if deductions for all contributions

made by such contributors to the foundation after February 28, 1913, had been disallowed.

(2) The aggregate increases in tax under chapter 1 (or the corresponding provisions of prior law) which would have been imposed with respect to the income of the private foundation for taxable years beginning after December 31, 1912, if (i) it had not been exempt from tax under section 501(a) (or the corresponding provisions of prior law), and (ii) in the case of a trust, deductions under section 642(c) (or the corresponding provisions of prior law) had been limited to 20 percent of the taxable income of the trust (computed without the benefit of section 642(c) but with the benefit of section 170(b)(1)(A)),

(3) The amount succeeded to from transferors under § 1.507-3(a) and section 507(b)(2), and

(4) Interest on the increases in tax determined under subparagraphs (1), (2), and (3) of this paragraph from the first date on which each such increase would have been due and payable to the date on which the organization ceases to be a private foundation.

(b) Contributions. In computing the amount of the aggregate increases in tax under subparagraph (1) of this paragraph, all deductions attributable to a particular contribution shall be included. For example, if a substantial contributor has taken deductions under sections 170 and 2522 (or the corresponding provisions of prior law) with respect to the same contribution, the amount of each deduction shall be included in the computations under section 507(d)(1)(A). Accordingly, the aggregate tax benefit may exceed the fair market value of the property transferred.

T.D. 7233, 12/20/72.

---

§ 1.507-6 Substantial contributor defined.

Caution: The Treasury has not yet amended Reg § 1.507-6 to reflect changes made by P.L. 98-369.

(a) Definition. *(1) In general.* Except as provided in subparagraph (2) of this paragraph, the term "substantial contributor" means, with respect to a private foundation, any person (within the meaning of section 7701(a)(1)), whether or not exempt from taxation under section 501(a), who contributed or bequeathed an aggregate amount of more than $5,000 to the private foundation, if such amount is more than 2 percent of the total contributions and bequests received by the private foundation before the close of the taxable year of the private foundation in which a contribution or bequest is received by the foundation from such person. In the case of a trust, the term "substantial contributor" also means the creator of the trust. Such term does not include a governmental unit described in section 170(c)(1).

(2) Special rules. For purposes of sections 170(b)(1)(E)(iii), 507(d)(1), 508(d), 509(a)(1) and (3), and chapter 42, the term "substantial contributor" shall not include an organization which is described in section 509(a)(1), (2), or (3) or any other organization which is wholly owned by such section 509(a)(1), (2), or (3) organization. Furthermore, taking section 4941 (relating to taxes on self-dealing) in context, it would unduly restrict the activities of private foundations if the term "substantial contributor" were to include any section 501(c)(3) organizations. It was not intended, for example, that a large grant for charitable purposes from one private foundation to another would forever preclude the latter from making any grants to, or otherwise dealing with, the former. Accordingly, for purposes of section 4941 only, the term "substantial contributor" shall not only include any organization which is described in section 501(c)(3) (other than an organization described in section 509(a)(4)).

(b) Determination of substantial contributor. *(1) In general.* In determining under paragraph (a) of this section whether the aggregate of contributions and bequests from a person exceeds 2 percent of the total contributions and bequests received by a private foundation, both the total of such amounts received by the private foundation, and the aggregate of such amounts contributed and bequeathed by such person, shall be determined as of the last day of each taxable year commencing with the first taxable year ending after October 9, 1969. Generally, under section 507(d)(2) and this section, except for purposes of valuation under section 507(d)(2)(B)(i), all contributions and bequests made before October 9, 1969, are deemed to have been made on October 9, 1969. For purposes of section 509(a)(2) and the support test described in § 1.509(a)-3(c), contributions and bequests before October 9, 1969, will be taken into account in the year when actually made. For example, in the case of a contribution or bequest of $6,000 in 1967, such contribution or bequest shall be treated as made by a substantial contributor in 1967 for purposes of section 509(a)(2) and § 1.509(a)-3(c) if such person met the $5,000—2 percent test as of December 31, 1967, and December 31, 1969 (in the case of a calendar year accounting period). Although the determination of the percentage of total contributions and bequests represented by a given donor's contributions and bequests is not made until the end of the foundation's taxable year, a donor is a substantial contributor as of the first date when the foundation received from him an amount sufficient to make him a substantial contributor. Except as otherwise provided in this subparagraph, such amount is treated for all purposes as made by a substantial contributor. Thus, the total contributions and bequests received by the private foundation from all persons, and the aggregate contributions and bequests made by a particular person, are to be determined as of December 31, 1969 (in the case of a calendar year organization which was in existence on that date), and the amounts included in each respective total would be all contributions and bequests received by the organization on or before that date, and all contributions and bequests made by the person on or before that date. Thereafter, a similar determination is to be made with respect to such private foundation as of the end of each of its succeeding taxable years. Status as a substantial contributor, however, will date from the time when the donor first met the $5,000 and 2 percent test. Once a person is a substantial contributor with respect to a private foundation, he remains a substantial contributor even though he might not be so classified if a determination were first made at some later date. For instance, even though the aggregate contributions and bequests of a person become less than 2 percent of the total received by a private foundation (for example, because of subsequent contributions and bequests by other persons), such person remains a substantial contributor with respect to the foundation.

(2) Example. The provisions of paragraph (a) of this section and this paragraph (b) may be illustrated by the following examples:

Example (1). On January 1, 1968, A, an individual, gave $4,500 to M, a private foundation on a calendar year basis. On June 1, 1969, A gave M the further sum of $1,500. Throughout its existence, through December 31, 1969, M has received $250,000 in contributions and bequests from all sources. As of June 1, 1969, A is a substantial contributor to M for purposes of section 509(a)(2).

Example (2). On September 9, 1966, B, an individual, gave $3,500 to N, a private foundation on a calendar year basis. On March 15, 1970, B gave N the further sum of $3,500. Throughout its existence through December 31, 1970, N has received $200,000 in contributions and bequests from all sources. B is a substantial contributor to N as of March 15, 1970, since that is the first date on which his contributions met the 2 percent-$5,000 test.

Example (3). On July 21, 1964, X, a corporation, gave $2,000 to O, a private foundation, on a calendar year basis. As of December 31, 1969, O had received $150,000 from all sources. On September 17, 1970, X gave O the further sum of $3,100. Through September 17, 1970, O had received $245,000 from all sources as total contributions and bequests. Between September 17, 1970, and December 31, 1970, however, O received $50,000 in contributions and bequests from others. X is not a substantial contributor to O, since X's contributions to O were not more than 2 percent of the total contributions and bequests received by O by December 31, 1970, the end of O's taxable year, even though X's contributions met that test at one point during the year.

Example (4). On September 16, 1970, C, an individual, gave $10,000 to P, a private foundation on a calendar year basis. Throughout its existence, and through December 31, 1970, the close of its taxable year, P had received a total of $100,000 in contributions and bequests. On January 3, 1971, P received a bequest of $1 million. C is a substantial contributor to P since he was a substantial contributor as of September 16, 1970, and therefore remains one even though he no longer meets the 2-percent test on a later date after the end of the taxable year of the foundation in which he first became a substantial contributor.

(c) Special rules. *(1) Contributions defined.* The term "contribution" shall, for purposes of section 507(d)(2), have the same meaning as such term has under section 170(c) and also include bequests, legacies, devises, and transfers within the meaning of section 2055 or 2106(a)(2). Thus, for purposes of section 507(d)(2), any payment of money or transfer of property without adequate consideration shall be considered a "contribution". Where payment is made or property transferred as consideration for admissions, sales of merchandise, performance of services, or furnishing of facilities to the donor, the qualification of all or any part of such payment or transfer as a contribution under section 170(c) shall determine whether and to what extent such payment or transfer constitutes a "contribution" under section 507(d)(2).

(2) Valuation of contributions and bequests. Each contribution or bequest to a private foundation shall be valued at fair market value when actually received by the private foundation.

(3) Contributions and bequests by a spouse. An individual shall be considered, for purposes of this section, to have made all contributions and bequests made by his spouse during the period of their marriage. Thus, for example, where W contributed $500,000 to P, a private foundation, in 1941 and that amount exceeded 2 percent of the total contributions received by P as of the end of P's first taxable year ending after October 9, 1969, H (W's spouse at the time of the 1941 gift) is considered to have made such contribution (even if W died prior to October 9, 1969, or their marriage was otherwise terminated prior to such date). Similarly, any bequest or devise shall be treated as having been made by the decedent's surviving spouse.

T.D. 7241, 12/28/72.

§ 1.507-7 Value of assets.

(a) In general. For purposes of section 507(c) the value of the net assets shall be determined at whichever time such value is higher:

(1) The first day on which action is taken by the organization which culminates in its ceasing to be a private foundation, or

(2) The date on which it ceases to be a private foundation.

(b) Valuation dates. *(1)* In the case of a termination under section 507(a)(1), the date referred to in paragraph (a)(1) of this section shall be the date on which the terminating foundation gives the notification described in section 507(a)(1).

(2) In the case of a termination under section 507(a)(2), the date referred to in paragraph (a)(1) of this section shall be the date of occurrence of the willful and flagrant act (or failure to act) or the first of the series of willful repeated acts (or failures to act) giving rise to liability for tax under chapter 42 and the imposition of tax under section 507(a)(2).

(c) Fair market value. For purposes of this section, fair market value shall be determined pursuant to the provisions of § 53.4942(a)-2(c)(4) of this chapter.

(d) Net assets. For purposes of section 507 and the regulations thereunder, the term "net assets" shall mean the gross assets of a private foundation reduced by all liabilities of the foundation, including appropriate estimated and contingent liabilities. Thus, a determination of net assets may reflect reductions for any liability or contingent liability for tax imposed upon the private foundation under chapter 42 with respect to acts or failures to act prior to termination, for any liability or contingent liability for failures to correct such acts or failures to act, or for any liability or estimated or contingent liability with respect to expenses associated with winding up the organization. If a private foundation's determination of net assets reflects any reduction for any estimated or contingent liability, such private foundation must establish, to the satisfaction of the Commissioner, the reasonableness of such reduction. If the amount of net assets reflects a reduction for any estimated or contingent liability, at the earlier of the final determination of the contingency or the termination of a reasonable time, any excess of the amount by which the gross assets was reduced over the amount of the liability shall be treated in the same manner as if such excess had been considered part of the net assets.

T.D. 7233, 12/20/72.

§ 1.507-8 Liability in case of transfers.

For purposes of determining liability for the tax imposed under section 507(c) in the case of assets transferred by the private foundation, such tax shall be deemed to have been imposed on the first day on which action is taken by the organization which culminates in its ceasing to be a private foundation. If an organization's private foundation status is terminated under section 507(a)(2), the first day on which action is taken which culminates in its ceasing to be a private foundation (within the meaning of section 507(f)) shall be the date described in § 1.507-7(b)(2). If an organization terminates its private foundation status under section 507(a)(1), the first day on which action is taken which culminates in its ceasing to be a private foundation (within the meaning of section 507(f)) shall be the date described in § 1.507-7(b)(1).

T.D. 7233, 12/20/72.

§ 1.507-9 Abatement of taxes.

(a) General rule. The Commissioner may at his discretion abate the unpaid portion of the assessment of any tax imposed by section 507(c), or any liability in respect thereof, if:

(1) The private foundation distributes all of its net assets to one or more organizations described in section 170(b)(1)(A) (other than in clauses (vii) or (viii)) each of which has been in existence and so described for a continuous period of at least 60 calendar months or

(2) Effective assurance is given to the Commissioner in accordance with paragraphs (b) and (c) of this section that the assets of the organization which are dedicated to charitable purposes will, in fact, be used for charitable purposes.

The provisions of § 1.507-2(a)(2), (3), and (7) shall apply to distributions under subparagraph (1) of this paragraph. Since section 507(g) provides only for the abatement of tax imposed under section 507(c), no tax imposed under any provision of chapter 42 shall be abated under section 507(g). Where the taxpayer files a petition with the Tax Court with respect to a notice of deficiency regarding any tax under section 507(c), such tax shall be treated as having been assessed for the purposes of abatement of such tax under section 507(g) and the regulations thereunder.

(b) State proceedings. *(1)* Commissioner may at his discretion abate the unpaid portion of the assessment of any tax imposed by section 507(c), or any liability in respect thereof, under the procedures outlined in subparagraphs (2) and (3) of this paragraph. Such tax may not be abated by the Commissioner unless he determines that corrective action as defined in paragraph (c) of this section has been taken. The Commissioner may not abate by reason of section 507(g) any amount of such tax which has already been collected since only the unpaid portion thereof can be abated.

(2) The appropriate State officer shall have 1 year from the date of notification prescribed in section 6104(c) that a notice of deficiency of tax imposed under section 507(c) has been issued with respect to a foundation, to advise the Commissioner that corrective action has been initiated pursuant to State law as may be ordered or approved by a court of competent jurisdiction. Corrective action may be initiated either by the appropriate State officer or by an organization described in section 509(a)(1), (2), or (3) which is a beneficiary of the private foundation and has enforceable rights against such foundation under State law. Copies of all pleadings and other documents filed with the court at the initial stages of the proceedings shall be attached to the notification made by the State officer to the Commissioner. Prior to notification by the appropriate State officer that corrective action has been initiated, the Commissioner shall follow those procedures which would apply with respect to the assessment and collection of the tax imposed under section 507(c) without regard to section 507(g)(2). Subsequent to notification by the appropriate State officer that corrective action has been initiated, the Commissioner shall suspend action with respect to the assessment or collection of tax imposed under section 507(c) until notified of the final determination of such corrective action, as long as any such resulting delay does not jeopardize the collection of such tax and does not cause collection to be barred by operation of law or any rule of law. In any case where collection of such tax is about to be barred by operation of section 6502 and the Commissioner has not been advised of the final determination of corrective action, the Commissioner should make every effort to obtain appropriate agreements with the foundation subject to such tax to extend the period of limitations under section 6502(a)(2). Where such agreements are obtained, action with respect to the assessment and collection of such tax may be suspended to the extent not inconsistent with this subparagraph.

(3) Upon receipt of certification from the appropriate State officer that action has been ordered or approved by a court of competent jurisdiction, the Commissioner may abate the unpaid portion of the assessment of tax imposed by section 507(c), or any liability in respect thereof, if in his judgment such action is corrective action within the meaning of paragraph (c) of this section. In the event that such action is not corrective action, the Commissioner may in his discretion again suspend action on the assessment and collection of such tax until corrective action is obtained, or if in his judgment corrective action cannot be obtained, he may resume the assessment and collection of such tax.

(c) Corrective action. The term "corrective action" referred to in paragraph (b) of this section means vigorous enforcement of State laws sufficient to assure implementation of the provisions of chapter 42 and insure that the assets of such private foundation are preserved for such charitable or other purposes specified in section 501(c)(3). Except where assets of the terminated private foundation are transferred to an organization described in section 509(a)(1) through (4) the State is required to take such action to assure that the provisions of section 508(e)(1)(A) and (B) are applicable to the terminated foundation (or any transferee) with respect to such assets as if such organization were a private foundation. Thus, the governing instrument of such organization must include provisions with respect to such assets:

(1) Requiring its income therefrom for each taxable year to be distributed at such time and in such manner as not to subject such organization to tax under section 4942 (as if the organization were a private foundation),

(2) Prohibiting such organization from engaging in any act of self-dealing (as defined in section 4941(d) as if the organization were a private foundation),

(3) Prohibiting such organization from retaining any excess business holdings (as defined in section 4943(c) as if the organization were a private foundation),

(4) Prohibiting such organization from making any investments in such manner as to subject such organization to tax under section 4944 (as if the organization were a private foundation), and

(5) Prohibiting such organization from making any taxable expenditures (as defined in section 4945(d) as if the organization were a private foundation).

Consequently, in cases where the preceding sentence applies, although the private foundation status of an organization is terminated for tax purposes, it is contemplated that its status under State law would remain unchanged, because the tax under section 507(c) has been abated solely because the Commissioner has been given effective assurance that there is vigorous enforcement of State laws sufficient to assure implementation of the provisions of chapter 42. Therefore, in such a case while chapter 42 will not apply to acts occurring subsequent to termination which previously would have resulted in the imposition of tax under chapter 42, it is contemplated that there will be vigorous enforcement of State laws (including laws made applicable by the provisions in the governing instrument) with respect to such acts. Notwithstanding the preceding three sentences, no amendment to the organization's governing instrument is necessary where there are provisions of State law which have the effect of requiring a terminated private foundation to which the rules of subparagraphs (1) through (5) of this paragraph apply to be subject to such rules whether or not there are such provisions in such terminated private foundation's governing instrument.

T.D. 7233, 12/20/72.

§ 1.508-1 Notices.

(a) New organizations must notify the Commissioner that they are applying for recognition of section 501(c)(3) status. *(1) In general.* Except as provided in subparagraph (3) of this paragraph, an organization that is organized after October 9, 1969, will not be treated as described in section 501(c)(3):

(i) Unless such organization has given the Commissioner notice in the manner prescribed in subparagraph (2) of this paragraph; or

(ii) For any period before the giving of such notice, unless such notice is given in the manner and within the time prescribed in subparagraph (2) of this paragraph.

No organization shall be exempt from taxation under section 501(a) by reason of being described in section 501(c)(3) whenever such organization is not treated as described in section 501(c)(3) by reason of section 508(a) and this paragraph. See section 508(d)(2)(B) and § 1.508-2(b) regarding the deductibility of charitable contributions to an organization during the period such organization is not exempt under section 501(a) as an organization described in section 501(c)(3) by reason of failing to file a notice under section 508(a) and this subparagraph. See also § 1.508-2(b)(1)(viii) regarding the deductibility of charitable contributions to trusts described in section 4947(a)(1).

(2) Filing of notice. (i) For purposes of subparagraph (1) of this paragraph, except as provided in subparagraph (3) of this paragraph, an organization seeking exemption under section 501(c)(3) must file the notice described in section 508(a) within 15 months from the end of the month in which the organization was organized, or before March 22, 1973, whichever comes later. Such notice is filed by submitting a properly completed and executed Form 1023, exemption application. Notice should be filed with the district director. A request for extension of time for the filing of such notice should be submitted to such district director. Such request may be granted if it demonstrates that additional time is required.

(ii) Although the information required by Form 1023 must be submitted to satisfy the notice required by this section, the failure to supply, within the required time, all of the information required to complete such form is not alone sufficient to deny exemption from the date of organization to the date such complete information is submitted by the organization. If the information which is submitted within the required time is incomplete, and the organization supplies the necessary additional information at the request of the Commissioner within the additional time period allowed by him, the original notice will be considered timely.

(iii) For purposes of subdivision (i) of this subparagraph and paragraph (b)(2)(i) of this section, an organization shall be considered "organized" on the date it becomes an organization described in section 501(c)(3) (determined without regard to section 508(a)).

(iv) Since a trust described in section 4947(a)(2) is not an organization described in section 501(c)(3), it is not required to file a notice described in section 508(a).

(v) For the treatment of community trusts, and the trusts or funds comprising them, under section 508, see the special rules under § 1.170A-9(e).

(vi) A foreign organization shall, for purposes of section 508, be treated in the same manner as a domestic organization, except that section 508 shall not apply to a foreign organization which is described in section 4948(b).

(3) Exceptions from notice. (i) Paragraphs (a)(1) and (2) of this section are inapplicable to the following organizations:

(a) Churches, interchurch organizations of local units of a church, conventions or associations of churches, or integrated auxiliaries of a church. See § 1.6033-2(h) regarding the definition of integrated auxiliary of a church;

(b) Any organization which is not a private foundation (as defined in section 509(a)) and the gross receipts of which in each taxable year are normally not more than $5,000 (as described in subdivision (ii) of this subparagraph);

(c) Subordinate organizations (other than private foundations) covered by a group exemption letter;

(d) Solely for purposes of sections 507, 508(d)(1), 508(d)(2)(A) and 508(d)(3), 508(e), 509 and chapter 42, a trust described in section 4947(a)(1). (However, a trust described in section 501(c)(3) which was organized after October 9, 1969, shall be exempt under section 501(a) by reason of being described in section 501(c)(3) only if it files such notice); and

(e) Any other class of organization that the Commissioner from time to time excludes from the requirement of filing notice under section 508(a).

(ii) For purposes of subdivision (i)(b) of this subparagraph and paragraph (b)(7)(ii) of this section, the gross receipts (as defined in subdivision (iii) of this subparagraph) of an organization are normally not more than $5,000 if:

(a) During the first taxable year of the organization the organization has received gross receipts of $7,500 or less;

(b) During its first 2 taxable years the aggregate gross receipts received by the organization are $12,000 or less; and

(c) In the case of an organization which has been in existence for at least 3 taxable years, the aggregate gross receipts received by the organization during the immediately preceding 2 taxable years, plus the current year are $15,000 or less.

If an organization fails to meet the requirements of (a), (b), or (c) of this subdivision, then with respect to the organization, such organization shall be required to file the notices described in section 508 (a) and (b) within 90 days after the end of the period described in (a), (b), or (c) of this subdivision or before March 22, 1973, whichever is later, in lieu of the period prescribed in subparagraph (2)(i) of this paragraph. Thus, for example, if an organization meets the $7,500 requirement of (a) of this subdivision for its first taxable year, but fails to meet the $12,000 requirement of (b) of this subdivision for the period ending with its second taxable year, then such organization shall meet the notification requirements of section 508(a)(1) and 508(b) and subparagraph (2)(i) of this paragraph if it files such notification within 90 days after the close of its second taxable year. If an organization which has been in existence at least 3 taxable years meets the requirements of (a), (b), and (c) with respect to all prior taxable years, but fails to meet the requirements of (c) of this subdivision with respect to the current taxable year, then even if the organization fails to make such notification within 90 days after the close of the current taxable year, section 508(a)(1) and 508(b) shall not apply with respect to its prior years. In such a case, the organization shall not be treated as described in section 501(c)(3) for a period beginning with such current taxable year and ending when such notice is given under section 508(a)(2).

(iii) For a definition of "gross receipts" for purposes of subdivision (i)(b) of this subparagraph and paragraph (b)(7)(ii) of this section, see § 1.6033-2(g)(4).

(4) Voluntary filings by new organizations excepted from filing notice. Any organization excepted from the requirement of filing notice under section 508(a) will be exempt from taxation under section 501(c)(3) if it meets the requirements of that section, whether or not it files such notice. However, in order to establish its exemption with the Internal Revenue Service and receive a ruling or determination letter recognizing its exempt status, an organization excepted from the notice requirement by reason of subparagraph (3) of this paragraph should file proof of its exemption in the manner prescribed in § 1.501(a)-1.

(b) Presumption that old and new organizations are private foundations. *(1) In general.* Except as provided in subparagraph (7) of this paragraph, any organization (including an organization in existence on October 9, 1969) which is described in section 501(c)(3), and which does not notify the Commissioner within the time and in the manner prescribed in subparagraph (2) that it is not a private foundation, will be presumed to be a private foundation.

(2) Filing of notice. (i) Except as provided in subparagraph (7) of this paragraph, an organization must file the notice described in section 508(b) and subparagraph (1) of this paragraph within 15 months from the end of the month in which such organization was organized, or before March 22, 1973, whichever comes later. See paragraph (a)(2)(iii) of this section, for rules pertaining to when an organization is "organized".

(ii) Any organization filing notice under this paragraph that has received a ruling or determination letter from the Internal Revenue Service dated on or before July 13, 1970, recognizing its exemption from taxation under section 501(c)(3) (or the corresponding provisions of prior law), shall file the notice described in section 508(b) by submitting a properly completed and executed Form 4653, Notification Concerning Foundation Status.

(iii) The financial schedule on Form 4653 need be completed only if the organization is, or thinks it might be, described in section 170(b)(1)(A)(iv) or (vi) or section 509(a)(2).

(iv) Any organization filing notice under this paragraph that has not received a ruling or determination letter from the Internal Revenue Service dated on or before July 13, 1970, recognizing its exemption from taxation under section 501(c)(3) (or the corresponding provisions of prior law), shall file its notice by submitting a properly completed and executed Form 1023 and providing information that it is not a private foundation. The organization shall also submit all information required by the regulations under section 170 or 509 (whichever is applicable) necessary to establish recognition of its classification as an organization described in section 509(a)(1), (2), (3), or (4). A Form 1023 submitted prior to July 14, 1970, will satisfy this requirement if the organization submits an additional statement that it is not a private foundation together with all pertinent additional information required. Any statement filed under this subdivision shall be accompanied by a written declaration by the principal officer, manager or authorized trustee that there is a reasonable basis in law and in fact for the statement that the organization so filing is not a private foundation, and that to the best of the knowledge and belief of such officer, manager or trustee, the information submitted is complete and correct.

(v) The notice filed under subdivision (ii) of this subparagraph should be filed in accordance with the instructions applicable to Form 4653. The notice required by subdivision (iv) of this subparagraph should be filed with the district director. An extension of time for the filing of such notice may be granted by the Director of the Internal Revenue Service Center or district director upon timely request by the organization to such person, if the organization demonstrates that additional time is required.

(3) Effect of notice upon the filing organization. (i) The notice filed under this paragraph may not be relied upon by the organization so filing unless and until the Internal Revenue Service notifies the organization that it is an organization described in paragraph (1), (2), (3), or (4), of section 509(a). For purposes of the preceding sentence, an organization that has filed notice under section 508(b), and has previously received a ruling that it is an organization described in section 170(b)(1)(A) (other than clauses (vii) and (viii) thereof), will be considered to have been notified by the Internal Revenue Service that it is an organization described in paragraph (1) of section 509(a) if (a) the facts and circumstances forming the basis for the issuance of such rulings have not substantially changed and (b) the ruling issued under that section has not been revoked expressly or by a subsequent change of the law or regulations under which the ruling was issued.

(ii) If an organization has filed a notice under section 508(b) stating that it is not a private foundation and designating only one paragraph of section 509(a) under which it claims recognition of its classification (such as an organization described in section 509(a)(2)), and if it has received a ruling or determination letter which recognizes that it is not a private foundation but which fails to designate the paragraph under section 509(a) in which it is described, then such organization will be treated as described under the paragraph designated by it, until such ruling or determination letter is modified or revoked. The rule in the preceding sentence shall not apply to an organization which indicated that it does not know its status under section 509(a) or which claimed recognition of its status under more than one paragraph of section 509(a).

(4) Effect of notice upon grantors or contributors to the filing organization. In the case of grants, contributions, or distributions made prior to:

(i) In the case of community trusts, 6 months after the date on which corrective and clarifying regulations designated as § 1.170A-9(e)(10) become final;

(ii) In the case of medical research organizations, 6 months after the date on which corrective and clarifying regulations designated as § 1.170A-9(b)(2), become final, and

(iii) In all other cases, January 1, 1976, any organization which has properly filed the notice described in section 508(b) prior to March 22, 1973 will not be treated as a private foundation for purposes of making any determination under the internal revenue laws with respect to a grantor, contributor or distributor (as for example, a private foundation distributing all of its net assets pursuant to a section 507(b)(1)(A) termination) thereto, unless the organization is controlled directly or indirectly by such grantor, contributor or distributor, if by the 30th day after the day on which such notice is filed, the organization has not been notified by the Commissioner that the notice filed by such organization has failed to establish that such organization is not a private foundation. See subparagraph (6) of this paragraph for the effect of an adverse notice by the Internal Revenue Service. For purposes of this subparagraph, an organization which has properly filed notice described in section 508(b) prior to March 22, 1973, and which has claimed recognition of its status under only one paragraph of section 509(a) in such notice, will be treated only for purposes of grantors, contributors or distributors as having the classification claimed in the notice if the provisions of this subparagraph are otherwise satisfied.

(5) Statement that old and new organizations are operating foundations. (i) Any organization (including an organization in existence on October 9, 1969) which is described in section 501(c)(3) may submit a statement, in the form and manner provided for notice in subparagraph (2) of this paragraph, that it is an operating foundation (as defined in section 4942(j)(3)) and include in such statement:

(a) Necessary supporting information as required by the regulations under section 4942(j)(3) to confirm such determination (including a statement identifying the clause of section 4942(j)(3)(B) that is applicable); and

(b) A written declaration by the principal officer, manager, or authorized trustee that there is a reasonable basis in law and in fact that the organization so filing is an operating foundation, and that to the best of the knowledge and belief of such officer, manager or trusts, the information submitted is complete and correct.

(ii) The statement filed under this subparagraph may not be relied upon by the organization so filing unless and until the Internal Revenue Service notifies the organization that it is an operating foundation described in section 4942(j)(3).

(iii) In the case of grants, contributions, or distributions made prior to March 22, 1973, any organization which has properly filed the statement described in this subparagraph prior to such date will be treated as an operating foundation for purposes of making any determination under the internal revenue laws with respect to a grantor, contributor, or distributor thereto, unless the organization is controlled directly or indirectly by such grantor, contributor, or distributor, if by the 30th day after the day on which such statement is filed, the organization has not been notified by the Commissioner or his delegate that its statement has failed to establish that such organization is an operating foundation. See subparagraph (6) of this paragraph for the effect of an adverse notice by the Internal Revenue Service.

(6) Effect of notice by Internal Revenue Service concerning organization's notice or statement. Subparagraph (4) and subdivision (iii) of subparagraph (5) of this paragraph shall have no effect:

(i) With respect to a grantor, contributor, or distributor to any organization for any period after the date on which the Internal Revenue Service makes notice to the public (such as by publication in the Internal Revenue Bulletin) that a grantor, contributor, or distributor to such organization can no longer rely upon the notice or statement submitted by such organization; and

(ii) Upon any grant, contribution, or distribution made to an organization on or after the date on which a grantor, contributor, or distributor acquired knowledge that the Internal Revenue Service has given notice to such organization that its notice or statement has failed to establish that such organization either is not a private foundation, or is an operating foundation, as the case may be.

(7) Exceptions from notice. Subparagraphs (1) and (2) of this paragraph are inapplicable to the following organizations:

(i) Churches, interchurch organizations of local units of a church, conventions or associations of churches, or integrated auxiliaries of a church, such as a men's or women's organization, religious school, mission society, or youth group;

(ii) Any organization which is not a private foundation (as defined in section 509(a)) and the gross receipts of which in each taxable year are normally not more than $5,000 (as determined under paragraph (a)(3)(ii) of this section);

(iii) Subordinate organizations (other than private foundations) covered by a group exemption letter but only if the parent or supervisory organization submits a notice covering the subordinates;

(iv) Trusts described in section 4947(a)(1); and

(v) Any other class of organization that the Commissioner from time to time excludes from the notification requirements of section 508(b).

(8) Voluntary filings by organizations excepted from filing notice. Any organization excepted from the requirement of filing notice under section 508(b) by reason of subdivisions (i), (ii), and (v) of subparagraph (7) of this paragraph may receive the benefits of subparagraph (4) of this paragraph by filing such notice.

T.D. 7232, 12/21/72, amend T.D. 7258, 2/9/73, T.D. 7300, 12/26/73, T.D. 7342, 1/6/75, T.D. 7395, 1/5/76, T.D. 8640, 12/19/95.

§ 1.508-2 Disallowance of certain charitable, etc., deductions.

(a) Gift or bequest to organizations subject to section 507(c) tax. *(1) General rule.* No gift or bequest made to an organization upon which the tax provided by section 507(c) has been imposed shall be allowed as a deduction under section 170, 545(b)(2), 556(b)(2), 642(c), 2055, 2106(a)(2), or 2522, if such gift or bequest is made:

(i) By any person after notification has been made by the organization under section 507(a)(1) or after notification has been made by the Commissioner under section 507(a)(2)(B), or

(ii) By a substantial contributor (as defined in section 507(d)(2)) in his taxable year which includes the first day on which action is taken by such organization which culminates in the imposition of tax under section 507(c) and any subsequent taxable year.

For purposes of subdivision (ii) of this subparagraph, the first day on which action is taken by an organization which culminates in the imposition of tax under section 507(c) shall be determined under the rules set forth in § 1.507-7(b)(1) and (2).

(2) Exception. Subparagraph (1) of this paragraph shall not apply if the entire amount of the unpaid portion of the tax imposed by section 507(c) is abated by the Commissioner under section 507(g).

(b) Gift or bequest to taxable private foundation, section 4947 trust, etc. *(1) General rule.* (i) Except as provided in subparagraph (2) of this paragraph, no gift or bequest made to an organization shall be allowed as a deduction under section 170, 545(b)(2), 556(b)(2), 642(c), 2055, 2106(a)(2), or 2522, if such gift or bequest is made:

(a) To a private foundation or a trust described in section 4947(a)(2) in a taxable year for which it fails to meet the requirements of section 508(e) (determined without regard to section 508(e)(2)(B) and (C)), or

(b) To any organization in a period for which it is not treated as an organization described in section 501(c)(3) by reason of section 508(a).

(ii) For purposes of subdivision (i)(a) of this subparagraph the term "taxable year" refers to the taxable year of the donee or beneficiary organization. In the event a bequest is made to a private foundation or trust described in section 4947(a)(2) which is not in existence at the date of the testator's death (but which is created under the terms of the testator's will), the term "taxable year" shall mean the first taxable year of the private foundation or trust.

(iii) For purposes of subdivision (i)(a) of this subparagraph, an organization does not fail to meet the requirements of section 508(e) for a taxable year, unless it fails to meet such requirements for the entire year. Therefore, even if a donee organization fails to meet the requirements of section 508(e) on the date it receives a grant from a donor, the donor's grant will not be disallowed by operation of section 508(d)(2)(A) and subdivision (i)(a) of this subparagraph, if the organization meets the requirements of section 508(e) (determined without regard to section 508(e)(2)(B) or (C)) by the end of its taxable year.

(iv) No deduction will be disallowed under section 508(d)(2)(A) with respect to a deduction under section 170, 545(b)(2), 556(b)(2), 642(c), 2055, 2106(a)(2), or 2522 if during the taxable year in question, the private foundation or trust described in section 4947(a)(2) has instituted a judicial proceeding which is necessary to reform its governing instrument or other instrument in order to meet the requirements of section 508(e)(1). This subdivision shall not apply unless within a reasonable time such judicial proceedings succeed in so reforming such instrument.

(v) No deduction will be disallowed under section 508(d)(2)(A) and subdivision (i)(a) of this subparagraph for any taxable year beginning before January 1, 1972, with respect to a private foundation or trust described in section 4947 organized before January 1, 1970. See also § 1.508-3(g) regarding transitional rules for extending compliance with section 508(e)(1).

(vi) (a) In the case of a contribution or bequest to a trust described in section 4947(a)(2) other than to a trust to which subdivision (vii) of this subparagraph applies, no deduction shall be disallowed by reason of section 508(d)(2)(A) on the grounds that such trust's governing instrument contains no provisions with respect to section 4942. Similarly, if for a taxable year such trust is also a trust described in section 4947(b)(3), no deduction for such year shall be so disallowed on the grounds that the governing instrument contains no provision with respect to section 4943 or 4944.

(b) This subdivision may be illustrated by the following example:

Example. H executes a will on January 1, 1977, establishing a charitable remainder trust (as described in section 664) with income payable to W, his wife, for life, remainder to X university, an organization described in section 170(b)(1)(A)(ii). The will provides that the trust is prohibited from engaging in activities which would subject itself, its foundation manager or a disqualified person to taxes under section 4941 or 4945 of the Code. The will is silent as to section 4942, 4943, and 4944. H dies February 12, 1978. Section 508(d)(2)(A) will not operate to disallow any deduction to H's estate under section 2055 with respect to such trust.

(vii) (a) In the case of a trust described in section 4947(a)(2) which by its terms will become a trust described in section 4947(a)(1) and the governing instrument of which is executed after March 22, 1973, the governing instrument shall not meet the requirements of section 508(e)(1) if it does not contain provisions to the effect that the trust must comply with the provisions of section 4942, or sections 4942, 4943, and 4944 (as the case may be) to the extent such section or sections shall become applicable to such trust.

(b) This subdivision may be illustrated by the following example:

Example. H executes a will on January 1, 1977, establishing a charitable remainder trust (as described in section 664) with income payable to W, his wife, for life, remainder in trust in perpetuity for the benefit of an organization described in section 170(c). By its terms the trust will become a trust described in section 4947(a)(1), and will become a private foundation. The will provides that the trust is prohibited from engaging in activities which would subject itself, its foundation manager or a disqualified person to taxes under section 4941 or 4945 of the Code. The will is silent as to sections 4942, 4943, and 4944. H dies February 12, 1978. Unless the trust's governing instrument is amended prior to the end of the trust's first taxable year, or judicial proceedings have been instituted under subdivision (iv) of this subparagraph, section 508(d)(2)(A) will operate to disallow any deduction to H's estate under section 2055 with respect to such trust.

(viii) Since a charitable trust described in section 4947(a)(1) is not required to file a notice under section 508(a), section 508(d)(2)(B) and subdivision (i)(b) of this subparagraph are not applicable to such a trust.

(2) Transitional rules. Any deduction which would otherwise be allowable under section 642(c)(2), 2106(a)(2), or 2055 shall not be disallowed under section 508(d)(2)(A) if such deduction is attributable to:

(i) Property passing under the term of a will executed on or before October 9, 1969,

(a) If the decedent dies after October 9, 1969, but before October 9, 1972, without having amended any dispositive provision of the will after October 9, 1969, by codicil or otherwise,

(b) If the decedent dies after October 9, 1969, and at no time after that date had the right to change the portions of the will which pertains to the passing of property to, or for the use of, an organization described in section 170(c)(2)(B) or 2055(a), or

(c) If no dispositive provision of the will is amended by the decedent, by codicil or otherwise, before October 9, 1972, and the decedent is on October 9, 1972, and at all times thereafter under a mental disability (as defined in § 1.642(c)-2(b)(3)(ii)) to amend the will by codicil or otherwise, or

(ii) Property transferred in trust on or before October 9, 1969,

(a) If the grantor dies after October 9, 1969, but before October 9, 1972, without having amended, after October 9, 1969, any dispositive provision of the instrument governing the disposition of the property,

(b) If the property transferred was an irrevocable interest to, or for the use of, an organization described in section 170(c)(2)(B) or 2055(a),

(c) In the case of a deduction under section 2106(a)(2) or 2055; if no dispositive provision of the instrument governing the disposition of the property is amended by the grantor before October 9, 1972, and the grantor is on October 9, 1972, and at all times thereafter under a mental disability (as defined in § 1.642(c)-2(b)(3)(ii)) to change the disposition of the property, or

(d) In the case of a deduction under section 642(c)(2)(A), if the grantor is at all times after October 9, 1969, and up to, and including, the last day of the taxable year for which the deduction under such section is claimed, under a mental disability (as defined in § 1.642(c)-2(b)(3)(ii)) to change the terms of the trust.

See also § 1.508-3(g) regarding the extension of time for compliance with section 508(e), § 1.664-1(f)(3)(ii) and (g) regarding the special transitional rules for charitable remainder annuity and unitrusts described in section 664 which were created prior to December 31, 1972, and § 20.2055-2(e)(4) of this chapter regarding the rules for determining if the dispositive provisions have been amended.

T.D. 7232, 12/21/72.

§ 1.508-3 Governing instruments.

(a) General rule. A private foundation shall not be exempt from taxation under section 501(a) for a taxable year unless by the end of such taxable year its governing instrument includes provisions the effects of which are:

(1) To require distributions at such times and in such manner as not to subject the foundation to tax under section 4942, and

(2) To prohibit the foundation from engaging in any act of self-dealing (as defined in section 4941(d)), from retaining any excess business holdings (as defined in section 4943(c)), from making any investments in such manner as to subject the foundation to tax under section 4944, and from making any taxable expenditures (as defined in section 4945(d)).

(b) Effect and nature of governing instrument. *(1) In general.* Except as provided in paragraph (d) of this section, the provisions of a foundation's governing instrument must require or prohibit, as the case may be, the foundation to act or refrain from acting so that the foundation, and any foundation managers or other disqualified persons with respect thereto, shall not be liable for any of the taxes imposed by sections 4941, 4942, 4943, 4944, and 4945 of the Code or, in the case of a split-interest trust described in section 4947(a)(2), any of the taxes imposed by those sections of chapter 42 made applicable under section 4947. Specific reference to these sections of the Code will generally be required to be included in the governing instrument, unless equivalent language is used which is deemed by the Commissioner to have the same full force and effect. However, a governing instrument which contains only language sufficient to satisfy the requirements of the organizational test under § 1.501(c)(3)-1(b) will not be considered as meeting the requirements of this subparagraph, regardless of the interpretation placed on such language as a matter of law by a State court in a particular jurisdiction, unless the requirements of paragraph (d) of this section are satisfied.

(2) Corpus. A governing instrument does not meet the requirements of paragraph (a)(1) of this section if it expressly prohibits the distribution of capital or corpus.

(3) Savings provisions. For purposes of section 508(d)(2)(A) and (e), a governing instrument need not include any provision which is inconsistent with section 101(l)(2), (3), (4) or (5) of the Tax Reform Act of 1969 (83 Stat. 533), as amended by sections 1301 and 1309 of the Tax Reform Act of 1976 (90 Stat. 1713, 1729), with respect to the organization. Accordingly, a governing instrument complying with the requirements of subparagraph (1) of this paragraph may incorporate any savings provision contained in section 101(l)(2), (3), (4) or (5) of the Tax Reform Act of 1969, as amended by sections 1301 and 1309 of the Tax Reform Act of 1976, as a specific exception to the general provisions of paragraph (a) of this section. In addition, in the absence of any express provisions to the contrary, the exceptions contained in such savings provisions will generally be regarded as contained in a governing instrument meeting the requirements of subparagraph (1) of this paragraph.

(4) Excess holdings. For purposes of paragraph (a)(2) of this section, the prohibition against "retaining any excess business holdings (as defined in section 4943(c))" shall be deemed only to prohibit the foundation from retaining any excess business holdings when such holdings would subject the foundation to tax under section 4943(a).

(5) Revoked ruling on status. In the case of an organization which—

(i) Has been classified as an organization described in section 509(a)(1), (2), (3), or (4), and

(ii) Subsequently receives a ruling or determination letter stating that it is no longer described in section 509(a)(1), (2), (3), or (4), but is a private foundation within the meaning of section 509,

such organization shall have 1 year from the date of receipt of such ruling or determination letter, or the final ruling or determination letter if a protest is filed to an earlier one, to meet the requirements of section 508(e). Section 508(d)(2)(A) shall not be applicable with respect to gifts and bequests made during this 1-year period if such requirements are met within the 1-year period.

(6) Judicial proceeding. For purposes of paragraphs (a), (b)(5), (d)(2), and (e)(3) of this section, an organization shall be deemed to have met the requirements of section 508(e) within a year, if a judicial proceeding which is necessary to reform its governing instrument or other instrument is instituted within the year and within a reasonable time the organization, in fact, meets the requirements of section 508(e). For purposes only of paragraphs (b)(5), (d)(2), and (e)(3) of this section, if an organization organized before January 1, 1970, institutes such a judicial proceeding within such 1-year period, section 508(e)(2)(C) shall be applied as if such proceeding had been instituted prior to January 1, 1972.

(c) Meaning of governing instrument. For purposes of section 508(e), the term "governing instrument" shall have the same meaning as the term "articles of organization" under § 1.501(c)(3)-1(b)(2). The bylaws of an organization shall not constitute its governing instrument for purposes of section 508(e).

(d) Effect of State law. *(1) In general.* A private foundation's governing instrument shall be deemed to conform with the requirements of paragraph (a) of this section if valid provisions of State law have been enacted which:

(i) Require it to act or refrain from acting so as not to subject the foundation to the taxes imposed by section 4941 (relating to taxes on self-dealing), 4942 (relating to taxes on failure to distribute income), 4943 (relating to taxes on excess business holdings), 4944 (relating to taxes on investments which jeopardize charitable purpose), and 4945 (relating to taxable expenditures); or

(ii) Treat the required provisions as contained in the foundation's governing instrument.

(2) Validity. (i) Any provision of State law described in subparagraph (1) of this paragraph shall be presumed valid as enacted, and in the absence of State provisions to the contrary, to apply with respect to any foundation that does not specifically disclaim coverage under State law (either by notification to the appropriate State official or by commencement of judicial proceedings) except as provided in subdivisions (ii) and (iii) of this subparagraph.

(ii) If such provision is declared invalid or inapplicable with respect to a class of foundations by the highest appellate court of the State or by the Supreme Court of the United States, the foundations covered by the determination must meet the requirements of section 508(e) within 1 year from the date on which the time for perfecting an application for review by the Supreme Court expires. If such application is filed, the requirements of section 508(e) must be met within a year from the date on which the Supreme Court disposes of the case, whether by denial of the application for review or decision on the merits.

(iii) In addition, if such provision of State law is declared invalid or inapplicable with respect to a class of foundations by any court of competent jurisdiction which decision is not reviewed by a court referred to in subdivision (ii) of this subparagraph, and the Commissioner makes notice to the general public (such as by publication in the Internal Revenue Bulletin) that such provision has been so declared invalid or inapplicable, then all foundations in such State must meet the requirements of section 508(e), without reliance upon such statute to the extent declared invalid or inapplicable by such decision, within 1 year from the date such notice is made public.

(iv) This subparagraph shall not apply to any foundation that is subject to a final judgment entered by a court of competent jurisdiction, holding the law invalid or inapplicable with respect to such foundation. See paragraph (b)(6) of this section for the effect of certain judicial proceedings that are brought within 1 year.

(3) Conflicting instrument. For taxable years beginning after March 22, 1973 in order for a private foundation or trust described in section 4947(a)(2) to receive the benefit of coverage under any State statute which makes applicable the requirements of section 508(e)(1)(A) and (B), where the statute by its terms does not apply to a governing instrument which contains a mandatory direction conflicting with any of such requirements, such organization must indicate on its annual return required to be filed under section 6033 (or section 6012 in the case of a trust described in section 4947(a)) that its governing instrument contains no mandatory directions which conflict with the requirements of section 508(e)(1)(A) or (B), as incorporated by the State statute. General language in a governing instrument empowering the trustee to make investments without being limited to those investments authorized by law will not be regarded as a mandatory conflicting direction.

(4) Exclusion from statute. (i) For any taxable year beginning after March 22, 1973 in the case of a private foundation or trust described in section 4947(a)(2) subject to a State statute which makes applicable the requirements of section 508(e)(1)(A) and (B) to the governing instruments of such organizations, other than those which take action to be excluded therefrom (such as by filing a notice of exclusion or by instituting appropriate judicial proceedings), an organization will receive the benefit of such State statute only if it indicates on its annual return required to be filed under section 6033 (or section 6012 in the case of a trust described in section 4947(a)) that it has not so taken action to be excluded.

(ii) This paragraph permits certain organizations that are subject to the provisions of such a State law, to avoid changing their governing instruments in order to meet the requirements of section 508(e)(1). Since an organization which avoids the application of a provision or provisions of State law, such as by filing a notice of exclusion, is not entitled to the benefits of this paragraph, such an organization must meet the requirements of section 508(e)(1) without regard to this paragraph and except as provided in section 508(e)(2)(C) or paragraph (g)(1)(iii) of this section must change its governing instrument to the extent inconsistent with section 508(e)(1).

(5) Treatment of prevailing conflicting clause. If provisions of State law are inapplicable to a clause in a governing instrument which is contrary to the provisions of section 508(e)(1), the requirements of section 508(e)(2)(C) and paragraph (g)(1)(iii) of this section are not satisfied by a provision of State law which purports to eliminate the need for litigation under such circumstances. Therefore, except as otherwise provided in this section unless the governing instrument is changed or litigation is commenced pursuant to section 508(e)(2)(B) by an organization organized before January 1, 1970, or pursuant to paragraph (g)(1)(ii) of this section, to amend the nonconforming provision to meet the requirements of section 508(e)(1)(A) and (B), then pursuant to section 508(e), such organization will not be exempt from taxation.

(6) Retroactive application to grants or bequests. If valid provisions of such a State law apply retroactively to a taxable year within which an organization has received a grant or request, section 508(d)(2)(A) shall not apply so as to disallow such grant or bequest, but only if such valid provisions of State law are enacted within 2 years of such grant or bequest.

(e) Effect of section 508(e) upon section 4947 trusts. *(1) Section 4947(a)(1) trusts.* A charitable trust described in section 4947(a)(1) (unless also described in paragraph of section 509(a)) is subject to all the provisions of paragraph (a) of this section.

(2) Section 4947(a)(2) trusts. A split-interest trust described in section 4947(a)(2), as long as it is so described, is subject to the provisions of paragraph (a)(2) of this section, except to the extent that section 4947 makes any such provisions inapplicable to certain trusts and certain amounts in trust. The governing instrument of a trust described in section 4947(a)(2) may except amounts described in section 4947(a)(2)(A), (B), and (C) from the requirements of paragraph (a)(2) of this section. In the case of a trust having amounts transferred to it both before May 27, 1969, and after May 26, 1969, its governing instrument may except from the provisions of paragraph (a)(2) of this section only those segregated amounts excluded from the application of section 4947(a)(2) by reason of section 4947(a)(2)(C) and the regulations thereunder. Also, the governing instrument of such a trust may exclude the application of sections 4943 and 4944 for any period during which such trust is described in section 4947(b)(3)(A) or (B). See § 53.4947-1(c) of this chapter for rules relating to the applicability of section 4947 to split-interest trusts and § 1.508-2(b)(1)(vi) and (vii) for rules re-

lating to the deductibility of grants or bequests to such trusts.

(3) A section 4947(a)(2) trust becoming a section 4947(a)(1) trust. If the governing instrument of a trust described in section 4947(a)(2) meets the applicable requirements of paragraph (a)(2) of this section and such trust ceases to be so described and becomes instead a trust described in section 4947(a)(1), then such governing instrument must meet, prior to the end of 12 months from the date such trust first becomes described in section 4947(a)(1) (except as otherwise provided in this section) all the requirements of paragraph (a) of this section in order to comply with section 508(e).

(f) Special rules for existing private foundations. *(1)* Pursuant to section 508(e)(2), section 508(e)(1) and paragraph (a) of this section shall not apply in the case of any organization whose governing instrument was executed before January 1, 1970:

(i) To any taxable year beginning before January 1, 1972;

(ii) To any period after December 31, 1971, during the pendency of any judicial proceeding begun before January 1, 1972, by the private foundation which is necessary to reform, or to excuse such foundation from compliance with, its governing instrument or any other instrument in order to meet the requirements of section 508(e)(1); and

(iii) To any period after the termination of any judicial proceeding described in subdivision (ii) of this subparagraph during which its governing instrument or any other instrument does not permit it to meet the requirements of section 508(e)(1).

(2) For purposes of subparagraph (1) of this paragraph, and § 1.508-2(b)(1)(vi)(a), a governing instrument will not be treated as executed before the applicable date, if, after such date the dispositive provisions of the instrument are amended (determined under rules similar to the rules set forth in § 20.2055-2(e)(4) of this chapter).

(3) For purposes of subparagraph (1)(ii) and (iii) of this paragraph, a private foundation will be treated as meeting the requirements of section 508(e)(2)(B) and (C) if it has commenced a necessary and timely proceeding in an appropriate court or original jurisdiction and such court has ruled that the foundation's governing instrument or any other instrument does not permit it to meet the requirements of section 508(e)(1). Such foundation is not required to commence proceedings in any court of appellate jurisdiction in order to comply with section 508(e)(2)(C). See also § 1.508-2(b)(2).

(g) Extension of time for compliance with section 508(e). *(1)* Except as provided in subparagraph (2) of this paragraph, section 508(e)(1) shall not apply to any private foundation (regardless of when organized) with respect:

(i) To any taxable year beginning before the transitional date,

(ii) To any period on or after the transitional date during the pendency of any judicial proceeding begun before the transitional date by the private foundation which is necessary to reform, or to excuse such foundation from compliance with, this subparagraph during which its governing instrument or any other instrument in order to meet the requirements of section 508(e)(1), and

(iii) To any period after the termination of any judicial proceeding described in subdivision (ii) of this subparagraph during which its governing instrument or any other instrument does not permit it to meet the requirements of section 508(e)(1).

(2) Subparagraph (1) of this paragraph shall apply only to gifts or bequests referred to in section 508(d)(2)(A) that are made before the transitional date.

(3) For purposes of this paragraph the term "transitional dates" means the earlier of the following dates:

(i) In the case of a medical research organization, May 21, 1976 or in the case of a community trust February 10, 1977, or

(ii) The 91st day after the date an organization receives a final ruling or determination letter that it is a private foundation under section 509(a).

T.D. 7232, 12/21/72, amend T.D. 7440, 11/11/76, T.D. 7678, 2/25/80.

§ 1.508-4 Effective date.

Except as otherwise provided, §§ 1.508-1 through 1.508-3 shall take effect on January 1, 1970.

T.D. 7232, 12/21/72.

§ 1.509(a)-1 Definition of private foundation.

In general. Section 509(a) defines the term "private foundation" to mean any domestic or foreign organization described in section 501(c)(3) other than an organization described in section 509(a)(1), (2), (3), or (4). Organizations which fall into the categories excluded from the definition of "private foundation" are generally those which either have broad public support or actively function in a supporting relationship to such organizations. Organizations which test for public safety are also excluded.

T.D. 7212, 10/16/72.

§ 1.509(a)-2 Exclusion for certain organizations described in section 170(b)(1)(A).

Caution: The Treasury has not yet amended Reg § 1.509(a)-2 to reflect changes made by P.L. 94-455, P.L. 94-81.

(a) General rule. Organizations described in section 170(b)(1)(A) (other than in clauses (vii) and (viii)) are excluded from the definition of "private foundation" by section 509(a)(1). For the requirements to be met by organizations described in section 170(b)(1)(A)(i) through (vi), see § 1.170A-9(a) through (e) and paragraph (b) of this section. For purposes of this section, the parenthetical language "other than in clauses (vii) and (viii)" used in section 509(a)(1) means "other than an organization which is described only in clause (vii) or (viii)." For purposes of this section, an organization may qualify as a section 509(a)(1) organization regardless of the fact that it does not satisfy section 170(c)(2) because:

(1) Its funds are not used within the United States or its possessions, or

(2) It was created or organized other than in, or under the law of, the United States, any State or territory, the District of Columbia, or any possession of the United States.

(b) Medical research organizations. In order to qualify under section 509(a)(1) as a medical research organization described in section 170(b)(1)(A)(iii), an organization must meet the requirements of section 170(b)(1)(A)(iii) and § 1.170A-9(c)(2), except that, solely for purposes of classification as a section 509(a)(1) organization, such organization need not be committed to spend every contribution for medical research before January 1 of the fifth calendar year which begins after the date such contribution is made.

T.D. 7212, 10/16/72.

§ 1.509(a)-3 Broadly, publicly supported organizations.

(a) In general. *(1) General rule.* Section 509(a)(2) excludes certain types of broadly, publicly supported organizations from private foundation status. An organization will be excluded under section 509(a)(2) if it meets the one-third support test under section 509(a)(2)(A) and the not-more-than-one-third support test under section 509(a)(2)(B).

(2) One-third support test. An organization will meet the one-third support test if it normally (within the meaning of paragraph (c), (d), or (e) of this section) receives more than one-third of its support in each taxable year from any combination of:

(i) Gifts, grants, contributions, or membership fees, and

(ii) Gross receipts from admissions, sales of merchandise, performance of services, or furnishing of facilities, in an activity which is not an unrelated trade or business (within the meaning of section 513), subject to certain limitations described in paragraph (b) of this section,

from permitted sources. For purposes of this section, governmental units, organizations described in section 509(a)(1) and persons other than disqualified persons with respect to the organization shall be referred to as permitted sources. For purposes of this section, the amount of support received from the sources described in subdivisions (i) and (ii) of this subparagraph (subject to the limitations referred to in this subparagraph) will be referred to as the numerator of the one-third support total amount of support received (as defined in section 509(d)) will be referred to as the denominator of the one-third support fraction. For purposes of section 509(a)(2), paragraph (f) of this section distinguishes gifts and contributions from gross receipts; paragraph (g) of this section distinguishes grants from gross receipts; paragraph (h) of this section defines membership fees; paragraph (i) of this section defines "any bureau or similar agency of a governmental unit"; paragraph (j) of this section describes the treatment of certain indirect forms of support; paragraph (k) of this section describes the method of accounting for support; paragraph (l) of this section describes the treatment of gross receipts from section 513(a)(1), (2), or (3) activities; and paragraph (m) of this section distinguishes gross receipts from gross investment income.

(3) Not-more-than-one-third support test. (i) In general. An organization will meet the not-more-than-one-third support test under section 509(a)(2)(B) if it normally (within the meaning of paragraph (c), (d), or (e) of this section) receives not more than one-third of its support in each taxable year from the sum of its gross investment income (as defined in section 509(e)) and the excess (if any) of the amount of its unrelated business taxable income (as defined in section 512) derived from trades or businesses which were acquired by the organization after June 30, 1975, over the amount of tax imposed on such income by section 511. For purposes of this section the amount of support received from items described in section 509(a)(2)(B) will be referred to as the numerator of the not-more-than-one-third support fraction, and the total amount of support (as defined in section 509(d)) will be referred to as the denominator of the not-more-than-one-third support fraction. For purposes of section 509(a)(2), paragraph (m) of this section distinguishes gross receipts from gross investment income. For purposes of section 509(e), gross investment income includes the items of investment income described in § 1.512(b)-1(a).

(ii) Trade or business. For purposes of section 509(a)(2)(B)(ii), a trade or business acquired after June 30, 1975, by an organization shall include, in addition to other trades or businesses:

(A) A trade or business acquired after such date from, or as a result of the liquidation of, an organization's subsidiary which is described in section 502 whether or not the subsidiary was held on June 30, 1975.

(B) A new trade or business commenced by an organization after such date.

(iii) Allocation of deductions between businesses acquired before, and businesses acquired after, June 30, 1975. Deductions which are allowable under section 512 but are not directly connected to a particular trade or business, such as deductions referred to in paragraphs (10) and (12) of section 512(b), shall be allocated in the proportion that the unrelated trade or business taxable income derived from trades or businesses acquired after June 30, 1975, bears to the organization's total unrelated business taxable income, both amounts being determined without regard to such deductions.

(iv) Allocation of tax. The tax imposed by section 511 shall be allocated in the same proportion as in paragraph (a)(3)(iii) of this section.

(4) Purposes. The one-third support test and the not-more-than-one-third support test are designed to insure that an organization which is excluded from private foundation status under section 509(a)(2) is responsive to the general public, rather than to the private interests of a limited number of donors or other persons.

(b) Limitation on gross receipts. *(1) General rule.* In computing the amount of support received from gross receipts under section 509(a)(2)(A)(ii) for purposes of the one-third support test of section 509(a)(2)(A), gross receipts from related activities received from any person, or from any bureau or similar agency of a governmental unit, are includible in any taxable year only to the extent that such receipts do not exceed the greater of $5,000 or 1 percent of the organization's support in such taxable year.

(2) Examples. The application of this paragraph may be illustrated by the examples set forth below. For purposes of these examples, the term "general public" is defined as persons other than disqualified persons and other than persons from whom the foundation receives gross receipts in excess of the greater of $5,000 or 1 percent of its support in any taxable year, and the term "gross receipts" is limited to receipts from activities which are not unrelated trade or business (within the meaning of section 513).

Example (1). For the taxable year 1970, X, an organization described in section 501(c)(3), received support of $10,000 [sic: should read "$100,000"] from the following sources:

Bureau M (a governmental bureau from which X received gross receipts for services rendered) . .	$ 25,000
Bureau N (a governmental bureau from which X received gross receipts for services rendered) . .	25,000
General public (gross receipts for services rendered.	20,000
Gross investment income	15,000
Contributions from individual substantial contributors (defined as disqualified persons under section 4946(a)(2)).	15,000
Total support.	100,000

Since the $25,000 received from each bureau amounts to more than the greater of $5,000 or 1 percent of X's support for 1970 (1% of $100,000 = $1,000) under section 509(a)(2)(A)(ii), each amount is includible in the numerator of the one-third support fraction only to the extent of $5,000. Thus, for the taxable year 1970, X received support from sources which are taken into account in meeting the one-third support test of section 509(a)(2)(A) computed as follows:

Bureau M	$5,000
Bureau N	5,000
General public	20,000
Total	30,000

Therefore, in making the computations required under paragraph (c), (d), or (e) of this section, only $30,000 is includible in the aggregate numerator and $100,000 is includible in the aggregate denominator of the support fraction.

Example (2). For the taxable year 1970, Y, an organization described in section 501(c)(3), received support of $600,000 from the following sources:

Bureau O (gross receipts for services rendered)	$10,000
Bureau P (gross receipts for services rendered)	10,000
General public (gross receipts for services rendered)	150,000
General public (contributions)	40,000
Gross investment income	150,000
Contributions from substantial contributors	240,000
Total support	600,000

Since the $10,000 received from each bureau amounts to more than the greater of $5,000 or 1 percent of Y's support for 1970 (1% of $600,000 = $6,000), each amount is includible in the numerator of the one-third support fraction only to the extent of $6,000. Thus, for the taxable year 1970, Y received support from sources required to meet the one-third support test of section 509(a)(2)(A) computed as follows:

Bureau O	$6,000
Bureau P	6,000
General public (gross receipts)	150,000
General public (contributions)	40,000
Total	202,000

Therefore, in making the computations required under paragraph (c), (d), or (e) of this section, $202,000 is includible in the aggregate numerator and $600,000 is includible in the aggregate denominator of the support fraction.

(c) "Normally." *(1) In general.* (i) Definition. The support tests set forth in section 509(a)(2) are to be computed on the basis of the nature of the organization's "normal" sources of support. An organization will be considered as "normally" receiving one-third of its support from any combination of gifts, grants, contributions, membership fees, and gross receipts from permitted sources (subject to the limitations described in paragraph (b) of this section) and not more than one-third of its support from items described in section 509(a)(2)(B) for its current taxable year and the taxable year immediately succeeding its current year, if, for the 4 taxable years immediately preceding the current taxable year, the aggregate amount of the support received during the applicable period from gifts, grants, contributions, membership fees, and gross receipts from permitted sources (subject to the limitations described in paragraph (b) of this section) is more than one-third, and the aggregate amount of the support received from items described in section 509(a)(2)(B) is not more than one-third of the total support of the organization for such 4-year period.

(ii) Exception for material changes in sources of support. If for the current taxable year there are substantial and material changes in an organization's sources of support other than changes arising from unusual grants excluded under subparagraph (3) of this paragraph, then in applying subdivision (i) of this subparagraph, neither the 4-year computation period applicable to such year as an immediately succeeding taxable year, not the 4-year computation period applicable to such year as a current taxable year shall apply, and in lieu of such computation periods there shall be applied a computation period consisting of the taxable year of substantial and material changes and the 4 taxable years immediately preceding such year. Thus, for example, if there are substantial and material changes in an organization's sources of support for taxable year 1976, then even though such organization meets the requirements of subdivision (i) of this subparagraph based on a computation period of taxable years 1971 through 1974 or 1972 through 1975, such an organization will not meet the requirements of section 509(a)(2) unless it meets the requirements of subdivision (i) of this subparagraph for a computation period of the taxable years 1972 through 1976. See example (3) in subparagraph (6) of this paragraph for an illustration of this subdivision. An example of a substantial and material change is the receipt of an unusually large contribution or bequest which does not qualify as an unusual grant under subparagraph (3) of this paragraph. See subparagraph (5)(ii) of this paragraph as to the procedure for obtaining a ruling whether an unusually large grant may be excluded as an unusual grant.

(iii) Status of grantors and contributors. (a) If as a result of subdivision (ii) of this subparagraph, an organization is not able to meet the requirements of either the one-third support test described in paragraph (a)(2) of this section or the not-more-than-one-third support test described in paragraph (a)(3) of this section for its current taxable year, its status (with respect to a grantor or contributor under section 170, 507, 545(b)(2), 556(b)(2), 642(c), 4942, 4945, 2055, 2106(a)(2), and 2522) will not be affected until notice of change of status under section 509(a)(2) is made to the public (such as by publication in the Internal Revenue Bulletin). The preceding sentence shall not apply, however, if the grantor or contributor was responsible for, or was aware of, the substantial and material change referred to in subdivision (ii) of this subparagraph, or acquired knowledge that the Internal Revenue Service had given notice to such organization that it would be deleted from classification as section 509(a)(2) organization.

(b) A grantor or contributor (other than one of the organization's founders, creators, or foundation managers (within the meaning of section 4946(b)) will not be considered to be responsible for, or aware of, the substantial and material change referred to in subdivision (ii) of this subparagraph if such grantor or contributor has made such grant or contribution in reliance upon a written statement by the grantee organization that such grant or contribution will not result in the loss of such organization's classification as not a private foundation under section 509(a). Such statement must be signed by a responsible officer of the grantee organization and must set forth sufficient information, including a summary of the pertinent financial data for the 4 preceding years, to assure a reasonably prudent man that his grant or contribution will not result in the loss of the grantee organization's classification as not a private foundation under section 509(a). If a reasonable doubt exists as to the effect of such grant or contribution, or if the grantor or contributor is one of the organization's founders, creators, or foundation managers, the procedure set forth in subparagraph (5)(ii) of this paragraph may be followed by the grantee organization for the protection of the grantor or contributor.

(iv) Special rule for new organizations. If an organization has been in existence for at least 1 taxable year consisting of at least 8 months, but for fewer than 5 taxable years, the number of years for which the organization has been in existence immediately preceding each current taxable year being tested will be substituted for the 4-year period described in subdivision (i) of this subparagraph to determine whether the organization "normally" meets the requirements of paragraph (a) of this section. However, if subdivision (ii) of this subparagraph applies, then the period consisting of the number of years for which the organization has been in existence (up to and including the current year) will be substituted for the 4-year period described in subdivision (i) of this subparagraph. An organization which has been in existence for at least 1 taxable year, consisting of 8 or more months, may be issued a ruling or determination letter if it "normally" meets the requirements of paragraph (a) of this section for the number of years described in this subdivision. Such an organization may apply for a ruling or determination letter under the provisions of this paragraph, rather than under the provisions of paragraph (d) of this section. The issuance of a ruling or determination letter will be discretionary with the Commissioner. See paragraph (e)(4) of this section as to the initial determination of the status of a newly created organization. This subdivision shall not apply to those organizations receiving an extended advance ruling under paragraph (d)(4) of this section.

(2) Terminations under section 507(b)(1)(B). For the special rules applicable to the term "normally" as applied to private foundations which elect to terminate their private foundation status pursuant to the 12-month or 60-month procedure provided in section 507(b)(1)(B), see the regulations under such section.

(3) Exclusion of unusual grants. For purposes of applying the 4-year aggregation test for support set forth in subparagraph (1) of this paragraph, one or more contributions (including contributions made prior to Jan. 1, 1970) may be excluded from the numerator of the one-third support fraction and from the denominator of both the one-third support and not-more-than-one-third support fractions only if such a contribution meets the requirements of this subparagraph. The exclusion provided by this subparagraph is generally intended to apply to substantial contributions and bequests from disinterested parties, which contributions or bequests:

(i) Are attracted by reason of the publicly supported nature of the organization;

(ii) Are unusual or unexpected with respect to the amount thereof; and

(iii) Would by reason of their size, adversely affect the status of the organization as normally meeting the one-third support test for any of the applicable periods described in paragraph (c), (d), or (e) of this section.

In the case of a grant (as defined in paragraph (g) of this section) which meets the requirements of this subparagraph, if the terms of the granting instrument (whether executed before or after 1969) require that the funds be paid to the recipient organization over a period of years, the amount received by the organization each year pursuant to the terms of such grant may be excluded for such year. However, no item described in section 509(a)(2)(B) may be excluded under this subparagraph. The provisions of this subparagraph shall apply to exclude unusual grants made during any of the applicable periods described in paragraph (c), (d), or (e) of this section. See subparagraph (5)(ii) of this paragraph as to reliance by a grantee organization upon an unusual grant ruling under this subparagraph.

(4) Determining factor. In determining whether a particular contribution may be excluded under subparagraph (3) of this paragraph, all pertinent facts and circumstances will be taken into consideration. No single factor will necessarily be determinative. Among the factors to be considered are:

(i) Whether the contribution was made by any person (or persons standing in a relationship to such person which is described in section 4946(a)(1)(C) through (G)) who created the organization, previously contributed a substantial part of its support or endowment, or stood in a position of authority, such as a foundation manager (within the meaning of section 4946(b)), with respect to the organization. A contribution made by a person other than those persons described in this subdivision will ordinarily be given more favorable consideration than a contribution made by a person described in this subdivision.

(ii) Whether the contribution was a bequest or an inter vivos transfer. A bequest will ordinarily be given more favorable consideration than an inter vivos transfer.

(iii) Whether the contribution was in the form of cash, readily marketable securities, or assets which further the exempt purposes of the organization, such as a gift of a painting to a museum.

(iv) Except in the case of a new organization, whether, prior to the receipt of the particular contribution, the organization (a) has carried on an actual program of public solicitation and exempt activities and (b) has been able to attract a significant amount of public support.

(v) Whether the organization may reasonably be expected to attract a significant amount of public support subsequent to the particular contribution. In this connection, continued reliance on unusual grants to fund an organization's current operating expenses (as opposed to providing new endowment funds) may be evidence that the organization cannot reasonably be expected to attract future support from the general public.

(vi) Whether, prior to the year in which the particular contribution was received, the organization met the one-third support test described in subparagraph (1) of this paragraph without the benefit of any exclusions of unusual grants pursuant to subparagraph (3) of this paragraph;

(vii) Whether neither the contributor nor any person standing in a relationship to such contributor which is described in section 4946(a)(1)(C) through (G) continues directly or indirectly to exercise control over the organization;

(viii) Whether the organization has a representative governing body as described in § 1.509(a)-3(d)(3)(i); and

(ix) Whether material restrictions or conditions (within the meaning of § 1.507-2(a)(8)) have been imposed by the transferor upon the transferee in connection with such transfer.

(5) Grantors and contributors. (i) As to the status of grants and contributions which result in substantial and material changes in the organization (as described in subparagraph (1)(ii) of this paragraph) and which fail to meet the requirements for exclusion under subparagraph (3) of this paragraph, see the rules prescribed in subparagraph (1)(iii) of this paragraph.

(ii) Prior to the making of any grant or contribution which will allegedly meet the requirements for exclusion under subparagraph (3) of this paragraph, a potential grantee organization may request a ruling whether such grant or contribution may be so excluded. Requests for such ruling may be filed by the grantee organization with the district director. The issuance of such ruling will be at the sole discretion of the Commissioner. The organization must submit all information necessary to make a determination of the applicability of subparagraph (3) of this paragraph, including all information relating to the factors described in subparagraph (4) of this paragraph. If a favorable ruling is issued, such ruling may be relied upon by the grantor or contributor of the particular contribution in question for purposes of sections 170, 507, 545(b)(2), 556(b)(2), 642(c), 4942, 4945, 2055, 2106(a)(2), and 2522 and by the grantee organization for purposes of subparagraph (3) of this paragraph.

(6) Examples. The application of the principles set forth in this paragraph is illustrated by the examples set forth below. For purposes of these examples, the term "general public" is defined as persons other than persons from whom the foundation received gross receipts in excess of the greater of $5,000 or 1 percent of its support in any taxable year, the term "gross investment income" is as defined in section 509(e), and the term "gross receipts" is limited to receipts from activities which are not unrelated trade or business (within the meaning of section 513).

Example (1). For the years 1970 through 1973, X, an organization exempt under section 501(c)(3) which makes scholarship grants to needy students of a particular city, received support from the following sources.

1970	
Gross receipts (general public)	$35,000
Contributions (substantial contributors)	36,000
Gross investment income	29,000
Total support	100,000

1971	
Gross receipts (general public)	34,000
Contributions (substantial contributors)	35,000
Gross investment income	31,000
Total support	100,000

1972	
Gross receipts (general public)	35,000
Contributions (substantial contributors)	30,000
Gross investment income	35,000
Total support	100,000

1973	
Gross receipts (general public)	30,000
Contributions (substantial contributors)	39,000
Gross investment income	31,000
Total support	100,000

In applying section 509(a)(2) to the taxable year 1974 on the basis of subparagraph (1)(i) of this paragraph, the total amount of support from gross receipts from the general public ($134,000) for the period 1970 through 1973 was more than one-third, and the total amount of support from gross investment income ($126,000) was less than one-third, of its total support for the same period ($400,000). For the taxable years 1974 and 1975, X is therefore considered "normally" to receive more than one-third of its support from the public sources described in section 509(a)(2)(A) and less than one-third of its support from items described in section 509(a)(2)(B) since due to the pattern of X's support, there are no substantial and material changes in the sources of the organization's support in these years. The fact that X received less than one-third of its support from section 509(a)(2)(A) sources in 1973 and more than one-third of its support from items described in section 509(a)(2)(B) in 1972 does not affect its status since it met the "normally" test over a 4-year period.

Example (2). Assume the same facts as in example (1) except that in 1973 X also received an unexpected bequest of $50,000 from A, an elderly widow who was interested in encouraging the work of X, but had no other relationship to it. Solely by reason of the bequest, A became a disqualified person. X used the bequest to create five new scholarships. Its operations otherwise remained the same. Under these circumstances X could not meet the 4-year support test since the total amount received from gross receipts from the general public ($134,000) would not be more than one-third of its total support for the 4-year period ($450,000). Since A is a disqualified person, her bequest cannot be included in the numerator of the one-third support test under section 509(a)(2)(A). However, based on the factors set forth in subparagraph (4) of this paragraph, A's bequest may be excluded as an unusual grant under subparagraph (3) of this paragraph. Therefore, X will be considered to have met the support test for taxable years 1974 and 1975.

Example (3). In 1970, Y, an organization described in section 501(c)(3), was created by A, the holder of all the common stock in M corporation, B, A's wife, and C, A's business associate. Each of the three creators made small cash contributions to Y to enable it to begin operations. The purpose of Y was to sponsor and equip athletic teams for underprivileged children in the community. Between 1970 and 1973, Y was able to raise small amounts of contributions through fund raising drives and selling admission to some of the sponsored sporting events. For its first year of operations, it was determined that Y was excluded from the definition of "private foundation" under the provisions of section 509(a)(2). A made small contributions to Y from time to time. At all times, the operations of Y were carried out on a small scale, usually being restricted to the sponsorship of two to four baseball teams of underprivileged children. In 1974, M recapitalized and created a first and second class of 6 percent non-voting preferred stock, most of which was held by A and B. A then contributed 49 percent of his common stock in M to Y. A, B, and C continued to be active participants in the affairs of Y from its creation through 1974. A's contribution of M's common stock was substantial and constituted 90 percent of Y's total support for 1974. Although Y could satisfy the one-third support test on the basis of the four taxable years prior to 1974, a combination of the facts and circumstances described in subparagraph (4) of this paragraph preclude A's contribution of M's common stock in 1974 from being excluded as an unusual grant under subparagraph (3) of this paragraph. A's contribution in 1974 constituted a substantial and material change in Y's sources of support within the meaning of subparagraph (1)(ii) of this paragraph and on the basis of the 5-year period prescribed in subparagraph (1)(ii) of this paragraph (1970 to 1974), Y would not be considered as "normally" meeting the one-third support test described in paragraph (a)(2) of this section for the taxable years 1974 (the current taxable year) and 1975 (the immediately succeeding taxable year).

Example (4). M, an organization described in section 501(c)(3), was organized in 1971 to promote the appreciation of ballet in a particular region of the United States. Its principal activities will consist of erecting a theater for the performance of ballet and the organization and operation of a ballet company. The governing body of M consists of 9 prominent unrelated citizens residing in the region who have either an expertise in ballet or a strong interest in encouraging appreciation of the art form. In order to provide sufficient capital for M to commence its activities, X, a private foundation, makes a grant of $500,000 in cash to M. Although A, the creator of X, is one of the nine members of M's governing body, was one of M's original founders, and continues to lend his prestige to M's activities and fund raising efforts, A does not, directly or indirectly, exercise any control over M. By the close of its first taxable year, M has also received a significant amount of support from a number of smaller contributions and pledges from other members of the general public. Upon the opening of its first season of ballet performances, M expects to charge admission to the general public. Under the above circumstances, the grant by X to M may be excluded as an unusual grant under subparagraph (3) of this paragraph for purposes of determining whether M meets the one-third support test under section 509(a)(2). Although A was a founder and member of the governing body of M, X's grant may be excluded.

Example (5). Assume the same facts as example (4). In 1974, during M's third season of operations, B, a widow, passed away and bequeathed $4 million to M. During 1971 through 1973, B had made small contributions to M, none exceeding $10,000 in any year. During 1971 through 1974, M had received approximately $550,000 from receipts for admissions and contributions from the general public. At the time of B's death, no person standing in a relationship to B described in section 4946(a)(1)(C) through (G) was a member of M's governing body. B's bequest was in the form of cash and readily marketable securities. The only condition placed upon the bequest was that it be used by M to advance the art of ballet. Under the above circumstances, the bequest of B to M may be excluded as an unusual grant under subparagraph (3) of this paragraph for purposes of determining whether M meets the one-third support test under section 509(a)(2).

Example (6). O is a research organization described in section 501(c)(3). O was created by A in 1971 for the purpose of carrying on economic studies primarily through persons receiving grants from O and engaging in the sale of economic publications. O's five-member governing body consists of A, A's sons, B, and C, and two unrelated economists. In 1971, A made a contribution to O of $100,000 to help establish the organization. During 1971 through 1974 A made annual contributions to O averaging $20,000 a year. During the same period, O received annual contributions from members of the general public averaging $15,000 per year and receipts from the sale of its publications averaging $50,000 per year. In 1974, B made an inter vivos contribution to O of $600,000 in cash and readily marketable securities. Under the above circumstances, B's contribution cannot be excluded as an unusual grant under subparagraph (3) of this paragraph for purposes of determining whether O meets the one-third support test.

Example (7). P is an educational organization described in section 501(c)(3). P was created in 1971. The governing body of P has 9 members, consisting of A, a prominent civic leader and 8 other unrelated civic leaders and educators in the community, who also participated in the creation of P. During 1971 through 1974, the principal source of income for P has been receipts from the sale of its educational periodicals. These sales have amounted to $200,000 for this period. Small contributions amounting to $50,000 have also been received during the same period from members of the governing body, including A, as well as other members of the general public. In 1974 A contributed $75,000 of the nonvoting stock of Y, a closely held corporation. A retained a substantial portion of the voting stock of Y. By a majority vote, the governing body decided to retain the Y stock for a period of at least 5 years. Under the above circumstances, A's contribution of the Y stock cannot be excluded as an unusual grant under subparagraph (3) of this paragraph for purposes of determining whether P meets the one-third support test.

(d) Advance rulings to newly created organizations. *(1) In general.* A ruling or determination letter that an organization is described in section 509(a)(2) will not be issued to a newly created organization prior to the close of its first taxable year consisting of at least 8 months. However, such organization may request a ruling or determination letter that it will be treated as a section 509(a)(2) organization for its first 2 taxable years (or its first 3 taxable years, if its first taxable year consists of less than 8 months). For purposes of this section such 2- or 3-year period, whichever is applicable, shall be referred to as the advance ruling period. Such an advance ruling or determination letter may be issued if the organization can reasonably be expected to meet the requirements of paragraph (a) of this section during the advance ruling period. The issuance of a ruling or determination letter will be discretionary with the Commissioner.

(2) Basic consideration. In determining whether an organization "can reasonably be expected" (within the meaning of subparagraph (1) of this paragraph) to meet the one-third support test under section 509(a)(2)(A) and the not-more-than-one-third support test under section 509(a)(2)(B) described in paragraph (a) of this section for its advance ruling period or extended advance ruling period as provided in subparagraph (4) of this paragraph, if applicable, the basic consideration is whether its organizational structure, proposed programs or activities, and intended method of operation are such as to attract the type of broadly based support from the general public, public charities, and governmental units which is necessary to meet such tests. While the factors which are relevant to this determination, and the weight accorded to each of them, may differ from case to case, depending on the nature and functions of the organization, a favorable determination will not be made where the facts indicate that an organization is likely during its advance or extended advance ruling period to receive less than one-third of its support from permitted sources (subject to the limitations of paragraph (b) of this section) or to receive more than one-third of its support from items described in section 509(a)(2)(B).

(3) Factors taken into account. All pertinent facts and circumstances shall be taken into account under subparagraph (2) of this paragraph in determining whether the organization structure, programs or activities, and method of operation of an organization are such as to enable it to meet the tests under section 509(a)(2) for its advance or extended advance ruling period. Some of the pertinent factors are:

(i) Whether the organization has or will have a governing body which is comprised of public officials, or individuals chosen by public officials acting in their capacity as such, of persons having special knowledge in the particular field or discipline in which the organization is operating, of community leaders, such has elected officials, clergymen, and educators, or, in the case of a membership organization of individuals elected pursuant to the organization's governing instrument or bylaws by a broadly based membership. This characteristic does not exist if the membership of the organization's governing body is such as to indicate that it represents the personal or private interests of disqualified persons, rather than the interests of the community or the general public.

(ii) Whether a substantial portion of the organization's initial funding is to be provided by the general public, by public charities, or by government grants, rather than by a limited number of grantors or contributors who are disqualified persons with respect to the organization. The fact that the organization plans to limit its activities to a particular community or region or to a special field which can be expected to appeal to a limited number of persons will be taken into consideration in determining whether those persons providing the initial support for the organization are representative of the general public. On the other hand, the subsequent sources of funding which the organization can reasonably expect to receive after it has become established and fully operational will also be taken into account.

(iii) Whether a substantial proportion of the organization's initial funds are placed, or will remain, in an endowment, and whether the investment of such funds is unlikely to result in more than one-third of its total support being received from items described in section 509(a)(2)(B).

(iv) In the case of an organization which carries on fund-raising activities, whether the organization has developed a concrete plan for solicitation of funds from the general public on a community or area-wide basis; whether any steps have been taken to implement such plan; whether any firm commitments of financial or other support have been made to the organization by civic, religious, charitable, or similar groups within the community; and whether the organization has made any commitments to, or established any working relationships with, those organizations or classes of persons intended as the future recipients of its funds.

(v) In the case of an organization which carries on community services, such as slum clearance and employment opportunities, whether the organization has a concrete program to carry out its work in the community; whether any steps have been taken to implement that program; whether it will receive any part of its funds from a public charity or governmental agency to which it is in some way held accountable as a condition of the grant or contribution; and whether it has enlisted the sponsorship or support of other civic or community leaders involved in community service programs similar to those of the organization.

(vi) In the case of an organization which carries on educational or other exempt activities for, or on behalf of, members, whether the solicitation for dues-paying members is designed to enroll a substantial number of persons in the community, area, profession, or field of special interest (depending on the size of the area and the nature of the organization's activities); whether membership dues for individual (rather than institutional) members have been fixed at rates designed to make membership available to a broad cross-section of the public rather than to restrict membership to a limited number of persons; and whether the activities of the organization will be likely to appeal to persons having some broad common interest or purpose, such as educational activities in the case of alumni associations, musical activities in the case of symphony societies, or civic affairs in the case of parent-teacher associations.

(vii) In the case of an organization which provides goods, services, or facilities, whether the organization is or will be required to make its services, facilities, performances, or products available (regardless of whether a fee is charged) to the general public, public charities or governmental units, rather than to a limited number of persons or organizations; whether the organization will avoid executing contracts to perform services for a limited number of firms or governmental agencies or bureaus; and whether the service to be provided is one which can be expected to meet a special or general need among a substantial portion of the general public.

(4) Extension of advance ruling period. (i) The advance ruling period described in subparagraph (1) of this paragraph shall be extended for a period of 3 taxable years after the close of the unextended advance ruling period if the organization so requests, but only if such organization's request accompanies its request for an advance ruling and is filed with a consent under section 6501(c)(4) to the effect that the period of limitation upon assessment under section 4940 for any taxable year within the extended advance ruling period shall not expire prior to 1 year after the date of the expiration of the time prescribed by law for the assessment of a deficiency for the last taxable year within the extended advance ruling period. An organization's extended advance ruling period is 5 taxable years if its first taxable year consists of at least 8 months, or is 6 taxable years if its first taxable year is less than 8 months.

(ii) Notwithstanding subdivision (i) of this subparagraph, an organization which has received or applied for an advance ruling prior to October 16, 1972, may file its request for the 3-year extension within 90 days from such date, but only if it files the consents required in this section.

(iii) See paragraph (e)(4)(i)(d) of this section for the effect upon the initial determination of status of an organization which receives an advance ruling for an extended advance ruling period.

(e) Status of newly created organization. *(1) Advance or extended advance ruling.* This subparagraph shall apply to a newly created organization which has received a ruling or determination letter under paragraph (d) of this section that it be treated as a section 509(a)(2) organization for its advance or extended advance ruling period. So long as such an organization's ruling or determination letter has not been terminated by the Commissioner before the expiration of the advance or extended advance ruling period, then whether or not such organization has satisfied the requirements of paragraph (a) of this section during such advance or extended advance ruling period, such an organization will be treated as an organization described in section 509(a)(2) in accordance with subparagraphs (2) and (3) of this paragraph, both for purposes of the organization and any grantor or contributor to such organization.

(2) Reliance period. Except as provided in subparagraphs (1) and (3) of this paragraph, an organization described in subparagraph (1) of this paragraph will be treated as an organization described in section 509(a)(2) for all purposes other than section 507(d) and 4940 for the period beginning with its inception and ending 90 days after its advance or extended advance ruling period. Such period will be extended until a final determination is made of such an organization's status only if the organization submits, within the 90-day period, information needed to determine whether it meets the requirements of paragraph (a) of this section for its advance ruling period (even if such organization fails to meet the requirements of such paragraph (a)). However, since this subparagraph does not apply to section 4940, if it is subsequently determined that the organization was a pri-

vate foundation from its inception, then the tax imposed by section 4940 shall be due without regard to the advance ruling or determination letter. Consequently, if any amount of tax under section 4940 in such a case is not paid on or before the last date prescribed for payment, the organization is liable for interest in accordance with section 6601. However, since any failure to pay such tax during the period referred to in this subparagraph is due to reasonable cause, the penalty under section 6651 with respect to the tax imposed by section 4940 shall not apply.

(3) Grantors or contributors. If a ruling or determination letter is terminated by the Commissioner prior to the expiration of the period described in subparagraph (2) of this paragraph, for purposes of sections 170, 507, 545(b)(2), 556(b)(2), 642(c), 4942, 4945, 2055, 2106(a)(2), and 2522 the status of grants or contributions with respect to grantors or contributors to such organizations will not be affected until notice of change of status of such organization is made to the public (such as by publication of the Internal Revenue Bulletin). The preceding sentence shall not apply, however, if the grantor or contributor was responsible for, or aware of the act or failure to act that resulted in the organization's loss of classification under section 509(a)(2) or acquired knowledge that the Internal Revenue Service had given notice to such organization that it would be deleted from such classification. See, however, § 1.509(a)-3 (c)(5)(ii) for the procedures to be followed to protect the grantor or contributor from being considered responsible for, or aware of, the act or failure to act resulting in the grantee's loss of classification under section 509(a)(2).

(4) Initial determination of status. (i) New organizations. (a) The initial determination of status of a newly created organization is the first determination (other than by issuance of an advance ruling or determination letter under paragraph (d) of this section) that the organization will be considered as "normally" meeting the requirements of paragraph (a) of this section for a period beginning with its first taxable year.

(b) In the case of a new organization whose first taxable year is at least 8 months, except as provided for in subdivision (i)(d) of this subparagraph, the initial determination of status shall be based on a computation period of either the first taxable year or the first and second taxable years.

(c) In the case of a new organization whose first taxable year is less than 8 taxable months, except as provided for in subdivision (i)(d) of this subparagraph, the initial determination of status shall be based on a computation period of either the first and second taxable years or the first, second and their taxable years.

(d) In the case of an organization which has received a ruling or determination letter for an extended advance ruling period under paragraph (d)(4) of this section, the initial determination of status shall be based on a computation period of all of the taxable years in the extended advance ruling period. However, where the ruling or determination letter for an extended advance ruling period under paragraph (d)(4) of this section is terminated by the Commissioner prior to the expiration of the period described in subparagraph (2) of this paragraph, the initial determination of status shall be based on a computation period of the period provided for in (b) or (c) of this subdivision or, if greater, the number of years to which the advance ruling applies.

(e) An initial determination that an organization will be considered as "normally" meeting the requirements of paragraph (a) of this section shall be effective for each taxable year in the computation period plus (except as provided by paragraph (c)(1)(ii) of this section relating to material changes in sources of support) the two taxable years immediately succeeding the computation period. Therefore, in the case of an organization referred to in (b) of this subdivision to which paragraph *(c)* (1)(ii) of this section does not apply, with respect to its first, second, and third taxable years, such an organization shall be described in section 509(a)(2) if it meets the requirements of paragraph (a) of this section for either its first taxable year or for its first and second taxable years on an aggregate basis. In addition, if it meets the requirements of paragraph (a) of this section for its first and second taxable years it shall be described in section 509(a)(2) for its fourth taxable year. Once an organization is considered as "normally" meeting the requirements of paragraph (a) for a period specified under this subdivision, paragraph (c)(1)(i), (ii), or (iv) of this section shall apply.

(f) The provisions of this subdivision may be illustrated by the following examples:

Example (1). X, a calendar year organization described in section 501(c)(3), is created in February 1972 for the purpose of displaying African art. The support X received from the public in 1972 satisfies the one-third support and not-more-than-one-third support tests described in section 509(a)(2) for its first taxable year, 1972. X may therefore get an initial determination that it meets the requirements of paragraph (a) of this section for its first taxable year beginning in February 1972 and ending on December 31, 1972. This determination will be effective for taxable years 1972, 1973, and 1974.

Example (2). Assume the same facts as in example (1) except that X also receives a substantial contribution from one individual in 1972 which is not excluded from the denominator of the one-third support fraction described in section 509(a)(2) by reason of the unusual grant provision of subparagraph (c)(3) of this section. Because of this substantial contribution, X fails to satisfy the one-third support test over its first taxable year, 1972. However, the support received from the public over X's first and second taxable years in the aggregate satisfies the one-third support and not-more-than-one-third support tests. X may therefore get an initial determination that it meets the requirements of paragraph (a) of this section for its first and second taxable years in the aggregate beginning in February 1972 and ending on December 31, 1973. This determination will be effective for taxable years 1972, 1973, 1974, and 1975.

Example (3). Y, a calendar year organization described in section 501(c)(3), is created in July 1972 for the encouragement of the musical arts. Y requests and receives an extended advance ruling period of five full taxable years plus its initial short taxable year of 6 months under subparagraph (d)(4) of this section. The extended advance ruling period begins in July 1972 and ends on December 31, 1977. The support received from the public over Y's first through sixth taxable years in the aggregate will satisfy the one-third support and not-more-than-one-third support tests described in section 509(a)(2). Therefore, Y in 1978 may get an initial determination that it meets the requirements of paragraph (a) of this section in the aggregate over all the taxable years in its extended advance ruling period beginning in July 1972 and ending on December 31, 1977. This determination will be effective for taxable years 1972 through 1979.

Example (4). Assume the same facts as in example (3) except that the ruling for the extended advance ruling period is terminated prospectively at the end of 1975, so that Y may not rely upon such ruling for 1976 or any so that Y may not rely upon such ruling for 1976 or any succeeding year. The support received from the public over Y's first through fourth taxable years (1972 through 1975) will not satisfy the one-third support and gross investment income tests described in section 509(a)(2). Because the ruling was terminated, the computation period for Y's initial determination of status is the period 1972 through 1975. Since Y has not met the requirements of paragraph (a) of this section for such computation period, Y is not described in section 509(a)(2) for purposes of its initial determination of status. If Y is not described in section 509(a) (1), (3), or (4), then Y is a private foundation. As of 1976, Y shall be treated as a private foundation for all purposes (except as provided in subparagraph (3) of this paragraph with respect to grantors and contributors), and as of July 1972 for purposes of the tax imposed by section 4940 and for purposes of section 507(d) (relating to aggregate tax benefit).

(ii) Advance rulings. Unless a newly created organization has obtained a ruling or determination letter under paragraph (d) of this section that it be treated as a section 509(a)(2) organization for its advance or extended advance ruling period, it can not rely upon the possibility it will meet the requirements of paragraph (a) of this section for a taxable year which begins before the close of either applicable computation period provided for in subdivision (i)(b) or (c) of this subparagraph. Therefore, an organization which has not obtained such a ruling or determination letter, in order to avoid the risks associated with subsequently being determined to be a private foundation, may comply with the rules applicable to private foundations, and may pay, for example, the tax imposed by section 4940. In that event, if the organization subsequently meets the requirements of paragraph (a) for either applicable computation period, it shall be treated as a section 509(a)(2) organization from its inception, and, therefore, any tax imposed under chapter 42 shall be refunded and section 509(b) shall not apply.

(iii) Penalties. If a newly created organization fails to obtain a ruling or determination letter under paragraph (d) of this section, and fails to meet the requirements of paragraph (a) of this section for the first applicable computation period provided for in subdivision (i)(b) or (c) of this subparagraph, see section 6651 for penalty for failure to file return and pay tax.

(iv) Examples. This subparagraph may be illustrated by the following examples:

Example (1). On January 1, 1972, A contributes $100,000 to X, an organization described in section 501(c)(3) which he created on such date. X is not described in section 509(a)(1), (3), or (4). X's governing instrument does not contain the provisions referred to in section 508(e). Therefore, A is not entitled to a deduction under section 170 for the $100,000 contribution by reason of section 508(d)(2)(A) unless X is described in section 509(a)(2). If X meets the requirements of section 509(a)(2) for 1972 and 1973 on an aggregate basis, then whether or not X met the requirements of section 509(a)(2) for 1972 based on the support received in 1972, X would not have to meet the governing instrument requirements of section 508(e), and section 508(d)(2)(A) would not prevent A from claiming the deduction under section 170 for 1972. If X fails to meet the requirements of section 509(a)(2) for both 1972 and, on an aggregate basis, 1972 and 1973, X would lose its exempt status under section 508(e) for both 1972 and 1973, and A would be barred by section 508(d)(2)(A) from claiming a deduction for the $100,000 contribution to X.

Example (2). Assume the same facts as in example (1) except that X's governing instrument contains provisions which meet the requirements of section 508(e) in the event X is a private foundation, but do not apply to X in the event X is not a private foundation. Whether or not X meets the requirements of section 509(a)(2) for 1972 based on the support received in 1972 or 1972 and 1973 on an aggregate basis, since X meets the requirements of section 508(e), section 508(d)(2)(A) would not bar A from claiming a deduction under section 170 for 1972 for the contribution to X.

(f) Gifts and contributions distinguished from gross receipts. *(1) In general.* In determining whether an organization normally receives more than one-third of its support from permitted sources, all "gifts" and "contributions" (within the meaning of section 509(a)(2)(A)(i)) received from permitted sources, are includible in the numerator of the support fraction in each taxable year. However, "gross receipts" (within the meaning of section 509(a)(2)(A)(ii)) from admissions, sales of merchandise, performance of services, or furnishing of facilities, in an activity which is not an unrelated trade or business, are includible in the numerator of the support fraction in any taxable year only to the extent that such gross receipts do not exceed the limitation with respect to the greater of $5,000 or 1 percent of support which is described in paragraph (b) of this section. The terms "gifts" and "contributions" shall, for purposes of section 509(a)(2), have the same meaning as such terms have under section 170(c) and also include bequests, legacies, devises, and transfers within the meaning of section 2055 or 2106(a)(2). Thus, for purposes of section 509(a)(2)(A), any payment of money or transfer of property without adequate consideration shall be considered a "gift" or "contribution." Where payment is made or property transferred as consideration for admissions, sales of merchandise, performance of services, or furnishing of facilities to the donor, the status of the payment or transfer under section 170(c) shall determine whether and to what extent such payment or transfer constitutes a "gift" or "contribution" under section 509(a)(2)(A)(i) as distinguished from "gross receipts" from related activities under section 509(a)(2)(A)(ii). For purposes of section 509(a)(2), the term contributions includes qualified sponsorship payments (as defined in § 1.513-4) in the form of money or property (but not services).

(2) Valuation of property. For purposes of section 509(a)(2), the amount includible in computing support with respect to gifts, grants or contributions of property or use of such property shall be the fair market or rental value of such property at the date of such gift or contribution.

(3) Examples. The provisions of this paragraph (f) may be illustrated by the following examples:

Example (1). P is a local agricultural club described in section 501(c)(3). In order to encourage interest and proficiency by young people in farming and raising livestock, it makes awards at its annual fair for outstanding specimens of produce and livestock. Most of these awards are cash or other property donated by local businessmen. When the awards are made, the donors are given recognition for their donations by being identified as the donor of the award. The recognition given to donors is merely incidental to the making of the award to worthy youngsters. For these reasons, the donations will constitute "contributions" for purposes of section 509(a)(2)(A)(i). The amount includible in computing support with respect to such contributions is equal to the cash contributed or the fair market value of other property on the dates contributed.

Example (2). Q, a performing arts center, enters into a contract with a large company to be the exclusive sponsor of the center's theatrical events. The company makes a payment of cash and products in the amount of $100,000 to Q, and in return, Q agrees to make a broadcast announcement thanking the company before each show and to provide $2,000 of advertising in the show's program (2% of $100,000 is $2,000). The announcement constitutes use or acknowledgment pursuant to section 513(i)(2). Because the value of the advertising does not exceed 2% of the total payment, the entire $100,000 is a qualified sponsorship payment under section 513(i), and $100,000 is treated as a contribution for purposes of section 509(a)(2)(A)(i).

Example (3). R, a charity, enters into a contract with a law firm to be the exclusive sponsor of the charity's outreach program. Instead of making a cash payment, the law firm agrees to perform $100,000 of legal services for the charity. In return, R agrees to acknowledge the law firm in all its informational materials. The total fair market value of the legal services, or $100,000, is a qualified sponsorship payment under section 513(i), but no amount is treated as a contribution under section 509(a)(2)(A)(i) because the contribution is of services.

(g) Grants distinguished from gross receipts. *(1) In general.* In determining whether an organization normally receives more than one-third of its support from public sources, all "grants" (within the meaning of section 509(a)(2)(A)(ii)) received from permitted sources are includible in full in the numerator of the support fraction in each taxable year. However, "gross receipts" (within the meaning of section 509(a)(2)(A)(ii)) from admissions, sales of merchandise, performance of services, or furnishing of facilities, in an activity which is not an unrelated trade or business, are includible in the numerator of the support fraction in any taxable year only to the extent that such gross receipts do not exceed the limitation with respect to the greater of $5,000 or 1 percent of support which is described in paragraph (b) of this section. A grant is normally made to encourage the grantee organization to carry on certain programs or activities in furtherance of its exempt purposes. It may contain certain terms and conditions imposed by the grantor to insure that the grantee's programs or activities are conducted in a manner compatible with the grantor's own programs and policies and beneficial to the public. The grantee may also perform a service or produce a work product which incidentally benefits the grantor. Because of the imposition of terms and conditions, the frequent similarity of public purposes of grantor and grantee, and the possibility of benefit resulting to the grantor, amounts received as grants "for" the carrying on of exempt activities are sometimes difficult to distinguish from amounts received as gross receipts "from" the carrying on of exempt activities. The fact that the agreement, pursuant to which payment is made, is designated a "contract" or a "grant" is not controlling for purposes of classifying the payment under section 509(a)(2).

(2) Distinguishing factors. For purposes of section 509(a)(2)(A)(ii), in distinguishing the term "gross receipts" from the term "grants," the term "gross receipts" means amounts received from an activity which is not an unrelated trade or business, if a specific service, facility, or product is provided to serve the direct and immediate needs of the payor, rather than primarily to confer a direct benefit upon the general public. In general, payments made primarily to enable the payor to realize or receive some economic or physical benefit as a result of the service, facility, or product obtained will be treated as "gross receipts" with respect to the payee. The fact that a profitmaking organization would, primarily for its own economic or physical betterment, contract with a nonprofit organization for the rendition of a comparable service, facility or product from such organization constitutes evidence that any payments received by the nonprofit payee organization (whether from a governmental unit, a nonprofit or a profitmaking organization) for such services, facilities or products are primarily for the economic or physical benefit of the payor and would therefore be considered "gross receipts," rather than "grants" with respect to the payee organization. For example, if a nonprofit hospital described in section 170(b)(1)(A)(iii) engages an exempt research and development organization to develop a more economical system of preparing food for its own patients and personnel, and it can be established that a hospital operated for profit might engage the services of such an organization to perform a similar benefit for its economic betterment, such fact would constitute evidence that the payments received by the research and development organization constitute "gross receipts," rather than "grants." Research leading to the development of tangible products for the use or benefit of the payor will generally be treated as a service provided to serve the direct and immediate needs of the payor, while basic research or studies carried on in the physical or social sciences will generally be treated as primarily to confer a direct benefit upon the general public.

(3) Examples. The application of this paragraph may be illustrated by the following examples:

Example (1). M, a nonprofit research organization described in section 501(c)(3), engages in some contract research. It receives funds from the government to develop a specific electronic device needed to perfect articles of space equipment. The initiative for the project came solely from the government. Furthermore, the government could have contracted with profitmaking research organizations which carry on similar activities. The funds received from the government for this project are gross receipts and do not constitute "grants" within the meaning of section 509(a)(2)(A)(i). M provided a specific product at the government's request and thus was serving the direct and immediate needs of the payor within the meaning of subparagraph (2) of this paragraph.

Example (2). N is a nonprofit educational organization described in section 501(c)(3). Its principal activity is to operate institutes to train employees of various industries in the principles of management and administration. The government pays N to set up a special institute for certain government employees and to train them over a 2-year period. Management training is also provided by profitmaking organizations. The funds received are included as "gross receipts." The particular services rendered were to serve the direct and immediate needs of the government in the training of its employees within the meaning of subparagraph (2) of this paragraph.

Example (3). The Office of Economic Opportunity makes a community action program grant to O, an organization described in section 509(a)(1). O serves as a "delegate agency" of OEO for purposes of financing a local community action program. As part of this program, O signs an agreement with X, an educational and charitable organization described in section 501(c)(3), to carry out a housing program for the benefit of poor families. Pursuant to this agreement, O pays X out of the funds provided by OEO to build or rehabilitate low income housing and to provide advisory services to other nonprofit organizations in order for them to meet similar housing objectives, all on a nonprofit basis. Payments made from O to X constitute "grants" for purposes of section 509(a)(2)(A) because such program is carried on primarily for the direct benefit of the community.

Example (4). P is an educational institute described in section 501(c)(3). It carries on studies and seminars to assist institutions of higher learning. It receives funds from the government to research and develop a program of black studies for institutions of higher learning. The performance of such a service confers a direct benefit upon the public. Because such program is carried on primarily for the direct benefit of the public, the funds are considered a "grant."

Example (5). Q is an organization described in section 501(c)(3) which carries on medical research. Its efforts have primarily been directed toward cancer research. Q sought funds from the government for a particular project being contemplated in connection with its work. In order to encourage its activities, the government gives Q the sum of $25,000. The research project sponsored by government funds is primarily to provide direct benefit to the general public, rather than to serve the direct and immediate needs of the government. The funds are therefore considered a "grant."

Example (6). R is a public service organization described in section 501(c)(3) and composed of State and local officials involved in public works activities. The Bureau of Solid Waste Management of the Department of Health, Education, and Welfare paid R to study the feasibility of a particular system for disposal of solid waste. Upon completion of the study, R was required to prepare a final report setting forth its findings and conclusions. Although R is providing the Bureau of Solid Waste Management with a final report, such report is the result of basic research and study in the physical sciences and is primarily to provide direct benefit to the general public by serving to further the general functions of government, rather than a direct and immediate governmental need. The funds paid to R are therefore a "grant" within the meaning of section 509(a)(2).

Example (7). R is the public service organization referred to in example (6). W, a municipality described in section 170(c)(1), decides to construct a sewage disposal plant. W pays R to study a number of possible locations for such plant and to make recommendations to W, based upon a number of factors, as to the best location. W instructed R that in making its recommendation, primary consideration should be given to minimizing the costs of the project to W. Since the study commissioned by W was primarily directed toward producing an economic benefit to W in the form of minimizing the costs of its project, the services rendered are treated as serving W's direct and immediate needs and are includible as "gross receipts" by R.

Example (8). S is an organization described in section 501(c)(3). It was organized and is operated to further African development and strengthen understanding between the United States and Africa. To further these purposes, S receives funds from the Agency for International Development and the Department of State under which S is required to carry out the following programs: Selection, transportation, orientation, counseling, and language training of African students admitted to American institutions of higher learning; payment of tuition, other fees, and maintenance of such students; and operation of schools and vocational training programs in underdeveloped countries for residents of those countries. Since the programs carried on by S are primarily to provide direct benefit to the general public, all of the funds received by S from the Federal agencies are considered "grants" within the meaning of section 509(a)(2).

(h) Definitions of membership fees. *(1) General rule.* For purposes of section 509(a)(2), the fact that a membership organization provides services, admissions, facilities, or merchandise to its members as part of its overall activities will not, in itself, result in the classification of fees received from members as "gross receipts" rather than "membership fees." If an organization uses membership fees as a means of selling admissions, merchandise, services, or the use of facilities to members of the general public who have no common goal or interest (other than the desire to purchase such admissions, merchandise, services, or use of facilities), then the income received from such fees shall not constitute "membership fees" under section 509(a)(2)(A)(i), but shall, if from a related activity, constitute "gross receipts" under section 509(a)(2)(A)(ii). On the other hand, to the extent the basic purpose for making the payment is to provide support for the organization rather than to purchase admissions, merchandise, services, or the use of facilities, the income received from such payment shall constitute "membership fees."

(2) Examples. The provisions of this paragraph may be illustrated by the following examples:

Example (1). M is a symphony society described in section 501(c)(3). Its primary purpose is to support the local symphony orchestra. The organization has three classes of membership. Contributing members pay annual dues of $10, sustaining members pay $25, and honorary members pay $100. The dues are placed in a maintenance fund which is used to provide financial assistance in underwriting the orchestra's annual deficit. Members have the privilege of purchasing subscriptions to the concerts before they go on sale to the general public, but must pay the same price as any other member of the public. They also are entitled to attend a number of rehearsals each season without charge. Under these circumstances, M's receipts from members constitute "membership fees" for purposes of section 509(a)(2)(A)(i).

Example (2). N is a theater association described in section 501(c)(3). Its purpose is to support a repertory company in the community in order to make live theatrical performances available to the public. The organization sponsors six plays each year. Members of the organization are entitled to a season subscription to the plays. The fee paid as dues approximates the retail price of the six plays, less a 10-percent discount. Tickets to each performance are also sold directly to the general public. The organization also holds a series of lectures on the theater which members may attend. Under these circumstances, the fees paid by members as dues will be considered "gross receipts" from a related activity. Although the fees are designated as membership fees, they are actually admissions to a series of plays.

(i) "Bureau" defined. *(1) In general.* The term "any bureau or similar agency of a governmental unit" (within the meaning of section 509(a)(2)(A)(ii)), refers to a specialized operating unit of the executive, judicial, or legislative branch of government where business is conducted under certain rules and regulations. Since the term "bureau" refers to a unit functioning at the operating, as distinct from the policymaking, level of government, it is normally descriptive of a subdivision of a department of government. The term "bureau," for purposes of section 509(a)(2)(A)(ii), would therefore not usually include those levels of government which are basically policymaking or administrative, such as the office of the Secretary or Assistant Secretary of a department, but would consist of the highest operational level under such policymaking or administrative levels. Each subdivision of a larger unit within the Federal Government, which is headed by a Presidential appointee holding a position at or above Level V of the Executive Schedule under 5 U.S.C. 5316, will normally be considered an administrative or policymaking, rather than an operating unit. Amounts received from a unit functioning at the policymaking or administrative level of government will be treated as received from one bureau or similar agency of such unit. Units of a governmental agency above the operating level shall be aggregated and considered a separate bureau for this purpose. Thus, an organization receiving gross receipts from both a policymaking administrative unit and an operational unit of a department will be treated as receiving gross receipts from two "bureaus" within the meaning of section 509(a)(2)(A)(ii). For purposes of this subparagraph, the Departments of Air Force, Army, and Navy are separate departments and each is considered as having its own policymaking, administrative, and operating units.

(2) Examples. The provisions of this paragraph may be illustrated by the following examples:

Example (1). The Bureau of Health Insurance is considered a "bureau" within the meaning of section 509(a)(2)(A)(ii). It is a part of the Department of Health, Education, and Welfare, whose Secretary performs a policymaking function, and is under the Social Security Administration, which is basically an administrative unit. The Bureau of Health Insurance is in the first operating level within the Social Security Administration. Similarly, the National Cancer Institute would be considered a "bureau," as it is an operating part of the National Institutes of Health within the Department of Health, Education, and Welfare.

Example (2). The Bureau for Africa and the Bureau for Latin America are considered "bureaus" within the meaning of section 509(a)(2)(A)(ii). Both are separate operating units under the Administrator of the Agency for International Development, a policymaking official. If an organization received gross receipts from both of these bureaus, the amount of gross receipts received from each would be subject to the greater of $5,000 or 1 percent limitation under section 509(a)(2)(A)(ii).

Example (3). The Bureau of International Affairs of the Civil Aeronautics Board is considered a "bureau" within the meaning of section 509(a)(2)(A)(ii). It is an operating unit under the administrative office of the Executive Director. The subdivisions of the Bureau of International Affairs are Geographic Areas and Project Development Staff. If an organization received gross receipts from these subdivisions, the total gross receipts from these subdivisions would be considered gross receipts from the same "bureau," the Bureau of International Affairs, and would be subject to the greater of $5,000 or 1 percent limitation under section 509(a)(2)(A)(ii).

Example (4). The Department of Mental Health, a State agency which is an operational part of State X's Department of Public Health, is considered a "bureau." The Department of Public Health is basically an administrative agency and the Department of Mental Health is at the first operational level within it.

Example (5). The Aeronautical Systems Division of the Air Force Systems Command, and other units on the same level, are considered separate "bureaus" with the meaning of section 509(a)(2)(A)(ii). They are part of the Department of the Air Force which is a separate department for this purpose, as are the Army and Navy. The Secretary and the Under Secretary of the Air Force perform the policymaking function, the Chief of Staff and the Air Force Systems Command are basically administrative, having a comprehensive complement of staff functions to provide administration for the various divisions. The Aeronautical Systems Division and other units on the same level are thus the first operating level, as evidenced by the fact that they are the units that let contracts and perform the various operating functions.

Example (6). The Division of Space Nuclear Systems, the Division of Biology and Medicine, and other units on the same level within the Atomic Energy Commission are each separate "bureaus" within the meaning of section 509(a)(2)(A)(ii). The Commissioners (which make up the Commission) are the policymakers. The general manager and the various assistant general managers perform the administrative function. The various divisions perform the operating function as evidenced by the fact that each has separate programs to pursue and contracts specifically for these various programs.

(j) Grants from public charities. *(1) General rule.* For purposes of the one-third support test in section 509(a)(2)(A), grants (as defined in paragraph (g) of this section) received from an organization described in section 509(a)(1) (hereinafter referred to in this subparagraph as a "public charity") are generally includible in full in computing the numerator of the recipient's support fraction of the taxable year in question. It is sometimes necessary to determine whether the recipient of a grant from a public charity has received such support from the public charity as a grant, or whether the recipient has in fact received such support as an indirect contribution from a donor to the public charity. If the amount received is considered a grant from the public charity, it is fully includable in the numerator of the support fraction under section 509(a)(2)(A). However, if the amount received is considered to be an indirect contribution from one of the public charity's donors which has passed through the public charity to the recipient organization, such amount will retain its character as a contribution from such donor and, if, for example, the donor is a substantial contributor (as defined in section 507(d)(2)) with respect to the ultimate recipient, such amount shall be excluded from the numerator of the support fraction under section 509(a)(2). If a public charity makes both an indirect contribution from its donor and an additional grant to the ultimate recipient, the indirect contribution shall be treated as made first.

(2) Indirect contributions. For purposes of subparagraph (1) of this paragraph, an indirect contribution is one which is expressly or impliedly earmarked by the donor as being for, or for the benefit of, a particular recipient (rather than for a particular purpose).

(3) Examples. The provisions of this paragraph may be illustrated by the following examples:

Example (1). M, a national foundation for the encouragement of the musical arts, is an organization described in section 170(b)(1)(A)(vi). A gives M a donation of $5,000 without imposing any restrictions or conditions upon the gift. M subsequently makes a $5,000 grant to X, an organization devoted to giving public performances of chamber music. Since the grant to X is treated as being received from M, it is fully includible in the numerator of X's support fraction for the taxable year of receipt.

Example (2). Assume M is the same organization described in example (1). B gives M a donation of $10,000, but requires that M spend the money for the purpose of supporting organizations devoted to the advancement of contemporary American music. M has complete discretion as to the organizations of the type described to which it will make a grant. M decides to make grants of $5,000 each to Y and Z, both being organizations described in section 501(c)(3) and devoted to furthering contemporary American music. Since the grants to Y and Z are treated as being received from M, Y and Z may each include one of the $5,000 grants in the numerator of its support fraction for purposes of section 509(a)(2)(A). Although the donation to M was conditioned upon the use of the funds for a particular purpose, M was free to select the ultimate recipient.

Example (3). N is a national foundation for the encouragement of art and is an organization described in section 170(b)(1)(A)(vi). Grants to N are permitted to be earmarked for particular purposes. O, which is an art workshop devoted to training young artists and claiming status under section 509(a)(2), persuades C, a private foundation, to make a grant of $25,000 to N. C is a disqualified person with respect to O. C made the grant to N with the understanding that N would be bound to make a grant to O in the sum of $25,000, in addition to a matching grant of N's funds to O in the sum of $25,000. Only the $25,000 received directly from N is considered a grant from N. The other $25,000 is deemed an indirect contribution from C to O and is to be excluded from the numerator of O's support fraction.

(k) Method of accounting. For purposes of section 509(a)(2), an organization's support will be determined solely on the cash receipts and disbursement method of accounting described in section 446(c)(1). For example, if a grantor makes a grant to an organization payable over a term of years, such grant will be includible in the support fraction of the grantee organization only when and to the extent amounts payable under the grant are received by the grantee.

(l) Gross receipts from section 513(a)(1), (2) or (3) activities. For purposes of section 509(a)(2)(A)(ii), gross receipts from activities described in section 513(a)(1), (2), or (3) will be considered gross receipts from activities which are not unrelated trade or business.

(m) Gross receipts distinguished from gross investment income. *(1)* For purposes of section 509(a)(2), where the charitable purpose of an organization described in section 501(c)(3) is accomplished through the furnishing of facilities for a rental fee or loans to a particular class of persons, such as aged, sick, or needy persons, the support received from such persons will be considered "gross receipts" (within the meaning of section 509(d)(2)) from an activity which is not an unrelated trade or business, rather than "gross investment income." However, if such organization also furnishes facilities or loans to persons who are not members of such class and such furnishing does not contribute importantly to the accomplishment of such organization's exempt purposes (aside from the need of such organization for income or funds or the use it makes of the profits derived), the support received from such furnishing will be considered "rents" or "interest" and therefore will be treated as "gross investment income" within the meaning of section 509(d)(4), unless such income is included in computing the tax imposed by section 511.

(2) The provisions of this paragraph may be illustrated by the following example:

Example. X, an organization described in section 501(c)(3), is organized and operated to provide living facilities for needy widows of deceased servicemen. X charges such widows a small rental fee for the use of such facilities. Since X is accomplishing its exempt purpose through the rental of such facilities, the support received from the widows is considered "gross receipts" within the meaning of section 509(d)(2). However, if X rents part of its facilities to persons having no relationship to X's exempt purpose, the support received from such rental will be considered "gross investment income" within the meaning of section 509(d)(4), unless such income is included in computing the tax imposed by section 511.

T.D. 7212, 10/16/72, amend T.D. 7784, 7/22/81, T.D. 8423, 7/28/92, T.D. 8991, 4/24/2002.

---

§ 1.509(a)-4 Supporting organizations.

Caution: The Treasury has not yet amended Reg § 1.509(a)-4 to reflect changes made by P.L. 109-280.

(a) In general. *(1)* Section 509(a)(3) excludes from the definition of "private foundation" those organizations which meet the requirements of subparagraphs (A), (B), and (C) thereof.

(2) Section 509(a)(3)(A) provides that a section 509(a)(3) organization must be organized, and at all times thereafter operated, exclusively for the benefit of, to perform the functions of, or to carry out the purposes of one or more specified organizations described in section 509(a)(1) or (2). Section 509(a)(3)(A) describes the nature of the support or benefit which a section 509(a)(3) organization must provide to one or more section 509(a)(1) or (2) organizations. For purposes of section 509(a)(3)(A), paragraph (b) of this section generally described the organizational and operational tests; paragraph (c) of this section describes permissible purposes under the organizational test; paragraph (d) of this section describes the requirement of supporting or benefiting one or more "specified" publicly supported organizations; and paragraph (e) of this section describes permissible beneficiaries and activities under the operational test.

(3) Section 509(a)(3)(B) provides that a section 509(a)(3) organization must be operated, supervised, or controlled by or in connection with one or more organizations described in section 509(a)(1) or (2). Section 509(a)(3)(B) and paragraph (f) of this section describe the nature of the relationship which must exist between the section 509(a)(3) and section 509(a)(1) or (2) organizations. For purposes of section 509(a)(3)(B), paragraph (g) of this section defines "operated, supervised, or controlled by"; paragraph (h) of this section defines "supervised or controlled in connection with;" and paragraph (i) of this section defines "operated in connection with."

(4) Section 509(a)(3)(C) provides that a section 509(a)(3) organization must not be controlled directly or indirectly by disqualified persons (other than foundation managers or organizations described in section 509(a)(1) or (2)). Section 509(a)(3)(C) and paragraph (j) of this section prescribe a limitation on the control over the section 509(a)(3) organization.

(5) For purposes of this section, the term "supporting organization" means either an organization described in section 509(a)(3) or an organization seeking section 509(a)(3) status, depending upon its context. For purposes of this section, the term "publicly supported organization" means an organization described in section 509(a)(1) or (2).

(b) Organizational and operational tests. *(1)* Under subparagraph (A) of section 509(a)(3), in order to qualify as a supporting organization, an organization must be both organized and operated exclusively "for the benefit of, to perform the functions of, or to carry out the purposes of" (hereinafter referred to in this section as being organized and operated "to support or benefit") one or more specified publicly supported organizations. If an organization fails to meet either the organizational or the operational test, it cannot qualify as a supporting organization.

(2) In the case of supporting organizations created prior to January 1, 1970, the organizational and operational tests shall apply as of January 1, 1970. Therefore, even though

the original articles of organization did not limit its purposes to those required under section 509(a)(3)(A) and even though it operated before January 1, 1970, for some purpose other than those required under section 509(a)(3)(A), an organization will satisfy the organizational and operational tests, if, on January 1, 1970, and at all times thereafter, it is so constituted as to comply with these tests. For the special rules pertaining to the application of the organizational and operational tests to organizations terminating their private foundation status under the 12-month or 60-month termination period provided under section 507(b)(1)(B) by becoming "public" under section 509(a)(3), see the regulations under section 507(b).

(c) Organizational test. *(1) In general.* An organization is organized exclusively for one or more of the purposes specified in section 509(a)(3)(A) only if its articles of organization (as defined in § 1.501(c)(3)-1(b)(2)):

(i) Limit the purposes of such organization to one or more of the purposes set forth in section 509(a)(3)(A);

(ii) Do not expressly empower the organization to engage in activities which are not in furtherance of the purposes referred to in subdivision (i) of this subparagraph;

(iii) State the specified publicly supported organizations on whose behalf such organization is to be operated (within the meaning of paragraph (d) of this section); and

(iv) Do not expressly empower the organization to operate to support or benefit any organization other than the specified publicly supported organizations referred to in subdivision (iii) of this subparagraph.

(2) Purposes. In meeting the organizational test, the organization's purposes, as stated in its articles, may be as broad as, or more specific than, the purposes set forth in section 509(a)(3)(A). Therefore, an organization which, by the terms of its articles, is formed "for the benefit of" one or more specified publicly supported organizations shall, if it otherwise meets the other requirements of this paragraph, be considered to have met the organizational test. Similarly, articles which state that an organization is formed "to perform the publishing functions" of a specified university are sufficient to comply with the organizational test. An organization which is "operated, supervised, or controlled by" (within the meaning of paragraph (g) of this section) or "supervised or controlled in connection with" (within the meaning of paragraph (h) of this section) one or more sections 509(a)(1) or (2) organizations to carry out the purposes of such organizations, will be considered as meeting the requirements of this paragraph if the purposes set forth in its articles are similar to, but no broader than, the purposes set forth in the articles of its controlling section 509(a)(1) or (2) organizations. If, however, the organization by which it is operated, supervised, or controlled is a publicly supported section 501(c)(4), (5), or (6) organization (deemed to be a section 509(a)(2) organization for purposes of section 509(a)(3) under the provisions of section 509(a)), the supporting organization will be considered as meeting the requirements of this paragraph if its articles require it to carry on charitable, etc., activities within the meaning of section 170(c)(2).

(3) Limitations. An organization is not organized exclusively for the purposes set forth in section 509(a)(3)(A) if its articles expressly permit it to operate to support or benefit any organization other than those specified publicly supported organizations referred to in subparagraph (1)(iii) of this paragraph. Thus, for example, an organization will not meet the organizational test under section 509(a)(3)(A) if its articles expressly empower it to pay over any part of its income to, or perform any service for, any organization other than those publicly supported organizations specified in its articles (within the meaning of paragraph (d) of this section). The fact that the actual operations of such organization have been exclusively for the benefit of the specified publicly supported organizations shall not be sufficient to permit it to meet the organizational test.

(d) Specified organizations. *(1) In general.* In order to meet the requirements of section 509(a)(3)(A), an organization must be organized and operated exclusively to support or benefit one or more "specified" publicly supported organizations. The manner in which the publicly supported organizations must be "specified" in the articles for purposes of section 509(a)(3)(A) will depend upon whether the supporting organization is "operated, supervised, or controlled by" or "supervised or controlled in connection with" (within the meaning of paragraphs (g) and (h) of this section) such organizations or whether it is "operated in connection with" (within the meaning of paragraph (i) of this section) such organizations.

(2) Nondesignated publicly supported organizations; requirements. (i) Except as provided in subdivision (iv) of this subparagraph, in order to meet the requirements of subparagraph (1) of this paragraph, the articles of the supporting organization must designate each of the "specified" organizations by name unless:

(a) The supporting organization is operated, supervised, or controlled by (within the meaning of paragraph (g) of this section), or is supervised or controlled in connection with (within the meaning of paragraph (h) of this section) one or more publicly supported organizations; and

(b) The articles of organization of the supporting organization require that it be operated to support or benefit one or more beneficiary organizations which are designated by class or purpose and which include:

(1) The publicly supported organizations referred to in (a) of this subdivision (without designating such organizations by name); or

(2) Publicly supported organizations which are closely related in purpose or function to those publicly supported organizations referred to in subdivision (i)(a) or this subparagraph (without designating such organization by name).

(ii) If a supporting organization is described in subdivision (i)(a) of this subparagraph, it will not be considered as failing to meet the requirements of subparagraph (1) of this paragraph that the publicly supported organizations be specified merely because its articles of organization permit the conditions described in subparagraphs (3)(i), (ii), and (iii) and (4)(i)(a) and (b) of this paragraph.

(iii) This subparagraph may be illustrated by the following examples:

Example (1). X is an organization described in section 501(c)(3) which operates for the benefit of institutions of higher learning in the State of Y. X is controlled by these institutions (within the meaning of paragraph (g) of this section) and such institutions are all section 509(a)(1) organizations. X's articles will meet the organizational test if they require X to operate for the benefit of institutions of higher learning or educational organizations in the State of Y (without naming each institution). X's articles would also meet the organizational test if they provided for the giving of scholarships to enable students to attend institutions of higher learning but only in the State of Y.

Example (2). M is an organization described in section 501(c)(3) which was organized and operated by representatives of N church to run a home for the aged. M is controlled (within the meaning of paragraph (g) of this section) by N church, a section 509(a)(1) organization. The care of the sick and the aged are long standing temporal functions and purposes of organized religion. By operating a home for the aged, M is operating to support or benefit N church in carrying out one of its temporal purposes. Thus M's articles will meet the organizational test if they require M to care for the aged since M is operating to support one of N church's purposes (without designating N church by name).

(iv) A supporting organization will meet the requirements of subparagraph (1) of this paragraph even though its articles do not designate each of the "specified" organizations by name if:

(a) There has been an historic and continuing relationship between the supporting organization and the section 509(a)(1) or (2) organizations, and

(b) By reason of such relationship, there has developed a substantial identity of interests between such organizations.

(3) Nondesignated publicly supported organizations; scope of rule. If the requirements of subparagraph (2)(i)(a) of this paragraph are met, a supporting organization will not be considered as failing the test of being organized for the benefit of "specified" organizations solely because its articles:

(i) Permit the substitution of one publicly supported organization within a designated class for another publicly supported organization either in the same or a different class designated in the articles;

(ii) Permit the supporting organization to operate for the benefit of new or additional publicly supported organizations of the same or a different class designated in the articles; or

(iii) Permit the supporting organization to vary the amount of its support among different publicly supported organizations within the class or classes of organizations designated by the articles. For example, X is an organization which operates for the benefit of private colleges in the State of Y. If X is controlled by these colleges (within the meaning of paragraph (g) of this section) and such colleges are all section 509(a)(1) organizations, X's articles will meet the organization test even if they permit X to operate for the benefit of any new colleges created in State Y in addition to the existing colleges or in lieu of one which has ceased to operate, or if they permit X to vary its support by paying more to one college than to another in a particular year.

(4) Designated publicly supported organizations. (i) If an organization is organized and operated to support one or more publicly supported organizations and it is "operated in connection with" such organization or organizations, then, except as provided in subparagraph (2)(iv) of this paragraph, its articles of organization must, for purposes of satisfying the organizational test under section 509(a)(3)(A), designate the "specified" organizations by name. Under the circumstances described in this subparagraph, a supporting organization which has one or more "specified" organizations designated by name in its articles, will not be considered as failing the test of being organized for the benefit of "specified" organizations solely because its articles:

(a) Permit a publicly supported organization which is designated by class or purpose, rather than by name, to be substituted for the publicly supported organization or organizations designated by name in the articles, but only if such substitution is conditioned upon the occurrence of an event which is beyond the control of the supporting organization, such as loss of exemption, substantial failure or abandonment of operations, or dissolution of the publicly supported organization or organizations designated in the articles;

(b) Permit the supporting organization to operate for the benefit of a beneficiary organization which is not a publicly supported organization, but only if such supporting organization is currently operating for the benefit of a publicly supported organization and the possibility of its operating for the benefit of other than a publicly supported organization is a remote contingency; or

(c) Permit the supporting organization to vary the amount of its support between different designated organizations, so long as it meets the requirements of the integral part test set forth in paragraph (i)(3) of this section with respect to at least one beneficiary organization.

(ii) If the beneficiary organization referred to in subdivision (i)(b) of this subparagraph is not a publicly supported organization, the supporting organization will not then meet the operational test of paragraph (e)(1) of this section. Therefore, if a supporting organization substituted in accordance with such subdivision (i)(b) a beneficiary other than a publicly supported organization and operated in support of such beneficiary organization, the supporting organization would not be described in section 509(a)(3).

(iii) This subparagraph may be illustrated by the following example:

Example. X is a charitable trust described in section 4947(a)(1) organized in 1968. Under the terms of its trust instrument, X's trustees are required to pay over all of X's annual income to M University Medical School for urological research. If M University Medical School is unable or unwilling to devote these funds to urological research, the trustees are required to pay all of such income to N University Medical School. However if N University Medical School is also unable or unwilling to devote these funds to urological research, X's trustees are directed to choose a similar organization willing to apply X's funds for urological research. From 1968 to 1973, X pays all of its net income to M University Medical School pursuant to the terms of the trust. M and N are publicly supported organizations. Although the contingent remainderman may not be a publicly supported organization, the possibility that X may operate for the benefit of other than a publicly supported organization is, in 1973, a remote possibility, and X will be considered as operating for the benefit of a "specified" publicly supported organization under subdivision (i) *(b)* of this subparagraph. However, if, at some future date, X actually substituted a nonpublicly supported organization as beneficiary, X would fail the requirements of the operational test set forth in paragraph (e)(1) of this section.

(e) Operational test. *(1) Permissible beneficiaries.* A supporting organization will be regarded as "operated exclusively" to support one or more specified publicly supported organizations (hereinafter referred to as the "operational test") only if it engages solely in activities which support or benefit the specified publicly supported organizations. Such activities may include making payments to or for the use of, or providing services or facilities for, individual members of the charitable class benefited by the specified publicly supported organization. A supporting organization may also, for example, make a payment indirectly through another unrelated organization to a member of a charitable class benefited by the specified publicly supported organization, but only if such a payment constitutes a grant to an individual rather than a grant to an organization. In determining whether a grant is indirectly to an individual rather than to an organization the same standard shall be applied as in

§ 53.4945-4(a)(4) of this chapter. Similarly, an organization will be regarded as "operated exclusively" to support or benefit one or more specified publicly supported organizations even if it supports or benefits an organization, other than a private foundation, which is described in section 501(c)(3) and is operated, supervised, or controlled directly by or in connection with such publicly supported organizations, or which is described in section 511(a)(2)(B). However, an organization will not be regarded as operated exclusively if any part of its activities is in furtherance of a purpose other than supporting or benefiting one or more specified publicly supported organizations.

(2) Permissible activities. A supporting organization is not required to pay over its income to the publicly supported organizations in order to meet the operational test. It may satisfy the test by using its income to carry on an independent activity or program which supports or benefits the specified publicly supported organizations. All such support must, however, be limited to permissible beneficiaries in accordance with subparagraph (1) of this paragraph. The supporting organization may also engage in fund raising activities, such as solicitations, fund raising dinners, and unrelated trade or business to raise funds for the publicly supported organizations, or for the permissible beneficiaries.

(3) Examples. The provisions of this paragraph may be illustrated by the following examples:

Example (1). M is a separately incorporated alumni association of X University and is an organization described in section 501(c)(3). X University is designated in M's articles as the sole beneficiary of its support. M uses all of its dues and income to support its own program of educational activities for alumni, faculty, and students of X University and to encourage alumni to maintain a close relationship with the university and to make contributions to it. M does not distribute any of its income directly to X for the latter's general purposes. M pays no part of its funds to, or for the benefit of, any organization other than X. Under these circumstances, M is considered as operated exclusively to perform the functions and carry out the purpose of X. Although it does not pay over any of its funds to X, it carries on a program which both supports and benefits X.

Example (2). N is a separately incorporated religious and educational organization described in section 501(c)(3). It was formed and is operated by Y Church to provide religious training for the members of the church. While it does not maintain a regular faculty, N conducts a Sunday school, weekly adult education lectures on religious subjects, and other similar activities for the benefit of the church members. All of its funds are disbursed in furtherance of such activities and no part of its funds is paid to, or for the benefit of, any organization other than Y Church. N is considered as operated exclusively to perform the educational functions of Y Church and to carry out its religious purposes by providing various forms of religious instruction.

Example (3). P is an organization described in section 501(c)(3). Its primary activity is providing financial assistance to S, a publicly supported organization which aids underdeveloped nations in Central America. P's articles of organization designate S as the principal recipient of P's assistance. However, P also makes a small annual general purpose grant to T, a private foundation engaged in work similar to that carried on by S. T performs a particular function that assists in the overall aid program carried on by S. Even though P is operating primarily for the benefit of S, a specified publicly supported organization, it is not considered as operated exclusively for the purposes set forth in section 509(a)(3)(A). The grant to T, a private foundation, prevents it from complying with the operational test under section 509(a)(3)(A).

Example (4). Assume the same facts as example (3), except that T is a section 501(c)(3) organization other than a private foundation and is operated in connection with S. Under these circumstances, P will be considered as operated exclusively to support S within the meaning of section 509(a)(3)(A).

Example (5). Assume the same facts as example (3) except that instead of the annual general purpose grant made to T, each grant made by P to T is specifically earmarked for the training of social workers and teachers, designated by name, from Central America. Under these circumstances, P's grants to T would be treated as grants to the individual social workers and teachers under section 4945(d)(3) and § 53.4945-4(a)(4), rather than as grants to T under section 4945(d)(4). These social workers and teachers are part of the charitable class benefitted by S. P would thus be considered as operating exclusively to support S within the meaning of section 509(a)(3)(A).

(f) Nature of relationship required between organizations. *(1) In general.* Section 509(a)(3)(B) describes the nature of the relationship required between a section 501(c)(3) organization and one or more publicly supported organizations in order for such section 501(c)(3) organization to qualify under the provisions of section 509(a)(3). To meet the requirements of section 509(a)(3), an organization must be operated, supervised, or controlled by or in connection with one or more publicly supported organizations. If an organization does not stand in one of such relationships (as provided in this paragraph) to one or more publicly supported organizations, it is not an organization described in section 509(a)(3).

(2) Types of relationships. Section 509(a)(3)(B) sets forth three different types of relationships, one of which must be met in order to meet the requirements of subparagraph (1) of this paragraph. Thus, a supporting organization may be:

(i) Operated, supervised, or controlled by,

(ii) Supervised or controlled in connection with, or

(iii) Operated in connection with, one or more publicly supported organizations.

(3) Requirements of relationships. Although more than one type of relationship may exist in any one case, any relationship described in section 509(a)(3)(B) must insure that:

(i) The supporting organization will be responsive to the needs of demands of one or more publicly supported organizations; and

(ii) The supporting organization will constitute an integral part of, or maintain a significant involvement in, the operations of one or more publicly supported organizations.

(4) General description of relationships. In the case of supporting organizations which are "operated, supervised, or controlled by" one or more publicly supported organizations, the distinguishing feature of this type of relationship is the presence of a substantial degree of direction by the publicly supported organizations over the conduct of the supporting organization, as described in paragraph (g) of this section. In the case of supporting organizations which are "supervised or controlled in connection with" one or more publicly supported organizations, the distinguishing feature is the presence of common supervision or control among the governing bodies of all organizations involved, such as the presence of common directors, as described in paragraph (h) of this sec-

tion. In the case of a supporting organization which is "operated in connection with" one or more publicly supported organizations, the distinguishing feature is that the supporting organization is responsive to, and significantly involved in the operations of, the publicly supported organization, as described in paragraph (i) of this section.

(g) Meaning of "operated, supervised, or controlled by". *(1)* (i) Each of the items "operated by," "supervised by," and "controlled by," as used in section 509(a)(3)(B), presupposes a substantial degree of direction over the policies, programs, and activities of a supporting organization by one or more publicly supported organizations. The relationship required under any one of these terms is comparable to that of a parent and subsidiary, where the subsidiary is under the direction of, and accountable or responsible to, the parent organization. This relationship is established by the fact that a majority of the officers, directors, or trustees of the supporting organization are appointed or elected by the governing body, members of the governing body, officers acting in their official capacity, or the membership of one or more publicly supported organizations.

(ii) A supporting organization may be "operated, supervised, or controlled by" one or more publicly supported organizations within the meaning of section 509(a)(3)(B) even though its governing body is not comprised of representatives of the specified publicly supported organizations for whose benefit it is operated within the meaning of section 509(a)(3)(A). A supporting organization may be "operated, supervised, or controlled by" one or more publicly supported organizations (within the meaning of section 509(a)(3)(B)) and be operated "for the benefit of" one or more different publicly supported organizations (within the meaning of section 509(a)(3)(A)) only if it can be demonstrated that the purposes of the former organizations are carried out by benefitting the latter organizations.

(2) The provisions of this paragraph may be illustrated by the following examples:

Example (1). X is a university press which is organized and operated as a nonstock educational corporation to perform the publishing and printing for M University, a publicly supported organization. Control of X is vested in a Board of Governors appointed by the Board of Trustees of M University upon the recommendation of the president of the university. X is considered to be operated, supervised, or controlled by M University within the meaning of section 509(a)(3)(B).

Example (2). Y Council was organized under the joint sponsorship of seven independent publicly supported organizations, each of which is dedicated to the advancement of knowledge in a particular field of social science. The sponsoring organizations organized Y Council as a means of pooling their ideas and resources for the attainment of common objectives, including the conducting of scholarly studies and formal discussions in various fields of social science. Under Y Council's by-laws, each of the seven sponsoring organizations elects three members to Y's board of trustees for 3-year terms. Y's board also includes the president of Y Council and eight other individuals elected at large by the board. Pursuant to policies established or approved by the board, Y Council engages in research, planning, and evaluation in the social sciences and sponsors or arranges conferences, seminars, and similar programs for scholars and social scientists. It carries out these activities through its own full-time professional staff, through a part-time committee of scholars, and through grant recipients. Under the above circumstances, Y Council is subject to a substantial degree of direction by the sponsoring publicly supported organizations. It is therefore considered to be operated, supervised, or controlled by such sponsoring organizations within the meaning of section 509(a)(3)(B).

Example (3). Z is a charitable trust created by A in 1972. It has three trustees, all of whom are appointed by M University, a publicly supported organization. The trust was organized and is operated to pay over all of its net income for medical research to N, O, and P, each of which is specified in the trust, is a hospital described in section 509(a)(1), and is located in the same city as M. Members of M's biology department are permitted to use the research facilities of N, O, and P. Under subparagraph (1)(ii) of this paragraph, Z is considered to be operated, supervised, or controlled by M within the meaning of section 509(a)(3)(B), even though it is operated for the benefit of N, O, and P within the meaning of section 509(a)(3)(A).

(h) Meaning of "supervised or controlled in connection with". *(1)* In order for a supporting organization to be "supervised or controlled in connection with" one or more publicly supported organizations, there must be common supervision or control by the persons supervising or controlling both the supporting organization and the publicly supported organizations to insure that the supporting organization will be responsive to the needs and requirements of the publicly supported organizations. Therefore, in order to meet such requirement, the control or management of the supporting organization must be vested in the same persons that control or manage the publicly supported organizations.

(2) A supporting organization will not be considered to be "supervised or controlled in connection with" one or more publicly supported organizations if such organization merely makes payments (mandatory or discretionary) to one or more named publicly supported organizations, even if the obligation to make payments to the named beneficiaries is enforceable under State law by such beneficiaries and the supporting organization's governing instrument contains provisions whose effect is described in section 508(e)(1)(A) and (B). Such arrangements do not provide a sufficient "connection" between the payor organization and the needs and requirements of the publicly supported organizations to constitute supervision or control in connection with such organizations.

(3) The provisions of this paragraph may be illustrated by the following examples;

Example (1). A, a philanthropist, founded X school for orphan boys (a publicly supported organization). At the same time A founded X school, he also established Y trust into which he transferred all of the operating assets of the school, together with a substantial endowment for it. Under the provisions of the trust instrument, the same persons who control and manage the school also control and manage the trust. The sole function of Y trust is to hold legal title to X school's operating and endowment assets, to invest the endowment assets and to apply the income from the endowment to the benefit of the school in accordance with direction from the school's governing body. Under these circumstances, Y trust is organized and operated "for the benefit of" X school and is "supervised or controlled in connection with" such organization within the meaning of section 509(a)(3). The fact that the same persons control both X and Y insures Y's responsiveness to X's needs.

Example (2). In 1972, B, a philanthropist, created P, a charitable trust for the benefit of Z, a symphony orchestra described in section 509(a)(2). B transferred 100 shares of common stock to P. Under the terms of the trust instrument, the trustees (none of whom is under the control of B) were required to pay over all of the income produced by the trust assets to Z. The governing instrument of P contains certain provisions whose effect is described in section 508(e)(1)(A) and (B). Under applicable State law, Z can enforce the provisions of the trust instrument and compel payment to Z in a court of equity. There is no relationship between the trustees of P and the governing body of Z. Under these circumstances P is not supervised or controlled in connection with a publicly supported organization. Because of the lack of any common supervision or control by the trustees of P and the governing body of Z, P is not supervised or controlled in connection with Z within the meaning of section 509(a)(3)(B).

Example (3). T is a charitable trust described in section 501(c)(3) and created under the will of D. Prior to his death, D was a leader and very active in C church, a publicly supported organization. D created T to perpetuate his interest in, and assistance to, C. The sole purpose of T was to provide financial support for C and its related institutions. All of the original named trustees of T are members of C, are leaders in C, and hold important offices in one or more of C's related institutions. Successor trustees of T are by the terms of the charitable trust instrument to be chosen by the remaining trustees and are also to be members of C. All of the original trustees have represented that any successor trustee will be a leader in C and will hold an important office in one or more of C's related institutions. By reason of the foregoing relationship T and its trustees are responsive to the needs and requirements of C and its related institutions. Under these circumstances, T trust is organized and operated "for the benefit of" C and is "supervised or controlled in connection with" C and its related institutions within the meaning of section 509(a)(3)(B).

(i) Meaning of "operated in connection with." *(1) General rule.* (i) Except as provided in subdivisions (ii) and (iii) of this subparagraph and subparagraph (4) of this paragraph, a supporting organization will be considered as being operated in connection with one or more publicly supported organizations only if it meets the "responsiveness test" which is defined in subparagraph (2) of this paragraph and the "integral part test" which is defined in subparagraph (3) of this paragraph.

(ii) In the case of an organization which was supporting or benefiting one or more publicly supported organizations before November 20, 1970, additional facts and circumstances, such as a historic and continuing relationship between organizations, may be taken into account, in addition to the factors described in subparagraph (2) of this paragraph, to establish compliance with the responsiveness test.

(iii) If—

(a) A supporting organization can establish that it has met the integral part test set forth in subparagraph (3)(iii) of this paragraph for any 5-year period,

(b) Such organization cannot meet the requirements of such test for its current taxable year solely because the amount received by one or more of the publicly supported beneficiary organizations from such supporting organization is no longer sufficient, with respect to such beneficiary organizations, to satisfy subparagraph (3)(iii) of this paragraph, and

(c) There has been a historic and continuing relationship of support between such organizations between the end of such 5-year period and the taxable year in question,

then such supporting organization will be considered as meeting the requirements of the integral part test in subparagraph (3)(iii) of this paragraph for such taxable year.

(2) Responsiveness test. (i) For purposes of this paragraph, a supporting organization will be considered to meet the "responsiveness test" if the organization is responsive to the needs or demands of the publicly supported organizations within the meaning of this subparagraph. In order to meet this test, either subdivision (ii) or subdivision (iii) of this subparagraph must be satisfied.

(ii) (a) One or more officers, directors, or trustees of the supporting organization are elected or appointed by the officers, directors, trustees, or membership of the publicly supported organizations;

(b) One or more members of the governing bodies of the publicly supported organizations are also officers, directors, or trustees of, or hold other important offices in, the supporting organization; or

(c) The officers, directors, or trustees of the supporting organization maintain a close continuous working relationship with the officers, directors, or trustees of the publicly supported organizations; and

(d) By reason of (a), (b), or (c) of this subdivision, the officers, directors or trustees of the publicly supported organizations have a significant voice in the investment policies of the supporting organization, the timing of grants, the manner of making them, and the selection of recipients by such supporting organization, and in otherwise directing the use of the income or assets of such supporting organization.

(iii) (a) The supporting organization is a charitable trust under State law;

(b) Each specified publicly supported organization is a named beneficiary under such charitable trust's governing instrument; and

(c) The beneficiary organization has the power to enforce the trust and compel an accounting under State law.

(3) Integral part test; general rule. (i) For purposes of this paragraph, a supporting organization will be considered to meet the "integral part test" if it maintains a significant involvement in the operations of one or more publicly supported organizations and such publicly supported organizations are in turn dependent upon the supporting organization for the type of support which it provides. In order to meet this test, either subdivision (ii) or subdivision (iii) of this subparagraph must be satisfied.

(ii) The activities engaged in for or on behalf of the publicly supported organizations are activities to perform the functions of, or to carry out the purposes of, such organizations, and, but for the involvement of the supporting organization, would normally be engaged in by the publicly supported organizations themselves.

(iii) (a) The supporting organization makes payments of substantially all of its income to or for the use of one or more publicly supported organizations, and the amount of support received by one or more of such publicly supported organizations is sufficient to insure the attentiveness of such organizations to the operations of the supporting organization. In addition, a substantial amount of the total support of the supporting organization must go to those publicly supported organizations which meet the attentiveness requirement of this subdivision with respect to such supporting organization. Except as provided in (b) of this subdivision, the amount of support received by a publicly supported organization must represent a sufficient part of the organization's total support so as to insure such attentiveness. In applying the preceding sentence, if such supporting organization makes payments to, or for the use of, a particular department or school of a university, hospital or church, the total support of the department or school shall be substituted for the total support of the beneficiary organization.

(b) Even where the amount of support received by a publicly supported beneficiary organization does not represent a sufficient part of the beneficiary organization's total support, the amount of support received from a supporting organization may be sufficient to meet the requirements of this subdivision if it can be demonstrated that in order to avoid the interruption of the carrying on of a particular function or activity, the beneficiary organization will be sufficiently attentive to the operations of the supporting organization. This may be the case where either the supporting organization or the beneficiary organization earmarks the support received from the supporting organization for a particular program or activity, even if such program or activity is not the beneficiary organization's primary program or activity so long as such program or activity is a substantial one.

(c) This subdivision may be illustrated by the following examples:

Example (1). X, an organization described in section 501(c)(3), pays over all of its annual net income to Y, a museum described in section 509(a)(2). X meets the responsiveness test described in subparagraph (2) of this paragraph. In recent years, Y has earmarked the income received from X to underwrite the cost of carrying on a chamber music series consisting of 12 performances a year which are performed for the general public free of charge at its premises. Because of the expense involved in carrying on these recitals, Y is dependent upon the income from X for their continuation. Under these circumstances, X will be treated as providing Y with a sufficient portion of Y's total support to assure Y's attentiveness to X's operations, even though the chamber music series is not the primary part of Y's activities.

Example (2). M, an organization described in section 501(c)(3), pays over all of its annual net income to the Law School of N University, a publicly supported organization. M meets the responsiveness test described in subparagraph (2) of this paragraph. M has earmarked the income paid over to N's Law School to endow a chair in its Department of International Law. Without M's continued support, N might not continue to maintain this chair. Under these circumstances, M will be treated as providing N with a sufficient portion of N's total support to assure N's attentiveness to M's operations.

(d) All pertinent factors, including the number of beneficiaries, the length and nature of the relationship between the beneficiary and supporting organization and the purpose to which the funds are put (as illustrated by subdivision (iii)(b) and (c) of this subparagraph), will be considered in determining whether the amount of support received by a publicly supported beneficiary organization is sufficient to insure the attentiveness of such organization to the operations of the supporting organization. Normally the attentiveness of a beneficiary organization is motivated by reason of the amounts received from the supporting organization. Thus, the more substantial the amount involved, in terms of a percentage of the publicly supported organization's total support the greater the likelihood that the required degree of attentiveness will be present. However, in determining whether the amount received from the supporting organization is sufficient to insure the attentiveness of the beneficiary organization to the operations of the supporting organization (including attentiveness to the nature and yield of such supporting organization's investments), evidence of actual attentiveness by the beneficiary organization is of almost equal importance. An example of acceptable evidence of actual attentiveness is the imposition of a requirement that the supporting organization furnish reports at least annually for taxable years beginning after December 31, 1971, to the beneficiary organization to assist such beneficiary organization in insuring that the supporting organization has invested its endowment in assets productive of a reasonable rate of return (taking appreciation into account) and has not engaged in any activity which would give rise to liability for a tax imposed under section 4941, 4943, 4944, or 4945 if such organization were a private foundation. The imposition of such requirement within 120 days after October 16, 1972, will be deemed to have retroactive effect to January 1, 1970, for purposes of determining whether a supporting organization has met the requirements of this subdivision for its first two taxable years beginning after December 31, 1969. The imposition of such requirement is, however, merely one of the factors in determining whether a supporting organization is complying with this subdivision and the absence of such requirement will not preclude an organization from classification as a supporting organization based on other factors.

(e) However, where none of the beneficiary organizations is dependent upon the supporting organization for a sufficient amount of the beneficiary organization's support within the meaning of this subdivision, the requirements of this subparagraph will not be satisfied, even though such beneficiary organizations have enforceable rights against such organization under State law.

(4) Integral part test; transitional rule. (i) A trust (whether or not exempt from taxation under section 501(a)) which on November 20, 1970, has met and continues to meet the requirements of subdivisions (ii) through (vi) of this subparagraph shall be treated as meeting the requirements of the integral part test (whether or not it meets the requirements of subparagraph (3)(ii) or (iii) of this paragraph) if for taxable years beginning after October 16, 1972, the trustee of such trust makes annual written reports to all of the beneficiary publicly supported organizations with respect to such trust setting forth a description of the assets of the trust, including a detailed list of the assets and the income produced by such assets. A trust organization which meets the requirements of this subparagraph may request a ruling that it is described in section 509(a)(3) in such manner as the Commissioner may prescribe.

(ii) All the unexpired interests in the trust are devoted to one or more purposes described in section 170(c)(1) or (2)(B) and a deduction was allowed with respect to such interests under section 170, 545(b)(2), 556(b)(2), 642(c), 2055, 2106(a)(2), 2522, or corresponding provisions of prior law (or would have been allowed such a deduction if the trust had not been created before 1913).

(iii) The trust was created prior to November 20, 1970, and did not receive any grant, contribution, bequest or other transfer on or after such date. For purpose of this subdivision, a split-interest trust described in section 4947(a)(2) which was created prior to November 20, 1970, which was irrevocable on such date, and which becomes a charitable trust described in section 4947(a)(1) after such date shall be treated as having been created prior to such date;

(iv) The trust is required by its governing instrument to distribute all of its net income currently to a designated publicly supported beneficiary organization. Where more than one publicly supported beneficiary organization is designated in the governing instrument of a trust, all of the net income must be distributable and must be distributed currently to each of such beneficiary organizations in fixed shares pursuant to such governing instrument. For purposes of this subdivision, the governing instrument of a charitable trust shall be treated as requiring distribution to a designated beneficiary organization where the trust instrument describes the charitable purpose of the trust so completely that such description can apply to only one existing beneficiary organization and is of sufficient particularity as to vest in such organization rights against the trust enforceable in a court possessing equitable powers;

(v) The trustee of the trust does not have discretion to vary either the beneficiaries or the amounts payable to the beneficiaries. For purposes of this subdivision, a trustee shall not be treated as having such discretion where the trustee has discretion to make payments of principal to the single section 509(a)(1) or (2) organization that is currently entitled to receive all of the trust's income or where the trust instrument provides that the trustee may cease making income payments to a particular charitable beneficiary in the event of certain specific occurrences, such as the loss of exemption under section 501(c)(3) or classification under section 509(a)(1) or (2) by the beneficiary or the failure of the beneficiary to carry out its charitable purpose properly;

(vi) None of the trustees would be disqualified persons within the meaning of section 4946(a) (other than foundation managers under 4946(a)(1)(B)) with respect to the trust if such trust were treated as a private foundation.

(5) Examples. The provisions of this paragraph may be illustrated by the following examples:

Example (1). N is a nonprofit publishing organization described in section 501(c)(3). It does all of the publishing and printing for the churches of a particular denomination (which are publicly supported organizations). Control of the organization is vested in a five-man Board of Directors, which includes one church official and four lay members of the congregations of that denomination. N does no other printing or publishing. It publishes all of the churches' religious as well as secular tracts and materials. Under these circumstances, N is considered as being "operated in connection with" a number of publicly supported organizations. Publishing religious literature is an integral part of the churches' activities; it is carried on by N on behalf of the churches, and there is sufficient direction of N's activities by the churches to insure responsiveness by N to their needs.

Example (2). O, an alumni association described in section 501(c)(3), was formed to promote a spirit of loyalty among graduates of Y University, a publicly supported organization, and to effect united action in promoting the general welfare of the university. A special committee of Y's governing board meets with O and makes recommendations as to the allocation of O's program of gifts and scholarships to the university and its students. O also provides certain functions which would otherwise be part of Y's functions, such as maintaining records of alumni. O publishes a bulletin to keep alumni aware of the activities of the university. Under these circumstances O is considered to be operated in connection with Y within the meaning of section 509(a)(3)(B).

Example (3). P is a trust created under the will of A for the purpose of furthering musician education. As a means of accomplishing its purposes P founded X, a school of music described in section 509(a)(1). The trust instrument is thereafter amended to name X specifically as the beneficiary of the trust. X can enforce its equitable rights as trust beneficiary under State law. Members of the governing body of X form a minority of the foundation managers of P. For many years the organizations have been operated in close association with each other. P provides the principal endowment fund for the operation of X. In addition, while the governing body of X concerns itself with artistic policies, the foundation managers of P handle the budgetary concerns of X. X's annual budget is prepared with the assistance of P's foundation managers and is approved by P. Under these circumstances, P is considered to be operated in connection with X within the meaning of section 509(a)(3)(B).

Example (4). Q is a charitable trust described in section 501(c)(3) and created under the will of C. Prior to his death, C built H Hospital and deeded it to I University for use as a training and clinical facility for I's medical school. Both H and I are publicly supported organizations. C created Q to perpetuate his interest in, and assistance to, H Hospital. The sole purpose of Q was to provide financial support for H, the beneficiary organization named in C's will. H can enforce its equitable rights as trust beneficiary under State law. After the death of C, Q continued to provide substantial support for H. It was primarily responsible for the erecting of a new hospital building, as well as the construction of other facilities for the hospital. In addition, each medical department of H indicates during the year what its greatest needs are. Once these requests are approved by the medical director of I University's Medical School, they are presented to Q, and subject to the amount of Q's income (all of which is applied to H), these requests are honored and the new equipment of [sic] facility is supplied through Q's funds. The governing body of Q and those of H and I are completely independent. However, based on the above facts, Q is responsive to the needs of H, Q maintains a substantial involvement in the conduct of H, and H is substantially dependent upon the receipt of support from Q. Accordingly, Q is operated in connection with one or more section 509(a)(1) organizations within the meaning of section 509(a)(3)(B).

Example (5). R is a charitable trust created under the will of B, who died in 1971. Its purpose is to hold assets as an endowment for S, a hospital, T, a university, and U, a national medical research organization (all being publicly supported organizations and specifically named in the trust instrument), and to distribute all of the income each year in equal shares among the three named beneficiaries. S, T, and U have certain enforceable rights against R under State law, including the right to compel an accounting. Except for making these annual payments, the trustees of R have no further contacts or relationships with S, T, or U. The payments by R to such organizations do not comprise a sufficient amount of support to meet the requirements of subparagraph (3) of this paragraph for any of these organizations. Although R meets the responsiveness test described in subparagraph (2) of this paragraph, it does not meet the integral part test described in subparagraph (3) of this paragraph. R is not, therefore, considered as operated in connection with one or more publicly supported organizations within the meaning of section 509(a)(3)(B). However, if B had died prior to November 20, 1970, R could, upon meeting all of the requirements of subparagraph (4) of this paragraph, be considered as operated in connection with one or more of publicly supported organizations within the meaning of section 509(a)(3)(B).

Example (6). S is a charitable trust described in section 501(c)(3). S was created under the will of C in 1910 for the purpose of providing aged and indigent women with care and shelter. Prior to his death in 1910, C helped to create T, a home for aged women, through a substantial inter vivos contribution. Although T is not specifically named in C's will, the trustees of S (who are completely independent of T) have paid over all of S's income to T in furtherance of the trust's purposes since the death of C. S establishes that between 1910 and 1955, the amount of support received by T from S was sufficient support to satisfy the provisions of § 1.509(a)-4(i)(3)(iii). In 1956, T merged with U, a home for aged and indigent men, and V, a nursing home. S continued to pay all its income to W, the organization resulting from the merger of T, U, and V. However, as a result of the merger and certain changes in the methods of financing the operations, the payments made by S after 1955 no longer was sufficient to satisfy the integral part test of § 1.509(a)-4(i)(3)(iii). W qualifies as an organization described in section 509(a)(2). For the taxable year 1971, S meets the responsiveness test under § 1.509(a)-4(i)(2)(ii). Although W is not a named beneficiary under S's governing instrument, pursuant to § 1.509(a)-4(i)(1)(ii) the historic and continuing relationship between the organizations will be taken into account to establish compliance with the responsiveness test. Furthermore, pursuant to § 1.509(a)-4(i)(1)(iii), under the facts set forth above, the integral part test under § 1.509(a)-4(i)(3)(iii) will be considered as being satisfied for the taxable year 1971. Thus S will be considered as "operated in connection with" W for the taxable year 1971.

(j) Control by disqualified persons. *(1) In general.* Under the provisions of section 509(a)(3)(C) a supporting organization may not be controlled directly or indirectly by one or more disqualified persons (as defined in section 4946) other than foundation managers and other than one or more publicly supported organizations. If a person who is a disqualified person with respect to a supporting organization, such as a substantial contributor to the supporting organization, is appointed or designated as a foundation manager of the supporting organization by a publicly supported beneficiary organization to serve as the representative of such publicly supported organization, then for purposes of this paragraph such person will be regarded as a disqualified person, rather than as a representative of the publicly supported organization. An organization will be considered "controlled," for purposes of section 509(a)(3)(C), if the disqualified persons, by aggregating their votes or positions or authority, may require such organization to perform any act which significantly affects its operations or may prevent such organization from performing such act. This includes, but is not limited to, the right of any substantial contributor or his spouse to designate annually the recipients, from among the publicly supported organizations of the income attributable to his contribution to the supporting organization. Except as provided in subparagraph (2) of this paragraph, a supporting organization will be considered to be controlled directly or indirectly by one or more disqualified persons if the voting power of such persons is 50 percent or more of the total voting power of the organization's governing body or if one or more of such persons have the right to exercise veto power over the actions of the organization. Thus, if the governing body of a foundation is composed of five trustees, none of whom has a veto power over the actions of the foundation, and no more than two trustees are at any time disqualified persons, such foundation will not be considered to be controlled directly or indirectly by one or more disqualified persons by reason of this fact alone. However, all pertinent facts and circumstances including the nature, diversity, and income yield of an organization's holdings, the length of time particular stocks, securities, or other assets are retained, and its manner of exercising its voting right with respect to stocks in which members of its governing body also have some interest, will be taken into consideration in determining whether a disqualified person does in fact indirectly control an organization.

(2) Proof of independent control. Notwithstanding subparagraph (1) of this paragraph, an organization shall be permitted to establish to the satisfaction of the Commissioner that disqualified persons do not directly or indirectly control it. For example, in the case of a religious organization operated in connection with a church, the fact that the majority of the organization's governing body is composed of lay persons who are substantial contributors to the organization will not disqualify the organization under section 509(a)(3)(C) if a representative of the church, such as a bishop or other official, has control over the policies and decisions of the organization.

(k) Organizations operated in conjunction with certain section 501(c)(4), (5), or (6) organizations. *(1)* For purposes of section 509(a)(3), an organization which is operated in conjunction with an organization described in section 501(c)(4), (5), or (6) (such as a social welfare organization, labor or agricultural organization, business league, or real estate board) shall, if it otherwise meets the requirements of section 509(a)(3), be considered an organization described in section 509(a)(3) if such section 501(c)(4), (5), or (6) organization would be described in section 509(a)(2) if it were an organization described in section 501(c)(3). The section 501(c)(4), (5), or (6) organization which the supporting organization is operating in conjunction with, must therefore meet the one-third tests of a publicly supported organization set forth in section 509(a)(2).

(2) This paragraph may be illustrated by the following example:

Example. X medical association, described in section 501(c)(6) is supported by membership dues and funds resulting from the performance of its exempt activities. This support, which is entirely from permitted sources, constitutes more than one-third of X's support. X does not normally receive more than one-third of its support from items described in section 509(a)(2)(B). X organized and operated an endowment fund for the sole purpose of furthering medical education. The fund is an organization described in section 501(c)(3). Since more than one-third of X's support is derived from membership dues and from funds resulting from the performance of exempt purposes (all of which are from permitted sources) and not more than one-third of its support is from items described in section 509(a)(2)(B), it would be a publicly supported organization described in section 509(a)(2) if it were described in section 501(c)(3) rather than section 501(c)(6). Accordingly, if the fund otherwise meets the requirements of section 509(a)(3) with respect to X, it will be considered an organization described in section 509(a)(3).

T.D. 7212, 10/16/72, amend T.D. 7784, 7/22/81.

§ 1.509(a)-5 Special rules of attribution.

Caution: The Treasury has not yet amended Reg § 1.509(a)-5 to reflect changes made by P.L. 109-280.

(a) Retained character of gross investment income. *(1)* For purposes of determining whether an organization meets the not-more-than-one-third support test set forth in section 509(a)(2)(B), amounts received by such organization from:

(i) An organization which seeks to be described in section 509(a)(3) by reason of its support of such organization; or

(ii) A charitable trust, corporation, fund, or association described in section 501(c)(3) (including a charitable trust described in section 4947(a)(1)) or a split interest trust described in section 4947(a)(2), which is required by its governing instrument or otherwise to distribute, or which normally does distribute, at least 25 percent of its adjusted net income (within the meaning of section 4942(f)) to such organization, and such distribution normally comprises at least 5 percent of such distributee organization's adjusted net income,

will retain their character as gross investment income (rather than gifts or contributions) to the extent that such amounts are characterized as gross investment income in the possession of the distributing organization described in subdivision (i) or (ii) of this subparagraph or, if the distributing organization is a split interest trust described in section 4947(a)(2), to the extent that such amounts would be characterized as gross investment income attributable to transfers in trust after May 26, 1969, if such trust were a private foundation. For purposes of this section, all income which is characterized as gross investment income in the possession of the distributing organization shall be deemed to be distributed first by such organization and shall retain its character as such in the possession of the recipient of amounts described in this paragraph. If an organization described in subdivision (i) or (ii) of this subparagraph makes distributions to more than one organization, the amount of gross investment income deemed distributed shall be prorated among the distributees.

(2) For purposes of subparagraph (1) of this paragraph, amounts paid by an organization to provide goods, services, or facilities for the direct benefit of an organization seeking section 509(a)(2) status (rather than for the direct benefit of the general public) shall be treated in the same manner as amounts received by the latter organization. Such amounts will be treated as gross investment income to the extent that such amounts are characterized as gross investment income in the possession of the organization spending such amounts. For example, X is an organization described in subparagraph (1)(i) of this paragraph. It uses part of its funds to provide Y, an organization seeking section 509(a)(2) status, with certain services which Y would otherwise be required to purchase on its own. To the extent that the funds used by X to provide such services for Y are characterized as gross investment income in the possession of X, such funds will be treated as gross investment income received by Y.

(3) An organization seeking section 509(a)(2) status shall file a separate statement with its return required by section 6033, setting forth all amounts received from organizations described in paragraph (a)(1)(i) or (ii) of this section.

(b) Relationships created for avoidance purposes. *(1)* If a relationship between an organization seeking section 509(a)(3) status and an organization seeking section 509(a)(2) status:

(i) Is established or availed of after October 9, 1969, and

(ii) One of the purposes of establishing or utilizing such relationship is to avoid classification as a private foundation with respect to either organization, the character and amount of support received by the section 509(a)(3) organization will be attributed to the section 509(a)(2) organization for purposes of determining whether the latter meets the one-third support test and the not-more-than-one-third support test under section 509(a)(2). If a relationship described in this subparagraph is established or utilized by an organization seeking section 509(a)(3) status and two or more organizations seeking section 509(a)(2) status, the amount of support received by the former organization will be prorated among the latter organizations and the character of each class of support (as defined in section 509(d)) will be attributed pro rata to each such organization. The provisions of this paragraph and of paragraph (a) of this section are not mutually exclusive.

(2) In determining whether a relationship between one or more organizations seeking section 509(a)(2) status (hereinafter referred to as "beneficiary organizations") and an organization seeking section 509(a)(3) status (hereinafter referred to as the "supporting organization") has been established or availed of to avoid classification as a private foundation (within the meaning of subparagraph (1) of this paragraph), all pertinent facts and circumstances, including the following, shall be taken into account as evidence that a relationship was not established or availed of to avoid classification as a private foundation:

(i) The supporting organization is operated to support or benefit several specified beneficiary organizations.

(ii) The beneficiary organization has a substantial number of dues-paying members (in relation to the public it serves and the nature of its activities) and such members have an effective voice in the management of both the supporting and beneficiary organizations.

(iii) The beneficiary organization is composed of several membership organizations, each of which has a substantial number of members (in relation to the public it serves and the nature of its activities), and such membership organizations have an effective voice in the management of the supporting and beneficiary organizations.

(iv) The beneficiary organization receives a substantial amount of support from the general public, public charities, or governmental grants.

(v) The supporting organization uses its funds to carry on a meaningful program of activities to support or benefit the beneficiary organization and such use would, if such supporting organization were a private foundation, be sufficient to avoid the imposition of any tax upon such organization under section 4942.

(vi) The supporting organization is not able to exercise substantial control or influence over the beneficiary organization by reason of the former's receiving support or holding assets which are disproportionately large in comparison with the support received or the assets held by the latter.

(vii) Different persons manage the operations of the beneficiary and supporting organizations and each organization performs a different function.

(3) The provisions of this paragraph may be illustrated by the following examples:

Example (1). M, an organization described in section 509(a)(2), is a council composed of 10 learned societies. Each member society has a large membership of scholars interested in a particular academic area. In 1970 M established N, an organization seeking section 509(a)(3) status, for the purpose of carrying on research and study projects of interest to the member societies. The principal source of funds for N's activities is from foundation and government grants and contracts. The principal source of funds for M's activities after the creation of N is membership dues. M continued to maintain a wide variety of activities for its members, such as publishing periodicals and carrying on seminars and conferences. N is subject to complete control by the governing body of M. Under these circumstances, the relationship between these organizations is not one which is described in subparagraph (1) of this paragraph.

Example (2). Q is a local medical research organization described in section 509(a)(2). Its fixed assets are negligible and it carries on research activities on a limited scale. It also makes a limited number of grants to scientists and doctors who are engaged in medical research of interest to Q. It receives support through small government grants and a few research contracts from private foundations. R is an organization described in section 501(c)(3). As of January 1, 1970, R was classified a private foundation under section 509. It has a substantial endowment which it uses to make grants to various charitable and scientific organizations described in section 501(c)(3). During 1970, R agrees to subsidize the research activities of Q. R amends its governing instrument to provide specifically that all of R's support will be used for research activities which are approved and supervised by Q. R also amends its bylaws to permit a minority of Q's board of directors to be members of R's governing body. R then gives timely notification under section 507(b)(1)(B)(ii) that R is terminating its private foundation status by meeting the requirements of section 509(a)(3) by the end of the 12-month period described in section 507(b)(1)(B)(i). For purposes of determining whether R has met the requirements of section 509(a)(3) by the end of the 12-month period, as well as determining Q's status under section 509(a)(2), the character and amount of support received by R will be attributed to Q.

(c) Effect on organizations claiming section 509(a)(3) status. If an organization claiming section 509(a)(2) status fails to meet either the one-third support test or the not-more-than-one-third support test under section 509(a)(2) by reason of the application of the provisions of paragraph (a) or (b) of this section, and such organization is one of the specified organizations (within the meaning of section 509(a)(3)(A)) for whose support or benefit an organization claiming section 509(a)(3) status is operated, the organization claiming section 509(a)(3) status will not be considered to be operated exclusively to support or benefit one or more section 509(a)(1) or (2) organizations.

T.D. 7212, 10/16/72, amend T.D. 7290, 11/16/73, T.D. 7784, 7/22/81.

§ 1.509(a)-6 Classification under section 509(a).

If an organization is described in section 509(a)(1) and also in another paragraph of section 509(a), it will be treated as described in section 509(a)(1). For purposes of this section, the parenthetical language "other than in clauses (vii) and (viii)" used in section 509(a)(1) shall be construed to mean "other than an organization which is described only in clause (vii) or (viii)". For example, X is an organization which is described in section 170(b)(1)(A)(vi), but could also meet the description of section 170(b)(1)(A)(viii) as an organization described in section 509(a)(2). For purposes of the one-third support test in section 509(a)(2)(A), contributions from X to other organizations will be treated as support from an organization described in section 170(b)(1)(A)(vi) rather than from an organization described in section 170(b)(1)(A)(viii).

T.D. 7212, 10/16/72.

§ 1.509(a)-7 Reliance by grantors and contributors to section 509(a)(1), (2), and (3) organizations.

(a) General rule. Once an organization has received a final ruling or determination letter classifying it as an organization described in section 509(a)(1), (2), or (3), the treatment of grants and contributions and the status of grantors and contributors to such organization under sections 170, 507, 545(b)(2), 556(b)(2), 642(c), 4942, 4945, 2055, 2106(a)(2), and 2522 will not be affected by reason of a subsequent revocation by the service of the organization's classification as described in section 509(a)(1), (2), or (3) until the date on which notice of change of status is made to the public (such as by publication in the Internal Revenue Bulletin) or another applicable date, if any, specified in such public notice. In appropriate cases, however, the treatment of grants and contributions and the status of grantors and contributors to an organization described in section 509(a)(1), (2), or (3) may be affected pending verification of the continued classification of such organization under section 509(a)(1), (2), or (3). Notice to this affect will be made in a public announcement by the service. In such cases the effect of grants and contributions made after the date of the announcement will depend upon the statutory qualification of the organization as an organization described in section 509(a)(1), (2), or (3),

(b) Exceptions. *(1)* Paragraph (a) of this section shall not apply if the grantor or contributor:

(i) Had knowledge of the revocation of the ruling or determination letter classifying the organization as an organization described in section 509(a)(1), (2), or (3), or

(ii) Was in part responsible for, or was aware of, the act, the failure to act, or the substantial and material change on the part of the organization which gave rise to the revocation of the ruling or determination letter classifying the organization as an organization described in section 509(a)(1), (2), or (3).

(2) Paragraph (a) of this section shall not apply where a different rule is otherwise expressly provided in the regulations under sections 170(b)(1)(A), 507(b)(1)(B), or 509.

T.D. 7212, 10/16/72.

§ 1.509(b)-1 Continuation of private foundation status.

(a) In general. If an organization is a private foundation (within the meaning of section 509(a)) on October 9, 1969, or becomes a private foundation on any subsequent date, such organization shall be treated as a private foundation for all periods after October 9, 1969, or after such subsequent date, unless its status as such is terminated under section 507. Therefore, if an organization was described in section 501(c)(3) and was a private foundation within the meaning of section 509(a) on October 9, 1969, it shall be treated as a private foundation for all periods thereafter, even though it may also satisfy the requirements of an organization described in some other paragraph of section 501(c). For example, if on October 9, 1969, an organization was described in section 501(c)(3), but because of its activities, it could also have qualified as an organization described in section 501(c)(4), such organization will continue to be treated as a private foundation, if it was a private foundation within the meaning of section 509(a) on October 9, 1969.

(b) Taxable private foundations. If an organization is a private foundation on October 9, 1969, and it is determined that it is not exempt under section 501(a) as an organization described in section 501(c)(3) as of any date after October 9, 1969, such organization, even though it may operate thereafter as a taxable entity, will continue to be treated as a private foundation unless its status as such is terminated under section 507. For example, X organization is a private foundation on October 9, 1969. It is subsequently determined that, as of July 1, 1972, X is no longer exempt under section 501(a) as an organization described in section 501(c)(3) because, for example, it has not conformed its governing instrument pursuant to section 508(e). X will continue to be treated as a private foundation after July 1, 1972, unless its status as such is terminated under section 507. However, if an organization is not exempt under section 501(a) as an organization described in section 501(c)(3) on October 9, 1969, then it will not be treated as a private foundation within the meaning of section 509(a) by reason of section 509(b), unless it becomes a private foundation on a subsequent date.

T.D. 7212, 10/16/72.

§ 1.509(c)-1 Status of organization after termination of private foundation status.

(a) In general. For purposes of Part II of Subchapter F of this chapter, an organization whose status as a private foundation is terminated under section 507 shall be treated as an organization created on the day after the date of such termination. An organization whose private foundation status has been terminated under the provisions of section 507(a) will, if it continues to operate, be treated as a new organization and must if it desires to be classified under section 501(c)(3), give notification that it is applying for recognition of section 501(c)(3) status pursuant to the provisions of section 508(a).

(b) Effect upon section 507(d)(1). If the private foundation status of an organization has been terminated under section 507(b)(1)(B) and the regulations thereunder, and:

(1) Such organization does not continue at all times thereafter to meet the requirements of section 509(a)(1), (2), or (3) (and is therefore no longer excluded from the definition of a private foundation); and

(2) The status of such organization as a private foundation is thereafter terminated under section 507(a),

then the tax imposed under section 507(c)(1) upon the aggregate tax benefit (described in section 507(d)(1)) resulting from section 501(c)(3) status shall be computed only upon the aggregate tax benefit resulting after the date on which the organization again becomes a private foundation under subparagraph (1) of this paragraph.

T.D. 7212, 10/16/72.

§ 1.509(d)-1 Definition of support.

For purposes of section 509(a)(2), the term "support" does not include amounts received in repayment of the principal of a loan or other indebtedness. See, however, section 509(e) as to amounts received as interest on a loan or other indebtedness.

T.D. 7212, 10/16/72.

§ 1.509(e)-1 Definition of gross investment income.

For the distinction between gross receipts and gross investment income, see § 1.509(a)-3(m).

T.D. 7212, 10/16/72.

§ 1.511-1 Imposition and rates of tax.

Caution: The Treasury has not yet amended Reg § 1.511-1 to reflect changes made by P.L. 100-647, P.L. 95-600, P.L. 95-30.

Section 511(a) imposes a tax upon the unrelated business taxable income of certain organizations otherwise exempt from Federal income tax. Under section 511(a)(1), organizations described in section 511(a)(2)(A) and in paragraph (a) of § 1.511-2 and organizations described in section 511(a)(2)(B) are subject to normal tax and surtax at the corporate rates provided by section 11. Under section 511(b)(1), trusts described in section 511(b)(2) are subject to tax at the individual rates prescribed in section 1(d) of the Code as amended by the Tax Reform Act of 1969 (section 1 for taxable years ending before Jan. 1, 1971). The deduction for personal exemption provided in section 642(b) in the case of a trust taxable under subchapter J, chapter 1 of the Code, is not allowed in computing unrelated business taxable income.

T.D. 6301, 7/8/58, amend T.D. 7117, 5/24/71.

§ 1.511-2 Organizations subject to tax.

(a) Organizations other than trusts and title holding companies. *(1)* (i) The taxes imposed by section 511(a)(1) apply in the case of any organization (other than a trust described in section 511(b)(2) or an organization described in section 501(c)(1)) which is exempt from taxation under section 501(a) (except as provided in sections 507 through 515). For special rules concerning corporations described in section 501(c)(2), see paragraph (c) of this section.

(ii) In the case of an organization described in section 501(c)(4), (7), (8), (9), (10), (11), (12), (13), (14)(A), (15), (16), or (18), the taxes imposed by section 511(a)(1) apply only for taxable years beginning after December 31, 1969. In the case of an organization described in section 501(c)(14)(B) or (C), the taxes imposed by section 511(a)(1) apply only for taxable years beginning after February 2, 1966.

(2) The taxes imposed by section 511(a) apply in the case of any college or university which is an agency or instrumentality of any government or any political subdivision thereof, or which is owned or operated by a government or any political subdivision thereof or by any agency or instrumentality of any one or more governments or political subdivisions. Such taxes also apply in the case of any corporation wholly owned by one or more such colleges or universities. As here used, the word "government" includes any foreign government (to the extent not contrary to any treaty obligation of the United States) and all domestic governments (the United States and any of its Territories or possessions, any State, and the District of Columbia). Elementary and secondary schools operated by such governments are not subject to the tax on unrelated business income.

(3) (i) For taxable years beginning before January 1, 1970, churches and associations or conventions of churches are exempt from the taxes imposed by section 511. The exemption is applicable only to an organization which itself is a church or an association or convention of churches. Subject to the provisions of subdivision (ii) of this subparagraph, religious organizations, including religious orders, if not themselves churches or associations or conventions of churches, and all other organizations which are organized or operated under church auspices, are subject to the tax imposed by section 511, whether or not they engage in religious, educational, or charitable activities approved by a church.

(ii) The term "church" includes a religious order or a religious organization if such order or organization (a) is an integral part of a church, and (b) is engaged in carrying out the functions of a church, whether as a civil law corporation or otherwise. In determining whether a religious order or organization is an integral part of a church, consideration will be given to the degree to which it is connected with, and controlled by, such church. A religious order or organization shall be considered to be engaged in carrying out the functions of a church if its duties include the ministration of sacerdotal functions and the conduct of religious worship. If a religious order or organization is not an integral part of a church, or if such an order or organization is not authorized to carry out the functions of a church (ministration of sacerdotal functions and conduct of religious worship) then it is subject to the tax imposed by section 511 whether or not it engages in religious, educational, or charitable activities approved by a church. What constitutes the conduct of religious worship or the ministration of sacerdotal functions depends on the tenets and practices of a particular religious body constituting a church. If a religious order or organization can fully meet the requirements stated in this subdivision, exemption from the tax imposed by section 511 will apply to all its activities, including those which it conducts through a separate corporation (other than a corporation described in section 501(c)(2)) or other separate entity which it wholly owns and which is not operated for the primary purpose of carrying on a trade or business for profit. Such exemption from tax will also apply to activities conducted through a separate corporation (other than a corporation described in section 501(c)(2)) or other separate entity which is wholly owned by more than one religious order or organization, if all such orders or organizations fully meet the requirements stated in this subdivision and if such corporation or other entity is not operated for the primary purpose or carrying on a trade or business for profit.

(iii) For taxable years beginning after December 31, 1969, churches and conventions or associations of churches are subject to the taxes imposed by section 511, unless otherwise entitled to the benefit of the transitional rules of section 512(b)(14) and § 1.512(b)-1(i).

(b) Trusts. *(1) In general.* The taxes imposed by section 511(b) apply in the case of any trust which is exempt from taxation under section 501(a) (except as provided in sections 507 through 515), and which, if it were not for such exemption, would be subject to the provisions of subchapter J, Chapter 1, of the Code. An organization which is considered as "trustee" of a stock bonus, pension, or profit-sharing plan described in section 401(a), a supplemental unemployment benefit trust described in section 501(c)(17) or a pension plan described in section 501(c)(18) (regardless of the form of such organization) is subject to the taxes imposed by section 511(b)(1) on its unrelated business income. However, if such an organization conducts a business which is a separate taxable entity on the basis of all the facts and circumstances, for example, an association taxable as a corporation, the business will be taxable as a feeder organization described in section 502.

(2) Effective dates. In the case of a trust described in section 501(c)(3), the taxes imposed by section 511(b) apply for taxable years beginning after December 31, 1953. In the case of a trust described in section 401(a), the taxes imposed by section 511 (b) apply for taxable years beginning after June 30, 1954. In the case of a trust described in section 501(c)(17), the taxes imposed by section 511(b) apply for taxable years beginning after December 31, 1959. In the case of any other trust described in subparagraph (1) of this paragraph, the taxes imposed by section 511(b) apply for taxable years beginning after December 31, 1959.

(c) Title holding companies. *(1) In general.* If a corporation described in section 501(c)(2) pays any amount of its net income for a taxable year to an organization exempt from taxation under section 501(a) (or would pay such an amount but for the fact that the expenses of collecting its income exceed its income), and if such corporation and such organization file a consolidated income tax return for such taxable year, then such corporation shall be treated, for purposes of the tax imposed by section 511(a), as being organized and operated for the same purposes as such organization, as well as for its title-holding purpose. Therefore, if an item of income of the section 501(c)(2) corporation is derived from a source which is related to the exempt function of the exempt organization to which such income is payable and with which such corporation files a consolidated return, such item is, together with all deductions directly connected therewith, excluded from the determination of unrelated business taxable income under section 512 and shall not be subject to the tax imposed by section 511(a). If, however, such item of income is derived from a source which is not so related, then such item, less all deductions directly connected therewith, is, subject to the modifications provided in section 512(b), unrelated business taxable income subject to the tax imposed by section 511(a).

(2) The provisions of subparagraph (1) of this paragraph may be illustrated by the following example:

Example. The income of X, a section 501(c)(2) corporation, is required to be distributed to exempt organization A. During the taxable year X realizes net income of $900,000 from source M and $100,000 from source N. Source M is related to A's exempt function, while source N is not so related. X and A file a consolidated return for such taxable year. X has net unrelated business income of $100,000, subject to the modifications in section 512(b).

(3) Cross reference. For rules relating generally to the filing of consolidated returns by certain organizations exempt from taxation under section 501(a), see section 1504(e) of the Code and § 1.1502-100.

(4) Effective dates. Subparagraphs (1) through (3) of this paragraph apply with respect to taxable years beginning after December 31, 1969. For taxable years beginning before January 1, 1970, a corporation described in section 501(c)(2) and otherwise exempt from taxation under section 501(a) is taxable upon its unrelated business taxable income only if such income is payable either—

(i) To a church or convention or association of churches, or

(ii) To any organization subject, for taxable years beginning before January 1, 1970, to the tax imposed by section 511(a)(1).

(d) The fact that any class of organizations exempt from taxation under section 501(a) is subject to the unrelated business income tax under section 511 and this section does not in any way enlarge the permissible scope of business activities of such class for purposes of the continued qualification of such class under section 501(a).

T.D. 6301, 7/8/58, amend T.D. 6972, 9/11/68, T.D. 7183, 4/20/72, T.D. 7632, 7/19/79.

---

§ 1.511-3 Provisions generally applicable to the tax on unrelated business income.

(a) Assessment and collections. Since the taxes imposed by section 511 are taxes imposed by subtitle A of the Code, all provisions of law and of the regulations applicable to the taxes imposed by subtitle A are applicable to the assessment and collection of the taxes imposed by section 511. Organizations subject to the tax imposed by section 511(a)(1) are subject to the same provisions, including penalties, as are provided in the case of the income tax of other corporations.

In the case of a trust subject to the tax imposed by section 511(b)(1), the fiduciaries for such trust are subject to the same provisions, including penalties, as are applicable to fiduciaries in the case of the income tax of other trusts. See section 6151, *et seq.*, and the regulations prescribed thereunder, for provisions relating to payment of tax.

(b) Returns. For requirements of filing annual returns with respect to unrelated business taxable income by organizations subject to the tax on such income, see section 6012, paragraph (e) of § 1.6012-2, and paragraph (a)(5) of § 1.6012-3.

(c) Taxable years, method of accounting, etc. The taxable year (fiscal year or calendar year, as the case may be) of an organization shall be determined without regard to the fact that such organization may have been exempt from tax during any prior period. See sections 441 and 446, and the regulations thereunder in this part, and section 7701 and the regulations in Part 301 of this chapter (Regulations on Procedure and Administration). Similarly, in computing unrelated business taxable income, the determination of the taxable year for which an item of income or expense is taken into account shall be made under the provisions of sections 441, 446, 451, and 461, and the regulations thereunder, whether or not the item arose during a taxable year beginning before, on, or after the effective date of the provisions imposing a tax upon unrelated business taxable income. If a method for treating bad debts was selected in a return of income (other than an information return) for a previous taxable year, the taxpayer must follow such method in its returns under section 511, unless such method is changed in accordance with the provisions of § 1.166-1. A taxpayer which has not previously selected a method for treating bad debts may, in its first return under section 511, exercise the option granted in § 1.166-1.

(d) Foreign tax credit. See section 515 for provisions applicable to the credit for foreign taxes provided in section 901.

T.D. 6301, 7/8/58.

---

§ 1.511-4 Minimum tax for tax preferences.

The tax imposed by section 56 applies to an organization subject to tax under section 511 with respect to items of tax preference which enter into the computation of unrelated business taxable income. For this purpose, only those items of income and those deductions entering into the determination of the tax imposed by this section are considered in the determination of the items of tax preference under section 57. For rules relating to the minimum tax for tax preferences, see sections 56 through 58 and the regulations thereunder.

T.D. 7564, 9/11/78.

---

§ 1.512(a)-1 Definition.

Caution: The Treasury has not yet amended Reg § 1.512(a)-1 to reflect changes made by P.L. 104-188.

(a) In general. Except as otherwise provided in § 1.512(a)-3, § 1.512(a)-4, or paragraph (f) of this section, section 512(a)(1) defines "unrelated business taxable income" as the gross income derived from any unrelated trade or business regularly carried on, less those deductions allowed by chapter 1 of the Code which are directly connected with the carrying on of such trade or business subject to certain modifications referred to in § 1.512(b)-1. To be deductible in computing unrelated business taxable income, therefore, expenses, depreciation, and similar items not only must qualify as deductions allowed by chapter 1 of the Code, but also must be directly connected with the carrying on of unrelated trade or business. Except as provided in paragraph (d)(2) of this section, to be "directly connected with" the conduct of unrelated business for purposes of section 512, an item of deduction must have proximate and primary relationship to the carrying on of that business. In the case of an organization which derives gross income from the regular conduct of two or more unrelated business activities, unrelated business taxable income is the aggregate of gross income from all such unrelated business activities less the aggregate of the deductions allowed with respect to all such unrelated business activities. For the treatment of amounts of income or loss of common trust funds, see § 1.584-2(c)(3).

(b) Expenses attributable solely to unrelated business activities. Expenses, depreciation, and similar items attributable solely to the conduct of unrelated business activities are proximately and primarily related to that business activity, and therefore qualify for deduction to the extent that they meet the requirements of section 162, section 167, or other relevant provisions of the Code, connected with the conduct of that activity and are deductible in computing unrelated business activities are directly connected with the conduct of that activity and are deductible in computing unrelated business taxable income if they otherwise qualify for deduction under the requirements of section 162. Similarly, depreciation of a building used entirely in the conduct of unrelated business activities would be an allowable deduction to the extent otherwise permitted by section 167.

(c) Dual use of facilities or personnel. Where facilities are used both to carry on exempt activities and to conduct unrelated trade or business activities, expenses, depreciation and similar items attributable to such facilities (as, for example, items of overhead), shall be allocated between the two uses on a reasonable basis. Similarly, where personnel are used both to carry on exempt activities and to conduct unrelated trade or business activities, expenses and similar items attributable to such personnel (as, for example, items of salary) shall be allocated between the two uses on a reasonable basis. The portion of any such item so allocated to the unrelated trade or business activity is proximately and primarily related to that business activity, and shall be allowable as a deduction in computing unrelated business taxable income in the manner and to the extent permitted by section 162, section 167, or other relevant provisions of the Code. Thus, for example, assume that X, an exempt organization subject to the provisions of section 511, pays its president a salary of $20,000 a year. X derives gross income from the conduct of unrelated trade or business activities. The president devotes approximately 10 percent of his time during the year to the unrelated business activity. For purposes of computing X's unrelated business taxable income, a deduction of $2,000 (10 percent of $20,000), would be allowable for the salary paid to its president.

(d) Exploitation of exempt activities. *(1) In general.* In certain cases, gross income is derived from an unrelated trade or business activity which exploits an exempt activity. One example of such exploitation is the sale of advertising in a periodical of an exempt organization which contains editorial material related to the accomplishment of the organization's exempt purpose. Except as specified in subparagraph (2) of this paragraph and paragraph (f) of this section, in such cases, expenses, depreciation and similar items attributable to the conduct of the exempt activities are not deductible in computing unrelated business taxable income. Since such items are incident to an activity which is carried on in furtherance of the exempt purpose of the organization, they do not possess the necessary proximate and primary relationship to the unrelated trade or business activity and are therefore not directly connected with that business activity.

(2) Allowable deductions. Where an unrelated trade or business activity is of a kind carried on for profit by taxable organizations and where the exempt activity exploited by the business is a type of activity normally conducted by taxable organizations in pursuance of such business, expenses, depreciation, and similar items which are attributable to the exempt activity qualify as directly connected with the carrying on of the unrelated trade or business activity to the extent that:

(i) The aggregate of such items exceeds the income (if any) derived from or attributable to the exempt activity; and

(ii) The allocation of such excess to the unrelated trade or business activity does not result in a loss from such unrelated trade or business activity.

Under the rule of the preceding sentence, expenses, depreciation and similar items paid or incurred in the performance of an exempt activity must be allocated first to the exempt activity to the extent of the income derived from or attributable to the performance of that activity. Furthermore, such items are in no event allocable to the unrelated trade or business activity exploiting such exempt activity to the extent that their deduction would result in a loss carryover or carryback with respect to that trade or business activity. Similarly, they may not be taken into account in computing unrelated business taxable income attributable to any unrelated trade or business activity not exploiting the same exempt activity. See paragraph (f) of this section for the application of these rules to periodicals published by exempt organizations.

(e) Examples. This section is illustrated by the following examples:

Example (1). W is an exempt business league with a large membership. Under an arrangement with an advertising agency W regularly mails brochures, pamphlets and other advertising materials to its members, charging the agency an agreed amount per enclosure. The distribution of the advertising materials does not contribute importantly to the accomplishment of the purpose for which W is granted exemption. Accordingly, the payments made to W by the advertising agency constitute gross income from an unrelated trade or business activity. In computing W's unrelated business taxable income, the expenses attributable solely to the conduct of the business, or allocable to such business under the rule of paragraph (c) of this section, are allowable as deductions in accordance with the provisions of section 162. Such deductions include the costs of handling and mailing, the salaries of personnel used full-time in the unrelated business activity and an allocable portion of the salaries of personnel used both to carry on exempt activities, and to conduct the unrelated business activity. However, costs of developing W's membership and carrying on its exempt activities are not deductible. Those costs are necessary to the maintenance of the intangible asset exploited in the unrelated business activity—W's membership—but are incurred primarily in connection with W's fundamental purpose as an exempt organization. As a consequence, they do not have proximate and primary relationship to the conduct of the unrelated business activity and do not qualify as directly connected with it.

Example (2). (i) P, a manufacturer of photographic equipment, underwrites a photography exhibition organized by M, an art museum described in section 501(c)(3). In return for a payment of $100,000, M agrees that the exhibition catalog sold by M in connection with the exhibit will advertise P's product. The exhibition catalog will also include educational material, such as copies of photographs included in the exhibition, interviews with photographers, and an essay by the curator of M's department of photography. For purposes of this example, assume that none of the $100,000 is a qualified sponsorship payment within the meaning of section 513(i) and § 1.513-4, that M's advertising activity is regularly carried on, and that the entire amount of the payment is unrelated business taxable income to M. Expenses directly connected with generating the unrelated business taxable income (i.e., direct advertising costs) total $25,000. Expenses directly connected with the preparation and publication of the exhibition catalog (other than direct advertising costs) total $110,000. M receives $60,000 of gross revenue from sales of the exhibition catalog. Expenses directly connected with the conduct of the exhibition total $500,000.

(ii) The computation of unrelated business taxable income is as follows:

(A) Unrelated trade or business (sale of advertising):

Income	$100,000	
Directly-connected expenses	(25,000)	
Subtotal	75,000	$75,000

(B) Exempt function (publication of exhibition catalog):

Income (from catalog sales)	60,000	
Directly-connected expenses	(110,000)	
Net exempt function income (loss)	(50,000)	(50,000)
Unrelated business taxable income		25,000

(iii) Expenses related to publication of the exhibition catalog exceed revenues by $50,000. Because the unrelated business activity (the sale of advertising) exploits an exempt activity (the publication of the exhibition catalog), and because the publication of editorial material is an activity normally conducted by taxable entities that sell advertising, the net loss from the exempt publication activity is allowed as a deduction from unrelated business income under paragraph (d)(2) of this section. In contrast, the presentation of an exhibition is not an activity normally conducted by taxable entities engaged in advertising and publication activity for purposes of paragraph (d)(2) of this section. Consequently, the $500,000 cost of presenting the exhibition is not directly connected with the conduct of the unrelated advertising activity and does not have a proximate and primary relationship to that activity. Accordingly, M has unrelated business taxable income of $25,000.

(f) Determination of unrelated business taxable income derived from sale of advertising in exempt organization periodicals. *(1) In general.* Under section 513 (relating to the definition of unrelated trade or business) and § 1.513-1, amounts realized by an exempt organization from the sale of advertising in a periodical constitute gross income from an unrelated trade or business activity involving the exploitation of an exempt activity, namely, the circulation and readership of the periodical developed through the production and distribution of the readership content of the periodical. Paragraph (d) of this section provides for the allowance of deductions attributable to the production and distribution of the readership content of the periodical. Thus, subject to the limitations of paragraph (d)(2) of this section, where the circulation and readership of an exempt organization periodical are utilized in connection with the sale of advertising in the periodical, expenses, depreciation, and similar items of deductions attributable to the production and distribution of the editorial or readership content of the periodical shall qualify as items of deductions directly connected with the unrelated advertising activity. Subparagraphs (2) through (6) of this paragraph provide rules for determining the amount of unrelated business taxable income attributable to the sale of advertising in exempt organization periodicals. Subparagraph (7) of this paragraph provides rules for determining when the unrelated business taxable income of two or more exempt organization periodicals may be determined on a consolidated basis.

(2) Computation of unrelated business taxable income attributable to sale of advertising. (i) Excess advertising costs. If the direct advertising costs of an exempt organization periodical (determined under subparagraph (6)(ii) of this paragraph) exceed gross advertising income (determined under subparagraph (3)(ii) of this paragraph), such excess shall be allowable as a deduction in determining unrelated business taxable income from any unrelated trade or business activity carried on by the organization.

(ii) Excess advertising income. If the gross advertising income of an exempt organization periodical exceeds direct advertising costs, paragraph (d)(2) of this section provides that items of deduction attributable to the production and distribution of the readership content of an exempt organization periodical shall qualify as items of deduction directly connected with unrelated advertising activity in computing the amount of unrelated business taxable income derived from the advertising activity to the extent that such items exceed the income derived from or attributable to such production and distribution, but only to the extent that such items do not result in a loss from such advertising activity. Furthermore, such items of deduction shall not qualify as directly connected with such advertising activity to the extent that their deduction would result in a loss carryback or carryover with respect to such advertising activity. Similarly, such items of deduction shall not be taken into account in computing unrelated business taxable income attributable to any unrelated trade or business activity other than such advertising activity. Thus—

(a) If the circulation income of the periodical (determined under subparagraph (3)(iii) of this paragraph) equals or exceeds the readership costs of such periodical (determined under subparagraph (6)(iii) of this paragraph), the unrelated business taxable income attributable to the periodical is the excess of the gross advertising income of the periodical over direct advertising costs; but

(b) If the readership costs of an exempt organization periodical exceed the circulation income of the periodical, the unrelated business taxable income is the excess, if any, of the total income attributable to the periodical (determined under subparagraph (3) of this paragraph) over the total periodical costs (as defined in subparagraph (6)(i) of this paragraph).

See subparagraph (7) of this paragraph for rules relating to the consolidation of two or more periodicals.

(iii) Examples. The application of this paragraph may be illustrated by the following examples. For purposes of these examples it is assumed that the production and distribution of the readership content of the periodical is related to the organization's exempt purpose.

Example (1). X, an exempt trade association, publishes a single periodical which carries advertising. During 1971, X realizes a total of $40,000 from the sale of advertising in the periodical (gross advertising income) and $60,000 from sales of the periodical to members and nonmembers (circulation income). The total periodical costs are $90,000 of which $50,000 is directly connected with the sale and publication of advertising (direct advertising costs) and $40,000 is attributable to the production and distribution of the readership content (readership costs). Since the direct advertising costs of the periodical ($50,000) exceed gross advertising income ($40,000), pursuant to subdivision (i) of this subparagraph, the unrelated business taxable income attributable to advertising is determined solely on the basis of the income and deductions directly connected with the production and sale of the advertising:

Gross advertising revenue	$40,000
Direct advertising costs	(50,000)
Loss attributable to advertising	(10,000)

X has realized a loss of $10,000 from its advertising activity. This loss is an allowable deduction in computing X's unrelated business taxable income derived from any other unrelated trade or business activity.

Example (2). Assume the facts as stated in example (1), except that the circulation income of X periodical is $100,000 instead of $60,000, and that of the total periodical costs, $25,000 are direct advertising costs, and $65,000 are readership costs. Since the circulation income ($100,000) exceeds the total readership costs ($65,000), pursuant to subdivision (ii)(a) of this subparagraph the unrelated business taxable income attributable to the advertising activity is $15,000, the excess of gross advertising income $40,000) over direct advertising costs ($25,000).

Example (3). Assume the facts as stated in example (1), except that of the total periodical costs, $20,000 are direct advertising costs and $70,000 are readership costs. Since the readership costs of the periodical ($70,000), exceed the circulation income ($60,000), pursuant to subdivision (ii)(b) of this subparagraph the unrelated business taxable income attributable to advertising is the excess of the total income attributable to the periodical over the total periodical costs. Thus, X has unrelated business taxable income attributable to the advertising activity of $10,000 ($100,000 total income attributable to the periodical less $90,000 total periodical costs).

Example (4). Assume the facts as stated in example (1), except that the total periodical costs are $120,000 of which $30,000 are direct advertising costs and $90,000 are readership costs. Since the readership costs of the periodical ($90,000), exceed the circulation income ($60,000), pursuant to subdivision (ii)(b) of this subparagraph the unrelated business taxable income attributable to advertising is the excess, if any, of the total income attributable to the periodical over the the total periodical costs. Since the total income of the periodical ($100,000) does not exceed the total periodical costs ($120,000), X has not derived any unrelated business taxable income from the advertising activity. Further, only $70,000 of the $90,000 of readership costs may be deducted in computing unrelated business taxable income since as provided in subdivision (ii) of this subparagraph, such costs may be deducted, to the extent they exceed circulation income, only to the extent they do not result in a loss from the advertising activity. Thus, there is no loss from such activity, and no amount may be deducted on this account in computing X's unrelated trade or business income derived from any other unrelated trade or business activity.

(3) Income attributable to exempt organization periodicals. (i) In general. For purposes of this paragraph the total income attributable to an exempt organization periodical is the sum of its gross advertising income and its circulation income.

(ii) Gross advertising income. The term "gross advertising income" means all amounts derived from the unrelated advertising activities of an exempt organization periodical (or for purposes of this paragraph in the case of a taxable organization, all amounts derived from the advertising activities of the taxable organization).

(iii) Circulation income. The term "circulation income" means the income attributable to the production, distribution or circulation of a periodical (other than gross advertising income) including all amounts realized from or attributable to the sale or distribution of the readership content of the periodical, such as amounts realized from charges made for reprinting or republishing articles and special items in the periodical and amounts realized from sales of back issues. Where the right to receive an exempt organization periodical is associated with membership or similar status in such organization for which dues, fees or other charges are received (hereinafter referred to as "membership receipts"), circulation income includes the portion of such membership receipts allocable to the periodical (hereinafter referred to as "allocable membership receipts"). Allowable membership receipts is the amount which would have been charged and paid if —

(a) The periodical was that of a taxable organization,

(b) The periodical was published for profit, and

(c) The member was an unrelated party dealing with the taxable organization at arm's length.

See subparagraph (4) of this paragraph for a discussion of the factors to be considered in determining allocable membership receipts of an exempt organization periodical under the standard described in the preceding sentence.

(4) Allocable membership receipts. The allocable membership receipts of an exempt organization periodical shall be determined in accordance with the following rules:

(i) Subscription price charged to nonmembers. If 20 percent or more of the total circulation of a periodical consist of sales to nonmembers, the subscription price charged to such nonmembers shall determine the price of the periodical purposes of allocating membership receipts to the periodical.

(ii) Subscription price to nonmembers. If paragraph (f)(4)(i) of this section does not apply and if the membership dues from 20 percent or more of the members of an exempt organization are less than those received from the other members because the former members do not receive the periodical, the amount of the reduction in membership dues for a member not receiving the periodical shall determine the price of the periodical for purposes of allocating membership receipts to the periodical.

(iii) Pro rata allocation of membership receipts. Since it may generally be assumed that membership receipts and gross advertising income are equally available for all the exempt activities (including the periodical) of the organization, the share of membership receipts allocated to the periodical, where paragraphs (f)(4)(i) and (ii) of this section do not apply, shall be an amount equal to the organization's membership receipts multiplied by a fraction the numerator of which is the total periodical costs and the denominator of which is such costs plus the cost of other exempt activities of the organization. For example, assume that an exempt organization has total periodical costs of $30,000 and other exempt costs of $70,000. Further assume that the membership receipts of the organization are $60,000 and that paragraphs (f)(4)(i) and (ii) of this section do not apply. Under these circumstances $18,000 ($60,000 times $30,000/$100,000) is allocated to the periodical's circulation income.

(5) Examples. The rules set forth in paragraph (f)(4) of this section may be illustrated by the following examples. For purposes of these examples it is assumed that the exempt organization periodical contains advertising, and that the production and distribution of the readership content of the periodical is related to the organization's exempt purpose.

Example (1). U is an exempt scientific organization with 10,000 members who pay annual dues of $15 per year. One of U's activities is the publication of a monthly periodical which is distributed to all of its members. U also distributes 5,000 additional copies of its periodical to nonmember subscribers at a cost of $10 per year. Pursuant to paragraph (f)(4)(i) of this section, since the nonmember circulation of U's periodical represents 33⅓ percent of its total circulation the subscription price charged to nonmembers will be used to determine the portion of U's membership receipts allocable to the periodical. Thus, U's allocable membership receipts will be $100,000 ($10 times 10,000 members), and U's total circulation income for the periodical will be $150,000 ($100,000 from members plus $50,000 from sales to nonmembers).

Example (2). Assume the facts as stated in example (1), except that U sells only 500 copies of its periodical to nonmembers, at a price of $10 per year. Assume further that U's members may elect not to receive the periodical, in which case their annual dues are reduced from $15 per year to $6 per year, and that only 3,000 members elect to receive the periodical and pay the full dues of $15 per year. U's stated subscription price to members of $9 consistently results in an excess of total income (including gross advertising income) attributable to the periodical over total costs of the periodical. Since the 500 copies of the periodical distributed to nonmembers represents only 14 percent of the 3,500 copies distributed, pursuant to paragraph (f)(4)(i) of this section, the $10 subscription price charged to nonmembers will not be used in determining the portion of membership receipts allocable to the periodical. On the other hand, since 70 percent of the members elect not to receive the periodical and pay $9 less per year in dues, pursuant to paragraph (f)(4)(ii) of this section, such $9 price will be used in determining the subscription price charged to members. Thus, the allocable membership receipts will be $9 per member, or $27,000 ($9 times 3,000 copies) and U's total circulation income will be $32,000 ($27,000 plus $5,000).

Example (3). (a) W, an exempt trade association, has 800 members who pay annual dues of $50 per year. W publishes a monthly journal the editorial content and advertising of which are directed to the business interests of its own members. The journal is distributed to all of W's members and no receipts are derived from nonmembers.

(b) W has total receipts of $100,000 of which $40,000 ($50 × 800) are membership receipts and $60,000 are gross advertising income. W's total costs for the journal and other exempt activities is $100,000. W has total periodical costs of $76,000 of which $41,000 are direct advertising costs and $35,000 are readership costs.

(c) Paragraph (f)(4)(i) of this section will not apply since no copies are available to nonmembers. Therefore, the allocation of membership receipts shall be made in accordance with paragraph (f)(4)(iii) of this section. Based upon pro rata allocation of membership receipts (40,000) by a fraction the numerator of which is total periodical costs ($76,000) and the denominator of which is the total costs of the journal and the other exempt activities ($100,000), $30,400 ($76,000/$100,000 times $40,000) of membership receipts is circulation income.

(6) Deductions attributable to exempt organization periodicals. (i) In general. For purposes of this paragraph the term "total periodical costs" means the total deductions attributable to the periodical. For purposes of this paragraph the total periodical costs of an exempt organization periodical are the sum of the direct advertising costs of the periodical (determined under subdivision (ii) of this subparagraph) and the readership costs of the periodical (determined under subdivision (iii) of this subparagraph). Items of deduction properly attributable to exempt activities other than the publication of an exempt organization periodical may not be allocated to such periodical. Where items are attributable both to an exempt organization periodical and to other activities of an exempt organization, the allocation of such items must be made on a reasonable basis which fairly reflects the portion of such item properly attributable to each such activity. The method of allocation will vary with the nature of the item, but once adopted, a reasonable method of allocation with respect to an item must be used consistently. Thus, for example, salaries may generally be allocated among various activities on the basis of the time devoted to each activity; occupancy costs such as rent, heat and electricity may be allocated on the basis of the portion of space devoted to each activity; and depreciation may be allocated on the basis of space occupied and the portion of the particular asset utilized in each activity. Allocations based on dollar receipts from various exempt activities will generally not be reasonable since such receipts are usually not an accurate reflection of the costs associated with activities carried on by exempt organizations.

(ii) Direct advertising costs. (a) The direct advertising costs of an exempt organization periodical include all expenses, depreciation, and similar items of deduction which are directly connected with the sale and publication of advertising as determined in accordance with paragraphs (a), (b), and (c) of this section. These items are allowable as deductions in the computation of unrelated business income of the organization for the taxable year to the extent they meet the requirements of section 162, section 167, or other relevant provisions of the Code. The items allowable as deductions under this subdivision do not include any items of deduction attributable to the production or distribution of the readership content of the periodical.

(b) The items allowable as deductions under this subdivision would include agency commissions and other direct selling costs, such as transportation and travel expenses, office salaries, promotion and research expenses, and direct office overhead directly connected with the sale of advertising lineage in the periodical. Also included would be other items of deduction commonly classified as advertising costs under standard account classification, such as art work and copy preparation, telephone, telegraph, postage, and similar costs directly connected with advertising.

(c) In addition to the items of deduction normally included in standard account classifications relating to advertising costs, it is also necessary to ascertain the portion of mechanical and distribution costs attributable to advertising lineage. For this purpose, the general account classifications of items includible in mechanical and distribution costs ordinarily employed in business-paper and consumer publication accounting provide a guide for the computation. Thus, the mechanical and distribution costs in such cases would include the portion of the costs and other expenses of composition, presswork, binding, mailing (including paper and wrappers used for mailing), and the bulk postage attributable to the advertising lineage of the publication. The portion of mechanical and distribution costs attributable to advertising lineage of the periodical will be determined on the basis of the ratio of advertising lineage to total lineage of the periodical, and the application of that ratio to the total mechanical and distribution costs of the periodical, where records are not kept in such a manner as to reflect more accurately the allocation of mechanical and distributions costs to advertising lineage of the periodical, and where there is no factor in the character of the periodical to indicate that such an allocation would be unreasonable.

(iii) Readership costs. The "readership costs" of an exempt organization periodical include expenses, depreciation or similar items which are directly connected with the production and distribution of the readership content of the periodical and which would otherwise be allowable as deductions in determining unrelated business taxable income under section 512 and the regulations thereunder if such production and distribution constituted an unrelated trade or business activity. Thus, readership costs include all the items of deduction attributable to an exempt organization periodical which are not allocated to direct advertising costs under subdivision (ii) of this subparagraph, including the portion of such items attributable to the readership content of the periodical, as opposed to the advertising content, and the portion of mechanical and distribution costs which is not attributable to advertising lineage in the periodical.

(7) Consolidation. (i) In general. Where an exempt organization subject to unrelated business income tax under section 511 publishes two or more periodicals for the production of income, it may treat the gross income from all (but not less than all) of such periodicals and the items of deduction directly connected with such periodicals (including readership costs of such periodicals), on a consolidated basis as if such periodicals were one periodical in determining the amount of unrelated business taxable income derived from the sale of advertising in such periodical. Such treatment must, however, be followed consistently and once adopted shall be binding unless the consent of the Commissioner is obtained as provided in section 446(e) and § 1.446-1(e).

(ii) Production of income. For purposes of this subparagraph, an exempt organization periodical is "published for the production of income" if—

(a) The organization generally receives gross advertising income from the periodical equal to at least 25 percent of the readership costs of such periodical, and

(b) The publication of such periodical is an activity engaged in for profit.

For purposes of the preceding sentence, the determination whether the publication of a periodical is an activity engaged in for profit is to be made by reference to objective standards taking into account all the facts and circumstances involved in each case. The facts and circumstances must indicate that the organization carries on the activity with the objective that the publication of the periodical will result in economic profit (without regard to tax consequences), although not necessarily in a particular year. Thus, an exempt organization periodical may be treated as having been published with such an objective even though in a particular year its total periodical costs exceed its total income. Similarly, if an exempt organization begins publishing a new periodical, the fact that the total periodical costs exceed the total income for the startup years because of a lack of advertising sales does not mean that the periodical was published without an objective of economic profit. The organization may establish that the activity was carried on with such an objective. This might be established by showing, for example, that there is a reasonable expectation that the total income, by reason of an increase in advertising sales, will exceed costs within a reasonable time. See § 1.183-2 for additional factors bearing on this determination.

(iii) Example. This subparagraph may be illustrated by the following example:

Example. Y, an exempt trade association, publishes three periodicals which it distributes to its members: a weekly newsletter, a monthly magazine, and quarterly journal. Both the monthly magazine and the quarterly journal contain advertising which accounts for gross advertising income equal to more than 25 percent of their respective readership costs. Similarly, the total income attributable to each such periodical has exceeded the total deductions attributable to each such periodical for substantially all the years they have been published. The newsletter carries no advertising and its annual subscription price is not intended to cover the cost of publication. The newsletter is a service of Y distributed to all of its members in an effort to keep them informed of changes occurring in the business world and is not engaged in for profit. Under these circumstances, Y may consolidate the income and deductions from the monthly and quarterly journals in computing its unrelated business taxable income, but may not consolidate the income and deductions attributable to the publication of the newsletter with the income and deductions of its other periodicals since the newsletter is not published for the production of income.

(g) Foreign organizations. *(1) In general.* The unrelated business taxable income of a foreign organization exempt from taxation under section 501(a) consists of:

(i) The organization's unrelated business taxable income which is derived from sources within the United States but which is not effectively connected with the conduct of a trade or business within the United States, plus

(ii) The organization's unrelated business taxable income effectively connected with the conduct of a trade or business within the United States (whether or not such income is derived from sources within the United States).

To determine whether income realized by a foreign organization is derived from sources within the United States or is effectively connected with the conduct of a trade or business within the United States, see part 1, subchapter N, chapter 1 of the Code (section 861 and following) and the regulations thereunder.

(2) Effective dates. Subparagraph (1) of this paragraph applies to taxable years beginning after December 31, 1969. For taxable years beginning on or before December 31, 1969, the unrelated business taxable income of a foreign organization exempt from taxation under section 501(a) consists of the organization's unrelated business taxable income which—

(i) For taxable years beginning after December 31, 1966, is effectively connected with the conduct of a trade or business within the United States, whether or not such income is derived from sources within the United States;

(ii) For taxable years beginning on or before December 31, 1966, is derived from sources within the United States.

(h) Effective date. Paragraphs (a) through (f) of this section are applicable with respect to taxable years beginning after December 12, 1967. However, if a taxpayer wishes to rely on the rules stated therein for taxable years beginning before December 13, 1967, he may do so.

T.D. 6939, 12/11/67, amend T.D. 7183, 4/20/72, T.D. 7392, 12/17/75, T.D. 7438, 10/7/76, T.D. 7935, 1/12/84, T.D. 8991, 4/24/2002.

---

§ 1.512(a)-2 Definition applicable to taxable years beginning before December 13, 1967.

(a) In general. The unrelated business taxable income which is subject to the tax imposed by section 511 is the gross income, derived by any organization to which section 511 applies, from any unrelated trade or business regularly carried on by it, less the deductions allowed by chapter 1 of the Code which are directly connected with the carrying on of such trade or business, subject to certain exceptions, additions, and limitations referred to below. In the case of an organization which regularly carries on two or more unrelated businesses, its unrelated business taxable income is the aggregate of its gross income from all such unrelated businesses, less the aggregate of the deductions allowed with respect to all such unrelated businesses. For provisions generally applicable to the unrelated business tax, see § 1.511-3, and for rules applicable to the determination of the adjusted basis of property, see paragraph (a)(2) of § 1.514(a)-1.

(b) Effective date. Except as provided in paragraph (f) of § 1.512(a)-1, this section is applicable with respect to taxable years beginning before December 13, 1967.

T.D. 6301, 7/8/58, amend T.D. 6939, 12/13/67.

---

§ 1.512(a)-4 Special rules applicable to war veterans organizations.

(a) In general. For taxable years beginning after December 31, 1969, this section provides special rules for the determination of the unrelated business taxable income of an organization described in section 501(c)(19). In general, the rules contained in sections 511 through 514 which are applicable to any organization listed in section 501(c) apply in determining the unrelated business taxable income of an organization described in section 501(c)(19). However, that amount which is paid by members of the organization for the purpose described in paragraph (b)(1) of this section, if set aside from other organizational monies and accounts in an insurance set aside, may be excluded from the unrelated business taxable income of the organization. The insurance set aside shall be used exclusively for providing insurance benefits, for the purposes specified in section 170(c)(4) of the Code, for the reasonable costs of administering the insurance program that are directly related to such set aside, or for the reasonable costs of distributing funds for section 170(c)(4) purposes. If an amount so set aside is used for any purposes other than those described in the preceding sentence, it shall be included in unrelated business taxable income without regard to any modifications provided by section 512(b), in the taxable year in which it is withdrawn from such set aside. Amounts will be considered to have been withdrawn from an insurance set aside if they are used in any manner inconsistent with providing insurance benefits, paying the reasonable costs of administering the insurance program for section 170(c)(4) purposes and for costs of distributing funds for section 170(c)(4) purposes. An example of a use of funds which would be considered a withdrawal would be the use of such funds as security for a loan.

(b) Insurance set aside. *(1) Purpose of payments by members.* Payments by members (including commissions on such payments earned by the set aside as agent for an insurance company) into an insurance set aside must be for the sole purpose of obtaining life, sick, accident or health insurance benefits from the organization or for the reasonable costs of administration of the insurance program, except that such purpose is not violated when excess funds from an experience gain are utilized for those purposes specified in section 170(c)(4) or the reasonable costs of distributing funds for such purposes. Funds for any other purpose may not be set aside in the insurance set aside.

(2) Income from set aside. In addition to the payments by members described in paragraph (b)(1) of this section, only income from amounts in the insurance set aside (including commissions earned as agent for an insurance company) may be so set aside. Moreover unless such income is used for providing insurance benefits, for those purposes specified in section 170(c)(4), or for reasonable costs of administration, such income must be set aside within the period described in paragraph (b)(3) of this section in order to avoid being included as an item of unrelated business taxable income under section 512(a)(4).

(3) Time within which income must be set aside. Income from amounts in the insurance set aside generally must be set aside in the taxable year in which it would be includible in gross income but for this section. However, income set aside on or before the date prescribed for filing the organization's return of unrelated business taxable income (whether or not it had such income) for the taxable year (including any extension of time) may, at the election of the organization, be treated as having been set aside in such taxable year.

(4) Computation of income from set aside. Income from amounts in the insurance set aside shall consist solely of items of investment income from, and other gains derived from dealings in, property in the set aside. The deductions allowed against such items of income or other gains are those amounts which are related to the production of such income or other gains. Only the amounts of income or other gain which are in excess of such deductions may be set aside in the insurance set aside.

(5) Requirements for set aside. An amount is not properly set aside if the organization commingles it with any amount which is not to be set aside. However, adequate records describing the amount set aside and indicating that it is to be used for the designated purpose are sufficient. Amounts that are set aside need not be permanently committed to such use either under state law or by contract. Thus, for example, it is not necessary that the organization place these funds in an irrevocable trust. Although set aside income may be accumulated, any accumulation which is unreasonable in amount or duration is evidence that the income was not accumulated for the purposes set forth. For purposes of the preceding sentence, accumulations which are reasonably necessary for the purpose of providing life, sick, health, or accident insurance benefits on the basis of recognized mortality or morbidity tables and assumed rates of interest under an actuarially acceptable method would not be unreasonable even though such accumulations are quite large and the time between the receipt by the organization of such amounts and the date of payment of the benefits is quite long. For example, an accumulation of income for 20 years or longer which is determined to be reasonably necessary to pay life insurance benefits to members, their dependents or designated beneficiaries, generally would not be an unreasonable accumulation. Income which has been set aside may be invested, pending the action contemplated by the set aside, without being regarded as having been used for other purposes.

T.D. 7438, 10/7/76.

§ 1.512(a)-5T Questions and answers relating to the unrelated business taxable income of organizations described in paragraphs (9), (17) or (20) of section 501(c) (temporary).

Caution: The Treasury has not yet amended Reg § 1.512(a)-5T to reflect changes made by P.L. 104-188.

Q-1. What does section 512(a)(3), as amended by the Tax Reform Act of 1984 (Act), provide with respect to organizations described in paragraphs (9), (17) or (20) of section 501(c)?

A-1. In general, section 512(a)(3), as amended by section 511 of the Act, extends the rules for determining the unrelated business income tax of voluntary employees' beneficiary associations (VEBAs) to supplemental unemployment compensation benefit trusts (SUBs) and group legal service organization (GLSOs). The section also restricts the amount of income that may be set aside by such organizations for exempt purposes.

Q-2. What is the effective date of the amendments to section 512(a)(3)?

A-2. The amendments to section 512(a)(3) will apply to income earned by VEBAs, SUBs or GLSOs after December 31, 1985, in the taxable years of such organizations ending after such date. For purposes of applying section 512(a)(3) to the first taxable year of such an organization ending after December 31, 1985, the income of the VEBA, SUB or GLSO earned after December 31, 1985, will be determined by allocating the total income earned for such taxable year on the basis of the calendar year 1985 and 1986 months in such taxable year. However, if a VEBA, SUB, or GLSO is a part of a plan that is maintained pursuant to one or more collective bargaining agreements (a) between employee representatives and one or more employers, and (b) which are in effect on July 1, 1985 (or ratified on or before that date), the amendments do not apply to income earned in a taxable year of a VEBA, SUB or GLSO beginning before the termination of the last of the collective bargaining agreements pursuant to which the plan is maintained (determined without regard to any extension of the contract agreed to after July 1, 1985). For purposes of the preceding sentence, any plan amendment made pursuant to a collective bargaining agreement relating to the plan which amends the plan solely to conform to any requirement added under section 511 of the Tax Reform Act 1984 (i.e., requirements under section 419, 419A, 512(a)(3)(E), and 4976) shall not be treated as a termination of such collective bargaining agreements.

Q-3. What amount of income may a VEBA, SUB or GLSO set aside for exempt purposes?

A-3. (a) Pursuant to section 512(a)(3)(E)(i), the amounts set aside in a VEBA, SUB, or GLSO (including a VEBA, SUB, or GLSO that is part of a 10 or more employer plan, as defined in section 419A(f)(6)(B)) as of the close of a taxable year of such VEBA, SUB, or GLSO to provide for the payment of life, sick, accident, or other benefits may not be taken into account for purposes of determining "exempt function income" to the extent that such amounts exceed the qualified asset account limit, determined under sections 419A(c) and 419A(f)(7), for such taxable year of the VEBA, SUB, or GLSO. In calculating the qualified asset account limit for this purpose, a reserve for post-retirement medical benefits under section 419A(c)(2)(A) is not to be taken into account.

(b) The exempt function income of a VEBA, SUB, or GLSO for a taxable year of such an organization, under section 512(a)(3)(B), includes: (1) Certain amounts paid by members of the VEBA, SUB, or GLSO within the meaning of the first sentence of section 512(a)(3)(B) ("member contributions"); and (2) other income of the VEBA, SUB, or GLSO (including earnings on member contributions) that is set aside for the payment of life, sick, accident, or other benefits to the extent that the total amount set aside in the VEBA, SUB or GLSO as of the close of the taxable year for any purpose (including member contributions and other income set aside in the VEBA, SUB, or GLSO as of the close of the year) does not exceed the qualified asset account limit for such taxable year of the organization. For purposes of section 512(c)(3)(B), member contributions include both employee contributions and employer contributions to the VEBA, SUB, or GLSO. In calculating the total amount set aside in a VEBA, SUB, or GLSO as of the close of a taxable year, certain assets with useful lives extending substantially beyond the end of the taxable year (e.g., buildings, and licenses) are not to be taken into account to the extent they are used in the provision of life, sick, accident, or other benefits. For example, cash and securities (and similar investments) held by a VEBA, SUB or GLSO are not disregarded in calculating the total amount set aside for this purpose because they are used to pay welfare benefits, rather than merely used in the provision of such benefits. Accordingly, the unrelated business taxable income of a VEBA, SUB, or GLSO for a taxable year of such an organization generally will equal the lesser of two amounts: the income of the VEBA, SUB, or GLSO for the taxable year (excluding member contributions), or the excess of the total amount set aside as of the close of the taxable year (including member contributions, and excluding certain assets with a useful life extending substantially beyond the end of the taxable year to the extent they are used in the provision of welfare benefits) over the qualified asset account limit (calculated without regard to the otherwise permitted reserve for post-retirement medical benefits) for the taxable year. See § 1.419A-2T for special rules relating to collectively bargained welfare benefit funds.

(c) The income of a VEBA, SUB, or GLSO for any taxable year includes gain realized by the organization on the sale or disposition of any asset during such year. The gain realized by a VEBA, SUB, or GLSO on the sale or disposition of an asset is equal to the amount realized by the organization over the basis of such asset (in the hands of the organization), reduced by any qualified direct costs attributable to such asset (under paragraphs (b), (c), and (d) of Q&A-6 of § 1.419-1T).

Q-4. What transition rules apply to "existing reserves for post-retirement medical or life insurance benefits"?

A-4. (a) Section 512(a)(3)(E)(iii)(I) provides that income that is either directly or indirectly attributable to "existing reserves for post-retirement medical or life insurance benefits" will not be treated as unrelated business taxable income. An "existing reserve for post-retirement medical or life insurance benefits" (as defined in section 512(a)(3)(E)(iii)(II)) is the total amount of assets actually set aside in a VEBA, SUB, or GLSO on July 18, 1984 (calculated in the manner set forth in Q&A-3 of the regulation, and adjusted under paragraph (c) of Q&A-11 of § 1.419-1T), reduced by employer contributions to the fund on or before such date to the extent such contributions are not deductible for the taxable year of the employer containing July 18, 1984, and for any prior taxable year of the employer, for purposes of providing such post-retirement benefits. For purposes of the preceding sentence only, an amount that was not actually set aside on July 18, 1984, will be treated as having been actually set aside on such date if (1) such amount was incurred by the employer (without regard to section 461(h)) as of the close of the last taxable year of the VEBA, SUB, or GLSO ending before July 18, 1984, and (2) such amount was actually contributed to the VEBA, SUB, or GLSO within 8½ months following the close of such taxable year.

(b) In addition, section 512(a)(3)(E)(iii)(I) applies to existing reserves for such post-retirement benefits only to the extent that such "existing reserves" do not exceed the amount that could be accumulated under the principles set forth in Revenue Rulings 69-382, 1969-2, C.B. 28; 69-478, 1969-2 C.B. 29; and 73-599, 1973-2 C.B. 40. Thus, amounts attributable to such excess "existing reserves" are not within this transition rule even though they were actually set aside on July 18, 1984.

(c) All post-retirement medical or life insurance benefits (or other benefits to the extent paid with amounts set aside to provide post-retirement medical or life insurance benefits) provided after July 18, 1984 (whether or not the employer has maintained a reserve or fund for such benefits) are to be charged, first, against the "existing reserves" within this transition rule (including amounts attributable to "existing reserves" within this transition rule) for post-retirement medical benefits or for post-retirement life insurance benefits (as the case may be) and, second, against all other amounts. For this purpose, the qualified direct cost of an asset with a useful life extending substantially beyond the end of the taxable year (as determined under Q&A-6 of § 1.419-1T) will be treated as a benefit provided and thus charged against the "existing reserve" based on the extent to which such asset is used in the provision of post-retirement medical benefits or post-retirement life insurance benefits (as the case may be). All plans of an employer providing post-retirement medical benefits are to be treated as one plan for purposes of section 512(a)(3)(E)(iii)(III), and all plans of an employer providing post-retirement life insurance benefits are to be treated as one plan for purposes of section 512(a)(3)(E)(iii)(III).

(d) In calculating the unrelated business taxable income of a VEBA, SUB, or GLSO for a taxable year of such organization, the total income of the VEBA, SUB, or GLSO for the taxable year is reduced by the income attributable to "existing reserves" within the transition rule before such income is compared to the excess of the total amount set aside as of the close of the taxable year over the qualified asset account limit for the taxable year. Thus, for example, assume that the total income of a VEBA for a taxable year is $1,000, and that the excess of the total amount of the VEBA set aside as of the close of the taxable year over the applicable qualified asset account limit is $600. Assume also that of the $1,000 of total income, $500 is attributable to "existing reserves" within the transition rule of section 512(a)(3)(E)(iii)(I). The unrelated business income of this VEBA for the taxable year is equal to the lesser of the following two amounts: (1) the total income of the VEBA for the taxable year ($1,000), reduced to the extent that such income is attributable to "existing reserves" within the transition rule ($500); or (2) the excess of the total amount set aside as of the close of the taxable year over the applicable qualified asset account limit ($600). Thus, the unrelated business income of this VEBA for the taxable year is $500.

T.D. 8073, 1/29/86.

§ 1.512(b)-1 Modifications.

Caution: The Treasury has not yet amended Reg § 1.512(b)-1 to reflect changes made by P.L. 105-34, P.L. 103-66, P.L. 101-508.

Whether a particular item of income falls within any of the modifications provided in section 512(b) shall be determined by all the facts and circumstances of each case. For example, if a payment termed "rent" by the parties is in fact a return of profits by a person operating the property for the benefit of the tax-exempt organization or is a share of the profits retained by such organization as a partner or a joint venturer, such payment is not within the modification for rents. The modifications provided in section 512(b) are as follows:

(a) Certain investment income. *(1) In general.* Dividends, interest, payments with respect to securities loans (as defined in section 512(a)(5)), annuities, income from notional principal contracts (as defined in Treasury Regulations 26 CFR 1.863-7 or regulations issued under section 446), other substantially similar income from ordinary and routine investments to the extent determined by the Commissioner, and all deductions directly connected with any of the foregoing items of income shall be excluded in computing unrelated business taxable income.

(2) Limitations. The exclusions under paragraph (a)(1) of this section do not apply to income derived from and deductions in connection with debt-financed property (as defined in section 514(b)). Moreover, the exclusions under paragraph (a)(1) of this section do not apply to gains or losses from the sale, exchange, or other disposition of any property, or to gains or losses from the lapse or termination of options to buy or sell securities. For rules regarding the treatment of these gains and losses, see section 512(b)(5) and § 1.512(b)-1(d). Furthermore, the exclusions under paragraph (a)(1) of this section do not apply to interest and annuities derived from and deductions in connection with controlled organizations. For rules regarding the treatment of such amounts, see section 512(b)(13) and § 1.512(b)-1(l). Finally, the exclusions under paragraph (a)(1) of this section of income from notional principal contracts and income that the Commissioner determines to be substantially similar income from ordinary and routine investments do not apply to income earned by brokers or dealers (including organizations that make a market in derivative financial products, as described in Treasury Regulations 26 CFR 1.954-2T(a)(4)(iii)(B)).

(3) Effective dates. The effective dates of the rules of paragraphs (a)(1) and (a)(2) of this section that were in effect prior to August 30, 1991 remain the same. The exclusion under paragraph (a)(1) of this section of income from notional principal contracts is effective for amounts received after August 30, 1991. However, an organization may apply the exclusion under paragraph (a)(1) of this section of income from notional principal contracts prior to that date, provided that such amounts are treated consistently for all open taxable years. Unless otherwise provided by the Commissioner, the exclusion under paragraph (a)(1) of this section of income that the Commissioner determines to be substantially similar income from ordinary and routine investments is effective for amounts received after the date of the Commissioner's determination.

(b) Royalties. Royalties, including overriding royalties, and all deductions directly connected with such income shall be excluded in computing unrelated business taxable income. However, for taxable years beginning after December 31, 1969, certain royalties from and certain deductions in connection with either, debt-financed property (as defined in section 514(b)) or controlled organizations (as defined in paragraph (1) of this section) shall be included in computing unrelated business taxable income. Mineral royalties shall be excluded whether measured by production or by gross or taxable income from the mineral property. However, where an organization owns a working interest in a mineral property, and is not relieved of its share of the development costs by the terms of any agreement with an operator, income received from such an interest shall not be excluded. To the extent not treated as a loan under section 636, payments in discharge of mineral production payments shall be treated in the same manner as royalty payments for the purpose of computing unrelated business taxable income. To the extent treated as a loan under section 636, the amount of any payment in discharge of a production payment which is the equivalent of interest shall be treated as interest for purposes of section 512(b)(1) and paragraph (a) of this section.

(c) Rents. *(1) Taxable years beginning before January 1, 1970.* For taxable years beginning before January 1, 1970, rents from real property (including personal property leased with the real property) and the deductions directly connected therewith shall also be excluded in computing unrelated business taxable income, except that certain rents from, and certain deductions in connection with, a business lease (as defined in section 514(f) shall be included in computing unrelated business taxable income. See subparagraph (5) of this paragraph for rules governing amounts received for the rendering of services.

(2) Taxable years beginning after December 31, 1969. (i) In general. For taxable years beginning after December 31, 1969, except as provided in subdivision (iii) of this subparagraph, rents from property described in subdivision (ii) of this subparagraph, and the deductions directly connected therewith, shall be excluded in computing unrelated business taxable income. However, notwithstanding subdivision (ii) of this subparagraph, certain rents from and certain deductions in connection with either debt-financed property (as defined in section 514(b)) or property rented to controlled organizations (as defined in paragraph (1) of this section) shall be included in computing unrelated business taxable income.

(ii) Excluded rents. The rents which are excluded from unrelated business income under section 512(b)(3)(A) and this paragraph are—

(a) Real property. All rents from real property; and

(b) Personal property. All rents from personal property leased with real property if the rents attributable to such personal property are an incidental amount of the total rents received or accrued under the lease, determined at the time the personal property is first placed in service by the lessee.

For purposes of the preceding sentence, rents attributable to personal property generally are not an incidental amount of the total rents if such rents exceed 10 percent of the total rents from all the property leased. For example, if the rents attributable to the personal property leased are determined to be $3,000 per year, and the total rents from all property leased are $10,000 per year, then such $3,000 amount is not to be excluded from the computation of unrelated business taxable income by operation of section 512(b)(3)(A)(ii) and this paragraph, since such amount is not an incidental portion of the total rents.

(iii) Exception. Subdivision (ii) of this subparagraph shall not apply, if either—

(a) Excess personal property rents. More than 50 percent of the total rents are attributable to personal property, determined at the time such personal property is first placed in service by the lessee; or

(b) Net profits. The determination of the amount of such rents depends in whole or in part on the income or profits derived by any person from the property leased, other than an amount based on a fixed percentage or percentages of the gross receipts or sales. For purposes of the preceding sentence, the rules contained in paragraph (b)(3) and (6) (other than paragraph (b)(6)(ii)) of § 1.856-4 shall apply.

(iv) Illustration. This subparagraph may be illustrated by the following example:

Example. A, an exempt organization, owns a printing factory which consists of a building housing two printing presses and other equipment necessary for printing. On January 1, 1971, A rents the building and the printing equipment to B for $10,000 a year. The lease states that $9,000 of such rent is for the building and $1,000 for the printing equipment. However, it is determined that notwithstanding the terms of the lease $4,000, or 40 percent ($4,000/$10,000), of the rent is actually attributable to the printing equipment. During 1971, A has $3,000 of deductions, all of which are properly allocable to the land and building. Under these circumstances, A shall not take into account in computing its unrelated business taxable income the $6,000 of rent attributable to the building and the $3,000 of deductions directly connected with such rent. However, the $4,000 of rent attributable to the printing equipment is not excluded from the computation of A's unrelated business taxable income by operation of section 512(b)(3)(A)(ii) or this paragraph since such rent represents more than an incidental portion of the total rents.

(3) Definitions and special rules. For purposes of subparagraph (2) of this paragraph—

(i) Real property defined. The term "real property" means all real property, including any property described in sections 1245(a)(3)(C) and 1250(c) and the regulations thereunder.

(ii) Personal property defined. The term "personal property" means all personal property, including any property described in section 1245(a)(3)(B) and the regulations thereunder.

(iii) Multiple leases. If separate leases are entered into with respect to real and personal property, and such properties have an integrated use (e.g., one or more leases for real property and another lease or leases for personal property to be used upon such real property), all such leases shall be considered as one lease.

(iv) Placed in service. Property is "placed in service" by the lessee when it is first subject to his use in accordance with the terms of the lease. For example, property subject to a lease entered into on November 1, 1971, for a term commencing on January 1, 1972, shall be considered as placed in service on January 1, 1972, regardless of when the property is first actually used by the lessee.

(v) Changes in rent charged or personal property rented. If—

(a) By reason of the placing of additional or substitute personal property in service, there is an increase of 100 percent or more in the rent attributable to all the personal property leased, or

(b) There is a modification of the lease by which there is a change in the rent charged (whether or not there is a change in the amount of personal property rented), the rent attributable to personal property shall be recomputed to determine whether the exclusion under subparagraph (2)(ii)(b) of this paragraph or the exception under subparagraph (2)(iii)(a) of this paragraph applies. Any change in the treatment of rents, attributable to a recomputation under this subdivision, shall be effective only with respect to rents for the period beginning with the event which occasioned the recomputation.

(4) Examples. Subparagraphs (2) and (3) of this paragraph may be illustrated by the following examples:

Example (1). On January 1, 1971, A, an exempt organization, executes two leases with B. One is for the rental of a computer, with a stated annual rental of $750. The other is for the rental of office space in which to use the computer, at a stated annual rental of $7,250. The total annual rent under both leases for 1971 is $8,000. At the time the computer is first placed in service, however, taking both leases into consideration, it is determined that notwithstanding the terms of the leases, $3,000, or 37.5 percent ($3,000/$8,000), of the rent is actually attributable to the computer. Therefore, for 1971, only the $5,000 ($8,000 – $3,000) attributable to the rental of the office space is excluded from the computation of A's unrelated business taxable income by operation of section 512(b)(3).

Example (2). Assume the facts as stated in example (1). Assume further that the leases to which the computer and office space are subject in example (1) provide that the rent may be increased or decreased, depending upon the prevailing rental value for similar computers and office space. On January 1, 1972, the total annual rent is increased in the computer lease to $2,000, and in the office space lease to $9,000. For 1972, it is determined that notwithstanding the terms of the leases $6,000, or 54.5 percent ($6,000/$11,000), of the total rent is actually attributable to the computer as of that time. Even though the rent attributable to personal property now exceeds 50 percent of the total rent, the rent attributable to real property will continue to be excluded, since there was no modification of the terms of the leases and since the increase in the rent was not attributable to the placing of new personal property in service. See subparagraph (3)(v) of this paragraph. Thus, for 1972 the $5,000 of rent attributable to the office space continues to be excluded from the computation of A's unrelated business taxable income by operation of section 512(b)(3).

Example (3). Assume the facts as stated in example (1), except that on January 1, 1973, B rents a second computer from A, which is placed in service on that date. The total rent is increased to $2,000 for the computer lease and to $10,000 for the office space lease. It is determined at the time the second computer is first placed in service that notwithstanding the terms of the leases $7,000 of the rent is actually attributable to the computers. Since the rent attributable to personal property has increased by more than 100 percent ($4,000/$8,000 = 133 percent), a redetermination must be made pursuant to subparagraph (3)(v)(a) of this paragraph. As a result, 58.3 percent ($7,000/$12,000) of the total rent is determined to be attributable to personal property. Accordingly, since more than 50 percent of the total rent A receives is attributable to the personal property leased, none of the rents are excluded from the computation of A's unrelated business taxable income by operation of section 512(b)(3).

Example (4). Assume the facts as stated in example (3), except that on June 30, 1975, the lease between B and A is modified. The total rent for the computer lease is reduced to $1,500 and the total rent for the office space lease is reduced to $7,500. Pursuant to subdivision (3)(v)(b)of this paragraph, a redetermination is made as of June 30, 1975. As of the modification date, it is determined that notwithstanding the terms of the leases, the rent actually attributable to the computers is $4,000, or 44.4 percent ($4,000/$9,000), of the total rent. Since less than 50 percent of the total rent is now attributable to personal property, the rent attributable to real property ($5,000), for periods after June 30, 1975, is excluded from the computation of A's unrelated business taxable income by operation of section 512(b)(3). However, the rent attributable to personal property ($4,000) is not excluded from unrelated business taxable income for such periods by operation of section 512(b)(3), since it represents more than an incidental portion of the total rent.

(5) Rendering of services. For purposes of this paragraph, payments for the use or occupancy of rooms and other space where services are also rendered to the occupant, such as for the use or occupancy of rooms or other quarters in hotels, boarding houses, or apartment houses furnishing hotel services, or in tourist camps or tourist homes, motor courts, or motels, or for the use or occupancy of space in parking lots, warehouses, or storage garages, does not constitute rent from real property. Generally, services are considered rendered to the occupant if they are primarily for his convenience and are other than those usually or customarily rendered in connection with the rental of rooms or other space for occupancy only. The supplying of maid service, for example, constitutes such service; whereas the furnishing of heat and light, the cleaning of public entrances, exits, stairways, and lobbies, the collection of trash, etc., are not considered as services rendered to the occupant. Payments for the use or occupancy of entire private residences or living quarters in duplex or multiple housing units, of offices in any office building, etc., are generally treated as rent from real property.

(d) Gains and losses from the sale, etc., of property. *(1)* There shall also be excluded from the computation of unrelated business taxable income gains or losses from the sale, exchange, or other disposition of property other than (i) stock in trade or other property of a kind which would properly be included in the inventory of the organization if on hand at the close of the taxable year, or (ii) property held primarily for sale to customers in the ordinary course of the trade or business. This exclusion does not apply with respect to the cutting of timber which is considered, upon the application of section 631(a), as a sale or exchange of such timber. In addition, for taxable years beginning after December 31, 1969, this exclusion does not apply to the gain derived from the sale or other disposition of debt-financed property (as defined in section 514(b)). Otherwise, the exclusion under section 512(b)(5) applies with respect to gains and losses from involuntary conversions, casualties, etc.

(2) There shall be excluded from the computation of unrelated business taxable income any gain from the lapse or termination after December 31, 1975, of options to buy or sell securities (as that term is defined in section 1236(c)). An option is considered terminated when the organization's obligation under the option ceases by any means other than by reason of the exercise or lapse of such option. If the exclusion is otherwise available it will apply whether or not the organization owns the securities upon which the option is written, that is, whether or not the option is "covered." However, income from the lapse or termination of an option is excludable only if the option is written in connection with the organization's investment activities. Thus, for example, if the securities upon which the options are written are held by the organization as inventory or for sale to customers in the ordinary course of a trade or business, the income from the lapse or termination will not be excludable under the provisions of this paragraph. Similarly, if an organization is engaged in the trade or business of writing options (whether or not such options are covered) the exclusion will not be available.

(e) Net operating losses. *(1)* The net operating loss deduction provided in section 172 shall be allowed in computing unrelated business taxable income. However, the net operating loss carryback or carryover (from a taxable year for which the taxpayer is subject to the provisions of section 511) shall be determined under section 172 without taking into account any amount of income or deduction which is not included under section 511 in computing unrelated business taxable income. For example, a loss attributable to an unrelated trade or business shall not be diminished by reason of the receipt of dividend income.

(2) For the purpose of computing the net operating loss deduction provided by section 172, any prior taxable year for which an organization was not subject to the provisions of section 511, or a corresponding provision of prior law, shall not be taken into account. Thus, if the organization was not subject to the provisions of section 511 or Supplement U of the Internal Revenue Code of 1939 for a preceding taxable year, the net operating loss is not a carryback to such preceding taxable year, and the net operating loss carryover to succeeding taxable years is not reduced by the taxable income for such preceding taxable year.

(3) A net operating loss carryback or carryover shall be allowed only from a taxable year for which the taxpayer is subject to the provisions of section 511, or a corresponding provision of prior law.

(4) In determining the span of years for which a net operating loss may be carried for purposes of section 172, taxable years in which an organization was not subject to the provisions of section 511 or a corresponding provision of prior law shall be taken into account. Thus, for example, if an organization is subject to the provisions of section 511 for the taxable year 1955 and has a net operating loss for that year, the last taxable year to which any part thereof may be carried over is the year 1960 regardless of whether the organization is subject to the provisions of section 511 in any of the intervening taxable years.

(f) Research. *(1)* Income derived from research for the United States or any of its agencies or instrumentalities or a State or political subdivision thereof, and all deductions directly connected with such income, shall be excluded in computing unrelated business taxable income.

(2) In the case of a college, university, or hospital, all income derived from research performed for any person and all deductions directly connected with such income, shall be excluded in computing unrelated business taxable income.

(3) In the case of an organization operated primarily for the purpose of carrying on fundamental research (as distinguished from applied research) the results of which are freely available to the general public, all income derived from research performed for any person and all deductions directly connected with such income shall be excluded in computing unrelated business taxable income.

(4) For the purpose of §§ 1.512(a)-1, 1.512(a)-2, and this section, the term "research" does not include activities of a type ordinarily carried on as an incident to commercial or industrial operations, for example, the ordinary testing or inspection of materials or products or the designing or construction of equipment, buildings, etc. The term "fundamental research" does not include research carried on for the primary purpose of commercial or industrial application.

(g) Charitable, etc., contributions. *(1)* In computing the unrelated business taxable income of an organization described in section 511(a)(2) the deduction from gross income allowed by section 170 (relating to charitable contributions and gifts) shall be allowed, whether or not the contribution is directly connected with the carrying on of the trade or business. Section 512(b)(10) provides that this deduction shall not exceed 5 percent of the organization's unrelated business taxable income computed without regard to that deduction. The provisions of section 170(b)(2) are not applicable to contributions by the organizations described in section 511(a)(2).

(2) In computing the unrelated business taxable income of a trust described in section 511(b)(2), the deduction allowed by section 170 (relating to charitable contributions and gifts) shall be allowed whether or not the contribution is directly connected with the carrying on of the trade or business. The deduction is limited as provided in section 170(b)(1)(A) and (B), except that the amounts so allowed are determined on the basis of unrelated business taxable income computed without regard to this deduction (rather than on the basis of adjusted gross income). For purposes of this deduction, a distribution by a trust described in section 511(b)(2) made pursuant to the trust instrument to a beneficiary described in section 170 shall be treated in the same manner as gifts or contributions.

(3) The contribution, whether made by a trust or other exempt organization, must be paid to another organization to be allowable. For example, a university described in section 501(c)(3) which is exempt from tax and which operates an unrelated business, shall be allowed a deduction, not in excess of 5 percent of its unrelated business taxable income, for gifts or contributions to another university described in section 501(c)(3) for educational work but shall not be allowed any deduction for amounts expended in administering its own educational program.

(h) Specific deduction. *(1) In general.* In computing unrelated business taxable income a specific deduction from gross income of $1,000 is allowed. However, for taxable years beginning after December 31, 1969, such specific deduction is not allowed in computing the net operating loss under section 172 and paragraph (6) of section 512(b).

(2) Special rule for a diocese, province of a religious order, or a convention or association of churches. (i) In the case of a diocese, province of a religious order, or a convention or association of churches, there shall be allowed with respect to each parish, individual church, district, or other local unit a specific deduction equal to the lower of $1,000 or the gross income derived from an unrelated trade or business regularly conducted by such local unit. However, a diocese, province of a religious order, or a convention or association of churches shall not be entitled to a specific deduction for a local unit which, for a taxable year, files a separate return. In the case of a local unit which, for a taxable year, files a separate return, such local unit may claim a specific deduction equal to the lower of $1,000 or the gross income derived from any unrelated trade or business which it regularly conducts.

(ii) The provisions of this subparagraph may be illustrated by the following example:

Example. X is an association of churches on the calendar year basis. X is divided into local units A, B, C, and D. During 1973, A, B, C, and D derive gross income of respectively, $1,200, $800, $1,500, and $700 from unrelated businesses which they regularly conduct. Furthermore, for such taxable year, D files a separate return. X may claim a specific deduction of $1,000 with respect to A, $800 with respect to B, and $1,000 with respect to C. X may not claim a specific deduction with respect to D. D, however, may claim a specific deduction of $700 on its return.

(i) Transitional period for churches. *(1)* (i) In the case of an unrelated trade or business (as defined in section 513) carried on before May 27, 1969, by a church or convention or association of churches (as defined in § 1.511-2(a)(3)(ii)), or by the predecessor of a church or convention or association of churches, all gross income derived from such unrelated trade or business and all deductions directly connected with the carrying on of such unrelated trade or business shall be excluded from the determination of unrelated business taxable income under section 512(a) for all taxable years beginning before January 1, 1976. Notwithstanding the preceding sentence, in the case of income from debt-financed property (and the deductions attributable thereto), as defined in section 514, of a church or convention or association of churches or by the predecessor of a church or convention or association of churches, the provisions of paragraphs (a) through (e) of section 514 and paragraph (4) of section 512(b) shall apply for taxable years beginning after December 31, 1969.

(ii) The provisions of subdivision (i) may be illustrated by the following example:

Example. X, a church as defined in § 1.151-2(a)(3)(ii), realizes gross income from an unrelated business (as defined in section 513) of $100,000 for calendar year 1972. X's predecessor church, Y, began conducting such unrelated business in January 1, 1968. Of the $100,000 realized for calendar year 1972, $40,000 is attributable to debt-financed property (as defined in section 514). Since the unrelated business was conducted by Y prior to May 27, 1969, and since X's taxable year begins before January 1, 1976, that amount of the income realized from such business (and all deductions directly connected therewith) which is not attributable to debt-financed property shall be excluded from the determination of unrelated business taxable income under section 512(a). Therefore, of the $100,000 realized, $60,000 ($100,000 less $40,000 attributable to debt-financed property), and all deductions directly connected therewith shall be excluded from the determination of such unrelated business taxable income for purposes of imposition of the tax under section 511(a). The remaining $40,000 and the deductions attributable thereto shall be subject to the provisions of paragraphs (a) through (e) of section 514 and paragraph (4) of section 512(b).

(2) This paragraph shall not apply in the case of income from property, or deductions directly connected with such income, if title to the property is held by a corporation described in section 501(c)(2) for a church or convention or association of churches. Thus, if such income is derived from an unrelated trade or business, the corporation shall be liable for tax imposed by section 511(a) on such income.

(j) Special rule for certain unrelated trades or businesses carried on by a religious order or by an educational institution maintained by such order. *(1)* Except as provided in subparagraph (2) of this paragraph, gross income realized by a religious order (or an educational organization described in section 170(b)(1)(A)(ii)) maintained by such order) from an unrelated trade or business, together with all deductions directly connected therewith, shall be excluded from the determination of unrelated business taxable income under section 512(a), if—

(i) The trade or business has been operated by such order or by such institution since before May 27, 1959,

(ii) The trade or business consists of providing services under a license issued by a Federal regulatory agency,

(iii) More than 90 percent of the net income from the business is, for each taxable year for which gross income from such business is so excluded by reason of section 512(b)(15) and this paragraph devoted to religious, charitable, or educational purposes, and

(iv) It is established to the satisfaction of an officer no lower than the Regional Commissioner that the rates or other charges for such services are fully competitive with rates or other charges charged for such services by persons not exempt from taxation. Rates or other charges for such services shall be considered as fully competitive with rates or other charges charged for such services by persons not exempt from taxation if the rates charged by such unrelated trade or business are neither materially higher nor materially lower than the rates charged by similar businesses operating in the same general area.

(2) The provisions of this paragraph shall not apply with respect to income from debt-financed property (as defined in section 514) and the deductions attributable thereto. For taxable years beginning after December 31, 1969, such income and deductions are subject to the provisions of paragraphs (a) through (e) of section 514 and paragraph (4) of section 512(b).

(k) Income and deductions from debt-financed property. For taxable years beginning after December 31, 1969, in the case of debt-financed property (as defined in section 514(b)), there shall be included in the unrelated business taxable income of an exempt organization, as an item of gross income derived from an unrelated trade or business, the amount of unrelated debt-financed income determined under section 514(a)(1) and § 1.514(a)-1(a), and there shall be allowed, as a deduction with respect to such income, the amount determined under section 514(a)(2) and § 1.514(a)-1(b).

(l) Interest, annuities, royalties, and rents from controlled organizations. *(1) In general.* For taxable years beginning after December 31, 1969, if an exempt organization (hereinafter referred to as the "controlling organization") has control (as defined in subparagraph (4) of this paragraph) of another organization (hereinafter referred to as the "controlled organization"), the controlling organization shall include as an item of gross income in computing its unrelated business taxable income, the amount of interest, annuities, royalties, and rents derived from the controlled organization determined under subparagraph (2) or (3) of this paragraph. The preceding sentence shall apply whether or not the activity conducted by the controlling organization to derive such amounts represents a trade or business or is regularly carried on. Thus, amounts received by a controlling organization from the rental of its real property to a controlled organization may be included in the unrelated business taxable income of the controlling organization, even though the rental of such property is not an activity regularly carried on by the controlling organization.

(2) Exempt controlled organization. (i) In general. If the controlled organization is exempt from taxation under section 501(a), the amount referred to in subparagraph (1) of this paragraph is an amount which bears the same ratio to the interest, annuities, royalties, and rents received by the controlling organization from the controlled organization as the unrelated business taxable income of the controlled organization bears to whichever of the following amounts is the greater—

(a) The taxable income of the controlled organization, computed as though the controlled organization were not exempt from taxation under section 501(a), or

(b) The unrelated business taxable income of the controlled organization,

both determined without regard to any amounts paid directly or indirectly to the controlling organization shall be allowed all deductions directly connected with amounts included in gross income under the preceding sentences.

(ii) Examples. This subparagraph may be illustrated by the following examples:

Example (1). A, an exempt scientific organization described in section 501(c)(3), owns all the stock of B, another exempt scientific organization described in section 501(c)(3). During 1971, A rents space for a laboratory to B for $15,000 a year. A's total deductions for 1971 with respect to the leased property are $3,000: $1,000 for maintenance and $2,000 for depreciation. If B were not an exempt organization, its total taxable income would be $300,000, disregarding rent paid to A. B's unrelated business taxable income, disregarding rent paid to A, is $100,000. Under these circumstances, $4,000 of the rent paid by B will be included by A as net rental income in determining its unrelated business taxable income, computed as follows:

B's unrelated business taxable income (disregarding rent paid to A)	$100,000
B's taxable income (computed as though B were not exempt and disregarding rent paid to A)	$300,000
Ratio ($100,000/$300,000)	⅓
Total rent	$ 15,000
Total deductions	$ 3,000
Rental income treated as gross income from an unrelated trade or business (⅓ of $15,000)	$ 5,000
Less deductions directly connected with such income (⅓ of $3,000)	$ 1,000
Net rental income included by A in computing its unrelated business taxable income	$ 4,000

Example (2). Assume the facts as stated in example (1), except that B's taxable income is $90,000 (computed as though B were not an exempt organization, and disregarding rents paid to A). B's unrelated business taxable income ($100,000) is therefore greater than its taxable income ($90,000). Thus, the ratio used to determine the portion of rent received by A which is to be taken into account is one since both the numerator and denominator of such ratio is B's unrelated business taxable income. Consequently, all the rent received by A from B ($15,000), and all the deductions directly connected therewith ($3,000), are included by A in computing its unrelated business taxable income.

(3) Nonexempt controlled organization. (i) In general. If the controlled organization is not exempt from taxation under section 501(a), the amount referred to in subparagraph (1) of this paragraph is an amount which bears the same ratio to the interest, annuities, royalties, and rents received by the controlling organization from the controlled organization as the "excess taxable income" (as defined in subdivision (ii) of this subparagraph) of the controlled organization bears to whichever of the following amounts is the greater—

(a) The taxable income of the controlled organization, or

(b) The excess taxable income of the controlled organization,

both determined without regard to any amount paid directly or indirectly to the controlling organization. The controlling organization shall be allowed all deductions which are directly connected with amounts included in gross income under the preceding sentence.

(ii) Excess taxable income. For purposes of this paragraph, the term "excess taxable income" means the excess of the controlled organization's taxable income over the amount of such taxable income which, if derived directly by the controlling organization, would not be unrelated business taxable income.

(iii) Examples. This subparagraph may be illustrated by the following examples:

Example (1). A, an exempt university described in section 501(c)(3), owns all the stock of M, a nonexempt organization. During 1971, M leases a factory and a dormitory from A for a total annual rental of $100,000. During the taxable year, M has $500,000 of taxable income, disregarding the rent paid to A: $150,000 from a dormitory for students of A university, and $350,000 from the operation of a factory which is a business unrelated to A's exempt purpose. A's deductions for 1971 with respect to the leased property are $4,000 for the dormitory and $16,000 for the factory. Under these circumstances, $56,000 of the rent paid by M will be included by A as net rental income in determining its unrelated business taxable income, computed as follows:

M's taxable income (disregarding rent paid to A)	$500,000
Less taxable income from dormitory	150,000
Excess taxable income	$350,000
Ratio ($350,000/$500,000)	7/10
Total rent paid to A	$100,000
Total deductions ($4,000 + $16,000)	20,000
Rental income treated as gross income from an unrelated trade or business (7/10 of $100,000)	$ 70,000
Less deductions directly connected with such income (7/10 of $20,000)	$ 14,000
Net rental income included by A in computing its unrelated business taxable income	$ 56,000

Example (2). Assume the facts as stated in example (1), except that M's taxable income (disregarding rent paid to A) is $300,000, consisting of $350,000 from the operation of the factory and a $50,000 loss from the operation of the dormitory. Thus, M's "excess taxable income" is also $300,000, since none of M's taxable income would be excluded from the computation of A's unrelated business taxable income if received directly by A. The ratio of M's "excess taxable income" to its taxable income is therefore one ($350,000/$300,000). Thus, all the rent received by A from M ($100,000), and all the deductions directly connected therewith ($20,000), are included in the computation of A's unrelated business taxable income.

(4) Control. (i) In general. For purposes of this paragraph—

(a) Stock corporation. In the case of an organization which is a stock corporation, the term "control" means ownership by an exempt organization of stock possessing at least 80 percent of the total combined voting power of all classes of stock entitled to vote and at least 80 percent of the total number of shares of all other classes of stock of such corporation.

(b) Nonstock organization. In the case of a nonstock organization, the term "control" means that at least 80 percent of the directors or trustees of such organization are either representatives of or directly or indirectly controlled by an exempt organization. A trustee or director is a representative of an exempt organization if he is a trustee, director, agent, or employee of such exempt organization. A trustee or director is controlled by an exempt organization if such organization has the power to remove such trustee or director and designate a new trustee or director.

(ii) Gain or loss of control. If control of an organization (as defined in subdivision (i) of this subparagraph) is acquired or relinquished during the taxable year, only the interest, annuities, royalties, and rents paid or accrued to the controlling organization in accordance with its method of accounting for that portion of the taxable year it has control shall be subject to the tax on unrelated business income.

(5) Amounts taxable under other provisions of the Code. (i) In general. Except as provided in subdivision (ii) of this subparagraph, section 512(b)(13) and this paragraph do not apply to amounts which are included in the computation of unrelated business taxable income by operation of any other section of the Code. However, amounts which are not included in unrelated business taxable income by operation of section 512(a)(1), or which are excluded by operation of section 512(b)(1), (2), or (3), may be included in unrelated business taxable income by operation of section 512(b)(13) and this paragraph.

(ii) Debt-financed property. Rents derived from the lease of debt-financed property by a controlling organization to a controlled organization are subject to the rules contained in section 512(b)(13) and this paragraph. Thus, if a controlling organization leases debt-financed property to a controlled organization, the amount of rents includible in the controlling organization's unrelated business taxable income shall first be determined under section 512(b)(13) and this paragraph, and only the portion of such rents not taken into account by operation of section 512(b)(13) are taken into account by operation of section 514. See example (3) of § 1.514(b)-1(b)(3).

T.D. 6301, 7/8/58, amend T.D. 6939, 12/11/67, T.D. 7177, 4/7/72, T.D. 7183, 4/20/72, T.D. 7261, 3/11/73, T.D. 7632, 7/19/79, T.D. 7767, 2/3/81, T.D. 8423, 7/28/92.

§ 1.512(c)-1 Special rules applicable to partnerships; in general.

Caution: The Treasury has not yet amended Reg § 1.512(c)-1 to reflect changes made by P.L. 100-203, P.L. 85-367.

In the event an organization to which section 511 applies is a member of a partnership regularly engaged in a trade or business which is an unrelated trade or business with respect to such organization, the organization shall include in computing its unrelated business taxable income so much of its share (whether or not distributed) of the partnership gross income as is derived from that unrelated business and its share of the deductions attributable thereto. For this purpose, both the gross income and the deductions shall be computed with the necessary adjustments for the exceptions, additions, and limitations referred to in section 512(b) and in § 1.512(b)-1. For example, if an exempt educational institution is a partner in a partnership which operates a factory and if such partnership also holds stock in a corporation, the exempt organization shall include in computing its unrelated business taxable income its share of the gross income from the operation of the factory, but not its share of any dividends received by the partnership from the corporation. If the taxable year of the organization differs from that of the partnership, the amounts included or deducted in computing unrelated business taxable income shall be based upon the income and deductions of the partnership for each taxable year of the partnership ending within or with the taxable year of the organization.

T.D. 6301, 7/8/58.

---

§ 1.513-1 Definition of unrelated trade or business.

(a) In general. As used in section 512 the term "unrelated business taxable income" means the gross income derived by an organization from any unrelated trade or business regularly carried on by it, less the deductions and subject to the modifications provided in section 512. Section 513 specifies with certain exceptions that the phrase "unrelated trade or business" means, in the case of an organization subject to the tax imposed by section 511, any trade or business the conduct of which is not substantially related (aside from the need of such organization for income or funds or the use it makes of the profits derived) to the exercise or performance by such organization of its charitable, educational, or other purpose or function constituting the basis for its exemption under section 501 (or, in the case of an organization described in section 511(a)(2)(B), to the exercise or performance of any purpose or function described in section 501(c)(3)). (For certain exceptions from this definition, see paragraph (e) of this section. For a special definition of "unrelated trade or business" applicable to certain trusts, see section 513(b).) Therefore, unless one of the specific exceptions of section 512 or 513 is applicable, gross income of an exempt organization subject to the tax imposed by section 511 is includible in the computation of unrelated business taxable income if: (1) It is income from trade or business; (2) such trade or business is regularly carried on by the organization; and (3) the conduct of such trade or business is not substantially related (other than through the production of funds) to the organization's performance of its exempt functions.

(b) Trade or business. The primary objective of adoption of the unrelated business income tax was to eliminate a source of unfair competition by placing the unrelated business activities of certain exempt organizations upon the same tax basis as the nonexempt business endeavors with which they compete. On the other hand, where an activity does not possess the characteristics of a trade or business within the meaning of section 162, such as when an organization sends out low-cost articles incidental to the solicitation of charitable contributions, the unrelated business income tax does not apply since the organization is not in competition with taxable organizations. However, in general, any activity of a section 511 organization which is carried on for the production of income and which otherwise possesses the characteristics required to constitute "trade or business" within the meaning of section 162—and which, in addition, is not substantially related to the performance of exempt functions—presents sufficient likelihood of unfair competition to be within the policy of the tax. Accordingly, for purposes of section 513 the term "trade or business" has the same meaning it has in section 162, and generally includes any activity carried on for the production of income from the sale of goods or performance of services. Thus, the term "trade or business" in section 513 is not limited to integrated aggregates of assets, activities and good will which comprise businesses for the purposes of certain other provisions of the Internal Revenue Code. Activities of producing or distributing goods or performing services from which a particular amount of gross income is derived do not lose identity as trade or business merely because they are carried on within a larger aggregate of similar activities or within a larger complex of other endeavors which may, or may not, be related to the exempt purposes of the organization. Thus, for example, the regular sale of pharmaceutical supplies to the general public by a hospital pharmacy does not lose identity as trade or business merely because the pharmacy also furnishes supplies to the hospital and patients of the hospital in accordance with its exempt purposes or in compliance with the terms of section 513(a)(2). Similarly, activities of soliciting, selling, and publishing commercial advertising do not lose identity as a trade or business even though the advertising is published in an exempt organization periodical which contains editorial matter related to the exempt purposes of the organization. However, where an activity carried on for the production of income constitutes an unrelated trade or business, no part of such trade or business shall be excluded from such classification merely because it does not result in profit.

(c) Regularly carried on. *(1) General principles.* In determining whether trade or business from which a particular amount of gross income derives is "regularly carried on," within the meaning of section 512, regard must be had to the frequency and continuity with which the activities productive of the income are conducted and the manner in which they are pursued. This requirement must be applied in light of the purpose of the unrelated business income tax to place exempt organization business activities upon the same tax basis as the nonexempt business endeavors with which they compete. Hence, for example, specific business activities of an exempt organization will ordinarily be deemed to be "regularly carried on" if they manifest a frequency and continuity, and are pursued in a manner, generally similar to comparable commercial activities of nonexempt organizations.

(2) Application of principles in certain cases. (i) Normal time span of activities. Where income producing activities are of a kind normally conducted by nonexempt commercial organizations on a year-round basis, the conduct of such activities by an exempt organization over a period of only a few weeks does not constitute the regular carrying on of trade or business. For example, the operation of a sandwich stand by a hospital auxiliary for only 2 weeks at a state fair

would not be the regular conduct of trade or business. However, the conduct of year-round business activities for one day each week would constitute the regular carrying on of trade or business. Thus, the operation of a commercial parking lot on Saturday of each week would be the regular conduct of trade or business. Where income producing activities are of a kind normally undertaken by nonexempt commercial organizations only on a seasonal basis, the conduct of such activities by an exempt organization during a significant portion of the season ordinarily constitutes the regular conduct of trade or business. For example, the operation of a track for horse racing for several weeks of a year would be considered the regular conduct of trade or business because it is usual to carry on such trade or business only during a particular season.

(ii) Intermittent activities; in general. In determining whether or not intermittently conducted activities are regularly carried on, the manner of conduct of the activities must be compared with the manner in which commercial activities are normally pursued by non-exempt organizations. In general, exempt organization business activities which are engaged in only discontinuously or periodically will not be considered regularly carried on if they are conducted without the competitive and promotional efforts typical of commercial endeavors. For example, the publication of advertising in programs for sports events or music or drama performances will not ordinarily be deemed to be the regular carrying on of business. Similarly, where an organization sells certain types of goods or services to a particular class of persons in pursuance of its exempt functions or "primarily for the convenience" of such persons within the meaning of section 513(a)(2) (as, for example, the sale of books by a college bookstore to students or the sale of pharmaceutical supplies by a hospital pharmacy to patients of the hospital), casual sales in the course of such activity which do not qualify as related to the exempt function involved or as described in section 513(a)(2) will not be treated as regular. On the other hand, where the nonqualifying sales are not merely casual, but are systematically and consistently promoted and carried on by the organization, they meet the section 512 requirement of regularity.

(iii) Intermittent activities; special rule in certain cases of infrequent conduct. Certain intermittent income producing activities occur so infrequently that neither their recurrence nor the manner of their conduct will cause them to be regarded as trade or business regularly carried on. For example, income producing or fund raising activities lasting only a short period of time will not ordinarily be treated as regularly carried on if they recur only occasionally or sporadically. Furthermore, such activities will not be regarded as regularly carried on merely because they are conducted on an annually recurrent basis. Accordingly, income derived from the conduct of an annual dance or similar fund raising event for charity would not be income from trade or business regularly carried on.

(d) Substantially related. *(1) In general.* Gross income derives from "unrelated trade or business," within the meaning of section 513(a), if the conduct of the trade or business which produces the income is not substantially related (other than through the production of funds) to the purposes for which exemption is granted. The presence of this requirement necessitates an examination of the relationship between the business activities which generate the particular income in question—the activities, that is, of producing or distributing the goods or performing the services involved—and the accomplishment of the organization's exempt purposes.

(2) Type of relationship required. Trade or business is "related" to exempt purposes, in the relevant sense, only where the conduct of the business activities has causal relationship to the achievement of exempt purposes (other than through the production of income); and it is "substantially related," for purposes of section 513, only if the causal relationship is a substantial one. Thus, for the conduct of trade or business from which a particular amount of gross income is derived to be substantially related to purposes for which exemption is granted, the production or distribution of the goods or the performance of the services from which the gross income is derived must contributed importantly to the accomplishment of those purposes. Where the production or distribution of the goods or the performance of the services does not contribute importantly to the accomplishment of the exempt purposes of an organization, the income from the sale of the goods or the performance of the services does not derive from the conduct of related trade or business. Whether activities productive of gross income contribute importantly to the accomplishment of any purpose for which an organization is granted exemption depends in each case upon the facts and circumstances involved.

(3) Size and extent of activities. In determining whether activities contribute importantly to the accomplishment of an exempt purpose, the size and extent of the activities involved must be considered in relation to the nature and extent of the exempt function which they purport to serve. Thus, where income is realized by an exempt organization from activities which are in part related to the performance of its exempt functions, but which are conducted on a larger scale than is reasonably necessary for performance of such functions, the gross income attributable to that portion of the activities in excess of the needs of exempt functions constitutes gross income from the conduct of unrelated trade or business. Such income is not derived from the production or distribution of goods or the performance of services which contribute importantly to the accomplishment of any exempt purpose of the organization.

(4) Application of principles. (i) Income from performance of exempt functions. Gross income derived from charges for the performance of exempt functions does not constitute gross income from the conduct of unrelated trade or business. The following examples illustrate the application of this principle:

Example (1). M, an organization described in section 501(c)(3), operates a school for training children in the performing arts, such as acting, singing, and dancing. It presents performances by its students and derives gross income from admission charges for the performances. The students' participation in performances before audiences is an essential part of their training. Since the income realized from the performances derives from activities which contribute importantly to the accomplishment of M's exempt purposes, it does not constitute gross income from unrelated trade or business. (For specific exclusion applicable in certain cases of contributed services, see section 513(a)(1) and paragraph (e)(1) of this section.)

Example (2). N is a trade union qualified for exemption under section 501(c)(5). To improve the trade skills of its members, N conducts refresher training courses and supplies handbooks and technical manuals. N receives payments from its members for these services and materials. However, the development and improvement of the skills of its members is one of the purposes for which exemption is granted N; and the activities described contribute importantly to that purpose. Therefore, the income derived from these activities does not constitute gross income from unrelated trade or business.

Example (3). O is an industry trade association qualified for exemption under section 501(c)(6). It presents a trade show in which members of its industry join in an exhibition of industry products. O derives income from charges made to exhibitors for exhibit space and admission fees charged patrons or viewers of the show. The show is not a sales facility for individual exhibitors; its purpose is the promotion and stimulation of interest in, and demand for, the industry's products in general, and it is conducted in a manner reasonably calculated to achieve that purpose. The stimulation of demand for the industry's products in general is one of the purposes for which exemption is granted O. Consequently, the activities productive of O's gross income from the show—that is, the promotion, organization and conduct of the exhibition—contribute importantly to the achievement of an exempt purpose, and the income does not constitute gross income from unrelated trade or business. See also section 513(d) and regulations thereunder regarding sales activity.

(ii) Disposition of product of exempt functions. Ordinarily, gross income from the sale of products which result from the performance of exempt functions does not constitute gross income from the conduct of unrelated trade or business if the product is sold in substantially the same state it is in on completion of the exemption functions. Thus, in the case of an organization described in section 501(c)(3) and engaged in a program of rehabilitation of handicapped persons, income from sale of articles made by such persons as a part of their rehabilitation training would not be gross income from conduct of unrelated trade or business. The income in such case would be from sale of products, the production of which contributed importantly to the accomplishment of purposes for which exemption is granted the organization— namely, rehabilitation of the handicapped. On the other hand, if a product resulting from an exempt function is utilized or exploited in further business endeavor beyond that reasonably appropriate or necessary for disposition in the state it is in upon completion of exempt functions, the gross income derived therefrom would be from conduct of unrelated trade or business. Thus, in the case of an experimental dairy herd maintained for scientific purposes by a research organization described in section 501(c)(3), income from sale of milk and cream produced in the ordinary course of operation of the project would not be gross income from conduct of unrelated trade or business. On the other hand, if the organization were to utilize the milk and cream in the further manufacture of food items such as ice cream pastries, etc., the gross income from the sale of such products would be from the conduct of unrelated trade or business unless the manufacturing activities themselves contribute importantly to the accomplishment of an exempt purpose of the organization.

(iii) Dual use of assets or facilities. In certain cases, an asset or facility necessary to the conduct of exempt functions may also be employed in a commercial endeavor. In such cases, the mere fact of the use of the asset or facility in exempt functions does not, by itself, make the income from the commercial endeavor gross income from related trade or business. The test, instead, is whether the activities productive of the income in question contribute importantly to the accomplishment of exempt purposes. Assume, for example, that a museum exempt under section 501(c)(3) has a theater auditorium which is specially designed and equipped for showing of educational films in connection with its program of public education in the arts and sciences. The theater is a principal feature of the museum and is in continuous operation during the hours the museum is open to the public. If the organization were to operate the theater as an ordinary motion picture theater for public entertainment during the evening hours when the museum was closed, gross income from such operation would be gross income from conduct of unrelated trade or business.

(iv) Exploitation of exempt functions. In certain cases, activities carried on by an organization in the performance of exempt functions may generate good will or other intangibles which are capable of being exploited in commercial endeavors. Where an organization exploits such an intangible in commercial activities, the mere fact that the resultant income depends in part upon an exempt function of the organization does not make it gross income from related trade or business. In such cases, unless the commercial activities themselves contribute importantly to the accomplishment of an exempt purpose, the income which they produce is gross income from the conduct of unrelated trade or business. The application of this subdivision is illustrated in the following examples:

Example (1). U, an exempt scientific organization, enjoys an excellent reputation in the field of biological research. It exploits this reputation regularly by selling endorsements of various items of laboratory equipment to manufacturers. The endorsing of laboratory equipment does not contribute importantly to the accomplishment of any purpose for which exemption is granted U. Accordingly, the income derived from the sale of endorsements is gross income from unrelated trade or business,

Example (2). V, an exempt university, has a regular faculty and a regularly enrolled student body. During the school year, V sponsors the appearance of professional theater companies and symphony orchestras which present drama and musical performances for the students and faculty members. Members of the general public are also admitted. V advertises these performances and supervises advance ticket sales at various places, including such university facilities as the cafeteria and the university bookstore. V derives gross income from the conduct of the performances. However, while the presentation of the performances make use of an intangible generated by V's exempt educational functions—the presence of the student body and faculty—the presentation of such drama and music events contributes importantly to the overall educational and cultural function of the university. Therefore, the income which V receives does not constitute gross income from the conduct of unrelated trade or business.

Example (3). W is an exempt business league with a large membership. Under an arrangement with an advertising agency, W regularly mails brochures, pamphlets and other commercial advertising materials to its members, for which service W charges the agency an agreed amount per enclosure. The distribution of the advertising materials does not contribute importantly to the accomplishment of any purpose for which W is granted exemption. Accordingly, the payments made to W by the advertising agency constitute gross income from unrelated trade or business.

Example (4). X, an exempt organization for the advancement of public interest in classical music, owns a radio station and operates it in a manner which contributes importantly to the accomplishment of the purposes for which the organization is granted exemption. However, in the course of the operation of the station the organization derives gross incomes from the regular sale of advertising time and services to commercial advertisers in the manner of an ordinary commercial station. Neither the sale of such time nor the performance of such services contributes importantly to the accomplishment of any purpose for which the organization is granted exemption. Notwithstanding the fact that the production of the advertising income depends upon the existence of the listening audience resulting from performance of exempt functions, such income is gross income from unrelated trade or business.

Example (5). Y, an exempt university, provides facilities, instruction and faculty supervision for a campus newspaper operated by its students. In addition to news items and editorial commentary, the newspaper publishes paid advertising. The solicitation, sale, and publication of the advertising are conducted by students, under the supervision and instruction of the university. Although the services rendered to advertisers are of a commercial character, the advertising business contributes importantly to the university's educational program through the training of the students involved. Hence, none of the income derived from publication of the newspaper constitutes gross income from unrelated trade or business. The same results would follow even though the newspaper is published by a separately incorporated section 501(c)(3) organization, qualified under the university rules for recognition of student activities, and even though such organization utilizes its own facilities and is independent of faculty supervision, but carries out its educational purposes by means of student instruction of other students in the editorial and advertising activities and student participation in those activities.

Example (6). Z is an association exempt under section 501(c)(6), formed to advance the interests of a particular profession and drawing its membership from the members of that profession. Z publishes a monthly journal containing articles and other editorial material which contribute importantly to the accomplishment of purposes for which exemption is granted the organization. Income from the sale of subscriptions to members and others in accordance with the organization's exempt purposes, therefore, does not constitute gross income from unrelated trade or business. In connection with the publication of the journal, Z also derives income from the regular sale of space and services for general consumer advertising, including advertising of such products as soft drinks, automobiles, articles of apparel, and home appliances. Neither the publication of such advertisements nor the performance of services for such commercial advertisers contributes importantly to the accomplishment of any purpose for which exemption is granted. Therefore, notwithstanding the fact that the production of income from advertising utilizes the circulation developed and maintained in performance of exempt functions, such income is gross income from unrelated trade or business.

Example (7). The facts are as described in the preceding example, except that the advertising in Z's journal promotes only products which are within the general area of professional interest of its members. Following a practice common among taxable magazines which publish advertising, Z requires its advertising to comply with certain general standards of taste, fairness, and accuracy; but within those limits the form, content, and manner of presentation of the advertising messages are governed by the basic objective of the advertisers to promote the sale of the advertised products. While the advertisements contain certain information, the informational function of the advertising is incidental to the controlling aim of stimulating demand for the advertised products and differs in no essential respect from the informational function of any commercial advertising. Like taxable publishers of advertising, Z accepts advertising only from those who are willing to pay its prescribed rates. Although continuing education of its members in matters pertaining to their profession is one of the purposes for which Z is granted exemption, the publication of advertising designed and selected in the manner of ordinary commercial advertising is not an educational activity of the kind contemplated by the exemption statute; it differs fundamentally from such an activity both in its governing objective and in its method. Accordingly, Z's publication of advertising does not contribute importantly to the accomplishment of its exempt purposes; and the income which it derives from advertising constitutes gross income from unrelated trade or business.

(e) Exceptions. Section 513(a) specifically states that the term "unrelated trade or business" does not include—

(1) Any trade or business in which substantially all the work in carrying on such trade or business is performed for the organization without compensation; or

(2) Any trade or business carried on by an organization described in section 501(c)(3) or by a governmental college or university described in section 511(a)(2)(B), primarily for the convenience of its members, students, patients, officers, or employees; or, any trade or business carried on by a local association of employees described in section 501(c)(4) organized before May 27, 1969, which consists of the selling by the organization of items of work related clothes and equipment and items normally sold through vending machines, through food dispensing facilities, or by snack bars, for the convenience of its members at their usual places of employment; or

(3) Any trade or business which consists of selling merchandise, substantially all of which has been received by the organization as gifts or contributions.

An example of the operation of the first of the exceptions mentioned above would be an exempt orphanage operating a retail store and selling to the general public, where substantially all the work in carrying on such business is performed for the organization by volunteers without compensation. An example of the first part of the second exception, relating to an organization described in section 501(c)(3) or a governmental college or university described in section 511(a)(2)(b), would be a laundry operated by a college for the purpose of laundering dormitory linens and the clothing of students. The latter part of the second exception, dealing with certain sales by local employee associations, will not apply to sales of these items at locations other than the usual place of employment of the employees; therefore sales at such other locations will continue to be treated as unrelated trade or business. The third exception applies to so-called "thrift shops" operated by a tax-exempt organization where those desiring to benefit such organization contribute old clothes, books, furniture, et cetera, to be sold to the general public with the proceeds going to the exempt organization.

(f) Special rule respecting publishing businesses prior to 1970. For a special rule for taxable years beginning before January 1, 1970, with respect to publishing businesses carried on by an organization, see section 513(c) of the Code prior to its amendment by section 121(c) of the Tax Reform Act of 1969 (83 Stat. 542).

(g) Effective date. This section is applicable with respect to taxable years beginning after December 12, 1967. However, if a taxpayer wishes to rely on the rules stated in this section for taxable years beginning before December 13, 1967, it may do so.

T.D. 6939, 12/11/67, amend T.D. 7107, 4/2/71, T.D. 7392, 12/17/75, T.D. 7896, 5/26/83.

§ 1.513-2 Definition of unrelated trade or business applicable to taxable years beginning before December 13, 1967.

(a) In general. *(1)* As used in section 512(a), the term unrelated business taxable income includes only income from an unrelated trade or business regularly carried on, and the term trade or business has the same meaning as it has in section 162.

(2) The income of an exempt organization is subject to the tax on unrelated business income only if two conditions are present with respect to such income. The first condition is that the income must be from a trade or business which is regularly carried on by the organization. The second condition is that the trade or business must not be substantially related (aside from the need of the organization for income or funds or the use it makes of the profits derived) to the exercise or performance by such organization of its charitable, educational, or other purpose or function constituting the basis for its exemption under section 501, or in the case of an organization described in section 511(a)(2)(B) (governmental colleges, etc.) to the exercise or performance of any purpose or function described in section 501(c)(3). Whether or not an organization is subject to the tax imposed by section 511 shall be determined by the application of these tests to the particular circumstances involved in each individual case. For certain exceptions from the term unrelated trade or business, see paragraph (b) of this section.

(3) A trade or business is regularly carried on when the activity is conducted with sufficient consistency to indicate a continuing purpose of the organization to derive some of its income from such activity. An activity may be regularly carried on even though its performance is infrequent or seasonal.

(4) Ordinarily, a trade or business is substantially related to the activities for which an organization is granted exemption if the principal purpose of such trade or business is to further (other than through the production of income) the purpose for which the organization is granted exemption. In the usual case the nature and size of the trade or business must be compared with the nature and extent of the activities for which the organization is granted exemption in order to determine whether the principal purpose of such trade or business is to further (other than through the production of income) the purpose for which the organization is granted exemption. For example, the operation of a wheat farm is substantially related to the exempt activity of an agricultural college if the wheat farm is operated as a part of the educational program of the college, and is not operated on a scale disproportionately large when compared with the educational program of the college. Similarly, a university radio station or press is considered a related trade or business if operated primarily as an integral part of the educational program of the university, but is considered an unrelated trade or business if operated in substantially the same manner as a commercial radio station or publishing house. A trade or business not otherwise related does not become substantially related to an organization's exempt purpose merely because incidental use is made of the trade or business in order to further the exempt purpose. For example, the manufacture and sale of a product by an exempt college would not become substantially related merely because students as part of their educational program perform clerical or bookkeeping functions in the business. In some cases, the business may be substantially related because it is a necessary part of the exempt activity. For example, in the case of an organization described in section 501(c)(3) and engaged in the rehabilitation of handicapped persons, the business of selling articles made by such persons as a part of their rehabilitation training would not be considered an unrelated business since such business is a necessary part of the rehabilitation program.

(5) If an organization receives a payment pursuant to a contract or agreement under which such organization is to perform research which constitutes an unrelated trade or business, the entire amount of such payment is income from an unrelated trade or business. See, however, section 512(b), (7), (8), and (9), relating to the exclusion from unrelated business taxable income of income derived from research for the United States, or any State, and of income derived from research performed for any person by a college, university, hospital, or organization operated primarily for the purpose of carrying on fundamental research the results of which are freely available to the general public.

(b) Exceptions. Section 513(a) specifically states that the term unrelated trade or business does not include:

(1) Any trade or business in which substantially all the work in carrying on such trade or business is performed for the organization without compensation; or

(2) Any trade or business carried on by an organization described in section 501(c)(3) or by a governmental college or university described in section 511(a)(2)(B), primarily for the convenience of its members, students, patients, officers, or employees; or

(3) Any trade or business which consists of selling merchandise, substantially all of which has been received by the organization as gifts or contributions.

An example of the operation of the first of the exceptions mentioned above would be an exempt orphanage operating a retail store and selling to the general public, where substantially all the work in carrying on such business is performed for the organization by volunteers without compensation. An example of the second exception would be a laundry operated by a college for the purpose of laundering dormitory linens and the clothing of students. The third exception applies to so-called thrift shops operated by a tax-exempt organization where those desiring to benefit such organization contribute old clothes, books, furniture, etc., to be sold to the general public with the proceeds going to the exempt organization.

(c) Special rules respecting publishing businesses. For a special rule with respect to publishing businesses carried on by an organization, see section 513(c) of the Code prior to its amendment by section 121(c) of the Tax Reform Act of 1969 (83 Stat. 542).

(d) Effective date. Except as provided in paragraph (g) of § 1.513-1, this section is applicable with respect to taxable years beginning before December 13, 1967.

T.D. 6939, 12/11/67, amend T.D. 7392, 12/17/75.

§ 1.513-3 Qualified convention and trade show activity.

Caution: The Treasury has not yet amended Reg § 1.513-3 to reflect changes made by P.L. 99-514.

(a) Introduction. *(1) In general.* Section 513(d) and § 1.513-3(b) provide that convention and trade show activities carried on by a qualifying organization in connection with a qualified convention or trade show will not be treated as unrelated trade or business. Consequently, income from qualified convention and trade show activities, derived by a qualifying organization that sponsors the qualified convention or trade show, will not be subject to the tax imposed by section 511. Section 1.513-3(c) defines qualifying organizations and qualified conventions or trade shows. Section 1.513-3(d) concerns the treatment of income derived from certain activities, including rental of exhibition space at a qualified convention or trade show where sales activity is permitted, and the treatment of supplier exhibits at qualified conventions and trade shows.

(2) Effective date. This section is effective for taxable years beginning after October 4, 1976.

(b) Qualified activities not unrelated. A convention or trade show activity, as defined in section 513(d)(3)(A) and § 1.513-3(c)(4), will not be considered unrelated trade or business if it is conducted by a qualifying organization described in section 513(d)(3)(C) and § 1.513-3(c)(1), in conjunction with a qualified convention or trade show, as defined in section 513(d)(3)(B) and § 1.513-3(c)(2), sponsored by the qualifying organization. Such an activity is a qualified convention or trade show activity. A convention or trade show activity which is conducted by an organization described in section 501(c)(5) or (6), but which otherwise is not so qualified under this section, will be considered unrelated trade or business.

(c) Definitions. *(1) Qualifying organization.* Under section 513(d)(3)(C), a qualifying organization is one which—

(i) Is described in either section 501(c)(5) or (6), and

(ii) Regularly conducts as one of its substantial exempt purposes a qualified convention or trade show.

(2) Qualified convention or trade show. For purposes of this section, the term "qualified convention or trade show" means a show that meets the following requirements:

(i) It is conducted by a qualifying organization described in section 513(d)(3)(C);

(ii) At least one purpose of the sponsoring organization in conducting the show is the education of its members, or the promotion and stimulation of interest in, and demand for, the products or services of the industry (or segment thereof) of the members of the qualifying organization; and

(iii) The show is designed to achieve that purpose through the character of a significant portion of the exhibits or the character of conferences and seminars held at a convention or meeting.

(3) Show. For purposes of this section, the term "show" includes an international, national, state, regional, or local convention, annual meeting or show.

(4) Convention and trade show activity. For purposes of this section, convention and trade show activity means any activity of a kind traditionally carried on at shows. It includes, but is not limited to—

(i) Activities designed to attract to the show members of the sponsoring organization, members of an industry in general, and members of the public, to view industry products or services and to stimulate interest in, and demand for such products or services;

(ii) Activities designed to educate persons in the industry about new products or services or about new rules and regulations affecting the industry; and

(iii) Incidental activities, such as furnishing refreshments, of a kind traditionally carried on at such shows.

(d) Certain activities. *(1) Rental of exhibition space.* The rental of display space to exhibitors (including exhibitors who are suppliers) at a qualified trade show or at a qualified convention and trade show will not be considered unrelated trade or business even though the exhibitors who rent the space are permitted to sell or solicit orders.

(2) Suppliers defined. For purposes of subparagraph (1), a supplier's exhibit is one in which the exhibitor displays goods or services that are supplied to, rather than by, the members of the qualifying organization in the conduct of such members' own trades or businesses.

(e) Example. The provisions of this section may be illustrated by the following examples:

Example (1). X, an organization described in section 501(c)(6), was formed to promote the construction industry. Its membership is made up of manufacturers of heavy construction machinery many of whom own, rent, or lease one or more digital computers produced by various computer manufacturers. X is a qualifying organization under section 513(d)(3)(C) that regularly holds an annual meeting. At this meeting a national industry sales campaign and methods of consumer financing for heavy construction machinery are discussed. In addition, new construction machinery developed for use in the industry is on display with representatives of the various manufacturers present to promote their machinery. Both members and nonmembers attend this portion of the conference. In addition, manufacturers of computers are present to educate X's members. While this aspect of the conference is a supplier exhibit (as defined in paragraph (d) of this section), income earned from such activity by X will not constitute unrelated business taxable income to X because the activity is conducted as part of a qualified trade show described in § 1.513-3(c).

Example (2). Assume the same facts as in Example 1, but the only goods or services displayed are those of suppliers, the computer manufacturers. Selling and order taking are permitted. No member exhibits are maintained. Standing alone, this supplier exhibit (as defined in paragraph (d)(2) of this section) would constitute a supplier show and not a qualified convention or trade show. In this situation, however, the rental of exhibition space to suppliers is not unrelated trade or business. It is conducted by a qualifying organization in conjunction with a qualified convention or trade show. The show (the annual meeting) is a qualified convention or trade show because one of its purposes is the promotion and stimulation of interest in, and demand for, the products or services of the industry through the character of the annual meeting.

Example (3). Y is an organization described in section 501(c)(6). The organization conducts an annual show at which its members exhibit their products and services in order to promote public interest in the line of business. Potential customers are invited to the show, and sales and order taking are permitted. The organization secures the exhibition facility, undertakes the planning and direction of the show, and maintains exhibits designed to promote the line of business in general. The show is a qualified convention or trade show described in paragraph (c)(2) of this section. The provision of exhibition space to individual members is a qualified trade show activity, and is not unrelated trade or business.

Example (4). Z is an organization described in section 501(c)(6) that sponsors an annual show. As the sole activity at the show, suppliers to the members of Z exhibit their products and services for the purpose of stimulating the sale of their products. Selling and order taking are permitted. The show is a supplier show and does not meet the definition of a qualified convention show as it does not satisfy any of the three alternative bases for qualification. First, the show does not stimulate interest in the members' products through the character of product exhibits as the only products exhibited are those of suppliers rather than members. Second, the show does not stimulate interest in members' products through conferences or seminars as no such conferences are held at the show. Third, the show does not meet the definition of a qualified show on the basis of educational activities as the exhibition of suppliers' products is designed primarily to stimulate interest in, and sale of, suppliers' products. Thus, the organization's provision of exhibition space is not a qualified convention or trade show activity. Income derived from rentals of exhibition space to suppliers will be unrelated business taxable income under section 512.

T.D. 7896, 5/26/83.

§ 1.513-4 Certain sponsorship not unrelated trade or business.

(a) In general. Under section 513(i), the receipt of qualified sponsorship payments by an exempt organization which is subject to the tax imposed by section 511 does not constitute receipt of income from an unrelated trade or business.

(b) Exception. The provisions of this section do not apply with respect to payments made in connection with qualified convention and trade show activities. For rules governing qualified convention and trade show activity, see § 1.513-3. The provisions of this section also do not apply to income derived from the sale of advertising or acknowledgments in exempt organization periodicals. For this purpose, the term periodical means regularly scheduled and printed material published by or on behalf of the exempt organization that is not related to and primarily distributed in connection with a specific event conducted by the exempt organization. For this purpose, printed material includes material that is published electronically. For rules governing the sale of advertising in exempt organization periodicals, see § 1.512(a)-1(f).

(c) Qualified sponsorship payment. *(1) Definition.* The term qualified sponsorship payment means any payment by any person engaged in a trade or business with respect to which there is no arrangement or expectation that the person will receive any substantial return benefit. In determining whether a payment is a qualified sponsorship payment, it is irrelevant whether the sponsored activity is related or unrelated to the recipient organization's exempt purpose. It is also irrelevant whether the sponsored activity is temporary or permanent. For purposes of this section, payment means the payment of money, transfer of property, or performance of services.

(2) Substantial return benefit. (i) In general. For purposes of this section, a substantial return benefit means any benefit other than a use or acknowledgment described in paragraph (c)(2)(iv) of this section, or disregarded benefits described in paragraph (c)(2)(ii) of this section.

(ii) Certain benefits disregarded. For purposes of paragraph (c)(2)(i) of this section, benefits are disregarded if the aggregate fair market value of all the benefits provided to the payor or persons designated by the payor in connection with the payment during the organization's taxable year is not more than 2% of the amount of the payment. If the aggregate fair market value of the benefits exceeds 2% of the amount of the payment, then (except as provided in paragraph (c)(2)(iv) of this section) the entire fair market value of such benefits, not merely the excess amount, is a substantial return benefit. Fair market value is determined as provided in paragraph (d)(1) of this section.

(iii) Benefits defined. For purposes of this section, benefits provided to the payor or persons designated by the payor may include:

(A) Advertising as defined in paragraph (c)(2)(v) of this section.

(B) Exclusive provider arrangements as defined in paragraph (c)(2)(vi)(B) of this section.

(C) Goods, facilities, services or other privileges.

(D) Exclusive or nonexclusive rights to use an intangible asset (e.g., trademark, patent, logo, or designation) of the exempt organization.

(iv) Use or acknowledgment. For purposes of this section, a substantial return benefit does not include the use or acknowledgment of the name or logo (or product lines) of the payor's trade or business in connection with the activities of the exempt organization. Use or acknowledgment does not include advertising as described in paragraph (c)(2)(v) of this section, but may include the following: exclusive sponsorship arrangements; logos and slogans that do not contain qualitative or comparative descriptions of the payor's products, services, facilities or company; a list of the payor's locations, telephone numbers, or Internet address; value-neutral descriptions, including displays or visual depictions, of the payor's product-line or services; and the payor's brand or trade names and product or service listings. Logos or slogans that are an established part of a payor's identity are not considered to contain qualitative or comparative descriptions. Mere display or distribution, whether for free or remuneration, of a payor's product by the payor or the exempt organization to the general public at the sponsored activity is not considered an inducement to purchase, sell or use the payor's product for purposes of this section and, thus, will not affect the determination of whether a payment is a qualified sponsorship payment.

(v) Advertising. For purposes of this section, the term advertising means any message or other programming material which is broadcast or otherwise transmitted, published, displayed or distributed, and which promotes or markets any trade or business, or any service, facility or product. Advertising includes messages containing qualitative or comparative language, price information or other indications of savings or value, an endorsement, or an inducement to purchase, sell, or use any company, service, facility or product. A single message that contains both advertising and an acknowledgment is advertising. This section does not apply to activities conducted by a payor on its own. For example, if a payor purchases broadcast time from a television station to advertise its product during commercial breaks in a sponsored program, the exempt organization's activities are not thereby converted to advertising.

(vi) Exclusivity arrangements. (A) Exclusive sponsor. An arrangement that acknowledges the payor as the exclusive sponsor of an exempt organization's activity, or the exclusive sponsor representing a particular trade, business or industry, generally does not, by itself, result in a substantial return benefit. For example, if in exchange for a payment, an organization announces that its event is sponsored exclusively by the payor (and does not provide any advertising or other substantial return benefit to the payor), the payor has not received a substantial return benefit.

(B) Exclusive provider. An arrangement that limits the sale, distribution, availability, or use of competing products, services, or facilities in connection with an exempt organization's activity generally results in a substantial return benefit. For example, if in exchange for a payment, the exempt organization agrees to allow only the payor's products to be sold in connection with an activity, the payor has received a substantial return benefit.

(d) Allocation of payment. *(1) In general.* If there is an arrangement or expectation that the payor will receive a substantial return benefit with respect to any payment, then only the portion, if any, of the payment that exceeds the fair market value of the substantial return benefit is a qualified sponsorship payment. However, if the exempt organization does not establish that the payment exceeds the fair market value of any substantial return benefit, then no portion of the payment constitutes a qualified sponsorship payment.

(i) Treatment of payments other than qualified sponsorship payments. The unrelated business income tax (UBIT) treatment of any payment (or portion thereof) that is not a qualified sponsorship payment is determined by application of sections 512, 513 and 514. For example, payments related to an exempt organization's providing facilities, services, or other privileges to the payor or persons designated by the payor, advertising, exclusive provider arrangements described in paragraph (c)(2)(vi)(B) of this section, a license to use intangible assets of the exempt organization, or other substantial return benefits, are evaluated separately in determining whether the exempt organization realizes unrelated business taxable income.

(ii) Fair market value. The fair market value of any substantial return benefit provided as part of a sponsorship arrangement is the price at which the benefit would be provided between a willing recipient and a willing provider of the benefit, neither being under any compulsion to enter into the arrangement and both having reasonable knowledge of relevant facts, and without regard to any other aspect of the sponsorship arrangement.

(iii) Valuation date. In general, the fair market value of the substantial return benefit is determined when the benefit is provided. However, if the parties enter into a binding, written sponsorship contract, the fair market value of any substantial return benefit provided pursuant to that contract is determined on the date the parties enter into the sponsorship contract. If the parties make a material change to a sponsorship contract, it is treated as a new sponsorship contract as of the date the material change is effective. A material change includes an extension or renewal of the contract, or a more than incidental change to any amount payable (or other consideration) pursuant to the contract.

(iv) Examples. The following examples illustrate the provisions of this section:

Example (1). On June 30, 2001, a national corporation and Z, a charitable organization, enter into a five-year binding, written contract effective for years 2002 through 2007. The contract provides that the corporation will make an annual payment of $5,000 to Z, and in return the corporation will receive no benefit other than advertising. On June 30, 2001, the fair market value of the advertising to be provided to the corporation in each year of the agreement is $75, which is less than the disregarded benefit amount provided for in paragraph (c)(2)(ii) of this section (2% of $5,000 is $100). In 2002, pursuant to the sponsorship contract, the corporation makes a payment to Z of $5,000, and receives the specified benefit (advertising). As of January 1, 2002, the fair market value of the advertising to be provided by Z each year has increased to $110. However, for purposes of this section, the fair market value of the advertising benefit is determined on June 30, 2001, the date the parties entered into the sponsorship contract. Therefore, the entire $5,000 payment received in 2002 is a qualified sponsorship payment.

Example (2). The facts are the same as Example 1, except that the contract provides for an initial payment by the corporation to Z of $5,000 in 2002, followed by annual payments of $1,000 during each of years 2003-2007. In 2003, pursuant to the sponsorship contract, the corporation makes a payment to Z of $1,000, and receives the specified advertising benefit. In 2003, the fair market value of the benefit provided ($75, as determined on June 30, 2001) exceeds 2% of the total payment received (2% of $1,000 is $20). Therefore, only $925 of the $1,000 payment received in 2003 is a qualified sponsorship payment.

(2) Anti-abuse provision. To the extent necessary to prevent avoidance of the rule stated in paragraphs (d)(1) and (c)(2) of this section, where the exempt organization fails to make a reasonable and good faith valuation of any substantial return benefit, the Commissioner (or the Commissioner's delegate) may determine the portion of a payment allocable to such substantial return benefit and may treat two or more related payments as a single payment.

(e) Special rules. *(1) Written agreements.* The existence of a written sponsorship agreement does not, in itself, cause a payment to fail to be a qualified sponsorship payment. The terms of the agreement, not its existence or degree of detail, are relevant to the determination of whether a payment is a qualified sponsorship payment. Similarly, the terms of the agreement and not the title or responsibilities of the individuals negotiating the agreement determine whether a payment (or any portion thereof) made pursuant to the agreement is a qualified sponsorship payment.

(2) Contingent payments. The term qualified sponsorship payment does not include any payment the amount of which is contingent, by contract or otherwise, upon the level of attendance at one or more events, broadcast ratings, or other factors indicating the degree of public exposure to the sponsored activity. The fact that a payment is contingent upon sponsored events or activities actually being conducted does not, by itself, cause the payment to fail to be a qualified sponsorship payment.

(3) Determining public support. Qualified sponsorship payments in the form of money or property (but not services) are treated as contributions received by the exempt organization for purposes of determining public support to the organization under section 170(b)(1)(A)(vi) or 509(a)(2). See §§ 1.509(a)-3(f)(1) and 1.170A-9(e)(6)(i). The fact that a payment is a qualified sponsorship payment that is treated as a contribution to the payee organization does not determine whether the payment is deductible by the payor under section 162 or 170.

(f) Examples. The provisions of this section are illustrated by the following examples. The tax treatment of any payment (or portion of a payment) that does not constitute a qualified sponsorship payment is governed by general UBIT principles. In these examples, the recipients of the payments at issue are section 501(c) organizations. The expectations or arrangements of the parties are those specifically indicated in the example. The examples are as follows:

Example (1). M, a local charity, organizes a marathon and walkathon at which it serves to participants drinks and other refreshments provided free of charge by a national corporation. The corporation also gives M prizes to be awarded to winners of the event. M recognizes the assistance of the corporation by listing the corporation's name in promotional fliers, in newspaper advertisements of the event and on T-shirts worn by participants. M changes the name of its event to include the name of the corporation. M's activities constitute acknowledgment of the sponsorship. The drinks, refreshments and prizes provided by the corporation are a qualified sponsorship payment, which is not income from an unrelated trade or business.

Example (2). N, an art museum, organizes an exhibition and receives a large payment from a corporation to help fund the exhibition. N recognizes the corporation's support by using the corporate name and established logo in materials publicizing the exhibition, which include banners, posters, brochures and public service announcements. N also hosts a dinner for the corporation's executives. The fair market value of the dinner exceeds 2% of the total payment. N's use of the corporate name and logo in connection with the exhibition constitutes acknowledgment of the sponsorship. However, because the fair market value of the dinner exceeds 2% of the total payment, the dinner is a substantial return benefit. Only that portion of the payment, if any, that N can demonstrate exceeds the fair market value of the dinner is a qualified sponsorship payment.

Example (3). O coordinates sports tournaments for local charities. An auto manufacturer agrees to underwrite the expenses of the tournaments. O recognizes the auto manufacturer by including the manufacturer's name and established logo in the title of each tournament as well as on signs, scoreboards and other printed material. The auto manufacturer receives complimentary admission passes and pro-am playing spots for each tournament that have a combined fair market value in excess of 2% of the total payment. Additionally, O displays the latest models of the manufacturer's premier luxury cars at each tournament. O's use of the manufacturer's name and logo and display of cars in the tournament area constitute acknowledgment of the sponsorship. However, the admission passes and pro-am playing spots are a substantial return benefit. Only that portion of the payment, if any, that O can demonstrate exceeds the fair market value of the admission passes and pro-am playing spots is a qualified sponsorship payment.

Example (4). P conducts an annual college football bowl game. P sells to commercial broadcasters the right to broadcast the bowl game on television and radio. A major corporation agrees to be the exclusive sponsor of the bowl game. The detailed contract between P and the corporation provides that in exchange for a $1,000,000 payment, the name of the bowl game will include the name of the corporation. In addition, the contract provides that the corporation's name and established logo will appear on player's helmets and uniforms, on the scoreboard and stadium signs, on the playing field, on cups used to serve drinks at the game, and on all related printed material distributed in connection with the game. P also agrees to give the corporation a block of game passes for its employees and to provide advertising in the bowl game program book. The fair market value of the passes is $6,000, and the fair market value of the program advertising is $10,000. The agreement is contingent upon the game being broadcast on television and radio, but the amount of the payment is not contingent upon the number of people attending the game or the television ratings. The contract provides that television cameras will focus on the corporation's name and logo on the field at certain intervals during the game. P's use of the corporation's name and logo in connection with the bowl game constitutes acknowledgment of the sponsorship. The exclusive sponsorship arrangement is not a substantial return benefit. Because the fair market value of the game passes and program advertising ($16,000) does not exceed 2% of the total payment (2% of $1,000,000 is $20,000), these benefits are disregarded and the entire payment is a qualified sponsorship payment, which is not income from an unrelated trade or business.

Example (5). Q organizes an amateur sports team. A major pizza chain gives uniforms to players on Q's team, and also pays some of the team's operational expenses. The uniforms bear the name and established logo of the pizza chain. During the final tournament series, Q distributes free of charge souvenir flags bearing Q's name to employees of the pizza chain who come out to support the team. The flags are valued at less than 2% of the combined fair market value of the uniforms and operational expenses paid. Q's use of the name and logo of the pizza chain in connection with the tournament constitutes acknowledgment of the sponsorship. Because the fair market value of the flags does not exceed 2% of the total payment, the entire amount of the funding and supplied uniforms are a qualified sponsorship payment, which is not income from an unrelated trade or business.

Example (6). R is a liberal arts college. A soft drink manufacturer enters into a binding, written contract with R that provides for a large payment to be made to the college's English department in exchange for R agreeing to name a writing competition after the soft drink manufacturer. The contract also provides that R will allow the soft drink manufacturer to be the exclusive provider of all soft drink sales on campus. The fair market value of the exclusive provider component of the contract exceeds 2% of the total payment. R's use of the manufacturer's name in the writing competition constitutes acknowledgment of the sponsorship. However, the exclusive provider arrangement is a substantial return benefit. Only that portion of the payment, if any, that R can demonstrate exceeds the fair market value of the exclusive provider arrangement is a qualified sponsorship payment.

Example (7). S is a noncommercial broadcast station that airs a program funded by a local music store. In exchange for the funding, S broadcasts the following message: "This program has been brought to you by the Music Shop, located at 123 Main Street. For your music needs, give them a call today at 555-1234. This station is proud to have the Music Shop as a sponsor." Because this single broadcast message contains both advertising and an acknowledgment, the entire message is advertising. The fair market value of the advertising exceeds 2% of the total payment. Thus, the advertising is a substantial return benefit. Unless S establishes that the amount of the payment exceeds the fair market value of the advertising, none of the payment is a qualified sponsorship payment.

Example (8). T, a symphony orchestra, performs a series of concerts. A program guide that contains notes on guest conductors and other information concerning the evening's program is distributed by T at each concert. The Music Shop makes a $1,000 payment to T in support of the concert series. As a supporter of the event, the Music Shop receives complimentary concert tickets with a fair market value of $85, and is recognized in the program guide and on a poster in the lobby of the concert hall. The lobby poster states that, "The T concert is sponsored by the Music Shop, located at 123 Main Street, telephone number 555-1234." The program guide contains the same information and also states, "Visit the Music Shop today for the finest selection of music CDs and cassette tapes." The fair market value of the advertisement in the program guide is $15. T's use of the Music Shop's name, address and telephone number in the lobby poster constitutes acknowledgment of the sponsorship.

However, the combined fair market value of the advertisement in the program guide and complimentary tickets is $100 ($15 + $85), which exceeds 2% of the total payment (2% of $1,000 is $20). The fair market value of the advertising and complimentary tickets, therefore, constitutes a substantial return benefit and only that portion of the payment, or $900, that exceeds the fair market value of the substantial return benefit is a qualified sponsorship payment.

Example (9). U, a national charity dedicated to promoting health, organizes a campaign to inform the public about potential cures to fight a serious disease. As part of the campaign, U sends representatives to community health fairs around the country to answer questions about the disease and inform the public about recent developments in the search for a cure. A pharmaceutical company makes a payment to U to fund U's booth at a health fair. U places a sign in the booth displaying the pharmaceutical company's name and slogan, "Better Research, Better Health," which is an established part of the company's identity. In addition, U grants the pharmaceutical company a license to use U's logo in marketing its products to health care providers around the country. The fair market value of the license exceeds 2% of the total payment received from the company. U's display of the pharmaceutical company's name and slogan constitutes acknowledgment of the sponsorship. However, the license granted to the pharmaceutical company to use U's logo is a substantial return benefit. Only that portion of the payment, if any, that U can demonstrate exceeds the fair market value of the license granted to the pharmaceutical company is a qualified sponsorship payment.

Example (10). V, a trade association, publishes a monthly scientific magazine for its members containing information about current issues and developments in the field. A textbook publisher makes a large payment to V to have its name displayed on the inside cover of the magazine each month. Because the monthly magazine is a periodical within the meaning of paragraph (b) of this section, the section 513(i) safe harbor does not apply. See § 1.512(a)-1(f).

Example (11). W, a symphony orchestra, maintains a website containing pertinent information and its performance schedule. The Music Shop makes a payment to W to fund a concert series, and W posts a list of its sponsors on its website, including the Music Shop's name and Internet address. W's website does not promote the Music Shop or advertise its merchandise. The Music Shop's Internet address appears as a hyperlink from W's website to the Music Shop's website. W's posting of the Music Shop's name and Internet address on its website constitutes acknowledgment of the sponsorship. The entire payment is a qualified sponsorship payment, which is not income from an unrelated trade or business.

Example (12). X, a health-based charity, sponsors a yearlong initiative to educate the public about a particular medical condition. A large pharmaceutical company manufactures a drug that is used in treating the medical condition, and provides funding for the initiative that helps X produce educational materials for distribution and post information on X's website. X's website contains a hyperlink to the pharmaceutical company's website. On the pharmaceutical company's website, the statement appears, "X endorses the use of our drug, and suggests that you ask your doctor for a prescription if you have this medical condition." X reviewed the endorsement before it was posted on the pharmaceutical company's website and gave permission for the endorsement to appear. The endorsement is advertising. The fair market value of the advertising exceeds 2% of the total payment received from the pharmaceutical company. Therefore, only the portion of the payment, if any, that X can demonstrate exceeds the fair market value of the advertising on the pharmaceutical company's website is a qualified sponsorship payment.

T.D. 8991, 4/24/2002.

---

§ 1.513-5 Certain bingo games not unrelated trade or business.

(a) In general. Under section 513(f), and subject to the limitations in paragraph (C) of this section, in the case of an organization subject to the tax imposed by section 511, the term "unrelated trade or business" does not include any trade or business that consists of conducting bingo games (as defined in paragraph (d) of this section).

(b) Exception. The provisions of this section shall not apply with respect to any bingo game otherwise excluded from the term "unrelated trade or business" by reason of section 513(a)(1) and § 1.513-1(e)(1) (relating to trades or businesses in which substantially all the work is performed without compensation).

(c) Limitations. *(1) Bingo games must be legal.* Paragraph (a) of this section shall not apply with respect to any bingo game conducted in violation of State or local law.

(2) No commercial competition. Paragraph (a) of this section shall not apply with respect to any bingo game conducted in a jurisdiction in which bingo games are ordinarily carried out on a commercial basis. Bingo games are "ordinarily carried out on a commercial basis" within a jurisdiction if they are regularly carried on (within the meaning of § 1.513-1(c)) by for-profit organizations in any part of that jurisdiction. Normally, the entire State will constitute the appropriate jurisdiction for determining whether bingo games are ordinarily carried out on a commercial basis. However, if State law permits local jurisdictions to determine whether bingo games may be conducted by for-profit organizations, or if State law limits or confines the conduct by for-profit organizations to specific local jurisdictions, then the local jurisdiction will constitute the appropriate jurisdiction for determining whether bingo games are ordinarily carried out on a commercial basis.

(3) Examples. The application of this paragraph is illustrated by the examples that follow. In each example, it is assumed that the bingo games referred to are operated by individuals who are compensated for their services. Accordingly, none of the bingo games would be excluded from the term "unrelated trade or business" under section 513(a)(1).

Example (1). Church Z, a tax-exempt organization, conducts weekly bingo games in State O. State and local laws in State O expressly provide that bingo games may be conducted by tax-exempt organizations. Bingo games are not conducted in State O by any for-profit businesses. Since Z's bingo games are not conducted in violation of State or local law and are not the type of activity ordinarily carried out on a commercial basis in State O, Z's bingo games do not constitute unrelated trade or business.

Example (2). Rescue Squad X, a tax-exempt organization, conducts weekly bingo games in State M. State M has a statutory provision that prohibits all forms of gambling including bingo games. However, that law generally is not enforced by State officials against local charitable organizations such as X that conduct bingo games to raise funds. Since bingo games are illegal under State law, X's bingo games constitute unrelated trade or business regardless of the degree to which the State law is enforced.

Example (3). Veteran's organizations Y and X, both tax-exempt organizations, are organized under the laws of State N. State N has a statutory provision that permits bingo games to be conducted by tax-exempt organizations. In addition, State N permits bingo games to be conducted by for-profit organizations in city S, a resort community located in county R. Several for-profit organizations conduct nightly bingo games in city S. Y conducts weekly bingo games in city S. X conducts weekly bingo games in county R. Since State law confines the conduct of bingo games by for-profit organizations to city S, and since bingo games are regularly carried on there by those organizations, Y's bingo games conducted in city S constitute unrelated trade or business. However, X's bingo games conducted in county R outside of city S do not constitute unrelated trade or business.

(d) Bingo game defined. A bingo game is a game of chance played with cards that are generally printed with five rows of five squares each. Participants place markers over randomly called numbers on the cards in an attempt to form a preselected pattern such as a horizontal, vertical, or diagonal line, or all four corners. The first participant to form the preselected pattern wins the game. As used in this section, the term "bingo game" means any game of bingo of the type described above in which wagers are placed, winners are determined, and prizes or other property is distributed in the presence of all persons placing wagers in that game. The term "bingo game" does not refer to any game of chance (including, but not limited to, keno games, dice games, card games, and lotteries) other than the type of game described in this paragraph.

(e) Effective date. Section 513(f) and this section apply to taxable years beginning after December 31, 1969.

T.D. 7699, 5/20/80.

§ 1.513-6 Certain hospital services not unrelated trade or business.

(a) In general. Under section 513(e), the furnishing of a service listed in section 501(e)(1)(A) by a hospital to one or more other hospitals will not constitute unrelated trade or business if—

(1) The service is provided solely to hospitals that have facilities to serve not more than 100 inpatients,

(2) The service would, if performed by the recipient hospital, constitute an activity consistent with that hospital's exempt purposes, and

(3) The service is provided at a fee not in excess of actual cost, including straight line depreciation and a reasonable rate of return on the capital goods used to provide the service. For purposes of this section, a rate of return on capital goods will be considered "reasonable" provided that it does not exceed, on an annual basis, the percentage described below which is based on the average of the rates of interest on special issues of public debt obligations issued to the Federal Hospital Insurance Trust Fund for each of the months included in the taxable year of the hospital during which the capital goods are used in providing the service. Determinations as to the cost of services and the applicable rate of return should be made as prescribed by 42 U.S.C. 1395x(v)(1)(A) and (B) and the regulations thereunder (permitting a health care facility to be reimbursed under the Medicare program for the "reasonable cost of (its) services," including, in the case of certain proprietary facilities, a "reasonable return on equity capital"). For taxable years beginning on or before May 14, 1986, the rate of return shall be one and one-half times the average of the rates of interest on public debt obligations described above which were in effect on or before April 20, 1983.

(b) Hospital defined. As used in this section the word "hospital" means a hospital described in section 170(b)(1)(A)(iii).

(c) Example. The provisions of this section are illustrated by the following example:

Example. A large metropolitan hospital provides various services to other hospitals. The hospital furnishes a purchasing service to hospitals N and O, a data processing service to hospitals R and S, and a food service to hospitals X and Y. All the hospitals are described in section 170(b)(1)(A)(iii). All the hospitals have facilities to serve not more than 100 inpatients except hospitals N. The services are furnished at cost to all hospitals except that hospital R is charged a fee in excess of cost for its use of the data processing service. The purchasing service constitutes unrelated trade or business because it is not provided solely to hospitals having facilities to serve not more than 100 inpatients.

The data processing service constitutes unrelated trade or business because it is provided at a fee in excess of cost. The food service satisfies all three requirements of paragraph (a) of this section and does not constitute unrelated trade or business.

(d) Effective date. Section 513(e) and this section apply to taxable years beginning after December 31, 1953.

T.D. 8075, 2/12/86.

§ 1.513-7 Travel and tour activities of tax exempt organizations.

(a) Travel tour activities that, constitute a trade or business, as defined in § 1.513-1(b), and that are not substantially related to the purposes for which exemption has been granted to the organization constitute an unrelated trade or business with respect to that organization. Whether travel tour activities conducted by an organization are substantially related to the organization's exempt purpose is determined by looking at all relevant facts and circumstances, including, but not limited to, how a travel tour is developed, promoted and operated. Section 513(c) and § 1.513-1(b) also apply to travel tour activity. Application of the rules of section 513(c) and § 1.513-1(b) may result in different treatment for individual tours within an organization's travel tour program.

(b) Examples. The provisions of this section are illustrated by the following examples. In all of these examples, the travel tours are priced to produce a profit for the exempt organization. The examples are as follows:

Example (1). O, a university alumni association, is exempt from federal income tax under section 501(a) as an educational organization described in section 501(c)(3). As part of its activities, O operates a travel tour program. The program is open to all current members of O and their guests. O works with travel agencies to schedule approximately 10 tours annually to various destinations around the world. Members of O pay $x to the organizing travel agency to participate in a tour. The travel agency pays O a per person fee for each participant. Although the literature advertising the tours encourages O's members to continue their lifelong learning by joining the tours, and a faculty member of O's related university frequently joins the tour as a guest of the alumni association, none of the tours includes any scheduled instruction or curriculum related to the destinations being visited. The travel tours made available to O's members do not contribute importantly to the accomplishment of O's educational purpose. Rather, O's program is designed to generate revenues for O by regularly offering its members travel services. Accordingly, O's tour program is an unrelated trade or business within the meaning of section 513(a).

Example (2). N is an organization formed for the purpose of educating individuals about the geography and culture of the United States. It is exempt from federal income tax under section 501(a) as an educational and cultural organization described in section 501(c)(3). N engages in a number of activities to accomplish its purposes, including offering courses and publishing periodicals and books. As one of its activities, N conducts study tours to national parks and other locations within the United States. The study tours are conducted by teachers and other personnel certified by the Board of Education of the State of P. The tours are directed toward students enrolled in degree programs at educational institutions in P, as reflected in the promotional materials, but are open to all who agree to participate in the required study program. Each tour's study program consists of instruction on subjects related to the location being visited on the tour. During the tour, five or six hours per day are devoted to organized study, preparation of reports, lectures, instruction and recitation by the students. Each tour group brings along a library of material related to the subject being studied on the tour. Examinations are given at the end of each tour and the P State Board of Education awards academic credit for tour participation. Because the tours offered by N include a substantial amount of required study, lectures, report preparation, examinations and qualify for academic credit, the tours are substantially related to N's educational purpose. Accordingly, N's tour program is not an unrelated trade or business within the meaning of section 513(a).

Example (3). R is a section 501(c)(4) social welfare organization devoted to advocacy on a particular issue. On a regular basis throughout the year, R organizes travel tours for its members to Washington, DC. While in Washington, the members follow a schedule according to which they spend substantially all of their time during normal business hours over several days attending meetings with legislators and government officials and receiving briefings on policy developments related to the issue that is R's focus. Members do have some time on their own in the evenings to engage in recreational or social activities of their own choosing. Bringing members to Washington to participate in advocacy on behalf of the organization and learn about developments relating to the organization's principal focus is substantially related to R's social welfare purpose. Therefore, R's operation of the travel tours does not constitute an unrelated trade or business within the meaning of section 513(a).

Example (4). S is a membership organization formed to foster cultural unity and to educate X Americans about X, their country of origin. It is exempt from federal income tax under section 501(a) and is described in section 501(c)(3) as an educational and cultural organization. Membership in S is open to all Americans interested in the X heritage. As part of its activities, S sponsors a program of travel tours to X. The tours are divided into two categories. Category A tours are trips to X that are designed to immerse participants in the X history, culture and language. Substantially all of the daily itinerary includes scheduled instruction on the X language, history and cultural heritage, and visits to destinations selected because of their historical or cultural significance or because of instructional resources they offer. Category B tours are also trips to X, but rather than offering scheduled instruction, participants are given the option of taking guided tours of various X locations included in their itinerary. Other than the optional guided tours, Category B tours offer no instruction or curriculum. Destinations of principally recreational interest, rather than historical or cultural interest, are regularly included on Category B tour itineraries. Based on the facts and circumstances, sponsoring Category A tours is an activity substantially related to S's exempt purposes, and does not constitute an unrelated trade or business within the meaning of section 513(a). However, sponsoring Category B tours does not contribute importantly to S's accomplishment of its exempt purposes and, thus, constitutes an unrelated trade or business within the meaning of section 513(a).

Example (5). T is a scientific organization engaged in environmental research. T is exempt from federal income tax under section 501(a) as an organization described in section 501(c)(3). T is engaged in a long-term study of how agricultural pesticide and fertilizer use affects the populations of various bird species. T collects data at several bases located in an important agricultural region of country U. The minutes of a meeting of T's Board of Directors state that, after study, the Board has determined that non-scientists can reliably perform needed data collection in the field, under supervision of T's biologists. The Board minutes reflect that the Board approved offering one-week trips to T's bases in U, where participants will assist T's biologists in collecting data for the study. Tour participants collect data during the same hours as T's biologists. Normally, data collection occurs during the early morning and evening hours, although the work schedule varies by season. Each base has rustic accommodations and few amenities, but country U is renowned for its beautiful scenery and abundant wildlife. T promotes the trips in its newsletter and on its Internet site and through various conservation organizations. The promotional materials describe the work schedule and emphasize the valuable contribution made by trip participants to T's research activities. Based on the facts and circumstances, sponsoring trips to T's bases in country U is an activity substantially related to T's exempt purpose, and, thus, does not constitute an unrelated trade or business within the meaning of section 513(a).

Example (6). V is an educational organization devoted to the study of ancient history and cultures and is exempt from federal income tax under section 501(a) as an organization described in section 501(c)(3). In connection with its educational activities, V conducts archaeological expeditions around the world, including in the Y region of country Z. In cooperation with the National Museum of Z, V recently presented an exhibit on ancient civilizations of the Y region of Z, including artifacts from the collection of the Z National Museum. V instituted a program of travel tours to V's archaeological sites located in the Y region. The tours were initially proposed by V staff members as a means of educating the public about ongoing field research conducted by V. V engaged a travel agency to handle logistics such as accommodations and transportation arrangements. In preparation for the tours, V developed educational materials relating to each archaeological site to be visited on the tour, describing in detail the layout of the site, the methods used by V's researchers in exploring the site, the discoveries made at the site, and their historical significance. V also arranged special guided tours of its exhibit on the Y region for individuals registered for the travel tours. Two archaeologists from V (both of whom had participated in prior archaeological expeditions in the Y region) accompanied the tours. These experts led guided tours of each site and explained the significance of the sites to tour participants. At several of the sites, tour participants also met with a working team of archaeologists from V and the National Museum of Z, who shared their experiences. V prepared promotional materials describing the educational nature of the tours, including the daily trips to V's archaeological sites and the educational background of the tour leaders, and providing a recommended reading list. The promotional materials do not refer to any particular recreational or sightseeing activities. Based on the facts and circumstances, sponsoring trips to the Y region is an activity substantially related to V's exempt purposes. The scheduled activities, which include tours of archaeological sites led by experts, are part of a coordinated educational program designed to educate tour participants about the ancient history of the Y region of Z and V's ongoing field research. Therefore, V's tour program does not constitute an unrelated trade or business within the meaning of section 513(a).

Example (7). W is an educational organization devoted to the study of the performing arts and is exempt from federal income tax under section 501(a) as an organization described in section 501(c)(3). In connection with its educational activities, W presents public performances of musical and theatrical works. Individuals become members of W by making an annual contribution to W of $q. Each year, W offers members an opportunity to travel as a group to one or more major cities in the United States or abroad. In each city, tour participants are provided tickets to attend a public performance of a play, concert or dance program each evening. W also arranges a sightseeing tour of each city and provides evening receptions for tour participants. W views its tour program as an important means to develop and strengthen bonds between W and its members, and to increase their financial and volunteer support of W. W engaged a travel agency to handle logistics such as accommodations and transportation arrangements. No educational materials are prepared by W or provided to tour participants in connection with the tours. Apart from attendance at the evening cultural events, the tours offer no scheduled instruction, organized study or group discussion. Although several members of W's administrative staff accompany each tour group, their role is to facilitate member interaction. The staff members have no special expertise in the performing arts and play no educational role in the tours. W prepared promotional materials describing the sightseeing opportunities on the tours and emphasizing the opportunity for members to socialize informally and interact with one another and with W staff members, while pursuing shared interests. Although W's tour program may foster goodwill among W members, it does not contribute importantly to W's educational purposes. W's tour program is primarily social and recreational in nature. The scheduled activities, which include sightseeing and attendance at various cultural events, are not part of a coordinated educational program. Therefore, W's tour program is an unrelated trade or business within the meaning of section 513(a).

T.D. 8874, 2/4/2000.

§ 1.514(a)-1 Unrelated debt-financed income and deductions.

(a) Income includible in gross income. *(1) Percentage of income taken into account.* (i) In general. For taxable years beginning after December 31, 1969, there shall be included with respect to each debt-financed property (as defined in section 514 and § 1.514(b)-1) as an item of gross income derived from an unrelated trade or business the amount of unrelated debt-financed income (as defined in subdivision (ii) of this subparagraph). See paragraph (a)(5) of § 1.514(c)-1 for special rules regarding indebtedness incurred before June 28, 1966, applicable for taxable years beginning before January 1, 1972, and for special rules applicable to churches or conventions or associations of churches.

(ii) Unrelated debt-financed income. The "unrelated debt-financed income" with respect to each debt-financed property is an amount which is the same percentage (but not in excess of 100 percent) of the total gross income derived during the taxable year from or on account of such property as—

(a) The average acquisition indebtedness (as defined in subparagraph (3) of this paragraph) with respect to the property is of

(b) The average adjusted basis of such property (as defined in subparagraph (2) of this paragraph).

(iii) Debt/basis percentage. The percentage determined under subdivision (ii) of this subparagraph is hereinafter referred to as the "debt-basis percentage".

(iv) Example. Subdivisions (i), (ii), and (iii) of this subparagraph are illustrated by the following example. For purposes of this example it is assumed that the property is debt-financed property.

Example. X, an exempt trade association, owns an office building which in 1971 produces $10,000 of gross rental income. The average adjusted basis of the building for 1971 is $100,000, and the average acquisition indebtedness with respect to the building for 1971 is $50,000. Accordingly, the debt/basis percentage for 1971 is 50 percent (the ratio of $50,000 to $100,000). Therefore, the unrelated debt-financed income with respect to the building for 1971 is $5,000 (50 percent of $10,000).

(v) Gain from sale or other disposition. If debt-financed property is sold or otherwise disposed of, there shall be included in computing unrelated business taxable income an amount with respect to such gain (or loss) which is the same percentage (but not in excess of 100 percent) of the total gain (or loss) derived from such sale or other disposition as—

(a) The highest acquisition indebtedness with respect to such property during the 12-month period, preceding the date of disposition, is of

(b) The average adjusted basis of such property. The tax on the amount of gain (or loss) included in unrelated business taxable income pursuant to the preceding sentence shall be determined in accordance with the rules set forth in Subchapter P, Chapter 1 of the Code (relating to capital gains and losses). See also section 511(d) and the regulations thereunder (relating to the minimum tax for tax preferences).

(2) Average adjusted basis. (i) In general. The "average adjusted basis" for debt-financed property is the average amount of the adjusted basis of such property during that portion of the taxable year it is held by the organization. This amount is the average of:

(a) The adjusted basis of such property as of the first day during the taxable year that the organization holds the property, and

(b) The adjusted basis of such property as of the last day during the taxable year that the organization holds the property.

See section 1011 and the regulations thereunder for determination of the adjusted basis of property.

(ii) Adjustments for prior taxable years. For purposes of subdivision (i) of this subparagraph, the determination of the average adjusted basis of debt-financed property is not affected by the fact that the organization was exempt from taxation for prior taxable years. Proper adjustment must be made under section 1011 for the entire period since the acquisition of the property. For example, adjustment must be made for depreciation for all prior taxable years whether or not the organization was exempt from taxation for any such years. Similarly, the fact that only a portion of the depreciation allowance may be taken into account in computing the percentage of depreciation allowable under section 514(a)(2) does not affect the amount of the adjustment for depreciation which is used in determining average adjusted basis.

(iii) Cross reference. For the determination of the basis of debt-financed property acquired in a complete or partial liquidation of a corporation in exchange for its stock, see § 1.514(d)-1.

(iv) Example. This subparagraph may be illustrated by the following example. For purposes of this example it is assumed that the property is debt-financed property.

Example. On July 10, 1970, X, an exempt educational organization, purchased an office building for $510,000, using $300,000 of borrowed funds. During 1970 the only adjustment to basis is $20,000 for depreciation. As of December 31, 1970, the adjusted basis of the building is $490,000 and the indebtedness is still $300,000, X files its return on a calendar year basis. Under these circumstances, the debt/basis percentage for 1970 is 60 percent, calculated in the following manner:

	Basis
As of July 10, 1970 (acquisition date)	$ 510,000
As of December 31, 1970	490,000
Total	$1,000,000

Average Adjusted basis:

$1,000,000 ÷ 2 = $500,000

Debt/basis percentage:

$$\frac{\text{Average acquisition indebtedness}}{\text{Average adjusted basis}} = \frac{\$\ 300{,}000}{\$500{,}000} = 60 \text{ percent}$$

For an illustration of the determination of the debt/basis percentage as changes in the acquisition indebtedness occur, see example (1) of subparagraph (3)(iii) of this paragraph.

(3) Average acquisition indebtedness. (i) In general. The "average acquisition indebtedness" with respect to debt-financed property is the average amount of the outstanding principal indebtedness during that portion of the taxable year the property is held by the organization.

(ii) Computation. The average acquisition indebtedness is computed by determining the amount of the outstanding principal indebtedness on the first day in each calendar month during the taxable year that the organization holds the property, adding these amounts together, and then dividing this sum by the total number of months during the taxable year that the organization held such property. A fractional part of a month shall be treated as a full month in computing average acquisition indebtedness.

(iii) Examples. The application of this subparagraph may be illustrated by the following examples. For purposes of these examples it is assumed that the property is debt-financed property.

Example (1). Assume the facts as stated in the example in subparagraph (2)(iv) of this paragraph, except that beginning July 20, 1970, the organization makes payments of $21,000 a month ($20,000 of which is attributable to principal and $1,000 to interest). In this situation, the average acquisition indebtedness for 1970 is $250,000. Thus, the debt/basis percentage for 1970 is 50 percent, calculated in the following manner:

Month:	Indebtedness on the first day in each calendar month that the property is held
July	$ 300,000
August	280,000
September	260,000
October	240,000
November	220,000
December	200,000
Total	1,500,000

Average acquisition indebtedness:

$1,500,000 ÷ 6 months = $250,000

Debt/basis percentage:

$$\frac{\text{Average acquisition indebtedness}}{\text{Average adjusted basis}} = \frac{\$250{,}000}{\$500{,}000} = 50 \text{ percent}$$

Example (2). Y, an exempt organization, owns stock in a corporation which it does not control. At the beginning of the year, Y has an outstanding principal indebtedness with respect to such stock of $12,000. Such indebtedness is paid off at the rate of $2,000 per month beginning January 30, so that it is retired at the end of 6 months. The average acquisition indebtedness for the taxable year is $3,500, calculated in the following manner:

Month:	Indebtedness on the first day in each calendar month that the property is held
January	$12,000
February	10,000
March	8,000
April	6,000
May	4,000
June	2,000
July thru December	0
Total	42,000

Average acquisition indebtedness:

$42,000 ÷ 12 months = $3,500

(4) Indeterminate price. (i) In general. If an exempt organization acquires (or improves) property for an indeterminate price, the initial acquisition indebtedness and the unadjusted basis shall be determined in accordance with subdivisions (ii) and (iii) of this paragraph, unless the organization has obtained the consent of the Commissioner to use another method to compute such amounts.

(ii) Unadjusted basis. For purposes of this subparagraph, the unadjusted basis of property (or of an improvement) is the fair market value of the property (or improvement) on the date of acquisition (or the date of completion of the improvement). The average adjusted basis of such property shall be determined in accordance with paragraph (a)(2) of this section.

(iii) Initial acquisition indebtedness. For purposes of this subparagraph, the initial acquisition indebtedness is the fair market value of the property (or improvement) on the date of acquisition (or the date of completion of the improvement) less any down payment or other initial payment applied to the principal indebtedness. The average acquisition indebtedness with respect to such property shall be computed in accordance with paragraph (a)(3) of this section.

(iv) Example. The application of this subparagraph may be illustrated by the following example. For purposes of this example it is assumed that the property is debt-financed property.

Example. On January 1, 1971, X, an exempt trade association, acquires an office building for a down payment of $310,000 and an agreement to pay 10 percent of the income generated by the building for 10 years. Neither the sales price nor the amount which X is obligated to pay in the future is certain. The fair market value of the building on the date of acquisition is $600,000. The depreciation allowance for 1971 is $40,000. Unless X obtains the consent of the Commissioner to use another method, the unadjusted basis of the property is $600,000 (the fair market value of the property on the date of acquisition), and the initial acquisition indebtedness is $290,000 (fair market value of $600,000 less initial payment of $310,000). Under these circumstances, the average adjusted basis of the property for 1971 is $580,000, calculated as follows:

$$\frac{\text{initial fair market value} + (\text{initial fair market value less depreciation})}{2} = \frac{\$600{,}000 + (\$600{,}000 - \$40{,}000)}{2} = \$580{,}000$$

If no payment other than the initial payment is made in 1971, the average acquisition indebtedness for 1971 is $290,000. Thus, the debt/basis percentage for 1971 is 50 percent, calculated as follows:

$$\frac{\text{average acquisition indebtedness}}{\text{average adjusted basis}} = \frac{\$290{,}000}{\$580{,}000} = 50 \text{ percent}$$

(b) Deductions. *(1) Percentage of deductions taken into account.* Except as provided in subparagraphs (4) and (5) of this paragraph, there shall be allowed as a deduction with respect to each debt-financed property an amount determined by applying the debt/basis percentage to the sum of the deductions allowable under subparagraph (2) of this paragraph.

(2) Deductions allowable. The deductions allowable are those items allowed as deductions by chapter 1 of the Code which are directly connected with the debt-financed property or the income therefrom (including the dividends received deductions allowed by sections 243, 244, and 245), except that—

(i) The allowable deductions are subject to the modifications provided by section 512(b) on computation of the unrelated business taxable income, and

(ii) If the debt-financed property is of a character which is subject to the allowance for depreciation provided in section 167, such allowance shall be computed only by use of the straight-line method of depreciation.

(3) Directly connected with. To be "directly connected with" debt-financed property or the income therefrom, an item of deduction must have proximate and primary relationship to such property or the income therefrom. Expenses, depreciation, and similar items attributable solely to such property are proximately and primarily related to such property or the income therefrom, and therefore qualify for deduction, to the extent they meet the requirements of subparagraph (2) of this paragraph. Thus, for example, if the straight-line depreciation allowance for an office building is $10,000 a year, an organization would be allowed a deduction for depreciation of $10,000 if the entire building were debt-financed property. However, if only one-half of the building were treated as debt-financed property, then the depreciation allowed as a deduction would be $5,000. (See example (2) of § 1.514(b)-1(b)(1)(iii).)

(4) Capital losses. (i) In general. If the sale or exchange of debt-financed property results in a capital loss, the amount of such loss taken into account in the taxable year in which the loss arises shall be computed in accordance with paragraph (a)(1)(v) of this section. If, however, any portion of such capital loss not taken into account in such year may be carried back or carried over to another taxable year, the debt/basis percentage is not applied to determine what portion of such capital loss may be taken as a deduction in the year to which such capital loss is carried.

(ii) Example. This subparagraph is illustrated by the following example. For purposes of this example it is assumed that the property is debt-financed property.

Example. X, an exempt educational organization, owns securities which are capital assets and which it has held for more than 6 months. In 1972 X sells the securities at a loss of $20,000. The debt/basis percentage with respect to computing the gain (or loss) derived from the sale of the securities is 40 percent. Thus, X has sustained a capital loss of $8,000 (40 percent of $20,000) with respect to the sale of the securities. For 1972 and the preceding three taxable years X has no other capital transactions. Under these circumstances, the $8,000 of capital loss may be carried over to the succeeding 5 taxable years without further application of the debt/basis percentage.

(5) Net operating loss. (i) In general. If, after applying the debt/basis percentage to the income derived from debt-financed property and the deductions directly connected with such income, such deductions exceed such income, the organization has sustained a net operating loss for the taxable year. This amount may be carried back or carried over to other taxable years in accordance with section 512(b)(6). However, the debt/basis percentage shall not be applied in such other years to determine the amounts that may be taken as a deduction in those years.

(ii) Example. This subparagraph may be illustrated by the following example. For purposes of this example it is assumed that the property is debt-financed property.

Example. During 1974, Y, an exempt organization, receives $20,000 of rent from a building which it owns. Y has no other unrelated business taxable income for 1974. For 1974 the deductions directly connected with this building are property taxes of $5,000, interest of $5,000 on the acquisition indebtedness, and salary of $15,000 to the manager of the building. The debt/basis percentage for 1974 with respect to the building is 50 percent. Under these circumstances, Y shall take into account in computing its unrelated business taxable income for 1974, $10,000 of income (50 percent of $20,000) and $12,500 (50 percent of $25,000) of the deductions directly connected with such income. Thus, for 1974 Y has sustained a net operating loss of $2,500 ($10,000 of income less $12,500 of deductions) which may be carried back or carried over to other taxable years without further application of the debt/basis percentage.

T.D. 6301, 7/8/58, amend T.D. 7229, 12/20/72.

§ 1.514(a)-2 Business lease rents and deductions for taxable years beginning before January 1, 1970.

(a) Effective date. This section applies to taxable years beginning before January 1, 1970.

(b) In general. *(1) Rents includible in gross income.* There shall be included with respect to each business lease, as an item of gross income derived from an unrelated trade or business, an amount which is the same percentage (but not in excess of 100 percent) of the total rents derived during the taxable year under such lease as—

(i) The amount of the business lease indebtedness at the close of the taxable year of the lessor tax-exempt organization, with respect to the premises covered by such lease, is of

(ii) The adjusted basis of such premises at the close of such taxable year.

For definition of business lease as a lease for a term of more than 5 years, and for rules for determining the computation of such 5-year term in certain specific situations, see § 1.514(f)-1. For definition of business lease indebtedness and allocation of business lease indebtedness where only a portion of the property is subject to a business lease, see § 1.514(g)-1.

(2) Determination of basis. For purposes of the unrelated business income tax the basis (unadjusted) of property is determined under section 1012, and the adjusted basis of property is determined under section 1011. The determination of the adjusted basis of property is not affected by the fact that the organization was exempt from tax for prior taxable years. Proper adjustment must be made under section 1011 for the entire period since the acquisition of the property. Thus adjustment must be made for depreciation for all taxable years whether or not the organization was exempt from tax for any of such years. Similarly, for taxable years during which the organization is subject to the tax on unrelated business taxable income the fact that only a portion of the deduction for depreciation is taken into account under paragraph (c)(1) of this section does not affect the amount of the adjustment for depreciation.

(3) Examples. The application of this paragraph may be illustrated by the following examples, in each of which it is assumed that the taxpayer makes its returns under section 511 on the basis of the calendar year, and that the lease is not substantially related to the purpose for which the organization is granted exemption from tax.

Example (1). Assume that a tax-exempt educational organization purchased property in 1952 for $600,000, using borrowed funds, and leased the building for a period of 20 years. Assume further that the adjusted basis of such building at the close of 1954 is $500,000 and that, at the close of 1954, $200,000 of the indebtedness incurred to acquire the property remains outstanding. Since the amount of the outstanding indebtedness is two-fifths of the adjusted basis of the building at the close of 1954, two-fifths of the gross rental received from the building during 1954 shall be included as an item of gross income in computing unrelated business taxable income. If, at the close of a subsequent taxable year, the outstanding indebtedness is $100,000 and the adjusted basis of the building is $400,000, one-fourth of the gross rental for such taxable year shall be included as an item of gross income in computing unrelated business taxable income for such taxable year.

Example (2). Assume that a tax-exempt organization owns a four-story building, that in 1954 it borrows $100,000 which it uses to improve the whole building, and that it thereafter in 1954 rents the first and second floors of the building under six-year leases at rentals of $4,000 a year. The third and fourth floors of the building are leased on a yearly basis during 1954. Assume, also, that the adjusted basis of the real property at the end of 1954 (after reflecting the expenditures for improving the building) is $200,000, allocable equally to each of the four stories. Under these facts, only one-half of the real property is subject to a business lease since only one-half is rented under a lease for more than 5 years. See § 1.514(f)-1. The percentage of the rent under such lease which is taken into account is determined by the ratio which the allocable part of the business lease indebtedness bears to the allocable part of the adjusted basis of the real property, that is, the ratio which one-half of the $100,000 of business lease indebtedness outstanding at the close of 1954, or $50,000 bears to one-half of the adjusted basis of the business lease premises at the close of 1954, or $100,000. The percentage of rent which is business lease income for 1954 is, therefore, one-half (the ratio of $50,000 to $100,000) of $8,000, or $4,000, and this amount of $4,000 is considered an item of gross income derived from an unrelated trade or business.

(c) Deductions. *(1) Deductions allowable against gross income.* The same percentage is used in determining both the portion of the rent and the portion of the deductions taken into account with respect to the business lease in computing unrelated business taxable income. Such percentage is applicable only to the sum of the following deductions allowable under section 161:

(i) Taxes and other expenses paid or accrued during the taxable year upon or with respect to the real property subject to the business lease;

(ii) Interest paid or accrued during the taxable year on the business lease indebtedness;

(iii) A reasonable allowance for exhaustion, wear and tear (including a reasonable allowance for obsolescence) of the real property subject to such lease. Where only a portion of the real property is subject to the business lease, there shall be taken into account only those amounts of the above-listed deductions which are properly allocable to the premises covered by such lease. Where only a portion of the real property is subject to the business lease, there shall be taken into account only those amounts of the above-listed deductions which are properly allocable to the premises covered by such lease.

(2) Excess deductions. The deductions allowable under subparagraph (1) of this paragraph with respect to a business lease are not limited by the amount included in gross income with respect to the rent from such lease. Any excess of such deductions over such gross income shall be applied against other items of gross income in computing unrelated business taxable income taxable under section 511(a).

(3) Example. The application of this paragraph may be illustrated by the following example:

Example. Assume the same facts as those in example (1) in paragraph (b)(3) of this section. Assume, also that for 1954 the organization pays taxes of $4,000 on the property, interest of $6,000 on its business lease indebtedness, and that the depreciation allowable for 1954 under section 167 is $10,000. Under the facts set forth in such example (1) and in this example, the deductions to be taken into account for 1954 in computing unrelated business taxable income would be two-fifths of the total of the deductions of $20,000, that is $8,000.

T.D. 6301, 7/8/58, amend T.D. 7229, 12/20/72.

---

§ 1.514(b)-1 Definition of debt-financed property.

Caution: The Treasury has not yet amended Reg § 1.514(b)-1 to reflect changes made by P.L. 100-647, P.L. 100-203, P.L. 99-514.

(a) In general. For purposes of section 514 and the regulations thereunder, the term "debt-financed property" means any property which is held to produce income (e.g., rental real estate, tangible personal property, and corporate stock), and with respect to which there is an acquisition indebtedness (determined without regard to whether the property is debt-financed property at any time during the taxable year. The term "income" is not limited to recurring income but applies as well to gains from the disposition of property. Consequently when any property held to produce income by an organization which is not used in a manner described in section 514(b)(1)(A), (B), (C), or (D) is disposed of at a gain during the taxable year, and there was an acquisition indebtedness outstanding with respect to such property at any time during the 12-month period preceding the date of disposition (even though such period covers more than 1 taxable year), such property is "debt-financed property". For example, assume that on June 1, 1972, an organization is given mortgaged, unimproved property which it does not use in a manner described in section 514(b)(1)(A), (B), (C), or (D) and that the organization assumes payment of the mortgage or such property. On July 15, 1972, the organization sells such property for a gain. Such property is "debt-financed property" and such gain is taxable as unrelated debt-financed income. See section 514(c) and § 1.514(c)-1 for rules relating to when there is acquisition indebtedness with respect to property. See paragraph (a) of § 1.514(a)-1 for rules determining the amount of income or gain from debt-financed property which is treated as unrelated debt-financed income.

(b) Exceptions. *(1) Property related to certain exempt purposes.* (i) To the extent that the use of any property is substantially related (aside from the need of the organization for income or funds or the use it makes of the profits derived) to the exercise or performance by an organization of its charitable, educational, or other purpose or function constituting its basis for exemption under section 501 (or, in the case of an organization described in section 511(a)(2)(B), to the exercise or performance of any purpose or function designated in section 501(c)(3)) such property shall not be treated as "debt-financed property". See § 1.513-1 for principles applicable in determining whether there is a substantial relationship to the exempt purpose of the organization.

(ii) If substantially all of any property is used in a manner described in subdivision (i) of this subparagraph, such property shall not be treated as "debt-financed property". In general the preceding sentence shall apply if 85 percent or more of the use of such property is devoted to the organization's exempt purpose. The extent to which property is used for a particular purpose shall be determined on the basis of all the facts and circumstances. These may include (where appropriate)—

(a) A comparison of the portion of time such property is used for exempt purposes with the total time such property is used,

(b) A comparison of the portion of such property that is used for exempt purposes with the portion of such property that is used for all purposes, or

(c) Both the comparisons described in *(a)* and *(b)* of this subdivision.

(iii) This subparagraph may be illustrated by the following examples. For purposes of these examples it is assumed that the indebtedness is acquisition indebtedness.

Example (1). W, an exempt organization, owns a computer with respect to which there is an outstanding principal indebtedness and which is used by W in the performance of its exempt purpose. W sells time for the use of the computer to M corporation on occasions when the computer is not in full-time use by W. W uses the computer in furtherance of its exempt purpose more than 85 percent of the time it is in use and M uses the computer less than 15 percent of the total time the computer is in use. In this situation, substantially all the use of the computer is related to the performance of W's exempt purpose. Therefore, no portion of the computer is treated as debt-financed property.

Example (2). X, an exempt college, owns a four story office building which has been purchased with borrowed funds. In 1971, the lower two stories of the building are used to house computers which are used by X for administrative purposes. The top two stories are rented to the public for purposes not described in section 514(b)(1)(A), (B), (C), or (D). The gross income derived by X from the building is $6,000, all of which is attributable to the rents paid by tenants. There are $2,000 of expenses, allocable equally to each use of the building. The average adjusted basis of the building for 1971 is $100,000, and the outstanding principal indebtedness throughout 1971 is $60,000. Thus, the average acquisition indebtedness for 1971 is $60,000. In accordance with subdivision (i) of this subparagraph, only the upper half of the building is debt-financed property. Consequently, only the rental income and the deductions directly connected with such income are to be taken into account in computing unrelated business taxable income. The portion of such amounts to be taken into account is determined by multiplying the $6,000 of rental income and $1,000 of deductions directly connected with such rental income by the debt/basis percentage. The debt/basis percentage is the ratio which the allocable part of the average acquisition indebtedness is of the allocable part of the average adjusted basis of the property, that is, the ratio which $30,000 (one-half of $60,000) bears to $50,000 (one-half of $100,000). Thus, the debt/basis percentage for 1971 is 60 percent (the ratio of $30,000 to $50,000). Under these circumstances, X shall include net rental income of $3,000 in its unrelated business taxable income for 1971, computed as follows:

Total rental income	$6,000
Deductions directly connected with rental income	$1,000
Debt/basis percentage ($30,000/$50,000)	60 percent
Rental income treated as gross income from an unrelated trade or business (60 percent of $6,000)	$3,600
Less the allowable portion of deductions directly connected with such income (60 percent of $1,000)	$ 600
Net rental income included by X in computing its unrelated business taxable income pursuant to section 514	$3,000

Example (3). Assume the facts as stated in example (2) except that on December 31, 1971, X sells the building and realizes a long-term capital gain of $10,000. This is X's only capital transaction for 1971. An allocable portion of this gain is subject to tax. This amount is determined by multiplying the gain related to the nonexempt use, $5,000 (one-half of $10,000), by the ratio which the allocable part of the highest acquisition indebtedness for the 12-month period preceding the date of sale. $30,000 (one-half of $60,000), is of the allocable part of the average adjusted basis, $50,000 (one-half of $100,000). Thus, the debt/basis percentage derived from the sale of the building is 60 percent (the ratio of $30,000 to $50,000). Consequently, $3,000 (60 percent of $5,000) is a net section 1201 gain (net capital gain for taxable years beginning after December 31, 1976). The portion of such gain which is taxable shall be determined in accordance with rules contained in subchapter P, chapter 1 of the Code (relating to capital gains and losses). See also section 511(d) and the regulations thereunder (relating to minimum tax for tax preferences).

(2) Property used in an unrelated trade or business. (i) In general. To the extent that the gross income from any property is treated as income from the conduct of an unrelated trade or business, such property shall not be treated as "debt-financed property." However, any gain on the disposition of such property which is not included in the income of an unrelated trade or business by reason of section 512(b)(5) is includible as gross income derived "from or on account of debt-financed property" under paragraph (a)(1) of § 1.514(a)-1.

(ii) Amounts specifically taxable under other provisions of the Code. Section 514 does not apply to amounts which are otherwise included in the computation of unrelated business taxable income, such as rents from personal property includible pursuant to section 512(b)(3) or rents and interest from controlled organizations includible pursuant to section 512(b)(13). See paragraph (1)(5) of § 1.512(b)-1 for the rules determining the manner in which amounts are taken into account where such amounts may be included in the computation of unrelated business taxable income by operation of more than one provision of the Code.

(3) Examples. Subparagraphs (1) and (2) of this paragraph may be illustrated by the following examples. For purposes of these examples it is assumed that the indebtedness is acquisition indebtedness.

Example (1). X, an exempt scientific organization, owns a 10-story office building. During 1972, four stories are occupied by X's administrative offices, and the remaining six stories are rented to the public for purposes not described in section 514(b)(1)(A), (B), (C), or (D). On December 31, 1972, the building is sold and X realizes a long-term capital gain of $100,000. This is X's only capital transaction for 1972. The debt/basis percentage with respect to computing the gain (or loss) derived from the sale of the building is 30 percent. Since 40 percent of the building was used for X's exempt purpose, only 60 percent of the building is debt-financed property. Thus, only $60,000 of the gain (60 percent of $100,000) is subject to this section. Consequently, the amount of gain treated as unrelated debt-financed income is $18,000 ($60,000 multiplied by the debt/basis percentage of 30 percent). The portion of such $18,000 which is taxable shall be determined in accordance with the rules contained in subchapter P, chapter 1 of the Code. See also section 511(d) and the regulations thereunder (relating to the minimum tax for tax preferences).

Example (2). Y, an exempt organization, owns two properties, a restaurant and an office building. In 1972, all the space in the office building, except for the portion utilized by Y to house the administrative offices of the restaurant, is rented to the public for purposes not described in section 514(b)(1)(A), (B), (C), or (D). The average adjusted basis of the office building for 1972 is $2 million. The outstanding principal indebtedness throughout 1972 is $1 million. Thus, the highest acquisition indebtedness in the calendar year of 1972 is $1 million. It is determined that 30 percent of the space in the office building is used for the administrative functions engaged in by the employees of the organization with respect to the restaurant. Since the income attributable to the restaurant is attributable to the conduct of an unrelated trade or business, only 70 percent of the building is treated as debt-financed property for purposes of determining the portion of the rental income which is unrelated debt-financed income. On December 31, 1972, the office building is sold and Y realizes a long-term capital gain of $250,000. This is Y's only capital transaction for 1972. In accordance with subparagraph (2)(i) of this paragraph, all the gain derived from this sale is taken into account in computing the amount of such gain subject to tax. The portion of such gain which is taxable is determined by multiplying the $250,000 gain by the debt/basis percentage. The debt/basis percentage is the ratio which the highest acquisition indebtedness for the 12-month period preceding the date of sale, $1 million, is of the average adjusted basis, $2 million. Thus, the debt/basis percentage with respect to computing the gain (or loss) derived from the sale of the building is 50 percent (the ratio of $1 million to $2 million). Consequently, $125,000 (50 percent of $250,000) is a net section 1201 gain (net capital gain for taxable years beginning after December 31, 1976). The amount of such gain which is taxable shall be determined in accordance with the rules contained in subchapter P, chapter 1 of the Code. See also section 511(d) and the regulations thereunder.

Example (3). (a) Z, an exempt university, owns all the stock of M, a nonexempt corporation. During 1971 M leases from Z University a factory unrelated to Z's exempt purpose and a dormitory for the students of Z, for a total annual rent of $100,000: $80,000 for the factory and $20,000 for the dormitory. During 1971, M has $500,000 of taxable income, disregarding the rent paid to Z: $150,000 from the dormitory and $850,000 from the factory. The factory is subject to a mortgage of $150,000. Its average adjusted basis for 1971 is determined to be $300,000. Z's deductions for 1971 with respect to the leased property are $4,000 for the dormitory and $16,000 for the factory. In accordance with subdivision (ii) of this subparagraph, section 514 applies only to that portion of the rent which is excluded from the computation of unrelated business taxable income by operation of section 512(b)(3) and not included in such computation pursuant to section 512(b)(13). Since all the rent received by Z is derived from real property, section 512(b)(3) would exclude all such rent from computation of Z's unrelated business taxable income. However, 70 percent of the rent paid to Z with respect to the factory and 70 percent of the deductions directly connected with such rent shall be taken into account by Z in determining its unrelated business taxable income pursuant to section 512(b)(13), computed as follows:

M's taxable income (disregarding rent paid to Z)	$ 500,000
Less taxable income from dormitory	$ 150,000
Excess taxable income	$3.550,000
Ratio ($3.550,000/$500,000)	7/10
Total rent paid to Z	$ 100,000
Total deductions ($4,000 + $16,000)	$ 20,000
Rental income treated under section 512(b)(15) as gross income from an unrelated trade or business (7/10 of $100,000)	$ 70,000
Less deductions directly connected with such income (7/10 of $20,000)	$ 14,000
Net rental income included by Z in computing its unrelated business taxable income pursuant to section 512(b)(13)	$ 56,000

(b) Since only that portion of the rent derived from the factory and the deductions directly connected with such rent not taken into account pursuant to section 512(b)(15) may be included in computing unrelated business taxable income by operation of section 514, only $10,000 ($80,000 minus $70,000) of rent and $2,000 ($16,000 minus $14,000) of deductions are so taken into account. The portion of such amounts to be taken into account is determined by multiplying the $10,000 of income and $2,000 of deductions by the debt/basis percentage. The debt/basis percentage is the ratio which the average acquisition indebtedness ($150,000) is of the average adjusted basis of the property ($300,000). Thus, the debt/basis percentage for 1971 is 50 percent (the ratio of $150,000 to $300,000). Under these circumstances, Z shall include net rental income of $4,000 in its unrelated business taxable income for 1971, computed as follows:

Total rents	$10,000
Deductions directly connected with such rents	$ 2,000
Debt/basis percentage ($150,000/$300,000)	50 percent
Rental income treated as gross income from an unrelated trade or business (50 percent of $10,000)	$ 5,000
Less the allowable portion of deductions directly connected with such income (50 percent of $2,000)	$ 1,000
Net rental income included by Z in computing its unrelated business taxable income pursuant to section 514	$ 4,000

(4) Property related to research activities. To the extent that the gross income from any property is derived from research activities excluded from the tax on unrelated business income by paragraph (7), (8), or (9) of section 512(b), such property shall not be treated as "debt-financed property".

(5) Property used in "thrift shops", etc. To the extent that property is used in any trade or business which is excepted from the definition of "unrelated trade or business" by paragraph (1), (2), or (3) of section 513(a), such property shall not be treated as "debt-financed property".

(6) Use by a related organization. For purposes of subparagraph (1), (4), or (5) of this paragraph, use of property by a related exempt organization (as defined in paragraph (c)(2)(ii) of this section) for a purpose described in such subparagraphs shall be taken into account in order to determine the extent to which such property is used for a purpose described in such subparagraphs.

(c) Special rules. *(1) Medical clinic.* Property is not debt-financed property if it is real property subject to a lease to a medical clinic, and the lease is entered into primarily for purposes which are substantially related (aside from the need of such organization for income or funds or the use it makes of the rents derived) to the exercise or performance by the lessor of its charitable, educational, or other purpose of function constituting the basis for its exemption under section 501. For example, assume that an exempt hospital leases all of its clinic space to an unincorporated association of physicians and surgeons who, by the provisions of the lease, agree to provide all of the hospital's out-patient medical and surgical services and to train all of the hospital's residents and interns. In this situation, the rents received by the hospital from this clinic are not to be treated as unrelated debt-financed income.

(2) Related exempt uses. (i) In general. Property owned by an exempt organization and used by a related exempt organization or by an exempt organization related to such related exempt organization shall not be treated as "debt-financed property" to the extent such property is used by either organization in furtherance of the purpose constituting the basis for its exemption under section 501. Furthermore, property shall not be treated as "debt-financed property" to the extent such property is used by a related exempt organization for a purpose described in paragraph (b)(4) or (5) of this section.

(ii) Related organizations. For purposes of subdivision (i) of this subparagraph, an exempt organization is related to another exempt organization only if—

(a) One organization is an exempt holding company described in section 501(c)(2) and the other organization receives the profits derived by such exempt holding company.

(b) One organization has control of the other organization within the meaning of paragraph (e)(4) of § 1.512(b)-1.

(c) More than 50 percent of the members of one organization are members of the other organization, or

(d) Each organization is a local organization which is directly affiliated with a common state, national, or international organization which is also exempt.

(iii) Examples. This subparagraph may be illustrated by the following examples. For purposes of these examples it is assumed that the indebtedness is acquisition indebtedness.

Example (1). M, an exempt trade association described in section 501(c)(6), leases 70 percent of the space of an office building for furtherance of its exempt purpose. The title to such building is held by N, an exempt holding company described in section 501(c)(2), which acquired title to the building with borrowed funds. The other 30 percent of the space in this office building is leased to L, a nonstock exempt trade association described in section 501(c)(6). L uses such office space in furtherance of its exempt purposes. The members of L's Board of Trustees serves for fixed terms and M's Board of Directors has the power to select all such members. N pays over to M all the profits it derives from the leasing of space in this building to M and L. Accordingly, M is "related" to N (as such term is defined in subdivision (ii) *(a)* of this subparagraph) and L is "related" to M (as such term is defined in subdivision (ii) *(b)* of this subparagraph). Under these circumstances, since all the available space in the building is leased to either an exempt organization related to the exempt organization holding title to the building or an exempt organization related to such related exempt organization, no portion of the building is treated as debt-financed property.

Example (2). W, an exempt labor union described in section 501(c)(5), owns a 10-story office building which has been purchased with borrowed funds. Five floors of the building are used by W in furtherance of its exempt purpose. Four of the other floors are rented to X which is an exempt voluntary employees' beneficiary association described in section 501(c)(9), operated for the benefit of W's members. X uses such office space in furtherance of its exempt purpose. Seventy percent of the members of W are also members of X. Accordingly, X is "related" to W (as such term is defined in subdivision (ii) *(c)* of this subparagraph). The remaining floor of the building is rented to the general public for purposes not described in section 514(b)(1) (A), (B), (C), or (D). Under these circumstances, no portion of this building is treated as debt-financed property since more than 85 percent of the office space available in this building is used either by W or X, an exempt organization related to W, in furtherance of their respective exempt purpose. See paragraph (b)(1) of this section for rules relating to the use of property substantially related to an exempt purpose. See paragraph (b)(6) of this section for rules relating to uses by related exempt organizations.

Example (3). Assume the same facts as in example (2), except that W and X are each exempt local labor unions described in section 501(c)(5) having no common membership and are each affiliated with N, an exempt international labor union described in section 501(c)(5). Under these circumstances, no portion of this building is treated as debt-financed property since more than 85 percent of the office space available in this building is used either by W or X, an exempt organization related to W, in furtherance of their respective exempt purpose.

Example (4). Assume the same facts as in example (3), except that W and X are directly affiliated with different exempt international labor unions and that W and X are not otherwise affiliated with, or members of, a common exempt organization, other than an association of international labor unions. Under these circumstances, the portions of this building which are rented to X and to the general public are treated as debt-financed property since X is not related to W and W uses less than 85 percent of the building for its exempt purpose.

(3) Life income contracts. (i) Property shall not be treated as "debt-financed property" when—

(a) An individual transfers property to a trust or a fund subject to a contract providing that the income is to be paid to him or other individuals or both for a period of time not to exceed the life of such individual or individuals in a transaction in which the payments to the individual or individuals do not constitute the proceeds of a sale or exchange of the property so transferred, and

(b) The remainder interest is payable to an exempt organization described in section 501(c)(3).

(ii) Subdivision (i) of this subparagraph is illustrated by the following example.

Example. On January 1, 1967, A transfers property to X, an exempt organization described in section 501(c)(3), which immediately places the property in a fund. On January 1, 1971, A transfers additional property to X, which property is also placed in the fund. In exchange for each transfer, A receives income participation fund certificates which entitle him to a proportionate part of the fund's income for his life and for the life of another individual. None of the payments made by X are treated by the recipients as the proceeds of a sale or exchange of the property transferred. In this situation, none of the property received by X from A is treated as debt-financed property.

(d) Property acquired for prospective exempt use. *(1) Neighborhood land.* (i) In general. If an organization acquires real property for the principal purpose of using the land in the exercise or performance of its exempt purpose, commencing within 10 years of the time of acquisition, such property will not be treated as debt-financed property, so long as *(a)* such property is in the neighborhood of other property owned by the organization which is used in the performance of its exempt purpose, and *(b)* the organization does not abandon its intent to use the land in such a manner within the 10-year period. The rule expressed in this subdivision is hereinafter referred to as the "neighborhood land rule."

(ii) "Neighborhood defined." Property shall be considered in the "neighborhood" of property owned and used by the organization in the performance of its exempt purpose if the acquired property is contiguous with the exempt purpose property or would be contiguous with such property except for the interposition of a road, street, railroad, stream, or similar property. If the acquired property is not contiguous with exempt function property, it may still be in the "neighborhood" of such property, but only if it is within 1 mile of such property and the facts and circumstances of the particular situation make the acquisition of contiguous property unreasonable. Some of the criteria to consider in determining this question include the availability of land and the intended future use of the land. For example, a university attempts to purchase land contiguous to its present campus but cannot do so because the owners either refuse to sell or ask unreasonable prices. The nearest land of sufficient size and utility is a block away from the campus. The university purchases such land. Under these circumstances, the continuity requirement is unreasonable and the land purchased would be considered "neighborhood land."

(iii) Exception. The neighborhood land rule shall not apply to any property after the expiration of 10 years from the date of acquisition. Further, the neighborhood land rule shall apply after the first 5 years of the 10-year period, only if the organization establishes to the satisfaction of the Commissioner that future use of the acquired land in furtherance of the organization's exempt purpose before the expiration of the 10-year period is reasonably certain. In order to satisfy the Commissioner, the organization does not necessarily have to show binding contracts. However, it must at least have a definite plan detailing a specific improvement and a completion date, and some affirmative action toward the fulfillment of such a plan. This information shall be forwarded to the Commissioner of Internal Revenue, Washington, D.C. 20224, for a ruling at least 90 days before the end of the fifth year after acquisition of the land.

(2) Actual use. If the neighborhood land rule is inapplicable because—

(i) The acquired land is not in the neighborhood of other property used by the organization in performance of its exempt purpose, or

(ii) The organization (for the period after the first 5 years of the 10-year period) is unable to establish to the satisfaction of the Commissioner that the use of the acquired land for its exempt purposes within the 10-year period is reasonably certain, but the land is actually used by the organization in furtherance of its exempt purpose within the 10-year period, such property (subject to the provisions of subparagraph (4) of this paragraph) shall not be treated as debt-financed property for any period prior to such conversion.

(3) Limitations. (i) Demolition or removal required. (a) Subparagraphs (1) and (2) of this paragraph shall apply with respect to any structure on the land when acquired by the organization, or to the land occupied by the structure, only so long as the intended future use of the land in furtherance of the organization's exempt purpose requires that the structure be demolished or removed in order to use the land in such a manner. Thus, during the first 5 years after acquisition (and for subsequent years if there is a favorable ruling in accordance with subparagraph (1)(iii) of this paragraph) improved property is not debt-financed so long as the organization does not abandon its intent to demolish the existing structures and use the land in furtherance of its exempt purpose. Furthermore, if there is an actual demolition of such structures, the use made of the land need not be the one originally intended. Therefore, the actual use requirement of this subdivision may be satisfied by using the land in any manner which furthers the exempt purpose of the organization.

(b) Subdivision (i)(a) of this subparagraph may be illustrated by the following examples. For purposes of the following examples it is assumed that but for the application of the neighborhood land rule such property would be debt-financed property.

Example (1). An exempt university acquires a contiguous tract of land on which there is an apartment building. The university intends to demolish the apartment building and build classrooms and does not abandon this intent during the first 4 years after acquisition. In the fifth year after acquisition it abandons the intent to demolish and sells the apartment building. Under these circumstances, such property is not debt-financed property for the first 4 years after acquisition even though there was no eventual demolition or use made of such land in furtherance of the university's exempt purpose. However, such property is debt-financed property as of the time in the fifth year that the intent to demolish the building is abandoned and any gain on the sale of the property is subject to section 514.

Example (2). Assume the facts as stated in Example (1) except that the university did not abandon its intent to demolish the existing building and construct a classroom building until the eighth year after acquisition when it sells the property. Assume further that the university did not receive a favorable ruling in accordance with subparagraph (1)(iii) of this paragraph. Under these circumstances, the building is debt-financed property for the sixth, seventh, and eighth years. It is not, however, treated as debt-financed property for the first 5 years after acquisition.

Example (3). Assume the facts as stated in Example (2) except that the university received a favorable ruling in accordance with subparagraph (1)(iii) of this paragraph. Under these circumstances, the building is not debt-financed property for the first 7 years after acquisition. It only becomes debt-financed property as of the time in the eighth year when the university abandoned its intent to demolish the existing structure.

Example (4). (1) Assume that a university acquires a contiguous tract of land containing an office building for the principal purpose of demolishing the office building and building a modern dormitory. Five years later the dormitory has not been constructed, and the university has failed to satisfy the Commissioner that the office building will be demolished and the land will be used in furtherance of its exempt purpose (and consequently has failed to obtain a favorable ruling under subparagraph (1)(iii) of this paragraph). In the ninth taxable year after acquisition the university converts the office building into an administration building. Under these circumstances, during the sixth, seventh, and eighth years after acquisition, the office building is treated as debt-financed property because the office building was not demolished or removed. Therefore, the income derived from such property during these years shall be subject to the tax on unrelated business income.

(2) Assume that instead of converting the office building to an administration building, the university demolishes the office building in the ninth taxable year after acquisition and then constructs a new administration building. Under these circumstances, the land would not be considered debt-financed property for any period following the acquisition, and the university would be entitled to a refund of taxes paid on the income derived from such property for the sixth through eighth taxable years after the acquisition in accordance with subparagraph (4) of this paragraph.

(ii) Subsequent construction. Subparagraphs (1) and (2) of this paragraph do not apply to structures erected on the land after the acquisition of the land.

(iii) Property subject to business lease. Subparagraphs (1) and (2) of this paragraph do not apply to property subject to a lease which is a business lease (as defined in § 1.514(f)-1) whether the organization acquired the property subject to the lease or whether it executed the lease subsequent to acquisition. If only a portion of the real property is subject to a lease, paragraph (c) of § 1.514(f)-1 applies in determining whether such lease is a business lease.

(4) Refund of taxes. (i) If an organization has not satisfied the actual use condition of subparagraph (2) of this paragraph or paragraph (e)(3) of this section before the date prescribed by law (including extensions) for filing the return for the taxable year, the tax for such year shall be computed without regard to the application of such actual use condition. However, if—

(a) A credit or refund of any overpayment of taxes is allowable for a prior taxable year as a result of the satisfaction of such actual use condition, and

(b) Such credit or refund is prevented by the operation of any law or rule of law (other than chapter 74, relating to closing agreements and compromises), such credit or refund may nevertheless be allowed or made, if a claim is filed within 1 year after the close of the taxable year in which such actual use condition is satisfied. For a special rule with respect to the payment of interest at the rate of 4 percent per annum, see section 514(b)(3)(D), prior to its amendment by section 7(b) of the Act of January 3, 1975 (Pub. L. 93-625, 88 Stat. 2115).

(ii) This subparagraph may be illustrated by the following example. For purposes of this example it is assumed that but for the neighborhood land rule such property would be debt-financed property.

Example. Y, a calendar year exempt organization, acquires real property in January 1970, which is contiguous with other property used by Y in furtherance of its exempt purpose. However, Y does not satisfy the Commissioner by January 1975, that the existing structure will be demolished and the land will be used in furtherance of its exempt purpose. In accordance with this subparagraph, from 1975 until the property is converted to an exempt use, the income derived from such property shall be subject to the tax on unrelated business income. During July 1979, Y demolishes the existing structure on the land and begins using the land in furtherance of its exempt purpose. At this time Y may file claims for refund for the open years 1976 through 1978. Further, in accordance with this subparagraph, Y may also file a claim for refund for 1975, even though a claim for such taxable year may be barred by the statute of limitations, provided such claim is filed before the close of 1980.

(e) Churches. *(1) In general.* If a church or association or convention of churches acquires real property, for the principal purpose of using the land in the exercise or performance of its exempt purpose, commencing within 15 years of the time of acquisition, such property shall not be treated as debt-financed property so long as the organization does not abandon its intent to use the land in such a manner within the 15-year period.

(2) Exception. This paragraph shall not apply to any property after the expiration of the 15-year period. Further, this paragraph shall apply after the first 5 years of the 15-year period only if the church or association or convention of churches establishes to the satisfaction of the Commissioner that use of the acquired land in furtherance of the organization's exempt purpose before the expiration of the 15-year period is reasonably certain. For purposes of the preceding sentence, the rules contained in paragraph (d)(1)(iii) of this section with respect to satisfying the Commissioner that the exempt organization intends to use the land within the prescribed time in furtherance of its exempt purpose shall apply.

(3) Actual use. If the church or association or convention of churches for the period after the first 5 years of the 15-year period is unable to establish to the satisfaction of the Commissioner that the use of the acquired land for its exempt purpose within the 15-year period is reasonably certain, but such land is in fact converted to an exempt use within the 15-year period, the land (subject to the provisions of paragraph (d)(4) of this section) shall not be treated as debt-financed property for any period prior to such convention.

(4) Limitations. The limitations stated in paragraph (d)(3)(i) and (ii) of this section shall similarly apply to the rules contained in this paragraph.

T.D. 6301, 7/8/58, amend T.D. 7229, 12/20/72, T.D. 7384, 10/21/75, T.D. 7632, 7/19/79, T.D. 7928, 11/3/80.

§ 1.514(c)-1 Acquisition indebtedness.

Caution: The Treasury has not yet amended Reg § 1.514(c)-1 to reflect changes made by P.L. 103-66, P.L. 100-647, P.L. 100-203, P.L. 99-514, P.L. 98-369, P.L. 96-605.

(a) In general. *(1) Definition of acquisition indebtedness.* For purposes of section 514 and the regulations thereunder, the term "acquisition indebtedness" means, with respect to any debt-financed property, the outstanding amount of—

(i) The principal indebtedness incurred by the organization in acquiring or improving such property;

(ii) The principal indebtedness incurred before the acquisition or improvement of such property if such indebtedness would not have been incurred but for such acquisition or improvement; and

(iii) The principal indebtedness incurred after the acquisition or improvement of such property if such indebtedness would not have been incurred but for such acquisition or improvement and the incurrence of such indebtedness was reasonably foreseeable at the time of such acquisition or improvement.

Whether the incurrence of an indebtedness is reasonably foreseeable depends upon the facts and circumstances of each situation. The fact that an organization did not actually foresee the need for the incurrence of an indebtedness prior to the acquisition or improvement does not necessarily mean that the subsequent incurrence of indebtedness was not reasonably foreseeable.

(2) Examples. The application of subparagraph (1) of this paragraph may be illustrated by the following examples:

Example (1). X, an exempt organization, pledges some of its investment securities with a bank for a loan and uses the proceeds of such loan to purchase an office building which it leases to the public for purposes other than those described in section 514(b)(1)(A), (B), (C), or (D). The outstanding principal indebtedness with respect to the loan constitutes acquisition indebtedness incurred prior to the acquisition which would not have been incurred but for such acquisition.

Example (2). Y, an exempt scientific organization, mortgages its laboratory to replace working capital used in remodeling an office building which Y rents to an insurance company for purposes not described in section 514(b)(1)(A), (B), (C), or (D). The indebtedness is "acquisition indebtedness" since such indebtedness, though incurred subsequent to the improvements of the office building, would not have been incurred but for such improvement, and the indebtedness was reasonably foreseeable when, to make such improvement, Y reduced its working capital below the amount necessary to continue current operations.

Example (3). (a) U, an exempt private preparatory school, as its sole educational facility owns a classroom building which no longer meets the needs of U's students. In 1971, U sells this building for $3 million to Y, a corporation which it does not control. U receives $1 million as a down payment from Y and takes back a purchase money mortgage of $2 million which bears interest at 10 percent per annum. At the time U became the mortgagee of the $2 million purchase money mortgage, U realized that it would have to construct a new classroom building and knew that it would have to incur an indebtedness in the construction of the new classroom building. In 1972, U builds a new classroom building for a cost of $4 million. In connection with the construction of this building, U borrows $2.5 million from X Bank pursuant to a deed of trust bearing interest at 6 percent per annum. Under these circumstances, $2 million of the $2.5 million borrowed to finance construction of the new classroom building would not have been borrowed but for the retention of the $2 million purchase money mortgage. Since such indebtedness was reasonably foreseeable, $2 million of the $2.5 million borrowed to finance the construction of the new classroom building is acquisition indebtedness with respect to the purchase money mortgage and the purchase money mortgage is debt-financed property.

(b) In 1972, U receives $200,000 in interest from Y (10 percent of $2 million) and makes a $150,000 interest payment to X (6 percent of $2.5 million). In addition, assume that for 1972 the debt/basis percentage is 100 percent ($2 million/$2 million). Accordingly, all the interest and all the deductions directly connected with such interest income are to be taken into account in computing unrelated business taxable income. Thus, $200,000 of interest income and $120,000 ($150,000 × $2 million/$2.5 million) of deductions directly connected with such interest income are taken into account. Under these circumstances, U shall include net interest income of $80,000 ($200,000 of income less $120,000 of deductions directly connected with such income) in its unrelated business taxable income for 1972.

Example (4). In 1972 X, an exempt organization, forms a partnership with A and B. The partnership agreement provides that all three partners shall share equally in the profits of the partnership, shall each invest $3 million, and that X shall be a limited partner. X invests $1 million of its own funds in the partnership and $2 million of borrowed funds. The partnership purchases as its sole asset an office building which is leased to the general public for purposes other than those described in section 514(b)(1)(A), (B), (C), or (D). The office building cost the partnership $24 million of which $15 million is borrowed from Y bank. This loan is secured by a mortgage on the entire office building. By agreement with Y bank, X is held not to be personally liable for payment of such mortgage. By reason of section 702(b) the character of any item realized by the partnership and included in the partner's distributive share shall be determined as if the partner realized such item directly from the source from which it was realized by the partnership and in the same manner. Therefore, a portion of X's income from the building is debt-financed income. Under these circumstances, since both the $2 million indebtedness incurred by X in acquiring its partnership interest and $5 million, the allocable portion of the partnership's indebtedness incurred with respect to acquiring the office building which is attributable to X in computing the debt/basis percentage (one-third of $15 million), were incurred in acquiring income-producing property, X has acquisition indebtedness of $7 million ($2 million plus $5 million). Similarly, the allocable portion of the partnership's adjusted basis in the office building which is attributable to X in computing the debt-basis percentage is $8 million (one-third of $24 million). Assuming no payment with respect to either indebtedness and no adjustments to basis in 1972, X's average acquisition indebtedness is $7 million and X's average adjusted basis is $8 million for such year. Therefore, X's debt/basis percentage with respect to its share of the partnership income for 1972 is 87.5 percent ($7 million/$8 million).

(3) Changes in use of property. Since property used in a manner described in section 514(b)(1)(A), (B), (C), or (D) is not considered debt-financed property, indebtedness with respect to such property is not acquisition indebtedness. However, if an organization converts such property to a use which is not described to section 514(b)(1)(A), (B), (C), or (D) and such property is otherwise treated as debt-financed property, the outstanding principal indebtedness with respect to such property will thereafter be treated as "acquisition indebtedness." For example, assume that in 1971 a university borrows funds to acquire an apartment building as housing for married students. In 1974 the university rents the apartment building to the public for purposes not described in section 514(b)(1)(A), (B), (C), or (D). The outstanding principal indebtedness is "acquisition indebtedness" as of the time in 1974 when the building is first rented to the public.

(4) Continued indebtedness. If—

(i) An organization sells or exchanges property, subject to an indebtedness (incurred in a manner described in subparagraph (1) of this paragraph),

(ii) Acquires another property without retiring the indebtedness, and

(iii) The newly acquired property is otherwise treated as debt-financed property,

the outstanding principal indebtedness with respect to the acquired property is "acquisition indebtedness," even though the original property was not debt-financed property. For example, to house its administrative offices, an exempt organization purchases a building with $609,000 of its own funds and $400,000 of borrowed funds secured by a pledge of its securities. It later sells the building for $1,000,000 without redeeming the pledge. It uses these proceeds to purchase an apartment building which it rents to the public for purposes not described in section 514(b)(1) (A), (B), (C), or (D). The indebtedness of $400,000 is "acquisition indebtedness" with respect to the apartment building even though the office building was not debt-financed property.

(5) Indebtedness incurred before June 28, 1966. For taxable years beginning before January 1, 1972, "acquisition indebtedness" does not include any indebtedness incurred before June 28, 1966, unless such indebtedness was incurred on rental real property subject to a business lease and such indebtedness constituted business lease indebtedness. Furthermore, in the case of a church or convention or association of churches, the preceding sentence applies without regard to whether the indebtedness incurred before June 28, 1966, constituted business lease indebtedness.

(b) Property acquired subject to lien. *(1) Mortgages.* Except as provided in subparagraphs (3) and (4) of this paragraph, whenever property is acquired subject to a mortgage, the amount of the outstanding principal indebtedness secured by such mortgage is treated as "acquisition indebtedness" with respect to such property even though the organization did not assume or agree to pay such indebtedness. The preceding sentence applies whether property is acquired by purchase, gift, devise, bequest, or any other means. Thus, for example, assume that an exempt organization pays $50,000 for real property valued at $150,000 and subject to a $100,000 mortgage. The $100,000 of outstanding principal indebtedness is "acquisition indebtedness" just as though the organization had borrowed $100,000 to buy the property.

(2) Other liens. For purposes of this paragraph, liens similar to mortgages shall be treated as mortgages. A lien is similar to a mortgage if title to property is encumbered by the lien for the benefit of a creditor. However, in the case where State law provides that a tax lien attaches to property prior to the time when such lien becomes due and payable, such lien shall not be treated as similar to a mortgage until after it has become due and payable and the organization has had an opportunity to pay such lien in accordance with State law. Liens similar to mortgages include (but are not limited to):

(i) Deeds of trust,

(ii) Conditional sales contracts,

(iii) Chattel mortgages,

(iv) Security interests under the Uniform Commercial Code,

(v) Pledges,

(vi) Agreements to hold title in escrow, and

(vii) Tax liens (other than those described in the third sentence of this subparagraph).

(3) Certain encumbered property acquired by gift, bequest or devise. (i) Bequest or devise. Where property subject to a mortgage is acquired by an organization by bequest or devise, the outstanding principal indebtedness secured by such mortgage is not to be treated as "acquisition indebtedness" during the 10-year period following the date of acquisition. For purposes of the preceding sentence, the date of acquisition is the date the organization receives the property.

(ii) Gifts. If an organization acquires property by gift subject to a mortgage, the outstanding principal indebtedness secured by such mortgage shall not be treated as "acquisition indebtedness" during the 10-year period following the date of such gift, so long as—

(a) The mortgage was placed on the property more than 5 years before the date of the gift, and

(b) The property was held by the donor for more than 5 years before the date of the gift. For purposes of the preceding sentence, the date of the gift is the date the organization receives the property.

(iii) Limitation. Subdivisions (i) and (ii) of this subparagraph shall not apply if—

(a) The organization assumes and agrees to pay all or any part of the indebtedness secured by the mortgage, or

(b) The organization makes any payment for the equity owned by the decedent or the donor in the property (other than a payment pursuant to an annuity excluded from the definition of "acquisition indebtedness" by paragraph (e) of this section).

Whether an organization has assumed and agreed to pay all or any part of an indebtedness in order to acquire the property shall be determined by the facts and circumstances of each situation.

(iv) Examples. The application of this subparagraph may be illustrated by the following examples:

Example (1). A dies on January 1, 1971. His will devises an office building subject to a mortgage to U, an exempt organization described in section 501(c)(3). U does not at any time assume the mortgage. For the period 1971 through 1980, the outstanding principal indebtedness secured by the mortgage is not acquisition indebtedness. However, after December 31, 1980, the outstanding principal indebtedness secured by the mortgage is acquisition indebtedness if the building is otherwise treated as debt-financed property.

Example (2). Assume the facts as stated in example (1) except that on January 1, 1975, U assumes the mortgage. After January 1, 1975, the outstanding principal indebtedness secured by the mortgage is acquisition indebtedness if the building is otherwise treated as debt-financed property.

(4) Bargain sale before October 9, 1969. Where property subject to a mortgage is acquired by an organization before October 9, 1969, the outstanding principal indebtedness secured by such mortgage is not to be treated as "acquisition indebtedness" during the 10-year period following the date of acquisition if—

(i) The mortgage was placed on the property more than 5 years before the purchase, and

(ii) The organization paid the seller a total amount no greater than the amount of the seller's cost (including attorney's fees) directly related to the transfer of such property to the organization, but in any event no more than 10 percent of the value of the seller's equity in the property transferred.

(c) Extension of obligations. *(1) In general.* An extension, renewal, or refinancing of an obligation evidencing a preexisting indebtedness is considered as a continuation of the old indebtedness to the extent the outstanding principal amount thereof is not increased. Where the principal amount of the modified obligation exceeds the outstanding principal amount of the preexisting indebtedness, the excess shall be treated as a separate indebtedness for purposes of section 514 and the regulations thereunder. For example, if the interest rate on an obligation incurred prior to June 28, 1966, by an exempt university is modified subsequent to such date, the modified obligation shall be deemed to have been incurred prior to June 28, 1966. Thus, such an indebtedness will not be treated as acquisition indebtedness for taxable years beginning before January 1, 1972, unless the original indebtedness was business lease indebtedness (as defined in § 1.514(g)-1).

(2) Extension or renewal. In general any modification or substitution of the terms of an obligation by the organization shall be an extension or renewal of the original obligation, rather than the creation of a new indebtedness to the extent that the outstanding principal amount of the indebtedness is not increased. The following are examples of acts which result in the extension or renewal of an obligation:

(i) Substitution of liens to secure the obligation;

(ii) Substitution of obligees, whether or not with the consent of the organization;

(iii) Renewal, extension or acceleration of the payment terms of the obligation; and

(iv) Addition, deletion, or substitution or sureties or other primary or secondary obligors.

(3) Allocation. In cases where the outstanding principal amount of the modified obligation exceeds the outstanding principal amount of the unmodified obligation and only a portion of such refinanced indebtedness is to be treated as acquisition indebtedness, payments on the amount of the refinanced indebtedness shall be apportioned pro-rata between the amount of the preexisting indebtedness and the excess amount. For example, assume that an organization has an outstanding principal indebtedness of $500,000 which is treated as acquisition indebtedness. It borrows another $100,000, which is not acquisition indebtedness, from the same lending institution and gives the lender a $600,000 note for its total obligation. In this situation, a payment of $60,000 on the amount of the total obligation would reduce the acquisition indebtedness by $50,000 and the excess indebtedness by $10,000.

(d) Indebtedness incurred in performing exempt purpose. "Acquisition indebtedness" does not include the incurrence of an indebtedness inherent in the performance or exercise of the purpose or function constituting the basis of the organization's exemption. Thus, "acquisition indebtedness" does not include the indebtedness incurred by an exempt credit union in accepting deposits from its members or the obligation incurred by an exempt organization in accepting payments from its members to provide such members with insurance, retirement or other similar benefits.

(e) Annuities. *(1) Requirements.* The obligation to make payment of an annuity is not "acquisition indebtedness" if the annuity meets all the following requirements—

(i) It must be the sole consideration (other than a mortgage to which paragraph (b)(3) of this section applies) issued in exchange for the property acquired;

(ii) At the time of the exchange, the present value of the annuity (determined in accordance with subparagraph (2) of this paragraph) must be less than 90 percent of the value of the prior owner's equity in the property received in the exchange:

(iii) The annuity must be payable over the life of one individual in being at the time the annuity is issued, or over the lives of two individuals in being at such time; and

(iv) The annuity must be payable under a contract which—

(a) Does not guarantee a minimum number of payments or specify a maximum number of payments, and

(b) Does not provide for any adjustment of the amount of the annuity payments by reference to the income received from the transferred property or any other property.

(2) Valuation. For purposes of this paragraph, the value of an annuity at the time of exchange shall be computed in accordance with section 1011(b), § 1.1011-2(e)(1)(iii)(b)(2), and section 3 of Rev. Rul. 62-216, C.B. 1962-2, 30.

(3) Examples. The application of this paragraph may be illustrated by the following examples. For purposes of these examples it is assumed that the property transferred is used for purposes other than those described in section 514(b)(1)(A), (B), (C), or (D).

Example (1). On January 1, 1971, X, an exempt organization receives property valued at $100,000 from donor A, a male aged 60. In return X promises to pay A $6,000 a year for the rest of A's life, with neither a minimum nor maximum number of payments specified. The annuity is payable on December 31 of each year. The amounts paid under the annuity are not dependent on the income derived from the property transferred to X. The present value of this annuity is $81,156, determined in accordance with Table A of Rev. Rul. 62-216. Since the value of the annuity is less than 90 percent of A's equity in the property transferred and the annuity meets all the other requirements of subparagraph (1) of this paragraph, the obligation to make annuity payments is not acquisition indebtedness.

Example (2). On January 1, 1971, B transfers an office building to Y, an exempt university, subject to a mortgage. In return Y agrees to pay B $5,000 a year for the rest of his life, with neither a minimum nor maximum number of payments specified. The amounts paid under the annuity are not dependent on the income derived from the property transferred to Y. It is determined that the actual value of the annuity is less than 90 percent of the value of B's equity in the property transferred. Y does not assume the mortgage. For the taxable years 1971 through 1980, the outstanding principal indebtedness secured by the mortgage is not treated as acquisition indebtedness. Further, Y's obligation to make annuity payments to B never constitutes acquisition indebtedness.

(f) Certain Federal financing. "Acquisition indebtedness" does not include an obligation to finance the purchase, rehabilitation, or construction of housing for low and moderate income persons to the extent that it is insured by the Federal Housing Administration. Thus, for example, to the extent that an obligation is insured by the Federal Housing Administration under section 221(d)(3) (12 U.S.C. 1715(1)(d)(3)) or section 236 (12 U.S.C. 1715z-1) of title II of the National Housing Act, as amended, the obligation is not "acquisition indebtedness."

(g) Certain obligations of charitable remainder trusts. For purposes of section 664(c) and § 1.664-1(c), a charitable remainder trust (as defined in § 1.664-1(a)(1)(iii)(a) does not incur "acquisition indebtedness" when the sole consideration it is required to pay in exchange for unencumbered property is an "annuity amount" or a "unitrust amount" (as defined in § 1.664-1(a)(1)(iii)(b) and (c)).

T.D. 6301, 7/8/58, amend T.D. 6972, 9/11/68, T.D. 7229, 12/20/72, T.D. 7698, 5/20/80.

---

§ 1.514(c)-2 Permitted allocations under section 514(c)(9)(E).

(a) Table of contents. This paragraph contains a listing of the major headings of this § 1.514(c)-2.

§ 1.512(c)-2 Permitted allocations under section 514(c)(9)(E).

(1) Partner nonrecourse deductions disregarded until actually allocated.

(2) Disproportionate allocation of partner nonrecourse deductions to a qualified organization.

(k) Special rules.

(1) Changes in partnership allocations arising from a change in the partners' interests.

(2) De minimis interest rule.

(i) In general.

(ii) Example.

(3) De minimis allocations disregarded.

(4) Anti-abuse rule.

(l) [Reserved]

(m) Tiered partnerships.

(1) In general.

(2) Examples.

(n) Effective date.

(1) In general.

(2) General effective date of the regulations.

(3) Periods after June 24, 1990, and prior to December 30, 1992.

(4) Periods prior to the issuance of Notice 90-41.

(5) Material modifications to partnership agreements.

(b) Application of section 514(c)(9)(E), relating to debt-financed real property held by partnerships. *(1) In general.* This § 1.514(c)-2 provides rules governing the application of section 514(c)(9)(E). To comply with section 514(c)(9)(E), the following two requirements must be met:

(i) The fractions rule. The allocation of items to a partner that is a qualified organization cannot result in that partner having a percentage share of overall partnership income for any partnership taxable year greater than that partner's fractions rule percentage (as defined in paragraph (c)(2) of this section).

(ii) Substantial economic effect. Each partnership allocation must have substantial economic effect. However, allocations that cannot have economic effect must be deemed to be in accordance with the partners' interests in the partnership pursuant to § 1.704-1(b)(4), or (if § 1.704-1(b)(4) does not provide a method for deeming the allocations to be in accordance with the partners' interests in the partnership) must otherwise comply with the requirements of § 1.704-1(b)(4). Allocations attributable to nonrecourse liabilities or partner nonrecourse debt must comply with the requirements of § 1.704-2(e) or § 1.704-2(i).

(2) Manner in which fractions rule is applied. (i) In general. A partnership must satisfy the fractions rule both on a prospective basis and on an actual basis for each taxable year of the partnership, commencing with the first taxable year of the partnership in which the partnership holds debt-financed real property and has a qualified organization as a partner. Generally, a partnership does not qualify for the unrelated business income tax exception provided by section 514(c)(9)(A) for any taxable year of its existence unless it satisfies the fractions rule for every year the fractions rule applies. However, if an actual allocation described in paragraph (e)(4), (h), (j)(2), or (m)(1)(ii) of this section (regarding certain allocations that are disregarded or not taken into account for purposes of the fractions rule until an actual allocation is made) causes the partnership to violate the fractions rule, the partnership ordinarily is treated as violating the fractions rule only for the taxable year of the actual allocation and subsequent taxable years. For purposes of applying the fractions rule, the term partnership agreement is defined in accordance with § 1.704-1(b)(2)(ii)(h), and informal understandings are considered part of the partnership agreement in appropriate circumstances. See paragraph (k) of this section for rules relating to changes in the partners' interests and de minimis exceptions to the fractions rule.

(ii) Subsequent changes. A subsequent change to a partnership agreement that causes the partnership to violate the fractions rule ordinarily causes the partnership's income to fail the exception provided by section 514(c)(9)(A) only for the taxable year of the change and subsequent taxable years.

(c) General definitions. *(1) Overall partnership income and loss.* Overall partnership income is the amount by which the aggregate items of partnership income and gain for the taxable year exceed the aggregate items of partnership loss and deduction for the year. Overall partnership loss is the amount by which the aggregate items of partnership loss and deduction for the taxable year exceed the aggregate items of partnership income and gain for the year.

(i) Items taken into account in determining overall partnership income and loss. Except as otherwise provided in this section, the partnership items that are included in computing overall partnership income or loss are those items of income, gain, loss, and deduction (including expenditures described in section 705(a)(2)(B)) that increase or decrease the partners' capital accounts under § 1.704-1(b)(2)(iv). Tax items allocable pursuant to section 704(c) or § 1.704-1(b)(2)(iv)(f)(4) are not included in computing overall partnership income or loss. Nonetheless, allocations pursuant to section 704(c) or § 1.704-1(b)(2)(iv)(f)(4) may be relevant in determining that this section is being applied in a manner that is inconsistent with the fractions rule. See paragraph (k)(4) of this section.

(ii) Guaranteed payments to qualified organizations. Except to the extent otherwise provided in paragraph (d) of this section—

(A) A guaranteed payment to a qualified organization is not treated as an item of partnership loss or deduction in computing overall partnership income or loss; and

(B) Income that a qualified organization may receive or accrue with respect to a guaranteed payment is treated as an allocable share of overall partnership income or loss for purposes of the fractions rule.

(2) Fractions rule percentage. A qualified organization's fractions rule percentage is that partner's percentage share of overall partnership loss for the partnership taxable year for which that partner's percentage share of overall partnership loss will be the smallest.

(3) Definitions of certain terms by cross reference to partnership regulations. Minimum gain chargeback, nonrecourse deduction, nonrecourse liability, partner nonrecourse debt, partner nonrecourse debt minimum gain, partner nonrecourse debt minimum gain chargeback, partner nonrecourse deduction, and partnership minimum gain have the meanings provided in § 1.704-2.

(4) Example. The following example illustrates the provisions of this paragraph (c).

Example. Computation of overall partnership income and loss for a taxable year.

(i) Taxable corporation TP and qualified organization QO form a partnership to own and operate encumbered real property. Under the partnership agreement, all items of income, gain, loss, deduction, and credit are allocated 50 percent to TP and 50 percent to QO. Neither partner is entitled to a preferred return. However, the partnership agreement provides for a $900 guaranteed payment for services to QO in each of the partnership's first two taxable years. No part of the guaranteed payments qualify as a reasonable guaranteed payment under paragraph (d) of this section.

(ii) The partnership violates the fractions rule. Due to the existence of the guaranteed payment, QO's percentage share of any overall partnership income in the first two years will exceed QO's fractions rule percentage. For example, the partnership might have bottom-line net income of $5,100 in its first taxable year that is comprised of $10,000 of rental income, $4,000 of salary expense, and the $900 guaranteed payment to QO. The guaranteed payment would not be treated as an item of deduction in computing overall partnership income or loss because it does not qualify as a reasonable guaranteed payment. See paragraph (c)(1)(ii)(A) of this section. Accordingly, overall partnership income for the year would be $6,000, which would consist of $10,000 of rental income less $4,000 of salary expense. See paragraph (c)(1)(i) of this section. The $900 QO would include in income with respect to the guaranteed payment would be treated as an allocable share of the $6,000 of overall partnership income. See paragraph (c)(1)(ii)(B) of this section. Therefore, QO's allocable share of the overall partnership income for the year would be $3,450, which would be comprised of the $900 of income pertaining to QO's guaranteed payment, plus QO's $2,550 allocable share of the partnership's net income for the year (50 percent of $5,100). QO's $3,450 allocable share of overall partnership income would equal 58 percent of the $6,000 of overall partnership income and would exceed QO's fractions rule percentage, which is less than 50 percent. (If there were no guaranteed payment, QO's fractions rule percentage would be 50 percent. However, the existence of the guaranteed payment to QO that is not disregarded for purposes of the fractions rule pursuant to paragraph (d) of this section means that QO's fractions rule percentage is less than 50 percent.)

(d) Exclusion of reasonable preferred returns and guaranteed payments. *(1) Overview.* This paragraph (d) sets forth requirements for disregarding reasonable preferred returns for capital and reasonable guaranteed payments for capital or services for purposes of the fractions rule. To qualify, the preferred return or guaranteed payment must be set forth in a binding, written partnership agreement.

(2) Preferred returns. Items of income (including gross income) and gain that may be allocated to a partner with respect to a current or cumulative reasonable preferred return for capital (including allocations of minimum gain attributable to nonrecourse liability (or partner nonrecourse debt) proceeds distributed to the partner as a reasonable preferred return) are disregarded in computing overall partnership income or loss for purposes of the fractions rule. Similarly, if a partnership agreement effects a reasonable preferred return with an allocation of what would otherwise be overall partnership income, those items comprising that allocation are disregarded in computing overall partnership income for purposes of the fractions rule.

(3) Guaranteed payments. A current or cumulative reasonable guaranteed payment to a qualified organization for capital or services is treated as an item of deduction in computing overall partnership income or loss, and the income that the qualified organization may receive or accrue from the current or cumulative reasonable guaranteed payment is not treated as an allocable share of overall partnership income or loss. The treatment of a guaranteed payment as reasonable for purposes of section 514(c)(9)(E) does not affect its possible characterization as unrelated business taxable income under other provisions of the Internal Revenue Code.

(4) Reasonable amount. (i) In general. A guaranteed payment for services is reasonable only to the extent the amount of the payment is reasonable under § 1.162-7 (relating to the deduction of compensation for personal services). A preferred return or guaranteed payment for capital is reasonable only to the extent it is computed, with respect to unreturned capital, at a rate that is commercially reasonable based on the relevant facts and circumstances.

(ii) Safe harbor. For purposes of this paragraph (d)(4), a rate is deemed to be commercially reasonable if it is no greater than four percentage points more than, or if it is no greater than 150 percent of, the highest long-term applicable federal rate (AFR) within the meaning of section 1274 (d), for the month the partner's right to a preferred return or guaranteed payment is first established or for any month in the partnership taxable year for which the return or payment on capital is computed. A rate in excess of the rates described in the preceding sentence may be commercially reasonable, based on the relevant facts and circumstances.

(5) Unreturned capital. (i) In general. Unreturned capital is computed on a weighted-average basis and equals the excess of—

(A) The amount of money and the fair market value of property contributed by the partner to the partnership (net of liabilities assumed, or taken subject to, by the partnership); over

(B) The amount of money and the fair market value of property (net of liabilities assumed, or taken subject to, by the partner) distributed by the partnership to the partner as a return of capital.

(ii) Return of capital. In determining whether a distribution constitutes a return of capital, all relevant facts and circumstances are taken into account. However, the designation of distributions in a written partnership agreement generally will be respected in determining whether a distribution constitutes a return of capital, so long as the designation is economically reasonable.

(6) Timing rules. (i) Limitation on allocations of income with respect to reasonable preferred returns for capital. Items of income and gain (or part of what would otherwise be overall partnership income) that may be allocated to a partner in a taxable year with respect to a reasonable preferred return for capital are disregarded for purposes of the fractions rule only to the extent the allocable amount will not exceed—

(A) The aggregate of the amount that has been distributed to the partner as a reasonable preferred return for the taxable year of the allocation and prior taxable years, on or before the due date (not including extensions) for filing the partnership's return for the taxable year of the allocation; minus

(B) The aggregate amount of corresponding income and gain (and what would otherwise be overall partnership income) allocated to the partner in all prior years.

(ii) Reasonable guaranteed payments may be deducted only when paid in cash. If a partnership that avails itself of paragraph (d)(3) of this section would otherwise be required (by virtue of its method of accounting) to deduct a reasonable guaranteed payment to a qualified organization earlier than the taxable year in which it is paid in cash, the partnership must delay the deduction of the guaranteed payment until the taxable year it is paid in cash. For purposes of this paragraph (d)(6)(ii), a guaranteed payment that is paid in cash on or before the due date (not including extensions) for filing the partnership's return for a taxable year may be treated as paid in that prior taxable year.

(7) Examples. The following examples illustrate the provisions of this paragraph (d).

Facts. Qualified organization QO and taxable corporation TP form a partnership. QO contributes $9,000 to the partnership and TP contributes $1,000. The partnership borrows $50,000 from a third party lender and purchases an office building for $55,000. At all relevant times the safe harbor rate described in paragraph (d)(4)(ii) of this section equals 10 percent.

Example (1). Allocations made with respect to preferred returns.

(i) The partnership agreement provides that in each taxable year the partnership's distributable cash is first to be distributed to QO as a 10 percent preferred return on its unreturned capital. To the extent the partnership has insufficient cash to pay QO its preferred return in any taxable year, the preferred return is compounded (at 10 percent) and is to be paid in future years to the extent the partnership has distributable cash. The partnership agreement first allocates gross income and gain 100 percent to QO, to the extent cash has been distributed to QO as a preferred return. All remaining profit or loss is allocated 50 percent to QO and 50 percent to TP.

(ii) The partnership satisfies the fractions rule. Items of income and gain that may be specially allocated to QO with respect to its preferred return are disregarded in computing overall partnership income or loss for purposes of the fractions rule because the requirements of paragraph (d) of this section are satisfied. After disregarding those allocations, QO's fractions rule percentage is 50 percent (see paragraph (c)(2) of this section), and under the partnership agreement QO may not be allocated more than 50 percent of overall partnership income in any taxable year.

(iii) The facts are the same as in paragraph (i) of this Example 1, except that QO's preferred return is computed on unreturned capital at a rate that exceeds a commercially reasonable rate. The partnership violates the fractions rule. The income and gain that may be specially allocated to QO with respect to the preferred return is not disregarded in computing overall partnership income or loss to the extent it exceeds a commercially reasonable rate. See paragraph (d) of this section. As a result, QO's fractions rule percentage is less than 50 percent (see paragraph (c)(2) of this section), and allocations of income and gain to QO with respect to its preferred return could result in QO being allocated more than 50 percent of the overall partnership income in a taxable year.

Example (2). Guaranteed payments and the computation of overall partnership income or loss.

(i) The partnership agreement allocates all bottom-line partnership income and loss 50 percent to QO and 50 percent to TP throughout the life of the partnership. The partnership agreement provides that QO is entitled each year to a 10 percent guaranteed payment on unreturned capital. To the extent the partnership is unable to make a guaranteed payment in any taxable year, the unpaid amount is compounded at 10 percent and is to be paid in future years.

(ii) Assuming the requirements of paragraph (d)(6)(ii) of this section are met, the partnership satisfies the fractions rule. The guaranteed payment is disregarded for purposes of the fractions rule because it is computed with respect to unreturned capital at the safe harbor rate described in paragraph (d)(4)(ii) of this section. Therefore, the guaranteed payment is treated as an item of deduction in computing overall partnership income or loss, and the corresponding income that QO may receive or accrue with respect to the guaranteed payment is not treated as an allocable share of overall partnership income or loss. See paragraph (d)(3) of this section. Accordingly, QO's fractions rule percentage is 50 percent (see paragraph (c)(2) of this section), and under the partnership agreement QO may not be allocated more than 50 percent of overall partnership income in any taxable year.

(e) Chargebacks and offsets. *(1) In general.* The following allocations are disregarded in computing overall partnership income or loss for purposes of the fractions rule—

(i) Allocations of what would otherwise be overall partnership income that may be made to chargeback (i.e., reverse) prior disproportionately large allocations of overall partnership loss (or part of the overall partnership loss) to a qualified organization, and allocations of what would otherwise be overall partnership loss that may be made to chargeback prior disproportionately small allocations of overall partnership income (or part of the overall partnership income) to a qualified organization;

(ii) Allocations of income or gain that may be made to a partner pursuant to a minimum gain chargeback attributable to prior allocations of nonrecourse deductions to the partner;

(iii) Allocations of income or gain that may be made to a partner pursuant to a minimum gain chargeback attributable to prior allocations of partner nonrecourse deductions to the partner and allocations of income or gain that may be made to other partners to chargeback compensating allocations of other losses, deductions, or section 705(a)(2)(B) expenditures to the other partners; and

(iv) Allocations of items of income or gain that may be made to a partner pursuant to a qualified income offset, within the meaning of § 1.704-1(b)(2)(ii)(d).

(v) Allocations made in taxable years beginning on or after January 1, 2002, that are mandated by statute or regulation other than subchapter K of chapter 1 of the Internal Revenue Code and the regulations thereunder.

(2) Disproportionate allocations. (i) In general. To qualify under paragraph (e)(1)(i) of this section, prior disproportionate allocations may be reversed in full or in part, and in any order, but must be reversed in the same ratio as originally made. A prior allocation is disproportionately large if the qualified organization's percentage share of that allocation exceeds its fractions rule percentage. A prior allocation is disproportionately small if the qualified organization's percentage share of that allocation is less than its fractions rule percentage. However, a prior allocation (or allocations) is not considered disproportionate unless the balance of the overall partnership income or loss for the taxable year of the allocation is allocated in a manner that would independently satisfy the fractions rule.

(ii) Limitation on chargebacks of partial allocations. Except in the case of a chargeback allocation pursuant to paragraph (e)(4) of this section, and except as otherwise provided by the Internal Revenue Service by revenue ruling, revenue procedure, or, on a case-by-case basis, by letter ruling, paragraph (e)(1)(i) of this section applies to a chargeback of an allocation of part of the overall partnership income or loss only if that part consists of a pro rata portion of each item of partnership income, gain, loss, and deduction (other than nonrecourse deductions, as well as partner nonrecourse deductions and compensating allocations) that is included in computing overall partnership income or loss.

(3) Minimum gain chargebacks attributable to nonrecourse deductions. Commencing with the first taxable year of the partnership in which a minimum gain chargeback (or partner nonrecourse debt minimum gain chargeback) occurs, a chargeback to a partner is attributable to nonrecourse deductions (or separately, on a debt-by-debt basis, to partner nonrecourse deductions) in the same proportion that the partner's percentage share of the partnership minimum gain (or separately, on a debt-by-debt basis, the partner nonrecourse debt minimum gain) at the end of the immediately preceding taxable year is attributable to nonrecourse deductions (or partner nonrecourse deductions). The partnership must determine the extent to which a partner's percentage share of the partnership minimum gain (or partner nonrecourse debt minimum gain) is attributable to deductions in a reasonable and consistent manner. For example, in those cases in which none of the exceptions contained in § 1.704-2(f)(2) through (5) are relevant, a partner's percentage share of the partnership minimum gain generally is attributable to nonrecourse deductions in the same ratio that—

(i) The aggregate amount of the nonrecourse deductions previously allocated to the partner but not charged back in prior taxable years; bears to

(ii) The sum of the amount described in paragraph (e)(3)(i) of this section, plus the aggregate amount of distributions previously made to the partner of proceeds of a nonrecourse liability allocable to an increase in partnership minimum gain but not charged back in prior taxable years.

(4) Minimum gain chargebacks attributable to distribution of nonrecourse debt proceeds. (i) Chargebacks disregarded until allocations made. Allocations of items of income and gain that may be made pursuant to a provision in the partnership agreement that charges back minimum gain attributable to the distribution of proceeds of a nonrecourse liability (or a partner nonrecourse debt) are taken into account for purposes of the fractions rule only to the extent an allocation is made. (See paragraph (d)(2) of this section, pursuant to which there is permanently excluded chargeback allocations of minimum gain that are attributable to proceeds distributed as a reasonable preferred return.)

(ii) Certain minimum gain chargebacks related to returns of capital. Allocations of items of income or gain that (in accordance with § 1.704-2(f)(1)) may be made to a partner pursuant to a minimum gain chargeback attributable to the distribution of proceeds of a nonrecourse liability are disregarded in computing overall partnership income or loss for purposes of the fractions rule to the extent that the allocations (subject to the requirements of paragraph (e)(2) of this section) also charge back prior disproportionately large allocations of overall partnership loss (or part of the overall partnership loss) to a qualified organization. This exception applies only to the extent the disproportionately large allocation consisted of depreciation from real property (other than items of nonrecourse deduction or partner nonrecourse deduction) that subsequently was used to secure the nonrecourse liability providing the distributed proceeds, and only if those proceeds were distributed as a return of capital and in the same proportion as the disproportionately large allocation.

(5) Examples. The following examples illustrate the provisions of this paragraph (e).

Example (1). Chargebacks of disproportionately large allocations of overall partnership loss.

(i) Qualified organization QO and taxable corporation TP form a partnership. QO contributes $900 to the partnership and TP contributes $100. The partnership agreement allocates overall partnership loss 50 percent to QO and 50 percent to TP until TP's capital account is reduced to zero; then 100 percent to QO until QO's capital account is reduced to zero; and thereafter 50 percent to QO and 50 percent to TP. Overall partnership income is allocated first 100 percent to QO to chargeback overall partnership loss allocated 100 percent to QO, and thereafter 50 percent to QO and 50 percent to TP.

(ii) The partnership satisfies the fractions rule. QO's fractions rule percentage is 50 percent. See paragraph (c)(2) of this section. Therefore, the 100 percent allocation of overall partnership loss to QO is disproportionately large. See paragraph (e)(2)(i) of this section. Accordingly, the 100 percent allocation to QO of what would otherwise be overall partnership income (if it were not disregarded), which charges back the disproportionately large allocation of overall partnership loss, is disregarded in computing overall partnership income and loss for purposes of the fractions rule. The 100 percent allocation is in the same ratio as the disproportionately large loss allocation, and the rest of the allocations for the taxable year of the disproportionately large loss allocation will independently satisfy the fractions rule. See paragraph (e)(2)(i) of this section. After disregarding the chargeback allocation of 100 percent of what would otherwise be overall partnership income, QO will not be allocated a percentage share of overall partnership income in excess of its fractions rule percentage for any taxable year.

Example (2). Chargebacks of disproportionately small allocations of overall partnership income.

(i) Qualified organization QO and taxable corporation TP form a partnership. QO contributes $900 to the partnership and TP contributes $100. The partnership purchases real property with money contributed by its partners and with money borrowed by the partnership on a recourse basis. In any year, the partnership agreement allocates the first $500 of overall partnership income 50 percent to QO and 50 percent to TP; the next $100 of overall partnership income 100 percent to TP (as an incentive for TP to achieve significant profitability in managing the partnership's operations); and all remaining overall partnership income 50 percent to QO and 50 percent to TP. Overall partnership loss is allocated first 100 percent to TP to chargeback overall partnership income allocated 100 percent to TP at any time in the prior three years and not reversed; and thereafter 50 percent to QO and 50 percent to TP.

(ii) The partnership satisfies the fractions rule. QO's fractions rule percentage is 50 percent because qualifying chargebacks are disregarded pursuant to paragraph (e)(1)(i) in computing overall partnership income or loss. See paragraph (c)(2) of this section. The zero percent allocation to QO of what would otherwise be overall partnership loss is a qualifying chargeback that is disregarded because it is in the same ratio as the income allocation it charges back, because the rest of the allocations for the taxable year of that income allocation will independently satisfy the fractions rule (see paragraph (e)(2)(i) of this section), and because it charges back an allocation of zero overall partnership income to QO, which is proportionately smaller (i.e., disproportionately small) than QO's 50 percent fractions rule percentage. After disregarding the chargeback allocation of 100 percent of what would otherwise be overall partnership loss, QO will not be allocated a percentage share of overall partnership income in excess of its fractions rule percentage for any taxable year.

Example (3). Chargebacks of partner nonrecourse deductions and compensating allocations of other items.

(i) Qualified organization QO and taxable corporation TP form a partnership to own and operate encumbered real property. QO and TP each contribute $500 to the partnership. In addition, QO makes a $300 nonrecourse loan to the partnership. The partnership agreement contains a partner nonrecourse debt minimum gain chargeback provision and a provision that allocates partner nonrecourse deductions to the partner who bears the economic burden of the deductions in accordance with § 1.704-2. The partnership agreement also provides that to the extent partner nonrecourse deductions are allocated to QO in any taxable year, other compensating items of partnership loss or deduction (and, if appropriate, section 705(a)(2)(B) expenditures) will first be allocated 100 percent to TP. In addition, to the extent items of income or gain are allocated to QO in any taxable year pursuant to a partner nonrecourse debt minimum gain chargeback of deductions, items of partnership income and gain will first be allocated 100 percent to TP. The partnership agreement allocates all other overall partnership income or loss 50 percent to QO and 50 percent to TP.

(ii) The partnership satisfies the fractions rule on a prospective basis. The allocations of the partner nonrecourse deductions and the compensating allocation of other items of loss, deduction, and expenditure that may be made to TP (but which will not be made unless there is an allocation of partner nonrecourse deductions to QO) are not taken into account for purposes of the fractions rule until a taxable year in which an allocation is made. See paragraph (j)(1) of this section. In addition, partner nonrecourse debt minimum gain chargebacks of deductions and allocations of income or gain to other partners that chargeback compensating allocations of other deductions are disregarded in computing overall partnership income or loss for purposes of the fractions rule. See paragraph (e)(1)(iii) of this section. Since all other overall partnership income and loss is allocated 50 percent to QO and 50 percent to TP, QO's fractions rule percentage is 50 percent (see paragraph (c)(2) of this section), and QO will not be allocated a percentage share of overall partnership income in excess of its fractions rule percentage for any taxable year.

(iii) The facts are the same as in paragraph (i) of this Example 3, except that the partnership agreement provides that compensating allocations of loss or deduction (and section 705(a)(2)(B) expenditures) to TP will not be charged back until year 10. The partners expect $300 of partner nonrecourse deductions to be allocated to QO in year 1 and $300 of income or gain to be allocated to QO in year 2 pursuant to the partner nonrecourse debt minimum gain chargeback provision.

(iv) The partnership fails to satisfy the fractions rule on a prospective basis under the anti-abuse rule of paragraph (k)(4) of this section. If the partners' expectations prove correct, at the end of year 2, QO will have been allocated $300 of partner nonrecourse deductions and an offsetting $300 of partner nonrecourse debt minimum gain. However, the $300 of compensating deductions and losses that may be allocated to TP will not be charged back until year 10. Thus, during the period beginning at the end of year 2 and ending eight years later, there may be $300 more of unreversed deductions and losses allocated to TP than to QO, which would be inconsistent with the purpose of the fractions rule.

Example (4). Minimum gain chargeback attributable to distributions of nonrecourse debt proceeds.

(i) Qualified organization QO and taxable corporation TP form a partnership. QO contributes $900 to the partnership and TP contributes $100. The partnership agreement generally allocates overall partnership income and loss 90 percent to QO and 10 percent to TP. However, the partnership agreement contains a minimum gain chargeback provision, and also provides that in any partnership taxable year in which there is a chargeback of partnership minimum gain to QO attributable to distributions of proceeds of nonrecourse liabilities, all other items comprising overall partnership income or loss will be allocated in a manner such that QO is not allocated more than 90 percent of the overall partnership income for the year.

(ii) The partnership satisfies the fractions rule on a prospective basis. QO's fractions rule percentage is 90 percent. See paragraph (c)(2) of this section. The chargeback that may be made to QO of minimum gain attributable to distributions of nonrecourse liability proceeds is taken into account for purposes of the fractions rule only to the extent an allocation is made. See paragraph (e)(4) of this section. Accordingly, that potential allocation to QO is disregarded in applying the fractions rule on a prospective basis (see paragraph (b)(2) of this section), and QO is treated as not being allocated a percentage share of overall partnership income in excess of its fractions rule percentage in any taxable year. (Similarly, QO is treated as not being allocated items of income or gain in a taxable year when the partnership has an overall partnership loss.)

(iii) In year 3, the partnership borrows $400 on a nonrecourse basis and distributes it to QO as a return of capital. In year 8, the partnership has $400 of gross income and cash flow and $300 of overall partnership income, and the partnership repays the $400 nonrecourse borrowing.

(iv) The partnership violates the fractions rule for year 8 and all future years. Pursuant to the minimum gain chargeback provision, the entire $400 of partnership gross income is allocated to QO. Accordingly, notwithstanding the curative provision in the partnership agreement that would allocate to TP the next $44 (($400 ÷ .9) × 10%) of income and gain included in computing overall partnership income, the partnership has no other items of income and gain to allocate to QO. Because the $400 of gross income actually allocated to QO is taken into account for purposes of the fractions rule in the year an allocation is made (see paragraph (e)(4) of this section), QO's percentage share of overall partnership income in year 8 is greater than 100 percent. Since this exceeds QO's fractions rule percentage (i.e., 90 percent), the partnership violates the fractions rule for year 8 and all subsequent taxable years. See paragraph (b)(2) of this section.

(f) Exclusion of reasonable partner-specific items of deduction or loss. Provided that the expenditures are allocated to the partners to whom they are attributable, the following partner-specific expenditures are disregarded in computing overall partnership income or loss for purposes of the fractions rule—

(1) Expenditures for additional record-keeping and accounting incurred in connection with the transfer of a partnership interest (including expenditures incurred in computing basis adjustments under section 743 (b));

(2) Additional administrative costs that result from having a foreign partner;

(3) State and local taxes or expenditures relating to those taxes; and

(4) Expenditures designated by the Internal Revenue Service by revenue ruling or revenue procedure, or, on a case-by-case basis, by letter ruling. (See § 601.601(d)(2)(ii)(b) of this chapter.)

(g) Exclusion of unlikely losses and deductions. Unlikely losses or deductions (other than items of nonrecourse deduction) that may be specially allocated to partners that bear the economic burden of those losses or deductions are disregarded in computing overall partnership income or loss for purposes of the fractions rule, so long as a principal purpose of the allocation is not tax avoidance. To be excluded under this paragraph (g), a loss or deduction must have a low likelihood of occurring, taking into account all relevant facts, circumstances, and information available to the partners (including bona fide financial projections). The types of events that may give rise to unlikely losses or deductions, depending on the facts and circumstances, include tort and other third-party litigation that give rise to unforeseen liabilities in excess of reasonable insurance coverage; unanticipated labor strikes; unusual delays in securing required permits or licenses; abnormal weather conditions (considering the season and the job site); significant delays in leasing property due to an unanticipated severe economic downturn in the geographic area; unanticipated cost overruns; and the discovery of environmental conditions that require remediation. No inference is drawn as to whether a loss or deduction is unlikely from the fact that the partnership agreement includes a provision for allocating that loss or deduction.

(h) Provisions preventing deficit capital account balances. A provision in the partnership agreement that allocates items of loss or deduction away from a qualified organization in instances where allocating those items to the qualified organization would cause or increase a deficit balance in its capital account that the qualified organization is not obligated to restore (within the meaning of § 1.704-1(b)(2)(ii)(b) or (d)), is disregarded for purposes of the fractions rule in taxable years of the partnership in which no such allocations are made pursuant to the provision. However, this exception applies only if, at the time the provision becomes part of the partnership agreement, all relevant facts, circumstances, and information (including bona fide financial projections) available to the partners reasonably indicate that it is unlikely that an allocation will be made pursuant to the provision during the life of the partnership.

(i) [Reserved]

(j) Exception for partner nonrecourse deductions. *(1) Partner nonrecourse deductions disregarded until actually allocated.* Items of partner nonrecourse deduction that may be allocated to a partner pursuant to § 1.704-2, and compensating allocations of other items of loss, deduction, and section 705(a)(2)(B) expenditures that may be allocated to other partners, are not taken into account for purposes of the fractions rule until the taxable years in which they are allocated.

(2) Disproportionate allocation of partner nonrecourse deductions to a qualified organization. A violation of the fractions rule will be disregarded if it arises because an allocation of partner nonrecourse deductions to a qualified organization that is not motivated by tax avoidance reduces another qualified organization's fractions rule percentage below what it would have been absent the allocation of the partner nonrecourse deductions.

(k) Special rules. *(1) Changes in partnership allocations arising from a change in the partners' interests.* A qualified organization that acquires a partnership interest from another qualified organization is treated as a continuation of the prior qualified organization partner (to the extent of that acquired interest) for purposes of applying the fractions rule. Changes in partnership allocations that result from other transfers or shifts of partnership interests will be closely scrutinized (to determine whether the transfer or shift stems from a prior agreement, understanding, or plan or could otherwise be expected given the structure of the transaction), but generally will be taken into account only in determining whether the partnership satisfies the fractions rule in the taxable year of the change and subsequent taxable years.

(2) De minimis interest rule. (i) In general. Section 514(c)(9)(B)(vi) does not apply to a partnership otherwise subject to that section if—

(A) Qualified organizations do not hold, in the aggregate, interests of greater than five percent in the capital or profits of the partnership; and

(B) Taxable partners own substantial interests in the partnership through which they participate in the partnership on substantially the same terms as the qualified organization partners.

(ii) Example. Partnership PRS has two types of limited partnership interests that participate in partnership profits and losses on different terms. Qualified organizations (QOs) only own one type of limited partnership interest and own no general partnership interests. In the aggregate, the QOs own less than five percent of the capital and profits of PRS. Taxable partners also own the same type of limited partnership interest that the QOs own. These limited partnership interests owned by the taxable partners are 30 percent of the capital and profits of PRS. Thirty percent is a substantial interest in the partnership. Therefore, PRS satisfies paragraph (k)(2) of this section and section 514(c)(9)(B)(vi) does not apply.

(3) De minimis allocations disregarded. A qualified organization's fractions rule percentage of the partnership's items of loss and deduction, other than nonrecourse and partner nonrecourse deductions, that are allocated away from the qualified organization and to other partners in any taxable year are treated as having been allocated to the qualified organization for purposes of the fractions rule if—

(i) The allocation was neither planned nor motivated by tax avoidance; and

(ii) The total amount of those items of partnership loss or deduction is less than both—

(A) One percent of the partnership's aggregate items of gross loss and deduction for the taxable year; and

(B) $50,000.

(4) Anti-abuse rule. The purpose of the fractions rule is to prevent tax avoidance by limiting the permanent or temporary transfer of tax benefits from tax-exempt partners to taxable partners, whether by directing income or gain to tax-exempt partners, by directing losses, deductions, or credits to taxable partners, or by some other similar manner. This section may not be applied in a manner that is inconsistent with the purpose of the fractions rule.

(l) [Reserved]

(m) Tiered partnerships. *(1) In general.* If a qualified organization holds an indirect interest in real property through one or more tiers of partnerships (a chain), the fractions rule is satisfied only if —

(i) The avoidance of tax is not a principal purpose for using the tiered-ownership structure (investing in separate real properties through separate chains of partnerships so that section 514(c)(9)(E) is, effectively, applied on a property-by-property basis is not, in and of itself, a tax avoidance purpose); and

(ii) The relevant partnerships can demonstrate under any reasonable method that the relevant chains satisfy the requirements of paragraphs (b)(2) through (k) of this section. For purposes of applying § 1.704-2(k) under the independent chain approach described in Example 3 of paragraph (m)(2) of this section, allocations of items of income or gain that may be made pursuant to a provision in the partnership agreement that charges back minimum gain are taken into account for purposes of the fractions rule only to the extent an allocation is made.

(2) Examples. The following examples illustrate the provisions of this paragraph (m).

Example (1). Tiered partnerships—collapsing approach.

(i) Qualified organization QO3 and taxable individual TP3 form upper-tier partnership P2. The P2 partnership agreement allocates overall partnership income 20 percent to QO3 and 80 percent to TP3. Overall partnership loss is allocated 30 percent to QO3 and 70 percent to TP3. P2 and taxable individual TP2 form lower-tier partnership P1. The P1 partnership agreement allocates overall partnership income 60 percent to P2 and 40 percent to TP2. Overall partnership loss is allocated 40 percent to P2 and 60 percent to TP2. The only asset of P2 (which has no outstanding debt) is its interest in P1. P1 purchases real property with money contributed by its partners and with borrowed money. There is no tax avoidance purpose for the use of the tiered-ownership structure, which is illustrated by the following diagram.

QO3 TP3
P2 TP2
P1

(ii) P2 can demonstrate that the P2/P1 chain satisfies the requirements of paragraphs (b)(2) through (k) of this section by collapsing the tiered-partnership structure. On a collapsed basis, QO3's fractions rule percentage is 12 percent (30 percent of 40 percent). See paragraph (c)(2) of this section. P2 satisfies the fractions rule because QO3 may not be allocated more than 12 percent (20 percent of 60 percent) of overall partnership income in any taxable year.

Example (2). Tiered partnerships—entity-by-entity approach.

(i) Qualified organization QO3A is a partner with taxable individual TP3A in upper-tier partnership P2A. Qualified organization QO3B is a partner with taxable individual TP3B in upper-tier partnership P2B. P2A, P2B, and taxable individual TP2 are partners in lower-tier partnership P1, which owns encumbered real estate. None of QO3A, QO3B, TP3A, TP3B or TP2 has a direct or indirect ownership interest in each other. P2A has been established for the purpose of investing in numerous real estate properties independently of P2B and its partners. P2B has been established for the purpose of investing in numerous real estate properties independently of P2A and its partners. Neither P2A nor P2B has outstanding debt. There is no tax avoidance purpose for the use of the tiered-ownership structure, which is illustrated by the following diagram.

QO3A TP3A QO3B TP3B
P2A TP2 P2B
P1

(ii) The P2A/P1 chain (Chain A) will satisfy the fractions rule if P1 and P2A can demonstrate in a reasonable manner that they satisfy the requirements of paragraphs (b)(2) through (k) of this section. The P2B/P1 chain (Chain B) will satisfy the fractions rule if P1 and P2B can demonstrate in a reasonable manner that they satisfy the requirements of paragraphs (b)(2) through (k) of this section. To meet its burden, P1 treats P2A and P2B as qualified organizations. Provided that the allocations that may be made by P1 would satisfy the fractions rule if P2A and P2B were direct qualified organization partners in P1, Chain A will satisfy the fractions rule (for the benefit of QO3A) if the allocations that may be made by P2A satisfy the requirements of paragraphs (b)(2) through (k) of this section. Similarly, Chain B will satisfy the fractions rule (for the benefit of QO3B) if the allocations that may be made by P2B satisfy the requirements of paragraphs (b)(2) through (k) of this section. Under these facts, QO3A does not have to know how income and loss may be allocated by P2B, and QO3B does not have to know how income and loss may be allocated by P2A. QO3A's and QO3B's burden would not change even if TP2 were not a partner in P1.

Example (3). Tiered partnerships—independent chain approach.

(i) Qualified organization QO3 and taxable corporation TP3 form upper-tier partnership P2. P2 and taxable corporation TP2 form lower-tier partnership P1A. P2 and qualified organization QO2 form lower-tier partnership P1B. P2 has no outstanding debt. P1A and P1B each purchase real property with money contributed by their respective partners and with borrowed money. Each partnership's real property is completely unrelated to the real property owned by the other partnership. P1B's allocations do not satisfy the requirements of paragraphs (b)(2) through (k) of this section because of allocations that may be made to QO2. However, if P2's interest in P1B were completely disregarded, the P2/P1A chain would satisfy the requirements of paragraphs (b)(2) through (k) of this section. There is no tax avoidance purpose for the use of the tiered-ownership structure, which is illustrated by the following diagram.

QO3 TP3
P2
TP2 QO2
P1A P1B

(ii) P2 satisfies the fractions rule with respect to the P2/P1A chain, but only if the P2 partnership agreement allocates those items allocated to P2 by P1A separately from those items allocated to P2 by P1B. For this purpose, allocations of items of income or gain that may be made pursuant to a provision in the partnership agreement that charges back minimum gain, are taken into account for purposes of the fractions rule only to the extent an allocation is made. See paragraph (m)(1)(ii) of this section. P2 does not satisfy the fractions rule with respect to the P2/P1B chain.

(n) Effective date. *(1) In general.* Section 514(c)(9)(E), as amended by sections 2004(h)(1) and (2) of the Technical and Miscellaneous Revenue Act of 1988, Pub. L. 100-647, applies generally with respect to property acquired by partnerships after October 13, 1987, and to partnership interests acquired after October 13, 1987.

(2) General effective date of the regulations. Section 1.514(c)-2(a) through (m) applies with respect to partnership agreements entered into after December 30, 1992, property acquired by partnerships after December 30, 1992, and partnership interests acquired by qualified organizations after December 30, 1992 (other than a partnership interest that at all times after October 13, 1987, and prior to the acquisition was held by a qualified organization). For this purpose, paragraphs (a) through (m) of this section will be treated as satisfied with respect to partnership agreements entered into on or before May 13, 1994, property acquired by partnerships on or before May 13, 1994, and partnership interests acquired by qualified organizations on or before May 13, 1994, if the guidance set forth in (paragraphs (a) through (m) of § 1.514(c)-2 of) PS-56-90, published at 1993-5 I.R.B. 42, February 1, 1993, is satisfied. (See § 601.601(d)(2)(ii)(b) of this chapter.)

(3) Periods after June 24, 1990, and prior to December 30, 1992. To satisfy the requirements of section 514(c)(9)(E) with respect to partnership agreements entered into after June 24, 1990, property acquired by partnerships after June 24, 1990, and partnership interests acquired by qualified organizations after June 24, 1990, (other than a partnership interest that at all times after October 13, 1987, and prior to the acquisition was held by a qualified organization) to which paragraph (n)(2) of this section does not apply, paragraphs (a) through (m) of this section must be satisfied as of the first day that section 514(c)(9)(E) applies with respect to the partnership, property, or acquired interest. For this purpose, paragraphs (a) through (m) of this section will be treated as satisfied if the guidance in sections I through VI of Notice 90-41, 90-1 C.B. 350, (see § 601.601(d)(2)(ii)(b) of this chapter) has been followed.

(4) Periods prior to the issuance of Notice 90-41. With respect to partnerships commencing after October 13, 1987, property acquired by partnerships after October 13, 1987, and partnership interests acquired by qualified organizations after October 13, 1987, to which neither paragraph (n)(2) nor (n)(3) of this section applies, the Internal Revenue Service will not challenge an interpretation of section 514(c)(9)(E) that is reasonable in light of the underlying purposes of section 514(c)(9)(E) (as reflected in its legislative history) and that is consistently applied as of the first day that section 514(c)(9)(E) applies with respect to the partnership, property, or acquired interest. A reasonable interpretation includes an interpretation that substantially follows the guidance in either sections I through VI of Notice 90-41 (see § 601.601(d)(2)(ii)(b) of this chapter) or paragraphs (a) through (m) of this section.

(5) Material modifications to partnership agreements. A material modification will cause a partnership agreement to be treated as a new partnership agreement in appropriate circumstances for purposes of this paragraph (n).

T.D. 8539, 5/11/94, amend T.D. 9047, 3/13/2003.

§ 1.514(d)-1 Basis of debt-financed property acquired in corporate liquidation.

(a) If debt-financed property is acquired by an exempt organization in a complete or partial liquidation of a corporation in exchange for its stock, the organization's basis in such property shall be the same as it would be in the hands of the transferor corporation, increased by the amount of gain recognized to the transferor corporation upon such distribution and by the amount of any gain which is includible, on account of such distribution, in the gross income of the organization as unrelated debt financed income.

(b) The application of this section may be illustrated by the following example:

Example. On July 1, 1970, T, an exempt trust, exchanges $15,000 of borrowed funds for 50 percent of the shares of M Corporation's stock. M uses $35,000 of borrowed funds in acquiring depreciable assets which are not used at any time for purposes described in section 514(b)(1)(A), (B), (C), or (D). On July 1, 1978, and for the 12-month period preceding this date, T's acquisition indebtedness with respect to M's stock has been $3,000. On this date, there is a complete liquidation of M Corporation to which section 331(a)(1) applies. In the liquidation T receives a distribution in kind of depreciable assets and assumes $7,000 of M's indebtedness which remains unpaid with respect to the depreciable assets. On this date, M's adjusted basis of these depreciable assets is $9,000, and such assets have a fair market value of $47,000. M recognizes gain of $6,000 with respect to this liquidation pursuant to sections 1245 and 1250. T realizes a gain of $25,000 (the difference between the excess of fair market value of the property received over the indebtedness assumed, $40,000 ($47,000 + $7,000) and T's basis in M's stock, $15,000). A portion of this gain is to be treated as unrelated debt-financed income. This amount is determined by multiplying T's gain of $25,000 by the debt/basis percentage. The debt/basis percentage is 20 percent, the ratio which the average acquisition indebtedness ($3,000) is of the average adjusted basis ($15,000). Thus, $5,000 (20 percent of $25,000) is unrelated debt-financed income. This amount and the gain recognized pursuant to sections 1245 and 1250 are added to M's basis to determine T's basis in the property received. Consequently, T's basis in the property received from M Corporation is $20,000, determined as follows:

M Corporation's adjusted basis	$9,000
Gain recognized by M Corporation on the distribution	6,000
Unrelated debt-financed income recognized by T with respect to the distribution	5,000
T's transferred basis	20,000

T.D. 7229, 12/20/72.

§ 1.514(e)-1 Allocation rules.

Caution: The Treasury has not yet amended Reg § 1.514(e)-1 to reflect changes made by P.L. 100-647, P.L. 100-203, P.L. 99-514.

Where only a portion of property is debt-financed property, proper allocation of the basis, indebtedness, income, and deduction with respect to such property must be made to determine the amount of income or gain derived from such property which is to be treated as unrelated debt-financed income. See examples (2) and (3) of paragraph (b)(1)(iii) of § 1.514(b)-1 and examples (1), (2), and (3) of paragraph (b)(3)(iii) of § 1.514(b)-1 for illustrations of proper allocation.

T.D. 7229, 12/20/72.

§ 1.514(f)-1 Definition of business lease.

Caution: The Treasury has not yet amended Reg § 1.514(f)-1 to reflect changes made by P.L. 94-455.

(a) In general. The term "business lease" means any lease, with certain exceptions discussed in paragraph (c) of this section, for a term of more than 5 years of real property by an organization subject to section 511 (or by a partnership of which it is a member) if at the close of the organization's taxable year there is a business lease indebtedness as defined in section 514(g) and § 1.514(g)-1 with respect to such property. For the purpose of this section the term "real property" and the term "premises" include personal property of the lessor tax-exempt organization leased by it to a lessee of its real estate if the lease of such personal property is made under, or in connection with, the lease of such real estate. For amounts of business lease rents and deductions to be included in computing unrelated business taxable income for taxable years beginning before January 1, 1970, see § 1.514(a)-2.

(b) Special rules. *(1)* In computing the term of the lease, the period for which a lease may be renewed or extended by reason of an option contained therein shall be considered as part of the term. For example, a 3-year lease with an option for renewal for another such period is considered a lease for a term of 6 years. Another example is the case of a 1-year lease with option of renewal for another such term, where the parties at the end of each year renew the arrangement. In this case, during the fifth year (but not during the first 4 years), the lease falls within the 5-year rule, since the lease then involves 5 years and there is an option for the sixth year. In determining the term of the lease, an option for renewal of the lease is taken into account whether or not the exercise of the option depends upon conditions or contingencies.

(2) If the property is acquired subject to a lease, the term of such lease shall be considered to begin on the date of such acquisition. For example, if an exempt organization purchases, in whole or in part with borrowed funds, real property subject to a 10-year lease which has 3 years left to run, and such lease contains no right of renewal or extension, the lease shall be considered a 3-year lease and hence does not meet the definition of a business lease in section 514(f) and paragraph (a) of this section. However, if this lease contains an option to renew for a period of 3 years or more, it is a business lease.

(3) Under the provisions of section 514(f)(2)(B) a lease is considered as continuing for more than 5 years if the same lessee has occupied the premises for a total period of more than 5 years, whether the occupancy is under one or more leases, renewals, extensions, or continuations. Continued occupancy shall be considered to be by the same lessee if the occupants during the period are so related that losses in respect of sales or exchanges of property between them would be disallowed under section 267(a). Such period shall be considered as commencing not earlier than the date of the acquisition of the property by the tax-exempt organization or trust. This rule is applicable only in the sixth and succeeding years of such occupancy by the same lessee. See, however, paragraph (c)(3) of this section.

(c) Exceptions. *(1)* A lease shall not be considered a business lease if such lease is entered into primarily for a purpose which is substantially related (aside from the need of such organization for income or funds, or the use it makes of the rents derived) to the exercise or performance by such organization of its charitable, educational, or other purposes or function constituting the basis for its exemption. For example, where a tax-exempt hospital leases real property owned by it to an association of doctors for use as a clinic, the rents derived under such lease would not be included in computing unrelated business taxable income if the clinic is substantially related to the carrying on of hospital functions. See § 1.513-1 for principles applicable in determining whether there is a substantial relationship to the exempt purpose of an organization.

(2) A lease is not a business lease if the lease is of premises in a building primarily designed for occupancy and occupied by the tax-exempt organization.

(3) If a lease for more than 5 years to a tenant is for only a portion of the real property, and space in the real property is rented during the taxable year under a lease for not more than 5 years to any other tenant of the tax-exempt organization, all leases of the real property for more than 5 years shall be considered as business leases during the taxable year only if—

(i) The rents derived from the real property during the taxable year under leases for more than 5 years represent 50 percent or more of the total rents derived during the taxable year from the real property; or the area of the premises occupied under leases for 5 years represents, at any time during the taxable year, 50 percent or more of the total area of the real property rented at such time; or

(ii) The rent derived from the real property during the taxable year from any tenant under a lease for more than 5 years, or from a group of tenants (under such leases) who are either members of an affiliated group (as defined in section 1504) or are partners, represents more than 10 percent of the total rents derived during the taxable years from such property; or the area of the premises occupied by any one such tenant, or by any such group of tenants, represents at any time during the taxable year more than 10 percent of the total area of the real property rented at such time.

In determining whether 50 percent or more of the total rents are derived from leases for more than 5 years, or whether 50 percent or more of the total area is occupied under leases for more than 5 years—

(iii) An occupancy which is considered to be a lease of more than 5 years solely by reason of the provisions of paragraph (b)(3) of this subparagraph shall not be treated as such a lease for purposes of subdivision (1) of this subparagraph, and

(iv) An occupancy which is considered to be a lease of more than 5 years solely by reason of the provisions of paragraph (b)(3) of this section shall be treated as such a lease for purposes of subdivision (ii) of this subparagraph, and

(v) If during the last half of the term of a lease a new lease is made to take effect after the expiration of such lease, the unexpired portion of the first lease will not be added to the second lease to determine whether such second lease is a lease for more than 5 years for purposes of subdivision (i) of this subparagraph.

(4) The application of subparagraph (3) of this paragraph may be illustrated by the following example:

Example. In 1954 an educational organization, which is on the calendar year basis, begins the erection of an 11-story apartment building using funds borrowed for that purpose, and immediately leases for a 10-year term the first floor to a real estate development company to sublet for stores and shops. As fast as the new apartments are completed, they are rented on an annual basis. At the end of 1959 all except the 10th and 11th floors are rented. Those two floors are completed during 1960 and rented. Assume that for 1954 and each subsequent taxable year through 1959, and for the taxable year 1963, the gross rental for the first floor represents more than 10 percent of the total gross rents derived during the taxable year from the building. Under this set of facts the 10-year lease of the first floor would be considered to be a business lease for all except the taxable years 1961, 1962, and 1964.

T.D. 7229, 12/20/72.

§ 1.514(g)-1 Business lease indebtedness.

Caution: The Treasury has not yet amended Reg § 1.514(g)-1 to reflect changes made by P.L. 94-455.

(a) Definition. The term "business lease indebtedness" means, with respect to any real property leased by a tax-exempt organization for a term of more than 5 years, the unpaid amount of—

(1) The indebtedness incurred by the lessor tax-exempt organization in acquiring or improving such property;

(2) The indebtedness incurred by the lessor tax-exempt organization prior to the acquisition or improvement of such property if such indebtedness would not have been incurred but for such acquisition or improvement; and

(3) The indebtedness incurred by the lessor tax-exempt organization subsequent to the acquisition or improvement of such property if such indebtedness would not have been incurred but for such acquisition or improvement and the incurrence of the indebtedness was reasonably foreseeable at the time of such acquisition or improvement.

See paragraph (i) of this section with respect to subsidiary corporations.

(b) Examples. The rules of section 514(g) respecting business leases also cover certain cases where the leased property itself is not subject to an indebtedness. For example, they apply to cases such as the following:

Example (1). A university pledges some of its investment securities with a bank for a loan and uses the proceeds of such loan to purchase (either directly or through a subsidiary corporation) a building, which building is subject to a lease that then has more than 5 years to run. This would be an example of a business lease indebtedness incurred prior to the acquisition of the property which would not have been incurred but for such acquisition.

Example (2). If the building itself in example (1) in this paragraph is later mortgaged to raise funds to release the pledged securities, the lease would continue to be a business lease.

Example (3). If a scientific organization mortgages its laboratory building to replace working capital used in remodelling another one of its buildings or a building held by its subsidiary corporation, which other building is free of indebtedness and is subject to a lease that then has more than 5 years to run, the lease would be a business lease inasmuch as the indebtedness though incurred subsequent to the improvement of such property would not have been incurred but for such improvement, and the incurrence of the indebtedness was reasonably foreseeable when, to make such improvement, the organization reduced its working capital below the amount necessary to continue current operations.

(c) Property acquired subject to lien. Where real property is acquired subject to a mortgage or similar lien, whether the acquisition be by gift, bequest, devise, or purchase, the amount of the indebtedness secured by such mortgage or lien is a business lease indebtedness (unless paragraph (d)(1) of this section applies) even though the lessor does not assume or agree to pay the indebtedness. For example, a university pays $100,000 for real estate valued at $300,000 and subject to a $200,000 mortgage. For the purpose of the tax on unrelated business taxable income, the result is the same as if $200,000 of borrowed funds had been used to buy the property.

(d) Certain property acquired by gifts, etc. *(1)* Where real property was acquired by gift, bequest, or devise, before July 1, 1950, subject to a mortgage or other similar lien, the amount of such mortgage or other similar lien shall not be considered as an indebtedness of the lessor tax-exempt organization incurred in acquiring such property. An indebtedness not otherwise covered by this exception is not brought within the exception by reason of a transfer of the property between a parent and its subsidiary corporation.

(2) Where real property was acquired by gift, bequest, or devise, before July 1, 1950, subject to a lease requiring improvements in such property upon the happening of stated contingencies, indebtedness incurred in improving such property in accordance with the terms of such lease shall not be considered as indebtedness described in section 514(g) and in this section. An indebtedness not otherwise covered by this exception is not brought within the exception by reason of a transfer of the property between a parent and its subsidiary corporation.

(e) Certain corporations described in section 501(c)(2). In the case of a title holding corporation described in section 501(c)(2), all of the stock of which was acquired before July 1, 1950, by an organization described in section 501(c)(3), (5), or (6) (and more than one-third of such stock was acquired by such organization by gift or bequest), any indebtedness incurred by such corporation before July 1, 1950, and any indebtedness incurred by such corporation on or after such date in improving real property in accordance with the terms of a lease entered into before such date, shall not be considered an indebtedness described in section 514(g) and in this section with respect to either such section 501(c)(2) corporation or such section 501(c)(3), (5), or (6) organization.

(f) Certain trusts described in section 401(a). In the case of a trust described in section 401(a), or in the case of a corporation described in section 501(c)(2) all of the stock of which was acquired before March 1, 1954, by such a trust, any indebtedness incurred by such trust or such corporation before such date, in connection with real property which is leased before such date, and any indebtedness incurred by such trust or such corporation on or after such date necessary to carry out the terms of such lease, shall not be considered as an indebtedness described in section 514(g) and in this section.

(g) Business lease on portion of property. Where only a portion of the real property is subject to a business lease, proper allocation of the indebtedness applicable to the whole property must be made to the premises covered by the lease. See example (2) of paragraph (b)(3) of § 1.514(a)-2.

(h) Special rule applicable to trusts described in section 401(a). If an employees' trust described in section 401(a) lends any money to another such employees' trust of the same employer, for the purposes of acquiring or improving real property, such loan will not be treated as an indebtedness of the borrowing trust except to the extent that the loaning trust—

(1) Incurs any indebtedness in order to make such loan;

(2) Incurred indebtedness before the making of such loan which would not have been incurred but for the making of such loan; or

(3) Incurred indebtedness after the making of such loan which would not have been incurred but for the making of such loan and which was reasonably foreseeable at the time of making such loan.

(i) Subsidiary corporations. The provisions of section 514(f), (g), and (h) are applicable whether or not a subsidiary corporation of the type described in section 501(c)(2) is availed of in making the business lease. For example, assume a parent organization borrows funds to purchase realty and sets up a separate section 501(c)(2) corporation as a subsidiary to hold the property. Such subsidiary corporation leases the property for a period of more than 5 years, collects the rents and pays over all of the income, less expenses, to the parent organization, the parent organization being liable for the indebtedness. Under these assumed facts, the lease by section 501(c)(2) subsidiary corporation would be a business lease with respect to such subsidiary corporation, and the rental income would be subject to the tax, whether or not the subsidiary itself assumes the indebtedness and whether or not the property is subject to the indebtedness.

(j) Certain trusts described in section 501(c)(17). *(1)* In the case of a supplemental unemployment benefit trust described in section 501(c)(17), or in the case of a corporation described in section 501(c)(2) all of the stock of which was acquired before January 1, 1960, by such a trust, any indebtedness incurred by such trust or such corporation before such date, in connection with real property which is leased before such date, and any indebtedness incurred by such trust or such corporation on or after such date necessary to carry out the terms of such lease, shall not be considered as an indebtedness described in section 514(g) and in this section.

(2) If a supplemental unemployment benefit trust described in section 501(c)(17) lends any money to another such supplemental unemployment benefit trust forming part of the same plan, for the purpose of acquiring or improving real property, such loan will not be treated as an indebtedness of the borrowing trust except to the extent that the loaning trust—

(i) Incurs any indebtedness in order to make such loan;

(ii) Incurred indebtedness before the making of such loan which would not have been incurred but for the making of such loan; or

(iii) Incurred indebtedness after the making of such loan which would not have been incurred but for the making of such loan and which was reasonably foreseeable at the time of making such loan.

T.D. 7229, 11/20/72.

---

§ 1.521-1 Farmers cooperative marketing and purchasing associations; requirements for exemption under section 521.

Caution: The Treasury has not yet amended Reg § 1.521-1 to reflect changes made by P.L. 99-272.

(a) *(1)* Cooperative associations engaged in the marketing of farm products for farmers, fruit growers, livestock growers, dairymen, etc., and turning back to the producers the proceeds of the sales of their products, less the necessary operating expenses, on the basis of either the quantity or the value of the products furnished by them, are exempt from income tax except as otherwise provided in section 522, or part I, subchapter T chapter 1 of the Code, and the regulations thereunder. For instance, cooperative dairy companies which are engaged in collecting milk and disposing of it or the products thereof and distributing the proceeds, less necessary operating expenses, among the producers upon the basis of either the quantity or the value of milk or of butterfat in the milk furnished by such producers, are exempt from the tax. If the proceeds of the business are distributed in any other way than on such a proportionate basis, the association does not meet the requirements of the Code and is not exempt. In other words, nonmember patrons must be treated the same as members insofar as the distribution of patronage dividends is concerned. Thus, if products are marketed for nonmember producers, the proceeds of the sale, less necessary operating expenses, must be returned to the patrons from the sale of whose goods such proceeds result, whether or not such patrons are members of the association. In order to show its cooperative nature and to establish compliance with the requirement of the Code that the proceeds of sales, less necessary expenses, be turned back to all producers on the basis of either the quantity or the value of the products furnished by them, it is necessary for such an association to keep permanent records of the business done both with members and nonmembers. The Code does not require, however, that the association keep ledger accounts with each producer selling through the association. Any permanent records which show that the association was operating during the taxable year on a cooperative basis in the distribution of patronage dividends to all producers will suffice. While under the Code patronage dividends must be paid to all producers on the same basis, this requirement is complied with if an association instead of paying patronage dividends to nonmember producers in cash, keeps permanent records from which the proportionate shares of the patronage dividends due to nonmember producers can be determined, and such shares are made applicable toward the purchase price of a share of stock or of a membership in the association. See, however, paragraph (c)(1) of § 1.1388-1 for the meaning of "payment in money" for purposes of qualifying a written notice of allocation.

(2) An association which has capital stock will not for such reason be denied exemption (i) if the dividend rate of such stock is fixed at not to exceed the legal rate of interest in the State of incorporation or 8 percent per annum, whichever is greater, on the value of the consideration for which the stock was issued, and (ii) if substantially all of such stock (with the exception noted below) is owned by producers who market their products or purchase their supplies and equipment through the association. Any ownership of stock by others than such actual producers must be satisfactorily explained in the association's application for exemption. The association will be required to show that the ownership of its capital stock has been restricted as far as possible to such actual producers. If by statutory requirement all officers of an association must be shareholders, the ownership of a share of stock by a nonproducer to qualify his as an officer will not destroy the association's exemption. Likewise, if a shareholder for any reason ceases to be a producer and the association is unable, because of a constitutional restriction or prohibition or other reason beyond the control of the association, to purchase or retire the stock of such nonproducer, the fact that under such circumstances a small amount of the outstanding capital stock is owned by shareholders who are no longer producers will not destroy the exemption. The restriction placed on the ownership of capital stock of an exempt cooperative association shall not apply to nonvoting

preferred stock, provided the owners of such stock are not entitled or permitted to participate, directly or indirectly, in the profits of the association, upon dissolution or otherwise, beyond the fixed dividends.

(3) The accumulation and maintenance of a reserve required by State statute, or the accumulation and maintenance of a reasonable reserve or surplus for any necessary purpose, such as to provide for he erection of buildings and facilities required in business or for the purchase and installation of machinery and equipment or to retire indebtedness incurred for such purposes, will not destroy the exemption. An association will not be denied exemption because it markets the products of nonmembers, provided the value of the products marketed for nonmembers does not exceed the value of products marketed for members. Anyone who shares in the profits of a farmers' cooperative marketing association, and is entitled to participate in the management of the association, must be regarded as a member of such association within the meaning of section 521.

(b) Cooperative associations engaged in the purchasing of supplies and equipment for farmers, fruit growers, livestock growers, dairymen, etc., and turning over such supplies and equipment to them at actual cost, plus the necessary operating expenses, are exempt. The term "supplies and equipment" as used in section 521 includes groceries and all other goods and merchandise used by farmers in the operation and maintenance of a farm or farmer's household. The provisions of paragraph (a) of this section relating to a reserve or surplus and to capital stock shall apply to associations coming under this paragraph. An association which purchases supplies and equipment for nonmembers will not for such reason be denied exemption, provided the value of the purchases for nonmembers does not exceed the value of the supplies and equipment purchased for members, and provided the value of the purchases made for nonmembers who are not producers does not exceed 15 percent of the value of all its purchases.

(c) In order to be exempt under either paragraph (a) or (b) of this section an association must establish that it has no taxable income for its own account other than that reflected in a reserve or surplus authorized in paragraph (a) of this section. An association engaged both in marketing farm products and in purchasing supplies and equipment is exempt if as to each of its functions it meets the requirements of the Code. Business done for the United States or any of its agencies shall be disregarded in determining the right to exemption under section 521 and this section. An association to be entitled to exemption must not only be organized but actually operated in the manner and for the purposes specified in section 521.

(d) Cooperative organizations engaged in occupations dissimilar from those of farmers, fruit growers, and the like, as not exempt.

(e) An organization is not exempt from taxation under this section merely because it claims that it complies with the requirements prescribed therein. In order to establish its exemption every organization claiming exemption under section 521 is required to file a Form 1028. The Form 1028, executed in accordance with the instructions on the form or issued therewith, should be filed with the district director for the internal revenue district in which is located the principal place of business or principal office of the organization. However, an organization which has been granted exemption under the provisions of the Internal Revenue Code of 1939 or prior law may rely on that ruling, unless affected by substantive changes in the Internal Revenue Code of 1954 or any changes in the character, purposes, or methods of operation of the organization, and it is not necessary in such case for the organization to request a new determination as to its exempt status.

(f) A cooperative association will not be denied exemption merely because it makes payments solely in nonqualified written notices of allocation to those patrons who do not consent as provided in section 1388 and § 1.1388-1, but makes payments of 20 percent in cash and the remainder in qualified written notices of allocation to those patrons who do so consent. Nor will such an association be denied exemption merely because, in the case of patrons who have so consented, payments of less than $5 are made solely in nonqualified written notices of allocation while payments of $5 or more are made in the form of 20 percent in cash and the remainder in qualified written notices of allocation. In addition, a cooperative association will not be denied exemption if it pays a smaller amount of interest or dividends on nonqualified written notices of allocation held by persons who have not consented as provided in section 1388 and § 1.1388-1 (or on per-unit retain certificates issued to patrons who are not qualifying patrons with respect thereto within the meaning of § 1.61-5(d)(2)) than it pays on qualified written notices of allocation held by persons who have so consented (or on per-unit retain certificates issued to patrons who are qualifying patrons with respect thereto) provided that the amount of the interest or dividend reduction is reasonable in relation to the fact that the association receives no tax benefit with respect to such nonqualified written notices of allocation (or such certificates issued to nonqualifying patrons) until redeemed. However, such an association will be denied exemption if it otherwise treats patrons who have not consented (or are not qualifying patrons) differently from patrons who have consented (or are qualifying patrons), either with regard to the original payment or allocation or with regard to the redemption of written notices of allocation or per-unit retain certificates. For example, if such an association pays patronage dividends in the form of written notices of allocation accompanied by qualified checks, and provides that any patron who does not cash his check within a specified time will forfeit the portion of the patronage dividend represented by such check, then the cooperative association will be denied exemption under this section as it does not treat all patrons alike.

T.D. 6301, 7/8/58, amend T.D. 6643, 4/1/63, T.D. 6855, 10/14/65.

§ 1.527-1 Political organizations; Generally.

Section 527 provides that a political organization is considered an organization exempt from income taxes for the purpose of any law which refers to organizations exempt from income taxes. A political organization is subject to tax only to the extent provided in section 527. In general, a political organization is an organization that is organized and operated primarily for an exempt function as defined in § 1.527-2(c). Section 527 provides that a political organization is taxed on its political organization taxable income (see § 1.527-4) which, in general, does not include the exempt function income (see § 1.527-3) of the political organization. Furthermore, section 527 provides that an exempt organization, other than a political organization, may be subject to tax under section 527 when it expends an amount for an exempt function, see § 1.527-6. The taxation of newsletter funds is provided under section 527(g) and § 1.527-7. A special rule for principal campaign committees is provided under section 527(h) and § 1.527-9.

T.D. 7744, 12/29/80, amend T.D. 8141, 7/29/85.

§ 1.527-2 Definitions.

For purposes of section 527 and these regulations—

(a) Political organization. *(1) In general.* A "political organization" is a party, committee, association, fund, or other organization (whether or not incorporated) organized and operated primarily for the purpose of directly or indirectly accepting contributions or making expenditures for an exempt function activity (as defined in paragraph (c) of this section). Accordingly, a political organization may include a committee or other group which accepts contributions or makes expenditures for the purpose of promoting the nomination of an individual for an elective public office in a primary election, or in a meeting or caucus of a political party. A segregated fund (as defined in paragraph (b) of this section) established and maintained by an individual may qualify as a political organization.

(2) Organizational test. A political organization meets the organizational test if its articles of organization provide that the primary purpose of the organization is to carry on one or more exempt functions. A political organization is not required to be formally chartered or established as a corporation, trust, or association. If an organization has no formal articles of organization, consideration is given to statements of the members of the organization at the time the organization is formed that they intend to operate the organization primarily to carry on one or more exempt functions.

(3) Operational test. A political organization does not have to engage exclusively in activities that are an exempt function. For example, a political organization may—

(i) Sponsor nonpartisan educational workshops which are not intended to influence or attempt to influence the selection, nomination, election, or appointment of any individual for public office,

(ii) Pay an incumbent's office expenses, or

(iii) Carry on social activities which are unrelated to its exempt function,

provided these are not the organization's primary activities. However, expenditures for purposes described in the preceding sentence are not for an exempt function. See § 1.527-2(c) and (d). Furthermore, it is not necessary that a political organization operate in accordance with normal corporate formalities as ordinarily established in bylaws or under state law.

(b) Segregated fund. *(1) General rule.* A "segregated fund" is a fund which is established and maintained by a political organization or an individual separate from the assets of the organization or the personal assets of the individual. The purpose of such a fund must be to receive and segregate exempt function income (and earnings on such income) for use only for an exempt function or for an activity necessary to fulfill an exempt function. Accordingly, the amounts in the fund must be dedicated for use only for an exempt function. Thus, expenditures for the establishment or administration of a political organization or the solicitation of political contributions may be made from the segregated fund, if necessary to fulfill an exempt function. The fund must be clearly identified and established for the purposes intended. A savings or checking account into which only contributions to the political organization are placed and from which only expenditures for exempt functions are made may be a segregated fund. If an organization that had designated a fund to be a segregated fund for purposes of segregating amounts referred to in section 527(c)(3) (A) through (D), expends more than an insubstantial amount from the segregated fund for activities that are not for an exempt function during a taxable year, the fund will not be treated as a segregated fund for such year. In such a case amounts referred to in section 527(c)(3)(A)–(D), segregated in such fund will not be exempt function income. Further, if more than insubstantial amounts segregated for an exempt function in prior years are expended for other than an exempt function the facts and circumstances may indicate that the fund was never a segregated fund as defined in this paragraph.

(2) Record keeping. The organization or individual maintaining a segregated fund must keep records that are adequate to verify receipts and disbursements of the fund and identify the exempt function activity for which each expenditure is made.

(c) Exempt function. *(1) Directly related expenses.* An "exempt function", as defined in section 527(e)(2), includes all activities that are directly related to and support the process of influencing or attempting to influence the selection, nomination, election, or appointment of any individual to public office or office in a political organization (the selection process). Whether an expenditure is for an exempt function depends upon all the facts and circumstances. Generally, where an organization supports an individual's campaign for public office, the organization's activities and expenditures in furtherance of the individual's election or appointment to that office are for an exempt function of the organization. The individual does not have to be an announced candidate for the office. Furthermore, the fact that an individual never becomes a candidate is not crucial in determining whether an organization is engaging in an exempt function. An activity engaged in between elections which is directly related to, and supports, the process of selection, nomination, or election of an individual in the next applicable political campaign is an exempt function activity.

(2) Indirect expenses. Expenditures that are not directly related to influencing or attempting to influence the selection process may also be an expenditure for an exempt function by a political organization. These are expenses which are necessary to support the directly related activities of the political organization. Activities which support the directly related activities are those which must be engaged in to allow the political organization to carry out the activity of influencing or attempting to influence the selection process. For example, expenses for overhead and record keeping are necessary to allow the political organization to be established and to engage in political activities. Similarly, expenses incurred in soliciting contributions to the political organization are necessary to support the activities of the political organization.

(3) Terminating activities. An exempt function includes an activity which is in furtherance of the process of terminating a political organization's existence. For example, where a political organization is established for a single campaign, payment of campaign debts after the conclusion of the campaign is an exempt function activity.

(4) Illegal expenditures. Expenditures which are illegal or are for a judicially determined illegal activity are not considered expenditures in furtherance of an exempt function, even though such expenditures are made in connection with the selection process.

(5) Examples. The following examples illustrate the principles of paragraph (c) of this section. The term "exempt function" when used in the following examples means exempt function within the meaning of section 527(e)(2).

(i) Example (1). A wants to run for election to public office in State X. A is not a candidate. A travels throughout X in order to rally support for A's intended candidacy. While in X, A attends a convention of an organization for the purpose of attempting to solicit its support. The amount expended for travel, lodging, food, and similar expenses are for an exempt function.

(ii) Example (2). B, a member of the United States House of Representatives, is a candidate for reelection. B travels with B's spouse to the district B represents. B feels it is important for B's reelection that B's spouse accompany B. While in the district, B makes speeches and appearances for the purpose of persuading voters to reelect B. The travel expenses of B and B's spouse are for an exempt function.

(iii) Example (3). C is a candidate for public office. In connection with C's campaign, C takes voice and speech lessons to improve C's skills. The expenses for these lessons are for an exempt function.

(iv) Example (4). D, an officeholder and candidate for reelection, purchases tickets to a testimonial dinner. D's attendance at the dinner is intended to aid D's reelection. Such expenditures are for an exempt function.

(v) Example (5). E, an officeholder, expends amounts for periodicals of general circulation in order to keep informed on national and local issues. Such expenditures are not for an exempt function.

(vi) Example (6). N is an organization described in section 501(c) and is exempt from taxation under section 501(a). F is employed as president of N. F, as a representative of N, testifies in response to a written request from a Congressional committee in support of the confirmation of an individual to a cabinet position. The expenditures by N that are directly related to F's testimony are not for an exempt function.

(vii) Example (7). P is a political organization described in section 527(e)(2). Between elections P does not support any particular individual for public office. However, P does train staff members for the next election, drafts party rules, implements party reform proposals, and sponsors a party convention. The expenditures for these activities are for an exempt function.

(viii) Example (8). Q is a political organization described in section 527(e)(2). Q finances seminars and conferences which are intended to influence persons who attend to support individuals to public office whose political philosophy is in harmony with the political philosophy of Q. The expenditures for these activities are for an exempt function.

(d) Public office. The facts and circumstances of each case will determine whether a particular Federal, State, or local office is a "public office." Principles consistent with those found under § 53.4946-1(g)(2) (relating to the definition of public office) will be applied.

(e) Principal campaign committee. A "principal campaign committee" is the political committee designated by a candidate for Congress as his or her principal campaign committee for purposes of section 302(e) of the Federal Election Campaign Act of 1971 (2 U.S.C. section 432(e)), as amended, and section 527(h) and § 1.527-9.

T.D. 7744, 12/29/80, amend T.D. 8041, 7/29/85.

---

§ 1.527-3 Exempt function income.

(a) General rule. *(1)* For purposes of section 527, exempt function income consists solely of amounts received as—

(i) Contributions of money or other property,

(ii) Membership dues, fees, or assessments from a member of a political organization, or

(iii) Proceeds from a political fund raising or entertainment event, or proceeds from the sale of political campaign materials, which are not received in the ordinary course of any trade or business,

but only to the extent such income is segregated for use only for exempt functions of the political organization.

(2) Income will be considered segregated for use only for an exempt function only if it is received into and disbursed from a segregated fund as defined in § 1.527-2(b).

(b) Contributions. The rules of section 271(b)(2) apply in determining whether the transfer of money or other property constitutes a contribution. Generally, money or other property, whether solicited personally, by mail, or through advertising, qualifies as a contribution. In addition, to the extent a political organization receives Federal, State, or local funds under the $1 "checkoff" provision (sections 9001–9013), or any other provision for financing of campaigns, such amounts are to be treated as contributions.

(c) Dues, fees, and assessments. Amounts received as membership fees and assessments from members of a political organization may constitute exempt function income to the political organization. Membership fees and assessments received in consideration for services, goods, or other items of value do not constitute exempt function income. However, filing fees paid by an individual directly or indirectly to a political party in order that the individual may run as a candidate in a primary election of the party (or run in a general election as a candidate of that party) are to be treated as exempt function income. For example, some States provide that a certain percentage of the first year's salary of the office sought must be paid to the State as a filing (or "qualifying") fee and party assessment. The State then transfers part of this fee to the candidate's party. In such a case, the entire amount transferred to the party is to be treated as exempt function income. Furthermore, amounts paid by an individual directly to the party as a qualification fee are treated similarly.

(d) Fund raising events. *(1) In general.* Amounts received from fund raising and entertainment events are eligible for treatment as exempt function income if the events are political in nature and are not carried on in the ordinary course of a trade or business. Whether an event is "political" in nature depends on all facts and circumstances. One factor that indicates an event is a political event is the extent to which the event is related to a political activity aside from the need of the organization for income or funds. For example, an event that is intended to rally and encourage support for an individual for public office would be a political fund raising event. Examples of political events can include dinners, breakfasts, receptions, picnics, dances, and athletic exhibitions.

(2) Ordinary course of any trade or business. Whether an activity is in the ordinary course of a trade or business depends on the facts and circumstances of each case. Generally, proceeds from casual, sporadic fund raising or entertainment events are not in the ordinary course of a trade or business. Factors to be taken into account in determining whether an activity is a trade or business include the frequency of the activity, the manner in which the activity is conducted, and the span of time over which the activity is carried on.

(e) Sale of campaign materials. Amounts received from the sale of campaign materials are eligible for treatment as exempt function income if the sale is not carried on in the ordinary course of a trade or business (as defined in paragraph (d)(2) of this section), and is related to a political activity of the organization aside from the need of such organization for income or funds. Proceeds from the sale of political memorabilia, bumper stickers, campaign buttons, hats, shirts, political posters, stationery, jewelry, or cookbooks are related to such a political activity where such items can be identified as relating to distributing political literature or organizing voters to vote for a candidate for public office.

T.D. 7744, 12/29/80.

§ 1.527-4 Special rules for computation of political organization taxable income.

(a) In general. Political organization taxable income is determined according to the provisions of section 527(b) and the rules set forth in this section.

(b) Limitation on capital losses. If for any taxable year a political organization has a net capital loss, the rules of sections 1211(a) and 1212(a) apply.

(c) Allowable deductions. *(1) In general.* To be deductible in computing political organization taxable income, expenses, depreciation, and similar items must not only qualify as deductions allowed by chapter 1 of the Code, but must also be directly connected with the production of political organization taxable income.

(2) "Directly connected with" defined. To be "directly connected with" the production of political organization taxable income, an item of deduction must have a proximate and primary relationship to the production of such income and have been incurred in the production of such income. Items of deduction attributable solely to items of political organization taxable income are proximately and primarily related to such income. Whether an item of deduction is incurred in the production of political organization taxable income is determined on the basis of all the facts and circumstances of each case.

(3) Dual use of facilities or personnel. Expenses, depreciation, and similar items that are attributable to the production of exempt function income and political organization taxable income shall be allocated between the two on a reasonable and consistent basis. For example, where facilities are used both for an exempt function of the organization and for the production of political organization taxable income, expenses, depreciation, and similar items attributable to such facilities (for example, items of overhead) shall be allocated between the two uses of a reasonable and consistent basis. Similarly, where personnel are employed both for an exempt function and for the production of political organization taxable income, expenses and similar items attributable to such personnel (for example, items of salary) shall be allocated between the activities on a reasonable and consistent basis. The portion of any such item so allocated to the production of political organization taxable income is directly connected with such income and is allowable as a deduction in computing political organization taxable income to the extent that it qualifies as an item of deduction allowed by chapter 1 of the Code. Thus, for example, assume that X, a political organization, pays its manager a salary of $10,000 a year and that it derives political organization taxable income. If 10 percent of the manager's time during the year is devoted to deriving X's gross income (other than exempt function income), a deduction of $1,000 (10 percent of $10,000) would generally be allowable for purposes of computing X's political organization taxable income.

T.D. 7744, 12/29/80.

§ 1.527-5 Activities resulting in gross income to an individual or political organization.

(a) In general. *(1) General rule.* Amounts expended by a political organization for an exempt function are not income to the individual or individuals on whose behalf such expenditures are made. However, where a political organization expends any other amount for the personal use of any individual, the individual on whose behalf the amount is expended will be in receipt of income. Amounts are expended for the personal use of an individual where a direct or indirect financial benefit accrues to such individual. For example, if a political organization pays a personal legal obligation of a candidate for public office, such as the candidate's federal income tax liability, the amount paid is includible in such candidate's gross income. Similarly, if a political organization expends any amount of its exempt function income for other than an exempt function, and the expenditure results in a direct or indirect financial benefit to the political organization, it must include the amount of such expenditure in its gross income. For example, if a political organization expends exempt function income for making an improvement or addition to its facilities, or for equipment, which is not necessary for or used in carrying out an exempt function, the amount of the expenditure will be included in the political organization's gross income. However, if a political organization expends exempt function income to make ordinary and necessary repairs on the facilities the political organization uses in conducting its exempt function, such amounts will not be included in the political organization's gross income.

(2) Expenditure for an illegal activity. Expenditures by a political organization that are illegal or for an activity that is judicially determined to be illegal are treated as amounts not segregated for use only for the exempt function and shall be included in the political organization's taxable income. However, expenses incurred in defense of civil or criminal suits against the organization are not treated as taxable to the organization. Similarly, voluntary reimbursement to the participants in the illegal activity for similar expenses incurred by them are not taxable to the organization if the organization can demonstrate that such payments do not constitute a part of the inducement to engage in the illegal activity or part of the agreed upon compensation therefor. However, if the organization entered into an agreement with the participants to defray such expenses as part of the inducement, such payments would be treated as an expenditure for an illegal activity. Except where necessary to prevent the period of limitation for assessment and collection of a tax from expiring, a notice of deficiency will not generally be issued until after there has been a final determination of illegality by an appropriate court in a criminal proceeding.

(b) Certain uses not treated as income to a candidate. Except as otherwise provided in paragraph (a) of this section, if a political organization—

(1) Contributes any amount to or for the use of any political organization described in section 527(e)(1) or newsletter fund described in section 527(g),

(2) Contributes any amount to or for the use of any organization described in paragraph (1) and (2) of section 509(a) which is exempt from taxation under section 501(a), or

(3) Deposits any amount in the general fund of the U.S. Treasury or in the general fund of any State or local government,

such amount shall not be treated as an amount expended for the personal use of a candidate or other person. No deduction shall be allowed under the Internal Revenue Code of 1954 for the contribution or deposit described in the preceding sentence.

(c) Excess funds. *(1) General rule.* Generally, funds controlled by a political organization or other person after a campaign or election are excess funds and are treated as expended for the personal use of the person having control over the ultimate use of such funds. However, such funds will not be treated as excess funds to the extent they are—

(i) Transferred within a reasonable period of time by the person controlling the funds in accordance with paragraph (b) of this section, or

(ii) Held in reasonable anticipation of being used by the political organization for future exempt functions.

(2) Excess funds transferred at death. Where excess funds are held by an individual who dies, and these funds go to the individual's estate or any other person (other than an organization or fund described in paragraph (b) of this section), the funds are income of the decedent and will be included in the decedent's gross estate unless the estate or other person receiving such funds transfers the funds within a reasonable period of time in accordance with paragraph (b) of this section.

This paragraph (c)(2) will not apply where the individual who dies provides that the funds be transferred to an organization or fund described in paragraph (b) of this section.

T.D. 7744, 12/29/80.

§ 1.527-6 Inclusion of certain amounts in the gross income of an exempt organization which is not a political organization.

(a) Exempt organizations. General rule. If an organization described in section 501(c) which is exempt from tax under section 501(a) expends any amount for an exempt function, it may be subject to tax. There is included in the gross income of such organization for the taxable year an amount equal to the lesser of—

(1) The net investment income of such organization for the taxable year, or

(2) The aggregate amount expended during the taxable year for an exempt function.

The amount included will be treated as political organization taxable income.

(b) Exempt function expenditures. *(1) Directly related expenses.* (i) Except as provided in this section, the term "exempt function" will generally have the same meaning it has in § 1.527-2(c). Thus, expenditures which are directly related to the selection process as defined in § 1.527-2(c)(1) are expenditures for an exempt function. Expenditures for indirect expenses as defined in § 1.527-2(c)(2), when made by a section 501(c) organization are for an exempt function only to the extent provided in paragraph (b)(2) of this section. Expenditures of a section 501(c) organization which are otherwise allowable under the Federal Election Campaign Act or similar State statute are for an exempt function only to the extent provided in paragraph (b)(3) of this section.

(ii) An expenditure may be made for an exempt function directly or through another organization. A section 501(c) organization will not be absolutely liable under section 527(f)(1) for amounts transferred to an individual or organization. A section 501(c) organization is, however, required to take reasonable steps to ensure that the transferee does not use such amounts for an exempt function.

(2) Indirect expenses.[Reserved].

(3) Expenditures allowed by Federal Election Campaign Act. [Reserved].

(4) Appointments or confirmations. Where an organization described in paragraph (a) of this section appears before any legislative body in response to a written request by such body for the purpose of influencing the appointment or confirmation of an individual to a public office, any expenditure directly related to such appearance is not treated as an expenditure for an exempt function.

(5) Nonpartisan activity. Expenditures for nonpartisan activities by an organization to which paragraph (a) of this section applies are not expenditures for an exempt function. Nonpartisan activities include voter registration and "get-out-the-vote" campaigns. To be nonpartisan voter registration and "get-out-the-vote" campaigns must not be specifically identified by the organization with any candidate or political party.

(c) Character of items included in gross income. *(1) General rule.* The items of income included in the gross income of an organization under paragraph (a) of this section retain their character as ordinary income or capital gain.

(2) Special rule in determining character of item. If the amount included in gross income is determined under paragraph (a)(2)(ii) of this section, the character of the items of income is determined by multiplying the total amount included in gross income under such paragraph by a fraction, the numerator of which is the portion of the organization's net investment income that is gain from the sale or exchange of a capital asset, and the denominator of which is the organization's net investment income. For example, if $5,000 is included in the gross income of an organization under paragraph (a)(2) of this section, and the organization had $100,000 of net investment income of which $10,000 is long term capital gain, then $500 would be treated as long term capital gain:

Capital gain / Net investment income	×	Amount Expended on an exempt function	=	Portion of income subject to tax under section 1201
$ 10,000 / $100,000	×	$5,000	=	$500

(d) Modifications. The modifications described in section 527(c)(2) apply in computing the tax under paragraph (a)(2) of this section. Thus, no net operating loss is allowed under section 172 nor is any deduction allowed under part VIII of subchapter B. However, there is allowed a specific deduction of $100.

(e) Transfer not treated as exempt function expenditures. Provided the provisions of this paragraph (e) are met, a transfer of political contributions or dues collected by a section 501(c) organization to a separate segregated fund as defined in paragraph (f) of this section is not treated as an expenditure for an exempt function (within the meaning of § 1.527-2(c)). Such transfers must be made promptly after the receipt of such amounts by the section 501(c) organization, and must be made directly to the separate segregated fund. A transfer is considered promptly and directly made if:

(1) The procedures followed by the section 501(c) organization satisfy the requirements of applicable Federal or State campaign law and regulations;

(2) The section 501(c) organization maintains adequate records to demonstrate that amounts transferred in fact consist of political contributions or dues, rather than investment income; and

(3) The political contributions or dues transferred were not used to earn investment income for the section 501(c) organization.

(f) Separate segregated fund. An organization or fund described in section 527(f)(3) is a separate segregated fund. To avoid the application of paragraph (a) of this section, an organization described in section 501(c) that is exempt from taxation under section 501(a) may, if it is consistent with its exempt status, establish and maintain such a separate segregated fund to receive contributions and make expenditures in a political campaign. If such a fund meets the requirements of § 1.527-2(a) (relating to the definition of a political organization), it shall be treated as a political organization subject to the provisions of section 527. A segregated fund established under the Federal Election Campaign Act will continue to be treated as a segregated fund when it engages in exempt function activities as defined in § 1.527-2(c), relating to State campaigns.

(g) Effect of expenditures on exempt status. Section 527(f) and this section do not sanction the intervention in any political campaign by an organization described in section 501(c) if such activity is inconsistent with its exempt status under section 501(c). For example, an organization described in section 501(c)(3) is precluded from engaging in any political campaign activities. The fact that section 527 imposes a tax on the exempt function (as defined in § 1.527-2(c)) expenditures of section 501(c) organizations and permits such organizations to establish separate segregated funds to engage in campaign activities does not sanction the participation in these activities by section 501(c)(3) organizations.

T.D. 7744, 12/29/80.

§ 1.527-7 Newsletter funds.

(a) In general. For purposes of this section, a fund established and maintained by an individual who holds, has been elected to, or is a candidate (within the meaning of section 41(c)(2)) for nomination or election to, any Federal, State, or local elective public office for the use by such individual exclusively for an exempt function, as defined in paragraph (c) of this section, shall be a newsletter fund. If assets of a newsletter fund are used for any purpose other than the exempt function of the newsletter fund as defined in paragraph (c) of this section, such amount shall be treated as expended for the personal use of the individual who established and maintained such fund. In addition, future contributions to such fund are treated as income to the individual who established and maintained the fund. In such a case, the facts and circumstances may indicate that the fund was never established and maintained exclusively for an exempt function as defined in paragraph (c) of this section.

(b) Determination of taxable income. A newsletter fund shall be treated as if it were a political organization for purposes of determining its taxable income. However, the specific $100 deduction provided by section 527(c)(2)(A) shall not be allowed.

(c) Exempt function. For purposes of this section, the exempt function of a newsletter fund consists solely of the preparation and circulation of the newsletter. Among the expenditures treated as preparation and circulation expenditures of the newsletter are—

(1) Secretarial services,

(2) Printing,

(3) Addressing, and

(4) Mailing.

(d) Nonexempt function purposes. Newsletter fund assets may not be used for campaign activities. Therefore, an exempt function of a newsletter fund does not include—

(1) Expenditures for an exempt function as defined in § 1.527-2(c) or

(2) Transfers of unexpended amounts to a political organization described in section 527(e)(1).

(e) Excess funds. Excess funds held by a newsletter fund which has ceased to engage in the preparation and circulation of the newsletter are treated as expended for the personal use of the individual who established and maintained such fund. However, to the extent such excess funds are within a reasonable period of time—

(1) Contributed to or for the use of any organization described in paragraph (1) or (2) of section 509(a) which is exempt from taxation under section 501(a),

(2) Deposited in the general fund of the U.S. Treasury or in the general fund of any State or local government (including the District of Columbia), or

(3) Contributed to any other newsletter fund as described in paragraph (a) of this section,

the excess funds are not treated as expended for the personal use of such individual. In such a case the individual is not allowed a deduction under the Internal Revenue Code of 1954 for such contribution or deposit.

T.D. 7744, 12/29/80.

§ 1.527-8 Effective date; filing requirements; and miscellaneous provisions.

(a) Assessment and collections. Since the taxes imposed by section 527 are taxes imposed by subtitle A of the Code, all provisions of law and of the regulations applicable to the taxes imposed by subtitle A are applicable to the assessment and collection of the taxes imposed by section 527. Organizations subject to the tax imposed by section 527 are subject to the same provisions, including penalties, as are provided for corporations, in general, except that the requirements of section 6154 concerning the payment of estimated tax do not apply. See, generally, sections 6151, et. seq., and the regulations prescribed thereunder, for provisions relating to payment of tax.

(b) Returns. For requirements of filing annual returns with respect to political organization taxable income, see section 6012(a)(6) and the applicable regulations.

(c) Taxable years, method of accounting, etc. The taxable year (fiscal year or calendar year, as the case may be) of a political organization is determined without regard to the fact that such organization may have been exempt from tax during any prior period. See sections 441 and 446, and the regulations thereunder in this part, and section 7701 and the regulations in Part 301 of this chapter (Regulations on Procedure and Administration). Similarly, in computing political organization taxable income, the determination of the taxable year for which an item of income or expense is taken into account is made under the provisions of sections 441, 446, 451, 461, and the regulations thereunder, whether or not the item arose during a taxable year beginning before, on, or after the effective date of the provisions imposing a tax upon political organization taxable income. If a method for treating bad debts was selected in a return of income (other than an information return) for a previous taxable year, the taxpayer must follow such method in its returns under section 527, unless such method is changed in accordance with the provisions of § 1.166-1. A taxpayer who has not previously selected a method for treating bad debts may, in its first return under section 6012(a)(6), exercise the option granted in § 1.166-1.

(d) Effective date. Except as provided in paragraph (b)(2) of § 1.527-6 and in paragraph (a) of § 1.527-9, the regulations under section 527 apply to taxable years beginning after December 31, 1974.

T.D. 7744, 12/29/80, amend T.D. 8041, 7/29/85.

§ 1.527-9 Special rule for principal campaign committees.

(a) In general. Effective with respect to taxable years beginning after December 31, 1981, the tax imposed by section 527(b) on the political organization taxable income of a principal campaign committee shall be computed by multiplying the political organization taxable income by the appropriate rates of tax specified in section 11(b). The political organization taxable income of a campaign committee not a principal campaign committee is taxed at the highest rate of tax specified in section 11(b). A candidate for Congress may designate one political committee to serve as his or her principal campaign committee for purposes of section 527(h)(1). If a designation is made, it shall be made in accordance with the requirements of paragraph (b) of this section. A candidate for Congress may have only one designation in effect at any time. Under 11 CFR 102.12, no political committee may be designated as the principal campaign committee of more than one candidate for Congress. Further, no political committee that supports or has supported more than one candidate for Congress may be designated as a principal campaign committee. No designation need be made where there is only one political campaign committee with respect to a candidate.

(b) Manner of designation. If a candidate for Congress elects to make a designation under section 527(h) and this section, he or she shall designate his or her principal campaign committee by appending a copy of his or her Statement of Candidacy (that is, the Federal Election Commission Form 2, or equivalent statement that the candidate filed with the Federal Election Commission under 11 CFR 101.1(a)), to the Form 1120-POL filed by the principal campaign committee for each taxable year for which the designation is effective. This designation may also be made by appending to the Form 1120-POL statement containing the following information: The name and address of the candidate for Congress; his or her taxpayer identification number; his or her party affiliation and the office sought; the district and State in which the office is sought; and the name and address of the principal campaign committee. This designation shall be made on or before the due date (as extended) for filing Form 1120-POL. Only a candidate for Congress may make a designation in accordance with this paragraph.

(c) Manner of revoking designation. A designation of a principal campaign committee that has been filed in accordance with this section may be revoked only with the consent of the Commissioner. In general, the Commissioner will grant such consent in every case where the candidate for Congress has revoked his or her designation in compliance with the requirements of the Federal Election Commission by filing an amended Statement of Organization or its equivalent pursuant to 11 CFR 102.2(a)(2). In the case of the revocation of the designation of a principal campaign committee by a candidate followed by the designation of another principal campaign committee by such candidate, for purposes of determining the appropriate rate of tax under section 11(b) for a taxable year, the political organization taxable income of the first principal campaign committee shall be treated as that of the subsequent principal campaign committee. In a case where consent to revoke a designation of a principal campaign committee is granted and a new designation is filed, the Commissioner may condition his consent upon the agreement of the candidate for Congress to insure compliance with the preceding sentence.

T.D. 8041, 7/29/85.

§ 1.528-1 Homeowners associations.

Caution: The Treasury has not yet amended Reg § 1.528-1 to reflect changes made by P.L. 105-34.

(a) In general. Section 528 only applies to taxable years of homeowners associations beginning after December 31, 1973. To qualify as a homeowners association an organization must either be a condominium management association or a residential real estate management association. For the purposes of Section 528 and the regulations under that section, the term "homeowners association" shall refer only to an organization described in section 528. Cooperative housing corporations and organizations based on a similar form of ownership are not eligible to be taxed as homeowners associations. As a general rule, membership in either a condominium management association or a residential real estate management association is confined to the developers and the owners of the units, residences, or lots. Furthermore, membership in either type of association is normally required as a condition of such ownership. However, if the membership of an organization consists of other homeowners associations, the owners of units, residences, or lots who are members of such other homeowners associations will be treated as the members of the organization for the purposes of the regulations under section 528.

(b) Condominium. The term "condominium" means an interest in real property consisting of an undivided interest in common in a portion of a parcel of real property (which may be a fee simple estate or an estate for years, such as a leasehold or subleasehold) together with a separate interest in space in a building located on such property. An interest in property is not a condominium unless the undivided interest in the common elements are vested in the unit holders. In addition, a condominium must meet the requirements of applicable state or local law relating to condominiums or horizontal property regimes.

(c) Residential real estate management association. Residential real estate management associations are normally composed of owners of single-family residential units located in a subdivision, development, or similar area. However, they may also include as members, owners of multiple-family dwelling units located in such areas. They are commonly formed to administer and enforce covenants relating to the architecture and appearance of the real estate development as well as to perform certain maintenance duties relating to common areas.

(d) Tenants. Tenants will not be considered members for purposes of meeting the source of income test under section

528(c)(1)(B) and § 1.528-5. However, the fact that tenants of members of a homeowners association are permitted to be members of the association will not disqualify an association under section 528(c)(1) if it otherwise meets the requirements of section 528(c) and these regulations.

T.D. 7692, 4/17/80.

§ 1.528-2 Organized and operated to provide for the acquisition, construction, management, maintenance and care of association property.

(a) Organized and operated. *(1) Organized.* To be treated as a homeowners association an organization must be organized and operated primarily for the purpose of carrying on one or more of the exempt functions of a homeowners association. For the purposes of section 528 and these regulations, the exempt functions of a homeowners association are the acquisition, construction, management, maintenance, and care of association property. In determining whether an organization is organized and operated primarily to carry on one or more exempt functions, all the facts and circumstances of each case shall be considered. For example, when an organization provides in its articles of organization that its sole purpose is to carry on one or more exempt functions, in the absence of other relevant factors it will be considered to have met the organizational test. (The term "articles of organization" means the organization's corporate charter, trust instruments, articles of association or other instrument by which it is created.)

(2) Operated. An organization will be treated as being operated for the purpose of carrying on one or more of the exempt functions of a homeowners association if it meets the provisions of §§ 1.528-5 and 1.528-6.

(b) Terms to be interpreted according to common meaning and usage. As used in section 528 and these regulations, the terms acquisition, construction, management, maintenance, and care are to be interpreted according to their common meaning and usage. For example, maintenance of association property includes the painting and repairing of such property as well as the gardening and janitorial services associated with its upkeep. Similarly, the term "construction" of association property includes covenants or other rules for preserving the architectural and general appearance of the area. The term also includes regulations relating to the location, color and allowable building materials to be used in all structures. (For the definition of association property see § 1.528-3)

T.D. 7692, 4/17/80.

§ 1.528-3 Association property.

Caution: The Treasury has not yet amended Reg § 1.528-3 to reflect changes made by P.L. 105-34.

(a) Property owned by the organization. "Association property" includes real and personal property owned by the organization or owned as tenants in common by the members of the organization. Such property must be available for the common benefit of all members of the organization and must be of a nature that tends to enhance the beneficial enjoyment of the private residences by their owners. If two or more facilities or items of property of a similar nature are owned by a homeowners association, and if the use of any particular facility or item is restricted to fewer than all association members, such facilities or items nevertheless will be considered association property if all association members are treated equitably and have similar rights with respect to comparable items or facilities. Among the types of property that ordinarily will be considered association property are swimming pools and tennis courts. On the other hand, facilities or areas set aside for the use of nonmembers, or in fact used primarily by nonmembers, are not association property for the purposes of this section. For example, property owned by an organization for the purpose of leasing it to groups consisting primarily of nonmembers to be used as a meeting place or a retreat will not be considered association property.

(b) Property normally owned by a governmental unit. "Association property" also includes areas and facilities traditionally recognized and accepted as being of direct governmental concern in the exercise of the powers and duties entrusted to governments to regulate community health, safety and welfare. Such areas and facilities would normally include roadways, parklands, sidewalks, streetlights and firehouses. Property described in this paragraph will be considered association property regardless of whether it is owned by the organization itself, by its members as tenants in common or by a governmental unit and used for the benefit of the residents of such unit including the members of the organization.

(c) Privately owned property. "Association property" may also include property owned privately by members of the organization. However, to be so included the condition of such property must affect the overall appearance or structure of the residential units which make up the organization. Such property may include the exterior walls and roofs of privately owned residences as well as the lawn and shrubbery on privately owned land and any other privately owned property the appearance of which may directly affect the appearance of the entire organization. However, privately owned property will not be considered association property unless—

(1) There is a covenant or similar requirement relating to exterior appearance or maintenance that applies on the same basis to all such property (or to a reasonable classification of such property);

(2) There is a pro rata mandatory assessment (at least once a year) on all members of the association for maintaining such property; and

(3) Membership in the organization is a condition of ownership of such property.

T.D. 7692, 4/17/80.

§ 1.528-4 Substantially test.

Caution: The Treasury has not yet amended Reg § 1.528-4 to reflect changes made by P.L. 105-34.

(a) In general. In order for an organization to be considered a condominium management association or a residential retail estate management association (and therefore in order for it to be considered a homeowners association), substantially all of its units, lots or buildings must be used by individuals for residences. For the purposes of applying paragraph (b) or (c) of this section, and organization which has attributes of both a condominium management association and a residential real estate management association shall be considered that association which, based on all the facts and circumstances, it more closely resembles. In addition, those paragraphs shall be applied based on conditions existing on the last day of the organization's taxable year.

(b) Condominium management associations. Substantially all of the units of a condominium management association will be considered as used by individuals for residences if at least 85% of the total square footage of all units within the project is used by individuals for residential purposes. If a completed unit has never been occupied, it will nonetheless be considered as used for residential purposes if, based on all the facts and circumstances, it appears to have been constructed for use as a residence. Similarly, a unit which is not occupied but which has been in the past will be considered as used for residential purposes if, based on all the facts and circumstances, it appears that it was constructed for use as a residence, and the last individual to occupy it did in fact use it as a residence. Units which are used for purposes auxiliary to residential use (such as laundry areas, swimming pools, tennis courts, storage rooms and areas used by maintenance personnel) shall be considered used for residential purposes.

(c) Residential real estate management associations. Substantially all of the lots or buildings of a residential real estate management association (including unimproved lots) will be considered as used by individuals as residences if at least 85% of the lots are zoned for residential purposes. Lots shall be treated as zoned for residential purposes even if under such zoning lots may be used for parking spaces, swimming pools, tennis courts, schools, fire stations, libraries, churches and other similar purposes which are auxiliary to residential use. However, commercial shopping areas (and their auxiliary parking areas) are not lots zoned for residential purposes.

(d) Exception. Notwithstanding any other provision of this section, a unit, or building will not be considered used for residential purposes, if for more than one-half the days in the association's taxable year, such unit, or building is occupied by a person or series of persons, each of whom so occupies such unit, or building for less than 30 days.

T.D. 7692, 4/17/80.

§ 1.528-5 Source of income test.

An organization cannot qualify as a homeowners association under section 528 for a taxable year unless 60 percent or more of its gross income for such taxable year is exempt function income as defined in § 1.528-9. The determination of whether an organization meets the provisions of this section shall be made after the close of the organization's taxable year.

T.D. 7692, 4/17/80.

§ 1.528-6 Expenditure test.

Caution: The Treasury has not yet amended Reg § 1.528-6 to reflect changes made by P.L. 105-34.

(a) In general. An organization cannot qualify as a homeowners association under section 528 for a taxable year unless 90 percent or more of its expenditures for such taxable year are qualifying expenditures as defined in paragraphs (b) and (c) of this section. The determination of whether an organization meets the provisions of this section shall be made after the close of the organization's taxable year. Investments or transfers of funds to be held to meet future costs shall not be taken into account as expenditures. For example, transfers to a sinking fund account for the replacement of a roof would not be considered an expenditure for the purposes of this section even if the roof is association property. In addition, excess assessments which are either rebated to members or applied against the members' following year's assessments will not be considered an expenditure for the purposes of this section.

(b) Qualifying expenditures. Qualifying expenditures are expenditures by an organization for the acquisition, construction, management, maintenance, and care of the organization's association property. They include both current operating and capital expenditures on association property. Qualifying expenditures include expenditures on association property despite the fact that such property may produce income which is not exempt function income. Thus expenditures on a swimming pool are qualifying expenditures despite the fact that fees from guests of members using the pool are not exempt function income. Where expenditures by an organization are used both for association property as well as other property, an allocation shall be made between the two uses on a reasonable basis. Only that portion of the expenditures which is properly allocable to the acquisition, construction, management, maintenance or care of association property, shall constitute qualifying expenditures.

(c) Examples of qualifying expenditures. Qualifying expenditures may include (but are not limited to) expenditures for—

(1) Salaries of an association manager and secretary;

(2) Paving of streets;

(3) Street signs;

(4) Security personnel;

(5) Legal fees;

(6) Upkeep of tennis courts;

(7) Swimming pools;

(8) Recreation rooms and halls;

(9) Replacement of common buildings, facilities, air conditioning, etc;

(10) Insurance premiums on association property;

(11) Accountant's fees;

(12) Improvement of private property to the extent it is association property; and

(13) Real estate and personal property taxes imposed on association property by a State or local government.

T.D. 7692, 4/17/80.

§ 1.528-7 Inurement.

An organization is not a homeowners association if any part of its net earnings inures (other than as a direct result of its engaging in one or more exempt functions) to the benefit of any private person. Thus, to the extent that members receive a benefit from the general maintenance, etc., of association property, this benefit generally would not constitute inurement. If an organization pays rebates from amounts other than exempt function income, such rebates will constitute inurement. In general, in determining whether an organization is in violation of this section, the principles used in making similar determinations under Section 501(c) will be applied.

T.D. 7692, 4/17/80.

§ 1.528-8 Election to be treated as a home-owners association.

(a) General rule. An organization wishing to be treated as a homeowners association under section 528 and this section for a taxable year must elect to be so treated. Except as otherwise provided in this section such election shall be made by the filing of a properly completed Form 1120-H (or such other form as the Secretary may prescribe). A separate election must be made for each taxable year.

(b) Taxable years ending after December 30, 1976. For taxable years ending after December 30, 1976, the election must be made not later than the time, including extensions, for filing an income tax return for the year in which the election is to apply.

(c) Taxable years ending before December 31, 1976, for which a return was filed before January 31, 1977. For taxable years ending before December 31, 1976, for which a return was filed before January 31, 1977, the election must be made not later than the time provided by law for filing a claim for credit or refund of overpayment of taxes for the year in which the election is to apply. Such an election shall be made by filing an amended return on Form 1120-H (or such other form as the Secretary may prescribe).

(d) Taxable years ending before December 31, 1976, for which a return was not filed before January 31, 1977. For taxable years ending before December 31, 1976, for which a return was not filed before January 31, 1977, the election must be made by October 20, 1980. Instead of making such an election in the manner described in paragraph (a) of this section, such an election may be made by a statement attached to the applicable income tax return or amended return for the year in which the elections made. The statement should identify the election being made, the period for which it applies and the taxpayer's basis for making the election.

(e) Revocation of exempt status. If an organization is notified after the close of a taxable year that its exemption for such taxable year under section 501(a) is being revoked retroactively, it may make a timely election under section 528 for such taxable year. Notwithstanding any other provisions of this section, such an election will be considered timely if it is made within 6 months after the date of revocation. The preceding sentence shall apply to revocations made after April 18, 1980. If the revocation was made on or before April 18, 1980, the election will be considered timely if it is made before the expiration of the period for filing a claim for credit or refund for the taxable year for which it is to apply.

(f) Effect of election. *(1) Revocation.* An election to be treated as an organization described in section 528 is binding on the organization for the taxable year and may not be revoked without the consent of the Commissioner.

(2) Exception. Notwithstanding paragraph (f)(1) of this section, an election under this section may be revoked prior to July 18, 1980. Such a revocation shall be made by filing a statement with the director of the Internal Revenue Service Center with whom the return of the organization for the year in which the revocation is to apply was filed. The statement shall include the following information.

(i) The name of the organization.

(ii) The fact that it is revoking an election made under section 528.

(iii) The taxable year for which the revocation is to apply.

T.D. 7692, 4/17/80.

---

§ 1.528-9 Exempt function income.

(a) General rule. For the purposes of section 528 exempt function income consists solely of income which is attributable to membership dues, fees, or assessments of owners of residential units or residential lots. It is not necessary that the source of income be labeled as membership dues, fees, or assessments. What is important is that such income be derived from owners of residential units or residential lots in their capacity as owner-members rather than in some other capacity such as customers for services. Generally, for the membership dues, fees, or assessments with respect to a residential unit or lot to be exempt function income, the unit must be used for (or the unit or lot must be expected to be used) for residential purposes. However, dues, fees, or assessments paid to an organization by a developer with respect to unfinished or finished but unsold units or lots shall be exempt function income even though the developer does not use the units or lots. If an assessment is more in the nature of a fee for the provision of services in the course of a trade or business than a fee for a common activity undertaken by a collective group of owners for the purpose of enhancing or maintaining the value of their residences, the assessment will not be considered exempt function income to the organization. Furthermore, income attributable to dues, fees, or assessments will not be considered exempt function income unless each member's liability for payment arises solely from membership in the association. Dues, fees, or assessments that are based on the extent, if any, to which a member avails him or herself of a facility or facilities are not exempt function income. For the purposes of section 528, dues, fees, or assessments which are based on the assessed value or size of property will be considered as arising solely as a result of membership in the organization. Regardless of the organization's method of accounting, excess assessments during a taxable year which are either rebated to the members or applied to their future assessments are not considered gross income and therefore will not be considered exempt function income for such taxable year. However, if such excess assessments are applied to a future year's assessments, they will be considered gross income and exempt function income for that future year. In addition, assessments in a taxable year, such as an assessment for a capital improvement, which are not treated as gross income do not enter into the determination of whether the organization meets the source of income test for that taxable year.

(b) Examples of exempt function income. Assessments which are considered more in the nature of a fee for common activity than for the providing of services and which will therefore generally be considered exempt function income include assessments made for the purpose of—

(1) Paying the principal and interest on debts incurred for the acquisition of association property;

(2) Paying real estate taxes on association property;

(3) Maintaining association property;

(4) Removing snow from public areas; and

(5) Removing trash.

(c) Examples of receipts which are not exempt function income. Exempt function income does not include—

(1) Amounts which are not includible in the organization's gross income other than by reason of section 528 (for example, tax-exempt interest);

(2) Amounts received from persons who are not members of the association;

(3) Amounts received from members for special use of the organization's facilities, the use of which is not available to all members as a result of having paid the dues, fees or assessments required to be paid by all members;

(4) Interest earned on amounts set aside in a sinking fund;

(5) Amounts received for work done on privately owned property which is not association property; or

(6) Amounts received from members in return for their transportation to or from shopping areas, work location, etc.

(d) Special Rule. Notwithstanding paragraphs (a) and (c)(3) of this section, amounts received from members or tenants of residential units owned by members (notwithstanding § 1.528-1(d)) for special use of an association's facilities will be considered exempt function income if—

(1) The amounts paid by the members are not paid more than once in any 12 month period; and

(2) The privilege obtained from the payment of such amounts lasts for the entire 12 month period or portion thereof in which the facility is commonly in use.

Thus, amounts received as the result of payments by members of a yearly fee for use of tennis courts or a swimming pool shall be considered exempt function income. However, amounts received for the use of a building for an evening, weekend, week, etc., shall not be considered exempt function income.

T.D. 7692, 4/17/80.

§ 1.528-10 Special rules for computation of homeowners association taxable income and tax.

(a) In general. Homeowners association taxable income shall be determined according to the provisions of section 528(d) and the rules set forth in this section.

(b) Limitation on capital losses. If for any taxable year a homeowners association has a net capital loss, the rules of sections 1211(a) and 1212(a) shall apply.

(c) Allowable deductions. *(1) In general.* To be deductible in computing the unrelated business taxable income of a homeowners association, expenses, depreciation and similar items must not only qualify as items of deduction allowed by chapter 1 of the Code but must also be directly connected with the production of gross income (excluding exempt function income). To be "directly connected with" the production of gross income (excluding exempt function income), an item of deduction must have both proximate and primary relationship to the production of such income and have been incurred in the production of such income. Items of deduction attributable solely to items of gross income (excluding exempt function income) are proximately and primarily related to such income. Whether an item of deduction is incurred in the production of gross income (excluding exempt function income) is determined on the basis of all the facts and circumstances involved in each case.

(2) Dual use of facilities or personnel. Where facilities are used both for exempt functions of the organization and for the production of gross income (excluding exempt function income), expenses, depreciation and similar items attributable to such facilities (for example, items of overhead) shall be allocated between the two uses on a reasonable basis. Similarly where personnel are employed both for exempt functions and for the production of gross income (excluding exempt function income), expenses and similar items attributable to such personnel (for example, items of salary) shall be allocated between the two activities on a reasonable basis. The portion of any such item so allocated to the production of gross income (excluding exempt function income) is directly connected with such income and shall be allowable as a deduction in computing homeowners association taxable income to the extent that it qualifies as an item of deduction allowed by chapter 1 of the Code. Thus, for example, assume that X, a homeowners association, pays its manager a salary of $10,000 a year and that it derives gross income other than exempt function income. If 10 percent of the manager's time during the year is devoted to deriving X's gross income (other than exempt function income), a deduction of $1,000 (10 percent of $10,000) would generally be allowable for purposes of computing X's homeowners association taxable income.

(d) Investment credit. A homeowners association is not entitled to an investment credit.

(e) Cross reference. For the definition of exempt function income, see § 1.528-9.

T.D. 7692, 4/17/80.

Proposed § 1.529-0 Table of contents. [*For Preamble, see ¶ 151,877*]

This section lists the following captions contained in §§ 1.529-1 through 1.529-6:

Proposed § 1.529-1 Qualified State tuition program, unrelated business income tax and definitions. [*For Preamble, see ¶ 151,877*]

(a) In general. A qualified State tuition program (QSTP) described in section 529 is exempt from income tax, except for the tax imposed under section 511 on the QSTP's unrelated business taxable income. A QSTP is not required to file Form 990, Return of Organization Exempt From Income Tax, Form 1041, U.S. Income Tax Return for Estates and Trusts, or Form 1120, U.S. Corporation Income Tax Return. A QSTP may be required to file Form 990-T, Exempt Organization Business Income Tax Return. See §§ 1.6012-2(e) and 1.6012-3(a)(5) for requirements for filing Form 990-T.

(b) Unrelated business income tax rules. For purposes of section 529, this section and §§ 1.529-2 through 1.529-6:

(1) Application of section 514. An interest in a QSTP shall not be treated as debt for purposes of section 514. Consequently, a QSTP's investment income will not constitute debt-financed income subject to the unrelated business income tax merely because the program accepts contributions and is obligated to pay out or refund such contributions and certain earnings attributable thereto to designated beneficiaries or to account owners. However, investment income of a QSTP shall be subject to the unrelated business income tax as debt-financed income to the extent the program incurs indebtedness when acquiring or improving income-producing property.

(2) Penalties and forfeitures. Earnings forfeited on prepaid educational arrangements or contracts and educational savings accounts and retained by a QSTP, or amounts collected by a QSTP as penalties on refunds or excess contributions are not unrelated business income to the QSTP.

(3) Administrative and other fees. Amounts paid, in order to open or maintain prepaid educational arrangements or contracts and educational savings accounts, as administrative or maintenance fees, and other similar fees including late fees, service charges, and finance charges, are not unrelated business income to the QSTP.

(c) Definitions. For purposes of section 529, this section and §§ 1.529-2 through 1.529-6:

Account means the formal record of transactions relating to a particular designated beneficiary when it is used alone without further modification in these regulations. The term includes prepaid educational arrangements or contracts described in section 529(b)(1)(A)(i) and educational savings accounts described in section 529(b)(1)(A)(ii).

Account owner means the person who, under the terms of the QSTP or any contract setting forth the terms under which contributions may be made to an account for the benefit of a designated beneficiary, is entitled to select or change the designated beneficiary of an account, to designate any person other than the designated beneficiary to whom funds may be paid from the account, or to receive distributions from the account if no such other person is designated.

Contribution means any payment directly allocated to an account for the benefit of a designated beneficiary or used to pay late fees or administrative fees associated with the account. In the case of a tax-free rollover, within the meaning of this paragraph (c), into a QSTP account, only the portion of the rollover amount that constituted investment in the account, within the meaning of this paragraph (c), is treated as a contribution to the account as required by § 1.529-3(a)(2).

Designated beneficiary means—

(1) The individual designated as the beneficiary of the account at the time an account is established with the QSTP;

(2) The individual who is designated as the new beneficiary when beneficiaries are changed; and

(3) The individual receiving the benefits accumulated in the account as a scholarship in the case of a QSTP account established by a State or local government or an organization described in section 501(c)(3) and exempt from taxation under section 501(a) as part of a scholarship program operated by such government or organization.

Distributee means the designated beneficiary or the account owner who receives or is treated as receiving a distribution from a QSTP. For example, if a QSTP makes a distribution directly to an eligible educational institution to pay tuition and fees for a designated beneficiary or a QSTP makes a distribution in the form of a check payable to both a designated beneficiary and an eligible educational institution, the distribution shall be treated as having been made in full to the designated beneficiary.

Distribution means any disbursement, whether in cash or in-kind, from a QSTP. Distributions include, but are not limited to, tuition credits or certificates, payment vouchers, tuition waivers or other similar items. Distributions also include, but are not limited to, a refund to the account owner, the designated beneficiary or the designated beneficiary's estate.

Earnings attributable to an account are the total account balance on a particular date minus the investment in the account as of that date.

Earnings ratio means the amount of earnings allocable to the account on the last day of the calendar year divided by the total account balance on the last day of that calendar year. The earnings ratio is applied to any distribution made during the calendar year. For purposes of computing the earnings ratio, the earnings allocable to the account on the last day of the calendar year and the total account balance on the last day of the calendar year include all distributions made during the calendar year and any amounts that have been forfeited from the account during the calendar year.

Eligible educational institution means an institution which is described in section 481 of the Higher Education Act of 1965 (20 U.S.C 1088) as in effect on August 5, 1997, and which is eligible to participate in a program under title IV of such Act. Such institutions generally are accredited post-secondary educational institutions offering credit toward a bachelor's degree, an associate's degree, a graduate level or professional degree, or another recognized post-secondary credential. Certain proprietary institutions and post-secondary vocational institutions also are eligible institutions. The institution must be eligible to participate in Department of Education student aid programs.

Final distribution means the distribution from a QSTP account that reduces the total account balance to zero.

Forfeit means that earnings and contributions allocable to a QSTP account are withdrawn by the QSTP from the account or deducted by the QSTP from a distribution to pay a penalty as required by § 1.529-2(e).

Investment in the account means the sum of all contributions made to the account on or before a particular date less the aggregate amount of contributions included in distributions, if any, made from the account on or before that date.

Member of the family means an individual who is related to the designated beneficiary as described in paragraphs (1) through (9) of this definition. For purposes of determining who is a member of the family, a legally adopted child of an individual shall be treated as the child of such individual by blood. The terms brother and sister include a brother or sister by the halfblood. Member of the family means—

(1) A son or daughter, or a descendant of either;

(2) A stepson or stepdaughter;

(3) A brother, sister, stepbrother, or stepsister;

(4) The father or mother, or an ancestor of either;

(5) A stepfather or stepmother;

(6) A son or daughter of a brother or sister;

(7) A brother or sister of the father or mother;

(8) A son-in-law, daughter-in-law, father-in-law, mother-in-law, brother-in-law, or sister-in-law; or

(9) The spouse of the designated beneficiary or the spouse of any individual described in paragraphs (1) through (8) of this definition.

Person has the same meaning as under section 7701(a)(1).

Qualified higher education expenses means—

(1) Tuition, fees, and the costs of books, supplies, and equipment required for the enrollment or attendance of a designated beneficiary at an eligible educational institution; and

(2) The costs of room and board (as limited by paragraph (2)(i) of this definition) of a designated beneficiary (who meets requirements of paragraph (2)(ii) of this definition) incurred while attending an eligible educational institution:

(i) The amount of room and board treated as qualified higher education expenses shall not exceed the minimum room and board allowance determined in calculating costs of attendance for Federal financial aid programs under section 472 of the Higher Education Act of 1965 (20 U.S.C. 1087ll) as in effect on August 5, 1997. For purposes of these regulations, room and board costs shall not exceed $1,500 per academic year for a designated beneficiary residing at home with parents or guardians. For a designated beneficiary residing in institutionally owned or operated housing, room and board costs shall not exceed the amount normally assessed most residents for room and board at the institution. For all other designated beneficiaries the amount shall not exceed $2,500 per academic year. For this purpose the term academic year has the same meaning as that term is given in 20 U.S.C. 1088(d) as in effect on August 5, 1997.

(ii) Room and board shall be treated as qualified higher education expenses for a designated beneficiary if they are incurred during any academic period during which the designated beneficiary is enrolled or accepted for enrollment in a degree, certificate, or other program (including a program of study abroad approved for credit by the eligible educational institution) that leads to a recognized educational credential awarded by an eligible educational institution. In addition, the designated beneficiary must be enrolled at least half-time. A student will be considered to be enrolled at least half-time if the student is enrolled for at least half the full-time academic workload for the course of study the student is pursuing as determined under the standards of the institution where the student is enrolled. The institution's standard for a full-time workload must equal or exceed the standard established by the Department of Education under the Higher Education Act and set forth in 34 CFR 674.2(b).

Rollover distribution means a distribution or transfer from an account of a designated beneficiary that is transferred to or deposited within 60 days of the distribution into an account of another individual who is a member of the family of the designated beneficiary. A distribution is not a rollover distribution unless there is a change in beneficiary. The new designated beneficiary's account may be in a QSTP in either the same State or a QSTP in another State.

Total account balance means the total amount or the total fair market value of tuition credits or certificates or similar benefits allocable to the account on a particular date. For purposes of computing the earnings ratio, the total account balance is adjusted as described in this paragraph (c).

Proposed § 1.529-2 Qualified State tuition program described. [*For Preamble, see ¶ 151,877*]

(a) In general. To be a QSTP, a program must satisfy the requirements described in paragraphs (a) through (i) of this section. A QSTP is a program established and maintained by a State or an agency or instrumentality of a State under which a person—

(1) May purchase tuition credits or certificates on behalf of a designated beneficiary that entitle the beneficiary to the waiver or payment of qualified higher education expenses of the beneficiary; or

(2) May make contributions to an account that is established for the purpose of meeting the qualified higher education expenses of the designated beneficiary of the account.

(b) Established and maintained by a State or agency or instrumentality of a State. *(1) Established.* A program is established by a State or an agency or instrumentality of a State if the program is initiated by State statute or regulation, or by an act of a State official or agency with the authority to act on behalf of the State.

(2) Maintained. A program is maintained by a State or an agency or instrumentality of a State if—

(i) The State or agency or instrumentality sets all of the terms and conditions of the program, including but not limited to who may contribute to the program, who may be a designated beneficiary of the program, what benefits the program may provide, when penalties will apply to refunds and what those penalties will be; and

(ii) The State or agency or instrumentality is actively involved on an ongoing basis in the administration of the program, including supervising all decisions relating to the investment of assets contributed to the program.

(3) Actively involved. Factors that are relevant in determining whether a State, agency or instrumentality is actively involved include, but are not limited to: whether the State provides services or benefits (such as tax, student aid or other financial benefits) to account owners or designated beneficiaries that are not provided to persons who are not account owners or designated beneficiaries; whether the State or agency or instrumentality establishes detailed operating rules for administering the program; whether officials of the State or agency or instrumentality play a substantial role in the operation of the program, including selecting, supervising, monitoring, auditing, and terminating any private contractors that provide services under the program; whether the State or agency or instrumentality holds the private contractors that provide services under the program to the same standards and requirements that apply when private contractors handle funds that belong to the State or provide services to the State; whether the State provides funding for the program; and, whether the State or agency or instrumentality acts as trustee or holds program assets directly or for the benefit of the account owners or designated beneficiaries. If the State or an agency or instrumentality thereof exercises the same authority over the funds invested in the program as it does over the investments in or pool of funds of a State employees' defined benefit pension plan, then the State or agency or instrumentality will be considered actively involved on an ongoing basis in the administration of the program.

(c) Permissible uses of contributions. Contributions to a QSTP can be placed into either a prepaid educational arrangement or contract described in section 529(b)(1)(A)(i) or an educational savings account described in section 529(b)(1)(A)(ii), or both, but cannot be placed into any other type of account.

(1) A prepaid educational services arrangement or contract is an account through which tuition credits or certificates or other rights are acquired that entitle the designated beneficiary of the account to the waiver or payment of qualified higher education expenses.

(2) An educational savings account is an account that is established exclusively for the purpose of meeting the qualified higher education expenses of a designated beneficiary.

(d) Cash contributions. A program shall not be treated as a QSTP unless it provides that contributions may be made only in cash and not in property. A QSTP may accept payment, however, in cash, or by check, money order, credit card, or similar methods.

(e) Penalties on refunds. *(1) General rule.* A program shall not be treated as a QSTP unless it imposes a more than de minimis penalty on the earnings portion of any distribution from the program that is not—

(i) Used exclusively for qualified higher education expenses of the designated beneficiary;

(ii) Made on account of the death or disability of the designated beneficiary;

(iii) Made on account of the receipt of a scholarship (or allowance or payment described in section 135(d)(1)(B) or (C)) by the designated beneficiary to the extent the amount of the distribution does not exceed the amount of the scholarship, allowance, or payment; or

(iv) A rollover distribution.

(2) More than de minimis penalty. (i) In general. A penalty is more than de minimis if it is consistent with a program intended to assist individuals in saving exclusively for qualified higher education expenses. Except as provided in paragraph (e)(2)(ii) of this section, whether any particular penalty is more than de minimis depends on the facts and circumstances of the particular program, including the extent to which the penalty offsets the federal income tax benefit from having deferred income tax liability on the earnings portion of any distribution.

(ii) Safe harbor. A penalty imposed on the earnings portion of a distribution is more than de minimis if it is equal to or greater than 10 percent of the earnings.

(3) Separate distributions. For purposes of applying the penalty, any single distribution described in paragraph (e)(1) of this section will be treated as a separate distribution and not part of a single aggregated annual distribution by the program, notwithstanding the rules under § 1.529-3 and §§ 1.529-4.

(4) Procedures for verifying use of distributions and imposing and collecting penalties. (i) In general. To be treated as imposing a more than de minimis penalty as required in paragraph (e)(1) of this section, a program must implement practices and procedures to identify whether a distribution is subject to a penalty and collect any penalty that is due.

(ii) Safe harbor. A program that falls within the safe harbor described in paragraphs (e)(4)(ii)(A) through (E) of this section will be treated as implementing practices and procedures to identify whether a more than de minimis penalty must be imposed as required in paragraph (e)(1) of this section.

(A) Distributions treated as payments of qualified higher education expenses. The program treats distributions as being used to pay for qualified higher education expenses only if—

(1) The distribution is made directly to an eligible educational institution;

(2) The distribution is made in the form of a check payable to both the designated beneficiary and the eligible educational institution;

(3) The distribution is made after the designated beneficiary submits substantiation to show that the distribution is a reimbursement for qualified higher education expenses that the designated beneficiary has already paid and the program has a process for reviewing the validity of the substantiation prior to the distribution; or

(4) The designated beneficiary certifies prior to the distribution that the distribution will be expended for his or her qualified higher education expenses within a reasonable time after the distribution; the program requires the designated beneficiary to provide substantiation of payment of qualified higher education expenses within 30 days after making the distribution and has a process for reviewing the substantiation; and the program retains an account balance that is large enough to collect any penalty owed on the distribution if valid substantiation is not produced.

(B) Treatment of all other distributions. The program collects a penalty on all distributions not treated as made to pay qualified higher education expenses except where—

(1) Prior to the distribution the program receives written third party confirmation that the designated beneficiary has died or become disabled or has received a scholarship (or allowance or payment described in section 135(d)(1)(B) or (C)) in an amount equal to the distribution; or

(2) Prior to the distribution the program receives a certification from the account owner that the distribution is being made because the designated beneficiary has died or become disabled or has received a scholarship (or allowance or payment described in section 135(d)(1)(B) or (C)) received by the designated beneficiary (and the distribution is equal to the amount of the scholarship, allowance, or payment) and the program withholds and reserves a portion of the distribution as a penalty. Any penalty withheld by the program may be refunded after the program receives third party confirmation that the designated beneficiary has died or become disabled or has received a scholarship or allowance (or payment described in section 135(d)(1)(B) or (C)).

(C) Refunds of penalties. The program will refund a penalty collected on a distribution only after the designated beneficiary substantiates that he or she had qualified higher education expenses greater than or equal to the distribution, and the program has reviewed the substantiation.

(D) Documentation of amounts refunded and not used for qualified higher education expenses. The program requires the distributee, defined in § 1.529-1(c), to provide a signed statement identifying the amount of any refunds received from eligible educational institutions at the end of each year in which distributions for qualified higher education expenses were made and of the next year.

(E) Procedures to collect penalty. The program collects required penalties by retaining a sufficient balance in the account to pay the amount of penalty, withholding an amount equal to the penalty from a distribution, or collecting the penalty on a State income tax return.

(f) Separate accounting. A program shall not be treated as a QSTP unless it provides separate accounting for each designated beneficiary. Separate accounting requires that contributions for the benefit of a designated beneficiary and any earnings attributable thereto must be allocated to the appropriate account. If a program does not ordinarily provide each account owner an annual account statement showing the total account balance, the investment in the account, earnings, and distributions from the account, the program must give this information to the account owner or designated beneficiary upon request. In the case of a prepaid educational arrangement or contract described in section 529(b)(1)(A)(i) the total account balance may be shown as credits or units of benefits instead of fair market value.

(g) No investment direction. A program shall not be treated as a QSTP unless it provides that any account owner in, or contributor to, or designated beneficiary under, such program may not directly or indirectly direct the investment of any contribution to the program or directly or indirectly direct the investment of any earnings attributable to contributions. A program does not violate this requirement if a person who establishes an account with the program is permitted to select among different investment strategies designed exclusively by the program, only at the time the initial contribution is made establishing the account. A program will not violate the requirement of this paragraph (g) if it permits a person who establishes an account to select between a prepaid educational services account and an educational savings account. A program also will not violate the requirement of this paragraph (g) merely because it permits its board members, its employees, or the board members or employees of a contractor it hires to perform administrative services to purchase tuition credits or certificates or make contributions as described in paragraph (c) of this section.

(h) No pledging of interest as security. A program shall not be treated as a QSTP unless the terms of the program or a state statute or regulation that governs the program prohibit any interest in the program or any portion thereof from being used as security for a loan. This restriction includes, but is not limited to, a prohibition on the use of any interest in the program as security for a loan used to purchase such interest in the program.

(i) Prohibition on excess contributions. *(1) In general.* A program shall not be treated as a QSTP unless it provides adequate safeguards to prevent contributions for the benefit of a designated beneficiary in excess of those necessary to provide for the qualified higher education expenses of the designated beneficiary.

(2) Safe harbor. A program satisfies this requirement if it will bar any additional contributions to an account as soon as the account reaches a specified account balance limit applicable to all accounts of designated beneficiaries with the same expected year of enrollment. The total contributions may not exceed the amount determined by actuarial esti-

mates that is necessary to pay tuition, required fees, and room and board expenses of the designated beneficiary for five years of undergraduate enrollment at the highest cost institution allowed by the program.

Proposed § 1.529-3 Income tax treatment of distributees. [*For Preamble, see ¶ 151,877*]

(a) Taxation of distributions. *(1) In general.* Any distribution, other than a rollover distribution, from a QSTP account must be included in the gross income of the distributee to the extent of the earnings portion of the distribution and to the extent not excluded from gross income under any other provision of chapter 1 of the Internal Revenue Code. If any amount of a distribution is forfeited under a QSTP as required by § 1.529-2(e), this amount is neither included in the gross income of the distributee nor deductible by the distributee.

(2) Rollover distributions. No part of a rollover distribution is included in the income of the distributee. Following the rollover distribution, that portion of the rollover amount that constituted investment in the account, defined in § 1.529-1(c), of the account from which the distribution was made is added to the investment in the account of the account that received the distribution. That portion of the rollover amount that constituted earnings of the account that made the distribution is added to the earnings of the account that received the distribution.

(b) Computing taxable earnings. *(1) Amount of taxable earnings in a distribution.* (i) Educational savings account. In the case of an educational savings account, the earnings portion of a distribution is equal to the product of the amount of the distribution and the earnings ratio, defined in § 1.529-1(c). The return of investment portion of the distribution is equal to the amount of the distribution minus the earnings portion of the distribution.

(ii) Prepaid educational services account. In the case of a prepaid educational services account, the earnings portion of a distribution is equal to the value of the credits, hours, or other units of education distributed at the time of distribution minus the return of investment portion of the distribution. The value of the credits, hours, or other units of education may be based on the tuition waived or the cash distributed. The return of investment portion of the distribution is determined by dividing the investment in the account at the end of the year in which the distribution is made by the number of credits, hours, or other units of education in the account at the end of the calendar year (including all credits, hours, or other units of education distributed during the calendar year), and multiplying that amount by the number of credits, hours, or other units of education distributed during the current calendar year.

(2) Adjustment for programs that treated distributions and earnings in a different manner for years beginning before January 1, 1999. For calendar years beginning after December 31, 1998, a QSTP must treat taxpayers as recovering investment in the account and earnings ratably with each distribution. Prior to January 1, 1999, a program may have treated distributions in a different manner and reported them to taxpayers accordingly. In order to adjust to the method described in this section, if distributions were treated as coming first from the investment in the account, the QSTP must adjust the investment in the account by subtracting the amount of the investment in the account previously treated as distributed. If distributions were treated as coming first from earnings, the QSTP must adjust the earnings portion of the account by subtracting the amount of earnings previously treated as distributed. After the adjustment is made, the investment in the account is recovered ratably in accordance with this section. If no previous distribution was made but earnings were treated as taxable to the taxpayer in the year they were allocated to the account, the earnings treated as already taxable are treated as additional contributions and added to the investment in the account.

(3) Examples. The application of this paragraph (b) is illustrated by the following examples. The rounding convention used (rounding to three decimal places) in these examples is for purposes of illustration only. A QSTP may use another rounding convention as long as it consistently applies the convention. The examples are as follows:

Example (1). (i) In 1998, an individual, A, opens a prepaid educational services account with a QSTP on behalf of a designated beneficiary. Through the account A purchases units of education equivalent to eight semesters of tuition for full-time attendance at a public four-year university covered by the QSTP. A contributes $16,000 that includes payment of processing fees to the QSTP. In 2011 the designated beneficiary enrolls at a public four-year university. The QSTP makes distributions on behalf of the designated beneficiary to the university in August for the fall semester and in December for the spring semester. Tuition for full-time attendance at the university is $7,500 per academic year in 2011 and 2012, $7,875 for the academic year in 2013, and $8,200 for the academic year in 2014. The only expense covered by the QSTP distribution is tuition for four academic years. The calculations are as follows:

2011

Investment in the account as of 12/31/2011	=	$16,000
Units in account	=	8
Per unit investment	=	$ 2,000
Units distributed in 2011	=	2
Investment portion of distribution in 2011 ($2,000 per unit × 2 units)	=	$ 4,000
Current value of two units distributed in 2011	=	$ 7,500
Earnings portion of distribution in 2011 ($7,500 - $4,000)	=	$ 3,500

2012

Investment in the account as of 12/31/2012 ($16,000-$4,000)	=	$12,000
Units in account	=	6
Per unit investment	=	$ 2,000
Units distributed in 2012	=	2
Investment portion of distribution in 2012 ($2,000 per unit X 2 units)	=	$ 4,000

Current value of two units distributed in 2012	=	$ 7,500
Earnings portion of distribution in 2012 ($7,500 - $4,000)	=	$ 3,500
2013		
Investment in the account as of 12/31/2013 ($12,000-$4000)	=	$ 8,000
Units in account	=	4
Per unit investment	=	$ 2,000
Units distributed in 2013	=	2
Investment portion of distribution in 2013 ($2,000 per unit X 2 units)	=	$ 4,000
Current value of two units distributed in 2013	=	$ 7,875
Earnings portion of distribution in 2013 ($7,875 - $4,000)	=	$ 3,875
2014		
Investment in the account as of 12/31/2014 ($8,000-$4000)	=	$ 4,000
Units in account	=	2
Per unit investment	=	$ 2,000
Units distributed in 2014	=	2
Investment portion of distribution in 2014 ($4,000 per unit X 2 units)	=	$ 4,000
Current value of two units distributed in 2014	=	$ 8,200
Earnings portion of distribution in 2014 ($8,200 - $4,000)	=	$ 4,200
12/31/2014 (after distributions)		
Investment in the account as of 12/31/2014 ($4,000-$4000)	=	0

(ii) In each year the designated beneficiary includes in his or her gross income the earnings portion of the distribution for tuition.

Example (2). (i) In 1998, an individual, B, opens a college savings account with a QSTP on behalf of a designated beneficiary. B contributes $18,000 to the account that includes payment of processing fees to the QSTP. On December 31, 2011, the total balance in the account for the benefit of the designated beneficiary is $30,000 (including distributions made during the year 2011). In 2011 the designated beneficiary enrolls at a four-year university. The QSTP makes distributions on behalf of the designated beneficiary to the university in August for the fall semester and in December for the spring semester. Tuition for full-time attendance at the university is $7,500 per academic year in 2011 and 2012, $7,875 for the academic year in 2013, and $8,200 for the academic year in 2014. The only expense covered by the QSTP distributions is tuition for four academic years. On the last day of the calendar year the account is allocated earnings of 5% on the total account balance on that day. Under the terms of the QSTP, a penalty of 15% is applied to the earnings not used to pay tuition. The calculations are as follows:

2011		
Investment in the account	=	$ 18,000
Total account balance as of 12/31/2011	=	$ 30,000
Earnings as of 12/31/2011	=	$ 12,000
Distributions in 2011	=	$ 7,500
Earnings ratio for 2011 ($12,000 / $30,000)	=	40%
Earnings portion of distributions in 2011 ($7,500 X .4)	=	$ 3,000
Return of investment portion of distributions in 2011 ($7,500 - $3,000)	=	$ 4,500
2012		
Investment in the account as of 12/31/2012 ($18,000 - $4,500)	=	$ 13,500
Total account balance as of 12/31/12 [($30,000-$7,500) x 105]	=	$ 23,625
Earnings as of 12/31/2012	=	$ 10,125
Distributions in 2012	=	$ 7,500
Earnings ratio for 2012 ($10,125 / $23,625)	=	42.9%
Earnings portion of distributions in 2012 ($7,500 X .429)	=	$ 3,217.50
Return of investment portion of distributions in 2012 ($7,500 - $3,217.50)	=	$ 4,282.50
2013		
Investment in the account as of 12/31/2013 ($13,500 - $4,282.50)	=	$ 9,217.50
Total account balance as of 12/31/13 [($23,625-$7,500) x 105%]	=	$16,931.25
Earnings as of 12/31/2013	=	$ 7,713.75
Distributions in 2013	=	$ 7,875
Earnings ratio for 2013 ($7,713.75 / $16,931.25)	=	45.6%

Earnings portion of distributions in 2013 ($7,875 X .456)	=	$ 3,591
Return of investment portion of distributions in 2013 ($7,875 - $3,591)	=	$ 4,284
2014		
Investment in the account as of 12/31/2014 ($9,217.50 - $4,284)	=	$ 4,933.50
Total account balance as of 12/31/14 [($16,931.25 - $7,875) x 105%]	=	$ 9,509.06
Earnings as of 12/31/2014	=	$ 4,575.56
Distributions in 2014 for qualified higher education expenses (QHEE)	=	$ 8,200
Distributions in 2014 not for qualified higher education expenses (Non-QHEE)	=	$ 1,309.06
Total distributions	=	$ 9,509.06
Earnings portion of QHEE distribution in 2014 [($8,200 / $9,509.06) X $4,575.56]	=	$ 3,945.68
Return of investment portion of QHEE distribution in 2014	=	$ 4,254.32
Earnings portion of Non-QHEE distribution subject to penalty [($1,309.06 / $9,509.06) X $4,575.56)]	=	$ 629.89
Return of investment portion of non-QHEE distribution in 2014	=	$ 679.17

(ii) In years 2011 through 2013 the designated beneficiary includes in gross income the earnings portion of the distributions for tuition. In year 2014 the designated beneficiary includes in gross income the earnings portion of the distribution for tuition, $3,945.68, plus the earnings portion of the distribution that was not used for tuition after reduction for the penalty, i.e. $535.41 ($629.89 minus a 15% penalty of $94.48).

(c) Change in designated beneficiaries. *(1) General rule.* A change in the designated beneficiary of a QSTP account is not treated as a distribution if the new designated beneficiary is a member of the family of the transferor designated beneficiary. However, any change of designated beneficiary not described in the preceding sentence is treated as a distribution to the account owner, provided the account owner has the authority to change the designated beneficiary. For rules related to a change in the designated beneficiary pursuant to a rollover distribution see §§ 1.529-1(c) and 1.529-3(a)(2).

(2) Scholarship program. Notwithstanding paragraph (c)(1) of this section, the requirement that the new beneficiary be a member of the family of the transferor beneficiary shall not apply to a change in designated beneficiary of an interest in a QSTP account purchased by a State or local government or an organization described in section 501(c)(3) as part of a scholarship program.

(d) Aggregation of accounts. If an individual is a designated beneficiary of more than one account under a QSTP, the QSTP shall treat all contributions and earnings as allocable to a single account for purposes of calculating the earnings portion of any distribution from that QSTP. For purposes of determining the effect of the distribution on each account, the earnings portion and return of investment in the account portion of the distribution shall be allocated pro rata among the accounts based on total account value as of the close of the current calendar year.

Proposed § 1.529-4 Time, form, and manner of reporting distributions from QSTPs and backup withholding. [*For Preamble, see ¶ 151,877*]

(a) Taxable distributions. The portion of any distribution made during the calendar year by a QSTP that represents earnings shall be reported by the payor as described in this section.

(b) Requirement to file return. *(1) Form of return.* A payor must file a return required by this section on Form 1099-G. A payor may use forms containing provisions similar to Form 1099-G if it complies with applicable revenue procedures relating to substitute Forms 1099. A payor must file a separate return for each distributee who receives a taxable distribution.

(2) Payor. For purposes of this section, the term "payor" means the officer or employee having control of the program, or their designee.

(3) Information included on return. A payor must include on Form 1099-G—

(i) The name, address, and taxpayer identifying number (TIN) (as defined in section 7701(a)(41)) of the payor;

(ii) The name, address, and TIN of the distributee;

(iii) The amount of earnings distributed to the distributee in the calendar year; and

(iv) Any other information required by Form 1099-G or its instructions.

(4) Time and place for filing return. A payor must file any return required by this paragraph (b) on or before February 28 of the year following the calendar year in which the distribution is made. A payor must file the return with the IRS office designated in the instructions for Form 1099-G.

(5) Returns required on magnetic media. If a payor is required to file at least 250 returns during the calendar year, the returns must be filed on magnetic media. If a payor is required to file fewer than 250 returns, the prescribed paper form may be used.

(6) Extension of time to file return. For good cause, the Commissioner may grant an extension of time in which to file Form 1099-G for reporting taxable earnings under section 529. The application for extension of time must be submitted in the manner prescribed by the Commissioner.

(c) Requirement to furnish statement to the distributee. *(1) In general.* A payor that must file a return under paragraph (b) of this section must furnish a statement to the distributee. The requirement to furnish a statement to the distributee will be satisfied if the payor provides the distributee with a copy of the Form 1099-G (or a substitute statement that complies with applicable revenue procedures) containing all the information filed with the Internal Revenue Service and all the legends required by paragraph (c)(2) of this section by the time required by paragraph (c)(3) of this section.

(2) Information included on statement. A payor must include on the statement that it must furnish to the distributee—

(i) The information required under paragraph (b)(3) of this section;

(ii) The telephone number of a person to contact about questions pertaining to the statement; and

(iii) A legend as required on the official Internal Revenue Service Form 1099-G.

(3) Time for furnishing statement. A payor must furnish the statement required by paragraph (c)(1) of this section to the distributee on or before January 31 of the year following the calendar year in which the distribution was made. The statement will be considered furnished to the distributee if it is mailed to the distributee's last known address.

(4) Extension of time to furnish statement. For good cause, the Commissioner may grant an extension of time to furnish statements to distributees of taxable earnings under section 529. The application for extension of time must be submitted in the manner prescribed by the Commissioner.

(d) Backup withholding. Distributions from a QSTP are not subject to backup withholding.

(e) Effective date. The reporting requirements set forth in this section apply to distributions made after December 31, 1998.

Proposed § 1.529-5 Estate, gift, and generation-skipping transfer tax rules relating to qualified State tuition programs. [*For Preamble, see ¶ 151,877*]

(a) Gift and generation-skipping transfer tax treatment of contributions after August 20, 1996, and before August 6, 1997. A contribution on behalf of a designated beneficiary to a QSTP (or to a program that meets the transitional rule requirements under § 1.529-6(b)) after August 20, 1996, and before August 6, 1997, is not treated as a taxable gift. The subsequent waiver of qualified higher education expenses of a designated beneficiary by an educational institution (or the subsequent payment of higher education expenses of a designated beneficiary to an educational institution) under a QSTP is treated as a qualified transfer under section 2503(e) and is not treated as a transfer of property by gift for purposes of section 2501. As such, the contribution is not subject to the generation-skipping transfer tax imposed by section 2601.

(b) Gift and generation-skipping transfer tax treatment of contributions after August 5, 1997. *(1) In general.* A contribution on behalf of a designated beneficiary to a QSTP (or to a program that meets the transitional rule requirements under § 1.529-6(b)) after August 5, 1997, is a completed gift of a present interest in property under section 2503(b) from the person making the contribution to the designated beneficiary. As such, the contribution is eligible for the annual gift tax exclusion provided under section 2503(b). The portion of a contribution excludible from taxable gifts under section 2503(b) also satisfies the requirements of section 2642(c)(2) and, therefore, is also excludible for purposes of the generation-skipping transfer tax imposed under section 2601. A contribution to a QSTP after August 5, 1997, is not treated as a qualified transfer within the meaning of section 2503(e).

(2) Contributions that exceed the annual exclusion amount. (i) Under section 529(c)(2)(B) a donor may elect to take certain contributions to a QSTP into account ratably over a five year period in determining the amount of gifts made during the calendar year. The provision is applicable only with respect to contributions not in excess of five times the section 2503(b) exclusion amount available in the calendar year of the contribution. Any excess may not be taken into account ratably and is treated as a taxable gift in the calendar year of the contribution.

(ii) The election under section 529(c)(2)(B) may be made by a donor and his or her spouse with respect to a gift considered to be made one-half by each spouse under section 2513.

(iii) The election is made on Form 709, Federal Gift Tax Return, for the calendar year in which the contribution is made.

(iv) If in any year after the first year of the five year period described in section 529(c)(2)(B), the amount excludible under section 2503(b) is increased as provided in section 2503(b)(2), the donor may make an additional contribution in any one or more of the four remaining years up to the difference between the exclusion amount as increased and the original exclusion amount for the year or years in which the original contribution was made.

(v) Example. The application of this paragraph (b)(2) is illustrated by the following example:

Example. In Year 1, when the annual exclusion under section 2503(b) is $10,000, P makes a contribution of $60,000 to a QSTP for the benefit of P's child, C. P elects under section 529(c)(2)(B) to account for the gift ratably over a five year period beginning with the calendar year of contribution. P is treated as making an excludible gift of $10,000 in each of Years 1 through 5 and a taxable gift of $10,000 in Year 1. In Year 3, when the annual exclusion is increased to $12,000, P makes an additional contribution for the benefit of C in the amount of $8,000. P is treated as making an excludible gift of $2,000 under section 2503(b); the remaining $6,000 is a taxable gift in Year 3.

(3) Change of designated beneficiary or rollover. (i) A transfer which occurs by reason of a change in the designated beneficiary, or a rollover of credits or account balances from the account of one beneficiary to the account of another beneficiary, is not a taxable gift and is not subject to the generation-skipping transfer tax if the new beneficiary is a member of the family of the old beneficiary, as defined in § 1.529-1(c), and is assigned to the same generation as the old beneficiary, as defined in section 2651.

(ii) A transfer which occurs by reason of a change in the designated beneficiary, or a rollover of credits or account balances from the account of one beneficiary to the account of another beneficiary, will be treated as a taxable gift by the old beneficiary to the new beneficiary if the new beneficiary is assigned to a lower generation than the old beneficiary, as defined in section 2651, regardless of whether the new beneficiary is a member of the family of the old beneficiary. The transfer will be subject to the generation-skipping transfer tax if the new beneficiary is assigned to a generation which is two or more levels lower than the generation assignment of the old beneficiary. The five year averaging rule described in paragraph (b)(2) of this section may be applied to the transfer.

(iii) Example. The application of this paragraph (b)(3) is illustrated by the following example:

Example. In Year 1, P makes a contribution to a QSTP on behalf of P's child, C. In Year 4, P directs that a distribution from the account for the benefit of C be made to an account for the benefit of P's grandchild, G. The rollover distribution is treated as a taxable gift by C to G, because, under section 2651, G is assigned to a generation below the generation assignment of C.

(c) Estate tax treatment for estates of decedents dying after August 20, 1996, and before June 9, 1997. The gross estate of a decedent dying after August 20, 1996, and before June 9, 1997, includes the value of any interest in any QSTP which is attributable to contributions made by the decedent to such program on behalf of a designated beneficiary.

(d) Estate tax treatment for estates of decedents dying after June 8, 1997. *(1) In general.* Except as provided in paragraph (d)(2) of this section, the gross estate of a decedent dying after June 8, 1997, does not include the value of any interest in a QSTP which is attributable to contributions made by the decedent to such program on behalf of any designated beneficiary.

(2) Excess contributions. In the case of a decedent who made the election under section 529(c)(2)(B) and paragraph (b)(3)(i) of this section who dies before the close of the five year period, that portion of the contribution allocable to calendar years beginning after the date of death of the decedent is includible in the decedent's gross estate.

(3) Designated beneficiary decedents. The gross estate of a designated beneficiary of a QSTP includes the value of any interest in the QSTP.

Proposed § 1.529-6 Transition rules. [*For Preamble, see ¶ 151,877*]

(a) Effective date. Section 529 is effective for taxable years ending after August 20, 1996, and applies to all contracts entered into or accounts opened on August 20, 1996, or later.

(b) Programs maintained on August 20, 1996. Transition relief is available to a program maintained by a State under which persons could purchase tuition credits, certification or similar rights on behalf of, or make contributions for educational expenses of, a designated beneficiary if the program was in existence on August 20, 1996. Such program must meet the requirements of a QSTP before the later of August 20, 1997, or the first day of the first calendar quarter after the close of the first regular session of the State legislature that begins after August 20, 1996. If a State has a two-year legislative session, each year of such session shall be deemed to be a separate regular session of the State legislature. The program, as in effect on August 20, 1996, shall be treated as a QSTP with respect to contributions (and earnings allocable thereto) pursuant to contracts entered into under the program. This relief is available for contributions (and earnings allocable thereto) made before, and the contracts entered into before, the first date on which the program becomes a QSTP. The provisions of the program, as in effect on August 20, 1996, shall apply in lieu of section 529(b) with respect to such contributions and earnings. A program shall be treated as meeting the transition rule if it conforms to the requirements of section 529, §§ 1.529-1 through 1.529-5 and this section, by the date this document is published as final regulations in the Federal Register.

(c) Retroactive effect. No income tax liability will be asserted against a QSTP for any period before the program meets the requirements of section 529, §§ 1.529-1 through 1.529-5 and this section, if the program qualifies for the transition relief described in paragraph (b) of this section.

(d) Contracts entered into and accounts opened before August 20, 1996. *(1) In general.* A QSTP may continue to maintain agreements in connection with contracts entered into and accounts opened before August 20, 1996, without jeopardizing its tax exempt status even if maintaining the agreements is contrary to section 529(b) provided that the QSTP operates in accordance with the restrictions contained in this paragraph (d). However, distributions made by the QSTP, regardless of the terms of any agreement executed before August 20, 1996, are subject to tax according to the rules of § 1.529-3 and subject to the reporting requirements of § 1.529-4.

(2) Interest in program pledged as security for a loan. An interest in the program, or a portion of an interest in the program, may be used as security for a loan if the contract giving rise to the interest was entered into or account was opened prior to August 20, 1996 and the agreement permitted such a pledge.

(3) Member of the family. In the case of an account opened or a contract entered into before August 20, 1996, the rules regarding a change in beneficiary, including the rollover rule in § 1.529-3(a) and the gift tax rule in § 1.529-5(b)(3), shall be applied by treating any transferee beneficiary permitted under the terms of the account or contract as a member of the family of the transferor beneficiary.

(4) Eligible educational institution. In the case of an account opened or contract entered into before August 20, 1996, an eligible educational institution is an educational institution in which the beneficiary may enroll under the terms of the account or contract.

§ 1.531-1 Imposition of tax.

Caution: The Treasury has not yet amended Reg § 1.531-1 to reflect changes made by P.L. 107-16, P.L. 103-66, P.L. 100-647.

Section 531 imposes (in addition to the other taxes imposed upon corporations by chapter 1 of the Code) a graduated tax on the accumulated taxable income of every corporation described in section 532 and § 1.532-1. In the case of an affiliated group which makes or is required to make a consolidated return see § 1.1502-43. All of the taxes on corporations under chapter 1 of the Code are treated as one tax for purposes of assessment, collection, payment, period of limitations, etc. See section 535 and §§ 1.535-1, 1.535-2, and 1.535-3 for the definition and determination of accumulated taxable income.

T.D. 6377, 5/12/59, amend T.D. 7244, 12/29/72, T.D. 7937, 1/26/84.

§ 1.532-1 Corporations subject to accumulated earnings tax.

Caution: The Treasury has not yet amended Reg § 1.532-1 to reflect changes made by P.L. 109-135, P.L. 99-514, P.L. 98-369.

(a) General rule. *(1)* The tax imposed by section 531 applies to any domestic or foreign corporation (not specifically excepted under section 532(b) and paragraph (b) of this section) formed or availed of to avoid or prevent the imposition of the individual income tax on its shareholders, or on the shareholders of any other corporation, by permitting earnings and profits to accumulate instead of dividing or distributing them. See section 533 and § 1.533-1, relating to evidence of purpose to avoid income tax with respect to shareholders.

(2) The tax imposed by section 531 may apply if the avoidance is accomplished through the formation or use of one corporation or a chain of corporations. For example, if the capital stock of the M Corporation is held by the N Corporation, the earnings and profits of the M Corporation would not be returned as income subject to the individual income tax until such earnings and profits of the M Corporation were distributed to the N Corporation and distributed in turn by the N Corporation to its shareholders. If either the M Corporation or the N Corporation was formed or is availed of for the purpose of avoiding or preventing the imposition of the individual income tax upon the shareholders of the N Corporation, the accumulated taxable income of the corporation so formed or availed of (M or N, as the case may be) is subject to the tax imposed by section 531.

(b) Exceptions. The accumulated earnings tax imposed by section 531 does not apply to a personal holding company (as defined in section 542), to a foreign personal holding company (as defined in section 552), or to a corporation exempt from tax under subchapter F, chapter 1 of the Code.

(c) Foreign corporations. Section 531 is applicable to any foreign corporation, whether resident or nonresident, with respect to any income derived from sources, within the United States, if any of its shareholders are subject to income tax on the distributions of the corporation by reason of being (1) citizens or residents of the United States, or (2) nonresident alien individuals to whom section 871 is applicable, or (3) foreign corporations if a beneficial interest therein is owned directly or indirectly by any shareholder specified in subparagraph (1) or (2) of this paragraph.

T.D. 6377, 5/12/59.

§ 1.533-1 Evidence of purpose to avoid income tax.

(a) In general. *(1)* The Commissioner's determination that a corporation was formed or availed of for the purpose of avoiding income tax with respect to shareholders is subject to disproof by competent evidence. Section 533(a) provides that the fact that earnings and profits of a corporation are permitted to accumulate beyond the reasonable needs of the business shall be determinative of the purpose to avoid the income tax with respect to shareholders unless the corporation, by the preponderance of the evidence, shall prove to the contrary. The burden of proving that earnings and profits have been permitted to accumulate beyond the reasonable needs of the business may be shifted to the Commissioner under section 534. See §§ 1.534-1 through 1.534-4. Section 533(b) provides that the fact that the taxpayer is a mere holding or investment company shall be prima facie evidence of the purpose to avoid income tax with respect to shareholders.

(2) The existence or nonexistence of the purpose to avoid income tax with respect to shareholders may be indicated by circumstances other than the conditions specified in section 533. Whether or not such purpose was present depends upon the particular circumstances of each case. All circumstances which might be construed as evidence of the purpose to avoid income tax with respect to shareholders cannot be outlined, but among other things, the following will be considered:

(i) Dealings between the corporation and its shareholders, such as withdrawals by the shareholders as personal loans or the expenditure of funds by the corporation for the personal benefit of the shareholders,

(ii) The investment by the corporation of undistributed earnings in assets having no reasonable connection with the business of the corporation (see § 1.537-3), and

(iii) The extent to which the corporation has distributed its earnings and profits.

The fact that a corporation is a mere holding or investment company or has an accumulation of earnings and profits in excess of the reasonable needs of the business is not absolutely conclusive against it if the taxpayer satisfies the Commissioner that the corporation was neither formed nor availed of for the purpose of avoiding income tax with respect to shareholders.

(b) General burden of proof and statutory presumptions. The Commissioner may determine that the taxpayer was formed or availed of to avoid income tax with respect to shareholders through the medium of permitting earnings and profits to accumulate. In the case of litigation involving any such determination (except where the burden of proof is on the Commissioner under section 534), the burden of proving such determination wrong by a preponderance of the evidence, together with the corresponding burden of first going forward with the evidence, is on the taxpayer under principles applicable to income tax cases generally. For the burden of proof in a proceeding before the Tax Court with respect to the allegation that earnings and profits have been permitted to accumulate beyond the reasonable needs of the business, see section 534 and §§ 1.534-2 through 1.534-4. For a definition of a holding or investment company, see paragraph (c) of this section. For determination of the reasonable needs of the business, see section 537 and §§ 1.537-1 through 1.537-3. If the taxpayer is a mere holding or investment company, and the Commissioner therefore determines that the corporation was formed or availed of for the purpose of avoiding income tax with respect to shareholders, then section 533(b) gives further weight to the presumption of correctness already arising from the Commissioner's determination by expressly providing an additional presumption of the existence of a purpose to avoid income tax with respect to shareholders. Further, if it is established (after complying with section 534 where applicable) that earnings and profits were permitted to accumulate beyond the reasonable needs of the business and the Commissioner has therefore determined that the corporation was formed or availed of for the purpose of avoiding income tax with respect to shareholders, then section 533(a) adds still more weight to the Commissioner's determination. Under such circumstances, the existence of such an accumulation is made determinative of the purpose to avoid income tax with respect to shareholders unless the taxpayer proves to the contrary by the preponderance of the evidence.

(c) Holding or investment company. A corporation having practically no activities except holding property and collecting the income therefrom or investment therein shall be considered a holding company within the meaning of section 533(b). If the activities further include, or consist substantially of, buying and selling stocks, securities, real estate, or other investment property (whether upon an outright or marginal basis) so that the income is derived not only from the investment yield but also from profits upon market fluctuations, the corporation shall be considered an investment company within the meaning of section 533(b).

(d) Small business investment companies. A corporation which is licensed to operate as a small business investment company under the Small Business Investment Act of 1958 (15 USC ch 14B) and the regulations thereunder (13 CFR Part 107) will generally be considered to be a "mere holding or investment company" within the meaning of section 533(b). However, the presumption of the existence of the purpose to avoid income tax with respect to shareholders which results from the fact that such a company is a "mere holding or investment company" will be considered overcome so long as such company—

(1) Complies with all the provisions of the Small Business Investment Act of 1958 and the regulations thereunder; and

(2) Actively engages in the business of providing funds to small business concerns through investment in the equity capital of, or through the disbursement of long-term loans to, such concerns in such manner and under such terms as the company may fix in accordance with regulations promulgated by the Small Business Administration (see secs. 304 and 305 of the Small Business Investment Act of 1958, as amended (15 USC 684, 685)).

On the other hand, if such a company violates or fails to comply with any of the provisions of the Small Business Investment Act of 1958, as amended, or the regulations thereunder, or ceases to be actively engaged in the business of providing funds to small business concerns in the manner provided in subparagraph (2) of this paragraph, it will not be considered to have overcome the presumption by reason of any rules provided in this paragraph.

T.D. 6377, 5/12/59, amend T.D. 6449, 1/27/60, T.D. 6652, 5/13/63.

§ 1.533-2 Statement required.

The corporation may be required to furnish a statement of its accumulated earnings and profits, the payment of dividends, the name and address of, and number of shares held by, each of its shareholders, the amounts that would be payable to each of the shareholders if the income of the corporation were distributed, and other information required under section 6042.

T.D. 6377, 5/12/59.

§ 1.534-1 Burden of proof as to unreasonable accumulations generally.

For purposes of applying the presumption provided for in section 533(a) and in determining the extent of the accumulated earnings credit under section 535(c)(1), the burden of proof with respect to an allegation by the Commissioner that all of any part of the earnings and profits of the corporation have been permitted to accumulate beyond the reasonable needs of the business may vary under section 534 as between litigation in the Tax Court and that in any other court. In case of a proceeding in a court other than the Tax Court, see paragraph (b) of § 1.533-1.

T.D. 6377, 5/12/59.

§ 1.534-2 Burden of proof as to unreasonable accumulations in cases before the Tax Court.

(a) Burden of proof on Commissioner. Under the general rule provided in section 534(a), in any proceeding before the Tax Court involving a notice of deficiency based in whole or in part on the allegation that all or any part of the earnings and profits have been permitted to accumulate beyond the reasonable needs of the business, the burden of proof with respect to such allegation is upon the Commissioner if—

(1) A notification, as provided for in section 534(b) and paragraph (c) of this section, has not been sent to the taxpayer; or

(2) A notification, as provided for in section 534(b) and paragraph (c) of this section, has been sent to the taxpayer and, in response to such notification, the taxpayer has submitted a statement, as provided in section 534(c) and paragraph (d) of this section, setting forth the ground or grounds (together with facts sufficient to show the basis thereof) on which it relies to establish that all or any part of its earnings and profits have not been permitted to accumulate beyond the reasonable needs of the business. However, the burden of proof in the latter case is upon the Commissioner only with respect to the relevant ground or grounds set forth in the statement submitted by the taxpayer, and only if such ground or grounds are supported by facts (contained in the statement) sufficient to show the basis thereof.

(b) Burden of proof on the taxpayer. The burden of proof in a Tax Court proceeding with respect to an allegation that all or any part of the earnings and profits have been permitted to accumulate beyond the reasonable needs of the business is upon the taxpayer if—

(1) A notification, as provided for in section 534(b) and paragraph (c) of this section, has been sent to the taxpayer and the taxpayer has not submitted a statement, in response to such notification, as provided in section 534(c) and paragraph (d) of this section; or

(2) A statement has been submitted by the taxpayer in response to such notification, but the ground or grounds on which the taxpayer relies are not relevant to the allegation or, if relevant, the statement does not contain facts sufficient to show the basis thereof.

(c) Notification to the taxpayer. Under section 534(b) a notification informing the taxpayer that the proposed notice of deficiency includes an amount with respect to the accumulated earnings tax imposed by section 531 may be sent by registered mail (or by certified or registered mail, if the notification is mailed after September 2, 1958) to the taxpayer at any time before the mailing of the notice of deficiency in the case of a taxable year beginning after December 31, 1953, and ending after August 16, 1954. See § 1.534-4 for rules relating to taxable years subject to the Internal Revenue Code of 1939. See section 534(d) and § 1.534-3 with respect to a notification in the case of a jeopardy assessment.

(d) Statement by taxpayer. *(1)* A taxpayer who has received a notification, as provided in section 534(b) and paragraph (c) of this section, that the proposed notice of deficiency includes an amount with respect to the accumulated earnings tax imposed by section 531, may, under section 534(c), submit a statement that all or any part of the earnings and profits of the corporation have not been permitted to accumulate beyond the reasonable needs of the business. Such statement shall set forth the ground or grounds (together with facts sufficient to show the basis thereof) on which the taxpayer relies to establish that there has been no accumulation of earnings and profits beyond the reasonable needs of the business. See paragraphs (a) and (b) of this section for rules concerning the effect of the statement with respect to burden of proof. See §§ 1.537-1 to 1.537-3, inclusive, relating to reasonable needs of the business.

(2) The taxpayer's statement, under section 534(c) and this paragraph, must be submitted to the Internal Revenue office which issued the notification (referred to in section 534(b) and paragraph (c) of this section) within 60 days after the mailing of such notification. If the taxpayer is unable, for good cause, to submit the statement within such 60-day period, an additional period not exceeding 30 days may be granted upon receipt in the Internal Revenue office concerned (before the expiration of the 60-day period provided herein) of a request from the taxpayer, setting forth the reasons for such request. See section 534(d) and § 1.534-3 with respect to a statement in the case of a jeopardy assessment.

T.D. 6377, 5/12/59.

§ 1.534-3 Jeopardy assessments in Tax Court cases.

In the case of a jeopardy assessment, a notice of deficiency is required to be sent to the taxpayer by registered mail (or by certified or registered mail, if the notice is mailed after September 2, 1958) within 60 days after the making of the assessment. See section 6861. If a jeopardy assessment is made before the mailing of the deficiency notice, then in the case of a proceeding in the Tax Court, if the deficiency notice informs the taxpayer that an amount of accumulated earnings tax is included in the deficiency, such notice shall constitute the notification provided for in section 534(b) and paragraph (c) of § 1.534-2. Under such circumstances the statement described in section 534(c) and paragraph (d) of § 1.534-2 shall instead be included in the taxpayer's petition to the Tax Court, if the taxpayer desires to submit such statement. See paragraph (b) of § 1.534-2, relating to burden of proof on the taxpayer.

T.D. 6377, 5/12/59.

§ 1.535-1 Definition.

Caution: The Treasury has not yet amended Reg § 1.535-1 to reflect changes made by P.L. 99-514, P.L. 98-369.

(a) The accumulated earnings tax is imposed by section 531 on the accumulated taxable income. Accumulated taxable income is the taxable income of the corporation with the adjustments prescribed by section 535(b) and § 1.535-2, minus the sum of the dividends paid deduction and the accumulated earnings credit. See section 561 and the regulations thereunder, relating to the definition of the deduction for dividends paid, and section 535(c) and § 1.535-3, relating to the accumulated earnings credit.

(b) In the case of a foreign corporation, whether resident or nonresident, which files or causes to be filed a return, the accumulated taxable income shall be the taxable income from sources within the United States with the adjustments prescribed by section 535(b) and § 1.535-2 minus the sum of the dividends paid deduction and the accumulated earnings credit. In the case of a foreign corporation which files no return, the accumulated taxable income shall be the gross income from sources within the United States without allowance of any deductions (including the accumulated earnings credit).

T.D. 6377, 5/12/59, amend T.D. 7244, 12/29/72.

§ 1.535-2 Adjustments to taxable income.

Caution: The Treasury has not yet amended Reg § 1.535-2 to reflect changes made by P.L. 109-135, P.L. 99-514, P.L. 98-369.

(a) Taxes. *(1) United States taxes.* In computing accumulated taxable income for any taxable year, there shall be allowed as a deduction the amount by which Federal income and excess profits taxes accrued during the taxable year exceed the credit provided by section 33 (relating to taxes of foreign countries and possessions of the United States), except that no deduction shall be allowed for (i) the accumulated earnings tax imposed by section 531 (or a corresponding section of a prior law), (ii) the personal holding company tax imposed by section 541 (or a corresponding section of a prior law), and (iii) the excess profits tax imposed by subchapter E, chapter 2 of the Internal Revenue Code of 1939, for taxable years beginning after December 31, 1940. The deduction is for taxes accrued during the taxable year, regardless of whether the corporation uses an accrual method of accounting, the cash receipts and disbursements method, or any other allowable method of accounting. In computing the amount of taxes accrued, an unpaid tax which is being contested is not considered accrued until the contest is resolved.

(2) Taxes of foreign countries and United States possessions. In determining accumulated taxable income for any taxable year, if the taxpayer chooses the benefits of section 901 for such taxable year, a deduction shall be allowed for—

(i) The income, war profits, and excess profits taxes imposed by foreign countries or possessions of the United States and accrued during such taxable year, and

(ii) In the case of a domestic corporation, the foreign income taxes deemed to be paid for such taxable year under section 902(a) in accordance with § 1.902-1 and 1.902-2 or section 960(a)(1) in accordance with § 1.960-7.

In no event shall the amount under subdivision (ii) of this subparagraph exceed the amount includible in gross income with respect to such taxes under section 78 and § 1.78-1. The credit for such taxes provided by section 901 shall not be allowed against the accumulated earnings tax imposed by section 531. See section 901(a).

(b) Charitable contributions. Section 535(b)(2) provides that, in computing the accumulated taxable income of a corporation, the deduction for charitable contributions shall be computed without regard to section 170(b)(2). Thus, the amount of charitable contributions made during the taxable year not allowable as a deduction under section 170 by reason of the limitations imposed by section 170(b)(2) shall be allowed as a deduction in computing accumulated taxable income for the taxable year. However, any excess of the amount of the charitable contributions made in a prior taxable year over the amount allowed as a deduction under section 170 for such year shall not be allowed as a deduction from taxable income in computing accumulated taxable income for the taxable year.

(c) Special deductions disallowed. Sections 241 through 248 provide for the allowance of special deductions for such items as partially tax-exempt interest, certain dividends received, dividends paid on certain preferred stock of public utilities, and organizational expenses. Such special deductions, except the deduction provided by section 248 (relating to organizational expenses) shall be disallowed in computing accumulated taxable income.

(d) Net operating loss. The net operating loss deduction provided in section 172 is not allowed for purposes of computing accumulated taxable income.

(e) Capital losses. *(1)* Losses from sales or exchanges of capital assets during the taxable year, which are disallowed as deductions under section 1211(a) in computing taxable income, shall be allowed as deductions in computing accumulated taxable income.

(2) The computation of the capital losses allowable as a deduction in computing accumulated taxable income may be illustrated by the following example:

Example. X Corporation has capital losses of $30,000 which are disallowed under section 1211(a) for the taxable year ended December 31, 1956. This amount represents a loss of $25,000 from the sale or exchange of capital assets during the taxable year ended December 31, 1956, plus a $5,000 capital loss carryover resulting from the sale or exchange of capital assets during the taxable year ended December 31, 1955. In computing accumulated taxable income for the taxable year ended December 31, 1956, only the loss of $25,000 arising from the sale or exchange of capital assets during that taxable year will be allowed as a deduction.

(f) Long-term capital gains. *(1)* There is allowed as a deduction in computing accumulated taxable income, the excess of the net long-term capital gain for the taxable year over the net short-term capital loss for such year (determined without regard to the capital loss carryover provided in section 1212) minus the taxes attributable to such excess as provided by section 535(b)(6). The tax attributable to such excess is the difference between—

(i) The taxes (except the accumulated earnings tax) imposed by subtitle A of the Code for such year, and

(ii) The taxes (except the accumulated earnings tax) imposed by subtitle A computing for such year as if taxable income were reduced by the excess of net long-term capital gain over net short-term capital loss (including the capital loss carryover to such year).

Where the tax (except the accumulated earnings tax) imposed by subtitle A includes an amount computed under section 1201(a)(2), the tax attributable to such excess is such amount computed under section 1201(a)(2).

(2) The application of the rule in subparagraph (1) of this paragraph may be illustrated by the following example:

Example. Assume that D Corporation, for the taxable year ended December 31, 1956, has taxable income of $103,000 of which $8,000 is the excess of net long-term capital gain over $12,000 over a net short-term capital loss of $9,000. The $9,000 net short-term capital loss includes a capital loss carryover of $5,000. The amount allowable as a deduction under section 535(b)(6) and subparagraph (1) of this paragraph is $7,250, computed as follows: Net long-term capital gain less net short-term capital loss (computed without regard to the capital loss carryover) is $8,000 (that is, $12,000 net long-term capital gain less $4,000 net short-term capital loss computed without regard to the capital loss carryover of $5,000). The tax attributable to the excess of net long-term capital gain over net short-term capital loss (computed by taking the capital loss carryover into account) is $750, that is, 25 percent of such excess of $3,000, computed under section 1201(a)(2). The difference of $7,250 ($8,000 less $750) is the amount allowable as a deduction in computing accumulated taxable income.

(3) Section 631(c) (relating to gain or loss in the case of disposal of coal or domestic iron ore) shall have no application in determining the amount of the deduction allowable under section 535(b)(6).

(g) Capital loss carrybacks and carryovers. Capital losses carried to a taxable year under section 1212(a) shall have no application for purposes of computing accumulated taxable income for such year.

(h) Bank affiliates. There is allowed the deduction provided by section 601 in the case of bank affiliates (as defined in section 2 of the Banking Act of 1933; 12 U. S. C. 221a(c)).

T.D. 6377, 5/12/59, amend T.D. 6805, 3/8/65, T.D. 6841, 7/26/65, T.D. 7301, 1/3/74, T.D. 7649, 10/17/79.

§ 1.535-3 Accumulated earnings credit.

Caution: The Treasury has not yet amended Reg § 1.535-3 to reflect changes made by P.L. 97-34.

(a) In general. As provided in section 535(a) and § 1.535-1, the accumulated earnings credit, provided by section 535(c), reduces taxable income in computing accumulated taxable income. In the case of a corporation, not a mere holding or investment company, the accumulated earnings credit is determined as provided in paragraph (b) of this section and, in the case of a holding or investment company, as provided in paragraph (c) of this section.

(b) Corporation which is not a mere holding or investment company. *(1) General rule.* (i) In the case of a corporation, not a mere holding or investment company, the accumulated earnings credit is the amount equal to such part of the earnings and profits of the taxable year which is retained for the reasonable needs of the business, minus the deduction allowed by section 535(b)(6) (see paragraph (f) of § 1.535-2, relating to the deduction for long-term capital gains). In no event shall the accumulated earnings credit be less than the minimum credit provided for in section 535(c)(2) and .subparagraph (2) of this paragraph. The amount of the earnings and profits for the taxable year retained is the amount by which the earnings and profits for the taxable year exceed the dividends paid deduction for such taxable year. See section 561 and §§ 1.561-1 and 1.561-2, relating to the deduction for dividends paid.

(ii) In determining whether any amount of the earnings and profits of the taxable year has been retained for the reasonable needs of the business, the accumulated earnings and profits of prior years will be taken into consideration. Thus, for example, if such accumulated earnings and profits of prior years are sufficient for the reasonable needs of the business, then any earnings and profits of the current taxable year which are retained will not be considered to be retained for the reasonable needs of the business. See section 537 and §§ 1.537-1 and 1.537-2.

(2) Minimum credit. Section 535(c)(2) provides for the allowance of a minimum accumulated earnings credit in the case of a corporation which is not a mere holding or investment company. Except as otherwise provided in section 243(b)(3) and § 1.243-5 (relating to effect of 100-percent dividends received deduction under section 243(b)) and sections 1561, 1562, and 1564 (relating to limitations on certain tax benefits in the case of certain controlled corporations), in the case of such a corporation, this minimum credit shall in no case be less than the amount by which $150,000 ($100,000 in the case of taxable years beginning before January 1, 1975) exceeds the accumulated earnings and profits of the corporation at the close of the preceding taxable year. See paragraph (d) of this section for the effect of dividends paid after the close of the taxable year in determining accumulated earnings and profits at the close of the preceding taxable year. In determining the amount of the minimum credit allowable under section 535(c)(2), the needs of the business are not taken into consideration. If the taxpayer has accumulated earnings and profits at the close of the preceding taxable year equal to or in excess of $150,000 ($100,000 in the case of taxable years beginning before January 1, 1975), the credit, if any, is determined without regard to section 535(c)(2). It is not intended that the provision for the minimum credit shall in any way create an inference that an accumulation in excess of $150,000 ($100,000 in the case of taxable years beginning before January 1, 1975) is unreasonable. The reasonable needs of the business may require the accumulation of more or less than $150,000 ($100,000 in the case of taxable years beginning before January 1, 1975), depending upon the circumstances in the case, but such needs shall not be taken into consideration to any extent in cases where the minimum accumulated earnings credit is applicable. For a discussion of the reasonable needs of the business, see section 537 and §§ 1.537-1, 1.537-2, and 1.537-3.

(3) Illustrations of accumulated earnings credit. The computation of the accumulated earnings credit provided by section 535(c) may be illustrated by the following examples:

Example (1). The X Corporation, which is not a mere holding or investment company, has accumulated earnings and profits in the amount of $125,000 as of December 31, 1974. Thus, the minimum credit provided by section 535(c)(2) exceeds the accumulated earnings and profits of X by $25,000. It has earnings and profits for the taxable year ended December 31, 1975, in the amount of $100,000 and has a dividends paid deduction under section 561 in the amount of $30,000 so that the earnings and profits for the taxable year which are retained in the business amount to $70,000. Assume that it has been determined that the earnings and profits for the taxable year which may be retained for the reasonable needs of the business amount to $55,000 and that a deduction has been allowed under section 535(b)(6) in the amount of $5,000. Since the amount by which $150,000 exceeds the accumulated earnings and profits at the close of the preceding taxable year is less than $50,000 ($55,000 − $5,000), the minimum credit provided by section 535(c)(2) will not apply and the accumulated earnings credit must be computed under section 535(c)(1) on the basis of the reasonable needs of the business. In this case, the accumulated earnings credit for the taxable year ended December 31, 1975, will be $50,000 computed as follows:

Earnings and profits of the taxable year determined to be retained for the reasonable needs of the business	$55,000
Less: The deduction for long-term capital gains (less applicable tax) allowed under section 535(b)(6)	5,000
Accumulated earnings credit allowable under section 535(c)(1)	50,000

Example (2). The Z Corporation which is not a mere holding or investment company, has accumulated earnings and profits in the amount of $45,000 as of December 31, 1974; it has earnings and profits for the taxable year ended December 31, 1975, in the amount of $115,000 and has a dividends paid deduction under section 561 in the amount of $10,000, so that the earnings and profits for the taxable year which are retained amount to $105,000. Assume that it has been determined that the accumulated earnings and profits of the taxable year which may be retained for the reasonable needs of the business amount to $20,000 and that no deduction is allowable for long-term capital gains under section 535(b)(6). The accumulated earnings credit allowable under section 535(c)(1) on the basis of the reasonable needs of the business is determined to be only $20,000. However, since the amount by which $150,000 exceeds the accumulated earnings and profits at the close of the preceding taxable year is more than $20,000, the minimum accumulated earnings credit provided by section 535(c)(2) is applicable. The allowable credit will be the amount by which $150,000 exceeds the accumulated earnings and profits at the close of the preceding taxable year *(i.e.,* $105,000, $150,000 less $45,000 of accumulated earnings and profits at the close of the preceding taxable year).

(c) Holding and investment companies. Section 535(c)(3) provides that, in the case of a mere holding or investment company, the accumulated earnings credit shall be the amount, if any, by which $150,000 ($100,000 in the case of taxable years beginning before January 1, 1975) exceeds the accumulated earnings and profits of the corporation at the close of the preceding taxable year. Thus, if such a corporation has accumulated earnings equal to or in excess of $150,000 ($100,000 in the case of taxable years beginning before January 1, 1975) at the close of its preceding taxable year, no accumulated earnings credit is allowable in computing the accumulated taxable income. See paragraph (c) of § 1.533-1 for a definition of a holding or investment company. For the accumulated earnings credit of a mere holding or investment company which is a member of an affiliated group which has elected the 100-percent dividends received deduction under section 243(b), see section 243(b)(3) and § 1.243-5. For the accumulated earnings credit of a mere holding or investment company which is a component member of a controlled group of corporations (as defined in section 1563), see sections 1561, 1562, and 1564.

(d) Accumulated earnings and profits. For the purposes of determining the minimum credit provided by section 535(c)(2) and paragraph (b)(2) of this section, and the credit provided by section 535(c)(3) and paragraph (c) of this section, dividends paid after the close of any taxable year which are considered paid during such taxable year, shall be deducted from the earnings and profits accumulated at the close of such taxable year. See section 563 and §§ 1.563-1 and 1.563-3, relating to dividends paid after the close of the taxable year.

T.D. 6377, 5/12/59, amend T.D. 6992, 1/17/69, T.D. 7181, 4/24/72, T.D. 7244, 12/29/72, T.D. 7376, 9/15/75, T.D. 7528, 12/27/77.

§ 1.536-1 Short taxable years.

Accumulated taxable income for a taxable year consisting of a period of less than 12 months shall not be placed on an annual basis for the purpose of the accumulated earnings tax imposed by section 531. In such cases accumulated taxable income shall be computed on the basis of the taxable income for such period of less than 12 months, adjusted in the manner provided by section 535(b) and § 1.535-2.

T.D. 6377, 5/12/59.

§ 1.537-1 Reasonable needs of the business.

(a) In general. The term "reasonable needs of the business" includes (1) the reasonable anticipated needs of the business (including product liability loss reserves, as defined in paragraph (f) of this section), (2) the section 303 redemption needs of the business, as defined in paragraph (c) of this section, and (3) the excess business holdings redemption needs of the business as described in paragraph (d) of this section. See paragraph (e) of this section for additional rules relating to the section 303 redemption needs and the excess business holdings redemption needs of the business. An accumulation of the earnings and profits (including the undistributed earnings and profits of prior years) is in excess of the reasonable needs of the business if it exceeds the amount that a prudent businessman would consider appropriate for the present business purposes and for the reasonable anticipated future needs of the business. The need to retain earnings and profits must be directly connected with the needs of the corporation itself and must be for bona fide business purposes. For purposes of this paragraph the section 303 redemption needs of the business and the excess business holdings redemption needs of the business are deemed to be directly connected with the needs of the business and for a bona fide business purpose. See § 1.537-3 for a discussion of what constitutes the business of the corporation. The extent to which earnings and profits have been distributed by the corporation may be taken into account in determining whether or not retained earnings and profits exceed the reasonable needs of the business. See § 1.537-2, relating to grounds for accumulation of earnings and profits.

(b) Reasonable anticipated needs. *(1)* In order for a corporation to justify an accumulation of earnings and profits for reasonably anticipated future needs, there must be an indication that the future needs of the business require such accumulation, and the corporation must have specific, definite, and feasible plans for the use of such accumulation. Such an accumulation need not be used immediately, nor must the plans for its use be consummated within a short period after the close of the taxable year, provided that such accumulation will be used within a reasonable time depending upon all the facts and circumstances relating to the future needs of the business. Where the future needs of the business are uncertain or vague, where the plans for the future use of an accumulation are not specific, definite, and feasible, or where the execution of such a plan is postponed indefinitely, an accumulation cannot be justified on the grounds of reasonably anticipated needs of the business.

(2) Consideration shall be given to reasonably anticipated needs as they exist on the basis of the facts at the close of the taxable year. Thus, subsequent events shall not be used for the purpose of showing that the retention of earnings or profits was unreasonable at the close of the taxable year if all the elements of reasonable anticipation are present at the close of such taxable year. However, subsequent events may be considered to determine whether the taxpayer actually intended to consummate or has actually consummated the plans for which the earnings and profits were accumulated. In this connection, projected expansion or investment plans shall be reviewed in the light of the facts during each year and as they exist as of the close of the taxable year. If a corporation has justified an accumulation for future needs by plans never consummated, the amount of such an accumulation shall be taken into account in determining the reasonableness of subsequent accumulations.

(c) Section 303 redemption needs of the business. *(1)* The term "section 303 redemption needs" means, with respect to the taxable year of the corporation in which a shareholder of the corporation died or any taxable year thereafter, the amount needed (or reasonably anticipated to be needed) to redeem stock included in the gross estate of such shareholder but not in excess of the amount necessary to effect a distribution to which section 303 applies. For purposes of this paragraph, the term "shareholder" includes an individual in whose gross estate stock of the corporation is includible upon his death for Federal estate tax purposes.

(2) This paragraph applies to a corporation to which section 303(c) would apply if a distribution described therein were made.

(3) If stock included in the gross estate of a decedent is stock of two or more corporations described in section 303(b)(2)(B), the amount needed by each such corporation for section 303 redemption purposes under this section shall, unless the particular facts and circumstances indicate otherwise, be that amount which bears the same ratio to the amount described in section 303(a) as the fair market value of such corporation's stock included in the gross estate of such decedent bears to the fair market value of all of the stock of such corporations included in the gross estate. For example, facts and circumstances indicating that the allocation prescribed by this subparagraph is not required would include notice given to the corporations by the executor or administrator of the decedent's estate that he intends to request the redemption of stock of only one of such corporations or the redemption of stock of such corporations in a ratio which is unrelated to the respective fair market values of the stock of the corporations included in the decedent's gross estate.

(4) The provisions of this paragraph apply only to taxable years ending after May 26, 1969.

(d) Excess business holdings redemption needs. *(1)* The term "excess business holdings redemption needs" means, with respect to taxable years of the corporation ending after May 26, 1969, the amount needed (or reasonably anticipated to be needed) to redeem from a private foundation stock which—

(i) Such foundation held on May 26, 1969 (or which was received by such foundation pursuant to a will or irrevocable trust to which section 4943(c)(5) applies), and either

(ii) Constituted excess business holdings on such date or would have constituted excess business holdings as of that date if there were taken into account (a) stock received pursuant to a will or trust described in subdivision (i) of this subparagraph and (b) the reduction in the total outstanding stock of the corporation which would have resulted solely from the redemption of stock held by the private foundation, or

(iii) Constituted stock redemption of which before January 1, 1975, or after October 4, 1976, and before January 1, 1977, is, by reason of section 101(l)(2)(B) of the Tax Reform Act of 1969, as amended by section 1309 of the Tax Reform Act of 1976, and § 53.4941(d)-4(b), permitted without imposition of tax under section 4941, but only to the extent such stock is to be redeemed before January 1, 1975 or after October 4, 1976, and before January 1, 1977, or is to be redeemed thereafter pursuant to the terms of a binding contract entered into on or before such date to redeem all of the stock of the corporation held by the private foundation on such date.

(2) The purpose of subparagraph (1) of this paragraph is to facilitate a private-foundation's disposition of certain excess business holdings, in order for the private foundation not to be liable for tax under section 4943. See section 4943(c) and the regulations thereunder for the definition of excess business holdings. For purposes of section 537(b)(2) and this paragraph, however, any determination of the existence of excess business holdings shall be made without taking into account the provisions of section 4943(c)(4) which treat certain excess business holdings as held by a disqualified person (rather than by the private foundation), except that the periods described in section 4943(c)(4)(B), (C), and (D), if applicable, shall be taken into account in determining the period during which an excess business holdings redemption need may be deemed to exist. Thus, an excess business holdings redemption need may, depending upon the facts and circumstances, be deemed to exist for a part or all of the 20-year, 15-year, or 10-year period specified in section 4943(c)(4)(B) during which the interest in the corporation held by the private foundation is treated as held by a disqualified person rather than by the private foundation, and, if applicable, (i) any suspension of such 20-year, 15-year, or 10-year period as provided by section 4943(c)(4)(C) and (ii) the 15-year "second phase" specified in section 4943(c)(4)(D). The foregoing sentence is not to be construed to prevent an accumulation of earnings and profits for the purpose of effecting a redemption of excess business holdings at a time or times prior to expiration of the periods described in such sentence. This subparagraph is not to be construed to prevent an accumulation of earnings and profits for the purpose of effecting a redemption described in subdivision (iii) of subparagraph (1) of this paragraph.

(3) The extent of an excess business holdings redemption need cannot exceed the total number of shares of stock so held or received by the private foundation (i) redemption of which alone would sufficiently reduce such private foundation's proportionate share of the corporation's total outstanding stock in order for the private foundation not to be liable for tax under section 4943, or (ii) redemption of which is, by reason of § 53.4941(d)-4(b), permitted without imposition of tax under section 4941 provided that such redemption is ac-

complished within the period and in the manner prescribed in subdivision (iii) of subparagraph (1) of this paragraph. Thus, excess business holdings of a private foundation attributable to an increase in the private foundation's proportionate share of the corporation's total outstanding stock by reason of a redemption of stock after May 26, 1969, from any person other than the private foundation do not give rise to an excess business holdings redemption need.

(4) For purposes of subdivision (ii) of subparagraph (1) of this paragraph, an excess business holdings redemption need can arise with respect to shares of the corporation's stock under section 537(a)(3) only following actual acquisition by the private foundation of such shares and their characterization as an excess business holding. Thus, this paragraph does not apply to an accumulation of earnings and profits in one taxable year in anticipation of redemption of excess business holdings to be acquired by a private foundation in a subsequent year pursuant to a will or irrevocable trust to which section 4943(c)(5) applies or in anticipation of shares held becoming excess business holdings of the private foundation in a subsequent year by reason of additional shares to be received by the private foundation in such subsequent year pursuant to a will or irrevocable trust to which section 4943(c)(5) applies. Once having arisen, however, an excess business holdings redemption need may continue until redemption of the private foundation's excess business holdings described in this paragraph or other disposition of such excess business holdings by the private foundation.

(5) Notwithstanding any other provision of this paragraph, an excess business holdings redemption need will not be deemed to exist with respect to stock held by a private foundation the redemption of which would subject any person to tax under section 4941.

(6) For purposes of subdivision (ii) of subparagraph (1) of this paragraph, the number of shares of stock held by a private foundation on May 26, 1969 (or received pursuant to a will or irrevocable trust to which section 4943(c)(5) applies), redemption of which alone would sufficiently reduce such foundation's proportionate share of a corporation's total outstanding stock in order for the foundation not to be liable for tax under section 4943 may be determined by application of the following formula:

$$X = \frac{PH-(Y \times SO)}{1-Y}$$

X =Number of shares to be redeemed.

Y =Maximum percentage of outstanding stock which private foundation can hold without being liable for tax under section 4943.

PH =Number of shares of stock held by private foundation on May 26, 1969, or received pursuant to a will or irrevocable trust to which section 4943(c)(5) applies.

SO =Total number of shares of stock outstanding unreduced by any redemption from a person other than the private foundation.

(7) The provisions of this paragraph may be illustrated by the following example:

Example. (i) On May 26, 1969, Private Foundation A holds 60 of the 100 outstanding shares of the capital stock of corporation X, which is not a disqualified person with respect to A. None of the remaining 40 shares is owned by a disqualified person within the meaning of section 4946(a). On June 1, 1975, X redeems 10 shares of its stock from individual B, thus reducing its outstanding stock to 90 shares. On June 1, 1976, A receives 20 additional shares of X stock by bequest under a will to which section 4943(c)(5) applies. As of June 1, 1976, then, A holds 80 of the 90 outstanding shares of X. Solely for purposes of this example and to illustrate the application of this paragraph, it will be assumed that in order not to be liable for the initial tax under section 4943, A must, before the close of the "second phase" described in section 4943(c)(4)(D), reduce its proportionate stock interest in X to 35 percent. A requests X to redeem from it a sufficient number of its shares to so reduce its proportionate stock interest in X to 35 percent, and X agrees to effect such a redemption.

(ii) As of May 26, 1969, A's excess business holdings are 25 shares of X, the number of shares which A would be required to dispose of to a person other than X in order to reduce its proportionate holdings in X to no more than 35 percent. If the disposition is to be by means of a redemption, however, A's excess holdings on May 26, 1969, for purposes of determining X's excess business holdings redemption needs, are 39 shares, i.e., the number of shares X would be required to redeem in order to reduce A's proportionate stock interest to 35 percent. Although the redemption of 10 shares from B on June 1, 1975, creates additional excess business holdings of A because it effectively increases A's proportionate stock interest in X, this increase does not create an additional excess business holdings redemption need because it resulted from a redemption from a person other than A. The bequest of 20 shares of X received by A on June 1, 1976, creates a further excess business holdings redemption need as of that date in the amount needed (or reasonably anticipated to be needed) to redeem an additional 31 shares from A, i.e., the number of shares which, when added to the excess business holdings of A on May 26, 1969, would have to be redeemed to reduce A's proportionate stock interest in X to 35 percent without taking the earlier redemption from B into account.

(e) *(1)* A determination whether and to what extent an amount is needed (or reasonably anticipated to be needed) for the purpose described in subparagraph (1) of paragraph (c) or (d) of this section is dependent upon the particular circumstances of the case, including the total amount of earnings and profits accumulated in prior years which may be available for such purpose and the existence of a reasonable expectation that a redemption described in paragraph (c) or (d) of this section will in fact be effected. Although paragraph (c) or (d) of this section may apply even though no redemption of stocks is in fact effected, the failure to effect such redemption may be taken into account in determining whether the accumulation was needed (or reasonably anticipated to be needed) for a purpose described in paragraph (c) or (d).

(2) In applying subparagraph (1) of paragraph (c) or (d) of this section, the discharge of an obligation incurred to make a redemption shall be treated as the making of the redemption.

(3) In determining whether an accumulation is in excess of the reasonable needs of the business for a particular year, the fact that one of the exceptions specified in paragraph (c) or (d) of this section applies in a subsequent year is not to give rise to an inference that the accumulation would not have been for the reasonable needs of the business in the prior year. Also, no inference is to be drawn from the enactment of section 537(a)(2) and (3) that accumulations in any prior year would not have been for the reasonable needs of the business in the absence of such provisions. Thus, the reasonableness of accumulations in years prior to a year in which one of the exceptions specified in paragraph (c) or (d) of this section applies is to be determined solely upon the

facts and circumstances existing at the times the accumulations occur.

(f) Product liability loss reserves. *(1)* The term "product liability loss reserve" means, with respect to taxable years beginning after September 30, 1979, reasonable amounts accumulated for the payment of reasonably anticipated product liability losses, as defined in section 172(j) and § 1.172-13(b)(1).

(2) For purposes of this paragraph, whether an accumulation for anticipated product liability losses is reasonable in amount and whether such anticipated product liability losses are likely to occur shall be determined in light of all facts and circumstances of the taxpayer making such accumulation. Some of the factors to be considered in determining the reasonableness of the accumulation include the taxpayer's previous product liability experience, the extent of the taxpayer's coverage by commercial product liability insurance, the income tax consequences of the taxpayer's ability to deduct product liability losses and related expenses, and the taxpayer's potential future liability due to defective products in light of the taxpayer's plans to expand the production of products currently being manufactured, provided such plans are specific, definite and feasible. Additionally, a factor to be considered in determining whether the accumulation is reasonable in amount is whether the taxpayer, in accounting for its potential future liability, took into account the reasonably estimated present value of the potential future liability.

(3) Only those accumulations made with respect to products that have been manufactured, leased, or sold shall be considered as accumulations made under this paragraph. Thus, for example, accumulations with respect to a product which has not progressed beyond the development stage are not reasonable accumulations under this paragraph.

T.D. 6377, 5/12/59, amend T.D. 7165, 3/8/72, T.D. 7678, 2/25/80, T.D. 8096, 8/26/86.

§ 1.537-2 Grounds for accumulation of earnings and profits.

(a) In general. Whether a particular ground or grounds for the accumulation of earnings and profits indicate that the earnings and profits have been accumulated for the reasonable needs of the business or beyond such needs is dependent upon the particular circumstances of the case. Listed below in paragraphs (b) and (c) of this section are some of the grounds which may be used as guides under ordinary circumstances.

(b) Reasonable accumulation of earnings and profits. Although the following grounds are not exclusive, one or more of such grounds, if supported by sufficient facts, may indicate that the earnings and profits of a corporation are being accumulated for the reasonable needs of the business provided the general requirements under §§ 1.537-1 and 1.537-3 are satisfied:

(1) To provide for bona fide expansion of business or replacement of plant;

(2) To acquire a business enterprise through purchasing stock or assets;

(3) To provide for the retirement of bona fide indebtedness created in connection with the trade or business, such as the establishment of a sinking fund for the purpose of retiring bonds issued by the corporation in accordance with contract obligations incurred on issue;

(4) To provide necessary working capital for the business, such as, for the procurement of inventories;

(5) To provide for investments or loans to suppliers or customers if necessary in order to maintain the business of the corporation; or

(6) To provide for the payment of reasonably anticipated product liability losses, as defined in section 172(j), § 1.172-13(b)(1), and § 1.537-1(f).

(c) Unreasonable accumulations of earnings and profits. Although the following purposes are not exclusive, accumulations of earnings and profits to meet any one of such objectives may indicate that the earnings and profits of a corporation are being accumulated beyond the reasonable needs of the business:

(1) Loans to shareholders, or the expenditure of funds of the corporation for the personal benefit of the shareholders;

(2) Loans having no reasonable relation to the conduct of the business made to relatives or friends of shareholders, or to other persons;

(3) Loans to another corporation, the business of which is not that of the taxpayer corporation, if the capital stock of such other corporation is owned, directly or indirectly, by the shareholder or shareholders of the taxpayer corporation and such shareholder or shareholders are in control of both corporations;

(4) Investments in properties, or securities which are unrelated to the activities of the business of the taxpayer corporation; or

(5) Retention of earnings and profits to provide against unrealistic hazards.

T.D. 6377, 5/12/59, amend T.D. 8096, 8/26/86.

§ 1.537-3 Business of the corporation.

(a) The business of a corporation is not merely that which it has previously carried on but includes, in general, any line of business which it may undertake.

(b) If one corporation owns the stock of another corporation and, in effect, operates the other corporation, the business of the latter corporation may be considered in substance, although not in legal form, the business of the first corporation. However, investment by a corporation of its earnings and profits in stock and securities of another corporation is not, of itself, to be regarded as employment of the earnings and profits in its business. Earnings and profits of the first corporation put into the second corporation through the purchase of stock or securities or otherwise, may, if a subsidiary relationship is established, constitute employment of the earnings and profits in its own business. Thus, the business of one corporation may be regarded as including the business of another corporation if such other corporation is a mere instrumentality of the first corporation; that may be established by showing that the first corporation owns at least 80 percent of the voting stock of the second corporation. If the taxpayer's ownership of stock is less than 80 percent in the other corporation, the determination of whether the funds are employed in a business operated by the taxpayer will depend upon the particular circumstances of the case. Moreover, the business of one corporation does not include the business of another corporation if such other corporation is a personal holding company, an investment company, or a corporation not engaged in the active conduct of a trade or business.

T.D. 6377, 5/12/59.

§ 1.541-1 Imposition of tax.

Caution: The Treasury has not yet amended Reg § 1.541-1 to reflect changes made by P.L. 107-16, P.L. 103-66.

(a) Section 541 imposes a graduated tax upon corporations classified as personal holding companies under section 542. This tax, if applicable, is in addition to the tax imposed upon corporations generally under section 11. Unless specifically excepted under section 542(c) the tax applies to domestic and foreign corporations and, to the extent provided by section 542(b), to an affiliated group of corporations filing a consolidated return. Corporations classified as personal holding companies are exempt from the accumulated earnings tax imposed under section 531 but are not exempt from other income taxes imposed upon corporations, generally, under any other provisions of the Code. Unlike the accumulated earnings tax imposed under section 531, the personal holding company tax imposed by section 541 applies to all personal holding companies as defined in section 542, whether or not they were formed or availed of to avoid income tax upon shareholders. See section 6501(f) and § 301.6501(f)-1 of this chapter (Regulations on Procedure and Administration) with respect to the period of limitation on assessment of personal holding company tax upon failure to file a schedule of personal holding company income.

(b) A foreign corporation, whether resident or nonresident, which is classified as a personal holding company is subject to the tax imposed under section 541 with respect to its income from sources within the United States, even though such income is not fixed or determinable annual or periodical income specified in section 881. A foreign corporation is not classified as a personal holding company subject to tax under section 541 if it is a foreign personal holding company as defined in section 552 or if it meets the requirements of the exception provided in section 542(c)(10).

T.D. 6308, 9/9/58.

§ 1.542-1 General rule.

A personal holding company is any corporation (other than one specifically excepted under section 542(c)) which, for the taxable year, meets—

(a) The gross income requirement specified in section 542(a)(1) and § 1.542-2, and

(b) The stock ownership requirement specified in section 542(a)(2) and § 1.542-3.

Both requirements must be satisfied with respect to each taxable year.

T.D. 6308, 9/9/58.

§ 1.542-2 Gross income requirement.

Caution: The Treasury has not yet amended Reg § 1.542-2 to reflect changes made by P.L. 99-514, P.L. 97-248, P.L. 96-589, P.L. 95-600, P.L. 93-480.

To meet the gross income requirement it is necessary that at least 80 percent of the total gross income of the corporation for the taxable year be personal holding company income as defined in section 543 and §§ 1.543-1 and 1.543-2. For the definition of "gross income" see section 61 and §§ 1.61-1 through 1.61-14. Under such provisions gross income is not necessarily synonymous with gross receipts. Further, in the case of transactions in stocks and securities and in commodities transactions, gross income for personal holding company tax purposes shall include only the excess of gains over losses from such transactions. See section 543(b), paragraph (b)(5) and (6) of § 1.543-1 and § 1.543-2. For determining the character of the amount includible in gross income under section 951(a), see paragraph (a) of § 1.951-1.

T.D. 6308, 9/9/58, amend T.D. 6795, 1/28/65.

§ 1.542-3 Stock ownership requirement.

Caution: The Treasury has not yet amended Reg § 1.542-3 to reflect changes made by P.L. 99-514, P.L. 97-248, P.L. 96-589, P.L. 95-600, P.L. 93-480.

(a) General rule. To meet the stock ownership requirement, it is necessary that at some time during the last half of the taxable year more than 50 percent in value of the outstanding stock of the corporation be owned, directly or indirectly, by or for not more than 5 individuals. Any organization or trust to which subparagraph (1) of this paragraph applies shall be considered as one individual for purposes of this stock ownership requirement subject, however, to the exception in subparagraph (2) of this paragraph which is applicable only to taxable years beginning after December 31, 1954. Thus, if an organization or trust which is considered as an individual owns 51 percent in value of the outstanding stock of the corporation at any time during the last half of the taxable year, the stock ownership requirement will be met by ownership of the required percentage by one individual. See section 544 and §§ 1.544-1 through 1.544-7 for the determination of stock ownership.

(1) An organization or trust considered as an individual. Any of the following organizations or trusts shall be considered as an individual:

(i) An organization to which section 503 applies, namely, any organization described in section 501(c)(3) (relating to charitable, etc., organizations) or section 401(a) (relating to employees' pension trust, etc.) other than an organization excepted from the application of section 503 by paragraphs (1) to (5) of section 503(b). Therefore, a religious organization (other than a trust) excepted under section 503(b)(1) is not considered an individual for purposes of the stock ownership requirement of section 542(a)(2).

(ii) A portion of a trust permanently set aside or to be used exclusively for the purposes described in section 642(c), relating to amounts set aside for charitable purposes, or described in a corresponding provision of the prior income tax law (such as section 162(a), Internal Revenue Code of 1939).

(2) Exception. For taxable years beginning after December 31, 1954, an organization or trust to which subparagraph (1) of this paragraph applies shall not be considered an individual if all of the following conditions are met:

(i) It was organized or created before July 1, 1950,

(ii) At all times on or after July 1, 1950, and before the close of the taxable year, it owned all of the common stock and at least 80 percent of the total number of shares of all other classes of stock of the corporation, and

(iii) For the taxable year it is not denied exemption under section 504(a) or the unlimited charitable deduction under section 681(c). In determining whether, for the purpose of section 542(a)(2), exemption is not denied under section 504(a) or the unlimited charitable deduction is not denied under section 681(c) all the income of the corporation which is available for distribution as dividends to its shareholders shall be deemed to have been distributed at the close of the taxable year whether or not any portion of such income was in fact distributed. If the amounts described in section 504(a) or section 681(c), increased by the income of the corporation deemed distributed pursuant to the preceding sentence, would be sufficient to deny exemption or the unlimited charitable deduction, the organization or trust will be considered to be an individual for the purpose of section 542(a)(2). For the purpose of this subdivision the restrictions in sections 504(a)(1) and 681(c)(1) against unreasonable accumulations will not apply to income attributable to property of a decedent dying before January 1, 1951, which was transferred during his lifetime to a trust or property that was transferred under his will to such trust.

(iv) This subparagraph is illustrated by the following example:

Example. The X Charitable Foundation (an organization described in section 501(c)(3) to which section 503 is applicable) has owned all of the stock of the Y Corporation since Y's organization in 1949. Both X and Y are calendar-year corporations. At the end of the year 1955, X has accumulated $100,000 out of income and has actually paid out only $75,000 of this amount, leaving a balance of $25,000 on December 31, 1955. X was not denied an exemption under section 504(a) for the year 1955. Y, during the calendar year 1955, has $400,000 taxable income of which $200,000 is available for distribution as dividends at the end of the year. X will be considered to have accumulated out of income during the calendar year 1955 the amount of $225,000 for the purpose of determining whether it would have been denied an exemption under section 504(a)(1). If X would have been denied an exemption under section 504(a)(1) by reason of having been deemed to have accumulated $225,000, the stock ownership requirement of section 542(a)(2) and this section will have been satisfied. If Y Corporation also satisfies the gross income requirement of section 542(a)(1) and § 1.542-2 it will be a personal holding company.

(b) Changes in stock outstanding. It is necessary to consider any change in the stock outstanding during the last half of the taxable year, whether in the number of shares or classes of stock, or in the ownership thereof. Stock subscribed and paid for will be considered as stock outstanding, whether or not such stock is evidenced by issued certificates. Treasury stock shall not be considered as stock outstanding.

(c) Value of stock outstanding. The value of the stock outstanding shall be determined in the light of all the circumstances. The value may be determined upon the basis of the company's net worth, earning and dividend paying capacity, appreciation of assets, together with such other factors as have a bearing upon the value of the stock. If the value of the stock is greatly at variance with that reflected by the corporate books, the evidence of such value should be filed with the return. In any case where there are two or more classes of stock outstanding, the total value of all the stock should be allocated among the different classes according to the relative value of each class.

T.D. 6308, 9/9/58, amend T.D. 6739, 6/16/64.

§ 1.542-4 Corporations filing consolidated returns.

Caution: The Treasury has not yet amended Reg § 1.542-4 to reflect changes made by P.L. 99-514, P.L. 97-248, P.L. 96-589, P.L. 95-600, P.L. 93-480, P.L. 89-809, P.L. 88-272.

(a) General rule. A consolidated return under section 1501 shall determine the application of the personal holding company tax to the group and to any member thereof on the basis of the consolidated gross income and consolidated personal holding company income of the group, as determined under the regulations prescribed pursuant to section 1502 (relating to consolidated returns); however, this rule shall not apply to either (1) an ineligible affiliated group as defined in section 542(b)(2) and paragraph (b) of this section, or (2) an affiliated group of corporations a member of which is excluded from the definition of a personal holding company under section 542(c) and paragraph (c) of this section. Thus, in the latter two instances the gross income requirement provided in section 542(a)(1) and § 1.542-2 shall apply to each individual member of the affiliated group of corporations.

(b) Ineligible affiliated group. *(1)* Except for certain affiliated railroad corporations, as provided in subparagraph (2) of this paragraph, an affiliated group of corporations is an ineligible affiliated group and therefore may not use its consolidated gross income and consolidated personal holding company income to determine the liability of the group or any member thereof for personal holding company tax (as provided in paragraph (a) of this section), if (i) any member of such group, including the common parent, derived gross income from sources outside the affiliated group for the taxable year in an amount equal to 10 percent or more of its gross income from all sources for that year and (ii) 80 percent or more of the gross income from sources outside the affiliated group consists of personal holding company income as defined in section 543 and §§ 1.543-1 and 1.543-2. For purposes of subdivision (i) of this subparagraph gross income shall not include certain dividend income received by a common parent from a corporation not a member of the affiliated group which qualifies under section 542(b)(4) and paragraph (d) of this section. See particularly the examples contained in paragraph (d)(2) of this section. Intercorporate dividends received by members of the affiliated group (including the common parent) are to be included in the gross income from all sources for purposes of the test in subdivision (i) of this subparagraph. For purposes of subdivision (ii) of this subparagraph, section 543 and paragraph (a) of § 1.543-1 shall be applied as if the amount of gross income derived from sources outside the affiliated group by a corporation which is a member of such group is the gross income of such corporation.

(2) An affiliated group of railroad corporations shall not be considered to be an ineligible affiliated group, notwithstanding any other provisions of section 542(b)(2) and this paragraph, if the common parent of such group would be eligible to file a consolidated return under section 141 of the Internal Revenue Code of 1939 prior to its amendment by the Revenue Act of 1942 (56 Stat. 798).

(3) See section 562(d) and § 1.562-3 for dividends paid deduction in the case of a distribution by a member of an ineligible affiliated group.

(4) The determination of whether an affiliated group of corporations is an ineligible group under section 542(b)(2) and this paragraph, may be illustrated by the following examples:

Example (1). Corporations X, Y, and Z constitute an affiliated group of corporations which files a consolidated return for the calendar year 1954; Corporations Y and Z are wholly-owned subsidiaries of Corporation X and derive no gross income from sources outside the affiliated group; Corporation X, the common parent, has gross income in the amount of $250,000 for the taxable year 1954. $200,000 of such gross income consists of dividends received from Corporations Y and Z. The remaining $50,000 was derived from sources outside the affiliated group, $40,000 of which represents personal holding company income as defined in section 543. The $50,000 included in the gross income of Corporation X and derived from sources outside the affiliated group is more than 10 percent of X's gross income ($50,000/$250,000) and the $40,000 which represents personal holding company income is 80 percent of $50,000 (the amount considered to be the gross income of Corporation X). Accordingly, Corporations X, Y, and Z would be an ineligible affiliated group and the gross income requirement under section 542(a)(1) and § 1.542-2 would be applied to each corporation individually.

Example (2). If, in the above example, only $30,000 of the $50,000 derived from sources outside the affiliated group by Corporation X represented personal holding company income, this group of affiliated corporations would not be an ineligible affiliated group. Although the $50,000 representing the gross income of Corporation X from sources outside the affiliated group is more than 10 percent of its total gross income, the amount of $30,000 representing personal holding company income is not 80 percent or more of the amount considered to be gross income for the purpose of this test. Under section 542(b)(2) and subparagraph (1) of this paragraph both the gross income and the personal holding company income requirements must be satisfied in determining that an affiliated group constitutes an ineligible group. Since both of these requirements have not been satisfied in this example this group of affiliated corporations would not be an ineligible group.

(c) Excluded corporations. The general rule for determining liability of an affiliated group under paragraph (a) of this section shall not apply if any member thereof is a corporation which is excluded, under section 542(c), from the definition of a personal holding company.

(d) Certain dividend income received by a common parent. *(1)* Dividends received by the common parent of an affiliated group from a corporation which is not a member of the affiliated group shall not be included in gross income or personal holding company income, for the purpose of the test under section 542(b)(2)—

(i) If such common parent owned, directly or indirectly, more than 50 percent of the outstanding voting stock of the dividend paying corporation at the time such common parent became entitled to the dividend, and

(ii) If the dividend paying corporation is not a personal holding company for the taxable year in which the dividends are paid.

Thus, if the tests in subdivisions (i) and (ii) of this subparagraph are met, the dividend income received by the common parent from such other corporation will not be considered gross income for purposes of the test in section 542(b)(2)(A) (paragraph (b) of this section), that is, either to determine gross income from sources outside the affiliated group or to determine gross income from all sources.

(2) The application of subparagraph (1) of this paragraph may be illustrated by the following examples:

Example (1). Corporation X is the common parent of Corporation Y and Corporation Z and together they constitute an affiliated group which files a consolidated return under section 1501. Corporation Y and Corporation Z derived no income from sources outside the affiliated group. Corporation X, the common parent, had gross income of $100,000 for the calendar year 1954 of which amount $20,000 represented a dividend received from Corporation W, and $4,000 represented interest from Corporation T. The remaining gross income of X, $76,000, was received from Corporations Y and Z. Corporation X, for its entire taxable year, owned 60 percent of the voting stock of Corporation W which was not a personal holding company for the calendar year 1954. For the purpose of the gross income and personal holding company income test under section 542(b)(2) and paragraph (b) of this section, the $20,000 dividend received from Corporation W would not be included in the gross income or personal holding company income of Corporation X. The affiliated group would not be an ineligible group under section 542(b)(2) because 10 percent or more of its gross income was not from sources outside the affiliated group as required by section 542(b)(2)(A). Inasmuch as the $20,000 dividend from Corporation W is not included in the gross income of Corporation X for purposes of section 542(b)(2) Corporation X only has $4,000 gross income from sources outside the affiliated group which is only 5 percent of its gross income from all sources, $80,000.

Example (2). If, in example (1), Corporation X owned 50 percent or less of the voting stock of Corporation W at the time X became entitled to the dividend, or if Corporation W had been a personal holding company for the taxable year in which the dividends were paid, the $20,000 dividends received by Corporation X would be included in gross income and personal holding company income of Corporation X for the purpose of the test under section 542(b)(2) and paragraph (b) of this section. Thus, the affiliated group would be an ineligible affiliated group under section 542(b)(2) because 24 percent of its gross income was from sources outside the affiliated group ($24,000/$100,000) and 100 percent of this $24,000 was personal holding company income.

T.D. 6308, 9/9/58.

§ 1.543-1 Personal holding company income.

Caution: The Treasury has not yet amended Reg § 1.543-1 to reflect changes made by P.L. 100-647, P.L. 99-514, P.L. 98-369, P.L. 94-455.

(a) General rule. The term "personal holding company income" means the portion of the gross income which consists of the classes of gross income described in paragraph (b) of this section. See section 543(b) and § 1.543-2 for special limitations on gross income and personal holding company income in cases of gains from stocks securities and commodities' transactions.

(b) Definitions. *(1) Dividends.* The term "dividends" includes dividends as defined in section 316 and amounts required to be included in gross income under section 551 and §§ 1.551-1–1.551-2 (relating to foreign personal holding company income taxed to United States shareholders).

(2) Interest. The term "interest" means any amounts, includible in gross income, received for the use of money loaned. However, (i) interest which constitutes "rent" shall not be classified as interest but shall be classified as "rents" (see subparagraph (10) of this paragraph) and (ii) interest on amounts set aside in a reserve fund under section 511 or 607 of the Merchant Marine Act, 1936 (46 USC 1161 or 1177), shall not be included in personal holding company income.

(3) Royalties (other than mineral, oil, or gas royalties or certain copyright royalties). The term "royalties" (other than mineral, oil, or gas royalties or certain copyright royalties) includes amounts received for the privilege of using patents, copyrights, secret processes and formulas, good will, trade marks, trade brands, franchises, and other like property. It does not, however, include rents. For rules relating to rents see section 543(a)(7) and subparagraph (10) of this para-

graph. For rules relating to mineral, oil, or gas royalties, see section 543(a)(8) and subparagraph (11) of this paragraph. For rules relating to certain copyright royalties for taxable years beginning after December 31, 1959, see section 543(a)(9) and subparagraph (12) of this paragraph.

(4) Annuities. The term "annuities" includes annuities only to the extent includible in the computation of gross income. See section 72 and §§ 1.72-1 – 1.72-14 for rules relating to the inclusion of annuities in gross income.

(5) Gains from the sale or exchange of stock or securities. (i) Except in the case of regular dealers in stocks or securities as provided in subdivision (ii) of this subparagraph, gross income and personal holding company income include the amount by which the gains exceed the losses from the sale or exchange of stock or securities. See section 543(b)(1) and § 1.543-2 for provisions relating to this limitation. For this purpose, there shall be taken into account all those gains includible in gross income (including gains from liquidating dividends and other distributions from capital) and all those losses deductible from gross income which are considered under chapter 1 of the Code to be gains or losses from the sale or exchange of stock or securities. The term "stock or securities" as used in section 543(a)(2) and this subparagraph includes shares or certificates of stock, stock rights or warrants, or interest in any corporation (including any joint stock company, insurance company, association, or other organization classified as a corporation by the Code, certificates of interest or participation in any profit-sharing agreement, or in any oil, gas, or other mineral property, or lease, collateral trust certificates, voting trust certificates, bonds, debentures, certificates of indebtedness, notes, car trust certificates, bills of exchange, obligations issued by or on behalf of a State, Territory, or political subdivision thereof.

(ii) In the case of "regular dealers in stock or securities" there shall not be included gains or losses derived from the sale or exchange of stock or securities made in the normal course of business. The term "regular dealer in stock or securities" means a corporation with an established place of business regularly engaged in the purchase of stock or securities and their resale to customers. However, such corporations shall not be considered as regular dealers with respect to stock or securities which are held for investment. See section 1236 and § 1.1236-1.

(6) Gains from futures transactions in commodities. Gross income and personal holding company income include the amount by which the gains exceed the losses from futures transactions in any commodity on or subject to the rules of a board of trade or commodity exchange. See § 1.543-2 for provisions relating to this limitation. In general, for the purpose of determining such excess, there are included all gains and losses on futures contracts which are speculative. However, for the purpose of determining such excess, there shall not be included gains or losses from cash transactions, or gains or losses by a producer, processor, merchant, or handler of the commodity, which arise out of bona fide hedging transactions reasonably necessary to the conduct of its business in the manner in which such business is customarily and usually conducted by others. See section 1233 and § 1.1233-1.

(7) Estates and trusts. Under section 543(a)(4) personal holding company income includes amounts includible in computing the taxable income of the corporation under Part I, subchapter J, chapter 1 of the Code (relating to estates, trusts, and beneficiaries); and any gain derived by the corporation from the sale or other disposition of any interest in an estate or trust.

(8) Personal service contracts. (i) Under section 543(a)(5) amounts received under a contract under which the corporation is to furnish personal services, as well as amounts received from the sale or other disposition of such contract, shall be included as personal holding company income if—

(a) Some person other than the corporation has the right to designate (by name or by description) the individual who is to perform the services, or if the individual who is to perform the services is designated (by name or by description) in the contract; and

(b) At any time during the taxable year 25 percent or more in value of the outstanding stock of the corporation is owned, directly or indirectly, by or for the individual who has performed, is to perform, or may be designated (by name or by description) as the one to perform, such services. For this purpose, the amount of stock outstanding and its value shall be determined in accordance with the rules set forth in the last two sentences of paragraph (b) and in paragraph (c) of § 1.542-3. It should be noted that the stock ownership requirement of section 543(a)(5) and this subparagraph relates to the stock ownership at any time during the taxable year. For rules relating to the determination of stock ownership, see section 544 and §§ 1.544-1 through 1.544-7.

(ii) If the contract, in addition to requiring the performance of services by a 25-percent stockholder who is designated or who could be designated (as specified in section 543(a)(5) and subdivision (i) of this subparagraph), requires the performance of services by other persons which are important and essential, then only that portion of the amount received under such contract which is attributable to the personal services of the 25-percent stockholder shall constitute personal holding company income. Incidental personal services of other persons employed by the corporation to facilitate the performance of the services by the 25-percent stockholder, however, shall not constitute important or essential services. Under section 482 gross income, deductions, credits, or allowances between or among organizations, trades, or businesses may be allocated if it is determined that allocation is necessary in order to prevent evasion of taxes or clearly to reflect the income of any such organizations, trades, or businesses.

(iii) The application of section 543(a)(5) and this subparagraph may be illustrated by the following examples:

Example (1). A, whose profession is that of an actor, owns all of the outstanding capital stock of the M Corporation. The M Corporation entered into a contract with A under which A was to perform personal services for the person or persons whom the M Corporation might designate, in consideration of which A was to receive $10,000 a year from the M Corporation. The M Corporation entered into a contract with the O Corporation in which A was designated to perform personal services for the O Corporation in consideration of which the O Corporation was to pay the M Corporation $500,000 a year. The $500,000 received by the M Corporation from the O Corporation constitutes personal holding company income.

Example (2). Assume the same facts as in example (1), except that, in addition to A's contract with the M Corporation, B, whose profession is that of a dancer and C, whose profession is that of a singer, were also under contract to the M Corporation to perform personal services for the person or persons whom the M Corporation might designate, in consideration of which they were each to receive $25,000 a year from the M Corporation. Neither B nor C were stockholders of the M Corporation. The contract entered into by the M Corporation with the O Corporation, in addition to designating that A was to perform personal services for the O Corporation, designated that B and C were also to perform personal services for the O Corporation. Although the O Corporation particularly desired the services of A for an entertainment program it planned, it also desired the services of B and C, who were prominent in their fields, to provide a good supporting cast for the program. The services of B and C required under the contract are determined to be important and essential; therefore, only that portion of the $500,000 received by the M Corporation which is attributable to the personal services of A constitutes personal holding company income. The same result would obtain although the dancer and the singer required by the contract were not designated by name but the contract gave the M Corporation discretion to select and provide the services of a singer and a dancer for the program and such services were provided.

Example (3). The N Corporation is engaged in engineering. Its entire outstanding capital stock is owned by four individuals. The N Corporation entered into a contract with the R Corporation to perform engineering services in consideration of which the R Corporation was to pay the N Corporation $50,000. The individual who was to perform the services was not designated (by name or by description) in the contract and no one but the N Corporation had the right to designate (by name or by description) such individual. The $50,000 received by the N Corporation from the R Corporation does not constitute personal holding company income.

(9) Compensation for use of property. Under section 543(a)(6) amounts received as compensation for the use of, or right to use, property of the corporation shall be included as personal holding company income if, at any time during the taxable year, 25 percent or more in value of the outstanding stock of the corporation is owned, directly or indirectly, by or for an individual entitled to the use of the property. Thus, if a shareholder who meets the stock ownership requirement of section 543(a)(6) and this subparagraph uses, or has the right to use, a yacht, residence, or other property owned by the corporation, the compensation to the corporation for such use, or right to use, the property constitutes personal holding company income. This is true even though the shareholder may acquire the use of, or the right to use, the property by means of a sublease or under any other arrangement involving parties other than the corporation and the shareholder. However, if the personal holding company income of the corporation (after excluding any such income described in section 543(a)(6) and this subparagraph, relating to compensation for use of property, and after excluding any such income described in section 543(a)(7) and subparagraph (10) of this paragraph, relating to rents) is not more than 10 percent of its gross income, compensation for the use of property shall not constitute personal holding company income. For purposes of the preceding sentence, in determining whether personal holding company income is more than 10 percent of gross income, copyright royalties constitute personal holding company income, regardless of whether such copyright royalties are excluded from personal holding company income under section 543(a)(9) and subparagraph (12)(ii) of this paragraph. For purposes of applying section 543(a)(6) and this subparagraph, the amount of stock outstanding and its value shall be determined in accordance with the rules set forth in the last two sentences of paragraph (b) and in paragraph (c) of § 1.542-3. It should be noted that the stock ownership requirement of section 543(a)(6) and this subparagraph relates to the stock outstanding at any time during the entire taxable year. For rules relating to the determination of stock ownership, see section 544 and §§ 1.544-1 through 1.544-7.

(10) Rents (including interest constituting rents). Rents which are to be included as personal holding company income consist of compensation (however designated) for the use, or right to use, property of the corporation. The term "rents" does not include amounts includible in personal holding company income under section 543(a)(6) and subparagraph (9) of this paragraph. The amounts considered as rents include charter fees, etc., for the use of, or the right to use, property, as well as interest on debts owed to the corporation (to the extent such debts represent the price for which real property held primarily for sale to customers in the ordinary course of the corporation's trade or business was sold or exchanged by the corporation). However, if the amount of the rents includible under section 543(a)(7) and this subparagraph constitutes 50 percent or more of the gross income of the corporation, such rents shall not be considered to be personal holding company income.

(11) Mineral, oil, or gas royalties. (i) The income from mineral, oil, or gas royalties is to be included as personal holding company income, unless (a) the aggregate amount of such royalties constitutes 50 percent or more of the gross income of the corporation for the taxable year and (b) the aggregate amount of deductions allowable under section 162 (other than compensation for personal services rendered by the shareholders of the corporation) equals 15 percent or more of the gross income of the corporation for the taxable year.

(ii) The term "mineral, oil, or gas royalties" means all royalties, including overriding royalties and, to the extent not treated as loans under section 636, mineral production payments, received from any interest in mineral, oil, or gas properties. The term "mineral" includes those minerals which are included within the meaning of the term "minerals" in the regulations under section 611.

(iii) The first sentence of subdivision (ii) of this subparagraph shall apply to overriding royalties received from the sublessee by the operating company which originally leased and developed the natural resource property in respect of which such overriding royalties are paid, and to mineral, oil, or gas production payments, only with respect to amounts received after September 30, 1958.

(12) Copyright royalties. (i) In general. The income from copyright royalties constitutes, generally, personal holding company income. However, for taxable years beginning after December 31, 1959, those copyright royalties which come within the definition of "copyright royalties" in section 543(a)(9) and subdivision (iv) of this subparagraph shall be excluded from personal holding company income only if the conditions set forth in subdivision (ii) of this subparagraph are satisfied.

(ii) Exclusion from personal holding company income. For taxable years beginning after December 31, 1959, copyright royalties (as defined in section 543(a)(9) and subdivision (iv) of this subparagraph) shall be excluded from personal holding company income only if the conditions set forth in (a), (b), and (c) of this subdivision are met.

(a) Such copyright royalties for the taxable year must constitute 50 percent or more of the corporation's gross income. For this purpose, copyright royalties shall be computed by excluding royalties received for the use of, or the right to use, copyrights or interests in copyrights in works created, in whole or in part, by any person who, at any time during the corporation's taxable year, is a shareholder.

(b) Personal holding company income for the taxable year must be 10 percent or less of the corporation's gross income.

For this purpose, personal holding company income shall be computed by excluding (1) copyright royalties (except that there shall be included royalties received for the use of, or the right to use, copyrights or interests in copyrights in works created, in whole or in part, by any shareholder owning, at any time during the corporation's taxable year, more than 10 percent in value of the outstanding stock of the corporation), and (2) dividends from any corporation in which the taxpayer owns, on the date the taxpayer becomes entitled to the dividends, at least 50 percent of all classes of stock entitled to vote and at least 50 percent of the total value of all classes of stock, provided the corporation which pays the dividends meets the requirements of subparagraphs (A), (B), and (C) of section 543(a)(9).

(c) The aggregate amount of the deductions allowable under section 162 must constitute 50 percent or more of the corporation's gross income for the taxable year. For this purpose, the deductions allowable under section 162 shall be computed by excluding deductions for compensation for personal services rendered by, and deductions for copyright and other royalties to, shareholders of the corporation.

(iii) Determination of stock value and stock ownership. For purposes of section 543(a)(9) and this subparagraph, the following rules shall apply:

(a) The amount and value of the outstanding stock of a corporation shall be determined in accordance with the rules set forth in the last two sentences of paragraph (b) and in paragraph (c) of § 1.542-3.

(b) The ownership of stock shall be determined in accordance with the rules set forth in section 544 and §§ 1.544-1 through 1.544-7.

(c) Any person who is considered to own stock within the meaning of section 544 and §§ 1.544-1 through 1.544-7 shall be a shareholder.

(iv) Copyright royalties defined. For purposes of section 543(a)(9) and this subparagraph, the term "copyright royalties" means compensation, however designated, for the use of, or the right to use, copyrights in works protected by copyright issued under Title 17 of the United States Code (other than by reason of section 2 or 6 thereof), and to which copyright protection is also extended by the laws of any foreign country as a result of any international treaty, convention, or agreement to which the United States is a signatory. Thus, "copyright royalties" includes not only royalties from sources within the United States under protection of United States laws relating to statutory copyrights but also royalties from sources within a foreign country with respect to United States statutory copyrights protected in such foreign country by any international treaty, convention, or agreement to which the United States is a signatory. The term "copyright royalties" includes compensation for the use of, or right to sue, an interest in any such copyrighted works as well as payments from any person for performing rights in any such copyrighted works.

(v) Compensation which is rent. Section 543(a)(9) and subdivisions (i) through (iv) of this subparagraph shall not apply to compensation which is "rent" within the meaning of the second sentence of section 543(a)(7).

T.D. 6308, 9/9/58, amend T.D. 6739, 6/16/64, T.D. 7261, 2/26/73.

§ 1.543-2 Limitation on gross income and personal holding company income in transactions involving stocks, securities and commodities.

Caution: The Treasury has not yet amended Reg § 1.543-2 to reflect changes made by P.L. 94-455.

(a) Under section 543(b)(1) the gains which are to be included in gross income, and in personal holding company income with respect to transactions described in section 543(a)(2) and paragraph (b)(5) of § 1.543-1, shall be the net gains from the sale or exchange of stock or securities. If there is an excess of losses over gains from such transactions, such excess (or net loss) shall not be used to reduce gross income or personal holding company income for purposes of the personal holding company tax. Similarly, under section 543(b)(2) the gains which are to be included in gross income, and in personal holding company income with respect to transactions described in section 543(a)(3) and paragraph (b)(6) of § 1.543-1, shall be the net gains from commodity transactions which reflect personal holding company income. Any excess of losses over gains from such transactions (resulting in a net loss) shall not be used to reduce gross income or personal holding company income. The capital loss carryover under section 1212 shall not be taken into account.

(b) The application of section 543(b) may be illustrated by the following examples:

Example (1). The P Corporation, not a regular dealer in stocks and securities, received rentals of $250,000 for its property from a 25-percent shareholder, and also had gains of $50,000 during the taxable year from the sale of stocks and securities. It also had losses on the sale of stocks and securities in the amount of $30,000. Accordingly, P Corporation had gross income during the taxable year of $270,000 ($250,000 plus $20,000 net gain from the sales of stocks and securities). It had personal holding company income of $20,000. (The rentals of $250,000 would not be personal holding company income under section 543(a)(6) since the personal holding company income of the corporation, $20,000 (after excluding any such income described in section 543(a)(6)), is not more than 10 percent of its gross income.)

Example (2). The R Corporation, not a regular dealer in stocks or securities, realized total gains during the taxable year of $900,000 from commodity futures transactions and $200,000 from the sales of stocks and securities. It also sustained total losses of $1,000,000 on such commodity futures transactions, resulting in a net gain for the taxable year of $100,000. None of the commodity futures transactions are hedging or other types of futures transactions excluded from the application of section 543(a)(3). No part of the loss on commodity futures transactions is to be taken into account in determining personal holding company income and gross income for personal holding company tax purposes for the taxable year. The full amount of the $200,000 in gains from the sales of stocks and securities is to be included in personal holding company income and in gross income for personal holding company tax purposes for the taxable year.

T.D. 6308, 9/9/58.

§ 1.543-12 Definitions.

(e) Adjusted income from mineral, oil, and gas royalties.

(2) Definition of mineral, oil, and gas royalties. For purposes of determining personal holding company income, the term "mineral, oil, and gas royalties" means all royalties, in-

cluding overriding royalties and, to the extent not treated as loans under section 636, mineral production payments, received from any interest in mineral, oil, or gas properties. The term "mineral" includes those minerals which are included within the meaning of the term "minerals" in the regulations under section 611. The term "overriding royalties" includes amounts received from the sublessee by the operating company which leased and developed the natural resource property in respect of which such overriding royalties are paid.

T.D. 7261, 2/26/73.

§ 1.544-1 Constructive ownership.

(a) Rules relating to the constructive ownership of stock are provided by section 544 for the purpose of determining whether the stock ownership requirements of the following sections are satisfied:

(1) Section 542(a)(2), relating to ownership of stock by five or fewer individuals.

(2) Section 543(a)(5), relating to personal holding company income derived from personal service contracts.

(3) Section 543(a)(6), relating to personal holding company income derived from property used by shareholders.

(4) Section 543(a)(9), relating to personal holding company income derived from copyright royalties.

(b) Section 544 provides four general rules with respect to constructive ownership. These rules are:

(1) Constructive ownership by reason of indirect ownership. See section 544(a)(1) and § 1.544-2.

(2) Constructive ownership by reason of family and partnership ownership. See section 544(a)(2), (4), (5), and (6), and § 1.544-3, 1.544-6, and 1.544-7.

(3) Constructive ownership by reason of ownership of options. See section 544(a)(3), (4), (5), and (6), and §§ 1.544-4, 1.544-6, and 1.544-7.

(4) Constructive ownership by reason of ownership of convertible securities. See section 544(b) and § 1.544-5.

Each of the rules referred to in subparagraphs (2), (3), and (4) of this paragraph is applicable only if it has the effect of satisfying the stock ownership requirement of the section to which applicable; that is, when applied to section 542(a)(2), its effect is to make the corporation a personal holding company, or when applied to section 543(a)(5), section 543(a)(6), or section 543(a)(9), its effect is to make the amounts described in such provisions includible as personal holding company income.

(c) All forms and classes of stock, however denominated, which represent the interests of shareholders, members, or beneficiaries in the corporation shall be taken into consideration in applying the constructive ownership rules of section 544.

(d) For rules applicable in treating constructive ownership, determined by one application of section 544, as actual ownership for purposes of a second application of section 544, see section 544(a)(5) and § 1.544-6.

T.D. 6308, 9/9/58, amend T.D. 6739, 6/16/64.

§ 1.544-2 Constructive ownership by reason of indirect ownership.

Caution: The Treasury has not yet amended Reg § 1.544-2 to reflect changes made by P.L. 88-272.

The following example illustrates the application of section 544(a)(1), relating to constructive ownership by reason of indirect ownership:

Example. A and B, two individuals, are the exclusive and equal beneficiaries of a trust or estate which owns the entire capital stock of the M Corporation. The M Corporation in turn owns the entire capital stock of the N Corporation. Under such circumstances the entire capital stock of both the M Corporation and the N Corporation shall be considered as being owned equally by A and B as the individuals owning the beneficial interest therein.

T.D. 6308, 9/9/58.

§ 1.544-3 Constructive ownership by reason of family and partnership ownership.

Caution: The Treasury has not yet amended Reg § 1.544-3 to reflect changes made by P.L. 88-272.

(a) The following example illustrates the application of section 544(a)(2), relating to constructive ownership by reason of family and partnership ownership.

Example. The M Corporation at some time during the last half of the taxable year, had 1,800 shares of outstanding stock, 450 of which were held by various individuals having no relationship to one another and none of whom were partners, and the remaining 1,350 were held by 51 shareholders as follows:

Relationships		Shares		Shares		Shares		Shares		Shares
An individual	A	100	B	20	C	20	D	20	E	20
His father	AF	10	BF	10	CF	10	DF	10	EF	10
His wife	AW	10	BW	40	CW	40	DW	40	EW	40
His brother	AB	10	BB	10	CB	10	DB	10	EB	10
His son	AS	10	BS	40	CS	40	DS	40	ES	40
His daughter by former marriage (son's half-sister)	ASHS	10	BSHS	40	CSHS	40	DSHS	40	ESHS	40
His brother's wife	ABW	10	BBW	10	CBW	10	DBW	160	EBW	10
His wife's father	AWF	10	BWF	10	CWF	110	DWF	10	EWF	10
His wife's brother	AWB	10	BWB	10	CWB	10	DWB	10	EWB	10
His wife's brother's wife	AWBW	10	BWBW	10	CWBW	10	DWBW	10	EWBW	110
Individual's partner	AP	10								

By applying the statutory rule provided in section 544(a)(2) five individuals own more than 50 percent of the outstanding stock as follows:

A (including AF, AW, AB, AS, ASHS, AP)	160
B (including BF, BW, BB, BS, BSHS)	160
CW (including C, CS, CWF, CWB)	220
DB (including D, DF, DBW)	200
EWB (including EW, EWF, EWBW)	170
Total, or more than 50 percent	910

Individual A represents the obvious case where the head of the family owns the bulk of the family stock and naturally is the head of the group. A's partner owns 10 shares of the stock. Individual B represents the case where he is still head of the group because of the ownership of stock by his immediate family. Individuals C and D represent cases where the individuals fall in groups headed in C's case by his wife and in D's case by his brother because of the preponderance of holdings on the part of relatives by marriage. Individual E represents the case where the preponderant holdings of others eliminate that individual from the group.

(b) For the restriction on the applicability of the family and partnership ownership rules of this section, see paragraph (b) of § 1.544-1. For rules relating to constructive ownership as actual ownership, see § 1.544-6.

T.D. 6308, 9/9/58.

§ 1.544-4 Options.

Caution: The Treasury has not yet amended Reg § 1.544-4 to reflect changes made by P.L. 88-272.

The shares of stock which may be acquired by reason of an option shall be considered to be constructively owned by the individual having the option to acquire such stock. For example: If C, an individual, on March 1, 1955, purchases an option, or otherwise comes into possession of an option, to acquire 100 shares of the capital stock of M Corporation, such 100 shares of stock shall be considered to be constructively owned by C as if C had actually acquired the stock on that date. If C has an option on an option (or one of a series of options) to acquire such stock, he shall also be considered to have constructive ownership of the stock which may be acquired by reason of the option (or the series of options). Under such circumstances, C shall be considered to have acquired constructive ownership of the stock on the date he acquired his option. For the restriction on the applicability of the rule of this section, see paragraph (b) of § 1.544-1.

T.D. 6308, 9/9/58.

§ 1.544-5 Convertible securities.

Caution: The Treasury has not yet amended Reg § 1.544-5 to reflect changes made by P.L. 88-272.

Under section 544(b) outstanding securities of a corporation such as bonds, debentures, or other corporate obligations, convertible into stock of the corporation (whether or not convertible during the taxable year) shall be considered as outstanding stock of the corporation. The consideration of convertible securities as outstanding stock is subject to the exception that, if some of the outstanding securities are convertible only after a later date than in the case of others, the class having the earlier conversion date may be considered as outstanding stock although the others are not so considered, but no convertible securities shall be considered as outstanding stock unless all outstanding securities having a prior conversion date are also so considered. For example, if outstanding securities are convertible in 1954, 1955 and 1956, those convertible in 1954 can be properly considered as outstanding stock without so considering those convertible in 1955 or 1956, and those convertible in 1954 and 1955 can be properly considered as outstanding stock without so considering those convertible in 1956. However, the securities convertible in 1955 could not be properly considered as outstanding stock without so considering those convertible in 1954 and the securities convertible in 1956 could not be properly considered as outstanding stock without so considering those convertible in 1954 and 1955. For the restriction on the applicability of the rule of this section, see paragraph (b) of § 1.544-1.

T.D. 6308, 9/9/58.

§ 1.544-6 Constructive ownership as actual ownership.

Caution: The Treasury has not yet amended Reg § 1.544-6 to reflect changes made by P.L. 88-272.

(a) General rules. *(1)* Stock constructively owned by a person by reason of the application of the rule provided in section 544(a)(1), relating to stock not owned by an individual, shall be considered as actually owned by such person for the purpose of again applying such rule or of applying the family and partnership rule provided in section 544(a)(2), in order to make another person the constructive owner of such stock, and

(2) Stock constructively owned by a person by reason of the application of the option rule provided in section 544(a)(3) shall be considered as actually owned by such person for the purpose of applying either the rule provided in section 544(a)(1), relating to stock not owned by an individual, or the family and partnership rule provided in section 544(a)(2) in order to make another person the constructive owner of such stock, but

(3) Stock constructively owned by an individual by reason of the application of the family and partnership rule provided in section 544(a)(2) shall not be considered as actually owned by such individual for the purpose of again applying such rule in order to make another individual the constructive owner of such stock.

(b) Examples. The application of this section may be illustrated by the following examples:

Example (1). A's wife, AW, owns all the stock of the M Corporation, which in turn owns all the stock of the O Corporation. The O Corporation in turn owns all the stock of the P Corporation. Under the rule provided in section 544(a)(1), relating to stock not owned by an individual, the stock in the P Corporation owned by the O Corporation is considered to be owned constructively by the M Corporation, the sole shareholder of the O Corporation. Such constructive ownership of the stock of the M Corporation is considered as actual ownership for the purpose of again applying such rule in order to make AW, the sole shareholder of the M Corporation, the constructive owner of the stock of the P Corporation. Similarly, the constructive ownership of the stock by AW is considered as actual ownership for the purpose of applying the family and partnership rule provided in section 544(a)(2) in order to make A the constructive owner of the stock of the P Corporation, if such application is necessary for any of the purposes set forth in paragraph (b) of § 1.544-1. But the stock thus constructively owned by A may not be considered as actual ownership for the purpose of again applying the family and partnership rule in order to make another member of A's family, for example, A's father, the constructive owner of the stock of the P Corporation.

Example (2). B, an individual, owns all the stock of the R Corporation which has an option to acquire all the stock of the S Corporation, owned by C, an individual, who is not related to B. Under the option rule provided in section 544(a)(3) the R Corporation may be considered as owning constructively the stock of the S Corporation owned by C. Such constructive ownership of the stock by the R Corporation is considered as actual ownership for the purpose of applying the rule provided in section 544(a)(1), relating to stock not owned by an individual, in order to make B, the sole shareholder of the R Corporation, the constructive owner of the stock of the S Corporation. The stock thus constructively owned by B by reason of the application of the rule provided in section 544(a)(1) likewise is considered as actual ownership for the purpose, if necessary, of applying the family and partnership rule provided in section 544(a)(2), in order to make another member of B's family, for example, B's wife, BW, the constructive owner of the stock of the S Corporation. However, the family and partnership rule could not again be applied so as to make still another individual the constructive owner of the stock of the S Corporation, that is, the stock constructively owned by BW could not be considered as actually owned by her in order to make BW's father the constructive owner of such stock by a second application of the family and partnership rule.

T.D. 6308, 9/9/58.

§ 1.544-7 Option rule in lieu of family and partnership rule.

Caution: The Treasury has not yet amended Reg § 1.544-7 to reflect changes made by P.L. 88-272.

(a) If, in determining the ownership of stock, such stock may be considered as constructively owned by an individual by an application of either the family and partnership rule (section 544(a)(2)) or the option rule (section 544(a)(3)), such stock shall be considered as owned constructively by the individual by reason of the application of the option rule.

(b) The application of this section may be illustrated by the following example:

Example. Two brothers, A and B, each own 10 percent of the stock of the M Corporation, and A's wife, AW, also owns 10 percent of the stock of such corporation. AW's husband, A, has an option to acquire the stock owned by her at any time. It becomes necessary, for one of the purposes stated in section 544(a)(4), to determine the stock ownership of B in the M Corporation. If the family and partnership rule were the only rule that applied in the case, B would be considered, under that rule, as owning 20 percent of the stock of the M Corporation, namely, his own stock plus the stock owned by his brother. In that event, B could not be considered as owning the stock held by AW since (1) AW is not a member of B's family and (2) the constructive ownership of such stock by A through the application of the family and partnership rule in his case is not considered as actual ownership so as to make B the constructive owner by a second application of the same rule with respect to the ownership of the stock. However, there is more than the family and partnership rule involved in this example. As the holder of an option upon the stock, A may be considered the constructive owner of his wife's stock by the application of the option rule and without reference to the family relationship between A and AW. If A is considered as owning the stock of his wife by application of the option rule, then such constructive ownership by A is regarded as actual ownership for the purpose of applying the family and partnership rule so as to make another member of A's family, for example, B, the constructive owner of the stock. Hence, since A may be considered as owning his wife's stock by applying either the family-partnership rule or the option rule, the provisions of section 544(a)(6) apply and accordingly A must be considered the constructive owner of his wife's stock under the option rule rather than the family-partnership rule. B thus becomes the constructive owner of 30 percent of the stock of the M Corporation, namely, his own 10 percent, A's 10 percent, and AW's 10 percent constructively owned by A as the holder of an option on the stock.

T.D. 6308, 9/9/58.

§ 1.545-1 Definition.

(a) Undistributed personal holding company income is the amount which is subject to the personal holding company tax imposed under section 541. Undistributed personal holding company income is the taxable income of the corporation adjusted in the manner described in section 545(b) and § 1.545-2 and section 545(c) and § 1.545-3, less the deduction for dividends paid. See part IV (section 561 and following), subchapter G, chapter 1 of the Code, and the regulations thereunder, relating to the dividends paid deduction.

(b) For purposes of the imposition of the personal holding company tax on a foreign corporation, resident or nonresident, which files or causes to be filed a return, the undistributed personal holding company income shall be computed on the basis of the taxable income from sources within the United States, and such income shall be adjusted in accordance with the principles of section 545(b) and § 1.545-2, and section 545(c) and § 1.545-3. For purposes of the imposition of such tax on a foreign corporation, resident or nonresident, which files no return, the undistributed personal holding company income shall be computed on the basis of the gross income from sources within the United States without allowance of any deductions. For purposes of this paragraph, a nonresident foreign corporation will be considered to have filed a return for any taxable year ending before September 9, 1958, if the return for any such taxable year is filed on or before February 5, 1960.

T.D. 6308, 9/9/58, amend T.D. 6427, 12/2/59, T.D. 6949, 4/8/68.

§ 1.545-2 Adjustments to taxable income.

Caution: The Treasury has not yet amended Reg § 1.545-2 to reflect changes made by P.L. 99-514, P.L. 97-448.

(a) Taxes. *(1) General rule.* (i) In computing undistributed personal holding company income for any taxable year, there shall be allowed as a deduction the amount by which Federal income and excess profits taxes accrued during the taxable year exceed the credit provided by section 33 (relating to taxes of foreign countries and possessions of the United States), and the income, war profits, and excess profits taxes of foreign countries and possessions of the United States accrued during the taxable year (to the extent provided by subparagraph (3) of this paragraph), except that no deduction shall be allowed for (a) the accumulated earnings tax imposed by section 531 (or a corresponding section of a prior law), (b) the personal holding company tax imposed by section 541 (or a corresponding section of a prior law), and (c) the excess profits tax imposed by subchapter E chapter 2 of the Internal Revenue Code of 1939 for taxable years beginning after December 31, 1940. The deduction is for taxes for the taxable year, determined under the accrual method of accounting, regardless of whether the corporation uses an accrual method of accounting, the cash receipts and disbursement method, or any other allowable method of accounting. In computing the amount of taxes accrued, an unpaid tax which is being contested is not considered accrued until the contest is resolved.

(ii) However, the taxpayer shall deduct taxes paid, rather than taxes accrued, if it used that method with respect to Federal taxes for each taxable year for which it was subject to the tax imposed by section 500 of the Internal Revenue Code of 1939, unless an election is made under subparagraph (2) of this paragraph to deduct taxes accrued.

(2) Election by taxpayer which deducted taxes paid. (i) If the corporation was subject to the personal holding company tax imposed by section 500 of the Internal Revenue Code of 1939 and, for the purpose of that tax, deducted Federal taxes paid rather than such taxes accrued for each taxable year for which it was subject to such taxes, the corporation may elect for any taxable year ending after June 30, 1954, to deduct taxes accrued, including taxes of foreign countries and possessions of the United States, rather than taxes paid, for the purposes of the tax imposed by section 541 of the Internal Revenue Code of 1954. The election shall be made by deducting such taxes accrued on Schedule PH, Form 1120, to be filed with the return. The schedule shall, in addition, contain a statement that the corporation has made such election and shall set forth the year to which such election was first applicable. The deduction of taxes accrued in the year of election precludes the deduction of taxes paid during such year. The election, if made, shall be irrevocable and the deduction for taxes accrued shall be allowed for the year of election and for all subsequent taxable years.

(ii) Pursuant to section 7851(a)(1)(C), the election provided for in subdivision (i) of this subparagraph may be made with respect to a taxable year ending after June 30, 1954, even though such taxable year is subject to the Internal Revenue Code of 1939.

(3) Taxes of foreign countries and United States possessions. In determining undistributed personal holding company income for any taxable year, if the taxpayer chooses the benefits of section 901 for such taxable year, a deduction shall be allowed for—

(i) The income, war profits, and excess profits taxes imposed by foreign countries or possessions of the United States and accrued (or paid, if required under subparagraph (1)(ii) of this paragraph) during such taxable year, and

(ii) In the case of a domestic corporation, the foreign income taxes deemed to be paid for such taxable year under section 902(a) in accordance with §§ 1.902-1 and 1.902-2 or section 960(a)(1) in accordance with 1.960-7.

In no event shall the amount under subdivision (ii) of this subparagraph exceed the amount includible in gross income with respect to such taxes under section 78 and § 1.78-1. The credit for such taxes provided by section 901 shall not be allowed against the personal holding company tax imposed by section 541. See section 901(a).

(b) Charitable contributions. *(1) Taxable years beginning before January 1, 1970* (i) Section 545(b)(2) provides that, in computing the deduction for charitable contributions for purposes of determining undistributed personal holding company income of a corporation for taxable years beginning before January 1, 1970, the limitations in section 170(b)(1)(A) and (B), relating to charitable contributions by individuals, shall apply and section 170(b)(2) and (5), relating to charitable contributions by corporations and carryover of certain excess charitable contributions made by individuals, respectively, shall not apply.

(ii) Although the limitations of section 170(b)(1)(A) and (B) are 10 and 20 percent, respectively, of the individual's adjusted gross income, the limitations are applied for purposes of section 545(b)(2) by using 10 and 20 percent, respectively, of the corporation's taxable income as adjusted for purposes of section 170(b)(2), that is, the same amount of taxable income to which the 5-percent limitation applied. Thus, the term "adjusted gross income" when used in section 170(b)(1) means the corporation's taxable income computed with the adjustments, other than the 5-percent limitation, provided in the first sentence of section 170(b)(2). However, a further adjustment for this purpose is that the taxable income shall also be computed without the deduction of the amount disallowed under section 545(b)(8), relating to expenses and depreciation applicable to property of the taxpayer. The carryover of charitable contributions made in a prior year, otherwise allowable as a deduction in computing taxable income to the extent provided in section 170(b)(2) and, with respect to contributions paid in taxable years beginning after December 31, 1963, in section 170(b)(5), shall not be allowed as a deduction in computing undistributed personal holding company income for any taxable year.

(iii) See § 1.170.2 with respect to the charitable contributions to which the 10-percent limitation is applicable and the charitable contributions to which the 20-percent limitation is applicable.

(2) Taxable years beginning after December 31, 1969. (i) Section 545(b)(2) provides that, in computing the deduction allowable for charitable contributions for purposes of determining undistributed personal holding company income of a corporation for taxable years beginning after December 31, 1969, the limitations in section 170(b)(1)(A), (B), and (D)(i) (relating to charitable contributions by individuals) shall apply, and section 170(b)(1)(D)(ii) (relating to excess charitable contributions by individuals of certain capital gain property, section 170(b)(2) (relating to the 5-percent limitation on charitable contributions by corporations), and section 170(d) (relating to carryovers of excess contributions of individuals and corporations) shall not apply.

(ii) Although the limitations of section 170(b)(1)(A), (B), and (D)(i) are 50, 20, and 30 percent, respectively, of an individual's contribution base, these limitations are applied for purposes of section 545(b)(2) by using 50, 20, and 30 percent respectively, of the corporation's taxable income as adjusted for purposes of section 170(b)(2), that is, the same amount of taxable income to which the 5-percent limitation applies. Thus, the term "contribution base" when used in section 170(b)(1) means the corporation's taxable income computed with the adjustments, other than the 5-percent limitation, provided in section 170(b)(2). However, a further adjustment for this purpose is that the taxable income shall also be computed without the deduction of the amount disallowed under section 545(b)(8), relating to expenses and depreciation applicable to property of the taxpayer. The carryover of charitable contributions made in a prior year, otherwise allowable as a deduction in computing taxable income to the extent provided in section 170(b)(1)(D)(ii) and (d), shall not be allowed as a deduction in computing undistributed personal holding company income for any taxable year.

(c) Special deductions disallowed. Part VIII, subchapter B, chapter 1 of the Code, allows corporations, in computing taxable income, special deductions for such matters as partially tax-exempt interest, certain dividends received, dividends paid on certain preferred stock of public utilities, organizational expenses, etc. See section 241. Such special deductions, except the deduction provided by section 248 (relating to organizational expenses) shall be disallowed in computing undistributed personal holding company income.

(d) Net operating loss. The net operating loss deduction provided in section 172 is not allowed for purposes of the computation of undistributed personal holding company income. For purposes of such a computation, however, there is allowed as a deduction the amount of the net operating loss (as defined in section 172(c)) for the preceding taxable year, except that, in computing undistributed personal holding company income for a taxable year beginning after December 31, 1957, the amount of such net operating loss shall be computed without the deductions provided in part VIII (section 241 and following, except section 248), subchapter B, chapter 1 of the Code.

(e) Long-term capital gains. *(1)* There is allowed as a deduction the excess of the net long-term capital gain for the taxable year over the net short-term capital loss for such year, minus the taxes attributable to such excess, as provided in section 545(b)(5).

(2) Section 631(c) (relating to gain or loss in the case of disposal of coal or domestic iron ore) shall have no application.

(f) Bank affiliates. There is allowed the deduction provided by section 601 in the case of bank affiliates (as defined in section 2 of the Banking Act of 1933; 12 U.S.C. 221a(c)).

(g) Payment of indebtedness incurred prior to January 1, 1934. *(1) General rule.* In computing undistributed personal holding company income, section 545(b)(7) provides that there shall be allowed as a deduction amounts used or irrevocably set aside to pay or to retire indebtedness of any kind incurred before January 1, 1934, if such amounts are reasonable with reference to the size and terms of such indebtedness. See § 1.545-3 for the deduction in computing undistributed personal holding company income of amounts used or irrevocably set aside to pay or retire qualified indebtedness (as defined in paragraph (d) of § 1.545-3).

(2) Indebtedness. The term "indebtedness" means an obligation absolute and not contingent, to pay on demand or within a given time, in cash or other medium, a fixed amount. The term "indebtedness" does not include the obligation of a corporation on its capital stock. The indebtedness must have been incurred (or, if incurred by assumption, assumed) by the taxpayer before January 1, 1934. An indebtedness evidenced by bonds, notes, or other obligations issued by a corporation is ordinarily incurred as of the date such obligations are issued and the amount of such indebtedness is the amount represented by the face value of the obligations. In the case of refunding, renewal, or other change in the form of an indebtedness, the giving of a new promise to pay by the taxpayer will not have the effect of changing the date the indebtedness was incurred.

(3) Amounts used or irrevocably set aside. The deduction is allowable, in any taxable year, only for amounts used or irrevocably set aside in that year. The use or irrevocable setting aside must be to effect the extinguishment or discharge of indebtedness. In the case of refunding, renewal, or other change in the form of an indebtedness, the mere giving of a new promise to pay by the taxpayer will not result in an allowable deduction. If amounts are set aside in one year, no deduction is allowable for such amounts for a later year in which actually paid. As long as all other conditions are satisfied, the aggregate amount allowable as a deduction for any taxable year includes all amounts (from whatever source) used and all amounts (from whatever source) irrevocably set aside, irrespective of whether in cash or other medium. Double deductions shall not be allowed.

(4) Reasonableness of the amounts with reference to the size and terms of the indebtedness. (i) The reasonableness of the amounts used or irrevocably set aside must be determined by reference to the size and terms of the particular indebtedness. Hence, all the facts and circumstances with respect to the nature, scope, conditions, amount, maturity, and other terms of the particular indebtedness must be shown in each case.

(ii) Ordinarily an amount used to pay or retire an indebtedness, in whole or in part, at or prior to the maturity and in accordance with the terms thereof will be considered reasonable, and may be allowable as a deduction for the year in which so used. However, if an amount has been set aside in a prior year for payment or retirement of the same indebtedness, the amount so set aside shall not be allowed as a deduction in the year of the payment.

(iii) All amounts irrevocably set aside for the payment or retirement of an indebtedness in accordance with and pursuant to the terms of the obligation, for example, the annual contribution to trustees required by the provisions of a mandatory sinking fund agreement, will be considered as complying with the requirement of reasonableness. To be considered reasonable, it is not necessary that the plan of retirement provide for a retroactive setting aside of amounts for years prior to that in which the plan is adopted. However, if a voluntary plan was adopted before 1934, no adjustment is allowable in respect of the amounts set aside in the years prior to 1934.

(5) Burden of proof. The burden of proof will rest upon the taxpayer to sustain the deduction claimed. Therefore, the taxpayer must furnish the information required by the return, and such other information as the district director may require in substantiation of the deduction claimed.

(6) Allowance to a successor corporation. For allowance of deduction for pre-1934 indebtedness to a successor corporation, see section 381(c)(15).

(h) Expenses and depreciation applicable to property of the taxpayer. *(1)* In computing undistributed personal holding company income in the case of a personal holding company which owns or operates property, section 545(b)(8) provides a specific limitation with respect to the allowance of deductions for trade or business expenses and depreciation allocable to the operation or maintenance of such property. Under this limitation, these deductions shall not be allowed in an amount in excess of the aggregate amount of the rent or other compensation received for the use of, or the right to use, the property, unless it is established to the satisfaction of the Commissioner—

(i) That the rent or other compensation received was the highest obtainable, or if none was received, that none was obtainable;

(ii) That the property was held in the course of a business carried on bona fide for profit; and

(iii) Either that there was reasonable expectation that the operation of the property would result in a profit, or that the property was necessary to the conduct of the business.

(2) The burden of proof will rest upon the taxpayer to sustain the deduction claimed. If, in computing undistributed personal holding company income, a personal holding company claims deductions for expenses and depreciation allocable to the operation and maintenance of property owned or operated by the company, in an aggregate amount in excess

of the rent or other compensation received for the use of, or the right to use, the property, it shall attach to its income tax return a statement setting forth its claim for allowance of the additional deductions, together with a complete statement of the facts and circumstances pertinent to its claim and the arguments on which it relies. Such statement shall set forth:

(i) A description of the property;

(ii) The cost or other basis to the corporation and the nature and value of the consideration paid for the property;

(iii) The name and address of the person from whom the property was acquired and the date the property was acquired;

(iv) The name and address of the person to whom the property is leased or rented, or the person permitted to use the property, and the number of shares of stock, if any, held by such person and the members of his family;

(v) The nature and gross amount of the rent or other compensation received for the use of, or the right to use, the property during the taxable year and for each of the five preceding years and the amount of the expenses incurred with respect to, and the depreciation sustained on, the property for such years;

(vi) Evidence that the rent or other compensation was the highest obtainable or, if none was received, a statement of the reasons therefor;

(vii) A copy of the contract, lease or rental agreement;

(viii) The purpose for which the property was used;

(ix) The business, carried on by the corporation, with respect to which the property was held and the gross income, expenses, and taxable income derived from the conduct of such business for the taxable year and for each of the five preceding years;

(x) A statement of any reasons which existed for expectation that the operation of the property would be profitable, or a statement of the necessity for the use of the property in the business of the corporation, and the reasons why the property was acquired; and

(xi) Any other information pertinent to the taxpayer's claim.

(i) Amount of a lien in favor of the United States. *(1)* If notices of lien are filed in the manner provided in section 6323(f), the amount of the liability to the United States outstanding at the close of the taxable year, and secured by such liens which are in effect at that time, shall be allowed as a deduction in computing undistributed personal holding company income. However, the amount of such deduction which may be allowed for any taxable year shall not exceed the taxable income (as adjusted for purposes of determining the undistributed personal holding company income, but without regard to the deduction under section 545(b)(9)) for such year. The fact that the amount of, or any part of, the outstanding obligation to the United States was deducted for one taxable year does not prevent its deduction for a subsequent taxable year to the extent the obligation is still outstanding at the close of the subsequent taxable year and is secured by a lien, notice of which has been filed.

(2) Subparagraph (1) of this paragraph may be illustrated by the following example:

Example. If the taxpayer (on the calendar year basis) is subject to a lien (notice of which has been properly filed) in the amount of $500,000 at the close of the calendar year 1954 and has taxable income of $400,000 for such taxable year, the deduction allowable by reason of the lien for the calendar year 1954 is $400,000. If, at the close of the taxable year ended December 31, 1955, the taxpayer is still subject to the same lien of $500,000 and it has taxable income of $450,000, a deduction is allowed by reason of such lien in the amount of $450,000.

(3) When the obligation secured by the lien in favor of the United States has been satisfied or released, the sum of the amounts which have been allowed as deductions under section 545(b)(9) in respect of such obligation shall be restored to taxable income for the year in which such lien is satisfied or released. If only a part of the obligation secured by the lien has been satisfied, the sum of the amounts which have been allowed as deductions under section 545(b)(9) in respect of such part shall be included in taxable income for the year of the satisfaction for the purpose of determining undistributed personal holding company income, It should be noted, however, that only the sum of the amounts which have been allowed as deductions under section 545(b)(9) and subparagraph (1) of this paragraph shall be included in taxable income. Thus, any amounts which were allowed as deductions under section 504(e) of the Internal Revenue Code of 1939 shall not be included as taxable income for any taxable year under section 545(b)(9) and subparagraph (1) of this paragraph.

(4) The application of subparagraph (3) of this paragraph may be illustrated by the following example:

Example. Assume the same facts as in the example in subparagraph (2) of this paragraph and assume further that the corporation has $100,000 taxable income both for 1956 (before including the $400,000 described below) and for 1957. In 1956, the corporation pays $200,000 of the obligation, thereby reducing its liability from $500,000 to $300,000. In such case, $400,000 is included in taxable income in computing its undistributed personal holding company income for 1956, that is, the sum of the $200,000 deduction for 1954 and the $200,000 deduction for 1955 in respect of the liability which is paid in 1956. In 1957, property of the corporation is discharged from the lien by reason of the fact that the value of the remaining property of the corporation exceeds double the outstanding liability. (See section 6325(b)(1).) Since this was not a release or satisfaction of the lien, no amount is added to taxable income for 1957 with respect to the property discharged from the lien. In 1958, the remaining property is released from the lien by reason of a bond being accepted under section 6325(a)(2). There is added to taxable income in computing undistributed personal holding company income for 1958, $850,000, that is, the sum of the deductions allowed for 1954, 1955, 1956, and 1957 in respect of the $300,000 liability, the lien for which was released in 1958. This amount of $850,000, is computed as follows:

Year	Outstanding liability	Taxable income	Deduction as limited by taxable income	Amount attributable to part payment of $200,000 in 1956	Amount attributable to release of lien in 1958
1954	$500,000	$400,000	$400,000	$200,000	$200,000
1955	500,000	450,000	450,000	200,000	250,000
1956	300,000	500,000	300,000		300,000
1957	300,000	100,000	100,000		100,000
Total					850,000

(5) (i) If an amount has been included in undistributed personal holding company income of the personal holding company by reason of section 545(b)(9), any shareholder of the company may elect to compute his income tax with respect to such of his dividends as are attributable to such amount as though such dividends were received ratably over the period the lien was in effect.

(ii) For purposes of section 545(b)(9), the dividends paid during the taxable year of the personal holding company (computed as of the close of such year) shall be deemed attributable first to undistributed personal holding company income by reason of section 545(b)(9) (computed as of the close of the taxable year of the personal holding company). If the period over which the lien was in effect consists of several taxable years of the personal holding company, the dividend deemed received for any taxable year shall be deemed received on the last day of such taxable year of the personal holding company.

(iii) Such election shall be made in a statement showing the amount of the deduction under section 545(b)(9) for each taxable year of the period in which the lien was in effect, the amount of such deduction, if any, which was added to undistributed personal holding company income in a later year or years as a result of partial satisfaction or release of such lien, and the details thereof, the taxable year or years to which such dividends are allocable, and a computation of tax, on the basis of the election, for all taxable years affected by such ratable allocation of the dividends. Further, the statement shall show the district director's office in which the returns, for the years to which the dividends are allocable, were filed, the kind of returns which were filed (separate returns or joint returns), and the name and address under which the returns were filed. The statement shall be attached to the shareholder's return for the taxable year for which the dividend would be reported but for such election.

(iv) The operation of this subparagraph may be illustrated as follows: If, in the example under subparagraph (4) of this paragraph, shareholder A owns 75 percent in value of the outstanding stock of the personal holding company, and receives a dividend of $540,000 from such company during 1958 (the total dividend distribution being $720,000) he may elect to compute his income tax with respect to the $540,000 in dividends for 1958 as if he had received $127,058,82 of such dividends for 1954 ($200,000/850,000 of $540,000), $158,823.53 of such dividends for 1955 ($250,000/850,000 of $540,000), $190,588.23 of such dividends for 1956 ($300,000/850,000 of $540,000), and $63,529.41 of such dividends for 1957 ($100,000/850,000 of $540,000). Accordingly, the tax computed for 1958 with respect to such dividends shall be the aggregate of the taxes attributable to such amounts had they been distributed in the respective years.

T.D. 6308, 9/9/58, amend T.D. 6376, 5/6/59, T.D. 6805, 3/8/65, T.D. 6841, 7/26/65, T.D. 6900, 11/16/66, T.D. 6949, 4/8/68, T.D. 7207, 10/3/72, T.D. 7429, 8/20/76, T.D. 7649, 10/17/79.

§ 1.545-3 Special adjustment to taxable income.

Caution: The Treasury has not yet amended Reg § 1.545-3 to reflect changes made by P.L. 101-508.

(a) In general. In computing undistributed personal holding company income for any taxable year beginning after December 31, 1963, section 545(c)(1) provides that, except as otherwise provided in section 545(c), there shall be allowed as a deduction amounts used or amounts irrevocably set aside (to the extent reasonable with reference to the size and terms of the indebtedness) during such year to pay or retire qualified indebtedness (as defined in section 545(c)(3) and paragraph (d) of this section). The reasonableness of amounts irrevocably set aside shall be determined under the rules of paragraph (g)(4) of § 1.545-2.

(b) Amounts used or irrevocably set aside. *(1) In general.* The deduction is allowable, in any taxable year, only for amounts used or irrevocably set aside in that year to extinguish or discharge qualified indebtedness. If amounts are set aside in 1 year, no deduction is allowable for a later year in which such amounts are actually paid. As long as all other conditions are satisfied, the aggregate amount allowable as a deduction for any taxable year includes all amounts (from whatever source) used and all amounts (from whatever source) irrevocably set aside, irrespective of whether in cash or other medium. The same item shall not be deducted more than once.

(2) Refunding, etc., of qualified indebtedness. (i) A refunding, renewal, or mere change in the form of a qualified indebtedness which does not involve a substantial change in the economic terms of the indebtedness will not result in an allowable deduction whether or not funds are obtained from such refunding, renewal, or change in form, and whether or not such funds are applied on the prior obligation, and will not constitute a reduction in the amount of such qualified indebtedness. For purposes of this section, if, in connection with a refunding, renewal, or other change in the form of an indebtedness, the rate of interest or principal amount of such debt, or the date when payment is due with respect to such debt or significantly changed, or if, after the refunding, renewal, or other change in the form of such debt, the creditor to whom such debt was owed before such refunding, renewal, or other change, nor a person standing in a relationship to such creditor described in section 267(b), then a substantial change in the economic terms of such indebtedness will normally have occurred.

(ii) The application of this subparagraph may be illustrated by the following examples:

Example (1). On December 31, 1963, M owes $10,000 to X represented by a 6-percent, 90-day note payable on January 31, 1964. On January 31, 1964, M renews the debt, giving X a new 6-percent, 90-day note (payable on April 30, 1964) and paying the accrued interest on the old note. Since the date when payment is due has been significantly changed, a substantial change in the economic terms of the indebtedness has occurred.

Example (2). On December 31, 1963, S owes $5,000 to T represented by a 6-percent note payable on January 1, 1965. On December 23, 1964, S liquidates the note, giving T a new note for $5,000 due on January 2, 1965, and bearing interest at 6 percent. Since the transaction does not involve a substantial change in the economic terms of the indebtedness, the transaction will not result in an allowable deduction, and the amount of the qualified indebtedness will not be reduced.

Example (3). (i) On December 31, 1963, Q owes $45,000 to R represented by a demand note. On July 1, 1964, Q renews $30,000 of the indebtedness by issuing a new demand not to R and liquidates $15,000 of the debt. Since the principal amount of the debt has been significantly changed, there has been a substantial change in the economic terms of the indebtedness.

(ii) If Q had issued renewal notes for $44,000 and had paid only $1,000 of the total indebtedness, then a significant change in the principal amount of the debt would not have occurred and Q would have been entitled to only a $1,000 deduction (the amount actually paid during the taxable year). In addition, the amount of qualified indebtedness would have been reduced to $44,000.

(c) Corporations to which applicable. Section 545(c)(2) describes the corporations to which section 545(c) applies. In order to qualify under Section 545(c)(2), the corporation must be one:

(1) Which for at least one of its two most recent taxable years ending before February 26, 1964, was not a personal holding company under section 542, but which would have been a personal holding company under section 542 for such taxable year if the law applicable for the first taxable year beginning after December 31, 1963, had been applicable to such taxable year; or

(2) Which is an acquiring corporation treated as a corporation described in subparagraph (1) of this paragraph by reason of section 381(c)(15) (relating to the carryover of certain indebtedness in corporate acquisitions), but only to the extent of the qualified indebtedness to which it has succeeded under section 381(c)(15) and the indebtedness referred to in paragraph (d)(1)(ii) of this section incurred to replace qualified indebtedness to which it has succeeded under section 381(c)(15). The law applicable for the first taxable year beginning after December 31, 1963, for purposes of this paragraph means part II (section 541 and following), subchapter G, chapter 1 of the Code as applicable to such year but does not include amendments to other parts of the Code first applicable with respect to such year. For an example of a corporation described in subparagraph (1) of this paragraph see paragraph (f)(1) of § 1.333-5.

(d) Qualified indebtedness. *(1) General definition.* Except as provided in subparagraphs (2), (3), and (4) of this paragraph the term "qualified indebtedness" means:

(i) The outstanding indebtedness (as defined in subparagraph (6) of this paragraph) incurred after December 31, 1933, and before January 1, 1964, by the taxpayer (or to which the taxpayer succeeded in a transaction to which section 381(c)(15) applies), and

(ii) The outstanding indebtedness (as defined in subparagraph (6) of this paragraph) incurred after December 31, 1963, by the taxpayer (or to which the taxpayer succeeded in a transaction to which section 381(c)15) applies) for the purpose of making a payment or set-aside referred to in paragraph (a) of this section in the same taxable year of the debtor in which such indebtedness was incurred. An indebtedness shall be deemed not to have been incurred for the purpose of making a payment or set-aside referred to in paragraph (a) of this section when such indebtedness is a consequence of a refunding, renewal, or mere change in the form of a qualified indebtedness which does not involve a substantial change in the economic terms of the qualified indebtedness. (See paragraph (b)(2) of this section for the meaning of "substantial change in the economic terms of the indebtedness.") In the case of such a payment or set-aside which is made on or after the first day of the first taxable year beginning after December 31, 1963, such indebtedness incurred after December 31, 1963, is treated as qualified indebtedness only to the extent that the deduction from taxable income otherwise allowed by section 545(c)(1) with respect to such payment or set-aside is treated as nondeductible by reason of the election referred to in paragraph (e) of this section.

(2) Exception for indebtedness owed to certain shareholders. For purposes of subparagraph (1) of this paragraph, qualified indebtedness does not include any amounts which were, at any time after December 31, 1963, and before the payment or set-aside to which this section applies, owed directly or indirectly to a person who at such time owned more than 10 percent in value of the taxpayer's outstanding stock. The rules of section 318(a) and the regulations thereunder apply for the purpose of determining ownership under this subparagraph. Amounts which cease to be qualified indebtedness by reason of this subparagraph may not subsequently become qualified indebtedness as a result of any change in the facts (for example, a subsequent sale of stock by the person to whom the amounts are directly or indirectly owed).

(3) Reduction for amounts irrevocably set aside. For purposes of subparagraph (1) of this paragraph, qualified indebtedness with respect to a particular contract is reduced when and to the extent that amounts are irrevocably set aside to pay or retire such indebtedness. An amount is not considered to be irrevocably set aside if any person could use such amount for any purpose other than the retirement of the qualified indebtedness with respect to which it was set aside. No deduction is allowed under section 545(c)(1) and this section for payments out of amounts previously set aside. Thus, for example if a corporation, which is a June 30 fiscal year taxpayer, incurs indebtedness of $1 million on February 1, 1962, and, in accordance with its contract of indebtedness, irrevocably sets aside $50,000 in a sinking fund on February 1, of each of the years 1963, 1964, and 1965, then its qualified indebtedness on January 1, 1964, is $950,000 ($1 million less one set-aside of $50,000 in 1963). The corporation is not allowed a deduction under section 545(c)(1) for the set-aside of $50,000 made during its taxable year ending on June 30, 1964, since section 545(c) is applicable only to taxable years beginning after December 31, 1963, but the qualified indebtedness is nevertheless reduced by such amount. The corporation is allowed a deduction of $50,000 for its taxable year ending June 30, 1965, as a result of the set-

aside made during such taxable year, and qualified indebtedness on July 1, 1965, is $850,000. No deduction is allowed to the corporation for a payment in any subsequent taxable year from the amounts so set aside.

(4) Reduction on disposition of certain property. (i) Section 545(c)(6) provides that the total amount of the taxpayer's qualified indebtedness (as determined under subdivision (ii) of this subparagraph) shall be reduced if property of a character subject to the allowance for exhaustion, wear and tear, obsolescence, amortization, or depletion is disposed of after December 31, 1963. The reduction is made pro rata (in accordance with subdivision (iii) of this subparagraph) for the taxable year of such disposition and is equal in total amount to the excess, if any, of:

(a) The adjusted basis of the property disposed of (determined under section 1011 and the regulations thereunder) immediately before such disposition; over

(b) The amount of qualified indebtedness which ceased to be qualified indebtedness with respect to the taxpayer by reason of the assumption of indebtedness by the transferee of the property disposed of (whether or not such indebtedness was incurred by the taxpayer in connection with the property disposed of:

For purposes of (b) of this subdivision, the transferee will be treated as having assumed qualified indebtedness if such transferee acquires real estate of which the taxpayer is the legal or equitable owner immediately before the transfer and which is subject to indebtedness that, with respect to the taxpayer, is qualified indebtedness immediately before the transfer, provided the taxpayer shows to the satisfaction of the Commissioner that under all the facts and circumstances it no longer bears the burden of discharging such indebtedness.

(ii) The indebtedness reduced under the rule of this subparagraph is the qualified indebtedness which is outstanding with respect to the taxpayer immediately after the disposition referred to in subdivision (i) of this subparagraph.

(iii) The reduction with respect to any particular contract of indebtedness under the rules of this subparagraph shall be determined by multiplying the total reduction (determined under subdivision (i) of this subparagraph) by the ratio which the amount of the qualified indebtedness owed with respect to such contract by the taxpayer on the date referred to in subdivision (ii) of this subparagraph bears to the aggregate qualified indebtedness owed by the taxpayer with respect to all contracts on such date.

(5) Total debt consisting of both qualified and nonqualified indebtedness. In any case where, with respect to a particular contract of indebtedness, a part of the total indebtedness owed with respect to such contract is qualified indebtedness and the other part is indebtedness which is not qualified indebtedness, then, any amount paid or irrevocably set aside with respect to such contract shall be allocated between both such parts pro rata unless the taxpayer clearly indicates in its return the part of the payment or set-aside which shall be allocated to the qualified indebtedness.

(6) Outstanding indebtedness. For purposes of determining qualified indebtedness, the term "indebtedness" has the same meaning that it has under section 545(b)(7) and paragraph (g)(2) of § 1.545-2. Indebtedness ceases to be outstanding when the taxpayer no longer has an obligation absolute and not contingent with respect to the payment of such debt. An indebtedness evidenced by bonds, notes, or other obligations issued by a corporation is ordinarily incurred as of the date such obligations are issued, and the amount of such indebtedness is the amount represented by the face value of the obligations. However, a refunding, renewal, or mere change in the form of an indebtedness which does not involve a substantial change in the economic terms of the indebtedness will not have the effect of changing the date the indebtedness was incurred. (See paragraph (b)(2) of this section for the meaning of "substantial change in the economic terms of the indebtedness.") For purposes of this section, the outstanding indebtedness of a taxpayer includes a mortgage or other security interest on real estate of which such taxpayer is the legal or equitable owner (even though the taxpayer is not directly liable on the underlying evidence of indebtedness secured by such mortgage or security interest) provided such taxpayer shows to the satisfaction of the Commissioner that under all of the facts and circumstances it bears the burden of discharging such indebtedness. Thus, for example, if X acquires from Y property which is subject to a mortgage (X not assuming the indebtedness underlying such mortgage) and if X actually bears the burden of discharging the indebtedness, then, after the date of acquisition, such underlying indebtedness is outstanding indebtedness with respect to X, and since Y's obligation to pay is in fact contingent upon X failing to discharge the indebtedness, such indebtedness is not outstanding indebtedness with respect to Y.

(7) Examples. The application of this paragraph may be illustrated by the following examples:

Example (1). M Corporation, a calendar year taxpayer has $600,000 of indebtedness outstanding on December 31, 1963 (which was incurred after 1933), represented by three demand notes. Individuals A and B (who are not shareholders) each hold one of M Corporation's notes in the amount of $150,000 and N Corporation (which is not a shareholder) holds M Corporation's note in the amount of $300,000. The note held by N Corporation is secured by a mortgage on certain depreciable real estate owned by M Corporation which has an adjusted basis to it on July 1, 1964, of $500,000. On July 1, 1964, M Corporation sells the depreciable real estate to O Corporation in consideration for $200,000 in cash and the assumption by O Corporation of the indebtedness on the note held by N Corporation. M Corporation borrows $200,000 on September 30, 1964, of which amount $150,000 is simultaneously applied to liquidate the note held by B. M Corporation's qualified indebtedness is reduced on July 1, 1964, by $300,000, the qualified indebtedness which ceased to be outstanding by reason of the transfer. In addition, the reduction (computed under section 545(c)(6) and subparagraph (4) of this paragraph) of M Corporation's qualified indebtedness by reason of the disposition of depreciable property on July 1, 1964, is as follows:

Outstanding qualified indebtedness after reduction of qualified indebtedness which ceased to be outstanding by reason of the transfer but before the sec. 545(c)(6) reduction	$300,000
Reduced by—	
The excess of the adjusted basis of depreciable real estate disposed of on July 1, 1964 ($500,000), over the amount of qualified indebtedness assumed by O Corporation ($300,000)	200,000
Qualified indebtedness after reductions from transfer and assumption of indebtedness	100,000

The pro-rata share of the reduction with respect to each debt is computed as follows:

Note held by A:

Qualified indebtedness owed by taxpayer on the note held by A before the disposition of depreciable property	$150,000
Less the pro-rata share of the total reduction computed under subparagraph (4) of this paragraph allocable to such	
$\$200,000 \times \frac{\$150,000}{\$300,000}$	100,000
Qualified indebtedness owed on the note held by A after the transfer	50,000

Note held by B:

Qualified indebtedness owed by taxpayer on the note held by B before the transfer of depreciable property	150,000
Less the pro-rata share of the total reduction computed under subparagraph (4) of this paragraph allocable to such	
$\$200,000 \times \frac{\$150,000}{\$300,000}$	100,000
Qualified indebtedness owed on the note held by B after the transfer	50,000

Of the $150,000 paid by M Corporation on September 30, 1964, to retire the note held by B only $50,000 qualified as a use of an amount to pay or retire qualified indebtedness and, thus, only $50,000 is allowable as a deduction for purposes of computing undistributed personal holding company income for 1964.

Example (2). The facts are the same as in example (1) except that M Corporation elects in accordance with paragraph (e) of this section not to deduct $25,000 of the $50,000 amount otherwise deductible. Then $25,000 of the $200,000 of new indebtedness incurred by M Corporation is qualified indebtedness. If the payment on the note held by B had not been made until January 1, 1965, then the new indebtedness would not be qualified indebtedness since the payment was not made in the taxable year in which the new indebtedness was incurred. If M Corporation pays $40,000 on April 1 and July 1, 1965, on the indebtedness incurred September 30, 1964, then (unless M indicates otherwise in its return for 1965 in accordance with subparagraph (5) of this paragraph) the payments made on such dates must be allocated between qualified and nonqualified indebtedness in the following manner:

	Qualified	Non-Qualified
April 1 payment		
$\$40,000 \times \frac{\$25,000 \text{ (qualified)}}{\$200,000 \text{ (total indebtedness)}} =$	$5,000	
$\$40,000 \times \frac{\$175,000 \text{ (nonqualified)}}{\$200,000 \text{ (total indebtedness)}} =$		$35,000
July 1 payment		
$\$40,000 \times \frac{\$20,000 \text{ (qualified)}}{\$160,000 \text{ (total indebtedness)}} =$	5,000	
$\$40,000 \times \frac{\$140,000 \text{ (nonqualified)}}{\$160,000 \text{ (total indebtedness)}} =$		35,000
Total	10,000	70,000

Thus, a total of $10,000 of the two payments would be considered used to pay or retire qualified indebtedness. The results in examples (1) and (2) would be the same if O Corporation purchased the real estate subject to the indebtedness (not assuming the indebtedness) on the note held by N Corporation, provided M Corporation does not bear the burden of discharging such indebtedness after July 1, 1964.

Example (3). C owns all of the 1,000 shares of outstanding capital stock of P Corporation. On December 31, 1963, P Corporation, a calendar year taxpayer, owes $200,000 of outstanding indebtedness to D and $500,000 of outstanding indebtedness to E. These debts were incurred after 1933. On January 15, 1964, P Corporation pays $100,000 in partial liquidation of the $500,000 indebtedness. On March 15, 1964, P Corporation pays $50,000 into a sinking fund with respect to the $200,000 indebtedness owed to D. On April 15, 1964, D purchases one-half of the shares owned by C, constituting 50 percent in value of P Corporation's outstanding stock. P Corporation, on June 15, 1964, pays $50,000 into a sinking fund with respect to the indebtedness owed to D. For purposes of the March 15, 1964, set-aside, the indebtedness owned to D ($200,000) is qualified indebtedness. However, the indebtedness owed to D is not qualified indebtedness for purposes of the June set-aside with respect to such indebtedness since D is a person who after December 31, 1963, and before the June set-aside, owned more than 10 percent in value of P Corporation's outstanding stock. Moreover, any subsequent set-asides made with respect to the indebtedness owed to D will not be made with respect to qualified indebtedness even if the shares owned by D are subsequently sold. Assuming no payments or set-asides are made by P Corporation after June 15, 1964, the P Corporation is entitled to a deduction of $150,000 under section 545(c)(1) for the calendar year 1964 for amounts paid and for amounts irrevocably set aside to pay or retire qualified indebtedness, and the total qualified indebtedness at the end of 1964 is $400,000. No additional deduction is allowed in subsequent taxable years for amounts paid out of the amounts set aside in 1964.

(e) Election not to deduct. *(1) In general.* Section 545(c)(4) provides that a taxpayer may elect to treat as nondeductible amounts otherwise deductible under section 545(c)(1) for the taxable year. The election shall be in the form of a statement of election filed on or before the 15th day of the third month following the close of the taxable year with respect to which the election applies. The election shall be irrevocable after such date.

(2) Statement of election. The statement of election referred to in subparagraph (1) of this paragraph shall be attached to the taxpayer's Schedule PH (Form 1120) for the year with respect to which such election applies, if such schedule is filed on or before the date referred to in subparagraph (1) of this paragraph. If the taxpayer's Schedule PH (Form 1120) is not filed on or before such date, then the statement of election shall clearly set forth the taxpayer's name, address, and employer identification number, shall be signed by an officer of the taxpayer who is authorized to sign a return of the taxpayer with respect to income, and shall be filed with the district director for the internal revenue district in which the taxpayer's income tax return (for the year with respect to which the election is applicable)

would be filed. The following information shall be included in the statement of election:

(i) A statement that the taxpayer wishes to elect in accordance with section 545(c)(4);

(ii) The amounts paid or set aside which are to be treated as nondeductible under section 545(c)(4) and this section;

(iii) All information necessary to identify the qualified indebtedness with respect to which such amounts were paid or set aside;

(iv) The date on which such payments or set-asides were made; and

(v) All information necessary to identify the indebtedness (referred to in section 545(c)(3)(A)(ii) and paragraph (d)(1)(ii) of this section) incurred for the purpose of making the payments or set-asides which the taxpayer elects to treat as nondeductible, including:

(a) The date on which such indebtedness was incurred;

(b) The amount of such indebtedness;

(c) The person or persons to whom such indebtedness is owed; and

(d) A statement that such person or persons do not own more than 10 percent in value of the taxpayer's outstanding stock.

(f) Limitation on deduction. *(1) In general.* Section 545(c)(5) provides certain limitation on the deduction otherwise allowed by section 545(c)(1). Such deduction is reduced by the sum of the following amounts:

(i) The amount, if any, by which—

(a) The deductions allowed for the taxable year and all preceding taxable years beginning after December 31, 1963, for exhaustion, wear and tear, obsolescence, amortization, or depletion (other than such deductions which are disallowed in computing undistributed personal holding company income under the rule of paragraph (h) of § 1.545-2), exceed

(b) Any reduction, by reason of section 545(c)(5)(A) and this subdivision (i), of the deductions otherwise allowed by section 545(c)(1) for such preceding years; and

(ii) The amount, if any, by which—

(a) The deductions allowed under section 545(b)(5) (relating to long-term capital gain deduction) in computing undistributed personal holding company income for the taxable year and all preceding taxable years beginning after December 31, 1963, exceed

(b) Any reduction, by reason of section 545(c)(5)(B) and this subdivision (ii), of the deductions otherwise allowed by section 545(c)(1) for such preceding years.

(2) Allocation of reduction. If the total reduction required by subparagraph (1) of this paragraph is greater than the amount of the payment or set-aside made in respect of qualified indebtedness in a taxable year, then the portion of the reduction which is attributable to either section 545(c)(5)(A) or section 545(c)(5)(B), as the case may be, is that portion which bears the same ratio to the total reduction as the total reduction available under either section 545(c)(5)(A) or section 545(c)(5)(B), respectively, bears to the total reduction available under both such sections.

(3) Example. The provisions of this paragraph may be illustrated by the following example:

Example. (i) Q Corporation, a calendar year taxpayer, has qualified indebtedness of $400,000 on January 1, 1964, with respect to which payments of $50,000 are made on April 15, 1964, and 1965, and $300,000 on April 15, 1966. In the years 1964 and 1966, Q Corporation is allowed a deduction under section 545(b)(5) of $50,000 for the excess of its net long-term capital gain over its net short-term capital loss, minus the taxes attributable to such excess. Q Corporation is allowed a depreciation deduction of $50,000 for each of its taxable years 1964 through 1966. Q Corporation is a personal holding company with taxable income of $200,000 in each of the years 1964 and 1966.

(ii) For 1964, in computing undistributed personal holding company income, Q Corporation's taxable income is reduced by $50,000 by reason of the deduction under section 545(b)(5). No part of the depreciation deduction is disallowed under the rule of paragraph (h) of § 1.545-2. Q Corporation's deduction for payment of qualified indebtedness otherwise allowable under section 545(c)(1) and this section is reduced to zero by reason of the depreciation deduction and the capital gains deduction. The reduction by reason of section 545(c)(5)(A) and subparagraph (1)(i) of this paragraph (depreciation) is

$$\$25{,}000\ \left(\frac{\$50{,}000}{\$100{,}000}\times \$50{,}000\right),$$

and the reduction by reason of section 545(c)(5)(B) and subparagraph (1)(ii) of this paragraph (capital gain) is

$$\$25{,}000\ \left(\frac{\$50{,}000}{\$100{,}000}\times \$50{,}000\right).$$

(iii) For 1966, Q Corporation is allowed a deduction for payment of qualified indebtedness of $100,000 computed as follows:

Amount paid in 1966 to retire qualified indebtedness			$300,000
Less the sum of:			
(a) Depreciation deductions allowed for 1964 through 1966 (3 × $50,000)	$150,000		
Reduction of deductions in proceeding taxable years (1964)	25,000		
		$125,000	
(b) Deduction allowed under section 545(b)(5) (relating to long-term capital gains) for 1964 through 1966	100,000		
Reduction of deductions in preceding taxable years (1964)	25,000		
		75,000	
			200,000
Deduction after reduction			100,000

(iv) If, in the year 1966, Q Corporation's depreciation deduction had been limited for purposes of computing undistributed personal holding company income to $25,000 by reason of section 545(b)(8), then Q Corporation's deduction for payment of qualified indebtedness would be $125,000, computed as follows:

Amounts paid in 1966 to retire qualified indebtedness			$300,000
Less the sum of:			
(a) Depreciation deductions allowed for 1964 through 1966	$125,000		
Reduction of deductions in preceding taxable year (1964)	25,000		
		$100,000	
(b) Deduction allowed under section 545(b)(5) (relating to long-term capital gains) for 1964 through 1966	100,000		
Reduction of deductions in preceding taxable years (1964)	25,000		
		75,000	
			175,000
Deduction after reduction			125,000

(g) Burden of proof. The burden of proof rests upon the taxpayer to sustain the deduction claimed under this section. In addition to any information required by this section, the taxpayer must furnish the information required by the return, and such other information as the district director may require in substantiation of the deduction claimed.

(h) Application of section 381(c)(15). Under section 381(c)(15), if an acquiring corporation assumes liability for qualified indebtedness in a transaction to which section 381(a) applies, then the acquiring corporation is considered to be the distributor or transferor corporation for purposes of section 545(c). Paragraph (c)(2) of this section reflects the application of section 381(c)(15) by including an acquiring corporation within the definition of corporation to which this section applies. Thus, the acquiring corporation is not required to meet the requirements of paragraph (c)(1) or paragraph (d)(1) of this section with respect to such acquired qualified indebtedness to which section 381(c)(15) is applicable. All the other provisions of this section apply in full to the acquiring corporation with respect to such acquired indebtedness.

T.D. 6949, 4/8/68.

§ 1.547-1 General rule.

Section 547 provides a method under which, by virtue of dividend distributions, a corporation may be relieved from the payment of a deficiency in the personal holding company tax imposed by section 541 (or by a corresponding provision of a prior income tax law), or may be entitled to a credit or refund of a part or all of any such deficiency which has been paid. The method provided by section 547 is to allow an additional deduction for a dividend distribution (which meets the requirements of this section) in computing undistributed personal holding company income for the taxable year for which a deficiency in personal holding company tax is determined. The additional deduction for deficiency dividends will not, however, be allowed for the purpose of determining interest, additional amounts, or assessable penalties, computed with respect to the personal holding company tax prior to the allowance of the additional deduction for deficiency dividends. Such amounts remain payable as if section 547 had not been enacted.

T.D. 6308, 9/9/58.

§ 1.547-2 Requirements for deficiency dividends.

(a) In general. There are certain requirements which must be fulfilled before a deduction is allowed for a deficiency dividend under section 547 and this section. These are—

(1) The taxpayer's liability for personal holding company tax shall be determined only in the manner provided in section 547(c) and paragraph (b)(1) of this section.

(2) The deficiency dividend shall be paid by the corporation on, or within 90 days after, the date of such determination and prior to the filing of a claim under section 547(e) and paragraph (b)(2) of this section for deduction for deficiency dividends. This claim must be filed within 120 days after such determination.

(3) The deficiency dividend must be of such a nature as would have permitted its inclusion in the computation of a deduction for dividends paid under section 561 for the taxable year with respect to which the liability for personal holding company tax exists, if it had been distributed during such year. See section 562 and §§ 1.562-1 through 1.562-3. In this connection, it should be noted that under section 316(b)(2), the term "dividend" means (in addition to the usual meaning under section 316(a)) any distribution of property (whether or not a dividend as defined in section 316(a)) made by a corporation to its shareholders, to the extent of its undistributed personal holding company income (determined under section 545 and §§ 1.545-1 and 1.545-2 without regard to section 316(b)(2)) for the taxable year in respect of which the distribution is made.

(b) Special rules. *(1) Nature and details of determination.* (i) A determination of a taxpayer's liability for personal holding company tax shall, for the purposes of section 547, be established in the manner specified in section 547(c) and this subparagraph.

(ii) The date of determination by a decision of the Tax Court of the United States is the date upon which such decision becomes final, as prescribed in section 7481.

(iii) The date upon which a judgment of a court becomes final, which is the date of the determination in such cases, must be determined upon the basis of the facts in the particular case. Ordinarily, a judgment of a United States district court becomes final upon the expiration of the time allowed for taking an appeal, if no such appeal is duly taken within such time; and a judgment of the United States Court of Claims becomes final upon the expiration of the time allowed for filing a petition for certiorari if no such petition is duly filed within such time.

(iv) The date of determination by a closing agreement, made under section 7121, is the date such agreement is approved by the Commissioner.

(v) A determination under section 547(c)(3) may be made by an agreement signed by the district director or such other official to whom authority to sign the agreement is delegated, and by or on behalf of the taxpayer. The agreement shall set forth the total amount of the liability for personal holding company tax for the taxable year or years. An agreement under this subdivision which is signed by the district director (or such other official to whom authority to sign the agreement is delegated) on or after July 15, 1963, shall be sent to the taxpayer at his last known address by either registered or certified mail. For further guidance regarding the definition of last known address, see § 301.6212-2 of this chapter. If registered mail is used for such purpose, the date of registration shall be treated as the date of determination; if certified mail is used for such purpose, the date of the postmark on the sender's receipt for such mail shall be treated as the date of determination. However, if a dividend is paid by the corporation before such registration or postmark date but on or after the date such agreement is signed by the district director or such other official to whom authority to sign the agreement is delegated, the date of determination shall be such date of signing.

(2) Claim for deduction. (i) Contents of claim. A claim for deduction for a deficiency dividend shall be made, with the requisite declaration, on Form 976 and shall contain the following information:

(a) The name and address of the corporation;

(b) The place and date of incorporation;

(c) The amount of the deficiency determined with respect to the tax imposed by section 541 (or a corresponding provision of a prior income tax law) and the taxable year or years involved; the amount of the unpaid deficiency or, if the deficiency has been paid in whole or in part, the date of payment and the amount thereof; a statement as to how the deficiency was established, if unpaid; or if paid in whole or in part, how it was established that any portion of the amount paid was a deficiency at the time when paid and, in either case whether it was by an agreement under section 547(c)(3), by a closing agreement under section 7121, or by a decision of the Tax Court or court judgment and the date thereof; if established by a final judgment in a suit against the United States for refund, the date of payment of the deficiency, the date the claim for refund was filed, and the date the suit was brought; if established by a Tax Court decision or court judgment, a copy thereof shall be attached, together with an explanation of how the decision became final; if established by an agreement under section 547(c)(3), a copy of such agreement shall be attached;

(d) The amount and date of payment of the dividend with respect to which the claim for the deduction for deficiency dividends is filed;

(e) A statement setting forth the various classes of stock outstanding, the name and address of each shareholder, the class and number of shares held by each on the date of payment of the dividend with respect to which the claim is filed, and the amount of such dividend paid to each shareholder;

(f) The amount claimed as a deduction for deficiency dividends; and

(g) Such other information as may be required by the claim form.

(ii) Filing of claim and corporate resolution. The claim together with a certified copy of the resolution of the board of directors or other authority, authorizing the payment of the dividend with respect to which the claim is filed, shall be filed with the district director for the internal revenue district in which the return is filed.

(iii) Carryover of deficiency dividends paid by acquiring corporation. In the case of the acquisition of assets of a corporation by another corporation in a distribution or transfer described in section 381(a), the distributor or transferor corporation shall be entitled to a deduction for any deficiency dividends (as defined in section 547(d)) paid by the acquiring corporation with respect to such distributor or transferor corporation. See section 381(c)(17).

T.D. 6308, 9/9/58, amend T.D. 6657, 6/11/63, T.D. 7604, 3/28/79, T.D. 8939, 1/11/2001.

§ 1.547-3 Claim for credit or refund.

(a) If a deficiency in personal holding company tax is asserted for any taxable year, and the corporation has paid any portion of such asserted deficiency, it is entitled to a credit or refund of such payment to the extent that such payment constitutes an overpayment as the result of a deduction for a deficiency dividend as provided in section 547 and §§ 1.547-1 through 1.547-7. It should be noted that a "determination" under section 547(c) and paragraph (b)(1) of § 1.547-2, of taxpayer's liability for personal holding company tax may take place subsequent to the time the deficiency was paid. To secure credit or refund of such overpayment, the taxpayer must file a claim on Form 843 in addition to the claim for the deduction for deficiency dividends required under section 547(e) and paragraph (b)(2) of § 1.547-2.

(b) No interest shall be allowed on such credit or refund.

(c) Such credit or refund will be allowed as if, on the date of the determination under section 547(c) and paragraph (b)(1) of § 1.547-2, two years remained before the expiration of the period of limitation on the filing of claim for refund for the taxable year to which the overpayment relates.

T.D. 6308, 9/9/58.

§ 1.547-4 Effect on dividends paid deduction.

The deficiency dividends deduction shall be allowed as of the date the claim is filed. No duplication of deductions with respect to any deficiency dividends is permitted. If a corporation claims and receives the benefit of the provisions of section 547 (or the corresponding section 506 of the Internal Revenue Code of 1939, or section 407 of the Revenue Act of 1938 (52 Stat. 447)), based upon a distribution of deficiency dividends, that distribution does not become a part of the dividends paid deduction under section 561. Likewise, it will not be made the basis of a dividends paid deduction under section 561 by reason of the application of section 563(b), relating to dividends paid after the close of the taxable year and on or before the 15th day of the third month following the close of such taxable year.

T.D. 6308, 9/9/58.

§ 1.547-5 Deduction denied in case of fraud or willful failure to file timely return.

No deduction for deficiency dividends shall be allowed under section 547(a) if the determination contains a finding that any part of the deficiency is due to fraud with intent to evade tax, or to wilful failure to file an income tax return within the time prescribed by law or prescribed by the Secretary or his delegate in pursuance of law. See § 1.547-7 for effective date.

T.D. 6308, 9/9/58.

§ 1.547-6 Suspension of statute of limitations and stay of collection.

(a) Statute of limitations. If the corporation files a claim for a deduction for deficiency dividends under section 547(e) and paragraph (b)(2) of § 1.547-2, the running of the statute of limitations upon assessment, distraint, and collection in court in respect of the deficiency, and all interest, additional amounts, or assessable penalties, shall be suspended for a period of two years after the date of the determination under section 547(c) and paragraph (b)(1) of § 1.547-2.

(b) Stay of collection. If a deficiency in personal holding company tax is established by a determination under section 547(c) and paragraph (b)(1) of § 1.547-2, collection by distraint or court proceeding (except in case of jeopardy), of the deficiency and all interest, additional amounts, and assessable penalties, shall be stayed for a period of 120 days after the date of such determination, and, to the extent any part of such deficiency remains after deduction for deficiency dividends, for an additional period until the date the claim is disallowed. After such claim is allowed or rejected, either in whole or in part, the amount of the deficiency which was not eliminated by the application of section 547, together with interest, additional amounts and assessable penalties, will be assessed and collected in the usual manner.

T.D. 6308, 9/9/58.

---

§ 1.547-7 Effective date.

The deduction for deficiency dividends, in computing personal holding company tax for any taxable year, is allowable only with respect to determinations under section 547(c) made after November 14, 1954 (the date falling 90 days after the date of enactment of the Internal Revenue Code of 1954). If the taxable year with respect to which the deficiency is asserted began before January 1, 1954, the deficiency dividends deduction shall include only the amounts which would have been includible in the computation of the basic surtax credit for such taxable year under the Internal Revenue Code of 1939. Section 547(g), relating to the denial of a deficiency dividends deduction if the determination contains a finding that any part of the deficiency is due to fraud, etc., shall apply only if the taxable year with respect to which the deficiency is asserted begins after December 31, 1953.

T.D. 6308, 9/9/58.

---

§ 1.551-1 General rule.

Caution: The Treasury has not yet amended Reg § 1.551-1 to reflect changes made by P.L. 108-357, P.L. 100-647.

Part III (section 551 and following), subchapter G, chapter 1 of the Code, does not impose a tax on foreign personal holding companies. The undistributed foreign personal holding company income of such companies, however, must be included in the manner and to the extent set forth in section 551, in the gross income of their "United States shareholders," that is, the shareholders who are individual citizens or residents of the United States, domestic corporations, domestic partnerships, and estates or trusts other than estates or trusts the gross income of which under subtitle A of the Code includes only income from sources within the United States.

T.D. 6308, 9/9/58.

---

§ 1.551-2 Amount included in gross income.

Caution: The Treasury has not yet amended Reg § 1.551-2 to reflect changes made by P.L. 108-357, P.L. 100-647, P.L. 99-514, P.L. 98-369.

(a) The undistributed foreign personal holding company income is included only in the gross income of the United States shareholders who were shareholders in the company on the last day of its taxable year on which a United States group (as defined in section 552(a)(2)) existed with respect to the company. Such United States shareholders, accordingly, are determined by the stock holdings as of such specified time. This rule applies to every United States shareholder who was a shareholder in the company at the specified time regardless of whether the United States shareholder is included within the United States group. For example, a domestic corporation which is a United States shareholder at the specified time must return its distributive share in the undistributed foreign personal holding company income even though the domestic corporation cannot be included within the United States group since, under section 554, the stock it owns in the foreign corporation is considered as being owned proportionately by its shareholders for the purpose of determining whether the foreign corporation is a foreign personal holding company.

(b) The United States shareholders must include in their gross income their distributive shares of that proportion of the undistributed foreign personal holding company income for the taxable year of the company which is equal in ratio to that which the portion of the taxable year up to and including the last day on which the United States group with respect to the company existed bears to the entire taxable year. Thus, if the last day in the taxable year on which the required United States group existed was also the end of the taxable year, the portion of the taxable year up to and including such last day would be equal to 100 percent and, in such case, the United States shareholders would be required to return their distributive shares in the entire undistributed foreign personal holding company income. But if the last day on which the required United States group existed was September 30, and the taxable year was a calendar year, the portion of the taxable year up to and including such last day would be equal to nine-twelfths and, in that case, the United States shareholders would be required to return their distributive shares in only nine-twelfths of the undistributed foreign personal holding company income.

(c) The amount which each United States shareholder must return is that amount which he would have received as a dividend if the above-specified portion of the undistributed foreign personal holding company income had in fact been distributed by the foreign personal holding company as a dividend on the last day of its taxable year on which the required United States group existed. Such amount is determined, therefore, by the interest of the United States shareholder in the foreign personal holding company, that is, by the number of shares of stock owned by the United States shareholder and the relative rights of his class of stock, if there are several classes of stock outstanding. Thus, if a foreign personal holding company has both common and preferred stock outstanding and the preferred shareholders are entitled to a specified dividend before any distribution may be made to the common shareholders, then the assumed distribution of the stated portion of the undistributed foreign personal holding company income must first be treated as a payment of the specified dividend on the preferred stock before any part may be allocated as a dividend on the common stock.

(d) The assumed distribution of the required portion of the undistributed foreign personal holding company income must be returned as dividend income by the United States shareholders for their respective taxable years in which or with which the taxable year of the foreign personal holding company ends. For example, if the M Corporation, whose taxable year is the calendar year, is a foreign personal holding company for 1954 and if A, one of its United States shareholders, makes returns on a calendar year basis, while B, another United States shareholder, makes returns on the basis of a fiscal year ending November 30, A must return his assumed dividend as income for the taxable year 1954 and B must return his distributive share as income for the fiscal year ending November 30, 1955. In applying this rule, the date as of which the United States group last existed with respect to the company is immaterial. Thus, in the foregoing example, if September 30, 1954, was the last day on which the United States group with respect to the M Corporation existed, B would still be required to return his assumed dividend as income for the fiscal year ending November 30, 1955, even though September 30, 1954, the date as of which the distribution is assumed to have been made, does not fall within such fiscal year.

(e) For the treatment of gain on the sale of certain stock, see section 306(f) and paragraph (h) of § 1.306-3.

T.D. 6308, 9/9/58.

§ 1.551-3 Deduction for obligations of the United States and its instrumentalities.

Caution: The Treasury has not yet amended Reg § 1.551-3 to reflect changes made by P.L. 108-357, P.L. 98-369, P.L. 94-455.

(a) Each United States shareholder required to return his distributive share of undistributed foreign personal holding company income for any taxable year shall take into account in computing the credit against tax under section 35, or the deduction under section 242, whichever is allowable to such shareholder, his proportionate share of whatever interest on obligations of the United States or its instrumentalities (as specified in section 35 or 242, as the case may be) may be included in the gross income of the company for such taxable year, with the exception of any such interest as may be so included by reason of the application of the provisions of section 555. For reduction of credit for such interest on account of amortizable bond premium, see section 171 and the regulations thereunder.

(b) The rule set forth in paragraph (a) of this section may be illustrated by the following example:

Example. The M Corporation is a foreign personal holding company which owns all the stock of the N Corporation, another foreign personal holding company. Both companies receive interest on obligations of the United States or its instrumentalities as specified in section 35. In determining the amount of the credit allowable under section 35 (if the shareholder is an individual) or the deduction allowable under section 242 (if the shareholder is a corporation), the United States shareholder of the M Corporation would be entitled to a credit or a deduction, as the case may be, only for his proportionate share of the interest received by that Company and not for any part of the interest received by the N Corporation, regardless of whether the interest received by the N Corporation is included in the gross income of the M Corporation as an actual dividend or is as a constructive dividend under section 555.

T.D. 6308, 9/9/58.

§ 1.551-4 Information in return.

Caution: The Treasury has not yet amended Reg § 1.551-4 to reflect changes made by P.L. 108-357.

The information required by section 551(d) in the returns of certain United States shareholders relates only to the taxable year of a foreign personal holding company for which any part of such corporation's undistributed foreign personal holding company income must be included in gross income by the United States shareholder of whom the information is required. The information shall be submitted as a part of the income tax return in the form of a statement attached to the return.

T.D. 6308, 9/9/58.

§ 1.551-5 Effect on capital account of foreign personal holding company and basis of stock in hands of shareholders.

Caution: The Treasury has not yet amended Reg § 1.551-5 to reflect changes made by P.L. 108-357, P.L. 98-369.

(a) Sections 551(e) and 551(f) are designed to prevent double taxation with respect to the undistributed foreign personal holding company income.

(b) The application of sections 551(e) and 551(f) may be illustrated by the following examples:

Example (1). The M Corporation is a foreign personal holding company. Seventy-five percent in value of its capital stock is owned by A, a citizen of the United States, and the remainder, or 25 percent, of its stock is owned by B, a nonresident alien individual. For the calendar year 1954 the M Corporation has an undistributed foreign personal holding company income of $100,000. A is required to include $75,000 of such income in gross income as a dividend in his return for the calendar year 1954. The $100,000 is treated as paid-in surplus or as a contribution to the capital of the M Corporation and its accumulated earnings and profits as of the close of the calendar year 1954 are correspondingly reduced. If after treating such $100,000 as paid-in surplus or as a contribution to capital, the M Corporation has no accumulated earnings and profits at the close of 1954, and if for the calendar year 1955, the M Corporation had no earnings and profits, but distributed $40,000, the amount so distributed would be a nontaxable distribution and would not be included in the gross income of either A or B for the calendar year 1955. If, however, after treating the $100,000 as paid-in surplus or as a contribution to capital, the M Corporation had accumulated earnings and profits of $100,000 at the close of 1954, the facts otherwise being the same, the distributions in 1955 would be taxable to A as a dividend, and the taxability of such distributions to B would depend upon the application of section 861(a)(2), relating to the treatment of dividends from a foreign corporation as income from sources within or without the United States.

Example (2). In example (1) assume the basis of A's stock to be $300,000. If A includes in gross income in his return for the calendar year 1954, $75,000 as a dividend from the M Corporation, the basis of his stock would be $375,000. After the nontaxable distribution of $30,000 to A by the M Corporation in 1955 (75 percent of the $40,000 distribution) the basis of A's stock, assuming no other changes, would be $345,000. If A failed to include the $75,000 as a dividend in gross income in his return for 1954 and his failure was not discovered until after the 6-year period of limitations had expired, the application of the rule would not increase the basis of A's stock. The subsequent nontaxable distribution of $30,000 to A in 1955 would reduce his basis of $300,000 to $270,000, thus tending to compensate for his failure to include the amount of $75,000 as a dividend in his gross income for 1954. If the undistributed foreign personal holding company income of the M Corporation is readjusted within the statutory period of limitations, thus increasing or decreasing the amount A would have to include in his gross income, proper adjustment is required to be made to the basis of A's stock on account of such readjustment.

T.D. 6308, 9/9/58.

§ 1.552-1 Definition of foreign personal holding company.

Caution: The Treasury has not yet amended Reg § 1.552-1 to reflect changes made by P.L. 108-357.

(a) A foreign personal holding company is any foreign corporation, other than a corporation exempt from taxation under subchapter F (section 501 and following), chapter 1 of the Code, and other than certain banking institutions which satisfy the requirements of section 552(b)(2) and paragraph (b) of § 1.552-4 which for the taxable year meets (1) the gross income requirement specified in section 552(a)(1); and (2) the stock ownership requirement specified in section 552(a)(2). Both requirements must be satisfied with respect to each taxable year.

(b) A foreign corporation which comes within the classification of a foreign personal holding company is not subject to taxation either under section 531 or section 541. See sections 532(b)(2) and 542(c)(5). The fact that a foreign corporation is a foreign personal holding company does not relieve the corporation from liability for the taxes imposed generally upon foreign corporations, such as the taxes imposed by sections 881 and 882, since such taxes apply regardless of the classification of the foreign corporation as a foreign personal holding company.

T.D. 6308, 9/9/58.

§ 1.552-2 Gross income requirement.

Caution: The Treasury has not yet amended Reg § 1.552-2 to reflect changes made by P.L. 108-357.

(a) To meet the gross income requirement, it is necessary that either of the following percentages of gross income of the corporation for the taxable year (including the additions to gross income provided in section 555(b) as required by section 555(c)(2)) be foreign personal holding company income as defined in section 553:

(1) 60 percent or more; or

(2) 50 percent or more if the foreign corporation has been classified as a foreign personal holding company for any taxable year ending after August 26, 1937, unless—

(i) A taxable year has intervened since the last taxable year for which it was so classified, during no part of which the stock ownership requirement specified in section 552(a)(2) exists; or

(ii) Three consecutive years have intervened since the last taxable year for which it was so classified, during each of which its foreign personal holding company income was less than 50 percent of its gross income.

(b) In determining whether the foreign personal holding company income is equal to the required percentage of the total gross income, the determination must not be made upon the basis of gross receipts, since gross income is not synonymous with gross receipts. For meaning of gross income in this part, see section 555 and § 1.555-1.

T.D. 6308, 9/9/58.

§ 1.552-3 Stock ownership requirement.

Caution: The Treasury has not yet amended Reg § 1.552-3 to reflect changes made by P.L. 108-357.

(a) To meet the stock ownership requirement, it is necessary that at some time in the taxable year more than 50 percent in value of the outstanding stock of the foreign corporation be owned, directly or indirectly, by or for not more than five individuals who are citizens or residents of the United States, herein referred to as "United States group." For the purpose of the requirement under section 552(a)(2), section 554 provides that the ownership of the stock must be determined under the rules prescribed by section 544 (relating to rules for determining stock ownership in the case of personal holding companies generally). Accordingly, section 544 and §§ 1.544-1 through 1.544-7 are applicable for purposes of section 552(a)(2) and this section as if each reference in section 544 and §§ 1.544-1 through 1.544-7 to a personal holding company or to part II (section 541 and following), subchapter G, chapter 1 of the Code, was a reference to a foreign personal holding company or to part III (section 551 and following), subchapter G, chapter 1 of the Code, as the case may be.

(b) It is necessary to consider any change in the stock outstanding during the taxable year, whether in the number of shares or classes of stock, or in the ownership thereof, since a corporation comes within the classification if the statutory conditions with respect to stock ownership are present at any time during the taxable year.

(c) In determining whether the statutory conditions with respect to stock ownership are present at any time during the taxable year, the phrase "in value" shall, in the light of all the circumstances, be deemed the value of the corporate stock outstanding at such time (not including treasury stock). This value may be determined upon the basis of the company's net worth, earning and dividend paying capacity, appreciation of assets, together with such other factors as have a bearing upon the value of the stock. If the value of the stock which is used is greatly at variance with that reflected by the corporate books, the evidence of such value should be filed with the return. In any case where there are two or more classes of stock outstanding, the total value of all the stock should be allocated among the different classes according to the relative value of each class therein.

T.D. 6308, 9/9/58.

§ 1.552-4 Certain excluded banks.

Caution: The Treasury has not yet amended Reg § 1.552-4 to reflect changes made by P.L. 108-357.

(a) A corporation is excluded from the definition of "foreign personal holding company" if it is organized and doing business under the banking and credit laws of a foreign country and if it establishes to the satisfaction of the Commissioner that it was not formed or availed of for the purpose of evading or avoiding United States income taxes which would otherwise be imposed on its shareholders. If this is established, the Commissioner, or such other official to whom authority may be delegated, will certify, by letter to the corporation, that it is not a foreign personal holding company.

(b) An application for certification under section 552(b)(2) shall be made in writing to the Commissioner of Internal Revenue, Washington 25, D. C., Attention: Director of International Operations. A separate application shall be filed for each taxable year for which certification is requested, and the application shall be accompanied by a completed Form 958 for the taxable year. See section 6035. The following information shall be set forth in, or submitted with, the application:

(1) A complete reference to the banking or credit laws of the foreign country under which the corporation operates;

(2) A statement as to the extent of the corporation's business in receiving deposits and making loans and discounts and similar banking and credit operations;

(3) A statement as to the extent of the operations of the corporation other than such banking and credit operations;

(4) A statement as to whether the banking and credit operations of the corporation are customary for it;

(5) A statement setting forth the degree and manner of supervision exercised over it by the foreign government under its banking and credit laws; a copy (in English) of the corporation's last annual financial statement, as submitted to the Government authority having jurisdiction over it, shall be submitted with the application;

(6) A statement setting forth the business reasons of the corporation for not distributing the amount which would be its undistributed foreign personal holding company income if the corporation were not excluded under section 552(b);

(7) A statement setting forth the extent of the corporation's profits which must be retained as reserves under the foreign law;

(8) A statement setting forth the date or dates when the corporation reasonably expects to distribute its undistributed foreign personal holding company income for the taxable year;

(9) A statement setting forth the name and address of each of the individuals described in section 552(a)(2), the extent of their stock ownership in the corporation, and the amount of distributions or other payments to such stockholders, including, but not limited to, dividends, compensation, interest, and rents; and

(10) Any other facts or information the corporation may wish to submit to show that it was not formed or availed of for the purpose of evading or avoiding United States income taxes which would otherwise be imposed on its shareholders.

The corporation shall also furnish such other information requested as necessary by the Director of International Operations. The application for certification, together with the information required by this paragraph, should be filed within 60 days after the close of the taxable year of the corporation or before November 9, 1958, whichever is later. However, if the corporation is unable, for good cause, to submit the application for certification within such 60-day period, additional time may be granted by the Director of International Operations upon receipt of a request from the corporation setting forth the reasons for such request.

T.D. 6308, 9/9/58.

§ 1.552-5 United States shareholder of excluded bank.

Caution: The Treasury has not yet amended Reg § 1.552-5 to reflect changes made by P.L. 108-357.

A copy of the certification issued to an excluded bank under section 552(b)(2) and § 1.552-4 shall be filed with, and made a part of, the income tax return for the taxable year of each United States shareholder of such foreign corporation, if he has been a shareholder of such corporation for any part of such year. If the certificate has not been issued at the time the return of the United States shareholder is filed, the shareholder shall compute the tax on his return by treating the bank as a foreign personal holding company. If a certificate is issued after the return is filed, the United States shareholder may file a claim for refund or an amended return, and shall attach thereto a copy of the certification.

T.D. 6308, 9/9/58.

§ 1.553-1 Foreign personal holding company income.

Caution: The Treasury has not yet amended Reg § 1.553-1 to reflect changes made by P.L. 108-357, P.L. 99-514.

Foreign personal holding company income shall consist of the items defined under section 543 and §§ 1.543-1 and 1.543-2, relating to personal holding company income, with the following exceptions:

(a) The entire amount received as "interest", whether or not treated as rent, shall be considered to be foreign personal holding company income. Thus, the exception in the second sentence of section 543(a)(1) and paragraph (b)(2) of § 1.543-1 (relating to interest treated as rent under section 543(a)(7) and paragraph (b)(10) of § 1.543-1), is inapplicable for the purpose of determining foreign personal holding company income. Similarly, section 543(a)(7) and paragraph (b)(10) of § 1.543-1 are applied for this purpose without regard to the interest described in that section.

(b) *(1)* The entire amount received as "royalties", whether or not mineral, oil, or gas royalties, or copyright royalties, shall be considered to be foreign personal holding company income. Thus, subparagraphs (A) and (B) of section 543(a)(8) and paragraph (b)(11)(i)(a) and (b) of § 1.543-1 (relating to mineral, oil, or gas royalties), and subparagraphs (A), (B), and (C) of section 543(a)(9) and paragraph (b)(12)(ii) of § 1.543-1 (relating to copyright royalties), are inapplicable for the purpose of determining foreign personal holding company income.

(2) In computing foreign personal holding company income, the first sentence of paragraph (b)(11)(ii) of § 1.543-1 shall apply to overriding royalties received from the sublessee by the operating company which originally leased and developed the natural resource property in respect of which such overriding royalties are paid, and to mineral, oil, or gas production payments, only with respect to amounts received after September 30, 1958.

T.D. 6308, 9/9/58, amend T.D. 6739, 6/16/64.

§ 1.555-1 General rule.

Caution: The Treasury has not yet amended Reg § 1.555-1 to reflect changes made by P.L. 108-357.

The gross income of a foreign corporation which is a foreign personal holding company is computed the same as if the foreign corporation were a domestic corporation which is a personal holding company. See section 542(a)(1) and § 1.542-2. The gross income of a foreign personal holding company thus includes income from all sources, whether within or without the United States, which is not specifically excluded from gross income under any other provisions of the Code. For example, the gross income of a foreign personal holding company includes all income from sources outside the United States even though the foreign personal holding company is a foreign corporation not engaged in trade or business within the United States. However, the gross income of a foreign corporation which is a foreign personal holding company shall not include, with respect to a United States shareholder described in section 951(b), dividends received by such corporation which are excluded under section 959(b) from the income of such corporation with respect to such shareholder.

T.D. 6308, 9/9/58, amend T.D. 6795, 1/28/65.

§ 1.555-2 Additions to gross income.

(a) If, for any taxable year—

(1) A foreign corporation meets the stock ownership requirement specified in section 552(a)(2) and § 1.552-3, regardless of whatever day in its taxable year is the last day on which the required United States group exists, and

(2) Such foreign corporation is a shareholder in a foreign personal holding company on any day of a taxable year of the second company which ends with or within the taxable year of the first company and such day is the last day in the taxable year of the second company in which the United States group exists with respect to the second company, then for the purpose of—

(i) Determining whether the first company meets the specified gross income requirement so as to come within the classification of a foreign personal holding company, and

(ii) Determining the undistributed foreign personal holding company income of the first company which (in the event the first company is a foreign personal holding company) is to be included, in whole or in part, in the gross income of its shareholders, whether United States shareholders or other foreign personal holding companies,

there shall be included as a dividend in the gross income of the first company for the taxable year in which or with which the taxable year of the second company ends, the amount the first company would have received as a dividend, if on the last day referred to in this subparagraph there had been distributed by the second company, and received by the shareholders, an amount which bears the same ratio to the undistributed foreign personal holding company income of the second company for its taxable year as the portion of such taxable year up to and including such last day bears to the entire taxable year. The foregoing rules apply to any chain of foreign corporations regardless of the number of corporations included in the chain.

(b) The application of section 555(b) may be illustrated by the following examples:

Example (1). The X Corporation is a foreign corporation whose stock is owned by A, a United States citizen. The X Corporation owns the entire stock of the Y Corporation, another foreign corporation. The taxable year of the X Corporation is the calendar year and the taxable year of the Y Corporation is the fiscal year ending June 30. For the fiscal year ending June 30, 1955, more than the required percentage of the Y Corporation's gross income consists of foreign personal holding company income and no part of the earnings for such year is distributed as dividends. On the basis of these facts the Y Corporation is a foreign personal holding company for the fiscal year ending June 30, 1955. The X Corporation meets the stock ownership requirement and constitutes a foreign personal holding company for 1955, if it also meets the gross income requirement. For the purpose of determining whether the X Corporation meets the gross income requirement, the entire undistributed foreign personal holding company income of the Y Corporation for the fiscal year ending June 30, 1955, must be included as a dividend in the gross income of the X Corporation for 1955, since—

(1) The X Corporation was a shareholder in the Y Corporation on a day (June 30, 1955) in the taxable year of the Y Corporation ending with or within the taxable year of the X Corporation, which day was the last day in the taxable year of the Y Corporation on which the United States group required with respect to the Y Corporation existed.

(2) Such last day was also the end of the Y Corporation's taxable year so that the portion of the taxable year of the Y Corporation up to and including such last day is equal to 100 percent of the taxable year of the Y Corporation, and, therefore, the portion of the undistributed foreign personal holding company income of the Y Corporation includible in the gross income of its shareholders is likewise equal to 100 percent,

(3) The X Corporation being the sole shareholder of the Y Corporation must include such portion in its gross income for 1955, the taxable year in which or with which the taxable year of the Y Corporation ends. If, after the inclusion of the presumptive dividend in its gross income, the X Corporation is a foreign personal holding company for 1955, then the undistributed foreign personal holding company income of the Y Corporation must also be included as a dividend in the gross income of the X Corporation in determining its undistributed foreign personal holding company income which is to be included in the gross income of A, the sole shareholder in the X Corporation. On the other hand, if, after including such presumptive dividend, the X Corporation does not constitute a foreign personal holding company, the undistributed foreign personal holding company income of the Y Corporation is not includible in the gross income of the X Corporation.

Example (2). The X Corporation referred to in example (1) sold the stock in the Y Corporation to other interests on September 30, 1955, so that after that date no United States group existed with respect to the Y Corporation. For the fiscal year ending June 30, 1956, more than the required percentage of the gross income of the Y Corporation consists of foreign personal holding company income. The taxable income of the Y Corporation for such fiscal year amounts to $1,000,000, of which $900,000 is distributed in dividends after September 30, 1955. The undistributed foreign personal holding company income of the Y Corporation for such fiscal year amounts to $100,000. Upon the basis of these facts the Y Corporation is a foreign personal holding company for the fiscal year ending June 30, 1956, since at one time in such fiscal year, or from July 1 to and including September 30, 1955, it meets the stock ownership requirement, and the gross income requirement is also satisfied. In determining whether the X Corporation constitutes a foreign personal holding company for 1956, a portion of the undistributed foreign personal holding company income of the Y Corporation for the fiscal year ending June 30, 1956 (three-twelfths of $100,000, or $25,000), must be included as a dividend in the gross income of the X Corporation, since—

(1) The X Corporation was a shareholder in the Y Corporation on September 30, 1955, or on a day in the taxable year of the Y Corporation ending with or within the taxable year of the X Corporation which day was the last day in the Y Corporation's taxable year on which the United States group required with respect to the Y Corporation existed.

(2) The portion of the taxable year of the Y Corporation up to and including such day is three-twelfths of the entire taxable year of the Y Corporation and, therefore, the portion of the undistributed foreign personal holding company income of the Y Corporation includible in the gross income of its shareholders also is equal to three-twelfths, and

(3) The X Corporation, being the sole shareholder of the Y Corporation at the time the United States group with respect to the Y Corporation last existed, must include all of such portion in its gross income for 1956, the taxable year of the X Corporation in which or with which the taxable year of the Y Corporation ends.

It is to be observed that three-twelfths of the undistributed foreign personal holding company income of the Y Corporation for the entire taxable year and not the earnings realized by the Y Corporation up to and including September 30, 1955, the last day on which the United States group with respect to the Y Corporation existed, must be included in the gross income of the X Corporation.

Example (3). The X Corporation referred to in example (1) sold the stock in the Y Corporation to other interests on September 30, 1955, so that after that date a different United States group existed with respect to the Y Corporation. Assuming that the Y Corporation is a foreign personal holding company for the fiscal year ending June 30, 1956, no part of the undistributed foreign personal holding company income of the Y Corporation for such fiscal year would, in this instance, be includible in the gross income of the X Corporation for the year 1956, in determining whether the X Corporation is a foreign personal holding company for that year. In such case, the undistributed foreign personal holding company income of the Y Corporation is includible in the gross income of the other foreign personal holding companies, if any, and of the United States shareholders who are shareholders in the Y Corporation the day after September 30, 1955, which was the last day in the taxable year of the Y Corporation on which the United States group with respect to the Y Corporation existed. If, however, the X Corporation sells 90 percent of its stock in the Y Corporation and thus is a minority shareholder in the Y Corporation on the last day of the taxable year of the Y Corporation on which the United States group with respect to the Y Corporation exists, the portion of the undistributed foreign personal holding company income allocable to the minority interests of the X Corporation would be includible in the gross income of the X Corporation, even though on such last day the United States group is not the same with respect to both corporations.

Example (4). If the Y Corporation in example (1) owns all of the stock of the Z Corporation, another foreign corporation, there would be a chain of three foreign corporations. In such case, assuming that the Z Corporation is a foreign personal holding company for a taxable year ending with or within the taxable year of the Y Corporation, the undistributed foreign personal holding company income of the Z Corporation would be included in the gross income of the Y Corporation for the purpose of determining whether the Y Corporation comes within the classification of a foreign personal holding company. If, after the inclusion of such presumptive dividend, the Y Corporation is a foreign personal holding company, the undistributed foreign personal holding company income of the Z Corporation would be included in the gross income of the Y Corporation in determining the undistributed foreign personal holding company income of the Y Corporation which is includible in the gross income of its shareholder, the X Corporation. The same process would be repeated with respect to determining whether the X Corporation is a foreign personal holding company and in determining its undistributed foreign personal holding company income. If all three corporations are foreign personal holding companies, the undistributed foreign personal holding company income of each would, in this manner, be reflected as a dividend in the gross income of A, the ultimate beneficial shareholder of the chain. In the event that after the inclusion of the undistributed foreign personal holding company income of the Z Corporation in the gross income of the Y Corporation, the Y Corporation is not a foreign personal holding company, then no part of the income of either the Z Corporation or the Y Corporation would be includible in the gross income of the X Corporation. In that event, whether the X Corporation is a foreign personal holding company, and its undistributed foreign personal holding company income, would be determined independently of the income of the Y Corporation and the Z Corporation.

T.D. 6308, 9/9/58.

§ 1.556-1 Definition.

Caution: The Treasury has not yet amended Reg § 1.556-1 to reflect changes made by P.L. 108-357.

Undistributed foreign personal holding company income is the amount which is to be included in the gross income of the United States shareholders under section 551(b) and § 1.551-2. Undistributed foreign personal holding company income is the taxable income of the foreign personal holding company, as defined in section 63(a) (computed without regard to subchapter N, chapter 1 of the Code), and adjusted in the manner described in section 556(b) and § 1.556-2, less the deduction for dividends paid (§§ 1.561 through 1.565-6). See § 1.556-3 for an illustration of the computation of undistributed foreign personal holding company income.

T.D. 6308, 9/9/58.

§ 1.556-2 Adjustments to taxable income.

Caution: The Treasury has not yet amended Reg § 1.556-2 to reflect changes made by P.L. 108-357.

(a) Taxes. *(1) General rule.* (i) In computing undistributed foreign personal holding company income for any taxable year, there shall be allowed as a deduction the Federal income and excess profits taxes accrued during the taxable year except that no deduction shall be allowed for (a) the accumulated earnings tax imposed by section 531 (or a corresponding section of a prior law), (b) the personal holding company tax imposed by section 541 (or a corresponding section of a prior law), and (c) the excess profits tax imposed by subchapter E, chapter 2 of the Internal Revenue Code of 1939 for taxable years beginning after December 31, 1940. The deduction is for taxes for the taxable year determined under the accrual method of accounting, regardless of whether the corporation uses an accrual method of accounting, the cash receipts and disbursements method, or any other allowable method of accounting. In computing the amount of taxes accrued, an unpaid tax which is being contested is not considered accrued until the contest is resolved.

(ii) However, the corporation shall deduct taxes paid, rather than taxes accrued, if it used that method with respect to Federal taxes for each taxable year for which it was subject to the provisions of supplement P, subchapter C, chapter 1 of the Internal Revenue Code of 1939, unless an election is made under subparagraph (2) of this paragraph to deduct taxes accrued.

(2) Election by corporation which deducted taxes paid. (i) If the corporation was subject to supplement P, subchapter C, chapter 1 of the Internal Revenue Code of 1939, and, for the purpose of computing undistributed supplement P net income under such Code, deducted Federal taxes paid, rather than such taxes accrued, for each taxable year for which it was subject to supplement P of the 1939 Code, the corporation may elect for any taxable year ending after August 16, 1954, to deduct taxes accrued, rather than taxes paid, for the purpose of computing its undistributed foreign personal holding company income. The election shall be made by deducting such taxes accrued in the return (Form 958) required to be filed for such taxable year. The return shall, in addition, contain a statement that the corporation has made such election and shall set forth the year to which such election was first applicable. The deduction of taxes accrued in the year of election precludes the deduction of taxes paid during such year. The election, if made, shall be irrevocable and the deduction for taxes accrued shall be allowed for the year of election and for all subsequent taxable years. See section 6035 and the regulations thereunder for rules relative to the filing of returns of officers, directors, and shareholders of foreign personal holding companies.

(ii) Pursuant to section 7851(a)(1)(C), the election provided for in subdivision (i) of this subparagraph may be made with respect to a taxable year ending after August 16, 1954, even though such taxable year is subject to the Internal Revenue Code of 1939.

(3) Taxes of foreign countries and United States possessions. In computing taxable income, a foreign personal holding company is allowed a deduction under section 164 for income, war profits, and excess-profits taxes paid or accrued during the taxable year to foreign countries or possessions of the United States, but is not allowed the foreign tax credit under section 901. Therefore, in computing undistributed foreign personal holding company income for any taxable year, no adjustment under section 556(b)(1) is allowed for such taxes.

(b) Charitable contributions. *(1) Taxable years beginning before January 1, 1970.* (i) Section 556(b)(2) provides that, in computing the deduction for charitable contributions for purposes of determining the undistributed foreign personal holding company income of a corporation for taxable years beginning before January 1, 1970, the limitations in section 170(b)(1)(A) and (B), relating to charitable contributions by individuals, shall apply and section 170(b)(2) and (5), relating to charitable contributions by corporations and carryover of certain excess charitable contributions made by individuals, respectively, shall not apply.

(ii) Although the limitations of section 170(b)(1)(A) and (B) are 10 and 20 percent, respectively, of the individual's adjusted gross income, the limitations are applied for purposes of section 556(b)(2) by using 10 and 20 percent, respectively, of the corporation's taxable income as adjusted for purposes of section 170(b)(2), that is, the same amount of taxable income to which the 5-percent limitation applied. Thus, the term "adjusted gross income" when used in section 170(b)(1) means the corporation's taxable income computed with the adjustments, other than the 5-percent limitation, provided in the first sentence of section 170(b)(2). However, a further adjustment for this purpose is that the taxable income shall also be computed without the deduction of the amount disallowed under section 556(b)(5), relating to expenses and depreciation applicable to property of the taxpayer, and section 556(b)(6), relating to taxes and contributions to pension trusts, and without the inclusion of the amounts includible as dividends under section 555(b), relating to the inclusion in gross income of a foreign personal holding company of its distributive share of the undistributed foreign personal holding company income of another company in which it is a shareholder. The carryover of charitable contributions made in a prior year, otherwise, allowable as a deduction in computing taxable income to the extent provided in section 170(b)(2) and, with respect to contributions paid in taxable years beginning after December 31, 1963, in section 170(b)(5), shall not be allowed as a deduction in computing undistributed foreign personal holding company income for any taxable year.

(iii) See § 1.170-2 with respect to the charitable contributions to which the 10-percent limitation is applicable and the charitable contributions to which the 20-percent limitation is applicable.

(2) Taxable years beginning after December 31, 1969. (i) Section 556(b)(2) provides that, in computing the deduction allowable for charitable contributions for purposes of determining the undistributed foreign personal holding company income of a corporation for taxable years beginning after December 31, 1969, the limitations in section 170(b)(1)(A), (B), and (D)(i) (relating to charitable contributions by individuals) shall apply, and section 170(b)(1)(D)(ii) (relating to excess charitable contributions by individuals of certain capital gain property), section 170(b)(2) (relating to the 5-percent limitation on charitable contributions by corporations), and section 170(d) (relating to carryovers of excess contributions of individuals and corporations) shall not apply.

(ii) Although the limitations of section 170(b)(1)(A), (B), and (D)(i) are 50, 20, and 30 percent respectively, of an individual's contribution base, these limitations are applied for purposes of section 556(b)(2) by using 50, 20, and 30 percent, respectively, of the corporation's taxable income as adjusted for purposes of section 170(b)(2), that is, the same amount of taxable income to which the 5-percent limitation applies. Thus, the term "contribution base" when used in section 170(b)(1) means the corporation's taxable income computed with the adjustments, other than the 5-percent limitation, provided in section 170(b)(2). However, a further adjustment for this purpose is that the taxable income shall also be computed without the deduction of the amount disallowed under section 556(b)(5), relating to expenses and depreciation applicable to property of the taxpayer, and section 556(b)(6), relating to taxes and contributions to pension trusts, and without the inclusion of the amounts includible as dividends under section 555(b), relating to the inclusion in gross income of a foreign personal holding company of its distributive share of the undistributed foreign personal holding company income of another company in which it is a shareholder. The carryover of charitable contributions made in a prior year, otherwise allowable as a deduction in computing taxable income to the extent provided in section 170(b)(1)(D)(ii) and (d), shall not be allowed as a deduction in computing undistributed foreign personal holding company income for any taxable year.

(iii) See § 1.170A-8 for the rules with respect to the charitable contributions to which the 50-, 20-, and 30-percent limitations apply.

(c) Special deductions disallowed. Part VIII, subchapter B, chapter 1 of the Code allows corporations special deductions in computing taxable income for such matters as partially tax-exempt interest, certain dividends received, dividends paid on certain preferred stock of public utilities, organizational expenses, etc. See section 241. For purposes of computing undistributed foreign personal holding company income, such special deductions, except the deduction provided by section 248 (relating to organizational expenditures) and, with respect to such a computation for a taxable year ending before January 1, 1958, the deduction provided by section 242 (relating to partially tax-exempt interest), shall be disallowed.

(d) Net operating loss. The net operating loss deduction provided in section 172 is not allowed for purposes of the computation of undistributed foreign personal holding company income. For purposes of such a computation, however, there is allowed as a deduction the amount of the net operating loss (as defined in section 172(c)) for the preceding taxable year, except that, in computing undistributed foreign personal holding company income for a taxable year ending after December 31, 1957, the amount of such net operating loss shall be computed without the deductions provided in part VIII (section 241 and following) except section 248, relating to organizational expenditures, subchapter B, chapter 1 of the Code.

(e) Expenses and depreciation applicable to property of the corporation. *(1)* Section 556(b)(5) provides a specific limitation in computing undistributed foreign personal holding company income, with respect to the allowance of deductions for trade or business expenses and depreciation which are allocable to the operation and maintenance of property owned or operated by a foreign personal holding company. Under this limitation these deductions shall not be allowed in excess of the aggregate amount of the rent or other compensation received for the use of, or the right to use, the property, unless it is established to the satisfaction of the Commissioner—

(i) That the rent or other compensation received was the highest obtainable, or if none was received, that none was obtainable;

(ii) That the property was held in the course of a business carried on bona fide for profit; and

(iii) Either that there was reasonable expectation that the operation of the property would result in a profit, or that the property was necessary to the conduct of the business.

(2) The burden of proof will rest upon the taxpayer to sustain the deduction claimed. If a United States shareholder, in computing his distributive share of undistributed foreign personal holding company income to be included in gross income in his individual return (see section 551, and §§ 1.551-1 and 1.551-2), claims deductions for expenses and depreciation allocable to the operation and maintenance of property owned or operated by the company, in an aggregate amount in excess of the rent or other compensation received for the use of, or the right to use, the property, he shall attach to his income tax return a statement setting forth his claim for allowance of the additional deductions, together with a complete statement of the facts and circumstances pertinent to his claim and the arguments on which he relies. Such statement shall set forth—

(i) A description of the property;

(ii) The cost or other basis to the corporation and the nature and value of the consideration paid for the property;

(iii) The name and address of the person from whom the property was acquired and the date the property was acquired;

(iv) The name and address of the person to whom the property is leased or rented, or the person permitted to use the property, and the number of shares of stock, if any, held by such person and the members of his family;

(v) The nature and gross amount of the rent or other compensation received for the use of, or the right to use, the property during the taxable year and for each of the five preceding years and the amount of the expenses incurred with respect to, and the depreciation sustained on, the property for such years;

(vi) Evidence that the rent or other compensation was the highest obtainable, or, if none was received, a statement of the reasons therefor;

(vii) In the case of a return for a taxable year beginning before January 1, 2003, a copy of the contract, lease, or rental agreement;

(viii) The purpose for which the property was used;

(ix) The business carried on by the corporation with respect to which the property was held and the gross income, expenses, and taxable income derived from the conduct of such business for the taxable year and for each of the five preceding years;

(x) A statement of any reasons which existed for expectation that the operation of the property would be profitable, or a statement of the necessity for the use of the property in the business of the corporation, and the reasons why the property was acquired; and

(xi) Any other information pertinent to the taxpayer's claim.

(3) If the statement described in § 1.556-2(e)(2) is attached to a taxpayer's income tax return for a taxable year beginning after December 31, 2002, a copy of the applicable contract, lease or rental agreement is not required to be submitted with the return, but must be retained by the taxpayer and kept available for inspection in the manner required by § 1.6001-1(e).

(f) Taxes and contributions to pension trusts. Section 164(e) provides for deduction by a corporation for taxes of a shareholder paid by it; section 404 provides for deduction by an employer for its contributions to an employees' trust, etc. For the purpose of computing undistributed foreign personal holding company income, neither of these deductions is allowable.

T.D. 6308, 9/9/58, amend T.D. 6376, 5/6/59, T.D. 6900, 11/16/66, T.D. 7207, 10/2/72, T.D. 9100, 12/18/2003, T.D. 9300, 12/7/2006.

§ 1.556-3 Illustration of computation of undistributed foreign personal holding company income.

Caution: The Treasury has not yet amended Reg § 1.556-3 to reflect changes made by P.L. 108-357.

The method of computation of the undistributed foreign personal holding company income may be illustrated by the following example:

Example. (a) The following facts exist with respect to the M Corporation, a foreign personal holding company, for the calendar year 1954:

(1) The gross income of the corporation as defined in section 555 amounts to $300,000, of which $85,000 represents its distributive share of the undistributed foreign personal holding company income of another foreign personal holding company in which it is a shareholder, $200,000 consists of dividends, $10,000 consists of fully taxable interest, and the remainder ($5,000) consists of rent received from the principal shareholder of the corporation for the use of property owned by the corporation.

(2) The expenses of the corporation amount to $85,000, of which $75,000 is allocable to the maintenance and operation of the property used by the principal shareholder and $10,000 consists of ordinary and necessary office expenses allowable as a deduction. The claim for deduction for the expenses of, and depreciation on, the rented property in excess of the rent received for its use is not established as provided in section 556(b)(5). The yearly depreciation on the rented property amounts to $30,000.

(3) Federal income tax withheld at the source on the income of the corporation from sources within the United States amounts to $59,125.

(4) No gain from the sale or exchange of stock or securities is realized during the taxable year, but losses in the amount of $10,000 are sustained from the sale of stock or securities which constitute capital assets. Such losses are not allowed as a deduction in any amount. See section 1211(a).

(5) Contributions, payment of which is made to or for the use of donees described in section 170(b)(1)(A) for the purposes therein specified, amount to $15,000, of which $5,000 is deductible in computing taxable income under section 63.

(6) Dividends paid by the corporation to its shareholders during the taxable year amount to $50,000.

(b) The taxable income of the corporation (including the distributive share of the undistributed foreign personal holding company income of the other foreign personal holding company) is $180,000, computed as follows (assuming for the purposes of this example only that the expenses of, and depreciation on, the rental property are deductible under sections 162 and 167):

Income (Section 61)

Dividends	$200,000
Interest	10,000
Rent	5,000
Gross income as defined in section 61	215,000
Add:	
Distributive share of undistributed income of the other foreign personal holding company (considered as a dividend)	85,000
Gross income as defined in section 555	300,000

Deductions (Section 161)

Expenses allocable to operation of the rented property	$ 75,000
Depreciation of the rented property	30,000
Ordinary and necessary expenses (office)	10,000
Contributions (within the 5-percent limitation specified in section 170(b)(2)	5,000
	120,000
Taxable income for purposes of computing undistributed foreign personal holding company income	180,000

(c)The undistributed foreign personal holding company income of the corporation is $160,875, computed as follows:

Taxable income for purposes of computing undistributed foreign personal holding company income	$180,000
Add (see section 556(b)):	
Contributions deductible in computing taxable income under section 63	5,000
Excess property expenses and depreciation over amount of rent received for use of property ($105,000 – $5,000)	100,000
Total	105,000
Deduct (see section 556(b)):	
Federal income taxes	59,125
Contributions (within the percentage limitations specified in section 170(b)(1)(A) and (B), determined under the rules provided in section 556(b)(2))	15,000
Total	74,125
Net additions under section 556(b)	30,875
Taxable incomes as adjusted under section 556(b)	210,875
Less: Deduction for dividends paid (see section 561)	50,000
Undistributed foreign personal holding company income	160,875

T.D. 6308, 9/9/58.

§ 1.561-1 Deduction for dividends paid.

(a) The deduction for dividends paid is applicable in determining accumulated taxable income under section 535, undistributed personal holding company income under section 545, undistributed foreign personal holding company income under section 556, investment company taxable income under section 852, and real estate investment trust taxable income under section 857. The deduction for dividends paid includes—

(1) The dividends paid during the taxable year;

(2) The consent dividends for the taxable year, determined as provided in section 565; and

(3) In the case of a personal holding company, the dividend carryover computed as provided in section 564.

(b) For dividends for which the dividends paid deduction is allowable, see section 562 and § 1.562-1. As to when dividends are considered paid, see § 1.561-2.

T.D. 6308, 9/9/58, amend T.D. 6598, 4/25/62.

§ 1.561-2 When dividends are considered paid.

Caution: The Treasury has not yet amended Reg § 1.561-2 to reflect changes made by P.L. 94-455, P.L. 87-403.

(a) In general. *(1)* A dividend will be considered as paid when it is received by the shareholder. A deduction for dividends paid during the taxable year will not be permitted unless the shareholder receives the dividend during the taxable year for which the deduction is claimed. See section 563 for special rule with respect to dividends paid after the close of the taxable year.

(2) If a dividend is paid by check and the check bearing a date within the taxable year is deposited in the mails, in a cover properly stamped and addressed to the shareholder at his last known address, at such time that in the ordinary handling of the mails the check would be received by the shareholder within the taxable year, a presumption arises that the dividend was paid to the shareholder in such year.

(3) The payment of a dividend during the taxable year to the authorized agent of the shareholder will be deemed payment of the dividend to the shareholder during such year.

(4) If a corporation, instead of paying the dividend directly to the shareholder, credits the account of the shareholder on the books of the corporation with the amount of the dividend, the deduction for a dividend paid will not be permitted unless it be shown to the satisfaction of the Commissioner that such crediting constituted payment of the dividend to the shareholder within the taxable year.

(5) A deduction will not be permitted for the amount of a dividend credited during the taxable year upon an obligation of the shareholder to the corporation unless it is shown to the satisfaction of the Commissioner that such crediting constituted payment of the dividend to the shareholder within the taxable year.

(6) If the dividend is payable in obligations of the corporation, they should be entered or registered in the taxable year on the books of the corporation, in the name of the shareholder (or his nominee or transferee), and, in the case of obligations payable to bearer, should be received in the taxable year by the shareholder (or his nominee or transferee) to constitute payment of the dividend within the taxable year.

(7) In the case of a dividend from which the tax has been deducted and withheld as required by chapter 3 (section 1441 and following), of the Code the dividend is considered as paid when such deducting and withholding occur.

(b) Methods of accounting. The determination of whether a dividend has been paid to the shareholder by the corporation during its taxable year is in no way dependent upon the method of accounting regularly employed by the corporation in keeping its books or upon the method of accounting upon the basis of which the taxable income of the corporation is computed.

(c) Records. Every corporation claiming a deduction for dividends paid shall keep such permanent records as are necessary (1) to establish that the dividends with respect to which such deduction is claimed were actually paid during the taxable year and (2) to supply the information required to be filed with the income tax return of the corporation. Such corporation shall file with its return (i) a copy of the dividend resolution; and (ii) a concise statement of the pertinent facts relating to the payment of the dividend, clearly specifying (a) the medium of payment and (b) if not paid in money, the fair market value and adjusted basis (or face value, if paid in its own obligations) on the date of distribution of the property distributed and the manner in which such fair market value and adjusted basis were determined. Canceled dividend checks and receipts obtained from shareholders acknowledging payment of dividends paid otherwise than by check need not be filed with the return but shall be kept by the corporation as a part of its records.

T.D. 6308, 9/9/58.

§ 1.562-1 Dividends for which the dividends paid deduction is allowable.

(a) General rule. Except as otherwise provided in section 562(b) and (d), the term "dividend", for purposes of determining dividends eligible for the dividends paid deduction, refers only to a dividend described in section 316 (relating to definition of dividends for purposes of corporate distributions). No distribution, however, which is preferential within the meaning of section 562(c) and § 1.562-2 shall be eligible for the dividends paid deduction. Moreover, when computing the dividends paid deduction with respect to a U.S. person (as defined in section 957(d)), no distribution which is excluded from the gross income of a foreign corporation under section 959(b) with respect to such person or from gross income of such person under section 959(a) shall be eligible for such deduction. Further, for purposes of the dividends paid deduction, the term "dividend" does not include a distribution in liquidation unless the distribution is treated as a dividend under section 316(b)(2) and paragraph (b)(2) of § 1.316-1, or under section 333(e)(1) and paragraph (c) of § 1.333-4 or paragraph (c)(2), (d)(1)(ii), or (d)(2) of § 1.333-5, or qualifies under section 562(b) and paragraph (b) of this section. If a dividend is paid in property (other than money) the amount of the dividends paid deduction with respect to such property shall be the adjusted basis of the property in the hands of the distributing corporation at the time of the distribution. See paragraph (b)(2) of this section for special rules with respect to liquidating distributions by personal holding companies occurring during a taxable year of the distributing corporation beginning after December 31, 1963. Also see section 563 for special rules with respect to dividends paid after the close of the taxable year.

(b) Distributions in liquidation. *(1) General rules.* (i) In general. In the case of amounts distributed in liquidation by any corporation during a taxable year of such corporation beginning before January 1, 1964, or by a corporation other than a personal holding company (as defined in section 542) or a foreign personal holding company (as defined in section 522) during a taxable year of such a corporation beginning after December 31, 1963, section 562(b) makes an exception to the general rule that a deduction for dividends paid is permitted only with respect to dividends described in section 316. In order to qualify under that exception, the distribution must be one either in complete or partial liquidation of a corporation pursuant to sections 331, 332, or 333. See subparagraph (2) of this paragraph for rules relating to the treatment of distributions in complete liquidation made by a corporation which is a personal holding company to corporate shareholders during a taxable year of such distributing corporation beginning after December 31, 1963. As provided by section 346(a), for the purpose of section 562(b), a partial liquidation includes a redemption of stock to which section 302 applies. Amounts distributed in liquidation in a transaction which is preceded, or followed, by a transfer to another corporation of all or part of the assets of the liquidating corporation, may not be eligible for the dividends paid deduction.

(ii) Amount of dividends paid deduction allowable (a) General rule. In the case of distributions in liquidation with respect to which a deduction for dividends paid is permissible under subdivision (i) of this subparagraph, the amount of the deduction is equal to the part of such distribution which is properly chargeable to the earnings and profits accumulated after February 28, 1913. To determine the amount properly chargeable to the earnings and profits accumulated after February 28, 1913, there must be deducted from the amount of the distribution that part allocable to capital account. The capital account, for the purposes of this subdivision, includes not only amounts representing the par or stated value of the stock with respect to which the liquidation distribution is made, but also that stock's proper share of the paid-in surplus, and such other corporate items, if any, which, for purposes of income taxation, are treated like capital in that they are not taxable dividends when distributed but are applied against and reduce the basis of the stock. The remainder of the distribution in liquidation is, ordinarily, properly chargeable to the earnings and profits accumulated after February 28, 1913. Thus, if there is a deficit in earnings and profits on the first day of a taxable year, and the earnings and profits for such taxable year do not exceed such deficit, no dividends paid deduction would be allowed for such taxable year with respect to a distribution in liquidation; if the earnings and profits for such taxable year exceed the deficit in earnings and profits which existed on the first day of such taxable year, then a dividends paid deduction would be allowed to the extent of such excess.

(b) Special rule. Section 562(b)(1)(B) provides that in the case of a complete liquidation occurring within 24 months after the adoption of a plan of liquidation the amount of the deduction is equal to the earnings and profits for each taxable year in which distributions are made. Thus, if there is a distribution in liquidation pursuant to section 333, or a distribution in complete liquidation pursuant to section 331(a)(1) or 332 which occurs within a 24-month period after the adoption of a plan of liquidation, a dividends paid deduction will be allowable to the extent of the current earnings and profits for the taxable year or years even though there was a deficit in earnings and profits on the first day of such taxable year or years. In computing the earnings and profits for the taxable year in which the distributions are made, computation shall be made with the inclusion of capital gains and without any deduction for capital losses.

(c) Examples. The application of this subparagraph may be illustrated by the following examples:

Example (1). The Y Corporation, which makes its income tax returns on the calendar year basis, was organized on January 1, 1910, with an authorized and outstanding capital stock of 2,000 shares of common stock of a par value of $100 each and 1,000 shares of participating preferred stock of a par value of $100 each. The preferred stock was to receive annual dividends of $7 per share and $100 per share on complete liquidation of the corporation in priority to any payments on common stock, and was to participate equally with the common stock in either instance after the common stock had received a similar amount. However, the preferred stock was redeemable in whole or in part at the option of the board of directors at any time at $106 per share plus its proportion of the earnings of the company at the time of such redemption. In 1910 the preferred stock was issued at $106 per share, for a total of $106,000 and the common stock was issued, at $100 per share, for a total of $200,000. On July 15, 1954, the company had a paid-in surplus of $6,000, consisting of the premium received on the preferred stock; earnings and profits of $30,000 accumulated prior to March 1, 1913; and earnings and profits accumulated since February 28, 1913, of $75,000. On July 15, 1954, the option with respect to the preferred stock was exercised and the entire amount of such stock was redeemed at $141 per share or a total of $141,000 in a transaction upon which gain or loss to the distributees resulting from the exchange was determined and recognized under section 302(a). The amount of the distribution allocable to capital account was $116,000 ($100,000 attributable to part value, $6,000 attributable to paid-in surplus, and $10,000 attributable to earnings and profits accumulated prior to March 1, 1913). The remainder, $25,000 ($141,000, the amount of the distribution, less $116,000, the amount allocable to capital account) is properly chargeable to the earnings and profits accumulated since February 28, 1913, and is deductible as dividends paid.

Example (2). The M Corporation, a calendar year taxpayer, is completely liquidated on November 1, 1955, pursuant to a plan of liquidation adopted April 1, 1955. On January 1, 1955, the M Corporation has a deficit in earnings and profits of $100,000. During the period January 1, 1955, to the date of liquidation, November 1, 1955, it has earnings and profits of $10,000. The M Corporation is entitled to a dividends paid deduction in the amount of $10,000 as a result of its distribution in complete liquidation on November 1, 1955.

Example (3). The N Corporation, a calendar year taxpayer, is completely liquidated on July 1, 1958, pursuant to a plan of liquidation adopted February 1, 1955. No distributions in liquidation were made pursuant to the plan of liquidation adopted February 1, 1955, until the distribution in complete liquidation on July 1, 1958. On January 1, 1958, N Corporation had a deficit in earnings and profits of $30,000. During the period January 1, 1958, to the date of liquidation, July 1, 1958, the N Corporation has earnings and profits of $5,000. The N Corporation is not entitled to any deduction for dividends paid as a result of the distribution in complete liquidation on July 1, 1958. If the earnings and profits for the period January 1, 1958, to July 1, 1958, had been $32,000, the N Corporation would have been entitled to a deduction for dividends paid in the amount of $2,000.

(2) Special rule. (i) Distributions to corporate shareholders. In the case of amounts distributed in complete liquidation of a personal holding company (as defined in section 542) within 24 months after the adoption of a plan of liquidation, section 562(b)(2) makes a further exception to the general rule that a deduction for dividends paid is permitted only with respect to dividends described in section 316. The exception referred to in the preceding sentence applies only to distributions made in any taxable year of the distributing corporation beginning after December 31, 1963. Under the exception, the amount of any distribution within the 24-month period pursuant to the plan shall be treated as a dividend for purposes of computing the dividends paid deduction, but:

(a) Only to the extent that such amount is distributed to corporate distributees, and

(b) Only to the extent that such amount represents such corporate distributees' allocable share of undistributed personal holding company income for the taxable year of such distribution (computed with regard to section 316(b)(2)(B) and section 562(b)(2)).

Amounts distributed in liquidation in a transaction which is preceded, or followed, by a transfer to another corporation of all or part of the assets of the liquidating corporation, may not be eligible for the dividends paid deduction.

(ii) Corporate distributees' allocable share. For purposes of subdivision (i)(b) of this subparagraph—

(a) Except as provided in (b) of this subdivision, the corporate distributees' allocable share of undistributed personal holding company income for the taxable year of the distribution (computed without regard to sections 316(b)(2)(B) and 562(b)(2)) shall be determined by multiplying such undistributed personal holding company income by the ratio which the aggregate value of the stock held by all corporate shareholders immediately before the record date of the last liquidating distribution in such year bears to the total value of all stock outstanding on such date. For rules applicable in a case where the distributing corporation has more than one class of stock, see (c) of this subdivision (ii).

(b) If more than one liquidating distribution was made during the year, and if, after the record date of the first distribution but before the record date of the last distribution, there was a change in the relative shareholdings as between corporate shareholders and noncorporate shareholders, then the corporate distributees' allocable share of undistributed personal holding company income for the taxable year of the distributions (computed without regard to sections 316(b)(2)(B) and 562(b)(2)) shall be determined as follows:

(1) First, allocate the corporation's undistributed personal holding company income for the taxable year among the distributions made during such year by reference to the ratio which the aggregate amount of each distribution bears to the total amount of all distributions during such year;

(2) Second, determine the corporate distributees' allocable share of the corporation's undistributed personal holding company income for each distribution by multiplying the amount determined under (1) of this subdivision (b) for each distribution by the ratio which the aggregate value of the stock held by all corporate shareholders immediately before the record date of such distribution bears to the total value of all stock outstanding on such date; and

(3) Last, determine the sum of the corporate distributees' allocable share of the corporation's undistributed personal holding company income for all such distributions. For rules applicable in a case where the distributing corporation has more than one class of stock, see (c) of this subdivision (ii).

(c) Where the distributing corporation has more than one class of stock—

(1) The undistributed personal holding company income for the taxable year in which, or in respect of which, the distribution was made shall be treated as a fund from which dividends may properly be paid and shall be allocated between or among the classes of stock in a manner consistent with the dividend rights of such classes under local law and the pertinent governing instruments, such as, for example, the distributing corporation's articles or certificate of incorporation and bylaws;

(2) The corporate distributee's allocable share of the undistributed personal holding company income for each class of stock shall be determined separately in accordance with the rules set forth in (a) and (b) of this subdivision (ii) as if each class of stock were the only class of stock outstanding; and

(3) The sum of the corporate distributee's allocable share of the undistributed personal holding company income for the taxable year in which, or in respect of which, the distribution was made shall be the sum of the corporate distributees' allocable share of the undistributed personal holding company income for all classes of stock.

(d) For purposes of this subdivision (ii), in any case where the record date of a liquidating distribution cannot be ascertained, the record date of the distribution shall be the date on which the liquidating distribution was actually made.

(iii) Example. The application of this subparagraph may be illustrated by the following example:

Example. O Corporation, a calendar year taxpayer is completely liquidated on December 31, 1964, pursuant to a plan of liquidation adopted July 1, 1964. No distributions in liquidation were made pursuant to the plan of liquidation adopted July 1, 1964, until the distribution in complete liquidation on December 31, 1964. O Corporation has undistributed personal holding company income of $300,000 for the year 1964 (computed without regard to section 316(b)(2)(B) and section 562(b)(2)). On December 31, 1964, immediately before the record date of the distribution in complete liquidation, P Corporation owns 100 shares of O Corporation's outstanding stock and individual A owns the remaining 200 shares. All shares are equal in value. The amount which represents P Corporation's allocable share of undistributed personal holding company income is

$$\$100,000 \left(\frac{100 \text{ shares}}{300 \text{ shares}} \times \$300,000 \right)$$

and for purposes of computing the dividends paid deduction, such amount is treated as a dividend under section 562(b)(2) provided that the liquidating distribution to P Corporation equals or exceeds $100,000. P Corporation does not treat the $100,000 distributed to it as a dividend to which section 301 applies. For an example of the treatment of the distribution to individual A see example (5) of paragraph (e) of § 1.316-1.

(iv) Distributions to noncorporate shareholders. For the rules for determining the extent to which distributions in complete liquidation made to noncorporate shareholders by a personal holding company are dividends within the meaning of section 562(a), see section 316(b)(2)(B) and paragraph (b)(2) of § 1.316-1.

(c) Special definition of dividend for nonliquidating distributions by personal holding companies. Section 316(b)(2)(A) provides that in the case of a corporation which, under the law applicable to the taxable year in which or in respect of which a distribution is made, is a personal holding company, the term "dividend" (in addition to the general meaning set forth in section 316(a)) also means a nonliquidating distribution to its shareholders to the extent of the corporation's undistributed personal holding company income (determined under section 545 without regard to such distributions) for the taxable year in which or in respect of which the distribution is made. See paragraph (b)(1) of § 1.316-1.

T.D. 6308, 9/9/58, amend T.D. 6795, 1/28/65, T.D. 6949, 4/8/68, T.D. 7767, 2/3/81.

§ 1.562-2 Preferential dividends.

(a) Section 562(c) imposes a limitation upon the general rule that a corporation is entitled to a deduction for dividends paid with respect to all dividends which it actually pays during the taxable year. Before a corporation may be entitled to any such deduction with respect to a distribution regardless of the medium in which the distribution is made, every shareholder of the class of stock with respect to which the distribution is made must be treated the same as every other shareholder of that class, and no class of stock may be treated otherwise than in accordance with its dividend rights as a class. The limitation imposed by section 562(c) is unqualified, except in the case of an actual distribution made in connection with a consent distribution (see section 565), if the entire distribution composed of such actual distribution and consent distribution is not preferential. The existence of a preference is sufficient to prohibit the deduction regardless of the fact (1) that such preference is authorized by all the shareholders of the corporation or (2) that the part of the distribution received by the shareholder benefited by the preference is taxable to him as a dividend. A corporation will not be entitled to a deduction for dividends paid with respect to any distribution upon a class of stock if there is distributed to any shareholder of such class (in proportion to the number of shares held by him) more or less than his pro rata part of the distribution as compared with the distribution made to any other shareholder of the same class. Nor will a corporation be entitled to a deduction for dividends paid in the case of any distribution upon a class of stock if there is distributed upon such class of stock more or less than the amount to which it is entitled as compared with any other class of stock. A preference exists if any rights to preference inherent in any class of stock are violated. The disallowance, where any preference in fact exists, extends to the entire amount of the distribution and not merely to a part of such distribution. As used in this section, the term "distribution" includes a dividend as defined in subchapter C, chapter 1 of the Code, and a distribution in liquidation referred to in section 562(b).

(b) The application of the provisions of section 562(c) may be illustrated by the following examples:

Example (1). A, B, C, and D are the owners of all the shares of class A common stock in the M Corporation, which makes its income tax returns on a calendar year basis. With the consent of all the shareholders, the M Corporation on July 15, 1954, declared a dividend of $5 a share payable in cash on August 1, 1954, to A. On September 15, 1954, it declared a dividend of $5 a share payable in cash on October 1, 1954, to B, C, and D. No allowance for dividends paid for the taxable year 1954 is permitted to the M Corporation with respect to any part of the dividends paid on August 1, 1954, and October 1, 1954.

Example (2). The N Corporation, which makes its income tax returns on the calendar year basis, has a capital of $100,000 (consisting of 1,000 shares of common stock of a par value of $100) and earnings or profits accumulated after February 28, 1913, in the amount of $50,000. In the year 1954, the N Corporation distributes $7,500 in cancellation of 50 shares of the stock owned by three of the four shareholders of the corporation. No deduction for dividends paid is permissible under section 562(c) and paragraph (a) of this section with respect to such distribution.

Example (3). The P Corporation has two classes of stock outstanding, 10 shares of cumulative preferred, owned by E, entitled to $5 per share and on which no dividends have been paid for two years, and 10 shares of common, owned by F. On December 31, 1954, the corporation distributes a dividend of $125, $50 to E, and $75 to F. The corporation is entitled to no deduction for any part of such dividend paid, since there has been a preference to F. If, however, the corporation had distributed $100 to E and $25 to F, it would have been entitled to include $125 as a dividend paid deduction.

T.D. 6308, 9/9/58.

§ 1.562-3 Distributions by a member of an affiliated group.

A personal holding company which files or is required to file a consolidated return with other members of an affiliated group may be required to file a separate personal holding company schedule by reason of the limitations and exceptions provided in section 542(b) and § 1.542-4. Section 562(d) provides that in such case the dividends paid deduction shall be allowed to the personal holding company, with respect to a distribution made to any member of the affiliated group, if such distribution would constitute a dividend if it were made to a shareholder which is not a member of the affiliated group.

T.D. 6308, 9/9/58.

§ 1.563-1 Accumulated earnings tax.

In the determination of the dividends paid deduction for purposes of the accumulated earnings tax imposed by section 531, a dividend paid after the close of any taxable year and on or before the 15th day of the third month following the close of such taxable year shall be considered as paid during such taxable year, and shall not be included in the computation of the dividends paid deduction for the year of payment. However, the rule provided in section 563(a) is not applicable to dividends paid during the first two and one-half months of the first taxable year of the corporation subject to tax under chapter 1 of the Internal Revenue Code of 1954.

T.D. 6308, 9/9/58.

§ 1.563-2 Personal holding company tax.

In the case of a personal holding company subject to the provisions of section 541 dividends paid after the close of the taxable year and before the 15th day of the third month thereafter shall be included in the computation of the dividends paid deduction for the taxable year only if the taxpayer so elects in its return for such taxable year. The election shall be made by including such dividends in computing its dividends paid deduction. The amount of such dividends which may be included in computing the dividends paid deduction for the taxable year shall not exceed either—

(a) The undistributed personal holding company income of the corporation for the taxable year, computed without regard to this section, or

(b) In the case of a taxable year beginning after December 31, 1969, 20 percent (10 percent, in the case of a taxable year beginning before Jan. 1, 1970) of the sum of the dividends paid during the taxable year (not including consent dividends), computed without regard to this section.

In computing the amount of the dividends paid deduction allowable for any taxable year, the amount allowed by reason of section 563(b) for any preceding taxable year is considered a dividend paid in such preceding taxable year and not in the year of actual distribution. Thus, a double deduction is not allowable.

T.D. 6308, 9/9/58, amend T.D. 7079, 12/7/70.

§ 1.563-3 Dividends considered as paid on last day of taxable year.

(a) General rule. Where a distribution made after the close of the taxable year is considered as paid during such taxable year, for purposes of applying section 562(a) the distribution shall be considered as made on the last day of such taxable year.

(b) Personal holding company tax. In the case of a corporation which under the law applicable to the taxable year in respect of which a distribution is made under section 563(b) and § 1.563-2 is a personal holding company under the law applicable to such taxable year, section 316(b)(2) provides that the term dividend means (in addition to the general rule under section 316(a)) any distribution to the extent of the corporation's undistributed personal holding company income (determined under section 545 without regard to distributions under section 316(b)(2)) for such year. See paragraph (b) of § 1.316-1.

(c) Dividends paid on or before December 15, 1955. The Act of June 15, 1955 (Public Law 74, 75th Cong., 69 Stat. 136), repealed sections 452 and 462 of the Code, relating to prepaid income and reserve for estimated expenses. Under section 4(c)(4) of that Act, dividends paid after the 15th day of the third month following the close of the taxable year and on or before December 15, 1955, may be treated as having been paid on the last day of the taxable year for purposes of the accumulated earnings tax or the personal holding company tax and in the case of regulated investment companies, but only to the extent that such dividends are attributable to an increase in taxable income for the taxable year by reason of the repeal of sections 452 and 462. See paragraph (b) of § 1.9000-8, relating to treatment of certain dividends, prescribed pursuant to section 4(c)(4) of the Act of June 15, 1955.

T.D. 6308, 9/9/58.

Proposed § 1.563-3 Foreign personal holding company tax; procedure for designation of a dividend as being taken into account under section 563(c). [*For Preamble, see ¶ 151,485*]

In determining the deduction for dividends paid under section 561, a foreign personal holding company may designate a dividend paid after the close of any taxable year beginning after July 10, 1989, and on or before the 15th day of the third month following the close of that taxable year, as being taken into account under section 563(c) and this section by making the designation on an attachment to Schedule N of Form 5471. The designation must set forth the date of the distribution and a statement indicating the extent to which the distribution is being taken into account under section 563(c), and any other information required by Form 5471 and the instructions to that form. The designation must be signed and dated by a duly authorized corporate officer of the foreign personal holding company. If a foreign personal holding company took a dividend paid into account under section 563(c) for any taxable year beginning after July 10, 1989, and ending prior to [INSERT DATE THAT IS 120 DAYS AFTER DATE OF PUBLICATION OF FINAL REGULATIONS IN THE FEDERAL REGISTER] but did not follow the procedures set forth in this paragraph, then a designation on an attachment to Schedule N of Form 5471 setting forth the information required above should be signed in a manner set forth above and attached to the first Form 5471 and, if applicable, Form 1120F, to be filed after [INSERT DATE THAT IS 120 DAYS AFTER DATE OF PUBLICATION OF FINAL REGULATIONS IN THE FEDERAL REGISTER].

§ 1.564-1 Dividend carryover.

Caution: The Treasury has not yet amended Reg § 1.564-1 to reflect changes made by P.L. 94-455.

(a) General rule. The dividend carryover from the two preceding years, allowable only to personal holding companies, is includible in the dividends paid deduction under section 561. It is computed as follows:

(1) If, for each of the preceding two years, the deduction for dividends paid under section 561 (determined without regard to the dividend carryover to each such year) exceeds the taxable income (adjusted as provided in section 545 for purposes of determining undistributed personal holding company income) then the dividend carryover to the taxable year is the sum of both such excess amounts.

(2) If the deduction for dividends paid under section 561 for the second preceding year (determined without regard to the dividend carryover to such year) exceeds the taxable income for such year (adjusted as provided in section 545), and if the taxable income for the first preceding year (as so adjusted) exceeds the dividends paid deduction for such first preceding year (as so determined), then the dividend carryover to the taxable year shall be such excess amount for the second preceding year, less such excess amount for the first preceding year.

(3) If for the first preceding year the deduction for dividends paid under section 561 (determined without regard to the dividend carryover to such year) exceeds the taxable income (adjusted as provided in section 545) for such year, and such excess is not present in the second preceding year, then the dividend carryover to the taxable year shall be such excess amount for the first preceding year.

(b) Dividend carryover from year in which payer was not a personal holding company. In computing the dividend carryover, the taxable income as adjusted under section 545 of any preceding taxable year shall be determined as if the corporation was, under the law applicable to such taxable year, a personal holding company.

(c) Dividend carryover from year in which taxpayer was subject to 1939 Code. In a case where the first or the second preceding taxable year began before the taxpayer's first taxable year under the Internal Revenue Code of 1954, the amount of the dividend carryover shall be determined under the Internal Revenue Code of 1939.

(d) Statement to be filed with return. Every corporation claiming a dividend carryover for any taxable year shall file with its return for such year a concise statement setting forth the amount of the dividend carryover claimed and all material and pertinent facts relative thereto, including a detailed schedule showing the computation of the dividend carryover claimed.

(e) Computation of dividend carryover. The computation of the dividend carryover may be illustrated by the following examples:

Example (1). The X Corporation, which files its income tax returns on the calendar year basis, has taxable income, adjusted as required by section 545, in the amount of $110,000 and has a dividends paid deduction of $150,000 for the year 1954. For 1955, its taxable income, adjusted as required by section 545, is $200,000 and its dividends paid deduction is $300,000. The dividend carryover to the year 1956 is $140,000, computed as follows:

Dividends paid deduction for 1954	$150,000
Taxable income for 1954	110,000
Dividend carryover from 1954	40,000
Dividends paid deduction for 1955	300,000
Taxable income for 1955	200,000
Dividend carryover from 1955	100,000
Dividend carryover for 2 preceding taxable years, allowable as a deduction for the year 1956	140,000

Example (2). The Y Corporation, which files its income tax returns on the calendar year basis, has taxable income, adjusted as required by section 545, in the amount of $100,000 and has a dividends paid deduction of $150,000 for the year 1954. For 1955, its taxable income, adjusted as required by section 545, is $200,000 and its dividends paid deduction is $170,000. The dividend carryover to the year 1956 is $20,000 computed as follows:

Dividends paid deduction for 1954	$150,000
Taxable income for 1954	100,000
Dividend carryover from 1954	50,000
Taxable income for 1955	200,000
Dividends paid deduction for 1955	170,000
Excess of taxable income over dividends paid deduction	30,000
Dividend carryover for second preceding taxable year, allowable as a deduction for the year 1956	20,000

T.D. 6308, 9/9/58.

§ 1.565-1 General rule.

(a) Consent dividends. The dividends paid deduction, as defined in section 561, includes the consent dividends for the taxable year. A consent dividend is a hypothetical distribution (as distinguished from an actual distribution) made by:

(1) A corporation that has a reasonable basis to believe that it is subject to the accumulated earnings tax imposed in part I of subchapter G, chapter 1 of the Code, or

(2) A corporation described in part II (personal holding companies or a corporation with adjusted income from rents described in section 543(a)(2)(A) which utilizes the consent dividends described in section 543(a)(2)(B)(iii) to avoid personal holding company status) or part III (foreign personal holding companies) of subchapter G or in part I (regulated investment companies) or part II (real estate investment trusts) of subchapter M, chapter 1 of the Code. A consent dividend may be made by a corporation described in this paragraph to any person who owns consent stock on the last day of the taxable year of such corporation and who agrees to treat the hypothetical distribution as an actual dividend, subject to the limitations in section 565, § 1.565-2, and paragraph (c)(2) of this section, by filing a consent at the time and in the manner specified in paragraph (b) of this section.

(b) Making and filing of consents. *(1)* A consent shall be made on Form 972 in accordance with this section and the instructions on the form issued therewith. It may be made only by or on behalf of a person who was the actual owner on the last day of the corporation's taxable year of any class of consent stock, that is, the person who would have been required to include in gross income any dividends on such stock actually distributed on the last day of such year. Form 972 shall contain or be verified by a written declaration that it is made under the penalties of perjury. In the consent such person must agree to include in gross income for his taxable year in which or with which the taxable year of the corporation ends a specific amount as a taxable dividend.

(2) See paragraph (c) of this section and § 1.565-2 for the rules as to when all or a portion of the amount so specified will be disregarded for tax purposes.

(3) A consent may be filed at any time not later than the due date (including extensions) of the corporation's income tax return for the taxable year for which the dividends paid deduction is claimed. With such return, and not later than the due date (including extensions) thereof, the corporation must file Forms 972 for each consenting shareholder, and a return on Form 973 showing by classes the stock outstanding on the first and last days of the taxable year, the dividend rights of such stock, distributions made during the taxable year to shareholders, and giving all the other information required by the form. For taxable years beginning before January 1, 2003, the Form 973 filed with the corporation's income tax return shall contain or be verified by a written declaration that is made under the penalties of perjury and the Forms 972 filed with the return must be duly executed by the consenting shareholders. For taxable years beginning after December 31, 2002, the Form 973 filed with the corporation's income tax return shall be verified by signing the return and the Forms 972 filed with the return must be duly executed by the consenting shareholders or, if unsigned, must contain the same information as the duly executed originals. If the corporation submits unsigned Forms 972 with its return for a taxable year beginning after December 31, 2002, the duly executed originals are records that the corporation must retain and keep available for inspection in the manner required by § 1.6001-1(e).

(c) Taxability of amounts specified in consents. *(1)* The filing of a consent is irrevocable, and except as otherwise provided in section 565(b), § 1.565-2, and paragraph (c)(2) of this section, the full amount specified in a consent filed by a shareholder of a corporation described in paragraph (a) of this section shall be included in the gross income of the shareholder as a taxable dividend. Where the shareholder is taxable on a dividend only if received from sources within the United States, the amount specified in the consent of the shareholder shall be treated as a dividend from sources within the United States in the same manner as if the dividend has been paid in money to the shareholder on the last day of the corporation's taxable year. See paragraph (b) of this section relating to the making and filing of consents, and section 565(e) and § 1.565-5, with respect to the payment requirement in the case of nonresident aliens and foreign corporations.

(2) To the extent that the Commissioner determines that the corporation making a consent dividend is not a corporation described in paragraph (a) of this section, the amount specified in the consent is not a consent dividend and the amount specified in the consent will not be included in the gross income of the shareholder. In addition, where a corporation is described in paragraph (a)(1) but not paragraph (a)(2) of this section, to the extent that the Commissioner determines that the amount specified in a consent is larger than the amount of earnings subject to the accumulated earnings tax imposed by part I of subchapter G, such excess is not a consent dividend under paragraph (a) of this section and will not be included in the gross income of the shareholder.

(3) Except as provided in section 565(b), § 1.565-2 and paragraph (c)(2) of this section, once a shareholder's consent is filed, the full amount specified in such consent must be included in the shareholder's gross income as a taxable dividend, and the ground upon which a deduction for consent dividends is denied the corporation does not affect the taxability of a shareholder whose consent has been filed for the amount specified in the consent. For example, although described in part I, II, or III of subchapter G, or part I or II of subchapter M, chapter 1 of the Code, the corporation's taxable income (as adjusted under section 535(b), 545(b), 556(b), 852(b)(2), or 857(b)(2), as appropriate) may be less than the total of the consent dividends.

(4) A shareholder who is a nonresident alien or a foreign corporation is taxable on the full amount of the consent dividend that otherwise qualifies under this section even though that payment has not been made as required by section 565(e) and § 1.565-5.

(5) Income of a foreign corporation is not subject to the tax on accumulated earnings under part I of subchapter G,

chapter 1 of the Code except to the extent of U.S. source income, adjusted as permitted under section 535. See section 535(b) and (d) and § 1.535-1(b). Therefore, foreign source earnings (other than those distributions subject to resourcing under section 535(d)) of a foreign corporation that is not described in paragraph (a)(2) of this section cannot qualify for consent dividend treatment. Accordingly, a consent dividend made by a foreign corporation described in paragraph (a)(1) of this section shall not be effective with respect to all of the corporation's earnings, but shall relate solely to earnings which would have been, in the absence of the consent dividend, subject to the accumulated earnings tax.

T.D. 8244, 3/13/89, amend T.D. 9100, 12/18/2003, T.D. 9300, 12/7/2006.

§ 1.565-2 Limitations.

(a) General rule. Amounts specified in consents filed by shareholders or other beneficial owners of a corporation described in § 1.565-1(a) are not treated as consent dividends to the extent that—

(1) They would constitute a preferential dividend or

(2) They would not constitute a dividend (as defined in section 316), if distributed in money to shareholders on the last day of the taxable year of the corporation. If any portion of any amount specified in a consent filed by a shareholder of a corporation described in the preceding sentence is not treated as a consent dividend under section 565(b) and this section, it is disregarded for all tax purposes. For example, it is not taxable to the consenting shareholder, and paragraph (c) of § 1.565-1 is not applicable to this portion of the amount specified in the consent.

(b) Preferential distribution. *(1)* A preferential distribution is an actual distribution, or a consent distribution, or a combination of the two, which involves a preference to one or more shares of stock as compared with other shares of the same class or to one class of stock as compared with any other class of stock. See section 562(c) and § 1.562-2.

(2) The application of section 565(b)(1) and § 1.565-2(b) may be illustrated by the following examples:

Example (1). The X Corporation, a personal holding company, which makes its income tax returns on the calendar year basis, has 200 shares of stock outstanding, owned by A and B in equal amounts. On December 15, 1987, the corporation distributes $600 to B and $100 to A. As a part of the same distribution, A executes a consent to include $500 in his gross income as a taxable dividend although such amount is not distributed to him. The X Corporation, assuming the other requirements of section 565 have been complied with, is entitled to a consent dividends deduction of $500. Although the consent dividend is deemed to have been paid on December 31, 1987, the last day of the taxable year of the corporation, the total amount of all distributions constitutes a single nonpreferential distribution of $1200.

Example (2). The Y corporation, a personal holding company, which makes its income tax returns on the calendar year basis, has one class of consent stock outstanding, owned in equal amounts by A, B, and C. If A and B each receive a distribution in cash of $5,000 and C consents to include $3,000 in gross income as a taxable dividend, the combined actual and consent distribution of $13,000 is preferential. See section 562(c) and § 1.562-2(a). Similarly, if no one receives a distribution in cash, but A and B each consents to include $5,000 as a taxable dividend in gross income and C agrees to include only $3,000, the entire consent distribution is preferential.

Example (3). The Z Corporation, which makes its income tax returns on the calendar year basis and is subject, for the taxable year in question, to the accumulated earnings tax, has only two classes of stock outstanding, each class being consent stock and consisting of 500 shares. Class A, with a par value of $40 per share, is entitled to two-thirds of any distribution of earnings and profits. Class B, with a par value of $20 per share, is entitled to one-third of any distribution of earnings and profits. On December 15, 1987, there is distributed on the class B stock $2 per share, or $1,000, and shareholders of the class A stock consent to include in gross income amounts equal to $2 per share, or $1,000. The entire distribution of $2,000 is preferential, inasmuch as the class B stock has received more than its pro rata share of the combined amounts of the actual distributions and the consent distributions.

(c) Section 316 Limitation. *(1)* An additional limitation under section 565(b) is that the amounts specified in consents which may be treated as consent dividends cannot exceed the amounts which would constitute a dividend (as defined in section 316) if the corporation had distributed the total specified amounts in money to shareholders on the last day of the taxable year of the corporation. If only a portion of such total would constitute a dividend, then only a corresponding portion of each specified amount is treated as a consent dividend.

(2) The application of section 565(b)(2) and § 1.565-2(c) may be illustrated by the following example:

Example. The X Corporation, a corporation described in § 1.565-(a)(1) or (2), which makes its income tax returns on the calendar year basis, has only one class of stock outstanding, owned in equal amounts by A and B. It makes no distributions during the taxable year 1987. Its earnings and profits for the calendar year 1987 amount to $8,000, there being at the beginning of such year no accumulated earnings or profits. A and B execute proper consents to include $5,000 each in their gross income as a dividend received by them on December 31, 1987. The sum of the amounts specified in the consents executed by A and B is $10,000, but if $10,000 had actually been distributed by the X corporation on December 31, 1987, only $8,000 would have constituted a dividend under section 316(a). The amount which could be considered as consent dividends in computing the dividends paid deduction for purposes of the accumulated earnings tax is limited to $8,000, or $4,000 of the $5,000 specified in each consent. The remaining $1,000 in each consent is disregarded for all tax purposes. (In the case of a personal holding company, see also the example in § 1.565-3(b).)

T.D. 8244, 3/13/89.

§ 1.565-3 Effect of consent.

(a) General Rule. The amount of the consent dividend that is described in paragraph (a) of § 1.565-1 shall be considered, for all purposes of the Code, as if it were distributed in money by the corporation to the shareholder on the last day of the taxable year of the corporation, received by the shareholder on such day, and immediately contributed by the shareholder as paid-in capital to the corporation on such day. Thus, the amount of the consent dividend will be treated by the shareholder as a dividend. The shareholder will be entitled to the dividends received deduction under section 243 or 245 with respect to such consent dividend. The basis of the shareholder's consent stock in a corporation will be increased by the amount thus treated in his hands as a dividend which he is considered as having contributed to the corporation as paid-in capital. The amount of the current dividend will also be treated as a dividend received from sources within the United States in the same manner as if the dividend had been paid in money to the shareholders. Among other effects of the consent dividend, the earnings and profits of the corporation will be decreased by the amount of the consent dividends. Moreover, if the shareholder is a corporation, its accumulated earnings and profits will be increased by the amount of the consent dividend with respect to which it makes a consent.

(b) Example. The application of section 565(c) may be illustrated by the following example:

Example. Corporation A, a personal holding company and a calendar year taxpayer, has one shareholder, individual B, whose consent to include $10,000 in his gross income for the calendar year 1987 has been timely filed. A has $8,000 of earnings and profits at the beginning of 1987. A has $10,000 of undistributed personal holding company income (determined without regard to distributions under section 316(b)(2)) for 1987. B must include $10,000 in his gross income as a taxable income and is treated as having immediately contributed $10,000 to A as paid-in capital. See section 316(b)(2).

T.D. 8244, 3/13/89.

§ 1.565-4 Consent dividends and other distributions.

Section 565(d) provides a rule applicable where a distribution is made in part in consent dividends and in part in money or other property. With respect to such a distribution the entire amount specified in the consents and the amount of such money or other property shall be considered together. Thus, if as a part of the same distribution consents are filed by some of the shareholders and cash is distributed to other shareholders, for example, those who may be unwilling to sign consents, the total amount of the cash and the amounts specified in the consents will be viewed as a single distribution to determine the tax effects of such distribution. For example, the total of such amounts must be considered to determine whether the distribution (including the amounts specified in the consents) is preferential and whether any part of such distribution would not be dividends if the total amounts specified in the consents were distributed in cash. See paragraph (b)(2) of § 1.565-2 for examples illustrating the treatment of distributions which consist in part of consent dividends and in part of other property.

T.D. 6308, 9/9/58.

§ 1.565-5 Nonresident aliens and foreign corporations.

(a) Withholding. In the event that a corporation makes a consent dividend, as described in § 1.565-1(a), to a shareholder that is subject to a withholding tax under section 1441 or 1442 on a distribution of cash or other property, the corporation must remit an amount of tax equal to the withholding tax that would be imposed under section 1441 or 1442 if an actual cash distribution equal to the consent dividend had been paid to the shareholder on the last day of the corporation's taxable year. Such payment must be in one of the following forms:

(1) Cash,

(2) United States postal money order,

(3) Certified check drawn on a domestic bank, provided that the law of the place where the bank is located does not permit the certification to be rescinded prior to presentation,

(4) A cashier's check of a domestic bank, or

(5) A draft on a domestic bank or a foreign bank maintaining a United States agency or branch and payable in United States funds.

The amount of such payment shall be credited against the tax imposed on the shareholder.

T.D. 8244, 3/13/89.

§ 1.565-6 Definitions.

(a) Consent stock. *(1)* The term "consent stock" includes what is generally known as common stock. It also includes participating preferred stock, the participation rights of which are unlimited.

(2) The definition of consent stock may be illustrated by the following example:

Example. If in the case of the X Corporation, a personal holding company, there is only one class of stock outstanding, it would all be consent stock. If, on the other hand, there were two classes of stock, class A and class B, and class A was entitled to 6 percent before any distribution could be made on class B, but class B was entitled to everything distributed after class A had received its 6 percent, only class B stock would be consent stock. Similarly, if class A, after receiving its 6 percent, was to participate equally or in some fixed proportion with class B until it had received a second 6 percent, after which class B alone was entitled to any further distributions, only class B stock would be consent stock. The same result would follow if the order of preferences were class A 6 percent, then class B 6 percent, then class A a second 6 percent, either alone or in conjunction with class B, then class B the remainder. If, however, class A stock is entitled to ultimate participation without limit as to amount, then it, too, may be consent stock. For example, if class A is to receive 3 percent and then share equally or in some fixed proportion with class B in the remainder of the earnings or profits distributed, both class A stock and class B stock are consent stock.

(b) Preferred dividends. *(1)* The term "preferred dividends" includes all fixed amounts (whether determined by percentage of par value, a stated return expressed in a certain number of dollars per share, or otherwise) the distribution of which on any class of stock is a condition precedent to a further distribution of earnings or profits (not including a distribution in partial or complete liquidation). A distribution, though expressed in terms of a fixed amount, is not a preferred dividend, however, unless it is preferred over a subsequent distribution within the taxable year upon some class or classes of stock other than one on which it is payable.

(2) The definition of preferred dividends may be illustrated by the following example:

Example. If, in the case of the X Corporation, there are only two classes of stock outstanding, class A and class B, and class A is entitled to a distribution of 6 percent of par, after which the balance of the earnings and profits are distributable on class B exclusively, class A's 6 percent is a preferred dividend. If the order of preferences is class A $6 per share, class B $6 per share, then class A and class B in fixed proportions until class A receives $3 more per share, then class B the remainder, all of class A's $9 per share and $6 per share of the amount distributable on class B are preferred dividends. The amount which class B is entitled to receive in conjunction with the payment to class A of its last $3 per share is not a preferred dividend, because the payment of such amount is preferred over no subsequent distribution except one made on class B itself. Finally, if a distribution must be $6 on class A, $6 on class B, then on class A and class B share and share alike, the distribution on class A of $6 and the distribution on class B of $6 are both preferred dividends.

T.D. 8244, 3/13/89.

§ 1.581-1 Banks.

(a) In order to be a bank as defined in section 581, an institution must be a corporation for federal tax purposes. See § 301.7701-2(b) of this chapter for the definition of a corporation.

(b) This section is effective as of January 1, 1997.

T.D. 6188, 7/5/56, amend T.D. 8697, 12/17/96.

§ 1.581-2 Mutual savings banks, building and loan associations, and cooperative banks.

Caution: The Treasury has not yet amended Reg § 1.581-2 to reflect changes made by P.L. 104-188.

(a) While the general principles for determining the taxable income of a corporation are applicable to a mutual savings bank, a building and loan association, and a cooperative bank not having capital stock represented by shares, there are certain exceptions and special rules governing the computation in the case of such institutions. See section 593 for special rules concerning additions to reserves for bad debts. See section 591 and § 1.591-1, relating to dividends paid by banking corporations, for special rules concerning deductions for amounts paid to, or credited to the accounts of, depositors or holders of withdrawable accounts as dividends. See also section 594 and § 1.594-1 for special rules governing the taxation of a mutual savings bank conducting a life insurance business.

(b) For the purpose of computing the net operating loss deduction provided in section 172, any taxable year for which a mutual savings bank, building and loan association, or a cooperative bank not having capital stock represented by shares was exempt from tax shall be disregarded. Thus, no net operating loss carryover shall be allowed from a taxable year beginning before January 1, 1952, and, in the case of any taxable year beginning after December 31, 1951, the amount of the net operating loss carryback or carryover from such year shall not be reduced by reference to the income of any taxable year beginning before January 1, 1952.

T.D. 6188, 7/5/56, amend T.D. 8697, 12/17/96.

PAR. 2. Section 1.581-2(b) is amended by removing the phrase "See section 593 and § 1.593-1" and inserting in its place "See section 593 and §§ 1.593-1 through 1.593-8".

Proposed § 1.581-2 Mutual savings banks, building and loan associations, and cooperative banks [Amended]. [*For Preamble, see ¶ 150,911*]

§ 1.582-1 Bad debts, losses, and gains with respect to securities held by financial institutions.

Caution: The Treasury has not yet amended Reg § 1.582-1 to reflect changes made by P.L. 104-188, P.L. 100-647, P.L. 99-514, P.L. 98-369, P.L. 94-455.

(a) Bad debt deduction for banks. A bank, as defined in section 581, is allowed a deduction for bad debts to the extent and in the manner provided by subsections (a), (b), and (c) of section 166 with respect to a debt which has become worthless in whole or in part and which is evidenced by a security (a bond, debenture, note, certificate, or other evidence of indebtedness to pay a fixed or determinable sum of money) issued by any corporation (including governments and their political subdivisions), with interest coupons or in registered form.

(b) Worthless stock in affiliated bank. For purposes of section 165(g)(1), relating to the deduction for losses involving worthless securities, if the taxpayer is a bank (as defined in section 581) and owns directly at least 80 percent of each class of stock of another bank, stock in such other bank shall not be treated as a capital asset.

(c) Pre-1970 sales and exchanges of bonds, etc., by banks. For taxable years beginning before July 12, 1969, with respect to the taxation under subtitle A of the Code of a bank (as defined in section 581), if the losses of the taxable year from sales or exchanges of bonds, debentures, notes, or certificates, or other evidences of indebtedness, issued by any corporation (including one issued by a government or political subdivision thereof), exceed the gains of the taxable year from such sales or exchanges, no such sale or exchange shall be considered a sale or exchange of a capital asset.

(d) Post-1969 sales and exchanges of securities by financial institutions. For taxable years beginning after July 11, 1969, the sale or exchange of a security is not considered the sale or exchange of a capital asset if such sale or exchange is made by a financial institution to which any of the following sections applies: Section 585 (relating to banks), 586 (relating to small business investment companies and business development corporations), or 593 (relating to mutual savings banks, domestic building and loan associations, and cooperative banks). This paragraph shall apply to determine the character of gain or loss from the sale or exchange of a security notwithstanding any other provision of subtitle A of the Code, such as section 1233 (relating to short sales). However, this paragraph shall have no effect in the determination of whether a security is a capital asset under section 1221 for purposes of applying any other provision of the Code, such as section 1232 (relating to original issue discount). For purposes of this paragraph, a security is a bond, debenture, note, or certificate or other evidence of indebtedness, issued by any person. See paragraphs (e) and (f) of this section for special transitional rules applicable, respectively, to banks and to small business investment companies and business development corporations.

(e) Transition rule for qualifying securities held by banks. *(1) In general.* Notwithstanding the provisions of paragraph (d) of this section, if the net long-term capital gain from sales and exchanges of qualifying securities exceeds the net short-term capital loss from such sales and exchanges in any taxable year beginning after July 11, 1969, such excess shall be treated as long-term capital gain, but in an amount not to exceed the net gain from sales and exchanges of securities in such year. For purposes of computing such net gain, a capital loss carried to the taxable year under section 1212 shall not be taken into account. See section 1222 and the regulations thereunder for definitions of the terms "net long-term capital gain" and "net short-term capital loss." For purposes of this paragraph:

(i) The term "security" means a security within the meaning of paragraph (d) of this section.

(ii) The term "qualifying security" means a security which is held by the bank on July 11, 1969, and continuously thereafter until it is first sold or exchanged by the bank.

See also subparagraph (4) of this paragraph for rules under which the time certain securities are held is deemed to include a period of time determined under section 1223 (1) and (2) with respect to such security.

(2) Computation of capital gain or loss. For purposes of this paragraph, the amount of gain or loss from the sale or exchange of a qualifying security treated as capital gain or loss is determined by multiplying the amount of gain or loss recognized from such sale or exchange by a fraction the numerator of which is the number of days before July 12, 1969, that such security was held by the bank and the denominator of which is the sum of the number of days included in the numerator and the number of days the security was held by the bank after July 11, 1969.

(3) Special rules. For purposes of subparagraphs (1) and (2) of this paragraph, the following items are not taken into account:

(i) Any amount treated as original issue discount under section 1232, and

(ii) Any amount which, without regard to section 582(c) and this section, would be treated as gain or loss from the sale or exchange of property which is not a capital asset, such as an amount which is realized from the sale or exchange of a security which is held by a bank as a dealer in securities.

(4) Holding period in certain cases. For purposes of this paragraph—

(i) The time a security received in an exchange is deemed to have been held by a bank includes a period of time determined under section 1223(1) with respect to such security.

(ii) The time a security transferred to a bank from another bank is deemed to have been held by the transferee bank includes a period of time determined under section 1223(2) with respect to such security.

For example, if a bank on December 3, 1972, surrendered an obligation of the United States which it held as a capital asset on July 11, 1969, in a transaction to which section 1037 applied, the time during which the newly received obligation is deemed to have been held includes the time during which the surrendered obligation was deemed to have been held by the bank. Because the surrendered obligation was held on July 11, 1969, the newly acquired obligation is deemed to have been held on that date and is a qualifying security. The period during which the surrendered obligation is deemed to have been held is taken into account in computing the fraction determined under subparagraph (2) of this paragraph with respect to the newly received obligation.

(5) Examples. The provisions of this paragraph may be illustrated by the following examples:

Example (1). Bank A, a calendar year taxpayer, purchased a qualifying security on July 14, 1968, and held it to maturity on August 20, 1970, when it was redeemed. The redemption resulted in a taxable gain of $10,000. The security was held by the bank for 363 days before July 12, 1969, and for a total of 768 days. During the taxable year, the bank had no other gains and no losses from sales or exchanges of qualifying securities, but had a net loss of $4,000 from sales of securities other than qualifying securities. The portion of the gain from the redemption of the qualifying security treated as capital gain under subparagraph (2) of this paragraph is $4,726.56 (363/768 × $10,000). Because the net gain of the taxable year from sales and exchanges of securities, $6,000 ($10,000 – $4,000), exceeds the portion of the gain on the sale of the qualifying security treated as capital gain under this paragraph, $4,726.56 is treated as long-term capital gain on the sale of the qualifying security for the taxable year.

Example (2). Assume the same facts as in example (1), except that the bank's net loss of the taxable year from the sale of securities other than qualifying securities was $7,000. The amount considered as long-term capital gain under this paragraph is limited by the amount of gain on the sale of securities to $3,000 ($10,000 – $7,000).

(f) Small business investment companies and business development corporations. *(1) Election.* In the case of a small business investment company or a business development corporation, described in section 586(a), section 582(c) does not apply for taxable years beginning after July 11, 1969, and before July 11, 1974, unless the taxpayer elects that such section shall apply. In the case of a small business investment company, see paragraph (a)(1) of § 1.1243-1 if such an election is made, but see paragraph (a)(2) of § 1.1243-1 if such an election is not made. Such election applies to all such taxable years and, except as provided in subparagraph (3) of this paragraph, is irrevocable. Such election must be made not later than (i) the time, including extensions thereof, prescribed by law for filing the taxpayer's income tax return for its first taxable year beginning after July 11, 1969, or (ii) June 8, 1970, whichever is later.

(2) Manner of making election. An election pursuant to the provisions of this paragraph is made by the taxpayer by a written statement attached to the taxpayer's income tax return (or an amended return) for its first taxable year beginning after July 11, 1969. Such statement shall indicate that the election is made pursuant to section 433(d) of the Tax Reform Act of 1969 (83 Stat. 624). The taxpayer shall attach to its income tax return for each subsequent taxable year to which such election is applicable a statement indicating that the election has been made and the amount to which it applies for such year.

(3) Revocation of election. An election made pursuant to subparagraph (2) of this paragraph shall be irrevocable unless—

(i) A written application for consent to revoke the election, setting forth the reasons therefor, is filed with the Commissioner within 90 days after the permanent regulations relating to section 433(d)(2) of the Tax Reform Act of 1969 (83 Stat. 624) are filed with the Office of the Federal Register, and

(ii) The Commissioner consents to the revocation.

The revocation is effective for all taxable years to which the election applied.

T.D. 6188, 7/5/56, amend T.D. 6362, 2/16/59, T.D. 7171, 3/16/72.

PAR. 14. In § 1.582-1, paragraphs (d) and (e)(3)(i) are amended by removing the phrase "section 1232" from each place that it appears and adding in its place the phrase "sections 1271 through 1275".

Proposed § 1.582-1 Bad debts, losses, and gains with respect to securities held by financial institutions [Amended]. [*For Preamble, see ¶ 151,065*]

§ 1.584-1 Common trust funds.

(a) Method of taxation. A common trust fund maintained by a bank is not subject to taxation under this chapter and is not considered a corporation. Its participants are taxed on their proportionate share of income from the common trust fund.

(b) Conditions for qualification. *(1)* For a fund to be qualified as a common trust fund it must be maintained by a bank (as defined in section 581) in conformity with the rules and regulations of the Comptroller of the Currency, exclusively for the collective investment and reinvestment of contributions to the fund by the bank. The bank may either act alone or with one or more other fiduciaries, but it must act solely in its capacity as one or a combination of the following: (i) As a trustee of a trust created by will, deed, agreement, declaration of trust, or order of court; (ii) as an executor of a will or as an administrator of an estate; (iii) as a guardian (by whatever name known under local law) of the estate of an infant, of an incompetent individual, or of an absent individual; or (iv) on or after October 3, 1976, as a custodian of a Uniform Gifts to Minors account. A Uniform Gifts to Minors account is an account established pursuant to a State law substantially similar to the Uniform Gifts to Minors Act. (See the Uniform Gifts to Minors Act of 1956 or the Uniform Gifts to Minors Act of 1966, as published by the National Conference of Commissioners on Uniform State Laws.) The Commissioner will publish a list of the States whose laws he determines to be substantially similar to such uniform acts. A bank that maintains a Uniform Gifts to Minors Act account must establish, to the satisfaction of the Commissioner or his delegate, that with respect to the account the bank has duties and responsibilities similar to the duties and responsibilities of a trustee or guardian.

(2) A common trust fund may be a participant in another common trust fund.

(c) Affiliated groups. For taxable years beginning after December 31, 1975, two or more banks that are members of the same affiliated group (within the meaning of section 1504) are treated, for purposes of section 584, as one bank for the period of their affiliation. A common trust fund may be maintained by one or by more than one member of an affiliated group. Any member of the group may, but need not, contribute to the fund. Further, for purposes of this paragraph, members of an affiliated group may be, but need not be, cotrustees of the common trust fund.

T.D. 6188, 7/5/56, amend T.D. 6651, 5/16/63, T.D. 7935, 1/12/84.

§ 1.584-2 Income of participants in common trust fund.

Caution: The Treasury has not yet amended Reg § 1.584-2 to reflect changes made by P.L. 108-27.

(a) Each participant in a common trust fund is required to include in computing its taxable income for its taxable year within which or with which the taxable year of the fund ends, whether or not distributed and whether or not distributable:

(1) Its proportionate share of short-term capital gains and losses, computed as provided in § 1.584-3;

(2) Its proportionate share of long-term capital gains and losses, computed as provided in § 1.584-3; and

(3) Its proportionate share of the ordinary taxable income or the ordinary net loss of the common trust fund, computed as provided in § 1.584-3.

(b) Any tax withheld at the source from income of the fund (e.g., under section 1441) is deemed to have been withheld proportionately from the participants to whom such income is allocated.

(c) *(1)* The proportionate share of each participant's short-term capital gains and losses, long-term capital gains and losses, ordinary taxable income or ordinary net loss, dividends and interest received, and tax withheld at the source shall be determined under the method of accounting adopted by the bank in accordance with the written plan by which the common trust fund is established and administered, provided such method clearly reflects the income of each participant.

(2) Items of income and deductions shall be allocated to the periods between valuation dates established by the plan within the taxable year in which they were realized. Ordinary taxable income or ordinary net loss, short-term capital gains and losses, long-term capital gains and losses, and tax withheld at the source shall be computed for each period. The participants' proportionate shares of income and losses for each period shall then be determined.

(3) For taxable years beginning on or after September 22, 1980, any amount of income or loss of the common trust fund which is included in the computation of a participant's taxable income for the taxable year shall be treated as income or loss from an unrelated trade or business to the extent that such amount would have been income or loss from an unrelated trade or business if such participant had made directly the investments of the common trust fund.

(4) The provisions of this paragraph may be illustrated by the following example:

Example. (i) The plan of a common trust fund provides for quarterly valuation dates and for the computation and the distribution of the income upon a quarterly basis, except that there shall be no distribution of capital gains. The participants are as follows: Trusts A, B, C, and D for the first quarter; Trusts A, B, C, and E for the second quarter; and Trusts A, B, F, and G for the third and fourth quarters, the participants having equal participating interests. As computed upon the quarterly basis, the ordinary taxable income, the short-term capital gain, and the long-term capital loss for the taxable year were as follows:

	First quarter	Second quarter	Third quarter	Fourth quarter	Total
Ordinary taxable income	$200	$300	$200	$400	$1,100
Short-term capital gain	200	100	200	100	600
Long-term capital loss	100	200	100	200	600

(ii) The participants shares or ordinary taxable income are as follows:

Participant's Shares of Ordinary Taxable income

Participant	First quarter	Second quarter	Third quarter	Fourth quarter	Total
A	$50	$75	$50	$100	$275
B	50	75	50	100	275
C	50	75			125
D	50				50
E		75			75
F			50	100	150
G			50	100	150
Total	200	300	200	400	1,100

(iii) The participants shares of the short-term capital gain are as follows:

Participants' Shares of Short-Term Capital Gain

Participant	First quarter	Second quarter	Third quarter	Fourth quarter	Total
A	$50	$25	$50	$25	$150
B	50	25	50	25	150
C	50	25			75
D	50				50
E		25			25
F			50	25	75
G			50	25	75
Total	200	100	200	100	600

(iv) The participants shares of the long-term capital loss are as follows:

Participants' Shares of Long-Term Capital Loss

Participant	First quarter	Second quarter	Third quarter	Fourth quarter	Total
A	$25	$50	$25	$50	$150
B	25	50	25	50	150
C	25	50			75
D	25				25
E		50			50
F			25	50	75
G			25	50	75
Total	100	200	100	200	600

(v) If in the above example the common trust fund also had short-term capital losses and long-term capital gains, the treatment of such gains or losses would be similar to that accorded to the short-term capital gains and long-term capital losses in the above example.

(vi) Assume in the above example that participant Trust A qualified as a trust forming part of a pension, profit sharing, or stock bonus plan under section 401(a). Assume further that 20 percent of the ordinary taxable income of the common trust fund would be unrelated business taxable income (as defined under section 512(a)(1)) if received directly by Trust A. Under paragraph (c)(3), participant Trust A, for purposes of computing its taxable income must treat its proportionate share of the common trust fund's ordinary taxable income as income from an unrelated trade or business to the extent such amount would have been income from an unrelated trade or business if Trust A had directly made the investments of the common trust fund. Therefore, participant Trust A must take into account 20 percent of its proportionate share of the common trust fund's ordinary taxable income as income from an unrelated trade or business.

(d) The provisions of part I, subchapter J, chapter 1 of the Code, or, as the case may be, the provisions of subchapters D, F, or H of chapter 1 of the Code are applicable in determining the extent to which each participant's proportionate share of any income or loss of the common trust fund is taxable to the participant, or to a person other than the participant.

T.D. 6188, 7/5/56, amend T.D. 6777, 12/15/64, T.D. 7935, 1/12/84, T.D. 8662, 5/1/96.

§ 1.584-3 Computation of common trust fund income.

The taxable income of the common trust fund shall be computed in the same manner and on the same basis as in the case of an individual, except that:

(a) No deduction shall be allowed under section 170 (relating to charitable, etc., contributions and gifts);

(b) The gains and losses from sales or exchanges of capital assets of the common trust fund are required to be segregated. A common trust fund is not allowed the benefit of the capital loss carryover provided by section 1212; and

(c) The ordinary taxable income (the excess of the gross income over deductions) or the ordinary net loss (the excess of the deductions over the gross income) shall be computed after excluding all items of gain and loss from sales or exchanges of capital assets.

T.D. 6188, 7/5/56, amend T.D. 7935, 1/12/84.

§ 1.584-4 Admission and withdrawal of participants in the common trust fund.

(a) Gain or loss. The common trust fund realizes no gain or loss by the admission or withdrawal of a participant, and the basis of the assets and the period for which they are deemed to have been held by the common trust fund for the purposes of section 1202 are unaffected by such admission or withdrawal. For taxable years of participants ending after April 7, 1976, and for transfers occurring after that date, the transfer of property by a participant to a common trust fund is treated as a sale or exchange of the property transferred. If a participant withdraws the whole or any part of its participating interest from the common trust fund, such withdrawal shall be treated as a sale or exchange by the participant of the participating interest or portion thereof which is so withdrawn. A participant is not deemed to have withdrawn any part of its participating interest in the common trust fund so as to have completed a closed transaction by reason of the segregation and administration of an investment of the fund, pursuant to the provisions of 12 CFR 9.18(b)(7) (or, for periods before September 28, 1962, 12 CFR 206.17(c)(7)), for the benefit of all the then participants in the common trust fund. Such segregated investment shall be considered as held by, or on behalf of, the common trust fund for the benefit ratably of all participants in the common trust fund at the time of segregation, and any income or loss arising from its administration and liquidation shall constitute income or loss to the common trust fund apportionable among the participants for whose benefit the investment was segregated. When a participating interest is transferred by a bank, or by two or more banks that are members of the same affiliated group (within the meaning of section 1504), as a result of the combination of two or more common trust funds or the division of a single common trust fund, the transfer to the surviving or divided fund is not considered to be an admission or a withdrawal if the combining, dividing, and resulting common trust funds have diversified portfolios. For purposes of this paragraph (a), a common trust fund has a diversified portfolio if it satisfies the 25 and 50-percent tests of section 368(a)(2)(F)(ii), applying the relevant provisions of section 368(a)(2)(F). However, Government securities are included in total assets for purposes of the deominator of the 25 and 50-percent tests (unless the government securities are acquired to meet the 25 and 50-percent tests), but are not treated as securities of an issuer for purposes of the numerator of the 25 and 50-percent tests. In addition, for a transfer of a participating interest in a division of a common trust fund not to be considered an admission or withdrawal, each participant's pro rata interest in each of the resulting common trust funds must be substantially the same as was the participant's pro rata interest in the dividing fund. However, in the case of the division of a common trust fund maintained by two or more banks that are members of the same affiliated group resulting from the termination of such affiliation, the division will be treated as meeting the requirements of the preceding sentence if the written plans of operation of the resulting common trust funds are substantially identical to the plan of operation of the dividing common trust fund, each of the assets of the dividing common trust fund are distributed substantially pro rata to each of the resulting common trust funds, and each participant's aggregate interest in the assets of the resulting common trust funds of which he or she is a participant in substantially the same as was the participant's pro rata interest in the assets of the dividing common trust fund. The plan of operation of a resulting common trust fund will not be considered to be substantially identical to that of the dividing common trust fund where, for example, the plan of operation of the resulting common trust fund contains restrictions as to the types of participants that may invest in the common trust fund where such restrictions were not present in the plan of operation of the dividing common trust fund.

(b) Basis for gain or loss upon withdrawal. The participant's gain or loss upon withdrawal of its participating interest or portion thereof shall be measured by the difference between the amount received upon such withdrawal and the adjusted basis of the participating interest or portion thereof withdrawn plus the additions prescribed in paragraph (c) of this section and minus the reductions prescribed in paragraph (d) of this section. The amount received by the participant shall be the sum of any money plus the fair market value of property (other than money) received upon such withdrawal. The basis of the participating interest or portion thereof withdrawn shall be the sum of any money plus the fair market value of any property (other than money) contributed by the participant to the common trust fund to acquire the participating interest or portion thereof withdrawn. Such basis shall not be reduced on account of the segregation of any investment in the common trust fund pursuant to the provisions of 12 CFR 9.18(b)(7) (or, for periods before September 28, 1962, 12 CFR 206.17(c)(7)). For the purpose of making the adjustments, additions, and reductions with respect to basis as prescribed in this paragraph, the ward, rather than the guardian, shall be deemed to be the participant; and the grantor, rather than the trust, shall be deemed to be the participant, to the extent that the income of the trust is taxable to the grantor under subpart E (section 671 and following), part I, subchapter J, chapter 1 of the Code.

(c) Additions to basis. As prescribed in paragraph (b) of this section, in computing the gain or loss upon the withdrawal of a participating interest or portion thereof, there shall be added to the basis of the participating interest or portion thereof withdrawn an amount equal to the aggregate of the following items (to the extent that they were properly allocated to the participant for a taxable year of the common trust fund and were not distributed to the participant prior to withdrawal):

(1) Wholly exempt income of the common trust fund for any taxable year,

(2) Net income of the common trust fund for the taxable years beginning after December 31, 1935, and prior to January 1, 1938.

(3) Net short-term capital gain of the common trust fund for each taxable year beginning after December 31, 1937,

(4) The excess of the gains over the losses recognized to the common trust fund upon sales or exchanges of capital assets held (i) for more than 18 months for taxable years beginning after December 31, 1937, and before January 1, 1942, (ii) for more than 6 months for taxable years beginning after December 31, 1941, and before January 1, 1977, (iii) for more than 9 months for taxable years beginning 1977, and (iv) for more than 1 year for taxable years beginning after December 31, 1977, and

(5) Ordinary net or taxable income of the common trust fund for each taxable year beginning after December 31, 1937.

(d) Reductions in basis. As prescribed in paragraph (b) of this section, in computing the gain or loss upon the withdrawal of a participating interest or portion thereof, the basis of the participating interest or portion thereof withdrawn shall be reduced by such portions of the following items as were allocable to the participant with respect to the participating interest or portion thereof withdrawn:

(1) The amount of the excess of the allowable deductions of the common trust fund over its gross income for the taxable years beginning after December 31, 1935, and before January 1, 1938, and

(2) The net amount of the net short-term capital loss, net long-term capital loss, and ordinary net loss of the common trust fund for each taxable year beginning after December 31, 1937.

(e) Effective date. The eighth sentence of paragraph (a) of this section is effective for combinations and divisions of common trust funds completed on or after May 2, 1996.

T.D. 6188, 7/5/56, amend T.D. 6651, 5/16/63, T.D. 7935, 1/12/84, T.D. 8662, 5/1/96.

§ 1.584-5 Returns of banks with respect to common trust funds.

For rules applicable to filing returns of common trust funds, see section 6032 and the regulations thereunder.

T.D. 6188, 7/5/56.

§ 1.584-6 Net operating loss deduction.

The net operating loss deduction is not allowed to a common trust fund. Each participant in a common trust fund, however, will be allowed the benefits of such deduction. In the computation of such deduction, a participant in a common trust fund shall take into account its pro rata share of items of income, gain, loss, deduction, or credit of the common trust fund. The character of any such item shall be determined as if the participant had realized such item directly from the source from which realized by the common trust fund, or incurred such item in the same manner as incurred by the common trust fund.

T.D. 6188, 7/5/56.

§ 1.585-1 Reserve for losses on loans of banks.

Caution: The Treasury has not yet amended Reg § 1.585-1 to reflect changes made by P.L. 104-188.

(a) General rule. As an alternative to a deduction from gross income under section 166(a) for specific debts which become worthless in whole or in part, a financial institution to which section 585 and this section apply shall be allowed a deduction under section 585(a) (or, for taxable years beginning before January 1,1987 section 166(c)) for a reasonable addition to a reserve for bad debts provided such financial institution has adopted or adopts the reserve method of treating bad debts in accordance with paragraph (b) of § 1.166-1. In the case of such a taxpayer the amount of the reasonable addition to such reserve for a taxable year beginning after July 11, 1969, shall be an amount determined by the taxpayer which does not exceed the amount computed under § 1.585-2. Such reasonable addition for the taxable year shall be an amount at least equal to the amount provided by § 1.585-2(a)(2). For each taxable year the taxpayer must include in its income tax return (or amended return) for that year a computation of the amount of the addition determined under this section showing the method used to determine that amount. The use of a particular method in the return for a taxable year is not a binding election by the taxpayer to apply such method either for such taxable year or for subsequent taxable years. A financial institution to which section 585 and this section apply which adopts the reserve method is not entitled to charge off any bad debts pursuant to section 166(a) with respect to a loan (as defined in § 1.585-2(e)(2)). Except as provided by § 1.585-3, the reserve for bad debts of a financial institution to which section 585 and this section apply shall be established and maintained in the same manner as is provided by section 585 (or, for taxable years beginning before January 1, 1987, section 166(c)) and the regulations under section 166 with respect to reserves for bad debts. Except as provided by this section, no deduction is allowable for an addition to a reserve for losses on loans as defined in § 1.585-2(e)(2) of financial institution to which section 585 and this section apply. For rules relating to deduction with respect to debts which are not loans (as defined in § 1.585-2(e)(2)), see section 166(a) and the regulations thereunder. For rules relating to a debt evidenced by a security (as defined in section 165(g)(2)(c)), see sections 166 and 582(a) and the regulations thereunder. For the definition of certain terms, see paragraph (e) of § 1.585-2. For rules relating to a transaction to which section 381(a) applies, see § 1.585-4. For rules relating to large banks, see §§ 1.585-5 through 1.585-8.

(b) Application of section. *(1) In general.* Except as provided in paragraph (b)(2) of this section, section 585 and this section apply to the following financial institutions—

(i) Any bank (as defined in section 581 and the regulations thereunder) other than a mutual savings bank, domestic building and loan association, or cooperative bank, to which section 593 applies; and

(ii) Any corporation to which paragraph (b)(1)(i) of this section would apply except for the fact that it is a foreign corporation and in the case of any such foreign corporation, the rules provided by section 585(a) and (b), this section, §§ 1.585-2, 1.585-3, and 1.585-4 apply only with respect to loans outstanding the interest on which is effectively connected with the conduct of a banking business within the United States.

(2) Exception. For taxable years beginning after December 31, 1986, section 585(a) and (b) and this section do not apply to any large bank (as defined in section 1.585-5(b)). For these years, a large bank may not deduct any amount under section 585 or any other section for an addition to a reserve for bad debts.

T.D. 7532, 1/18/78, amend T.D. 8513, 12/28/93.

§ 1.585-2 Addition to reserve.

(a) In general. *(1) Maximum addition.* For taxable years beginning before January 1, 1988, the maximum reasonable addition to the reserve for losses on loans as defined in paragraph (e)(2) of this section is the amount allowable under the percentage method provided by paragraph (b) of this section or the experience method provided by paragraph (c) of this section, whichever is greater. For taxable years beginning after December 31, 1987, the maximum reasonable addition to the reserve for losses on loans is the amount determined under the experience method provided by paragraph (c) of this section.

(2) Minimum addition. For taxable years beginning before December 31, 1976, and before January 1, 1988, a taxpayer to which this section applies shall make a minimum addition to the reserve for losses on loans as defined in paragraph (e)(2) of this section. For purposes of this subparagraph, the term "minimum addition" means an addition to the reserve for losses on loans in an amount equal to the lesser of (i) the amount allowable under section 585(b)(3)(A) and paragraph (c)(1)(ii) of this section, or (ii) the maximum amount allowable under section 585(b)(2) and paragraph (b) of this section. For taxable years beginning after December 31, 1987, a taxpayer to which this section applies shall make a minimum addition to the reserve for losses on loans for each taxable year in an amount equal to the amount allowable under section 585(b)(3)(A) and paragraph (c)(1)(ii) of this section.

(b) Percentage method. *(1) In general.* (i) Maximum addition. Except as limited under subparagraph (2) of this paragraph, the maximum reasonable additional to the reserve for losses on loans under the percentage method for a taxable year is the amount determined under paragraph (b)(1)(ii), (iii), or (iv) of this section, whichever is applicable. For purposes of this paragraph, the term "allowable percentage" means 1.8 percent for taxable years beginning before 1976; 1.2 percent for taxable years beginning after 1975 but before 1982; 1.0 percent for taxable years beginning in 1982; and 0.6 percent for taxable years beginning after 1982 and before 1988. This paragraph does not apply for taxable years beginning after 1987.

(ii) Reserve less than allowable percentage of eligible loans. (A) If the reserve for losses on loans as of the close of the base year is less than the allowable percentage for the taxable year multiplied by the eligible loans outstanding at the close of the base year, the amount determined under this subdivision for the taxable year is the amount necessary to increase the balance of the reserve for losses on loans as of the close of the taxable year to an amount equal to the allowable percentage for the taxable year multiplied by the eligible loans outstanding at the close of that year, except that the amount determined with respect to the reserve deficiency shall not exceed one-fifth of the reserve deficiency. For purposes of this section, the term "reserve deficiency" means the excess of the allowable percentage for the taxable year multiplied by the eligible loans outstanding at the close of the base year over the reserve for losses on loans as of the close of the base year. Where a taxpayer has recoveries of bad debts for a taxable year which exceed the bad debts sustained for such year, the taxpayer is not required to reduce its otherwise permissible current addition by the amount of the net recovery. A reasonable addition attributable to an increase in eligible loans outstanding at the close of the taxable year over eligible loans outstanding at the close of the base year may be made only for the portion of such increase which does not exceed the excess of eligible loans outstanding at the close of the taxable year over the sum of the amount of eligible loans outstanding at the close of the base year and the amount of previous increases in such loans for which an addition was made in taxable years ending after the close of the base year. For purposes of this subdivision, the order in which the factors which make up the annual reserve addition shall be claimed is:

(1) An amount equal to one-fifth of the reserve deficiency;

(2) Net bad debts charged to the reserve; and

(3) An amount attributable to an increase in the amount of eligible loans outstanding.

(B) For its first taxable year, a newly organized financial institution to which § 1.585-1 and this section apply shall be considered to have no reserve deficiency. For example, a new financial institution would compute its annual reserve addition by including in such addition an amount not in excess of the sum of *(1)* the amount of its net bad debts charged to the reserve for the taxable year, and (2) the allowable percentage of the increase in its eligible loans outstanding at the close of the taxable year over the amount of its loans outstanding (zero) at the end of the year preceding its first taxable year. Such amount would be subject to the 0.6 percent limitations provided in subparagraph (2) of this paragraph.

(C) The application of the rules provided by this subdivision may be illustrated by the following example:

Example. The X Bank is a commercial bank which has a calendar year as its taxable year. X adopted the reserve method of accounting for bad debts in 1950. On December 31, 1969, X has $1,000,000 of outstanding eligible loans and a balance of $13,000 in its reserve for losses on loans. The base year is 1969 and, consequently, X has a reserve deficiency of $5,000 ((1.8% × $1,000,000) – $13,000).

(a) During 1970, X has net bad debts of $1,000 charged to the reserve for losses on loans. On December 31, 1970, X has $1,050,000 of outstanding eligible loans. The maximum reasonable addition under the percentage method is $2,900 which consists of $1,000 of reserve deficiency (⅕ × $5,000), the $1,000 in net bad debts charged to the reserve for losses on loans, and $900 attributable to the increase in the balance of eligible loans (1.8% × $1,050,000 – $1,000,000). Assuming that X makes an addition to the reserve for losses on loans of $2,900 for the year, the balance of the reserve as of December 31, 1970 is $14,900 ($13,000 – $1,000 + $2,900).

(b) During 1971, X has net debts of $1,000 charged to the reserve for losses on loans. On December 31, 1971, X has $800,000 of outstanding eligible loans. The allowable percentage of eligible loans is $14,400 (1.8% × $800,000). The maximum reasonable addition under the percentage method is $500 which is a portion of one-fifth of the reserve deficiency. Assuming that X makes an addition to the reserve for losses on loans of $500 for the year, the balance of the reserve as of December 31, 1971, is $14,400 ($14,900 – $1,000 + $500).

(c) During 1972, X has net bad debts of $600 charged to the reserve for losses on loans. On December 31, 1972, X has $850,000 of outstanding eligible loans. The allowable percentage of eligible loans is $15,300 (1.8% × $850,000). The maximum reasonable addition under the percentage method is $1,500 which consists of $1,000 of reserve deficiency (⅕ × $5,000) and $500 of the net bad debts charged to the reserve for losses on loans in 1971. Even though the full addition with respect to the reserve deficiency in 1971 was not made, the amount of the addition that can be made in 1972 with respect to the reserve deficiency is limited to one-fifth of such deficiency. Assuming that X makes an addition to the reserve for losses on loans of $1,500 for the year, the balance of the reserve as of December 31, 1972, is $15,300 ($14,400 – $600 + $1,500).

(d) During 1973, X did not have any net bad debts charged to the reserve for losses on loans. On December 31, 1973, X has $1,000,000 of outstanding eligible loans. The allowable percentage of eligible loans is $18,000 (1.8% × $1,000,000). The maximum reasonable addition under the percentage method is $2,100 which consists of $1,000 of reserve deficiency (⅕ × $5,000), $500 of net bad debts charged to the reserve for losses in 1971, and $600 of net bad debts charged to the reserve in 1972. Although outstanding eligible loans increased from $850,000 in 1972 to $1,000,000 in 1973, no addition is permitted with respect to the increase because the amount of eligible loans outstanding at the close of 1973 ($1,000,000) does not exceed the sum of the amount of such loans at the close of the base year ($1,000,000) and the amount of previous increases in such loans for which an addition was made in taxable years ending after the close of the base year ($50,000 loan increase in 1970). Assuming that X makes an addition to the reserve for losses on loans of $2,100, the balance of the reserve as of December 31, 1973, is $17,400 ($15,300 + $2,100).

(iii) Reserve equal to or greater than allowable percentage and eligible loans have not declined. If the reserve for losses on loans as of the close of the base year is equal to or greater than the allowable percentage for the taxable year multiplied by the eligible loans outstanding at the close of the base year and if the amount of eligible loans outstanding at the close of the taxable year is equal to or greater than the amount of eligible loans outstanding at the close of the base year, the amount determined under this subdivision is the amount necessary to increase the reserve to the greater of (A) the allowable percentage for the taxable year multiplied by the eligible loans outstanding at the close of the year, or (B) the balance of the reserve as of the close of the base year. The application of the rule provided by this subdivision may be illustrated by the following example:

Example. The M Bank is a commercial bank which has a calendar year as its taxable year. M adopted the reserve method of accounting for bad debts in 1950. On December 31, 1969, M has $1,000,000 of outstanding eligible loans and a balance of $20,000 in its reserve for losses on loans.

(a) During 1970, M has net bad debts of $1,000 charged to the reserve for losses on loans. On December 31, 1970, M has $1,100,000 of outstanding eligible loans. The allowable percentage of eligible loans is $19,800 (1.8% × $1,100,000). The maximum reasonable addition under the percentage method is $1,000 which is the amount sufficient to increase the balance of the reserve as of the close of the taxable year to the balance of the reserve as of the close of the 1969 base year ($20,000). Assuming that M makes an addition to the reserve for losses on loans of $1,000 for the year, the balance of the reserve as of December 31, 1970, is $20,000 ($20,000 – $1,000 + $1,000).

(b) During 1971, M has net bad debts of $1,000 charged to the reserve for losses on loans. On December 31, 1971, M has $1,300,000 of outstanding eligible loans. The allowable percentage of eligible loans is $23,400 (1.8% × $1,300,000). The maximum reasonable addition under the percentage method is $4,400 which is the amount sufficient to increase the balance of the reserve to the allowable percentage of eligible loans outstanding at the close of the taxable year. Assuming that M makes an addition to the reserve for losses on loans of $4,400 for the year, the balance of the reserve as of December 31, 1971, is $23,400 ($20,000 – $1,000 + $4,400).

(c) During 1972, M has net bad debts of $1,000 charged to the reserve for losses on loans. On December 31, 1972, M has $1,200,000 of outstanding eligible loans. The allowable percentage of eligible loans is $21,600 (1.8% × $1,200,000). No reasonable addition may be made under the percentage method because the reserve for losses on loans ($22,400, i.e., $23,400 – $1,000) is greater than the allowable percentage of eligible loans outstanding at the close of the taxable year ($21,600) and the balance of the reserve as of the close of the base year ($20,000). Assuming that no amount is added under the experience method provided by paragraph (c) of this section, the balance of the reserve for losses on loans as of December 31, 1972, is $22,400 ($23,400 – $1,000).

(d) During 1973, M has net bad debts of $1,000 charged to the reserve for losses on loans. On December 31, 1973, M has $1,200,000 of outstanding eligible loans. The allowable percentage of eligible loans of $21,600 (1.8% × $1,200,000). The maximum reasonable addition under the percentage method is $200 which is the amount sufficient to increase the reserve for losses on loans to the allowable percentage of eligible loans outstanding at the close of the taxable year. Assuming that M makes an addition to the reserve for losses on loans of $200 for the year, the balance of the reserve as of December 31, 1973, is $21,600 ($22,400 – $1,000 + $200).

(iv) Reserve greater than allowable percentage and eligible loans have declined. If the reserve for losses on loans as of the close of the base year is equal to or greater than the allowable percentage of eligible loans outstanding at such time and if the amount of eligible loans at the close of the taxable year is less than the amount of eligible loans outstanding at the close of the base year, the amount determined under this subdivision is the amount necessary to increase the balance of the reserve to the amount which bears the same ratio to eligible loans outstanding at the close of the taxable year as the balance of the reserve as of the close of the base year bears to the amount of eligible loans outstanding at the close of the base year. The application of the rule provided by this subdivision may be illustrated by the following example:

Example. The N Bank is a commercial bank which has a calendar year as its taxable year. N adopted the reserve method of accounting for bad debts in 1950. On December 31, 1969, N has $1,000,000 of outstanding eligible loans and a balance of $20,000 in its reserve for losses on loans.

(a) During 1970, N has net bad debts of $3,000 charged to the reserve for losses on loans. On December 31, 1970, N has $900,000 of outstanding eligible loans. The maximum reasonable addition under the percentage method is $1,000, which is the amount necessary to increase the balance of the reserve to the amount ($18,000) which bears the same ratio to eligible loans outstanding at the close of the taxable year ($900,000) as the balance of the reserve as of the close of the base year ($20,000) bears to the amount of the eligible loans outstanding at the close of the base year ($1,000,000). Assuming that N makes an addition to the reserve for losses on loans of $1,000 for the year, the balance of the reserve as of December 31, 1970, is $18,000 ($20,000 – $3,000 + $1,000).

(b) During 1971, N has net bad debts of $1,000 charged to the reserve for losses on loans. On December 31, 1971, N has $1,100,000 of outstanding eligible loans. The maximum reasonable addition under the percentage method, determined under subdivision (111) of this subparagraph, is $3,000 which is the amount necessary to increase the balance of the reserve to the greater of the allowable percentage of eligible loans outstanding at the close of the taxable year ($19,800) or the balance of the reserve at the close of the base year ($20,000). Assuming that N makes an addition to the reserve for loses on loans of $3,000 for the year, the balance of the reserve as of December 31, 1971, is $20,000 ($18,000 – $1,000 + $3,000).

(2) *Limitations.* Notwithstanding any other provision of this paragraph, the maximum reasonable addition to the reserve for losses on loans under the percentage method shall not exceed the greater of—

(i) Six-tenths of 1 percent of the eligible loans outstanding at the close of the taxable year, or

(ii) An amount sufficient to increase the reserve for losses on loans at the close of the taxable year to six-tenths of 1 percent of the eligible loans outstanding at the close of the taxable year.

The application of the rules provided by this subparagraph may be illustrated by the following example:

Example. The Y Bank begins business as a commercial bank on July 1, 1974. Y adopts the calendar year as its taxable year and the reserve method of accounting for bad debts.

(a) During 1974, Y has net bad debts of $1,000. On December 31, 1974, Y has $1,000,000 maximum reasonable addition under subparagraph (1)(ii)(B) of this paragraph, because Y is a newly-organized financial institution, there is no reserve deficiency. Except for the limitations of this subparagraph, the maximum reasonable addition under subparagraph (1)(ii)(A) of this paragraph would be the amount of net bad debts charged to the reserve for losses ($1,000) plus the allowable percentage of outstanding eligible loans at the close of the taxable year $18,000 (1.8% × $1,000,000). However, because of the limitations of this subparagraph, the maximum reasonable addition to the reserve for losses on loans under the percentage method is an amount sufficient to increase the balance of the reserve for losses on loans to $6,000 which is 0.6 percent of the eligible loans outstanding at the close of the taxable year. Assuming that Y makes an addition to the reserve for losses on loans of $7,000 for the year, the balance of the reserve as of December 31, 1974, is $6,000 ($7,000 – $1,000). The $7,000 consists of the $1,000 in net bad debts and $6,000 attributable to the increase in eligible loans outstanding.

(b) During 1975, Y has net bad debts of $1,000 charged to the reserve for losses on loans. On December 31, 1975, Y has $1,000,000 of outstanding eligible loans. Except for the limitations of this subparagraph, the maximum reasonable addition under subparagraph (1)(ii)(A) of this paragraph would be the amount of net bad debts charged to the reserve for losses ($1,000) plus an amount attributable to the increase in the amount of eligible loans outstanding with respect to which no reasonable addition was allowed in 1974 ($12,000, *i.e.*, $18,000 – $6,000). However, because of the limitations of this paragraph, the maximum reasonable addition to the reserve for losses on loans under the percentage method is $6,000 which is an amount equal to 0.6 percent of the eligible loans outstanding at the close of the taxable year. This amount consists of net bad debts of $1,000 and $5,000 attributable to a portion of the increase in eligible loans in 1974 with respect to which no reasonable addition was allowable for 1974. Assuming that Y makes an addition to the reserve for losses on loans of $6,000 for the year, the balance of the reserve as of December 31, 1975, is $11,000 ($6,000 – $1,000 + $6,000).

(c) During 1976, Y has net bad debts charged to the reserve for losses on loans of $1,000. On December 31, 1976, Y has $1,000,000 in outstanding eligible loans. At the close of 1975 (Y's base year for 1976), the amount of outstanding eligible loans was also $1,000,000. Consequently, there is a reserve deficiency of $1,000 ((1.2% × $1,000,000) – $11,000). The maximum reasonable addition to the reserve for losses under subparagraph (1)(ii)(A) of this paragraph is

$1,200 which consists of one-fifth of the reserve deficiency ($1,000 × 1/5 = $200) and the net bad debts charged to the reserve for losses on loans for the year ($1,000). Because that amount is less than 0.6 percent of the eligible loans outstanding at the close of the taxable year (0.6% × $1,000,000 = $6,000), the limitations of this subparagraph do no apply. Assuming that Y makes an addition to the reserve for losses on loans of $1,200 for the year, the balance of the reserve as of December 31, 1976, is $11,200 ($11,000 − $1,000 + $1,200).

(c) Experience method: *(1) In general.* (i) Maximum addition. The amount determined under this paragraph for a taxable year is the amount necessary to increase the balance of the reserve for losses on loans (as of the close of the taxable year) to the greater of the amount determined under subdivision (ii) or (iii) of this subparagraph. For special rules for a new financial institution, see subparagraph (2) of this paragraph.

(ii) Six-year moving average amount. The amount determined under this subdivision is the amount which bears the same ratio to loans outstanding at the close of the taxable year as (A) the total bad debts sustained during the taxable year and the 5 preceding taxable years (or, with the approval of the Commissioner, a shorter period), adjusted for recoveries of bad debts during such period, bears to (B) the sum of the loans outstanding at the close of such 6 (or fewer) taxable years. For purposes of applying this subdivision, a period shorter than 6 years generally would be appropriate only where there is a change in the type of a substantial portion of the loans outstanding such that the risk of loss is substantially increased. For example, if the major portion of a bank's portfolio of loans changes from agricultural loans to industrial loans which results in a substantial increase in the risk of loss, a period shorter than 6 years may be appropriate. Similarly, a bank which has recently altered its lending practices to include in its portfolio of loans consumer-installment loans, when it had previously made only commercial loans, may also qualify to use a period shorter than six years. A decline in the general economic conditions in the area, which substantially increase the risk of loss, is a relevant factor which may be considered. In any case, however, approval to use a shorter period will not be granted unless the taxpayer supplies specific evidence that the loans outstanding at the close of the taxable years for the shorter period requested are not comparable in nature and risk to loans outstanding at the close of the six taxable years. The fact that a bank's bad debt experience has shown a substantial increase is not, by itself, sufficient to justify use of a shorter period. If approval is granted to use a shorter period, the experience for those taxable years which are excluded shall not be used for any subsequent year. A request for approval to exclude the experience of a prior taxable year shall not be considered unless it is sent to the Commissioner at least 30 days before the close of the first taxable year for which such approval is requested.

(iii) Base year amount. The amount determined under this subdivision is the lower of (A) the balance of the reserve as of the close of the base year, or (B) if the amount of loans outstanding at the close of the taxable year is less than the amount of loans outstanding at the close of the base year, the amount which bears the same ratio to loans outstanding at the close of the taxable year as the balance of the reserve as of the close of the base year bears to the amount of loans outstanding at the close of the base year.

(2) Special rules for new financial institutions. (i) In general. In the case of any taxable year preceded by less than 5 authorization years (as defined in paragraph (e)(5) of this section), subparagraph (1) of this paragraph shall be applied with the adjustments provided by subdivision (ii) of this subparagraph.

(ii) Adjustments. (A) The total bad debts for the 6-year period computed under subparagraph (1)(ii)(A) of this paragraph shall be the sum of:

(1) The bad debts sustained by the taxpayer during its authorization years, adjusted for recoveries of bad debts for such years, and

(2) That fraction of the total bad debts sustained by a comparable bank (as defined in paragraph (e)(7) of this section) during the comparison years (as defined in paragraph (e)(6) of this section), adjusted for recoveries of bad debts for such years, which bears the same ratio to such total as the average loans outstanding of the taxpayer during the authorization years bears to the average loans outstanding of the comparable bank during the comparison years.

(B) The total amount of loans outstanding during the 6-year period computed under subparagraph (1)(ii)(B) of this paragraph shall be six times the average loans outstanding of the taxpayer during the authorization years.

(d) Change in accounting method from specific charge-off method to reserve method of treating bad debts. *(1) In general.* If a bank is granted permission in accordance with § 1.446-1(e)(3) to change its method of accounting for bad debts from a method under which specific bad debt items are deducted to the reserve method of treating bad debts, the taxpayer shall effect the change as provided in subparagraphs (2) and (3) of this paragraph.

(2) Initial balance of the reserve. The initial balance of the reserve at the close of the year of change shall be no less than the minimum addition as described in paragraph (a)(2) of this section and shall be no larger than the greater of—

(i) The allowable percentage of eligible loans outstanding at the close of the taxable year of change, or

(ii) The amount which bears the same ratio to loans outstanding at the close of the taxable year as the total bad debts sustained during the taxable year and the 5 preceding taxable years (or, with the approval of the Commissioner, a shorter period), adjusted for recoveries of bad debts during such period, bears to the sum of the loans outstanding at the close of such 6 or fewer taxable years.

In the case of taxable years beginning after 1987, the initial balance of the reserve at the end of the year of change shall be the amount specified in subdivision (ii) of this subparagraph.

(3) Deduction with respect to initial balance. The deduction with respect to the initial balance of the reserve at the close of the taxable year of change, determined under subparagraph (2) of this paragraph, is allowable ratably over a period of 10 years commencing with the taxable year of change (or a shorter period as may be approved by the Commissioner). Thus, the bad debt deduction under section 166 for the taxable year of change will consist of the amount of debts determined to be wholly or partially worthless and charged-off during such taxable year plus one-tenth (if a 10-year period is used) of the amount of the reserve determined under subparagraph (2) of this paragraph. For each of the 9 taxable years following the taxable year of change, the bad debt deduction will consist of the reasonable addition to the reserve for bad debts for each such year as provided by section 585, as otherwise determined, plus one-tenth of the amount determined to be the initial balance of the reserve under subparagraph (2) of this paragraph. The amount estab-

lished as a bad debt reserve for the taxable year of change under subparagraph (2) of this paragraph shall be considered as the balance of the reserve for purposes of determining the amount of subsequent additions to such reserve, even though the entire amount of the reserve may not have been deducted under section 585(a)(1) or former section 166(c) because of the requirement that it be deducted over a number of years.

(e) Definitions. *(1) Base year.* (i) Percentage method. For purposes of paragraph (b) of this section (relating to the percentage method), the term "base year" means: For years beginning before 1976, the last taxable year beginning on or before July 11, 1969; for taxable years beginning after 1975 but before 1983, the last taxable year beginning before 1976; and, for taxable years beginning after 1982, the last taxable year beginning before 1983. However, for purposes of section 585(b)(2)(A) the term "base year" means the last taxable year before the most recent adoption of the percentage method, if later than the base year as determined under the preceding sentence.

(ii) Experience method. For purposes of paragraph (c) of this section (relating to the experience method), the term "base year" means (A) the last taxable year before the most recent adoption of the experience method, or (B) the last taxable year beginning on or before July 11, 1969, which ever is later; and for taxable years beginning after 1987, the last taxable year beginning before 1988.

(iii) Example. The application of the rules provided by this subparagraph may be illustrated by the following example:

Example. The T Bank is a commercial bank which has a calendar year as its taxable year. T adopted the reserve method of accounting for bad debts in 1950. On December 31, 1969, T has $1,000,000 of outstanding eligible loans and a balance of $19,300 in its reserve for losses on loans.

(a) During 1970, T has net bad debts of $1,000 charged to the reserve for losses on loans. On December 31, 1970, T has $1,050,000 of outstanding eligible loans. T elects the percentage method. The base year is 1969. The maximum reasonable addition under the percentage method of $1,000 which is the amount sufficient to increase the balance of the reserve as of the close of the taxable year to the balance of the reserve as of the close of the base year 1969 ($19,300). Assuming that T makes an addition to the reserve for losses on loans of $1,000 for the year, the balance of the reserve for losses on loans as of December 31, 1970, is $19,300 ($19,300 – $1,000 + $1,000).

(b) During 1971, T has net bad debts of $8,000 charged to the reserve for losses on loans. On December 31, 1971, T has $1,100,000 of outstanding eligible loans. T elects the experience method. The base year is 1970. The maximum reasonable addition under the experience method is $8,000 which is the amount sufficient to increase the balance of the reserve as of the close of the taxable year to the balance of the reserve as of the close of the 1970 base year ($19,300). Assuming that T makes an addition to the reserve for losses on loans of $8,000 for the year, the balance of the reserve for losses on loans as of December 31, 1971, is $19,300 ($19,300 – $8,000 + $8,000).

(c) During 1972, T has net bad debts of $1,000 charged to the reserve for losses on loans. On December 31, 1972, T has $1,200,000 of outstanding eligible loans. T elects the percentage method. The base year is 1971 and there is a reserve deficiency of $500 ((1.8% × $1,100,000) – $19,300). The maximum reasonable addition under the percentage method is $2,900 which consists of $100 of reserve deficiency (⅕ × $500), the $1,000 in net bad debts charged to the reserve for losses on loans, and $1,800 attributable to the increase in the balance of eligible loans (1.8% × ($1,200,000 – $1,100,000)). Assuming that T makes an addition to the reserve for losses on loans of $2,900 for the year, the balance of the reserve for losses on loans as of December 31, 1972 is $21,200 ($19,300 – $1,000 + $2,900).

(2) Loan. (i) General rule. For purposes of this section and §§ 1.585-1, 1.585-3, and 1.585-4, the term "loan" means debt as the term "debt" is used in section 166 and the regulations thereunder. The term "loan" includes (but is not limited to) the following items:

(A) An overdraft in one or more deposit accounts by a customer in good faith whether or not other deposit accounts of the same customer have balances in excess of the overdraft;

(B) A bankers acceptance purchased or discounted by a bank; and

(C) A loan participation to the extent that the taxpayer bears a risk of loss.

For purposes of (B) of this subdivision (i), a bankers acceptance shall be considered as a loan made by the bank which purchased or discounted the bankers acceptance and not a loan made by the originating bank.

(ii) Exceptions. Notwithstanding the provisions of subdivision (i) of this subparagraph, the term "loan" does not include the following items:

(A) Discount or interest receivable reflected in the face amount of an outstanding loan, which discount or interest has not been included in gross income;

(B) For taxable years beginning after December 31, 1976, commercial paper, however acquired by the bank, including, for example, short-term promissory notes which may be purchased on the open market;

(C) For taxable years beginning after December 31, 1976, a debt evidenced by a security (as defined in section 165(g)(2)(C) and the regulations thereunder);

(D) Any loan which is entered into or acquired for the primary purpose of enlarging the otherwise available bad debt deduction;

(E) Loans which have been contractually committed to the extent that funds have not been disbursed to the borrower or disbursed on behalf of the borrower; and

(F) Any transaction which is in violation of a Federal or State statute that governs the activities of the financial institution.

(3) Eligible loan. (i) General rule. For purposes of this section and §§ 1.585-3 and 1.585-4, the term "eligible loan" means a loan (as defined in subparagraph (2) of this paragraph) which is incurred in the course of the normal customer loan activities of a financial institution and which is not a loan described in subdivision (ii) of this subparagraph. Nothing within the preceding sentence will be construed to exclude from the term "eligible loan" a bona fide loan in a new market or under a novel repayment arrangement if the likelihood of nonrepayment is at least as great as that of other customer loans of the financial institution.

(ii) Exceptions. Loans which do not constitute eligible loans include:

(A) A loan to a bank (as defined in section 581 and the regulations thereunder) or to a domestic branch of a foreign corporation to which § 1.585-1 applies, including a repurchase transaction or other similar transaction;

(B) Bank funds on deposit in any bank (foreign or domestic) such as a deposit represented by a certificate of deposit or any other form of instrument evidencing the deposit of a sum of money with the issuing bank that will be available on or after a stated date or period of time;

(C) A sale or loan of Federal funds irrespective of the purchaser or borrower;

(D) A loan, to the extent that it is directly or indirectly made to, guaranteed by, or insured by the United States, a possession or instrumentality thereof, or a State or political subdivision thereof;

(E) A loan which is secured by a deposit in the lending financial institution or in a bank as defined in section 581 or a domestic branch of a foreign corporation to which this section applies to the extent that the financial institution has control over withdrawal of such deposit.

(iii) Definition of loan which is secured by a deposit. For purposes of subdivision (ii)(E) of this subparagraph—

(A) A loan is considered secured if the loan is on the security of any instrument which makes the deposit specific security for the payment of the loan, provided that such instrument is of such a nature that in the event of default the deposit could be subjected to the satisfaction of the loan;

(B) A deposit includes a guarantee deposit in the form of a "holdback", pledged collateral that has been reduced to cash, and loan payments that are maintained in a separate account; and

(C) Control over the withdrawal of a deposit is evidenced by possession of a passbook, certificate of deposit, note, or other similar instrument the possession of which is normally required to permit withdrawal. The lending financial institution does not have control over withdrawal of the deposit if the deposit can be withdrawn without consent of the lending financial institution. Thus, the lending financial institution normally does not have control over the withdrawal of a deposit in an account merely because the borrower agrees to maintain a minimum, average, or compensating balance.

(4) Predecessor. For purposes of this section, the term "predecessor" means (i) any taxpayer which transferred more than 50 percent of the total amount of its assets to the taxpayer and is described in § 1.585-1, or (i) any predecessor of such predecessor.

(5) Authorization years. For purposes of this section, the term "authorization years" means the number of years, containing 12 complete months, between (i) the first day of the first full taxable year of the taxpayer for which it (or any predecessor) was authorized to do business as a financial institution described in § 1.585-1, and (ii) the taxable year.

(6) Comparison years. For purposes of this section, the term "comparison years" means those consecutive taxable years containing 12 complete months of a comparable bank, the last of which ends within 12 months immediately preceding the beginning of the first taxable year of the taxpayer, which are equal in number to six minus the number of authorization years of the taxpayer.

(7) Comparable bank. For purposes of this section, the term "comparable bank" means all the financial institutions described in § 1.585-1 located within the same Federal Reserve district.

(8) Average loans outstanding. For purposes of this section, the term "average loans outstanding" means the sum of the loans outstanding at the close of each taxable year of a period divided by the number of taxable years in such period.

(9) Adjusted for recoveries of bad debts. For purposes of this section, the term "adjusted for recoveries of bad debts" means an adjustment for the full amount recovered with respect to bad debts previously charged to the reserve during any of the applicable taxable years.

T.D. 7532, 1/18/78, amend T.D. 7835, 9/24/82, T.D. 8513, 12/28/93.

§ 1.585-3 Special rules.

(a) Treatment of reserve. For taxable years beginning after July 11, 1969, if a financial institution to which section 585 and § 1.585-1 apply establishes a reserve pursuant to section 585(a) (or, for taxable years beginning before January 1, 1987, section 166(c)), any bad debt in respect of a loan (whether or not such loan is an eligible loan) must be charged to the reserve for losses on loans provided for by § 1.585-1 for the taxable year in which the bad debt occurs. For such a year, any recovery of a bad debt previously charged to the reserve account in respect of a loan (whether or not such loan is an eligible loan) must be credited to such reserve in the taxable year of recovery regardless of whether such credit causes the reserve to exceed the permissible amount. If, as a result of net recoveries during the taxable year, the reserve balance exceeds the permissible amount, a taxpayer is not required to report the excess as taxable income. In such a case, the excess over the otherwise permissible amount in the reserve account precludes current reasonable additions to the reserve and may affect future reasonable additions. Recoveries of bad debts which were not charged to the reserve shall not be credited to such reserve, but shall be treated as taxable income subject to the provisions of § 1.111. No item other than a loan as defined in § 1.585-2(e)(2) shall be charged to the reserve for losses on loans.

(b) Accounting for reserve. A financial institution to which section 585 and § 1.585-1 apply which establishes a reserve pursuant to section 585(a) (or, for taxable years beginning before January 1, 1987, section 166(c)) shall establish and maintain a permanent record of such reserve. Copies of Federal income tax returns and amended returns with attached schedules satisfy the requirements of this paragraph provided that such returns are permanently maintained by the financial institution and the balance of the reserve for losses on loans established pursuant to section 585(a) (or former section 166(c)) can be readily reconciled with the reserve for losses on loans maintained by the financial institution for financial statement purposes. The requirements of this paragraph would also be satisfied if a financial institution establishes and maintains a permanent subsidiary ledger reflecting an account for the reserve for losses on loans established pursuant to section 585(a) (or former section 166(c)) provided the balance in such account can be readily reconciled with the balance of the reserve for losses on loans for financial statement purposes maintained in any other ledger. The permanent records maintained pursuant to this section must reflect any changes in the amount initially added to the reserve for losses on loans and the amount finally determined by the taxpayer to be a reasonable addition to the reserve for losses on loans.

T.D. 7532, 1/18/78, amend T.D. 8513, 12/28/93.

§ 1.585-4 Reorganizations and asset acquisitions.

Caution: The Treasury has not yet amended Reg § 1.585-4 to reflect changes made by P.L. 100-647, P.L. 100-203, P.L. 99-514.

(a) In general. In computing a reasonable addition to the reserve for losses on loans for the first taxable year ending after a transaction to which section 381(a) applies and for subsequent taxable years, the separate reserves for losses on loans, the amount of loans outstanding, the total bad debts sustained (adjusted for recoveries), and the amount of eligible loans outstanding of the distributor or transferor corporation and the acquiring corporation (or, in the case of a consolidation, the transferor corporations) shall be combined for all applicable years. Thus, for example, in applying § 1.585-2(c)(1)(i) for the first taxable year ending after the distribution or transfer, the total bad debts sustained during the 5 preceding taxable years are the sum of the bad debts sustained by the acquiring corporation for the 5 preceding taxable years and bad debts sustained by the distributor or transferor corporation for the taxable year ending on the date of distribution or transfer and the 4 preceding taxable years.

(b) Base year and base year amounts of acquiring corporation. *(1) Base year.* For transactions to which section 381(a) applies, the base year of the acquiring corporation for the first taxable year ending after the date of distribution or transfer shall be the last taxable year ending on or before the date of distribution or transfer. The balance of the reserve, the amount of loans outstanding, and the amount of eligible loans outstanding at the close of such base year shall be determined in accordance with the provisions of subparagraph (2)(i) of this paragraph. For taxable years subsequent to the first taxable year ending after the date of distribution or transfer, the base year of the acquiring corporation shall be the more recent of the base year provided by the first sentence of this subparagraph or the base year provided by § 1.585-2(e)(1). If § 1.585-2(e)(1) provides the more recent base year, the balance of the reserve for losses on loans, the amount of loans outstanding, and the amount of eligible loans outstanding shall be determined at the close of such base year without regard to this paragraph.

(2) Base year amounts. (i) Method of determination. The balance of the reserve for losses on loans, the amount of loans outstanding, and the amount of eligible loans outstanding at the close of the base year provided by the first sentence of subparagraph (1) of this paragraph shall be the total of such amounts of the distributor or transferor corporation and the acquiring corporation (or, in the case of a consolidation, the transferor corporations) at the close of what would have been their respective base years determined under § 1.585-2(e)(1) if the distribution or transfer to which section 381(a) applies had not occurred, except that the method (experience or percentage) used or adopted by the acquiring corporation to determine its reasonable addition to a reserve for losses on loans for the first taxable year ending after the date of the distribution or transfer shall be considered to be the method that the distributor or transferor corporation (or, in the case of a consolidation, that the transferor corporations) would have used or adopted for its first taxable year ending after the date of distribution or transfer if the distribution or transfer had not occurred.

(ii) Examples. The application of the rule provided by this subparagraph may be illustrated by the following examples:

Example (1). The X corporation and the Y Corporation are commercial banks both of which have a calendar year as a taxable year. Both X and Y adopted the reserve method of accounting for bad debts prior to July 11, 1969. For the taxable year 1970 through 1973, X and Y determined their reasonable additions to a reserve for losses on loans as defined in § 1.585-2(e)(2) under the percentage method. On June 30, 1974, the X Bank is merged into the Y Bank; for its short taxable year ending on June 30, 1974, X determines its reasonable addition under the percentage method. If, for the taxable year ending on December 31, 1974 (the first taxable year ending after the date of distribution or transfer) Y determines its reasonable addition to a reserve for losses on loans under the percentage method, then at the close of the base year the reserve balance, the amount of outstanding loans, and the amount of eligible loans outstanding are the sum of X's and Y's respective amounts at the close of the taxable year ending December 31, 1969 (the base year of both X and Y determined under § 1.585-2(e)(1) as if the distribution or transfer had not taken place). If, instead of the above, Y adopts the experience method of determining its reasonable addition to a reserve for losses for the taxable year 1974, then at the close of the base year (1973) the reserve balances, the amount of loans outstanding, and the amount of eligible loans outstanding are the sum of X's respective amounts at the close of its short taxable year ending on June 30, 1974 (X's last taxable year before its (Y's) most recent adoption of the experience method) and of Y's respective amounts at the close of its taxable year 1973 (Y's last taxable year before its most recent adoption of the experience method).

Example (2). The M Corporation and the N Corporation are commercial banks. M has a fiscal year ending September 30, as its taxable year and N has a calendar year as its taxable year. Both M and N adopted the reserve method of accounting for bad debts prior to July 11, 1969. For the taxable years ending in 1970, 1971, and 1972, M determined its reasonable addition to a reserve for losses under the percentage method; for the taxable year ending in 1973 M adopted the experience method. For the taxable years 1970 through 1973 N determined its reasonable addition under the percentage method. M is merged into N on June 30, 1974, and for its short taxable year ending on June 30, 1974, M determines its reasonable addition under the experience method. If, for the taxable year ending on December 31, 1974 (the first taxable year ending after the date of distribution or transfer), N determines its reasonable addition to a reserve for losses under the percentage method, then at the close of the base year (1973) the reserve balance, the amount of loans outstanding, and the amount of eligible loans outstanding are the sum of M's respective amounts at the close of (a) if M had a reserve deficiency as of June 30, 1974, its short taxable year ending on June 30, 1974 (M's last taxable year before its (N's) most recent adoption of the percentage method) or (b) if M did not have a reserve deficiency, the taxable year ending on September 30, 1969, and N's respective amounts at the close of its taxable year 1969. If, instead of the above, N adopts the experience method for the taxable year 1974, then at the close of the base year the reserve balance, the amount of outstanding loans, and the amount of eligible loans outstanding are the sum of M's respective amounts at the close of its taxable year ending on September 30, 1972 (the last taxable year before M's most recent adoption of the experience method) and N's respective amounts at the close of the taxable year 1973 (the last taxable year ending before N's most recent adoption of the experience method).

T.D. 7532, 1/18/78.

§ 1.585-5 Denial of bad debt reserves for large banks.

Caution: The Treasury has not yet amended Reg § 1.585-5 to reflect changes made by P.L. 104-188.

(a) General rule. For taxable years beginning after December 31, 1986, a large bank (as defined in paragraph (b) of this section) may not deduct any amount under section 585 or any other section for an addition to a reserve for bad debts. However, for these years, except as provided in § 1.585-7, a large bank may deduct amounts allowed under section 166(a) for specific debts that become worthless in whole or in part. Any large bank that maintained a reserve for bad debts under section 585 for the taxable year immediately preceding its disqualification year (as defined in paragraph (d)(1) of this section) must follow the rules prescribed by § 1.585-6 or § 1.585-7 for changing from the reserve method of accounting for bad debts that is allowed by section 585, to the specific charge-off method of accounting for bad debts, in its disqualification year. However, except as may be provided otherwise in regulations prescribed under section 593, the rules prescribed by §§ 1.585-6 and 1.585-7 do not apply to a large bank that maintained a reserve for bad debts under section 593 for the taxable year immediately preceding its disqualification year.

(b) Large bank. *(1) General definition.* For purposes of this section, a large bank is any institution described in § 1.585-1(b)(1)(i) or (ii) if, for the taxable year (or for any preceding taxable year beginning after December 31, 1986)—

(i) The average total assets of the institution (determined under paragraph (c) of this section) exceed $500,000,000; or

(ii) The institution is a member of a parent-subsidiary controlled group (as defined in paragraph (d)(2) of this section) and the average total assets of the group exceed $500,000,000.

(2) Large bank resulting from transfer by large bank. (i) In general. If a corporation acquires the assets of a large bank (as defined in this paragraph (b)) in an acquisition to which paragraph (b)(2)(ii), (iii) or (iv) of this section applies, the acquiring corporation (the acquiror) is treated as a large bank for any taxable year ending after the date of the acquisition in which it is an institution described in § 1.585-1(b)(1)(i) or (ii).

(ii) Transfer of significant portion of assets where control is retained. This paragraph (b)(2)(ii) applies to any direct or indirect acquisition of a significant portion of a large bank's assets if, after the acquisition, the transferor large bank owns more than 50 percent (by vote or value) of the outstanding stock of the acquiror. For this purpose, stock of an acquiror is considered owned by a transferor bank if the stock is owned by any member of a parent-subsidiary controlled group (as defined in paragraph (d)(2) of this section) of which the bank is a member, by any related party within the meaning of section 267(b) or 707(b), or by any person that received the stock in a transaction to which section 355 applies.

(iii) Transfer to which section 381 applies. This paragraph (b)(2)(iii) applies to any acquisition to which section 381(a) applies if, immediately after the acquisition, the acquiror's principal method of accounting for bad debts (determined under § 1.381(c)(4)-1(c)(2)) with respect to its banking business is the specific charge-off method. In applying § 1.381(c)(4)-1(c)(2) for this purpose, the following rules apply: a transferor large bank is considered to use the specific charge-off method for all of its loans immediately before the acquisition; and all banking businesses of the acquiror immediately after the acquisition are treated as one integrated business. See §§ 1.585-6(c)(3) and 1.585-7(d)(2) for rules on the treatment of assets acquired from large banks in section 381(a) transactions.

(iv) Transfer of substantially all assets to related party. This paragraph (b)(2)(iv) applies to any direct or indirect acquisition of substantially all of a large bank's assets if the transferor large bank and the acquiror are related parties before or after the acquisition and a principal purpose of the acquisition is to avoid treating the acquired assets as those of a large bank. A transferor bank and an acquiror are considered to be related parties for this purpose if they are members of the same parent-subsidiary controlled group (as defined in paragraph (d)(2) of this section) or related parties within the meaning of section 267(b) or 707(b).

(3) Examples. The following examples illustrate the principles of this paragraph (b):

Example (1). Bank M, a calendar year taxpayer, is an institution described in § 1.585-1(b)(1)(i). For its taxable year beginning on January 1, 1987, M has average total assets of $600 million. Since M's average total assets for 1987 exceed $500 million, M is a large bank for that year. Pursuant to § 1.585-5(d)(1), 1987 is M's disqualification year. If M maintained a bad debt reserve under section 585 for its immediately preceding taxable year (1986), M must change in 1987 to the specific charge-off method of accounting for bad debts, in accordance with § 1.585-6 or § 1.585-7.

Example (2). Assume the same facts as in Example 1. Also assume that in 1988 M disposes of a portion of its assets and, as a result, M's average total assets for taxable year 1988 fall to $400 million. M remains a large bank for taxable year 1988 and succeeding taxable years, since its average total assets for a preceding taxable year (1987) beginning after December 31, 1986, exceeded $500 million.

Example (3). Bank P, a calendar year taxpayer, is an institution described in § 1.585-1(b)(1)(i). P has average total assets of $300 million for its taxable year beginning on January 1, 1988. For the same year, P is a member of a parent-subsidiary controlled group (within the meaning of § 1.585-5(d)(2)) that has average total assets of $800 million. In February 1989, the group sells its stock in P to several individual investors. P is a large bank for taxable year 1988 because it is a member of a group described in § 1.585-5(b)(1)(ii) for that year. P also is a large bank for taxable year 1989 and succeeding taxable years because it was a member of a group described in § 1.585-5(b)(1)(ii) for a preceding taxable year (1988) beginning after December 31, 1986.

Example (4). Assume the same facts as in Example 3, except that P's stock is purchased by a corporation that is not a large bank under § 1.585-5(b). Also assume that the purchasing corporation elects under section 338 to treat the stock purchase as an asset acquisition. Under section 338, P is considered to have sold all of its assets on the purchase date and is treated as a new corporation that purchased these assets on the next day. Since P is treated as a new corporation, its prior membership in a group described in § 1.585-5(b)(1)(ii) does not cause it to be treated as a large bank for taxable years ending after the date of its sale by the group. However, P may be treated as a large bank because of new membership in such a group or pursuant to § 1.585-5(b)(1)(i) or (b)(2).

Example (5). Bank Q is a large bank, within the meaning of § 1.585-5(b)(1), for its taxable year beginning on January 1, 1988, and hence for all later years. On March 1, 1989, Q transfers $200 million of its $600 million of assets to Bank R, a newly created subsidiary, in a transaction to which section 351 applies; these assets are R's only assets. On the same day, Q then spins off R in a transaction to which section 355 applies. After these transactions, the shareholders of

Q own more than 50 percent of R's outstanding stock. Although R's average total assets do not exceed $500 million, R becomes a large bank on March 1, 1989, pursuant to § 1.585-5(b)(2)(ii). These transactions do not affect Q's status as a large bank.

Example (6). Bank S is a large bank, within the meaning of § 1.585-5(b)(1)(ii), for its taxable year beginning on January 1, 1987. As a result, S changes to the specific charge-off method of accounting for bad debts in that year. Bank T, which is not a large bank under § 1.585-5(b), uses the reserve method of accounting for bad debts. On June 30, 1988, T acquires substantially all of S's assets in a transaction to which section 381(a) applies. Immediately before the acquisition, S's banking business has total assets of $200 million, and T's has total assets of $250 million. To determine whether T is a large bank under § 1.585-5(b)(2)(iii) for taxable years ending after the acquisition, it is necessary to determine T's principal method of accounting for bad debts with respect to its banking business immediately after the acquisition. This determination requires an application of § 1.381(c)(4)-1(c)(2). For this purpose, T's original and acquired banking businesses are treated as an integrated business. Applying § 1.381(c)(4)-1(c)(2), it is determined that the business's principal method of accounting for bad debts immediately after the acquisition is the reserve method. Hence, the acquisition does not cause T to become a large bank under § 1.585-5(b)(2)(iii).

(c) Average total assets. *(1) In general.* For purposes of paragraph (b)(1) of this section, and except as otherwise provided in paragraph (c)(3)(ii) of this section, the average total assets of an institution or group for any taxable year are determined by—

(i) Computing, for each report date (as defined in paragraph (c)(2) of this section) within the taxable year, the amount of total assets (as defined in paragraph (c)(3) of this section) held by the institution or group as of the close of business on the report date;

(ii) Adding these amounts; and

(iii) Dividing the sum of these amounts by the number of report dates within the taxable year.

(2) Report date. (i) Institutions. (A) In general. A report date for an institution generally is the last day of the regular period for which the institution must report to its primary Federal regulatory agency. However, an institution that is required to report to its primary Federal regulatory agency more frequently than quarterly may choose the last day of the calendar quarter as its report date, and an institution that is required to report to its primary Federal regulatory agency less frequently than quarterly must choose the last day of the calendar quarter as its report date. If an institution does not have a Federal regulatory agency, its primary State regulatory agency is considered its primary Federal regulatory agency for purposes of this paragraph (c)(2)(i)(A). In the case of a short taxable year that does not otherwise include a report date, the first or last day of the taxable year is the institution's report date for the year.

(B) Alternative report date. In lieu of the report date prescribed by paragraph (c)(2)(i)(A) of this section, for any taxable year an institution may choose as its report date the last day of any regular interval in the taxable year that is more frequent than quarterly (such as bi-monthly, monthly, weekly, or daily).

(ii) Groups. If all members of a parent-subsidiary controlled group have the same taxable year, a report date for the group is the report date, determined under paragraph (c)(2)(i) of this section, for any one member of the group that is an institution described in § 1.585-1(b)(1)(i) or (ii). The same report date must be used in applying paragraph (b)(1)(ii) of this section to all members of the group for a taxable year. If all members of a parent-subsidiary controlled group do not have the same taxable year, a report date for the group must be determined under similar principles.

(iii) Member of group for only part of taxable year. If an institution is a member of a parent-subsidiary controlled group for only part of a taxable year, paragraph (b)(1)(ii) of this section is applied to the institution for that year on the basis of the group's average total assets for the portion of the year that the institution is a member of the group. Thus, only the group's report dates (as determined under paragraph (c)(2)(ii) of this section) that are included in that portion of the year are taken into account in determining the group's average total assets for purposes of applying paragraph (b)(1)(ii) of this section to the institution. If no report date of the group is included in that portion of the year, the first or last day of that portion of the year must be treated as the group's report date for purposes of this paragraph (c)(2)(iii).

(3) Total assets. (i) All corporations. The amount of total assets held by an institution or group is the amount of cash, plus the sum of the adjusted bases of all other assets, held by the institution or group. For this purpose, the adjusted basis of an asset generally is its basis for Federal income tax purposes, determined under sections 1012, 1016 and other applicable sections of the Internal Revenue Code. In determining the amount of total assets held by a group, any asset of a member of the group that is an interest in another member of the group is not to be counted.

(ii) Foreign corporations. In determining the amount of total assets held by a foreign corporation, all of the corporation's assets are taken into account, including those that are not effectively connected with the conduct of a banking business within the United States. In the case of a foreign corporation that is not engaged in a trade or business in the United States, the adjusted basis of an asset must be determined substantially in accordance with United States tax principles as provided in regulations under section 964. In the case of a foreign corporation that is engaged in a trade or business in the United States, the amount of its average total assets for a taxable year (within the meaning of paragraph (c)(1) of this section) is the amount of the corporation's average worldwide assets used for purposes of computing the interest expense deduction allowable under section 882 and § 1.882-5 for the taxable year.

(4) Estimated adjusted tax bases. (i) In general. The amount of the adjusted Federal income tax bases (tax bases) of assets held on a report date may be estimated, for purposes of applying paragraph (c)(3) of this section. This estimate must be based on the adjusted bases of the assets on that date as determined by reference to the asset holder's books and records maintained for financial reporting purposes (book bases). The estimate must reflect any change in the ratio between the asset holder's tax and book bases of assets that occurs during the taxable year, and the estimate must assume that this change occurs ratably. If an institution or group member estimates the tax bases of assets held on any report date during a taxable year, it must do so for all assets (other than cash) held on that report date, and it must do so for all other report dates during the year. However, the tax bases of assets may not be estimated for any report date that is the first or last day of the taxable year or that is determined under paragraph (c)(2)(i)(B) of this section.

(ii) Formulas.

The estimated amount of the tax bases of assets held on any report date during a taxable year is based on the following variables: the total book bases of the assets on the report date (B); the asset holder's tax/book ratio as of the close of the preceding taxable year (R); and the result (whether positive or negative) obtained when R is subtracted from the asset holder's tax/book ratio as of the close of the current taxable year (Y). For purposes of determining R and Y, an asset holder's tax/book ratio is the ratio of the total tax bases of all of the holder's assets (other than cash), to the total book bases of those assets. If an asset holder's taxable year is the calendar year and its report date is the last day of the calendar quarter, its estimated tax bases of assets held on the first three report dates of the year are determined under the following formulas:

1st Report Date = B × (R + ¼Y)

2nd Report Date = B × (R + ½Y)

3rd Report Date = B × (R + ¾Y)

(5) Examples. The following examples illustrate the principles of this paragraph (c):

Example (1). Bank U is a fiscal year taxpayer, and its fiscal year ends on January 31. U reports to its primary Federal regulatory agency as of the last day of the calendar quarter. U does not choose under § 1.585-5(c)(2)(i)(B) a report date more frequent than quarterly. Thus, U's report dates under § 1.585-5(c)(2)(i)(A) are March 31, June 30, September 30, and December 31. For its taxable year beginning on February 1, 1987, U has total assets (within the meaning of § 1.585-5(c)(3)) of $480 million on March 31, $490 million on June 30, $510 million on September 30, and $540 million on December 31. Thus, pursuant to § 1.585-5(c)(1), U's average total assets for its taxable year beginning on February 1, 1987, are $505 million.

Example (2). Bank W is a calendar year taxpayer, and its report date (within the meaning of § 1.585-5(c)(2)(i)(A)) is the last day of the calendar quarter. Pursuant to § 1.585-5(c)(4), W chooses to estimate the tax bases of its assets for 1990. Therefore, W must estimate the tax bases of all of its assets (other than cash) for its first three report dates in 1990. Since W's fourth report date (December 31) is the last day of its taxable year, the tax bases of its assets may not be estimated for this date. The adjusted tax bases of all of W's assets (other than cash) are $450z on December 31, 1989, and $480z on December 31, 1990. The book bases of those assets are $500z on December 31, 1989; $520z on March 31, 1990; $540z on June 30, 1990; $560z on September 30, 1990; and $600z on December 31, 1990. Applying the formulas provided in § 1.585-5(c)(4)(ii), W's tax/book ratio as of the close of 1989 (R), is 0.9 (450z/500z). W's tax/book ratio as of the close of 1990 is 0.8 (480z/600z). Thus, Y is -0.1. The estimated adjusted tax bases of all of W's assets (other than cash) on the first three report dates of 1990 are as follows:

1st
= B × (R + ¼Y)
= $520z × [0.9 + ¼(– 0.1)]
= $455z

2nd
= B × (R + ½Y)
= $540z × [0.9 + ½(– 0.1)]
= $459z

3rd
= B × (R + ¾Y)
= $560z × [0.9 + ¾(– 0.1)]
= $462z

(d) Definitions. The following definitions apply for purposes of this section and §§ 1.585-6, 1.585-7 and 1.585-8:

(1) Disqualification year. A bank's disqualification year is its first taxable year beginning after December 31, 1986, for which the bank is a large bank within the meaning of paragraph (b) of this section.

(2) Parent-subsidiary controlled group. A parent-subsidiary controlled group includes all of the members of a controlled group of corporations described in section 1563(a)(1). The members of such a group are determined without regard to whether any member is an *excluded member* described in section 1563(b)(2), a foreign entity, or a commercial bank.

(3) Example. The following example illustrates the principles of this paragraph (d):

Example. Bank X is a large bank within the meaning of § 1.585-5(b)(1)(i). Bank Y is not a large bank under § 1.585-5(b), and it maintains a bad debt reserve under section 585. In 1988, X purchases all of the stock of Y. If the acquisition causes Y to become a member of a parent-subsidiary controlled group described in § 1.585-5(b)(1)(ii), Y is a large bank beginning in its first taxable year that ends after the date of the acquisition. Pursuant to § 1.585-5(d)(1), this year is Y's disqualification year. Y must change in this year to the specific charge-off method of accounting for bad debts, in accordance with § 1.585-6 or § 1.585-7.

T.D. 8513, 12/28/93.

§ 1.585-6 Recapture method of changing from the reserve method of section 585.

(a) General rule. This section applies to any large bank (as defined in § 1.585-5(b)) that maintained a reserve for bad debts under section 585 for the taxable year immediately preceding its disqualification year (as defined in § 1.585-5(d)(1)) and that does not elect the cut-off method set forth in § 1.585-7. Except as otherwise provided in paragraphs (c) and (d) of this section, any bank to which this section applies must include in income the amount of its net section 481(a) adjustment (as defined in paragraph (b)(3) of this section) over the four-year period beginning with the bank's disqualification year. If a bank follows the rules prescribed by this section, its change to the specific charge-off method of accounting for bad debts in its disqualification year will be treated as a change in accounting method that is made with the consent of the Commissioner. Paragraph (b) of this section specifies the portion of the net section 481(a) adjustment to be included in income in each year of the recapture period; paragraph (c) of this section provides rules on the effect of disposing of loans; and paragraph (d) of this section provides rules on the suspension of recapture by financially troubled banks.

(b) Four-year spread of net section 481(a) adjustment. *(1) In general.* If a bank to which this section applies does not make the election allowed by paragraph (b)(2) of this section, the bank must include in income the following portions of its net section 481(a) adjustment in each year of the four-year recapture period: 10 percent in the bank's disqualification year; 20 percent in its first taxable year after its disqualification year; 30 percent in its second taxable year after its disqualification year; and 40 percent in its third taxable year after its disqualification year.

(2) Election to include more than 10 percent in disqualification year. A bank to which this section applies may elect to include in income, in its disqualification year, any percentage of its net section 481(a) adjustment that is larger than 10 percent. Any such election must be made at the time

and in the manner prescribed by § 1.585-8. If a bank makes such an election, the bank must include in income the remainder, if any, of its net section 481(a) adjustment in the following portions: 2/9 of the remainder in the bank's first taxable year after its disqualification year; 1/3 of the remainder in its second taxable year after its disqualification year; and 4/9 of the remainder in its third taxable year after its disqualification year. For this purpose, the remainder of a bank's net section 481(a) adjustment is any portion of the adjustment that the bank does not elect to include in income in its disqualification year.

(3) Net section 481(a) adjustment. For purposes of this section, the amount of a bank's net section 481(a) adjustment is the amount of the bank's reserve for bad debts as of the close of the taxable year immediately preceding its disqualification year. Since the change from the reserve method of section 585 is initiated by the taxpayer, the amount of the bank's bad debt reserve for this purpose is not reduced by amounts attributable to taxable years beginning before 1954.

(4) Examples. The following examples illustrate the principles of this paragraph (b):

Example (1). Bank M is a large bank within the meaning of § 1.585-5(b). M's disqualification year is its taxable year beginning on January 1, 1989, and M maintained a bad debt reserve under section 585 for the preceding taxable year. Pursuant to § 1.585-5(a), M must change from the reserve method of accounting for bad debts to the specific charge-off method in its disqualification year. M does not elect the cut-off method set forth in § 1.585-7. Thus, M must follow the recapture method set forth in this § 1.585-6. M's net section 481(a) adjustment, as defined in § 1.585-6(b)(3), is $2 million. M does not make the election allowed by § 1.585-6(b)(2). Pursuant to § 1.585-6(b)(1), M must include the following amounts in income: $200,000 in taxable year 1989; $400,000 in 1990; $600,000 in 1991; and $800,000 in 1992.

Example (2). Assume the same facts as in Example 1, except that M elects under § 1.585-6(b)(2) to recapture 55 percent of its net section 481(a) adjustment in its disqualification year. Pursuant to § 1.585-6(b)(2), M must include the following amounts in income: $1,100,000 in taxable year 1989; $200,000 in 1990; $300,000 in 1991; and $400,000 in 1992.

(c) Effect of disposing of loans. *(1) In general.* Except as provided in paragraphs (c)(2) and (c)(3) of this section, if a bank to which this section applies sells or otherwise disposes of any of its outstanding loans on or after the first day of its disqualification year, the disposition does not affect the bank's obligation under this section to include in income the amount of its net section 481(a) adjustment, and the disposition does not affect the amount of this adjustment.

(2) Cessation of banking business. (i) In general. If a bank to which this section applies ceases to engage in the business of banking before it is otherwise required to include in income the full amount of its net section 481(a) adjustment, the bank must include in income the remaining amount of the adjustment in the taxable year in which it ceases to engage in the business of banking. For this purpose, and except as provided in paragraph (c)(2)(ii) of this section, whether a bank ceases to engage in the business of banking is determined under the principles of § 1.446-1(e)(3)(ii) and its administrative procedures.

(ii) Transition rule. A bank that ceases to engage in the business of banking as the result of a transaction to which section 381(a) applies is not treated as ceasing to engage in the business of banking if, on or before March 30, 1994, either the transaction occurs or the bank enters into a binding written agreement to carry out the transaction.

(3) Certain section 381 transactions. This paragraph (c)(3) applies if a bank to which this section applies transfers outstanding loans to another corporation on or after the first day of the bank's disqualification year (and before it has included in income the full amount of its net section 481(a) adjustment) in a transaction to which section 381(a) applies, and under paragraph (c)(2)(i) or (ii) of this section the transferor bank is not treated as ceasing to engage in the business of banking as a result of the transaction. If this paragraph (c)(3) applies, the acquiring corporation (the acquiror) steps into the shoes of the transferor with respect to using the recapture method prescribed by this section and assumes all of the transferor's rights and obligations under paragraph (b) of this section. The unrecaptured balance of the transferor's net section 481(a) adjustment carries over in the transaction to the acquiror, and the acquiror must complete the four-year recapture procedure begun by the transferor. In applying this procedure, the transferor's taxable year that ends on or includes the date of the acquisition and the acquiror's first taxable year ending after the date of the acquisition represent two consecutive taxable years within the four-year recapture period.

(4) Examples. The following examples illustrate the principles of this paragraph (c):

Example (1). Bank P is a bank to which this § 1.585-6 applies. P's disqualification year is its taxable year beginning on January 1, 1989, and P recaptures 10 percent of its net section 481(a) adjustment in that year pursuant to § 1.585-6(b)(1). In July 1990 P disposes of a portion of its loan portfolio in a transaction to which section 381(a) does not apply, and P continues to engage in the business of banking. Pursuant to § 1.585-6(c)(1), the disposition does not affect P's obligation under § 1.585-6(b)(1) to recapture the remainder of its net section 481(a) adjustment in 1990, 1991 and 1992. Nor does the disposition affect the amount of the adjustment.

Example (2). Assume the same facts as in Example 1, except that P ceases to engage in the business of banking in 1990, as determined under the principles of § 1.446-1(e)(3)(ii) and its administrative procedures. Pursuant to § 1.585-6(c)(2)(i), in 1990 P must include in income the remaining 90 percent of its net section 481(a) adjustment.

Example (3). Assume the same facts as in Example 1, except that P's 1990 disposition of loans is a transaction to which section 381(a) applies, P ceases to engage in the business of banking as a result of the transaction, and P's taxable year ends on the date of the transaction. Thus, in the transaction, P transfers substantially all of its loans to an acquiring corporation (Q). Q is a calendar year taxpayer. Because the transaction occurred before March 30, 1994, the transition rule of § 1.585-6(c)(2)(ii) applies, and P is not treated as ceasing to engage in the business of banking. Pursuant to § 1.585-6(c)(3), Q steps into P's shoes with respect to using the recapture method prescribed by § 1.585-6. The unrecaptured balance of P's net section 481(a) adjustment carries over to Q in the section 381(a) transaction, and Q must complete the four-year recapture procedure begun by P. Pursuant to § 1.585-6(b) and 1.585-6(c)(3), P includes 20 percent of its net section 481(a) adjustment in income in its taxable year ending on the date of the section 381(a) transaction, and Q includes 30 percent of the adjustment in income in 1990 and 40 percent in 1991.

Example (4). Assume the same facts as in Example 3. Assume also that Q becomes a large bank under § 1.585-5(b) as a result of the transaction and maintained a bad debt reserve immediately before the transaction. Q must change to the specific charge-off method for all of its loans in the first taxable year that it is a large bank. Thus, Q not only completes the recapture procedure begun by P but also follows the rules prescribed by § 1.585-6 or § 1.585-7 with respect to its own reserve.

Example (5). Assume the same facts as in Example 3. Assume also that Q is not a large bank after the transaction and properly establishes a bad debt reserve for the loans it receives in the transaction. This establishment of the reserve results in a new negative section 481(a) adjustment. Thus, Q not only completes the recapture procedure begun by P but also takes into account the new negative adjustment as required under section 381.

(d) Suspension of recapture by financially troubled banks. *(1) In general.* Except as provided in paragraph (d)(2) of this section, a bank that is financially troubled (within the meaning of paragraph (d)(3) of this section) for any taxable year must not include any amount in income under paragraphs (a) and (b) of this section for that taxable year and disregard that taxable year in applying paragraphs (a) and (b) of this section to other taxable years. See paragraph (d)(4) of this section for rules on determining estimated tax payment of financially troubled banks, and see paragraph (d)(5) of this section for examples illustrating this paragraph (d).

(2) Election to recapture. A bank that is financially troubled (within the meaning of paragraph (d)(3) of this section) for its disqualification year may elect to include in income, in one taxable year, any percentage of its net section 481(a) adjustment that is greater than 10 percent. This election may be made for the bank's disqualification year, for the first taxable year after the disqualification year in which the bank is not financially troubled (within the meaning of paragraph (d)(3) of this section), or for any intervening taxable year. Any such election must be made at the time and in the manner prescribed by § 1.585-8. A bank that makes this election must include an amount in income under paragraphs (a) and (b) of this section in the year for which the election is made (election year) and must not disregard this year in applying paragraphs (a) and (b) of this section to other taxable years. Such a bank must follow the rules of paragraph (b)(2) of this section in applying paragraph (b) of this section to later taxable years, treating the election year as the disqualification year for purposes of applying paragraph (b)(2) of this section. However, if the bank is financially troubled for any year after its election year, the bank must not include any amount in income under paragraphs (a) and (b) of this section for the later year and must disregard the later year in applying paragraphs (a) and (b) of this section to other taxable years.

(3) Definition of financially troubled. (i) In general. For purposes of this section, a bank is considered financially troubled for any taxable year if the bank's nonperforming loan percentage for that year exceeds 75 percent. For this purpose, a bank's nonperforming loan percentage is the percentage determined by dividing the sum of the outstanding balances of the bank's nonperforming loans (as defined in paragraph (d)(3)(iii) of this section) as of the close of each quarter of the taxable year, by the sum of the amounts of the bank's equity (as defined in paragraph (d)(3)(iv) of this section) as of the close of each such quarter. The quarters for a short taxable year of at least 3 months are the same as those of the bank's annual accounting period, except that quarters ending before or after the short year are disregarded. If a taxable year consists of less than 3 months, the first or last day of the taxable year is treated as the last day of its only quarter. In lieu of determining its nonperforming loan percentage on the basis of loans and equity as of the close of each quarter of the taxable year, a bank may, for all years, determine this percentage on the basis of loans and equity as of the close of each report date (as defined in § 1.585-5(c)(2), without regard to § 1.585-5(c)(2)(i)(B))). In the case of a bank that is a foreign corporation, all nonperforming loans and equity that are not effectively connected with the conduct of a banking business within the United States.

(ii) Parent-subsidiary controlled groups. (A) In general. If a bank is a member of a parent-subsidiary controlled group (as defined in § 1.585-5(d)(2)) for the taxable year, the nonperforming loans and the equity of all members of the bank's financial group (as determined under paragraph (d)(3)(ii)(B) of this section) are treated as the nonperforming loans and the equity of the bank for purposes of paragraph (d)(3)(i) of this section. However, any equity interest that a member of a bank's financial group holds in another member of this group is not to be counted in determining equity. Similarly, any loan that a member of a bank's financial group makes to another member of the group is not to be counted in determining nonperforming loans. All banks that are members of the same parent-subsidiary controlled group must (for all taxable years that they are members of this group) determine their nonperforming loan percentage on the basis of the close of each quarter of the taxable year, or all must (for all such taxable years) determine this percentage on the basis of the close of each report date (as determined under § 1.585-5(c)(2)(ii), applied without regard to § 1.585-5(c)(2)(i)(B)).

(B) Financial group. (1) In general. All banks that are members of the same parent-subsidiary controlled group must (for all taxable years that they are members of this group) determine their financial group under paragraph (d)(3)(ii)(B)(2) of this section, or all must (for all such taxable years) determine their financial group under paragraph (d)(3)(ii)(B)(3) of this section.

(2) Financial institution members of parent-subsidiary controlled group. A bank's financial group, determined under this paragraph (d)(3)(ii)(B)(2), consists of all financial institutions within the meaning of section 265(b)(5) (and comparable foreign financial institutions) that are members of the parent-subsidiary controlled group of which the bank is a member.

(3) All members of parent-subsidiary controlled group. A bank's financial group, determined under this paragraph (d)(3)(ii)(B)(3), consists of all members of the parent-subsidiary controlled group of which the bank is a member.

(iii) Nonperforming loan. (A) In general. For purposes of this section, a nonperforming loan is any loan (as defined in paragraph (d)(3)(iii)(B) of this section) that is considered to be nonperforming by the holder's primary Federal regulatory agency. Nonperforming loans include the following types of loans as defined by the Federal Financial Institutions Examination Council: loans that are past due 90 days or more and still accruing; loans that are in nonaccrual status; and loans that are restructured troubled debt. A loan is not considered to be nonperforming merely because it is past due, if it is past due less than 90 days. The outstanding balances of nonperforming loans are determined on the basis of amounts that are required to be reported to the holder's primary Federal regulatory agency. For purposes of this paragraph (d)(3)(iii)(A), a holder that does not have a Federal regulatory agency is treated as Federally regulated under the standards prescribed by the Federal Financial Institutions Examination Council.

(B) Loan. For purposes of paragraph (d)(3)(iii)(A) of this section, a loan is any extension of credit that is defined and treated as a loan under the standards prescribed by the Federal Financial Institutions Examination Council. (Accordingly, a troubled debt restructuring that is in substance a foreclosure or repossession is not considered a loan.) In addition, a debt evidenced by a security issued by a foreign government is treated as a loan if the security is issued as an integral part of a restructuring of one or more troubled loans to the foreign government (or an agency or instrumentality thereof). Similarly, a deposit with the central bank of a foreign country is treated as a loan if the deposit is made under a deposit facility agreement that is entered into as an integral part of a restructuring of one or more troubled loans to the foreign country's government (or an agency or instrumentality thereof).

(iv) Equity. For purposes of this section, the equity of a bank or other financial institution is its equity (i.e., assets minus liabilities) as required to be reported to the institution's primary Federal regulatory agency (or, if the institution does not have a Federal regulatory agency, as required under the standards prescribed by the Federal Financial Institutions Examination Council). The balance in a reserve for bad debts is not treated as equity.

(4) Estimated tax payments of financially troubled banks. For purposes of applying section 6655(e)(2)(A)(i) with respect to any installment of estimated tax, a bank that is financially troubled as of the due date of the installment is treated as if no amount will be included in income under paragraphs (a) and (b) of this section for the taxable year. For this purpose, a bank is considered financially troubled as of the due date of an installment of estimated tax only if its nonperforming loan percentage (computed under paragraph (d)(3) of this section) would exceed 75 percent for a short taxable year ending on that date. For purposes of computing this nonperforming loan percentage, the ending of such a short taxable year would not cause the last day of that year to be treated as the last day of a quarter of the taxable year.

(5) Examples. The following examples illustrate the principles of this paragraph (d):

Example (1). Bank R is a bank to which this § 1.585-6 applies. R's disqualification year is its taxable year beginning on January 1, 1987. R is not financially troubled (within the meaning of § 1.585-6(d)(3)) for taxable year 1987 or for any taxable year after 1989, but it is financially troubled for taxable years 1988 and 1989. Since R is not financially troubled for its disqualification year, R must include an amount in income under § 1.585-6(a) and (b) for that year (taxable year 1987). R may make the election allowed by § 1.585-6(b)(2) for that year. Since R is financially troubled for taxable years 1988 and 1989, pursuant to § 1.585-6(d)(1) R does not include any amount in income under § 1.585-6(a) and (b) for these years, and it treats taxable years 1990, 1991 and 1992 as the first, second and third taxable years after its disqualification year for purposes of applying § 1.585-6(a) and (b).

Example (2). Assume the same facts as in Example 1, except that R is financially troubled for taxable year 1987 (its disqualification year). R may make the election allowed by § 1.585-6(d)(2) for 1987 (the disqualification year), for 1990 (the first year after the disqualification year in which R is not financially troubled), or for 1988 or 1989 (the intervening years). R elects to include 60 percent of its net section 481(a) adjustment in income in 1987. Thus, the remainder of the adjustment, for purposes of applying the rules of § 1.585-6(b)(2), is 40 percent. R must include in income 2/9 of the remainder in 1990, 1/3 of the remainder in 1991, and 4/9 of the remainder in 1992.

Example (3). Bank S, which is not a member of a parent-subsidiary controlled group, is a bank to which this § 1.585-6 applies. S's disqualification year is its taxable year beginning on January 1, 1987. S determines its nonperforming loan percentage under § 1.585-6(d)(3) on a quarterly basis. S is not financially troubled for taxable year 1987 and includes 10 percent of its net section 481(a) adjustment in income in that year. S's outstanding balance of nonperforming loans (as defined in § 1.585-6(d)(3)(iii)) is $80 million on March 31, 1988; $68 million on June 30, 1988; and $59 million on September 30, 1988. The amount of S's equity (as defined in § 1.585-6(d)(3)(iv)) is $100 million on each of these three dates. Thus, S's nonperforming loan percentage, computed under § 1.585-6(d)(3), would be 80 percent (80/100) for a short taxable year ending on April 15 or June 15, 74 percent [(80 + 68) ÷ 200] for a short taxable year ending on September 15, and 69 percent [(80 + 68 + 59) ÷ 300] for a short taxable year ending on December 15. Since S's nonperforming loan percentage for a short taxable year ending on April 15 or June 15 would exceed 75 percent, pursuant to § 1.585-6(d)(4) S is considered financially troubled as of these dates. Thus, S is treated as if no amount will be included in income under § 1.585-6(a) and (b) for the year for purposes of applying section 6655(e)(2)(A)(i) with respect to the installments of estimated tax that are due on April 15, 1988, and June 15, 1988. However, since S's nonperforming loan percentage for a short taxable year ending on September 15 or December 15 would not exceed 75 percent, S is not considered financially troubled as of these dates. Thus, S is treated as if 20 percent of its net section 481(a) adjustment will be included in income under § 1.585-6(a) and (b) for the year for purposes of applying section 6655(e)(2)(A)(i) with respect to the installments of estimated tax that are due on September 15, 1988, and December 15, 1988.

T.D. 8513, 12/28/93.

---

§ 1.585-7 Elective cut-off method of changing from the reserve method of section 585.

(a) General rule. Any large bank (as defined in § 1.585-5(b)) that maintained a reserve for bad debts under section 585 for the taxable year immediately preceding its disqualification year (as defined in § 1.585-5(d)(1)) may elect to use the cut-off method set forth in this section. Any such election must be made at the time and in the manner prescribed by § 1.585-8. If a bank makes this election, the bank must maintain its bad debt reserve for its pre-disqualification loans, as prescribed in paragraph (b) of this section, and the bank must include in income any excess balance in this reserve, as required by paragraph (c) of this section. The bank may not deduct, for its disqualification year or any subsequent taxable year, any amount allowed under section 166(a) for pre-disqualification loans (as defined in paragraph (b)(2) of this section) that become worthless in whole or in part, except as allowed by paragraph (b)(1) of this section. However, except as provided in paragraph (d)(3) of this section, the bank may deduct, for its disqualification year or any subsequent taxable year, amounts allowed under section 166(a) for loans that the bank originates or acquires on or after the first day of its disqualification year and that become worthless in whole or in part. If a bank makes the election allowed by this paragraph (a), its change to the specific charge-off method of accounting for bad debts in its disqualification year does not give rise to a section 481(a) adjustment.

(b) Maintaining reserve for pre-disqualification loans. *(1) In general.* A bank that makes the election allowed by paragraph (a) of this section must maintain its bad debt reserve for its pre-disqualification loans (as defined in paragraph (b)(2) of this section). Except as provided in paragraph (d)(3) of this section, the bank must charge against the reserve the amount of any losses resulting from these loans (including losses resulting from the sale or other disposition of these loans), and the bank must add to the reserve the amount of recoveries with respect to these loans. In general, the reserve must be maintained in the manner provided by former section 166(c) of the Internal Revenue Code and the regulations thereunder. However, after the balance in the reserve is reduced to zero, the bank is to account for any losses and recoveries with respect to outstanding pre-disqualification loans under the specific charge-off method of accounting for bad debts, as if the bank always had accounted for these loans under this method.

(2) Definition of pre-disqualification loans. For purposes of this section, a pre-disqualification loan of a bank is any loan that the bank held on the last day of its taxable year immediately preceding its disqualification year (as defined in § 1.585-5(d)(1)). If the amount of a pre-disqualification loan is increased during or after the disqualification year, the amount of the increase is not treated as a pre-disqualification loan.

(c) Amount to be included in income when reserve balance exceeds loan balance. If, as of the close of any taxable year, the balance in a bank's reserve that is maintained under paragraph (b) of this section exceeds the balance of the bank's outstanding pre-disqualification loans, the bank must include in income the amount of the excess for the taxable year. The balance in the reserve is then reduced by the amount of this excess. See paragraph (d) of this section for rules on the application of this paragraph (c) when a bank disposes of loans.

(d) Effect of disposing of loans. *(1) In general.* Except as provided in paragraphs (d)(2) and (d)(3) of this section, if a bank that makes the election allowed by paragraph (a) of this section sells or otherwise disposes of any of its outstanding pre-disqualification loans, the bank is to reduce the balance of its outstanding pre-disqualification loans by the amount of the loans disposed of, for purposes of applying paragraph (c) of this section.

(2) Section 381 transactions. If a bank that makes the election allowed by paragraph (a) of this section transfers outstanding pre-disqualification loans to another corporation in a transaction to which section 381(a) applies, the acquiring corporation (the acquiror) must follow the rules of paragraph (d)(2)(i) or (ii) of this section.

(i) Acquiror completes cut-off method of change. Except as provided in paragraph (d)(2)(ii) of this section, the acquiror steps into the shoes of the transferor in the section 381(a) transaction with respect to using the cut-off method of change. Thus, the transferor's bad debt reserve immediately before the section 381(a) transaction carries over to the acquiror, and the acquiror must complete the cut-off method begun by the transferor. For purposes of completing the transferor's cut-off method, the acquiror's balance of outstanding pre-disqualification loans immediately after the section 381(a) transaction is the balance of these loans that it receives in the transaction, and the acquiror assumes all of the transferor's rights and obligations under this section.

(ii) Acquiror uses reserve method. If the acquiror is not a large bank (within the meaning of § 1.585-5(b)) immediately after the section 381(a) transaction and uses a reserve method of accounting for bad debts attributable to the pre-disqualification loans (and any other loans) received in the transaction, the acquiror does not step into the shoes of the transferor with respect to using the cut-off method of change. The transferor's bad debt reserve immediately before the section 381(a) transaction carries over to the acquiror, but the acquiror does not continue the cut-off method begun by the transferor. If the six-year moving average amount (as defined in § 1.585-2(c)(1)(ii)) for all of the loans received in the transaction exceeds the balance of the reserve that carries over to the acquiror, the acquiror increases this balance by the amount of the excess. Any such increase in the reserve results in a negative section 481(a) adjustment that is taken into account as required under section 381.

(3) Dispositions intended to change the status of pre-disqualification loans. This paragraph (d)(3) applies if a bank that makes the election allowed by paragraph (a) of this section sells, exchanges, or otherwise disposes of a significant amount of its pre-disqualification loans (as defined in paragraph (b)(2) of this section) and a principal purpose of the transaction is to avoid the provisions of this section by increasing the amount of loans for which deductions are allowable under the specific charge-off method. If this paragraph (d)(3) applies, the District Director may disregard the disposition for purposes of paragraphs (b)(1) and (d)(1) of this section or treat the replacement loans as pre-disqualification loans. If loans are so treated as pre-disqualification loans, no deductions are allowable under the specific charge-off method for the loans, except as provided in paragraph (b)(1) of this section, and the disposition that causes the loans to be so treated may be disregarded for purposes of paragraphs (b)(1) and (d)(1) of this section. If a bank sells pre-disqualification loans and uses the proceeds of the sale to originate new loans, this paragraph (d)(3) does not apply to the transaction.

(e) Examples. The following examples illustrate the principles of this section:

Example (1). Bank M is a bank that properly elects to use the cut-off method set forth in this § 1.585-7. M's disqualification year is its taxable year beginning on January 1, 1987. On December 31, 1986, M had outstanding loans of $700 million (pre-disqualification loans), and the balance in its bad debt reserve was $10 million. M must maintain its reserve for its pre-disqualification loans in accordance with § 1.585-7(b), and it may not deduct any addition to this reserve for taxable year 1987 or any later year. For these years, M may deduct amounts allowed under section 166(a) for loans that it originates or acquires after December 31, 1986, and that become worthless in whole or in part.

Example (2). Assume the same facts as in Example 1. Also assume that in 1987 M collects $150 million of its pre-disqualification loans, M determines that $2 million of its pre-disqualification loans are worthless, and M recovers $1 million of pre-disqualification loans that it had previously charged against the reserve as worthless. On December 31, 1987, the balance in M's bad debt reserve is $9 million ($10 million − $2 million + $1 million), and the balance of its outstanding pre-disqualification loans is $548 million ($700 million − $150 million − $2 million).

Example (3). Assume the same facts as in Examples 1 and 2. Also assume that on December 31, 1990, the balance in M's bad debt reserve is $5 million and the balance of its outstanding pre-disqualification loans is $25 million. In 1991

M collects $21 million of its outstanding pre-disqualification loans and determines that $1 million of its outstanding pre-disqualification loans are worthless. Thus, on December 31, 1991, the balance in M's bad debt reserve is $4 million ($5 million – $1 million), and the balance of its outstanding pre-disqualification loans is $3 million ($25 million – $21 million – $1 million). Accordingly, M must include $1 million ($4 million – $3 million) in income in taxable year 1991, pursuant to § 1.585-7(c). On January 1, 1992, the balance in M's reserve is $3 million ($4 million – $1 million).

Example (4). Assume the same facts as in Examples 1 through 3. Also assume that in 1992 M transfers substantially all of its assets to another corporation (N) in a transaction to which section 381(a) applies, and N is treated as a large bank under § 1.585-5(b)(2) for taxable years ending after the date of the transaction. Pursuant to § 1.585-7(d)(2)(i), N steps into M's shoes with respect to using the cut-off method. M's bad debt reserve immediately before the section 381(a) transaction carries over to N, and N must complete the cut-off procedure begun by M. For this purpose, N's balance of outstanding pre-disqualification loans immediately after the section 381(a) transaction is the balance of these loans that it receives from M.

Example (5). Assume the same facts as in Examples 1 through 4, except that N is not treated as a large bank after the section 381(a) transaction. Also assume that N uses the reserve method of section 585 and plans to use this method for all of the loans it acquires from M (including loans that were not pre-disqualification loans). Pursuant to § 1.585-7(d)(2)(ii), M's bad debt reserve immediately before the section 381(a) transaction carries over to N in the transaction; however, N does not continue the cut-off procedure begun by M and does not treat any loan as a pre-disqualification loan. If the six-year moving average amount (as defined in § 1.585-2(c)(1)(ii)) for all of N's newly acquired loans exceeds the balance of the reserve that carries over to N, N increases this balance by the amount of the excess. Any such increase in the reserve results in a negative section 481(a) adjustment that is taken into account as required under section 381.

T.D. 8513, 12/28/93.

§ 1.585-8 Rules for making and revoking elections under § 1.585-6 and 1.585-7.

(a) Time of making elections. *(1) In general.* Any election under § 1.585-6(b)(2), § 1.585-6(d)(2) or § 1.585-7(a) must be made on or before the later of—

(i) February 28, 1994; or

(ii) The due date (taking extensions into account) of the electing bank's original tax return for its disqualification year (as defined in § 1.585-5(d)(1)) or, for elections under § 1.585-6(d)(2), the year for which the election is made.

(2) No extension of time for payment. Payments of tax due must be made in accordance with chapter 62 of the Internal Revenue Code. However, if an election under § 1.585-6(b)(2), § 1.585-6(d)(2) or § 1.585-7(a) is made or revoked on or before February 24, 1994 and the making or revoking of the election results in an underpayment of estimated tax (within the meaning of section 6655(a)) with respect to an installment of estimated tax due on or before the date the election was so made or revoked, no addition to tax will be imposed under section 6655(a) with respect to the amount of the underpayment attributable to the making or revoking of the election.

(b) Manner of making elections. *(1) In general.* Except as provided in paragraph (b)(2) of this section, an electing bank must make any election under § 1.585-6(b)(2), § 1.585-6(d)(2) or § 1.585-7(a) by attaching a statement to its tax return (or amended return) for its disqualification year or, for elections under § 1.585-6(d)(2), the year for which the election is made. This statement must contain the following information:

(i) The name, address and taxpayer identification number of the electing bank;

(ii) The nature of the election being made (i.e., whether the election is to include in income more than 10 percent of the bank's net section 481(a) adjustment under § 1.585-6(b)(2) or (d)(2) or to use the cut-off method under § 1.585-7); and

(iii) If the election is under § 1.585-6(b)(2) or (d)(2), the percentage being elected.

(2) Certain tax returns filed before December 29, 1993. A bank is deemed to have made an election under § 1.585-6(b)(2) or (d)(2) if the bank evidences its intent to make an election under section 585(c)(3)(A)(iii)(I) or section 585(c)(3)(B)(ii) for its disqualification year (or, for elections under § 1.585-6(d)(2), the election year), by designating a specific recapture amount on its tax return or amended return for that year (or attaching a statement in accordance with § 301.9100-7T(a)(3)(i) of this chapter), and the return is filed before December 29, 1993. A bank is deemed to have made an election under § 1.585-7(a) if the bank evidences its intent to make an election under section 585(c)(4) for its disqualification year by attaching a statement in accordance with § 301.9100-7T(a)(3)(i) of this chapter to its tax return or amended return for that year, and the return is filed before December 29, 1993.

(c) Revocation of elections. *(1) On or before final date for making election.* An election under § 1.585-6(b)(2), § 1.585-6(d)(2) or § 1.585-7(a) may be revoked without the consent of the Commissioner on or before the final date prescribed by paragraph (a)(1) of this section for making the election. To do so, the bank that made the election must file an amended tax return for its disqualification year (or, for elections under § 1.585-6(d)(2), the year for which the election was made) and attach a statement that—

(i) Includes the bank's name, address and taxpayer identification number;

(ii) Identifies and withdraws the previous election; and

(iii) If the bank is making a new election under § 1.585-6(b)(2), § 1.585-6(d)(2) or § 1.585-7(a), contains the information described in paragraphs (b)(1)(ii) and (b)(1)(iii) of this section.

(2) After final date for making election. An election under § 1.585-6(b)(2), § 1.585-6(d)(2) or § 1.585-7(a) may be revoked only with the consent of the Commissioner after the final date prescribed by paragraph (a)(1) of this section for making the election. The Commissioner will grant this consent only in extraordinary circumstances.

(d) Elections by banks that are members of parent-subsidiary controlled groups. In the case of a bank that is a member of a parent-subsidiary controlled group (as defined in § 1.585-5(d)(2)), any election under § 1.585-6(b)(2), § 1.585-6(d)(2) or § 1.585-7(a) with respect to the bank is to be made separately by the bank. An election made by one member of such a group is not binding on any other member of the group.

(e) Elections made or revoked by amended return on or before February 28, 1994. This paragraph (e) applies to any election that a bank seeks to make under paragraph (b) of this section, or revoke under paragraph (c) of this section, by means of an amended return that is filed on or before February 28, 1994. To make or revoke an election to which this paragraph (e) applies, a bank must file (before expiration of each applicable period of limitations under section 6501) this amended return and amended returns for all taxable years after the taxable year for which the election is made or revoked by amended return, to any extent necessary to report the bank's tax liability in a manner consistent with the making or revoking of the election by amended return.

T.D. 8513, 12/28/93.

---

§ 1.586-1 Reserve for losses on loans of small business investment companies, etc.

Caution: The Treasury has not yet amended Reg § 1.586-1 to reflect changes made by P.L. 99-514.

(a) General rule. As an alternative to a deduction from gross income under section 166(a) for specific debts which become worthless in whole or in part, a taxpayer which is a financial institution to which section 586 and this section apply is allowed a deduction under section 166(c) for a reasonable addition to a reserve for bad debts provided such financial institution has adopted or adopts the reserve method of treating bad debts in accordance with paragraph (b) of § 1.166-1. In the case of such a taxpayer, the amount of the reasonable addition to such reserve for a taxable year beginning after July 11, 1969, shall be an amount determined by the taxpayer which does not exceed the amount computed under § 1.586-2. A financial institution to which section 586 and this section apply which adopts the reserve method is not entitled to charge-off any bad debts pursuant to section 166(a) with respect to a loan (as defined in § 1.586-2(c)(2)). Except as provided by § 1.586-2, regarding the manner of computation of the addition to the reserve for bad debts, the reserve for bad debts of a financial institution to which this section applies shall be maintained in the same manner as is provided by section 166(c) and the regulations thereunder with respect to reserves for bad debts. Except as provided by this section, no deduction is allowable for an addition to a reserve for bad debts of a financial institution to which section 586 and this section apply. For rules relating to deduction with respect to debts which are not loans (as defined in § 1.586-2(c)(2)), see section 166(a) and the regulations thereunder.

(b) Application of section. Section 586 and this section shall apply only to the following financial institutions—

(1) Any small business investment company operating under the Small Business Investment Act of 1958 as amended and supplemented (72 Stat. 689), and

(2) Any business development corporation, which for purposes of this section, means a corporation which was created by or pursuant to an act of a State legislature for purposes of promoting, maintaining, and assisting the economy and industry within such State on a regional or statewide basis by making loans which would generally not be made by banks (as defined in section 581 and the regulations thereunder) within such region or State in the ordinary course of their businesses (except on the basis of a partial participation), and which is operated primarily for such purposes.

T.D. 7444, 12/6/76.

---

§ 1.586-2 Addition to reserve.

Caution: The Treasury has not yet amended Reg § 1.586-2 to reflect changes made by P.L. 99-514.

(a) General rule. Except as provided by paragraph (b) of this section, the amount computed under this section is the amount necessary to increase the balance of the reserve for bad debts (as of the close of the taxable year) to the greater of—

(1) The amount which bears the same ratio to loans outstanding at the close of the taxable year as (i) the total bad debts sustained during the taxable year and the 5 preceding taxable years (or, with the approval of the Commissioner, a shorter period), adjusted for recoveries of bad debts during such period, bears to (ii) the sum of the loans outstanding at the close of such 6 or fewer taxable years, or

(2) the lower of—

(i) The balance of the reserve as of the close of the base year, or

(ii) If the amount of loans outstanding at the close of the taxable year is less than the amount of loans outstanding at the close of the base year, the amount which bears the same ratio to loans outstanding at the close of the taxable year as the balance of the reserve as of the close of the base year bears to the amount of loans outstanding at the close of the base year.

For purposes of subparagraph (2) of this paragraph, the term "base year" means the last taxable year beginning on or before July 11, 1969. For purposes of applying this paragraph, a period shorter than the 6 years generally would be appropriate only where there is a change in the type of a substantial portion of the loans outstanding such that the risk of loss is substantially increased. For example, if the major portion of a business development corporation's portfolio of loans changes from agricultural loans to industrial loans which results in a substantial increase in the risk of loss, a period shorter than the 6 years may be appropriate. If approval is granted to use a shorter period, the experience for those taxable years which are excluded shall not be used for any subsequent year. A request for approval to exclude the experience of a prior taxable year shall not be considered unless it is sent to the Commissioner at least 30 days before the close of the current taxable year. The request shall include a statement of the reasons such experience should be excluded.

(b) New financial institutions *(1) Small business investment companies.* In the case of a new financial institution which is a small business investment company to which section 586 applies, the amount computed under this section is the greater of the amount computed under paragraph (a) of this section or the amount necessary to increase the balance of the reserve for bad debts as of the close of the taxable year to the amount which bears the same ratio to loans outstanding at the close of the taxable year as—

(i) The total bad debts (as determined by the Commissioner) sustained by all such small business investment companies during the 12-month period ending on March 31 that ends with or within the taxpayer's previous taxable year, and during the five 12-month periods ending on March 31 that precede such 12-month period, adjusted for recoveries of bad debts during such periods (as determined by the Commissioner), bears to

(ii) The sum of the loans outstanding (as determined by the Commissioner) by all such small business investment companies at the close of each of such six 12-month periods ending on March 31.

(2) Business development corporations. In the case of a new financial institution which is a business development corporation to which section 586 applies, the amount computed under this section is the greater of the amount computed under paragraph (a) of this section or the amount necessary to increase the balance of the reserve for bad debts as of the close of the taxable year to the amount which bears the same ratio to loans outstanding at the close of the taxable year as—

(i) The total bad debts (as determined by the Commissioner) sustained by all such business development corporations during the calendar year ending with or within the taxpayer's previous taxable year and during the 5 calendar years preceding such calendar year, adjusted for recoveries of bad debts during such period (as determined by the Commissioner), bears to

(ii) The sum of the loans outstanding (as determined by the Commissioner) by all such business development corporations at the close of each of such 6 calendar years.

(c) Definitions. For purposes of this section—

(1) New financial institution. A financial institution is a new financial institution for any taxable year beginning less than 10 years after the day on which it (or any predecessor) was authorized to do business as a financial institution described in the applicable subparagraph of § 1.586-1(b). For this purpose, the term "predecessor" means (i) any taxpayer which transferred more than 50 percent of the total amount of its assets to the taxpayer and is described in the same subparagraph of § 1.586-1(b) which describes the taxpayer, or (ii) any predecessor of such predecessor.

(2) Loan. (i) The term "loan" means debt, as the term "debt" is used in section 166 and the regulations thereunder.

(ii) The term "loan" does not include the following items:

(A) Discount or interest receivable reflected in the face amount of an outstanding loan, which discount or interest has not been included in gross income;

(B) A debt evidenced by a security (as defined in section 165(g)(2)(C) and the regulations thereunder); and

(C) Any loan which is entered into or acquired for the primary purpose of enlarging the otherwise available bad debt deduction.

T.D. 7444, 12/6/76.

---

§ 1.591-1 Deduction for dividends paid on deposits.

Caution: The Treasury has not yet amended Reg § 1.591-1 to reflect changes made by P.L. 97-34.

(a) In general. *(1)* In the case of a taxpayer described in paragraph (c)(1) or (2) of this section, whichever is applicable, there are allowed as deductions from gross income amounts which during the taxable year are paid to, or credited to the accounts of, depositors or holders of accounts as dividends or interest on their deposits or withdrawable accounts, if such amounts paid or credited are withdrawable on demand subject only to customary notice of intention to withdraw.

(2) The deduction provided in section 591 is applicable to the taxable year in which amounts credited as dividends or interest become withdrawable by the depositor or holder of an account subject only to customary notice of intention to withdraw. Thus, amounts which, as of the last day of the taxable year, are credited as dividends or interest, but which are not withdrawable by depositors or holders of accounts until the following business day, are deductible under section 591 in the year subsequent to the taxable year in which they were so credited. A deduction under this section will not be denied by reason of the fact that amounts credited as dividends or interest, otherwise deductible under section 591, are subject to the terms of a pledge agreement between the taxpayer and the depositor or holder of an account. In the case of a domestic building and loan association having nonwithdrawable capital stock represented by shares, no deduction is allowable under this section for amounts paid or credited as dividends on such shares. In the case of a taxable year ending after December 31, 1962, for special rules governing the treatment of dividends or interest paid or credited for periods representing more than 12 months, see section 461(e).

(b) Serial associations, bonus plans, etc. If a taxpayer described in paragraph (c)(1) or (2) of this section, whichever is applicable, operates in whole or in part as a serial association, maintains a bonus plan, or issues shares, or accepts deposits, subject to fines, penalties, forfeitures, or other withdrawal fees, it may deduct under section 591 the total amount credited as dividends or interest upon such shares or deposits, credited to a bonus account for such shares or deposits, or allocated to a series of shares for the taxable year, notwithstanding that as a customary condition of withdrawal:

(1) Amounts invested in, and earnings credited to, series shares must be withdrawn in multiples of even shares, or

(2) Such taxpayer has the right, pursuant to bylaw, contract, or otherwise, to retain or recover a portion of the total amount invested in, or credited as earnings upon, such shares or deposits, such bonus account, or series of shares, as a fine, penalty, forfeiture, or other withdrawal fee.

In any taxable year in which the right referred to in subparagraph (2) of this paragraph is exercise, there is includible in the gross income of such taxpayer for such taxable year amounts retained or recovered by the taxpayer pursuant to the exercise of such right. If the provisions of paragraph (a) of § 1.163-4 (relating to deductions for original issue discount) apply to deposits made with respect to a certificate of deposit, time deposit, bonus plan or other deposit arrangement, the provisions of this paragraph shall not apply.

(c) Effective date. The provisions of paragraphs (a) and (b) of this section shall apply to—

(1) Dividends or interest paid or credited after October 16, 1962, by any taxpayer which (at the time of such payment or credit) qualifies as (i) a mutual savings bank not having capital stock represented by shares, (ii) a domestic building and loan association (as defined in section 7701(a)(19)), (iii) a cooperative bank (as defined in section 7701(a)(32)), or (iv) any other savings institution chartered and supervised as a savings and loan or similar association under Federal or State law; and

(2) Dividends paid or credited before October 17, 1962, by any taxpayer which (at the time of such payment or credit) qualifies as (i) a mutual savings bank not having capital stock represented by shares, (ii) a cooperative bank without capital stock organized and operated for mutual purposes and without profit, or (iii) a domestic building and loan association (as defined in section 7701(a)(19) before amendment by section 6(c) of the Revenue Act of 1962 (76 Stat. 982)).

T.D. 6188, 7/5/56, amend T.D. 6728, 5/4/64, T.D. 7154, 12/27/71.

PAR. 3. Section 1.591-1 is amended as follows:

1. Paragraph (a)(2) is amended by inserting "or a mutual savings bank described in section 591(b)" after "domestic building and loan association".

2. Paragraph (c)(2) is removed and paragraph (c)(1) is redesignated as paragraph (c)(2).

3. Paragraph (c)(2) as so redesignated is amended by inserting "and before the first day of the taxpayer's first taxable year ending after August 13, 1981," after "October 16, 1962," and by removing "; and" and inserting a period in lieu thereof.

4. A new paragraph (c)(1) is added which reads as follows:

Proposed § 1.591-1 Deduction for dividends paid on deposits [Amended]. [*For Preamble, see ¶ 150,911*]

(c) Effective date. * * * *(1)* Dividends or interest paid or credited during a taxable year ending after August 13, 1981, by any taxpayer which (at the time of such payment or credit) qualifies as (i) a mutual savings bank (including a mutual savings bank which has capital stock represented by shares and which is subject to, and operates under, Federal or State laws relating to mutual savings banks), (ii) a domestic building and loan association (as defined in section 7701(a)(19)), (iii) a cooperative bank (as defined in section 7701(a)(32)), or (iv) any other savings institution chartered and supervised as a savings and loan or similar association under Federal or State law; and

* * * * *

Proposed § 1.591-1 Deduction for dividends paid on deposits. [*For Preamble, see ¶ 150,911*]

* * * * *

(c) Effective date. * * *

(1) Dividends or interest paid or credited during a taxable year ending after August 13, 1981, by any taxpayer which (at the time of such payment or credit) qualifies as (i) a mutual savings bank (including a mutual savings bank which has capital stock represented by shares and which is subject to, and operates under, Federal of State laws relating to mutual savings banks), (ii) a domestic building and loan association (as defined in section 7701(a)(19)), (iii) a cooperative bank (as defined in section 7701(a)(32)), or (iv) any other savings institution chartered and supervised as a savings and loan or similar association under Federal or State law; and

* * * * *

§ 1.593-1 Additions to reserve for bad debts.

(a) In general. A mutual savings bank not having capital stock represented by shares, a domestic building and loan association, and a cooperative bank without capital stock organized and operated for mutual purposes and without profit may, as an alternative to a deduction from gross income under section 166(a) for specific debts which become worthless in whole or in part, deduct amounts credited to a reserve for bad debts in the manner and under the circumstances prescribed in this section and § 1.593-2. In the case of such an institution, the selection of either of the alternative methods for treating bad debts may be made by the taxpayer in the return for its first taxable year beginning after December 31, 1951. The method selected shall be subject to the approval of the Commissioner upon examination of the return. If the method selected is approved, it must be followed in returns for subsequent years, unless permission is granted by the Commissioner to change to another method. Application for permission to change the method of treating bad debts shall be made at least 30 days prior to the close of the taxable year for which the change is to be effective.

(b) Addition to reserve. Except as otherwise provided in § 1.593-2, the reasonable addition to a reserve for bad debts shall be any amount determined by the taxpayer which does not exceed the lesser of:

(1) The amount of its taxable income for the taxable year, computed without regard to section 593 and without regard to any section providing for a deduction the amount of which is dependent upon the amount of taxable income (such as section 170, relating to charitable, etc., contributions and gifts), or

(2) The amount by which 12 percent of the total deposits or withdrawable accounts of its depositors at the close of such year exceeds the sum of its surplus, undivided profits, and reserves at the beginning of the taxable year.

(c) Adjustments to reserve. Bad debt losses sustained during the taxable year shall be charged against the bad debt reserve. Recoveries of debts charged against the bad debt reserve during a prior taxable year in which the institution was subject to tax under chapter 1 of the Internal Revenue Code of 1954 or under chapter 1 of the Internal Revenue Code of 1939 shall be credited to the bad debt reserve. The establishment of such reserve and all adjustments made thereto must be reflected on the regular books of account of the institution at the close of the taxable year, or as soon as practicable thereafter. Minimum amounts credited in compliance with Federal or State statutes, regulations, or supervisory orders to reserve or similar accounts, or additional amounts credited to such reserve or similar accounts and permissive under such statutes, regulations, or orders, against which charges may be made for the purpose of absorbing losses sustained by an institution, will be deemed to have been credited to the bad debt reserve.

(d) Definitions. When used in this section and in § 1.593-2:

(1) Institution. The term institution means either a mutual savings bank not having capital stock represented by shares, a domestic building and loan association as defined in section 7701(a)(19), or a cooperative bank without capital stock organized and operated for mutual purposes and without profit.

(2) Surplus, undivided profits, and reserves. (i) The phrase surplus, undivided profits, and reserves means the amount by which the total assets of an institution exceed the amount of the total liabilities of such an institution.

(ii) For this purpose the term total assets means the sum of money, plus the aggregate of the adjusted basis of the property other than money, held by an institution. Such adjusted basis for any asset is its adjusted basis for determining gain upon sale or exchange for Federal income tax purposes. (See sections 1011 through 1022, and the regulations thereunder. For special rules with respect to adjustments to basis for prior taxable years during which the institution was exempt from tax, see section 1016(a)(3) and the regulations thereunder.) The determination of the total assets of any taxpayer shall conform to the method of accounting employed by such taxpayer in determining taxable income and to the rules applicable in determining its earnings and profits.

(iii) The term total liabilities means all liabilities of the taxpayer, which are fixed and determined, absolute and not contingent, and includes those items which constitute liabilities in the sense of debts or obligations. The total deposits or withdrawable accounts, as defined in subparagraph (3) of this paragraph, shall be considered a liability. In the case of a building and loan association having permanent nonwithdrawable capital stock represented by shares, the paid-in amount of such stock shall also be considered a liability. Reserves for contingencies and other reserves, however, which are mere appropriations of surplus, are not liabilities.

(3) Total deposits or withdrawable accounts. The phrase total deposits or withdrawable accounts means the aggregate of (i) amounts placed with an institution for deposit or investment and (ii) earnings outstanding on the books of account of the institution at the close of the taxable year which have been credited as dividends upon such accounts prior to the close of the taxable year, except that such term, in the case of a building and loan association, does not include permanent nonwithdrawable capital stock represented by shares, or earnings credited thereon.

(e) Examples. The provisions of this section may be illustrated by the following examples:

Example (1).

(i) Institution X, which keeps its books on the basis of the calendar year, has surplus, reserves, and undivided profits of $800,000 as of January 1, 1955, and total deposits or withdrawable accounts of $10,000,000 as of December 31, 1955. During 1955 the institution credits $30,000, as required by a Federal agency, to a Federal insurance reserve for the sole purpose of absorbing losses. Likewise, it credits $25,000, as permitted by State statute, to another reserve fund for the purpose of absorbing losses. In 1955 Institution X charges $5,000 against its bad debt reserve for losses sustained during the taxable year.

(ii) The taxable income of Institution X for the taxable year 1955, computed without regard to section 593 and without regard to any section providing for a deduction the amount of which is dependent upon the amount of taxable income, is $200,000.

(iii) Upon the basis of the facts as stated in subdivision (i) of this example, the amount by which 12 percent of the total deposits or withdrawable accounts of Institution X at the close of taxable year 1955 exceeds the sum of such institution's surplus, undivided profits, and reserves at the beginning of the taxable year is $400,000 (12 percent of $10,000,000, minus $800,000).

(iv) Institution X, therefore, may deduct, for the taxable year 1955, as an addition to a reserve for bad debts, any amount it may determine that does not exceed the lesser of the amounts determined in subdivision (ii) or (iii) of this example. That amount is $200,000 (as determined in subdivision (ii) of this example). Since under paragraph (c) of this section, the $30,000 credited to the reserve as required by the Federal agency and the $25,000 credited to the reserve as permitted by the State statute are regarded as amounts credited to a reserve for bad debts account Institution X can credit an additional $145,000 ($200,000 minus $55,000) to a general reserve for bad debts account at any time during the taxable year.

(v) The loss of $5,000 charged to the bad debt reserve during the taxable year does not affect the amount of the addition to the bad debt reserve provided for in paragraph (b) of this section. It is of significance only in determining the surplus, undivided profits, and reserves of Institution X as of January 1, 1956.

Example (2). The taxable income of Institution Y for the taxable year 1955, computed without regard to the deduction under section 593 and without regard to any section providing for a deduction the amount of which is dependent upon the amount of taxable income, is determined to be $250,000. The amount by which 12 percent of the total deposits or withdrawable accounts of Institution Y at the close of the taxable year exceeds the sum of such institution's surplus, undivided profits, and reserves at the beginning of the taxable year is $500,000. Institution Y credits $250,000 to its bad debt reserve in 1955. In 1957, it is determined that the correct taxable income of Institution Y for 1955, computed without regard to any deduction under section 593 and without regard to any section providing for a deduction the amount of which is dependent upon the amount of taxable income, is $275,000 and not $250,000. Assuming that Institution Y credits the additional $25,000 to its bad debt reserve, $275,000 is allowable as a deduction from gross income for such institution for the taxable year 1955.

PAR. 4. Section 1.593-1 is removed.

Proposed § 1.593-1 Additions to reserve for bad debts [Removed]. [*For Preamble, see ¶ 150,911*]

Caution: The Treasury has not yet amended Reg § 1.593-1 to reflect changes made by P.L. 104-188.

Proposed § 1.593-1 Organizations to which section 593 applies. [*For Preamble, see ¶ 150,911*]

Caution: The Treasury has not yet amended Reg § 1.593-1 to reflect changes made by P.L. 104-188.

The provisions of section 593 and §§ 1.593-2 through 1.593-8 (except 1.593-7), for taxable years ending after December 31, 1962, apply to (1) a mutual savings bank (including, for taxable years ending after August 13, 1981, a mutual savings bank described in section 591(b)), (2) a domestic building and loan association, or (3) a cooperative bank without capital stock organized and operated for mutual purposes and without profit. The term "thrift institution", as used in this section and §§ 1.593-2 through 1.593-8, refers to any such financial institution. For definition of the terms "domestic building and loan association" and "cooperative bank", see paragraphs (19) and (32), respectively, of section 7701(a).

§ 1.593-2 Additions to reserve for bad debts where surplus, reserves, and undivided profits equal or exceed 12 percent of deposits or withdrawable accounts.

Where 12 percent of the total deposits or withdrawable accounts of an institution at the close of the taxable year is equal to or less than the sum of such institution's surplus, undivided profits, and reserves at the beginning of the taxable year, a reasonable addition to the reserve for bad debts as determined under the general provisions of section 166(c) may be allowable as a deduction from gross income. In making such determination, there shall be taken into account (a) surplus or bad debt reserves existing at the close of December 31, 1951 (i.e., the amount of surplus, undivided profits, and reserves accumulated prior to January 1, 1952, and in existence at the close of December 31, 1951), and (b) changes in the surplus, undivided profits, and reserves of the institution from December 31, 1951, until the beginning of the taxable year. A deduction for an addition to the reserve for bad debts pursuant to this section will be authorized only in those cases where the institution proves to the satisfaction of the Commissioner that the bad debt experience of the institution warrants an addition to the reserve for bad debts in excess of that provided in paragraph (b) of § 1.593-1. For definitions, see paragraph (d) of § 1.593-1.

PAR. 5.

Section 1.593-2 is removed.

Proposed § 1.593-2 Additions to reserve for bad debts where surplus, reserves, and undivided profits equal or exceed 12 percent of deposits or withdrawable accounts [Removed]. [*For Preamble, see ¶ 150,911*]

PAR. 8.

Section 1.593-5 is redesignated as § 1.593-2 and is revised to read as follows:

Proposed § 1.593-2 Addition to reserves for bad debts. [*For Preamble, see ¶ 150,911*]

Caution: The Treasury has not yet amended Reg § 1.593-2 to reflect changes made by P.L. 104-188.

(a) In general. As an alternative to a deduction from gross income under section 166(a) for specific debts which become worthless in whole or in part, a thrift institution is allowed a deduction under section 166(c) for a reasonable addition to a reserve for bad debts provided that the thrift institution adopts or has adopted the reserve method of treating bad debts in accordance with paragraph (b) of § 1.166-1. The amount of the reasonable addition shall not exceed a maximum addition computed under § 1.593-3(a) and, for taxable years begining after sixty days after the publication of this notice as a final Treasury decision, shall be an amount at least equal to the amount computed under § 1.593-3(b). For each taxable year the thrift institution shall include in its income tax return (or amended return) a computation of the amount of the addition determined under section 593 and the regulations thereunder showing the method used to determine that amount. The use of a particular method in the return for a taxable year is not a binding election by the taxpayer to apply that method either for that taxable year or for subsequent taxable years. A thrift institution which adopts the reserve method is not entitled to charge off any bad debts under section 166(a) with respect to a loan (as defined in § 1.593-8(a)).

(b) Crediting to reserves. The amount of the reasonable addition to a reserve for bad debts computed under §§ 1.593-3 and 1.593-4 shall be credit to a reserve for losses on qualifying real property loans or to a reserve for losses on nonqualifying loans, whichever is applicable. The reserves for bad debts of a thrift institution shall be established and maintained in accordance with the rules set forth in § 1.593-5.

§ 1.593-3 Taxable years affected.

Sections 1.593-1 and 1.593-2 apply only to taxable years beginning after December 31, 1953, and ending after August 16, 1954, but before January 1, 1963, and all references to sections of the Code are to the Internal Revenue Code of 1954 before amendment by the Revenue Act of 1962. Sections 1.593-4 through 1.593-11 apply only to taxable years ending after December 31, 1962, and all references to sections of the Code are to the Internal Revenue Code of 1954 after amendment by the Revenue Act of 1962.

T.D. 6728, 5/5/64.

PAR. 6.

Section 1.593-3 is removed.

Proposed § 1.593-3 Amount of addition to reserves [Removed]. [*For Preamble, see ¶ 150,911*]

Proposed § 1.593-3 Amount of addition to reserves. [*For Preamble, see ¶ 150,911*]

Caution: The Treasury has not yet amended Reg § 1.593-3 to reflect changes made by P.L. 104-188.

(a) Maximum addition. The maximum reasonable addition to the reserve for losses on nonqualifying loans of a thrift institution is an amount computed, with respect to such nonqualifying loans, in the manner provided under section 585(b)(3) and § 1.585-2(c). The maximum addition to the reserve for losses on qualifying real property loans is an amount equal to the larger of (i) the amount allowable under section 593(b)(2) and § 1.593-4(b) (relating to the percentage of taxable income method); (ii) the amount allowable under section 593(b)(3) and § 1.593-4(c) (relating to percentage method); or (iii) the amount allowable under sections 593(b)(4), 585(b)(3) and § 1.585-2(c)(1) (relating to the experience method), computed taking into account only qualifying real property loans.

(b) Minimum addition. For taxable years beginning after sixty days from the date of publication of this notice as a final Treasury decision, a thrift institution shall make a minimum addition to the reserve for losses on qualifying real property loans and a minimum addition to the reserve for losses on nonqualifying loans. The minimum addition to the reserve for losses on nonqualifying loans is an amount computed in the manner provided in section 585(b)(3)(A) and § 1.585-2(c)(1)(ii). The minimum addition to the reserve for losses on qualifying real property loans is an amount equal to the lesser of (1) the amount allowable under section 593(b)(2) and § 1.593-4(b) (relating to the percentage of taxable income method); (2) the amount allowable under section 593(b)(3) and § 1.593-4(c) (relating to the percentage method); or (3) the amount allowable under section 585(b)(3)(A) and § 1.585-2(c)(1)(ii) (relating to the experience method) computed taking into account only qualifying real property loans. In the event that the lesser of the amounts referred to in the preceding sentence is zero, the minimum addition to the reserve for losses on qualifying real property loans is zero.

§ 1.593-4 Organizations to which section 593 applies.

Caution: The Treasury has not yet amended Reg § 1.593-4 to reflect changes made by P.L. 104-188, P.L. 100-647, P.L. 99-514, P.L. 97-34.

The provisions of section 593 and §§ 1.593-5 through 1.593-11 (except subsection (f) of section 593 and § 1.593-10) apply to any mutual savings bank not having capital stock represented by shares, any domestic building and loan association, and any cooperative bank without capital stock organized and operated for mutual purposes and without profit. The term "thrift institution", as used in this section and §§ 1.593-5 through 1.593-11, refers to any such financial institution. For definition of the terms "domestic building and loan association" and "cooperative bank", see paragraphs (19) and (32), respectively, of section 7701(a).

T.D. 6728, 5/4/64, amend T.D. 7549, 5/17/78.

PAR. 7. Section 1.593-4 is redesignated as § 1.593-1. Section 1.593-1 as so redesignated is revised to read as follows:

Proposed § 1.593-4 [Redesignated as § 1.593-1] [*For Preamble, see ¶ 150,911*]

PAR. 11. Section 1.593-6A is redesignated as § 1.593-4. Section 1.593-4 as so redesignated is amended as follows:

1. Its caption is revised to read "Addition to reserve for losses on qualifying real property loans".

2. Paragraph (b)(3) is amended by inserting "(which is not described in section 593(b))" after "mutual savings bank" in each of the two places where it appears, and by removing "paragraph (a)(1)(i) of § 1.593-5" and inserting "§ 1.593-2(a)" in lieu thereof in each of the two places where it appears.

3. Paragraph (b)(5)(i) is amended by removing "§ 1.593-10" and inserting "§ 1.593-7" in lieu thereof.

4. Paragraph (b)(5)(iv) is amended by inserting "(eighteen forty-sixths, for taxable years ending after December 31, 1978)" after "three-eighths" in each of the two places where it appears.

5. Paragraph (e) is amended by removing "paragraph (a)(1)(i) of § 1.593-5" and inserting "§ 1.593-2(a)" in lieu thereof and by removing the last sentence of paragraph (e).

6. Paragraphs (a)(1) and (b)(2)(i) are revised as set forth below. Paragraph (b)(2)(ii) is amended by redesignating the example therein as "Example (1)", and by adding new examples (2) and (3) immediately following example (1) as so redesignated and by adding new paragraph (f) immediately following paragraph (e). The revised and added provisions read as follows:

Proposed § 1.593-4 Addition to reserve for losses on qualifying real property loans. [*For Preamble, see ¶ 150,911*]

Caution: The Treasury has not yet amended Reg § 1.593-4 to reflect changes made by P.L. 104-188.

(a) In general. *(1) Amount of additional determined for the taxable year.* For purposes of paragraph § 1.593-2(a), the amount of the addition to the reserve for losses on qualifying real property loans for any taxable year beginning after July 11, 1969, is the amount which the taxpayer determines to constitute a reasonable addition to such reserve for such year. However, the amount so determined for such year shall be determined without regard to any amount charged for any taxable year against the reserve for losses on qualifying real property loans pursuant to § 1.593-7 (relating to certain distributions to shareholders by a domestic building and loan association). The addition to the reserve shall be determined under section 593(b)(2), (3), or (4) (relating, respectively, to the percentage of taxable income method, the percentage method, and the experience method). See § 1.593-3, for the maximum and minimum additions allowed. For each taxable year the taxpayer must include in its income tax return (or amended return) for such year a computation of the amount of the addition determined under this section. The use of a particular method in the return for a taxable year is not a binding election by the taxpayer to apply such method either for such taxable year or for subsequent taxable years. Thus, for example, in the case of a subsequent adjustment with respect to the income tax return (whether initiated by the taxpayer or by the Commissioner) which has the effect of increasing or decreasing taxable income, the amount of the addition to the reserve for losses on qualifying real property loans may be recomputed (subject to the rules of § 1.593-3) under whichever method the taxpayer selects for the purpose of such recomputation, irrespective of the method initially applied for such taxable year.

* * * * *

(b) Percentage of taxable income method. * * *

(2) Reduction of applicable percentage in certain cases. (i) General rules. If for the taxable year the percentage of the assets of a thrift institution, which are assets described in section 7701(a)(19)(C) (relating to assets of a domestic building and loan association) is less than—

(a) 82 percent of the total assets in the case of a thrift institution other than a mutual savings bank which is not described in section 591(b), the applicable percentage for such year provided by subparagraph (1) of this paragraph is reduced by three-fourths of 1 percentage point for each 1 percentage point of such difference; or

(b) 72 percent of the total assets in the case of a thrift institution which is a mutual savings bank which is not described in section 591(b), the applicable percentage for such year provided by subparagraph (1) of this paragraph is reduced by 1 1/2 percentage points for each 1 percentage point of such difference.

If such percentage is less than 60 percent (50 percent for a taxable year beginning before 1973 in the case of a mutual savings bank not described in section 591(b)) of the total assets in the case of any thrift institution, section 593(b)(2) and this paragraph are not applicable. The percentage of total assets specified in this subparagraph is computed as of the close of the taxable year or, at the option of the taxpayer, may be computed on the basis of the average assets outstanding during the taxable year. Such average is determined by computing such percentage either as of the close of each month, as of the close of each quarter, or as of the close of each semiannual period during the taxable year and by using the yearly average of the monthly, quarterly, or semiannual percentages. A thrift institution which is a mutual savings bank (as defined in section 591) and which determines the amount of the reasonable addition for the taxable year to the reserve for losses on qualifying real property loans under this paragraph shall file for such taxable year a statement which shall show the amount of assets defined in paragraph (e) of § 301.7701-13A as of the close of the taxable year and a brief description and the amount of all other assets, together with a description of the method used in determining such amounts. If the percentage specified in this subparagraph is computed by such thrift institution on the basis of the average assets outstanding during the taxable year, the statement shall also show such information as of the end of each month, each quarter, or each semiannual period and the manner of calculating the average.

(ii) Examples. The provisions of this subparagraph may be illustrated by the following examples:

Example (1). * * *

Example (2). N is a mutual savings bank which has capital stock represented by shares (as defined in section 591(b)) to which section 593 applies. For its taxable year beginning in 1983, 80.5 percent of N's assets (computed as of the close of that year) constitute assets described in section 7701(a)(19)(C). N's assets which are assets described in section 7701(a)(19)(C), when computed on semiannual, quarterly, and monthly bases, constitute 79.8, 79.6 and 79.5 percent, respectively, of its total assets computed on the corresponding bases. N's applicable percentage for 1983 is 39.25 percent, determined as follows:

	Percents
Percentage of total assets specified in *(a)* of subdivision (i) of this subparagraph	82.0
Percentage of total assets constituting assets described in section 7701(a)(19)(C)	80.5
Difference	1.15
Applicable percentage determined under table in subparagraph (1) of this paragraph	40.0

Reduction of applicable percentage required by *(a)* of subdivision (i) of this subparagraph (¾ of 1 percentage point for each full percentage point of difference)	.75
Applicable percentage	39.25

Example (3). Assume the same facts as in example (2) except that N is a mutual savings bank other than a mutual savings bank described in section 593(b) and 70.5 percent of N's assets (computed as of the close of that year) constitute assets described in section 7701(a)(19)(C). N's assets which are assets described in section 7701(a)(19)(C), when computed on semiannual, quarterly, and monthly bases, constitute 69.8, 69.6 and 69.5 percent, respectively, of its total assets computed on the corresponding bases. N's applicable percentage for 1983 is 38.5 percent, determined as follows:

	Percent
Percentage of total assets specified in *(b)* of subdivision (i) of this subparagraph	72.0
Percentage of total assets constituting assets described in section 7701(a)(19)(C)	70.5
Difference	1.5
Applicable percentage determined under table in subparagraph (1) of this paragraph	40.0
Reduction of applicable percentage required by *(b)* of subdivision (i) of this subparagraph (1½ percentage points for each full percentage point of difference)	1.5
Applicable percentage	38.5

* * * * *

(f) Definitions. For purposes of this section—

(1) Surplus, undivided profits, and reserves. The term "surplus, undivided profits, and reserves" means the amount by which the total assets of the taxpayer exceed its total liabilities. The determination of such total assets and total liabilities shall conform to the method of accounting employed by the taxpayer in determining taxable income and to the rules applicable in determining its earnings and profits. Total deposits or withdrawable accounts (as defined in subparagraph (3) of this paragraph but determined as of the beginning of the taxable year) shall be considered a liability. In the case of a domestic building and loan association or a mutual savings bank described in section 591(b) having permanent nonwithdrawable capital stock represented by shares, the paid-in amount of such stock shall also be considered a liability. However, reserves for contingencies and other reserves which are mere appropriations of surplus are not liabilities for purposes of this section.

(2) Total assets. The term "total assets" means the sum of money (including time or demand deposits with, or withdrawable accounts in, any financial institution), plus the aggregate of the adjusted basis (determined under § 1.1011-1) of the property other than money held by the taxpayer. For special rules with respect to adjustments to basis in the case of property acquired by the taxpayer in a transaction described in section 595(a), see section 595.

(3) Total deposits or withdrawable accounts. The term "total deposits or withdrawable accounts" means the total of the amounts placed with the taxpayer for deposit or investment. Such term also includes earnings outstanding on the books of account of the taxpayer at the close of the taxable year which have been credited as dividends or interest upon such deposits or withdrawable accounts prior to the close of such taxable year, and which are withdrawable on demand subject only to customary notice of intention to withdraw. In the case of a domestic building and loan association or a mutual savings bank described in section 591(b), however, such phrase does not include permanent notwithdrawable capital stock represented by shares, or earnings credited thereon.

§ 1.593-5 Addition to reserves for bad debts.

Caution: The Treasury has not yet amended Reg § 1.593-5 to reflect changes made by P.L. 100-647, P.L. 99-514, P.L. 97-34.

(a) Amount of addition. As an alternative to a deduction from gross income under section 166(a) for specific debts which become worthless in whole or in part, a thrift institution is allowed a deduction under section 166(c) for a reasonable addition to a reserve for bad debts. In the case of a thrift institution, the amount of the reasonable addition to such reserve for a taxable year may not exceed:

(1) For taxable years beginning after July 11, 1969, the sum of (i) the amount determined to be the reasonable addition to the reserve for losses on nonqualifying loans, determined in the same manner as is provided with respect to additions to the reserve for losses on qualifying real property loans under paragraph (d) of § 1.593-6A (relating to the experience method), and (ii) the amount determined under § 1.593-6A to be the reasonable addition to the reserve for losses on qualifying real property loans, or

(2) For taxable years beginning before July 12, 1969, the sum of (i) the amount determined under § 1.166-4 to be the reasonable addition to the reserve for losses on nonqualifying loans, and (ii) the amount determined under § 1.593-6 to be the reasonable addition to the reserve for losses on qualifying real property loans.

(b) Crediting to reserves required. *(1) In general.* The amounts referred to in paragraph (a)(1) and (2) of this section must be credited, respectively, to the reserve for losses on nonqualifying loans and to the reserve for losses on qualifying real property loans by the close of the taxable year, or as soon as practicable thereafter. For rules with respect to accounting for such reserves, see paragraph (a)(2) of § 1.593-7.

(2) Subsequent adjustments. If an adjustment with respect to the income tax return for a taxable year is made, and if such adjustment (whether initiated by the taxpayer or the Commissioner) has the effect of permitting an increase, or requiring a reduction, in the amount claimed on such return as an addition to the reserve for losses on non-qualifying loans or to the reserve for losses on qualifying real property loans, then the amount initially credited to such reserve for such year pursuant to subparagraph (1) of this paragraph may have to be increased or decreased, as the case may be, to the extent necessary to reflect such adjustment.

(c) Transition year. For rules governing the computation of taxable income in the case of a taxable year beginning in 1962 and ending in 1963, see § 1.593-9.

T.D. 6728, 5/4/64, amend T.D. 7549, 5/17/78.

PAR. 8. Section 1.593-5 is redesignated as § 1.593-2 and is revised to read as follows:

Proposed § 1.593-5 [Redesignated as § 1.593-2] [*For Preamble, see ¶ 150,911*]

Proposed § 1.593-2 Addition to reserves for bad debts. [*For Preamble, see ¶ 150,911*]

Caution: The Treasury has not yet amended Reg § 1.593-2 to reflect changes made by P.L. 104-188.

(a) In general. As an alternative to a deduction from gross income under section 166(a) for specific debts which become worthless in whole or in part, a thrift institution is allowed a deduction under section 166(c) for a reasonable addition to a reserve for bad debts provided that the thrift institution adopts or has adopted the reserve method of treating bad debts in accordance with paragraph (b) of § 1.166-1. The amount of the reasonable addition shall not exceed a maximum addition computed under § 1.593-3(a) and, for taxable years begining after sixty days after the publication of this notice as a final Treasury decision, shall be an amount at least equal to the amount computed under § 1.593-3(b). For each taxable year the thrift institution shall include in its income tax return (or amended return) a computation of the amount of the addition determined under section 593 and the regulations thereunder showing the method used to determine that amount. The use of a particular method in the return for a taxable year is not a binding election by the taxpayer to apply that method either for that taxable year or for subsequent taxable years. A thrift institution which adopts the reserve method is not entitled to charge off any bad debts under section 166(a) with respect to a loan (as defined in § 1.593-8(a)).

(b) Crediting to reserves. The amount of the reasonable addition to a reserve for bad debts computed under §§ 1.593-3 and 1.593-4 shall be credit to a reserve for losses on qualifying real property loans or to a reserve for losses on nonqualifying loans, whichever is applicable. The reserves for bad debts of a thrift institution shall be established and maintained in accordance with the rules set forth in § 1.593-5.

§ 1.593-6 Pre-1970 addition to reserve for losses on qualifying real property loans.

(a) In general. For purposes of paragraph (a)(2)(ii) of § 1.593-5, the amount of the addition to the reserve for losses on qualifying real property loans for any taxable year beginning before July 12, 1969, is the amount which the taxpayer determines to constitute a reasonable addition to such reserve for such year. However, the amount so determined for such year—

(1) Cannot exceed the largest of the amounts computed under one of the three methods described (b), (c), or (d) of this section (relating, respectively, to the percentage of taxable income method, the percentage of real property loans method, and the experience method),

(2) Cannot exceed the maximum permissible addition described in paragraph (e) of this section (if applicable), and

(3) Shall be determined without regard to any amount charged for any taxable year against the reserve for losses on qualifying real property loans pursuant to § 1.593-10 (relating to certain distributions to shareholders by a domestic building and loan association).

For each taxable year the taxpayer must include in its income tax return for such year a computation of the addition under this section. The use of a particular method in the return for a taxable year is not a binding election by the taxpayer to apply such method either for such taxable year or for subsequent taxable years. Thus, in the case of a subsequent adjustment described in paragraph (b)(2) of § 1.593-5 which has the effect of permitting an increase, or requiring a reduction, in the amount claimed in the return for a taxable year as an addition to the reserve for losses on qualifying real property loans, the amount of such addition may be recomputed under whichever method the taxpayer selects for the purposes of such recomputation, irrespective of the method initially applied for such taxable year. However, a taxpayer may not subsequently reduce the amount claimed in the return for a taxable year for the purpose of obtaining a larger deduction in a later year.

(b) Percentage of taxable income method. *(1) In general.* The amount determined under the percentage of taxable income method for any taxable year is an amount equal to 60 percent of the taxable income for such year, minus the amount determined under § 1.166-4 as a reasonable addition for such year to the reserve for losses on nonqualifying loans. However, the amount determined under such method shall not exceed the amount necessary to increase the balance (as of the close of the taxable year) of the reserve for losses on qualifying real property loans to an amount equal to 6 percent of such loans outstanding at such time.

(2) Taxable income defined. For purposes of this paragraph, taxable income shall be computed—

(i) By excluding from gross income any amount included therein by reason of the application of § 1.593-10 (relating to certain distributions to shareholders by a domestic building and loan association);

(ii) Without regard to any deduction allowable under section 166(c) for an addition to a reserve for bad debts;

(iii) Without regard to any section providing for a deduction the amount of which is dependent upon the amount of taxable income (such as section 170, relating to charitable, etc., contributions and gifts), other than sections 243, 244, and 245 (relating to deductions for dividends received); and

(iv) Without regard to any net operating loss carryback to such year under section 172.

In computing the deductions under sections 243, 244, and 245, section 246(b) (relating to limitation on aggregate amount of deduction) shall not apply. For purposes of subdivision (iii) of this subparagraph, a net operating loss deduction under section 172 is not a deduction the amount of which is dependent upon the amount of taxable income.

(c) Percentage of real property loans method. *(1) General rule.* The amount determined under the percentage of real property loans method for any taxable year is the amount necessary to increase the balance (as of the close of such year) of the reserve for losses on qualifying real property loans to—

(i) An amount equal to 3 percent of such loans outstanding at such time, plus

(ii) In the case of a taxpayer described in subparagraph (2) of this paragraph, an amount equal to—

(a) The lesser of 2 percent of such loans outstanding at such time, or $80,000, reduced (but not below zero) by

(b) The balance as of the close of such year, if any, of such taxpayer's supplemental reserve for losses on loans.

(2) Certain new companies. (i) Subparagraph (1)(ii) of this paragraph applies only in the case of a taxpayer which is a new company, and which does not have capital stock with respect to which distributions of property (as defined in section 317(a)) are not allowable as a deduction under section 591.

(ii) For purposes of this subparagraph, a taxpayer is a new company for any taxable year only if such year begins not more than 10 calendar years after the first day on which such taxpayer, or any predecessor of such taxpayer, was authorized by Federal or State law to do business as (a) a mutual savings bank not having capital stock represented by shares, (b) a domestic building and loan association, (c) a cooperative bank without capital stock organized and operated for mutual purposes and without profit, or (d) any other savings institution chartered and supervised as a savings and loan or similar association under Federal or State law.

(iii) As used in subdivision (ii) of this subparagraph, the term "calendar year" has the meaning assigned to such term in section 441 (relating to the period for computation of taxable income); and the term "predecessor" means any organization which transferred more than 50 percent of the total amount of its assets to the taxpayer, and which, prior to the time of such transfer, was (a) authorized by Federal or State law to do business as a mutual savings bank not having capital stock represented by shares, a domestic building and loan association, or a cooperative bank without capital stock organized and operated for mutual purposes and without profit, or (b) any other savings institution chartered and supervised as a savings and loan or similar association under Federal or State law. The term "predecessor" also means any predecessor of such predecessor.

(d) Experience method. The amount determined under the experience method for any taxable year is the amount determined under § 1.166-4 to be a reasonable addition for such year to the reserve for losses on qualifying real property loans.

(e) Maximum permissible addition where percentage of taxable income method or percentage of real property loans method is applied. *(1) 12 percent of deposits limitation.* If, for the taxable year, the taxpayer uses either the percentage of taxable income method described in paragraph (b) of this section or the percentage of real property loans method described in paragraph (c) of this section, then (unless subparagraph (2) of this paragraph applies) the maximum permissible addition for such year is equal to the lesser of—

(i) The amount determined under such paragraph (b) or (c), or

(ii) An amount which, when added to the amount determined under § 1.166-4 as an addition for such year to the reserve for losses on nonqualifying loans, equals the amount by which 12 percent of the total deposits or of depositors of the taxpayer at the close of such year exceeds the sum of the taxpayer's surplus, undivided profits, and reserves at the beginning of such year (taking into account any portion thereof which is attributable to the period before the first taxable year beginning after December 31, 1951).

For definition of the terms "surplus, undivided profits, and reserves" and "total deposits or withdrawable accounts", see paragraph (f) of this section.

(2) Special rule where a domestic building and loan association or corporative bank exceeds certain assets limitations. If, for the taxable year, the taxpayer uses either the percentage of taxable income method described in paragraph (b) of this section or the percentage of real property loans method described in paragraph (c) of this section, and if for such year such taxpayer qualifies as a domestic building and loan association under the first sentence of paragraph (19) of section 7701(a) (or as a cooperative bank under paragraph (32) thereof) solely by reason of the application of the second sentence of such paragraph (19) (that is, solely by reason of the fact that for such year more than 36 percent, but not more than 41 percent, of the amount of the total assets of such association or bank consists of assets other than assets described in section 7701(a)(19)(D)(ii)), then the maximum permissible addition for such year is equal to the amount determined under subparagraph (1) of this paragraph, reduced in accordance with the following table:

If the percentage of the taxpayer's assets which are not assets described in section 7701(a)(19)(D)(ii) exceeds—	But does not exceed—	The reduction shall be the following proportion of the amount determined under such subparagraph (1)—
Percent	Percent	
36	37	1/12
37	38	1/6
38	39	1/4
39	40	1/3
40	41	5/12

(f) Definitions. For purposes of this section—

(1) Surplus, undivided profits, and reserves. The term "surplus, undivided profits, and reserves" means the amount by which the total assets of the taxpayer exceed its total liabilities. The determination of such total assets and total liabilities shall conform to the method of accounting employed by the taxpayer in determining taxable income and to the rules applicable in determining its earnings and profits. Total deposits or withdrawable accounts (as defined in subparagraph (3) of this paragraph but determined as of the beginning of the taxable year) shall be considered a liability. In the case of a domestic building and loan association having permanent nonwithdrawable capital stock represented by shares, the paid-in amount of such stock shall also be considered a liability. However, reserves for contingencies and other reserves which are mere appropriations of surplus are not liabilities for purposes of this section.

(2) Total assets. The term "total assets" means the sum of money (including time or demand deposits with, or withdrawable accounts in, any financial institution), plus the aggregate of the adjusted basis (determined under § 1.1011-1) of the property other than money held by the taxpayer. For special rules with respect to adjustments to basis in the case of property acquired by the taxpayer in a transaction described in section 595(a), see section 595.

(3) Total deposits or withdrawable accounts. The term "total deposits or withdrawable accounts" means the total of the amounts placed with the taxpayer for deposit or investment. Such term also includes earnings outstanding on the books of account of the taxpayer at the close of the taxable year which have been credited as dividends or interest upon such deposits or withdrawable accounts prior to the close of such taxable year, and which are withdrawable on demand subject only to customary notice of intention to withdraw. In the case of a domestic building and loan association, however, such phrase does not include permanent nonwithdrawable capital stock represented by shares, or earnings credited thereon.

(g) Examples. The provisions of this section may be illustrated by the following examples:

Example (1). (i) Facts. X is a domestic building and loan association which was organized in 1947 and which makes its returns on the basis of the calendar year and the reserve method of accounting for bad debts. X's accounts contain the following entries:

Account	Balance as of— Jan. 1, 1965	Dec. 31, 1965
Total deposits or withdrawable accounts	$1,000,000	$1,200,000
Nonqualifying loans	50,000	60,000
Qualifying real property loans	900,000	940,000
Reserve for losses on nonqualifying loans	200	160*
Reserve for losses on qualifying real property loans	24,000	21,000*
Supplemental reserve for losses on loans	60,800	60,800
Surplus, undivided profits, and other reserves	15,000	18,040

* Computed before any addition for 1965 under section 166(c).

X's taxable income for 1965 (before any deductible addition to a reserve for bad debts and without regard to charitable contributions of $200) is $20,000, computed as follows:

Interest and other income	$19,940
Dividends received from Y Corporation, a domestic corporation subject to taxation under chapter 1 of the Code	400
	20,340
Deduction for 85 percent of dividends received computed without regard to the limitation of section 246(b)	340
Taxable income	20,000

It is assumed that under § 1.166-4 X's addition for 1965 to its reserve for losses on nonqualifying loans is $80.

(ii) Computation of addition to reserve for losses on qualifying real property loans.

(a) In general. X determines that the reasonable addition for 1965 to its reserve for losses on qualifying real property loans is $11,920. Such amount, computed under the percentage of taxable income method, is the largest of the amounts determined under (b), (c), and (d) of this subdivision, and does not exceed the 12 percent of deposits limitation computed under (e) of this subdivision.

(b) Percentage of taxable income method. The amount determined under the percentage of taxable income method is $11,920, that is, 60 percent of the taxable income for 1965, or $12,000 (60 percent of $20,000), minus $80, the addition for such year to the reserve for losses on nonqualifying loans. This amount is not subject to reduction under the 6 percent of qualifying real property loans limitation described in paragraph (b)(1) of this section since the addition of $11,920 to the $21,000 balance of the reserve for losses on qualifying real property loans at the close of 1965 will not increase such balance to an amount in excess of $56,400, that is, 6 percent of such loans of $940,000 outstanding at such time.

(c) Percentage of real property loans method. Since X is not a new company within the meaning of paragraph (c)(2) of this section, the amount determined under the percentage of real property loans method is $7,200, that is, the amount necessary to increase the balance of the reserve for losses on qualifying real property loans at the close of 1965 from $21,000 to an amount equal to 3 percent of such loans outstanding at such time, or $28,200 (3 percent of $940,000).

(d) Experience method. The amount determined under the experience method is zero since it is assumed that the $21,000 balance of the reserve for losses on qualifying real property loans at the close of 1965 before any addition for such year exceeds the maximum amount to which such reserve could be increased under such method.

(e) 12 percent of deposits limitation. The amount determined under the 12 percent of deposits limitation is $43,920, that is, $44,000 (the excess of 12 percent of $1,200,000 of deposits at the close of 1965, or $144,000, over the $100,000 of surplus, undivided profits, and reserves at the beginning of such year), minus $80, the addition for such year to the reserve for losses on non-qualifying loans. Since such $43,920 is greater than $11,920 (the amount determined under (b) of this subdivision), the 12 percent of deposits limitation does not apply for 1965.

(iii) Computation of taxable income for 1965. X's taxable income for 1965, after deducting the additions for such year to its reserves for losses on nonqualifying loans and on qualifying real property loans, after deducting the charitable contributions which were not taken into account in computing taxable income for purposes of the addition to the reserve for losses on qualifying real property loans, after including in taxable income dividends received from Y Corporation, and after taking into account the deduction for dividends received under section 243 (subject to the limitation in section 246(b)), is $7,800, computed as follows:

Interest and other income	$19,940	
Dividends received from Y Corporation	400	
		$20,340
Less:		
Deduction for charitable contributions	200	
85 percent of dividends received from Y Corporation	340	
Additions to reserves for bad debts	12,000	
		12,540
Taxable income		7,800

Example (2). Assume the same facts as in example (1), except that X Corporation was organized in 1957, and qualifies for the taxable year 1965 as a new company within the meaning of paragraph (c)(2) of this section. The maximum permissible addition for 1965 to X's reserve for losses on qualifying real property loans is $18,000, the amount computed under the percentage of real property loans method, since such amount is greater than (i) $11,920, the amount computed under the percentage of taxable income method, or (ii) zero, the amount computed under the experience method. The $18,000 amount (as computed under the percentage of real property loans method) is the amount necessary to increase the reserve for losses on qualifying real property loans from the $21,000 closing balance to $39,000, computed as follows:

3 percent of $940,000 of qualifying real property loans at close of 1965		$28,200
Plus:		
Lesser of $80,000 or $18,800 2 percent of such loans of $940,000)	$18,800	
Reduced by the balance of supplemental reserve for losses on loans	8,000	
		10,800
		39,000

Example (3). Assume the same facts as in example (1), except that for 1965, 38.4 percent of X's total assets consist of assets other than the assets described in section 7701(a)(19)(D)(ii). In such case, the maximum permissible addition of $11,920 for such year to the reserve for losses on qualifying real property loans (as determined under subdivision (ii) of example (1)) would be reduced by $2,980 (¼ of $11,920) to $8,940.

T.D. 6728, 5/4/64, amend T.D. 7549, 5/17/78.

PAR. 10. Section 1.593-6 is removed.

Proposed § 1.593-6 Pre-1970 addition to reserve for losses on qualifying real property loans [Removed].

[For Preamble, see ¶ 150,911]

§ 1.593-6A Post-1969 addition to reserve for losses on qualifying real property loans.

Caution: The Treasury has not yet amended Reg § 1.593-6A to reflect changes made by P.L. 104-188, P.L. 100-647, P.L. 99-514, P.L. 97-34.

(a) In general. *(1) Amount of addition determined for the taxable year.* For purposes of paragraph (a)(1)(ii) of § 1.593-5, the amount of the addition to the reserve for losses on qualifying real property loans for any taxable year beginning after July 11, 1969, is the amount which the taxpayer determines to constitute a reasonable addition to such reserve for such year. However, the amount so determined for such year—

(i) Cannot exceed the largest of the amount determined under section 593(b)(2), (3), or (4) (relating, respectively, to the percentage of taxable income method, the percentage method, and the experience method), and

(ii) Shall be determined without regard to any amount charged for any taxable year against the reserve for losses on qualifying real property loans pursuant to § 1.593-10 (relating to certain distributions to shareholders by a domestic building and loan association).

For each taxable year the taxpayer must include in its income tax return for such year a computation of the amount of the addition determined under this section. The use of a particular method in the return for a taxable year is not a binding election by the taxpayer to apply such method either for such taxable year or for subsequent taxable years. Thus, in the case of a subsequent adjustment described in paragraph (b)(2) of § 1.593-5 which has the effect of permitting an increase, or requiring a reduction, in the amount claimed in the return for a taxable year as an addition to the reserve for losses on qualifying real property loans, the amount of such addition may be recomputed under whichever method the taxpayer selects for the purpose of such recomputation, irrespective of the method initially applied for such taxable year.

(2) Method of determination. For purposes of this section and § 1.596-1 (relating to limitation on dividends received deduction), a thrift institution is deemed to have determined the addition to its reserve for losses on qualifying real property loans for the taxable year under the percentage of taxable income method provided by section 593(b)(2) and paragraph (b) of this section if the amount finally determined to be a reasonable addition for such year to such reserve exceeds the amount determined for such year under section 593(b)(3) (relating to the percentage method) and exceeds the amount determined for such year under section 593(b)(4) (relating to the experience method).

(b) Percentage of taxable income method. *(1) In general.* Subject to the limitations described in subparagraph (4) of this paragraph and in paragraph (e) of this section, the amount determined under section 593(b)(2) and this paragraph for the taxable year, if such section and paragraph are applicable, is an amount equal to the applicable percentage of the taxable income for such year, reduced by the amount determined under subparagraph (3) of this paragraph. For this purpose, taxable income is computed as provided in subparagraph (5) of this paragraph, and the applicable percentage (except as reduced under subparagraph (2) of this paragraph) is determined under the following table:

For a table year beginning in	The applicable percentage under this subparagraph is
1969	60 percent.
1970	57 percent.
1971	54 percent.
1972	51 percent.
1973	49 percent.
1974	47 percent.
1975	45 percent.
1976	43 percent.
1977	42 percent.
1978	41 percent.
1979 or thereafter	40 percent.

(2) Reduction of applicable percentage in certain cases. (i) General rule. If for the taxable year the percentage of the assets of a thrift institution, which are assets described in section 7701(a)(19)(C) (relating to assets of a domestic building and loan association) is less than—

(a) 82 percent of the total assets in the case of a thrift institution other than a mutual savings bank, the applicable percentage for such year provided by subparagraph (1) of this paragraph is reduced by three-fourths of 1 percentage point for each 1 percentage point of such difference; or

(b) 72 percent of the total assets in the case of a thrift institution which is a mutual savings bank, the applicable percentage for such year provided by subparagraph (1) of this paragraph is reduced by 1½ percentage points for each 1 percentage point of such difference.

If such percentage is less than 60 percent of the total assets in the case of any thrift institution (less than 50 percent of the total assets for a taxable year beginning before 1973 in the case of a thrift institution which is a mutual savings bank), section 593(b)(2) and this paragraph are not applicable. The percentage of total assets specified in this subparagraph is computed as of the close of the taxable year or, at the option of the taxpayer, may be computed on the basis of the average assets outstanding during the taxable year. Such average is determined by computing such percentage either as of the close of each month, as of the close of each quarter, or as of the close of each semiannual period during the taxable year and by using the yearly average of the monthly, quarterly, or semiannual percentages. A thrift institution which is a mutual savings bank and which determines the amount of the reasonable addition for the taxable year to the reserve for losses on qualifying real property loans under this paragraph shall file for such taxable year a statement which shall show the amount of assets defined in paragraph (e) of § 402.1-2 (Temporary Regulations On Procedure and Administration under Tax Reform Act of 1969) as of the close of the taxable year and a brief description and the amount of all other assets, together with a description of the method used in determining such amounts. If the percentage specified in this subparagraph is computed by such thrift institution on the basis of the average assets outstanding during the taxable year, the statement shall also show such information as of the end of each month, each quarter, or each semiannual period and the manner of calculating the average.

(ii) Example. The provisions of this subparagraph may be illustrated by the following example:

Example. M is a cooperative bank to which section 593 applies. For its taxable year beginning in 1970, 80.4 percent of M's assets (computed as of the close of such year) constitute assets described in section 7701(a)(19)(C). M's assets which are assets described in section 7701(a)(19)(C), when computed on semiannual, quarterly, and monthly bases, constitute 79.8, 79.6, and 79.5 percent, respectively, of its total assets computed on the corresponding bases. M's applicable percentage for 1970 is 56.25 percent, determined as follows:

	Percent
Percentage of total assets specified in *(a)* of subdivision (i) of this subparagraph	82.0
Percentage of total assets constituting assets described in section 7701(a)(19)(C)	80.4
Difference	1.6
Applicable percentage determined under table in subparagraph (1) of this paragraph	57.0
Reduction of applicable percentage required by *(a)* of subdivision (i) of this subparagraph (¾ of 1 percentage point for each full percentage point of difference)	.75
Applicable percentage	56.25

(3) Reduction for addition to reserve for nonqualifying loans. (i) General rule. Subparagraph (1) of this paragraph provides that, subject to certain limitations, the amount determined under the percentage of taxable income method provided by section 593(b)(2) and this paragraph for the taxable year is an amount equal to the applicable percentage of the taxable income for such year, reduced by the amount determined under this subparagraph. In the case of a thrift institution other than a mutual savings bank, the amount determined under this subparagraph is an amount equal to the amount determined under paragraph (a)(1)(i) of § 1.593-5 to be a reasonable addition for the taxable year to the reserve for losses on nonqualifying loans multiplied by a fraction—

(a) The numerator of which is 18 percent, and

(b) The denominator of which is the percentage (in no case less than 18 percent) of the assets of the taxpayer for such year which are not assets defined in paragraph (e) of § 402.1-2 of this chapter.

In the case of a thrift institution which is a mutual savings bank, the amount determined under this subparagraph is an amount determined in the manner described in the preceding sentence, except that the numerator of the fraction described therein is 28 percent, and the denominator of such fraction shall not be less than 28 percent. For purposes of this subparagraph, the percentage of assets for a taxable year which are not assets defined in paragraph (e) of § 402.1-2 of this chapter is determined upon the same annual or average basis as is used in determining the percentage specified in subparagraph (2) of this paragraph.

(ii) Examples. The provisions of this subparagraph may be illustrated by the following examples:

Example (1). K is a domestic building and loan association to which section 593 applies. The amount determined under subparagraph (1) of this paragraph (before reduction by the amount determined under this subparagraph) to be the reasonable addition for the taxable year to K's reserve for losses on qualifying real property loans is $100,000. The amount determined under paragraph (a)(1)(i) of § 1.593-5 as the reasonable addition for the taxable year to the association's reserve for losses on nonqualifying loans is $10,000. The percentage of K's assets which are not assets defined in paragraph (e) of § 402.1-2 is 24 percent. The amount determined under subparagraph (1) of this paragraph ($100,000) must be reduced by $7,500.

$10,000 × 18 percent/24 percent.

Therefore, subject to the limitations described in subparagraph (4) of this paragraph and in paragraph (e) of this section, the amount determined under this paragraph to be the reasonable addition for the taxable year to K's reserve for losses on qualifying real property loans is $92,500 ($100,000 less $7,500).

Example (2). The facts are the same as in example (1), except that the percentage of K's assets which are not assets defined in paragraph (e) of § 402.1-2 is 12 percent. The amount determined under subparagraph (1) of this paragraph (before reduction by the amount determined under this subparagraph) to be the reasonable addition for the taxable year to K's reserve for losses on qualifying real property loans must be reduced by $10,000.

$10,000 × 18 percent/18 percent.

Because the denominator of the fraction may not be less than 18 percent, the fraction used in determining the amount of such reduction is equal to 1.

(4) Overall limitation. The amount determined under this paragraph shall not exceed the amount necessary to increase the balance (as of the close of the taxable year) of the reserve for losses on qualifying real property loans to 6 percent of such loans outstanding at such time.

(5) Computation of taxable income. For purposes of this paragraph, taxable income is computed—

(i) By excluding from gross income any amount included therein by reason of the application of section 593(e) and § 1.593-10 (relating to certain distributions to shareholders by a domestic building and loan association).

(ii) Without regard to any deduction allowable under section 166(c) (whether or not determined under section 593) and the regulations thereunder for an addition to a reserve for bad debts.

(iii) (a) By excluding from gross income an amount equal to the excess (if any) or (1) the total gains of the taxable year arising from sales and exchanges at a gain of (i) obligations the interest on which is excludable from gross income under section 103, and (ii) corporate stock, over (2) the total losses of such year arising from sales and exchanges at a loss of such obligations and stock.

(b) The provisions of this subdivision (iii) may be illustrated by the following example:

Example. For its taxable year beginning in 1971, the gains and losses of a domestic building and loan association from sales of stock and securities (all of which were made on December 31, 1971) were as follows:

	Gain	Loss
Municipal bonds acquired July 1, 1969, the interest on which is excludable from income under sec. 103	$25,000	.....
Stock of Corporation A, acquired July 14, 1971	.....	$6,000

Stock of Corporation B, acquired Dec. 22, 1970................ $ 3,000 .....

For purposes of this paragraph, the association's taxable income for 1971 is computed by excluding $22,000 ($25,000 + $3,000 − $6,000) from its gross income.

(iv) By excluding from gross income an amount equal to the lesser of (a) three-eighths of the net long-term capital gain for the taxable year or (b) three-eighths of the net long-term capital gain for the taxable year from the sale or exchange of property other than property described in subdivision (iii) of this subparagraph.

(v) (a) By excluding from gross income so much of the amount of dividends with respect to which a deduction is allowable under part VIII, subchapter B, chapter 1, subtitle A of the Code (section 241 and following) as is in excess of the applicable percentage (determined under subparagraphs (1) and (2) of this paragraph) of the dividends received deduction (determined under part VIII, subchapter B, chapter 1, subtitle A of the Code, without regard to section 596) for the taxable year.

(b) The provisions of this subdivision (v) may be illustrated by the following example:

Example. For its taxable year beginning in 1977, a domestic building and loan association receives dividends of $100 with respect to which a dividends received deduction of $85 is allowable under section 243(a)(1). The association receives no other dividends for the taxable year. The association's applicable percentage for the taxable year, as determined under subparagraphs (1) and (2) of this paragraph, is 42 percent. For purposes of this paragraph, the association's taxable income is computed by excluding from gross income the excess of the amount of dividends received ($100) over the applicable percentage of the allowable dividends received deduction (42 percent of $85, or $35.70), computed without regard to section 596. Thus, for purposes of this paragraph, $64.30 ($100 less $35.70) is excluded from gross income. See section 596 and § 1.596-1 with respect to the computation of the dividends received deduction for purposes of determining taxable income under section 63(a).

(vi) For taxable years beginning before January 1, 1978, without regard to any deduction the amount of which is computed upon, or may be subject to a limitation computed upon, the amount of taxable income, and without regard to any net operating loss carryback to such year from a taxable year beginning before January 1, 1979. (For purposes of this subparagraph, a net operating loss deduction under section 172 is not a deduction the amount of which may be subject to a limitation computed upon the amount of taxable income.)

(vii) For taxable years beginning after December 31, 1977, by taking into account any deduction the amount of which is computed upon or may be subject to a limitation computed upon the amount of taxable income, and any other deduction or loss allowed under subtitle A of the Code, such as any deduction allowable under section 172 or any loss allowable under section 1212(a), unless otherwise provided in this subparagraph.

(c) Percentage method. [Reserved]

(d) Experience method. [Reserved]

(e) Percentage of deposits limitation where percentage of taxable income method or percentage method is applied. If the amount determined by the taxpayer to constitute a reasonable addition for the taxable year to the reserve for losses on qualifying real property loans is greater than the amount determined under paragraph (d) of this section (relating to the experience method), the amount so determined cannot exceed an amount which, when added to the amount determined under paragraph (a)(1)(i) of § 1.593-5 to be a reasonable addition for such year to the reserve for losses on nonqualifying loans, equals the amount by which 12 percent of the total deposits or withdrawable accounts of depositors of the taxpayer at the close of such year exceeds the sum of the taxpayer's surplus, undivided profits, and reserves at the beginning of such year (taking into account any portion thereof which is attributable to the period before the first taxable year beginning after December 31, 1951. The terms "surplus, undivided profit, and reserves" and "total deposits or withdrawable accounts" have the same meanings as are assigned to them in paragraph (f) of § 1.593-6.

T.D. 7549, 5/17/78, amend T.D. 7626, 5/31/79.

PAR. 11. Section 1.593-6A is redesignated as § 1.593-4. Section 1.593-4 as so redesignated is amended as follows:

1. Its caption is revised to read "Addition to reserve for losses on qualifying real property loans".

2. Paragraph (b)(3) is amended by inserting "(which is not described in section 593(b))" after "mutual savings bank" in each of the two places where it appears, and by removing "paragraph (a)(1)(i) of § 1.593-5" and inserting "§ 1.593-2(a)" in lieu thereof in each of the two places where it appears.

3. Paragraph (b)(5)(i) is amended by removing "§ 1.593-10" and inserting "§ 1.593-7" in lieu thereof.

4. Paragraph (b)(5)(iv) is amended by inserting "(eighteen forty-sixths, for taxable years ending after December 31, 1978)" after "three-eighths" in each of the two places where it appears.

5. Paragraph (e) is amended by removing "paragraph (a)(1)(i) of § 1.593-5" and inserting "§ 1.593-2(a)" in lieu thereof and by removing the last sentence of paragraph (e).

6. Paragraphs (a)(1) and (b)(2)(i) are revised as set forth below. Paragraph (b)(2)(ii) is amended by redesignating the example therein as "Example (1)", and by adding new examples (2) and (3) immediately following example (1) as so redesignated and by adding new paragraph (f) immediately following paragraph (e). The revised and added provisions read as follows:

Proposed § 1.593-6A [Redesignated as 1.593-4 and amended] [*For Preamble, see ¶ 150,911*]

§ 1.593-7 Establishment and treatment of reserves for bad debts.

Caution: The Treasury has not yet amended Reg § 1.593-7 to reflect changes made by P.L. 104-188, P.L. 100-647, P.L. 99-514, P.L. 97-34.

(a) Establishment of reserves. *(1) In general.* A taxpayer described in § 1.593-4 shall establish and maintain a reserve for losses on nonqualifying loans, a reserve for losses on qualifying real property loans, and, if required under paragraph (b)(4) or (c)(3)(i)(c) of this section, a supplemental reserve for losses on loans. For rules governing the crediting of additions to the reserve for losses on nonqualifying loans and the reserve for losses on qualifying real property loans, see paragraph (b) of § 1.593-5.

(2) Accounting for reserves. (i) The taxpayer shall establish and maintain as a permanent part of its regular books of account an account for each of the reserves established pursuant to subparagraph (1) of this paragraph. For purposes of the preceding sentence, a taxpayer may establish and main-

tain a permanent subsidiary ledger containing an account for each of such reserves. If a taxpayer maintains such a permanent subsidiary ledger, the total of the reserve accounts in such ledger and the total of the reserve accounts in any other ledger must be reconciled.

(ii) Any credit or charge to a reserve established pursuant to subparagraph (1) of this paragraph must be made to such reserve irrespective of whether the amount thereof is also credited or charged to any surplus, reserve, or other account which the taxpayer may be required or permitted to maintain pursuant to any Federal or State statute, regulation, or supervisory order. Minimum amounts credited in compliance with such Federal or State statutes, regulations, or supervisory orders to reserve or similar accounts, or additional amounts credited to such reserve or similar accounts and permissible under such statutes, regulations, or orders, against which charges may be made for the purpose of absorbing losses sustained by the taxpayer, may also be credited to the reserve for losses on nonqualifying loans or the reserve for losses on qualifying real property loans, provided that the total of the amounts so credited to the reserve for losses on nonqualifying loans, or to the reserve for losses on qualifying real property loans, for any taxable years does not exceed the amount described in subparagraph (1) or (2) of § 1.593-5(a) (whichever applies) as the addition to such reserve for such year.

(b) Allocation of pre-1963 reserves. *(1) In general.* In the case of a taxpayer described in § 1.593-4, the pre-1963 reserves, if any, of such taxpayer shall be allocated to (and constitute the opening balance of) the reserve for losses on nonqualifying loans, the reserve for losses on qualifying real property loans, and, if required under subparagraph (4) of this paragraph, the supplemental reserve for losses on loans. The term "pre-1963 reserves" means the net amount (determined as of the close of December 31, 1962) accumulated for taxable years beginning after December 31, 1951, in the taxpayer's reserve for bad debts pursuant to section 166(c) of the Internal Revenue Code of 1954 and section 23(k)(1) of the Internal Revenue Code of 1939 (including the amount of any bad debt reserves acquired from another taxpayer). For purposes of the preceding sentence in the case of a taxable year beginning before January 1, 1963, and ending after December 31, 1962, the part of such year occurring before January 1, 1963, shall be treated as a taxable year. Thus, the pre-1963 reserves of the taxpayer shall be an amount equal to—

(i) The sum of the amounts allowed as deductions for additions to a reserve for bad debts for taxable years beginning after December 31, 1951, and ending before January 1, 1963, plus

(ii) In the case of a taxable year beginning before January 1, 1963, and ending after December 31, 1962, the amount (determined under § 1.593-1 or 1.593-2) which would be allowable under section 166(c) as a deduction for an addition to a reserve for bad debts for the part of such year occurring before January 1, 1963, if such part year constituted a taxable year, minus

(iii) The total amount of bad debts charged against a reserve for bad debts during the period which begins with the opening of the first taxable year beginning after December 31, 1951, and which ends at the close of December 31, 1962, plus

(iv) The total amount of recoveries, during the period described in subdivision (iii) of this subparagraph, on bad debts charged against a reserve for bad debts in a taxable year beginning after December 31, 1951.

(2) Allocation to opening balance of reserve for losses on nonqualifying loans. (i) As of the close of December 31, 1962, the pre-1963 reserves shall first be allocated to (and constitute the opening balance of) the reserve for losses on nonqualifying loans in an amount equal to the lesser of (a) the amount of such pre-1963 reserves, or (b) the amount determined under subdivision (ii) of this subparagraph.

(ii) The amount referred to in subdivision (i)(b) of this subparagraph shall be the amount which would constitute a reasonable addition to the reserve for losses on nonqualifying loans under § 1.166-4 for a period in which the taxpayer's nonqualifying loans increased from zero to the amount thereof outstanding at the close of December 31, 1962.

(3) Allocation to opening balance of reserve for losses on qualifying real property loans. (i) Any portion of the pre-1963 reserves remaining after the allocation provided in subparagraph (2) of this paragraph shall, as of the close of December 31, 1962, be allocated to (and constitute the opening balance of) the reserve for losses on qualifying real property loans in an amount equal to the lesser of (a) the amount of such remaining portion, or (b) the amount determined under subdivision (ii) of this subparagraph. If the amount described in (a) of the preceding sentence is less than the amount described in (b) thereof, see § 1.593-8 for allocation of pre-1952 surplus, if any, to the opening balance of such reserve.

(ii) The amount referred to in subdivision (i)(b) of this subparagraph shall be an amount equal to the greater of—

(a) 3 percent of the taxpayer's qualifying real property loans outstanding at the close of December 31, 1962, or

(b) The amount which would constitute a reasonable addition to the reserve for losses on such loans under § 1.166-4 for a period in which the amount of such loans increased from zero to the amount thereof outstanding at the close of December 31, 1962.

(4) Allocation to supplemental reserve for losses on loans. Any portion of the pre-1963 reserves remaining after the allocations provided in subparagraphs (2) and (3) of this paragraph shall be allocated in its entirety to the supplemental reserve for losses on loans.

(5) Examples. This paragraph may be illustrated by the following examples:

Example (1). (i) Facts. X Corporation, a domestic building and loan association organization organized on April 1, 1954, makes its returns on the basis of a taxable year ending March 31 and the reserve method of accounting for bad debts. For its taxable years ending March 31, 1955, through March 31, 1962, X was allowed a total of $750,000 as deductible additions to its reserve for bad debts under section 166(c). For its taxable year ending March 31, 1963, X was allowed a deduction under section 166(c) for an addition to a reserve for bad debts. Of such deduction $46,000 was determined under § 1.593-1 (relating to additions to reserve for bad debts) by reference to § 1.593-9 (relating to taxable income for taxable years beginning in 1962 and ending in 1963) as the amount which would be allowable for the period April 1 through December 31, 1962, if such period constituted a taxable year. During the taxable years ending March 31, 1955, through March 31, 1963, X charged bad debts of $55,000 against its reserve for bad debts and made recoveries on such debts of $10,000. Of such bad debt charges and recoveries, $50,000 was charged off and $9,000 was recovered prior to January 1, 1963. At the close of December 31, 1962, X had outstanding nonqualifying loans of $500,000 and outstanding qualifying real property loans of

$10 million. It is assumed that, under § 1.166-4, $2,000 would constitute a reasonable addition to the reserve for losses on nonqualifying loans for a period in which such loans increased from zero to $500,000 and $20,000 would constitute a reasonable addition to the reserve for losses on qualifying real property loans for a period in which such loans increased from zero to $10 million.

(ii) Pre-1963 reserves determined. X's pre-1963 reserves are $755,000, computed as follows:

Deductible additions to reserve for bad debts:

Deductible additions to reserve for bad debts:		
Years ending March 31, 1955, through March 31, 1962	$750,000	
Period April 1 through December 31, 1962	46,000	
		$796,000
Less:		
Net bad debt losses for period April 1, 1954, through December 31, 1962:		
Bad debts	50,000	
Recoveries	(9,000)	41,000
		755,000

(iii) Allocation to opening balance of reserve for losses on nonqualifying loans. The portion of the $755,000 of pre-1963 reserves to be allocated to the reserve for losses on nonqualifying loans as the opening balance thereof is $2,000 since such amount would constitute a reasonable addition to the reserve for losses on nonqualifying loans under § 1.166-4 for a period in which the amount of such loans increased from zero to $500,000.

(iv) Allocation to opening balance of reserve for losses on qualifying real property loans. Of the $753,000 ($755,000 minus $2,000) of pre-1963 reserves remaining after the allocation described in subdivision (iii) of this example, $300,000 (3 percent of $10 million, the total amount of qualifying real property loans outstanding at the close of December 31, 1962) is allocated to the opening balance of the reserve for losses on qualifying real property loans, since such amount is greater than $20,000, the amount which would constitute a reasonable addition to the reserve for losses on such loans under § 1.166-4 for a period in which the amount of such loans increased from zero to $10 million.

(v) Allocation to supplemental reserve for losses on loans. The balance of the pre-1963 reserves, or $453,000 ($755,000 minus the sum of $2,000 and $300,000), is allocated in its entirety to the supplemental reserve for losses on loans.

Example (2). Assume the same facts as in example (1), except that X was organized in 1936, and on December 31, 1962, had pre-1963 reserves of only $15,000 (rather than $755,000). In such case, $2,000 of such pre-1963 reserves would be allocated to, and constitute the opening balance of, the reserve for losses on nonqualifying loans, and $13,000 ($15,000 minus $2,000) would be allocated to and constitute part of the opening balance of the reserve for losses on qualifying real property loans. However, since such $13,000 is less than $300,000 (3 percent of $10 million), the opening balance of the reserve for losses on qualifying real property loans must be increased by so much of the taxpayer's pre-1952 surplus as is necessary to increase such opening balance to $300,000. For rules on the allocation of pre-1952 surplus to the opening balance of the reserve for losses on qualifying real property loans, see § 1.593-8.

(c) Treatment of reserves. *(1) In general.* Except as provided in paragraph (d) of § 1.593-8 (relating to the allocation of pre-1952 surplus), each of the reserves established pursuant to paragraph (a) of this section shall be treated, for purposes of subtitle A of the Code, as a reserve for bad debts, except that no deduction shall be allowed under section 166 for any addition to the supplemental reserve for losses on loans. Accordingly, if in any taxable year the taxpayer charges any of the reserves established pursuant to paragraph (a) of this section for an item other than a bad debt, gross income for such year shall be increased by the amount of such charge. For special rules in case of certain nondeductible distributions to shareholders by a domestic building and loan association, see § 1.593-10.

(2) Bad debt losses. Any bad debt in respect of a nonqualifying loan shall be charged against the reserve for losses on nonqualifying loans, and any bad debt in respect of a qualifying real property loan shall be charged against the reserve for losses on qualifying real property loans. At the option of the taxpayer, however, any bad debt in respect of either class of loans may be charged in whole or in part against the supplemental reserve for losses on loans.

(3) Recoveries of bad debts. Any amount recovered after December 31, 1962, in respect of a bad debt shall be credited to the reserves established pursuant to paragraph (a) of this section in the following manner:

(i) If the recovery is in respect of a bad debt which was charged prior to January 1, 1963, against a reserve for bad debts established pursuant to section 166(c) of the Internal Revenue Code of 1954, or section 23(k)(1) of the Internal Revenue Code of 1939, then the amount recovered shall be credited—

(a) First, to the reserve for losses on nonqualifying loans in an amount equal to the amount, if any, by which the amount determined under subdivision (ii) of paragraph (b)(2) of this section exceeds the opening balance of such reserve (determined under such paragraph (b)(2)),

(b) Second, to the reserve for losses on qualifying real property loans in an amount equal to the amount, if any, by which the amount determined under subdivision (ii) of paragraph (b)(3) of this section exceeds the opening balance of such reserve (determined under such paragraph (b)(3)), and

(c) Finally, to the supplemental reserve for losses on loans.

For purposes of determining the amounts of the credits under (a) and (b) of this subdivision, the opening balances of the reserve for losses on nonqualifying loans and the reserve for losses on qualifying real property loans shall be deemed to include the sum of the amounts of any prior credits made to such reserves pursuant to this subdivision.

(ii) If the recovery is in respect of a bad debt which is charged after December 31, 1962, against only one of the reserves established pursuant to paragraph (a) of this section, the entire amount recovered shall be credited to the reserve so charged.

(iii) If the recovery is in respect of a bad debt which is charged after December 31, 1962, against more than one of the reserves established pursuant to paragraph (a) of this section, then the amount recovered shall be credited to each of the reserves so charged in the ratio which the amount of the bad debt charged against such reserve bears to the total amount of such bad debt charged against both such reserves.

(iv) Subdivision (i) of this subparagraph may be illustrated by the following example:

Example. In 1962, the taxpayer sustained a bad debt of $10,000, which was charged against a reserve for bad debts established pursuant to section 166(c). As of the close of December 31, 1962, the balance of the taxpayer's reserve for losses on nonqualifying loans was $2,000, the amount determined under paragraph (b)(2)(ii) of this section. As of the same time, the balance of the taxpayer's reserve for losses on qualifying real property loans was $100,000, but the amount determined under paragraph (b)(3)(ii) of this section was $106,000. In 1963, the taxpayer recovers $8,000 of the $10,000 charged off in 1962. Of the $8,000 recovered in 1963, $6,000 ($106,000 minus $100,000) is credited to the reserve for losses on qualifying real property loans, and the balance of $2,000 is credited to the supplemental reserve for losses on loans.

T.D. 6728, 5/4/64, amend T.D. 7549, 5/17/78.

PAR. 12. Section 1.593-7 is redesignated as § 1.593-5. Section 1.593-5 as so redesignated is amended as follows:

1. Paragraph (a)(1) is amended by removing "paragraph (b) of § 1.593-5"; and inserting in its place "§ 1.593-2".

2. Paragraph (a)(2)(ii) is amended by removing "subparagraph (1) or (2) of § 1.593-5(a) (whichever applies) as the addition to such reserve for such year year" and inserting "§ 1.593-3" in lieu thereof.

3. Paragraph (b)(1)(ii) is amended by removing "(determined under § 1.593-1 or § 1.593-2)" and inserting "(determined under section 593)" in lieu thereof.

4. Example (1)(i) of paragraph (b)(5) is amended by removing "under § 1.593-1 (relating to additions to reserve for bad debts) by reference to § 1.593-9 (relating to taxable income for taxable years beginning in 1962 and ending in 1963)".

5. Also, in § 1.593-5 as so redesignated, the references "§ 1.593-4", "§ 1.593-5", "§ 1.593-8", and "§ 1.593-10" are removed and "§ 1.593-1", "§ 1.593-2", "§ 1.593.6", and "§ 1.593-7", respectively, are inserted in lieu thereof in each place they appear as a reference.

Proposed § 1.593-7 [Redesignated as 1.593-5 and amended] [*For Preamble, see ¶ 150,911*]

PAR. 15. Section 1.593-10 is redesignated as § 1.593-7. Section 1.593-7 as so redesignated is amended as follows:

1. Paragraph (b)(1) and (2) is amended by inserting "or institution" after "association" in both places that "association" appears.

2. Paragraph (b)(3)(i) is amended by removing "§ 1.593-6 or § 1.593-6A (whichever is applicable)" and inserting "§ 1.593-4" in lieu thereof.

3. Paragraph (b)(3)(ii)(b) is amended by removing "paragraph (d) of § 1.593-6 or paragraph (d) of § 1.593-6A, whichever is applicable" and inserting "§ 1.593-4" in lieu thereof.

4. Examples (1)(i), (2)(i), and (3)(i) of paragraph (d) are amended by removing the phrase "described in paragraph (d) of § 1.593-6".

5. The references "section 593(f)", "§ 1.593-7", and "§ 1.593-8" are removed and "section 593(e)", "§ 1.593-5", and "§ 1.593-6", respectively, are inserted in lieu thereof in each place that they appear as a reference or as part of a reference in § 1.593-7 as so redesignated.

6. Paragraph (a) is revised to read as follows:

Proposed § 1.593-7 Certain distributions to shareholders by a domestic building and loan association. [*For Preamble, see ¶ 150,911*]

Caution: The Treasury has not yet amended Reg § 1.593-7 to reflect changes made by P.L. 104-188.

(a) In general. Section 593(e) provides that if a domestic building and loan association (as defined in section 7701(a)(19) and the regulations thereunder) distributes property after December 31, 1962, or an institution that is treated as a mutual savings bank under section 591(b) distributes property during a taxable year ending after August 13, 1981, to a shareholder with respect to its stock and if the amount of such distribution is not allowable to the association as a deduction under section 591 (relating to deduction for dividends paid on deposits), then, notwithstanding any other provision of the Code, the distribution shall be treated as provided in paragraphs (b) and (c) of this section. For purposes of the preceding sentence, the term " distribution" includes any distribution in redemption of stock to which section 302(a) or 303 applies, or in partial or complete liquidation of the association or institution, as well as any other distribution which the association or institution may make to a shareholder with respect to its stock. For definition of the term "property", see section 317(a). For determination of the amount of a distribution, see section 301(b). For taxable years beginning after July 11, 1969, this paragraph is not applicable to any transaction to which section 381 (relating to carryovers in certain corporate acquisitions) and the regulations thereunder apply. This paragraph also does not apply to any distribution made on or after January 1, 1981, to the Federal Savings and Loan Insurance Corporation in redemption of an interest in an association, if the interest was originally received by the Federal Savings and Loan Insurance Corporation in exchange for financial assistance under section 406(f) of the National Housing Act (12 U.S.C. 1729(f)).

* * * * *

§ 1.593-8 Allocation of pre-1952 surplus to opening balance of reserve for losses on qualifying real property loans.

(a) General rule. In the case of a taxpayer described in § 1.593-4, if the amount of pre-1963 reserves allocated (under paragraph (b)(3)(i) of § 1.593-7) to the opening balance of the reserve for losses on qualifying real property loans is less than an amount equal to the greater of—

(1) The total amount of qualifying real property loans outstanding at the close of December 31, 1962, multiplied by 3 percent, or

(2) The amount which would constitute a reasonable addition to the reserve for losses on such loans under § 1.166-4 for a period in which the amount of such loans increased from zero to the amount thereof outstanding at the close of December 31, 1962,

then such opening balance shall be increased by an amount equal to so much of the "pre-1952 surplus" of the taxpayer as is necessary to increase such opening balance to the greater of the amounts described in subparagraph (1) or (2) of this paragraph. The amount of such increase shall be deemed to be included in such opening balance solely for the limited purpose described in paragraph (d) of this section.

(b) Pre-1952 surplus defined. *(1) In general.* For purposes of this section and § 1.593-7, the term "pre-1952 surplus" means an amount equal to—

(i) The sum of the taxpayer's surplus, undivided profits, and reserves determined (under the principles of paragraph (d)(2) of § 1.593-1) as of the close of the taxpayer's last taxable year beginning before January 1, 1952 (including any amount acquired from another taxpayer), minus

(ii) The amount of any impairments of such sum (as determined under paragraph (c) of this section).

(2) Reduction for certain excludable interest. (i) The amount otherwise determined under subparagraph (1) of this paragraph may, at the option of the taxpayer, be reduced by the portion, if any, of such amount which is attributable to interest which would have been excludable from gross income of such taxpayer under section 22(b)(4) of the Internal Revenue Code of 1939 (relating to interest on governmental obligations) or the corresponding provisions of prior revenue laws, had such taxpayer been subject, when such interest was received or accrued, to the income tax imposed by such Code or prior revenue laws.

(ii) For purposes of subdivision (i) of this subparagraph, the portion of the amount otherwise determined under subparagraph (1) of this paragraph which is attributable to interest which would have been excludable from gross income shall be determined by multiplying such amount by the ratio which—

(a) The total amount of such excludable interest for the period before the taxpayer's first taxable year beginning after December 31, 1951, bears to

(b) The total amount of the taxpayer's gross income, plus the total amount of such excludable interest, for such period.

If the amount determined under subparagraph (1)(i) of this paragraph includes any amount acquired from another taxpayer, then the gross income and excludable interest of the taxpayer for the period before its first taxable year beginning after December 31, 1951, shall include the gross income and excludable interest (for the same period) of such other taxpayer.

(c) Impairment of surplus, undivided profits, and reserves. *(1) General rule.* In the case of a taxable year beginning after December 31, 1951, and ending before January 1, 1963, if for such year—

(i) The amount described in paragraph (b)(1)(i) of this section (as decreased under subparagraph (3)(i) of this paragraph), exceeds

(ii) The sum of the taxpayer's surplus, undivided profits, and reserves (excluding the amount of any pre-1963 reserves) determined as of the close of such year under the principles of paragraph (d)(2) of § 1.593-1,

then the amount described in paragraph (b)(1)(i) of this section may, at the option of the taxpayer, be reduced by the amount of such excess.

(2) Transition year. In the case of a taxable year beginning before January 1, 1963, and ending after December 31, 1962, the part of such year which occurs before January 1, 1963, shall be considered to be a taxable year for purposes of subparagraph (1) of this paragraph.

(3) Rules for applying subparagraph (1). (i) For purposes of subparagraph (1)(i) of this paragraph, the amount described in paragraph (b)(1)(i) of this section shall be decreased by the total of any reductions under subparagraph (1) of this paragraph for prior taxable years; and

(ii) For purposes of subparagraph (1)(ii) of this paragraph, the term "pre-1963 reserves" means the amount determined under the principles of paragraph (b)(1) of § 1.593-7 for the period which begins with the first day of the first taxable year beginning after December 31, 1951, and which ends at the close of the taxable year with respect to which the computation under subparagraph (1) is being made.

(d) Treatment of pre-1952 surplus. Any portion of the taxpayer's pre-1952 surplus which, pursuant to paragraph (a) of this section, is deemed to be included in the opening balance of the reserve for losses on qualifying real property loans shall not be treated as a reserve for bad debts for any purpose other than computing for any taxable year the amount determined under the method described in paragraph (b), (c), or (d) of § 1.593-6 (relating, respectively, to the percentage of taxable income method, the percentage of real property loans method, and the experience method) or paragraph (b), (c), or (d) of § 1.593-6A (relating, respectively, to the percentage of taxable income method, the percentage method, and the experience method). For such limited purpose, such portion shall be deemed to remain in, and constitute a part of, the reserve for losses on qualifying real property loans. For all other purposes, such portion will retain its character as part of the taxpayer's pre-1952 surplus.

(e) Example. The provisions of this section may be illustrated by the following example:

Example. (1) Facts. X Corporation, a mutual savings bank organized in 1934, makes its returns on the basis of the calendar year and the reserve method of accounting for bad debts. For the taxable years 1934 through 1951, X's gross income was $2.7 million, in addition to which X received $300,000 of interest which would have been excludable from gross income under section 22(b)(4) of the Internal Revenue Code of 1939, or the corresponding provisions of prior revenue laws, if X had been subject to the income tax imposed by such Code or prior revenue laws when such interest was received. At the close of 1951, the sum of X's surplus, undivided profits, and reserves was $650,000. At the close of 1954, X had pre-1963 reserves of $10,000, and surplus, undivided profits, and reserves of $630,000. At the close of 1955, X had pre-1963 reserves of $15,000, and surplus, undivided profits, and reserves of $625,000. At the close of 1962, X had pre-1963 reserves of $55,000, nonqualifying loans of $4 million, and qualifying real property loans of $10 million. It is assumed that, under § 1.166-4, $16,000 would constitute a reasonable addition to the reserve for losses on nonqualifying loans for a period in which such loans increased from zero to $4 million and $20,000 would constitute a reasonable addition to the reserve for losses on qualifying real property loans for a period in which such loans increased from zero to $10 million.

(2) Impairment of surplus, undivided profits, and reserves for 1954. The sum of X's surplus, undivided profits, and reserves at the close of 1951 was impaired during 1954 by $30,000, computed as follows:

Sum of surplus, undivided profits, and reserves at close of 1951	$650,000
Less:	
Sum of surplus, undivided profits, and reserves at close of 1954, excluding pre-1963 reserves at close of such year ($630,000 minus $10,000)	620,000
	30,000

(3) Impairment of surplus, undivided profits, and reserves for 1955. The sum of X's surplus, undivided profits, and reserves at the close of 1951 was further impaired during 1955 by $10,000, computed as follows:

Sum of surplus, undivided profits, and reserves at close of 1951, decreased by amount of 1954 impairment ($650,000 minus $30,000)		$620,000
Less:		
Sum of surplus, undivided profits, and reserves at close of 1955, excluding pre-1963 reserves at close of such year ($625,000 minus $15,000)		610,000
		10,000

(4) Pre-1952 surplus. X's pre-1952 surplus is $549,000, computed as follows:

Sum of surplus, undivided profits and reserves at close of 1951	$650,000	
Less:		
Sum of impairments for 1954 and 1955 ($30,000 plus $10,000)	40,000	
		$610,000
Less:		
Portion of such $610,000 which is attributable to excludable interest ($610,000 multiplied by $300,000/$3 million)		61,000
		$549,000

(5) Allocation of pre-1963 reserves to reserve for losses on nonqualifying loans and to reserve for losses on qualifying real property loans. Of the $55,000 of pre-1963 reserves at the close of 1962, $16,000 (the amount which would constitute a reasonable addition to the reserve for losses on nonqualifying loans for a period in which such loans increased from zero to $4 million) shall be allocated to, and constitute the opening balance of, the reserve for losses on nonqualifying loans, and the balance of $39,000 ($55,000 minus $16,000) shall be allocated to, and constitute a part of the opening balance of, the reserve for losses on qualifying real property loans.

(6) Allocation of pre-1952 surplus to reserve for losses on qualifying real property loans. X's pre-1963 reserves are not sufficient to bring the opening balance of the reserve for losses on qualifying real property loans to $300,000, which is an amount equal to the greater of—

(i) $300,000 i.e., $10 million of qualifying real property loans outstanding at the close of 1962, multiplied by 3 percent), or

(ii) $20,000 (the amount which would constitute a reasonable addition to the reserve for losses on such loans under § 1.166-4 for a period in which the amount of such loans increased from zero to the $10 million).

Therefore, $261,000 ($300,000 minus $39,000) of X's pre-1952 surplus of $549,000 shall be deemed to be included in the opening balance of such reserve in order to increase such opening balance to $300,000.

T.D. 6728, 5/4/64, amend T.D. 7549, 5/17/78.

PAR. 13. Section 1.593-8 is redesignated as § 1.593-6. Section 1.593-6 as so redesignated is amended as follows:

1. The references "§ 1.593-4" and "§ 1.593-7" are removed and "§ 1.593-1" and "§ 1.593-5", respectively, are inserted in lieu thereof in each place that they appear as a reference in § 1.593-6 as so redesignated.

2. Paragraph (b)(1)(i) is amended by removing the phrase "(under the principles of paragraph (d)(2) of § 1.593-1)".

3. Paragraph (c)(1)(ii) is amended by removing the phrase "(under the principles of paragraph (d)(2) of § 1.593-1".

4. The first sentence of paragraph (d) is removed and the following new sentence is inserted in its place: "Any portion of the taxpayer's pre-1952 surplus which, under paragraph (a) of this section, is deemed to be included in the opening balance of the reserve for losses on qualifying real property loans shall not be treated as a reserve for bad debts for any purpose other than computing for any taxable year the amount determined under the method described in paragraph (b), (c), or (d) of § 1.593-4 (relating, respectively, to the percentage of taxable income method, the percentage method, and the experience method).".

Proposed § 1.593-8 [Redesignated as 1.593-6 and amended] [*For Preamble, see ¶ 150,911*]

PAR. 14. Section 1.593-9 is removed.

Proposed § 1.593-9 [Removed] [*For Preamble, see ¶ 150,911*]

§ 1.593-10 Certain distributions to shareholders by a domestic building and loan association.

Caution: The Treasury has not yet amended Reg § 1.593-10 to reflect changes made by P.L. 104-188, P.L. 100-647, P.L. 99-514, P.L. 97-34.

(a) In general. Section 593(f) provides that if a domestic building and loan association (as defined in section 7701(a)(19) and the regulations thereunder) distributes property after December 31, 1962, to a shareholder with respect to its stock and if the amount of such distribution is not allowable to the association as a deduction under section 591 (relating to deduction for dividends paid on deposits), then, notwithstanding any other provision of the Code, the distribution shall be treated as provided in paragraphs (b) and (c) of this section. For purposes of the preceding sentence, the term "distribution" includes any distribution in redemption of stock to which section 302(a) or 303 applies, or in partial or complete liquidation of the association, as well as any other distribution which the association may make to a shareholder with respect to its stock. For definition of the term "property", see section 317(a). For determination of the amount of a distribution, see section 301(b). For taxable years beginning after July 11, 1969, this paragraph is not applicable to any transaction to which section 381 (relating to carryovers in certain corporate acquisitions) and the regulations thereunder apply.

(b) Distributions out of certain reserves. *(1) Distributions not in exchange for stock.* If the distribution is not a redemption to which section 302(a) or 303 applies or in partial or complete liquidation of the association, then to the extent that the distribution is not out of earnings and profits of the taxable year (within the meaning of section 316(a)(2)) or out of earnings and profits accumulated in taxable years beginning after December 31, 1951, the distribution shall be treated as made out of—

(i) First, the reserve for losses on qualifying real property loans (determined under subparagraph (3) of this paragraph), to the extent thereof,

(ii) Second, the supplemental reserve for losses on loans, to the extent thereof, and

(iii) Finally, such other accounts as may be proper.

(2) Distributions in redemption of stock or in liquidation. If the distribution is a redemption to which section 302(a) or 303 applies, or in partial or complete liquidation of the association, the distribution shall be treated as made out of—

(i) First, the reserve for losses on qualifying real property loans (as determined under subparagraph (3) of this paragraph), to the extent thereof,

(ii) Second, the supplemental reserve for losses on loans, to the extent thereof,

(iii) Third, earnings and profits of the taxable year (within the meaning of section 316(a)(2)),

(iv) Fourth, earnings and profits accumulated in taxable years beginning after December 31, 1951, and

(v) Finally, such other accounts as may be proper.

(3) Special rule. For purposes of subparagraphs (1)(i) and (2)(i) of this paragraph, the reserve for losses on qualifying real property loans shall be an amount equal to—

(i) The balance of such reserve determined as of the close of the taxable year after all adjustments for such year have been made (including the addition for such year determined under § 1.593-6 or § 1.593-6A (whichever is applicable)), minus

(ii) The sum of—

(a) The amount which would have constituted the opening balance of such reserve (at the close of December 31, 1962) if such opening balance had been determined under the experience method described in paragraph (b)(3)(ii)(b) of § 1.593-7 (relating to allocation of pre-1963 reserves to the opening balance of the reserve for losses on qualifying real property loans), and

(b) The total amount of the annual additions which would have been made to such reserve under section 166(c) for taxable years ending after December 31, 1962, if each such addition had been determined under the experience method described in paragraph (d) of § 1.593-6 or paragraph (d) of § 1.593-6A, whichever is applicable for the taxable year of such addition.

For purposes of subdivision (i) of this subparagraph, the balance of the reserve for losses on qualifying real property loans shall include the total amount of any pre-1963 reserves allocated thereto under paragraph (b)(3) of § 1.593-7, but shall not include any pre-1952 surplus which is deemed to be included therein under paragraph (a) of § 1.593-8 (relating to allocation of pre-1952 surplus to the opening balance of the reserve for losses on qualifying real property loans).

(c) Amount charged against reserve and included in gross income. *(1) In general.* If a distribution is treated under paragraph (b)(1) or (2) of this section as having been made out of the reserve for losses on qualifying real property loans or out of the supplemental reserve for losses on loans, such reserves shall be charged with, and gross income for the taxable year shall be increased by, an amount equal to the lesser of—

(i) The amount of such reserves, or

(ii) The amount which, when reduced by the amount of income tax imposed by chapter 1 of the Code and attributable to the inclusion of such amount in gross income, is equal to the amount of such distribution.

(2) Special rule. For purposes of subparagraph (1)(ii) of this paragraph, in determining the income tax attributable to the inclusion of an amount in gross income, taxable income shall be determined without regard to any net operating loss carryback to the taxable year under section 172.

(d) Examples. This section may be illustrated by the following examples:

Example (1). (i) Facts. X Corporation, a domestic building and loan association having nonwithdrawable capital stock represented by shares, was organized in 1946, and makes its returns on the basis of the calendar year and the reserve method of accounting for bad debts. As of the close of December 31, 1962, X had $6,900 of earnings and profits accumulated in taxable years beginning after December 31, 1951. X's taxable income for 1963 is $30,000 (computed prior to the inclusion of any amount in gross income for such year under section 593(f)) and during such year X received tax-exempt interest of $500. X's earnings and profits for 1963 (computed at the close of the taxable year without diminution by reason of any distributions made during the taxable year) is $20,400. The opening balance of X's reserve for losses on qualifying real property loans as of the close of December 31, 1962 (determined under paragraph (b)(3)(ii)(a) of § 1.593-7) was $24,500. Pre-1963 reserves of $22,500 were included in such opening balance, but it is assumed that pre-1963 reserves of only $2,500 would have been included in the opening balance if the opening balance had been determined under the experience method described in paragraph (b)(3)(ii)(b) of § 1.593-7. Pre-1952 surplus of $2,000 was deemed included in such opening balance under paragraph (a) of § 1.593-8. The deductible addition to such reserve for 1963 is $47,000. It is assumed that the addition to such reserve for 1963 would have been $2,200 if such addition had been computed under the experience method described in paragraph (d) of § 1.593-6. On each of four dates during 1963 (January 1, April 1, July 1, and October 1), X made a $12,000 distribution (which was not a redemption to which section 302(a) or 303 applied or in partial or complete liquidation of X) to its shareholders with respect to its stock.

(ii) Reserve for losses on qualifying real property loans. For purposes of paragraph (b)(1)(i) of this section, X's reserve for losses on qualifying real property loans is $64,800, computed as follows:

Closing balance of reserve for losses on qualifying real property loans after addition for 1963 ($24,500 opening balance plus $47,000 addition)		$71,500
Minus:		
Amount of pre-1963 reserves which would have been included in opening balance under experience method	$2,500	
Total additions which would have been made under experience method	2,200	
Pre-1952 surplus included in opening balance	2,000	$ 6,700
		$64,800

(iii) Treatment of distributions. Of each $12,000 quarterly distribution, $5,100 ($20,400 earnings and profits of the taxable year divided by 4) is out of X's earnings and profits of the taxable year (within the meaning of section 316(a)(2)); the remainder of the January 1 distribution, $6,900 ($12,000 minus $5,100), is out of X's earnings and profits accumulated in taxable years beginning after December 31, 1951. Since $20,700 ($6,900 multiplied by 3) is not out of X's earnings and profits, such amount shall be treated as made out of X's reserve for losses on qualifying real property loans (as determined under subdivision (ii) of this example).

(iv) Amount charged against reserve for losses on qualifying real property loans and included in gross income. The reserve for losses on qualifying real property loans is charged with, and X's gross income for 1963 is increased by, $43,124, which is the lesser of—

(a) $64,800 (the reserve as of December 31, 1963, as determined under subdivision (ii) of this example), or

(b) $43,124, i.e., the amount which, when reduced by the amount of income tax attributable to the inclusion of such amount in gross income, $22,424 ($43,124 multiplied by a tax rate of 52 percent), is equal to the amount of such distribution, $20,700.

Example (2). (i) Facts. Assume the same facts as in example (1) and the following additional facts: X's taxable income for 1964 is $6,000. The deductible addition to the reserve for losses on qualifying real property loans for 1964 is $11,000, but it is assumed that only $2,676 would have been the addition to such reserve for 1964 if such addition had been computed under the experience method described in paragraph (d) of § 1.593-6. On December 31, 1964, X makes a $10,000 distribution in a redemption to which section 302(a) applies.

(ii) Reserve for losses on qualifying real property loans. For purposes of paragraph (b)(2)(i) of this section, X's reserve for losses on qualifying real property loans is $30,000, computed as follows:

Closing balance of reserve for losses on qualifying real property loans after addition for 1964 ($71,500 opening balance plus $11,000 addition)		$82,500
Minus:		
Amount of pre-1963 reserves which would have been included in opening balance under the experience method	$2,500	
Total additions which would have been made under the experience method ($2,200 for 1963 plus $2,676 for 1964)	4,876	
Pre-1952 surplus included in opening balance	2,000	$ 9,376
		$73,124
Less charge against reserve under subdivision (iv) of example (1) for 1963 distribution		43,124
		$30,000

(iii) Treatment of distribution. The $10,000 distribution in a redemption to which section 302 (a) applies shall be treated as made out of X's reserve for losses on qualifying real property loans (as determined under subdivision (ii) of this example).

(iv) Amount charged against reserve for losses on qualifying real property loans and included in gross income. The reserve for losses on qualifying real property loans is charged with, and X's gross income for 1964 is increased by, $12,820, which is the lesser of—

(a) $30,000 (the reserve as of December 31, 1964, as determined under subdivision (ii) of this example), or

(b) $12,820, i.e., the amount which, when reduced by the amount of income tax attributable to the inclusion of such amount in gross income, $2,820 ($12,820 multiplied by a tax rate of 22 percent), is equal to the amount of such distribution, $10,000.

Example (3). (i) Facts. X Corporation, a domestic building and loan association having nonwithdrawable capital stock represented by shares, was organized in 1946, and makes its returns on the basis of the calendar year and the reserve method of accounting for bad debts. As of the close of December 31, 1962, X had $6,900 of earnings and profits accumulated in taxable years beginning after December 31, 1951. X's taxable income for 1963 is $30,000 (computed prior to the inclusion of any amount in gross income for such year under section 593(f)) and during such year X received tax-exempt interest of $500. X's earnings and profits for 1963 (computed at the close of the taxable year without diminution by reason of any distributions made during the taxable year) is $20,400. The opening balance of X's reserve for losses on qualifying real property loans as of the close of December 31, 1962 (determined under paragraph (b)(3)(ii)(a) of § 1.593-7) was $24,500. Pre-1963 reserves of $24,500 were included in such opening balance, but it is assumed that pre-1963 reserves of only $4,500 would have been included in the opening balance if the opening balance had been determined under the experience method described in paragraph (b)(3)(ii)(b) of § 1.593-7. The deductible addition to such reserve for 1963 is $500. It is assumed that the addition to such reserve for 1963 would have been $100 if such addition had been computed under the experience method described in paragraph (d) of § 1.593-6. As of December 31, 1963, the balance of X's supplemental reserve for losses on loans is $30,000. On each of four dates during 1963 (January 1, April 1, July 1, and October 1), X made a $12,000 distribution (which was not a redemption to which section 302(a) or 303 applied or in partial or complete liquidation of X) to its shareholders with respect to its stock.

(ii) Reserve for losses on qualifying real property loans. For purposes of paragraph (b)(1)(i) of this section, X's reserve for losses on qualifying real property loans is $20,400, computed as follows:

Closing balance of reserve for losses on qualifying real property loans after addition for 1963 ($24,500 opening balance plus $500 addition)		$25,000
Minus:		
Amount of pre-1963 reserves which would have been included in opening balance under experience method	$4,500	
Total additions which would have been made under experience method	100	4,600
		$20,400

(iii) Treatment of distributions. Of each $12,000 quarterly distribution, $5,100 ($20,400 earnings and profits of the taxable year divided by 4) is out of X's earnings and profits of the taxable year (within the meaning of section 316(a)(2)); the remainder of the January 1 distribution, $6,900 ($12,000 minus $5,100), is out of X's earnings and profits accumulated in taxable years beginning after December 31, 1951. Since $20,700 ($6,900 multiplied by 3) is not out of X's earnings and profits, $20,400 of such amount shall be treated as made out of X's reserve for losses on qualifying real property loans (as determined under subdivision (ii) of this example) and $300 ($20,700 minus $20,400) shall be treated as made out of X's supplemental reserve for losses on loans.

(iv) Amount included in gross income. X's gross income for 1963 is increased by $43,124, which is the lesser of—

(a) $50,400 ($20,400, the reserve for losses on qualifying real property loans, as determined under subdivision (ii) of this example, plus $30,000, the supplemental reserve for losses on loans), or

(b) $43,124, i.e., the amount which, when reduced by the amount of income tax attributable to the inclusion of such amount in gross income, $22,424 ($43,124 multiplied by a tax rate of 52 percent), is equal to the amount of such distribution, $20,700.

(v) Amount charged against reserve for losses on qualifying real property loans and supplemental reserve for losses on loans. The reserve for losses on qualifying real property loans is charged with $20,400 (the balance of the reserve as of December 31, 1963, as determined under subdivision (ii) of this example), and the supplemental reserve for losses on loans is charged with $22,724 ($43,124, the amount included in gross income under subdivision (iv) of this example, minus $20,400).

T.D. 6728, 5/4/64, amend T.D. 7549, 5/17/78.

PAR. 15. Section 1.593-10 is redesignated as § 1.593-7. Section 1.593-7 as so redesignated is amended as follows:

1. Paragraph (b)(1) and (2) is amended by inserting "or institution" after "association" in both places that "association" appears.

2. Paragraph (b)(3)(i) is amended by removing "§ 1.593-6 or § 1.593-6A (whichever is applicable)" and inserting "§ 1.593-4" in lieu thereof.

3. Paragraph (b)(3)(ii)(b) is amended by removing "paragraph (d) of § 1.593-6 or paragraph (d) of § 1.593-6A, whichever is applicable" and inserting "§ 1.593-4" in lieu thereof.

4. Examples (1)(i), (2)(i), and (3)(i) of paragraph (d) are amended by removing the phrase "described in paragraph (d) of § 1.593-6".

5. The references "section 593(f)", "§ 1.593-7", and "§ 1.593-8" are removed and "section 593(e)", "§ 1.593-5", and "§ 1.593-6", respectively, are inserted in lieu thereof in each place that they appear as a reference or as part of a reference in § 1.593-7 as so redesignated.

6. Paragraph (a) is revised to read as follows:

Proposed § 1.593-10 [Redesignated as 1.593-7 and amended] [*For Preamble, see ¶ 150,911*]

§ 1.593-11 Qualifying real property loan and nonqualifying loan defined.

Caution: The Treasury has not yet amended Reg § 1.593-11 to reflect changes made by P.L. 104-188.

(a) Loan defined. For purposes of this section, the term "loan" means debt, as the term "debt" is used in section 166 and the regulations thereunder. The term "loan" also includes a redeemable ground rent (as defined in section 1055(c)) which is owned by the taxpayer, and any property acquired by the taxpayer in a transaction described in section 595(a). For determination of the amount of a loan, see paragraph (d) of this section.

(b) Qualifying real property loan defined. *(1) General rule.* For purposes of §§ 1.593-4 through 1.593-10, the term "qualifying real property loan" means any loan (other than a loan described in subparagraph (5) of this paragraph) which is secured by an interest in qualifying real property. For purposes of this section, the term "real property" means any property which, under the law of the jurisdiction in which such property is situated, constitutes real property. The term "real property" also includes a mobile unit which is permanently fixed to real property. The determination of whether a mobile unit is permanently fixed to real property shall be made on the basis of facts and circumstances in each particular case. For example, a mobile unit is permanently fixed to real property during a taxable year if, except for a brief period during which the unit is transported to a site, such unit was placed upon a foundation at a site with wheels and axles removed, affixed to the ground by means of straps, and connected to water, sewer, gas, and electric facilities. See paragraph (e) of this section for the treatment of a REMIC interest as a qualifying real property loan.

(2) Meaning of "secured". A loan will be considered as "secured" only if the loan is on the security of any instrument (such as a mortgage, deed of trust, or land contract) which makes the interest of the debtor in the property described therein specific security for the payment of the loan, provided that such instrument is of such a nature that, in the event of default, the property could be subjected to the satisfaction of the loan with the same priority as a mortgage or deed of trust in the jurisdiction in which the property is situated.

(3) Meaning of "interest". The word "interest" means an interest in real property which, under the law of the jurisdiction in which such property is situated, constitutes either (i) an interest in fee in such property (or in the case of a mobile unit, an ownership interest), (ii) a leasehold interest in such property extending or renewable automatically for a period of at least 30 years, or at least 10 years beyond the date scheduled for the final payment on the loan secured by such interest, (iii) a leasehold interest in improved residential real property consisting of a structure or structures containing, in the aggregate, no more than four family units extending for a period of at least 2 years beyond the date scheduled for the final payment on the loan secured by such interest, or (iv) a leasehold interest in such property held subject to a redeemable ground rent defined in section 1055(c).

(4) Meaning of "qualifying real property". The term "qualifying real property" means any real property which is improved real property, or which from the proceeds of the loan will become improved real property. As used in the preceding sentence, the term "improved real property" means—

(i) Land on which is located any building of a permanent nature (such as a house, mobile unit, apartment house, office building, hospital, shopping center, warehouse, garage, or other similar permanent structure), provided that the value of such building is substantial in relation to the value of such land,

(ii) Any building lot or site which, by reason of installations and improvements that have been completed in keeping with applicable governmental requirements and with general practice in the community, is a building lot or site ready for the construction of any building of a permanent nature within the meaning of paragraph (b)(4)(i) of this section,

(iii) Real property which, because of its state of improvement, produces sufficient income to maintain such real property and retire the loan in accordance with the terms thereof, or

(iv) A mobile unit which is permanently fixed to real property.

(5) Loans not included. The term "qualifying real property loan" does not include—

(i) Any loan evidenced by a security as defined in section 165(g)(2)(C),

(ii) Any loan (whether or not evidenced by a security as so defined) the primary obligor on which is (a) a government or a political subdivision or instrumentality thereof, (b) a bank (as defined in section 581), or (c) another member of the same affiliated group,

(iii) Any loan to the extent such loan is secured by a deposit in or share of the taxpayer (including a share of non-withdrawable capital stock), determined as of the close of the taxable year, and

(iv) Any loan which (within a 60-day period beginning in one taxable year of the taxpayer and ending in the next taxable year of such taxpayer) is made or acquired, and then repaid or disposed of, unless both the transaction by which the loan is made or acquired and the transaction by which the loan is repaid or disposed of are established to the satisfaction of the district director to be for bona fide business purposes.

As used in subdivision (ii)(c) of this subparagraph, the term "affiliated group" shall have the meaning assigned to such term by section 1504(a) (relating to the definition of an affiliated group), except that the phrase "more than 50 percent" shall be substituted for the phrase "at least 80 percent" each place the latter phrase appears in section 1504(a), and all corporations shall be treated as includible corporations (without regard to any of the exclusions provided in section 1504(b)).

(c) Nonqualifying loan defined. For purposes of §§ 1.593-4 through 1.593-9, the term "nonqualifying loan" means any loan which is not a qualifying real property loan.

(d) Amount of loan determined. *(1) General rule.* Except as provided in subparagraph (2) of this paragraph, the amount of any qualifying real property loan or nonqualifying loan, for purposes of section 593, is the adjusted basis of such loan as determined under § 1.1011-1. However, the adjusted basis, determined under § 1.1011-1, of any "loan in process" does not include the unadvanced portion of such loan. For the basis of a redeemable ground rent reserved or created by the taxpayer before April 11, 1963, see section 1055(b)(3); and for the basis of a loan represented by property acquired by the taxpayer in a transaction described in section 595(a), see section 595(c).

(2) Limitation. If the total amount advanced on any loan exceeds the loan value of any interest in qualifying real property which secures such loan, then the portion of such loan which, as of the close of any taxable year, will be considered as a qualifying real property loan shall be determined under the principles of section 7701(a)(19) and the regulations thereunder.

(e) Treatment of REMIC interests as qualifying real property loans. *(1) In general.* For purposes of section 593 and §§ 1.593-4 through 1.593-10, if, for any calendar quarter, at least 95 percent of a REMIC's assets (as determined in accordance with § 1.860F-4(e)(1)(ii) or § 1.6049-7(f)(3)) are qualifying real property loans (as defined in paragraph (b) of this section), then, for that calendar quarter, all the regular and residual interests in that REMIC are treated as qualifying real property loans. If less than 95 percent of a REMIC's assets are qualifying real property loans, then a percentage of each regular or residual interest is treated as a qualifying real property loan. The percentage equals the percentage of the REMIC's assets that are qualifying real property loans. See § 1.860F-4(e)(1)(ii)(B) and § 1.6049-7(f)(3) for information required to be provided to regular and residual interest holders if the 95-percent test is not met.

(2) Treatment of REMIC assets for section 593 purposes. (i) Manufactured housing treated as qualifying real property. For purposes of paragraph (e)(1) of this section, the term "qualifying real property" includes manufactured housing treated as a single family residence under section 25(e)(10).

(ii) Status of cash flow investments. For purposes of paragraph (e)(1) of this section, cash flow investments (as defined in section 860G(a)(6) and § 1.860G-2(g)(1)) are treated as qualifying real property loans.

T.D. 6728, 5/4/64, amend T.D. 7549, 5/17/78, T.D. 8458, 12/23/92.

PAR. 16. Section 1.593-11 is redesignated as § 1.593-8. In paragraph (b)(1) of § 1.593-8 as so redesignated, the phrase "For purposes of §§ 1.593-4 through 1.593-10," is removed and the phrase "For purposes of §§ 1.593-1 through 1.593-7," is inserted in its place. In paragraph (c) of § 1.593-8 as so redesignated, the phrase "For purposes of §§ 1.593-4 through 1.593-9," is removed and the phrase "For purposes of §§ 1.593-1 through 1.593-6," is inserted in its place.

Proposed § 1.593-11 [Redesignated as 1.593-8 and amended] [*For Preamble, see ¶ 150,911*]

§ 1.594-1 Mutual savings banks conducting life insurance business.

Caution: The Treasury has not yet amended Reg § 1.594-1 to reflect changes made by P.L. 98-369.

(a) Scope of application. Section 594 applies to the case of a mutual savings bank not having capital stock represented by shares which conducts a life insurance business, if:

(1) The conduct of the life insurance business is authorized under State law,

(2) The life insurance business is carried on in a separate department of the bank,

(3) The books of account of the life insurance business are maintained separately from other departments of the bank, and

(4) The life insurance department of the bank would, if it were treated as a separate corporation, qualify as a life insurance company under section 801.

(b) Computation of tax. In the case of a mutual savings bank conducting a life insurance business to which section 594 is applicable, the tax upon such bank consists of the sum of the following:

(1) A partial tax computed under section 11 upon the taxable income of the bank determined without regard to any items of income or deduction properly allocable to the life insurance department, and

(2) A partial tax computed on the income (or, in the case of taxable years beginning before January 1, 1955, the taxable income (as defined in section 803)) of the life insurance department determined without regard to any items of income or deduction not properly allocable to such department, at the rates and in the manner provided in subchapter L (section 801 and following), chapter 1 of the Code, with respect to life insurance companies.

T.D. 6188, 7/5/56.

§ 1.595-1 Treatment of foreclosed property by certain creditors.

Caution: The Treasury has not yet amended Reg § 1.595-1 to reflect changes made by P.L. 104-188.

(a) Nonrecognition of gain or loss on the acquisition of security property by certain creditors. *(1) In general.* Section 595(a) provides that in the case of a creditor which is an organization described in section 593(a) (that is, a mutual savings bank not having capital stock represented by shares, a domestic building and loan association, or a cooperative bank without capital stock organized and operated for mutual purposes and without profit), no gain or loss shall be recognized, and no debt shall be considered as becoming worthless or partially worthless for purposes of section 166 (relating to bad debts), as the result of a transaction by which such creditor bids in at foreclosure, or reduces to ownership or possession by agreement or process of law, any property (whether real or personal, tangible or intangible) which was security for the payment of any indebtedness (whether or not a qualifying real property loan as defined in section 593(e)(1)). The treatment provided by section 595(a) is mandatory (regardless of whether such creditor utilizes the specific deduction or reserve method of accounting for bad debts) if, for the taxable year in which the property is bid in at foreclosure, or reduced to ownership or possession by agreement or process of law, the creditor is an organization described in section 593(a), even though the creditor subsequently becomes an organization not described in section 593(a). For definition of the terms "domestic building and loan association" and "cooperative bank" for taxable years beginning after October 16, 1962, see paragraphs (19) and (32), respectively, of section 7701(a).

(2) Effective date. Section 595 applies to any transaction (described in subparagraph (1) of this paragraph) occurring after December 31, 1962, except that such section does not apply to any such transaction in which the taxable event determined without regard to section 595 (that is, the sale or exchange to the creditor of the security property by reason of the default or anticipated default of the debtor) occurred before January 1, 1963.

(b) Rules for determining when security property is reduced to ownership or possession by agreement or process of law. *(1) Ownership or possession.* For purposes of this section, security property shall be considered as reduced to ownership or possession by agreement or process of law on the earliest date on which the creditor, by reason of the default or anticipated default of the debtor—

(i) Acquires, by agreement or process of law, a title to, or a right or interest in, the security property which under local law is indefeasible and which the creditor can validly dispose of apart from the indebtedness which the property secures, or

(ii) Acquires, by agreement or process of law, an enforceable right to direct the use to which the security property shall be put, including, in the case of real property, whether or not the property shall continue to be occupied by the debtor who has defaulted (regardless of whether such creditor has obtained indefeasible title to the property), or

(iii) Sells or otherwise disposes of the security property or any interest therein.

(2) Agreement or process of law. The reduction of security property to ownership or possession by agreement includes, where valid under local law, such methods as voluntary conveyance from the debtor (including a conveyance directly to the Federal Housing Commissioner) and abandonment to the creditor. The reduction of security property to ownership or possession by process of law includes foreclosure proceedings in which a competitive bid is entered, such as foreclosure by judicial sale or by power of sale contained in the loan agreement without recourse to the courts, as well as those types of foreclosure proceedings in which a competitive bid is not entered, such as strict foreclosure and foreclosure by entry and possession, by writ of entry, or by publication or notice.

(c) Examples. The provisions of paragraphs (a) and (b) of this section may be illustrated by the following examples:

Example (1). On January 31, 1963, X, a creditor which is an organization described in section 593(a), purchases at a foreclosure sale residential real property which was security for a debt owing to X, and with respect to which the debtor has defaulted. Under local law, there is a 1-year statutory redemption period (during which period the debtor is entitled to remain in possession) so that X must wait until February 1, 1964, to obtain indefeasible title to the property. No gain or loss is recognized by reason of the purchase at the foreclosure sale on January 31, 1963. However, the date on which the security property is considered as reduced to ownership or possession by agreement or process of law is February 1, 1964. If, under local law, there were no statutory redemption period so that X obtained indefeasible title to the security property at the foreclosure sale, the date on which the security property would be considered as so reduced is January 31, 1963. Furthermore, with respect to either of the preceding situations, if the foreclosure sale had occurred on November 1, 1962 (instead of on January 31, 1963), section 595 would not apply to the transaction since the taxable event in respect of such transaction occurred prior to January 1, 1963.

Example (2). The facts are the same as in example (1), except that instead of purchasing the property at a foreclosure sale, X, pursuant to the provisions of local law, enters upon the security property on January 31, 1963, and acquires an enforceable right to direct whether the property shall continue to be occupied by the debtor. X does not obtain indefeasible title to the property until February 1, 1964. The date on which the security property is considered as reduced to ownership or possession by agreement or process of law is January 31, 1963.

(d) Basis of acquired property. Section 595(c) provides that the basis of any property to which section 595(a) applies (hereinafter referred to as "acquired property") shall be the adjusted basis of the indebtedness for which such property was security, determined as of the date of acquisition of such property, properly increased for costs of acquisition. The date of acquisition is the date, determined under paragraph (b) of this section, on which the security property is reduced to ownership or possession by agreement or process of law. Costs of acquisition are expenditures incurred by the creditor (for example, fees for an attorney, master, trustee, auctioneer, for publication, acquiring title, clearing liens, filing and recording, and court costs) which are directly related to the foreclosure sale or proceeding, or to the other process used to reduce the security property to ownership or possession, or both, by agreement or process of law. For purposes of determining the adjusted basis of the indebtedness for which the acquired property was security, there shall be included the amount of any unpaid interest with respect to such indebtedness, but only to the extent that it has been included in gross income. The basis of the acquired property, as determined under this paragraph, shall be adjusted in accordance with the rules provided in paragraph (e) of this section.

(e) Characteristics of acquired property. *(1) Depreciation: decline in fair market value.* Section 595(b) provides, in part, that for purposes of section 166 (relating to bad debts) acquired property shall be considered as property having the same characteristics as the indebtedness for which such property was security. Thus, no deduction for exhaustion, wear and tear, obsolescence, amortization, or depletion shall be allowed to a creditor with respect to acquired property. However, if, at any time, the adjusted basis of the acquired property exceeds the fair market value of such property (determined by proper appraisal and without regard to any outstanding right of redemption), and the creditor can establish (in the same manner as worthlessness in whole or in part is established for purposes of section 166) that an amount equal to any portion of such excess will not be collected with respect to the indebtedness for which such property was security, the creditor may treat such portion, under the provisions of section 166, as a worthless debt. In such case, the basis of the acquired property shall be reduced by the amount treated as a worthless debt.

(2) Example. The provisions of subparagraph (1) of this paragraph may be illustrated by the following example:

Example. X Corporation, a creditor which is an organization described in section 593(a), makes its returns on the basis of the calendar year and the reserve method of accounting for bad debts. In 1963, A defaults in his payments on a debt owed to X which is secured by residential real property. X reduces the property to ownership or possession by agreement or process of law by bidding it in at a foreclosure sale for $23,000. The adjusted basis of the indebtedness at the date of acquisition of the property (increased for costs of acquisition) is $25,000, and this amount becomes the basis of the acquired property. X obtains a deficiency judgment against A for $2,000. Later in 1963, a proper appraisal enables X to establish that the fair market value of the property is $18,000. X is also able to establish (under the rules of section 166 and the regulations thereunder) that due to A's poor financial condition only $1,000 can be collected on the outstanding deficiency judgment. For the year 1963, X may charge its bad debt reserve for $6,000, computed as follows:

Basis of acquired property	$25,000
Less: Fair market value of acquired property	18,000
Excess	7,000
Less: Collectible portion of deficiency judgment	1,000
Portion of excess treated as worthless debt	6,000

(3) Capital improvements made after date of acquisition not treated as acquired property. Except as provided in subparagraph (4) of this paragraph, the term "acquired property" does not include capital improvements made after the date of acquisition (within the meaning of paragraph (d) of this section) of the property. Thus, the applicable deduction for exhaustion, wear and tear, obsolescence, amortization, or depletion shall be allowed, if otherwise allowable, for improvements which are made by the creditor with respect to acquired property and which are properly chargeable to the capital account. If the creditor sells or otherwise disposes of the acquired property with such capital improvements, any amount realized by reason of such sale or other disposition shall be allocated in proportion to the respective fair market values of the acquired property and such capital improvements. The portion of the amount realized which is allocable to the acquired property shall be treated in accordance with the rules prescribed in subparagraph (6) of this paragraph. The portion of the amount realized which is allocable to such capital improvements shall be treated under the applicable rules governing the sale or other disposition of such property and without regard to section 595.

(4) Treatment of minor capital improvements as acquired property. A creditor may treat any minor capital improvements which it makes to a particular acquired property after the date of acquisition (within the meaning of paragraph (d) of this section) in the same manner as the acquired property, provided such creditor treats all minor capital improvements with respect to that particular acquired property in such manner. For purposes of section 595, a capital improvement shall be considered as "minor" only if the cost of such improvement does not exceed $3,000.

(5) Records for capital improvements. For purposes of subparagraphs (3) and (4) of this paragraph, the creditor must maintain such records as are necessary to clearly reflect, with respect to each particular acquired property, the cost of each capital improvement and whether the taxpayer treated minor capital improvements with respect to such property in the same manner as the acquired property.

(6) Amounts realized with respect to acquired property. Section 595(b) provides, in part, that any amount realized with respect to acquired property shall be treated as a payment on account of the indebtedness for which such property was security, and any loss with respect thereto shall be treated as a bad debt to which the provisions of section 166 (relating to bad debts) apply. An amount realized with respect to acquired property means an amount representing a recovery of capital, such as proceeds from the sale or other disposition of the property, payments on the original indebtedness made by or on behalf of the debtor (including amounts received under an insurance contract with the Federal Housing Administration or a guarantee by the Veterans' Administration), and collections on a deficiency judgment obtained against the debtor (other than amounts treated as interest under applicable local law). Amounts realized with respect to acquired property include amounts which otherwise would be treated in the manner prescribed in section 351 (relating to transfer to a corporation controlled by transferor), section 354 (relating to exchanges of stock and securities in certain reorganizations), section 453 (relating to installment method), section 1031 (relating to exchange of property held for productive use or for investment), or section 1033 (relating to involuntary conversions). For purposes of section 595(b), if a corporation distributes acquired property in a distribution to which section 311 (relating to taxability of corporation on distribution) or section 336 (relating to nonrecognition of gain or loss to a corporation on distribution of its property in partial or complete liquidation) applies, the fair market value of the acquired property at the time of the distribution shall be treated as an amount realized with respect to such property. However, no amount shall be considered realized by reason of the distribution or transfer of acquired property in a transaction to which section 381(a) (relating to carry-overs in certain corporate acquisitions) applies, and in the case of such a distribution or transfer the acquired property shall be treated by the distributee or transferee as having the same characteristics as it had in the hands of the distributor or transferor at the time of such distribution or transfer. The following rules shall apply to amounts realized with respect to acquired property:

(i) Any amount realized shall be applied against and reduce the adjusted basis of the acquired property, and to the extent that such amount exceeds the adjusted basis, it shall, in the case of a creditor using the specific deduction method of accounting for bad debts, be included in gross income as ordinary income, or, in the case of a creditor using the reserve method of accounting for bad debts, be credited to the appropriate bad debt reserve (that is, the reserve for losses on qualifying real property loans or the reserve for losses on nonqualifying loans). Any amounts credited during the taxable year to a reserve for bad debts pursuant to this subdivision shall not be considered as a part of the addition under section 593 for such year, but shall be included in the balance of the reserve for purposes of computing such addition to the reserve for such taxable year. Thus, for example, an amount credited to the reserve for losses on qualifying real property loans during a taxable year shall not be considered as a part of the addition to such reserve computed under the percentage of taxable income method. However, the amount of such credit shall be included in the balance of such reserve for the purpose of determining the amount necessary to increase the balance of such reserve (as of the close of such taxable year) to an amount equal to 3 percent of qualifying real property loans and for the purpose of determining whether such balance exceeds 6 percent of such loans.

(ii) If an amount realized on the sale or other disposition of the acquired property is insufficient to restore to the creditor the adjusted basis of the property, the difference between such adjusted basis and such amount realized shall be treated as a bad debt to which the provisions of section 166 apply. If the creditor subsequently realizes an additional amount with respect to the original indebtedness or the acquired property, such additional amount shall be treated as the recovery of a bad debt.

(7) Treatment of rents, similar amounts and expenses. Section 595 does not change the treatment of rents, royalties, dividends, interest, or similar amounts received or accrued by the creditor with respect to acquired property, nor does it change the treatment of expenses incurred with respect to such property. (See, however, subparagraph (1) of this paragraph for treatment of depreciation, etc.) Thus, for example, if the acquired property is a governmental obligation within the meaning of section 103 (relating to interest on certain governmental obligations), interest payments received by the creditor with respect to such obligation would not be included in gross income.

(8) Examples. The provisions of subparagraphs (6) and (7) of this paragraph may be illustrated by the following examples:

Example (1). (i) Facts. X Corporation, a creditor which is an organization described in section 593(a), uses the reserve method of accounting for bad debts. On May 1, 1964, X reduces to ownership or possession by agreement or process of law improved real property which is security for an indebtedness of A which is in default. On the date of acquisition there remains unpaid on the indebtedness $20,000 principal and $700 interest. X has previously included the $700 interest in gross income. Subsequent to acquisition, X incurs expenses totaling $500 for maintenance, and during the period June 1 through September 30, 1964, rents the property for a total rental of $400. Under local law, X is accountable to A for the rents received and A is accountable to X for the expenses incurred. There are no other receipts or expenses until October 1, 1964, at which time X sells the acquired property for $22,000. Under local law, A is not entitled to any portion of the sales proceeds.

(ii) Treatment of rents, expenses, and sales proceeds. X would treat rents, expenses, and sales proceeds in the following manner:

Basis of acquired property at acquisition (adjusted basis of indebtedness, i.e., $20,000 principal plus $700 interest)	$20,700
Plus: Expenses charged to debtor	500
	21,200
Less: Rents credited to debtor	400
Adjusted basis of acquired property at sale	20,800
Less: Portion of $22,000 sales proceeds applied in reduction of adjusted basis of acquired property	20,800
	0
Portion of sales proceeds credited to reserve for losses on qualifying real property loans ($22,000 minus $20,800)	1,200

(iii) Creditor using specific deduction method. If instead of using the reserve method of accounting for bad debts X used the specific deduction method, the $1,200 portion of the sales proceeds would be treated as ordinary income.

Example (2). (i) Facts. The facts are the same as in example (1) except that under local law X is not accountable to A for any portion of the rents received and A is not accountable to X for the expenses incurred by X.

(ii) Treatment of rents and expenses. X includes in gross income the total rent receipts of $400 and deducts (if otherwise allowable) the expenses of $500.

(iii) Treatment of sales proceeds. As the result of the sale of the acquired property, X credits $1,300 to the reserve for losses on qualifying real property loans, computed as follows:

Basis of acquired property at acquisition and at date of sale (adjusted basis of indebtedness, i.e., $20,000 principal plus $700 interest)	$20,700
Less: Portion of $22,000 sales proceeds applied in reduction of adjusted basis of acquired property	20,700
	0
Portion of sales proceeds credited to reserve for losses on qualifying real property loans ($22,000 minus $20,700)	1,300

(iv) Creditor using specific deduction method. If instead of using the reserve method of accounting for bad debts X used the specific deduction method, the $1,300 portion of the sales proceeds would be treated as ordinary income.

Example (3). (i) Facts. The facts are the same in example (1) except that X sells the acquired property for $15,000.

(ii) Treatment of rents, expenses, and sales proceeds. X would treat rents, expenses, and sales proceeds in the following manner:

Basis of acquired property at acquisition (adjusted basis of indebtedness, i.e., $20,000 principal plus $700 interest)	$20,700
Plus: Expenses charged to debtor	500
	21,200
Less: Rents credited to debtor	400
Adjusted basis of acquired property at sale	20,800
Less: Portion of $15,000 sales proceeds applied in reduction of adjusted basis of acquired property	15,000
Amount charged to reserve for losses on qualifying real property loans	5,800

(iii) Creditor using specific deduction method. If instead of using the reserve method of accounting for bad debts X used the specific deduction method, the excess of $5,800 would be allowed as a specific bad debt deduction.

T.D. 6814, 4/6/65.

§ 1.596-1 Limitation on dividends received deduction.

Caution: The Treasury has not yet amended Reg § 1.596-1 to reflect changes made by P.L. 104-188, P.L. 99-514.

(a) In general. For taxable years beginning after July 11, 1969, in the case of mutual savings banks, domestic building and loan associations, and cooperative banks, if the addition to the reserve for losses on qualifying real property loans for the taxable year is determined under section 593(b)(2) (relating to the percentage of taxable income method), the total amount allowed as a deduction with respect to dividends received under part VIII, subchapter B, chapter 1, subtitle A of the Code (section 241 *et seq.*) (determined without regard to section 596 and this section) for such taxable year is reduced as provided by this section. In such case, the dividends received deduction otherwise determined under part VIII, subchapter B, chapter 1, subtitle A of the Code, is reduced by an amount equal to the applicable percentage for such year (determined solely under subparagraphs (A) and (B) of section 593(b)(2) and the regulations thereunder) of such total amount. For the rule under which a mutual savings bank, domestic building and loan association, or cooperative bank is deemed to have determined the addition to its reserve for losses on qualifying real property loans for the taxable year under section 593(b)(2), see § 1.593-6A(a)(2).

(b) Example. The provisions of this section may be illustrated by the following example:

Example. X Corporation, a domestic building and loan association, determines the addition to its reserve for losses on qualifying real property loans under section 593(b)(2) for its taxable year beginning in 1971. During that taxable year, X Corporation received a total of $100,000 as dividends from domestic corporations subject to tax under chapter 1 of the Code. X Corporation received no other dividends during the taxable year. Under part VIII, subchapter B, chapter 1, subtitle A of the Code, a deduction, determined without regard to section 596 and this section, of $85,000 would be allowed with respect to the dividends. For the taxable year, the applicable percentage, determined under subparagraphs (A) and (B) of section 593(b)(2), is 54 percent. Under section 596 and this section, the amount allowed as a deduction under section 243 and the regulations thereunder is reduced by $45,900 (54 percent of $85,000) to $39,100 ($85,000 less $45,900).

(c) Dividends received by members of a controlled group. If a thrift institution that computes a deduction under section 593(b)(2) is a member of a controlled group of corporations (within the meaning of section 1563 (a), determined by substituting "50 percent" for "80 percent" each place it appears therein) and if the thrift institution, without a bona fide business purpose, transfers stock, directly or indirectly, to another member of the group, the Commissioner may allocate any dividends with respect to the stock to the thrift institution.

T.D. 7149, 11/1/71, amend T.D. 7631, 7/10/79.

---

§ 1.597-1 Definitions.

For purposes of the regulations under section 597—

(a) Unless the context otherwise requires, the terms consolidated group, member and subsidiary have the meanings provided in § 1.1502-1; and

(b) The following terms have the meanings provided below—

Acquiring. The term *Acquiring* means a corporation that is a transferee in a Taxable Transfer, other than a deemed transferee in a Taxable Transfer described in § 1.597-5(b).

Agency. The term *Agency* means the Resolution Trust Corporation, the Federal Deposit Insurance Corporation, any similar instrumentality of the United States government, and any predecessor or successor of the foregoing (including the Federal Savings and Loan Insurance Corporation).

Agency control. An Institution or entity is under Agency Control if Agency is conservator or receiver of the Institution or entity, or if Agency has the right to appoint any of the Institution's or entity's directors.

Agency Obligation. The term *Agency Obligation* means a debt instrument that Agency issues to an Institution or to a direct or indirect owner of an Institution.

Bridge Bank. The term *Bridge Bank* means an Institution that is organized by Agency to hold assets and liabilities of another Institution and that continues the operation of the other Institution's business pending its acquisition or liquidation, and that is any of the following—

(1) A national bank chartered by the Comptroller of the Currency under section 11(n) of the Federal Deposit Insurance Act (12 U.S.C. 1821(n)) or section 21A(b)(10)(A) of the Federal Home Loan Bank Act (12 U.S.C. 1441a(b)(10)(A)) or any successor sections;

(2) A Federal savings association chartered by the Director of the Office of Thrift Supervision under section 21A(b)(10)(A) of the Federal Home Loan Bank Act (12 U.S.C. 1441a(b)(10)(A)) or any successor section; or

(3) A similar Institution chartered under any other statutory provisions.

Consolidated Subsidiary. The term *Consolidated Subsidiary* means a member of the consolidated group of which an Institution is a member that bears the same relationship to the Institution that the members of a consolidated group bear to their common parent under section 1504(a)(1).

Continuing Equity. An Institution has *Continuing Equity* for any taxable year if, on the last day of the taxable year, the Institution is not (1) a Bridge Bank, (2) in Agency receivership, or (3) treated as a New Entity.

Controlled Entity. The term *Controlled Entity* means an entity under Agency Control.

Federal Financial Assistance (FFA). The term *Federal Financial Assistance (FFA)*, as defined by section 597(c), means any money or property provided by Agency to an Institution or to a direct or indirect owner of stock in an Institution under section 406(f) of the National Housing Act (12 U.S.C. 1729(f)), section 21A(b)(4) of the Federal Home Loan Bank Act (12 U.S.C. 1441a(b)(4)), section 11(f) or 13(c) of the Federal Deposit Insurance Act (12 U.S.C. 1821(f), 1823(c)), or under any similar provision of law. Any such money or property is FFA, regardless of whether the Institution or any of its affiliates issues Agency a note or other obligation, stock, warrants, or other rights to acquire stock in connection with Agency's provision of the money or property. FFA includes Net Worth Assistance, Loss Guarantee payments, yield maintenance payments, cost to carry or cost of funds reimbursement payments, expense reimbursement or indemnity payments, and interest (including original issue discount) on an Agency Obligation.

Institution. The term *Institution* means an entity that is, or immediately before being placed under Agency Control was, a bank or domestic building and loan association within the meaning of section 597 (including a Bridge Bank). Except as otherwise provided in the regulations under section 597, the term Institution includes a New Entity or Acquiring that is a bank or domestic building and loan association within the meaning of section 597.

Loss Guarantee. The term *Loss Guarantee* means an agreement pursuant to which Agency or a Controlled Entity guarantees or agrees to pay an Institution a specified amount upon the disposition or charge-off (in whole or in part) of specific assets, an agreement pursuant to which an Institution has a right to put assets to Agency or a Controlled Entity at a specified price, or a similar arrangement.

Net Worth Assistance. The term *Net Worth Assistance* means money or property (including an Agency Obligation to the extent it has a fixed principal amount) that Agency provides as an integral part of a Taxable Transfer, other than FFA that accrues after the date of the Taxable Transfer. For example, Net Worth Assistance does not include Loss Guarantee payments, yield maintenance payments, cost to carry or cost of funds reimbursement payments, or expense reimbursement or indemnity payments. An Agency Obligation is considered to have a fixed principal amount notwithstanding an agreement providing for its adjustment after issuance to reflect a more accurate determination of the condition of the Institution at the time of the acquisition.

New Entity. The term New Entity means the new corporation that is treated as purchasing all of the assets of an Old Entity in a Taxable Transfer described in § 1.597-5(b).

Old Entity. The term *Old Entity* means the Institution or Consolidated Subsidiary that is treated as selling all of its assets in a Taxable Transfer described in § 1.597-5(b).

Residual Entity. The term *Residual Entity* means the entity that remains after an Institution transfers deposit liabilities to a Bridge Bank.

Taxable Transfer. The term *Taxable Transfer* has the meaning provided in § 1.597-5(a)(1).

T.D. 8641, 12/20/95.

---

§ 1.597-2 Taxation of Federal financial assistance.

Caution: The Treasury has not yet amended Reg § 1.597-2 to reflect changes made by P.L. 104-188.

(a) Inclusion in income. *(1) In general.* Except as otherwise provided in the regulations under section 597, all FFA is includible as ordinary income to the recipient at the time the FFA is received or accrued in accordance with the recipient's method of accounting. The amount of FFA received or accrued is the amount of any money, the fair market value of any property (other than an Agency Obligation), and the issue price of any Agency Obligation (determined under § 1.597-3(c)(2)). An Institution (and not the nominal recipient) is treated as receiving directly any FFA that Agency provides in a taxable year to a direct or indirect shareholder of the Institution, to the extent money or property is transferred to the Institution pursuant to an agreement with Agency.

(2) Cross references. See paragraph (c) of this section for rules regarding the timing of inclusion of certain FFA. See paragraph (d) of this section for additional rules regarding the treatment of FFA received in connection with transfers of money or property to Agency or a Controlled Entity, or paid pursuant to a Loss Guarantee. See § 1.597-5(c)(1) for additional rules regarding the inclusion of Net Worth Assistance in the income of an Institution.

(b) Basis of property that is FFA. If FFA consists of property, the Institution's basis in the property equals the fair market value of the property (other than an Agency Obligation) or the issue price of the Agency Obligation, as determined under § 1.597-3(c)(2).

(c) Timing of inclusion of certain FFA. *(1) Scope.* This paragraph (c) limits the amount of FFA an Institution must include in income currently under certain circumstances and provides rules for the deferred inclusion in income of amounts in excess of those limits. This paragraph (c) does not apply to a New Entity or Acquiring.

(2) Amount currently included in income by an institution without continuing equity. The amount of FFA an Institution without Continuing Equity must include in income in a taxable year under paragraph (a)(1) of this section is limited to the sum of—

(i) The excess at the beginning of the taxable year of the Institution's liabilities over the adjusted bases of the Institution's assets; and

(ii) The amount by which the excess for the taxable year of the Institution's deductions allowed by chapter 1 of the Internal Revenue Code (other than net operating and capital loss carryovers) over its gross income (determined without regard to FFA) is greater than the excess at the beginning of the taxable year of the adjusted bases of the Institution's assets over the Institution's liabilities.

(3) Amount currently included in income by an institution with Continuing Equity. The amount of FFA an Institution with Continuing Equity must include in income in a taxable year under paragraph (a)(1) of this section is limited to the sum of—

(i) The excess at the beginning of the taxable year of the Institution's liabilities over the adjusted bases of the Institution's assets;

(ii) The greater of—

(A) The excess for the taxable year of the Institution's deductions allowed by chapter 1 of the Internal Revenue Code (other than net operating and capital loss carryovers) over its gross income (determined without regard to FFA); or

(B) The excess for the taxable year of the deductions allowed by chapter 1 of the Internal Revenue Code (other than net operating and capital loss carryovers) of the consolidated group of which the Institution is a member on the last day of the Institution's taxable year over the group's gross income (determined without regard to FFA); and

(iii) The excess of the amount of any net operating loss carryover of the Institution (or in the case of a carryover from a consolidated return year of the Institution's current consolidated group, the net operating loss carryover of the group) to the taxable year over the amount described in paragraph (c)(3)(i) of this section.

(4) Deferred FFA. (i) Maintenance of account. An Institution must establish a deferred FFA account commencing in the first taxable year in which it receives FFA that is not currently included in income under paragraph (c)(2) or (c)(3) of this section, and must maintain that account in accordance with the requirements of this paragraph (c)(4). The Institution must add the amount of any FFA that is not currently included in income under paragraph (c)(2) or (c)(3) of this section to its deferred FFA account. The Institution must decrease the balance of its deferred FFA account by the amount of deferred FFA included in income under paragraphs (c)(4)(ii), (iv) and (v) of this section. (See also paragraph (d)(5)(i)(B) of this section for other adjustments

that decrease the deferred FFA account.) If, under paragraph (c)(3) of this section, FFA is not currently included in income in a taxable year, the Institution thereafter must maintain its deferred FFA account on a FIFO (first in, first out) basis (e.g., for purposes of the first sentence of paragraph (c)(4)(iv) of this section).

(ii) Deferred FFA recapture. In any taxable year in which an Institution has a balance in its deferred FFA account, it must include in income an amount equal to the lesser of the amount described in paragraph (c)(4)(iii) of this section or the balance in its deferred FFA account.

(iii) Annual recapture amount. (A) Institutions without Continuing Equity. (1) In general. In the case of an Institution without Continuing Equity, the amount described in this paragraph (c)(4)(iii) is the amount by which—

(i) The excess for the taxable year of the Institution's deductions allowed by chapter 1 of the Internal Revenue Code (other than net operating and capital loss carryovers) over its gross income (taking into account FFA included in income under paragraph (c)(2) of this section); is greater than

(ii) The Institution's remaining equity as of the beginning of the taxable year.

(2) Remaining equity. The Institution's remaining equity is—

(i) The amount at the beginning of the taxable year in which the deferred FFA account was established equal to the adjusted bases of the Institution's assets minus the Institution's liabilities (which amount may be positive or negative); plus

(ii) The Institution's taxable income (computed without regard to any carryover from any other year) in any subsequent taxable year or years; minus

(iii) The excess in any subsequent taxable year or years of the Institution's deductions allowed by chapter 1 of the Internal Revenue Code (other than net operating and capital loss carryovers) over its gross income.

(B) Institutions with Continuing Equity. In the case of an Institution with Continuing Equity, the amount described in this paragraph (c)(4)(iii) is the amount by which the Institution's deductions allowed by chapter 1 of the Internal Revenue Code (other than net operating and capital loss carryovers) exceed its gross income (taking into account FFA included in income under paragraph (c)(3) of this section).

(iv) Additional deferred FFA recapture by an Institution with Continuing Equity. To the extent that, as of the end of a taxable year, the cumulative amount of FFA deferred under paragraph (c)(3) of this section that an Institution with Continuing Equity has recaptured under this paragraph (c)(4) is less than the cumulative amount of FFA deferred under paragraph (c)(3) of this section that the Institution would have recaptured if that FFA had been included in income ratably over the six taxable years immediately following the taxable year of deferral, the Institution must include that difference in income for the taxable year. An Institution with Continuing Equity must include in income the balance of its deferred FFA account in the taxable year in which it liquidates, ceases to do business, transfers (other than to a Bridge Bank) substantially all of its assets and liabilities, or is deemed to transfer all of its assets under § 1.597-5(b).

(v) Optional accelerated recapture of deferred FFA. An Institution that has a deferred FFA account may include in income the balance of its deferred FFA account on its timely filed (including extensions) original income tax return for any taxable year that it is not under Agency Control. The balance of its deferred FFA account is income on the last day of that year.

(5) Exceptions to limitations on use of losses. In computing an Institution's taxable income or alternative minimum taxable income for a taxable year, sections 56(d)(1), 382 and 383 and §§ 1.1502-15, 1.1502-21 and 1.1502-22 (or §§ 1.1502-15A, 1.1502-21A, and 1.1502-22A, as appropriate) do not limit the use of the attributes of the Institution to the extent, if any, that the inclusion of FFA (including recaptured FFA) in income results in taxable income or alternative minimum taxable income (determined without regard to this paragraph (c)(5)) for the taxable year. This paragraph (c)(5) does not apply to any limitation under section 382 or 383 or § 1.1502-15, 1.1502-21 or 1.1502-22 (or §§ 1.1502-15A, 1.1502-21A or 1.1502-22A, as appropriate) that arose in connection with or prior to a corporation becoming a Consolidated Subsidiary of the Institution.

(6) Operating rules. (i) Bad debt reserves. For purposes of paragraphs (c)(2), (c)(3) and (c)(4) of this section, the adjusted bases of an Institution's assets are reduced by the amount of the Institution's reserves for bad debts under section 585 or 593, other than supplemental reserves under section 593.

(ii) Aggregation of Consolidated Subsidiaries. For purposes of this paragraph (c), an Institution is treated as a single entity that includes the income, expenses, assets, liabilities, and attributes of its Consolidated Subsidiaries, with appropriate adjustments to prevent duplication.

(iii) Alternative minimum tax. To compute the alternative minimum taxable income attributable to FFA of an Institution for any taxable year under section 55, the rules of this section, and related rules, are applied by using alternative minimum tax basis, deductions, and all other items required to be taken into account. All other alternative minimum tax provisions continue to apply.

(7) Earnings and profits. FFA that is not currently included in income under this paragraph (c) is included in earnings and profits for all purposes of the Internal Revenue Code to the extent and at the time it is included in income under this paragraph (c).

(d) Transfers of money or property to Agency, and property subject to a Loss Guarantee. *(1) Transfers of property to Agency.* The transfer of property to Agency or a Controlled Entity is a taxable sale or exchange in which the Institution is treated as realizing an amount equal to—

(i) The property's fair market value; or

(ii) For property subject to a Loss Guarantee, the greater of the property's fair market value or the guaranteed value or price at which the property can be put at the time of transfer.

(2) FFA with respect to property covered by a Loss Guarantee other than on transfer to Agency. (i) FFA provided pursuant to a Loss Guarantee with respect to covered property is included in the amount realized with respect to the property to the extent the total amount realized does not exceed the greater of—

(A) The property's fair market value; or

(B) The guaranteed value or price at which the property can be put at the time of transfer.

(ii) For the purposes of this paragraph (d)(2), references to an amount realized include amounts obtained in whole or partial satisfaction of loans, amounts obtained by virtue of charging off or marking to market covered property, and other amounts similarly related to property, whether or not disposed of.

(3) Treatment of FFA received in exchange for property. FFA included in the amount realized for property under this paragraph (d) is not includible in income under paragraph (a)(1) of this section. The amount realized is treated in the same manner as if realized from a person other than Agency or a Controlled Entity. For example, gain attributable to FFA received with respect to a capital asset retains its character as capital gain. Similarly, FFA received with respect to property that has been charged off for income tax purposes is treated as a recovery to the extent of the amount previously charged off. Any FFA provided in excess of the amount realized under this paragraph (d) is includible in income under paragraph (a)(1) of this section.

(4) Adjustment to FFA. (i) In general. If an Institution pays or transfers money or property to Agency or a Controlled Entity, the amount of money and fair market value of the property is an adjustment to its FFA to the extent the amount paid and transferred exceeds the amount of money and fair market value of property Agency or a Controlled Entity provides in exchange.

(ii) Deposit insurance. This paragraph (d)(4) does not apply to amounts paid to Agency with respect to deposit insurance.

(iii) Treatment of an interest held by Agency or a Controlled Entity. (A) In general. For purposes of this paragraph (d), an interest described in § 1.597-3(b) is not treated as property when transferred by the issuer to Agency or a Controlled Entity nor when acquired from Agency or a Controlled Entity by the issuer.

(B) Dispositions to persons other than issuer. On the date Agency or a Controlled Entity transfers an interest described in § 1.597-3(b) to a holder other than the issuer, Agency or a Controlled Entity, the issuer is treated for purposes of this paragraph (d)(4) as having transferred to Agency an amount of money equal to the sum of the amount of money and the fair market value of property that was paid by the new holder as consideration for the interest.

(iv) Consolidated groups. For purposes of this paragraph (d), an Institution will be treated as having made any transfer to Agency or a Controlled Entity that was made by any other member of its consolidated group. The consolidated group must make appropriate investment basis adjustments to the extent the member transferring money or other property is not the member that received FFA.

(5) Manner of making adjustments to FFA. (i) Reduction of FFA and deferred FFA. An Institution adjusts its FFA under paragraph (d)(4) of this section by reducing in the following order and in an aggregate amount not greater than the adjustment—

(A) The amount of any FFA that is otherwise includible in income for the taxable year (before application of paragraph (c) of this section); and

(B) The balance (but not below zero) in the deferred FFA account, if any, maintained under paragraph (c)(4) of this section.

(ii) Deduction of excess amounts. If the amount of the adjustment exceeds the sum of the amounts described in paragraph (d)(5)(i) of this section, the Institution may deduct the excess to the extent the deduction does not exceed the amount of FFA included in income for prior taxable years reduced by the amount of deductions allowable under this paragraph (d)(5)(ii) in prior taxable years.

(iii) Additional adjustments. Any adjustment to FFA in excess of the sum of the amounts described in paragraphs (d)(5)(i) and (ii) of this section is treated—

(A) By an Institution other than a New Entity or Acquiring, as a deduction of the amount in excess of FFA received that is required to be transferred to Agency under section 11(g) of the Federal Deposit Insurance Act (12 U.S.C. 1821(g)); or

(B) By a New Entity or Acquiring, as an adjustment to the purchase price paid in the Taxable Transfer (see § 1.338(b)-7).

(e) Examples. The following examples illustrate the provisions of this section:

Example (1). Timing of inclusion of FFA in income.

(i) Institution M, a calendar year taxpayer without Continuing Equity because it is in Agency receivership, is not a member of a consolidated group and has not been acquired in a Taxable Transfer. On January 1, 1997, M has assets with a total adjusted basis of $100 million and total liabilities of $120 million. M's deductions do not exceed its gross income (determined without regard to FFA) for 1997. Agency provides $30 million of FFA to M in 1997. The amount of this FFA that M must include in income in 1997 is limited by § 1.597-2(c)(2) to $20 million, the amount by which M's liabilities ($120 million) exceed the total adjusted basis of its assets ($100 million) at the beginning of the taxable year. Pursuant to § 1.597-2(c)(4)(i), M must establish a deferred FFA account for the remaining $10 million.

(ii) If Agency instead lends M the $30 million, M's indebtedness to Agency is disregarded and the results are the same as in paragraph (i) of this Example 1. Section 597(c); §§ 1.597-1(b) (defining FFA) and 1.597-3(b).

Example (2). Transfer of property to Agency.

(i) Institution M, a calendar year taxpayer without Continuing Equity because it is in Agency receivership, is not a member of a consolidated group and has not been acquired in a Taxable Transfer. At the beginning of 1998, M's remaining equity is $0 and M has a deferred FFA account of $10 million. Agency does not provide any FFA to M in 1998. During the year, M transfers property not covered by a Loss Guarantee to Agency and does not receive any consideration. The property has an adjusted basis of $5 million and a fair market value of $1 million at the time of the transfer. M has no other taxable income or loss in 1998.

(ii) Under § 1.597-2(d)(1), M is treated as selling the property for $1 million, its fair market value, thus recognizing a $4 million loss ($5 million – $1 million). In addition, because M did not receive any consideration from Agency, under § 1.597-2(d)(4) M has an adjustment to FFA of $1 million, the amount by which the fair market value of the transferred property ($1 million) exceeds the consideration M received from Agency ($0). Because no FFA is provided to M in 1998, this adjustment reduces the balance of M's deferred FFA account to $9 million ($10 million – $1 million). Section 1.597-2(d)(5)(i)(B). Because M's $4 million loss causes M's deductions to exceed its gross income by $4 million in 1998 and M has no remaining equity, under § 1.597-2(c)(4)(iii)(A) M must include $4 million of deferred FFA in income, and must decrease the remaining $9 million balance of its deferred FFA account by the same amount, leaving a balance of $5 million.

Example (3). Loss guarantee. Institution Q, a calendar year taxpayer, sells an asset covered by a Loss Guarantee to an unrelated third party for $4,000. Q's adjusted basis in the asset at the time of sale and the asset's guaranteed value are both $10,000. Pursuant to the Loss Guarantee, Agency pays Q $6,000 ($10,000 – $4,000). Q's amount realized from the sale of the asset is $10,000 ($4,000 from the third party and $6,000 from Agency). Section 1.597-2(d)(2). Q realizes no gain or loss on the sale ($10,000 – $10,000 = $0), and therefore includes none of the $6,000 of FFA it receives pursuant to the Loss Guarantee in income. Section 1.597-2(d)(3).

T.D. 8641, 12/20/95, amend T.D. 8677, 6/26/96, T.D. 8823, 6/25/99, T.D. 8858, 1/5/2000, T.D. 8940, 2/12/2001.

§ 1.597-3 Other rules.

(a) Ownership of assets. For all income tax purposes, an Institution is treated as the owner of all assets covered by a Loss Guarantee, yield maintenance agreement, or cost to carry or cost of funds reimbursement agreement, regardless of whether Agency (or a Controlled Entity) otherwise would be treated as the owner under general principles of income taxation.

(b) Debt and equity interests received by Agency. Debt instruments, stock, warrants, or other rights to acquire stock of an Institution (or any of its affiliates) that Agency or a Controlled Entity receives in connection with a transaction in which FFA is provided are not treated as debt, stock or other equity interests of or in the issuer for any purpose of the Internal Revenue Code while held by Agency or a Controlled Entity. On the date Agency or a Controlled Entity transfers an interest described in this paragraph (b) to a holder other than Agency or a Controlled Entity, the interest is treated as having been newly issued by the issuer to the holder with an issue price equal to the sum of the amount of money and the fair market value of property paid by the new holder in exchange for the interest.

(c) Agency obligations. *(1) In general.* Except as otherwise provided in this paragraph (c), the original issue discount rules of sections 1271 et seq. apply to Agency Obligations.

(2) Issue price of Agency Obligations provided as Net Worth Assistance. The issue price of an Agency Obligation that is provided as Net Worth Assistance and that bears interest at either a single fixed rate or a qualified floating rate (and provides for no contingent payments) is the lesser of the sum of the present values of all payments due under the obligation, discounted at a rate equal to the applicable Federal rate (within the meaning of section 1274(d)(1) and (3)) in effect for the date of issuance, or the stated principal amount of the obligation. The issue price of an Agency Obligation that bears a qualified floating rate of interest (within the meaning of § 1.1275-5(b)) is determined by treating the obligation as bearing a fixed rate of interest equal to the rate in effect on the date of issuance under the obligation.

(3) Adjustments to principal amount. Except as provided in § 1.597-5(d)(2)(iv), this paragraph (c)(3) applies if Agency modifies or exchanges an Agency Obligation provided as Net Worth Assistance (or a successor obligation). The issue price of the modified or new Agency Obligation is determined under paragraphs (c)(1) and (2) of this section. If the issue price is greater than the adjusted issue price of the existing Agency Obligation, the difference is treated as FFA. If the issue price is less than the adjusted issue price of the existing Agency Obligation, the difference is treated as an adjustment to FFA under § 1.597-2(d)(4).

(d) Successors. To the extent necessary to effectuate the purposes of the regulations under section 597, an entity's treatment under the regulations applies to its successor. A successor includes a transferee in a transaction to which section 381(a) applies or a Bridge Bank to which another Bridge Bank transfers deposit liabilities.

(e) [Reserved].

(f) Losses and deductions with respect to covered assets. Prior to the disposition of an asset covered by a Loss Guarantee, the asset cannot be charged off, marked to a market value, depreciated, amortized, or otherwise treated in a manner that supposes an actual or possible diminution of value below the greater of the asset's highest guaranteed value or the highest price at which the asset can be put.

(g) Anti-abuse rule. The regulations under section 597 must be applied in a manner consistent with the purposes of section 597. Accordingly, if, in structuring or engaging in any transaction, a principal purpose is to achieve a tax result that is inconsistent with the purposes of section 597 and the regulations thereunder, the Commissioner can make appropriate adjustments to income, deductions and other items that would be consistent with those purposes.

T.D. 8641, 12/20/95, amend T.D. 9048, 3/11/2003.

§ 1.597-4 Bridge Banks and Agency Control.

> ***Caution:*** The Treasury has not yet amended Reg § 1.597-4 to reflect changes made by P.L. 104-193, P.L. 104-188.

(a) Scope. This section provides rules that apply to a Bridge Bank or other Institution under Agency Control and to transactions in which an Institution transfers deposit liabilities (whether or not the Institution also transfers assets) to a Bridge Bank.

(b) Status as taxpayer. A Bridge Bank or other Institution under Agency Control is a corporation within the meaning of section 7701(a)(3) for all purposes of the Internal Revenue Code and is subject to all Internal Revenue Code provisions that generally apply to corporations, including those relating to methods of accounting and to requirements for filing returns, even if Agency owns stock of the Institution.

(c) No section 382 ownership change. The imposition of Agency Control, the cancellation of Institution stock by Agency, a transaction in which an Institution transfers deposit liabilities to a Bridge Bank, and an election under paragraph (g) of this section are disregarded in determining whether an ownership change has occurred within the meaning of section 382(g).

(d) Transfers to Bridge Banks. *(1) In general.* Except as otherwise provided in paragraph (g) of this section, the rules of this paragraph (d) apply to transfers to Bridge Banks. In general, a Bridge Bank and its associated Residual Entity are together treated as the successor entity to the transferring Institution. If an Institution transfers deposit liabilities to a Bridge Bank (whether or not it also transfers assets), the Institution recognizes no gain or loss on the transfer and the Bridge Bank succeeds to the transferring Institution's basis in any transferred assets. The associated Residual Entity retains its basis in any assets it continues to hold. Immediately after the transfer, the Bridge Bank succeeds to and takes into account the transferring Institution's items described in section 381(c) (subject to the conditions and limitations specified in section 381(c)), taxpayer identification number ("TIN"), deferred FFA account, and account receivable for future FFA as described in paragraph (g)(4)(ii) of this section. The Bridge Bank also succeeds to and continues the transferring Institution's taxable year.

(2) Transfers to a Bridge Bank from multiple Institutions. If two or more Institutions transfer deposit liabilities to the same Bridge Bank, the rules in paragraph (d)(1) of this section are modified to the extent provided in this paragraph (d)(2). The Bridge Bank succeeds to the TIN and continues the taxable year of the Institution that transfers the largest amount of deposits. The taxable years of the other transferring Institutions close at the time of the transfer. If all the transferor Institutions are members of the same consolidated group, the Bridge Bank's carryback of losses to the Institution that transfers the largest amount of deposits is not limited by section 381(b)(3). The limitations of section 381(b)(3) do apply to the Bridge Bank's carrybacks of losses to all other transferor Institutions. If the transferor Institutions are not all members of the same consolidated group, the limitations of section 381(b)(3) apply with respect to all transferor Institutions. See paragraph (g)(6)(ii) of this section for additional rules that apply if two or more Institutions that are not members of the same consolidated group transfer deposit liabilities to the same Bridge Bank.

(e) Treatment of Bridge Bank and Residual Entity as a single entity. A Bridge Bank and its associated Residual Entity or Entities are treated as a single entity for income tax purposes and must file a single combined income tax return. The Bridge Bank is responsible for filing all income tax returns and statements for this single entity and is the agent of each associated Residual Entity to the same extent as if the Bridge Bank were the common parent of a consolidated group including the Residual Entity. The term Institution includes a Residual Entity that files a combined return with its associated Bridge Bank.

(f) Rules applicable to members of consolidated groups. *(1) Status as members.* Unless an election is made under paragraph (g) of this section, Agency Control of an Institution does not terminate the Institution's membership in a consolidated group. Stock of a subsidiary that is canceled by Agency is treated as held by the members of the consolidated group that held the stock prior to its cancellation. If an Institution is a member of a consolidated group immediately before it transfers deposit liabilities to a Bridge Bank, the Bridge Bank succeeds to the Institution's status as the common parent or, unless an election is made under paragraph (g) of this section, as a subsidiary of the group. If a Bridge Bank succeeds to an Institution's status as a subsidiary, its stock is treated as held by the shareholders of the transferring Institution, and the stock basis or excess loss account of the Institution carries over to the Bridge Bank. A Bridge Bank is treated as owning stock owned by its associated Residual Entities, including for purposes of determining membership in an affiliated group.

(2) No 30-day election to be excluded from consolidated group. Neither an Institution nor any of its Consolidated Subsidiaries may be excluded from a consolidated group for a taxable year under § 1.1502-76(b)(5)(ii), as contained in 26 CFR part 1 edition revised April 1, 1994, if the Institution is under Agency Control at any time during the year.

(3) Coordination with consolidated return regulations. The provisions of the regulations under section 597 take precedence over conflicting provisions in the regulations under section 1502.

(g) Elective disaffiliation. *(1) In general.* A consolidated group of which an Institution is a subsidiary may elect irrevocably not to include the Institution in its affiliated group if the Institution is placed in Agency receivership (whether or not assets or deposit liabilities of the Institution are transferred to a Bridge Bank). See paragraph (g)(6) of this section for circumstances under which a consolidated group is deemed to make this election.

(2) Consequences of election. If the election under this paragraph (g) is made with respect to an Institution, the following consequences occur immediately before the subsidiary Institution to which the election applies is placed in Agency receivership (or, in the case of a deemed election under paragraph (g)(6) of this section, immediately before the consolidated group is deemed to make the election) and in the following order—

(i) All adjustments of the Institution and its Consolidated Subsidiaries under section 481 are accelerated;

(ii) Deferred intercompany gains and losses with respect to the Institution and its Consolidated Subsidiaries are taken into account and the Institution and its Consolidated Subsidiaries take into account any other items required under the regulations under section 1502 for members that become nonmembers within the meaning of § 1.1502-32(d)(4);

(iii) The taxable year of the Institution and its Consolidated Subsidiaries closes and the Institution includes the amount described in paragraph (g)(3) of this section in income as ordinary income as its last item for that taxable year;

(iv) The members of the consolidated group owning the common stock of the Institution include in income any excess loss account with respect to the Institution's stock under § 1.1502-19 and any other items required under the regulations under section 1502 for members that own stock of corporations that become nonmembers within the meaning of § 1.1502-32(d)(4); and

(v) If the Institution's liabilities exceed the aggregate fair market value of its assets on the date the Institution is placed in Agency receivership (or, in the case of a deemed election under paragraph (g)(6) of this section, on the date the consolidated group is deemed to make the election), the members of the consolidated group treat their stock in the Institution as worthless. (See §§ 1.337(d)-2 and 1.1502-35(f) for rules applicable when a member of a consolidated group is entitled to a worthless stock deduction with respect to stock of another member of the group.) In all other cases, the consolidated group will be treated as owning stock of a nonmember corporation until such stock is disposed of or becomes worthless under rules otherwise applicable.

(3) Toll charge. The amount described in this paragraph (g)(3) is the excess of the Institution's liabilities over the adjusted bases of its assets immediately before the Institution is placed in Agency receivership (or, in the case of a deemed election under paragraph (g)(6) of this section, immediately before the consolidated group is deemed to make the election). In computing this amount, the adjusted bases of an Institution's assets are reduced by the amount of the Institution's reserves for bad debts under section 585 or 593, other than supplemental reserves under section 593. For purposes of this paragraph (g)(3), an Institution is treated as a single entity that includes the assets and liabilities of its Consolidated Subsidiaries, with appropriate adjustments to prevent duplication. The amount described in this paragraph (g)(3) for alternative minimum tax purposes is determined using alternative minimum tax basis, deductions, and all other items required to be taken into account. In computing the increase in the group's taxable income or alternative minimum taxable income, sections 56(d)(1), 382 and 383 and §§ 1.1502-15, 1.1502-21 and 1.1502-22 (or §§ 1.1502-15A, 1.1502-21A and 1.1502-22A, as appropriate) do not limit the use of the attributes of the Institution and its Con-

solidated Subsidiaries to the extent, if any, that the inclusion of the amount described in this paragraph (g)(3) in income would result in the group having taxable income or alternative minimum taxable income (determined without regard to this sentence) for the taxable year. The preceding sentence does not apply to any limitation under section 382 or 383 or §§ 1.1502-15, 1.1502-21, or 1.1502-22 (or §§ 1.1502-15A, 1.1502-21A, or 1.1502-22A, as appropriate) that arose in connection with or prior to a corporation becoming a Consolidated Subsidiary of the Institution.

(4) Treatment of Institutions after disaffiliation. (i) In general. If the election under this paragraph (g) is made with respect to an Institution, immediately after the Institution is placed in Agency receivership (or, in the case of a deemed election under paragraph (g)(6) of this section, immediately after the consolidated group is deemed to make the election), the Institution and each of its Consolidated Subsidiaries are treated for income tax purposes as new corporations that are not members of the electing group's affiliated group. Each new corporation retains the TIN of the corresponding disaffiliated corporation and is treated as having received the assets and liabilities of the corresponding disaffiliated corporation in a transaction to which section 351 applies (and in which no gain was recognized under section 357(c) or otherwise). Thus, the new corporation has no net operating or capital loss carryforwards. An election under this paragraph (g) does not terminate the single entity treatment of a Bridge Bank and its Residual Entities provided in paragraph (e) of this section.

(ii) FFA. A new Institution is treated as having a non-interest bearing, nontransferable account receivable for future FFA with a basis equal to the amount described in paragraph (g)(3) of this section. If a disaffiliated Institution has a deferred FFA account at the time of its disaffiliation, the corresponding new Institution succeeds to and takes into account that deferred FFA account.

(iii) Filing of consolidated returns. If a disaffiliated Institution has Consolidated Subsidiaries at the time of its disaffiliation, the corresponding new Institution is required to file a consolidated income tax return with the subsidiaries in accordance with the regulations under section 1502.

(iv) Status as Institution. If an Institution is disaffiliated under this paragraph (g), the resulting new corporation is treated as an Institution for purposes of the regulations under section 597 regardless of whether it is a bank or domestic building and loan association within the meaning of section 597.

(v) Loss carrybacks. To the extent a carryback of losses would result in a refund being paid to a fiduciary under section 6402(i), an Institution or Consolidated Subsidiary with respect to which an election under this paragraph (g) (other than under paragraph (g)(6)(ii) of this section) applies is allowed to carry back losses as if the Institution or Consolidated Subsidiary had continued to be a member of the consolidated group that made the election.

(5) Affirmative election. (i) Original Institution. (A) Manner of making election. Except as otherwise provided in paragraph (g)(6) of this section, a consolidated group makes the election provided by this paragraph (g) by sending a written statement by certified mail to the affected Institution on or before the later of 120 days after its placement in Agency receivership or May 31, 1996. The statement must contain the following legend at the top of the page: "THIS IS AN ELECTION UNDER § 1.597-4(g) TO EXCLUDE THE BELOW-REFERENCED INSTITUTION AND CONSOLIDATED SUBSIDIARIES FROM THE AFFILIATED GROUP," and must include the names and taxpayer identification numbers of the common parent and of the Institution and Consolidated Subsidiaries to which the election applies, and the date on which the Institution was placed in Agency receivership. The consolidated group must send a similar statement to all subsidiary Institutions placed in Agency receivership during the consistency period described in paragraph (g)(5)(ii) of this section. (Failure to satisfy the requirement in the preceding sentence, however, does not invalidate the election with respect to any subsidiary Institution placed in Agency receivership during the consistency period described in paragraph (g)(5)(ii) of this section.) The consolidated group must include a copy of any election statement and accompanying certified mail receipt as part of its first income tax return filed after the due date under this paragraph (g)(5) for such statement. A statement must be attached to this return indicating that the individual who signed the election was authorized to do so on behalf of the consolidated group. Agency cannot make this election under the authority of section 6402(i) or otherwise.

(B) Consistency limitation on affirmative elections. A consolidated group may make an affirmative election under this paragraph (g)(5) with respect to a subsidiary Institution placed in Agency receivership only if the group made, or is deemed to have made, the election under this paragraph (g) with respect to every subsidiary Institution of the group placed in Agency receivership on or after May 10, 1989 and within five years preceding the date the subject Institution was placed in Agency receivership.

(ii) Effect on Institutions placed in receivership simultaneously or subsequently. An election under this paragraph (g), other than under paragraph (g)(6)(ii) of this section, applies to the Institution with respect to which the election is made or deemed made (the original Institution) and each subsidiary Institution of the group placed in Agency receivership or deconsolidated in contemplation of Agency Control or the receipt of FFA simultaneously with the original Institution or within five years thereafter.

(6) Deemed election. (i) Deconsolidations in contemplation. If one or more members of a consolidated group deconsolidate (within the meaning of § 1.1502-19(c)(1)(ii)(B)) a subsidiary Institution in contemplation of Agency Control or the receipt of FFA, the consolidated group is deemed to make the election described in this paragraph (g) with respect to the Institution on the date the deconsolidation occurs. A subsidiary Institution is conclusively presumed to have been deconsolidated in contemplation of Agency Control or the receipt of FFA if either event occurs within six months after the deconsolidation.

(ii) Transfers to a Bridge Bank from multiple groups. On the day an Institution's transfer of deposit liabilities to a Bridge Bank results in the Bridge Bank holding deposit liabilities from both a subsidiary Institution and an Institution not included in the subsidiary Institution's consolidated group, each consolidated group of which a transferring Institution or the Bridge Bank is a subsidiary is deemed to make the election described in this paragraph (g) with respect to its subsidiary Institution. If deposit liabilities of another Institution that is a subsidiary member of any consolidated group subsequently are transferred to the Bridge Bank, the consolidated group of which the Institution is a subsidiary is deemed to make the election described in this paragraph (g) with respect to that Institution at the time of the subsequent transfer.

(h) Examples. The following examples illustrate the provisions of this section:

Facts. Corporation X, the common parent of a consolidated group, owns all the stock (with a basis of $4 million) of Institution M, an insolvent Institution with no Consolidated Subsidiaries. At the close of business on April 30, 1996, M has $4 million of deposit liabilities, $1 million of other liabilities, and assets with an adjusted basis of $4 million and a fair market value of $3 million.

Example (1). Effect of receivership on consolidation. On May 1, 1996, Agency places M in receivership and begins liquidating M. X does not make an election under § 1.597-4(g). M remains a member of the X consolidated group after May 1, 1996. Section 1.597-4(f)(1).

Example (2). Effect of Bridge Bank on consolidation (i) Additional facts. On May 1, 1996, Agency places M in receivership and causes M to transfer all of its assets and deposit liabilities to Bridge Bank MB.

(ii) Consequences without an election to disaffiliate. M recognizes no gain or loss from the transfer and MB succeeds to M's basis in the transferred assets, M's items described in section 381(c) (subject to the conditions and limitations specified in section 381(c)) and TIN. Section 1.597-4(d)(1). (If M had a deferred FFA account, MB would also succeed to that account. Section 1.597-4(d)(1).) MB continues M's taxable year and succeeds to M's status as a member of the X consolidated group after May 1, 1996. Section 1.597-4(d)(1) and (f). MB and M are treated as a single entity for income tax purposes. Section 1.597-4(e).

(iii) Consequences with an election to disaffiliate. If, on July 1, 1996, X makes an election under § 1.597-4(g) with respect to M, the following consequences are treated as occurring immediately before M was placed in Agency receivership. M must include $1 million ($5 million of liabilities – $4 million of adjusted basis) in income as of May 1, 1996. Section 1.597-4(g)(2) and (3). M is then treated as a new corporation that is not a member of the X consolidated group and that has assets (including a $1 million account receivable for future FFA) with a basis of $5 million and $5 million of liabilities received from disaffiliated corporation M in a section 351 transaction. New corporation M retains the TIN of disaffiliated corporation M. Section 1.597-4(g)(4). Immediately after the disaffiliation, new corporation M is treated as transferring its assets and deposit liabilities to Bridge Bank MB. New corporation M recognizes no gain or loss from the transfer and MB succeeds to M's TIN and taxable year. Section 1.597-4(d)(1). Bridge Bank MB is treated as a single entity that includes M and has $5 million of liabilities, an account receivable for future FFA with a basis of $1 million, and other assets with a basis of $4 million. Section 1.597-4(d)(1).

T.D. 8641, 12/20/95, amend T.D. 8677, 6/26/96, T.D. 8823, 6/25/99, T.D. 9048, 3/11/2003, T.D. 9187, 3/2/2005, T.D. 9254, 3/9/2006.

PAR. 18. For each section listed in the table, remove the language in the "Remove" column and add in its place the language in the "Add" column as set forth below:

Section	Remove	Add
§ 1.267(f)-1(k)	§ 1.337(d)-2; § 1.1502-35	§ 1.1502-36.
§ 1.597-4(g)(2)(v)	§§ 1.337(d)-2 and § 1.1502-35(f)	§ 1.1502-36.
§ 1.1502-11(b)(3)(ii)(c)	§§ 1.337(d)-2 and § 1.1502-35	§ 1.1502-36.
§ 1.1502-12(r)	§§ 1.337(d)-2 and § 1.1502-35	§ 1.1502-36.
§ 1.1502-15(b)(2)(iii)	§§ 1.337(d)-2, 1.1502-35, or	§ 1.1502-36.
§ 1.1502-32(b)(3)(iii)(B)	§ 1.1502-35(b) or (f)(2).	

Proposed § 1.597-4 [*For Preamble, see ¶ 152,831*]

• ***Caution:*** This Notice of Proposed Rulemaking was partially finalized by TD 9341, 07/17/2007. Proposed Regs. 1.267(f)-1, 1.337(d)-1, 1.337(d)-2, 1.358-6, 1.597-4, 1.1502-11, 1.1502-12, 1.1502-13, 1.1502-15, 1.1502-19, 1.1502-20, 1.1502-21, 1.1502-30, 1.1502-31, 1.1502-32, 1.1502-33, 1.1502-35, 1.1502-35T, 1.1502-36, 1.1502-91 remain proposed.

§ 1.597-5 Taxable transfers.

(a) Taxable Transfers. *(1) Defined.* The term *Taxable Transfer* means—

(i) A transaction in which an entity transfers to a transferee other than a Bridge Bank—

(A) Any deposit liability (whether or not the Institution also transfers assets), if FFA is provided in connection with the transaction; or

(B) Any asset for which Agency or a Controlled Entity has any financial obligation (e.g., pursuant to a Loss Guarantee or Agency Obligation); or

(ii) A deemed transfer of assets described in paragraph (b) of this section.

(2) Scope. This section provides rules governing Taxable Transfers. Rules applicable to both actual and deemed asset acquisitions are provided in paragraphs (c) and (d) of this section. Special rules applicable only to deemed asset acquisitions are provided in paragraph (e) of this section.

(b) Deemed asset acquisitions upon stock purchase. *(1) In general.* In a deemed transfer of assets under this paragraph (b), an Institution (including a Bridge Bank or a Residual Entity) or a Consolidated Subsidiary of the Institution (the Old Entity) is treated as selling all of its assets in a single transaction and is treated as a new corporation (the New Entity) that purchases all of the Old Entity's assets at the close of the day immediately preceding the occurrence of an event described in paragraph (b)(2) of this section. However, such an event results in a deemed transfer of assets under this paragraph (b) only if it occurs—

(i) In connection with a transaction in which FFA is provided;

(ii) While the Old Entity is a Bridge Bank;

(iii) While the Old Entity has a positive balance in a deferred FFA account (see § 1.597-2(c)(4)(v) regarding the optional accelerated recapture of deferred FFA); or

(iv) With respect to a Consolidated Subsidiary, while the Institution of which it is a Consolidated Subsidiary is under Agency Control.

(2) Events. A deemed transfer of assets under this paragraph (b) results if the Old Entity—

(i) Becomes a non-member within the meaning of § 1.1502-32(d)(4) of its consolidated group (other than pursuant to an election under § 1.597-4(g));

(ii) Becomes a member of an affiliated group of which it was not previously a member (other than pursuant to an election under § 1.597-4(g)); or

(iii) Issues stock such that the stock that was outstanding before the imposition of Agency Control or the occurrence of any transaction in connection with the provision of FFA represents 50 percent or less of the vote or value of its outstanding stock (disregarding stock described in section 1504(a)(4) and stock owned by Agency or a Controlled Entity).

(3) Bridge Banks and Residual Entities. If a Bridge Bank is treated as selling all of its assets to a New Entity under this paragraph (b), each associated Residual Entity is treated as simultaneously selling its assets to a New Entity in a Taxable Transfer described in this paragraph (b).

(c) Treatment of transferor. *(1) FFA in connection with a Taxable Transfer.* A transferor in a Taxable Transfer is treated as having directly received immediately before a Taxable Transfer any Net Worth Assistance that Agency provides to the New Entity or Acquiring in connection with the transfer. (See § 1.597-2(a) and (c) for rules regarding the inclusion of FFA in income and § 1.597-2(a)(1) for related rules regarding FFA provided to shareholders.) The Net Worth Assistance is treated as an asset of the transferor that is sold to the New Entity or Acquiring in the Taxable Transfer.

(2) Amount realized in a Taxable Transfer. In a Taxable Transfer described in paragraph (a)(1)(i) of this section, the amount realized is determined under section 1001(b) by reference to the consideration paid for the assets. In a Taxable Transfer described in paragraph (a)(1)(ii) of this section, the amount realized is the sum of the grossed-up basis of the stock acquired in connection with the Taxable Transfer (excluding stock acquired from the Old or New Entity), plus the amount of liabilities assumed or taken subject to in the deemed transfer, plus other relevant items. The grossed-up basis of the acquired stock equals the acquirors' basis in the acquired stock divided by the percentage of the Old Entity's stock (by value) attributable to the acquired stock.

(3) Allocation of amount realized. (i) In general. The amount realized under paragraph (c)(2) of this section is allocated among the assets transferred in the Taxable Transfer in the same manner as amounts are allocated among assets under §§ 1.338(b)-6(b), (c)(1) and (2).

(ii) Modifications to general rule. This paragraph (c)(3)(ii) modifies certain of the allocation rules of paragraph (c)(3)(i) of this section. Agency Obligations and assets covered by Loss Guarantees in the hands of the New Entity or Acquiring are treated as Class II assets. Stock of a Consolidated Subsidiary is treated as a Class II asset to the extent the fair market value of the Consolidated Subsidiary's Class I and Class II assets exceeds the amount of its liabilities. The fair market value of an Agency Obligation is deemed to equal its adjusted issue price immediately before the Taxable Transfer. The fair market value of an asset covered by a Loss Guarantee immediately after the Taxable Transfer is deemed to be not less than the greater of the asset's highest guaranteed value or the highest price at which the asset can be put.

(d) Treatment of a New Entity and Acquiring. *(1) Purchase price.* The purchase price for assets acquired in a Taxable Transfer described in paragraph (a)(1)(i) of this section is the cost of the assets acquired. See § 1.1060-1T(c)(1). The purchase price for assets acquired in a Taxable Transfer described in paragraph (a)(1)(ii) of this section is the sum of the grossed-up basis of the stock acquired in connection with the Taxable Transfer (excluding stock acquired from the Old or New Entity), plus the amount of liabilities assumed or taken subject to in the deemed transfer, plus other relevant items. The grossed-up basis of the acquired stock equals the acquirors' basis in the acquired stock divided by the percentage of the Old Entity's stock (by value) attributable to the acquired stock. FFA provided in connection with a Taxable Transfer is not included in the New Entity's or Acquiring's purchase price for the acquired assets. Any Net Worth Assistance so provided is treated as an asset of the transferor sold to the New Entity or Acquiring in the Taxable Transfer.

(2) Allocation of basis. (i) In general. Except as otherwise provided in this paragraph (d)(2), the purchase price determined under paragraph (d)(1) of this section is allocated among the assets transferred in the Taxable Transfer in the same manner as amounts are allocated among assets under § 1.338(b)-6(b), (c)(1) and (2).

(ii) Modifications to general rule. The allocation rules contained in paragraph (c)(3)(ii) of this section apply to the allocation of basis among assets acquired in a Taxable Transfer. No basis is allocable to Agency's agreement to provide Loss Guarantees, yield maintenance payments, cost to carry or cost of funds reimbursement payments, or expense reimbursement or indemnity payments. A New Entity's basis in assets it receives from its shareholders is determined under general principles of income taxation and is not governed by this paragraph (d).

(iii) Allowance and recapture of additional basis in certain cases. If the fair market value of the Class I and Class II assets acquired in a Taxable Transfer is greater than the New Entity's or Acquiring's purchase price for the acquired assets, the basis of the Class I and Class II assets equals their fair market value. The amount by which the fair market value of the Class I and Class II assets exceeds the purchase price is included ratably as ordinary income by the New Entity or Acquiring over a period of six taxable years beginning in the year of the Taxable Transfer. The New Entity or Acquiring must include as ordinary income the entire amount remaining to be recaptured under the preceding sentence in the taxable year in which an event occurs that would accelerate inclusion of an adjustment under section 481.

(iv) Certain post-transfer adjustments. (A) Agency Obligations. If an adjustment to the principal amount of an Agency Obligation or cash payment to reflect a more accurate determination of the condition of the Institution at the time of the Taxable Transfer is made before the earlier of the date the New Entity or Acquiring files its first post-transfer income tax return or the due date of that return (including extensions), the New Entity or Acquiring must adjust its basis in its acquired assets to reflect the adjustment. In making adjustments to the New Entity's or Acquiring's basis in its acquired assets, paragraph (c)(3)(ii) of this section is applied by treating an adjustment to the principal amount of an Agency Obligation pursuant to the first sentence of this paragraph (d)(2)(iv)(A) as occurring immediately before the Taxable Transfer. (See § 1.597-3(c)(3) for rules regarding other adjustments to the principal amount of an Agency Obligation.)

(B) Assets covered by a Loss Guarantee. If, immediately after a Taxable Transfer, an asset is not covered by a Loss

Guarantee but the New Entity or Acquiring has the right to designate specific assets that will be covered by a Loss Guarantee, the New Entity or Acquiring must treat any asset so designated as having been subject to the Loss Guarantee at the time of the Taxable Transfer. The New Entity or Acquiring must adjust its basis in the covered assets and in its other acquired assets to reflect the designation in the manner provided by paragraph (d)(2) of this section. The New Entity or Acquiring must make appropriate adjustments in subsequent taxable years if the designation is made after the New Entity or Acquiring files its first post-transfer income tax return or the due date of that return (including extensions) has passed.

(e) Special rules applicable to Taxable Transfers that are deemed asset acquisitions. *(1) Taxpayer identification numbers.* Except as provided in paragraph (e)(3) of this section, a New Entity succeeds to the TIN of the transferor in a deemed sale under paragraph (b) of this section.

(2) Consolidated subsidiaries. (i) In general. A Consolidated Subsidiary that is treated as selling its assets in a Taxable Transfer under paragraph (b) of this section is treated as engaging immediately thereafter in a complete liquidation to which section 332 applies. The consolidated group of which the Consolidated Subsidiary is a member does not take into account gain or loss on the sale, exchange, or cancellation of stock of the Consolidated Subsidiary in connection with the Taxable Transfer.

(ii) Certain minority shareholders. Shareholders of the Consolidated Subsidiary that are not members of the consolidated group that includes the Institution do not recognize gain or loss with respect to shares of Consolidated Subsidiary stock retained by the shareholder. The shareholder's basis for that stock is not affected by the Taxable Transfer.

(3) Bridge Banks and Residual Entities. (i) In general. A Bridge Bank or Residual Entity's sale of assets to a New Entity under paragraph (b) of this section is treated as made by a single entity under § 1.597-4(e). The New Entity deemed to acquire the assets of a Residual Entity under paragraph (b) of this section is not treated as a single entity with the Bridge Bank (or with the New Entity acquiring the Bridge Bank's assets) and must obtain a new TIN.

(ii) Treatment of consolidated groups. At the time of a Taxable Transfer described in paragraph (a)(1)(ii) of this section, treatment of a Bridge Bank as a subsidiary member of a consolidated group under § 1.597-4(f)(1) ceases. However, the New Entity deemed to acquire the assets of a Residual Entity is a member of the selling consolidated group after the deemed sale. The group's basis or excess loss account in the stock of the New Entity that is deemed to acquire the assets of the Residual Entity is the group's basis or excess loss account in the stock of the Bridge Bank immediately before the deemed sale, as adjusted for the results of the sale.

(4) Certain returns. If an Old Entity without Continuing Equity is not a subsidiary of a consolidated group at the time of the Taxable Transfer, the controlling Agency must file all income tax returns for the Old Entity for periods ending on or prior to the date of the deemed sale described in paragraph (b) of this section that are not filed as of that date.

(5) Basis limited to fair market value. If all of the stock of the corporation is not acquired on the date of the Taxable Transfer, the Commissioner may make appropriate adjustments under paragraphs (c) and (d) of this section to the extent using a grossed-up basis of the stock of a corporation results in an aggregate amount realized for, or basis in, the assets other than the aggregate fair market value of the assets.

(f) Examples. The following examples illustrate the provisions of this section:

Example (1). Branch sale resulting in Taxable Transfer.

(i) Institution M is a calendar year taxpayer in Agency receivership. M is not a member of a consolidated group. On January 1, 1997, M has $200 million of liabilities (including deposit liabilities) and assets with an adjusted basis of $100 million. M has no income or loss for 1997 and, except as described below, receives no FFA. On September 30, 1997, Agency causes M to transfer six branches (with assets having an adjusted basis of $1 million) together with $120 million of deposit liabilities to N. In connection with the transfer, Agency provides $121 million in cash to N.

(ii) The transaction is a Taxable Transfer in which M receives $121 million of Net Worth Assistance. Section 1.597-5(a)(1). (M is treated as directly receiving the $121 million of Net Worth Assistance immediately before the Taxable Transfer. Section 1.597-5(c)(1).) M transfers branches having a basis of $1 million and is treated as transferring $121 million in cash (the Net Worth Assistance) to N in exchange for N's assumption of $120 million of liabilities. Thus, M realizes a loss of $2 million on the transfer. The amount of the FFA M must include in its income in 1997 is limited by § 1.597-2(c) to $102 million, which is the sum of the $100 million excess of M's liabilities ($200 million) over the total adjusted basis of its assets ($100 million) at the beginning of 1997, plus the $2 million excess for the taxable year, which results from the Taxable Transfer, of M's deductions (other than carryovers) over its gross income other than FFA. M must establish a deferred FFA account for the remaining $19 million of FFA. Section 1.597-2(c)(4).

(iii) N, as Acquiring, must allocate its $120 million purchase price for the assets acquired from M among those assets. Cash is a Class I asset. The branch assets are in Classes III and IV. N's adjusted basis in the cash is its amount, i.e., $121 million. Section 1.597-5(d)(2). Because this amount exceeds N's purchase price for all of the acquired assets by $1 million, N allocates no basis to the other acquired assets and, under § 1.597-5(d)(2), must recapture the $1 million excess at an annual rate of $166,667 in the six consecutive taxable years beginning with 1997 (subject to acceleration for certain events).

Example (2). Stock issuance by Bridge Bank causing Taxable Transfer.

(i) On April 1, 1996, Institution P is placed in receivership and caused to transfer assets and liabilities to Bridge Bank PB. On August 31, 1996, the assets of PB consist of $20 million in cash, loans outstanding with an adjusted basis of $50 million and a fair market value of $40 million, and other non-financial assets (primarily branch assets and equipment) with an adjusted basis of $5 million. PB has deposit liabilities of $95 million and other liabilities of $5 million. P, the Residual Entity, holds real estate with an adjusted basis of $10 million and claims in litigation having a zero basis. P retains no deposit liabilities and has no other liabilities (except its liability to Agency for having caused its deposit liabilities to be satisfied).

(ii) On September 1, 1996, Agency causes PB to issue 100 percent of its common stock for $2 million cash to X. On the same day, Agency issues a $25 million note to PB. The note bears a fixed rate of interest in excess of the applicable federal rate in effect for September 1, 1996. Agency provides Loss Guarantees guaranteeing PB a value of $50 million for PB's loans outstanding.

(iii) The stock issuance is a Taxable Transfer in which PB is treated as selling all of its assets to a new corporation, New PB. Section 1.597-5(b)(1). PB is treated as directly receiving $25 million of Net Worth Assistance (the issue price of the Agency Obligation) immediately before the Taxable Transfer. Section 1.597-3(c)(2); § 1.597-5(c)(1). The amount of FFA PB must include in income is determined under § 1.597-2(a) and (c). PB in turn is deemed to transfer the note to New PB in the Taxable Transfer, together with $20 million of cash, all its loans outstanding (with a basis of $50 million) and its other non-financial assets (with a basis of $5 million). The amount realized by PB from the sale is $100 million, the amount of PB's liabilities deemed to be assumed by New PB. This amount realized equals PB's basis in its assets and thus, PB realizes no gain or loss on the transfer to New PB.

(iv) Residual Entity P also is treated as selling all its assets (consisting of real estate and claims in litigation) for $0 (the amount of consideration received by P) to a new corporation (New P) in a Taxable Transfer. Section 1.597-5(b)(3). (P's only liability is to Agency and a liability to Agency is not treated as a debt under § 1.597-3(b).) Thus, P realizes a $10 million loss on the transfer to New P. The combined return filed by PB and P for 1996 will reflect a total loss on the Taxable Transfer of $10 million ($0 for PB and $10 million for P). Section 1.597-5(e)(3). That return also will reflect FFA income from the Net Worth Assistance, determined under § 1.597-2(a) and (c).

(v) New PB is treated as having acquired the assets it acquired from PB for $100 million, the amount of liabilities assumed. In allocating basis among these assets, New PB treats the Agency note and the loans outstanding (which are covered by Loss Guarantees) as Class II assets. For the purpose of allocating basis, the fair market value of the Agency note is deemed to equal its adjusted issue price immediately before the transfer, $25 million. The fair market value of the loans is deemed not to be less than the guaranteed value of $50 million.

(vi) New P is treated as having acquired its assets for no consideration. Thus its basis in its assets immediately after the transfer is zero. New PB and New P are not treated as a single entity. Section 1.597-5(e)(3).

Example (3). Taxable Transfer of previously disaffiliated Institution.

(i) Corporation X, the common parent of a consolidated group, owns all the stock of Institution M, an insolvent Institution with no Consolidated Subsidiaries. On April 30, 1996, M has $4 million of deposit liabilities, $1 million of other liabilities, and assets with an adjusted basis of $4 million and a fair market value of $3 million. On May 1, 1996, Agency places M in receivership. X elects under § 1.597-4(g) to disaffiliate M. Accordingly, as of May 1, 1996, new corporation M is not a member of the X consolidated group. On May 1, 1996, Agency causes M to transfer all of its assets and liabilities to Bridge Bank MB. Under § 1.597-4(e), MB and M are thereafter treated as a single entity which has $5 million of liabilities, an account receivable for future FFA with a basis of $1 million, and other assets with a basis of $4 million. Section 1.597-4(g)(4).

(ii) During May 1996, MB earns $25,000 of interest income and accrues $20,000 of interest expense on depositor accounts and there is no net change in deposits other than the additional $20,000 of interest expense accrued on depositor accounts. MB pays $5,000 of wage expenses and has no other items of income or expense.

(iii) On June 1, 1996, Agency causes MB to issue 100 percent of its stock to corporation Y. In connection with the stock issuance, Agency provides an Agency Obligation for $2 million and no other FFA.

(iv) The stock issuance results in a Taxable Transfer. Section 1.597-5(b). MB is treated as receiving the Agency Obligation immediately prior to the Taxable Transfer. Section 1.597-5(c)(1). MB has $1 million of basis in its account receivable for FFA. This receivable is treated as satisfied, offsetting $1 million of the $2 million of FFA provided by Agency in connection with the Taxable Transfer. The status of the remaining $1 million of FFA as includible income is determined as of the end of the taxable year under § 1.597-2(c). However, under § 1.597-2(b), MB obtains a $2 million basis in the Agency Obligation received as FFA.

(v) Under § 1.597-5(c)(2), in the Taxable Transfer, Old Entity MB is treated as selling, to New Entity MB, all of Old Entity MB's assets, having a basis of $6,020,000 (the original $4 million of asset basis as of April 30, 1996, plus $20,000 net cash from May 1996 activities, plus $2 million in the Agency Obligation received as FFA), for $5,020,000, the amount of Old Entity MB's liabilities assumed by New Entity MB pursuant to the Taxable Transfer. Therefore, Old Entity MB recognizes, in the aggregate, a loss of $1 million from the Taxable Transfer.

(vi) Because this $1 million loss causes Old Entity MB's deductions to exceed its gross income (determined without regard to FFA) by $1 million, Old Entity MB must include in its income the $1 million of FFA not offset by the FFA receivable. Section 1.597-2(c). (As of May 1, 1996, Old Entity MB's liabilities ($5,000,000) did not exceed MB's $5 million adjusted basis of its assets. For the taxable year, MB's deductions of $1,025,000 ($1,000,000 loss from the Taxable Transfer, $20,000 interest expense and $5,000 of wage expense) exceeded its gross income (disregarding FFA) of $25,000 (interest income) by $1,000,000. Thus, under § 1.597-2(c), MB includes in income the entire $1,000,000 of FFA not offset by the FFA receivable.)

(vii) Therefore, Old Entity MB's taxable income for the taxable year ending on the date of the Taxable Transfer is $0.

(viii) Residual Entity M is also deemed to engage in a deemed sale of its assets to New Entity M under § 1.597-5(b)(3), but there are no tax consequences as M has no assets or liabilities at the time of the deemed sale.

(ix) Under § 1.597-5(d)(1), New Entity MB is treated as purchasing Old Entity MB's assets for $5,020,000, the amount of New Entity MB's liabilities. Of this, $2,000,000 is allocated to the $2 million Agency Obligation, and $3,020,000 is allocated to the other assets New Entity MB is treated as purchasing in the Taxable Transfer.

Example (4). Loss sharing. Institution N acquires assets and assumes liabilities of another Institution in a Taxable Transfer. Among the assets transferred are three parcels of real estate. In the hands of the transferring Institution, these assets had book values of $100,000 each. In connection with the Taxable Transfer, Agency agrees to reimburse Institution N for 80 percent of any loss (based on the original book value) realized on the disposition or charge-off of the three properties. This arrangement constitutes a Loss Guarantee. Thus, in allocating basis, Institution N treats the three parcels as Class II assets. By virtue of the arrangement with the Agency, Institution N is assured that the parcels will not be worth less to it than $80,000 each, because even if the properties are worthless, Agency will reimburse 80 percent of the loss. Although Institution could obtain payments under the Loss Guarantee if the properties are worth more, it is not guaranteed that it will realize more than $80,000. Accordingly, $80,000 is the highest guaranteed value of the three parcels. Institution N will allocate basis to the Class II assets up to their fair market value. For this purpose, the fair market value of the three parcels is not less than $80,000 each. Section 1.597-5(d)(2)(ii); § 1.597-5(c)(3)(ii).

T.D. 8641, 12/20/95, amend T.D. 8858, 1/5/2000, T.D. 8940, 2/12/2001.

§ 1.597-6 Limitation on collection of income tax.

(a) Limitation on collection where tax is borne by Agency. If an Institution without Continuing Equity (or any of its Consolidated Subsidiaries) is liable for income tax that is attributable to the inclusion in income of FFA or gain from a Taxable Transfer, the tax will not be collected if it would be borne by Agency. The final determination of whether the tax would be borne by Agency is within the sole discretion of the Commissioner. In determining whether tax would be borne by Agency, the Commissioner will disregard indemnity, tax-sharing, or similar obligations of Agency, an Institution, or its Consolidated Subsidiaries. Collection of the several income tax liability under § 1.1502-6 from members of an Institution's consolidated group other than the Institution or its Consolidated Subsidiaries is not affected by this section. Income tax will continue to be subject to collection except as specifically limited in this section. This section does not apply to taxes other than income taxes.

(b) Amount of tax attributable to FFA or gain on a Taxable Transfer. For purposes of paragraph (a) of this section, the amount of income tax in a taxable year attributable to the inclusion of FFA or gain from a Taxable Transfer in the income of an Institution (or a Consolidated Subsidiary) is the excess of the actual income tax liability of the Institution (or the consolidated group in which the Institution is a member); over the income tax liability of the Institution (or the consolidated group in which the Institution is a member) determined without regard to FFA or gain or loss on the Taxable Transfer.

(c) Reporting of uncollected tax. A taxpayer must specify on the front page of Form 1120 (U.S. Corporate Income Tax Return), to the left of the space provided for "Total Tax," the amount of income tax for the taxable year that is potentially not subject to collection under this section. If an Institution is a subsidiary member of a consolidated group, the amount specified as not subject to collection is zero.

(d) Assessments of tax to offset refunds. Income tax that is not collected under this section will be assessed and, thus, used to offset any claim for refund made by or on behalf of the Institution, the Consolidated Subsidiary or any other corporation with several liability for the tax.

(e) Collection of taxes from Acquiring or a New Entity. *(1) Acquiring.* No income tax liability (including the several liability for taxes under § 1.1502-6) of a transferor in a Taxable Transfer will be collected from Acquiring.

(2) New Entity. Income tax liability (including the several liability for taxes under § 1.1502-6) of a transferor in a Taxable Transfer will be collected from a New Entity only if stock that was outstanding in the Old Entity remains outstanding as stock in the New Entity or is reacquired or exchanged for consideration.

(f) Effect on section 7507. This section supersedes the application of section 7507, and the regulations thereunder, for the assessment and collection of income tax attributable to FFA.

T.D. 8641, 12/20/95.

§ 1.597-7 Effective date.

(a) FIRREA effective date. Section 597, as amended by section 1401 of the Financial Institutions Reform, Recovery, and Enforcement Act of 1989 (FIRREA), Public Law 101-73, is generally effective for any FFA received or accrued by an Institution on or after May 10, 1989, and for any transaction in connection with which such FFA is provided, unless the FFA is provided in connection with an acquisition occurring prior to May 10, 1989. See § 1.597-8 for rules regarding FFA received or accrued on or after May 10, 1989, that relates to an acquisition that occurred before May 10, 1989.

(b) Effective date of regulations. Except as otherwise provided in this section, §§ 1.597-1 through 1.597-6 apply to taxable years ending on or after April 22, 1992. However, the provisions of §§ 1.597-1 through 1.597-6 do not apply to FFA received or accrued for taxable years ending on or after April 22, 1992, in connection with an Agency assisted acquisition within the meaning of Notice 89-102 (1989-2 C.B. 436; see § 601.601(d)(2)) (which does not include a transfer to a Bridge Bank), that occurs before April 22, 1992. Taxpayers not subject to §§ 1.597-1 through 1.597-6 must comply with an interpretation of the statute that is reasonable in light of the legislative history and applicable administrative pronouncements. For this purpose, the rules contained in Notice 89-102 apply to the extent provided in the Notice.

(c) Elective application to prior years and transactions. *(1) In general.* Except as limited in this paragraph (c), an election is available to apply §§ 1.597-1 through 1.597-6 to taxable years prior to the general effective date of these regulations. A consolidated group may elect to apply §§ 1.597-1 through 1.597-6 for all members of the group in all taxable years to which section 597, as amended by FIRREA, applies. The common parent makes the election for the group. An entity that is not a member of a consolidated group may elect to apply §§ 1.597-1 through 1.597-6 to all taxable years to which section 597, as amended by FIRREA, applies for which it is not a member of a consolidated group. The election is irrevocable.

(2) Election unavailable in certain cases. (i) Statute of limitations closed. The election cannot be made if the period for assessment and collection of tax has expired under the rules of section 6501 for any taxable year in which §§ 1.597-1 through 1.597-6 would affect the determination of the electing entity's or group's income, deductions, gain, loss, basis, or other items.

(ii) No section 338 election under Notice 89-102. The election cannot be made with respect to an Institution if, under Notice 89-102, it was a Target with respect to which a qualified stock purchase was made, a timely election under section 338 was not made, and on April 22, 1992, a timely election under section 338 could not be made.

(iii) Inconsistent treatment of Institution that would be New Entity. If, under § 1.597-5(b), an Institution would become a New Entity before April 22, 1992, the election cannot be made with respect to that Institution unless elections are made by all relevant persons such that §§ 1.597-1 through § 1.597-6 apply both before and after the deemed sale under § 1.597-5. However, this requirement does not apply if, under §§ 1.597-1 through § 1.597-6, the Institution would not have Continuing Equity prior to the deemed sale.

(3) Expense reimbursements. Notice 89-102, 1989-2 C.B. 436, provides that reimbursements paid or accrued pursuant to an expense reimbursement or indemnity arrangement are not included in income but the taxpayer may not deduct, or otherwise take into account, the item of cost or expense to which the reimbursement or indemnity payment relates. With respect to an Agency assisted acquisition within the meaning of Notice 89-102 that occurs before April 22, 1992, a taxpayer that elects to apply these regulations retroactively under this paragraph (c) may continue to account for these items under the rules of Notice 89-102.

(4) Procedural rules. (i) Manner of making election. An Institution or consolidated group makes the election provided by this paragraph (c) by attaching a written statement to, and including it as a part of, the taxpayer's or consolidated group's first annual income tax return filed on or after March 15, 1996. The statement must contain the following legend at the top of the page: "THIS IS AN ELECTION UNDER § 1.597-7(c)," and must contain the name, address and employer identification number of the taxpayer or common parent making the election. The statement must include a declaration that "TAXPAYER AGREES TO EXTEND THE STATUTE OF LIMITATIONS ON ASSESSMENT FOR THREE YEARS FROM THE DATE OF THE FILING OF THIS ELECTION UNDER § 1.597-7(c), IF THE LIMITATIONS PERIOD WOULD EXPIRE EARLIER WITHOUT SUCH EXTENSION, FOR ANY ITEMS AFFECTED IN ANY TAXABLE YEAR BY THE FILING OF THIS ELECTION," and a declaration that either "AMENDED RETURNS WILL BE FILED FOR ALL TAXABLE YEARS AFFECTED BY THE FILING OF THIS ELECTION WITHIN 180 DAYS OF MAKING THIS STATEMENT, UNLESS SUCH REQUIREMENT IS WAIVED IN WRITING BY THE DISTRICT DIRECTOR OR HIS DELEGATE" or "ALL RETURNS PREVIOUSLY FILED ARE CONSISTENT WITH THE PROVISIONS OF §§ 1.597-1 THROUGH 1.597-6," and be signed by an individual who is authorized to make the election under this paragraph (c) on behalf of the taxpayer. An election with respect to a consolidated group must be made by the common parent of the group, not Agency, and applies to all members of the group.

(ii) Effect of elective disaffiliation. To make the affirmative election described in § 1.597-4(g)(5) for an Institution placed in Agency receivership in a taxable year ending before April 22, 1992, the consolidated group must send the affected Institution the statement described in § 1.597-4(g)(5) on or before May 31, 1996. Notwithstanding the requirements of paragraph (c)(4)(i) of this section, a consolidated group sending such a statement is deemed to make the election described in, and to agree to the conditions contained in, this paragraph (c). The consolidated group must nevertheless attach the statement described in paragraph (c)(4)(i) of this section to its first annual income tax return filed on or after March 15, 1996.

(d) Reliance on prior guidance. *(1) Notice 89-102.* Taxpayers may rely on Notice 89-102, 1989-2 C.B. 436, to the extent they acted in reliance on that Notice prior to April 22, 1992. Such reliance must be reasonable and transactions with respect to which taxpayers rely must be consistent with the overriding policies of section 597, as expressed in the legislative history.

(2) Notice FI-46-89. (i) In general. Notice FI-46-89 was published in the Federal Register on April 23, 1992 (57 FR 14804). Taxpayers may rely on the provisions of §§ 1.597-1 through 1.597-6 of that notice to the extent they acted in reliance on those provisions prior to December 21, 1995. Such reliance must be reasonable and transactions with respect to which taxpayers rely must be consistent with the overriding policies of section 597, as expressed in the legislative history, as well as the overriding policies of notice FI-46-89.

(ii) Taxable Transfers. Any taxpayer described in this paragraph (d) that, under notice FI-46-89, would be a New Entity or Acquiring with respect to a Taxable Transfer on or after April 22, 1992, and before December 21, 1995, may apply the rules of that notice with respect to such transaction.

T.D. 8641, 12/20/95.

---

§ 1.597-8 Transitional rules for Federal financial assistance.

(a) Scope. This section provides transitional rules for the tax consequences of Federal financial assistance received or accrued on or after May 10, 1989, if the assistance payment relates to an acquisition that occurred before that date.

(b) Transitional rules. The tax consequences of any payment of Federal financial assistance received or accrued on or after May 10, 1989, are governed by the applicable provisions of section 597 that were in effect prior to the Financial Institutions Reform, Recovery, and Enforcement Act of 1989 ("FIRREA") if either—

(1) The payment—

(i) Is pursuant to an acquisition of a bank or domestic building and loan association before May 10, 1989,

(ii) Is provided pursuant to an assistance agreement executed before May 10, 1989,

(iii) Is provided to a party to that agreement or to such other party as the Commissioner may determine appropriate by letter ruling or other written guidance, and

(iv) Would, if provided before May 10, 1989, have been governed by applicable provisions of section 597 that were in effect prior to FIRREA; or

(2) The payment—

(i) Represents a prepayment of (or a payment in lieu of) a fixed or contingent right to Federal financial assistance that would have satisfied the conditions of paragraphs (b)(1)(i), (ii) and (iv) of this section, and

(ii) Is provided to a party described in paragraph (b)(1)(iii) of this section.

(c) Definition of Federal financial assistance. Federal financial assistance for purposes of this section has the meaning prescribed by section 597(c) as amended by FIRREA.

(d) Examples. The following examples illustrate the provisions of this section:

Example (1). X corporation acquired Y, a domestic building and loan association on September 10, 1988. Pursuant to a written agreement executed at the time of the acquisition, Y received Federal financial assistance that included a note bearing a market rate of interest, the right to future payments if certain assets were sold at a loss, and the right to future payments if the income produced by certain assets was less than an agreed upon amount. On December 1, 1991, an agreement was executed in which Y relinquished its rights to Federal financial assistance under the September 10, 1988 agreement in return for a lump sum payment. The lump sum payment represented a prepayment of the principal and accrued but unpaid interest for the note, and the rights to the contingent future loss and income payments. The entire prepayment is excluded from the income of Y because it is a prepayment of Federal financial assistance and the assistance (i) would have been provided pursuant to an acquisition that occurred before May 10, 1989, would have been provided pursuant to an assistance agreement executed before May 10, 1989, and would, if it had been provided prior to May 10, 1989, have been governed by a pre-FIRREA version of section 597; and (ii) the prepayment is paid to a party to the assistance agreement.

Example (2). The facts are the same as those in Example 1, except that the note bears an above market rate of interest and part of the lump sum represents a premium payment for the note. The portion of the lump sum allocable to the premium payment is also excluded from the income of Y because the payment represents the present value of the right to future Federal financial assistance in the form of interest.

Example (3). The facts are the same as those in Example 1, except that a portion of the lump sum payment represents compensation for additional expenses Y may incur in the future because of termination of the September 10, 1988 agreement. The portion of the lump sum payment allocable to the compensation for additional expenses must be included in the income of Y because it is not a prepayment of Federal financial assistance provided for by a written agreement entered into prior to May 10, 1989.

Example (4). The facts are the same as those in Example 1, except that instead of a new assistance agreement, the September 10, 1988 assistance agreement was modified on December 1, 1991. The modified agreement provided new Federal financial assistance in addition to the amounts previously agreed to. None of the new Federal financial assistance is governed by this regulation because the new assistance was not provided for by a written agreement entered into prior to May 10, 1989. The modification does not, however, affect the tax treatment of assistance provided for by the agreement prior to its modification.

(e) Effective date. This section is effective April 23, 1992 for assistance received or accrued on or after May 10, 1989 in connection with acquisitions before that date.

T.D. 8406, 4/22/92, amend T.D. 8471, 4/7/93.

§ 1.601-1 Special deduction for bank affiliates.

Caution: The Treasury has not yet amended Reg § 1.601-1 to reflect changes made by P.L. 94-455.

(a) The special deduction described in section 601 is allowed:

(1) To a holding company affiliate of a bank, as defined in section 2 of the Banking Act of 1933 (12 U.S.C. 221a), which holding company affiliate holds, at the end of the taxable year, a general voting permit granted by the Board of Governors of the Federal Reserve System.

(2) In the amount of the earnings or profits of such holding company affiliate which, in compliance with section 5144 of the Revised Statutes (12 U.S.C. 61), has been devoted by it during the taxable year to the acquisition of readily marketable assets other than bank stock.

(3) Upon certification by the Board of Governors of the Federal Reserve System to the Commissioner that such an amount of the earnings or profits has been so devoted by such affiliate during the taxable year.

No deduction is allowable under section 601 for the amount of readily marketable assets in excess of what is required by section 5144 of the Revised Statutes (12 U.S.C. 61) to be acquired by such affiliate, or in excess of the taxable income for the taxable year computed without regard to the special deductions for corporations provided in part VIII (section 241 and following), subchapter B, chapter 1 of the Code. Nor may the aggregate of the deductions allowable under section 601 and the credits allowable under the corresponding provision of any prior income tax law for all taxable years exceed the amount required to be devoted under such section 5144 to the acquisition of readily marketable assets other than bank stock.

(b) Every taxpayer claiming a deduction provided for in section 601 shall attach to its return a supplementary statement setting forth all the facts and information upon which the claim is predicated, including such facts and information as the Board of Governors of the Federal Reserve System may prescribe as necessary to enable it, upon the request of the Commissioner subsequent to the filing of the return, to certify to the Commissioner the amount of earnings or profits devoted to the acquisition of such readily marketable assets. A certified copy of such supplementary statement shall be forwarded by the taxpayer to the Board of Governors at the time of the filing of the return. The holding company affiliate shall also furnish the Board of Governors such further information as the Board shall require. For the requirements with respect to the amount of such readily marketable assets which must be acquired and maintained by a holding company affiliate to which a voting permit has been granted, see section 5144(b) and (c) of the Revised Statutes (12 U.S.C. 61).

T.D. 6188, 7/5/56.

§ 1.611-0 Regulatory authority.

Sections 1.611-1 through 1.614-8, inclusive, are prescribed under the authority granted the Secretary or his delegate by section 611(a) of the Code to prescribe regulations under which a reasonable allowance for depletion and depreciation of improvements shall be allowed, according to the peculiar conditions in each case, in the case of mines, oil and gas wells, other natural deposits and timber.

T.D. 6965, 7/25/68.

§ 1.611-1 Allowance of deduction for depletion.

(a) Depletion of mines, oil and gas wells, other natural deposits, and timber. *(1) In general.* Section 611 provides that there shall be allowed as a deduction in computing taxable income in the case of mines, oil and gas wells, other natural deposits, and timber, a reasonable allowance for depletion. In the case of standing timber, the depletion allowance shall be computed solely upon the adjusted basis of the property. In the case of other exhaustible natural resources the allowance for depletion shall be computed upon either the adjusted depletion basis of the property (see section 612, relating to cost depletion) or upon a percentage of gross income from the property (see section 613, relating to percentage depletion), whichever results in the greater allowance for depletion for any taxable year. In no case will depletion based upon discovery value be allowed.

(2) See § 1.611-5 for methods of depreciation relating to improvements connected with mineral or timber properties.

(3) See paragraph (d) of this section for definition of terms.

(b) Economic interest. *(1)* Annual depletion deductions are allowed only to the owner of an economic interest in mineral deposits or standing timber. An economic interest is possessed in every case in which the taxpayer has acquired by investment any interest in mineral in place or standing timber and secures, by any form of legal relationship, income derived from the extraction of the mineral or severance of the timber, to which he must look for a return of his capital. For an exception in the case of certain mineral production payments, see section 636 and the regulations thereunder. A person who has no capital investment in the mineral deposit or standing timber does not possess an economic interest merely because through a contractual relation he possesses a mere economic or pecuniary advantage derived from production. For example, an agreement between the owner of an economic interest and another entitling the latter to purchase or process the product upon production or entitling the latter to compensation for extraction or cutting does not convey a depletable economic interest. Further, depletion deductions with respect to an economic interest of a corporation are allowed to the corporation and not to its shareholders.

(2) No depletion deduction shall be allowed the owner with respect to any timber, coal, or domestic iron ore that such owner has disposed of under any form of contract by virtue of which he retains an economic interest in such timber, coal, or iron ore, if such disposal is considered a sale of timber, coal, or domestic iron ore under section 631(b) or (c).

(c) Special rules. *(1) In general.* For the purpose of the equitable apportionment of depletion among the several owners of economic interests in a mineral deposit or standing timber, if the value of any mineral or timber must be ascertained as of any specific date for the determination of the basis for depletion, the values of such several interests therein may be determined separately, but, when determined as of the same date, shall together never exceed the value at that date of the mineral or timber as a whole.

(2) Leases. In the case of a lease, the deduction for depletion under section 611 shall be equitably apportioned between the lessor and lessee. In the case of a lease or other contract providing for the sharing of economic interests in a mineral deposit or standing timber, such deduction shall be computed by each taxpayer by reference to the adjusted basis of his property determined in accordance with sections 611 and 612, or computed in accordance with section 613, if applicable, and the regulations thereunder.

(3) Life tenant and remainderman. In the case of property held by one person for life with remainder to another person, the deduction for depletion under section 611 shall be computed as if the life tenant were the absolute owner of the property so that he will be entitled to the deduction during his life, and thereafter the deduction, if any, shall be allowed to the remainderman.

(4) Mineral or timber property held in trust. If a mineral property or timber property is held in trust, the allowable deduction for depletion is to be apportioned between the income beneficiaries and the trustee on the basis of the trust income from such property allocable to each, unless the governing instrument (or local law) requires or permits the trustee to maintain a reserve for depletion in any amount. In the latter case, the deduction is first allocated to the trustee to the extent that income is set aside for a depletion reserve, and any part of the deduction in excess of the income set aside for the reserve shall be apportioned between the income beneficiaries and the trustee on the basis of the trust income (in excess of the income set aside for the reserve) allocable to each. For example:

(i) If under the trust instrument or local law the income of a trust computed without regard to depletion is to be distributed to a named beneficiary, the beneficiary is entitled to the deduction to the exclusion of the trustee.

(ii) If under the trust instrument or local law the income of a trust is to be distributed to a named beneficiary, but the trustee is directed to maintain a reserve for depletion in any amount, the deduction is allowed to the trustee (except to the extent that income set aside for the reserve is less than the allowable deduction). The same result would follow if the trustee sets aside income for a depletion reserve pursuant to discretionary authority to do so in the governing instrument. No effect shall be given to any allocation of the depletion deduction which gives any beneficiary or the trustee a share of such deduction greater than his pro rata share of the trust income, irrespective of any provisions in the trust instrument, except as otherwise provided in this paragraph when the trust instrument or local law requires or permits the trustee to maintain a reserve for depletion.

(5) Mineral or timber property held by estate. In the case of a mineral property or timber property held by an estate, the deduction for depletion under section 611 shall be apportioned between the estate and the heirs, legatees, and devisees on the basis of income of the estate from such property which is allocable to each.

(d) Definitions. As used in this part, and the regulations thereunder, the term—

(1) "Property" means. (i) in the case of minerals, each separate economic interest owned in each mineral deposit in each separate tract or parcel of land or an aggregation or combination of such mineral interests permitted under section 614(b), (c), (d), or (e); and (ii) in the case of timber, an economic interest in standing timber in each tract or block representing a separate timber account (see paragraph (d) of § 1.611-3). For rules with respect to waste or residue of prior mining, see paragraph (c) of § 1.614-1. When, in the regulations under this part, either the word "mineral" or "timber" precedes the word "property", such adjectives are used only to classify the type of "property" involved. For further explanation of the term "property", see section 614 and the regulations thereunder.

(2) "Fair market value" of a property is that amount which would induce a willing seller to sell and a willing buyer to purchase.

(3) "Mineral enterprise" is the mineral deposit or deposits and improvements, if any, used in mining or in the production of oil and gas, and only so much of the surface of the land as is necessary for purposes of mineral extraction. The value of the mineral enterprise is the combined value of its component parts.

(4) "Mineral deposit" refers to minerals in place. When a mineral enterprise is acquired as a unit, the cost of any interest in the mineral deposit or deposits is that proportion of the total cost of the mineral enterprise which the value of the interest in the deposit or deposits bears to the value of the entire enterprise at the time of its acquisition.

(5) "Minerals" includes ores of the metals, coal, oil, gas, and all other natural metallic and nonmetallic deposits, except minerals derived from sea water, the air, or from similar inexhaustible sources. It includes but is not limited to all of the minerals and other natural deposits subject to depletion based upon a percentage of gross income from the property under section 613 and the regulations thereunder.

T.D. 6446, 1/20/60, amend T.D. 6841, 7/26/65, T.D. 7261, 2/26/73.

§ 1.611-2 Rules applicable to mines, oil and gas wells, and other natural deposits.

(a) Computation of cost depletion of mines, oil and gas wells, and other natural deposits. *(1)* The basis upon which cost depletion is to be allowed in respect of any mineral property is the basis provided for in section 612 and the regulations thereunder. After the amount of such basis applicable to the mineral property has been determined for the taxable year, the cost depletion for that year shall be computed by dividing such amount by the number of units of mineral remaining as of the taxable year (see subparagraph (3) of this paragraph), and by multiplying the depletion unit, so determined, by the number of units of mineral sold within the taxable year (see subparagraph (2) of this paragraph). In the selection of a unit of mineral for depletion, preference shall be given to the principal or customary unit or units paid for in the products sold, such as tons of ore, barrels of oil, or thousands of cubic feet of natural gas.

(2) As used in this paragraph, the phrase "number of units sold within the taxable year"—

(i) In the case of a taxpayer reporting income on the cash receipts and disbursements method, includes units for which payments were received within the taxable year although produced or sold prior to the taxable year, and excludes units sold but not paid for in the taxable year, and

(ii) In the case of a taxpayer reporting income on the accrual method, shall be determined from the taxpayer's inventories kept in physical quantities and in a manner consistent with his method of inventory accounting under section 471 or 472. The phrase does not include units with respect to which depletion deductions were allowed or allowable prior to the taxable year.

(3) "The number of units of mineral remaining as of the taxable year" is the number of units of mineral remaining at the end of the year to be recovered from the property (including units recovered but not sold) plus the "number of units sold within the taxable year" as defined in this section.

(4) In the case of a natural gas well where the annual production is not metered and is not capable of being estimated with reasonable accuracy, the taxpayer may compute the cost depletion allowance in respect of such property for the taxable year by multiplying the adjusted basis of the property by a fraction, the numerator of which is equal to the decline in rock pressure during the taxable year and the denominator of which is equal to the expected total decline in rock pressure from the beginning of the taxable year to the economic limit of production. Taxpayers computing depletion by this method must keep accurate records of periodical pressure determinations.

(5) If an aggregation of two or more separate mineral properties is made during a taxable year under section 614, cost depletion for each such property shall be computed separately for that portion of the taxable year ending immediately before the effective date of the aggregation. Cost depletion with respect to the aggregated property shall be computed for that portion of the taxable year beginning on such effective date. The allowance for cost depletion for the taxable year shall be the sum of such cost depletion computations. For purposes of this paragraph, each such portion of the taxable year shall be considered as a taxable year. Similar rules shall be applied where a separate mineral property is properly removed from an existing aggregation during a taxable year. See section 614 and the regulations thereunder for rules relating to the effective date of an aggregation of mineral interests and for rules relating to the adjusted basis of an aggregation.

(6) The apportionment of the deduction among the several owners of economic interests in the mineral deposit or deposits will be made as provided in paragraph (c) of § 1.611-1.

(b) Depletion accounts of mineral property. *(1)* Every taxpayer claiming and making a deduction for depletion of mineral property shall keep a separate account in which shall be accurately recorded the cost or other basis provided by section 1012, of such property together with subsequent allowable capital additions to each account and all the other adjustments required by section 1016.

(2) Mineral property accounts shall thereafter be credited annually with the amounts of the depletion computed in accordance with section 611 or 613 and the regulations thereunder; or the amounts of the depletion so computed shall be credited to depletion reserve accounts. No further deductions for cost depletion shall be allowed when the sum of the credits for depletion equals the cost or other basis of the property, plus allowable capital additions. However, depletion deductions may be allowable thereafter computed upon a percentage of gross income from the property. See section 613 and the regulations thereunder. In no event shall percentage depletion in excess of cost or other basis of the property be credited to the improvements account or the depreciation reserve account.

(c) Determination of mineral contents of deposits. *(1)* If it is necessary to estimate or determine with respect to any mineral deposit as of any specific date the total recoverable units (tons, pounds, ounces, barrels, thousands of cubic feet, or other measure) of mineral products reasonably known, or on good evidence believed, to have existed in place as of that date, the estimate or determination must be made according to the method current in the industry and in the light of the most accurate and reliable information obtainable. In the selection of a unit of estimate, preference shall be given to the principal unit (or units) paid for in the product marketed. The estimate of the recoverable units of the mineral products in the deposit for the purposes of valuation and depletion shall include as to both quantity and grade:

(i) The ores and minerals "in sight", "blocked out", "developed", or "assured", in the usual or conventional meaning of these terms with respect to the type of the deposits, and

(ii) "Probable" or "prospective" ores or minerals (in the corresponding sense), that is, ores or minerals that are believed to exist on the basis of good evidence although not actually known to occur on the basis of existing development. Such "probable" or "prospective" ores or minerals may be estimated:

(a) As to quantity, only in case they are extensions of known deposits or are new bodies or masses whose existence is indicated by geological surveys or other evidence to a high degree of probability, and

(b) As to grade, only in accordance with the best indications available as to richness.

(2) If the number of recoverable units of mineral in the deposit has been previously estimated for the prior year or years, and if there has been no known change in the facts upon which the prior estimate was based, the number of recoverable units of mineral in the deposit as of the taxable year will be the number remaining from the prior estimate. However, for any taxable year for which it is ascertained ei-

ther by the taxpayer or the district director from any source, such as operations or development work prior to the close of the taxable year, that the remaining recoverable mineral units as of the taxable year are materially greater or less than the number remaining from the prior estimate, then the estimate of the remaining recoverable units shall be revised, and the annual cost depletion allowance with respect to the property for the taxable year and for subsequent taxable years will be based upon the revised estimate until a change in the facts requires another revision. Such revised estimate will not, however, change the adjusted basis for depletion.

(d) Determination of fair market value of mineral properties, and improvements, if any. *(1)* If the fair market value of the mineral property and improvements at a specified date is to be determined for the purpose of ascertaining the basis, such value must be determined, subject to approval or revision by the district director, by the owner of such property and improvements in the light of the conditions and circumstances known at that date, regardless of later discoveries or developments or subsequent improvements in methods of extraction and treatment of the mineral product. The district director will give due weight and consideration to any and all factors and evidence having a bearing on the market value, such as cost, actual sales and transfers of similar properties and improvements, bona fide offers, market value of stock or shares, royalties and rentals, valuation for local or State taxation, partnership accountings, records of litigation in which the value of the property and improvements was in question, the amount at which the property and improvements may have been inventoried or appraised in probate or similar proceedings, and disinterested appraisals by approved methods.

(2) If the fair market value must be ascertained as of a certain date, analytical appraisal methods of valuation, such as the present value method will not be used:

(i) If the value of a mineral property and improvements, if any, can be determined upon the basis of cost or comparative values and replacement value of equipment, or

(ii) If the fair market value can reasonably be determined by any other method.

(e) Determination of the fair market value of mineral property by the present value method. *(1)* To determine the fair market value of a mineral property and improvements by the present value method, the essential factors must be determined for each mineral deposit. The essential factors in determining the fair market value of mineral deposits are:

(i) The total quantity of mineral in terms of the principal or customary unit (or units) paid for in the product marketed,

(ii) The quantity of mineral expected to be recovered during each operating period,

(iii) The average quality or grade of the mineral reserves,

(iv) The allocation of the total expected profit to the several processes or operations necessary for the preparation of the mineral for market,

(v) The probable operating life of the deposit in years,

(vi) The development cost,

(vii) The operating cost,

(viii) The total expected profit,

(ix) The rate at which this profit will be obtained, and

(x) The rate of interest commensurate with the risk for the particular deposit.

(2) If the mineral deposit has been sufficiently developed, the valuation factors specified in subparagraph (1) of this paragraph may be determined from past operating experience. In the application of factors derived from past experience, full allowance should be made for probable future variations in the rate of exhaustion, quality or grade of the mineral, percentage of recovery, cost of development, production, interest rate, and selling price of the product marketed during the expected operating life of the mineral deposit. Mineral deposits for which these factors cannot be determined with reasonable accuracy from past operating experience may also be valued by the present value method; but the factors must be deduced from concurrent evidence, such as the general type of the deposit, the characteristics of the district in which it occurs, the habit of the mineral deposits, the intensity of mineralization, the oil-gas ratio, the rate at which additional mineral has been disclosed by exploitation, the stage of the operating life of the deposit, and any other evidence tending to establish a reasonable estimate of the required factors.

(3) Mineral deposits of different grades, locations, and probable dates of extraction should be valued separately. The mineral content of a deposit shall be determined in accordance with paragraph (c) of this section. In estimating the average grade of the developed and prospective mineral, account should be taken of probable increases or decreases as indicated by the operating history. The rate of exhaustion of a mineral deposit should be determined with due regard to the limitations imposed by plant capacity, by the character of the deposit, by the ability to market the mineral product, by labor conditions, and by the operating program in force or reasonably to be expected for future operations. The operating life of a mineral deposit is that number of years necessary for the exhaustion of both the developed and prospective mineral content at the rate determined as above. The operating life of oil and gas wells is also influenced by the natural decline in pressure and flow, and by voluntary or enforced curtailment of production. The operating cost includes all current expense of producing, preparing, and marketing the mineral product sold (due consideration being given to taxes) exclusive of allowable capital additions, as described in §§ 1.612-2 and 1.612-4, and deductions for depreciation and depletion, but including cost of repairs. This cost of repairs is not to be confused with the depreciation deduction by which the cost of improvements is returned to the taxpayer free from tax. In general, no estimates of these factors will be approved by the district director which are not supported by the operating experience of the property or which are derived from different and arbitrarily selected periods.

(4) The value of each mineral deposit is measured by the expected gross income (the number of units of mineral recoverable in marketable form multiplied by the estimated market price per unit) less the estimated operating cost, reduced to a present value as of the date for which the valuation is made at the rate of interest commensurate with the risk for the operating life, and further reduced by the value at that date of the improvements and of the capital additions, if any, necessary to realize the profits. The degree of risk is generally lowest in cases where the factors of valuation are fully supported by the operating record of the mineral enterprise before the date for which the valuation is made. On the other hand, higher risks ordinarily attach to appraisals upon any other basis.

(f) Revaluation of mineral property not allowed. No revaluation of a mineral property whose value as of any specific date has been determined and approved will be made or allowed during the continuance of the ownership under which the value was so determined and approved, except in the case of misrepresentation or fraud or gross error as to any facts known on the date as of which the valuation was made. Revaluation on account of misrepresentation or fraud or such gross error will be made only with the written approval of the Commissioner.

(g) Statement to be attached to return when valuation, depletion, or depreciation of mineral property or improvements are claimed. *(1)* For the first taxable year ending before December 31, 1967, for which a taxpayer asserts a value for any mineral property or improvement as of a specific date or claims a deduction for depletion, or depreciation, there shall be attached to the return of the taxpayer for such taxable year a statement setting forth, in complete, summary form, the pertinent information required by this paragraph with respect to each such mineral property or improvement (including oil and gas properties or improvements). The summary statement shall be deemed a part of the income tax return to which it relates. In addition to such summary statement, the taxpayer must assemble, segregate and have readily available at his principal place of business, all the supporting data (listed in subparagraphs (2), (3), and (4) of this paragraph) which is used in compiling the summary statement. For taxable years after such first taxable year, and ending before December 31, 1967, the taxpayer need attach to his return only an explanation of the changes, if any, in the information previously furnished. For example, when a taxpayer has filed adequate maps with the district director he may be relieved of filing further maps of the same area, if all additional information necessary for keeping the maps up-to-date is filed each year. In any case in which any of the information required by this paragraph has been previously filed by the taxpayer (including information furnished in accordance with corresponding provisions of prior regulations), such information need not be filed again, but a statement should be attached to the return of the taxpayer indicating clearly when and in what form such information was previously filed. For provisions relating to the data which shall be submitted with returns for taxable years ending on or after December 31, 1967, see subparagraph (5) of this paragraph.

(2) The information referred to in subparagraph (1) of this paragraph is as follows:

(i) An adequate map showing the name, description, location, date of surveys, and identification of the deposit or deposits;

(ii) A description of the character of the taxpayer's property, accompanied by a copy of the instrument or instruments by which it was acquired;

(iii) The date of acquisition of the property, the exact terms and dates of expiration of all leases involved, and if terminated, the reasons therefor;

(iv) The cost of the mineral property and improvements, stating the amount paid to each vendor, with his name and address;

(v) The date as of which the mineral property and improvements are valued, if a valuation is necessary to establish the basis as provided by section 1012;

(vi) The value of the mineral property and improvements on that date with a statement of the precise method by which it was determined;

(vii) An allocation of the cost or value among the mineral property, improvements and the surface of the land for purposes other than mineral production;

(viii) The estimated number of units of each kind of mineral at the end of the taxable year, and also at the date of acquisition, if acquired during the taxable year or at the date as of which any valuation is made, together with an explanation of the method used in the estimation, the name and address of the person making the estimate, and an average analysis which will indicate the quality of the mineral valued, including the grade or gravity in the case of oil;

(ix) The number of units sold and the number of units for which payment was received or accrued during the year for which the return is made (in the case of newly developed oil and gas deposits it is desirable that this information be furnished by months);

(x) The gross amount received from the sale of mineral;

(xi) The amount of depreciation for the taxable year and the amount of cost depletion for the taxable year;

(xii) The amounts of depletion and depreciation, if any, stated separately, which for each and every prior year:

(a) Were allowed (see section 1016(a)(2)),

(b) Were allowable, and

(c) Would have been allowable without reference to percentage or discovery depletion;

(xiii) The fractions (however measured) of gross production from the deposit or deposits to which the taxpayer and other persons are entitled together with the names and addresses of such other persons; and

(xiv) Any other data which will be helpful in determining the reasonableness of the valuation asserted or of the deductions claimed.

(3) In the case of oil and gas properties, the following information with respect to each property is required in addition to that information set forth in subparagraph (2) of this paragraph:

(i) The number of acres of producing oil or gas land and, if additional acreage is claimed to be proven, the amount of such acreage and the reasons for believing it to be proven;

(ii) The number of wells producing at the beginning and end of the taxable year;

(iii) The date of completion of each well finished during the taxable year;

(iv) The date of abandonment of each well abandoned during the taxable year;

(v) Maps showing the location of the tracts or leases and of the producing and abandoned wells, dry holes, and proven oil and gas lands (the maps should show depth, initial production, and date of completion of each well, etc., to the extent that these data are available);

(vi) The number of pay sands and average thickness of each pay sand or zone;

(vii) The average depth to the top of each of the different pay sands;

(viii) The annual production of the deposit or of the individual wells, if the latter information is available, from the beginning of its productivity to the end of the taxable year, the average number of wells producing during each year, and the initial daily production of each well (the extent to which oil or gas is used for fuel on the premises should be stated with reasonable accuracy);

(ix) All available data regarding change in operating conditions, such as unit operation, proration, flooding, use of air-gas lift, vacuum, shooting, and similar information, which have a direct effect on the production of the deposit; and

(x) Available geological information having a probable bearing on the oil and gas content; information with respect to edge water, water drive, bottom hole pressures, oil-gas ratio, porosity of reservoir rock, percentage of recovery, expected date of cessation of natural flow, decline in estimated potential, and characteristics similar to characteristics of other known fields.

(4) For rules relating to an additional statement to be attached to the return when the depletion deduction is computed upon a percentage of gross income from the property, see § 1.613-6.

(5) A taxpayer who claims a total deduction of more than $200 for depletion of mines, oil and gas wells, or other natural deposits for the taxable year ending on or after December 31, 1967, and before December 31, 1968, shall submit with his return for such taxable year a filled-out Form M (Mines and Other Natural Deposits—Depletion Data) or Form O (Oil and Gas Depletion Data). See section 6011(a). For the purpose of this subparagraph, the determination under section 631(c) of gain or loss upon the disposition of coal or domestic iron ore with a retained economic interest shall not be regarded as the claiming of a deduction for depletion. Such forms shall be filed for any subsequent taxable year if the Commissioner determines that the forms are required for such year. Where appropriate, both Form M and Form O shall be filed. Forms M and O shall be deemed to be part of the return to which they relate. If a taxpayer mines more than one mineral, a separate Form M shall be filed for each such mineral. If a taxpayer has both domestic and foreign properties, separate forms shall be filed for each country in which a taxpayer's properties are located. All data relating to a taxpayer's domestic oil and gas properties shall be summarized on a single Form O, and data relating to a taxpayer's domestic mineral properties (other than oil and gas properties) shall be summarized on a single Form M for each mineral. Similarly, all data relating to a taxpayer's oil and gas properties in a specific foreign country shall be summarized on a single Form O, and data relating to a taxpayer's mineral properties (other than oil and gas properties) in a specific foreign country shall be summarized on a single Form M for each mineral. In addition, the taxpayer shall assemble, segregate, and have readily available at his principal place of business, the data listed in subparagraphs (2), (3), and (4) of this paragraph.

T.D. 6446, 1/20/60, amend T.D. 6938, 12/6/67, T.D. 7170, 3/10/72.

§ 1.611-3 Rules applicable to timber.

(a) Capital recoverable through depletion allowance in case of timber. In general, the capital remaining in any year recoverable through depletion allowances is the basis provided by section 612 and the regulations thereunder. For the method of determining fair market value and quantity of timber, see paragraphs (d), (e), and (f) of this section. For capitalization of carrying charges, see section 1016(a)(1)(A). Amounts paid or incurred in connection with the planting of timber (including planting for Christmas tree purposes) shall be capitalized and recoverable through depletion allowances. Such amounts include, for example, expenditures made for the preparation of the timber site for planting or for natural seeding and the cost of seedlings. The apportionment of deductions between the several owners of economic interests in standing timber will be made as provided in paragraph (c) of § 1.611-1.

(b) Computation of allowance for depletion of timber for taxable year. *(1)* The depletion of timber takes place at the time timber is cut, but the amount of depletion allowable with respect to timber that has been cut may be computed when the quantity of cut timber is first accurately measured in the process of exploitation. To the extent that depletion is allowable in a particular taxable year with respect to timber the products of which are not sold during such year, the depletion so allowable shall be included as an item of cost in the closing inventory of such products for such year.

(2) The depletion unit of the timber for a given timber account in a given year shall be the quotient obtained by dividing (i) the basis provided by section 1012 and adjusted as provided by section 1016, of the timber on hand at the beginning of the year plus the cost of the number of units of timber acquired during the year plus proper additions to capital, by (ii) the total number of units of timber on hand in the given account at the beginning of the year plus the number of units acquired during the year plus (or minus) the number of units required to be added (or deducted) by way of correcting the estimate of the number of units remaining available in the account. The number of units of timber of a given timber account cut during any taxable year multiplied by the depletion unit of that timber account applicable to such year shall be the amount of depletion allowable for the taxable year. Those taxpayers who keep their accounts on a monthly basis may, at their option, keep their depletion accounts on such basis, in which case the amount allowable on account of depletion for a given month will be determined in the manner outlined herein for a given year. The total amount of the allowance for depletion in any taxable year shall be the sum of the amounts allowable for the several timber accounts. For a description of timber accounts, see paragraphs (c) and (d) of this section.

(3) When a taxpayer has elected to treat the cutting of timber as a sale or exchange of such timber under the provisions of section 631(a), he shall reduce the timber account containing such timber by an amount equal to the adjusted depletion basis of such timber. In computing any further gain or loss on such timber, see paragraph (e) of § 1.631-1.

(c) Timber depletion accounts on books. *(1)* Every taxpayer claiming or expecting to claim a deduction for depletion of timber property shall keep accurate ledger accounts in which shall be recorded the cost or other basis provided by section 1012 of the property and land together with subsequent allowable capital additions in each account and all other adjustments provided by section 1016 and the regulations thereunder.

(2) In such accounts there shall be set up separately the quantity of timber, the quantity of land, and the quantity of other resources, if any, and a proper part of the total cost or value shall be allocated to each after proper provision for immature timber growth. See paragraph (d) of this section. The timber accounts shall be credited each year with the amount of the charges to the depletion accounts computed in accordance with paragraph (b) of this section or the amount of the charges to the depletion accounts shall be credited to depletion reserve accounts. When the sum of the credits for depletion equals the cost or other basis of the timber property, plus subsequent allowable capital additions, no further deduction for depletion will be allowed.

(d) Aggregating timber and land for purposes of valuation and accounting. *(1)* With a view to logical and reasonable valuation of timber, the taxpayer shall include his timber in one or more accounts. In general, each such account shall include all of the taxpayer's timber which is located in one "block". A block may be an operation unit which includes all the taxpayer's timber which would logically go to a single given point of manufacture. In those cases in which the point of manufacture is at a considerable distance, or in which the logs or other products will probably be sold in a log or other market, the block may be a logging unit which includes all of the taxpayer's timber which would logically be removed by a single logging development. Blocks may also be established by geographical or political boundaries or by logical management areas. Timber acquired under cutting contracts should be carried in separate accounts and shall not constitute part of any block. In exceptional cases, provided there are good and substantial reasons, and subject to approval or revision by the district director on audit, the taxpayer may divide the timber in a given block into two or more accounts. For example, timber owned on February 28, 1913, and that purchased subsequently may be kept in separate accounts, or timber owned on February 28, 1913, and the timber purchased since that date in several distinct transactions may be kept in several distinct accounts. Individual tree species or groups of tree species may be carried in distinct accounts, or special timber products may be carried in distinct accounts. Blocks may be divided into two or more accounts based on the character of the timber or its accessibility, or scattered tracts may be included in separate accounts. If such a division is made, a proper portion of the total value or cost, as the case may be, shall be allocated to each account.

(2) The timber accounts mentioned in subparagraph (1) of this paragraph shall not include any part of the value or cost, as the case may be, of the land. In a manner similar to that prescribed in subparagraph (1) of this paragraph, the land in a given "block" may be carried in a single land account or may be divided into two or more accounts on the basis of its character or accessibility. When such a division is made, a proper portion of the total value or cost, as the case may be, shall be allocated to each account.

(3) The total value or total cost, as the case may be, of land and timber shall be equitably allocated to the timber and land accounts, respectively. In cases in which immature timber growth is a factor, a reasonable portion of the total value or cost shall be allocated to such immature timber, and when the timber becomes merchantable such value or cost shall be recoverable through depletion allowances.

(4) Each of the several land and timber accounts carried on the books of the taxpayer shall be definitely described as to their location on the ground either by maps or by legal descriptions.

(5) For good and substantial reasons satisfactory to the district director, or as required by the district director on audit, the timber or the land accounts may be readjusted by dividing individual accounts, by combining two or more accounts, or by dividing and recombining accounts.

(e) Determination of quantity of timber. Each taxpayer claiming or expecting to claim a deduction for depletion is required to estimate with respect to each separate timber account the total units (feet board measure, log scale, cords, or other units) of timber reasonably known, or on good evidence believed, to have existed on the ground on March 1, 1913, or on the date of acquisition of the property, whichever date is applicable in determining the basis for cost depletion. This estimate shall state as nearly as possible the number of units which would have been found present by careful estimate made on the specified date with the object of determining 100 percent of the quantity of timber which the area covered by the specific account would have produced on that date if all of the merchantable timber had been cut and utilized in accordance with the standards of utilization prevailing in that region at that time. If subsequently during the ownership of the taxpayer making the return, as the result of the growth of the timber, of changes in standards of utilization, of losses not otherwise accounted for, of abandonment of timber, or of operations or development work, it is ascertained either by the taxpayer or the district director that there remain on the ground, available for utilization, more or less units of timber at the close of the taxable year (or at the close of the month if the taxpayer keeps his depletion accounts on a monthly basis) than remain in the timber account or accounts on the basis of the original estimate, then the original estimate (but not the basis for depletion) shall be revised. The depletion unit shall be changed when such revision has been made. The annual charge to the depletion account with respect to the property shall be computed by using such revised unit for the taxable year for which the revision is made and all subsequent taxable years until a change in facts requires another revision.

(f) Determination of fair market value of timber property. *(1)* If the fair market value of the property at a specified date is the basis for depletion deductions, such value shall be determined, subject to approval or revision by the district director upon audit, by the owner of the property in the light of the most reliable and accurate information available with reference to the condition of the property as it existed at that date, regardless of all subsequent changes, such as changes in surrounding circumstances, and methods of exploitation, in degree of utilization, etc. Such factors as the following will be given due consideration:

(i) Character and quality of the timber as determined by species, age, size, condition, etc.;

(ii) The quantity of timber per acre, the total quantity under consideration, and the location of the timber in question with reference to other timber;

(iii) Accessibility of the timber (location with reference to distance from a common carrier, the topography and other features of the ground upon which the timber stands and over which it must be transported in process of exploitation, the probable cost of exploitation and the climate and the state of industrial development of the locality); and

(iv) The freight rates by common carrier to important markets.

(2) The timber in each particular case will be valued on its own merits and not on the basis of general averages for regions; however, the value placed upon it, taking into consideration such factors as those mentioned in this paragraph, will be consistent with that of other similar timber in the region. The district director will give weight and consideration to any and all facts and evidence having a bearing on the market value, such as cost, actual sales and transfers of similar properties, the margin between the cost of production and the price realized for timber products, market value of stock or shares, royalties and rentals, valuation for local or State taxation, partnership accountings, records of litigation in which the value of the property has been involved, the amount at which the property may have been inventoried or appraised in probate or similar proceedings, disinterested appraisals by approved methods, and other factors.

(g) Revaluation of timber property not allowed. No revaluation of a timber property whose value as of any specific date has been determined and approved will be made or allowed during the continuance of the ownership under which the value was so determined and approved, except in the case of misrepresentation or fraud or gross error as to any facts known on the date as of which the valuation was made. Revaluation on account of misrepresentation or fraud or such gross error will be made only with the written approval of the Commissioner. The depletion unit shall be revised when such a revaluation of a timber property has been made and the annual charge to the depletion account with respect to the property shall be computed by using such revised unit for the taxable year for which such revision is made and for all subsequent taxable years.

(h) Reporting and recordkeeping requirements. *(1) Taxable years beginning before January 1, 2002.* A taxpayer claiming a deduction for depletion of timber for a taxable year beginning before January 1, 2002, shall attach to the income tax return of the taxpayer a filled-out Form T (Timber) for the taxable year covered by the income tax return, including the following information—

(i) A map where necessary to show clearly timber and land acquired, timber cut, and timber and land sold;

(ii) Description of, cost of, and terms of purchase of timberland or timber, or cutting rights, including timber or timber rights acquired under any type of contract;

(iii) Profit or loss from sale of land, or timber, or both;

(iv) Description of timber with respect to which claim for loss, if any, is made;

(v) Record of timber cut;

(vi) Changes in each timber account as a result of purchase, sale, cutting, reestimate, or loss;

(vii) Changes in improvements accounts as the result of additions to or deductions from capital and depreciation, and computation of profit or loss on sale or other disposition of such improvements;

(viii) Operation data with respect to raw and finished material handled and inventoried;

(ix) Statement as to application of the election under section 631(a) and pertinent information in support of the fair market value claimed thereunder;

(x) Information with respect to land ownership and capital investment in timberland; and

(xi) Any other data which will be helpful in determining the reasonableness of the depletion or depreciation deductions claimed in the return.

(2) Taxable years beginning after December 31, 2001. A taxpayer claiming a deduction for depletion of timber on a return filed for a taxable year beginning after December 31, 2001, shall attach to the income tax return of the taxpayer a filled-out Form T (Timber) for the taxable year covered by the income tax return. In addition, the taxpayer must retain records sufficient to substantiate the right of the taxpayer to claim the deduction, including a map, where necessary, to show clearly timber and land acquired, timber cut, and timber and land sold for as long as their contents may become material in the administration of any internal revenue law.

T.D. 6446, 1/20/60, amend T.D. 8989, 4/23/2002, T.D. 9040, 1/30/2003.

§ 1.611-4 Depletion as a factor in computing earnings and profits for dividend purposes.

For rules with respect to computation of earnings and profits where depletion is a factor in the case of corporations, see paragraph (c)(1) of § 1.312-6.

T.D. 6446, 1/20/60.

§ 1.611-5 Depreciation of improvements.

(a) In general. Section 611 provides in the case of mines, oil and gas wells, other natural deposits, and timber that there shall be allowed as a deduction a reasonable allowance for depreciation of improvements. Such allowance shall include exhaustion, wear and tear, and obsolescence. The deduction allowed under section 611 shall be determined under the provisions of section 167 and the regulations thereunder. For purposes of section 167 the unit of production method may, under appropriate circumstances, be considered a reasonable method under section 167(a), and therefore, not subject to the limitations prescribed by section 167(b).

(b) Special rules for mines, oil and gas wells, other natural deposits and timber. *(1)* For principles governing the apportioning of depreciation allowances under sections 611 and 167 in the case of property held by one person for life with remainder to another or in the case of property held in trust or by an estate, see § 1.167(h)-1.

(2) A reasonable allowance for depreciation on account of obsolescence or decay shall be required in an appropriate case during periods when the improvement is not used in production or is used in producing at a rate below its normal capacity. This rule is applicable whether or not the taxpayer uses the unit of production method.

(3) See sections 615 and 616 and the regulations thereunder for special rules for treatment of allowances for depreciation of improvements with respect to the exploration and development of a mine or other natural deposit (other than oil or gas).

(4) In the case of operating oil or gas properties, the deduction for depreciation shall be allowed for those costs of improvements such as machinery, tools, equipment, pipes, and other similar items and the costs of installation which are not treated as a deductible expense under section 263(c). See § 1.612-4.

(c) Accounting and record keeping. See § 1.167(a)-7 for accounting and record keeping requirements for taxpayers claiming deductions under section 611 and this section.

T.D. 6446, 1/20/60, amend T.D. 6712, 3/23/64, T.D. 6836, 7/14/65.

§ 1.612-1 Basis for allowance of cost depletion.

(a) In general. The basis upon which the deduction for cost depletion under section 611 is to be allowed in respect of any mineral or timber property is the adjusted basis provided in section 1011 for the purpose of determining gain upon the sale or other disposition of such property except as provided in paragraph (b) of this section. The adjusted basis of such property is the cost or other basis determined under section 1012, relating to the basis of property, adjusted as provided in section 1016, relating to adjustments to basis, and the regulations under such sections. In the case of the sale of a part of such property, the unrecovered basis thereof shall be allocated to the part sold and the part retained.

(b) Special rules. *(1)* The basis for cost depletion of mineral or timber property does not include:

(i) Amounts recoverable through depreciation deductions, through deferred expenses, and through deductions other than depletion, and

(ii) The residual value of land and improvements at the end of operations.

In the case of any mineral property the basis for cost depletion does not include amounts representing the cost or value of land for purposes other than mineral production. Furthermore, in the case of certain mineral properties, such basis does not include exploration or development expenditures which are treated under section 615(b) or 616(b) as deferred expenses to be taken into account as deductions on a ratable basis as the units of minerals benefited thereby are produced and sold. However, there shall be included in the basis for cost depletion of oil and gas property the amounts of capitalized drilling and development costs which, as provided in § 1.612-4, are recoverable through depletion deductions. In the case of timber property, the basis for cost depletion does not include amounts representing the cost or value of land.

(2) Where a taxpayer elects to treat the cutting of timber as a sale or exchange of such timber, the basis for cost depletion shall be the fair market value of such timber as of the first day of the taxable year in which such timber is cut and such value shall be considered for such taxable year and all subsequent taxable years as the cost of such timber for all purposes for which such cost is a necessary factor. See section 631(a).

(c) Cross references. In cases where the valuation, revaluation, or mineral content of deposits is a factor, see paragraphs (c), (d), (e), and (f) of § 1.611-2. In cases where the valuation, revaluation, or quantity of timber is a factor, see paragraphs (e), (f), and (g) of § 1.611-3. For definitions of the terms "property", "fair market value", "mineral enterprise", "mineral deposit", and "minerals", see paragraph (d) of § 1.611-1. For rules with respect to treatment of depletion accounts on taxpayers' books, see paragraph (b) of § 1.611-2 in the case of mineral property, and paragraph (c) of § 1.611-3 in the case of timber property.

T.D. 6446, 1/20/60.

§ 1.612-2 Allowable capital additions in case of mines.

(a) In general. Expenditures for improvements and for replacements, not including expenditures for ordinary and necessary maintenance and repairs, shall ordinarily be charged to capital account recoverable through depreciation deductions. Expenditures for equipment (including its installation and housing) and for replacements thereof, which are necessary to maintain the normal output solely because of the recession of the working faces of the mine and which—

(1) Do not increase the value of the mine, or

(2) Do not decrease the cost of production of mineral units, or

(3) Do not represent an amount expended in restoring property or in making good the exhaustion thereof for which an allowance is or has been made shall be deducted as ordinary and necessary business expenses.

(b) Special rule. For special provisions applicable to treatment of expenditures for certain exploration and development costs (other than for the acquisition, restoration, or betterment of improvements) with respect to minerals other than oil or gas, see sections 615 and 616 and the regulations thereunder.

T.D. 6446, 1/20/60.

§ 1.612-3 Depletion; treatment of bonus and advanced royalty.

(a) Bonus. *(1)* If a bonus in addition to royalties is received upon the grant of an economic interest in a mineral deposit, or standing timber, there shall be allowed to the payee as a cost depletion deduction in respect of the bonus an amount equal to that proportion of his basis for depletion as provided in section 612 and § 1.612-1 which the amount of the bonus bears to the sum of the bonus and the royalties expected to be received. Such allowance shall be deducted from the payee's basis for depletion and the remainder of the basis is recoverable through depletion deductions as the royalties are thereafter received. (But see paragraph (e) of this section.) For example, a taxpayer leases mineral property to another reserving a one-eighth royalty and in addition receives a bonus of $10,000. Assuming that the taxpayer's basis with respect to the mineral property is $21,000 and that the royalties expected to be received are estimated to total $20,000, the depletion on the bonus would be $7,000

$$\left(\frac{\$21{,}000\text{ (basis)} \times \$10{,}000\text{ (bonus)}}{\$30{,}000\text{ (bonus plus estimated royalties)}}\right)$$

The remaining $14,000 of basis will be recovered through depletion as the royalties are received.

(2) If the grant of an economic interest in a mineral deposit or standing timber with respect to which a bonus was received expires, terminates, or is abandoned before there has been any income derived from the extraction of mineral or cutting of timber, the payee shall adjust his capital account by restoring thereto the depletion deduction taken on the bonus and a corresponding amount must be returned as income in the year of such expiration, termination, or abandonment.

(3) In the case of the payor, payment of the bonus constitutes a capital investment made for the acquisition of an economic interest in a mineral deposit or standing timber recoverable through the depletion allowance. See paragraph (c)(5)(ii) of § 1.613-2 in cases in which percentage depletion is used.

(b) Advanced royalties. *(1)* If the owner of an operating interest in a mineral deposit or standing timber is required to pay royalties on a specified number of units of such mineral or timber annually whether or not extracted or cut within the year, and may apply any amounts paid on account of units not extracted or cut within the year, and may apply any amounts paid on account of units not extracted or cut within the year against the royalty on the mineral or timber thereafter extracted or cut, the payee shall compute cost depletion on the number of units so paid for in advance of extraction or cutting and shall treat the amount so determined as an allowable deduction for depletion from the gross income of the year in which such payment or payments are made. No deduction for depletion by such payee shall be claimed or allowed in any subsequent year on account of the extraction or cutting in such year of any mineral or timber so paid for in advance and for which deduction has once been made. (But see paragraph (e) of this section.)

(2) If the right to extract minerals or to cut timber against which the advanced royalties may be applied expires, terminates, or is abandoned before all such minerals or timber have been extracted or cut, the payee shall adjust his capital account by restoring thereto the depletion deductions made in prior years on account of any units of mineral or timber paid for in advance but not extracted or cut, and a corresponding amount must be returned as income for the year of such expiration, termination or abandonment. (But see paragraph (e) of this section.)

(3) The payor shall treat the advanced royalties paid or accrued in connection with mineral property as deductions from gross income for the year the mineral product, in re-

spect of which the advanced royalties were paid or accrued, is sold. For purposes of the preceding sentence, in the case of mineral sold before production the mineral product is considered to be sold when the mineral is produced (i.e., when a mineral product first exists). However, in the case of advanced mineral royalties paid or accrued in connection with mineral property as a result of a minimum royalty provision, the payor, at his option, may instead treat the advanced royalties as deductions from gross income for the year in which the advanced royalties are paid or accrued. See section 446 (relating to general rule for methods of accounting) and the regulations thereunder. For purposes of this paragraph, a minimum royalty provision requires that a substantially uniform amount of royalties be paid at least annually either over the life of the lease or for a period of at least 20 years, in the absence of mineral production requiring payment of aggregate royalties in a greater amount. For purposes of the preceding sentence, in the case of a lease which is subject to renewal or extension, the period for which it can be renewed or extended shall be treated as part of the term of the original lease. For special rules applicable when the payor is a sublessor of coal or domestic iron ore, see paragraph (b)(3) of § 1.631-3. Every taxpayer who pays or accrues advanced royalties resulting from a minimum royalty provision must make an election as to the treatment of all such advanced royalties in his return for the first taxable year ending after December 31, 1939, in which the advanced royalties are paid or accrued. The taxpayer's treatment of the advanced royalties for the first year shall be deemed to be the exercise of the election. Accordingly, a failure to deduct the advanced royalties for that year will constitute an election to have all the advanced royalties treated as deductions for the year of the sale of the mineral product in respect of which the advanced royalties are paid or accrued. See section 7807(b)(2). For additional rules relating to elections in the case of partners and partnerships, see section 703(b) and the regulations thereunder. The provisions of this subparagraph do not allow as deductions from gross income amounts disallowed as deductions under other provisions of the Code, such as section 461 (relating to general rule for taxable year of deduction), section 465 (relating to deductions limited to amount at risk in case of certain activities), or section 704(d) (relating to limitation on allowance to partners of partnership losses).

(4) The application of subparagraphs (2) and (3) of this paragraph may be illustrated by the following examples:

Example (1). B leased certain mineral lands from A under a lease in which A reserved a royalty of 10 cents a ton on minerals mined and sold by B. The lease also provided that B had to pay an annual minimum royalty of $10,000 representing the amount due on 100,000 tons of the particular mineral whether or not B mined and sold that amount. It was further provided that, if B did not mine and sell 100,000 tons in any year, he could mine and sell in any subsequent year the amount of mineral on which he had paid the royalty without the payment of any additional royalty. However, this right of recoupment was limited to minerals mined and sold in any later year in excess of the 100,000 tons represented by the $10,000 minimum royalty required to be paid for that later year. Assume that in 1956 B paid A the minimum royalty of $10,000, but mined and sold only 60,000 tons of the mineral and that in 1957 he abandoned the lease without any further production. Since the $10,000 represents royalties on 100,000 tons of mineral and only 60,000 tons were mined and sold, A must restore in 1957 to his capital account the depletion deductions taken in 1956 on $4,000 on account of the 40,000 tons paid for in advance but not mined and sold, and must also return the corresponding amount as income in 1957.

Example (2). Assume that B, under the lease in example (1), paid the $10,000 minimum royalty and mined no minerals in 1956 but that in 1957 B mined and sold 200,000 tons of mineral. If this is B's first such expenditure, B has an option, for the purpose of computing taxable income under section 63, to deduct in 1956 the $10,000 paid in that year although no mineral was mined, or to take the deduction in 1957 when the mineral, for which the $10,000 was paid in 1956, was mined and sold. (For treatment under percentage depletion, see example in paragraph (c)(5)(iii) of § 1.613-2.)

(c) Delay rental. *(1)* A delay rental is an amount paid for the privilege of deferring development of the property and which could have been avoided by abandonment of the lease, or by commencement of development operations, or by obtaining production.

(2) Since a delay rental is in the nature of rent it is ordinary income to the payee and not subject to depletion. The payor may at his election deduct such amount as an expense, or under section 266 and the regulations thereunder, charge it to depletable capital account.

(d) Percentage depletion deduction with respect to bonus and advanced royalty. In lieu of the allowance based on cost depletion computed under paragraphs (a) and (b) of this section, the payees referred to therein may be allowed a depletion deduction in respect of any bonus or advanced royalty for the taxable year in an amount computed on the basis of the percentage of gross income from the property as provided in section 613 and the regulations thereunder. However, for special rules applicable to certain bonuses and advanced royalties received in connection with oil or gas properties, see paragraph (j) of § 1.613A-3.

(e) Cross reference. In the case of bonuses and advanced royalties received in connection with a contract of disposal of timber covered by section 631(b) or coal or iron ore covered by section 631(c), see that section and the regulations thereunder.

T.D. 6446, 1/20/60, amend T.D. 6841, 7/26/65, T.D. 7523, 12/14/77, T.D. 8348, 5/10/91.

PAR. 2. In § 1.612-3, the second sentence of paragraph (c)(2) is removed and two sentences are added in its place to read as follows:

Proposed § 1.612-3 Depletion; treatment of bonus and advanced royalty. [*For Preamble, see ¶ 152,051*]

* * * * *

(c) * * *

(2) * * * To the extent the delay rental is not required to be capitalized under section 263A and the regulations thereunder, the payor may at his election deduct such amount or under section 266 and the regulations thereunder, charge it to depletable capital account. The second sentence of this paragraph (c)(2) applies to delay rentals paid with respect to leasing transactions entered into on or after the date these regulations are published as final regulations in the Federal Register.

* * * * *

§ 1.612-4 Charges to capital and to expense in case of oil and gas wells.

(a) Option with respect to intangible drilling and development costs. In accordance with the provisions of section 263(c), intangible drilling and development costs incurred by an operator (one who holds a working or operating interest in any tract or parcel of land either as a fee owner or under a lease or any other form of contract granting working or operating rights) in the development of oil and gas properties may at his option be chargeable to capital or to expense. This option applies to all expenditures made by an operator for wages, fuel, repairs, hauling, supplies, etc., incident to and necessary for the drilling of wells and the preparation of wells for the production of oil or gas. Such expenditures have for convenience been termed intangible drilling and development costs. They include the cost to operators of any drilling or development work (excluding amounts payable only out of production or gross or net proceeds from production, if such amounts are depletable income to the recipient, and amounts properly allocable to cost of depreciable property) done for them by contractors under any form of contract, including turnkey contracts. Examples of items to which this option applies are, all amounts paid for labor, fuel, repairs, hauling, and supplies, or any of them, which are used—

(1) In the drilling, shooting, and cleaning of wells,

(2) In such clearing of ground, draining, road making, surveying, and geological works as are necessary in preparation for the drilling of wells, and

(3) In the construction of such derricks, tanks, pipelines, and other physical structures as are necessary for the drilling of wells and the preparation of wells for the production of oil or gas. In general, this option applies only to expenditures for those drilling and developing items which in themselves do not have a salvage value. For the purpose of this option, labor, fuel, repairs, hauling, supplies, etc., are not considered as having a salvage value, even though used in connection with the installation of physical property which has a salvage value. Included in this option are all costs of drilling and development undertaken (directly or through a contract) by an operator of an oil and gas property whether incurred by him prior or subsequent to the formal grant or assignment to him of operating rights (a leasehold interest, or other form of operating rights, or working interest); except that in any case where any drilling or development project is undertaken for the grant or assignment of a fraction of the operating rights, only that part of the costs thereof which is attributable to such fractional interest is within this option. In the excepted cases, costs of the project undertaken, including depreciable equipment furnished, to the extent allocable to fractions of the operating rights held by others, must be capitalized as the depletable capital cost of the fractional interest thus acquired.

(b) Recovery of optional items, if capitalized. *(1) Items returnable through depletion.* If the taxpayer charges such expenditures as fall within the option to capital account, the amounts so capitalized and not deducted as a loss are returnable through depletion insofar as they are not represented by physical property. For the purposes of this section the expenditures for clearing ground, draining, road making, surveying, geological work, excavation, grading, and the drilling, shooting, and cleaning of wells, are considered not to be represented by physical property, and when charged to capital account are returnable through depletion.

(2) Items returnable through depreciation. If the taxpayer charges such expenditures as fall within the option to capital account, the amounts so capitalized and not deducted as a loss are returnable through depreciation insofar as they are represented by physical property. Such expenditures are amounts paid for wages, fuel, repairs, hauling, supplies, etc., used in the installation of casing and equipment and in the construction on the property of derricks and other physical structures.

(3) In the case of capitalized intangible drilling and development costs incurred under a contract, such costs shall be allocated between the foregoing classes of items specified in subparagraphs (1) and (2) for the purpose of determining the depletion and depreciation allowances.

(4) Option with respect to cost of nonproductive wells. If the operator has elected to capitalize intangible drilling and development costs, then an additional option is accorded with respect to intangible drilling and development costs incurred in drilling a nonproductive well. Such costs incurred in drilling a nonproductive well may be deducted by the taxpayer as an ordinary loss provided a proper election is made in the return for the first taxable year beginning after December 31, 1942, in which such a nonproductive well is completed. Such election with respect to intangible drilling and development costs of nonproductive wells is a new election, and, when made, shall be binding for all subsequent years. Any taxpayer who incurs optional drilling and development costs in drilling in nonproductive well must make a clear statement of election under this option in the return for the first taxable year beginning after December 31, 1942, in which such nonproductive well is completed. The absence of a clear indication in such return of an election to deduct as ordinary losses intangible drilling and development costs of nonproductive wells shall be deemed to be an election to recover such costs through depletion to the extent that they are not represented by physical property, and through depreciation to the extent that they are represented by physical property.

(c) Nonoptional items distinguished. *(1) Capital items.* The option with respect to intangible drilling and development costs does not apply to expenditures by which the taxpayer acquires tangible property ordinarily considered as having a salvage value. Examples of such items are the costs of the actual materials in those structures which are constructed in the wells and on the property, and the cost of drilling tools, pipe, casing, tubing, tanks, engines, boilers, machines, etc. The option does not apply to any expenditure for wages, fuel, repairs, hauling, supplies, etc., in connection with equipment, facilities, or structures, not incident to or necessary for the drilling of wells, such as structures for storing or treating oil or gas. These are capital items and are returnable through depreciation.

(2) Expense items. Expenditures which must be charged off as expense, regardless of the option provided by this section, are those for labor, fuel, repairs, hauling, supplies, etc., in connection with the operation of the wells and of other facilities on the property for the production of oil or gas.

(d) Manner of making election. The option granted in paragraph (a) of this section to charge intangible drilling and development costs to expense may be exercised by claiming intangible drilling and development costs as a deduction on the taxpayer's return for the first taxable year in which the taxpayer pays or incurs such costs; no formal statement is necessary. If the taxpayer fails to deduction such costs as expenses in such return, he shall be deemed to have elected to recover such costs through depletion to the extent that they are not represented by physical property, and through depreciation to the extent that they are represented by physical property.

(e) Effect of option and election. This section does not grant a new option under paragraph (a) of this section or new election under paragraph (b) of this section. Section 3 of the Act of October 23, 1962 (Public Law 87-863, 76 Stat

1142) granted any taxpayer who had exercised an option to capitalize intangible drilling and development costs under Regulations 111, § 29.23(m)-16 (1939 Code) or Regulations 118, § 39.23(m)-16 (1939 Code) a new option for the first taxable year ending after October 22, 1962, to deduct such costs as expenses. Unless he has exercised the new option granted by such Act, any taxpayer who exercised an option or made an election under the regulations described in the preceding sentence is, by such option or election, bound with respect to all intangible drilling and development costs (whether made before January 1, 1954, or after December 31, 1953) in connection with oil and gas properties. See section 7807(b)(2). Any taxpayer who has not made intangible drilling and development expenditures in any taxable year beginning after December 31, 1942, prior to his first taxable year beginning after December 31, 1953, and ending after August 16, 1954, must exercise the option granted in paragraph (a) of this section in the return for the first taxable year in which the taxpayer pays or incurs such expenditures. If such return is required by law (including extensions thereof) to be filed before November 1, 1965, the option under paragraph (a) of this section, or the election under paragraph (b) of this section, may be exercised or changed not later than November 1, 1965. The exercise of or change in such option or election shall be effective with respect to the earliest taxable year to which the option or election is applicable in respect of which assessment of a deficiency or credit or refund of an overpayment, as the case may be, resulting from such exercise or change is not prevented by any law or rule of law on the date such option is exercised or such election is made. Any such option or election shall be binding upon the taxpayer for the first taxable year for which it is effective and for all subsequent taxable years.

T.D. 6836, 7/14/65.

---

§ 1.612-5 Charges to capital and to expense in case of geothermal wells.

(a) Option with respect to intangible drilling and development costs. In accordance with the provisions of section 263(c), intangible drilling and development costs incurred by an operator (one who holds a working or operating interest in any tract or parcel of land either as a fee owner or under a lease or any other form of contract granting working or operating rights) in the development of a geothermal deposit (as defined in section 613(e)(3) and the regulations thereunder) may at the operator's option be chargeable to capital or to expense. This option applies to all expenditures made by an operator for wages, fuel, repairs, hauling, supplies, etc., incident to and necessary for the drilling of wells and the preparation of wells for the production of geothermal steam or hot water. Such expenditures have for convenience been termed intangible drilling and development costs. They include the cost to operators of any drilling or development work (excluding amounts payable only out of production of gross or net proceeds from production, if such amounts are depletable income to the recipient, and amounts properly allocable to cost of depreciable property) done for them by contractors under any form of contract, including turnkey contracts. Examples of items to which this option applies are all amounts paid for labor, fuel, repairs, hauling, and supplies, or any of them, which are used—

(1) In the drilling, shooting and cleaning of wells,

(2) In such clearing of ground, draining, road making, surveying, and geological work as are necessary in preparation for the drilling of wells, and

(3) In the construction of such derricks, tanks, pipelines, and other physical structures as are necessary for the drilling of wells and the preparation of wells for the production of geothermal steam or hot water.

In general, this option applies only to expenditures for those drilling and developing items which in themselves do *not* have a salvage value. For the purpose of *this* option, labor, fuel, repairs, hauling, supplies, etc. are not considered as having a salvage value, even though used in connection with the installation of physical property which has a salvage value. Included in this option are all costs of drilling and development undertaken (directly or through a contract) by an operator of a geothermal property whether incurred by the operator prior or subsequent to the formal grant or assignment of operating rights (a leasehold interest, or other form of operating rights, or working interest); except that in any case where any drilling or development project is undertaken for the grant or assignment of fraction of the operation rights, only that part of the costs thereof which is attributable to such fractional interest is within this option. In the excepted cases, costs of the project undertaken, including depreciable equipment furnished, to the extent allocable to fractions of the operating rights held by others, must be capitalized as the depletable capital cost of the fractional interest thus acquired.

(b) Recovery of optional items, if capitalized. *(1)* Items recoverable through depletion: If the taxpayer charges such expenditures as fall within the option to capital account, the amounts so capitalized and not deducted as a loss are recoverable through depletion insofar as they are not represented by physical property. For the purposes of this section the expenditures for clearing ground, draining, road making, surveying, geological work, excavation, grading, and the drilling, shooting, and cleaning of wells, are considered not to be represented by physical property, and when charged to capital account are recoverable through depletion.

(2) Items recoverable through depreciation: If the taxpayer charges such expenditures as fall within the option to capital account, the amounts so capitalized and not deducted as a loss are recoverable through depreciation insofar as they are represented by physical property. Such expenditures are amounts paid for wages, fuel, repairs, hauling, supplies, etc. used in the installation of casing and equipment and in the construction on the property of derricks and other physical structures.

(3) In the case of capitalized intangible drilling and development costs incurred under a contract, such costs shall be allocated between the foregoing classes of items specified in paragraphs (b)(1) and (2) of this section for the purpose of determining the depletion and depreciation allowances.

(4) Option with respect to cost of nonproductive wells: If the operator has elected to capitalize intangible drilling and development costs; then an additional option is accorded with respect to intangible drilling and development costs incurred in drilling a nonproductive well. Such costs incurred in drilling a nonproductive well may be deducted by the taxpayer as an ordinary loss provided a proper election is made in the taxpayer's original or amended return for the first taxable year ending on or after October 1, 1978, in which such a nonproductive well is completed. The taxpayer must make a clear statement of election under this option in the return or amended return. The election may be revoked by the filing of an amended return that does not contain such a statement. The absence of a clear indication in such return of an election to deduct as ordinary losses intangible drilling and development costs of nonproductive wells shall be deemed

to be an election to recover such costs through depletion to the extent that they are not represented by physical property, and through depreciation to the extent that they are represented by physical property. Upon the expiration of the time for filing a claim for credit or refund of any overpayment of tax imposed by chapter 1 of the Code with respect to the first taxable year ending on or after October 1, 1978 in which a nonproductive well is completed, the taxpayer is bound for all subsequent years by his exercise of the option to deduct intangible drilling and development costs of nonproductive wells as an ordinary loss or his deemed election to recover such costs through depletion or depreciation.

(c) Nonoptional items distinguished. *(1) Capital Items:* The option with respect to intangible drilling and development costs does not apply to expenditures by which the taxpayer acquires tangible property ordinarily considered as having a salvage value. Examples of such items are the costs of the actual materials in those structures which are constructed in the wells and on the property, and the cost of drilling tools, pipe, casing, tubing, tanks, engines, boilers, machines, etc. The option does not apply to any expenditure for wages, fuel, repairs, hauling, supplies, etc., in connection with equipment, facilities, or structures, not incident to or necessary for the drilling of wells, such as structures for treating geothermal steam or hot water. These are capital items and are recoverable through depreciation.

(2) Expense items: Expenditures which must be charged off as expense, regardless of the option provided by this section, are those for labor, fuel, repairs, hauling, supplies, etc., in connection with the operation of the wells and of other facilities on the property for the production of geothermal steam or hot water.

(d) Manner of making election. The option granted in paragraph (a) of this section to charge intangible drilling and development costs to expense may be exercised by claiming intangible drilling and development costs as a deduction on the taxpayer's original or amended return for the first taxable year ending on or after October 1, 1978, in which the taxpayer pays or incurs such costs with respect to a geothermal well commenced on or after that date. No formal statement is necessary. The exercise of the option may be revoked by the filing of an amended return that does not claim such a deduction. If the taxpayer fails to deduct such costs as expenses in any such return, he shall be deemed to have elected to recover such costs through depletion to the extent that they are not represented by physical property, and through depreciation to the extent that they are represented by physical property. Upon the expiration of the time for filing a claim for credit or refund of any overpayment of tax imposed by chapter 1 of the Code with respect to the first taxable year ending on or after October 1, 1978, in which the taxpayer pays or incurs intangible drilling and development costs with respect to a geothermal well commenced on or after that date, the taxpayer is bound by his exercise of the option to charge such costs to expense or his deemed election to recover such costs through depletion or depreciation for that year and for all subsequent years.

(e) Effective date. The option granted by paragraph (a) of this section is available only for taxable years ending on or after October 1, 1978, with respect to geothermal wells commenced on or after that date.

T.D. 7806, 1/27/82.

§ 1.613-1 Percentage depletion; general rule.

Caution: The Treasury has not yet amended Reg § 1.613-1 to reflect changes made by P.L. 108-357.

(a) In general. In the case of a taxpayer computing the deduction for depletion under section 611 with respect to minerals on the basis of a percentage of gross income from the property, as defined in section 613(c) and §§ 1.613-3 and 1.613-4, the deduction shall be the percentage of the gross income as specified in section 613(b) and § 1.613-2. The deduction shall not exceed 50 percent (100 percent in the case of oil and gas properties for taxable years beginning after December 31, 1990) of the taxpayer's taxable income from the property (computed without regard to the allowance for depletion). The taxable income shall be computed in accordance with § 1.613-5. In no case shall the deduction for depletion computed under this section be less than the deduction computed upon the cost or other basis of the property provided in section 612 and the regulations thereunder. The apportionment of the deduction between the several owners of economic interests in a mineral deposit will be made as provided in paragraph (c) of § 1.611-1. For rules with respect to "gross income from the property" and for definition of the term "mining," see §§ 1.613-3 and 1.613-4. For definitions of the terms "property," "mineral deposit," and "minerals," see paragraph (d) of § 1.611-1.

(b) Denial of percentage depletion in case of oil and gas wells. Except as otherwise provided in section 613A and the regulations thereunder, in the case of oil or gas which is produced after December 31, 1974, and to which gross income is attributable after that date, the allowance for depletion shall be computed without regard to section 613.

T.D. 6446, 1/20/60, amend T.D. 7170, 3/10/72, T.D. 8348, 5/10/91, T.D. 8437, 9/23/92.

§ 1.613-2 Percentage depletion rates.

Caution: The Treasury has not yet amended Reg § 1.613-2 to reflect changes made by P.L. 95-618.

(a) In general. Subject to the provisions of paragraph (b) of this section and as provided in section 613(b), in the case of mines, wells, or other natural deposits, a taxpayer may deduct as an allowance for depletion under section 611 the percentages of gross income from the property as set forth in subparagraphs (1), (2), and (3) of this paragraph.

(1) Without regard to situs of deposits. The following rates are applicable to the minerals listed in this subparagraph regardless of the situs of the deposits from which the minerals are produced:

(i) 27½ percent—Gas wells, oil wells.

(ii) 23 percent—Sulfur, uranium.

(iii) 15 percent—Ball clay, bentonite, china clay, metal mines,[1] sagger clay, rock asphalt, vermiculite.

(iv) 10 percent—Asbestos, brucite, coal, lignite, perlite, sodium chloride, wollastonite.

(v) 5 percent—Brick and tile clay, gravel, mollusk shells (including clam shells and oyster shells), peat, pumice, sand, scoria, shale, stone (except dimension or ornamental stone). If from brine wells—Bromine, calcium chloride, magnesium chloride.

1. Not applicable if the rate prescribed in subparagraph (2) of this paragraph is applicable.

(2) Production from United States deposits. A rate of 23 percent is applicable to the minerals listed in this subparagraph if produced from deposits within the United States:

Anorthosite.[2]	Ilmenite.
Asbestos.	Kyanite.
Bauxite.	Mica.
Beryl.[3]	Olivine.
Celestite.	Quartz crystals (radio grade).
Chromite.	Rutile.
Corundum.	Block steatite talc.
Fluorspar.	Zircon.
Graphite.	

Ores of the following metals—

Antimony.	Nickel.
Beryllium.[4]	Platinum.
Bismuth.	Platinum group metals.
Cadmium.	Tantalum.
Cobalt.	Thorium.
Columbium.	Tin.
Lead.	Titanium.
Lithium.	Tungsten.
Manganese.	Vanadium.
Mercury.	Zinc.

[2] The rate prescribed in this subparagraph does not apply except to the extent that alumina and aluminum compounds are extracted therefrom.

[3] Applicable only for taxable years beginning before January 1, 1964.

[4] Applicable only for taxable years beginning after December 31, 1963.

(3) Other minerals. A rate of 15 percent is applicable to the minerals listed in this subparagraph regardless of the situs of the deposits from which the minerals are produced, provided the minerals are not used or sold for use by the mine owner or operator as rip rap, ballast, road material, rubble, concrete aggregates, or for similar purposes. If, however, such minerals are sold or used for the purposes described in the preceding sentence, a rate of 5 percent is applicable to any of such minerals unless sold on bid in direct competition with a bona fide bid to sell any of the minerals listed in subdivision (iii) of subparagraph (1) of this paragraph, in which case the rate is 15 percent. In addition, the provisions of this subparagraph are not applicable with respect to any of the minerals listed herein if the rate prescribed in subparagraph (2) of this paragraph is applicable.

Aplite.	Limestone.
Barite.	Magnesite.
Bauxite.	Magnesium carbonates.
Beryl.[5]	Marble.
Borax.	Mica.
Calcium carbonates.	Phosphate rock.
Clay, refractory and fire.[6]	Potash.
	Quartzite.
Diatomaceous earth.	Slate.
Dolomite.	Soapstone.
Feldspar.	Spodumene.
Flake Graphite.	Stone (dimension or ornamental).[7]
Fluorspar.	
Fullers earth.	Talc (including pyrophyllite).
Garnet.	
Gilsonite.	Thenardite.
Granite.	Tripoli.
Lepidolite.	Trona.
	All other minerals.

[5] Applicable only for taxable years beginning before January 1, 1964.

[6] Not applicable for taxable years beginning after December 31, 1960.

[7] The 15-percent rate is applicable only to stone used or sold for use by the mine owner or operator as dimension stone or ornamental stone.

(b) Definition of terms. *(1)* For purposes of this section, the minerals indicated below shall have the following meanings:

(i) Clay, brick and tile—Clay used or sold for use in the manufacture of common brick, drain and roofing tile, sewer pipe, flower pots, and kindred products (other than clay specifically identified as a clay for which a 15 percent rate of percentage allowance is provided).

(ii) Clay, refractory and fire—Clay which has a pyrometric cone equivalent of 19 or higher.

(iii) Pumice—All pumice including pumicite.

(iv) Scoria—Only scoria produced from natural deposits.

(2) For purposes of this section, the term "United States" means the States and the District of Columbia. See section 7701(a)(9).

(3) For purposes of this section, the term "dimension stone" means blocks and slabs of natural stone, subsequently cut to definite shapes and sizes and used or sold for such uses as building stone (excluding rubble), monumental stone, paving blocks, curbing and flagging. For purposes of this section, "ornamental stone" means blocks and slabs of natural stone, subsequently cut to definite shapes and sizes and used or sold for use for making ornaments or statues.

(4) For purposes of this section, the term "all other minerals" does not include (i) soil, sod, dirt, turf, water, or mosses; or (ii) minerals from sea water, the air, or similar inexhaustible sources. However, the term "all other minerals" is not limited in meaning to the minerals listed in section 613(b), but includes all other minerals (except those to which a specific percentage rate applies under subparagraphs (1), (2), (3), (4), and (5) of section 613(b)): For example, gypsum, novaculite, natural mineral pigments, quartz sand and quartz pebbles, graphite and kyanite (if section 613(b)(2)(B) does not apply), and anorthosite to the extent that alumina and aluminum compounds are not extracted therefrom. The 15-percent rate applies to such "all other minerals" when used or sold for use by the mine owner or operator for purposes other than as rip rap, ballast, road material, rubble, concrete aggregates, or for similar purposes. When any such minerals are used or sold for use by the mine owner or operator as rip rap, ballast, road material, rubble, concrete aggregates, or for similar purposes, the 5-percent rate applies except that, when sold for such use by the mine owner or operator on a bid in direct competition with a bona fide bid to sell a mineral listed in section 613(b)(3), the 15-percent rate applies. For example, limestone sold on a bid in direct competition with a bona fide bid to sell rock asphalt for road building purposes may be entitled to a 15-percent rate. In every case the taxpayer must establish to the satisfaction of the district director that there was a bona fide bid to sell a mineral listed under section 613(b)(3) by a person other than the taxpayer, and that the mineral sold by the taxpayer was sold on a bid in direct competition with such bona fide bid to sell such other material.

(c) Rules for application of paragraph (a) of this section. *(1)* In no case may the allowance for depletion computed upon the basis of a percentage of gross income from the property exceed 50 percent of the taxpayer's taxable income from the property (computed without allowance for depletion). For rules relating to the computation of such taxable income, see § 1-613-5.

(2) In cases in which there are produced from a mineral property two or more minerals, each entitled to a different percentage depletion rate under section 613(b) and this section or any of which is entitled to cost depletion only, the percentage depletion allowance is the sum of the results obtained by applying the percentage applicable to each mineral (zero, if not entitled to percentage depletion) to the "gross income from the property" attributable to such mineral. The sum so computed is subject to the limitation provided in section 613(a) and § 1.613-1, that is, 50 percent of the taxpayer's taxable income from the property (computed without allowance for depletion). Such taxable income (computed in accordance with § 1.613-4) is the total taxable income resulting from the sale of all minerals produced from the mineral property (as defined in section 614 and the regulations thereunder). The provisions of this subparagraph may be illustrated by the following examples:

Example (1). Pyrite, an iron sulfide, may be sold for either its sulfur content or its iron content, or both. Sulfur is entitled to a percentage depletion deduction based on 23 percent of gross income from the property whereas the percentage depletion deduction for iron is based on 15 percent of such gross income. Therefore, in the case of a taxpayer who sells pyrite for both its sulfur and iron content, 23 percent of his gross income from sulfur plus 15 percent of his gross income from iron would be his maximum allowable percentage depletion deduction. However, this maximum deduction would be subject to the limitation provided for in section 613(a), i.e., 50 percent of "taxable income from the property (computed without allowance for depletion)", such taxable income being the overall taxable income resulting from the sale of both minerals contained in the deposit.

Example (2). Oil and gas are produced from a single mineral property of a taxpayer who operates a retail outlet for the sale of oil products within the meaning of section 613A(d)(2). The taxpayer is not entitled to percentage depletion on the gross income attributable to the oil, but is entitled to percentage depletion on the gross income attributable to gas which is regulated gas under section 613A(b)(2)(B). Accordingly, the taxpayer's maximum allowable percentage depletion deduction would be zero percent of gross income from the property with respect to oil, plus 22 percent (see section 613A(b)(1)) of gross income from the property with respect to gas. This maximum deduction would be subject to the limitation provided for in section 613(a), i.e., 50 percent of "taxable income from the property (computed without allowance for depletion)," such taxable income being the overall taxable income resulting from the sale of both oil and gas. However, in the case of oil or gas production which qualifies for percentage depletion under section 613A(c), see the special allocation rules contained in section 613A(c)(7)(C) and (E) and § 1.613A-4.

(3) Except as provided in section 613(d) and the regulations thereunder relating to special rules for determining rates of depletion for taxable years ending after December 31, 1953, to which the Internal Revenue Code of 1939 applies—

(i) The percentage rates set forth in this section are applicable only for taxable years beginning after December 31, 1953, and ending after August 16, 1954; and

(ii) The percentage rates set forth in 26 CFR (1939) 39.23(m)-5 (Regulations 118) are applicable for taxable years beginning before January 1, 1954, or ending before August 17, 1954.

(4) Percentage depletion is not allowable with respect to the income from a disposal of coal (including lignite) or domestic iron ore (as defined in paragraph (e) of § 1.631-3) with a retained economic interest to the extent that such income is treated as from a sale of coal or iron ore under section 631(c) and § 1.631-3. Rents or royalties paid or incurred by a taxpayer with respect to coal (including lignite) or domestic iron ore shall be excluded by such taxpayer in determining "gross income from the property" without regard to the treatment under section 631(c) of such rents and royalties in the hands of the recipient.

(5) (i) In all cases there shall be excluded in determining the "gross income from the property" an amount equal to any rents or royalties (which are depletable income to the payee) which are paid or incurred by the taxpayer in respect of the property and are not otherwise excluded from "gross income from the property." The following example illustrates this rule:

Example. A leases coal-bearing lands to B on condition that B will annually pay a royalty of 25 cents a ton on coal mined and sold by B. During the year 1956, B mines and sells f.o.b. mine 100,000 tons of coal for $600,000. In computing "gross income from the property" for the year 1956, B will exclude $25,000 (100,000 tons × $0.25) in computing his allowable percentage depletion deduction. B's allowable percentage depletion deduction (without reference to the limitation based on taxable income from the property) for the year 1956 will be $57,500 (($600,000 − $25,000) × 10 percent).

(ii) If bonus payments have been paid in respect of the property in any taxable year or any prior taxable years, there shall be excluded in determining the "gross income from the property," an amount equal to that part of such payments which is allocable to the product sold (or otherwise giving rise to gross income) for the taxable year. For purposes of the preceding sentence, bonus payments include payments by the lessee with respect to a production payment which is treated as a bonus under section 636(c). Such a production payment is equally allocable to all mineral from the mineral property burdened thereby. The following examples illustrate the provisions of this subdivision:

Example (1). In 1956, A leases oil bearing lands to B, receiving $200,000 as a bonus and reserving a royalty of one-eighth of the proceeds of all oil produced and sold. It is estimated at the time the lease is entered into that there are 1,000,000 barrels of oil recoverable. In 1956, B produces and sells 100,000 barrels for $240,000. In computing his "gross income from the property" for the year 1956, B will exclude $30,000 (⅛ of $240,000), the royalty paid to A, and $20,000 (100,000 bbls. sold/1,000,000 bbls. estimated to be available × $200,000 bonus), the portion of the bonus allocable to the oil produced and sold during the year. However, in computing B's taxable income under section 63, the $20,000 attributable to the bonus payment shall not be either excluded or deducted from B's gross income computed under section 61. (See paragraph (a)(3) of § 1.612-3.)

Example (2). In 1971, C leases to D oil bearing lands estimated to contain 1,000,000 barrels of oil, reserving a royalty of one-eighth of the proceeds of all oil produced and sold and a $500,000 production payment payable out of 50 percent of the first oil produced and sold attributable to the seven-eighths operating interest. In 1972, D produces and sells 100,000 barrels of oil. In computing his "gross income from the property" for the year 1972, D will exclude, in addition to the royalty paid to C, $50,000 (100,000 bbls. sold/1,000,000 bbls. estimated to be available × $500,000 treated under section 636(c) as a bonus), the portion of the production payment allocable to the oil produced and sold during the taxable year. However, in computing D's taxable income under section 63, the $50,000 attributable to the retained production payment shall not be either excluded or deducted from D's gross income computed under section 61.

(iii) If advanced royalties have been paid in respect of the property in any taxable year, the amount excluded from "gross income from the property" of the payor for the current taxable year on account of such payment shall be an amount equal to the deduction for such taxable year taken on account of such payment pursuant to paragraph (b)(3) of § 1.612-3.

Example. If B in example (2) in paragraph (b)(4) of § 1.612-3, elects to deduct in 1956 the $10,000 paid to A in that year, he must exclude the same amount from "gross income from the property" in 1956; however, if B elects to defer the deduction until 1957 when he mined and sold the mineral, he must exclude the $10,000 from "gross income from the property" in 1957.

T.D. 6446, 1/20/60, amend T.D. 6841, 7/26/65, T.D. 7170, 3/10/72, T.D. 7261, 2/26/73, T.D. 7487, 5/12/77.

§ 1.613-3 Gross income from the property.

Oil and gas wells. In the case of oil and gas wells, "gross income from the property," as used in section 613(c)(1), means the amount for which the taxpayer sells the oil or gas in the immediate vicinity of the well. If the oil or gas is not sold on the premises but is manufactured or converted into a refined product prior to sale, or is transported from the premises prior to sale, the gross income from the property shall be assumed to be equivalent to the representative market or field price of the oil or gas before conversion or transportation.

T.D. 6446, 1/20/60, amend T.D. 6965, 7/25/68, T.D. 8474, 4/26/93.

§ 1.613-4 Gross income from the property in the case of minerals other than oil and gas.

Caution: The Treasury has not yet amended Reg § 1.613-4 to reflect changes made by P.L. 95-618.

(a) In general. The rules contained in this section are applicable to the determination of gross income from the property in the case of minerals other than oil and gas and the rules contained in § 1.613-3 are not applicable to such determination, notwithstanding provisions to the contrary in § 1.613-3. The term "gross income from the property," as used in section 613(c)(1), means, in the case of a mineral property other than an oil or gas property, gross income from mining. "Gross income from mining" is that amount of income which is attributable to the extraction of the ores or minerals from the ground and the application of mining processes, including mining transportation. For the purpose of this section, "ordinary treatment processes" (applicable to the taxable years beginning before January 1, 1961) and "treatment processes considered as mining" (applicable to the taxable years beginning after December 31, 1960) will be referred to as "mining processes." Processes, including packaging and transportation, which do not qualify as mining will be referred to as "nonmining processes." Also for the purpose of this section, transportation which qualifies as "mining" will be referred to as "mining transportation" and transportation which does not qualify as "mining" will be referred to as "nonmining transportation." See paragraph (f) of this section for the definition of the term "mining" and paragraph (g) of this section for rules relating to nonmining processes.

(b) Sales prior to the application of nonmining processes including nonmining transportation. *(1)* Subject to the adjustments required by paragraph (e)(1) of this section, gross income from mining means (except as provided in subparagraph (2) of this paragraph) the actual amount for which the ore or mineral is sold if the taxpayer sells the ore or mineral—

(i) As it emerges from the mine, prior to the application of any process other than a mining process or any transportation, or

(ii) After application of only mining processes, including mining transportation, and before any nonmining transportation.

If the taxpayer sells his ore or mineral in more than one form, and if only mining processes are applied to the ore or mineral, gross income from mining is the actual amount for which the various forms of the ore or mineral are sold, after any adjustments required by paragraph (e)(1) of this section. For example, if, at his mine or quarry, a taxpayer sells several sizes of crushed gypsum and also sells gypsum fines produced as an incidental by-product of his crushing operations, without applying any nonmining processes, gross income from mining will ordinarily be the total amount for which such crushed gypsum and fines are actually sold. See paragraphs (f) and (g) of this section for provisions defining mining and nonmining processes for various minerals.

(2) In the case of sales between members of a controlled group (including sales as to which the district director exercises his authority under section 482 and the regulations thereunder), the prices for such sales (which shall be deemed to be the actual amount for which the ore or mineral is sold) shall be determined, if possible, by use of the representative market or field price method, as described in paragraph (c) of this section; otherwise such prices shall be determined by the appropriate pricing method as provided in paragraph (d)(1) of this section. For the definitions of the terms "controlled" and "group," see paragraph (j)(1) and (2) of this section.

(c) Cases where a representative market or field price for the taxpayer's ore or mineral can be ascertained. *(1) General rule.* If the taxpayer processes the ore or mineral before sale by the application of nonmining processes (including nonmining transportation), or uses it in his operations, gross income from mining shall be computed by use of the representative market or field price of an ore or mineral of like kind and grade as the taxpayer's ore or mineral after the application of the mining processes actually applied (if any), including mining transportation (if any), and before any nonmining transportation, subject to any adjustments required by paragraph (e)(1) of this section. See paragraph (e)(2)(i) of this section for certain other situations in which this paragraph shall apply. The objective in computing gross income from mining by the representative market or field price method is to ascertain, on the basis of an analysis of actual competitive sales by the taxpayer or others, the dollar figure or amount which most nearly represents the approximate price at which the taxpayer, in light of market conditions, could have sold his ores or minerals if, prior to the application of nonmining processes, the taxpayer had sold the quantities and types of ores and minerals to which he applied nonmining processes. If it is possible to determine a market or field price under the provisions of this paragraph, and if that price is determined to be representative, the taxpayer's gross income from mining shall be determined on the basis of that price and not under the provisions of paragraph (d) of this section. The taxpayer's own actual sales prices for ores or minerals of like kind and grade shall be taken into account when establishing market or field prices, provided that those sales are determined to be representative.

(2) *Criteria for determining whether an ore or mineral is of like kind and grade as the taxpayer's ore or mineral.* An ore or mineral will be considered to be of like kind and grade as the taxpayer's ore or mineral if, in common commercial practice, it is sufficiently similar in chemical, mineralogical, or physical characteristics to the taxpayer's ore or mineral that it is used, or is commercially suitable for use, for essentially the same purposes as the uses to which the taxpayer's ore or mineral is put. Whether an ore or mineral is of like kind and grade as the taxpayer's ore or mineral will generally be determined by reference to industrial or commercial specifications and by consideration of chemical and physical data relating to the minerals and deposits in question. The fact that the taxpayer applies slightly different size reduction processes, or the fact that the taxpayer uses slightly different beneficiation processes, or the fact that the taxpayer sells his ore or mineral for different purposes, will not, in itself, prevent another person's ore or mineral from being considered to be of like kind and grade as the taxpayer's ore or mineral. On the other hand, the fact that the taxpayer's ore or mineral is suitable for the same general commercial use as another person's ore or mineral will not cause the two ores or minerals to be considered to be of like kind and grade if the desirable natural constituents of the two ores or minerals are markedly different substances. For example, anthracite coal will not be considered to be of like kind as bituminous coal merely because both types of coal can be used as fuel. Similarly, bituminous coal which does not possess coking qualities will not be considered to be of like grade as bituminous coking coal. However, in the case of a taxpayer who mines and uses his bituminous coal in the production of coke, all bituminous coals in the same marketing area will be considered to be of like kind, and all such bituminous coals having the same or similar coking quality suitable for commercial use by coke producers will be considered to be of like grade as the coal mined and used by the taxpayer.

Fine distinctions between various grades of minerals are to be avoided unless those distinctions are clearly shown to have genuine commercial significance.

(3) *Factors to be considered in determining the representative market or field price for the taxpayer's ore or mineral.* In determining the representative market or field price for the taxpayer's ore or mineral, consideration shall be given only to prices of ores or minerals of like kind and grade as the taxpayer's ore or mineral and with which, under commercially accepted standards, the taxpayer's ore or mineral would be considered to be in competition if it were sold under the conditions described in paragraph (b)(1) of this section. A weighted average of the competitive selling prices of ores or minerals of like kind and grade as the taxpayer's, beneficiated only by mining processes, if any, in the relevant markets, although not determinative of the representative market or field price, is an important factor in the determination of that price. The taxpayer's own competitive sales prices for minerals which have been subjected only to mining processes shall be taken into account in computing such a weighted average. For purposes of the preceding sentence, if the district director has exercised his authority under section 482 and the regulations thereunder and has determined the appropriate price with respect to specific sales transactions by the taxpayer, that price shall be deemed to be a competitive sales price for those transactions. Sales or purchases, including the taxpayer's, of ores or minerals of like kind and grade as the taxpayer's, will be taken into consideration in determining the representative market or field price for the taxpayer's ore or mineral only if those sales or purchases are the result of competitive transactions. The identity of the taxpayer's relevant markets (including their accessibility to the taxpayer), and the representative market or field price within those markets, are necessarily factual determinations to be made on the basis of the facts and circumstances of each individual case. For the purpose of determining the representative market or field price for the taxpayer's ore or mineral, exceptional, insignificant, unusual, tie-in, or accommodation sales shall be disregarded. Except as provided above, representative market or field prices shall not be determined by reference to prices established between members of a controlled group. See paragraph (j) of this section for the definitions of the terms "controlled" and "group."

(4) *Use of prices of mineral of different grade.* If there is no representative market or field price for a mineral of like kind and grade as the taxpayer's representative market or field prices for an ore or mineral which is of like kind but which is not of like grade as his ore or mineral may be used, with appropriate adjustments for differences in mineral content. Representative market or field prices of an ore or mineral of like kind but not of like grade may be used only if such adjustments are readily ascertainable. For example, it may be appropriate in a particular case to establish the representative market or field price for an ore having 50 percent X mineral content by reference to the representative market or field price for the same kind of ore having 60 percent X mineral content with an appropriate adjustment for the differences in the valuable mineral content of the two ores, any differences in processing costs attributable to impurities, and any other relevant factors.

(5) *Information to be furnished by a taxpayer computing gross income from mining by use of a representative market or field price.* A taxpayer who computes his gross income from mining pursuant to the provisions of this paragraph shall attach to his return a summary statement indicating the prices used by him in computing gross income from mining under this paragraph and the source of his information as to those prices, and the relevant supporting data shall be assembled, segregated, and made readily available at the taxpayer's principal place of business.

(6) *Limitation on gross income from mining computed under the provisions of this paragraph.* It shall be presumed that a price is not a representative market or field price for the taxpayer's ore or mineral if the sum of such price plus the total of all costs of the nonmining processes (including nonmining transportation) which the taxpayer applies to his ore or mineral regularly exceeds the taxpayer's actual sales price of his product. For example, if on a regular basis the total of all costs of nonmining processes applied by the taxpayer to coal for the purpose of making coke is $12 per ton, and if the taxpayer's actual sale price for such coke is $18 per ton, a price of $7 per ton would not be a representative market or field price for the taxpayer's coal which is used for making coke. In order to rebut the presumption set forth in the first sentence of this subparagraph, it must be estab-

lished that the loss on nonmining operations is directly attributable to unusual, peculiar and nonrecurring factors rather than to the use of a market or field price which is not representative. For example, the first sentence of this subparagraph shall not apply if the taxpayer establishes in an appropriate case that the loss on nonmining operations is directly attributable to an event such as a fire, flood, explosion, earthquake, or strike.

(d) Cases where a representative market or field price cannot be ascertained. *(1) General rule.* (i) If it is impossible to determine a representative market or field price as described in paragraph (c) of this section then, except as provided in subdivision (ii) of this subparagraph, gross income from mining shall be computed by use of the proportionate profits method as set forth in subparagraph (4) of this paragraph. A method of computing gross income from mining under the provisions of this paragraph shall not be deemed to be a method of accounting for purposes of paragraph (e) of § 1.446-1.

(ii) (a) The Office of the Assistant Commissioner (Technical) may determine that a method of computation is more appropriate than the proportionate profits method or the method being used by the taxpayer. The taxpayer may request such a determination (see (d) of this subdivision (ii)). If the taxpayer is using a method of computation which has been determined by the Office of Assistant Commissioner (Technical) to be more appropriate than the proportionate profits method, such method shall continue to be used until it is determined by the Office of Assistant Commissioner (Technical) that either the proportionate profits method or another method is more appropriate.

(b) The proportionate profits method is more appropriate than the method being used under (a) if, under the particular facts and circumstances, the method being used under (a) consistently fails to clearly reflect gross income from mining and the proportionate profits method more clearly reflects gross income from mining for the taxable year.

(c) An alternative method (a method other than the method being used under (a) (if any) and the proportionate profits method) is more appropriate than the method being used under (a) (if any) and the proportionate profits method if, under the particular facts and circumstances, the latter methods consistently fail to clearly reflect gross income from mining, and the alternative method being considered more clearly reflects gross income from mining on a consistent basis than the method being used under (a) (if any) and the proportionate profits method. When determining whether a method of computation clearly reflects gross income from mining, it is relevant to compare the gross income from mining produced by such method with the gross income from mining, on an equivalent amount of production, which results from the computation methods used by competitors. When determining the acceptability of proposed alternative methods, primary consideration will be given to computation methods based upon representative charges for ores, minerals, products, or services. See paragraph (c) of this section for principles determining the representative character of a charge.

(d) Application for permission to compute gross income from mining by use of an alternative method shall be made by submitting a request to the Commissioner of Internal Revenue, Attention: Assistant Commissioner (Technical), Washington, D.C. 20224.

(e) Among the alternative methods of computation to which consideration will be given, provided that the requirements of this subdivision (ii) are met, are the methods listed in subparagraphs (5), (6), and (7) of this paragraph. The order in which these methods are listed is not significant, and the listing of these methods does not preclude a request to make use of a method which is not listed.

(iii) Approval and continued use of any method of computation under this paragraph depends upon all the facts and circumstances in each case, and shall be subject to such terms and conditions as may be necessary in the opinion of the Commissioner to reflect clearly the gross income from mining. Accordingly, the use of such a method for any taxable year shall be subject to review and change.

(2) Costs to be used in computing gross income from mining by use of methods based on the taxpayer's costs. In determining the taxpayer's gross income from mining by use of methods based on the taxpayer's costs, only costs actually paid or incurred shall be taken into consideration. In general, if the taxpayer has consistently employed a reasonable method of determining the costs of the various individual phases of his mining and nonmining processes (such as extraction, loading for shipment, calcining, packaging, etc.), such method shall not be disturbed. The amount of any particular item to be taken into account shall, for taxable years beginning after November 30, 1968, be the amount used in determining the taxpayer's income for tax purposes. For example, the depreciation lives, methods, and records used for tax purposes, if different from those used for book purposes, shall be the basis for determining the amount of depreciation to be used. However, a taxpayer may continue to use a reasonable method for determining those costs on the basis of the amounts computed for cost control or similar financial or accounting books and records if that method has been used consistently and is applied to the determination of all those costs.

(3) Treatment of particular items in computing gross income from the mining by use of methods based on the taxpayer's costs. (i) Except as specifically provided elsewhere in this section, when determining gross income from mining by use of methods based on the taxpayer's costs, the costs attributable to mining transportation shall be treated as nonmining costs. Accordingly, except as specifically provided elsewhere in this section, all profits attributable to mining transportation shall be treated as mining profits, and all profits attributable to nonmining transportation shall be treated as nonmining profits. For this purpose mining transportation means so much of the transportation of ores or minerals (whether or not by common carrier) from the point of extraction from the ground to plants or mills in which other mining processes are applied thereto as is not in excess of 50 miles or, if the taxpayer files an application pursuant to paragraph (h) of this section and the Commissioner finds that both the physical and other requirements are such that the ores or minerals must be transported a greater distance to such plants or mills, the transportation over the greater distance. Further, for this purpose, nonmining transportation includes the transportation (whether or not by common carrier) of ores, minerals, or the products produced therefrom, from the point of extraction from the ground to nonmining facilities or from a mining facility to a nonmining facility, or from one nonmining facility to another, or from a nonmining facility to the customers who purchase the taxpayer's first marketable product or group of products. See paragraph (e)(2) of this section for provisions relating to purchased transportation to the customer and paragraph (g)(3) of this section for provisions relating to transportation the primary purpose of which is marketing or distribution. In the absence of other methods which clearly reflect the costs of the vari-

ous phases of transportation, the cost attributable to nonmining transportation shall be an amount which is in the same ratio to the costs incurred for the total transportation as the distance of the nonmining transportation is to the distance of the total transportation. As an example, where the plants or mills in which mining processes are applied to ores or minerals are in excess of 50 miles from the point of extraction from the ground (or in excess of a greater distance approved by the Commissioner), the costs incurred for transportation to those plants or mills in excess of 50 miles (or of that greater distance) shall be treated as nonmining costs in determining gross income from mining. Accordingly, all profits attributable to that excess transportation are treated as nonmining profits. However, except in the case of transportation performed in conveyances owned or leased by the taxpayer, the preceding sentence shall apply only to taxable years beginning after November 30, 1968.

(ii) In determining gross income from mining by use of methods based on the taxpayer's costs, a process shall not be considered as a mining process to the extent it is applied to ores, minerals, or other materials with respect to which the taxpayer is not entitled to a deduction for depletion under section 611. The costs of such nondepletable ores, minerals, or materials; the costs of the processes (including blending, size reduction, etc.) applied thereto; and the transportation costs thereof, if any, shall be considered as nonmining costs in determining gross income from mining. If a mining process is applied to an admixture of depletable and nondepletable material, the cost of the process and the cost of transportation, if any, attributable to the nondepletable material shall be considered as nonmining costs in determining gross income from mining. Accordingly, all profits attributable thereto are treated as nonmining profits. In the absence of other methods which clearly reflect the cost attributable to the processing and transportation, if any, of the nondepletable admixed material, that cost shall be deemed to be that proportion of the costs which the tonnage of nondepletable material bears to the total tonnage of both depletable and nondepletable material.

(iii) In determining gross income from mining by use of methods based on the taxpayer's costs—

(a) The costs attributable to containers, bags, packages, pallets, and similar items as well as the costs of materials and labor attributable to bagging, packaging, palletizing, or similar operations shall be considered as nonmining costs.

(b) The costs attributable to the bulk loading of manufactured products shall be considered as nonmining costs.

(c) The costs attributable to the operation of warehouses or distribution terminals for manufactured products shall be considered as nonmining costs.

Accordingly, all profits attributable thereto are treated as nonmining profits.

(iv) In computing gross income from mining by the use of methods based on the taxpayer's costs, the principles set forth in paragraph (c) of § 1.613-5 shall apply when determining whether selling expenses and trade association dues are to be treated, in whole or in part, as mining costs or as nonmining costs. To the extent that selling expenses and trade association dues are treated as nonmining costs, all profits attributable thereto are treated as nonmining profits.

(v) See paragraph (e)(1) of this section for provisions excluding certain allowances from the taxpayer's gross sales and costs of his first marketable product or group of products.

(4) Proportionate profits method. (i) The objective of the "proportionate profits method" of computation is to ascertain gross income from mining by applying the principle that each dollar of the total costs paid or incurred to produce, sell, and transport the first marketable product or group of products (as defined in subdivision (iv) of this subparagraph) earns the same percentage of profit. Accordingly, in the proportionate profits method no ranking of costs is permissible which results in excluding or minimizing the effect of any costs incurred to produce, sell, and transport the first marketable product or group of products. For purposes of this subparagraph, members of a controlled group shall be treated as divisions of a single taxpayer. See paragraph (j) of this section for the definitions of the terms "controlled" and "group."

(ii) The proportionate profits method of computation is applied by multiplying the taxpayer's gross sales (actual or constructive) of his first marketable product or group of products (after making the adjustments required by paragraph (e) of this section) by a fraction whose numerator is the sum of all the costs allocable to those mining processes which are applied to produce, sell, and transport the first marketable product or group of products, and whose denominator is the total of all the mining and nonmining costs paid or incurred to produce, sell, and transport the first marketable product or group of products (after making the adjustments required by this paragraph and paragraph (e) of this section). The method as described herein is merely a restatement of the method formerly set forth in the second sentence of Regulations 118, section 39.23(m)-1(e)(3) (1939 Code). The proportionate profits method of computation may be illustrated by the following equation:

$$\frac{\text{Mining Costs}}{\text{Total Costs}} \times \frac{\text{Gross}}{\text{Sales}} = \frac{\text{Gross income}}{\text{from mining}}$$

(iii) Those costs which are paid or incurred by the taxpayer to produce, sell, and transport the first marketable product or group of products, and which are not directly identifiable with either a particular mining process or a particular nonmining process shall, in the absence of a specific provision of this section providing an apportionment method, be apportioned to mining and to nonmining by use of a method which is reasonable under the circumstances. One method which may be reasonable in a particular case is an allocation based on the proportion that the direct costs of mining processes and the direct costs of nonmining processes bear to each other. For example, the salary of a corporate officer engaged in overseeing all of the taxpayer's processes is an expense which may reasonably be apportioned on the basis of the ratio between the direct costs of mining and nonmining processes. On the other hand, an expense such as workmen's compensation premiums would normally be apportioned on the basis of direct labor costs. For the rule relating to selling expenses, see paragraph (c)(4) of § 1.613-5.

(iv) As used in this section, the term "first marketable product or group of products" means the product (or group of essentially the same products) produced by the taxpayer as a result of the application of nonmining processes, in the form or condition in which such product or products are first marketed in significant quantities by the taxpayer or by others in the taxpayer's marketing area. For this purpose, bulk and packaged products are considered to be essentially the same product. Sales between members of a controlled group (as defined in paragraph (j) of this section) shall not be considered in making a determination under this subdivision. The first marketable product or group of products does not include any product which results from additional manufacturing or other nonmining processes applied to the product or products first marketed in significant quantities by the taxpayer or others in the taxpayer's marketing area. For example, if a cement manufacturer sells his own finished cement in bulk and bags and also sells concrete blocks or dry ready-mix aggregates containing additives, the finished cement, in bulk and bags, constitutes the first marketable product or group of products produced by him. Similarly, if an integrated iron ore and steel producer sells both pig iron in various sizes and rolled sheet iron or shapes, his first marketable product is the pig iron in its various sizes. Further, if an integrated clay and brick producer sells both unglazed bricks and tiles of various shapes and sizes and additionally manufactured bricks and tiles which are specially glazed, the unglazed products, both packaged and unpackaged, constitute his first marketable product or group of products.

(v) (a) As used in this subparagraph, the term "gross sales (actual or constructive)" means the total of the taxpayer's actual competitive sales to others of the first marketable product or group of products, plus the taxpayer's constructive sales of the first marketable product or group of products used or retained for use in his own subsequent operations, subject to the adjustments required by paragraph (e) of this section. See (b) of this subdivision in the case of actual sales between members of controlled groups and in the case of constructive sales. A "constructive sale" occurs when a miner-manufacturer is deemed, for percentage depletion purposes, to be selling the first marketable product or group of products to himself.

(b) In the case of sales between members of a controlled group as to which the district director has exercised his authority under section 482 and the regulations thereunder and has determined the appropriate price with respect to specific sales transactions, that price shall be deemed for those transactions, to be actual amount for which the first marketable product or group of products is sold for purposes of this subdivision (v). In the case of all other sales between members of a controlled group, and in the case of constructive sales, the prices for such sales shall be determined by use of the principles set forth in paragraph (c) of this section, subject to the adjustments required by paragraph (e) of this section. In the case of constructive sales, see paragraph (c)(4) of this section for rules relating to information to be furnished by the taxpayer.

(vi) The provisions of this subparagraph may be illustrated by the following examples:

Example (1). (a) Facts. A is engaged in the mining of a mineral to which section 613 applies and in the application thereto of nonmining processes. During 1968, A incurred extraction costs of $35,000; other mining costs of $56,000; $150,000 for manufacturing costs; $46,000 for other nonmining processes; and $14,000 for the company president's salary and similar costs resulting from both nonmining and mining processes. During that year, A produced and sold 70,000 tons of his first marketable product for an actual gross sales price of $420,000, after the adjustments required by paragraph (e) of this section. A representative market or field price for A's mineral before the application of nonmining processes cannot be established.

(b) Computation.

(1) The computation of A's gross income from mining by use of the proportionate profits method involves two steps. The first is to apportion A's costs to mining and to nonmining. A apportions the company president's salary and similar costs to mining and to nonmining in the manner described in the second and third sentences of subdivision (iii) of this subparagraph, and apportions his remaining costs as follows:

Cost	Mining	Nonmining	Total
Extraction	$35,000		$ 35,000
Other mining processes	56,000		56,000
Manufacturing ...		$150,000	150,000
Other nonmining processes	-	46,000	46,000
Subtotal	91,000	196,000	287,000
President's salary and similar costs	4,439	9,561	14,000
Total costs ...	$95,439	$205,561	$301,000

(2) The second step is to apply the proportionate profits fraction so as to compute A's gross income from mining. To do this, A first computes his gross sales of his first marketable group of products, in this case $420,000. A multiplies his actual gross sales of $420,000 by the proportionate profits fraction, whose numerator consists of his total mining costs ($95,439) and whose denominator consists of his total costs ($301,000). Thus, A's gross income from mining is $133,170 (i.e., $95,439/301,000ths of A's actual gross sales of $420,000).

Example (2). B, who leases a mineral property from C, is engaged in the mining of a mineral to which section 613 applies and in the application thereto of nonmining processes. Pursuant to the terms of the lease, B is required to pay C 10 cents for each ton of mineral which B mines. During 1971, B extracted 100,000 tons of mineral. He sold his first marketable product for an actual gross sales price of $225,000 after the adjustments required by paragraph (e) of this section. A representative market or field price for B's mineral before the application of nonmining processes cannot be established. During 1971, with respect to the 100,000 tons of mineral extracted, B incurred mining costs of $50,000 and nonmining costs of $100,000, and paid $10,000 to C as C's royalty. Since the royalty payment is considered to be C's share of the gross income from mining under section 613(a), it is not considered to be either a mining cost or a nonmining cost of B. B's gross income from mining is $65,000 under the proportionate profits method, determined as follows: The $225,000 gross receipts must be multiplied by the proportionate profits fraction which is $50,000 mining costs over $150,000 total costs ($50,000 + $100,000 nonmining costs). Since the resulting $75,000 is the total gross income from mining with respect to the property, it must be allocated between B's lease interest and C's royalty interest. The $10,000 paid to C must be subtracted from the $75,000 leaving $65,000 which represents B's gross income from mining. C's gross income from mining is the royalty he received or $10,000.

(5) Representative schedule method. The "representative schedule method" is a pricing formula which uses representative finished product prices, penalties, charges and adjustments, established in arms-length transactions between unrelated parties, to determine the market or field price for a crude mineral product. The representative character of a price, penalty, charge or adjustment shall be determined by applying the principles set forth in paragraph (c) of this section. The representative schedule method is principally intended for use in those industries in which such a schedule-

type pricing method is in general use to determine the price paid to unintegrated mineral producers for their crude mineral product. For example, if unintegrated producers of copper concentrate in a particular field or market customarily sell their product at prices which are determined in accordance with a schedule-type pricing formula, consideration will be given to the determination of concentrate prices for integrated copper producers in accordance with the same pricing formula. The representative schedule method shall not be used if it is impossible to determine one or more of the elements in the representative schedule formula by reference to prices, penalties, charges, or adjustments established in representative transactions between unrelated parties. See paragraph (c) of this section for principles determining the representative character of a charge.

(6) Method using prices outside the taxpayer's market. Under the "other market method" the taxpayer uses representative market or field prices established outside his markets, provided that conditions there are substantially the same as in his markets. For example, it may be appropriate in a particular case to establish the representative market or field price for pellets containing 60 percent iron which are produced and used in market area X by reference to the representative market or field price for pellets containing 60 percent iron which are produced and sold in adjacent market area Y, provided that conditions in the two marketing areas are shown to be substantially the same.

(7) Rate of return on investment method. [Reserved]

(e) Reductions of sales price in computing gross income from mining. *(1) Discounts.* If a taxpayer computes gross income from mining under the provisions of paragraph (b)(1) of this section, trade discounts and, for taxable years beginning after November 30, 1968, cash discounts actually allowed by the taxpayer shall be subtracted from the sale price of the taxpayer's ore or mineral. If a taxpayer computes gross income from mining under the provisions of paragraph (c) of this section, any such discounts actually allowed (if not otherwise taken into account) by the person or persons making the sales on the basis of which the representative market or field price for the taxpayer's ore or mineral is to be determined shall be subtracted from the sale price in computing such representative market or field price. If a taxpayer computes gross income from mining under the provisions of paragraph (d) of this section, such discounts actually allowed (if not otherwise taken into account) shall be subtracted from the gross sales (actual or constructive), and shall not be considered a cost, of the first marketable product or group of products. The provisions of this subparagraph shall apply to arrangements which have the same effect as trade or cash discounts, regardless of the form of the arrangements.

(2) Purchased transportation to the customer. (1) A taxpayer who computes gross income from mining under the provisions of paragraph (c) of this section and who sells his ore or mineral after the application of only mining processes but after nonmining transportation shall use as the representative market or field price his delivered price (if otherwise representative) reduced by costs paid or incurred by him for purchased transportation to the customer as defined in subdivision (iii) of this subparagraph. If the transportation by the taxpayer is not purchased transportation to the customer, or if the taxpayer does not sell the ore or mineral until after the application of nonmining processes, and if other producers in the taxpayer's marketing area sell significant quantities of an ore or mineral of like kind and grade after the application of only mining processes but after purchased transportation to the customer, the representative delivered price at which the ore or mineral is sold by those other producers reduced by representative costs of purchased transportation to the customer paid or incurred by those producers shall be used by the taxpayer as the representative market or field price for his ore or mineral in applying paragraph (c) of this section. Furthermore, appropriate adjustments shall be made to take into account differences in mode of transportation and distance. When applying this subdivision, the representative market or field price so computed shall not exceed the taxpayer's delivered prices less his actual costs of transportation to the customer. For purposes of this subdivision, any delivered price shall be adjusted as provided in subparagraph (1) of this paragraph.

(ii) If a taxpayer computes gross income from mining under the provisions of paragraph (d) of this section, the cost of purchased transportation to the customer (as defined in subdivision (iii) of this subparagraph) shall be excluded from the gross sales of his first marketable product or group of products (after any adjustments required by subparagraph (1) of this paragraph), and from the denominator of the proportionate profits fraction, so as not to attribute profits to the cost of that transportation. Similar transportation cost adjustments may be made, if appropriate in the case of other methods of computation which are based on the taxpayer's costs. For the treatment of costs and profits attributable to transportation which is not purchased transportation to the customer as defined in subdivision (iii) of this subparagraph, see paragraph (d)(3)(i) of this section.

(iii) For purposes of this section, the term "purchased transportation to the customer" means in general, nonmining transportation of the taxpayer's minerals or mineral products to the customer—

(a) Which is not performed in conveyances owned or leased directly or indirectly, in whole or in part, by the taxpayer.

(b) Which is performed solely to deliver the taxpayer's minerals or mineral products to the customer, rather than to transport such minerals or products for packaging or other additional processing by the taxpayer (other than incidental storage or handling), and

(c) With respect to which the taxpayer ordinarily does not earn any profit. For purposes of the preceding sentence, transportation which is performed by a person controlling or controlled by the taxpayer (within the meaning of paragraph (j)(1) of this section) shall be deemed to have been performed in conveyances owned or leased by the taxpayer unless it is established by the taxpayer that the price charged by the controlling or controlled person for such transportation constitutes an arm's-length charge (under the standard described in paragraph (b)(1) of § 1.482-1). The term "purchased transportation to the customer" includes transportation to a warehouse, terminal, or distribution facility owned or operated by the taxpayer, provided that such transportation is performed under the conditions described in the first sentence of this subdivision. A taxpayer will not be deemed ordinarily to earn a profit on transportation merely because charges for the transportation are included in the stated selling price, rather than being separately stated or segregated from other billing. A taxpayer will not be deemed ordinarily to earn a profit on transportation if the rates for the transportation constitute an arm's-length charge ordinarily paid by shippers of the same product in similar circumstances. If a taxpayer computes gross income from mining under the provisions of paragraph (d) of this section, the term "purchased transportation to the customer" refers to transportation which conforms to the other requirements of this subdivision and which is performed to transport the taxpayer's first marketable product or group of products (as defined in paragraph (d)(4)(iv) of this section) rather than to transport minerals or mineral products which do not yet constitute the taxpayer's first marketable product or group of products.

(iv) The provisions of this subparagraph may be illustrated by the following examples:

Example (1). A is engaged in the mining of an ore of mineral M and in the production and sale of M concentrate. A retains a portion of his concentrate for use in his own nonmining operations. During 1968, A sold 100,000 tons of M concentrate of ore mined and processed by him, which sales constituted a significant portion of his total production. Eighty thousand tons of that concentrate were sold by A on the basis of a representative price (after adjustments required by subparagraph (1) of this paragraph) of $30 per ton f.o.b. mine or plant, resulting in gross income from mining of $2,400,000. The remaining 20,000 tons were sold by A, both directly and through terminals, on the basis of a delivered price (after adjustments required by subparagraph (1) of this paragraph) at City X of $40 per ton. The delivered price included $15 per ton cost of purchased transportation from the mine or plant to customers in City X. The representative market or field price of the concentrate sold by A on the basis of a delivered price is $25 per ton, determined by subtracting the cost of the purchased transportation to the customer ($15 per ton) from the delivered price for the concentrate ($40 per ton). Accordingly, A's gross income from mining with respect to the 20,000 tons of M concentrate sold on a delivered basis is $500,000. The representative market or field price for the concentrate retained by A and used in his own nonmining operations may be computed by reference to the weighted average price for both A's f.o.b. mine and A's delivered sales of concentrate, with the delivered sales prices reduced in the manner described above. On this basis, the representative market or field price for the retained concentrate is $29 per ton.

Example (2). B is engaged in the mining of an ore of mineral N and in the production of N concentrate. B retained all but an insignificant amount of his concentrate for use in his own nonmining operations. Other producers in B's marketing area sell significant amounts of N concentrate of like kind and grade, both on an f.o.b. mine or plant basis and on a delivered basis. In this case, the prices for both the f.o.b. and the delivered sales made by other producers (after any adjustments required by subparagraph (1) of this paragraph), after reduction of the delivered prices by the cost of purchased transportation to the customer, shall, if such prices are otherwise representative, be taken into account in establishing the representative market or field price for the N concentrate produced and used by B.

(f) Definition of mining. *(1) In general.* The the term "mining" includes only—

(i) The extraction of ores or minerals from the ground;

(ii) Mining processes, as described in subparagraphs (2) through (6) of this paragraph; and

(iii) So much of the transportation (whether or not by common carrier) of ores or minerals from the point of extraction of the ores or minerals from the ground to the plants or mills in which the processes referred to in subdivision (ii) of this subparagraph are applied thereto as is not in excess of 50 miles, and, if the Commissioner finds that both the physical and other requirements are such that the ores or minerals must be transported a greater distance to such plants or mills, the transportation over such greater distance as the Commissioner authorizes. See paragraph (h) of this section for rules relating to the filing of applications to treat as mining any transportation in excess of 50 miles.

(2) Definition of mining processes. (i) As used in subparagraph (1)(ii) of this paragraph, the term "mining processes" means, for taxable years beginning before January 1, 1961, the ordinary treatment processes normally applied by mine owners or operators in order to obtain the commercially marketable mineral product or products, including the following processes (and the processes necessary or incidental thereto), and, for taxable years beginning after December 31, 1960, the following processes (and the processes necessary or incidental thereto):

(a) In the case of coal—cleaning, breaking, sizing, dust allaying, treating to prevent freezing, and loading for shipment;

(b) In the case of sulfur recovered by the Frasch process—cleaning, pumping to vats, cooling, breaking, and loading for shipment;

(c) In the case of iron ore, bauxite, ball and sagger clay, rock asphalt, and ores or minerals which are customarily sold in the form of a crude mineral product (as defined in subparagraph (3)(iv) of this paragraph)—

(1) Where applied for the purpose of bringing to shipping grade and form (as defined in subparagraph (3)(iii) of this paragraph)—sorting, concentrating, sintering, and substantially equivalent processes, and

(2) Loading for shipment.

(d) In the case of lead, zinc, copper, gold, silver, uranium, or fluorspar ores, potash, and ores or minerals which are not customarily sold in the form of the crude mineral product—crushing, grinding, and beneficiation by concentration (gravity, flotation, amalgamation, electrostatic, or magnetic), cyanidation, leaching, crystallization, precipitation (but not including electrolytic deposition, roasting thermal or electric smelting, or refining), or by substantially equivalent processes or combination of processes used in the separation or extraction of the product or products from the ore or the mineral or minerals from other material from the mine or other natural deposit; and

(e) In the case of the following ores or minerals—

(1) The furnacing of quicksilver ores,

(2) The pulverization of talc,

(3) The burning of magnesite, and

(4) The sintering and nodulizing of phosphate

(ii) The term "mining processes" also includes the following processes (and, except as otherwise provided in this subdivision, the processes necessary or incidental thereto):

(a) For taxable years beginning after December 31, 1960, in the case of calcium carbonates and other minerals when used in making cement—all processes (other than preheating the kiln feed) applied prior to the introduction of the kiln feed into the kiln, but not including any subsequent process;

(b) For taxable years beginning after December 31, 1960, and before November 14, 1966, in the case of clay to which former section 613(b)(5)(B) applied, and for taxable years beginning after November 13, 1966, in the case of clay to which section 613(b)(5) or (6)(B) applies—crushing, grinding, and separating the clay from waste, but not including any subsequent process;

(c) For taxable years beginning after October 9, 1969, in the case of minerals (other than sodium chloride) extracted from brines pumped from a saline perennial lake (as defined in paragraph (b) of § 1.613-2 —the extraction of such minerals from the brines, but in no case including any further processing or refining of such extracted minerals; and

(d) For taxable years beginning after December 30, 1969, in the case of oil shale (as defined in paragraph (b) of § 1.613-2$extraction from the ground, crushing, loading into the retort, and retorting, but in no case hydrogenation, refining, or any other process subsequent to retorting.

(iii) A process is "necessary" to another related process if it is prerequisite to the performance of the other process. For example, if the concentrating of low-grade iron ores to bring to shipping grade and form cannot be effectively accomplished without fine pulverization, such pulverization shall be treated as a process which is "necessary" to the concentration process. Accordingly, because concentration is a mining process, such pulverization is also a mining process. Furthermore, if mining processes cannot be effectively applied to a mineral without storage of the mineral while awaiting the application of such processes, such storage shall be treated as a process which is "necessary" to the accomplishment of such mining processes. A process is "incidental" to another related process if the cost thereof is insubstantial in relation to the cost of the other process, or if the process is merely the coincidental result of the application of the other process. For example, the sprinkling of coal, prior to loading for shipment, with dots of paper to identify the coal for trade-name purposes will be considered incidental to the loading where the cost of that sprinkling is insubstantial in relation to the cost of the loading process. Also, where crushing of a crude mineral is treated as a mining process, the production of fines as a byproduct is ordinarily the coincidental result of the application of a mining process. If a taxpayer demonstrates that, as a factual matter, a particular process is necessary or incidental to a process named as a mining process in section 613(c)(4) of this paragraph, the necessary or incidental process will also be considered a mining process.

(iv) The term "mining" does not include purchasing minerals from another. Accordingly, the processes listed in this paragraph shall be considered as mining processes only to the extent that they are applied by a mine owner or operator to an ore or mineral in respect of which he is entitled to a deduction for depletion under section 611. The application of these processes to purchased ores, minerals, or materials does not constitute mining.

(3) Processes recognized as mining for ores or minerals covered by section 613(c)(4)(C). (i) As used in section 613(c)(4)(C) and subparagraph (2)(i)*(c)* of this paragraph, the terms "sorting" and "concentrating" mean the process of eliminating substantial amounts of the impurities or foreign matter associated with the ores or minerals in their natural state, or of separating two or more valuable minerals or ores, without changing the physical or chemical identity of the ores or minerals. Examples of sorting and concentrating processes are hand or mechanical sorting, magnetic separation, gravity concentration, jigging, the use of shaking or concentrating tables, the use of spiral concentrators, the use of sluices or sluice boxes, sink-and-float processes, classifiers, hydrotators and flotation processes. Under section 613(c)(4)(C), sorting and concentration will be considered mining processes only where they are applied to bring an ore or mineral to shipping grade and form.

(ii) As used in section 613(c)(4)(C) and subparagraph (2)(i)*(c)* of this paragraph, the term "sintering" means the agglomeration of fine particles by heating to a temperature at which incipient, but not complete, fusion occurs. Sintering will be considered a mining process only where it is applied to an ore or mineral, or a concentrate of an ore or mineral, as an auxiliary process necessary to bring the ore or mineral to shipping form. A thermal action which is applied in the manufacture of a finished product will not be considered to be a mining process even though such thermal action may cause the agglomeration of fine particles by incipient fusion, and even though such action does not cause a chemical change in the agglomerated particles. For example, the sintering of finely ground iron ore concentrate, prior to shipment from the concentration plant, for the purpose of preventing the risk of loss of the finely divided particles during shipment is considered a mining process. On the other hand, for example, a heating process applied to expand or harden clay, shale, perlite, vermiculite, or other materials in the course of the manufacture of lightweight aggregate or other building materials is not considered to be a mining process.

(iii) As used in section 613(c)(4)(C) and this section, to "bring to shipping grade and form" means, with respect to taxable years beginning after December 31, 1960, to bring (by the application of mining processes at the mine or concentration plant) the quality or size of an ore or mineral to the stage or stages at which the ore or mineral is shipped to customers or used in nonmining processes (as defined in paragraph (g) of this section) by the taxpayer.

(iv) An ore or mineral is "customarily sold in the form of a crude mineral product", within the meaning of section 613(c)(4)(C), if a significant portion of the production thereof is sold or used in a nonmining process prior to the alteration of its inherent mineral content by some form of beneficiation, concentration, or ore dressing. An ore or mineral does not lose its classification as a crude mineral product by reason of the fact that, before sale or use in a nonmining process, the ore or mineral may be crushed or subjected to other processes which do not alter its inherent mineral content. Whether the portion of production sold or used in the form of a crude mineral product is a significant portion of the total production of an ore or mineral is a question of fact.

(4) Type of processes recognized as mining for ores or minerals covered by section 613(c)(4)(D). Cyanidation, leaching, crystallization, and precipitation, which are listed in section 613(c)(4)(D) as treatment processes considered as mining, and the processes (or combination of processes) which are substantially equivalent thereto, will be recognized as mining only to the extent that they are applied to the taxpayer's ore or mineral for the purpose of separation or extraction of the valuable mineral product or products from the ore, or for the purpose of separation or extraction of the mineral or minerals from other material extracted from the mine or other natural deposit. A process, no matter how denominated, will not be recognized as mining if the process beneficiates the ore or mineral to the degree that such process, in effect, constitutes smelting, refining, or any other nonmining process within the meaning of paragraph (g) of this section. As used in section 613(c)(4)(D) and subparagraph (2)(i) *(d)* of this paragraph, the term "concentration" has the meaning set forth in the first two sentences of subparagraph (3)(i) of this paragraph.

(5) Processes recognized as mining under section 613(c)(4)(I). Under the authority granted the Secretary or his delegate in section 613(c)(4)(I), the processes (i) through (iv) of this subparagraph, and the processes necessary or incidental thereto, are recognized as mining processes for taxable

years beginning after December 31, 1960. The processes described in subdivisions (i) through (iv) of this subparagraph are in addition to the specific processes recognized as mining under section 613(c)(4). Such additional processes are:

(i) Crushing and grinding, but not fine pulverization (as defined in paragraph (g)(6)(v) of this section);

(ii) Size classification processes applied to the products of an allowable mining process;

(iii) Drying to remove free water, provided that such drying does not change the physical or chemical identity or composition of the mineral; and

(iv) Washing or cleaning the surface of mineral particles (including the washing of sand and gravel and the treatment of kaolin particles to remove surface stains), provided that such washing or cleaning does not activate or otherwise change the physical or chemical structure of the mineral particles.

(6) In the case of a process applied subsequent to a nonmining process, see paragraph (g)(2) of this section.

(g) Nonmining processes. *(1) General rule.* Unless they are otherwise provided for in paragraph (f) of this section as mining processes (or are necessary or incidental to processes listed therein), the following processes are not considered to be mining processes— electrolytic deposition, roasting, calcining, thermal or electric smelting, refining, polishing, fine pulverization, blending with other materials, treatment effecting a chemical change, thermal action, and molding or shaping. See subparagraph (6) of this paragraph for definitions of certain of these terms.

(2) Processes subsequent to nonmining processes. Notwithstanding any other provision of this section, a process applied subsequent to a nonmining process (other than nonmining transportation) shall also be considered to be a nonmining process. Exceptions to this rule shall be made, however, in those instances in which the rule would discriminate between similarly situated producers of the same mineral. For example, roasting is specifically designated in subparagraph (1) of this paragraph as a nonmining process, but in the case of minerals referred to in section 613(c)(4)(C) sintering is recognized as a mining process. If certain impurities in an ore can only be removed by roasting in order to bring it to the same shipping grade and form as a competitive sintered ore of the same kind which requires no roasting, the subsequent sintering of the roasted ore will be treated as a mining process. In that case, however, the roasting of the ore will nonetheless continue to be treated as a nonmining process.

(3) Transportation for the purpose of marketing or distribution; storage. Transportation the primary purpose of which is marketing, distribution, or delivery for the application of only nonmining processes shall not be considered as mining. Nor shall transportation be considered as mining merely because, during the course of such transportation, some extraneous matter is removed from the ore or mineral by the operation of forces of nature, such as evaporation, drainage, or gravity flow. Similarly, storage or warehousing of manufactured products shall not be considered as mining. The preceding sentence shall apply even though, during the course of such storage or warehousing, some extraneous matter is removed from the ore or mineral by the operation of forces of nature, such as evaporation, drainage, or gravity flow.

(4) Manufacturing, etc. The production, packaging, distribution, and marketing of manufactured products, and the processes necessary or incidental thereto, are nonmining processes.

(5) Transformation processes. Processes which effect a substantial physical or chemical change in a crude mineral product, or which transform a crude mineral product into new or different mineral products, or into refined or manufactured products, are nonmining processes except to the extent that such processes are allowed as mining processes under section 613(c) or under paragraph (f) of this section.

(6) Definitions. As used in section 613(c)(5) and this section—

(i) The term "calcining" refers to processes used to expel the volatile portions of a mineral by the application of heat, as, for example, the burning of carbonate rock to produce lime, the heating of gypsum to produce calcined gypsum or plaster of Paris, or the heating of clays to reduce water or crystallization.

(ii) The term "thermal smelting" refers to processes which reduce, separate, or remove impurities from ores or minerals by the application of heat, as, for example, the furnacing of copper concentrates, the heating of iron ores, concentrates, or pellets in a blast furnace to produce pig iron, or the heating of iron ores or concentrates in a direct reduction kiln to produce a feed for direct conversion into steel.

(iii) The term "refining" refers to processes (other than mining processes designated in section 613(c)(4) or this section) used to eliminate impurities or foreign matter from smelted or partially processed metallic and nonmetallic ores and minerals, as, for example, the refining of blister copper. In general, a refining process is designed to achieve a high degree of purity by removing relatively small amounts of impurities or foreign matter from smelted or partially processed ores or minerals.

(iv) The term "polishing" refers to processes used to smooth the surface of minerals, as, for example, sawing applied to finish rough cut blocks of stone, sand finishing, buffing, or otherwise smoothing blocks of stone.

(v) The term "fine pulverization" refers to any grinding or other size reduction process applied to reduce the normal topsize of a mineral product to less than .0331 inches, which is the size opening in a No. 20 Screen (U.S. Standard Sieve Series). A mineral product will be considered to have a normal topsize of .0331 inches if at least 98 percent of the product will pass through a No. 20 Screen (U.S. Standard Sieve Series), provided that at least 5 percent of the product is retained on a No. 45 Screen (U.S. Standard Sieve Series). Compliance with the normal topsize test may also be demonstrated by other tests which are shown to be reasonable in the circumstances. The normal topsize test shall be applied to the product of the operation of each separate and distinct piece of size reduction equipment utilized (such as a roller mill), rather than to the final products for sale. Fine pulverization includes the repeated recirculation of material through crushing or grinding equipment to accomplish fine pulverization. Separating or screening the product of a fine pulverization process (including separation by air or water flotation) shall be treated as a nonmining process.

(vi) The term "blending with other materials" refers to processes used to blend different kinds of minerals with one another, as, for example, blending iodine with common salt for the purpose of producing iodized table salt.

(vii) The term "treatment effecting a chemical change" refers to processes which transform or modify the chemical composition of a crude mineral, as, for example, the coking of coal. The term does not include the use of chemicals to clean the surface of mineral particles provided that such cleaning does not make any change in the physical or chemical structure of the mineral particles.

(viii) The term "thermal action" refers to processes which involve the application of artificial heat to ores or minerals, such as, for example, the burning of bricks, the coking of coal, the expansion or popping of perlite, the exfoliation of vermiculite, the heat treatment of garnet, and the heating of shale, clay, or slate to produce lightweight aggregates. The term does not include drying to remove free water.

(h) Application to treat, as mining, transportation in excess of 50 miles. If a taxpayer desires to include in the computation of his gross income from mining transportation in excess of 50 miles from the point of extraction of the minerals from the ground, he shall file an original and one copy of an application for the inclusion of such greater distance with the Commissioner of Internal Revenue, Washington, D.C. 20224. The application must include a statement setting forth in detail the facts concerning the physical and other requirements which prevented the construction and operation of the plant (in which mining processes, as defined in paragraph (f) of this section, are applied) at a place nearer to the point of extraction from the ground. These facts must be sufficient to apprise the Commissioner of the exact basis of the application. If the taxpayer's return is filed prior to receipt of notice of the Commissioner's action upon the application, a copy of such application shall be attached to the return. If after an application is approved by the Commissioner, there is a material change in any of the facts relied upon in such application, a new application must be submitted by the taxpayer.

(i) Extraction from waste or residue. "Extraction of ores or minerals from the ground" means not only the extraction of ores or minerals from a deposit, but also the extraction by mine owners or operators of ores or minerals from waste or residue of their prior mining. It is immaterial whether the waste or residue results from the process of extraction from the ground or from application of mining processes as defined in paragraph (f) of this section. However, extraction of ores or minerals from waste or residue which results from processes which are not allowable as mining processes is not treated as mining. "Extraction of ores or minerals from the ground" does not include extraction of ores or minerals by the purchaser of waste or residue or the purchaser of the rights to extract ores or minerals from waste or residue. The term "purchaser" does not apply to any person who acquires a mineral property, including waste or residue, in a tax-free exchange, such as a corporate reorganization, from a person who was entitled to a depletion allowance upon ores or minerals produced from such waste or residue, or from a person who would have been entitled to such depletion allowance had section 613(c)(3) been in effect at the time of the transfer. The term "purchaser" also does not apply to a lessee who has renewed a mineral lease if the lessee was entitled to a depletion allowance (or would have been so entitled had section 613(c)(3) been in effect at the time of the renewal) upon ores or minerals produced from waste or residue before renewal of the lease. It is not necessary, for purposes of the preceding sentence, that the mineral lease contain an option for renewal. The term "purchaser" does include a person who acquires waste or residue in a taxable transaction, even though such waste or residue is acquired merely as an incidental part of the entire mineral enterprise. For special rules with respect to certain corporate acquisitions referred to in section 381(a), see section 381(c)(18) and the regulations thereunder.

(j) Definition of controlled group. When used in this section—

(1) The term "controlled" includes any kind of control, direct or indirect, whether or not legally enforceable, and however exercisable or exercised. It is the reality of the control which is decisive, not its form or the mode of its exercise. A presumption of control arises if income or deductions have been arbitrarily shifted.

(2) The term "group" means the organizations, trades, or businesses owned or controlled by the same interests.

T.D. 7170, 3/10/72.

§ 1.613-5 Taxable income from the property.

(a) In general. The term "taxable income from the property (computed without allowance for depletion)" as used in section 613 and this part, means "gross income from the property" as defined in section 613(c) and §§ 1.613-3 and 1.613-4 less allowable deductions (excluding any deduction for depletion) which are attributable to the mineral processes, including mining transportation, with respect to which depletion is claimed. These deductible items include operating expenses, certain selling expenses, administrative and financial overhead, depreciation, taxes deductible under section 162 or 164, losses sustained, intangible drilling and development costs, exploration and development expenditures, etc. See paragraph (c) of this section for special rules relating to discounts and to certain of these deductible items. Expenditures which may be attributable both to the mineral property upon which depletion is claimed and to other activities shall be properly apportioned to the mineral property and to such other activities. Furthermore, where a taxpayer has more than one mineral property, deductions which are not directly attributable to a specific mineral property shall be properly apportioned among the several properties. In determining the taxpayer's taxable income from the property, the amount of any particular item to be taken into account shall be determined in accordance with the principles set forth in paragraph (d)(2) and (3) of § 1.613-4.

(b) Special rule; decrease in mining expenses resulting from gain recognized under section 1245(a)(1). *(1)* If during any taxable year beginning after December 31, 1962, the taxpayer disposes of an item of section 1245 property (as defined in section 1245(a)(3)) which has been used in connection with a mineral property, then for the purpose of computing the taxable income from such mineral property for such taxable year, the allowable deductions taken into account with respect to expenses of mining (that is, expenses attributable to a mineral property other than an oil and gas property) shall be decreased by an amount equal to the portion of any gain recognized under section 1245(a)(1) (relating to treatment of gain from dispositions of certain depreciable property as ordinary income) which is properly allocable to such mineral property in respect of which the taxable income is being computed. The portion of such gain which is properly allocable to such mineral property shall bear the same ratio to the total of such gain as—

(i) The portion of the "adjustments reflected in the adjusted basis" (as such term is defined in paragraph (a)(2) of § 1.1245-2, relating to definition of recomputed basis) of such section 1245 property, which were allowable as deductions from the "gross income from the property" (as defined in section 613(c) and § 1.613-3) in computing the taxable income from such mineral property, bears to

(ii) The total of the "adjustments reflected in the adjusted basis" of such section 1245 property.

(2) For the purposes of this paragraph, the adjustments reflected in the adjusted basis of the section 1245 property disposed of shall be deemed to have been taken into account in computing the taxable income from the mineral property for any taxable year notwithstanding that for the taxable year the allowance for depletion was determined without reference to percentage depletion under section 613.

(3) If the amount of gain described in subparagraph (1) of this paragraph allocable to a mineral property for a taxable year exceeds the allowable deductions otherwise taken into account in computing the taxable income from the mineral property for the taxable year, the excess may not be taken into account in computing the taxable income from the mineral property for any other taxable year.

(4) To the extent that the adjustments reflected in the adjusted basis of the section 1245 property are allocable to mineral property which the taxpayer no longer owns in the taxable year in which he disposes of the section 1245 property, the gain recognized under section 1245 property, the gain recognized under section 1245(a)(1) does not result in any tax benefit to the taxpayer under this paragraph since he has no taxable income from the mineral property for such year. However, if a taxpayer has, in the taxable year in which he disposes of an item of section 1245 property, only a portion of the original mineral property to which gain described in subparagraph (1) of this paragraph with respect to the section 1245 property is properly allocable, the entire amount of that gain shall nevertheless be taken into account in computing the taxable income of the remaining portion of the mineral property. Furthermore, the fact that a mineral property to which section 1245 gain is properly allocable is (in the taxable year in which the taxpayer disposes of an item of section 1245 property) no longer in existence merely because the mineral property has been made a part of an aggregation or has been deaggregated will not result in the loss of tax benefits under this section. Accordingly,

(i) If a taxpayer has made an aggregation of mineral properties (see section 614 and the regulations thereunder), the amount of any gain described in subparagraph (1) of this paragraph which is properly allocable to the aggregation shall include the portion of any gain which would be properly allocable to the mineral properties which existed separately prior to the aggregation and of which the aggregation is or was composed, if the prior mineral properties had not been aggregated; and

(ii) If a taxpayer has deaggregated a mineral property, the amount of any gain described in subparagraph (1) of this paragraph which is properly allocable to each of the resulting mineral properties shall include a part of the portion of any gain which would be properly allocable to the prior aggregation if the aggregation had not been deaggregated, the part properly allocable to each of the resulting properties being determined by allocating the gain between the resulting properties in the same manner as basis is allocated between them for tax purposes (see paragraph (a)(2) of § 1.614-6 and example (5) of subparagraph (7) of this paragraph).

(5) In any case in which it is necessary to determine the portion of any gain recognized under section 1245(a)(1) which is properly allocable to the mineral property in respect of which the taxable income is being computed, the taxpayer shall have available permanent records of all the facts necessary to determine with reasonable accuracy the amount of such portion. In the absence of such records, none of the gain recognized under section 1245(a)(1) shall be allocable to such mineral property.

(6) As used in this paragraph, the term "mineral property" has the meaning assigned to it by section 614 and § 1.614-1.

(7) The provisions of this paragraph may be illustrated by the following examples:

Example (1). A, who uses the calendar year as his taxable year, operated and treated as separate properties mines Nos. 1 and 2. On January 1, 1963, A acquired a truck which was section 1245 property. During 1963 and 1964 the truck was used 25 percent of the time at mine No. 1 and 75 percent of the time at mine No. 2. For each such year the depreciation adjustments allowed in respect of the truck were $800 (the amount allowable). In computing the taxable income from mines Nos. 1 and 2 for each such year, $200 (25 percent of $800) of the depreciation adjustments was allocated by A to mine No. 1 and $600 (75 percent of $800) to mine No. 2. Thus, for the 2 years, the total of the depreciation adjustments on the truck was $1,600, of which $400 was allocated to mine No. 1 and $1,200 to mine No. 2. On January 1, 1965, A recognized upon sale of the truck a gain of $500 to which section 1245 (a)(1) applied. During 1965, A did not recognize any other gain to which section 1245(a)(1) applied. In computing taxable income from the mines for 1965, the expenses otherwise required to be taken into account are reduced by $125 (that is $400/$1,600 of $500) for mine No. 1 and by $375 (that is $1,200/$1,600 of $500) for mine No. 2.

Example (2). The situation is the same as in example (1), except that the truck in question is used 25 percent of the time at mine No. 1, and 75 percent of the time in a nonmining business owned by A. Accordingly, in computing taxable income from A's mines for 1965, the expenses for mine No. 1 otherwise required to be taken into account are reduced by $125 (that is $400/$1,600 of $500), but no reduction is made in the expenses for mine No. 2, since the truck in question was not used in connection with that mineral property.

Example (3). The situation is the same as in example (1), except that the truck in question was used exclusively at mine No. 1 in 1963. On January 1, 1964, the truck was transferred to mine No. 2, and was used exclusively at mine No. 2 during the remaining period prior to its sale.

However, A continued to own and operate mine No. 1. for the 2 years 1963 and 1964, the total of the depreciation adjustments on the truck was $1,600, of which $800 was allocated to mine No. 1 and $800 to mine No. 2. In computing taxable income from A's mines for 1965, the expenses for mines Nos. 1 and 2 otherwise required to be taken into account are reduced by $250 each (that is $800/$1,600 of $500). If A had sold mine No. 1 on January 1, 1964, no reduction in expenses would be allowable as a result of the operation of the truck at mine No. 1, since A would no longer have owned mine No. 1 in the year in which the truck was sold.

Example (4). On January 1, 1963, B, who uses the calendar year as his taxable year and who normally allocates depreciation costs to mines according to the percentage of time which the depreciable asset is used with respect to the mines, acquired a truck which was section 1245 property. During 1963 the truck was used exclusively on mine No. 1, which B operated and treated as a separate property. The depreciation adjustments allowed in respect of the truck for 1963 were $1,000 (the amount allowable), which amount was allocated to mine No. 1 in computing the taxable income therefrom. On January 1, 1964, B acquired and began operating mine No. 2 and elected under section 614(c) to aggregate and treat as one property mines Nos. 1 and 2. During 1964 B used the truck 60 percent of the time for mine

No. 1 and 40 percent of the time for mine No. 2. For 1964 the depreciation adjustments allowed in respect of the truck were $1,000 (the amount allowable), which amount was allocated to the aggregation of mines Nos. 1 and 2 in computing the taxable income therefrom. On December 31, 1964, B sold mine No. 2. For 1965 the depreciation adjustments allowed in respect to the truck were $1,000 (the amount allowable), which amount was allocated to mine No. 1 in computing the taxable income therefrom. On January 1, 1966, B recognized gain upon sale of the truck of $600 to which section 1245(a)(1) applied. In computing the taxable income from mine No. 1 for 1966, the expenses otherwise required to be taken into account are reduced by $600, since all the depreciation adjustments allowed with respect to the truck, including those allowed with respect to the use of the truck at mine No. 2 ($400 for 1964), relate to the same mineral property from which B had taxable income in 1966, the taxable year in which he sold the truck.

Example (5). On January 1, 1962, A, who uses the calendar year as his taxable year, elected under section 614(c) to aggregate and treat as one mineral property his operating mineral interests in mines Nos. 1 and 2. On January 1, 1963, A acquired a truck which was section 1245 property, to be used at both mine No. 1 and mine No. 2. A later elected (with the consent of the Commissioner) to deaggregate mines Nos. 1 and 2, and this deaggregation became effective on January 1, 1964. At the time of deaggregation, half of the tax basis of the aggregated property was allocated to mine No. 1, and the other half to mine No. 2. During each of the years 1963 and 1964, the truck was used 25 percent of the time on mine No. 1 and 75 percent of the time on mine No. 2, and the depreciation adjustments allowed in respect of the truck were $800 (the amount allowable). On January 1, 1965, A recognized upon sale of the truck a gain of $500 to which section 1245(a)(1) applied. In computing taxable income from A's mines for 1965, the expenses otherwise required to be taken into account are reduced by $187.50 (that is half of $250 for 1963 and $200/$800 of $250 for 1964) for mine No. 1 and by $312.50 (that is half of $250 for 1963 and $600/$800 of $250 for 1964) for mine No. 2.

(c) Treatment of particular items in computing taxable income from the property. In determining taxable income from the property under the provisions of paragraph (a) of this section—

(1) Trade or cash discounts (or allowances determined to have the same effect as trade or cash discounts) which are actually allowed to the taxpayer in connection with the acquisition of property, supplies, or services shall not be included in the cost of such property, supplies, or services.

(2) Intangible drilling and development costs which are deducted under section 263(c) and § 1.612-4 shall be subtracted from the gross income from the property.

(3) Exploration and development expenditures which are deducted for the taxable year under sections 615, 616, or 617 shall be subtracted from the gross income from the property.

(4) (i) Selling expenses, if any, paid or incurred with respect to a raw mineral product shall be subtracted from gross income from the property. See subdivision (iii) of this subparagraph for the definition of the term "raw mineral product." For example, the selling expenses paid or incurred by a producer of raw mineral products with respect to products such as crude oil, raw gas, coal, iron ore, or crushed dolomite shall be subtracted from gross income from the property.

(ii) A reasonable portion of the expenses of selling a refined, manufactured, or fabricated product shall be subtracted from gross income from the property. Such reasonable portion shall be equivalent to the typical selling expenses which are incurred by unintegrated miners or producers in the same mineral industry so as to maintain equality in the tax treatment of unintegrated miners or producers in comparison with integrated miner-manufacturers or producer-manufacturers. If unintegrated miners or producers in the same mineral industry do not typically incur any selling expenses, then no portion of the expenses of selling a refined, manufactured, or fabricated product shall be subtracted from gross income from the property when determining the taxpayer's taxable income from the property.

(iii) For purposes of this subparagraph, a product will be considered to be a raw mineral product if (in the case of oil and gas) it is sold in the immediate vicinity of the well or if (in the case of minerals other than oil and gas) it is sold under the conditions described in paragraph (b)(1) of § 1.613-4. In addition, a product will be considered to be a raw mineral product if only insubstantial value is added to the product by nonmining processes (or, in the case of oil and gas, by conversion or transportation processes). For example, in the case of a producer of crushed granite poultry grit, both bulk and bagged grit will be deemed to be a raw mineral product for purposes of the selling expense rule set forth in this subparagraph.

(iv) The term "selling expenses," for purposes of this subparagraph, includes sales management salaries, rent of sales offices, sales clerical expenses, salesmen's salaries, sales commissions and bonuses, advertising expenses, sales traveling expenses, and similar expenses, together with an allocable share of the costs of supporting services, but the term does not include delivery expenses.

(5) Taxes which are taken as a credit rather than as a deduction or which are capitalized shall not be subtracted from the gross income from the property.

(6) Trade association dues paid or incurred by a producer of crude oil or gas or a raw mineral product shall be subtracted from the gross income from the property. See subparagraph (4)(iii) of this paragraph for the definition of the term "raw mineral product." In addition, a reasonable portion of the trade association dues incurred by a producer of a refined, manufactured, or fabricated product shall also be subtracted from gross income from the property if the activities of the association relate to production, treatment and marketing of the crude oil or gas or raw mineral product. One reasonable method of allocating the trade association dues described in the preceding sentence is an allocation based on the proportion that the direct costs of mining processes and the direct costs of nonmining processes (or, in the case of oil and gas, conversion and transportation processes) bear to each other. The foregoing rules shall apply even though one of the principal purposes of an association is to advise, promote, or assist in the production, marketing, or sale of refined, manufactured, or fabricated products. For example, a reasonable portion of the trade association dues paid to an association which promotes the sale of cement, refined petroleum, or copper products shall be subtracted from gross income from the property.

T.D. 6446, 1/20/60, amend T.D. 6836, 7/14/65, T.D. 6955, 5/8/68, T.D. 7170, 3/10/72.

§ 1.613-6 Statement to be attached to return when depletion is claimed on percentage basis.

In addition to the requirements set forth in paragraph (g) of § 1.611-2, a taxpayer who claims the percentage depletion deduction under section 613 for any taxable year shall attach to his return for such year a statement setting forth in complete, summary form, with respect to each property for which such deduction is allowable, the following information:

(a) All data necessary for the determination of the "gross income from the property", as defined in § 1.613-3, including—

(1) Amounts paid as rents or royalties including amounts which the recipient treats under section 631(c).

(2) Proportion and amount of bonus excluded, and

(3) Amounts paid to holders of other interests in the mineral deposit.

(b) All additional data necessary for the determination of the "taxable income from the property (computed without the allowance for depletion)", as defined in § 1.613-4.

T.D. 6446, 1/20/60, amend T.D. 7170, 3/10/72.

§ 1.613A-0 Limitations on percentage depletion in the case of oil and gas wells; table of contents.

This section lists the paragraphs contained in §§ 1.613A-0 through 1.613A-7.

(g) Crude oil.

(h) Depletable oil quantity.

(i) Depletable natural gas quantity.

(j) Barrel.

(k) Secondary or tertiary production.

(l) Controlled group of corporations.

(m) Related person.

(n) Transfer.

(o) Transferee.

(p) Interest in proven oil or gas property.

(q) Amount disallowed.

(r) Retailer.

(s) Refiner.

T.D. 8348, 5/10/91, amend T.D. 8437, 9/23/92.

§ 1.613A-1 Post-1974 limitations on percentage depletion in case of oil and gas wells; general rule.

Except as otherwise provided in section 613A and the regulations thereunder, in the case of oil or gas which is produced after December 31, 1974, and to which gross income from the property is attributable after such year, the allowance for depletion under section 611 with respect to any oil or gas well shall be computed without regard to section 613. In the case of a taxable year beginning before January 1, 1975, and ending after that date, the percentage depletion allowance (but not the cost depletion allowance) with respect to oil and gas wells for such taxable year shall be determined by treating the portion thereof in 1974 as if it were a short taxable year for purposes of section 613 and the portion thereof in 1975 as if it were a short taxable year for purposes of section 613A.

T.D. 7487, 5/12/77.

§ 1.613A-2 Exemption for certain domestic gas wells.

(a) The allowance for depletion under section 611 shall be computed in accordance with section 613 with respect to:

(1) Regulated natural gas (as defined in paragraph (c) of § 1.613A-7),

(2) Natural gas sold under a fixed contract (as defined in paragraph (d) of § 1.613A-7), and

(3) Any geothermal deposit in the United States or in a possession of the United States that is determined to be a gas well within the meaning of former section 613(b)(1)(A) (as in effect before enactment of the Tax Reduction Act of 1975) for taxable years ending after December 31, 1974, and before October 1, 1978 (see section 613(e) for depletion on geothermal deposits thereafter),

and 22 percent shall be deemed to be specified in section 613(b) for purposes of section 613(a).

(b) For taxable years ending after September 30, 1978, the allowance for depletion under section 611 shall be computed in accordance with section 613 with respect to any qualified natural gas from geopressured brine (as defined in paragraph (e) of § 1.613A-7), and 10 percent shall be deemed to be specified in section 613(b) for purposes of section 613(a).

(c) For special rules applicable to partnerships, S corporations, trusts, and estates, see paragraphs (e), (f), and (g) of § 1.613A-3.

(d) The provisions of this section may be illustrated by the following examples:

Example (1). A is a producer of natural gas which is sold by A under a contract in effect on February 1, 1975. The contract provides for an increase in the price of the gas sold under the contract to the highest price paid to a producer for natural gas in the area. The gas sold by A qualifies under section 613A(b)(1)(B) for percentage depletion as gas sold under a fixed contract until its price increases, but is presumed not to qualify thereafter unless A demonstrates by clear and convincing evidence that the price increase in no event takes increases in tax liabilities into account.

Example (2). B is a producer of natural gas which is sold by B under a contract in effect on February 1, 1975. The contract provides that beginning January 1, 1980, the price of the gas may be renegotiated. Such a provision does not disqualify gas from qualifying for the exemption under section 613A(b)(1)(B) with respect to the gas sold prior to January 1, 1980. However, gas sold on or after January 1, 1980, does not qualify for the exemption whether or not the price of the gas is renegotiated.

T.D. 8348, 5/10/91, amend T.D. 8437, 9/23/92.

§ 1.613A-3 Exemption for independent producers and royalty owners.

Caution: The Treasury has not yet amended Reg § 1.613A-3 to reflect changes made by P.L. 106-170.

(a) General rules. *(1)* Except as provided in section 613A(d) and § 1.613A-4, the allowance for depletion under section 611 with respect to oil or gas which is produced after December 31, 1974, and to which gross income from the property is attributable after that date, shall be computed in accordance with section 613 with respect to:

(i) So much of the taxpayer's average daily production (as defined in paragraph (f) of § 1.613A-7) of domestic crude oil (as defined in paragraphs (a) and (g) of § 1.613A-7) as does not exceed the taxpayer's depletable oil quantity (as defined in paragraph (h) of § 1.613A-7), and

(ii) So much of the taxpayer's average daily production of domestic natural gas (as defined in paragraphs (a) and (b) of § 1.613A-7) as does not exceed the taxpayer's depletable natural gas quantity (as defined in paragraph (i) of § 1.613A-7), and the applicable percentage (determined in accordance with the table in paragraph (c) of this section shall be deemed to be specified in section 613(b) for purposes of section 613(a).

(2) Except as provided in section 613A(d) and § 1.613A-4, the allowance for depletion under section 611 with respect to oil or gas which is produced after December 31, 1974, and to which gross income from the property is attributable after that date and before January 1, 1984, shall be computed in accordance with section 613 with respect to:

(i) So much of the taxpayer's average daily secondary or tertiary production (as defined in paragraph (k) of § 1.613A-7) of domestic crude oil as does not exceed the taxpayer's depletable oil quantity (determined without regard to section 613A(c)(3)(A)(ii), as in effect prior to the Revenue Reconciliation Act of 1990), and

(ii) So much of the taxpayer's average daily secondary or tertiary production of domestic natural gas as does not exceed the taxpayer's depletable natural gas quantity (determined without regard to section 613A(c)(3)(A)(ii), as in effect prior to the Revenue Reconciliation Act of 1990), and 22 percent shall be deemed to be specified in section 613(b) for purposes of section 613(a).

(3) For purposes of this section, there shall not be taken into account any production with respect to which percentage depletion is allowed pursuant to section 613A(b) or is not allowable by reason of section 613A(c)(9), as in effect prior to the Revenue Reconciliation Act of 1990.

(4) The provisions of this paragraph may be illustrated by the following examples:

Example (1). A, a calendar year taxpayer, owns an oil producing property with 100,000 barrels of production to which income was attributable for 1975 and a gas producing property with 1,200,000,000 cubic feet of production to which income was attributable for 1975. Under section 613A(c)(4), the oil equivalent of 1,200,000,000 cubic feet of gas is 200,000 barrels, bringing A's total production of oil and gas to which income was attributable for 1975 to the equivalent of 300,000 barrels of oil. A's average daily production was 821.92 barrels (300,000 barrels ÷ 365 days) which is less than the depletable oil quantity (2,000 barrels) before reduction for any election by A under section 613A(c)(4). Accordingly, A may make an election with respect to A's entire gas production and thereby be entitled to percentage depletion with respect to A's entire 1975 income from production of oil and gas. A's allowable depletion pursuant to section 613A(c) for A's oil and gas properties would be the amount determined under section 613(a) computed at the 22 percent rate specified in section 613A(c)(5), as in effect prior to the Revenue Reconciliation Act 1990, for 1975.

Example (2). B, a calendar year taxpayer, owns oil producing properties with 365,000 barrels of production to which income was attributable for 1975. B was a retailer of oil and gas for only the last 3 months of 1975. B's average daily production for 1975 was 1,000 barrels (365,000 barrels ÷ 365 days).

Example (3). C, a calendar year taxpayer, owns property X with 500,000 barrels of primary production to which income was attributable for 1975 and property Y with 200,000 barrels of primary production to which income was attributable for 1975. Property Y had been transferred to C on January 1, 1975, on which date it was a proven property. Therefore, the exemption under section 613A(c)(1) does not apply to C with respect to production from property Y. In determining C's depletable oil quantity for the year, the production from property Y is not taken into account. Thus, C's average daily production for 1975 was 1,369.86 barrels (500,000 barrels ÷ 365).

Example (4). D owns an oil property with producing wells X and Y on it. In 1975 D converts well X into an injection well. Prior to the application of the secondary process, it is estimated that without the application of the process the annual production from well X would have been 50x barrels of oil and from well Y would have been 100x barrels of oil. For the taxable year in which injection is commenced production from well X is 10x barrels and from well Y is 180x barrels. Forty x barrels of oil [190x barrels of oil (actual production from the property) − 150x barrels (estimate of primary production from the property)] qualify as secondary production.

Example (5). E, a calendar year taxpayer, owns a domestic oil well which produced 100,000 barrels of oil in 1980. The proceeds from the sale of 15,000 barrels of that production are not includible in E's income until 1981. The 15,000 barrels produced in 1980 are included in E's average daily production for 1981 and excluded from such production for 1980. The tentative quantity and the percentage depletion rate for 1981 are applicable to the 15,000 barrels of oil.

(b) Phase-out table. For purposes of section 613A(c)(3)(A)(i) and § 1.613A-7(h) (relating to depletable oil quantity)—

In the case of production after 1974 and to which gross income from the property is attributable for the calendar year:	The tentative quantity in barrels per day is:
1975	2,000
1976	1,800
1977	1,600
1978	1,400
1979	1,200
1980 and thereafter	1,000

(c) Applicable percentage. For purposes of section 613A(c)(1) and paragraph (2) of this section—

In the case of production after 1974 and to which gross income from the property is attributable for the calendar year	The applicable percentage is:
1975	22
1976	22
1977	22
1978	22
1979	22
1980	22
1981	20
1982	18
1983	16
1984 and thereafter	15

(d) Production in excess of depletable quantity. *(1) Primary production.* (i) If the taxpayer's average daily production of domestic crude oil exceeds his depletable oil quantity, the allowance for depletion pursuant to section 613A(c)(1)(A) and paragraph (a)(1)(i) of this section with respect to oil produced during the taxable year from each property in the United States shall be that amount which bears the same ratio to the amount of depletion which would have been allowable under section 613(a) for all of the taxpayer's oil produced from the property during the taxable year (computed as if section 613 applied to all of the production at the rate specified in paragraph (c) of this section) as the amount of his depletable oil quantity bears to the aggregate number of barrels representing the average daily production of domestic crude oil of the taxpayer for such year.

(ii) If the taxpayer's average daily production of domestic natural gas exceeds his depletable natural gas quantity, the allowance for depletion pursuant to section 613A(c)(1)(B) and paragraph (a)(1)(ii) of this section with respect to natural gas produced during the taxable year from each property in the United States shall be that amount which bears the same ratio to the amount of depletion which would have been allowable pursuant to section 613(a) for all of the taxpayer's natural gas produced from the property during the taxable year (computed as if section 613 applied to all of the production at the rate specified in paragraph (c) of this section) as the amount of his depletable natural gas quantity in cubic feet bears to the aggregate number of cubic feet representing the average daily production of domestic natural gas of the taxpayer for such year.

(2) Secondary or tertiary production. (i) If the taxpayer's average daily secondary or tertiary production of domestic crude oil exceeds his depletable oil quantity (determined

without regard to section 613A(c)(3)(A)(ii), as in effect prior to the Revenue Reconciliation Act of 1990), the allowance for depletion pursuant to section 613A(c)(6)(A)(i), as in effect prior to the Revenue Reconciliation Act of 1990, and paragraph (a)(2)(i) of this section with respect to oil produced during the taxable year from each property in the United States shall be that amount which bears the same ratio to the amount of depletion which would have been allowable pursuant to section 613(a) for all of the taxpayer's secondary or tertiary production of oil from the property during the taxable year (computed as if section 613 applied to all of the production at the rate specified in paragraph (a)(2) of this section) as the amount of his depletable oil quantity (determined without regard to section 613A(c)(3)(A)(ii), as in effect prior to the Revenue Reconciliation Act of 1990) bears to the aggregate number of barrels representing the average daily secondary or tertiary production of domestic crude oil of the taxpayer for such year.

(ii) If the taxpayer's average daily secondary or tertiary production of domestic natural gas exceeds his depletable natural gas quantity (determined without regard to section 613A(c)(3)(A)(ii), as in effect prior to the Revenue Reconciliation Act of 1990), the allowance for depletion pursuant to section 613A(c)(6)(A)(ii), as in effect prior to the Revenue Reconciliation Act of 1990, and paragraph (a)(2)(ii) of this section with respect to natural gas produced during the taxable year from each property in the United states shall be that amount which bears the same ratio to the amount of depletion which would have been allowable pursuant to section 613(a) for all of the taxpayer's secondary or tertiary production of natural gas from the property during the taxable year (computed as if section 613 applied to all of the production at the rate specified in paragraph (a)(2) of this section) as the amount of his depletable natural gas quantity in cubic feet (determined without regard to section 613A(c)(3)(A)(ii), as in effect prior to the Revenue Reconciliation Act of 1990) bears to the aggregate number of cubic feet representing the average daily secondary or tertiary production of domestic natural gas of the taxpayer for such year.

(iii) This paragraph (d)(2) shall not apply after December 31, 1983.

(3) Taxable income from the property. If both oil and gas are produced from the property during the taxable year, then for purposes of section 613A(c)(7)(A) and (B) and paragraph (d) of this section the taxable income from the property, in applying the taxable income limitation in section 613(a), shall be allocated between the oil production and the gas production in proportion to the gross income from the property during the taxable year from each. If both gas with respect to which section 613A(b) and § 1.613A-2 apply and oil or gas with respect to which section 613A(c) and this section apply are produced from the property during the taxable year, then for purposes of section 613A(d)(1) and paragraph (a) of § 1.613A-4 the taxable income from the property, in applying the taxable income limitation in section 613(a), shall also be so allocated. In addition, if both primary production and secondary or tertiary production (to which gross income from the property is attributable before January 1, 1984) are produced from the property during the taxable year and the total amount of production is in excess of the depletable quantity, then for purposes of paragraph (d) of this section the taxable income from the property, in applying the taxable income limitation in section 613(a), shall also be so allocated.

(4) Examples. The application of this paragraph may be illustrated by the following examples:

Example (1). A owns Y and Z oil producing properties. With respect to properties Y and Z, the percentage depletion allowable pursuant to section 613(a) (computed as if section 613 applied to all of the production at the rate specified in section 613A(c)(5)) for 1975 was 5100x and 5200x, respectively. A's average daily production for 1975 was 4,000 barrels. A's allowable depletion pursuant to section 613A(c) with respect to property Y was $50x: [$100x depletion (2,000 depletable oil quantity/4,000 average daily production)]. A's allowable depletion pursuant to section 613A(c) with respect to property Z was $100x ($200x depletion × 2,000 depletable oil quantity/4,000 average daily production).

Example (2). B owns gas producing properties which had secondary gas production for 1975 of 3,285,000,000 cubic feet, which under section 613A(c)(4) is equivalent to 547,500 barrels of oil. B's average daily secondary production of gas for 1975 was equivalent to 1,500 barrels (547,500 barrels ÷ 365). B elected to have section 613A(c)(4) apply to the gas production. With respect to the production, the percentage depletion allowable pursuant to section 613(a) (computed at the rate specified in section 613A(c)(6)(A), as in effect prior to the Revenue Reconciliation Act of 1990) was $150x. B also owns an oil producing property which had primary oil production for 1975 of 365,000 barrels. B's average daily production of oil for 1975 was 1,000 barrels (365,000 ÷ 365). With respect to the oil property, the percentage depletion allowable pursuant to section 613(a) (computed as if section 613 applied to all of the production at the rate specified in section 613A(c)(5), as in effect prior to the Revenue Reconciliation Act of 1990) was $100x. B's depletable oil quantity for 1975 was 500 barrels (2,000 barrels tentative quantity − 1,500 barrels average daily secondary production). B's allowable depletion pursuant to section 613A(c) with respect to the oil property was $50x ($100x depletion x 500 depletable oil quantity/1,000 average daily production).

Example (3). Assume the same facts as in Example 2 except that B's primary production was 6,000,000 cubic feet of natural gas daily rather than its equivalent under section 613A(c)(4) of 1,000 barrels of oil and that B elected to have that section apply to such gas. B's allowable depletion pursuant to section 613A(c) with respect to B's primary production is $50x, the same as in example (2).

Example (4). C is a partner with a one-third interest in partnerships CDE and CFG with each partnership owning a single oil property. C's percentage depletion allowable under section 613(a) (computed as if section 613 applied to all of the production at the rate specified in section 613A(c)(5), as in effect prior to the Revenue Reconciliation Act of 1990) for 1975 was $20x with respect to 495,000 barrels (his allocable share of Partnership CDE production) and $40x with respect to 600,000 barrels (his allocable share of partnership CFG production). C's average daily production is 3,000 barrels (1,095,000 total production ÷ 365 days). C's allowable depletion pursuant to section 613A(c) with respect to C's share of the production of partnership CDE is $13.33x ($20x depletion x 2,000 depletable oil quantity/3,000 average daily production). C's allowable depletion pursuant to section 613A(c) with respect to C's share of the production of partnership CFG is $26.67x ($40x depletion × 2,000 depletable oil quantity/3,000 average daily production). See § 1.613A-3(e) for the rules on computing depletion in the case of a partnership.

Example (5). H owns a property which, during H's fiscal year which began on June 1, 1975, and ended on May 31,

1976, produced gas qualifying under section 613A(b) and oil qualifying under section 613A(c). For the fiscal year H's gross income from the property was $400x, of which $100x was from gas and $300x was from oil. For the oil his gross income from the property for the period beginning June 1, 1975, and ending December 31, 1975, was $100x and for the 1976 portion of the fiscal year was $200x. The percentage depletion allowance (before applying the 50 percent limitation of section 613(a) or the 65 percent limitation of section 613A(d)(1)) was $22x for the gas, $22x for the oil in 1975, and $44x for the oil in 1976. H's taxable income from the property for the fiscal year was $100x. In accordance with paragraph (d)(3) of this section, the taxable income from the property is allocated $25x to the gas:

$$[\$100x \text{ taxable income from the property} \left(\frac{\$100x \text{ gross income from gas from the property}}{\$400x \text{ total gross income from the property}}\right)$$

$25x to the 1975 oil:

$$[\$100x \text{ taxable income from the property} \left(\frac{\$100x \text{ gross income from 1975 oil from the property}}{\$400x \text{ total gross income from the property}}\right)$$

and $50x to the 1976 oil:

$$[\$100x \text{ taxable income from the property} \left(\frac{\$200x \text{ gross income from 1976 oil from the property}}{\$400x \text{ total gross income from the property}}\right)$$

With the application of the 50 percent of taxable income from the property limitation, the allowable percentage depletion (computed without reference to section 613A) is limited to $12.50x for the gas, $12.50x for the oil in 1975, and $25x for the oil in 1976.

(e) Partnerships. *(1) General rule.* In the case of a partnership, the depletion allowance under section 611 with respect to production from domestic oil and gas properties shall be computed separately by the partners and not by the partnership. The determination of whether cost or percentage depletion is applicable is to be made at the partner level. The partnership must allocate to each partner the partner's proportionate share of the adjusted basis of each partnership oil or gas property in accordance with the provisions of paragraphs (e)(2) through (e)(6) of this section. This allocation of the adjusted basis of oil or gas property does not affect a partner's adjusted basis in his or her partnership interest.

(2) Initial allocation of adjusted basis of oil or gas property among partners. (i) General rule. Each partner shall be allocated his or her proportionate share of the adjusted basis of each partnership domestic oil or gas property. The initial allocation of adjusted basis is to be made as of the later of the date of acquisition of the oil or gas property by the partnership or January 1, 1975.

(ii) Allocation methods. Except as otherwise provided in paragraph (e)(5) of this section, the provisions of this paragraph (e)(2)(ii) govern the determination under paragraph (e)(2)(i) of this section of a partner's proportionate share of the adjusted basis of oil or gas property. Each partner's proportionate share is determined in accordance with the partner's proportionate interest in partnership capital at the time of the allocation unless both—

(A) The partnership agreement provides that a partner's share of the adjusted basis of one or more properties is determined in accordance with his or her proportionate interest in partnership income; and

(B) At the time of allocation under the partnership agreement the share of each partner in partnership income is reasonably expected to be substantially unchanged throughout the life of the partnership, other than changes merely to reflect the admission of a new partner, an increase in a partner's interest in consideration for money, property, or services, or a partial or complete withdrawal of an existing partner. If the requirements of paragraph (e)(2)(ii)(A) and (B) of this section are met, a partner's proportionate share is determined in accordance with his or her proportionate interest in partnership income. The partners' shares of adjusted basis are determined on a property-by-property basis. Accordingly, the basis of one property may be allocated in proportion to capital and the basis of another property may be allocated in proportion to income. See §§ 1.613A-3(e)(5) and 1.704-1(b)(4)(v) for special rules concerning allocation of the adjusted basis of oil and gas properties.

(3) Adjustments by partnership to allocated adjusted bases. (i) Capital expenditures by partnership. Appropriate adjustments shall be made to the partners' adjusted bases in any domestic oil and gas property for any partnership capital expenditures relating to such property that are made after the initial allocation. These adjustments shall be allocated among the partners in accordance with the principles set forth in paragraph (e)(2)(ii) of this section.

(ii) Admission of a new partner or increase in partner's interest. (A) In general. Upon a contribution of money, other property, or services to the partnership by a new or existing partner ("contributing partner") as consideration for an interest in the partnership, the partnership shall allocate, in accordance with paragraph (e)(3)(ii)(B) of this section, a share of the partnership's basis in each existing oil and gas property to the contributing partner, and each existing partner shall reduce, in accordance with paragraph (e)(3)(ii)(C) of this section, his or her share of the partnership's basis in such property.

(B) Allocation of basis to contributing partner. The partnership shall allocate to a contributing partner his or her proportionate share (determined under paragraph (e)(2)(ii) of this section in accordance with the partner's proportionate interest in partnership capital or income) of the partnership's adjusted basis in each existing partnership oil or gas property. For purposes of this allocation, the partnership's adjusted basis in such property equals the aggregate of its partners' adjusted bases in the property, as determined under paragraph (e)(3)(iii) of this section.

(C) Reduction of existing partners' bases. Each existing partner's basis in each existing partnership oil or gas property is reduced by the percentage of the partnership's aggregate basis in the property that is allocated to the contributing partner. Thus, if one third of the partnership's aggregate basis in a property is allocated to a contributing partner because the contributing partner has a one-third interest in partnership capital, after the admission of the contributing partner each existing partner's basis (including the contributing partner's pre-existing basis if such partner is also an existing partner) in each property equals the partner's basis (prior to the admission) reduced by one-third.

(iii) Determination of aggregate of partners' adjusted bases in the property. (A) In general. To determine the aggregate of its partners' adjusted bases for purposes of this paragraph (e)(3), the partnership must determine each partner's adjusted basis under either paragraph (e)(3)(iii)(B) (written data) or paragraph (e)(3)(iii)(C) (assumptions) of this section. The partnership is permitted to determine the bases of some partners under paragraph (e)(3)(iii)(B) of this section and of others under paragraph (e)(3)(iii)(C) of this section. For this purpose, a partner's basis in an oil or gas property does not include any basis adjustment under section 743(b).

(B) Written data. A partnership may determine a partner's basis in an oil or gas property by using written data provided by a partner stating the amount of the partner's adjusted basis or depletion deductions with respect to the property unless the partnership knows or has reason to know that the written data is inaccurate. In determining depletion deductions, a partner must treat as actually deducted any amount disallowed and carried over as a result of the 65 percent-of-income limitation of section 613A(d)(1). If a partnership does not receive written data upon which it may rely, the partnership must use the assumptions provided in paragraph (e)(3)(iii)(C) of this section in determining a partner's adjusted basis in an oil or gas property.

(C) Assumptions. Except as provided in paragraph (e)(3)(iv)(B) of this section, a partnership that does not use written data pursuant to paragraph (e)(3)(iii)(B) of this section to determine a partner's basis must use the following assumptions to determine the partner's adjusted basis in an oil or gas property:

(1) The partner deducted his or her share of deductions under section 263(c) in the first year in which the partner could claim a deduction for such amounts, unless the partnership elected to capitalize such amounts;

(2) The partner was not subject to the 65 percent-of-income limitation of section 613A(d)(1) with respect to the partner's depletion allowance under section 611; and

(3) The partner was not subject to the following limitations, with respect to the partner's depletion allowance under section 611, except to the extent a limitation applied at the partnership level: the taxable income limitation of section 613(a); the depletable quantity limitations of section 613A(c); the prohibition against claiming percentage depletion on transferred proven property under section 613A(c)(9), prior to its repeal; or the limitations of section 613A(d)(2), (3), and (4) (exclusion of retailers and refiners).

(iv) Withdrawal of partner or decrease in partner's interest. (A) In general. Upon a distribution of money or other property to a withdrawing partner as consideration for an interest in the partnership, the withdrawing partner's adjusted basis in each domestic oil or gas property that continues to be held by the partnership is allocated to the remaining partners in proportion to their proportionate interest in partnership capital or income after taking into account any increase or decrease as a result of the event giving rise to the reallocation. A similar rule shall apply in the case of a diminution of a continuing partner's interest in the partnership.

(B) Special rule for determining a withdrawing partner's basis in the property. If a partnership is required to determine a withdrawing partner's adjusted basis using the assumptions under paragraph (e)(3)(iii)(C) of this section, the partnership may rebut the assumption in paragraph (e)(3)(iii)(C)(3) of this section that the withdrawing partner was not subject to the limitations of sections 613A(d)(2), (3), and (4) (exclusion of retailers and refiners) by demonstrating that the withdrawing partner was subject to the limitations of sections 613A(d)(2), (3), or (4).

(v) Effective date. The provisions of § 1.613A-3(e)(3)(i) through (iv) are effective for taxable years beginning after May 13, 1991. However, a partnership may elect to apply these provisions to taxable years beginning on or before May 13, 1991.

(4) Determination of a partner's interest in partnership capital or income. For purposes of this paragraph (e), a partner's interest in partnership capital or income is determined by taking into account all facts and circumstances relating to the economic arrangement of the partners. See the factors listed in § 1.704-1(b)(3)(ii).

(5) Special rules on allocation of adjusted basis to partners. An allocation or reallocation of the adjusted basis of oil or gas property is pursuant to this paragraph (e) of this section deemed to be in accordance with the partner's proportionate interest in partnership capital or income for purposes of this paragraph (e) where so provided in § 1.704-1(b)(4)(v). In addition, in connection with a revaluation described in § 1.704-1(b)(2)(iv)(f), the basis of an oil or gas property is allocated among the partners based on the principles used under § 1.704-1(b)(4)(i) of allocating tax items to take into account variations between the adjusted basis of the property and its fair market value. In the case of an oil or gas property contributed to a partnership by a partner, section 704(c) is taken into account in determining the partner's share of the adjusted basis.

(6) Miscellaneous rules. (i) Each partner must separately keep records of his or her share of the adjusted basis in each domestic oil or gas property of the partnership, adjust his or her share of such basis pursuant to section 1016 (including adjustments for any depletion allowed or allowable with respect to such property), and use that adjusted basis each year in the computation of his or her cost depletion or in the computation of his or her gain or loss on the disposition (including abandonment) of the property by the partnership.

(ii) The adjusted basis of a partner's interest in a partnership is decreased (but not below zero) pursuant to section 705(a)(3) by the amount of the depletion deduction allowed or allowable to the partner with respect to a domestic oil or gas property to the extent such deduction does not exceed the proportionate share of the adjusted basis of such property allocated to the partner under section 613A(c)(7)(D), as adjusted by the partner after the initial allocation. Section 705(a)(1)(C) does not apply to depletion deductions that are not included in a partner's distributive share under section 702. Accordingly, the adjusted basis of a partner's interest in a partnership is not increased under section 705(a)(1)(C) with respect to depletion of oil or gas properties. See § 1.705-1(a)(2)(iii).

(iii) Upon the disposition of an oil or gas property by the partnership, each partner must subtract the partner's adjusted basis in the property from his or her allocable portion of the amount realized from the sale of the property to determine gain or loss. The partner's allocable portion of amount realized must, except to the extent governed by section 704(c) (or related principles under § 1.704-1(b)(4)(i)), be determined in accordance with § 1.704-1(b)(4)(v). Except as otherwise provided (e.g., section 751), the sale of a partnership interest is not treated as a sale of an oil and gas property.

(iv) In the case of a transfer of an interest in a partnership, the transferor partner's adjusted basis in each partnership oil or gas property carries over to the transferee partner. If an election under section 754 (relating to optional adjustment to the basis of partnership property) is in effect, such basis is adjusted in accordance with section 743.

(v) For purposes of section 732 (relating to basis of distributed property other than money) and section 734(b) (relating to optional adjustment to basis of partnership property), the partnership's adjusted basis in oil and gas property is an amount equal to the aggregate of its partners' adjusted bases in the property as determined under the rules provided in paragraph (e)(3) of this section.

(7) Examples. The provisions of this paragraph may be illustrated by the following examples:

Example (1). A, B, and C have equal interests in capital in Partnership ABC. On January 1, 1992, the partnership acquired a producing domestic oil property. The partnership's basis in the property was $90x. The partnership allocated the adjusted basis of the property to each partner in proportion to the partner's interest in partnership capital. Accordingly, each partner was allocated an adjusted basis of $30x. Each partner must separately compute his or her depletion allowance. The amount of percentage depletion allowable for each partner for 1992 was $10x. On January 1, 1993, each partner's adjusted basis in the property was $20x ($30x minus $10x). On January 1, 1993, the oil property was sold for $150x. Each partner's gain was $30x ($50x allocable share of amount realized minus the partner's adjusted basis of $20x). Each partner must adjust the partner's adjusted basis in his or her partnership interest to reflect the gain.

Example (2). The facts are the same as in Example 1 except that on January 1, 1993, the property was not sold but transferred by the partnership to partner A. A's basis in the property was $60x (the sum of A's, B's, and C's adjusted bases in the property).

Example (3). The facts are the same as in Example 1 with the exception that in 1992 C was a retailer of oil and gas and was only entitled to a cost depletion deduction of $5x. C's gain from the sale of the mineral property on January 1, 1993, was $25x ($50x allocable share of amount realized minus C's adjusted basis of $25x ($30x minus $5x)).

Example (4). D, a calendar year taxpayer, is a partner in Partnership DEF which owns a domestic producing oil property. On January 1, 1993, the partnership's adjusted basis in the property was $900x. On January 1, 1993, D's adjusted basis in D's partnership interest was $300x and D's adjusted basis in the partnership's oil property was $300x. D's allowable percentage depletion for 1993 with respect to production from the oil property was $50x. On January 1, 1994, D's adjusted basis in D's partnership interest was $250x and D's adjusted basis in the partnership's oil property was $250x ($300x minus $50x).

Example (5). On January 1, 1990, G has an adjusted basis of $5x in partnership GH's proven domestic oil property, which is the sole asset of the partnership. On January 1, 1990 G sells G's partnership interest to I for $100x when the election under section 754 is in effect. I has a special basis adjustment for the oil property of $95x (the difference between I's basis, $100x, and I's share of the basis of the partnership property, $5x). I is not entitled to percentage depletion with respect to I's distributive share of the oil property income because I is a transferee of an interest in a proven oil property. However, I is entitled to cost depletion and for this purpose I's interest in the oil property has an adjusted basis to I of $100x ($5x, plus I's special basis adjustment of $95x).

Example (6). On January 1, 1960, Partnership JK acquired a domestic producing oil property. On January 1, 1990, the partnership's adjusted basis in the property was zero. On January 1, 1990, L is admitted as a partner to the partnership. Since the partnership's adjusted basis in the oil property is zero, L's proportionate share of the basis in the property is also zero. L is not entitled to percentage depletion because L is a transferee of a proven oil property (see paragraph (g) of this section). Since the property's basis is zero, L is also not entitled to any cost depletion with respect to production from the property.

Example (7). (i) O and P have equal interests in capital in Partnership OP. On January 1, 1991, the partnership acquired an unproven domestic oil property X the basis of which is $200x to the partnership. The partnership allocates $100x of the basis of the property to each partner in accordance with each partner's proportionate interest in partnership capital. For the 1991 taxable year, O has a $10x cost depletion allowance and P has a $25x percentage depletion allowance. Accordingly, at the end of the 1991 taxable year, O's adjusted basis in the property is $90x, and P's adjusted basis in the property is $75x. On January 1, 1992, Q is admitted as an equal partner. The partnership does not use written data from the partners and must therefore assume that each partner was entitled to $25x depletion based on the assumptions provided in § 1.613A-3(e)(3)(iii). This would result in a $50x combined depletion allowance for the partners and an aggregate adjusted basis in the oil property of $150x. Accordingly, the partnership allocates $50x of the basis of the property to Q, one-third of the aggregate adjusted basis determined by the partnership. O and P must each reduce their basis in the property by one-third. Accordingly, after the admission of Q, O's adjusted basis in the property is $60x ($90x minus $30x), and P's adjusted basis in the property is $50x ($75x minus $25x).

(ii) Assume the same facts as in paragraph (i) of this Example 7 except that O informs the partnership that its adjusted basis in the property is $90x (determined without regard to section 613A(d)(1)). The partnership uses the written data provided by O and determines the aggregate adjusted basis in the property to be $165x ($90x + $75X). Accordingly, the partnership allocates $55x (⅓ of $165x) of the basis of the property to Q, and O and P must each reduce their adjusted basis in the property by one-third, as in paragraph (i) of this Example 7. Thus, after the admission of Q, O's adjusted basis in the property is $60x and P's adjusted basis in the property is $50x.

(f) S corporations. For purposes of section 613A(c)(13), adjustments to shareholders' adjusted bases in any domestic oil or gas property to reflect capital expenditures by S corporations, the addition of a new shareholder or an increase in a shareholder's interest by reason of a contribution to the S corporation, the redemption of a shareholder's interest, or other appropriate transaction shall be made in accordance with principles similar to the principles under § 1.613A-3(e) applicable to the entry or withdrawal of a partner.

(g) Trusts and estates. *(1)* In the case of production from domestic oil and gas properties held by a trust or estate, the depletion allowance under section 611 shall be computed initially by the trust or estate. The determination of whether cost or percentage depletion is applicable shall be made at the trust or estate level, but such determination shall not result in the disallowance of cost depletion to a beneficiary of a trust or estate for whom cost depletion exceeds percentage depletion. The limitations contained in section 613A(c) and (d), other than section 613A(d)(1), shall be applied at the trust or estate level in its computation of percentage depletion pursuant to section 613A and shall also be applied by a beneficiary with respect to any percentage depletion apportioned to the beneficiary by the trust or estate. The limitation of section 613A(d)(1) shall be applied by each taxpayer (i.e., trust, estate or beneficiary) only with respect to its allocable share of percentage depletion under section 611(b)(3) or (4). For purposes of adjustments to the basis of oil or gas properties held by a trust or estate, in the absence of clear and convincing evidence to the contrary, it shall be presumed that no beneficiary is affected by any section 613A(d) limitations or by the rules contained in section 613A(c)(8) and (9) (relating to businesses under common control and members of the same family and to transfers, respectively), as in effect prior to the Revenue Reconciliation Act of 1990, or has any oil or gas production from sources other than the trust or estate.

(2) The provisions of this paragraph may be illustrated by the following examples.

Example (1). A is the income beneficiary of a trust the only asset of which is a domestic producing oil property. The trust instrument requires that an amount which equals 10 percent of the gross income from the property be set aside annually as a reserve for depletion. In 1975 the property had production of 1,095,000 barrels of oil. The trust's gross income from the property in 1975 was $30,000x. In that year, after setting aside $3,000x of income for the reserve for depletion, the trustee distributed the remaining income to A which represented 80 percent of the trust's net income. The percentage depletion computed by the trust with respect to the production (computed as if section 613 applied to all of the production at the rate specified in section 613A(c)(5), as in effect prior to the Revenue Reconciliation Act of 1990) for 1975 was $6,600x. The trust's average daily production for 1975 was 3,000 barrels (1,095,000 ÷ 365 days). The trust's allowable depletion pursuant to section 613A(c) with respect to the production was $4,400x:

$$\$6{,}600x \text{ depletion} \left(\frac{2{,}000 \text{ depletable oil quantity}}{3{,}000 \text{ average daily production}} \right)$$

Pursuant to § 1.611-1(c)(4)(ii), the percentage depletion of $4,400x was apportioned between the trustee and A so that the trustee received $3,000x (an amount equal to the amount of income set aside for the reserve for depletion) and A received $1,400x of the depletion deduction. The $1,400x depletion received by A is attributable to 80 percent of the trust's depletable oil quantity, i.e., 1,600 barrels per day.

Example (2). B, a retailer of oil and gas, is the income beneficiary of a trust the only asset of which is a domestic producing oil property. In 1975 the trustee distributed one-half of the trust's net income and accumulated the other one-half for the benefit of the remainderman. One-half of the percentage depletion computed by the trust with respect to the production from the property was apportioned to B. Since B is a retailer of oil and gas, B is not entitled to deduct any of the percentage depletion apportioned to B. However, B is entitled to take cost depletion with respect to one-half of the production from the oil property, notwithstanding the fact that depletion was computed at the trust level on the basis of percentage depletion.

(h) Businesses under common control; members of the same family. *(1) Component members of a controlled group.* For purposes of only the depletable quantity limitations contained in section 613A(c) and this section, component members of a controlled group of corporations (as defined in paragraph (1) of § 1.613A-7) shall be treated as one taxpayer. Accordingly, the group shares the depletable oil (or natural gas) quantity prescribed for a taxpayer for the taxable year and the secondary production (to which gross income from the property is attributable before January 1, 1984) of a member of the group will reduce the other members' share of the group's depletable quantity.

(2) Aggregation of business entities under common control. If 50 percent or more of the beneficial interest in any two or more entities (i.e., corporations, trusts, or estates) is owned by the same or related persons (taking into account only each person who owns at least 5 percent of the beneficial interest in an entity and with respect to such person his or her entire interest) as defined in paragraph (m)(2) of § 1.613A-7, the tentative quantity determined under the table in section 613A(c)(3)(B) (as in effect prior to the Revenue Reconciliation Act of 1990) for a taxpayer for the taxable year shall be allocated among all such entities in proportion to their respective production. This paragraph (h)(2) shall not apply to component members of a controlled group of corporations (as defined in § 1.613A-7(1)). For purposes of determining ownership interest, an interest owned by or for a corporation, partnership, trust, or estate shall be considered as owned directly both by itself and proportionately by its shareholders, partners, or beneficiaries, as the case may be.

(3) Allocation among members of the same family. In the case of individuals who are members of the same family, the tentative quantity determined under the table in section 613A(c)(3)(B) (as in effect prior to the Revenue Reconciliation Act of 1990) for a taxpayer for the taxable year shall be allocated among such individuals in proportion to the respective production of barrels of domestic crude oil (and the equivalent in barrels to the cubic feet of natural gas determined under paragraph (h)(4)(ii) of this section) during the period in question by such individuals.

(4) Special rules. For purposes of section 613A(c)(8) and this section—

(i) The family of an individual includes only his spouse and minor children, and

(ii) Each 6,000 cubic feet of domestic natural gas shall be treated as 1 barrel of domestic crude oil.

(5) Examples. The application of this paragraph may be illustrated by the following examples:

Example (1). A owns 50 percent of the stock of Corporation M and 50 percent of the stock of Corporation N. Both corporations are calendar year taxpayers. For 1975 Corporation M's production of domestic crude oil was 8,000,000 barrels (365,000 of which was secondary production) and Corporation N's was 2,000,000 barrels (all of which was primary production). The tentative quantity (2,000 barrels per day) determined under the table in section 613A(c)(3)(B) (as in effect prior to the Revenue Reconciliation Act of 1990) must be allocated between the two corporations in proportion to their respective barrels of production of domestic crude oil during the taxable year. Corporation M's allocable share of the tentative quantity is 1,600 barrels:

$$2{,}000 \left(\frac{8{,}000{,}000}{10{,}000{,}000} \right)$$

and Corporation N's allocable share is 400 barrels:

$$2{,}000 \left(\frac{2{,}000{,}000}{10{,}000{,}000} \right)$$

With respect to M's primary production, M's depletable oil quantity is 600 barrels (1,600 barrels − 1,000 barrels

[365,000 secondary production ÷ 365 days]). N's depletable oil quantity, unaffected by M's secondary production, is 400 barrels.

Example (2). Assume the same facts as in Example 1 except that Corporation M is a retailer and Corporation N is not selling its oil through Corporation M. Because Corporation M is a retailer, no portion of the tentative quantity is allocated to Corporation M. Accordingly, Corporation N's depletable oil quantity is the entire 2,000 barrels per day because section 613A(c), which contains the allocation requirements, is inapplicable to retailers.

Example (3). Corporations O and P are members of a controlled group and are treated as one taxpayer as provided in paragraph (h)(1) of this section. Corporation O owns oil properties A and B. Property A had primary production for 1975 of 800,000 barrels of oil. Property B had secondary production for 1975 of 365,000 barrels of oil. Corporation P owns oil property C which had primary production of 660,000 barrels for 1975. The allowable percentage depletion with respect to property B's secondary production was $360x. The controlled group's average daily production was 4,000 barrels [(800,000 + 660,000) ÷ 365]. The controlled group's depletable oil quantity was 1,000 barrels [2,000 tentative quantity − 1,000 average daily secondary production (365,000 ÷ 365)]. The allowable percentage depletion pursuant to section 613(a) (computed as if section 613 applied to all of the production at the rate specified in section 613A(c)(5), as in effect prior to the Revenue Reconciliation Act of 1990) was $800x with respect to production from property A and $660x with respect to production from property C. Corporation O's allowable depletion pursuant to section 613A(c) with respect to property B's secondary production (for which depletion is allowable before primary production) for 1975 was $360x. Corporation O's allowable depletion pursuant to section 613A(c) with respect to property A was $200x:

$$\$800x \text{ depletion} \left(\frac{1{,}000 \text{ depletable oil quantity}}{4{,}000 \text{ average daily production}} \right)$$

Therefore, Corporation O's allowable depletion pursuant to section 613A(c) was $560x ($360x relating to property B plus $200x relating to property A). Corporation P's allowable depletion pursuant to section 613A(c) with respect to property C was $165x:

$$\$660x \text{ depletion} \left(\frac{1{,}000 \text{ depletable oil quantity}}{4{,}000 \text{ average daily production}} \right)$$

(i) Transfer of oil or gas property. *(1) General rule.* (i) In general. Except as provided in paragraph (i)(2) of this section, in the case of a transfer (as defined in paragraph (n) of § 1.613A-7) of an interest in any proven oil or gas property (as defined in paragraph (p) of § 1.613A-7), paragraph (a)(1) of this section shall not apply to a transferee (as defined in paragraph (o) of § 1.613A-7) with respect to production of crude oil or natural gas attributable to such interest, and such production shall not be taken into account for any computation by the transferee under this section.

(ii) Examples. The provisions of this subparagraph may be illustrated by the following examples:

Example (1). On January 1, 1975, Individual A transfers proven oil properties to Corporation M in an exchange to which section 351 applies for shares of its stock. Since there is no allocation requirement pursuant to section 613A(c)(8) between A (the transferor) and Corporation M (the transferee), the transfer of the proven properties by A is a transfer for purposes of section 613A(c)(9) (as in effect prior to the Revenue Reconciliation Act of 1990) and percentage depletion is not allowable to Corporation M with respect to such properties.

Example (2). On January 1, 1975, Corporation N sells proven oil property to Corporation O, its wholly-owned subsidiary. Because the transfer was made between corporations which are members of the same controlled group of corporations, Corporation O is entitled to percentage depletion with respect to production from the property so long as the tentative oil quantity is allocated between the two corporations. If Corporation N were a retailer, the tentative oil quantity would not be required to be allocated between the two corporations (see example (2) of § 1.613A-3(h)(5)), and Corporation O would not be entitled to percentage depletion on the production from the property.

Example (3). B, owner of a proven oil property, died on January 1, 1975. Pursuant to the provisions of B's will, B's estate transferred the oil property on April 1, 1975, into a trust. On July 1, 1976, pursuant to a requirement in B's will, the trustee distributed the oil property to C. The transfer of the oil property by the estate to the trust and the later distribution of the property by the trust to C are transfers at death. Therefore, the trust was entitled to compute percentage depletion with respect to the production from the oil property when the property was owned by the trust and C is entitled to percentage depletion with respect to production from the oil property after the trust distributes the property to C.

Example (4). On January 1, 1975, property which produces oil resulting from secondary processes was transferred to D. The exemption under section 613A(c) applies to D because section 613A(c)(9) (relating to transfers of oil or gas property), as in effect in 1975, does not apply with respect to secondary production. In addition, even if at the time of the transfer the production from the property was primary and D applied secondary processes to the property transferred and obtained secondary production, D would be entitled to percentage depletion with respect to the secondary production.

Example (5). On July 1, 1975, E and F entered into a contract whereby F is given the privilege of drilling a well on E's unproven property, and if F does so F is to own the entire working interest in the property until F has recovered all the costs of drilling, equipping, and operating the well. Thereafter, 50 percent of the working interest would revert to E. In accordance with the contract, 50 percent of the working interest reverted to E on July 1, 1976. F is entitled to percentage depletion because the transfer of the working interest to F occurred when the property was unproven on July 1, 1975, which is the date of the contract establishing F's right to the working interest. E is entitled to percentage depletion with respect to this working interest since the reversion of such interest with respect to which E was eligible for percentage depletion is not a transfer. However, if on the date of the contract E's property was proven (although not proven when E acquired the property), F would not be entitled to claim percentage depletion with respect to any of the working interest income. Nonetheless, E would still be entitled to percentage depletion with respect to E's working interest since the reversion of the interest is not a transfer.

Example (6). On January 1, 1975, G subleased an oil property to X, retaining a ⅛ royalty interest with the option to convert G's royalty into a 50 percent working interest. On July 1, 1975, the property was proven and on July 1, 1976, G exercised G's option. G is entitled to claim percentage depletion with respect to G's working interest since the conversion of the royalty interest which is eligible for percentage depletion pursuant to section 613A(c) into an interest which constituted part of an interest previously owned by G is not a transfer pursuant to § 1.613A-7(n)(8).

Example (7). I and J (both of whom are minors) are beneficiaries of a trust which owned a proven oil property. The oil property was transferred to the trust on January 1, 1975, by the father of I and J. For 1975, the trustee allocated all the income from the oil property to I. For 1976, the trustee allocated all the income from such property to J. On January 1, 1977, the trustee distributed the property to I and J as equal tenants in common. Since I, J, and their father are members of the same family within the meaning of section 613A(c)(8)(C), the transfer of the property to the trust by the father, the shifting of income between I and J, and the distribution of the oil property by the trust to I and J are not transfers for purposes of section 613A(c)(9) (as in effect prior to the Revenue Reconciliation Act of 1990). However, the distribution of the oil property will constitute a transfer to each distributee on the date on which the distributee reaches majority under state law.

Example (8). In 1975, K transferred a proven oil property productive at 5,000 feet to L. Subsequent to the transfer, L drilled new wells on the property finding another reservoir at 10,000 feet. The two zones were combined under section 614 as a single property. L is not entitled to percentage depletion on the gross income attributable to the production from the productive zone at 5,000 feet, but is entitled to percentage depletion on the gross income attributable to the production from the productive zone at 10,000 feet because that zone was not part of the proven property until the date of development expenses by L, which is after the date of the transfer. Accordingly, L's maximum allowable percentage depletion deduction for 1975 would be zero percent of gross income from the property with respect to the production from 5,000 feet, plus 22 percent of gross income from the property with respect to the production from 10,000 feet. This maximum deduction would be subject to the limitation provided for in section 613(a), i.e., 50 percent of "taxable income from the property (computed without allowance for depletion)," such taxable income being the overall taxable income resulting from the sale of production from both zones, and would also be subject to the limitations provided in section 613A. The production from the productive zone at 5,000 feet is not taken into account in determining K's depletable oil quantity for the year.

Example (9). On July 1, 1975, M transferred an oil property with a fair market value of $100x to N. On February 1, 1976, N commenced production of oil from the property. The fair market value of the property on February 1, 1976, as reduced by actual costs incurred by N for equipment and intangible drilling and development costs, was $300x. Because the value of the property on transfer was not 50 percent or more of the value on February 1, 1976, the property transferred to N was not a proven property (see § 1.613A-7(p)). However, if there had been only marginal production from the property so that the fair market value of the property on February 1, 1976, was $40x rather than 5300x, the property transferred to N would have been a proven property provided the other requirements of a proven property were met.

Example (10). O is the owner of a remainder interest in a trust created January 1, 1970. On that date, the trust held oil and gas properties. On January 1, 1976, O's interest for the first time entitled O to the trust's income from oil and gas production from the properties. The reversion of the remainder interest to O is not a transfer (see § 1.613A-7(n)(7)). Accordingly, the transfer of the interest in oil and gas property to O is deemed to have occurred on January 1, 1970, the date O's interest was created.

Example (11). On January 1, 1976, P, Q, and R entered into a partnership for the acquisition of oil and gas leases. It was agreed that the sharing of income will be divided equally among P, Q, and R. However, it was further agreed that with respect to the first production obtained from each property acquired P will receive 80 percent thereof and Q and R each will receive 10 percent thereof until $100x has been received by P. Assume these allocations have substantial economic effect under section 704 of the Code and the regulations thereunder. On February 1, 1976, Partnership PQR acquired an unproven property and production therefrom was shared pursuant to the partnership agreement. P is entitled to percentage depletion with respect to the production allocated to him since the transfer of right to the production is deemed to have been made on the date the partnership agreement became applicable to the specific property, at which time the property was unproven. See § 1.613A-7(n) for rules relating to the definition of transfer. Similarly, when $100x has been obtained and Q and R each commence receiving 33⅓ percent of the revenue, Q and R are entitled to percentage depletion with respect to their entire interests. However, if the property had been proven when acquired by the partnership, P, Q, and R would not be entitled to claim any percentage depletion with respect to production from the property.

Example (12). On December 30, 1960, S placed producing oil property in trust for the benefit of S's nephew, T, and executed a trust agreement which required the trustee of the trust to transfer the oil property to T on January 1, 1975. The trustee's transfer of the oil property to T on January 1, 1975, is deemed to have occurred on December 30, 1960 (see § 1.613A-7(n)). Since the transfer is deemed to have occurred before January 1, 1975, section 613A(c) applies with respect to the production from the oil property. Moreover, if the trustee was not required to transfer the oil property on a specific date but was given discretion to select the date of transfer, the transfer of such property would still be deemed to have occurred on December 30, 1960. However, the result would be different if the trust agreement had provided that the trustee, at the trustee's discretion, may transfer the oil property to T on January 1, 1975, but is not under any obligation to transfer the property to T on January 1, 1975, or on any other date. Since the transfer was discretionary, the date of the actual transfer governs.

Example (13). On January 1, 1974, U acquired an oil property. On February 1, 1974, U granted V an option to purchase the oil property. V exercised V's option on March 2, 1975, and subsequently the oil property was conveyed to V. The date of the transfer was March 2, 1975, the day V exercised V's option (on which date both parties were bound).

Example (14). On July 1, 1974, W executed a deed conveying oil and gas property to X. W delivered the deed to X on January 1, 1975. Under state law, the mere execution of the deed without delivery did not give X any rights in the property. Title to the oil property passed to X on the date of delivery. Therefore, the date of transfer was January 1, 1975.

Example (15). Y, owner of a proven oil property, transferred Y's interest therein on July 25, 1975, to a revocable trust of which Y is treated as the owner under section 676. Y is not deemed a transferee and section 613A(c) applies to Y because immediately preceding the transfer Y was entitled to percentage depletion on the production from the property.

Example (16). On January 1, 1975, a proven oil property was transferred to Z; therefore, section 613A(c)(1) did not apply with respect to the production from such property. After Z's death, neither Z's estate nor its beneficiaries are entitled to percentage depletion with respect to the decedent's oil property since Z was a transferee of proven property.

Example (17). Partnership ABC, owner of proven oil and gas properties, admitted D as a partner in 1975 in consideration of cash. The shares of partners A, B, and C of the partnership income were proportionately reduced so that D had a 25 percent interest in the income. D is not entitled to percentage depletion with respect to D's share of partnership oil and gas income because D is a transferee for purposes of section 613A(c)(9) (as in effect prior to the Revenue Reconciliation Act of 1990). See § 1.613A-7(n).

Example (18). On January 1, 1975, E and F formed partnership EF to which E contributed proven oil property. For 1975, pursuant to the partnership agreement 70 percent of the mineral income from the property was allocated to E and 30 percent of the mineral income from the property was allocated F. F is not entitled to percentage depletion with respect to production from the property because F is a transferee of an interest in proven property. However, E is not a transferee of an interest in proven property because E was entitled to percentage depletion on the oil produced with respect to the property immediately before the transfer. Therefore, E is entitled to percentage depletion with respect to the income allocated to E. However, if in 1976 the partnership agreement were revised so that E's interest in the income was increased by 10 percent, E would not be entitled to percentage depletion with respect to the additional 10 percent interest because E is a transferee with respect thereto.

Example (19). G is the owner of a ⅓ interest in a partnership owning a proven oil property, and as such is entitled to ⅓ of the income from the property. G received a distribution on July 1, 1975, from the partnership of a ⅓ interest in the proven oil property. Although the transfer of such interest is a transfer for purposes of section 613A(c)(9) (as in effect prior to the Revenue Reconciliation Act of 1990), G is still entitled to percentage depletion with respect to the ⅓ interest in the oil production from the property since G was entitled to percentage depletion on such production with respect to such property immediately before the transfer. If the entire property were distributed to G, G's percentage depletion allowance would still be based on only ⅓ of the oil produced.

Example (20). H and I contributed property X and property Y respectively to Partnership HI. The partnership agreement provides that all the gross income from property X is to be allocated to H and all the gross income from property Y is to be allocated to I. Assume these allocations have substantial economic effect under section 704 of the Code and the regulations thereunder. For 1975 H and I each received 100x gross income. Although the contributions of the properties by H and I are transfers for purposes of section 613A(c)(9) (as in effect prior to the Revenue Reconciliation Act of 1990), both H and I are entitled to percentage depletion with respect to the $100x income received since each was entitled to a percentage depletion allowance with respect to the property contributed immediately before the transfer. However, if no special allocation of income were made but H and I are to share equally in the income from both properties, each would be entitled to a depletion allowance based on only one-half of the production with respect to the property he had contributed. If property X produces $100x of gross income from the property and property Y produces $200x of gross income from the property, H would be entitled to percentage depletion but only with respect to $50x (50 percent of $100x) of gross income from the property and I would be entitled to percentage depletion with respect to $100x (50 percent of $200x) of gross income from the property.

(2) Transfers after October 11, 1990. (i) General rule. Section 613A(c)(9) and (10), as in effect prior to the Revenue Reconciliation Act of 1990 (relating to prohibition of percentage depletion on transferred proven properties) has been repealed effective for transfers after October 11, 1990. Accordingly, a transferee of a proven oil or gas property transferred after October 11, 1990 is permitted to claim percentage depletion with respect to production from the property. For purposes of transfers of property occurring before October 12, 1990 under section 613A(c)(10), prior to its repeal, the disposition of stock after October 11, 1990 by a transferor will not result in a reduction in the depletable quantity of the transferee corporation under section 613A(c)(10)(F).

(ii) Transfer. The term "transfer" has the same meaning as under § 1.613A-7(n).

(iii) Transferee. A person shall not be treated as a transferee with respect to a transferred property to the extent that such person held an interest in the property but was not entitled to a percentage depletion allowance on mineral produced with respect to the property immediately before the transfer. Thus, for example, if a taxpayer who is not entitled to claim percentage depletion on a proven property transfers the property to a partnership for an interest in the partnership, the taxpayer is not a transferee with respect to the property in the hands of the partnership.

(iv) Effective date. The provisions of paragraph (i)(2) of § 1.613A-3 are effective for transfers occurring after May 13, 1991. However, a taxpayer may elect to apply these provisions to transfers occurring after October 11, 1990 and on or before May 13, 1991.

(v) Examples. The examples below illustrate the provisions of this subparagraph. The examples ignore the application of any restriction on percentage depletion other than the proven property transfer rule.

Example (1). On December 31, 1991, A transfers a proven oil property to B. B may claim percentage depletion with respect to production from the property regardless of whether production from the property was eligible for percentage depletion in A's hands (even if A were a retailer or refiner of oil or gas).

Example (2). On October 10, 1990, A transfers a proven oil property to B. B may not claim percentage depletion with respect to production from the property.

Example (3). On January 1, 1990, C purchases a proven oil property. Because C is a transferee of a proven property, production from the property is not eligible for percentage depletion in C's hands. On December 31, 1991, C contributes the property to Corporation M, an S corporation in which C owns 100 percent of the stock. The contribution of the property is a transfer, but C is not a transferee with respect to the property in the hands of the corporation. Accordingly, C may not claim percentage depletion with respect to production from the property. However, if prior to the contribution C had been entitled to claim percentage depletion with respect to production from the property, C would be entitled to claim percentage depletion with respect to production from the property after the contribution.

Example (4). On December 31, 1991, C contributes a proven oil property (with respect to which C is not entitled to claim percentage depletion) to Corporation N, an S corporation in which C owns 30 percent and D owns 70 percent of the stock. The contribution of the property is a transfer, but C is not a transferee with respect to the property in the hands of the corporation. Accordingly, C may not claim percentage depletion with respect to C's share of the production from the property. D is a transferee with respect to the property in the hands of Corporation N, and may claim percentage depletion with respect to D's share of production from the property.

Example (5). On December 31, 1991, D transfers a proven oil property (with respect to which D is not entitled to claim percentage depletion) to DE, an equal partnership between D and E. E is a transferee with respect to the property and may claim percentage depletion with respect to production from the property allocated to E under the DE partnership agreement. D is not a transferee with respect to the property, and may not claim percentage depletion with respect to production from the property allocated to D under the DE partnership agreement. However, if D had been entitled to claim percentage depletion with respect to production from the property, then D would be entitled to claim percentage depletion with respect to production from the property in the hands of DE.

Example (6). On January 1, 1990, Corporation P contributes a proven property to Corporation O, its wholly owned subsidiary. Under § 1.613A-7(n)(4), the contribution is not treated as a transfer, but only for so long as the tentative quantity is required under section 613A(c)(8) to be allocated between P and O. On December 31, 1991, P sells 90% of the O stock to an unrelated person; accordingly, the tentative quantity is no longer required under section 613A(c)(8) to be allocated between P and O. After the sale of O stock, production from the property in O's hands is eligible for percentage depletion because a transfer of a proven property is deemed to occur upon the transfer of the stock.

Example (7). On October 10, 1990, G transfers a proven oil property to his minor son, H. G had been entitled to claim percentage depletion with respect to production from the property. Under § 1.613A-7(n)(5), H is permitted to claim percentage depletion for so long as G and H are related persons under section 613A(c)(8)(C). On December 31, 1991, H reaches majority and is no longer related to G under section 613A(c)(8)(C). H is entitled to continue to claim percentage depletion on production from the property because the property is treated as being transferred to H on December 31, 1991.

Example (8). On December 31, 1991, I sells a proven property to J, her husband. I had not been entitled to claim percentage depletion with respect to production from the property. Under § 1.613A-7(n)(5), the sale is not a transfer because it is made between persons related under section 613A(c)(8). Accordingly, J may not claim percentage depletion with respect to production from the property. If, however, I had been entitled to claim percentage depletion with respect to production from the property, J would be entitled to claim percentage depletion with respect to production from the property.

Example (9). On December 31, 1991, L inherits a proven property from K. K had not been entitled to claim percentage depletion with respect to production from the property. Under § 1.613A-7(n)(1), the inheritance is not a transfer. Accordingly, L may not claim percentage depletion with respect to production from the property. If, however, K had been entitled to claim percentage depletion with respect to production from the property, L would be entitled to claim percentage depletion with respect to production from the property.

Example (10). On December 31, 1991, Corporation R, a calendar year taxpayer, made an S election effective for the taxable year beginning January 1, 1992 and succeeding taxable years. Since Corporation R is deemed to have transferred its oil and gas properties on January 1, 1992, the shareholders of Corporation R are eligible to claim percentage depletion with respect to the production from the properties.

Example (11). Assume the same facts as in Example 10 except that Corporation R makes the S election on December 31, 1989, effective for the taxable year beginning January 1, 1990 and succeeding taxable years. Since Corporation R is deemed to have transferred its oil and gas properties on January 1, 1990, the shareholders of Corporation R are not eligible to claim percentage depletion with respect to the production from the properties.

(j) Percentage depletion with respect to bonuses and advanced royalties. *(1) Amounts received or accrued after August 16, 1986.* In computing the percentage depletion allowance pursuant to section 613A(c) with respect to amounts received or accrued after August 16, 1986, there shall not be taken into account any advance royalty (to the extent that actual production during the taxable year is insufficient to earn such royalty), lease bonus, or other amount payable without regard to production, even though the amount may be taken into account for purposes of sections 61 and 612 (relating to definitions of gross income and cost depletion, respectively).

(2) Amounts received or accrued before August 17, 1986. (i) A lease bonus or advanced royalty received or accrued before August 17, 1986, with respect to oil or gas property shall be taken into account for purposes of percentage depletion in the taxable year such payment is includible in income. percentage depletion shall be determined according to the depletion rate and depletable oil and natural gas limitations of section 613A(c)(1) and § 1.613A-3(a) applicable on the date of such inclusion. The payee of the bonus or advanced royalty shall apply the depletable oil and natural gas quantity limitations by attributing a specific number of barrels of oil or cubic feet of natural gas to the lease bonus or advanced royalty. The determination of the number of barrels of oil or cubic feet of natural gas shall be based on the average price of oil or gas produced from the property during the taxable year. If oil or gas is not produced from the property during that year, or if the oil or gas is not sold before conversion or transportation from the premises, the number of barrels of oil or cubic feet of gas shall be based on a price (as of the date of the bonus or advanced royalty) determined under the constructive pricing principles applicable under section 613(a), generally the representative market or field price. In the case where no oil or gas has been produced in such year, the constructive price applicable to the type of production expected to be produced from the property shall apply. However, if the first actual production from the property in a later year is different from the type of production upon which the conversion of the bonus or advanced royalty into barrels of oil or cubic feet of gas was based and the period of limitations on assessment has not expired (see section 6501) for the year in which the lease bonus or advanced royalty is includible in income, the taxpayer should promptly file an amended return, if necessary. In the amended return the conversion shall be recomputed taking into account the pricing applicable to the actual production. For purposes of paragraph (f) of § 1.613A-7, the number of barrels of oil or cubic feet of natural gas attributed to a lease bonus or advanced royalty is deemed to have been extracted

on the date the bonus or advanced royalty is includible in the payee's income.

(ii) For purposes of applying the depletable oil and natural gas quantity limitations in taxable years after the year in which the advanced royalty payment is included in income, the payee of an advanced royalty which is recouped out of future production shall not include production which recoups the advanced royalty in such later years. The payor of a bonus or advanced royalty that is not recouped from future production may reduce the production to be taken into account for purposes of applying the depletable quantity limitations in each year in which the payor's gross income from the property is adjusted under § 1.613-2(c)(5)(ii) to reflect the bonus paid by an amount determined by dividing the portion of the bonus required to be excluded from the payor's gross income from the property by the price of oil or gas applicable to the payee for converting the bonus into barrels of oil or cubic feet of gas.

(iii) See § 1.612-3(a)(2) and (b)(2) for rules relating to the requirement that certain depletion deductions allowed with respect to lease bonuses and advanced royalties be restored to income.

(k) Special rules for fiscal year taxpayers. In applying this section to a taxable year which is not a calendar year, each portion of such taxable year which occurs during a single calendar year shall be treated as if it were a short taxable year.

(l) Information furnished by partnerships, trusts, estates, and operators. Each partnership, trust, or estate producing domestic crude oil or natural gas, and each operator of a well from which domestic crude oil or natural gas was produced, shall provide each partner, beneficiary, or person holding a nonoperating interest, as the case may be, with all information in its possession necessary to determine the amount of his depletion deduction allowable with respect to such crude oil or natural gas. For example, for each property a partnership is required to provide each partner with partnership information relating to the partner's allocable share of gross income from the property, the partner's allocable share of operating expenses, the partner's allocable share of depreciation, the partner's share of allocated overhead, the partner's share of estimated reserves, the partner's share of production in barrels or cubic feet for the taxable year, the partner's original share of the partnership adjusted basis of properties producing domestic crude oil or domestic natural gas, the partner's allocable share of any adjustments made to the basis of such properties by the partnership, and the percentage by which existing partners must reduce their bases in a partnership oil or gas property upon entry of a partner by contribution. In addition, upon the disposition of an oil or gas property by the partnership, the partnership shall inform each partner of his allocable portion of the amount realized from the sale of the property.

T.D. 8348, 5/10/91, amend T.D. 8437, 9/23/92.

Section 1.613A-3 of the notice of proposed rulemaking appearing in the FEDERAL REGISTER for May 13, 1977 (42 FR 24279—is revised by redesignating paragraphs (i) and (j) as paragraphs (j) and (k), respectively, and by inserting new paragraph (i), to read as follows:

Proposed § 1.613A-3 Exemption for independent producers and royalty owners. [*For Preamble, see ¶ 150,991*]

*   *   *   *   *

(i) Treatment of transfer of oil or gas property by individuals to corporations. *(1) In general.* Paragraph (h) of this section shall not apply to a transfer by an individual of qualified property (as defined in paragraph (i)(5) of this section) to a qualified transferee corporation (as defined in paragraph (i)(4) of this section) solely in exchange for stock in the corporation.

(2) 1,000-barrel limit for corporation. A tentative quantity, not exceeding 1,000 barrels per day, shall be determined for the qualified transferee corporation under this section.

(3) Transferor's tentative quantity reduced. (i) In general. The tentative quantity for the transferor (and his family as defined in paragraph (i)(7)(ii) of this section) for any period shall be reduced by the transferor's pro rata share of the corporation's depletable quantity for such period.

(ii) Pro rata share. For purposes of paragraph (i)(3)(i) of this section, a transferor's pro rata share for any period shall be—

(A) In the case of production from property (including property transferred by other transferors) to which paragraph (i)(1) of this section applies, that portion of the corporation's depletable quantity which is allocable to production from such property, and

(B) In the case of production from all other property, that portion of the corporation's depletable quantity which is allocable to the production from such property, multiplied by a fraction the numerator of which is the fair market value of the transferor's stock in the corporation, and the denominator of which is the fair market value of all stock in the corporation.

(iii) Depletable quantity. For purposes of this paragraph, a corporation's depletable quantity for any period is the lesser of—

(A) Such corporation's tentative quantity for such period (determined under paragraphs (b) and (g) of this section), or

(B) Such corporation's average daily production for such period. The corporation's depletable quantity is subject to reduction under paragraph (i)(6) of this section.

(iv) The provisions of this subparagraph may be illustrated by the following examples:

Example (1). On January 1, 1981, A and B, two unrelated individuals, transferred qualified property to a newly formed corporation in a transaction which satisfies the requirements under section 613A(c)(10) of the Code and § 1.613A-3(i). A and B timely file their respective elections under paragraph (i)(9) of this section. A transferred \$20X worth of unproven oil property and received 20 percent of the stock of the corporation having a fair market value of \$20X. B transferred \$80X worth of proven oil property and received 80 percent of the stock of the corporation having a fair market value of \$80X. In 1981 the corporation had an average daily production of 600 barrels from the transferred property. During 1981 the corporation had no oil and gas property other than the property transferred under paragraph (i) of this section. Under paragraph (i)(3)(iii) of this section the corporation's depletable quantity is 600 barrels per day. Both A and B would each have their respective tentative quantities reduced by 600 barrels per day under paragraph (i)(3)(ii)(A) of this section.

Example (2). In 1982, the corporation in example (1) purchased unproven oil property and in 1983 the property came into production. The corporation had an average daily oil production of 800 barrels in 1983. The average daily quantity was made up of 600 barrels per day from qualified property and 200 barrels per day from the "other property" purchased in 1982. The corporation's depletable oil quantity is 800 barrels per day under paragraph (i)(3)(iii) of this section. Both A and B would each have their respective tentative quantities reduced by 600 barrels per day under paragraph (i)(3)(ii)(A) of this section. Under paragraph (i)(3)(ii)(B) of this section, A would have his depletable quantity reduced by an additional 40 barrels per day (20 percent (A's allocable share of the fair market value of all the stock in the corporation) of the 200 barrels per day production from "other property") for a total reduction of 640 barrels per day. Similarly B would have his depletable quantity reduced by an additional 160 barrels per day (80 percent (B's allocable share of the fair market value of all the stock in the corporation) of the 200 barrels per day production from "other property") for a total reduction of 760 barrels per day.

(4) Qualified transferee corporation defined. For purposes of this paragraph, the term "qualified transferee corporation" means a corporation all of the outstanding stock of which has been issued to individuals solely in exchange for qualified property held by such individuals. Stock of a " qualified transferee corporation" may at no time be issued for property which is not "qualified property." Where property is transferred to a corporation by two or more persons in exchange for stock, the stock received by each must be in proportion to his interest in the property immediately prior to the transfer (including cash contribution within the limits prescribed in paragraph (i)(5) of this section). If the stock is received in disproportion to such interest, the requirement that stock be issued by the corporation to the transferor solely in exchange for qualified property will not be met. For purposes of this paragraph, an otherwise "qualified transferee corporation" which subsequently issues stock in exchange for nonqualified property will be treated as if it never had been a qualified transferee corporation. For example, if a corporation issues stock to its employees in exchange for services, the corporation will not be a " qualified transferee corporation." Any percentage depletion deductions previously taken by the corporation on the transferred proven property will be disallowed. In addition, the transferor's tentative quantity shall be treated as if it was never subject to any reduction by reason of paragraph (i)(3) of § 1.613A-3.

(5) Qualified property defined. For purposes of this paragraph, the term "qualified property" includes both proven oil or gas property (as defined in paragraph (p) of § 1.613A-7) and unproven oil or gas property with respect to which the transferor has made an election to have this paragraph apply (see paragraph (i)(9) of this section). The term "oil and gas property" has the same meaning as under section 614 of the Code. However, the term "qualified property" does not include proven oil or gas property to which there has been a prior transfer to which paragraph (h) of this section applied. The term also includes cash (not to exceed $1,000 in the aggregate) which one or more individuals transfers to the corporation and necessary production equipment associated with a well which is in place when the well is transferred. The term "necessary production equipment" includes, for example, the "Christmas tree", casings, pumping equipment, flowlines, separators, storage tanks, salt water disposal equipment, and other equipment essential for the efficient and effective production of oil and gas from a well.

(6) Transferor must retain stock during lifetime. If at any time during his lifetime any transferor disposes of stock in the corporation (other than to a member of his family), then the depletable quantity of the corporation (determined without regard to this subparagraph) shall be reduced (for all periods on or after the date of the disposition) by an amount which bears the same ratio to such quantity as the fair market value the stock so disposed bears to the aggregate fair market value of all stock of the corporation on such date of disposition. Disposition of stock in the corporation by reason of the death of a transferor will not reduce the depletable quantity of the corporation. Reduction of the corporation's depletable quantity is not required even if the recipient (other than the transferor's spouse) of such stock disposes of the stock. However, if stock transferred to the transferor's spouse by reason of the death of the transferor ceases to be held by the spouse, the transferor shall be treated as having disposed of such stock at the time of such cessation for purposes of this subparagraph.

(7) Special rules relating to family of transferor. (i) In general. For purposes of this paragraph—

(A) The issuance of stock to a member of the family of the transferor shall be treated as issuance of stock to the transferor, and

(B) During the lifetime of the transferor, stock transferred to a member of the family of the transferor shall be treated as held by the transferor.

If stock described in the preceding sentence ceases to be held (whether or not by reason of death) by a member of the family of the transferor, the transferor shall be treated as having disposed of such stock at the time of such cessation.

(ii) Family defined. For purposes of this paragraph, the members of the family of an individual include only his spouse and minor children (and only so long as they maintain that status).

(8) Property subject to liabilities. For purposes of this paragraph, section 357 of the Code shall be applied as if—

(i) References to section 351 of the Code include references to paragraph (i)(1) of this section, and

(ii) The reference in subsection (a)(1) of section 357 of the Code to the nonrecognition of gain includes a reference to the nonapplication of paragraph (h) of this section.

(9) Election. (i) In general. The election under this paragraph is made by filing a statement with the director of the Internal Revenue Service Center with whom the transferor files his or her return. The statement, headed "SECTION 613A(c)(10)—ELECTION" must indicate that the taxpayer is electing to apply the provisions of section 613A(c)(10). The statement also must include the taxpayer's and any other transferor's name, address and identification number of the transferee corporation, and the due date, including extensions, for filing the Federal income tax return of the transferee corporation. The taxpayer must provide the transferee corporation a copy of the statement of election, which the corporation shall attach to its Federal income tax return. The election by the individual taxpayer (transferor) must be made on or before the due date, including extensions, for filing the transferee corporation's income tax return for the first taxable year ending after the date of the transfer (or if later, December 28, 1980) of the qualified property to the qualified transferee corporation.

(ii) Multiple transferors. If there is more than one transferor, each of the transferors must make the election. If one of the transferors does not make the election, then the corporation would not be a "qualified transferee corporation" since not all of its stock would have been issued solely in exchange for qualified property. See paragraph (i)(5) of § 1.613A-3 for a definition of qualified property.

(iii) Subsequent transferor. If there is a later transfer of property to a qualified transferee corporation, the subsequent transferor must make the election. Earlier transferors do not need to make the election at that time if they are not then making a transfer.

(10) Effective date. The provisions of this paragraph apply to transfers in taxable years ending after December 31, 1974, but only for purposes of applying section 613A of the Code to periods after December 31, 1979.

* * * * *

§ 1.613A-4 Limitations on application of § 1.613A-3 exemption.

(a) Limitation based on taxable income. *(1)* The aggregate amount of a taxpayer's deductions allowed pursuant to section 613A(c) for the taxable year shall not exceed 65 percent of the taxpayer's taxable income (reduced in the case of an individual by the zero bracket amount for taxable years beginning after December 31, 1976, and before January 1, 1987) for the year, adjusted to eliminate the effects of:

(i) Any depletion with respect to an oil or gas property (other than a gas property with respect to which the depletion allowance for all production is determined pursuant to section 613A(b)) for which percentage depletion would exceed cost depletion in the absence of the depletable quantity limitations contained in section 613A(c)(1) and (6) (as in effect prior to the Revenue Reconciliation Act of 1990) or the taxable income limitation contained in section 613A(d)(1);

(ii) Any net operating loss carryback to the taxable year under section 172;

(iii) Any capital loss carryback to the taxable year under section 1212; and

(iv) In the case of a trust, any distributions to its beneficiaries, except in the case of any trust where any beneficiary of such trust is a member of the family (as defined in section 267(c)(4)) of a settlor who created inter vivos and testamentary trusts for members of the family and such settlor died within the last 6 days of the 5th month in 1970, and the law in the jurisdiction in which such trust was created requires all or a portion of the gross or net proceeds of any royalty or other interest in oil, gas, or other mineral representing any percentage depletion allowance to be allocated to the principal of the trust.

The amount disallowed (as defined in paragraph (q) of § 1.613A-7) shall be carried over to the succeeding year and treated as an amount allowable as a deduction pursuant to section 613A(c) for such succeeding year, subject to the 65-percent limitation of section 613A(d)(1). For rules relating to corporations filing a consolidated return, see the regulations under section 1502. With respect to fiscal year taxpayers, except as provided in § 1.613A-1 for taxable years beginning before January 1, 1975, and ending after that date, the limitation shall be calculated on the entire fiscal year and not applied with respect to each short period included in a fiscal year. For purposes of basis adjustments and determining whether cost depletion exceeds percentage depletion with respect to the production from a property, any amount disallowed as a deduction after the application of this paragraph shall be allocated to the respective properties from which the oil or gas was produced in proportion to the percentage depletion otherwise allowable to such properties pursuant to section 613A(c). Accordingly, the maximum amount which may be allowable as a deduction pursuant to section 613A(c) after application of this paragraph (65 percent × adjusted taxable income) shall be allocated to properties for which percentage depletion pursuant to section 613A(c) would be allowed in the absence of the limitation contained in section 613A(d)(1) by application of the same proportion. However, once it is determined that after application of this paragraph cost depletion exceeds percentage depletion with respect to a property, the maximum amount determined under the preceding sentence shall be reallocated among the remaining properties, and the portion of the amount disallowed which is allocable to such property shall be the amount by which percentage depletion pursuant to section 613A(c) before application of this paragraph exceeds cost depletion. See Example 1 of paragraph (a)(2) of this section. If the taxpayer becomes entitled to the deduction in a later year (i.e., because the disallowed depletion does not exceed 65 percent of the taxpayer's taxable income for that year after taking account of any percentage depletion deduction otherwise allowable for that year), then the basis of the taxpayer's properties must be adjusted downward (but not below zero) by the amount of the deduction in proportion to the portion of the amount disallowed to the respective properties in the year of the disallowance. However, if the property in question was disposed of by the taxpayer prior to the beginning of such later year, the amount of the deduction in such later year shall be reduced by the difference between the taxpayer's adjusted basis in the property at the time it is disposed of and the adjusted basis which the taxpayer would have had in the property in the absence of the 65-percent limitation.

(2) The application of this paragraph may be illustrated by the following examples:

Example (1). A owns producing oil properties M, N, and O. With respect to property M, the depletion allowable pursuant to section 613A(c) for 1975 without regard to section 613A(d)(1) was $60x (cost depletion would have been $40x). With respect to property N, the depletion allowable pursuant to section 613A(c) for 1975 without regard to section 613A(d)(1) was $90x (cost depletion would have been zero). With respect to property O, the depletion pursuant to section 613A(c) for 1975 without regard to section 613A(d)(1) was $50x (cost depletion would have been $10x). A's taxable income (as adjusted under § 1.613A-4(a)(1)) for 1975 was $100x; accordingly, A's percentage depletion pursuant to section 613A(c) for 1975 must be reduced from $200x to $65x (65 percent × $100x taxable income). Of that amount, $19.5x:

$$\$65x \text{ dollars} \left(\frac{\$60x}{\$60x + \$90x + 50x} \right) \text{ is}$$

tentatively allocated to property M, $29.25x:

$$\$65x \text{ dollars} \left(\frac{\$90x}{\$90x + \$60x + \$50x} \right) \text{ is}$$

tentatively allocated to property N, $16.25x:

$$\$65x \text{ dollars} \left(\frac{\$50x}{\$50x + \$90x + \$60x} \right) \text{ is}$$

tentatively allocated to property O.

Since cost depletion of $40x with respect to property M exceeded the percentage depletion of $19.5x allowable on such property, A claimed the cost depletion. Accordingly, the only percentage depletion deduction allowable to A pursuant to section 613A(c) for 1975 is with respect to properties N and O. Therefore, the $65x ceiling applies to the percentage depletion allowable on properties N and O. Of that amount, $41.79x:

$$\$65x \text{ dollars} \left(\frac{\$90x}{\$90x + \$50x} \right) \text{ is allocated to}$$

property N, and \$23.21x:

$$\$65x \text{ dollars} \left(\frac{\$50x}{\$50x + \$90x} \right) \text{ is allocated}$$

to property O.

Accordingly, A is allowed a total depletion deduction of \$105x (\$40x cost depletion on property M + \$41.79x percentage depletion on property N + \$23.21x percentage depletion on property O). The amount disallowed to A under section 613A(d)(1) is \$95x (\$200x aggregate depletion allowable before application of section 613A(d)(1) − \$105x [\$40x cost depletion allowable on property M + \$41.79x percentage depletion allowable on property N after application of section 613A(d)(1) + \$23.21x depletion allowable on property O after application of section 613A(d)(1)]). For purposes of basis adjustments, \$20x (\$60x percentage depletion before limitation − \$40x cost depletion allowed) of the amount disallowed is allocated to property M. The balance of the amount disallowed of \$75x is allocated \$48.21x:

$$\$75x \text{ dollars} \left(\frac{\$90x}{\$90x + \$50x} \right)$$

to property N, and

$$\$75x \text{ dollars} \left(\frac{\$50x}{\$50x + \$90x} \right)$$

to property O.

Example (2). The amount disallowed to B as a deduction under this paragraph is \$50x for 1975 and \$125x for 1976 (including the \$50x carried over from 1975). B may carry forward the \$125x as a deduction to 1977 and subsequent years.

Example (3). C is a fiscal year taxpayer whose fiscal year ended on May 31, 1975. For purposes of applying the 65 percent of taxable income limitation, the period beginning January 1, 1975, and ending May 31, 1975, is treated as a short taxable year. The depletion allowable pursuant to section 613A(c) without regard to section 613A(d)(1) for such short taxable year was \$80x and A's taxable income (as adjusted under § 1.613A-4(a)(1)) during such short taxable year was \$100x. Only \$65x (65 percent × \$100x adjusted taxable income) of the deduction pursuant to section 613A(c) was deductible for such portion of 1975, in addition to any percentage depletion allowable for June 1, 1974, through December 31, 1974. With respect to the taxable year commencing June 1, 1975, and ending May 31, 1976, the 65 percent limitation is applied to the taxable income for the entire taxable year.

Example (4). Under the trust law of State X, a trustee is required to allocate 22 percent of gross mineral income to the principal of a trust for purposes of maintaining a reserve for depletion and the depletion deduction is entirely allocated to the trustee. In 1975 the gross income of a trust in State X the only assets of which were oil properties was \$1,000. The trust's allowable percentage depletion pursuant to section 613A(c) without regard to section 613A(d)(1) was \$220. The trust incurred expenses of \$150 for the taxable year and made distributions to beneficiaries (who are not described in the exception for family members set forth in paragraph (a)(1)(iv) of this section) of \$630 (\$1,000 gross income − \$220 allocated to principal − \$150 expenses). The trust's deduction for personal exemption under section 642(b) is \$300. For purposes of applying the 65 percent limitation, the trust's taxable income was \$550 (\$1,000 gross income − \$150 expenses − \$300 exemption). The limitation under section 613A(d)(1) was \$357.50 (65% × \$550 taxable income). Accordingly, the trust's percentage depletion allowance was unaffected by the 65 percent limitation.

Example (5). In 1980 the gross income of the estate of D was \$1,000. The only assets of the estate were oil properties. The estate's adjusted basis in the oil properties was \$0. The estate's allowable percentage depletion pursuant to section 613A(c) without regard to section 613A(d)(1) was \$220. The estate incurred expenses of \$150 for the taxable year and made distributions to beneficiaries of \$425. The distributions thus equaled one half of the net income of the estate (ignoring depletion). Under section 611(b)(4), the percentage depletion is apportioned equally between the estate and its beneficiary. The distribution amount of \$425 is deductible under section 661(a) in computing the taxable income of the estate. For purposes of applying the 65 percent limitation to the percentage depletion apportioned to the estate, the estate's taxable income was \$0 (\$1,000 gross income − \$150 expenses − \$425 distribution − \$600 exemption). The limitation under section 613A(d)(1) was therefore also \$0 (65% × \$0 taxable income). Accordingly, the \$110 amount is disallowed to the estate for the taxable year but may be carried forward by the estate as a deduction to 1981 and subsequent years. The beneficiaries shall apply the 65 percent limitation to the \$110 percentage depletion apportioned to them based on their respective taxable incomes.

Example (6). In 1975 E sold an oil property for which E's adjusted basis was \$20x. The amount disallowed for 1975 to E under section 613A(d) was \$10x. The amount of the carryover under that section to 1976 was \$0 (\$10x disallowed amount − \$10x [\$20x adjusted basis of property on sale − \$10x adjusted basis which taxpayer would have had in the property in the absence of the 65-percent limitation]). However, if the adjusted basis of the property on disposition had been \$0, the amount of the carryover to 1976 would have been \$10x (\$10x disallowed amount − \$0 adjusted basis of property on sale).

Example (7). In 1975 F owned producing properties M, N, O, P, Q, and R. With respect to property M, the allowable cost depletion was \$100x (the allowable percentage depletion pursuant to section 613A(c) without regard to the depletable quantity and taxable income limitations contained in section 613A(c)(1), (6) and (d)(1) would have been \$90x). With respect to property N, the allowable percentage depletion pursuant to section 613A(c) before applying section 613A(d)(1) was \$80x (cost depletion would have been \$0). With respect to property O, the allowable cost depletion was \$60x (the allowable percentage depletion pursuant to section 613A(c) would have been \$70x, except that the application of section 613A(d)(1) reduced allowable percentage depletion to less than \$60x). With respect to property P, the allowable percentage depletion pursuant to section 613A(b) was \$55x (cost depletion would have been \$40x). With respect to property Q, which produces both gas subject to section 613A(b)(1)(B) and oil subject to section 613A(c), the allowable percentage depletion was \$45x (cost depletion would have been \$40x). With respect to property R, the allowable cost depletion was \$40x (the allowable percentage depletion pursuant to section 613A(c) would have been \$50x, except that the application of section 613A(c)(7)(A) reduced allowable percentage depletion to less than \$40x). Under paragraph (a)(1)(i) of this section, for purposes of applying the 65 percent limitation under section 613A(d)(1), F's taxable income must be reduced by the allowable depletion with respect to property M (for which cost depletion exceeded percentage depletion even in the absence of section

613A(c)(1), (6), and (d)) and property P (for which all depletion is determined pursuant to section 613A(b)), but shall not be reduced by the allowable depletion with respect to properties N, O, Q, and R.

(b) Retailers excluded. *(1)* Section 613A(c) and § 1.613A-3 shall not apply in the case of any taxpayer who is a retailer as defined in paragraph (r) of § 1.613A-7.

(2) The application of this paragraph may be illustrated by the following examples (those that involve sales through retail outlets assume, unless otherwise stated, that the $5,000,000 gross receipts requirement of section 613A(d)(2) is met):

Example (1). A, owner of producing oil and gas properties, also owns 5 percent in value of the stock of Corporation M, a retailer of oil and gas. None of A's production is sold through Corporation M. Since A may benefit from Corporation M's sales of oil and gas through A's ownership interest in Corporation M, A is considered to be selling oil or natural gas through Corporation M, a related person. Accordingly, the exemption under section 613A(c) does not apply to A, even though none of A's production is sold through Corporation M.

Example (2). Assume the same facts as in Example 1 except that A has gross receipts of $2 million from sales of oil for the taxable year from A's retail outlets and Corporation M has gross receipts of $4 million from sales of oil for the taxable year from its retail outlets. For purposes of the $5 million gross receipts requirement of section 613A(d)(2), A is treated as having gross receipts of $6 million. Accordingly, the exemption under section 613A(c) does not apply to A.

Example (3). Corporation N, a retailer of oil and gas, owns 5 percent in value of the stock of Corporation O, owner of producing oil and gas properties. None of Corporation O's production is sold through Corporation N. Since Corporation O has no direct or indirect ownership interest in Corporation N, and therefore does not benefit from Corporation N's sales of oil and gas, and since none of Corporation O's production is sold through Corporation N, the exemption under section 613A(c) applies to Corporation O.

Example (4). Corporation P, a producer of oil, owns 70 percent in value of the stock of Corporation Q. Corporation Q owns 30 percent in value of the stock of Corporation R. Corporation R owns 30 percent in value of the stock of Corporation S, a retailer of oil and gas. P indirectly owns 6.3 percent (70 percent × 30 percent × 30 percent) in value of the stock of Corporation S. Since P may benefit from Corporation S's sales of oil and gas through P's indirect ownership interest in Corporation S, P is not entitled to percentage depletion.

Example (5). B is the owner of certain oil and gas properties in Texas and is also the owner of a service station in Washington, D.C., which B leases to Corporation T. None of B's production is sold to Corporation T. The exemption under section 613A(c) applies to B. However, if sales of B's production were made to Corporation T and the gross receipts from such sales of B's production to Corporation T exceed 5 million dollars, the exemption under section 613A(c) would not apply to B because B is selling oil or natural gas to a person given authority to occupy a retail outlet leased by the taxpayer, B.

Example (6). C has a ⅛ royalty interest and Corporation U has a ⅞ working interest in an oil property. Corporation V, a retailer of oil, owns 5 percent in value of the stock of Corporation U. C has no interest in either corporation. All of the production from the property is sold through Corporation V, C receiving from Corporation U ⅛ of its receipts therefrom. The exemption under section 613A(c) does not apply to Corporation U because Corporation U is selling oil or natural gas through Corporation V, a related person that is a retailer. However, the exemption applies to C because C, as owner of a nonoperating mineral interest, is not treated as an operator of a retail outlet merely because C's oil or gas is sold on C's behalf through a retail outlet operated by an unrelated person.

Example (7). D owns and operates retail grocery stores where refined oil may be purchased. D also owns oil and gas producing properties. If the sales of refined oil at each store location constitute less than 5 percent of the gross receipts from all sales made at that store, D is not considered a retailer by reason of such sales.

Example (8). Lessee E sells natural gas to lessor F directly from a wellhead gathering pipeline system for F's local agricultural use, in transactions incidental to the acquisition of a natural gas lease. The sales of natural gas to F are not sales through a retail outlet.

Example (9). Corporation W produces natural gas, some of which it sells at retail. For purposes of determining whether Corporation W is a retailer selling gas through a retail outlet within the meaning of § 1.613A-7(r), the business office of Corporation W where a purchaser would normally contact the corporation with respect to its sales to the purchaser is considered the place at which those sales of natural gas are made.

Example (10). G, husband, is the sole owner and operator of a retail outlet which sells oil and gas. H, wife, owns producing oil and gas properties. G is not related to H for purposes of section 613A(d).

Example (11). I, husband, and J, wife, are community property owners of 10 percent in value of the stock of Corporation X which is a retailer of oil and gas. I and J are each treated as owning 5 percent of Corporation X. Therefore, neither I nor J qualify for the exemption under section 613A(c).

Example (12). Corporation Y, an electing small business corporation as defined in section 1371 (as in effect prior to the enactment of the subchapter S Revision Act of 1982), owns producing oil and gas properties. K, a retailer of oil and gas, is a 50 percent interest shareholder of Corporation Y's production is sold through K. Corporation Y is eligible for percentage depletion.

Example (13). Corporation Z, a producer of natural gas, makes bulk sales of natural gas to industrial users. For purposes of determining whether Corporation Z is a retailer under § 1.613A-7(r), the bulk sales are disregarded.

Example (14). L, a calendar year taxpayer, is the owner of a producing oil property. On September 1, 1976, L purchased a chain of gasoline service stations. Therefore, L was a retailer of oil and gas for the last 122 days of 1976. L's gross income from the oil property for the taxable year was $150x and L's taxable income from the property was $30x. L is treated as a retailer with respect to $50x of gross income from the property ($150x × 122/366) and $10x of taxable income from the property ($30x × 122/366). Therefore, L is entitled to percentage depletion with respect to $100x of gross income from the property ($150x minus $50x). However, the allowable percentage depletion is limited by the 50 percent of taxable income from the property limitation to $10x (50 percent times $20x taxable income ($30x minus $10x)).

Example (15). Corporation M is a partner in Partnership MNO which is the owner of an operating interest in a producing oil property. Corporation P, a retailer of oil and gas, owns 5 percent in value of the stock of Corporation M. Partnership MNO sells its production to Corporation P. Corporation M is retailing oil through Corporation P, a related person, because its share of the oil is being sold on its behalf by the partnership through a retail outlet operated by a person related to Corporation M. Therefore, the exemption under section 613A(c) does not apply to Corporation M.

Example (16). AA and BB are beneficiaries of a trust which is a retailer of oil and gas. AA has an interest in the income of the trust for AA's lifetime which, actuarially determined, represents more than 5 percent of the beneficial interests in the trust. BB's interest in the trust, which entitles BB to 5 percent of the corpus of the trust 5 years after AA's death, represents less than 5 percent of the beneficial interests in the trust prior to AA's death and represents more than 5 percent after AA's death. The trust is a related person of AA but not BB while AA is alive. Accordingly, during AA's lifetime BB is not disqualified from the exemption provided by section 613A(c), but AA is.

Example (17). Assume the same facts as in Example 16, except that AA's interest in the income of the trust represents 4 percent of the beneficial interests in the trust. AA is disqualified from the exemption provided by section 613A(c) with respect to the income from the trust but not with respect to income from other sources.

(c) Certain refiners excluded. *(1)* Section 613A(c) and § 1.613A-3 shall not apply in the case of any taxpayer who is a refiner as defined in paragraph (s) of § 1.613A-7.

(2) The provisions of this paragraph may be illustrated by the following examples:

Example (1). Corporation M owns a refinery which has refinery runs in excess of 50,000 barrels on at least one day during the taxable year. Corporation M also owns a 5 percent interest in Corporation N, owner of producing oil and gas properties. None of Corporation N's production is sold to Corporation M. The exemption under section 613A(c) does not apply to Corporation N because Corporation M, a related person of Corporation N, engages in the refining of crude oil.

Example (2). A and B are equal partners in Partnership AB, which owns oil and gas producing properties. A owns a refinery which has refinery runs in excess of 50,000 barrels on at least one day during the taxable year and which buys all of Partnership AB's production. B has no ownership interest in any refinery. B is not a refiner.

T.D. 8348, 5/10/91.

---

§ 1.613A-5 Election under section 613A(c)(4).

The election under section 613A(c)(4) is an annual election which the taxpayer may make by claiming percentage depletion deductions for the taxable year based upon such election. The election may be made, on an original or amended tax return or a claim for credit or refund, at any time prior to the expiration of the statutory period (including any extensions thereof) for the filing of a claim for credit or refund by the taxpayer. The election may be changed by the taxpayer by filing an amended return or a claim for credit or refund. The election allows the taxpayer to treat as his depletable natural gas quantity an amount equal to 6,000 cubic feet multiplied by the number of barrels of the taxpayer's depletable oil quantity to which the election applies. The election applies to secondary or tertiary production, as well as primary production, but in determining the taxpayer's depletable natural gas quantity with respect to secondary or tertiary production the taxpayer's depletable oil quantity shall be determined without regard to section 613A(c)(3)(A)(ii) with respect to production from secondary or tertiary processes.

T.D. 7487, 5/12/77.

---

§ 1.613A-6 Recordkeeping requirements.

(a) Principal value of property demonstrated. In the case of a transfer (as defined in § 1.613A-7(n)) after December 31, 1974, of an interest in an oil or gas property (as defined in § 1.613A-7(p)), the transferee (as defined in section 1.613A-7(o)) shall keep records showing the terms of the transfer, any geological and geophysical data in the possession of the transferee or other exploratory data with respect to the property transferred, and any other information which bears upon the question of whether at the time of the transfer the principal value of the property transferred had been demonstrated by prospecting, exploration, and discovery work.

(b) Production from secondary or tertiary processes. Every taxpayer who claims depletion with respect to oil or gas produced by secondary or tertiary processes (as defined in § 1.613A-7(k)) shall keep records of the secondary and tertiary processes applied and maintain records of the amount of production so resulting.

(c) Retention of records. The records required by this section shall be kept at all times available for inspection by authorized Internal Revenue officers or employees, and shall be retained so long as the contents may become material in the administration of any Internal Revenue law.

T.D. 7487, 5/12/77.

---

§ 1.613A-7 Definitions.

For purposes of section 613A and the regulations thereunder—

(a) Domestic. The term "domestic," as applied to oil and gas wells (or to production from such wells), refers to wells located in the United States or in a possession of the United States, as defined in section 638 and the regulations thereunder.

(b) Natural gas. The term "natural gas" means any product (other than crude oil as defined in paragraph (g) of this section) of an oil or gas well if a deduction for depletion is allowable under section 611 with respect to such product.

(c) Regulated natural gas. Natural gas is considered to be "regulated" only if all of the following requirements are met:

(1) The gas must be domestic gas produced and sold by the producer (whether for himself or on behalf of another person) before July 1, 1976,

(2) The price for which the gas is sold by the producer must not be adjusted to reflect to any extent the increase in liability of the seller for tax under chapter 1 of the Code by reason of the repeal of percentage depletion for gas,

(3) The sale of the gas must have been subject to the jurisdiction of the Federal Power Commission for regulatory purposes,

(4) An order or certificate of the Federal Power Commission must be in effect (or a proceeding to obtain such an order or certificate must have been instituted), and

(5) The price at which the gas is sold must be taken into account, directly or indirectly, in the issuance of the order or certificate by the Federal Power Commission. Price increases after February 1, 1975, are presumed to take increases in tax liabilities into account unless the taxpayer demonstrates to the contrary by clear and convincing evidence that the increases are wholly attributable to a purpose or purposes unrelated to the repeal of percentage depletion for gas (e.g., where the record of the Federal Power Commission clearly establishes that the Commission did not take the repeal into account). Increases to reflect additional State and local real property or severance taxes, increases for additional operating costs (such as costs of secondary or tertiary processes), adjustments for inflation, increases for additional drilling and related costs, or increases to reflect changes in the quality of gas sold, are some examples of increases that are not attributable to the repeal of percentage depletion for gas. In the absence of a statement in writing by the Federal Power Commission that the price of the gas in question was not in fact regulated, the requirement of paragraph (c)(5) of this section is deemed to have been met in any case in which the Federal Power Commission issued an order or certificate approving the sale to an interstate pipeline company or, in a case in which it is established by the taxpayer that the Federal Power Commission has influenced the price of such gas, an order or certificate permitting the interstate transportation of such gas. In addition, an "emergency" sale of natural gas to an interstate pipeline, which, pursuant to the authority contained in 18 CFR 2.68, 2.70, 157.22, and 157.29, may be made without prior order approving the sale, is deemed to have met the requirements of paragraph (c)(3), (4), and (5) of this section. For purposes of meeting the requirements under this paragraph, it is not necessary that the total gas production from a property qualify as "regulated natural gas." The determination of whether mineral production is "regulated natural gas" shall be made with respect to each sale of the mineral or minerals produced.

(d) Natural gas sold under a fixed contract. The term "natural gas sold under a fixed contract" means domestic natural gas sold by the producer (whether for himself or on behalf of another person) under a contract, in effect on February 1, 1975, and at all times thereafter before such sale, under which the price for the gas during such period cannot be adjusted to reflect to any extent the increase in liabilities of the seller for tax under chapter 1 of the Code by reason of the repeal of percentage depletion for gas. The term may include gas sold under a fixed contract even though production sold under the contract had previously been treated as regulated natural gas. Price increases after February 1, 1975, are presumed to take increases in tax liabilities into account unless the taxpayer demonstrates to the contrary by clear and convincing evidence. Paragraph (c) of this section provides examples of increases which do not take increases in tax liabilities into account. However, if an adjustment provided for in the contract permits the possible increase in federal income tax liability of the seller to be taken into account to any extent, the gas sold under the contract after such an increase becomes permissible is not gas sold under a fixed contract. If the adjustment provided for in the contract provides for an increase in the price of the contract to the highest price paid to a producer for natural gas in the area, or if the price may be renegotiated, then gas sold under the contract after such an increase becomes permissible is presumed not to be sold under a fixed contract unless the taxpayer demonstrates by clear and convincing evidence that the price increase in no event takes increases in tax liabilities into account. For purposes of meeting the requirements of this paragraph, it is not necessary that the total gas production from a property qualify as "natural gas sold under a fixed contract," for the determination of "natural gas sold under a fixed contract" is to be made with respect to each sale of each type of natural gas sold pursuant to each contract.

(e) Qualified natural gas from geopressured brine. The term "qualified natural gas from geopressured brine" means any natural gas which is determined in accordance with section 503 of the Natural Gas Policy Act of 1978 to be produced from geopressured brine and which is produced from any well the drilling of which began after September 30, 1978, and before January 1, 1984.

(f) Average daily production. *(1)* The term "average daily production" means the taxpayer's aggregate production of domestic crude oil or natural gas, as the case may be, which is extracted after December 31, 1974, and to which gross income from the property is attributable during the taxable year divided by the number of days in such year. As used in the preceding sentence the term "taxpayer" includes a small business corporation as defined in section 1371 (as in effect prior to the enactment of the Subchapter S Revision Act of 1982) and the regulations thereunder.

Notwithstanding the provisions of § 1.612-3 and except as provided in § 1.613A-3(j)(2), in computing the average daily production for a taxable year only oil or gas which has been actually produced by the close of such taxable year is taken into account. Average daily production does not include production resulting from secondary or tertiary processes to which gross income from the property is attributable before January 1, 1984.

(2) In the case of a fiscal-year taxpayer, paragraph (f)(1) of this section shall be applied separately to each short taxable year under section 613A(c)(11), as in effect prior to the Revenue Reconciliation Act of 1990.

(3) In the case of a taxpayer holding a partial interest in the production from any property (including an interest of a partner in property of a partnership or a net profit interest) such taxpayer's production shall be considered to be that amount of such production determined by multiplying the total production (which is produced after December 31, 1974, and to which gross income from the property is attributable during the taxable year) of the property by the taxpayer's percentage participation in the gross revenues from the property during the year. However, the portion of trust (or estate) production allocable to a beneficiary shall not exceed that amount of the trust's (or estate's) depletable oil quantity determined by multiplying such quantity by the beneficiary's percentage interest in the trust's (or estate's) gross income from the property.

(g) Crude oil. For purposes of section 613A and the regulations thereunder, the term "crude oil" means—

(1) A mixture of hydrocarbons which existed in the liquid phase in natural underground reservoirs and which remains liquid at atmospheric pressure after passing through surface separating facilities,

(2) Hydrocarbons which existed in the gaseous phase in natural underground reservoirs but which are liquid at atmospheric pressure after being recovered from oil well (casinghead) gas in lease separators, and

(3) Natural gas liquid recovered from gas well effluent in lease separators or field facilities before any conversion process has been applied to such production.

(h) Depletable oil quantity. The taxpayer's depletable oil quantity, within the meaning of section 613A(c)(1)(A), shall be equal to the tentative quantity determined under the table contained in section 613A(c)(3)(B) and paragraph (b) of § 1.613A-3 (except that, in the case of determinations with respect to days prior to January 1, 1984, such quantity shall be reduced (but not below zero) by the taxpayer's average daily secondary or tertiary production for the taxable year).

(i) Depletable natural gas quantity. The taxpayer's depletable natural gas quantity, within the meaning of section 613A(c)(1)(B), shall be equal to 6,000 cubic feet multiplied by the number of barrels of the taxpayer's depletable oil quantity to which the taxpayer elects to have section 613A(c)(4) apply. The taxpayer's depletable oil quantity for any taxable year shall be reduced (in addition to any reduction required to be made under paragraph (h) of this section) by the number of barrels with respect to which an election under section 613A(c)(4) for natural gas has been made. See § 1.613A-5.

(j) Barrel. The term "barrel" means 42 United States gallons.

(k) Secondary or tertiary production. For purposes of section 613A the term "secondary or tertiary production" means the increased production of domestic crude oil or natural gas from a property at any time after the application of a secondary or tertiary process. The increased production is the excess of actual production over the maximum primary production which would have resulted during the taxable year if the secondary or tertiary process had not been applied. The increased production may be due to an increase in either the rate or the duration of recovery. A secondary or tertiary process is a process applied for the recovery of hydrocarbons in which liquids, gases, or other matter is injected into the reservoir to supplement or augment the natural forces required to move the hydrocarbons through the reservoir. However, no process which must be introduced early in the productive life of the mineral property in order to be reasonably effective (such as cycling of gas in the case of a gas-condensate reservoir) is a secondary or tertiary process. A process (such as fire flooding or miscible fluid injection) introduced early in the productive life of the mineral property will not be disqualified as a secondary or tertiary process if a later introduction of the process in the property would still have been reasonably effective.

(l) Controlled group of corporations. The term "controlled group of corporations" has the meaning given to such term by section 1563(a), except that section 1563(b)(2) shall not apply and except that "more than 50 percent" shall be substituted for "at least 80 percent" each place it appears in section 1563(a).

(m) Related person. *(1)* A person is a "related person" to another person, within the meaning of section 613A(d)(2) and (4), paragraphs (b) and (c) of § 1.613A-4, and paragraphs (r) and (s) of this section, if either a significant ownership interest in such person is held by the other, or a third person has a significant ownership interest in both such persons. For purposes of determining a significant ownership interest, an interest owned by or for a corporation, partnership, trust, or estate shall be considered as owned directly both by itself and proportionately by its shareholders, partners, or beneficiaries, as the case may be. The term "significant ownership" means—

(i) With respect to any corporation, direct or indirect ownership of 5 percent or more in value of the outstanding stock of such corporation,

(ii) With respect to a partnership, direct or indirect ownership of 5 percent or more interest in the profits or capital of such partnership, and

(iii) With respect to an estate or trust, direct or indirect ownership of 5 percent or more of the beneficial interests in such estate or trust. The relative percentage ownership of beneficiaries of an estate or trust in the beneficial interests therein shall be determined under actuarial principles.

(2) A person is a "related person" to another person, within the meaning of section 613A(c)(8)(B) and paragraph (h)(2) of § 1.613A-3, if such persons are members of the same controlled group of corporations or if the relationship between such persons would result in a disallowance of losses under section 267 or 707(b), except that for this purpose the family of an individual includes only the individual's spouse and minor children.

(n) Transfer. The term "transfer" means any change in ownership for federal tax purposes after December 31, 1974, by sale, exchange, gift, lease, sublease, assignment, contract, or other disposition (including any contribution to or any distribution by a corporation, partnership, or trust), any change in the membership of a partnership or the beneficiaries of a trust, or any other change by which a taxpayer's proportionate share of the income subject to depletion of an oil or gas property is increased. For taxable years beginning after 1982, the term "transfer" includes an election by a C corporation to be an S corporation (properties deemed transferred by the C corporation on the day the election first becomes effective) and a termination of an S election (each shareholder's pro rata share of assets of S corporation deemed transferred to C corporation on the day that the termination first becomes effective). However, the term does not include—

(1) A transfer of property at death (including a distribution by an estate, whether or not a pro rata distribution),

(2) An exchange to which section 351 applies,

(3) A change of beneficiaries of a trust by reason of the death, birth, or adoption of any vested beneficiary if the transferee was a beneficiary of the trust or is a lineal descendant of the settlor or any other vested beneficiary of the trust, except in the case of any trust where any beneficiary of the trust is a member of the family (as defined in section 267(c)(4)) of a settlor who created inter vivos and testamentary trusts for members of the family and the settlor died within the last six days of the fifth month in 1970, and the law in the jurisdiction in which the trust was created requires all or a portion of the gross or net proceeds of any royalty or other interest in oil, gas, or other mineral representing any percentage depletion allowance to be allocated to the principal of the trust,

(4) A transfer of property between corporations which are members of the same controlled group of corporations (as defined in section 613A(c)(8)(D)(i)),

(5) A transfer of property between business entities which are under common control (within the meaning of section 613A(c)(8)(B)) or between related persons in the same family (within the meaning of section 613A(c)(8)(C)),

(6) A transfer of property between a trust and members of the same family (within the meaning of section 613A(c)(8)(C)) to the extent that both (i) the beneficiaries of the trust are and continue to be members of the family that transferred the property, and (ii) the tentative oil quantity is allocated among the members of such family,

(7) A reversion of all or part of an interest with respect to which the taxpayer was eligible for percentage depletion pursuant to section 613A(c), or

(8) A conversion of a retained interest which is eligible for such depletion into an interest which constituted all or

part of an interest previously owned by the taxpayer also eligible for such depletion.

However, paragraph (n)(2), (4), and (5) of this section shall apply only so long as the tentative quantity determined under the table contained in section 613A(c)(3)(B) (as in effect prior to the Revenue Reconciliation Act of 1990) is required to be allocated under section 613A(c)(8) between the transferor and transferee, or among members of a controlled group of corporations. In the case of an individual transferor, the allocation test of the preceding sentence shall not be failed merely because of the death of the transferor. For purposes of paragraph (n)(3) and (6), an individual adopted by a beneficiary is a lineal descendant of that beneficiary. For purposes of paragraph (n)(7) and (8), a taxpayer previously ineligible for percentage depletion solely by reason of section 613A(d)(2) or (4) will be considered to have been eligible for such depletion. A transfer is deemed to occur on the day on which a contract or other commitment to transfer the property becomes binding upon both the transferor and transferee, or, if no such contract or commitment is made, on the day on which ownership of the interest in oil or gas property passes to the transferee.

(o) Transferee. The term "transferee," as used in section 613A(c)(9), paragraph (i)(1) of § 1.613A-3, and this section includes the original transferee of proven property and his or her successors in interest (excluding successors in interest of proven property transferred after October 11, 1990). A person shall not be treated as a transferee of an interest in a proven oil or gas property to the extent that such person was entitled to a percentage depletion allowance on mineral produced with respect to the property immediately before the transfer. However, a person shall be treated as a transferee of an interest in a proven property to the extent that the interest such person receives is greater than the interest in the property the person held immediately before the transfer. For example, where the owner of a proven oil property transfers his or her entire interest therein to a partnership of which he or she is a member and, as a consequence, becomes entitled to a depletion allowance based on only one-third of the oil produced with respect to that property, the owner (the transferor) is not denied percentage depletion with respect to the one-third interest in oil production which the owner still possesses. If the partnership agreement had made an effective allocation (under section 704 and § 1.704-1) of all the income in respect of such property to the transferor partner, that partner would be entitled to percentage depletion on the entire oil production from that property. For this purpose, a person who has transferred oil or gas property pursuant to a unitization or pooling agreement shall be treated as having been entitled to a depletion allowance immediately before the transfer to that person of the interest in the unit or pool with respect to all of the mineral in respect of which the person receives gross income from the property pursuant to the unitization or pooling agreement, except to the extent such income is attributable to consideration paid by that person for such interest in addition to that person's contribution of the oil or gas property and equipment affixed thereto.

(p) Interest in proven oil or gas property. The term "interest in an oil or gas property" means an economic interest in oil or gas property. An economic interest includes working or operating interests, royalties, overriding royalties, net profits interests, and, to the extent not treated as loans under section 636, production payments from oil or gas properties. The term also includes an interest in a partnership, S corporation, small business corporation, or trust holding an economic interest in oil or gas property but does not include shares of stock in a corporation (other than an S corporation and small business corporation) owning such an interest. An oil or gas property is "proven" if its principal value has been demonstrated by prospecting, exploration, or discovery work. The principal value of the property has been demonstrated by prospecting, exploration, or discovery work only if at the time of the transfer—

(1) Any oil or gas has been produced from a deposit, whether or not produced by the taxpayer or from the property transferred;

(2) Prospecting, exploration, or discovery work indicate that it is probable that the property will have gross income from oil or gas from the deposit sufficient to justify development of the property; and

(3) The fair market value of the property is 50 percent or more of the fair market value of the property, minus actual expenses of the transferee for equipment and intangible drilling and development costs, at the time of the first production from the property subsequent to the transfer and before the transferee transfers his or her interest.

For purposes of this paragraph, the property is to be determined by applying section 614 and the regulations thereunder to the transferee at the time of the transfer. If the transfer is of an interest in a partnership, S corporation, small business corporation, or trust, the determination shall be made with respect to each property owned by the partnership, S corporation, small business corporation, or trust. The term "prospecting, exploration, or discovery work" includes activities which produce information relating to the existence, location, extent, or quality of any deposit of oil or gas, such as seismograph surveys and drilling activities (whether for exploration or for the production of oil or gas).

(q) Amount disallowed. The amount disallowed, within the meaning of section 613A(d)(1) and paragraph (a) of § 1.613A-4, is the excess of the amount of the aggregate of the taxpayer's allowable depletion deductions (whether based upon cost or percentage depletion) computed without regard to section 613A(d)(1) over the amount of the aggregate of such deductions computed with regard to such section. The disallowed amount shall be carried over to the succeeding year and treated as an amount allowable as a deduction pursuant to section 613A(c) for the succeeding year, subject to the 65-percent limitation of section 613A(d)(1) and the rules contained in § 1.613A-4(a).

(r) Retailer. *(1)* Except as otherwise provided in paragraph (r)(2) of this section, the term "retailer" means any taxpayer who directly, or through a related person (as defined in paragraph (m)(1) of this section), sells oil or natural gas, or any product derived from oil or natural gas—

(i) Through any retail outlet operated by the taxpayer or a related person, or

(ii) To any person—

(A) Obligated under an agreement or contract with the taxpayer or a related person to use a trademark, trade name, or service mark or name owned by such taxpayer or a related person, in marketing or distributing oil or natural gas or any product derived from oil or natural gas, or

(B) Given authority, pursuant to an agreement or contract with the taxpayer or a related person, to occupy any retail outlet owned, leased, or in any way controlled by the taxpayer or a related person.

For purposes of the preceding sentence, bulk sales (i.e., sales in very large quantities) of oil or natural gas (but not bulk sales of any product derived from oil or natural gas) to commercial or industrial users shall be disregarded. Bulk sales made after September 18, 1982, of aviation fuels to the Department of Defense shall be also disregarded. In addition, sales of oil or natural gas (whether or not produced by the taxpayer), or of any product derived from oil or natural gas, which are made outside the United States shall be disregarded if no domestic production of oil, natural gas (or products derived therefrom) of the taxpayer or a related person is exported during the taxable year or the immediately preceding taxable year.

(2) Notwithstanding paragraph (r)(1) of this section, the taxpayer shall not be considered a retailer in any case where, during the taxable year of the taxpayer, the combined gross receipts from sales (excluding sales for resale) of oil or natural gas, or products derived therefrom, of all retail outlets taken into account under paragraph (r)(1) of this section (including sales through a retail outlet of oil, natural gas, or a product derived from oil or natural gas which had previously been the subject of a sale described in paragraph (r)(1)(ii) of this section) do not exceed $5 million. If the taxpayer's combined gross receipts for the taxable year exceed $5 million, the taxpayer will be treated as a retailer as of the first day in which a retail sale was made. For purposes of paragraph (r)(1) of this section, a taxpayer shall be deemed to be selling oil or natural gas (or a product derived therefrom) through a related person in any case in which any sale of oil or natural gas (or a derivative product) by the related person produces gross income from which the taxpayer may benefit by reason of the taxpayer's direct or indirect ownership interest in the related person. In such cases (and in any other case in which the taxpayer is selling through a retail outlet referred to in section 613A(d)(2)(A) or is selling such items to a person described in section 613A(d)(2)(B)), it is immaterial whether the oil or natural gas which is sold, or from which is derived a product which is sold, was produced by the taxpayer. A taxpayer shall be deemed to be selling oil or natural gas (or a derivative product) through a retail outlet operated by a related person in any case in which a related person who operates a retail outlet acquires for resale oil or natural gas (or a derivative product) which the taxpayer produced or caused to be made available for acquisition by the related person pursuant to an arrangement whereby some or all of the taxpayer's production is marketed. An owner of a nonoperating mineral interest (such as a royalty) shall not be treated as an operator of a retail outlet merely because the owner's oil or gas is sold on the owner's behalf through a retail outlet operated by an unrelated person. In addition, the mere fact that a member of a partnership is a retailer shall not result in characterization of the remaining partners as retailers. However, any partner of a partnership who has a 5 percent or more interest in any entity actually engaging in retail activities (including the partnership or another entity to which the partnership is related) is treated as a retailer. See paragraph (m)(1) of this section for rules on the ownership interest by partners in an entity related to a partnership. Similarly, if a trust or estate is a retailer, only its beneficiaries having a 5 percent or more current income interest from the trust or estate are treated as retailers. A person who is a retailer during a portion of the taxable year shall be treated as a retailer with respect to a fraction of that person's gross and taxable income from oil or gas properties for the taxable year, the numerator of which is the number of days during the taxable year in which the taxpayer is a retailer and the denominator of which is the total number of days during the taxable year; except that a person who ceases to be a retailer during the taxable year before the first production of oil or gas during such year shall not be treated as a retailer for any portion of such year.

(3) For purposes of this paragraph (r), the term "any product derived from oil or natural gas" means gasoline, kerosene, Number 2 fuel oil, refined lubricating oils, diesel fuel, butane, propane, and similar products which are recovered from petroleum refineries or extracted from natural gas in field facilities or natural gas processing plants. The term "retail outlet" means any place where sales of oil or natural gas (excluding bulk sales of such items to commercial or industrial users), or a product of oil or natural gas (excluding bulk sales of aviation fuels to the Department of Defense), accounting for more than 5 percent of the gross receipts from all sales made at such place during the taxpayer's taxable year, are systematically made for any purpose other than for resale. For this purpose, sales of oil or natural gas, or any product derived from oil or natural gas, to a person for refining are considered as sales made for resale.

(s) Refiner. A person is a refiner if such person or a related person (as defined in paragraph (m)(1) of this section) engages in the refining of crude oil (whether or not owned by such person or related person) and if the total refinery runs of such person and any related persons exceed 50,000 barrels on any day during the taxable year. A refinery run is the volume of inputs of crude oil (excluding any product derived from oil) into the refining stream. For purposes of this paragraph, crude oil refined outside the United States shall be taken into account. Refining is any operation by which the physical or chemical characteristics of crude oil are changed, exclusive of such operations as passing crude oil through separators to remove gas, placing crude oil in settling tanks to recover basic sediment and water, dehydrating crude oil, and blending of crude oil products.

T.D. 8348, 5/10/91, amend T.D. 8437, 9/23/92.

§ 1.614-0 Introduction.

Caution: The Treasury has not yet amended Reg § 1.614-0 to reflect changes made by P.L. 95-618.

Section 614 relates to the definition of property and to the various special rules by means of which taxpayers are permitted to aggregate or combine separate properties or to treat such properties as separate. These rules are set forth in detail in §§ 1.614-1 through 1.614-8. Section 1.614-1 sets forth rules under section 614(a) relating to the definition of the term "property." Section 1.614-2 contains the rules relating to the election under section 614(b), as it existed prior to its amendment by section 226(a) of the Revenue Act of 1964, to aggregate operating mineral interests. In the case of mines, the rules contained in § 1.614-2 are applicable only to taxable years beginning before January 1, 1958, to which the Internal Revenue Code of 1954 applies. In the case of oil and gas wells, the rules contained in § 1.614-2 are applicable only to taxable years beginning before January 1, 1964, to which the Internal Revenue Code of 1954 applies. In the case of oil and gas wells, the taxpayer may, however, for taxable years beginning before January 1, 1964, treat any operating mineral interests as if section 614(a) and (b) (as it existed prior to its amendment by section 226(a) of the Revenue Act of 1964) had not been enacted. If any operating mineral interests are so treated, the rules contained in § 1.614-2 are not applicable to such interests and such interests are, in respect of taxable years beginning before January 1, 1964, treatment of separate operating mineral interests in the case of oil and gas wells. Section 1.614-3 prescribes the rules relating to the election under section 614(c)(1) permitting the aggregation of operating mineral interests in the cases of mines for taxable years beginning after December 31, 1957. Section 1.614-3 also sets forth rules relating to the election under section 614(c)(2) in the case of mines by means of which a taxpayer is permitted to treat a single operating mineral interest as more than one such interest for taxable years beginning after December 31, 1957. At the election of the taxpayer with respect to an operating unit, the rules contained in § 1.614-3 are also applicable to taxable years beginning before January 1, 1958, to which the Internal Revenue Code of 1954 applies. If the taxpayer makes such an election, the rules contained in § 1.614-2 are not applicable to any of the operating mineral interests which are part of the operating unit with respect to which the election described in § 1.614-3 is made. Section 1.614-5 sets forth the rules relating to the aggregation of nonoperating mineral interests. Section 1.614-6 contains the rules relating to basis, holding period, and abandonment and casualty losses where properties have been aggregated or combined. Section 1.614-7 relates to the extension of time for performing certain acts. Section 1.614-8 contains the rules relating to the elections under section 614(b) as amended by section 226(a) of the Revenue Act of 1964 to treat separate operating mineral interests in the case of oil and gas wells as separate properties or in combination for taxable years beginning after December 31, 1963.

T.D. 6524, 1/9/61, amend T.D. 6859, 10/27/65.

§ 1.614-1 Definition of property.

Caution: The Treasury has not yet amended Reg § 1.614-1 to reflect changes made by P.L. 95-618.

(a) General rule. *(1)* For purposes of subtitle A of the Code, in the case of mines, wells, and other natural deposits, the term "property" means each separate interest owned by the taxpayer in each mineral deposit in each separate tract or parcel of land.

(2) The term "interest" means an economic interest in a mineral deposit. See paragraph (b) of § 1.611-1. The term includes working or operating interests, royalties, overriding royalties, net profits interests, and, to the extent not treated as loans under section 636, production payments.

(3) The term "tract or parcel of land" is merely descriptive of the physical scope of the land to which the taxpayer's interest relates. It is not descriptive of the nature of his rights or interests in the land. All contiguous areas (even though separately described) included in a single conveyance or grant or in separate conveyances or grants at the same time from the same owner constitute a single separate tract or parcel of land. Areas included in separate conveyances or grants (whether or not at the same time) from separate owners are separate tracts or parcels of land even though the areas described may be contiguous. If the taxpayer's rights or interests within the same tract or parcel of land are dissimilar, then each such dissimilar interest constitutes a separate property. If the taxpayer's rights or interests (whether or not dissimilar) within the same tract or parcel of land relate to more than one separate mineral deposit, then his interest with respect to each such separate deposit is a separate property.

(4) Upon the transfer of a "property" in any transaction in which the basis of such property in the hands of the transferee is determined by reference to the basis of such property in the hands of the transferor, such property shall, notwithstanding the provisions of subparagraph (3) of this paragraph, retain the same status and identity in the hands of the transferee as it had in the hands of the transferor. See paragraph (c) of § 1.614-6 if the transferor has made a binding election to treat a separate mineral interest as a separate property, to treat a separate mineral interest as more than one property under section 614(c), or to treat two or more separate mineral interests as an aggregated or combined property under section 614(b) (as it existed either before or after its amendment by section 226(a) of the Revenue Act of 1964), (c), or (e).

(5) The provisions of this paragraph may be illustrated by the following examples:

Example (1). A taxpayer owns one tract of land under which lie three separate and distinct seams of coal. Therefore, the taxpayer owns three separate mineral interests each of which constitutes a separate property.

Example (2). A taxpayer conducts mining operations on eight tracts of land as a single unit. He acquired his interests in each of the eight tracts from separate owners. Even if each tract of land contains part of the same mineral deposit, the taxpayer owns eight separate mineral interests each of which constitutes a separate property.

Example (3). A taxpayer owns a tract of land under which lies one mineral deposit. The taxpayer operates a well on part of the tract and leases to another operator the mineral rights in the remainder retaining a royalty interest therein. The taxpayer thereafter owns two separate mineral interests each of which constitutes a separate property.

Example (4). In 1954, a taxpayer acquires from a single owner, in a single deed, three noncontiguous tracts of mineral land for a single consideration. Even if each tract contains part of the same mineral deposit, the taxpayer owns three separate mineral interests each of which constitutes a separate property.

Example (5). In 1954, taxpayer A simultaneously acquires in fee two contiguous tracts of mineral land from two separate owners. The same mineral deposit underlies both tracts. Thereafter, taxpayer A owns two separate mineral interests each of which constitutes a separate property.

Example (6). Assume that in 1955, taxpayer A, in example (5), leases the two contiguous tracts of mineral land that he acquired in 1954 to taxpayer B by means of a single lease. Thereafter, taxpayer B owns one mineral interest which constitutes a separate property for such time as the lease continues in existence.

Example (7). Assume that in 1955, taxpayer A, in example (5), sells at the same time all the mineral land he acquired in 1954 to taxpayer B. Thereafter, taxpayer B owns one mineral interest which constitutes a separate property. If taxpayer B acquires the mineral land in a transaction in which the basis of such mineral land in his hands is determined by reference to the basis of such mineral land in the hands of taxpayer A, then taxpayer B owns two separate mineral interests each of which constitutes a separate property.

Example (8). In 1954, taxpayer A simultaneously acquires two contiguous leasehold interests from two separate owners. The same mineral deposit underlies both tracts. Thereafter, taxpayer A owns two separate mineral interests each of which constitutes a separate property.

Example (9). In 1955, taxpayer A, in example (8), simultaneously assigns the two leases to taxpayer B. Thereafter, taxpayer B owns two separate mineral interests each of which constitutes a separate property.

(b) Separation of interests treated as "single property" under prior regulations. Each separate mineral interest which, in accordance with paragraph (a) of this section, is a separate property shall be so treated, notwithstanding the fact that the taxpayer under paragraph (i) of § 39.23(m)-1 of this chapter (Regulations 118) and corresponding provisions of prior regulations may have treated more than one of such interests as a "single property." The basis of each such separate property must be established by a reasonable method. See, however, section 614(b) and (d) (as they existed prior to amendment by section 226 of the Revenue Act of 1964), section 614(c) and (e), and §§ 1.614-2, 1.614-3, 1.614-4, and 1.614-5 for special rules relating to the treatment of two or more separate mineral interests as a single property.

(c) Treatment of a waste bank or residue. A waste bank or residue of prior mining, the extraction of ores or minerals from which is treated as mining under section 613(c)(3), shall not be considered to be a separate mineral deposit but is a part of the mineral deposit from which it was extracted. However, if the owner of such waste bank or residue has disposed of the deposit from which the waste bank or residue was accumulated, or if the waste bank or residue cannot practicably be attributed to a particular deposit of the owner, the waste bank or residue will be regarded as a separate deposit.

T.D. 6524, 1/9/61, amend T.D. 6859, 10/27/65, T.D. 7261, 2/26/73.

§ 1.614-2 Election to aggregate separate operating mineral interests under section 614(b) prior to its amendment by Revenue Act of 1964.

(a) General rule. *(1)* The provisions of this section relate to the election, under section 614(b) prior to its amendment by section 226(a) of the Revenue Act of 1964, to aggregate separate operating mineral interests, and, unless otherwise indicated, all references in this section to section 614(b) or any paragraph or subparagraph thereof are references to section 614(b) or a paragraph or subparagraph thereof as it existed prior to such amendment. Notwithstanding the preceding sentence, the definitions contained in paragraphs (b) and (c) of this section shall apply both before and after such amendment. All references in this section to section 614(d) are references to section 614(d) as it existed prior to its amendment by section 226(b)(3) of the Revenue Act of 1964.

(2) A taxpayer who owns two or more separate operating mineral interests, which constitute part or all of an operating unit, may elect under section 614(b) and this section to form one aggregation of any two or more of such operating mineral interests and to treat such aggregation as one property. Any operating mineral interest which the taxpayer does not elect to include within the aggregation within the time prescribed in paragraph (d) of this section shall be treated as a separate property. The aggregation of separate properties which results from exercising the election shall be considered as one property for all purposes of subtitle A of the Code. The preceding sentence does not preclude the use of more than one account under a single method of computing depreciation or the use of more than one method of computing depreciation under section 167, if otherwise proper. Any reasonable and consistently applied method or methods of computing depreciation of the improvements made with respect to the separate properties aggregated may be continued in accordance with section 167 and the regulations thereunder. Operating interests in different minerals which comprise part or all of the same operating unit may be included in the aggregation. It is not necessary for purposes of the aggregation that the separate operating mineral interests be included in a single tract or parcel of land or in contiguous tracts or parcels of land so long as such interests are a part of the same operating unit. Under section 614(b), a taxpayer cannot elect to form more than one aggregation of separate operating mineral interests within one operating unit. For definitions of "operating mineral interest" and "operating unit" see respectively paragraphs (b) and (c) of this section.

(b) Operating mineral interest defined. The term "operating mineral interest" means a separate mineral interest as described in section 614(a), in respect of which the costs of production are required to be taken into account by the taxpayer for purposes of computing the limitation of 50 percent of the taxable income from the property in determining the deduction for percentage depletion computed under section 613, or such costs would be so required to be taken into account if the mine, well, or other natural deposit were in the production stage. The term does not include royalty interests or similar interests, such as production payments or net profits interests. For the purpose of determining whether a mineral interest is an operating mineral interest, "costs of production" do not include intangible drilling and development costs, exploration expenditures under section 615, or development expenditures under section 616. Taxes, such as production taxes, payable by holders of nonoperating interests are not considered costs of production for this purpose. A taxpayer may not aggregate operating mineral interests and nonoperating mineral interests such as royalty interests.

(c) Operating unit defined. *(1)* The term "operating unit" refers to the operating mineral interests which are operated together for the purpose of producing minerals. An "operating unit" of a particular taxpayer must be determined on the basis of his own operations. It is recognized that operating units may not be uniform in the various natural resources industries or in any one of the natural resources industries, such as coal, oil and gas, and the like. As to a particular taxpayer, business reasons may require the formation of operating units that vary in size and content. The term "operating unit" refers to a producing unit, and not to an administrative or sales organization. Among the factors which indicate that mineral interests are operated together as a unit are—

(i) Common field or operating personnel,

(ii) Common supply and maintenance facilities,

(iii) Common processing or treatment plants, and

(iv) Common storage facilities.

However, operating mineral interests which are geographically widespread may not be treated as parts of the same operating unit merely because a single set of accounting records, a single executive organization, or a single sales force is maintained by the taxpayer with respect to such interests, or merely because the products of such interests are processed at the same treatment plant.

(2) If aggregated, an undeveloped operating mineral interest shall be aggregated only with those interests with which it will be operated as a unit when it reaches the production stage.

(3) While a taxpayer may operate an operating mineral interest through an agent, a coowner may aggregate only his operating mineral interests that are actually operated as a unit. For example, if A owned and actually operated the entire working interest in lease X and also owned an undivided fraction of lease Y in which B owned the remaining interest and which B actually operated as a unit with lease Z, A may

not aggregate his interest in lease X with his undivided interest in lease Y, since they are not actually operated as a unit.

(4) The determination of the taxpayer as to what constitutes an operating unit is to be accepted unless there is a clear and convincing basis for a change in such determination.

(d) Manner and scope of election. *(1) Election; when made.* (i) Except as provided in subparagraph (2)(ii) of this paragraph, the election under section 614(b) and paragraph (a) of this section to treat an operating mineral interest as part of an aggregation shall be made not later than the time prescribed by law for filing the taxpayer's income tax return (including extensions thereof), for whichever of the following taxable years is the later:

(a) The first taxable year beginning after December 31, 1953, and ending after August 16, 1954, or

(b) The first taxable year in which any expenditure for exploration, development, or operation in respect of the separate operating mineral interest is made by the taxpayer after the acquisition of such interest.

See, however, paragraph (c) of § 1.614-6 as to the binding effect of an election where the basis of a separate operating mineral interest in the hands of the taxpayer is determined by reference to the basis in the hands of a transferor. The election under section 614(b) may not be made with respect to any taxable year beginning after December 31, 1957, except in the case of oil and gas wells. See paragraph (e) of this section for rules with respect to the termination of the election under section 614(b) except in the case of oil and gas wells. If an expenditure has been made in respect of a separate operating mineral interest, it is immaterial whether or not any proven deposit has been discovered with respect to such interest when such expenditure has been made. The provisions of this subdivision may be illustrated by the following example:

Example. Taxpayer A is producing from an oil and gas horizon and in 1958 he drills for the purpose of locating a deeper horizon which will be operated in the same operating unit as the upper producing horizon. At the end of the taxable year 1958 he has expended $50,000 drilling for the purpose of locating a deeper horizon although at such time there is no assurance that such a horizon will be found. If taxpayer A desires to aggregate the deeper horizon, if found, with the upper horizon under section 614(b), he must elect to do so in his return for 1958. If the election to aggregate the upper and lower horizons as one property is made, the drilling expenditures with respect to the prospective lower horizon must be taken into account along with the income and expenses with respect to the upper producing horizon in computing the depletion allowance on the aggregated property.

However, where expenditures for development of, or production from, a particular mineral deposit result in the discovery of another mineral deposit, the election with respect to such other deposit shall be made for the taxable year in which it is discovered and not for the taxable year in which the expenditures were first made which resulted in such discovery.

(ii) Except in the case of oil and gas wells, if a taxpayer fails to make an election under section 614(b) to aggregate a particular operating mineral interest on or before the time prescribed for the making of such election, such interest will be treated as if an election had been made under section 614(b) to treat it as a separate property and it cannot be included in any aggregation within the operating unit of which it is a part unless the taxpayer obtains the consent of the Commissioner. However, where the taxpayer owns more than one property within an operating unit, but has elected to treat such properties separately and one of more additional operating mineral interests are subsequently acquired, any one or more of the latter may be aggregated with one of the existing separate properties within the operating unit but not with more than one of them since they cannot be validly aggregated with each other.

(iii) In the case of oil and gas wells, if the taxpayer fails to make an election under section 614(b) with respect to a particular operating mineral interest on or before the time prescribed for the making of such election, the taxpayer shall be deemed to have treated such interest under the provisions of section 614(d). See section 614(d) and § 1.614-4.

(iv) For purposes of section 614(b), the acquisition of an option to acquire an economic interest in minerals in place does not constitute the acquisition of a mineral interest. Thus, a taxpayer who makes expenditures for the exploration of minerals on a particular tract under an option to acquire an economic interest in minerals in place is not required to make an election with respect to such interest at that time. Furthermore, the election need not be made in the taxable year in which payments are made for the acquisition of a lease, such as the payment of a bonus, unless exploratory, development, or operation expenditures are made thereafter with respect to the property in that year.

(2) Election; how made. (i) The election under section 614(b) must be made by a statement attached to the income tax return of the taxpayer for the first taxable year for which the election is made. This statement shall indicate that the taxpayer is making an aggregation of separate operating mineral interests within an operating unit under section 614(b) and shall contain a description of the aggregation and describe the operating mineral interests within the operating unit which are to be treated as separate properties apart from the aggregation. A general description, accompanied by maps appropriately marked, which accurately circumscribes the scope of the aggregation and identifies the properties which are to be treated separately will be sufficient. The statement shall also contain a description of the operating unit in sufficient detail to show that the aggregated operating mineral interests are properly within a single operating unit. See paragraph (c) of this section. The taxpayer shall maintain adequate records and maps in support of the above information. In the event expenditures are first made on an operating mineral interest within an operating unit after an election with respect to the aggregation of interests in that operating unit has been made, the taxpayer shall furnish only information describing such operating mineral interest, its location in the operating unit, and whether it is to be included within the aggregation.

(ii) If the taxpayer made or did not make the election under section 614(b) with respect to a particular operating mineral interest and the last day prescribed by law for filing the return (including extensions of time therefor) on which the election was required to be made falls on or before May 1, 1961, consent is hereby given to the taxpayer to make or change the election not later than May 1, 1961. Any such election or change of such election shall be effective with respect to the earliest taxable year to which the election is applicable in respect of which assessment of a deficiency or credit or refund of an overpayment, as the case may be, resulting from such election or change is not prevented by any law or rule of law on the date such election or change is made. An election or change of election made pursuant to this subdivision shall be binding upon the taxpayer for the first taxable year for which it is effective and for all subsequent taxable years unless consent to a different treatment is obtained from the Commissioner. (See, however, paragraph (e) of this section for rules relating to the termination and nonapplicability of the election under section 614(b) except in the case of oil and gas wells.) Such election or change shall be made in the form of a statement setting forth the nature of the election or change, including information substantially the same as that required by subdivision (i) of this subparagraph, and shall be accompanied by an amended return or returns if necessary or, if appropriate, a claim for refund or credit. The appropriate documents must be filed on or before May 1, 1961, with the district director for the district in which the original return was filed.

(3) Election; when effective. If a taxpayer has elected to aggregate an operating mineral interest, the date on which the aggregation becomes effective is the earliest date within the taxable year affected, on which the taxpayer incurred any expenditure for exploration, development, or operation of such interest. The application of this rule may be illustrated by the following examples:

Example (1). In 1953, a taxpayer owned and operated mineral interests Nos. 1, 2, and 3. All three interests form one operating unit. The taxpayer, who files his return on a calendar year basis, continued to own and operate these interests during the year 1954, and in his return for that year, filed on April 15, 1955, elected to aggregate these three interests. As the result of this election, the aggregation was effective for all purposes of subtitle A of the Code as of January 1, 1954.

Example (2). Assume that, on March 1, 1955, the taxpayer described in example (1) acquired operating mineral interest No. 4 which was also a part of the operating unit composed of operating mineral interests Nos. 1, 2, and 3, that he made his first expenditure for exploration with respect to operating mineral interest No. 4 on September 1, 1955, and that, in his return filed on April 15, 1956, he elected to aggregate operating mineral interest No. 4 with the aggregation consisting of Nos. 1, 2, and 3. As the result of that election, operating mineral interest No. 4 became a part of the aggregation for all purposes of subtitle A of the Code on September 1, 1955.

(4) Election; binding effect. A valid election made under section 614(b) and this section shall be binding upon the taxpayer for the taxable year for which made and all subsequent taxable years unless consent to make a change is obtained from the Commissioner. However, see paragraph (e) of this section for rules with respect to the termination of the election under section 614(b) except in the case of oil and gas wells. For rules relating to the binding effect of an election where the basis of a separate or an aggregated property in the hands of the transferee is determined by reference to the basis in the hands of the transferor, see paragraph (c) of § 1.614-6. A taxpayer can neither include within the aggregation a separate operating mineral interest which he had previously elected to treat separately, nor exclude from the aggregation a separate operating mineral interest previously included therein unless consent to do so is obtained from the Commissioner. A change in tax consequences alone is not sufficient to obtain consent to change the treatment of an operating mineral interest. However, consent may be appropriate where, for example, there has been a substantial change in the taxpayer's operations so that a major part of an aggregation becomes a part of another operating unit. Applications for consent shall be made in writing to the Commissioner of Internal Revenue, Washington 25, D.C. The application must be accompanied by a statement indicating the reason or reasons for the change and furnishing the information required under subdivision (i) of subparagraph (2) of this paragraph, unless such information has been previously filed and is current.

(5) Invalid aggregations. (i) In general. In addition to aggregations which are invalid under section 614(b) because of the failure to make timely elections, aggregations may be invalid under such section in situations which may be divided into two general categories. The first category involves basic aggregations which were timely but otherwise initially invalid. The second category involves invalid additions of operating mineral interests to basic aggregations which additions became subject to the election in years subsequent to the year in which the initial basic aggregation or aggregations were formed.

(ii) Invalid basic aggregations. The term "invalid basic aggregations" refers to those aggregations which are initially invalid. Generally, such basic aggregations will be invalid because more than one aggregation has been formed within an operating unit or because operating mineral interests in two or more operating units have been improperly aggregated. For any year in which an invalid basic aggregation exists, each operating mineral interest included in such aggregation shall be treated for all purposes as a separate property unless consent is obtained from the Commissioner to treat any such interest in a different manner. Consent will be granted in appropriate cases as, for example, where the taxpayer demonstrates that he inadvertently formed an invalid basic aggregation. The provisions of this subdivision may be illustrated by the following examples:

Example (1). In 1953, taxpayer A owned six operating mineral interests, designated No. 1 through No. 6, and he continued to own and operate such interests during 1954. He acquired no other operating mineral interests during such year. All six of these operating mineral interests form one operating unit. Assume that A elected under section 614(b) to aggregate operating mineral interests Nos. 1 through 3 into one aggregation and Nos. 4 through 6 into another aggregation. Since A has formed two aggregations in one operating unit, they are invalid basic aggregations. Therefore, interests Nos. 1 through 6 must be treated as separate properties for 1954 and all subsequent taxable years unless consent is obtained from the Commissioner to treat any of such interests in a different manner.

Example (2). Assume the same facts as in example (1) and assume also that, in his return for 1954, A correctly elected to aggregate all six operating mineral interests into one aggregation under section 614(b). Assume further that all these operating mineral interests continued to be in one operating unit for the years 1954, 1955, and 1956 but that, because of changes in the facts and circumstances of A's operations, in 1957 operating mineral interests Nos. 1, 2, and 3 became a part of one operating unit and Nos. 4, 5, and 6 became a part of another operating unit. Notwithstanding the change in operations, the election made by A shall continue to be binding unless consent to change such election is obtained from the Commissioner.

(iii) Invalid additions. The term "additions" refers to the additions that a taxpayer makes by electing to aggregate an operating mineral interest with an aggregation formed in a previous year. Such additions will be invalid where the taxpayer either elected to aggregate an operating mineral interest which is part of one operating unit with an aggregation of operating mineral interests which is a part of another operating unit. An operating mineral interest which is invalidly added to either a valid basic aggregation or to an invalid basic aggregation shall be considered as a separate property unless consent is obtained from the Commissioner to treat such interest in a different manner. The following are examples of invalid additions:

Example (1). In 1953, taxpayer A owned six operating mineral interests designated No. 1 through No. 6 and he continued to own and operate such interests during 1954. He acquired no other operating mineral interests during that year. Nos. 1 through 3 formed one operating unit and Nos. 4 through 6 formed another operating unit. In his return for 1954, A incorrectly elected to aggregate all six operating mineral interests into one aggregation under section 614(b). In 1955, A acquired and commenced development of operating mineral interest No. 7 which is correctly a part of the operating unit of which operating mineral interests Nos. 1, 2, and 3 are a part. A elected under section 614(b), for the year 1955, to aggregate operating mineral interest No. 7 with the invalid basic aggregation composed of Nos. 1 through 6. Since operating mineral interest No. 7 was aggregated with an invalid basic aggregation, it is an invalid addition and must be treated as a separate property unless consent is obtained from the Commissioner to treat it in a different manner.

Example (2). In 1953, taxpayer A owned nine operating mineral interests designated No. 1 through No. 9. During 1954, he continued to own and operate such interests and acquired no other operating mineral interest. Interest No. 1 through No. 3 form one operating unit, Nos. 4 through 6 form another operating unit, and Nos. 7 through 9 form a third operating unit. For the year 1954, A elected under section 614(b) to aggregate operating mineral interests Nos. 1, 2, 3, and 4 into one aggregation, to treat Nos. 5 and 6 as separate properties, and to aggregate Nos. 7, 8, and 9 into another aggregation. Assume that in 1955 A acquired and commenced development of operating mineral interest No. 10 which was a part of the operating unit composed of Nos. 1, 2, and 3. Assume further that he elected under section 614(b) to aggregate No. 10 with the aggregation composed of Nos. 7, 8, and 9. This would be an invalid addition to a valid basic aggregation since operating mineral interest No. 10 was not properly a part of the operating unit formed by Nos. 7, 8, and 9. Therefore, interest No. 10 must be treated as a separate property for 1955 and all subsequent taxable years unless consent is obtained from the Commissioner to treat it in a different manner. However, the valid basic aggregation composed of interests Nos. 7 through 9 is not affected by the invalid addition of interest No. 10.

Example (3). Assume the same facts as in example (2) except that A elected under section 614(b) in 1955 to aggregate No. 10 with the aggregation of Nos. 1 through 4. This would also be an invalid addition because the aggregation composed of Nos. 1 through 4 is an invalid basic aggregation since operating mineral interest No. 4 is not a part of the operating unit consisting of Nos. 1, 2, and 3. Therefore, interest No. 10 must be treated as a separate property for 1955 and all subsequent taxable years unless consent is obtained from the Commissioner to treat such interest in a different manner.

(e) **Termination of election.** *(1) Taxable years beginning after December 31, 1963, in the case of oil and gas wells.* In the case of oil and gas wells, the election provided for under section 614(b) and paragraph (a) of this section to form an aggregation of separate operating mineral interests shall not apply with respect to any taxable year beginning after December 31, 1963. In addition, if a taxpayer treated certain separate operating mineral interests in a single tract or parcel of land as separate rather than as an aggregation and decides to continue such treatment for taxable years beginning after December 31, 1963, he must make an appropriate election under section 614(b) as amended by the Revenue Act of 1964. See § 1.614-8.

(2) Taxable years beginning after December 31, 1957, in the case of mines. Except in the case of oil and gas wells, the election provided for under section 614(b) and paragraph (a) of this section to form an aggregation of separate operating mineral interests shall not apply with respect to any taxable year beginning after December 31, 1957. Thus, if a taxpayer makes a binding election under section 614(b) to form an aggregation of separate operating mineral interests within an operating unit for taxable years beginning before January 1, 1958, he must make a new election for the first taxable year beginning after December 31, 1957, under section 614(c) within the time prescribed in § 1.614-3 if he wishes to aggregate any separate operating mineral interests within such operating unit. A new election must be made under section 614(c) notwithstanding the fact that the aggregation formed under section 614(b) would constitute a valid aggregation under section 614(c). Failure to make such an election within the time prescribed shall constitute an election to treat each separate operating mineral interest within the operating unit as a separate property for taxable years beginning after December 31, 1957.

(3) Taxable years beginning before January 1, 1958, in the case of mines. An election made under section 614(b) and paragraph (a) of this section to form an aggregation of separate operating mineral interests within a particular operating unit shall not apply with respect to any taxable year beginning prior to January 1, 1958, for which the taxpayer makes an election under section 614(c)(3)(B) and paragraph (f)(2) of § 1.614-3 which is applicable to any separate operating mineral interest within the same operating unit. The provisions of this subparagraph may be illustrated by the following examples:

Example (1). In 1953, taxpayer A owned six separate operating mineral interests, designated No. 1 through No. 6, which he operated as a unit. Operating mineral interest Nos. 1 through 5 comprise a mine, and operating mineral interest No. 6 represents one mineral deposit in a single tract of land which is being extracted by means of two mines. Taxpayer A previously made a binding election under section 614(b) to aggregate operating mineral interests Nos. 1 through 5 and to treat operating mineral interest No. 6 as a separate property. Under section 614(c)(2) and (3)(B) taxpayer A makes an election which is applicable for the taxable year 1954 and all subsequent taxable years to treat operating mineral interest No. 6 as two separate operating mineral interests. Therefore, the previous election of taxpayer A to aggregate operating mineral interests Nos. 1 through 5 under section 614(b) does not apply. Unless taxpayer A also makes an election to aggregate operating mineral interests Nos. 1 through 5 as one property under section 614(c)(1) and (3)(B) within the time prescribed in paragraph (f)(2) of § 1.614-3, he shall be deemed to have made an election to treat each of such interests as a separate property for 1954 and all subsequent taxable years.

Example (2). In 1953, taxpayer B owned six separate operating mineral interests, designated No. 1 through No. 6, which he operated as a unit. Operating mineral interests Nos. 1 through 3 comprise a mine and Nos. 4 through 6 comprise a second mine. Taxpayer B previously made a binding election under section 614(b) to aggregate operating mineral interests Nos. 1 through 3 and to treat Nos. 4 through 6 as separate properties. Under section 614(c)(1) and (3)(B) taxpayer B makes an election which is applicable for the taxable year 1954 and all subsequent taxable years to aggregate operating mineral interests Nos. 4 through 6 as one property. The previous election of the taxpayer under section 614(b) to aggregate operating mineral interests Nos. 1 through 3 does not apply even though such aggregation would constitute a valid aggregation if formed under section 614(c)(1). Therefore, if taxpayer B wishes to continue to treat operating mineral interests Nos. 1 through 3 as one property, he must also make an election to do so under section 614(c)(1) and (3)(B) within the time prescribed in paragraph (f)(2) of § 1.614-3.

(4) Bases of separate operating mineral interests. If an aggregation formed under section 614(b) is terminated by reason of the provisions of section 614(b)(4)(A), is terminated under section 614(b)(4)(B) for any taxable year after the first taxable year to which the election under section 614(b) applies, or is terminated by reason of the provisions of section 614(b) as amended by the Revenue Act of 1964, the bases of the separate operating mineral interests (and combinations thereof) included in such aggregation shall be determined in accordance with the rules contained in paragraph (a)(2) of § 1.614-6 as of the first day of the first taxable year for which the termination is effective. However, if by reason of the provisions of section 614(b)(4)(B), an election to aggregate under section 614(b) does not apply for any taxable year for which such election was made, the bases of the separate operating mineral interests included in the aggregation formed under section 614(b) shall be determined without regard to the election under section 614(b).

(f) Alternative treatment of separate operating mineral interests in the case of oil and gas wells. For rules relating to an alternative treatment of separate operating mineral interests in the case of oil and gas wells, see § 1.614-4.

T.D. 6524, 1/9/61, amend T.D. 6859, 10/27/65.

§ 1.614-3 Rules relating to separate operating mineral interests in the case of mines.

Caution: The Treasury has not yet amended Reg § 1.614-3 to reflect changes made by P.L. 95-618.

(a) Election to aggregate separate operating mineral interests. *(1) General rule.* Except in the case of oil and gas wells, a taxpayer who owns two or more separate operating mineral interests, which constitute part or all of the same operating unit, may elect under section 614(c)(1) and this paragraph to form an aggregation of all such operating mineral interests which comprise any one mine or any two or more mines and to treat such aggregation as one property. The aggregated property which results from the exercise of such election shall be considered as one property for all purposes of subtitle A of the Code. The preceding sentence does not preclude the use of more than one account under a single method of computing depreciation or the use of more than one method of computing depreciation under section 167, if otherwise proper. Any reasonable and consistently applied method or methods of computing depreciation of the improvements made with respect to the separate properties aggregated may be continued in accordance with section 167 and the regulations thereunder. It is not necessary for purposes of the aggregation that the separate operating mineral interests be included in a single tract or parcel of land or in contiguous tracts or parcels of land so long as such interests constitute part or all of the same operating unit. A taxpayer may elect to form more than one aggregation of separate operating mineral interests within one operating unit so long as each aggregation consists of all the separate operating mineral interests which compromise any one mine or any two or more mines. Thus, no aggregation may include any separate operating mineral interest which is a part of a mine without including all of the separate operating mineral interests which comprise such mine in the first taxable year for which the election to aggregate is effective. Any separate operating mineral interest which becomes a part of such mine in a subsequent taxable year must also be included in such aggregation as of the taxable year that such interest becomes a part of such mine. The taxable year in which such interest becomes a part of such mine shall be determined upon the basis of the facts and circumstances of the particular case. If a taxpayer fails to make an election under this paragraph to aggregate a particular operating mineral interest (other than an interest which becomes a part of a mine with respect to which the interests have been aggregated in a prior taxable year) on or before the last day prescribed for making such an election, such interest shall be treated as if an election had been made to treat it as a separate property. A taxpayer may not aggregate operating mineral interests and nonoperating mineral interests such as royalty interests. For definitions of the terms "operating mineral interest", "operating unit", and "mine", see respectively paragraphs (c), (d), and (e) of this section.

(2) Aggregation in subsequent taxable years. If the taxpayer has made an election under section 614(c)(1) for a particular taxable year with respect to any operating mineral interest or interests within a particular operating unit, and if, for a subsequent taxable year, the taxpayer desires to make an election with respect to an additional operating mineral interest within the same operating unit, then whether or not the taxpayer may elect to include such additional interest in an aggregation or treat it as a separate property depends upon the nature of such additional interest and of the taxpayer's previous elections. If the additional interest is a part of a mine with respect to which the other interests have been aggregated, the additional interest must be included in such aggregation. If the additional interest is a part of a mine with respect to which the other interests have been treated as separate properties, the additional interest must be treated as a separate property. If the additional interest is part of a mine which previously consisted of only a single interest which has not been aggregated with any other mine, such additional interest may be aggregated or treated as a separate property. If the additional interest is an entire mine, it may, at the election of the taxpayer, (i) be added to any aggregation within the same operating unit, (ii) be aggregated with any other single interest which is an entire mine provided both interests are within the same operating unit even though such single interest has previously been treated as a separate property, or (iii) be treated as a separate property.

(b) Election to treat a single operating mineral interest as more than one property. *(1) General rule.* Except in the case of oil and gas wells, a taxpayer who owns a separate operating mineral interest in a mineral deposit in a single tract or parcel of land may elect under section 614(c)(2) and this paragraph to treat such interest as two or more separate operating mineral interests if such mineral deposit is being developed or extracted by means of two or more mines. In order for this election to be applicable, there must be at least two mines with respect to each of which an expenditure for development or operation has been made by the taxpayer. The election under section 614(c)(2) may also be made with respect to a separate operating mineral interest formed by a previous election under section 614(c)(2) at such time as the mineral deposit previously allocated to such interest is being developed or extracted by means of two or more mines. If there is more than one mineral deposit in a single tract or parcel of land, an election under section 614(c)(2) with respect to any one of such mineral deposits has no application to the other mineral deposits. The election under section 614(c)(2) may not be made with respect to an aggregated property or with respect to any operating mineral interest which is a part of any aggregation formed by the taxpayer unless the taxpayer obtains consent from the Commissioner. Such consent will not be granted where the principal purpose for the request to make the election is based on tax consequences. Application for such consent shall be made in writing to the Commissioner of Internal Revenue, Washington, D.C. The application must be accompanied by a statement setting forth in detail the reason or reasons for the request to exercise the election with respect to an aggregated property.

(2) Allocation of mineral deposit. If the taxpayer elects to treat a separate operating mineral interest in a mineral deposit in a single tract or parcel of land as more than one separate operating mineral interest, then all of such mineral deposit therein and all of the portion of the tract or parcel of land allocated thereto must be allocated to the newly formed separate operating mineral interests. A portion of such mineral deposit and such tract or parcel of land must be allocated to each such newly formed separate operating mineral interest. There must be at least one mine, with respect to which an expenditure for development or operation has been made by the taxpayer, with respect to each such portion. The extent of the portion to be allocated to each newly formed separate operating mineral interest is to be determined upon the basis of the facts and circumstances of the particular case.

(3) Bases of newly formed separate operating mineral interests. The adjusted basis of each of the separate operating mineral interests formed by the making of the election under section 614(c)(2) shall be determined by apportioning the adjusted basis of the separate operating mineral interest with respect to which such election was made between (or among) the newly formed separate operating mineral interests in the same proportion as the fair market value of each such newly formed interest (as of the date on which the election becomes effective) bears to the total fair market value of the interest with respect to which the election was made as of such date.

(4) Aggregation of newly formed separate operating mineral interests. Any separate operating mineral interest formed by the making of the election under section 614(c)(2) may be included as a part of an aggregation subject to the requirements of paragraph (a) of this section, provided that the time for making the election under section 614(c)(1) to include such separate operating mineral interest in such aggregation has not expired. See paragraph (f) of this section. The provisions of this subparagraph may be illustrated by the following example:

Example. In 1958, taxpayer A acquired two separate operating mineral interests designated No. 1 and No. 2. Each is an interest in a single mineral deposit in a single tract of land. In the same year, taxpayer A made his first development expenditure with respect to a mine on operating mineral interest No. 1 and a mine on operating mineral interest No. 2. Operating mineral interests Nos. 1 and 2 are operated as a unit. Taxpayer A did not elect to aggregate operating mineral interests Nos. 1 and 2 under section 614 (c)(1) within the time prescribed for making such an election. In 1960 taxpayer A made his first development expenditure with respect to a second mine on operating mineral interest No. 2. Taxpayer A elected under section 614(c)(2) to treat operating mineral interest No. 2 as two separate operating mineral interests, designated as Nos. 2(a) and 2(b), for the taxable year 1960 and all subsequent taxable years. No. 2(a) contained the mine for which the first development expenditure was made in 1958, and No. 2(b) contained the mine for which the first development expenditure was made in 1960. If taxpayer A wishes to do so, he may elect to aggregate mineral interests Nos. 1 and 2(b) under section 614(c)(1) for the taxable year 1960 and all subsequent taxable years since the first development expenditure with respect to the mine on operating mineral interest No. 2(b) was made during the taxable year 1960. Taxpayer A may not elect to aggregate mineral interests Nos. 1 and 2(a) under such section since the time for making such an election has expired.

(c) Operating mineral interest defined. For the definition of the term "operating mineral interest" as used in this section, see paragraph (b) of § 1.614-2.

(d) Operating unit defined. For the definition of the term "operating unit" as used in this section, see paragraph (c) of § 1.614-2.

(e) Mine defined. For purposes of this section, the term "mine" means any excavation or other workings or series of related excavations or related workings, as the case may be, for the purpose of extracting any known mineral deposit except oil and gas deposits. For the purpose of the preceding sentence, the term "excavations" or "workings" includes quarries, pots, shafts, and wells (except oil and gas wells). The number of excavations or workings that constitute a mine is to be determined upon the basis of the facts and circumstances of the particular case such as the nature and position of the mineral deposit or deposits, the method of mining the mineral, the location of the excavations or other workings in relation to the mineral deposit or deposits, and the topography of the area. The determination of the taxpayer as to the composition of a mine is to be accepted unless there is a clear and convincing basis for a change in such determination.

(f) Manner and scope of election. *(1) Election to apply section 614(c)(1) and (2) for taxable years beginning after December 31, 1957.* Except as provided in subparagraphs (2) and (3) of this paragraph, the election under section 614(c)(1) and paragraph (a) of this section to treat an operating mineral interest as part of an aggregation shall be made under section 614(c)(3)(A) not later than the time prescribed by law for filing the taxpayer's income tax return (including extensions thereof) for whichever of the following taxable years is the later:

(i) The first taxable year beginning after December 31, 1957, or

(ii) The first taxable year in which any expenditure for development or operation in respect of the separate operating mineral interest is made by the taxpayer after the acquisition of such interest. Except as provided in subparagraphs (2) and (3) of this paragraph, the election under section 614(c)(2) and paragraph (b) of this section to treat a single operating mineral interest as more than one operating mineral interest shall be made under section 614(c)(3)(A) not later than the time prescribed by law for filing the taxpayer's income tax return (including extensions thereof) for whichever of the following taxable years is the later:

(iii) The first taxable year beginning after December 31, 1957, or

(iv) The first taxable year in which expenditures for development or operation of more than one mine in respect of the separate operating mineral interest are made by the taxpayer after the acquisition of such interest.

However, if the latest time at which an election may be made under this subparagraph falls on or before May 1, 1961, such election may be made or modified at any time on or before May 1, 1961. See paragraph (c) of § 1.614-6 as to the binding effect of an election where the basis of a separate operating mineral interest in the hands of the taxpayer is determined by reference to the basis in the hands of a transferor.

(2) Election to apply section 614(c)(1) and (2) for taxable years beginning before January 1, 1958. In accordance with section 614(c)(3)(B), the election under section 614(c)(1) and paragraph (a) of this section to treat an operating mineral interest as part of an aggregation may, at the election of the taxpayer, be made not later than the time prescribed by law for filing the taxpayer's income tax return (including extensions thereof) for whichever of the following taxable years is the later:

(i) The first taxable year beginning after December 31, 1953, and ending after August 16, 1954, for which assessment of a deficiency or credit or refund of an overpayment, as the case may be, resulting from an election under section 614(c)(1), is not prevented on September 2, 1958, by the operation of any law or rule of law, or

(ii) The first taxable year in which any expenditure for development or operation in respect of the separate operating mineral interest is made by the taxpayer after the acquisition of such interest. In accordance with section 614(c)(3)(B), the election under section 614(c)(2) and paragraph (b) of this section to treat an operating mineral interest as more than one operating mineral interest may, at the election of the taxpayer, be made not later than the time prescribed by law for filing the taxpayer's income tax return (including extensions thereof) for whichever of the following taxable years is the later:

(iii) The first taxable year beginning after December 31, 1953, and ending after August 16, 1954, for which assessment of a deficiency or credit or refund of an overpayment, as the case may be, resulting from an election under section 614(c)(2), is not prevented on September 2, 1958, by the operation of any law or rule of law, or

(iv) The first taxable year in which expenditures for development or operation of more than one mine in respect of the separate operating mineral interest are made by the taxpayer after the acquisition of such interest.

However, if the latest time at which an election may be made under this subparagraph falls on or before May 1, 1961, such election may be made or modified at any time on or before May 1, 1961. See paragraph (c) of § 1.614-6 as to the binding effect of an election where the basis of a separate operating mineral interest in the hands of the taxpayer is determined by reference to the basis in the hands of a transferor.

(3) Limitation. If the taxpayer makes an election under section 614(c)(1) or (2) in accordance with section 614(c)(3)(B) and subparagraph (2) of this paragraph with respect to any operating mineral interest which constitutes part or all of an operating unit, such taxpayer may not make any election under section 614(c)(1) or (2) in accordance with section 614(c)(3)(A) and subparagraph (1) of this paragraph with respect to any operating mineral interest which constitutes part or all of such operating unit. The provisions of this subparagraph may be illustrated by the following example:

Example. In 1953, taxpayer A owned six separate operating mineral interests, designated No. 1 through No. 6, which he operated as a unit. Operating mineral interests Nos. 1 through 5 comprise a mine, and operating mineral interest No. 6 represents one mineral deposit in a single tract of land which is being extracted by means of two mines. In accordance with section 614(c)(3)(B) and subparagraph (2) of this paragraph, taxpayer A elects under section 614(c)(2) to treat operating mineral interest No. 6 as two separate operating mineral interests for the taxable year 1954 and all subsequent taxable years. Unless taxpayer A also makes an election under section 614(c)(1) to aggregate operating mineral interests Nos. 1 through 5 for the taxable year 1954 and all subsequent taxable years in accordance with section 614(c)(3)(B) and subparagraph (2) of this paragraph, he shall be deemed to have made an election to treat each of such interests as a separate property. Taxpayer A may not elect, under section 614(c)(1) and (3)(A), to aggregate operating mineral interests Nos. 1 through 5 for the taxable year 1958 or any subsequent taxable year.

(4) Statute of limitations. If the taxpayer makes any election in accordance with section 614(c)(3)(B) and subparagraph (2) of this paragraph and if assessment of any deficiency for any taxable year resulting from such election is prevented on May 1, 1961, or at any time within one year after May 1, 1961, by the operation of any law or rule of law, such assessment may, nevertheless, be made within one year after May 1, 1961. Any election by a taxpayer in accordance with section 614(c)(3)(B) shall constitute consent to the assessment of any deficiency resulting from any such election. If refund or credit of any overpayment of income tax resulting from any election made in accordance with section 614(c)(3)(B) is prevented on May 1, 1961, or at any time within one year after May 1, 1961, by the operation of any law or rule of law, refund or credit of such overpayment may, nevertheless, be made or allowed but only if claim therefor is filed within one year after May 1, 1961. This subparagraph shall not apply with respect to any taxable year of a taxpayer for which an assessment of a deficiency resulting from an election made in accordance with section 614(c)(3)(B) or a refund or credit of an overpayment resulting from any such election, as the case may be, is prevented by the operation of any law or rule of law on September 2, 1958.

(5) Elections—how made. (i) General rule. Except as provided in subdivision (ii) of this subparagraph, an election under section 614(c)(1) or (2) and paragraph (a) or (b) of this section must be made by a statement attached to the income tax return of the taxpayer for the first taxable year for which the election is made. The statement shall contain the following information:

(a) Whether the taxpayer is making an election or elections with respect to the operating unit in accordance with section 614(c)(3)(A) or (B);

(b) A description of the operating unit of the taxpayer in sufficient detail to identify the operating mineral interests which are included within such operating unit;

(c) A description of each aggregation to be formed within the operating unit in sufficient detail to show that each aggregation consists of all the separate operating mineral interests which comprise any one mine or any two or more mines;

(d) A description of each separate operating mineral interest within the operating unit which is to be treated as a separate property in sufficient detail to show that such interest is not a part of any mine for which an election to aggregate has been made;

(e) The taxable year in which the first expenditure for development or operation was made by the taxpayer with respect to each separate operating mineral interest within the operating unit, but if the first expenditure for development or operation has not been made with respect to a separate operating mineral interest before the close of the taxable year for which the election under this section is made, such information should also be included;

(f) A description of each separate operating mineral interest within the operating unit which the taxpayer elects to treat as more than one such interest under section 614(c)(2) in sufficient detail to show that the separate operating mineral interest was not a part of an aggregation formed by the taxpayer under section 614(c)(1) for any taxable year prior to the taxable year for which the election under section 614(c)(2) is made, and to show that the mineral deposit representing the separate operating mineral interest is being developed or extracted by means of two or more mines;

(g) The taxable year in which the first expenditure for development or operation was made by the taxpayer with respect to each mine on the separate operating mineral interest that the taxpayer is electing to treat as more than one such interest; and

(h) The allocation of the mineral deposit representing the separate operating mineral interest between (or among) the newly formed interests and the method by which such allocation was made. For the purpose of applying subdivisions (e) and (g) of this subdivision, if the first expenditure for development or operation with respect to a separate operating mineral interest or a mine was made prior to the first taxable year for which the election with respect to such interest or mine is applicable, the taxpayer may state that such is the case in lieu of identifying the exact taxable year in which such first expenditure was made. In any case where part of the information required under this subdivision can be adequately supplied by means of appropriately marked maps, the statement may be accompanied by such maps and may omit the required descriptive material to the extent replaced by the maps. The taxpayer shall maintain adequate records and maps in support of the above information. In the event that the first expenditure for development or operation with respect to a separate operating mineral interest is made by the taxpayer in a taxable year subsequent to the taxable year for which an election under this section has been made with respect to the operating unit of which such interest is a part, the taxpayer shall furnish information describing such interest in sufficient detail to identify it as a part of such operating unit, to show whether it is a part of a mine with respect to which the interests have previously been aggregated or have previously been treated as separate properties, and to indicate whether it is to be included within an aggregation.

(ii) Special rule. If the last day prescribed by law for filing the taxpayer's income tax return (including extensions thereof) for the first taxable year for which an election under section 614(c)(1) or (2) is made falls before May 1, 1961, the statement of election or modification thereof for such taxable year must be filed on or before May 1, 1961, with the district director for the district in which such return was filed. The statement must contain the information as required in subdivision (i) of this subparagraph, must indicate the first taxable year for which the election contained therein is made, and shall be accompanied by an amended return or returns if necessary or, if appropriate, a claim for refund or credit.

(6) Elections; when effective. If the taxpayer has elected to form an aggregation under section 614(c)(1) and this section, the date on which the aggregation becomes effective is the first day of the first taxable year for which the election is made; except that if any separate operating mineral interest included in such aggregation was acquired after such first day, the date on which the inclusion of such interest in such aggregation becomes effective is the date of its acquisition. If the taxpayer elects to add another operating mineral interest to such aggregation for a subsequent taxable year, the date on which aggregation of the additional interest becomes effective is the first day of such subsequent taxable year or the date of acquisition of such interest, whichever is later. If an operating mineral interest is required to be included in the aggregation for a subsequent taxable year because such interest becomes a part of a mine which the taxpayer has previously elected to aggregate, the date on which the inclusion of such interest in the aggregation becomes effective is the first day of the subsequent taxable year or the date of acquisition of such interest, whichever is later. If the taxpayer has elected to treat a separate operating mineral interest as more than one such interest, the date on which the election becomes effective is the first day of the first taxable year for which the election is made or the earliest date on which the first expenditure for development or operation has been made by the taxpayer with respect to a mine on each newly formed separate operating mineral interest, whichever is later.

(7) Elections; binding effect. A valid election under section 614(c)(1) or (2) whether made in accordance with section 614(c)(3)(A) or (B) shall be binding upon the taxpayer for the taxable year for which made and for all subsequent taxable years unless consent to change the treatment of an operating mineral interest with respect to which an election has been made is obtained from the Commissioner. For rules relating to the binding effect of an election where the basis of a separate or an aggregated property in the hands of the transferee is determined by reference to the basis in the hands of the transferor, see paragraph (c) of § 1.614-6. A taxpayer can neither include within an aggregation a separate operating mineral interest which he has previously elected to treat as a separate property, nor exclude from an aggregation a separate operating mineral interest which he has properly elected to include within such aggregation unless consent to do so is obtained from the Commissioner. A change in tax consequences alone is not sufficient to obtain consent to change the treatment of an operating mineral interest. However, consent may be appropriate where, for example, there has been a substantial change in the taxpayer's operations so that a major part of an aggregation becomes a part of another operating unit. Applications for consent shall be made in writing to the Commissioner of Internal Revenue, Washington 25, D.C. The application must be accompanied by a statement indicating the reason or reasons for the change and furnishing the information required in subparagraph (5)(i) of this paragraph, unless such information has been previously filed and is current.

(8) Invalid aggregations. (i) General rule. In addition to aggregations which are invalid under this section because of the failure to make timely elections, aggregations may be invalid under this section in situations which may be divided into two general categories. The first category involves invalid basic aggregations. The second category involves invalid additions to basic aggregations.

(ii) Invalid basic aggregations. The term "invalid basic aggregations" refers to aggregations which are initially invalid.

Generally, a basic aggregation is initially invalid because it does not include all the separate operating mineral interests which comprise a complete mine or mines or because it includes separate operating mineral interests which are not part of the same operating unit. If the taxpayer makes an invalid basic aggregation, each of the separate operating mineral interests included in such aggregation shall be treated as a separate property for the first taxable year for which the election is made and for all subsequent taxable years unless consent is obtained from the Commissioner to treat any such interest in a different manner. Consent will be granted in appropriate cases. For example, assume that the taxpayer elects to form an aggregation of the operating mineral interests which comprise one or more complete mines. If the taxpayer demonstrates that he inadvertently failed to include a minor part of one of the aggregated mines or inadvertently included a minor part of another mine that is not a part of the aggregation, consent will ordinarily be granted to maintain the aggregation by including the part omitted or by excluding the part included. The provisions of this subdivision may be illustrated by the following examples:

Example (1). In 1958, taxpayer A owned ten operating mineral interests, designated No. 1 through No. 10, which he operated as a unit. Interests Nos. 1 through 5 comprised mine X, and interests Nos. 6 through 10 comprised mine Y. Taxpayer A had made his first development expenditure with respect to each of the ten interests before January 1, 1958. Taxpayer A elected under section 614(c)(1) and (3)(A) to aggregate interests Nos. 1 through 8 for 1958 and all subsequent taxable years. The aggregation formed by taxpayer A is an invalid basic aggregation because it does not include all the operating mineral interests which comprise a complete mine or mines. Therefore, interests Nos. 1 through 8 must be treated as separate properties for 1958 and all subsequent taxable years unless consent is obtained from the Commissioner to treat any of such interests in a different manner.

Example (2). In 1958, taxpayer B owned ten operating mineral interests designated No. 1 through No. 10. Interests Nos. 1 through 5 comprised mine X, and interests Nos. 6 through 10 comprised mine Y. Taxpayer B had made his first development expenditure with respect to each of the ten interests before January 1, 1958. Taxpayer B elected under section 614(c)(1) and (3)(A) to aggregate interests Nos. 1 through 10 for 1958 and all subsequent taxable years. Upon audit, it was determined that mines X and Y were in two separate operating units. Therefore, the aggregation formed by taxpayer B is invalid, and interests Nos. 1 through 10 must be treated as separate properties for 1958 and all subsequent taxable years unless consent is obtained from the Commissioner to treat any of such interests in a different manner.

(iii) Invalid additions. The term "invalid addition" refers to an operating mineral interest which is invalidly aggregated with an existing aggregation. Generally, an addition is invalid because it is a part of a mine and is aggregated with an aggregation which does not include other interests which are parts of the same mine, or because it is in one operating unit and is included as part of an aggregation which is in another operating unit. If an invalid addition is properly a part of a mine with respect to which other interests have been validly aggregated for a taxable year prior to the first taxable year for which the election to aggregate the invalid addition is made, then the invalid addition shall be included in the aggregation of which it is properly a part for such first taxable year and all subsequent taxable years. Any other invalid addition shall be treated as a separate property for the first taxable year for which the election to aggregate such addition is made and for all subsequent taxable years unless consent is obtained from the Commissioner to treat any such interest in a different manner. The provisions of this subdivision may be illustrated by the following examples:

Example (1). In 1958, taxpayer A owned six operating mineral interests, designated No. 1 through No. 6, which he operated as a unit. Interests Nos. 1 through 3 comprised mine X, and interests Nos. 4 through 6 comprised mine Y. Taxpayer A had made his first development expenditure with respect to each of the six interests before January 1, 1958. Taxpayer A elected under section 614(c)(1) and (3)(A) to aggregate interests Nos. 1 through 3 for 1958 and all subsequent taxable years. He elected to treat interests Nos. 4 through 6 as separate properties for 1958 and all subsequent taxable years. In 1959, taxpayer A acquired and made his first development expenditure with respect to interest No. 7. Interest No. 7 was a part of the mine composed of interests Nos. 4 through 6. Taxpayer A elected under section 614(c)(1) and (3)(A) to aggregate interest No. 7 with the aggregation of interests Nos. 1 through 3 for 1959 and all subsequent taxable years. Interest No. 7 is an invalid addition and must be treated as a separate property for 1959 and all subsequent taxable years. It cannot be aggregated with interests Nos. 4 through 6 since taxpayer A has previously elected to treat such interests as separate properties. However, the valid basic aggregation composed of interests Nos. 1 through 3 is not affected by the invalid addition of interest No. 7.

Example (2). Assume the same facts as in example (1) except that taxpayer A elected under section 614(c)(1) and (3)(A) to aggregate interests Nos. 1 through 3 as one aggregation and interests Nos. 4 through 6 as another aggregation for 1958 and all subsequent taxable years. The aggregation of interest No. 7 with the aggregation consisting of interests Nos. 1 through 3 constitutes an invalid addition. Interest No. 7 must be included in the aggregation consisting of interests Nos. 4 through 6 for 1959 and all subsequent taxable years.

Example (3). In 1958, taxpayer B owned three operating mineral interests, designated No. 1 through No. 3, which comprised mine X. Taxpayer B had made his first development expenditure with respect to each of the three interests before January 1, 1958. Taxpayer B elected under section 614(c)(1) and (3)(A) to aggregate interests Nos. 1 through 3 for 1958 and all subsequent taxable years. In 1959, taxpayer B acquired interests Nos. 4 through 7 which comprised mine Y. Taxpayer B made his first development expenditure with respect to each of the four interests during 1959. Taxpayer B elected under section 614(c)(1) and (3)(A) to aggregate interests Nos. 4 through 6 and to aggregate interest No. 7 with the aggregation consisting of interests Nos. 1 through 3 for 1959 and all subsequent taxable years. The aggregation consisting of interests Nos. 4 through 6 is an invalid basic aggregation, and the aggregation of interest No. 7 is an invalid addition. Interests Nos. 4 through 7 must be treated as separate properties for 1959 and all subsequent taxable years unless consent is obtained from the Commissioner to treat such interests in a different manner.

(g) Special rule as to deductions under section 615(a) prior to aggregation. *(1) General rule.* If an aggregation of operating mineral interests under section 614(c)(1) and paragraph (a) of this section includes any interest or interests in respect of which exploration expenditures, paid or incurred after the acquisition of such interest or interests, were deducted by the taxpayer under section 615(a) for any taxable year which precedes the date on which such aggregation becomes effective, then the tax imposed by chapter 1 of the Code for the taxable year or years in which such exploration expenditures were so deducted shall be recomputed in accordance with the rules contained in this paragraph. If an operating mineral interest is added to such aggregation for a subsequent taxable year and exploration expenditures made with respect to such interest after its acquisition were deducted by the taxpayer under section 615(a) for any taxable year which precedes the date on which the aggregation of such additional interest becomes effective, then the tax imposed by chapter 1 of the Code for the taxable year or years in which such exploration expenditures were so deducted shall be recomputed. For purposes of this paragraph, such taxable year or years shall be referred to as the taxable year or years for which a recomputation is required to be made. See paragraph (f)(6) of this section for rules relating to the date on which an aggregation becomes effective or the date on which the aggregation of an additional interest to an aggregation becomes effective. See subparagraph (3) of this paragraph for rules relating to the method of recomputation of tax. The provisions of this subparagraph may be illustrated by the following examples:

Example (1). In 1954, taxpayer A owned two operating mineral interests designated Nos. 1 and 2. Interest No. 1 was in the production stage prior to 1954. The first exploration expenditures with respect to interest No. 2 were made by taxpayer A in 1954 and were deducted under section 615(a) on his return for that year. In 1955, taxpayer A made his first development expenditure with respect to interest No. 2, and thereafter it was operated with interest No. 1 as a unit. Taxpayer A elected under section 614(c)(1) and (3)(B) to form an aggregation of interests Nos. 1 and 2 for 1955 and all subsequent taxable years. Taxpayer A must recompute his tax for 1954 in accordance with this paragraph.

Example (2). Assume the same facts as in example (1) except that, in 1957, taxpayer A acquired another operating mineral interest, designated No. 3, made his first exploration expenditures with respect to such interest in that year, and deducted such expenditures under section 615(a) on his return for that year. In 1958, taxpayer A made his first development expenditure with respect to interest No. 3. Interest No. 3 was part of the same operating unit as interests Nos. 1 and 2. Taxpayer A elected under section 614(c)(1) and (3)(B) to add interest No. 3 to his aggregation of interests Nos. 1 and 2 for 1958 and all subsequent taxable years. Taxpayer A must recompute his tax for 1957 in accordance with this paragraph.

(2) Exceptions. (i) Taxable years beginning before January 1, 1958. In the case of exploration expenditures deducted by the taxpayer with respect to an operating mineral interest for any taxable year beginning before January 1, 1958, subparagraph (1) of this paragraph shall apply only if the taxpayer has made an election under section 614(c)(1) or (2) with respect to the operating unit of which such interest is a part and such election applies to the taxable year for which such exploration expenditures were deducted. Thus, if the taxpayer does not make an election with respect to the operating unit under section 614(c)(1) or (2) and (3)(B), subparagraph (1) of this paragraph does not apply in the case of exploration expenditures deducted with respect to any operating mineral interest which is a part of such operating unit for any taxable year beginning before January 1, 1958. The provisions of this subdivision may be illustrated by the following examples:

Example (1). In 1956, taxpayer A acquired two operating mineral interests designated Nos. 1 and 2. Interest No. 1 was in the production stage at that time. Taxpayer A made his first exploration expenditures with respect to interest No. 2 in 1956, 1957, and 1958 and deducted such expenditures under section 615(a) on his returns for such years. In 1959, taxpayer A made his first development expenditure with respect to interest No. 2. Interests Nos. 1 and 2 were operated as a unit. Taxpayer A elected under section 614(c)(1) and (3)(A) to aggregate interests Nos. 1 and 2 for 1959 and all subsequent taxable years. Only the exploration expenditures deducted by the taxpayer for 1958 must be taken into account for purposes of applying subparagraph (1) of this paragraph.

Example (2). In 1954, taxpayer B owned two operating mineral interests, designated Nos. 1 and 2, which he operated as a unit. Interest No. 1 was in the production stage at that time, and interest No. 2 represented one mineral deposit in a single tract of land which was being extracted by means of two mines. Under section 614(c)(2) and (3)(B), taxpayer B elects to treat interest No. 2 as two separate operating mineral interests, designated as Nos. 2(a) and 2(b), for 1954 and all subsequent taxable years. In 1955, taxpayer B acquired operating mineral interest No. 3. He made his first exploration expenditures with respect to interest No. 3 in 1955, 1956, and 1957 and deducted such expenditures under section 615(a) on his returns for such years. In 1958, taxpayer B made his first development expenditure with respect to interest No. 3, and thereafter it was operated with interests Nos. 1, 2(a), and 2(b) as a unit. Taxpayer B elects under section 614(c)(1) and (3)(B) to aggregate interests Nos. 1 and 3 for 1958 and all subsequent taxable years. The exploration expenditures deducted by the taxpayer for 1955, 1956, and 1957 must be taken into account for purposes of applying subparagraph (1) of this paragraph since the taxpayer has made an election under section 614(c)(2) with respect to the operating unit of which interest No. 3 is a part and such election applies to the taxable years 1955, 1956, and 1957.

(ii) Interests formed pursuant to an election under section 614(c)(2). In the case of exploration expenditures deducted with respect to an operating mineral interest which the taxpayer elects to treat as more than one such interest under section 614(c)(2) and paragraph (b) of this section, subparagraph (1) of this paragraph shall not apply. Thus, if the taxpayer deducts exploration expenditures with respect to an operating mineral interest, subsequently elects to treat such interest as more than one interest under section 614(c)(2), and includes one of the newly formed interests in an aggregation under section 614(c)(1), subparagraph (1) of this paragraph does not apply in the case of the exploration expenditures deducted with respect to the interest which the taxpayer elected to treat as more than one interest. The provisions of this subdivision may be illustrated by the following examples:

Example (1). In 1958, taxpayer A acquired two operating mineral interests, designated Nos. 1 and 2, which he operated as a unit. Each interest was an interest in a single mineral deposit in a single tract or parcel of land. There was a mine in the production stage on each of the two interests at that time. Taxpayer A elected under section 614(c)(1)(B) to treat interests Nos. 1 and 2 as separate properties. In 1959 and 1960, taxpayer A made exploration expenditures with respect to interest No. 2 for the purpose of extracting the mineral by means of a second mine, and he deducted such expenditures on his returns for such years. In 1961, taxpayer A made his first development expenditure with respect to a second mine on interest No. 2. Taxpayer A elected under section 614(c)(2) to treat interest No. 2 as two separate operating mineral interests, designated as Nos. 2(a) and 2(b), for 1961 and all subsequent taxable years. Interest No. 2(a) contained the producing mine and interest No. 2(b) contained the subsequently developed mine. In his return for 1961, taxpayer A also elected under section 614(c)(1)(A) to aggregate interests Nos. 1 and 2(b) for 1961 and all subsequent taxable years. The exploration expenditures deducted with respect to interest No. 2 prior to the effective date of the formation of interests Nos. 2(a) and 2(b) need not be taken into account for purposes of applying subparagraph (1) of this paragraph.

Example (2). In 1954, taxpayer B owned two operating mineral interests designated Nos. 1 and 2. Interest No. 1 was an interest in a single mineral deposit in a single tract of land which was being extracted by means of two mines. Taxpayer B elected under section 614(c)(2) and (3)(B) to treat interest No. 1 as two separate operating mineral interests, designated as Nos. 1(a) and 1(b), for 1954 and all subsequent taxable years. In 1955, 1956, and 1957, taxpayer B made exploration expenditures with respect to interest No. 2 and deducted such expenditures on his returns for such years. In 1958, taxpayer B made his first development expenditure with respect to interest No. 2, and, on his return for that year, taxpayer B elected to aggregate interests Nos. 1(a) and 2 under section 614(c)(1) for 1958 and all subsequent taxable years. The exploration expenditures deducted with respect to interest No. 2 for 1955, 1956, and 1957 shall be taken into account for purposes of applying subparagraph (1) of this paragraph since such exploration expenditures were deducted with respect to an interest to which this subdivision does not apply.

(3) Recomputation of tax. (i) General rule. In the case of an aggregation formed under section 614(c)(1) and paragraph (a) of this section in respect of which a recomputation of tax is required to be made under the provisions of subparagraphs (1) and (2) of this paragraph for any taxable year or years, the tax imposed by chapter 1 of the Code shall be recomputed for each such taxable year as if—

(a) The taxpayer had elected to form an aggregation for the taxable year for which the recomputation is required to be made, and

(b) Such aggregation had included all the interests included in the aggregation formed, under section 614(c)(1) except those interests which the taxpayer did not own during the taxable year for which the recomputation is required to be made and those interests in respect of which the taxpayer had made no expenditures for exploration, development, or operation before or during the taxable year for which the recomputation is required to be made.

If a recomputation of tax is required to be made for any taxable year in the case of the aggregation of an additional interest to an existing aggregation under section 614(c)(1), such recomputation shall be made as if—

(c) The taxpayer had elected to form an aggregation for the taxable year for which the recomputation is required to be made, and

(d) Such aggregation had included all the interests included in the aggregation formed under section 614(c)(1) (including any interest which the taxpayer had disposed of prior to the date on which the aggregation of the additional interest becomes effective) except those interests which the taxpayer did not own during the taxable year for which the recomputation is required to be made and those interests in respect of which the taxpayer had made no expenditures for exploration, development, or operation before or during the taxable year for which the recomputation is required to be made.

For purposes of this paragraph, any aggregation which is treated as having been formed under subdivisions (a) and (b) or under subdivisions (c) and (d) shall be referred to as the "constructed aggregated property".

(ii) Recomputation of depletion allowance. The taxpayer shall compute the depletion allowance with respect to the constructed aggregated property for the taxable year for which the recomputation is required to be made. In making this computation, cost depletion for such taxable year shall be computed with reference to the depletion unit for the constructed aggregated property. See paragraph (a) of § 1.611-2. Percentage depletion for such taxable year shall not exceed 50 percent of the taxable income from the constructed aggregated property computed in accordance with § 1.613-5. If a recomputation is required to be made for the same taxable year with respect to any other aggregation or aggregations formed by the taxpayer under section 614(c)(1), the depletion allowance with respect to the other constructed aggregated property or properties shall be similarly computed. If, for a taxable year in respect of which a recomputation is required, the sum of the depletion allowance or allowances as computed under this subdivision is less than the sum of the depletion allowance or allowances actually deducted for such taxable year with respect to all the properties required to be taken into account in making the computation under this subdivision, then the total depletion allowance deducted by the taxpayer for such taxable year shall be reduced by the difference. The taxable income or net operating loss of the taxpayer for such taxable year shall be adjusted to reflect such reduction for purposes of the recomputation of tax. However, if for a taxable year in respect of which a recomputation is required, the sum of the depletion allowance or allowances as computed under this subdivision exceeds the sum of the depletion allowance or allowances actually deducted for such taxable year with respect to all the properties required to be taken into account in making the computation under this subdivision, the recomputation of tax for such taxable year is disregarded for purposes of applying section 614(c)(4)(B), (C), and (D).

(iii) Effect of recomputation with respect to items based on amount of income. In making the recomputation of tax under this subparagraph for any taxable year, any deduction, credit, or other allowance which is based upon the adjusted gross income or taxable income of the taxpayer for such year shall be recomputed taking into account the adjustment required under subdivision (ii) of this subparagraph. For example, if a corporate taxpayer's taxable income is increased under the provisions of such subdivision, then the amount of charitable contributions which may be deducted under the limitation contained in section 170(b)(2) shall be correspondingly increased for purposes of the recomputation. Moreover, the effect that the recomputation of any deduction, credit, or other allowance for a taxable year has on the tax imposed for any other taxable year shall also be taken into account for purposes of the recomputation of tax under this subparagraph. Any change in items of tax preferences (as defined in section 57 and the regulations thereunder) must also be taken into account for purposes of the recomputation under this subparagraph.

(iv) Effect of recomputation with respect to a net operating loss and a net operating loss deduction. If the recomputation of tax under this subparagraph for the taxable year for which the recomputation is required to be made results in a reduction of a net operating loss for such year, then the taxpayer shall take into account the effect of such reduction on the tax imposed by chapter 1 of the Internal Revenue Code of 1954 (or by corresponding provisions of the Internal Revenue Code of 1939) for any taxable year affected by such reduction. If the recomputation of tax for the taxable year for which the recomputation is required to be made results in an increase in taxable income as defined in section 172(b)(2) for such year, then the taxpayer shall take into account the effect of such increase on the tax imposed by chapter 1 of the Internal Revenue Code of 1954 (or by corresponding provisions of the Internal Revenue Code of 1939) for any taxable year affected by such increase. Furthermore, in making the recomputation of tax for any taxable year for which the recomputation is required to be made, the taxpayer shall take into account any change in the net operating loss deduction for such year resulting from the recomputation of tax for any other taxable year for which a recomputation is required to be made. For provisions relating to the net operating loss deduction, see section 172 and the regulations thereunder. For rules relating to the effect of the net operating loss deduction on the minimum tax for tax preferences see section 56 and the regulations thereunder and § 1.58-7.

(v) Determination of increase in tax. If the taxpayer elects to form an aggregation or aggregations for a taxable year under section 614(c)(1) and if a recomputation of tax is required to be made under this paragraph for any prior taxable year or years, then the taxpayer shall compute the difference between the tax, including the tax imposed by section 56 (relating to the minimum tax for tax preferences), as recomputed under this subparagraph for such prior taxable year or years (and other taxable years affected by the recomputation) and the tax liability previously determined (computed without regard to section 614(c)(4)) with respect to such prior taxable year or years (and other taxable years affected by the recomputation). If the taxpayer is subsequently required to make a recomputation with respect to any taxable year or years for which he has previously made a recomputation, then the taxpayer shall compute the difference between the tax as subsequently recomputed for such taxable year or years (and other taxable years affected by the subsequent recomputation) and the tax as previously recomputed for such taxable year or years (and other taxable years affected by the subsequent recomputation). For treatment of the increase in tax resulted from the recomputation of tax under this subparagraph, see subparagraph (4) of this paragraph.

(4) Treatment of increase in tax. (i) General rule. If the taxpayer elects to form an aggregation or aggregations for a taxable year under section 614(c)(1) and if a recomputation of tax is required to be made for any prior taxable year or years, then the total increase in tax resulting from such recomputation determined under subparagraph (3)(v) of this paragraph shall be taken into account in the first taxable year to which the election to form such aggregation or aggregations is applicable and in each succeeding taxable year until the full amount of such total increase in tax has been taken into account. The number of taxable years over which such total increase shall be taken into account shall be equal to the number of taxable years for which a recomputation of tax is required to be made under subparagraph (1) of this paragraph as limited by subparagraph (2) of this paragraph and for which such recomputation results in a reduction of the taxpayer's depletion allowance under subparagraph (3)(ii) of this paragraph. The amount of the increase in tax which is to be taken into account in a taxable year is determined by dividing the total increase in tax by the number of taxable years over which such total increase is to be taken into account. The tax imposed by chapter 1 of the Code for each of the taxable years over which the total increase in tax is to be taken into account shall be increased by the amount determined in accordance with the preceding sentence. However, such increase in tax for each of such taxable years shall have no effect upon the determination of the amount of any credit against the tax for any of such taxable years. For example, the amount of such increase shall not affect the computation of the limitation on the foreign tax credit under section 904. The amount of the increase in tax which is required to be taken into account by the taxpayer in a particular taxable year under section 614(c)(4)(C) shall be treated as a tax imposed with respect to such taxable years even though, without regard to section 614(c)(4) and this paragraph, such taxpayer would otherwise have no tax liability for such taxable year.

(ii) Increase in tax not determinable as of first taxable year of aggregation. If the recomputation of tax under subparagraph (3) of this paragraph, for any taxable year or years prior to the first taxable year to which the election to form an aggregation or aggregations under section 614(c)(1) applies, results in a reduction of any net operating loss carryover to a taxable year subsequent to such first taxable year, then the total increase in tax resulting from the recomputation is not determinable as of such first taxable year. In such case, the total increase in tax shall be taken into account in equal installments in the first taxable year for which such total increase is determinable and in each succeeding taxable year for which a portion of the increase in tax would have been taken into account under subdivision (i) of this subparagraph if the total increase had been determinable as of the first taxable year to which the election to form the aggregation or aggregations under section 614(c)(1) applies. The provisions of this subdivision may be illustrated by the following example:

Example. Assume that taxpayer A elects under section 614(c)(1) to form an aggregation for 1960 and all subsequent taxable years. Assume further that taxpayer A is required to recompute his tax for four prior taxable years under subparagraphs (1) and (2) of this paragraph and that the recomputation for each of such taxable years results in a reduction of taxpayer A's depletion allowance. Under subdivision (i) of this subparagraph, the total increase in tax resulting from the recomputation is to be taken into account in equal installments in 1960, 1961, 1962, and 1963. However, if the total increase in tax is not determinable until 1961 because the recomputation for the prior taxable years results in the reduction of a net operating loss carryover to 1961, then the total increase shall be taken into account in equal installments in 1961, 1962, and 1963. In like manner, if the total increase in tax is not determinable until 1962, it shall be taken into account in equal installments in 1962 and 1963.

(iii) Death or cessation of existence of taxpayer. If the taxpayer dies or ceases to exist, the portion of the increase in tax determined under subparagraph (3)(v) of this paragraph which has not been taken into account under subdivision (i) or (ii) of this subparagraph for taxable years prior to the taxable year of the occurrence of such death or such cessation of existence, as the case may be, shall be taken into account for the taxable year in which such death or such cessation of existence, as the case may be, occurs.

(5) Adjustments to basis of aggregated property. If the taxpayer elects to form an aggregated property or properties under section 614(c)(1) for a taxable year and if a recomputation of tax is required to be made for any taxable year

which results in reduction of the depletion allowance previously deducted by the taxpayer for such year, then proper adjustments shall be made with respect to the adjusted basis of such aggregated property or properties. In such a case—

(i) If the sum of the depletion allowances actually deducted with respect to the interests included in a constructed aggregated property exceeds the depletion allowance computed under subparagraph (3)(ii) of this paragraph with respect to such constructed aggregated property, the adjusted basis of the aggregated property formed under section 614(c)(1) shall be increased by such excess, and

(ii) If the depletion allowance computed under subparagraph (3)(ii) of this paragraph with respect to a constructed aggregated property exceeds the sum of the depletion allowances actually deducted with respect to the interests included in such constructed aggregated property, the adjusted basis of the aggregated property formed under section 614(c)(1) shall be reduced (but not below zero) by such excess.

However, the adjusted basis of an aggregated property formed under section 614(c)(1) may be increased only to the extent such excess would have resulted in an increase in such adjusted basis if taken into account under paragraph (a) of § 1.614-6. Thus, if depletion previously allowed with respect to the separate operating mineral interests included in the aggregation formed under section 614(c)(1) exceeds the total of the unadjusted bases of such interests by $5,000, and if the recomputation of tax required to be made under this paragraph results in a depletion allowance which is $7,000 less than the depletion actually deducted with respect to such interests, then the adjusted basis of such aggregation may be increased by only $2,000. If, with respect to the same aggregated property formed under section 614(c)(1), adjustments to adjusted basis are required under this subparagraph as a result of recomputation of tax for two or more taxable years, the total or net amount of such adjustments shall be taken into account. Any adjustment to the adjusted basis of an aggregation required by this subparagraph shall be taken into account as of the effective date of the election to form such aggregation under section 614(c)(1) and shall be effective for all purposes of subtitle A of the Code. For other rules relating to the determination of the adjusted basis of an aggregated property, see paragraph (a) of § 1.614-6.

T.D. 6524, 1/9/61, amend T.D. 7170, 3/10/72, T.D. 7564, 9/11/78.

---

§ 1.614-4 Treatment under the Internal Revenue Code of 1939 with respect to separate operating mineral interests for taxable years beginning before January 1, 1964, in the case of oil and gas wells.

(a) General rule. *(1)* All references in this section to section 614(b) or any paragraph or subparagraph thereof are references to section 614(b) or a paragraph or subparagraph thereof as it existed prior to its amendment by section 226(a) of the Revenue Act of 1964. All references in this section to section 614(d) are references to section 614(d) as it existed prior to its amendment by section 226(b)(3) of the Revenue Act of 1964.

(2) For taxable years beginning before January 1, 1964, in the case of oil and gas wells, a taxpayer may treat under section 614(d) and this section any property as if section 614(a) and (b) had not been enacted. For purposes of this section, the term "property" means each separate operating mineral interest owned by the taxpayer in each mineral deposit in each separate tract or parcel of land. Separate tracts or parcels of land exist not only when areas of land are separated geographically, but also when areas of land are separated by means of the execution of conveyances or leases. If the taxpayer treats any property or properties under this section, the taxpayer must treat each such property as a separate property except that the taxpayer may treat any two or more properties that are included within the same tract or parcel of land as a single property provided such treatment is consistently followed. If the taxpayer treats two or more properties as a single property under this section, such properties shall be considered as a single property for all purposes of subtitle A of the Internal Revenue Code of 1954. The taxpayer may not make more than one combination of properties within the same tract or parcel of land. Thus, if the taxpayer treats two or more properties that are included within the same tract or parcel of land as a single property, each of the remaining properties included within such tract or parcel of land shall be treated as a separate property. If the taxpayer has treated two or more properties that are included within the same tract or parcel of land as a single property and subsequently discovers or acquires an additional mineral deposit within the same tract or parcel of land, he may include his interest in such deposit with the two or more properties which are being treated as a single property or he may treat his interest in such deposit as a separate property. If the taxpayer has treated each property included within a tract or parcel of land as a separate property and subsequently discovers or acquires an additional mineral deposit within the same tract or parcel of land, he may combine his interest in such deposit with any one of the separate properties included within the tract or parcel of land, but not with more than one of them since they cannot be validly combined with each other. The taxpayer may not combine properties which are included within different tracts or parcels of land under this section irrespective of whether such tracts or parcels of land are contiguous. The treatment of a property as a separate property or the treatment of two or more properties included within a single tract or parcel of land as a single property under this section shall be binding upon the taxpayer for the first taxable year for which such treatment is effective and for all subsequent taxable years beginning before January 1, 1964. For the continuation of such treatment under § 1.614-8 for taxable years beginning after December 31, 1963, see paragraph (d) of § 1.614-8. For provisions relating to the first taxable year for which treatment under this section becomes effective, see paragraph (d) of this section.

(b) Treatment consistent with treatment for taxable years prior to 1954. If the taxpayer has treated properties in a manner consistent with the rules contained in paragraph (a) of this section for taxable years to which the Internal Revenue Code of 1939 applies and if the taxpayer desires to treat such properties under section 614(d), then such properties must continue to be treated in the same manner. The provisions of this paragraph may be illustrated by the following examples:

Example (1). In 1950, taxpayer A owned two separate tracts of land designated No. 1 and No. 2. Each tract contained three mineral deposits. In the case of tract No. 1, taxpayer A treated the three mineral deposits as a single property. In the case of tract No. 1, taxpayer A treated the first mineral deposit as a separate property and treated the second and third mineral deposits as a single property. This treatment was consistently followed for the taxable years 1950, 1951, 1952, and 1953. Taxpayer A desires, for 1954 and subsequent taxable years, to treat the properties in tracts Nos. 1 and 2 as if section 614(a) and (b) had not been enacted. For 1954 and subsequent taxable years, the three deposits in tract No. 1 must be treated as a single property; the first deposit in tract No. 2 must be treated as a separate property; and the second and third deposits in tract No. 2 must be treated as a single property.

Example (2). Assume the same facts as in example (1) except that, at the time the treatment under this section is adopted, assessment of any deficiency or credit or refund of any overpayment for the taxable years 1954 and 1955 resulting from the treatment of properties under this section is prevented by the operation of the statute of limitations. For 1956 and subsequent taxable years, the three deposits in tract No. 1 must be treated as a single property; the first deposit in tract No. 2 must be treated as a separate property; and the second and third deposits in tract No. 2 must be treated as a single property.

(c) Bases of separate properties previously included in an aggregation under section 614(b). If the taxpayer has made an election under section 614(b) to form an aggregation of operating mineral interests and if such taxpayer subsequently revokes such election for all taxable years for which it was made and treats the properties that are included within such aggregation under section 614(d) and this section by filing the statement required by paragraph (e) of this section, then the adjusted basis of each separate property (as defined in paragraph (a) of this section) that is a part of such aggregation shall be determined as if the taxpayer had made no election under section 614(b). However, if, at the time of the filing of the statement revoking the election under section 614(b), assessment of any deficiency or credit or refund of any overpayment, as the case may be, resulting from such revocation is prevented by the operation of any law or rule of law for any taxable year or years for which the election under section 614(b) was made, then the adjusted basis of each separate property that is a part of the aggregation shall be determined in accordance with the provisions contained in paragraph (a)(2) of § 1.614-6 as of the first day of the first taxable year for which the revocation is effective. After determining the adjusted basis of each separate property included within the aggregation, the taxpayer may treat such properties in any manner which is in accordance with paragraph (a) of this section. See, however, paragraph (b) of this section. The provisions of this paragraph may be illustrated by the following examples:

Example (1). Taxpayer A owns two separate tracts of land, designated No. 1 and No. 2, each of which contains three mineral deposits. The interests in the two tracts of land constitute an operating unit as defined in paragraph (c) of § 1.614-2. Taxpayer A elects under section 614(b) to form an aggregation of all the interests in the operating unit for 1954 and all subsequent taxable years. Subsequently, taxpayer A revokes such election by filing a statement in accordance with paragraph (e) of this section. Such revocation is effective for 1956 and subsequent taxable years because, at the time of the filing of the statement of revocation, assessment of any deficiency or credit or refund of any overpayment for the taxable years 1954 and 1955 resulting from such revocation is prevented by the operation of the statute of limitations. The adjusted bases of the six properties that are included within the aggregation shall be determined in accordance with paragraph (a)(2) of § 1.614-6 as of the beginning of the taxable year 1956.

Example (2). Assume the same facts as in example (1) and, in addition, assume that for taxable years to which the Internal Revenue Code of 1939 is applicable, taxpayer A treated the three deposits in tract No. 1 as a single property and the three deposits in tract No. 2 as a single property. After determining the adjusted basis of each of the six properties as illustrated in example (1), the adjusted bases of the three properties in tract No. 1 must be combined and the adjusted basis of the three properties in tract No. 2 must be combined since the manner in which such properties were treated for taxable years to which the Internal Revenue Code of 1939 is applicable is consistent with the rules contained in paragraph (a) of this section.

(d) Treatment; when effective. If a taxpayer treats any property in accordance with this section, then such treatment shall be effective for whichever of the following taxable years is the later:

(1) The latest taxable year for which an election could have been made with respect to such property under section 614(b); or

(2) The first taxable year beginning after December 31, 1953, and ending after August 16, 1954, in respect of which assessment of a deficiency or credit or refund of an overpayment, as the case may be, resulting from the treatment of such property under this section, is not prevented by the operation of any law or rule of law on the date such treatment is adopted.

(e) Manner of adopting the treatment of properties under this section. If the taxpayer does not make an election under section 614(b) with respect to a property within the time prescribed for making such an election, then the taxpayer shall be deemed to have treated such property under this section. In such case, the manner in which such property is treated in filing the taxpayer's income tax return for the first taxable year for which the treatment of such property is effective under paragraph (d) of this section shall establish the treatment which must be consistently followed with respect to such property for subsequent taxable years. However, if the income tax return for such first taxable year is filed prior to May 1, 1961, then the taxpayer may adopt the treatment provided for under this section with respect to the property by filing a statement at any time on or before May 1, 1961, with the district director for the district in which the taxpayer's income tax return was filed for the first taxable year for which the treatment of such property is effective under paragraph (d) of this section. Such statement shall set forth the first taxable year for which the treatment of the property under this section is effective, shall revoke any previous elections made with respect to such property under section 614(b), shall state the manner in which such property was treated for taxable years subject to the Internal Revenue Code of 1939 shall state the manner in which such property is to be treated under this section, and shall be accompanied by an amended return or returns if necessary.

(f) Certain treatment under this section precludes election to aggregate under section 614(b) with respect to the same operating unit. If the taxpayer's treatment of any properties that are included within an operating unit (as defined in paragraph (c) of § 1.614-2) under section 614(d) and this section would constitute an aggregation under section 614(b) and if such taxpayer elects, or has elected, to form an aggregation within the same operating unit under section 614(b) for any taxable year for which the treatment under section 614(d) is effective, then the election made under section 614(b) shall not apply for any such taxable year.

T.D. 6524, 1/9/61, amend T.D. 6859, 10/27/65.

§ 1.614-5 Special rules as to aggregating nonoperating mineral interests.

(a) Aggregating nonoperating mineral interests for taxable years beginning before January 1, 1958. Upon proper showing to the Commissioner, a taxpayer who owns two or more separate nonoperating mineral interests in a single tract or parcel of land, or in two or more contiguous tracts or parcels of land, shall be permitted to aggregate all such interests in each separate kind of mineral deposit and treat them as one property. Permission will be granted by the Commissioner only if the taxpayer establishes that he will sustain an undue hardship if such nonoperating mineral interests are not treated as one property. Such hardship may exist, for example, if it is impossible for the taxpayer to determine the boundaries, source, or costs of the separate interests, or if a taxpayer who owns a single royalty interest, production payment, or net profits interest cannot determine the separate deposits from which his payments will be derived. In no event shall undue hardship be deemed to exist solely by reason of tax disadvantage. The treatment of such interests as one property shall be applicable for all purposes of subtitle A of the Internal Revenue Code of 1954. In no event may nonoperating mineral interests in tracts or parcels of land which are not contiguous be treated as one property. The term "two or more contiguous tracts or parcels or land" means tracts or parcels of land which have common boundaries. Common boundaries include survey lines, public roads, or similar easements for the use of land without the existence of an intervening mineral right between the tracts or parcels of land. Tracts or parcels of land which touch only at a common corner are not contiguous. For the definition of "nonoperating mineral interests", see paragraph (g) of this section.

(b) Manner and scope of election. *(1) Time for filing application for permission to aggregate separate nonoperating mineral interests under paragraph (a) of this section.* The application for permission to aggregate separate nonoperating mineral interests under paragraph (a) of this section shall be filed at any time on or before May 1, 1961. Such application shall indicate the first taxable year for which the aggregation is to be formed. If, prior to January 10, 1961, an application has been filed, the taxpayer need file only a supplemental application containing such additional information as is necessary to comply with the requirements of subparagraph (2) of this paragraph.

(2) Contents of application and returns under permission. The application for permission to aggregate nonoperating mineral interests under paragraph (a) of this section shall include a complete statement of the facts upon which the taxpayer relies to show the undue hardship which would result if such an aggregation were not permitted. Such application shall also include a description of the nonoperating mineral interests owned by the taxpayer within the tract or tracts of land involved. A general description, accompanied by maps appropriately marked, which accurately circumscribes the scope of the aggregation and shows that the taxpayer is aggregating all the nonoperating mineral interests in a particular kind of mineral deposit within the tract or tracts of land involved will be sufficient. If the Commissioner grants permission, a copy of the letter granting such permission shall be filed with the district director for the district in which the taxpayer's income tax return was filed for the first taxable year for which such permission applies, and shall be accompanied by an amended return or returns if necessary.

(3) Election; binding effect. The election to aggregate separate nonoperating mineral interests under paragraph (a) of this section shall be binding upon the taxpayer for the first taxable year for which made and all subsequent taxable years beginning before January 1, 1958, unless consent to make a change is obtained from the Commissioner. The application for consent to make a change must set forth in detail the reason or reasons for such change. Consent to a different treatment shall not be granted where the principal purpose for such change is due to tax consequences. For rules relating to the binding effect of an election where the basis of an aggregated property in the hands of the transferee is determined by reference to the basis in the hands of the transferor, see paragraph (c) of § 1.614-6.

(4) Aggregations under the Internal Revenue Code of 1939. An application for permission to aggregate nonoperating mineral interests under paragraph (a) of this section shall be submitted in accordance with the requirements of this paragraph notwithstanding the fact that the taxpayer may have aggregated such interests for taxable years to which the Internal Revenue Code of 1939 is applicable. If such interests were aggregated for taxable years to which the Internal Revenue Code of 1939 applies and the aggregation was approved by the Internal Revenue Service for such years after full consideration thereof on its merits, such approval will generally be accepted as evidence that undue hardship would result if the aggregation were not permitted.

(c) Termination of aggregation of nonoperating mineral interests. *(1) General rule.* Any aggregation of nonoperating mineral interests formed under paragraphs (a) and (b) of this section shall not apply with respect to any taxable year beginning after December 31, 1957. Thus, if a taxpayer makes a binding election to form such an aggregation for taxable years beginning before January 1, 1958, then in order to form an aggregation with respect to any taxable year beginning after December 31, 1957, he must obtain permission in accordance with the rules prescribed in paragraphs (d) and (e) of this section.

(2) Bases of separate nonoperating mineral interests. If a taxpayer forms an aggregation of nonoperating mineral interests under paragraphs (a) and (b) of this section which is terminated under subparagraph (1) of this paragraph, the adjusted bases of the separate nonoperating mineral interests included in such aggregation shall be determined in accordance with paragraph (a)(2) of § 1.614-6.

(d) Aggregating nonoperating mineral interests for taxable years beginning after December 31, 1957, or for earlier taxable years. Upon proper showing to the Commissioner, a taxpayer who owns two or more separate nonoperating mineral interests in a single tract or parcel of land, or in two or more adjacent tracts or parcels of land, shall be permitted, under 614(e), to form an aggregation of all of such interests in each separate kind of mineral deposit and treat such aggregation as one property. Permission shall be granted by the Commissioner only if the taxpayer establishes that a principal purpose in forming the aggregation is not the avoidance of tax. The fact that the aggregation of nonoperating mineral interests will result in a substantial reduction in tax is evidence that avoidance of tax is a principal purpose of the taxpayer. An aggregation formed under the provisions of this paragraph shall be considered as one property for all purposes of the Code. In no event may nonoperating mineral interests in tracts or parcels of land which are not adjacent be aggregated and treated as one property. The term "two or more adjacent tracts or parcels of land" means tracts or parcels of land that are in reasonably close proximity to each other depending on the facts and circumstances of each case. Adjacent tracts or parcels of land do not necessarily have any common boundaries, and may be separated by intervening mineral rights. For the definition of "nonoperating mineral interests", see paragraph (g) of this section.

(e) Manner and scope of election. *(1) Time for filing application for permission to aggregate separate nonoperating mineral interests under section 614(e).* The application for permission to aggregate separate nonoperating mineral interests under section 614(e) and paragraph (d) of this section shall be made in writing to the Commissioner of Internal Revenue, Washington 25, D.C. Such application shall be filed within 90 days after the beginning of the first taxable year beginning after December 31, 1957, for which aggregation is desired or within 90 days after the acquisition of one of the nonoperating mineral interests which is to be included in the aggregation, whichever is later. However, if the last day on which the application may be filed under this paragraph falls before May 1, 1961, such application may be filed at any time on or before May 1, 1961. If, prior to January 10, 1961, an application has been filed, the taxpayer need file only a supplemental application containing such additional information as is necessary to comply with subparagraph (4) of this paragraph.

(2) Election to apply section 614(e) retroactively. The application for permission to aggregate separate nonoperating mineral interests under section 614(e) and paragraph (d) of this section may be filed, at the election of the taxpayer, for any taxable year beginning before January 1, 1958, to which the Internal Revenue Code of 1954 is applicable. In such case, the application may be filed at any time on or before May 1, 1961. Such application shall designate the first taxable year for which the aggregation is to be formed. If, prior to January 10, 1961, an application has been filed, the taxpayer need file only a supplemental application containing such additional information as is necessary to comply with the requirements of subparagraph (4) of this paragraph.

(3) Limitation. If the taxpayer forms any aggregation of nonoperating mineral interests under subparagraph (2) of this paragraph, then any aggregation of nonoperating mineral interests formed under paragraphs (a) and (b) of this section shall not apply for any taxable year. The provisions of this subparagraph may be illustrated by the following example:

Example. In 1954, taxpayer A owns six separate nonoperating mineral interests designated No. 1 through No. 6. Interests Nos. 1 through 3 are royalty interests in contiguous tracts of land. Interests Nos. 4 through 6, which are located in an entirely different area from interests Nos. 1 through 3, are royalty interests in tracts of land which are not contiguous but which are adjacent to each other. In 1959 taxpayer A obtains permission and elects under section 614(e) and subparagraph (2) of this paragraph to form an aggregation of interests Nos. 4 through 6 for 1956 and all subsequent taxable years. Taxpayer A may not elect to form an aggregation of interests Nos. 1 through 3 under paragraphs (a) and (b) of this section for 1954 or any subsequent taxable year. If taxpayer A wishes to form an aggregation of interests Nos. 1 through 3, he must obtain permission under paragraph (d) of this section and this paragraph.

(4) Contents of application and returns under permission. The application for permission to aggregate nonoperating mineral interests under section 614(e) and paragraph (d) of this section shall include a complete statement of the facts upon which the taxpayer relies to show that avoidance of tax is not a principal purpose of forming the aggregation. Such application shall also include a description of the nonoperating mineral interests within the tract or tracts of land involved. A general description, accompanied by maps appropriately marked, which accurately circumscribes the scope of the aggregation and shows that the taxpayer is aggregating all the nonoperating mineral interests in a particular kind of mineral deposit within the tract or tracts of land involved will be sufficient. If the Commissioner grants permission, a copy of the letter granting such permission shall be attached to the taxpayer's income tax return for the first taxable year for which such permission applies. If the taxpayer has already filed such return, a copy of the letter of permission shall be filed with the district director for the district in which such return was filed and shall be accompanied by an amended return or returns if necessary or, if appropriate, a claim for credit or refund.

(5) Election; binding effect. The election to aggregate separate nonoperating mineral interests under section 614(e) and paragraph (d) of this section shall be binding upon the taxpayer for the first taxable year for which made and for all subsequent taxable years unless consent to make a change is obtained from the Commissioner. The application for consent to make a change must set forth in detail the reason or reasons for such change. Consent to a different treatment shall not be granted where the principal purpose for such change is due to tax consequences. For rules relating to the binding effect of an election where the basis of an aggregated property in the hands of the transferee is determined by reference to the basis in the hands of the transferor, see paragraph (c) of § 1.614-6.

(6) Aggregations under the Internal Revenue Code of 1939. An application for permission to aggregate nonoperating mineral interests under section 614(e) and paragraph (d) of this section shall be submitted in accordance with the requirements of this paragraph notwithstanding the fact that the taxpayer may have aggregated such interests for taxable years to which the Internal Revenue Code of 1939 is applicable. If such interests were aggregated for taxable years to which the Internal Revenue Code of 1939 applies and the aggregation was approved by the Internal Revenue Service for such years after full consideration thereof on its merits, such approval will generally be accepted as evidence that avoidance of tax is not a principal purpose of forming the aggregation.

(f) Elections; when effective. If the taxpayer has elected to form an aggregation under either paragraph (a) or paragraph (d) of this section, the date on which the aggregation becomes effective is the first day of the first taxable year for which the election is made; except that if any separate nonoperating mineral interest included in such aggregation was acquired after such first day, the date on which the inclusion of such interest in such aggregation becomes effective is the date of its acquisition.

(g) Definition of nonoperating mineral interests. For purposes of this section, "nonoperating mineral interests" includes only those interests described in section 614(a) which are not operating mineral interests within the meaning of paragraph (b) of § 1.614-2. The taxpayer who holds the operating or working rights in a mineral deposit, but is not actually conducting operations with respect to such deposit, does not have a nonoperating mineral interest in such deposit notwithstanding the fact that he intends to transfer such operating rights at a later time.

T.D. 6524, 1/9/61.

§ 1.614-6 Rules applicable to basis, holding period, and abandonment losses where mineral interests have been aggregated or combined.

(a) Basis of property resulting from aggregation or combination. *(1) General rule.* (i) When a taxpayer has aggregated as one property two or more interests under section

614(b) (prior to its amendment by section 226(a) of the Revenue Act of 1964), (c), or (e), the unadjusted basis of such aggregated property shall be the sum of the unadjusted bases of the various mineral interests aggregated. The adjusted basis of the aggregated property on the effective date of the aggregation shall be the unadjusted basis of the aggregated property, adjusted by the total of all adjustments to the bases of the several mineral interests aggregated as required by section 1016 to the effective date of aggregation. Thereafter, the adjustments to basis required by section 1016 shall apply to the total adjusted basis of the aggregated property for all purposes of subtitle A of the Code.

(ii) When a taxpayer has combined as one property two or more interests under section 614(b) (as amended by section 226(a) of the Revenue Act of 1964), the adjusted basis of such combined property shall be the sum of—

(a) The unadjusted bases of all such interests which have never been included in an aggregation; and

(b) The adjusted bases of all such interests which at some time have been included in an aggregation, as of the date on which they ceased to participate in an aggregation;

adjusted by the total of all adjustments to the bases of the several mineral interests combined, as required by section 1016,

(c) In the case of interests described in (a), for the entire period of the taxpayer's ownership of such interest; and

(d) In the case of interests described in (b), for the period, if any, between the time of deaggregation and the time of combination.

Thereafter, the adjustments to basis required by section 1016 shall apply to the total adjusted basis of the combined property for all purposes of subtitle A of the Code.

(2) Bases upon disposition of part of, or termination of, or change in, an aggregated or combined property. (i) In general. (a) When a taxpayer has aggregated or combined two or more separate mineral interests as one property under section 614(b) (either before or after its amendment by section 226(a) of the Revenue Act of 1964), (c), or (e) and thereafter sells, exchanges, or otherwise disposes of part of such property, the total adjusted basis of the property as of the date of sale, exchange, or other disposition shall be apportioned to determine the adjusted basis of the part disposed of and the part retained for purposes of computing gain or loss, depletion and for all other purposes of subtitle A of the Code. Such adjusted basis shall be determined by apportioning the total adjusted basis of the property between the part of the property disposed of and the part retained in the same proportion as the fair market value of each part (as of the date of sale, exchange, or other disposition) bears to the total fair market value of the property as of such date. For determining gain or loss on the sale or exchange of any part of the aggregated or combined property, the adjusted basis of the aggregated or combined property (from which the adjusted basis of the part is determined) shall not be reduced below zero.

(b) If, for any taxable year after the first taxable year for which an aggregation under section 614(b) (prior to its amendment by section 226(a) of the Revenue Act of 1964), (c), or (e), is effective—

(1) Any such aggregation is terminated for any reason other than the expiration of an aggregation by reason of section 614(b) as amended by section 226(a) of the Revenue Act of 1964 (see subdivision (ii) of this subparagraph), or

(2) The treatment of any mineral interests in any such aggregation is changed after obtaining the consent of the Commissioner,

then the adjusted basis of the aggregated property as of the first day of the first taxable year for which such termination or change is effective shall be apportioned to determine the adjusted bases of the resultant separate mineral interests, as of such first day, for purposes of computing gain or loss, depletion, and for all other purposes of subtitle A of the Code. The adjusted bases of such separate mineral interests shall be determined by apportioning the adjusted basis of the aggregated property (as of the first day of the first taxable year for which such termination or change is effective) between or among such interests in the same proportion as the fair market value of each such interest (as of such first day) bears to the total fair market value of the aggregated property as of such first day. For the purpose of determining the adjusted bases of the separate mineral interests, the adjusted basis of the aggregated property (from which the adjusted basis of each separate mineral interest is determined) shall not be reduced below zero.

(ii) Allocation of basis of aggregation of operating mineral interests in oil and gas wells as of the first day of the first taxable year beginning after December 31, 1963. (a) Fair market value method. Unless the taxpayer elects to use the allocation of adjustments method of determining basis provided in (b) of this subdivision (ii), the adjusted basis as of the first day of the first taxable year beginning after December 31, 1963, of each interest which was participating in an aggregation of operating mineral interests on the day preceding such first day shall be determined by multiplying the adjusted basis of the aggregation by a fraction the numerator of which is the fair market value of such interest and the denominator of which is the fair market value of such aggregation. For purposes of this subdivision (a), the adjusted basis and the fair market value of such interest, shall be determined as of the day preceding the first day of the first taxable year which begins after December 31, 1963. Unless the taxpayer elects to use the allocation of adjustments method, he shall obtain accurate and reliable information, and keep records with respect thereto, establishing all facts necessary for making the computation prescribed in this subdivision (a). See example (5) of subparagraph (3) of this paragraph.

(b) Allocation of adjustments method. (i) The taxpayer may elect to determine basis by an allocation of adjustments in lieu of the fair market value method prescribed in (a) of this subdivision (ii). In such a case, the adjusted basis (as of the first day of the first taxable year beginning after December 31, 1963) of each interest which was participating in an aggregation of operating mineral interests on the day preceding such first day is the unadjusted basis of such interest immediately after its acquisition by the taxpayer, adjusted by the total of all adjustments to its basis as required by section 1016 to the effective date of aggregation, and by that portion of those section 1016 adjustments to the basis of the aggregation which is reasonably attributable to such interest. For this purpose, two or more interests which are being combined upon deaggregation shall be treated as one interest. An adjustment to the basis of the aggregation is reasonably attributable to such interest to the extent that the adjustment thereto resulted from inclusion of the interest in the aggregation, even though such interest would not have been entitled to the adjustment to the same extent if such interest had been treated separately because of the 50 percent of taxable income limitation or for any other reason. In a case in which the amount of a percentage depletion deduction which was allowed with respect to an aggregation was limited by the 50 percent of taxable income limitation of section 613(a), the portion of such amount which is attributable to each of the interests in the aggregation shall be determined by multiplying such amount by a fraction, the numerator of which is the gross income from such interest and the denominator of which is the gross income from the aggregation. The determination as to which property a particular adjustment is attributable may be based upon records of production or any other facts which establish the reasonableness of the determination. See example (6) of subparagraph (3) of this paragraph.

(ii) If, under the adjustment described in (i) of this subdivision (b), the total of the adjusted bases of the interests which were included in the aggregation exceeds the adjusted basis of the aggregation, the adjusted bases of the interests shall be further adjusted so that the total of the adjusted bases of the interests equals the adjusted basis of the aggregation. This further adjustment shall be made by reducing the basis of each interest (other than an interest having a basis of zero) by an amount which is determined by multiplying such excess by a fraction, the numerator of which is the adjusted basis of such interest after making the adjustment described in (i) of this subdivision (b) and the denominator of which is the total of the adjusted bases of all such interests after making the adjustment described in (i) of this subdivision (b). See example (6) of subparagraph (3) of this paragraph.

(ii) The election provided for in this subdivision (b) shall be made not later than the time prescribed by law for filing the taxpayer's income tax return (including extensions thereof) for the first taxable year beginning after December 31, 1963, and shall be made in a statement attached to such return.

(3) The application of subparagraphs (1) and (2) of this paragraph may be illustrated by the following examples:

Example (1). A taxpayer owning three operating mineral interests, designated Nos. 1, 2, and 3, within a single operating unit, properly elects to aggregate such properties under section 614(b) for the calendar year 1954 in his income tax return filed on April 15, 1955. The unadjusted bases and adjustments under section 1016 for depletion through December 31, 1953, in respect of such properties are as follows:

	Unadjusted basis	Adjustments under section 1016
No. 1	$25,000	$27,000
No. 2	18,000	10,000
No. 3	15,000	4,000
Total	58,000	41,000

Example (2). Assume the same facts as in example (1), except that a portion of the aggregated property is sold on June 1, 1956, for $15,000 which is also the fair market value of such portion on the date of sale. In order to determine the gain or loss from this sale as well as the adjusted basis of the retained property, an apportionment must be made. The aggregated property had a fair market value of $25,000 on the date of sale. From January 1, 1954, through May 31, 1956, $10,000 of depletion has been allowed with respect to the aggregated property. The adjusted basis of the portion sold is determined as follows:

$$\$7{,}000 \text{ (adjusted basis of aggregated property)} \times \frac{\$15{,}000}{\$25{,}000} = \$4{,}200 \text{ (adjusted basis of portion sold)}$$

Therefore, the gain on this sale of the portion sold is $10,800 ($15,000 – $4,200). The adjusted basis of the property retained is $2,800 ($7,000 – $4,200).

Example (3). Assume the same facts as in example (2), except that instead of selling, the taxpayer subleases one of the leases making up the aggregated property, retaining a one-eighth royalty interest therein. The fair market value of such lease is $15,000 on the date of the sublease. The adjusted basis of such royalty interest is $4,200 which is computed as follows:

$$\$7{,}000 \text{ (adjusted basis of aggregated property)} \times \frac{\$15{,}000 \text{ (FMV of portion transferred)}}{\$25{,}000 \text{ (FMV of aggregated property)}}$$

Example (4). In 1953, a taxpayer owned mineral interests Nos. 1, 2, and 3 which he operated as a unit. He owned no other operating interests during that year. The unadjusted bases of these properties were $10,000, $15,000, and $20,000, respectively, and depletion allowed through December 31, 1953, was $5,000 with respect to each property. The taxpayer operated these properties during the year 1954 and, in addition, operated as part of the unit mineral interest No. 4 which he acquired on July 1, 1954, on which date he made the first exploration expenditure with respect thereto. He paid $20,000 for No. 4. In his return for the calendar year 1954, the taxpayer elected under section 614(b) to aggregate all of these mineral interests. The taxpayer must compute cost depletion for the calendar year 1954 on the basis of an aggregated property with an adjusted basis of $30,000 ($45,000 – $15,000) for the period from January 1 to June 30, and with an adjusted basis of $50,000 (less depletion for the first six months) for the period from July 1 to December 31. If applicable, the taxpayer must compute percentage depletion on the basis of gross income and taxable income from the aggregated property for the entire year, including the gross income and deductions with respect to operating mineral interest No. 4 for the period from July 1 to December 31. If a portion of the aggregated property is sold during the first six months, its adjusted basis must be determined at the time of sale with an adjustment for depletion to the date of sale. If percentage depletion is applicable, it must be allocated on an equitable basis to the periods prior and subsequent to the date of sale in order to determine the adjustment for depletion to the date of sale.

Example (5). A taxpayer owns two operating mineral interests in oil wells, designated Nos. 1 and 2, in tract A, and another such interest, designated No. 3, in tract B. All three interests are in the same operating unit (as defined in paragraph (c) of § 1.614-2). The taxpayer, who is on a calendar year basis, has properly elected under § 1.614-2 to aggregate such interests for the calendar years 1954 through 1963. The unadjusted bases and adjustments under section 1016 for depletion through December 31, 1953, in respect of such interests are as follows:

	Unadjusted basis	Adjustments under section 1016
No. 1	$42,000	$11,000
No. 2	37,000	4,000
No. 3	19,000	23,000
Total	98,000	38,000

The adjusted basis of the aggregated property as of January 1, 1954, is therefore $60,000 ($98,000 minus $38,000). The taxpayer properly elects under section 614(b) and § 1.614-8 to treat Nos. 1 and 2 as separate properties for the calendar year 1964 and thereafter and does not elect to use the allocation of adjustments method of determining basis provided in subparagraph (2)(ii)(b) of this paragraph. No. 3 will be treated as a separate property, also, because it is in a different tract than the taxpayer's other interests. From January 1, 1954, through December 31, 1963, $50,000 of depletion has been allowed with respect to the aggregated property, leaving an adjusted basis of $10,000 ($60,000 minus $50,000) on January 1, 1964. On December 31, 1963, the aggregated property has a fair market value of $40,000. Nos. 1, 2, and 3 have fair market values of $16,000, $22,000, and $2,000, respectively. Accordingly, the adjusted bases of Nos. 1, 2, and 3 on January 1, 1964, are $4,000

$$\left(\$10{,}000 \text{ (adjusted basis of aggregated property} \times \frac{16{,}000}{40{,}000}\right),$$

$$\$5{,}500 \left(\$10{,}000 \times \frac{22{,}000}{40{,}000}\right),$$

$$\text{and } \$500 \left(\$10{,}000 \times \frac{2{,}000}{40{,}000}\right), \text{ respectively.}$$

Example (6). A taxpayer owns four operating mineral interests in oil wells, designated Nos. 1, 2, 3, and 4. All four interests are in the same operating unit and the same tract or parcel of land. The taxpayer, who is on a calendar year basis, has properly elected under § 1.614-2 to aggregate such interests for the calendar years 1954 through 1963. The taxpayer properly elects under section 614(b) and paragraph (a) of § 1.614-8 to treat Nos. 1 and 2 as separate properties for the calendar year 1964 and thereafter. The taxpayer also properly elects to use the allocation of adjustments method of determining basis as provided in subparagraph (2)(ii)(b) of this paragraph. The unadjusted bases of Nos. 1, 2, and combined 3 and 4, the adjustments attributable to each, and the deaggregated basis of each (prior to further adjustment as provided in subparagraph (2)(ii)(b) (ii) of this paragraph) are as follows:

	Basis upon acquisition	Adjustments to time or aggregation	Attributable adjustments during aggregation	Basis upon deaggregation after first adjustment
No. 1 ...	$35,000	$1,000	$16,000	$18,000
No. 2 ...	30,000	11,000	23,000	0
No. 3 ...	25,000	3,000	5,000	6,000
No. 4 ...	10,000	12,000	9,000	
Total	100,000	27,000	53,000	24,000

The total of the adjusted bases (prior to further adjustment) of the interests which were included in the aggregation is $24,000 while the adjusted basis of the aggregation is $20,000 ($100,000 minus the sum of $27,000 and $53,000). Therefore the adjusted bases of the interests are further reduced by 4,000 ($24,000 minus $20,000). The adjusted basis of No. 1 of $18,000 is further reduced by $3,000

$$\left(\$4{,}000 \times \frac{18{,}000}{24{,}000}\right) \text{ to } \$15{,}000.$$

Similarly, the adjusted basis of combined Nos. 3 and 4 of $6,000 is further reduced by $1,000

$$\left(\$4{,}000 \times \frac{6{,}000}{24{,}000}\right) \text{ to } \$5{,}000.$$

Assume further that the taxpayer also owns interest No. 5 in the same tract or parcel of land, that such interest was not a part of any aggregation, that such interest had a basis of $15,000 upon acquisition and had subsequent adjustments in reduction of basis totaling $17,000, and that the taxpayer does not elect to treat such interest as a separate property. In such case, Nos. 3, 4, and 5 will be combined. The combination will have an adjusted basis of $3,000, determined by adding the unadjusted basis of No. 5, 3 and 4 upon deaggregation ($5,000), and subtracting from the total thereof ($20,000) the adjustments to No. 5 ($17,000).

(4) Basis for gain and loss where mineral interests acquired before March 1, 1913, are included in an aggregation. Where mineral interests acquired before March 1, 1913, are included in an aggregation under section 614(b), (c), or (e), the aggregated property has two bases, one for the determination of gain and another for the determination of loss upon the disposition of the whole or a part of the aggregated property. For the purpose of determining gain, the adjusted basis of the aggregated property on the effective date of aggregation shall be the sum of—

(i) The unadjusted bases of those mineral interests acquired on or after March 1, 1913, plus

(ii) The cost of any interest acquired before March 1, 1913 (adjusted for the period before March 1, 1913), or the fair market value of such interest as of March 1, 1913, whichever is greater, and such sum shall be adjusted by the total of all adjustments to the bases of the several mineral interests aggregated as required by section 1016 to the effective date of aggregation. For the purpose of determining loss, the adjusted basis of the aggregated property on the effective date of aggregation shall be the sum of—

(iii) The unadjusted bases of those mineral interests acquired on or after March 1, 1913, plus

(iv) The cost of those interests acquired before March 1, 1913, adjusted for the period before March 1, 1913,

and such sum shall be adjusted by the total of all adjustments to the bases of the several mineral interests aggregated as required by section 1016 to the effective date of aggregation. Thereafter, the adjustments to basis required by section 1016 shall apply to the total adjusted basis of the aggregated property for all purposes of the Code. Upon disposition of a part of the aggregated property or upon termination of the aggregation for any reason, or upon change in the treatment of any mineral interests in the aggregation with consent of the Commissioner, the adjusted basis for determining gain and the adjusted basis for determining loss with respect to each resultant part of the aggregated property shall be determined in accordance with subparagraph (2) of this paragraph. The provisions of this subparagraph may be illustrated by the following examples:

Example (1). At the close of 1953 a taxpayer owned two operating mineral interests designated as Nos. 1 and 2 in the same operating unit. Operating mineral interest No. 1 was acquired by the taxpayer before March 1, 1913, and on such date its basis with reference to its fair market value was $50,000 and its adjusted basis with reference to its cost was $44,000. The unadjusted basis to operating mineral interest No. 2, acquired after March 1, 1913, was $30,000. Adjustments under section 1016 for depletion from March 1, 1913, through December 31, 1953, were $37,000 for operating mineral interest No. 1 and $20,000 for operating mineral interest No. 2. Assume that the taxpayer elected for the taxable year 1954 to aggregate operating mineral interests Nos. 1 and 2. The adjusted basis of the aggregated property as of January 1, 1954, for the purpose of determining gain would be $23,000 ($50,000 plus $30,000) minus ($37,000 plus $20,000). For the purpose of determining loss, the adjusted basis would be $17,000 ($44,000 plus $30,000) minus ($37,000 plus $20,000).

Example (2). Assume the same facts as in example (1) and further assume that for the taxable years 1954 and 1955, the taxpayer was allowed $5,000 of depletion on the aggregated property, that on January 1, 1956, he sold a portion of the aggregated property for $20,000, and that, as of January 1, 1956, the aggregated property had a fair market value of $24,000. At the time of sale, the adjusted basis of the aggregated property for the purpose of determining gain was $18,000 ($23,000 – $5,000); and the adjusted basis for the purpose of determining loss was $12,000 ($17,000 – $5,000). The adjusted basis of the portion sold would be computed as follows:

$$\frac{\$20{,}000 \text{ (FMV of portion sold)}}{\$24{,}000 \text{ (FMV of aggregated property)}} \times \$18{,}000 \text{ (adjusted basis for gain)} = \$15{,}000 \text{ (adjusted basis of portion sold)}$$

Taxpayer's gain would then be computed as follows:

	$20,000	amount received for portion sold
Less:	15,000	adjusted basis of portion sold
	$ 5,000	gain on portion sold

The adjusted basis of the portion retained as of January 1, 1956, for the purpose of determining gain is $3,000 ($18,000 – $15,000). For the purpose of determining loss, the adjusted basis is $2,000 ($12,000 – $10,000).

Example (3). Assume the same facts as in example (2), except that a portion of the aggregated property was sold for $5,000 and that the fair market value of the aggregated property at the time of sale was $10,000. The adjusted basis of the portion sold would be computed as follows:

$$\frac{\$5{,}000 \text{ (FMV of portion sold)}}{\$10{,}000 \text{ (FMV of aggregated property)}} \times \$12{,}000 \text{ (adjusted basis for loss)} = \$6{,}000 \text{ (adjusted basis of portion sold)}$$

Taxpayer's loss would then be computed as follows:

	$5,000	amount received for portion sold
Less:	6,000	adjusted basis of portion sold
	(1,000)	loss on portion sold

(5) Basis for gain and loss where mineral interests acquired before March 1, 1913, are included in a combination and one or more of such interests have not previously been included in an aggregation. Where mineral interests acquired before March 1, 1913, are included in a combination under section 614(b) and § 1.614-8 and one or more of such interests have not previously been included in an aggregation, the combined property has two bases, one for the determination of gain and another for the determination of loss upon the disposition of the whole or a part of the combined property. For the purpose of determining gain, the adjusted basis of the combined property on the effective date of combination shall be the sum of—

(i) The adjusted bases at the time of deaggregation, as determined under subparagraph (2) of this paragraph, of all interests which have previously been included in an aggregation,

(ii) The unadjusted bases of other mineral interests acquired on or after March 1, 1913, and

(iii) The cost of each other interest acquired before March 1, 1913 (adjusted for the period before March 1, 1913), or the fair market value of such interest as of March 1, 1913, whichever is greater,

and such sum shall be adjusted by the total of all adjustments to the bases of the mineral interests as required by section 1016 to the effective date of combination. For the purpose of determining loss, the adjusted basis of the combined property on the effective date of combination shall be the sum of—

(iv) The adjusted bases at the time of deaggregation, as determined under subparagraph (2) of this paragraph, of all interests which have previously been included in an aggregation,

(v) The unadjusted bases of other mineral interests acquired on or after March 1, 1913, and

(vi) The cost of other mineral interests acquired before March 1, 1913, adjusted for the period before March 1, 1913,

and such sum shall be adjusted by the total of all adjustments to the bases of the mineral interests as required by section 1016 to the effective date of combination. Thereafter, the adjustments to basis required by section 1016 shall apply to the total adjusted basis of the combined property for all purposes of the Code. Upon disposition of a part of the combined property, the adjusted basis for determining gain and the adjusted basis for determining loss with respect to each resultant part of the combined property shall be determined in accordance with subparagraph (2) of this paragraph.

(b) Holding period of aggregated or combined properties. Where a taxpayer sells or exchanges either a part or all of an aggregated or combined property which includes part or all of a mineral interest which the taxpayer has held for 1 year (6 months for taxable years beginning before 1977; 9 months for taxable years beginning in 1977) or less, thc sales price and adjusted basis attributable to the interest sold must be apportioned in proportion to the relative fair market values as of the date of sale to determine the amount of income represented by the sale of property held for 1 year (6 months for taxable years beginning before 1977; 9 months for taxable years beginning in 1977) or less. The application of this rule may be illustrated by the following example:

Example. Taxpayer A owns operating mineral interests Nos. 1, 2, and 3. He acquired interests Nos. 1 and 2 in 1953 but purchased and made development expenditures on interest No. 3 on December 1, 1954. In his return for the taxable year 1954, taxpayer A elects to aggregate interests Nos. 1, 2, and 3 which are operated as a unit. On May 1, 1955, taxpayer A sells the north half of the aggregated property which includes portions of interests Nos. 1, 2, and 3. The sales price of the north half was $80,000; the adjusted basis of the aggregated property as of the date of sale was $20,000; and the fair market value of the aggregated property as of the date of sale was $100,000. The adjusted basis applicable to the north half is computed as follows:

$$\frac{\$80{,}000 \text{ (FMV of portion sold)}}{\$100{,}000 \text{ (FMV of aggregated property)}} \times \$20{,}000 \text{ (adjusted basis of aggregated property)} = \$16{,}000 \text{ (adjusted basis of portion sold)}$$

The total gain on the sale is $64,000 ($80,000 – $16,000).

The gain attributable to the sale of the portion held for six months or less is computed as follows (assuming that the fair market value of the portion of No. 3 included in the sale as of the date of sale was $30,000):

$$\frac{\$30{,}000 \text{ (FMV of portion of No. 3 sold)}}{\$80{,}000 \text{ (FMV of north half)}} \times \$16{,}000 \text{ (adjusted basis of north half)} = \$6{,}000 \text{ (adjusted basis of portion of No. 3 sold)}$$

The gain on the portion of No. 3 sold is $24,000 ($30,000 – $6,000).

(c) Acquisition of property with transferor's basis. If a separate property or an aggregated or combined property is acquired in a transaction in which the basis of such property in the hands of the taxpayer is determined by reference to the basis of such property in the hands of a transferor, then the election of such transferor as to the treatment of such separate, aggregated, or combined property shall be binding upon the taxpayer for all taxable years ending after the transfer unless, in the case of an aggregation, the aggregation terminates or consent to make a change is obtained under paragraph (d)(4) of § 1.614-2, paragraph (f)(7) of § 1.614-3, or paragraph (b)(3) or (e)(5) of § 1.614-5, whichever is applicable.

(d) Abandonment and casualty losses. In the case of mineral interests which are aggregated or combined as one property, no losses resulting from worthlessness or abandonment are allowable until all the mineral rights in the entire aggregated or combined property are proven to be worthless or until the entire aggregated or combined property is disposed of or abandoned. Casualty losses are allowable in accordance with the rules applicable to casualty losses in general. For rules applicable to losses in general, see section 165 and the regulations thereunder.

T.D. 6524, 1/9/61, amend T.D. 6859, 10/27/65, T.D. 7728, 10/31/80.

§ 1.614-7 Extension of time for performing certain acts.

Sections 1.614-2 to 1.614-5, inclusive, require certain acts to be performed on or before May 1, 1961 (the first day of the first month which begins more than 90 days after the regulations under section 614 were published in the FEDERAL REGISTER as a Treasury decision). The district director may, upon good cause shown, extend for a period not exceeding 6 months the period within which such acts are to be performed, and shall, if the interests of the Government would otherwise be jeopardized thereby, grant such an extension only if the taxpayer and the district director agree in writing to a corresponding or greater extension of the period prescribed for the assessment of the tax, or in the case of taxable years described in section 614(c)(3)(E), the assessment of the tax resulting from the exercise or change in an election.

T.D. 6561, 4/24/61.

§ 1.614-8 Elections with respect to separate operating mineral interests for taxable years beginning after December 31, 1963, in the case of oil and gas wells.

Caution: The Treasury has not yet amended Reg § 1.614-8 to reflect changes made by P.L. 95-618.

(a) Election to treat separate operating mineral interests as separate properties. *(1) General rule.* If a taxpayer has more than one operating mineral interest in oil and gas wells in one tract or parcel of land, he may elect to treat one or more of such interests as separate properties for taxable years beginning after December 31, 1963. Any such interests with respect to which the taxpayer does not so elect shall be combined and treated as one property. Nonoperating mineral interests may not be included in such combination. There may be only one such combination in one tract or parcel. Any such combination of interests shall be considered as one property for all purposes of subtitle A of the Code for the period to which the election applies. The preceding sentence does not preclude the use of more than one account under a single method of computing depreciation or the use of more than one method of computing depreciation under section 167, if otherwise proper. Any reasonable and consistently applied method or methods of computing depreciation of the improvements made with respect to the separate interests which are combined may be continued in accordance with section 167 and the regulations thereunder. Except as provided in paragraph (b) of this section, such an interest in one tract or parcel may not be combined with such an interest in another tract or parcel. For rules with respect to the allocation of the basis of an aggregation of separate operating mineral interests under this section among such interests as of the first day of the first taxable year beginning after December 31, 1963, see paragraph (a)(2)(ii) of § 1.614-6. For the definition of "operating mineral interest" see paragraph (b) of § 1.614-2.

(2) Election in respect of newly discovered or acquired interest or interest ceasing to participate in cooperative or unit plan of operation. (i) If the taxpayer makes an election under this paragraph in respect of an operating mineral interest in a tract or parcel of land and, after the taxable year for which such election is made, an additional operating mineral interest in the same tract or parcel is discovered or acquired by the taxpayer or is the subject of an election under this paragraph because it ceases to participate in a cooperative or unit plan of operation to which paragraph (b) of this section applies, the additional operating mineral interest shall be treated—

(a) If there is no combination of interests in such tract or parcel, as a separate property unless the taxpayer elects to combine it with another interest, or

(b) If there is a combination of interests in such tract or parcel, as part of such combination unless the taxpayer elects to treat it as a separate property.

(ii) The application of this subparagraph may be illustrated by the following example:

Example. Prior to 1964 a taxpayer acquired, and incurred development expenditures with respect to, three operating mineral interests in oil, designated Nos. 1, 2, and 3. All three interests are in the same tract or parcel of land. For the taxable year 1964, the taxpayer elects to treat such interests as three separate properties. During the taxable year 1965, the taxpayer discovers and incurs development costs with respect to a fourth operating mineral interest, No. 4, in the same tract of land. During the taxable year 1966, the taxpayer discovers and incurs development costs with respect to a fifth operating mineral interest, No. 5, in the same tract of land. If the taxpayer makes no election relative to No. 4 for 1965, such interest will thereafter be treated as a separate property. Alternatively, the taxpayer may make an election 1965 to combine No. 4 with any one (and only one) of the three other interests and to treat such combination as one property. If, for example, he elects to combine No. 4 with No. 3, then in 1966, No. 5 will automatically become part of the combination of Nos. 3 and 4 if no election is made to treat it as a separate property. After the combination of Nos. 3 and 4 is formed, Nos. 1 and 2, which were acquired or discovered prior to the formation of the combination and which were not included in such combination within the time prescribed, may not be included in that or any other combination. However, see subparagraph (3)(iv) of this paragraph.

(3) Manner and scope of election. (i) Election; when made. Except as provided hereafter in this subdivision (i), any election under subparagraph (1) or (2) of this paragraph shall be made for each operating mineral interest not later than the time prescribed by law for filing the income tax return (including extensions thereof) for whichever of the following taxable years is later:

(a) The first taxable year beginning after December 31, 1963; or

(b) The first taxable year in which any expenditure for development or operation in respect of such operating mineral interest is made by the taxpayer after his acquisition of such interest.

Notwithstanding the provisions of (a) and (b), if it is determined that the operating mineral interest in respect of which the election is to be made was, during what would otherwise be the entire effective period of the election insofar as it would apply to the appropriate taxable year determined under (a) and (b), participating in a cooperative or unit plan of operation to which section 614(b)(3) applies, the election shall be made not later than the time prescribed by law for filing the income tax return (including extensions thereof) for the taxable year in which the interest ceases to participate in the cooperative or unit plan. See subdivision (iii) of this subparagraph for provisions relating to the effective date of an election and paragraph (b) of this section for provisions relating to certain unitization or pooling arrangements. For purposes of this subparagraph, expenditures for development include any intangible drilling or development costs within the purview of section 263(c). Delay rentals are not considered as expenditures for development. For purposes of this subparagraph, the acquisition of an option to acquire an economic interest in minerals in place does not constitute the acquisition of a mineral interest.

(ii) Election; how made. Any election under this paragraph shall be made by a statement attached to the income tax return of the taxpayer for the first taxable year for which the election is made. This statement shall identify by name, code number, or other means the operating mineral interests within the same tract or parcel of land which the taxpayer is electing to treat as separate properties or in combination, as the case may be. The statement shall also identify by name, code number, or other means the tract or parcel and shall set forth the facts upon which its treatment as a single and entire tract or parcel is based. See paragraph (a)(3) of § 1.614-1. However, if the taxpayer is electing to treat all of his operating mineral interests in a tract or parcel as separate properties, a blanket election with respect to all of such interests in that tract or parcel which are owned by the taxpayer at the time the election is made will suffice and only the tract or parcel itself need be so identified. The taxpayer shall maintain and have available records and maps sufficient to clearly define the tract or parcel and all of the taxpayer's operating mineral interests therein.

(iii) Election; when combination effective (a) If, by reason of the exercise or nonexercise of an election under this paragraph, a combination is formed of two or more operating mineral interests, all of which are owned and operated by a taxpayer on the first day of the first taxable year beginning after December 31, 1963, and are not participating in a cooperative or unit plan of operation to which paragraph (b) of this section applies on such first day, the combination is effective on such first day.

(b) If, by reason of the exercise or nonexercise of an election under this paragraph, a combination of operating mineral interests not described in (a) of this subdivision (including a combination described in (a) to which another operating mineral interest is added) is formed, the date on which each operating mineral interest which is being combined by the taxpayer for the first time enters into the combination is the later of (1) the earliest date within the taxable year affected on which the taxpayer incurred any expenditure for development or operation of such interest at a time when such interest was not participating in a cooperative or unit plan of operation to which paragraph (b) of this section applies, or (2) the earliest date on which the taxpayer incurred any expenditure for development or operation of any other interest with which such interest is to be combined at a time when such other interest was not participating in a cooperative or unit plan of operation to which paragraph (b) of this section applies.

(c) The application of these provisions may be illustrated by the following examples:

Example (1). In 1963, a taxpayer owned and operated mineral interests Nos. 1 and 2, both of which are in the same tract or parcel of land. Neither No. 1 nor No. 2 participates in a cooperative or unit plan of operation. The taxpayer, who is on a calendar year basis, continued to own and operate these interests during the year 1964, and made no election with respect to such interests in his income tax return for that year. As a result, Nos. 1 and 2 are combined as of January 1, 1964.

Example (2). Assume that the taxpayer described in example (1) discovered operating mineral interests Nos. 3 and 4 in the same tract or parcel of land as Nos. 1 and 2, that he made his first expenditures for the development of No. 3 on June 1, 1964, and of No. 4 on September 1, 1964, and that, in a timely return for 1964, he elected to treat No. 3 as a separate property and made no election with respect to No. 4. As a result, No. 3 is treated as a separate property and No. 4 joins the combination of Nos. 1 and 2 as of September 1, 1964.

Example (3). On March 1, 1964, a taxpayer acquired a tract or parcel of land containing operating mineral interests Nos. 1 and 2. The taxpayer made his first operating expenditures on No. 1 on April 1, 1964. On October 1, 1964, the taxpayer made his first development expenditures with respect to operating mineral interest No. 2. The taxpayer made no election with respect to these interests. As a result, Nos. 1 and 2 enter into a combination as of October 1, 1964.

(iv) Election; binding effect. A valid election made under section 614(b) and this subparagraph shall be binding upon the taxpayer for the first taxable year for which made and for all subsequent taxable years. However, notwithstanding the preceding sentence, an election to treat one or more operating mineral interests as separate properties shall not prevent the making of a later election to combine a newly discovered or acquired operating mineral interest with one of such interests, if no other combination exists in the tract or parcel of land on the date when the later election would become effective under subdivision (iii) of this subparagraph. Nor will an election to treat an operating mineral interest as a separate property prevent its treatment with another interest as a single property under paragraph (b) of this section if such interest later participates in a cooperative or unit plan of operation to which paragraph (b) applies. For rules relating to the binding effect of an election in certain cases in which the basis of a separate or combined property in the hands of the transferee is determined by reference to the basis in the hands of the transferor, see paragraph (c) of § 1.614-6.

(b) Certain unitization or pooling arrangements. *(1)* Except as provided in this paragraph, if one or more of the taxpayer's operating mineral interests, or a part or parts thereof, participate, under a voluntary or compulsory unitization or pooling agreement as defined in subparagraph (6) of this paragraph, in a single cooperative or unit plan of operation, then for the period of such participation in taxable years beginning after December 31, 1963, such interest or interests, and part or parts thereof, included in such unit, shall be treated for purposes of subtitle A of the Code as one property, separate from the interest or interests, or part or parts thereof, not included in such unit.

(2) Subparagraph (1) of this paragraph shall apply to a voluntary agreement only if all the operating mineral interests covered by the agreement are in the same deposit or are in two or more deposits, the joint development or production of which is logical, without taking tax benefits into account, from the standpoint of geology, convenience, economy, or conservation, and which are in tracts or parcels of land which are contiguous or in close proximity. Operating mineral interests under a voluntary agreement to which subparagraph (1) does not apply are subject to the rules contained in paragraph (a) of this section. For purposes of this paragraph an agreement is voluntary unless required by the laws or rulings of any State or any agency of any State.

(3) Notwithstanding the provisions of subparagraph (1) of this paragraph, if the taxpayer, for the last taxable year beginning before January 1, 1964, treated as separate properties two or more operating mineral interests which participate, under a voluntary or compulsory unitization or pooling agreement entered into in any taxable year beginning before January 1, 1964, in a single cooperative or unit plan of operation, and if it is determined that such treatment was proper under the law applicable to such taxable year, the taxpayer may continue to treat all such interests in a consistent manner for the period of such participation. If it is determined that such treatment was not proper under the law applicable to such taxable year, or if the taxpayer does not continue to treat all such interests in a manner consistent with the treatment of them for the last taxable year beginning before January 1, 1964, the treatment of the interests shall be in accordance with the provisions of subparagraph (1).

(4) If only a part of an operating mineral interest, which interest is not being treated under paragraph (a) of this section as part of a combination of interests, participates in a unit or pool, such part shall, for the period of its participation in the unit or pool, be treated for purposes of this section as being separate from the nonparticipating portion of the operating mineral interest of which it is a part. A portion of the adjusted basis and of the units of mineral of such operating mineral interest remaining at the beginning of the period described in the preceding sentence shall be allocated to the participating part in accordance with the principles contained in paragraph (a)(2)(i)(a) of § 1.614-6 as if such participating part had been sold. If participation in the unit or pool ends, the separate status of the participating part shall immediately terminate. At such time the adjusted basis of such part and the units of mineral with respect to such part remaining at the time of termination shall be added to the adjusted basis and to the remaining units of mineral of the nonparticipating portion of the operating mineral interest. During the period of participation in the unit or pool such participating part shall not be treated separately from the nonparticipating portion of the operating mineral interest in applying section 165.

(5) Where an operating mineral interest which is being treated under paragraph (a) of this section as part of a combination of interests begins participation in a unit or pool, the combination shall remain in force but the treatment of such participating interest as a part of the combination shall be suspended for the period of its participation in the unit or pool. If, for example, a taxpayer owns operating mineral interests Nos. 1, 2, and 3 in a single tract or parcel of land, elects to treat No. 1 as a separate property (with mineral interests Nos. 2 and 3 thus being combined), is later required by an agency of a State to place No. 2 in a unit, and subsequently discovers operating mineral interest No. 4 in the same tract or parcel of land, then under paragraph (a)(2)(i)(b) of this section No. 4 will automatically be combined with No. 3 unless the taxpayer elects to treat it as a separate property. Under this subparagraph, an interest may be treated as part of a combination for a portion of a taxable year and as part of a unit or pool for a portion of a taxable year. At the commencement of participation in the unit or pool, a portion of the adjusted basis of the combination and a portion of the units of mineral with respect to the combination remaining at that time shall be allocated to such participating interest in accordance with the principles contained in paragraph (a)(2)(i)(a) of § 1.614-6 as if such interest had been sold. During the period of participation in the unit or pool such participating interest is nevertheless treated as a part of the combination for purposes of paragraph (d) of § 1.614-6. If participation in the unit or pool ends, the treatment of such interest as participating in the unit or pool shall immediately terminate. At such time, the adjusted basis of the participating interest and the units of mineral with respect to such interest remaining at the time of termination shall be added to the adjusted basis and to the remaining units of mineral of the nonparticipating portion of the com-

bination. In determining the adjusted basis of the participating interest at the time of termination there shall be taken into account any section 1016 adjustments attributable to such interest for the period of its participation in the unit or pool. If two or more operating mineral interests of the taxpayer participate in a unit or pool and are treated as one property under subparagraph (1) of this paragraph, and if participation by such interests in the unit or pool terminates, the adjusted basis of each such interest at the time of termination shall be separately determined. If the total of the adjusted bases of such interests upon termination of their participation in the unit or pool exceeds the adjusted basis of such one property, then the adjusted bases of such interests shall be further adjusted by applying the principles contained in paragraph (a)(2)(ii)(b)(ii) of § 1.614-6 so that the total of the adjusted bases of such interests equals the adjusted basis of such one property. In addition, the units of oil and gas estimated to be attributable to a participating interest at the time of termination of participation shall be restored to the units of oil and gas of the combination of which it is a part. The rules stated in this subparagraph with respect to an operating mineral interest which is being treated under paragraph (a) of this section as part of a combination and which begins participation in a unit or pool shall also apply to a portion of an operating mineral interest which is being treated under paragraph (a) as part of a combination if such portion begins participation in a unit or pool.

(6) As used in this paragraph, the term "unitization or pooling agreement" means an agreement under which two or more persons owning operating mineral interests agree to have the interests operated on a unified basis and further agree to share in production on a stipulated percentage or fractional basis regardless of from which interest or interests the oil or gas is produced. In addition, in a situation in which one person owns operating mineral interests in several leases, an agreement of such person with his several royalty owners to determine the royalties payable to each on a stipulated percentage basis regardless of from which lease or leases oil or gas is obtained is also considered to be a unitization or pooling agreement. No formal cross-conveyance of properties is necessary. An agreement between co-owners of a tract or parcel of land or a part thereof for the development of the property by one of such co-owners for the account of all is not a unitization or pooling agreement, provided that the agreement does not affect ownership of minerals or entitle any such co-owner to share in production from any operating mineral interests other than his own.

(c) Operating mineral interest defined. For the definition of the term "operating mineral interest" as used in this section, see paragraph (b) of § 1.614-2.

(d) Alternative treatment under Internal Revenue Code of 1939. If, on the day preceding the first day of the first taxable year beginning after December 31, 1963, the taxpayer has any operating mineral interests which he treats under section 614(d) (as in effect before the amendments made by the Revenue Act of 1964) and § 1.614-4, such treatment shall be continued and shall be deemed to have been adopted pursuant to the provisions of section 614(b) and paragraph (a) of this section. Accordingly, a taxpayer, who has four operating mineral interests in a single tract or parcel of land, and who has treated two of such interests as one property and two of such interests as separate properties under section 614(d) prior to the first day of the first taxable year beginning after December 31, 1963, is deemed to have adopted such treatment pursuant to the provisions of section 614(b) and paragraph (a) of this section. Hence, in the absence of an election to the contrary, a fifth operating mineral interest in the same tract or parcel acquired by the taxpayer in a taxable year beginning after December 31, 1963, will, after an expenditure for development or operation, be combined with the combination of two interests made under section 614(d). Furthermore, an election which was made for a taxable year beginning before January 1, 1964, under section 614(d) as then in effect will be binding for all taxable years beginning after December 31, 1963, even though the time for making an election under section 614(b) and paragraph (a) of this section has not elapsed.

T.D. 6859, 10/27/65.

§ 1.616-1 Development expenditures.

Caution: The Treasury has not yet amended Reg § 1.616-1 to reflect changes made by P.L. 99-514.

(a) General rule. Section 616 prescribes rules for treating expenditures paid or incurred during the taxable year by the taxpayer for the development of a mine or other natural deposit (other than an oil or gas well). Development expenditures under section 616 are those which are made after such time when, in consideration of all the facts and circumstances (including actions of the taxpayer), deposits of ore or other mineral are shown to exist in sufficient quantity and quality to reasonably justify commercial exploitation by the taxpayer. Under section 616(a), a taxpayer is allowed a deduction for development expenditures whether or not such expenditures are made in the development or production stage of the mine or other natural deposit. Under section 616(b), the taxpayer may elect to defer development expenditures made in the development or producing stage and to deduct such expenditures ratably as the minerals or ores benefited are sold. While the mine or other natural deposit is in the development stage, the election applies only to that portion of the development expenditures which is in excess of net receipts from the mine or other natural deposit. See § 1.616-2 for rules with respect to the election to defer. It is not necessary that the taxpayer incur the development costs directly. He may engage a contractor to make the expenditures on his behalf.

(b) Expenditures to which section 616 is not applicable. *(1)* Section 616 is not applicable to development expenditures which are deductible for the taxable year under any other provision of the internal revenue laws.

(2) Section 616 is not applicable to expenditures which are reflected in improvements subject to allowances for depreciation under sections 167 and 611. However, allowance for depreciation of such improvements which are used in the development of ores or minerals are considered development expenditures under section 616. If such improvements are used only in part for development during a taxable year, an allocable portion of the allowance for depreciation shall be treated as a development expenditure.

(3) Section 616 is applicable to development expenditures paid or incurred by a taxpayer in connection with the acquisition of a fractional share of the working or operating interest to the extent of the fractional interest so acquired. The expenditure attributable to the remaining fractional share shall be considered as part of the cost of his acquired interest and shall be capitalized and recovered through depletion allowances. For example, taxpayer A owns mineral leases on undeveloped mineral lands. A agrees to convey an undivided three-fourths (¾) interest in such leases to B, provided B will pay all of the expenditures incurred during the development stage of the deposits on these leases. B may deduct

three-fourths (¾) of such amount under section 616, but shall treat one-fourth of such amount as part of the cost of his interest, recoverable through depletion.

(4) The provisions of section 616 do not apply to costs of development paid or incurred by a prior owner which are reflected in the amount which the taxpayer paid or incurred to acquire the property. Such provisions apply only to costs paid or incurred by the taxpayer for development undertaken directly or through contract by the taxpayer. See, however, section 381(a) and 381(c)(10) for special rules with respect to deferred development expenditures in certain corporate acquisitions.

(c) Mine or other natural deposit. Section 616 has reference to expenditures made for the development of a mine or other natural deposit. Within an aggregated property, as that term is defined in section 614(b) and (c), or within a single tract or parcel of land, there may be more than one mine or other natural deposit. Where a property, as determined under section 614, contains more than one mine or other natural deposit, the taxpayer may deduct under section 616(a) the development expenditures made with respect to one of such mines or deposits, and may defer under section 616(b) the development expenditures made with respect to another of such mines or deposits. Where there is more than one mine with respect to a single underlying deposit, the taxpayer may deduct under section 616(a) the development expenditures made with respect to one of such mines, and may defer under section 616(b) the development expenditures made with respect to another of such mines. The taxpayer must treat consistently all development expenditures with respect to each such mine or other natural deposit in a taxable year. The taxpayer must make a separate determination of the units of minerals or ores benefited in a mine or other natural deposit (regardless of the computation of the depletion allowance) in order that deferred expenditures with respect to such mine or deposit may be deducted on a ratable basis. See paragraph (f) of § 1.616-2.

T.D. 6446, 1/20/60.

§ 1.616-2 Election to defer.

(a) General rule. In lieu of taking a deduction under section 616(a), in the taxable year when the development expenditures are paid or incurred, a taxpayer may elect under section 616(b) to treat such expenditures with respect to each mine or other natural deposit as deferred expenses to be deducted ratably as the units of the produced ore or minerals benefited by such expenditures are sold. Section 616(b) is applicable to development expenditures paid or incurred both in the development and producing stage of the mine or other natural deposit. However, in the case of such expenditures made in the development stage, this election is applicable only to the excess of the amount of such expenditures over the net receipts from the ore or minerals from such mine or deposit received or accrued during the development stage and in the same taxable year as the expenditures were paid or incurred. Such development expenditures not in excess of such net receipts shall be subject to the provisions of section 616(a).

(b) Producing stage; definition of. The mine or other natural deposit will be considered to be in a producing stage when the major portion of the mineral production is obtained from workings other than those opened for the purpose of development, or when the principal activity of the mine or other natural deposit is the production of developed ores or minerals rather than the development of additional ores or minerals for mining.

(c) Expenditures made by the owner who retains a nonoperating interest. *(1)* A taxpayer who elects to defer development expenditures and thereafter transfers his interest in the mine or other natural deposit, retaining an economic interest therein, shall deduct an amount attributable to such interest on a pro rata basis as the interest pays out. For example, a taxpayer who defers development expenditures and then leases his deposit, retaining a royalty interest therein, shall deduct the deferred expenditures ratably as he receives the royalties. If the taxpayer receives a bonus or advanced royalties in connection with the transfer of his interest, he shall deduct the deferred expenditures allocable to such bonus or advanced royalties in an amount which is in the same proportion to the total of such costs as the bonus or advanced royalties bears to the bonus and total royalties expected to be received. Also, in the case of a transfer of a mine or other natural deposit by a taxpayer who retains a production payment therein, he may deduct the development expenditures ratably over the payments expected to be received.

(2) Where a taxpayer receives an amount, in addition to retaining an economic interest, which amount is treated as from the sale or exchange of a capital asset or property treated under section 1231 (except coal or iron ore to which section 631(c) applies), the deferred development expenditures shall be allocated between the interest sold and the interest retained in proportion to the fair market value of each interest as of the date of sale. The amount allocated to the interest sold may not be deducted, but shall be a part of the basis of such interest for the purpose of determining gain or loss upon the sale thereof.

(d) Losses from abandonment. Section 165 and the regulations thereunder contain general rules relating to the treatment of losses resulting from abandonment.

(e) Effect of election. *(1)* The election to defer development expenditures shall apply only to expenditures for the taxable year for which made. However, once made, the election shall be binding with respect to the expenditures for that taxable year. Thus, a taxpayer cannot revoke his election for any reason whatsoever.

(2) The election shall be made for each mine or other natural deposit by a clear indication on the return or by a statement filed with the district director with whom the return was filed, not later than the time prescribed by law for filing such return (including extensions thereof) for the taxable year to which such election is applicable.

(f) Computation of amount of deduction. The amount of the deduction allowable during the taxable year is an amount A, which bears the same ratio to B (the total deferred development expenditures for a particular mine or other natural deposit reduced by the amount of such expenditures deducted in prior taxable years) as C (the number of units of the ore or mineral benefited by such expenditures sold during the taxable year) bears to D (the number of units of ore or mineral benefited by such expenditures remaining as of the taxable year). For the purposes of this proportion, the "number of units of ore or mineral benefited by such expenditures remaining as of the taxable year" is the number of units of ore or mineral benefited by the deferred development expenditures remaining at the end of the year to be recovered from the mine or other natural deposit (including units benefited by such expenditures recovered but not sold) plus the number of units benefited by such expenditures sold within the taxable year. The principles outlined in § 1.611-2 are applicable in estimating the number of units remaining as of the taxable year and the number of units sold during the taxable year. The estimate is subject to revision in accordance with that section in the event it is ascertained, from any source, such as operations or development work, that the remaining units are materially greater or less than the number of units remaining from a prior estimate.

T.D. 6446, 1/20/60, amend T.D. 6841, 7/26/65.

§ 1.616-3 Time for making election with respect to returns due on or before May 2, 1960.

In the case of any taxable year beginning after December 31, 1953, and ending after August 16, 1954, the income tax return for which is due not later than May 2, 1960, the time to deduct or defer development expenditures for such a year under section 616(a) or (b) shall expire on May 2, 1960.

T.D. 6446, 1/20/60.

§ 1.617-1 Exploration expenditures.

Caution: The Treasury has not yet amended Reg § 1.617-1 to reflect changes made by P.L. 99-514.

(a) General rule. Section 617 prescribes rules for the treatment of expenditures paid or incurred after September 12, 1966, for ascertaining the existence, location, extent, or quality of any deposit of ore or other mineral for which a deduction for depletion is allowable under section 613 (other than oil or gas) paid or incurred by the taxpayer before the beginning of the development stage of the mine or other natural deposit. Such expenditures hereinafter in the regulations under section 617 will be referred to as exploration expenditures. The development stage of the mine or other natural deposit will be deemed to begin at the time when, in consideration of all the facts and circumstances (including the actions of the taxpayer), deposits of ore or other mineral are disclosed in sufficient quantity and quality to reasonably justify commercial exploitation by the taxpayer. For example, core drilling expenditures paid or incurred by the taxpayer to ascertain the existence of commercially marketable ore are exploration expenditures within the meaning of this section. Also, expenditures for exploratory drilling from within a producing mine to ascertain the existence of what appears (on the basis of all the facts and circumstances known at the time of the expenditure) to be a different ore deposit are exploration expenditures within the meaning of this section. Expenditures paid or incurred in connection with core drilling to further delineate the extent and location of an existing commercially marketable deposit to facilitate its development are development expenditures. Under section 617(a), a taxpayer may deduct exploration expenditures paid or incurred for the exploration of any deposit of ore or other mineral subject to the limitation of section 617(h). Under section 617(b), a taxpayer shall recapture the exploration expenditures previously deducted under section 617(a) either through including in income an amount equal to the amount of the adjusted exploration expenditures (as defined in section 617(f)) or through disallowance of the deduction for depletion under section 611. Certain rules are provided in section 617(c) for recapture of exploration expenditures made with respect to property for which the taxpayer later receives a bonus or royalty. Under section 617(d), gain from dispositions of mining property, with respect to which exploration expenditures have been previously deducted, is to be recognized notwithstanding certain other provisions of the Code.

(b) Expenditures to which section 617 is not applicable. *(1)* Section 617 is not applicable to expenditures which would be allowed as deductions for the taxable year without regard to section 617.

(2) Section 617 is not applicable to expenditures which are reflected in improvements subject to allowances for depreciation under sections 167 and 611. However, allowances for depreciation of such improvements which are used in the exploration of ores or minerals are considered exploration expenditures under section 617. If such improvements are used only in part for exploration during the taxable year, an allocable portion of the allowance for depreciation shall be treated as an exploration expenditure.

(3) Section 617 is applicable to exploration expenditures paid or incurred by a taxpayer in connection with the acquisition of a fractional share of the working or operating interest to the extent of the fractional interest so acquired by the taxpayer. The expenditures attributable to the remaining fractional share shall be considered as the cost of his acquired interest and shall be recovered through depletion allowances. For example, taxpayer A owns mineral leases on unexplored mineral lands and agrees to convey an undivided three-fourths (¾) interest in such leases to taxpayer B provided B will pay all of the expenses for ascertaining the existence, location, extent, or quality of any deposit of ore or other mineral which will be incurred before the beginning of the development stage. B may elect to treat three-fourths of such amount under section 617. B must treat one-fourth of such amount as part of the cost of his interest, recoverable through depletion.

(4) Section 617 is not applicable to costs of exploration which are reflected in the amount which the taxpayer paid or incurred to acquire the property. Section 617 applies only to costs paid or incurred by the taxpayer for exploration undertaken directly or through a contract by the taxpayer. See, however, sections 381(a) and 381(c)(10) for special rules with respect to deferred exploration expenditures in certain corporate acquisitions.

(5) Section 617 is not applicable to amounts paid or incurred for the purpose of ascertaining the existence, location, extent, or quality of any deposit of oil or gas or of any mineral with respect to which a deduction for percentage depletion is not allowable under section 613. The purpose of the expenditure shall be determined by reference to the facts and circumstances at the time the expenditure is paid or incurred.

(c) Elections. *(1) Election to deduct under section 617(a).* (i) The election to deduct exploration expenditures under section 617(a) may be made by deducting such expenditures in the taxpayer's income tax return for his first taxable year ending after September 12, 1966, for which the taxpayer desires to deduct exploration expenditures which are paid or incurred by him during such taxable year and after September 12, 1966. This election may be exercised by deducting such exploration expenditures either in the taxpayer's return for such taxable year or in an amended return filed before the expiration of the period for filing a claim for credit or refund of income tax for such taxable year. Where the election is made in an amended return for a taxable year prior to the most recent year for which the taxpayer has filed a return, the taxpayer shall file amended income tax returns, reflecting any increase or decrease in tax attributable to the election, for all subsequent taxable years affected by the election for which he has filed income tax returns before making the election. See section 617(a)(2)(C) and subparagraph (4) of this paragraph for provisions relating to extension of the period of limitations for the assessment of any deficiency for any taxable year to the extent the deficiency is attributable to an election or revocation of an election under section 617(a). In applying the election to the years affected, there shall be taken into account the effect that any adjustments resulting from the election shall have on other items affected thereby (such as the deduction for charitable contributions, the foreign tax credit, net operating loss, and other deductions or credits the amount of which is limited by the taxpayer's income) and the effect that adjustments of any such items have on items of other taxable years. Amended returns filed for taxable years subsequent to the taxable year for which the election under section 617(a) is made by amended return shall, where appropriate, apply the recapture rules of subsections (b), (c), and (d) of section 617. See §§ 1.617-3 and 1.617-4.

(ii) A taxpayer who makes or has made an election under section 617(a) shall state clearly on his income tax return for each taxable year for which he deducts exploration expenditures the amount of the deduction claimed under section 617(a) with respect to each property or mine. Such property or mine shall be identified by a description adequate to permit application of the recapture rules of section 617(b), (c), and (d).

(iii) A taxpayer who has made an election under section 617(a) may not make an election under section 615(e) unless, within the period set forth in section 615(e), he revokes his election under section 617(a). A taxpayer who has made and has not revoked an election under section 617(a) may not, in his return for the taxable year for which the election is made or for any subsequent taxable year, charge to capital account any exploration expenditures which are deductible by him under section 617(a); and he must deduct all such expenditures as expenses in computing adjusted gross income. Any exploration expenditures paid or incurred after December 31, 1969, which are not deductible by the taxpayer under section 617(a) solely because of the application of section 617(h) shall be charged to capital account.

(2) Time for making elections. The election under section 617(a) may be made at any time before the expiration of the period prescribed for filing a claim for credit or refund of the tax imposed by chapter 1 for the first taxable year for which the taxpayer desires to deduct exploration expenditures under section 617(a).

(3) Revocation of election to deduct. (i) A taxpayer may revoke an election made by him under section 617(a) by filing with the Internal Revenue service center with which the taxpayer's income tax return is required to be filed, within the period set forth in subdivision (ii) of this subparagraph, a statement, signed by the taxpayer or his authorized representative, which sets forth that the taxpayer is revoking the section 617(a) election previously made by him and states with whom and where the document making the election was filed. A taxpayer revoking a section 617(a) election shall file amended income tax returns which reflect any increase or decrease in tax attributable to the revocation of election for all taxable years affected by the revocation of election for which he has filed income tax returns before revoking the election. See section 617(a)(2)(C) and subparagraph (4) of this paragraph for provisions relating to extension of the period of limitations for the assessment of any deficiency attributable to an election or revocation of an election under section 617(a). In applying the revocation of election to the years affected, there shall be taken into account the effect that any adjustments resulting from the revocation of election shall have on other items affected thereby (such as the deduction for charitable contributions, the foreign tax credit, net operating loss, and other deductions or credits the amount of which is limited by the taxpayer's income) and the effect that adjustments of any such items have on items of other taxable years.

(ii) An election under section 617(a) may be revoked before the expiration of the last day of the third month following the month in which the final regulations under section 617(a) are published in the Federal Register. After the expiration of this period, a taxpayer who has made an election under section 617(a) may not revoke that election unless he obtains the prior consent of the Commissioner of Internal Revenue. Consent will not be granted where a principal purpose for the revocation of the election is to circumvent the recapture provisions of section 517(b), (c), or (d). The request for consent shall be made in writing to the Commissioner of Internal Revenue, Attention T:I:E, Washington, D.C. 20224. The request shall include in detail:

(a) The reason or reasons for the revocation of election under section 617(a);

(b) An itemization of the taxpayer's deductions under section 617(a);

(c) A description of all properties and detailed information of the exploration activities with respect to which the taxpayer has taken deductions under section 617(a);

(d) A description of any development or production activities on all properties with respect to which exploration expenditures were deducted under section 617(a); and

(e) A recomputation of the tax for each prior taxable year affected by the revocation. A letter setting forth the Commissioner's determination will be mailed to the taxpayer. If consent is granted, a copy of the letter granting such consent shall be filed with the director of the Internal Revenue service center with which the taxpayer's income tax return is required to be filed and shall be accompanied by an amended return or returns, if necessary.

(iii) If, before revoking his election, the taxpayer has transferred any mineral property with respect to which he deducted exploration expenditures under section 617(a), to another person in a transaction as a result of which the basis of such property in the hands of the transferee is determined in whole or in part by reference to the basis in the hands of the transferor, the statement submitted pursuant to subdivision (i) of this paragraph shall state that such property has been so transferred, shall identify the transferee, the property transferred, the date of the transfer, and shall indicate the amount of the adjusted exploration expenditures with respect to such property on such date.

(4) Deficiency attributable to election or revocation of election. The statutory period for the assessment of any deficiency for any taxable year, to the extent such deficiency is attributable to an election or revocation of an election under section 617(a), shall not expire before the last day of the 2-year period which begins on the day after the date on which such election or revocation of election is made; and such deficiency may be assessed at any time before the expiration of such 2-year period, notwithstanding any law or rule which would otherwise prevent such assessment.

T.D. 7192, 6/29/72.

§ 1.617-2 Limitation on amount deductible.

Caution: The Treasury has not yet amended Reg § 1.617-2 to reflect changes made by P.L. 99-514.

(a) Expenditures paid or incurred before January 1, 1970. In the case of expenditures paid or incurred before

January 1, 1970, a taxpayer may deduct exploration expenditures paid or incurred during the taxable year with respect to any deposit of ore or other mineral for which a deduction for percentage depletion is allowable under section 613 (other than oil or gas) in the United States or on the Outer Continental Shelf (within the meaning of section 2 of the Outer Continental Shelf Lands Act, as amended and supplemented; 43 U.S.C. 1331).

(b) Expenditures paid or incurred after December 31, 1969. In the case of exploration expenditures paid or incurred after December 31, 1969, with respect to any deposit of ore or other mineral for which a deduction for percentage depletion is allowable under section 613 (other than oil or gas), a taxpayer may deduct—

(1) The amount of such expenditures paid or incurred during the taxable year with respect to any such deposit in the United States (as defined in section 638 and the regulations thereunder), and

(2) With respect to any such deposit located outside the United States (as defined in section 638 and the regulations thereunder) the lesser of:

(i) The amount of the exploration expenditures paid or incurred with respect to such deposits during the taxable year, or

(ii) $400,000 minus the sum of the amount to be deducted under subparagraph (1) of this paragraph for the taxable year and all amounts deducted or treated as deferred expenses during all preceding taxable years under section 617 and section 615 of the Internal Revenue Code of 1954 and section 23(ff) of the Internal Revenue Code of 1939. See paragraph (d) of this section for application of the limitation in the case of a transferee of a mining property.

(c) Examples. The application of the provisions of paragraphs (a) and (b) of this section may be illustrated by the following examples:

Example (1). A, a calendar-year taxpayer who has claimed the benefits of section 615, expended $100,000 for exploration expenditures during the year 1966. For each of the years 1967, 1968, 1969, and 1970 A had exploration costs of $80,000 all with respect to coal deposits located within the United States. A deducted or deferred the maximum amounts ($80,000). The $80,000 of exploration expenditures for 1970 may be deducted under section 617 by A.

Example (2). B, a calendar-year taxpayer claimed deductions of $100,000 per year under section 615 for the years 1968 and 1969. In 1970, B deducted $150,000 under section 617 for exploration conducted with respect to coal deposits in the United States. In 1971, B paid $150,000 with respect to exploration of tin deposits outside the United States. The maximum amount B may deduct with respect to the foreign exploration in 1971 is $50,000 computed as follows:

(a) Add all amounts deducted or deferred for exploration expenditures by B for all years:

Year	Expenditures	Deducted or deferred
1968	$100,000	$100,000
1969	100,000	100,000
1970	150,000	150,000
Total		350,000

(b) Subtract from $400,000 (the maximum amount allowable to B for deduction of foreign exploration expenditures) the sum of the amounts obtained in (a) $350,000:

Maximum amount allowable to taxpayer	$400,000
Sum of amounts obtained in (a)	350,000
	50,000

Example (3). Assume the same facts as in example (2) except that in 1971 in addition to the $150,000 paid with respect to exploration outside the United States, B paid $100,000 with respect to exploration within the United States. As the following computation indicates, B may not deduct any amount with respect to the foreign exploration:

(a) Add all amounts deducted or deferred for exploration expenditures in prior years and the exploration expenditures with respect to exploration in the United States to be deducted in 1971:

Year	Expenditures	Deducted or deferred
1968	$100,000	$100,000
1969	100,000	100,000
1970	150,000	150,000
1971	250,000[1]	100,000
Total		450,000

[1] Domestic.

(b) Because the sum of the amounts obtained in (a), $450,000, exceeds $400,000 no deduction would be allowable to B with respect to foreign exploration expenditures for 1971.

(d) Transferee of mineral property. *(1)* Where an individual or corporation transfers any mining property to the taxpayer, the taxpayer shall take into account for purposes of the $400,000 limitation described in paragraph (b)(ii) of this section all amounts deducted and amounts treated as deferred expenses by the transferor if—

(i) The taxpayer acquired any mineral property from the transferor in a transaction described in section 23(ff)(3) of the Internal Revenue Code of 1939, excluding the reference therein to section 113(a)(13),

(ii) The taxpayer acquired any mineral property by reason of the acquisition of assets of a corporation in a transaction described in section 381(a) as a result of which the taxpayer succeeds to and takes into account the items described in section 381(c),

(iii) The taxpayer acquired any mineral property under circumstances which make applicable any of the following sections of the Internal Revenue Code:

(a) Section 334(b)(1), relating to the liquidation of a subsidiary where the basis of the property in the hands of the distributee is the same as it would be in the hands of the transferor.

(b) Section 362(a) and (b), relating to property acquired by a corporation as paid-in surplus or as a contribution to capital, or in connection with a transaction to which section 351 applies.

(c) Section 372(a), relating to reorganization in certain receiverships and bankruptcy proceedings.

(d) Section 373(b)(1), relating to property of a railroad corporation acquired in certain bankruptcy or receivership proceedings.

(e) Section 1051, relating to property acquired by a corporation that is a member of an affiliated group.

(f) Section 1082, relating to property acquired pursuant to a Securities Exchange Commission order.

(2) For purposes of applying the limitations imposed by section 617(h):

(i) The partner, and not the partnership, shall be considered as the taxpayer (see paragraph (a)(8)(iii) of § 1.702-1), and

(ii) An electing small business corporation, as defined in section 1371(b), and not its shareholders, shall be considered as the taxpayer.

(3) For purposes of subparagraph (1)(iii)(b) of this paragraph, relating to a transaction to which section 362(a) and (b) applies or to which section 351 applies:

(i) If mineral property is acquired from a partnership, the transfer shall be considered as having been made by the individual partners so that the amounts which each partner has deducted or deferred under sections 615 and 617 of the Internal Revenue Code of 1954 and section 23(ff) of the Internal Revenue Code of 1939 shall be taken into account, or

(ii) If an interest in a partnership having mineral property is transferred, the transfer shall be considered as a transfer of mineral property by the partner or partners relinquishing an interest, so that the amounts which each such partner has deducted or deferred under sections 615 and 617 of the Internal Revenue Code of 1954 and section 23(ff) of the Internal Revenue Code of 1939 shall be taken into account.

(e) Examples. The application of the provisions of this section may be illustrated by the following examples:

Example (1). A calendar year taxpayer (who has never claimed the benefits of section 617) received in 1970 a mineral deposit from X Corporation upon a distribution in complete liquidation of the latter under conditions which make the provisions of section 334(b)(1) applicable in determining the basis of the property in the hands of the taxpayer. During the year 1969, X Corporation expended $60,000 for exploration expenditures which it elected to treat under section 615(b) as deferred expenses. Subsequent to the transfer the taxpayer made similar expenditures for domestic exploration of $250,000 and $140,000, for the years 1970, and 1971, respectively, which the taxpayer elected to deduct. In 1972, the taxpayer made expenditures for domestic exploration of $100,000 and for foreign exploration of $50,000. The taxpayer may deduct the $100,000 domestic exploration expenditures but may not deduct any portion of the $50,000 of foreign exploration expenditures because the $400,000 limitation of section 617(h) applies.

Example (2). In 1971, A and B transfer assets to a corporation in a transfer to which section 351 applied. Among the assets transferred by A is a mineral lease with respect to certain coal lands. A has deducted exploration expenditures under section 615 for the years 1968 and 1969 in the amounts of $50,000 and $100,000, respectively, made with respect to other deposits not included in the transfer to the corporation. The corporation is required to take into account the deductions previously made by A for purposes of applying the $400,000 limitation on deduction of foreign exploration expenditures. Thus, if in 1970 the corporation incurred $400,000 of foreign exploration expenditures, the maximum which it could deduct under section 617(a) is $250,000.

T.D. 7192, 6/29/72.

§ 1.617-3 Recapture of exploration expenditures.

Caution: The Treasury has not yet amended Reg § 1.617-3 to reflect changes made by P.L. 99-514.

(a) In general. *(1)* (i) Except as provided in subparagraphs (2) and (3) of this paragraph, if in any taxable year any mine (as defined in paragraph (c) of this section) with respect to which deductions have been allowed under section 617(a) reaches the producing stage (as defined in paragraph (c) of this section) the deduction for depletion under section 611 (whether determined under § 1.611-2 or under section 613) with respect to the property shall be disallowed for the taxable year and each subsequent taxable year until the aggregate amount of depletion which would be allowable but for section 617(b)(1)(B) and this subparagraph equals the amount of the adjusted exploration expenditures (determined under section 617(f)(1) and paragraph (d) of this section) attributable to the mine. The preceding sentence shall apply notwithstanding the fact that such mine is not in the producing stage at the close of such taxable year. In the case of a taxpayer who owns more than one property in a mine with respect to which he has been allowed deductions under section 617(a), the depletion deduction described in the second preceding sentence shall be disallowed with respect to all of the properties until the aggregate amount of depletion disallowed under section 617(b)(1)(B) is equal to the adjusted exploration expenditures with respect to the mine. In the case of a taxpayer who elects under section 614(c)(1) to aggregate a mine, with respect to which he has been allowed deductions under section 617(a), with another mine, no deduction for depletion will be allowable under section 611 with respect to the aggregated property until the amount of depletion disallowed under section 617(b)(1)(B) equals the adjusted exploration expenditures attributable to all of the producing mines included in the aggregated property.

(ii) If a taxpayer who has made an election under section 617(a) receives or accrues a bonus or royalty with respect to a mining property with respect to which deductions have been allowed under section 617(a), the deduction for depletion under section 611 with respect to such bonus or royalty (whether determined under § 1.611-2 or under section 613) shall be disallowed for the taxable year of receipt or accrual and each subsequent taxable year until the aggregate amount of the depletion disallowed under section 617(c) and this section equals the amount of the adjusted exploration expenditures with respect to the property to which the bonus or royalty relates. The preceding sentence shall not apply if the bonus or royalty is paid with respect to a mineral for which a deduction is not allowable under section 617(a). In the case of the disposal of coal or domestic iron ore with a retained economic interest, see paragraph (a)(2) of § 1.617-4.

(2) If the taxpayer so elects with respect to all mines as to which deductions have been allowed under section 617(a) and which reach the producing stage during the taxable year, he shall include in gross income (but not "gross income from the property" for purposes of section 613) for such taxable year an amount equal to the adjusted exploration expenditures (determined under section 617(f)(1) and paragraph (d) of this section) with respect to all of such mines. The amount so included in income shall be treated for purposes of subtitle A of the Internal Revenue Code as expenditures which are paid or incurred on the respective dates on which the mines reach the producing stage and which are properly chargeable to capital account. The fact that a taxpayer does not make the election described in this subparagraph for a taxable year during which mines with respect to which deductions have been allowed under section 617(a) reach the producing stage shall not preclude the taxpayer from making the election with respect to other mines which reach the producing stage during subsequent taxable years. However, the election described in this subparagraph may not be made for any taxable year with respect to any mines

which reached the producing stage during the preceding taxable year.

(3) The provisions of section 617(b)(1) and subparagraphs (1) and (2) of this paragraph do not apply in the case of any deposit of oil or gas. For example, A in exploring for sulphur incurred $500,000 of exploration expenditures which he deducted under section 617(a). In the following year, A did not find sulphur but on the same mineral property located commercially marketable quantities of oil and gas. In computing the depletion allowance with respect to the oil and gas, no depletion would be disallowed because of section 617(b)(1).

(4) In the case of exploration expenditures which are paid or incurred with respect to a mining property which contains more than one mine, the provisions of subparagraphs (1) and (2) of this paragraph shall apply only to the amount of the adjusted exploration expenditures properly chargeable to the mine or mines which reach the producing stage during the taxable year. For example, A owns a mining property which contains mines X, Y, and Z. For 1970, A deducted under section 617(a), $250,000 with respect to X, $100,000 with respect to Y and $70,000 with respect to Z. In 1971, mine X reaches the producing stage. At that time, A will only have to recapture the $250,000 attributable to mine X.

(b) Manner and time for making election. *(1)* A taxpayer will be deemed not to have elected pursuant to section 617(b)(1)(A) and paragraph (a)(2) of this section unless he clearly indicates such election on his income tax return for the taxable year in which the mine with respect to which deductions were allowed under section 617(a) reaches the producing stage.

(2) The election described in paragraph (a)(2) of this section may be made (or changed) not later than the time prescribed by law for filing the return (including extensions thereof) for the taxable year in which the mine with respect to which deductions were allowed under section 617(a) reaches the producing stage.

(c) Definitions. *(1) Mine.* The term "mine" includes all quarries, pits, shafts, and wells, and any other excavations or workings for the purpose of extracting any known deposit of ore or other mineral.

(2) Producing stage. A mine will be considered to have reached the producing stage when (i) the major portion of the mineral production is obtained from workings other than those opened for the purpose of development, or (ii) the principal activity of the mine is the production of developed ores or minerals rather than the development of additional ores or minerals for mining.

(3) Mining property. The term "mining property" means any property (as the term is defined in section 614(a) after the application of subsections (c) and (e) thereof) with respect to which any expenditures allowed as deductions under section 617(a) are properly chargeable.

(d) Adjusted exploration expenditures. *(1) In general.* The term "adjusted exploration expenditures" means, with respect to any property or mine—

(i) The aggregate amount of the expenditures allowed as deductions under section 617(a) for the taxable year and all preceding taxable years to the taxpayer or any other person which are properly chargeable to such property or mine and which (but for the election under section 617(a)) would be reflected in the adjusted basis of such property or mine, reduced by

(ii) The excess, if any, of the amount which would have been allowable for all taxable years under section 613 but for the deduction of such expenditures over the amount allowable for depletion under section 611 (determined without regard to section 617(b)(1)(B)). The amount determined under the preceding sentence shall be reduced by the aggregate of the amounts included in gross income for the taxable year and all preceding taxable years under section 617(b) or (c) and the amount treated under section 617(d) as gain from the sale or exchange of the property which is neither a capital asset nor property described in section 1231.

(iii) If a taxpayer pays or incurs exploration expenditures on a property which contains a producing mine and if such taxpayer deducts any portion of such expenditures under section 617(a), an amount equal to the amount so deducted shall be taken into account in computing the taxpayer's "taxable income from the property" for the purposes of the limitation on the percentage depletion deduction under section 613(a) and the regulations thereunder. The amount of the adjusted exploration expenditures with respect to the producing mine shall be reduced by an amount equal to the amount by which the taxpayer's deduction under 617(a) (described in the preceding sentence) reduces the taxpayer's deduction for depletion for the taxable year. See example (1) in subparagraph (6) of this paragraph.

(iv) For purposes of § 1.617-4, the aggregate amount of adjusted exploration expenditures with respect to a mining property includes the aggregate amount of adjusted exploration expenditures properly allocable to all mines on such property.

(v) (a) For purposes of paragraph (a)(1) of this section, the aggregate amount of the adjusted exploration expenditures is determined as of the close of the taxpayer's taxable year.

(b) For purposes of § 1.617-4, the aggregate amount of the adjusted exploration expenditures is determined as of the date of the operation of the mining property or portion thereof.

(2) Adjustments for certain expenditures of other taxpayers or in respect of other property. (i) For purposes of subparagraph (1) of this paragraph, the exploration expenditures which must be taken into account in determining the adjusted exploration expenditures with respect to any property or mine are not limited to those expenditures with respect to the property disposed of or which entered the production stage nor are such expenditures limited to those deducted by the taxpayer. For the manner of determining the amount of adjusted exploration expenditures immediately after certain dispositions, see subparagraph (4) of this paragraph.

(ii) If a transferee who at the time of the transfer has not made an election under section 617(a) (including a transferee who has made an election under section 615(e)) receives mineral property in a transaction in which the basis of such property in his hands is determined in whole or in part by reference to its basis in the hands of the transferor and with respect to such property the transferor has deducted exploration expenditures under section 617(a), the adjusted exploration expenditures immediately after such transfer shall be treated as exploration expenditures allowed as deductions under section 617(a) to the transferee.

(iii) If a transferee who makes an election under section 617(a) receives mineral property in a transaction in which the basis of such property in his hands is determined in whole or in part by reference to the basis of such property in the hands of the transferor and the transferor had in effect at the time of the transfer an election under section 615(e), an amount equal to the total of the amounts allowed as deductions to the transferor under section 615 with respect to the transferred property shall be treated as expenditures allowed as deductions under section 617(a) to the transferee. The preceding sentence shall not apply to expenditures which could not have been reflected in the basis of the property in the hands of the transferee had the transferor not made the section 615(e) election.

(iv) The provisions of this subparagraph may be illustrated by the following examples:

Example (1). On July 14, 1969, A purchased mineral property Z for $10,000. After deducting exploration expenditures of $20,000 under section 617(a), A transferred the property to his son as a gift on July 9, 1970. Since the exception for gifts in section 617(d)(3) (by incorporation by reference of the provisions of section 1245(b)(1)) applies, A does not recognize gain under section 617(d). On September 30, 1972, after deducting exploration expenditures of $150,000 under section 617(a), the son transfers the mineral property to corporation X in a transaction under which no gain is recognized by the son under section 351. Since the exception of section 617(d)(3) (by incorporation by reference of the provisions of section 1245(b)(3)) applies, the son does not recognize gain under section 617(d). On November 14, 1972, corporation X sells the mineral property. No deductions for exploration expenditures were taken by corporation X. The amount of the adjusted exploration expenditures with respect to mineral property Z to be recaptured by corporation X upon such sale is $170,000 (the total amount deducted by A and the son).

Example (2). Assume the same facts as in example (1) except that A deducted the $20,000 of exploration expenditures under section 615(a). The amount of the adjusted exploration expenditures with respect to mineral property Z in corporation X's hands is $170,000 (the $20,000 deducted under section 615(a) by A plus the $150,000 deducted under section 617(a) by the son).

(3) Allocation of certain expenditures. A project area consists of that territory which the taxpayer has determined by analysis of certain variables (the size and topography of the area to be explored, existing information with respect to that area and nearby areas, and the quantity of equipment, men, and money available) can be explored advantageously as a single integrated operation. If exploration expenditures are paid or incurred with respect to a project area and one or more areas of interest are identified within such project area, the entire amount of such expenditures shall be allocated equally to each such area of interest. If an area of interest contains one or more mines or deposits the expenditures allocable to such area of interest shall be allocated (i) if only one mine or deposit is located or identified, entirely to such mine or deposit, or (ii) if more than one mine or deposit is located or identified, equally among the various mines or deposits located. For purposes of this subparagraph, the term "area of interest" means each separable, noncontiguous portion of the project area which is identified as possessing sufficient mineral-producing potential to merit further exploration. The provisions of this subparagraph may be illustrated by the following example: A pays $100,000 for the exploration of a project area which results in the identification of two areas of interest. A pays an additional $60,000 for the exploration of one of the areas of interest in which he locates mineral deposit X and mineral deposit Y. With respect to the exploration of deposit X he incurs an additional $100,000 of expenses and with respect to deposit Y he incurs an additional $200,000 of expenses. The exploration expenditures properly attributable to deposit X would be $155,000 ($100,000 plus one-half of $50,000 plus one-half of $60,000) and the exploration expenditures properly attributable to deposit Y would be $255,000 ($200,000 plus one-half of $50,000 plus one-half of $60,000).

(4) Partnership distributions. The adjusted exploration expenditures with respect to any property or mine received by a taxpayer in a distribution with respect to all or part of his interest in a partnership (i) include the adjusted exploration expenditures (not otherwise included under section 617(f)(1)) with respect to such property or mine immediately prior to such distribution and (ii) shall be reduced by the amount of gain to which section 751(b) applies realized by the partnership (as constituted after the distribution) on the distribution of such property or mine. In the case of any property or mine held by a partnership after a distribution to a partner to which section 751(b) applies, the adjusted exploration expenditures with respect to such property or mine shall be reduced by the amount of gain (if any) to which section 751(b) applies realized by such partner with respect to such distribution on account of such property or mine.

(5) Amount of transferee's adjusted exploration expenditures immediately after certain acquisitions. (i) Transactions in which basis is determined by reference to the cost or fair market value of the property transferred. (a) If on the date a person acquires mining property his basis for the property is determined solely by reference to its cost (within the meaning of section 1012), then on such date the amount of the adjusted exploration expenditures for the mining property in such person's hands is zero.

(b) If on the date a person acquires mining property his basis for the property is determined solely by reason of the application of section 301(d) (relating to basis of property received in corporate distribution) or section 334(a) (relating to basis of property received in a liquidation in which gain or loss is recognized), then on such date the amount of the adjusted exploration expenditures for the mining property in such person's hands is zero.

(c) If on the date a person acquires mining property his basis for the property is determined solely under the provisions of section 334(b)(2) or (c) (relating to basis of property received in certain corporate liquidations), then on such date the amount of the adjusted exploration expenditures for the mining property in such person's hands is zero.

(d) If on the date a person acquires mining property from a decedent such person's basis is determined, by reason of the application of section 1014(a), solely by reference to the fair market value of the property on the date of the decedent's death or on the applicable date provided in section 2032 (relating to alternate valuation date), then on the date of acquisition the amount of the adjusted exploration expenditures for the mining property in such person's hands is zero.

(ii) Gifts and certain tax-free transactions. (a) If mining property is disposed of in a transaction described in (b) of this subdivision (ii), then the amount of the adjusted exploration expenditures for the mining property in the hands of a transferee immediately after the disposition shall be an amount equal to—

(1) The amount of the adjusted exploration expenditures with respect to the mining property in the hands of the transferor immediately before the disposition, minus

(2) The amount of any gain taken into account under section 617(d) by the transferor upon the disposition.

(b) The transactions referred to in *(a)* of this subdivision (ii) are—

(1) A disposition which is in part a sale or exchange and in part a gift, or

(2) A disposition which is described in section 617(d) through the incorporation by reference of the provisions of section 1245(b)(3) (relating to certain tax free transactions).

(iii) Property acquired from a decedent. If mining property is acquired in a transfer at death to which section 617(d) applies through incorporation by reference of the provisions of section 1245(b)(2), the amount of the adjusted exploration expenditures with respect to the mining property in the hands of the transferee immediately after the transfer shall include the amount, if any, of the exploration expenditures deducted by the transferee before the decedent's death, to the extent that the basis of the mining property (determined under section 1014(a)) is required to be reduced under the second sentence of section 1014(b)(9) (relating to adjustments to basis where the property is acquired from a decedent prior to his death).

(6) Examples. The provisions of this paragraph may be illustrated by the following examples:

Example (1). A owns the working interest in a large tract of land located in the United States. A's interest in the entire tract of land constitutes one property for purposes of section 614. In the northwest corner of this tract is an operating mine, X, producing an ore of beryllium, which is entitled to a percentage depletion rate of 22 percent under section 613(b)(2)(B). During 1971, A conducts an exploration program in the southeast corner of this same tract of land, and he incurs $400,000 of expenditures to which section 617(a)(1) applies in connection with this exploration program. A elects to deduct this amount as expenses under section 617(a). During 1971, A's "gross income from the property" computed under section 613 was $1 million, with respect to the property encompassing mine X and the area in which exploration was conducted. A's "taxable income from the property" computed under section 613, before adjustment to reflect the deductions taken with respect to the property during the year under section 617, was $400,000. The cost depletion deduction allowable and deducted with respect to the property during 1971 was $50,000. The amount of adjusted exploration expenditures chargeable to the exploratory mine (hereinafter referred to as mine Y) at the close of 1971 is $250,000, computed as follows:

Expenditures allowed as deductions under sec. 617(a)		$400,000
Gross income from the property	$1,000,000	
22 percent thereof	220,000	
Taxable income from the property, before adjustment to reflect deductions allowed under sec. 617 during year	400,000	
50 percent thereof—tentative deduction	200,000	
Taxable income from the property after adjustment to reflect deductions allowed under sec. 617 during year ($400,000 minus $400,000)	0	
Cost depletion allowed for year	50,000	
Amount by which allowance for depletion under sec. 611 was reduced on account of deductions under sec. 617 ($200,000 minus $50,000) . .		150,000
Adjusted exploration expenditures at end of 1971		250,000

Example (2). Assume the same facts as in example 1. Assume further that mine Y, with respect to which exploration expenditures were deducted in 1971, enters the producing stage in 1972, and that no deductions were taken under section 617 with respect to that mine after 1971. A does not make an election under section 617(b)(1)(A) during 1972. Assume that the depletion deduction which would be allowable for 1972 with respect to the property (which includes both mines) but for the application of section 617(b)(1)(B) is $100,000. Pursuant to section 617(b)(1)(B), this depletion deduction is disallowed. Therefore, the amount of adjusted exploration expenditures with respect to mine Y at the end of 1972 is $150,000 ($250,000 less $100,000).

T.D. 7192, 6/29/72.

§ 1.617-4 Treatment of gain from disposition of certain mining property.

Caution: The Treasury has not yet amended Reg § 1.617-4 to reflect changes made by P.L. 99-514.

(a) In general. *(1)* In general, section 617(d)(1) provides, that, upon a disposition of mining property, the lower of (i) the "adjusted exploration expenditures" (as defined in section 617(f)(1) and paragraph (d) of § 1.617-3) with respect to the property, or (ii) the amount, if any, by which the amount realized on the sale, exchange, or involuntary conversion (or the fair market value of the property on any other disposition, exceeds the adjusted basis of the property, shall be treated as gain from the sale of exchange of property which is neither a capital asset nor property described in section 1231 (that is, shall be recognized as ordinary income). However, any amount recognized under the preceding sentence shall not be included by the taxpayer in his "gross income from the property" for purposes of section 613. Generally, the ordinary income treatment applies even though in the absence of section 617(d) no gain would be recognized under any other provision of the Code. For example, if a corporation distributes mining property as a dividend, gain may be recognized as ordinary income to the corporation even though, in the absence of section 617, section 311(a) would preclude any recognition of gain to the corporation. For an exception to the recognition of gain with respect to dispositions which involve mineral production payments, see section 636 and the regulations thereunder. For the definition of the term "mining property", see section 617(f)(2) and paragraph (c)(3), of § 1.617-3. For exceptions and limitations to the application of section 617(d)(1), see section 617(d)(3) and paragraph (c) of this section.

(2) In the case of a sale, exchange, or involuntary conversion of mining property, the gain to which section 617(d)(1) applies is the lower of the adjusted exploration expenditures with respect to such property or the excess of the amount realized upon the disposition of the property over the adjusted basis of the property. In the case of a disposition of mining property other than by a manner described in the preceding sentence, the gain to which section 617(d)(1) applies is the lower of the adjusted exploration expenditures with respect to such property or the excess of the fair market value of the

property on the date of disposition over the adjusted basis of the property. In the case of a disposal of coal or domestic iron ore subject to a retained economic interest to which section 631(c) applies, the excess of the amount realized over the adjusted basis of the mining property shall be treated as equal to the gain, if any, referred to in section 631(c). For determination of the amount realized upon a disposition of mining property and nonmining property, see paragraph (c)(3)(i) of this section.

(3) The provisions of this paragraph may be illustrated by the following examples:

Example (1). On July 14, 1970, A purchased undeveloped mining property for $100,000. During 1970, A incurred with respect to the property, $50,000 of exploration expenditures which he deducts under section 617(a). In 1971, A incurred $150,000 of exploration expenditures with respect to the property which he deducts on his income tax return. On January 2, 1972, A sells the mining property to B for $250,000. A's gain on the sale is $150,000 ($250,000 amount realized minus $100,000 basis). Since the excess of the amount realized over the adjusted basis of the mining property is less than the adjusted exploration expenditures with respect to the property ($200,000), the entire gain is treated as ordinary income under section 617(d)(1).

Example (2). Assume the same facts as in example (1) except that A sells the mining property to B for $400,000, thereby realizing gain of $300,000 ($400,000 minus $100,000 basis). Since the amount of adjusted exploration expenditures with respect to the mining property ($200,000) is less than the amount realized upon its disposition ($300,000), an amount equal to the amount of adjusted exploration expenditures is treated as ordinary income under section 617(d)(1). The remaining $100,000 is treated by A without regard to section 617(d)(1).

(4) Section 617(d) does not apply to losses. Thus, section 617(d) does not apply if a loss is realized upon a sale, exchange, or involuntary conversion of mining property, nor does section 617(d) apply to a disposition of mining property other than by way of sale, exchange, or involuntary conversion if at the time of the disposition the fair market value of such property is not greater than its adjusted basis.

(b) Disposition of portion of mining property. *(1)* For purposes of section 617(d)(1) and paragraph (a) of this section, except as provided in subparagraph (3) of this paragraph, in the case of the disposition of a portion of a mining property (other than an undivided interest), the entire amount of the adjusted exploration expenditures with respect to such property shall be treated as attributable to such portion to the extent of the amount of the gain to which section 617(d)(1) applies. If the amount of the gain to which section 617(d)(1) applies is less than the amount of the adjusted exploration expenditures with respect to the property, the balance of the adjusted exploration expenditures shall remain subject to recapture in the hands of the taxpayer under the provisions of section 617(b), (c), and (d). The disposition of a portion of a mining property (other than an undivided interest) includes the disposition of a geographical portion of a mining property. For example, assume that A owns an 80-acre tract of land with respect to which he has deducted exploration expenditures under section 617(a). If A were to sell the north 40 acres, the entire amount of the adjusted exploration expenditures with respect to the 80-acre tract would be treated as attributable to the 40-acre portion sold (to the extent of the amount of the gain to which section 617(d)(1) applies).

(2) For purposes of section 617(d)(1), except as provided in subparagraph (3) of this paragraph, in the case of the disposition of an undivided interest in a mining property (or portion thereof) a proportionate part of the adjusted exploration expenditures with respect to such property shall be treated as attributable to such undivided interest to the extent of the amount of the gain to which section 617(d)(1) applies. For example, assume that A owns an 80-acre tract of land with respect to which he has deducted exploration expenditures under section 617(a). If A were to sell an undivided 40 percent interest in such tract, 40 percent of the adjusted exploration expenditures with respect to the 80-acre tract would be treated as attributable to the 40 percent of the 80-acre tract disposed of (to the extent of the amount of the gain to which section 617(d)(1) applies).

(3) Section 617(d)(2) and subparagraphs (1) and (2) of this paragraph shall not apply to any expenditure to the extent that such expenditure relates neither to the portion (or interest therein) disposed of nor to any mine, in the property held by the taxpayer before the disposition, which has reached the producing stage. In any case where a taxpayer disposes of a mining property (or interest therein) and treats adjusted exploration expenditures with respect to the mining property as if they relate neither to the portion (or interest therein) disposed of nor to any mine, in the property held by the taxpayer before the disposition, which has reached the producing stage, the taxpayer shall attach to its return for the taxable year in which the disposition occurred, a statement which includes:

(i) A description of the portion (or interest therein) disposed of;

(ii) A description of the mineral property which included the portion (or interest therein) disposed of;

(iii) An itemization of all expenditures deducted under sections 617 and 615 with respect to such mineral property; and

(iv) A description of the location of all producing mines on such mineral property.

(c) Exceptions. *(1)* (i) Section 617(d)(3) provides, through incorporation by reference of the provisions of section 1245(b)(1), that no gain shall be recognized under section 617(d) upon a disposition by gift of mining property. For purposes of this subparagraph, the term "gift" means, except to the extent that subdivision (ii) of this subparagraph applies, a transfer of mining property which, in the hands of the transferee, has a basis determined under the provisions of section 1015 (a) or (d) (relating to basis of property acquired by gift). For reduction in amount of the charitable contribution in case of a gift of section 617 property, see section 170(e) and paragraph (c)(3) of § 1.170-1.

(ii) Where a disposition of mining property is in part a sale or exchange and in part a gift, the gain to which section 617(d) applies is the lower of the adjusted exploration expenditures with respect to such property or the excess of the amount realized upon the disposition of the property over the adjusted basis of such property.

(2) Section 617(d)(3) provides, through incorporation by reference of the provisions of section 1245(b)(2), that, except as provided in section 691 (relating to income in respect to a decedent), no gain shall be recognized under section 617(d) upon a transfer at death. For purposes of this paragraph, the term "transfer at death" means a transfer of mining property which property, in the hands of the transferee, has a basis determined under the provisions of section 1014(a) (relating to basis of property acquired from a decedent) because of the death of the transferor.

(3) (i) Section 617(d) provides, through incorporation by reference of the provisions of section 1245(b)(3), that upon a transfer of property described in subdivision (ii) of this subparagraph, the amount of gain taken into account by the transferor under section 617(d) shall not exceed the amount of gain recognized to the transferor on the transfer (determined without regard to section 617). For purposes of this subdivision, in case of a transfer of mining property and nonmining property in one transaction, the amount realized from the disposition of the mining property shall be deemed to be equal to the amount which bears the same ratio to the total amount realized as the fair market value of the mining property bears to the aggregate fair market value of all of the property transferred. The preceding sentence shall be applied solely for purposes of computing the portion of the total gain (determined without regard to section 617) which shall be recognized as ordinary income under section 617(d). Section 617(d)(3) does not apply to a disposition of mining property to an organization (other than a cooperative described in section 521) which is exempt from the tax imposed by chapter 1 of the Code.

(ii) The transfers referred to in subdivision (i) of this subparagraph are transfers of mining property in which the basis of the mining property in the hands of the transferee is determined by reference to its basis in the hands of the transferor by reason of the application of any of the following provisions:

(a) Section 332 (relating to distributions in complete liquidation of an 80-percent-or-more controlled subsidiary corporation). See subdivision (iii) of this subparagraph.

(b) Section 351 (relating to transfer to a corporation controlled by transferor).

(c) Section 361 (relating to exchanges pursuant to certain corporate reorganizations).

(d) Section 371(a) (relating to exchanges pursuant to certain receivership and bankruptcy proceedings).

(e) Section 374(a) (relating to exchanges pursuant to certain railroad reorganizations).

(f) Section 721 (relating to transfers to a partnership in exchange for a partnership interest).

(g) Section 731 (relating to distributions by a partnership to a partner).

(iii) In the case of a distribution in complete liquidation of an 80-percent-or-more controlled subsidiary to which section 332 applies, the limitation provided in section 617(d)(3), through incorporation by reference of the provisions of section 1245(b)(3), is confined to instances in which the basis of the mining property in the hands of the transferee is determined under section 334(b)(1), by reference to its basis in the hands of the transferor. Thus, for example, the limitation may apply in respect of a liquidating distribution of mining property by an 80-percent-or-more controlled corporation to the parent corporation, but does not apply in respect of a liquidating distribution of mining property to a minority shareholder. Section 617(d)(3) does not apply to a liquidating distribution of property by an 80-percent-or-more controlled subsidiary to its parent if the parent's basis for the property is determined, under section 334(b)(2), by reference to its basis in the stock of the subsidiary.

T.D. 7192, 6/29/72.

---

§ 1.621-1 Payments to encourage exploration, development, and mining for defense purposes.

Caution: The Treasury has not yet amended Reg § 1.621-1 to reflect changes made by P.L. 101-508.

(a) General rule. *(1)* Under section 621, a taxpayer shall exclude from gross income amounts which are paid to him:

(i) By the United States or by an agency or instrumentality of the United States,

(ii) As a grant, gift, bounty, bonus, premium, incentive, subsidy, loan, or advance,

(iii) For the encouragement of exploration for, or development or mining of, a critical and strategic mineral or metal,

(iv) Pursuant to or in connection with an undertaking by the taxpayer to explore for, or develop or produce, such mineral or metal and to expend or use any amounts so received for the purpose and in accordance with the terms and conditions upon which such amounts are paid, which undertaking has been approved by the United States or by an agency or instrumentality of the United States, and

(v) For which the taxpayer has accounted, or is required to account, to an appropriate agency of the United States Government for the expenditure or use thereof for the purpose and in accordance with the terms and conditions upon which such amounts are paid.

In order for section 621 to apply, such amount must qualify under each of the foregoing subdivisions of this paragraph. Under section 621, there shall also be excluded from gross income any income attributable to the forgiveness or discharge of any indebtedness arising from amounts to which such section applies.

(2) Section 621 is applicable whether or not the payee is obligated to repay to the United States any portion or all of the amount so received. However, such section is not applicable to any loan or advance for the repayment of which the borrower's liability is unconditional and legally enforceable.

(3) Except as provided in paragraph (e) of this section any expenditure attributable to an amount received by a taxpayer to which section 621 applies shall not be deductible by the taxpayer as an expense under subtitle A of the Code, nor shall any such expenditure increase the basis of the taxpayer's property either for determining gain or loss on sale, exchange, or other disposition, or for computing depletion or depreciation (including amortization under section 168).

(b) Allowance as part of purchase price. *(1)* Section 621 is not applicable to any part of the purchase price of a critical and strategic mineral or metal which amount is received, whether before, on, or after delivery from the United States or any agency or instrumentality thereof, and irrespective of whether such purchase price is below, at, or above the currently prevailing market price.

(2) However, a payment of a separate and specific amount for the encouragement of exploration for, or development or mining of, a critical and strategic mineral or metal shall not be considered to be a part of the purchase price of such mineral or metal merely because such payment is added to, or included with, the payment of such purchase price.

(c) Payments for expenditures previously deducted or capitalized. *(1)* Where amounts described in section 621 and this section are paid to a taxpayer in reimbursement for expenditures previously allowed as a deduction, the taxpayer shall include in gross income that portion of such amounts which is equivalent to the deduction for such expenditures allowed to the taxpayer and which deduction resulted in a reduction for any taxable year of the taxpayer's taxes under subtitle A of the Code (other than chapter 2, relating to tax on self-employment income), or prior income, war-profits, or excess-profits tax laws.

(2) Where amounts described in section 621 and this section are paid to the taxpayer in reimbursement for expenditures which have been deferred under sections 615 and 616 (relating to exploration and development expenditures) the taxpayer shall include in gross income that portion of such amounts which is equivalent to any deduction for such expenditures allowed to the taxpayer and which deduction resulted in a reduction for any taxable year of the taxpayer's taxes under subtitle A of the Code (other than chapter 2, relating to tax on self-employment income), or prior income, war-profits, or excess-profits tax laws. The portion of such amounts, equivalent to expenditures which are reflected in the adjusted basis of the assets to which charged, shall be excluded from gross income, and such adjusted basis shall be decreased by the amount of such exclusion.

(3) Where amounts described in section 621 and this section are paid to the taxpayer in reimbursement for expenditures which have been charged to capital account (either to a depletable or depreciable account), there shall be included in the taxpayer's gross income that portion of such amounts which is equivalent to such capital expenditures that have been recovered through cost depletion or depreciation deductions and which deductions have resulted in a reduction of the taxpayer's taxes for any taxable year under subtitle A of the Code (other than chapter 2, relating to tax on self-employment income), or prior income, war-profits, or excess-profits tax laws. The portion of such amounts which is equivalent to the expenditures which are reflected in the adjusted basis of the asset to which charged shall be excluded from gross income. The adjusted basis of such assets shall be reduced by the amount of such exclusion from gross income.

(4) Where amounts described in section 621 and this section are paid to the taxpayer in reimbursement for expenditures which have been charged to a depletable capital account, such amounts shall be excluded to the extent such expenditures are recovered through depletion deductions computed under section 613 (relating to percentage depletion).

(5) The amount of reimbursed expenditures charged to an account (depletable or depreciable) and recovered through depletion or depreciation deductions for any taxable year shall be that proportion of the total deductions allowed with respect to such account that such reimbursed expenditures bear to the total amount in the account. For example, in 1956 A incurs exploration expenditures of $12,000 which he charges to a depletable capital account. This brings the total amount in this account to $36,000 which is the adjusted basis of the property on January 1, 1957. In 1957, A is allowed a deduction for cost depletion of $9,000 which resulted in a reduction of A's income taxes. One-third of this deduction is attributable to the $12,000 of exploration expenditures since they were a third of the total in the capital account on January 1, 1957. Therefore, on January 1, 1958, these exploration expenditures make up $9,000 of the remaining $27,000 in the account. If on January 1, 1958, A receives $12,000, which qualifies under section 621, in reimbursement for these exploration expenditures, he must report $3,000 as income and reduce the capital account by $9,000.

(d) Definition. As used in section 621 and this section, the term "critical and strategic minerals or metals" means minerals and metals which are considered by those departments, agencies, and instrumentalities of the United States charged with the encouragement of exploration for, and development and mining of, critical and strategic minerals and metals, to constitute critical and strategic minerals and metals for defense purposes. See, for example, 30 CFR 301.3 (Regulations for Obtaining Federal Assistance in Financing Explorations for Mineral Reserves, Excluding Organic Fuels, in the United States, its Territories and Possessions).

(e) Repayments of amounts excluded under section 621. Upon the repayment by the taxpayer of any portion of any amount to which section 621 applies and which portion has been expended for the purpose and in accordance with the terms and conditions upon which it was paid to the taxpayer, any expenditures attributable to such amount made by the taxpayer shall be treated as if such expenditures had been made at the time of such repayment. Such expenditures shall to the extent of the repayment be expensed or capitalized, as the case may be, in the order in which they were actually made or in such other manner as may be adopted by the taxpayer with the approval of the Commissioner.

T.D. 6446, 1/20/60.

§ 1.631-1 Election to consider cutting as sale or exchange.

Caution: The Treasury has not yet amended Reg § 1.631-1 to reflect changes made by P.L. 108-357, P.L. 98-369.

(a) Effect of election. *(1)* Section 631(a) provides an election to certain taxpayers to treat the difference between the actual cost or other basis of certain timber cut during the taxable year and its fair market value as standing timber on the first day of such year as gain or loss from a sale or exchange under section 1231. Thereafter, any subsequent gain or loss shall be determined in accordance with paragraph (e) of this section.

(2) For the purposes of section 631(a) and this section, timber shall be considered cut at the time when in the ordinary course of business the quantity of timber felled is first definitely determined.

(3) The election may be made with respect to any taxable year even though such election was not made with respect to a previous taxable year. If an election has been made under the provisions of section 631(a), or corresponding provisions of prior internal revenue laws, such election shall be binding upon the taxpayer not only for the taxable year for which the election is made but also for all subsequent taxable years, unless the Commissioner on showing by the taxpayer of undue hardship permits the taxpayer to revoke his election for such subsequent taxable years. If the taxpayer has revoked a previous election, such revocation shall preclude any further elections unless the taxpayer obtains the consent of the Commissioner.

(4) Such election shall apply with respect to all timber which the taxpayer has owned, or has had a contract right to cut, for a period of more than 1 year (6 months for taxable years beginning before 1977; 9 months for taxable years beginning in 1977) prior to when such timber is cut for sale or for use in the taxpayer's trade or business, irrespective of whether such timber or contract right was acquired before or after the election. (For purposes of the preceding sentence, the rules with respect to the holding period of property contained in section 1223 shall be applicable.) However, timber which is not cut for sale or for use in the taxpayer's trade or business (for example, firewood cut for the taxpayer's own

household consumption) shall not be considered to have been sold or exchanged upon the cutting thereof.

(b) Who may make election. *(1)* A taxpayer who has owned, or has held a contract right to cut, timber for a period of more than 1 year (6 months for taxable years beginning before 1977; 9 months for taxable years beginning in 1977) prior to when the timber is cut may elect under section 631(a) to consider the cutting of such timber during such year for sale or for use in the taxpayer's trade or business as a sale or exchange of the timber so cut. In order to have a "contract right to cut timber" within the meaning of section 631(a) and this section, a taxpayer must have a right to sell the timber cut under the contract on his own account or to use such cut timber in his trade or business.

(2) For purposes of section 631(a) and this section, the term "timber" includes evergreen trees which are more than six years old at the time severed from their roots and are sold for ornamental purposes, such as Christmas decorations. Section 631(a) is not applicable to evergreen trees which are sold in a live state, whether or not for ornamental purposes. Tops and other parts of standing timber are not considered as evergreen trees within the meaning of section 631(a). The term "evergreen trees" is used in its commonly accepted sense and includes pine, spruce, fir, hemlock, cedar, and other coniferous trees.

(c) Manner of making election. The election under section 631(a) must be made by the taxpayer in his income tax return for the taxable year for which the election is applicable, and such election cannot be made in an amended return for such year. The election in the return shall take the form of a computation under the provisions of section 631(a) and section 1231.

(d) Computation of gain or loss under the election. *(1)* If the cutting of timber is considered as a sale or exchange pursuant to an election made under section 631(a), gain or loss shall be recognized to the taxpayer in an amount equal to the difference between the adjusted basis for depletion in the hands of the taxpayer of the timber which has been cut during the taxable year and the fair market value of such timber as of the first day of the taxable year in which such timber is cut. The adjusted basis for depletion of the cut timber shall be based upon the number of units of timber cut during the taxable year which are considered to be sold or exchanged and upon the depletion unit of the timber in the timber account or accounts pertaining to the timber cut, and shall be computed in the same manner as is provided in section 611 and the regulations thereunder with respect to the computation of the allowance for depletion.

(2) The fair market value of the timber as of the first day of the taxable year in which such timber is cut shall be determined, subject to approval or revision by the district director upon examination of the taxpayer's return, by the taxpayer in the light of the most reliable and accurate information available with reference to the condition of the property as it existed at that date, regardless of all subsequent changes, such as changes in surrounding circumstances, methods of exploitation, degree of utilization, etc. The value sought will be the selling price, assuming a transfer between a willing seller and a willing buyer as of that particular day. Due consideration will be given to the factors and the principles involved in the determination of the fair market value of timber as described in the regulations under section 611.

(3) The fair market value as of the beginning of the taxable year of the standing timber cut during the year shall be considered to be the cost of such timber, in lieu of the actual cost or other basis of such timber, for all purposes for which such cost is a necessary factor. See paragraph (e) of this section.

(4) For any taxable year for which the cutting of timber is considered to be a sale or exchange of such timber under section 631(a), the timber so cut shall be considered as property used in the trade or business for the purposes of section 1231, along with other property of the taxpayer used in the trade or business as defined in section 1231(b), regardless of whether such timber is property of a kind which would properly be includible in the inventory of the taxpayer if on hand at the close of the taxable year or property held by the taxpayer primarily for sale to customers in the ordinary course of his trade or business. Whether the gain or loss considered to have resulted from the cutting of the timber will be considered to be gain or loss resulting from the sale or exchange of capital assets held for more than 1 year (6 months for taxable years beginning before 1977; 9 months for taxable years beginning in 1977) depends upon the application of section 1231 to the taxpayer for the taxable year. See section 1231 and the regulations thereunder.

(e) Computation of subsequent gain or loss. *(1)* In case the products of the timber are sold after cutting, either in the form of logs or lumber or in the form of manufactured products, the income from such actual sales shall be considered ordinary income. When the election under section 631(a) is in effect, the cost of standing timber cut during the taxable year is determined as if the taxpayer had purchased such timber on the first day of the taxable year. Thus, in determining the cost of the products so sold, the cost of the timber shall be the fair market value on the first day of the taxable year in which the standing timber was cut, in lieu of the actual cost or other basis of such timber.

(2) This is also the rule in case the products of the timber cut during one taxable year, with respect to which an election has been made under section 631(a), are sold during a subsequent taxable year, whether or not the election provided in section 631(a) is applicable with respect to such subsequent year. If the products of the timber cut during a taxable year with respect to which an election under section 631(a) was made were not sold during such year and are included in inventory at the close of such year, the fair market value as of the beginning of the year of the timber cut during the year shall be used in lieu of the actual cost of such timber in computing the closing inventory for such year and the opening inventory for the succeeding year. With respect to the costs applicable in the determination of the amount of such inventories, there shall be included the fair market value of the timber cut, the costs of cutting, logging, and all other expenses incident to the cost of converting the standing timber into the products in inventory. See section 471 and the regulations thereunder. The fact that the fair market value as of the first day of the taxable year in which the timber is cut is deemed to be the cost of such timber shall not preclude the taxpayer from computing its inventories upon the basis of cost or market, whichever is lower, if such is the method used by the taxpayer. Nor shall it preclude the taxpayer from computing its inventories under the last-in, first-out inventory method provided by section 472 if such section is applicable to, and has been elected by, the taxpayer.

T.D. 6281, 12/20/57, amend T.D. 7728, 10/31/80.

§ 1.631-2 Gain or loss upon the disposal of timber under cutting contract.

Caution: The Treasury has not yet amended Reg § 1.631-2 to reflect changes made by P.L. 108-357, P.L. 98-369.

(a) In general. *(1)* If an owner disposes of timber held for more than 1 year (6 months for taxable years beginning before 1977; 9 months for taxable years beginning in 1977) before such disposal, under any form or type of contract whereby he retains an economic interest in such timber, the disposal shall be considered to be a sale of such timber. The difference between the amounts realized from disposal of such timber in any taxable year and the adjusted basis for depletion thereof shall be considered to be a gain or loss upon the sale of such timber for such year. Such adjusted basis shall be computed in the same manner as provided in section 611 and the regulations thereunder with respect to the allowance for depletion. See paragraph (e)(2) of this section for definition of "owner". For the purpose of determining whether or not the timber disposed of was held for more than 1 year (6 months for taxable years beginning before 1977; 9 months for taxable years beginning in 1977) before such disposal the rules with respect to the holding period of property contained in section 1223 shall be applicable.

(2) In the case of such a disposal, the provisions of section 1231 apply and such timber shall be considered to be property used in the trade or business for the taxable year in which it is considered to have been sold, along with other property of the taxpayer used in the trade or business as defined in section 1231(b), regardless of whether such timber is property held by the taxpayer primarily for sale to customers in the ordinary course of his trade or business. Whether gain or loss resulting from the disposition of the timber which is considered to have been sold will be deemed to be gain or loss resulting from a sale of a capital asset held for more than 1 year (6 months for taxable years beginning before 1977; 9 months for taxable years beginning in 1977) will depend upon the application of section 1231 to the taxpayer for the taxable year.

(b) Determination of date of disposal. *(1)* For purposes of section 631(b) and this section, the date of disposal of timber shall be deemed to be the date such timber is cut. However, if payment is made to the owner under the contract for timber before such timber is cut the owner may elect to treat the date of payment as the date of disposal of such timber. Such election shall be effective only for purposes of determining the holding period of such timber. Neither section 631(b) nor the election thereunder has any effect on the time of reporting gain or loss. See subchapter E, chapter 1 of the Code and the regulations thereunder. See paragraph (c)(2) of this section for the effect of exercising the election with respect to the payment for timber held for 1 year (6 months for taxable years beginning before 1977; 9 months for taxable years beginning in 1977) or less. See paragraph (d) of this section for the treatment of payments received in advance of cutting.

(2) For purposes of section 631(b) and this section, the "date such timber is cut" means the date when in the ordinary course of business the quantity of timber felled is first definitely determined.

(c) Manner and effect of election to treat date of payment as the date of disposal. *(1)* The election to treat the date of payment as the date of disposal of timber shall be evidenced by a statement attached to the taxpayer's income tax return filed on or before the due date (including extensions thereof) for the taxable year in which the payment is received. The statement shall specify the advance payments which are subject to the election and shall identify the contract under which the payments are made. However, in no case shall the time for making the election under section 631(b) expire before the close of March 21, 1958.

(2) Where the election to treat the date of payment as the date of disposal is made with respect to a payment made in advance of cutting, and such payment is made 1 year (6 months for taxable years beginning before 1977; 9 months for taxable years beginning in 1977) or less from the date the timber disposed of was acquired, section 631(b) shall not apply to such payment, irrespective of the date such timber is cut, since the timber was not held for more than 1 year (6 months for taxable years beginning before 1977; 9 months for taxable years beginning in 1977) prior to disposal.

(d) Payments received in advance of cutting. *(1)* Where the conditions of paragraph (a) of this section are met, amounts received or accrued prior to cutting (such as advance royalty payments or minimum royalty payments) shall be treated under section 631(b) as realized from the sale of timber if the contract of disposal provides that such amounts are to be applied as payment for timber subsequently cut. Such amounts will be so treated irrespective of whether or not an election has been made under paragraph (c) of this section to treat the date of payment as the date of disposal. For example, if no election has been made under paragraph (c) of this section, amounts received or accrued prior to cutting will be treated as realized from the sale of timber, provided the timber paid for is cut more than 1 year (6 months for taxable years beginning before 1977; 9 months for taxable years beginning in 1977) after the date of acquisition of such timber.

(2) However, if the right to cut timber under the contract expires, terminates, or is abandoned before the timber which has been paid for is cut, the taxpayer shall treat payments attributable to the uncut timber as ordinary income and not as received from the sale of timber under section 631(b). Accordingly, the taxpayer shall recompute his tax liability for the taxable year in which such payments were received or accrued. The recomputation shall be made in the form of an amended return where necessary.

(3) (i) Bonuses received or accrued by an owner in connection with the grant of a contract of disposal shall be treated under section 631(b) as amounts realized from the sale of timber to the extent attributable to timber held for more than 1 year (6 months for taxable years beginning before 1977; 9 months for taxable years beginning in 1977)

(ii) The adjusted depletion basis attributable to the bonus shall be determined under the provisions of section 612 and the regulations thereunder. This subdivision may be illustrated as follows:

Example. Taxpayer A has held timber having a depletion basis of $90,000 for two months when he enters into a contract of disposal with B. B pays A a bonus of $5,000 upon the execution of the contract and agrees to pay X dollars per unit of timber to A as the timber is cut. A does not exercise the election to treat the date of payment as the date of disposal. It is estimated that there are 50,000 units of timber subject to the contract and that the total estimated royalties to be paid to A will be $95,000. A must report the bonus in the taxable year it is received or accrued by him. The portion of the basis of the timber attributable to the bonus is determined by the following formula:

$$\frac{\text{Bonus}}{\text{Bonus + amount of expected royalties}} \times \text{Basis of timber} = \text{Basis attributable to bonus}$$

$$\frac{\$5,000}{\$100,000} \times \$90,000 = \$4,500$$

(iii) To the extent attributable to timber not held for more than six months, such bonuses shall be treated as ordinary income subject to depletion. In order to determine the amount of the bonus allocable to timber not held for more than six months, the bonus shall be apportioned ratably over the estimated number of units of timber covered by the contract of disposal. This subdivision may be illustrated as follows:

Example. Assume under the facts stated in the example in subdivision (ii) of this subparagraph that B cuts 10,000 units of timber that have been held by A for six months or less. The amount of the bonus (as well as the royalties) attributable to these units must be reported as ordinary income subject to depletion. The amount of the bonus attributable to these units is determined by the following formula:

$$\frac{\text{Number of units cut held for six months or less}}{\text{Total units covered by the contract}} \times \text{Amount of bonus} = \text{Amount of bonus treated as ordinary income subject to depletion}$$

$$\frac{10,000}{50,000} \times \$5,000 = \$1,000$$

The amount of the depletion attributable to the portion of the bonus received for timber held for six months or less is determined by the following formula:

$$\frac{\text{Amount of bonus attributable to timber held for six months or less}}{\text{Total bonus}} \times \text{Adjusted basis for depletion of bonus} = \text{Depletion allowance on timber held for six months or less.}$$

$$\frac{\$1,000}{\$5,000} \times \$4,500 = \$900$$

The amount of the bonus attributable to timber held for more than six months, and which is treated under section 631(b) as realized from the sale of timber would be $4,000. The gain on such amount is $400 ($4,000 – $3,600).

(iv) If the right to cut timber under the contract of disposal expires, terminates, or is abandoned before any timber is cut, the taxpayer shall treat the bonus received under such contract as ordinary income, not subject to depletion. Accordingly, the taxpayer shall recompute his tax liability for the taxable year in which such bonus was received. The recomputation shall be made in the form of an amended return where necessary.

(e) Other rules for application of section. *(1)* Amounts paid by the lessee for timber or the acquisition of timber cutting rights, whether designated as such or as a rental, royalty, or bonus, shall be treated as the cost of timber and constitute part of the lessee's depletable basis of the timber, irrespective of the treatment accorded such payments in the hands of the lessor.

(2) The provisions of section 631(b) apply only to an owner of timber. An owner of timber means any person who owns an interest in timber, including a sublessor and a holder of a contract to cut timber. Such owner of timber must have a right to cut timber for sale on his own account or for use in his trade or business in order to own an interest in timber within the meaning of section 631(b).

(3) For purposes of section 631(b) and this section, the term "timber" includes evergreen trees which are more than 6 years old at the time severed from their roots and are sold for ornamental purposes such as Christmas decorations. Tops and other parts of standing timber are not considered as evergreen trees within the meaning of section 631(b). The term "evergreen trees" is used in its commonly accepted sense and includes pine, spruce, fir, hemlock, cedar, and other coniferous trees.

T.D. 6281, 12/20/57, amend T.D. 7728, 10/31/80.

§ 1.631-3 Gain or loss upon the disposal of coal or domestic iron ore with a retained economic interest.

Caution: The Treasury has not yet amended Reg § 1.631-3 to reflect changes made by P.L. 99-514, P.L. 98-369.

(a) In general. *(1)* The provisions of section 631(c) apply to an owner who disposes of coal (including lignite), or iron ore mined in the United States, held for more than 1 year (6 months for taxable years beginning before 1977; 9 months for taxable years beginning in 1977) before such disposal under any form or type of contract whereby he retains an economic interest in such coal or iron ore. The difference between the amount realized from disposal of the coal or iron ore in any taxable year, and the adjusted depletion basis thereof plus the deductions disallowed for the taxable year under section 272, shall be gain or loss upon the sale of the coal or iron ore. See paragraph (b)(4) of this section for the definition of "owner." See paragraph (e) of this section for special rules relating to iron ore.

(2) In the case of such a disposal, the provisions of section 1231 apply, and the coal or iron ore shall be considered to be property used in the trade or business for the taxable year in which it is considered to have been sold, along with other property of the taxpayer used in the trade or business as defined in section 1231(b), regardless of whether the coal or iron ore is property held by the taxpayer primarily for sale to customers in the ordinary course of his trade or business. Whether gain or loss resulting from the disposition of the coal or iron ore which is considered to have been sold will be deemed to be gain or loss resulting from a sale of a capital asset held for more than 1 year (6 months for taxable years beginning before 1977; 9 months for taxable years beginning in 1977) will depend on the application of section 1231 to the taxpayer for the taxable year; i.e., if the gains do not exceed the losses, they shall not be considered as gains and losses from sales or exchanges of capital assets but shall be treated as ordinary gains and losses.

(b) Rules for application of section. *(1)* For purposes of section 631(c) and this section, the date of disposal of the coal or iron ore shall be deemed to be the date the coal or iron ore is mined. If the coal or iron ore has been held for more than 1 year (6 months for taxable years beginning before 1977; 9 months for taxable years beginning in 1977) on the date it is mined, it is immaterial that it had not been held for more than 1 year (6 months for taxable years beginning before 1977; 9 months for taxable years beginning in 1977) on the date of the contract. There shall be no allowance for percentage depletion provided in section 613 with respect to amounts which are considered to be realized from the sale of coal or iron ore under section 631(c).

(2) The term "adjusted depletion basis" as used in section 631(c) and this section means the basis for allowance of cost depletion provided in section 612 and the regulations thereunder. Such "adjusted depletion basis" shall include exploration or development expenditures treated as deferred expenses under section 615(b) or 616(b), or corresponding provisions of prior income tax laws, and be reduced by adjustments under section 1016(a)(9) and (10), or corresponding provisions of prior income tax laws, relating to deductions of deferred expenses for exploration or development expenditures in the taxable year or any prior taxable years. The depletion unit of the coal or iron ore disposed of shall be determined under the rules provided in the regulations under section 611, relating to cost depletion.

(3) (i) In determining the gross income, the adjusted gross income, or the taxable income of the lessee, the deductions allowable with respect to rents and royalties (except rents and royalties paid by a lessee with respect to coal or iron ore disposed of by the lessee as an "owner" under section 631(c)) shall be determined without regard to the provisions of section 631(c). Thus, the amounts of rents and royalties paid or incurred by a lessee with respect to coal or iron ore shall be excluded from the lessee's gross income from the property for the purpose of determining his percentage depletion without regard to the treatment of such rents or royalties in the hands of the recipient under this section. See section 613 and the regulations thereunder.

(ii) (a) However, a lessee who is also a sublessor may dispose of coal or iron ore as an "owner" under section 631(c). Rents and royalties paid with respect to coal or iron ore disposed of by such a lessee under section 631(c) shall increase the adjusted depletion basis of the coal or iron ore and are not otherwise deductible.

(b) The provisions of this subdivision may be illustrated by the following example:

Example. B is a sublessor of a coal lease; A is the lessor; and C is the sublessee. B pays A a royalty of 50 cents per ton. C pays B a royalty of 60 cents per ton. The amount realized by B under section 631(c) is 60 cents per ton and will be reduced by the adjusted depletion basis of 50 cents per ton, leaving a gain of 10 cents per ton taxable under section 631(c).

(4) (i) The provisions of this section apply only to an owner who has disposed of coal or iron ore and retained an economic interest. For the purposes of section 631(c) and this section, the word "owner" means any person who owns an economic interest in coal or iron ore in place, including a sublessor thereof. A person who merely acquires an economic interest and has not disposed of coal or iron ore under a contract retaining an economic interest does not qualify under section 631(c). A successor to the interest of a person who has disposed of coal or iron ore under a contract by virtue of which he retained an economic interest in such coal or iron ore is also entitled to the benefits of this section. Section 631(c) and this section shall not apply with respect to any income realized by any owner as co-adventurer, partner, or principal in the mining of such coal or iron ore.

(ii) The provisions of this subparagraph may be illustrated by the following examples:

Example (1). A owns a tract of coal land in fee. A leases to B the right to mine all the coal in this tract in return for a royalty of 30 cents per ton. B subleases his right to mine coal in this tract to C, who agrees to pay A 30 cents per ton and to pay to B an additional royalty of 10 cents per ton. Section 631(c) applies to the royalties of both A and B, if the other requisites of the section have been met.

Example (2). Assume the same facts as in example (1), except that A dies leaving his royalty interest to D. D has an economic interest in the coal in place and qualifies for section 631(c) treatment with respect to his share of the royalties since he is a successor in title to A.

Example (3). Assume the same facts as in example (1), except that E agrees to pay a sum of money to C in return for 10 cents per ton on the coal mined by C. E has an economic interest, since he must look solely to the extraction of the coal for the return of his investment. However, E has not made a disposal of coal under a contract wherein he retains an economic interest, and, therefore, does not qualify under section 631(c). E is entitled to depletion on his royalties.

(c) Payments received in advance of mining. *(1)* (i) Where the conditions of paragraph (a) of this section are met, amounts received or accrued prior to mining shall be treated under section 631(c) as received from the sale of coal or iron ore if the contract of disposal provides that such amounts are to be applied as payment for coal or iron ore subsequently mined. For example, advance royalty payments or minimum royalty payments received by an owner of coal or iron ore qualify under section 631(c) where the contract of disposal grants the lessee the right to apply such royalties in payment of coal or iron ore mined at a later time.

(ii) The provisions of this subparagraph may be illustrated by the following example:

Example. A acquires coal rights on January 1. On January 30, A enters into a contract of disposal providing that mining shall begin July 2, and mining actually begins no earlier. Any advance payments which A receives qualify under section 631(c).

(2) However, if the right to mine coal or iron ore under the contract expires, terminates, or is abandoned before the coal or iron ore which had been paid for is mined, the taxpayer shall treat payments attributable to the unmined coal or iron ore as ordinary income and not as received from the sale of coal or iron ore under section 631(c). Accordingly, the taxpayer shall recompute his tax liability for the taxable year in which such payments were received. The recomputation shall be made in the form of an amended return where necessary.

(3) Bonuses received or accrued by an owner in connection with the grant of a contract of disposal shall be treated under section 631(c) as received from the sale of coal or iron ore to the extent attributable to coal or iron ore held for more than 1 year (6 months for taxable years beginning before 1977; 9 months for taxable years beginning in 1977). The rules contained in paragraph (d) of § 1.631-2 relating to bonuses in the case of contracts for the disposal of timber shall be equally applicable in the case of bonuses received for the grant of a contract of disposal of coal or iron ore under this section.

(d) Nonapplication of section. Section 631(c) shall not affect the application of the provisions of subchapter G, chapter 1 of the Code, relating to corporations used to avoid income tax on shareholders. For example, for the purposes of applying section 543 (relating to personal holding companies), the amounts received from a disposal of coal or iron ore subject to section 631(c) shall be considered as mineral royalties. The determination of whether an amount received under a contract to which section 631(c) applies is "personal holding company income" shall be made in accordance with section 543 and the regulations thereunder, without regard to section 631(c) or this section. See also paragraph (e) of § 1.272-1.

(e) Special rules with regard to iron ore. *(1)* With regard to iron ore, section 631(c) and this section apply only to amounts received or accrued in taxable years beginning after December 31, 1963, attributable to iron ore mined in such taxable years.

(2) Section 631(c) and this section apply only to disposals of iron ore mined in the United States.

(3) For the purposes of section 631(c) and this section, iron ore is any ore which is used as a source of iron, including but not limited to taconite and jaspilite.

(4) Section 631(c) shall not apply to any disposal of iron ore to a person whose relationship to the person disposing of such iron ore would result in the disallowance of losses under section 267 or 707(b).

(5) Section 631(c)(2) results in the denial of section 631(c) treatment in the case of a contract for disposal of iron ore entered into with a person owned or controlled, directly or indirectly, by the same interests which own or control the person disposing of the iron ore, even though section 631(c) treatment would not be denied under the provisions of section 631(c)(1). For example, section 631(c) treatment is denied in the case of a contract for disposal of iron ore entered into between two "brother and sister" corporations, or a parent corporation and its subsidiary. The presence or absence of control shall be determined by applying the same standards as are applied under section 482 (relating to the allocation of income and deductions between taxpayers).

T.D. 6281, 12/20/57, amend T.D. 6841, 7/26/65, T.D. 7728, 10/31/80.

§ 1.636-1 Treatment of production payments as loans.

(a) In general. *(1)* (i) For purposes of subtitle A of the Internal Revenue Code of 1954, a production payment (as defined in paragraph (a) of § 1.636-3) to which this section applies shall be treated as a loan on the mineral property (or properties) burdened thereby and not as an economic interest in mineral in place, except to the extent that § 1.636-2 or paragraph (b) of this section applies. See paragraph (b) of § 1.611-1. A production payment carved out of mineral property which remains in the hands of the person carving out the production payment immediately after the transfer of such production payment shall be treated as a mortgage loan on the mineral property burdened thereby. A production payment created and retained upon the transfer of the mineral property burdened by such production payment shall be treated as a purchase money mortgage loan on the mineral property burdened thereby. Such production payments will be referred to hereinafter in the regulations under section 636 as carved-out production payments and retained production payments, respectively. Moreover, in the case of a transaction involving a production payment treated as a loan pursuant to this section, the production payment shall constitute an item of income (not subject to depletion), consideration for a sale or exchange, a contribution to capital, or a gift if in the transaction a debt obligation used in lieu of the production payment would constitute such an item of income, consideration, contribution to capital, or gift, as the case may be. For the definition of the term "transfer" see paragraph (c) of § 1.636-3.

(ii) The payer of a production payment treated as a loan pursuant to this section shall include the proceeds from (or, if paid in kind, the value of) the mineral produced and applied to the satisfaction of the production payment in his gross income and "gross income from the property" (see section 613(a)) for the taxable year so applied. The payee shall include in his gross income (but not "gross income from the property") amounts received with respect to such production payment to the extent that such amounts would be includible in gross income if such production payment were a loan. The payer and payee shall determine their allowable deductions as if such production payment were a loan. See section 483, relating to interest on certain deferred payments in the case of a production payment created and retained upon the transfer of the mineral property burdened thereby, or in the case of a production payment transferred in exchange for property. See section 1232 in the case of a production payment which is originally transferred by a corporation at a discount and is a capital asset in the hands of the payee. In the case of a carved-out production payment treated as a mortgage loan pursuant to this section, the consideration received for such production payment by the taxpayer who created it is not included in either gross income or "gross income from the property" by such taxpayer.

(2) If a production payment is treated as a loan pursuant to this section, no transfer of such production payment or any property burdened thereby (other than a transfer between the payer and payee of the production payment which, if the production payment were a loan, would extinguish the loan) shall cause it to cease to be so treated. For example, A sells operating mineral interest X to B for $100,000, subject to a $500,000 retained production payment payable out of X. Subsequently, A sells the production payments to C, and B sells X to D. C and D must treat the production payment as a purchase money mortgage loan.

(3) The provisions of this paragraph may be illustrated by the following examples:

Example (1). On December 22, 1972, A, a cash-basis calendar-year taxpayer who owns operating mineral interest X, carves out of X a production payment in favor of B for $300,000 plus interest, payable out of 50 percent of the first oil produced and sold from X. In 1972, A treats the $300,000 received from B for the production payment as the proceeds of a mortgage loan on X. In 1973, A produces and sells 125,000 barrels of oil for $373,500. A pays B $186,750 with respect to the production payment, $168,750 being principal and $18,000 being interest. In computing his gross income and "gross income from the property" for the year 1973, A includes the $373,500 and takes as deductions the allowable expenses paid in production of such mineral. A also takes a deduction under section 163 for the $18,000 interest paid with respect to the production payment. For 1973, B would treat $18,000 as ordinary income not subject to the allowance for depletion under section 611.

Example (2). Assume the same facts as in example (1) except that the principal amount of the production payment is to be increased by the amount of the ad valorem tax on the mineral attributable to the production payment which is paid by B. Under State law, the ad valorem tax with respect to the mineral attributable to the production payment is a liability of the owner of the production payment. For 1973, B includes the amount received with respect to such taxes as income and takes a deduction under section 164 for the taxes paid by him. Since the ad valorem taxes paid by B are his liability under State law, A may not take a deduction under section 164 for such taxes.

Example (3). On December 31, 1974, C, a calendar-year taxpayer and owner of the operating mineral interest Y, sells Y to D for $10,000 cash and retains a $40,000 production payment payable out of Y. At the time D acquires the property, it is estimated that 500,000 tons of mineral are recoverable from the property. In 1975, D produces a total of 50,000 tons from the property. D's cost depletion for 1975 is $5,000 determined as follows:

Basis in property: $50,000
Total recoverable units: 500,000
Rate of depletion per ton: $0.10 $\left(\frac{\$50,000}{500,000}\right)$

Cost depletion for year: $5,000 ($0.10 × 50,000)

(b) Exception. *(1)* A production payment carved out of a mineral property (or properties) for exploration or development of such property (or properties) shall not be treated as a mortgage loan under section 636(a) and this section to the extent "gross income from the property" (for purposes of section 613) would not be realized by the taxpayer creating such production payment, under the law existing at the time of the creation of such production payment, in the absence of section 636(a). See section 83 and the regulations thereunder, relating to property transferred in connection with the performance of services. For purposes of section 636(a) and this paragraph, an expenditure is for exploration or development to the extent that it is necessary for ascertaining the existence, location, extent, or quality of any deposit of mineral or is incident to and necessary for the preparation of a deposit for the production of mineral. However, an expenditure which relates primarily to the production of mineral (as, for example, in the case of a pilot water flood program with respect to the secondary recovery of oil) is not for exploration or development as those terms are used in section 636(a) and this paragraph. Whether or not a production payment is carved out for exploration or development shall be determined in light of all relevant facts and circumstances, including any prior production of mineral from the mineral deposit burdened by the production payment. However, a production payment shall not be treated as carved out for exploration or development to the extent that the consideration for the production payment—

(i) Is not pledged for use in the future exploration or development of the mineral property (or properties) which is burdened by the production payment;

(ii) May be used for the exploration or development of any other property, or for any other purpose than that described in subdivision (i) of this subparagraph;

(iii) Does not consist of a binding obligation of the payee of the production payment to pay expenses of the exploration or development described in subdivision (i) of this subparagraph; or

(iv) Does not consist of a binding obligation of the payee of the production payment to provide services, materials, supplies, or equipment for the exploration or development described in subdivision (i) of this subparagraph.

(2) In the case of a carved-out production payment only a portion of which is subject to the exception provided in this paragraph, the rules contained in paragraph (a) of this section with respect to the treatment of income and deductions where a production payment is treated as a loan shall apply to the portion of the taxpayer's income or expenses attributable to the production payment which bears the same ratio to the total amount of such income or expenses, as the case may be, as the amount of the consideration for the production payment which would have been realized as income in the absence of section 636(a), by the taxpayer creating such production payment, bears to the total consideration to the taxpayer for the production payment. For example, A, owner of a mineral property, carves out a production payment in favor of B for $600,000 plus interest in return for $600,000 cash. A pledges to use $400,000 for the development of the burdened mineral property. In each of the payout years loan treatment applies to one-third of the income and expenses of A and B attributable to the production payment.

(c) Treatment upon disposition or termination of mineral property burdened by production payment. *(1)* (i) In the case of a sale or other disposition of the mineral property burdened by a production payment treated as a loan pursuant to this section, there shall be included in determining the amount realized upon such disposition an amount equal to the outstanding principal balance of such production payment on the date of such disposition. However, if such a production payment is created in connection with the disposition, the amount to be so included shall be the fair market value of the production payment, rather than its principal amount, if the fair market value is established by clear and convincing evidence to be an amount which differs from the principal amount. See section 1001 and the regulations thereunder. In determining the cost of the transferred mineral property to the transferee for purposes of section 1012, the outstanding principal balance of the production payment shall be included in the cost.

(ii) The provisions of this subparagraph may be illustrated by the following examples:

Example (1). A, the owner of mineral property X which is burdened by a carved-out production payment to which section 636(a) applies having an outstanding principal balance of $10,000, sells property X to B, an individual, for $100,000 cash. The amount realized by A on the sale of property X is $110,000. B's basis in property X for cost depletion and other purposes is also $110,000.

Example (2). Assume the same facts as in example (1) except that the production payment is retained by A in connection with the sale of property X to B, that section 636(b) applies to the production payment, that the production payment includes, in addition to the $10,000 principal amount, an additional amount equivalent to interest at a rate which precludes application of section 483, and that the fair market value of the production payment is $9,000. The amount realized by A on the sale of property X is $109,000. B's basis in property X for cost depletion and other purposes is $110,000, A's basis in the retained production payment is $9,000. If the production payment is paid in full, A realizes income of $1,000 plus the amount equivalent to interest, which income is includible in A's gross income at the time when such amounts would be so includible if such production payment were a loan.

Example (3). C, the owner of mineral property Y, sells the mineral property to D for $500,000 cash. Property Y is burdened by a carved-out production payment with an outstanding principal balance of $600,000, 40 percent of the consideration for which was pledged for the development of property Y. The amount realized by C on the sale is $860,000 ($500,000 plus $600,000 × .60). D's basis in property Y for cost depletion and other purposes is $860,000.

(2) In the case of the expiration, termination, or abandonment of a mineral property burdened by a production payment treated as a loan pursuant to this section, for purposes of determining the amount of any loss under section 165 with respect to the burdened mineral property the adjusted basis of such property shall be reduced (but not below zero) by an amount equal to the outstanding principal balance of such production payment on the date of such expiration, termination, or abandonment. Thus, in example (2) in subparagraph (1)(ii) of this paragraph, if B abandons the mineral property at a time when $5,000 of the principal amount of the production payment remains unsatisfied, B's adjusted basis immediately before the abandonment would be reduced by $5,000 for determining his loss on abandonment under section 165.

(3) In the case of a transfer of a portion of the mineral property burdened by a production payment treated as a loan pursuant to this section, such production payment shall be apportioned between the transferred portion and the retained portion by allocating to such transferred portion that part of the outstanding principal balance of the production payment which bears the same ratio to such balance as the value of such transferred portion (exclusive of any value not related to the burdened mineral) bears to the total value of the burdened mineral property (exclusive of any value not related to the burdened mineral).

(4) In general, the entire amount of gain or loss realized pursuant to this paragraph shall be recognized in the taxable year of such realization. See section 1211 for limitation on capital losses. This subparagraph shall not affect the applicability of rules providing exceptions to the recognition of gain or loss which has been realized (e.g., a transfer to which section 351 or 1031 applies). However, see section 357(c) with respect to the assumption of liabilities in excess of basis in certain tax-free exchanges. Furthermore, in the case of a transaction which otherwise qualifies, gain realized on a transfer of a mineral property to which section 636(b) applies may be returned on the installment method under section 453.

T.D. 7261, 2/26/73.

PAR. 15. In § 1.636-1, paragraph (a)(1)(ii) is amended by removing the phrase "section 1232" and adding in its place the phrase "section 1271".

Proposed § 1.636-1 [Amended] [*For Preamble, see ¶ 151,065*]

§ 1.636-2 Production payments retained in leasing transactions.

(a) Treatment by lessee. In the case of a production payment (as defined in paragraph (a) of § 1.636-3) which is retained by the lessor in a leasing transaction (including a sublease or the exercise of an option to acquire a lease or sublease), the lessee (or his successors in interest) shall treat the retained production payment for purposes of subtitle A of the Code as if it were a bonus granted by the lessee to the lessor payable in installments. Accordingly, the lessee shall include the proceeds from (or, if paid in kind, the value of) the mineral produced and applied to the satisfaction of the production payment in his gross income for the taxable year so applied. The lessee shall capitalize each payment (including any interest and any amounts added on to the production payment other than amounts for which the lessee would be liable in the absence of the production payment) paid or incurred with respect to such production payment. See paragraph (c)(5)(ii) of § 1.613-2 for rules relating to computation of percentage depletion with respect to a mineral property burdened by a production payment treated as a bonus under section 636(c) and this section.

(b) Treatment by lessor. The lessor who retains a production payment in a leasing transaction (or his successors in interest) shall treat the production payment without regard to the provisions of section 636 and § 1.636-1. Thus, the production payment will be treated as an economic interest in the mineral in place in the hands of the lessor (or his successors in interest) and the receipts in discharge of the production payment will constitute ordinary income subject to depletion.

(c) Example. The provisions of this section may be illustrated by the following example:

Example. In 1971, A leases a mineral property to B reserving a one-eighth royalty and a production payment (as defined in § 1.636-3(a)) with a principal amount of $300,000 plus an amount equivalent to interest. In 1972, B pays A $60,000 with respect to the principal amount of the production payment plus $16,350 equivalent to interest. The adjusted basis of the property in the hands of B for cost depletion and other purposes for 1972 and subsequent years will include (subject to proper adjustment under section 1016) the $76,350 paid to A. In 1973, B pays to A $60,000 with respect to the principal amount of the production payment plus $12,750 equivalent to interest. The adjusted basis of the property in the hands of B for cost depletion and other purposes for 1973 and subsequent years will include (subject to proper adjustment under section 1016) the $72,750 paid to A. The $76,350 received by A in 1972, and the $72,750 received by A in 1973, will constitute ordinary income subject to depletion in the hands of A in the years of receipt of such amounts by A.

T.D. 7261, 2/26/73.

§ 1.636-3 Definitions.

For purposes of section 636 and the regulations thereunder—

(a) Production payment. *(1)* The term "production payment" means, in general, a right to a specified share of the production from mineral in place (if, as, and when produced), or the proceeds from such production. Such right must be an economic interest in such mineral in place. It may burden more than one mineral property, and the burdened mineral property need not be an operating mineral interest. Such right must have an expected economic life (at the time of its creation) of shorter duration than the economic life of one or more of the mineral properties burdened thereby. A right to mineral in place which can be required to be satisfied by other than the production of mineral from the burdened mineral property is not an economic interest in mineral in place. A production payment may be limited by a dollar amount, a quantum of mineral, or a period of time. A right to mineral in place has an economic life of shorter duration than the economic life of a mineral property burdened thereby only if such right may not reasonably be expected to extend in substantial amounts over the entire productive life of such mineral property. The term "production payment" includes payments which are commonly referred to as "in-oil payments," "gas payments," or "mineral payments."

(2) A right which is in substance economically equivalent to a production payment shall be treated as a production payment for purposes of section 636 and the regulations thereunder, regardless of the language used to describe such right, the method of creation of such right, or the form in

which such right is cast (even though such form is that of an operating mineral interest). Whether or not a right is in substance economically equivalent to a production payment shall be determined from all the facts and circumstances. An example of an interest which is to be treated as a production payment under this subparagraph is that portion of a "royalty" which is attributable to so much of the rate of the royalty which exceeds the lowest possible rate of the royalty at any subsequent time (disregarding any reductions in the rate of the royalty which are based solely upon changes in volume of production within a specified period of no more than 1 year). For example, assume that A creates a royalty with respect to a mineral property owned by A equal to 5 percent for 5 years and thereafter equal to 4 percent for the balance of the life of the property. An amount equal to 1 percent for 5 years shall be treated as a production payment. On the other hand, if A leases a coal mine to B in return for a royalty of 30 cents per ton on the first 500,000 tons of coal produced from the mine in each year and 20 cents per ton on all coal in excess of 500,000 tons produced from the mine in each year, the fact that the royalty may decline to 20 cents per ton on some of the coal in each year does not result in a production payment of 10 cents per ton of coal on the first 500,000 tons in any year. Another example of an interest which is to be treated as a production payment under this subparagraph is the interest in a partnership engaged in operating oil properties of a partner who provides capital for the partnership if such interest is subject to a right of another person or persons to acquire or terminate it upon terms which merely provide for such partner's recovery of his capital investment and a reasonable return thereon.

(b) Property. The term "property" has the meaning assigned to it in section 614(a), without the application of section 614(b), (c), or (e).

(c) Transfer. The term "transfer" means any sale, exchange, gift, bequest, devise, or other disposition (including a distribution by an estate or a contribution to or distribution by a corporation, partnership, or trust).

T.D. 7261, 2/26/73.

---

§ 1.636-4 Effective dates of section 636.

(a) In general. Except as provided hereinafter in this section, section 636 and §§ 1.636-1, 1.636-2, and 1.636-3 apply to production payments created on or after August 7, 1969, other than production payments created before January 1, 1971, pursuant to a binding contract entered into before August 7, 1969.

(b) Election. Under section 503(c)(2) of the Tax Reform Act of 1969, if the taxpayer so elects, section 636(a) of the Code and §§ 1.636-1 and 1.636-3 apply to all production payments carved out by him after the beginning of his last taxable year ending before August 7, 1969, including such production payments created after such date pursuant to a binding contract entered into before such date. No interest shall be allowed on any refund or credit of any overpayment of tax resulting from an election under section 503(c)(2) for any taxable year ending before August 7, 1969. The provisions of this paragraph may be illustrated by the following example:

Example. A, a fiscal-year taxpayer whose taxable year ends on October 31, carved out and sold (from a producing property) production payments on October 1, 1967, and on July 9, 1969. On August 1, 1969, A entered into a binding contract to create another carved-out production payment (from a different producing property) and the production payment was carved out on December 22, 1969. If A elects under section 503(c)(2), the production payments carved out on July 9, 1969, and December 22, 1969, are treated as mortgage loans under section 636(a). The production payment carved out on October 1, 1967, is not treated as a mortgage loan under section 636(a) because it was carved out before the beginning of A's last taxable year ending before August 7, 1969.

(c) Time and manner of making election. *(1)* Any election under section 503(c)(2) of the Tax Reform Act of 1969 must be made not later than May 30, 1973.

(2) An election under section 503(c)(2) shall be made by a statement attached to the taxpayer's income tax return (or amended return) for the first taxable year in which the taxpayer created a production payment (i) to which the election applies, and (ii) which, in the absence of section 636, would not have been treated as a loan. A statement shall also be attached to an amended return for each subsequent taxable year for which he has filed his income tax return before making the election, but only if his tax liability for such year is affected by the election. Each such statement shall indicate the taxpayer's election under section 503(c)(2), and shall identify by date, amount, parties, and burdened mineral properties all production payments described in subdivisions (i) and (ii) of this subparagraph which have been created by the date on which the statement is filed. However, a taxpayer who, prior to the date on which permanent regulations under this section are published in the FEDERAL REGISTER, made a valid election under section 503(c)(2) pursuant to §§ 301.9100-17T and 301.9100-18T of this chapter are not required to amend statements previously furnished which meet the requirements of § 301.9100-17T(b)(1)(ii) of this chapter unless requested to do so by the district director. In applying the election to the taxable years affected, there shall be taken into account the effect that any adjustments resulting therefrom have on other items affected thereby and the effect that adjustments of any such items have on other taxable years. In the case of a member of a consolidated return group (as defined in paragraph (a) of § 1.1502-1), section 503(c)(2) and paragraphs (b), (c), and (d) of this section shall be applied as if such member field a separate return.

(d) Revocation of election. A valid election under section 503(c)(2) shall be binding upon the taxpayer unless consent to revoke the election is obtained from the Commissioner. The application to revoke such election must be made in writing to the Commissioner of Internal Revenue, Washington, D.C. 20224, not later than May 30, 1973. Such application must set forth the reasons therefor and a recomputation of the tax reflecting such revocation for each prior taxable year affected by the revocation, whether or not the period of limitations for credit or refund or assessment and collection has expired with respect to such taxable year. Consent shall not be given in any case in which the revocation would result in an increase in the taxpayer's tax liability for a taxable year for which such period of limitations has expired unless the taxpayer waives his right to assert the statute of limitations.

(e) Special rule. *(1)* Except as provided in subparagraph (2) of this paragraph, in the case of a taxpayer who does not make the election provided in section 503(c)(2) of the Tax Reform Act of 1969, section 636 of the Code applies to production payments carved out during the taxable year which includes August 7, 1969, as provided in paragraph (a) of this section, only to the extent that the aggregate amount of such production payments exceeds the lesser of—

(i) The excess of—

(a) The aggregate amount of production payments carved out and sold by the taxpayer during the 12-month period immediately preceding his taxable year which includes August 7, 1969, over

(b) The aggregate amount of production payments carved out and sold before August 7, 1969, by the taxpayer during his taxable year which includes such date, or

(ii) The amount necessary to increase the amount of the taxpayer's gross income within the meaning of chapter 1 of subtitle A of the Code, for his taxable year which includes August 7, 1969, to an amount equal to the amount of his deductions (other than any deduction under section 172) allowable for such year under such chapter.

In applying the preceding sentence, production payments carved out for exploration or development are to be taken into account only to the extent, if any, that "gross income from the property" (for purposes of section 613) would have been realized by the taxpayer creating such production payment under the law existing at the time of the creation of such production payment, in the absence of section 636(a).

(2) Subparagraph (1) of this paragraph shall not apply for any taxable year for purposes of determining the amount of any deduction for cost or percentage depletion allowable under section 611 or the limitation on any foreign tax credit under section 904.

(3) The application of this paragraph may be illustrated by the following examples:

Example (1). (a) A, a calendar-year taxpayer who does not make the election provided in section 503(c)(2) of the Tax Reform Act of 1969, carves out and sells on December 31, 1968, a $500,000 production payment. Further, A carves out and sells on March 4, 1969, a $300,000 production payment, and on November 14, 1969, a $150,000 production payment. None of the production payments are carved out for exploration or development. During 1969, A has gross income of $600,000 (determined initially for this purpose by treating the $150,000 production payment carved out on November 14, 1969, as a loan) and allowable deductions of $700,000.

(b) The provisions of section 636 do not apply to a portion of the November 14, 1969, production payment for purposes other than section 611 and section 904 of the Code, determined as follows:

(1) Amount of production payment carved out in 1969 on or after August 7, 1969	$150,000
(2) Amount of production payment carved out during 1969	500,000
(3) Amount of production payment carved out during 1969 taxable year before August 7, 1969	300,000
(4) Item (2) minus item (3)	200,000
(5) Excess of allowable deductions over gross income for 1969	100,000
(6) Amount of production payment carved out in 1969 on or after August 7, 1969, to which section 636 does not apply (lesser of items (1), (4), and (5))	100,000

Thus, A will not treat $100,000 of the consideration received for the production payment carved out on November 14, 1969, as a loan and as a result his gross income for 1969 will be $700,000. However, in computing percentage depletion, A will not include the $100,000 in "gross income from property" and in computing cost depletion A will not include the mineral units attributable thereto. Nor, will A include the $100,000 in determining the limitation on foreign tax credit under section 904.

Example (2). Assume the same facts as in example (1) except that for taxable year 1969 A's gross income (determined initially for this purpose by treating the November 14, 1969, production payment as a loan) exceeds the amount of his allowable deductions under chapter 1 of subtitle A of the Code. The entire amount of the November 14, 1969, production payment is treated as a mortgage loan under section 636(a).

T.D. 7261, 2/26/73, amend T.D. 8435, 9/18/92.

§ 1.638-1 Continental Shelf areas.

(a) General rule. For purposes of applying any provision of Chapter 1, 2, 3, or 24 (including section 861(a)(3), 862(a)(3), 1441, 3402, or other provisions dealing with the performance of personal services), with respect to mines, oil and gas wells, and other natural deposits—

(1) United States and possession of the United States. The terms "United States" and "possession of the United States" when used in a geographical sense include the seabed and subsoil of those submarine areas which are adjacent to the territorial waters of the United States or such possession and over which the United States has exclusive rights, in accordance with international law, with respect to the exploration for, and exploitation of, natural resources. The terms "Continental Shelf of the United States" and "Continental Shelf of a possession of the United States," as used in this section, refer to the seabed and subsoil included, respectively, in the terms "United States" and "possession of the United States," as provided in the preceding sentence.

(2) Foreign country. The term "foreign country" when used in a geographical sense includes the seabed and subsoil of those submarine areas which are adjacent to the territorial waters of the foreign country and over which such foreign country has exclusive rights, in accordance with international law, with respect to the exploration for, and exploitation of, natural resources, but this sentence applies only if such foreign country exercises, directly or indirectly, taxing jurisdiction with respect to such exploration or exploitation. The term "foreign continental shelf," as used in this section, refers to the seabed and subsoil described in the preceding sentence. A foreign country is not to be treated as a country contiguous to the United States by reason of the application of section 638 and this section.

(b) Exercise of taxing jurisdiction. For purposes of paragraph (a)(2) of this section, the exercise, directly or indirectly, of taxing jurisdiction with respect to the exploration for, or exploitation of, natural resources is deemed to include (but is not limited to) those cases in which a foreign country—

(1) Imposes a tax upon assets, equipment, or other property connected with or income derived from such exploration or exploitation, or

(2) Requires natural resources referred to in paragraph (a)(2) of this section to be transported to points within its landward boundaries and then levies a tax upon such natural resources or upon the income derived from the sale thereof.

A foreign country which, for purposes of paragraph (a)(2) of this section, exercises taxing jurisdiction by the imposition of tax upon any person, property, or activity engaged in or related to the exploration for, or exploitation of, natural resources in the seabed or subsoil referred to in paragraph (a)(2) of this section, or the income therefrom of any taxpayer, is deemed to exercise taxing jurisdiction over all such persons, property, and activities and over all income therefrom of all such taxpayers; thus, for example, a foreign country which imposes tax upon a person engaged in exploitation of oil and gas wells in its seabed and subsoil referred to in paragraph (a)(2) of this section is deemed to exercise taxing jurisdiction over property related to exploration for other natural deposits in such seabed and subsoil. A foreign country is deemed to be imposing tax upon a person, property, activity, or income described in the preceding sentence if such foreign country exempts all persons, property, and activities or income from tax for a period not in excess of 10 years from the commencement of such exploration or exploitation. Except in the case of a foreign country which is deemed under the preceding sentence to impose tax by virtue of an exemption for a period not in excess of 10 years, a foreign country which exempts all persons, property, and activities engaged in or related to the exploration for, or exploitation of, natural resources in the seabed or subsoil referred to in paragraph (a)(2) of this section and the income therefrom, from taxation is deemed not to be exercising, directly or indirectly, taxing jurisdiction for purposes of paragraph (a)(2) of this section. For purposes of paragraph (a)(2) of this section, the exercise of taxing jurisdiction with respect to any type of tax constitutes the exercise of taxing jurisdiction with respect to all types of taxes. However, a royalty or other charge (whether payable in a lump sum or over a period of time or in amounts dependent upon the volume of production of natural resources) for the right to explore for or exploit natural resources does not constitute a tax.

(c) Scope. *(1)* for purposes of applying this section, persons, property, or activities which are engaged in or related to the exploration for, or exploitation of, mines, oil and gas wells, or other natural deposits need not be physically upon, connected, or attached to the seabed or subsoil referred to in subparagraph (1) or (2) of paragraph (a) of this section to be deemed to be within the United States, a possession of the United States, or a foreign country, as the case may be, to the extent provided in subparagraph (2) or (3) and subparagraph (4) of this paragraph.

(2) Persons, property, or activities which are not in a foreign country (determined without regard to section 638 or this section), and which are engaged in or related to the exploration for, or exploitation of, mines, oil and gas wells, or other natural deposits of the seabed or subsoil referred to in paragraph (a)(1) of this section, are generally within the United States or a possession of the United States, as the case may be, unless such persons, property, or activities are solely involved in or constitute transportation to (or from) the site of exploration or exploitation from (or to) a foreign country, other than transportation on a regular basis from (or to) a base of operations.

(3) Persons, property, or activities which are not in the United States or in a third country (determined in each case without regard to section 638 or this section), and which are engaged in or related to the exploration for, or exploitation of, mines, oil and gas wells, or other natural deposits of the seabed or subsoil of a foreign country referred to in paragraph (a)(2) of this section, are generally within such foreign country, unless such persons, property, or activities are solely involved in or constitute transportation to (or from) the site of exploration or exploitation from (or to) the United States or a possession of the United States or a third country, as the case may be, other than transportation on a regular basis from (or to) a base of operations.

(4) Persons, property, or activities are within the United States, a possession of the United States, or a foreign country, as the case may be, pursuant to this paragraph, only to the extent such persons, property, or activities are engaged in or related to the exploration for, or exploitation of, mines, oil and gas wells, or other natural deposits.

(d) Natural deposits and natural resources. For purposes of this section, the terms "natural deposits" and "natural resources" mean nonliving resources to which section 611(a) applies. Such terms do not include sedentary species (organisms which, at the harvestable stage, either are immovable on or under the seabed or are unable to move except in constant physical contact with the seabed or subsoil), fish or other animal or plant life.

(e) Rights under international law. Nothing in this section shall prejudice or affect the freedoms of the high seas and other rights under international law, or the exercise of such freedoms and rights by the United States or foreign countries.

(f) Examples. The application of the provisions of section 638 and this section may be illustrated by the following examples:

Example (1). A, a citizen of the United States employed as an engineer, is engaged in the exploitation of oil and is physically present on an offshore oil drilling platform operated by employees of L Corporation. Such platform is affixed to the foreign continental shelf of foreign country X. Assuming that foreign country X exercises taxing jurisdiction as provided in paragraph (b) of this section. A is to be treated as being employed in foreign country X with respect to compensation for his employment for purposes of chapters 1 and 24.

Example (2). The facts are the same as in example (1) except that B, a citizen of the United States engaged in the private practice of law, is physically present on such platform for the sole purpose of interviewing his client, A, whom he represents in a domestic relations matter. Since B is not engaged in activities related to the exploration for, or exploitation of, natural deposits, he is not to be treated as being in foreign country X for purposes of chapters 1 and 2.

Example (3). The facts are the same as in example (1) except that C, a citizen of the United States engaged in the private practice of medicine, is physically present on such platform for the purpose of making routine physical examinations of L Corporation's employees who are engaged in the exploitation of oil on the platform. C is paid by L Corporation to give such examinations on the platform at regular intervals in order to determine whether the state of any employee's health is such that he should not continue work on the platform. The balance of C's medical practice is conducted at his office on the U.S. mainland. Since C is engaged in activities related to the exploitation of oil, he is treated as being in foreign country X under section 638 and this section while making physical examinations on L Corporation's platform, provided that foreign country X exercise taxing jurisdiction as provided in paragraph (b) of this section. For purposes of chapters 1 and 2, amounts paid by L Corporation to C are treated as derived from sources within foreign country X.

Example (4). C, a nonresident alien individual employed as an engineer in a foreign country, designs equipment for use on oil drilling platforms affixed to the continental shelf of the United States and engaged in the exploitation of oil. Although C's activities in this respect are related to the exploitation of oil, C is not treated as being in the United

States under section 638 and this section by reason of such activities.

Example (5). M Corporation, a domestic corporation, chartered a ship from N Corporation, also a domestic corporation, under a time charter under which N Corporation's personnel continued to navigate and manage the ship. M Corporation equipped the ship with special oil exploration equipment and furnished its personnel to operate the equipment. The ship then commenced to explore for oil in the foreign Continental Shelf of foreign country Y. Foreign country Y exercises taxing jurisdiction as provided in paragraph (b) of this section. The ship is treated as being within foreign country Y under section 638 and this section for the period it was engaged in the exploration for oil in such foreign Continental Shelf. Thus, the entire income derived during such period by N Corporation from the chapter is income derived from sources within foreign country Y, since N Corporation had property and employees engaged in the exploration for oil in such foreign Continental Shelf.

Example (6). The facts are the same as in example (5) except that C, a citizen of the United States, was employed by N Corporation as a cook and was physically present on the ship. C's sole duties consisted of cooking meals for personnel aboard such ship. In such case, as C's activities are related to the exploration for oil, C is to be treated as being in foreign country Y under section 638 and this section for the period he was aboard such ship while it was engaged in activities relating to the exploration for oil in the foreign Continental Shelf referred to in example (5). For purposes of chapters 1 and 24, C's compensation as a cook for such period is treated as derived from sources without the United States.

Example (7). Z Corporation, a foreign corporation, entered into a contract with Y Corporation, a United States corporation, to engage in exploratory oil drilling activities on a leasehold held by Y Corporation. Such leasehold was located in the Continental Shelf of the United States. Since Z Corporation is engaged in and has property and activities which are engaged in the exploration for oil, such property and activities are to be treated as being in the United States under section 638 and this section for the period such property and activities were engaged in or related to the exploration for oil in the Continental Shelf of the United States and were not in a foreign country. For purposes of chapters 1 and 3, amounts paid to Z Corporation pursuant to the contract are treated as derived from sources within the United States.

Example (8). M Corporation is a controlled foreign corporation (within the meaning of section 957(b)) for its entire taxable year beginning in 1972. During such taxable year, M Corporation issues a policy of insurance relating to fire damage to an offshore oil drilling platform, owned by N Corporation (a foreign corporation), which is attached to the Continental Shelf of the United States. The income attributable to the issuing of such policy would be taxed under subchapter L, chapter 1, subtitle A of the Code (as modified, for this purpose, by section 953(b)(1), (2), and (3)) if such income were the income of a domestic insurance corporation. Since N Corporation's oil drilling platform is located within the United States under section 638 and this section, M Corporation's income attributable to the issuing of the insurance in connection with such platform is income derived from the insurance of United States risks, within the meaning of section 953(a)(1)(A).

T.D. 7277, 5/14/73.

§ 1.638-2 Effective date.

The specific requirements and limitations of § 1.638-1 apply on and after December 30, 1969.

T.D. 7277, 5/14/73.

§ 1.641(a)-0 Scope of subchapter J.

(a) In general. Subchapter J (section 641 and following), Chapter 1 of the Code, deals with the taxation of income of estates and trusts and their beneficiaries, and of income in respect of decedents. Part I of Subchapter J contains general rules for taxation of estates and trusts (Subpart A), specific rules relating to trusts which distribute current income only (Subpart B), estates and trusts which may accumulate income or which distribute corpus (Subpart C), treatment of excess distributions by trusts (Subpart D), grantors and other persons treated as substantial owners (Subpart E), and miscellaneous provisions relating to limitations on charitable deductions, income of an estate or trust in case of divorce, and taxable years to which the provisions of Subchapter J are applicable (Subpart F). Part I has no application to any organization which is not to be classified for tax purposes as a trust under the classification rules of §§ 301.7701-2, 301.7701-3, and 301.7701-4, of this chapter (Regulations on Procedure and Administration). Part II of Subchapter J relates to the treatment of income in respect of decedents. However, the provisions of Subchapter J do not apply to employees trusts subject to Subchapters D and F, Chapter 1 of the Code, and common trust funds subject to Subchapter H, Chapter 1 of the Code.

(b) Scope of subparts A, B, C, and D. Subparts A, B, C, and D (section 641 and following), part I, subchapter J, chapter 1 of the Code, relate to the taxation of estates and trusts and their beneficiaries. These subparts have no application to any portion of the corpus or income of a trust which is to be regarded, within the meaning of the Code, as that of the grantor or others treated as its substantial owners. See subpart E (section 671 and following), part I, subchapter J, chapter 1 of the Code, and the regulations thereunder for rules for the treatment of any portion of a trust where the grantor (or another person) is treated as the substantial owner. So-called alimony trusts are treated under subparts A, B, C, and D, except to the extent otherwise provided in section 71 or section 682. These subparts have no application to beneficiaries of nonexempt employees' trusts. See section 402(b) and the regulations thereunder.

(c) Multiple trusts. Multiple trusts that have—

(1) No substantially independent purposes (such as independent dispositive purposes),

(2) The same grantor and substantially the same beneficiary, and

(3) The avoidance of mitigation of (a) the progressive rates of tax (including mitigation as a result of deferral of tax) or (b) the minimum tax for tax preferences imposed by section 56 as their principal purpose, shall be consolidated and treated as one trust for the purposes of subchapter J.

T.D. 6217, 12/19/56, amend T.D. 6989, 1/16/69, T.D. 7204, 8/24/72.

§ 1.641(a)-1 Imposition of tax; application of tax.

Caution: The Treasury has not yet amended Reg § 1.641(a)-1 to reflect changes made by P.L. 95-30.

For taxable years beginning after December 31, 1970, section 641 prescribes that the taxes imposed by section 1(d), as amended by the Tax Reform Act of 1969, shall apply to the income of estates or of any kind of property held in trust. For taxable years ending before January 1, 1971, section 641 prescribes that the taxes imposed upon individuals by chapter 1 of the Code apply to the income of estates or of any kind of property held in trust. The rates of tax, the statutory provisions respecting gross income, and, with certain exceptions, the deductions and credits allowed to individuals apply also to estates and trust.

T.D. 6217, 12/19/56, amend T.D. 7117, 5/24/71.

§ 1.641(a)-2 Gross income of estates and trusts.

Caution: The Treasury has not yet amended Reg § 1.641(a)-2 to reflect changes made by P.L. 99-514, P.L. 94-455.

The gross income of an estate or trust is determined in the same manner as that of an individual. Thus, the gross income of an estate or trust consists of all items of gross income received during the taxable year, including:

(a) Income accumulated in trust for the benefit of unborn or unascertained persons or persons with contingent interests;

(b) Income accumulated or held for future distribution under the terms of the will or trust;

(c) Income which is to be distributed currently by the fiduciary to the beneficiaries, and income collected by a guardian of an infant which is to be held or distributed as the court may direct;

(d) Income received by estates of deceased persons during the period of administration or settlement of the estate; and

(e) Income which, in the discretion of the fiduciary, may be either distributed to the beneficiaries or accumulated. The several classes of income enumerated in this section do not exclude others which also may come within the general purposes of section 641.

T.D. 6217, 12/19/56.

§ 1.641(b)-1 Computation and payment of tax; deductions and credits of estates and trusts.

Generally, the deductions and credits allowed to individuals are also allowed to estates and trusts. However, there are special rules for the computation of certain deductions and for the allocation between the estate or trust and the beneficiaries of certain credits and deductions. See section 642 and the regulations thereunder. In addition, an estate or trust is allowed to deduct, in computing its taxable income, the deductions provided by sections 651 and 661 and regulations thereunder, relating to distributions to beneficiaries.

T.D. 6217, 12/19/56.

§ 1.641(b)-2 Filing of returns and payment of the tax.

(a) The fiduciary is required to make and file the return and pay the tax on the taxable income of an estate or of a trust. Liability for the payment of the tax on the taxable income of an estate attaches to the person of the executor or administrator up to and after his discharge if, prior to distribution and discharge, he had notice of his tax obligations or failed to exercise due diligence in ascertaining whether or not such obligations existed. For the extent of such liability, see section 3467 of the Revised Statutes, as amended by section 518 of the Revenue Act of 1934 (31 U.S.C. 192). Liability for the tax also follows the assets of the estate distributed to heirs, devisees, legatees, and distributees, who may be required to discharge the amount of the tax due and unpaid to the extent of the distributive shares received by them. See section 6901. The same considerations apply to trusts.

(b) The estate of an infant, incompetent, or other person under a disability, or, in general, of an individual or corporation in receivership or a corporation in bankruptcy is not a taxable entity separate from the person for whom the fiduciary is acting, in that respect differing from the estate of a deceased person or of a trust. See section 6012(b)(2) and (3) for provisions relating to the obligation of the fiduciary with respect to returns of such persons.

T.D. 6217, 12/19/56, amend T.D. 6580, 12/4/61.

§ 1.641(b)-3 Termination of estates and trusts.

(a) The income of an estate of a deceased person is that which is received by the estate during the period of administration or settlement. The period of administration or settlement is the period actually required by the administrator or executor to perform the ordinary duties of administration, such as the collection of assets and the payment of debts, taxes, legacies, and bequests, whether the period required is longer or shorter than the period specified under the applicable local law for the settlement of estates. For example, where an executor who is also named as trustee under a will fails to obtain his discharge as executor, the period of administration continues only until the duties of administration are complete and he actually assumes his duties as trustee, whether or not pursuant to a court order. However, the period of administration of an estate cannot be unduly prolonged. If the administration of an estate is unreasonably prolonged, the estate is considered terminated for Federal income tax purposes after the expiration of a reasonable period for the performance by the executor of all the duties of administration. Further, an estate will be considered as terminated when all the assets have been distributed except for a reasonable amount which is set aside in good faith for the payment of unascertained or contingent liabilities and expenses (not including a claim by a beneficiary in the capacity of beneficiary). Notwithstanding the above, if the estate has joined in making a valid election under section 645 to treat a qualified revocable trust, as defined under section 645(b)(1), as part of the estate, the estate shall not terminate under this paragraph prior to the termination of the section 645 election period. See section 645 and the regulations thereunder for rules regarding the termination of the section 645 election period.

(b) Generally, the determination of whether a trust has terminated depends upon whether the property held in trust has been distributed to the persons entitled to succeed to the property upon termination of the trust rather than upon the technicality of whether or not the trustee has rendered his final accounting. A trust does not automatically terminate upon the happening of the event by which the duration of the trust is measured. A reasonable time is permitted after such event for the trustee to perform the duties necessary to complete the administration of the trust. Thus, if under the terms of the governing instrument, the trust is to terminate upon the death of the life beneficiary and the corpus is to be distributed to the remainderman, the trust continues after the death of the life beneficiary for a period reasonably necessary to a proper winding up of the affairs of the trust. However, the winding up of a trust cannot be unduly postponed and if the distribution of the trust corpus is unreasonably delayed, the trust is considered terminated for Federal income tax purposes after the expiration of a reasonable period for the trustee to complete the administration of the trust. Further, a trust will be considered as terminated when all the assets have been distributed except for a reasonable amount which is set aside in good faith for the payment of unascertained or contingent liabilities and expenses (not including a claim by a beneficiary in the capacity of beneficiary).

(c) *(1)* Except as provided in subparagraph (2) of this paragraph, during the period between the occurrence of an event which causes a trust to terminate and the time when the trust is considered as terminated under this section, whether or not the income and the excess of capital gains over capital losses of the trust are to be considered as amounts required to be distributed currently to the ultimate distributee for the year in which they are received depends upon the principles stated in § 1.651(a)-2. See §§ 1.663 *et seq.* for application of the separate share rule.

(2) (i) Except in cases to which the last sentence of this subdivision applies, for taxable years of a trust ending before September 1, 1957, subparagraph (1) of this paragraph shall not apply and the rule of subdivision (ii) of this subparagraph shall apply unless the trustee elects to have subparagraph (1) of this paragraph apply. Such election shall be made by the trustee in a statement filed on or before April 15, 1959, with the district director with whom such trust's return for any such taxable year was filed. The election provided by this subdivision shall not be available if the treatment given the income and the excess of capital gains over capital losses for taxable years for which returns have been filed was consistent with the provisions of subparagraph (1) of this paragraph.

(ii) The rule referred to in subdivision (i) of this subparagraph is as follows: During the period between the occurrence of an event which causes a trust to terminate and the time when a trust is considered as terminated under this section, the income and the excess of capital gains over capital losses of the trust are in general considered as amounts required to be distributed for the year in which they are received. For example, a trust instrument provides for the payment of income to A during her life, and upon her death for the payment of the corpus to B. The trust reports on the basis of the calendar year. A dies on November 1, 1955, but no distribution is made to B until January 15, 1956. The income of the trust and the excess of capital gains over capital losses for the entire year 1955, to the extent not paid, credited, or required to be distributed to A or A's estate, are treated under sections 661 and 662 as amounts required to be distributed to B for the year 1955.

(d) If a trust or the administration or settlement of an estate is considered terminated under this section for Federal income tax purposes (as for instance, because administration has been unduly prolonged), the gross income, deductions, and credits of the estate or trust are, subsequent to the termination, considered the gross income, deductions, and credits of the person or persons succeeding to the property of the estate or trust.

T.D. 6217, 12/19/56, amend T.D. 6353, 1/13/59, T.D. 6462, 5/5/60, T.D. 9032, 12/23/2002.

§ 1.641(c)-0 Table of contents.

This section lists the major captions contained in § 1.641(c)-1.

T.D. 8994, 5/13/2002.

§ 1.641(c)-1 Electing small business trust.

Caution: The Treasury has not yet amended Reg § 1.641(c)-1 to reflect changes made by P.L. 110-28.

(a) In general. An electing small business trust (ESBT) within the meaning of section 1361(e) is treated as two separate trusts for purposes of chapter 1 of the Internal Revenue Code. The portion of an ESBT that consists of stock in one or more S corporations is treated as one trust. The portion of an ESBT that consists of all the other assets in the trust is treated as a separate trust. The grantor or another person may be treated as the owner of all or a portion of either or both such trusts under subpart E, part I, subchapter J, chapter 1 of the Internal Revenue Code. The ESBT is treated as a single trust for administrative purposes, such as having one taxpayer identification number and filing one tax return. See § 1.1361-1(m).

(b) Definitions. *(1) Grantor portion.* The grantor portion of an ESBT is the portion of the trust that is treated as owned by the grantor or another person under subpart E.

(2) S portion. The S portion of an ESBT is the portion of the trust that consists of S corporation stock and that is not treated as owned by the grantor or another person under subpart E.

(3) Non-S portion. The non-S portion of an ESBT is the portion of the trust that consists of all assets other than S corporation stock and that is not treated as owned by the grantor or another person under subpart E.

(c) Taxation of grantor portion. The grantor or another person who is treated as the owner of a portion of the ESBT includes in computing taxable income items of income, deductions, and credits against tax attributable to that portion of the ESBT under section 671.

(d) Taxation of S portion. *(1) In general.* The taxable income of the S portion is determined by taking into account only the items of income, loss, deduction, or credit specified in paragraphs (d)(2), (3), and (4) of this section, to the extent not attributable to the grantor portion.

(2) Section 1366 amounts. (i) In general. The S portion takes into account the items of income, loss, deduction, or credit that are taken into account by an S corporation shareholder pursuant to section 1366 and the regulations thereunder. Rules otherwise applicable to trusts apply in determining the extent to which any loss, deduction, or credit may be taken into account in determining the taxable income of the S portion. See § 1.1361-1(m)(3)(iv) for allocation of those items in the taxable year of the S corporation in which the trust is an ESBT for part of the year and an eligible shareholder under section 1361(a)(2)(A)(i) through (iv) for the rest of the year.

(ii) Special rule for charitable contributions. If a deduction described in paragraph (d)(2)(i) of this section is attributable to an amount of the S corporation's gross income that is paid by the S corporation for a charitable purpose specified in section 170(c) (without regard to section 170(c)(2)(A)), the contribution will be deemed to be paid by the S portion pursuant to the terms of the trust's governing instrument within the meaning of section 642(c)(1). The limitations of section 681, regarding unrelated business income, apply in determining whether the contribution is deductible in computing the taxable income of the S portion.

(iii) Multiple S corporations. If an ESBT owns stock in more than one S corporation, items of income, loss, deduction, or credit from all the S corporations are aggregated for purposes of determining the S portion's taxable income.

(3) Gains and losses on disposition of S stock. (i) In general. The S portion takes into account any gain or loss from the disposition of S corporation stock. No deduction is allowed under section 1211(b)(1) and (2) for capital losses that exceed capital gains.

(ii) Installment method. If income from the sale or disposition of stock in an S corporation is reported by the trust on the installment method, the income recognized under this method is taken into account by the S portion. See paragraph (g)(3) of this section for the treatment of interest on the installment obligation. See § 1.1361-1(m)(5)(ii) regarding treatment of a trust as an ESBT upon the sale of all S corporation stock using the installment method.

(iii) Distributions in excess of basis. Gain recognized under section 1368(b)(2) from distributions in excess of the ESBT's basis in its S corporation stock is taken into account by the S portion.

(4) State and local income taxes and administrative expenses. (i) In general. State and local income taxes and administrative expenses directly related to the S portion and those allocated to that portion in accordance with paragraph (h) are taken into account by the S portion.

(ii) Special rule for certain interest. Interest paid by the trust on money borrowed by the trust to purchase stock in an S corporation is allocated to the S portion but is not a deductible administrative expense for purposes of determining the taxable income of the S portion.

(e) Tax rates and exemption of S portion. *(1) Income tax rate.* Except for capital gains, the highest marginal trust rate provided in section 1(e) is applied to the taxable income of the S portion. See section 1(h) for the rates that apply to the S portion's net capital gain.

(2) Alternative minimum tax exemption. The exemption amount of the S portion under section 55(d) is zero.

(f) Adjustments to basis of stock in the S portion under section 1367. The basis of S corporation stock in the S portion must be adjusted in accordance with section 1367 and the regulations thereunder. If the ESBT owns stock in more than one S corporation, the adjustments to the basis in the S corporation stock of each S corporation must be determined separately with respect to each S corporation. Accordingly, items of income, loss, deduction, or credit of an S corporation that are taken into account by the ESBT under section 1366 can only result in an adjustment to the basis of the stock of that S corporation and cannot affect the basis in the stock of the other S corporations held by the ESBT.

(g) Taxation of non-S portion. *(1) In general.* The taxable income of the non-S portion is determined by taking into account all items of income, deduction, and credit to the extent not taken into account by either the grantor portion or the S portion. The items attributable to the non-S portion are taxed under subparts A through D of part I, subchapter J, chapter 1 of the Internal Revenue Code. The non-S portion may consist of more than one share pursuant to section 663(c).

(2) Dividend income under section 1368(c)(2). Any dividend income within the meaning of section 1368(c)(2) is includible in the gross income of the non-S portion.

(3) Interest on installment obligations. If income from the sale or disposition of stock in an S corporation is reported by the trust on the installment method, the interest on the installment obligation is includible in the gross income of the non-S portion. See paragraph (d)(3)(ii) of this section for the treatment of income from such a sale or disposition.

(4) Charitable deduction. For purposes of applying section 642(c)(1) to payments made by the trust for a charitable purpose, the amount of gross income of the trust is limited to the gross income of the non-S portion. See paragraph (d)(2)(ii) of this section for special rules concerning charitable contributions paid by the S corporation that are deemed to be paid by the S portion.

(h) Allocation of state and local income taxes and administration expenses. Whenever state and local income taxes or administration expenses relate to more than one portion of an ESBT, they must be allocated between or among the portions to which they relate. These items may be allocated in any manner that is reasonable in light of all the circumstances, including the terms of the governing instrument, applicable local law, and the practice of the trustee with respect to the trust if it is reasonable and consistent. The taxes and expenses apportioned to each portion of the ESBT are taken into account by that portion.

(i) Treatment of distributions from the trust. Distributions to beneficiaries from the S portion or the non-S portion, including distributions of the S corporation stock, are deductible under section 651 or 661 in determining the taxable income of the non-S portion, and are includible in the gross income of the beneficiaries under section 652 or 662. However, the amount of the deduction or inclusion cannot exceed the amount of the distributable net income of the non-S portion. Items of income, loss, deduction, or credit taken into account by the grantor portion or the S portion are excluded for purposes of determining the distributable net income of the non-S portion of the trust.

(j) Termination or revocation of ESBT election. If the ESBT election of the trust terminates pursuant to § 1.1361-1(m)(5) or the ESBT election is revoked pursuant to § 1.1361-1(m)(6), the rules contained in this section are thereafter not applicable to the trust. If, upon termination or revocation, the S portion has a net operating loss under section 172; a capital loss carryover under section 1212; or deductions in excess of gross income; then any such loss, carryover, or excess deductions shall be allowed as a deduction, in accordance with the regulations under section 642(h), to the trust, or to the beneficiaries succeeding to the property of the trust if the entire trust terminates.

(k) Effective date. This section generally is applicable for taxable years of ESBTs beginning on and after May 14, 2002. However, paragraphs (a), (b), (c), and (l) Example 1 of this section are applicable for taxable years of ESBTs that end on and after December 29, 2000. ESBTs may apply paragraphs (d)(4) and (h) of this section for taxable years of ESBTs beginning after December 31, 1996.

(l) Examples. The following examples illustrate the rules of this section:

Example (1). Comprehensive example.

(i) Trust has a valid ESBT election in effect. Under section 678, B is treated as the owner of a portion of Trust consisting of a 10% undivided fractional interest in Trust. No other person is treated as the owner of any other portion of Trust under subpart E. Trust owns stock in X, an S corporation, and in Y, a C corporation. During 2000, Trust receives a distribution from X of $5,100, of which $5,000 is applied against Trust's adjusted basis in the X stock in accordance with section 1368(c)(1) and $100 is a dividend under section 1368(c)(2). Trust makes no distributions to its beneficiaries during the year.

(ii) For 2000, Trust has the following items of income and deduction:

Ordinary income attributable to X under section 1366	$5,000
Dividend income from Y	$900
Dividend from X representing C corporation earnings and profits	$100
Total trust income	$6,000
Charitable contributions attributable to X under section 1366	$300
Trustee fees	$200
State and local income taxes	$100

(iii) Trust's items of income and deduction are divided into a grantor portion, an S portion, and a non-S portion for purposes of determining the taxation of those items. Income is allocated to each portion as follows: B must take into account the items of income attributable to the grantor portion, that is, 10% of each item, as follows:

Ordinary income from X	$500
Dividend income from Y	$90
Dividend income from X	$10
Total grantor portion income	$600

The total income of the S portion is $4,500, determined as follows:

Ordinary income from X	$5,000
Less: Grantor portion	($500)
Total S portion income	$4,500

The total income of the non-S portion is $900 determined as follows:

Dividend income from Y (less grantor portion)	$810
Dividend income from X (less grantor portion)	$90
Total non-S portion income	$900

(iv) The administrative expenses and the state and local income taxes relate to all three portions and under state law would be allocated ratably to the $6,000 of trust income. Thus, these items would be allocated 10% (600/6000) to the grantor portion, 75% (4500/6000) to the S portion and 15% (900/6000) to the non-S portion.

(v) B must take into account the following deductions attributable to the grantor portion of the trust:

Charitable contributions from X	$30
Trustee fees	$20
State and local income taxes	$10

(vi) The taxable income of the S portion is $4,005, determined as follows:

Ordinary income from X	$4,500
Less: Charitable contributions from X (less grantor portion)	($270)
75% of trustee fees	($150)
75% of state and local income taxes	($75)
Taxable income of S portion	$4,005

(vii) The taxable income of the non-S portion is $755, determined as follows:

Dividend income from Y	$810
Dividend income from X	$90
Total non-S portion income	$900
Less: 15% of trustee fees	($30)
15% state and local income taxes	($15)
Personal exemption	($100)
Taxable income of non-S portion	$755

Example (2). Sale of S stock. Trust has a valid ESBT election in effect and owns stock in X, an S corporation. No person is treated as the owner of any portion of Trust under subpart E. In 2003, Trust sells all of its stock in X to a person who is unrelated to Trust and its beneficiaries and realizes a capital gain of $5,000. This gain is taken into account by the S portion and is taxed using the appropriate capital gain rate found in section 1(h).

Example (3). (i) Sale of S stock for an installment note. Assume the same facts as in Example 2, except that Trust sells its stock in X for a $400,000 installment note payable with stated interest over ten years. After the sale, Trust does not own any S corporation stock.

(ii) Loss on installment sale. Assume Trust's basis in its X stock was $500,000. Therefore, Trust sustains a capital loss of $100,000 on the sale. Upon the sale, the S portion terminates and the excess loss, after being netted against the other items taken into account by the S portion, is made available to the entire trust as provided in section 641(c)(4).

(iii) Gain on installment sale. Assume Trust's basis in its X stock was $300,000 and that the $100,000 gain will be recognized under the installment method of section 453. Interest income will be recognized annually as part of the installment payments. The portion of the $100,000 gain recognized annually is taken into account by the S portion. However, the annual interest income is includible in the gross income of the non-S portion.

Example (4). Charitable lead annuity trust. Trust is a charitable lead annuity trust which is not treated as owned by the grantor or another person under subpart E. Trust acquires stock in X, an S corporation, and elects to be an ESBT. During the taxable year, pursuant to its terms, Trust pays $10,000 to a charitable organization described in section 170(c)(2). The non-S portion of Trust receives an income tax deduction for the charitable contribution under section 642(c) only to the extent the amount is paid out of the gross income of the non-S portion. To the extent the amount is paid from the S portion by distributing S corporation stock, no charitable deduction is available to the S portion.

Example (5). ESBT distributions.

(i) As of January 1, 2002, Trust owns stock in X, a C corporation. No portion of Trust is treated as owned by the grantor or another person under subpart E. X elects to be an S corporation effective January 1, 2003, and Trust elects to be an ESBT effective January 1, 2003. On February 1, 2003, X makes an $8,000 distribution to Trust, of which $3,000 is treated as a dividend from accumulated earnings and profits under section 1368(c)(2) and the remainder is applied against Trust's basis in the X stock under section 1368(b). The trustee of Trust makes a distribution of $4,000 to Beneficiary during 2003. For 2003, Trust's share of X's section 1366 items is $5,000 of ordinary income. For the year, Trust has no other income and no expenses or state or local taxes.

(ii) For 2003, Trust has $5,000 of taxable income in the S portion. This income is taxed to Trust at the maximum rate provided in section 1(e). Trust also has $3,000 of distributable net income (DNI) in the non-S portion. The non-S portion of Trust receives a distribution deduction under section 661(a) of $3,000, which represents the amount distributed to Beneficiary during the year ($4,000), not to exceed the amount of DNI ($3,000). Beneficiary must include this amount in gross income under section 662(a). As a result, the non-S portion has no taxable income.

T.D. 8994, 5/13/2002.

§ 1.642(a)(1)-1 Partially tax-exempt interest.

Caution: The Treasury has not yet amended Reg § 1.642(a)(1)-1 to reflect changes made by P.L. 94-455.

An estate or trust is allowed the credit against tax for partially tax-exempt interest provided by section 35 only to the extent that the credit does not relate to interest properly allocable to a beneficiary under section 652 or 662 and the regulations thereunder. A beneficiary of an estate or trust is allowed the credit against tax for partially tax-exempt interest provided by section 35 only to the extent that the credit relates to interest properly allocable to him under section 652 or 662 and the regulations thereunder. If an estate or trust holds partially tax-exempt bonds and elects under section 171 to treat the premium on the bonds as amortizable, the credit allowable under section 35, with respect to the bond interest (whether allowable to the estate or trust or to the beneficiary), is reduced under section 171(a)(3) by reducing the shares of the interest allocable, respectively, to the estate or trust and its beneficiary by the portion of the amortization deduction attributable to the shares.

T.D. 6217, 12/19/56.

§ 1.642(a)(2)-1 Foreign taxes.

Caution: The Treasury has not yet amended Reg § 1.642(a)(2)-1 to reflect changes made by P.L. 94-455.

An estate or trust is allowed the credit against tax for taxes imposed by foreign countries and possessions of the United States to the extent allowed by section 901 only for so much of those taxes as are not properly allocable under that section to the beneficiaries. See section 901(b)(4). For purposes of section 901(b)(4), the term "beneficiaries" includes charitable beneficiaries.

T.D. 6217, 12/19/56.

§ 1.642(a)(3)-1 Dividends received by an estate or trust.

Caution: The Treasury has not yet amended Reg § 1.642(a)(3)-1 to reflect changes made by P.L. 88-272.

An estate or trust is allowed a credit against the tax for dividends received on or before December 31, 1964 (see section 34), only for so much of the dividends as are not properly allocable to any beneficiary under section 652 or 662. Section 642(a)(3), and this section do not apply to amounts received as dividends after December 31, 1964. For treatment of the credit in the hands of the beneficiary, see § 1.652(b)-1.

T.D. 6217, 12/19/56, amend T.D. 6777, 12/15/64.

§ 1.642(a)(3)-2 Time of receipt of dividends by beneficiary.

Caution: The Treasury has not yet amended Reg § 1.642(a)(3)-2 to reflect changes made by P.L. 88-272.

In general, dividends are deemed received by a beneficiary in the taxable year in which they are includible in his gross income under section 652 or 662. For example, a simple trust, reporting on the basis of a fiscal year ending October 30, receives quarterly dividends on November 3, 1954, and February 3, May 3, and August 3, 1955. These dividends are all allocable to beneficiary A, reporting on a calendar year basis, under section 652 and are deemed received by A in 1955. See section 652(c). Accordingly, A may take all these dividends into account in determining his credit for dividends received under section 34 and his dividends exclusion under section 116. However, solely for purposes of determining whether dividends deemed received by individuals from trusts or estates qualify under the time limitations of section 34(a) or section 116(a), section 642(a)(3) provides that the time of receipt of the dividends by the trust or estate is also considered the time of receipt by the beneficiary. For example, a simple trust reporting on the basis of a fiscal year ending October 30 receives quarterly dividends on December 3, 1953, and March 3, June 3, and September 3, 1954. These dividends are all allocable to beneficiary A, reporting on the calendar year basis, under section 652 and are includible in his income for 1954. However, for purposes of section 34(a) or section 116(a), these dividends are deemed received by A on the same dates that the trust received them. Accordingly, A may take into account in determining the credit under section 34 only those dividends received by the trust on September 3, 1954, since the dividend received credit is not allowed under section 34 for dividends received before August 1, 1954 (or after December 31, 1964). Section 642(a)(3) and this section do not apply to amounts received by an estate or trust as dividends after December 31, 1964. However, the rules in this section relating to time of receipt of dividends by a beneficiary are applicable to dividends received by an estate or trust prior to January 1, 1965, and accordingly, such dividends are deemed to be received by the beneficiary (even though received after December 31, 1964) on the same dates that the estate or trust received them for purposes of determining the credit under section 34 or the exclusion under section 116.

T.D. 6217, 12/19/56, amend T.D. 6777, 12/15/64.

§ 1.642(a)(3)-3 Cross reference.

Caution: The Treasury has not yet amended Reg § 1.642(a)(3)-3 to reflect changes made by P.L. 88-272.

See § 1.683-2(c) for examples relating to the treatment of dividends received by an estate or trust during a fiscal year beginning in 1953 and ending in 1954.

T.D. 6217, 12/19/56.

§ 1.642(b)-1 Deduction for personal exemption.

Caution: The Treasury has not yet amended Reg § 1.642(b)-1 to reflect changes made by P.L. 94-455.

In lieu of the deduction for personal exemptions provided by section 151:

(a) An estate is allowed a deduction of $600,

(b) A trust which, under its governing instrument, is required to distribute currently all of its income for the taxable year is allowed a deduction of $300, and

(c) All other trusts are allowed a deduction of $100. A trust which, under its governing instrument, is required to distribute all of its income currently is allowed a deduction of $300, even though it also distributes amounts other than income in the taxable year and even though it may be required to make distributions which would qualify for the charitable contributions deduction under section 642(c) (and therefore does not qualify as a "simple trust" under sections 651-652). A trust for the payment of an annuity is allowed a deduction of $300 in a taxable year in which the amount of the annuity required to be paid equals or exceeds all the income of the trust for the taxable year. For the meaning of the term "income required to be distributed currently", see § 1.651(a)-2.

T.D. 6217, 12/19/56.

§ 1.642(c)-0 Effective dates.

Caution: The Treasury has not yet amended Reg § 1.642(c)-0 to reflect changes made by P.L. 94-455.

The provisions of section 642(c) (other than section 642(c)(5)) and of §§ 1.642(c)-1 through 1.642(c)-4 apply to amounts paid, permanently set aside, or to be used for a charitable purpose in taxable years beginning after December 31, 1969. The provisions of section 642(c)(5) and of §§ 1.642(c)-5 through 1.642(c)-7 apply to transfers in trust made after July 31, 1969. For provisions relating to amounts paid, permanently set aside, or to be used for a charitable purpose in taxable years beginning before January 1, 1970, see 26 CFR 1.642(c) through 1.642(c)-4 (Rev. as of Jan. 1, 1971).

T.D. 7357, 5/30/75.

§ 1.642(c)-1 Unlimited deduction for amounts paid for a charitable purpose.

Caution: The Treasury has not yet amended Reg § 1.642(c)-1 to reflect changes made by P.L. 94-455.

(a) In general. *(1)* Any part of the gross income of an estate or trust which, pursuant to the terms of the governing instrument is paid (or treated under paragraph (b) of this section as paid) during the taxable year for a purpose specified in section 170(c) shall be allowed as a deduction to such estate or trust in lieu of the limited charitable contributions deduction authorized by section 170(a). In applying this paragraph without reference to paragraph (b) of this section, a deduction shall be allowed for an amount paid during the taxable year in respect of gross income received in a previous taxable year, but only if no deduction was allowed for any previous taxable year to the estate or trust, or in the case of a section 645 election, to a related estate, as defined under § 1.645-1(b), for the amount so paid.

(2) In determining whether an amount is paid for a purpose specified in section 170(c)(2) the provisions of section 170(c)(2)(A) shall not be taken into account. Thus, an amount paid to a corporation, trust, or community chest, fund, or foundation otherwise described in section 170(c)(2) shall be considered paid for a purpose specified in section 170(c) even though the corporation, trust, or community chest, fund, or foundation is not created or organized in the United States, any State, the District of Columbia, or any possession of the United States.

(3) See section 642(c)(6) and § 1.642(c)-4 for disallowance of a deduction under this section to a trust which is, or is treated under section 4947(a)(1) as though it were, a private foundation (as defined in section 509(a) and the regulations thereunder) and not exempt from taxation under section 501(a).

(b) Election to treat contributions as paid in preceding taxable year. *(1) In general.* For purposes of determining the deduction allowed under paragraph (a) of this section, the fiduciary (as defined in section 7701(a)(6)) of an estate or trust may elect under section 642(c)(1) to treat as paid during the taxable year (whether or not such year begins before January 1, 1970) any amount of gross income received during such taxable year or any preceding taxable year which is otherwise deductible under such paragraph and which is paid after the close of such taxable year but on or before the last day of the next succeeding taxable year of the estate or trust. The preceding sentence applies only in the case of payments actually made in a taxable year which is a taxable year beginning after December 31, 1969. No election shall be made, however, in respect of any amount which was deducted for any previous taxable year or which is deducted for the taxable year in which such amount is paid.

(2) Time for making election. The election under subparagraph (1) of this paragraph shall be made not later than the time, including extensions thereof, prescribed by law for filing the income tax return for the succeeding taxable year. Such election shall, except as provided in subparagraph (4) of this paragraph, become irrevocable after the last day prescribed for making it. Having made the election for any taxable year, the fiduciary may, within the time prescribed for making it, revoke the election without the consent of the Commissioner.

(3) Manner of making the election. The election shall be made by filing with the income tax return (or an amended return) for the taxable year in which the contribution is treated as paid a statement which—

(i) States the name and address of the fiduciary,

(ii) Identifies the estate or trust for which the fiduciary is acting,

(iii) Indicates that the fiduciary is making an election under section 642(c)(1) in respect of contributions treated as paid during such taxable year,

(iv) Gives the name and address of each organization to which any such contribution is paid, and

(v) States the amount of each contribution and date of actual payment or, if applicable, the total amount of contributions paid to each organization during the succeeding taxable year, to be treated as paid in the preceding taxable year.

(4) Revocation of certain elections with consent. An application to revoke with the consent of the Commissioner any election made on or before June 8, 1970, must be in writing and must be filed not later than September 2, 1975.

No consent will be granted to revoke an election for any taxable year for which the assessment of a deficiency is prevented by the operation of any law or rule of law. If consent to revoke the election is granted, the fiduciary must attach a copy of the consent to the return (or amended return) for each taxable year affected by the revocation. The application must be addressed to the Commissioner of Internal Revenue, Washington, D.C. 20224, and must indicate—

(i) The name and address of the fiduciary and the estate or trust for which he was acting,

(ii) The taxable year for which the election was made,

(iii) The office of the district director, or the service center, where the return (or amended return) for the year of election was filed, and

(iv) The reason for revoking the election.

T.D. 6217, 12/19/56, amend T.D. 7357, 5/30/75, T.D. 9032, 12/23/2002.

PAR. 2. Paragraph (a)(1) of § 1.642(c)-1 is amended by revising the first sentence to read as set forth below.

Proposed § 1.642(c)-1 Unlimited deduction for amounts paid for charitable purpose. [*For Preamble, see ¶ 151,114*]

(a) In general. (1) Any part of the gross income of an estate or trust which, pursuant to the terms of the governing instrument, is paid (or treated under paragraph (b) of this section as paid) during the taxable year for a purpose specified in section 170(c) shall be allowed as a deduction to such estate or trust in lieu of the limited charitable contributions deduction authorized by section 170(a) (provided that the recordkeeping and return requirements for charitable contribution deductions contained in § 1.170A-13 are satisfied). * * *

§ 1.642(c)-2 Unlimited deduction for amounts permanently set aside for a charitable purpose.

Caution: The Treasury has not yet amended Reg § 1.642(c)-2 to reflect changes made by P.L. 94-455.

(a) Estates. Any part of the gross income of an estate which pursuant to the terms of the will—

(1) Is permanently set aside during the taxable year for a purpose specified in section 170(c), or

(2) Is to be used (within or without the United States or any of its possessions) exclusively for religious, charitable, scientific, literary, or educational purposes, or for the prevention of cruelty to children or animals, or for the establishment, acquisition, maintenance, or operation of a public cemetery not operated for profit,

shall be allowed as a deduction to the estate in lieu of the limited charitable contributions deduction authorized by section 170(a).

(b) Certain trusts. *(1) In general.* Any part of the gross income of a trust to which either subparagraph (3) or (4) of this paragraph applies, that by the terms of the governing instrument—

(i) Is permanently set aside during the taxable year for a purpose specified in section 170(c), or

(ii) Is to be used (within or without the United States or any of its possessions) exclusively for religious, charitable, scientific, literary, or educational purposes, or for the prevention of cruelty to children or animals, or for the establishment, acquisition, maintenance, or operation of a public cemetery not operated for profit, shall be allowed, subject to the limitation provided in subparagraph (2) of this paragraph, as a deduction to the trust in lieu of the limited charitable contributions deduction authorized by section 170(a). The preceding sentence applies only to a trust which is required by the terms of its governing instrument to set amounts aside. See section 642(c)(6) and § 1.642(c)-4 for disallowance of a deduction under this section to a trust which is, or is treated under section 4947(a)(1) as though it were, a private foundation (as defined in section 509(a) and the regulations thereunder) that is not exempt from taxation under section 501(a).

(2) Limitation of deduction. Subparagraph (1) of this paragraph applies only to the gross income earned by a trust with respect to amounts transferred to the trust under a will executed on or before October 9, 1969, and satisfying the requirements of subparagraph (4) of this paragraph or transferred to the trust on or before October 9, 1969. For such purposes, any income, gains, or losses, which are derived at any time from the amounts so transferred to the trust shall also be taken into account in applying subparagraph (1) of this paragraph. If any such amount so transferred to the trust is invested or reinvested at any time, any asset received by the trust upon such investment or reinvestment shall also be treated as an amount which was so transferred to the trust. In the case of a trust to which this paragraph applies which contains (i) amounts transferred pursuant to transfers described in the first sentence of this subparagraph and (ii)

amounts transferred pursuant to transfers not so described, subparagraph (1) of this paragraph shall apply only if the amounts described in subdivision (i) of this subparagraph, together with all income, gains, and losses derived therefrom, are separately accounted for from the amounts described in subdivision (ii) of this subparagraph, together with all income, gains, and losses derived therefrom. Such separate accounting shall be carried out consistently with the principles of paragraph (c)(4) of § 53.4947-1 of this chapter (Foundation Excise Tax Regulations), relating to accounting for segregated amounts of split-interest trusts.

(3) Trusts created on or before October 9, 1969. A trust to which this subparagraph applies is a trust, testamentary or otherwise, which was created on or before October 9, 1969, and which qualifies under either subdivision (i) or (ii) of this subparagraph.

(i) Transfer of irrevocable remainder interest to charity. To qualify under this subdivision the trust must have been created under the terms of an instrument granting an irrevocable remainder interest in such trust to or for the use of an organization described in section 170(c). If the instrument granted a revocable remainder interest but the power to revoke such interest terminated on or before October 9, 1969, without the remainder interest having been revoked, the remainder interest will be treated as irrevocable for purposes of the preceding sentence.

(ii) Grantor under a mental disability to change terms of trust. (A) To qualify under this subdivision (ii) the trust must have been created by a grantor who was at all times after October 9, 1969, under a mental disability to change the terms of the trust. The term "mental disability" for this purpose means mental incompetence to change the terms of the trust, whether or not there has been an adjudication of mental incompetence and whether or not there has been an appointment of a committee, guardian, fiduciary, or other person charged with the care of the person or property of the grantor.

(B) If the grantor has not been adjudged mentally incompetent, the trustee must obtain from a qualified physician a certificate stating that the grantor of the trust has been mentally incompetent at all times after October 9, 1969, and that there is no reasonable probability that the grantor's mental capacity will ever improve to the extent that he will be mentally competent to change the terms of the trust. A copy of this certification must be filed with the first return on which a deduction is claimed by reason of this subdivision (ii) and subparagraph (1) of this paragraph. Thereafter, a statement referring to such medical opinion must be attached to any return for a taxable year for which such a deduction is claimed and during which the grantor's mental incompetence continues. The original certificate must be retained by the trustee of the trust.

(C) If the grantor has been adjudged mentally incompetent, a copy of the judgment or decree, and any modification thereof, must be filed with the first return on which a deduction is claimed by reason of this subdivision (ii) and subparagraph (1) of this paragraph. Thereafter, a statement referring to such judgment or decree must be attached to any return for a taxable year for which such a deduction is claimed and during which the grantor's mental incompetence continues. A copy of such judgment or decree must also be retained by the trustee of the trust.

(D) This subdivision (ii) applies even though a person charged with the care of the person or property of the grantor has the power to change the terms of the trust.

(4) Testamentary trust established by will executed on or before October 9, 1969. A trust to which this subparagraph applies is a trust which was established by will executed on or before October 9, 1969, and which qualifies under either subdivision (i), (ii), or (iii) of this subparagraph. This subparagraph does not apply, however, to that portion of any trust, not established by a will executed on or before October 9, 1969, which was transferred to such trust by a will executed on or before October 9, 1969. Nor does it apply to that portion of any trust, not established by a will executed on or before October 9, 1969, which was subject to a testamentary power of appointment that fails by reason of the testator's nonexercise of the power in a will executed on or before October 9, 1969.

(i) Testator dying within 3 years without republishing his will. To qualify under this subdivision the trust must have been established by the will of a testator who died after October 9, 1969, but before October 9, 1972, without having amended any dispositive provision of the will after October 9, 1969, by codicil or otherwise.

(ii) Testator having no right to change his will. To qualify under this subdivision the trust must have been established by the will of a testator who died after October 9, 1969, and who at no time after that date had the right to change any portion of such will pertaining to such trust. This subdivision could apply, for example, where a contract has been entered into for the execution of wills containing reciprocal provisions as well as provisions for the benefit of an organization described in section 170(c) and under applicable local law the surviving testator is prohibited from revoking his will because he has accepted the benefit of the provision of the will of the other contracting party.

(iii) Testator under a mental disability to republish his will. To qualify under this subdivision the trust must have been established by the will of a testator who died after October 8, 1972, without having amended any dispositive provision of such will after October 9, 1969, October 9, 1972 by codicil or otherwise, and who is under a mental disability at all times after October 8, 1972, to amend such will, by codicil or otherwise. The provisions of subparagraph (3)(ii) of this paragraph with respect to mental incompetence apply for purposes of this subdivision.

(iv) Amendment of dispositive provisions. The provision of paragraph (e)(4) and (5) of § 20.2055-2 of this chapter (Estate Tax Regulations) are to be applied under subdivisions (i) and (iii) of this subparagraph in determining whether there has been an amendment of a dispositive provision of a will.

(c) Pooled income funds. Any part of the gross income of a pooled income fund to which § 1.642(c)-5 applies for the taxable year that is attributable to net long-term capital gain (as defined in section 1222(7)) which, pursuant to the terms of the governing instrument, is permanently set aside during the taxable year for a purpose specified in section 170(c) shall be allowed as a deduction to the fund in lieu of the limited charitable contributions deduction authorized by section 170(a). No amount of net long-term capital gain shall be considered permanently set aside for charitable purposes if, under the terms of the fund's governing instrument and applicable local law, the trustee has the power, whether or not exercised, to satisfy the income beneficiaries' right to income by the payment of either: an amount equal to a fixed percentage of the fair market value of the fund's assets (whether determined annually or averaged on a multiple year basis); or any amount that takes into account unrealized appreciation in the value of the fund's assets. In addition, no amount of net long-term capital gain shall be considered permanently set aside for charitable purposes to the extent the trustee distributes proceeds from the sale or exchange of the fund's assets as income within the meaning of § 1.642(c)-5(a)(5)(i). No deduction shall be allowed under this paragraph for any portion of the gross income of such fund which is (1) attributable to income other than net long-term capital gain or (2) earned with respect to amounts transferred to such fund before August 1, 1969. However, see paragraph (b) of this section for a deduction (subject to the limitations of such paragraph) for amounts permanently set aside by a pooled income fund which meets the requirements of that paragraph. The principles of paragraph (b)(2) of this section with respect to investment, reinvestment, and separate accounting shall apply under this paragraph in the case of amounts transferred to the fund after July 31, 1969.

(d) Disallowance of deduction for certain amounts not deemed to be permanently set aside for charitable purposes. No amount will be considered to be permanently set aside, or to be used, for a purpose described in paragraph (a) or (b)(1) of this section unless under the terms of the governing instrument and the circumstances of the particular case the possibility that the amount set aside, or to be used, will not be devoted to such purpose or use is so remote as to be negligible. Thus, for example, where there is possibility of the invasion of the corpus of a charitable remainder trust, as defined in § 1.664-1(a)(1)(ii), in order to make payment of the annuity amount or unitrust amount, no deduction will be allowed under paragraph (a) of this section in respect of any amount set aside by an estate for distribution to such a charitable remainder trust.

For treatment of distributions by an estate to a charitable remainder trust, see paragraph (a)(5)(iii) of § 1.664-1.

(e) Effective dates. Generally, the second sentence of paragraph (c) of this section, concerning the loss of any charitable deduction for long-term capital gains if the fund's income may be determined by a fixed percentage of the fair market value of the fund's assets or by any amount that takes into account unrealized appreciation in the value of the fund's assets, applies for taxable years beginning after January 2, 2004. In a state whose statute permits income to be determined by reference to a fixed percentage of, or the unrealized appreciation in, the value of the fund's assets, net long-term capital gain of a pooled income fund may be considered to be permanently set aside for charitable purposes if the fund's governing instrument is amended or reformed to eliminate the possibility of determining income in such a manner and if income has not been determined in this manner. For this purpose, a judicial proceeding to reform the fund's governing instrument must be commenced, or a nonjudicial reformation that is valid under state law must be completed, by the date that is nine months after the later of January 2, 2004 or the effective date of the state statute authorizing determination of income in such a manner.

T.D. 6217, 12/19/56, amend T.D. 7357, 5/30/75, T.D. 9102, 12/30/2003.

PAR. 3. Section 1.642(c)-2 is amended by adding a new paragraph (e) immediately after paragraph (d) to read as set forth below.

Proposed § 1.642(c)-2 Unlimited deduction for amounts permanently set aside for a charitable purpose. [*For Preamble, see ¶ 151,114*]

* * * * *

(e) Substantiation requirements. No deduction shall be allowed under paragraphs (a), (b)(2), or (c) of this section unless the recordkeeping and return requirements for charitable contribution deductions contained in § 1.170A-13 are satisfied.

§ 1.642(c)-3 Adjustments and other special rules for determining unlimited charitable contributions deduction.

Caution: The Treasury has not yet amended Reg § 1.642(c)-3 to reflect changes made by P.L. 103-66, P.L. 99-514.

(a) Income in respect of a decedent. For purposes of §§ 1.642(c)-1 and 1.642(c)-2, an amount received by an estate or trust which is includible in its gross income under section 691(a)(1) as income in respect of a decedent shall be included in the gross income of the estate or trust.

(b) Reduction of charitable contributions deduction by amounts not included in gross income. *(1)* If an estate, pooled income fund, or other trust pays, permanently sets aside, or uses any amount of its income for a purpose specified in section 642(c)(1), (2) or (3) and that amount includes any items of estate or trust income not entering into the gross income of the estate or trust, the deduction allowable under § 1.642(c)-1 or § 1.642(c)-2 is limited to the gross income so paid, permanently set aside, or used. In the case of a pooled income fund for which a deduction is allowable under paragraph (c) of § 1.642(c)-2 for amounts permanently set aside, only the gross income of the fund which is attributable to net long-term capital gain (as defined in section 1222(7) shall be taken into account.

(2) In determining whether the amounts of income so paid, permanently set aside, or used for a purpose specified in section 642(c)(1), (2), or (3) include particular items of income of an estate or trust not included in gross income, the specific provision controls if the governing instrument specifically provides as to source out of which amounts are to be paid, permanently set aside, or used for such a purpose.

In the absence of specific provisions in the governing instrument, an amount to which section 642(c)(1), (2) or (3) applies is deemed to consist of the same proportion of each class of the items of income of the estate or trust as the total of each class bears to the total of all classes. See paragraph (b) of § 1.643(a)-5 for the method of determining the allocable portion of exempt income and foreign income.

(3) For examples showing the determination of the character of an amount deductible under § 1.642(c)-1 or § 1.642(c)-2, see examples (1) and (2) in § 1.662(b)-2 and paragraph (e) of the example in § 1.662(c)-4.

(4) For the purpose of this paragraph, the provision of section 116 are not to be taken into account.

(c) Capital gains included in charitable contribution. Where any amount of the income paid, permanently set aside, or used for a purpose specified in section 642(c)(1), (2), or (3), is attributable to net long-term capital gain (as defined in section 1222(7)), the amount of the deduction otherwise allowable under § 1.642(c)-1 or § 1.642(c)-2, must be adjusted for any deduction provided in section 1202 of 50 percent of the excess, if any, of the net long-term capital gain over net short-term capital loss. For determination of the extent to which the contribution to which § 1.642(c)-1 or § 1.642(c)-2 applies is deemed to consist of net long-term capital gains, see paragraph (b) of this section. The application of this paragraph may be illustrated by the following examples:

Example (1). Under the terms of the trust instrument, the income of a trust described in § 1.642(c)-2(b)(3)(i) is currently distributable to A during his life and capital gains are allocable to corpus. No provision is made in the trust instrument for the invasion of corpus for the benefit of A. Upon A's death the corpus of the trust is to be distributed to M University, an organization described in section 501(c)(3) which is exempt from taxation under section 501(a). During the taxable year ending December 31, 1970, the trust has long-term capital gains of $100,000 for property transferred to it on or before October 9, 1969, which are permanently set aside for charitable purposes. The trust includes $100,000 in gross income but is allowed a deduction of $50,000 under section 1202 for the long-term capital gains and a charitable contributions deduction of $50,000 under section 642(c)(2) ($100,000 permanently set aside for charitable purposes less $50,000 allowed as a deduction under section 1202 with respect to such $100,000).

Example (2). Under the terms of the will, $200,000 of the income (including $100,000 capital gains) for the taxable year 1972 of an estate is distributed, one-quarter to each of two individual beneficiaries and one-half to N University, an organization described in section 501(c)(3) which is exempt from taxation under section 501(a). During 1972 the estate has ordinary income of $200,000, long-term capital gains of $100,000, and no capital losses. It is assumed that for 1972 the estate has no other items of income or any deductions other than those discussed herein. The entire capital gains of $100,000 are included in the gross income of the estate for 1972, and N University receives $100,000 from the estate in such year. However, the amount allowable to the estate under section 642(c)(1) is subject to appropriate adjustment for the deduction allowable under section 1202. In view of the distributions of $25,000 of capital gains to each of the individual beneficiaries, the deduction allowable to the estate under section 1202 is limited by such section to $25,000 [($100,000 capital gains less $50,000 capital gains includible in income of individual beneficiaries under section 662) × 50%]. Since the whole of this $25,000 deduction under section 1202 is attributable to the distribution of $50,000 of capital gains to N University, the deduction allowable to the estate in 1972 under section 642(c)(1) is $75,000 [$100,000 (distributed to N) less $25,000 (proper adjustment for section 1202 deduction)].

Example (3). Under the terms of the trust instrument, 30 percent of the gross income (exclusive of capital gains) of a trust described in § 1.642(c)-2(b)(3)(i) is currently distributed to B, the sole income beneficiary. Net capital gains (capital gain net income for taxable years beginning after December 31, 1976) and undistributed ordinary income are allocable to corpus. No provision is made in the trust instrument for the invasion of corpus for the benefit of B. Upon B's death the remainder of the trust is to be distributed to M Church. During the taxable year 1972, the trust has ordinary income of $100,000, long-term capital gains of $15,000, short-term capital gains of $1,000, long-term capital losses of $5,000, and short-term capital losses of $2,500. It is assumed that the trust has no other items of income or any deductions other than those discussed herein. All the ordinary income and capital gains and losses are attributable to amounts transferred to the trust before October 9, 1969. The trust includes in gross income for 1972 the total amount of $116,000 [$100,000 (ordinary income) + $16,000 (total capital gains determined without regard to capital losses)]. Pursuant to the terms of the governing instrument the trust distributes to B in 1972 the amount of $30,000 ($100,000 × 30%). The balance of $78,500 [($116,000 less $7,500 capital losses) − $30,000 distribution] is available for the set-aside for charitable purposes. In determining taxable income for 1972 the capital losses of $7,500 ($5,000 + $2,500) are allowable in full under section 1211(b)(1). The net capital gain (capital gain net income for taxable years beginning after December 31, 1976) of $8,500 ($16,000 less $7,500) is the excess of the net long-term capital gain of $10,000 ($15,000 less $5,000) over the net short-term capital loss of $1,500 ($2,500 less $1,000). The deduction under section 1202 is $4,250 ($8,500 × 50%), all of which is attributable to the set-aside for charitable purposes. Accordingly, for 1972 the deduction allowable to the trust under section 642(c)(2) is $74,250 [$78,500 (set-aside for M) less $4,250 (proper adjustment for section 1202 deduction)].

Example (4). During the taxable year a pooled income fund, as defined in § 1.642(c)-5, has in addition to ordinary income long-term capital gains of $150,000, short-term capital gains of $15,000, long-term capital losses of $100,000, and short-term capital losses of $10,000. Under the Declaration of Trust and pursuant to State law net long-term capital gain is allocable to corpus and net short-term capital gain is to be distributed to the income beneficiaries of the fund. All the capital gains and losses are attributable to amounts transferred to the fund after July 31, 1969. In view of the distribution of the net short-term capital gain of $5,000 ($15,000 less $10,000) to the income beneficiaries, the deduction allowed to the fund under section 1202 is limited by such section to $25,000 [($150,000 (long-term capital gains) less $100,000 (long-term capital losses)) × 50%]. Since the whole of this deduction under section 1202 is attributable to the set-aside for charitable purposes, the deduction of $50,000 ($150,000 less $100,000) otherwise allowable under section 642(c)(3) is subject to appropriate adjustment under section 642(c)(4) for the deduction allowable under section 1202. Accordingly, the amount of the set-aside deduction is $25,000 [$50,000 (set-aside for public charity) less $25,000 (proper adjustment for section 1202 deduction)].

Example (5). The facts are the same as in example (4) except that under the Declaration of Trust and pursuant to State law all the net capital gain (capital gain net income for taxable years beginning after December 31, 1976) for the taxable year is allocable to corpus of the fund. The fund would thus include in gross income total capital gains of $165,000 ($150,000 + $15,000). In determining taxable income for the taxable year the capital losses of $110,000 ($100,000 + $10,000) are allowable in full under section 1211(b)(1). The net capital gain (capital gain net income for taxable years beginning after December 31, 1976) of $55,000 ($165,000 less $110,000) is available for the set-aside for charitable purposes under section 642(c)(3) only in the amount of the net long-term capital gain of $50,000 ($150,000 long-term gains less $100,000 long-term losses). The deduction under section 1202 is $25,000 ($50,000 × 50%), all of which is attributable to the set-aside for charitable purposes. Accordingly, the deduction allowable to the fund under section 642(c)(3) is $25,000 [$50,000 (set-aside for public charity) less $25,000 (proper adjustment for section 1202 deduction)]. The $5,000 balance of net capital gain (capital gain net income for taxable years beginning after December 31, 1976) is taken into account in determining taxable income of the pooled income fund for the taxable year.

(d) Disallowance of deduction for amounts allocable to unrelated business income. In the case of a trust, the deduction otherwise allowable under § 1.642(c)-1 or § 1.642(c)-2 is disallowed to the extent of amounts allocable to the trust's unrelated business income. See section 681(a) and the regulations thereunder.

(e) Disallowance of deduction in certain cases. For disallowance of certain deductions otherwise allowable under section 642(c)(1), (2), or (3), see sections 508(d) and 4948(c)(4).

(f) Information returns. For rules applicable to the annual information return that must be filed by trusts claiming a deduction under section 642(c) for the taxable year, see section 6034 and the regulations thereunder.

T.D. 6217, 12/19/56, amend T.D. 7357, 5/30/75, T.D. 7728, 10/31/80.

§ 1.642(c)-4 Nonexempt private foundations.

Caution: The Treasury has not yet amended Reg § 1.642(c)-4 to reflect changes made by P.L. 94-455.

In the case of a trust which is, or is treated under section 4947(a)(1) as though it were, a private foundation (as defined in section 509(a) and the regulations thereunder) that is not exempt from taxation under section 501(a) for the taxable year, a deduction for amounts paid or permanently set aside, or used for a purpose specified in section 642(c)(1) or (2), shall not be allowed under § 1.642(c)-1 or § 1.642(c)-2, but such trust shall, subject to the provisions applicable to individuals, be allowed a deduction under section 170 for charitable contributions paid during the taxable year. Section 642(c)(6) and this section do not apply to a trust described in section 4947(a)(1) unless such trust fails to meet the requirements of section 508(e). However, if on October 9, 1969, or at any time thereafter, a trust is recognized as being exempt from taxation under section 501(a) as an organization described in section 501(c)(3), if at such time such trust is a private foundation, and if at any time thereafter such trust is determined not to be exempt from taxation under section 501(a) as an organization described in section 501(c)(3), section 642(c)(6) and this section will apply to such trust. See § 1.509(b)-1(b).

T.D. 6217, 12/19/56, amend T.D. 7357, 5/30/75.

§ 1.642(c)-5 Definition of pooled income fund.

Caution: The Treasury has not yet amended Reg § 1.642(c)-5 to reflect changes made by P.L. 100-647, P.L. 99-514, P.L. 98-369.

(a) In general. *(1) Application of provisions.* Section 642(c)(5) prescribes certain rules for the valuation of contributions involving transfers to certain funds described in that section as pooled income funds. This section sets forth the requirements for qualifying as a pooled income fund and provides for the manner of allocating the income of the fund to the beneficiaries. Section 1.642(c)-6 provides for the valuation of a remainder interest in property transferred to a pooled income fund. Section 1.642(c)-7 provides transitional rules under which certain funds may be amended so as to qualify as pooled income funds in respect to transfers of property occurring after July 31, 1969.

(2) Tax status of fund and its beneficiaries. Notwithstanding any other provision of this chapter, a fund which meets the requirements of a pooled income fund, as defined in section 642(c)(5) and paragraph (b) of this section, shall not be treated as an association within the meaning of section 7701(a)(3). Such a fund, which need not be a trust under local law, and its beneficiaries shall be taxable under part I, subchapter J, chapter 1 of the Code, but the provisions of subpart E (relating to grantors and others treated as substantial owners) of such part shall not apply to such fund.

(3) Recognition of gain or loss on transfers to fund. No gain or loss shall be recognized to the donor on the transfer of property to a pooled income fund. In such case, the fund's basis and holding period with respect to property transferred to the fund by a donor shall be determined as provided in sections 1015(b) and 1223(2). If, however, a donor transfers property to a pooled income fund and, in addition to creating or retaining a life income interest therein, receives property from the fund, or transfers property to the fund which is subject to an indebtedness, this subparagraph shall not apply to the gain realized by reason of (i) the receipt of such property or (ii) the amount of such indebtedness, whether or not assumed by the pooled income fund, which is required to be treated as an amount realized on the transfer. For applicability of the bargain sale rules, see section 1011(b) and the regulations thereunder.

(4) Charitable contributions deduction. A charitable contributions deduction for the value of the remainder interest, as determined under § 1.642(c)-6, may be allowed under section 170, 2055, 2106, or 2522, where there is a transfer of property to a pooled income fund. For a special rule relating to the reduction of the amount of a charitable contribution of certain ordinary income property or capital gain property, see section 170(e)(1)(A) or (B)(i) and the regulations thereunder.

(5) Definitions. For purposes of this section, § 1.642(c)-6, and § 1.642(c)-7—

(i) The term income has the same meaning as it does under section 643(b) and the regulations thereunder, except that income generally may not include any long-term capital gains. However, in conformance with the applicable state statute, income may be defined as or satisfied by a unitrust amount, or pursuant to a trustee's power to adjust between income and principal to fulfill the trustee's duty of impartiality, if the state statute both provides for a reasonable apportionment between the income and remainder beneficiaries of the total return of the trust and meets the requirements of § 1.643(b)-1. In exercising a power to adjust, the trustee must allocate to principal, not to income, the proceeds from the sale or exchange of any assets contributed to the fund by any donor or purchased by the fund at least to the extent of the fair market value of those assets on the date of their contribution to the fund or of the purchase price of those assets purchased by the fund. This definition of income applies for taxable years beginning after January 2, 2004.

(ii) The term "donor" includes a decedent who makes a testamentary transfer of property to a pooled income fund.

(iii) The term "governing instrument" means either the governing plan under which the pooled income fund is established and administered or the instrument of transfer, as the context requires.

(iv) The term "public charity" means an organization described in clause (i) to (vi) of section 170(b)(1)(A). If an organization is described in clause (i) to (vi) of section 170(b)(1)(A) and is also described in clause (viii) of such section, it shall be treated as a public charity.

(v) The term "fair market value," when used with respect to property, means its value in excess of the indebtedness or charges against such property.

(vi) The term "determination date" means each day within the taxable year of a pooled income fund on which a valuation is made of the property in the fund. The property in the fund shall be valued on the first day of the taxable year of the fund and on at least 3 other days within the taxable year. The period between any two consecutive determination dates within the taxable year shall not be greater than 3 calendar months. In the case of a taxable year of less than 12 months, the property in the fund shall be valued on the first day of such taxable year and on such other days within such year as occur at successive intervals of no greater than 3 calendar months. Where a valuation date falls on a Saturday, Sunday, or a legal holiday (as defined in section 7503 and the regulations thereunder), the valuation may be made on either the next preceding day which is not a Saturday, Sunday, or legal holiday or the next succeeding day which is not a Saturday, Sunday, or legal holiday, so long as the next such preceding day or next such succeeding day is consistently used where the valuation date falls on a Saturday, Sunday, or legal holiday.

(6) Cross references. (i) See section 4947(a)(2) and section 4947(b)(3)(B) for the application to pooled income funds of the provisions relating to private foundations and section 508(e) for rules relating to provisions required in the governing instrument prohibiting certain activities specified in section 4947(a)(2).

(ii) For rules for postponing the time for deduction of a charitable contribution of a future interest in tangible personal property, see section 170(a)(3) and the regulations thereunder.

(b) Requirements for qualification as a pooled income fund. A pooled income fund to which this section applies must satisfy all of the following requirements:

(1) Contribution of remainder interest to charity. Each donor must transfer property to the fund and contribute an irrevocable remainder interest in such property to or for the use of a public charity, retaining for himself, or creating for another beneficiary or beneficiaries, a life income interest in the transferred property. A contingent remainder interest shall not be treated as an irrevocable remainder interest for purposes of this subparagraph.

(2) Creation of life income interest. Each donor must retain for himself for life an income interest in the property transferred to such fund, or create an income interest in such property for the life of one or more beneficiaries, each of whom must be living at the time of the transfer of the property to the fund by the donor. The term "one or more beneficiaries" includes those members of a named class who are alive and can be ascertained at the time of transfer of the property to the fund. In the event more than one beneficiary of the income interest is designated, such beneficiaries may enjoy their shares of income concurrently, consecutively, or both concurrently and consecutively. The donor may retain the power exercisable only by will to revoke or terminate the income interest of any designated beneficiary other than the public charity. The governing instrument must specify at the time of the transfer the particular beneficiary or beneficiaries to whom the income is payable and the share of income distributable to each person so specified. The public charity to or for the use of which the remainder interest is contributed may also be designated as one of the beneficiaries of an income interest. The donor need not retain or create a life interest in all the income from the property transferred to the fund provided any income not payable under the terms of the governing instrument to an income beneficiary is contributed to, and within the taxable year in which it is received is paid to, the same public charity to or for the use of which the remainder interest is contributed. No charitable contributions deduction shall be allowed to the donor for the value of such income interest of the public charity or for the amount of any such income paid to such organization.

(3) Commingling of property required. The property transferred to the fund by each donor must be commingled with, and invested or reinvested with, other property transferred to the fund by other donors satisfying the requirements of subparagraphs (1) and (2) of this paragraph. The governing instrument of the pooled income fund must contain a provision requiring compliance with the preceding sentence. The public charity to or for the use of which the remainder interest is contributed may maintain more than one pooled income fund, provided that each such fund is maintained by the organization and is not a device to permit a group of donors to create a fund which may be subject to their manipulation. The fund must not include property transferred under arrangements other than those specified in section 642(c)(5) and this paragraph. However, a fund shall not be disqualified as a pooled income fund under this paragraph because any portion of its properties is invested or reinvested jointly with other properties, not a part of the pooled income fund, which are held by, or for the use of, the public charity which maintains the fund, as for example, with securities in the general endowment fund of the public charity to or for the use of which the remainder interest is contributed. Where such joint investment or reinvestment of properties occurs, records must be maintained which sufficiently identify the portion of the total fund which is owned by the pooled income fund and the income earned by, and attributable to, such portion. Such a joint investment or reinvestment of properties shall not be treated as an association or partnership for purposes of the Code. A bank which serves as trustee of more than one pooled income fund may maintain a common trust fund to which section 584 applies for the collective investment and reinvestment of moneys of such funds.

(4) Prohibition against exempt securities. The property transferred to the fund by any donor must not include any securities, the income from which is exempt from tax under subtitle A of the Code, and the fund must not invest in such securities. The governing instrument of the fund must contain specific prohibitions against accepting or investing in such securities.

(5) Maintenance by charitable organization required. The fund must be maintained by the same public charity to or for the use of which the irrevocable remainder interest is contributed. The requirement of maintenance will be satisfied where the public charity exercises control directly or indirectly over the fund. For example, this requirement of control shall ordinarily be met when the public charity has the power to remove the trustee or trustees of the fund and designate a new trustee or trustees. A national organization which carries out its purposes through local organizations, chapters, or auxiliary bodies with which it has an identity of aims and purposes may maintain a pooled income fund (otherwise satisfying the requirements of this paragraph) in which one or more local organizations, chapters, or auxiliary bodies which are public charities have been named as recipients of the remainder interests. For example, a national church body may maintain a pooled income fund where donors have transferred property to such fund and contributed an irrevocable remainder interest therein to or for the use of various local churches or educational institutions of such body. The fact that such local organizations or chapters have been separately incorporated from the national organization is immaterial.

(6) Prohibition against donor or beneficiary serving as trustee. The fund must not have, and the governing instru-

ment must prohibit the fund from having, as a trustee a donor to the fund or a beneficiary (other than the public charity to or for the use of which the remainder interest is contributed) of an income interest in any property transferred to such fund. Thus, if a donor or beneficiary (other than such public charity) directly or indirectly has general responsibilities with respect to the fund which are ordinarily exercised by a trustee, such fund does not meet the requirements of section 642(c)(5) and this paragraph. The fact that a donor of property to the fund, or a beneficiary of the fund, is a trustee, officer, director, or other official of the public charity to or for the use of which the remainder interest is contributed ordinarily will not prevent the fund from meeting the requirements of section 642(c)(5) and this paragraph.

(7) Income of beneficiary to be based on rate of return of fund. Each beneficiary entitled to income of any taxable year of the fund must receive such income in an amount determined by the rate of return earned by the fund for such taxable year with respect to his income interest, computed as provided in paragraph (c) of this section. The governing instrument of the fund shall direct the trustee to distribute income currently or within the first 65 days following the close of the taxable year in which the income is earned. Any such payment made after the close of the taxable year shall be treated as paid on the last day of the taxable year. A statement shall be attached to the return of the pooled income fund indicating the date and amount of such payments after the close of the taxable year. Subject to the provisions of part I, subchapter J, chapter 1 of the Code, the beneficiary shall include in his gross income all amounts properly paid, credited, or required to be distributed to the beneficiary during the taxable year or years of the fund ending within or with his taxable year. The governing instrument shall provide that the income interest of any designated beneficiary shall either terminate with the last regular payment which was made before the death of the beneficiary or be pro-rated to the date of his death.

(8) Termination of life income interest. Upon the termination of the income interest retained or created by any donor, the trustee shall sever from the fund an amount equal to the value of the remainder interest in the property upon which the income interest is based. The value of the remainder interest for such purpose may be either (i) its value as of the determination date next succeeding the termination of the income interest or (ii) its value as of the date on which the last regular payment was made before the death of the beneficiary if the income interest is terminated on such payment date. The amount so severed from the fund must either be paid to, or retained for the use of, the designated public charity, as provided in the governing instrument. However, see subparagraph (3) of this paragraph for rules relating to commingling of property.

(c) Allocation of income to beneficiary. *(1) In general.* Every income interest retained or created in property transferred to a pooled income fund shall be assigned a proportionate share of the annual income earned by the fund, such share, or unit of participation, being based on the fair market value of such property on the date of transfer, as provided in this paragraph.

(2) Units of participation. (i) Unit plan. (a) On each transfer of property by a donor to a pooled income fund, one or more units of participation in the fund shall be assigned to the beneficiary or beneficiaries of the income interest retained or created in such property, the number of units of participation being equal to the number obtained by dividing the fair market value of the property by the fair market value of a unit in the fund at the time of the transfer.

(b) The fair market value of a unit in the fund at the time of the transfer shall be determined by dividing the fair market value of all property in the fund at such time by the number of units then in the fund. The initial fair market value of a unit in a pooled income fund shall be the fair market value of the property transferred to the fund divided by the number of units assigned to the income interest in that property. The value of each unit of participation will fluctuate with each new transfer of property to the fund in relation to the appreciation or depreciation in the fair market value of the property in the fund, but all units in the fund will always have equal value.

(c) The share of income allocated to each unit of participation shall be determined by dividing the income of the fund for the taxable year by the outstanding number of units in the fund at the end of such year, except that, consistently with paragraph (b)(7) of this section, income shall be allocated to units outstanding during only part of such year by taking into consideration the period of time such units are outstanding. For this purpose the actual income of such part of the taxable year, or a prorated portion of the annual income, may be used, after making such adjustments as are reasonably necessary to reflect fluctuations during the year in the fair market value of the property in the fund.

(ii) Other plans. The governing instrument of the fund may provide any other reasonable method not described in subdivision (i) of this subparagraph for assigning units of participation in the fund and allocating income to such units which reaches a result reasonably consistent with the provisions of such subdivision.

(iii) Transfers between determination dates. For purposes of subdivision (i) and (ii) of this subparagraph, if a transfer of property to the fund by a donor occurs on other than a determination date, the number of units of participation assigned to the income interest in such property may be determined by using the fair market value of the property in the fund on the determination date immediately preceding the date of transfer (determined without regard to the property so transferred), subject, however, to appropriate adjustments on the next succeeding determination date. Such adjustments may be made by any reasonable method, including the use of a method whereby the fair market value of the property in the fund at the time of the transfer is deemed to be the average of the fair market values of the property in the fund on the determination dates immediately preceding and succeeding the date of transfer. For purposes of determining such average any property transferred to the fund between such preceding and succeeding dates, or on such succeeding date, shall be excluded. The application of this subdivision may be illustrated by the following example:

Example. The determination dates of a pooled income fund are the first day of each calendar month. On April 1, 1971, the fair market value of the property in the fund is $100,000, at which time 1,000 units of participation are outstanding with a value of $100 each. On April 15, 1971, B transfers property with a fair market value of $50,000 to the fund, retaining for himself for life an income interest in such property. No other property is transferred to the fund after April 1, 1971. On May 1, 1971, the fair market value of the property in the fund, including the property transferred by B, is $160,000. The average of the fair market values of the property in the fund (excluding the property transferred by B) on April 1 and May 1, 1971, is $105,000 ($100,000 + [$160,000 − $50,000] ÷ 2). Accordingly, the fair market value of a unit of participation in the fund on April 15, 1971, at the time of B's transfer may be deemed to be $105 ($105,000/1,000 units), and B is assigned 476.19 units of participation in the fund ($50,000/$105).

(3) Special rule for partial allocation of income to charity. Notwithstanding subparagraph (2) of this paragraph, the governing instrument may provide that a unit of participation is entitled to share in the income of the fund in a lesser amount than would otherwise be determined under such subparagraph, provided that the income otherwise allocable to the unit under such subparagraph is paid within the taxable year in which it is received to the public charity to or for the use of which the remainder interest is contributed under the governing instrument.

(4) Illustrations. The application of this paragraph may be illustrated by the following examples:

Example (1). On July 1, 1970, A and B transfer separate properties with a fair market value of $20,000 and $10,000, respectively, to a newly created pooled income fund which is maintained by Y University and uses as its taxable year the fiscal year ending June 30. A and B each retain in themselves for life an income interest in such property, the remainder interest being contributed to Y University. The pooled income fund assigns an initial value of $100 to each unit of participation in the fund, and under the governing instruments A receives 200 units, and B receives 100 units, in the fund. On October 1, 1970, which is a determination date, C transfers property to the fund with a fair market value of $12,000, retaining in himself for life an income interest in such property and contributing the remainder interest to Y University. The fair market value of the property in the fund at the time of C's transfer is $36,000. The fair market value of A's and B's units at the time of such transfer is $120 each ($36,000/300). By reason of his transfer of property C is assigned 100 units of participation in the fund ($12,000/$120).

Example (2). Assume that the pooled income fund in example (1) earns $2,600 for its taxable year ending June 30, 1971, and there are no further contributions of property to the fund in such year. Further assume $300 is earned in the first quarter ending September 30, 1970. Therefore, the fund earns $1 per unit for the first quarter ($300 divided by 300 units outstanding) and $5.75 per unit for the remainder of the taxable year ([$2,600 – $300] divided by 400 units outstanding). If the fund distributes its income for the year based on its actual earnings per quarter, the income must be distributed as follows:

Beneficiary	Share of income
A	$1,350 ([200 × $1] + [200 × $5.75]).
B	$ 675 ([100 × $1] + [100 × $5.75]).
C	$ 575 (100 × $575).

Example (3). (a) On July 1, 1970, A and B transfer separate properties with a fair market value of $10,000 and $20,000, respectively, to a newly created pooled income fund which is maintained by X University and uses as its taxable year the fiscal year ending June 30. A and B each retain in themselves an income interest for life in such property, the remainder interest being contributed to X University. The governing instrument provides that each unit of participation in the fund shall have a value of not more than its initial fair market value; the instrument also provides that the income allocable to appreciation in the fair market value of such unit (to the extent in excess of its initial fair market value) at the end of each quarter of the fiscal year is to be distributed currently to X University. On October 1, 1970, which is a determination date, C contributes to the fund property with a fair market value of $60,000 and retains in himself an income interest for life in such property, the remainder interest being contributed to X University. The initial fair market value of the units assigned to A, B, and C is $100. A, B, and C's units of participation are as follows:

Beneficiary	Units of participation
A	100 ($10,000 divided by $100).
B	200 ($20,000 divided by $100).
C	600 ($60,000 divided by $100).

(b) The fair market value of the property in the fund at the time of C's contribution is $40,000. Assuming the fair market value of the property in the fund is $100,000 on December 31, 1970, and that the income of the fund for the second quarter ending December 31, 1970, is $2,000, the income is shared by the income beneficiaries and X University as follows:

Beneficiary	Allocation of income
A, B, and C	90% ($90,000 divided by $100,000).
X University	10% ($10,000 divided by $100,000).

(c) For the quarter ending December 31, 1970, each unit of participation is allocated $2 (90 percent × $2,000 divided by 900) of the income earned for that quarter. A, B, C, and X University share in the income as follows:

Beneficiary	Share of income
A	$200 (100 × $2).
B	$400 (200 × $2).
C	$1,200 (600 × $2).
X University	$200 (10% × $2,000).

T.D. 7105, 4/5/71, amend T.D. 7125, 6/7/71, T.D. 7357, 5/30/75, T.D. 7633, 7/19/79, T.D. 9102, 12/30/2003.

§ 1.642(c)-6 Valuation of a remainder interest in property transferred to a pooled income fund.

(a) In general. *(1)* For purposes of sections 170, 2055, 2106, and 2522, the fair market value of a remainder interest in property transferred to a pooled income fund is its present value determined under paragraph (d) of this section.

(2) The present value of a remainder interest at the time of the transfer of property to the pooled income fund is determined by computing the present value (at the time of the transfer) of the life income interest and subtracting that value from the fair market value of the transferred property on the valuation date. The fact that the income beneficiary may not receive the last income payment, as provided in paragraph (b)(7) of section 1.642(c)-5, is not taken into account for purposes of determining the value of the life income interest. For purposes of this section, the valuation date is the date on which property is transferred to the fund by the donor except that, for purposes of section 2055 or 2106, it is the alternate valuation date, if elected, under the provisions and limitations set forth in section 2032 and the regulations thereunder.

(3) Any claim for a deduction on any return for the value of the remainder interest in property transferred to a pooled income fund must be supported by a statement attached to

the return showing the computation of the present value of the interest.

(b) Actuarial computations by the Internal Revenue Service. The regulations in this and in related sections provide tables of actuarial factors and examples that illustrate the use of the tables in determining the value of remainder interests in property. Section 1.7520-1(c)(2) refers to government publications that provide additional tables of factors and examples of computations for more complex situations. If the computation requires the use of a factor that is not provided in this section, the Commissioner may supply the factor upon a request for a ruling. A request for a ruling must be accompanied by a recitation of the facts including the pooled income fund's highest yearly rate of return for the 3 taxable years immediately preceding the date of transfer, the date of birth of each measuring life, and copies of the relevant documents. A request for a ruling must comply with the instructions for requesting a ruling published periodically in the Internal Revenue Bulletin (see sections 601.201 and 601.601(d)(2)(ii)(b) of this chapter) and include payment of the required user fee. If the Commissioner furnishes the factor, a copy of the letter supplying the factor should be attached to the tax return in which the deduction is claimed. If the commissioner does not furnish the factor, the taxpayer must furnish a factor computed in accordance with the principles set forth in this section.

(c) Computation of pooled income fund's yearly rate of return. *(1)* For purposes of determining the present value of the life income interest, the yearly rate of return earned by a pooled income fund for a taxable year is the percentage obtained by dividing the amount of income earned by the pooled income fund for the taxable year by an amount equal to—

(i) The average fair market value of the property in such fund for that taxable year; less

(ii) The corrective term adjustment.

(2) The average fair market value of the property in a pooled income fund for a taxable year shall be the sum of the amounts of the fair market value of all property held by the pooled income fund on each determination date, as defined in paragraph (a)(5)(vi) of § 1.642(c)-5, of such taxable year divided by the number of determination dates in such taxable year. For such purposes the fair market value of property held by the fund shall be determined without including any income earned by the fund.

(3) (i) The corrective term adjustment shall be the sum of the products obtained by multiplying each income payment made by the pooled income fund within its taxable year by the percentage set forth in column (2) of the following table opposite the period within such year, set forth in column (1), which includes the date on which that payment is made:

Table

(1) Payment period	(2) Percentage of payment
Last week of 4th quarter	0
Balance of 4th quarter	25
Last week of 3d quarter	25
Balance of 3d quarter	50
Last week of 2d quarter	50
Balance of 2d quarter	75
Last week of 1st quarter	75
Balance of 1st quarter	100

(ii) If the taxable year of the fund consists of less than 12 months, the corrective term adjustment shall be the sum of the products obtained by multiplying each income payment made by the pooled income fund within such taxable year by the percentage obtained by subtracting from 1 a fraction the numerator of which is the number of days from the first day of such taxable year to the date of such income payment and the denominator of which is 365.

(4) A pooled income fund's method of calculating its yearly rate of return must be supported by a full statement attached to the income tax return of the pooled income fund for each taxable year.

(5) The application of this paragraph may be illustrated by the following examples:

Example (1). (a) The pooled income fund maintained by W University has established determination dates on the first day of each calendar quarter. The pooled income fund is on a calendar-year basis. The pooled income fund earned $5,000 of income during 1971. The fair market value of its property (determined without including any income earned by the fund), and the income paid out, on the first day of each calendar quarter in 1971 are as follows:

Date	Fair market value of property	Income payment
Jan. 1	$100,000	$1,200
Apr. 1	105,000	1,200
July 1	95,000	1,200
Oct. 1	100,000	1,400
	400,000	5,000

(b) The average fair market value of the property in the fund for 1971 is $100,000 ($400,000, divided by 4).

(c) The corrective term adjustment for 1971 is $3,050, determined by applying the percentages obtained in column (2) of the table in subparagraph (3) of this paragraph:

Multiplication	Product
100% × $1,200	$1,200
75% × $1,200	900
50% × $1,200	600
25% × $1,400	350
Sum of products	3,050

(d) The pooled income fund's yearly rate of return for 1971 is 5.157 percent, determined as follows:

$$\frac{\$5{,}000}{\$100{,}000 - \$3{,}050} = 0.05157$$

Example (2). (a) The pooled income fund maintained by X University has established determination dates on the first day of each calendar quarter. The pooled income fund is on a calendar-year basis. The pooled income fund earned $5,000 of income during 1971 and paid out $3,000 on December 15, 1971, and $2,000 on January 15, 1972, the last amount being treated under paragraph (b)(7) of § 1.642(c)-5 as paid on December 31, 1971. The fair market value of its property (determined without including any income earned by the fund) on the determination dates in 1971 and the income paid out during 1971 are as follows:

Date	Fair market value of property	Income payment
Jan. 1	$125,000	
Apr. 1	125,000	
July 1	75,000	
Oct. 1	75,000	
Dec. 15		$3,000
Dec. 31		2,000
	400,000	5,000

(b) The average fair market value of the property in the fund for 1971 is $100,000 ($400,000 divided by 4).

(c) The corrective term adjustment for 1971 is $750, determined by applying the percentages obtained in column (2) of the table in subparagraph (3) of this paragraph:

Multiplication	Product
0% × $2,000	$....
25% × $3,000	750
Sum of products	750

(d) The pooled income fund's yearly rate of return for 1971 is 5.038 percent, determined as follows:

$$\frac{\$5{,}000}{\$100{,}000 - \$750} = 0.05038$$

(d) Valuation. The present value of the remainder interest in property transferred to a pooled income fund after April 30, 1999, is determined under paragraph (e) of this section. The present value of the remainder interest in property transferred to a pooled income fund for which the valuation date is before May 1, 1999, is determined under the following sections:

Valuation Dates		Applicable regulations
After	Before	
	01-01-52	1.642(c)-6A(a)
12-31-51	01-01-71	1.642(c)-6A(b)
12-31-70	12-01-83	1.642(c)-6A(c)
11-30-83	05-01-89	1.642(c)-6A(d)
04-30-89	05-01-99	1.642(c)-6A(e)

(e) Present value of the remainder interest in the case of transfers to pooled income funds for which the valuation date is after April 30, 1999. *(1) In general.* In the case of transfers to pooled income funds for which the valuation date is after April 30, 1999, the present value of a remainder interest is determined under this section. See, however, § 1.7520-3(b) (relating to exceptions to the use of prescribed tables under certain circumstances). The present value of a remainder interest that is dependent on the termination of the life of one individual is computed by the use of Table S in paragraph (e)(6) of this section. For purposes of the computations under this section, the age of an individual is the age at the individual's nearest birthday.

(2) Transitional rules for valuation of transfers to pooled income funds. (i) For purposes of sections 2055, 2106, or 2624, if on May 1, 1999, the decedent was mentally incompetent so that the disposition of the property could not be changed, and the decedent died after April 30, 1999, without having regained competency to dispose of the decedent's property, or the decedent died within 90 days of the date that the decedent first regained competency after April 30, 1999, the present value of a remainder interest is determined as if the valuation date with respect to the decedent's gross estate is either before May 1, 1999, or after April 30, 1999, at the option of the decedent's executor.

(ii) For purposes of sections 170, 2055, 2106, 2522, or 2624, in the case of transfers to a pooled income fund for which the valuation date is after April 30, 1999, and before July 1, 1999, the present value of the remainder interest under this section is determined by use of the section 7520 interest rate for the month in which the valuation date occurs (see §§ 1.7520-1(b) and 1.7520-2(a)(2)) and the appropriate actuarial tables under either paragraph (e)(6) of this section or § 1.642(c)-6A(e)(5), at the option of the donor or the decedent's executor, as the case may be.

(iii) For purposes of paragraphs (e)(2)(i) and (ii) of this section, where the donor or decedent's executor is given the option to use the appropriate actuarial tables under either paragraph (e)(6) of this section or § 1.642(c)-6A(e)(5), the donor or decedent's executor must use the same actuarial table with respect to each individual transaction and with respect to all transfers occurring on the valuation date (for example, gift and income tax charitable deductions with respect to the same transfer must be determined based on the same tables, and all assets includible in the gross estate and/or estate tax deductions claimed must be valued based on the same tables).

(3) Present value of a remainder interest. The present value of a remainder interest in property transferred to a pooled income fund is computed on the basis of—

(i) Life contingencies determined from the values of lx that are set forth in Table 90CM in § 20.2031-7(d)(7) of this chapter (see § 20.2031-7A of this chapter for certain prior periods); and

(ii) Discount at a rate of interest, compounded annually, equal to the highest yearly rate of return of the pooled income fund for the 3 taxable years immediately preceding its taxable year in which the transfer of property to the fund is made. For purposes of this paragraph (e), the yearly rate of return of a pooled income fund is determined as provided in paragraph (c) of this section unless the highest rate of return is deemed to be the rate described in paragraph (e)(4) of this section for funds in existence less than 3 taxable years. For purposes of this paragraph (e)(3)(ii), the first taxable year of a pooled income fund is considered a taxable year even though the taxable year consists of less than 12 months. However, appropriate adjustments must be made to annualize the rate of return earned by the fund for that period. Where it appears from the facts and circumstances that the highest yearly rate of return of the fund for the 3 taxable years immediately preceding the taxable year in which the transfer of property is made has been purposely manipulated to be substantially less than the rate of return that would otherwise be reasonably anticipated with the purpose of obtaining an excessive charitable deduction, that rate of return may not be used. In that case, the highest yearly rate of return of the fund is determined by treating the fund as a pooled income fund that has been in existence for less than 3 preceding taxable years.

(4) Pooled income funds in existence less than 3 taxable years. If a pooled income fund has been in existence less than 3 taxable years immediately preceding the taxable year in which the transfer is made to the fund and the transfer to the fund is made after April 30, 1989, the highest rate of return is deemed to be the interest rate (rounded to the nearest two-tenths of one percent) that is 1 percent less than the highest annual average of the monthly section 7520 rates for the 3 calendar years immediately preceding the calendar year

in which the transfer to the pooled income fund is made. The deemed rate of return for transfers to new pooled income funds is recomputed each calendar year using the monthly section 7520 rates for the 3-year period immediately preceding the calendar year in which each transfer to the fund is made until the fund has been in existence for 3 taxable years and can compute its highest rate of return for the 3 taxable years immediately preceding the taxable year in which the transfer of property to the fund is made in accordance with the rules set forth in the first sentence of paragraph (e)(3)(ii) of this section.

(5) Computation of value of remainder interest. The factor that is used in determining the present value of a remainder interest that is dependent on the termination of the life of one individual is the factor from Table S in paragraph (e)(6) of this section under the appropriate yearly rate of return opposite the number that corresponds to the age of the individual upon whose life the value of the remainder interest is based (see § 1.642(c)-6A for certain prior periods). The tables in paragraph (e)(6) of this section include factors for yearly rates of return from 4.2 to 14 percent. Many actuarial factors not contained in the tables in paragraph (e)(6) of this section are contained in Table S in Internal Revenue Service Publication 1457, "Actuarial Values, Book Aleph," (7-1999). A copy of this publication is available for purchase from the Superintendent of Documents, United States Government Printing Office, Washington, DC 20402. For other situations, see paragraph (b) of this section. If the yearly rate of return is a percentage that is between the yearly rates of return for which factors are provided, a linear interpolation must be made. The present value of the remainder interest is determined by multiplying the fair market value of the property on the valuation date by the appropriate remainder factor. This paragraph (e)(5) may be illustrated by the following example:

Example. A, who is 54 years and 8 months, transfers $100,000 to a pooled income fund, and retains a life income interest in the property. The highest yearly rate of return earned by the fund for its 3 preceding taxable years is 9.47 percent. In Table S, the remainder factor opposite 55 years under 9.4 percent is .17449 and under 9.6 percent is .17001. The present value of the remainder interest is $17,292.00, computed as follows:

Factor at 9.4 percent for age 55	.17449
Factor at 9.6 percent for age 55	.17001
Difference	.00448

Interpolation adjustment:

$$\frac{9.47\% - 9.4\%}{0.2\%} = \frac{x}{.00448}$$

x = .00157

Factor at 9.4 percent for age 55	.17449
Less: Interpolation adjustment	.00157
Interpolated factor	.17292
Present value of remainder interest:	
($100,000 × .17292)	$17,292.00

(6) Actuarial tables. In the case of transfers for which the valuation date is after April 30, 1999, the present value of a remainder interest dependent on the termination of one life in the case of a transfer to a pooled income fund is determined by use of the following Table S:

Table S.--Based on Life Table 90CM Single Life Remainder Factors

Applicable After April 30, 1999

Age	[Interest rate] 4.2%	4.4%	4.6%	4.8%	5.0%	5.2%	5.4%	5.6%	5.8%	6.0%
0	.06752	.06130	.05586	.05109	.04691	.04322	.03998	.03711	.03458	.03233
1	.06137	.05495	.04932	.04438	.04003	.03620	.03283	.02985	.02721	.02487
2	.06325	.05667	.05088	.04580	.04132	.03737	.03388	.03079	.02806	.02563
3	.06545	.05869	.05275	.04752	.04291	.03883	.03523	.03203	.02920	.02668
4	.06784	.06092	.05482	.04944	.04469	.04048	.03676	.03346	.03052	.02791
5	.07040	.06331	.05705	.05152	.04662	.04229	.03845	.03503	.03199	.02928
6	.07310	.06583	.05941	.05372	.04869	.04422	.04025	.03672	.03357	.03076
7	.07594	.06849	.06191	.05607	.05089	.04628	.04219	.03854	.03528	.03236
8	.07891	.07129	.06453	.05853	.05321	.04846	.04424	.04046	.03709	.03407
9	.08203	.07423	.06731	.06115	.05567	.05079	.04643	.04253	.03904	.03592
10	.08532	.07734	.07024	.06392	.05829	.05326	.04877	.04474	.04114	.03790
11	.08875	.08059	.07331	.06683	.06104	.05587	.05124	.04709	.04336	.04002
12	.09233	.08398	.07653	.06989	.06394	.05862	.05385	.04957	.04572	.04226
13	.09601	.08748	.07985	.07304	.06693	.06146	.05655	.05214	.04816	.04458
14	.09974	.09102	.08322	.07624	.06997	.06435	.05929	.05474	.05064	.04694
15	.10350	.09460	.08661	.07946	.07303	.06725	.06204	.05735	.05312	.04930
16	.10728	.09818	.09001	.08268	.07608	.07014	.06479	.05996	.05559	.05164
17	.11108	.10179	.09344	.08592	.07916	.07306	.06755	.06257	.05807	.05399
18	.11494	.10545	.09691	.08921	.08227	.07601	.07034	.06521	.06057	.05636
19	.11889	.10921	.10047	.09259	.08548	.07904	.07322	.06794	.06315	.05880
20	.12298	.11310	.10417	.09610	.08881	.08220	.07622	.07078	.06584	.06135
21	.12722	.11713	.10801	.09976	.09228	.08550	.07935	.07375	.06866	.06403
22	.13159	.12130	.11199	.10354	.09588	.08893	.08260	.07685	.07160	.06682
23	.13613	.12563	.11612	.10748	.09964	.09250	.08601	.08009	.07468	.06975
24	.14084	.13014	.12043	.11160	.10357	.09625	.08958	.08349	.07793	.07284
25	.14574	.13484	.12493	.11591	.10768	.10018	.09334	.08708	.08135	.07611
26	.15084	.13974	.12963	.12041	.11199	.10431	.09728	.09085	.08496	.07956
27	.15615	.14485	.13454	.12513	.11652	.10865	.10144	.09484	.08878	.08322

Age	[Interest rate] 4.2%	4.4%	4.6%	4.8%	5.0%	5.2%	5.4%	5.6%	5.8%	6.0%
28	.16166	.15016	.13965	.13004	.12124	.11319	.10580	.09901	.09279	.08706
29	.16737	.15567	.14497	.13516	.12617	.11792	.11035	.10339	.09699	.09109
30	.17328	.16138	.15048	.14047	.13129	.12286	.11510	.10796	.10138	.09532
31	.17938	.16728	.15618	.14599	.13661	.12799	.12004	.11272	.10597	.09974
32	.18568	.17339	.16210	.15171	.14214	.13333	.12520	.11769	.11076	.10435
33	.19220	.17972	.16824	.15766	.14790	.13889	.13058	.12289	.11578	.10920
34	.19894	.18627	.17460	.16383	.15388	.14468	.13618	.12831	.12102	.11426
35	.20592	.19307	.18121	.17025	.16011	.15073	.14204	.13399	.12652	.11958
36	.21312	.20010	.18805	.17691	.16658	.15701	.14814	.13990	.13225	.12514
37	.22057	.20737	.19514	.18382	.17331	.16356	.15450	.14608	.13825	.13096
38	.22827	.21490	.20251	.19100	.18031	.17038	.16113	.15253	.14452	.13705
39	.23623	.22270	.21013	.19845	.18759	.17747	.16805	.15927	.15108	.14344
40	.24446	.23078	.21805	.20620	.19516	.18487	.17527	.16631	.15795	.15013
41	.25298	.23915	.22626	.21425	.20305	.19259	.18282	.17368	.16514	.15715
42	.26178	.24782	.23478	.22262	.21125	.20062	.19069	.18138	.17267	.16450
43	.27087	.25678	.24360	.23129	.21977	.20898	.19888	.18941	.18053	.17220
44	.28025	.26603	.25273	.24027	.22860	.21766	.20740	.19777	.18873	.18023
45	.28987	.27555	.26212	.24953	.23772	.22664	.21622	.20644	.19724	.18858
46	.29976	.28533	.27179	.25908	.24714	.23591	.22536	.21542	.20606	.19725
47	.30987	.29535	.28171	.26889	.25682	.24546	.23476	.22468	.21518	.20621
48	.32023	.30563	.29190	.27897	.26678	.25530	.24447	.23425	.22460	.21549
49	.33082	.31615	.30234	.28931	.27702	.26543	.25447	.24412	.23434	.22509
50	.34166	.32694	.31306	.29995	.28756	.27586	.26479	.25432	.24441	.23502
51	.35274	.33798	.32404	.31085	.29838	.28658	.27541	.26482	.25479	.24528
52	.36402	.34924	.33525	.32200	.30946	.29757	.28630	.27561	.26547	.25584
53	.37550	.36070	.34668	.33339	.32078	.30882	.29746	.28667	.27643	.26669
54	.38717	.37237	.35833	.34500	.33234	.32031	.30888	.29801	.28766	.27782
55	.39903	.38424	.37019	.35683	.34413	.33205	.32056	.30961	.29918	.28925
56	.41108	.39631	.38227	.36890	.35617	.34405	.33250	.32149	.31099	.30097
57	.42330	.40857	.39455	.38118	.36844	.35629	.34469	.33363	.32306	.31297
58	.43566	.42098	.40699	.39364	.38089	.36873	.35710	.34600	.33538	.32522
59	.44811	.43351	.41956	.40623	.39350	.38133	.36968	.35855	.34789	.33768
60	.46066	.44613	.43224	.41896	.40624	.39408	.38243	.37127	.36058	.35033
61	.47330	.45887	.44505	.43182	.41914	.40699	.39535	.38418	.37347	.36318
62	.48608	.47175	.45802	.44485	.43223	.42011	.40848	.39732	.38660	.37629
63	.49898	.48478	.47115	.45807	.44550	.43343	.42184	.41069	.39997	.38966
64	.51200	.49793	.48442	.47143	.45895	.44694	.43539	.42427	.41357	.40326
65	.52512	.51121	.49782	.48495	.47255	.46062	.44912	.43805	.42738	.41709
66	.53835	.52461	.51137	.49862	.48634	.47449	.46307	.45206	.44143	.43118
67	.55174	.53818	.52511	.51250	.50034	.48860	.47727	.46633	.45576	.44556
68	.56524	.55188	.53899	.52654	.51452	.50291	.49168	.48083	.47034	.46020
69	.57882	.56568	.55299	.54071	.52885	.51737	.50627	.49552	.48513	.47506
70	.59242	.57951	.56703	.55495	.54325	.53193	.52096	.51034	.50004	.49007
71	.60598	.59332	.58106	.56918	.55767	.54651	.53569	.52520	.51503	.50516
72	.61948	.60707	.59504	.58338	.57206	.56108	.55043	.54009	.53004	.52029
73	.63287	.62073	.60895	.59751	.58640	.57561	.56513	.55495	.54505	.53543
74	.64621	.63435	.62282	.61162	.60073	.59015	.57985	.56984	.56009	.55061
75	.65953	.64796	.63671	.62575	.61510	.60473	.59463	.58480	.57523	.56591
76	.67287	.66160	.65063	.63995	.62954	.61940	.60952	.59989	.59050	.58135
77	.68622	.67526	.66459	.65419	.64404	.63415	.62450	.61509	.60590	.59694
78	.69954	.68892	.67856	.66845	.65858	.64895	.63955	.63036	.62140	.61264
79	.71278	.70250	.69246	.68265	.67308	.66372	.65457	.64563	.63690	.62836
80	.72581	.71588	.70618	.69668	.68740	.67833	.66945	.66077	.65227	.64396
81	.73857	.72899	.71962	.71045	.70147	.69268	.68408	.67566	.66741	.65933
82	.75101	.74178	.73274	.72389	.71522	.70672	.69840	.69024	.68225	.67441
83	.76311	.75423	.74553	.73700	.72864	.72044	.71240	.70451	.69678	.68919
84	.77497	.76645	.75809	.74988	.74183	.73393	.72618	.71857	.71110	.70377
85	.78665	.77848	.77047	.76260	.75487	.74728	.73982	.73250	.72530	.71823
86	.79805	.79025	.78258	.77504	.76764	.76036	.75320	.74617	.73925	.73245
87	.80904	.80159	.79427	.78706	.77998	.77301	.76615	.75940	.75277	.74624
88	.81962	.81251	.80552	.79865	.79188	.78521	.77865	.77220	.76584	.75958
89	.82978	.82302	.81636	.80980	.80335	.79699	.79072	.78455	.77847	.77248
90	.83952	.83309	.82676	.82052	.81437	.80831	.80234	.79645	.79064	.78492
91	.84870	.84260	.83658	.83064	.82479	.81902	.81332	.80771	.80217	.79671

Age	[Interest rate] 4.2%	4.4%	4.6%	4.8%	5.0%	5.2%	5.4%	5.6%	5.8%	6.0%
92	.85716	.85136	.84563	.83998	.83441	.82891	.82348	.81812	.81283	.80761
93	.86494	.85942	.85396	.84858	.84326	.83801	.83283	.82771	.82266	.81767
94	.87216	.86690	.86170	.85657	.85149	.84648	.84153	.83664	.83181	.82704
95	.87898	.87397	.86902	.86412	.85928	.85450	.84977	.84510	.84049	.83592
96	.88537	.88060	.87587	.87121	.86659	.86203	.85751	.85305	.84864	.84427
97	.89127	.88672	.88221	.87775	.87335	.86898	.86467	.86040	.85618	.85200
98	.89680	.89245	.88815	.88389	.87968	.87551	.87138	.86730	.86326	.85926
99	.90217	.89803	.89393	.88987	.88585	.88187	.87793	.87402	.87016	.86633
100	.90738	.90344	.89953	.89567	.89183	.88804	.88428	.88056	.87687	.87322
101	.91250	.90876	.90504	.90137	.89772	.89412	.89054	.88699	.88348	.88000
102	.91751	.91396	.91045	.90696	.90350	.90007	.89668	.89331	.88997	.88666
103	.92247	.91912	.91579	.91249	.90922	.90598	.90276	.89957	.89640	.89326
104	.92775	.92460	.92148	.91839	.91532	.91227	.90924	.90624	.90326	.90031
105	.93290	.92996	.92704	.92415	.92127	.91841	.91558	.91276	.90997	.90719
106	.93948	.93680	.93415	.93151	.92889	.92628	.92370	.92113	.91857	.91604
107	.94739	.94504	.94271	.94039	.93808	.93579	.93351	.93124	.92899	.92675
108	.95950	.95767	.95585	.95404	.95224	.95045	.94867	.94689	.94512	.94336
109	.97985	.97893	.97801	.97710	.97619	.97529	.97438	.97348	.97259	.97170

Age	6.2%	6.4%	6.6%	6.8%	7.0%	7.2%	7.4%	7.6%	7.8%	8.0%
0	.03034	.02857	.02700	.02559	.02433	.02321	.02220	.02129	.02047	.01973
1	.02279	.02094	.01929	.01782	.01650	.01533	.01427	.01331	.01246	.01168
2	.02347	.02155	.01983	.01829	.01692	.01569	.01458	.01358	.01268	.01187
3	.02444	.02243	.02065	.01905	.01761	.01632	.01516	.01412	.01317	.01232
4	.02558	.02349	.02163	.01996	.01846	.01712	.01590	.01481	.01382	.01292
5	.02686	.02469	.02275	.02101	.01945	.01804	.01677	.01562	.01458	.01364
6	.02825	.02600	.02398	.02217	.02053	.01906	.01773	.01653	.01544	.01445
7	.02976	.02742	.02532	.02343	.02172	.02019	.01880	.01754	.01640	.01536
8	.03137	.02894	.02675	.02479	.02301	.02140	.01995	.01864	.01744	.01635
9	.03311	.03059	.02832	.02627	.02442	.02274	.02122	.01985	.01859	.01745
10	.03499	.03237	.03001	.02788	.02595	.02420	.02262	.02118	.01987	.01867
11	.03700	.03428	.03183	.02961	.02760	.02578	.02413	.02262	.02125	.02000
12	.03913	.03632	.03377	.03146	.02937	.02748	.02575	.02418	.02275	.02144
13	.04135	.03843	.03579	.03339	.03122	.02924	.02744	.02580	.02431	.02294
14	.04359	.04057	.03783	.03534	.03308	.03102	.02915	.02744	.02587	.02444
15	.04584	.04270	.03986	.03728	.03493	.03279	.03083	.02905	.02742	.02593
16	.04806	.04482	.04187	.03919	.03674	.03452	.03248	.03063	.02892	.02736
17	.05029	.04692	.04387	.04108	.03855	.03623	.03411	.03218	.03040	.02877
18	.05253	.04905	.04588	.04299	.04036	.03795	.03574	.03373	.03187	.03017
19	.05484	.05124	.04796	.04496	.04222	.03972	.03742	.03532	.03339	.03161
20	.05726	.05354	.05013	.04702	.04418	.04158	.03919	.03700	.03498	.03313
21	.05980	.05595	.05242	.04920	.04625	.04354	.04105	.03877	.03667	.03473
22	.06246	.05847	.05482	.05147	.04841	.04559	.04301	.04063	.03844	.03642
23	.06524	.06112	.05734	.05387	.05069	.04777	.04508	.04260	.04032	.03821
24	.06819	.06392	.06001	.05642	.05312	.05008	.04728	.04470	.04232	.04012
25	.07131	.06690	.06285	.05913	.05570	.05255	.04964	.04695	.04447	.04218
26	.07460	.07005	.06586	.06200	.05845	.05518	.05215	.04936	.04677	.04438
27	.07810	.07340	.06907	.06508	.06140	.05800	.05485	.05195	.04925	.04676
28	.08179	.07693	.07246	.06833	.06451	.06098	.05772	.05469	.05189	.04929
29	.08566	.08065	.07603	.07176	.06780	.06414	.06075	.05761	.05469	.05198
30	.08973	.08456	.07978	.07536	.07127	.06748	.06396	.06069	.05766	.05483
31	.09398	.08865	.08372	.07915	.07491	.07098	.06733	.06394	.06078	.05785
32	.09843	.09294	.08785	.08313	.07875	.07468	.07089	.06737	.06409	.06103
33	.10310	.09745	.09220	.08732	.08279	.07858	.07466	.07100	.06759	.06441
34	.10799	.10217	.09676	.09173	.08705	.08269	.07862	.07483	.07129	.06798
35	.11314	.10715	.10157	.09638	.09155	.08704	.08283	.07890	.07522	.07179
36	.11852	.11236	.10662	.10127	.09628	.09162	.08726	.08319	.07938	.07581
37	.12416	.11783	.11193	.10641	.10126	.09645	.09194	.08772	.08377	.08006
38	.13009	.12359	.11751	.11183	.10652	.10155	.09689	.09253	.08843	.08459
39	.13629	.12962	.12338	.11753	.11206	.10693	.10212	.09761	.09337	.08938
40	.14281	.13597	.12955	.12355	.11791	.11262	.10766	.10299	.09860	.09447
41	.14966	.14264	.13606	.12989	.12409	.11864	.11352	.10870	.10417	.09989
42	.15685	.14966	.14291	.13657	.13061	.12500	.11972	.11475	.11006	.10564

Age	6.2%	6.4%	6.6%	6.8%	7.0%	7.2%	7.4%	7.6%	7.8%	8.0%
43	.16437	.15702	.15010	.14360	.13747	.13171	.12627	.12115	.11631	.11174
44	.17224	.16472	.15764	.15098	.14469	.13876	.13317	.12789	.12290	.11819
45	.18042	.17274	.16550	.15867	.15223	.14615	.14040	.13496	.12982	.12496
46	.18893	.18110	.17370	.16671	.16011	.15387	.14796	.14238	.13708	.13207
47	.19775	.18975	.18220	.17505	.16830	.16190	.15584	.15010	.14466	.13950
48	.20688	.19873	.19102	.18373	.17682	.17027	.16406	.15817	.15258	.14727
49	.21633	.20804	.20018	.19274	.18568	.17898	.17262	.16658	.16084	.15539
50	.22612	.21769	.20969	.20210	.19490	.18805	.18155	.17536	.16948	.16388
51	.23625	.22769	.21955	.21182	.20448	.19749	.19084	.18452	.17849	.17275
52	.24669	.23799	.22973	.22186	.21438	.20726	.20047	.19400	.18784	.18196
53	.25742	.24861	.24022	.23222	.22461	.21735	.21043	.20383	.19753	.19151
54	.26845	.25952	.25101	.24290	.23516	.22777	.22072	.21399	.20756	.20140
55	.27978	.27074	.26212	.25389	.24604	.23853	.23136	.22450	.21793	.21166
56	.29140	.28227	.27355	.26522	.25725	.24963	.24233	.23535	.22867	.22227
57	.30333	.29411	.28529	.27686	.26879	.26106	.25365	.24656	.23976	.23324
58	.31551	.30621	.29731	.28878	.28061	.27278	.26528	.25807	.25116	.24453
59	.32790	.31854	.30956	.30095	.29269	.28477	.27716	.26986	.26284	.25610
60	.34050	.33107	.32202	.31334	.30500	.29699	.28929	.28190	.27478	.26794
61	.35331	.34384	.33473	.32598	.31757	.30948	.30170	.29422	.28701	.28007
62	.36639	.35688	.34772	.33892	.33044	.32229	.31443	.30687	.29958	.29255
63	.37974	.37020	.36101	.35216	.34363	.33542	.32750	.31986	.31250	.30539
64	.39334	.38378	.37456	.36568	.35711	.34884	.34087	.33317	.32574	.31857
65	.40718	.39761	.38838	.37947	.37087	.36257	.35455	.34681	.33932	.33208
66	.42128	.41172	.40249	.39357	.38496	.37663	.36858	.36079	.35326	.34597
67	.43569	.42616	.41694	.40803	.39941	.39107	.38299	.37518	.36761	.36028
68	.45038	.44089	.43170	.42281	.41419	.40585	.39777	.38994	.38235	.37499
69	.46531	.45587	.44672	.43786	.42927	.42094	.41286	.40503	.39743	.39006
70	.48040	.47103	.46194	.45312	.44456	.43626	.42820	.42038	.41278	.40540
71	.49558	.48629	.47727	.46851	.46000	.45174	.44371	.43591	.42832	.42095
72	.51082	.50162	.49268	.48399	.47554	.46733	.45934	.45157	.44401	.43666
73	.52607	.51697	.50813	.49952	.49114	.48299	.47506	.46733	.45981	.45249
74	.54139	.53241	.52367	.51515	.50686	.49879	.49092	.48325	.47578	.46849
75	.55683	.54798	.53936	.53095	.52276	.51477	.50698	.49938	.49197	.48474
76	.57243	.56373	.55524	.54696	.53888	.53100	.52330	.51579	.50846	.50130
77	.58819	.57965	.57132	.56318	.55523	.54747	.53988	.53247	.52523	.51815
78	.60408	.59572	.58755	.57957	.57177	.56414	.55668	.54939	.54225	.53527
79	.62001	.61184	.60385	.59604	.58840	.58092	.57360	.56644	.55943	.55256
80	.63582	.62786	.62007	.61244	.60497	.59765	.59048	.58347	.57659	.56985
81	.65142	.64367	.63608	.62864	.62135	.61421	.60721	.60034	.59361	.58701
82	.66673	.65920	.65182	.64458	.63748	.63052	.62368	.61698	.61041	.60395
83	.68175	.67444	.66728	.66024	.65334	.64656	.63991	.63338	.62696	.62066
84	.69657	.68950	.68256	.67574	.66904	.66246	.65599	.64964	.64340	.63727
85	.71128	.70446	.69775	.69116	.68467	.67830	.67204	.66587	.65982	.65386
86	.72576	.71919	.71272	.70636	.70010	.69394	.68789	.68193	.67606	.67029
87	.73981	.73349	.72726	.72114	.71511	.70917	.70333	.69757	.69190	.68632
88	.75342	.74735	.74137	.73548	.72968	.72396	.71833	.71279	.70732	.70194
89	.76658	.76076	.75503	.74938	.74381	.73832	.73290	.72757	.72231	.71712
90	.77928	.77371	.76823	.76281	.75748	.75221	.74702	.74190	.73684	.73186
91	.79131	.78600	.78075	.77557	.77046	.76542	.76044	.75553	.75068	.74589
92	.80246	.79737	.79235	.78740	.78250	.77767	.77290	.76818	.76353	.75893
93	.81274	.80788	.80307	.79832	.79363	.78899	.78441	.77989	.77542	.77100
94	.82232	.81766	.81306	.80850	.80401	.79956	.79517	.79082	.78653	.78228
95	.83141	.82695	.82254	.81818	.81387	.80961	.80539	.80122	.79710	.79302
96	.83996	.83569	.83147	.82729	.82316	.81907	.81503	.81103	.80707	.80315
97	.84787	.84378	.83973	.83573	.83176	.82784	.82396	.82012	.81632	.81255
98	.85530	.85138	.84750	.84366	.83985	.83609	.83236	.82867	.82502	.82140
99	.86255	.85880	.85508	.85140	.84776	.84415	.84057	.83703	.83353	.83005
100	.86960	.86601	.86246	.85894	.85546	.85200	.84858	.84519	.84183	.83849
101	.87655	.87313	.86974	.86638	.86305	.85975	.85648	.85324	.85003	.84684
102	.88338	.88012	.87689	.87369	.87052	.86738	.86426	.86116	.85809	.85505
103	.89015	.88706	.88399	.88095	.87793	.87494	.87197	.86903	.86611	.86321
104	.89737	.89446	.89157	.88871	.88586	.88304	.88024	.87745	.87469	.87195
105	.90443	.90170	.89898	.89628	.89360	.89094	.88830	.88568	.88307	.88049
106	.91351	.91101	.90852	.90605	.90359	.90115	.89873	.89632	.89392	.89154
107	.92452	.92230	.92010	.91791	.91573	.91356	.91141	.90927	.90714	.90502

Age	6.2%	6.4%	6.6%	6.8%	7.0%	7.2%	7.4%	7.6%	7.8%	8.0%
108	.94161	.93987	.93814	.93641	.93469	.93298	.93128	.92958	.92790	.92622
109	.97081	.96992	.96904	.96816	.96729	.96642	.96555	.96468	.96382	.96296

Age	8.2%	8.4%	8.6%	8.8%	9.0%	9.2%	9.4%	9.6%	9.8%	10.0%
0	.01906	.01845	.01790	.01740	.01694	.01652	.01613	.01578	.01546	.01516
1	.01098	.01034	.00977	.00924	.00876	.00833	.00793	.00756	.00722	.00691
2	.01113	.01046	.00986	.00930	.00880	.00834	.00791	.00753	.00717	.00684
3	.01155	.01084	.01020	.00962	.00909	.00860	.00816	.00775	.00737	.00702
4	.01211	.01137	.01069	.01008	.00952	.00900	.00853	.00810	.00770	.00733
5	.01279	.01201	.01130	.01065	.01006	.00952	.00902	.00856	.00814	.00775
6	.01356	.01274	.01199	.01131	.01068	.01011	.00959	.00910	.00865	.00824
7	.01442	.01356	.01277	.01205	.01140	.01079	.01023	.00972	.00925	.00881
8	.01536	.01446	.01363	.01287	.01218	.01154	.01096	.01041	.00991	.00945
9	.01641	.01546	.01460	.01380	.01307	.01240	.01178	.01120	.01068	.01019
10	.01758	.01659	.01567	.01484	.01407	.01336	.01270	.01210	.01154	.01103
11	.01886	.01781	.01686	.01598	.01517	.01442	.01373	.01310	.01251	.01196
12	.02024	.01915	.01814	.01721	.01636	.01558	.01485	.01419	.01357	.01299
13	.02168	.02054	.01948	.01851	.01762	.01679	.01603	.01533	.01467	.01407
14	.02313	.02193	.02083	.01981	.01887	.01801	.01721	.01646	.01578	.01514
15	.02456	.02330	.02214	.02107	.02009	.01918	.01834	.01756	.01684	.01617
16	.02593	.02462	.02340	.02229	.02126	.02030	.01942	.01860	.01785	.01714
17	.02728	.02590	.02463	.02346	.02238	.02138	.02046	.01960	.01880	.01806
18	.02861	.02717	.02584	.02462	.02348	.02243	.02146	.02056	.01972	.01894
19	.02998	.02847	.02708	.02580	.02461	.02351	.02249	.02154	.02066	.01984
20	.03142	.02984	.02839	.02704	.02580	.02465	.02357	.02258	.02165	.02079
21	.03295	.03130	.02978	.02837	.02706	.02585	.02473	.02368	.02271	.02180
22	.03455	.03283	.03124	.02976	.02839	.02712	.02594	.02484	.02382	.02286
23	.03626	.03446	.03279	.03124	.02981	.02847	.02723	.02608	.02500	.02400
24	.03809	.03620	.03446	.03283	.03133	.02993	.02863	.02741	.02628	.02522
25	.04005	.03808	.03625	.03456	.03298	.03151	.03014	.02887	.02768	.02656
26	.04216	.04010	.03819	.03641	.03476	.03322	.03178	.03044	.02919	.02802
27	.04444	.04229	.04029	.03843	.03670	.03508	.03357	.03217	.03085	.02962
28	.04687	.04463	.04254	.04059	.03877	.03708	.03550	.03402	.03263	.03133
29	.04946	.04712	.04493	.04289	.04099	.03922	.03756	.03600	.03455	.03318
30	.05221	.04976	.04748	.04534	.04335	.04149	.03975	.03812	.03659	.03515
31	.05511	.05255	.05017	.04794	.04585	.04390	.04208	.04037	.03876	.03725
32	.05818	.05551	.05302	.05069	.04851	.04647	.04455	.04276	.04107	.03948
33	.06144	.05866	.05606	.05363	.05135	.04921	.04720	.04532	.04355	.04188
34	.06489	.06200	.05928	.05674	.05436	.05212	.05002	.04805	.04619	.04444
35	.06857	.06555	.06273	.06007	.05758	.05524	.05304	.05097	.04902	.04718
36	.07246	.06932	.06638	.06361	.06101	.05856	.05626	.05409	.05205	.05012
37	.07659	.07332	.07025	.06737	.06466	.06210	.05969	.05742	.05528	.05325
38	.08098	.07758	.07439	.07138	.06855	.06588	.06336	.06099	.05874	.05662
39	.08563	.08210	.07878	.07565	.07270	.06992	.06729	.06480	.06245	.06023
40	.09059	.08692	.08347	.08021	.07714	.07423	.07149	.06889	.06643	.06411
41	.09586	.09206	.08848	.08509	.08189	.07886	.07600	.07329	.07072	.06828
42	.10147	.09753	.09381	.09029	.08696	.08381	.08083	.07800	.07531	.07277
43	.10742	.10334	.09948	.09583	.09237	.08909	.08598	.08304	.08024	.07758
44	.11373	.10950	.10551	.10172	.09813	.09472	.09148	.08841	.08549	.08272
45	.12035	.11599	.11185	.10792	.10420	.10066	.09730	.09410	.09106	.08817
46	.12732	.12281	.11853	.11447	.11061	.10694	.10345	.10013	.09696	.09395
47	.13460	.12995	.12553	.12133	.11733	.11353	.10991	.10646	.10317	.10004
48	.14223	.13743	.13287	.12853	.12439	.12046	.11671	.11313	.10972	.10646
49	.15020	.14526	.14056	.13608	.13181	.12774	.12385	.12015	.11661	.11322
50	.15855	.15347	.14862	.14401	.13960	.13540	.13138	.12754	.12388	.12037
51	.16727	.16205	.15707	.15232	.14777	.14344	.13929	.13532	.13153	.12789
52	.17634	.17098	.16587	.16097	.15630	.15183	.14755	.14345	.13953	.13577
53	.18576	.18027	.17501	.16999	.16518	.16057	.15616	.15194	.14789	.14400
54	.19552	.18990	.18451	.17935	.17441	.16968	.16514	.16078	.15661	.15260
55	.20564	.19989	.19437	.18908	.18402	.17915	.17449	.17001	.16571	.16157
56	.21613	.21025	.20461	.19919	.19400	.18901	.18422	.17962	.17519	.17093
57	.22698	.22098	.21522	.20968	.20436	.19925	.19434	.18961	.18507	.18069
58	.23816	.23204	.22616	.22051	.21507	.20984	.20481	.19996	.19530	.19080
59	.24962	.24339	.23740	.23163	.22608	.22073	.21558	.21062	.20584	.20123

Age	8.2%	8.4%	8.6%	8.8%	9.0%	9.2%	9.4%	9.6%	9.8%	10.0%
60	.26136	.25502	.24892	.24304	.23738	.23192	.22666	.22158	.21669	.21196
61	.27339	.26695	.26075	.25477	.24900	.24343	.23806	.23288	.22787	.22304
62	.28578	.27925	.27295	.26687	.26100	.25533	.24985	.24456	.23945	.23451
63	.29854	.29192	.28553	.27935	.27339	.26762	.26205	.25666	.25145	.24641
64	.31164	.30494	.29846	.29221	.28615	.28030	.27463	.26915	.26384	.25870
65	.32508	.31831	.31177	.30543	.29930	.29336	.28761	.28203	.27663	.27140
66	.33891	.33208	.32547	.31906	.31285	.30684	.30101	.29536	.28987	.28456
67	.35318	.34630	.33963	.33316	.32689	.32081	.31491	.30918	.30363	.29823
68	.36785	.36093	.35422	.34770	.34138	.33524	.32928	.32349	.31787	.31240
69	.38290	.37595	.36920	.36265	.35628	.35009	.34408	.33824	.33256	.32703
70	.39823	.39127	.38450	.37791	.37151	.36529	.35924	.35335	.34762	.34204
71	.41378	.40681	.40003	.39343	.38701	.38076	.37467	.36875	.36298	.35736
72	.42950	.42253	.41575	.40914	.40271	.39644	.39034	.38438	.37858	.37293
73	.44535	.43840	.43162	.42502	.41858	.41231	.40619	.40022	.39440	.38872
74	.46139	.45446	.44771	.44112	.43469	.42842	.42230	.41632	.41049	.40479
75	.47769	.47080	.46408	.45752	.45111	.44485	.43874	.43277	.42693	.42123
76	.49430	.48747	.48079	.47427	.46790	.46167	.45558	.44963	.44380	.43811
77	.51123	.50447	.49786	.49139	.48506	.47888	.47282	.46690	.46111	.45543
78	.52845	.52177	.51523	.50884	.50257	.49645	.49044	.48457	.47881	.47317
79	.54584	.53926	.53282	.52650	.52032	.51426	.50833	.50251	.49681	.49122
80	.56325	.55678	.55044	.54423	.53813	.53216	.52630	.52056	.51492	.50939
81	.58054	.57419	.56797	.56186	.55587	.54999	.54422	.53856	.53300	.52754
82	.59762	.59140	.58530	.57931	.57343	.56766	.56198	.55641	.55094	.54557
83	.61448	.60840	.60243	.59657	.59081	.58515	.57958	.57411	.56874	.56346
84	.63124	.62531	.61949	.61376	.60813	.60259	.59715	.59179	.58652	.58134
85	.64800	.64224	.63657	.63099	.62550	.62010	.61478	.60955	.60441	.59934
86	.66461	.65902	.65351	.64810	.64276	.63751	.63233	.62724	.62222	.61728
87	.68083	.67541	.67008	.66483	.65965	.65455	.64953	.64458	.63970	.63489
88	.69663	.69140	.68624	.68116	.67615	.67121	.66634	.66154	.65680	.65213
89	.71201	.70696	.70199	.69708	.69224	.68747	.68276	.67811	.67353	.66900
90	.72694	.72209	.71730	.71257	.70791	.70330	.69876	.69427	.68984	.68547
91	.74117	.73650	.73190	.72735	.72286	.71842	.71404	.70972	.70545	.70123
92	.75439	.74991	.74548	.74110	.73678	.73251	.72829	.72412	.72000	.71593
93	.76664	.76233	.75806	.75385	.74969	.74557	.74150	.73748	.73350	.72957
94	.77809	.77394	.76983	.76578	.76177	.75780	.75388	.75000	.74616	.74237
95	.78899	.78500	.78106	.77715	.77329	.76947	.76569	.76195	.75826	.75460
96	.79928	.79544	.79165	.78790	.78418	.78050	.77686	.77326	.76970	.76617
97	.80883	.80514	.80149	.79787	.79430	.79075	.78725	.78377	.78033	.77693
98	.81781	.81427	.81075	.80727	.80382	.80041	.79703	.79368	.79036	.78708
99	.82661	.82320	.81982	.81648	.81316	.80988	.80662	.80340	.80020	.79704
100	.83519	.83192	.82868	.82547	.82228	.81913	.81600	.81290	.80982	.80678
101	.84368	.84055	.83744	.83437	.83131	.82829	.82529	.82231	.81936	.81643
102	.85203	.84904	.84607	.84313	.84021	.83731	.83444	.83159	.82876	.82596
103	.86034	.85748	.85465	.85184	.84906	.84629	.84355	.84082	.83812	.83544
104	.86923	.86653	.86385	.86119	.85855	.85593	.85333	.85074	.84818	.84563
105	.87792	.87537	.87283	.87032	.86782	.86534	.86287	.86042	.85799	.85557
106	.88918	.88683	.88450	.88218	.87987	.87758	.87530	.87304	.87079	.86855
107	.90291	.90082	.89873	.89666	.89460	.89255	.89051	.88849	.88647	.88447
108	.92455	.92288	.92123	.91958	.91794	.91630	.91468	.91306	.91145	.90984
109	.96211	.96125	.96041	.95956	.95872	.95788	.95704	.95620	.95537	.95455

Age	10.2%	10.4%	10.6%	10.8%	11.0%	11.2%	11.4%	11.6%	11.8%	12.0%
0	.01488	.01463	.01439	.01417	.01396	.01377	.01359	.01343	.01327	.01312
1	.00662	.00636	.00612	.00589	.00568	.00548	.00530	.00513	.00497	.00482
2	.00654	.00626	.00600	.00576	.00554	.00533	.00514	.00496	.00479	.00463
3	.00670	.00641	.00613	.00588	.00564	.00542	.00522	.00502	.00484	.00468
4	.00699	.00668	.00639	.00612	.00587	.00563	.00542	.00521	.00502	.00484
5	.00739	.00706	.00675	.00646	.00620	.00595	.00571	.00550	.00529	.00510
6	.00786	.00751	.00718	.00687	.00659	.00633	.00608	.00585	.00563	.00543
7	.00841	.00803	.00769	.00736	.00706	.00678	.00652	.00627	.00604	.00582
8	.00902	.00863	.00826	.00791	.00759	.00730	.00702	.00675	.00651	.00628
9	.00973	.00931	.00892	.00856	.00822	.00790	.00760	.00733	.00706	.00682
10	.01055	.01010	.00969	.00930	.00894	.00861	.00829	.00799	.00772	.00746
11	.01146	.01099	.01055	.01014	.00976	.00940	.00907	.00875	.00846	.00818

Age	10.2%	10.4%	10.6%	10.8%	11.0%	11.2%	11.4%	11.6%	11.8%	12.0%
12	.01246	.01196	.01150	.01106	.01066	.01028	.00993	.00960	.00928	.00899
13	.01351	.01298	.01249	.01204	.01161	.01121	.01084	.01049	.01016	.00985
14	.01455	.01400	.01348	.01300	.01255	.01213	.01173	.01136	.01102	.01069
15	.01555	.01497	.01443	.01392	.01345	.01300	.01259	.01220	.01183	.01148
16	.01648	.01587	.01530	.01477	.01427	.01380	.01336	.01295	.01257	.01220
17	.01737	.01673	.01612	.01556	.01504	.01455	.01408	.01365	.01324	.01286
18	.01822	.01754	.01691	.01632	.01576	.01525	.01476	.01430	.01387	.01347
19	.01908	.01837	.01770	.01708	.01650	.01595	.01544	.01495	.01450	.01407
20	.01999	.01924	.01854	.01788	.01726	.01669	.01615	.01564	.01516	.01471
21	.02096	.02017	.01943	.01874	.01809	.01748	.01691	.01637	.01586	.01539
22	.02197	.02114	.02036	.01963	.01895	.01830	.01770	.01713	.01660	.01610
23	.02306	.02218	.02136	.02059	.01987	.01919	.01855	.01795	.01739	.01686
24	.02424	.02331	.02245	.02163	.02087	.02016	.01948	.01885	.01825	.01769
25	.02552	.02455	.02364	.02278	.02197	.02122	.02051	.01984	.01920	.01861
26	.02692	.02589	.02493	.02403	.02318	.02238	.02162	.02091	.02025	.01961
27	.02846	.02738	.02636	.02541	.02451	.02367	.02287	.02212	.02141	.02074
28	.03012	.02898	.02791	.02690	.02595	.02506	.02422	.02342	.02267	.02196
29	.03190	.03070	.02957	.02851	.02751	.02656	.02567	.02483	.02404	.02329
30	.03381	.03254	.03135	.03023	.02917	.02817	.02723	.02634	.02551	.02471
31	.03583	.03450	.03324	.03206	.03094	.02989	.02890	.02796	.02707	.02623
32	.03799	.03659	.03527	.03402	.03284	.03173	.03068	.02968	.02874	.02785
33	.04031	.03883	.03744	.03612	.03488	.03371	.03260	.03155	.03055	.02961
34	.04279	.04123	.03976	.03838	.03707	.03583	.03465	.03354	.03249	.03149
35	.04545	.04382	.04227	.04081	.03943	.03812	.03688	.03571	.03459	.03354
36	.04830	.04658	.04495	.04341	.04196	.04058	.03927	.03803	.03685	.03573
37	.05134	.04953	.04782	.04620	.04467	.04321	.04183	.04052	.03928	.03809
38	.05462	.05272	.05092	.04921	.04760	.04606	.04461	.04322	.04191	.04066
39	.05812	.05613	.05424	.05245	.05075	.04913	.04760	.04614	.04475	.04343
40	.06190	.05981	.05782	.05594	.05415	.05245	.05083	.04929	.04783	.04643
41	.06597	.06378	.06170	.05972	.05784	.05605	.05435	.05272	.05118	.04970
42	.07035	.06806	.06587	.06380	.06182	.05994	.05815	.05644	.05481	.05326
43	.07505	.07265	.07036	.06818	.06611	.06414	.06225	.06045	.05874	.05710
44	.08008	.07757	.07518	.07290	.07072	.06865	.06667	.06478	.06298	.06125
45	.08542	.08279	.08029	.07791	.07563	.07346	.07138	.06940	.06750	.06569
46	.09108	.08834	.08573	.08324	.08085	.07858	.07640	.07432	.07233	.07043
47	.09705	.09419	.09147	.08886	.08637	.08399	.08172	.07954	.07745	.07545
48	.10335	.10038	.09754	.09482	.09222	.08973	.08735	.08507	.08288	.08078
49	.10999	.10690	.10394	.10111	.09840	.09581	.09332	.09093	.08864	.08644
50	.11701	.11380	.11073	.10778	.10496	.10225	.09965	.09716	.09477	.09247
51	.12441	.12108	.11789	.11482	.11189	.10907	.10636	.10376	.10126	.09886
52	.13217	.12871	.12540	.12222	.11916	.11623	.11341	.11071	.10810	.10560
53	.14028	.13670	.13327	.12997	.12680	.12375	.12082	.11801	.11529	.11268
54	.14875	.14505	.14150	.13808	.13480	.13163	.12859	.12566	.12284	.12012
55	.15760	.15378	.15011	.14657	.14317	.13989	.13674	.13370	.13077	.12794
56	.16684	.16290	.15911	.15546	.15194	.14855	.14528	.14213	.13909	.13615
57	.17648	.17242	.16851	.16474	.16111	.15760	.15422	.15096	.14781	.14477
58	.18647	.18229	.17827	.17438	.17064	.16702	.16353	.16015	.15689	.15374
59	.19678	.19249	.18835	.18435	.18049	.17676	.17316	.16968	.16631	.16305
60	.20740	.20300	.19875	.19464	.19066	.18682	.18311	.17952	.17604	.17268
61	.21837	.21385	.20949	.20527	.20119	.19724	.19341	.18971	.18613	.18266
62	.22973	.22511	.22064	.21631	.21212	.20807	.20414	.20033	.19664	.19306
63	.24152	.23680	.23222	.22779	.22350	.21934	.21530	.21139	.20760	.20392
64	.25372	.24890	.24422	.23969	.23529	.23103	.22690	.22289	.21899	.21521
65	.26633	.26141	.25664	.25201	.24752	.24316	.23893	.23482	.23083	.22695
66	.27940	.27439	.26953	.26481	.26023	.25577	.25145	.24724	.24316	.23918
67	.29299	.28790	.28296	.27815	.27348	.26894	.26453	.26024	.25606	.25200
68	.30709	.30193	.29691	.29202	.28728	.28265	.27816	.27378	.26952	.26537
69	.32166	.31643	.31134	.30639	.30157	.29687	.29230	.28785	.28351	.27928
70	.33661	.33133	.32618	.32116	.31628	.31152	.30688	.30235	.29794	.29364
71	.35188	.34654	.34134	.33627	.33133	.32651	.32181	.31722	.31275	.30838
72	.36742	.36204	.35679	.35168	.34668	.34181	.33706	.33241	.32788	.32345
73	.38317	.37776	.37248	.36733	.36229	.35738	.35257	.34788	.34330	.33882
74	.39923	.39380	.38849	.38330	.37823	.37328	.36844	.36370	.35908	.35455
75	.41566	.41021	.40489	.39968	.39459	.38961	.38474	.37997	.37531	.37074
76	.43254	.42709	.42176	.41655	.41144	.40645	.40156	.39677	.39208	.38749

Age	10.2%	10.4%	10.6%	10.8%	11.0%	11.2%	11.4%	11.6%	11.8%	12.0%
77	.44988	.44444	.43912	.43391	.42880	.42380	.41891	.41411	.40940	.40479
78	.46765	.46224	.45694	.45174	.44665	.44166	.43677	.43197	.42726	.42265
79	.48574	.48037	.47510	.46993	.46487	.45990	.45502	.45024	.44554	.44094
80	.50397	.49865	.49343	.48830	.48327	.47834	.47349	.46873	.46406	.45947
81	.52219	.51693	.51176	.50669	.50171	.49682	.49201	.48729	.48265	.47809
82	.54029	.53510	.53000	.52499	.52007	.51523	.51047	.50580	.50120	.49667
83	.55826	.55315	.54813	.54319	.53834	.53356	.52886	.52424	.51969	.51522
84	.57624	.57123	.56629	.56144	.55666	.55195	.54732	.54277	.53828	.53386
85	.59435	.58944	.58460	.57984	.57516	.57054	.56599	.56151	.55710	.55275
86	.61241	.60762	.60289	.59824	.59365	.58913	.58468	.58029	.57596	.57170
87	.63015	.62548	.62087	.61633	.61185	.60744	.60309	.59880	.59456	.59039
88	.64753	.64299	.63851	.63409	.62973	.62543	.62118	.61700	.61287	.60879
89	.66454	.66013	.65579	.65150	.64726	.64308	.63895	.63488	.63086	.62689
90	.68115	.67689	.67268	.66853	.66442	.66037	.65637	.65241	.64851	.64465
91	.69706	.69294	.68887	.68486	.68089	.67696	.67309	.66925	.66547	.66173
92	.71190	.70792	.70399	.70011	.69627	.69247	.68872	.68501	.68134	.67771
93	.72569	.72184	.71804	.71429	.71057	.70689	.70326	.69967	.69611	.69259
94	.73861	.73490	.73123	.72759	.72400	.72044	.71692	.71344	.71000	.70659
95	.75097	.74739	.74384	.74033	.73686	.73342	.73002	.72665	.72331	.72001
96	.76267	.75922	.75579	.75240	.74905	.74572	.74243	.73917	.73595	.73275
97	.77356	.77022	.76691	.76363	.76039	.75718	.75399	.75084	.74772	.74463
98	.78382	.78059	.77740	.77423	.77110	.76799	.76491	.76186	.75884	.75584
99	.79390	.79079	.78771	.78465	.78162	.77862	.77565	.77270	.76978	.76688
100	.80376	.80076	.79779	.79485	.79193	.78904	.78617	.78333	.78051	.77771
101	.81353	.81066	.80780	.80497	.80217	.79938	.79662	.79388	.79117	.78847
102	.82318	.82042	.81768	.81496	.81227	.80960	.80694	.80431	.80170	.79911
103	.83278	.83014	.82752	.82491	.82233	.81977	.81723	.81470	.81220	.80971
104	.84310	.84059	.83810	.83563	.83317	.83073	.82831	.82591	.82352	.82115
105	.85318	.85079	.84843	.84607	.84374	.84142	.83911	.83682	.83455	.83229
106	.86633	.86413	.86193	.85975	.85758	.85543	.85329	.85116	.84904	.84694
107	.88247	.88049	.87852	.87656	.87460	.87266	.87073	.86881	.86690	.86500
108	.90825	.90666	.90507	.90350	.90193	.90037	.89881	.89727	.89572	.89419
109	.95372	.95290	.95208	.95126	.95045	.94964	.94883	.94803	.94723	.94643

Age	12.2%	12.4%	12.6%	12.8%	13.0%	13.2%	13.4%	13.6%	13.8%	14.0%
0	.01298	.01285	.01273	.01261	.01250	.01240	.01230	.01221	.01212	.01203
1	.00468	.00455	.00443	.00431	.00420	.00410	.00400	.00391	.00382	.00374
2	.00448	.00435	.00421	.00409	.00398	.00387	.00376	.00366	.00357	.00348
3	.00452	.00437	.00423	.00410	.00398	.00386	.00375	.00365	.00355	.00345
4	.00468	.00452	.00437	.00423	.00410	.00397	.00386	.00375	.00364	.00354
5	.00493	.00476	.00460	.00445	.00431	.00418	.00405	.00393	.00382	.00371
6	.00524	.00506	.00489	.00473	.00458	.00444	.00430	.00418	.00406	.00394
7	.00562	.00543	.00525	.00508	.00492	.00477	.00462	.00449	.00436	.00423
8	.00606	.00586	.00566	.00548	.00531	.00515	.00499	.00485	.00471	.00458
9	.00659	.00637	.00616	.00597	.00579	.00561	.00545	.00529	.00514	.00500
10	.00721	.00698	.00676	.00655	.00636	.00617	.00600	.00583	.00567	.00552
11	.00792	.00767	.00744	.00722	.00701	.00682	.00663	.00645	.00628	.00612
12	.00871	.00845	.00821	.00797	.00775	.00754	.00735	.00716	.00698	.00681
13	.00955	.00928	.00902	.00877	.00854	.00831	.00810	.00790	.00771	.00753
14	.01038	.01009	.00981	.00955	.00930	.00907	.00885	.00864	.00843	.00824
15	.01116	.01085	.01056	.01028	.01002	.00977	.00954	.00932	.00910	.00890
16	.01186	.01153	.01123	.01094	.01066	.01040	.01015	.00992	.00969	.00948
17	.01250	.01215	.01183	.01152	.01124	.01096	.01070	.01045	.01022	.00999
18	.01308	.01272	.01238	.01206	.01175	.01147	.01119	.01093	.01068	.01044
19	.01367	.01329	.01293	.01259	.01227	.01196	.01167	.01140	.01113	.01088
20	.01428	.01388	.01350	.01314	.01280	.01248	.01217	.01188	.01161	.01134
21	.01494	.01451	.01411	.01373	.01337	.01303	.01271	.01240	.01211	.01183
22	.01562	.01517	.01475	.01435	.01397	.01361	.01326	.01294	.01263	.01233
23	.01635	.01588	.01543	.01501	.01460	.01422	.01386	.01351	.01319	.01287
24	.01716	.01665	.01618	.01573	.01530	.01489	.01451	.01415	.01380	.01347
25	.01804	.01751	.01701	.01653	.01608	.01565	.01524	.01485	.01448	.01413
26	.01902	.01845	.01792	.01741	.01693	.01648	.01604	.01563	.01524	.01487
27	.02011	.01951	.01895	.01841	.01790	.01742	.01696	.01652	.01610	.01571
28	.02129	.02066	.02006	.01949	.01895	.01844	.01795	.01748	.01704	.01662

Age	12.2%	12.4%	12.6%	12.8%	13.0%	13.2%	13.4%	13.6%	13.8%	14.0%
29	.02258	.02191	.02127	.02067	.02009	.01955	.01903	.01853	.01806	.01762
30	.02396	.02325	.02257	.02193	.02132	.02074	.02019	.01966	.01916	.01869
31	.02543	.02467	.02396	.02328	.02263	.02201	.02143	.02087	.02034	.01983
32	.02701	.02621	.02545	.02472	.02404	.02338	.02276	.02217	.02160	.02106
33	.02871	.02786	.02706	.02629	.02556	.02487	.02420	.02357	.02297	.02240
34	.03054	.02964	.02879	.02797	.02720	.02646	.02576	.02509	.02445	.02383
35	.03253	.03158	.03067	.02981	.02898	.02820	.02745	.02674	.02606	.02541
36	.03467	.03366	.03269	.03178	.03090	.03007	.02928	.02852	.02779	.02710
37	.03697	.03590	.03488	.03391	.03298	.03209	.03125	.03044	.02967	.02893
38	.03947	.03833	.03725	.03622	.03524	.03430	.03340	.03254	.03172	.03094
39	.04217	.04096	.03982	.03873	.03768	.03669	.03573	.03482	.03395	.03312
40	.04510	.04383	.04262	.04146	.04035	.03930	.03828	.03732	.03639	.03550
41	.04830	.04695	.04567	.04445	.04327	.04215	.04108	.04005	.03907	.03812
42	.05177	.05035	.04900	.04770	.04646	.04527	.04413	.04304	.04200	.04100
43	.05553	.05404	.05261	.05123	.04992	.04866	.04746	.04630	.04520	.04413
44	.05960	.05802	.05651	.05506	.05368	.05235	.05107	.04985	.04867	.04754
45	.06395	.06229	.06069	.05917	.05770	.05630	.05495	.05365	.05241	.05121
46	.06860	.06685	.06517	.06356	.06202	.06053	.05911	.05774	.05643	.05516
47	.07353	.07169	.06992	.06823	.06660	.06504	.06353	.06209	.06070	.05936
48	.07877	.07684	.07498	.07320	.07149	.06984	.06826	.06673	.06527	.06385
49	.08433	.08231	.08036	.07849	.07669	.07495	.07329	.07168	.07013	.06864
50	.09026	.08814	.08609	.08413	.08224	.08042	.07867	.07698	.07535	.07378
51	.09655	.09433	.09219	.09013	.08815	.08624	.08440	.08262	.08091	.07926
52	.10318	.10086	.09863	.09647	.09439	.09239	.09046	.08860	.08680	.08506
53	.11017	.10774	.10541	.10315	.10098	.09888	.09686	.09491	.09302	.09120
54	.11750	.11498	.11254	.11019	.10792	.10572	.10361	.10156	.09958	.09767
55	.12522	.12258	.12005	.11759	.11522	.11294	.11072	.10859	.10652	.10451
56	.13332	.13059	.12794	.12539	.12292	.12054	.11823	.11599	.11383	.11174
57	.14183	.13899	.13624	.13359	.13102	.12853	.12613	.12380	.12154	.11936
58	.15070	.14775	.14490	.14215	.13948	.13689	.13439	.13197	.12962	.12734
59	.15990	.15685	.15389	.15103	.14826	.14558	.14298	.14046	.13801	.13564
60	.16942	.16626	.16321	.16024	.15737	.15459	.15189	.14927	.14673	.14426
61	.17929	.17603	.17287	.16981	.16684	.16395	.16115	.15844	.15580	.15324
62	.18960	.18623	.18297	.17980	.17673	.17375	.17085	.16803	.16530	.16264
63	.20035	.19688	.19352	.19025	.18708	.18400	.18100	.17809	.17525	.17250
64	.21154	.20797	.20451	.20114	.19787	.19469	.19159	.18859	.18566	.18281
65	.22318	.21951	.21595	.21249	.20912	.20584	.20265	.19955	.19652	.19358
66	.23532	.23156	.22790	.22434	.22088	.21751	.21422	.21102	.20791	.20487
67	.24804	.24419	.24044	.23679	.23324	.22977	.22640	.22311	.21990	.21678
68	.26133	.25740	.25356	.24983	.24618	.24263	.23917	.23579	.23250	.22929
69	.27516	.27114	.26723	.26341	.25969	.25605	.25251	.24905	.24567	.24237
70	.28945	.28536	.28137	.27747	.27367	.26996	.26633	.26279	.25934	.25596
71	.30412	.29996	.29590	.29193	.28806	.28427	.28057	.27696	.27343	.26998
72	.31913	.31491	.31078	.30675	.30281	.29895	.29519	.29150	.28790	.28438
73	.33444	.33016	.32597	.32188	.31788	.31396	.31013	.30638	.30271	.29913
74	.35012	.34579	.34155	.33741	.33335	.32938	.32549	.32168	.31795	.31430
75	.36628	.36190	.35762	.35343	.34932	.34530	.34136	.33750	.33372	.33001
76	.38299	.37858	.37427	.37004	.36589	.36183	.35784	.35394	.35011	.34636
77	.40028	.39585	.39151	.38725	.38307	.37898	.37496	.37103	.36716	.36337
78	.41812	.41368	.40933	.40506	.40086	.39675	.39271	.38874	.38485	.38103
79	.43641	.43198	.42762	.42334	.41914	.41502	.41096	.40698	.40308	.39924
80	.45496	.45054	.44619	.44192	.43772	.43360	.42954	.42556	.42164	.41779
81	.47360	.46920	.46487	.46061	.45643	.45231	.44827	.44429	.44038	.43653
82	.49223	.48785	.48355	.47932	.47516	.47106	.46703	.46307	.45916	.45532
83	.51081	.50648	.50221	.49802	.49388	.48982	.48581	.48187	.47799	.47416
84	.52951	.52523	.52101	.51686	.51277	.50874	.50477	.50086	.49701	.49321
85	.54847	.54425	.54009	.53600	.53196	.52798	.52406	.52019	.51638	.51262
86	.56749	.56335	.55926	.55523	.55126	.54734	.54348	.53966	.53591	.53220
87	.58627	.58221	.57820	.57425	.57035	.56650	.56270	.55895	.55526	.55161
88	.60477	.60079	.59688	.59301	.58919	.58542	.58170	.57802	.57439	.57081
89	.62297	.61909	.61527	.61149	.60776	.60408	.60044	.59685	.59330	.58979
90	.64084	.63707	.63335	.62968	.62604	.62246	.61891	.61540	.61194	.60851
91	.65803	.65437	.65076	.64719	.64366	.64017	.63672	.63330	.62993	.62659
92	.67412	.67058	.66707	.66360	.66017	.65678	.65342	.65010	.64682	.64357
93	.68911	.68567	.68227	.67890	.67557	.67227	.66901	.66578	.66258	.65942

Age	12.2%	12.4%	12.6%	12.8%	13.0%	13.2%	13.4%	13.6%	13.8%	14.0%
94	.70321	.69988	.69657	.69330	.69006	.68686	.68369	.68055	.67744	.67437
95	.71674	.71351	.71031	.70713	.70399	.70088	.69781	.69476	.69174	.68875
96	.72959	.72646	.72335	.72028	.71724	.71422	.71123	.70828	.70534	.70244
97	.74156	.73853	.73552	.73254	.72959	.72666	.72376	.72089	.71804	.71522
98	.75287	.74993	.74702	.74413	.74126	.73842	.73561	.73282	.73006	.72732
99	.76401	.76117	.75834	.75555	.75277	.75002	.74730	.74459	.74191	.73926
100	.77494	.77219	.76946	.76676	.76408	.76142	.75878	.75616	.75357	.75099
101	.78580	.78315	.78052	.77791	.77532	.77275	.77021	.76768	.76517	.76268
102	.79654	.79399	.79146	.78894	.78645	.78397	.78152	.77908	.77666	.77426
103	.80724	.80479	.80236	.79994	.79755	.79517	.79280	.79046	.78813	.78582
104	.81879	.81646	.81413	.81183	.80954	.80726	.80501	.80276	.80054	.79832
105	.83005	.82782	.82560	.82340	.82121	.81904	.81688	.81474	.81260	.81049
106	.84485	.84277	.84071	.83866	.83662	.83459	.83257	.83057	.82857	.82659
107	.86311	.86124	.85937	.85751	.85566	.85382	.85199	.85017	.84835	.84655
108	.89266	.89114	.88963	.88812	.88662	.88513	.88364	.88216	.88068	.87922
109	.94563	.94484	.94405	.94326	.94248	.94170	.94092	.94014	.93937	.93860

(f) Effective dates. This section applies after April 30, 1999.

T.D. 7105, 4/5/71, amend T.D. 7955, 5/10/84, T.D. 8540, 6/9/94, T.D. 8819, 4/29/99, T.D. 8886, 6/9/2000.

§ 1.642(c)-6A Valuation of charitable remainder interests for which the valuation date is before May 1, 1999.

(a) Valuation of charitable remainder interests for which the valuation date is before January 1, 1952. There was no provision for the qualification of pooled income funds under section 642 until 1969. See § 20.2031-7A(a) of this chapter (Estate Tax Regulations) for the determination of the present value of a charitable remainder interest created before January 1, 1952.

(b) Valuation of charitable remainder interests for which the valuation date is after December 31, 1951, and before January 1, 1971. No charitable deduction is allowable for a transfer to a pooled income fund for which the valuation date is after the effective dates of the Tax Reform Act of 1969 unless the pooled income fund meets the requirements of section 642(c)(5). See § 20.2031-7A(b) of this chapter (Estate Tax Regulations) for the determination of the present value of a charitable remainder interest for which the valuation date is after December 31, 1951, and before January 1, 1971.

(c) Present value of remainder interest in the case of transfers to pooled income funds for which the valuation date is after December 31, 1970, and before December 1, 1983. For the determination of the present value of a remainder interest in property transferred to a pooled income fund for which the valuation date is after December 31, 1970, and before December 1, 1983, see § 20.2031-7A(c) of this chapter (Estate Tax Regulations) and former § 1.642(c)-6(e) (as contained in the 26 CFR part 1 edition revised as of April 1, 1994).

(d) Present value of remainder interest dependent on the termination of one life in the case of transfers to pooled income funds made after November 30, 1983, for which the valuation date is before May 1, 1989. *(1) In general.* For transfers to pooled income funds made after November 30, 1983, for which the valuation date is before May 1, 1989, the present value of the remainder interest at the time of the transfer of property to the fund is determined by computing the present value (at the time of the transfer) of the life income interest in the transferred property (as determined under paragraph (d)(2) of this section) and subtracting that value from the fair market value of the transferred property on the valuation date. The present value of a remainder interest that is dependent on the termination of the life of one individual is computed by use of Table G in paragraph (d)(4) of this section. For purposes of the computation under this section, the age of an individual is to be taken as the age of the individual at the individual's nearest birthday.

(2) Present value of life income interest. The present value of the life income interest in property transferred to a pooled income fund shall be computed on the basis of:

(i) Life contingencies determined from the values of 1x that are set forth in Table LN of § 20.2031-7A(d)(6) of this chapter (Estate Tax Regulations); and

(ii) Discount at a rate of interest, compounded annually, equal to the highest yearly rate of return of the pooled income fund for the 3 taxable years immediately preceding its taxable year in which the transfer of property to the fund is made. For purposes of this paragraph (d)(2), the yearly rate of return of a pooled income fund is determined as provided in § 1.642(c)-6(c) unless the highest yearly rate of return is deemed to be 9 percent. For purposes of this paragraph (d)(2), the first taxable year of a pooled income fund is considered a taxable year even though the taxable year consists of less than 12 months. However, appropriate adjustments must be made to annualize the rate of return earned by the fund for that period. Where it appears from the facts and circumstances that the highest yearly rate of return for the 3 taxable years immediately preceding the taxable year in which the transfer of property is made has been purposely manipulated to be substantially less than the rate of return that would otherwise be reasonably anticipated with the purpose of obtaining an excessive charitable deduction, that rate of return may not be used. In that case, the highest yearly rate of return of the fund is determined by treating the fund as a pooled income fund that has been in existence for less than 3 preceding taxable years. If a pooled income fund has been in existence less than 3 taxable years immediately preceding the taxable year in which the transfer of property to the fund is made, the highest yearly rate of return is deemed to be 9 percent.

(3) Computation of value of remainder interest. The factor which is used in determining the present value of the remainder interest is the factor under the appropriate yearly rate of return in column (2) of Table G opposite the number

in column (1) which corresponds to the age of the individual upon whose life the value of the remainder interest is based. If the yearly rate of return is a percentage which is between yearly rates of return for which factors are provided in Table G, a linear interpolation must be made. The present value of the remainder interest is determined by multiplying, by the factor determined under this paragraph (d)(3), the fair market value on the appropriate valuation date. If the yearly rate of return is below 2.2 percent or above 14 percent, see § 1.642(c)-6(b). This paragraph (d)(3) may be illustrated by the following example:

Example. A, who will be 50 years old on April 15, 1985, transfers $100,000 to a pooled income fund on January 1, 1985, and retains a life income interest in such property. The highest yearly rate of return earned by the fund for its 3 preceding taxable years is 9.9 percent. In Table G the figure in column (2) opposite 50 years under 9.8 percent is .15653 and under 10 percent is .15257. The present value of the remainder interest is $15,455, computed as follows:

Factor at 9.8 percent for person aged 50	.15653
Factor at 10 percent for person aged 50	.15257
Difference	.00396

Interpolation adjustment:

$$\frac{9.9\% - 9.8\%}{.2\%} = \frac{X}{.00396}$$

$$X \times .00198$$

Factor at 9.8 percent for person aged 50	0.15653
Less:	
Interpolation adjustment	.00198
Interpolated factor	.15455
Present value of remainder interest ($100,000 = .15455	$15,455

(4) Actuarial tables. The following tables shall be used in the application of the provisions of this section.

Table G—Single Life, Unisex—Table Showing the Present Worth of the Remainder Interest in Property Transferred to a Pooled Income Fund Having the Yearly Rate of Return Shown—Applicable for Transfers after November 30, 1983, and before May 1, 1989

(1) Age	(2) Yearly Rate of Return 2.2%	2.4%	2.6%	2.8%	3.0%	3.2%	3.4%	3.6%	3.8%	4.0%
0	.23930	.21334	.19077	.17112	.15401	.13908	.12603	.11461	.10461	.09583
1	.22891	.20224	.17903	.15880	.14114	.12570	.11220	.10036	.08998	.08086
2	.23297	.20610	.18265	.16218	.14429	.12862	.11489	.10284	.09225	.08293
3	.23744	.21035	.18669	.16600	.14787	.13198	.11802	.10576	.09496	.08544
4	.24212	.21485	.19098	.17006	.15171	.13559	.12141	.10893	.09793	.08821
5	.24701	.21955	.19547	.17434	.15577	.13943	.12503	.11234	.10112	.09121
6	.25207	.22442	.20015	.17880	.16001	.14345	.12884	.11593	.10451	.09439
7	.25726	.22944	.20497	.18342	.16441	.14763	.13280	.11968	.10805	.09773
8	.26259	.23461	.20995	.18820	.16898	.15198	.13694	.12360	.11176	.10125
9	.26809	.23995	.21511	.19315	.17373	.15652	.14126	.12771	.11567	.10495
10	.27373	.24544	.22043	.29828	.17865	.16123	.14576	.13200	.11975	.10883
11	.27953	.25110	.22592	.20358	.18375	.16613	.15045	.13648	.12402	.11290
12	.28546	.25690	.23156	.20904	.18902	.17119	.15531	.14113	.12847	.11715
13	.29149	.26280	.23731	.21462	.19440	.17638	.16029	.14591	.13304	.12152
14	.29757	.26877	.24312	.22026	.19986	.18164	.16535	.15076	.13769	.12597
15	.30368	.27476	.24896	.22593	.20535	.18693	.17044	.15565	.14238	.13045
16	.30978	.28075	.25481	.23161	.21085	.19224	.17554	.16055	.14707	.13494
17	.31589	.28676	.26068	.23732	.21637	.19756	.18066	.16547	.15178	.13945
18	.32204	.29280	.26659	.24306	.22193	.20294	.18584	.17044	.15655	.14401
19	.32825	.29892	.27257	.24889	.22759	.20840	.19110	.17550	.16140	.14866
20	.33457	.30514	.27867	.25484	.23336	.21399	.19650	.18069	.16639	.15344
21	.34099	.31148	.28489	.26092	.23927	.21972	.20203	.18602	.17152	.15836
22	.34751	.31794	.29124	.26712	.24532	.22559	.20771	.19151	.17680	.16344
23	.35416	.32452	.29773	.27348	.25152	.23162	.21356	.19716	.18225	.16869
24	.36096	.33127	.30439	.28002	.25791	.23784	.21960	.20301	.18791	.17414
25	.36793	.33821	.31124	.28676	.26452	.24429	.22588	.20910	.19380	.17984
26	.37509	.34535	.31832	.29374	.27136	.25098	.23240	.21545	.19996	.18581
27	.38244	.35269	.32560	.30093	.27844	.25792	.23918	.22206	.20639	.19205
28	.38998	.36023	.33311	.30836	.28577	.26512	.24623	.22894	.21310	.19858
29	.39767	.36795	.34080	.31599	.29330	.27253	.25350	.23605	.22004	.20534
30	.40553	.37584	.34868	.32382	.30104	.28016	.26100	.24341	.22724	.21236
31	.41352	.38388	.35672	.33182	.30897	.28799	.26871	.25097	.23464	.21961
32	.42165	.39208	.36494	.34001	.31710	.29603	.27664	.25877	.24230	.22710
33	.42993	.40044	.37333	.34839	.32543	.30428	.28478	.26679	.25018	.23484
34	.43834	.40894	.38188	.35694	.33395	.31273	.29314	.27504	.25830	.24280
35	.44689	.41760	.39060	.36567	.34266	.32139	.30172	.28351	.26665	.25102
36	.45556	.42640	.39947	.37458	.35156	.33024	.31050	.29220	.27523	.25948
37	.46435	.43534	.40850	.38365	.36063	.33929	.31949	.30111	.28404	.26816
38	.47325	.44440	.41767	.39288	.36987	.34851	.32867	.31022	.29305	.27707
39	.48226	.45358	.42696	.40225	.37927	.35791	.33804	.31953	.30228	.28620
40	.49136	.46288	.43640	.41177	.38884	.36749	.34759	.32904	.31172	.29555
41	.50056	.47228	.44596	.42143	.39856	.37724	.35733	.33874	.32137	.30512

42	.50988	.48182	.45566	.43125	.40846	.38717	.36727	.34866	.33124	.31493
43	.51927	.49145	.46547	.44120	.41850	.39727	.37739	.35877	.34132	.32495
44	.52874	.50118	.47540	.45128	.42869	.40752	.38768	.36906	.35159	.33518
45	.53828	.51099	.48543	.46146	.43899	.41791	.39811	.37952	.36204	.34560
46	.54788	.52088	.49554	.47176	.44943	.42844	.40871	.39014	.37267	.35621
47	.55754	.53083	.50574	.48216	.45998	.43910	.41944	.40092	.38347	.36701
48	.56726	.54087	.51604	.49267	.47065	.44990	.43034	.41188	.39446	.37801
49	.57703	.55097	.52652	.50327	.48144	.46083	.44137	.42299	.40562	.38929
50	.58685	.56114	.53677	.51398	.49234	.47189	.45256	.43427	.41695	.40056
51	.59670	.57136	.54740	.52476	.50333	.48306	.46386	.44567	.42844	.41209
52	.60658	.58161	.55798	.53560	.51441	.49432	.47528	.45721	.44006	.42378
53	.61647	.59189	.56859	.54651	.52556	.50567	.48679	.46886	.45182	.43562
54	.62635	.60217	.57923	.55744	.53675	.51708	.49838	.48060	.46367	.44756

Table G—Continued (1) Single Life, Unisex—Table Showing the Present Worth of the Remainder Interest in Property Transferred to a Pooled Income Fund Having the Yearly Rate of Return Shown—Applicable for Transfers after November 30, 1983, and before May 1, 1989

(1) Age	(2) Yearly Rate of Return									
	2.2%	2.4%	2.6%	2.8%	3.0%	3.2%	3.4%	3.6%	3.8%	4.0%
55	.63622	.61246	.58987	.56840	.54798	.52854	.51004	.49242	.47563	.45962
56	.64606	.62273	.60052	.57937	.55923	.54004	.52175	.50430	.48766	.47177
57	.65589	.63299	.61117	.59037	.57052	.55159	.53352	.51626	.49978	.48402
58	.66569	.64324	.62181	.60136	.58183	.56316	.54533	.52827	.51196	.49636
59	.67546	.65347	.63246	.61237	.59316	.57478	.55719	.54036	.52424	.50879
60	.68521	.66368	.64309	.62338	.60450	.58643	.56910	.55250	.53658	.52131
61	.69492	.67388	.65372	.63440	.61587	.59811	.58107	.56471	.54901	.53393
62	.70461	.68406	.66434	.64542	.62726	.60982	.59307	.57697	.56150	.54662
63	.71425	.69420	.67494	.65643	.63865	.62155	.60510	.58928	.57405	.55940
64	.72384	.70430	.68550	.66742	.65002	.63327	.61714	.60161	.58664	.57222
65	.73336	.71434	.69602	.67837	.66137	.64498	.62918	.61395	.59926	.58508
66	.74281	.72431	.70647	.68926	.67267	.67666	.64120	.62628	.61188	.59796
67	.75216	.73419	.71684	.70009	.68391	.66829	.65319	.63859	.62448	.61083
68	.76143	.74399	.72714	.71085	.69509	.67986	.66512	.65086	.63706	.62370
69	.77060	.75370	.73735	.72153	.70622	.69139	.67702	.66311	.64963	.63656
70	.77969	.76334	.74750	.73215	.71728	.70286	.68888	.67533	.66218	.64942
71	.78870	.77290	.75758	.74272	.72830	.71431	.70073	.68754	.67474	.66231
72	.79764	.78240	.76760	.75323	.73928	.72572	.71255	.69974	.68730	.67520
73	.80646	.79178	.77751	.76364	.75016	.73704	.72429	.71188	.69980	.68805
74	.81511	.80099	.78725	.77387	.76086	.74819	.73586	.72384	.71214	.70075
75	.82353	.80995	.79674	.78386	.77132	.75909	.74718	.73557	.72424	.71320
76	.83169	.81866	.80596	.79357	.78149	.76971	.75822	.74700	.73606	.72538
77	.83960	.82710	.81491	.80301	.79139	.78004	.76897	.75815	.74758	.73726
78	.84727	.83530	.82360	.81218	.80101	.79010	.77944	.76902	.75883	.74886
79	.85473	.84328	.83207	.82112	.81041	.79993	.78968	.77965	.76984	.76023
80	.86201	.85106	.84034	.82986	.81960	.80955	.79971	.79008	.78064	.77140
81	.86905	.85861	.84837	.83835	.82853	.81891	.80948	.80024	.79118	.78230
82	.87585	.86589	.85612	.84655	.83717	.82796	.81894	.81009	.80140	.79288
83	.88239	.87291	.86360	.85447	.84552	.83672	.82810	.81962	.81131	.80314
84	.88873	.87971	.87085	.86216	.85362	.84524	.83700	.82891	.82096	.81314
85	.89487	.88630	.87789	.86963	.86150	.85352	.84567	.83795	.83037	.82291
86	.90070	.89258	.88459	.87674	.86901	.86141	.85394	.84659	.83936	.83224
87	.90609	.89838	.89079	.88332	.87597	.86874	.86162	.85461	.84771	.84092
88	.91106	.90372	.89650	.88939	.88234	.87549	.86870	.86201	.85542	.84893
89	.91570	.90872	.90184	.89507	.88839	.88182	.87534	.86895	.86266	.85645
90	.92014	.91350	.90696	.90051	.89416	.88789	.88171	.87562	.86961	.86369
91	.92435	.91804	.91182	.90569	.89964	.89367	.88779	.88198	.87625	.87059
92	.92822	.92222	.91630	.91045	.90469	.89900	.89338	.88784	.88237	.87697
93	.93170	.92597	.92032	.91474	.90923	.90379	.89842	.89312	.88788	.88271
94	.93477	.92929	.92387	.91853	.91325	.90803	.90288	.89780	.89277	.88781
95	.93743	.93216	.92695	.92181	.91673	.91171	.90675	.90185	.89701	.89223
96	.93967	.93458	.92955	.92458	.91966	.91481	.91001	.90527	.90058	.89594
97	.94167	.93674	.93186	.92704	.92228	.91757	.91291	.90831	.90376	.89926
98	.94342	.93863	.93389	.92921	.92457	.91999	.91546	.91098	.90655	.90217
99	.94508	.94041	.93580	.93124	.92673	.92227	.91786	.91349	.90917	.90490
100	.94672	.94218	.93770	.93326	.92887	.92453	.92023	.91598	.91177	.90761
101	.94819	.94377	.93940	.93508	.93080	.92656	.92236	.91821	.91410	.91003
102	.94979	.94550	.94125	.93704	.93288	.92875	.92467	.92063	.91662	.91266
103	.95180	.94766	.94357	.93952	.93550	.93152	.92758	.92367	.91980	.91597
104	.95377	.94979	.94585	.94194	.93806	.93423	.93042	.92665	.92291	.91920

105	.95663	.95288	.94916	.94547	.94181	.93818	.93458	.93101	.92747	.92395
106	.96101	.95762	.95425	95091	.94760	.94430	.94104	.93779	.93457	.93137
107	.96688	.96398	.96110	.95824	.95539	.95256	.94975	.94696	.94418	.94143
108	.97569	.97354	.97141	.96928	.96717	.96507	.96298	.96090	.95883	.95676
109	.98924	.98828	.98733	.98638	.98544	.98450	.98356	.98263	.98170	.98077

Table G—Continued (2) Single Life, Unisex—Table Showing the Present Worth of the Remainder Interest in Property Transferred to a Pooled Income Fund Having the Yearly Rate of Return Shown—Applicable for Transfers after November 30, 1983, and before May 1, 1989

(1) Age	(2) Yearly Rate of Return									
	4.2%	4.4%	4.6%	4.8%	5.0%	5.2%	5.4%	5.6%	5.8%	6.0%
0	.08811	.08132	.07534	.07006	.06539	.06126	.05759	.05433	.05143	.04884
1	.07283	.06576	.05952	.05400	.04912	.04480	.04096	.03754	.03450	.03179
2	.07471	.06746	.06106	.05539	.05037	.04591	.04194	.03841	.03527	.03246
3	.07704	.06962	.06304	.05722	.05205	.04745	.04336	.03972	.03646	.03355
4	.07962	.07202	.06528	.05930	.05398	.04924	.04502	.04125	.03789	.03487
5	.08243	.07464	.06773	.06159	.05612	.05124	.04689	.04300	.03952	.03639
6	.08542	.07745	.07037	.06406	.05844	.05342	.04893	.04492	.04131	.03808
7	.08857	.08042	.07316	.06669	.06091	.05574	.05112	.04697	.04324	.03990
8	.09189	.08355	.07612	.06948	.06354	.05822	.05346	.04918	.04533	.04186
9	.09540	.08687	.07926	.07245	.06635	.06089	.05598	.05156	.04759	.04400
10	.09908	.09037	.08258	.07560	.06934	.06372	.05866	.05411	.05000	.04630
11	.10296	.09406	.08609	.07894	.07251	.06673	.06153	.05684	.05260	.04877
12	.10701	.09793	.08977	.08245	.07586	.06992	.06457	.05973	.05536	.05141
13	.11119	.10191	.09358	.08608	.07932	.07322	.06772	.06274	.05824	.05415
14	.11544	.10597	.09745	.08978	.08285	.07659	.07093	.06581	.06117	.05695
15	.11972	.11007	.10136	.09350	.08640	.07998	.07417	.06890	.06411	.05976
16	.12402	.11416	.10527	.09723	.08995	.08337	.07739	.07197	.06704	.06255
17	.12832	.11827	.10919	.10096	.09351	.08675	.08062	.07504	.06996	.06533
18	.13268	.12243	.11315	.10474	.09711	.09018	.08387	.07813	.07290	.06813
19	.13712	.12667	.11720	.10860	.10078	.09367	.08720	.08130	.07591	.07099
20	.14170	.13105	.12138	.11259	.10459	.09730	.09065	.08458	.07904	.07397
21	.14642	.13557	.12570	.11671	.10853	.10106	.09423	.08800	.08229	.07707
22	.15129	.14024	.13017	.12099	.11261	.10496	.09796	.09155	.08568	.08030
23	.15634	.14508	.13481	.12544	.11687	.10903	.10185	.09526	.08923	.08368
24	.16159	.15013	.13967	.13009	.12133	.11330	.10594	.09918	.09297	.08726
25	.16709	.15543	.14477	.13500	.12604	.11782	.11028	.10334	.09696	.09108
26	.17286	.16101	.15014	.14018	.13103	.12262	.11489	.10778	.10122	.09518
27	.17891	.16686	.15580	.14564	.13630	.12771	.11979	.11249	.10576	.09955
28	.18525	.17301	.16175	.15140	.14187	.13309	.12499	.11751	.11060	.10421
29	.19183	.17940	.16796	.15742	.14700	.13873	.13044	.12278	.11570	.10914
30	.19867	.18606	.17443	.16370	.15380	.14464	.13617	.12833	.12107	.11433
31	.20574	.19295	.13114	.17023	.16013	.15079	.14214	.13412	.12668	.11977
32	.21307	.20010	.18811	.17702	.16674	.15722	.14838	.14018	.13256	.12548
33	.22064	.20751	.19535	.18407	.17362	.16391	.15490	.14652	.13873	.13147
34	.22846	.21516	.20283	.19138	.18075	.17087	.16168	.15312	.14515	.13772
35	.23653	.22307	.21058	.19896	.18816	.17811	.16874	.16001	.15186	.14426
36	.24484	.23124	.21859	.20681	.19584	.18562	.17608	.16717	.15886	.15108
37	.25340	.23966	.22685	.21492	.20379	.19340	.18369	.17462	.16613	.15819
38	.26219	.24831	.23536	.22328	.21199	.20144	.19157	.18233	.17368	.16557
39	.27120	.25720	.24411	.23188	.22044	.20974	.19971	.19031	.18149	.17322
40	.28045	.26633	.25311	.24075	.22916	.21830	.20812	.19856	.18959	.18115
41	.28992	.27569	.26236	.24986	.23814	.22714	.21681	.20710	.19797	.18938
42	.29965	.28532	.27188	.25926	.24741	.23627	.22579	.21594	.20665	.19791
43	.30960	.29518	.28163	.26890	.25693	.24566	.23606	.22505	.21562	.20673
44	.31977	.30527	.29164	.27880	.26671	.25532	.24458	.23445	.22488	.21585
45	.33013	.31557	.30185	.28892	.27673	.26522	.25436	.24410	.23440	.22523
46	.34071	.32609	.31230	.29929	.28700	.27538	.26441	.25402	.24420	.23490
47	.35148	.33681	.32296	.30988	.29750	.28579	.27471	.26421	.25427	.24484
48	.36246	.34777	.33387	.32072	.30826	.29647	.28529	.27469	.26463	.25508
49	.37364	.35893	.34499	.33179	.31927	.30739	.29613	.28543	.27527	.26562
50	.38503	.37030	.35634	.34310	.33053	.31859	.30724	.29646	.28620	.27645
51	.39659	.38187	.36790	.35462	.34201	.33001	.31860	.30774	.29740	.28755
52	.40832	.39362	.37965	.36636	.35371	.34167	.33020	.31928	.30886	.29893
53	.42021	.40554	.39158	.37829	.36562	.35355	.34204	.33105	.32057	.31056
54	.43222	.41760	.40367	.39039	.37771	.36562	.35407	.34304	.33250	.32243

Table G—Continued (3) Single Life, Unisex—Table Showing the Present Worth of the Remainder Interest in Property Transferred to a Pooled Income Fund Having the Yearly Rate of Return Shown—Applicable for Transfers after November 30, 1983, and before May 1, 1989

(1)	(2) Yearly Rate of Return									
Age	4.2%	4.4%	4.6%	4.8%	5.0%	5.2%	5.4%	5.6%	5.8%	6.0%
55	.44436	.42980	.41591	.41264	.38997	.37787	.36630	.35523	.34465	.33452
56	.45660	.44212	.42828	.41504	.40239	.39029	.37870	.36761	.35699	.34682
57	.46897	.45456	.44079	.42760	.41498	.40289	.39130	.38020	.36956	.35935
58	.48142	.46712	.45342	.44030	.42771	.41565	.40408	.39297	.38231	.37208
59	.49399	.47980	.46620	.45314	.44062	.42859	.41704	.40595	.39529	.38504
60	.50666	.49260	.47910	.46613	.45367	.44170	.43019	.41912	.40847	.39822
61	.51944	.50552	.49214	.47927	.46690	.45499	.44353	.43250	.42187	.41164
62	.53232	.51856	.50531	.49256	.48028	.46845	.45706	.44607	.43548	.42527
63	.54529	.53169	.51860	.50598	.49381	.48208	.47076	.45984	.44930	.43913
64	.55832	.54491	.53198	.51950	.50746	.49583	.48461	.47377	.46329	.45317
65	.57140	.55819	.54544	.53312	.52121	.50971	.49859	.48784	.47744	.46738
66	.58451	.57152	.55895	.54681	.53506	.52369	.51269	.50204	.49173	.48175
67	.59763	.58486	.57251	.56054	.54896	.53774	.52688	.51635	.50614	.49625
68	.61076	.59823	.58609	.57432	.56292	.55187	.54115	.53075	.52066	.51088
69	.62390	.61162	.59971	.58816	.57695	.56607	.55551	.54526	.53530	.52563
70	.63705	.62503	.61337	.60204	.59104	.58035	.56997	.55987	.55006	.54053
71	.65023	.63849	.62709	.61600	.60522	.59474	.58455	.57463	.56498	.55559
72	.66344	.65199	.64086	.63003	.61949	.60923	.59924	.58952	.58004	.57082
73	.67661	.66547	.65463	.64407	.63378	.62375	.61398	.60446	.59518	.58613
74	.68964	.67882	.66827	.65798	.64796	.63818	.62864	.61933	.61026	.60140
75	.70243	.69193	.68168	.67168	.66192	.65240	.64310	.63402	.62515	.61649
76	.71495	.70477	.69482	.68411	.67563	.66636	.65731	.64836	.63981	.63135
77	.72717	.71731	.70768	.69826	.68905	.68005	.57124	.66263	.65420	.64596
78	.73912	.72959	.72026	.71114	.70221	.69347	.68492	.67655	.66836	.66033
79	.75083	.74163	.73262	.72379	.71515	.70669	.69840	.69028	.68232	.67452
80	.76235	.75348	.74479	.73627	.72792	.71973	.71171	.70384	.69613	.68856
81	.77360	.76506	.75669	.74848	.74043	.73252	.72377	.71717	.70970	.70237
82	.78452	.77632	.76827	.76036	.75260	.74499	.73751	.73016	.72295	.71587
83	.79513	.78725	.77952	.77192	.76446	.75713	.74992	.74284	.73589	.72905
84	.80547	.79792	.79051	.78322	.77606	.76901	.76208	.75527	.74857	.74198
85	.81557	.80836	.80126	.79429	.78742	.78067	.77402	.76748	.76104	.75471
86	.82524	.81835	.81157	.80489	.79832	.79185	.78548	.77921	.77304	.76695
87	.83423	.82764	.82115	.81477	.80847	.80228	.79617	.79015	.78423	.77838
88	.84253	.83623	.83002	.82390	.81787	.81193	.80607	.80029	.79460	.78899
89	.85033	.84430	.83836	.83250	.82672	.82102	.81540	.80985	.80438	.79899
90	.85784	.85208	.84639	.84079	.83525	.82979	.82441	.81909	.81384	.80867
91	.86502	.85951	.85408	.84871	.84342	.83820	.83304	.82795	.82292	.81796
92	.87164	.86638	.86118	.85605	.85098	.84598	.84104	.83616	.83134	.82657
93	.87761	.87257	.86759	.86267	.85781	.85300	.84826	.84357	.83894	.83437
94	.88290	.87806	.87327	.86854	.86386	.85924	.85468	.85017	.84570	.84130
95	.88750	.88282	.87820	.87364	.86913	.86466	.86025	.85589	.85158	.84732
96	.89136	.88683	.88236	.87793	.87355	.86922	.86494	.86071	.85652	.85238
97	.89481	.89041	.88606	.88176	.87750	.87329	.86913	.86501	.86093	.85690
98	.89783	.89354	.88930	.88511	.88096	.87685	.87279	.86877	.86479	.86085
99	.90067	.89649	.89235	.88826	.88420	.88019	.87622	.87230	.86814	.86456
100 ...	.90349	.89941	.89538	.89138	.88743	.88351	.87964	.87580	.87200	.86824
101 ...	.90600	.90202	.89807	.89416	.89029	.88646	.88267	.87891	.87519	.87150
102 ...	.90873	.90484	.90099	.89717	.89339	.88965	.88594	.88227	.87863	.87503
103 ...	.91217	.90841	.90468	.90099	.89733	.89370	.89011	.88654	.88301	.87952
104 ...	.91553	.91188	.90827	.90469	.90114	.89763	.89414	.89068	.88725	.88385
105 ...	.92047	.91701	.91358	.91018	.90680	.90345	.90013	.89683	.89356	.89032
106 ...	.92819	.92504	.92191	.91880	.91571	.91265	.90961	.90658	.90358	.90060
107 ...	.93868	.93596	.93325	.93056	.92788	.92522	.92258	.91995	.91734	.91474
108 ...	.95471	.95267	.95064	.94862	.94661	.94461	.94262	.94063	.93866	.93670
109 ...	.97985	.97893	.97801	.97710	.97619	.97529	.97438	.97348	.97259	.97170

Table G—Continued (4) Single Life, Unisex—Table Showing the Present Worth of the Remainder Interest in Property Transferred to a Pooled Income Fund Having the Yearly Rate of Return Shown—Applicable for Transfers after November 30, 1983, and before May 1, 1989

(1)	(2) Yearly Rate of Return									
Age	6.2%	6.4%	6.6%	6.8%	7.0%	7.2%	7.4%	7.6%	7.8%	8.0%
0	.04653	.04447	.04262	.04095	.03946	.03811	.03689	.03579	.03479	.03388
1	.02937	.02720	.02525	.02351	.02194	.02052	.01924	.01809	.01704	.01609
2	.02994	.02769	.02567	.02385	.02221	.02074	.01940	.01819	.01710	.01611
3	.03094	.02860	.02650	.02460	.02290	.02136	.01996	.01870	.01756	.01652
4	.03216	.02973	.02755	.02558	.02380	.02219	.02074	.01942	.01822	.01713
5	.03359	.03106	.02879	.02674	.02488	.02321	.02169	.02031	.01905	.01791
6	.03517	.03255	.03019	.02805	.02612	.02437	.02278	.02134	.02003	.01883
7	.93688	.03416	.03171	.02949	.02747	.02565	.02399	.02248	.02111	.01986
8	.03874	.03592	.03337	.03106	.02896	.02706	.02533	.02376	.02232	.02101
9	.04077	.03784	.03519	.03279	.03061	.02863	.02682	.02518	.02367	.02230
10	.04295	.03992	.03717	.03467	.03240	.03034	.02846	.02674	.02517	.02373
11	.04531	.04217	.03931	.03672	.03436	.03221	.03025	.02846	.02682	.02532
12	.04782	.04457	.04161	.03892	.03647	.03424	.03219	.03032	.02861	.02704
13	.05045	.04708	.04402	.04122	.03868	.03635	.03422	.03228	.03049	.02885
14	.05312	.04964	.04646	.04357	.04093	.03851	.03630	.03427	.03240	.03069
15	.05581	.05220	.04891	.04591	.04317	.04066	.03836	.03624	.03430	.03252
16	.05847	.05474	.05134	.04822	.04538	.04277	.04037	.03817	.03615	.03429
17	.06111	.05726	.05374	.05051	.04756	.04485	.04236	.04007	.03796	.03602
18	.06378	.05979	.05615	.05280	.04974	.04693	.04434	.04196	.03976	.03773
19	.06650	.06238	.05861	.05514	.05196	.04904	.04635	.04387	.04159	.03947
20	.06933	.06507	.06117	.05758	.05429	.05125	.04845	.04588	.04349	.04129
21	.07228	.06788	.06384	.06013	.05671	.05356	.05065	.04797	.04549	.04319
22	.07535	.07081	.06664	.06279	.05925	.05597	.05295	.05016	.04758	.04519
23	.07858	.07389	.06958	.06559	.06192	.05853	.05539	.05248	.04979	.04730
24	.08201	.07717	.07270	.06858	.06477	.06125	.05799	.05497	.05217	.04957
25	.08567	.08067	.07606	.07179	.06785	.06420	.06081	.05767	.05475	.05205
26	.08960	.08444	.07968	.07527	.07118	.06739	.06388	.06062	.05758	.05476
27	.09380	.08849	.08357	.07901	.07478	.07086	.06721	.06382	.06067	.05773
28	.09830	.09283	.08775	.08304	.07867	.07460	.07082	.06730	.06402	.06097
29	.10306	.09742	.09218	.08732	.08280	.07859	.07467	.07102	.06762	.06444
30	.10808	.10228	.09688	.09187	.08720	.08284	.07879	.07500	.07146	.06815
31	.11335	.10738	.10182	.09665	.09182	.08733	.08312	.07920	.07553	.07209
32	.11889	.11275	.10704	.10170	.09672	.09207	.08773	.08366	.07986	.07629
33	.12471	.11840	.11252	.10703	.10189	.09709	.09260	.08829	.08445	.08075
34	.13079	.12432	.11827	.11261	.10732	.10237	.09773	.09338	.08929	.08546
35	.13716	.13052	.12431	.11849	.11305	.10794	.10315	.09865	.09442	.09045
36	.14381	.13701	.13063	.12465	.11905	.11379	.10884	.10420	.09983	.09572
37	.15075	.14378	.13724	.13110	.12534	.11992	.11483	.11003	.10552	.10126
38	.15796	.15083	.14412	.13782	.13190	.12633	.12108	.11614	.11148	.10708
39	.16545	.15815	.15129	.14483	.13875	.13302	.12762	.12253	.11772	.11318
40	.17322	.16576	.15874	.15212	.14589	.14000	.13445	.12921	.12425	.11957
41	.18129	.17367	.16649	.15971	.15332	.14728	.14158	.13619	.13109	.12626
42	.18967	.18190	.17456	.16763	.16108	.15490	.14904	.14350	.13825	.13328
43	.19834	.19041	.18293	.17585	.16915	.16281	.15680	.15111	.14572	.14060
44	.20731	.19924	.19160	.18437	.17753	.17104	.16488	.15905	.15351	.14825
45	.21655	.20834	.20055	.19318	.18619	.17955	.17326	.16727	.16159	.15619
46	.22608	.21773	.20981	.20229	.19516	.18838	.18194	.17582	.16999	.16445
47	.23690	.22741	.21935	.21170	.20443	.19751	.19093	.18467	.17870	.17302
48	.24602	.23741	.22922	.22144	.21403	.20698	.20026	.19386	.18776	.18194
49	.25644	.24770	.23939	.23148	.22394	.21676	.20991	.20338	.19715	.19119
50	.26716	.25831	.24989	.24185	.23419	.22689	.21991	.21325	.20689	.20080
51	.27816	.26921	.26068	.25253	.24475	.23732	.23023	.22344	.21695	.21074
52	.28945	.28040	.27176	.26351	.25562	.24808	.24086	.23396	.22735	.22102
53	.30100	.29187	.28313	.27478	.26679	.25914	.25181	.24479	.23807	.23162
54	.31279	.30357	.29475	.28631	.27822	.27047	.26304	.25591	.24908	.24252

Table G—Continued (5) Single Life, Unisex—Table Showing the Present Worth of the Remainder Interest in Property Transferred to a Pooled Income Fund Having the Yearly Rate of Return Shown—Applicable for Transfers after November 30, 1983, and before May 1, 1989

(1)	(2) Yearly Rate of Return									
Age	6.2%	6.4%	6.6%	6.8%	7.0%	7.2%	7.4%	7.6%	7.8%	8.0%
55	.32482	.31553	.30663	.29810	.28992	.28208	.27455	.26733	.26039	.25372
56	.33707	.32771	.31875	.31014	.30188	.29395	.28633	.27901	.27197	.26521
57	.34955	.34015	.33112	.32244	.31411	.30610	.29840	.29099	.28386	.27700
58	.36225	.35280	.34372	.33499	.32659	.31851	.31074	.30325	.29604	.28909
59	.37519	.36571	.35659	.34781	.33936	.33122	.32337	.31581	.30853	.30150
60	.38836	.37886	.36971	.36089	.35239	.34420	.33630	.32867	.32132	.31422
61	.41077	.39226	.38309	.37425	.36572	.35748	.34953	.34185	.33444	.32727
62	.41542	.40591	.39674	.38788	.37932	.37106	.36307	.35535	.34788	.34066
63	.42930	.41981	.41064	.40178	.39321	.38492	.37691	.36915	.36165	.35438
64	.44338	.43392	.42477	.41591	.40734	.39905	.39102	.38324	.37571	.36841
65	.45765	.44823	.43910	.43027	.42171	.41342	.40539	.39760	.39005	.38272
66	.47208	.46271	.45364	.44483	.43630	.42803	.42000	.41221	.40465	.39731
67	.48666	.47736	.46834	.45958	.45108	.44283	.43483	.42705	.41949	.41215
68	.50138	.49215	.48320	.47450	.46605	.45784	.44987	.44211	.43457	.42724
69	.51624	.50711	.49824	.48961	.48122	.47307	.46513	.45741	.44990	.44259
70	.53125	.52223	.51345	.50491	.49660	.48851	.48063	.47296	.46549	.45821
71	.54645	.53755	.52899	.52045	.51223	.50422	.49641	.48880	.48139	.47416
72	.56183	.55307	.54453	.53621	.52809	.52018	.51246	.50493	.49758	.49042
73	.57731	.56870	.56030	.55211	.54412	.53631	.52870	.52126	.51400	.50691
74	.59275	.58431	.57606	.56801	.56015	.55247	.54497	.53764	.53048	.52347
75	.60803	.59976	.59168	.58379	.57607	.56852	.56115	.55393	.54687	.53997
76	.62308	.61500	.60709	.59936	.59179	.58439	.57714	.57005	.56311	.55632
77	.63789	.63000	.62227	.61470	.60730	.60005	.59294	.58599	.57917	.57249
78	.65247	.64477	.63723	.62984	.62261	.61551	.60856	.60174	.59506	.58851
79	.66687	.65938	.65203	.64483	.63777	.63084	.62405	.61739	.61085	.60443
80	.68114	.67386	.66672	.65971	.65284	64609	.63946	.63296	.62657	.62030
81	.69518	.68812	.68119	.67438	.66770	.66114	.65469	.64836	.64213	.63602
82	.70891	.70207	.69535	.68875	.68227	.67589	.66963	.66347	.65742	.65146
83	.72232	.71572	.70922	.70283	.69655	.69037	.68429	.67831	.67342	.66664
84	.73550	.72913	.72285	.71668	.71061	.70463	.69875	.69296	.68726	.68165
85	.74847	.74234	.73630	.73035	.72449	.71872	.71304	.70745	.70194	.69654
86	.76096	.75506	.74925	.74353	.73789	.73233	.72685	.72146	.71614	.71089
87	.77263	.76696	.76137	.75585	.75042	.74507	.73978	.73458	.72944	.72438
88	.78345	.77799	.77261	.76730	.76207	.75691	.75181	.74679	.74183	.73694
89	.79367	.78842	.78323	.77812	.77308	.76810	.76319	.75834	.75355	.74883
90	.80356	.79851	.79353	.78862	.78376	.77897	.77424	.76957	.76496	.76040
91	.81306	.80821	.80344	.79871	.79405	.78945	.78490	.78040	.77596	.77158
92	.82187	.81722	.81263	.80810	.80361	.79919	.79481	.79048	.78621	.78198
93	.82984	.82538	.82096	.81659	.81228	.80801	.80380	.79963	.79550	.79143
94	.83694	.83263	.32837	.83416	.81999	.81587	.81180	.80777	.80379	.79985
95	.84310	.83893	.83481	.83073	.82670	.82271	.81877	.81487	.81100	.80719
96	.84829	.84424	.84023	.83626	.83234	.82846	.82462	.83083	.81707	.81335
97	.85291	.84897	.84506	.84120	.83738	.83360	.82985	.82615	.82248	.81885
98	.85696	.85310	.84929	.84551	.84177	.83808	.83441	.83079	.82720	.82365
99	.86075	.85698	.85325	.84956	.84590	.84228	.83869	.83514	.83163	.82815
100 ...	.86452	.86084	.85719	.85357	.85000	.84645	.84294	.83947	.83603	.83262
101 ...	.86785	.86424	.86066	.85711	.85360	.85012	.84668	.84327	.83988	.83653
102 ...	.87146	.86792	.86442	.86094	.85750	.85409	.85072	.84737	.84405	.84077
103 ...	.87605	.87261	.86921	.86583	.86248	.85917	.85588	.85262	.84939	.84619
104 ...	.88047	.87713	.87382	.87053	.86727	.86403	.86083	.85765	.85449	.85136
105 ...	.88710	.88390	.88073	.87758	.87446	.87136	.86829	.86524	.86221	.85921
106 ...	.89764	.89471	.89179	.88889	.88601	.88315	.88032	.87750	.87470	.87192
107 ...	.91216	.90960	.90705	.90451	.90199	.89949	.89700	.89452	.89206	.88961
108 ...	.93474	.93280	.93086	.92894	.92702	.92511	.92321	.92132	.91944	.91757
109 ...	.97081	.96992	.96904	.96816	.96729	.96642	.96555	.96468	.96382	.96296

Table G—Continued (6) Single Life, Unisex—Table Showing the Present Worth of the Remainder Interest in Property Transferred to a Pooled Income Fund Having the Yearly Rate of Return Shown—Applicable for Transfers after November 30, 1983, and before May 1, 1989

(1) Age	(2) Yearly Rate of Return 8.2%	8.4%	8.6%	8.8%	9.0%	9.2%	9.4%	9.6%	9.8%	10.0%
0	.03305	.03230	.03161	.03098	.03040	.02987	.02938	.02893	.02851	.02812
1	.01523	.01444	.01372	.01307	.01247	.01192	.01141	.01094	.01051	.01012
2	.01520	.01438	.01362	.01294	.01230	.01173	.01119	.01070	.01025	.00983
3	.01557	.01470	.01391	.01319	.01253	.01192	.01136	.01084	.01036	.00992
4	.01613	.01522	.01439	.01363	.01294	.01229	.01170	.01116	.01066	.01019
5	.01687	.01591	.01504	.01424	.01351	.01283	.01221	.01164	.01111	.01062
6	.01774	.01674	.01582	.01498	.01421	.01350	.01284	.01224	.01168	.01116
7	.01871	.01766	.01670	.01581	.01500	.01425	.01356	.01292	.01233	.01178
8	.01980	.01870	.01769	.01676	.01591	.01512	.01439	.01372	.01309	.01252
9	.02104	.01989	.01883	.01785	.01695	.01612	.01535	.01464	.01398	.01337
10	.02241	.02120	.02009	.01906	.01812	.01724	.01644	.01569	.01499	.01435
11	.02394	.02267	.02150	.02042	.01943	.01851	.01766	.01688	.01615	.01547
12	.02560	.02427	.02305	.02192	.02088	.01991	.01902	.01819	.01742	.01671
13	.02734	.02595	.02467	.02349	.02240	.02139	.02045	.01958	.01877	.01802
14	.02912	.02766	.02632	.02509	.02394	.02288	.02190	.02098	.02013	.01934
15	.03087	.02935	.02795	.02666	.02546	.02435	.02331	.02235	.02146	.02063
16	.03257	.03099	.02952	.02817	.02691	.02575	.02466	.02366	.02272	.20185
17	.03423	.03257	.03104	.02962	.02831	.02709	.02595	.02490	.02391	.02300
18	.03586	.03414	.03253	.03105	.02967	.02839	.02721	.02610	.02507	.02410
19	.03752	.03572	.03414	.03249	.03105	.02971	.02846	.02730	.02621	.02520
20	.03925	.03737	.03562	.03399	.03248	.03108	.02977	.02855	.02741	.02635
21	.04107	.03910	.03727	.03557	.03398	.03251	.03114	.02986	.02866	.02755
22	.04297	.04091	.03899	.03722	.03556	.03402	.03258	.03123	.02998	.02880
23	.04498	.04283	.04083	.03897	.03723	.03562	.03410	.03269	.03137	.03014
24	.04715	.04491	.04282	.04087	.03905	.03735	.03577	.03428	.03290	.03159
25	.04953	.04718	.04499	.04295	.04105	.03927	.03761	.03605	.03459	.03322
26	.05213	.04968	.04740	.04527	.04327	.04141	.03966	.03803	.03649	.03505
27	.05499	.05243	.05005	.04782	.04573	.04377	.04194	.04023	.03861	.03710
28	.05811	.05545	.05295	.05062	.04844	.04639	.04447	.04267	.04098	.03938
29	.06146	.05868	.05608	.05365	.05136	.04922	.04721	.04532	.04354	.04187
30	.06506	.06217	.05945	.05691	.05452	.05228	.05017	.04819	.04633	.04457
31	.06888	.06586	.06303	.06038	.05789	.05554	.05334	.05126	.04930	.04746
32	.07295	.06981	.06687	.06410	.06149	.05904	.05674	.05456	.05251	.05058
33	.07728	.07401	.07095	.06806	.06535	.06279	.06038	.05810	.05595	.05392
34	.08185	.07846	.07527	.07227	.06944	.06677	.06425	.06187	.05962	.05750
35	.08671	.08319	.07988	.07675	.07380	.07102	.06839	.06590	.06355	.06132
36	.09184	.08819	.08475	.08150	.07843	.07553	.07278	.07019	.06773	.06540
37	.09725	.09347	.08989	.08652	.08332	.08030	.07745	.07474	.07217	.06974
38	.10293	.09901	.09531	.09180	.08848	.08534	.08237	.07955	.07687	.07433
39	.10889	.01483	.10099	.09736	.09391	.09065	.08755	.08462	.08182	.07917
40	.11514	.11094	.10697	.10320	.09963	.09624	.09302	.08996	.08706	.08429
41	.12168	.11735	.11324	.10934	.10564	.10212	.09878	.09560	.09258	.08970
42	.12856	.12409	.11984	.11581	.11197	.10833	.10486	.10156	.09842	.09543
43	.13574	.13113	.12675	.12258	.11862	.11484	.11125	.10783	.10456	.10145
44	.14325	.13850	.13398	.12967	.12558	.12167	.11795	.11441	.11102	.10779
45	.15105	.14616	.14150	.13706	.13283	.12880	.12495	.12128	.11777	.11442
46	.15917	.15414	.14935	.14478	.14041	.13625	.13227	.12847	.12484	.12137
47	.16760	.16244	.15751	.15280	.14831	.14402	.13991	.13599	.13223	.12863
48	.17639	.17109	.16602	.16119	.15656	.15214	.14791	.14385	.13997	.13626
49	.18551	.18007	.17488	.16991	.16516	.16060	.15625	.15207	.14806	.14422
50	.19499	.18942	.18410	.17900	.17412	.16944	.16496	.16065	.15653	.15257
51	.20480	.19911	.19366	.18844	.18343	.17862	.17401	.16959	.16534	.16126
52	.21495	.20914	.20357	.19822	.19309	.18816	.18343	.17888	.17451	.17031
53	.22544	.21951	.21381	.20835	.20309	.19805	.19320	.18853	.18404	.17972
54	.23622	.23018	.22437	.21878	.21341	.20825	.20328	.19850	.19390	.18946

Table G—Continued (7) Single Life, Unisex—Table Showing the Present Worth of the Remainder Interest in Property Transferred to a Pooled Income Fund Having the Yearly Rate of Return Shown—Applicable for Transfers after November 30, 1983, and before May 1, 1989

(1) Age	(2) Yearly Rate of Return 8.2%	8.4%	8.6%	8.8%	9.0%	9.2%	9.4%	9.6%	9.8%	10.0%
55	.24732	.24116	.23524	.22954	.22406	.21878	.21370	.20881	.20409	.19954
56	.25870	.25244	.24641	.24060	.23501	.22963	.22443	.21943	.21460	.20994
57	.27040	.26404	.25791	.25200	.24630	.24081	.23551	.23040	.22546	.22069
58	.28239	.27594	.26971	.26370	.25791	.25231	.24691	.24170	.23665	.23178
59	.29472	.28817	.28186	.27576	.26987	.26418	.25868	.25336	.24822	.24325
60	.30736	.30074	.29434	.28816	.28218	.27640	.27081	.26540	.26016	.25509
61	.32035	.31365	.30718	.30092	.29486	.28899	.28332	.27782	.27249	.26733
62	.33368	.32692	.32038	.31405	.30791	.30197	.29622	.29064	.28523	.27998
63	.34735	.34054	.33394	.32754	.32134	.31533	.30950	.30385	.29836	.29304
64	.36133	.35448	.34783	.34138	.33612	.32905	.32316	.31743	.31188	.30648
65	.37562	.36873	.36204	.35554	.34924	.34311	.33716	.33138	.32576	.32030
66	.39019	.38327	.37655	.37002	.36367	.35751	.35151	.34568	.34001	.33449
67	.40502	.39809	.39134	.38479	.37841	.37221	.36618	.36030	.35459	.34902
68	.42011	.41317	.40642	.39985	.39345	.38723	.38116	.37526	.36950	.36390
69	.43547	.42854	.42179	.41522	.40882	.40257	.39649	.39056	.38478	.37914
70	.45112	.44421	.43748	.43091	.42451	.41826	.41217	.40623	.40043	.39478
71	.46711	.46023	.45352	.44698	.44059	.43435	.42827	.42233	.41642	.41086
72	.48342	.47659	.46992	.46341	.45705	.45084	.44478	.43885	.43305	.42739
73	.49998	.49321	.48660	.48014	.47382	.46765	.46161	.45571	.44994	.44429
74	.51663	.50994	.50339	.49699	.49073	.48460	.47861	.47274	.46700	.64138
75	.53322	.52661	.52014	.51381	.50762	.50155	.49561	.48979	.48409	.47851
76	.54967	.54315	.53678	.53053	.52440	.51841	.41253	.50677	.50112	.49559
77	.56595	.55954	.55326	.54710	.54106	.53514	.52934	.52364	.51806	.51258
78	.58209	.57579	.56961	.56355	.55761	.55177	.54605	.54043	.53492	.52951
79	.59814	.59196	.58590	.57995	.57410	.56837	.56273	.55720	.55177	.54643
80	.61415	.60810	.60217	.59633	59060	.58497	.57944	.57401	.56866	.56341
81	.63001	.62410	.61830	.61260	.60699	.60148	.59606	.59073	.58548	.58033
82	.64561	.63985	.63419	.62862	.62314	.61775	.61245	.60723	.60210	.59705
83	.66095	.65535	.64983	.64441	.63907	.63381	.62863	.62354	.61852	.61358
84	.67612	.67068	.66533	.66005	.65486	.64974	.64470	.63973	.63484	.63002
85	.69116	.68589	.68070	.67559	.67055	.66558	.66068	.65586	.65110	.64641
86	.70573	.70063	.69561	.69066	.68578	.68096	.67622	.67154	.66692	.66236
87	.71939	.71466	.70961	.70481	.70009	.69542	.69082	.68628	.68180	.67738
88	.73211	.72735	.72265	.71801	.71343	.70891	.70445	.70005	.69570	.69141
89	.74417	.73956	.73501	.73053	.72609	.72172	.71739	.71312	.70891	.70474
90	.75590	.75146	.74707	.74273	.73845	.73422	.73004	.72591	.72182	.71779
91	.76724	.76296	.75873	.75454	.75041	.74632	.74229	.73829	.73435	.73045
92	.77781	.77368	.76960	.76556	.76158	.75763	.75373	.74988	.74606	.74229
93	.78740	.78342	.77948	.77558	.77173	.76791	.76414	.76042	.75673	.75308
94	.79596	.79210	.78829	.78452	.78079	.77710	.77345	.76983	.76626	.76272
95	.80341	.79967	.79597	.79231	.78869	.78510	.78155	.77304	.77457	.77113
96	.80967	.80603	.80242	.79885	.79532	.79183	.78837	.78494	.78155	.77819
97	.81526	.81170	.80818	.80470	.80125	.79783	.79445	.79110	.78779	.78450
98	.82013	.81665	.81320	.80979	.80641	.80306	.79975	.79647	.79322	.79000
99	.82470	.82129	.81791	.81456	.81125	.80797	.80471	.80149	.79830	.79514
100 ...	.82924	.82590	.82258	.81930	.81605	.81283	.80964	.80648	.80335	.80025
101 ...	.83322	.82993	.82667	.82344	.82024	.81708	.81394	.81082	.80774	.80468
102 ...	.83751	.83428	.83108	.82791	.82477	.82165	.81856	.81550	.81247	.80946
103 ...	.84301	.83986	.83674	.83365	.83058	.82754	.82452	.82153	.81857	.81563
104 ...	.84826	.84518	.84213	.83910	.83610	.83312	.83017	.82723	.82433	.82144
105 ...	.85623	.85327	.85033	.84741	.84452	.84165	.83880	.83597	.83316	.83038
106 ...	.86915	.86641	.86369	.86098	.85829	.85562	.85297	.85034	.84772	.84512
107 ...	.88718	.88476	.88236	.87997	.87759	.87523	.87288	.87054	.86822	.86591
108 ...	.91571	.91385	.91201	.91017	.90834	.90652	.90471	.90291	.90111	.89932
109 ...	.96211	.96125	.96041	.95966	.95872	.95788	.95704	.95620	.95537	.95455

Table G—Continued (8) Single Life, Unisex—Table Showing the Present Worth of the Remainder Interest in Property Transferred to a Pooled Income Fund Having the Yearly Rate of Return Shown—Applicable for Transfers after November 30, 1983, and before May 1, 1989

(1) Age	(2) Yearly Rate of Return 10.2%	10.4%	10.6%	10.8%	11.0%	11.2%	11.4%	11.6%	11.8%	12.0%
0	.02776	.02743	.02712	.02682	.02655	.02630	.02606	.02583	.02562	.02542
1	.00975	.00941	.00909	.00880	.00852	.00827	.00803	.00780	.00759	.00739
2	.00945	.00909	.00875	.00844	.00816	.00789	.00763	.00740	.00718	.00697
3	.00952	.00914	.00879	.00846	.00815	.00787	.00760	.00736	.00712	.00690
4	.00976	.00936	.00899	.00865	.00832	.00802	.00774	.00748	.00723	.00700
5	.01016	.00974	.00935	.00898	.00864	.00832	.00802	.00774	.00748	.00724
6	.01068	.01023	.00981	.00943	.00907	.00873	.00841	.00812	.00784	.00758
7	.01128	.01080	.01036	.00995	.00957	.00921	.00888	.00856	.00827	.00799
8	.01198	.01148	.01101	.01058	.01017	.00979	.00944	.00910	.00879	.00850
9	.01281	.01228	.01179	.01133	.01090	.01049	.01012	.00976	.00943	.00912
10	.01375	.01319	.01267	.01219	.01173	.01131	.01091	.01053	.01018	.00985
11	.01483	.01425	.01370	.01318	.01270	.01225	.01183	.01143	.01106	.01070
12	.01604	.01542	.01484	.01430	.01379	.01331	.01286	.01244	.01205	.01168
13	.01732	.01666	.01605	.01548	.01494	.01444	.01397	.01352	.01311	.01271
14	.01860	.01792	.01727	.01667	.01610	.01558	.01508	.01461	.01417	.01375
15	.01986	.01913	.01845	.01782	.01723	.01667	.01614	.01565	.01519	.01475
16	.02103	.02027	.01956	.01889	.01827	.01768	.01713	.01661	.01612	.01566
17	.02214	.02134	.02059	.01989	.01923	.01862	.01803	.01749	.01697	.01649
18	.02320	.02236	.02157	.02084	.02014	.01949	.01888	.01831	.01776	.01725
19	.02426	.02337	.02254	.02177	.02104	.02035	.01971	.01910	.01853	.01799
20	.02536	.02442	.02355	.02273	.02197	.02124	.02056	.01992	.01932	.01875
21	.02650	.02552	.02460	.02374	.02293	.02217	.02145	.02078	.02014	.01954
22	.02770	.02667	.02570	.02479	.02394	.02313	.02238	.02166	.02099	.02035
23	.02898	.02789	.02687	.02591	.02501	.02416	.02336	.02261	.02190	.02122
24	.03037	.02923	.02815	.02714	.02619	.02529	.02445	.02365	.02290	.02218
25	.03194	.03073	.02960	.02853	.02752	.02657	.02568	.02484	.02404	.02328
26	.03370	.03243	.03123	.03010	.02904	.02804	.02710	.02620	.02536	.02456
27	.05688	.03434	.03307	.03188	.03076	.02970	.02870	.02776	.02686	.02601
28	.03789	.03647	.03614	.03389	.03271	.03159	.03053	.02953	.02858	.02768
29	.04029	.03880	.03740	.03608	.03483	.03365	.03253	.03147	.03047	.02951
30	.04291	.04135	.03987	.03848	.03716	.03591	.03473	.03361	.03255	.03154
31	.04572	.04407	.04252	.04105	.03966	.03834	.03709	.03591	.03478	.03372
32	.04875	.04702	.04538	.04384	.04237	.04098	.03966	.03841	.03722	.03610
33	.05200	.05019	.04847	.04684	.04530	.40383	.04244	.04112	.03987	.03867
34	.05548	.05358	.05177	.05006	.04843	.04689	.04543	.04403	.04271	.04145
35	.05921	.05722	.05532	.05352	.05181	.05019	.04865	.04718	.04578	.04445
36	.06319	.06110	.05911	.05722	.05543	.05372	.05210	.05055	.04907	.04767
37	.06743	.06524	.06315	.06117	.05929	.05749	.05578	.05416	.05260	.05112
38	.07191	.06962	.06744	.06536	.06338	.06150	.05970	.05799	.05636	.05480
39	.07665	.07425	.07197	.06980	.06773	.06575	.06387	.06207	.06035	.05871
40	.08166	.07916	.07677	.07450	.07233	.07026	.06828	.06639	.06459	.06286
41	.08696	.08434	.08185	.07947	.07721	.07504	.07297	.07099	.06909	.06728
42	.09257	.08985	.08725	.08477	.08239	.08018	.07796	.07589	.07390	.07200
43	.09848	.09564	.09293	.09034	.08787	.08550	.08323	.08106	.07898	.07699
44	.10470	.10175	.09893	.09623	.09365	.09118	.08881	.08654	.08437	.08228
45	.11121	.10815	.10522	.10241	.09972	.09714	.09467	.09230	.09003	.08784
46	.11805	.11486	.11182	.10890	.10610	.10341	.10084	.09837	.09599	.09371
47	.12519	.12189	.11873	.11569	.11279	.10999	.10731	.10473	.10226	.09988
48	.13269	.12927	.12600	.12285	.11983	.11693	.11414	.11145	.10888	.10639
49	.14054	.13700	.13361	.13035	.12721	.12721	.12130	.11852	.11583	.11325
50	.14876	.14511	.14160	.13822	.13497	.13185	.12884	.12595	.12316	.12047
51	.15734	.15356	.14994	.14645	.14309	.13985	.13674	.13373	.13084	.12805
52	.16627	.16238	.15864	.15504	.15156	.14822	.14499	.14188	.13888	.13598
53	.17557	.17156	.16770	.16399	.16040	.15695	.15361	.15039	.14729	.14428
54	.18519	.18107	.17710	.17327	.16957	.16601	.16256	.15924	.15602	.15292

Table G—Continued (9) Single Life, Unisex—Table Showing the Present Worth of the Remainder Interest in Property Transferred to a Pooled Income Fund Having the Yearly Rate of Return Shown—Applicable for Transfers after November 30, 1983, and before May 1, 1989

(1)	(2) Yearly Rate of Return									
Age	10.2%	10.4%	10.6%	10.8%	11.0%	11.2%	11.4%	11.6%	11.8%	12.0%
55	.19515	.19092	.18684	.18290	.17909	.17542	.17186	.16843	.16511	.16190
56	.20544	.20110	.19691	.19286	.18894	.18516	.18150	.17796	.17454	.17122
57	.21609	.21164	.20734	.20318	.19916	.19527	.19150	.18786	.18733	.18091
58	.22707	.22252	.21811	.21385	.20972	.20573	.20186	.19811	.19448	.19096
59	.23844	.23378	.22928	.22491	.22068	.21659	.21262	.20877	.20504	.20142
60	.25018	.24543	.24082	.23636	.23203	.22784	.22377	.21982	.21599	.21227
61	.26233	.25749	.25279	.24823	.24381	.23952	.23535	.23131	.22738	.22357
62	.27490	.26996	.26517	.26052	.25601	.25163	.24737	.24324	.23922	.23531
63	.28787	.28286	.27798	.27325	.26865	.26418	.25984	.25561	.25151	.24751
64	.30124	.29615	.29120	.28639	.28171	.27716	.27273	.26842	.26423	.26015
65	.31500	.30983	.30481	.29993	.29517	.29054	.28604	.28165	.27738	.27322
66	.32912	.32390	.31881	.31386	.30904	.30434	.29976	.29530	.29096	.28672
67	.34360	.33832	.33318	.32817	.32328	.31852	.31388	.30935	.30494	.30063
68	.35843	.35311	.34791	.34285	.33791	.33310	.32840	.32381	.31933	.31496
69	.37365	.36828	.36305	.35794	.35296	.34809	.34334	.33870	.33417	.32975
70	.38925	.38386	.37860	.37346	.36844	.36353	.35874	.35405	.34948	.34500
71	.40532	.39991	.39463	.38945	.38442	.37948	.37466	.36994	.36532	.36081
72	.42185	.41644	.41115	.40597	.40091	.39595	.39111	.38636	.38172	.37718
73	.43876	.43336	.42807	.42289	.41782	.41286	.40801	.40325	.39859	.39403
74	.45588	.45050	.44522	.44005	.43499	.43004	.42518	.42042	.41575	.41118
75	.47304	.46769	.46244	.45729	.45225	.44730	.44245	.43770	.43304	.42846
76	.49016	.48485	.47963	.47451	.46949	.46457	.45974	.45500	.45035	.44579
77	.50721	.50193	.49676	.49168	.48670	.48181	.47700	.47229	.46766	.46311
78	.52419	.51898	.51385	.50882	.50388	.49903	.49426	.48958	.48497	.48045
79	.54119	.53604	.64097	.52600	.52111	.51631	.51159	.50694	.50238	.49789
80	.55825	.55318	.54819	.54328	.53846	.53371	.52905	.52446	.41994	.51550
81	.57526	.57027	.56536	.56053	.55578	.55110	.54650	.54197	.53752	.53313
82	.59208	.58718	.58236	.57762	.57295	.56835	.56382	.55937	.55497	.55065
83	.60871	.60392	.59920	.59455	.58997	.58546	.58101	.57663	.57231	.56806
84	.62527	.62959	.62597	.61143	.60695	.50253	.59817	.59388	.58965	.58547
85	.64179	.63723	.63273	.62830	.62393	.61961	.61536	.61116	.60703	.60294
86	.65787	.65344	.64907	.64475	.64050	.63630	.63215	.62806	.62402	.62004
87	.67302	.66871	.66446	.66026	.65612	.65203	.64800	.64401	.64007	.63619
88	.68717	.68298	.67885	.67477	.67074	.66676	.66282	.65894	.65510	.65131
89	.70063	.69656	.69255	.68858	.68466	.68079	.67696	.67318	.66944	.66574
90	.71380	.70986	.70597	.70212	.69831	.69455	.69084	.68716	.68353	.67993
91	.72659	.72278	.71901	.71528	.71160	.70795	.70435	.70078	.69726	.69377
92	.78356	.73488	.73123	.72762	.72405	.72052	.71703	.71357	.71015	.70677
93	.74947	.74590	.74236	.73887	.73541	.73198	.72860	.72524	.72192	.71864
94	.75922	.75575	.75233	.74893	.74557	.74225	.73896	.73570	.73248	.72928
95	.76773	.76436	.76102	.75772	.75445	.75121	.74801	.74483	.74169	.73858
96	.77487	.77158	.76832	.76510	.76190	.75874	.75561	.75250	.74943	.74639
97	.78125	.77803	.77485	.77169	.76856	.76546	.76240	.75936	.75635	.75336
98	.78681	.78365	.78052	.77742	.77435	.77131	.76830	.76531	.76235	.75942
99	.79201	.78891	.78583	.78279	.77977	.77678	.77382	.77088	.76798	.76509
100 ...	.79717	.79412	.79111	.78811	.78515	.78221	.77930	.77642	.77356	.77072
101 ...	.80165	.79865	.79568	.79273	.78981	.78691	.78404	.78119	.77837	.77557
102 ...	.80648	.80353	.80060	.79769	.79481	.79196	.78912	.78632	.78353	.78077
103 ...	.81271	.80982	.80695	.80411	.80129	.79849	.79572	.79297	.79024	.78753
104 ...	.81858	.81574	.81292	.81013	.80736	.80460	.80188	.79917	.79648	.79381
105 ...	.82761	.82487	.82214	.81943	.81675	.81408	.81143	.80881	.80620	.80361
106 ...	.84254	.83998	.83743	.83490	.83238	.82989	.82740	.82494	.82249	.82006
107 ...	.86362	.86133	.85906	.85681	.85456	.85233	.85012	.84791	.84572	.84353
108 ...	.89755	.89577	.89401	.89226	.89051	.88877	.88704	.88532	.88361	.88190
109 ...	.95372	.95290	.95208	.95126	.95045	.94964	.94883	.94803	.94723	.94643

Table G—Continued (10) Single Life, Unisex—Table Showing the Present Worth of the Remainder Interest in Property Transferred to a Pooled Income Fund Having the Yearly Rate of Return Shown—Applicable for Transfers after November 30, 1983, and before May 1, 1989

(1) Age	(2) Yearly Rate of Return									
	12.2%	12.4%	12.6%	12.8%	13.0%	13.2%	13.4%	13.6%	13.8%	14.0%
0	.02523	.02505	.02488	.02472	.02456	.02442	.02428	.02414	.02402	.02389
1	.00721	.00703	.00687	.00671	.00657	.00643	.00629	.00617	.00605	.00594
2	.00678	.00659	.00642	.00626	.00610	.00596	.00582	.00569	.00556	.00544
3	.00670	.00650	.00632	.00615	.00599	.00583	.00569	.00555	.00542	.00529
4	.00678	.00658	.00638	.00620	.00603	.00586	.00571	.00556	.00542	.00529
5	.00701	.00679	.00658	.00639	.00620	.00603	.00587	.00571	.00556	.00542
6	.00733	.00710	.00688	.00668	.00648	.00630	.00612	.00595	.00580	.00565
7	.00773	.00748	.00725	.00703	.00682	.00663	.00644	.00626	.00610	.00594
8	.00822	.00796	.00771	.00748	.00726	.00705	.00685	.00666	.00648	.00631
9	.00882	.00854	.00828	.00803	.00780	.00757	.00736	.00716	.00697	.00679
10	.00953	.00924	.00896	.00869	.00844	.00821	.00798	.00777	.00756	.00737
11	.01037	.01006	.00976	.00948	.00922	.00896	.00872	.00850	.00828	.00807
12	.01132	.01099	.01068	.01038	.01010	.00983	.00958	.00934	.00911	.00889
13	.01234	.01199	.01166	.01134	.01104	.01076	.01049	.01024	.00999	.00976
14	.01336	.01299	.01264	.01231	.01199	.01170	.01141	.01114	.01088	.01064
15	.01434	.01395	.01358	.01323	.01289	.01258	.01228	.01200	.01172	.01147
16	.01552	.01481	.01442	.01405	.01371	.01337	.01306	.01275	.01247	.01220
17	.01603	.01559	.01518	.01480	.01443	.01408	.01375	.01343	.01313	.01284
18	.01677	.01631	.01588	.01547	.01508	.01471	.01436	.01403	.01371	.01341
19	.01748	.01700	.01654	.01611	.01570	.01531	.01494	.01459	.01426	.01394
20	.01821	.01770	.01722	.01677	.01633	.01592	.01553	.01516	.01481	.01447
21	.01897	.01843	.01792	.01744	.01698	.01655	.01614	.01574	.01537	.01502
22	.01975	.01918	.01864	.01813	.01765	.01719	.01675	.01634	.01594	.01557
23	.02059	.01998	.01941	.01887	.01836	.01787	.01741	.01697	.01655	.01615
24	.02151	.02087	.02027	.01970	.01915	.01863	.01814	.01768	.01723	.01681
25	.02257	.02189	.02125	.02064	.02006	.01952	.01899	.01850	.01802	.01757
26	.02380	.02308	.02240	.02175	.02114	.02056	.02000	.01947	.01897	.01849
27	.02521	.02445	.02373	.02304	.02239	.02177	.02118	.02061	.02008	.01956
28	.02683	.02602	.02525	.02452	.02382	.02317	.02254	.02194	.02137	.02082
29	.02861	.02775	.02694	.02616	.02543	.02472	.02405	.02342	.02281	.02223
30	.03058	.02967	.03881	.02798	.02720	.02645	.02574	.02506	.02441	.02379
31	.03270	.03174	.03082	.02995	.02911	.02832	.02756	.02684	.02615	.02549
32	.03502	.03400	.03303	.03210	.03122	.03037	.02957	.02880	.02806	.02736
33	.03754	.03646	.03543	.03444	.03350	.03261	.03175	.03093	.03015	.02940
34	.04025	.03910	.03801	.03697	.03597	.03502	.03411	.03324	.03241	.03162
35	.04318	.04197	.04081	.03971	.03865	.03764	.03668	.03576	.03488	.03403
36	.04633	.04505	.04383	.04266	.04154	.04048	.03945	.03847	.03754	.03664
37	.04971	.04836	.04707	.04583	.04465	.04352	.04244	.04140	.04040	.03945
38	.05331	.05188	.05052	.04922	.04797	.04677	.04563	.04453	.04347	.04246
39	.05714	.05564	.05420	.05282	.05150	.05024	.04903	.04787	.04675	.04568
40	.06121	.05963	.05812	.05667	.05528	.05394	.05266	.04143	.05025	.04912
41	.06554	.06388	.06229	.06076	.05929	.05789	.05653	.05524	.05399	.05279
42	.07018	.06843	.06675	.06514	.06360	.06212	.06069	.05932	.05800	.05674
43	.07508	.07324	.07148	.06979	.06817	.06661	.06511	.06366	.06227	.06093
44	.08028	.07835	.07651	.07473	.07303	.07138	.06980	.06828	.06682	.06541
45	.08575	.08373	.08180	.07993	.07814	.07642	.07476	.07316	.07162	.07013
46	.09152	.08941	.08738	.08543	.08355	.08174	.08000	.07832	.07670	.07514
47	.09759	.09539	.09326	.09122	.08926	.08736	.08553	.08377	.08207	.08042
48	.10410	.10171	.09949	.09735	.09530	.09331	.09140	.08955	.08776	.08604
49	.11076	.10836	.10605	.10382	.10167	.09959	.09759	.09565	.09378	.09198
50	.11788	.11538	.11297	.11065	.10840	.10624	.10414	.10212	.10016	.09827
51	.12535	.12276	.12025	.11782	.11548	.11322	.11104	.10892	.10688	.10490
52	.13319	.13049	.12788	.12536	.12292	.12057	.11829	.11608	.11395	.11188
53	.14139	.13858	.13588	.13326	.13072	.12827	.12590	.12360	.12138	.11922
54	.14992	.14701	.14420	.14149	.13885	.13631	.13384	.13145	.12913	.12689

Table G—Continued (11) Single Life, Unisex—Table Showing the Present Worth of the Remainder Interest in Property Transferred to a Pooled Income Fund Having the Yearly Rate of Return Shown—Applicable for Transfers after November 30, 1983, and before May 1, 1989

(1) Age	(2) Yearly Rate of Return 12.2%	12.4%	12.6%	12.8%	13.0%	13.2%	13.4%	13.6%	13.8%	14.0%
55	.15880	.15579	.15288	.15006	.14733	.14469	.14213	.13964	.13724	.13490
56	.16801	.16491	.16190	.15898	.15615	.15341	.15075	.14817	.14567	.14324
57	.17760	.17439	.17128	.16827	.16534	.16250	.15975	.15708	.15448	.15196
58	.18755	.18424	.18103	.17792	.17489	.17196	.16911	.16634	.16365	.16104
59	.19790	.19450	.19119	.18798	.18486	.18183	.17888	.17602	.17324	.17053
60	.20866	.20516	.20175	.19844	.19523	.19210	.18906	.18611	.18323	.18043
61	.21986	.21626	.21276	.20936	.20695	.20283	.19970	.19665	.19368	.19079
62	.23151	.22782	.22423	.22073	.21733	.21402	.21079	.20766	.20460	.20162
63	.24362	.23984	.23616	.23257	.22908	.22568	.22237	.21914	.21600	.21293
64	.25617	.25231	.24854	.24487	.24129	.23780	.23440	.23109	.22786	.22471
65	.26917	.26522	.26137	.25761	.25395	.25038	.24690	.24350	.24019	.23695
66	.28259	.27857	.27464	.27081	.26707	.26342	.25986	.25638	.25298	.24967
67	.29643	.29233	.28833	.28443	.28061	.27689	.27325	.26970	.26623	.26284
68	.31070	.30653	.30246	.29849	.29461	.29081	.28711	.28348	.27994	.27647
69	.32542	.32120	.31707	.31303	.30908	.30523	.30145	.29776	.29415	.29062
70	.34063	.33635	.33217	.32807	.32407	.32015	.31632	.31257	.30890	.30530
71	.35639	.35207	.34784	.34370	.33965	.33568	.33179	.32799	.32426	.32061
72	.37273	.36837	.36410	.35993	.35583	.35182	.34789	.34404	.34027	.33657
73	.38955	.38517	.38088	.37667	.37255	.36815	.36455	.36066	.35685	.35311
74	.40670	.40230	.39799	.39377	.38962	.38555	.38156	.37765	.37381	.37004
75	.42398	.41958	.41526	.41102	.40686	.40278	.39877	.39484	.39098	.38719
76	.44131	.43691	.43259	.42835	.42419	.42010	.41608	.41213	.40826	.40445
77	.45864	.45425	.44994	.44571	.44155	.43746	.43344	.42949	.42561	.42179
78	.47601	.47164	.46734	.46312	.45897	.45489	.45088	.44693	.44305	.43923
79	.49348	.48914	.48487	.48067	.47654	.47248	.46848	.46454	.46067	.45686
80	.51112	.50682	.50259	.49842	.49432	.49028	.48631	.48240	.47854	.47475
81	.52881	.52455	.52036	.51624	.51218	.50818	.50423	.50035	.49653	.49276
82	.54639	.54219	.53805	.53398	.52996	.52600	.52210	.51826	.51447	.51074
83	.56386	.55973	.55566	.55164	.54768	.54377	.53992	.53613	.53238	.52869
84	.58136	.57730	.57329	.56934	.56545	.56160	.55781	.55407	.55038	.54674
85	.59891	.59494	.59102	.58715	.58333	.57956	.57584	.57216	.56854	.56496
86	.61610	.61222	.60839	.60460	.60086	.59717	.59353	.58993	.58638	.58287
87	.63235	.62856	.62481	.62111	.61746	.61385	.61028	.61676	.60328	.59984
88	.64757	.64386	.64021	.63659	.63302	.62950	.62601	.62256	.61915	.61578
89	.66209	.65848	.65491	.65149	.64790	.64445	.64104	.63767	.63434	.63105
90	.67638	.67387	.66939	.66596	.66256	.62920	.65588	.65259	.64934	.64612
91	.69032	.68691	.68353	.68019	.67689	.67362	.67039	.66719	.66402	.66089
92	.70342	.70011	.69683	.69359	.69038	.68720	.68405	.68094	.67786	.67481
93	.71539	.71217	.70899	.70584	.70271	.69962	.69657	.69354	.69054	.68757
94	.72612	.72299	.71989	.71683	.71379	.71078	.70780	.70485	.70193	.69903
95	.73550	.73245	.73943	.72643	.72347	.72053	.71763	.71475	.71189	.70906
96	.74337	.74039	.73743	.73450	.73160	.73872	.72587	.72305	.72026	.71748
97	.75041	.74748	.74458	.74171	.73886	.73604	.73325	.73048	.72773	.72501
98	.75652	.75364	.75079	.74797	.74517	.74329	.73964	.73692	.73422	.73154
99	.76224	.75941	.75660	.75882	.75106	.74833	.74562	.74294	.74028	.73764
100 ...	.76791	.76521	.76237	.75963	.75692	.75423	.75156	.74892	.74630	.74370
101 ...	.77280	.77005	.75732	.76462	.76194	.75928	.75664	.75403	.75144	.74887
102 ...	.77804	.77532	.77263	.76996	.76732	.76469	.76209	.75950	.75694	.75440
103 ...	.78485	.78218	.77954	.77692	.77432	.77174	.76918	.76664	.76413	.76163
104 ...	.79117	.78854	.78594	.78335	.78078	.77824	.77571	.77320	.77071	.76824
105 ...	.80103	.79848	.79595	.79343	.79093	.78845	.78599	.78354	.78111	.77870
106 ...	.81764	.81524	.81285	.81048	.80813	.80579	.80346	.80115	.79885	.79657
107 ...	.84137	.83921	.83706	.83493	.83281	.83070	.82860	.82652	.82444	.82238
108 ...	.88020	.87851	.87682	.87515	.87348	.87182	.87016	.86852	.86688	.86525
109 ...	.94563	.94484	.94405	.94326	.94248	.94170	.94092	.94014	.93937	.93860

(e) Present value of the remainder interest in the case of transfers to pooled income funds for which the valuation date is after April 30, 1989, and before May 1, 1999. *(1) In general.* In the case of transfers to pooled income funds for which the valuation date is after April 30, 1989, and before May 1, 1999, the present value of a remainder interest is determined under this section. See, however, section 1.7520-3(b) (relating to exceptions to the use of prescribed tables under certain circumstances). The present value of a remainder interest that is dependent on the termination of the life of one individual is computed by the use of Table S in paragraph (e)(5) of this section. For purposes of the computation's under this section, the age of an individual is the age at the individual's nearest birthday. If the valuation date of a transfer to a pooled income fund is after April 30, 1989, and before June 10, 1994, a transferor can rely on Notice 89-24, 1989-1 C.B. 660, or Notice 89-60, 1989-1 C.B. 700, in valuing the transferred interest. (See section 601.601(d)(2)(ii)(b) of this chapter.)

(2) Present value of a remainder interest. The present value of a remainder interest in property transferred to a pooled income fund is computed on the basis of—

(i) Life contingencies determined from the values of 1x that are set forth in Table 80CNSMT in section 20.2031-7A(e)(4) of this chapter (Estate Tax Regulations); and

(ii) Discount at a rate of interest, compounded annually, equal to the highest yearly rate of return of the pooled income fund for the 3 taxable years immediately preceding its taxable year in which the transfer of property to the fund is made. The provisions of § 1.642(c)-6(c) apply for determining the yearly rate of return. However, where the taxable year is less than 12 months, the provisions of § 1.642(c)-6(e)(3)(ii) apply for the determining the yearly rate of return.

(3) Pooled income funds in existence less than 3 taxable years. The provisions of § 1.642(c)-6(e)(4) apply for determining the highest yearly rate of return when the pooled income fund has been in existence less than three taxable years.

(4) Computation of value of remainder interest. The factor that is used in determining the present value of a remainder interest that is dependent on the termination of the life of one individual is the factor from Table S in paragraph (e)(5) of this section under the appropriate yearly rate of return opposite the number that corresponds to the age of the individual upon whose life the value of the remainder interest is based. Table S in paragraph (e)(5) of this section includes factors for yearly rates of return from 4.2 to 14 percent. Many actuarial factors not contained in Table S in paragraph (e)(5) of this section are contained in Table S in Internal Revenue Service Publication 1457, "Actuarial Values, Alpha Volume," (8-89). Publication 1457 is no longer available for purchase from the Superintendent of Documents, United States Government Printing Office, Washington, DC 20402. However, pertinent factors in this publication may be obtained by a written request to: CC:DOM:CORP:R (IRS Publication 1457), room 5226, Internal Revenue Service, POB 7604, Ben Franklin Station, Washington, DC 20044. For other situations, see § 1.642(c)-6(b). If the yearly rate of return is a percentage that is between the yearly rates of return for which factors are provided, a linear interpolation must be made. The present value of the remainder interest is determined by multiplying the fair market value of the property on the valuation date by the appropriate remainder factor. For an example of a computation of the present value of a remainder interest requiring a linear interpolation adjustment, see § 1.642(c)-6(e)(5).

(5) Actuarial tables. In the case of transfers for which the valuation date is after April 30, 1989, and before May 1, 1999, the present value of a remainder interest dependent on the termination of one life in the case of a transfer to a pooled income fund is determined by use of the following tables:

TABLE S

BASED ON LIFE TABLE 80CNSMT SINGLE LIFE REMAINDER FACTORS [APPLICABLE AFTER APRIL 30, 1989, AND BEFORE MAY 1, 1999]

	INTEREST RATE									
AGE	4.2%	4.4%	4.6%	4.8%	5.0%	5.2%	5.4%	5.6%	5.8%	6.0%
0	.07389	.06749	.06188	.05695	.05261	.04879	.04541	.04243	.03978	.03744
1	.06494	.05832	.05250	.04738	.04287	.03889	.03537	.03226	.02950	.02705
2	.06678	.05999	.05401	.04874	.04410	.03999	.03636	.03314	.03028	.02773
3	.06897	.06200	.05587	.05045	.04567	.04143	.03768	.03435	.03139	.02875
4	.07139	.06425	.05796	.05239	.04746	.04310	.03922	.03578	.03271	.02998
5	.07401	.06669	.06023	.05451	.04944	.04494	.04094	.03738	.03421	.03137
6	.07677	.06928	.06265	.05677	.05156	.04692	.04279	.03911	.03583	.03289
7	.07968	.07201	.06521	.05918	.05381	.04903	.04477	.04097	.03757	.03453
8	.08274	.07489	.06792	.06172	.05621	.05129	.04689	.04297	.03945	.03630
9	.08597	.07794	.07079	.06443	.05876	.05370	.04917	.04511	.04148	.03821
10	.08936	.08115	.07383	.06730	.06147	.05626	.05159	.04741	.04365	.04027
11	.09293	.08453	.07704	.07035	.06436	.05900	.05419	.04988	.04599	.04250
12	.09666	.08807	.08040	.07354	.06739	.06188	.05693	.05248	.04847	.04486
13	.10049	.09172	.08387	.07684	.07053	.06487	.05977	.05518	.05104	.04731
14	.10437	.09541	.08738	.08017	.07370	.06788	.06263	.05791	.05364	.04978
15	.10827	.09912	.09090	.08352	.07688	.07090	.06551	.06064	.05623	.05225
16	.11220	.10285	.09445	.08689	.08008	.07394	.06839	.06337	.05883	.05472
17	.11615	.10661	.09802	.09028	.08330	.07699	.07129	.06612	.06144	.05719
18	.12017	.11043	.10165	.09373	.08656	.08009	.07422	.06890	.06408	.05969
19	.12428	.11434	.10537	.09726	.08992	.08327	.07724	.07177	.06679	.06226
20	.12850	.11836	.10919	.10089	.09337	.08654	.08035	.07471	.06959	.06492
21	.13282	.12248	.11311	.10462	.09692	.08991	.08355	.07775	.07247	.06765
22	.13728	.12673	.11717	.10848	.10059	.09341	.08686	.08090	.07546	.07049
23	.14188	.13113	.12136	.11248	.10440	.09703	.09032	.08418	.07858	.07345
24	.14667	.13572	.12575	.11667	.10839	.10084	.09395	.08764	.08187	.07659
25	.15167	.14051	.13034	.12106	.11259	.10486	.09778	.09130	.08536	.07991
26	.15690	.14554	.13517	.12569	.11703	.10910	.10184	.09518	.08907	.08346
27	.16237	.15081	.14024	.13056	.12171	.11359	.10614	.09930	.09302	.08724
28	.16808	.15632	.14555	.13567	.12662	.11831	.11068	.10366	.09720	.09125

29	.17404	.16208	.15110	.14104	.13179	.12329	.11547	.10827	.10163	.09551
30	.18025	.16808	.15692	.14665	.13721	.12852	.12051	.11313	.10631	.10002
31	.18672	.17436	.16300	.15255	.14291	.13403	.12584	.11827	.11127	.10480
32	.19344	.18090	.16935	.15870	.14888	.13980	.13142	.12367	.11650	.10985
33	.20044	.18772	.17598	.16514	.15513	.14587	.13730	.12936	.12201	.11519
34	.20770	.19480	.18287	.17185	.16165	.15221	.14345	.13533	.12780	.12080

TABLE S

BASED ON LIFE TABLE 80CNSMT SINGLE LIFE REMAINDER FACTORS APPLICABLE AFTER APRIL 30, 1989

	INTEREST RATE									
AGE	4.2%	4.4%	4.6%	4.8%	5.0%	5.2%	5.4%	5.6%	5.8%	6.0%
35	.21522	.20215	.19005	.17884	.16846	.15883	.14989	.14159	.13388	.12670
36	.22299	.20974	.19747	.18609	.17552	.16571	.15660	.14812	.14022	.13287
37	.23101	.21760	.20516	.19360	.18286	.17288	.16358	.15492	.14685	.13933
38	.23928	.22572	.21311	.20139	.19048	.18032	.17085	.16201	.15377	.14607
39	.24780	.23409	.22133	.20945	.19837	.18804	.17840	.16939	.16097	.15310
40	.25658	.24273	.22982	.21778	.20654	.19605	.18624	.17706	.16847	.16043
41	.26560	.25163	.23858	.22639	.21499	.20434	.19436	.18502	.17627	.16806
42	.27486	.26076	.24758	.23525	.22370	.21289	.20276	.19326	.18434	.17597
43	.28435	.27013	.25683	.24436	.23268	.22172	.21143	.20177	.19270	.18416
44	.29407	.27975	.26633	.25373	.24191	.23081	.22038	.21057	.20134	.19265
45	.30402	.28961	.27608	.26337	.25142	.24019	.22962	.21966	.21028	.20144
46	.31420	.29970	.28608	.27326	.26120	.24983	.23913	.22904	.21951	.21053
47	.32460	.31004	.29632	.28341	.27123	.25975	.24892	.23870	.22904	.21991
48	.33521	.32058	.30679	.29379	.28151	.26992	.25897	.24862	.23883	.22957
49	.34599	.33132	.31746	.30438	.29201	.28032	.26926	.25879	.24888	.23949
50	.35695	.34224	.32833	.31518	.30273	.29094	.27978	.26921	.25918	.24966
51	.36809	.35335	.33940	.32619	.31367	.30180	.29055	.27987	.26973	.26010
52	.37944	.36468	.35070	.33744	.32486	.31292	.30158	.29081	.28057	.27083
53	.39098	.37622	.36222	.34892	.33629	.32429	.31288	.30203	.29170	.28186
54	.40269	.38794	.37393	.36062	.34795	.33590	.32442	.31349	.30308	.29316
55	.41457	.39985	.38585	.37252	.35983	.34774	.33621	.32522	.31474	.30473
56	.42662	.41194	.39796	.38464	.37193	.35981	.34824	.33720	.32666	.31658
57	.43884	.42422	.41028	.39697	.38426	.37213	.36053	.34945	.33885	.32872
58	.45123	.43668	.42279	.40951	.39682	.38468	.37307	.36196	.35132	.34114
59	.46377	.44931	.43547	.42224	.40958	.39745	.38584	.37471	.36405	.35383
60	.47643	.46206	.44830	.43513	.42250	.41040	.39880	.38767	.37699	.36674
61	.48916	.47491	.46124	.44814	.43556	.42350	.41192	.40080	.39012	.37985
62	.50196	.48783	.47427	.46124	.44874	.43672	.42518	.41408	.40340	.39314
63	.51480	.50081	.48736	.47444	.46201	.45006	.43856	.42749	.41684	.40658
64	.52770	.51386	.50054	.48773	.47540	.46352	.45208	.44105	.43043	.42019
65	.54069	.52701	.51384	.50115	.48892	.47713	.46577	.45480	.44422	.43401
66	.55378	.54029	.52727	.51472	.50262	.49093	.47965	.46876	.45824	.44808
67	.56697	.55368	.54084	.52845	.51648	.50491	.49373	.48293	.47248	.46238
68	.58026	.56717	.55453	.54231	.53049	.51905	.50800	.49729	.48694	.47691
69	.59358	.58072	.56828	.55624	.54459	.53330	.52238	.51179	.50154	.49160
70	.60689	.59427	.58205	.57021	.55874	.54762	.53683	.52638	.51624	.50641

TABLE S

BASED ON LIFE TABLE 80CNSMT SINGLE LIFE REMAINDER FACTORS APPLICABLE AFTER APRIL 30, 1989

	INTEREST RATE									
AGE	4.2%	4.4%	4.6%	4.8%	5.0%	5.2%	5.4%	5.6%	5.8%	6.0%
71	.62014	.60778	.59578	.58415	.57287	.56193	.55131	.54100	.53099	.52126
72	.63334	.62123	.60948	.59808	.58700	.57624	.56579	.55563	.54577	.53617
73	.64648	.63465	.62315	.61198	.60112	.59056	.58029	.57030	.56059	.55113
74	.65961	.64806	.63682	.62590	.61527	.60492	.59485	.58504	.57550	.56620
75	.67274	.66149	.65054	.63987	.62948	.61936	.60950	.59990	.59053	.58140
76	.68589	.67495	.66429	.65390	.64377	.63390	.62427	.61487	.60570	.59676
77	.69903	.68841	.67806	.66796	.65811	.64849	.63910	.62993	.62097	.61223
78	.71209	.70182	.69179	.68199	.67242	.66307	.65393	.64501	.63628	.62775
79	.72500	.71507	.70537	.69588	.68660	.67754	.66867	.65999	.65151	.64321
80	.73768	.72809	.71872	.70955	.70058	.69180	.68320	.67479	.66655	.65849
81	.75001	.74077	.73173	.72288	.71422	.70573	.69741	.68926	.68128	.67345
82	.76195	.75306	.74435	.73582	.72746	.71926	.71123	.70335	.69562	.68804

83	.77346	.76491	.75654	.74832	.74026	.73236	.72460	.71699	.70952	.70219
84	.78456	.77636	.76831	.76041	.75265	.74503	.73756	.73021	.72300	.71592
85	.79530	.78743	.77971	.77212	.76466	.75733	.75014	.74306	.73611	.72928
86	.80560	.79806	.79065	.78337	.77621	.76917	.76225	.75544	.74875	.74216
87	.81535	.80813	.80103	.79404	.78717	.78041	.77375	.76720	.76076	.75442
88	.82462	.81771	.81090	.80420	.79760	.79111	.78472	.77842	.77223	.76612
89	.83356	.82694	.82043	.81401	.80769	.80147	.79533	.78929	.78334	.77747
90	.84225	.83593	.82971	.82357	.81753	.81157	.80570	.79991	.79420	.78857
91	.85058	.84455	.83861	.83276	.82698	.82129	.81567	.81013	.80466	.79927
92	.85838	.85263	.84696	.84137	.83585	.83040	.82503	.81973	.81449	.80933
93	.86557	.86009	.85467	.84932	.84405	.83884	.83370	.82862	.82360	.81865
94	.87212	.86687	.86169	.85657	.85152	.84653	.84160	.83673	.83192	.82717
95	.87801	.87298	.86801	.86310	.85825	.85345	.84872	.84404	.83941	.83484
96	.88322	.87838	.87360	.86888	.86420	.85959	.85502	.85051	.84605	.84165
97	.88795	.88328	.87867	.87411	.86961	.86515	.86074	.85639	.85208	.84782
98	.89220	.88769	.88323	.87883	.87447	.87016	.86589	.86167	.85750	.85337
99	.89612	.89176	.88745	.88318	.87895	.87478	.87064	.86656	.86251	.85850
100	.89977	.89555	.89136	.88722	.88313	.87908	.87506	.87109	.86716	.86327
101	.90326	.89917	.89511	.89110	.88712	.88318	.87929	.87543	.87161	.86783
102	.90690	.90294	.89901	.89513	.89128	.88746	.88369	.87995	.87624	.87257
103	.91076	.90694	.90315	.89940	.89569	.89200	.88835	.88474	.88116	.87760
104	.91504	.91138	.90775	.90415	.90058	.89704	.89354	.89006	.88661	.88319
105	.92027	.91681	.91337	.90996	.90658	.90322	.89989	.89659	.89331	.89006
106	.92763	.92445	.92130	.91816	.91506	.91197	.90890	.90586	.90284	.89983
107	.93799	.93523	.93249	.92977	.92707	.92438	.92170	.91905	.91641	.91378
108	.95429	.95223	.95018	.94814	.94611	.94409	.94208	.94008	.93809	.93611
109	.97985	.97893	.97801	.97710	.97619	.97529	.97438	.97348	.97259	.97170

TABLE S

BASED ON LIFE TABLE 80CNSMT SINGLE LIFE REMAINDER FACTORS APPLICABLE AFTER APRIL 30, 1989

	INTEREST RATE									
AGE	6.2%	6.4%	6.6%	6.8%	7.0%	7.2%	7.4%	7.6%	7.8%	8.0%
0	.03535	.03349	.03183	.03035	.02902	.02783	.02676	.02579	.02492	.02413
1	.02486	.02292	.02119	.01963	.01824	.01699	.01587	.01486	.01395	.01312
2	.02547	.02345	.02164	.02002	.01857	.01727	.01609	.01504	.01408	.01321
3	.02640	.02429	.02241	.02073	.01921	.01785	.01662	.01552	.01451	.01361
4	.02753	.02535	.02339	.02163	.02005	.01863	.01735	.01619	.01514	.01418
5	.02883	.02656	.02453	.02269	.02105	.01956	.01822	.01700	.01590	.01490
6	.03026	.02790	.02578	.02387	.02215	.02060	.01919	.01792	.01677	.01572
7	.03180	.02935	.02714	.02515	.02336	.02174	.02027	.01894	.01773	.01664
8	.03347	.03092	.02863	.02656	.02469	.02300	.02146	.02007	.01881	.01766
9	.03528	.03263	.03025	.02810	.02615	.02438	.02278	.02133	.02000	.01880
10	.03723	.03449	.03201	.02977	.02774	.02590	.02423	.02271	.02133	.02006
11	.03935	.03650	.03393	.03160	.02949	.02757	.02583	.02424	.02279	.02147
12	.04160	.03865	.03598	.03356	.03136	.02936	.02755	.02589	.02438	.02299
13	.04394	.04088	.03811	.03560	.03331	.03123	.02934	.02761	.02603	.02458
14	.04629	.04312	.04025	.03764	.03527	.03311	.03113	.02933	.02768	.02617
15	.04864	.04536	.04238	.03968	.03721	.03496	.03290	.03103	.02930	.02773
16	.05099	.04759	.04451	.04170	.03913	.03679	.03466	.03270	.03090	.02926
17	.05333	.04982	.04662	.04370	.04104	.03861	.03638	.03434	.03247	.03075
18	.05570	.05207	.04875	.04573	.04296	.04044	.03812	.03599	.03404	.03225
19	.05814	.05438	.05095	.04781	.04494	.04231	.03990	.03769	.03565	.03378
20	.06065	.05677	.05321	.04996	.04698	.04424	.04173	.03943	.03731	.03535
21	.06325	.05922	.05554	.05217	.04907	.04623	.04362	.04122	.03901	.03697
22	.06594	.06178	.05797	.05447	.05126	.04831	.04559	.04309	.04078	.03865
23	.06876	.06446	.06051	.05688	.05355	.05048	.04766	.04505	.04265	.04042
24	.07174	.06729	.06321	.05945	.05599	.05281	.04987	.04715	.04465	.04233
25	.07491	.07031	.06609	.06219	.05861	.05530	.05224	.04941	.04680	.04438
26	.07830	.07355	.06918	.06515	.06142	.05799	.05481	.05187	.04915	.04662
27	.08192	.07702	.07250	.06832	.06446	.06090	.05759	.05454	.05170	.04906
28	.08577	.08071	.07603	.07171	.06772	.06402	.06059	.05740	.05445	.05170
29	.08986	.08464	.07981	.07534	.07120	.06736	.06380	.06049	.05742	.05456
30	.09420	.08882	.08383	.07921	.07492	.07095	.06725	.06381	.06061	.05763
31	.09881	.09327	.08812	.08335	.07891	.07479	.07095	.06738	.06405	.06095
32	.10369	.09797	.09267	.08774	.08315	.07888	.07491	.07120	.06774	.06451

33	.10885	.10297	.09750	.09241	.08767	.08325	.07913	.07529	.07170	.06834
34	.11430	.10824	.10261	.09736	.09246	.08790	.08363	.07964	.07592	.07243

TABLE S

BASED ON LIFE TABLE 80CNSMT SINGLE LIFE REMAINDER FACTORS APPLICABLE AFTER APRIL 30, 1989

	INTEREST RATE									
AGE	6.2%	6.4%	6.6%	6.8%	7.0%	7.2%	7.4%	7.6%	7.8%	8.0%
35	.12002	.11380	.10800	.10259	.09754	.09282	.08841	.08428	.08041	.07679
36	.12602	.11963	.11366	.10809	.10288	.09800	.09344	.08917	.08516	.08140
37	.13230	.12574	.11961	.11387	.10850	.10347	.09876	.09433	.09018	.08628
38	.13887	.13214	.12584	.11994	.11441	.10922	.10436	.09978	.09549	.09145
39	.14573	.13883	.13237	.12630	.12061	.11527	.11025	.10553	.10109	.09690
40	.15290	.14583	.13920	.13297	.12712	.12162	.11644	.11157	.10698	.10266
41	.16036	.15312	.14633	.13994	.13393	.12827	.12294	.11792	.11318	.10871
42	.16810	.16071	.15375	.14720	.14103	.13522	.12973	.12456	.11967	.11505
43	.17614	.16858	.16146	.15475	.14842	.14245	.13682	.13149	.12645	.12169
44	.18447	.17675	.16948	.16261	.15613	.15000	.14421	.13873	.13355	.12864
45	.19310	.18524	.17780	.17078	.16414	.15787	.15192	.14630	.14096	.13591
46	.20204	.19402	.18644	.17926	.17247	.16604	.15995	.15418	.14870	.14350
47	.21128	.20311	.19538	.18806	.18112	.17454	.16830	.16238	.15676	.15141
48	.22080	.21249	.20462	.19716	.19007	.18335	.17696	.17090	.16513	.15964
49	.23059	.22214	.21413	.20653	.19930	.19244	.18591	.17970	.17379	.16816
50	.24063	.23206	.22391	.21617	.20881	.20180	.19514	.18879	.18274	.17697
51	.25095	.24225	.23398	.22610	.21861	.21147	.20466	.19818	.19199	.18609
52	.26157	.25275	.24436	.23636	.22874	.22147	.21453	.20791	.20159	.19556
53	.27249	.26357	.25505	.24694	.23919	.23180	.22474	.21799	.21154	.20537
54	.28369	.27466	.26604	.25782	.24995	.24244	.23526	.22839	.22181	.21552
55	.29518	.28605	.27734	.26900	.26103	.25341	.24611	.23912	.23243	.22601
56	.30695	.29774	.28893	.28050	.27242	.26469	.25728	.25019	.24338	.23685
57	.31902	.30973	.30084	.29232	.28415	.27632	.26881	.26161	.25469	.24805
58	.33138	.32203	.31306	.30446	.29621	.28829	.28069	.27339	.26637	.25962
59	.34402	.33461	.32558	.31691	.30859	.30059	.29290	.28550	.27839	.27155
60	.35690	.34745	.33836	.32963	.32124	.31317	.30540	.29792	.29073	.28379
61	.36999	.36050	.35137	.34259	.33414	.32601	.31817	.31062	.30334	.29633
62	.38325	.37374	.36458	.35576	.34726	.33907	.33117	.32356	.31621	.30912
63	.39669	.38717	.37799	.36913	.36060	.35236	.34441	.33674	.32933	.32217
64	.41031	.40078	.39159	.38272	.37415	.36588	.35789	.35016	.34270	.33548
65	.42416	.41464	.40545	.39656	.38798	.37968	.37166	.36390	.35639	.34912
66	.43825	.42876	.41958	.41070	.40211	.39380	.38576	.37797	.37043	.36312
67	.45260	.44315	.43399	.42513	.41655	.40824	.40019	.39238	.38482	.37749
68	.46720	.45779	.44868	.43985	.43129	.42299	.41494	.40713	.39956	.39221
69	.48197	.47263	.46357	.45478	.44625	.43798	.42995	.42215	.41458	.40722
70	.49686	.48760	.47861	.46988	.46140	.45316	.44516	.43738	.42983	.42248

TABLE S

BASED ON LIFE TABLE 80CNSMT SINGLE LIFE REMAINDER FACTORS APPLICABLE AFTER APRIL 30, 1989

	INTEREST RATE									
AGE	6.2%	6.4%	6.6%	6.8%	7.0%	7.2%	7.4%	7.6%	7.8%	8.0%
71	.51182	.50265	.49374	.48508	.47666	.46847	.46051	.45276	.44523	.43790
72	.52685	.51778	.50896	.50038	.49203	.48390	.47599	.46829	.46079	.45349
73	.54194	.53298	.52426	.51578	.50751	.49946	.49161	.48397	.47652	.46926
74	.55714	.54832	.53972	.53134	.52317	.51520	.50744	.49986	.49247	.48527
75	.57250	.56382	.55536	.54710	.53904	.53118	.52351	.51601	.50870	.50156
76	.58803	.57951	.57120	.56308	.55515	.54740	.53984	.53245	.52522	.51817
77	.60369	.59535	.58720	.57923	.57144	.56383	.55639	.54912	.54200	.53504
78	.61942	.61126	.60329	.59549	.58787	.58040	.57310	.56596	.55896	.55212
79	.63508	.62713	.61935	.61174	.60428	.59698	.58983	.58283	.57597	.56925
80	.65059	.64285	.63527	.62785	.62058	.61345	.60646	.59961	.59290	.58632
81	.66579	.65827	.65090	.64368	.63659	.62965	.62283	.61615	.60959	.60316
82	.68061	.67332	.66616	.65914	.65226	.64550	.63886	.63235	.62595	.61968
83	.69499	.68793	.68099	.67418	.66749	.66092	.65447	.64813	.64191	.63579
84	.70896	.70213	.69541	.68881	.68233	.67595	.66969	.66353	.65748	.65153
85	.72256	.71596	.70947	.70308	.69681	.69063	.68456	.67859	.67271	.66693
86	.73569	.72931	.72305	.71688	.71081	.70484	.69896	.69318	.68748	.68188

87	.74818	.74204	.73599	.73003	.72417	.71839	.71271	.70711	.70159	.69616
88	.76011	.75419	.74836	.74261	.73695	.73137	.72588	.72046	.71512	.70986
89	.77169	.76599	.76037	.75484	.74938	.74400	.73870	.73347	.72831	.72323
90	.78302	.77755	.77215	.76683	.76158	.75640	.75129	.74625	.74128	.73638
91	.79395	.78870	.78352	.77842	.77337	.76840	.76349	.75864	.75385	.74913
92	.80423	.79920	.79423	.78933	.78449	.77971	.77499	.77033	.76572	.76118
93	.81377	.80894	.80417	.79946	.79481	.79022	.78568	.78120	.77677	.77239
94	.82247	.81784	.81325	.80873	.80425	.79983	.79547	.79115	.78688	.78266
95	.83033	.82586	.82145	.81709	.81278	.80852	.80431	.80014	.79602	.79195
96	.83729	.83298	.82872	.82451	.82034	.81622	.81215	.80812	.80414	.80019
97	.84361	.83944	.83532	.83124	.82721	.82322	.81927	.81537	.81151	.80769
98	.84929	.84525	.84126	.83730	.83339	.82952	.82569	.82190	.81815	.81443
99	.85454	.85062	.84674	.84290	.83910	.83534	.83161	.82792	.82427	.82066
100	.85942	.85561	.85184	.84810	.84440	.84074	.83711	.83352	.82997	.82644
101	.86408	.86037	.85670	.85306	.84946	.84589	.84236	.83886	.83539	.83196
102	.86894	.86534	.86177	.85823	.85473	.85126	.84782	.84442	.84104	.83770
103	.87408	.87060	.86714	.86371	.86032	.85695	.85362	.85031	.84703	.84378
104	.87980	.87644	.87311	.86980	.86653	.86328	.86005	.85686	.85369	.85054
105	.88684	.88363	.88046	.87731	.87418	.87108	.86800	.86494	.86191	.85890
106	.89685	.89389	.89095	.88804	.88514	.88226	.87940	.87656	.87374	.87094
107	.91117	.90858	.90600	.90344	.90089	.89836	.89584	.89334	.89085	.88838
108	.93414	.93217	.93022	.92828	.92634	.92442	.92250	.92060	.91870	.91681
109	.97081	.96992	.96904	.96816	.96729	.96642	.96555	.96468	.96382	.96296

TABLE S

BASED ON LIFE TABLE 80CNSMT SINGLE LIFE REMAINDER FACTORS APPLICABLE AFTER APRIL 30, 1989

	INTEREST RATE									
AGE	8.2%	8.4%	8.6%	8.8%	9.0%	9.2%	9.4%	9.6%	9.8%	10.0%
0	.02341	.02276	.02217	.02163	.02114	.02069	.02027	.01989	.01954	.01922
1	.01237	.01170	.01108	.01052	.01000	.00953	.00910	.00871	.00834	.00801
2	.01243	.01172	.01107	.01048	.00994	.00944	.00899	.00857	.00819	.00784
3	.01278	.01203	.01135	.01073	.01016	.00964	.00916	.00872	.00832	.00795
4	.01332	.01253	.01182	.01116	.01056	.01001	.00951	.00904	.00862	.00822
5	.01400	.01317	.01241	.01172	.01109	.01051	.00998	.00949	.00904	.00862
6	.01477	.01390	.01310	.01238	.01171	.01110	.01054	.01002	.00954	.00910
7	.01563	.01472	.01389	.01312	.01242	.01178	.01118	.01064	.01013	.00966
8	.01660	.01564	.01477	.01396	.01322	.01254	.01192	.01134	.01081	.01031
9	.01770	.01669	.01577	.01492	.01414	.01342	.01276	.01216	.01159	.01107
10	.01891	.01785	.01688	.01599	.01517	.01442	.01372	.01308	.01249	.01194
11	.02026	.01915	.01814	.01720	.01634	.01555	.01481	.01414	.01351	.01293
12	.02173	.02056	.01950	.01852	.01761	.01678	.01601	.01529	.01463	.01402
13	.02326	.02204	.02092	.01989	.01895	.01807	.01726	.01651	.01582	.01517
14	.02478	.02351	.02234	.02126	.02027	.01935	.01850	.01771	.01698	.01630
15	.02628	.02495	.02372	.02259	.02155	.02058	.01969	.01886	.01810	.01738
16	.02774	.02635	.02507	.02388	.02279	.02178	.02084	.01997	.01917	.01842
17	.02917	.02772	.02637	.02513	.02399	.02293	.02194	.02103	.02018	.01940
18	.03059	.02907	.02767	.02637	.02517	.02406	.02302	.02207	.02118	.02035
19	.03205	.03046	.02899	.02763	.02637	.02521	.02412	.02312	.02218	.02131
20	.03355	.03188	.03035	.02892	.02760	.02638	.02524	.02419	.02320	.02229
21	.03509	.03334	.03173	.03024	.02886	.02758	.02638	.02527	.02424	.02328
22	.03669	.03487	.03318	.03162	.03017	.02882	.02757	.02640	.02532	.02430
23	.03837	.03646	.03470	.03306	.03154	.03013	.02881	.02759	.02644	.02538
24	.04018	.03819	.03634	.03463	.03303	.03155	.03016	.02888	.02767	.02655
25	.04214	.04006	.03812	.03633	.03465	.03309	.03164	.03029	.02902	.02784
26	.04428	.04210	.04008	.03820	.03644	.03481	.03328	.03186	.03052	.02928
27	.04662	.04434	.04223	.04025	.03841	.03670	.03509	.03360	.03219	.03088
28	.04915	.04677	.04456	.04249	.04056	.03876	.03708	.03550	.03403	.03264
29	.05189	.04941	.04709	.04493	.04291	.04102	.03925	.03760	.03604	.03458
30	.05485	.05226	.04984	.04757	.04546	.04348	.04162	.03988	.03825	.03671
31	.05805	.05535	.05282	.05045	.04824	.04616	.04421	.04238	.04067	.03905
32	.06149	.05867	.05603	.05356	.05124	.04906	.04702	.04510	.04329	.04160
33	.06520	.06226	.05950	.05692	.05449	.05221	.05007	.04806	.04616	.04438
34	.06916	.06609	.06322	.06052	.05799	.05560	.05336	.05125	.04926	.04738

TABLE S

BASED ON LIFE TABLE 80CNSMT SINGLE LIFE REMAINDER FACTORS APPLICABLE AFTER APRIL 30, 1989

	INTEREST RATE									
AGE	8.2%	8.4%	8.6%	8.8%	9.0%	9.2%	9.4%	9.6%	9.8%	10.0%
35	.07339	.07020	.06720	.06439	.06174	.05925	.05690	.05469	.05260	.05063
36	.07787	.07455	.07143	.06850	.06573	.06313	.06068	.05836	.05617	.05411
37	.08262	.07917	.07593	.07287	.06999	.06727	.06470	.06228	.05999	.05783
38	.08765	.08407	.08069	.07751	.07451	.07167	.06899	.06646	.06407	.06180
39	.09296	.08925	.08574	.08243	.07931	.07635	.07356	.07092	.06841	.06604
40	.09858	.09472	.09109	.08765	.08440	.08132	.07841	.07565	.07303	.07055
41	.10449	.10050	.09673	.09316	.08978	.08658	.08355	.08067	.07794	.07535
42	.11069	.10656	.10265	.09895	.09544	.09212	.08896	.08596	.08312	.08041
43	.11718	.11291	.10887	.10503	.10140	.09794	.09466	.09154	.08858	.08576
44	.12399	.11958	.11540	.11143	.10766	.10407	.10067	.09743	.09434	.09141
45	.13111	.12656	.12224	.11814	.11423	.11052	.10699	.10362	.10042	.09736
46	.13856	.13387	.12941	.12516	.12113	.11728	.11362	.11013	.10680	.10363
47	.14633	.14150	.13690	.13252	.12835	.12438	.12059	.11697	.11352	.11022
48	.15442	.14945	.14471	.14020	.13589	.13179	.12787	.12412	.12055	.11713
49	.16280	.15769	.15281	.14816	.14373	.13949	.13544	.13157	.12787	.12433
50	.17147	.16622	.16121	.15643	.15186	.14749	.14331	.13931	.13548	.13182
51	.18045	.17507	.16993	.16501	.16030	.15580	.15150	.14737	.14342	.13963
52	.18979	.18427	.17899	.17394	.16911	.16448	.16004	.15579	.15172	.14780
53	.19947	.19383	.18842	.18324	.17828	.17352	.16896	.16458	.16038	.15635
54	.20950	.20372	.19819	.19288	.18779	.18291	.17822	.17372	.16940	.16524
55	.21986	.21397	.20831	.20288	.19767	.19266	.18785	.18322	.17878	.17450
56	.23058	.22457	.21879	.21324	.20791	.20278	.19785	.19310	.18854	.18414
57	.24167	.23554	.22965	.22399	.21854	.21329	.20824	.20338	.19870	.19419
58	.25314	.24690	.24090	.23512	.22956	.22420	.21904	.21407	.20927	.20464
59	.26497	.25863	.25252	.24664	.24097	.23550	.23023	.22515	.22024	.21551
60	.27712	.27068	.26448	.25849	.25272	.24716	.24178	.23659	.23158	.22674
61	.28956	.28304	.27674	.27067	.26480	.25913	.25366	.24837	.24325	.23831
62	.30228	.29567	.28929	.28312	.27717	.27141	.26584	.26045	.25524	.25020
63	.31525	.30857	.30211	.29586	.28982	.28397	.27832	.27284	.26754	.26240
64	.32851	.32176	.31522	.30890	.30278	.29685	.29111	.28555	.28016	.27493
65	.34209	.33528	.32868	.32229	.31610	.31010	.30429	.29865	.29317	.28787
66	.35604	.34918	.34253	.33609	.32983	.32377	.31788	.31217	.30663	.30124
67	.37037	.36347	.35678	.35028	.34398	.33786	.33191	.32614	.32053	.31508
68	.38508	.37815	.37142	.36489	.35854	.35237	.34638	.34055	.33488	.32937
69	.40008	.39313	.38638	.37982	.37344	.36724	.36120	.35533	.34961	.34405
70	.41533	.40838	.40162	.39504	.38864	.38241	.37634	.37043	.36468	.35907

TABLE S

BASED ON LIFE TABLE 80CNSMT SINGLE LIFE REMAINDER FACTORS APPLICABLE AFTER APRIL 30, 1989

	INTEREST RATE									
AGE	8.2%	8.4%	8.6%	8.8%	9.0%	9.2%	9.4%	9.6%	9.8%	10.0%
71	.43076	.42382	.41705	.41047	.40405	.39780	.39171	.38578	.38000	.37436
72	.44638	.43945	.43269	.42611	.41969	.41344	.40733	.40138	.39558	.38991
73	.46218	.45527	.44854	.44197	.43556	.42931	.42321	.41725	.41143	.40575
74	.47823	.47137	.46466	.45812	.45173	.44549	.43940	.43345	.42763	.42195
75	.49459	.48777	.48112	.47462	.46826	.46205	.45598	.45004	.44424	.43856
76	.51127	.50452	.49793	.49148	.48517	.47900	.47297	.46706	.46129	.45563
77	.52823	.52157	.51505	.50867	.50243	.49632	.49033	.48447	.47873	.47311
78	.54541	.53885	.53242	.52613	.51996	.51392	.50800	.50220	.49652	.49094
79	.56267	.55621	.54989	.54369	.53762	.53166	.52582	.52009	.51448	.50897
80	.57987	.57354	.56733	.56125	.55527	.54941	.54366	.53802	.53248	.52705
81	.59685	.59065	.58457	.57860	.57274	.56699	.56134	.55579	.55035	.54499
82	.61351	.60746	.60151	.59567	.58993	.58429	.57875	.57331	.56796	.56270
83	.62978	.62387	.61806	.61236	.60675	.60123	.59581	.59047	.58523	.58007
84	.64567	.63992	.63426	.62869	.62321	.61783	.61253	.60731	.60218	.59713
85	.66125	.65565	.65014	.64472	.63938	.63413	.62896	.62387	.61886	.61392
86	.67636	.67092	.66557	.66030	.65511	.65000	.64496	.64000	.63511	.63030
87	.69081	.68554	.68034	.67522	.67018	.66520	.66031	.65548	.65071	.64602
88	.70468	.69957	.69453	.68956	.68466	.67983	.67507	.67037	.66574	.66117

89	.71821	.71326	.70838	.70357	.69882	.69414	.68952	.68495	.68045	.67601
90	.73153	.72676	.72204	.71739	.71280	.70827	.70379	.69938	.69502	.69071
91	.74447	.73986	.73532	.73083	.72640	.72202	.71770	.71343	.70921	.70504
92	.75669	.75225	.74787	.74354	.73927	.73504	.73087	.72674	.72267	.71864
93	.76807	.76379	.75957	.75540	.75127	.74719	.74317	.73918	.73524	.73135
94	.77849	.77437	.77030	.76627	.76229	.75835	.75446	.75061	.74680	.74303
95	.78792	.78394	.78001	.77611	.77226	.76845	.76468	.76096	.75727	.75362
96	.79630	.79244	.78863	.78485	.78112	.77742	.77377	.77015	.76657	.76303
97	.80391	.80016	.79646	.79280	.78917	.78559	.78203	.77852	.77504	.77160
98	.81076	.80712	.80352	.79996	.79643	.79294	.78948	.78606	.78267	.77931
99	.81709	.81354	.81004	.80657	.80313	.79972	.79635	.79302	.78971	.78644
100	.82296	.81950	.81609	.81270	.80934	.80602	.80273	.79947	.79624	.79304
101	.82855	.82518	.82185	.81854	.81526	.81201	.80880	.80561	.80245	.79932
102	.83438	.83110	.82785	.82462	.82142	.81826	.81512	.81200	.80892	.80586
103	.84056	.83737	.83420	.83106	.82795	.82487	.82181	.81878	.81577	.81279
104	.84743	.84433	.84127	.83822	.83521	.83221	.82924	.82630	.82338	.82048
105	.85591	.85295	.85001	.84709	.84419	.84132	.83846	.83563	.83282	.83003
106	.86816	.86540	.86266	.85993	.85723	.85454	.85187	.84922	.84659	.84397
107	.88592	.88348	.88105	.87863	.87623	.87384	.87147	.86911	.86676	.86443
108	.91493	.91306	.91119	.90934	.90749	.90566	.90383	.90201	.90020	.89840
109	.96211	.96125	.96041	.95956	.95872	.95788	.95704	.95620	.95537	.95455

TABLE S

BASED ON LIFE TABLE 80CNSMT SINGLE LIFE REMAINDER FACTORS APPLICABLE AFTER APRIL 30, 1989

	INTEREST RATE									
AGE	10.2%	10.4%	10.6%	10.8%	11.0%	11.2%	11.4%	11.6%	11.8%	12.0%
0	.01891	.01864	.01838	.01814	.01791	.01770	.01750	.01732	.01715	.01698
1	.00770	.00741	.00715	.00690	.00667	.00646	.00626	.00608	.00590	.00574
2	.00751	.00721	.00693	.00667	.00643	.00620	.00600	.00580	.00562	.00544
3	.00760	.00728	.00699	.00671	.00646	.00622	.00600	.00579	.00560	.00541
4	.00786	.00752	.00721	.00692	.00665	.00639	.00616	.00594	.00573	.00554
5	.00824	.00788	.00755	.00724	.00695	.00668	.00643	.00620	.00598	.00578
6	.00869	.00832	.00796	.00764	.00733	.00705	.00678	.00654	.00630	.00608
7	.00923	.00883	.00846	.00811	.00779	.00749	.00720	.00694	.00669	.00646
8	.00986	.00943	.00904	.00867	.00833	.00801	.00771	.00743	.00716	.00692
9	.01059	.01014	.00972	.00933	.00897	.00863	.00831	.00801	.00773	.00747
10	.01142	.01095	.01051	.01009	.00971	.00935	.00901	.00869	.00840	.00812
11	.01239	.01189	.01142	.01098	.01057	.01019	.00983	.00950	.00918	.00889
12	.01345	.01292	.01243	.01197	.01154	.01113	.01075	.01040	.01007	.00975
13	.01457	.01401	.01349	.01300	.01255	.01212	.01172	.01135	.01100	.01067
14	.01567	.01508	.01453	.01402	.01354	.01309	.01267	.01227	.01190	.01155
15	.01672	.01610	.01552	.01498	.01448	.01400	.01356	.01314	.01275	.01238
16	.01772	.01707	.01646	.01589	.01536	.01486	.01439	.01396	.01354	.01315
17	.01866	.01798	.01734	.01674	.01618	.01566	.01516	.01470	.01427	.01386
18	.01958	.01886	.01818	.01755	.01697	.01641	.01590	.01541	.01495	.01452
19	.02050	.01974	.01903	.01837	.01775	.01717	.01662	.01611	.01563	.01517
20	.02143	.02064	.01989	.01919	.01854	.01793	.01735	.01681	.01630	.01582
21	.02238	.02154	.02075	.02002	.01933	.01868	.01807	.01750	.01696	.01646
22	.02336	.02247	.02164	.02087	.02014	.01946	.01882	.01821	.01764	.01711
23	.02438	.02345	.02257	.02176	.02099	.02027	.01959	.01895	.01835	.01778
24	.02550	.02451	.02359	.02273	.02192	.02115	.02044	.01976	.01913	.01853
25	.02673	.02569	.02472	.02381	.02295	.02214	.02138	.02067	.01999	.01936
26	.02811	.02701	.02598	.02502	.02411	.02326	.02246	.02170	.02098	.02031
27	.02965	.02849	.02741	.02639	.02543	.02452	.02367	.02287	.02211	.02140
28	.03134	.03013	.02898	.02790	.02689	.02593	.02503	.02418	.02338	.02262
29	.03322	.03193	.03072	.02958	.02851	.02750	.02654	.02564	.02479	.02398
30	.03527	.03391	.03264	.03143	.03030	.02923	.02821	.02726	.02635	.02550
31	.03753	.03610	.03475	.03348	.03228	.03115	.03008	.02907	.02811	.02720
32	.04000	.03849	.03707	.03573	.03446	.03326	.03213	.03105	.03004	.02907
33	.04269	.04111	.03961	.03819	.03685	.03558	.03438	.03325	.03217	.03115
34	.04561	.04394	.04236	.04087	.03946	.03812	.03685	.03565	.03451	.03342

TABLE S

BASED ON LIFE TABLE 80CNSMT SINGLE LIFE REMAINDER FACTORS APPLICABLE AFTER APRIL 30, 1989

	INTEREST RATE									
AGE	10.2%	10.4%	10.6%	10.8%	11.0%	11.2%	11.4%	11.6%	11.8%	12.0%
35	.04877	.04702	.04535	.04378	.04229	.04087	.03953	.03826	.03706	.03591
36	.05215	.05031	.04856	.04690	.04533	.04384	.04242	.04108	.03980	.03859
37	.05578	.05384	.05200	.05025	.04860	.04703	.04553	.04411	.04276	.04148
38	.05965	.05761	.05568	.05385	.05211	.05045	.04888	.04738	.04595	.04460
39	.06379	.06165	.05962	.05770	.05587	.05412	.05247	.05089	.04939	.04795
40	.06820	.06596	.06383	.06181	.05989	.05806	.05631	.05465	.05307	.05155
41	.07288	.07054	.06832	.06620	.06418	.06226	.06042	.05868	.05701	.05541
42	.07784	.07539	.07306	.07085	.06873	.06671	.06479	.06295	.06119	.05952
43	.08308	.08052	.07808	.07576	.07355	.07143	.06941	.06748	.06564	.06387
44	.08861	.08594	.08340	.08097	.07865	.07644	.07432	.07230	.07036	.06851
45	.09445	.09167	.08901	.08648	.08406	.08174	.07953	.07741	.07538	.07343
46	.10060	.09770	.09494	.09230	.08977	.08735	.08503	.08281	.08068	.07865
47	.10707	.10406	.10119	.09843	.09579	.09327	.09085	.08853	.08630	.08417
48	.11386	.11073	.10774	.10487	.10213	.09949	.09697	.09455	.09222	.08999
49	.12094	.11769	.11458	.11160	.10874	.10600	.10337	.10084	.09842	.09609
50	.12831	.12494	.12172	.11862	.11565	.11280	.11006	.10743	.10490	.10247
51	.13600	.13251	.12917	.12596	.12288	.11991	.11706	.11432	.11169	.10915
52	.14405	.14044	.13698	.13366	.13046	.12738	.12442	.12157	.11883	.11619
53	.15247	.14875	.14517	.14172	.13841	.13522	.13215	.12919	.12635	.12360
54	.16124	.15740	.15370	.15014	.14671	.14341	.14023	.13717	.13421	.13136
55	.17039	.16642	.16261	.15893	.15539	.15198	.14868	.14551	.14244	.13948
56	.17991	.17583	.17190	.16811	.16445	.16092	.15752	.15423	.15106	.14799
57	.18984	.18564	.18160	.17769	.17392	.17029	.16677	.16338	.16010	.15692
58	.20018	.19587	.19172	.18770	.18382	.18007	.17645	.17295	.16956	.16628
59	.21093	.20652	.20225	.19812	.19414	.19028	.18655	.18294	.17945	.17606
60	.22206	.21753	.21316	.20893	.20483	.20087	.19703	.19332	.18972	.18624
61	.23353	.22890	.22442	.22009	.21589	.21182	.20788	.20407	.20037	.19678
62	.24532	.24059	.23601	.23158	.22728	.22311	.21907	.21515	.21135	.20767
63	.25742	.25260	.24793	.24339	.23900	.23473	.23060	.22658	.22268	.21890
64	.26987	.26495	.26019	.25556	.25107	.24671	.24248	.23837	.23438	.23050
65	.28271	.27771	.27286	.26815	.26357	.25912	.25480	.25059	.24651	.24254
66	.29601	.29093	.28600	.28120	.27654	.27200	.26760	.26331	.25913	.25507
67	.30978	.30462	.29961	.29474	.29000	.28539	.28090	.27653	.27227	.26813
68	.32401	.31879	.31371	.30877	.30396	.29927	.29471	.29027	.28593	.28171
69	.33863	.33336	.32822	.32322	.31835	.31359	.30896	.30445	.30005	.29576
70	.35361	.34829	.34310	.33804	.33311	.32830	.32361	.31903	.31457	.31021

TABLE S

BASED ON LIFE TABLE 80CNSMT SINGLE LIFE REMAINDER FACTORS APPLICABLE AFTER APRIL 30, 1989

	INTEREST RATE									
AGE	10.2%	10.4%	10.6%	10.8%	11.0%	11.2%	11.4%	11.6%	11.8%	12.0%
71	.36886	.36349	.35826	.35316	.34818	.34332	.33858	.33394	.32942	.32500
72	.38439	.37899	.37373	.36858	.36356	.35866	.35387	.34919	.34461	.34015
73	.40021	.39479	.38950	.38432	.37927	.37433	.36950	.36478	.36016	.35565
74	.41639	.41096	.40565	.40046	.39538	.39042	.38556	.38081	.37616	.37161
75	.43301	.42758	.42226	.41706	.41198	.40699	.40212	.39734	.39267	.38809
76	.45009	.44467	.43937	.43417	.42908	.42410	.41921	.41443	.40974	.40514
77	.46761	.46221	.45693	.45175	.44667	.44170	.43682	.43203	.42734	.42274
78	.48548	.48013	.47488	.46973	.46468	.45972	.45486	.45009	.44541	.44082
79	.50356	.49826	.49306	.48795	.48294	.47802	.47319	.46845	.46379	.45922
80	.52171	.51647	.51133	.50628	.50132	.49644	.49166	.48695	.48233	.47779
81	.53974	.53457	.52950	.52451	.51961	.51479	.51006	.50541	.50083	.49633
82	.55753	.55245	.54745	.54254	.53771	.53296	.52828	.52369	.51917	.51472
83	.57500	.57001	.56510	.56026	.55551	.55083	.54623	.54170	.53724	.53285
84	.59216	.58726	.58245	.57770	.57304	.56844	.56391	.55945	.55506	.55074
85	.60906	.60428	.59956	.59492	.59034	.58583	.58139	.57702	.57270	.56845
86	.62555	.62088	.61627	.61173	.60725	.60284	.59849	.59420	.58997	.58580
87	.64139	.63683	.63233	.62790	.62352	.61921	.61495	.61076	.60661	.60253
88	.65666	.65221	.64783	.64350	.63923	.63502	.63086	.62675	.62270	.61871

89	.67163	.66730	.66304	.65882	.65466	.65055	.64650	.64249	.63854	.63463
90	.68646	.68226	.67812	.67402	.66998	.66599	.66204	.65814	.65430	.65049
91	.70093	.69686	.69285	.68888	.68496	.68108	.67725	.67347	.66973	.66604
92	.71466	.71073	.70684	.70300	.69920	.69545	.69173	.68806	.68444	.68085
93	.72750	.72370	.71994	.71622	.71254	.70890	.70530	.70174	.69822	.69474
94	.73931	.73562	.73198	.72838	.72481	.72129	.71780	.71434	.71093	.70755
95	.75001	.74644	.74291	.73941	.73595	.73253	.72914	.72579	.72247	.71919
96	.75953	.75606	.75262	.74923	.74586	.74253	.73924	.73598	.73275	.72955
97	.76819	.76481	.76147	.75816	.75489	.75165	.74844	.74526	.74211	.73899
98	.77599	.77270	.76944	.76621	.76302	.75986	.75672	.75362	.75054	.74750
99	.78319	.77998	.77680	.77365	.77053	.76744	.76437	.76134	.75833	.75535
100	.78987	.78673	.78362	.78054	.77748	.77446	.77146	.76849	.76555	.76263
101	.79622	.79315	.79010	.78708	.78409	.78113	.77819	.77528	.77239	.76953
102	.80283	.79983	.79685	.79390	.79097	.78807	.78519	.78234	.77951	.77671
103	.80983	.80690	.80399	.80111	.79825	.79541	.79260	.78981	.78705	.78430
104	.81760	.81475	.81192	.80912	.80633	.80357	.80083	.79810	.79541	.79273
105	.82726	.82451	.82178	.81907	.81638	.81371	.81106	.80843	.80582	.80322
106	.84137	.83879	.83623	.83368	.83115	.82863	.82614	.82366	.82119	.81874
107	.86211	.85981	.85751	.85523	.85297	.85071	.84847	.84624	.84403	.84182
108	.89660	.89481	.89304	.89127	.88950	.88775	.88601	.88427	.88254	.88081
109	.95372	.95290	.95208	.95126	.95045	.94964	.94883	.94803	.94723	.94643

TABLE S

BASED ON LIFE TABLE 80CNSMT SINGLE LIFE REMAINDER FACTORS APPLICABLE AFTER APRIL 30, 1989

	INTEREST RATE									
AGE	12.2%	12.4%	12.6%	12.8%	13.0%	13.2%	13.4%	13.6%	13.8%	14.0%
0	.01683	.01669	.01655	.01642	.01630	.01618	.01607	.01596	.01586	.01576
1	.00559	.00544	.00531	.00518	.00506	.00494	.00484	.00473	.00464	.00454
2	.00528	.00513	.00499	.00485	.00473	.00461	.00449	.00439	.00428	.00419
3	.00524	.00508	.00493	.00479	.00465	.00453	.00441	.00429	.00419	.00408
4	.00536	.00519	.00503	.00488	.00473	.00460	.00447	.00435	.00423	.00412
5	.00558	.00540	.00523	.00507	.00492	.00477	.00464	.00451	.00439	.00427
6	.00588	.00569	.00550	.00533	.00517	.00502	.00487	.00473	.00460	.00448
7	.00624	.00604	.00584	.00566	.00549	.00532	.00517	.00502	.00488	.00475
8	.00668	.00646	.00626	.00606	.00588	.00570	.00554	.00538	.00523	.00509
9	.00722	.00699	.00677	.00656	.00636	.00617	.00600	.00583	.00567	.00552
10	.00785	.00761	.00737	.00715	.00694	.00674	.00655	.00637	.00620	.00604
11	.00861	.00835	.00810	.00786	.00764	.00743	.00723	.00704	.00686	.00668
12	.00946	.00918	.00891	.00866	.00843	.00820	.00799	.00779	.00760	.00741
13	.01035	.01006	.00978	.00951	.00927	.00903	.00880	.00859	.00839	.00819
14	.01122	.01091	.01061	.01034	.01007	.00982	.00958	.00936	.00914	.00894
15	.01203	.01171	.01140	.01110	.01082	.01056	.01031	.01007	.00985	.00963
16	.01279	.01244	.01211	.01181	.01151	.01123	.01097	.01072	.01048	.01025
17	.01347	.01311	.01276	.01244	.01213	.01184	.01156	.01130	.01104	.01081
18	.01411	.01373	.01336	.01302	.01270	.01239	.01210	.01182	.01155	.01130
19	.01474	.01434	.01396	.01359	.01325	.01293	.01262	.01233	.01205	.01178
20	.01537	.01494	.01454	.01415	.01379	.01345	.01313	.01282	.01252	.01224
21	.01598	.01553	.01510	.01470	.01432	.01396	.01361	.01329	.01298	.01268
22	.01660	.01613	.01568	.01525	.01485	.01446	.01410	.01375	.01343	.01312
23	.01725	.01674	.01627	.01581	.01539	.01498	.01460	.01423	.01388	.01355
24	.01796	.01742	.01692	.01644	.01599	.01556	.01515	.01476	.01439	.01404
25	.01876	.01819	.01765	.01714	.01666	.01621	.01577	.01536	.01497	.01460
26	.01967	.01907	.01850	.01796	.01745	.01696	.01650	.01606	.01565	.01525
27	.02072	.02008	.01948	.01890	.01836	.01784	.01735	.01688	.01644	.01601
28	.02190	.02122	.02057	.01996	.01938	.01883	.01831	.01781	.01734	.01689
29	.02322	.02249	.02181	.02116	.02054	.01996	.01940	.01887	.01836	.01788
30	.02469	.02392	.02319	.02250	.02184	.02122	.02062	.02006	.01952	.01900
31	.02634	.02552	.02475	.02401	.02331	.02264	.02201	.02140	.02083	.02028
32	.02816	.02729	.02647	.02568	.02494	.02423	.02355	.02291	.02229	.02170
33	.03018	.02926	.02838	.02755	.02675	.02600	.02528	.02459	.02393	.02331
34	.03239	.03142	.03048	.02960	.02875	.02795	.02718	.02645	.02575	.02508

TABLE S

BASED ON LIFE TABLE 80CNSMT SINGLE LIFE REMAINDER FACTORS APPLICABLE AFTER APRIL 30, 1989

	INTEREST RATE									
AGE	12.2%	12.4%	12.6%	12.8%	13.0%	13.2%	13.4%	13.6%	13.8%	14.0%
35	.03482	.03378	.03279	.03185	.03095	.03009	.02928	.02850	.02775	.02704
36	.03743	.03633	.03528	.03428	.03333	.03242	.03155	.03072	.02992	.02916
37	.04026	.03909	.03798	.03692	.03591	.03494	.03401	.03313	.03228	.03147
38	.04330	.04207	.04089	.03977	.03869	.03767	.03668	.03574	.03484	.03398
39	.04658	.04528	.04403	.04284	.04170	.04061	.03957	.03857	.03762	.03670
40	.05011	.04873	.04741	.04615	.04495	.04379	.04269	.04163	.04061	.03964
41	.05389	.05244	.05104	.04971	.04844	.04721	.04604	.04492	.04384	.04281
42	.05791	.05638	.05491	.05350	.05216	.05086	.04962	.04844	.04729	.04620
43	.06219	.06057	.05902	.05754	.05612	.05475	.05344	.05218	.05098	.04981
44	.06673	.06503	.06340	.06184	.06034	.05890	.05752	.05619	.05491	.05368
45	.07157	.06978	.06806	.06642	.06484	.06332	.06186	.06046	.05911	.05781
46	.07669	.07481	.07301	.07128	.06962	.06802	.06649	.06501	.06358	.06221
47	.08212	.08015	.07826	.07645	.07470	.07302	.07140	.06984	.06834	.06690
48	.08784	.08578	.08380	.08190	.08006	.07830	.07660	.07496	.07338	.07186
49	.09384	.09169	.08961	.08762	.08570	.08384	.08206	.08034	.07868	.07708
50	.10013	.09787	.09570	.09361	.09160	.08966	.08779	.08598	.08424	.08256
51	.10671	.10436	.10209	.09991	.09780	.09577	.09381	.09192	.09009	.08832
52	.11365	.11120	.10883	.10655	.10435	.10222	.10017	.09819	.09628	.09442
53	.12095	.11840	.11593	.11355	.11126	.10904	.10689	.10482	.10282	.10088
54	.12860	.12595	.12338	.12090	.11851	.11619	.11396	.11179	.10970	.10767
55	.13663	.13386	.13120	.12862	.12613	.12372	.12138	.11912	.11694	.11482
56	.14503	.14217	.13940	.13672	.13413	.13162	.12919	.12683	.12456	.12235
57	.15385	.15089	.14801	.14523	.14254	.13994	.13741	.13496	.13259	.13029
58	.16311	.16004	.15706	.15418	.15139	.14868	.14606	.14352	.14105	.13866
59	.17279	.16961	.16654	.16355	.16066	.15786	.15514	.15250	.14994	.14745
60	.18286	.17958	.17640	.17332	.17033	.16743	.16462	.16188	.15922	.15664
61	.19330	.18992	.18665	.18347	.18038	.17738	.17447	.17164	.16889	.16622
62	.20409	.20061	.19724	.19396	.19078	.18768	.18467	.18175	.17891	.17614
63	.21522	.21165	.20818	.20480	.20152	.19833	.19523	.19221	.18928	.18642
64	.22672	.22306	.21949	.21602	.21265	.20937	.20617	.20306	.20003	.19708
65	.23867	.23491	.23125	.22769	.22423	.22085	.21757	.21437	.21125	.20821
66	.25112	.24727	.24353	.23988	.23632	.23286	.22948	.22619	.22299	.21986
67	.26409	.26016	.25633	.25260	.24896	.24541	.24195	.23857	.23528	.23206
68	.27760	.27359	.26968	.26586	.26214	.25851	.25497	.25151	.24814	.24484
69	.29157	.28748	.28350	.27961	.27581	.27211	.26849	.26495	.26150	.25812
70	.30596	.30181	.29775	.29379	.28992	.28614	.28245	.27884	.27532	.27187

TABLE S

BASED ON LIFE TABLE 80CNSMT SINGLE LIFE REMAINDER FACTORS APPLICABLE AFTER APRIL 30, 1989

	INTEREST RATE									
AGE	12.2%	12.4%	12.6%	12.8%	13.0%	13.2%	13.4%	13.6%	13.8%	14.0%
71	.32069	.31648	.31236	.30833	.30440	.30055	.29679	.29312	.28952	.28600
72	.33578	.33151	.32733	.32325	.31925	.31535	.31152	.30778	.30412	.30054
73	.35123	.34691	.34269	.33855	.33450	.33054	.32666	.32286	.31914	.31550
74	.36715	.36279	.35852	.35434	.35024	.34623	.34230	.33845	.33468	.33098
75	.38360	.37921	.37491	.37069	.36656	.36250	.35853	.35464	.35082	.34708
76	.40064	.39623	.39190	.38765	.38349	.37941	.37540	.37148	.36762	.36384
77	.41823	.41381	.40947	.40521	.40103	.39692	.39290	.38895	.38507	.38126
78	.43632	.43189	.42755	.42329	.41910	.41499	.41095	.40698	.40309	.39926
79	.45473	.45032	.44599	.44173	.43755	.43344	.42940	.42543	.42153	.41770
80	.47333	.46894	.46463	.46040	.45623	.45213	.44811	.44414	.44025	.43642
81	.49191	.48755	.48328	.47907	.47493	.47085	.46684	.46290	.45902	.45520
82	.51034	.50603	.50179	.49762	.49351	.48947	.48549	.48157	.47772	.47392
83	.52852	.52427	.52008	.51595	.51189	.50788	.50394	.50006	.49623	.49246
84	.54648	.54228	.53815	.53407	.53006	.52610	.52221	.51836	.51458	.51084
85	.56426	.56013	.55606	.55205	.54810	.54420	.54035	.53656	.53282	.52913
86	.58169	.57764	.57364	.56970	.56581	.56197	.55818	.55445	.55076	.54713
87	.59850	.59452	.59060	.58673	.58291	.57913	.57541	.57174	.56811	.56453
88	.61476	.61086	.60702	.60322	.59947	.59577	.59212	.58851	.58494	.58142

89	.63078	.62697	.62321	.61950	.61583	.61220	.60862	.60508	.60159	.59813
90	.64674	.64302	.63935	.63573	.63215	.62861	.62511	.62165	.61823	.61485
91	.66238	.65877	.65520	.65167	.64819	.64474	.64133	.63795	.63462	.63132
92	.67730	.67379	.67032	.66689	.66350	.66014	.65682	.65354	.65029	.64708
93	.69130	.68789	.68452	.68119	.67789	.67463	.67140	.66820	.66504	.66191
94	.70421	.70090	.69762	.69438	.69118	.68800	.68486	.68175	.67867	.67563
95	.71594	.71272	.70954	.70639	.70326	.70017	.69712	.69409	.69109	.68812
96	.72638	.72325	.72014	.71707	.71403	.71101	.70803	.70507	.70215	.69925
97	.73590	.73285	.72982	.72682	.72385	.72090	.71799	.71510	.71224	.70941
98	.74448	.74149	.73853	.73560	.73269	.72981	.72696	.72414	.72134	.71856
99	.75240	.74948	.74658	.74371	.74086	.73805	.73525	.73248	.72974	.72702
100	.75974	.75687	.75403	.75121	.74842	.74566	.74292	.74020	.73751	.73484
101	.76669	.76388	.76109	.75833	.75559	.75287	.75018	.74751	.74486	.74223
102	.77393	.77117	.76844	.76573	.76304	.76037	.75773	.75511	.75251	.74993
103	.78158	.77888	.77620	.77355	.77091	.76830	.76571	.76313	.76058	.75805
104	.79007	.78743	.78482	.78222	.77964	.77709	.77455	.77203	.76953	.76705
105	.80065	.79809	.79556	.79304	.79054	.78805	.78559	.78314	.78071	.77829
106	.81631	.81389	.81149	.80911	.80674	.80438	.80204	.79972	.79741	.79511
107	.83963	.83745	.83529	.83313	.83099	.82886	.82674	.82463	.82254	.82045
108	.87910	.87739	.87569	.87400	.87232	.87064	.86897	.86731	.86566	.86401
109	.94563	.94484	.94405	.94326	.94248	.94170	.94092	.94014	.93937	.93860

T.D. 8540, 6/9/94, amend T.D. 8819, 4/29/99, T.D. 8886, 6/9/2000.

§ 1.642(c)-7 Transitional rules with respect to pooled income funds.

(a) In general. *(1) Amendment of certain funds.* A fund created before May 7, 1971, and not otherwise qualifying as a pooled income fund may be treated as a pooled income fund to which § 1.642(c)-5 applies if on July 31, 1969, or on each date of transfer of property to the fund occurring after July 31, 1969, it possessed the initial characteristics described in paragraph (b) of this section and is amended, in the time and manner provided in paragraph (c) of this section, to meet all the requirements of section 642(c)(5) and § 1.642(c)-5. If a fund to which this subparagraph applies is amended in the time and manner provided in paragraph (c) of this section it shall be treated as provided in paragraph (d) of this section for the period beginning on August 1, 1969, or, if later, on the date of its creation and ending the day before the date on which it meets the requirements of section 642(c)(5) and § 1.642(c)-5.

(2) Severance of a portion of a fund. Any portion of a fund created before May 7, 1971, which consists of property transferred to such fund after July 31, 1969, may be severed from such fund consistently with the principles of paragraph (c)(2) of this section and established before January 1, 1972, as a separate pooled income fund, provided that on and after the date of severance the severed fund meets all the requirements of section 642(c)(5) and § 1.642(c)-5. A separate fund which is established pursuant to this subparagraph shall be treated as provided in paragraph (d) of this section for the period beginning on the day of the first transfer of property which becomes part of the separate fund and ending the day before the day on which the separate fund meets the requirements of section 642(c)(5) and § 1.642(c)-5.

(b) Initial characteristics required. A fund described in paragraph (a)(1) of this section shall not be treated as a pooled income fund to which section 642(c)(5) applies, even though it is amended as provided in paragraph (c) of this section, unless it possessed the following characteristics on July 31, 1969, or on each date of transfer of property to the fund occurring after July 31, 1969:

(1) It satisfied the requirements of section 642(c)(5)(A) other than that the fund be a trust;

(2) It was constituted in a way to attract and contain commingled properties transferred to the fund by more than one donor satisfying such requirements; and

(3) Each beneficiary of a life income interest which was retained or created in any property transferred to the fund was entitled to receive, but not less often than annually, a proportional share of the annual income earned by the fund, such share being based on the fair market value of the property in which such life interest was retained or created.

(c) Amendment requirements. *(1)* A fund described in paragraph (a)(1) of this section and possessing the initial characteristics described in paragraph (b) of this section on the date prescribed therein shall be treated as a pooled income fund if it is amended to meet all the requirements of section 642(c)(5) and § 1.642(c)-5 before January 1, 1972, or, if later, on or before the 30th day after the date on which any judicial proceedings commenced before January 1, 1972, which are required to amend its governing instrument or any other instrument which does not permit it to meet such requirements, becomes final. However, see paragraph (d) of this section for limitation on the period in which a claim for credit or refund may be filed.

(2) In addition, if the transferred property described in paragraph (b)(2) of this section is commingled with other property, the transferred property must be separated on or before the date specified in subparagraph (1) of this paragraph from the other property and allocated to the fund in accordance with the transferred property's percentage share of the fair market value of the total commingled property on the date of separation. The percentage share shall be the ratio which the fair market value of the transferred property on the date of separation bears to the fair market value of the total commingled property on that date and shall be computed in a manner consistent with paragraph (c) of § 1.642(c)-5. The property which is so allocated to the fund shall be treated as property received from transfers which meet the requirements of section 642(c)(5), and such transfers shall be treated as made on the dates on which the properties giving rise to such allocation were transferred to the fund by the respective donors. The property so allocated to the fund must be representative of all the commingled property other than securities the income from which is exempt from tax under subtitle A of the Code; compensating increases in other commingled property allocated to the fund

shall be made where such tax-exempt securities are not allocated to the fund. The application of this subparagraph may be illustrated by the following example:

Example. (a) The trustees of X fund are in the process of amending it in order to qualify as a pooled income fund. The property transferred to the X fund was commingled with other property transferred to the organization by which the fund was established. After taking into account the various transfers and the appreciation in the fair market value of all the properties, the fair market value of the property allocated to the fund on the various transfer dates is set forth in the following schedule and determined in the manner indicated:

TRANSFERS

Date of transfer	Value of all property before transfer (1)	Trust property (2)	Other property (3)	Value of all property after transfer (4)	Property allocated to fund (5)
January 1, 1968		$100,000	$100,000	$200,000	$100,000[1]
September 30, 1968	$300,000	100,000		400,000	250,000[2]
January 15, 1969	480,000	60,000		540,000	360,000[3]
November 11, 1969	600,000	200,000		800,000	600,000[4]

[1] $100,000 = (the amount in column (2)).
[2] 250,000 = ([$100,000/$200,000 × $300,000] + $100,000).
[3] 360,000 = ([$250,000/$400,000 × $480,000] + $60,000).
[4] 600,000 = ([$360,000/$540,000 × $600,000] + $200,000).

(b) On September 30, 1970, the trustees decide to separate the property of X fund from the other property. The fair market value of all the commingled property is $1 million on September 30, 1970, and there were no additional transfers to the fund after November 11, 1969. Accordingly, the fair market value of the property required to be allocated to X fund must be $750,000 ($600,000/$800,000 × $100,000), and X fund's percentage share of the commingled property is 75 percent ($750,000/$100,000). Accordingly, assuming that the commingled property consists of Y stock with a fair market value of $800,000 and Z bonds with a fair market value of $200,000, there must be allocated to X fund at the close of September 30, 1970, Y stock with a value of $600,000 ($800,000 = 75%) and Z bonds with a value of $150,000 ($200,000 × 75%).

(d) Transactions before amendment of or severance from fund. *(1)* A fund which is amended pursuant to paragraph (c) of this section, or is severed from a fund pursuant to paragraph (a)(2) of this section, shall be treated for all purposes, including the allowance of a deduction for any charitable contribution, as if it were before its amendment or severance a pooled income fund to which section 642(c)(5) and § 1.642(c)-5 apply. Thus, for example, where a donor transferred property in trust to such an amended or severed fund on August 1, 1969, but before its amendment or severance under this section, a charitable contributions deduction for the value of the remainder interest may be allowed under section 170, 2055, 2106, or 2522. The deduction may not be allowed, however, until the fund is amended or severed pursuant to this section and shall be allowed only if a claim for credit or refund is filed within the period of limitation prescribed by section 6511(a).

(2) For purposes of determining under § 1.642(c)-6 the highest yearly rate of return earned by a fund (which is amended pursuant to paragraph (c) of this section) for the 3 preceding taxable years, taxable years of the fund preceding its taxable year in which the fund is so amended and qualifies as a pooled income fund under this section shall be used provided that the fund did not at any time during such preceding years hold any investments in securities the income from which is exempt from tax under subtitle A of the Code. If any such tax-exempt securities were held during such period by such amended fund, or if the fund consists of a portion of a fund which is severed pursuant to paragraph (a)(2) of this section, the highest yearly rate of return under § 1.642(c)-6 shall be determined by treating the fund as a pooled income fund which has been in existence for less than 3 taxable years preceding the taxable year in which the transfer of property to the fund is made.

(3) Property transferred to a fund before its amendment pursuant to paragraph (c) of this section, or before its severance under paragraph (a)(2) of this section, shall be treated as property received from transfers which meet the requirements of section 642(c)(5).

T.D. 7105, 4/5/71, amend T.D. 7125, 6/7/71, T.D. 8540, 6/9/94.

§ 1.642(d)-1 Net operating loss deduction.

Caution: The Treasury has not yet amended Reg § 1.642(d)-1 to reflect changes made by P.L. 94-455.

The net operating loss deduction allowed by section 172 is available to estates and trusts generally, with the following exceptions and limitations:

(a) In computing gross income and deductions for the purposes of section 172, a trust shall exclude that portion of the income and deductions attributable to the grantor or another person under sections 671 through 678 (relating to grantors and others treated as substantial owners).

(b) An estate or trust shall not, for the purposes of section 172, avail itself of the deductions allowed by section 642(c) (relating to charitable contributions deductions) and sections 651 and 661 (relating to deductions for distributions).

T.D. 6217, 12/19/56.

§ 1.642(e)-1 Depreciation and depletion.

Caution: The Treasury has not yet amended Reg § 1.642(e)-1 to reflect changes made by P.L. 101-508, P.L. 97-34, P.L. 94-455.

An estate or trust is allowed the deductions for depreciation and depletion, but only to the extent the deductions are not apportioned to beneficiaries under sections 167(h) and

611(b). For purposes of sections 167(h) and 611(b), the term "beneficiaries" includes charitable beneficiaries. See the regulations under those sections.

T.D. 6217, 12/19/56, amend T.D. 6712, 3/23/64.

§ 1.642(f)-1 Amortization deductions.

Caution: The Treasury has not yet amended Reg § 1.642(f)-1 to reflect changes made by P.L. 103-66, P.L. 101-508, P.L. 97-34.

An estate or trust is allowed amortization deductions with respect to an emergency facility as defined in section 168(d), with respect to a certified pollution control facility as defined in section 169(d), with respect to qualified railroad rolling stock as defined in section 184(d), with respect to certified coal mine safety equipment as defined in section 187(d), with respect to on-the-job training and child care facilities as defined in section 188(b), and with respect to certain rehabilitations of certified historic structures as defined in section 191, in the same manner and to the same extent as in the case of an individual. However, the principles governing the apportionment of the deductions for depreciation and depletion between fiduciaries and the beneficiaries of an estate or trust (see sections 167(h) and 611(b) and the regulations thereunder) shall be applicable with respect to such amortization deductions.

T.D. 6217, 12/19/56, amend T.D. 6712, 3/23/64, T.D. 7116, 5/17/71, T.D. 7599, 3/12/79, T.D. 7700, 6/4/80.

§ 1.642(g)-1 Disallowance of double deductions; in general.

Caution: The Treasury has not yet amended Reg § 1.642(g)-1 to reflect changes made by P.L. 101-239, P.L. 94-455, P.L. 89-621.

Amounts allowable under section 2053(a)(2) (relating to administration expenses) or under section 2054 (relating to losses during administration) as deductions in computing the taxable estate of a decedent are not allowed as deductions in computing the taxable income of the estate unless there is filed a statement, in duplicate, to the effect that the items have not been allowed as deductions from the gross estate of the decedent under section 2053 or 2054 and that all rights to have such items allowed at any time as deductions under section 2053 or 2054 are waived. The statement should be filed with the return for the year for which the items are claimed as deductions or with the district director for the internal revenue district in which the return was filed, for association with the return. The statement may be filed at any time before the expiration of the statutory period of limitation applicable to the taxable year for which the deduction is sought. Allowance of a deduction in computing an estate's taxable income is not precluded by claiming a deduction in the estate tax return, so long as the estate tax deduction is not finally allowed and the statement is filed. However, after a statement is filed under section 642(g) with respect to a particular item or portion of an item, the item cannot thereafter be allowed as a deduction for estate tax purposes since the waiver operates as a relinquishment of the right to have the deduction allowed at any time under section 2053 or 2054.

T.D. 6217, 12/19/56.

§ 1.642(g)-2 Deductions included.

Caution: The Treasury has not yet amended Reg § 1.642(g)-2 to reflect changes made by P.L. 101-239, P.L. 94-455.

It is not required that the total deductions, or the total amount of any deduction, to which section 642(g) is applicable be treated in the same way. One deduction or portion of a deduction may be allowed for income tax purposes if the appropriate statement is filed, while another deduction or portion is allowed for estate tax purposes. Section 642(g) has no application to deductions for taxes, interest, business expenses, and other items accrued at the date of a decedent's death so that they are allowable as a deduction under section 2053(a)(3) for estate tax purposes as claims against the estate, and are also allowable under section 691(b) as deductions in respect of a decedent for income tax purposes. However, section 642(g) is applicable to deductions for interest, business expenses, and other items not accrued at the date of the decedent's death so that they are allowable as deductions for estate tax purposes only as administration expenses under section 2053(a)(2). Although deductible under section 2053(a)(3) in determining the value of the taxable estate of a decedent, medical, dental, etc., expenses of a decedent which are paid by the estate of the decedent are not deductible in computing the taxable income of the estate. See section 213(d) and the regulations thereunder for rules relating to the deductibility of such expenses in computing the taxable income of the decedent.

T.D. 6217, 12/19/56.

§ 1.642(h)-1 Unused loss carryovers on termination of an estate or trust.

Caution: The Treasury has not yet amended Reg § 1.642(h)-1 to reflect changes made by P.L. 99-514.

(a) If, on the final termination of an estate or trust, a net operating loss carryover under section 172 or a capital loss carryover under section 1212 would be allowable to the estate or trust in a taxable year subsequent to the taxable year of termination but for the termination, the carryover or carryovers are allowed under section 642(h)(1) to the beneficiaries succeeding to the property of the estate or trust. See § 1.641(b)-3 for the determination of when an estate or trust terminates.

(b) The net operating loss carryover and the capital loss carryover are the same in the hands of a beneficiary as in the estate or trust, except that the capital loss carryover in the hands of a beneficiary which is a corporation is a short-term loss irrespective of whether it would have been a long-term or short-term capital loss in the hands of the estate or trust. The net operating loss carryover and the capital loss carryover are taken into account in computing taxable income, adjusted gross income, and the tax imposed by section 56 (relating to the minimum tax for tax preferences). The first taxable year of the beneficiary to which the loss shall be carried over is the taxable year of the beneficiary in which or with which the estate or trust terminates. However, for purposes of determining the number of years to which a net operating loss, or a capital loss under paragraph (a) of § 1.1212-1, may be carried over by a beneficiary, the last taxable year of the estate or trust (whether or not a short taxable year) and the first taxable year of the beneficiary to which a loss is carried over each constitute a taxable year, and, in the case of a beneficiary of an estate or trust that is a corporation, capital losses carried over by the estate or trust to any taxable year of the estate or trust beginning after December 31, 1963, shall be treated as if they were incurred in the last taxable year of the estate or trust (whether or not a short taxable year). For the treatment of the net operating loss carryover when the last taxable year of the estate or trust is the last taxable year to which such loss can be carried over, see § 1.642(h)-2.

(c) The application of this section may be illustrated by the following examples:

Example (1). A trust distributes all of its assets to A, the sole remainderman, and terminates on December 31, 1954, when it has a capital loss carryover of $10,000 attributable to transactions during the taxable year 1952. A, who reports on the calendar year basis, otherwise has ordinary income of $10,000 and capital gains of $4,000 for the taxable year 1954. A would offset his capital gains of $4,000 against the capital loss of the trust and, in addition, deduct under section 1211(b) $1,000 on his return for the taxable year 1954. The balance of the capital loss carryover of $5,000 may be carried over only to the years 1955 and 1956, in accordance with paragraph (a) of § 1.1212-1 and the rules of this section.

Example (2). A trust distributes all of its assets, one-half to A, an individual, and one-half to X, a corporation, who are the sole remaindermen, and terminates on December 31, 1966, when it has a short-term capital loss carryover of $20,000 attributable to short-term transactions during the taxable years 1964, 1965, and 1966, and a long-term capital loss carryover of $12,000 attributable to long-term transactions during such years. A, who reports on the calendar year basis, otherwise has ordinary income of $15,000, short-term capital gains of $4,000 and long-term capital gains of $6,000, for the taxable year 1966. A would offset his short-term capital gains of $4,000 against his share of the short-term capital loss carryover of the trust, $10,000 (one-half of $20,000), and, in addition deduct under section 1211(b) $1,000 (treated as a short-term gain for purposes of computing capital loss carryovers) on his return for the taxable year 1966. A would also offset his long-term capital gains of $6,000 against his share of the long-term capital loss carryover of the trust, $6,000 (one-half of $12,000). The balance of A's share of the short-term capital loss carryover, $5,000, may be carried over as a short-term capital loss carryover to the succeeding taxable year and treated as a short-term capital loss incurred in such succeeding taxable year in accordance with paragraph (b) of § 1.1212-1. X, which also reports on the calendar year basis, otherwise has capital gains of $4,000 for the taxable year 1966. X would offset its capital gains of $4,000 against its share of the capital loss carryovers of the trust, $16,000 (the sum of one-half of each the short-term carryover and the long-term carryover of the trust), on its return for the taxable year 1966. The balance of X's share, $12,000, may be carried over as a short-term capital loss only to the years 1967, 1968, 1969, and 1970, in accordance with paragraph (a) of § 1.1212-1 and the rules of this section.

T.D. 6217, 12/19/56, amend T.D. 6828, 6/16/65, T.D. 7564, 9/11/78.

§ 1.642(h)-2 Excess deductions on termination of an estate or trust.

(a) If, on the termination of an estate or trust, the estate or trust has for its last taxable year deductions (other than the deductions allowed under section 642(b) (relating to personal exemption) or section 642(c) (relating to charitable contributions)) in excess of gross income, the excess is allowed under section 642(h)(2) as a deduction to the beneficiaries succeeding to the property of the estate or trust. The deduction is allowed only in computing taxable income and must be taken into account in computing the items of tax preference of the beneficiary; it is not allowed in computing adjusted gross income. The deduction is allowable only in the taxable year of the beneficiary in which or with which the estate or trust terminates, whether the year of termination of the estate or trust is of normal duration or is a short taxable year. For example: Assume that a trust distributes all of its assets to B and terminates on December 31, 1954. As of that date it has excess deductions, for example, because of corpus commissions on termination, of $18,000. B, who reported on the calendar year basis, could claim the $18,000 as a deduction for the taxable year 1954. However, if the deduction (when added to his other deductions) exceeds his gross income, the excess may not be carried over to the year 1955 or subsequent years.

(b) A deduction based upon a net operating loss carryover will never be allowed to beneficiaries under both paragraphs (1) and (2) of section 642(h). Accordingly, a net operating loss deduction which is allowable to beneficiaries succeeding to the property of the estate or trust under the provisions of paragraph (1) of section 642(h) cannot also be considered a deduction for purposes of paragraph (2) of section 642(h) and paragraph (a) of this section. However, if the last taxable year of the estate or trust is the last year in which a deduction on account of a net operating loss may be taken, the deduction, to the extent not absorbed in that taxable year by the estate or trust, is considered an "excess deduction" under section 642(h)(2) and paragraph (a) of this section.

(c) Any item of income or deduction, or any part thereof, which is taken into account in determining the net operating loss or capital loss carryover of the estate or trust for its last taxable year shall not be taken into account again in determining excess deductions on termination of the trust or estate within the meaning of section 642(h)(2) and paragraph (a) of this section (see example in § 1.642(h)-5).

T.D. 6217, 12/19/56, amend T.D. 7564, 9/11/78.

§ 1.642(h)-3 Meaning of "beneficiaries succeeding to the property of the estate or trust".

Caution: The Treasury has not yet amended Reg § 1.642(h)-3 to reflect changes made by P.L. 94-455.

(a) The phrase "beneficiaries succeeding to the property of the estate or trust" means those beneficiaries upon termination of the estate or trust who bear the burden of any loss for which a carryover is allowed, or of any excess of deductions over gross income for which a deduction is allowed, under section 642(h).

(b) With reference to an intestate estate, the phrase means the heirs and next of kin to whom the estate is distributed, or if the estate is insolvent, to whom it would have been distributed if it had not been insolvent. If a decedent's spouse is entitled to a specified dollar amount of property before any distribution to other heirs and next of kin, and if the estate is less than that amount, the spouse is the beneficiary succeeding to the property of the estate or trust to the extent of the deficiency in amount.

(c) In the case of a testate estate, the phrase normally means the residuary beneficiaries (including a residuary trust), and not specific legatees or devisees, pecuniary legatees, or other nonresiduary beneficiaries. However, the phrase does not include the recipient of a specific sum of money even though it is payable out of the residue, except to the extent that it is not payable in full. On the other hand, the phrase includes a beneficiary (including a trust) who is not strictly a residuary beneficiary but whose devise or bequest is determined by the value of the decedent's estate as reduced by the loss or deductions in question. Thus the phrase includes:

(1) A beneficiary of a fraction of a decedent's net estate after payment of debts, expenses, etc.;

(2) A nonresiduary legatee or devisee, to the extent of any deficiency in his legacy or devise resulting from the insufficiency of the estate to satisfy it in full;

(3) A surviving spouse receiving a fractional share of an estate in fee under a statutory right of election, to the extent that the loss or deductions are taken into account in determining the share. However, the phrase does not include a recipient of dower or curtesy, or any income beneficiary of the estate or trust from which the loss or excess deduction is carried over.

(d) The principles discussed in paragraph (c) of this section are equally applicable to trust beneficiaries. A remainderman who receives all or a fractional share of the property of a trust as a result of the final termination of the trust is a beneficiary succeeding to the property of the trust. For example, if property is transferred to pay the income to A for life and then to pay $10,000 to B and distribute the balance of the trust corpus to C, C and not B is considered to be the succeeding beneficiary except to the extent that the trust corpus is insufficient to pay B $10,000.

T.D. 6217, 12/19/56.

§ 1.642(h)-4 Allocation.

Caution: The Treasury has not yet amended Reg § 1.642(h)-4 to reflect changes made by P.L. 94-455.

The carryovers and excess deductions to which section 642(h) applies are allocated among the beneficiaries succeeding to the property of an estate or trust (see § 1.642(h)-3) proportionately according to the share of each in the burden of the loss or deductions. A person who qualified as a beneficiary succeeding to the property of an estate or trust with respect to one amount and does not qualify with respect to another amount is a beneficiary succeeding to the property of the estate or trust as to the amount with respect to which he qualifies. The application of this section may be illustrated by the following example:

Example. A decedent's will leaves $100,000 to A, and the residue of his estate equally to B and C. His estate is sufficient to pay only $90,000 to A, and nothing to B and C. There is an excess of deductions over gross income for the last taxable year of the estate or trust of $5,000, and a capital loss carryover of $15,000, to both of which section 642(h) applies. A is a beneficiary succeeding to the property of the estate to the extent of $10,000, and since the total of the excess of deductions and the loss carryover is $20,000, A is entitled to the benefit of one half of each item, and the remaining half is divided equally between B and C.

T.D. 6217, 12/19/56.

§ 1.642(h)-5 Example.

Caution: The Treasury has not yet amended Reg § 1.642(h)-5 to reflect changes made by P.L. 94-455.

The application of section 642(h) may be illustrated by the following example:

Example. (a) A decedent dies January 31, 1954, leaving a will which provides for distributing all her estate equally to A and an existing trust for B. The period of administration of the estate terminates on December 31, 1954, at which time all the property of the estate is distributed to A and the trust. A reports his income for tax purposes on a calendar year basis, and the trust reports its income on the basis of a fiscal year ending August 31. During the period of the administration, the estate has the following items of income and deductions:

Taxable interest	$ 2,500
Business income	3,000
Total	5,500
Business expenses (including administrative expense allocable to business income)	5,000
Administrative expenses and corpus commissions not allocable to business income	9,800
Total deductions	14,800

(b) Under section 642(h)(1), an unused net operating loss carryover of the estate on termination of $2,000 will be allowable to: A to the extent of $1,000 for his taxable year 1954 and the next four taxable years in accordance with section 172; and to the trust to the extent of $1,000 for its taxable year ending August 31, 1955, and its next four taxable years. The amount of the net operating loss carryover is computed as follows:

Deductions of estate for 1954	$14,800
Less adjustment under section 172(d)(4) (deductions not attributable to a trade or business ($9,800) allowable only to extent of gross income not derived from such trade or business ($2,500)	7,300
Deductions as adjusted	7,500
Gross income of estate for 1954	5,500
Net operating loss of estate for 1954	2,000

Neither A nor the trust will be allowed to carry back any part of the net operating loss made available to them under section 642(h)(1).

(c) Under section 642(h)(2), excess deductions of the estate of $7,300 will be allowed as a deduction to A to the extent of $3,650 for the calendar year 1954 and to the trust to the extent of $3,650 for the taxable year ending August 31, 1955. The deduction of $7,300 for administrative expenses and corpus commissions is the only amount which was not taken into account in determining the net operating loss of the estate ($9,800 of such expenses less $2,500 taken into account).

(d) Under section 642(h)(1), there will be allowable to A a capital loss carryover of $2,500 for his taxable year 1954 and for his next 4 taxable years in accordance with paragraph (a) of § 1.1212-1. There will be allowable to the trust a similar capital loss carryover of $2,500 for its taxable year ending August 31, 1955, and its next 4 taxable years (but see paragraph (b) of § 1.643(a)-3). (For taxable years beginning after December 31, 1963, net capital losses may be carried over indefinitely by beneficiaries other than corporations, in accordance with § 1.642(h)-1 and paragraph (b) of § 1.1212-1.)

(e) The carryovers and excess deductions are not allowable directly to B, the trust beneficiary, but to the extent the distributable net income of the trust is reduced by the carry-overs and excess deductions B may receive indirect benefit.

T.D. 6217, 12/19/56, amend T.D. 6828, 6/16/65.

§ 1.642(i)-1 Certain distributions by cemetery perpetual care funds.

(a) In general. Section 642(i) provides that amounts distributed during taxable years ending after December 31, 1963, by a cemetery perpetual care fund trust for the care and maintenance of gravesites shall be treated as distributions solely for purposes of sections 651 and 661. The deduction for such a distribution is allowable only if the fund is taxable as a trust. In addition, the fund must have been created pursuant to local law by a taxable cemetery corporation (as defined in § 1.642(i)-2(a)) expressly for the care and maintenance of cemetery property. A care fund will be treated as having been created by a taxable cemetery corporation ("cemetery") if the distributee cemetery is taxable, even though the care fund was created by the distributee cemetery in a year that it was tax-exempt or by a predecessor of such distributee cemetery which was tax-exempt in the year the fund was established. The deduction is the amount of the distributions during the fund's taxable year to the cemetery corporation for such care and maintenance that would be otherwise allowable under section 651 or 661, but in no event is to exceed the limitations described in paragraphs (b) and (c) of this section. The provisions of this paragraph shall not have the effect of extending the period of limitations under section 6511.

(b) Limitation on amount of deduction. The deduction in any taxable year may not exceed the product of $5 multiplied by the aggregate number of gravesites sold by the cemetery corporation before the beginning of the taxable year of the trust. In general, the aggregate number of gravesites sold shall be the aggregate number of interment rights sold by the cemetery corporation (including gravesites sold by the cemetery before a care fund trust law was enacted). In addition, the number of gravesites sold shall include gravesites used to make welfare burials. Welfare burials and pre-trust fund law gravesites shall be included only to the extent that the cemetery cares for and maintains such gravesites. For purposes of this section, a gravesite is sold as of the date on which the purchaser acquires interment rights enforceable under local law. The aggregate number of gravesites includes only those gravesites with respect to which the fund or taxable cemetery corporation has an obligation for care and maintenance.

(c) Requirements for deductibility of distributions for care and maintenance. *(1) Obligation for care and maintenance.* A deduction is allowed only for distributions for the care and maintenance of gravesites with respect to which the fund or taxable cemetery corporation has an obligation for care and maintenance. Such obligation may be established by the trust instrument, by local law, or by the cemetery's practice of caring for and maintaining gravesites, such as welfare burial plots or gravesites sold before the enactment of a care fund trust law.

(2) Distribution actually used for care and maintenance. The amount of a deduction otherwise allowable for care fund distributions in any taxable year shall not exceed the portion of such distributions expended by the distributee cemetery corporation for the care and maintenance of gravesites before the end of the fund's taxable year following the taxable year in which it makes the distributions. A 6-month extension of time for filing the trust's return may be obtained upon request under section 6081. The failure of a cemetery to expend the care fund's distributions within a reasonable time before the due date for filing the return will be considered reasonable grounds for granting a 6-month extension of time for section 6081. For purposes of this paragraph, any amount expended by the care fund directly for the care and maintenance of gravesites shall be treated as an additional care fund distribution which is expended on the day of distribution by the cemetery corporation. The fund shall be allowed a deduction for such direct expenditure in the fund's taxable year during which the expenditure is made.

(3) Example. The application of paragraph (c)(2) of this section is illustrated by the following example:

A, a calendar year perpetual care fund trust, meeting the requirements of section 642(i), makes a $10,000 distribution on December 1, 1978 to X, a taxable cemetery corporation operating on a May 31 fiscal year. From this $10,000 distribution, the cemetery makes the following expenditures for the care and maintenance of gravesites: $2,000 on December 20, 1978; $4,000 on June 1, 1979; $2,000 on October 1, 1979; and $1,000 on April 1, 1980. In addition, as authorized by the trust instrument, A itself makes a direct $1,000 payment to a contractor on September 1, 1979 for qualifying care and maintenance work performed. As a result of these transactions, A will be allowed an $8,000 deduction for its 1978 taxable year attributable to the cemetery's expenditures, and a $1,000 deduction for its 1979 taxable year attributable to the fund's direct payment. A will not be allowed a deduction for its 1978 taxable year for the cemetery's expenditure of either the $1,000 expended on April 1, 1980 or the remaining unspent portion of the original $10,000 distribution. The trustee may request a 6-month extension in order to allow the fund until October 15, 1979 to file its return for 1978.

(d) Certified statement made by cemetery officials to fund trustees. A trustee of a cemetery perpetual care fund shall not be held personally liable for civil or criminal penalties resulting from false statements on the trust's tax return to the extent that such false statements resulted from the trustee's reliance on a certified statement made by the cemetery specifying the number of interments sold by the cemetery or the amount of the cemetery's expenditures for care and maintenance. The statement must indicate the basis upon which the cemetery determined what portion of its expenditures were made for the care and maintenance of gravesites. The statement must be certified by an officer or employee of the cemetery who has the responsibility to make or account for expenditures for care and maintenance. A copy of this statement shall be retained by the trustee along with the trust's return and shall be made available for inspection upon request by the Secretary. This paragraph does not relieve the care fund trust of its liability to pay the proper amount of tax due and to maintain adequate records to substantiate each of its deductions, including the deduction provided in section 642(i) and this section.

T.D. 7651, 10/25/79.

§ 1.642(i)-2 Definitions.

(a) Taxable cemetery corporation. For purposes of section 642(i) and this section, the meaning of the term "taxable cemetery corporation" is limited to a corporation (within the meaning of section 7701(a)(3)) engaged in the business of owning and operating a cemetery that either (1) is not exempt from Federal tax, or (2) is subject to tax under section 511 with respect to its cemetery activities.

(b) Pursuant to local law. A Cemetery perpetual care fund is created pursuant to local law if:

(1) The governing law of the relevant jurisdiction (State, district, county, parish, etc.) requires or expressly permits the creation of such a find, or

(2) The legally enforceable bylaws or contracts of a taxable cemetery corporation require a perpetual care fund.

(c) Gravesite. A gravesite is any type of interment right that has been sold by a cemetery, including, but not limited to, a burial lot, mausoleum, lawn crypt, niche, or scattering ground. For purposes of § 1.642(i)-1, the term "gravesites" includes only those gravesites with respect to which the care fund or cemetery has an obligation for care and maintenance within the meaning of § 1.642(i)-1(c)(1).

(d) Care and maintenance. For purposes of section 642(i) and this section, the term "care and maintenance of gravesite" shall be generally defined in accordance with the definition of such term under the local law pursuant to which the cemetery perpetual care fund is created. If the applicable local law contains no definition, care and maintenance of gravesites may include the upkeep, repair and preservation of those portions of cemetery property in which gravesites (as defined in paragraph (c) of this section) have been sold; including gardening, road maintenance, water line and drain repair and other activities reasonably necessary to the preservation of cemetery property. The costs for care and maintenance include, but are not limited to, expenditures for the maintenance, repair and replacement of machinery, tools, and equipment, compensation of employees performing such work, insurance premiums, reasonable payments for employees' pension and other benefit plans, and the costs of maintaining necessary records of lot ownership, transfers and burials. However, if some of the expenditures of the cemetery corporation, such as officers' salaries, are for both care and maintenance and for other purposes, the expenditures must be properly allocated between care and maintenance of gravesites and the other purposes. Only those expenditures that are properly allocable to those portions of cemetery property in which gravesites have been sold qualify as expenditures for care and maintenance of gravesites.

T.D. 7651, 10/25/79.

§ 1.643(a)-0 Distributable net income; deduction for distributions; in general.

Caution: The Treasury has not yet amended Reg § 1.643(a)-0 to reflect changes made by P.L. 101-239, P.L. 100-647, P.L. 99-514, P.L. 98-369, P.L. 97-448, P.L. 97-34, P.L. 96-223, P.L. 94-455, P.L. 87-834.

The term "distributable net income" has no application except in the taxation of estates and trusts and their beneficiaries. It limits the deductions allowable to estates and trusts for amounts paid, credited, or required to be distributed to beneficiaries and is used to determine how much of an amount paid, credited, or required to be distributed to a beneficiary will be includible in his gross income. It is also used to determine the character of distributions to the beneficiaries. Distributable net income means for any taxable year, the taxable income (as defined in section 63) of the estate or trust, computed with the modifications set forth in §§ 1.643(a)-1 through 1.643(a)-7.

T.D. 6217, 12/19/56.

§ 1.643(a)-1 Deduction for distributions.

Caution: The Treasury has not yet amended Reg § 1.643(a)-1 to reflect changes made by P.L. 101-239, P.L. 100-647, P.L. 99-514, P.L. 98-369, P.L. 97-448, P.L. 97-34, P.L. 96-223, P.L. 94-455, P.L. 87-834.

The deduction allowable to a trust under section 651 and to an estate or trust under section 661 for amounts paid, credited, or required to be distributed to beneficiaries is not allowed in the computation of distributable net income.

T.D. 6217, 12/19/56.

§ 1.643(a)-2 Deduction for personal exemption.

The deduction for personal exemption under section 642(b) is not allowed in the computation of distributable net income.

T.D. 6217, 12/19/56.

§ 1.643(a)-3 Capital gains and losses.

Caution: The Treasury has not yet amended Reg § 1.643(a)-3 to reflect changes made by P.L. 103-66, P.L. 101-239, P.L. 100-647, P.L. 99-514, P.L. 98-369, P.L. 97-448, P.L. 97-34, P.L. 96-223, P.L. 94-455, P.L. 87-834.

(a) In general. Except as provided in § 1.643(a)-6 and paragraph (b) of this section, gains from the sale or exchange of capital assets are ordinarily excluded from distributable net income and are not ordinarily considered as paid, credited, or required to be distributed to any beneficiary.

(b) Capital gains included in distributable net income. Gains from the sale or exchange of capital assets are included in distributable net income to the extent they are, pursuant to the terms of the governing instrument and applicable local law, or pursuant to a reasonable and impartial exercise of discretion by the fiduciary (in accordance with a power granted to the fiduciary by applicable local law or by the governing instrument if not prohibited by applicable local law)—

(1) Allocated to income (but if income under the state statute is defined as, or consists of, a unitrust amount, a discretionary power to allocate gains to income must also be exercised consistently and the amount so allocated may not be greater than the excess of the unitrust amount over the amount of distributable net income determined without regard to this subparagraph § 1.643(a)-3(b));

(2) Allocated to corpus but treated consistently by the fiduciary on the trust's books, records, and tax returns as part of a distribution to a beneficiary; or

(3) Allocated to corpus but actually distributed to the beneficiary or utilized by the fiduciary in determining the amount that is distributed or required to be distributed to a beneficiary.

(c) Charitable contributions included in distributable net income. If capital gains are paid, permanently set aside, or to be used for the purposes specified in section 642(c), so that a charitable deduction is allowed under that section in respect of the gains, they must be included in the computation of distributable net income.

(d) Capital losses. Losses from the sale or exchange of capital assets shall first be netted at the trust level against any gains from the sale or exchange of capital assets, except for a capital gain that is utilized under paragraph (b)(3) of this section in determining the amount that is distributed or required to be distributed to a particular beneficiary. See § 1.642(h)-1 with respect to capital loss carryovers in the year of final termination of an estate or trust.

(e) Examples. The following examples illustrate the rules of this section:

Example (1). Under the terms of Trust's governing instrument, all income is to be paid to A for life. Trustee is given discretionary powers to invade principal for A's benefit and to deem discretionary distributions to be made from capital gains realized during the year. During Trust's first taxable year, Trust has $5,000 of dividend income and $10,000 of capital gain from the sale of securities. Pursuant to the terms of the governing instrument and applicable local law, Trustee allocates the $10,000 capital gain to principal. During the year, Trustee distributes to A $5,000, representing A's right to trust income. In addition, Trustee distributes to A $12,000, pursuant to the discretionary power to distribute principal. Trustee does not exercise the discretionary power to deem the discretionary distributions of principal as being paid from capital gains realized during the year. Therefore, the capital gains realized during the year are not included in distributable net income and the $10,000 of capital gain is taxed to the trust. In future years, Trustee must treat all discretionary distributions as not being made from any realized capital gains.

Example (2). The facts are the same as in Example 1, except that Trustee intends to follow a regular practice of treating discretionary distributions of principal as being paid first from any net capital gains realized by Trust during the year. Trustee evidences this treatment by including the $10,000 capital gain in distributable net income on Trust's federal income tax return so that it is taxed to A. This treatment of the capital gains is a reasonable exercise of Trustee's discretion. In future years Trustee must treat all discretionary distributions as being made first from any realized capital gains.

Example (3). The facts are the same as in Example 1, except that Trustee intends to follow a regular practice of treating discretionary distributions of principal as being paid from any net capital gains realized by Trust during the year from the sale of certain specified assets or a particular class of investments. This treatment of capital gains is a reasonable exercise of Trustee's discretion.

Example (4). The facts are the same as in Example 1, except that pursuant to the terms of the governing instrument (in a provision not prohibited by applicable local law), capital gains realized by Trust are allocated to income. Because the capital gains are allocated to income pursuant to the terms of the governing instrument, the $10,000 capital gain is included in Trust's distributable net income for the taxable year.

Example (5). The facts are the same as in Example 1, except that Trustee decides that discretionary distributions will be made only to the extent Trust has realized capital gains during the year and thus the discretionary distribution to A is $10,000, rather than $12,000. Because Trustee will use the amount of any realized capital gain to determine the amount of the discretionary distribution to the beneficiary, the $10,000 capital gain is included in Trust's distributable net income for the taxable year.

Example (6). Trust's assets consist of Blackacre and other property. Under the terms of Trust's governing instrument, Trustee is directed to hold Blackacre for ten years and then sell it and distribute all the sales proceeds to A. Because Trustee uses the amount of the sales proceeds that includes any realized capital gain to determine the amount required to be distributed to A, any capital gain realized from the sale of Blackacre is included in Trust's distributable net income for the taxable year.

Example (7). Under the terms of Trust's governing instrument, all income is to be paid to A during the Trust's term. When A reaches 35, Trust is to terminate and all the principal is to be distributed to A. Because all the assets of the trust, including all capital gains, will be actually distributed to the beneficiary at the termination of Trust, all capital gains realized in the year of termination are included in distributable net income. See § 1.641(b)-3 for the determination of the year of final termination and the taxability of capital gains realized after the terminating event and before final distribution.

Example (8). The facts are the same as Example 7, except Trustee is directed to pay B $10,000 before distributing the remainder of Trust assets to A. Because the distribution to B is a gift of a specific sum of money within the meaning of section 663(a)(1), none of Trust's distributable net income that includes all of the capital gains realized during the year of termination is allocated to B's distribution.

Example (9). The facts are the same as Example 7, except Trustee is directed to distribute one-half of the principal to A when A reaches 35 and the balance to A when A reaches 45. Trust assets consist entirely of stock in corporation M with a fair market value of $1,000,000 and an adjusted basis of $300,000. When A reaches 35, Trustee sells one-half of the stock and distributes the sales proceeds to A. All the sales proceeds, including all the capital gain attributable to that sale, are actually distributed to A and therefore all the capital gain is included in distributable net income.

Example (10). The facts are the same as Example 9, except when A reaches 35, Trustee sells all the stock and distributes one-half of the sales proceeds to A. If authorized by the governing instrument and applicable state statute, Trustee may determine to what extent the capital gain is distributed to A. The $500,000 distribution to A may be treated as including a minimum of $200,000 of capital gain (and all of the principal amount of $300,000) and a maximum of $500,000 of the capital gain (with no principal). Trustee evidences the treatment by including the appropriate amount of capital gain in distributable net income on Trust's federal income tax return. If Trustee is not authorized by the governing instrument and applicable state statutes to determine to what extent the capital gain is distributed to A, one-half of the capital gain attributable to the sale is included in distributable net income.

Example (11). The applicable state statute provides that a trustee may make an election to pay an income beneficiary an amount equal to four percent of the fair market value of the trust assets, as determined at the beginning of each taxable year, in full satisfaction of that beneficiary's right to income. State statute also provides that this unitrust amount shall be considered paid first from ordinary and tax-exempt income, then from net short-term capital gain, then from net long-term capital gain, and finally from return of principal. Trust's governing instrument provides that A is to receive each year income as defined under state statute. Trustee makes the unitrust election under state statute. At the beginning of the taxable year, Trust assets are valued at $500,000. During the year, Trust receives $5,000 of dividend income and realizes $80,000 of net long-term gain from the sale of capital assets. Trustee distributes to A $20,000 (4% of $500,000) in satisfaction of A's right to income. Net long-term capital gain in the amount of $15,000 is allocated to income pursuant to the ordering rule of the state statute and is included in distributable net income for the taxable year.

Example (12). The facts are the same as in Example 11, except that neither state statute nor Trust's governing instrument has an ordering rule for the character of the unitrust amount, but leaves such a decision to the discretion of Trustee. Trustee intends to follow a regular practice of treating principal, other than capital gain, as distributed to the beneficiary to the extent that the unitrust amount exceeds Trust's ordinary and tax-exempt income. Trustee evidences this treatment by not including any capital gains in distributable net income on Trust's Federal income tax return so that the entire $80,000 capital gain is taxed to Trust. This treatment of the capital gains is a reasonable exercise of Trustee's discretion. In future years Trustee must consistently follow this treatment of not allocating realized capital gains to income.

Example (13). The facts are the same as in Example 11, except that neither state statutes nor Trust's governing instrument has an ordering rule for the character of the unitrust amount, but leaves such a decision to the discretion of Trustee. Trustee intends to follow a regular practice of treating net capital gains as distributed to the beneficiary to the extent the unitrust amount exceeds Trust's ordinary and tax-exempt income. Trustee evidences this treatment by including $15,000 of the capital gain in distributable net income on Trust's Federal income tax return. This treatment of the capital gains is a reasonable exercise of Trustee's discretion. In future years Trustee must consistently treat realized capital gain, if any, as distributed to the beneficiary to the extent that the unitrust amount exceeds ordinary and tax-exempt income.

Example (14). Trustee is a corporate fiduciary that administers numerous trusts. State statutes provide that a trustee may make an election to distribute to an income beneficiary an amount equal to four percent of the annual fair market value of the trust assets in full satisfaction of that beneficiary's right to income. Neither state statutes nor the governing instruments of any of the trusts administered by Trustee has an ordering rule for the character of the unitrust amount, but leaves such a decision to the discretion of Trustee. With respect to some trusts, Trustee intends to follow a regular practice of treating principal, other than capital gain, as distributed to the beneficiary to the extent that the unitrust amount exceeds the trust's ordinary and tax-exempt income. Trustee will evidence this treatment by not including any capital gains in distributable net income on the Federal income tax returns for those trusts. With respect to other trusts, Trustee intends to follow a regular practice of treating any net capital gains as distributed to the beneficiary to the extent the unitrust amount exceeds the trust's ordinary and tax-exempt income. Trustee will evidence this treatment by including net capital gains in distributable net income on the Federal income tax returns filed for these trusts. Trustee's decision with respect to each trust is a reasonable exercise of Trustee's discretion and, in future years, Trustee must treat the capital gains realized by each trust consistently with the treatment by that trust in prior years.

(f) Effective date. This section applies for taxable years of trusts and estates ending after January 2, 2004.

T.D. 6217, 12/19/56, amend T.D. 6989, 1/16/69, T.D. 7357, 5/30/75, T.D. 9102, 12/30/2003.

§ 1.643(a)-4 Extraordinary dividends and taxable stock dividends.

Caution: The Treasury has not yet amended Reg § 1.643(a)-4 to reflect changes made by P.L. 101-239, P.L. 100-647, P.L. 99-514, P.L. 98-369, P.L. 97-448, P.L. 97-34, P.L. 96-223, P.L. 94-455.

In the case solely of a trust which qualifies under Subpart B (section 651 and following) as a "simple trust," there are excluded from distributable net income extraordinary dividends (whether paid in cash or in kind) or taxable stock dividends which are not distributed or credited to a beneficiary because the fiduciary in good faith determines that under the terms of the governing instrument and applicable local law such dividends are allocable to corpus. See section 665(e), paragraph (b) of § 1.665(e)-1A for the treatment of such dividends upon subsequent distribution.

T.D. 6217, 12/19/56, amend T.D. 6989, 1/16/69, T.D. 7204, 8/24/72.

§ 1.643(a)-5 Tax-exempt interest.

Caution: The Treasury has not yet amended Reg § 1.643(a)-5 to reflect changes made by P.L. 101-239, P.L. 100-647, P.L. 99-514, P.L. 98-369, P.L. 97-448, P.L. 97-34, P.L. 96-223, P.L. 94-455, P.L. 87-834.

(a) There is included in distributable net income any tax-exempt interest excluded from gross income under section 103, reduced by disbursements allocable to such interest which would have been deductible under section 212 but for the provisions of section 265 (relating to disallowance of deductions allocable to tax-exempt income).

(b) If the estate or trust is allowed a charitable contributions deduction under section 642(c), the amounts specified in paragraph (a) of this section and § 1.643(a)-6 are reduced by the portion deemed to be included in income paid, permanently set aside, or to be used for the purposes specified in section 642(c). If the governing instrument specifically provides as to the source out of which amounts are paid, permanently set aside, or to be used for such charitable purposes, the specific provisions control. In the absence of specific provisions in the governing instrument, an amount to which section 642(c) applies is deemed to consist of the same proportion of each class of the items of income of the estate or trust as the total of each class bears to the total of all classes. For illustrations showing the determination of the character of an amount deductible under section 642(c), see examples (1) and (2) of § 1.662(b)-2 and paragraph (e) of § 1.662(c)-4.

T.D. 6217, 12/19/56.

§ 1.643(a)-6 Income of foreign trust.

Caution: The Treasury has not yet amended Reg § 1.643(a)-6 to reflect changes made by P.L. 101-239, P.L. 100-647, P.L. 99-514, P.L. 98-369, P.L. 97-448, P.L. 97-34, P.L. 94-455.

(a) Distributable net income of a foreign trust. In the case of a foreign trust (see section 7701(a)(31)), the determination of distributable net income is subject to the following rules:

(1) There is included in distributable net income the amounts of gross income from sources without the United States, reduced by disbursements allocable to such foreign income which would have been deductible but for the provisions of section 265 (relating to disallowance of deductions

allocable to tax exempt income). See paragraph (b) of § 1.643(a)-5 for rules applicable when an estate or trust is allowed a charitable contributions deduction under section 642(c).

(2) In the case of a distribution made by a trust before January 1, 1963, for purposes of determining the distributable net income of the trust for the taxable year in which the distribution is made, or for any prior taxable year;

(i) Gross income from sources within the United States is determined by taking into account the provisions of section 894 (relating to income exempt under treaty); and

(ii) Distributable net income is determined by taking into account the provisions of section 643(a)(3) (relating to exclusion of certain gains from the sale or exchange of capital assets).

(3) In the case of a distribution made by a trust after December 31, 1962, for purposes of determining the distributable net income of the trust for any taxable year, whether ending before January 1, 1963, or after December 31, 1962;

(i) Gross income (for the entire foreign trust) from sources within the United States is determined without regard to the provisions of section 894 (relating to income exempt under treaty);

(ii) In respect of a foreign trust created by a U.S. person (whether such trust constitutes the whole or only a portion of the entire foreign trust) (see section 643(d) and § 1.643(d)-1), there shall be included in gross income gains from the sale or exchange of capital assets reduced by losses from such sales or exchanges to the extent such losses do not exceed gains from such sales or exchanges, and the deduction under section 1202 (relating to deduction for capital gains) shall not be taken into account; and

(iii) In respect of a foreign trust created by a person other than a U.S. person (whether such trust constitutes the whole or only a portion of the entire foreign trust) (see section 643(d) and § 1.643(d)-1), distributable net income is determined by taking into account all of the provisions of section 643 except section 643(a)(6)(C) (relating to gains from the sale or exchange of capital assets by a foreign trust created by a U.S. person).

(b) The application of this section showing the computation of distributable net income for one of the taxable years for which such a computation must be made, may be illustrated by the following examples:

Example (1). (1) A trust created in 1952 under the laws of Country X by the transfer to a trustee in Country X of money and property by a U.S. person. The entire trust constitutes a foreign trust created by a U.S. person. The income from the trust corpus is to be accumulated until the beneficiary, a resident citizen of the United States who was born in 1944, reaches the age of 21 years, and upon his reaching that age, the corpus and accumulated income are to be distributed to him. The trust instrument provides that capital gains are to be allocated to corpus and are not to be paid, credited, or required to be distributed to any beneficiary during the taxable year or paid, permanently set aside, or to be used for the purposes specified in section 642(c). Under the terms of a tax convention between the United States and Country X interest income received by the trust from U.S. sources is exempt from U.S. taxation. In 1965 the corpus and accumulated income are distributed to the beneficiary. During the taxable year 1964, the trust has the following items of income, loss, and expense:

Interest on bonds of a U.S. corporation	$10,000
Net long-term capital gain from U.S. sources	30,000
Gross income from investments in Country X	40,000
Net short-term capital loss from U.S. sources	5,000
Expenses allocable to gross income from investments in Country X	5,000

(2) The distributable net income for the taxable year 1964 of the foreign trust created by a U.S. person, determined under section 643(a), is $70,000, computed as follows:

Interest on bonds of a U.S. corporation		$10,000
Gross income from investments in Country X		40,000
Net long-term capital gain from U.S. sources	$30,000	
Less: Net short-term capital loss from U.S. sources	5,000	
Excess of net long-term capital gain over net short-term capital loss		25,000
Total		75,000
Less: Expenses allocable to income from investments in Country X		5,000
Distributable net income		70,000

(3) In determining the distributable net income of $70,000, the taxable income of the trust is computed with the following modifications: No deduction is allowed for the personal exemption of the trust (section 643(a)(2)); the interest received on bonds of a U.S. corporation is included in the trust gross income despite the fact that such interest is exempt from U.S. tax under the provisions of the tax treaty between Country X and the United States (section 643(a)(6)(B)); the excess of net long-term capital gain over net short-term capital loss allocable to corpus is included in distributable net income, but such excess is not subject to the deduction under section 1202 (section 643(a)(6)(C)); and the amount representing gross income from investments in Country X is included, but such amount is reduced by the amount of the disbursements allocable to such income (section 643(a)(6)(A)).

Example (2). (1) The facts are the same as in example (1) except that money or property has also been transferred to the trust by a person other than a U.S. person and, pursuant to the provisions of § 1.643(d)-1, during 1964 only 60 percent of the entire trust constitutes a foreign trust created by a U.S. person.

(2) The distributable net income for the taxable year 1964 of the foreign trust created by a U.S. person, determined under section 643(a), is $42,000 computed as follows:

Interest on bonds of a U.S. corporation (60 percent of $10,000)		$ 6,000
Gross income from investments in Country X (60 percent of $40,000)		24,000
Net long-term capital gain from U.S. sources (60 percent of $30,000)	$18,000	
Less: Net short-term capital loss from U.S. sources (60 percent of $5,000)	3,000	
		15,000
Total		45,000
Less: Expenses allocable to income from investments in Country X (60 percent of $5,000)		3,000
Distributable net income		42,000

(3) The distributable net income for the taxable year 1964 of the portion of the entire foreign trust which does not constitute a foreign trust created by a U.S. person, determined under section 643(a), is $18,000, computed as follows:

Interest on bonds of a U.S. corporation (40 percent of $10,000)	$ 4,000
Gross income from investments in Country X (40 percent of $40,000)	16,000
Total	20,000
Less: Expenses allocable to income from investments in Country X (40 percent of $5,000)	2,000
Distributable net income	18,000

(4) The distributable net income of the entire foreign trust for the taxable year 1964 is $60,000, computed as follows:

Distributable net income of the foreign trust created by a U.S. person	$42,000
Distributable net income of that portion of the entire foreign trust which does not constitute a foreign trust created by a U.S. person	18,000
Distributable net income of the entire foreign trust	60,000

It should be noted that the difference between the $70,000 distributable net income of the foreign trust in example (1) and the $60,000 distributable net income of the entire foreign trust in this example is due to the $10,000 (40 percent of $25,000) net capital gain (capital gain net income for taxable years beginning after December 31, 1976) which under section 643(a)(3) is excluded from the distributable net income of that portion of the foreign trust in example (2) which does not constitute a foreign trust created by a U.S. person.

T.D. 6217, 12/19/56, amend T.D. 6989, 1/16/69, T.D. 7728, 10/31/80.

§ 1.643(a)-7 Dividends.

Caution: The Treasury has not yet amended Reg § 1.643(a)-7 to reflect changes made by P.L. 101-239, P.L. 100-647, P.L. 99-514, P.L. 98-369, P.L. 97-448, P.L. 97-34, P.L. 96-223, P.L. 94-455, P.L. 87-834.

Dividends excluded from gross income under section 116 (relating to partial exclusion of dividends received) are included in distributable net income. For this purpose, adjustments similar to those required by § 1.643(a)-5 with respect to expenses allocable to tax-exempt income and to income included in amounts paid or set aside for charitable purposes are not made. See the regulations under section 642(c).

T.D. 6217, 12/19/56, amend T.D. 7357, 5/30/75.

§ 1.643(a)-8 Certain distributions by charitable remainder trusts.

(a) Purpose and scope. This section is intended to prevent the avoidance of the purposes of the charitable remainder trust rules regarding the characterizations of distributions from those trusts in the hands of the recipients and should be interpreted in a manner consistent with this purpose. This section applies to all charitable remainder trusts described in section 664 and the beneficiaries of such trusts.

(b) Deemed sale by trust. *(1)* For purposes of section 664(b), a charitable remainder trust shall be treated as having sold, in the year in which a distribution of an annuity or unitrust amount is made from the trust, a pro rata portion of the trust assets to the extent that the distribution of the annuity or unitrust amount would (but for the application of this paragraph (b)) be characterized in the hands of the recipient as being from the category described in section 664(b)(4) and exceeds the amount of the previously undistributed

(i) Cash contributed to the trust (with respect to which a deduction was allowable under section 170, 2055, 2106, or 2522); plus

(ii) Basis in any contributed property (with respect to which a deduction was allowable under section 170, 2055, 2106, or 2522) that was sold by the trust.

(2) Any transaction that has the purpose or effect of circumventing the rules in this paragraph (b) shall be disregarded.

(3) For purposes of paragraph (b)(1) of this section, trust assets do not include cash or assets purchased with the proceeds of a trust borrowing, forward sale, or similar transaction.

(4) Proper adjustment shall be made to any gain or loss subsequently realized for gain or loss taken into account under paragraph (b)(1) of this section.

(c) Examples. The following examples illustrate the rules of paragraph (b) of this section:

Example (1). Deemed sale by trust. Donor contributes stock having a fair market value of $2 million to a charitable remainder unitrust with a unitrust amount of 50 percent of the net fair market value of the trust assets and a two-year term. The stock has a total adjusted basis of $400,000. In Year 1, the trust receives dividend income of $20,000. As of the valuation date, the trust's assets have a net fair market value of $2,020,000 ($2 million in stock, plus $20,000 in cash). To obtain additional cash to pay the unitrust amount to the noncharitable beneficiary, the trustee borrows $990,000 against the value of the stock. The trust then distributes $1,010,000 to the beneficiary before the end of Year 1. Under section 664(b)(1), $20,000 of the distribution is characterized in the hands of the beneficiary as dividend income. The rest of the distribution, $990,000, is attributable to an amount received by the trust that did not represent either cash contributed to the trust or a return of basis in any contributed asset sold by the trust during Year 1. Under paragraph (b)(3) of this section, the stock is a trust asset because it was not purchased with the proceeds of the borrowing. Therefore, in Year 1, under paragraph (b)(1) of this section, the trust is treated as having sold $990,000 of stock and as having realized $792,000 of capital gain (the trust's basis in the shares deemed sold is $198,000). Thus, in the hands of the beneficiary, $792,000 of the distribution is characterized as capital gain under section 664(b)(2) and $198,000 is characterized as a tax-free return of corpus under section 664(b)(4). No part of the $990,000 loan is treated as acquisition indebtedness under section 514(c) because the entire loan has been recharacterized as a deemed sale.

Example (2). Adjustment to trust's basis in assets deemed sold. The facts are the same as in Example 1. During Year 2, the trust sells the stock for $2,100,000. The trustee uses a portion of the proceeds of the sale to repay the outstanding loan, plus accrued interest. Under paragraph (b)(4) of this section, the trust's adjusted basis in the stock is $1,192,000 ($400,000 plus the $792,000 of gain recognized in Year 1). Therefore, the trust recognizes capital gain (as described in section 664(b)(2)) in Year 2 of $908,000.

Example (3). Distribution of cash contributions. Upon the death of D, the proceeds of a life insurance policy on D's life are payable to T, a charitable remainder annuity trust. The terms of the trust provide that, for a period of three years commencing upon D's death, the trust shall pay an annuity amount equal to $x annually to A, the child of D. After the expiration of such three-year period, the remainder interest in the trust is to be transferred to charity Z. In Year 1, the trust receives payment of the life insurance proceeds and pays the appropriate pro rata portion of the $x annuity to A from the insurance proceeds. During Year 1, the trust has no income. Because the entire distribution is attributable to a cash contribution (the insurance proceeds) to the trust for which a charitable deduction was allowable under section 2055 with respect to the present value of the remainder interest passing to charity, the trust will not be treated as selling a pro rata portion of the trust assets under paragraph (b)(1) of this section. Thus, the distribution is characterized in A's hands as a tax-free return of corpus under section 664(b)(4).

(d) Effective date. This section is applicable to distributions made by a charitable remainder trust after October 18, 1999.

T.D. 8926, 1/4/2001.

§ 1.643(b)-1 Definition of income.

Caution: The Treasury has not yet amended Reg § 1.643(b)-1 to reflect changes made by P.L. 101-239, P.L. 100-647, P.L. 99-514, P.L. 98-369, P.L. 97-448, P.L. 97-34, P.L. 96-223, P.L. 94-455.

For purposes of subparts A through D, part I, subchapter J, chapter 1 of the Internal Revenue Code, "income," when not preceded by the words "taxable," "distributable net," "undistributed net," or "gross," means the amount of income of an estate or trust for the taxable year determined under the terms of the governing instrument and applicable local law. Trust provisions that depart fundamentally from traditional principles of income and principal will generally not be recognized. For example, if a trust instrument directs that all the trust income shall be paid to the income beneficiary but defines ordinary dividends and interest as principal, the trust will not be considered one that under its governing instrument is required to distribute all its income currently for purposes of section 642(b) (relating to the personal exemption) and section 651 (relating to simple trusts). Thus, items such as dividends, interest, and rents are generally allocated to income and proceeds from the sale or exchange of trust assets are generally allocated to principal. However, an allocation of amounts between income and principal pursuant to applicable local law will be respected if local law provides for a reasonable apportionment between the income and remainder beneficiaries of the total return of the trust for the year, including ordinary and tax-exempt income, capital gains, and appreciation. For example, a state statute providing that income is a unitrust amount of no less than 3% and no more than 5% of the fair market value of the trust assets, whether determined annually or averaged on a multiple year basis, is a reasonable apportionment of the total return of the trust. Similarly, a state statute that permits the trustee to make adjustments between income and principal to fulfill the trustee's duty of impartiality between the income and remainder beneficiaries is generally a reasonable apportionment of the total return of the trust. Generally, these adjustments are permitted by state statutes when the trustee invests and manages the trust assets under the state's prudent investor standard, the trust describes the amount that may or must be distributed to a beneficiary by referring to the trust's income, and the trustee after applying the state statutory rules regarding the allocation of receipts and disbursements to income and principal, is unable to administer the trust impartially. Allocations pursuant to methods prescribed by such state statutes for apportioning the total return of a trust between income and principal will be respected regardless of whether the trust provides that the income must be distributed to one or more beneficiaries or may be accumulated in whole or in part, and regardless of which alternate permitted method is actually used, provided the trust complies with all requirements of the state statute for switching methods. A switch between methods of determining trust income authorized by state statute will not constitute a recognition event for purposes of section 1001 and will not result in a taxable gift from the trust's grantor or any of the trust's beneficiaries. A switch to a method not specifically authorized by state statute, but valid under state law (including a switch via judicial decision or a binding non-judicial settlement) may constitute a recognition event to the trust or its beneficiaries for purposes of section 1001 and may result in taxable gifts from the trust's grantor and beneficiaries, based on the relevant facts and circumstances. In addition, an allocation to income of all or a part of the gains from the sale or exchange of trust assets will generally be respected if the allocation is made either pursuant to the terms of the governing instrument and applicable local law, or pursuant to a reasonable and impartial exercise of a discretionary power granted to the fiduciary by applicable local law or by the governing instrument, if not prohibited by applicable local law. This section is effective for taxable years of trusts and estates ending after January 2, 2004.

T.D. 6217, 12/19/56, amend T.D. 9102, 12/30/2003.

§ 1.643(b)-2 Dividends allocated to corpus.

Caution: The Treasury has not yet amended Reg § 1.643(b)-2 to reflect changes made by P.L. 101-239, P.L. 100-647, P.L. 99-514, P.L. 98-369, P.L. 97-448, P.L. 97-34, P.L. 96-223, P.L. 94-455.

Extraordinary dividends or taxable stock dividends which the fiduciary, acting in good faith, determines to be allocable to corpus under the terms of the governing instrument and applicable local law are not considered "income" for purposes of Subpart A, B, C, or D, Part I, Subchapter J, Chapter 1 of the Code. See section 643(a)(4), § 1.643(a)-4, § 1.643(d)-2, section 665(e) and paragraph (b) of § 1.665(e)-1A for the treatment of such items in the computation of distributable net income.

T.D. 6217, 12/19/56, amend T.D. 6989, 1/16/69, T.D. 7204, 8/24/72.

§ 1.643(c)-1 Definition of "beneficiary".

Caution: The Treasury has not yet amended Reg § 1.643(c)-1 to reflect changes made by P.L. 101-239, P.L. 100-647, P.L. 99-514, P.L. 98-369, P.L. 97-448, P.L. 97-34, P.L. 96-223, P.L. 94-455.

An heir, legatee, or devisee (including an estate or trust) is a beneficiary. A trust created under a decedent's will is a beneficiary of the decedent's estate. The following persons are treated as beneficiaries:

(a) Any person with respect to an amount used to discharge or satisfy that person's legal obligation as that term is used in § 1.662(a)-4.

(b) The grantor of a trust with respect to an amount applied or distributed for the support of a dependent under the circumstances specified in section 677(b) out of corpus or out of other than income for the taxable year of the trust.

(c) The trustee or cotrustee of a trust with respect to an amount applied or distributed for the support of a dependent under the circumstances specified in section 678(c) out of corpus or out of other than income for the taxable year of the trust.

T.D. 6217, 12/19/56.

---

§ 1.643(d)-1 Definition of "foreign trust created by a United States person."

Caution: The Treasury has not yet amended Reg § 1.643(d)-1 to reflect changes made by P.L. 101-239, P.L. 100-647, P.L. 99-514, P.L. 98-369, P.L. 97-448, P.L. 97-34, P.L. 96-223, P.L. 94-455.

(a) In general. For the purpose of Part I, subchapter J, chapter 1 of the Internal Revenue Code, the term "foreign trust created by a United States person" means that portion of a foreign trust (as defined in section 7701(a)(31)) attributable to money or property (including all accumulated earnings, profits, or gains attributable to such money or property) of a U.S. person (as defined in section 7701(a)(30)) transferred directly or indirectly, or under the will of a decedent who at the date of his death was a U.S. citizen or resident, to the foreign trust. A foreign trust created by a person who is not a U.S. person, to which a U.S. person transfers his money or property, is a foreign trust created by a U.S. person to the extent that the fair market value of the entire foreign trust is attributable to money or property of the U.S. person transferred to the foreign trust. The transfer of money or property to the foreign trust may be made either directly or indirectly by a U.S. person. Transfers of money or property to a foreign trust do not include transfers of money or property pursuant to a sale or exchange which is made for a full and adequate consideration. Transfers to which section 643(d) and this section apply are transfers of money or property which establish or increase the corpus of a foreign trust. The rules set forth in this section with respect to transfers by a U.S. person to a foreign trust also are applicable with respect to transfers under the will of a decedent who at the date of his death was a U.S. citizen or resident. For provisions relating to the information returns which are required to be filed with respect to the creation of or transfers to foreign trusts, see section 6048 and § 16.3-1 of this chapter (Temporary Regulations under the Revenue Act of 1962).

(b) Determination of a foreign trust created by a U.S. person. *(1) Transfers of money or property only by a U.S. person.* If all the items of money or property constituting the corpus of a foreign trust are transferred to the trust by a U.S. person, the entire foreign trust is a foreign trust created by a U.S. person.

(2) Transfers of money or property by both a U.S. person and a person other than a U.S. person; transfers required to be treated as separate funds. Where there are transfers of money or property by both a U.S. person and a person other than a U.S. person to a foreign trust, and it is necessary, either by reason of the provisions of the governing instrument of the trust or by reason of some other requirement such as local law, that the trustee treat the entire foreign trust as composed of two separate funds, one consisting of the money or property (including all accumulated earnings, profits, or gains attributable to such money or property) transferred by the U.S. person and the other consisting of the money or property (including all accumulated earnings, profits, or gains attributable to such money or property) transferred by the person other than the U.S. person, the foreign trust created by a U.S. person shall be the fund consisting of the money or property transferred by the U.S. person. See example (1) in paragraph (c) of this section.

(3) Transfers of money or property by both a U.S. person and a person other than a U.S. person; transfers not required to be treated as separate funds. Where the corpus of a foreign trust consists of money or property transferred to the trust (simultaneously or at different times) by a U.S. person and by a person who is not a U.S. person, the foreign trust created by a U.S. person within the meaning of section 643(d) is that portion of the entire foreign trust which, immediately after any transfer of money or property to the trust, the fair market value of money or property (including all accumulated earnings, profits, or gains attributable to such money or property) transferred to the foreign trust by the U.S. person bears to the fair market value of the corpus (including all accumulated earnings, profits, or gains attributable to the corpus) of the entire foreign trust.

(c) Examples. The provisions of paragraph (b) of this section may be illustrated by the following examples.

Example (1) illustrates the application of paragraph (b)(2) of this section. Example (2) illustrates the application of paragraph (b)(3) of this section in a case where there is no provision in the governing instrument of the trust or elsewhere which would require the trustee to treat the corpus of the trust as composed of more than one fund.

Example (1). On January 1, 1964, the date of the creation of a foreign trust, a U.S. person transfers to it stock of a U.S. corporation with a fair market value of $50,000. On the same day, a person other than a U.S. person transfers to the trust Country X bonds with a fair market value of $25,000. The governing instrument of the trust provides that the income from the stock of the U.S. corporation is to be accumulated until A, a U.S. beneficiary, reaches the age of 21 years, and upon his reaching that age, the stock and income accumulated thereon are to be distributed to him. The governing instrument of the trust further provides that the income from the Country X bonds is to be accumulated until B, a U.S. beneficiary, reaches the age of 21 years, and upon his reaching that age, the bonds and income accumulated thereon are to be distributed to him. To comply with the provisions of the governing instrument of the trust that the income from the stock of the U.S. corporation be accumulated and distributed to A and that the income from the Country X bonds be accumulated and distributed to B, it is necessary that the trustee treat the transfers as two separate funds. The fund consisting of the stock of the U.S. corporation is a foreign trust created by a U.S. person.

Example (2). On January 1, 1964, the date of the creation of a foreign trust, a U.S. person transfers to it property having fair market value of $60,000 and a person other than a U.S. person transfers to it property having a fair market value of $40,000. Immediately after these transfers, the foreign trust created by a U.S. person is 60 percent of the entire foreign trust, determined as follows:

$$\frac{\$60{,}000 \text{ (Value of property transferred by U.S. person)}}{\$100{,}000 \text{ (Value of entire property transferred to trust)}} = 60 \text{ percent}$$

The undistributed net income for the calendar years 1964 and 1965 is $20,000 which increases the value of the entire foreign trust to $120,000 ($100,000 plus $20,000). Accordingly, as of December 31, 1965, the portion of the foreign trust created by the U.S. person is $72,000 (60 percent of $120,000). On January 1, 1966, the U.S. person transfers property having a fair market value of $40,000 increasing the value of the entire foreign trust to $160,000 ($120,000 plus $40,000) and increasing the value of the portion of the foreign trust created by the U.S. person to $112,000

($72,000 plus $40,000). Immediately, after this transfer, the foreign trust created by the U.S. person is 70 percent of the entire foreign trust, determined as follows:

$$\frac{\$112{,}000 \text{ (Value of property transferred by U.S. person)}}{\$160{,}000 \text{ (Value of entire property transferred to the trust)}} = 70 \text{ percent}$$

T.D. 6989, 1/16/69.

§ 1.643(d)-2 Illustration of the provisions of section 643.

Caution: The Treasury has not yet amended Reg § 1.643(d)-2 to reflect changes made by P.L. 103-66, P.L. 101-239, P.L. 100-647, P.L. 99-514, P.L. 98-369, P.L. 97-448, P.L. 97-34, P.L. 96-223, P.L. 94-455.

(a) The provisions of section 643 may be illustrated by the following example:

Example. (1) Under the terms of the trust instrument, the income of a trust is required to be currently distributed to W during her life. Capital gains are allocable to corpus and all expenses are charges against corpus. During the taxable year the trust has the following items of income and expenses:

Dividends from domestic corporations	$30,000
Extraordinary dividends allocated to corpus by the trustee in good faith	20,000
Taxable interest	10,000
Tax-exempt interest	10,000
Long-term capital gains	10,000
Trustee's commissions and miscellaneous expenses allocable to corpus	5,000

(2) The "income" of the trust determined under section 643(b) which is currently distributable to W is $50,000. consisting of dividends of $30,000, taxable interest of $10,000, and tax-exempt interest of $10,000. The trustee's commissions and miscellaneous expenses allocable to tax-exempt interest amount to $1,000 (10,000/50,000 × $5,000).

(3) The "distributable net income" determined under section 643(a) amounts to $45,000, computed as follows:

Dividends from domestic corporations		$30,000
Taxable interest		10,000
Nontaxable interest	$10,000	
Less: Expenses allocable thereto	1,000	
		9,000
Total		49,000
Less: Expenses ($5,000 less $1,000 allocable to tax-exempt interest)		4,000
Distributable net income		45,000

In determining the distributable net income of $45,000, the taxable income of the trust is computed with the following modifications: No deductions are allowed for distributions to W and for personal exemption of the trust (section 643(a)(1) and (2)); capital gains allocable to corpus are excluded and the deduction allowable under section 1202 is not taken into account (section 643(a)(3)): the extraordinary dividends allocated to corpus by the trustee in good faith are excluded (sections 643(a)(4)); and the tax-exempt interest (as adjusted for expenses) and the dividend exclusion of $50 are included (section 643(a)(5) and (7)).

(b) See paragraph (c) of the example in § 1.661(c)-2 for the computation of distributable net income where there is a charitable contributions deduction.

T.D. 6217, 12/19/56, amend T.D. 6989, 1/16/69.

§ 1.643(h)-1 Distributions by certain foreign trusts through intermediaries.

(a) In general. *(1) Principal purpose of tax avoidance.* Except as provided in paragraph (b) of this section, for purposes of part I of subchapter J, chapter 1 of the Internal Revenue Code, and section 6048, any property (within the meaning of paragraph (f) of this section) that is transferred to a United States person by another person (an intermediary) who has received property from a foreign trust will be treated as property transferred directly by the foreign trust to the United States person if the intermediary received the property from the foreign trust pursuant to a plan one of the principal purposes of which was the avoidance of United States tax.

(2) Principal purpose of tax avoidance deemed to exist. For purposes of paragraph (a)(1) of this section, a transfer will be deemed to have been made pursuant to a plan one of the principal purposes of which was the avoidance of United States tax if the United States person—

(i) Is related (within the meaning of paragraph (e) of this section) to a grantor of the foreign trust, or has another relationship with a grantor of the foreign trust that establishes a reasonable basis for concluding that the grantor of the foreign trust would make a gratuitous transfer (within the meaning of § 1.671-2(e)(2)) to the United States person;

(ii) Receives from the intermediary, within the period beginning twenty-four months before and ending twenty-four months after the intermediary's receipt of property from the foreign trust, either the property the intermediary received from the foreign trust, proceeds from such property, or property in substitution for such property; and

(iii) Cannot demonstrate to the satisfaction of the Commissioner that—

(A) The intermediary has a relationship with the United States person that establishes a reasonable basis for concluding that the intermediary would make a gratuitous transfer to the United States person;

(B) The intermediary acted independently of the grantor and the trustee of the foreign trust;

(C) The intermediary is not an agent of the United States person under generally applicable United States agency principles; and

(D) The United States person timely complied with the reporting requirements of section 6039F, if applicable, if the intermediary is a foreign person.

(b) Exceptions. *(1) Nongratuitous transfers.* Paragraph (a) of this section does not apply to the extent that either the transfer from the foreign trust to the intermediary or the transfer from the intermediary to the United States person is a transfer that is not a gratuitous transfer within the meaning of § 1.671-2(e)(2).

(2) Grantor as intermediary. Paragraph (a) of this section does not apply if the intermediary is the grantor of the portion of the trust from which the property that is transferred is derived. For the definition of grantor, see § 1.671-2(e).

(c) Effect of disregarding intermediary. *(1) General rule.* Except as provided in paragraph (c)(2) of this section, the intermediary is treated as an agent of the foreign trust, and the property is treated as transferred to the United States person in the year the property is transferred, or made available, by the intermediary to the United States person. The fair market value of the property transferred is determined as of the date of the transfer by the intermediary to the United States person. For purposes of section 665(d)(2), the term taxes imposed on the trust includes any income, war profits, and excess profits taxes imposed by any foreign country or possession of the United States on the intermediary with respect to the property transferred.

(2) Exception. If the Commissioner determines, or if the taxpayer can demonstrate to the satisfaction of the Commissioner, that the intermediary is an agent of the United States person under generally applicable United States agency principles, the property will be treated as transferred to the United States person in the year the intermediary receives the property from the foreign trust. The fair market value of the property transferred will be determined as of the date of the transfer by the foreign trust to the intermediary. For purposes of section 901(b), any income, war profits, and excess profits taxes imposed by any foreign country or possession of the United States on the intermediary with respect to the property transferred will be treated as having been imposed on the United States person.

(3) Computation of gross income of intermediary. If property is treated as transferred directly by the foreign trust to a United States person pursuant to this section, the fair market value of such property is not taken into account in computing the gross income of the intermediary (if otherwise required to be taken into account by the intermediary but for paragraph (a) of this section).

(d) Transfers not in excess of $10,000. This section does not apply if, during the taxable year of the United States person, the aggregate fair market value of all property transferred to such person from all foreign trusts either directly or through one or more intermediaries does not exceed $10,000.

(e) Related parties. For purposes of this section, a United States person is treated as related to a grantor of a foreign trust if the United States person and the grantor are related for purposes of section 643(i)(2)(B), with the following modifications--

(1) For purposes of applying section 267 (other than section 267(f)) and section 707(b)(1), "at least 10 percent" is used instead of "more than 50 percent" each place it appears; and

(2) The principles of section 267(b)(10), using "at least 10 percent" instead of "more than 50 percent," apply to determine whether two corporations are related.

(f) Definition of property. For purposes of this section, the term property includes cash.

(g) Examples. The following examples illustrate the rules of this section. In each example, FT is an irrevocable foreign trust that is not treated as owned by any other person and the fair market value of the property that is transferred exceeds $10,000. The examples are as follows:

Example (1). Principal purpose of tax avoidance. FT was created in 1980 by A, a nonresident alien, for the benefit of his children and their descendants. FT's trustee, T, determines that 1000X of accumulated income should be distributed to A's granddaughter, B, who is a resident alien. Pursuant to a plan with a principal purpose of avoiding the interest charge that would be imposed by section 668, T causes FT to make a gratuitous transfer (within the meaning of § 1.671-2(e)(2)) of 1000X to I, a foreign person. I subsequently makes a gratuitous transfer of 1000X to B. Under paragraph (a)(1) of this section, FT is deemed to have made an accumulation distribution of 1000X directly to B.

Example (2). United States person unable to demonstrate that intermediary acted independently. GM and her daughter, M, are both nonresident aliens. M's daughter, D, is a resident alien. GM creates and funds FT for the benefit of her children. On July 1, 2001, FT makes a gratuitous transfer of XYZ stock to M. M immediately sells the XYZ stock and uses the proceeds to purchase ABC stock. On January 1, 2002, M makes a gratuitous transfer of the ABC stock to D. D is unable to demonstrate that M acted independently of GM and the trustee of FT in making the transfer to D. Under paragraph (a)(2) of this section, FT is deemed to have distributed the ABC stock to D. Under paragraph (c)(1) of this section, M is treated as an agent of FT, and the distribution is deemed to have been made on January 1, 2002.

Example (3). United States person demonstrates that specified conditions are satisfied. Assume the same facts as in Example 2, except that M receives 1000X cash from FT instead of XYZ stock. M gives 1000X cash to D on January 1, 2002. Also assume that M receives annual income of 5000X from her own investments and that M has given D 1000X at the beginning of each year for the past ten years. Based on this and additional information provided by D, D demonstrates to the satisfaction of the Commissioner that M has a relationship with D that establishes a reasonable basis for concluding that M would make a gratuitous transfer to D, that M acted independently of GM and the trustee of FT, that M is not an agent of D under generally applicable United States agency principles, and that D timely complied with the reporting requirements of section 6039F. FT will not be deemed under paragraph (a)(2) of this section to have made a distribution to D.

Example (4). Transfer to United States person less than 24 months before transfer to intermediary. Several years ago, A, a nonresident alien, created and funded FT for the benefit of his children and their descendants. A has a close friend, C, who also is a nonresident alien. A's granddaughter, B, is a resident alien. On December 31, 2001, C makes a gratuitous transfer of 1000X to B. On January 15, 2002, FT makes a gratuitous transfer of 1000X to C. B is unable to demonstrate that C has a relationship with B that would establish a reasonable basis for concluding that C would make a gratuitous transfer to B or that C acted independently of A and the trustee of FT in making the transfer to B. Under paragraph (a)(2) of this section, FT is deemed to have distributed 1000X directly to B. Under paragraph (c)(1) of this section, C is treated as an agent of FT, and the distribution is deemed to have been made on December 31, 2001.

Example (5). United States person receives property in substitution for property transferred to intermediary. GM and her son, S, are both nonresident aliens. S's daughter, GD, is a resident alien. GM creates and funds FT for the benefit of her children and their descendants. On July 1, 2001, FT makes a gratuitous transfer of ABC stock with a fair market value of approximately 1000X to S. On January 1, 2002, S makes a gratuitous transfer of DEF stock with a fair market value of approximately 1000X to GD. GD is unable to demonstrate that S acted independently of GM and the trustee of FT in transferring the DEF stock to GD. Under paragraph (a)(2) of this section, FT is deemed to have distributed the DEF stock to GD. Under paragraph (c)(1) of this section, S is treated as an agent of FT, and the distribution is deemed to have been made on January 1, 2002.

Example (6). United States person receives indirect loan from foreign trust. Several years ago, A, a nonresident alien, created and funded FT for the benefit of her children and their descendants. A's daughter, B, is a resident alien. B needs funds temporarily while she is starting up her own business. If FT were to loan money directly to B, section 643(i) would apply. FT deposits 500X with FB, a foreign bank, on June 30, 2001. On July 1, 2001, FB loans 400X to B. Repayment of the loan is guaranteed by FT's 500X deposit. B is unable to demonstrate to the satisfaction of the Commissioner that FB has a relationship with B that establishes a reasonable basis for concluding that FB would make a loan to B or that FB acted independently of A and the trustee of FT in making the loan. Under paragraph (a)(2) of this section, FT is deemed to have loaned 400X directly to B on July 1, 2001. Under paragraph (c)(1) of this section, FB is treated as an agent of FT. For the treatment of loans from foreign trusts, see section 643(i).

Example (7): United States person demonstrates that specified conditions are satisfied. GM, a nonresident alien, created and funded FT for the benefit of her children and their descendants. One of GM's children is M, who is a resident alien. During the year 2001, FT makes a gratuitous transfer of 500X to M. M reports the 500X on Form 3520 as a distribution received from a foreign trust. During the year 2002, M makes a gratuitous transfer of 400X to her son, S, who also is a resident alien. M files a Form 709 treating the gratuitous transfer to S as a gift. Based on this and additional information provided by S, S demonstrates to the satisfaction of the Commissioner that M has a relationship with S that establishes a reasonable basis for concluding that M would make a gratuitous transfer to S, that M acted independently of GM and the trustee of FT, and that M is not an agent of S under generally applicable United States agency principles. FT will not be deemed under paragraph (a)(2) of this section to have made a distribution to S.

Example (8). Intermediary as agent of trust; increase in FMV. A, a nonresident alien, created and funded FT for the benefit of his children and their descendants. On December 1, 2001, FT makes a gratuitous transfer of XYZ stock with a fair market value of 85X to B, a nonresident alien. On November 1, 2002, B sells the XYZ stock to a third party in an arm's length transaction for 100X in cash. On November 1, 2002, B makes a gratuitous transfer of 98X to A's grandson, C, a resident alien. C is unable to demonstrate to the satisfaction of the Commissioner that B acted independently of A and the trustee of FT in making the transfer. Under paragraph (a)(2) of this section, FT is deemed to have made a distribution directly to C. Under paragraph (c)(1) of this section, B is treated as an agent of FT, and FT is deemed to have distributed 98X to C on November 1, 2002.

Example (9). Intermediary as agent of United States person; increase in FMV. Assume the same facts as in Example 8, except that the Commissioner determines that B is an agent of C under generally applicable United States agency principles. Under paragraph (c)(2) of this section, FT is deemed to have distributed 85X to C on December 1, 2001. C must take the gain of 15X into account in the year 2002.

Example (10). Intermediary as agent of trust; decrease in FMV. Assume the same facts as in Example 8, except that the value of the XYZ stock on November 1, 2002, is only 80X. Instead of selling the XYZ stock to a third party and transferring cash to C, B transfers the XYZ stock to C in a gratuitous transfer. Under paragraph (c)(1) of this section, FT is deemed to have distributed XYZ stock with a value of 80X to C on November 1, 2002.

Example (11). Intermediary as agent of United States person; decrease in FMV. Assume the same facts as in Example 10, except that the Commissioner determines that B is an agent of C under generally applicable United States agency principles. Under paragraph (c)(2) of this section, FT is deemed to have distributed XYZ stock with a value of 85X to C on December 1, 2001.

(h) Effective date. The rules of this section are applicable to transfers made to United States persons after August 10, 1999.

T.D. 8831, 8/5/99, amend T.D. 8890, 7/3/2000.

---

§ 1.645-1 Election by certain revocable trusts to be treated as part of estate.

(a) In general. If an election is filed for a qualified revocable trust, as defined in paragraph (b)(1) of this section, in accordance with the rules set forth in paragraph (c) of this section, the qualified revocable trust is treated and taxed for purposes of subtitle A of the Internal Revenue Code as part of its related estate, as defined in paragraph (b)(5) of this section (and not as a separate trust) during the election period, as defined in paragraph (b)(6) of this section. Rules regarding the use of taxpayer identification numbers (TINs) and the filing of a Form 1041, "U.S. Income Tax Return for Estates and Trusts," for a qualified revocable trust are in paragraph (d) of this section. Rules regarding the tax treatment of an electing trust and related estate and the general filing requirements for the combined entity during the election period are in paragraph (e)(2) of this section. Rules regarding the tax treatment of an electing trust and its filing requirements during the election period if no executor, as defined in paragraph (b)(4) of this section, is appointed for a related estate are in paragraph (e)(3) of this section. Rules for determining the duration of the section 645 election period are in paragraph (f) of this section. Rules regarding the tax effects of the termination of the election are in paragraph (h) of this section. Rules regarding the tax consequences of the appointment of an executor after a trustee has made a section 645 election believing that an executor would not be appointed for a related estate are in paragraph (g) of this section.

(b) Definitions. For purposes of this section:

(1) Qualified revocable trust. A qualified revocable trust (QRT) is any trust (or portion thereof) that on the date of death of the decedent was treated as owned by the decedent under section 676 by reason of a power held by the decedent (determined without regard to section 672(e)). A trust that was treated as owned by the decedent under section 676 by reason of a power that was exercisable by the decedent only with the approval or consent of a nonadverse party or with the approval or consent of the decedent's spouse is a QRT. A trust that was treated as owned by the decedent under section 676 solely by reason of a power held by a nonadverse party or by reason of a power held by the decedent's spouse is not a QRT.

(2) Electing trust. An electing trust is a QRT for which a valid section 645 election has been made. Once a section 645 election has been made for the trust, the trust shall be treated as an electing trust throughout the entire election period.

(3) Decedent. The decedent is the individual who was treated as the owner of the QRT under section 676 on the date of that individual's death.

(4) Executor. An executor is an executor, personal representative, or administrator that has obtained letters of appointment to administer the decedent's estate through formal or informal appointment procedures. Solely for purposes of

this paragraph (b)(4), an executor does not include a person that has actual or constructive possession of property of the decedent unless that person is also appointed or qualified as an executor, administrator, or personal representative of the decedent's estate. If more than one jurisdiction has appointed an executor, the executor appointed in the domiciliary or primary proceeding is the executor of the related estate for purposes of this paragraph (b)(4).

(5) Related estate. A related estate is the estate of the decedent who was treated as the owner of the QRT on the date of the decedent's death.

(6) Election period. The election period is the period of time during which an electing trust is treated and taxed as part of its related estate. The rules for determining the duration of the election period are in paragraph (f) of this section.

(c) The election. *(1) Filing the election if there is an executor.* (i) Time and manner for filing the election. If there is an executor of the related estate, the trustees of each QRT joining in the election and the executor of the related estate make an election under section 645 and this section to treat each QRT joining in the election as part of the related estate for purposes of subtitle A of the Internal Revenue Code by filing a form provided by the IRS for making the election (election form) properly completed and signed under penalties of perjury, or in any other manner prescribed after December 24, 2002 by forms provided by the Internal Revenue Service (IRS), or by other published guidance for making the election. For the election to be valid, the election form must be filed not later than the time prescribed under section 6072 for filing the Form 1041 for the first taxable year of the related estate (regardless of whether there is sufficient income to require the filing of that return). If an extension is granted for the filing of the Form 1041 for the first taxable year of the related estate, the election form will be timely filed if it is filed by the time prescribed for filing the Form 1041 including the extension granted with respect to the Form 1041.

(ii) Conditions to election. In addition to providing the information required by the election form, as a condition to a valid section 645 election, the trustee of each QRT joining in the election and the executor of the related estate agree, by signing the election form under penalties of perjury, that:

(A) With respect to a trustee—

(1) The trustee agrees to the election;

(2) The trustee is responsible for timely providing the executor of the related estate with all the trust information necessary to permit the executor to file a complete, accurate, and timely Form 1041 for the combined electing trust(s) and related estate for each taxable year during the election period;

(3) The trustee of each QRT joining the election and the executor of the related estate have agreed to allocate the tax burden of the combined electing trust(s) and related estate for each taxable year during the election period in a manner that reasonably reflects the tax obligations of each electing trust and the related estate; and

(4) The trustee is responsible for insuring that the electing trust's share of the tax obligations of the combined electing trust(s) and related estate is timely paid to the Secretary.

(B) With respect to the executor—

(1) The executor agrees to the election;

(2) The executor is responsible for filing a complete, accurate, and timely Form 1041 for the combined electing trust(s) and related estate for each taxable year during the election period;

(3) The executor and the trustee of each QRT joining in the election have agreed to allocate the tax burden of the combined electing trust(s) and related estate for each taxable year during the election period in a manner that reasonably reflects the tax obligations of each electing trust and the related estate;

(4) The executor is responsible for insuring that the related estate's share of the tax obligations of the combined electing trust(s) and related estate is timely paid to the Secretary.

(2) Filing the election if there is no executor. (i) Time and manner for filing the election. If there is no executor for a related estate, an election to treat one or more QRTs of the decedent as an estate for purposes of subtitle A of the Internal Revenue Code is made by the trustees of each QRT joining in the election, by filing a properly completed election form, or in any other manner prescribed after December 24, 2002 by forms provided by the IRS, or by other published guidance for making the election. For the election to be valid, the election form must be filed not later than the time prescribed under section 6072 for filing the Form 1041 for the first taxable year of the trust, taking into account the trustee's election to treat the trust as an estate under section 645 (regardless of whether there is sufficient income to require the filing of that return). If an extension is granted for the filing of the Form 1041 for the first taxable year of the electing trust, the election form will be timely filed if it is filed by the time prescribed for filing the Form 1041 including the extension granted with respect to the filing of the Form 1041.

(ii) Conditions to election. In addition to providing the information required by the election form, as a condition to a valid section 645 election, the trustee of each QRT joining in the election agrees, by signing the election form under penalties of perjury, that—

(A) The trustee agrees to the election;

(B) If there is more than one QRT joining in the election, the trustees of each QRT joining in the election have appointed one trustee to be responsible for filing the Form 1041 for the combined electing trusts for each taxable year during the election period (filing trustee) and the filing trustee has agreed to accept that responsibility;

(C) If there is more than one QRT, the trustees of each QRT joining in the election have agreed to allocate the tax liability of the combined electing trusts for each taxable year during the election period in a manner that reasonably reflects the tax obligations of each electing trust;

(D) The trustee agrees to:

(1) Timely file a Form 1041 for the electing trust(s) for each taxable year during the election period; or

(2) If there is more than one QRT and the trustee is not the filing trustee, timely provide the filing trustee with all of the electing trust's information necessary to permit the filing trustee to file a complete, accurate, and timely Form 1041 for the combined electing trusts for each taxable year during the election period;

(3) Insure that the electing trust's share of the tax burden is timely paid to the Secretary;

(E) There is no executor and, to the knowledge and belief of the trustee, one will not be appointed; and

(F) If an executor is appointed after the filing of the election form and the executor agrees to the section 645 election, the trustee will complete and file a revised election form with the executor.

(3) Election for more than one QRT. If there is more than one QRT, the election may be made for some or all of the QRTs. If there is no executor, one trustee must be appointed by the trustees of the electing trusts to file Forms 1041 for the combined electing trusts filing as an estate during the election period.

(d) TIN and filing requirements for a QRT. *(1) Obtaining a TIN.* Regardless of whether there is an executor for a related estate and regardless of whether a section 645 election will be made for the QRT, a TIN must be obtained for the QRT following the death of the decedent. See § 301.6109-1(a)(3) of this chapter. The trustee must furnish this TIN to the payors of the QRT. See § 301.6109-1(a)(5) of this chapter for the definition of payor.

(2) Filing a Form 1041 for a QRT. (i) Option not to file a Form 1041 for a QRT for which a section 645 election will be made. If a section 645 election will be made for a QRT, the executor of the related estate, if any, and the trustee of the QRT may treat the QRT as an electing trust from the decedent's date of death until the due date for the section 645 election. Accordingly, the trustee of the QRT is not required to file a Form 1041 for the QRT for the short taxable year beginning with the decedent's date of death and ending December 31 of that year. However, if a QRT is treated as an electing trust under this paragraph from the decedent's date of death until the due date for the section 645 election but a valid section 645 election is not made for the QRT, the QRT will be subject to penalties and interest for failing to timely file a Form 1041 and pay the tax due thereon.

(ii) Requirement to file a Form 1041 for a QRT if paragraph (d)(2)(i) of this section does not apply. (A) Requirement to file Form 1041. If the trustee of the QRT and the executor of the related estate, if any, do not treat the QRT as an electing trust as provided under paragraph (d)(2)(i) of this section, or if the trustee of the electing trust and the executor, if any, are uncertain whether a section 645 election will be made for a QRT, the trustee of the QRT must file a Form 1041 for the short taxable year beginning with the decedent's death and ending December 31 of that year (unless the QRT is not required to file a Form 1041 under section 6012 for this period).

(B) Requirement to amend Form 1041 if a section 645 election is made. (1) If there is an executor. If there is an executor and a valid section 645 election is made for a QRT after a Form 1041 has been filed for the QRT as a trust (see paragraph (d)(2)(ii)(A) of this section), the trustee must amend the Form 1041. The QRT's items of income, deduction, and credit must be excluded from the amended Form 1041 filed under this paragraph and must be included on the Form 1041 filed for the first taxable year of the combined electing trust and related estate under paragraph (e)(2)(ii)(A) of this section.

(2) If there is no executor. If there is no executor and a valid section 645 election is made for a QRT after a Form 1041 has been filed for the QRT as a trust (see paragraph (d)(2)(ii)(A) of this section) for the short taxable year beginning with the decedent's death and ending December 31 of that year, the trustee must file an amended return for the QRT. The amended return must be filed consistent with paragraph (e)(3) of this section and must be filed by the due date of the Form 1041 for the QRT, taking into account the trustee's election under section 645.

(e) Tax treatment and general filing requirements of electing trust and related estate during the election period. *(1) Effect of election.* The section 645 election once made is irrevocable.

(2) If there is an executor. (i) Tax treatment of the combined electing trust and related estate. If there is an executor, the electing trust is treated, during the election period, as part of the related estate for all purposes of subtitle A of the Internal Revenue Code. Thus, for example, the electing trust is treated as part of the related estate for purposes of the set-aside deduction under section 642(c)(2), the subchapter S shareholder requirements of section 1361(b)(1), and the special offset for rental real estate activities in section 469(i)(4).

(ii) Filing requirements. (A) Filing the Form 1041 for the combined electing trust and related estate during the election period. If there is an executor, the executor files a single income tax return annually (assuming a return is required under section 6012) under the name and TIN of the related estate for the combined electing trust and the related estate. Information regarding the name and TIN of each electing trust must be provided on the Form 1041 as required by the instructions to that form. The period of limitations provided in section 6501 for assessments with respect to an electing trust and the related estate starts with the filing of the return required under this paragraph. Except as required under the separate share rules of section 663(c), for purposes of filing the Form 1041 under this paragraph and computing the tax, the items of income, deduction, and credit of the electing trust and related estate are combined. One personal exemption in the amount of $600 is permitted under section 642(b), and the tax is computed under section 1(e), taking into account section 1(h), for the combined taxable income.

(B) Filing a Form 1041 for the electing trust is not required. Except for any final Form 1041 required to be filed under paragraph (h)(2)(i)(B) of this section, if there is an executor, the trustee of the electing trust does not file a Form 1041 for the electing trust during the election period. Although the trustee is not required to file a Form 1041 for the electing trust, the trustee of the electing trust must timely provide the executor of the related estate with all the trust information necessary to permit the executor to file a complete, accurate and timely Form 1041 for the combined electing trust and related estate. The trustee must also insure that the electing trust's share of the tax obligations of the combined electing trust and related estate is timely paid to the Secretary. In certain situations, the trustee of a QRT may be required to file a Form 1041 for the QRT's short taxable year beginning with the date of the decedent's death and ending December 31 of that year. See paragraph (d)(2) of this section.

(iii) Application of the separate share rules. (A) Distributions to beneficiaries (other than to a share (or shares) of the combined electing trust and related estate). Under the separate share rules of section 663(c), the electing trust and related estate are treated as separate shares for purposes of computing distributable net income (DNI) and applying the distribution provisions of sections 661 and 662. Further, the electing trust share or the related estate share may each contain two or more shares. Thus, if during the taxable year, a distribution is made by the electing trust or the related estate, the DNI of the share making the distribution must be determined and the distribution provisions of sections 661 and 662 must be applied using the separately determined DNI applicable to the distributing share.

(B) Adjustments to the DNI of the separate shares for distributions between shares to which sections 661 and 662 would apply. A distribution from one share to another share to which sections 661 and 662 would apply if made to a beneficiary other than another share of the combined electing trust and related estate affects the computation of the DNI of the share making the distribution and the share receiving the distribution. The share making the distribution reduces its DNI by the amount of the distribution deduction that it would be entitled to under section 661 (determined without regard to section 661(c)), had the distribution been made to another beneficiary, and, solely for purposes of calculating DNI, the share receiving the distribution increases its gross income by the same amount. The distribution has the same character in the hands of the recipient share as in the hands of the distributing share. The following example illustrates the provisions of this paragraph (e)(2)(iii)(B):

Example. (i) A's will provides that, after the payment of debts, expenses, and taxes, the residue of A's estate is to be distributed to Trust, an electing trust. The sole beneficiary of Trust is C. The estate share has $15,000 of gross income, $5,000 of deductions, and $10,000 of taxable income and DNI for the taxable year based on the assets held in A's estate. During the taxable year, A's estate distributes $15,000 to Trust. The distribution reduces the DNI of the estate share by $10,000.

(ii) For the same taxable year, the trust share has $25,000 of gross income and $5,000 of deductions. None of the modifications provided for under section 643(a) apply. In calculating the DNI for the trust share, the gross income of the trust share is increased by $10,000, the amount of the reduction in the DNI of the estate share as a result of the distribution to Trust. Thus, solely for purposes of calculating DNI, the trust share has gross income of $35,000, and taxable income of $30,000. Therefore, the trust share has $30,000 of DNI for the taxable year.

(iii) During the same taxable year, Trust distributes $35,000 to C. The distribution deduction reported on the Form 1041 filed for A's estate and Trust is $30,000. As a result of the distribution by Trust to C, C must include $30,000 in gross income for the taxable year. The gross income reported on the Form 1041 filed for A's estate and Trust is $40,000.

(iv) Application of the governing instrument requirement of section 642(c). A deduction is allowed in computing the taxable income of the combined electing trust and related estate to the extent permitted under section 642(c) for—

(A) Any amount of the gross income of the related estate that is paid or set aside during the taxable year pursuant to the terms of the governing instrument of the related estate for a purpose specified in section 170(c); and

(B) Any amount of gross income of the electing trust that is paid or set aside during the taxable year pursuant to the terms of the governing instrument of the electing trust for a purpose specified in section 170(c).

(3) If there is no executor. (i) Tax treatment of the electing trust. If there is no executor, the trustee treats the electing trust, during the election period, as an estate for all purposes of subtitle A of the Internal Revenue Code. Thus, for example, an electing trust is treated as an estate for purposes of the set-aside deduction under section 642(c)(2), the subchapter S shareholder requirements of section 1361(b)(1), and the special offset for rental real estate activities under section 469(i)(4). The trustee may also adopt a taxable year other than a calendar year.

(ii) Filing the Form 1041 for the electing trust. If there is no executor, the trustee of the electing trust must, during the election period, file a Form 1041, under the TIN obtained by the trustee under § 301.6109-1(a)(3) of this chapter upon the death of the decedent, treating the trust as an estate. If there is more than one electing trust, the Form 1041 must be filed by the filing trustee (see paragraph (c)(2)(ii)(B) of this section) under the name and TIN of the electing trust of the filing trustee. Information regarding the names and TINs of the other electing trusts must be provided on the Form 1041 as required by the instructions to that form. Any return filed in accordance with this paragraph shall be treated as a return filed for the electing trust (or trusts, if there is more than one electing trust) and not as a return filed for any subsequently discovered related estate. Accordingly, the period of limitations provided in section 6501 for assessments with respect to a subsequently discovered related estate does not start until a return is filed with respect to the related estate. See paragraph (g) of this section.

(4) Application of the section 6654(l)(2) to the electing trust. Each electing trust and related estate (if any) is treated as a separate taxpayer for all purposes of subtitle F of the Internal Revenue Code, including, without limitation, the application of section 6654. The provisions of section 6654(l)(2)(A) relating to the two year exception to an estate's obligation to make estimated tax payments, however, will apply to each electing trust for which a section 645 election has been made.

(f) Duration of election period. *(1) In general.* The election period begins on the date of the decedent's death and terminates on the earlier of the day on which both the electing trust and related estate, if any, have distributed all of their assets, or the day before the applicable date. The election does not apply to successor trusts (trusts that are distributees under the trust instrument).

(2) Definition of applicable date. (i) Applicable date if no Form 706 "United States Estate (and Generation Skipping Transfer) Tax Return" is required to be filed. If a Form 706 is not required to be filed as a result of the decedent's death, the applicable date is the day which is 2 years after the date of the decedent's death.

(ii) Applicable date if a Form 706 is required to be filed. If a Form 706 is required to be filed as a result of the decedent's death, the applicable date is the later of the day that is 2 years after the date of the decedent's death, or the day that is 6 months after the date of final determination of liability for estate tax. Solely for purposes of determining the applicable date under section 645, the date of final determination of liability is the earliest of the following—

(A) The date that is six months after the issuance by the Internal Revenue Service of an estate tax closing letter, unless a claim for refund with respect to the estate tax is filed within twelve months after the issuance of the letter;

(B) The date of a final disposition of a claim for refund, as defined in paragraph (f)(2)(iii) of this section, that resolves the liability for the estate tax, unless suit is instituted within six months after a final disposition of the claim;

(C) The date of execution of a settlement agreement with the Internal Revenue Service that determines the liability for the estate tax;

(D) The date of issuance of a decision, judgment, decree, or other order by a court of competent jurisdiction resolving the liability for the estate tax unless a notice of appeal or a petition for certiorari is filed within 90 days after the issuance of a decision, judgment, decree, or other order of a court; or

(E) The date of expiration of the period of limitations for assessment of the estate tax provided in section 6501.

(iii) Definition of final disposition of claim for refund. For purposes of paragraph (f)(2)(ii)(B) of this section, a claim for refund shall be deemed finally disposed of by the Secretary when all items have been either allowed or disallowed. If a waiver of notification with respect to disallowance is filed with respect to a claim for refund prior to disallowance of the claim, the claim for refund will be treated as disallowed on the date the waiver is filed.

(iv) Examples. The application of this paragraph (f)(2) is illustrated by the following examples:

Example (1). A died on October 20, 2002. The executor of A's estate and the trustee of Trust, an electing trust, made a section 645 election. A Form 706 is not required to be filed as a result of A's death. The applicable date is October 20, 2004, the day that is two years after A's date of death. The last day of the election period is October 19, 2004. Beginning October 20, 2004, Trust will no longer be treated and taxed as part of A's estate.

Example (2). Assume the same facts as Example 1, except that a Form 706 is required to be filed as the result of A's death. The Internal Revenue Service issues an estate tax closing letter accepting the Form 706 as filed on March 15, 2005. The estate does not file a claim for refund by March 15, 2006, the day that is twelve months after the date of issuance of the estate tax closing letter. The date of final determination of liability is September 15, 2005, and the applicable date is March 15, 2006. The last day of the election period is March 14, 2006. Beginning March 15, 2006, Trust will no longer be treated and taxed as part of A's estate.

Example (3). Assume the same facts as Example 1, except that a Form 706 is required to be filed as the result of A's death. The Form 706 is audited, and a notice of deficiency authorized under section 6212 is mailed to the executor of A's estate as a result of the audit. The executor files a petition in Tax Court. The Tax Court issues a decision resolving the liability for estate tax on December 14, 2005, and neither party appeals within 90 days after the issuance of the decision. The date of final determination of liability is December 14, 2005. The applicable date is June 14, 2006, the day that is six months after the date of final determination of liability. The last day of the election period is June 13, 2006. Beginning June 14, 2006, Trust will no longer be treated and taxed as part of A's estate.

(g) Executor appointed after the section 645 election is made. *(1) Effect on the election.* If an executor for the related estate is not appointed until after the trustee has made a valid section 645 election, the executor must agree to the trustee's election, and the IRS must be notified of that agreement by the filing of a revised election form (completed as required by the instructions to that form) within 90 days of the appointment of the executor, for the election period to continue past the date of appointment of the executor. If the executor does not agree to the election or a revised election form is not timely filed as required by this paragraph, the election period terminates the day before the appointment of the executor. If the IRS issues other guidance after December 24, 2002 for notifying the IRS of the executor's agreement to the election, the IRS must be notified in the manner provided in that guidance for the election period to continue.

(2) Continuation of election period. (i) Correction of returns filed before executor appointed. If the election period continues under paragraph (g)(1) of this section, the executor of the related estate and the trustee of each electing trust must file amended Forms 1041 to correct the Forms 1041 filed by the trustee before the executor was appointed. The amended Forms 1041 must be filed under the name and TIN of the electing trust and must reflect the items of income, deduction, and credit of the related estate and the electing trust. The name and TIN of the related estate must be provided on the amended Forms 1041 as required in the instructions to that Form. The amended return for the taxable year ending immediately before the executor was appointed must indicate that this Form 1041 is a final return. If the period of limitations for making assessments has expired with respect to the electing trust for any of the Forms 1041 filed by the trustee, the executor must file Forms 1041 for any items of income, deduction, and credit of the related estate that cannot be properly included on amended forms for the electing trust. The personal exemption under section 642(b) is not permitted to be taken on these Forms 1041 filed by the executor.

(ii) Returns filed after the appointment of the executor. All returns filed by the combined electing trust and related estate after the appointment of the executor are to be filed under the name and TIN of the related estate in accordance with paragraph (e)(2) of this section. Regardless of the change in the name and TIN under which the Forms 1041 for the combined electing trust and related estate are filed, the combined electing trust and related estate will be treated as the same entity before and after the executor is appointed.

(3) Termination of the election period. If the election period terminates under paragraph (g)(1) of this section, the executor must file Forms 1041 under the name and TIN of the estate for all taxable years of the related estate ending after the death of the decedent. The trustee of the electing trust is not required to amend any returns filed for the electing trust during the election period. Following termination of the election period, the trustee of the electing trust must obtain a new TIN. See § 301.6109-1(a)(4) of this chapter.

(h) Treatment of an electing trust and related estate following termination of the election. *(1) The share (or shares) comprising the electing trust is deemed to be distributed upon termination of the election period.* On the close of the last day of the election period, the combined electing trust and related estate, if there is an executor, or the electing trust, if there is no executor, is deemed to distribute the share (or shares, as determined under section 663(c)) comprising the electing trust to a new trust in a distribution to which sections 661 and 662 apply. All items of income, including net capital gains, that are attributable to the share (or shares) comprising the electing trust are included in the calculation of the distributable net income of the electing trust and treated as distributed by the combined electing trust and related estate, if there is an executor, or by the electing trust, if there is no executor, to the new trust. The combined electing trust and related estate, if there is an executor, or the electing trust, if there is no executor, is entitled to a distribution deduction to the extent permitted under section 661 in the taxable year in which the election period terminates as a result of the deemed distribution. The new trust shall include the amount of the deemed distribution in gross income to the extent required under section 662.

(2) Filing of the Form 1041 upon the termination of the section 645 election. (i) If there is an executor. (A) Filing the Form 1041 for the year of termination. If there is an executor, the Form 1041 filed under the name and TIN of the related estate for the taxable year in which the election terminates includes—

(1) The items of income, deduction, and credit of the electing trust attributable to the period beginning with the first day of the taxable year of the combined electing trust and related estate and ending with the last day of the election period;

(2) The items of income, deduction, and credit, if any, of the related estate for the entire taxable year; and

(3) A deduction for the deemed distribution of the share (or shares) comprising the electing trust to the new trust as provided for under paragraph (h)(1) of this section.

(B) Requirement to file a final Form 1041 under the name and TIN of the electing trust. If the electing trust terminates during the election period, the trustee of the electing trust must file a Form 1041 under the name and TIN of the electing trust and indicate that the return is a final return to notify the IRS that the electing trust is no longer in existence. The items of income, deduction, and credit of the trust are not reported on this final Form 1041 but on the appropriate Form 1041 filed for the combined electing trust and related estate.

(ii) If there is no executor. If there is no executor, the taxable year of the electing trust closes on the last day of the election period. A Form 1041 is filed in the manner prescribed under paragraph (e)(3)(ii) of this section reporting the items of income, deduction, and credit of the electing trust for the short period ending with the last day of the election period. The Form 1041 filed under this paragraph includes a distribution deduction for the deemed distribution provided for under paragraph (h)(1) of this section. The Form 1041 must indicate that it is a final return.

(3) Use of TINs following termination of the election. (i) If there is an executor. Upon termination of the section 645 election, a former electing trust may need to obtain a new TIN. See § 301.6109-1(a)(4) of this chapter. If the related estate continues after the termination of the election period, the related estate must continue to use the TIN assigned to the estate during the election period.

(ii) If there is no executor. If there is no executor, the former electing trust must obtain a new TIN if the trust will continue after the termination of the election period. See § 301.6109-1(a)(4) of this chapter.

(4) Taxable year of estate and trust upon termination of the election. (i) Estate. Upon termination of the section 645 election period, the taxable year of the estate is the same taxable year used during the election period.

(ii) Trust. Upon termination of the section 645 election, the taxable year of the new trust is the calendar year. See section 644.

(i) Reserved.

(j) Effective date. Paragraphs (a), (b), (c), (d), (f), and (g) of this section apply to trusts and estates of decedents dying on or after December 24, 2002. Paragraphs (e) and (h) of this section apply to taxable years ending on or after December 24, 2002.

T.D. 9032, 12/23/2002.

§ 1.651(a)-1 Simple trusts; deduction for distributions; in general.

Section 651 is applicable only to a trust the governing instruments of which:

(a) Requires that the trust distribute all of its income currently for the taxable year, and

(b) Does not provide that any amounts may be paid, permanently set aside, or used in the taxable year for the charitable, etc., purposes specified in section 642(c),

and does not make any distribution other than of current income. A trust to which section 651 applies is referred to in this part as a "simple" trust. Trusts subject to section 661 are referred to as "complex" trusts. A trust may be a simple trust for one year and a complex trust for another year. It should be noted that under section 651 a trust qualifies as a simple trust in a taxable year in which it is required to distribute all of its income currently and makes no other distributions, whether or not distributions of current income are in fact made. On the other hand a trust is not a complex trust by reason of distributions of amounts other than income unless such distributions are in fact made during the taxable year, whether or not they are required in that year.

T.D. 6217, 12/19/56.

§ 1.651(a)-2 Income required to be distributed currently.

(a) The determination of whether trust income is required to be distributed currently depends upon the terms of the trust instrument and the applicable local law. For this purpose, if the trust instrument provides that the trustee in determining the distributable income shall first retain a reserve for depreciation or otherwise make due allowance for keeping the trust corpus intact by retaining a reasonable amount of the current income for that purpose, the retention of current income for that purpose will not disqualify the trust from being a "simple" trust. The fiduciary must be under a duty to distribute the income currently even if, as a matter of practical necessity, the income is not distributed until after the close of the trust's taxable year. For example: Under the terms of the trust instrument, all of the income is currently distributable to A. The trust reports on the calendar year basis and as a matter of practical necessity makes distribution to A of each quarter's income on the fifteenth day of the month following the close of the quarter. The distribution made by the trust on January 15, 1955, of the income for the fourth quarter of 1954 does not disqualify the trust from treatment in 1955 under section 651, since the income is required to be distributed currently. However, if the terms of a trust require that none of the income be distributed until after the year of its receipt by the trust, the income of the trust is not required to be distributed currently and the trust is not a simple trust. For definition of the term "income" see section 643(b) and § 1.643(b)-1.

(b) It is immaterial, for purposes of determining whether all the income is required to be distributed currently, that the amount of income allocated to a particular beneficiary is not specified in the instrument. For example, if the fiduciary is required to distribute all the income currently, but has discretion to "sprinkle" the income among a class of beneficiaries, or among named beneficiaries in such amount as he may see fit, all the income is required to be distributed currently, even though the amount distributable to a particular beneficiary is unknown until the fiduciary has exercised his discretion.

(c) If in one taxable year of a trust its income for that year is required or permitted to be accumulated, and in another taxable year its income for the year is required to be distributed currently (and no other amounts are distributed), the trust is a simple trust for the latter year. For example, a trust under which income may be accumulated until a beneficiary is 21 years old, and thereafter must be distributed currently, is a simple trust for taxable years beginning after the beneficiary reaches the age of 21 years in which no other amounts are distributed.

(d) If a trust distributes property in kind as part of its requirement to distribute currently all the income as defined under section 643(b) and the applicable regulations, the trust shall be treated as having sold the property for its fair market value on the date of distribution. If no amount in excess of the amount of income as defined under section 643(b) and the applicable regulations is distributed by the trust during the year, the trust will qualify for treatment under section 651 even though property in kind was distributed as part of a distribution of all such income. This paragraph (d) applies for taxable years of trusts ending after January 2, 2004.

T.D. 6217, 12/19/56, amend T.D. 9102, 12/30/2003.

§ 1.651(a)-3 Distribution of amounts other than income.

(a) A trust does not qualify for treatment under section 651 for any taxable year in which it actually distributes corpus. For example, a trust which is required to distribute all of its income currently would not qualify as a simple trust under section 651 in the year of its termination since in that year actual distributions of corpus would be made.

(b) A trust otherwise qualifying under section 651, which may make a distribution of corpus in the discretion of the trustee, or which is required under the terms of its governing instrument to make a distribution of corpus upon the happening of a specified event, will be disqualified for treatment under section 651 only for the taxable year in which an actual distribution of corpus is made. For example: Under the terms of a trust, which is required to distribute all of its income currently, half of the corpus is to be distributed to beneficiary A when he becomes 30 years of age. The trust reports on the calendar year basis. On December 28, 1954, A becomes 30 years of age and the trustee distributes half of the corpus of the trust to him on January 3, 1955. The trust will be disqualified for treatment under section 651 only for the taxable year 1955, the year in which an actual distribution of corpus is made.

(c) See section 661 and the regulations thereunder for the treatment of trusts which distribute corpus or claim the charitable contributions deduction provided by section 642(c).

T.D. 6217, 12/19/56.

§ 1.651(a)-4 Charitable purposes.

A trust is not considered to be a trust which may pay, permanently set aside, or use any amount for charitable, etc., purposes for any taxable year for which it is not allowed a charitable, etc., deduction under section 642(c). Therefore, a trust with a remainder to a charitable organization is not disqualified for treatment as a simple trust if either (a) the remainder is subject to a contingency, so that no deduction would be allowed for capital gains or other amounts added to corpus as amounts permanently set aside for a charitable, etc., purpose under section 642(c), or (b) the trust receives no capital gains or other income added to corpus for the taxable year for which such a deduction would be allowed.

T.D. 6217, 12/19/56.

§ 1.651(a)-5 Estates.

Subpart B has no application to an estate.

T.D. 6217, 12/19/56.

§ 1.651(b)-1 Deduction for distributions to beneficiaries.

In computing its taxable income, a simple trust is allowed a deduction for the amount of income which is required under the terms of the trust instrument to be distributed currently to beneficiaries. If the amount of income required to be distributed currently exceeds the distributable net income, the deduction allowable to the trust is limited to the amount of the distributable net income. For this purpose the amount of income required to be distributed currently, or distributable net income, whichever is applicable, does not include items of trust income (adjusted for deductions allocable thereto) which are not included in the gross income of the trust. For determination of the character of the income required to be distributed currently, see § 1.652(b)-2. Accordingly, for the purposes of determining the deduction allowable to the trust under section 651, distributable net income is computed without the modifications specified in paragraphs (5), (6), and (7) of section 643 (a), relating to tax-exempt interest, foreign income, and excluded dividends. For example: Assume that the distributable net income of a trust as computed under section 643 (a) amounts to $99,000 but includes nontaxable income of $9,000. Then distributable net income for the purpose of determining the deduction allowable under section 651 is $90,000 ($99,000 less $9,000 nontaxable income).

T.D. 6217, 12/19/56.

§ 1.652(a)-1 Simple trusts; inclusion of amounts in income of beneficiaries.

Subject to the rules in §§ 1.652(a)-2 and 1.652(b)-1, a beneficiary of a simple trust includes in his gross income for the taxable year the amounts of income required to be distributed to him for such year, whether or not distributed. Thus, the income of a simple trust is includible in the beneficiary's gross income for the taxable year in which the income is required to be distributed currently even though, as a matter of practical necessity, the income is not distributed until after the close of the taxable year of the trust. See § 1.642(a)(3)-2 with respect to time of receipt of dividends. See § 1.652(c)-1 for treatment of amounts required to be distributed where a beneficiary and the trust have different taxable years. The term "income required to be distributed currently" includes income required to be distributed currently which is in fact used to discharge or satisfy any person's legal obligation as that term is used in § 1.662(a)-4.

T.D. 6217, 12/19/56.

§ 1.652(a)-2 Distributions in excess of distributable net income.

If the amount of income required to be distributed currently to beneficiaries exceeds the distributable net income of the trust (as defined in section 643(a)), each beneficiary includes in his gross income an amount equivalent to his proportionate share of such distributable net income. Thus, if beneficiary A is to receive two-thirds of the trust income and B is to receive one-third, and the income required to be distributed currently is $99,000, A will receive $66,000 and B, $33,000. However, if the distributable net income, as determined under section 643(a) is only $99,000, A will include his two-thirds ($60,000) of that sum in his gross income, and B will include one-third ($30,000) in his gross income. See §§ 1.652(b)-1 and 1.652(b)-2, however, for amounts which are not includible in the gross income of a beneficiary because of their tax-exempt character.

T.D. 6217, 12/19/56.

§ 1.652(b)-1 Character of amounts.

In determining the gross income of a beneficiary, the amounts includible under § 1.652(a)-1 have the same character in the hands of the beneficiary as in the hands of the trust. For example, to the extent that the amounts specified in § 1.652(a)-1 consist of income exempt from tax under section 103, such amounts are not included in the beneficiary's gross income. Similarly, dividends distributed to a beneficiary retain their original character in the beneficiary's hands for purposes of determining the availability to the beneficiary of the dividends received credit under section 34 (for dividends received on or before December 31, 1964) and the dividend exclusion under section 116. Also, to the extent that the amounts specified in § 1.652(a)-1 consist of "earned income" in the hands of the trust under the provisions of section 1348 such amount shall be treated under section 1348 as "earned income" in the hands of the beneficiary. Similarly, to the extent such amounts consist of an amount received as a part of a lump sum distribution from a qualified plan and to which the provisions of section 72(n) would apply in the hands of the trust, such amount shall be treated as subject to such section in the hands of the beneficiary except where such amount is deemed under section 666(a) to have been distributed in a preceding taxable year of the trust and the partial tax described in section 668(a)(2) is determined under section 668(b)(1)(B). The tax treatment of amounts determined under § 1.652(a)-1 depends upon the beneficiary's status with respect to them not upon the status of the trust. Thus, if a beneficiary is deemed to have received foreign income of a foreign trust, the includibility of such income in his gross income depends upon his taxable status with respect to that income.

T.D. 6217, 12/9/56, amend T.D. 6777, 12/15/64, T.D. 7204, 8/24/72.

PAR. 18.

Section 1.652(b)-1 is amended by deleting "72(n)" and inserting in lieu thereof "402(a)(2)". As amended, § 1.652(b)-1 reads as follows:

Proposed § 1.652(b)-1 Character of amounts. [*For Preamble, see ¶ 150,135*]

In determining the gross income of a beneficiary, the amounts includible under § 1.652(a)-1 have the same character in the hands of the beneficiary as in the hands of the trust. For example, to the extent that the amounts specified in § 1.652(a)-1 consist of income exempt from tax under section 103, such amounts are not included in the beneficiary's gross income. Similarly, dividends distributed to a beneficiary retain their original character in the beneficiary's hands for purposes of determining the availability to the beneficiary of the dividends received credit under section 34 (for dividends received on or before December 31, 1964) and the dividend exclusion under section 116. Also, to the extent that the amounts specified in § 1.652(a)-1 consist of "earned income" in the hands of the trust under the provisions of section 1348 such amount shall be treated under section 1348 as "earned income" in the hands of the beneficiary. Similarly, to the extent the amounts specified in § 1.652(a)-1 consist of an amount received as a part of a lump sum distribution from a qualified plan and to which the provisions of section 402(a)(2) would apply in the hands of the trust, such amount shall be treated as subject to such section in the hands of the beneficiary except where such amount is deemed under section 666(a) to have been distributed in a preceding taxable year of the trust and the partial tax described in section 668(a)(2) is determined under section 668(b)(1)(B). The tax treatment of amounts determined under § 1.652(a)-1 depends upon the beneficiary's status with respect to them, not upon the status of the trust. Thus, if a beneficiary is deemed to have received foreign income of a foreign trust, the includibility of such income in his gross income depends upon his taxable status with respect to that income.

§ 1.652(b)-2 Allocation of income items.

Caution: The Treasury has not yet amended Reg § 1.652(b)-2 to reflect changes made by P.L. 99-514.

(a) The amounts specified in § 1.652(a)-1 which are required to be included in the gross income of a beneficiary are treated as consisting of the same proportion of each class of items entering into distributable net income of the trust (as defined in section 643(a)) as the total of each class bears to such distributable net income, unless the terms of the trust specifically allocate different classes of income to different beneficiaries, or unless local law requires such an allocation. For example: Assume that under the terms of the governing instrument, beneficiary A is to receive currently one-half of the trust income and beneficiaries B and C are each to receive currently one-quarter, and the distributable net income of the trust (after allocation of expenses) consists of dividends of $10,000, taxable interest of $10,000 and tax-exempt interest of $4,000. A will be deemed to have received $5,000 of dividends, $5,000 of taxable interest, and $2,000 of tax-exempt interest; B and C will each be deemed to have received $2,500 of dividends, $2,500 of taxable interest, and $1,000 of tax-exempt interest. However, if the terms of the trust specifically allocate different classes of income to different beneficiaries, entirely or in part, or if local law requires such an allocation, each beneficiary will be deemed to have received those items of income specifically allocated to him.

(b) The terms of the trust are considered specifically to allocate different classes of income to different beneficiaries only to the extent that the allocation is required in the trust instrument, and only to the extent that it has an economic effect independent of the income tax consequences of the allocation. For example:

(1) Allocation pursuant to a provision in a trust instrument granting the trustee discretion to allocate different classes of income to different beneficiaries is not a specific allocation by the terms of the trust.

(2) Allocation pursuant to a provision directing the trustee to pay all of one income to A, or $10,000 out of the income to A, and the balance of the income to B, but directing the trustee first to allocate a specific class of income to A's share (to the extent there is income of that class and to the extent it does not exceed A's share) is not a specific allocation by the terms of the trust.

(3) Allocation pursuant to a provision directing the trustee to pay half the class of income (whatever it may be) to A, and the balance of the income to B, is a specific allocation by the terms of the trust.

T.D. 6217, 12/19/56.

Character of amounts in the hands of the beneficiaries	17,075	50,000	24,025	91,100[1]

[1] Distributable net income.

Inasmuch as the income of the trust is to be distributed equally to A and B, each is deemed to have received one-half of each item of income; that is, rents of $8,537.50, dividends of $25,000, and tax-exempt interest of $12,012.50. The dividends of $25,000 allocated to each beneficiary are to be aggregated with his other dividends (if any) for purposes of the dividend exclusion provided by section 116 and the dividend received credit allowed under section 34. Also, each beneficiary is allowed a deduction of $2,500 for depreciation of rental property attributable to the portion (one-half) of the income of the trust distributed to him.

T.D. 6217, 12/19/56, amend T.D. 6712, 3/23/64.

§ 1.661(a)-1 Estates and trusts accumulating income or distributing corpus; general.

Subpart C, part I, subchapter J, chapter 1 of the Code, is applicable to all decedents' estates and their beneficiaries, and to trusts other than trusts subject to the provisions of subpart B of such part I (relating to trusts which distribute current income only, or "simple" trusts). A trust which is required to distribute amounts other than income during the taxable year may be subject to subpart B, and not subpart C, in the absence of an actual distribution of amounts other than income during the taxable year. See §§ 1.651(a)-1 and 1.651(a)-3. A trust to which subpart C is applicable is referred to as a "complex" trust in this part. Section 661 has no application to amounts excluded under section 663(a).

T.D. 6217, 12/19/56.

§ 1.661(a)-2 Deduction for distributions to beneficiaries.

Caution: The Treasury has not yet amended Reg § 1.661(a)-2 to reflect changes made by P.L. 98-369.

(a) In computing the taxable income of an estate or trust there is allowed under section 661(a) as a deduction for distributions to beneficiaries the sum of:

(1) The amount of income for the taxable year which is required to be distributed currently, and

(2) Any other amounts properly paid or credited or required to be distributed for such taxable year.

However, the total amount deductible under section 661(a) cannot exceed the distributable net income as computed under section 643(a) and as modified by section 661(c). See § 1.661(c)-1.

(b) The term "income required to be distributed currently" includes any amount required to be distributed which may be paid out of income or corpus (such as an annuity), to the extent it is paid out of income for the taxable year. See § 1.651(a)-2 which sets forth additional rules which are applicable in determining whether income of an estate or trust is required to be distributed currently.

(c) The term "any other amounts properly paid or credited or required to be distributed" includes all amounts properly paid, credited, or required to be distributed by an estate or trust during the taxable year other than income required to be distributed currently. Thus, the term includes the payment of an annuity to the extent it is not paid out of income for the taxable year, and a distribution of property in kind (see paragraph (f) of this section). However, see section 663(a) and regulations thereunder for distributions which are not included. Where the income of an estate or trust may be accumulated or distributed in the discretion of the fiduciary, or where the fiduciary has a power to distribute corpus to a beneficiary, any such discretionary distribution would qualify under section 661(a)(2). The term also includes an amount applied or distributed for the support of a dependent of a grantor or of a trustee or cotrustee under the circumstances described in section 677(b) or section 678(c) out of corpus or out of other than income for the taxable year.

(d) The terms "income required to be distributed currently" and "any other amounts properly paid or credited or required to be distributed" also include any amount used to discharge or satisfy any person's legal obligation as that term is used in § 1.662(a)-4.

(e) The terms "income required to be distributed currently" and "any other amounts properly paid or credited or required to be distributed" include amounts paid, or required to be paid, during the taxable year pursuant to a court order or decree or under local law, by a decedent's estate as an allowance or award for the support of the decedent's widow or other dependent for a limited period during the administration of the estate. The term "any other amounts properly paid or credited or required to be distributed" does not include the value of any interest in real estate owned by a decedent, title to which under local law passes directly from the decedent to his heirs or devisees.

(f) Gain or loss is realized by the trust or estate (or the other beneficiaries) by reason of a distribution of property in kind if the distribution is in satisfaction of a right to receive a distribution of a specific dollar amount, of specific property other than that distributed, or of income as defined under section 643(b) and the applicable regulations, if income is required to be distributed currently. In addition, gain or loss is realized if the trustee or executor makes the election to recognize gain or loss under section 643(e). This paragraph applies for taxable years of trusts and estates ending after January 2, 2004.

T.D. 6217, 12/19/56, amend T.D. 7287, 9/26/73, T.D. 9102, 12/30/2003.

§ 1.661(b)-1 Character of amounts distributed; in general.

In the absence of specific provisions in the governing instrument for the allocation of different classes of income, or unless local law requires such an allocation, the amount deductible for distributions to beneficiaries under section 661(a) is treated as consisting of the same proportion of each class of items entering into the computation of distributable net income as the total of each class bears to the total distributable net income. For example, if a trust has distributable net income of $20,000, consisting of $10,000 each of taxable interest and royalties and distributes $10,000 to beneficiary A, the deduction of $10,000 allowable under section 661(a) is deemed to consist of $5,000 each of taxable interest and royalties, unless the trust instrument specifically provides for the distribution or accumulation of different classes of income or unless local law requires such an allocation. See also § 1.661(c)-1.

T.D. 6217, 12/19/56.

§ 1.661(b)-2 Character of amounts distributed when charitable contributions are made.

In the application of the rule stated in § 1.661(b)-1, the items of deduction which enter into the computation of distributable net income are allocated among the items of income which enter into the computation of distributable net income in accordance with the rules set forth in § 1.652(b)-3, except that, in the absence of specific provisions in the governing instrument, or unless local law requires a different apportionment, amounts paid, permanently set aside, or to be used for the charitable, etc., purposes specified in section 642(c) are first ratably apportioned among each class of items of income entering into the computation of the distributable net income of the estate or trust, in accordance with the rules set out in paragraph (b) of § 1.643(a)-5.

T.D. 6217, 12/19/56.

§ 1.661(c)-1 Limitation on deduction.

An estate or trust is not allowed a deduction under section 661(a) for any amount which is treated under section 661(b) as consisting of any item of distributable net income which is not included in the gross income of the estate or trust. For example, if in 1962, a trust, which reports on the calendar year basis, has distributable net income of $20,000, which is deemed to consist of $10,000 of dividends and $10,000 of tax-exempt interest, and distributes $10,000 to beneficiary A, the deduction allowable under section 661(a) (computed without regard to section 661(c)) would amount to $10,000 consisting of $5,000 of dividends and $5,000 of tax-exempt interest. The deduction actually allowable under section 661(a) as limited by section 661(c) is $4,975, since no deduction is allowable for the $5,000 of tax-exempt interest and the $25 deemed distributed out of the $50 of dividends excluded under section 116, items of distributable net income which are not included in the gross income of the estate or trust.

T.D. 6217, 12/19/56, amend T.D. 6777, 12/15/64.

§ 1.661(c)-2 Illustration of the provisions of section 661.

The provisions of section 661 may be illustrated by the following example:

Example. (a) Under the terms of a trust, which reports on the calendar year basis, $10,000 a year is required to be paid out of income to a designated charity. The balance of the income may, in the trustee's discretion, be accumulated or distributed to beneficiary A. Expenses are allocable against income and the trust instrument requires a reserve for depreciation. During the taxable year 1955 the trustee contributes $10,000 to charity and in his discretion distributes $15,000 of income to A. The trust has the following items of income and expense for the taxable year 1955:

Dividends	$10,000
Partially tax-exempt interest	10,000
Fully tax-exempt interest	10,000
Rents	20,000
Rental expenses	2,000
Depreciation of rental property	3,000
Trustee's commissions	5,000

(b) The income of the trust for fiduciary accounting purposes is $40,000, computed as follows:

Dividends		$10,000
Partially tax-exempt interest		10,000
Fully tax-exempt interest		10,000
Rents		20,000
Total		50,000
Less:		
Rental expenses	$2,000	
Depreciation	3,000	
Trustee's commissions	5,000	
		10,000
Income as computed under section 643(b)		40,000

(c) The distributable net income of the trust as computed under section 643(a) is $30,000, determined as follows:

Rents			$20,000
Dividends			10,000
Partially tax-exempt interest			10,000
Fully tax-exempt interest		$10,000	
Less:			
Expenses allocable thereto (10,000/50,000 × $5,000)	$1,000		
Charitable contributions allocable thereto (10,000/50,000 × $10,000)	2,000		
		3,000	
			7,000
Total			47,000
Deductions:			
Rental expenses		$ 2,000	
Depreciation of rental property		3,000	
Trustee's commissions ($5,000 less $1,000 allocated to tax-exempt interest)		4,000	
Charitable contributions ($10,000 less $2,000 allocated to tax-exempt interest)		8,000	
			17,000
Distributable net income (section 643(a))			30,000

(d) The character of the amounts distributed under section 661(a), determined in accordance with the rules prescribed in §§ 1.661(b)-1 and 1.661 (b)-2 is shown by the following table (for the purpose of this allocation, it is assumed that the trustee elected to allocate the trustee's commissions to rental income except for the amount required to be allocated to tax-exempt interest):

	Rental income	Taxable dividends	Excluded dividends	Partially tax-exempt interest	Tax-exempt interest	Total
Trust income	$20,000	$9,950	$50	$10,000	$10,000	$50,000
Less:						
Charitable contributions	4,000	2,000		2,000	2,000	10,000
Rental expenses	2,000					2,000
Depreciation	3,000					3,000
Trustee's commissions	4,000				1,000	5,000
Total deductions	13,000	2,000	0	2,000	3,000	20,000
Distributable net income	7,000	7,950	50	8,000	7,000	30,000
Amounts deemed distributed under section 661(a) before applying the limitation of section 661(c)	3,500	3,975	25	4,000	3,500	15,000

In the absence of specific provisions in the trust instrument for the allocation of different classes of income, the charitable contribution is deemed to consist of a pro rata portion of the gross amount of each item of income of the trust (except dividends excluded under section 116) and the trust is deemed to have distributed to A a pro rata portion (one-half) of each item of income included in distributable net income.

(e) The taxable income of the trust is $11,375 computed as follows:

Rental income		$20,000
Dividends ($10,000 less $50 exclusion)		9,950
Partially tax-exempt interest		10,000
Gross income		39,950
Deductions:		
Rental expenses	$2,000	
Depreciation of rental property	3,000	
Trustee's commissions	4,000	
Charitable contributions	8,000	
Distributions to A	11,475	
Personal exemption	100	
		28,575
Taxable income		11,375

In computing the taxable income of the trust no deduction is allowable for the portions of the charitable contributions deduction ($2,000) and trustee's commissions ($1,000) which are treated under section 661(b) as attributable to the tax-exempt interest excludable from gross income. Also, of the dividends of $4,000 deemed to have been distributed to A under section 661(a), $25 (25/50ths of $50) is deemed to have been distributed from the excluded dividends and is not an allowable deduction to the trust. Accordingly, the deduction allowable under section 661 is deemed to be composed of $3,500 rental income, $3,975 of dividends, and $4,000 partially tax-exempt interest. No deduction is allowable for the portion of tax-exempt interest or for the portion of the excluded dividends deemed to have been distributed to the beneficiary.

(f) The trust is entitled to the credit allowed by section 34 with respect to dividends of $5,975 ($9,950 less $3,975 distributed to A) included in gross income. Also, the trust is allowed the credit provided by section 35 with respect to partially tax-exempt interest of $6,000 ($10,000 less $4,000 deemed distributed to A) included in gross income.

(g) Dividends of $4,000 allocable to A are to be aggregated with his other dividends (if any) for purposes of the dividend exclusion under section 116 and the dividend received credit under section 34.

T.D. 6217, 12/19/56.

§ 1.662(a)-1 Inclusion of amounts in gross income of beneficiaries of estates and complex trusts; general.

There is included in the gross income of a beneficiary of an estate or complex trust the sum of:

(1) Amounts of income required to be distributed currently to him, and

(2) All other amounts properly paid, credited, or required to be distributed to him by the estate or trust. The preceding sentence is subject to the rules contained in § 1.662(a)-2 (relating to currently distributable income), § 1.662(a)-3 (relating to other amounts distributed), and §§ 1.662(b)-1 and 1.662(b)-2 (relating to character of amounts). Section 662 has no application to amounts excluded under section 663(a).

T.D. 6217, 12/19/56.

§ 1.662(a)-2 Currently distributable income.

(a) There is first included in the gross income of each beneficiary under section 662(a)(1) the amount of income for the taxable year of the estate or trust required to be distributed currently to him, subject to the provisions of paragraph (b) of this section. Such amount is included in the beneficiary's gross income whether or not it is actually distributed.

(b) If the amount of income required to be distributed currently to all beneficiaries exceeds the distributable net income (as defined in section 643(a) but computed without taking into account the payment, crediting, or setting aside of an amount for which a charitable contributions deduction is allowable under section 642(c)) of the estate or trust, then there is included in the gross income of each beneficiary an amount which bears the same ratio to distributable net income (as so computed) as the amount of income required to be distributed currently to the beneficiary bears to the amount required to be distributed currently to all beneficiaries.

(c) The phrase "the amount of income for the taxable year required to be distributed currently" includes any amount required to be paid out of income or corpus to the extent the amount is satisfied out of income for the taxable year. Thus, an annuity required to be paid in all events (either out of income or corpus) would qualify as income required to be distributed currently to the extent there is income (as defined in section 643(b)) not paid, credited, or required to be distributed to other beneficiaries for the taxable year. If an annuity or a portion of an annuity is deemed under this paragraph to be income required to be distributed currently, it is treated in all respects in the same manner as an amount of income actually required to be distributed currently. The phrase "the amount of income for the taxable year required to be distributed currently" also includes any amount required to be paid during the taxable year in all events (either out of income or corpus) pursuant to a court order or decree or under local law, by a decedent's estate as an allowance or award for the support of the decedent's widow or other dependent for a limited period during the administration of the estate to the extent there is income (as defined in section 643(b)) of the estate for the taxable year not paid, credited, or required to be distributed to other beneficiaries.

(d) If an annuity is paid, credited, or required to be distributed tax free, that is, under a provision whereby the executor or trustee will pay the income tax of the annuitant resulting from the receipt of the annuity, the payment of or for the tax by the executor or trustee will be treated as income paid, credited, or required to be distributed currently to the extent it is made out of income.

(e) The application of the rules stated in this section may be illustrated by the following examples:

Example (1). (1) Assume that under the terms of the trust instrument $5,000 is to be paid to X charity out of income each year; that $20,000 of income is currently distributable to A; and that an annuity of $12,000 is to be paid to B out of income or corpus. All expenses are charges against income and capital gains are allocable to corpus. During the taxable year the trust had income of $30,000 (after the payment of expenses) derived from taxable interest and made the payments to X charity and distributions to A and B as required by the governing instrument.

(2) The amounts treated as distributed currently under section 662(a)(1) total $25,000 ($20,000 to A and $5,000 to B). Since the charitable contribution is out of income, the amount of income available for B's annuity is only $5,000. The distributable net income of the trust computed under section 643(a) without taking into consideration the charitable contributions deduction of $5,000 as provided by section 661(a)(1), is $30,000. Since the amounts treated as distributed currently of $25,000 do not exceed the distributable net income (as modified) of $30,000, A is required to include $20,000 in his gross income and B is required to include $5,000 in his gross income under section 662(a)(1).

Example (2). Assume the same facts as in paragraph (1) of example (1), except that the trust has, in addition, $10,000 of administration expenses, commissions, etc., chargeable to corpus. The amounts treated as distributed currently under section 662(a)(1) total $25,000 ($20,000 to A and $5,000 to B), since trust income under section 643(b) remains the same as in example (1). Distributable net income of the trust computed under section 643(a) but without taking into account the charitable contributions deduction of $5,000 as provided by section 662(a)(1) is only $20,000. Since the amounts treated as distributed currently of $25,000 exceed the distributable net income (as so computed) of $20,000, A is required to include $16,000 (20,000/25,000 of $20,000) in his gross income and B is required to include $4,000 (5,000/25,000 of $20,000) in his gross income under section 662(a)(1). Because A and B are beneficiaries of amounts of income required to be distributed currently, they do not benefit from the reduction of distributable net income by the charitable contributions deduction.

T.D. 6217, 12/19/56, amend T.D. 7287, 9/26/73.

§ 1.662(a)-3 Other amounts distributed.

(a) There is included in the gross income of a beneficiary under section 662(a)(2) any amount properly paid, credited, or required to be distributed to the beneficiary for the taxable year, other than (1) income required to be distributed currently, as determined under § 1.662(a)-2, (2) amounts excluded under section 663(a) and the regulations thereunder, and (3) amounts in excess of distributable net income (see paragraph (c) of this section). An amount which is credited or required to be distributed is included in the gross income of a beneficiary whether or not it is actually distributed.

(b) Some of the payments to be included under paragraph (a) of this section are: (1) A distribution made to a beneficiary in the discretion of the fiduciary; (2) a distribution required by the terms of the governing instrument upon the happening of a specified event; (3) an annuity which is required to be paid in all events but which is payable only out of corpus; (4) a distribution of property in kind (see paragraph (f) of § 1.661(a)-2; (5) an amount applied or distributed for the support of a dependent of a grantor or a trustee or cotrustee under the circumstances specified in section 677(b) or section 678(c) out of corpus or out of other than income for the taxable year; and (6) an amount required to be paid during the taxable year pursuant to a court order or decree or under local law, by a decedent's estate as an allowance or award for the support of the decedent's widow or other dependent for a limited period during the administration of the estate which is payable only out of corpus of the estate under the order or decree or local law.

(c) If the sum of the amounts of income required to be distributed currently (as determined under § 1.662(a)-2) and other amounts properly paid, credited, or required to be distributed (as determined under paragraph (a) of this section) exceeds distributable net income (as defined in section 643(a)), then such other amounts properly paid, credited, or required to be distributed are included in gross income of the beneficiary but only to the extent of the excess of such distributable net income over the amounts of income required to be distributed currently. If the other amounts are paid, credited, or required to be distributed to more than one beneficiary, each beneficiary includes in gross income his proportionate share of the amount includible in gross income pursuant to the preceding sentence. The proportionate share is an amount which bears the same ratio to distributable net income (reduced by amounts of income required to be distributed currently) as the other amounts (as determined under paragraphs (a) and (d) of this section) distributed to the beneficiary bear to the other amounts distributed to all beneficiaries. For treatment of excess distributions by trusts, see sections 665 to 668, inclusive, and the regulations thereunder.

(d) The application of the rules stated in this section may be illustrated by the following example:

Example. The terms of a trust require the distribution annually of $10,000 of income to A. If any income remains, it may be accumulated or distributed to B, C, and D in amounts in the trustee's discretion. He may also invade corpus for the benefit of A, B, C, or D. In the taxable year, the trust has $20,000 of income after the deduction of all expenses. Distributable net income is $20,000. The trustee distributes $10,000 of income to A. Of the remaining $10,000 of income, he distributes $3,000 each to B, C, and D, and also distributes an additional $5,000 to A. A includes $10,000 in income under section 662(a)(1). The "other amounts distributed" amount to $14,000, includible in the income of the recipients to the extent of $10,000, distributable net income less the income currently distributable to A. A will include an additional $3,571 (5,000/14,000 × $10,000) in income under this section, and B, C, and D will each include $2,143 (3,000/14,000 × $10,000).

T.D. 6217, 12/19/56, amend T.D. 7287, 9/26/73.

§ 1.662(a)-4 Amounts used in discharge of a legal obligation.

Any amount which, pursuant to the terms of a will or trust instrument, is used in full or partial discharge or satisfaction of a legal obligation of any person is included in the gross income of such person under section 662(a)(1) or (2), whichever is applicable, as though directly distributed to him as a beneficiary, except in cases to which section 71 (relating to alimony payments) or section 682 (relating to income of a trust in case of divorce, etc.) applies. The term "legal obligation" includes a legal obligation to support another person if, and only if, the obligation is not affected by the adequacy of the dependent's own resources. For example, a parent has a "legal obligation" within the meaning of the preceding sentence to support his minor child if under local law property or income from property owned by the child cannot be used for his support so long as his parent is able to support him. On the other hand, if under local law a mother may use the resources of a child for the child's support in lieu of supporting him herself, no obligation of support exists within the meaning of this paragraph, whether or not income is actually used for support. Similarly, since under local law a child ordinarily is obligated to support his parent only if the parent's earnings and resources are insufficient for the purpose, no obligation exists whether or not the parent's earnings and resources are sufficient. In any event, the amount of trust income which is included in the gross income of a person obligated to support a dependent is limited by the extent of his legal obligation under local law. In the case of a parent's obligation to support his child, to the extent that the parent's legal obligation of support, including education, is determined under local law by the family's station in life and by the means of the parent, it is to be determined without consideration of the trust income in question.

T.D. 6217, 12/19/56.

§ 1.662(b)-1 Character of amounts; when no charitable contributions are made.

In determining the amount includible in the gross income of a beneficiary, the amounts which are determined under section 662(a) and §§ 1.662(a)-1 through 1.662(a)-4 shall have the same character in the hands of the beneficiary as in the hands of the estate or trust. The amounts are treated as consisting of the same proportion of each class of items entering into the computation of distributable net income as the total of each class bears to the total distributable net income of the estate or trust unless the terms of the governing instrument specifically allocate different classes of income to different beneficiaries, or unless local law requires such an allocation. For this purpose, the principles contained in § 1.652(b)-1 shall apply.

T.D. 6217, 12/19/56.

§ 1.662(b)-2 Character of amounts; when charitable contributions are made.

Caution: The Treasury has not yet amended Reg § 1.662(b)-2 to reflect changes made by P.L. 99-514.

When a charitable contribution is made, the principles contained in §§ 1.652(b)-1 and 1.662(b)-1 generally apply. However, before the allocation of other deductions among the items of distributable net income, the charitable contributions deduction allowed under section 642(c) is (in the absence of specific allocation under the terms of the governing instrument or the requirement under local law of a different allocation) allocated among the classes of income entering into the computation of estate or trust income in accordance with the rules set forth in paragraph (b) of § 1.643(a)-5. In the application of the preceding sentence, for the purpose of allocating items of income and deductions to beneficiaries to whom income is required to be distributed currently, the amount of the charitable contributions deduction is disregarded to the extent that it exceeds the income of the trust for the taxable year reduced by amounts for the taxable year required to be distributed currently. The application of this section may be illustrated by the following examples (of which example (1) is illustrative of the preceding sentence):

Example (1). (a) A trust instrument provides that $30,000 of its income must be distributed currently to A, and the balance may either be distributed to B, distributed to a designated charity, or accumulated. Accumulated income may be distributed to B and to the charity. The trust for its taxable year has $40,000 of taxable interest and $10,000 of tax-exempt income, with no expenses. The trustee distributed $30,000 to A, $50,000 to charity X, and $10,000 to B.

(b) Distributable net income for the purpose of determining the character of the distribution to A is $30,000 (the charitable contributions deduction, for this purpose, being taken into account only to the extent of $20,000, the difference between the income of the trust for the taxable year, $50,000, and the amount required to be distributed currently, $30,000).

(c) The charitable contributions deduction taken into account, $20,000, is allocated proportionately to the items of income of the trust, $16,000 to taxable interest and $4,000 to tax-exempt income.

(d) Under section 662(a)(1), the amount of income required to be distributed currently to A is $30,000, which consists of the balance of these items, $24,000 of taxable interest and $6,000 of tax-exempt income.

(e) In determining the amount to be included in the gross income of B under section 662 for the taxable year, however, the entire charitable contributions deduction is taken into account, with the result that there is no distributable net income and therefore no amount to be included in gross income.

(f) See subpart D (section 665 and following), part I, subchapter J, chapter 1 of the Code for application of the throwback provisions to the distribution made to B.

Example (2). The net income of a trust is payable to A for life, with the remainder to a charitable organization. Under the terms of the trust instrument and local law capital gains are added to corpus. During the taxable year the trust receives dividends of $10,000 and realized a long-term capital gain of $10,000, for which a long-term capital gain deduction of $5,000 is allowed under section 1202. Since under the trust instrument and local law the capital gains are allocated to the charitable organization, and since the capital gain deduction is directly attributable to the capital gain, the charitable contributions deduction and the capital gain deduction are both allocable to the capital gain, and dividends in the amount of $10,000 are allocable to A.

T.D. 6217, 12/19/56.

§ 1.662(c)-1 Different taxable years.

Caution: The Treasury has not yet amended Reg § 1.662(c)-1 to reflect changes made by P.L. 99-514.

If a beneficiary has a different taxable year (as defined in section 441 or 442) from the taxable year of an estate or trust, the amount he is required to include in gross income in accordance with section 662(a) and (b) is based upon the distributable net income of the estate or trust and the amounts properly paid, credited, or required to be distributed to the beneficiary for any taxable year or years of the estate or trust ending with or within his taxable year. This rule applies as to so-called short taxable years as well as taxable years of normal duration. Income of an estate or trust for its taxable year or years is determined in accordance with its method of accounting and without regard to that of the beneficiary.

T.D. 6217, 12/19/56.

§ 1.662(c)-2 Death of individual beneficiary.

If an amount specified in section 662(a)(1) or (2) is paid, credited, or required to be distributed by an estate or trust for a taxable year which does not end with or within the last taxable year of a beneficiary (because of the beneficiary's death), the extent to which the amount is included in the gross income of the beneficiary for his last taxable year or in the gross income of his estate is determined by the computations under section 662 for the taxable year of the estate or trust in which his last taxable year ends. Thus, the distributable net income and the amounts paid, credited, or required to be distributed for the taxable year of the estate or trust, determine the extent to which the amounts paid, credited, or required to be distributed to the beneficiary are included in his gross income for his last taxable year or in the gross income of his estate. (Section 662(c) does not apply to such amounts.) The gross income for the last taxable year of a beneficiary on the cash basis includes only income actually distributed to the beneficiary before his death. Income required to be distributed, but in fact distributed to his estate, is included in the gross income of the estate as income in respect of a decedent under section 691. See paragraph (e) of § 1.663(c)-3 with respect to separate share treatment for the periods before and after the death of a trust's beneficiary.

T.D. 6217, 12/19/56.

§ 1.662(c)-3 Termination of existence of other beneficiaries.

If the existence of a beneficiary which is not an individual terminates, the amount to be included under section 662(a) in its gross income for the last taxable year is computed with reference to §§ 1.662(c)-1 and 1.662(c)-2 as if the beneficiary were a deceased individual, except that income required to be distributed prior to the termination but actually distributed to the beneficiary's successor in interest is included in the beneficiary's income for its last taxable year.

T.D. 6217, 12/19/56.

§ 1.662(c)-4 Illustration of the provisions of sections 661 and 662.

Caution: The Treasury has not yet amended Reg § 1.662(c)-4 to reflect changes made by P.L. 99-514.

The provisions of sections 661 and 662 may be illustrated in general by the following example:

Example. (a) Under the terms of a testamentary trust one-half of the trust income is to be distributed currently to W, the decedent's wife, for her life. The remaining trust income may, in the trustee's discretion, either be paid to D, the grantor's daughter, paid to designated charities, or accumulated. The trust is to terminate at the death of W and the principal will then be payable to D. No provision is made in the trust instrument with respect to depreciation of rental property. Capital gains are allocable to the principal account under the applicable local law. The trust and both beneficiaries file returns on the calendar year basis. The records of the fiduciary show the following items of income and deduction for the taxable year 1955:

Rents	$50,000
Dividends of domestic corporations	50,000
Tax-exempt interest	20,000
Partially tax-exempt interest	10,000
Capital gains (long term)	20,000
Depreciation of rental property	10,000
Expenses attributable to rental income	15,400
Trustee's commissions allocable to income account	2,800
Trustee's commissions allocable to principal account	1,100

(b) The income for trust accounting purposes is $111,800, and the trustee distributes one-half ($55,900) to W and in his discretion makes a contribution of one-quarter ($27,950) to charity X and distributes the remaining one-quarter ($27,950) to D. The total of the distributions to beneficiaries is $83,850, consisting of (1) income required to be distributed currently to W of $55,900 and (2) other amounts properly paid or credited to D of $27,950. The income for trust accounting purposes of $111,800 is determined as follows:

Rents		$50,000
Dividends		50,000
Tax-exempt interest		20,000
Partially tax-exempt interest		10,000
Total		130,000
Less:		
Rental expenses	$15,400	
Trustee's commissions allocable to income account	2,800	
		18,200
Income as computed under section 643(b)		111,800

(c) The distributable net income of the trust as computed under section 643(a) is $82,750, determined as follows:

Rents			$ 50,000
Dividends			50,000
Partially tax-exempt interest			10,000
Tax-exempt interest		$20,000	
Less:			
Trustee's commissions allocable thereto (20,000/130,000 of $3,900)	$ 600		
Charitable contributions allocable thereto (20,000/130,000 of $27,950)	4,300		
		4,900	
			15,100
Total			125,100
Deductions:			
Rental expenses		$15,400	
Trustee's commissions ($3,900 less $600 allocated to tax-exempt interest)		3,300	
Charitable deduction ($27,95 u0 less $4,300 attributable to tax-exempt interest)		23,650	
			42,350
Distributable net income			82,750

In computing the distributable net income of $82,750, the taxable income of the trust was computed with the following modifications: No deductions were allowed for distributions to beneficiaries and for personal exemption of the trust (section 643 (a)(1) and (2)); capital gains were excluded and no deduction under section 1202 (relating to the 50 percent deduction for long-term capital gains) was taken in account (section 643(a)(3)); and the tax-exempt interest (as adjusted for expenses and charitable contributions) and the dividend exclusion of $50 were included (section 643(a)(5) and (7)).

(d) Inasmuch as the distributable net income of $82,750 as determined under section 643(a) is less than the sum of the amounts distributed to W and D of $83,850, the deduction allowable to the trust under section 661(a) is such distributable net income as modified under section 661(c) to exclude therefrom the items of income not included in the gross income of the trust, as follows:

Distributable net income		$82,750
Less:		
Tax-exempt interest (as adjusted for expenses and the charitable contributions)	$15,100	
Dividend exclusion allowable under section 116	$ 50	
		$15,150
Deduction allowable under section 661(a)		67,600

(e) For the purpose of determining the character of the amounts deductible under section 642(c) and section 661(a), the trustee elected to offset the trustee's commissions (other than the portion required to be allocated to tax-exempt interest) against the rental income. The following table shows the determination of the character of the amounts deemed distributed to beneficiaries and contributed to charity:

	Rental income	Taxable dividends	Excluded dividends	Partially tax-exempt interest	Tax-exempt interest	Total
Trust income	$50,000	$49,950	$50	$20,000	$10,000	$130,000
Less:						
Charitable contributions	10,750	10,750		4,300	2,150	27,950
Rental expenses	15,400					15,400
Trustee's commissions	3,300			600		3,900
Total deductions	29,450	10,750	0	4,900	2,150	47,250
Amounts distributable to beneficiaries	20,550	39,200	50	15,100	7,850	82,750

The character of the charitable contribution is determined by multiplying the total charitable contribution ($27,950) by a fraction consisting of each item of trust income, respectively, over the total trust income, except that no part of the dividends excluded from gross income are deemed included in the charitable contribution. For example, the charitable contribution is deemed to consist of rents of $10,750 (50,000/130,000 × $27,950).

(f) The taxable income of the trust is $9,900 determined as follows:

Rental income		$ 50,000
Dividends ($50,000 less $50 exclusion)		49,950
Partially tax-exempt interest		10,000
Capital gains		20,000
Gross income		129,950
Deductions:		
Rental expenses	$15,400	
Trustee's commissions	3,300	
Charitable contributions	23,650	
Capital gain deduction	10,000	
Distributions to beneficiaries	67,600	
Personal exemption	100	
		120,050
Taxable income		9,900

(g) In computing the amount includible in W's gross income under section 662(a)(1), the $55,900 distribution to her is deemed to be composed of the following proportions of the items of income deemed to have been distributed to the beneficiaries by the trust (see paragraph (e) of this example):

Rents (20,550/82,750 × $55,900)	$13,882
Dividends (39,250/82,750 × $55,900)	26,515
Partially tax-exempt interest (7,850/82,750 × $55,900)	5,303
Tax-exempt interest (15,100/82,750 × $55,900)	10,200
Total	55,900

Accordingly, W will exclude $10,200 of tax-exempt interest from gross income and will receive the credits and exclusion for dividends received and for partially tax-exempt interest provided in sections 34, 116, and 35, respectively, with respect to the dividends and partially tax-exempt interest deemed to have been distributed to her, her share of the dividends being aggregated with other dividends received by her for purposes of the dividend credit and exclusion. In addition, she may deduct a share of the depreciation deduction proportionate to the trust income allocable to her; that is, one-half of the total depreciation deduction, or $5,000.

(h) Inasmuch as the sum of the amount of income required to be distributed currently to W ($55,900) and the other amounts properly paid, credited, or required to be distributed to D ($27,950) exceeds the distributable net income ($82,750) of the trust as determined under section 643(a), D is deemed to have received $26,850 ($82,750 less $55,900) for income tax purposes. The character of the amounts deemed distributed to her is determined as follows:

Rents (20,550/82,750 × $26,850)	$ 6,668
Dividends (39,250/82,750 × $26,850)	12,735
Partially tax-exempt interest (7,850/82,750 × $26,850)	2,547
Tax-exempt interest (15,100/82,750 × $26,850)	4,900
Total	26,850

Accordingly, D will exclude $4,900 of tax-exempt interest from gross income and will receive the credits and exclusion for dividends received and for partially tax-exempt interest provided in sections 34, 116, and 35, respectively, with respect to the dividends and partially tax-exempt interest deemed to have been distributed to her, her share of the dividends being aggregated with other dividends received by her for purposes of the dividend credit and exclusion. In addition, she may deduct a share of the depreciation deduction proportionate to the trust income allocable to her; that is, one-fourth of the total depreciation deduction, or $2,500.

(i) [Reserved]

(j) The remaining $2,500 of the depreciation deduction is allocated to the amount distributed to charity X and is hence nondeductible by the trust, W, or D. (See § 1.642(e)-1.)

T.D. 6217, 12/19/56.

§ 1.663(a)-1 Special rules applicable to sections 661 and 662; exclusions; gifts, bequests, etc.

Caution: The Treasury has not yet amended Reg § 1.663(a)-1 to reflect changes made by P.L. 91-172.

(a) In general. A gift or bequest of a specific sum of money or of specific property, which is required by the specific terms of the will or trust instrument and is properly paid or credited to a beneficiary, is not allowed as a deduction to an estate or trust under section 661 and is not included in the gross income of a beneficiary under section 662, unless under the terms of the will or trust instrument the gift or bequest is to be paid or credited to the recipient in more than three installments. Thus, in order for a gift or bequest to be excludable from the gross income of the recipient, (1) it must qualify as a gift or bequest of a specific sum of money or of specific property (see paragraph (b) of this section), and (2) the terms of the governing instrument must not provide for its payment in more than three installments (see paragraph (c) of this section). The date when the estate came into existence or the date when the trust was created is immaterial.

(b) Definition of a gift or bequest of a specific sum of money or of specific property. *(1)* In order to qualify as a gift or bequest of a specific sum of money or of specific property under section 663(a), the amount of money or the identity of the specific property must be ascertainable under the terms of a testator's will as of the date of his death, or under the terms of an inter vivos trust instrument as of the date of the inception of the trust. For example, bequests to a decedent's son of the decedent's interest in a partnership and to his daughter of a sum of money equal to the value of the partnership interest are bequests of specific property and of a specific sum of money, respectively. On the other hand, a bequest to the decedent's spouse of money or property, to be selected by the decedent's executor, equal in value to a fraction of the decedent's "adjusted gross estate" is neither a bequest of a specific sum of money or of specific property. The identity of the property and the amount of money specified in the preceding sentence are dependent both on the exercise of the executor's discretion and on the payment of administration expenses and other charges, neither of which are facts existing on the date of the decedent's death. It is immaterial that the value of the bequest is determinable after the decedent's death before the bequest is satisfied (so that gain or loss may be realized by the estate in the transfer of property in satisfaction of it).

(2) The following amounts are not considered as gifts or bequests of a sum of money or of specific property within the meaning of this paragraph:

(i) An amount which can be paid or credited only from the income of an estate or trust, whether from the income for the year of payment or crediting, or from the income accumulated from a prior year;

(ii) An annuity, or periodic gifts of specific property in lieu of or having the effect of an annuity;

(iii) A residuary estate or the corpus of a trust; or

(iv) A gift or bequest paid in a lump sum or in not more than three installments, if the gift or bequest is required to be paid in more than three installments under the terms of the governing instrument.

(3) The provisions of subparagraphs (1) and (2) of this paragraph may be illustrated by the following examples, in which it is assumed that the gift or bequest is not required to be made in more than three installments (see paragraph (c)):

Example (1). Under the terms of a will, a legacy of $5,000 was left to A, 1,000 shares of X company stock was left to W, and the balance of the estate was to be divided equally between W and B. No provision was made in the will for the disposition of income of the estate during the period of administration. The estate had income of $25,000 during the taxable year 1954, which was accumulated and added to corpus for estate accounting purposes. During the taxable year, the executor paid the legacy of $5,000 in a lump sum to A, transferred the X company stock to W, and made no other distributions to beneficiaries. The distributions to A and W qualify for the exclusion under section 663(a)(1).

Example (2). Under the terms of a will, the testator's estate was to be distributed to A. No provision was made in the will for the distribution of the estate's income during the period of administration. The estate had income of $50,000 for the taxable year. The estate distributed to A stock with a basis of $40,000 and with a fair market value of $40,000 on the date of distribution. No other distributions were made during the year. The distribution does not qualify for the exclusion under section 663(a)(1), because it is not a specific gift to A required by the terms of the will. Accordingly, the fair market value of the property ($40,000) represents a distribution within the meaning of sections 661(a) and 662(a) (see § 1.661(a)-2(c)).

Example (3). Under the terms of a trust instrument, trust income is to be accumulated for a period of 10 years. During the eleventh year, the trustee is to distribute $10,000 to B, payable from income or corpus, and $10,000 to C, payable out of accumulated income. The trustee is to distribute the balance of the accumulated income to A. Thereafter, A is to receive all the current income until the trust terminates. Only the distribution to B would qualify for the exclusion under section 663(a)(1).

(4) A gift or bequest of a specific sum of money or of specific property is not disqualified under this paragraph solely because its payment is subject to a condition. For example, provision for a payment by a trust to beneficiary A of $10,000 when he reaches age 25, and $10,000 when he reaches age 30, with payment over to B of any amount not paid to A because of his death, is a gift to A of a specific sum of money payable in two installments, within the meaning of this paragraph, even though the exact amount payable to A cannot be ascertained with certainty under the terms of the trust instrument.

(c) Installment payments. *(1)* In determining whether a gift or bequest of a specific sum of money or of specific property, as defined in paragraph (b) of this section, is required to be paid or credited to a particular beneficiary in more than three installments—

(i) Gifts or bequests of articles for personal use (such as personal and household effects, automobiles, and the like) are disregarded.

(ii) Specifically devised real property, the title to which passes directly from the decedent to the devisee under local law, is not taken into account, since it would not constitute an amount paid, credited, or required to be distributed under section 661 (see paragraph (e) of § 1.661(a)-2).

(iii) All gifts and bequests under a decedent's will (which are not disregarded pursuant to subdivisions (i) and (ii) of this subparagraph) for which no time of payment or crediting is specified, and which are to be paid or credited in the ordinary course of administration of the decedent's estate, are considered as required to be paid or credited in a single installment.

(iv) All gifts and bequests (which are not disregarded pursuant to subdivisions (i) and (ii) of this subparagraph) payable at any one specified time under the terms of the governing instrument are taken into account as a single installment.

For purposes of determining the number of installments paid or credited to a particular beneficiary, a decedent's estate and a testamentary trust shall each be treated as a separate entity.

(2) The application of the rules stated in subparagraph (1) of this paragraph may be illustrated by the following examples:

Example (1). (i) Under the terms of a decedent's will, $10,000 in cash, household furniture, a watch, an automobile, 100 shares of X company stock, 1,000 bushels of grain, 500 head of cattle, and a farm (title to which passed directly to A under local law) are bequeathed or devised outright to A. The will also provides for the creation of a trust for the benefit of A, under the terms of which there are required to be distributed to A, $10,000 in cash and 100 shares of Y company stock when he reaches 25 years of age, $25,000 in cash and 200 shares of Y company stock when he reaches 30 years of age, and $50,000 in cash and 300 shares of Y company stock when he reaches 35 years of age.

(ii) The furniture, watch, automobile, and the farm are excluded in determining whether any gift or bequest is required to be paid or credited to A in more than three installments. These items qualify for the exclusion under section 663(a)(1) regardless of the treatment of the other items of property bequeathed to A.

(iii) The $10,000 in cash, the shares of X company stock, the grain, the cattle and the assets required to create the trust, to be paid or credited by the estate to A and the trust are considered as required to be paid or credited in a single installment to each, regardless of the manner of payment or distribution by the executor, since no time of payment or crediting is specified in the will. The $10,000 in cash and shares of Y company stock required to be distributed by the trust to A when he is 25 years old are considered as required to be paid or distributed as one installment under the trust. Likewise, the distributions to be made by the trust to A when he is 30 and 35 years old are each considered as one installment under the trust. Since the total number of installments to be made by the estate does not exceed three, all of the items of money and property distributed by the estate qualify for the exclusion under section 663(a)(1). Similarly, the three distributions by the trust qualify.

Example (2). Assume the same facts as in example (1), except that another distribution of a specified sum of money is required to be made by the trust to A when he becomes 40 years old. This distribution would also qualify as an installment, thus making four installments in all under the trust. None of the gifts to A under the trust would qualify for the exclusion under section 663(a)(1). The situation as to the estate, however, would not be changed.

Example (3). A trust instrument provides that A and B are each to receive $75,000 in installments of $25,000, to be paid in alternate years. The trustee distributes $25,000 to A in 1954, 1956, and 1958, and to B in 1955, 1957, and 1959. The gifts to A and B qualify for exclusion under section 663(a)(1), although a total of six payments is made. The gifts of $75,000 to each beneficiary are to be separately treated.

T.D. 6217, 12/19/56, amend T.D. 8849, 12/27/99.

§ 1.663(a)-2 Charitable, etc., distributions.

Any amount paid, permanently set aside, or to be used for the charitable, etc., purposes specified in section 642(c) and which is allowable as a deduction under that section is not allowed as a deduction to an estate or trust under section 661 or treated as an amount distributed for purposes of determining the amounts includible in gross income of beneficiaries under section 662. Amounts paid, permanently set aside, or to be used for charitable, etc., purposes are deductible by estates or trusts only as provided in section 642(c). For purposes of this section, the deduction provided in section 642(c) is computed without regard to the provisions of section 508(d), section 681, or section 4948(c)(4) (concerning unrelated business income private foundations).

T.D. 6217, 12/19/56, amend T.D. 7428, 8/13/76.

§ 1.663(a)-3 Denial of double deduction.

Caution: The Treasury has not yet amended Reg § 1.663(a)-3 to reflect changes made by P.L. 91-172.

No amount deemed to have been distributed to a beneficiary in a preceding year under section 651 or 661 is included in amounts falling within section 661(a) or 662(a). For example, assume that all of the income of a trust is required to be distributed currently to beneficiary A and both the trust and A report on the calendar year basis. For administrative convenience, the trustee distributes in January and February 1956 a portion of the income of the trust required to be distributed in 1955. The portion of the income for 1955 which was distributed by the trust in 1956 may not be claimed as a deduction by the trust for 1956 since it is deductible by the trust and includible in A's gross income for the taxable year 1955.

T.D. 6217, 12/19/56.

§ 1.663(b)-1 Distributions in first 65 days of taxable year; scope.

Caution: The Treasury has not yet amended Reg § 1.663(b)-1 to reflect changes made by P.L. 105-34.

(a) Taxable years beginning after December 31, 1968. *(1) General rule.* With respect to taxable years beginning after December 31, 1968, the fiduciary of a trust may elect under section 633(b) to treat any amount or portion thereof that is properly paid or credited to a beneficiary within the first 65 days following the close of the taxable year as an amount that was properly paid or credited on the last day of such taxable year.

(2) Effect of election. (i) An election is effective only with respect to the taxable year for which the election is made. In the case of distributions made after May 8, 1972, the amount to which the election applies shall not exceed—

(a) The amount of income of the trust (as defined in § 1.643(b)-1) for the taxable year for which the election is made or,

(b) The amount of distributable net income of the trust (as defined in §§ 1.643(a)-1 through 1.643(a)-7) for such taxable year, if greater, reduced by any amounts paid, credited, or required to be distributed in such taxable year other than those amounts considered paid or credited in a preceding taxable year by reason of section 663(b) and this section. An election shall be made for each taxable year for which the treatment is desired. The application of this paragraph may be illustrated by the following example:

Example. X Trust, a calendar year trust, has $1,000 of income (as defined in § 1.643(b)-1) and $800 of distributable net income (as defined in §§ 1.643(a)-1 through 1.643(a)-7) in 1972. The trust properly pays $550 to A, a beneficiary, on January 15, 1972, which the trustee elects to treat under section 663(b) as paid on December 31, 1971. The trust also properly pays to A $600 on July 19, 1972, and $450 on January 17, 1973. For 1972, the maximum amount that may be elected under this subdivision to be treated as properly paid or credited on the last day of 1972 is $400 ($1,000 – $600). The $550 paid on January 15, 1972, does not reduce the maximum amount to which the election may apply, because that amount is treated as properly paid on December 31, 1971.

(ii) If an election is made with respect to a taxable year of a trust, this section shall apply only to those amounts which are properly paid or credited within the first 65 days following such year and which are so designated by the fiduciary in his election. Any amount considered under section 663(b) as having been distributed in the preceding taxable year shall be so treated for all purposes. For example, in determining the beneficiary's tax liability, such amount shall be considered as having been received by the beneficiary in his taxable year in which or with which the last day of the preceding taxable year of the trust ends.

(b) Taxable years beginning before January 1, 1969. With respect to taxable years of a trust beginning before January 1, 1969, the fiduciary of the trust may elect under section 663(b) to treat distributions within the first 65 days following such taxable year as amounts which were taxable year, if:

(1) The trust was in existence prior to January 1, 1954;

(2) An amount in excess of the income of the immediately preceding taxable year may not (under the terms of the governing instrument) be distributed in any taxable year; and

(3) The fiduciary elects (as provided in § 1.663(b)-2) to have section 663(b) apply.

T.D. 6217, 12/19/56, amend T.D. 7204, 8/24/72.

§ 1.663(b)-2 Election.

Caution: The Treasury has not yet amended Reg § 1.663(b)-2 to reflect changes made by P.L. 105-34.

(a) Manner and time of election; irrevocability. *(1) When return is required to be filed.* If a trust return is required to be filed for the taxable year of the trust for which the election is made, the election shall be made in the appropriate place on such return. The election under this subparagraph shall be made not later than the time prescribed by law for filing such return (including extensions thereof). Such election shall become irrevocable after the last day prescribed for making it.

(2) When no return is required to be filed. If no return is required to be filed for the taxable year of the trust for which the election is made, the election shall be made in a statement filed with the internal revenue office with which a return by such trust would be filed if such trust were required to file a return for such taxable year. See section 6091 and the regulations thereunder for place for filing returns. The election under this subparagraph shall be made not later than the time prescribed by law for filing a return if such time prescribed by law for filing a return if such trust were required to file a return for such taxable year. Such election shall become irrevocable after the last day prescribed for making it.

(b) Elections under prior law. Elections made pursuant to section 663(b) prior to its amendment by section 331(b) of the Tax Reform Act of 1969 (83 Stat. 598), which, under prior law, were irrevocable for the taxable year for which the election was made and all subsequent years, are not effective for taxable years beginning after December 31, 1968. In the case of a trust for which an election was made under prior law, the fiduciary shall make the election for each taxable year beginning after December 31, 1968, for which the treatment provided by section 663(b) is desired.

T.D. 6217, 12/19/56, amend T.D. 7204, 8/24/72.

§ 1.663(c)-1 Separate shares treated as separate trusts or as separate estates; in general.

Caution: The Treasury has not yet amended Reg § 1.663(c)-1 to reflect changes made by P.L. 91-172.

(a) If a single trust (or estates) has more than one beneficiary, and if different beneficiaries have substantially separate and independent shares, their shares are treated as separate trusts (or estates) for the sole purpose of determining the amount of distributable net income allocable to the respective beneficiaries under sections 661 and 662. Application of this rule will be significant in, for example, situations in which income is accumulated for beneficiary A but a distribution is made to beneficiary B of both income and corpus in an amount exceeding the share of income that would be distributable to B had there been separate trusts (or estates). In the absence of a separate share rule B would be taxed on income which is accumulated for A. The division of distributable net income into separate shares will limit the tax liability of B. Section 663(c) does not affect the principles of applicable law in situations in which a single trust (or estate) instrument creates not one but several separate trusts (or estates), as opposed to separate shares in the same trust (or estate) within the meaning of this section.

(b) The separate share rule does not permit the treatment of separate shares as separate trusts (or estates) for any purpose other than the application of distributable net income. It does not, for instance, permit the treatment of separate shares as separate trusts (or estates) for purposes of:

(1) The filing of returns and payment of tax,

(2) The deduction of personal exemption under section 642(b), and

(3) The allowance to beneficiaries succeeding to the trust (or estate) property of excess deductions and unused net operating loss and capital loss carryovers on termination of the trust (or estate) under section 642(h).

(c) The separate share rule may be applicable even though separate and independent accounts are not maintained and are not required to be maintained for each share on the books of account of the trust (or estate), and even though no physical segregation of assets is made or required.

(d) Separate share treatment is not elective. Thus, if a trust (or estate) is properly treated as having separate and independent shares, such treatment must prevail in all taxable years of the trust (or estate) unless an event occurs as a result of which the terms of the trust instrument and the requirements of proper administration require different treatment.

T.D. 6217, 12/19/56, amend T.D. 8849, 12/27/99.

§ 1.663(c)-2 Computation of distributable net income.

Caution: The Treasury has not yet amended Reg § 1.663(c)-2 to reflect changes made by P.L. 91-172.

(a) When separate shares come into existence. A separate share comes into existence upon the earliest moment that a fiduciary may reasonably determine, based upon the known facts, that a separate economic interest exists.

(b) Computation of distributable net income for each separate share. *(1) General rule.* The amount of distributable net income for any share under section 663(c) is computed as if each share constituted a separate trust or estate. Accordingly, each separate share shall calculate its distributable net income based upon its portion of gross income that is includible in distributable net income and its portion of any applicable deductions or losses.

(2) Section 643(b) income. This paragraph (b)(2) governs the allocation of the portion of gross income includible in distributable net income that is income within the meaning of section 643(b). Such gross income is allocated among the separate shares in accordance with the amount of income that each share is entitled to under the terms of the governing instrument or applicable local law.

(3) Income in respect of a decedent. This paragraph (b)(3) governs the allocation of the portion of gross income includible in distributable net income that is income in respect of a decedent within the meaning of section 691(a) and is not income within the meaning of section 643(b). Such gross income is allocated among the separate shares that could potentially be funded with these amounts irrespective of whether the share is entitled to receive any income under the terms of the governing instrument or applicable local law. The amount of such gross income allocated to each share is based on the relative value of each share that could potentially be funded with such amounts.

(4) Gross income not attributable to cash. This paragraph (b)(4) governs the allocation of the portion of gross income includible in distributable net income that is not attributable to cash received by the estate or trust (for example, original issue discount, a distributive share of partnership tax items, and the pro rata share of an S corporation's tax items). Such gross income is allocated among the separate shares in the same proportion as section 643(b) income from the same source would be allocated under the terms of the governing instrument or applicable local law.

(5) Deductions and losses. Any deduction or any loss which is applicable solely to one separate share of the trust or estate is not available to any other share of the same trust or estate.

(c) Computations and valuations. For purposes of calculating distributable net income for each separate share, the fiduciary must use a reasonable and equitable method to make the allocations, calculations, and valuations required by paragraph (b) of this section.

T.D. 6217, 12/19/56, amend T.D. 8849, 12/27/99.

§ 1.663(c)-3 Applicability of separate share rule to certain trusts.

Caution: The Treasury has not yet amended Reg § 1.663(c)-3 to reflect changes made by P.L. 105-34.

(a) The applicability of the separate share rule provided by section 663(c) to trusts other than qualified revocable trusts within the meaning of section 645(b)(1) will generally depend upon whether distributions of the trust are to be made in substantially the same manner as if separate trusts had been created. Thus, if an instrument directs a trustee to divide the testator's residuary estate into separate shares (which under applicable law do not constitute separate trusts) for each of the testator's children and the trustee is given discretion, with respect to each share, to distribute or accumulate income or to distribute principal or accumulated income, or to do both, separate shares will exist under section 663(c). In determining whether separate shares exist, it is immaterial whether the principal and any accumulated income of each share is ultimately distributable to the beneficiary of such share, to his descendants, to his appointees under a general or special power of appointment, or to any other beneficiaries (including a charitable organization) designated to receive his share of the trust and accumulated income upon termination of the beneficiary's interest in the share. Thus, a separate share may exist if the instrument provides that upon the death of the beneficiary of the share, the share will be added to the shares of the other beneficiaries of the trust.

(b) Separate share treatment will not be applied to a trust or portion of a trust subject to a power to:

(1) Distribute, apportion, or accumulate income, or

(2) Distribute corpus

to or for one or more beneficiaries within a group or class of beneficiaries, unless payment of income, accumulated income, or corpus of a share of one beneficiary cannot affect the proportionate share of income, accumulated income, or corpus of any shares of the other beneficiaries, or unless substantially proper adjustment must thereafter be made (under the governing instrument) so that substantially separate and independent shares exist.

(c) A share may be considered as separate even though more than one beneficiary has an interest in it. For example, two beneficiaries may have equal, disproportionate, or indeterminate interests in one share which is separate and independent from another share in which one or more beneficiaries have an interest. Likewise, the same person may be a beneficiary of more than one separate share.

(d) Separate share treatment may be given to a trust or portion of a trust otherwise qualifying under this section if the trust or portion of a trust is subject to a power to pay out to a beneficiary of a share (of such trust or portion) an amount of corpus in excess of his proportionate share of the corpus of the trust if the possibility of exercise of the power is remote. For example, if the trust is subject to a power to invade the entire corpus for the health, education, support, or maintenance of A, separate share treatment is applied if exercise of the power requires consideration of A's other income which is so substantial as to make the possibility of exercise of the power remote. If instead it appears that A and B have separate shares in a trust, subject to a power to invade the entire corpus for the comfort, pleasure, desire, or happiness of A, separate share treatment shall not be applied.

(e) For taxable years ending before January 1, 1979, the separate share rule may also be applicable to successive interests in point of time, as for instance in the case of a trust providing for a life estate to A and a second life estate or outright remainder to B. In such a case, in the taxable year of a trust in which a beneficiary dies items of income and deduction properly allocable under trust accounting principles to the period before a beneficiary's death are attributed to one share, and those allocable to the period after the beneficiary's death are attributed to the other share. Separate share treatment is not available to a succeeding interest, however, with respect to distributions which would otherwise be deemed distributed in a taxable year of the earlier interest under the throwback provisions of subpart D (section 665 and following), part I, subchapter J, chapter 1 of the Code. The application of this paragraph may be illustrated by the following example:

Example. A trust instrument directs that the income of a trust is to be paid to A for her life. After her death income may be distributed to B or accumulated. A dies on June 1, 1956. The trust keeps its books on the basis of the calendar year. The trust instrument permits invasions of corpus for the benefit of A and B, and an invasion of corpus was in fact made for A's benefit in 1956. In determining the distributable net income of the trust for the purpose of determining the amounts includible in A's income, income and deductions properly allocable to the period before A's death are treated as income and deductions of a separate share, and for that purpose no account is taken of income and deductions allocable to the period after A's death.

T.D. 6217, 12/19/56, amend T.D. 7633, 7/19/79, T.D. 8849, 12/27/99.

§ 1.663(c)-4 Applicability of separate share rule to estates and qualified revocable trusts.

(a) General rule. The applicability of the separate share rule provided by section 663(c) to estates and qualified revocable trusts within the meaning of section 645(b)(1) will generally depend upon whether the governing instrument and applicable local law create separate economic interests in one beneficiary or class of beneficiaries of such estate or trust. Ordinarily, a separate share exists if the economic interests of the beneficiary or class of beneficiaries neither affect nor are affected by the economic interests accruing to another beneficiary or class of beneficiaries. Separate shares include, for example, the income on bequeathed property if the recipient of the specific bequest is entitled to such income and a surviving spouse's elective share that under local law is entitled to income and appreciation or depreciation. Furthermore, a qualified revocable trust for which an election is made under section 645 is always a separate share of the estate and may itself contain two or more separate shares. Conversely, a gift or bequest of a specific sum of money or of property as defined in section 663(a)(1) is not a separate share.

(b) Special rule for certain types of beneficial interests. Notwithstanding the provisions of paragraph (a) of this section, a surviving spouse's elective share that under local law is determined as of the date of the decedent's death and is not entitled to income or any appreciation or depreciation is a separate share. Similarly, notwithstanding the provisions of paragraph (a) of this section, a pecuniary formula bequest that, under the terms of the governing instrument or applicable local law, is not entitled to income or to share in appreciation or depreciation constitutes a separate share if the governing instrument does not provide that it is to be paid or credited in more than three installments.

(c) Shares with multiple beneficiaries and beneficiaries of multiple shares. A share may be considered as separate even though more than one beneficiary has an interest in it. For example, two beneficiaries may have equal, disproportionate, or indeterminate interests in one share which is economically separate and independent from another share in which one or more beneficiaries have an interest. Moreover, the same person may be a beneficiary of more than one separate share.

T.D. 8849, 12/27/99.

§ 1.663(c)-5 Examples.

Section 663(c) may be illustrated by the following examples:

Example (1). (a) A single trust was created in 1940 for the benefit of A, B, and C, who were aged 6, 4, and 2, respectively. Under the terms of the instrument, the trust income is required to be divided into three equal shares. Each beneficiary's share of the income is to be accumulated until he becomes 21 years of age. When a beneficiary reaches the age of 21, his share of the income may thereafter be either accumulated or distributed to him in the discretion of the trustee. The trustee also has discretion to invade corpus for the benefit of any beneficiary to the extent of his share of the trust estate, and the trust instrument requires that the beneficiary's right to future income and corpus will be proportionately reduced. When each beneficiary reaches 35 years of age, his share of the trust estate shall be paid over to him. The interest in the trust estate of any beneficiary dying without issue and before he has attained the age of 35 is to be equally divided between the other beneficiaries of the trust. All expenses of the trust are allocable to income under the terms of the trust instrument.

(b) No distributions of income or corpus were made by the trustee prior to 1955, although A became 21 years of age on June 30, 1954. During the taxable year 1955, the trust has income from royalties of $20,000 and expenses of $5,000. The trustee in his discretion distributes $12,000 to A. Both A and the trust report on the calendar year basis.

(c) The trust qualifies for the separate share treatment under section 663(c) and the distributable net income must be divided into three parts for the purpose of determining the amount deductible by the trust under section 661 and the amount includible in A's gross income under section 662.

(d) The distributable net income of each share of the trust is $5,000 ($6,667 less $1,667). Since the amount ($12,000) distributed to A during 1955 exceeds the distributable net income of $5,000 allocated to his share, the trust is deemed to have distributed to him $5,000 of 1955 income and $7,000 of amounts other than 1955 income. Accordingly, the trust is allowed a deduction of $5,000 under section 661. The taxable income of the trust for 1955 is $9,900, computed as follows:

Royalties		$20,000
Deductions:		
Expenses	$5,000	
Distribution to A	5,000	
Personal exemption	100	
		10,100
Taxable income		9,900

(e) In accordance with section 662, A must include in his gross income for 1955 an amount equal to the portion ($5,000) of the distributable net income of the trust allocated to his share. Also, the excess distribution of $7,000 made by the trust is subject to the throwback provisions of subpart D (section 665 and following), part I, subchapter J, chapter 1 of the Code, and the regulations thereunder.

Example (2). (i) Facts. Testator, who dies in 2000, is survived by a spouse and two children. Testator's will contains a fractional formula bequest dividing the residuary estate between the surviving spouse and a trust for the benefit of the children. Under the fractional formula, the marital bequest constitutes 60% of the estate and the children's trust constitutes 40% of the estate. During the year, the executor makes a partial proportionate distribution of $1,000,0000, ($600,000 to the surviving spouse and $400,000 to the children's trust) and makes no other distributions. The estate receives dividend income of $20,000, and pays expenses of $8,000 that are deductible on the estate's federal income tax return.

(ii) Conclusion. The fractional formula bequests to the surviving spouse and to the children's trust are separate shares. Because Testator's will provides for fractional formula residuary bequests, the income and any appreciation in the value of the estate assets are proportionately allocated between the marital share and the trust's share. Therefore, in determining the distributable net income of each share, the income and expenses must be allocated 60% to the marital share and 40% to the trust's share. The distributable net income is $7,200 (60% of income less 60% of expenses) for the marital share and $4,800 (40% of income less 40% of expenses) for the trust's share. Because the amount distributed in partial satisfaction of each bequest exceeds the distributable net income of each share, the estate's distribution deduction under section 661 is limited to the sum of the distributable net income for both shares. The estate is allowed a distribution deduction of $12,000 ($7,200 for the marital share and $4,800 for the trust's share). As a result, the estate has zero taxable income ($20,000 income less $8,000 expenses and $12,000 distribution deduction). Under section 662, the surviving spouse and the trust must include in gross income $7,200 and $4,800, respectively.

Example (3). The facts are the same as in Example 2, except that in 2000 the executor makes the payment to partially fund the children's trust but makes no payment to the surviving spouse. The fiduciary must use a reasonable and equitable method to allocate income and expenses to the trust's share. Therefore, depending on when the distribution is made to the trust, it may no longer be reasonable or equitable to determine the distributable net income for the trust's share by allocating to it 40% of the estate's income and expenses for the year. The computation of the distributable net income for the trust's share should take into consideration that after the partial distribution the relative size of the trust's separate share is reduced and the relative size of the spouse's separate share is increased.

Example (4). (i) Facts. Testator, who dies in 2000, is survived by a spouse and one child. Testator's will provides for a pecuniary formula bequest to be paid in not more than three installments to a trust for the benefit of the child of the largest amount that can pass free of Federal estate tax and a bequest of the residuary to the surviving spouse. The will provides that the bequest to the child's trust is not entitled to any of the estate's income and does not participate in appreciation or depreciation in estate assets. During the 2000 taxable year, the estate receives dividend income of $200,000 and pays expenses of $15,000 that are deductible on the estate's federal income tax return. The executor partially funds the child's trust by distributing to it securities that have an adjusted basis to the estate of $350,000 and a fair market value of $380,000 on the date of distribution. As a result of this distribution, the estate realizes long-term capital gain of $30,000.

(ii) Conclusion. The estate has two separate shares consisting of a formula pecuniary bequest to the child's trust and a residuary bequest to the surviving spouse. Because, under the terms of the will, no estate income is allocated to the bequest to the child's trust, the distributable net income for that trust's share is zero. Therefore, with respect to the $380,000 distribution to the child's trust, the estate is allowed no deduction under section 661, and no amount is included in the trust's gross income under section 662. Because no distributions were made to the spouse, there is no need to compute the distributable net income allocable to the marital share. The taxable income of the estate for the 2000 taxable year is $214,400 ($200,000 (dividend income) plus $30,000 (capital gain) minus $15,000 (expenses) and minus $600 (personal exemption)).

Example (5). The facts are the same as in Example 4, except that during 2000 the estate reports on its federal income tax return a pro rata share of an S corporation's tax items and a distributive share of a partnership's tax items allocated on Form K-1s to the estate by the S corporation and by the partnership, respectively. Because, under the terms of the will, no estate income from the S corporation or the partnership would be allocated to the pecuniary bequest to child's trust, none of the tax items attributable to the S corporation stock or the partnership interest is allocated to the trust's separate share. Therefore, with respect to the $380,000 distribution to the trust, the estate is allowed no deduction under section 661, and no amount is included in the trust's gross income under section 662.

Example (6). The facts are the same as in Example 4, except that during 2000 the estate receives a distribution of $900,000 from the decedent's individual retirement account that is included in the estate's gross income as income in respect of a decedent under section 691(a). The entire $900,000 is allocated to corpus under applicable local law. Both the separate share for the child's trust and the separate share for the surviving spouse may potentially be funded with the proceeds from the individual retirement account. Therefore, a portion of the $900,000 gross income must be allocated to the trust's separate share. The amount allocated to the trust's share must be based upon the relative values of the two separate shares using a reasonable and equitable method. The estate is entitled to a deduction under section 661 for the portion of the $900,000 properly allocated to the trust's separate share, and the trust must include this amount in income under section 662.

Example (7). (i) Facts. Testator, who dies in 2000, is survived by a spouse and three adult children. Testator's will divides the residue of the estate equally among the three children. The surviving spouse files an election under the applicable state's elective share statute. Under this statute, a surviving spouse is entitled to one-third of the decedent's estate after the payment of debts and expenses. The statute also provides that the surviving spouse is not entitled to any of the estate's income and does not participate in appreciation or depreciation of the estate's assets. However, under the statute, the surviving spouse is entitled to interest on the elective share from the date of the court order directing the payment until the executor actually makes payment. During the estate's 2001 taxable year, the estate distributes to the surviving spouse $5,000,000 in partial satisfaction of the elective share and pays $200,000 of interest on the delayed payment of the elective share. During that year, the estate receives dividend income of $3,000,000 and pays expenses of $60,000 that are deductible on the estate's federal income tax return.

(ii) Conclusion. The estate has four separate shares consisting of the surviving spouse's elective share and each of the three children's residuary bequests. Because the surviving spouse is not entitled to any estate income under state law, none of the estate's gross income is allocated to the spouse's separate share for purposes of determining that share's distributable net income. Therefore, with respect to the $5,000,000 distribution, the estate is allowed no deduction under section 661, and no amount is included in the spouse's gross income under section 662. The $200,000 of interest paid to the spouse must be included in the spouse's gross income under section 61. Because no distributions were made to any other beneficiaries during the year, there is no need to compute the distributable net income of the other three separate shares. Thus, the taxable income of the estate for the 2000 taxable year is $2,939,400 ($3,000,000 (dividend income) minus $60,000 (expenses) and $600 (personal exemption)). The estate's $200,000 interest payment is a nondeductible personal interest expense described in section 163(h).

Example (8). The will of Testator, who dies in 2000, directs the executor to distribute the X stock and all dividends therefrom to child A and the residue of the estate to child B. The estate has two separate shares consisting of the income on the X stock bequeathed to A and the residue of the estate bequeathed to B. The bequest of the X stock meets the definition of section 663(a)(1) and therefore is not a separate share. If any distributions, other than shares of the X stock, are made during the year to either A or B, then for purposes of determining the distributable net income for the separate shares, gross income attributable to dividends on the X stock must be allocated to A's separate share and any other income must be allocated to B's separate share.

Example (9). The will of Testator, who dies in 2000, directs the executor to divide the residue of the estate equally between Testator's two children, A and B. The will directs the executor to fund A's share first with the proceeds of Testator's individual retirement account. The date of death value of the estate after the payment of debts, expenses, and estate taxes is $9,000,000. During 2000, the $900,000 balance in Testator's individual retirement account is distributed to the estate. The entire $900,000 is allocated to corpus under applicable local law. This amount is income in respect of a decedent within the meaning of section 691(a). The estate has two separate shares, one for the benefit of A and one for the benefit of B. If any distributions are made to either A or B during the year, then, for purposes of determining the distributable net income for each separate share, the $900,000 of income in respect of a decedent must be allocated to A's share.

Example (10). The facts are the same as in Example 9, except that the will directs the executor to fund A's share first with X stock valued at $3,000,000, rather than with the proceeds of the individual retirement account. The estate has two separate shares, one for the benefit of A and one for the benefit of B. If any distributions are made to either A or B during the year, then, for purposes of determining the distributable net income for each separate share, the $900,000 of gross income attributable to the proceeds from the individual retirement account must be allocated between the two shares to the extent that they could potentially be funded with those proceeds. The maximum amount of A's share that could potentially be funded with the income in respect of decedent is $1,500,000 ($4,500,000 value of share less $3,000,000 to be funded with stock) and the maximum amount of B's share that could potentially be funded with income in respect of decedent is $4,500,000. Based upon the relative values of these amounts, the gross income attributable to the proceeds of the individual retirement account is allocated $225,000 (or one-fourth) to A's share and $675,000 (or three-fourths) to B's share.

Example (11). The will of Testator, who dies in 2000, provides that after the payment of specific bequests of money, the residue of the estate is to be divided equally among the Testator's three children, A, B, and C. The will also provides that during the period of administration one-half of the income from the residue is to be paid to a designated charitable organization. After the specific bequests of money are paid, the estate initially has three equal separate shares. One share is for the benefit of the charitable organization and A, another share is for the benefit of the charitable organization and B, and the last share is for the benefit of the charitable organization and C. During the period of administration, payments of income to the charitable organization are deductible by the estate to the extent provided in section 642(c) and are not subject to the distribution provisions of sections 661 and 662.

T.D. 6217, 12/19/56, amend T.D. 8849, 12/27/99.

§ 1.663(c)-6 Effective dates.

Sections 1.663(c)-1 through 1.663(c)-5 are applicable for estates and qualified revocable trusts within the meaning of section 645(b)(1) with respect to decedents who die on or after December 28, 1999. However, for estates and qualified revocable trusts with respect to decedents who died after the date that section 1307 of the Tax Reform Act of 1997 became effective but before December 28, 1999, the IRS will accept any reasonable interpretation of the separate share provisions, including those provisions provided in 1999-11 I.R.B. 41 (see § 601.601(d)(2)(ii)(b) of this chapter). For trusts other than qualified revocable trusts, § 1.663(c)-2 is applicable for taxable years of such trusts beginning after December 28, 1999.

T.D. 8849, 12/27/99.

§ 1.664-1 Charitable remainder trusts.

Caution: The Treasury has not yet amended Reg § 1.664-1 to reflect changes made by P.L. 109-432, P.L. 99-514, P.L. 98-369, P.L. 94-455, P.L. 93-483.

(a) In general. *(1) Introduction.* (i) General description of a charitable remainder trust. Generally, a charitable remainder trust is a trust which provides for a specified distribution, at least annually, to one or more beneficiaries, at least one of which is not a charity, for life or for a term of years, with an irrevocable remainder interest to be held for the benefit of, or paid over to, charity. The specified distribution to be paid at least annually must be a sum certain which is not less than 5 percent of the initial net fair market value of all property placed in trust (in the case of a charitable remainder annuity trust) or a fixed percentage which is not less than 5 percent of the net fair market value of the trust assets, valued annually (in the case of a charitable remainder unitrust). A trust created after July 31, 1969, which is a charitable remainder trust is exempt from all of the taxes imposed by subtitle A of the Code for any taxable year of the trust except a taxable year in which it has unrelated business taxable income.

(ii) Scope. This section provides definitions, general rules governing the creation and administration of a charitable remainder trust, and rules governing the taxation of the trust and its beneficiaries. For the application of certain foundation rules to charitable remainder trusts, see paragraph (b) of this section. If the trust has unrelated business taxable income, see paragraph (c) of this section. For the treatment of distributions to recipients, see paragraph (d) of this section. For the treatment of distributions to charity, see paragraph (e) of this section. For the time limitations for amendment of governing instruments, see paragraph (f) of this section. For transitional rules under which particular requirements are inapplicable to certain trusts, see paragraph (g) of this section. Section 1.664-2 provides rules relating solely to a charitable remainder annuity trust. Section 1.664-3 provides rules relating solely to a charitable remainder unitrust. Section 1.664-4 provides rules governing the calculation of the fair market value of the remainder interest in a charitable remainder unitrust. For rules relating to the filing of returns for a charitable remainder trust, see paragraph (a)(6) of § 1.6012-3 and section 6034 and the regulations thereunder.

(iii) Definitions. As used in this section and §§ 1.664-2, 1.664-3, and 1.664-4:

(a) Charitable remainder trust. The term "charitable remainder trust" means a trust with respect to which a deduction is allowable under section 170, 2055, 2106, or 2522 and which meets the description of a charitable remainder annuity trust (as described in § 1.664-2) or a charitable remainder unitrust (as described in § 1.664-3).

(b) Annuity amount. The term "annuity amount" means the amount described in paragraph (a)(1) of § 1.664-2 which is payable, at least annually, to the beneficiary of a charitable remainder annuity trust.

(c) Unitrust amount. The term "unitrust amount" means the amount described in paragraph (a)(1) of § 1.664-3 which is payable, at least annually, to the beneficiary of a charitable remainder unitrust.

(d) Recipient. The term "recipient" means the beneficiary who receives the possession or beneficial enjoyment of the annuity amount or unitrust amount.

(e) Governing instrument. The term "governing instrument" has the same meaning as in section 508(e) and the regulations thereunder.

(2) Requirement that the trust must be either a charitable remainder annuity trust or a charitable remainder unitrust. A trust is a charitable remainder trust only if it is either a charitable remainder annuity trust in every respect or a charitable remainder unitrust in every respect. For example, a trust which provides for the payment each year to a noncharitable beneficiary of the greater of a sum certain or a fixed percentage of the annual value of the trust assets is not a charitable remainder trust inasmuch as the trust is neither a charitable remainder annuity trust (for the reason that the payment for the year may be a fixed percentage of the annual value of the trust assets which is not a "sum certain") nor a charitable remainder unitrust (for the reason that the payment for the year may be a sum certain which is not a "fixed percentage" of the annual value of the trust assets).

(3) Restrictions on investments. A trust is not a charitable remainder trust if the provisions of the trust include a provision which restricts the trustee from investing the trust assets in a manner which could result in the annual realization of a reasonable amount of income or gain from the sale or disposition of trust assets. In the case of transactions with, or for the benefit of, a disqualified person, see section 4941(d) and the regulations thereunder for rules relating to the definition of self-dealing.

(4) Requirement that trust must meet definition of and function exclusively as a charitable remainder trust from its creation. In order for a trust to be a charitable remainder trust, it must meet the definition of and function exclusively as a charitable remainder trust from the creation of the trust. Solely for the purposes of section 664 and the regulations thereunder, the trust will be deemed to be created at the earliest time that neither the grantor nor any other person is treated as the owner of the entire trust under subpart E, part

1, subchapter J, subtitle A of the Code (relating to grantors and others treated as substantial owners), but in no event prior to the time property is first transferred to the trust. For purposes of the preceding sentence, neither the grantor nor his spouse shall be treated as the owner of the trust under such subpart E merely because the grantor or his spouse is named as a recipient. See examples 1 through 3 of subparagraph (6) of this paragraph for illustrations of the foregoing rule.

(5) Rules applicable to testamentary transfers. (i) Deferral of annuity or unitrust amount. Notwithstanding subparagraph (4) of this paragraph and §§ 1.664-2 and 1.664-3, for purposes of sections 2055 and 2106 a charitable remainder trust shall be deemed created at the date of death of the decedent (even though the trust is not funded until the end of a reasonable period of administration or settlement) if the obligation to pay the annuity or unitrust amount with respect to the property passing in trust at the death of the decedent begins as of the date of death of the decedent, even though the requirement to pay such amount is deferred in accordance with the rules provided in this subparagraph. If permitted by applicable local law or authorized by the provisions of the governing instrument, the requirement to pay such amount may be deferred until the end of the taxable year of the trust in which occurs the complete funding of the trust. Within a reasonable period after such time, the trust must pay (in the case of an underpayment) or must receive from the recipient (in the case of an overpayment) the difference between—

(a) Any annuity or unitrust amounts actually paid, plus interest on such amounts computed at the rate of interest specified in paragraph (a)(5)(iv) of this section compounded annually, and

(b) The annuity or unitrust amounts payable, plus interest on such amounts computed at the rate of interest specified in paragraph (a)(5)(iv) of this section, compounded annually.

The amounts payable shall be retroactively determined by using the taxable year, valuation method, and valuation dates which are ultimately adopted by the charitable remainder trust. See subdivision (ii) of this subparagraph for rules relating to retroactive determination of the amount payable under a charitable remainder unitrust. See paragraph (d)(4) of this section for rules relating to the year of inclusion in the case of an underpayment to a recipient and the allowance of a deduction in the case of an overpayment to a recipient.

(ii) For purposes of retroactively determining the amount under subdivision (i)(b) of this subparagraph, the governing instrument of a charitable remainder unitrust may provide that the amount described in subdivision (i)(b) of this subparagraph with respect to property passing in trust at the death of the decedent for the period which begins on the date of death of the decedent and ends on the earlier of the date of death of the last recipient or the end of the taxable year of the trust in which occurs the complete funding of the trust shall be computed by multiplying—

(a) The sum of (1) the value, on the earlier of the date of death of the last recipient or the last day in such taxable year, of the property held in trust which is attributable to property passing to the trust at the death of the decedent, (2) any distributions in respect of unitrust amounts made by the trust or estate before such date, and (3) interest on such distributions computed at the rate of interest specified in paragraph (a)(5)(iv) of this section, compounded annually, from the date of distribution to such date by—

(b) (1) In the case of transfers made after November 30, 1983, for which the valuation date is before May 1, 1989, a factor equal to 1.000000 less the factor under the appropriate adjusted payout rate in Table D in § 1.664-4(e)(6) opposite the number of years in column 1 between the date of death of the decedent and the date of the earlier of the death of the last recipient or the last day of such taxable year.

(2) In the case of transfers for which the valuation date is after April 30, 1989, a factor equal to 1.000000 less the factor under the appropriate adjusted payout rate in Table D in § 1.664-4(e)(6) opposite the number of years in column 1 between the date of death of the decedent and the date of the earlier of the death of the last recipient or the last day of such taxable year. The appropriate adjusted payout rate is determined by using the appropriate Table F contained in § 1.664-4(e)(6) for the section 7520 rate for the month of the valuation date.

(3) If the number of years between the date of death and the date of the earlier of the death of the last recipient or the last day of such taxable year is between periods for which factors are provided, a linear interpolation must be made.

(iii) Treatment of distributions. The treatment of a distribution to a charitable remainder trust, or to a recipient in respect of an annuity or unitrust amount, paid, credited, or required to be distributed by an estate, or by a trust which is not a charitable remainder trust, shall be governed by the rules of subchapter J, chapter 1, subtitle A of the Code other than section 664. In the case of a charitable remainder trust which is partially or fully funded during the period of administration of an estate or settlement of a trust (which is not a charitable remainder trust), the treatment of any amount paid, credited, or required to be distributed by the charitable remainder trust shall be governed by the rules of section 664.

(iv) Rate of interest. The following rates of interest shall apply for purposes of paragraphs (a)(5)(i) through (ii) of this section:

(a) The section 7520 rate for the month in which the valuation date with respect to the transfer is (or one of the prior two months if elected under section 1.7520-2(b)) after April 30, 1989;

(b) 10 percent for instruments executed or amended (other than in the case of a reformation under section 2055(e)(3)) on or after August 9, 1984, and before May 1, 1989, and not subsequently amended;

(c) 6 percent or 10 percent for instruments executed or amended (other than in the case of a reformation under section 2055(e)(3)) after October 24, 1983, and before August 9, 1984; and

(d) 6 percent for instruments executed before October 25, 1983, and not subsequently amended (other than in the case of a reformation under section 2055(e)(3)).

(6) Examples. The application of the rules in paragraphs (a)(4) and (a)(5) of this section require the use of actuarial factors contained in §§ 1.664-4(e) and 1.664-4A(d) and (e) and may be illustrated by use of the following examples:

Example (1). On September 19, 1971, H transfers property to a trust over which he retains an inter vivos power of revocation. The trust is to pay W 5 percent of the value of the trust assets, valued annually, for her life, remainder to charity. The trust would satisfy all of the requirements of section 664 if it were irrevocable. For purposes of section 664, the trust is not deemed created in 1971 because H is treated as the owner of the entire trust under subpart E. On May 26, 1975, H predeceases W at which time the trust becomes irrevocable. For purposes of section 664, the trust is deemed created on May 26, 1975, because that is the earliest date on which H is not treated as the owner of the entire trust under subpart E. The trust becomes a charitable remainder trust on May 26, 1975, because it meets the definition of a charitable remainder trust from its creation.

Example (2). The facts are the same as in example (1), except that H retains the inter vivos power to revoke only one-half of the trust. For purposes of section 664, the trust is deemed created on September 19, 1971, because on that date the grantor is not treated as the owner of the entire trust under subpart E. Consequently, a charitable deduction is not allowable either as the creation of the trust or at H's death because the trust does not meet the definition of a charitable remainder trust from the date of its creation. The trust does not meet the definition of a charitable remainder trust from the date of its creation because the trust is subject to a partial power to revoke on such date.

Example (3). The facts are the same as in example (1), except that the residue of H's estate is to be paid to the trust and the trust is required to pay H's debts. The trust is not a charitable remainder trust at H's death because it does not function exclusively as a charitable remainder trust from the date of its creation which, in this case, is the date it becomes irrevocable.

Example (4). (i) In 1971, H transfers property to Trust A over which he retains an inter vivos power of revocation. Trust A, which is not a charitable remainder trust, is to provide income or corpus to W until the death of H. Upon H's death the trust is required by its governing instrument to pay the debts and administration expenses of H's estate, and then to terminate and distribute all of the remaining assets to a separate Trust B which meets the definition of a charitable remainder annuity trust.

(ii) Trust B will be charitable remainder trust from the date of its funding because it will function exclusively as a charitable remainder trust from its creation. For purposes of section 2055, Trust B will be deemed created at H's death if the obligation to pay the annuity amount begins on the date of H's death. For purposes of section 664, Trust B becomes a charitable remainder trust as soon as it is partially or completely funded. Consequently, unless Trust B has unrelated business taxable income, the income of the trust is exempt from all taxes imposed by subtitle A of the Code, and any distributions by the trust, even before it is completely funded, are governed by the rules of section 664. Any distributions made by Trust A, including distributions to a recipient in respect of annuity amounts, are governed by the rules of subchapter J, chapter 1, subtitle A of the Code other than section 664.

Example (5). In 1973, H dies testate leaving the net residue of his estate (after payment by the estate of all debts and administration expenses) to a trust which meets the definition of a charitable remainder unitrust. For purposes of section 2055, the trust is deemed created at H's death if the requirement to pay the unitrust amount begins on H's death and is a charitable remainder trust even though the estate is obligated to pay debts and administration expenses.

For purposes of section 664, the trust becomes a charitable remainder trust as soon as it is partially or completely funded. Consequently, unless the trust has unrelated business taxable income, the income of the trust is exempt from all taxes imposed by subtitle A of Code, and any distributions by the trust, even before it is completely funded, are governed by the rules of section 664. Any distributions made by H's estate, including distributions to a recipient in respect of unitrust amounts, are governed by the rules of subchapter J, chapter 1, subtitle A of the Code other than section 664.

Example (6). (i) On January 1, 1974, H dies testate leaving the residue of his estate to a charitable remainder unitrust. The governing instrument provides that, beginning at H's death, the trustee is to make annual payments to W, on December 31 of each year of 5 percent of the net fair market value of the trust assets, valued as of December 31 of each year, for W's life and to pay the remainder to charity at the death of W. The governing instrument also provides that the actual payment of the unitrust amount need not be made until the end of the taxable year of the trust in which occurs the complete funding of the trust. The governing instrument also provides that the amount payable with respect to the period between the date of death and the end of such taxable year shall be computed under the special method provided in subparagraph (5)(ii) of this paragraph. The governing instrument provides that, within a reasonable period after the end of the taxable year of the trust in which occurs the complete funding of the trust, the trustee shall pay (in the case of an underpayment) or shall receive from the recipient (in the case of an overpayment) the difference between the unitrust amounts paid (plus interest at 6 percentage compounded annually) and the amount computed under the special method. The trust is completely funded on September 20, 1976. No amounts were paid before June 30, 1977. The trust adopts a fiscal year of July 1 to June 30. The net fair market value of the trust assets on June 30, 1977, is $100,000.

(ii) Because no amounts were paid prior to the end of the taxable year in which the trust was completely funded, the amount payable at the end of such taxable year is equal to the net fair market value of the trust assets on the last day of such taxable year (June 30, 1977) multiplied by a factor equal to 1.0 minus the factor in Table D corresponding to the number of years in the period between the date of death and the end of such taxable year. The adjusted payout rate (determined under § 1.664-4A(c)) is 5 percent. Because the last day of the taxable year in which the trust is completely funded is June 30, 1977, there are 3-181/365 years in such period. Because there is no factor given in Table D for such a period, a linear interpolation must be made:

1.0 minus 0.814506 (factor at 5 percent for 4 years)	0.185494
1.0 minus 0.857375 (factor at 5 percent for 3 years)	.142625
Difference	.042869

$$\frac{181}{365} = \frac{X}{0.042869}$$

$$X = 0.021258$$

1.0 minus 0.857375 (factor at 5 percent for 3 years)	0.142625
Plus: X	.021258
Interpolated factor	.163883

Thus, the amount payable for the period from January 1, 1974, to June 30, 1977, is $16,388.30 ($100,000 × 0.163883). Thereafter, the trust assets must be valued on December 31 of each year and 5 percent of such value paid annually to W for her life.

(7) Valuation of unmarketable assets. (i) In general. If unmarketable assets are transferred to or held by a trust, the trust will not be a trust with respect to which a deduction is available under section 170, 2055, 2106, or 2522, or will be treated as failing to function exclusively as a charitable remainder trust unless, whenever the trust is required to value such assets, the valuation is—

(a) Performed exclusively by an independent trustee; or

(b) Determined by a current qualified appraisal, as defined in § 1.170A-13(c)(3), from a qualified appraiser, as defined in § 1.170A-13(c)(5).

(ii) Unmarketable assets. Unmarketable assets are assets that are not cash, cash equivalents, or other assets that can be readily sold or exchanged for cash or cash equivalents. For example, unmarketable assets include real property, closely-held stock, and an unregistered security for which there is no available exemption permitting public sale.

(iii) Independent trustee. An independent trustee is a person who is not the grantor of the trust, a noncharitable beneficiary, or a related or subordinate party to the grantor, the grantor's spouse, or a noncharitable beneficiary (within the meaning of section 672(c) and the applicable regulations).

(b) Application of certain foundation rules to charitable remainder trusts. See section 4947(a)(2) and section 4947(b)(3)(B) and the regulations thereunder for the application to charitable remainder trusts of certain provisions relating to private foundations. See section 508(e) for rules relating to required provisions in governing instruments prohibiting certain activities specified in section 4947(a)(2).

(c) Taxation of nonexempt charitable remainder trusts. If the charitable remainder trust has any unrelated business taxable income (within the meaning of section 512 and the regulations thereunder, determined as if part III, subchapter F, chapter 1, subtitle A of the Code applied to such trust) for any taxable year, the trust is subject to all of the taxes imposed by subtitle A of the Code for such taxable year. For taxable years beginning after December 31, 1969, unrelated business taxable income includes debt-financed income. The taxes imposed by subtitle A of the Code upon a nonexempt charitable remainder trust shall be computed under the rules prescribed by subparts A and C, part 1, subchapter J, chapter 1, subtitle A of the Code for trusts which may accumulate income or which distribute corpus. The provisions of subpart E, part 1 of such subchapter J are not applicable, with respect to a nonexempt charitable remainder trust. The application of the above rules may be illustrated by the following example:

Example. In 1975, a charitable remainder trust which has a calendar year as its taxable year has $1,000 of ordinary income, including $100 of unrelated business taxable income, and no deductions other than under sections 642(b) and 661(a). The trust is required to pay out $700 for 1975 to a noncharitable recipient. Because the trust has some unrelated business taxable income in 1975, it is not exempt for such year. Consequently, the trust is taxable on all of its income as a complex trust. Under section 661(a) of the Code, the trust is allowed a deduction of $700. Under section 642(b) of the Code, the trust is allowed a deduction of $100. Consequently, the taxable income of the trust for 1975 is $200 ($1,000 – $700 – $100).

(d) Treatment of annual distributions to recipients. *(1) Character of distributions.* (i) Assignment of income to categories and classes at the trust level. (a) A trust's income, including income includible in gross income and other income, is assigned to one of three categories in the year in which it is required to be taken into account by the trust. These categories are—

(1) Gross income, other than gains and amounts treated as gains from the sale or other disposition of capital assets (referred to as the ordinary income category);

(2) Gains and amounts treated as gains from the sale or other disposition of capital assets (referred to as the capital gains category); and

(3) Other income (including income excluded under part III, subchapter B, chapter 1, subtitle A of the Internal Revenue Code).

(b) Items within the ordinary income and capital gains categories are assigned to different classes based on the Federal income tax rate applicable to each type of income in that category in the year the items are required to be taken into account by the trust. For example, for a trust with a taxable year ending December 31, 2004, the ordinary income category may include a class of qualified dividend income as defined in section 1(h)(11) and a class of all other ordinary income, and the capital gains category may include separate classes for short-term and long-term capital gains and losses, such as a short-term capital gain class, a 28-percent long-term capital gain class (gains and losses from collectibles and section 1202 gains), an unrecaptured section 1250 long-term capital gain class (long-term gains not treated as ordinary income that would be treated as ordinary income if section 1250(b)(1) included all depreciation), a qualified 5-year long-term capital gain class as defined in section 1(h)(9) prior to amendment by the Jobs and Growth Tax Relief Reconciliation Act of 2003 (JGTRRA), Public Law 108-27 (117 Stat. 752), and an all other long-term capital gain class. After items are assigned to a class, the tax rates may change so that items in two or more classes would be taxed at the same rate if distributed to the recipient during a particular year. If the changes to the tax rates are permanent, the undistributed items in those classes are combined into one class. If, however, the changes to the tax rates are only temporary (for example, the new rate for one class will sunset in a future year), the classes are kept separate.

(ii) Order of distributions. (a) The categories and classes of income (determined under paragraph (d)(1)(i) of this section) are used to determine the character of an annuity or unitrust distribution from the trust in the hands of the recipient irrespective of whether the trust is exempt from taxation under section 664(c) for the year of the distribution. The determination of the character of amounts distributed or deemed distributed at any time during the taxable year of the trust shall be made as of the end of that taxable year. The tax rate or rates to be used in computing the recipient's tax on the distribution shall be the tax rates that are applicable, in the year in which the distribution is required to be made, to the classes of income deemed to make up that distribution, and not the tax rates that are applicable to those classes of income in the year the income is received by the trust. The character of the distribution in the hands of the annuity or unitrust recipient is determined by treating the distribution as being made from each category in the following order:

(1) First, from ordinary income to the extent of the sum of the trust's ordinary income for the taxable year and its undistributed ordinary income for prior years.

(2) Second, from capital gain to the extent of the trust's capital gains determined under paragraph (d)(1)(iv) of this section.

(3) Third, from other income to the extent of the sum of the trust's other income for the taxable year and its undistributed other income for prior years.

(4) Finally, from trust corpus (with corpus defined for this purpose as the net fair market value of the trust assets less the total undistributed income (but not loss) in paragraphs (d)(1)(i)(a) (1) through (3) of this section).

(b) If the trust has different classes of income in the ordinary income category, the distribution from that category is treated as being made from each class, in turn, until exhaustion of the class, beginning with the class subject to the highest Federal income tax rate and ending with the class subject to the lowest Federal income tax rate. If the trust has different classes of net gain in the capital gains category, the distribution from that category is treated as being made first from the short-term capital gain class and then from each class of long-term capital gain, in turn, until exhaustion of the class, beginning with the class subject to the highest Federal income tax rate and ending with the class subject to the lowest rate. If two or more classes within the same category are subject to the same current tax rate, but at least one of those classes will be subject to a different tax rate in a future year (for example, if the current rate sunsets), the order of that class in relation to other classes in the category with the same current tax rate is determined based on the future rate or rates applicable to those classes. Within each category, if there is more than one type of income in a class, amounts treated as distributed from that class are to be treated as consisting of the same proportion of each type of income as the total of the current and undistributed income of that type bears to the total of the current and undistributed income of all types of income included in that class. For example, if rental income and interest income are subject to the same current and future Federal income tax rate and, therefore, are in the same class, a distribution from that class will be treated as consisting of a proportional amount of rental income and interest income.

(iii) Treatment of losses at the trust level. (a) Ordinary income category. A net ordinary loss for the current year is first used to reduce undistributed ordinary income for prior years that is assigned to the same class as the loss. Any excess loss is then used to reduce the current and undistributed ordinary income from other classes, in turn, beginning with the class subject to the highest Federal income tax rate and ending with the class subject to the lowest Federal income tax rate. If any of the loss exists after all the current and undistributed ordinary income from all classes has been offset, the excess is carried forward indefinitely to reduce ordinary income for future years and retains its class assignment. For purposes of this section, the amount of current income and prior years' undistributed income shall be computed without regard to the deduction for net operating losses provided by section 172 or 642(d).

(b) Other income category. A net loss in the other income category for the current year is used to reduce undistributed income in this category for prior years and any excess is carried forward indefinitely to reduce other income for future years.

(iv) Netting of capital gains and losses at the trust level. Capital gains of the trust are determined on a cumulative net basis under the rules of this paragraph (d)(1) without regard to the provisions of section 1212. For each taxable year, current and undistributed gains and losses within each class are netted to determine the net gain or loss for that class, and the classes of capital gains and losses are then netted against each other in the following order. First, a net loss from a class of long-term capital gain and loss (beginning with the class subject to the highest Federal income tax rate and ending with the class subject to the lowest rate) is used to offset net gain from each other class of long-term capital gain and loss, in turn, until exhaustion of the class, beginning with the class subject to the highest Federal income tax rate and ending with the class subject to the lowest rate. Second, either—

(a) A net loss from all the classes of long-term capital gain and loss (beginning with the class subject to the highest Federal income tax rate and ending with the class subject to the lowest rate) is used to offset any net gain from the class of short-term capital gain and loss; or

(b) A net loss from the class of short-term capital gain and loss is used to offset any net gain from each class of long-term capital gain and loss, in turn, until exhaustion of the class, beginning with the class subject to the highest Federal income tax rate and ending with the class subject to the lowest Federal income tax rate.

(v) Carry forward of net capital gain or loss by the trust. If, at the end of a taxable year, a trust has, after the application of paragraph (d)(1)(iv) of this section, any net loss or any net gain that is not treated as distributed under paragraph (d)(1)(ii)(a)(2) of this section, the net gain or loss is carried over to succeeding taxable years and retains its character in succeeding taxable years as gain or loss from its particular class.

(vi) Special transitional rules. To be eligible to be included in the class of qualified dividend income, dividends must meet the definition of section 1(h)(11) and must be received by the trust after December 31, 2002. Long-term capital gain or loss properly taken into account by the trust before January 1, 1997, is included in the class of all other long-term capital gains and losses. Long-term capital gain or loss properly taken into account by the trust on or after January 1, 1997, and before May 7, 1997, if not treated as distributed in 1997, is included in the class of all other long-term capital gains and losses. Long-term capital gain or loss (other than 28-percent gain (gains and losses from collectibles and section 1202 gains), unrecaptured section 1250 gain (long-term gains not treated as ordinary income that would be treated as ordinary income if section 1250(b)(1) included all depreciation), and qualified 5-year gain as defined in section 1(h)(9) prior to amendment by JGTRRA), properly taken into account by the trust before January 1, 2003, and distributed during 2003 is treated as if it were properly taken into account by the trust after May 5, 2003. Long-term capital gain or loss (other than 28-percent gain, unrecaptured section 1250 gain, and qualified 5-year gain), properly taken into account by the trust on or after January 1, 2003, and before May 6, 2003, if not treated as distributed during 2003, is included in the class of all other long-term capital gain. Qualified 5-year gain properly taken into account by the trust after December 31, 2000, and before May 6, 2003, if not treated as distributed by the trust in 2003 or a prior year, must be maintained in a separate class within the capital gains category until distributed. Qualified 5-year gain properly taken into account by the trust before January 1, 2003, and deemed distributed during 2003 is subject to the same current tax rate as deemed distributions from the class of all other long-term capital gain realized by the trust after May 5, 2003. Qualified 5-year gain properly taken into account by the trust on or after January 1, 2003, and before May 6, 2003, if treated as distributed by the trust in 2003, is subject to the tax rate in effect prior to the amendment of section 1(h)(9) by JGTRRA.

(vii) Application of section 643(a)(7). For application of the anti-abuse rule of section 643(a)(7) to distributions from charitable remainder trusts, see § 1.643(a)-8.

(viii) Examples. The following examples illustrate the rules in this paragraph (d)(1):

Example (1). (i) X, a charitable remainder annuity trust described in section 664(d)(1), is created on January 1, 2003. The annual annuity amount is $100. X's income for the 2003 tax year is as follows:

Interest income	$80
Qualified dividend income	50
Capital gains and losses	0
Tax-exempt income	0

(ii) In 2003, the year this income is received by the trust, qualified dividend income is subject to a different rate of Federal income tax than interest income and is, therefore, a separate class of income in the ordinary income category. The annuity amount is deemed to be distributed from the classes within the ordinary income category, beginning with the class subject to the highest Federal income tax rate and ending with the class subject to the lowest rate. Because during 2003 qualified dividend income is taxed at a lower rate than interest income, the interest income is deemed distributed prior to the qualified dividend income. Therefore, in the hands of the recipient, the 2003 annuity amount has the following characteristics:

Interest income	$80
Qualified dividend income	20

(iii) The remaining $30 of qualified dividend income that is not treated as distributed to the recipient in 2003 is carried forward to 2004 as undistributed qualified dividend income.

Example (2). (i) The facts are the same as in Example 1, and at the end of 2004, X has the following classes of income:

Interest income class	$5
Qualified dividend income class ($10 from 2004 and $30 carried forward from 2003)	40
Net short-term capital gain class	15
Net long-term capital loss in 28-percent class	(325)
Net long-term capital gain in unrecaptured section 1250 gain class	175
Net long-term capital gain in all other long-term capital gain class	350

(ii) In 2004, gain in the unrecaptured section 1250 gain class is subject to a 25-percent Federal income tax rate, and gain in the all other long-term capital gain class is subject to a lower rate. The net long-term capital loss in the 28-percent gain class is used to offset the net capital gains in the other classes of long-term capital gain and loss, beginning with the class subject to the highest Federal income tax rate and ending with the class subject to the lowest rate. The $325 net loss in the 28-percent gain class reduces the $175 net gain in the unrecaptured section 1250 gain class to $0. The remaining $150 loss from the 28-percent gain class reduces the $350 gain in the all other long-term capital gain class to $200. As in Example 1, qualified dividend income is taxed at a lower rate than interest income during 2004. The annuity amount is deemed to be distributed from all the classes in the ordinary income category and then from the classes in the capital gains category, beginning with the class subject to the highest Federal income tax rate and ending with the class subject to the lowest rate. In the hands of the recipient, the 2004 annuity amount has the following characteristics:

Interest income	$ 5
Qualified dividend income	40
Net short-term capital gain	15
Net long-term capital gain in all other long-term capital gain class	40

(iii) The remaining $160 gain in the all other long-term capital gain class that is not treated as distributed to the recipient in 2004 is carried forward to 2005 as gain in that same class.

Example (3). (i) The facts are the same as in Examples 1 and 2, and at the end of 2005, X has the following classes of income:

Interest income class	$ 5
Qualified dividend income	20
Net loss in short-term capital gain class	(50)
Net long-term capital gain in 28-percent gain class	10
Net long-term capital gain in unrecaptured section 1250 gain class	135
Net long-term capital gain in all other long-term capital gain class (carried forward from 2004)	160

(ii) There are no long-term capital losses to net against the long-term capital gains. Thus, the net short-term capital loss is used to offset the net capital gains in the classes of long-term capital gain and loss, in turn, until exhaustion of the class, beginning with the class subject to the highest Federal income tax rate and ending with the class subject to the lowest rate. The $50 net short-term loss reduces the $10 net gain in the 28-percent gain class to $0. The remaining $40 net loss reduces the $135 net gain in the unrecaptured section 1250 gain class to $95. As in Examples 1 and 2, during 2005, qualified dividend income is taxed at a lower rate than interest income; gain in the unrecaptured section 1250 gain class is taxed at 25 percent; and gain in the all other long-term capital gain class is taxed at a rate lower than 25 percent. The annuity amount is deemed to be distributed from all the classes in the ordinary income category and then from the classes in the capital gains category, beginning with the class subject to the highest Federal income tax rate and ending with the class subject to the lowest rate. Therefore, in the hands of the recipient, the 2005 annuity amount has the following characteristics:

Interest income	$ 5
Qualified dividend income	20
Unrecaptured section 1250 gain	75

(iii) The remaining $20 gain in the unrecaptured section 1250 gain class and the $160 gain in the all other long-term capital gain class that are not treated as distributed to the recipient in 2005 are carried forward to 2006 as gains in their respective classes.

Example (4). (i) The facts are the same as in Examples 1, 2 and 3, and at the end of 2006, X has the following classes of income:

Interest income class	$95
Qualified dividend income class	10
Net loss in short-term capital gain class	(20)
Net long-term capital loss in 28-percent gain class	(350)
Net long-term capital gain in unrecaptured section 1250 gain class (carried forward from 2005)	20
Net long-term capital gain in all other long-term capital gain class (carried forward from 2005)	160

(ii) A net long-term capital loss in one class is used to offset the net capital gains in the other classes of long-term capital gain and loss, in turn, until exhaustion of the class, beginning with the class subject to the highest Federal income tax rate and ending with the class subject to the lowest rate. The $350 net loss in the 28-percent gain class reduces the $20 net gain in the unrecaptured section 1250 gain class to $0. The remaining $330 net loss reduces the $160 net gain in the all other long-term capital gain class to $0. As in Examples 1, 2 and 3, during 2006, qualified dividend income is taxed at a lower rate than interest income. The annuity amount is deemed to be distributed from all the classes in the ordinary income category and then from the classes in the capital gains category, beginning with the class subject to the highest Federal income tax rate and ending with the class subject to the lowest rate. In the hands of the recipient, the 2006 annuity amount has the following characteristics:

Interest income	$95
Qualified dividend income	5

(iii) The remaining $5 of qualified dividend income that is not treated as distributed to the recipient in 2006 is carried forward to 2007 as qualified dividend income. The $20 net loss in the short-term capital gain class and the $170 net loss in the 28-percent gain class are carried forward to 2007 as net losses in their respective classes.

Example (5). (i) X, a charitable remainder annuity trust described in section 664(d)(1), is created on January 1, 2002. The annual annuity amount is $100. Except for qualified 5-year gain of $200 realized before May 6, 2003, but not distributed, X has no other gains or losses carried over from former years. X's income for the 2007 tax year is as follows:

Interest income class	$10
Net gain in short-term capital gain class	5
Net long-term capital gain in 28-percent gain class	5
Net long-term capital gain in unrecaptured section 1250 gain class	10
Net long-term capital gain in all other long-term capital gain class	10

(ii) The annuity amount is deemed to be distributed from all the classes in the ordinary income category and then from the classes in the capital gains category, beginning with the class subject to the highest Federal income tax rate and ending with the class subject to the lowest rate. In 2007, gains distributed to a recipient from both the qualified 5-year gain class and the all other long-term capital gains class are taxed at a 15/5 percent tax rate. Since after December 31, 2008, gains distributed from the qualified 5-year gain class will be taxed at a lower rate than gains distributed from the other classes of long-term capital gain and loss, distributions from the qualified 5-year gain class are made after distributions from the other classes of long-term capital gain and loss. In the hands of the recipient, the 2007 annuity amount has the following characteristics:

Interest income	$10
Short-term capital gain	5
28-percent gain	5
Unrecaptured section 1250 gain	10
All other long-term capital gain	10
Qualified 5-year gain (taxed as all other long-term capital gain)	60

(iii) The remaining $140 of qualified 5-year gain that is not treated as distributed to the recipient in 2007 is carried forward to 2008 as qualified 5-year gain.

(ix) Effective dates. The rules in this paragraph (d)(1) that require long-term capital gains to be distributed in the following order: first, 28-percent gain (gains and losses from collectibles and section 1202 gains); second, unrecaptured section 1250 gain (long-term gains not treated as ordinary income that would be treated as ordinary income if section 1250(b)(1) included all depreciation); and then, all other long-term capital gains are applicable for taxable years ending on or after December 31, 1998. The rules in this paragraph (d)(1) that provide for the netting of capital gains and losses are applicable for taxable years ending on or after December 31, 1998. The rule in the second sentence of paragraph (d)(1)(vi) of this section is applicable for taxable years ending on or after December 31, 1998. The rule in the third sentence of paragraph (d)(1)(vi) of this section is applicable for distributions made in taxable years ending on or after December 31, 1998. All other provisions of this paragraph (d)(1) are applicable for taxable years ending after November 20, 2003.

(2) Allocation of deductions. Items of deduction of the trust for a taxable year of the trust which are deductible in determining taxable income (other than the deduction permitted by sections 642(b), 642(c), 661, and 1202) which are directly attributable to one or more classes of items within a category of income (determined under paragraph (d)(1)(i)(a) of this section) or to corpus shall be allocated to such classes of items or to corpus. All other allowable deductions for such taxable year which are not directly attributable to one or more classes of items within a category of income or to corpus (other than the deductions permitted by sections 642(b), 642(c), 661, and 1202) shall be allocated among the classes of items within the category (excluding classes of items with net losses) on the basis of the gross income of such classes for such taxable year reduced by the deductions allocated thereto under the first sentence of this subparagraph, but in no event shall the amount of expenses allocated to any class of items exceed such income of such class for the taxable year. Items of deduction which are not allocable under the above two sentences (other than the deductions permitted by sections 642(b), 642(c), 661, and 1202) may be allocated in any manner. All taxes imposed by subtitle A of the Code for which the trust is liable because it has unrelated business taxable income and all taxes imposed by chapter 42 of the Code shall be allocated to corpus. Any expense which is not deductible in determining taxable income and which is not allocable to any class of items described in paragraph (d)(1)(i)(a)(3) of this section shall be allocated to corpus. The deductions allowable to a trust under sections 642(b), 642(c), 661, and 1202 are not allowed in determining the amount or character of any class of items within a category of income described in paragraph (d)(1)(i)(a) of this section or to corpus.

(3) Allocation of income among recipients. If there are two or more recipients, each will be treated as receiving his pro rata portion of the categories of income and corpus. The application of this rule may be illustrated by the following

Example. X transfers $40,000 to a charitable remainder annuity trust which is to pay $3,000 per year to X and $2,000 per year to Y for a term of 5 years. During the first taxable year the trust has $3,000 of ordinary income, $500 of capital gain, and $500 of tax-exempt income after allocation of all expenses. X is treated as receiving ordinary income of $1,800 ($3,000 – $5,000 × $3,000), capital gain of $300 ($3,000/$5,000 × $500), tax exempt income of $300 ($3,000/$5,000 × $500), and corpus of $600 ($3,000/$5,000 × [$5,000 – $4,000]). Y is treated as receiving ordinary income of $1,200 ($2,000/$5,000 × $3,000), capital gain of $200 ($2,000/$5,000 × $500), tax exempt income of $200 ($2,000/$5,000 × $500), and corpus of $400 ($2,000/$5,000 × [$5,000 – $4,000]).

(4) Year of inclusion. (i) General rule. To the extent required by this paragraph, the annuity or unitrust amount is includible in the recipient's gross income for the taxable year in which the annuity or unitrust amount is required to be distributed even though the annuity or unitrust amount is not distributed until after the close of the taxable year of the trust. If a recipient has a different taxable year (as defined in section 441 or 442) from the taxable year of the trust, the

amount he is required to include in gross income to the extent required by this paragraph shall be included in his taxable year in which or with which ends the taxable year of the trust in which such amount is required to be distributed.

(ii) Payments resulting from incorrect valuations. Notwithstanding subdivision (i) of this subparagraph, any payments which are made or required to be distributed by a charitable remainder trust pursuant to paragraph (a)(5) of this section, under paragraph (f)(3) of this section because of an amendment to the governing instrument, or under paragraphs (a)(1) of §§ 1.664-2 and 1.664-3 because of an incorrect valuation, shall, to the extent required by this paragraph, be included in the gross income of the recipient in his taxable year in which or with which ends the taxable year of the trust in which the amount is paid, credited, or required to be distributed. For rules relating to required adjustments of underpayments and overpayments of the annuity or unitrust amounts in respect of payments made prior to the amendment of a governing instrument, see paragraph (f)(3) of this section. There is allowable to a recipient a deduction from gross income for any amounts repaid to the trust because of an overpayment during the reasonable period of administration or settlement or until the trust is fully funded, because of an amendment, or because of an incorrect valuation, to the extent such amounts were included in his gross income. See section 1341 and the regulations thereunder for rules relating to the computation of tax where a taxpayer restores substantial amounts held under a claim of right.

(iii) Rules applicable to year of recipient's death. If the taxable year of the trust does not end with or within the last taxable year of the recipient because of the recipient's death, the extent to which the annuity or unitrust amount required to be distributed to him is included in the gross income of the recipient for his last taxable year, or in the gross income of his estate, is determined by making the computations required under this paragraph for the taxable year of the trust in which his last taxable year ends. (The last sentence of subdivision (i) of this subparagraph does not apply to such amounts.) The gross income for the last taxable year of a recipient on the cash basis includes (to the extent required by this paragraph) amounts actually distributed to the recipient before his death. Amounts required to be distributed which are distributed to his estate, are included (to the extent required by this paragraph) in the gross income of the estate as income in respect of a decedent under section 691.

(5) Distributions in kind. The annuity or unitrust amount may be paid in cash or in other property. In the case of a distribution made in other property, the amount paid, credited, or required to be distributed shall be considered as an amount realized by the trust from the sale or other disposition of property. The basis of the property in the hands of the recipient is its fair market value at the time it was paid, credited, or required to be distributed. The application of these rules may be illustrated by the following example:

Example. On January 1, 1971, X creates a charitable remainder annuity trust, whose taxable year is the calendar year, under which X is to receive $5,000 per year. During 1971, the trust receives $500 of ordinary income. On December 31, 1971, the trust distributed cash of $500 and a capital asset of the trust having a fair market value of $4,500 and a basis of $2,200. The trust is deemed to have realized a capital gain of $2,300. X treats the distribution of $5,000 as being ordinary income of $500, capital gain of $2,300 and trust corpus of $2,200. The basis of the distributed property is $4,500 in the hands of X.

(e) Other distributions. *(1) Character of distributions.* An amount distributed by the trust to an organization described in section 170(c) other than the annuity or unitrust amount shall be considered as a distribution of corpus and of those categories of income specified in paragraph (d)(1)(i)(a) of this section in an order inverse to that prescribed in such paragraph. The character of such amount shall be determined as of the end of the taxable year of the trust in which the distribution is made after the character of the annuity or unitrust amount has been determined.

(2) Distributions in kind. In the case of a distribution of an amount to which subparagraph (1) of this paragraph applies, no gain or loss is realized by the trust by reason of a distribution in kind unless such distribution is in satisfaction of a right to receive a distribution of a specific dollar amount or in specific property other than that distributed.

(f) Effective date. *(1) General rule.* The provisions of this section are effective with respect to transfers in trust made after July 31, 1969. Any trust created (within the meaning of applicable local law) prior to August 1, 1969, is not a charitable remainder trust even if it otherwise satisfies the definition of á charitable remainder trust.

(2) Transfers to pre-1970 trusts. Property transferred to a trust created (within the meaning of applicable local law) before August 1, 1969, whose governing instrument provides that an organization described in section 17(c) receives an irrevocable remainder interest in such trust, shall, for purposes of subparagraphs (1) and (3) of this paragraph, be deemed transferred to a trust created on the date of such transfer provided that the transfer occurs after July 31, 1969, and prior to October 18, 1971, and the transferred property and any undistributed income therefrom is severed and placed in a separate trust before the 30th day after the date on which any judicial proceedings begun before December 31, 1972, which are required to sever such property, become final.

(3) Amendment of post-1969 trusts. A trust created (within the meaning of applicable local law) subsequent to July 31, 1969, and prior to December 31, 1972, which is not a charitable remainder trust at the date of its creation, may be treated as a charitable remainder trust from the date it would be deemed created under § 1.664-1(a)(4) and (5)(i) for all purposes: Provided, that all the following requirements are met:

(i) At the time of the creation of the trust, the governing instrument provides that an organization described in section 170(c) receives an irrevocable remainder interest in such trust.

(ii) The governing instrument of the trust is amended so that the trust will meet the definition of a charitable remainder trust and, if applicable, will meet the requirement of paragraph (a)(5)(i) of this section that obligation to make payment of the annuity or unitrust amount with respect to property passing at death begin as of the date of death, before December 31, 1972, or if later, on or before the 30th day after the date on which any judicial proceedings which are begun before December 31, 1972, and which are required to amend its governing instrument, become final. In the case of a trust created (within the meaning of applicable local law) subsequent to July 31, 1969, and prior to December 31, 1972, the provisions of section 508(d)(2)(A) shall not apply if the governing instrument of the trust is amended so as to comply with the requirements of section 508(e) before December 31, 1972, or if later, on or before the 30th day after the date on which any judicial proceeding which are begun before December 31, 1972, and which are required to amend its governing instrument, become final. Notwithstanding the provisions of paragraphs (a)(3) and (a)(4) of §§ 1.664-2 and 1.664-3, the governing instrument may grant to the trustee a power to amend the governing instrument for the sole purpose of complying with the requirements of this section and § 1.664-2 or § 1.664-3; Provided, That at the creation of the trust, the governing instrument (a) provides for the payment of a unitrust amount described in § 1.664-3(a) (1)(i) or an annuity which meets the requirements of paragraph (a)(2) of § 1.664-2 or § 1.664-3, (b) designates the recipients of the trust and the period for which the amount described in (a) of this subdivision (ii) is to be paid, and (c) provides that an organization described in section 170(c) receives an irrevocable remainder interest in such trust. The mere granting of such a power is not sufficient to meet the requirements of this subparagraph that the government instrument be amended in the manner and within the time limitations of this subparagraph.

(iii) (a) Where the amount of the distributions which would have been made by the trust to a recipient if the amended provisions of such trust had been in effect from the time of creation of such trust exceeds the amount of the distributions made by the trust prior to its amendment, the trust pays an amount equal to such excess to the recipient.

(b) Where the amount of distributions made to exceeds the amount of the distributions which would have been made by such trust if the amended provisions of such trust had been in effect from the time of creation of such trust, such excess is repaid to the trust by the recipient.

See paragraph (d)(4) of this section for rules relating to the year of inclusion in the case of an underpayment to a recipient and the allowance of a deduction in the case of an overpayment to a recipient. A deduction for a transfer to a charitable remainder trust shall not be allowed until the requirements of this paragraph are met and then only if the deduction is claimed on a timely filed return (including extensions) or on a claim for refund filed within the period of limitations prescribed by section 6511(a).

(4) Valuation of unmarketable assets. The rules contained in paragraph (a)(7) of this section are applicable for trusts created on or after December 10, 1998. A trust in existence as of December 10, 1998, whose governing instrument requires that an independent trustee value the trust's unmarketable assets may be amended or reformed to permit a valuation method that satisfies the requirements of paragraph (a)(7) of this section for taxable years beginning on or after December 10, 1998.

(g) Transitional effective date. Notwithstanding any other provision of this section, § 1.664-2 or § 1.664-3, the requirement of paragraph (a)(5)(i) of this section that interest accrue on overpayments and underpayments, the requirement of paragraph (a)(5)(ii) of this section that the unitrust amount accruing under the formula provided therein cease with the death of the last recipient, and the requirement that the governing instrument of the trust contain the provisions specified in paragraph (a)(1)(iv) of § 1.664-2 (relating to computation of the annuity amount in certain circumstances), paragraph (a)(1)(v) of § 1.664-3 (relating to computation of the unitrust amount in certain circumstances), paragraphs (b) of §§ 1.664-2 and 1.664-3 (relating to additional contributions), and paragraph (a)(1)(iii) of § 1.664-3 (relating to incorrect valuations), paragraphs (a)(6)(iv) of §§ 1.664-2 and 1.664-3 relating to alternative remaindermen) shall not apply to:

(1) A will executed on or before December 31, 1972, if:

(i) The testator dies before December 31, 1975, without having republished the will after December 31, 1972, by codicil or otherwise,

(ii) The testator at no time after December 31, 1972, had the right to change the provisions of the will which pertain to the trust, or

(iii) The will is not republished by codicil or otherwise before December 31, 1975, and the testator is on such date and at all times thereafter under a mental disability to republish the will by codicil or otherwise, or

(2) A trust executed in or before December 31, 1972, if:

(i) The grantor dies before December 31, 1975, without having amended the trust after December 31, 1972.

(ii) The trust is irrevocable on December 31, 1972, or

(iii) The trust is not amended before December 31, 1975, and the grantor is on such date and at all times thereafter under a mental disability to change the terms of the trust.

T.D. 7202, 8/22/72, amend T.D. 7955, 5/10/84, T.D. 8540, 6/9/94, T.D. 8791, 12/09/98, T.D. 8819, 4/29/99, T.D. 8926, 1/4/2001, T.D. 9190, 3/15/2005.

PARAGRAPH 1. Paragraph (f) of § 1.664-1 is amended by revising the heading of subparagraph (3) and by adding a new subparagraph (4) at the end thereof. These revised and added provisions read as follows:

Proposed § 1.664-1 Charitable remainder trusts. [*For Preamble, see ¶ 150,177*]

* * * * *

(f) Effective date. * * *

(3) Amendment of certain trusts created after July 31, 1969. * * *

(4) Certain wills and trusts in existence on September 21, 1974. (i) In the case of a will executed before September 21, 1974, or a trust created (within the meaning of applicable local law) after July 31, 1969, and before September 21, 1974, which is amended pursuant to section 2055(e)(3) and § 20.2055-2(g), a charitable remainder trust resulting from such amendment will be treated as a charitable remainder trust from the date it would be deemed created under § 1.664-1(a)(4) and (5), whether or not such date is after September 20, 1974.

(ii) Property transferred to a trust created (within the meaning of applicable local law) before August 1, 1969, whose governing instrument provides that an organization described in section 170(c) receives an irrevocable remainder interest in such trust shall be deemed transferred to a trust created on the date of such transfer, provided that the transfer occurs after July 31, 1969, and prior to October 18, 1971, and pursuant to an amendment provided in § 20.2055-2(g), the transferred property and any undistributed income therefrom is severed and placed in a separate trust as of the date of the amendment.

§ 8.1 Charitable remainder trusts.

Caution: The Treasury has not yet amended Reg § 8.1 to reflect changes made by P.L. 100-647, P.L. 98-369, P.L. 96-605, P.L. 96-222, P.L. 95-600.

(a) Certain wills and trusts in existence on September 21, 1974. In the case of a will executed before September 21, 1974, or a trust created (within the meaning of applicable local law) after July 31, 1969, and before September 21, 1974, which is amended pursuant to section 2055(e)(3) and

§ 24.1 of this Chapter (Temporary Estate Tax Regulations), a charitable remainder trust resulting from such amendment will be treated as a charitable remainder trust from the date it would be deemed created under § 1.664-1(a) (4) and (5) of this chapter (Income Tax Regulations), whether or not such date is after September 20, 1974.

(b) Certain transfers to trusts created before August 1, 1969. Property transferred to a trust created (within the meaning of applicable local law) before August 1, 1969, whose governing instrument provides that an organization described in section 170(c) receives an irrevocable remainder interest in such trust shall be deemed transferred to a trust created on the date of such transfer, provided that the transfer occurs after July 31, 1969 and prior to October 18, 1971, and pursuant to an amendment provided in § 24.1 of this chapter (Temporary Estate Tax Regulations), the transferred property and any undistributed income therefrom is severed and placed in a separate trust as of the date of the amendment.

T.D. 7393, 12/16/75.

---

§ 1.664-2 Charitable remainder annuity trust.

Caution: The Treasury has not yet amended Reg § 1.664-2 to reflect changes made by P.L. 105-34, P.L. 98-369.

(a) Description. A charitable remainder annuity trust is a trust which complies with the applicable provisions of § 1.664-1 and meets all of the following requirements:

(1) Required payment of annuity amount. (i) Payment of sum certain at least annually.

The governing instrument provides that the trust will pay a sum certain not less often than annually to a person or persons described in paragraph (a)(3) of this section for each taxable year of the period specified in paragraph (a)(5) of this section.

(a) General rule applicable to all trusts. A trust will not be deemed to have engaged in an act of self-dealing (within the meaning of section 4941), to have unrelated debt-financed income (within the meaning of section 514), to have received an additional contribution (within the meaning of paragraph (b) of this section), or to have failed to function exclusively as a charitable remainder trust (within the meaning of § 1.664-1(a)(4)) merely because the annuity amount is paid after the close of the taxable year if such payment is made within a reasonable time after the close of such taxable year and the entire annuity amount in the hands of the recipient is characterized only as income from the categories described in section 664(b)(1), (2), or (3), except to the extent it is characterized as corpus described in section 664(b)(4) because—

(1) The trust pays the annuity amount by distributing property (other than cash) that it owned at the close of the taxable year to pay the annuity amount, and the trustee elects to treat any income generated by the distribution as occurring on the last day of the taxable year in which the annuity amount is due;

(2) The trust pays the annuity amount by distributing cash that was contributed to the trust (with respect to which a deduction was allowable under section 170, 2055, 2106, or 2522); or

(3) The trust pays the annuity amount by distributing cash received as a return of basis in any asset that was contributed to the trust (with respect to which a deduction was allowable under section 170, 2055, 2106, or 2522), and that is sold by the trust during the year for which the annuity amount is due.

(b) Special rule for trusts created before December 10, 1998. In addition, to the circumstances described in paragraph (a)(1)(i)(a) of this section, a trust created before December 10, 1998, will not be deemed to have engaged in an act of self-dealing (within the meaning of section 4941), to have unrelated debt-financed income (within the meaning of section 514), to have received an additional contribution (within the meaning of paragraph (b) of this section), or to have failed to function exclusively as a charitable remainder trust (within the meaning of § 1.664-1(a)(4)) merely because the annuity amount is paid after the close of the taxable year if such payment is made within a reasonable time after the close of such taxable year and the sum certain to be paid each year as the annuity amount is 15 percent or less of the initial net fair market value of the property irrevocably passing in trust as determined for federal tax purposes.

(c) Reasonable time. For this paragraph (a)(1)(i), a reasonable time will not ordinarily extend beyond the date by which the trustee is required to file Form 5227, "Split-Interest Trust Information Return," (including extensions) for the taxable year.

(d) Example. The following example illustrates the rules in paragraph (a)(1)(i)(a) of this section:

Example. X is a charitable remainder annuity trust described in section 664(d)(1) that was created after December 10, 1998. The prorated annuity amount payable from X for Year 1 is $100. The trustee does not pay the annuity amount to the recipient by the close of Year 1. At the end of Year 1, X has only $95 in the ordinary income category under section 664(b)(1) and no income in the capital gain or tax-exempt income categories under section 664(b)(2) or (3), respectively. By April 15 of Year 2, in addition to $95 in cash, the trustee distributes to the recipient of the annuity a capital asset with a $5 fair market value and a $2 adjusted basis to pay the $100 annuity amount due for Year 1. The trust owned the asset at the end of Year 1. Under § 1.664-1(d)(5), the distribution is treated as a sale by X, resulting in X recognizing a $3 capital gain. The trustee elects to treat the capital gain as occurring on the last day of Year 1. Under § 1.664-1(d)(1), the character of the annuity amount for Year 1 in the recipient's hands is $95 of ordinary income, $3 of capital gain income, and $2 of trust corpus. For Year 1, X satisfied paragraph (a)(1)(i)(a) of this section.

(e) Effective date. This paragraph (a)(1)(i) is applicable for taxable years ending after April 18, 1997. However, paragraphs (a)(1)(i)(a)(2) and (3) of this section apply only to distributions made on or after January 5, 2001.

(ii) Definition of sum certain. A sum certain is a stated dollar amount which is the same either as to each recipient or as to the total amount payable for each year of such period. For example, a provision for an amount which is the same every year to A until his death and concurrently an amount which is the same every year to B until his death, with the amount to each recipient to terminate at his death, would satisfy the above rule. Similarly, provisions for an amount to A and B for their joint lives and then to the survivor would satisfy the above rule. In the case of a distribution to an organization described in section 170(c) at the death of a recipient or the expiration of a term of years, the governing instrument may provide for a reduction of the stated amount payable after such a distribution: Provided, That:

(a) The reduced amount payable is the same either as to each recipient or as to the total amount payable for each year of the balance of such period, and

(b) The requirements of subparagraph (2)(ii) of this paragraph are met.

(iii) Sum certain stated as a fraction or percentage. The stated dollar amount may be expressed as a fraction or a percentage of the initial net fair market value of the property irrevocably passing in trust as finally determined for Federal tax purposes. If the stated dollar amount is so expressed and such market value is incorrectly determined by the fiduciary, the requirement of this subparagraph will be satisfied if the governing instrument provides that in such event the trust shall pay to the recipient (in the case of an undervaluation) or be repaid by the recipient (in the case of an overvaluation) an amount equal to the difference between the amount which the trust should have paid the recipient if the correct value were used and the amount which the trust actually paid the recipient. Such payments or repayments must be made within a reasonable period after the final determination of such value. Any payment due to a recipient by reason of such incorrect valuation shall be considered to be a payment required to be distributed at the time of such final determination for purposes of paragraph (d)(4)(ii) of § 1.664-1. See paragraph (d)(4) of § 1.664-1 for rules relating to the year of inclusion of such payments and the allowance of a deduction for such repayments. See paragraph (b) of this section for rules relating to future contributions. For rules relating to required adjustments for underpayments or overpayments of the amount described in this paragraph in respect of payments made during a reasonable period of administration, see paragraph (a)(5) of § 1.664-1. The application of the rule permitting the stated dollar amount to be expressed as a fraction or a percentage of the initial net fair market value of the property irrevocably passing in trust as finally determined for Federal tax purposes may be illustrated by the following example:

Example. The will of X provides for the transfer of one-half of his residuary estate to a charitable remainder annuity trust which is required to pay to W for life an annuity equal to 5 percent of the initial net fair market value of the interest passing in trust as finally determined for Federal tax purposes. The annuity is to be paid on December 31 of each year computed from the date of X's death. The will also provides that if such initial net fair market value is incorrectly determined, the trust shall pay to W, in the case of an undervaluation, or be repaid by W, in the case of an overvaluation, an amount equal to the difference between the amount which the trust should have paid if the correct value were used and the amount which the trust actually paid. X dies on March 1, 1971. The executor files an estate tax return showing the value of the residuary estate as $250,000 before reduction for taxes and expenses of $50,000. The executor paid to W $4,192 ([$250,000 − $50,000] × ½ × 5 percent × 306/365) on December 31, 1971. On January 1, 1972, the executor transfers one-half of the residue of the estate to the trust. The trust adopts the calendar year as its taxable year. The value of the residuary estate is finally determined for Federal tax purposes to be $240,000 ($290,000 − $50,000). Accordingly, the amount which the executor should have paid to W is $5,030 ([$290,000 − $50,000] × ½ × 5 percent × 306/365). Consequently, an additional amount of $838 ($5,030 − $4,192) must be paid to W within a reasonable period after the final determination of value for Federal tax purposes.

(iv) Computation of annuity amount in certain circumstances. (a) Short taxable years. The governing instrument provides that, in the case of a taxable year which is for a period of less than 12 months other than the taxable year in which occurs the end of the period specified in subparagraph (5) of this paragraph, the annuity amount determined under subdivision (i) of this subparagraph shall be the amount otherwise determined under that subdivision multiplied by a fraction the numerator of which is the number of days in the taxable year of the trust and the denominator of which is 365 (366 if February 29 is a day included in the numerator).

(b) Last taxable year of period. The governing instrument provides that, in the case of the taxable year in which occurs the end of the period specified in subparagraph (5) of this paragraph, the annuity amount which must be distributed under subdivision (i) of this subparagraph shall be the amount otherwise determined under that subdivision multiplied by a fraction the numerator of which is the number of days in the period beginning on the first day of such taxable year and ending on the last day of the period specified in subparagraph (5) of this paragraph and the denominator of which is 365 (366 if February 29 is a day included in the numerator). See subparagraph (5) of this paragraph for a special rule allowing termination of payment of the annuity amount with the regular payment next preceding the termination of the period specified therein.

(2) Minimum annuity amount. (i) General rule. The total amount payable under subparagraph (1) of this paragraph is not less than 5 percent of the initial net fair market value of the property placed in trust as finally determined for Federal tax purposes.

(ii) Reduction of annuity amount in certain cases. A trust will not fail to meet the requirements of this subparagraph by reason of the fact that it provides for a reduction of the stated amount payable upon the death of a recipient or the expiration of a term of years provided that:

(a) A distribution is made to an organization described in section 170(c) at the death of such recipient or the expiration of such term of years,, and

(b) The total amounts payable each year under subparagraph (1) of this paragraph after such distribution are not less than a stated dollar amount which bears the same ratio to 5 percent of the initial net fair market value of the trust assets as the net fair market value of the trust assets immediately after such distribution bears to the net fair market value of the trust assets immediately before such distribution.

(iii) Rule applicable to inter vivos trust which does not provide for payment of minimum annuity amount. In the case where the grantor of an inter vivos trust underestimates in good faith the initial net fair market value of the property placed in trust as finally determined for Federal tax purposes and specifies a fixed dollar amount for the annuity which is less than 5 percent of the initial net fair market value of the property placed in trust as finally determined for Federal tax purposes, the trust will be deemed to have met the 5 percent requirement if the grantor or his representative consents, by appropriate agreement with the District Director, to accept an amount equal to 20 times the annuity as the fair market value of the property placed in trust for purposes of determining the appropriate charitable contributions deduction.

(3) Permissible recipients. (i) General rule. The amount described in subparagraph (1) of this paragraph is payable to or for use of a named person or persons, at least one of which is not an organization described in section 170(c). If the amount described in subparagraph (1) of this paragraph

is to be paid to an individual or individuals, all such individuals must be living at the time of the creation of the trust. A named person or persons may include members of a named class provided that, in the case of a class which includes any individual, all such individuals must be alive and ascertainable at the time of the creation of the trust unless the period for which the annuity amount is to be paid to such class consists solely of a term of years. For example, in the case of a testamentary trust, the testator's will may provide that an amount shall be paid to his children living at his death.

(ii) Power of alter amount paid to recipients, A trust is not a charitable remainder annuity trust if any person has the power to alter the amount to be paid to any named person other than an organization described in section 170(c) if such power would cause any person to be treated as the owner of the trust, or any portion thereof, if subpart E, Part 1, subchapter J, chapter 1, subtitle A of the Code were applicable to such trust. See paragraph (a)(4) of this section for a rule permitting the retention by a grantor of a testamentary power to revoke or terminate the interest of any recipient other than an organization described in section 170(c). For example, the governing instrument may not grant the trustee the power to allocate the annuity among members of a class unless such power falls within one of the exceptions to section 674(a).

(4) Other payments. No amount other than the amount described in subparagraph (1) of this paragraph may be paid to or for the use of any person other than an organization described in section 170(c). An amount is not paid to or for the use of any person other than an organization described in section 170(c) if the amount is transferred for full and adequate consideration. The trust may not be subject to a power to invade, alter, amend, or revoke for the beneficial use of a person other than an organization described in section 170(c). Notwithstanding the preceding sentence, the grantor may retain the power exercisable only by will to revoke or terminate the interest of any recipient other than an organization described in section 170(c). The governing instrument may provide that any amount other than the amount described in subparagraph (1) of this paragraph shall be paid (or may be paid in the discretion of the trustee) to an organization described in section 170(c) provided that in the case of distributions in kind, the adjusted basis of the property distributed is fairly representative of the adjusted basis of the property available for payment on the date of payment. For example, the governing instrument may provide that a portion of the trust assets may be distributed currently, or upon the death of one or more recipients, to an organization described in section 170(c).

(5) Period of payment of annuity amount. (i) General rules. The period for which an amount described in subparagraph (1) of this paragraph is payable begins with the first year of the charitable remainder trust and continues either for the life or lives of a named individual or individuals or for a term of years not to exceed 20 years. Only an individual or an organization described in section 170(c) may receive an amount for the life of an individual. If an individual receives an amount for life, it must be solely for his life. Payment of the amount described in subparagraph (1) of this paragraph may terminate with the regular payment next preceding the termination of the period described in this subparagraph. The fact that the recipient may not receive such last payment shall not be taken into account for purposes of determining the present value of the remainder interest. In the case of an amount payable for a term of years, the length of the term of years shall be ascertainable with certainty at the time of the creation of the trust, except that the term may be terminated by the death of the recipient or by the grantor's exercise by will of a retained power to revoke or terminate the interest of any recipient other than an organization described in section 170(c). In any event, the period may not extend beyond either the life or lives of a named individual or individuals or a term of years not to exceed 20 years. For example, the governing instrument may not provide for the payment of an annuity amount to A for his life and then to B for a term of years because it is possible for the period to last longer than either the lives of recipients in being at the creation of the trust or a term of years not to exceed 20 years. On the other hand, the governing instrument may provide for the payment of an annuity amount to A for his life and then to B for his life or a term of years (not to exceed 20 years), whichever is shorter (but not longer), if both A and B are in being at the creation of the trust because it is not possible for the period to last longer than the lives of recipients in being at the creation of the trust.

(ii) Relationship to 5 percent requirement. The 5 percent requirement provided in subparagraph (2) of this paragraph must be met until the termination of all of the payments described in subparagraph (1) of this paragraph. For example, the following provisions would satisfy the above rules:

(a) An amount equal to at least 5 percent of the initial net fair market value of the property placed in trust to A and B for their joint lives and then to the survivor for his life;

(b) An amount equal to at least 5 percent of the initial net fair market value of the property placed in trust to A for life or for a term of years not longer than 20 years, whichever is longer (or shorter);

(c) An amount equal to at least 5 percent of the initial net fair market value of the property placed in trust to A for a term of years not longer than 20 years and then to B for life (provided B was living at the date of creation of the trust);

(d) An amount to A for his life and concurrently an amount to B for his life (the amount to each recipient to terminate at his death) if the amount given to each individual is not less than 5 percent of the initial net fair market value of the property placed in trust; or

(e) An amount to A for his life and concurrently an equal amount to B for his life, and at the death of the first to die, the trust to distribute one-half of the then value of its assets to an organization described in section 170(c), if the total of the amounts given to A and B is not less than 5 percent of the initial net fair market value of the property placed in trust.

(6) Permissible remaindermen. (i) General rule. At the end of the period specified in subparagraph (5) of this paragraph the entire corpus of the trust is required to be irrevocably transferred, in whole or in part, to or for the use of one or more organizations described in section 170(c) or retained, in whole or in part, for such use.

(ii) Treatment of trust. If all of the trust corpus is to be retained for such use, the taxable year of the trust shall terminate at the end of the period specified in subparagraph (5) of this paragraph and the trust shall cease to be treated as a charitable remainder trust for all purposes. If all or any portion of the trust corpus is to be transferred to or for the use of such organization or organizations, the trustee shall have a reasonable time after the period specified in subparagraph (5) of this paragraph to complete the settlement of the trust. During such time, the trust shall continue to be treated as a charitable remainder trust for all purposes, such as sections 664, 4947(a)(2), and 4947(b)(3)(B). Upon the expiration of such period, the taxable year of the trust shall terminate and the trust shall cease to be treated as a charitable remainder trust for all purposes. If the trust continues in existence, it will be subject to the provisions of section 4947(a)(1) unless the trust is exempt from taxation under section 501(a). For purposes of determining whether the trust is exempt under section 501(a) as an organization described in section 501(c)(3), the trust shall be deemed to have been created at the time it ceases to be treated as a charitable remainder trust.

(iii) Concurrent or successive remaindermen. Where interests in the corpus of the trust are given to more than one organization described in section 170(c) such interests may be enjoyed by them either concurrently or successively.

(iv) Alternative remaindermen. The governing instrument shall provide that if an organization to or for the use of which the trust corpus is to be transferred or for the use of which the trust corpus is to be retained is not an organization described in section 170(c) at the time any amount is to be irrevocably transferred to or for the use of such organization, such amount shall be transferred to or for the use of one or more alternative organizations which are described in section 170(c) at such time or retained for such use. Such alternative organization or organizations may be selected in any manner provided by the terms of the governing instrument.

(b) Additional contributions. A trust is not a charitable remainder annuity trust unless its governing instrument provides that no additional contributions may be made to the charitable remainder annuity trust after the initial contribution. For purposes of this section, all property passing to a charitable remainder annuity trust by reason of death of the grantor shall be considered one contribution.

(c) Calculation of the fair market value of the remainder interest of a charitable remainder annuity trust. For purposes of sections 170, 2055, 2106, and 2522, the fair market value of the remainder interest of a charitable remainder annuity trust (as described in this section) is the net fair market value (as of the appropriate valuation date) of the property placed in trust less the present value of the annuity. For purposes of this section, valuation date means, in general, the date on which the property is transferred to the trust by the donor regardless of when the trust is created. In the case of transfers to a charitable remainder annuity trust for which the valuation date is after April 30, 1999, if an election is made under section 7520 and § 1.7520-2(b) to compute the present value of the charitable interest by use of the interest rate component for either of the 2 months preceding the month in which the transfer is made, the month so elected is the valuation date for purposes of determining the interest rate and mortality tables. For purposes of section 2055 or 2106, the valuation date is the date of death unless the alternate valuation date is elected in accordance with section 2032, in which event, and within the limitations set forth in section 2032 and the regulations thereunder, the valuation date is the alternate valuation date. If the decedent's estate elects the alternate valuation date under section 2032 and also elects, under section 7520 and § 1.7520-2(b), to use the interest rate component for one of the 2 months preceding the alternate valuation date, the month so elected is the valuation date for purposes of determining the interest rate and mortality tables. The present value of an annuity is computed under § 20.2031-7(d) of this chapter (Estate Tax Regulations) for transfers for which the valuation date is after April 30, 1989, or under § 20.2031-7A(a) through (e) of this chapter, whichever is applicable, for transfers for which the valuation date is before May 1, 1999. See, however, § 1.7520-3(b) (relating to exceptions to the use of prescribed tables under certain circumstances). If the valuation date of a transfer to a charitable remainder annuity trust is after April 30, 1989, and before June 10, 1994, a transferor can rely on Notice 89-24, 1989-1 C.B. 660, or Notice 89-60, 1989-1 C.B. 700 (See § 601.601(d)(2)(ii)(b) of this chapter), in valuing the transferred interest.

(d) Deduction for transfers to a charitable remainder annuity trust. For rules relating to a deduction for transfers to a charitable remainder annuity trust, see sections 170, 2055, 2106, or 2522 and the regulations thereunder. Any claim for deduction on any return for the value of a remainder interest in a charitable remainder annuity trust must be supported by a full statement attached to the return showing the computation of the present value of such interest. The deduction allowed by section 170 is limited to the fair market value of the remainder interest of a charitable remainder annuity trust regardless of whether an organization described in section 170(c) also receives a portion of the annuity. For a special rule relating to the reduction of the amount of a charitable contribution deduction with respect to a contribution of certain ordinary income property or capital gain property, see sections 170(e)(1)(A) or 170(e)(1)(B)(i) and the regulations thereunder. For rules for postponing the time for deduction of a charitable contribution of a future interest in tangible personal property, see section 170(a)(3) and the regulations thereunder.

T.D. 7202, 8/22/72, amend T.D. 7955, 5/10/84, T.D. 8540, 6/9/94, T.D. 8791, 12/09/98, T.D. 8926, 1/4/2001.

§ 1.664-3 Charitable remainder unitrust.

Caution: The Treasury has not yet amended Reg § 1.664-3 to reflect changes made by P.L. 105-34, P.L. 98-369, P.L. 94-455.

(a) Description. A charitable remainder unitrust is a trust which complies with the applicable provisions of § 1.664-1 and meets all of the following requirements:

(1) Required payment of unitrust amount. (i) Payment of fixed percentage at least annually. (a) General rule. The governing instrument provides that the trust will pay not less often than annually a fixed percentage of the net fair market value of the trust assets determined annually to a person or persons described in paragraph (a)(3) of this section for each taxable year of the period specified in paragraph (a)(5) of this section. This paragraph (a)(1)(i)(a) is applicable for taxable years ending after April 18, 1997.

(b) Income exception. Instead of the amount described in (a) of this subdivision (i), the governing instrument may provide that the trust shall pay for any year either the amount described in (1) or the total of the amounts described in (1) and (2) of this subdivision (b).

(1) The amount of trust income for a taxable year to the extent that such amount is not more than the amount required to be distributed under paragraph (a)(1)(i)(a) of this section.

(2) An amount of trust income for a taxable year that is in excess of the amount required to be distributed under paragraph (a)(1)(i)(a) of this section for such year to the extent that (by reason of paragraph (a)(1)(i)(b)(1) of this section) the aggregate of the amounts paid in prior years was less than the aggregate of such required amounts.

(3) For purposes of this paragraph (a)(1)(i)(b), trust income generally means income as defined under section 643(b) and the applicable regulations. However, trust income may not be determined by reference to a fixed percentage of the annual fair market value of the trust property, notwith-

standing any contrary provision in applicable state law. Proceeds from the sale or exchange of any assets contributed to the trust by the donor must be allocated to principal and not to trust income at least to the extent of the fair market value of those assets on the date of their contribution to the trust. Proceeds from the sale or exchange of any assets purchased by the trust must be allocated to principal and not to trust income at least to the extent of the trust's purchase price of those assets. Except as provided in the two preceding sentences, proceeds from the sale or exchange of any assets contributed to the trust by the donor or purchased by the trust may be allocated to income, pursuant to the terms of the governing instrument, if not prohibited by applicable local law. A discretionary power to make this allocation may be granted to the trustee under the terms of the governing instrument but only to the extent that the state statute permits the trustee to make adjustments between income and principal to treat beneficiaries impartially.

(4) The rules in paragraph (a)(1)(i)(b)(1) and (2) of this section are applicable for taxable years ending after April 18, 1997. The rule in the first sentence of paragraph (a)(1)(i)(b)(3) is applicable for taxable years ending after April 18, 1997. The rules in the second, fourth, and fifth sentences of paragraph (a)(1)(i)(b)(3) are applicable for taxable years ending after January 2, 2004. The rule in the third sentence of paragraph (a)(1)(i)(b)(3) is applicable for sales or exchanges that occur after April 18, 1997. The rule in the sixth sentence of paragraph (a)(1)(i)(b)(3) is applicable for trusts created after January 2, 2004.

(c) Combination of methods. Instead of the amount described in paragraph (a)(1)(i)(a) or (b) of this section, the governing instrument may provide that the trust will pay not less often than annually the amount described in paragraph (a)(1)(i)(b) of this section for an initial period and then pay the amount described in paragraph (a)(1)(i)(a) of this section (calculated using the same fixed percentage) for the remaining years of the trust only if the governing instrument provides that—

(1) The change from the method prescribed in paragraph (a)(1)(i)(b) of this section to the method prescribed in paragraph (a)(1)(i)(a) of this section is triggered on a specific date or by a single event whose occurrence is not discretionary with, or within the control of, the trustees or any other persons;

(2) The change from the method prescribed in paragraph (a)(1)(i)(b) of this section to the method prescribed in paragraph (a)(1)(i)(a) of this section occurs at the beginning of the taxable year that immediately follows the taxable year during which the date or event specified under paragraph (a)(1)(i)(c)(1) of this section occurs; and

(3) Following the trust's conversion to the method described in paragraph (a)(1)(i)(a) of this section, the trust will pay at least annually to the permissible recipients the amount described only in paragraph (a)(1)(i)(a) of this section and not any amount described in paragraph (a)(1)(i)(b) of this section.

(d) Triggering event. For purposes of paragraph (a)(1)(i)(c)(1) of this section, a triggering event based on the sale of unmarketable assets as defined in § 1.664-1(a)(7)(ii), or the marriage, divorce, death, or birth of a child with respect to any individual will not be considered discretionary with, or within the control of, the trustees or any other persons.

(e) Examples. The following examples illustrate the rules in paragraph (a)(1)(i)(c) of this section. For each example, assume that the governing instrument of charitable remainder unitrust Y provides that Y will initially pay not less often than annually the amount described in paragraph (a)(1)(i)(b) of this section and then pay the amount described in paragraph (a)(1)(i)(a) of this section (calculated using the same fixed percentage) for the remaining years of the trust and that the requirements of paragraphs (a)(1)(i)(c)(2) and (3) of this section are satisfied. The examples are as follows:

Example (1). Y is funded with the donor's former personal residence. The governing instrument of Y provides for the change in method for computing the annual unitrust amount as of the first day of the year following the year in which the trust sells the residence. Y provides for a combination of methods that satisfies paragraph (a)(1)(i)(c) of this section.

Example (2). Y is funded with cash and an unregistered security for which there is no available exemption permitting public sale under the Securities and Exchange Commission rules. The governing instrument of Y provides that the change in method for computing the annual unitrust amount is triggered on the earlier of the date when the stock is sold or at the time the restrictions on its public sale lapse or are otherwise lifted. Y provides for a combination of methods that satisfies paragraph (a)(1)(i)(c) of this section.

Example (3). Y is funded with cash and with a security that may be publicly traded under the Securities and Exchange Commission rules. The governing instrument of Y provides that the change in method for computing the annual unitrust amount is triggered when the stock is sold. Y does not provide for a combination of methods that satisfies the requirements of paragraph (a)(1)(i)(c) of this section because the sale of the publicly-traded stock is within the discretion of the trustee.

Example (4). S establishes Y for her granddaughter, G, when G is 10 years old. The governing instrument of Y provides for the change in method for computing the annual unitrust amount as of the first day of the year following the year in which G turns 18 years old. Y provides for a combination of methods that satisfies paragraph (a)(1)(i)(c) of this section.

Example (5). The governing instrument of Y provides for the change in method for computing the annual unitrust amount as of the first day of the year following the year in which the donor is married. Y provides for a combination of methods that satisfies paragraph (a)(1)(i)(c) of this section.

Example (6). The governing instrument of Y provides that if the donor divorces, the change in method for computing the annual unitrust amount will occur as of the first day of the year following the year of the divorce. Y provides for a combination of methods that satisfies paragraph (a)(1)(i)(c) of this section.

Example (7). The governing instrument of Y provides for the change in method for computing the annual unitrust amount as of the first day of the year following the year in which the noncharitable beneficiary's first child is born. Y provides for a combination of methods that satisfies paragraph (a)(1)(i)(c) of this section.

Example (8). The governing instrument of Y provides for the change in method for computing the annual unitrust amount as of the first day of the year following the year in which the noncharitable beneficiary's father dies. Y provides for a combination of methods that satisfies paragraph (a)(1)(i)(c) of this section.

Example (9). The governing instrument of Y provides for the change in method for computing the annual unitrust amount as of the first day of the year following the year in which the noncharitable beneficiary's financial advisor determines that the beneficiary should begin receiving payments under the second prescribed payment method. Because the change in methods for paying the unitrust amount is triggered by an event that is within a person's control, Y does not provide for a combination of methods that satisfies paragraph (a)(1)(i)(c) of this section.

Example (10). The governing instrument of Y provides for the change in method for computing the annual unitrust amount as of the first day of the year following the year in which the noncharitable beneficiary submits a request to the trustee that the trust convert to the second prescribed payment method. Because the change in methods for paying the unitrust amount is triggered by an event that is within a person's control, Y does not provide for a combination of methods that satisfies paragraph (a)(1)(i)(c) of this section.

(f) Effective date. (1) General rule. Paragraphs (a)(1)(i)(c), (d), and (e) of this section are applicable for charitable remainder trusts created on or after December 10, 1998.

(2) General rule regarding reformations of combination of method unitrusts. If a trust is created on or after December 10, 1998, and contains a provision allowing a change in calculating the unitrust amount that does not comply with the provisions of paragraph (a)(1)(i)(c) of this section, the trust will qualify as a charitable remainder unitrust only if it is amended or reformed to use the initial method for computing the unitrust amount throughout the term of the trust, or is reformed in accordance with paragraph (a)(1)(i)(f)(3) of this section. If a trust was created before December 10, 1998, and contains a provision allowing a change in calculating the unitrust amount that does not comply with the provisions of paragraph (a)(1)(i)(c) of this section, the trust may be reformed to use the initial method for computing the unitrust amount throughout the term of the trust without causing the trust to fail to function exclusively as a charitable remainder unitrust under § 1.664-1(a)(4), or may be reformed in accordance with paragraph (a)(1)(i)(f)(3) of this section. Except as provided in paragraph (a)(1)(i)(f)(3) of this section, a qualified charitable remainder unitrust will not continue to qualify as a charitable remainder unitrust if it is amended or reformed to add a provision allowing a change in the method for calculating the unitrust amount.

(3) Special rule for reformations of trusts that begin by June 8, 1999. Notwithstanding paragraph (a)(1)(i)(f)(2) of this section, if a trust either provides for payment of the unitrust amount under a combination of methods that is not permitted under paragraph (a)(1)(i)(c) of this section, or provides for payment of the unitrust amount under only the method prescribed in paragraph (a)(1)(i)(b) of this section, then the trust may be reformed to allow for a combination of methods permitted under paragraph (a)(1)(i)(c) of this section without causing the trust to fail to function exclusively as a charitable remainder unitrust under § 1.664-1(a)(4) or to engage in an act of self-dealing under section 4941 if the trustee begins legal proceedings to reform by June 8, 1999. The triggering event under the reformed governing instrument may not occur in a year prior to the year in which the court issues the order reforming the trust, except for situations in which the governing instrument prior to reformation already provided for payment of the unitrust amount under a combination of methods that is not permitted under paragraph (a)(1)(i)(c) of this section and the triggering event occurred prior to the reformation.

(g) Payment under general rule for fixed percentage trusts. When the unitrust amount is computed under paragraph (a)(1)(i)(a) of this section, a trust will not be deemed to have engaged in an act of self-dealing (within the meaning of section 4941), to have unrelated debt-financed income (within the meaning of section 514), to have received an additional contribution (within the meaning of paragraph (b) of this section), or to have failed to function exclusively as a charitable remainder trust (within the meaning of § 1.664-1(a)(4)) merely because the unitrust amount is paid after the close of the taxable year if such payment is made within a reasonable time after the close of such taxable year and the entire unitrust amount in the hands of the recipient is characterized only as income from the categories described in section 664(b)(1), (2), or (3), except to the extent it is characterized as corpus described in section 664(b)(4) because—

(1) The trust pays the unitrust amount by distributing property (other than cash) that it owned at the close of the taxable year, and the trustee elects to treat any income generated by the distribution as occurring on the last day of the taxable year in which the unitrust amount is due;

(2) The trust pays the unitrust amount by distributing cash that was contributed to the trust (with respect to which a deduction was allowable under section 170, 2055, 2106, or 2522); or

(3) The trust pays the unitrust amount by distributing cash received as a return of basis in any asset that was contributed to the trust (with respect to which a deduction was allowable under section 170, 2055, 2106, or 2522), and that is sold by the trust during the year for which the unitrust amount is due.

(h) Special rule for fixed percentage trusts created before December 10, 1998. When the unitrust amount is computed under paragraph (a)(1)(i)(a) of this section, a trust created before December 10, 1998, will not be deemed to have engaged in an act of self-dealing (within the meaning of section 4941), to have unrelated debt-financed income (within the meaning of section 514), to have received an additional contribution (within the meaning of paragraph (b) of this section), or to have failed to function exclusively as a charitable remainder trust (within the meaning of § 1.664-1(a)(4)) merely because the unitrust amount is paid after the close of the taxable year if such payment is made within a reasonable time after the close of such taxable year and the fixed percentage to be paid each year as the unitrust amount is 15 percent or less of the net fair market value of the trust assets as determined under paragraph (a)(1)(iv) of this section.

(i) Example. The following example illustrates the rules in paragraph (a)(1)(i)(g) of this section:

Example. X is a charitable remainder unitrust that calculates the unitrust amount under paragraph (a)(1)(i)(a) of this section. X was created after December 10, 1998. The prorated unitrust amount payable from X for Year 1 is $100. The trustee does not pay the unitrust amount to the recipient by the end of the Year 1. At the end of Year 1, X has only $95 in the ordinary income category under section 664(b)(1) and no income in the capital gain or tax-exempt income categories under section 664(b)(2) or (3), respectively. By April 15 of Year 2, in addition to $95 in cash, the trustee distributes to the unitrust recipient a capital asset with a $5 fair market value and a $2 adjusted basis to pay the $100 unitrust amount due for Year 1. The trust owned the asset at the end of Year 1. Under § 1.664-1(d)(5), the distribution is treated as a sale by X, resulting in X recognizing a $3 capital gain. The trustee elects to treat the capital gain as occurring on the last day of Year 1. Under § 1.664-1(d)(1), the character of the unitrust amount for Year 1 in the recipient's hands is $95 of ordinary income, $3 of capital gain income, and $2 of trust corpus. For Year 1, X satisfied paragraph (a)(1)(i)(g) of this section.

(j) Payment under income exception. When the unitrust amount is computed under paragraph (a)(1)(i)(b) of this section, a trust will not be deemed to have engaged in an act of self-dealing (within the meaning of section 4941), to have unrelated debt-financed income (within the meaning of section 514), to have received an additional contribution (within the meaning of paragraph (b) of this section), or to have failed to function exclusively as a charitable remainder trust (within the meaning of § 1.664-1(a)(4)) merely because payment of the unitrust amount is made after the close of the taxable year if such payment is made within a reasonable time after the close of such taxable year.

(k) Reasonable time. For paragraphs (a)(1)(i)(g), (h), and (j) of this section, a reasonable time will not ordinarily extend beyond the date by which the trustee is required to file Form 5227, "Split-Interest Trust Information Return," [including extensions] for the taxable year.

(l) Effective date. Paragraphs (a)(1)(i)(g), (h), (i), (j), and (k) of this section are applicable for taxable years ending after April 18, 1997. Paragraphs (a)(1)(i)(g)(2) and (3) apply only to distributions made on or after January 5, 2001.

(ii) Definition of fixed percentage. The fixed percentage may be expressed either as a fraction or as a percentage and must be payable each year in the period specified in subparagraph (5) of this paragraph. A percentage is fixed if the percentage is the same either as to each recipient or as to the total percentage payable each year of such period. For example, provision for a fixed percentage which is the same every year to A until his death and concurrently a fixed percentage which is the same every year to B until his death, the fixed percentage to each recipient to terminate at his death, would satisfy the rule. Similarly, provision for a fixed percentage to A and B for their joint lives and then to the survivor would satisfy the rule. In the case of a distribution to an organization described in section 170(c) at the death of a recipient or the expiration of a term of years, the governing instrument may provide for a reduction of the fixed percentage payable after such distribution provided that:

(a) The reduced fixed percentage is the same either as to each recipient or as to the total amount payable for each year of the balance of such period, and

(b) The requirements of subparagraph (2)(ii) of this paragraph are met.

(iii) Rules applicable to incorrect valuations. The governing instrument provides that in the case where the net fair market value of the trust assets is incorrectly determined by the fiduciary, the trust shall pay to the recipient (in the case of an undervaluation) or be repaid by the recipient (in the case of an overvaluation) an amount equal to the difference between the amount which the trust should have paid the recipient if the correct value were used and the amount which the trust actually paid the recipient. Such payments or repayments must be made within a reasonable period after the final determination of such value. Any payment due to a recipient by reason of such incorrect valuation shall be considered to be a payment required to be distributed at the time of such final determination for purposes of paragraph (d)(4)(ii) of § 1.664-1. See paragraph (d)(4) of § 1.664-1 for rules relating to the year of inclusion of such payments and the allowance of a deduction for such repayments. See paragraph (b) of this section for rules relating to additional contributions.

(iv) Rules applicable to valuation. In computing the net fair market value of the trust assets there shall be taken into account all assets and liabilities without regard to whether particular items are taken into account in determining the income of the trust. The net fair market value of the trust assets may be determined on any one date during the taxable year of the trust, or by taking the average of valuations made on more than one date during the taxable year of the trust, so long as the same valuation date or dates and valuation methods are used each year. If the governing instrument does not specify the valuation date or dates, the trustee must select such date or dates and indicate the selection on the first return on Form 5227, "Split-Interest Trust Information Return," that the trust must file. The amount described in subdivision (i)(a) of this subparagraph which must be paid each year must be based upon the valuation for such year.

(v) Computation of unitrust amount in certain circumstances. (a) Short taxable years. The governing instrument provides that, in the case of a taxable year which is for a period of less than 12 months other than the taxable year in which occurs the end of the period specified in subparagraph (5) of this paragraph:

(1) The amount determined under subdivision (i)(a) of this subparagraph shall be the amount otherwise determined under that subdivision multiplied by a fraction the numerator of which is the number of days in the taxable year of the trust and the denominator of which is 365 (366 if February 29 is a day included in the numerator),

(2) The amount determined under subdivision (i)(b) of this subparagraph shall be computed by using the amount determined under subdivision (a)(1) of this subdivision (v), and

(3) If no valuation date occurs before the end of the taxable year of the trust, the trust assets shall be valued as of the last day of the taxable year of the trust.

(b) Last taxable year of period. (1) The governing instrument provides that, in the case of the taxable year in which occurs the end of the period specified in subparagraph (5) of this paragraph:

(i) The unitrust amount which must be distributed under subdivision (i)(a) of this subparagraph shall be the amount otherwise determined under that subdivision multiplied by a fraction the numerator of which is the number of days in the period beginning on the first day of such taxable year and ending on the last day of the period specified in subparagraph (5) of this paragraph and the denominator of which is 365 (366 if February 29 is a day included in the numerator).

(ii) The amount determined under subdivision (i)(b) of this subparagraph shall be computed by using the amount determined under (b)(1)(i) of this subdivision (v), and

(iii) If no valuation date occurs before the end of such period, the trust assets shall be valued as of the last day of such period.

(2) See subparagraph (5) of this paragraph for a special rule allowing termination of payment of the unitrust amount with the regular payment next preceding the termination of the period specified therein.

(2) Minimum unitrust amount. (i) General rule. The fixed percentage described in subparagraph (1)(i) of this paragraph with respect to all beneficiaries taken together is not less than 5 percent.

(ii) Reduction of unitrust amount in certain cases. A trust will not fail to meet the requirements of this subparagraph by reason of the fact that it provides for a reduction of the fixed percentage payable upon the death of a recipient or the expiration of a term of years provided that:

(a) A distribution is made to an organization described in section 170(c) at the death of such recipient or the expiration of such term of years, and

(b) The total of the percentage payable under subparagraph (1) of this paragraph after such distribution is not less than 5 percent.

(3) Permissible recipients. (i) General rule. The amount described in subparagraph (1) of this paragraph is payable to or for the use of a named person or persons, at least one of which is not an organization described in section 170(c). If the amount described in subparagraph (1) of this paragraph is to be paid to an individual or individuals, all such individuals must be living at the time of creation of the trust. A named person or persons may include members of a named class except in the case of a class which includes any individual, all such individuals must be alive and ascertainable at the time of the creation of the trust unless the period for which the unitrust amount is to be paid to such class consists solely of a term of years. For example, in the case of a testamentary trust, the testator's will may provide that the required amount shall be paid to his children living at his death.

(ii) Power to alter amount paid to recipients. A trust is not a charitable remainder unitrust if any person has the power to alter the amount to be paid to any named person other than an organization described in section 170(c) if such power would cause any person to be treated as the owner of the trust, or any portion thereof, if subpart E, part 1, subchapter J, chapter 1, subtitle A of the Code were applicable to such trust. See paragraph (a)(4) of this section for a rule permitting the retention by a grantor of a testamentary power to revoke or terminate the interest of any recipient other than an organization described in section 170(c). For example, the governing instrument may not grant the trustee the power to allocate the fixed percentage among members of a class unless such power falls within one of the exceptions to section 674(a).

(4) Other payments. No amount other than the amount described in subparagraph (1) of this paragraph may be paid to or for the use of any person other than an organization described in section 170(c). An amount is not paid to or for the use of any person other than an organization described in section 170(c) if the amount is transferred for full and adequate consideration. The trust may not be subject to a power to invade, alter, amend, or revoke for the beneficial use of a person other than an organization described in section 170(c). Notwithstanding the preceding sentence, the grantor may retain the power exercisable only by will to revoke or terminate the interest of any recipient other than an organization described in section 170(c). The governing instrument may provide that any amount other than the amount described in subparagraph (1) of this paragraph shall be paid (or may be paid in the discretion of the trustee) to an organization described in section 170(c) provided that, in the case of distributions in kind, the adjusted basis of the property distributed is fairly representative of the adjusted basis of the property available for payment on the date of payment. For example, the governing instrument may provide that a portion of the trust assets may be distributed currently, or upon the death of one or more recipients, to an organization described in section 170(c).

(5) Period of payment of unitrust amount. (i) General rules. The period for which an amount described in subparagraph (1) of this paragraph is payable begins with the first year of the charitable remainder trust and continues either for the life or lives of a named individual or individuals or for a term of years not to exceed 20 years. Only an individual or an organization described in section 170(c) may receive an amount for the life of an individual. If an individual receives an amount for life, it must be solely for his life. Payment of the amount described in subparagraph (1) of this paragraph may terminate with the regular payment next preceding the termination of the period described in this subparagraph. The fact that the recipient may not receive such last payment shall not be taken into account for purposes of determining the present value of the remainder interest. In the case of an amount payable for a term of years, the length of the term of years shall be ascertainable with certainty at the time of the creation of the trust, except that the term may be terminated by the death of the recipient or by the grantor's exercise by will of a retained power to revoke or terminate the interest of any recipient other than an organization described in section 170(c). In any event, the period may not extend beyond either the life or lives of a named individual or individuals or a term of years not to exceed 20 years. For example, the governing instrument may not provide for the payment of a unitrust amount to A for his life and then to B for a term of years because it is possible for the period to last longer than either the lives of recipients in being at the creation of the trust or a term of years not to exceed 20 years. On the other hand, the governing instrument may provide for the payment of a unitrust amount to A for his life and then to B for his life or a term of years (not to exceed 20 years), whichever is shorter (but not longer), if both A and B are in being at the creation of the trust because it is not possible for the period to last longer than the lives of recipients in being at the creation of the trust.

(ii) Relationship to 5 percent requirement. The 5 percent requirement provided in subparagraph (2) of this paragraph must be met until the termination of all of the payments described in subparagraph (1) of this paragraph. For example, the following provisions would satisfy the above rules:

(a) A fixed percentage of at least 5 percent to A and B for their joint lives and then to the survivor for his life;

(b) A fixed percentage of at least 5 percent to A for life or for a term of years not longer than 20 years, whichever is longer (or shorter);

(c) A fixed percentage of at least 5 percent to A for a term of years not longer than 20 years and then to B for life (provided B was living at the creation of the trust);

(d) A fixed percentage to A for his life and concurrently a fixed percentage to B for his life (the percentage to each recipient to terminate at his death) if the percentage given to each individual is not less than 5 percent;

(e) A fixed percentage to A for his life and concurrently an equal percentage to B for his life, and at the death of the first to die, the trust to distribute one-half of the then value of its assets to an organization described in section 170(c) if the total of the percentage is not less than 5 percent for the entire period described in this subparagraph.

(6) Permissible remaindermen. (i) General rule. At the end of the period specified in subparagraph (5) of this paragraph, the entire corpus of the trust is required to be irrevocably transferred, in whole or in part, to or for the use of one or more organizations described in section 170(c) or retained, in whole or in part, for such use.

(ii) Treatment of trust. If all of the trust corpus is to be retained for such use, the taxable year of the trust shall terminate at the end of the period specified in subparagraph (5) of this paragraph and the trust shall cease to be treated as a charitable remainder trust for all purposes. If all or any portion of the trust corpus is to be transferred to or for the use of such organization or organizations, the trustee shall have a reasonable time after the period specified in subparagraph (5) of this paragraph to complete the settlement of the trust. During such time, the trust shall continue to be treated as a charitable remainder trust for all purposes, such as section 664, 4947(a)(2), and 4947(b)(3)(B). Upon the expiration of such period, the taxable year of the trust shall terminate and the trust shall cease to be treated as a charitable remainder trust for all purposes. If the trust continues in existence, it will be subject to the provisions of section 4947(a)(1) unless the trust is exempt from taxation under section 501(a). For purposes of determining whether the trust is exempt under section 501(a) as an organization described in section 501(c)(3), the trust shall be deemed to have been created at the time it ceases to be treated as a charitable remainder trust.

(iii) Concurrent or successive remaindermen. Where interests in the corpus of the trust are given to more than one organization described in section 170(c) such interests may be enjoyed by them either concurrently or successively.

(iv) Alternative remaindermen. The governing instrument shall provide that if an organization to or for the use of which the trust corpus is to be transferred or for the use of which the trust corpus is to be retained is not an organization described in section 170(c) at the time any amount is to be irrevocably transferred to or for the use of such organization, such amount shall be transferred to or for the use of or retained for the use of one or more alternative organizations which are described in section 170(c) at such time. Such alternative organization or organizations may be selected in any manner provided by the terms of the governing instrument.

(b) Additional contributions. A trust is not a charitable remainder unitrust unless its governing instrument either prohibits additional contributions to the trust after the initial contribution or provides that for the taxable year of the trust in which the additional contribution is made:

(1) Where no valuation date occurs after the time of the contribution and during the taxable year in which the contribution is made, the additional property shall be valued as of the time of contribution; and

(2) The amount described in paragraph (a)(1)(i)(a) of this section shall be computed by multiplying the fixed percentage by the sum of (i) the net fair market value of the trust assets (excluding the value of the additional property and any earned income from and any appreciation on such property after its contribution), and (ii) that proportion of the value of the additional property (that was excluded under subdivision (i) of this paragraph), which the number of days in the period which begins with the date of contribution and ends with the earlier of the last day of such taxable year or the last day of the period described in paragraph (a)(5) of this section bears to the number of days in the period which begins with the first day of such taxable year and ends with the earlier of the last day of such taxable year or the last day of the period described in paragraph (a)(5) of this section.

For purposes of this section, all property passing to a charitable remainder unitrust by reason of death of the grantor shall be considered one contribution. The application of the preceding rules may be illustrated by the following examples:

Example (1). On March 2, 1971, X makes an additional contribution of property to a charitable remainder unitrust. The taxable year of the trust is the calendar year and the regular valuation date is January 1 of each year. For purposes of computing the required payout with respect to the additional contribution for the year of contribution, the additional contribution is valued on March 2, 1971, the time of contribution. The property had a value on that date of $5,000. Income from such property in the amount of $250 was received on December 31, 1971. The required payout with respect to the additional contribution for the year of contribution is $208 (5 percent × $5,000 × 305/365). The income earned after the date of the contribution and after the regular valuation date does not enter into the computation.

Example (2). On July 1, 1971, X makes an additional contribution of $10,000 to a charitable remainder unitrust. The taxable year of the trust is the calendar year and the regular valuation date is December 31 of each year. The fixed percentage is 5 percent. Between July 1, 1971, and December 31, 1971, the additional property appreciates in value to $12,500 and earns $500 of income. Because the regular valuation date for the year of contribution occurs after the date of the additional contribution, the additional contribution including income earned by it is valued on the regular valuation date. Thus, the required payment with respect to the additional contribution is $325.87 (5 percent × [$12,500 + $500] × 183/365).

(c) Calculation of the fair market value of the remainder interest of a charitable remainder unitrust. See § 1.664-4 for rules relating to the calculation of the fair market value of the remainder interest of a charitable remainder unitrust.

(d) Deduction for transfers to a charitable remainder unitrust. For rules relating to a deduction for transfers to a charitable remainder unitrust, see sections 170, 2055, 2106, or 2522 and the regulations thereunder. The deduction allowed by section 170 for transfers to charity is limited to the fair market value of the remainder interest of a charitable remainder unitrusts regardless of whether an organization described in section 170(c) also receives a portion of the amount described in § 1.664-3(a)(1). For a special rule relating to the reduction of the amount of a charitable contribution deduction with respect to a contribution of certain ordinary income property or capital gain property, see section 170(e)(1)(A) or (B)(i) and the regulations thereunder. For rules for postponing the time for deduction of a charitable contribution of a future interest in tangible personal property, see section 170(a)(3) and the regulations thereunder.

T.D. 7202, 8/22/72, amend T.D. 8791, 12/09/98, T.D. 8926, 1/4/2001, T.D. 9102, 12/30/2003.

§ 1.664-4 Calculation of the fair market value of the remainder interest in a charitable remainder unitrust.

(a) Rules for determining present value. For purposes of sections 170, 2055, 2106, and 2522, the fair market value of a remainder interest in a charitable remainder unitrust (as described in § 1.664-3) is its present value determined under paragraph (d) of this section. The present value determined under this section shall be computed on the basis of —

(1) Life contingencies determined as to each life involved, from the values of lx set forth in Table 90CM contained in § 20.2031-7(d)(7) of this chapter in the case of transfers for which the valuation date is after April 30, 1999; or from Ta-

ble 80CNSMT contained § 20.2031-7A(e)(4) of this chapter in the case of transfer for which the valuation date is after April 30, 1989, and before May 1, 1999. See § 20.2031-7A(a) through (d) of this chapter, whichever is applicable, for transfers for which the valuation date is before May 1, 1989;

(2) Interest at the section 7520 rate in the case of transfers for which the valuation date is after April 30, 1989, or 10 percent in the case of transfers to charitable remainder unitrusts made after November 30, 1983, for which the valuation date is before May 1, 1989. See § 20.2031-7A(a) through (c) of this chapter, whichever is applicable, for transfers for which the valuation date is before December 1, 1983; and

(3) The assumption that the amount described in § 1.664-3(a)(1)(i)(a) is distributed in accordance with the payout sequence described in the governing instrument. If the governing instrument does not prescribe when the distribution is made during the period for which the payment is made, for purposes of this section, the distribution is considered payable on the first day of the period for which the payment is made.

(b) Actuarial computations by the Internal Revenue Service. The regulations in this and in related sections provide tables of actuarial factors and examples that illustrate the use of the tables in determining the value of remainder interests in property. Section 1.7520-1(c)(2) refers to government publications that provide additional tables of factors and examples of computations for more complex situations. If the computation requires the use of a factor that is not provided in this section, the Commissioner may supply the factor upon a request for a ruling. A request for a ruling must be accompanied by a recitation of the facts including the date of birth of each measuring life, and copies of the relevant documents. A request for a ruling must comply with the instructions for requesting a ruling published periodically in the Internal Revenue Bulletin (See § 601.601(d)(2)(ii)(b) of this chapter) and include payment of the required user fee. If the Commissioner furnishes the factor, a copy of the letter supplying the factor should be attached to the tax return in which the deduction is claimed. If the Commissioner does not furnish the factor, the taxpayer must furnish a factor computed in accordance with the principles set forth in this section.

(c) Statement supporting deduction required. Any claim for a deduction on any return for the value of a remainder interest in a charitable remainder unitrust must be supported by a full statement attached to the return showing the computation of the present value of such interest.

(d) Valuation. The fair market value of a remainder interest in a charitable remainder unitrust (as described in § 1.664-3) for transfers for which the valuation date is after April 30, 1999, is its present value determined under paragraph (e) of this section. The fair market value of a remainder interest in a charitable remainder unitrust (as described in § 1.664-3) for transfers for which the valuation date is before May 1, 1999, is its present value determined under the following sections:

Valuation dates		Applicable Regulations
After	Before	
	01-01-52	1.664-4A(a)
12-31-51	01-01-71	1.664-4A(b)
12-31-70	12-01-83	1.664-4A(c)
11-30-83	05-01-89	1.664-4A(d)
04-30-89	05-01-99	1.664-4A(e)

(e) Valuation of charitable remainder unitrusts having certain payout sequences for transfers for which the valuation date is after April 30, 1999. *(1) In general.* Except as otherwise provided in paragraph (e)(2) of this section, in the case of transfers for which the valuation date is after April 30, 1999, the present value of a remainder interest is determined under paragraphs (e)(3) through (e)(7) of this section, provided that the amount of the payout as of any payout date during any taxable year of the trust is not larger than the amount that the trust could distribute on such date under § 1.664-3(a)(1)(v) if the taxable year of the trust were to end on such date. See, however, § 1.7520-3(b) (relating to exceptions to the use of the prescribed tables under certain circumstances).

(2) Transitional rules for valuation of charitable remainder unitrusts. (i) For purposes of sections 2055, 2106, or 2624, if on May 1, 1999, the decedent was mentally incompetent so that the disposition of the property could not be changed, and the decedent died after April 30, 1999, without having regained competency to dispose of the decedent's property, or the decedent died within 90 days of the date that the decedent first regained competency after April 30, 1999, the present value of a remainder interest under this section is determined as if the valuation date with respect to the decedent's gross estate is either before May 1, 1999, or after April 30, 1999, at the option of the decedent's executor.

(ii) For purposes of sections 170, 2055, 2106, 2522, or 2624, in the case of transfers to a charitable remainder unitrust for which the valuation date is after April 30, 1999, and before July 1, 1999, the present value of a remainder interest based on one or more measuring lives is determined under this section by use of the section 7520 interest rate for the month in which the valuation date occurs (see §§ 1.7520-1(b) and 1.7520-2(a)(2)) and the appropriate actuarial tables under either paragraph (e)(7) of this section or § 1.664-4A(e)(6), at the option of the donor or the decedent's executor, as the case may be.

(iii) For purposes of paragraphs (e)(2)(i) and (ii) of this section, where the donor or decedent's executor is given the option to use the appropriate actuarial tables under either paragraph (e)(7) of this section or § 1.664-4A(e)(6), the donor or decedent's executor must use the same actuarial table with respect to each individual transaction and with respect to all transfers occurring on the valuation date (for example, gift and income tax charitable deductions with respect to the same transfer must be determined based on the same tables, and all assets includible in the gross estate and/or estate tax deductions claimed must be valued based on the same tables).

(3) Adjusted payout rate. For transfers for which the valuation date is after April 30, 1989, the adjusted payout rate is determined by using the appropriate Table F in paragraph (e)(6) of this section, for the section 7520 interest rate applicable to the transfer. If the interest rate is between 4.2 and 14 percent, see paragraph (e)(6) of this section. If the interest rate is below 4.2 percent or greater than 14 percent, see paragraph (b) of this section. The adjusted payout rate is determined by multiplying the fixed percentage described in § 1.664-3(a)(1)(i)(a) by the factor describing the payout sequence of the trust and the number of months by which the valuation date for the first full taxable year of the trust precedes the first payout date for such taxable year. If the governing instrument does not prescribe when the distribution or

distributions shall be made during the taxable year of the trust, see paragraph (a) of this section. In the case of a trust having a payout sequence for which no figures have been provided by the appropriate table, and in the case of a trust that determines the fair market value of the trust assets by taking the average of valuations on more than one date during the taxable year, see paragraph (b) of this section.

(4) Period is a term of years. If the period described in § 1.664-3(a)(5) is a term of years, the factor that is used in determining the present value of the remainder interest for transfers for which the valuation date is after November 30, 1983, is the factor under the appropriate adjusted payout rate in Table D of paragraph (e)(6) of this section corresponding to the number of years in the term. If the adjusted payout rate is an amount that is between adjusted payout rates for which factors are provided in Table D, a linear interpolation must be made. The present value of the remainder interest is determined by multiplying the net fair market value (as of the appropriate valuation date) of the property placed in trust by the factor determined under this paragraph. For purposes of this section, the valuation date is, in the case of an inter vivos transfer, the date on which the property is transferred to the trust by the donor. However, if an election is made under section 7520 and § 1.7520-2(b) to compute the present value of the charitable interest by use of the interest rate component for either of the 2 months preceding the month in which the date of transfer falls, the month so elected is the valuation date for purposes of determining the interest rate and mortality tables. In the case of a testamentary transfer under section 2055, 2106, or 2624, the valuation date is the date of death, unless the alternate valuation date is elected under section 2032, in which event, and within the limitations set forth in section 2032 and the regulations thereunder, the valuation date is the alternate valuation date. If the decedent's estate elects the alternate valuation date under section 2032 and also elects, under section 7520 and § 1.7520-2(b), to use the interest rate component for one of the 2 months preceding the alternate valuation date, the month so elected is the valuation date for purposes of determining the interest rate and mortality tables. The application of this paragraph (e)(4) may be illustrated by the following example:

Example. D transfers $100,000 to a charitable remainder unitrust on January 1. The trust instrument requires that the trust pay 8 percent of the fair market value of the trust assets as of January 1st for a term of 12 years to D in quarterly payments (March 31, June 30, September 30, and December 31). The section 7520 rate for January (the month that the transfer occurred) is 9.6 percent. Under Table F(9.6) in paragraph(e)(6) of this section, the appropriate adjustment factor is .944628 for quarterly payments payable at the end of each quarter. The adjusted payout rate is 7.557 (8% × .944628). Based on the remainder factors in Table D in paragraph(e)(6) of this section, the present value of the remainder interest is $38,950.30, computed as follows:

Factor at 7.4 percent for 12 years	.397495
Factor at 7.6 percent for 12 years	.387314
Difference	.010181

Interpolation adjustment:

$$\frac{7.557\% - 7.4\%}{0.2\%} = \frac{x}{.010181}$$

x = .007992

Factor at 7.4 percent for 12 years	.397495
Less: Interpolation adjustment	.007992
Interpolated factor	.389503

Present value of remainder interest:

($100,000 × .389503) $38,950.30

(5) Period is the life of one individual. If the period described in § 1.664-3(a)(5) is the life of one individual, the factor that is used in determining the present value of the remainder interest for transfers for which the valuation date is after April 30, 1999, is the factor in Table U(1) in paragraph (e)(7) of this section under the appropriate adjusted payout. For purposes of the computations described in this paragraph, the age of an individual is the age of that individual at the individual's nearest birthday. If the adjusted payout rate is an amount that is between adjusted payout rates for which factors are provided in the appropriate table, a linear interpolation must be made. The present value of the remainder interest is determined by multiplying the net fair market value (as of the valuation date as determined in paragraph (e)(4) of this section) of the property placed in trust by the factor determined under this paragraph (e)(5). If the adjusted payout rate is between 4.2 and 14 percent, see paragraph (e)(7) of this section. If the adjusted payout rate is below 4.2 percent or greater than 14 percent, see paragraph (b) of this section. The application of this paragraph (e)(5) may be illustrated by the following example:

Example. A, who is 44 years and 11 months old, transfers $100,000 to a charitable remainder unitrust on January 1st. The trust instrument requires that the trust pay to A semiannually (on June 30 and December 31) 9 percent of the fair market value of the trust assets as of January 1st during A's life. The section 7520 rate for January is 9.6 percent. Under Table F(9.6) in paragraph (e)(6) of this section, the appropriate adjustment factor is .933805 for semiannual payments payable at the end of the semiannual period. The adjusted payout rate is 8.404 (9% × .933805). Based on the remainder factors in Table U(1) in paragraph (e)(7) of this section, the present value of the remainder interest is $10,109.00, computed as follows:

Factor at 8.4 percent at age 45	.10117
Factor at 8.6 percent at age 45	.09715
Difference	.00402

Interpolation adjustment:

$$\frac{8.404\% - 8.4\%}{0.2\%} = \frac{x}{.00402}$$

x = .00008

Factor at 8.4 percent at age 45	.10117
Less: Interpolation adjustment	.00008
Interpolated Factor	.10109

Present value of remainder interest:

($100,000 × .10109)..........$10,109.00

(6) Actuarial Table D and F (4.2 through 14.0) for transfers for which the valuation date is after April 30, 1989. For transfers for which the valuation date is after April 30, 1989, the present value of a charitable remainder unitrust interest that is dependent upon a term of years is determined by using the section 7520 rate and the tables in this paragraph (e)(6). For transfers for which the valuation date is after April 30, 1999, where the present value of a charitable remainder unitrust interest is dependent on the termination of a life interest, see paragraph (e)(5) of this section. See, however, § 1.7520-3(b) (relating to exceptions to the use of pre-

scribed tables under certain circumstances). Many actuarial factors not contained in the following tables are contained in Internal Revenue Service Publication 1458, "Actuarial Values, Book Beth," (1999). A copy of this publication is available for purchase from the Superintendent of Documents, United States Government Printing Office, Washington, DC 20402.

TABLE D

SHOWING THE PRESENT WORTH OF A REMAINDER INTEREST POSTPONED FOR A TERM CERTAIN IN A CHARITABLE REMAINDER UNITRUST APPLICABLE AFTER APRIL 30, 1989

	ADJUSTED PAYOUT RATE									
YEARS	4.2%	4.4%	4.6%	4.8%	5.0%	5.2%	5.4%	5.6%	5.8%	6.0%
1	.958000	.956000	.954000	.952000	.950000	.948000	.946000	.944000	.942000	.940000
2	.917764	.913936	.910116	.906304	.902500	.898704	.894916	.891136	.887364	.883600
3	.879218	.873723	.868251	.862801	.857375	.851971	.846591	.841232	.835897	.830584
4	.842291	.835279	.828311	.821387	.814506	.807669	.800875	.794123	.787415	.780749
5	.806915	.798527	.790209	.781960	.773781	.765670	.757627	.749652	.741745	.733904
6	.773024	.763392	.753859	.744426	.735092	.725855	.716716	.707672	.698724	.689870
7	.740557	.729802	.719182	.708694	.698337	.688111	.678013	.668042	.658198	.648478
8	.709454	.697691	.686099	.674677	.663420	.652329	.641400	.630632	.620022	.609569
9	.679657	.666993	.654539	.642292	.630249	.618408	.606765	.595317	.584061	.572995
10	.651111	.637645	.624430	.611462	.598737	.586251	.573999	.561979	.550185	.538615
11	.623764	.609589	.595706	.582112	.568800	.555766	.543003	.530508	.518275	.506298
12	.597566	.582767	.568304	.554170	.540360	.526866	.513681	.500800	.488215	.475920
13	.572469	.557125	.542162	.527570	.513342	.499469	.485942	.472755	.459898	.447365
14	.548425	.532611	.517222	.502247	.487675	.473496	.459701	.446281	.433224	.420523
15	.525391	.509177	.493430	.478139	.463291	.448875	.434878	.421289	.408097	.395292
16	.503325	.486773	.470732	.455188	.440127	.425533	.411394	.397697	.384427	.371574
17	.482185	.465355	.449079	.433339	.418120	.403405	.389179	.375426	.362131	.349280
18	.461933	.444879	.428421	.412539	.397214	.382428	.368163	.354402	.341127	.328323
19	.442532	.425304	.408714	.392737	.377354	.362542	.348282	.334555	.321342	.308624
20	.423946	.406591	.389913	.373886	.358486	.343690	.329475	.315820	.302704	.290106

TABLE D

SHOWING THE PRESENT WORTH OF A REMAINDER INTEREST POSTPONED FOR A TERM CERTAIN IN A CHARITABLE REMAINDER UNITRUST APPLICABLE AFTER APRIL 30, 1989

	ADJUSTED PAYOUT RATE									
YEARS	6.2%	6.4%	6.6%	6.8%	7.0%	7.2%	7.4%	7.6%	7.8%	8.0%
1	.938000	.936000	.934000	.932000	.930000	.928000	.926000	.924000	.922000	.920000
2	.879844	.876096	.872356	.868624	.864900	.861184	.857476	.853776	.850084	.846400
3	.825294	.820026	.814781	.809558	.804357	.799179	.794023	.788889	.783777	.778688
4	.774125	.767544	.761005	.754508	.748052	.741638	.735265	.728933	.722643	.716393
5	.726130	.718421	.710779	.703201	.695688	.688240	.680855	.673535	.666277	.659082
6	.681110	.672442	.663867	.655383	.646990	.638687	.630472	.622346	.614307	.606355
7	.638881	.629406	.620052	.610817	.601701	.592701	.583817	.575048	.566391	.557847
8	.599270	.589124	.579129	.569282	.559582	.550027	.540615	.531344	.522213	.513219
9	.562115	.551420	.540906	.530571	.520411	.510425	.500609	.490962	.481480	.472161
10	.527264	.516129	.505206	.494492	.483982	.473674	.463564	.453649	.443925	.434388
11	.494574	.483097	.471863	.460866	.450104	.439570	.429260	.419171	.409298	.399637
12	.463910	.452179	.440720	.429527	.418596	.407921	.397495	.387314	.377373	.367666
13	.435148	.423239	.411632	.400320	.389295	.378550	.368081	.357879	.347938	.338253
14	.408169	.396152	.384465	.373098	.362044	.351295	.340843	.330680	.320799	.311193
15	.382862	.370798	.359090	.347727	.336701	.326002	.315620	.305548	.295777	.286297
16	.359125	.347067	.335390	.324082	.313132	.302529	.292264	.282326	.272706	.263394
17	.336859	.324855	.313254	.302044	.291213	.280747	.270637	.260870	.251435	.242322
18	.315974	.304064	.292579	.281505	.270828	.260533	.250610	.241044	.231823	.222936
19	.296383	.284604	.273269	.262363	.251870	.241775	.232065	.222724	.213741	.205101
20	.278008	.266389	.255233	.244522	.234239	.224367	.214892	.205797	.197069	.188693

TABLE D

SHOWING THE PRESENT WORTH OF A REMAINDER INTEREST POSTPONED FOR A TERM CERTAIN IN A CHARITABLE REMAINDER UNITRUST APPLICABLE AFTER APRIL 30, 1989

	ADJUSTED PAYOUT RATE									
YEARS	8.2%	8.4%	8.6%	8.8%	9.0%	9.2%	9.4%	9.6%	9.8%	10.0%
1	.918000	.916000	.914000	.912000	.910000	.908000	.906000	.904000	.902000	.900000
2	.842724	.839056	.835396	.831744	.828100	.824464	.820836	.817216	.813604	.810000
3	.773621	.768575	.763552	.758551	.753571	.748613	.743677	.738763	.733871	.729000
4	.710184	.704015	.697886	.691798	.685750	.679741	.673772	.667842	.661951	.656100
5	.651949	.644878	.637868	.630920	.624032	.617205	.610437	.603729	.597080	.590490
6	.598489	.590708	.583012	.575399	.567869	.560422	.553056	.545771	.538566	.531441
7	.549413	.541089	.532873	.524764	.516761	.508863	.501069	.493377	.485787	.478297
8	.504361	.495637	.487046	.478585	.470253	.462048	.453968	.446013	.438180	.430467
9	.463003	.454004	.445160	.436469	.427930	.419539	.411295	.403196	.395238	.387420
10	.425037	.415867	.406876	.398060	.389416	.380942	.372634	.364489	.356505	.348678
11	.390184	.380934	.371885	.363031	.354369	.345895	.337606	.329498	.321567	.313811
12	.358189	.348936	.339902	.331084	.322475	.314073	.305871	.297866	.290054	.282430
13	.328817	.319625	.310671	.301949	.293453	.285178	.277119	.269271	.261628	.254187
14	.301854	.292777	.283953	.275377	.267042	.258942	.251070	.243421	.235989	.228768
15	.277102	.268184	.259533	.251144	.243008	.235119	.227469	.220053	.212862	.205891
16	.254380	.245656	.237213	.229043	.221137	.213488	.206087	.198928	.192001	.185302
17	.233521	.225021	.216813	.208887	.201235	.193847	.186715	.179830	.173185	.166772
18	.214372	.206119	.198167	.190505	.183124	.176013	.169164	.162567	.156213	.150095
19	.196794	.188805	.181125	.173741	.166643	.159820	.153262	.146960	.140904	.135085
20	.180657	.172946	.165548	.158452	.151645	.145117	.138856	.132852	.127096	.121577

TABLE D

SHOWING THE PRESENT WORTH OF A REMAINDER INTEREST POSTPONED FOR A TERM CERTAIN IN A CHARITABLE REMAINDER UNITRUST APPLICABLE AFTER APRIL 30, 1989

	ADJUSTED PAYOUT RATE									
YEARS	10.2%	10.4%	10.6%	10.8%	11.0%	11.2%	11.4%	11.6%	11.8%	12.0%
1	.898000	.896000	.894000	.892000	.890000	.888000	.886000	.884000	.882000	.880000
2	.806404	.802816	.799236	.795664	.792100	.788544	.784996	.781456	.777924	.774400
3	.724151	.719323	.714517	.709732	.704969	.700227	.695506	.690807	.686129	.681472
4	.650287	.644514	.638778	.633081	.627422	.621802	.616219	.610673	.605166	.599695
5	.583958	.577484	.571068	.564708	.558406	.552160	.545970	.539835	.533756	.527732
6	.524394	.517426	.510535	.503720	.496981	.490318	.483729	.477214	.470773	.464404
7	.470906	.463613	.456418	.449318	.442313	.435402	.428584	.421858	.415222	.408676
8	.422874	.415398	.408038	.400792	.393659	.386637	.379726	.372922	.366226	.359635
9	.379741	.372196	.364786	.357506	.350356	.343334	.336437	.329663	.323011	.316478
10	.341007	.333488	.326118	.318896	.311817	.304881	.298083	.291422	.284896	.278501
11	.306224	.298805	.291550	.284455	.277517	.270734	.264102	.257617	.251278	.245081
12	.274989	.267729	.260645	.253734	.246990	.240412	.233994	.227734	.221627	.215671
13	.246941	.239886	.233017	.226331	.219821	.213486	.207319	.201317	.195475	.189791
14	.221753	.214937	.208317	.201887	.195641	.189575	.183684	.177964	.172409	.167016
15	.199134	.192584	.186236	.180083	.174121	.168343	.162744	.157320	.152065	.146974
16	.178822	.172555	.166495	.160634	.154967	.149488	.144191	.139071	.134121	.129337
17	.160582	.154609	.148846	.143286	.137921	.132746	.127754	.122939	.118295	.113817
18	.144203	.138530	.133069	.127811	.122750	.117878	.113190	.108678	.104336	.100159
19	.129494	.124123	.118963	.114007	.109247	.104676	.100286	.096071	.092024	.088140
20	.116286	.111214	.106353	.101694	.097230	.092952	.088853	.084927	.081166	.077563

TABLE D

SHOWING THE PRESENT WORTH OF A REMAINDER INTEREST POSTPONED FOR A TERM CERTAIN IN A CHARITABLE REMAINDER UNITRUST APPLICABLE AFTER APRIL 30, 1989

	ADJUSTED PAYOUT RATE									
YEARS	12.2%	12.4%	12.6%	12.8%	13.0%	13.2%	13.4%	13.6%	13.8%	14.0%
1	.878000	.876000	.874000	.872000	.870000	.868000	.866000	.864000	.862000	.860000
2	.770884	.767376	.763876	.760384	.756900	.753424	.749956	.746496	.743044	.739600
3	.676836	.672221	.667628	.663055	.658503	.653972	.649462	.644973	.640504	.636056
4	.594262	.588866	.583507	.578184	.572898	.567648	.562434	.557256	.552114	.547008
5	.521762	.515847	.509985	.504176	.498421	.492718	.487068	.481469	.475923	.470427
6	.458107	.451882	.445727	.439642	.433626	.427679	.421801	.415990	.410245	.404567
7	.402218	.395848	.389565	.383368	.377255	.371226	.365279	.359415	.353631	.347928
8	.353147	.346763	.340480	.334297	.328212	.322224	.316332	.310535	.304830	.299218
9	.310063	.303764	.297579	.291507	.285544	.279690	.273944	.268302	.262764	.257327
10	.272236	.266098	.260084	.254194	.248423	.242771	.237235	.231813	.226502	.221302
11	.239023	.233102	.227314	.221657	.216128	.210725	.205446	.200286	.195245	.190319
12	.209862	.204197	.198672	.193285	.188032	.182910	.177916	.173047	.168301	.163675
13	.184259	.178877	.173640	.168544	.163588	.158766	.154075	.149513	.145076	.140760
14	.161779	.156696	.151761	.146971	.142321	.137809	.133429	.129179	.125055	.121054
15	.142042	.137266	.132639	.128158	.123819	.119618	.115550	.111611	.107798	.104106
16	.124713	.120245	.115927	.111754	.107723	.103828	.100066	.096432	.092922	.089531
17	.109498	.105334	.101320	.097450	.093719	.090123	.086657	.083317	.080098	.076997
18	.096139	.092273	.088554	.084976	.081535	.078227	.075045	.071986	.069045	.066217
19	.084410	.080831	.077396	.074099	.070936	.067901	.064989	.062196	.059517	.056947
20	.074112	.070808	.067644	.064614	.061714	.058938	.056280	.053737	.051303	.048974

TABLE F(4.2), WITH INTEREST AT 4.2 PERCENT, SHOWING FACTORS FOR COMPUTATION OF THE ADJUSTED PAYOUT RATE FOR CERTAIN VALUATIONS APPLICABLE AFTER APRIL 30, 1989

1 Number Of Months By Which The Valuation Date for the First Full Taxable Year of the Trust Precedes The First Payout		2 Factors For Payout At The End Of Each Period			
At Least	But Less Than	Annual Period	Semiannual Period	Quarterly Period	Monthly Period
....	1	1.000000	.989820	.984755	.981389
1	2	.996577	.986432	.981385	.978030
2	3	.993166	.983056	.978026	
3	4	.989767	.979691	.974679	
4	5	.986380	.976338		
5	6	.983004	.972996		
6	7	.979639	.969666		
7	8	.976286			
8	9	.972945			
9	10	.969615			
10	11	.966296			
11	12	.962989			
12	....	.959693			

TABLE F(4.4), WITH INTEREST AT 4.4 PERCENT, SHOWING FACTORS FOR COMPUTATION OF THE ADJUSTED PAYOUT RATE FOR CERTAIN VALUATIONS APPLICABLE AFTER APRIL 30, 1989

1 Number Of Months By Which The Valuation Date for the First Full Taxable Year of the Trust Precedes The First Payout		2 Factors For Payout At The End Of Each Period			
At Least	But Less Than	Annual Period	Semiannual Period	Quarterly Period	Monthly Period

At Least	But Less Than	Annual Period	Semiannual Period	Quarterly Period	Monthly Period
....	1	1.000000	.989350	.984054	.980533
1	2	.996418	.985806	.980529	.977021
2	3	.992849	.982275	.977017	
3	4	.989293	.978757	.973517	
4	5	.985749	.975251		
5	6	.982219	.971758		
6	7	.978700	.968277		
7	8	.975195			
8	9	.971702			
9	10	.968221			
10	11	.964753			
11	12	.961298			
12	....	.957854			

TABLE F(4.6), WITH INTEREST AT 4.6 PERCENT, SHOWING FACTORS FOR COMPUTATION OF THE ADJUSTED PAYOUT RATE FOR CERTAIN VALUATIONS APPLICABLE AFTER APRIL 30, 1989

1 Number Of Months By Which The Valuation Date for the First Full Taxable Year of the Trust Precedes The First Payout		2 Factors For Payout At The End Of Each Period			
At Least	But Less Than	Annual Period	Semiannual Period	Quarterly Period	Monthly Period
....	1	1.000000	.988882	.983354	.979680
1	2	.996259	.985183	.979676	.976015
2	3	.992532	.981498	.976011	
3	4	.988820	.977826	.972360	
4	5	.985121	.974168		
5	6	.981436	.970524		
6	7	.977764	.966894		
7	8	.974107			
8	9	.970463			
9	10	.966832			
10	11	.963216			
11	12	.959613			
12	....	.956023			

TABLE F(4.8), WITH INTEREST AT 4.8 PERCENT, SHOWING FACTORS FOR COMPUTATION OF THE ADJUSTED PAYOUT RATE FOR CERTAIN VALUATIONS APPLICABLE AFTER APRIL 30, 1989

1 Number Of Months By Which The Valuation Date for the First Full Taxable Year of the Trust Precedes The First Payout		2 Factors For Payout At The End Of Each Period			
At Least	But Less Than	Annual Period	Semiannual Period	Quarterly Period	Monthly Period
....	1	1.000000	.988415	.982657	.978830
1	2	.996101	.984561	.978825	.975013
2	3	.992217	.980722	.975008	
3	4	.988348	.976898	.971206	
4	5	.984494	.973089		
5	6	.980655	.969294		
6	7	.976831	.965515		
7	8	.973022			
8	9	.969228			
9	10	.965448			
10	11	.961684			
11	12	.957934			
12	....	.954198			

TABLE F(5.0), WITH INTEREST AT 5.0 PERCENT, SHOWING FACTORS FOR COMPUTATION OF THE ADJUSTED PAYOUT RATE FOR CERTAIN VALUATIONS APPLICABLE AFTER APRIL 30, 1989

1 Number Of Months By Which The Valuation Date for the First Full Taxable Year of the Trust Precedes The First Payout		2 Factors For Payout At The End Of Each Period			
At Least	But Less Than	Annual Period	Semiannual Period	Quarterly Period	Monthly Period
....	1	1.000000	.987950	.981961	.977982
1	2	.995942	.983941	.977977	.974014
2	3	.991901	.979949	.974009	
3	4	.987877	.975973	.970057	
4	5	.983868	.972013		
5	6	.979876	.968069		
6	7	.975900	.964141		
7	8	.971940			
8	9	.967997			
9	10	.964069			
10	11	.960157			
11	12	.956261			
12	....	.952381			

TABLE F(5.2), WITH INTEREST AT 5.2 PERCENT, SHOWING FACTORS FOR COMPUTATION OF THE ADJUSTED PAYOUT RATE FOR CERTAIN VALUATIONS APPLICABLE AFTER APRIL 30, 1989

1 Number Of Months By Which The Valuation Date for the First Full Taxable Year of the Trust Precedes The First Payout		2 Factors For Payout At The End Of Each Period			
At Least	But Less Than	Annual Period	Semiannual Period	Quarterly Period	Monthly Period
....	1	1.000000	.987486	.981268	.977137
1	2	.995784	.983323	.977132	.973018
2	3	.991587	.979178	.973012	
3	4	.987407	.975050	.968911	
4	5	.983244	.970940		
5	6	.979099	.966847		
6	7	.974972	.962771		
7	8	.970862			
8	9	.966769			
9	10	.962694			
10	11	.958636			
11	12	.954594			
12	....	.950570			

TABLE F(5.4), WITH INTEREST AT 5.4 PERCENT, SHOWING FACTORS FOR COMPUTATION OF THE ADJUSTED PAYOUT RATE FOR CERTAIN VALUATIONS APPLICABLE AFTER APRIL 30, 1989

1 Number Of Months By Which The Valuation Date for the First Full Taxable Year of the Trust Precedes The First Payout		2 Factors For Payout at the End of Each Period			
At Least	But Less Than	Annual Period	Semiannual Period	Quarterly Period	Monthly Period

At Least	But Less Than	Annual Period	Semiannual Period	Quarterly Period	Monthly Period
....	1	1.000000	.987023	.980577	.976295
1	2	.995627	.982707	.976289	.972026
2	3	.991273	.978409	.972019	
3	4	.986938	.974131	.967769	
4	5	.982622	.969871		
5	6	.978325	.965629		
6	7	.974047	.961407		
7	8	.969787			
8	9	.965546			
9	10	.961323			
10	11	.957119			
11	12	.952934			
12	....	.948767			

TABLE F(5.6), WITH INTEREST AT 5.6 PERCENT, SHOWING FACTORS FOR COMPUTATION OF THE ADJUSTED PAYOUT RATE FOR CERTAIN VALUATIONS APPLICABLE AFTER APRIL 30, 1989

1 Number Of Months By Which The Valuation Date for the First Full Taxable Year of the Trust Precedes The First Payout		2 Factors for Payout at the End of Each Period			
At Least	But Less Than	Annual Period	Semiannual Period	Quarterly Period	Monthly Period
....	1	1.000000	.986562	.979888	.975455
1	2	.995470	.982092	.975449	.971036
2	3	.990960	.977643	.971029	
3	4	.986470	.973214	.966630	
4	5	.982001	.968805		
5	6	.977552	.964416		
6	7	.973124	.960047		
7	8	.968715			
8	9	.964326			
9	10	.959958			
10	11	.955609			
11	12	.951279			
12	....	.946970			

TABLE F(5.8), WITH INTEREST AT 5.8 PERCENT, SHOWING FACTORS FOR COMPUTATION OF THE ADJUSTED PAYOUT RATE FOR CERTAIN VALUATIONS APPLICABLE AFTER APRIL 30, 1989

1 Number Of Months By Which The Valuation Date for the First Full Taxable Year of the Trust Precedes The First Payout		2 Factors for Payout at the End of Each Period			
At Least	But Less Than	Annual Period	Semiannual Period	Quarterly Period	Monthly Period
....	1	1.000000	.986102	.979201	.974618
1	2	.995313	.981480	.974611	.970050
2	3	.990647	.976879	.970043	
3	4	.986004	.972300	.965496	
4	5	.981382	.967743		
5	6	.976782	.963206		
6	7	.972203	.958692		
7	8	.967646			
8	9	.963111			
9	10	.958596			
10	11	.954103			
11	12	.949631			
12	....	.945180			

TABLE F(6.0), WITH INTEREST AT 6.0 PERCENT, SHOWING FACTORS FOR COMPUTATION OF THE ADJUSTED PAYOUT RATE FOR CERTAIN VALUATIONS APPLICABLE AFTER APRIL 30, 1989

1 Number Of Months By Which The Valuation Date for the First Full Taxable Year of the Trust Precedes The First Payout		2 Factors for Payout at the End of Each Period			
At Least	But Less Than	Annual Period	Semiannual Period	Quarterly Period	Monthly Period
....	1	1.000000	.985643	.978516	.973784
1	2	.995156	.980869	.973776	.969067
2	3	.990336	.976117	.969059	
3	4	.985538	.971389	.964365	
4	5	.980764	.966684		
5	6	.976014	.962001		
6	7	.971286	.957341		
7	8	.966581			
8	9	.961899			
9	10	.957239			
10	11	.952603			
11	12	.947988			
12	....	.943396			

TABLE F(6.2), WITH INTEREST AT 6.2 PERCENT, SHOWING FACTORS FOR COMPUTATION OF THE ADJUSTED PAYOUT RATE FOR CERTAIN VALUATIONS APPLICABLE AFTER APRIL 30, 1989

1 Number Of Months By Which The Valuation Date for the First Full Taxable Year of the Trust Precedes The First Payout		2 Factors for Payout at the End of Each Period			
At Least	But Less Than	Annual Period	Semiannual Period	Quarterly Period	Monthly Period
....	1	1.000000	.985185	.977833	.972952
1	2	.995000	.980259	.972944	.968087
2	3	.990024	.975358	.968079	
3	4	.985074	.970481	.963238	
4	5	.980148	.965628		
5	6	.975247	.960799		
6	7	.970371	.955995		
7	8	.965519			
8	9	.960691			
9	10	.955887			
10	11	.951107			
11	12	.946352			
12	....	.941620			

TABLE F(6.4), WITH INTEREST AT 6.4 PERCENT, SHOWING FACTORS FOR COMPUTATION OF THE ADJUSTED PAYOUT RATE FOR CERTAIN VALUATIONS APPLICABLE AFTER APRIL 30, 1989

1 Number Of Months By Which The Valuation Date for the First Full Taxable Year of the Trust Precedes The First Payout		2 Factors for Payout at the End of Each Period			
At Least	But Less Than	Annual Period	Semiannual Period	Quarterly Period	Monthly Period

At Least	But Less Than	Annual Period	Semiannual Period	Quarterly Period	Monthly Period
....	1	1.000000	.984729	.977152	.972122
1	2	.994844	.979652	.972114	.967110
2	3	.989714	.974600	.967101	
3	4	.984611	.969575	.962115	
4	5	.979534	.964576		
5	6	.974483	.959602		
6	7	.969458	.954654		
7	8	.964460			
8	9	.959487			
9	10	.954539			
10	11	.949617			
11	12	.944721			
12	....	.939850			

TABLE F(6.6), WITH INTEREST AT 6.6 PERCENT, SHOWING FACTORS FOR COMPUTATION OF THE ADJUSTED PAYOUT RATE FOR CERTAIN VALUATIONS APPLICABLE AFTER APRIL 30, 1989

1 Number Of Months By Which The Valuation Date for the First Full Taxable Year of the Trust Precedes The First Payout		2 Factors for Payout at the End of Each Period			
At Least	But Less Than	Annual Period	Semiannual Period	Quarterly Period	Monthly Period
....	1	1.000000	.984274	.976473	.971295
1	2	.994688	.979046	.971286	.966136
2	3	.989404	.973845	.966127	
3	4	.984149	.968672	.960995	
4	5	.978921	.963527		
5	6	.973721	.958408		
6	7	.968549	.953317		
7	8	.963404			
8	9	.958286			
9	10	.953196			
10	11	.948132			
11	12	.943096			
12	....	.938086			

TABLE F(6.8), WITH INTEREST AT 6.8 PERCENT, SHOWING FACTORS FOR COMPUTATION OF THE ADJUSTED PAYOUT RATE FOR CERTAIN VALUATIONS APPLICABLE AFTER APRIL 30, 1989

1 Number Of Months By Which The Valuation Date for the First Full Taxable Year of the Trust Precedes The First Payout		2 Factors for Payout at the End of Each Period			
At Least	But Less Than	Annual Period	Semiannual Period	Quarterly Period	Monthly Period
....	1	1.000000	.983821	.975796	.970471
1	2	.994533	.978442	.970461	.965165
2	3	.989095	.973092	.965156	
3	4	.983688	.967772	.959879	
4	5	.978309	.962481		
5	6	.972961	.957219		
6	7	.967641	.951985		
7	8	.962351			
8	9	.957089			
9	10	.951857			
10	11	.946653			
11	12	.941477			
12	....	.936330			

TABLE F(7.0), WITH INTEREST AT 7.0 PERCENT, SHOWING FACTORS FOR COMPUTATION OF THE ADJUSTED PAYOUT RATE FOR CERTAIN VALUATIONS APPLICABLE AFTER APRIL 30, 1989

1 Number Of Months By Which The Valuation Date for the First Full Taxable Year of the Trust Precedes The First Payout		2 Factors for Payout at the End of Each Period			
At Least	But Less Than	Annual Period	Semiannual Period	Quarterly Period	Monthly Period
....	1	1.000000	.983368	.975122	.969649
1	2	.994378	.977839	.969639	.964198
2	3	.988787	.972342	.964187	
3	4	.983228	.966875	.958766	
4	5	.977700	.961439		
5	6	.972203	.956033		
6	7	.966736	.950658		
7	8	.961301			
8	9	.955896			
9	10	.950522			
10	11	.945178			
11	12	.939864			
12	....	.934579			

TABLE F(7.2), WITH INTEREST AT 7.2 PERCENT, SHOWING FACTORS FOR COMPUTATION OF THE ADJUSTED PAYOUT RATE FOR CERTAIN VALUATIONS APPLICABLE AFTER APRIL 30, 1989

1 Number Of Months By Which The Valuation Date for the First Full Taxable Year of the Trust Precedes The First Payout		2 Factors for Payout at the End of Each Period			
At Least	But Less Than	Annual Period	Semiannual Period	Quarterly Period	Monthly Period
....	1	1.000000	.982917	.974449	.968830
1	2	.994223	.977239	.968819	.963233
2	3	.988479	.971593	.963222	
3	4	.982769	.965980	.957658	
4	5	.977091	.960400		
5	6	.971446	.954851		
6	7	.965834	.949335		
7	8	.960255			
8	9	.954707			
9	10	.949192			
10	11	.943708			
11	12	.938256			
12	....	.932836			

TABLE F(7.4), WITH INTEREST AT 7.4 PERCENT, SHOWING FACTORS FOR COMPUTATION OF THE ADJUSTED PAYOUT RATE FOR CERTAIN VALUATIONS APPLICABLE AFTER APRIL 30, 1989

1 Number Of Months By Which The Valuation Date for the First Full Taxable Year of the Trust Precedes The First Payout		2 Factors for Payout at the End of Each Period			
At Least	But Less Than	Annual Period	Semiannual Period	Quarterly Period	Monthly Period

At Least	But Less Than	Annual Period	Semiannual Period	Quarterly Period	Monthly Period
....	1	1.000000	.982467	.973778	.968013
1	2	.994068	.976640	.968002	.962271
2	3	.988172	.970847	.962260	
3	4	.982311	.965088	.956552	
4	5	.976484	.959364		
5	6	.970692	.953673		
6	7	.964935	.948017		
7	8	.959211			
8	9	.953521			
9	10	.947866			
10	11	.942243			
11	12	.936654			
12	..	.931099			

TABLE F(7.6), WITH INTEREST AT 7.6 PERCENT, SHOWING FACTORS FOR COMPUTATION OF THE ADJUSTED PAYOUT RATE FOR CERTAIN VALUATIONS APPLICABLE AFTER APRIL 30, 1989

1 Number Of Months By Which The Valuation Date for the First Full Taxable Year of the Trust Precedes The First Payout		2 Factors for Payout at the End of Each Period			
At Least	But Less Than	Annual Period	Semiannual Period	Quarterly Period	Monthly Period
....	1	1.000000	.982019	.973109	.967199
1	2	.993914	.976042	.967187	.961313
2	3	.987866	.970103	.961301	
3	4	.981854	.964199	.955451	
4	5	.975879	.958331		
5	6	.969940	.952499		
6	7	.964037	.946703		
7	8	.958171			
8	9	.952340			
9	10	.946544			
10	11	.940784			
11	12	.935058			
12	....	.929368			

TABLE F(7.8), WITH INTEREST AT 7.8 PERCENT, SHOWING FACTORS FOR COMPUTATION OF THE ADJUSTED PAYOUT RATE FOR CERTAIN VALUATIONS APPLICABLE AFTER APRIL 30, 1989

1 Number Of Months By Which The Valuation Date for the First Full Taxable Year of the Trust Precedes The First Payout		2 Factors for Payout at the End of Each Period			
At Least	But Less Than	Annual Period	Semiannual Period	Quarterly Period	Monthly Period
....	1	1.000000	.981571	.972442	.966387
1	2	.993761	.975447	.966374	.960357
2	3	.987560	.969361	.960345	
3	4	.981398	.963312	.954353	
4	5	.975275	.957302		
5	6	.969190	.951329		
6	7	.963143	.945393		
7	8	.957133			
8	9	.951161			
9	10	.945227			
10	11	.939329			
11	12	.933468			
12	....	.927644			

TABLE F(8.0), WITH INTEREST AT 8.0 PERCENT, SHOWING FACTORS FOR COMPUTATION OF THE ADJUSTED PAYOUT RATE FOR CERTAIN VALUATIONS APPLICABLE AFTER APRIL 30, 1989

1 Number Of Months By Which The Valuation Date for the First Full Taxable Year of the Trust Precedes The First Payout		2 Factors for Payout at the End of Each Period			
At Least	But Less Than	Annual Period	Semiannual Period	Quarterly Period	Monthly Period
....	1	1.000000	.981125	.971777	.965578
1	2	.993607	.974853	.965564	.959405
2	3	.987255	.968621	.959392	
3	4	.980944	.962429	.953258	
4	5	.974673	.956276		
5	6	.968442	.950162		
6	7	.962250	.944088		
7	8	.956099			
8	9	.949987			
9	10	.943913			
10	11	.937879			
11	12	.931883			
12	....	.925926			

TABLE F(8.2), WITH INTEREST AT 8.2 PERCENT, SHOWING FACTORS FOR COMPUTATION OF THE ADJUSTED PAYOUT RATE FOR CERTAIN VALUATIONS APPLICABLE AFTER APRIL 30, 1989

1 Number Of Months By Which The Valuation Date for the First Full Taxable Year of the Trust Precedes The First Payout		2 Factors for Payout at the End of Each Period			
At Least	But Less Than	Annual Period	Semiannual Period	Quarterly Period	Monthly Period
....	1	1.000000	.980680	.971114	.964771
1	2	.993454	.974261	.964757	.958455
2	3	.986951	.967883	.958441	
3	4	.980490	.961547	.952167	
4	5	.974072	.955253		
5	6	.967695	.949000		
6	7	.961361	.942788		
7	8	.955068			
8	9	.948816			
9	10	.942605			
10	11	.936434			
11	12	.930304			
12	....	.924214			

TABLE F(8.4), WITH INTEREST AT 8.4 PERCENT, SHOWING FACTORS FOR COMPUTATION OF THE ADJUSTED PAYOUT RATE FOR CERTAIN VALUATIONS APPLICABLE AFTER APRIL 30, 1989

1 Number Of Months By Which The Valuation Date for the First Full Taxable Year of the Trust Precedes The First Payout		2 Factors for Payout at the End of Each Period			
At Least	But Less Than	Annual Period	Semiannual Period	Quarterly Period	Monthly Period

....	1	1.000000	.980237	.970453	.963966
1	2	.993301	.973670	.963952	.957509
2	3	.986647	.967148	.957494	
3	4	.980037	.960669	.951080	
4	5	.973472	.954233		
5	6	.966951	.947841		
6	7	.960473	.941491		
7	8	.954039			
8	9	.947648			
9	10	.941300			
10	11	.934994			
11	12	.928731			
12	....	.922509			

TABLE F(8.6), WITH INTEREST AT 8.6 PERCENT, SHOWING FACTORS FOR COMPUTATION OF THE ADJUSTED PAYOUT RATE FOR CERTAIN VALUATIONS APPLICABLE AFTER APRIL 30, 1989

1 Number Of Months By Which The Valuation Date for the First Full Taxable Year of the Trust Precedes The First Payout		2 Factors For Payout At The End Of Each Period			
At Least	But Less Than	Annual Period	Semiannual Period	Quarterly Period	Monthly Period
....	1	1.000000	.979794	.969794	.963164
1	2	.993148	.973081	.963149	.956565
2	3	.986344	.966414	.956550	
3	4	.979586	.959793	.949996	
4	5	.972874	.953217		
5	6	.966209	.946686		
6	7	.959589	.940199		
7	8	.953014			
8	9	.946484			
9	10	.940000			
10	11	.933559			
11	12	.927163			
12	....	.920810			

TABLE F(8.8), WITH INTEREST AT 8.8 PERCENT, SHOWING FACTORS FOR COMPUTATION OF THE ADJUSTED PAYOUT RATE FOR CERTAIN VALUATIONS APPLICABLE AFTER APRIL 30, 1989

1 Number Of Months By Which The Valuation Date for the First Full Taxable Year of the Trust Precedes The First Payout		2 Factors For Payout At The End Of Each Period			
At Least	But Less Than	Annual Period	Semiannual Period	Quarterly Period	Monthly Period
....	1	1.000000	.979353	.969136	.962364
1	2	.992996	.972494	.962349	.955624
2	3	.986041	.965683	.955609	
3	4	.979135	.958919	.948916	
4	5	.972278	.952203		
5	6	.965468	.945534		
6	7	.958706	.938912		
7	8	.951992			
8	9	.945324			
9	10	.938703			
10	11	.932129			
11	12	.925600			
12	....	.919118			

TABLE F(9.0), WITH INTEREST AT 9.0 PERCENT, SHOWING FACTORS FOR COMPUTATION OF THE ADJUSTED PAYOUT RATE FOR CERTAIN VALUATIONS APPLICABLE AFTER APRIL 30, 1989

1 Number Of Months By Which The Valuation Date for the First Full Taxable Year of the Trust Precedes The First Payout		2 Factors For Payout At The End Of Each Period			
At Least	But Less Than	Annual Period	Semiannual Period	Quarterly Period	Monthly Period
....	1	1.000000	.978913	.968481	.961567
1	2	.992844	.971908	.961551	.954686
2	3	.985740	.964954	.954670	
3	4	.978686	.958049	.947839	
4	5	.971683	.951193		
5	6	.964730	.944387		
6	7	.957826	.937629		
7	8	.950972			
8	9	.944167			
9	10	.937411			
10	11	.930703			
11	12	.924043			
12	....	.917431			

TABLE F(9.2), WITH INTEREST AT 9.2 PERCENT, SHOWING FACTORS FOR COMPUTATION OF THE ADJUSTED PAYOUT RATE FOR CERTAIN VALUATIONS APPLICABLE AFTER APRIL 30, 1989

1 Number Of Months By Which The Valuation Date for the First Full Taxable Year of the Trust Precedes The First Payout		2 Factors For Payout At The End Of Each Period			
At Least	But Less Than	Annual Period	Semiannual Period	Quarterly Period	Monthly Period
....	1	1.000000	.978474	.967827	.960772
1	2	.992693	.971324	.960755	.953752
2	3	.985439	.964226	.953734	
3	4	.978238	.957180	.946765	
4	5	.971089	.950186		
5	6	.963993	.943242		
6	7	.956949	.936350		
7	8	.949956			
8	9	.943014			
9	10	.936123			
10	11	.929283			
11	12	.922492			
12	....	.915751			

TABLE F(9.4), WITH INTEREST AT 9.4 PERCENT, SHOWING FACTORS FOR COMPUTATION OF THE ADJUSTED PAYOUT RATE FOR CERTAIN VALUATIONS APPLICABLE AFTER APRIL 30, 1989

1 Number Of Months By Which The Valuation Date for the First Full Taxable Year of the Trust Precedes The First Payout		2 Factors For Payout At The End Of Each Period			
At Least	But Less Than	Annual Period	Semiannual Period	Quarterly Period	Monthly Period

At Least	But Less Than	Annual Period	Semiannual Period	Quarterly Period	Monthly Period
....	1	1.000000	.978037	.967176	.959980
1	2	.992541	.970742	.959962	.952820
2	3	.985138	.963501	.952802	
3	4	.977790	.956315	.945695	
4	5	.970497	.949182		
5	6	.963258	.942102		
6	7	.956074	.935075		
7	8	.948942			
8	9	.941865			
9	10	.934839			
10	11	.927867			
11	12	.920946			
12	....	.914077			

TABLE F(9.6), WITH INTEREST AT 9.6 PERCENT, SHOWING FACTORS FOR COMPUTATION OF THE ADJUSTED PAYOUT RATE FOR CERTAIN VALUATIONS APPLICABLE AFTER APRIL 30, 1989

1 Number Of Months By Which The Valuation Date for the First Full Taxable Year of the Trust Precedes The First Payout		2 Factors For Payout At The End Of Each Period			
At Least	But Less Than	Annual Period	Semiannual Period	Quarterly Period	Monthly Period
....	1	1.000000	.977600	.966526	.959190
1	2	.992390	.970161	.959171	.951890
2	3	.984838	.962778	.951872	
3	4	.977344	.955452	.944628	
4	5	.969906	.948181		
5	6	.962526	.940965		
6	7	.955201	.933805		
7	8	.947932			
8	9	.940718			
9	10	.933560			
10	11	.926455			
11	12	.919405			
12	....	.912409			

TABLE F(9.8), WITH INTEREST AT 9.8 PERCENT, SHOWING FACTORS FOR COMPUTATION OF THE ADJUSTED PAYOUT RATE FOR CERTAIN VALUATIONS APPLICABLE AFTER APRIL 30, 1989

1 Number Of Months By Which The Valuation Date for the First Full Taxable Year of the Trust Precedes The First Payout		2 Factors For Payout At The End Of Each Period			
At Least	But Less Than	Annual Period	Semiannual Period	Quarterly Period	Monthly Period
....	1	1.000000	.977165	.965878	.958402
1	2	.992239	.969582	.958382	.950964
2	3	.984539	.962057	.950945	
3	4	.976898	.954591	.943565	
4	5	.969317	.947183		
5	6	.961795	.939832		
6	7	.954331	.932539		
7	8	.946924			
8	9	.939576			
9	10	.932284			
10	11	.925049			
11	12	.917870			
12	....	.910747			

TABLE F(10.0), WITH INTEREST AT 10.0 PERCENT, SHOWING FACTORS FOR COMPUTATION OF THE ADJUSTED PAYOUT RATE FOR CERTAIN VALUATIONS APPLICABLE AFTER APRIL 30, 1989

1 Number Of Months By Which The Valuation Date for the First Full Taxable Year of the Trust Precedes The First Payout		2 Factors For Payout At The End Of Each Period			
At Least	But Less Than	Annual Period	Semiannual Period	Quarterly Period	Monthly Period
....	1	1.000000	.976731	.965232	.957616
1	2	.992089	.969004	.957596	.950041
2	3	.984240	.961338	.950021	
3	4	.976454	.953733	.942505	
4	5	.968729	.946188		
5	6	.961066	.938703		
6	7	.953463	.931277		
7	8	.945920			
8	9	.938436			
9	10	.931012			
10	11	.923647			
11	12	.916340			
12	....	.909091			

TABLE F(10.2), WITH INTEREST AT 10.2 PERCENT, SHOWING FACTORS FOR COMPUTATION OF THE ADJUSTED PAYOUT RATE FOR CERTAIN VALUATIONS APPLICABLE AFTER APRIL 30, 1989

1 Number Of Months By Which The Valuation Date for the First Full Taxable Year of the Trust Precedes The First Payout		2 Factors For Payout At The End Of Each Period			
At Least	But Less Than	Annual Period	Semiannual Period	Quarterly Period	Monthly Period
....	1	1.00000	.976298	.964588	.956833
1	2	.991939	.968428	.956812	.949120
2	3	.983943	.960622	.949099	
3	4	.976011	.952878	.941448	
4	5	.968143	.945196		
5	6	.960338	.937577		
6	7	.952597	.930019		
7	8	.944918			
8	9	.937301			
9	10	.929745			
10	11	.922250			
11	12	.914816			
12	....	.907441			

TABLE F(10.4), WITH INTEREST AT 10.4 PERCENT, SHOWING FACTORS FOR COMPUTATION OF THE ADJUSTED PAYOUT RATE FOR CERTAIN VALUATIONS APPLICABLE AFTER APRIL 30, 1989

1 Number Of Months By Which The Valuation Date for the First Full Taxable Year of the Trust Precedes The First Payout		2 Factors For Payout At The End Of Each Period			
At Least	But Less Than	Annual Period	Semiannual Period	Quarterly Period	Monthly Period

....	1	1.000000	.975867	.963946	.956052
1	2	.991789	.967854	.956031	.948202
2	3	.983645	.959907	.948181	
3	4	.975568	.952025	.940395	
4	5	.967558	.944208		
5	6	.959613	.936455		
6	7	.951734	.928765		
7	8	.943919			
8	9	.936168			
9	10	.928481			
10	11	.920858			
11	12	.913296			
12	....	.905797			

TABLE F(10.6), WITH INTEREST AT 10.6 PERCENT, SHOWING FACTORS FOR COMPUTATION OF THE ADJUSTED PAYOUT RATE FOR CERTAIN VALUATIONS APPLICABLE AFTER APRIL 30, 1989

1 Number Of Months By Which The Valuation Date for the First Full Taxable Year of the Trust Precedes The First Payout		2 Factors For Payout At The End Of Each Period			
At Least	But Less Than	Annual Period	Semiannual Period	Quarterly Period	Monthly Period
....	1	1.000000	.975436	.963305	.955274
1	2	.991639	.967281	.955252	.947287
2	3	.983349	.959194	.947265	
3	4	.975127	.951174	.939345	
4	5	.966974	.943222		
5	6	.958890	.935336		
6	7	.950873	.927516		
7	8	.942923			
8	9	.935039			
9	10	.927222			
10	11	.919470			
11	12	.911782			
12	..	.904159			

TABLE F(10.8), WITH INTEREST AT 10.8 PERCENT, SHOWING FACTORS FOR COMPUTATION OF THE ADJUSTED PAYOUT RATE FOR CERTAIN VALUATIONS APPLICABLE AFTER APRIL 30, 1989

1 Number Of Months By Which The Valuation Date for the First Full Taxable Year of the Trust Precedes The First Payout		2 Factors For Payout At The End Of Each Period			
At Least	But Less Than	Annual Period	Semiannual Period	Quarterly Period	Monthly Period
....	1	1.000000	.975007	.962667	.954498
1	2	.991490	.966710	.954475	.946375
2	3	.983052	.958483	.946352	
3	4	.974687	.950327	.938299	
4	5	.966392	.942239		
5	6	.958168	.934221		
6	7	.950014	.926271		
7	8	.941930			
8	9	.933914			
9	10	.925966			
10	11	.918086			
11	12	.910273			
12	..	.902527			

TABLE F(11.0), WITH INTEREST AT 11.0 PERCENT, SHOWING FACTORS FOR COMPUTATION OF THE ADJUSTED PAYOUT RATE FOR CERTAIN VALUATIONS APPLICABLE AFTER APRIL 30, 1989

1 Number Of Months By Which The Valuation Date for the First Full Taxable Year of the Trust Precedes The First Payout		2 Factors For Payout At The End Of Each Period			
At Least	But Less Than	Annual Period	Semiannual Period	Quarterly Period	Monthly Period
....	1	1.000000	.974579	.962030	.953724
1	2	.991341	.966140	.953700	.945466
2	3	.982757	.957774	.945442	
3	4	.974247	.949481	.937255	
4	5	.965811	.941260		
5	6	.957449	.933109		
6	7	.949158	.925029		
7	8	.940939			
8	9	.932792			
9	10	.924715			
10	11	.916708			
11	12	.908770			
12	....	.900901			

TABLE F(11.2), WITH INTEREST AT 11.2 PERCENT, SHOWING FACTORS FOR COMPUTATION OF THE ADJUSTED PAYOUT RATE FOR CERTAIN VALUATIONS APPLICABLE AFTER APRIL 30, 1989

1 Number Of Months By Which The Valuation Date for the First Full Taxable Year of the Trust Precedes The First Payout		2 Factors For Payout At The End Of Each Period			
At Least	But Less Than	Annual Period	Semiannual Period	Quarterly Period	Monthly Period
....	1	1.000000	.974152	.961395	.952952
1	2	.991192	.965572	.952927	.944559
2	3	.982462	.957068	.944534	
3	4	.973809	.948638	.936215	
4	5	.965232	.940283		
5	6	.956731	.932001		
6	7	.948304	.923792		
7	8	.939952			
8	9	.931673			
9	10	.923467			
10	11	.915333			
11	12	.907272			
12	....	.899281			

TABLE F(11.4), WITH INTEREST AT 11.4 PERCENT, SHOWING FACTORS FOR COMPUTATION OF THE ADJUSTED PAYOUT RATE FOR CERTAIN VALUATIONS APPLICABLE AFTER APRIL 30, 1989

1 Number Of Months By Which The Valuation Date for the First Full Taxable Year of the Trust Precedes The First Payout		2 Factors For Payout At The End Of Each Period			
At Least	But Less Than	Annual Period	Semiannual Period	Quarterly Period	Monthly Period

At Least	But Less Than	Annual Period	Semiannual Period	Quarterly Period	Monthly Period
....	1	1.000000	.973726	.960762	.952183
1	2	.991044	.965005	.952157	.943655
2	3	.982168	.956363	.943630	
3	4	.973372	.947798	.935178	
4	5	.964654	.939309		
5	6	.956015	.930896		
6	7	.947452	.922559		
7	8	.938967			
8	9	.930557			
9	10	.922223			
10	11	.913964			
11	12	.905778			
12	....	.897666			

TABLE F(11.6), WITH INTEREST AT 11.6 PERCENT, SHOWING FACTORS FOR COMPUTATION OF THE ADJUSTED PAYOUT RATE FOR CERTAIN VALUATIONS APPLICABLE AFTER APRIL 30, 1989

1 Number Of Months By Which The Valuation Date for the First Full Taxable Year of the Trust Precedes The First Payout		2 Factors For Payout At The End Of Each Period			
At Least	But Less Than	Annual Period	Semiannual Period	Quarterly Period	Monthly Period
....	1	1.000000	.973302	.960130	.951416
1	2	.990896	.964440	.951389	.942754
2	3	.981874	.955660	.942728	
3	4	.972935	.946959	.934145	
4	5	.964077	.938338		
5	6	.955300	.929795		
6	7	.946603	.921330		
7	8	.937985			
8	9	.929445			
9	10	.920984			
10	11	.912599			
11	12	.904290			
12	....	.896057			

TABLE F(11.8), WITH INTEREST AT 11.8 PERCENT, SHOWING FACTORS FOR COMPUTATION OF THE ADJUSTED PAYOUT RATE FOR CERTAIN VALUATIONS APPLICABLE AFTER APRIL 30, 1989

1 Number Of Months By Which The Valuation Date for the First Full Taxable Year of the Trust Precedes The First Payout		2 Factors For Payout At The End Of Each Period			
At Least	But Less Than	Annual Period	Semiannual Period	Quarterly Period	Monthly Period
....	1	1.000000	.972878	.959501	.950651
1	2	.990748	.963877	.950624	.941855
2	3	.981582	.954959	.941828	
3	4	.972500	.946124	.933114	
4	5	.963502	.937370		
5	6	.954588	.928698		
6	7	.945756	.920105		
7	8	.937006			
8	9	.928337			
9	10	.919748			
10	11	.911238			
11	12	.902807			
12	....	.894454			

TABLE F(12.0), WITH INTEREST AT 12.0 PERCENT, SHOWING FACTORS FOR COMPUTATION OF THE ADJUSTED PAYOUT RATE FOR CERTAIN VALUATIONS APPLICABLE AFTER APRIL 30, 1989

1 Number Of Months By Which The Valuation Date for the First Full Taxable Year of the Trust Precedes The First Payout		2 Factors For Payout At The End Of Each Period			
At Least	But Less Than	Annual Period	Semiannual Period	Quarterly Period	Monthly Period
....	1	1.000000	.972456	.958873	.949888
1	2	.990600	.963315	.949860	.940960
2	3	.981289	.954260	.940932	
3	4	.972065	.945290	.932087	
4	5	.962928	.936405		
5	6	.953877	.927603		
6	7	.944911	.918884		
7	8	.936029			
8	9	.927231			
9	10	.918515			
10	11	.909882			
11	12	.901329			
12	....	.892857			

TABLE F(12.2), WITH INTEREST AT 12.2 PERCENT, SHOWING FACTORS FOR COMPUTATION OF THE ADJUSTED PAYOUT RATE FOR CERTAIN VALUATIONS APPLICABLE AFTER APRIL 30, 1989

1 Number Of Months By Which The Valuation Date for the First Full Taxable Year of the Trust Precedes The First Payout		2 Factors For Payout At The End Of Each Period			
At Least	But Less Than	Annual Period	Semiannual Period	Quarterly Period	Monthly Period
....	1	1.000000	.972034	.958247	.949128
1	2	.990453	.962754	.949099	.940067
2	3	.980997	.953563	.940038	
3	4	.971632	.944460	.931063	
4	5	.962356	.935443		
5	6	.953168	.926512		
6	7	.944069	.917667		
7	8	.935056			
8	9	.926129			
9	10	.917287			
10	11	.908530			
11	12	.899856			
12	....	.891266			

TABLE F(12.4), WITH INTEREST AT 12.4 PERCENT, SHOWING FACTORS FOR COMPUTATION OF THE ADJUSTED PAYOUT RATE FOR CERTAIN VALUATIONS APPLICABLE AFTER APRIL 30, 1989

1 Number Of Months By Which The Valuation Date for the First Full Taxable Year of the Trust Precedes The First Payout		2 Factors For Payout At The End Of Each Period			
At Least	But Less Than	Annual Period	Semiannual Period	Quarterly Period	Monthly Period

At Least	But Less Than	Annual Period	Semiannual Period	Quarterly Period	Monthly Period
....	1	1.000000	.971614	.957623	.948370
1	2	.990306	.962195	.948340	.939176
2	3	.980706	.952868	.939147	
3	4	.971199	.943631	.930043	
4	5	.961785	.934484		
5	6	.952461	.925425		
6	7	.943228	.916454		
7	8	.934085			
8	9	.925030			
9	10	.916063			
10	11	.907183			
11	12	.898389			
12	....	.889680			

TABLE F(12.6), WITH INTEREST AT 12.6 PERCENT, SHOWING FACTORS FOR COMPUTATION OF THE ADJUSTED PAYOUT RATE FOR CERTAIN VALUATIONS APPLICABLE AFTER APRIL 30, 1989

1 Number Of Months By Which The Valuation Date for the First Full Taxable Year of the Trust Precedes The First Payout		2 Factors For Payout At The End Of Each Period			
At Least	But Less Than	Annual Period	Semiannual Period	Quarterly Period	Monthly Period
....	1	1.000000	.971195	.957000	.947614
1	2	.990159	.961638	.947583	.938289
2	3	.980416	.952175	.938258	
3	4	.970768	.942805	.929025	
4	5	.961215	.933527		
5	6	.951756	.924341		
6	7	.942390	.915245		
7	8	.933117			
8	9	.923934			
9	10	.914842			
10	11	.905840			
11	12	.896926			
12	....	.888099			

TABLE F(12.8), WITH INTEREST AT 12.8 PERCENT, SHOWING FACTORS FOR COMPUTATION OF THE ADJUSTED PAYOUT RATE FOR CERTAIN VALUATIONS APPLICABLE AFTER APRIL 30, 1989

1 Number Of Months By Which The Valuation Date for the First Full Taxable Year of the Trust Precedes The First Payout		2 Factors For Payout At The End Of Each Period			
At Least	But Less Than	Annual Period	Semiannual Period	Quarterly Period	Monthly Period
....	1	1.000000	.970777	.956379	.946860
1	2	.990013	.961082	.946828	.937403
2	3	.980126	.951484	.937372	
3	4	.970337	.941981	.928011	
4	5	.960647	.932574		
5	6	.951053	.923260		
6	7	.941554	.914040		
7	8	.932151			
8	9	.922842			
9	10	.913625			
10	11	.904501			
11	12	.895468			
12	....	.886525			

TABLE F(13.0), WITH INTEREST AT 13.0 PERCENT, SHOWING FACTORS FOR COMPUTATION OF THE ADJUSTED PAYOUT RATE FOR CERTAIN VALUATIONS APPLICABLE AFTER APRIL 30, 1989

1 Number Of Months By Which The Valuation Date for the First Full Taxable Year of the Trust Precedes The First Payout		2 Factors For Payout At The End Of Each Period			
At Least	But Less Than	Annual Period	Semiannual Period	Quarterly Period	Monthly Period
	1	1.000000	.970360	.955760	.946108
1	2	.989867	.960528	.946075	.936521
2	3	.979836	.950795	.936489	
3	4	.969908	.941160	.926999	
4	5	.960079	.931623		
5	6	.950351	.922183		
6	7	.940721	.912838		
7	8	.931188			
8	9	.921753			
9	10	.912412			
10	11	.903167			
11	12	.894015			
12	..	.884956			

TABLE F(13.2), WITH INTEREST AT 13.2 PERCENT, SHOWING FACTORS FOR COMPUTATION OF THE ADJUSTED PAYOUT RATE FOR CERTAIN VALUATIONS APPLICABLE AFTER APRIL 30, 1989

1 Number Of Months By Which The Valuation Date for the First Full Taxable Year of the Trust Precedes The First Payout		2 Factors For Payout At The End Of Each Period			
At Least	But Less Than	Annual Period	Semiannual Period	Quarterly Period	Monthly Period
....	1	1.000000	.969945	.955143	.945359
1	2	.989721	.959975	.945325	.935641
2	3	.979548	.950107	.935608	
3	4	.969479	.940341	.925991	
4	5	.959514	.930675		
5	6	.949651	.921109		
6	7	.939889	.911641		
7	8	.930228			
8	9	.920667			
9	10	.911203			
10	11	.901837			
11	12	.892567			
12	....	.883392			

TABLE F(13.4), WITH INTEREST AT 13.4 PERCENT, SHOWING FACTORS FOR COMPUTATION OF THE ADJUSTED PAYOUT RATE FOR CERTAIN VALUATIONS APPLICABLE AFTER APRIL 30, 1989

1 Number Of Months By Which The Valuation Date for the First Full Taxable Year of the Trust Precedes The First Payout		2 Factors For Payout At The End Of Each Period			
At Least	But Less Than	Annual Period	Semiannual Period	Quarterly Period	Monthly Period

At Least	But Less Than	Annual Period	Semiannual Period	Quarterly Period	Monthly Period
....	1	1.000000	.969530	.954527	.944611
1	2	.989575	.959423	.944577	.934764
2	3	.979260	.949422	.934730	
3	4	.969051	.939524	.924986	
4	5	.958949	.929730		
5	6	.948953	.920038		
6	7	.939060	.910447		
7	8	.929271			
8	9	.919584			
9	10	.909998			
10	11	.900511			
11	12	.891124			
12	....	.881834			

TABLE F(13.6), WITH INTEREST AT 13.6 PERCENT, SHOWING FACTORS FOR COMPUTATION OF THE ADJUSTED PAYOUT RATE FOR CERTAIN VALUATIONS APPLICABLE AFTER APRIL 30, 1989

1 Number Of Months By Which The Valuation Date for the First Full Taxable Year of the Trust Precedes The First Payout		2 Factors For Payout At The End Of Each Period			
At Least	But Less Than	Annual Period	Semiannual Period	Quarterly Period	Monthly Period
....	1	1.000000	.969117	.953913	.943866
1	2	.989430	.958873	.943831	.933890
2	3	.978972	.948738	.933854	
3	4	.968624	.938710	.923984	
4	5	.958386	.928788		
5	6	.948256	.918971		
6	7	.938233	.909257		
7	8	.928316			
8	9	.918504			
9	10	.908796			
10	11	.899190			
11	12	.889686			
12	....	.880282			

TABLE F(13.8), WITH INTEREST AT 13.8 PERCENT, SHOWING FACTORS FOR COMPUTATION OF THE ADJUSTED PAYOUT RATE FOR CERTAIN VALUATIONS APPLICABLE AFTER APRIL 30, 1989

1 Number Of Months By Which The Valuation Date for the First Full Taxable Year of the Trust Precedes The First Payout		2 Factors For Payout At The End Of Each Period			
At Least	But Less Than	Annual Period	Semiannual Period	Quarterly Period	Monthly Period
....	1	1.000000	.968704	.953301	.943123
1	2	.989285	.958325	.943087	.933018
2	3	.978685	.948056	.932982	
3	4	.968199	.937898	.922985	
4	5	.957824	.927849		
5	6	.947561	.917907		
6	7	.937408	.908072		
7	8	.927364			
8	9	.917428			
9	10	.907598			
10	11	.897873			
11	11	.888252			
12	....	.878735			

TABLE F(14.0), WITH INTEREST AT 14.0 PERCENT, SHOWING FACTORS FOR COMPUTATION OF THE ADJUSTED PAYOUT RATE FOR CERTAIN VALUATIONS APPLICABLE AFTER APRIL 30, 1989

1 Number Of Months By Which The Valuation Date for the First Full Taxable Year of the Trust Precedes The First Payout		2 Factors For Payout At The End Of Each Period			
At Least	But Less Than	Annual Period	Semiannual Period	Quarterly Period	Monthly Period
....	1	1.000000	.968293	.952691	.942382
1	2	.989140	.957778	.942345	.932148
2	3	.978399	.947377	.932111	
3	4	.967774	.937088	.921989	
4	5	.957264	.926912		
5	6	.946868	.916846		
6	7	.936586	.906889		
7	8	.926415			
8	9	.916354			
9	10	.906403			
10	11	.896560			
11	12	.886824			
12	....	.877193			

(7) *Actuarial Table U(1) for transfers for which the valuation date is after April 30, 1999.* For transfers for which the valuation date is after April 30, 1999, the present value of a charitable remainder unitrust interest that is dependent on the termination of a life interest is determined by using the section 7520 rate, Table U(1) in this paragraph (e)(7), and Table F(4.2) through (14.0) in paragraph (e)(6) of this section. See, however, § 1.7520-3(b) (relating to exceptions to the use of prescribed tables under certain circumstances). Many actuarial factors not contained in the following tables are contained in Internal Revenue Service Publication 1458, "Actuarial Values, Book Beth," (7-1999). A copy of this publication is available for purchase from the Superintendent of Documents, United States Government Printing Office, Washington, DC 20402.

Table U(1).--Based on Life Table 90CM Unitrust Single Life Remainder

Factors Applicable For Transfers After April 30, 1999

	[Adjusted payout rate]									
Age	4.2%	4.4%	4.6%	4.8%	5.0%	5.2%	5.4%	5.6%	.8%	6.0%
0	.06177	.05580	.05061	.04609	.04215	.03871	.03570	.03307	.03075	.02872
1	.05543	.04925	.04388	.03919	.03509	.03151	.02838	.02563	.02321	.02109
2	.05716	.05081	.04528	.04045	.03622	.03252	.02927	.02642	.02391	.02170
3	.05920	.05268	.04699	.04201	.03765	.03382	.03046	.02750	.02490	.02260
4	.06143	.05475	.04889	.04376	.03926	.03530	.03182	.02876	.02605	.02366
5	.06384	.05697	.05095	.04567	.04103	.03694	.03334	.03016	.02735	.02487
6	.06637	.05933	.05315	.04771	.04292	.03870	.03497	.03168	.02876	.02618
7	.06905	.06183	.05547	.04987	.04494	.04058	.03673	.03332	.03029	.02761
8	.07186	.06445	.05792	.05216	.04708	.04258	.03859	.03506	.03192	.02914
9	.07482	.06722	.06052	.05460	.04936	.04471	.04060	.03694	.03369	.03079
10	.07793	.07015	.06327	.05718	.05179	.04700	.04274	.03896	.03559	.03259
11	.08120	.07323	.06617	.05991	.05435	.04942	.04502	.04111	.03762	.03450
12	.08461	.07645	.06920	.06277	.05706	.05197	.04744	.04339	.03978	.03655
13	.08812	.07976	.07234	.06574	.05985	.05461	.04993	.04576	.04202	.03867
14	.09168	.08313	.07552	.06874	.06269	.05729	.05247	.04815	.04428	.04081
15	.09527	.08652	.07872	.07176	.06554	.05999	.05501	.05055	.04655	.04296
16	.09886	.08991	.08192	.07478	.06839	.06267	.05754	.05294	.04880	.04508
17	.10249	.09334	.08515	.07782	.07126	.06537	.06008	.05533	.05105	.04720
18	.10616	.09680	.08842	.08090	.07415	.06809	.06264	.05774	.05332	.04933
19	.10994	.10037	.09178	.08407	.07714	.07091	.06529	.06023	.05566	.05153
20	.11384	.10406	.09527	.08737	.08025	.07383	.06805	.06283	.05811	.05384
21	.11790	.10790	.09891	.09080	.08349	.07690	.07094	.06555	.06068	.05626
22	.12208	.11188	.10267	.09436	.08686	.08008	.07395	.06839	.06336	.05879
23	.12643	.11601	.10659	.09808	.09038	.08342	.07710	.07138	.06618	.06146
24	.13095	.12031	.11069	.10197	.09408	.08692	.08042	.07452	.06915	.06427
25	.13567	.12481	.11497	.10605	.09795	.09060	.08392	.07784	.07230	.06726

[Adjusted payout rate]

Age	4.2%	4.4%	4.6%	4.8%	5.0%	5.2%	5.4%	5.6%	.8%	6.0%
26	.14058	.12950	.11945	.11032	.10202	.09447	.08760	.08134	.07563	.07042
27	.14571	.13442	.12415	.11481	.10631	.09856	.09149	.08505	.07916	.07379
28	.15104	.13953	.12904	.11949	.11078	.10284	.09558	.08895	.08288	.07733
29	.15656	.14484	.13414	.12438	.11546	.10731	.09986	.09304	.08679	.08106
30	.16229	.15034	.13943	.12946	.12034	.11198	.10433	.09732	.09089	.08498
31	.16821	.15605	.14493	.13474	.12541	.11685	.10900	.10179	.09517	.08909
32	.17433	.16196	.15063	.14023	.13069	.12193	.11387	.10647	.09966	.09339
33	.18068	.16810	.15655	.14595	.13620	.12723	.11897	.11137	.10437	.09791
34	.18724	.17446	.16270	.15189	.14193	.13275	.12430	.11650	.10930	.10265
35	.19405	.18107	.16910	.15808	.14791	.13853	.12987	.12187	.11448	.10764
36	.20109	.18791	.17574	.16451	.15414	.14456	.13569	.12749	.11990	.11287
37	.20838	.19500	.18263	.17120	.16062	.15083	.14177	.13337	.12558	.11835
38	.21593	.20236	.18979	.17816	.16739	.15739	.14813	.13953	.13154	.12412
39	.22374	.20998	.19723	.18540	.17443	.16423	.15477	.14597	.13779	.13017
40	.23183	.21789	.20496	.19294	.18177	.17138	.16172	.15272	.14434	.13653
41	.24021	.22611	.21299	.20079	.18943	.17885	.16899	.15980	.15123	.14322
42	.24889	.23463	.22134	.20896	.19741	.18665	.17660	.16721	.15845	.15025
43	.25786	.24344	.23000	.21744	.20572	.19477	.18453	.17496	.16601	.15762
44	.26712	.25257	.23896	.22625	.21435	.20322	.19281	.18305	.17391	.16534
45	.27665	.26196	.24821	.23534	.22328	.21198	.20139	.19145	.18213	.17338
46	.28644	.27163	.25774	.24472	.23251	.22105	.21028	.20018	.19068	.18174
47	.29647	.28155	.26754	.25438	.24201	.23040	.21947	.20919	.19952	.19041
48	.30676	.29173	.27760	.26431	.25181	.24004	.22896	.21852	.20868	.19941
49	.31729	.30217	.28794	.27453	.26190	.24999	.23876	.22817	.21817	.20873
50	.32808	.31289	.29856	.28505	.27229	.26026	.24889	.23814	.22799	.21839
51	.33912	.32387	.30946	.29585	.28299	.27083	.25933	.24845	.23815	.22840
52	.35038	.33507	.32060	.30691	.29395	.28168	.27005	.25904	.24861	.23872
53	.36185	.34651	.33198	.31821	.30517	.29280	.28106	.26993	.25937	.24934
54	.37352	.35815	.34358	.32976	.31664	.30418	.29234	.28110	.27042	.26026
55	.38539	.37002	.35542	.34155	.32836	.31583	.30390	.29256	.28177	.27149
56	.39746	.38209	.36748	.35358	.34034	.32774	.31574	.30431	.29342	.28303
57	.40971	.39437	.37976	.36584	.35257	.33992	.32785	.31634	.30536	.29488
58	.42212	.40682	.39222	.37829	.36500	.35231	.34019	.32862	.31756	.30699
59	.43464	.41939	.40482	.39090	.37759	.36488	.35272	.34109	.32996	.31932
60	.44726	.43207	.41754	.40364	.39034	.37761	.36542	.35375	.34257	.33186
61	.45999	.44488	.43041	.41655	.40326	.39053	.37833	.36662	.35540	.34463
62	.47286	.45785	.44345	.42964	.41639	.40367	.39146	.37974	.36848	.35767
63	.48589	.47098	.45667	.44293	.42972	.41703	.40484	.39311	.38184	.37100
64	.49903	.48426	.47005	.45638	.44324	.43060	.41843	.40671	.39544	.38458
65	.51229	.49766	.48357	.47001	.45694	.44435	.43223	.42054	.40927	.39841
66	.52568	.51121	.49726	.48381	.47084	.45833	.44626	.43461	.42337	.41252
67	.53924	.52495	.51115	.49784	.48498	.47256	.46056	.44898	.43778	.42696
68	.55293	.53883	.52521	.51205	.49932	.48701	.47511	.46360	.45246	.44169
69	.56671	.55283	.53940	.52640	.51382	.50165	.48985	.47844	.46738	.45666
70	.58052	.56687	.55365	.54084	.52843	.51639	.50473	.49342	.48245	.47181
71	.59431	.58091	.56791	.55529	.54306	.53118	.51966	.50847	.49761	.48707
72	.60804	.59490	.58213	.56973	.55768	.54598	.53461	.52357	.51283	.50239
73	.62168	.60881	.59629	.58411	.57227	.56076	.54955	.53866	.52806	.51774
74	.63528	.62268	.61042	.59848	.58686	.57555	.56453	.55380	.54335	.53316
75	.64887	.63657	.62458	.61290	.60151	.59041	.57959	.56904	.55875	.54872
76	.66249	.65049	.63880	.62739	.61625	.60538	.59478	.58443	.57432	.56446
77	.67612	.66446	.65307	.64194	.63108	.62046	.61009	.59995	.59005	.58037
78	.68975	.67843	.66736	.65654	.64596	.63561	.62548	.61558	.60590	.59643
79	.70330	.69233	.68160	.67109	.66081	.65074	.64088	.63123	.62178	.61253
80	.71666	.70605	.69566	.68548	.67550	.66573	.65615	.64676	.63755	.62853
81	.72975	.71950	.70946	.69961	.68995	.68047	.67117	.66205	.65310	.64433
82	.74250	.73263	.72293	.71342	.70407	.69490	.68589	.67705	.66837	.65984
83	.75493	.74542	.73608	.72690	.71788	.70902	.70031	.69175	.68333	.67506
84	.76712	.75798	.74900	.74016	.73147	.72292	.71451	.70624	.69810	.69010
85	.77913	.77037	.76175	.75326	.74491	.73668	.72859	.72061	.71276	.70503
86	.79086	.78248	.77423	.76610	.75808	.75019	.74241	.73474	.72719	.71974
87	.80218	.79418	.78628	.77850	.77083	.76326	.75580	.74844	.74118	.73402
88	.81307	.80544	.79790	.79047	.78313	.77589	.76874	.76169	.75473	.74786

[Adjusted payout rate]

Age	4.2%	4.4%	4.6%	4.8%	5.0%	5.2%	5.4%	5.6%	.8%	6.0%
89	.82355	.81628	.80909	.80200	.79500	.78808	.78125	.77450	.76783	.76125
90	.83360	.82668	.81985	.81309	.80642	.79982	.79330	.78685	.78048	.77418
91	.84308	.83650	.83000	.82357	.81721	.81092	.80470	.79855	.79246	.78645
92	.85182	.84556	.83937	.83325	.82718	.82119	.81525	.80937	.80356	.79780
93	.85985	.85390	.84800	.84215	.83637	.83064	.82497	.81936	.81379	.80829
94	.86732	.86164	.85601	.85044	.84491	.83944	.83402	.82865	.82333	.81806
95	.87437	.86895	.86359	.85827	.85300	.84778	.84260	.83746	.83237	.82733
96	.88097	.87582	.87070	.86563	.86060	.85561	.85066	.84575	.84088	.83605
97	.88708	.88216	.87727	.87243	.86762	.86285	.85811	.85341	.84875	.84413
98	.89280	.88810	.88343	.87880	.87420	.86964	.86511	.86061	.85614	.85171
99	.89836	.89388	.88943	.88501	.88062	.87626	.87193	.86763	.86336	.85911
100	.90375	.89948	.89525	.89103	.88685	.88269	.87856	.87445	.87037	.86632
101	.90905	.90500	.90097	.89696	.89298	.88902	.88509	.88118	.87729	.87342
102	.91424	.91040	.90658	.90278	.89900	.89524	.89150	.88778	.88408	.88040
103	.91939	.91575	.91214	.90854	.90496	.90139	.89785	.89432	.89081	.88732
104	.92485	.92144	.91805	.91467	.91131	.90796	.90463	.90131	.89800	.89471
105	.93020	.92701	.92383	.92067	.91751	.91437	.91125	.90813	.90502	.90193
106	.93701	.93411	.93122	.92834	.92546	.92260	.91974	.91689	.91405	.91122
107	.94522	.94268	.94013	.93760	.93507	.93254	.93002	.92750	.92499	.92249
108	.95782	.95583	.95385	.95187	.94989	.94791	.94593	.94396	.94199	.94002
109	.97900	.97800	.97700	.97600	.97500	.97400	.97300	.97200	.97100	.97000

Age	6.2%	6.4%	6.6%	6.8%	7.0%	7.2%	7.4%	7.6%	7.8%	8.0%
0	.02693	.02534	.02395	.02271	.02161	.02063	.01976	.01898	.01828	.01765
1	.01922	.01756	.01610	.01480	.01365	.01263	.01171	.01090	.01017	.00951
2	.01975	.01802	.01650	.01514	.01393	.01286	.01190	.01104	.01028	.00959
3	.02056	.01876	.01717	.01575	.01449	.01336	.01235	.01145	.01064	.00992
4	.02155	.01967	.01800	.01652	.01520	.01401	.01296	.01201	.01116	.01039
5	.02266	.02071	.01896	.01741	.01603	.01479	.01368	.01269	.01179	.01098
6	.02389	.02184	.02003	.01841	.01696	.01566	.01450	.01345	.01251	.01166
7	.02522	.02309	.02120	.01950	.01799	.01663	.01540	.01431	.01332	.01242
8	.02665	.02444	.02246	.02069	.01910	.01768	.01640	.01524	.01420	.01326
9	.02821	.02590	.02384	.02199	.02033	.01884	.01750	.01629	.01520	.01421
10	.02990	.02750	.02535	.02342	.02169	.02013	.01872	.01745	.01631	.01526
11	.03172	.02922	.02698	.02497	.02316	.02153	.02006	.01872	.01752	.01643
12	.03365	.03106	.02872	.02663	.02474	.02303	.02149	.02010	.01884	.01769
13	.03566	.03297	.03054	.02835	.02638	.02460	.02299	.02154	.02021	.01901
14	.03770	.03490	.03237	.03010	.02804	.02619	.02450	.02298	.02159	.02033
15	.03973	.03682	.03419	.03182	.02968	.02775	.02599	.02439	.02294	.02162
16	.04173	.03871	.03598	.03352	.03129	.02926	.02743	.02576	.02424	.02286
17	.04372	.04059	.03775	.03519	.03287	.03076	.02884	.02710	.02551	.02406
18	.04573	.04248	.03953	.03686	.03444	.03224	.03024	.02842	.02676	.02524
19	.04780	.04443	.04137	.03859	.03607	.03378	.03169	.02978	.02804	.02646
20	.04997	.04647	.04329	.04040	.03778	.03539	.03321	.03122	.02940	.02773
21	.05226	.04862	.04532	.04232	.03958	.03709	.03481	.03274	.03083	.02909
22	.05465	.05088	.04745	.04432	.04148	.03888	.03650	.03433	.03234	.03052
23	.05716	.05325	.04969	.04645	.04348	.04077	.03830	.03603	.03394	.03203
24	.05983	.05578	.05208	.04871	.04562	.04280	.04021	.03784	.03566	.03367
25	.06266	.05846	.05463	.05112	.04791	.04497	.04227	.03980	.03752	.03543
26	.06566	.06131	.05734	.05369	.05035	.04729	.04448	.04189	.03951	.03732
27	.06887	.06436	.06024	.05646	.05298	.04979	.04686	.04416	.04168	.03939
28	.07225	.06758	.06331	.05938	.05577	.05245	.04940	.04658	.04398	.04159
29	.07581	.07099	.06656	.06248	.05873	.05528	.05210	.04916	.04645	.04394
30	.07956	.07457	.06998	.06575	.06186	.05827	.05495	.05189	.04906	.04644
31	.08348	.07833	.07358	.06920	.06515	.06142	.05797	.05478	.05182	.04908
32	.08761	.08228	.07736	.07282	.06863	.06475	.06116	.05783	.05475	.05189
33	.09195	.08645	.08136	.07666	.07231	.06828	.06454	.06108	.05786	.05488
34	.09651	.09082	.08557	.08070	.07619	.07200	.06812	.06452	.06117	.05805
35	.10131	.09545	.09002	.08498	.08030	.07596	.07193	.06818	.06469	.06144
36	.10635	.10031	.09470	.08949	.08465	.08015	.07596	.07206	.06842	.06503
37	.11165	.10542	.09963	.09424	.08923	.08457	.08022	.07617	.07238	.06885
38	.11722	.11081	.10484	.09927	.09409	.08926	.08475	.08054	.07661	.07293
39	.12308	.11648	.11032	.10458	.09922	.09422	.08955	.08518	.08109	.07726

Age	6.2%	6.4%	6.6%	6.8%	7.0%	7.2%	7.4%	7.6%	7.8%	8.0%
40	.12925	.12246	.11612	.11020	.10466	.09949	.09465	.09011	.08587	.08189
41	.13575	.12877	.12225	.11614	.11043	.10508	.10007	.09537	.09097	.08683
42	.14259	.13542	.12871	.12243	.11654	.11101	.10583	.10097	.09640	.09210
43	.14977	.14242	.13552	.12905	.12298	.11729	.11193	.10690	.10217	.09771
44	.15731	.14976	.14269	.13604	.12979	.12391	.11838	.11318	.10828	.10367
45	.16516	.15743	.15017	.14334	.13691	.13086	.12516	.11979	.11472	.10994
46	.17334	.16544	.15800	.15099	.14438	.13816	.13228	.12674	.12150	.11656
47	.18184	.17375	.16613	.15895	.15217	.14576	.13972	.13400	.12860	.12349
48	.19066	.18240	.17461	.16724	.16029	.15371	.14749	.14161	.13604	.13077
49	.19981	.19138	.18342	.17588	.16875	.16201	.15562	.14956	.14383	.13839
50	.20931	.20072	.19259	.18489	.17759	.17067	.16412	.15790	.15199	.14639
51	.21917	.21042	.20212	.19426	.18679	.17971	.17299	.16660	.16054	.15477
52	.22933	.22043	.21198	.20395	.19633	.18909	.18220	.17566	.16943	.16350
53	.23981	.23076	.22216	.21399	.20621	.19881	.19176	.18506	.17867	.17258
54	.25060	.24141	.23267	.22434	.21642	.20886	.20166	.19480	.18826	.18201
55	.26171	.25239	.24351	.23504	.22697	.21927	.21192	.20491	.19821	.19182
56	.27313	.26369	.25468	.24608	.23787	.23003	.22254	.21538	.20854	.20199
57	.28487	.27531	.26618	.25746	.24912	.24114	.23351	.22621	.21923	.21254
58	.29688	.28722	.27798	.26914	.26067	.25257	.24481	.23738	.23025	.22343
59	.30913	.29937	.29002	.28107	.27249	.26427	.25639	.24882	.24157	.23461
60	.32159	.31175	.30231	.29325	.28457	.27623	.26823	.26055	.25317	.24608
61	.33429	.32437	.31485	.30571	.29692	.28848	.28037	.27257	.26507	.25786
62	.34728	.33730	.32770	.31847	.30960	.30106	.29285	.28495	.27734	.27001
63	.36057	.35053	.34087	.33157	.32262	.31400	.30569	.29769	.28998	.28255
64	.37412	.36404	.35433	.34498	.33596	.32726	.31887	.31078	.30298	.29545
65	.38794	.37783	.36809	.35868	.34961	.34085	.33239	.32422	.31633	.30871
66	.40205	.39193	.38216	.37272	.36361	.35479	.34628	.33804	.33008	.32238
67	.41650	.40639	.39661	.38715	.37800	.36915	.36059	.35230	.34428	.33651
68	.43126	.42117	.41139	.40193	.39277	.38390	.37530	.36697	.35890	.35108
69	.44628	.43622	.42648	.41703	.40787	.39898	.39037	.38201	.37391	.36604
70	.46150	.45149	.44178	.43236	.42321	.41433	.40571	.39735	.38922	.38132
71	.47683	.46689	.45723	.44785	.43873	.42987	.42126	.41290	.40476	.39685
72	.49225	.48238	.47279	.46346	.45439	.44556	.43697	.42862	.42048	.41257
73	.50770	.49793	.48841	.47915	.47013	.46135	.45280	.44447	.43635	.42844
74	.52324	.51358	.50416	.49498	.48603	.47731	.46880	.46051	.45242	.44454
75	.53894	.52939	.52008	.51100	.50214	.49349	.48505	.47681	.46877	.46092
76	.55483	.54543	.53624	.52728	.51852	.50996	.50160	.49344	.48546	.47766
77	.57091	.56167	.55263	.54380	.53516	.52671	.51845	.51038	.50247	.49475
78	.58716	.57809	.56922	.56053	.55203	.54372	.53557	.52760	.51980	.51216
79	.60346	.59459	.58590	.57738	.56904	.56086	.55286	.54501	.53732	.52978
80	.61969	.61102	.60252	.59419	.58601	.57800	.57014	.56243	.55487	.54745
81	.63571	.62726	.61897	.61082	.60283	.59499	.58729	.57974	.57232	.56503
82	.65146	.64324	.63515	.62722	.61942	.61176	.60423	.59683	.58957	.58242
83	.66693	.65893	.65108	.64335	.63575	.62828	.62093	.61371	.60660	.59962
84	.68222	.67447	.66684	.65934	.65195	.64468	.63753	.63049	.62356	.61674
85	.69742	.68993	.68255	.67528	.66812	.66106	.65411	.64727	.64053	.63389
86	.71241	.70517	.69805	.69102	.68410	.67727	.67054	.66390	.65736	.65091
87	.72696	.72000	.71313	.70635	.69967	.69307	.68656	.68014	.67381	.66756
88	.74108	.73438	.72777	.72125	.71480	.70845	.70217	.69597	.68985	.68380
89	.75475	.74832	.74198	.73571	.72951	.72339	.71734	.71137	.70547	.69963
90	.76796	.76180	.75572	.74971	.74376	.73788	.73207	.72633	.72065	.71503
91	.78049	.77460	.76878	.76302	.75732	.75168	.74610	.74058	.73512	.72972
92	.79211	.78647	.78089	.77537	.76990	.76449	.75913	.75383	.74858	.74338
93	.80283	.79743	.79208	.78679	.78154	.77634	.77119	.76610	.76105	.75604
94	.81283	.80765	.80253	.79744	.79240	.78741	.78247	.77756	.77270	.76789
95	.82233	.81737	.81245	.80757	.80274	.79795	.79320	.78849	.78382	.77918
96	.83126	.82651	.82180	.81712	.81248	.80788	.80332	.79880	.79431	.78985
97	.83953	.83498	.83046	.82597	.82152	.81710	.81271	.80836	.80404	.79976
98	.84731	.84294	.83860	.83429	.83002	.82577	.82155	.81737	.81321	.80908
99	.85490	.85071	.84656	.84243	.83832	.83425	.83020	.82618	.82219	.81822
100	.86229	.85828	.85431	.85035	.84642	.84252	.83864	.83478	.83095	.82714
101	.86958	.86575	.86195	.85818	.85442	.85069	.84698	.84329	.83962	.83597
102	.87674	.87310	.86947	.86587	.86229	.85873	.85518	.85166	.84815	.84466
103	.88384	.88038	.87694	.87351	.87010	.86671	.86334	.85998	.85663	.85331
104	.89143	.88817	.88492	.88169	.87847	.87526	.87207	.86889	.86573	.86258

Age	6.2%	6.4%	6.6%	6.8%	7.0%	7.2%	7.4%	7.6%	7.8%	8.0%
105	.89885	.89578	.89272	.88967	.88664	.88361	.88060	.87760	.87461	.87163
106	.90840	.90559	.90278	.89999	.89720	.89442	.89165	.88888	.88613	.88338
107	.91999	.91750	.91501	.91253	.91005	.90758	.90511	.90265	.90019	.89774
108	.93805	.93609	.93412	.93216	.93020	.92824	.92629	.92434	.92239	.92044
109	.96900	.96800	.96700	.96600	.96500	.96400	.96300	.96200	.96100	.96000

Age	8.2%	8.4%	8.6%	8.8%	9.0%	9.2%	9.4%	9.6%	9.8%	10.0%
0	.01709	.01658	.01612	.01570	.01532	.01497	.01466	.01437	.01410	.01386
1	.00892	.00839	.00791	.00747	.00708	.00672	.00639	.00609	.00582	.00557
2	.00896	.00840	.00790	.00744	.00702	.00664	.00629	.00598	.00569	.00542
3	.00926	.00867	.00814	.00765	.00721	.00681	.00644	.00611	.00580	.00552
4	.00970	.00908	.00851	.00800	.00753	.00711	.00672	.00636	.00604	.00574
5	.01026	.00960	.00900	.00846	.00796	.00751	.00710	.00672	.00637	.00606
6	.01089	.01019	.00956	.00899	.00846	.00799	.00755	.00715	.00678	.00644
7	.01161	.01088	.01021	.00960	.00905	.00854	.00808	.00765	.00726	.00690
8	.01241	.01163	.01093	.01029	.00970	.00917	.00867	.00822	.00781	.00743
9	.01331	.01249	.01175	.01107	.01045	.00988	.00936	.00889	.00845	.00804
10	.01432	.01346	.01268	.01196	.01131	.01071	.01016	.00965	.00918	.00875
11	.01543	.01453	.01370	.01295	.01226	.01162	.01104	.01051	.01001	.00956
12	.01664	.01569	.01482	.01403	.01330	.01263	.01202	.01145	.01093	.01045
13	.01791	.01691	.01600	.01516	.01440	.01369	.01304	.01245	.01190	.01139
14	.01918	.01813	.01717	.01629	.01548	.01474	.01406	.01343	.01285	.01231
15	.02041	.01931	.01831	.01738	.01653	.01576	.01504	.01437	.01376	.01320
16	.02160	.02044	.01938	.01841	.01752	.01670	.01595	.01525	.01460	.01401
17	.02274	.02152	.02041	.01940	.01846	.01760	.01680	.01607	.01539	.01476
18	.02386	.02258	.02142	.02035	.01936	.01846	.01762	.01685	.01613	.01547
19	.02500	.02367	.02245	.02132	.02029	.01933	.01845	.01764	.01689	.01619
20	.02621	.02481	.02353	.02235	.02126	.02025	.01933	.01847	.01768	.01694
21	.02749	.02603	.02468	.02344	.02229	.02124	.02026	.01936	.01852	.01774
22	.02884	.02730	.02589	.02458	.02338	.02227	.02124	.02029	.01940	.01859
23	.03028	.02867	.02718	.02581	.02454	.02337	.02229	.02128	.02035	.01949
24	.03183	.03013	.02857	.02713	.02580	.02456	.02342	.02236	.02138	.02047
25	.03350	.03172	.03008	.02857	.02717	.02587	.02467	.02355	.02251	.02155
26	.03530	.03344	.03172	.03013	.02865	.02729	.02602	.02484	.02375	.02273
27	.03727	.03532	.03351	.03183	.03028	.02885	.02751	.02627	.02511	.02404
28	.03937	.03732	.03543	.03367	.03204	.03052	.02911	.02780	.02658	.02545
29	.04162	.03947	.03748	.03564	.03392	.03233	.03084	.02946	.02818	.02698
30	.04401	.04176	.03967	.03773	.03593	.03425	.03269	.03124	.02988	.02861
31	.04654	.04419	.04200	.03996	.03807	.03630	.03466	.03312	.03169	.03035
32	.04923	.04676	.04447	.04233	.04034	.03849	.03676	.03514	.03363	.03221
33	.05210	.04952	.04711	.04487	.04278	.04083	.03901	.03731	.03571	.03422
34	.05515	.05245	.04993	.04758	.04538	.04333	.04142	.03962	.03794	.03637
35	.05841	.05558	.05295	.05048	.04818	.04603	.04401	.04212	.04035	.03869
36	.06187	.05892	.05616	.05358	.05116	.04890	.04678	.04480	.04293	.04118
37	.06555	.06247	.05958	.05688	.05435	.05198	.04975	.04766	.04570	.04385
38	.06949	.06627	.06325	.06043	.05777	.05528	.05295	.05075	.04868	.04674
39	.07368	.07032	.06717	.06421	.06143	.05882	.05637	.05406	.05189	.04984
40	.07816	.07465	.07137	.06827	.06537	.06263	.06006	.05764	.05535	.05320
41	.08295	.07930	.07587	.07264	.06960	.06674	.06405	.06150	.05910	.05683
42	.08807	.08427	.08069	.07733	.07415	.07116	.06833	.06567	.06315	.06077
43	.09352	.08957	.08585	.08233	.07902	.07589	.07294	.07014	.06750	.06500
44	.09932	.09521	.09134	.08768	.08423	.08096	.07787	.07495	.07218	.06956
45	.10543	.10117	.09715	.09334	.08974	.08634	.08311	.08005	.07716	.07441
46	.11189	.10747	.10329	.09933	.09559	.09204	.08867	.08548	.08245	.07958
47	.11866	.11408	.10974	.10564	.10174	.09805	.09454	.09121	.08805	.08504
48	.12577	.12103	.11654	.11228	.10823	.10439	.10074	.09727	.09397	.09083
49	.13323	.12833	.12368	.11926	.11506	.11107	.10728	.10366	.10022	.09695
50	.14107	.13601	.13120	.12663	.12228	.11813	.11419	.11043	.10685	.10344
51	.14928	.14407	.13910	.13437	.12987	.12558	.12149	.11758	.11386	.11031
52	.15785	.15248	.14735	.14247	.13781	.13337	.12913	.12508	.12122	.11752
53	.16678	.16124	.15597	.15093	.14612	.14153	.13714	.13294	.12893	.12509
54	.17606	.17037	.16493	.15974	.15478	.15004	.14550	.14116	.13700	.13302
55	.18570	.17986	.17428	.16893	.16382	.15893	.15424	.14976	.14546	.14134
56	.19573	.18974	.18400	.17851	.17325	.16821	.16338	.15875	.15430	.15004

Age	8.2%	8.4%	8.6%	8.8%	9.0%	9.2%	9.4%	9.6%	9.8%	10.0%
57	.20613	.20000	.19412	.18848	.18307	.17789	.17291	.16814	.16355	.15914
58	.21688	.21060	.20458	.19880	.19325	.18792	.18280	.17788	.17316	.16861
59	.22793	.22151	.21535	.20943	.20374	.19827	.19301	.18795	.18309	.17840
60	.23927	.23272	.22642	.22036	.21454	.20893	.20354	.19834	.19334	.18851
61	.25092	.24425	.23782	.23163	.22567	.21993	.21440	.20907	.20393	.19898
62	.26295	.25616	.24961	.24329	.23721	.23134	.22568	.22021	.21494	.20985
63	.27538	.26847	.26180	.25537	.24916	.24316	.23738	.23179	.22639	.22117
64	.28817	.28116	.27438	.26783	.26150	.25539	.24949	.24377	.23825	.23291
65	.30134	.29423	.28735	.28069	.27426	.26803	.26201	.25618	.25054	.24508
66	.31493	.30772	.30075	.29399	.28746	.28113	.27500	.26906	.26331	.25774
67	.32899	.32170	.31464	.30780	.30118	.29475	.28852	.28248	.27663	.27095
68	.34349	.33614	.32901	.32209	.31538	.30887	.30256	.29643	.29047	.28469
69	.35841	.35100	.34381	.33683	.33005	.32346	.31707	.31085	.30481	.29894
70	.37366	.36620	.35896	.35193	.34509	.33844	.33197	.32568	.31957	.31362
71	.38916	.38167	.37440	.36732	.36043	.35372	.34720	.34084	.33466	.32864
72	.40486	.39736	.39006	.38295	.37602	.36927	.36270	.35629	.35005	.34396
73	.42074	.41323	.40591	.39878	.39182	.38504	.37843	.37198	.36568	.35955
74	.43685	.42934	.42202	.41488	.40791	.40110	.39446	.38798	.38165	.37547
75	.45326	.44577	.43846	.43132	.42435	.41754	.41088	.40438	.39802	.39181
76	.47004	.46259	.45530	.44818	.44122	.43442	.42776	.42125	.41488	.40865
77	.48718	.47979	.47255	.46547	.45853	.45175	.44511	.43861	.43225	.42601
78	.50467	.49735	.49017	.48314	.47626	.46951	.46290	.45643	.45008	.44386
79	.52239	.51515	.50806	.50110	.49427	.48758	.48102	.47459	.46828	.46209
80	.54018	.53304	.52603	.51916	.51242	.50580	.49930	.49292	.48666	.48052
81	.55788	.55085	.54396	.53718	.53053	.52399	.51757	.51126	.50507	.49898
82	.57540	.56851	.56173	.55506	.54851	.54207	.53574	.52951	.52339	.51737
83	.59274	.58598	.57933	.57279	.56635	.56001	.55378	.54765	.54161	.53567
84	.61002	.60341	.59690	.59049	.58418	.57796	.57184	.56582	.55988	.55403
85	.62734	.62090	.61454	.60828	.60211	.59603	.59004	.58414	.57832	.57258
86	.64455	.63828	.63210	.62600	.61999	.61406	.60821	.60244	.59675	.59113
87	.66139	.65531	.64930	.64337	.63752	.63175	.62605	.62043	.61488	.60939
88	.67783	.67194	.66612	.66037	.65469	.64908	.64354	.63807	.63267	.62733
89	.69387	.68817	.68254	.67698	.67148	.66605	.66068	.65537	.65012	.64493
90	.70947	.70398	.69855	.69318	.68786	.68261	.67742	.67228	.66719	.66217
91	.72437	.71908	.71385	.70867	.70354	.69847	.69345	.68848	.68357	.67870
92	.73823	.73314	.72810	.72310	.71816	.71326	.70841	.70361	.69886	.69415
93	.75109	.74618	.74132	.73650	.73173	.72700	.72232	.71768	.71308	.70852
94	.76312	.75839	.75370	.74905	.74445	.73988	.73536	.73087	.72643	.72202
95	.77459	.77004	.76552	.76104	.75660	.75220	.74783	.74350	.73920	.73494
96	.78543	.78105	.77670	.77238	.76810	.76386	.75964	.75546	.75131	.74720
97	.79550	.79128	.78709	.78293	.77880	.77470	.77063	.76659	.76258	.75860
98	.80498	.80091	.79687	.79286	.78888	.78492	.78099	.77709	.77322	.76937
99	.81428	.81036	.80647	.80261	.79877	.79496	.79117	.78741	.78367	.77995
100	.82336	.81959	.81586	.81214	.80845	.80478	.80113	.79751	.79390	.79032
101	.83234	.82873	.82515	.82158	.81804	.81451	.81101	.80753	.80406	.80062
102	.84119	.83774	.83431	.83089	.82750	.82412	.82076	.81742	.81409	.81078
103	.84999	.84670	.84342	.84016	.83691	.83368	.83046	.82726	.82408	.82091
104	.85944	.85632	.85321	.85011	.84703	.84396	.84090	.83786	.83483	.83182
105	.86866	.86570	.86276	.85982	.85690	.85399	.85109	.84820	.84532	.84245
106	.88065	.87792	.87520	.87248	.86978	.86708	.86440	.86172	.85905	.85638
107	.89530	.89286	.89042	.88799	.88557	.88315	.88073	.87833	.87592	.87352
108	.91849	.91654	.91460	.91266	.91072	.90879	.90685	.90492	.90299	.90106
109	.95900	.95800	.95700	.95600	.95500	.95400	.95300	.95200	.95100	.95000

Age	10.2%	10.4%	10.6%	10.8%	11.0%	11.2%	11.4%	11.6%	11.8%	12.0%
0	.01363	.01342	.01323	.01305	.01288	.01272	.01258	.01244	.01231	.01219
1	.00534	.00512	.00493	.00474	.00458	.00442	.00427	.00414	.00401	.00389
2	.00518	.00495	.00474	.00455	.00437	.00421	.00405	.00391	.00377	.00365
3	.00526	.00502	.00480	.00459	.00440	.00422	.00406	.00391	.00376	.00363
4	.00546	.00521	.00497	.00475	.00455	.00436	.00419	.00402	.00387	.00373
5	.00576	.00549	.00524	.00501	.00479	.00459	.00440	.00423	.00406	.00391
6	.00613	.00584	.00557	.00532	.00509	.00488	.00468	.00449	.00432	.00415
7	.00657	.00626	.00598	.00571	.00547	.00524	.00502	.00482	.00464	.00446
8	.00707	.00675	.00644	.00616	.00590	.00565	.00542	.00521	.00501	.00482

Age	10.2%	10.4%	10.6%	10.8%	11.0%	11.2%	11.4%	11.6%	11.8%	12.0%
9	.00766	.00732	.00699	.00669	.00641	.00615	.00591	.00568	.00547	.00527
10	.00835	.00798	.00764	.00732	.00702	.00675	.00649	.00624	.00602	.00580
11	.00913	.00874	.00838	.00804	.00772	.00743	.00715	.00689	.00665	.00642
12	.01000	.00959	.00920	.00884	.00851	.00819	.00790	.00762	.00737	.00712
13	.01091	.01048	.01007	.00969	.00933	.00900	.00869	.00840	.00813	.00787
14	.01181	.01135	.01092	.01052	.01014	.00979	.00947	.00916	.00887	.00860
15	.01267	.01218	.01173	.01130	.01091	.01054	.01019	.00987	.00956	.00928
16	.01345	.01294	.01246	.01201	.01160	.01121	.01084	.01050	.01018	.00988
17	.01418	.01364	.01313	.01266	.01222	.01181	.01143	.01107	.01073	.01041
18	.01486	.01429	.01375	.01326	.01279	.01236	.01196	.01158	.01122	.01088
19	.01554	.01494	.01438	.01385	.01336	.01291	.01248	.01208	.01170	.01135
20	.01626	.01562	.01503	.01448	.01396	.01348	.01303	.01260	.01220	.01183
21	.01702	.01635	.01573	.01514	.01460	.01409	.01361	.01316	.01274	.01235
22	.01782	.01711	.01645	.01584	.01526	.01472	.01422	.01374	.01330	.01288
23	.01868	.01793	.01724	.01658	.01597	.01540	.01487	.01437	.01390	.01345
24	.01962	.01883	.01809	.01740	.01675	.01615	.01558	.01505	.01455	.01408
25	.02065	.01981	.01903	.01830	.01762	.01698	.01638	.01581	.01528	.01478
26	.02178	.02089	.02006	.01929	.01856	.01789	.01725	.01665	.01609	.01556
27	.02303	.02209	.02122	.02040	.01963	.01891	.01824	.01760	.01700	.01644
28	.02439	.02339	.02247	.02160	.02079	.02002	.01931	.01863	.01800	.01740
29	.02585	.02480	.02382	.02290	.02204	.02123	.02047	.01976	.01908	.01845
30	.02742	.02631	.02527	.02430	.02339	.02253	.02172	.02096	.02025	.01957
31	.02910	.02793	.02683	.02579	.02482	.02391	.02306	.02225	.02149	.02077
32	.03089	.02965	.02849	.02739	.02636	.02540	.02449	.02363	.02282	.02206
33	.03282	.03151	.03028	.02912	.02803	.02701	.02604	.02513	.02427	.02346
34	.03489	.03350	.03220	.03097	.02982	.02873	.02771	.02674	.02583	.02497
35	.03713	.03567	.03429	.03299	.03177	.03061	.02953	.02850	.02753	.02661
36	.03953	.03798	.03653	.03515	.03386	.03263	.03148	.03039	.02936	.02838
37	.04211	.04048	.03894	.03748	.03611	.03481	.03359	.03243	.03134	.03030
38	.04490	.04318	.04155	.04001	.03856	.03719	.03589	.03466	.03350	.03239
39	.04791	.04609	.04437	.04274	.04120	.03975	.03837	.03707	.03583	.03466
40	.05116	.04924	.04742	.04571	.04408	.04254	.04108	.03970	.03839	.03714
41	.05469	.05267	.05075	.04894	.04722	.04559	.04405	.04258	.04119	.03987
42	.05851	.05638	.05436	.05245	.05063	.04891	.04728	.04573	.04425	.04285
43	.06263	.06039	.05827	.05625	.05433	.05252	.05079	.04915	.04759	.04610
44	.06707	.06472	.06248	.06035	.05834	.05642	.05459	.05286	.05121	.04963
45	.07180	.06933	.06698	.06474	.06262	.06059	.05867	.05684	.05509	.05342
46	.07685	.07425	.07178	.06943	.06720	.06507	.06304	.06110	.05926	.05750
47	.08218	.07946	.07687	.07440	.07205	.06981	.06768	.06564	.06369	.06183
48	.08784	.08499	.08228	.07969	.07722	.07487	.07262	.07047	.06842	.06646
49	.09382	.09085	.08801	.08530	.08271	.08024	.07788	.07562	.07346	.07140
50	.10018	.09707	.09410	.09127	.08856	.08597	.08349	.08112	.07885	.07667
51	.10691	.10367	.10057	.09761	.09477	.09206	.08946	.08697	.08459	.08231
52	.11399	.11061	.10738	.10429	.10132	.09849	.09577	.09316	.09066	.08826
53	.12142	.11791	.11454	.11132	.10823	.10526	.10242	.09969	.09707	.09456
54	.12921	.12556	.12206	.11870	.11548	.11239	.10942	.10657	.10383	.10120
55	.13738	.13359	.12995	.12646	.12311	.11989	.11679	.11382	.11096	.10820
56	.14595	.14202	.13824	.13462	.13113	.12778	.12456	.12146	.11847	.11560
57	.15491	.15084	.14693	.14317	.13955	.13607	.13272	.12949	.12638	.12338
58	.16424	.16004	.15599	.15209	.14834	.14473	.14125	.13789	.13465	.13153
59	.17390	.16955	.16537	.16134	.15746	.15371	.15010	.14662	.14325	.14001
60	.18387	.17939	.17507	.17091	.16689	.16302	.15927	.15566	.15217	.14880
61	.19420	.18958	.18513	.18084	.17669	.17268	.16881	.16506	.16145	.15795
62	.20494	.20020	.19561	.19119	.18691	.18277	.17877	.17490	.17115	.16753
63	.21613	.21126	.20654	.20199	.19758	.19331	.18918	.18518	.18131	.17757
64	.22774	.22274	.21791	.21322	.20869	.20429	.20004	.19592	.19192	.18805
65	.23979	.23467	.22971	.22490	.22025	.21573	.21135	.20710	.20299	.19899
66	.25233	.24709	.24202	.23709	.23231	.22767	.22318	.21881	.21457	.21045
67	.26543	.26009	.25489	.24985	.24496	.24021	.23560	.23111	.22676	.22252
68	.27908	.27363	.26833	.26319	.25819	.25332	.24860	.24400	.23954	.23519
69	.29324	.28769	.28230	.27705	.27195	.26699	.26216	.25746	.25288	.24843
70	.30783	.30219	.29671	.29137	.28618	.28112	.27619	.27139	.26672	.26216
71	.32277	.31706	.31150	.30608	.30079	.29564	.29063	.28573	.28096	.27631
72	.33803	.33225	.32661	.32112	.31575	.31052	.30542	.30044	.29559	.29084
73	.35356	.34772	.34201	.33645	.33101	.32571	.32053	.31547	.31053	.30571

Age	10.2%	10.4%	10.6%	10.8%	11.0%	11.2%	11.4%	11.6%	11.8%	12.0%
74	.36943	.36354	.35778	.35215	.34666	.34129	.33604	.33091	.32590	.32100
75	.38574	.37980	.37400	.36833	.36278	.35735	.35205	.34686	.34178	.33681
76	.40256	.39660	.39076	.38505	.37947	.37400	.36864	.36340	.35827	.35324
77	.41991	.41394	.40808	.40235	.39674	.39124	.38585	.38056	.37539	.37032
78	.43777	.43180	.42594	.42020	.41457	.40906	.40365	.39834	.39314	.38803
79	.45602	.45007	.44422	.43849	.43287	.42735	.42193	.41661	.41139	.40627
80	.47449	.46856	.46275	.45704	.45143	.44592	.44051	.43519	.42997	.42484
81	.49300	.48712	.48134	.47566	.47008	.46460	.45921	.45391	.44870	.44357
82	.51145	.50563	.49990	.49427	.48873	.48328	.47792	.47265	.46746	.46235
83	.52983	.52407	.51841	.51284	.50735	.50195	.49663	.49139	.48624	.48116
84	.54828	.54261	.53702	.53151	.52609	.52075	.51549	.51030	.50519	.50015
85	.56693	.56135	.55586	.55044	.54510	.53983	.53464	.52952	.52447	.51949
86	.58560	.58013	.57474	.56943	.56418	.55901	.55390	.54886	.54389	.53898
87	.60398	.59864	.59337	.58817	.58303	.57795	.57294	.56799	.56310	.55828
88	.62206	.61685	.61170	.60662	.60159	.59663	.59173	.58688	.58209	.57736
89	.63980	.63474	.62972	.62477	.61987	.61503	.61024	.60551	.60083	.59620
90	.65719	.65227	.64741	.64259	.63783	.63312	.62846	.62385	.61928	.61477
91	.67388	.66912	.66440	.65973	.65511	.65053	.64600	.64152	.63708	.63269
92	.68949	.68487	.68030	.67577	.67129	.66685	.66245	.65809	.65378	.64950
93	.70401	.69954	.69511	.69072	.68637	.68205	.67778	.67355	.66935	.66519
94	.71765	.71332	.70902	.70477	.70055	.69636	.69222	.68810	.68403	.67998
95	.73072	.72653	.72237	.71825	.71416	.71010	.70608	.70209	.69813	.69421
96	.74311	.73906	.73504	.73105	.72709	.72316	.71926	.71539	.71155	.70774
97	.75465	.75073	.74684	.74297	.73914	.73533	.73155	.72780	.72407	.72037
98	.76555	.76175	.75798	.75424	.75052	.74683	.74317	.73953	.73591	.73232
99	.77626	.77260	.76895	.76534	.76174	.75817	.75462	.75109	.74759	.74411
100	.78676	.78323	.77971	.77622	.77274	.76929	.76586	.76245	.75906	.75569
101	.79719	.79379	.79040	.78703	.78368	.78035	.77704	.77375	.77048	.76722
102	.80749	.80422	.80096	.79772	.79450	.79130	.78811	.78494	.78178	.77864
103	.81775	.81461	.81149	.80838	.80529	.80221	.79914	.79609	.79306	.79003
104	.82881	.82582	.82284	.81988	.81693	.81399	.81106	.80815	.80525	.80236
105	.83959	.83674	.83391	.83108	.82826	.82546	.82267	.81988	.81711	.81435
106	.85373	.85108	.84844	.84581	.84319	.84058	.83797	.83537	.83278	.83020
107	.87113	.86875	.86636	.86399	.86161	.85925	.85689	.85453	.85218	.84984
108	.89913	.89721	.89529	.89337	.89145	.88953	.88762	.88571	.88380	.88189
109	.94900	.94800	.94700	.94600	.94500	.94400	.94300	.94200	.94100	.94000

Age	12.2%	12.4%	12.6%	12.8%	13.0%	13.2%	13.4%	13.6%	13.8%	14.0%
0	.01208	.01197	.01187	.01177	.01168	.01159	.01151	.01143	.01135	.01128
1	.00378	.00367	.00358	.00348	.00340	.00331	.00323	.00316	.00309	.00302
2	.00353	.00342	.00331	.00322	.00312	.00304	.00295	.00288	.00280	.00273
3	.00350	.00339	.00327	.00317	.00307	.00298	.00289	.00281	.00273	.00265
4	.00359	.00347	.00335	.00324	.00313	.00303	.00294	.00285	.00276	.00268
5	.00377	.00363	.00351	.00339	.00327	.00317	.00306	.00297	.00288	.00279
6	.00400	.00386	.00372	.00359	.00347	.00335	.00325	.00314	.00305	.00295
7	.00430	.00414	.00400	.00386	.00373	.00360	.00349	.00338	.00327	.00317
8	.00465	.00448	.00432	.00417	.00403	.00390	.00378	.00366	.00354	.00344
9	.00508	.00490	.00473	.00457	.00442	.00428	.00414	.00402	.00389	.00378
10	.00560	.00541	.00523	.00506	.00490	.00475	.00460	.00446	.00433	.00421
11	.00620	.00600	.00581	.00563	.00546	.00529	.00514	.00499	.00485	.00472
12	.00689	.00668	.00647	.00628	.00610	.00593	.00576	.00560	.00545	.00531
13	.00763	.00740	.00718	.00698	.00678	.00660	.00642	.00626	.00610	.00595
14	.00834	.00810	.00787	.00766	.00745	.00726	.00707	.00689	.00673	.00657
15	.00901	.00875	.00851	.00828	.00807	.00786	.00767	.00748	.00730	.00714
16	.00959	.00932	.00907	.00883	.00860	.00839	.00818	.00799	.00780	.00762
17	.01011	.00983	.00956	.00930	.00907	.00884	.00862	.00842	.00822	.00804
18	.01057	.01027	.00999	.00972	.00947	.00923	.00900	.00879	.00858	.00839
19	.01101	.01070	.01040	.01012	.00985	.00960	.00936	.00914	.00892	.00871
20	.01148	.01115	.01083	.01054	.01026	.00999	.00974	.00950	.00927	.00905
21	.01197	.01162	.01129	.01098	.01068	.01040	.01014	.00988	.00964	.00941
22	.01249	.01211	.01176	.01143	.01112	.01082	.01054	.01027	.01002	.00978
23	.01304	.01264	.01227	.01192	.01159	.01127	.01098	.01069	.01042	.01017
24	.01364	.01322	.01283	.01246	.01210	.01177	.01145	.01115	.01087	.01060
25	.01431	.01387	.01345	.01306	.01268	.01233	.01199	.01168	.01137	.01109

Age	12.2%	12.4%	12.6%	12.8%	13.0%	13.2%	13.4%	13.6%	13.8%	14.0%
26	.01506	.01459	.01415	.01373	.01333	.01295	.01260	.01226	.01194	.01163
27	.01591	.01541	.01494	.01449	.01407	.01367	.01329	.01293	.01259	.01226
28	.01684	.01631	.01580	.01533	.01488	.01445	.01405	.01367	.01330	.01296
29	.01785	.01728	.01675	.01624	.01577	.01531	.01488	.01447	.01408	.01372
30	.01893	.01833	.01776	.01723	.01672	.01623	.01578	.01534	.01493	.01453
31	.02010	.01946	.01885	.01828	.01773	.01722	.01673	.01627	.01582	.01540
32	.02134	.02066	.02002	.01940	.01883	.01828	.01776	.01726	.01679	.01634
33	.02270	.02197	.02128	.02063	.02002	.01943	.01887	.01835	.01784	.01736
34	.02415	.02338	.02265	.02195	.02130	.02067	.02008	.01951	.01897	.01846
35	.02574	.02492	.02414	.02340	.02270	.02203	.02140	.02080	.02022	.01967
36	.02746	.02658	.02575	.02496	.02422	.02350	.02283	.02218	.02157	.02098
37	.02932	.02838	.02750	.02666	.02586	.02510	.02438	.02369	.02303	.02241
38	.03135	.03035	.02941	.02851	.02766	.02685	.02608	.02534	.02464	.02397
39	.03355	.03249	.03149	.03053	.02962	.02876	.02793	.02715	.02640	.02568
40	.03596	.03484	.03377	.03275	.03178	.03086	.02998	.02914	.02833	.02757
41	.03861	.03742	.03628	.03520	.03416	.03318	.03224	.03134	.03048	.02966
42	.04152	.04025	.03903	.03788	.03678	.03573	.03473	.03377	.03285	.03198
43	.04468	.04333	.04205	.04082	.03965	.03853	.03746	.03644	.03546	.03453
44	.04813	.04670	.04533	.04403	.04278	.04159	.04045	.03936	.03832	.03732
45	.05183	.05032	.04887	.04748	.04616	.04489	.04368	.04252	.04141	.04034
46	.05582	.05421	.05267	.05121	.04980	.04846	.04717	.04593	.04475	.04362
47	.06006	.05836	.05673	.05518	.05369	.05226	.05089	.04958	.04832	.04711
48	.06459	.06279	.06107	.05943	.05785	.05634	.05488	.05349	.05216	.05087
49	.06942	.06752	.06571	.06397	.06230	.06070	.05916	.05768	.05626	.05490
50	.07459	.07259	.07068	.06884	.06708	.06538	.06376	.06219	.06069	.05924
51	.08012	.07801	.07599	.07406	.07220	.07041	.06869	.06703	.06544	.06391
52	.08596	.08375	.08163	.07959	.07763	.07574	.07392	.07218	.07049	.06887
53	.09214	.08982	.08759	.08544	.08338	.08139	.07948	.07763	.07586	.07415
54	.09867	.09623	.09389	.09164	.08946	.08737	.08536	.08342	.08154	.07974
55	.10556	.10301	.10055	.09819	.09591	.09371	.09159	.08955	.08757	.08567
56	.11283	.11016	.10759	.10511	.10272	.10042	.09819	.09605	.09397	.09197
57	.12050	.11771	.11502	.11243	.10993	.10751	.10518	.10293	.10075	.09864
58	.12852	.12562	.12281	.12011	.11749	.11496	.11252	.11016	.10787	.10567
59	.13687	.13385	.13092	.12810	.12537	.12273	.12017	.11770	.11531	.11299
60	.14554	.14240	.13935	.13641	.13356	.13080	.12813	.12555	.12305	.12063
61	.15457	.15130	.14813	.14507	.14210	.13923	.13644	.13375	.13113	.12860
62	.16402	.16063	.15734	.15415	.15107	.14808	.14518	.14237	.13964	.13699
63	.17393	.17042	.16700	.16370	.16049	.15738	.15437	.15144	.14860	.14584
64	.18429	.18065	.17712	.17369	.17036	.16714	.16400	.16096	.15800	.15513
65	.19511	.19135	.18769	.18415	.18070	.17735	.17410	.17094	.16787	.16488
66	.20645	.20257	.19880	.19513	.19157	.18810	.18473	.18146	.17827	.17517
67	.21841	.21441	.21052	.20673	.20305	.19947	.19599	.19259	.18929	.18608
68	.23096	.22685	.22284	.21895	.21515	.21146	.20786	.20436	.20094	.19762
69	.24409	.23987	.23575	.23175	.22784	.22404	.22033	.21672	.21320	.20976
70	.25772	.25339	.24918	.24507	.24106	.23715	.23333	.22961	.22598	.22244
71	.27178	.26735	.26304	.25882	.25471	.25070	.24679	.24296	.23923	.23559
72	.28622	.28170	.27729	.27298	.26877	.26467	.26065	.25673	.25290	.24915
73	.30100	.29639	.29189	.28749	.28320	.27899	.27489	.27087	.26694	.26310
74	.31621	.31152	.30694	.30246	.29807	.29378	.28959	.28548	.28146	.27753
75	.33195	.32719	.32253	.31797	.31351	.30914	.30486	.30067	.29657	.29255
76	.34832	.34350	.33877	.33415	.32961	.32517	.32082	.31656	.31238	.30828
77	.36535	.36047	.35570	.35101	.34642	.34192	.33750	.33317	.32892	.32475
78	.38302	.37811	.37329	.36856	.36392	.35937	.35490	.35051	.34621	.34198
79	.40124	.39630	.39145	.38669	.38201	.37742	.37291	.36848	.36413	.35985
80	.41980	.41485	.40998	.40520	.40050	.39588	.39134	.38688	.38249	.37818
81	.43854	.43358	.42871	.42392	.41921	.41457	.41001	.40553	.40112	.39678
82	.45733	.45238	.44752	.44273	.43802	.43338	.42881	.42431	.41989	.41553
83	.47616	.47123	.46638	.46161	.45690	.45227	.44770	.44320	.43877	.43441
84	.49519	.49030	.48548	.48073	.47604	.47143	.46688	.46239	.45797	.45361
85	.51458	.50974	.50496	.50025	.49560	.49102	.48650	.48204	.47763	.47329
86	.53413	.52935	.52463	.51998	.51538	.51084	.50636	.50194	.49758	.49327
87	.55351	.54881	.54416	.53957	.53503	.53055	.52613	.52176	.51744	.51317
88	.57268	.56806	.56349	.55898	.55451	.55010	.54574	.54144	.53718	.53296
89	.59162	.58710	.58262	.57819	.57382	.56949	.56520	.56097	.55678	.55263
90	.61030	.60588	.60151	.59718	.59290	.58866	.58447	.58032	.57621	.57214

Age	12.2%	12.4%	12.6%	12.8%	13.0%	13.2%	13.4%	13.6%	13.8%	14.0%
91	.62834	.62403	.61977	.61554	.61136	.60722	.60312	.59907	.59505	.59107
92	.64527	.64107	.63692	.63280	.62872	.62468	.62068	.61672	.61279	.60890
93	.66107	.65699	.65294	.64893	.64495	.64101	.63711	.63323	.62940	.62559
94	.67597	.67200	.66806	.66415	.66027	.65643	.65262	.64884	.64509	.64138
95	.69031	.68645	.68262	.67881	.67504	.67130	.66759	.66390	.66025	.65662
96	.70396	.70021	.69648	.69279	.68912	.68548	.68186	.67828	.67471	.67118
97	.71670	.71305	.70943	.70584	.70227	.69872	.69520	.69171	.68824	.68480
98	.72875	.72521	.72169	.71819	.71472	.71127	.70784	.70444	.70106	.69770
99	.74065	.73721	.73379	.73040	.72703	.72368	.72035	.71704	.71375	.71048
100	.75234	.74901	.74570	.74241	.73914	.73589	.73265	.72944	.72625	.72307
101	.76399	.76077	.75757	.75438	.75122	.74807	.74494	.74183	.73873	.73565
102	.77552	.77241	.76932	.76625	.76319	.76015	.75712	.75411	.75111	.74813
103	.78703	.78404	.78106	.77809	.77514	.77221	.76929	.76638	.76348	.76060
104	.79948	.79662	.79377	.79093	.78810	.78528	.78248	.77969	.77691	.77414
105	.81159	.80885	.80612	.80340	.80069	.79799	.79530	.79262	.78995	.78729
106	.82763	.82506	.82250	.81995	.81741	.81488	.81235	.80983	.80732	.80482
107	.84749	.84516	.84283	.84051	.83819	.83587	.83356	.83126	.82896	.82666
108	.87999	.87808	.87618	.87428	.87238	.87049	.86859	.86670	.86481	.86293
109	.93900	.93800	.93700	.93600	.93500	.93400	.93300	.93200	.93100	.93000

(f) Effective dates. This section applies after April 30, 1999.

T.D. 7202, 8/22/72, amend T.D. 7955, 5/10/84, T.D. 8540, 6/9/94, T.D. 8819, 4/29/99, T.D. 8886, 6/9/2000.

§ 1.664-4A Valuation of charitable remainder interests for which the valuation date is before May 1, 1999.

(a) Valuation of charitable remainder interests for which the valuation date is before January 1, 1952. There was no provision for the qualification of a charitable remainder unitrust under section 664 until 1969. See § 20.2031-7A(a) of this chapter (Estate Tax Regulations) for the determination of the present value of a charitable interest for which the valuation date is before January 1, 1952.

(b) Valuation of charitable remainder interests for which the valuation date is after December 31, 1951, and before January 1, 1971. No charitable deduction is allowable for a transfer to a unitrust for which the valuation date is after the effective dates of the Tax Reform Act of 1969 unless the unitrust meets the requirements of section 664. See § 20.2031-7A(b) of this chapter (Estate Tax Regulations) for the determination of the present value of a charitable remainder interest for which the valuation date is after December 31, 1951, and before January 1, 1971.

(c) Valuation of charitable remainder unitrusts having certain payout sequences for transfers for which the valuation date is after December 31, 1970, and before December 1, 1983. For the determination of the present value of a charitable remainder unitrust for which the valuation date is after December 31, 1970, and before December 1, 1983, see § 20.2031-7A(c) of this chapter (Estate Tax Regulations) and former § 1.664-4(d) (as contained in the 26 CFR part 1 edition revised as of April 1, 1994).

(d) Valuation of charitable remainder unitrusts having certain payout sequences for transfers for which the valuation date is after November 30, 1983, and before May 1, 1989. *(1) In general.* Except as otherwise provided in paragraph (d)(2) of this section, in the case of transfers made after November 30, 1983, for which the valuation date is before May 1, 1989, the present value of a remainder interest that is dependent on a term of years or the termination of the life of one individual is determined under paragraphs (d)(3) through (d)(6) of this section, provided that the amount of the payout as of any payout date during any taxable year of the trust is not larger than the amount that the trust could distribute on such date under § 1.664-3(a)(1)(v) if the taxable year of the trust were to end on such date. The present value of the remainder interest in the trust is determined by computing the adjusted payout rate (as defined in paragraph (d)(3) of this section) and following the procedure outlined in paragraph (d)(4) or (d)(5) of this section, whichever is applicable. The present value of a remainder interest that is dependent on a term of years is computed under paragraph (d)(4) of this section. The present value of a remainder interest that is dependent on the termination of the life of one individual is computed under paragraph (d)(5) of this section. See paragraph (d)(2) of this section for testamentary transfers for which the valuation date is after November 30, 1983, and before August 9, 1984.

(2) Rules for determining the present value for testamentary transfers where the decedent dies after November 30, 1983, and before August 9, 1984. For purposes of section 2055 or 2106, if—

(i) The decedent dies after November 30, 1983, and before August 9, 1984; or

(ii) On December 1, 1983, the decedent was mentally incompetent so that the disposition of the property could not be changed, and the decedent died after November 30, 1983, without regaining competency to dispose of the decedent's property, or died within 90 days of the date on which the decedent first regained competency, the present value determined under this section of a remainder interest is determined in accordance with paragraph (d)(1) and paragraphs (d)(3) through (d)(6) of this section, or § 1.664-4A(c), at the option of the taxpayer.

(3) Adjusted payout rate. The adjusted payout rate is determined by multiplying the fixed percentage described in paragraph (a)(1)(i)(a) of § 1 664-3 by the figure in column (2) of Table F(1) which describes the payout sequence of the trust opposite the number in column (1) of Table F(1) which corresponds to the number of months by which the valuation date for the first full taxable year of the trust precedes the first payout date for such taxable year. If the governing instrument does not prescribe when the distribution shall be made during the taxable year of the trust, see § 1.664-4(a).

In the case of a trust having a payout sequence for which no figures have been provided by Table F(1) and in the case of a trust which determines the fair market value of the trust assets by taking the average of valuations on more than one date during the taxable year, see § 1.664-4(b).

(4) Period is a term of years. If the period described in § 1.664-3(a)(5) is a term of years, the factor which is used in determining the present value of the remainder interest is the factor under the appropriate adjusted payout rate in Table D in § 1.664-4(e)(6) that corresponds to the number of years in the term. If the adjusted payout rate is an amount which is between adjusted payout rates for which factors are provided in Table D, a linear interpolation must be made. The present value of the remainder interest is determined by multiplying the net fair market value (as of the appropriate valuation date) of the property placed in trust by the factor determined under this paragraph (d)(4). For purposes of this section, the term "appropriate valuation date" means the date on which the property is transferred to the trust by the donor except that, for purposes of section 2055 or 2106, it means the date of death unless the alternate valuation date is elected in accordance with section 2032 and the regulations thereunder in which event it means the alternate valuation date. If the adjusted payout rate is greater than 14 percent, see § 1.664-4(b). The application of this paragraph (d)(4) may be illustrated by the following example:

Example. D transfers $100,000 to a charitable remainder unitrust on January 1, 1985. The trust instrument requires that the trust pay to D semiannually (on June 30 and December 31) 10 percent of the fair market value of the trust assets as of June 30th for a term of 15 years. The adjusted payout rate is 9.767 percent (10% x 0.976731). The present value of the remainder interest is $21,404.90, computed as follows:

Factor at 9.6 percent for 15 years	0.220053
Factor at 9.8 percent for 15 years	.212862
Difference	.007191

$$\frac{9.767\% - 9.6\%}{0.2\%} = \frac{X}{.007191}$$

$$X = .006004$$

Factor at 9.6 percent for 15 years	0.220053
Less: X	.006004
Interpolated factor	.214049

Present value of remainder interest =
$100,000 × 0.214049 = $21,404.90

(5) Period is the life of one individual. If the period described in paragraph (a)(5) of § 1.664-3 is the life of one individual, the factor that is used in determining the present value of the remainder interest is the factor under the appropriate adjusted payout rate in column (2) of Table E in paragraph (d)(6) of this section opposite the number in column (1) that corresponds to the age of the individual whose life measures the period. For purposes of the computations described in this paragraph (b)(5), the age of an individual is to be taken as the age of that individual at the individual's nearest birthday. If the adjusted payout rate is an amount which is between adjusted payout rates for which factors are provided for in Table E, a linear interpolation must be made. The present value of the remainder interest is determined by multiplying the net fair market value (as of the appropriate valuation date) of the property placed in trust by the factor determined under this paragraph (b)(5). If the adjusted payout rate is greater than 14 percent, see § 1.664-4(b). The application of this paragraph may be illustrated by the following example:

Example. A, who will be 50 years old on April 15, 1985, transfers $100,000 to a charitable remainder unitrust on January 1, 1985. The trust instrument requires that the trust pay to A at the end of each taxable year of the trust 10 percent of the fair market value of the trust assets as of the beginning of each taxable year of the trust. The adjusted payout rate is 9.091 percent (10 percent × .909091). The present value of the remainder interest is $15,259.00 computed as follows:

Factor at 9 percent at age 50	0.15472
Factor at 9.2 percent at age 50	0.15003
Difference	.00469

$$9.091\% - 9\% + 0.2\% = X \div 0.00469$$

$$X = 0.00213$$

Factor at 9 percent at age 50	.15472
Less: X	.00213
Interpolated factor	.15259

Present value of remainder interest =
$100,000 × 0.15259 = $15,259.00

(6) Actuarial tables for transfers for which the valuation date is after November 30, 1983, and before May 1, 1989. Table D in § 1.664-4(e)(6) and the following tables shall be used in the application of the provisions of this section:

TABLE E

TABLE E—SINGLE LIFE, UNISEX—TABLE SHOWING THE PRESENT WORTH OF THE REMAINDER INTEREST IN PROPERTY TRANSFERRED TO A UNITRUST HAVING THE ADJUSTED PAYOUT RATE SHOWN—APPLICABLE FOR TRANSFERS AFTER NOVEMBER 30, 1983, AND BEFORE MAY 1, 1989

(1)	(2) Adjusted Payout Rate									
Age	2.2%	2.4%	2.6%	2.8%	3.0%	3.2%	3.4%	3.6%	3.8%	4.0%
0	.23253	.20635	.18364	.16394	.14683	.13196	.11901	.10774	.09791	.08933
1	.22196	.19506	.17170	.15139	.13372	.11834	.10493	.09324	.08303	.07410
2	.22597	.19884	.17523	.15468	.13676	.12113	.10749	.09557	.08514	.07601
3	.23039	.20304	.17920	.15840	.14024	.12437	.11050	.09835	.08770	.07837
4	.23053	.20747	.18340	.16237	.14397	.12787	.11376	.10138	.09052	.08098
5	.23988	.21211	.18783	.16656	.14793	.13159	.11725	.10465	.09357	.08382
6	.24489	.21693	.19243	.17094	.15207	.13549	.12092	.10810	.09680	.08684
7	.25004	.22189	.19718	.17546	.15637	.13956	.12476	.11171	.10019	.09002
8	.25534	.22701	.20209	.18016	.16084	.14380	.12877	.11549	.10376	.09337
9	.26080	.23230	.20718	.18503	.16549	.14822	.13296	.11946	.10751	.09691
10	.26640	.23774	.21243	.19008	.17031	.15282	.13734	.12361	.11144	.10063
11	.27217	.24335	.21786	.19530	.17532	.15761	.14190	.12795	.11556	.10454

12	.27807	.24911	.22344	.20068	.18049	.16257	.14663	.13247	.11986	.10863
13	.28407	.25497	.22913	.20618	.18579	.16764	.15149	.13711	.12428	.11283
14	.29013	.26089	.23489	.21175	.19115	.17279	.15643	.14182	.12878	.11712
15	.29621	.26684	.24067	.21735	.19655	.17798	.16140	.14657	.13331	.12143
16	.30229	.27279	.24647	.22296	.20196	.18318	.16638	.15133	.13785	.12576
17	.30838	.27876	.25228	.22859	.20739	.18840	.17138	.15611	.14241	.13010
18	.31451	.28477	.25813	.23427	.21287	.19367	.17643	.16094	.14702	.13449
19	.32070	.29085	.26407	.24003	.21844	.19903	.18157	.16586	.15172	.13897
20	.32699	.29704	.27012	.24591	.22413	.20452	.18685	.17092	.15655	.14358
21	.33339	.30335	.27629	.25192	.22996	.21014	.19226	.17612	.16153	.14833
22	.33991	.30977	.28259	.25807	.23592	.21591	.19783	.18146	.16665	.15324
23	.34655	.31634	.28904	.26437	.24205	.22185	.20356	.18698	.17195	.15832
24	.35334	.32306	.29566	.27085	.24836	.22798	.20949	.19270	.17746	.16361
25	.36031	.32998	.30248	.27754	.25490	.23434	.21565	.19866	.18321	.16914
26	.36746	.33710	.30952	.28446	.26167	.24094	.22207	.20489	.18922	.17494
27	.37481	.34443	.31678	.29161	.26869	.24780	.22875	.21138	.19551	.18102
28	.38236	.35197	.32427	.29901	.27596	.25492	.23570	.21814	.20208	.18739
29	.39006	.35968	.33194	.30660	.28344	.26226	.24288	.22514	.20889	.19400
30	.39793	.36757	.33980	.31439	.29113	.26982	.25029	.23239	.21596	.20088
31	.40594	.37561	.34783	.32237	.29902	.27759	.25792	.23985	.22324	.20798
32	.41410	.38383	.35605	.33054	.30711	.28557	.26577	.24755	.23078	.21533
33	.42240	.39220	.36444	.33890	.31541	.29377	.27385	.25548	.23855	.22293
34	.43084	.40072	.37299	.34744	.32389	.30217	.28214	.26364	.24656	.23077
35	.43942	.40941	.38172	.35617	.33258	.31079	.29065	.27203	.25481	.23887
36	.44813	.41824	.39061	.36508	.34146	.31961	.29939	.28065	.26330	.24721
37	.45696	.42720	.39966	.37416	.35053	.32863	.30833	.28950	.27202	.25579
38	.46591	.43630	.40885	.38339	.35977	.33784	.31747	.29855	.28096	.26460
39	.47496	.44552	.41818	.39378	.36917	.34722	.32680	.30780	.29011	.27363
40	.48412	.45486	.42765	.40232	.37875	.35679	.33633	.31727	.29948	.28290
41	.49338	.46432	.43725	.41201	.38849	.36654	.34606	.32693	.30908	.29239
42	.50275	.47391	.44700	.42187	.39840	.37648	.35599	.33683	.31890	.30213
43	.51221	.48360	.45686	.43186	.40847	.38659	.36610	.34691	.32894	.31209
44	.52175	.49340	.46685	.44199	.41870	.39687	.37640	.35720	.33918	.32227
45	.53136	.50327	.47693	.45223	.42905	.40728	.38685	.36765	.34961	.33265
46	.54104	.51323	.48712	.46259	.43953	.41785	.39746	.37828	.36023	.34323
47	.55077	.52327	.49739	.47305	.45013	.42856	.40823	.38908	.37103	.35400
48	.56058	.53339	.50777	.48363	.46087	.43941	.41917	.40006	.38202	.36499
49	.57043	.54358	.51823	.49432	.47173	.45040	.43025	.41121	.39320	.37617
50	.58035	.55384	.52879	.50510	.48271	.46153	.44149	.42252	.40457	.38756
51	.59029	.56415	.53940	.51597	.49379	.47277	.45286	.43398	.41609	.39911
52	.60027	.57450	.55008	.52692	.50496	.48412	.46435	.44558	.42776	.41084
53	.61026	.58488	.56080	.53793	.51620	.49556	.47595	.45731	.43958	.42272
54	.62025	.59528	.57154	.54897	.52750	.50707	.48763	.46913	.45151	.43473

TABLE E—Continued (1) SINGLE LIFE, UNISEX—TABLE SHOWING THE PRESENT WORTH OF THE REMAINDER INTEREST IN PROPERTY TRANSFERRED TO A UNITRUST HAVING THE ADJUSTED PAYOUT RATE SHOWN—APPLICABLE FOR TRANSFERS AFTER NOVEMBER 30, 1983, AND BEFORE MAY 1, 1989

(1)	(2)									
	Adjusted Payout Rate									
Age	2.2%	2.4%	2.6%	2.8%	3.0%	3.2%	3.4%	3.6%	3.8%	4.0%
55	.63022	.60567	.58230	.56004	.53884	.51864	.49939	.48104	.46354	.44685
56	.64018	.61606	.59306	.57113	.55021	.53026	.51121	.49303	.47567	.45908
57	.65012	.62644	.60384	.58225	.56163	.54192	.52310	.50510	.48789	.47143
58	.66004	.63681	.61461	.59337	.57306	.55363	.53503	.51723	.50019	.48387
59	.66993	.64717	.62538	.60452	.58453	.56538	.54703	.52945	.51258	.49642
60	.67979	.65751	.63615	.61567	.59602	.57717	.55909	.54173	.52506	.50906
61	.68963	.66784	.64692	.62683	.60754	.58901	.57120	.55408	.53763	.52181
62	.69944	.67815	.65769	.63801	.61908	.60087	.58336	.56650	.55028	.53466
63	.70922	.68844	.66843	.64918	.63063	.61277	.59556	.57898	.56300	.54760
64	.71893	.69868	.67915	.66032	.64217	.62467	.60778	.59149	.57577	.56060
65	.72859	.70886	.68982	.67144	.65369	.63655	.62000	.60402	.58857	.57365
66	.73817	.71897	.70043	.68250	.66517	.64842	.63221	.61654	.60139	.58672
67	.74766	.72901	.71096	.69350	.67660	.66023	.64439	.62905	.61420	.59980
68	.75706	.73896	.72142	.70443	.68796	.67200	.65653	.64154	.62699	.61289
69	.76637	.74882	.73181	.71530	.69928	.68373	.66865	.65400	.63978	.62598
70	.77559	.75861	.74212	.72610	.71053	.69541	.68072	.66645	.65257	.63908
71	.78475	.76833	.75237	.73685	.72176	.70708	.69279	.67890	.66538	.65222
72	.79383	.77799	.76257	.74756	.73294	.71870	.70484	.69134	.67819	.66538
73	.80279	.78753	.77266	.75816	.74403	.73025	.71682	.70372	.69095	.67850
74	.81158	.79689	.78256	.76858	.75494	.74163	.72863	.71595	.70356	.69147

75	.82013	.80602	.79223	.77876	.76561	.75275	.74019	.72792	.71593	.70421
76	.82844	.81488	.80163	.78867	.77599	.76360	.75147	.73962	.72802	.71667
77	.83648	.82347	.81075	.79829	.78609	.77415	.76246	.75102	.73981	.72883
78	.84428	.83182	.81961	.80764	.79592	.78443	.77318	.76214	.75133	.74073
79	.85187	.83994	.82824	.81677	.80552	.79448	.78365	.77303	.76261	.75238
80	.85927	.84787	.83668	.82569	.81491	.80432	.79392	.78371	.77369	.76384
81	.86645	.85556	.84487	.83437	.82404	.81390	.80393	.79413	.78450	.77504
82	.87336	.86299	.85278	.84275	.83288	.82317	.81362	.80423	.79499	.78590
83	.88003	.87014	.86042	.85084	.84142	.83214	.82301	.81402	.80517	.79645
84	.88648	.87708	.86782	.85870	.84971	.84086	.83214	.42355	.81508	.80674
85	.89273	.88381	.87501	.86633	.85778	.84935	.84104	.83284	.82476	.81679
86	.89868	.89021	.88185	.87360	.86547	.85745	.84953	.84172	.83401	.82540
87	.90417	.89613	.88818	.88034	.87260	.86496	.85741	.84996	.84260	.83533
88	.90923	.90158	.89402	.88655	.87917	.87189	.86468	.85757	.85054	.84359
89	.91396	.90668	.89948	.89237	.88533	.87838	.87150	.86471	.85799	.85135
90	.91849	.91156	.90471	.89794	.89124	.88461	.87806	.87157	.86516	.85881
91	.92278	.91620	.90968	.90324	.89686	.89055	.88430	.87812	.87200	.86594
92	.92673	.92046	.91426	.90812	.90204	.89602	.89006	.88416	.87831	.87252
93	.93027	.92429	.91837	.91251	.90670	.90094	.89524	.88959	.88400	.87846
94	.93341	.92768	.92201	.91639	.91082	.90530	.89983	.89441	.88904	.88372
95	.93612	.93062	.92516	.91976	.91440	.90908	.90381	.89859	.89341	.88828
96	.93841	.93309	.92782	.92259	.91740	.91226	.90716	.90211	.89709	.89212
97	.94044	.93529	.93018	.92512	.92009	.91510	.91015	.90525	.90038	.89555
98	.94223	.93723	.93226	.92733	.92244	.91759	.91277	.90800	.90326	.89855
99	.94392	.93905	.93421	.92942	.92466	.91993	.91524	.81058	.90596	.90137
100 ...	.94559	.94086	.93615	.93149	.92685	.92225	.91768	.91315	.90865	.90417
101 ...	.94709	.94248	.93790	.93334	.92882	.92433	.91987	.91544	.91104	.90667
102 ...	.94873	.94424	.93979	.93536	.93096	.92659	.92225	.91793	.91364	.90938
103 ...	.95077	.94645	.94216	.93789	.93365	.92943	.92524	.92107	.91692	.91280
104 ...	.95278	.94862	.94449	.94037	.93628	.93221	.92816	.92413	.92012	.91614
105 ...	.95570	.95178	.94787	.94399	.94012	.93627	.93244	.92863	.92483	.92105
106 ...	.96017	.95662	.95309	.94957	.94607	.94257	.93909	.93562	.93217	.92872
107 ...	.96616	.96313	.96010	.95709	.95408	.95107	.94808	.84509	.94211	.93914
108 ...	.97515	.97291	.97067	.96843	.96620	.96396	.96173	.95950	.95728	.95505
109 ...	.98900	.98800	.98700	.98600	.98500	.98400	.98300	.98200	.98100	.98000

TABLE E—Continued (2) SINGLE LIFE, UNISEX—TABLE SHOWING THE PRESENT WORTH OF THE REMAINDER INTEREST IN PROPERTY TRANSFERRED TO A UNITRUST HAVING THE ADJUSTED PAYOUT RATE SHOWN—APPLICABLE FOR TRANSFERS AFTER NOVEMBER 30, 1983, AND BEFORE MAY 1, 1989

(1)	(2) Adjusted Payout Rate									
Age	4.2%	4.4%	4.6%	4.8%	5.0%	5.2%	5.4%	5.6%	5.8%	6.0%
0	.08183	.07527	.06952	.06448	.06005	.05615	.05272	.04969	.04701	.04464
1	.06629	.05945	.05344	.04817	.04354	.03945	.03585	.03268	.02986	.02737
2	.06801	.06098	.05481	.04939	.04460	.04039	.03667	.03337	.03046	.02787
3	.07017	.06297	.05663	.05104	.04611	.04176	.03791	.03450	.03147	.02879
4	.07259	.06520	.05868	.05294	.04786	.04336	.03938	.03585	.03272	.02993
5	.07523	.06765	.06096	.05505	.04982	.04518	.04107	.03741	.03416	.03127
6	.07805	.07029	.06342	.05734	.05195	.04717	.04292	.03914	.03577	.03276
7	.08103	.07307	.06603	.05978	.05423	.04929	.04490	.04099	.03750	.03438
8	.08418	.07603	.06880	.06238	.05666	.05158	.04704	.04300	.03938	.03615
9	.08752	.07917	.07175	.06516	.05928	.05404	.04936	.04518	.04143	.03808
10	.09103	.08249	.07488	.06811	.06206	.05666	.05183	.04751	.04364	.04016
11	.09473	.08600	.07820	.07125	.06503	.05947	.05449	.05003	.04602	.04242
12	.09861	.08968	.08169	.07456	.06817	.06245	.05731	.05271	.04856	.04484
13	.10261	.09348	.08530	.07799	.07142	.06554	.06025	.05549	.05121	.04735
14	.10669	.09735	.08899	.08148	.07474	.06869	.06324	.05834	.05391	.04992
15	.11080	.10126	.09269	.08500	.07808	.07186	.06625	.06119	.05662	.05250
16	.11491	.10516	.09640	.08852	.08142	.07502	.06924	.05403	.05931	.05504
17	.11903	.10908	.10012	.09204	.08475	.07817	.07223	.06685	.06199	.05757
18	.12321	.11304	.10387	.09560	.08812	.08136	.07524	.06970	.06468	.06012
19	.12747	.11709	.10771	.09923	.09156	.08462	.07832	.07261	.06743	.06272
20	.13186	.12126	.11168	.10300	.095$3	.08800	.08152	.07564	.07029	.06542
21	.13639	.12558	.11578	.10690	.09883	.09151	.08485	.07879	.07327	.06824
22	.14108	.13005	.12004	.11094	.10268	.09516	.08831	.08207	.07638	.07119
23	.14594	.13469	.12446	.11516	.10669	.09897	.09193	.08551	.07964	.07428
24	.15101	.13954	.12910	.11958	.11091	.10299	.09576	.08915	.08310	.07756
25	.15632	.14464	.13398	.12426	.11537	.10725	.09982	.09302	.08679	.08108
26	.16191	.15001	.13914	.12920	.12011	.11179	.10416	.09717	.09075	.08486
27	.16778	.15567	.14459	.13444	.12514	.11661	.10878	.10160	.09500	.08892

28	.17394	.16162	.15032	.13997	.13046	.12173	.11370	.10632	.09953	.09328
29	.18035	.16782	.15632	.14575	.13604	.12710	.11888	.11130	.10432	.09788
30	.18702	.17429	.16259	.15181	.14189	.13276	.12433	.11656	.10938	.10276
31	.19393	.18100	.16909	.15811	.14799	.13865	.13002	.12205	.11469	.10787
32	.20109	.18797	.17586	.16468	.15436	.14482	.13599	.12783	.12026	.11326
33	.20851	.19520	.18290	.17152	.16100	.15126	.14223	.13387	.12612	.11892
34	.21618	.20268	.19018	.17861	.16789	.15796	.14874	.14018	.13223	.12485
35	.22411	.21043	.19775	.18599	.17508	.16494	.15553	.14678	.13864	.13107
36	.23228	.21844	.20558	.19363	.18253	.17221	.16260	.15366	.14533	.13757
37	.24071	.22670	.21367	.20154	.19026	.17975	.16996	.16082	.15231	.14435
38	.24938	.23521	.22201	.20971	.19825	.18756	.17758	.16826	.15955	.15142
39	.25827	.24396	.23060	.21814	.20650	.19563	.18547	.17597	.16708	.15875
40	.26741	.25295	.23945	.22682	.21502	.20397	.19364	.18395	.17488	.16638
41	.27679	.26220	.24855	.23577	.22381	.21259	.20209	.19223	.18298	.17430
42	.28642	.27172	.25793	.24501	.23289	.22152	.21084	.20082	.19140	.18254
43	.29629	.28147	.26756	.25450	.24224	.23071	.21988	.20969	.20010	.19107
44	.30639	.29147	.27745	.26426	.25186	.24019	.22920	.21885	.20910	.19991
45	.31669	.30169	.28756	.27426	.26173	.24992	.23878	.22828	.21837	.20902
46	.32722	.31213	.29791	.28450	.27185	.25991	.24864	.23799	.22793	.21842
47	.33795	.32280	.30849	.29498	.28222	.27016	.25876	.24798	.23777	.22812
48	.34890	.33370	.31932	.30573	.29287	.28070	.26918	.25826	.24792	.23812
49	.36007	.34482	.33039	.31672	.30377	.39150	.27987	.26883	.25837	.24843
50	.37144	.35617	.34170	.32797	.31494	.30258	.29084	.27970	.26911	.25905
51	.38301	.36773	.35322	.33944	.32635	.31391	.30208	.29084	.28014	.26996
52	.39476	.37948	.36495	.35113	.33799	.32548	.31358	.30224	.29144	.28115
53	.40668	.39141	.37688	.36304	.34896	.33729	.32532	.31390	.30302	.29263
54	.41874	.40350	.38897	.37512	.36191	.34931	.33728	.32579	.31482	.30434

TABLE E—Continued (3) SINGLE LIFE, UNISEX—TABLE SHOWING THE PRESENT WORTH OF THE REMAINDER INTEREST IN PROPERTY TRANSFERRED TO A UNITRUST HAVING THE ADJUSTED PAYOUT RATE SHOWN—APPLICABLE FOR TRANSFERS AFTER NOVEMBER 30, 1983, AND BEFORE MAY 1, 1989

(1)	(2)									
	Adjusted Payout Rate									
Age	4.2%	4.4%	4.6%	4.8%	5.0%	5.2%	5.4%	5.6%	5.8%	6.0%
55	.43093	.41574	.40123	.38739	.37416	.36152	.34945	.33790	.32686	.31631
56	.44324	.42811	.41364	.39980	.38657	.37392	.36181	.35022	.33912	.32850
57	.45568	.44062	.42620	.41240	.39918	.38652	.37438	.36276	.35162	.34093
58	.48623	.45325	.43890	.42514	.41194	.39929	.38715	.37550	.36432	.35359
59	.48091	.46603	.45175	.43805	.42489	.41226	.40013	.38847	.37727	.36650
60	.49370	.47893	.46475	.45112	.43802	.42542	.41331	.40165	.39044	.37965
61	.50661	.49198	.47790	.46436	.45133	.43878	.42670	.41506	.40386	.39306
62	.51963	.50515	.49120	.47776	.46481	.45233	.44029	.42869	.41750	.40671
63	.53275	.51844	.50463	.49131	.47846	.46606	.45409	.44253	.43138	.42060
64	.54596	.53182	.51817	.50498	.49225	.47994	.46805	.45656	.44545	.43471
65	.55922	.54528	.53180	.51877	.50616	.49397	.48217	.47076	.45971	.44902
66	.57253	.55880	.54551	.53264	.52018	.50811	.49642	.48510	.47413	.46350
67	.58586	.57235	.55926	.54657	.53427	.52235	.51079	.49957	.48869	.47814
68	.59921	.58594	.57306	.56057	.54845	.53668	.52525	.51416	.50339	.49293
69	.61258	.59956	.58692	.57463	.56270	.55110	.53983	.52888	.51823	.50788
70	.62597	.61322	.60082	.58877	.57704	.56563	.55453	.54373	.53322	.52299
71	.63941	.62695	.61481	.60300	.59149	.58029	.56938	.55875	.54839	.53830
72	.65289	.64073	.62887	.61731	.60605	.59507	.58436	.57392	.56374	.55380
73	.66635	.65449	.64293	.63165	.62064	.60990	.59941	.58917	.57918	.56942
74	.67967	.66814	.65688	.64588	.63514	.62465	.61439	.60437	.59458	.58502
75	.69275	.68156	.67061	.65990	.64944	.63920	.62919	.61940	.60983	.60046
76	.70557	.69470	.68407	.67366	.66348	.65351	.64375	.63419	.62484	.61568
77	.71809	.70756	.69724	.68714	.67724	.66755	.65804	.64873	.63961	.63066
78	.73033	.72014	.71015	.70036	.69075	.68133	.67209	.66303	.65414	.64542
79	.74235	.73251	.72284	.71336	.70405	.69492	.68595	.67714	.66850	.66001
80	.74417	.74468	.73535	.72619	.71718	.70834	.69965	.69111	.68272	.67448
81	.76573	.75659	.74759	.73875	.73006	.72151	.71311	.70484	.69671	.68872
82	.77696	.76816	.75951	.75099	.74261	.73436	.72624	.71825	.71039	.70265
83	.78787	.77942	.77110	.86291	.75484	.74689	.73906	.73135	.72376	.71627
84	.79852	.79042	.78243	.77457	.76681	.75917	.75163	.74421	.73688	.72967
85	.80893	.80118	.79353	.78599	.77856	.77122	.76398	.75685	.74980	.74286
86	.81889	.81148	.80417	.79695	.78983	.78280	.77586	.76901	.76224	.75556
87	.82816	.82107	.81408	.80716	.80034	.79359	.78693	.78036	.77386	.76744
88	.83673	.82994	.82324	.81662	.81007	.80360	.79720	.79088	.78463	.77846
89	.84478	.83829	.83186	.82551	.81923	.81302	.80688	.80081	.79480	.78886
90	.85253	.84632	.84018	.83410	.82808	.82213	.81624	.81041	.80465	.79894

91	.85994	.85401	.84813	.84232	.83656	.83086	.82522	.81963	.81410	.80862
92	.86679	.86111	.85549	.84993	.84441	.83895	.83354	.82818	.82287	.81762
93	.87296	.86752	.86213	.85679	.85150	.84626	.84106	.83591	.83081	.82575
94	.87844	.87321	.86803	.86289	.85780	.85275	.84774	.84278	.83787	.83299
95	.88319	.87815	.87314	.86818	.86327	.85839	.85355	.84876	.84400	.83929
96	.88719	.88230	.87745	.87264	.86787	.86313	.85844	.85378	.84916	.84458
97	.89076	.88601	.88129	.87661	.87197	.86737	.86280	.85826	.85377	.84930
98	.89388	.88925	.88465	.88009	.87556	.87107	.86661	.86218	.85779	.85343
99	.89682	.89230	.88781	.88336	.87894	.87455	.87019	.86586	.86157	.85730
100 ...	.89973	.89533	.89095	.88660	.88228	.87800	.87374	.86951	.86532	.86115
101 ...	.90233	.89802	.89374	.88948	.88526	.88106	.87689	.87275	.86863	.86455
102 ...	.90515	.90094	.89676	.89260	.88848	.88437	.88030	.87625	.87222	.86822
103 ...	.90871	.90464	.90059	.89656	.89256	.88858	.88463	.88070	.87679	.87290
104 ...	.91217	.90823	.90431	.90040	.89652	.89266	.88882	.88500	.88120	.87741
105 ...	.91729	.91354	.90981	.90610	.90240	.89872	.89506	.89141	.88778	.88417
106 ...	.92529	.92187	.91846	.91507	.91169	.90832	.90496	.90161	.89828	.89496
107 ...	.93617	.93322	.93027	.92732	.92439	.92146	.91854	.91562	.91271	.90981
108 ...	.95283	.95062	.94840	.94619	.94398	.94177	.93956	.93736	.93516	.93296
109 ...	.97900	.97800	.97700	.97600	.97500	.97400	.97300	.97200	.97100	.97000

TABLE E—Continued (4) SINGLE LIFE, UNISEX—TABLE SHOWING THE PRESENT WORTH OF THE REMAINDER INTEREST IN PROPERTY TRANSFERRED TO A UNITRUST HAVING THE ADJUSTED PAYOUT RATE SHOWN—APPLICABLE FOR TRANSFERS AFTER NOVEMBER 30, 1983, AND BEFORE MAY 1, 1989

(1)	(2)									
	Adjusted Payout Rate									
Age	6.2%	6.4%	6.6%	6.8%	7.0%	7.2%	7.4%	7.6%	7.8%	8.0%
0	.04253	.04066	.03899	.03751	.03618	.03499	.03392	.03296	.03209	.03130
1	.02516	.02320	.02145	.01989	.01850	.01725	.01613	.01513	.01422	.01340
2	.02557	.02353	.02171	.02008	.01862	.01732	.01615	.01509	.01414	.01329
3	.02640	.02427	.02237	.02067	.01915	.01778	.01656	.01545	.01446	.01356
4	.02744	.02523	.02325	.02147	.01988	.01846	.01717	.01601	.01497	.01402
5	.02868	.02638	.02431	.02246	.02080	.01930	.01796	.01674	.01565	.01465
6	.03008	.02767	.02552	.02359	.02185	.02029	.01888	.01761	.01645	.01541
7	.03159	.02909	.02685	.02483	.02302	.02138	.01991	.01857	.01736	.01627
8	.03325	.03065	.02831	.02621	.02432	.02261	.02106	.01966	.01839	.01724
9	.03507	.03236	.02993	.02774	.02576	.02397	.02236	.02089	.01956	.01835
10	.03704	.03423	.03170	.02941	.02735	.02548	.02379	.02225	.02086	.01959
11	.03918	.03626	.03363	.03125	.02910	.02715	.02538	.02377	.02231	.02098
12	.04148	.03845	.03571	.03323	.03099	.02895	.02710	.02542	.02389	.02240
13	.04387	.04073	.03788	.03531	.03297	.03085	.02892	.02716	.02556	.02410
14	.04632	.04305	.04010	.03742	.03499	.03278	.03076	.02893	.02725	.02572
15	.04876	.04538	.04231	.03953	.03699	.03469	.03259	.03067	.02892	.02732
16	.05118	.04767	.04449	.04159	.03896	.03656	.03437	.03237	.03054	.02286
17	.05357	.04994	.04663	.04362	.04088	.03838	.03610	.03401	.03210	.03035
18	.05598	.05221	.04878	.04565	.04280	.04020	.03782	.03564	.03364	.03181
19	.05843	.05453	.05097	.04772	.04476	.04204	.03956	.03729	.03520	.03328
20	.06099	.05694	.05325	.04988	.04679	.04397	.04138	.03901	.03683	.03483
21	.06265	.05946	.05564	.05213	.04893	.04599	.04329	.04081	.03853	.03644
22	.06644	.06210	.05813	.05449	.05116	.04810	.04529	.04270	.04032	.03813
23	.06937	.06488	.06076	.05699	.05352	.05033	.04740	.04470	.04222	.03992
24	.07249	.06784	.06357	.05965	.05605	.05273	.04968	.04686	.04427	.04187
25	.07584	.07103	.06660	.06254	.05879	.05534	.05216	.04922	.04651	.04400
26	.07945	.07447	.06989	.06567	.06178	.05819	.05488	.05182	.04899	.04636
27	.08334	.07819	.07345	.06907	.06503	.06130	.05785	.05466	.05170	.04896
28	.08751	.08219	.07729	.07275	.06856	.06468	.06109	.05777	.05468	.05182
29	.09194	.08634	.08137	.07667	.07233	.06830	.06457	.06110	.05789	.05490
30	.09663	.09096	.08572	.08086	.07635	.07217	.06829	.06469	.06134	.05822
31	.10156	.09572	.09030	.08527	.08060	.07627	.07224	.06849	.06500	.06174
32	.10677	.10074	.09515	.08995	.08512	.08062	.07644	.07254	.06891	.06552
33	.11224	.10604	.10027	.09490	.08990	.08524	.08090	.07686	.07308	.06955
34	.11798	.11159	.10564	.10010	.09494	.09012	.08562	.08142	.07749	.07382
35	.12401	.11744	.11131	.10560	.10026	.09528	.09062	.08626	.08218	.07836
36	.13033	.12357	.11727	.11137	.10586	.10071	.09589	.09137	.08714	.08317
37	.13693	.12999	.12350	.11743	.11175	.10643	.10144	.09676	.09237	.08825
38	.14380	.13668	.13002	.12377	.11791	.11242	.10727	.10243	.09788	.09361
39	.15096	.14366	.13681	.13038	.12436	.11869	.11337	.10837	.10366	.09923
40	.15841	.15092	.14390	.13729	.13109	.12526	.11977	.11460	.10973	.10514
41	.16615	.15848	.15128	.14450	.13812	.13212	.12646	.12113	.11609	.11135
42	.17421	.16637	.15899	.15204	.14549	.13931	.13349	.12799	.12279	.11789
43	.18257	.17456	.16700	.15988	.15316	.14681	.14082	.13515	.12980	.12473

44	.19124	.18306	.17533	.16804	.16115	.15463	.14847	.14264	.13712	.13189
45	.20018	.19184	.18395	.17649	.16943	.16274	.15642	.15042	.14474	.13935
46	.20943	.20092	.19287	.18524	.17802	.17117	.16468	.15853	.15268	.14713
47	.21897	.21030	.20209	.19431	.18692	.17991	.17326	.16694	.16094	.15523
48	.22883	.22001	.21165	.20371	.19616	.18900	.18219	.17571	.16955	.16368
49	.23900	.23004	.22152	.21343	.20573	.19841	.19145	.18481	.17850	.17248
50	.24948	.24039	.23173	.22349	.21565	.20818	.20106	.19428	.18781	.18163
51	.26027	.25104	.24225	.23387	.22589	.21827	.21101	.20407	.19745	.19113
52	.27135	.26200	.25308	.24457	.23645	.22869	.22129	.21421	.20745	.20098
53	.28271	.27325	.26421	.25558	.24733	.23944	.23190	.22468	.21778	.21117
54	.29433	.28476	.27561	.26686	.25848	.25047	.24280	.23545	.22841	.22167

TABLE E—Continued (5) SINGLE LIFE, UNISEX—TABLE SHOWING THE PRESENT WORTH OF THE REMAINDER INTEREST IN PROPERTY TRANSFERRED TO A UNITRUST HAVING THE ADJUSTED PAYOUT RATE SHOWN—APPLICABLE FOR TRANSFERS AFTER NOVEMBER 30, 1983, AND BEFORE MAY 1, 1989

(1)	(2)									
	Adjusted Payout Rate									
Age	6.2%	6.4%	6.6%	6.8%	7.0%	7.2%	7.4%	7.6%	7.8%	8.0%
55	.30621	.29654	.28728	.27842	.26993	.26180	.25400	.24653	.23936	.23249
56	.31832	.30856	.29921	.29025	.28165	.27341	.26550	.25790	.25061	.24361
57	.33068	.32085	.31142	.30236	.29367	.28532	.27729	.26959	.26218	.25505
58	.34329	.33339	.32388	.31474	.30595	.29751	.28938	.28157	.27405	.26681
59	.35615	.34620	.33662	.32741	.31855	.31001	.30180	.29388	.28626	.27892
60	.36927	.35927	.34964	.34037	.33143	.32282	.31452	.30652	.29880	.29136
61	.38265	.37262	.37295	.35362	.34463	.33595	.32758	.31950	.31169	.30416
62	.39630	.38625	.37655	.36718	.35814	.34941	.34097	.33282	.32494	.31733
63	.41020	.40014	.39043	.38104	.37196	.36318	.35469	.34648	.33854	.33085
64	.42432	.41428	.40456	.39516	.38606	.37725	.36872	.36046	.35246	.34472
65	.43866	.42864	.41893	.40953	.40042	.39159	.38304	.37474	.36670	.35891
66	.45320	.44321	.43353	.42414	.41503	.40620	.39763	.38931	.38124	.37340
67	.46790	.45796	.44832	.43896	.42987	.42104	.41247	.40414	.39605	.38819
68	.48277	.47289	.46330	.45398	.44492	.43611	.42755	.41923	.41113	.40326
69	.49781	.48802	.47849	.46923	.46021	.45144	.44290	.43459	.42650	.41863
70	.51303	.50333	.49389	.48470	.47574	.46702	.45852	.45025	.44218	.43432
71	.52847	.51888	.50954	.50044	.49156	.48291	.47447	.46623	.45820	.45037
72	.54412	.53466	.52544	.51644	.50766	.49909	.49072	.48255	.47458	.46679
73	.55990	.55059	.54151	.53263	.52396	.51549	.50721	.49912	.49122	.48349
74	.57566	.56652	.55758	.54885	.54030	.53195	.52377	.51578	.50796	.50031
75	.59129	.58232	.57354	.56496	.55655	.54832	.54027	.53238	.52466	.51710
76	.60671	.59792	.58932	.58089	.57263	.56454	.55661	.54884	.54123	.53377
77	.62189	.61330	.60487	.59661	.58851	.58057	.57278	.56514	.55765	.55030
78	.63687	.62847	.62024	.61215	.60422	.59644	.58879	.58129	.57393	.56670
79	.65168	.64349	.63546	.62756	.61981	.61219	.60471	.59736	.59013	.58304
80	.66637	.65841	.65058	.64289	.63532	.62788	.62057	.61338	.60632	.59936
81	.68085	.67312	.66551	.65802	.65066	.64341	.63628	.62926	.62236	.61556
82	.69503	.68753	.68014	.67287	.66571	.65866	.65172	.64488	.63815	.63151
83	.70890	.70164	.69448	.68743	.68048	.67364	.66689	.66024	.65369	.64723
84	.72255	.71553	.70861	.70179	.69506	.68843	.68189	.67544	.66907	.66279
85	.73600	.72924	.72257	.71598	.70948	.70307	.69674	.69050	.68433	.67825
86	.74897	.74246	.73603	.72969	.72342	.71723	.71112	.70508	.69912	.69323
87	.76109	.75483	.74864	.74252	.73647	.73050	.72460	.71877	.71300	.70731
88	.77235	.76631	.76035	.75445	.74862	.74285	.73715	.73151	.72593	.72042
89	.78298	.77717	.77142	.76573	.76011	.75454	.74903	.74358	.73819	.73286
90	.79329	.78770	.78217	.77669	.77127	.76591	.76060	.75534	.75014	.74499
91	.80320	.79783	.79252	.78725	.78204	.77688	.77176	.76670	.76169	.75672
92	.81241	.80725	.80214	.79708	.79206	.78709	.78217	.77729	.77245	.76766
93	.83074	.81578	.81086	.80598	.80115	.79635	.79160	.78690	.78223	.77761
94	.82816	.82337	.81862	.81391	.80924	.80461	.80002	.79547	.79096	.78648
95	.83461	.82997	.82537	.82081	.81629	.81180	.80735	.80294	.79856	.79421
96	.84003	.83552	.83105	.82661	.82221	.81784	.81351	.80921	.80494	.80071
97	.84487	.84048	.83612	.83179	.82750	.82324	.81901	.81481	.81065	.80651
98	.84910	.84481	.84054	.83631	.83211	.82794	.82380	.81969	.81562	.81157
99	.85307	.84887	.84469	.84055	.83644	.83235	.82830	.82427	.82028	.81631
100 ...	.85701	.85290	.84882	.84476	.84803	.83674	.83276	.82882	.82490	.82101
101 ...	.86049	.85645	.85244	.84846	.84451	.84058	.83668	.83280	.82895	.82512
102 ...	.86424	.86029	.85637	.85247	.84859	.84474	.84091	.83710	.83332	.82956
103 ...	.86904	.86520	.86138	.85758	.85381	.85006	.84633	.84262	.83893	.83526
104 ...	.87365	.86991	.86619	.86249	.85880	.85514	.85150	.84787	.84427	.84068
105 ...	.88058	.87700	.87343	.86988	.86635	.86284	.85934	.85585	.85239	.84893
106 ...	.89165	.88835	.88506	.88179	.87852	.87527	.87204	.86881	.86559	.86239

107 . . .	.90692	.90404	.90116	.89829	.89542	.89257	.88972	.88688	.88404	.88121
108 . . .	.93077	.92858	.92639	.92420	.92201	.91983	.91765	.91547	.91330	.91113
109 . . .	.96900	.96800	.96700	.96600	.96500	.96400	.96300	.96200	.96100	.96000

TABLE E—Continued (6) SINGLE LIFE, UNISEX—TABLE SHOWING THE PRESENT WORTH OF THE REMAINDER INTEREST IN PROPERTY TRANSFERRED TO A UNITRUST HAVING THE ADJUSTED PAYOUT RATE SHOWN—APPLICABLE FOR TRANSFERS AFTER NOVEMBER 30, 1983, AND BEFORE MAY 1, 1989

(1)	(2)									
	Adjusted Payout Rate									
Age	8.2%	8.4%	8.6%	8.8%	9.0%	9.2%	9.4%	9.6%	9.8%	10.0%
0	.03059	.02995	.02936	.02882	.02833	.02788	.02747	.02709	.02673	.02641
1	.01267	.01200	.01139	.01084	.01033	.00987	.00945	.00906	.00871	.00838
2	.01251	.01181	.01117	.01059	.01006	.00957	.00913	.00872	.00835	.00800
3	.01274	.01200	.01133	.01072	.01016	.00965	.00918	.00875	.00836	.00799
4	.01316	.01239	.01168	.01103	.01044	.00991	.00941	.00896	.00854	.00815
5	.01375	.01293	.01218	.01150	.01088	.01031	.00979	.00931	.00887	.00846
6	.01446	.01360	.01281	.01209	.01144	.01084	.01028	.00978	.00931	.00888
7	.01527	.01436	.01353	.01277	.01208	.01144	.01086	.01032	.00983	.00937
8	.01619	.01523	.01436	.01356	.01283	.01216	.01154	.01097	.01044	.00996
9	.01725	.01624	.01532	.01448	.01370	.01299	.01234	.01174	.01118	.01067
10	.01843	.01737	.01640	.01551	.01470	.01395	.01326	.01262	.01204	.01149
11	.01976	.01865	.01763	.01669	.01583	.01504	.01432	.01364	.01302	.01245
12	.02122	.02055	.01898	.01800	.01709	.01626	.01549	.01478	.01413	.01352
13	.22076	.02153	.02041	.01937	.01842	.01755	.01674	.01599	.01530	.01466
14	.02432	.02303	.02185	.02077	.01977	.01885	.01800	.01721	.01648	.01581
15	.02585	.02451	.02327	.02213	.02108	.02011	.01922	.01839	.01762	.01691
16	.02732	.02591	.02462	.02342	.02232	.02130	.02036	.01949	.01869	.01794
17	.02874	.02726	.02590	.02465	.02349	.02243	.02144	.02052	.01967	.01888
18	.03013	.02858	.02715	.02584	.02462	.02350	.02246	.02150	.02061	.01978
19	.03152	.02990	.02841	.02703	.02575	.02457	.02348	.02247	.02153	.02065
20	.03298	.03128	.02971	.02826	.02692	.02569	.02454	.02347	.02248	.02156
21	.03451	.03272	.03108	.02956	.02815	.02685	.02564	.02452	.02347	.02250
22	.03611	.03424	.03251	.03091	.02944	.02806	.02679	.02561	.02451	.02348
23	.03781	.03585	.03404	.03236	.03081	.02936	.02802	.02677	.02561	.02453
24	.03965	.03760	.03570	.03393	.03230	.03078	.02937	.02805	.02683	.02569
25	.04168	.03953	.03753	.03568	.03396	.03236	.03087	.02949	.02820	.02699
26	.04393	.04168	.03958	.03764	.03583	.03415	.03258	.03112	.02975	.02848
27	.04642	.04406	.04186	.03982	.03792	.03615	.03450	.03295	.03151	.03017
28	.04916	.04669	.04439	.04224	.04025	.03838	.03664	.03502	.03350	.03208
29	.05212	.04953	.04712	.04487	.04277	.04081	.03898	.03727	.03567	.03416
30	.05531	.05260	.05008	.04772	.04552	.04346	.04154	.03973	.03804	.03646
31	.05871	.05588	.05324	.05077	.04846	.04630	.04427	.04237	.04059	.03892
32	.06236	.05940	.05663	.05405	.05163	.04936	.04723	.04523	.04335	.04159
33	.06625	.06316	.06027	.05756	.05502	.05264	.05041	.04831	.04633	.04448
34	.07038	.06716	.06414	.06131	.05865	.05615	.05381	.05160	.04952	.04757
35	.07478	.07142	.06827	.06531	.06253	.05992	.05746	.05514	.05296	.05090
36	.07944	.07595	.07266	.06957	.06667	.06393	.06135	.05892	.05663	.05447
37	.08438	.08074	.07732	.07410	.07106	.06820	.06550	.06295	.06055	.05828
38	.08958	.08580	.08223	.07888	.07571	.07272	.06990	.06723	.06471	.06233
39	.09506	.09112	.08742	.08392	.08061	.07749	.07454	.07175	.06912	.06662
40	.10081	.09673	.09288	.08924	.08580	.08254	.07946	.07655	.07379	.07117
41	.10687	.10263	.09863	.09484	.09126	.08787	.08466	.08162	.07873	.07599
42	.11325	.10886	.10471	.10078	.09705	.09352	.09018	.08700	.08399	.08112
43	.11993	.11539	.11109	.10701	.10314	.09947	.09599	.09268	.08953	.08654
44	.12694	.12224	.11779	.11356	.10955	.10573	.10211	.09866	.09539	.09227
45	.13424	.12939	.12478	.12040	.11624	.11229	.10852	.10494	.10152	.09827
46	.14186	.13686	.13210	.12757	.12326	.11916	.11525	.11153	.10798	.10459
47	.14980	.14464	.13973	.13505	.13059	.12634	.12229	.11843	.11474	.11122
48	.15810	.15278	.14772	.14289	.13828	.13388	.12969	.12568	.12186	.11820
49	.16674	.16127	.15605	.15107	.14631	.14177	.13743	.13329	.12932	.12553
50	.17574	.17012	.16475	.15962	.15472	.15003	.14555	.14126	.13716	.13322
51	.18150	.17932	.17381	.16853	.16348	.15865	.15402	.14959	.14534	.14127
52	.19480	.18888	.18322	.17779	.17260	.16763	.16286	.15828	.15390	.14969
53	.20484	.19878	.19298	.18741	.18208	.17696	.17205	.16734	.16281	.15847
54	.21520	.20901	.20306	.19735	.19188	.18662	.18157	.17672	.17206	.16758

TABLE E—Continued (7) SINGLE LIFE, UNISEX—TABLE SHOWING THE PRESENT WORTH OF THE REMAINDER INTEREST IN PROPERTY TRANSFERRED TO A UNITRUST HAVING THE ADJUSTED PAYOUT RATE SHOWN—APPLICABLE FOR TRANSFERS AFTER NOVEMBER 30, 1983, AND BEFORE MAY 1, 1989

(1)	(2)									
	Adjusted Payout Rate									
Age	8.2%	8.4%	8.6%	8.8%	9.0%	9.2%	9.4%	9.6%	9.8%	10.0%
55	.22589	.21955	.21347	.20763	.20202	.19662	.19144	.18645	.18165	.17703
56	.23688	.23041	.22420	.21822	.21248	.20695	.20163	.19651	.19157	.18682
57	.24820	.24161	.23527	.22917	.22329	.21763	.21218	.20693	.20186	.19698
58	.25984	.25313	.24667	.24044	.23444	.22865	.22307	.21769	.21250	.20749
59	.27184	.26501	.25843	.25209	.24596	.24005	.23435	.22885	.22353	.21839
60	.28417	.27724	.27055	.26409	.25786	.25183	.24601	.24038	.23494	.22969
61	.29688	.28985	.28306	.27650	.27015	.26401	.25808	.25234	.24678	.24141
62	.30996	.30284	.29596	.28929	.28285	.27661	.27056	.26471	.25905	.25356
63	.32341	.31621	.30924	.30249	.29595	.28961	.28347	.27752	.27175	.26615
64	.33721	.32994	.32289	.31605	.30943	.30300	.29677	.29072	.28486	.27916
65	.35134	.34401	.33689	.32999	.32329	.31678	.31046	.30433	.29837	.29259
66	.36580	.35841	.35124	.34427	.33750	.33093	.32454	.31832	.31228	.30641
67	.38055	.37312	.36590	.35889	.35206	.34542	.33897	.33268	.32657	.32062
68	.39559	.38814	.38089	.37383	.36696	.36027	.35376	.34742	.34124	.33522
69	.41096	.40349	.39622	.38913	.38222	.37550	.36894	.36255	.35632	.35024
70	.42665	.41918	.41190	.40480	.39787	.39111	.38452	.37809	.37182	.36570
71	.44273	.43527	.42799	.42089	.41395	.40719	.40058	.39412	.38782	.38166
72	.45919	.45176	.44450	.43741	.43049	.42372	.41710	.41064	.40432	.39814
73	.47594	.46856	.46134	.45428	.44738	.44062	.43402	.42756	.42124	.41506
74	.49283	.48550	.47834	.47132	.46446	.45774	.45116	.44471	.43840	.43223
75	.50969	.50244	.49534	.48838	.48157	.47489	.46834	.46193	.45565	.44949
76	.52646	.51929	.51226	.50537	.49862	.49199	.48550	.47913	.47288	.46675
77	.54309	.53601	.52907	.52226	.51558	.50902	.50258	.49626	.49006	.48397
78	.55960	.55263	.54579	.53907	.53247	.52598	.51962	.51336	.50721	.50117
79	.57606	.56921	.56248	.55586	.54935	.54295	.53667	.53049	.52441	.51843
80	.59253	.58580	.57919	.57269	.56629	.55999	.55380	.54771	.54171	.53581
81	.60887	.60229	.59581	.58943	.58315	.57697	.57088	.56489	.55899	.55317
82	.62498	.61855	.61221	.60597	.59982	.59375	.58778	.58190	.57610	.57039
83	.64086	.63459	.62840	.62230	.61629	.61036	.60451	.59875	.59306	.58746
84	.65660	.65049	.64447	.63852	.63266	.62687	.62116	.61553	.60997	.60448
85	.67224	.66631	.66046	.65468	.64898	.64335	.63779	.63230	.62688	.62152
86	.68742	.68167	.67600	.67040	.66486	.65939	.65398	.64864	.64337	.63816
87	.70168	.69611	.69061	.68518	.67980	.67449	.66924	.66405	.65892	.65384
88	.71497	.70958	.70425	.69897	.69376	.68860	.68350	.67845	.67346	.66852
89	.72758	.72236	.71720	.71208	.70702	.70202	.69706	.69216	.68731	.68250
90	.63989	.73484	.72985	.72490	.72000	.71515	.71035	.70559	.70088	.69622
91	.75180	.74693	.74210	.73732	.73259	.72790	.72325	.71865	.71409	.70957
92	.76292	.75821	.75355	.74894	.74436	.73982	.73533	.73087	.72646	.72208
93	.77302	.76848	.76397	.75951	.75508	.75069	.74634	.74202	.73774	.73350
94	.78204	.77764	.77328	.76895	.76466	.76040	.75618	.75199	.74784	.74372
95	.78991	.78563	.78139	.77719	.77302	.76888	.76477	.76070	.75666	.75265
96	.79651	.79234	.78821	.78411	.78003	.77599	.77199	.76801	.76406	.76014
97	.80241	.79834	.79430	.79029	.78630	.78235	.77843	.77454	.77067	.76684
98	.80755	.80356	.79960	.79567	.79176	.78789	.78404	.78022	.77642	.77266
99	.81236	.80845	.80456	.80071	.79687	.79307	.78929	.78554	.78181	.77811
100 ...	.81715	.81331	.80949	.80571	.80195	.79821	.79450	.79081	.78715	.78351
101 ...	.82132	.81754	.81379	.81006	.80636	.80268	.79902	.79539	.79178	.78819
102 ...	.82582	.82211	.81842	.81476	.81111	.80749	.80389	.80031	.79676	.79322
103 ...	.83162	.82799	.82439	.82080	.81724	.81370	.81018	.80668	.80319	.79973
104 ...	.83711	.83356	.83003	.82652	.82302	.81955	.81609	.81265	.80923	.80582
105 ...	.84550	.84208	.83867	.83528	.83191	.82855	.82520	.82187	.81856	.81526
106 ...	.85920	.85602	.85285	.84969	.84655	.84341	.84029	.83718	.83408	.83099
107 ...	.87839	.87558	.87277	.86997	.86718	.86439	.86162	.85884	.85608	.85332
108 ...	.90896	.90679	.90463	.90246	.90030	.89815	.89599	.89384	.89169	.88955
109 ...	.95900	.95800	.95700	.95600	.95500	.95400	.95300	.95200	.95100	.95000

TABLE E—Continued (8) SINGLE LIFE, UNISEX—TABLE SHOWING THE PRESENT WORTH OF THE REMAINDER INTEREST IN PROPERTY TRANSFERRED TO A UNITRUST HAVING THE ADJUSTED PAYOUT RATE SHOWN—APPLICABLE FOR TRANSFERS AFTER NOVEMBER 30, 1983, AND BEFORE MAY 1, 1989

(1)	(2) Adjusted Payout Rate									
Age	10.2%	10.4%	10.6%	10.8%	11.0%	11.2%	11.4%	11.6%	11.8%	12.0%
0	.02610	.02582	.02556	.02531	.02508	.02487	.02466	.02447	.02429	.02412
1	.00807	.00779	.00753	.00729	.00707	.00686	.00666	.00648	.00631	.00615
2	.00769	.00739	.00712	.00686	.00663	.00641	.00620	.00601	.00583	.00566
3	.00766	.00735	.00706	.00679	.00654	.00631	.00609	.00589	.00570	.00552
4	.00780	.00747	.00716	.00688	.00662	.00637	.00614	.00593	.00573	.00554
5	.00808	.00773	.00741	.00711	.00683	.00657	.00633	.00610	.00588	.00568
6	.00848	.00811	.00776	.00744	.00715	.00687	.00661	.00637	.00614	.00593
7	.00894	.00855	.00819	.00785	.00753	.00724	.00696	.00670	.00646	.00623
8	.00951	.00909	.00871	.00835	.00801	.00770	.00740	.00713	.00687	.00633
9	.01019	.00975	.00934	.00896	.00860	.00827	.00795	.00766	.00739	.00713
10	.01099	.01052	.01008	.00967	.00930	.00894	.00861	.00830	.00800	.00773
11	.01191	.01142	.01095	.01052	.01012	.00974	.00939	.00906	.00875	.00846
12	.01295	.01243	.01194	.01148	.01106	.01066	.01029	.00993	.00961	.00929
13	.01406	.01351	.01299	.01251	.01206	.01164	.01124	.01087	.01052	.01019
14	.01518	.01459	.01405	.01354	.01306	.01262	.01220	.01181	.01144	.01109
15	.01625	.01563	.01506	.01452	.01402	.01355	.01311	.01270	.01231	.01194
16	.01724	.01659	.01599	.01542	.01489	.01440	.01394	.01350	.01309	.01271
17	.01815	.01747	.01683	.01624	.01568	.01516	.01467	.01421	.01378	.01337
18	.01901	.01829	.01761	.01699	.01640	.01585	.01534	.01485	.01440	.01397
19	.01984	.01908	.01837	.01771	.01709	.01651	.01597	.01546	.01498	.01453
20	.02070	.01990	.01915	.01846	.01780	.01719	.01662	.01608	.01557	.01510
21	.02160	.02075	.01996	.01923	.01854	.01789	.01728	.01672	.01618	.01568
22	.02253	.02164	.02080	.02003	.01930	.01861	.01797	.01737	.01680	.01627
23	.02352	.02258	.02170	.02088	.02010	.01938	.01870	.01806	.01746	.01689
24	.02462	.02362	.02269	.02182	.02100	.02023	.01951	.01883	.01819	.01759
25	.02586	.02481	.02382	.02289	.02203	.02121	.02045	.01973	.01905	.01841
26	.02729	.02617	.02512	.02414	.02322	.02236	.02155	.02078	.02006	.01938
27	.02891	.02772	.02662	.02558	.02460	.02368	.02282	.02200	.02124	.02051
28	.03074	.02949	.02832	.02722	.02618	.02521	.02429	.02342	.02261	.02183
29	.03276	.03143	.03019	.02902	.02792	.02689	.02591	.02499	.02412	.02330
30	.03497	.03357	.03225	.03102	.02985	.02875	.02772	.02674	.02581	.02494
31	.03735	.03587	.03448	.03317	.03193	.03076	.02966	.02863	.02764	.02671
32	.03993	.03837	.03690	.03551	.03420	.03297	.03180	.03070	.02965	.02866
33	.04273	.04108	.03952	.03806	.03667	.03536	.03412	.03295	.03184	.03079
34	.04572	.04399	.04234	.04079	.03933	.03794	.03663	.03539	.03421	.03309
35	.04896	.04713	.04539	.04376	.04221	.04074	.03935	.03803	.03678	.03559
36	.05243	.05049	.04867	.04694	.04530	.04375	.04228	.04089	.03956	.03830
37	.05613	.05410	.05217	.05035	.04862	.04699	.04543	.04395	.04255	.04122
38	.06007	.05793	.05591	.05399	.05217	.05044	.04879	.04723	.04575	.04433
39	.06425	.06200	.05987	.05785	.05593	.05411	.05238	.05073	.04916	.04766
40	.06869	.06633	.06409	.06197	.05995	.05802	.05620	.05445	.05279	.05121
41	.07339	.07092	.06857	.06634	.06421	.06219	.06026	.05843	.05668	.05500
42	.07840	.07581	.07335	.07101	.06878	.06665	.06462	.06269	.06084	.05908
43	.08370	.08099	.07841	.07595	.07361	.07138	.06924	.06721	.06526	.06341
44	.08930	.08646	.08377	.08119	.07874	.07639	.07415	.07202	.06997	.06801
45	.09517	.09222	.08940	.08670	.08413	.08168	.07933	.07708	.07493	.07287
46	.10136	.09828	.09533	.09252	.08983	.08726	.08480	.08244	.08018	.07802
47	.10786	.10464	.10157	.09864	.09582	.09313	.09056	.08809	.08572	.08345
48	.11470	.11136	.10816	.10510	.10216	.09935	.09666	.09408	.09160	.08922
49	.12189	.11842	.11509	.11190	.10884	.10591	.10309	.10039	.09780	.09531
50	.12946	.12585	.12239	.11907	.11588	.11282	.10989	.10707	.10436	.10176
51	.13737	.13363	.13003	.12659	.12327	.12009	.11703	.11409	.11127	.10855
52	.14565	.14177	.13805	.13447	.13103	.12772	.12454	.12147	.11853	.11569
53	.15429	.15028	.14642	.14271	.13914	.13571	.13240	.12922	.12615	.12319
54	.16327	.15912	.15513	.15129	.14759	.14403	.14060	.13729	.13410	.13102

TABLE E—Continued (9) SINGLE LIFE, UNISEX—TABLE SHOWING THE PRESENT WORTH OF THE REMAINDER INTEREST IN PROPERTY TRANSFERRED TO A UNITRUST HAVING THE ADJUSTED PAYOUT RATE SHOWN—APPLICABLE FOR TRANSFERS AFTER NOVEMBER 30, 1983, AND BEFORE MAY 1, 1989

(1)	(2)									
	Adjusted Payout Rate									
Age	10.2%	10,4%	10.6%	10.8%	11.0%	11.2%	11.4%	11.6%	11.8%	12.0%
55	.17259	.16831	.16419	.16022	.15639	.15270	.14914	.14571	.14240	.13920
56	.18225	.17784	.17358	.16948	.16553	.16171	.15802	.15447	.15103	.14771
57	.19227	.18773	.18335	.17912	.17503	.17109	.16728	.16360	.16004	.15660
58	.20265	.19798	.19347	.18911	.18490	.18083	.17690	.17309	.16941	.16585
59	.21343	.20863	.20400	.19951	.19518	.19098	.18692	.18299	.17919	.17551
60	.22460	.21968	.21492	.21032	.20586	.20154	.19736	.19331	.18938	.18558
61	.23620	.23117	.22629	.22156	.21698	.21254	.20824	.20407	.20003	.19610
62	.24824	.24309	.23810	.23325	.22856	.22400	.21958	.21530	.21113	.20709
63	.26073	.25546	.25036	.24540	.24060	.23593	.23139	.22699	.22272	.21856
64	.27364	.26827	.26306	.25800	.25308	.24830	.24366	.23915	.23476	.23050
65	.28696	.28150	.27619	.27103	.26601	.26113	.25638	.25176	.24727	.24290
66	.30070	.29515	.28974	.28449	.27937	.27439	.26955	.26483	.26023	.25576
67	.31483	.30919	.30371	.29836	.29316	.28808	.28314	.27833	.27364	.26906
68	.32936	.32365	.31808	.31266	.30737	.30221	.29718	.29228	.28750	.20283
69	.34432	.33854	.33290	.32741	.32204	.31681	.31170	.30672	.30185	.29710
70	.35972	.35389	.34820	.34264	.33721	.33190	.32673	.32167	.31672	.31189
71	.37565	.36977	.36403	.35842	.35294	.34758	.34234	.33721	.33220	.32731
72	.39210	.38619	.38042	.37477	.36924	.36384	.35855	.35337	.34831	.34335
73	.40900	.40308	.39728	.39161	.38605	.38061	.37529	.37007	.36496	.35996
74	.42618	.42025	.41444	.40876	.40318	.39772	.39237	.38713	.38199	.37695
75	.44345	.43753	.43173	.42604	.42046	.41499	.40962	.40436	.39920	.39413
76	.46073	.45483	.44904	.44336	.43779	.43232	.42695	.42168	.41650	.41142
77	.47799	.47212	.46635	.46069	.45513	.44967	.44431	.43905	.43386	.42878
78	.49524	.48941	.48368	.47805	.47252	.46708	.46173	.45647	.45130	.44622
79	.51256	.50678	.50110	.49551	.49001	.48460	.47928	.47405	.46890	.46383
80	.53001	.52429	.51867	.51313	.50769	.50232	.49705	.49185	.48673	.48169
81	.54745	.54181	.53626	.53079	.52541	.52010	.51487	.50973	.50465	.49965
82	.56476	.55921	.55374	.54835	.54303	.53779	.53263	.52754	.52252	.51757
83	.58193	.57648	.57110	.56579	.56056	.55540	.55031	.54529	.54033	.53544
84	.55907	.59373	.58845	.58325	.57811	.57304	.56804	.56309	.55822	.55340
85	.61624	.61102	.60586	.60077	.59574	.59077	.58586	.58102	.57623	.57150
86	.63300	.62791	.62289	.61791	.61300	.60815	.60335	.59860	.59392	.58928
87	.64883	.64387	.63896	.63411	.62932	.62458	.61989	.61525	.61066	.60613
88	.66363	.65880	.65402	.64929	.64461	.63998	.63540	.63086	.62638	.62194
89	.67775	.67304	.66838	.66377	.65921	.65469	.65022	.64579	.64141	.63707
90	.69160	.68703	.68250	.67802	.67357	.66918	.66482	.66050	.65623	.65199
91	.70509	.70066	.69626	.69191	.68760	.68332	.67909	.67489	.67073	.66661
92	.71775	.71345	.70919	.70496	.70078	.69662	.69251	.68843	.68439	.68038
93	.72929	.72512	.72099	.71689	.71282	.70879	.70479	.70082	.69689	.69299
94	.73964	.73559	.63157	.72758	.72362	.71970	.71581	.71195	.70812	.70432
95	.74867	.74472	.74081	.73692	.73306	.72924	.72544	.72167	.71793	.71422
96	.75625	.75239	.74856	.74476	.74099	.73724	.73353	.72984	.72618	.72254
97	.76303	.75925	.75550	.75177	.74807	.74440	.74076	.73714	.73354	.72998
98	.76892	.76521	.76152	.75786	.75422	.75061	.74703	.74347	.73994	.73643
99	.77443	.77078	.76715	.76355	.75998	.75642	.75290	.74939	.74591	.74245
100 ...	.77990	.77631	.77275	.76921	.76569	.76219	.75872	.75527	.75184	.74844
101 ...	.78463	.78109	.77757	.77407	.77060	.76715	.76372	.76031	.75692	.65356
102 ...	.78971	.78622	.78275	.77930	.77587	.77246	.76908	.76571	.76236	.75904
103 ...	.79629	.79287	.78947	.78608	.78272	.77937	.77605	.77274	.76945	.76618
104 ...	.80244	.79907	.79572	.79239	.78907	.78577	.78249	.77923	.77598	.77275
105 ...	.81198	.80871	.80546	.80222	.79900	.79579	.79259	.78941	.78625	.78310
106 ...	.82792	.82485	.82180	.81876	.81572	.81270	.80969	.80670	.80371	.80073
107 ...	.85057	.84783	.84509	.84237	.83964	.83693	.83422	.83152	.82883	.82614
108 ...	.88740	.88526	.88312	.88098	.87885	.87672	.87459	.87246	.87034	.86822
109 ...	.94900	.94800	.94700	.94600	.94500	.94400	.94300	.94200	.94100	.94000

TABLE E—Continued (10) SINGLE LIFE, UNISEX—TABLE SHOWING THE PRESENT WORTH OF THE REMAINDER INTEREST IN PROPERTY TRANSFERRED TO A UNITRUST HAVING THE ADJUSTED PAYOUT RATE SHOWN—APPLICABLE FOR TRANSFERS AFTER NOVEMBER 30, 1983, AND BEFORE MAY 1, 1989

(1)	(2)									
	Adjusted Payout Rate									
Age	12.2%	12.4%	12.6%	12.8%	13.0%	13.2%	13.4%	13.6%	13.8%	14.0%
0	.02396	.02380	.02366	.02352	.02338	.02325	.02313	.02301	.02290	.02279
1	.00600	.00585	.00572	.00559	.00547	.00536	.00525	.00514	.00505	.00495
2	.00550	.00535	.00521	.00508	.00495	.00484	.00472	.00462	.00451	.00442
3	.00536	.00520	.00505	.00491	.00478	.00465	.00453	.00442	.00431	.00421
4	.00536	.00519	.00504	.00489	.00475	.00461	.00449	.00437	.00426	.00415
5	.00549	.00532	.00515	.00499	.00484	.00470	.00457	.00444	.00432	.00421
6	.00572	.00554	.00536	.00519	.00503	.00488	.00474	.00460	.00447	.00435
7	.00602	.00582	.00563	.00545	.00528	.00512	.00496	.00482	.00468	.00455
8	.00640	.00618	.00598	.00579	.00561	.00543	.00527	.00512	.00497	.00483
9	.00688	.00665	.00644	.00623	.00604	.00585	.00568	.00551	.00536	.00521
10	.00747	.00723	.00699	.00678	.00657	.00637	.00619	.00601	.00584	.00568
11	.00818	.00792	.00767	.00744	.00722	.00701	.00681	.00662	.00644	.00627
12	.00900	.00873	.00846	.00822	.00798	.00776	.00755	.00735	.00716	.00697
13	.00988	.00959	.00931	.00905	.00880	.00857	.00834	.00813	.00793	.00773
14	.01077	.01046	.01017	.00989	.00963	.00938	.00914	.00892	.00870	.00850
15	.01160	.01127	.01097	.01067	.01040	.01014	.00989	.00965	.00942	.00921
16	.01234	.01200	.01167	.01137	.01108	.01080	.01054	.01029	.01005	.00983
17	.01299	.01263	.01229	.01197	.01166	.01137	.01109	.01083	.01058	.01035
18	.01357	.01319	.01283	.01249	.01217	.01186	.01157	.01130	.01103	.01078
19	.01410	.01370	.01332	.01297	.01263	.01230	.01200	.01171	.01143	.01117
20	.01465	.01422	.01382	.01345	.01309	.01275	.01243	.01212	.01183	.01155
21	.01520	.01475	.01433	.01393	.01355	.01319	.01285	.01253	.01222	.01193
22	.01576	.01529	.01484	.01442	.01402	.01364	.01328	.01293	.01261	.01230
23	.01636	.01586	.01538	.01493	.01450	.01410	.01372	.01336	.01301	.01268
24	.01703	.01649	.01599	.01551	.01505	.01463	.01422	.01383	.01347	.01312
25	.01781	.01724	.01670	.01619	.01571	.01525	.01482	.01441	.01401	.01364
26	.01874	.01813	.01756	.01701	.01650	.01601	.01555	.01511	.01469	.01430
27	.01983	.01918	.01857	.01799	.01744	.01692	.01643	.01596	.01551	.01509
28	.02111	.02042	.01976	.01915	.01856	.01800	.01748	.01697	.01650	.01604
29	.02253	.02179	.02110	.02044	.01981	.01922	.01865	.01812	.01760	.01712
30	.02411	.02333	.02259	.02188	.02121	.02058	.01998	.01940	.01886	.01833
31	.02583	.02500	.02421	.02345	.02274	.02206	.02142	.02080	.02022	.01966
32	.02772	.02683	.02599	.02519	.02443	.02370	.02301	.02236	.02173	.02113
33	.02979	.02885	.02795	.02709	.02628	.02550	.02477	.02407	.02340	.02276
34	.03203	.03102	.03006	.02915	.02829	.02746	.02667	.02592	.02521	.02452
35	.03447	.03340	.03238	.03141	.03048	.02960	.02876	.02796	.02719	.02646
36	.03710	.03597	.03488	.03385	.03286	.03193	.03103	.03017	.02936	.02858
37	.03995	.03874	.03758	.03649	.03544	.03444	.03348	.03257	.03170	.03087
38	.04299	.04170	.04048	.03931	.03820	.03714	.03612	.03515	.03422	.03333
39	.04623	.04487	.04358	.04234	.04115	.04002	.03894	.03791	.03692	.03597
40	.04970	.04826	.04689	.04558	.04432	.04312	.04197	.04087	.03981	.03880
41	.05341	.05189	.05043	.04904	.04771	.04643	.04521	.04404	.04292	.04185
42	.05739	.05578	.05424	.05277	.05136	.05001	.04871	.04747	.04628	.04514
43	.06163	.05993	.05830	.05674	.05525	.05382	.05245	.05113	.04987	.04865
44	.06614	.06435	.06263	.06099	.05941	.05789	.05644	.05505	.05371	.05242
45	.07090	.06901	.06720	.06547	.06380	.06220	.06067	.05919	.05777	.05641
46	.07595	.07396	.07206	.07023	.06847	.06678	.06516	.06360	.06210	.06065
47	.08128	.07919	.07718	.07525	.07340	.07162	.06991	.06826	.06668	.06514
48	.08693	.08474	.08263	.08061	.07866	.07678	.07498	.07324	.07157	.06999
49	.09291	.09061	.08840	.08627	.08423	.08225	.08035	.07852	.07676	.07506
50	.09925	.09684	.09452	.09229	.09014	.08807	.08607	.08415	.08229	.08050
51	.10593	.10341	.10098	.09864	.09638	.09421	.09211	.09009	.08814	.08625
52	.11296	.11032	.10778	.10534	.10297	.10070	.09850	.09637	.09432	.09234
53	.12034	.11759	.11494	.11238	.10991	.10753	.10523	.10300	.10085	.09877
54	.12805	.12519	.12243	.11976	.11718	.11468	.11227	.10994	.10769	.10551

TABLE E—Continued (11) SINGLE LIFE, UNISEX—TABLE SHOWING THE PRESENT WORTH OF THE REMAINDER INTEREST IN PROPERTY TRANSFERRED TO A UNITRUST HAVING THE ADJUSTED PAYOUT RATE SHOWN—APPLICABLE FOR TRANSFERS AFTER NOVEMBER 30, 1983, AND BEFORE MAY 1, 1989

(1)	(2)									
	Adjusted Payout Rate									
Age	12.2%	12.4%	12.6%	12.8%	13.0%	13.2%	13.4%	13.6%	13.8%	14.0%
55	.13611	.13313	.13025	.12747	.12478	.12218	.11966	.11722	.11487	.11258
56	.14451	.14141	.13841	.13551	.13271	.12999	.12737	.12483	.12236	.11998
57	.15327	.15005	.14694	.14393	.14101	.13818	.13545	.13279	.13022	.12773
58	.16240	.15906	.15583	.15270	.14967	.14673	.14388	.14112	.13844	.13584
59	.17194	.16848	.16513	.16189	.15874	.15568	.15272	.14985	.14706	.14435
60	.18189	.17831	.17485	.17148	.16822	.16505	.16198	.15899	.15609	.15327
61	.19230	.18860	.18502	.18154	.17816	.17488	.17169	.16859	.16558	.16265
62	.20317	.19936	.19566	.19207	.18857	.18518	.18187	.17866	.17554	.17251
63	.21453	.21060	.20679	.20308	.19947	.19596	.19255	.18923	.18600	.18285
64	.22635	.22231	.21839	.21457	.21085	.20723	.20371	.20028	.19694	.19368
65	.23864	.23450	.23046	.22653	.22271	.21893	.21535	.21181	.20836	.20500
66	.25140	.24715	.24301	.23898	.23505	.23121	.22748	.22383	.22028	.21681
67	.26461	.26026	.25602	.25188	.24785	.24392	.24008	.23633	.23267	.22910
68	.27828	.27384	.26950	.26527	.26114	.25711	.25317	.24932	.24556	.24189
69	.29246	.28793	.28350	.27918	.27496	.27083	.26680	.26285	.25900	.25523
70	.30718	.30256	.29805	.29364	.28933	.28512	.28100	.27697	.27302	.26916
71	.32251	.31783	.31324	.30876	.30437	.30007	.29587	.29176	.28773	.28378
72	.33850	.33375	.32910	.32455	.32009	.31572	.31145	.30726	.30315	.29913
73	.35506	.35026	.34555	.34094	.33642	.33199	.32765	.32340	.31923	.31514
74	.37201	.36716	.36241	.35776	.35319	.34871	.34431	.34000	.33577	.33162
75	.38916	.38429	.37950	.37481	.37020	.36568	.36124	.35688	.35260	.34840
76	.40644	.40154	.39673	.39200	.38737	.38281	.37833	.37393	.36961	.36537
77	.42378	.41887	.41404	.40930	.40464	.40006	.39555	.39113	.38677	.38249
78	.44123	.43631	.43148	.42673	.42205	.41745	.41293	.40848	.40410	.39980
79	.45885	.45394	.44911	.44436	.43969	.43508	.43055	.42609	.42170	.41737
80	.47673	.47184	.46703	.46229	.45763	.45303	.44850	.44404	.43964	.43531
81	.49473	.48987	.48509	.48037	.47573	.47115	.46663	.46218	.45779	.45347
82	.51269	.50787	.50313	.49845	.49383	.48928	.48479	.48036	.47599	.47168
83	.53062	.52586	.52116	.51653	.51195	.50744	.50298	.49858	.49424	.48995
84	.54864	.54395	.53931	.53473	.53021	.52575	.52134	.51698	.51268	.50843
85	.56683	.56221	.55765	.55314	.54869	.54429	.53994	.53564	.53139	.52720
86	.58470	.58017	.57570	.57127	.56689	.56257	.55829	.55406	.54988	.54574
87	.60164	.59720	.59281	.58847	.58417	.57993	.57572	.57156	.56745	.56338
88	.61754	.61320	.60889	.60464	.60042	.59625	.59212	.58804	.58399	.57999
89	.63277	.62851	.62430	.62013	.61600	.61191	.60786	.60384	.59987	.59594
90	.64780	.64364	.63953	.63545	.63141	.62741	.62344	.61952	.61562	.61177
91	.66252	.65848	.65446	.65049	.64655	.64264	.63877	.63493	.63113	.62736
92	.67640	.67246	.66856	.66468	.66084	.65703	.65326	.64951	.64580	.64212
93	.68912	.68528	.68148	.67770	.67396	.67024	.66656	.66291	.65928	.65568
94	.70055	.69680	.69309	.68941	.68576	.68213	.67854	.67497	.67142	.66791
95	.71054	.70689	.70326	.69966	.69609	.69255	.68903	.68554	.68207	.67863
96	.71893	.71535	.71180	.70827	.70476	.70128	.69783	.69440	.69100	.68762
97	.72643	.62292	.71943	.71596	.71252	.70910	.70570	.70233	.69899	.69566
98	.73294	.72948	.72604	.72263	.71924	.71587	.71252	.70920	.70590	.70263
99	.73902	.73561	.73222	.72886	.72551	.72219	.71889	.71562	.71236	.70913
100 ...	.74506	.74170	.73836	.73504	.73174	.72847	.72522	.72198	.71877	.71558
101 ...	.75021	.74689	.74359	.74030	.73704	.73380	.73058	.72738	.72420	.72104
102 ...	.75573	.75244	.74918	.74593	.74270	.73949	.73630	.73313	.72998	.72685
103 ...	.76293	.75970	.75649	.75329	.75011	.74695	.74381	.74068	.73758	.73449
104 ...	.76954	.76634	.76316	.76000	.75685	.75372	.75060	.74751	.74442	.74136
105 ...	.77996	.77684	.77373	.77064	.76756	.76449	.76144	.75840	.75538	.75237
106 ...	.79777	.79481	.79187	.78894	.78602	.78311	.78021	.77732	.77444	.77157
107 ...	.82346	.82078	.81812	.81546	.81281	.81016	.80752	.80489	.80227	.79965
108 ...	.86610	.86398	.86187	.85976	.85765	.85554	.85344	.85134	.84924	.84715
109 ...	.93900	.93800	.93700	.93600	.93500	.93400	.93300	.93200	.93100	.93000

TABLE F(1)—10 PERCENT—TABLE SHOWING FACTORS FOR COMPUTATIONS OF THE ADJUSTED PAYOUT RATE FOR CERTAIN VALUATIONS AND PAYOUT SEQUENCES—APPLICABLE FOR TRANSFERS AFTER NOVEMBER 30, 1983, AND BEFORE MAY 1, 1989

1 Number Of Months By Which the Valuation Date Precedes The First Payout		2 Factors For Payout At The End Of Each			
At Least	But Less Than	Annual Period	Semiannual Period	Quarterly Period	Monthly Period
....	1	....	.976731	.965232	.957616
1	2	.992089	.969004	.957596	.950041
2	3	.984240	.961338	.950021	
3	4	.976454	.953733	.942505	
4	5	.968729	.946488		
5	6	.961066	.938703		
6	7	.953463	.931277		
7	8	.945920			
8	9	.938436			
9	10	.931012			
10	11	.923647			
11	12	.916340			
12	....	.909091			

(e) Valuation of charitable remainder unitrusts having certain payout sequences for transfers for which the valuation date is after April 30, 1989, and before May 1, 1999. *(1) In general.* Except as otherwise provided in paragraph (e)(2) of this section, in the case of transfers for which the valuation date is after April 30, 1989, and before May 1, 1999, the present value of a remainder interest is determined under paragraphs (e)(3) through (e)(6) of this section, provided that the amount of the payout as of any payout date during any taxable year of the trust is not larger than the amount that the trust could distribute on such date under § 1.664-3(a)(1)(v) if the taxable year of the trust were to end on such date. See, however, § 1.7520-3(b) (relating to exceptions to the use of the prescribed tables under certain circumstances).

(2) Transitional rules for valuation of charitable remainder unitrusts. (i) If the valuation date of a transfer to a charitable remainder unitrust is after April 30, 1989, and before June 10, 1994, a transferor can rely upon Notice 89-24, 1989-1 C.B. 660, or Notice 89-60, 1989-1 C.B. 700, in valuing the transferred interest. (See § 601.601(d)(2)(ii)(b) of this chapter.)

(ii) For purposes of sections 2055, 2106, or 2624, if on May 1, 1989, the decedent was mentally incompetent so that the disposition of the property could not be changed, and the decedent died after April 30, 1989, without having regained competency to dispose of the decedent's property, or the decedent died within 90 days of the date that the decedent first regained competency after April 30, 1989, the present value of a remainder interest determined under this section is determined as if the valuation date with respect to the decedent's gross estate is either before May 1, 1989, or after April 30, 1989, at the option of the decedent's executor.

(3) Adjusted payout rate. For transfers for which the valuation date is after April 30, 1989, and before May 1, 1999, the adjusted payout rate is determined by using the appropriate Table F, contained in § 1.664-4(e)(6), for the section 7520 interest rate applicable to the transfer. If the interest rate is between 4.2 and 14 percent, see § 1.664-4(e)(6). If the interest rate is below 4.2 percent or greater than 14 percent, see § 1.664-4(b). See § 1.664-4(e) for rules applicable in determining the adjusted payout rate.

(4) Period is a term of years. If the period described in § 1.664-3(a)(5) is a term of years, the factor that is used in determining the present value of the remainder interest for transfers for which the valuation date is after April 30, 1989, and before May 1, 1999, is the factor under the appropriate adjusted payout rate in Table D in § 1.664-4(e)(6) corresponding to the number of years in the term. If the adjusted payout rate is an amount that is between adjusted payout rates for which factors are provided in Table D, a linear interpolation must be made. The present value of the remainder interest is determined by multiplying the net fair market value (as of the appropriate valuation date) of the property placed in trust by the factor determined under this paragraph. Generally, for purposes of this section, the valuation date is, in the case of an inter vivos transfer, the date on which the property is transferred to the trust by the donor, and, in the case of a testamentary transfer under sections 2055, 2106, or 2624, the valuation date is the date of death. See § 1.664-4(e)(4) for additional rules regarding the valuation date. See § 1.664-4(e)(4) for an example that illustrates the application of this paragraph (e)(4).

(5) Period is the life of one individual. If the period described in § 1.664-3(a)(5) is the life of one individual, the factor that is used in determining the present value of the remainder interest for transfers for which the valuation date is after April 30, 1989, and before May 1, 1999, is the factor in Table U(1) in paragraph (e)(6) of this section under the appropriate adjusted payout. For purposes of the computations described in this paragraph (e)(5), the age of an individual is the age of that individual at the individual's nearest birthday. If the adjusted payout rate is an amount that is between adjusted payout rates for which factors are provided in the appropriate table, a linear interpolation must be made. The rules provided in § 1.664-4(e)(5) apply for determining the present value of the remainder interest. See § 1.664-4(e)(5) for an example illustrating the application of this paragraph (e)(5)(using current actuarial tables).

(6) Actuarial tables for transfers for which the valuation date is after April 30, 1989, and before May 1, 1999. For

transfers for which the valuation date is after April 30, 1989, and before May 1, 1999, the present value of a charitable remainder unitrust interest that is dependent on a term of years or the termination of a life interest is determined by using the section 7520 rate and Table D, Tables F(4.2) through F(14.0) in § 1.664-4(e)(6) and Table U(1) of this paragraph (e)(6), as applicable. See, however, § 1.7520-3(b) (relating to exceptions to the use of prescribed tables under certain circumstances). Many actuarial factors not contained in the following tables are contained in Internal Revenue Service Publication 1458, "Actuarial Values, Beta Volume," (8-89). Publication 1458 is no longer available for purchase from the Superintendent of Documents, United States Government Printing Office, Washington, DC 20402. However, pertinent factors in this publication may be obtained by a written request to: CC:DOM:CORP:R (IRS Publication 1458), room 5226, Internal Revenue Service, POB 7604, Ben Franklin Station, Washington, DC 20044.

TABLE U(1)

UNITRUST SINGLE LIFE REMAINDER FACTORS BASED ON LIFE TABLE 80CNSMT [APPLICABLE FOR TRANSFERS AFTER APRIL 30, 1989, AND BEFORE MAY 1, 1999]

				ADJUSTED PAYOUT RATE						
AGE	4.2%	4.4%	4.6%	4.8%	5.0%	5.2%	5.4%	5.6%	5.8%	6.0%
0	.06797	.06181	.05645	.05177	.04768	.04410	.04096	.03820	.03578	.03364
1	.05881	.05243	.04686	.04199	.03773	.03400	.03072	.02784	.02531	.02308
2	.06049	.05394	.04821	.04319	.03880	.03494	.03155	.02856	.02593	.02361
3	.06252	.05579	.04990	.04473	.04020	.03621	.03270	.02961	.02688	.02446
4	.06479	.05788	.05182	.04650	.04183	.03771	.03408	.03087	.02804	.02553
5	.06724	.06016	.05393	.04845	.04363	.03937	.03562	.03230	.02936	.02675
6	.06984	.06257	.05618	.05054	.04557	.04117	.03729	.03385	.03080	.02809
7	.07259	.06513	.05856	.05276	.04764	.04310	.03909	.03552	.03236	.02954
8	.07548	.06784	.06109	.05513	.04985	.04517	.04102	.03733	.03405	.03113
9	.07854	.07071	.06378	.05765	.05221	.04738	.04310	.03928	.03588	.03285
10	.08176	.07374	.06663	.06033	.05473	.04976	.04533	.04138	.03786	.03471
11	.08517	.07695	.06966	.06319	.05743	.05230	.04772	.04364	.04000	.03673
12	.08872	.08031	.07284	.06619	.06026	.05498	.05026	.04604	.04227	.03889
13	.09238	.08378	.07612	.06929	.06320	.05776	.05289	.04853	.04463	.04113
14	.09608	.08728	.07943	.07243	.06616	.06056	.05554	.05104	.04701	.04338
15	.09981	.09081	.08276	.07557	.06914	.06337	.05820	.05356	.04938	.04563
16	.10356	.09435	.08612	.07874	.07213	.06619	.06086	.05607	.05176	.04787
17	.10733	.09792	.08949	.08192	.07513	.06902	.06353	.05858	.05413	.05010
18	.11117	.10155	.09291	.08515	.07817	.07189	.06623	.06113	.05652	.05236
19	.11509	.10526	.09642	.08847	.08130	.07484	.06901	.06375	.05899	.05469
20	.11913	.10908	.10003	.09188	.08452	.07788	.07188	.06645	.06154	.05708
21	.12326	.11300	.10375	.09539	.08784	.08101	.07483	.06923	.06416	.05955
22	.12753	.11705	.10758	.09902	.09127	.08426	.07789	.07212	.06688	.06212
23	.13195	.12125	.11156	.10279	.09484	.08763	.08109	.07514	.06973	.06481
24	.13655	.12563	.11573	.10675	.09860	.09119	.08446	.07833	.07274	.06766
25	.14136	.13022	.12010	.11091	.10255	.09495	.08802	.08171	.07595	.07069
26	.14640	.13504	.12471	.11530	.10674	.09893	.09181	.08531	.07937	.07394
27	.15169	.14011	.12956	.11994	.11117	.10316	.09584	.08915	.08302	.07742
28	.15721	.14542	.13465	.12482	.11583	.10762	.10010	.09322	.08691	.08112
29	.16299	.15097	.13999	.12994	.12075	.11233	.10461	.09753	.09104	.08507
30	.16901	.15678	.14559	.13533	.12592	.11729	.10937	.10210	.09541	.08926
31	.17531	.16287	.15146	.14099	.13137	.12254	.11441	.10694	.10006	.09372
32	.18186	.16921	.15759	.14691	.13709	.12804	.11972	.11205	.10497	.09844
33	.18869	.17584	.16401	.15312	.14309	.13384	.12531	.11744	.11017	.10345
34	.19578	.18273	.17070	.15961	.14937	.13992	.13119	.12312	.11565	.10874
35	.20315	.18990	.17767	.16637	.15593	.14628	.13735	.12908	.12142	.11431
36	.21076	.19732	.18490	.17340	.16276	.15291	.14377	.13531	.12745	.12016
37	.21863	.20501	.19239	.18071	.16987	.15982	.15049	.14182	.13377	.12628
38	.22676	.21296	.20016	.18828	.17725	.16701	.15748	.14862	.14037	.13269
39	.23515	.22118	.20820	.19614	.18492	.17448	.16476	.15571	.14727	.13940
40	.24379	.22967	.21652	.20428	.19288	.18225	.17234	.16310	.15447	.14641
41	.25270	.23842	.22511	.21270	.20112	.19031	.18021	.17078	.16197	.15372
42	.26184	.24742	.23395	.22137	.20962	.19864	.18836	.17875	.16975	.16132

TABLE U(1)

UNITRUST SINGLE LIFE REMAINDER FACTORS BASED ON LIFE TABLE 80CNSMT [APPLICABLE FOR TRANSFERS AFTER APRIL 30, 1989, AND BEFORE MAY 1, 1999]

43	.27123	.25666	.24305	.23031	.21840	.20724	.19679	.18700	.17782	.16921
44	.28085	.26616	.25241	.23952	.22745	.21613	.20551	.19554	.18618	.17739
45	.29072	.27591	.26203	.24901	.23678	.22530	.21452	.20438	.19485	.18589
46	.30082	.28591	.27191	.25875	.24639	.23476	.22381	.21352	.20382	.19468
47	.31116	.29616	.28204	.26877	.25626	.24449	.23340	.22295	.21309	.20379
48	.32171	.30663	.29241	.27902	.26640	.25449	.24326	.23265	.22264	.21318
49	.33245	.31730	.30300	.28950	.27676	.26473	.25336	.24262	.23246	.22285
50	.34338	.32816	.31379	.30020	.28735	.27521	.26371	.25283	.24253	.23277
51	.35449	.33923	.32479	.31112	.29818	.28593	.27431	.26331	.25287	.24297
52	.36582	.35053	.33603	.32230	.30927	.29692	.28520	.27408	.26352	.25349
53	.37736	.36205	.34751	.33372	.32063	.30819	.29637	.28514	.27446	.26431
54	.38909	.37376	.35921	.34537	.33221	.31970	.30780	.29647	.28569	.27542
55	.40099	.38568	.37111	.35724	.34404	.33146	.31949	.30807	.29719	.28681
56	.41308	.39779	.38322	.36934	.35610	.34348	.33143	.31994	.30898	.29851
57	.42536	.41011	.39555	.38167	.36841	.35575	.34366	.33210	.32106	.31051
58	.43781	.42262	.40810	.39422	.38096	.36828	.35615	.34454	.33344	.32281
59	.45043	.43530	.42083	.40698	.39373	.38104	.36888	.35724	.34609	.33540
60	.46318	.44813	.43372	.41992	.40668	.39400	.38183	.37017	.35898	.34824
61	.47602	.46107	.44674	.43299	.41979	.40713	.39497	.38329	.37207	.36129
62	.48893	.47410	.45986	.44617	.43303	.42039	.40825	.39657	.38534	.37454
63	.50190	.48720	.47306	.45946	.44638	.43379	.42168	.41001	.39878	.38796
64	.51494	.50038	.48636	.47286	.45986	.44733	.43526	.42362	.41240	.40158
65	.52808	.51368	.49980	.48641	.47350	.46104	.44903	.43743	.42624	.41544
66	.54134	.52711	.51338	.50013	.48733	.47496	.46302	.45148	.44033	.42956
67	.55471	.54068	.52712	.51401	.50134	.48908	.47723	.46577	.45467	.44394
68	.56820	.55437	.54100	.52805	.51552	.50339	.49165	.48027	.46925	.45858
69	.58172	.56812	.55495	.54219	.52982	.51783	.50620	.49494	.48401	.47341
70	.59526	.58190	.56894	.55637	.54417	.53234	.52086	.50971	.49889	.48838

TABLE U(1)

UNITRUST SINGLE LIFE REMAINDER FACTORS BASED ON LIFE TABLE 80CNSMT [APPLICABLE FOR TRANSFERS AFTER APRIL 30, 1989, AND BEFORE MAY 1, 1999]

	ADJUSTED PAYOUT RATE									
AGE	4.2%	4.4%	4.6%	4.8%	5.0%	5.2%	5.4%	5.6%	5.8%	6.0%
71	.60874	.59564	.58291	.57055	.55854	.54687	.53554	.52453	.51382	.50342
72	.62218	.60934	.59685	.58471	.57291	.56143	.55026	.53939	.52882	.51854
73	.63557	.62301	.61078	.59887	.58728	.57600	.56501	.55431	.54389	.53373
74	.64896	.63669	.62472	.61307	.60171	.59064	.57985	.56932	.55906	.54906
75	.66237	.65040	.63872	.62733	.61622	.60538	.59480	.58447	.57439	.56455
76	.67581	.66416	.65279	.64168	.63083	.62023	.60988	.59977	.58989	.58023
77	.68925	.67793	.66688	.65606	.64550	.63516	.62506	.61517	.60551	.59605
78	.70263	.69166	.68093	.67044	.66016	.65010	.64026	.63062	.62119	.61195
79	.71585	.70525	.69486	.68468	.67471	.66495	.65538	.64600	.63681	.62780
80	.72885	.71860	.70856	.69872	.68906	.67959	.67031	.66120	.65227	.64350
81	.74150	.73162	.72193	.71242	.70308	.69392	.68492	.67609	.66742	.65890
82	.75376	.74425	.73490	.72572	.71671	.70785	.69915	.69059	.68219	.67393
83	.76559	.75643	.74744	.73859	.72989	.72134	.71293	.70466	.69652	.68852
84	.77700	.76821	.75955	.75104	.74266	.73441	.72629	.71831	.71044	.70270
85	.78805	.77961	.77130	.76311	.75505	.74711	.73929	.73158	.72399	.71652
86	.79866	.79056	.78258	.77472	.76697	.75933	.75180	.74438	.73707	.72985
87	.80870	.80094	.79329	.78574	.77829	.77095	.76370	.75656	.74951	.74255
88	.81825	.81081	.80348	.79623	.78908	.78202	.77506	.76818	.76139	.75469
89	.82746	.82035	.81332	.80638	.79952	.79275	.78606	.77945	.77292	.76647
90	.83643	.82963	.82291	.81627	.80971	.80322	.79681	.79047	.78420	.77801
91	.84503	.83854	.83212	.82578	.81950	.81330	.80716	.80109	.79509	.78915
92	.85308	.84689	.84076	.83470	.82870	.82276	.81689	.81107	.80532	.79963
93	.86052	.85460	.84875	.84295	.83721	.83152	.82590	.82033	.81481	.80935
94	.86729	.86163	.85602	.85046	.84496	.83951	.83412	.82877	.82348	.81823
95	.87338	.86795	.86257	.85723	.85195	.84672	.84153	.83639	.83129	.82624
96	.87877	.87354	.86836	.86323	.85814	.85309	.84809	.84313	.83822	.83334
97	.88365	.87861	.87362	.86867	.86375	.85888	.85405	.84926	.84450	.83979
98	.88805	.88318	.87835	.87356	.86880	.86409	.85941	.85477	.85016	.84559
99	.89210	.88739	.88271	.87807	.87347	.86890	.86436	.85986	.85539	.85095
100	.89588	.89131	.88678	.88227	.87780	.87337	.86896	.86459	.86024	.85593
101	.89949	.89506	.89066	.88629	.88195	.87764	.87336	.86911	.86488	.86069

102	.90325	.89897	.89471	.89047	.88627	.88209	.87794	.87381	.86971	.86564
103	.90724	.90311	.89900	.89491	.89085	.88681	.88279	.87880	.87484	.87089
104	.91167	.90770	.90376	.89983	.89593	.89205	.88819	.88435	.88053	.87673
105	.91708	.91333	.90959	.90587	.90217	.89848	.89481	.89116	.88752	.88391
106	.92470	.92126	.91782	.91440	.91100	.90760	.90422	.90085	.89749	.89414
107	.93545	.93246	.92948	.92650	.92353	.92057	.91762	.91467	.91173	.90880
108	.95239	.95016	.94792	.94569	.94346	.94123	.93900	.93678	.93456	.93234
109	.97900	.97800	.97700	.97600	.97500	.97400	.97300	.97200	.97100	.97000

TABLE U(1)

UNITRUST SINGLE LIFE REMAINDER FACTORS BASED ON LIFE TABLE 80CNSMT [APPLICABLE FOR TRANSFERS AFTER APRIL 30, 1989, AND BEFORE MAY 1, 1999]

				ADJUSTED PAYOUT RATE						
AGE	6.2%	6.4%	6.6%	6.8%	7.0%	7.2%	7.4%	7.6%	7.8%	8.0%
0	.03176	.03009	.02861	.02730	.02613	.02509	.02416	.02333	.02258	.02191
1	.02110	.01936	.01781	.01644	.01522	.01413	.01316	.01229	.01150	.01080
2	.02156	.01974	.01812	.01669	.01541	.01427	.01325	.01234	.01152	.01078
3	.02233	.02043	.01875	.01725	.01591	.01471	.01364	.01268	.01182	.01105
4	.02330	.02132	.01956	.01800	.01660	.01535	.01422	.01322	.01231	.01149
5	.02443	.02237	.02054	.01890	.01743	.01612	.01494	.01389	.01293	.01208
6	.02568	.02353	.02162	.01990	.01837	.01700	.01576	.01465	.01365	.01275
7	.02704	.02480	.02280	.02102	.01941	.01798	.01668	.01552	.01446	.01351
8	.02852	.02619	.02411	.02224	.02057	.01906	.01770	.01648	.01537	.01437
9	.03014	.02772	.02554	.02360	.02184	.02027	.01885	.01756	.01640	.01535
10	.03190	.02938	.02711	.02508	.02325	.02160	.02012	.01877	.01755	.01645
11	.03381	.03119	.02883	.02672	.02481	.02308	.02153	.02012	.01884	.01768
12	.03585	.03313	.03068	.02847	.02648	.02468	.02305	.02157	.02023	.01902
13	.03798	.03515	.03260	.03030	.02822	.02635	.02464	.02310	.02170	.02042
14	.04012	.03718	.03453	.03213	.02997	.02801	.02623	.02462	.02315	.02181
15	.04225	03919	.03644	.03395	.03169	.02965	.02779	.02611	.02457	.02317
16	.04436	.04120	.03833	.03574	.03339	.03126	.02932	.02756	.02595	.02449
17	.04647	.04319	.04021	.03752	.03507	.03285	.03082	.02898	.02730	.02577
18	.04860	.04519	.04210	.03930	.03675	.03443	.03232	.03040	.02864	.02703
19	.05079	.04725	.04404	.04113	.03847	.03606	.03386	.03185	.03001	.02833
20	.05304	.04938	.04604	.04301	.04025	.03773	.03543	.03333	.03141	.02965
21	.05537	.05157	.04811	.04495	.04208	.03945	.03705	.03486	.03285	.03101
22	.05779	.05385	.05025	.04698	.04398	.04125	.03874	.03645	.03435	.03242
23	.06032	.05623	.05250	.04910	.04598	.04313	.04052	.03812	.03592	.03390
24	.06302	.05878	.05491	.05136	.04812	.04515	.04242	.03992	.03762	.03550
25	.06589	.06150	.05748	.05380	.05042	.04733	.04448	.04187	.03946	.03725
26	.06897	.06442	.06025	.05643	.05292	.04969	.04673	.04400	.04148	.03916
27	.07228	.06757	.06325	.05928	.05563	.05227	.04917	.04632	.04369	.04126
28	.07582	.07094	.06646	.06234	.05854	.05504	.05182	.04884	.04609	.04355
29	.07958	.07454	.06990	.06562	.06167	.05804	.05468	.05157	.04870	.04604
30	.08360	.07838	.07357	.06913	.06504	.06125	.05775	.05452	.05152	.04874
31	.08788	.08249	.07751	.07291	.06866	.06472	.06108	.05771	.05457	.05167
32	.09242	.08685	.08170	.07694	.07252	.06844	.06465	.06113	.05786	.05483
33	.09724	.09149	.08617	.08124	.07666	.07242	.06848	.06482	.06141	.05824
34	.10234	.09641	.09091	.08581	.08107	.07667	.07257	.06876	.06521	.06191

TABLE U(1)

UNITRUST SINGLE LIFE REMAINDER FACTORS BASED ON LIFE TABLE 80CNSMT [APPLICABLE FOR TRANSFERS AFTER APRIL 30, 1989, AND BEFORE MAY 1, 1999]

				ADJUSTED PAYOUT RATE						
AGE	6.2%	6.4%	6.6%	6.8%	7.0%	7.2%	7.4%	7.6%	7.8%	8.0%
35	.10773	.10161	.09594	.09066	.08575	.08119	.07694	.07298	.06928	.06583
36	.11338	.10708	.10122	.09577	.09070	.08597	.08156	.07744	.07360	.07001
37	.11932	.11283	.10680	.10117	.09592	.09102	.08645	.08217	.07818	.07444
38	.12554	.11887	.11265	.10685	.10142	.09636	.09162	.08719	.08304	.07915
39	.13206	.12521	.11880	.11282	.10722	.10198	.09708	.09249	.08818	.08414
40	.13888	.13184	.12526	.11909	.11332	.10791	.10284	.09808	.09361	.08942
41	.14601	.13878	.13201	.12567	.11972	.11414	.10890	.10398	.09935	.09499
42	.15342	.14601	.13906	.13254	.12641	.12066	.11525	.11016	.10537	.10086
43	.16112	.15353	.14640	.13970	.13340	.12747	.12189	.11663	.11168	.10701

44	.16913	.16136	.15406	.14718	.14070	.13460	.12885	.12342	.11830	.11347
45	.17745	.16951	.16202	.15497	.14832	.14204	.13612	.13053	.12525	.12025
46	.18608	.17796	.17030	.16308	.15625	.14981	.14372	.13796	.13251	.12735
47	.19501	.18673	.17890	.17150	.16451	.15790	.15164	.14571	.14010	.13478
48	.20425	.19579	.18780	.18024	.17308	.16630	.15987	.15378	.14800	.14252
49	.21375	.20514	.19698	.18926	.18193	.17499	.16840	.16214	.15620	.15056
50	.22352	.21476	.20644	.19856	.19107	.18396	.17721	.17080	.16470	.15890
51	.23358	.22467	.21620	.20816	.20051	.19325	.18634	.17976	17350	.16755
52	.24396	.23490	.22628	.21809	.21030	.20288	.19581	.18908	.18267	.17655
53	.25465	.24545	.23670	.22836	.22042	.21285	.20563	.19875	.19218	.18592
54	.26563	.25631	.24742	.23895	.23086	.22315	.21579	.20876	.20204	.19562
55	.27692	.26747	.25846	.24986	.24164	.23379	.22628	.21911	.21225	.20568
56	.28850	.27895	.26982	.26109	.25275	.24476	.23712	.22981	.22281	.21611
57	.30041	.29076	.28152	.27267	.26421	.25610	.24833	.24089	.23376	.22691
58	.31263	.30288	.29355	.28460	.27602	.26780	.25991	.25234	.24508	.23811
59	.32515	.31532	.30590	.29685	.28817	.27984	.27184	.26416	.25677	.24968
60	.33793	.32803	.31853	.30940	.30062	.29219	.28409	.27630	.26880	.26159
61	.35093	.34098	.33141	.32220	.31335	.30483	.29663	.28873	.28113	.27381
62	.36414	.35414	.34451	.33524	.32631	.31771	.30942	.30144	.29374	.28631
63	.37754	.36750	.35783	.34850	.33951	.33084	.32247	.31440	.30661	.29910
64	.39115	.38108	.37137	.36200	.35296	.34422	.33579	.32765	.31978	.31217
65	.40500	.39493	.38519	.37579	.36670	.35792	.34943	.34122	.33328	.32560
66	.41914	.40906	.39932	.38990	.38079	.37197	.36343	.35517	.34717	.33943
67	.43355	.42350	.41376	.40434	.39521	.38636	.37780	.36950	.36145	.35365
68	.44824	.43822	.42851	.41909	.40996	.40111	.39252	.38419	.37611	.36827
69	.46313	.45316	.44348	.43409	.42498	.41613	.40754	.39919	.39109	.38322
70	.47818	.46827	.45864	.44929	.44020	.43137	.42279	.41445	.40634	.39845

TABLE U(1)

UNITRUST SINGLE LIFE REMAINDER FACTORS BASED ON LIFE TABLE 80CNSMT [APPLICABLE FOR TRANSFERS AFTER APRIL 30, 1989, AND BEFORE MAY 1, 1999]

	ADJUSTED PAYOUT RATE									
AGE	6.2%	6.4%	6.6%	6.8%	7.0%	7.2%	7.4%	7.6%	7.8%	8.0%
71	.49331	.48348	.47391	.46461	.45557	.44677	.43821	.42988	.42177	.41388
72	.50853	.49879	.48930	.48007	.47108	.46233	.45380	.44550	.43741	.42952
73	.52384	.51421	.50482	.49566	.48674	.47805	.46957	.46130	.45324	.44538
74	.53930	.52979	.52050	.51145	.50261	.49399	.48557	.47736	.46934	.46152
75	.55495	.54557	.53641	.52747	.51873	.51020	.50187	.49372	.48577	.47799
76	.57079	.56157	.55256	.54374	.53513	.52670	.51847	.51041	.50253	.49483
77	.58680	.57775	.56890	.56024	.55176	.54346	.53534	.52739	.51960	.51198
78	.60291	.59405	.58537	.57687	.56855	.56040	.55241	.54458	.53691	.52940
79	.61898	.61032	.60184	.59353	.58537	.57738	.56954	.56185	.55431	.54691
80	.63491	.62647	.61819	.61007	.60210	.59428	.58660	.57907	.57167	.56441
81	.65054	.64234	.63427	.62636	.61858	.61094	.60344	.59606	.58882	.58170
82	.66582	.65784	.65000	.64229	.63472	.62727	.61994	.61274	.60566	.59870
83	.68065	.67291	.66530	.65781	.65044	.64319	.63605	.62903	.62212	.61532
84	.69508	.68758	.68020	.67293	.66577	.65872	.65178	.64495	.63821	.63158
85	.70915	.70190	.69475	.68770	.68076	.67392	.66718	.66054	.65399	.64754
86	.72274	.71573	.70882	.70200	.69528	.68865	.68212	.67567	.66931	.66304
87	.73569	.72892	.72224	.71565	.70915	.70273	.69639	.69014	.68397	.67788
88	.74807	.74154	.73509	.72872	.72243	.71622	.71009	.70403	.69805	.69214
89	.76010	.75381	.74759	.74144	.73537	.72937	.72344	.71758	.71179	.70607
90	.77189	.76584	.75985	.75394	.74809	.74230	.73659	.73093	.72534	.71981
91	.78327	.77746	.77171	.76603	.76040	.75484	.74933	.74388	.73850	.73316
92	.79399	.78841	.78289	.77743	.77202	.76667	.76137	.75613	.75093	.74579
93	.80394	.79858	.79328	.78803	.78283	.77768	.77258	.76753	.76252	.75757
94	.81303	.80788	.80278	.79773	.79272	.78776	.78284	.77797	.77315	.76837
95	.82124	.81628	.81136	.80649	.80166	.79687	.79213	.78742	.78276	.77814
96	.82851	.82372	.81897	.81426	.80959	.80496	.80036	.79581	.79129	.78682
97	.83512	.83048	.82588	.82132	.81679	.81230	.80785	.80343	.79905	.79471
98	.84106	.83656	.83210	.82767	.82328	.81892	.81459	.81030	.80604	.80181
99	.84655	.84218	.83785	.83354	.82927	.82503	.82082	.81664	.81249	.80837
100	.85165	.84740	.84318	.83899	.83483	.83070	.82660	.82252	.81848	.81446
101	.85652	.85238	.84827	.84419	.84013	.83611	.83210	.82813	.82418	.82026
102	.86159	.85757	.85358	.84960	.84566	.84174	.83784	.83397	.83012	.82630

103	.86697	.86307	.85920	.85535	.85152	.84771	.84392	.84016	.83642	.83270
104	.87295	.86919	.86544	.86172	.85802	.85434	.85068	.84704	.84341	.83981
105	.88030	.87672	.87315	.86959	.86605	.86253	.85903	.85554	.85207	.84861
106	.89081	.88749	.88418	.88088	.87760	.87433	.87106	.86782	.86458	.86135
107	.90588	.90296	.90005	.89715	.89425	.89137	.88849	.88561	.88275	.87989
108	.93013	.92791	.92570	.92350	.92129	.91909	.91689	.91469	.91250	.91031
109	.96900	.96800	.96700	.96600	.96500	.96400	.96300	.96200	.96100	.96000

TABLE U(1)

UNITRUST SINGLE LIFE REMAINDER FACTORS BASED ON LIFE TABLE 80CNSMT [APPLICABLE FOR TRANSFERS AFTER APRIL 30, 1989, AND BEFORE MAY 1, 1999]

	ADJUSTED PAYOUT RATE									
AGE	8.2%	8.4%	8.6%	8.8%	9.0%	9.2%	9.4%	9.6%	9.8%	10.0%
0	.02130	.02075	.02025	.01980	.01939	.01901	.01867	.01835	.01806	.01779
1	.01017	.00960	.00908	.00861	.00819	.00780	.00745	.00712	.00683	.00655
2	.01011	.00951	.00897	.00848	.00803	.00762	.00725	.00690	.00659	.00630
3	.01035	.00971	.00914	.00862	.00815	.00771	.00732	.00696	.00663	.00632
4	.01076	.01009	.00948	.00894	.00843	.00798	.00756	.00718	.00683	.00650
5	.01130	.01059	.00996	.00938	.00885	.00836	.00792	.00752	.00714	.00680
6	.01193	.01119	.01051	.00990	.00934	.00883	.00836	.00793	.00754	.00717
7	.01265	.01187	.01116	.01051	.00992	.00938	.00888	.00842	.00800	.00762
8	.01347	.01264	.01189	.01121	.01058	.01001	.00948	.00900	.00856	.00815
9	.01440	.01353	.01274	.01201	.01135	.01075	.01019	.00968	.00921	.00877
10	.01544	.01453	.01369	.01293	.01223	.01159	.01101	.01046	.00997	.00950
11	.01662	.01566	.01478	.01398	.01324	.01257	.01195	.01137	.01085	.01036
12	.01791	.01690	.01597	.01513	.01435	.01364	.01298	.01238	.01182	.01131
13	.01926	.01820	.01722	.01634	.01552	.01477	.01408	.01344	.01285	.01231
14	.02059	.01948	.01846	.01752	.01667	.01588	.01515	.01448	.01386	.01328
15	.02189	.02072	.01965	.01867	.01777	.01694	.01617	.01547	.01481	.01421
16	.02315	.02192	.02080	.01977	.01882	.01795	.01714	.01640	.01572	.01508
17	.02436	.02308	.02190	.02082	.01982	.01891	.01806	.01728	.01656	.01589
18	.02556	.02422	.02298	.02184	.02080	.01983	.01894	.01812	.01736	.01665
19	.02679	.02537	.02408	.02288	.02178	.02077	.01983	.01897	.01817	.01742
20	.02804	.02656	.02519	.02394	.02278	.02172	.02073	.01982	.01898	.01819
21	.02932	.02776	.02633	.02501	.02380	.02268	.02164	.02068	.01979	.01896
22	.03065	.02902	.02751	.02613	.02485	.02367	.02258	.02157	.02063	.01976
23	.03204	.03033	.02876	.02730	.02595	.02471	.02356	.02249	.02150	.02058
24	.03356	.03176	.03010	.02857	.02716	.02585	.02463	.02351	.02246	.02149
25	.03520	.03332	.03158	.02997	.02848	.02710	.02582	.02463	.02352	.02249
26	.03702	.03504	.03321	.03152	.02995	.02850	.02714	.02589	.02472	.02363
27	.03902	.03695	.03502	.03324	.03159	.03006	.02863	.02730	.02607	.02492
28	.04120	.03902	.03700	.03513	.03339	.03178	.03027	.02887	.02757	.02635
29	.04358	.04129	.03917	.03720	.03537	.03367	.03208	.03061	.02923	.02794
30	.04616	.04376	.04154	.03947	.03754	.03575	.03408	.03251	.03106	.02969
31	.04897	.04646	.04413	.04195	.03993	.03804	.03627	.03463	.03309	.03165
32	.05200	.04938	.04693	.04465	.04252	.04053	.03867	.03693	.03531	.03378
33	.05529	.05254	.04998	.04758	.04534	.04325	.04130	.03946	.03775	.03614
34	.05883	.05595	.05326	.05075	.04840	.04620	.04414	.04221	.04040	.03870

TABLE U(1)

UNITRUST SINGLE LIFE REMAINDER FACTORS BASED ON LIFE TABLE 80CNSMT [APPLICABLE FOR TRANSFERS AFTER APRIL 30, 1989, AND BEFORE MAY 1, 1999]

	ADJUSTED PAYOUT RATE									
AGE	8.2%	8.4%	8.6%	8.8%	9.0%	9.2%	9.4%	9.6%	9.8%	10.0%
35	.06262	.05961	.05680	.05417	.05170	.04939	.04723	.04520	.04329	.04149
36	.06665	.06351	.06057	.05781	.05523	.05280	.05053	.04839	.04638	.04449
37	.07094	.06766	.06459	.06171	.05900	.05646	.05407	.05182	.04971	.04771
38	.07550	.07208	.06888	.06586	.06303	.06037	.05786	.05550	.05327	.05118
39	.08034	.07678	.07344	.07029	.06733	.06454	.06191	.05943	.05709	.05489
40	.08547	.08177	.07828	.07499	.07190	.06898	.06623	.06363	.06118	.05886
41	.09090	.08704	.08341	.07998	.07675	.07371	.07083	.06811	.06553	.06310
42	.09661	.09260	.08882	.08525	.08188	.07870	.07569	.07284	.07015	.06760
43	.10260	.09844	.09451	.09080	.08729	.08397	.08083	.07785	.07503	.07236
44	.10891	.10459	.10051	.09666	.09300	.08954	.08626	.08316	.08021	.07741

45	.11553	.11106	.10683	.10282	.09902	.09542	.09201	.08876	.08568	.08276
46	.12247	.11784	.11346	.10930	.10536	.10161	.09806	.09468	.09146	.08841
47	.12974	.12496	.12042	.11611	.11202	.10813	.10443	.10091	.09756	.09438
48	.13732	.13238	.12769	.12323	.11899	.11495	.11111	.10745	.10397	.10065
49	.14520	.14011	.13526	.13064	.12625	.12207	.11809	.11429	.11066	.10721
50	.15338	.14812	.14312	.13836	.13381	.12948	.12535	.12141	.11765	.11405
51	.16187	.15646	.15130	.14639	.14169	.13721	.13294	.12885	.12495	.12121
52	.17072	.16516	.15985	.15478	.14993	.14531	.14088	.13665	.13261	.12873
53	.17993	.17422	.16876	.16353	.15854	.15377	.14920	.14482	.14064	.13662
54	.18949	.18362	.17801	.17264	.16750	.16258	.15787	.15335	.14902	.14486
55	.19940	.19339	.18763	.18212	.17683	.17176	.16690	.16224	.15777	.15348
56	.20968	.20353	.19762	.19196	.18654	.18132	.17632	.17152	.16691	.16247
57	.22035	.21406	.20802	.20222	.19665	.19129	.18615	.18121	.17646	.17189
58	.23142	.22499	.21881	.21287	.20717	.20168	.19640	.19132	.18643	.18172
59	.24286	.23630	.23000	.22393	.21809	.21247	.20705	.20184	.19682	.19198
60	.25465	.24797	.24154	.23534	.22938	.22363	.21808	.21274	.20759	.20262
61	.26676	.25996	.25341	.24710	.24101	.23513	.22946	.22399	.21871	.21361
62	.27916	.27225	.26559	.25916	.25295	.24695	.24117	.23557	.23017	.22495
63	.29184	.28483	.27806	.27152	.26520	.25909	.25319	.24748	.24196	.23661
64	.30483	.29772	.29085	.28421	.27779	.27157	.26555	.25973	.25409	.24863
65	.31817	.31098	.30402	.29729	.29076	.28444	.27832	.27240	.26665	.26108
66	.33192	.32466	.31762	.31079	.30418	.29777	.29155	.28552	.27968	.27400
67	.34609	.33876	.33164	.32474	.31805	.31156	.30525	.29913	.29319	.28742
68	.36066	.35328	.34610	.33914	.33238	.32581	.31943	.31323	.30720	.30134
69	.37558	.36815	.36093	.35391	.34709	.34045	.33400	.32773	.32163	.31569
70	.39078	.38332	.37606	.36900	.36213	.35545	.34894	.34260	.33643	.33042

TABLE U(1)

UNITRUST SINGLE LIFE REMAINDER FACTORS BASED ON LIFE TABLE 80CNSMT [APPLICABLE FOR TRANSFERS AFTER APRIL 30, 1989, AND BEFORE MAY 1, 1999]

				ADJUSTED PAYOUT RATE						
AGE	8.2%	8.4%	8.6%	8.8%	9.0%	9.2%	9.4%	9.6%	9.8%	10.0%
71	.40620	.39872	.39144	.38435	.37744	.37071	.36415	.35776	.35153	.34547
72	.42184	.41435	.40706	.39994	.39301	.38625	.37965	.37322	.36694	.36082
73	.43771	.43023	.42293	.41581	.40886	.40207	.39545	.38899	.38267	.37651
74	.45387	.44641	.43912	.43201	.42505	.41826	.41163	.40514	.39881	.39261
75	.47039	.46296	.45570	.44861	.44167	.43488	.42824	.42175	.41541	.40920
76	.48729	.47991	.47269	.46563	.45872	.45196	.44534	.43886	.43251	.42630
77	.50452	.49722	.49006	.48305	.47619	.46946	.46287	.45642	.45009	.44389
78	.52203	.51481	.50773	.50079	.49399	.48732	.48078	.47437	.46808	.46191
79	.53966	.53254	.52556	.51870	.51198	.50538	.49891	.49255	.48632	.48019
80	.55728	.55028	.54340	.53665	.53002	.52351	.51712	.51083	.50466	.49860
81	.57471	.56784	.56109	.55445	.54792	.54151	.53521	.52901	.52292	.51692
82	.59186	.58512	.57850	.57199	.56558	.55927	.55307	.54697	.54097	.53506
83	.60863	.60204	.59556	.58918	.58289	.57671	.57062	.56462	.55872	.55290
84	.62505	.61862	.61228	.60604	.59989	.59383	.58786	.58198	.57618	.57047
85	.64118	.63491	.62873	.62263	.61663	.61070	.60486	.59911	.59343	.58783
86	.65685	.65075	.64473	.63879	.63294	.62716	.62145	.61583	.61027	.60479
87	.67187	.66594	.66008	.65430	.64859	.64296	.63739	.63190	.62647	.62112
88	.68631	.68054	.67485	.66923	.66367	.65818	.65276	.64740	.64211	.63688
89	.70042	.69483	.68930	.68384	.67845	.67311	.66784	.66262	.65747	.65237
90	.71434	.70894	.70359	.69830	.69307	.68790	.68278	.67772	.67271	.66775
91	.72789	.72266	.71750	.71239	.70733	.70232	.69736	.69246	.68760	.68280
92	.74070	.73567	.73068	.72574	.72085	.71601	.71121	.70647	.70176	.69711
93	.75266	.74780	.74298	.73821	.73348	.72880	.72417	.71957	.71502	.71051
94	.76363	.75893	.75428	.74967	.74510	.74057	.73608	.73163	.72722	.72285
95	.77356	.76901	.76451	.76005	.75562	.75123	.74688	.74257	.73829	.73405
96	.78237	.77797	.77360	.76927	.76497	.76071	.75648	.75229	.74813	.74401
97	.79039	.78612	.78187	.77766	.77348	.76934	.76523	.76115	.75710	.75308
98	.79762	.79345	.78932	.78522	.78115	.77711	.77310	.76913	.76518	.76126
99	.80429	.80023	.79620	.79220	.78823	.78429	.78038	.77649	.77264	.76881
100	.81047	.80651	.80258	.79867	.79479	.79094	.78712	.78332	.77955	.77580
101	.81636	.81249	.80865	.80483	.80104	.79727	.79352	.78981	.78611	.78244
102	.82250	.81872	.81497	.81124	.80754	.80386	.80020	.79656	.79295	.78936
103	.82900	.82532	.82167	.81804	.81442	.81083	.80726	.80371	.80018	.79667

104	.83622	.83266	.82911	.82558	.82207	.81858	.81510	.81165	.80821	.80479
105	.84517	.84174	.83833	.83494	.83156	.82819	.82485	.82151	.81820	.81489
106	.85814	.85494	.85175	.84857	.84540	.84225	.83911	.83598	.83286	.82975
107	.87704	.87420	.87136	.86853	.86571	.86290	.86009	.85729	.85450	.85171
108	.90812	.90593	.90375	.90156	.89939	.89721	.89504	.89286	.89070	.88853
109	.95900	.95800	.95700	.95600	.95500	.95400	.95300	.95200	.95100	.95000

TABLE U(1)

UNITRUST SINGLE LIFE REMAINDER FACTORS BASED ON LIFE TABLE 80CNSMT [APPLICABLE FOR TRANSFERS AFTER APRIL 30, 1989, AND BEFORE MAY 1, 1999]

	ADJUSTED PAYOUT RATE									
AGE	10.2%	10.4%	10.6%	10.8%	11.0%	11.2%	11.4%	11.6%	11.8%	12.0%
0	.01754	.01731	.01710	.01690	.01671	.01654	.01638	.01622	.01608	.01594
1	.00630	.00607	.00585	.00565	.00547	.00530	.00514	.00499	.00485	.00472
2	.00604	.00579	.00557	.00536	.00516	.00498	.00481	.00465	.00451	.00437
3	.00604	.00578	.00554	.00532	.00511	.00492	.00474	.00458	.00442	.00427
4	.00621	.00593	.00568	.00544	.00522	.00502	.00483	.00465	.00448	.00433
5	.00648	.00619	.00592	.00567	.00544	.00522	.00502	.00483	.00465	.00449
6	.00684	.00653	.00624	.00597	.00572	.00549	.00528	.00507	.00489	.00471
7	.00726	.00693	.00663	.00634	.00608	.00583	.00560	.00539	.00518	.00499
8	.00777	.00742	.00709	.00679	.00651	.00624	.00600	.00577	.00555	.00535
9	.00837	.00800	.00765	.00733	.00703	.00675	.00649	.00625	.00602	.00580
10	.00908	.00868	.00832	.00797	.00765	.00736	.00708	.00682	.00657	.00634
11	.00991	.00949	.00910	.00874	.00840	.00808	00779	.00751	.00725	.00700
12	.01083	.01039	.00997	.00959	.00923	.00890	.00858	.00829	.00801	.00775
13	.01181	.01134	.01090	.01049	.01012	.00976	.00943	.00912	.00883	.00855
14	.01275	.01226	.01180	.01137	.01097	.01060	.01025	.00992	.00961	.00932
15	.01365	.01313	.01264	.01219	.01177	.01138	.01101	.01066	.01034	.01003
16	.01449	.01394	.01343	.01295	.01251	.01209	.01171	.01134	.01100	.01068
17	.01526	.01469	.01415	.01365	.01318	.01274	.01233	.01195	.01159	.01125
18	.01600	.01539	.01482	.01430	.01380	.01334	.01291	.01251	.01213	.01177
19	.01673	.01609	.01550	.01494	.01442	.01393	.01348	.01305	.01265	.01227
20	.01747	.01679	.01616	.01557	.01502	.01451	.01403	.01358	.01316	.01276
21	.01820	.01748	.01682	.01620	.01562	.01508	.01457	.01409	.01365	.01323
22	.01895	.01819	.01749	.01683	.01622	.01565	.01511	.01461	.01414	.01369
23	.01972	.01893	.01818	.01749	.01684	.01624	.01567	.01514	.01464	.01417
24	.02058	.01974	.01895	.01822	.01753	.01689	.01629	.01572	.01519	.01469
25	.02154	.02064	.01981	.01903	.01830	.01762	.01698	.01638	.01582	.01529
26	.02262	.02167	.02079	.01996	.01919	.01847	.01779	.01715	.01655	.01599
27	.02385	.02284	.02191	.02103	.02021	.01944	.01872	.01804	.01740	.01680
28	.02521	.02415	.02316	.02222	.02135	.02053	.01977	.01904	.01836	.01772
29	.02673	.02561	.02455	.02357	.02264	.02177	.02095	.02018	.01946	.01877
30	.02842	.02723	.02611	.02506	.02407	.02315	.02227	.02146	.02068	.01996
31	.03030	.02903	.02784	.02673	.02568	.02470	.02377	.02290	.02207	.02130
32	.03235	.03101	.02976	.02857	.02746	.02641	.02543	.02450	.02362	.02279
33	.03463	.03321	.03188	.03062	.02944	.02833	.02728	.02629	.02535	.02447
34	.03711	.03561	.03419	.03286	.03161	.03043	.02931	.02826	.02726	.02632

TABLE U(1)

UNITRUST SINGLE LIFE REMAINDER FACTORS BASED ON LIFE TABLE 80CNSMT [APPLICABLE FOR TRANSFERS AFTER APRIL 30, 1989, AND BEFORE MAY 1, 1999]

	ADJUSTED PAYOUT RATE									
AGE	10.2%	10.4%	10.6%	10.8%	11.0%	11.2%	11.4%	11.6%	11.8%	12.0%
35	.03981	.03822	.03672	.03531	.03398	.03273	.03154	.03042	.02936	.02836
36	.04271	.04103	.03945	.03796	.03655	.03522	.03396	.03277	.03164	.03057
37	.04584	.04407	.04239	.04081	.03932	.03791	.03657	.03531	.03411	.03297
38	.04920	.04733	.04556	.04389	.04231	.04082	.03940	.03806	.03679	.03558
39	.05280	.05083	.04897	.04721	.04554	.04396	.04246	.04103	.03968	.03840
40	.05667	.05459	.05263	.05077	.04901	.04733	.04575	.04424	.04280	.04144
41	.06080	.05861	.05655	.05459	.05272	.05096	.04928	.04768	.04617	.04472
42	.06518	.06289	.06071	.05864	.05668	.05482	.05305	.05136	.04975	.04822
43	.06982	.06742	.06513	.06296	.06089	.05893	.05706	.05528	.05358	.05196
44	.07475	.07223	.06983	.06754	.06537	.06330	.06133	.05945	.05766	.05595
45	.07998	.07733	.07481	.07242	.07014	.06796	.06588	.06390	.06202	.06021

46	.08550	.08273	.08010	.07758	.07519	.07290	.07072	.06864	.06665	.06474
47	.09134	.08845	.08569	.08306	.08055	.07815	.07586	.07367	.07157	.06957
48	.09748	.09446	.09158	.08882	.08619	.08368	.08128	.07898	.07678	.07467
49	.10391	.10076	.09775	.09487	.09212	.08949	.08697	.08456	.08225	.08003
50	.11062	.10734	.10420	.10120	.09832	.09557	.09293	.09041	.08798	.08566
51	.11764	.11423	.11096	.10783	.10483	.10195	.09919	.09655	.09401	.09158
52	.12503	.12148	.11807	.11481	.11168	.10868	.10581	.10304	.10039	.09784
53	.13278	.12909	.12556	.12216	.11891	.11578	.11278	.10989	.10712	.10445
54	.14088	.13706	.13339	.12986	.12648	.12322	.12009	.11709	.11419	.11141
55	.14936	.14540	.14159	.13793	.13442	.13103	.12778	.12464	.12163	.11872
56	.15821	.15412	.15018	.14639	.14274	.13923	.13584	.13258	.12944	.12642
57	.16749	.16326	.15918	.15526	.15148	.14784	.14433	.14094	.13768	.13453
58	.17719	.17282	.16862	.16456	.16065	.15688	.15324	.14973	.14634	.14306
59	.18731	.18281	.17847	.17429	.17025	.16634	.16258	.15894	.15543	.15203
60	.19782	.19319	.18872	.18440	.18023	.17621	.17231	.16855	.16491	.16139
61	.20869	.20393	.19934	.19489	.19060	.18644	.18242	.17854	.17477	.17113
62	.21990	.21502	.21029	.20573	.20131	.19703	.19289	.18887	.18499	.18123
63	.23144	.22644	.22159	.21690	.21236	.20796	.20370	.19956	.19556	.19167
64	.24335	.23823	.23326	.22845	.22379	.21927	.21489	.21063	.20651	.20250
65	.25568	.25045	.24537	.24044	.23566	.23103	.22653	.22216	.21791	.21379
66	.26850	.26316	.25797	.25293	.24804	.24329	.23868	.23420	.22984	.22560
67	.28182	.27637	.27108	.26594	.26095	.25609	.25137	.24678	.24231	.23797
68	.29565	.29011	.28472	.27949	.27439	.26943	.26461	.25991	.25534	.25089
69	.30991	.30429	.29882	.29349	.28830	.28325	.27833	.27354	.26887	.26432
70	.32457	.31887	.31332	.30791	.30264	.29750	.29249	.28760	.28284	.27820

TABLE U(1)

UNITRUST SINGLE LIFE REMAINDER FACTORS BASED ON LIFE TABLE 80CNSMT [APPLICABLE FOR TRANSFERS AFTER APRIL 30, 1989, AND BEFORE MAY 1, 1999]

	ADJUSTED PAYOUT RATE									
AGE	10.2%	10.4%	10.6%	10.8%	11.0%	11.2%	11.4%	11.6%	11.8%	12.0%
71	.33955	.33378	.32816	.32267	.31732	.31210	.30701	.30204	.29719	.29246
72	.35485	.34902	.34333	.33778	.33236	.32707	.32190	.31686	.31193	.30711
73	.37049	.36461	.35887	.35326	.34778	.34242	.33719	.33207	.32707	.32218
74	.38656	.38064	.37485	.36920	.36366	.35825	.35296	.34778	.34272	.33776
75	.40312	.39717	.39136	.38566	.38009	.37464	.36930	.36407	.35895	.35394
76	.42022	.41426	.40842	.40271	.39711	.39163	.38625	.38099	.37583	.37077
77	.43782	.43187	.42603	.42031	.41470	.40920	.40380	.39851	.39332	.38823
78	.45586	.44992	.44410	.43839	.43278	.42728	.42188	.41658	.41138	.40627
79	.47418	.46828	.46248	.45679	.45120	.44572	.44033	.43503	.42983	.42472
80	.49264	.48679	.48103	.47538	.46982	.46436	.45900	.45372	.44853	.44343
81	.51103	.50524	.49954	.49394	.48843	.48301	.47768	.47243	.46727	.46219
82	.52925	.52352	.51789	.51235	.50690	.50153	.49624	.49104	.48591	.48087
83	.54718	.54154	.53598	.53051	.52512	.51981	.51459	.50943	.50436	.49936
84	.56484	.55930	.55383	.54844	.54313	.53789	.53273	.52764	.52262	.51767
85	.58231	.57686	.57149	.56619	.56096	.55581	.55072	.54571	.54076	.53588
86	.59939	.59405	.58878	.58358	.57845	.57339	.56839	.56346	.55858	.55377
87	.61583	.61061	.60545	.60035	.59532	.59035	.58545	.58060	.57581	.57108
88	.63171	.62661	.62156	.61658	.61165	.60678	.60196	.59721	.59251	.58786
89	.64733	.64235	.63742	.63255	.62774	.62298	.61827	.61361	.60900	.60444
90	.66285	.65801	.65321	.64847	.64377	.63913	.63453	.62998	.62548	.62103
91	.67804	.67334	.66868	.66407	.65950	.65498	.65050	.64607	.64169	.63735
92	.69250	.68793	.68341	.67893	.67450	.67011	.66575	.66144	.65718	.65295
93	.70604	.70162	.69723	.69288	.68858	.68431	.68008	.67589	.67174	.66762
94	.71852	.71422	.70997	.70575	.70156	.69742	.69331	.68923	.68519	.68119
95	.72984	.72567	.72154	.71744	.71337	.70934	.70534	.70137	.69744	.69354
96	.73992	.73586	.73183	.72784	.72388	.71995	.71605	.71218	.70835	.70454
97	.74910	.74514	.74122	.73733	.73346	.72963	.72582	.72205	.71830	.71458
98	.75737	.75351	.74967	.74587	.74209	.73835	.73463	.73093	.72727	.72363
99	.76501	.76123	.75748	.75376	.75007	.74640	.74276	.73914	.73555	.73198
100	.77208	.76838	.76471	.76107	.75745	.75385	.75028	.74673	.74321	.73971
101	.77879	.77517	.77157	.76800	.76444	.76092	.75741	.75392	.75046	.74702
102	.78579	.78224	.77871	.77521	.77173	.76827	.76483	.76141	.75801	.75463
103	.79318	.78971	.78626	.78283	.77942	.77604	.77266	.76931	.76598	.76267
104	.80139	.79801	.79464	.79129	.78796	.78465	.78136	.77808	.77482	.77157

105	.81161	.80834	.80508	.80184	.79861	.79540	.79220	.78902	.78585	.78270
106	.82665	.82357	.82049	.81743	.81438	.81134	.80831	.80530	.80229	.79930
107	.84893	.84616	.84340	.84064	.83789	.83515	.83241	.82969	.82696	.82425
108	.88637	.88421	.88205	.87989	.87774	.87559	.87344	.87129	.86915	.86701
109	.94900	.94800	.94700	.94600	.94500	.94400	.94300	.94200	.94100	.94000

TABLE U(1)

UNITRUST SINGLE LIFE REMAINDER FACTORS BASED ON LIFE TABLE 80CNSMT [APPLICABLE FOR TRANSFERS AFTER APRIL 30, 1989, AND BEFORE MAY 1, 1999]

	ADJUSTED PAYOUT RATE									
AGE	12.2%	12.4%	12.6%	12.8%	13.0%	13.2%	13.4%	13.6%	13.8%	14.0%
0	.01581	.01569	.01557	.01546	.01536	.01526	.01516	.01507	.01499	.01490
1	.00459	.00448	.00437	.00426	.00417	.00407	.00399	.00390	.00382	.00375
2	.00424	.00412	.00400	.00389	.00379	.00369	.00360	.00352	.00343	.00335
3	.00414	.00401	.00389	.00377	.00366	.00356	.00346	.00337	.00328	.00320
4	.00418	.00404	.00391	.00379	.00368	.00357	.00347	.00337	.00327	.00319
5	.00433	.00418	.00405	.00391	.00379	.00368	.00357	.00346	.00336	.00327
6	.00454	.00439	.00424	.00410	.00397	.00384	.00372	.00361	.00351	.00341
7	.00482	.00465	.00449	.00434	.00420	.00407	.00394	.00382	.00371	.00360
8	.00516	.00498	.00481	.00465	.00450	.00436	.00422	.00410	.00397	.00386
9	.00560	.00541	.00523	.00505	.00489	.00474	.00459	.00446	.00433	.00420
10	.00613	.00592	.00573	.00555	.00537	.00521	.00505	.00491	.00477	.00463
11	.00677	.00655	.00635	.00615	.00597	.00580	00563	.00547	.00532	.00518
12	.00751	.00728	.00706	.00685	.00666	.00647	.00629	.00613	.00597	.00581
13	.00829	.00805	.00782	.00760	.00739	.00719	.00701	.00683	.00666	.00650
14	.00905	.00879	.00854	.00831	.00809	.00789	.00769	.00750	.00732	.00715
15	.00974	.00947	.00921	.00897	.00874	.00852	.00831	.00811	.00793	.00775
16	.01037	.01009	.00982	.00956	.00932	.00909	.00887	.00866	.00846	.00827
17	.01093	.01063	.01034	.01007	.00982	.00958	.00935	.00913	.00892	.00873
18	.01143	.01112	.01082	.01053	.01027	.01001	.00977	.00954	.00933	.00912
19	.01192	.01159	.01127	.01097	.01069	.01043	.01017	.00993	.00970	.00949
20	.01239	.01204	.01170	.01139	.01109	.01081	.01055	.01029	.01005	.00983
21	.01283	.01246	.01211	.01178	.01147	.01117	.01089	.01063	.01037	.01013
22	.01328	.01288	.01251	.01216	.01183	.01152	.01122	.01094	.01067	.01042
23	.01372	.01331	.01292	.01254	.01219	.01186	.01155	.01125	.01097	.01070
24	.01422	.01378	.01336	.01297	.01260	.01225	.01191	.01160	.01130	.01101
25	.01479	.01432	.01388	.01346	.01306	.01269	.01233	.01200	.01168	.01138
26	.01545	.01495	.01448	.01404	.01362	.01322	.01284	.01248	.01214	.01182
27	.01623	.01570	.01520	.01472	.01427	.01385	.01344	.01306	.01270	.01235
28	.01712	.01655	.01601	.01551	.01503	.01457	.01414	.01373	.01334	.01298
29	.01813	.01752	.01695	.01641	.01589	.01541	.01494	.01451	.01409	.01370
30	.01927	.01862	.01801	.01743	.01688	.01635	.01586	.01539	.01495	.01452
31	.02056	.01987	.01922	.01859	.01801	.01745	.01692	.01642	.01594	.01548
32	.02201	.02127	.02057	.01990	.01927	.01868	.01811	.01757	.01706	.01657
33	.02363	.02284	.02209	.02138	.02071	.02007	.01946	.01888	.01833	.01781
34	.02543	.02458	.02378	.02302	.02230	.02162	.02096	.02034	.01975	.01919

TABLE U(1)

UNITRUST SINGLE LIFE REMAINDER FACTORS BASED ON LIFE TABLE 80CNSMT [APPLICABLE FOR TRANSFERS AFTER APRIL 30, 1989, AND BEFORE MAY 1, 1999]

	ADJUSTED PAYOUT RATE									
AGE	12.2%	12.4%	12.6%	12.8%	13.0%	13.2%	13.4%	13.6%	13.8%	14.0%
35	.02741	.02651	.02565	.02484	.02407	.02333	.02264	.02197	.02134	.02073
36	.02956	.02859	.02768	.02681	.02599	.02520	.02446	.02374	.02307	.02242
37	.03189	.03087	.02990	.02897	.02809	.02725	.02645	.02569	.02496	.02427
38	.03443	.03334	.03230	.03131	.03037	.02948	.02862	.02781	.02703	.02628
39	.03718	.03602	.03491	.03386	.03285	.03190	.03099	.03011	.02928	.02849
40	.04015	.03891	.03774	.03662	.03555	.03453	.03355	.03262	.03173	.03088
41	.04335	.04204	.04079	.03959	.03846	.03737	.03633	.03534	.03439	.03348
42	.04677	.04538	.04405	.04278	.04157	.04042	.03931	.03825	.03724	.03627
43	.05042	.04894	.04754	.04619	.04491	.04368	.04250	.04138	.04030	.03926
44	.05432	.05276	.05127	.04984	.04848	.04718	.04593	.04473	.04358	.04248
45	.05849	.05684	.05526	.05375	.05231	.05092	.04960	.04832	.04710	.04593
46	.06292	.06118	.05952	.05792	.05639	.05492	.05352	.05217	.05087	.04963

47	.06765	.06581	.06405	.06237	.06075	.05920	.05771	.05628	.05491	.05359
48	.07265	.07071	.06886	.06708	.06537	.06373	.06216	.06064	.05919	.05779
49	.07791	.07587	.07392	.07204	.07024	.06851	.06685	.06525	.06371	.06223
50	.08343	.08129	.07923	.07726	.07536	.07354	.07178	.07009	.06847	.06690
51	.08924	.08699	.08483	.08276	.08076	.07884	.07699	.07520	.07349	.07183
52	.09539	.09303	.09076	.08858	.08648	.08446	.08251	.08064	.07883	.07708
53	.10189	.09942	.09704	.09475	.09255	.09043	.08838	.08640	.08450	.08266
54	.10872	.10614	.10365	.10126	.09894	.09672	.09456	.09249	.09049	.08855
55	.11592	.11322	.11062	.10811	.10569	.10335	.10110	.09892	.09682	.09478
56	.12350	.12068	.11796	.11534	.11281	.11036	.10800	.10571	.10350	.10137
57	.13148	.12855	.12572	.12298	.12033	.11777	.11530	.11291	.11060	.10836
58	.13990	.13685	.13389	.13104	.12828	.12561	.12303	.12053	.11811	.11576
59	.14875	.14557	.14250	.13953	.13665	.13387	.13118	.12856	.12604	.12359
60	.15799	.15469	.15150	.14841	.14542	.14253	.13972	.13700	.13436	.13180
61	.16761	.16419	.16088	.15768	.15457	.15156	.14864	.14580	.14305	.14039
62	.17758	.17404	.17062	.16729	.16407	.16094	.15791	.15496	.15210	.14932
63	.18791	.18425	.18071	.17726	.17392	.17068	.16753	.16447	.16150	.15861
64	.19862	.19484	.19118	.18762	.18417	.18081	.17754	.17437	.17129	.16829
65	.20979	.20590	.20212	.19845	.19487	.19140	.18802	.18474	.18154	.17843
66	.22149	.21748	.21359	.20980	.20612	.20253	.19904	.19564	.19233	.18911
67	.23374	.22962	.22562	.22172	.21792	.21423	.21062	.20712	.20370	.20037
68	.24656	.24234	.23822	.23422	.23031	.22651	.22280	.21919	.21566	.21222
69	.25988	.25556	.25134	.24724	.24323	.23932	.23551	.23179	.22816	.22461
70	.27367	.26925	.26493	.26073	.25662	.25261	.24870	.24488	.24115	.23750

TABLE U(1)

UNITRUST SINGLE LIFE REMAINDER FACTORS BASED ON LIFE TABLE 80CNSMT [APPLICABLE FOR TRANSFERS AFTER APRIL 30, 1989, AND BEFORE MAY 1, 1999]

	ADJUSTED PAYOUT RATE									
AGE	12.2%	12.4%	12.6%	12.8%	13.0%	13.2%	13.4%	13.6%	13.8%	14.0%
71	.28784	.28333	.27892	.27462	.27042	.26631	.26230	.25839	.25456	.25082
72	.30241	.29781	.29332	.28893	.28464	.28044	.27634	.27233	.26841	.26457
73	.31740	.31272	.30815	.30368	.29930	.29502	.29084	.28674	.28273	.27880
74	.33291	.32817	.32352	.31897	.31452	.31016	.30589	.30171	.29762	.29361
75	.34903	.34422	.33951	.33490	.33038	.32595	.32161	.31735	.31318	.30909
76	.36581	.36095	.35619	.35152	.34694	.34245	.33805	.33373	.32949	.32533
77	.38324	.37835	.37354	.36883	.36420	.35966	.35520	.35083	.34654	.34232
78	.40126	.39634	.39150	.38676	.38210	.37752	.37302	.36861	.36427	.36001
79	.41970	.41476	.40992	.40515	.40047	.39587	.39135	.38690	.38253	.37823
80	.43842	.43348	.42864	.42387	.41918	.41456	.41002	.40556	.40117	.39685
81	.45719	.45228	.44744	.44267	.43799	.43337	.42883	.42436	.41996	.41562
82	.47590	.47101	.46619	.46145	.45677	.45217	.44764	.44317	.43877	.43443
83	.49443	.48957	.48478	.48007	.47542	.47084	.46632	.46187	.45748	.45315
84	.51279	.50798	.50324	.49856	.49394	.48939	.48490	.48048	.47611	.47180
85	.53106	.52630	.52161	.51698	.51241	.50790	.50345	.49906	.49473	.49045
86	.54902	.54434	.53971	.53514	.53062	.52616	.52176	.51741	.51312	.50888
87	.56640	.56178	.55722	.55271	.54826	.54386	.53951	.53521	.53097	.52677
88	.58326	.57872	.57423	.56979	.56541	.56107	.55678	.55254	.54834	.54420
89	.59994	.59548	.59107	.58671	.58240	.57813	.57391	.56973	.56560	.56152
90	.61662	.61226	.60794	.60367	.59944	.59526	.59112	.58702	.58296	.57894
91	.63305	.62879	.62457	.62040	.61627	.61217	.60812	.60411	.60013	.59619
92	.64876	.64461	.64050	.63643	.63239	.62839	.62443	.62051	.61662	.61277
93	.66355	.65950	.65550	.65153	.64759	.64369	.63983	.63600	.63220	.62843
94	.67722	.67328	.66938	.66551	.66167	.65786	.65409	.65035	.64664	.64296
95	.68967	.68583	.68203	.67825	.67451	.67079	.66711	.66345	.65983	.65623
96	.70076	.69701	.69330	.68961	.68595	.68231	.67871	.67513	.67158	.66806
97	.71089	.70722	.70359	.69998	.69640	.69284	.68931	.68581	.68234	.67888
98	.72001	.71642	.71286	.70933	.70582	.70233	.69887	.69544	.69203	.68864
99	.72844	.72492	.72143	.71796	.71452	.71110	.70770	.70433	.70098	.69765
100	.73623	.73278	.72935	.72594	.72256	.71920	.71586	.71254	.70924	.70597
101	.74361	.74021	.73684	.73349	.73016	.72685	.72356	.72029	.71704	.71382
102	.75128	.74794	.74463	.74133	.73806	.73480	.73157	.72835	.72515	.72198
103	.75938	.75610	.75284	.74961	.74639	.74319	.74000	.73684	.73369	.73056
104	.76835	.76514	.76194	.75877	.75561	.75246	.74934	.74623	.74313	.74005
105	.77956	.77643	.77332	.77023	.76714	.76408	.76102	.75798	.75496	.75195

106	.79632	.79334	.79038	.78743	.78449	.78157	.77865	.77575	.77285	.76997
107	.82154	.81884	.81615	.81346	.81079	.80811	.80545	.80279	.80014	.79750
108	.86487	.86274	.86061	.85848	.85635	.85423	.85210	.84998	.84787	.84575
109	.93900	.93800	.93700	.93600	.93500	.93400	.93300	.93200	.93100	.93000

T.D. 8540, 6/9/94, amend T.D. 8819, 4/29/99, T.D. 8886, 6/9/2000.

§ 1.665(a)-0A Excess distributions by trusts; scope of subpart D.

Caution: The Treasury has not yet amended Reg § 1.665(a)-0A to reflect changes made by P.L. 105-34, P.L. 99-514, P.L. 95-600, P.L. 94-455.

(a) In general. *(1)* Subpart D (section 665 and following), part I, subchapter J, chapter 1 of the Code as amended by the Tax Reform Act of 1969, is designed to tax the beneficiary of a trust that accumulates, rather than distributes, all or part of its income currently (i.e., an accumulation trust), in most cases, as if the income had been currently distributed to the beneficiary instead of accumulated by the trusts. Accordingly, subpart D provides special rules for the treatment of amounts paid, credited, or required to be distributed by a complex trust (one that is subject to subpart C (section 661 and following) of such part I) in any year in excess of "distributable net income" (as defined in section 643 (a)) for that year. Such an excess distribution is an "accumulation distribution" (as defined in section 665(b)). The special rules of subpart D are generally inapplicable to amounts paid, credited, or required to be distributed by a trust in a taxable year in which it qualifies as a simple trust (one this is subject to subpart B (section 651 and following) of such part I). However, see § 1.665(e)-1A(b) for rules relating to the treatment of a simple trust as a complex trust.

(2) An accumulation distribution is deemed to consist of, first, "undistributed net income" (as defined in section 665(a)) of the trust from preceding taxable years, and, after all the undistributed net income for all preceding taxable years has been deemed distributed, "undistributed capital gain" (as defined in section 665(f)) of the trust for all preceding taxable years commencing with the first year such amounts were accumulated. An accumulation distribution of undistributed capital gain is a "capital gain distribution" (as defined in section 665(g)). To the extent an accumulation distribution exceeds the "undistributed net income" and "undistributed capital gain" so determined, it is deemed to consist of corpus.

(3) The accumulation distribution is "thrown back" to the earliest "preceding taxable year" of the trust, which, in the case of distributions made for a taxable year beginning after December 31, 1973, from a trust (other than a foreign trust created by a U.S. person), is any taxable year beginning after December 31, 1968. Special transitional rules apply for distributions made in taxable years beginning before January 1, 1974. In the case of a foreign trust created by a U.S. person, a "preceding taxable year" is any year of the trust to which the Code applies.

(4) A distribution of undistributed net income (included in an accumulation distribution) and a capital gain distribution will be included in the income of the beneficiary in the year they are actually paid, credited, or required to be distributed to him. The tax on the distribution will be approximately the amount of tax the beneficiary would have paid with respect to the distribution had the income and capital gain been distributed to the beneficiary in the year earned by the trust. An additional amount equal to the "taxes imposed on the trust" for the preceding year is also deemed distributed. To prevent double taxation, however, the beneficiary receives a credit for such taxes.

(b) Effective dates. All regulations sections under subpart D (sections 665 through 669) which have an "A" suffix (such as §§ 1.665(a)A and 1.666(b)-1A) are applicable to taxable years beginning on or after January 1, 1969, and all references therein to sections 665 through 669 are references to such sections as amended by the Tax Reform Act of 1969. Sections without the "A" suffix (such as §§ 1.665(a) and 1.666(b)-1) are applicable only to taxable years beginning before January 1, 1969, and all references therein to sections 665 through 669 are references to such sections before amendment by the Tax Reform Act of 1969.

(c) Examples. Where examples contained in the regulations under subpart D refer to tax rates for years after 1968, such tax rates are not necessarily the actual rates for such years, but are only used for example purposes.

(d) Applicability to estates. Subpart D does not apply to any estate.

T.D. 7204, 8/24/72.

§ 1.665(a)-1A Undistributed net income.

Caution: The Treasury has not yet amended Reg § 1.665(a)-1A to reflect changes made by P.L. 105-34, P.L. 99-514, P.L. 95-600, P.L. 94-455.

(a) Domestic trusts. The term "undistributed net income", in the case of a trust (other than a foreign trust created by a U.S. person) means, for any taxable year beginning after December 31, 1968, the distributable net income of the trust for that year (as determined under section 643(a)), less

(1) The amount of income required to be distributed currently and any other amounts properly paid or credited or required to be distributed to beneficiaries in the taxable year as specified in section 661(a), and

(2) The amount of taxes imposed on the trust attributable to such distributable net income, as defined in § 1.665(d)-1A. The application of the rule in this paragraph to a taxable year of a trust in which income is accumulated may be illustrated by the following example.

Example. Under the terms of the trust, $10,000 of income is required to be distributed currently to A and the trustee has discretion to make additional distributions to A. During the taxable year 1971 the trust had distributable net income of $30,100 derived from royalties and the trustee made distributions of $20,000 to A. The taxable income of the trust is $10,000 on which a tax of $2,190 is paid. The undistributed net income of the trust for the taxable year 1971 is $7,910, computed as follows:

Distributable net income		$30,100
Less:		
Income currently distributable to A . . .	$10,000	
Other amounts distributable to A	10,000	
Taxes imposed on the trust attributable to the undistributed net income (see § 1.665(d)-1(A)	2,190	

Total	22,190
Undistributed net income	7,910

(b) Foreign trusts. The undistributed net income of a foreign trust created by a U.S. person for any taxable year is the distributable net income of such trust (see § 1.643(a)-6 and the examples set forth in paragraph (b) thereof), less:

(1) The amount of income required to be distributed currently and any other amounts properly paid or credited or required to be distributed to beneficiaries in the taxable year as specified in section 661(a), and

(2) The amount of taxes imposed on such trust by chapter 1 of the Internal Revenue Code, which are attributable to items of income which are required to be included in such distributable net income.

For purposes of subparagraph (2) of this paragraph, the amount of taxes imposed on the trust for any taxable year by chapter 1 of the Internal Revenue Code is the amount of taxes imposed pursuant to section 871 (relating to tax on non-resident alien individuals) which is properly allocable to the undistributed portion of the distributable net income. See § 1.665(d)-1A. The amount of taxes imposed pursuant to section 871 is the difference between the total tax imposed pursuant to that section on the foreign trust created by a U.S. person for the year and the amount which would have been imposed on such trust had all the distributable net income, as determined under section 643(a), been distributed. The application of the rule is this paragraph may be illustrated by the following example:

Example (1). A trust was created in 1952 under the laws of Country X by the transfer to a trustee in Country X of property by a U.S. person. The entire trust constitutes a foreign trust created by a U.S. person. The governing instrument of the trust provides that $7,000 of income is required to be distributed currently to a U.S. beneficiary and gives the trustee discretion to make additional distributions to the beneficiary. During the taxable year 1973 the trust had income of $10,000 from dividends of a U.S. corporation (on which Federal income taxes of $3,000 were imposed pursuant to section 871 and withheld under section 1441, resulting in the receipt by the trust of cash in the amount of $7,000), $20,000 in capital gains from the sale of stock of a Country Y corporation and $30,000 from dividends of a Country X corporation, none of the gross income of which was derived from sources within the United States. No income taxes were required to be paid to Country X or Country Y in 1973. The trustee did not file a U.S. income tax return for the taxable year 1973. The distributable net income of the trust before distributions to the beneficiary for 1973 is $60,000 ($57,000 of which is cash). During 1973 the trustee made distributions to the U.S. beneficiary equaling one-half of the trust's distributable net income. Thus, the U.S. beneficiary is treated as having had distributed to him $5,000 (composed of $3,500 as a cash distribution and $1,500 as the tax imposed pursuant to section 871 and withheld under section 1441), representing one-half of the income from U.S. sources; $10,000 in cash, representing one-half of the capital gains from the sale of stock of the Country Y corporation; and $15,000 in cash, representing one-half of the income from Country X sources for a total of $30,000. The undistributed net income of the trust at the close of taxable year 1973 is $28,500 computed as follows:

Distributable net income		$60,000
Less:		
(1) Amounts distributed to the beneficiary:		
Income currently distributed to the beneficiary	$ 7,000	
Other amounts distributed to the beneficiary	21,500	
Taxes under sec. 871 deemed distributed to the beneficiary	1,500	
Total amounts distributed to the beneficiary	30,000	
(2) Amount of taxes imposed on the trust under chapter 1 of the Code attributable to the undistributed net income (See § 1.665(d)-1A) $3,000 less $1,500)	1,500	
Total		31,500
Undistributed net income		28,500

Example (2). The facts are the same as in example (1) except that property has been transferred to the trust by a person other than a U.S. person, and during 1973 the foreign trust created by a U.S. person was 60 percent of the entire foreign trust. The trustee paid no income taxes to Country X or Country Y in 1973.

(1) The undistributed net income of the portion of the entire trust which is a foreign trust created by a U.S. person for 1973 is $17,100, computed as follows:

Distributable net income (60% of each item of gross income of entire trust)		
60% of $10,000 U.S. dividends		$ 6,000
60% of $20,000 Country X capital gains		12,000
60% of $30,000 Country X dividends		18,000
Total		36,000
Less:		
(i) Amounts distributed to the beneficiary—		
Income currently distributed to the beneficiary (60% of $7,000)	$ 4,200	
Other amounts distributed to the beneficiary (60% of $21,500)	12,900	
Taxes under sec. 871 deemed distributed to the beneficiary (60% of $1,500)	900	
Total amounts distributed to the beneficiary	18,000	
(ii) Amount of taxes imposed on the trust under chapter 1 of the Code attributable to the undistributed net income (see § 1.665(d)-1A) (60% of $1,500)	900	
Total		18,900
Undistributed net income		17,100

(2) The undistributed net income of the portion of the entire trust which is not a foreign trust created by a U.S. person for 1973 is $11,400, computed as follows:

Distributable net income (40% of each item of gross income of entire trust)		
40% of $10,000 U.S. dividends		$ 4,000
40% of $20,000 Country X capital gains		8,000
40% of $30,000 Country X dividends		12,000
Total		24,000
Less:		
(i) Amounts distributed to the beneficiary—		

Income currently distributed to the beneficiary (40% of $7,000)	$ 2,800
Other amounts distributed to the beneficiary (40% of $21,500)	8,600
Taxes under sec. 871 deemed distributed to the beneficiary (40% of $1,500)	600
Total amounts distributed to the beneficiary	12,000
(ii) Amount of taxes imposed on the trust under chapter 1 of the Code attributable to the undistributed net income (see § 1.665(d)-1A) (40% of $1,500)	600
Total	12,600
Undistributed net income	11,400

(c) Effect of prior distributions. The undistributed net income for any year to which an accumulation distribution for a later year may be thrown back will be reduced by accumulation distributions in intervening years that are required to be thrown back to such year. For example, if a trust has undistributed net income for 1975, and an accumulation distribution is made in 1980, there must be taken into account the effect on undistributed net income for 1975 of any accumulation distribution made in 1976, 1977, 1978, or 1979. However, undistributed net income for any year will not be reduced by any distributions in any intervening years that are excluded under section 663(a)(1), relating to gifts, bequests, etc. See paragraph (d) of § 1.666(a)-1A for an illustration of the reduction of undistributed net income for any year by a subsequent accumulation distribution.

(d) Distributions made in taxable years beginning before January 1, 1974. For special rules relating to accumulation distributions of undistributed net income made in taxable years of the trust beginning before January 1, 1974, see § 1.665(b)-2A.

T.D. 7204, 8/24/72.

§ 1.665(b)-1A Accumulation distributions.

Caution: The Treasury has not yet amended Reg § 1.665(b)-1A to reflect changes made by P.L. 99-514, P.L. 95-600, P.L. 94-455.

(a) In general. *(1)* For any taxable year of a trust the term "accumulation distribution" means an amount by which the amounts properly paid, credited, or required to be distributed within the meaning of section 661(a)(2) (i.e., all amounts properly paid, credited, or required to be distributed to the beneficiary other than income required to be distributed currently within the meaning of section 661(a)(1)) for that year exceed the distributable net income (determined under section 643(a)) of the trust, reduced (but not below zero) by the amount of income required to be distributed currently. To the extent provided in section 663(b) and the regulations thereunder, distributions made within the first 65 days following a taxable year may be treated as having been distributed on the last day of such taxable year.

(2) An accumulation distribution also includes, for a taxable year of the trust, any amount to which section 661(a)(2) and the preceding paragraph are inapplicable and which is paid, credited, or required to be distributed during the taxable year of the trust by reason of the exercise of a power to appoint, distribute, consume, or withdraw corpus of the trust or income of the trust accumulated in a preceding taxable year. No accumulation distribution is deemed to be made solely because the grantor or any other person is treated as owner of a portion of the trust by reason of an unexercised power to appoint, distribute, consume, or withdraw corpus or accumulated income of the trust. Nor will an accumulation distribution be deemed to have been made by reason of the exercise of a power that may affect only taxable income previously attributed to the holders of such power under subpart E (section 671 and following). See example 4 of paragraph (d) of this section for an example of an accumulation distribution occurring as a result of the exercise of a power of withdrawal.

(3) Although amounts properly paid or credited under section 661(a) do not exceed the income of the trust during the taxable year, an accumulation distribution may result if the amounts properly paid or credited under section 661(a)(2) exceed distributable net income reduced (but not below zero) by the amount required to be distributed currently under section 661(a)(1). This may occur, for example, when expenses, interest, taxes, or other items allocable to corpus are taken into account in determining taxable income and hence causing distributable net income to be less than the trust's income.

(b) Payments that are accumulation distributions. The following are some instances in which an accumulation distribution may arise:

(1) One trust to another. A distribution from one trust to another trust is generally an accumulation distribution. See § 1.643(c)-1. This general rule will apply regardless of whether the distribution is to an existing trust or to a newly created trust and regardless of whether the trust to which the distribution is made was created by the same person who created the trust from which the distribution is made or a different person. However, a distribution made from one trust to a second trust will be deemed an accumulation distribution by the first trust to an ultimate beneficiary of the second trust if the primary purpose of the distribution to the second trust is to avoid the capital gain distribution provisions (see section 669 and the regulations thereunder). An amount passing from one separate share of a trust to another separate share of the same trust is not an accumulation distribution. See § 1.665(g)-2A. For rules relating to the computation of the beneficiary's tax under section 668 by reason of an accumulation distribution from the second trust, see paragraphs (b)(1) and (c)(1)(i) of § 1.668(b)-1A and paragraphs (b)(1) and (c)(1)(i) of § 1.669(b)-1A.

(2) Income accumulation during minority. A distribution of income accumulated during the minority of the beneficiary is generally an accumulation distribution. For example, if a trust accumulates income until the beneficiary's 21st birthday, and then distributes the income to the beneficiary, such a distribution is an accumulation distribution. However, see § 1.665(b)-2A for rules governing income accumulated in taxable years beginning before January 1, 1969.

(3) Amounts paid for support. To the extent that amounts forming all or part of an accumulation distribution are applied or distributed for the support of a dependent under the circumstances specified in section 677(b) or section 678(c) or are used to discharge or satisfy any person's legal obligation as that term is used in § 1.662(a)-4, such amounts will be considered as having been distributed directly to the person whose obligation is being satisfied.

(c) Payments that are not accumulation distributions. *(1) Gifts, bequests, etc., described in section 663(a)(1).* A gift or bequest of a specific sum of money or of specific property described in section 663(a)(1) is not an accumulation distribution.

(2) Charitable payments. Any amount paid, permanently set aside, or used for the purposes specified in section 642(c) is not an accumulation distribution, even though no charitable deduction is allowed under such section with respect to such payment.

(3) Income required to be distributed currently. No accumulation distribution will arise by reason of a payment of income required to be distributed currently even though such income exceeds the distributable net income of the trust because the payment is an amount specified in section 661(a)(1).

(d) Examples. The provisions of this section may be illustrated by the following examples:

Example (1). A trustee properly makes a distribution to a beneficiary of $20,000 during the taxable year 1976, of which $10,000 is income required to be distributed currently to the beneficiary. The distributable net income of the trust is $15,000. There is an accumulation distribution of $5,000 computed as follows.

Total distribution		$20,000
Less: Income required to be distributed currently (section 661(a)(1))		10,000
Other amounts distributed (section 661(a)(2))		10,000
Distributable net income	$15,000	
Less: Income required to be distributed currently	10,000	
Balance of distributable net income		5,000
Accumulation distribution		5,000

Example (2). Under the terms of the trust instrument, an annuity of $15,000 is required to be paid to A out of income each year and the trustee may in his discretion make distributions out of income or corpus to B. During the taxable year the trust had income of $18,000, as defined in section 643(b), and expenses allocable to corpus of $5,000. Distributable net income amounted to $13,000. The trustee distributed $15,000 of income to A and, in the exercise of his discretion, paid $5,000 to B. There is an accumulation distribution of $5,000 computed as follows:

Total distribution		$20,000
Less: Income required to be distributed currently (section 661(a)(1))		15,000
Other amounts distributed (section 661(a)(2))		5,000
Distributable net income	$13,000	
Less: Income required to be distributed currently to A	15,000	
Balance of distributable net income		0
Accumulation distribution to B		5,000

Example (3). Under the terms of a trust instrument, the trustee may either accumulate the trust income or make distributions to A and B. The trustee may also invade corpus for the benefit of A and B. During the taxable year, the trust had income as defined in section 643(b) of $22,000 and expenses of $5,000 allocable to corpus. Distributable net income amounts to $17,000. The trustee distributed $10,000 each to A and B during the taxable year. There is an accumulation distribution of $3,000 computed as follows:

Total distribution		$20,000
Less: Income required to be distributed currently		0
Other amounts distributed (section 661(a)(2))		20,000
Distributable net income	$17,000	
Less: Income required to be distributed currently	0	
Balance of distributable net income		17,000
Accumulation distribution		3,000

Example (4). A dies in 1974 and bequeaths one-half the residue of his estate in trust. His widow, W, is given a power, exercisable solely by her, to require the trustee to pay her each year of the trust $5,000 from corpus. W's right to exercise such power was exercisable at any time during the year but was not cumulative, so that, upon her failure to exercise it before the end of any taxable year of the trust, her right as to that year lapsed. The trust's taxable year is the calendar year. During the calendar years 1975 and 1976, W did not exercise her right and it lapsed as to those years. In the calendar years 1977 and 1978, in which years the trust had not distributable net income, she exercised her right and withdrew $4,000 in 1977 and $5,000 in 1978. No accumulation distribution was made by the trust in the calendar years 1975 and 1976. An accumulation distribution of $4,000 was made in 1977 and an accumulation distribution of $5,000 was made in 1978. The accumulation distribution for the years 1977 and 1978 is not reduced by any amount of income of the trust attributable to her under section 678 by reason of her power of withdrawal.

T.D. 7204, 8/24/72.

§ 1.665(b)-2A Special rules for accumulation distributions made in taxable years beginning before January 1, 1974.

Caution: The Treasury has not yet amended Reg § 1.665(b)-2A to reflect changes made by P.L. 99-514, P.L. 95-600, P.L. 94-455.

(a) General rule. Section 331(d)(2)(A) of the Tax Reform Act of 1969 excludes certain accumulated income from the tax imposed by section 668(a)(2) by providing certain exceptions from the definition of an "accumulation distribution." Any amount paid, credited, or required to be distributed by a trust (other than a foreign trust created by a U.S. person) during a taxable year of the trust beginning after December 31, 1968, and before January 1, 1974, shall not be subject to the tax imposed by section 668(a)(2) to the extent of the portion of such amount that (1) would be allocated under section 666(a) to a preceding taxable year of the trust beginning before January 1, 1969, and (2) would not have been deemed an accumulation distribution because of the provisions of paragraphs (1), (2), (3), or (4) of section 665(b) as in effect on December 31, 1968, had the trust distributed such amounts on the last day of its last taxable year beginning before January 1, 1969. However, the $2,000 de minimis exception formerly in section 665(b) does not apply in the case of any distribution made in a taxable year of a trust beginning after December 31, 1968. Amounts to which this exclusion applies shall reduce the undistributed net income of the trust for the preceding taxable year or years to which such amounts would be allocated under section 666(a). However, since section 668(a)(2) does not apply to such amounts, no amount of taxes imposed on the trust allocable to such undistributed net income is deemed distributed under section 666(b) and (c).

(b) Application of general rule. The rule expressed in paragraph (a) of this section is applied to the exceptions formerly in section 665(b) as follows:

(1) Distributions from amounts accumulated while beneficiary is under 21. (i) Paragraph (1) of section 665(b) as in

effect on December 31, 1968, provided that amounts paid, credited, or required to be distributed to a beneficiary as income accumulated before the birth of such beneficiary or before such beneficiary attains the age of 21 were not to be considered to be accumulation distributions. If an accumulation distribution is made in a taxable year of the trust beginning after December 31, 1968, and before January 1, 1974, and under section 666(a) such accumulation distribution would be allocated to a preceding taxable year beginning before January 1, 1969, no tax shall be imposed under section 668(a)(2) to the extent the income earned by the trust for such preceding taxable year would be deemed under § 1.665(b)-2(b)(1) to have been accumulated before the beneficiary's birth or before his 21st birthday. The provisions of this subparagraph may be illustrated by the following example:

Example. A trust on the calendar year basis was established on January 1, 1965, to accumulate the income during the minority of B, and to pay the accumulated income over to B upon his attaining the age of 21. B's 21st birthday is January 1, 1973. On January 2, 1973, the trustee pays over to B all the accumulated income of the trust. The distribution is an accumulation distribution that may be allocated under section 666(a) to 1968, 1969, 1970, 1971, and 1972 (the 5 preceding taxable years as defined in § 1.665(e)-1A). To the extent the distribution is allocated to 1968, no tax is imposed under section 668(a)(2).

(ii) As indicated in paragraph (a) of this section, a distribution of an amount excepted from the tax otherwise imposed under section 668(a)(2) will reduce undistributed net income for the purpose of determining the effect of a future distribution. Thus, under the facts of the example in subdivision (i) of this subparagraph, the undistributed net income for the trust's taxable year 1968 would be reduced by the amount of the distribution allocated to that year under section 666(a).

(2) Emergency distributions. Paragraph (2) of section 665(b) as in effect on December 31, 1968, provided an exclusion from the definition of an accumulation distribution for amounts properly paid or credited to a beneficiary to meet his emergency needs. Therefore, if an accumulation distribution is made from a trust in a taxable year beginning before January 1, 1974, and under section 666(a) such accumulation distribution would be allocated to a preceding taxable year of the trust beginning before January 1, 1969, no tax shall be imposed under section 668(a)(2) if such distribution would have been considered an emergency distribution under § 1.665(b)-2(b)(2) had it been made in a taxable year of the trust beginning before January 1, 1969. For example, assume a trust on a calendar year basis in 1972 makes an accumulation distribution which under § 1.665(b)-2(b)(2) would be considered an emergency distribution and under section 666(a) the distribution would be allocated to the years 1967, 1968, and 1969. To the extent such amount is allocated to 1967 and 1968, no tax would be imposed under section 668(a)(2).

(3) Certain distributions at specified ages. Paragraph (3) of section 665(b) as in effect on December 31, 1968, provided an exclusion (in the case of certain trusts created before January 1, 1954) from the definition of an accumulation distribution for amounts properly paid or credited to a beneficiary upon his attaining a specified age or ages, subject to certain restrictions (see § 1.665(b)-2(b)(3)). Therefore, a distribution from a trust in a taxable year beginning after December 31, 1968, will not be subject to the tax imposed under section 668(a)(2) to the extent such distribution would be allocated to a preceding taxable year of the trust beginning before January 1, 1969, if such distribution would have qualified under the provisions of § 1.665(b)-2(b)(3) had it been made in a taxable year of the trust to which such section was applicable.

(4) Certain final distributions. Paragraph (4) of section 665(b) as in effect on December 31, 1968, provided an exclusion from the definition of an accumulation distribution for amounts properly paid or credited to a beneficiary as a final distribution of the trust if such final distribution was made more than 9 years after the date of the last transfer to such trust. Therefore, amounts properly paid or credited to a beneficiary as a final distribution of a trust in a taxable year of a trust beginning after December 31, 1968, and before January 1, 1974, will not be subject to the tax imposed under section 668(a)(2) to the extent such distribution would be allocated to a preceding taxable year of the trust beginning before January 1, 1969, if such final distribution was made more than 9 years after the date of the last transfer to such trust. The provisions of this subparagraph may be illustrated by the following example:

Example. A trust on a calendar-year basis was established on January 1, 1958, and no additional transfers were made to it. On January 1, 1973, the trustee terminates the trust and on the same day he makes a final distribution to the beneficiary, B. The distribution is an accumulation distribution that may be allocated under section 666(a) to 1968, 1969, 1970, 1971, and 1972 (the 5 preceding taxable years as defined in § 1.665(e)-1A). Because more than 9 years elapsed between the date of the last transfer to the trust and the date of final distribution, the distribution is not taxed under section 668(a)(2) to the extent it would be allocated to 1968 under section 666(a).

T.D. 7204, 8/24/72.

§ 1.665(c)-1A Special rule applicable to distributions by certain foreign trusts.

Caution: The Treasury has not yet amended Reg § 1.665(c)-1A to reflect changes made by P.L. 99-514, P.L. 95-600, P.L. 94-455.

(a) In general. Except as provided in paragraph (b) of this section, for purposes of section 665 any amount paid to a U.S. person which is from a payor who is not a U.S. person and which is derived directly or indirectly from a foreign trust created by a U.S. person shall be deemed in the year of payment to the U.S. person to have been directly paid to the U.S. person by the trust. For example, if a nonresident alien receives a distribution from a foreign trust created by a U.S. person and then pays the amount of the distribution over to a U.S. person, the payment of such amount to the U.S. person represents an accumulation distribution to the U.S. person from the trust to the extent that the amount received would have been an accumulation distribution had the trust paid the amount directly to the U.S. person in the year in which the payment was received by the U.S. person. This section also applies in a case where a nonresident alien receives indirectly an accumulation distribution from a foreign trust created by a U.S. person and then pays it over to a U.S. person. An example of such a transaction is one where the foreign trust created by a U.S. person makes the distribution to an intervening foreign trust created by either a U.S. person or a person other than a U.S. person and the intervening trust distributes the amount received to a nonresident alien who in turn pays it over to a U.S. person. Under these circumstances, it is deemed that the payment received by the

U.S. person was received directly from a foreign trust created by a U.S. person.

(b) Limitation. In the case of a distribution to a beneficiary who is a U.S. person, paragraph (a) of this section does not apply if the distribution is received by such beneficiary under circumstances indicating lack of intent on the part of the parties to circumvent the purposes for which section 7 of the Revenue Act of 1962 (76 Stat. 985) was enacted.

T.D. 7204, 8/24/72.

§ 1.665(d)-1A Taxes imposed on the trust.

Caution: The Treasury has not yet amended Reg § 1.665(d)-1A to reflect changes made by P.L. 99-514, P.L. 95-600, P.L. 94-455.

(a) In general. *(1)* For purposes of subpart D, the term "taxes imposed on the trust" means the amount of Federal income taxes properly imposed for any taxable year on the trust that are attributable to the undistributed portions of distributable net income and gains in excess of losses from the sales or exchanges of capital assets. Except as provided in paragraph (c)(2) of this section, the minimum tax for tax preferences imposed by section 56 is not a tax attributable to the undistributed portions of distributable net income and gains in excess of losses from the sales or exchanges of capital assets. See section 56 and the regulations thereunder.

(2) In the case of a trust that has received an accumulation distribution from another trust, the term "taxes imposed on the trust" also includes the amount of taxes deemed distributed under §§ 1.666(b)-1A, 1.666(c)-1A, 1.669(d)-1A, and 1.669(e)-1A (whichever are applicable) as a result of such accumulation distribution, to the extent that they were taken into account under paragraphs (b)(2) or (c)(1)(vi) of § 1.668(b)-1A and (b)(2) or (c)(1)(vi) of § 1.669(b)-1A in computing the partial tax on such accumulation distribution. For example, assume that trust A, a calendar year trust, makes an accumulation distribution in 1975 to trust B, also on the calendar year basis, in connection with which $500 of taxes are deemed under § 1.666(b)-1A to be distributed to trust B. The partial tax on the accumulation distribution is computed under paragraph (b) of § 1.668(b)-1A (the exact method) to be $600 and all of the $500 is used under paragraph (b)(2) of § 1.668(b)-1A to reduce the partial tax to $100. The taxes imposed on trust B for 1975 will, in addition to the $100 partial tax, also include the $500 used to reduce the partial tax.

(b) Taxes imposed on the trust attributable to undistributed net income. *(1)* For the purpose of subpart D, the term "taxes imposed on the trust attributable to the undistributed net income" means the amount of Federal income taxes for the taxable year properly allocable to the undistributed portion of the distributable net income for such taxable year. This amount is (i) an amount that bears the same relationship to the total taxes of the trust for the year (other than the minimum tax for tax preferences imposed by section 56), computed after the allowance of credits under section 642(a), as (a) the taxable income of the trust, other than the capital gains not included in distributable net income less their share of section 1202 deduction, bears to (b) the total taxable income of the trust for such year or, (ii) if the alternative tax computation under section 1201(b) is used and there are no net short-term gains, an amount equal to such total taxes less the amount of the alternative tax imposed on the trust and attributable to the capital gain. Thus, for the purposes of subpart D, in determining the amount of taxes imposed on the trust attributable to the undistributed net income, that portion of the taxes paid by the trust attributable to capital gain allocable to corpus is excluded. The rule stated in this subparagraph may be illustrated by the following example, which assumes that the alternative tax computation is not used:

Example. (1) Under the terms of a trust, which reports on the calendar year basis, the income may be accumulated or distributed to A in the discretion of the trustee and capital gains are allocable to corpus. During the taxable year 1974, the trust had income of $20,000 from royalties, long-term capital gains of $10,000, and expenses of $2,000. The trustee in his discretion made a distribution of $10,000 to A. The taxes imposed on the trust for such year attributable to the undistributed net income are $2,319, determined as shown below.

(2) The distributable net income of the trust computed under section 643(a) is $18,000 (royalties of $20,000 less expenses of $2,000). The total taxes paid by the trust are $3,787, computed as follows:

Royalties		$20,000
Capital gain allocable to corpus		10,000
Gross income		30,000
Deductions:		
Expenses	$ 2,000	
Distributions to A	10,000	
Capital gain deduction	5,000	
Personal exemption	100	
		17,100
Taxable income		12,900
Total income taxes		3,787

(3) Taxable income other than capital gains less the section 1202 deduction is $7,900 ($12,900 – ($10,000 – $5,000)). Therefore, the amount of taxes imposed on the trust attributable to the undistributed net income is $2,319, computed as follows:

$3,787 (total taxes) × $7,900 (taxable income other than capital gains not included in d.n.i. less the 1202 deduction) divided by $12,900 (taxable income)	$2,319

(2) If in any taxable year an accumulation distribution of undistributed net income is made by the trust which results in a throwback to a prior year, the taxes of the year imposed on the trust attributable to any remaining undistributed net income of such prior year are the taxes prescribed in subparagraph (1) of this paragraph reduced by the taxes of the prior year deemed distributed under section 666(b) or (c). The provisions of this subparagraph may be illustrated by the following example:

Example. Assume the same facts as in the example in subparagraph (1) of this paragraph. In 1975 the trust makes an accumulation distribution, of which an amount of undistributed net income is deemed distributed in 1974. Taxes imposed on the trust (in the amount of $1,000) attributable to the undistributed net income are therefore deemed distributed in such year. Consequently, the taxes imposed on the trust subsequent to the 1975 distribution attributable to the remaining undistributed net income are $1,319 ($2,319 less $1,000).

(c) Taxes imposed on the trust attributable to undistributed capital gain. *(1) Regular tax.* For the purpose of subpart D the term "taxes imposed on the trust attributable to undistributed capital gain" means the amount of Federal income taxes for the taxable year properly attributable to that portion of the excess of capital gains over capital losses of the trust that is allocable to corpus for such taxable year. Such amount is the total of—

(i) The amount computed under subparagraph (2) of this paragraph (the minimum tax), plus

(ii) The amount that bears the same relationship to the total taxes of the trust for the year (other than the minimum tax), computed after the allowance of credits under section 642(a), as (a) the excess of capital gains over capital losses for such year that are not included in distributable net income, computed after its share of the deduction under section 1202 (relating to the deduction for capital gains) has been taken into account, bears to the greater of (b) the total taxable income of the trust for such year, or (c) the amount of capital gains computed under (a) of this subdivision.

However, if the alternative tax computation under section 1201(b) is used and there are no net short-term gains, the amount is the amount of the alternative tax imposed on the trust and attributable to the capital gain. The application of this subparagraph may be illustrated by the following example, which assumes that the alternative tax computation is not used:

Example. Assume the same facts as in the example in paragraph (b)(1). The capital gains not included in d.n.i. are $10,000, and the deduction under section 1202 is $5,000. The amount of taxes imposed on the trust attributable to undistributed capital gain is $1,468, computed as follows:

$3,787 (total taxes) × $5,000 (capital gains not included in d.n.i. less section 1202 deductions) divided by $12,900 (taxable income) $1,468

(2) Minimum tax. The term "taxes imposed on the trust attributable to the undistributed capital gain" also includes the minimum tax for tax preferences imposed on the trust by section 56 with respect to the undistributed capital gain. The amount of such minimum tax so included bears the same relation to the total amount of the minimum tax imposed on the trust by section 56 for the taxable year as one-half of the net capital gain (net section 1201 gain for taxable years beginning before January 1, 1977) (as defined in section 1222(11)) from such taxable year bears to the sum of the items of tax preference of the trust for such taxable year which are apportioned to the trust in accordance with § 1.58-3(a)(1).

(3) Reduction for prior distribution. If in any taxable year a capital gain distribution is made by the trust which results in a throwback to a prior year, the taxes of the prior year imposed on the trust attributable to any remaining undistributed capital gain of the prior year are the taxes prescribed in subparagraph (1) of this paragraph reduced by the taxes of the prior year deemed distributed under section 669(d) or (e). The provisions of this subparagraph may be illustrated by the following example:

Example. Assume the same facts as in the example in subparagraph (1) of this paragraph. In 1976, the trust makes a capital gain distribution, of which an amount of undistributed capital gain is deemed distributed in 1974. Taxes imposed on the trust (in the amount of $500) attributable to the undistributed capital gain are therefore deemed distributed in such year. Consequently, the taxes imposed on the trust attributable to the remaining undistributed capital gain are $968 ($1,468 less $500).

T.D. 7204, 8/24/72, amend T.D. 7728, 10/31/80.

§ 1.665(e)-1A Preceding taxable year.

Caution: The Treasury has not yet amended Reg § 1.665(e)-1A to reflect changes made by P.L. 101-508, P.L. 99-514, P.L. 95-600, P.L. 94-455.

(a) Definition. *(1) Domestic trusts.* (i) In general. For purposes of subpart D, in the case of a trust other than a foreign trust created by a U.S. person, the term "preceding taxable year" serves to identify and limit the taxable years of a trust to which an accumulation distribution consisting of undistributed net income or undistributed capital gain may be allocated (or "thrown back") under section 666(a) and 669(a). An accumulation distribution consisting of undistributed net income or undistributed capital gain may not be allocated or "thrown back" to a taxable year of a trust if such year is not a "preceding taxable year."

(ii) Accumulation distributions. In the case of an accumulation distribution consisting of undistributed net income made in a taxable year beginning before January 1, 1974, any taxable year of the trust that precedes by more than 5 years the taxable year of the trust in which such accumulation distribution was made is not a "preceding taxable year." Thus, for a domestic trust on a calendar year basis, calendar year 1967 is not a "preceding taxable year" with respect to an accumulation distribution made in calendar year 1973, whereas calendar year 1968 is a "preceding taxable year." In the case of an accumulation distribution made during a taxable year beginning after December 31, 1973, any taxable year of the trust that begins before January 1, 1969, is not a "preceding taxable year." Thus, for a domestic trust on a calendar year basis, calendar year 1968 is not a "preceding taxable year" with respect to an accumulation distribution made in calendar year 1975, whereas calendar year 1969 is a "preceding taxable year."

(iii) Capital gain distributions. In the case of an accumulation distribution that is a capital gain distribution, any taxable year of the trust that (a) begins before January 1, 1969, or (b) is prior to the first year in which income is accumulated, whichever occurs later, is not a "preceding taxable year." Thus, for the purpose of capital gain distributions and section 669, only taxable years beginning after December 31, 1968, can be "preceding taxable years." See § 1.688(a)-1A(c).

(2) Foreign trusts created by U.S. persons. For purposes of subpart D, in the case of a foreign trust created by a U.S. person, the term "preceding taxable year" does not include any taxable year to which part I of subchapter J does not apply. See section 683 and regulations thereunder. Accordingly, the provisions of subpart D may not, in the case of a foreign trust created by a U.S. person, be applied to any taxable year which begins before 1954 or ends before August 17, 1954. For example, if a foreign trust created by a U.S. person (reporting on the calendar year basis) makes a distribution during the calendar year 1970 of income accumulated during prior years, the earliest year of the trust to which the accumulation distribution may be allocated under such subpart D is 1954, but it may not be allocated to 1953 and prior years, since the Internal Revenue Code of 1939 applies to those years.

(b) Simple trusts. A taxable year of a trust during which the trust was a simple trust (that is, was subject to subpart B) for the entire year shall not be considered a "preceding taxable year" unless during such year the trust received "outside income" or unless the trustee did not distribute all of the income of the trust that was required to be distributed currently for such year. In such event, undistributed net income for such year shall not exceed the greater of the "outside income" or income not distributed during such year. For purposes of this paragraph, the term "outside income" means amounts that are included in distributable net income of the trust for the year but are not "income" of the trust as that term is defined in § 1.643(b)-1. Some examples of "outside income" are:

(1) Income taxable to the trust under section 691;

(2) Unrealized accounts receivable that were assigned to the trust; and

(3) Distributions from another trust that include distributable net income or undistributed net income of such other trust.

The term "outside income," however, does not include amounts received as distributions from an estate, other than income specified in (1) and (2), for which the estate was allowed a deduction under section 661(a). The application of this paragraph may be illustrated by the following examples:

Example (1). By his will D creates a trust for his widow W. The terms of the trust require that the income be distributed currently (i.e., it is a simple trust), and authorize the trustee to make discretionary payments of corpus to W. Upon W's death the trust corpus is to be distributed to D's then living issue. The executor of D's will makes a $10,000 distribution of corpus to the trust that carries out estate income consisting of dividends and interest to the trust under section 662(a)(2). The trust reports this income as its only income on its income tax return for its taxable year in which ends the taxable year of the estate in which the $10,000 distribution was made, and pays a tax thereon of $2,106. Thus, the trust has undistributed net income of $7,894 ($10,000 – $2,106). Several years later the trustee makes a discretionary corpus payment of $15,000 to W. This payment is an accumulation distribution under section 665(b). However, since the trust had no "outside income" in the year of the estate distribution, such year is not a preceding taxable year. Thus, W is not treated as receiving undistributed net income of $7,894 and taxes thereon of $2,106 for the purpose of including the same in her gross income under section 668. The result would be the same if the invasion power were not exercised and the accumulation distribution occurred as a result of the distribution of the corpus to D's issue upon the death of W.

Example (2). Trust A, a simple trust on the calendar year basis, received in 1972 extraordinary dividends or taxable stock dividends that the trustee in good faith allocated to corpus, but that are determined in 1974 to have been currently distributable to the beneficiary. See section 643(a)(4) and § 1.643(a)-4. Trust A would qualify for treatment under subpart C for 1974, the year of distribution of the extraordinary dividends or taxable stock dividends, because the distribution is not out of income of the current taxable year and is treated as an other amount properly paid or credited or required to be distributed for such taxable year within the meaning of section 661(a)(2). Also, the distribution in 1974 qualifies as an accumulation distribution for the purposes of subpart D. For purposes only of such subpart D, trust A would be treated as subject to the provisions of such subpart C for 1972, the preceding taxable year in which the extraordinary or taxable stock dividends were received, and, in computing undistributed net income for 1972, the extraordinary or taxable stock dividends would be included in distributable net income under section 643(a). The rule stated in the preceding sentence would also apply if the distribution in 1974 was made out of corpus without regard to a determination that the extraordinary dividends or taxable stock dividends in question were currently distributable to the beneficiary.

T.D. 7204, 8/24/72.

§ 1.665(f)-1A Undistributed capital gain.

Caution: The Treasury has not yet amended Reg § 1.665(f)-1A to reflect changes made by P.L. 99-514, P.L. 95-600, P.L. 94-455.

(a) Domestic trusts. *(1)* The term "undistributed capital gain" means (in the case of a trust other than a foreign trust created by a U.S. person), for any taxable year of the trust beginning after December 31, 1968, the gains in excess of losses for that year from the sale or exchange of capital assets of the trust less:

(i) The amount of such gains that are included in distributable net income under section 643(a)(3) and § 1.643(a)-3.

(ii) The amount of taxes imposed on the trust for such year attributable to such gains, as defined in § 1.665(d)-1A, and

(iii) In the case of a trust that does not use the alternative method for computing taxes on capital gains of the taxable year, the excess of deductions (other than deductions allowed under section 642(b) relating to personal exemption or section 642(c) relating to charitable contributions) over distributable net income for such year to the extent such excess deductions are properly allowable in determining taxable income for such year.

For purposes of computing the amount of capital gain under this paragraph, no deduction under section 1202, relating to deduction for excess of capital gains over capital losses, shall be taken into account. The application of this subparagraph may be illustrated by the following example:

Example. Under the terms of the trust, the trustee must distribute all income currently and has discretion to distribute capital gain to A or to allocate it to corpus. During the taxable year 1971 the trust recognized capital gain in the amount of $15,000, and capital losses of $5,000, and had interest income (after expenses) of $6,000. The trustee distributed $8,000 to A, consisting of $6,000 of interest and $2,000 of capital gain. The $2,000 of gain distributed to A is included in the computation of distributable net income under § 1.643(a)-3. The balance of the capital gain is not included in distributable net income since it is allocated to corpus and not paid, credited, or required to be distributed to any beneficiary. The trust paid taxes of $671, all of which are attributable under § 1.665(d)-1A to the undistributed capital gain. The amount of undistributed capital gain of the trust for 1971 is therefore $7,329, computed as follows:

Total capital gains	$15,000
Less: Capital losses	5,000
Gains in excess of losses	10,000
Less:	
Amount of capital gain included in distributable net income	2,000
Taxes imposed on the trust attributable to the undistributed capital gain (see § 1.665(d)-1A)	671
	2,671
Undistributed capital gain	7,329

(2) For purposes of subparagraph (1) of this paragraph, the term "losses for that year" includes losses of the trusts from the sale or exchange of capital assets in preceding taxa-

ble years not included in the computation of distributable net income of any year, reduced by such losses taken into account in a subsequent preceding taxable year in computing undistributed capital gain but not reduced by such losses taken into account in determining the deduction under section 1211. See section 1212(b)(2) and the regulations thereunder. For example, assume that a trust had a net long-term capital loss in 1970 of $5,000. During the years 1971 through 1975, the trust had no capital gains or capital losses. In 1976, it has a long-term capital gain of $8,000, which it allocates to corpus and does not distribute to a beneficiary, but has no taxes attributable to such gain. The undistributed capital gain for 1976 is $8,000 − $5,000, or $3,000, even though all or a part of the $5,000 loss was claimed under section 1211 as a deduction in years 1970 through 1975.

(b) Foreign trusts. Distributable net income for a taxable year of a foreign trust created by a U.S. person includes capital gains in excess of capital losses for such year (see § 1.643(a)-6(a)(3)). Thus, a foreign trust created by a U.S. person can never have any undistributed capital gain.

T.D. 7204, 8/24/72.

§ 1.665(g)-1A Capital gain distribution.

Caution: The Treasury has not yet amended Reg § 1.665(g)-1A to reflect changes made by P.L. 99-514, P.L. 95-600, P.L. 94-455.

For any taxable year of a trust, the term "capital gain distribution" means, to the extent of the undistributed capital gain of the trust, that portion of an accumulation distribution that exceeds the amount of such accumulation distribution deemed under section 666(a) to be undistributed net income of the trust for all preceding taxable years. See § 1.665(b)-1A for the definition of "accumulation distribution". For any such taxable year the undistributed capital gain includes the total undistributed capital gain for all years of the trust beginning with the first taxable year beginning after December 31, 1968, in which income (as determined under section 643(b)) is accumulated, and ending before such taxable year. See § 1.665(g)-2A for application of the separate share rule. The application of this section may be illustrated by the following example:

Example. A trust on the calendar year basis made the following accumulations. For purposes of this example, the undistributed net income is the same as income under applicable local law. No income was accumulated prior to 1970.

Year	Undistributed net income	Undistributed capital gain
1969	None	$10,000
1970	$1,000	3,000
1971	None	4,000

The trust has distributable net income in 1972 of $2,000 and recognizes capital gains of $4,500 that are allocable to corpus. On December 31, 1972, the trustee makes a distribution of $20,000 to the beneficiary. There is an accumulation distribution of $18,000 ($20,000 distribution less $2,000 d.n.i.,) that consists of undistributed net income of $1,000 (see § 1.666(a)-1A) and a capital gain distribution of $7,000. The capital gain distribution is computed as follows:

Accumulation distribution	$18,000
Less: Undistributed net income	1,000
Balance	17,000
Capital gain distribution (undistributed capital gain of the trust for 1972 ($3,000 from 1970 and $4,000 from 1971))	7,000
Balance (corpus)	10,000

No undistributed capital gain is deemed distributed from 1969 because 1969 is a year prior to the first year in which income is accumulated (1970). The accumulation distribution is not deemed to consist of any part of the capital gains recognized in 1972.

T.D. 7204, 8/24/72.

§ 1.665(g)-2A Application of separate share rule.

Caution: The Treasury has not yet amended Reg § 1.665(g)-2A to reflect changes made by P.L. 99-514, P.L. 95-600, P.L. 94-455.

(a) In general. If the separate share rule of section 663(c) is applicable for any taxable year of a trust, subpart D is applied as if each share were a separate trust except as provided in paragraph (c) of this section and in § 1.668(a)-1A(c). Thus, the amounts of an "accumulation distribution," "undistributed net income," "undistributed capital gain," and "capital gain distribution" are computed separately for each share.

(b) Allocation of taxes—undistributed net income. The "taxes imposed on the trust attributable to the undistributed net income" are allocated as follows:

(1) There is first allocated to each separate share that portion of the "taxes imposed on the trust attributable to the undistributed net income" (as defined in § 1.665(d)-1A(b)), computed before the allowance of any credits under section 642(a), that bears the same relation to the total of such taxes that the distributable net income of the separate share bears to the distributable net income of the trust, adjusted for this purpose as follows:

(i) There is excluded from distributable net income of the trust and of each separate share any tax-exempt interest, foreign income of a foreign trust, and excluded dividends, to the extent such amounts are included in distributable net income pursuant to section 643(a)(5), (6), and (7); and

(ii) The distributable net income of the trust is reduced by any deductions allowable under section 661 for amounts paid, credited, or required to be distributed during the taxable year, and the distributable net income of each separate share is reduced by any such deduction allocable to that share.

(2) The taxes so determined for each separate share are then reduced by that portion of the credits against tax allowable to the trust under section 642(a) in computing the "taxes imposed on the trust" that bears the same relation to the total of such credits that the items of distributable net income allocable to the separate share with respect to which the credit is allowed bear to the total of such items of the trust.

(c) Allocation of taxes—undistributed capital gain. The "taxes imposed on the trust attributable to undistributed capital gain" are allocated as follows:

(1) There is first allocated to each separate share that portion of the "taxes imposed on the trust attributable to undistributed capital gain" (as defined in § 1.665(d)-1A(c)), computed before the allowance of any credits under section 642(a), that bears the same relation to the total of such taxes that the undistributed capital gain (prior to the deduction of

taxes under section 665(c)(2)) of the separate share bears to the total such undistributed capital gain of the trust.

(2) The taxes so determined for each separate share are then reduced by that portion of the credits against tax allowable to the trust under section 642(a) in computing the "taxes imposed on the trust" that bears the same relation to the total of such credits that the capital gain allocable to the separate share with respect to which the credit is allowed bear to the total of such capital gain of the trust.

(d) Termination of a separate share. *(1)* If upon termination of a separate share, an amount is properly paid, credited or required to be distributed by the trust under section 661(a)(2) to a beneficiary from such share, an accumulation distribution will be deemed to have been made to the extent of such amount. In determining the distributable net income of such share, only those items of income and deduction for the taxable year of the trust in which such share terminates, properly allocable to such share, shall be taken into consideration.

(2) No accumulation distribution will be deemed to have been made upon the termination of a separate share to the extent that the property constituting such share, or a portion thereof, continues to be held as a part of the same trust. The undistributed net income, undistributed capital gain, and the taxes imposed on the trust attributable to such items, if any, for all preceding taxable years (reduced by any amounts deemed distributed under sections 666(a) and 669(a) by reason of any accumulation distribution of undistributed net income or undistributed capital gain in prior years or the current taxable year), which were allocable to the terminating share shall be treated as being applicable to the trust itself. However, no adjustment will be made to the amounts deemed distributed under sections 666 and 669 by reason of an accumulation distribution of undistributed net income or undistributed capital gain from the surviving share or shares made in years prior to the year in which the terminating share was added to such surviving share or shares.

(3) The provisions of this paragraph may be illustrated by the following example:

Example. A trust was established under the will of X for the benefit of his wife and upon her death the property was to continue in the same trust for his two sons, Y and Z. The separate share rule is applicable to this trust. The trustee had discretion to pay or accumulate the income to the wife, and after her death was to pay each son's share to him after he attained the age of 25. When the wife died, Y was 23 and Z was 28.

(1) Upon the death of X's widow, there is no accumulation distribution. The entire trust is split into two equal shares, and therefore the undistributed net income and the undistributed capital gain of the trust are split into two shares.

(2) The distribution to Z of his share after his mother's death is an accumulation distribution of his separate share of one-half of the undistributed net income and undistributed capital gain.

T.D. 7204, 8/24/72.

---

§ 1.666(a)-1A Amount allocated.

Caution: The Treasury has not yet amended Reg § 1.666(a)-1A to reflect changes made by P.L. 95-600, P.L. 94-455.

(a) In general. In the case of a trust that is subject to subpart C of part I of subchapter J of chapter 1 of the Code (relating to estates and trusts that may accumulate income or that distribute corpus), section 666(a) prescribes rules for determining the taxable years from which an accumulation distribution will be deemed to have been made and the extent to which the accumulation distribution is considered to consist of undistributed net income. In general, an accumulation distribution made in taxable years beginning after December 31, 1969, is deemed to have been made first from the earliest preceding taxable year of the trust for which there is undistributed net income. An accumulation distribution made in a taxable year beginning before January 1, 1970, is deemed to have been made first from the most recent preceding taxable year of the trust for which there is undistributed net income. See § 1.665(e)-1A for the definition of "preceding taxable year."

(b) Distributions by domestic trusts. *(1) Taxable years beginning after December 31, 1973.* An accumulation distribution made by a trust (other than a foreign trust created by a U.S. person) in any taxable year beginning after December 31, 1973, is allocated to the preceding taxable years of the trust (defined in § 1.665(e)-1A(a)(1)(ii) as those beginning after December 31, 1968) according to the amount of undistributed net income of the trust for such years. For this purpose, an accumulation distribution is first to be allocated to the earliest such preceding taxable year in which there is undistributed net income and shall then be allocated, beginning with the next earliest, to any remaining preceding taxable years of the trust. The portion of the accumulation distribution portion of the accumulation distribution allocated to the earliest preceding taxable year is the amount of the undistributed net income for that preceding taxable year. The portion of the accumulation distribution allocated to any preceding taxable year subsequent to the earliest such preceding taxable year is the excess of the accumulation distribution over the aggregate of the undistributed net income for all earlier preceding taxable years. See paragraph (d) of this section for adjustments to undistributed net income for prior distributions. The provisions of this subparagraph may be illustrated by the following example:

Example. In 1977, a domestic trust reporting on the calendar year basis makes an accumulation distribution of $33,000. Therefore, years before 1969 are ignored. In 1969, the trust had $6,000 of undistributed net income; in 1970, $4,000; in 1971, none; in 1972, $7,000; in 1973, $5,000; in 1974, $8,000; in 1975, $6,000; and $4,000 in 1976. The accumulation distribution is deemed distributed $6,000 in 1969, $4,000 in 1970, none in 1971, $7,000 in 1972, $5,000 in 1973, $8,000 in 1974, and $3,000 in 1975.

(2) Taxable years beginning after December 31, 1969, and before January 1, 1974. If a trust (other than a foreign trust created by a U.S. person) makes an accumulation distribution in a taxable year beginning after December 31, 1969, and before January 1, 1974, the distribution will be deemed distributed in the same manner as accumulation distributions qualifying under subparagraph (1) of this paragraph, except that the first year to which the distribution may be thrown back cannot be earlier than the fifth taxable year of the trust preceding the year in which the accumulation distribution is made. Thus, for example, in the case of an accumulation distribution made in the taxable year of a domestic trust which begins on January 1, 1972, the taxable year of the trust beginning on January 1, 1967, would be the first year in which the distribution was deemed made, assuming that there was undistributed net income for 1967. See also § 1.665(e)-1A(a)(1). The provisions of this subparagraph may be illustrated by the following example:

Example. In 1973, a domestic trust, reporting on the calendar year basis, makes an accumulation distribution of $25,000. In 1968, the fifth year preceding 1973, the trust had $7,000 of undistributed net income; in 1969, none; in 1970, $12,000; in 1971, $4,000; in 1972, $4,000. The accumulation distribution is deemed distributed in the amounts of $7,000 in 1968, none in 1969, $12,000 in 1970, $4,000 in 1971, and $2,000 in 1972.

(3) Taxable years beginning after December 31, 1968, and before January 1, 1970. Accumulation distributions made in taxable years of the trust beginning after December 31, 1968, and before January 1, 1970, are allocated to prior years according to § 1.666(a)-1.

(c) Distributions by foreign trusts. *(1) Foreign trusts created solely by U.S. persons.* (i) Taxable years beginning after December 31, 1969. If a foreign trust created by a U.S. person makes an accumulation distribution in any taxable year beginning after December 31, 1969, the distribution is allocated to the trust's preceding taxable years (defined in § 1.665(e)-1A(a)(2) as those beginning after Dec. 31, 1953, and ending after Aug. 16, 1954) according to the amount of undistributed net income of the trust for such years. For this purpose, an accumulation distribution is first allocated to the earliest such preceding taxable year in which there is undistributed net income and shall then be allocated in turn, beginning with the next earliest, to any remaining preceding taxable years of the trust. The portion of the accumulation distribution allocated to the earliest preceding taxable year is the amount of the undistributed net income for that preceding taxable year. The portion of the accumulation distribution allocated to any preceding taxable year subsequent to the earliest such preceding taxable year is the excess of the accumulation distribution over the aggregate of the undistributed net income for all earlier preceding taxable years. See paragraph (d) of this section for adjustments to undistributed net income for prior distributions. The provisions of this subdivision may be illustrated by the following example:

Example. In 1971, a foreign trust created by a U.S. person, reporting on the calendar year basis, makes an accumulation distribution of $50,000. In 1961, the trust had $12,000 of undistributed net income; in 1962, none; in 1963, $10,000; in 1964, $8,000; in 1965, $5,000; in 1966, $14,000; in 1967, none; in 1968, $8,000; in 1969, $2,000; and in 1970, $1,000. The accumulation distribution is deemed distributed in the amounts of $12,000 in 1961, none in 1962, $10,000 in 1963, $8,000 in 1964, $5,000 in 1965, $14,000 in 1966, none in 1967, and $1,000 in 1968.

(ii) Taxable years beginning after December 31, 1968, and before January 1, 1970. Accumulation distributions made in taxable years of the trust beginning after December 31, 1968, and before January 1, 1970, are allocated to prior years according to § 1.666(a)-1.

(2) Foreign trusts created partly by U.S. persons. (i) Taxable years beginning after December 31, 1969. If a trust that is in part a foreign trust created by a U.S. person and in part a foreign trust created by a person other than a U.S. person makes an accumulation distribution in any year after December 31, 1969, the distribution is deemed made from the undistributed net income of the foreign trust created by a U.S. person in the proportion that the total undistributed net income for all preceding years of the foreign trust created by the U.S. person bears to the total undistributed net income for all years of the entire foreign trust. In addition, such distribution is deemed made from the undistributed net income of the foreign trust created by a person other than a U.S. person in the proportion that the total undistributed net income for all preceding years of the foreign trust created by a person other than a U.S. person bears to the total undistributed net income for all years of the entire foreign trust. Accordingly, an accumulation distribution of such a trust is composed of two portions with one portion relating to the undistributed net income of the foreign trust created by the U.S. person and the other portion relating to the undistributed net income of the foreign trust created by the person other than a U.S. person. For these purposes, each portion of an accumulation distribution made in any taxable year is first allocated to each of such preceding taxable years in turn, beginning with the earliest preceding taxable year, as defined in § 1.665(e)-1A(a), of the applicable foreign trusts, to the extent of the undistributed net income for the such trust for each of these years. Thus, each portion of an accumulation distribution is deemed to have been made from the earliest accumulated income of the applicable trust. If the foreign trust created by a U.S. person makes an accumulation distribution in any year beginning after December 31, 1969, the distribution is included in the beneficiary's income for that year to the extent of the undistributed net income of the trust for the trust's preceding taxable years which began after December 31, 1953, and ended after August 16, 1954. The provisions of this subdivision may be illustrated by the following example:

Example. A trust is created in 1962 under the laws of Country X by the transfer to a trustee in Country X of property by both a U.S. person and a person other than a U.S. person. Both the trust and the only beneficiary of the trust (who is a U.S. person) report their taxable income on a calendar year basis. On March 31, 1974, the trust makes an accumulation distribution of $150,000 to the beneficiary. The distributable net income of both the portion of the trust which is a foreign trust created by a U.S. person and the portion of the trust which is a foreign trust created by a person other than a U.S. person for each year is computed in accordance with the provisions of paragraph (b)(3) of § 1.643(d)-1 and the undistributed net income for each portion of the trust for each year is computed as described in paragraph (b) of § 1.665(a)-1A. For taxable years 1962 through 1973, the portion of the trust which is a foreign trust created by a U.S. person and the portion of the trust which is a foreign trust created by a person other than a U.S. person had the following amounts of undistributed net income:

Year	Undistributed net income portion of the trust created by a U.S. person	Undistributed net income-portion of the trust created by a person other than a U.S. person
1962	$ 7,000	$ 4,000
1963	12,000	7,000
1964	None	None
1965	11,000	5,000
1966	8,000	3,000
1967	None	None
1968	4,000	2,000
1969	17,000	8,000
1970	16,000	9,000
1971	None	None
1972	25,000	12,000
1973	20,000	10,000
Totals	120,000	60,000

The accumulation distribution in the amount of $150,000 is deemed to have been distributed in the amount of $100,000 (120,000/180,000 × $150,000) from the portion of the trust which is a foreign trust created by a U.S. person and in the amount of $39,000, which is less than $50,000 (60,000/180,000 × $150,000), from the portion of the trust which is a foreign trust created by a person other than a U.S. person computed as follows:

Year	Throwback to preceding years of foreign trust created by a U.S. person	Throwback to preceding years of portion of the entire foreign trust which is not a foreign trust created by a U.S. person
1962	$ 7,000	None
1963	12,000	None
1964	None	None
1965	11,000	None
1966	8,000	None
1967	None	None
1968	4,000	None
1969	17,000	$ 8,000
1970	16,000	9,000
1971	None	None
1972	25,000	12,000
1973	None	10,000
Totals	100,000	39,000

Pursuant to this paragraph, the accumulation distribution in the amount of $100,000 from the portion of the trust which is a foreign trust created by a U.S. person is included in the beneficiary's income for 1974, as the amount represents undistributed net income of the trust for the trust's preceding taxable years which began after December 31, 1953, and ended after August 16, 1954. The accumulation distribution in the amount of $50,000 from the portion of the trust which is a foreign trust created by a person other than a U.S. person is included in the beneficiary's income for 1974 to the extent of the undistributed net income of the trust for the preceding years beginning after December 31, 1968. Accordingly, with respect to the portion of the trust which is a foreign trust created by a person other than a U.S. person, only the undistributed net income for the years 1969 through 1973, which totals $39,000, is includible in the beneficiary's income for 1974. Thus, of the $150,000 distribution made in 1974, the beneficiary is required to include a total of $139,000 in his income for 1974. The balance of $11,000 is deemed to represent a distribution of corpus.

(ii) Taxable years beginning after December 31, 1968, and before January 1, 1970. Accumulation distributions made in taxable years of the trust beginning after December 31, 1968, and before January 1, 1970, are allocated to prior years according to § 1.666(a)-1.

(3) Foreign trusts created by non-U.S. persons. To the extent that a foreign trust is a foreign trust created by a person other than a U.S. person, an accumulation distribution is included in the beneficiary's income for the year paid, credited, or required to be distributed to the extent provided under paragraph (b) of this section.

(d) Reduction of undistributed net income for prior accumulation distributions. For the purposes of allocating to any preceding taxable year an accumulation distribution of the taxable year, the undistributed net income of such preceding taxable year is reduced by the amount from such year deemed distributed in any accumulation distribution of undistributed net income made in any taxable year intervening between such preceding taxable year and the taxable year. Accordingly, for example, if a trust has undistributed net income for 1974 and makes accumulation distributions during the taxable years 1978 and 1979, in determining that part of the 1979 accumulation distribution that is thrown back to 1974 the undistributed net income for 1974 is first reduced by the amount of the undistributed net income for 1974 deemed distributed in the 1979 accumulation distribution.

(e) Rule when no undistributed net income. If, before the application of the provisions of subpart D to an accumulation distribution for the taxable year, there is no undistributed net income for a preceding taxable year, then no portion of the accumulation distribution is undistributed net income deemed distributed on the last day of such preceding taxable year. Thus, if an accumulation distribution is made during the taxable year 1975 from a trust whose earliest preceding taxable year is taxable year 1970, and the trust had no undistributed net income for 1970, then no portion of the 1975 accumulation distribution is undistributed net income deemed distributed on the last day of 1970.

T.D. 7204, 8/24/72.

§ 1.666(b)-1A Total taxes deemed distributed.

Caution: The Treasury has not yet amended Reg § 1.666(b)-1A to reflect changes made by P.L. 95-600, P.L. 94-455.

(a) If an accumulation distribution is deemed under § 1.666(a)-1A to be distributed on the last day of a preceding taxable year and the amount is not less than the undistributed net income for such preceding taxable year, then an additional amount equal to the "taxes imposed on the trust attributable to the undistributed net income" (as defined in § 1.665(d)-1A(b)) for such preceding taxable year is also deemed distributed under section 661(a)(2). For example, a trust has undistributed net income of $8,000 for the taxable year 1974. The taxes imposed on the trust attributable to the undistributed net income are $3,032. During the taxable year 1977, an accumulation distribution of $8,000 is made to the beneficiary, which is deemed under § 1.666(a)-1A to have been distributed on the last day of 1974. The 1977 accumulation distribution is not less than the 1974 undistributed net income. Accordingly, the taxes of $3,032 imposed on the trust attributable to the undistributed net income for 1974 are also deemed to have been distributed on the last day of 1974. Thus, a total of $11,032 will be deemed to have been distributed on the last day of 1974.

(b) For the purpose of paragraph (a) of this section, the undistributed net income of any preceding taxable year and the taxes imposed on the trust for such preceding taxable year attributable to such undistributed net income are computed after taking into account any accumulation distributions of taxable years intervening between such preceding taxable year and the taxable year. See paragraph (d) of § 1.666(a)-1A.

T.D. 7204, 8/24/72.

§ 1.666(c)-1A Pro rata portion of taxes deemed distributed.

Caution: The Treasury has not yet amended Reg § 1.666(c)-1A to reflect changes made by P.L. 96-222, P.L. 95-600, P.L. 94-455.

(a) If an accumulation distribution is deemed under § 1.666(a)-1A to be distributed on the last day of a preceding taxable year and the amount is less than the undistributed net income for such preceding taxable year, then an additional amount is also deemed distributed under section 661(a)(2). The additional amount is equal to the "taxes imposed on the trust attributable to the undistributed net income" (as defined in § 1.665(a)-1A(b)) for such preceding taxable year, multiplied by a fraction, the numerator of which is the amount of the accumulation distribution allocated to such preceding taxable year and the denominator of which is the undistributed net income for such preceding taxable year. See paragraph (b) of example (1) and paragraphs (c) and (f) of example (2) in § 1.666(c)-2A for illustrations of this paragraph.

(b) For the purpose of paragraph (a) of this section, the undistributed net income of any preceding taxable year and the taxes imposed on the trust for such preceding taxable year attributable to such undistributed net income are computed after taking into account any accumulation distributions of any taxable years intervening between such preceding taxable year and the taxable year. See paragraph (d) of § 1.666(a)-1A and paragraph (c) of example (1) and paragraphs (e) and (h) of example (2) in § 1.666(c)-2A.

T.D. 7204, 8/24/72.

§ 1.666(c)-2A Illustration of the provisions of section 666(a), (b), and (c).

Caution: The Treasury has not yet amended Reg § 1.666(c)-2A to reflect changes made by P.L. 95-600, P.L. 94-455.

The application of the provisions of §§ 1.666(a)-1A, 1.666(b)-1A, and 1.666(c)-1A may be illustrated by the following examples:

Example (1). (a) A trust created on January 1, 1974, makes accumulation distributions as follows:

1979	$ 7,000
1980	26,000

For 1974 through 1978, the undistributed portion of distributable net income, taxes imposed on the trust attributable to the undistributed net income, and undistributed net income are as follows:

Year	Undistributed portion of distributable net income	Taxes imposed on the trust attributable to the undistributed net income	Undistributed net income
1974	$12,100	$3,400	$ 8,700
1975	16,100	5,200	10,900
1976	6,100	1,360	4,740
1977	None	None	None
1978	10,100	2,640	7,460

The trust has no undistributed capital gain.

(b) Since the entire amount of the accumulation distribution for 1979 ($7,000) is less than the undistributed net income for 1974 ($8,700), an additional amount of $2,736 (7,000/8,700 × $3,400) is deemed distributed under section 666(c).

(c) In allocating the accumulation distribution for 1980, the amount of undistributed net income for 1974 will reflect the accumulation distribution for 1979. The undistributed net income for 1974 will then be $1,700 and the taxes imposed on the trust for 1974 will be $664, determined as follows:

Undistributed net income as of the close of 1974 ...	$8,700
Less: Accumulation distribution (1979)	7,000
Balance (undistributed net income as of the close of 1979)	1,700
Taxes imposed on the trust attributable to the undistributed net income as of the close of 1979 (1,700/8,700 × $3,400)	664

(d) The accumulation distribution of $26,000 for 1980 is deemed to have been made on the last day of the preceding taxable years of the trust to the extent of $24,800, the total of the undistributed net income for such years, as shown in the tabulation below. In addition, $9,864, the total taxes imposed on the trust attributable to the undistributed net income for such years is also deemed to have been distributed on the last day of such years, as shown below:

Year	Undistributed net income	Taxes imposed on the trust
1974	$ 1,700	$664
1975	10,900	5,200
1976	4,740	1,360
1977	None	None
1978	7,460	2,640
1979	None	None

Example (2). (a) Under the terms of a trust instrument, the trustee has discretion to accumulate or distribute the income to X and to invade corpus for the benefit of X. The entire income of the trust is from royalties. Both X and the trust report on the calendar year basis. All of the income for 1974 was accumulated. The distributable net income of the trust for the taxable year 1974 is $20,100 and the income taxes paid by the trust for 1974 attributable to the undistributed net income are $7,260. All of the income for 1975 and 1976 was distributed and in addition the trustee made accumulation distributions within the meaning of section 665(b) of $5,420 for each year.

(b) The undistributed net income of the trust determined under section 665(a) as of the close of 1974, is $12,840, computed as follows:

Distributable net income	$20,100
Less: Taxes imposed on the trust attributable to the undistributed net income	7,260
Undistributed net income as of the close of 1974	12,840

(c) The accumulation distribution of $5,420 made during the taxable year 1975 is deemed under section 666(a) to have been made on December 31, 1974. Since this accumulation distribution is less than the 1974 undistributed net income of $12,840, a portion of the taxes imposed on the trust for 1974 is also deemed under section 666(c) to have been distributed on December 31, 1974. The total amount deemed to have been distributed to X on December 31, 1974 is $8,484, computed as follows:

Accumulation distribution	$5,420
Taxes deemed distributed (5,420/12,840 × $7,260)	3,064
Total	8,484

(d) After the application of the provisions of subpart D to the accumulation distribution of 1975, the undistributed net income of the trust for 1974 is $7,420, computed as follows:

Undistributed net income as of the close of 1974	$12,840
Less: 1975 accumulation distribution deemed distributed on December 31, 1974 (paragraph (c) of this example)	5,420
Undistributed net income for 1974 as of the close of 1975	7,420

(e) The taxes imposed on the trust attributable to the undistributed net income for the taxable year 1974, as adjusted to give effect to the 1975 accumulation distribution, amount to $4,196, computed as follows:

Taxes imposed on the trust attributable to undistributed net income as of the close of 1974	$7,260
Less: Taxes deemed distributed in 1974	3,064
Taxes attributable to the undistributed net income determined as of the close of 1975	4,196

(f) The accumulation distribution of $5,420 made during the taxable year 1976 is, under section 666(a), deemed a distribution to X on December 31, 1974, within the meaning of section 661(a)(2). Since the accumulation distribution is less than the 1974 adjusted undistributed net income of $7,420, the trust is deemed under section 666(c) also to have distributed on December 31, 1974, a portion of the taxes imposed on the trust for 1974. The total amount deemed to be distributed on December 31, 1974, with respect to the accumulation distribution made in 1976, is $8,484, computed as follows:

Accumulation distribution	$5,420
Taxes deemed distributed (5,420/7,420 × $4,196)	3,064
Total	8,484

(g) After the application of the provisions of subpart D to the accumulation distribution of 1976, the undistributed net income of the trust for 1974 is $2,000, computed as follows:

Undistributed net income for 1974 as of the close of 1975	$7,420
Less: 1976 accumulation distribution deemed distributed on December 31, 1974 (paragraph (f) of this example)	5,420
Undistributed net income for 1974 as of the close of 1976	2,000

(h) The taxes imposed on the trust attributable to the undistributed net income of the trust for the taxable year 1974, determined as of the close of the taxable year 1976, amount to $1,132 ($4,196 less $3,064).

T.D. 7204, 8/24/72.

§ 1.666(d)-1A Information required from trusts.

Caution: The Treasury has not yet amended Reg § 1.666(d)-1A to reflect changes made by P.L. 95-600, P.L. 94-455.

(a) Adequate records required. For all taxable years of a trust, the trustee must retain copies of the trust's income tax return as well as information pertaining to any adjustments in the tax shown as due on the return. The trustee shall also keep the records of the trust required to be retained by section 6001 and the regulations thereunder for each taxable year as to which the period of limitations on assessment of tax under section 6501 has not expired. If the trustee fails to produce such copies and records, and such failure is due to circumstances beyond the reasonable control of the trustee or any predecessor trustee, the trustee may reconstruct the amount of corpus, accumulated income, etc., from competent sources (including, to the extent permissible, Internal Revenue Service records). To the extent that an accurate reconstruction can be made for a taxable year, the requirements of this paragraph shall be deemed satisfied for such year.

(b) Rule when information is not available. *(1)* Accumulation distributions. If adequate records (as required by paragraph (a) of this section) are not available to determine the proper application of subpart D to an accumulation distribution made in a taxable year by a trust, such accumulation distribution shall be deemed to consist of undistributed net income earned during the earliest preceding taxable year (as defined in § 1.665(e)-1A) of the trust in which it can be established that the trust was in existence. If adequate records are available for some years, but not for others, the accumulation distribution shall be allocated first to the earliest preceding taxable year of the trust for which there are adequate records and then to each subsequent preceding taxable year for which there are adequate records. To the extent that the distribution is not allocated in such manner to years for which adequate records are available, it will be deemed distributed on the last day of the earliest preceding taxable year of the trust in which it is established that the trust was in existence and for which the trust has no records. The provisions of this subparagraph may be illustrated by the following example:

Example. A trust makes a distribution in 1975 of $100,000. The trustee has adequate records for 1973, 1974, and 1975. The records show that the trust is on the calendar year basis, had distributable net income in 1975 of $20,000, and undistributed net income in 1974 of $15,000, and in 1973 of $16,000. The trustee has no other records of the trust except for a copy of the trust instrument showing that the trust was established on January 1, 1965. He establishes that the loss of the records was due to circumstances beyond his control. Since the distribution is made in 1975, the earliest "preceding taxable year", as defined in § 1.665(e)-1A, is 1969. Since $80,000 of the distribution is an accumulation distribution, and $31,000 thereof is allocated to 1974 and 1973, $49,000 is deemed to have been distributed on the last day of 1969.

(2) Taxes. (i) If an amount is deemed under this paragraph to be undistributed net income allocated to a preceding taxable year for which adequate records are not available, there shall be deemed to be "taxes imposed on the trust" for such preceding taxable year an amount equal to the taxes that the trust would have paid if the deemed undistributed net income were the amount remaining when the taxes were subtracted from taxable income of the trust for such year. For example, assume that an accumulation distribution in 1975 of $100,000 is deemed to be undistributed net income from 1971, and that the taxable income required to produce $100,000 after taxes in 1971 would be $284,965. Therefore the amount deemed to be "taxes imposed on the trust" for such preceding taxable year is $184,966.

(ii) The credit allowed by section 667(b) shall not be allowed for any amount deemed under this subparagraph to be "taxes imposed on the trust."

T.D. 7204, 8/24/72.

§ 1.667(a)-1A Denial of refund to trusts.

Caution: The Treasury has not yet amended Reg § 1.667(a)-1A to reflect changes made by P.L. 99-514, P.L. 95-600, P.L. 94-455.

If an amount is deemed under section 666 or 669 to be an amount paid, credited, or required to be distributed on the last day of a preceding taxable year, the trust is not allowed a refund or credit of the amount of "taxes imposed on the trust", as defined in § 1.665(d)-1A. However, such taxes imposed on the trust are allowed as a credit under section 667(b) against the tax of certain beneficiaries who are treated as having received the distributions in the preceding taxable year.

T.D. 7204, 8/24/72.

§ 1.667(b)-1A Authorization of credit to beneficiary for taxes imposed on the trust.

Caution: The Treasury has not yet amended Reg § 1.667(b)-1A to reflect changes made by P.L. 99-514, P.L. 95-600, P.L. 94-455.

(a) Determination of credit. *(1) In general.* Section 667(b) allows under certain circumstances a credit (without interest) against the tax imposed by subtitle A of the Code on the beneficiary for the taxable year in which the accumulation distribution is required to be included in income under section 668(a). In the case of an accumulation distribution consisting only of undistributed net income, the amount of such credit is the total of the taxes deemed distributed to such beneficiary under section 666(b) and (c) as a result of such accumulation distribution for preceding taxable years of the trust on the last day of which such beneficiary was in being, less the amount of such taxes for such preceding taxable years taken into account in reducing the amount of partial tax determined under § 1.668(b)-1A. In the case of an accumulation distribution consisting only of undistributed capital gain, the amount of such credit is the total of the taxes deemed distributed as a result of the accumulation distribution to such beneficiary under section 669(d) and (e) for preceding taxable years of the trust on the last day of which such beneficiary was in being, less the amount of such taxes for such preceding taxable years taken into account in reducing the amount of partial tax determined under § 1.669(b)-1A. In the case of an accumulation distribution consisting of both undistributed net income and undistributed capital gain, a credit will not be available unless the total taxes deemed distributed to the beneficiary for all preceding taxable years as a result of the accumulation distribution exceeds the beneficiary's partial tax determined under §§ 1.668(b)-1A and 1.669(b)-1A without reference to the taxes deemed distributed. A credit is not allowed for any taxes deemed distributed as a result of an accumulation distribution to a beneficiary by reason of sections 666(b) and (c) or sections 669(d) and (e) for a preceding taxable year of the trust before the beneficiary was born or created. However, if as a result of an accumulation distribution the total taxes deemed distributed under sections 668(a)(2) and 668(a)(3) in preceding taxable years before the beneficiary was born or created exceed the partial taxes attributable to amounts deemed distributed in such years, such excess may be used to offset any liability for partial taxes attributable to amounts deemed distributed as a result of the same accumulation distribution in preceding taxable years after the beneficiary was born or created.

(2) Exact method. In the case of the tax computed under the exact method provided in §§ 1.668(b)-1A(b) and 1.669(b)-1A(b), the credit allowed by this section is computed as follows:

(i) Compute the total taxes deemed distributed under §§ 1.666(b)-1A and 1.666(c)-1A or §§ 1.669(d)-1A and 1.669(e)-1A, whichever are appropriate, for the preceding taxable years of the trust on the last day of which the beneficiary was in being.

(ii) Compute the total of the amounts of tax determined under § 1.668(b)-1A(b)(1) or § 1.669(b)-1A(b)(1), whichever is appropriate, for the prior taxable years of the beneficiary in which he was in being.

If the amount determined under subdivision (i) of this subparagraph does not exceed the amount determined under subdivision (ii) of this subparagraph, no credit is allowable. If the amount determined under subdivision (i) of this subparagraph exceeds the amount determined under subdivision (ii) of this subparagraph, the credit allowable is the lesser of the amount of such excess or the amount of taxes deemed distributed to the beneficiary for all preceding taxable years to the extent that such taxes are not used in § 1.668(b)-1A(b)(2) or § 1.669(b)-1A(b)(2) in determining the beneficiary's partial tax under section 668(a)(2) or 668(a)(3). The application of this subparagraph may be illustrated by the following example:

Example. An accumulation distribution made in 1975 is deemed distribution in 1973 and 1974, years in which the beneficiary was in being. The taxes deemed distributed in such years are $4,000 and $2,000, respectively, totaling $6,000. The amounts of tax computed under § 1.668(b)-1A(b)(1) attributable to the amounts thrown back are $3,000 and $2,000, respectively, totaling $5,000. The credit allowable under this subparagraph is therefore $1,000 ($6,000 less $5,000).

(3) Short-cut method. In the case of the tax computed under the short-cut method provided in § 1.668(b)-1A(c) or 1.669(b)-1A(c), the credit allowed by this section is computed as follows:

(i) Compute the total taxes deemed distributed in all preceding taxable years of the trust under §§ 1.666(b)-1A and 1.666(c)-1A or §§ 1.669(d)-1A and 1.669(e)-1A, whichever are appropriate.

(ii) Compute the beneficiary's partial tax determined under either § 1.668(b)-1A(c)(1)(v) or § 1.669(b)-1A(c)(1)(v), whichever is appropriate.

If the amount determined under subdivision (i) of this subparagraph does not exceed the amount determined under subdivision (ii) of this subparagraph, no credit is allowable. If the amount determined under subdivision (i) of this subparagraph exceeds the amount determined under subdivision (ii) of this subparagraph.

(iii) Compute the total taxes deemed distributed under §§ 1.666(b)-1A and 1.666(c)-1A or §§ 1.669(d)-1A and 1.669(e)-1A, which are appropriate, for the preceding taxable years of the trust on the last day of which the beneficiary was in being.

(iv) Multiply the amount by which subdivision (i) of this subparagraph exceeds subdivision (ii) of this subparagraph by a fraction, the numerator of which is the amount determined under subdivision (iii) of this subparagraph and the denominator of which is the amount determined under subdivision (i) of this subparagraph.

The result is the allowable credit. The application of this subparagraph may be illustrated by the following example:

Example. An accumulation distribution that consists only of undistributed net income is made in 1975. The taxes deemed distributed in the preceding years under §§ 1.666(b)-1A and 1.666(c)-1A are $15,000. The amount determined under § 1.668(b)-1A(c)(1)(v) is $12,000. The beneficiary was in being on the last day of all but one preceding taxable year in which the accumulation distribution was deemed made, and the taxes deemed distributed in those years was $10,000. Therefore, the excess of the subdivision (i) amount over the subdivision (ii) amount is $3,000, and is multiplied by 10,000/15,000, resulting in an answer of $2,000, which is the credit allowable when computed under the short-cut method.

(b) Year of credit. The credit to which a beneficiary is entitled under this section is allowed for the taxable year in which the accumulation distribution (to which the credit relates) is required to be included in the income of the beneficiary under section 668(a). Any excess over the total tax liability of the beneficiary for such year is treated as an overpayment of tax by the beneficiary. See section 6401(b) and the regulations thereunder.

T.D. 7204, 8/24/72.

§ 1.668(a)-1A Amounts treated as received in prior taxable years; inclusion in gross income.

Caution: The Treasury has not yet amended Reg § 1.668(a)-1A to reflect changes made by P.L. 94-455.

(a) Section 668(a) provides that the total of the amounts treated under sections 666 and 669 as having been distributed by the trust on the last day of a preceding taxable year of the trust shall be included in the income of the beneficiary or beneficiaries receiving them. The total of such amounts is includable in the income of each beneficiary to the extent the amounts would have been included under section 662(a)(2) and (b) as if the total had actually been an amount properly paid by the trust under section 661(a)(2) on the last day of such preceding taxable year. The total is included in the income of the beneficiary for the taxable year of the beneficiary in which such amounts are in fact paid, credited, or required to be distributed unless the taxable year of the beneficiary differs from the taxable year of the trust (see section 662(c) and the regulations thereunder). The character of the amounts treated as received by a beneficiary in prior taxable years, including taxes deemed distributed, in the hands of the beneficiary is determined by the rules set forth in section 662(b) and the regulations thereunder.

(b) Any deduction allowed to the trust in computing distributable net income for a preceding taxable year (such as depreciation, depletion, etc.) is not deemed allocable to a beneficiary because of amounts included in a beneficiary's gross income under this section since the deduction has already been utilized in reducing the amount included in beneficiary's income.

(c) For purposes of applying section 668(a)(3), a trust shall be considered to be other than a "trust which is not required to distribute all of its income currently" for each taxable year prior to the first taxable year beginning after December 31, 1968, and ending after November 30, 1969, in which income is accumulated. Income will not be deemed to have been accumulated for purposes of applying section 668(a)(3) in a year if the trustee makes a determination, as evidenced by a statement on the return, to distribute all of the trust's income for such year and also makes a good faith determination as to the amount of such income and actually distributed for such year the entire amount so determined. The term "income," as used in the preceding two sentences is defined in §§ 1.643(b)-1 and 1.643(b)-2. Since, under such definitions, certain items may be included in distributable net income but are not, under applicable local law, "income" (as, for example, certain extraordinary dividends), a trust that has undistributed net income from such sources might still qualify as a trust that has not accumulated income. Also, for example, if a trust establishes a reserve for depreciation or depletion and applicable local law permits the deduction for such reserve in the computation of "income," amounts so added to the reserve do not constitute an accumulation of income. If a trust has separate shares, and any share accumulates income, all shares of the trust will be considered to have accumulated income for the purposes of section 668(a)(3). Amounts retained by a trust or a portion of a trust that is subject to subpart E (sections 671–678) shall not be considered accumulated income.

(d) See section 1302(a)(2)(B) to the effect that amounts included in the income of a beneficiary of a trust under section 668(a) are not eligible for income averaging.

T.D. 7204, 8/24/72.

§ 1.668(a)-2A Allocation among beneficiaries; in general.

Caution: The Treasury has not yet amended Reg § 1.668(a)-2A to reflect changes made by P.L. 94-455.

The portion of the total amount includible in income under § 1.668(a)-1A which is includible in the income of a particular beneficiary is based upon the ratio determined under the second sentence of section 662(a)(2) for the taxable year (and not for the preceding taxable year). This section may be illustrated by the following example:

Example. (a) Under the terms of a trust instrument, the trustee may accumulate the income or make distributions to A and B. The trustee may also invade corpus for the benefit of A and B. The distributable net income of the trust for taxable year 1975 is $10,000. The trust had undistributed net income for taxable year 1973, the first year of the trust, of $5,000, to which a tax of $1,100 was allocable. On May 1, 1975, the trustee distributes $10,000 to A, and on November 29, 1975, he distributes $5,000 to B. Thus, of the total distribution of $15,000, A received two-thirds and B receives one-third.

(b) For the purposes of determining the amounts includible in the beneficiaries' gross income for 1975, the trust is deemed to have made the following distributions:

Amount distributed out of 1975 income (distributable net income)	$10,000
Accumulation distribution deemed distributed by the trust on the last day of 1973 under section 666(a)	5,000
Taxes imposed on the trust attributable to the undistributed net income deemed distributed under section 666(b)	1,100

(c) A will include in his income for 1975 two-thirds of each item shown in paragraph (b) of this example. Thus, he will include in gross income $6,666.67 (10,000/15,000 × $10,000) of the 1975 distributable net income of the trust as provided in section 662(a)(2) (which is not an amount includable in his income under § 1.668(a)-1A(a)). He will include in his income $3,333.33 (10,000/15,000 × $5,000) of the accumulation distribution and $733.33 (10,000/15,000 × $1,100) of the taxes imposed on the trust, as provided in section 668(a).

(d) B will include in his income for 1975 one-third of each item shown in paragraph (b) of this example, computed in the manner shown in paragraph (c) of this example.

(e) To the extent the total accumulation distribution consists of undistributed net income and undistributed capital gain. A and B shall be treated as receiving a pro rata share of each for the preceding taxable year 1973.

T.D. 7204, 8/24/72.

§ 1.668(a)-3A Determination of tax.

Caution: The Treasury has not yet amended Reg § 1.668(a)-3A to reflect changes made by P.L. 94-455.

In a taxable year in which an amount is included in a beneficiary's income under § 1.668(a)-1A(a), the tax on the beneficiary for such taxable year is determined only as provided in section 668 and consists of the sum of—

(a) A partial tax computed on (1) the beneficiary's taxable income reduced by (2) an amount equal to the total amounts includible in his income under § 1.668(a)-1A(a), at the rate and in the manner as if section 668 had not been enacted,

(b) A partial tax determined as provided in § 1.668(b)-1A, and

(c) In the case of a beneficiary of a trust which is not required to distribute all of its income currently, a partial tax determined as provided in § 1.669(b)-1A.

T.D. 7204, 8/24/72.

§ 1.668(b)-1A Tax on distribution.

Caution: The Treasury has not yet amended Reg § 1.668(b)-1A to reflect changes made by P.L. 94-455.

(a) In general. The partial tax imposed on the beneficiary by section 668(a)(2) shall be the lesser of—

(1) The tax computed under paragraph (b) of this section (the "exact" method), or

(2) The tax computed under paragraph (c) of this section (the "short-cut" method),

except as provided in § 1.668(b)-4A (relating to failure to furnish proper information) and paragraph (d) of this section (relating to disallowance of short-cut method). For purposes of this paragraph, the method used in the return shall be accepted as the method that produces the lesser tax. The beneficiary's choice of the two methods is not dependent upon the method that he uses to compute his partial tax imposed by section 668(a)(3).

(b) Computation of partial tax by the exact method. The partial tax referred to in paragraph (a)(1) of this section is computed as follows:

(1) First, compute the tax attributable to the section 666 amounts for each of the preceding taxable years. For purposes of this paragraph, the "section 666 amounts" for a preceding taxable year are the amounts deemed distributed under section 666(a) on the last day of the preceding taxable year, plus the amount of taxes deemed distributed on such day under section 666(b) or (c). The tax attributable to such amounts in each prior taxable year of the beneficiary is the difference between the tax for such year computed with the inclusion of the section 666 amounts in the beneficiary's gross income and the tax for such year computed without including them in such gross income. Tax computations for each such year shall reflect a taxpayer's marital, dependency, exemption, and filing status for such year. To the extent the undistributed net income of a trust deemed distributed in an accumulation distribution includes amounts received as an accumulation distribution from another trust, for purposes of this paragraph they shall be considered as amounts deemed distributed by the trust under section 666(a) on the last day of each of the preceding taxable years in which such amounts were accumulated by such other trust. For example, assume trust Z, a calendar year trust, received in its taxable year 1975 an accumulation distribution from trust Y, a calendar year trust, that included undistributed net income and taxes of trust Y for the taxable years 1972, 1973, and 1974. To the extent an accumulation distribution made by trust Z in its taxable year 1976 includes such undistributed net income and taxes, it shall be considered an accumulation distribution by trust Z in the taxable year 1976 and under section 666(a) will be deemed and distributed on the last day of the preceding taxable years 1972, 1973, and 1974.

(2) From the sum of the taxes for the prior taxable years attributable to the section 666 amounts (computed in accordance with subparagraph (1) of this paragraph), subtract so much of the amount of taxes deemed distributed to the beneficiary under §§ 1.666(b)-1A and 1.666(c)-1A as does not exceed such sum. The resulting amount, if any, is the partial tax, computed under the exact method, for the taxable year in which the accumulation distribution is paid, credited, or required to be distributed to the beneficiary.

(3) The provisions of this paragraph may be illustrated by the following example:

Example. (i) Assume that in 1979 a trust makes an accumulation distribution of $15,000 to A. The accumulation distribution is allocated under section 666(a) in the amounts of $5,000 to 1971, $4,000 to 1972, and $6,000 to 1973. Under section 666(b) and (c), taxes in the amounts of $935, $715, and $1,155 (totaling $2,805) are deemed distributed in 1971, 1972, and 1973 respectively.

(ii) A, the beneficiary, had taxable income and paid income tax in 1971-72 as follows:

Year	Taxable income	Tax
1971	$10,000	$2,190
1972	12,000	2,830
1973	14,000	3,550

(iii) Taxes attributable to the section 666 amounts (paragraph (i) of this example) are $6,979, computed as follows:

1971

Taxable income including section 666 amounts ($10,000 + $5,000 + $935)	$15,935	
Tax on $15,935	$ 4,305	
Less: Tax paid by A in 1971	2,190	
Tax attributable to 1971 section 666 amounts	2,115	

1972

Taxable income including section 666 amounts ($12,000 + $4,000 + $715)	$16,715	
Tax on $16,715		$4,620
Less: Tax paid by A in 1972		2,830
Tax attributable to 1972 section 666 amounts		1,790

1973

Taxable income including section 666 amounts ($14,000 + $6,000 + $1,155)	$21,155	
Tax on $21,155		$6,624
Less: Tax paid by A in 1973		3,550
Tax attributable to 1973 section 666 amounts		3,074
Total tax attributable to section 666 amounts:		
1971	$ 2,115	
1972	1,790	
1973	3,074	
Total	6,979	

(iv) The partial tax computed under the exact method is $4,174, computed by subtracting the taxes deemed distributed ($2,805) from the tax attributable to the section 666 amounts ($6,979).

(c) Computation of tax by the short-cut method. *(1)* The tax referred to in paragraph (a)(2) of this section is computed as follows:

(i) First, determine the number of preceding taxable years of the trust on the last day of which an amount is deemed under section 666(a) to have been distributed. For purposes of the preceding sentence, the preceding taxable years of a trust that has received an accumulation distribution from another trust shall include the taxable years of such other trust in which an amount was deemed distributed in such accumulation distribution. For example, assume trust Z, a calendar year trust, received in its taxable year 1975 an accumulation distribution from trust Y, a calendar year trust, that included undistributed net income of trust Y for the taxable years 1972, 1973, and 1974. To the extent an accumulation distribution made by trust Z in its taxable year 1976 includes such undistributed net income, it shall be considered an accumulation distribution by trust Z in the taxable year 1976 and under section 666(a) will be deemed distributed on the last day of the preceding taxable years 1972, 1973, and 1974. For purposes of this subparagraph, such number of preceding taxable years of the trust shall not include any preceding taxable year of the trust in which the undistributed net income deemed distributed is less than 25 percent of (a) the total amounts deemed under section 666(a) to be undistributed net income from preceding taxable years divided by (b) the number of such preceding taxable years of the trust on the last day of which an amount is deemed under section 666(a) to have been distributed without application of this sentence. For example, assume that an accumulation distribution of $90,000 made to a beneficiary in 1979 is deemed distributed in the amounts of $29,000 in each of the years 1972, 1973, and 1974, and $3,000 in 1975. The number of preceding taxable years on the last day of which an amount was deemed distributed without reference to the second sentence of this subparagraph is four. However, the distribution deemed made in 1975 ($3,000) is less than $5,625, which is 25 percent of (a) the total undistributed net income deemed distributed under section 666(a) ($90,000) divided by (b) the number of such preceding taxable years (4), or $22,500. Therefore, for purposes of this subparagraph the accumulation distribution is deemed distributed in only 3 preceding taxable years (1973, 1973, and 1974).

(ii) Second, divide the amount (representing the accumulation distribution and taxes deemed distributed) required under section 668(a) to be included in the income of the beneficiary for the taxable year by the number of preceding taxable years of the trust on the last day of which an amount is deemed under section 666(a) to have been distributed (determined as provided in subdivision (i) of this subparagraph). The amount determined under this subdivision, including taxes deemed distributed, consists of the same proportion of each class of income as the total of each class of income deemed distributed in the accumulation distribution bears to the total undistributed net income from such preceding taxable years deemed distributed in the accumulation distribution. For example, assume that an amount of $50,000 is deemed distributed under section 666(a) from undistributed net income of 5 preceding taxable years of the trust and consists of $25,000 of interest, $15,000 of dividends, and $10,000 of net rental income. Taxes attributable to such amounts in the amount of $10,000 are also deemed distributed. The amount determined under this subdivision, $12,000 ($50,000 income plus $10,000 tax divided by 5 years), is deemed to consist of $6,000 in interest, $3,600 in dividends, and $2,400 in net rental income.

(iii) Third, compute the tax of the beneficiary for each of the 3 taxable years immediately preceding the year in which the accumulation distribution is paid, credited, or required to be distributed to him.

(a) With the inclusion in gross income of the beneficiary for each of such 3 years of the amount determined under subdivision (ii) of this subparagraph, and

(b) Without such inclusion.

The difference between the amount of tax computed under (a) of this subdivision for each year and the amount computed under (b) of this subdivision for that year is the additional tax resulting from the inclusion in gross income for that year of the amount determined under subdivision (ii) of this subparagraph. For example, assume that a distribution of $12,000, is includable in the income of each of the beneficiary's 3 preceding taxable years when his income (without the inclusion of the accumulation distribution) was $20,000, $30,000, and $40,000. The inclusion of $12,000 in income would produce taxable income of $32,000, $42,000, and $52,000, and the tax attributable to such increases would be $4,000, $5,000, and $6,000, respectively.

(iv) Fourth, add the additional taxes resulting from the application of subdivision (iii) of this subparagraph and then divide this amount by 3. For example, if these additional taxes are $4,000, $5,000, and $6,000 for the 3 preceding taxable years, this amount would be $5,000 ($4,000 + $5,000 + $6,000 divided by 3).

(v) Fifth, the resulting amount is then multiplied by the number of preceding taxable years of the trust on the last day of which an amount is deemed under section 666(a) to have been distributed (previously determined under subdivision (i) of this subparagraph). For example, if an amount is deemed distributed for 5 preceding taxable years, the resulting amount would be five times the $5,000 amount.

(vi) Sixth, the resulting amount, less so much of the amount of taxes deemed distributed to the beneficiary under §§ 1.666(b)-1A and 1.666(c)-1A as does not exceed such resulting amount, is the tax under the short-cut method provided in section 668(b)(1)(B).

(2) The computation of the tax by the short-cut method may be illustrated by the following example:

Example. In 1971, X creates a trust which is to accumulate its income and pay the income to Y when Y reaches 30. Y is 19. Over the 11 years of the trust, the trust earns $1,200 of interest income annually and has expenses each year of $100 allocable to the production of income. The trust pays a total tax of $1,450 on the accumulated income. In 1981, when Y reaches 30, the $9,550 of accumulated undistributed net income and the $1,100 of current net income are distributed to Y. Y is treated as having received a total distribution of $11,000 (the $9,550 accumulation distribution plus the taxes paid by the trust which are deemed to have been distributed to Y). The income of the current year (1981) is taxed directly to Y. The computation is as follows: $11,000 accumulation distribution plus taxes) divided by 10 (number of years out of which distribution was made) equals $1,100. The $1,100 added to the income of the beneficiary's preceding 3 years produces increases in tax as follows:

1980	$350
1979	300
1978	250
Total	$900

$900 (total additional tax) divided by 3 equals $300 (average annual increase in tax). $300 (average annual increase in tax) times 10 equals $3,000, from which is deducted the amount of taxes ($1,450) paid by the trust attributable to the undistributed net income deemed distributed. The amount of tax to be paid currently under the short-cut method is therefore $1,550.

(d) Disallowance of short-cut method. If, in any prior taxable year the beneficiary in which any part of the accumulation distribution of undistributed net income is deemed to have been distributed under section 666(a) to such beneficiary, any part of prior accumulation distributions of undistributed net income by each of two or more other trusts is deemed under section 666(a) to have been distributed to such beneficiary, then the short-cut method under paragraph (c) of this section may not be used and the partial tax imposed by section 668(a)(2) shall be computed only under the exact method under paragraph (b) of this section. For example, assume that, in 1978, trust X makes an accumulation distribution of undistributed net income to A, who is on the calendar year basis, and part of the accumulation distribution is deemed under section 666(a) to have been distributed on March 31, 1974. In 1977, A had received an accumulation distribution of undistributed net income from both trust Y and trust Z. Part of the accumulation distribution from trust Y was deemed under section 666(a) to have been distributed to A on June 30, 1974, and part of the accumulation distribution from trust Z was deemed under section 666(a) to have been distributed to A on December 31, 1974. Because there were portions of accumulation distributions of undistributed net income from two other trusts deemed distributed within the same prior taxable year of A (1974), the 1978 accumulation distribution from trust X may not be computed under the short-cut method provided in paragraph (c) of this section. Therefore the exact method under paragraph (b) of this section must be used to compute the tax imposed by section 666(a)(2).

T.D. 7204, 8/24/72.

§ 1.668(b)-2A Special rules applicable to section 668.

Caution: The Treasury has not yet amended Reg § 1.668(b)-2A to reflect changes made by P.L. 94-455.

(a) Rule when beneficiary not in existence on the last day of a taxable year. If a beneficiary was not in existence on the last day of preceding taxable year of the trust with respect to which a distribution is deemed made under section 666(a), it shall be assumed, for purposes of the computations under paragraphs (b) and (c) of § 1.668(b)-1A, that the beneficiary—

(1) Was in existence on such last day,

(2) Was a calendar year taxpayer,

(3) Had no gross income other than the amounts deemed distributed to him from such trust in his calendar year in which such last day occurred and from all other trusts from which amounts are deemed to have been distributed to him in such calendar year,

(4) If an individual, was unmarried and had no dependents,

(5) Had no deductions other than the standard deduction, if applicable, under section 141 for such calendar year, and

(6) Was entitled to the personal exemption under section 151 or 642(b).

For example, assume that part of an accumulation distribution made in 1980 is deemed under section 666(a) to have been distributed to the beneficiary, A, in 1973; $10,000 of a prior accumulation distribution was deemed distributed in 1973. A was born on October 9, 1975. It will be assumed for purposes of § 1.668(b)-1A that A was alive in 1973, was on the calendar year basis, had no income other than (i) the $10,000 from the earlier accumulation distribution deemed distributed in 1973, and (ii) the part of the 1980 distribution deemed distributed in 1973, and had no deductions other than the personal exemption provided in section 151. It should be noted that the standard deduction for 1973 will be available to A with respect to the distribution only to the extent it qualifies as "earned income" in the hands of the trust. See section 141(e) and the regulations thereunder and § 1.652(b)-1. If A were a trust or estate created after 1973, the same assumptions would apply, except that the trust or estate would not be entitled to the standard deduction and would receive the personal exemption provided under section 642(b) in the same manner as allowed under such section for A's first actual taxable year.

(b) Effect of other distributions. The income of the beneficiary, for any of his prior taxable years for which a tax is being recomputed under § 1.668(b)-1A, shall include any amounts of prior accumulation distributions (including prior capital gain distributions) deemed distributed under sections 666 and 669 in such prior taxable year. For purposes of the preceding sentence, a "prior accumulation distribution" is a distribution from the same or another trust which was paid, credited, or required to be distributed in a prior taxable year of the beneficiary. The term "prior accumulation distribution" also includes accumulation distributions of other trusts which were paid, credited, or required to be distributed to the beneficiary in the same taxable year and which the beneficiary has determined under paragraph (c) of this section to treat as having been distributed before the accumulation distribution for which tax is being computed under § 1.668(b)-1A. Any capital gain distribution from the same trust paid, credited, or required to be distributed in the same taxable year of the beneficiary shall not be considered under this paragraph to be a "prior capital gain distribution."

(c) Multiple distributions in the same taxable year. For purposes of paragraph (b) of this section, accumulation distributions made from more than one trust in the same taxable year of the beneficiary, regardless of when in the taxable year they were actually made, shall be treated as having been made consecutively, in whichever order the beneficiary may determine. However, the beneficiary must treat them as having been made in the same order for the purpose of computing the partial tax on the several accumulation distributions. The beneficiary shall indicate the order he has determined to deem the accumulation distributions to have been received by him on his return for the taxable year. A failure by him so to indicate, however, shall not affect his right to make such determination. The purpose of this rule is to assure that the tax resulting from the later (as so deemed under this paragraph) distribution is computed with the inclusion of the earlier distribution in the taxable base and that the tax resulting from the earlier (as so deemed under this paragraph) distribution is computed with the later distribution excluded from the taxable base.

(d) Examples. The provisions of paragraphs (b) and (c) of this section may be illustrated by the following examples:

Example (1). In 1978, trust X made an accumulation distribution of undistributed net income to A, a calendar year taxpayer, of which $3,000 was deemed to have been distributed in 1974. In 1980, trust X makes another accumulation distribution of undistributed net income to A, $10,000 of which is deemed under section 666 to have been distributed in 1974. Also in 1980, trust Y makes an accumulation distribution of undistributed net income to A, of which $5,000 is deemed under section 666 to have been distributed in 1974. A determines to treat the 1980 distribution from trust Y as having been made prior to the 1980 distribution from trust X. In computing the tax on the 1980 trust Y distribution, A's gross income for 1974 includes (i) the $3,000 deemed distributed from the 1978 distribution, and (ii) the $5,000 deemed distributed in 1974 from the 1980 trust Y accumulation distribution. To compute A's tax under the exact method for 1974 on the $10,000 from the 1980 trust X accumulation distribution deemed distributed in 1974, A's gross income for 1974 includes (i) the $10,000, (ii) the $3,000 previously deemed distributed in 1974 from the 1978 trust X accumulation distribution, and (iii) the $5,000 deemed distribution in 1974 from the 1980 trust Y accumulation distribution.

Example (2). In 1978, trust T makes all accumulation distribution of undistributed net income to B, a calendar year taxpayer. Determination of the tax on the accumulation distribution under the short-cut method requires the use of B's gross income for 1975, 1976, and 1977. In 1977, B received an accumulation distribution of undistributed net income from trust U, of which $2,000 was deemed to have been distributed in 1975, and $3,000 in 1976. B's gross income for 1975, for purposes of using the short-cut method to determine the tax from the trust accumulation distribution, will be deemed to include the $2,000 deemed distributed in 1975 by trust U, and his gross income for 1976 will be deemed to include the $3,000 deemed distributed by trust U in 1976.

T.D. 7204, 8/24/72.

§ 1.668(b)-3A Computation of the beneficiary's income and tax for a prior taxable year.

Caution: The Treasury has not yet amended Reg § 1.668(b)-3A to reflect changes made by P.L. 94-455.

(a) Basis for computation. *(1)* The beneficiary's income and tax paid for any prior taxable year for which a recomputation is involved under either the exact method or the short-cut method shall be determined by reference to the information required to be furnished by him under § 1.668(b)-4A(a). The gross income, related deductions, and taxes paid for a prior taxable year of the beneficiary as finally determined shall be used for computation purposes. The term "as finally determined" has reference to the final status of the gross income, deductions, credits, and taxes of the taxable year after the expiration of the period of limitations or after completion of any court action regarding the tax for the taxable year.

(2) If any computations rely on the beneficiary's return for a prior taxable year for which the applicable period of limitations on assessment under section 6501 has expired, and such return shows a mathematical error on its face which resulted in the wrong amount of tax being paid for such year, the determination of both the tax for such year computed with the inclusion of the section 666 amount in the beneficiary's gross income and the tax for such year computed without including such amounts in such gross income shall be based upon the return after the correction of such mathematical errors, and the beneficiary shall be credited for the correct amount of tax that should have been properly paid.

(b) Effect of allocation of undistributed net income on items based on amount of income and with respect to a net operating loss, a charitable contributions carryover, or a capital loss carryover. *(1)* In computing the tax for any taxable year under either the exact method or the short-cut method, any item which depends upon the amount of gross income, adjusted gross income, or taxable income shall be recomputed to take into consideration the amount of undistributed net income allocated to such year. For example, if $1,000 of undistributed net income is allocated to 1970, adjusted gross income for 1970 is increased from $5,000 to $6,000. The allowable 50 percent charitable deduction under section 170(b)(1)(A) is then increased and the amount of the nondeductible medical expenses under section 213 (3 percent of adjusted gross income) is also increased.

(2) In computing the tax attributable to the undistributed net income deemed distributed to the beneficiary in any of his prior taxable years under either the exact method or the short-cut method, the effect of amounts of undistributed net income on a net operating loss carryback or a carryover, a charitable contributions carryover, or a capital loss carryback or carryover, shall be taken into account. In determining the amount of tax attributable to such deemed distribution, a computation shall also be made for any taxable year which is affected by a net operating loss carryback or carryover, by a charitable contributions carryover, or by a capital loss carryback or carryover determined by reference to the taxable year to which amounts are allocated under either method and which carryback or carryover is reduced or increased by such amounts so allocated. The provisions of this subparagraph may be illustrated by the following example:

Example. In 1978, a trust makes an accumulation distribution of undistributed net income to X of $50,000 that is deemed under section 666(a) to have been distributed in 1972. X had income in 1972, 1973, and 1974, and had a net operating loss in 1975 that offset his taxable income (computed as provided in § 1.172-5) for those years, as follows:

Year	Actual income (or loss)	Income after net operating loss carryback (n.o.l.c.b.)
1972	$10,000	$0
1973	50,000	0
1974	50,000	10,000
1975	(100,000)	0

As a result of the allocation of the 1978 accumulation distribution to 1972, X's income for 1972, 1973, 1974, and 1975, after taking into account the 1975 n.o.l.c.b., is deemed to be as follows:

Year	Income deemed to have been earned after consideration of n.o.l.c.b., and accumulation distribution
1972	0 ($10,000 + $50,000 − $60,000 n.o.l.c.b.).
1973	$10,000 ($50,000 − $40,000 balance of n.o.l.c.b.).
1974	$50,000.
1975	0.

Therefore, the tax on the 1978 accumulation distribution to X is the tax X would have paid in 1973 and 1974 had he had the above income in such years.

(c) Averaging. A beneficiary who uses the exact method may recompute his tax for a prior taxable year by using income averaging for all of his actual income for that year, plus the amount deemed distributed in that year under section 666, even though he may not have actually used section 1301 to determine his income tax for such taxable year. For purposes of such recomputation, the beneficiary's income for all other taxable years involved must include any amounts deemed distributed in such years from the current and all prior accumulation distributions. See § 1.668(b)-4A(c)(3) for additional information requirements. The beneficiary may not apply the provisions of this paragraph to a taxable year in which an amount is deemed to be income by reason of § 1.666(d)-1A(b). The accumulation distribution itself is not eligible for income averaging in the years in which it is paid, credited, or required to be distributed. See section 1302(a)(2)(B) and the regulations thereunder.

T.D. 7204, 8/24/72.

§ 1.668(b)-4A Information requirements with respect to beneficiary.

Caution: The Treasury has not yet amended Reg § 1.668(b)-4A to reflect changes made by P.L. 94-455.

(a) Information to be supplied by beneficiary: *(1) In general.* The beneficiary must supply the information required by subparagraph (3) of this paragraph for any prior taxable year for which a recomputation is required under either the exact method or the short-cut method. Such information shall be filed with the beneficiary's return for the year in which the tax under section 668(a)(2) is imposed.

(2) Failure to furnish. If the beneficiary fails to furnish the information required by this paragraph for any prior year involved in the exact method, he may not use such method and the tax computed under paragraph (c) of § 1.668(b)-1A (the short-cut method) shall be deemed to be the amount of partial tax imposed by section 668(a)(2). See, however, paragraph (b) of this section for an exception to this rule where the short-cut method is not permitted. If he cannot furnish the information required for a prior year involved in the short-cut method, such year will be recomputed on the basis of the best information available.

(3) Information required. The beneficiary shall file the following items with his income tax return for the taxable year in which the accumulation distribution is included in income:

(i) A statement showing the gross income, adjustments, deductions, credits, taxes paid, and computations for each of his taxable years for which a computation is required under the method by which he computes his partial tax imposed by section 668(a)(2). Such statement shall include such amounts for the taxable year as adjusted by any events subsequent to such year, such as any adjustment resulting from the determination of a deficiency or an overpayment, or from a court action regarding the tax.

(ii) A copy of the statement required by this subparagraph to be furnished by the beneficiary for any prior taxable year in which an accumulation distribution was received by him which was also deemed distributed in whole or in part in the prior taxable year for which the statement under subdivision (i) of this subparagraph is required.

(iii) A copy of any statements furnished the beneficiary by the trustee (such as schedules E and J of Form 1041, etc.) with regard to the current taxable year or any prior taxable year for which a statement is furnished under subdivision (i) of this subparagraph.

(b) Exception. If by reason of § 1.668(b)-1A(e) the beneficiary may not compute the partial tax on the accumulation distribution under § 1.668(b)-1A(c) (the short-cut method), the provisions of subparagraph (2) of paragraph (a) of this section shall not apply. In such case, if the beneficiary fails to provide the information required by subparagraph (3) of paragraph (a) of this section for any prior taxable year, the district director shall, by utilizing whatever information is available to him (including information supplied by the beneficiary), determine the beneficiary's income and related expenses for such prior taxable year.

(c) Records to be supplied by the beneficiary. *(1) Year when return was filed.* If the beneficiary filed an income tax return for a taxable year for which a recomputation is necessary, and the period of limitations on assessment under section 6501 for such year has expired as of the filing of the return for the year in which the accumulation distribution was made, then a copy of such return, plus proof of any changes of liability for such year due to the determination of a deficiency or an overpayment, court action, etc., shall, to the extent they verify the statements required under paragraph (a) of this section, serve as proof of such statements. If the period of limitations on assessment under section 6501 for a prior taxable year has not expired as of the filing of the beneficiary's return for the year in which the accumulation distribution was received, then the records required by section 6001 to be retained by the beneficiary for such prior taxable year shall serve as the basis of proof of the statements required to be filed under paragraph (a) of this section.

(2) Year for which no return was filed. If the beneficiary did not file a return for a taxable year for which a recomputation is necessary, he shall be deemed to have had in such year, in the absence of proof to the contrary, gross income in the amount equal to the maximum amount of gross income that he could have received without having had to file a return under section 6012 for such year.

(3) Distributions deemed averaged. In order for a beneficiary to use income averaging with respect to a prior taxable year (see § 1.668(b)-3A((c)), he must furnish all the information that would support the computation under section 1301 as if the distribution were actually received and averaged in such prior taxable year, even if a portion of the information relates to years in which no amount was deemed distributed to the beneficiary.

T.D. 7204, 8/24/72.

§ 1.669(a)-1A Amount allocated.

Caution: The Treasury has not yet amended Reg § 1.669(a)-1A to reflect changes made by P.L. 94-455.

(a) In general. After a trust has distributed all of its undistributed net income, the rules concerning the treatment of capital gain distributions (prescribed under section 669) may become applicable to an accumulation distribution. This section prescribes rules to determine from which years capital gain distributions are considered to be made. For the definition of "capital gain distribution," see § 1.665(g)-1A. Section 669 does not apply to a trust that has distributed all of its income currently since its inception. See § 1.668(a)-1A(c). Capital gain retains its character in the hands of the beneficiary. See § 1.669(f)-1A. A capital gain distribution to more than one beneficiary will be allocated among them. See § 1.668(a)-2A.

(b) First-in, first-out rule. A capital gain distribution is allocated to the preceding taxable years of the trust (as defined in § 1.665(e)-1A(a)(1)(iii)), according to the undistributed capital gain of the trust for such years. For this purpose, a capital gain distribution is first allocated to the earliest such preceding taxable year in which there is undistributed capital gain and shall then be allocated in turn, beginning with the next earliest, to any remaining preceding taxable years of the trust. The portion of the capital gain distribution allocated to the earliest preceding taxable year is the amount of undistributed capital gain for that preceding taxable year. The portion of the capital gain distribution allocated to any preceding taxable year subsequent to the earliest such preceding taxable year is the excess of the capital gain distribution over the aggregate of the undistributed capital gain for all earlier preceding taxable years. See paragraph (c) of this section for adjustments to undistributed capital gain for prior distributions.

(c) Reduction of undistributed capital gain for prior capital gain distributions. For the purposes of allocating to any preceding taxable year a capital gain distribution of the taxable year, the undistributed capital gain of such preceding taxable year is reduced by the amount from such year deemed distributed in any capital gain distribution made in any taxable year intervening between such preceding taxable year and the taxable year. Accordingly, for example, if a trust subject to the capital gain throwback has no undistributed net income but has undistributed capital gain for 1974, and makes capital gain distributions during the taxable years 1978 and 1979, then in determining that part of the 1979 capital gain distribution that is thrown back to 1974, the undistributed capital gain for 1974 is reduced by the amount of such undistributed capital gain for 1974 deemed distributed in the 1978 capital gain distribution.

(d) Rule when no undistributed capital gain. If, before the application of the provisions of subpart D to a capital gain distribution for the taxable year, there is no undistributed capital gain for a preceding taxable year, then no portion of the capital gain distribution is deemed distributed on the last day of such preceding taxable year. Thus, for example, if a capital gain distribution is made during the taxable year 1975 from a trust whose earliest preceding taxable year is taxable year 1970, and the trust had no undistributed capital gain for 1970, then no portion of the 1975 capital gain distribution is deemed distributed on the last day of 1970.

(e) Example. The provisions of this section may be illustrated by the following example:

Example. In 1977, a trust reporting on the calendar year basis makes a capital gain distribution of $33,000. In 1969, the trust had $6,000 of undistributed capital gain; in 1970, $4,000; in 1971, none; in 1972, $7,000; in 1973, $5,000; in 1974, $8,000; in 1975, $6,000; in 1976, $4,000; and $6,000 in 1977. The capital gain distribution is deemed distributed $6,000 in 1969, $4,000 in 1970, none in 1971, $7,000 in 1972, $5,000 in 1973, $8,000 in 1974, and $3,000 in 1975.

T.D. 7204, 8/24/72.

§ 1.669(b)-1A Tax on distribution.

Caution: The Treasury has not yet amended Reg § 1.669(b)-1A to reflect changes made by P.L. 94-455.

(a) In general. The partial tax imposed on the beneficiary by section 668(a)(3) shall be the lesser of—

(1) The tax computed under paragraph (b) of this section (the "exact" method), or

(2) The tax computed under paragraph (c) of this section (the "short-cut" method),

except as provided in § 1.669(c)-3A (relating to failure to furnish proper information) and paragraph (d) of this section (relating to disallowance of short-cut method). For purposes of this paragraph, the method used in the return shall be accepted as the method that produces the lesser tax. The beneficiary's choice of the two methods is not dependent upon the method that he uses to compute his partial tax imposed by section 668(a)(2).

(b) Computation of partial tax by the exact method. The partial tax referred to in paragraph (a)(1) of this section is computed as follows:

(1) First, compute the tax attributable to the section 669 amounts for each of the preceding taxable years. For purposes of this paragraph, the "section 669 amounts" for a preceding taxable year are the amounts deemed distributed under section 669(a) on the last day of such preceding taxable year, plus the amount of taxes deemed distributed on such day under section 669(d) or (e). The tax attributable to such amounts in each prior taxable year of the beneficiary is the difference between the tax for such year computed with the inclusion of the section 669 amounts in the beneficiary's gross income and the tax for such year computed without including them in such gross income. Tax computations for each such year shall reflect a taxpayer's marital, dependency, exemption, and filing status for such year. To the extent the undistributed capital gain of a trust deemed distributed in a capital gain distribution includes amounts received as a capital gain distribution from another trust, for purposes of this paragraph they shall be considered as amounts deemed distributed by the trust under section 669(a) on the last day of each of the preceding taxable years in which such amounts were accumulated by such other trust. For example, assume trust Z, a calendar year trust received in its taxable year 1975 a capital gain distribution from trust Y, a calendar year trust, that included undistributed capital gain of trust Y for the taxable years 1972, 1973, and 1974. To the extent a capital gain distribution made by trust Z in its taxable year 1976 includes such undistributed capital gain, it shall be considered a capital gain distribution by trust Z in the taxable year 1976 and under section 669(a) will be deemed distributed on the last day of the preceding taxable years 1972, 1973, and 1974.

(2) From the sum of the taxes for the prior taxable years attributable to the section 669(a) amounts (computed in ac-

cordance with subparagraph (1) of this paragraph), subtract so much of the amount of taxes deemed distributed to the beneficiary under §§ 1.669(d)-1A and 1.669(e)-1A as does not exceed such sum. The resulting amount, if any, is the partial tax on the beneficiary, computed under the exact method, for the taxable year in which the capital gain distribution is paid, credited, or required to be distributed to the beneficiary.

(c) Computation of tax by the short-cut method. *(1)* The tax referred to in paragraph (a)(2) of this section is computed as follows:

(i) First, determine the number of preceding taxable years of the trust on the last day of which an amount is deemed under section 669(a) to have been distributed. For purposes of the preceding sentence, the preceding taxable years of a trust that has received a capital gain distribution from another trust shall include the taxable years of such other trust in which an amount was deemed distributed in such capital gain distribution. For example, assume trust Z, a calendar year trust, received in its taxable year 1975 a capital gain distribution from trust Y, a calendar year trust, that included undistributed capital gain of trust Y for the taxable years 1972, 1973, and 1974. To the extent a capital gain distribution made by trust Z in its taxable year 1976 includes such undistributed capital gain, it shall be considered a capital gain distribution by trust Z in the taxable year 1976 and under section 669(a) will be deemed distributed on the last day of the preceding taxable years 1972, 1973, and 1974. For purposes of this subparagraph, such number of preceding taxable years of the trust shall not include any preceding taxable year of the trust in which the undistributed capital gain deemed distributed is less than 25 percent of (a) the total amounts deemed under section 669(a) to be undistributed capital gain from preceding taxable years, divided by (b) the number of such preceding taxable years of the trust on the last day of which an amount is deemed under section 669(a) to have been distributed without application of this sentence. For example, assume that a capital gain distribution of $90,000 made to a beneficiary in 1979 is deemed distributed in the amounts of $29,000 in each of the years 1972, 1973, and 1974, and $3,000 in 1975. The number of preceding taxable years on the last day of which an amount was deemed distributed without reference to the second sentence of this subparagraph is 4. However, the distribution deemed made in 1975 ($3,000) is less than $5,625, which is 25 percent of (a) the total undistributed capital gain deemed distributed under section 669(a) ($90,000) divided by (b) the number of such preceding taxable years (4), or $22,500. Therefore, for purposes of this subparagraph, the capital gain distribution is deemed distributed in only 3 preceding taxable years (1972, 1973, and 1974).

(ii) Second, divide the amount (representing the capital gain distribution and taxes deemed distributed) required under section 668(a) to be included in the income of the beneficiary for the taxable year by the number of preceding taxable years of the trust on the last day of which an amount is deemed under section 669(a) to have been distributed (determined as provided in subdivision (i) of this paragraph). The amount determined under this subdivision, including taxes deemed distributed, consists of the same proportion of long-term and short-term capital gain as the total of each type of capital gain deemed distributed in the capital gain distribution bears to the total undistributed capital gain from such preceding taxable years deemed distributed in the capital gain distribution. For example, assume that an amount of $50,000 is deemed distributed under section 669(a) from undistributed capital gain of 5 preceding taxable years of the trust, and consists of $30,000 of long-term capital gain and $20,000 of short-term capital gain. Taxes attributable to such amounts in the amount of $10,000 are also deemed distributed. The amount determined under this subdivision, $12,000 ($50,000 income plus $10,000 tax, divided by 5 years), is deemed to consist of $7,200 of long-term capital gain and $4,800 in short-term capital gain.

(iii) Third, compute the tax of the beneficiary for each of the 3 taxable years immediately preceding the year in which the capital gain distribution is paid, credited, or required to be distributed to him,

(a) With the inclusion in gross income of the beneficiary for each of such 3 years of the amount determined under subdivision (ii) of this subparagraph, and

(b) Without such inclusion.

The difference between the amount of tax computed under (a) of this subdivision for each year and the amount computed under (b) of this subdivision for that year is the additional tax resulting from the inclusion in gross income for that year of the amount determined under subdivision (ii) of this subparagraph.

(iv) Fourth, add the additional taxes resulting from the application of subdivision (iii) of this subparagraph and then divide this amount by 3.

(v) Fifth, the resulting amount is then multiplied by the number of preceding taxable years of the trust on the last day of which an amount is deemed under section 669(a) to have been distributed (previously determined under subdivision (i) of this subparagraph).

(vi) The resulting amount, less so much of the amount of taxes deemed distributed to the beneficiary under §§ 1.669(d)-1A and 1.669(e)-1A as does not exceed such resulting amount, is the tax under the short-cut method provided in section 669(b)(1)(B).

(2) See § 1.668(b)-1A(c) for examples of the short-cut method in the context of an accumulation distribution.

(d) Disallowance of short-cut method. If, in any prior taxable year of the beneficiary in which any part of the capital gain distribution is deemed to have been distributed under section 669(a) to such beneficiary, any part of prior capital gain distributions by each of two or more other trusts is deemed under section 669(a) to have been distributed to such beneficiary, then the short-cut method under paragraph (c) of this section may not be used and the partial tax imposed by section 668(a)(3) shall be computed only under the exact method under paragraph (b) of this section. For example, assume that, in 1978, trust X makes a capital gain distribution to A, who is on the calendar year basis, and part of the distribution is deemed under section 669(a) to have been distributed on March 31, 1974. In 1977, A had received a capital gain distribution from both trust Y and trust Z. Part of the capital gain distribution from trust Y was deemed under section 669(a) to have been distributed to A on June 30, 1974, and part of the capital gain distribution from trust Z was deemed under section 669(a) to have been distributed to A on December 31, 1974. Because there were portions of capital gain distributions from two other trusts deemed distributed within the same prior taxable year of A (1974), the 1978 capital gain distribution from trust X may not be computed under the short-cut method provided in paragraph (c) of this section. Therefore the exact method under paragraph (b) of this section must be used to compute the tax imposed by section 668(a)(3).

T.D. 7204, 8/24/72.

§ 1.669(c)-1A Special rules applicable to section 669.

Caution: The Treasury has not yet amended Reg § 1.669(c)-1A to reflect changes made by P.L. 94-455.

(a) Effect of other distributions. The income of the beneficiary, for any of his prior taxable years for which a tax is being recomputed under § 1.669(b)-1A, shall include any amounts of prior accumulation distributions (including prior capital gain distributions) deemed distributed under sections 666 and 669 in such prior taxable year. For purposes of the preceding sentence, a "prior accumulation distribution" is a distribution from the same or another trust which was paid, credited, or required to be distributed in a prior taxable year of the beneficiary. The term "prior accumulation distribution" also includes accumulation distributions of the same or other trusts which were distributed to the beneficiary in the same taxable year. The term "prior capital gain distribution" also includes capital gain distributions of other trusts which were paid, credited, or required to be distributed to the beneficiary in the same taxable year and which the beneficiary has determined under paragraph (b) of this section to treat as having been distributed before the capital gain distribution for which tax is being computed under § 1.669(b)-1A.

(b) Multiple distributions in the same taxable year. For purposes of paragraph (a) of this section, capital gain distributions made from more than one trust in the same taxable year of the beneficiary, regardless of when in the taxable year they were actually made, shall be treated as having been made consecutively, in whichever order the beneficiary may determine. However, the beneficiary must treat them as having been made in the same order for the purpose of computing the partial tax on the several capital gain distributions. The beneficiary shall indicate the order he has determined to deem the capital gain distributions to have been received by him on his return for the taxable year. A failure by him so to indicate, however, shall not affect his right to make such determination. The purpose of this rule is to assure that the tax resulting from the later (as so deemed under this paragraph) distribution is computed with the inclusion of the earlier distribution in the taxable base and that the tax resulting from the earlier (as so deemed under this paragraph) distribution is computed when the later distribution excluded from the taxable base.

(c) Rule when beneficiary not in existence on the last day of a taxable year. If a beneficiary was not in existence on the last day of a preceding taxable year of the trust with respect to which a distribution is deemed made under section 669(a), it shall be assumed, for purposes of the computations under paragraphs (b) and (c) of § 1.669(b)-1A, that the beneficiary—

(1) Was in existence on such last day,

(2) Was a calendar year taxpayer,

(3) Had no gross income other than the amounts deemed distributed to him from such trust in his calendar year in which such last day occurred and from all other trusts from which amounts are deemed to have been distributed to him in such calendar year,

(4) If an individual was unmarried and had no dependents,

(5) Had no deductions other than the standard deduction, if applicable, under section 141 for such calendar year, and

(6) Was entitled to the personal exemption under section 151 or 642(b).

For example, assume that part of a capital gain distribution made in 1980 is deemed under section 669(a) to have been distributed to the beneficiary, A, in 1973. $10,000 of a prior accumulation distribution was deemed distributed in 1973. A was born on October 9, 1975. It will be assumed for purposes of § 1.669(b)-1A that A was alive in 1973, was on the calendar year basis, had no income other than (i) the $10,000 from the accumulation distribution deemed distributed in 1973 and (ii) the part of the 1980 distribution deemed distributed in 1973, and had no deductions other than the personal exemption provided in section 151. If A were a trust or estate created after 1973, the same assumptions would apply, except that the trust or estate would not be entitled to the standard deduction and would receive the personal exemption provided under section 642(b) in the same manner as allowed under such section for A's first actual taxable year.

(d) Examples. The provisions of paragraphs (a) and (b) of this section may be illustrated by the following examples:

Example (1). In 1978, trust X made a capital gain distribution to A, a calendar year taxpayer, of which $3,000 was deemed to have been distributed in 1974. In 1980, trust X makes another capital gain distribution to A, $10,000 of which is deemed under section 669(a) to have been distributed in 1974. Also in 1980, trust Y makes a capital gain distribution to A, of which $5,000 is deemed under section 669(a) to have been distributed in 1974. A determines to treat the 1980 distribution from trust Y as having been made prior to the 1980 distribution from trust X. In computing the tax on the 1980 Trust Y distribution A's gross income for 1973 includes (i) the $3,000 deemed distributed from the 1978 distribution, and (ii) the $5,000 deemed distributed in 1974 from the 1980 Trust Y capital gain distribution. To compute A's tax under the exact method for 1974 on the $10,000 from the 1980 trust X capital gain distribution deemed distributed in 1974. A's gross income for 1974 includes (i) the $10,000, (ii) the $3,000 previously deemed distributed in 1974 from the 1978 trust X capital gain distribution, and (iii) the $5,000 deemed distributed in 1974 from the 1980 trust Y capital gain distribution.

Example (2). In 1978, trust T makes a capital gain distribution to B, a calendar year taxpayer. Determination of the tax on the distribution under the short-cut method requires the use of B's gross income for 1975, 1976, and 1977. In 1977, B received an accumulation distribution from trust U, of which $2,000 was deemed to have been distributed in 1975, and $3,000 in 1976. B's gross income for 1975, for purposes of using the shortcut method to determine the tax from the trust T capital gain distribution, will be deemed to include the $2,000 deemed distributed in 1975 by trust U, and his gross income for 1976 will be deemed to include the $3,000 deemed distributed by trust U in 1976.

T.D. 7204, 8/24/72.

§ 1.669(c)-2A Computation of the beneficiary's income and tax for a prior taxable year.

Caution: The Treasury has not yet amended Reg § 1.669(c)-2A to reflect changes made by P.L. 94-455.

(a) Basis for computation. *(1)* The beneficiary's income and tax paid for any prior taxable year for which a recomputation is involved under either the exact method or the short-cut method shall be determined by reference to the information required to be furnished by him under § 1.669(c)-3A(a). The gross income, related deductions, and taxes paid for a prior taxable year of the beneficiary as finally determined shall be used for recomputation purposes. The term "as finally determined" shall have the same meaning for purposes of this section as in § 1.668(b)-3A(a).

(2) If any computations rely on the beneficiary's return for a prior taxable year for which the applicable period of limitations on assessment under section 6501 has expired, and such return shows a mathematical error on its face which resulted in the wrong amount of tax being paid for such year, the determination of both the tax for such year computed with the inclusion of the section 669 amounts in the beneficiary's gross income, and the tax for such year computed without including such amounts in such gross income, shall be based upon the return after the correction of such mathematical errors.

(b) Effect of allocation of undistributed capital gain on items based on amount of income and with respect to a net operating loss, a charitable contributions carryover, or a capital loss carryover. *(1)* In computing the tax for any taxable year under either the exact method or the short-cut method, any item which depends upon the amount of gross income, adjusted gross income, or taxable income shall be recomputed to take into consideration the amount of undistributed capital gain allocated to such year. For example, if $2,000 of undistributed long-term capital gain is allocated to 1970, adjusted gross income for 1970 is increased from $5,000 to $6,000. The allowable 50 percent charitable deduction under section 170(b)(1)(A) is then increased and the amount of the nondeductible medical expenses under section 213 (3 percent of adjusted gross income) is also increased.

(2) In computing the tax attributable to the undistributed capital gain deemed distributed to the beneficiary in any of his prior taxable years under either the exact method or the short-cut method, the effect of amounts of undistributed capital gain on a net operating loss carryback or carryover, a charitable contributions carryover, or a capital loss carryback or carryover, shall be taken into account. In determining the amount of tax attributable to such deemed distribution, a computation shall also be made for any taxable year which is affected by a net operating loss carryback or carryover, by a charitable contributions carryover, or by a capital loss carryback or carryover determined by reference to the taxable year to which amounts are allocated under either method and which carryback or carryover is reduced or increased by such amounts so allocated.

T.D. 7204, 8/24/72.

§ 1.669(c)-3A Information requirements with respect to beneficiary.

Caution: The Treasury has not yet amended Reg § 1.669(c)-3A to reflect changes made by P.L. 94-455.

(a) Information to be supplied by beneficiary. *(1) Use of exact method.* The beneficiary must supply the information required by subparagraph (3) of § 1.668(b)-4A(a) for any prior taxable year for which a recomputation is required under either the exact method or the short-cut method. Such information shall be filed with the beneficiary's return for the year in which the tax under section 668(a)(3) is imposed.

(2) Failure to furnish. If the beneficiary fails to furnish the information required by this paragraph for any prior year involved in the exact method, he may not use such method and the tax computed under paragraph (c) of § 1.669(b)-1A (the short-cut method) shall be deemed to be the amount of partial tax imposed by section 668(a)(3). See, however, paragraph (b) of this section for an exception to this rule where the short-cut method is not permitted. If he cannot furnish the information required for a prior year involved in the short-cut method, such year will be recomputed on the basis of the best information available.

(b) Exception. If, by reason of § 1.669(b)-1A(e), the beneficiary may not compute the partial tax on the capital gain distribution under § 1.669(b)-1A(c) (the short-cut method), the provisions of subparagraph (2) of paragraph (a) of this section shall not apply. In such case, if the beneficiary fails to provide the information required by § 1.668(b)-4A(a)(3) for any prior taxable year, the district director shall, by utilizing whatever information is available to him (including information supplied by the beneficiary), determine the beneficiary's income and related expenses for such prior taxable year.

T.D. 7204, 8/24/72.

§ 1.669(d)-1A Total taxes deemed distributed.

Caution: The Treasury has not yet amended Reg § 1.669(d)-1A to reflect changes made by P.L. 94-455.

(a) If a capital gain distribution is deemed under § 1.669(a)-1A to be distributed on the last day of a preceding taxable year and the amount is not less than the undistributed capital gain for such preceding taxable year, then an additional amount equal to the "taxes imposed on the trust attributable to the undistributed capital gain" (as defined in § 1.665(d)-1A(c)) for such preceding taxable year is also deemed to have been properly distributed. For example, assume a trust has no distributable net income and has undistributed capital gain of $18,010 for the taxable year 1974. The taxes imposed on the trust attributable to the undistributed capital gain are $2,190. During the taxable year 1977, a capital gain distribution of $18,010 is made to the beneficiary which is deemed under § 1.669(a)-1A to have been distributed on the last day of 1974. The 1977 capital gain distribution is not less than the 1974 undistributed capital gain. Accordingly, taxes of $2,190 imposed on the trust attributable to the undistributed capital gain for 1974 are also deemed to have been distributed on the last day of 1974. Thus, a total of $20,200 will be deemed to have been distributed on the last day of 1974.

(b) For the purpose of paragraph (a) of this section, the undistributed capital gain of any preceding taxable year and the taxes imposed on the trust for such preceding taxable year attributable to such undistributed capital gain are computed after taking into account any capital gain distributions of taxable years intervening between such preceding taxable year and the taxable year. See paragraph (c) of § 1.669(a)-1A.

T.D. 7204, 8/24/72.

§ 1.669(e)-1A Pro rata portion of taxes deemed distributed.

Caution: The Treasury has not yet amended Reg § 1.669(e)-1A to reflect changes made by P.L. 94-455.

(a) If a capital gain distribution is deemed under § 1.669(a)-1A to be distributed on the last day of a preceding taxable year and the amount is less than the undistributed capital gain for such preceding taxable year, then an additional amount is also deemed to have been properly distributed. The additional amount is equal to the "taxes imposed on the trust attributable to the undistributed capital gain" (as defined in § 1.665(d)-1A(c) for such preceding taxable year, multiplied by a fraction, the numerator of which is the amount of the capital gain distribution allocated to such preceding taxable year and the denominator of which is the undistributed capital gain for such preceding taxable year. See paragraph (b) of example (1) and paragraphs (c) and (f) of example (2) in § 1.669(e)-2A for illustrations of this paragraph.

(b) For the purpose of paragraph (a) of this section, the undistributed capital gain of any preceding taxable year and the taxes imposed on the trust for such preceding taxable year attributable to such undistributed capital gain are computed after taking into account any capital gain distributions of any taxable years intervening between such preceding taxable year and the taxable year. See paragraph (c) of § 1.669(a)-1A, paragraph (c) of example (1) and paragraphs (e) and (h) of example (2) in § 1.669(e)-2A.

T.D. 7204, 8/24/72.

§ 1.669(e)-2A Illustration of the provisions of section 669.

Caution: The Treasury has not yet amended Reg § 1.669(e)-2A to reflect changes made by P.L. 94-455.

The application of the provisions of §§ 1.669(a)-1A, 1.669(d)-1A, and 1.669(e)-1A may be illustrated by the following examples:

Example (1). (a) A trust created on January 1, 1974, makes capital gain distributions as follows:

1979	$14,000
1980	60,000

The trust had accumulated income in 1974.

For 1974 through 1978, the undistributed portion of capital gain, taxes imposed on the trust attributable to the undistributed capital gain, and undistributed capital gain are as follows:

Year	Undistributed portion of capital gain	Taxes imposed on the trust attributable to the undistributed capital gain	Undistributed capital gain
1974	$24,200	$2,830	$21,370
1975	32,200	4,330	27,870
1976	12,200	1,130	11,070
1977	None	None	None
1978	10,200	910	9,290

(b) Since the entire amount of the capital gain distribution for 1979 ($14,000), determined without regard to the capital gain distribution for 1980, is less than the undistributed capital gain for 1974 ($21,370), an additional amount of $1,864 (14,000/21,370 × $2,830) is deemed distributed under section 669(e).

(c) In allocating the capital gain distribution for 1980, the amount of undistributed capital gain for 1974 will reflect the capital gain distribution for 1979. The undistributed capital gain for 1974 will then be $7,370 and the taxes imposed on the trust for 1974 will be $976, determined as follows:

Undistributed capital gain as of the close of 1974	$21,370
Less: Capital gain distribution (1979)	14,000
Balance (undistributed capital gain as of the close of 1979)	7,370
Taxes imposed on the trust attributable to the undistributed capital gain as of the close of 1979 (7,370/21,370 × 2,830)	976

(d) The capital gain distribution of $60,000 for 1980 is deemed to have been made on the last day of the preceding taxable years of the trust to the extent of $55,600, the total of the undistributed capital gain for such years, as shown in the tabulation below. In addition, $7,346, the total taxes imposed on the trust attributable to the undistributed capital gain for such years is also deemed to have been distributed on the last day of such years, as shown below:

Year	Undistributed capital gain	Taxes imposed on the trust attributable to the undistributed capital gain
1974	$7,370	$976
1975	27,870	4,330
1976	11,070	1,130
1977	None	None
1978	9,290	910
1979	None	None
Total	55,600	7,346

Example (2). (a) Under the terms of a trust instrument, the trustee has discretion to accumulate or distribute the income to X and to invade corpus for the benefit of X. The trust is subject to capital gain throwback. Both X and the trust report on the calendar year basis. All of the income for 1974 was distributed and the capital gain was accumulated. The capital gain of the trust for the taxable year 1974 is $40,200 and the income taxes paid by the trust for 1974 attributable to the undistributed capital gain are $6,070. All of the income and capital gains for 1975 and 1976 were distributed and in addition the trustee made capital gain distributions within the meaning of section 665(g) of $8,000 for each year.

(b) The undistributed capital gain of the trust determined under section 665(f) as of the close of 1974 is $34,130, computed as follows:

Capital gain	$40,200
Less: Taxes imposed on the trust attributable to the undistributed capital gain	6,070
Undistributed capital gain as of the close of 1974	34,130

(c) The capital gain distribution of $8,000 made during the taxable year 1975 is deemed under section 669(a) to have been made on December 31, 1974. Since this capital gain distribution is less than the 1974 undistributed capital gain of $34,130, a portion of the taxes imposed on the trust for 1974 is also deemed under section 669(e) to have been distributed on December 31, 1974. The total amount deemed to have been distributed to X on December 31, 1974, is $9,486, computed as follows:

Capital gain distribution	$8,000
Taxes deemed distributed (8,000/34,130 × $6,070)	1,423
Total	9,423

(d) After the application of the provisions of subpart D to the capital gain distribution of 1975, the undistributed capital gain of the trust for 1974 is $26,130, computed as follows:

Undistributed capital gain as of the close of 1974	$34,130
Less: 1975 capital gain distribution deemed distributed on December 31, 1974 (paragraph (c) of this example)	8,000
Undistributed capital gain for 1974 as of the close of 1975	26,130

(e) The taxes imposed on the trust attributable to the undistributed capital gain for the taxable year 1974, as adjusted to give effective to the 1975 capital gain distribution, amount to $4,647, computed as follows:

Taxes imposed on the trust attributable to undistributed capital gain as of the close of 1974	$6,070
Less: Taxes deemed distributed in 1974	1,423
Taxes attributable to the undistributed capital gain determined as of the close of 1975	4,647

(f) The capital gain distribution of $8,000 made during the taxable year 1976 is, under section 669(a), deemed an amount properly distributed to X on December 31, 1974. Since the capital gain distribution is less than the 1974 adjusted undistributed capital gain of $26,130, the trust is deemed under section 669(e) also to have distributed on December 31, 1974, a portion of the taxes imposed on the trust for 1974. The total amount deemed to be distributed on December 31, 1974, with respect to the capital gain distribution made in 1976, is $9,423, computed as follows:

Capital gain distribution	$8,000
Taxes deemed distributed (8,000/26,130 × $4,647)	1,423
Total	9,423

(g) After the application of the provisions of subpart D to the capital gain distribution of 1976, the undistributed capital gain of the trust for 1974 is $18,130, computed as follows:

Undistributed capital gain for 1974 as of the close of 1975	$26,130
Less:	
1976 capital gain distribution deemed distributed on December 31, 1974 (paragraph (f) of this example)	8,000
Undistributed capital gain for 1974 as of the close of 1976	18,130

(h) The taxes imposed on the trust attributable to the undistributed capital gain of the trust for the taxable year 1974, determined as of the close of the taxable year 1976, amount to $3,224 ($4,647 less $1,423).

T.D. 7204, 8/24/72.

§ 1.669(f)-1A Character of capital gain.

Caution: The Treasury has not yet amended Reg § 1.669(f)-1A to reflect changes made by P.L. 94-455.

Amounts distributed as a capital gain distribution and the taxes attributable thereto (determined under § 1.665(d)-1A(c) retain the character that the gain had with respect to the trust. Thus, a capital gain that was taxed to the trust as a "long-term" capital gain and the pro rata amount of taxes attributable to such long-term gain shall be treated to the beneficiary as a "long-term" capital gain when they are deemed distributed as part of a capital gain distribution. If a trust has different types of capital gain for the same taxable year, and all of the capital gains are not deemed distributed for such year under section 669(a), the amount deemed distributed from such year (including taxes deemed distributed) shall be treated as consisting of the different types of gains in the ratio that the total of each such type of gains of the trust bears to the total of all such gains for the taxable year. For example, assume that in 1975 a trust had net long-term capital gains of $4,000 and net short-term capital gains of $2,000. Taxes attributable to such undistributed capital gain were $700. Therefore, undistributed capital gain for 1975 is $5,300. In 1980, the trust distributed $2,650 that is deemed to be undistributed capital gain from 1975. Such distribution is deemed to consist of long-term gain of $1,766.67 and short-term gain of $883.33. The taxes deemed distributed of $350 consist of long-term gain of $233.33 and short-term gain of $116.67.

T.D. 7204, 8/24/72.

§ 1.669(f)-2A Exception for capital gain distributions from certain trusts.

Caution: The Treasury has not yet amended Reg § 1.669(f)-2A to reflect changes made by P.L. 94-455.

(a) General rule. If a capital gain distribution is paid, credited, or required to be distributed before January 1, 1973, from a trust that was in existence on December 31, 1969, section 669 shall not apply and no tax shall be imposed on such capital gain distribution under section 663(a)(3). If capital gain distributions from more than one such trust are paid, credited, or required to be distributed to a beneficiary before January 1, 1973, the exception under the preceding sentence shall apply only to the capital gain distributions from one of the trusts. The beneficiary shall indicate on his income tax return for the taxable year in which the distribution would otherwise be included in income under section 668(a) the trust to which the exception provided by this section shall apply.

(b) Special rule for section 2056(b)(5) trust. A capital gain distribution paid, credited, or required to be distributed by a trust that qualifies under section 2056(b)(5) of the Code (commonly known as a "marital deduction trust") to a surviving spouse shall, in general, not be taxed under section 668(a)(3) since such a trust is required to distribute all of its income annually or more often. See section 2056(b)(5) and the regulations thereunder.

(c) Effect of exception. If this section applies to a capital gain distribution from a trust, such distribution shall reduce the undistributed capital gain of the trust. Since section 669 does not apply to such capital gain distribution, no amount of taxes paid by the trust attributable to such capital gain distribution are deemed distributed under section 669(d) and (e).

T.D. 7204, 8/24/72.

§ 1.671-1 Grantors and others treated as substantial owners; scope.

(a) Subpart E (section 671 and following), part I, subchapter J, chapter 1 of the Code, contains provisions taxing income of a trust to the grantor or another person under certain circumstances even though he is not treated as a beneficiary under subparts A through D (section 641 and following) of such part I. Sections 671 and 672 contain general provisions relating to the entire subpart. Sections 673 through 677 define the circumstances under which income of a trust is taxed to a grantor. These circumstances are in general as follows:

(1) If the grantor has retained a reversionary interest in the trust, within specified time limits (section 673);

(2) If the grantor or a nonadverse party has certain powers over the beneficial interests under the trust (section 674);

(3) If certain administrative powers over the trust exist under which the grantor can or does benefit (section 675);

(4) If the grantor or a nonadverse party has a power to revoke the trust or return the corpus to the grantor (section 676); or

(5) If the grantor or a nonadverse party has the power to distribute income to or for the benefit of the grantor or the grantor's spouse (section 677).

Under section 678, income of a trust is taxed to a person other than the grantor to the extent that he has the sole power to vest corpus or income in himself.

(b) Sections 671 through 677 do not apply if the income of a trust is taxable to a grantor's spouse under section 71 or 682 (relating respectively to alimony and separate maintenance payments, and the income of an estate or trust in the case of divorce, etc.).

(c) Except as provided in such subpart E, income of a trust is not included in computing the taxable income and credits of a grantor or another person solely on the grounds of his dominion and control over the trust. However, the provisions of subpart E do not apply in situations involving an assignment of future income, whether or not the assignment is to a trust. Thus, for example, a person who assigns his right to future income under an employment contract may be taxed on that income even though the assignment is to a trust over which the assignor has retained none of the controls specified in sections 671 through 677. Similarly, a bondholder who assigns his right to interest may be taxed on interest payments even though the assignment is to an uncontrolled trust. Nor are the rules as to family partnerships affected by the provisions of subpart E, even though a partnership interest is held in trust. Likewise, these sections have no application in determining the right of a grantor to deductions for payments to a trust under a transfer and lease-back arrangement. In addition, the limitation of the last sentence of section 671 does not prevent any person from being taxed on the income of a trust when it is used to discharge his legal obligation. See § 1.662(a)-4. He is then treated as a beneficiary under subparts A through D or treated as an owner under section 677 because the income is distributed for his benefit, and not because of his dominion or control over the trust.

(d) The provisions of subpart E are not applicable with respect to a pooled income fund as defined in paragraph (5) of section 642(c) and the regulations thereunder, a charitable remainder annuity trust as defined in paragraph (1) of section 664(d) and the regulations thereunder, or a charitable remainder unitrust as defined in paragraph (2) of section 664(d) and the regulations thereunder.

(e) For the effective date of subpart E see section 683 and the regulations thereunder.

(f) For rules relating to the treatment of liabilities resulting on the sale or other disposition of encumbered trust property due to a renunciation of powers by the grantor or other owner, see § 1.1001-2.

T.D. 6217, 12/19/56, amend T.D. 7148, 10/28/71, T.D. 7741, 12/11/80.

PAR. 2. Section 1.671-1 is amended by adding paragraphs (g) and (h) to read as follows:

Proposed § 1.671-1 Grantors and others treated as substantial owners; scope. [*For Preamble, see ¶ 151,755*]

* * * * *

(g) Domestic nonexempt employees' trust. *(1) General rule.* An employer is not treated as an owner of any portion of a nonexempt employees' trust described in section 402(b) that is part of a deferred compensation plan, and that is not a foreign trust within the meaning of section 7701(a)(31), regardless of whether the employer has a power or interest described in sections 673 through 677 over any portion of the trust. See section 402(b)(3) and § 1.402(b)-1(b)(6) for rules relating to treatment of a beneficiary of a nonexempt employees' trust as the owner of a portion of the trust.

(2) Example. The following example illustrates the rules of paragraph (g)(1) of this section:

Example. Employer X provides nonqualified deferred compensation through Plan A to certain of its management employees. Employer X has created Trust T to fund the benefits under Plan A. Assets of Trust T may not be used for any purpose other than to satisfy benefits provided under Plan A until all plan liabilities have been satisfied. Trust T is classified as a trust under § 301.7701-4 of this chapter, and is not a foreign trust within the meaning of section 7701(a)(31). Under § 1.83-3(e), contributions to Trust T are considered transfers of property to participants within the meaning of section 83. On these facts, Trust T is a nonexempt employees' trust described in section 402(b). Because Trust T is a nonexempt employees' trust described in section 402(b) that is part of a deferred compensation plan, and that is not a foreign trust within the meaning of section 7701(a)(31), Employer X is not treated as an owner of any portion of Trust T.

(h) Foreign employees' trust. *(1) General rules.* Except as provided under section 679 or as provided under this paragraph (h)(1), an employer is not treated as an owner of any portion of a foreign employees' trust (as defined in paragraph (h)(2) of this section), regardless of whether the employer has a power or interest described in sections 673 through 677 over any portion of the trust.

(i) Plan of CFC employer. If a controlled foreign corporation (as defined in section 957) maintains a deferred compensation plan funded through a foreign employees' trust, then, with respect to the controlled foreign corporation, the provisions of subpart E apply to the portion of the trust that is the fractional interest described in paragraph (h)(3) of this section.

(ii) Plan of U.S. employer. If a United States person (as defined in section 7701(a)(30)) maintains a deferred compensation plan that is funded through a foreign employees' trust, then, with respect to the U.S. person, the provisions of subpart E apply to the portion of the trust that is the fractional interest described in paragraph (h)(3) of this section.

(iii) Plan of U.S.-related foreign partnership employer. (A) General rule. If a U.S.-related foreign partnership (as defined in paragraph (h)(1)(iii)(B) of this section) maintains a deferred compensation plan funded through a foreign employees' trust, then, with respect to the U.S.-related foreign partnership, the provisions of subpart E apply to the portion of the trust that is the fractional interest described in paragraph (h)(3) of this section.

(B) U.S.-related foreign partnership. For purposes of this paragraph (h), a U.S.-related foreign partnership is a foreign partnership in which a U.S. person or a controlled foreign corporation owns a partnership interest either directly or indirectly through one or more partnerships.

(iv) Application of § 1.1297-4 to plan of foreign non-CFC employer. A foreign employer that is not a controlled foreign corporation may be treated as an owner of a portion of a foreign employees' trust as provided in § 1.1297-4.

(v) Application to employer entity. The rules of paragraphs (h)(1)(i) through (h)(1)(iv) of this section apply to the employer whose employees benefit under the deferred compensation plan funded through a foreign employees' trust, or, in the case of a deferred compensation plan covering independent contractors, the recipient of services performed by those independent contractors, regardless of whether the plan is maintained through another entity. Thus, for example, where a deferred compensation plan benefitting employees of a controlled foreign corporation is funded through a foreign employees' trust, the controlled foreign corporation is considered to be the grantor of the foreign employees' trust for purposes of applying paragraph (h)(1)(i) of this section.

(2) Foreign employees' trust. A foreign employees' trust is a nonexempt employees' trust described in section 402(b) that is part of a deferred compensation plan, and that is a foreign trust within the meaning of section 7701(a)(31).

(3) Fractional interest for paragraph (h)(1). (i) In general. The fractional interest for a foreign employees' trust used for purposes of paragraph (h)(1) of this section for a taxable year of the employer is an undivided fractional interest in the trust for which the fraction is equal to the relevant amount for the employer's taxable year divided by the fair market value of trust assets for the employer's taxable year.

(ii) Relevant amount. (A) In general. For purposes of applying paragraph (h)(3)(i) of this section, and except as provided in paragraph (h)(3)(iii) of this section, the relevant amount for the employer's taxable year is the amount, if any, by which the fair market value of trust assets, plus the fair market value of any assets available to pay plan liabilities that are held in the equivalent of a trust within the meaning of section 404A(b)(5)(A), exceed the plan's accrued liability. The following rules apply for this purpose:

(1) The plan's accrued liability is determined using a projected unit credit funding method that satisfies the requirements of § 1.412(c)(3)-1, taking into account only liabilities relating to services performed through the measurement date for the employer or a predecessor employer.

(2) The plan's accrued liability is reduced (but not below zero) by any liabilities that are provided for under annuity contracts held to satisfy plan liabilities.

(3) Any amount held under an annuity contract that exceeds the amount that is needed to satisfy the liabilities provided for under the contract (e.g., the value of a participation right under a participating annuity contract) is added to the fair market value of any assets available to pay plan liabilities that are held in the equivalent of a trust.

(4) If the relevant amount as determined under this paragraph (h)(3)(ii), without regard to this paragraph (h)(3)(ii)(A)(4), is greater than the fair market value of trust assets, then the relevant amount is equal to the fair market value of trust assets.

(B) Permissible actuarial assumptions for accrued liability. For purposes of paragraph (h)(3)(ii)(A) of this section, a plan's accrued liability must be calculated using an interest rate and other actuarial assumptions that the Commissioner determines to be reasonable. It is appropriate in determining this interest rate to look to available information about rates implicit in current prices of annuity contracts, and to look to rates of return on high-quality fixed-income investments currently available and expected to be available during the period prior to maturity of the plan benefits. If the qualified business unit computes its income or earnings and profits in dollars pursuant to the dollar approximate separate transactions method under § 1.985-3, the employer must use an exchange rate that can be demonstrated to clearly reflect income, based on all relevant facts and circumstances, including appropriate rates of inflation and commercial practices.

(iii) Exception for reasonable funding. The relevant amount does not include an amount that the taxpayer demonstrates to the Commissioner is attributable to amounts that were properly contributed to the trust pursuant to a reasonable funding method, applied using actuarial assumptions that the Commissioner determines to be reasonable, or any amount that the taxpayer demonstrates to the Commissioner is attributable to experience that is favorable relative to any actuarial assumptions used that the Commissioner determines to be reasonable. For this paragraph (h)(3)(iii) to apply to a controlled foreign corporation employer described in paragraph (h)(1)(i) of this section, the taxpayer must indicate on a statement attached to a timely filed Form 5471 that the taxpayer is relying on this rule. For purposes of this paragraph (h)(3)(iii), an amount is considered contributed pursuant to a reasonable funding method if the amount is contributed pursuant to a funding method permitted to be used under section 412 (e.g., the entry age normal funding method) that is consistently used to determine plan contributions. In addition, for purposes of this paragraph (h)(3)(iii), if there has been a change to that method from another funding method, an amount is considered contributed pursuant to a reasonable funding method only if the prior funding method is also a funding method described in the preceding sentence that was consistently used to determine plan contributions. For purposes of this paragraph (h)(3)(iii), a funding method is considered reasonable only if the method provides for any initial unfunded liability to be amortized over a period of at least 6 years, and for any net change in accrued liability resulting from a change in funding method to be amortized over a period of at least 6 years.

(iv) Reduction for transition amount. The relevant amount is reduced (but not below zero) by any transition amount described in paragraphs (h)(5), (h)(6), or (h)(7) of this section.

(v) Fair market value of assets. For purposes of paragraphs (h)(3)(i) and (ii) of this section, for a taxable year of the employer, the fair market value of trust assets, and the fair market value of other assets held in the equivalent of a trust within the meaning of section 404A(b)(5)(A), equals the fair market value of those assets, as of the measurement date for the employer's taxable year, adjusted to include contributions made after the measurement date and by the end of the employer's taxable year.

(vi) Annual valuation. For purposes of determining the relevant amount for a taxable year of the employer, the fair market value of plan assets, and the plan's accrued liability as described in paragraphs (h)(3)(ii) and (iii) of this section, and the normal cost as described in paragraph (h)(4) of this section, must be determined as of a consistently used annual measurement date within the employer's taxable year.

(vii) Special rule for plan funded through multiple trusts. In cases in which a plan is funded through more than one foreign employees' trust, the fractional interest determined under paragraph (h)(3)(i) of this section in each trust is determined by treating all of the trusts as if their assets were held in a single trust for which the fraction is determined in accordance with the rules of this paragraph (h)(3).

(4) De minimis exception. If the relevant amount is not greater than the plan's normal cost for the plan year ending with or within the employer's taxable year, computed using a funding method and actuarial assumptions as described in paragraph (h)(3)(ii) of this section or as described in paragraph (h)(3)(iii) of this section if the requirements of that paragraph are met, that are used to determine plan contributions, then the relevant amount is considered to be zero for purposes of applying paragraph (h)(3)(i) of this section.

(5) General rule for transition amount. (i) General rule. If paragraphs (h)(6) and (h)(7) of this section do not apply to the employer, the transition amount for purposes of paragraph (h)(3)(iv) of this section is equal to the preexisting amount multiplied by the applicable percentage for the year in which the employer's taxable year begins.

(ii) Preexisting amount. The preexisting amount is equal to the relevant amount of the trust, determined without regard to paragraphs (h)(3)(iv) and (h)(4) of this section, computed as of the measurement date that immediately precedes September 27, 1996, disregarding contributions to the trust made after the measurement date.

(iii) Applicable percentage. The applicable percentage is equal to 100 percent for the employer's first taxable year ending after this document is published as a final regulation in the Federal Register and prior taxable years of the employer, and is reduced (but not below zero) by 10 percentage points for each subsequent taxable year of the employer.

(6) Transition amount for new CFCs. (i) General rule. In the case of a new controlled foreign corporation employer, the transition amount for purposes of paragraph (h)(3)(iv) is equal to the pre-change amount multiplied by the applicable percentage for the year in which the new controlled foreign corporation employer's taxable year begins.

(ii) Pre-change amount. The pre-change amount for purposes of paragraph (h)(6)(i) is equal to the relevant amount of the trust, determined without regard to paragraphs (h)(3)(iv) and (h)(4) of this section and disregarding contributions to the trust made after the measurement date, for the new controlled foreign corporation employer's last taxable year ending before the corporation becomes a new controlled foreign corporation employer.

(iii) Applicable percentage. (A) General rule. Except as provided in paragraph (h)(6)(iii)(B) of this section, the applicable percentage is equal to 100 percent for a new controlled foreign corporation employer's first taxable year ending after the corporation becomes a controlled foreign corporation. The applicable percentage is reduced (but not below zero) by 10 percentage points for each subsequent taxable year of the new controlled foreign corporation.

(B) Interim rule. For any taxable year of a new controlled foreign corporation employer that ends on or before the date this document is published as a final regulation in the Federal Register, the applicable percentage is equal to 100 percent. The applicable percentage is reduced by 10 percentage points for each subsequent taxable year of the new controlled foreign corporation employer that ends after the date this document is published as a final regulation in the Federal Register.

(iv) New CFC employer. For purposes of paragraph (h)(6) of this section, a new controlled foreign corporation employer is a corporation that first becomes a controlled foreign corporation within the meaning of section 957 after September 27, 1996. A new controlled foreign corporation employer includes a corporation that was a controlled foreign corporation prior to, but not on, September 26, 1996, and that first becomes a controlled foreign corporation again after September 27, 1996.

(v) Anti-stuffing rule. Notwithstanding paragraph (h)(6)(iii) of this section, if, prior to becoming a controlled foreign corporation, a corporation contributes amounts to a foreign employees' trust with a principal purpose of obtaining tax benefits by increasing the pre-change amount, the applicable percentage with respect to those amounts is 0 percent for all taxable years of the new controlled foreign corporation employer.

(7) Transition amount for new U.S.-related foreign partnerships. (i) General rule. In the case of a new U.S.-related foreign partnership employer, the transition amount for purposes of paragraph (h)(3)(iv) of this section is equal to the pre-change amount multiplied by the applicable percentage for the year in which the new U.S.-related foreign partnership employer's taxable year begins.

(ii) Pre-change amount. The pre-change amount for purposes of paragraph (h)(7)(i) of this section is equal to the relevant amount of the trust, determined without regard to paragraphs (h)(3)(iv) and (h)(4) of this section and disregarding contributions to the trust made after the measurement date, for the entity's last taxable year ending before the entity becomes a new U.S.-related foreign partnership employer.

(iii) Applicable percentage. (A) General rule. Except as provided in paragraph (h)(7)(iii)(B) of this section, the applicable percentage is equal to 100 percent for a new U.S.-related foreign partnership employer's first taxable year ending after the entity becomes a new U.S.-related foreign partnership employer. The applicable percentage is reduced (but not below zero) by 10 percentage points for each subsequent taxable year of the new U.S.-related foreign partnership employer.

(B) Interim rule. For any taxable year of a new U.S.-related foreign partnership employer that ends on or before the date this document is published as a final regulation in the Federal Register, the applicable percentage is equal to 100 percent. The applicable percentage is reduced by 10 percentage points for each subsequent taxable year of the new U.S.-related foreign partnership employer that ends after the date this document is published as a final regulation in the Federal Register.

(iv) New U.S.-related foreign partnership employer. For purposes of paragraph (h)(7) of this section, a new U.S.-related foreign partnership employer is an entity that was a foreign corporation other than a controlled foreign corporation, or that was a foreign partnership other than a U.S.-related foreign partnership, and that changes from this status to a U.S.-related foreign partnership after September 27, 1996. A new U.S.-related foreign partnership employer includes a corporation that was a U.S.-related foreign partnership prior to, but not on, September 27, 1996, and that first becomes a U.S.-related foreign partnership again after September 27, 1996.

(v) Anti-stuffing rule. Notwithstanding paragraph (h)(7)(iii) of this section, if, prior to becoming a new U.S.-related foreign partnership employer, an entity contributes amounts to a foreign employees' trust with a principal purpose of obtaining tax benefits by increasing the pre-change amount, the applicable percentage with respect to those amounts is 0 percent for all taxable years of the new U.S.-related foreign partnership employer.

(8) Examples. The following examples illustrate the rules of paragraph (h) of this section. In each example, the employer has a power or interest described in sections 673 through 677 over the foreign employees' trust, and the monetary unit is the applicable functional currency (FC) determined in accordance with section 985(b) and the regulations thereunder.

Example (1). (i) Employer X is a controlled foreign corporation (as defined in section 957). Employer X maintains a defined benefit retirement plan for its employees. Employer X's taxable year is the calendar year. Trust T, a foreign employees' trust, is the sole funding vehicle for the plan. Both the plan year of the plan and the taxable year of Trust T are the calendar year.

(ii) As of December 31, 1997, Trust T's measurement date, the fair market value (as described in paragraph (h)(3)(iv) of this section) of Trust T's assets is FC 1,000,000, and the amount of the plan's accrued liability is FC 800,000, which includes a normal cost for 1997 of FC 50,000. The preexisting amount for Trust T is FC 40,000. Thus, the relevant amount for 1997 is FC 160,000 (which is greater than the plan's normal cost for the year). Employer X's shareholder does not indicate on a statement attached to a timely filed Form 5471 that any of the relevant amount qualifies for the exception described in paragraph (h)(3)(iii) of this section. Therefore, the fractional interest for Employer X's taxable year ending on December 31, 1997, is 16 percent. Employer X is treated as the owner for federal income tax purposes of an undivided 16 percent interest in each of Trust T's assets for the period from January 1, 1997 through December 31, 1997. Employer X must take into account a 16 percent pro rata share of each item of income, deduction or credit of Trust T during this period in computing its federal income tax liability.

Example (2). Assume the same facts as in Example 1, except that Employer X's shareholder indicates on a statement attached to a timely filed Form 5471 and can demonstrate to the satisfaction of the Commissioner that, in reliance on paragraph (h)(3)(iii) of this section, FC 100,000 of the fair market value of Trust T's assets is attributable to favorable experience relative to reasonable actuarial assumptions used. Accordingly, the relevant amount for 1997 is FC 60,000. Because the plan's normal cost for 1997 is less than FC 60,000, the de minimis exception of paragraph (h)(4) of this section does not apply. Therefore, the fractional interest for Employer X's taxable year ending on December 31, 1997, is 6 percent. Employer X is treated as the owner for federal income tax purposes of an undivided 6 percent interest in each of Trust T's assets for the period from January 1, 1997, through December 31, 1997. Employer X must take into account a 6 percent pro rata share of each item of income, deduction or credit of Trust T during this period in computing its federal income tax liability.

(9) Effective date. Paragraphs (g) and (h) of this section apply to taxable years of an employer ending after September 27, 1996.

§ 1.671-2 Applicable principles.

Caution: The Treasury has not yet amended Reg § 1.671-2 to reflect changes made by P.L. 100-647, P.L. 99-514.

(a) Under section 671 a grantor or another person includes in computing his taxable income and credits those items of income, deduction, and credit against tax which are attributable to or included in any portion of a trust of which he is treated as the owner. Sections 673 through 678 set forth the rules for determining when the grantor or another person is treated as the owner of any portion of a trust. The rules for determining the items of income, deduction, and credit against tax that are attributable to or included in a portion of the trust are set forth in § 1.671-3.

(b) Since the principle underlying subpart E (section 671 and following), part I, subchapter J, chapter 1 of the Code, is in general that income of a trust over which the grantor or another person has retained substantial dominion or control should be taxed to the grantor or other person rather than to the trust which receives the income or to the beneficiary to whom the income may be distributed, it is ordinarily immaterial whether the income involved constitutes income or corpus for trust accounting purposes. Accordingly, when it is stated in the regulations under subpart E that "income" is attributed to the grantor or another person, the reference, unless specifically limited, is to income determined for tax purposes and not to income for trust accounting purposes. When it is intended to emphasize that income for trust accounting purposes (determined in accordance with the provisions set forth in § 1.643(b)-1 is meant, the phrase "ordinary income" is used.

(c) An item of income, deduction, or credit included in computing the taxable income and credits of a grantor or another person under section 671 is treated as if it had been received or paid directly by the grantor or other person (whether or not an individual). For example, a charitable contribution made by a trust which is attributed to the grantor (an individual) under sections 671 through 677 will be aggregated with his other charitable contributions to determine their deductibility under the limitations of section 170(b)(1). Likewise, dividends received by a trust from sources in a particular foreign country which are attributed to a grantor or another person under subpart E will be aggregated with his other income from sources within that country to determine whether the taxpayer is subject to the limitations of section 904 with respect to credit for the tax paid to that country.

(d) Items of income, deduction, and credit not attributed to or included in any portion of a trust of which the grantor or another person is treated as the owner under subpart E are subject to the provisions of subparts A through D (section 641 and following), of such part I.

(e) *(1)* For purposes of part I of subchapter J, chapter 1 of the Internal Revenue Code, a grantor includes any person to the extent such person either creates a trust, or directly or indirectly makes a gratuitous transfer (within the meaning of paragraph (e)(2) of this section) of property to a trust. For purposes of this section, the term property includes cash. If a person creates or funds a trust on behalf of another person, both persons are treated as grantors of the trust. (See section 6048 for reporting requirements that apply to grantors of foreign trusts.) However, a person who creates a trust but makes no gratuitous transfers to the trust is not treated as an owner of any portion of the trust under sections 671 through 677 or 679. Also, a person who funds a trust with an amount that is directly reimbursed to such person within a reasonable period of time and who makes no other transfers to the trust that constitute gratuitous transfers is not treated as an owner of any portion of the trust under sections 671 through 677 or 679. See also § 1.672(f)-5(a).

(2) (i) A gratuitous transfer is any transfer other than a transfer for fair market value. A transfer of property to a trust may be considered a gratuitous transfer without regard to whether the transfer is treated as a gift for gift tax purposes.

(ii) For purposes of this paragraph (e), a transfer is for fair market value only to the extent of the value of property received from the trust, services rendered by the trust, or the right to use property of the trust. For example, rents, royalties, interest, and compensation paid to a trust are transfers for fair market value only to the extent that the payments reflect an arm's length price for the use of the property of, or for the services rendered by, the trust. For purposes of this determination, an interest in the trust is not property received from the trust. In addition, a person will not be treated as making a transfer for fair market value merely because the transferor recognizes gain on the transaction. See, for example, section 684 regarding the recognition of gain on certain transfers to foreign trusts.

(iii) For purposes of this paragraph (e), a gratuitous transfer does not include a distribution to a trust with respect to an interest held by such trust in either a trust described in paragraph (e)(3) of this section or an entity other than a trust.

For example, a distribution to a trust by a corporation with respect to its stock described in section 301 is not a gratuitous transfer.

(3) A grantor includes any person who acquires an interest in a trust from a grantor of the trust if the interest acquired is an interest in certain investment trusts described in § 301.7701-4(c) of this chapter, liquidating trusts described in § 301.7701-4(d) of this chapter, or environmental remediation trusts described in § 301.7701-4(e) of this chapter.

(4) If a gratuitous transfer is made by a partnership or corporation to a trust and is for a business purpose of the partnership or corporation, the partnership or corporation will generally be treated as the grantor of the trust. For example, if a partnership makes a gratuitous transfer to a trust in order to secure a legal obligation of the partnership to a third party unrelated to the partnership, the partnership will be treated as the grantor of the trust. However, if a partnership or a corporation makes a gratuitous transfer to a trust that is not for a business purpose of the partnership or corporation but is for the personal purposes of one or more of the partners or shareholders, the gratuitous transfer will be treated as a constructive distribution to such partners or shareholders under federal tax principles and the partners or the shareholders will be treated as the grantors of the trust. For example, if a partnership makes a gratuitous transfer to a trust that is for the benefit of a child of a partner, the gratuitous transfer will be treated as a distribution to the partner under section 731 and a subsequent gratuitous transfer by the partner to the trust.

(5) If a trust makes a gratuitous transfer of property to another trust, the grantor of the transferor trust generally will be treated as the grantor of the transferee trust. However, if a person with a general power of appointment over the transferor trust exercises that power in favor of another trust, then such person will be treated as the grantor of the transferee trust, even if the grantor of the transferor trust is treated as the owner of the transferor trust under subpart E of part I, subchapter J, chapter 1 of the Internal Revenue Code.

(6) The following examples illustrate the rules of this paragraph (e). Unless otherwise indicated, all trusts are domestic trusts, and all other persons are United States persons. The examples are as follows:

Example (1). A creates and funds a trust, T, for the benefit of her children. B subsequently makes a gratuitous transfer to T. Under paragraph (e)(1) of this section, both A and B are grantors of T.

Example (2). A makes an investment in a fixed investment trust, T, that is classified as a trust under § 301.7701-4(c)(1) of this chapter. A is a grantor of T. B subsequently acquires A's entire interest in T. Under paragraph (e)(3) of this section, B is a grantor of T with respect to such interest.

Example (3). A, an attorney, creates a foreign trust, FT, on behalf of A's client, B, and transfers $100 to FT out of A's funds. A is reimbursed by B for the $100 transferred to FT. The trust instrument states that the trustee has discretion to distribute the income or corpus of FT to B and B's children. Both A and B are treated as grantors of FT under paragraph (e)(1) of this section. In addition, B is treated as the owner of the entire trust under section 677. Because A is reimbursed for the $100 transferred to FT on behalf of B, A is not treated as transferring any property to FT. Therefore, A is not an owner of any portion of FT under sections 671 through 677 regardless of whether A retained any power over or interest in FT described in sections 673 through 677. Furthermore, A is not treated as an owner of any portion of FT under section 679. Both A and B are responsible parties for purposes of the requirements in section 6048.

Example (4). A creates and funds a trust, T. A does not retain any power or interest in T that would cause A to be treated as an owner of any portion of the trust under sections 671 through 677. B holds an unrestricted power, exercisable solely by B, to withdraw certain amounts contributed to the trust before the end of the calendar year and to vest those amounts in B. B is treated as an owner of the portion of T that is subject to the withdrawal power under section 678(a)(1). However, B is not a grantor of T under paragraph (e)(1) of this section because B neither created T nor made a gratuitous transfer to T.

Example (5). A transfers cash to a trust, T, through a broker, in exchange for units in T. The units in T are not property for purposes of determining whether A has received fair market value under paragraph (e)(2)(ii) of this section. Therefore, A has made a gratuitous transfer to T, and, under paragraph (e)(1) of this section, A is a grantor of T.

Example (6). A borrows cash from T, a trust. A has not made any gratuitous transfers to T. Arm's length interest payments by A to T will not be treated as gratuitous transfers under paragraph (e)(2)(ii) of this section. Therefore, under paragraph (e)(1) of this section, A is not a grantor of T with respect to the interest payments.

Example (7). A, B's brother, creates a trust, T, for B's benefit and transfers $50,000 to T. The trustee invests the $50,000 in stock of Company X. C, B's uncle, purportedly sells property with a fair market value of $1,000,000 to T in exchange for the stock when it has appreciated to a fair market value of $100,000. Under paragraph (e)(2)(ii) of this section, the $900,000 excess value is a gratuitous transfer by C. Therefore, under paragraph (e)(1) of this section, A is a grantor with respect to the portion of the trust valued at $100,000, and C is a grantor of T with respect to the portion of the trust valued at $900,000. In addition, A or C or both will be treated as the owners of the respective portions of the trust of which each person is a grantor if A or C or both retain powers over or interests in such portions under sections 673 through 677.

Example (8). G creates and funds a trust, T1, for the benefit of G's children and grandchildren. After G's death, under authority granted to the trustees in the trust instrument, the trustees of T1 transfer a portion of the assets of T1 to another trust, T2, and retain a power to revoke T2 and revest the assets of T2 in T1. Under paragraphs (e)(1) and (5) of this section, G is the grantor of T1 and T2. In addition, because the trustees of T1 have retained a power to revest the assets of T2 in T1, T1 is treated as the owner of T2 under section 678(a).

Example (9). G creates and funds a trust, T1, for the benefit of B. G retains a power to revest the assets of T1 in G within the meaning of section 676. Under the trust agreement, B is given a general power of appointment over the assets of T1. B exercises the general power of appointment with respect to one-half of the corpus of T1 in favor of a trust, T2, that is for the benefit of C, B's child. Under paragraph (e)(1) of this section, G is the grantor of T1, and under paragraphs (e)(1) and (5) of this section, B is the grantor of T2.

(7) The rules of this section are applicable to any transfer to a trust, or transfer of an interest in a trust, on or after August 10, 1999.

T.D. 6217, 12/19/56, amend T.D. 8831, 8/5/99, T.D. 8890, 7/3/2000.

PAR. 3. Section 1.671-2 is amended by adding paragraph (f) to read as follows:

Proposed § 1.671-2 Applicable principles. [*For Preamble, see ¶ 151,755*]

* * * * *

(f) For purposes of subtitle A of the Internal Revenue Code, a person that is treated as the owner of any portion of a trust under subpart E is considered to own the trust assets attributable to that portion of the trust.

§ 1.671-3 Attribution or inclusion of income, deductions, and credits against tax.

(a) When a grantor or another person is treated under subpart E (section 671 and following) as the owner of any portion of a trust, there are included in computing his tax liability those items of income, deduction, and credit against tax attributable to or included in that portion. For example:

(1) If a grantor or another person is treated as the owner of an entire trust (corpus as well as ordinary income), he takes into account in computing his income tax liability all items of income, deduction, and credit (including capital gains and losses) to which he would have been entitled had the trust not been in existence during the period he is treated as owner.

(2) If the portion treated as owned consists of specific trust property and its income, all items directly related to that property are attributable to the portion. Items directly related to trust property not included in the portion treated as owned by the grantor or other person are governed by the provisions of subparts A through D (section 641 and following), part I, subchapter J, chapter 1 of the Code. Items that relate both to the portion treated as owned by the grantor and to the balance of the trust must be apportioned in a manner that is reasonable in the light of all the circumstances of each case, including the terms of the governing instrument, local law, and the practice of the trustee if it is reasonable and consistent.

(3) If the portion of a trust treated as owned by a grantor or another person consists of an undivided fractional interest in the trust, or of an interest represented by a dollar amount, a pro rata share of each item of income, deduction, and credit is normally allocated to the portion. Thus, where the portion owned consists of an interest in or a right to an amount of corpus only, a fraction of each item (including items allocated to corpus, such as capital gains) is attributed to the portion. The numerator of this fraction is the amount which is subject to the control of the grantor or other person and the denominator is normally the fair market value of the trust corpus at the beginning of the taxable year in question. The share not treated as owned by the grantor or other person is governed by the provisions of subparts A through D. See the last three sentences of paragraph (c) of this section for the principles applicable if the portion treated as owned consists of an interest in part of the ordinary income in contrast to an interest in corpus alone.

(b) If a grantor or another person is treated as the owner of a portion of a trust, that portion may or may not include both ordinary income and other income allocable to corpus. For example—

(1) Only ordinary income is included by reason of an interest in or a power over ordinary income alone. Thus, if a grantor is treated under section 673 as an owner by reason of a reversionary interest in ordinary income only, items of income allocable to corpus will not be included in the portion he is treated as owning. Similarly, if a grantor or another person is treated under sections 674-678 as an owner of a portion by reason of a power over ordinary income only, items of income allocable to corpus are not included in that portion. (See paragraph (c) of this section to determine the treatment of deductions and credits when only ordinary income is included in the portion.)

(2) Only income allocable to corpus is included by reason of an interest in or a power over corpus alone, if satisfaction of the interest or an exercise of the power will not result in an interest in or the exercise of a power over ordinary income which would itself cause that income to be included. For example, if a grantor has a reversionary interest in a trust which is not such as to require that he be treated as an owner under section 673, he may nevertheless be treated as an owner under section 677(a)(2) since any income allocable to corpus is accumulated for future distribution to him, but items of income included in determining ordinary income are not included in the portion he is treated as owning. Similarly, he may have a power over corpus which is such that he is treated as an owner under section 674 or 676(a), but ordinary income will not be included in the portion he owns, if his power can only affect income received after a period of time such that he would not be treated as an owner of the income if the power were a reversionary interest. (See paragraph (c) of this section to determine the treatment of deductions and credits when only income allocated to corpus is included in the portion.)

(3) Both ordinary income and other income allocable to corpus are included by reason of an interest in or a power over both ordinary income and corpus, or an interest in or a power over corpus alone which does not come within the provisions of subparagraph (2) of this paragraph. For example, if a grantor is treated under section 673 as the owner of a portion of a trust by reason of a reversionary interest in corpus, both ordinary income and other income allocable to

corpus are included in the portion. Further, a grantor includes both ordinary income and other income allocable to corpus in the portion he is treated as owning if he is treated under section 674 or 676 as an owner because of a power over corpus which can affect income received within a period such that he would be treated as an owner under section 673 if the power were a reversionary interest. Similarly, a grantor or another person includes both ordinary income and other income allocable to corpus in the portion he is treated as owning if he is treated as an owner under section 675 or 678 because of a power over corpus.

(c) If only income allocable to corpus is included in computing a grantor's tax liability, he will take into account in that computation only those items of income, deduction, and credit which would not be included under subparts A through D in the computation of the tax liability of the current income beneficiaries if all distributable net income had actually been distributed to those beneficiaries. On the other hand, if the grantor or another person is treated as an owner solely because of his interest in or power over ordinary income alone, he will take into account in computing his tax liability those items which would be included in computing the tax liability of a current income beneficiary, including expenses allocable to corpus which enter into the computation of distributable net income. If the grantor or other person is treated as an owner because of his power over or right to a dollar amount of ordinary income, he will first take into account a portion of those items of income and expense entering into the computation of ordinary income under the trust instrument or local law sufficient to produce income of the dollar amount required. There will then be attributable to him a pro rata portion of other items entering into the computation of distributable net income under subparts A through D, such as expenses allocable to corpus, and a pro rata portion of credits of the trust. For examples of computations under this paragraph, see paragraph (g) of § 1.677(a)-1.

T.D. 6217, 12/19/56, amend T.D. 6989, 1/16/69.

§ 1.671-4 Method of reporting.

(a) Portion of trust treated as owned by the grantor or another person. Except as otherwise provided in paragraph (b) of this section and § 1.671-5, items of income, deduction, and credit attributable to any portion of a trust that, under the provisions of subpart E (section 671 and following), part I, subchapter J, chapter 1 of the Internal Revenue Code, is treated as owned by the grantor or another person, are not reported by the trust on Form 1041, "U.S. Income Tax Return for Estates and Trusts," but are shown on a separate statement to be attached to that form. Section 1.671-5 provides special reporting rules for widely held fixed investment trusts. Section 301.7701-4(e)(2) of this chapter provides guidance regarding the application of the reporting rules in this paragraph (a) to an environmental remediation trust.

(b) A trust all of which is treated as owned by one or more grantors or other persons. *(1) In general.* In the case of a trust all of which is treated as owned by one or more grantors or other persons, and which is not described in paragraph (b)(6) or (7) of this section, the trustee may, but is not required to, report by one of the methods described in this paragraph (b) rather than by the method described in paragraph (a) of this section. A trustee may not report, however, pursuant to paragraph (b)(2)(i)(A) of this section unless the grantor or other person treated as the owner of the trust provides to the trustee a complete Form W-9 or acceptable substitute Form W-9 signed under penalties of perjury. See section 3406 and the regulations thereunder for the information to include on, and the manner of executing, the Form W-9, depending upon the type of reportable payments made.

(2) A trust all of which is treated as owned by one grantor or by one other person. (i) In general. In the case of a trust all of which is treated as owned by one grantor or one other person, the trustee reporting under this paragraph (b) must either—

(A) Furnish the name and taxpayer identification number (TIN) of the grantor or other person treated as the owner of the trust, and the address of the trust, to all payors during the taxable year, and comply with the additional requirements described in paragraph (b)(2)(ii) of this section; or

(B) Furnish the name, TIN, and address of the trust to all payors during the taxable year, and comply with the additional requirements described in paragraph (b)(2)(iii) of this section.

(ii) Additional obligations of the trustee when name and TIN of the grantor or other person treated as the owner of the trust and the address of the trust are furnished to payors. (A) Unless the grantor or other person treated as the owner of the trust is the trustee or a co-trustee of the trust, the trustee must furnish the grantor or other person treated as the owner of the trust with a statement that —

(1) Shows all items of income, deduction, and credit of the trust for the taxable year;

(2) Identifies the payor of each item of income;

(3) Provides the grantor or other person treated as the owner of the trust with the information necessary to take the items into account in computing the grantor's or other person's taxable income; and

(4) Informs the grantor or other person treated as the owner of the trust that the items of income, deduction and credit and other information shown on the statement must be included in computing the taxable income and credits of the grantor or other person on the income tax return of the grantor or other person.

(B) The trustee is not required to file any type of return with the Internal Revenue Service.

(iii) Additional obligations of the trustee when name, TIN, and address of the trust are furnished to payors. (A) Obligation to file forms 1099. The trustee must file with the Internal Revenue Service the appropriate Forms 1099, reporting the income or gross proceeds paid to the trust during the taxable year, and showing the trust as the payor and the grantor or other person treated as the owner of the trust as the payee. The trustee has the same obligations for filing the appropriate Forms 1099 as would a payor making reportable payments, except that the trustee must report each type of income in the aggregate, and each item of gross proceeds separately. See paragraph (b)(5) of this section regarding the amounts required to be included on any Forms 1099 filed by the trustee.

(B) Obligation to furnish statement. (1) Unless the grantor or other person treated as the owner of the trust is the trustee or a co-trustee of the trust, the trustee must also furnish to the grantor or other person treated as the owner of the trust a statement that—

(i) Shows all items of income, deduction, and credit of the trust for the taxable year;

(ii) Provides the grantor or other person treated as the owner of the trust with the information necessary to take the items into account in computing the grantor's or other person's taxable income; and

(iii) Informs the grantor or other person treated as the owner of the trust that the items of income, deduction and credit and other information shown on the statement must be included in computing the taxable income and credits of the grantor or other person on the income tax return of the grantor or other person.

(2) By furnishing the statement, the trustee satisfies the obligation to furnish statements to recipients with respect to the Forms 1099 filed by the trustee.

(iv) Examples. The following examples illustrate the provisions of this paragraph (b)(2):

Example (1). G, a United States citizen, creates an irrevocable trust which provides that the ordinary income is to be payable to him for life and that on his death the corpus shall be distributed to B, an unrelated person. Except for the right to receive income, G retains no right or power which would cause him to be treated as an owner under sections 671 through 679. Under the applicable local law, capital gains must be added to corpus. Since G has a right to receive income, he is treated as an owner of a portion of the trust under section 677. The tax consequences of any items of capital gain of the trust are governed by the provisions of subparts A, B, C, and D (section 641 and following), part I, subchapter J, chapter 1 of the Internal Revenue Code. Because not all of the trust is treated as owned by the grantor or another person, the trustee may not report by the methods described in paragraph (b)(2) of this section.

Example (2). (i)

(A) On January 2, 1996, G, a United States citizen, creates a trust all of which is treated as owned by G. The trustee of the trust is T. During the 1996 taxable year the trust has the following items of income and gross proceeds:

Interest	$2,500
Dividends	3,205
Proceeds from the sale of B stock	2,000

(B) The trust has no items of deduction or credit.

(ii)

(A) The payors of the interest paid to the trust are X ($2,000), Y ($300), and Z ($200). The payors of the dividends paid to the trust are A ($3,200), and D ($5). The payor of the gross proceeds paid to the trust is D, a brokerage firm, which held the B stock as the nominee for the trust. The B stock was purchased by T for $1,500 on January 3, 1996, and sold by T on November 29, 1996. T chooses to report pursuant to paragraph (b)(2)(i)(B) of this section, and therefore furnishes the name, TIN, and address of the trust to X, Y, Z, A, and D. X, Y, and Z each furnish T with a Form 1099-INT showing the trust as the payee. A furnishes T with a Form 1099-DIV showing the trust as the payee. D does not furnish T with a Form 1099-DIV because D paid a dividend of less than $10 to T. D furnishes T with a Form 1099-B showing the trust as the payee.

(B) On or before February 28, 1997, T files a Form 1099-INT with the Internal Revenue Service on which T reports interest attributable to G, as the owner of the trust, of $2,500; a Form 1099-DIV on which T reports dividends attributable to G, as the owner of the trust, of $3,205; and a Form 1099-B on which T reports gross proceeds from the sale of B stock attributable to G, as the owner of the trust, of $2,000. On or before April 15, 1997, T furnishes a statement to G which lists the following items of income and information necessary for G to take the items into account in computing G's taxable income:

Interest	$2,500
Dividends	3,205
Gain from sale of B stock	500
Information regarding sale of B stock:	
Proceeds	$2,000
Basis	1,500
Date acquired	1/03/96
Date sold	11/29/96

(C) T informs G that any items of income, deduction and credit and other information shown on the statement must be included in computing the taxable income and credits of the grantor or other person on the income tax return of the grantor or other person.

(D) T has complied with T's obligations under this section.

(iii)

(A) Same facts as paragraphs (i) and (ii) of this Example 2, except that G contributed the B stock to the trust on January 2, 1996. On or before April 15, 1997, T furnishes a statement to G which lists the following items of income and information necessary for G to take the items into account in computing G's taxable income:

Interest	$2,500
Dividends	3,205
Information regarding sale of B stock:	
Proceeds	$2,000
Date sold	11/29/96

(B) T informs G that any items of income, deduction and credit and other information shown on the statement must be included in computing the taxable income and credits of the grantor or other person on the income tax return of the grantor or other person.

(C) T has complied with T's obligations under this section.

Example (3). (i) (A) On January 2, 1996, G, a United States citizen, creates a trust all of which is treated as owned by G. The trustee of the trust is T. The only asset of the trust is an interest in C, a common trust fund under section 584(a). T chooses to report pursuant to paragraph (b)(2)(i)(B) of this section and therefore furnishes the name, TIN, and address of the trust to C. C files a Form 1065 and a Schedule K-1 (Partner's Share of Income, Credits, Deductions, etc.) showing the name, TIN, and address of the trust with the Internal Revenue Service and furnishes a copy to T. Because the trust did not receive any amounts described in paragraph (b)(5) of this section, T does not file any type of return with the Internal Revenue Service. On or before April 15, 1997, T furnishes G with a statement that shows all items of income, deduction, and credit of the trust for the 1996 taxable year. In addition, T informs G that any items of income, deduction and credit and other information shown on the statement must be included in computing the taxable income and credits of the grantor or other person on the income tax return of the grantor or other person. T has complied with T's obligations under this section.

(3) A trust all of which is treated as owned by two or more grantors or other persons. (i) In general. In the case of a trust all of which is treated as owned by two or more grantors or other persons, the trustee must furnish the name, TIN, and address of the trust to all payors for the taxable year, and comply with the additional requirements described in paragraph (b)(3)(ii) of this section.

(ii) Additional obligations of trustee. (A) Obligation to file Forms 1099. The trustee must file with the Internal Revenue Service the appropriate Forms 1099, reporting the items of income paid to the trust by all payors during the taxable year attributable to the portion of the trust treated as owned by each grantor or other person, and showing the trust as the payor and each grantor or other person treated as an owner of the trust as the payee. The trustee has the same obligations for filing the appropriate Forms 1099 as would a payor making reportable payments, except that the trustee must report each type of income in the aggregate, and each item of gross proceeds separately. See paragraph (b)(5) of this section regarding the amounts required to be included on any Forms 1099 filed by the trustee.

(B) Obligation to furnish statement. (1) The trustee must also furnish to each grantor or other person treated as an owner of the trust a statement that—

(i) Shows all items of income, deduction, and credit of the trust for the taxable year attributable to the portion of the trust treated as owned by the grantor or other person;

(ii) Provides the grantor or other person treated as an owner of the trust with the information necessary to take the items into account in computing the grantor's or other person's taxable income; and

(iii) Informs the grantor or other person treated as the owner of the trust that the items of income, deduction and credit and other information shown on the statement must be included in computing the taxable income and credits of the grantor or other person on the income tax return of the grantor or other person.

(2) Except for the requirements pursuant to section 3406 and the regulations thereunder, by furnishing the statement, the trustee satisfies the obligation to furnish statements to recipients with respect to the Forms 1099 filed by the trustee.

(4) Persons treated as payors. (i) In general. For purposes of this section, the term payor means any person who is required by any provision of the Internal Revenue Code and the regulations thereunder to make any type of information return (including Form 1099 or Schedule K-1) with respect to the trust for the taxable year, including persons who make payments to the trust or who collect (or otherwise act as middlemen with respect to) payments on behalf of the trust.

(ii) Application to brokers and customers. For purposes of this section, a broker, within the meaning of section 6045, is considered a payor. A customer, within the meaning of section 6045, is considered a payee.

(5) Amounts required to be included on Forms 1099 filed by the trustee. (i) In general. The amounts that must be included on any Forms 1099 required to be filed by the trustee pursuant to this section do not include any amounts that are reportable by the payor on an information return other than Form 1099. For example, in the case of a trust which owns an interest in a partnership, the trust's distributive share of the income and gain of the partnership is not includible on any Forms 1099 filed by the trustee pursuant to this section because the distributive share is reportable by the partnership on Schedule K-1.

(ii) Example. The following example illustrates the provisions of this paragraph (b)(5):

Example. (i)

(A) On January 2, 1996, G, a United States citizen, creates a trust all of which is treated as owned by G. The trustee of the trust is T. The assets of the trust during the 1996 taxable year are shares of stock in X, an S corporation, a limited partnership interest in P, shares of stock in M, and shares of stock in N. T chooses to report pursuant to paragraph (b)(2)(i)(B) of this section and therefore furnishes the name, TIN, and address of the trust to X, P, M, and N. M furnishes T with a Form 1099-DIV showing the trust as the payee. N does not furnish T with a Form 1099-DIV because N paid a dividend of less than $10 to T. X and P furnish T with Schedule K-1 (Shareholder's Share of Income, Credits, Deductions, etc.) and Schedule K-1 (Partner's Share of Income, Credits, Deductions, etc.), respectively, showing the trust's name, TIN, and address.

(B) For the 1996 taxable year the trust has the following items of income and deduction:

Dividends paid by M	$ 12
Dividends paid by N	6
Administrative expense	$ 20
Items reported by X on Schedule K-1 attributable to trust's shares of stock in X:	
Interest	$ 20
Dividends	35
Items reported by P on Schedule K-1 attributable to trust's limited partnership interest in P:	
Ordinary income	$300

(ii)

(A) On or before February 28, 1997, T files with the Internal Revenue Service a Form 1099-DIV on which T reports dividends attributable to G as the owner of the trust in the amount of $18. T does not file any other returns.

(B) T has complied with T's obligation under paragraph (b)(2)(iii)(A) of this section to file the appropriate Forms 1099.

(6) Trusts that cannot report under this paragraph (b). The following trusts cannot use the methods of reporting described in this paragraph (b)—

(i) A Common trust fund as defined in section 584(a);

(ii) A trust that has its situs or any of its assets located outside the United States;

(iii) A trust that is a qualified subchapter S trust as defined in section 1361(d)(3);

(iv) A trust all of which is treated as owned by one grantor or one other person whose taxable year is a fiscal year;

(v) A trust all of which is treated as owned by one grantor or one other person who is not a United States person; or

(vi) A trust all of which is treated as owned by two or more grantors or other persons, one of whom is not a United States person.

(7) Grantors or other persons who are treated as owners of the trust and are exempt recipients for information reporting purposes. (i) Trust treated as owned by one grantor or one other person. The trustee of a trust all of which is treated as owned by one grantor or one other person may not report pursuant to this paragraph (b) if the grantor or other person is an exempt recipient for information reporting purposes.

(ii) Trust treated as owned by two or more grantors or other persons. The trustee of a trust, all of which is treated as owned by two or more grantors or other persons, may not report pursuant to this paragraph (b) if one or more grantors or other persons treated as owners are exempt recipients for information reporting purposes unless —

(A) At least one grantor or one other person who is treated as an owner of the trust is a person who is not an exempt recipient for information reporting purposes; and

(B) The trustee reports without regard to whether any of the grantors or other persons treated as owners of the trust are exempt recipients for information reporting purposes.

(8) Husband and wife who make a single return jointly. A trust all of which is treated as owned by a husband and wife who make a single return jointly of income taxes for the taxable year under section 6013 is considered to be owned by one grantor for purposes of this paragraph (b).

(c) Due date for Forms 1099 required to be filed by trustee. The due date for any Forms 1099 required to be filed with the Internal Revenue Service by a trustee pursuant to this section is the due date otherwise in effect for filing Forms 1099.

(d) Due date and other requirements with respect to statement required to be furnished by trustee. *(1) In general.* The due date for the statement required to be furnished by a trustee to the grantor or other person treated as an owner of the trust pursuant to this section is the date specified by section 6034A(a). The trustee must maintain in its records a copy of the statement furnished to the grantor or other person treated as an owner of the trust for a period of three years from the due date for furnishing such statement specified in this paragraph (d).

(2) Statement for the taxable year ending with the death of the grantor or other person treated as the owner of the trust. If a trust ceases to be treated as owned by the grantor, or other person, by reason of the death of that grantor or other person (decedent), the due date for the statement required to be furnished for the taxable year ending with the death of the decedent shall be the date specified by section 6034A(a) as though the decedent had lived throughout the decedent's last taxable year. See paragraph (h) of this section for special reporting rules for a trust or portion of the trust that ceases to be treated as owned by the grantor or other person by reason of the death of the grantor or other person.

(e) Backup withholding requirements. *(1) Trustee reporting under paragraph (b)(2)(i)(A) of this section.* In order for the trustee to be able to report pursuant to paragraph (b)(2)(i)(A) of this section and to furnish to all payors the name and TIN of the grantor or other person treated as the owner of the trust, the grantor or other person must provide a complete Form W-9 to the trustee in the manner provided in paragraph (b)(1) of this section, and the trustee must give the name and TIN shown on that Form W-9 to all payors. In addition, if the Form W-9 indicates that the grantor or other person is subject to backup withholding, the trustee must notify all payors of reportable interest and dividend payments of the requirement to backup withhold. If the Form W-9 indicates that the grantor or other person is not subject to backup withholding, the trustee does not have to notify the payors that backup withholding is not required. The trustee should not give the Form W-9, or a copy thereof, to a payor because the Form W-9 contains the address of the grantor or other person and paragraph (b)(2)(i)(A) of this section requires the trustee to furnish the address of the trust to all payors and not the address of the grantor or other person. The trustee acts as the agent of the grantor or other person for purposes of furnishing to the payors the information required by this paragraph (e)(1). Thus, a payor may rely on the name and TIN provided to the payor by the trustee, and, if given, on the trustee's statement that the grantor is subject to backup withholding.

(2) Other backup withholding requirements. Whether a trustee is treated as a payor for purposes of backup withholding is determined pursuant to section 3406 and the regulations thereunder.

(f) Penalties for failure to file a correct form 1099 or furnish a correct statement. A trustee who fails to file a correct Form 1099 or to furnish a correct statement to a grantor or other person treated as an owner of the trust as required by paragraph (b) of this section is subject to the penalties provided by sections 6721 and 6722 and the regulations thereunder.

(g) Changing reporting methods *(1) Changing from reporting by filing form 1041 to a method described in paragraph (b) of this section.* If the trustee has filed a Form 1041 for any taxable year ending before January 1, 1996 (and has not filed a final Form 1041 pursuant to § 1.671-4(b)(3) (as contained in the 26 CFR part 1 edition revised as of April 1, 1995)), or files a Form 1041 for any taxable year thereafter, the trustee must file a final Form 1041 for the taxable year which ends after January 1, 1995, and which immediately precedes the first taxable year for which the trustee reports pursuant to paragraph (b) of this section, on the front of which form the trustee must write: "Pursuant to § 1.671-4(g), this is the final Form 1041 for this grantor trust.".

(2) Changing from reporting by a method described in paragraph (b) of this section to the filing of a form 1041. The trustee of a trust who reported pursuant to paragraph (b) of this section for a taxable year may report pursuant to paragraph (a) of this section for subsequent taxable years. If the trustee reported pursuant to paragraph (b)(2)(i)(A) of this section, and therefore furnished the name and TIN of the grantor to all payors, the trustee must furnish the name, TIN, and address of the trust to all payors for such subsequent taxable years. If the trustee reported pursuant to paragraph (b)(2)(i)(B) or (b)(3)(i) of this section, and therefore furnished the name and TIN of the trust to all payors, the trustee must indicate on each Form 1096 (Annual Summary and Transmittal of U.S. Information Returns) that it files (or appropriately on magnetic media) for the final taxable year for which the trustee so reports that it is the final return of the trust.

(3) Changing between methods described in paragraph (b) of this section. (i) Changing from furnishing the TIN of the grantor to furnishing the TIN of the trust. The trustee of a trust who reported pursuant to paragraph (b)(2)(i)(A) of this section for a taxable year, and therefore furnished the name and TIN of the grantor to all payors, may report pursuant to paragraph (b)(2)(i)(B) of this section, and furnish the name and TIN of the trust to all payors, for subsequent taxable years.

(ii) Changing from furnishing the TIN of the trust to furnishing the TIN of the grantor. The trustee of a trust who reported pursuant to paragraph (b)(2)(i)(B) of this section for a taxable year, and therefore furnished the name and TIN of the trust to all payors, may report pursuant to paragraph (b)(2)(i)(A) of this section, and furnish the name and TIN of the grantor to all payors, for subsequent taxable years. The trustee, however, must indicate on each Form 1096 (Annual Summary and Transmittal of U.S. Information Returns) that it files (or appropriately on magnetic media) for the final taxable year for which the trustee reports pursuant to paragraph (b)(2)(i)(B) of this section that it is the final return of the trust.

(4) Example. The following example illustrates the provisions of paragraph (g) of this section:

Example. (i) On January 3, 1994, G, a United States citizen, creates a trust all of which is treated as owned by G. The trustee of the trust is T. On or before April 17, 1995, T files with the Internal Revenue Service a Form 1041 with an attached statement for the 1994 taxable year showing the items of income, deduction, and credit of the trust. On or before April 15, 1996, T files with the Internal Revenue Service a Form 1041 with an attached statement for the 1995 taxable year showing the items of income, deduction, and credit of the trust. On the Form 1041, T states that "pursuant to § 1.671-4(g), this is the final Form 1041 for this grantor trust." T may report pursuant to paragraph (b) of this section for the 1996 taxable year.

(ii) T reports pursuant to paragraph (b)(2)(i)(B) of this section, and therefore furnishes the name, TIN, and address of the trust to all payors, for the 1996 and 1997 taxable years. T chooses to report pursuant to paragraph (a) of this section for the 1998 taxable year. On each Form 1096 (Annual Summary and Transmittal of U.S. Information Returns) which T files for the 1997 taxable year (or appropriately on magnetic media), T indicates that it is the trust's final return. On or before April 15, 1999, T files with the Internal Revenue Service a Form 1041 with an attached statement showing the items of income, deduction, and credit of the trust. On the Form 1041, T uses the same TIN which T used on the Forms 1041 and Forms 1099 it filed for previous taxable years. T has complied with T's obligations under paragraph (g)(2) of this section.

(h) Reporting rules for a trust, or portion of a trust, that ceases to be treated as owned by a grantor or other person by reason of the death of the grantor or other person. *(1) Definition of decedent.* For purposes of this paragraph (h), the decedent is the grantor or other person treated as the owner of the trust, or portion of the trust, under subpart E, part I, subchapter J, chapter 1 of the Internal Revenue Code on the date of death of that person.

(2) In general. The provisions of this section apply to a trust, or portion of a trust, treated as owned by a decedent for the taxable year that ends with the decedent's death. Following the death of the decedent, the trust or portion of a trust that ceases to be treated as owned by the decedent, by reason of the death of the decedent, may no longer report under this section. A trust, all of which was treated as owned by the decedent, must obtain a new TIN upon the death of the decedent, if the trust will continue after the death of the decedent. See § 301.6109-1(a)(3)(i) of this chapter for rules regarding obtaining a TIN upon the death of the decedent.

(3) Special rules. (i) Trusts reporting pursuant to paragraph (a) of this section for the taxable year ending with the decedent's death. The due date for the filing of a return pursuant to paragraph (a) of this section for the taxable year ending with the decedent's death shall be the due date provided for under § 1.6072-1(a)(2). The return filed under this paragraph for a trust all of which was treated as owned by the decedent must indicate that it is a final return.

(ii) Trust reporting pursuant to paragraph (b)(2)(B) of this section for the taxable year of the decedent's death. A trust that reports pursuant to paragraph (b)(2)(B) of this section for the taxable year ending with the decedent's death must indicate on each Form 1096 "Annual Summary and Transmittal of the U.S. Information Returns" that it files (or appropriately on magnetic media) for the taxable year ending with the death of the decedent that it is the final return of the trust.

(iii) Trust reporting under paragraph (b)(3) of this section. If a trust has been reporting under paragraph (b)(3) of this section, the trustee may not report under that paragraph if any portion of the trust has a short taxable year by reason of the death of the decedent and the portion treated as owned by the decedent does not terminate on the death of the decedent.

(i) Effective date and transition rule. *(1) Effective date.* The trustee of a trust any portion of which is treated as owned by one or more grantors or other persons must report pursuant to paragraphs (a), (b), (c), (d)(1), (e), (f), and (g) of this section for taxable years beginning on or after January 1, 1996.

(2) Transition rule. For taxable years beginning prior to January 1, 1996, the Internal Revenue Service will not challenge the manner of reporting of —

(i) A trustee of a trust all of which is treated as owned by one or more grantors or other persons who did not report in accordance with § 1.671-4(a) (as contained in the 26 CFR part 1 edition revised as of April 1, 1995) as in effect for taxable years beginning prior to January 1, 1996, but did report in a manner substantially similar to one of the reporting methods described in paragraph (b) of this section; or

(ii) A trustee of two or more trusts all of which are treated as owned by one or more grantors or other persons who filed a single Form 1041 for all of the trusts, rather than a separate Form 1041 for each trust, provided that the items of income, deduction, and credit of each trust were shown on a statement attached to the single Form 1041.

(3) Effective date for paragraphs (d)(2) and (h) of this section. Paragraphs (d)(2) and (h) of this section apply for taxable years ending on or after December 24, 2002.

(j) Cross-reference. For rules relating to employer identification numbers, and to the obligation of a payor of income or proceeds to the trust to furnish to the payee a statement to recipient, see § 301.6109-1(a)(2) of this chapter.

T.D. 6217, 12/19/56, amend T.D. 7796, 11/23/81, T.D. 8633, 12/20/95, T.D. 8668, 4/30/96, T.D. 9032, 12/23/2002, T.D. 9241, 1/23/2006.

§ 1.671-5 Reporting for widely held fixed investment trusts.

(a) Table of contents. This table of contents lists the major paragraph headings for this section.

§ 1.671-5(a)

(iii) Inclusion of information with respect to all calculation periods.

(5) Requesting information from a WHFIT.

(i) In general.

(ii) Manner of requesting information.

(iii) Period of time during which a requesting person may request WHFIT information.

(6) Trustee's requirement to retain records.

(d) Form 1099 requirement for trustees and middlemen.

(1) Obligation to file Form 1099 with the IRS.

(i) In general.

(ii) Forms 1099 not required for exempt recipients.

(iii) Reporting and withholding with respect to foreign persons.

(2) Information to be reported.

(i) Determining amounts to be provided on Forms 1099.

(ii) Information to be provided on Forms 1099.

(3) Time and manner of filing Forms 1099.

(i) Time and place.

(ii) Reporting trust sales proceeds, redemption asset proceeds, redemption proceeds, sales asset proceeds, sales proceeds, and non pro-rata partial principal payments.

(e) Requirement to furnish a written tax information statement to the TIH.

(1) In general.

(2) Information required.

(i) WHFIT information.

(ii) Identification of the person furnishing the statement.

(iii) Items of income, expense, and credit.

(iv) Non pro-rata partial principal payments.

(v) Asset sales and dispositions.

(vi) Redemption or sale of a trust interest.

(vii) Information regarding market discount and bond premium.

(viii) Other information.

(ix) Required statement.

(3) Due date and other requirements.

(4) Requirement to retain records.

(f) Safe harbor for providing information for certain NMWHFITs.

(1) Safe harbor for trustee reporting of NMWHFIT information.

(i) In general.

(ii) Reporting NMWHFIT income and expenses.

(iii) Reporting non pro-rata partial principal payments under the safe harbor.

(iv) Reporting sales and dispositions of NMWHFIT assets under the safe harbor.

(v) Reporting redemptions under the safe harbor.

(vi) Reporting the sale of a trust interest under the safe harbor.

(vii) Reporting OID information under the safe harbor.

(viii) Reporting market discount information under the safe harbor.

(xi) Reporting bond premium information under the safe harbor.

(x) Reporting additional information.

(2) Use of information provided by trustees under the safe harbor for NMWHFITs.

(i) In general.

(ii) Determining NMWHFIT income and expenses under the safe harbor.

(iii) Reporting non pro-rata partial principal payments under the safe harbor.

(iv) Reporting sales and dispositions of NMWHFIT assets under the safe harbor.

(v) Reporting redemptions under the safe harbor.

(vi) Reporting sales of trust interests under the safe harbor.

(vii) Reporting OID information under the safe harbor.

(viii) Reporting market discount information under the safe harbor.

(ix) Reporting bond premium information under the safe harbor.

(3) Example of the use of the safe harbor for NMWHFITs.

(i) Facts.

(ii) Trustee reporting.

(iii) Brokers' use of information provided by Trustee.

(g) Safe Harbor for certain WHMTs.

(1) Safe harbor for trustees of certain WHMTs for reporting information.

(i) In general.

(ii) Requirements.

(iii) Reporting WHMT income, expenses, non pro-rata partial principal payments, and sales and dispositions under the safe harbor.

(iv) Reporting OID information under the safe harbor.

(v) Reporting market discount information under the safe harbor.

(vi) Reporting bond premium information under the safe harbor.

(2) Use of information provided by a trustee under the safe harbor.

(i) In general.

(ii) Reporting WHMT income, expenses, non pro-rata partial principal payments, and sales and dispositions under the safe harbor.

(iii) Reporting OID information under the safe harbor.

(iv) Requirement to provide market discount information under the safe harbor.

(v) Requirement to provide bond premium information under the safe harbor.

(3) Example of safe harbor in paragraph (g)(1) of this section.

(i) Facts.

(ii) Trustee reporting.

(iii) Broker's use of the information provided by Trustee.

(h) Additional safe harbors.

(1) Temporary safe harbors.

(2) Additional safe harbors provided by other published guidance.

(i) Reserved.

(j) Requirement that middlemen furnish information to beneficial owners that are exempt recipients and non calendar year beneficial owners.

(1) In general.

(2) Time for providing information.

(3) Manner of providing information.

(4) Clearing organization.

(k) Coordination with other information reporting rules.

(l) Backup withholding requirements.

(m) Penalties for failure to comply.

(n) Effective date.

(b) Definitions. Solely for purposes of this section:

(1) An asset includes any real or personal, tangible or intangible property held by the trust, including an interest in a contract.

(2) An affected expense is an expense described in § 1.67-2T(i)(1).

(3) A beneficial owner is a trust interest holder (TIH) (as defined in paragraph (b)(20) of this section) that holds a beneficial interest in a widely held fixed investment trust (WHFIT) (as defined in paragraph (b)(22) of this section.)

(4) The calculation period is the period the trustee chooses under paragraph (c)(1)(ii) of this section for calculating the trust information required to be provided under paragraph (c) of this section.

(5) The cash held for distribution is the amount of cash held by the WHFIT (other than trust sales proceeds and proceeds from sales described in paragraphs (c)(2)(iv)(D)(4), (G), and (H) of this section) less reasonably required reserve funds as of the date that the amount of a distribution is required to be determined under the WHFIT's governing document.

(6) A clean-up call is the redemption of all trust interests in termination of the WHFIT when the administrative costs of the WHFIT outweigh the benefits of maintaining the WHFIT.

(7) An exempt recipient is—

(i) Any person described in § 1.6049-4(c)(1)(ii);

(ii) A middleman (as defined in paragraph (b)(10) of this section);

(iii) A real estate mortgage investment conduit (as defined in section 860(D)(a)) (REMIC);

(iv) A WHFIT; or

(v) A trust or an estate for which the trustee or middleman of the WHFIT is also required to file a Form 1041, "U.S. Income Tax Return for Estates and Trusts," in its capacity as a fiduciary of that trust or estate.

(8) An in-kind redemption is a redemption in which a beneficial owner receives a pro-rata share of each of the assets of the WHFIT that the beneficial owner is deemed to own under section 671. For example, for purposes of this paragraph (b)(8), if beneficial owner A owns a one percent interest in a WHFIT that holds 100 shares of X corporation stock, so that A is considered to own a one percent interest in each of the 100 shares, A's pro-rata share of the X corporation stock for this purpose is one share of X corporation stock.

(9) An item refers to an item of income, expense, or credit as well as any trust event (for example, the sale of an asset) or any characteristic or attribute of the trust that affects the income, deductions, and credits reported by a beneficial owner in any taxable year that the beneficial owner holds an interest in the trust. An item may refer to an individual item or a group of items depending on whether the item must be reported separately under paragraphs (c)(1)(i) and (e)(1) of this section.

(10) A middleman is any TIH, other than a qualified intermediary as defined in § 1.1031(k)-1(g), who, at any time during the calendar year, holds an interest in a WHFIT on behalf of, or for the account of, another TIH, or who otherwise acts in a capacity as an intermediary for the account of another person. A middleman includes, but is not limited to—

(i) A custodian of a person's account, such as a bank, financial institution, or brokerage firm acting as custodian of an account;

(ii) A nominee;

(iii) A joint owner of an account or instrument other than—

(A) A joint owner who is the spouse of the other owner; and

(B) A joint owner who is the beneficial owner and whose name appears on the Form 1099 filed with respect to the trust interest under paragraph (d) of this section; and

(iv) A broker (as defined in section 6045(c)(1) and § 1.6045-1(a)(1)), holding an interest for a customer in street name.

(11) A mortgage is an obligation that is principally secured by an interest in real property within the meaning of § 1.860G-2(a)(5), except that a mortgage does not include an interest in another WHFIT or mortgages held by another WHFIT.

(12) A non-mortgage widely held fixed investment trust (NMWHFIT) is a WHFIT other than a widely held mortgage trust (as defined in paragraph (b)(23) of this section).

(13) A non pro-rata partial principal payment is any partial payment of principal received on a debt instrument which does not retire the debt instrument and which is not a pro-rata prepayment described in § 1.1275-2(f)(2).

(14) The redemption asset proceeds equal the redemption proceeds (as defined in paragraph (b)(15) of this section) less the cash held for distribution with respect to the redeemed trust interest.

(15) The redemption proceeds equal the total amount paid to a redeeming TIH as the result of a redemption of a trust interest.

(16) A requesting person is—

(i) A middleman;

(ii) A beneficial owner who is a broker;

(iii) A beneficial owner who is an exempt recipient who holds a trust interest directly and not through a middleman;

(iv) A noncalendar-year beneficial owner who holds a trust interest directly and not through a middleman; or

(v) A representative or agent of a person specified in this paragraph (b)(16).

(17) The sales asset proceeds equal the sales proceeds (as defined in paragraph (b)(18) of this section) less the cash held for distribution with respect to the sold trust interest at the time of the sale.

(18) The sales proceeds equal the total amount paid to a selling TIH in consideration for the sale of a trust interest.

(19) The start-up date is the date on which substantially all of the assets have been deposited with the trustee of the WHFIT.

(20) A trust interest holder (TIH) is any person who holds a direct or indirect interest, including a beneficial interest, in a WHFIT at any time during the calendar year.

(21) Trust sales proceeds equal the amount paid to a WHFIT for the sale or disposition of an asset held by the WHFIT, including principal payments received by the WHFIT that completely retire a debt instrument (other than a final scheduled principal payment) and pro-rata partial principal prepayments described under § 1.1275-2(f)(2). Trust sales proceeds do not include amounts paid for any interest income that would be required to be reported under § 1.6045-1(d)(3). Trust sales proceeds also do not include amounts paid to a NMWHFIT as the result of pro-rata sales of trust assets to effect a redemption described in paragraph (c)(2)(iv)(G) of this section or the value of assets received as a result of a tax-free corporate reorganization as described in paragraph (c)(2)(iv)(H) of this section.

(22) A widely held fixed investment trust (WHFIT) is an arrangement classified as a trust under § 301.7701-4(c) of this chapter, provided that—

(i) The trust is a United States person under section 7701(a)(30)(E);

(ii) The beneficial owners of the trust are treated as owners under subpart E, part I, subchapter J, chapter 1 of the Internal Revenue Code; and

(iii) At least one interest in the trust is held by a middleman.

(23) A widely held mortgage trust (WHMT) is a WHFIT, the assets of which consist only of one or more of the following—

(i) Mortgages;

(ii) Regular interests in a REMIC;

(iii) Interests in another WHMT;

(iv) Reasonably required reserve funds;

(v) Amounts received on the assets described in paragraphs (b)(23)(i), (ii), (iii), and (iv) of this section pending distribution to TIHs; and

(vi) During a brief initial funding period, cash and short-term contracts for the purchase of the assets described in paragraphs (b)(23)(i), (ii), and (iii).

(c) Trustee's obligation to report information. *(1) In general.* Upon the request of a requesting person (as defined in paragraph (b)(16) of this section), a trustee of a WHFIT must report the information described in paragraph (c)(2) of this section to the requesting person. The trustee must determine such information in accordance with the following rules—

(i) Calculation. WHFIT information may be calculated in any manner that enables a requesting person to determine with reasonable accuracy the WHFIT items described in paragraph (c)(2) of this section that are attributable (or, if permitted under paragraphs (c)(2)(iv)(B) or (f)(2)(iii) of this section, distributed) to a beneficial owner for the taxable year of that owner. The manner of calculation must generally conform with industry practice for calculating the WHFIT items described in paragraph (c)(2) of this section for the type of asset or assets held by the WHFIT, and must enable a requesting person to separately state any WHFIT item that, if taken into account separately by a beneficial owner, would result in an income tax liability different from that which would result if the owner did not take the item into account separately.

(ii) Calculation period—WHFIT information may be calculated on the basis of a calendar month, calendar quarter, or half or full calendar year, provided that a trustee uses the same calculation period for the life of the WHFIT and the information provided by the trustee meets the requirements of paragraph (c)(1)(i) of this section. Regardless of the calculation period chosen by the trustee, the trustee must provide information requested by a requesting person under paragraph (c)(5) on a calendar year basis. The trustee may provide additional information to requesting persons throughout the calendar year at the trustee's discretion.

(iii) Accounting method. (A) General rule. WHFIT information must be calculated and reported using the cash receipts and disbursements method of accounting unless another method is required by the Internal Revenue Code or regulations with respect to a specific trust item. Accordingly, a trustee must provide information necessary for TIHs to comply with the rules of subtitle A, chapter 1, subchapter P, part V, subpart A of the Internal Revenue Code, which require the inclusion of accrued amounts with respect to OID, and section 860B(b), which requires the inclusion of accrued amounts with respect to a REMIC regular interest.

(B) Exception for WHFITs marketed predominantly to taxpayers on the accrual method. If the trustee or the trust's sponsor knows or reasonably should know that a WHFIT is marketed primarily to accrual method TIHs and the WHFIT holds assets for which the timing of the recognition of income is materially affected by the use of the accrual method of accounting, the trustee must calculate and report trust information using the accrual method of accounting.

(iv) Gross income requirement. The amount of income required to be reported by the trustee is the gross income (as defined in section 61) generated by the WHFIT's assets. Thus, in the case of a WHFIT that receives a payment of income from which an expense (or expenses) has been deducted, the trustee, in calculating the income to be reported under paragraph (c)(2)(ii) of this section, must report the income earned on the trusts assets unreduced by the deducted expense or expenses and separately report the deducted expense or expenses. See paragraph (c)(2)(iv) of this section regarding reporting with respect to sales and dispositions.

(2) Information to be reported by all WHFITs. With respect to all WHFITs—

(i) Trust identification and calculation period chosen. The trustee must report information identifying the WHFIT, including—

(A) The name of the WHFIT;

(B) The employer identification number of the WHFIT;

(C) The name and address of the trustee;

(D) The Committee on Uniform Security Identification Procedure (CUSIP) number, account number, serial number, or other identifying number of the WHFIT;

(E) The classification of the WHFIT as either a WHMT or NMWHFIT; and

(F) The calculation period used by the trustee.

(ii) Items of income, expense, and credit. The trustee must report information detailing—

(A) All items of gross income (including OID, except than OID is not required to be included for a WHMT that has a start-up date (as defined in paragraph (b)(19) of this section) prior to August 13, 1998).

(B) All items of expense (including affected expenses); and

(C) All items of credit.

(iii) Non pro-rata partial principal payments. The trustee must report information detailing non pro-rata partial principal payments (as defined in paragraph (b)(13) of this section) received by the WHFIT.

(iv) Asset sales and dispositions. The trustee must report information regarding sales and dispositions of WHFIT assets as required in this paragraph (c)(2)(iv). For purposes of this paragraph (c)(2)(iv), a payment (other than a final scheduled payment) that completely retires a debt instrument (including a mortgage held by a WHMT) or a pro-rata prepayment on a debt instrument (see § 1.1275-2(f)(2)) held by a WHFIT must be reported as a full or partial sale or disposition of the debt instrument. Pro-rata sales of trust assets to effect redemptions, as defined in paragraph (c)(2)(iv)(G) of this section, or exchanges of trust assets as the result of a corporate reorganization under paragraph (c)(2)(iv)(H) of this section, are not reported as sales or dispositions under this paragraph (c)(2)(iv).

(A) General rule. Except as provided in paragraph (c)(2)(iv)(B) (regarding the exception for certain NMWHFITs) or paragraph (c)(2)(iv)(C) (regarding the exception for certain WHMTs) of this section, the trustee must report with respect to each sale or disposition of a WHFIT asset --

(1) The date of each sale or disposition;

(2) Information that enables a requesting person to determine the amount of trust sales proceeds (as defined in paragraph (b)(21) of this section) attributable to a beneficial owner as a result of each sale or disposition; and

(3) Information that enables a beneficial owner to allocate, with reasonable accuracy, a portion of the owner's basis in its trust interest to each sale or disposition.

(B) Exception for certain NMWHFITs. If a NMWHFIT meets paragraph (c)(2)(iv)(D)(1)(regarding the general de minimis test), paragraph (c)(2)(iv)(E) (regarding the qualified NMWHFIT exception), or paragraph (c)(2)(iv)(F) (regarding the NMWHFIT final calendar year exception) of this section, the trustee is not required to report under paragraph (c)(2)(iv)(A) of this section. Instead, the trustee must report sufficient information to enable a requesting person to determine the amount of trust sales proceeds distributed to a beneficial owner during the calendar year with respect to each sale or disposition of a trust asset. The trustee also must provide requesting persons with a statement that the NMWHFIT is permitted to report under this paragraph (c)(2)(iv)(B).

(C) Exception for certain WHMTs. If a WHMT meets either the general or the special de minimis test of paragraph (c)(2)(iv)(D) of this section for the calendar year, the trustee is not required to report under paragraph (c)(2)(iv)(A) of this section. Instead, the trustee must report information to enable a requesting person to determine the amount of trust sales proceeds attributable to a beneficial owner as a result of the sale or disposition. The trustee also must provide requesting persons with a statement that the WHMT is permitted to report under this paragraph (c)(2)(iv)(C).

(D) De minimis tests. (1) General WHFIT de minimis test. The general WHFIT de minimis test is satisfied if trust sales proceeds for the calendar year are not more than five percent of the net asset value of the trust (aggregate fair market value of the trust's assets less the trust's liabilities) as of the later of January 1 and the start-up date (as defined paragraph (b)(19) of this section); or, if the trustee chooses, the later of January 1 and the measuring date. The measuring date is the date of the last deposit of assets into the WHFIT (not including any deposit of assets into the WHFIT pursuant to a distribution reinvestment program), not to exceed 90 days after the date the registration statement of the WHFIT becomes effective under the Securities Act of 1933.

(2) Special WHMT de minimis test. A WHMT that meets the asset requirement of paragraph (g)(1)(ii)(E) of this section satisfies the special WHMT de minimis test in this paragraph (c)(2)(iv)(D)(2) if trust sales proceeds for the calendar year are not more than five percent of the aggregate outstanding principal balance of the WHMT (as defined in paragraph (g)(1)(iii)(D) of this section) as of the later of January 1 of that year or the trust's start-up date. For purposes of applying the special WHMT de minimis test in this paragraph (c)(2)(iv)(D)(2), amounts that result from the complete or partial payment of the outstanding principal balance of the mortgages held by the trust are not included in the amount of trust sales proceeds. The IRS and the Treasury Department may provide by revenue ruling, or by other published guidance, that the special de minimis test of this paragraph (c)(2)(iv)(D)(2) may be applied to WHFITs holding debt instruments other than those described in paragraph (g)(1)(ii)(E) of this section.

(3) Effect of clean-up call. If a WHFIT fails to meet either de minimis test described in this paragraph (c)(2)(iv)(D) solely as the result of a clean-up call, as defined in paragraph (b)(6) of this section, the WHFIT will be treated as having met the de minimis test.

(4) Exception for certain fully reported sales. (i) Rule. If a trustee of a NMWHFIT reports the sales described in paragraph (c)(2)(iv)(D)(4)(ii) of this section as provided under paragraph (c)(2)(iv)(A) of this section (regardless of whether the general minimis test in paragraph (c)(2)(iv)(D)(1) of this section is satisfied for a particular calendar year) consistently throughout the life of the WHFIT, a trustee may exclude the trust sales proceeds received by the WHFIT as a result of those sales from the trust sales proceeds used to determine whether a WHFIT has satisfied the general de minimis test in paragraph (c)(2)(iv)(D)(1) of this section.

(ii) Applicable sales and dispositions. This paragraph (c)(2)(iv)(D)(4) applies to sales and dispositions resulting from corporate reorganizations and restructurings for which the trust receives cash, the sale of assets received by the trust in corporate reorganizations and restructurings (including conversions of closed-end investment companies to open-end investment companies), principal prepayments, bond calls, bond maturities, and the sale of securities by the trustee as required by the governing document or applicable law governing fiduciaries in order to maintain the sound investment character of the trust, and any other nonvolitional dispositions of trust assets.

(iii) Certain small sales and dispositions. If the amount of trust sales proceeds from a sale or disposition described in paragraph (c)(2)(iv)(D)(4)(ii) of this section is less than .01 percent of the net fair market value of the WHFIT as determined for applying the de minimis test for the calendar year, the trustee is not required to report the sale or disposition under paragraph (c)(2)(iv)(A) of this section provided the trustee includes the trust sales proceeds, received for purposes of determining whether the trust has met the general de minimis test of paragraph (c)(2)(iv)(D)(1) of this section.

(E) Qualified NMWHFIT exception. The qualified NMWHFIT exception is satisfied if --

(1) The NMWHFIT has a start-up date (as defined in paragraph (b)(19) of this section) before February 23, 2006;

(2) The registration statement of the NMWHFIT becomes effective under the Securities Act of 1933, as amended (15 U.S.C. 77a, et. seq.) and trust interests are offered for sale to the public before February 23, 2006; or

(3) The registration statement of the NMWHFIT becomes effective under the Securities Act of 1933 and trust interests are offered for sale to the public on or after February 23, 2006, and before July 31, 2006, and the NMWHFIT is fully funded before October 1, 2006. For purposes of determining whether a NMWHFIT is fully funded under this paragraph (c)(2)(iv)(E), deposits to the NMWHFIT after October 1, 2006, that are made pursuant to a distribution reinvestment program that is consistent with the requirements of § 301.7701-4(c) of this chapter are disregarded.

(F) NMWHFIT final calendar year exception. The NMWHFIT final calendar year exception is satisfied if --

(1) The NMWHFIT terminates on or before December 31 of the year for which the trustee is reporting;

(2) Beneficial owners exchange their interests for cash or are treated as having exchanged their interests for cash upon termination of the trust; and

(3) The trustee makes reasonable efforts to engage in pro-rata sales of trust assets to effect redemptions.

(G) Pro-rata sales of trust assets to effect a redemption. (1) Rule. Pro-rata sales of trust assets to effect redemptions are not required to be reported under this paragraph (c)(2)(iv).

(2) Definition. Pro-rata sales of trust assets to effect redemptions occur when --

(i) One or more trust interests are tendered for redemption;

(ii) The trustee identifies the pro-rata shares of the trust assets that are deemed to be owned by the trust interest or interests tendered for redemption (See paragraph (b)(8) of this section for a description of how pro-rata is to be applied for purposes of this paragraph (c)(2)(iv)(G)) and sells those assets as soon as practicable;

(iii) Proceeds from the sales of the assets identified in paragraph (c)(2)(iv)(G)(2)(ii) of this section are used solely to effect redemptions; and

(iv) The redemptions are reported as required under paragraph (c)(2)(v) of this section by the trustee.

(3) Additional rules. (i) Calendar month aggregation. The trustee may compare the aggregate pro-rata share of the assets deemed to be owned by the trust interests tendered for redemption during the calendar month with the aggregate sales of assets to effect redemptions for the calendar month to determine the pro-rata sales of trust assets to effect redemptions for the calendar month. If the aggregate pro-rata share of an asset deemed to be owned by the trust interests tendered for redemption for the month is a fractional amount, the trustee may round that number up to the next whole number for the purpose of determining the pro-rata sales to effect redemptions for the calendar month;

(ii) Sales of assets to effect redemptions may be combined with sales of assets for other purposes. Sales of assets to effect redemptions may be combined with the sales of assets to obtain cash for other purposes but the proceeds from the sales of assets to effect redemptions must be used solely to provide cash for redemptions and the sales of assets to obtain cash for other purposes must be reported as otherwise provided in this paragraph (c)(2)(iv). For example, if a trustee sells assets and the proceeds are used by the trustee to pay trust expenses, these amounts are to be included in the amounts reported under paragraph (c)(2)(iv)(A) or (B), as appropriate.

(4) Example. (i) January 1, 2008. Trust has one million trust interests and all interests have equal value and equal rights. The number of shares of stock in corporations A through J and the pro-rata share of each stock that a trust interest is deemed to own as of the January 1, 2008, is as follows:

Stock	Total shares	Per trust interest
A	24,845	.024845
B	28,273	.028273
C	35,575	.035575
D	13,866	.013866
E	25,082	.025082
F	39,154	.039154
G	16,137	.016137
H	14,704	.014704
I	17,436	.017436
J	31,133	.031133

(ii) Transactions of January 2, 2008. On January 2, 2008, 50,000 trust interests are tendered for redemption. The deemed pro-rata ownership of stocks A through J represented by the 50,000 redeemed trust interests and the stocks sold to provide cash for the redemptions are set out in the following table:

Stock	Deemed pro-rata ownership	Shares sold
A	1,242.25	1,242
B	1,413.65	1,413
C	1,778.75	1,779
D	693.30	694
E	1,254.10	1,254
F	1,957.70	1,957
G	806.85	807
H	735.20	735
I	871.80	872
J	1,556.65	1,557

(iii) Transactions on January 15 through 17 2008. On January 15, 2008, 10,000 trust interests are tendered for redemption. Trustee lends money to Trust for redemptions. On January 16, B merges into C at a rate of .55 per share. On January 17, Trustee sells stock to obtain cash to be reimbursed the cash loaned to Trust to effect the redemptions. The pro-rata share of the stock deemed to be owned by the 10,000 redeemed trust interests and the stock sold by the trustee to effect the redemptions are set out in the following table:

Stock	Deemed pro-rata ownership	Shares sold
A	248.45	249
B	00	00
C	511.25	512
D	138.66	138
E	250.82	251
F	391.54	392
G	161.37	162
H	147.04	148
I	174.36	174
J	311.33	311

(iv) Transactions on January 28 and 29, 2008. On January 28, 2008, the value of the H stock is $30.00 per share and Trustee, pursuant to Trust's governing document, sells the H stock to preserve the financial integrity of Trust and receives $414, 630. Trustee intends to report this sale under paragraph (c)(2)(iv)(A) of this section and to distribute the proceeds of the sale pro-rata to trust interest holders on Trust's next scheduled distribution date. On January 29, 2008, while trustee still holds the proceeds from the January 28 sale, 10,000 trust interests are tendered for redemption. The pro-rata share of the stock deemed to be owned by the 10,000 redeemed trust interests and the stock sold by the trustee to effect the redemptions are set out in the following table:

Stock	Deemed pro-rata ownership	Shares sold
A	248.45	248
B	0	0
C	511.25	511
D	138.66	139
E	250.82	251
F	391.54	391
G	161.37	161
H	0 [1]	0
I	174.36	175
J	311.33	312

[1] Share of cash proceeds: $4,458.39.

(v) Monthly amounts. To determine the pro-rata sales to effect redemptions for January, trustee compares the aggregate pro-rata share of stocks A through J (rounded to the next whole number) deemed to be owned by the trust interests tendered for redemption during the month of January with the sales of stocks A through J to effect redemptions:

Stock	Deemed pro-rata ownership	Shares sold
A	1740	1739
B	0	0
C	3579	3579
D	971	971
E	1756	1756
F	2741	2741
G	1130	1130
H	883	883
I	1221	1221
J	2180	2180

(vi) Pro-rata sales to effect redemptions for the month of January. For the month of January, the deemed pro-rata ownership of shares of stocks A through J equal or exceed the sales of stock to effect redemptions for the month. Accordingly, all of the sales to effect redemptions during the month of January are considered to be pro-rata and are not required to be reported under this paragraph (c)(2)(iv).

(H) Corporate Reorganizations. The exchange of trust assets for other assets of equivalent value pursuant to a tax free corporate reorganization is not required to be reported as a sale or disposition under this paragraph (c)(2)(iv).

(v) Redemptions and sales of WHFIT interests. (A) Redemptions. (1) In general. Unless paragraph (c)(2)(v)(C) of this section applies, for each date on which the amount of a redemption proceeds for the redemption of a trust interest is determined, the trustee must provide information to enable a requesting person to determine --

(i) The redemption proceeds (as defined in paragraph (b)(15) of this section) per trust interest on that date;

(ii) The redemption asset proceeds (as defined in paragraph (b)(14) of this section) per trust interest on that date; and

(iii) The gross income that is attributable to the redeeming beneficial owner for the portion of the calendar year that the redeeming beneficial owner held its interest (including income earned by the WHFIT after the date of the last income distribution.

(2) In kind redemptions. The value of the assets received with respect to an in-kind redemption (as defined in paragraph (b)(8) of this section) is not required to be reported under this paragraph (c)(2)(v)(A). Information regarding the income attributable to a redeeming beneficial owner must, however, be reported under paragraph (c)(2)(v)(A)(1)(iii) of this section.

(B) Sale of a trust interest. Under paragraph (c)(2)(v)(C) of this section applies, if a secondary market for interests in the WHFIT is established, the trustee must provide, for each day of the calendar year, information to enable requesting persons to determine --

(1) The sale assets proceeds (as defined in paragraph (b)(17) of this section) per trust interest on that date; and

(2) The gross income that is attributable to a selling beneficial owner and to a purchasing beneficial owner for the portion of the calendar year that each held the trust interest.

(C) Simplified Reporting for Certain NMWHFITs. (1) In general. The trustee of a NMWHFIT described in paragraph (c)(2)(v)(C)(2) of this section is not required to report the information described in paragraph (c)(2)(v)(A) of this section (regarding redemptions) or (c)(2)(v)(B) of this section (regarding sales). However, the trustee must report to requesting persons, for each date on which the amount of redemption proceeds to be paid for the redemption of a trust interest is determined, information that will enable requesting persons to determine the redemption proceeds per trust interest on that date. The trustee also must provide requesting persons with a statement that this paragraph applies to the NMWHFIT.

(2) NMWHFITs that qualify for the exception. This paragraph (c)(2)(v)(C) applies to a NMWHFIT if --

(i) Substantially all the assets of the NMWHFIT produce income that is treated as interest income (but only if these assets trade on a recognized exchange or securities market without a price component attributable to accrued interest) or produce dividend income (as defined in section 6042(b) and the regulations under that section). (Trust sales proceeds and gross proceeds from sales described in paragraphs (c)(2)(iv)(G) and (H) of this section are ignored for the purpose of determining if substantially all of a NMWHFIT's assets produce dividend or the interest income described in this paragraph); and

(ii) The qualified NMWHFIT exception of paragraph (c)(2)(iv)(E) of this section is satisfied, or the trustee is required by the governing document of the NMWHFIT to determine and distribute all cash held for distribution (as defined in paragraph (b)(5) of this section) no less frequently than monthly. A NMWHFIT will be considered to have satisfied this paragraph (c)(2)(v)(C)(2)(i) notwithstanding that the governing document of the NMWHFIT permits the trustee to forego making a required monthly or more frequent distribution, if the cash held for distribution is less than 0.1 percent of the aggregate net asset value of the trust as of the date specified in the governing document for calculating the amount of the monthly distribution.

(vi) Information regarding bond premium. The trustee generally must report information that enables a beneficial owner to determine, in any manner that is reasonably consistent with section 171, the amount of the beneficial owner's amortizable bond premium, if any, for each calendar year. However, if a NMWHFIT meets the general de minimis test in paragraph (c)(2)(iv)(D)(1) of this section, the qualified NMWHFIT exception of paragraph (c)(2)(iv)(E) of this section, or the NMWHFIT final calendar year exception of paragraph (c)(2)(iv)(F) of this section, the trustee of the NMWHFIT is not required to report information regarding bond premium.

(vii) Information regarding market discount. The trustee generally must report information that enables a beneficial owner to determine, in any manner reasonably consistent with section 1276 (including section 1276(a)(3)), the amount of market discount that has accrued during the calendar year. However, if a NMWHFIT meets the general de minimis test in paragraph (c)(2)(iv)(D) of this section, the qualified NMWHFIT exception of paragraph (c)(2)(iv)(E) of this section, or the NMWHFIT final calendar year exception of paragraph (c)(2)(iv)(F) of this section, the trustee of such NMWHFIT is not required to provide information regarding market discount.

(viii) Other information. The trustee must provide any other information necessary for a beneficial owner of a trust interest to report, with reasonable accuracy, the items (as defined in paragraph (b)(9) of this section) attributable to the portion of the trust treated as owned by the beneficial owner under section 671.

(3) Identifying the representative who will provide trust information. The trustee must identify a representative of the WHFIT who will provide the information specified in this paragraph (c). The trustee also may identify an Internet website at which the trustee will provide the information specified in this paragraph (c). This information must be—

(i) Printed in a publication generally read by, and available to, requesting persons;

(ii) Stated in the trust's prospectus; or

(iii) Posted at the trustee's Internet website.

(4) Time and manner of providing information. (i) Time. (A) In general. Except as provided in paragraph (c)(4)(i)(B) of this section, a trustee must provide the information specified in this paragraph (c) to requesting persons on or before the later of—

(1) The 30th day after the close of the calendar year to which the request relates; or

(2) The day that is 14 days after the receipt of the request.

(B) Trusts holding interests in other WHFITs or in REMICs. If the WHFIT holds an interest in one or more other WHFITs or holds one or more REMIC regular interests, or holds both, a trustee must provide the information specified in this paragraph (c) to requesting persons on or before the later of—

(1) The 44th day after the close of the calendar year to which the request relates; or

(2) The day that is 28 days after the receipt of the request.

(ii) Manner. The information specified in this paragraph (c) must be provided—

(A) By written statement sent by first class mail to the address provided by the requesting person;

(B) By causing it to be printed in a publication generally read by and available to requesting persons and by notifying requesting persons in writing of the publication in which it will appear, the date on which it will appear, and, if possible, the page on which it will appear;

(C) By causing it to be posted at an Internet website, provided the trustee identifies the website under paragraph (c)(3) of this section;

(D) By electronic mail provided that the requesting person requests that the trustee furnish the information by electronic mail and the person furnishes an electronic address; or

(E) By any other method agreed to by the trustee and the requesting person.

(iii) Inclusion of information with respect to all calculation periods. If a trustee calculates WHFIT information using a calculation period other than a calendar year, the trustee must provide information for each calculation period that falls within the calendar year requested.

(5) Requesting information from a WHFIT. (i) In general. Requesting persons may request the information specified in this paragraph (c) from a WHFIT.

(ii) Manner of requesting information. In requesting WHFIT information, a requesting person must specify the WHFIT and the calendar year for which information is requested.

(iii) Period of time during which a requesting person may request WHFIT information. For the life of the WHFIT and for five years following the date of the WHFIT's termination, a requesting person may request the information specified in this paragraph (c) for any calendar year of the WHFIT's existence beginning with the 2007 calendar year.

(6) Trustee's requirement to retain records. For the life of the WHFIT and for five years following the date of termination of the WHFIT, the trustee must maintain in its records a copy of the information required to be provided to requesting persons this paragraph (c) for each calendar year beginning with the 2007 calendar year. For a period of five years following the close of the calendar year to which the data pertains, the trustee also must maintain in its records such supplemental data as may be necessary to establish that the information provided to requesting persons is correct and meets the requirements of this paragraph (c).

(d) Form 1099 requirement for trustees and middlemen. *(1) Obligation to file Form 1099 with the IRS.* (i) In general. Except as provided in paragraphs (d)(1)(ii) and (iii) of this section—

(A) The trustee must file with the IRS the appropriate Forms 1099, reporting the information specified in paragraph (d)(2) of this section with respect to any TIH who holds an interest in the WHFIT directly and not through a middleman; and

(B) Every middleman must file with the IRS the appropriate Forms 1099, reporting the information specified in paragraph (d)(2) of this section with respect to any TIH on whose behalf or account the middleman holds an interest in the WHFIT or acts as an intermediary.

(ii) Forms 1099 not required for exempt recipients. (A) In general. A Form 1099 is not required with respect to a TIH who is an exempt recipient (as defined in paragraph (b)(7) of this section), unless the trustee or middleman backup withholds under section 3406 on payments made to an exempt recipient (because, for example, the exempt recipient has failed to furnish a Form W-9 on request). If the trustee or middleman backup withholds, then the trustee or middleman is required to file a Form 1099 under this paragraph (d) unless the trustee or middleman refunds the amount withheld in accordance with § 31.6413(a)-3 of this chapter.

(B) Exempt recipients must include WHFIT information in computing taxable income. A beneficial owner who is an exempt recipient must obtain WHFIT information and must include the items (as defined in paragraph (b)(9) of this section) of the WHFIT in computing its taxable income on its federal income tax return. Paragraphs (c)(3) and (h) of this section provide rules for exempt recipients to obtain information from a WHFIT.

(iii) Reporting and withholding with respect to foreign persons. The items of the WHFIT attributable to a TIH who is not a United States person must be reported, and amounts must be withheld, as provided under subtitle A, chapter 3 of the Internal Revenue Code (sections 1441 through 1464) and the regulations thereunder and not reported under this paragraph (d).

(2) Information to be reported. (i) Determining amounts to be provided on Forms 1099. The amounts reported to the IRS for a calendar year by a trustee or middleman on the appropriate Form 1099 must be consistent with the information provided by the trustee under paragraph (c) of this section and must reflect with reasonable accuracy the amount of each item required to be reported on a Form 1099 that is attributable (or if permitted under paragraphs (d)(2)(ii)(D) and (E) of this section, distributed) to the TIH. If the trustee, in providing WHFIT information, uses the safe harbors in paragraph (f)(1) or (g)(1) of this section, then the trustee or middleman must calculate the information to be provided to the IRS on the Forms 1099 in accordance with paragraph (f)(2) or (g)(2) of this section, as appropriate.

(ii) Information to be provided on Forms 1099. The trustee or middleman must include on the appropriate Forms 1099: (A) Taxpayer information. The name, address, and taxpayer identification number of the TIH;

(B) Information regarding the person filing the Form 1099. The name, address, taxpayer identification number, and telephone number of the person required to file the Form 1099;

(C) Gross income. All items of gross income of the WHFIT attributable to the TIH for the calendar year (including OID (unless the exception for certain WHMTs applies (see paragraph (c)(2)(ii)(A) of this section)) and all amounts of income attributable to a selling, purchasing, or redeeming TIH for the portion of the calendar year that the TIH held its interest (unless paragraph (c)(2)(v)(C) of this section (regarding an exception for certain NMWHFITs) applies));

(D) Non pro-rata partial principal payments. All non pro-rata partial principal payments (as defined in paragraph (b)(13) of this section) received by the WHFIT that are attributable (or distributed, in the case of a trustee or middleman reporting under paragraph (f)(2)(iii) of this section) to the TIH;

(E) Trust sales proceeds. All trust sales proceeds (as defined in paragraph (b)(21) of this section) that are attributable to the TIH for the calendar year, if any, or, if paragraph (c)(2)(iv)(B) of this section (regarding certain NMWHFITs) applies, the amount of trust sales proceeds distributed to the TIH for the calendar year;

(F) Reporting Redemptions. All redemption asset proceeds (as defined in paragraph (b)(14) of this section) paid to the TIH for the calendar year, if any, or if paragraph (c)(2)(v)(C) of this section (regarding an exception for certain NMWHFITs) applies, all redemption proceeds (as defined in paragraph (b)(15) of this section) paid to the TIH for the calendar year;

(G) Reporting sales of a trust interest on a secondary market. All sales asset proceeds (as defined in paragraph (b)(17) of this section) paid to the TIH for the sale of a trust interest or interests on a secondary market established for the NMWHFIT for the calendar year, if any, or, if paragraph (c)(2)(v)(C) of this section (regarding an exception for certain NMWHFITs) applies, all sales proceeds (as defined in paragraph (b)(18) of this section) paid to the TIH for the calendar year; and

(H) Other information. Any other information required by the Form 1099.

(3) Time and manner of filing Forms 1099. (i) Time and place. The Forms 1099 required to be filed under this paragraph (d) must be filed on or before February 28 (March 31, if filed electronically) of the year following the year for which the Forms 1099 are being filed. The returns must be filed with the appropriate Internal Revenue Service Center, at the address listed in the instructions for the Forms 1099. For extensions of time for filing returns under this section, see § 1.6081-1, the instructions for the Forms 1099, and applicable revenue procedures (see § 601.601(d)(2) of this chapter). For magnetic media filing requirements, see § 301.6011-2 of this chapter.

(ii) Reporting trust sales proceeds, redemption asset proceeds, redemption proceeds, sale asset proceeds, sales proceeds and non pro-rata partial principal payments. (A) Form to be used. Trust sales proceeds, redemption asset proceeds, redemption proceeds, sale asset proceeds, sales proceeds, and non pro-rata partial principal payments are to be reported on the same type of Form 1099 as that required for reporting gross proceeds under section 6045.

(B) Appropriate reporting for in-kind redemptions. The value of the assets distributed with respect to an in-kind redemption is not required to be reported to the IRS. Unless paragraph (c)(2)(v)(C) of this section applies, the trustee or middleman must report the gross income attributable to the redeemed trust interest for the calendar year up to the date of the redemption under paragraph (d)(2)(ii)(C) of this section.

(e) Requirement to furnish a written tax information statement to the TIH. *(1) In general.* Every trustee or middleman required to file appropriate Forms 1099 under paragraph (d) of this section with respect to a TIH must furnish to that TIH (the person whose identifying number is required to be shown on the form) a written tax information statement showing the information described in paragraph (e)(2) of this section. The amount of a trust item reported to a TIH under this paragraph (e) must be consistent with the information reported to the IRS with respect to the TIH under paragraph (d) of this section. Information provided in this written statement must be determined in accordance with the rules provided in paragraph (d)(2)(i) of this section (regardless of whether the information was required to be provided on a Form 1099). Further, the trustee or middleman must separately state on the written tax information statement any items that, if taken into account separately by that TIH, would result in an income tax liability that is different from the income tax liability that would result if the items were not taken into account separately.

(2) Information required. For the calendar year, the written tax information statement must meet the following requirements:

(i) WHFIT information. The written tax information statement must include the name of the WHFIT and the identifying number of the WHFIT ;

(ii) Identification of the person furnishing the statement. The written tax information statement must include the name, address, and taxpayer identification number of the person required to furnish the statement;

(iii) Items of income, expense, and credit. The written tax information statement must include information regarding the items of income (that is, the information required to be reported to the IRS on Forms 1099), expense (including affected expenses), and credit that are attributable to the TIH for the calendar year;

(iv) Non pro-rata partial principal payments. The written tax information statement must include the information required to be reported to the IRS on Forms 1099 under paragraph (d)(2)(ii)(D) of this section (regarding the non pro-rata partial principal payments that are attributable (or distributed, in the case of a trustee or middleman reporting under paragraph (f)(2)(iii) of this section) to the TIH for the calendar year).

(v) Asset sales and dispositions. (A) General rule. Unless paragraph (c)(2)(iv)(B) (regarding the exception for certain NMWHFITs) or (c)(2)(iv)(C) (regarding the exception for certain WHMTs) of this section applies, the written tax information statement must include, with respect to each sale or disposition of a WHFIT asset for the calendar year—

(1) The date of sale or disposition;

(2) Information regarding the trust sales proceeds that are attributable to the TIH as a result of the sale or disposition; and

(3) Information that will enable the TIH to allocate with reasonable accuracy a portion of the TIH's basis in the TIH's trust interest to the sale or disposition.

(B) Special rule for certain NMWHFITs and WHMTs. In the case of a NMWHFIT to which paragraph (c)(2)(iv)(B) of this section applies or in the case of a WHMT to which paragraph (c)(2)(iv)(C) of this section applies, the written tax information statement must include, with respect to asset sales and dispositions, only the information required to be reported to the IRS on Form 1099 under paragraph (d)(2)((ii)(E) of this section.

(vi) Redemption or sale of a trust interest. The written tax information statement must include the information required to be reported to the IRS on Forms 1099 under paragraphs (d)(2)(ii)(F) and (G) of this section (regarding the sales and redemptions of trust interests made by the TIH for the calendar year);

(vii) Information regarding market discount and bond premium. The written tax information statement must include the information required to be reported by the trustee under paragraphs (c)(2)(vi) and (vii) of this section (regarding bond premium and market discount);

(viii) Other information. The written tax information statement must include any other information necessary for the TIH to report, with reasonable accuracy for the calendar year, the items (as defined in paragraph (b)(9) of this section) attributable to the portion of the trust treated as owned by the TIH under section 671. The written tax information statement may include information with respect to a trust item on a per trust interest basis if the trustee has reported (or calculated) the information with respect to that item on a per trust interest basis and information with respect to that item is not required to be reported on a Form 1099; and

(ix) Required statement. The written tax information statement must inform the TIH that the items of income, deduction, and credit, and any other information shown on the statement must be taken into account in computing the taxable income and credits of the TIH on the Federal income tax return of the TIH. If the written tax information statement reports that an amount of qualified dividend income is attributable to the TIH, the written tax information statement also must inform the TIH that the TIH must meet the requirements of section 1(h)(11)(B)(iii) to treat the dividends as qualified dividends.

(3) Due date and other requirements. The written tax information statement must be furnished to the TIH on or before March 15 of the year following the calendar year for which the statement is being furnished.

(4) Requirement to retain records. For a period of no less than five years from the due date for furnishing the written tax information statement, a trustee or middleman must maintain in its records a copy of any written tax information statement furnished to a TIH, and such supplemental data as may be required to establish the correctness of the statement.

(f) Safe harbor for providing information for certain NMWHFITs. *(1) Safe harbor for trustee reporting of NMWHFIT information.* The trustee of a NMWHFIT that meets the requirements of paragraph (f)(1)(i) of this section is deemed to satisfy paragraph (c)(1)(i) of this section, if the trustee calculates and provides WHFIT information in the manner described in this paragraph (f) and provides a statement to a requesting person giving notice that information has been calculated in accordance with this paragraph (f)(1).

(i) In general. (A) Eligibility to report under this safe harbor. Only NMWHFITs that meet the requirements set forth in paragraphs (f)(1)(i)(A)(1) and (2) of this section may report under this safe harbor. For purposes of determining whether the requirements of paragraph (f)(1)(i)(A)(1) of this section are met, trust sales proceeds and gross proceeds from sales described in paragraphs (c)(2)(iv)(G) and (H) of this section are ignored.

(1) Substantially all of the NMWHFIT's income is from dividends or interest; and

(2) All trust interests have identical value and rights

(B) Consistency requirements. The trustee must—

(1) Calculate all trust items subject to the safe harbor consistent with the safe harbor; and, (2) Report under this paragraph (f)(1) for the life of the NMWHFIT; or, if the NMWHFIT has a start-up date before January 1, 2007, the NMWHFIT must begin reporting under this paragraph (f)(1) as of January 1, 2007 and must continue to report under this paragraph for the life of the NMWHFIT.

(ii) Reporting NMWHFIT income and expenses. A trustee must first determine the total amount of NMWHFIT distributions (both actual and deemed) for the calendar year and then express each income or expense item as a fraction of the total amount of NMWHFIT distributions. These fractions (hereinafter referred to as factors) must be accurate to at least four decimal places.

(A) Step One: Determine the total amount of NMWHFIT distributions for the calendar year. The trustee must determine the total amount of NMWHFIT distributions (actual and deemed) for the calendar year. If the calculation of the total amount of NMWHFIT distributions under this paragraph (f)(1)(ii)(A) results in a zero or a negative number, the trustee may not determine income and expense information under this paragraph (f)(1)(ii)(A) (but may report all other applicable items under this paragraph (f)(1)). The total amount of NMWHFIT distributions equals the amount of NMWHFIT funds paid out to all TIHs (including all trust sales proceeds, all principal receipts, and all redemption proceeds) for the calendar year—

(1) Increased by—

(i) All amounts that would have been distributed during the calendar year, but were instead reinvested pursuant to a reinvestment plan; and

(ii) All cash held for distribution to TIHs as of December 31 of the year for which the trustee is reporting; and

(2) Decreased by—

(i) All cash distributed during the current year that was included in a year-end cash allocation factor (see paragraph (f)(1)(ii)(C)(1) of this section) for a prior year;

(ii) All redemption asset proceeds paid for the calendar year, or if paragraph (c)(2)(v)(C) of this section applies to the NMWHFIT, all redemption proceeds paid for the calendar year;

(iii) All trust sales proceeds distributed during the calendar year; and

(iv) All non pro-rata partial principal payments distributed during the calendar year.

(3) For the purpose of determining the amount of all redemption asset proceeds or redemption proceeds paid for the calendar year with respect to paragraph (f)(1)(ii)(A)(2)(ii) of this section, the value of the assets (not including cash) distributed with respect to an in-kind redemption is disregarded. Any cash distributed as part of the redemption must be included in the total amount of NMWHFIT distributions.

(B) Step Two: Determine factors that express the ratios of NMWHFIT income and expenses to the total amount of NMWHFIT distributions. The trustee must determine factors that express the ratios of NMWHFIT income and expenses to the total amount of NMWHFIT distributions as follows:

(1) Income factors. For each item of income generated by the NMWHFIT's assets for the calendar year, the trustee must determine the ratio of the gross amount of that item of income to the total amount of NMWHFIT distributions for the calendar year; and

(2) Expense factors. For each item of expense paid by a NMWHFIT during the calendar year, the trustee must determine the ratio of the gross amount of that item of expense to the total amount of NMWHFIT distributions for the calendar year.

(C) Step Three: Determine adjustments for reconciling the total amount of NMWHFIT distributions (determined under Step One) with amounts actually paid to TIHs. Paragraph (f)(1)(ii)(B) of this section (Step Two) requires an item of income or expense to be expressed as a ratio of that item to the total amount of NMWHFIT distributions as determined in paragraph (f)(1)(ii)(A) of this section (Step One). A TIH's share of the total amount of NMWHFIT distributions may differ from the amount actually paid to that TIH. A trustee, therefore, must provide information that can be used to compute a TIH's share of the total amount of NMWHFIT distributions based on the amount actually paid to the TIH. A trustee satisfies this requirement by providing a current year-end cash allocation factor, a prior year cash allocation factor, and the date on which the prior year cash was distributed to TIHs (prior year cash distribution date).

(1) The current year-end cash allocation factor. The current year-end cash allocation factor is the amount of cash held for distribution to TIHs by the NMWHFIT as of December 31 of the calendar year for which the trustee is reporting, divided by the number of trust interests outstanding as of that date.

(2) The prior year cash allocation factor. The prior year cash allocation factor is the amount of the distribution during the calendar year for which the trustee is reporting that was included in determining a year-end cash allocation factor for a prior year, divided by the number of trust interests outstanding on the date of the distribution.

(iii) Reporting non pro-rata partial principal payments under the safe harbor. The trustee must provide a list of dates on which non pro-rata partial principal payments were distributed by the trust, and the amount distributed, per trust interest.

(iv) Reporting sales and dispositions of NMWHFIT assets under the safe harbor. (A) NMWHFITs that must report under the general rule. (1) In general. If a NMWHFIT must report under the general rule of paragraph (c)(2)(iv)(A) of this section, the trustee must provide a list of dates (from earliest to latest) on which sales or dispositions of NMWHFIT assets occurred during the calendar year for which the trustee is reporting and, for each date identified, provide—

(i) The trust sales proceeds received by the trust, per trust interest, with respect to the sales and dispositions, on that date;

(ii) The trust sales proceeds distributed to TIHs, per trust interest, with respect to the sales and dispositions on that date, and the date that the trust sales proceeds were distributed to the TIHs; and

(iii) The ratio (expressed as a percentage) of the assets sold or disposed of on that date to all assets held by the NMWHFIT.

(2) Determination of the portion of all assets held by the NMWHFIT that the assets sold or disposed of represented—

(i) If a NMWHFIT terminates within twenty-four months of its start-up date, the ratio of the assets sold or disposed of on that date to all assets held by the NMWHFIT is based on the fair market value of the NMWHFIT's assets as of the start-up date; or

(ii) If a NMWHFIT terminates more than twenty-four months after its start-up date, the ratio of the assets sold or disposed of on that date to all assets held by the NMWHFIT is based on the fair market value of the NMWHFIT's assets as of the date of the sale or disposition.

(B) NMWHFITs excepted from the general rule. If paragraph (c)(2)(iv)(B) of this section applies to the NMWHFIT, the trustee must provide a list of dates on which trust sales proceeds were distributed, and the amount of trust sales proceeds, per trust interest, that were distributed on that date. The trustee also must also provide requesting persons with the statement required by paragraph (c)(2)(iv)(B) of this section.

(v) Reporting redemptions under the safe harbor. (A) In general. The trustee must:

(1) Provide a list of dates on which the amount of redemption proceeds paid for the redemption of a trust interest was determined and the amount of the redemption asset proceeds determined per trust interest on that date, or if paragraph (c)(2)(v)(C) of this section applies to the NMWHFIT, the amount of redemption proceeds determined on that date; or

(2) Provide to each requesting person that held (either for its own behalf or for the behalf of a TIH) a trust interest that was redeemed during the calendar year, the date of the redemption and the amount of the redemption asset proceeds per trust interest determined on that date, or if paragraph (c)(2)(v)(C) of this section applies to the NMWHFIT, the amount of the redemption proceeds determined for that date; and

(B) Paragraph (c)(2)(v)(C) statement. If paragraph (c)(2)(v)(C) of this section applies to the NMWHFIT, the trustee must provide a statement to requesting persons to the effect that the trustee is providing information consistent with paragraph (c)(2)(v)(C) of this section.

(vi) Reporting the sale of a trust interest under the safe harbor. If paragraph (c)(2)(v)(C) of this section does not apply to the NMWHFIT, the trustee must provide, for each day of the calendar year, the amount of cash held for distribution, per trust interest, by the NMWHFIT on that date. If the trustee is able to identify the date on which trust interests were sold on the secondary market, the trustee alternatively may provide information for each day on which sales of trust interests occurred rather than for each day during the calendar year. If paragraph (c)(2)(v)(C) of this section applies to the NMWHFIT, the trustee is not required to provide any information under this paragraph (f)(1)(vi), other than a statement that the NMWHFIT meets the requirements to report under paragraph (c)(2)(v)(C) of this section.

(vii) Reporting OID information under the safe harbor. The trustee must provide, for each calculation period, the average aggregate daily accrual of OID per $1,000 of original principal amount.

(viii) Reporting market discount information under the safe harbor. (A) In general. (1) Trustee required to provide market discount information. If the trustee is required to provide information regarding market discount under paragraph (c)(2)(vii) of this section, the trustee must provide --

(i) The information required to be provided under paragraph (f)(1)(iv)(A)(1)(iii) of this section; and

(ii) If the NMWHFIT holds debt instruments with OID, a list of the aggregate adjusted issue prices of the debt instruments per trust interest calculated as of the start-up date or measuring date (see paragraph (c)(2)(iv)(D)(4) of this section) (whichever provides more accurate information) and as of January 1 for each subsequent year of the NMWHFIT.

(2) Trustee not required to provide market discount information. If the trustee is not required to provide market discount information under paragraph (c)(2)(vii) of this section (because the NMWHFIT meets the general de minimis test of paragraph (c)(2)(iv)(D)(1) of this section, the qualified NMWHFIT exception of paragraph (c)(2)(iv)(E) of this section, or the NMWHFIT final year exception of paragraph (c)(2)(iv)(F) of this section), the trustee is not required under this paragraph (f) to provide any information regarding market discount.

(B) Reporting market discount information under the safe harbor when the yield of the debt obligations held by the WHFIT is expected to be affected by prepayments. [Reserved.]

(ix) Reporting bond premium information under the safe harbor. [Reserved.]

(x) Reporting additional information. If a requesting person cannot use the information provided by the trustee under paragraphs (f)(1)(ii) through (ix) of this section to determine with reasonable accuracy the trust items that are attributable to a TIH, the requesting person must request, and the trustee must provide, additional information to enable the requesting person to determine the trust items that are attributable to the TIH. See, for example, paragraph (f)(2)(ii)(A)(4) of this section which requires a middleman to request additional information from the trustee when the total amount of WHFIT distributions attributable to a TIH equals zero or less.

(2) Use of information provided by trustees under the safe harbor for NMWHFITs. (i) In general. If a trustee reports NMWHFIT items in accordance with paragraph (f)(1) of this section, the information provided with respect to those items on the Forms 1099 required under paragraph (d) of this section to be filed with the IRS and on the statement required under paragraph (e) of this section to be furnished to the TIH must be determined as provided in this paragraph (f)(2).

(ii) Determining NMWHFIT income and expense under the safe harbor. The trustee or middleman must determine the amount of each item of income and expense attributable to a TIH as follows—

(A) Step One: Determine the total amount of NMWHFIT distributions attributable to the TIH. To determine the total amount of NMWHFIT distributions attributable to a TIH for the calendar year, the total amount paid to, or credited to the account of, the TIH during the calendar year (including amounts paid as trust sales proceeds or partial non-pro rata principal payments, redemption proceeds, and sales proceeds) is—

(1) Increased by—

(i) All amounts that would have been distributed during the calendar year to the TIH, but that were reinvested pursuant to a reinvestment plan (unless another person (for example, the custodian of the reinvestment plan) is responsible for reporting these amounts under paragraph (d) of this section); and

(ii) An amount equal to the current year-end cash allocation factor (provided by the trustee in accordance with paragraph (f)(1)(ii)(C)(1) of this section) multiplied by the number of trust interests held by the TIH as of December 31 of the calendar year for which the trustee is reporting; and

(2) Decreased by—

(i) An amount equal to the prior year cash allocation factor (provided by the trustee in accordance with paragraph (f)(1)(ii)(C)(2) of this section) multiplied by the number of trust interests held by the TIH on the date of the distribution;

(ii) An amount equal to all redemption asset proceeds paid to the TIH for the calendar year, or if paragraph (c)(2)(v)(C) of this section applies to the NMWHFIT, an amount equal to all redemption proceeds paid to the TIH for the calendar year;

(iii) An amount equal to all sale asset proceeds paid to the TIH for the calendar year, or if paragraph (c)(2)(v)(C) of this section applies to the NMWHFIT, the amount of sales proceeds paid to the TIH for the calendar year;

(iv) In the case of a TIH that purchased a trust interest in a NMWHFIT to which paragraph (c)(2)(v)(C) of this section does not apply, an amount equal to the cash held for distribution per trust interest on the date that the TIH acquired its interest, multiplied by the trust interests acquired on that date;

(v) The amount of the trust sales proceeds distributed to the TIH, calculated as provided in paragraph (f)(2)(iv)(A)(3) of this section; and

(vi) The amount of non pro-rata partial principal prepayments distributed to the TIH during the calendar year, calculated as provided in paragraph (f)(2)(iii) of this section.

(3) Treatment of in-kind distributions under this paragraph (f)(2)(i). The value of the assets (not including cash) received with respect to an in-kind redemption is not included in the amount used in paragraph (f)(2)(ii)(A)(2)(ii) of this section. The cash distributed as part of the redemption, however, must be included in the total amount of NMWHFIT distributions paid to the TIH.

(4) The total amount of distributions attributable to a TIH calculated under this paragraph (f)(2)(i)(A) equals zero or less. If the total amount of distributions attributable to a TIH, calculated under this paragraph (f)(2)(i)(A), equals zero or less, the trustee or middleman may not report the income and expense attributable to the TIH under this paragraph (f)(2)(i). The trustee or middleman must request additional information from the trustee of the NMWHFIT to enable the trustee or middleman to determine with reasonable accuracy the items of income and expense that are attributable to the TIH. The trustee or middleman must report the other items subject to paragraph (f)(1) of this section in accordance with this paragraph (f)(2).

(B) Step Two: Apply the factors provided by the trustee to determine the items of income and expense that are attributable to the TIH. The amount of each item of income (other than OID) and each item of expense attributable to a TIH is determined as follows—

(1) Application of income factors. For each income factor, the trustee or middleman must multiply the income factor by the total amount of NMWHFIT distributions attributable to the TIH for the calendar year (as determined in paragraph (f)(2)(i)(A) of this section).

(2) Application of expense factors. For each expense factor, the trustee or middleman must multiply the expense factor by the total amount of NMWHFIT distributions attributable to the TIH for the calendar year (as determined in paragraph (f)(2)(i)(A) of this section).

(iii) Reporting non pro-rata partial principal payments under the safe harbor. To determine the amount of non pro-rata partial principal payments that are distributed to a TIH for the calendar year, the trustee or middleman must aggregate the amount of non pro-rata partial principal payments distributed to a TIH for each day that non pro-rata principal payments were distributed. To determine the amount of non pro-rata principal payments that are distributed to a TIH on each distribution date, the trustee or middleman must multiply the amount of non-pro rata principal payments per trust interest distributed on that date by the number of trust interests held by the TIH.

(iv) Reporting sales and dispositions of NMWHFIT assets under the safe harbor.

(A) Reporting under the safe harbor if the general rules apply to the NMWHFIT. Unless paragraph (c)(2)(iv)(B) of this section applies, the trustee or middleman must comply with paragraphs (f)(2)(iv)(A)(1), (2), and (3) of this section.

(1) Form 1099. The trustee or middleman must report the amount of trust sales proceeds attributable to the TIH for the calendar year on Form 1099. To determine the amount of trust sales proceeds attributable to a TIH for the calendar year, the trustee or middleman must aggregate the total amount of trust sales proceeds attributable to the TIH for each date on which the NMWHFIT sold or disposed of an asset or assets. To determine the total amount of trust sales proceeds attributable to a TIH for each date that the NMWHFIT sold or disposed of an asset or assets, the trustee or middleman multiplies the amount of trust sales proceeds received by the NMWHFIT per trust interest on that date by the number of trust interests held by the TIH on that date.

(2) The written tax information statement furnished to the TIH. The written tax information statement required to be furnished to the TIH under paragraph (e) of this section must include a list of dates (in order, from earliest to latest) on which sales or dispositions of trust assets occurred during the calendar year and provide, for each date identified—

(i) The trust sales proceeds received by the trust, per trust interest, with respect to the sales or dispositions of trust assets on that date; and

(ii) The information provided by the trustee under paragraph (f)(1)(iv)(B)(2) of this section regarding the ratio of the assets sold or disposed of on that date to all the assets of the NMWHFIT held on that date, prior to such sale or disposition.

(3) Calculating the total amount of trust sales proceeds distributed to the TIH. To determine the total amount of NMWHFIT distributions attributable to a TIH, the trustee or middleman must calculate the amount of trust sales proceeds distributed to the TIH for the calendar year. (See paragraph (f)(2)(ii)(A)(2)(v) of this section.) To determine the amount of trust sales proceeds distributed to a TIH for the calendar year, the trustee or middleman must aggregate the total amount of trust sales proceeds distributed to the TIH for each date on which the NMWHFIT distributed trust sales proceeds. To determine the total amount of trust sales proceeds distributed to a TIH for each date that the NMWHFIT distributed trust sales proceeds, the trustee or middleman must multiply the amount of trust sales proceeds distributed by the NMWHFIT per trust interest on that date by the number of trust interests held by the TIH on that date.

(B) Reporting under the safe harbor if paragraph (c)(2)(iv)(B) of this section applies to the NMWHFIT. If paragraph (c)(2)(iv)(B) of this section applies, the trustee or middleman must calculate, in the manner provided in paragraph (f)(2)(iv)(A)(3) of this section, the amount of trust sales proceeds distributed to the TIH for the calendar year. The trustee or middleman must report this amount on the Form 1099 filed for the TIH and on the written tax information statement furnished to the TIH.

(v) Reporting redemptions under the safe harbor. (A) Except as provided in paragraph (f)(2)(v)(B) or (C) of this section, if the trustee has provided a list of dates for which the amount of the redemption proceeds to be paid for the redemption of a trust interest was determined and the redemption asset proceeds paid for that date, the trustee or middleman must multiply the redemption asset proceeds determined per trust interest for that date by the number of trust interests redeemed by the TIH on that date.

(B) If paragraph (c)(2)(v)(C) of this section applies, and the trustee has provided a list of dates for which the amount of the redemption proceeds to be paid for the redemption of a trust interest was determined and the redemption proceeds determined per trust interest on each date, the trustee or middleman must multiply the redemption proceeds per trust interest for each date by the number of trust interests redeemed by the TIH on that date.

(C) If the trustee has provided the requesting person with information regarding the redemption asset proceeds paid for each redemption of a trust interest held by the middleman for the calendar year, or if paragraph (c)(2)(v)(C) of this section applies and the trustee has provided the amount of redemption proceeds paid for each redemption of a trust interest held by the middleman during the calendar year, the requesting person may use this information to determine the amount of the redemption asset proceeds or redemption proceeds paid to the TIH for the calendar year.

(vi) Reporting sales of trust interests under the safe harbor. (A) Except as provided in paragraph (f)(2)(vi)(B) of this section, the trustee or middleman must subtract the amount of cash held for distribution per trust interest on the date of the sale from the sales proceeds paid to the TIH to determine the sale asset proceeds that are to be reported to the TIH for each sale of a trust interest.

(B) If paragraph (c)(2)(v)(C) of this section applies, the trustee or middleman must report the sales proceeds paid to the TIH as a result of each sale of a trust interest.

(vii) Reporting OID information under the safe harbor—The trustee or middleman must aggregate the amounts of OID that are allocable to each trust interest held by a TIH for each calculation period. The amount of OID that is allocable to a trust interest, with respect to each calculation period, is determined by multiplying—

(A) The product of the OID factor and the original principal balance of the trust interest, divided by 1,000; by

(B) The number of days during the OID calculation period in that calendar year that the TIH held the trust interest.

(viii) Reporting market discount information under the safe harbor. (A) Except as provided in paragraph (f)(2)(viii)(B) of this section, the trustee or middleman must provide the TIH with the information provided under paragraph (f)(1)(viii) of this section.

(B) If paragraph (c)(2)(iv)(B) of this section applies, the trustee and middleman are not required under this paragraph (f)(2) to provide any information regarding market discount.

(ix) Reporting bond premium information under the safe harbor. [Reserved]

(3) Example of the use of the safe harbor for NMWHFITs. The following example illustrates the use of the factors in this paragraph (f) to calculate and provide NMWHFIT information:

Example. (i) Facts. (A) In general. (1) Trust is a NMWHFIT that holds common stock in ten different corporations and has 100 trust interests outstanding. The start-up date for Trust is December 15, 2006, and Trust's registration statement under the Securities Act of 1933 became effective after July 31, 2006. Trust terminates on March 15, 2008. The agreement governing Trust requires Trust to distribute cash held by Trust reduced by accrued but unpaid expenses on April 15, July 15, and October 15 of the 2007 calendar year. The agreement also provides that the trust interests will be redeemed by the Trust for an amount equal to the value of the trust interest, as of the close of business, on the day the trust interest is tendered for redemption. There is no reinvestment plan. A secondary market for interests in Trust will be created by Trust's sponsor and Trust's sponsor will provide Trustee with a list of dates on which sales occurred on this secondary market.

(2) As of December 31, 2006, Trust holds $12x for distribution to TIHs on the next distribution date and has no accrued but unpaid expenses. Trustee includes the $12x in determining the year-end cash allocation factor for December 31, 2006.

(B) Events occurring during the 2007 calendar year. (1) As of January 1, 2007, Broker1 holds ten trust interests in Trust in street name for each of J and A and Broker2 holds ten trust interests in Trust in street name for S. J, A, and S; are individual, cash method taxpayers.

(2) As of January 1, 2007, the fair market value of the Trust's assets equals $10,000x.

(3) During 2007, Trust receives $588x in dividend income. Trustee determines that $400x of the dividend income received during 2007 meets the definition of a qualified dividend in section 1(h)(11)(B)(i) and the holding period requirement in section 1(h)(11)(B)(iii) with respect to the Trust. During 2007, Trust also receives $12x in interest income from investment of Trust's funds pending distribution to TIHs, and pays $45x in expenses, all of which are affected expenses.

(4) On April 15, 2007, Trustee distributes $135x, which includes the $12x included in determining the year-end cash allocation factor for December 31, 2006. As a result of the distribution, Broker1 credits J's account and A's account for $13.50x each. Broker2 credits S's account for $13.50x.

(5) On June 1, 2007, Trustee sells shares of stock for $1000x to preserve the soundness of the trust. The stock sold on June 1, 2007, equaled 20% of the aggregate fair market value of the assets held by Trust on the start-up date of Trust. Trustee has chosen not to report sales described in paragraph (c)(2)(iv)(4)(ii) of Trust's assets under paragraph (c)(2)(iv)(D)(4) of this section.

(6) On July 15, 2007, Trustee distributes $1,135x, which includes the $1,000x of trust sales proceeds received by Trust for the sale of assets on June 1, 2007. As a result of the distribution, Broker1 credits J's account and A's account for $113.50x each. Broker 2 credits S's account for $113.50x.

(7) On September 30 2007, J, through Trust's sponsor, sells a trust interest to S for $115.35x. Trustee determines that the cash held for distribution per trust interest on September 30 is $1.35x. As a result of the sale, Broker1 credits J's account for $115.35x.

(8) On October 15, 2007, Trustee distributes $123x. As a result of the distribution, Broker1 credits J's account for $11.07x and A's account for $12.30x. Broker2 credits S's account for $13.53x.

(9) On December 10, 2007, J tenders a trust interest to Trustee for redemption through Broker1. Trustee determines that the amount of the redemption proceeds to be paid for a trust interest that is tendered for redemption on December 10, 2007 is $116x, of which $115x represents the redemption asset proceeds. Trustee pays this amount to Broker1 on J's behalf. On December 12, 2007, trustee engages in a non pro-rata sale of shares of common stock for $115x to effect J's redemption of a trust interest. The stock sold on December 12, 2007, equals 2% of the aggregate fair market value of all the assets of Trust as of the start-up date.

(10) On December 10, 2007, J, through Trust's sponsor, also sells a trust interest to S for $116x. Trustee determines that the cash held for distribution per trust interest on that date is $1x. As a result of the sale, Broker1 credits J's account for $116x.

(11) As of December 31, 2007, Trust holds cash of $173x and has incurred $15x in expenses that Trust has not paid. J is the only TIH to redeem a trust interest during the calendar year. The sale of two trust interests in Trust by J to S are the only sales that occurred on the secondary market established by Trust's sponsor during 2007.

(ii) Trustee reporting. (A) Summary of information provided by Trustee. Trustee meets the requirements of paragraph (f)(1) of this section if Trustee provides the following information to requesting persons: (1) Income and expense information:

Factor for ordinary dividend income	0.3481
Factor for qualified dividend income	0.7407
Factor for interest income	0.0222
Factor for affected expenses	0.0833
Current year-end cash allocation factor	1.5960
Prior year cash allocation factor	0.1200
Prior year cash distribution date	April 15

(2) Information regarding asset sales and distributions:

Date of sale	Trust sales proceeds received distributed	Trust sales proceeds distributed and date	Percent of trust sold
June 1	$10.0000x	$10.0000x (July 15)	20
December 12	1.1616x	0.0000x	2

(3) Information regarding redemptions:

Date	Redemption asset proceeds
December 10	$115x

(4) Information regarding sales of trust interests

Date	Cash held for distribution per trust interest
September 30	$1.35x
December 10	1.00x

(B) Trustee determines this information as follows:

(1) Step One: Trustee determines the total amount of NMWHFIT distributions for the calendar year. The total amount of NMWHFIT distributions (actual and deemed) for the calendar year for purposes of determining the safe harbor factors is $540x. This amount consists of the amounts paid on each scheduled distribution date during the calendar year ($1135x, $135x, and $123x), plus the total amount paid to J as a result of J's redemption of a trust interest ($116x) ($1,135x + $135x + $123x + $116x = $1,509x)— (i) Increased by all cash held for distribution to TIHs as of December 31, 2007 ($158x), which is the cash held as of December 31, 2007 ($173x) reduced by the accrued but unpaid expenses as of December 31, 2007 ($15x), and

(ii) Decreased by all amounts distributed during the calendar year but included in the year-end cash allocation factor from a prior year ($12x); all redemption asset proceeds paid for the calendar year ($115x); and all trust sales proceeds distributed during the calendar year ($1,000x).

(2) Step Two: Trustee determines factors that express the ratio of NMWHFIT income (other than OID) and expenses to the total amount of NMWHFIT distributions. Trustee determines the factors for each item of income earned by Trust and each item of expense as follows:

(i) Ordinary dividend income factor. The ordinary dividend income factor is 0.3481, which represents the ratio of the gross amount of ordinary dividends ($188x) to the total amount of NMWHFIT distributions for the calendar year ($540x).

(ii) Qualified dividend income factor. The qualified dividend income factor is 0.7407 which represents the ratio of the gross amount of qualified dividend income ($400x) to the total amount of NMWHFIT distributions for the calendar year ($540x).

(iii) Interest income factor. The interest income factor is 0.0222, which represents the ratio of the gross amount of interest income ($12x) to the total amount of NMWHFIT distributions for the calendar year ($540x).

(iv) Expense factor. The affected expenses factor is 0.0833, which represents the ratio of the gross amount of affected expenses paid by Trust for the calendar year ($45x) to the total amount of NMWHFIT distributions for the calendar year ($540x).

(3) Step Three: Trustee determines adjustments for reconciling the total amount of NMWHFIT distributions with amounts paid to TIHs. To enable requesting persons to determine the total amount of NMWHFIT distributions that are attributable to a TIH based on amounts actually paid to the TIH, the trustee must provide both a current year-end cash allocation factor and a prior year cash allocation factor.

(i) Current year-end cash allocation factor. The adjustment factor for cash held by Trust at year end is 1.5960, which represents the cash held for distribution as of December 31, 2007 ($158x) (the amount of cash held by Trust on December 31, 2007 ($173x) reduced by accrued, but unpaid, expenses ($15x)), divided by the number of trust interests outstanding at year-end (99).

(ii) Prior Year Cash Allocation Factor. The adjustment factor for distributions of year-end cash from the prior year is 0.1200, which represents the amount of the distribution during the current calendar year that was included in a year-end cash allocation factor for a prior year ($12x), divided by the number of trust interests outstanding at the time of the distribution (100). The prior year cash distribution date is April 15, 2007.

(4) Reporting sales and dispositions of trust assets. (i) Application of the de minimis test. The aggregate fair market value of the assets of Trust as of January 1, 2007, was $10,000x. During the 2007 calendar year, Trust received trust sales proceeds of $1115x. The trust sales proceeds received by Trust for the 2007 calendar year equal 11.15% of Trust's fair market value as of January 1, 2007. Accordingly, the de minimis test is not satisfied for the 2007 calendar year. The qualified NMWHFIT exception in paragraph (c)(2)(iv)(E) of this section and the NMWHFIT final calendar year exception in (c)(2)(iv)(F) of this section also do not apply to Trust for the 2007 calendar year.

(ii) Information to be provided. To satisfy the requirements of paragraph (f)(1) of this section with respect to sales and dispositions of Trust's assets, Trustee provides a list of dates on which trust assets were sold during the calendar year, and provides, for each date: the trust sales proceeds (per trust interest) received on that date; the trust sales proceeds distributed to TIHs (per trust interest) with respect to sales or dispositions on that date; the date those trust sales proceeds were distributed, and the ratio of the assets sold or disposed of on that day to all the assets held by Trust. Because Trust will terminate within 15 months of its start-up date, Trustee must use the fair market value of the assets as of the start-up date to determine the portion of Trust sold or disposed of on any particular date.

(5) Reporting redemptions. Because Trust is not required to make distributions at least as frequently as monthly, and Trust does not satisfy the qualified NMWHFIT exception in paragraph (c)(2)(iv)(E) of this section, the exception in paragraph (c)(2)(v)(C) does not apply to Trust. To satisfy the requirements of paragraph (f)(1) of this section, Trustee provides a list of dates for which the redemption proceeds to be paid for the redemption of a trust interest was determined for the 2007 calendar year and the redemptions asset proceeds

paid for each date. During 2007, Trustee only determined the amount of redemption proceeds paid for the redemption of a trust interest once, for December 10, 2007 and the redemption asset proceeds determined for that date was $115x.

(6) Reporting sales of trust interests. Because trust is not required to make distributions at least as frequently as monthly, and Trust does not satisfy the qualified NMWHFIT exception in paragraph (c)(2)(iv)(E) of this section, the exception in paragraph (c)(2)(v)(C) of this section does not apply to Trust. Sponsor, in accordance with the trust agreement, provides Trustee with a list of dates on which sales on the secondary market occurred. To satisfy the requirements of paragraph (f)(1) of this section, Trustee provides requesting persons with a list of dates on which sales on the secondary market occurred and the amount of cash held for distribution, per trust interest, on each date. The first sale during the 2007 calendar year occurred on September 30, 2007, and the amount of cash held for distribution, per trust interest, on that date is $1.35x. The second sale occurred on December 10, 2007, and the amount of cash held for distribution, per trust interest, on that date is $1.00x.

(1) Brokers' use of information provided by Trustee. (A) Broker1 and Broker2 use the information furnished by Trustee under the safe harbor to determine that the following items are attributable to J, A, and S—

With respect to J	
Ordinary Dividend Income	$17.89x
Qualified Dividend Income	38.07x
Interest Income	1.14x
Affected Expenses	4.28x
Trust sales proceeds reported on Form 1099	108.13x
Redemption asset proceeds	
For redemption on December 10	115.00x
Sale asset proceeds	
For sale on September 30	114.00x
For sale on December 10	115.00x
With respect to A	
Ordinary Dividend Income	18.82x
Qualified Dividend Income	40.04x
Interest Income	1.20x
Affected Expenses	4.50x
Trust sales proceeds reported on Form 1099	11.62x
With respect to S	
Ordinary Dividend Income	19.54x
Qualified Dividend Income	41.58x
Interest Income	1.25x
Affected Expenses	4.68x
Trust sales proceeds reported on Form 1099	113.94x

With respect to J, A, and S (regarding the sales and dispositions executed by Trust during the calendar year)

Date	Trust sales proceeds received per trust interest	Percent of trust sold
June 15	$10.0000x	20
December 12	1.1616x	2

(B) The brokers determine the information provided to J, A, and S as follows—

(1) Step One: Brokers determine the total amount of NMWHFIT distributions attributable to J, A, and S. Broker1 determines that the total amount of NMWHFIT distributions attributable to J is $51.39x and the total amount of NMWHFIT distributions attributable to A is $54.06x. Broker2 determines that the total amount of NMWHFIT distributions attributable to S is $56.13x. (i) To calculate these amounts the brokers begin by determining the total amount paid to J, A, and S for the calendar year—

(A) The total amount paid to J for the calendar year equals $485.42x and includes the April 15, 2007, distribution of $13.50x, the July 15, 2007, distribution of $113.50x, the sales proceeds for the September 30, 2007, sale of $115.35x, the October 15, 2007, distribution of $11.07x, and the redemption proceeds of $116x and sales proceeds of $116x for the redemption and sale on December 10, 2007.

(B) The total amount paid to A for the calendar year equals $139.30x and includes the April 15, 2007, distribution of $13.50x, the July 15, 2007, distribution of $113.50x and the October 15, 2007, distribution of $12.30x.

(C) The total amount paid to S for the calendar year equals $140.53x and includes the April 15, 2007, distribution of $13.50x, the July 15, 2007, distribution of $113.50x and the October 15, 2007, distribution of $13.53x.

(ii) The brokers increase the total amount paid to J, A, and S by an amount equal to the current year-end cash allocation factor (1.5960) multiplied by the number of trust interests held by J (7), A (10), and S (12) as of December 31, 2007; that is for J, $11.17x; for A, $15.96x; and for S, $19.15x.

(iii) The brokers reduce the amount paid to J, A, and S as follows—

(A) An amount equal to the prior year cash allocation factor (0.1200), multiplied by the number of trust interests held by J (10), A (10), and S (10) on the date of the prior year cash distribution; that is for J, A, and S, $1.20x, each;

(B) An amount equal to all redemption asset proceeds paid to a TIH for the calendar year; that is, for J, $115x;

(C) An amount equal to all sales asset proceeds attributable to the TIH for the calendar year; that is for J, $229x (for the September 30, 2007, sale: $115.35x-1.35x (cash held for distribution per trust interest on that date)-$114x; and for the December 10, 2007, sale: $116x-1.00 (cash held for distribution per trust interest on that date)=$115x));

(D) In the case of a purchasing TIH, an amount equal to the amount of cash held for distribution per trust interest at the time the TIH purchased its trust interest, multiplied by the number of trust interests purchased; that is for S, $2.35x ($1.35x with respect to the September 30, 2007, sale and $1x with respect to the December 10, 2007, sale);

(E) All amounts of trust sales proceeds distributed to the TIH for the calendar year; that is for J, A, and S, $100. ($100 each, with respect to the June 15, 2007, sale of assets by Trust, and $0 each, with respect to the December 12, 2007, sale of assets by Trust).

(2) Step two: The brokers apply the factors provided by Trustee to determine the Trust's income and expenses that are attributable to J, A, and S. The amounts of each item of income (other than OID) and expense that are attributable to J, A, and S are determined by multiplying the factor for that type of income or expense by the total amount of NMWHFIT distributions attributable to J, A, and S as follows:

(i) Application of factor for ordinary dividends. The amount of ordinary dividend income attributable to J is $17.89x, to A is $18.82x, and to S is $19.54x. The brokers determine these amounts by multiplying the total amount of NMWHFIT distributions attributable to J, A, and S ($51.39x, $54.06x, and $56.13x, respectively) by the factor for ordinary dividends (0.3481).

(ii) Application of factor for qualified dividend income. The amount of qualified dividend income attributable to J is $38.07x, to A is $40.04x, and to S is $41.58x. The brokers determine these amounts by multiplying the total amount of NMWHFIT distributions attributable to J, A, and S ($51.39x, $54.06x, and $56.13x, respectively) by the factor for qualified dividends (0.7407).

(iii) Application of factor for interest income. The amount of interest income attributable to J is $1.14x, to A is $1.20x, and to S is $1.25x. The brokers determine these amounts by multiplying the total amount of NMWHFIT distributions attributable to J, A, and S ($51.39x, $54.06x, and $56.13x, respectively) by the factor for interest (0.0222).

(iv) Application of factor for affected expenses. The amount of affected expenses attributable to J is $4.28x, to A is $4.50x, and to S is $4.68x. The brokers determine these amounts by multiplying the total amount of NMWHFIT distributions attributable to J, A, and S ($51.39x, $54.06x, and $56.13x, respectively) by the factor for affected expenses (0.0833).

(3) Brokers reporting of sales and dispositions of trust assets—(i) Determining the amount of trust sales proceeds to be reported on Form 1099 for J, A, and S. The amount of trust sales proceeds to be reported on Form 1099 with respect to J is $108.13x, to A is $111.62x, and to S is $113.94x. To determine these amounts, the brokers aggregate the amount of trust sales proceeds attributable to J, A, and S for each date on which Trust sold or disposed of assets. The brokers determine the amount of trust sales proceeds to be reported with respect to the June 15, 2007, asset sale by multiplying the number of trust interests held by J (10), A (10) and S (10) on that date by the trust sales proceeds received per trust interest on that date ($10x). The brokers determine the amount of trust sales proceeds to be reported with respect to the December 12, 2007, asset sale by multiplying the number of trust interests held by J (7), A (10) and S (12) on that date by the trust sales proceeds received per trust interest on that date ($1.1616x).

(ii) Information provided on the tax information statements furnished to J, A, and S. The tax information statements furnished to J, A, and S must include the dates of each sale or disposition (June 15, 2007, and December 12, 2007); the amount of trust sales proceeds per trust interest received on those dates ($10.00x and $1.1616x, respectively); and, the percentage of Trust sold or disposed of on that date (20% and 2%, respectively).

(4) Reporting redemptions. Broker1 reports on Form 1099 and on the written tax information statement furnished to J that J received $115x in redemption asset proceeds for the calendar year.

(5) Reporting sales of trust interests on the secondary market. Broker1 reports on J's two sales of trust interests. With respect to the sale on September 30, 2007, the sale asset proceeds equals $114x ($115.35x sale proceeds—$1.35x cash held for distribution on that date) and with respect to the sale on December 10, 2007, the sale asset proceeds equal $115x ($116x sale proceeds—$1x cash held for distribution on that date). Broker1 reports these amounts on Form 1099 and on the tax information statement furnished to J.

(g) Safe Harbor for certain WHMTs. *(1) Safe harbor for trustee of certain WHMTs for reporting information.* (i) In general. The trustee of a WHMT that meets the requirements of paragraph (g)(1)(ii) of this section is deemed to satisfy paragraph (c)(1)(i) of this section, if the trustee calculates and provides WHFIT information in the manner described in this paragraph (g) and provides a statement to the requesting person giving notice that information has been calculated in accordance with this paragraph (g)(1).

(ii) Requirements. A WHMT must meet the following requirements—

(A) The WHMT must make monthly distributions of the income and principal payments received by the WHMT to its TIHs;

(B) All trust interests in the WHMT must represent the right to receive an equal pro-rata share of both the income and the principal payments received by the WHMT on the mortgages it holds (for example, a WHMT that holds or issues trust interests that qualify as stripped interests under section 1286 may not report under this safe harbor);

(C) The WHMT must—

(1) Report under this paragraph (g)(1)(ii) for the life of the WHMT; or

(2) If the WHMT has a start-up date before January 1, 2007, the WHMT must begin reporting under this paragraph (g)(1)(ii) as of January 1, 2007, and must continue to report under this paragraph for the life of the WHMT;

(D) The WHMT must calculate all items subject to the safe harbor consistent with the safe harbor;

(E) The assets of the WHMT must be limited to—

(1) Mortgages with uniform characteristics;

(2) Reasonably required reserve funds; and

(3) Amounts received on mortgages or reserve funds and held for distribution to TIHs; and

(F) The aggregate outstanding principal balance (as defined in paragraph (g)(1)(iii)(D) of this section) as of the WHMT's start-up date must equal the aggregate of the original face amounts of all issued trust interests.

(iii) Reporting WHMT income, expenses, non pro-rata partial principal payments, and sales and dispositions under the safe harbor. A trustee must comply with each step provided in this paragraph (g)(1)(iii).

(A) Step One: Determine monthly pool factors. The trustee must, for each month of the calendar year and for January of the following calendar year, calculate and provide the ratio (expressed as a decimal carried to at least eight places and called a pool factor) of—

(1) The amount of the aggregate outstanding principal balance of the WHMT as of the first business day of the month; to

(2) The amount of the aggregate outstanding principal balance of the WHMT as of the start-up date.

(B) Step Two: Determine monthly expense factors. For each month of the calendar year and for each item of expense paid by the WHMT during that month, the trustee must calculate and provide the ratio (expressed as a decimal carried to at least eight places and called an expense factor) of—

(1) The gross amount, for the month, of each item of expense; to

(2) The amount that represents the aggregate outstanding principal balance of the WHMT as of the start-up date, divided by 1,000.

(C) Step Three: Determine monthly income factors. For each month of the calendar year and for each item of gross income earned by the WHMT during that month, the trustee must calculate and provide the ratio (expressed as a decimal carried to at least eight places and called an income factor) of—

(1) The gross amount, for the month, of each item of income, to

(2) The amount that represents the aggregate outstanding principal balance of the WHMT as of the start-up date, divided by 1,000.

(D) Definition of aggregate outstanding principal balance. For purposes of this paragraph (g)(1)(iii), the amount of the aggregate outstanding principal balance of a WHMT is the aggregate of—

(1) The outstanding principal balance of all mortgages held by the WHMT;

(2) The amounts received on mortgages as principal payments and held for distribution by the WHMT; and

(3) The amount of the reserve fund (exclusive of undistributed income).

(iv) Reporting OID information under the safe harbor. (A) Reporting OID prior to the issuance of final regulations under section 1272(a)(6)(C)(iii). (1) For calendar years prior to the effective date of final regulations under section 1272(a)(6)(C)(iii), the trustee must provide, for each month during the calendar year, the aggregate daily accrual of OID per $1,000 of aggregate outstanding principal balance as of the start-up date (daily portion). For purposes of this paragraph (g)(1)(iv), the daily portion of OID is determined by allocating to each day of the month its ratable portion of the excess (if any) of—

(i) The sum of the present value (determined under section 1272(a)(6)(B)) of all remaining payments under the mortgages held by the WHMT at the close of the month, and the payments during the month of amounts included in the stated redemption price of the mortgages, over

(ii) The aggregate of each mortgage's adjusted issue price as of the beginning of the month.

(2) In calculating the daily portion of OID, the trustee must use the prepayment assumption used in pricing the original issue of trust interests. If the WHMT has a start-up date prior to January 24, 2006, and the trustee, after a good faith effort to ascertain that information, does not know the prepayment assumption used in pricing the original issue of trust interests, the trustee may use any reasonable prepayment assumption to calculate OID provided it continues to use the same prepayment assumption consistently thereafter.

(B) Reporting OID after the issuance of final regulations under section 1272(a)(6)(C)(iii). [Reserved.]

(v) Reporting market discount information under the safe harbor— (A) Reporting market discount information prior to the issuance of final regulations under sections 1272(a)(6)(C)(iii) and 1276(b)(3). For calendar years prior to the effective date of final regulations under sections 1272(a)(6)(C)(iii) and 1276(b)(3), the trustee must provide—

(1) In the case of a WHMT holding mortgages issued with OID, the ratio (expressed as a decimal carried to at least eight places) of—

(i) The OID accrued during the month (calculated in accordance with paragraph (g)(1)(iv) of this section); to

(ii) The total remaining OID as of the beginning of the month (as determined under paragraph (g)(1)(v)(A)(3) of this section); or

(2) In the case of a WHMT holding mortgages issued without OID, the ratio (expressed as a decimal carried to at least eight places) of—

(i) The amount of stated interest paid to the WHMT during the month; to

(ii) The total amount of stated interest remaining to be paid to the WHMT as of the beginning of the month (as determined under paragraph (g)(1)(v)(A)(3) of this section).

(3) Computing the total amount of stated interest remaining to be paid and the total remaining OID at the beginning of the month. To compute the total amount of stated interest remaining to be paid to the WHMT as of the beginning of the month and the total remaining OID as of the beginning of the month, the trustee must use the prepayment assumption used in pricing the original issue of trust interests. If the WHMT has a start-up date prior to January 24, 2006, and the trustee, after a good faith effort to ascertain that information, does not know the prepayment assumption used in pricing the original issue of trust interests, the trustee may use any reasonable prepayment assumption to calculate these amounts provided it continues to use the same prepayment assumption consistently thereafter.

(B) Reporting market discount information under the safe harbor following the issuance of final regulations under sections 1272(a)(6)(C)(iii) and 1276(b)(3). [Reserved.]

(vi) Reporting bond premium information under the safe harbor. [Reserved.]

(2) Use of information provided by a trustee under the safe harbor. (i) In general. If a trustee reports WHMT items in accordance with paragraph (g)(1) of this section, the information provided with respect to those items on the Forms 1099 required to be filed with the IRS under paragraph (d)

of this section and on the statement required to be furnished to the TIH under paragraph (e) of this section must be determined as provided in this paragraph (g)(2).

(ii) Reporting WHMT income, expenses, non pro-rata partial principal payments, and sales and dispositions under the safe harbor. The amount of each item of income, the amount of each item of expense, and the combined amount of non pro-rata partial principal payments and trust sales proceeds that are attributable to a TIH for each month of the calendar year must be computed as follows:

(A) Step One: Determine the aggregate of the non pro-rata partial principal payments and trust sales proceeds that are attributable to the TIH for the calendar year. For each month of the calendar year that a trust interest was held on the record date—

(1) Determine the monthly amounts per trust interest. The trustee or middleman must determine the aggregate amount of non pro-rata partial principal payments and the trust sales proceeds that are attributable to each trust interest for each month by multiplying—

(i) The original face amount of the trust interest; by

(ii) The difference between the pool factor for the current month and the pool factor for the following month.

(2) Determine the amount for the calendar year. The trustee or middleman must multiply the monthly amount per trust interest by the number of trust interests held by the TIH on the record date of each month. The trustee or middleman then must aggregate these monthly amounts, and report the aggregate amount on the Form 1099 filed with the IRS and on the tax information statement furnished to the TIH as trust sales proceeds. No other information is required to be reported to the IRS or the TIH to satisfy the requirements of paragraphs (d) and (e) of this section under this paragraph (g) with respect to sales and dispositions and non pro-rata partial principal payments.

(B) Step Two: Determine the amount of each item of expense that is attributable to a TIH. (i) Determine the monthly amounts per trust interest. For each month of the calendar year that a trust interest was held on the record date, the trustee or middleman must determine the amount of each item of expense that is attributable to each trust interest by multiplying—

(i) The original face amount of the trust interest, divided by 1000; by

(ii) The expense factor for that month and that item of expense.

(2) Determine the amount for the calendar year. The trustee or middleman must multiply the monthly amount of each item of expense per trust interest by the number of trust interests held by the TIH on the record date of each month. The trustee or middleman then must aggregate the monthly amounts for each item of expense to determine the total amount of each item of expense that is attributable to the TIH for the calendar year.

(C) Step Three: Determine the amount of each item of income that is attributable to the TIH for the calendar year. (1) Determine the monthly amounts per trust interest. For each month of the calendar year that a trust interest was held on the record date, the trustee or middleman must determine the amount of each item of income that is attributable to each trust interest by multiplying—

(i) The original face amount of the trust interest, divided by 1,000; by

(ii) The income factor for that month and that item of income.

(2) Determine the amount for the calendar year. The trustee or middleman must multiply the monthly amount of each item of income per trust interest by the number of trust interests held by the TIH on the record date of each month. The trustee or middleman then must aggregate the monthly amounts for each item of income to determine the total amount of each item of income that is attributable to the TIH for the calendar year.

(D) Definitions for this paragraph (g)(2). For purposes of this paragraph (g)(2)(ii)—

(1) The record date is the date used by the WHMT to determine the owner of the trust interest for the purpose of distributing the payment for the month.

(2) The original face amount of the trust interest is the original principal amount of a trust interest on its issue date.

(iii) Reporting OID information under the safe harbor. With respect to each month, trustee or middleman must determine the amount of OID that is attributable to each trust interest held by a TIH by multiplying—

(A) The product of the OID factor multiplied by the original face amount of the trust interest, divided by 1,000; by

(B) The number of days during the month that the TIH held the trust interest.

(iv) Requirement to provide market discount information under the safe harbor. The trustee or middleman must provide the market discount information in accordance with paragraph (g)(1)(v) of this section to the TIH in, or with, the written statement required to be furnished to the TIH under paragraph (e) of this section.

(v) Requirement to provide bond premium information under the safe harbor. [Reserved]

(3) Example of safe harbor in paragraph (g)(1) of this section. The following example illustrates the use of the factors in this paragraph (g) to calculate and provide WHMT information:

Example. (i) Facts. (A) In general. X is a WHMT. X's start-up date is January 1, 2007. As of that date, X's assets consist of 100 15-year mortgages, each having an unpaid principal balance of $125,000 and a fixed, annual interest rate of 7.25 percent. None of the mortgages were issued with OID. X's TIHs are entitled to monthly, pro-rata distributions of the principal payments received by X. X's TIHs are also entitled to monthly, pro-rata distributions of the interest earned on the mortgages held by X, reduced by expenses. Trust interests are issued in increments of $5,000 with a $25,000 minimum. The prepayment assumption used in pricing the original issue of trust interests is six percent. Broker holds a trust interest in X, with an original face amount of $25,000, in street name, for C during the entire 2007 calendar year.

(B) Trust events during the 2007 calendar year. During the 2007 calendar year, X collects all interest and principal payments when due and makes all monthly distributions when due. One mortgage is repurchased from X in July 2007 for $122,249, the mortgage's unpaid principal balance plus accrued, but unpaid, interest at the time. During November 2007, another mortgage is prepaid in full. X earns $80 interest income each month from the temporary investment of X's funds pending distribution to the TIHs. All of X's expenses are affected expenses. The aggregate outstanding principal balance of X's mortgages, X's interest income, and X's expenses, for each month of the 2007 calendar year, along with the aggregate outstanding principal balance of X as of January 2008, are as follows:

Month	Principal balance	Income	Expenses
January	$12,500,000	$75,601	$5,288
February	12,461,413	75,368	5,273
March	12,422,593	75,133	5,256
April	12,383,538	74,897	5,240
May	12,344,247	74,660	5,244
June	12,304,719	74,421	5,207
July	12,264,952	74,181	5,191
August	12,102,696	73,200	5,122
September	12,062,849	72,960	5,106
October	12,022,762	72,718	5,089
November	11,982,432	72,474	5,073
December	11,821,234	71,500	5,006
January	11,780,829	......	....

(ii) Trustee reporting. (A) Trustee, X's fiduciary, comes within the safe harbor of paragraph (g)(1)(ii) of this section by providing the following information to requesting persons:

Month	Pool factor	Income factor	Expense factor
January	1.00000000	6.04806667	0.42304000
February	0.99691304	6.02941628	0.42184000
March	0.99380744	6.01065328	0.42048000
April	0.99068304	5.99177670	0.41920000
May	0.98753976	5.97278605	0.41952000
June	0.98437752	5.95368085	0.41656000
July	0.98119616	5.93446013	0.41528000
August	0.96821564	5.85603618	0.40976000
September	0.96502792	5.83677704	0.40848000
October	0.96182096	5.81740161	0.40712000
November	0.95859459	5.79790896	0.40584000
December	0.94569875	5.71999659	0.40048000
January	0.94246631	....	....

(B) Trustee determines this information as follows:

(1) Step One: Trustee determines monthly pool factors. Trustee calculates and provides X's pool factor for each month of the 2007 calendar year. For example, for the month of January 2007 the pool factor is 1.0, which represents the ratio of — (i) The amount that represents the aggregate outstanding principal balance of X ($12,500,000) as of the first business day of January; divided by

(ii) The amount that represents the aggregate outstanding principal balance of X ($12,500,000) as of the start-up day.

(2) Step Two: Trustee determines monthly expense factors. Trustee calculates and provides the expense factors for each month of the 2007 calendar year. During 2007, X has only affected expenses, and therefore, will have only one expense factor for each month. For example, the expense factor for the month of January 2007 is 0.42304000, which represents the ratio of—

(i) The gross amount of expenses paid during January by X ($5,288); divided by

(ii) The amount that represents the aggregate outstanding principal balance of X as of the start-up date ($12,500,000) divided by 1,000 ($12,500).

(3) Step Three: Trustee determines monthly income factors. Trustee calculates and provides the income factors for each month of the 2007 calendar year. During 2007, X has only interest income, and therefore, will have only one income factor for each month. For example, the income factor for the month of January 2007 is 6.04806667, which represents the ratio of—

(i) The gross amount of interest income earned by X during January ($75,601); divided by

(ii) The amount that represents that aggregate outstanding principal balance of X as of the start-up date ($12,500,000), divided by 1,000 ($12,500).

(4) Step Four: Trustee calculates and provides monthly market discount fractions. Trustee calculates and provides a market discount fraction for each month of the 2007 calendar year using a prepayment assumption of 6% and a stated interest rate of 7.25%.

(iii) Broker's use of the information provided by Trustee. (A) Broker uses the information provided by Trustee under paragraph (g) of this section to determine that the following trust items are attributable to C:

Month	Aggregate trust sales proceeds and non pro-rata partial principal payments	Affected expenses	Gross interest income
January	$ 77.17	$ 10.58	$ 151.20
February	77.64	10.55	150.74
March	78.11	10.51	150.27
April	78.58	10.48	149.79
May	79.06	10.49	149.32
June	79.53	10.41	148.84
July	324.51	10.38	148.36
August	79.69	10:24	146.40
September	80.17	10.21	145.92
October	80.66	10.18	145.43
November	322.40	10.15	144.95
December	80.81	10.01	143.00
Total	1438.33	124.19	1774.22

(B) Broker determines this information as follows:

(1) Step One: Broker determines the amount of the non pro-rata partial principal payments and trust sales proceeds received by X that are attributable to C for the 2007 calendar year. Broker determines the amount of the non pro-rata partial principal payments and trust sales proceeds received by X that are attributable to C for each month of the 2007 calendar year. For example, for the month of January, Broker determines that the amount of principal receipts and the amount of trust sales proceeds that are attributable to C is $77.17. Broker determines this by multiplying the original face amount of C's trust interest ($25,000) by 0.00308696, the difference between the pool factor for January 2007 (1.00000000) and the pool factor for the following month of February 2007 (0.99691304). Broker reports the aggregate of the monthly amounts of non pro-rata partial principal payments and trust sales proceeds that are attributable to C for the 2007 calendar year as trust sales proceeds on the Form 1099 filed with the IRS.

(2) Step Two: Broker applies the expense factors provided by Trustee to determine the amount of expenses that are attributable to C for the 2007 calendar year. Broker determines the amount of X's expenses that are attributable to C for each month of the calendar year. For example, for the month of January 2007, Broker determines that the amount of expenses attributable to C is $10.58. Broker determines this by multiplying the original face amount of C's trust interest ($25,000), divided by 1,000 ($25) by the expense factor for January 2007 (0.42304000). Broker determines the expenses that are attributable to C for the 2007 calendar year by aggregating the monthly amounts.

(3) Step Three: Broker applies the income factors provided by Trustee to determine the amount of gross interest income attributable to C for the 2007 calendar year. Broker determines the amount of gross interest income that is attributable to C for each month of the calendar year. For example, for the month of January 2007, Broker determines that the amount of gross interest income attributable to C is $151.20. Broker determines this by multiplying the original face amount of C's trust interest ($25,000), divided by 1,000 ($25), by the income factor for January 2007 (6.04806667). Broker determines the amount of the gross interest income that is attributable to C for the 2007 calendar year by aggregating the monthly amounts.

(4) Step Four: Broker provides market discount information to C. Broker provides C with the market discount fractions calculated and provided by the trustee of X under paragraph (g)(3)(ii)(D) of this section.

(h) Additional safe harbors. *(1) Temporary safe harbor for WHMTs.* (i) Application. Pending the issuance of additional guidance, the safe harbor in this paragraph applies to trustees and middlemen of WHMTs that are not eligible to report under the WHMT safe harbor in paragraph (g) of this section because they hold interests in another WHFIT, in a REMIC, or hold or issue stripped interests.

(ii) Safe harbor. A trustee is deemed to satisfy the requirements of paragraph (c) of this section, if the trustee calculates and provides trust information in a manner that enables a requesting person to provide trust information to a beneficial owner of a trust interest that enables the owner to reasonably accurately report the tax consequences of its ownership of a trust interest on its federal income tax return. Additionally, to be deemed to satisfy the requirements of paragraph (c) of this section, the trustee must calculate and provide trust information regarding market discount and OID by any reasonable manner consistent with section 1272(a)(6). A middleman or a trustee may satisfy its obligation to furnish information to the IRS under paragraph (d) of this section and to the trust interest holder under paragraph (e) of this section by providing information consistent with the information provided under this paragraph by the trustee.

(2) Additional safe harbors provided by other published guidance. The IRS and the Treasury Department may provide additional safe harbor reporting procedures for complying with this section or a specific paragraph of this section by other published guidance (see § 601.601(d)(2) of this chapter).

(i) [Reserved.]

(j) Requirement that middlemen furnish information to beneficial owners that are exempt recipients and non-calendar-year beneficial owners. *(1) In general.* A middleman that holds a trust interest on behalf of, or for the account of, either a beneficial owner that is an exempt recipient defined in paragraph (b)(7) of this section or a non-calendar-year beneficial owner, must provide to such beneficial owner, upon request, the information provided by the trustee to the middleman under paragraph (c) of this section.

(2) Time for providing information. The middleman must provide the requested information to any beneficial owner making a request under paragraph (h)(1) of this section on or before the later of the 44th day after the close of the calendar year for which the information was requested, or the day that is 28 days after the receipt of the request. A middleman must provide information with respect to a WHFIT holding an interest in another WHFIT, or a WHFIT holding an interest in a REMIC, on or before the later of the 58th day after the close of the calendar year for which the information was requested, or the 42nd day after the receipt of the request.

(3) Manner of providing information. The requested information must be provided—

(i) By written statement sent by first class mail to the address provided by the person requesting the information;

(ii) By electronic mail provided that the person requesting the information requests that the middleman furnish the information by electronic mail and the person furnishes an electronic address;

(iii) At an Internet website of the middleman or the trustee, provided that the beneficial owner requesting the information is notified that the requested information is available at the Internet website and is furnished the address of the site; or

(iv) Any other manner agreed to by the middleman and the beneficial owner requesting the information.

(4) Clearing organization. A clearing organization described in § 1.163-5(c)(2)(i)(D)(8) is not required to furnish information to exempt recipients or non-calendar-year TIHs under this paragraph (h).

(k) Coordination with other information reporting rules. In general, in cases in which reporting is required for a WHFIT under both this section and subpart B, part III, subchapter A, chapter 61 of the Internal Revenue Code (Sections 6041 through 6050S) (Information Reporting Sections), the reporting rules for WHFITs under this section must be applied. The provisions of the Information Reporting Sections and the regulations thereunder are incorporated into this section as applicable, but only to the extent that such provisions are not inconsistent with the provisions of this section.

(l) Backup withholding requirements. Every trustee and middleman required to file a Form 1099 under this section is a payor within the meaning of § 31.3406(a)-2, and must backup withhold as required under section 3406 and any regulations thereunder.

(m) Penalties for failure to comply. *(1) In general.* Every trustee or middleman who fails to comply with the reporting obligations imposed by this section is subject to penalties under sections 6721, 6722, and any other applicable penalty provisions.

(2) Penalties not imposed on trustees and middlemen of certain WHMTs for failure to report OID. Penalties will not be imposed as a result of a failure to provide OID information for a WHMT that has a start-up date on or after August 13, 1998 and on or before January 24, 2006, if the trustee of the WHMT does not have the historic information necessary to provide this information and the trustee demonstrates that it has attempted in good faith, but without success, to obtain this information. For purposes of calculating a market discount fraction under paragraph (g)(1)(v) of this section, for a WHMT described in this paragraph, it may be assumed that the WHMT is holding mortgages that were issued without OID. A trustee availing itself of this paragraph must include a statement to that effect when providing information to requesting persons under paragraph (c) of these regulations.

(n) Effective date. These regulations are applicable January 1, 2007. Trustees must calculate and provide trust information with respect to the 2007 calendar year and all subsequent years consistent with these regulations. Information returns required to be filed with the IRS and the tax information statements required to be furnished to trust interest holders after December 31, 2007 must be consistent with these regulations.

T.D. 9241, 1/23/2006, amend T.D. 9279, 7/28/2006, T.D. 9308, 12/26/2006.

---

§ 1.672(a)-1 Definition of adverse party.

Caution: The Treasury has not yet amended Reg § 1.672(a)-1 to reflect changes made by P.L. 100-647, P.L. 99-514.

(a) Under section 672(a) an adverse party is defined as any person having a substantial beneficial interest in a trust which would be adversely affected by the exercise or nonexercise of a power which he possesses respecting the trust. A trustee is not an adverse party merely because of his interest as trustee. A person having a general power of appointment over the trust property is deemed to have a beneficial interest in the trust. An interest is a substantial interest if its value in relation to the total value of the property subject to the power is not insignificant.

(b) Ordinarily, a beneficiary will be an adverse party, but if his right to share in the income or corpus of a trust is limited to only a part, he may be an adverse party only as to that part. Thus, if A, B, C, and D are equal income beneficiaries of a trust and the grantor can revoke with A's consent, the grantor is treated as the owner of a portion which represents three-fourths of the trust; and items of income, deduction, and credit attributable to that portion are included in determining the tax of the grantor.

(c) The interest of an ordinary income beneficiary of a trust may or may not be adverse with respect to the exercise of a power over corpus. Thus, if the income of a trust is payable to A for life, with a power (which is not a general power of appointment) in A to appoint the corpus to the grantor either during his life or by will, A's interest is adverse to the return of the corpus to the grantor during A's life, but is not adverse to a return of the corpus after A's death. In other words, A's interest is adverse as to ordinary income but is not adverse as to income allocable to corpus. Therefore, assuming no other relevant facts exist, the grantor would not be taxable on the ordinary income of the trust under section 674, 676, or 677, but would be taxable under section 677 on income allocable to corpus (such as capital gains), since it may in the discretion of a nonadverse party be accumulated for future distribution to the grantor. Similarly, the interest of a contingent income beneficiary is adverse to a return of corpus to the grantor before the termination of his interest but not to a return of corpus after the termination of his interest.

(d) The interest of a remainderman is adverse to the exercise of any power over the corpus of a trust, but not to the exercise of a power over any income interest preceding his remainder. For example, if the grantor creates a trust which provides for income to be distributed to A for 10 years and then for the corpus to go to X if he is then living, a power exercisable by X to revest corpus in the grantor is a power exercisable by an adverse party; however, a power exercisable by X to distribute part or all of the ordinary income to the grantor may be a power exercisable by a nonadverse party (which would cause the ordinary income to be taxed to the grantor).

T.D. 6217, 12/19/56.

§ 1.672(b)-1 Nonadverse party.

Caution: The Treasury has not yet amended Reg § 1.672(b)-1 to reflect changes made by P.L. 100-647, P.L. 99-514.

A "nonadverse party" is any person who is not an adverse party.

T.D. 6217, 12/19/56.

§ 1.672(c)-1 Related or subordinate party.

Caution: The Treasury has not yet amended Reg § 1.672(c)-1 to reflect changes made by P.L. 104-188, P.L. 100-647, P.L. 99-514.

Section 672(c) defines the term "related or subordinate party". The term, as used in sections 674(c) and 675(3), means any nonadverse party who is the grantor's spouse if living with the grantor; the grantor's father, mother, issue, brother or sister; an employee of the grantor; a corporation or any employee of a corporation in which the stock holdings of the grantor and the trust are significant from the viewpoint of voting control; or a subordinate employee of a corporation in which the grantor is an executive. For purposes of sections 674(c) and 675(3), these persons are presumed to be subservient to the grantor in respect of the exercise or nonexercise of the powers conferred on them unless shown not to be subservient by a preponderance of the evidence.

T.D. 6217, 12/19/56.

§ 1.672(d)-1 Power subject to condition precedent.

Caution: The Treasury has not yet amended Reg § 1.672(d)-1 to reflect changes made by P.L. 100-647, P.L. 99-514.

Section 672(d) provides that a person is considered to have a power described in subpart E (section 671 and following), part I, subchapter J, chapter 1 of the Code, even though the exercise of the power is subject to a precedent giving of notice or takes effect only after the expiration of a certain period of time. However, although a person may be considered to have such a power, the grantor will nevertheless not be treated as an owner by reason of the power if its exercise can only affect beneficial enjoyment of income received after the expiration of a period of time such that, if the power were a reversionary interest, he would not be treated as an owner under section 673. See sections 674(b)(2), 676(b), and the last sentence of section 677(a). Thus, for example, if a grantor creates a trust for the benefit of his son and retains a power to revoke which takes effect only after the expiration of 2 years from the date of exercise, he is treated as an owner from the inception of the trust. However, if the grantor retains a power to revoke, exercisable at any time, which can only affect the beneficial enjoyment of the ordinary income of a trust received after the expiration of 10 years commencing with the date of the transfer in trust, or after the death of the income beneficiary, the power does not cause him to be treated as an owner with respect to ordinary income during the first 10 years of the trust or during the income beneficiary's life, as the case may be. See section 676(b).

T.D. 6217, 12/19/56.

§ 1.672(f)-1 Foreign persons not treated as owners.

(a) General rule. *(1) Application of the general rule.* Section 672(f)(1) provides that subpart E of part I, subchapter J, chapter 1 of the Internal Revenue Code (the grantor trust rules) shall apply only to the extent such application results in an amount (if any) being currently taken into account (directly or through one or more entities) in computing the income of a citizen or resident of the United States or a domestic corporation. Accordingly, the grantor trust rules apply to the extent that any portion of the trust, upon application of the grantor trust rules without regard to section 672(f), is treated as owned by a United States citizen or resident or domestic corporation. The grantor trust rules do not apply to any portion of the trust to the extent that, upon application of the grantor trust rules without regard to section 672(f), that portion is treated as owned by a person other than a United States citizen or resident or domestic corporation, unless the person is described in § 1.672(f)-2(a) (relating to certain foreign corporations treated as domestic corporations), or one of the exceptions set forth in § 1.672(f)-3 is met, (relating to: trusts where the grantor can revest trust assets; trusts where the only amounts distributable are to the grantor or the grantor's spouse; and compensatory trusts). Section 672(f) applies to domestic and foreign trusts. Any portion of the trust that is not treated as owned by a grantor or another person is subject to the rules of subparts A through D (section 641 and following), part I, subchapter J, chapter 1 of the Internal Revenue Code.

(2) Determination of portion based on application of the grantor trust rules. The determination of the portion of a trust treated as owned by the grantor or other person is to be made based on the terms of the trust and the application of the grantor trust rules and section 671 and the regulations thereunder.

(b) Example. The following example illustrates the rules of this section:

Example. (i) A, a nonresident alien, funds an irrevocable domestic trust, DT, for the benefit of his son, B, who is a United States citizen, with stock of Corporation X. A's brother, C, who also is a United States citizen, contributes stock of Corporation Y to the trust for the benefit of B. A has a reversionary interest within the meaning of section 673 in the X stock that would cause A to be treated as the owner of the X stock upon application of the grantor trust rules without regard to section 672(f). C has a reversionary interest within the meaning of section 673 in the Y stock that would cause C to be treated as the owner of the Y stock upon application of the grantor trust rules without regard to section 672(f). The trustee has discretion to accumulate or currently distribute income of DT to B.

(ii) Because A is a nonresident alien, application of the grantor trust rules without regard to section 672(f) would not result in the portion of the trust consisting of the X stock being treated as owned by a United States citizen or resident. None of the exceptions in § 1.672(f)-3 applies because A cannot revest the X stock in A, amounts may be distributed during A's lifetime to B, who is neither a grantor nor a spouse of a grantor, and the trust is not a compensatory trust. Therefore, pursuant to paragraph (a)(1) of this section, A is not treated as an owner under subpart E of part I, subchapter J, chapter 1 of the Internal Revenue Code, of the portion of the trust consisting of the X stock. Any distributions from such portion of the trust are subject to the rules of subparts A through D (641 and following), part I, subchapter J, chapter 1 of the Internal Revenue Code.

(iii) Because C is a United States citizen, paragraph (a)(1) of this section does not prevent C from being treated under section 673 as the owner of the portion of the trust consisting of the Y stock.

(c) Effective date. The rules of this section are applicable to taxable years of a trust beginning after August 10, 1999.

T.D. 8831, 8/5/99.

---

§ 1.672(f)-2 Certain foreign corporations.

Caution: The Treasury has not yet amended Reg § 1.672(f)-2 to reflect changes made by P.L. 108-357.

(a) Application of general rule. Subject to the provisions of paragraph (b) of this section, if the owner of any portion of a trust upon application of the grantor trust rules without regard to section 672(f) is a controlled foreign corporation (as defined in section 957), a passive foreign investment company (as defined in section 1297), or a foreign personal holding company (as defined in section 552), the corporation will be treated as a domestic corporation for purposes of applying the rules of § 1.672(f)-1.

(b) Gratuitous transfers to United States persons. *(1) Transfer from trust to which corporation made a gratuitous transfer.* If a trust (or portion of a trust) to which a controlled foreign corporation, passive foreign investment company, or foreign personal holding company has made a gratuitous transfer (within the meaning of § 1.671-2(e)(2)), makes a gratuitous transfer to a United States person, the controlled foreign corporation, passive foreign investment company, or foreign personal holding company, as the case may be, is treated as a foreign corporation for purposes of § 1.672(f)-4(c), relating to gratuitous transfers from trusts (or portions of trusts) to which a partnership or foreign corporation has made a gratuitous transfer.

(2) Transfer from trust over which corporation has a section 678 power. If a trust (or portion of a trust) that a controlled foreign corporation, passive foreign investment company, or foreign personal holding company is treated as owning under section 678 makes a gratuitous transfer to a United States person, the controlled foreign corporation, passive foreign investment company, or foreign personal holding company, as the case may be, is treated as a foreign corporation that had made a gratuitous transfer to the trust (or portion of a trust) and the rules of § 1.672(f)-4(c) apply.

(c) Special rules for passive foreign investment companies. *(1) Application of section 1297.* For purposes of determining whether a foreign corporation is a passive foreign investment company as defined in section 1297, the grantor trust rules apply as if section 672(f) had not come into effect.

(2) References to renumbered Internal Revenue Code section. For taxable years of shareholders beginning on or before December 31, 1997, and taxable years of passive foreign investment companies ending with or within such taxable years of the shareholders, all references in this § 1.672(f)-2 to section 1297 are deemed to be references to section 1296.

(d) Examples. The following examples illustrate the rules of this section. In each example, FT is an irrevocable foreign trust, and CFC is a controlled foreign corporation. The examples are as follows:

Example (1). Application of general rule. CFC creates and funds FT. CFC is the grantor of FT within the meaning of § 1.671-2(e). CFC has a reversionary interest in FT within the meaning of section 673 that would cause CFC to be treated as the owner of FT upon application of the grantor trust rules without regard to section 672(f). Under paragraph (a) of this section, CFC is treated as a domestic corporation for purposes of applying the general rule of § 1.672(f)-1. Thus, § 1.672(f)-1 does not prevent CFC from being treated as the owner of FT under section 673.

Example (2). Distribution from trust to which CFC made gratuitous transfer. A, a nonresident alien, owns 40 percent of the stock of CFC. A's brother B, a resident alien, owns the other 60 percent of the stock of CFC. CFC makes a gratuitous transfer to FT. FT makes a gratuitous transfer to A's daughter, C, who is a resident alien. Under paragraph (b)(1) of this section, CFC will be treated as a foreign corporation for purposes of § 1.672(f)-4(c). For further guidance, see § 1.672(f)-4(g) Example 2 through Example 4.

(e) Effective date. The rules of this section are generally applicable to taxable years of shareholders of controlled foreign corporations, passive foreign investment companies, and foreign personal holding companies beginning after August 10, 1999, and taxable years of controlled foreign corporations, passive foreign investment companies, and foreign personal holding companies ending with or within such taxable years of the shareholders.

T.D. 8831, 8/5/99, amend T.D. 8890, 7/3/2000.

---

§ 1.672(f)-3 Exceptions to general rule.

(a) Certain revocable trusts. *(1) In general.* Subject to the provisions of paragraph (a)(2) of this section, the general rule of § 1.672(f)-1 does not apply to any portion of a trust for a taxable year of the trust if the power to revest absolutely in the grantor title to such portion is exercisable solely by the grantor (or, in the event of the grantor's incapacity, by a guardian or other person who has unrestricted authority to exercise such power on the grantor's behalf) without the approval or consent of any other person. If the grantor can exercise such power only with the approval of a related or subordinate party who is subservient to the grantor, such power is treated as exercisable solely by the grantor. For the definition of grantor, see § 1.671-2(e). For the definition of related or subordinate party, see § 1.672(c)-1. For purposes of this paragraph (a), a related or subordinate party is subservient to the grantor unless the presumption in the last sentence of § 1.672(c)-1 is rebutted by a preponderance of the evidence. A trust (or portion of a trust) that fails to qualify for the exception provided by this paragraph (a) for a particular taxable year of the trust will be subject to the general rule of § 1.672(f)-1 for that taxable year and all subsequent taxable years of the trust.

(2) 183-day rule. For purposes of paragraph (a)(1) of this section, the grantor is treated as having a power to revest for a taxable year of the trust only if the grantor has such power for a total of 183 or more days during the taxable year of the trust. If the first or last taxable year of the trust (including the year of the grantor's death) is less than 183 days, the grantor is treated as having a power to revest for purposes of paragraph (a)(1) of this section if the grantor has such power for each day of the first or last taxable year, as the case may be.

(3) Grandfather rule for certain revocable trusts in existence on September 19, 1995. Subject to the rules of paragraph (d) of this section (relating to separate accounting for

gratuitous transfers to the trust after September 19, 1995), the general rule of § 1.672(f)-1 does not apply to any portion of a trust that was treated as owned by the grantor under section 676 on September 19, 1995, as long as the trust would continue to be so treated thereafter. However, the preceding sentence does not apply to any portion of the trust attributable to gratuitous transfers to the trust after September 19, 1995.

(4) Examples. The following examples illustrate the rules of this paragraph (a):

Example (1). Grantor is owner. FP1, a foreign person, creates and funds a revocable trust, T, for the benefit of FP1's children, who are resident aliens. The trustee is a foreign bank, FB, that is owned and controlled by FP1 and FP2, who is FP1's brother. The power to revoke T and revest absolutely in FP1 title to the trust property is exercisable by FP1, but only with the approval or consent of FB. The trust instrument contains no standard that FB must apply in determining whether to approve or consent to the revocation of T. There are no facts that would suggest that FB is not subservient to FP1. Therefore, the exception in paragraph (a)(1) of this section is applicable.

Example (2). Death of grantor. Assume the same facts as in Example 1, except that FP1 dies. After FP1's death, FP2 has the power to withdraw the assets of T, but only with the approval of FB. There are no facts that would suggest that FB is not subservient to FP2. However, the exception in paragraph (a)(1) of this section is no longer applicable, because FP2 is not a grantor of T within the meaning of § 1.671-2(e).

Example (3). Trustee is not related or subordinate party. Assume the same facts as in Example 1, except that neither FP1 nor any member of FP1's family has any substantial ownership interest or other connection with FB. FP1 can remove and replace FB at any time for any reason. Although FP1 can replace FB with a related or subordinate party if FB refuses to approve or consent to FP1's decision to revest the trust property in himself, FB is not a related or subordinate party. Therefore, the exception in paragraph (a)(1) of this section is not applicable.

Example (4). Unrelated trustee will consent to revocation. FP, a foreign person, creates and funds an irrevocable trust, T. The trustee is a foreign bank, FB, that is not a related or subordinate party within the meaning of § 1.672(c)-1. FB has the discretion to distribute trust income or corpus to beneficiaries of T, including FP. Even if FB would in fact distribute all the trust property to FP if requested to do so by FP, the exception in paragraph (a)(1) of this section is not applicable, because FP does not have the power to revoke T.

(b) Certain trusts that can distribute only to the grantor or the spouse of the grantor. *(1) In general.* The general rule of § 1.672(f)-1 does not apply to any trust (or portion of a trust) if at all times during the lifetime of the grantor the only amounts distributable (whether income or corpus) from such trust (or portion thereof) are amounts distributable to the grantor or the spouse of the grantor. For purposes of this paragraph (b), payments of amounts that are not gratuitous transfers (within the meaning of § 1.671-2(e)(2)) are not amounts distributable. For the definition of grantor, see § 1.671-2(e).

(2) Amounts distributable in discharge of legal obligations. (i) In general. A trust (or portion of a trust) does not fail to satisfy paragraph (b)(1) of this section solely because amounts are distributable from the trust (or portion thereof) in discharge of a legal obligation of the grantor or the spouse of the grantor. Subject to the provisions of paragraph (b)(2)(ii) of this section, an obligation is considered a legal obligation for purposes of this paragraph (b)(2)(i) if it is enforceable under the local law of the jurisdiction in which the grantor (or the spouse of the grantor) resides.

(ii) Related parties. (A) In general. Except as provided in paragraph (b)(2)(ii)(B) of this section, an obligation to a person who is a related person for purposes of § 1.643(h)-1(e) (other than an individual who is legally separated from the grantor under a decree of divorce or of separate maintenance) is not a legal obligation for purposes of paragraph (b)(2)(i) of this section unless it was contracted bona fide and for adequate and full consideration in money or money's worth (see § 20.2043-1 of this chapter).

(B) Exceptions. (1) Amounts distributable in support of certain individuals. Paragraph (b)(2)(ii)(A) of this section does not apply with respect to amounts that are distributable from the trust (or portion thereof) to support an individual who—

(i) Would be treated as a dependent of the grantor or the spouse of the grantor under section 152(a)(1) through (9), without regard to the requirement that over half of the individual's support be received from the grantor or the spouse of the grantor; and

(ii) Is either permanently and totally disabled (within the meaning of section 22(e)(3)), or less than 19 years old.

(2) Certain potential support obligations. The fact that amounts might become distributable from a trust (or portion of a trust) in discharge of a potential obligation under local law to support an individual other than an individual described in paragraph (b)(2)(ii)(B)(1) of this section is disregarded if such potential obligation is not reasonably expected to arise under the facts and circumstances.

(3) Reinsurance trusts. [Reserved]

(3) Grandfather rule for certain section 677 trusts in existence on September 19, 1995. Subject to the rules of paragraph (d) of this section (relating to separate accounting for gratuitous transfers to the trust after September 19, 1995), the general rule of § 1.672(f)-1 does not apply to any portion of a trust that was treated as owned by the grantor under section 677 (other than section 677(a)(3)) on September 19, 1995, as long as the trust would continue to be so treated thereafter. However, the preceding sentence does not apply to any portion of the trust attributable to gratuitous transfers to the trust after September 19, 1995.

(4) Examples. The following examples illustrate the rules of this paragraph (b):

Example (1). Amounts distributable only to grantor or grantor's spouse. H and his wife, W, are both nonresident aliens. H is 70 years old, and W is 65. H and W have a 30-year-old child, C, a resident alien. There is no reasonable expectation that H or W will ever have an obligation under local law to support C or any other individual. H creates and funds an irrevocable trust, FT, using only his separate property. H is the grantor of FT within the meaning of § 1.671-2(e). Under the terms of FT, the only amounts distributable (whether income or corpus) from FT as long as either H or W is alive are amounts distributable to H or W. Upon the death of both H and W, C may receive distributions from FT. During H's lifetime, the exception in paragraph (b)(1) of this section is applicable.

Example (2). Effect of grantor's death. Assume the same facts as in Example 1. H predeceases W. Assume that W would be treated as owning FT under section 678 if the grantor trust rules were applied without regard to section

672(f). The exception in paragraph (b)(1) of this section is no longer applicable, because W is not a grantor of FT within the meaning of § 1.671-2(e).

Example (3). Amounts temporarily distributable to person other than grantor or grantor's spouse. Assume the same facts as in Example 1, except that C (age 30) is a law student at the time FT is created and the trust instrument provides that, as long as C is in law school, amounts may be distributed from FT to pay C's expenses. Thereafter, the only amounts distributable from FT as long as either H or W is alive will be amounts distributable to H or W. Even assuming there is an enforceable obligation under local law for H and W to support C while he is in school, distributions from FT in payment of C's expenses cannot qualify as distributions in discharge of a legal obligation under paragraph (b)(2) of this section, because C is neither permanently and totally disabled nor less than 19 years old. The exception in paragraph (b)(1) of this section is not applicable. After C graduates from law school, the exception in paragraph (b)(1) still will not be applicable, because amounts were distributable to C during the lifetime of H.

Example (4). Fixed investment trust. FC, a foreign corporation, invests in a domestic fixed investment trust, DT, that is classified as a trust under § 301.7701-4(c)(1) of this chapter. Under the terms of DT, the only amounts that are distributable from FC's portion of DT are amounts distributable to FC. The exception in paragraph (b)(1) of this section is applicable to FC's portion of DT.

Example (5). Reinsurance trust. A domestic insurance company, DI, reinsures a portion of its business with an unrelated foreign insurance company, FI. To satisfy state regulatory requirements, FI places the premiums in an irrevocable domestic trust, DT. The trust funds are held by a United States bank and may be used only to pay claims arising out of the reinsurance policies, which are legally enforceable under the local law of the jurisdiction in which FI resides. On the termination of DT, any assets remaining will revert to FI. Because the only amounts that are distributable from DT are distributable either to FI or in discharge of FI's legal obligations within the meaning of paragraph (b)(2)(i) of this section, the exception in paragraph (b)(1) of this section is applicable.

Example (6). Trust that provides security for loan. FC, a foreign corporation, borrows money from B, an unrelated bank, to finance the purchase of an airplane. FC creates a foreign trust, FT, to hold the airplane as security for the loan from B. The only amounts that are distributable from FT while the loan is outstanding are amounts distributable to B in the event that FC defaults on its loan from B. When FC repays the loan, the trust assets will revert to FC. The loan is a legal obligation of FC within the meaning of paragraph (b)(2)(i) of this section, because it is enforceable under the local law of the country in which FC is incorporated. Paragraph (b)(2)(ii) of this section is not applicable, because B is not a related person for purposes of § 1.643(h)-1(e). The exception in paragraph (b)(1) of this section is applicable.

(c) Compensatory trusts. *(1) In general.* The general rule of § 1.672(f)-1 does not apply to any portion of—

(i) A nonexempt employees' trust described in section 402(b), including a trust created on behalf of a self-employed individual;

(ii) A trust, including a trust created on behalf of a self-employed individual, that would be a nonexempt employees' trust described in section 402(b) but for the fact that the trust's assets are not set aside from the claims of creditors of the actual or deemed transferor within the meaning of § 1.83-3(e); and

(iii) Any additional category of trust that the Commissioner may designate in revenue procedures, notices, or other guidance published in the Internal Revenue Bulletin (see § 601.601(d)(2) of this chapter).

(2) Exceptions. The Commissioner may, in revenue rulings, notices, or other guidance published in the Internal Revenue Bulletin (see § 601.601(d)(2) of this chapter), designate categories of compensatory trusts to which the general rule of paragraph (c)(1) of this section does not apply.

(d) Separate accounting for gratuitous transfers to grandfathered trusts after September 19, 1995. If a trust that was treated as owned by the grantor under section 676 or 677 (other than section 677(a)(3)) on September 19, 1995, contains both amounts held in the trust on September 19, 1995, and amounts that were gratuitously transferred to the trust after September 19, 1995, paragraphs (a)(3) and (b)(3) of this section apply only if the amounts that were gratuitously transferred to the trust after September 19, 1995, are treated as a separate portion of the trust that is accounted for under the rules of § 1.671-3(a)(2). If the amounts that were gratuitously transferred to the trust after September 19, 1995 are not so accounted for, the general rule of § 1.672(f)-1 applies to the entire trust. If such amounts are so accounted for, and without regard to whether there is physical separation of the assets, the general rule of § 1.672(f)-1 does not apply to the portion of the trust that is attributable to amounts that were held in the trust on September 19, 1995.

(e) Effective date. The rules of this section are generally applicable to taxable years of a trust beginning after August 10, 1999. The initial separate accounting required by paragraph (d) of this section must be prepared by the due date (including extensions) for the tax return of the trust for the first taxable year of the trust beginning after August 10, 1999.

T.D. 8831, 8/5/99, amend T.D. 8890, 7/3/2000.

§ 1.672(f)-4 Recharacterization of purported gifts.

(a) In general. *(1) Purported gifts from partnerships.* Except as provided in paragraphs (b), (e), and (f) of this section, and without regard to the existence of any trust, if a United States person (United States donee) directly or indirectly receives a purported gift or bequest (as defined in paragraph (d) of this section) from a partnership, the purported gift or bequest must be included in the United States donee's gross income as ordinary income.

(2) Purported gifts from foreign corporations. Except as provided in paragraphs (b), (e), and (f) of this section, and without regard to the existence of any trust, if a United States donee directly or indirectly receives a purported gift or bequest (as defined in paragraph (d) of this section) from any foreign corporation, the purported gift or bequest must be included in the United States donee's gross income as if it were a distribution from the foreign corporation. If the foreign corporation is a passive foreign investment company (within the meaning of section 1297), the rules of section 1291 apply. For purposes of section 1012, the United States donee is not treated as having basis in the stock of the foreign corporation. However, for purposes of section 1223, the United States donee is treated as having a holding period in the stock of the foreign corporation on the date of the deemed distribution equal to the weighted average of the holding periods of the actual interest holders (other than any interest holders who treat the portion of the purported gift at-

tributable to their interest in the foreign corporation in the manner described in paragraph (b)(1) of this section). For purposes of section 902, a United States donee that is a domestic corporation is not treated as owning any voting stock of the foreign corporation.

(b) Exceptions. *(1) Partner or shareholder treats transfer as distribution and gift.* Paragraph (a) of this section does not apply to the extent the United States donee can demonstrate to the satisfaction of the Commissioner that either—

(i) A United States citizen or resident alien individual who directly or indirectly holds an interest in the partnership or foreign corporation treated and reported the purported gift or bequest for United States tax purposes as a distribution to such individual and a subsequent gift or bequest to the United States donee; or

(ii) A nonresident alien individual who directly or indirectly holds an interest in the partnership or foreign corporation treated and reported the purported gift or bequest for purposes of the tax laws of the nonresident alien individual's country of residence as a distribution to such individual and a subsequent gift or bequest to the United States donee, and the United States donee timely complied with the reporting requirements of section 6039F, if applicable.

(2) All beneficial owners of domestic partnership are United States citizens or residents or domestic corporations. Paragraph (a)(1) of this section does not apply to a purported gift or bequest from a domestic partnership if the United States donee can demonstrate to the satisfaction of the Commissioner that all beneficial owners (within the meaning of § 1.1441-1(c)(6)) of the partnership are United States citizens or residents or domestic corporations.

(3) Contribution to capital of corporate United States donee. Paragraph (a) of this section does not apply to the extent a United States donee that is a corporation can establish that the purported gift or bequest was treated for United States tax purposes as a contribution to the capital of the United States donee to which section 118 applies.

(4) Charitable transfers. Paragraph (a) of this section does not apply if either—

(i) The United States donee is described in section 170(c); or

(ii) The transferor has received a ruling or determination letter, which has been neither revoked nor modified, from the Internal Revenue Service recognizing its exempt status under section 501(c)(3), and the transferor made the transfer pursuant to an exempt purpose for which the transferor was created or organized. For purposes of the preceding sentence, a ruling or determination letter recognizing exemption may not be relied upon if there is a material change, inconsistent with exemption, in the character, the purpose, or the method of operation of the organization.

(c) Certain transfers from trusts to which a partnership or foreign corporation has made a gratuitous transfer. *(1) Generally treated as distribution from partnership or foreign corporation.* Except as provided in paragraphs (c)(2) and (3) of this section, if a United States donee receives a gratuitous transfer (within the meaning of § 1.671-2(e)(2)) from a trust (or portion of a trust) to which a partnership or foreign corporation has made a gratuitous transfer, the United States donee must treat the transfer as a purported gift or bequest from the partnership or foreign corporation that is subject to the rules of paragraph (a) of this section (including the exceptions in paragraphs (b) and (f) of this section). This paragraph (c) applies without regard to who is treated as the grantor of the trust (or portion thereof) under § 1.671-2(e)(4).

(2) Alternative rule. Except as provided in paragraph (c)(3) of this section, if the United States tax computed under the rules of paragraphs (a) and (c)(1) of this section does not exceed the United States tax that would be due if the United States donee treated the transfer as a distribution from the trust (or portion thereof), paragraph (c)(1) of this section does not apply and the United States donee must treat the transfer as a distribution from the trust (or portion thereof) that is subject to the rules of subparts A through D (section 641 and following), part I, subchapter J, chapter 1 of the Internal Revenue Code. For purposes of paragraph (f) of this section, the transfer is treated as a purported gift or bequest from the partnership or foreign corporation that made the gratuitous transfer to the trust (or portion thereof).

(3) Exception. Neither paragraph (c)(1) of this section nor paragraph (c)(2) of this section applies to the extent the United States donee can demonstrate to the satisfaction of the Commissioner that the transfer represents an amount that is, or has been, taken into account for United States tax purposes by a United States citizen or resident or a domestic corporation. A transfer will be deemed to be made first out of amounts that have not been taken into account for United States tax purposes by a United States citizen or resident or a domestic corporation, unless the United States donee can demonstrate to the satisfaction of the Commissioner that another ordering rule is more appropriate.

(d) Definition of purported gift or bequest. *(1) In general.* Subject to the provisions of paragraphs (d)(2) and (3) of this section, a purported gift or bequest for purposes of this section is any transfer of property by a partnership or foreign corporation other than a transfer for fair market value (within the meaning of § 1.671-2(e)(2)(ii)) to a person who is not a partner in the partnership or a shareholder of the foreign corporation (or to a person who is a partner in the partnership or a shareholder of a foreign corporation, if the amount transferred is inconsistent with the partner's interest in the partnership or the shareholder's interest in the corporation, as the case may be). For purposes of this section, the term property includes cash.

(2) Transfers for less than fair market value. (i) Excess treated as purported gift or bequest. Except as provided in paragraph (d)(2)(ii) of this section, if a transfer described in paragraph (d)(1) of this section is for less than fair market value, the excess of the fair market value of the property transferred over the value of the property received, services rendered, or the right to use property is treated as a purported gift or bequest.

(ii) Exception for transfers to unrelated parties. No portion of a transfer described in paragraph (d)(1) of this section will be treated as a purported gift or bequest for purposes of this section if the United States donee can demonstrate to the satisfaction of the Commissioner that the United States donee is not related to a partner or shareholder of the transferor within the meaning of § 1.643(h)-1(e) or does not have another relationship with a partner or shareholder of the transferor that establishes a reasonable basis for concluding that the transferor would make a gratuitous transfer to the United States donee.

(e) Prohibition against affirmative use of recharacterization by taxpayers. A taxpayer may not use the rules of this section if a principal purpose for using such rules is the avoidance of any tax imposed by the Internal Revenue Code. Thus, with respect to such taxpayer, the Commissioner may depart from the rules of this section and recharacterize (for all purposes of the Internal Revenue Code) the transfer in accordance with its form or its economic substance.

(f) Transfers not in excess of $10,000. This section does not apply if, during the taxable year of the United States donee, the aggregate amount of purported gifts or bequests that is transferred to such United States donee directly or indirectly from all partnerships or foreign corporations that are related (within the meaning of section 643(i)) does not exceed $10,000. The aggregate amount must include gifts or bequests from persons that the United States donee knows or has reason to know are related to the partnership or foreign corporation (within the meaning of section 643(i)).

(g) Examples. The following examples illustrate the rules of this section. In each example, the amount that is transferred exceeds $10,000. The examples are as follows:

Example (1). Distribution from foreign corporation. FC is a foreign corporation that is wholly owned by A, a nonresident alien who is resident in Country C. FC makes a gratuitous transfer of property directly to A's daughter, B, who is a resident alien. Under paragraph (a)(2) of this section, B generally must treat the transfer as a dividend from FC to the extent of FC's earnings and profits and as an amount received in excess of basis thereafter. If FC is a passive foreign investment company, B must treat the amount received as a distribution under section 1291. B will be treated as having the same holding period as A. However, under paragraph (b)(1)(ii) of this section, if B can establish to the satisfaction of the Commissioner that, for purposes of the tax laws of Country C, A treated (and reported, if applicable) the transfer as a distribution to himself and a subsequent gift to B, B may treat the transfer as a gift (provided B timely complied with the reporting requirements of section 6039F, if applicable).

Example (2). Distribution of corpus from trust to which foreign corporation made gratuitous transfer. FC is a foreign corporation that is wholly owned by A, a nonresident alien who is resident in Country C. FC makes a gratuitous transfer to a foreign trust, FT, that has no other assets. FT immediately makes a gratuitous transfer in the same amount to A's daughter, B, who is a resident alien. Under paragraph (c)(1) of this section, B must treat the transfer as a transfer from FC that is subject to the rules of paragraph (a)(2) of this section. Under paragraph (a)(2) of this section, B must treat the transfer as a dividend from FC unless she can establish to the satisfaction of the Commissioner that, for purposes of the tax laws of Country C, A treated (and reported, if applicable) the transfer as a distribution to himself and a subsequent gift to B and that B timely complied with the reporting requirements of section 6039F, if applicable. The alternative rule in paragraph (c)(2) of this section would not apply as long as the United States tax computed under the rules of paragraph (a)(2) of this section is equal to or greater than the United States tax that would be due if the transfer were treated as a distribution from FT.

Example (3). Accumulation distribution from trust to which foreign corporation made gratuitous transfer. FC is a foreign corporation that is wholly owned by A, a nonresident alien. FC is not a passive foreign investment company (as defined in section 1297). FC makes a gratuitous transfer of 100X to a foreign trust, FT, on January 1, 2001. FT has no other assets on January 1, 2001. Several years later, FT makes a gratuitous transfer of 1000X to A's daughter, B, who is a United States resident. Assume that the section 668 interest charge on accumulation distributions will apply if the transfer is treated as a distribution from FT. Under the alternative rule of paragraph (c)(2) of this section, B must treat the transfer as an accumulation distribution from FT, because the resulting United States tax liability is greater than the United States tax that would be due if the transfer were treated as a transfer from FC that is subject to the rules of paragraph (a) of this section.

Example (4). Transfer from trust that is treated as owned by United States citizen. Assume the same facts as in Example 3, except that A is a United States citizen. Assume that A treats and reports the transfer to FT as a constructive distribution to himself, followed by a gratuitous transfer to FT, and that A is properly treated as the grantor of FT within the meaning of § 1.671-2(e). A is treated as the owner of FT under section 679 and, as required by section 671 and the regulations thereunder, A includes all of FT's items of income, deductions, and credit in computing his taxable income and credits. Neither paragraph (c)(1) nor paragraph (c)(2) of this section is applicable, because the exception in paragraph (c)(3) of this section applies.

Example (5). Transfer for less than fair market value. FC is a foreign corporation that is wholly owned by A, a nonresident alien. On January 15, 2001, FC transfers property directly to A's daughter, B, a resident alien, in exchange for 90X. The Commissioner later determines that the fair market value of the property at the time of the transfer was 100X. Under paragraph (d)(2)(i) of this section, 10X will be treated as a purported gift to B on January 15, 2001.

(h) Effective date. The rules of this section are generally applicable to any transfer after August 10, 1999, by a partnership or foreign corporation, or by a trust to which a partnership or foreign corporation makes a gratuitous transfer after August 10, 1999.

T.D. 8831, 8/5/99, amend T.D. 8890, 7/3/2000.

---

§ 1.672(f)-5 Special rules.

(a) Transfers by certain beneficiaries to foreign grantor. *(1) In general.* If, but for section 672(f)(5), a foreign person would be treated as the owner of any portion of a trust, any United States beneficiary of the trust is treated as the grantor of a portion of the trust to the extent the United States beneficiary directly or indirectly made transfers of property to such foreign person (without regard to whether the United States beneficiary was a United States beneficiary at the time of any transfer) in excess of transfers to the United States beneficiary from the foreign person. The rule of this paragraph (a) does not apply to the extent the United States beneficiary can demonstrate to the satisfaction of the Commissioner that the transfer by the United States beneficiary to the foreign person was wholly unrelated to any transaction involving the trust. For purposes of this paragraph (a), the term property includes cash, and a transfer of property does not include a transfer that is not a gratuitous transfer (within the meaning of § 1.671-2(e)(2)). In addition, a gift is not taken into account to the extent such gift would not be characterized as a taxable gift under section 2503(b). For a definition of United States beneficiary, see section 679.

(2) Examples. The following examples illustrate the rules of this section:

Example (1). A, a nonresident alien, contributes property to FC, a foreign corporation that is wholly owned by A. FC creates a foreign trust, FT, for the benefit of A and A's children. FT is revocable by FC without the approval or consent of any other person. FC funds FT with the property received from A. A and A's family move to the United States. Under paragraph (a)(1) of this section, A is treated as a grantor of

FT. (A may also be treated as an owner of FT under section 679(a)(4).)

Example (2). B, a United States citizen, makes a gratuitous transfer of $1 million to B's uncle, C, a nonresident alien. C creates a foreign trust, FT, for the benefit of B and B's children. FT is revocable by C without the approval or consent of any other person. C funds FT with the property received from B. Under paragraph (a)(1) of this section, B is treated as a grantor of FT. (B also would be treated as an owner of FT as a result of section 679.)

(b) Entity characterization. Entities generally are characterized under United States tax principles for purposes of § 1.672(f)-1 through 1.672(f)-5. See §§ 301.7701-1 through 301.7701-4 of this chapter. However, solely for purposes of § 1.672(f)-4, a transferor that is a wholly owned business entity is treated as a corporation, separate from its single owner.

(c) Effective date. The rules in paragraph (a) of this section are applicable to transfers to trusts on or after August 10, 1999. The rules in paragraph (b) of this section are applicable August 10, 1999.

T.D. 8831, 8/5/99, amend T.D. 8890, 7/3/2000.

§ 1.673(a)-1 Reversionary interests; income payable to beneficiaries other than certain charitable organizations; general rule.

Caution: The Treasury has not yet amended Reg § 1.673(a)-1 to reflect changes made by P.L. 100-647, P.L. 99-514.

(a) Under section 673(a), a grantor, in general, is treated as the owner of any portion of a trust in which he has a reversionary interest in either the corpus or income if, as of the inception of that portion of the trust, the grantor's interest will or may reasonably be expected to take effect in possession or enjoyment within 10 years commencing with the date of transfer of that portion of the trust. However, the following types of reversionary interests are excepted from the general rule of the preceding sentence:

(1) A reversionary interest after the death of the income beneficiary of a trust (see paragraph (b) of this section); and

(2) Except in the case of transfers in trust made after April 22, 1969, a reversionary interest in a charitable trust meeting the requirements of section 673(b) (see § 1.673(b)-1).

Even though the duration of the trust may be such that the grantor is not treated as its owner under section 673, and therefore is not taxed on the ordinary income, he may nevertheless be treated as an owner under section 677(a)(2) if he has a reversionary interest in the corpus. In the latter case, items of income, deduction, and credit allocable to corpus, such as capital gains and losses, will be included in the portion he owns. See § 1.671-3 and the regulations under section 677. See § 1.673(d)-1 with respect to a postponement of the date specified for reacquisition of a reversionary interest.

(b) Section 673(c) provides that a grantor is not treated as the owner of any portion of a trust by reason of section 673 if his reversionary interest in the portion is not to take effect in possession or enjoyment until the death of the person or persons to whom the income of the portion is payable, regardless of the life expectancies of the income beneficiaries. If his reversionary interest is to take effect on or after the death of an income beneficiary or upon the expiration of a specific term of years, whichever is earlier, the grantor is treated as the owner if the specific term of years is less than 10 years (but not if the term is 10 years or longer).

(c) Where the grantor's reversionary interest in a portion of a trust is to take effect in possession or enjoyment by reason of some event other than the expiration of a specific term of years or the death of the income beneficiary, the grantor is treated as the owner of the portion if the event may reasonably be expected to occur within 10 years from the date of transfer of that portion, but he is not treated as the owner under section 673 if the event may not reasonably be expected to occur within 10 years from that date. For example, if the reversionary interest in any portion of a trust is to take effect on or after the death of the grantor (or any person other than the person to whom the income is payable) the grantor is treated under section 673 as the owner of the portion if the life expectancy of the grantor (or other person) is less than 10 years on the date of transfer of the portion, but not if the life expectancy is 10 years or longer. If the reversionary interest in any portion is to take effect on or after the death of the grantor (or any person other than the person to whom the income is payable) or upon the expiration of a specific term of years, whichever is earlier, the grantor is treated as the owner of the portion if on the date of transfer of the portion either the life expectancy of the grantor (or other person) or the specific term is less than 10 years; however, if both the life expectancy and the specific term are 10 years or longer the grantor is not treated as the owner of the portion under section 673. Similarly, if the grantor has a reversionary interest in any portion which will take effect at the death of the income beneficiary or the grantor, whichever is earlier, the grantor is not treated as an owner of the portion unless his life expectancy is less than 10 years.

(d) It is immaterial that a reversionary interest in corpus or income is subject to a contingency if the reversionary interest may, taking the contingency into consideration, reasonably be expected to take effect in possession or enjoyment within 10 years. For example, the grantor is taxable where the trust income is to be paid to the grantor's son for 3 years, and the corpus is then to be returned to the grantor if he survives that period, or to be paid to the grantor's son if he is already deceased.

(e) See section 671 and §§ 1.671-2 and 1.671-3 for rules for treatment of items of income, deduction, and credit when a person is treated as the owner of all or only a portion of a trust.

T.D. 6217, 12/19/56, amend T.D. 7357, 5/30/75.

§ 1.673(b)-1 Income payable to charitable beneficiaries (before amendment by Tax Reform Act of 1969).

(a) Pursuant to section 673(b) a grantor is not treated as an owner of any portion of a trust under section 673, even though he has a reversionary interest which will take effect within 10 years, to the extent that, under the terms of the trust, the income of the portion is irrevocably payable for a period of at least 2 years (commencing with the date of the transfer) to a designated beneficiary of the type described in section 170(b)(1)(A).

(b) Income must be irrevocably payable to a designated beneficiary for at least 2 years commencing with the date of the transfer before the benefit of section 673(b) will apply. Thus, section 673(b) will not apply if income of a trust is irrevocably payable to University A for 1 year and then to University B for the next year; or if income of a trust may be allocated among two or more charitable beneficiaries in the discretion of the trustee or any other person. On the other hand, section 673(b) will apply if half the income of a trust is irrevocably payable to University A and the other half is irrevocably payable to University B for two years.

(c) Section 673(b) applies to the period of 2 years or longer during which income is paid to a designated beneficiary of the type described in section 170(b)(1)(A)(i), (ii), or (iii), even though the trust term is to extend beyond that period. However, the other provisions of section 673 apply to the part of the trust term, if any, that extends beyond that period. This paragraph may be illustrated by the following example:

Example. G transfers property in trust with the ordinary income payable to University C (which qualifies under section 170(b)(1)(A)(ii) for 3 years, and then to his son, B, for 5 years. At the expiration of the term the trust reverts to G. G is not taxed under section 673 on the trust income payable to University C for the first 3 years because of the application of section 673(b). However, he is taxed on income for the next 5 years because he has a reversionary interest which will take effect within 10 years commencing with the date of the transfer. On the other hand, if the income were payable to University C for 3 years and then to B for 7 years so that the trust corpus would not be returned to G within 10 years, G would not be taxable under section 673 on income payable to University C for the first 3 years because of the application of section 673(b). However, he and to B during any part of the term.

(d) This section does not apply to transfers in trust made after April 22, 1969.

T.D. 6217, 12/19/56, amend T.D. 6605, 8/14/62, T.D. 7357, 5/30/75.

§ 1.673(c)-1 Reversionary interest after income beneficiary's death.

Caution: The Treasury has not yet amended Reg § 1.673(c)-1 to reflect changes made by P.L. 100-647, P.L. 99-514.

The subject matter of section 673(c) is covered in paragraph (b) of § 1.673(a)-1.

T.D. 6217, 12/19/56.

§ 1.673(d)-1 Postponement of date specified for reacquisition.

Caution: The Treasury has not yet amended Reg § 1.673(d)-1 to reflect changes made by P.L. 100-647, P.L. 99-514.

Any postponement of the date specified for the reacquisition of possession or enjoyment of any reversionary interest is considered a new transfer in trust commencing with the date on which the postponement is effected and terminating with the date prescribed by the postponement. However, the grantor will not be treated as the owner of any portion of a trust for any taxable year by reason of the foregoing sentence if he would not be so treated in the absence of any postponement. The rules contained in this section may be illustrated by the following example:

Example. G places property in trust for the benefit of his son B. Upon the expiration of 12 years or the earlier death of B the property is to be paid over to G or his estate. After the expiration of 9 years G extends the term of the trust for an additional 2 years. G is considered to have made a new transfer in trust for a term of 5 years (the remaining 3 years of the original transfer plus the 2-year extension). However, he is not treated as the owner of the trust under section 673 for the first 3 years of the new term because he would not be so treated if the term of the trust had not been extended. G is treated as the owner of the trust, however, for the remaining 2 years.

T.D. 6217, 12/19/56.

§ 1.674(a)-1 Power to control beneficial enjoyment; scope of section 674.

Caution: The Treasury has not yet amended Reg § 1.674(a)-1 to reflect changes made by P.L. 100-647, P.L. 99-514.

(a) Under section 674, the grantor is treated as the owner of a portion of trust if the grantor or a nonadverse party has a power, beyond specified limits, to dispose of the beneficial enjoyment of the income or corpus, whether the power is a fiduciary power, a power of appointment, or any other power. Section 674(a) states in general terms that the grantor is treated as the owner in every case in which he or a nonadverse party can affect the beneficial enjoyment of a portion of a trust, the limitations being set forth as exceptions in subsections (b), (c), and (d) of section 674. These exceptions are discussed in detail in §§ 1.674(b)-1 through 1.674(d)-1. Certain limitations applicable to section 674(b), (c), and (d) are set forth in § 1.674(d)-2. Section 674(b) describes powers which are excepted regardless of who holds them. Section 674(c) describes additional powers of trustees which are excepted if at least half the trustees are independent, and if the grantor is not a trustee. Section 674(d) describes a further power which is excepted if it is held by trustees other than the grantor or his spouse (if living with the grantor).

(b) In general terms the grantor is treated as the owner of a portion of a trust if he or a nonadverse party or both has a power to dispose of the beneficial enjoyment of the corpus or income unless the power is one of the following:

(1) Miscellaneous powers over either ordinary income or corpus. (i) A power that can only affect the beneficial enjoyment of income (including capital gains) received after a period of time such that the grantor would not be treated as an owner under section 673 if the power were a reversionary interest (section 674(b)(2));

(ii) A testamentary power held by anyone (other than a testamentary power held by the grantor over accumulated income) (section 674(b)(3));

(iii) A power to choose between charitable beneficiaries or to affect the manner of their enjoyment of a beneficial interest (section 674(b)(4));

(iv) A power to allocate receipts and disbursements between income and corpus (section 674(b)(8)).

(2) Powers of distribution primarily affecting only one beneficiary. (i) A power to distribute corpus to or for a current income beneficiary, if the distribution must be charged against the share of corpus from which the beneficiary may receive income (section 674(b)(5)(B));

(ii) A power to distribute income to or for a current income beneficiary or to accumulate it either (a) if accumulated income must either be payable to the beneficiary from whom it was withheld or as described in paragraph (b)(6) of § 1.674(b)-1 (section 674(b)(6)); (b) if the power is to apply income to the support of a dependent of the grantor, and the income is not so applied (section 674(b)(1)); or (c) if the beneficiary is under 21 or under a legal disability and accumulated income is added to corpus (section 674(b)(7)).

(3) Powers of distribution affecting more than one beneficiary. A power to distribute corpus or income to or among

one or more beneficiaries or to accumulate income, either (i) if the power is held by a trustee or trustees other than the grantor, at least half of whom are independent (section 674(c)), or (ii) if the power is limited by a reasonably definite standard in the trust instrument, and in the case of a power over income, if in addition the power is held by a trustee or trustees other than the grantor and the grantor's spouse living with the grantor (section 674(b)(5)(A) and (d)). (These powers include both powers to "sprinkle" income or corpus among current beneficiaries, and powers to shift income of corpus between current beneficiaries and remaindermen; however, certain of the powers described under subparagraph (2) of this paragraph can have the latter effect incidentally.)

(c) See section 671 and §§ 1.671-2 and 1.671-3 for rules for the treatment of income, deductions, and credits when a person is treated as the owner of all or only a portion of a trust.

T.D. 6217, 12/19/56.

§ 1.674(b)-1 Excepted powers exercisable by any person.

Caution: The Treasury has not yet amended Reg § 1.674(b)-1 to reflect changes made by P.L. 100-647, P.L. 99-514.

(a) Paragraph (b)(1) through (8) of this section sets forth a number of powers which may be exercisable by any person without causing the grantor to be treated as an owner of a trust under section 674(a). Further, with the exception of powers described in paragraph (b)(1) of this section, it is immaterial whether these powers are held in the capacity of trustee. It makes no difference under section 674(b) that the person holding the powers is the grantor, or a related or subordinate party (with the qualifications noted in paragraph (b)(1) and (3) of this section).

(b) The exceptions referred to in paragraph (a) of this section are as follows (see, however, the limitations set forth in § 1.674(d)-2):

(1) Powers to apply income to support of a dependent. Section 674(b)(1) provides, in effect, that regardless of the general rule of section 674(a), the income of a trust will not be considered as taxable to the grantor merely because in the discretion of any person (other than a grantor who is not acting as a trustee or co-trustee) it may be used for the support of a beneficiary whom the grantor is legally obligated to support, except to the extent that it is in fact used for that purpose. See section 677(b) and the regulations thereunder.

(2) Powers affecting beneficial enjoyment only after a period. Section 674(b)(2) provides an exception to section 674(a) if the exercise of a power can only affect the beneficial enjoyment of the income of a trust received after a period of time which is such that a grantor would not be treated as an owner under section 673 if the power were a reversionary interest. See §§ 1.673(a)-1 and 1.673(b)-1. For example, if a trust created on January 1, 1955, provides for the payment of income to the grantor's son, and the grantor reserves the power to substitute other beneficiaries of income or corpus in lieu of his son on or after January 1, 1965, the grantor is not treated under section 674 as the owner of the trust with respect to ordinary income received before January 1, 1965. But the grantor will be treated as an owner on and after that date unless the power is relinquished. If the beginning of the period during which the grantor may substitute beneficiaries is postponed, the rules set forth in § 1.673(d)-1 are applicable in order to determine whether the grantor should be treated as an owner during the period following the postponement.

(3) Testamentary powers. Under paragraph (3) of section 674(b) a power in any person to control beneficial enjoyment exercisable only by will does not cause a grantor to be treated as an owner under section 674(a). However, this exception does not apply to income accumulated for testamentary disposition by the grantor or to income which may be accumulated for such distribution in the discretion of the grantor or a nonadverse party, or both, without the approval or consent of any adverse party. For example, if a trust instrument provides that the income is to be accumulated during the grantor's life and that the grantor may appoint the accumulated income by will, the grantor is treated as the owner of the trust. Moreover, if a trust instrument provides that the income is payable to another person for his life, but the grantor has a testamentary power of appointment over the remainder, and under the trust instrument and local law capital gains are added to corpus, the grantor is treated as the owner of a portion of the trust and capital gains and losses are included in that portion. (See § 1.671-3.)

(4) Powers to determine beneficial enjoyment of charitable beneficiaries. Under paragraph (4) of section 674(b) a power in any person to determine the beneficial enjoyment of corpus or income which is irrevocably payable (currently or in the future) for purposes specified in section 170(c) (relating to definition of charitable contributions) will not cause the grantor to be treated as an owner under section 674(a). For example, if a grantor creates a trust, the income of which is irrevocably payable solely to educational or other organizations that qualify under section 170(c), he is not treated as an owner under section 674 although he retains the power to allocate the income among such organizations.

(5) Powers to distribute corpus. Paragraph (5) of section 674(b) provides an exception to section 674(a) for powers to distribute corpus, subject to certain limitations, as follows:

(i) If the power is limited by a reasonably definite standard which is set forth in the trust instrument, it may extend to corpus distributions to any beneficiary or beneficiaries or class of beneficiaries (whether income beneficiaries or remaindermen) without causing the grantor to be treated as an owner under section 674. See section 674(b)(5)(A). It is not required that the standard consist of the needs and circumstances of the beneficiary. A clearly measurable standard under which the holder of a power is legally accountable is deemed a reasonably definite standard for this purpose. For instance, a power to distribute corpus for the education, support, maintenance, or health of the beneficiary; for his reasonable support and comfort; or to enable him to maintain his accustomed standard of living; or to meet an emergency, would be limited by a reasonably definite standard. However, a power to distribute corpus for the pleasure, desire, or happiness of a beneficiary is not limited by a reasonably definite standard. The entire context of a provision of a trust instrument granting a power must be considered in determining whether the power is limited by a reasonably definite standard. For example, if a trust instrument provides that the determination of the trustee shall be conclusive with respect to the exercise or nonexercise of a power, the power is not limited by a reasonably definite standard. However, the fact that the governing instrument is phrased in discretionary terms is not in itself an indication that no reasonably definite standard exists.

(ii) If the power is not limited by a reasonably definite standard set forth in the trust instrument, the exception applies only if distributions of corpus may be made solely in favor of current income beneficiaries, and any corpus distribution to the current income beneficiary must be chargeable against the proportionate part of corpus held in trust for payment of income to that beneficiary as if it constituted a separate trust (whether or not physically segregated). See section 674(b)(5)(B).

(iii) This subparagraph may be illustrated by the following examples:

Example (1). A trust instrument provides for payment of the income to the grantor's two brothers for life, and for payment of the corpus to the grantor's nephews in equal shares. The grantor reserves the power to distribute corpus to pay medical expenses that may be incurred by his brothers or nephews. The grantor is not treated as an owner by reason of this power because section 674(b)(5)(A) excepts a power, exercisable by any person, to invade corpus for any beneficiary, including a remainderman, if the power is limited by a reasonably definite standard which is set forth in the trust instrument. However, if the power were also exercisable in favor of a person (for example, a sister) who was not otherwise a beneficiary of the trust, section 674(b)(5)(A) would not be applicable.

Example (2). The facts are the same as in example (1) except that the grantor reserves the power to distribute any part of the corpus to his brothers or to his nephews for their happiness. The grantor is treated as the owner of the trust. Paragraph (5)(A) of section 674(b) is inapplicable because the power is not limited by a reasonably definite standard. Paragraph (5)(B) is inapplicable because the power to distribute corpus permits a distribution of corpus to persons other than current income beneficiaries.

Example (3). A trust instrument provides for payment of the income to the grantor's two adult sons in equal shares for 10 years, after which the corpus is to be distributed to his grandchildren in equal shares. The grantor reserves the power to pay over to each son up to one-half of the corpus during the 10-year period, but any such payment shall proportionately reduce subsequent income and corpus payments made to the son receiving the corpus. Thus, if one-half of the corpus is paid to one son, all the income from the remaining half is thereafter payable to the other son. The grantor is not treated as an owner under section 674(a) by reason of this power because it qualifies under the exception of section 674(b)(5)(B).

(6) Powers to withhold income temporarily. (i) Section 674(b)(6) excepts a power which, in general, enables the holder merely to effect a postponement in the time when the ordinary income is enjoyed by a current income beneficiary. Specifically, there is excepted a power to distribute or apply ordinary income to or for a current income beneficiary or to accumulate the income, if the accumulated income must ultimately be payable either:

(a) To the beneficiary from whom it was withheld, his estate, or his appointees (or persons designated by name, as a class, or otherwise as alternate takers in default of appointment) under a power of appointment held by the beneficiary which does not exclude from the class of possible appointees any person other than the beneficiary, his estate, his creditors, or the creditors of his estate (section 674(b)(6)(A));

(b) To the beneficiary from whom it was withheld, or if he does not survive a date of distribution which could reasonably be expected to occur within his lifetime, to his appointees (or alternate takers in default of appointment) under any power of appointment, general or special, or if he has no power of appointment to one or more designated alternate takers (other than the grantor or the grantor's estate) whose shares have been irrevocably specified in the trust instrument (section 674(b)(6)(A) and the flush material following); or

(c) On termination of the trust, or in conjunction with a distribution of corpus which is augmented by the accumulated income, to the current income beneficiaries in shares which have been irrevocably specified in the trust instrument, or if any beneficiary does not survive a date of distribution which would reasonably be expected to occur within his lifetime, to his appointees (or alternate takers in default of appointment) under any power of appointment, general or special, or if he has no power of appointment to one or more designated alternate takers (other than the grantor or the grantor's estate) whose shares have been irrevocably specified in the trust instrument (section 674(b)(6)(B) and the flush material following). (In the application of (a) of this subdivision, if the accumulated income of a trust is ultimately payable to the estate of the current income beneficiary, or is ultimately payable to his appointees, or takers in default of appointment, under a power of the type described in (a) of this subdivision, it need not be payable to the beneficiary from whom it was withheld under any circumstances. Furthermore, if a trust otherwise qualifies for the exception in (a) of this subdivision the trust income will not be considered to be taxable to the grantor under section 677 by reason of the existence of the power of appointment referred to in (a) of this subdivision.) In general, the exception in section 674(b)(6) is not applicable if the power is in substance one to shift ordinary income from one beneficiary to another. Thus, a power will not qualify for this exception if ordinary income may be distributed to beneficiary A, or may be added to corpus which is ultimately payable to beneficiary B, a remainderman who is not a current income beneficiary. However, section 674(b)(6)(B), and (c) of this subdivision, permit a limited power to shift ordinary income among current income beneficiaries, as illustrated in example (1) of this subparagraph.

(ii) The application of section 674(b)(6) may be illustrated by the following examples:

Example (1). A trust instrument provides that the income shall be paid in equal shares to the grantor's two adult daughters but the grantor reserves the power to withhold from either beneficiary any part of that beneficiary's share of income and to add it to the corpus of the trust until the younger daughter reaches the age of 30 years. When the younger daughter reaches the age of 30, the trust is to terminate and the corpus is to be divided equally between the two daughters or their estates. Although exercise of this power may permit the shifting of accumulated income from one beneficiary to the other (since the corpus with the accumulations is to be divided equally) the power is excepted under section 674(b)(6)(B) and subdivision (i)(c) of this subparagraph.

Example (2). The facts are the same as in example (1), except that the grantor of the trust reserves the power to distribute accumulated income to the beneficiaries in such shares as he chooses. The combined powers are not excepted by section 674(b)(6)(B) since income accumulated pursuant to the first power is neither required to be payable only in conjunction with a corpus distribution nor required to be payable in shares specified in the trust instrument. See, however, section 674(c) and § 1.674(c)-1 for the effect of such a power if it is exercisable only by independent trustees.

Example (3). A trust provides for payment of income to the grantor's adult son with the grantor retaining the power to accumulate the income until the grantor's death, when all accumulations are to be paid to the son. If the son predeceases the grantor, all accumulations are, at the death of the grantor, to be paid to his daughter, or if she is not living, to alternate takers (which do not include the grantor's estate) in specified shares. The power is excepted under section 674(b)(6)(A) since the date of distribution (the date of the grantor's death) may, in the usual case, reasonably be expected to occur during the beneficiary's (the son's) lifetime. It is not necessary that the accumulations be payable to the son's estate or his appointees if he should predecease the grantor for this exception to apply.

(7) Power to withhold income during disability. Section 674(b)(7) provides an exception for a power which, in general, will permit ordinary income to be withheld during the legal disability of an income beneficiary or while he is under 21. Specifically, there is excepted a power, exercisable only during the existence of a legal disability of any current income beneficiary or the period during which any income beneficiary is under the age of 21 years, to distribute or apply ordinary income to or for that beneficiary or to accumulate the income and add it to corpus. To qualify under this exception it is not necessary that the income ultimately be payable to the income beneficiary from whom it was withheld, his estate, or his appointees; that is, the accumulated income may be added to corpus and ultimately distributed to others. For example, the grantor is not treated as an owner under section 674 if the income of a trust is payable to his son for life, remainder to his grandchildren, although he reserves the power to accumulate income and add it to corpus while his son is under 21.

(8) Powers to allocate between corpus and income. Paragraph (8) of section 674(b) provides that a power to allocate receipts and disbursements between corpus and income, even though expressed in broad language, will not cause the grantor to be treated as an owner under the general rule of section 674(a).

T.D. 6217, 12/19/56.

§ 1.674(c)-1 Excepted powers exercisable only by independent trustees.

Caution: The Treasury has not yet amended Reg § 1.674(c)-1 to reflect changes made by P.L. 100-647, P.L. 99-514.

Section 674(c) provides an exception to the general rule of section 674(a) for certain powers that are exercisable by independent trustees. This exception is in addition to those provided for under section 674(b) which may be held by any person including an independent trustee. The powers to which section 674(c) apply are powers (a) to distribute, apportion, or accumulate income to or for a beneficiary or beneficiaries, or to, for, or within a class of beneficiaries, or (b) to pay out corpus to or for a beneficiary or beneficiaries or to or for a class of beneficiaries (whether or not income beneficiaries). In order for such a power to fall within the exception of section 674(c) it must be exercisable solely (without the approval or consent of any other person) by a trustee or trustees none of whom is the grantor and no more than half of whom are related or subordinate parties who are subservient to the wishes of the grantor. (See section 672(c) for definitions of these terms.) An example of the application of section 674(c) is a trust whose income is payable to the grantor's three adult sons with power in an independent trustee to allocate without restriction the amounts of income to be paid to each son each year. Such a power does not cause the grantor to be treated as the owner of the trust. See, however, the limitations set forth in § 1.674(d)-2.

T.D. 6217, 12/19/56.

§ 1.674(d)-1 Excepted powers exercisable by any trustee other than grantor or spouse.

Caution: The Treasury has not yet amended Reg § 1.674(d)-1 to reflect changes made by P.L. 100-647, P.L. 99-514.

Section 674(d) provides an additional exception to the general rule of section 674(a) for a power to distribute, apportion, or accumulate income to or for a beneficiary or beneficiaries or to, for, or within a class of beneficiaries, whether or not the conditions of section 674(b)(6) or (7) are satisfied, if the power is solely exercisable (without the approval or consent of any other person) by a trustee or trustees none of whom is the grantor or spouse living with the grantor, and if the power is limited by a reasonably definite external standard set forth in the trust instrument (see paragraph (b)(5) of § 1.674(b)-1 with respect to what constitutes a reasonably definite standard). See, however, the limitations set forth in § 1.674(d)-2.

T.D. 6217, 12/19/56.

§ 1.674(d)-2 Limitations on exceptions in section 674(b), (c), and (d).

Caution: The Treasury has not yet amended Reg § 1.674(d)-2 to reflect changes made by P.L. 100-647, P.L. 99-514.

(a) Power to remove trustee. A power in the grantor to remove, substitute, or add trustees (other than a power exercisable only upon limited conditions which do not exist during the taxable year, such as the death or resignation of, or breach of fiduciary duty by, an existing trustee) may prevent a trust from qualifying under section 674(c) or (d). For example, if a grantor has an unrestricted power to remove an independent trustee and substitute any person including himself as trustee, the trust will not qualify under section 674(c) or (d). On the other hand if the grantor's power to remove, substitute, or add trustees is limited so that its exercise could not alter the trust in a manner that would disqualify it under section 674(c) or (d), as the case may be, the power itself does not disqualify the trust. Thus, for example, a power in the grantor to remove or discharge an independent trustee on the condition that he substitute another independent trustee will not prevent a trust from qualifying under section 674(c).

(b) Power to add beneficiaries. The exceptions described in section 674(b)(5), (6), and (7), (c), and (d) are not applicable if any person has a power to add to the beneficiary or beneficiaries or to a class of beneficiaries designated to receive the income or corpus, except where the action is to provide for after-born or after-adopted children. This limitation does not apply to a power held by a beneficiary to substitute other beneficiaries to succeed to his interest in the trust (so that he would be an adverse party as to the exercise or nonexercise of that power). For example, the limitation does not apply to a power in a beneficiary of a nonspendthrift trust to assign his interest. Nor does the limitation apply to a power held by any person which would qualify as an exception under section 674(b)(3) (relating to testamentary powers).

T.D. 6217, 12/19/56.

§ 1.675-1 Administrative powers.

Caution: The Treasury has not yet amended Reg § 1.675-1 to reflect changes made by P.L. 100-647, P.L. 99-514.

(a) General rule. Section 675 provides in effect that the grantor is treated as the owner of any portion of a trust if under the terms of the trust instrument or circumstances attendant on its operation administrative control is exercisable primarily for the benefit of the grantor rather than the beneficiaries of the trust. If a grantor retains a power to amend the administrative provisions of a trust instrument which is broad enough to permit an amendment causing the grantor to be treated as the owner of a portion of the trust under section 675, he will be treated as the owner of the portion from its inception. See section 671 and §§ 1.671-2 and 1.671-3 for rules for treatment of items of income, deduction, and credit when a person is treated as the owner of all or only a portion of a trust.

(b) Prohibited controls. The circumstances which cause administrative controls to be considered exercisable primarily for the benefit of the grantor are specifically described in paragraphs (1) through (4) of section 675 as follows:

(1) The existence of a power, exercisable by the grantor or a nonadverse party, or both, without the approval or consent of any adverse party, which enables the grantor or any other person to purchase, exchange, or otherwise deal with or dispose of the corpus or the income of the trust for less than adequate consideration in money or money's worth. Whether the existence of the power itself will constitute the holder an adverse party will depend on the particular circumstances.

(2) The existence of a power exercisable by the grantor or a nonadverse party, or both, which enables the grantor to borrow the corpus or income of the trust, directly or indirectly, without adequate interest or adequate security. However, this paragraph does not apply where a trustee (other than the grantor acting alone) is authorized under a general lending power to make loans to any person without regard to interest or security. A general lending power in the grantor, acting alone as trustee, under which he has power to determine interest rates and the adequacy of security is not in itself an indication that the grantor has power to borrow the corpus or income without adequate interest or security.

(3) The circumstance that the grantor has directly or indirectly borrowed the corpus or income of the trust and has not completely repaid the loan, including any interest, before the beginning of the taxable year. The preceding sentence does not apply to a loan which provides for adequate interest and adequate security, if it is made by a trustee other than the grantor or a related or subordinate trustee subservient to the grantor. See section 672(c) for definition of "a related or subordinate party".

(4) The existence of certain powers of administration exercisable in a nonfiduciary capacity by any nonadverse party without the approval or consent of any person in a fiduciary capacity. The term "powers of administration" means one or more of the following powers:

(i) A power to vote or direct the voting of stock or other securities of a corporation in which the holdings of the grantor and the trust are significant from the viewpoint of voting control;

(ii) A power to control the investment of the trust funds either by directing investments or reinvestments, or by vetoing proposed investments or reinvestments, to the extent that the trust funds consist of stocks or securities of corporations in which the holdings of the grantor and the trust are significant from the viewpoint of voting control; or

(iii) A power to reacquire the trust corpus by substituting other property of an equivalent value. If a power is exercisable by a person as trustee, it is presumed that the power is exercisable in a fiduciary capacity primarily in the interests of the beneficiaries. This presumption may be rebutted only by clear and convincing proof that the power is not exercisable primarily in the interests of the beneficiaries. If a power is not exercisable by a person as trustee, the determination of whether the power is exercisable in a fiduciary or a nonfiduciary capacity depends on all the terms of the trust and the circumstances surrounding its creation and administration.

(c) Authority of trustee. The mere fact that a power exercisable by a trustee is described in broad language does not indicate that the trustee is authorized to purchase, exchange, or otherwise deal with or dispose of the trust property or income for less than an adequate and full consideration in money or money's worth, or is authorized to lend the trust property or income to the grantor without adequate interest. On the other hand, such authority may be indicated by the actual administration of the trust.

T.D. 6217, 12/19/56.

§ 1.676(a)-1 Power to revest title to portion of trust property in grantor; general rule.

Caution: The Treasury has not yet amended Reg § 1.676(a)-1 to reflect changes made by P.L. 100-647, P.L. 99-514.

If a power to revest in the grantor title to any portion of a trust is exercisable by the grantor or a nonadverse party, or both, without the approval or consent of an adverse party, the grantor is treated as the owner of that portion, except as provided in section 676(b) (relating to powers affecting beneficial enjoyment of income only after the expiration of certain periods of time). If the title to a portion of the trust will revest in the grantor upon the exercise of a power by the grantor or a nonadverse party, or both, the grantor is treated as the owner of that portion regardless of whether the power is a power to revoke, to terminate, to alter or amend, or to appoint. See section 671 and §§ 1.671-2 and 1.671-3 for rules for treatment of items of income, deduction, and credit when a person is treated as the owner of all or only a portion of a trust.

T.D. 6217, 12/19/56.

§ 1.676(b)-1 Powers exercisable only after a period of time.

Caution: The Treasury has not yet amended Reg § 1.676(b)-1 to reflect changes made by P.L. 100-647, P.L. 99-514.

Section 676(b) provides an exception to the general rule of section 676(a) when the exercise of a power can only affect the beneficial enjoyment of the income of a trust received after the expiration of a period of time which is such that a grantor would not be treated as an owner under section 673 if the power were a reversionary interest. See §§ 1.673(a)-1 and 1.673(b)-1. Thus, for example, a grantor is excepted from the general rule of section 676(a) with respect to ordinary income if exercise of a power to revest corpus in him cannot affect the beneficial enjoyment of the income received within 10 years after the date of transfer of that portion of the trust. It is immaterial for this purpose that the power is vested at the time of the transfer. However, the grantor is subject to the general rule of section 676(a) after the expiration of the period unless the power is relinquished. Thus, in the above example, the grantor may be treated as the owner and be taxed on all income in the eleventh and succeeding years if exercise of the power can affect beneficial enjoyment of income received in those years. If the beginning of the period during which the grantor may revest is postponed, the rules set forth in § 1.673(d)-1 are applicable to determine whether the grantor should be treated as an owner during the period following the postponement.

T.D. 6217, 12/19/56.

§ 1.677(a)-1 Income for benefit of grantor; general rule.

Caution: The Treasury has not yet amended Reg § 1.677(a)-1 to reflect changes made by P.L. 100-647, P.L. 99-514.

(a) *(1) Scope.* Section 677 deals with the treatment of the grantor of a trust as the owner of a portion of the trust because he has retained an interest in the income from that portion. For convenience, "grantor" and "spouse" are generally referred to in the masculine and feminine genders, respectively, but if the grantor is a woman the reference to "grantor" is to her and the reference to "spouse" is to her husband. Section 677 also deals with the treatment of the grantor of a trust as the owner of a portion of the trust because the income from property transferred in trust after October 9, 1969, or may be, distributed to his spouse or applied to the payment of premiums on policies of insurance on the life of his spouse. However, section 677 does not apply when the income of a trust is taxable to a grantor's spouse under section 71 (relating to alimony and separate maintenance payments) or section 682 (relating to income of an estate or trust in case of divorce, etc.). See section 671-1(b).

(2) Cross references. See section 671 and §§ 1.671-2 and 1.671-3 for rules for treatment of items of income, deduction, and credit when a person is treated as the owner of all or a portion of a trust.

(b) Income for benefit of grantor or his spouse; general rule. *(1) Property transferred in trust prior to October 10, 1969.* With respect to property transferred in trust prior to October 10, 1969, the grantor is treated, under section 677, in any taxable year as the owner (whether or not he is treated as an owner under section 674) of a portion of a trust of which the income for the taxable year or for a period not within the exception described in paragraph (e) of this section is, or in the discretion of the grantor or a nonadverse party, or both (without the approval or consent of any adverse party) may be:

(i) Distributed to the grantor;

(ii) Held or accumulated for future distribution to the grantor; or

(iii) Applied to the payment or premiums on policies of insurance on the life of the grantor, except policies of insurance irrevocably payable for a charitable purpose specified in section 170(c).

(2) Property transferred in trust after October 9, 1969. With respect to property transferred in trust after October 9, 1969, the grantor is treated, under section 677, in any taxable year as the owner (whether or not he is treated as an owner under section 674) of a portion of a trust of which the income for the taxable year or for a period not within the exception described in paragraph (e) of this section is, or in the discretion of the grantor, or his spouse, or a nonadverse party, or any combination thereof (without the approval or consent of any adverse party other than the grantor's spouse) may be:

(i) Distributed to the grantor or the grantor's spouse;

(ii) Held or accumulated for future distribution to the grantor or the grantor's spouse; or

(iii) Applied to the payment of premiums on policies of insurance on the life of the grantor or the grantor's spouse, except policies of insurance irrevocably payable for a charitable purpose specified in section 170(c).

With respect to the treatment of a grantor as the owner of a portion of a trust solely because its income is, or may be, distributed or held or accumulated for future distributions to a beneficiary who is his spouse or applied to the payment of premiums for insurance on the spouse's life, section 677(a) applies to the income of a trust solely during the period of the marriage of the grantor to a beneficiary. In the case of divorce or separation, see sections 71 and 682 and the regulations thereunder.

(c) Constructive distribution; cessation of interest. Under section 677 the grantor is treated as the owner of a portion of a trust if he has retained any interest which might, without the approval or consent of an adverse party, enable him to have the income from that portion, distributed to him at some time, either actually or constructively (subject to the exception described in paragraph (e) of this section). In the case of a transfer in trust after October 9, 1969, the grantor is also treated as the owner of a portion of a trust if he has granted or retained any interest which might, without the approval or consent of an adverse party (other than the grantor's spouse), enable his spouse to have the income from the portion at some time, whether or not within the grantor's lifetime, distributed to the spouse either actually or constructively. See paragraph (b)(2) of this section for additional rules relating to the income of a trust prior to the grantor's marriage to a beneficiary. Constructive distribution to the grantor or to his spouse includes payment on behalf of the grantor or his spouse to another in obedience to his or her direction and payment of premiums upon policies of insurance on the grantor's, or his spouse's, life (other than policies of insurance irrevocably payable for charitable purposes specified in section 170(c)). If the grantor (in the case of property transferred prior to Oct. 10, 1969) or the grantor and his spouse (in the case of property transferred after Oct. 9, 1969) are divested permanently and completely of every interest described in this paragraph, the grantor is not treated as an owner under section 677 after that divesting. The word "interest" as used in this paragraph does not include the possibility that the grantor or his spouse might receive back from a beneficiary an interest in a trust by inheritance. Further, with respect to transfers in trust prior to October 10, 1969, the word "interest" does not include the possibility that the grantor might receive back from a beneficiary an interest in a trust as a surviving spouse under a statutory right of election or a similar right.

(d) Discharge of legal obligation of grantor or his spouse. Under section 677 a grantor is, in general, treated as owner of a portion of a trust whose income is, or in the discretion of the grantor or a nonadverse party, or both, may be applied in discharge of a legal obligation of the grantor (or his spouse in the case of property transferred in trust by the grantor after October 9, 1969). However, see § 1.677(b)-1 for special rules for trusts whose income may not be applied for the discharge of any legal obligation of the grantor or the grantor's spouse other than the support or maintenance of a beneficiary (other than the grantor's spouse) whom the grantor is legally obligated to support. See § 301.7701-4(e) of this chapter for rules on the classification of and application of section 677 to an environmental remediation trust.

(e) Exception for certain discretionary rights affecting income. The last sentence of section 677(a) provides that a grantor shall not be treated as the owner when a discretionary right can only affect the beneficial enjoyment of the income of a trust received after a period of time during which a grantor would not be treated as an owner under section 673 if the power were a reversionary interest. See §§ 1.673(a)-1 and 1.673(b)-1. For example, if the ordinary income of a trust is payable to B for 10 years and then in the grantor's discretion income or corpus may be paid to B or to the grantor (or his spouse in the case of property transferred in trust by the grantor after October 9, 1969), the grantor is not treated as an owner with respect to ordinary income under section 677 during the first 10 years. He will be treated as an owner under section 677 after the expiration of the 10-year period unless the power is relinquished. If the beginning of the period during which the grantor may substitute beneficiaries is postponed, the rules set forth in § 1.673(d)-1 are applicable in determining whether the grantor should be treated as an owner during the period following the postponement.

(f) Accumulation of income. If income is accumulated in any taxable year for future distribution to the grantor (or his spouse in the case of property transferred in trust by the grantor after Oct. 9, 1969), section 677(a)(2) treats the grantor as an owner for that taxable year. The exception set forth in the last sentence of section 677(a) does not apply merely because the grantor (or his spouse in the case of property transferred in trust by the grantor after Oct. 9, 1969) must await the expiration of a period of time before he or she can receive or exercise discretion over previously accumulated income of the trust, even though the period is such that the grantor would not be treated as an owner under section 673 if a reversionary interest were involved. Thus, if income (including capital gains) of a trust is to be accumulated for 10 years and then will be, or at the discretion of the grantor, or his spouse in the case of property transferred in trust after October 9, 1969, or a nonadverse party, may be, distributed to the grantor (or his spouse in the case of property transferred in trust after Oct. 9, 1969), the grantor is treated as the owner of the trust from its inception. If income attributable to transfers after October 9, 1969 is accumulated in any taxable year during the grantor's lifetime for future distribution to his spouse, section 677(a)(2) treats the grantor as an owner for that taxable year even though his spouse may not receive or exercise discretion over such income prior to the grantor's death.

(g) Examples. The application of section 677(a) may be illustrated by the following examples:

Example (1). G creates an irrevocable trust which provides that the ordinary income is to be payable to him for life and that on his death the corpus shall be distributed to B, an unrelated person. Except for the right to receive income, G retains no right or power which would cause him to be treated as an owner under sections 671 through 677. Under the applicable local law capital gains must be applied to corpus. During the taxable year 1970 the trust has the following items of gross income and deductions:

Dividends	$5,000
Capital gain	1,000
Expenses allocable to income	200
Expenses allocable to corpus	100

Since G has a right to receive income he is treated as an owner of a portion of the trust under section 677. Accordingly, he should include the $5,000 of dividends, $200 income expense, and $100 corpus expense in the computation of his taxable income for 1970. He should not include the $1,000 capital gain since that is not attributable to the portion of the trust that he owns. See § 1.671-3(b). The tax consequences of the capital gain are governed by the provisions of subparts A, B, C, and D (section 641 and following), part I, subchapter J, chapter 1 of the Code. Had the trust sustained a capital loss in any amount the loss would likewise not be included in the computation of G's taxable income, but would also be governed by the provisions of such subparts.

Example (2). G creates a trust which provides that the ordinary income is payable to his adult son. Ten years and one day from the date of transfer or on the death of his son, whichever is earlier, corpus is to revert to G. In addition, G retains a discretionary right to receive $5,000 of ordinary income each year. (Absent the exercise of this right all the ordinary income is to be distributed to his son.) G retained no other right or power which would cause him to be treated as an owner under subpart E (section 671 and following). Under the terms of the trust instrument and applicable local law capital gains must be applied to corpus. During the taxable year 1970 the trust had the following items of income and deductions:

Dividends	$10,000
Capital gain	2,000
Expenses allocable to income	400
Expenses allocable to corpus	200

Since the capital gain is held or accumulated for future distributions to G, he is treated under section 677(a)(2) as an owner of a portion of the trust to which the gain is attributable. See § 1.671-3(b).

Therefore, he must include the capital gain in the computation of his taxable income. (Had the trust sustained a capital loss in any amount, G would likewise include that loss in the computation of his taxable income.) In addition, because of G's discretionary right (whether exercised or not) he is treated as the owner of a portion of the trust which will permit a distribution of income to him of $5,000. Accordingly, G includes dividends of $5,208.33 and income expenses of $208.33 in computing his taxable income, determined in the following manner:

Total dividends	$10,000.00
Less:	
Expenses allocable to income	400.00
Distributable income of the trust	9,600.00
Portion of dividends attributable to G (5,000/9,600 × $10,000)	5,208.33
Portion of income expenses attributable to G (5,000/9,600 × $400)	208.33
Amount of income subject to discretionary right	5,000.00

In accordance with paragraph 1.671-3(c), G also takes into account $104.17 (5,000/9,600 × $200) of corpus expenses in computing his tax liability. The portion of the dividends and expenses of the trust not attributable to G are governed by the provisions of subparts A through D.

T.D. 6217, 12/19/56, amend T.D. 7148, 10/28/71, T.D. 8668, 4/30/96.

§ 1.677(b)-1 Trusts for support.

Caution: The Treasury has not yet amended Reg § 1.677(b)-1 to reflect changes made by P.L. 100-647, P.L. 99-514.

(a) Section 677(b) provides that a grantor is not treated as the owner of a trust merely because its income may in the discretion of any person other than the grantor (except when he is acting as trustee or cotrustee) be applied or distributed for the support or maintenance of a beneficiary (other than the grantor's spouse in the case of income from property transferred in trust after October 9, 1969), such as the child of the grantor, whom the grantor or his spouse is legally obligated to support. If income of the current year of the trust is actually so applied or distributed the grantor may be treated as the owner of any portion of the trust under section 677 to that extent, even though it might have been applied or distributed for other purposes. In the case of property transferred to a trust before October 10, 1969, for the benefit of the grantor's spouse, the grantor may be treated as the owner to the extent income of the current year is actually applied for the support or maintenance of his spouse.

(b) If any amount applied or distributed for the support of a beneficiary including the grantor's spouse in the case of property transferred in trust before October 10, 1969, whom the grantor is legally obligated to support is paid out of corpus or out of other than income of the current year, the grantor is treated as a beneficiary of the trust, and the amount applied or distributed is considered to be an amount paid within the meaning of section 661(a)(2), taxable to the grantor under section 662. Thus, he is subject to the other relevant portions of subparts A through D (section 641 and following), part I, subchapter J, chapter 1 of the Code. Accordingly, the grantor may be taxed on an accumulation distribution or a capital gain distribution under subpart D (section 665 and following) of such part I. Those provisions, including the exceptions in section 665, are applied on the basis that the grantor is the beneficiary.

(c) For the purpose of determining the items of income, deduction, and credit of a trust to be included under this section in computing the grantor's tax liability, the income of the trust for the taxable year of distribution will be deemed to have been first distributed. For example, in the case of a trust reporting on the calendar year basis, a distribution made on January 1, 1956, will be deemed to have been made out of ordinary income of the trust for the calendar year 1956 to the extent of the income for that year even though the trust had received no income as of January 1, 1956. Thus, if a distribution of $10,000 is made on January 1, 1956, for the support of the grantor's dependent, the grantor will be treated as the owner of the trust for 1956 to that extent. If the trust received dividends of $5,000 and incurred expenses of $1,000 during that year but subsequent to January 1, he will take into account dividends of $5,000 and expenses of $1,000 in computing his tax liability for 1956. In addition, the grantor will be treated as a beneficiary of the trust with respect to the $6,000 ($10,000 less distributable income of $4,000 (dividends of $5,000 less expenses of $1,000)) paid out of corpus or out of other than income of the current year. See paragraph (b) of this section.

(d) The exception provided in section 677(b) relates solely to the satisfaction of the grantor's legal obligation to support or maintain a beneficiary. Consequently, the general rule of section 677(a) is applicable when in the discretion of the grantor or nonadverse parties income of a trust may be applied in discharge of a grantor's obligations other than his obligation of support or maintenance falling within section 677(b). Thus, if the grantor creates a trust the income of which may in the discretion of a nonadverse party be applied in the payment of the grantor's debts, such as the payment of his rent or other household expenses, he is treated as an owner of the trust regardless of whether the income is actually so applied.

(e) The general rule of section 677(a), and not section 677(b), is applicable if discretion to apply or distribute income of a trust rests solely in the grantor, or in the grantor in conjunction with other persons, unless in either case the grantor has such discretion as trustee or cotrustee.

(f) The general rule of section 677(a), and not section 677(b), is applicable to the extent that income is required, without any discretionary determination, to be applied to the support of a beneficiary whom the grantor is legally obligated to support.

T.D. 6217, 12/19/56, amend T.D. 7148, 10/28/71.

§ 1.678(a)-1 Person other than grantor treated as substantial owner; general rule.

Caution: The Treasury has not yet amended Reg § 1.678(a)-1 to reflect changes made by P.L. 100-647, P.L. 99-514.

(a) Where a person other than the grantor of a trust has a power exercisable solely by himself to vest the corpus or the income of any portion of a testamentary or inter vivos trust in himself, he is treated under section 678(a) as the owner of that portion, except as provided in section 678(b) (involving taxation of the grantor) and section 678(c) (involving an obligation of support). The holder of such a power also is treated as an owner of the trust even though he has partially released or otherwise modified the power so that he can no longer vest the corpus or income in himself, if he has retained such control of the trust as would, if retained by a grantor, subject the grantor to treatment as the owner under sections 671 to 677, inclusive. See section 671 and §§ 1.671-2 and 1.671-3 for rules for treatment of items of income, deduction, and credit where a person is treated as the owner of all or only a portion of a trust.

(b) Section 678(a) treats a person as an owner of a trust if he has a power exercisable solely by himself to apply the income or corpus for the satisfaction of his legal obligations, other than an obligation to support a dependent (see § 1.678(c)-1) subject to the limitation of section 678(b). Section 678 does not apply if the power is not exercisable solely by himself. However, see § 1.662(a)-4 for principles applicable to income of a trust which, pursuant to the terms of the trust instrument, is used to satisfy the obligations of a person other than the grantor.

T.D. 6217, 12/19/56.

§ 1.678(b)-1 If grantor is treated as the owner.

Caution: The Treasury has not yet amended Reg § 1.678(b)-1 to reflect changes made by P.L. 94-455.

Section 678(a) does not apply with respect to a power over income, as originally granted or thereafter modified, if the grantor of the trust is treated as the owner under sections 671 to 677, inclusive.

T.D. 6217, 12/19/56.

§ 1.678(c)-1 Trusts for support.

Caution: The Treasury has not yet amended Reg § 1.678(c)-1 to reflect changes made by P.L. 94-455.

(a) Section 678(a) does not apply to a power which enables the holder, in the capacity of trustee or cotrustee, to apply the income of the trust to the support or maintenance of a person whom the holder is obligated to support, except to the extent the income is so applied. See paragraphs (a), (b), and (c) of § 1.677(b)-1 for applicable principles where any amount is applied for the support or maintenance of a person whom the holder is obligated to support.

(b) The general rule in section 678(a) (and not the exception in section 678(c)) is applicable in any case in which the holder of a power exercisable solely by himself is able, in any capacity other than that of trustee or cotrustee, to apply the income in discharge of his obligation of support or maintenance.

(c) Section 678(c) is concerned with the taxability of income subject to a power described in section 678(a). It has no application to the taxability of income which is either required to be applied pursuant to the terms of the trust instrument or is applied pursuant to a power which is not described in section 678(a), the taxability of such income being governed by other provisions of the Code. See § 1.662(a)-4.

T.D. 6217, 12/19/56.

§ 1.678(d)-1 Renunciation of power.

Caution: The Treasury has not yet amended Reg § 1.678(d)-1 to reflect changes made by P.L. 94-455.

Section 678(a) does not apply to a power which has been renounced or disclaimed within a reasonable time after the holder of the power first became aware of its existence.

T.D. 6217, 12/19/56.

§ 1.679-0 Outline of major topics.

This section lists the major paragraphs contained in §§ 1.679-1 through 1.679-7 as follows:

§ 1.679-1 U.S. transferor treated as owner of foreign trust.

(a) In general.

(b) Interaction with sections 673 through 678.

(c) Definitions.

(1) U.S. transferor.

(2) U.S. person.

(3) Foreign trust.

(4) Property.

(5) Related person.

(6) Obligation.

(d) Examples.

§ 1.679-2 Trusts treated as having a U.S. beneficiary.

(a) Existence of U.S. beneficiary.

(1) In general.

(2) Benefit to a U.S. person.

(i) In general.

(ii) Certain unexpected beneficiaries.

(iii) Examples.

(3) Changes in beneficiary's status.

(i) In general.

(ii) Examples.

(4) General rules.

(i) Records and documents.

(ii) Additional factors.

(iii) Examples.

(b) Indirect U.S. beneficiaries.

(1) Certain foreign entities.

(2) Other indirect beneficiaries.

(3) Examples.

(c) Treatment of U.S. transferor upon foreign trust's acquisition or loss of U.S. beneficiary.

(1) Trusts acquiring a U.S. beneficiary.

(2) Trusts ceasing to have a U.S. beneficiary.

(3) Examples.

§ 1.679-3 Transfers.

(a) In general.

(b) Transfers by certain trusts.

(1) In general.

(2) Example.

(c) Indirect transfers.

(1) Principal purpose of tax avoidance.

(2) Principal purpose of tax avoidance deemed to exist.

(3) Effect of disregarding intermediary.

(i) In general.

(ii) Special rule.

(iii) Effect on intermediary.

(4) Related parties.

(5) Examples.

(d) Constructive transfers.

(1) In general.

(2) Examples.

(e) Guarantee of trust obligations.

(1) In general.

(2) Amount transferred.

(3) Principal repayments.

(4) Guarantee.

(5) Examples.

(f) Transfers to entities owned by a foreign trust.

(1) General rule.

(2) Examples.

§ 1.679-4 Exceptions to general rule.

(a) In general.

(b) Transfers for fair market value.

(1) In general.

(2) Special rule.

(i) Transfers for partial consideration.

(ii) Example.

(c) Certain obligations not taken into account.

(d) Qualified obligations.

(1) In general.

(2) Additional loans.

(3) Obligations that cease to be qualified.

(4) Transfers resulting from failed qualified obligations.

(5) Renegotiated loans.

T.D. 8955, 7/19/2001.

§ 1.679-1 U.S. transferor treated as owner of foreign trust.

(a) In general. A U.S. transferor who transfers property to a foreign trust is treated as the owner of the portion of the trust attributable to the property transferred if there is a U.S. beneficiary of any portion of the trust, unless an exception in § 1.679-4 applies to the transfer.

(b) Interaction with sections 673 through 678. The rules of this section apply without regard to whether the U.S. transferor retains any power or interest described in sections 673 through 677. If a U.S. transferor would be treated as the owner of a portion of a foreign trust pursuant to the rules of this section and another person would be treated as the owner of the same portion of the trust pursuant to section 678, then the U.S. transferor is treated as the owner and the other person is not treated as the owner.

(c) Definitions. The following definitions apply for purposes of this section and §§ 1.679-2 through 1.679-7:

(1) U.S. transferor. The term U.S. transferor means any U.S. person who makes a transfer (as defined in § 1.679-3) of property to a foreign trust.

(2) U.S. person. The term U.S. person means a United States person as defined in section 7701(a)(30), a nonresident alien individual who elects under section 6013(g) to be treated as a resident of the United States, and an individual who is a dual resident taxpayer within the meaning of § 301.7701(b)-7(a) of this chapter.

(3) Foreign trust. Section 7701(a)(31)(B) defines the term foreign trust. See also § 301.7701-7 of this chapter.

(4) Property. The term property means any property including cash.

(5) Related person. A person is a related person if, without regard to the transfer at issue, the person is—

(i) A grantor of any portion of the trust (within the meaning of § 1.671-2(e)(1));

(ii) An owner of any portion of the trust under sections 671 through 679;

(iii) A beneficiary of the trust; or

(iv) A person who is related (within the meaning of section 643(i)(2)(B)) to any grantor, owner or beneficiary of the trust.

(6) Obligation. The term obligation means any bond, note, debenture, certificate, bill receivable, account receivable, note receivable, open account, or other evidence of indebtedness, and, to the extent not previously described, any annuity contract.

(d) Examples. The following examples illustrate the rules of paragraph (a) of this section. In these examples, A is a resident alien, B is A's son, who is a resident alien, C is A's father, who is a resident alien, D is A's uncle, who is a nonresident alien, and FT is a foreign trust. The examples are as follows:

Example (1). Interaction with section 678. A creates and funds FT. FT may provide for the education of B by paying for books, tuition, room and board. In addition, C has the power to vest the trust corpus or income in himself within the meaning of section 678(a)(1). Under paragraph (b) of this section, A is treated as the owner of the portion of FT attributable to the property transferred to FT by A and C is not treated as the owner thereof.

Example (2). U.S. person treated as owner of a portion of FT. D creates and funds FT for the benefit of B. D retains a power described in section 676 and § 1.672(f)-3(a)(1). A transfers property to FT. Under sections 676 and 672(f), D is treated as the owner of the portion of FT attributable to the property transferred by D. Under paragraph (a) of this section, A is treated as the owner of the portion of FT attributable to the property transferred by A.

T.D. 8955, 7/19/2001.

§ 1.679-2 Trusts treated as having a U.S. beneficiary.

(a) Existence of U.S. beneficiary. *(1) In general.* The determination of whether a foreign trust has a U.S. beneficiary is made on an annual basis. A foreign trust is treated as having a U.S. beneficiary unless during the taxable year of the U.S. transferor—

(i) No part of the income or corpus of the trust may be paid or accumulated to or for the benefit of, directly or indirectly, a U.S. person; and

(ii) If the trust is terminated at any time during the taxable year, no part of the income or corpus of the trust could be paid to or for the benefit of, directly or indirectly, a U.S. person.

(2) Benefit to a U.S. person. (i) In general. For purposes of paragraph (a)(1) of this section, income or corpus may be paid or accumulated to or for the benefit of a U.S. person during a taxable year of the U.S. transferor if during that year, directly or indirectly, income may be distributed to, or accumulated for the benefit of, a U.S. person, or corpus may be distributed to, or held for the future benefit of, a U.S. person. This determination is made without regard to whether income or corpus is actually distributed to a U.S. person during that year, and without regard to whether a U.S. person's interest in the trust income or corpus is contingent on a future event.

(ii) Certain unexpected beneficiaries. Notwithstanding paragraph (a)(2)(i) of this section, for purposes of paragraph (a)(1) of this section, a person who is not named as a beneficiary and is not a member of a class of beneficiaries as defined under the trust instrument is not taken into consideration if the U.S. transferor demonstrates to the satisfaction of the Commissioner that the person's contingent interest in the trust is so remote as to be negligible. The preceding sentence does not apply with respect to persons to whom distributions could be made pursuant to a grant of discretion to the trustee or any other person. A class of beneficiaries generally does not include heirs who will benefit from the trust under the laws of intestate succession in the event that the named beneficiaries (or members of the named class) have all deceased (whether or not stated as a named class in the trust instrument).

(iii) Examples. The following examples illustrate the rules of paragraphs (a)(1) and (2) of this section. In these examples, A is a resident alien, B is A's son, who is a resident alien, C is A's daughter, who is a nonresident alien, and FT is a foreign trust. The examples are as follows:

Example (1). Distribution of income to U.S. person. A transfers property to FT. The trust instrument provides that all trust income is to be distributed currently to B. Under paragraph (a)(1) of this section, FT is treated as having a U.S. beneficiary.

Example (2). Income accumulation for the benefit of a U.S. person. In 2001, A transfers property to FT. The trust instrument provides that from 2001 through 2010, the trustee of FT may distribute trust income to C or may accumulate the trust income. The trust instrument further provides that in 2011, the trust will terminate and the trustee may distribute the trust assets to either or both of B and C, in the trustee's discretion. If the trust terminates unexpectedly prior to 2011, all trust assets must be distributed to C. Because it is possible that income may be accumulated in each year, and that the accumulated income ultimately may be distributed to B, a U.S. person, under paragraph (a)(1) of this section FT is treated as having a U.S. beneficiary during each of A's tax years from 2001 through 2011. This result applies even though no U.S. person may receive distributions from the trust during the tax years 2001 through 2010.

Example (3). Corpus held for the benefit of a U.S. person. The facts are the same as in Example 2, except that from 2001 through 2011, all trust income must be distributed to C. In 2011, the trust will terminate and the trustee may distribute the trust corpus to either or both of B and C, in the trustee's discretion. If the trust terminates unexpectedly prior to 2011, all trust corpus must be distributed to C. Because during each of A's tax years from 2001 through 2011 trust corpus is held for possible future distribution to B, a U.S. person, under paragraph (a)(1) of this section FT is treated as having a U.S. beneficiary during each of those years. This result applies even though no U.S. person may receive distributions from the trust during the tax years 2001 through 2010.

Example (4). Distribution upon U.S. transferor's death. A transfers property to FT. The trust instrument provides that all trust income must be distributed currently to C and, upon A's death, the trust will terminate and the trustee may distribute the trust corpus to either or both of B and C. Because B may receive a distribution of corpus upon the termination of FT, and FT could terminate in any year, FT is treated as having a U.S. beneficiary in the year of the transfer and in subsequent years.

Example (5). Distribution after U.S. transferor's death. The facts are the same as in Example 4, except the trust instrument provides that the trust will not terminate until the year following A's death. Upon termination, the trustee may distribute the trust assets to either or both of B and C, in the trustee's discretion. All trust assets are invested in the stock of X, a foreign corporation, and X makes no distributions to FT. Although no U.S. person may receive a distribution until the year after A's death, and FT has no realized income during any year of its existence, during each year in which A is living corpus may be held for future distribution to B, a U.S. person. Thus, under paragraph (a)(1) of this section FT is treated as having a U.S. beneficiary during each of A's tax years from 2001 through the year of A's death.

Example (6). Constructive benefit to U.S. person. A transfers property to FT. The trust instrument provides that no income or corpus may be paid directly to a U.S. person. However, the trust instrument provides that trust corpus may be used to satisfy B's legal obligations to a third party by making a payment directly to the third party. Under paragraphs (a)(1) and (2) of this section, FT is treated as having a U.S. beneficiary.

Example (7). U.S. person with negligible contingent interest. A transfers property to FT. The trust instrument provides that all income is to be distributed currently to C, and upon C's death, all corpus is to be distributed to whomever of C's three children is then living. All of C's children are nonresident aliens. Under the laws of intestate succession that would apply to FT, if all of C's children are deceased at the time of C's death, the corpus would be distributed to A's heirs. A's living relatives at the time of the transfer consist solely of two brothers and two nieces, all of whom are nonresident aliens, and two first cousins, one of whom, E, is a U.S. citizen. Although it is possible under certain circumstances that E could receive a corpus distribution under the applicable laws of intestate succession, for each year the trust is in existence A is able to demonstrate to the satisfaction of the Commissioner under paragraph (a)(2)(ii) of this section that E's contingent interest in FT is so remote as to be negligible. Provided that paragraph (a)(4) of this section does not require a different result, FT is not treated as having a U.S. beneficiary.

Example (8). U.S. person with non-negligible contingent interest. A transfers property to FT. The trust instrument provides that all income is to be distributed currently to D, A's uncle, who is a nonresident alien, and upon A's death, the corpus is to be distributed to D if he is then living. Under the laws of intestate succession that would apply to FT, B and C would share equally in the trust corpus if D is not living at the time of A's death. A is unable to demonstrate to the satisfaction of the Commissioner that B's contingent interest in the trust is so remote as to be negligible. Under paragraph (a)(2)(ii) of this section, FT is treated as having a U.S. beneficiary as of the year of the transfer.

Example (9). U.S. person as member of class of beneficiaries. A transfers property to FT. The trust instrument provides that all income is to be distributed currently to D, A's uncle, who is a nonresident alien, and upon A's death, the corpus is to be distributed to D if he is then living. If D is not then living, the corpus is to be distributed to D's descendants. D's grandson, E, is a resident alien. Under paragraph (a)(2)(ii) of this section, FT is treated as having a U.S. beneficiary as of the year of the transfer.

Example (10). Trustee's discretion in choosing beneficiaries. A transfers property to FT. The trust instrument provides that the trustee may distribute income and corpus to, or accumulate income for the benefit of, any person who is pursuing the academic study of ancient Greek, in the trustee's discretion. Because it is possible that a U.S. person will receive distributions of income or corpus, or will have income accumulated for his benefit, FT is treated as having a U.S. beneficiary. This result applies even if, during a tax year, no distributions or accumulations are actually made to or for the benefit of a U.S. person. A may not invoke paragraph (a)(2)(ii) of this section because a U.S. person could benefit pursuant to a grant of discretion in the trust instrument.

Example (11). Appointment of remainder beneficiary. A transfers property to FT. The trust instrument provides that the trustee may distribute current income to C, or may accumulate income, and, upon termination of the trust, trust assets are to be distributed to C. However, the trust instrument further provides that D, A's uncle, may appoint a different remainder beneficiary. Because it is possible that a U.S. person could be named as the remainder beneficiary, and because corpus could be held in each year for the future benefit of that U.S. person, FT is treated as having a U.S. beneficiary for each year.

Example (12). Trust not treated as having a U.S. beneficiary. A transfers property to FT. The trust instrument provides that the trustee may distribute income and corpus to, or accumulate income for the benefit of C. Upon termination of the trust, all income and corpus must be distributed to C. Assume that paragraph (a)(4) of this section is not applicable under the facts and circumstances and that A establishes to the satisfaction of the Commissioner under paragraph (a)(2)(ii) of this section that no U.S. persons are reasonably expected to benefit from the trust. Because no part of the income or corpus of the trust may be paid or accumulated to or for the benefit of, either directly or indirectly, a U.S. person, and if the trust is terminated no part of the income or corpus of the trust could be paid to or for the benefit of, either directly or indirectly, a U.S. person, FT is not treated as having a U.S. beneficiary.

Example (13). U.S. beneficiary becomes non-U.S. person. In 2001, A transfers property to FT. The trust instrument provides that, as long as B remains a U.S. resident, no distributions of income or corpus may be made from the trust to B. The trust instrument further provides that if B becomes a nonresident alien, distributions of income (including previously accumulated income) and corpus may be made to him. If B remains a U.S. resident at the time of FT's termination, all accumulated income and corpus is to be distributed to C. In 2007, B becomes a nonresident alien and remains so thereafter. Because income may be accumulated during the years 2001 through 2007 for the benefit of a person who is a U.S. person during those years, FT is treated as having a U.S. beneficiary under paragraph (a)(1) of this section during each of those years. This result applies even though B cannot receive distributions from FT during the years he is a resident alien and even though B might remain a resident alien who is not entitled to any distribution from FT. Provided that paragraph (a)(4) of this section does not require a different result and that A establishes to the satisfaction of the Commissioner under paragraph (a)(2)(ii) of this section that no other U.S. persons are reasonably expected to benefit from the trust, FT is not treated as having a U.S. beneficiary under paragraph (a)(1) of this section during tax years after 2007.

(3) Changes in beneficiary's status. (i) In general. For purposes of paragraph (a)(1) of this section, the possibility that a person that is not a U.S. person could become a U.S. person will not cause that person to be treated as a U.S. person for purposes of paragraph (a)(1) of this section until the tax year of the U.S. transferor in which that individual actually becomes a U.S. person. However, if a person who is not a U.S. person becomes a U.S. person for the first time more than 5 years after the date of a transfer to the foreign trust by a U.S. transferor, that person is not treated as a U.S. person for purposes of applying paragraph (a)(1) of this section with respect to that transfer.

(ii) Examples. The following examples illustrate the rules of paragraph (a)(3) of this section. In these examples, A is a resident alien, B is A's son, who is a resident alien, C is A's daughter, who is a nonresident alien, and FT is a foreign trust. The examples are as follows:

Example (1). Non-U.S. beneficiary becomes U.S. person. In 2001, A transfers property to FT. The trust instrument provides that all income is to be distributed currently to C and that, upon the termination of FT, all corpus is to be distributed to C. Assume that paragraph (a)(4) of this section is not applicable under the facts and circumstances and that A establishes to the satisfaction of the Commissioner under paragraph (a)(2)(ii) of this section that no U.S. persons are reasonably expected to benefit from the trust. Under paragraph (a)(3)(i) of this section, FT is not treated as having a U.S. beneficiary during the tax years of A in which C remains a nonresident alien. If C first becomes a resident alien in 2004, FT is treated as having a U.S. beneficiary commencing in that year under paragraph (a)(3) of this section. See paragraph (c) of this section regarding the treatment of A upon FT's acquisition of a U.S. beneficiary.

Example (2). Non-U.S. beneficiary becomes U.S. person more than 5 years after transfer. The facts are the same as in Example 1, except C first becomes a resident alien in 2007. FT is treated as not having a U.S. beneficiary under paragraph (a)(3)(i) of this section with respect to the property transfer by A. However, if C had previously been a U.S. person during any prior period, the 5-year exception in paragraph (a)(3)(i) of this section would not apply in 2007 because it would not have been the first time C became a U.S. person.

(4) General rules. (i) Records and documents. Even if, based on the terms of the trust instrument, a foreign trust is not treated as having a U.S. beneficiary within the meaning of paragraph (a)(1) of this section, the trust may nevertheless be treated as having a U.S. beneficiary pursuant to paragraph (a)(1) of this section based on the following—

(A) All written and oral agreements and understandings relating to the trust;

(B) Memoranda or letters of wishes;

(C) All records that relate to the actual distribution of income and corpus; and

(D) All other documents that relate to the trust, whether or not of any purported legal effect.

(ii) Additional factors. For purposes of determining whether a foreign trust is treated as having a U.S. beneficiary within the meaning of paragraph (a)(1) of this section, the following additional factors are taken into account—

(A) If the terms of the trust instrument allow the trust to be amended to benefit a U.S. person, all potential benefits that could be provided to a U.S. person pursuant to an amendment must be taken into account;

(B) If the terms of the trust instrument do not allow the trust to be amended to benefit a U.S. person, but the law applicable to a foreign trust may require payments or accumulations of income or corpus to or for the benefit of a U.S. person (by judicial reformation or otherwise), all potential benefits that could be provided to a U.S. person pursuant to the law must be taken into account, unless the U.S. transferor demonstrates to the satisfaction of the Commissioner that the law is not reasonably expected to be applied or invoked under the facts and circumstances; and

(C) If the parties to the trust ignore the terms of the trust instrument, or if it is reasonably expected that they will do so, all benefits that have been, or are reasonably expected to be, provided to a U.S. person must be taken into account.

(iii) Examples. The following examples illustrate the rules of paragraph (a)(4) of this section. In these examples, A is a resident alien, B is A's son, who is a resident alien, C is A's daughter, who is a nonresident alien, and FT is a foreign trust. The examples are as follows:

Example (1). Amendment pursuant to local law. A creates and funds FT for the benefit of C. The terms of FT (which, according to the trust instrument, cannot be amended) provide that no part of the income or corpus of FT may be paid or accumulated during the taxable year to or for the benefit of any U.S. person, either during the existence of FT or at the time of its termination. However, pursuant to the applicable foreign law, FT can be amended to provide for additional beneficiaries, and there is an oral understanding between A and the trustee that B can be added as a beneficiary. Under paragraphs (a)(1) and (a)(4)(ii)(B) of this section, FT is treated as having a U.S. beneficiary.

Example (2). Actions in violation of the terms of the trust. A transfers property to FT. The trust instrument provides that no U.S. person can receive income or corpus from FT during the term of the trust or at the termination of FT. Notwithstanding the terms of the trust instrument, a letter of wishes directs the trustee of FT to provide for the educational needs of B, who is about to begin college. The letter of wishes contains a disclaimer to the effect that its contents are only suggestions and recommendations and that the trustee is at all times bound by the terms of the trust as set forth in the trust instrument. Under paragraphs (a)(1) and (a)(4)(ii)(C) of this section, FT is treated as having a U.S. beneficiary.

(b) Indirect U.S. beneficiaries. *(1) Certain foreign entities.* For purposes of paragraph (a)(1) of this section, an amount is treated as paid or accumulated to or for the benefit of a U.S. person if the amount is paid to or accumulated for the benefit of—

(i) A controlled foreign corporation, as defined in section 957(a);

(ii) A foreign partnership, if a U.S. person is a partner of such partnership; or

(iii) A foreign trust or estate, if such trust or estate has a U.S. beneficiary (within the meaning of paragraph (a)(1) of this section).

(2) Other indirect beneficiaries. For purposes of paragraph (a)(1) of this section, an amount is treated as paid or accumulated to or for the benefit of a U.S. person if the amount is paid to or accumulated for the benefit of a U.S. person through an intermediary, such as an agent or nominee, or by any other means where a U.S. person may obtain an actual or constructive benefit.

(3) Examples. The following examples illustrate the rules of this paragraph (b). Unless otherwise noted, A is a resident alien. B is A's son and is a resident alien. FT is a foreign trust. The examples are as follows:

Example (1). Trust benefitting foreign corporation. A transfers property to FT. The beneficiary of FT is FC, a foreign corporation. FC has outstanding solely 100 shares of common stock. B owns 49 shares of the FC stock and FC2, also a foreign corporation, owns the remaining 51 shares. FC2 has outstanding solely 100 shares of common stock. B owns 49 shares of FC2 and nonresident alien individuals own the remaining 51 FC2 shares. FC is a controlled foreign corporation (as defined in section 957(a), after the application of section 958(a)(2)). Under paragraphs (a)(1) and (b)(1)(i) of this section, FT is treated as having a U.S. beneficiary.

Example (2). Trust benefitting another trust. A transfers property to FT. The terms of FT permit current distributions of income to B. A transfers property to another foreign trust, FT2. The terms of FT2 provide that no U.S. person can benefit either as to income or corpus, but permit current distributions of income to FT. Under paragraph (a)(1) of this section, FT is treated as having a U.S. beneficiary and, under paragraphs (a)(1) and (b)(1)(iii) of this section, FT2 is treated as having a U.S. beneficiary.

Example (3). Trust benefitting another trust after transferor's death. A transfers property to FT. The terms of FT require that all income from FT be accumulated during A's lifetime. In the year following A's death, a share of FT is to be distributed to FT2, another foreign trust, for the benefit of B. Under paragraphs (a)(1) and (b)(1)(iii) of this section, FT is treated as having a U.S. beneficiary beginning with the year of A's transfer of property to FT.

Example (4). Indirect benefit through use of debit card. A transfers property to FT. The trust instrument provides that no U.S. person can benefit either as to income or corpus. However, FT maintains an account with FB, a foreign bank, and FB issues a debit card to B against the account maintained by FT and B is allowed to make withdrawals. Under paragraphs (a)(1) and (b)(2) of this section, FT is treated as having a U.S. beneficiary.

Example (5). Other indirect benefit. A transfers property to FT. FT is administered by FTC, a foreign trust company. FTC forms IBC, an international business corporation formed under the laws of a foreign jurisdiction. IBC is the beneficiary of FT. IBC maintains an account with FB, a foreign bank. FB issues a debit card to B against the account maintained by IBC and B is allowed to make withdrawals. Under paragraphs (a)(1) and (b)(2) of this section, FT is treated as having a U.S. beneficiary.

(c) Treatment of U.S. transferor upon foreign trust's acquisition or loss of U.S. beneficiary. *(1) Trusts acquiring a U.S. beneficiary.* If a foreign trust to which a U.S. transferor has transferred property is not treated as having a U.S. beneficiary (within the meaning of paragraph (a) of this section) for any taxable year of the U.S. transferor, but the trust is treated as having a U.S. beneficiary (within the meaning of paragraph (a) of this section) in any subsequent taxable year, the U.S. transferor is treated as having additional income in the first such taxable year of the U.S. transferor in which the trust is treated as having a U.S. beneficiary. The amount of the additional income is equal to the trust's undistributed net income, as defined in section 665(a), at the end of the U.S. transferor's immediately preceding taxable year and is subject to the rules of section 668, providing for an interest charge on accumulation distributions from foreign trusts.

(2) Trusts ceasing to have a U.S. beneficiary. If, for any taxable year of a U.S. transferor, a foreign trust that has received a transfer of property from the U.S. transferor ceases to be treated as having a U.S. beneficiary, the U.S. transferor ceases to be treated as the owner of the portion of the trust attributable to the transfer beginning in the first taxable year following the last taxable year of the U.S. transferor during which the trust was treated as having a U.S. beneficiary (unless the U.S. transferor is treated as an owner thereof pursuant to sections 673 through 677). The U.S. transferor is treated as making a transfer of property to the foreign trust on the first day of the first taxable year following the last taxable year of the U.S. transferor during which the trust was treated as having a U.S. beneficiary. The amount of the property deemed to be transferred to the trust is the portion

of the trust attributable to the prior transfer to which paragraph (a)(1) of this section applied. For rules regarding the recognition of gain on transfers to foreign trusts, see section 684.

(3) Examples. The rules of this paragraph (c) are illustrated by the following examples. A is a resident alien, B is A's son, and FT is a foreign trust. The examples are as follows:

Example (1). Trust acquiring U.S. beneficiary.

(i) In 2001, A transfers stock with a fair market value of $100,000 to FT. The stock has an adjusted basis of $50,000 at the time of the transfer. The trust instrument provides that income may be paid currently to, or accumulated for the benefit of, B and that, upon the termination of the trust, all income and corpus is to be distributed to B. At the time of the transfer, B is a nonresident alien. A is not treated as the owner of any portion of FT under sections 673 through 677. FT accumulates a total of $30,000 of income during the taxable years 2001 through 2003. In 2004, B moves to the United States and becomes a resident alien. Assume paragraph (a)(4) of this section is not applicable under the facts and circumstances.

(ii) Under paragraph (c)(1) of this section, A is treated as receiving an accumulation distribution in the amount of $30,000 in 2004 and immediately transferring that amount back to the trust. The accumulation distribution is subject to the rules of section 668, providing for an interest charge on accumulation distributions.

(iii) Under paragraphs (a)(1) and (3) of this section, beginning in 2005, A is treated as the owner of the portion of FT attributable to the stock transferred by A to FT in 2001 (which includes the portion attributable to the accumulated income deemed to be retransferred in 2004).

Example (2). Trust ceasing to have U.S. beneficiary.

(i) The facts are the same as in Example 1. In 2008, B becomes a nonresident alien. On the date B becomes a nonresident alien, the stock transferred by A to FT in 2001 has a fair market value of $125,000 and an adjusted basis of $50,000.

(ii) Under paragraph (c)(2) of this section, beginning in 2009, FT is not treated as having a U.S. beneficiary, and A is not treated as the owner of the portion of the trust attributable to the prior transfer of stock. For rules regarding the recognition of gain on the termination of ownership status, see section 684.

T.D. 8955, 7/19/2001.

§ 1.679-3 Transfers.

(a) In general. A transfer means a direct, indirect, or constructive transfer.

(b) Transfers by certain trusts. *(1) In general.* If any portion of a trust is treated as owned by a U.S. person, a transfer of property from that portion of the trust to a foreign trust is treated as a transfer from the owner of that portion to the foreign trust.

(2) Example. The following example illustrates this paragraph (b):

Example. In 2001, A, a U.S. citizen, creates and funds DT, a domestic trust. A has the power to revest absolutely in himself the title to the property in DT and is treated as the owner of DT pursuant to section 676. In 2004, DT transfers property to FT, a foreign trust. A is treated as having transferred the property to FT in 2004 for purposes of this section.

(c) Indirect transfers. *(1)* Principal purpose of tax avoidance. A transfer to a foreign trust by any person (intermediary) to whom a U.S. person transfers property is treated as an indirect transfer by a U.S. person to the foreign trust if such transfer is made pursuant to a plan one of the principal purposes of which is the avoidance of United States tax.

(2) Principal purpose of tax avoidance deemed to exist. For purposes of paragraph (c)(1) of this section, a transfer is deemed to have been made pursuant to a plan one of the principal purposes of which was the avoidance of United States tax if—

(i) The U.S. person is related (within the meaning of paragraph (c)(4) of this section) to a beneficiary of the foreign trust, or has another relationship with a beneficiary of the foreign trust that establishes a reasonable basis for concluding that the U.S. transferor would make a transfer to the foreign trust; and

(ii) The U.S. person cannot demonstrate to the satisfaction of the Commissioner that—

(A) The intermediary has a relationship with a beneficiary of the foreign trust that establishes a reasonable basis for concluding that the intermediary would make a transfer to the foreign trust;

(B) The intermediary acted independently of the U.S. person;

(C) The intermediary is not an agent of the U.S. person under generally applicable United States agency principles; and

(D) The intermediary timely complied with the reporting requirements of section 6048, if applicable.

(3) Effect of disregarding intermediary. (i) In general. Except as provided in paragraph (c)(3)(ii) of this section, if a transfer is treated as an indirect transfer pursuant to paragraph (c)(1) of this section, then the intermediary is treated as an agent of the U.S. person, and the property is treated as transferred to the foreign trust by the U.S. person in the year the property is transferred, or made available, by the intermediary to the foreign trust. The fair market value of the property transferred is determined as of the date of the transfer by the intermediary to the foreign trust.

(ii) Special rule. If the Commissioner determines, or if the taxpayer can demonstrate to the satisfaction of the Commissioner, that the intermediary is an agent of the foreign trust under generally applicable United States agency principles, the property will be treated as transferred to the foreign trust in the year the U.S. person transfers the property to the intermediary. The fair market value of the property transferred will be determined as of the date of the transfer by the U.S. person to the intermediary.

(iii) Effect on intermediary. If a transfer of property is treated as an indirect transfer under paragraph (c)(1) of this section, the intermediary is not treated as having transferred the property to the foreign trust.

(4) Related parties. For purposes of this paragraph (c), a U.S. transferor is treated as related to a U.S. beneficiary of a foreign trust if the U.S. transferor and the beneficiary are related for purposes of section 643(i)(2)(B), with the following modifications—

(i) For purposes of applying section 267 (other than section 267(f)) and section 707(b)(1), "at least 10 percent" is used instead of "more than 50 percent" each place it appears; and

(ii) The principles of section 267(b)(10), using "at least 10 percent" instead of "more than 50 percent," apply to determine whether two corporations are related.

(5) Examples. The rules of this paragraph (c) are illustrated by the following examples:

Example (1). Principal purpose of tax avoidance. A, a U.S. citizen, creates and funds FT, a foreign trust, for the benefit of A's children, who are U.S. citizens. In 2004, A decides to transfer an additional 1000X to the foreign trust. Pursuant to a plan with a principal purpose of avoiding the application of section 679, A transfers 1000X to I, a foreign person. I subsequently transfers 1000X to FT. Under paragraph (c)(1) of this section, A is treated as having made a transfer of 1000X to FT.

Example (2). U.S. person unable to demonstrate that intermediary acted independently. A, a U.S. citizen, creates and funds FT, a foreign trust, for the benefit of A's children, who are U.S. citizens. On July 1, 2004, A transfers XYZ stock to D, A's uncle, who is a nonresident alien. D immediately sells the XYZ stock and uses the proceeds to purchase ABC stock. On January 1, 2007, D transfers the ABC stock to FT. A is unable to demonstrate to the satisfaction of the Commissioner, pursuant to paragraph (c)(2) of this section, that D acted independently of A in making the transfer to FT. Under paragraph (c)(1) of this section, A is treated as having transferred the ABC stock to FT. Under paragraph (c)(3) of this section, D is treated as an agent of A, and the transfer is deemed to have been made on January 1, 2007.

Example (3). Indirect loan to foreign trust. A, a U.S. citizen, previously created and funded FT, a foreign trust, for the benefit of A's children, who are U.S. citizens. On July 1, 2004, A deposits 500X with FB, a foreign bank. On January 1, 2005, FB loans 450X to FT. A is unable to demonstrate to the satisfaction of the Commissioner, pursuant to paragraph (c)(2) of this section, that FB has a relationship with FT that establishes a reasonable basis for concluding that FB would make a loan to FT or that FB acted independently of A in making the loan. Under paragraph (c)(1) of this section, A is deemed to have transferred 450X directly to FT on January 1, 2005. Under paragraph (c)(3) of this section, FB is treated as an agent of A. For possible exceptions with respect to qualified obligations of the trust, and the treatment of principal repayments with respect to obligations of the trust that are not qualified obligations, see § 1.679-4.

Example (4). Loan to foreign trust prior to deposit of funds in foreign bank. The facts are the same as in Example 3, except that A makes the 500X deposit with FB on January 2, 2005, the day after FB makes the loan to FT. The result is the same as in Example 3.

(d) Constructive transfers. *(1) In general.* For purposes of paragraph (a) of this section, a constructive transfer includes any assumption or satisfaction of a foreign trust's obligation to a third party.

(2) Examples. The rules of this paragraph (d) are illustrated by the following examples. In each example, A is a U.S. citizen and FT is a foreign trust. The examples are as follows:

Example (1). Payment of debt of foreign trust. FT owes 1000X to Y, an unrelated foreign corporation, for the performance of services by Y for FT. In satisfaction of FT's liability to Y, A transfers to Y property with a fair market value of 1000X. Under paragraph (d)(1) of this section, A is treated as having made a constructive transfer of the property to FT.

Example (2). Assumption of liability of foreign trust. FT owes 1000X to Y, an unrelated foreign corporation, for the performance of services by Y for FT. A assumes FT's liability to pay Y. Under paragraph (d)(1) of this section, A is treated as having made a constructive transfer of property with a fair market value of 1000X to FT.

(e) Guarantee of trust obligations. *(1) In general.* If a foreign trust borrows money or other property from any person who is not a related person (within the meaning of § 1.679-1(c)(5)) with respect to the trust (lender) and a U.S. person (U.S. guarantor) that is a related person with respect to the trust guarantees (within the meaning of paragraph (e)(4) of this section) the foreign trust's obligation, the U.S. guarantor is treated for purposes of this section as a U.S. transferor that has made a transfer to the trust on the date of the guarantee in an amount determined under paragraph (e)(2) of this section. To the extent this paragraph causes the U.S. guarantor to be treated as having made a transfer to the trust, a lender that is a U.S. person shall not be treated as having transferred that amount to the foreign trust.

(2) Amount transferred. The amount deemed transferred by a U.S. guarantor described in paragraph (e)(1) of this section is the guaranteed portion of the adjusted issue price of the obligation (within the meaning of § 1.1275-1(b)) plus any accrued but unpaid qualified stated interest (within the meaning of § 1.1273-1(c)).

(3) Principal repayments. If a U.S. person is treated under this paragraph (e) as having made a transfer by reason of the guarantee of an obligation, payments of principal to the lender by the foreign trust with respect to the obligation are taken into account on and after the date of the payment in determining the portion of the trust attributable to the property deemed transferred by the U.S. guarantor.

(4) Guarantee. For purposes of this section, the term guarantee—

(i) Includes any arrangement under which a person, directly or indirectly, assures, on a conditional or unconditional basis, the payment of another's obligation;

(ii) Encompasses any form of credit support, and includes a commitment to make a capital contribution to the debtor or otherwise maintain its financial viability; and

(iii) Includes an arrangement reflected in a comfort letter, regardless of whether the arrangement gives rise to a legally enforceable obligation. If an arrangement is contingent upon the occurrence of an event, in determining whether the arrangement is a guarantee, it is assumed that the event has occurred.

(5) Examples. The rules of this paragraph (e) are illustrated by the following examples. In all of the examples, A is a U.S. resident and FT is a foreign trust. The examples are as follows:

Example (1). Foreign lender. X, a foreign corporation, loans 1000X of cash to FT in exchange for FT's obligation to repay the loan. A guarantees the repayment of 600X of FT's obligation. Under paragraph (e)(2) of this section, A is treated as having transferred 600X to FT.

Example (2). Unrelated U.S. lender. The facts are the same as in Example 1, except X is a U.S. person that is not a related person within the meaning of § 1.679-1(c)(5). The result is the same as in Example 1.

(f) Transfers to entities owned by a foreign trust. *(1) General rule.* If a U.S. person is a related person (as defined in § 1.679-1(c)(5)) with respect to a foreign trust, any transfer of property by the U.S. person to an entity in which the foreign trust holds an ownership interest is treated as a transfer of such property by the U.S. person to the foreign trust followed by a transfer of the property from the foreign trust to the entity owned by the foreign trust, unless the U.S. person demonstrates to the satisfaction of the Commissioner that the transfer to the entity is properly attributable to the U.S. person's ownership interest in the entity.

(2) Examples. The rules of this paragraph (f) are illustrated by the following examples. In all of the examples, A is a U.S. citizen, FT is a foreign trust, and FC is a foreign corporation. The examples are as follows:

Example (1). Transfer treated as transfer to trust. A creates and funds FT, which is treated as having a U.S. beneficiary under § 1.679-2. FT owns all of the outstanding stock of FC. A transfers property directly to FC. Because FT is the sole shareholder of FC, A is unable to demonstrate to the satisfaction of the Commissioner that the transfer is properly attributable to A's ownership interest in FC. Accordingly, under this paragraph (f), A is treated as having transferred the property to FT, followed by a transfer of such property by FT to FC. Under § 1.679-1(a), A is treated as the owner of the portion of FT attributable to the property treated as transferred directly to FT. Under § 1.367(a)-1T(c)(4)(ii), the transfer of property by FT to FC is treated as a transfer of the property by A to FC.

Example (2). Transfer treated as transfer to trust. The facts are the same as in Example 1, except that FT is not treated as having a U.S. beneficiary under § 1.679-2. Under this paragraph (f), A is treated as having transferred the property to FT, followed by a transfer of such property by FT to FC. A is not treated as the owner of FT for purposes of § 1.679-1(a). For rules regarding the recognition of gain on the transfer, see section 684.

Example (3). Transfer not treated as transfer to trust. A creates and funds FT. FC has outstanding solely 100 shares of common stock. FT owns 50 shares of FC stock, and A owns the remaining 50 shares. On July 1, 2001, FT and A each transfer 1000X to FC. A is able to demonstrate to the satisfaction of the Commissioner that A's transfer to FC is properly attributable to A's ownership interest in FC. Accordingly, under this paragraph (f), A's transfer to FC is not treated as a transfer to FT.

T.D. 8955, 7/19/2001.

§ 1.679-4 Exceptions to a general rule.

(a) In general. Section 1.679-1 does not apply to—

(1) Any transfer of property to a foreign trust by reason of the death of the transferor;

(2) Any transfer of property to a foreign trust described in sections 402(b), 404(a)(4), or 404A;

(3) Any transfer of property to a foreign trust described in section 501(c)(3) (without regard to the requirements of section 508(a)); and

(4) Any transfer of property to a foreign trust to the extent the transfer is for fair market value.

(b) Transfers for fair market value. *(1) In general.* For purposes of this section, a transfer is for fair market value only to the extent of the value of property received from the trust, services rendered by the trust, or the right to use property of the trust. For example, rents, royalties, interest, and compensation paid to a trust are transfers for fair market value only to the extent that the payments reflect an arm's length price for the use of the property of, or for the services rendered by, the trust. For purposes of this determination, an interest in the trust is not property received from the trust. For purposes of this section, a distribution to a trust with respect to an interest held by such trust in an entity other than a trust or an interest in certain investment trusts described in § 301.7701-4(c) of this chapter, liquidating trusts described in § 301.7701-4(d) of this chapter, or environmental remediation trusts described in § 301.7701-4(e) of this chapter is considered to be a transfer for fair market value.

(2) Special rule. (i) Transfers for partial consideration. For purposes of this section, if a person transfers property to a foreign trust in exchange for property having a fair market value that is less than the fair market value of the property transferred, the exception in paragraph (a)(4) of this section applies only to the extent of the fair market value of the property received.

(ii) Example. This paragraph (b) is illustrated by the following example:

Example. A, a U.S. citizen, transfers property that has a fair market value of 1000X to FT, a foreign trust, in exchange for 600X of cash. Under this paragraph (b), § 1.679-1 applies with respect to the transfer of 400X (1000X less 600X) to FT.

(c) Certain obligations not taken into account. Solely for purposes of this section, in determining whether a transfer by a U.S. transferor that is a related person (as defined in § 1.679-1(c)(5)) with respect to the foreign trust is for fair market value, any obligation (as defined in § 1.679-1(c)(6)) of the trust or a related person (as defined in § 1.679-1(c)(5)) that is not a qualified obligation within the meaning of paragraph (d)(1) of this section shall not be taken into account.

(d) Qualified obligations. *(1) In general.* For purposes of this section, an obligation is treated as a qualified obligation only if—

(i) The obligation is reduced to writing by an express written agreement;

(ii) The term of the obligation does not exceed five years (for purposes of determining the term of an obligation, the obligation's maturity date is the last possible date that the obligation can be outstanding under the terms of the obligation);

(iii) All payments on the obligation are denominated in U.S. dollars;

(iv) The yield to maturity is not less than 100 percent of the applicable Federal rate and not greater that 130 percent of the applicable Federal rate (the applicable Federal rate for an obligation is the applicable Federal rate in effect under section 1274(d) for the day on which the obligation is issued, as published in the Internal Revenue Bulletin (see § 601.601(d)(2) of this chapter));

(v) The U.S. transferor extends the period for assessment of any income or transfer tax attributable to the transfer and any consequential income tax changes for each year that the obligation is outstanding, to a date not earlier than three years after the maturity date of the obligation (this extension is not necessary if the maturity date of the obligation does not extend beyond the end of the U.S. transferor's taxable year for the year of the transfer and is paid within such period); when properly executed and filed, such an agreement is deemed to be consented to for purposes of § 301.6501(c)-1(d) of this chapter; and

(vi) The U.S. transferor reports the status of the loan, including principal and interest payments, on Form 3520 for every year that the loan is outstanding.

(2) Additional loans. If, while the original obligation is outstanding, the U.S. transferor or a person related to the trust (within the meaning of § 1.679-1(c)(5)) directly or indirectly obtains another obligation issued by the trust, or if the U.S. transferor directly or indirectly obtains another obligation issued by a person related to the trust, the original obligation is deemed to have the maturity date of any such subsequent obligation in determining whether the term of the original obligation exceeds the specified 5-year term. In addition, a series of obligations issued and repaid by the trust (or a person related to the trust) is treated as a single obligation if the transactions giving rise to the obligations are structured with a principal purpose to avoid the application of this provision.

(3) Obligations that cease to be qualified. If an obligation treated as a qualified obligation subsequently fails to be a qualified obligation (e.g., renegotiation of the terms of the obligation causes the term of the obligation to exceed five years), the U.S. transferor is treated as making a transfer to the trust in an amount equal to the original obligation's adjusted issue price (within the meaning of § 1.1275-1(b)) plus any accrued but unpaid qualified stated interest (within the meaning of § 1.1273-1(c)) as of the date of the subsequent event that causes the obligation to no longer be a qualified obligation. If the maturity date is extended beyond five years by reason of the issuance of a subsequent obligation by the trust (or person related to the trust), the amount of the transfer will not exceed the issue price of the subsequent obligation. The subsequent obligation is separately tested to determine if it is a qualified obligation.

(4) Transfers resulting from failed qualified obligations. In general, a transfer resulting from a failed qualified obligation is deemed to occur on the date of the subsequent event that causes the obligation to no longer be a qualified obligation. However, based on all of the facts and circumstances, the Commissioner may deem a transfer to have occurred on any date on or after the issue date of the original obligation. For example, if at the time the original obligation was issued, the transferor knew or had reason to know that the obligation would not be repaid, the Commissioner could deem the transfer to have occurred on the issue date of the original obligation.

(5) Renegotiated loans. Any loan that is renegotiated, extended, or revised is treated as a new loan, and any transfer of funds to a foreign trust after such renegotiation, extension, or revision under a pre-existing loan agreement is treated as a transfer subject to this section.

(6) Principal repayments. The payment of principal with respect to any obligation that is not treated as a qualified obligation under this paragraph is taken into account on and after the date of the payment in determining the portion of the trust attributable to the property transferred.

(7) Examples. The rules of this paragraph (d) are illustrated by the following examples. In the examples, A and B are U.S. residents and FT is a foreign trust. The examples are as follows:

Example (1). Demand loan. A transfers 500X to FT in exchange for a demand note that permits A to require repayment by FT at any time. A is a related person (as defined in § 1.679-1(c)(5)) with respect to FT. Because FT's obligation to A could remain outstanding for more than five years, the obligation is not a qualified obligation within the meaning of paragraph (d) of this section and, pursuant to paragraph (c) of this section, it is not taken into account for purposes of determining whether A's transfer is eligible for the fair market value exception of paragraph (a)(4) of this section. Accordingly, § 1.679-1 applies with respect to the full 500X transfer to FT.

Example (2). Private annuity. A transfers 4000X to FT in exchange for an annuity from the foreign trust that will pay A 100X per year for the rest of A's life. A is a related person (as defined in § 1.679-1(c)(5)) with respect to FT. Because FT's obligation to A could remain outstanding for more than five years, the obligation is not a qualified obligation within the meaning of paragraph (d)(1) of this section and, pursuant to paragraph (c) of this section, it is not taken into account for purposes of determining whether A's transfer is eligible for the fair market value exception of paragraph (a)(4) of this section. Accordingly, § 1.679-1 applies with respect to the full 4000X transfer to FT.

Example (3). Loan to unrelated foreign trust. B transfers 1000X to FT in exchange for an obligation of the trust. The term of the obligation is fifteen years. B is not a related person (as defined in § 1.679-1(c)(5)) with respect to FT. Because B is not a related person, the fair market value of the obligation received by B is taken into account for purposes of determining whether B's transfer is eligible for the fair market value exception of paragraph (a)(4) of this section, even though the obligation is not a qualified obligation within the meaning of paragraph (d)(1) of this section.

Example (4). Transfer for an obligation with term in excess of 5 years. A transfers property that has a fair market value of 5000X to FT in exchange for an obligation of the trust. The term of the obligation is ten years. A is a related person (as defined in § 1.679-1(c)(5)) with respect to FT. Because the term of the obligation is greater than five years, the obligation is not a qualified obligation within the meaning of paragraph (d)(1) of this section and, pursuant to paragraph (c) of this section, it is not taken into account for purposes of determining whether A's transfer is eligible for the fair market value exception of paragraph (a)(4) of this section. Accordingly, § 1.679-1 applies with respect to the full 5000X transfer to FT.

Example (5). Transfer for a qualified obligation. The facts are the same as in Example 4, except that the term of the obligation is 3 years. Assuming the other requirements of paragraph (d)(1) of this section are satisfied, the obligation is a qualified obligation and its adjusted issue price is taken into account for purposes of determining whether A's transfer is eligible for the fair market value exception of paragraph (a)(4) of this section.

Example (6). Effect of subsequent obligation on original obligation. A transfers property that has a fair market value of 1000X to FT in exchange for an obligation that satisfies the requirements of paragraph (d)(1) of this section. A is a related person (as defined in § 1.679-1(c)(5)) with respect to FT. Two years later, A transfers an additional 2000X to FT and receives another obligation from FT that has a maturity date four years from the date that the second obligation was issued. Under paragraph (d)(2) of this section, the original obligation is deemed to have the maturity date of the second obligation. Under paragraph (a) of this section, A is treated as having made a transfer in an amount equal to the original obligation's adjusted issue price (within the meaning of § 1.1275-1(b)) plus any accrued but unpaid qualified stated interest (within the meaning of § 1.1273-1(c)) as of the date of issuance of the second obligation. The second obligation is tested separately to determine whether it is a qualified obligation for purposes of applying paragraph (a) of this section to the second transfer.

T.D. 8955, 7/19/2001.

§ 1.679-5 Pre-immigration trusts.

(a) In general. If a nonresident alien individual becomes a U.S. person and the individual has a residency starting date (as determined under section 7701(b)(2)(A)) within 5 years after directly or indirectly transferring property to a foreign trust (the original transfer), the individual is treated as having transferred to the trust on the residency starting date an amount equal to the portion of the trust attributable to the property transferred by the individual in the original transfer.

(b) Special rules. *(1) Change in grantor trust status.* For purposes of paragraph (a) of this section, if a nonresident alien individual who is treated as owning any portion of a trust under the provisions of subpart E of part I of subchapter J, chapter 1 of the Internal Revenue Code, subsequently ceases to be so treated, the individual is treated as having made the original transfer to the foreign trust immediately before the trust ceases to be treated as owned by the individual.

(2) Treatment of undistributed income. For purposes of paragraph (a) of this section, the property deemed transferred to the foreign trust on the residency starting date includes undistributed net income, as defined in section 665(a), attributable to the property deemed transferred. Undistributed net income for periods before the individual's residency starting date is taken into account only for purposes of determining the amount of the property deemed transferred.

(c) Examples. The rules of this section are illustrated by the following examples:

Example (1). Nonresident alien becomes resident alien. On January 1, 2002, A, a nonresident alien individual, transfers property to a foreign trust, FT. On January 1, 2006, A becomes a resident of the United States within the meaning of section 7701(b)(1)(A) and has a residency starting date of January 1, 2006, within the meaning of section 7701(b)(2)(A). Under paragraph (a) of this section, A is treated as a U.S. transferor and is deemed to transfer the property to FT on January 1, 2006. Under paragraph (b)(2) of this section, the property deemed transferred to FT on January 1, 2006, includes the undistributed net income of the trust, as defined in section 665(a), attributable to the property originally transferred.

Example (2). Nonresident alien loses power to revest property. On January 1, 2002, A, a nonresident alien individual, transfers property to a foreign trust, FT. A has the power to revest absolutely in himself the title to such property transferred and is treated as the owner of the trust pursuant to sections 676 and 672(f). On January 1, 2008, the terms of FT are amended to remove A's power to revest in himself title to the property transferred, and A ceases to be treated as the owner of FT. On January 1, 2010, A becomes a resident of the United States. Under paragraph (b)(1) of this section, for purposes of paragraph (a) of this section A is treated as having originally transferred the property to FT on January 1, 2008. Because this date is within five years of A's residency starting date, A is deemed to have made a transfer to the foreign trust on January 1, 2010, his residency starting date. Under paragraph (b)(2) of this section, the property deemed transferred to the foreign trust on January 1, 2010, includes the undistributed net income of the trust, as defined in section 665(a), attributable to the property deemed transferred.

T.D. 8955, 7/19/2001.

§ 1.679-6 Outbound migrations of domestic trusts.

(a) In general. Subject to the provisions of paragraph (b) of this section, if an individual who is a U.S. person transfers property to a trust that is not a foreign trust, and such trust becomes a foreign trust while the U.S. person is alive, the U.S. individual is treated as a U.S. transferor and is deemed to transfer the property to a foreign trust on the date the domestic trust becomes a foreign trust.

(b) Amount deemed transferred. For purposes of paragraph (a) of this section, the property deemed transferred to the trust when it becomes a foreign trust includes undistributed net income, as defined in section 665(a), attributable to the property previously transferred. Undistributed net income for periods prior to the migration is taken into account only for purposes of determining the portion of the trust that is attributable to the property transferred by the U.S. person.

(c) Example. The following example illustrates the rules of this section. For purposes of the example, A is a resident alien, B is A's son, who is a resident alien, and DT is a domestic trust. The example is as follows:

Example. Outbound migration of domestic trust. On January 1, 2002, A transfers property to DT, for the benefit of B. On January 1, 2003, DT acquires a foreign trustee who has the power to determine whether and when distributions will be made to B. Under section 7701(a)(30)(E) and § 301.7701-7(d)(ii)(A) of this chapter, DT becomes a foreign trust on January 1, 2003. Under paragraph (a) of this section, A is treated as transferring property to a foreign trust on January 1, 2003. Under paragraph (b) of this section, the property deemed transferred to the trust when it becomes a foreign trust includes undistributed net income, as defined in section 665(a), attributable to the property deemed transferred.

T.D. 8955, 7/19/2001.

§ 1.679-7 Effective dates.

(a) In general. Except as provided in paragraph (b) of this section, the rules of §§ 1.679-1, 1.679-2, 1.679-3, and 1.679-4 apply with respect to transfers after August 7, 2000.

(b) Special rules. *(1)* The rules of § 1.679-4(c) and (d) apply to an obligation issued after February 6, 1995, whether or not in accordance with a pre-existing arrangement or understanding. For purposes of the rules of § 1.679-4(c) and (d), if an obligation issued on or before February 6, 1995, is modified after that date, and the modification is a significant modification within the meaning of § 1.1001-3, the obligation is treated as if it were issued on the date of the modification. However, the penalty provided in section 6677 applies only to a failure to report transfers in exchange for obligations issued after August 20, 1996.

(2) The rules of § 1.679-5 apply to persons whose residency starting date is after August 7, 2000.

(3) The rules of § 1.679-6 apply to trusts that become foreign trusts after August 7, 2000.

T.D. 8955, 7/19/2001.

§ 1.681(a)-1 Limitations on charitable contributions deduction of trusts; scope of section 681.

Caution: The Treasury has not yet amended Reg § 1.681(a)-1 to reflect changes made by P.L. 91-172.

Under section 681, the unlimited charitable contributions deduction otherwise allowable to a trust under section 642(c) is, in general, subject to percentage limitations, corresponding to those applicable to contributions by an individual under section 170(b)(1)(A) and (B), under the following circumstances:

(a) To the extent that the deduction is allocable to "unrelated business income";

(b) For taxable years beginning before January 1, 1970, if the trust has engaged in a "prohibited transaction";

(c) For taxable years beginning before January 1, 1970, if income is accumulated for a charitable purpose and the accumulation is (1) unreasonable, (2) substantially diverted to a noncharitable purpose, or (3) invested against the interests of the charitable beneficiaries.

Further, if the circumstance set forth in paragraph (a) or (c) of this section is applicable, the deduction is limited to income actually paid out for charitable purposes, and is not allowed for income only set aside or to be used for those purposes. If the circumstance set forth in paragraph (b) of this section is applicable, deductions for contributions to the trust may be disallowed. The provisions of section 681 are discussed in detail in §§ 1.681(a)-2 through 1.681(c)-1. For definition of the term "income", see section 643(b) and § 1.643(b)-1.

T.D. 6269, 11/15/57, amend T.D. 7428, 8/13/76.

§ 1.681(a)-2 Limitation on charitable contributions deduction of trusts with trade or business income.

Caution: The Treasury has not yet amended Reg § 1.681(a)-2 to reflect changes made by P.L. 91-172.

(a) In general. No charitable contributions deduction is allowable to a trust under section 642(c) for any taxable year for amounts allocable to the trust's unrelated business income for the taxable year. For the purpose of section 681(a) the term "unrelated business income" of a trust means an amount which would be computed as the trust's unrelated business taxable income under section 512 and the regulations thereunder, if the trust were an organization exempt from tax under section 501(a) by reason of section 501(c)(3). For the purpose of the computation under section 512, the term "unrelated trade or business" includes a trade or business carried on by a partnership of which a trust is a member, as well as one carried on by the trust itself. While the charitable contributions deduction under section 642(c) is entirely disallowed by section 681(a) for amounts allocable to "unrelated business income", a partial deduction is nevertheless allowed for such amounts by the operation of section 512(b)(11), as illustrated in paragraphs (b) and (c) of this section. This partial deduction is subject to the percentage limitations applicable to contributions by an individual under section 170(b)(1)(A) and (B), and is not allowed for amounts set aside or to be used for charitable purposes but not actually paid out during the taxable year. Charitable contributions deductions otherwise allowable under section 170, 545(b)(2), or 642(c) for contributions to a trust are not disallowed solely because the trust has unrelated business income.

(b) Determination of amounts allocable to unrelated business income. In determining the amount for which a charitable contributions deduction would otherwise be allowable under section 642(c) which are allocable to unrelated business income, and therefore not allowable as a deduction, the following steps are taken:

(1) There is first determined the amount which would be computed as the trust's unrelated business taxable income under section 512 and the regulations thereunder if the trust were an organization exempt from tax under section 501(a) by reason of section 501(c)(3), but without taking the charitable contributions deduction allowed under section 512(b)(11).

(2) The amount for which a charitable contributions deduction would otherwise be allowable under section 642(c) is then allocated between the amount determined in subparagraph (1) of this paragraph and any other income of the trust. Unless the facts clearly indicate to the contrary, the allocation to the amount determined in subparagraph (1) of this paragraph is made on the basis of the ratio (but not in excess of 100 percent) of the amount determined in subparagraph (1) of this paragraph to the taxable income of the trust, determined without the deduction for personal exemption under section 642(b), the charitable contributions deduction under section 642(c), or the deduction for distributions to beneficiaries under section 661(a).

(3) The amount for which a charitable contributions deduction would otherwise be allowable under section 642(c) which is allocable to unrelated business income as determined in subparagraph (2) of this paragraph, and therefore not allowable as a deduction, is the amount determined in subparagraph (2) of this paragraph reduced by the charitable contributions deduction which would be allowed under section 512(b)(11) if the trust were an organization exempt from tax under section 501(a) by reason of section 501(c)(3).

(c) Examples. *(1)* The application of this section may be illustrated by the following examples, in which it is assumed that the Y charity is not a charitable organization qualifying under section 170(b)(1)(A) (see subparagraph (2) of this paragraph):

Example (1). The X trust has income of $50,000. There is included in this amount a net profit of $31,000 from the operation of a trade or business. The trustee is required to pay half of the trust income to A, an individual, and the balance of the trust income to the Y charity, an organization described in section 170(c)(2). The trustee pays each beneficiary $25,000. Under these facts, the unrelated business income of the trust (computed before the charitable contributions deduction which would be allowed under section 512(b)(11)) is $30,000 ($31,000 less the deduction of $1,000 allowed by section 512(b)(12)). The deduction otherwise allowable under section 642(c) is $25,000, the amount paid to the Y charity. The portion allocable to the unrelated business income (computed as prescribed in paragraph (b)(2) of this section) is $15,000, that is, an amount which bears the same ratio to $25,000 as $30,000 bears to $50,000. The portion allocable to the unrelated business income, and therefore disallowed as a deduction, is $15,000 reduced by $6,000 (20 percent of $30,000, the charitable contributions deduction which would be allowable under section 512(b)(11)), or $9,000.

Example (2). Assume the same facts as in example (1), except that the trustee has discretion as to the portion of the trust income to be paid to each beneficiary, and the trustee pays $40,000 to A and $10,000 to the Y charity. The deduction otherwise allowable under section 642(c) is $10,000. The portion allocable to the unrelated business income computed as prescribed in paragraph (b)(2) of this section is $6,000, that is, an amount which bears the same ratio to $10,000 as $30,000 bears to $50,000. Since this amount does not exceed the charitable contributions deduction which would be allowable under section 512(b)(11) ($6,000, determined as in example (1)), no portion of it is disallowed as a deduction.

Example (3). Assume the same facts as in example (1), except that the terms of the trust instrument require the trustee to pay to the Y charity the trust income, if any, derived from the trade or business, and to pay to A all the trust income derived from other sources. The trustee pays $31,000 to the Y charity and $19,000 to A. The deduction otherwise allowable under section 642(c) is $31,000. Since the entire income from the trade or business is paid to Y charity, the amount allocable to the unrelated business income computed before the charitable contributions deduction under section 512(b)(11) is $30,000 ($31,000 less the deduction of $1,000 allowed by section 512(b)(12)). The amount allocable to the unrelated business income and therefore disallowed as a deduction is $24,000 ($30,000 less $6,000).

Example (4). (i) Under the terms of the trust, the trustee is required to pay half of the trust income to A, an individual, for his life, and the balance of the trust income to the Y charity, an organization described in section 170(c)(2). Capital gains are allocable to corpus and upon A's death the trust is to terminate and the corpus is to be distributed to the Y charity. The trust has taxable income of $50,000 computed without any deduction for personal exemption, charitable contributions, or distributions. The amount of $50,000 includes $10,000 capital gains, $30,000 ($31,000 less the $1,000 deduction allowed under section 512(b)(12)) unrelated business income (computed before the charitable contributions deduction which would be allowed under section 512(b)(11)) and other income of $9,000. The trustee pays each beneficiary $20,000.

(ii) The deduction otherwise allowable under section 642(c) is $30,000 ($20,000 paid to Y charity and $10,000 capital gains allocated to corpus and permanently set aside for charitable purposes). The portion allocable to the unrelated business income is $15,000, that is, an amount which bears the same ratio to $20,000 (the amount paid to Y charity) as $30,000 bears to $40,000 ($50,000 less $10,000 capital gains allocable to corpus). The portion allocable to the unrelated business income, and therefore disallowed as a deduction, is $15,000 reduced by $6,000 (the charitable contributions deduction which would be allowable under section 512(b)(11)), or $9,000.

(2) If, in the examples in subparagraph (1) of this paragraph, the Y charity were a charitable organization qualifying under section 170(b)(1)(A), then the deduction allowable under section 512(b)(11) would be computed at a rate of 30 percent.

T.D. 6269, 11/15/57, amend T.D. 6605, 8/14/62.

---

§ 1.681(b)-1 Cross reference.

For disallowance of certain charitable, etc., deductions otherwise allowable under section 642(c), see sections 508(d) and 4948(c)(4). See also 26 CFR §§ 1.681(b)-1 and 1.681(c)-1 (rev. as of Apr. 1, 1974) for provisions applying before January 1, 1970.

T.D. 6269, 11/15/57, amend T.D. 6605, 8/14/62, T.D. 7428, 8/13/76.

---

§ 1.682(a)-1 Income of trust in case of divorce, etc.

Caution: The Treasury has not yet amended Reg § 1.682(a)-1 to reflect changes made by P.L. 98-369.

(a) In general. *(1)* Section 682(a) provides rules in certain cases for determining the taxability of income of trust as between spouses who are divorced, or who are separated under a decree of separate maintenance or a written separation agreement. In such cases, the spouse actually entitled to receive payments from the trust is considered the beneficiary rather than the spouse in discharge of whose obligations the payments are made, except to the extent that the payments are specified to be for the support of the obligor spouse's minor children in the divorce or separate maintenance decree, the separation agreement or the governing trust instrument. For convenience, the beneficiary spouse will hereafter in this section and in § 1.682(b)-1 be referred to as the "wife" and the obligor spouse from whom she is divorced or legally separated as the "husband". (See section 7701(a)(17).) Thus, under section 682(a) income of a trust—

(i) Which is paid, credited, or required to be distributed to the wife in a taxable year of the wife, and

(ii) Which, except for the provisions of section 682, would be includible in the gross income of her husband,

is includible in her gross income and is not includible in his gross income.

(2) Section 682(a) does not apply in any case to which section 71 applies. Although section 682(a) and section 71 seemingly cover some of the same situations, there are important differences between them. Thus, section 682(a) applies, for example, to a trust created before the divorce or separation and not in contemplation of it, while section 71 applies only if the creation of the trust or payments by a previously created trust are in discharge of an obligation imposed upon or assumed by the husband (or made specific) under the court order or decree divorcing or legally separating the husband and wife, or a written instrument incident to the divorce status or legal separation status, or a written separation agreement. If section 71 applies, it requires inclusion in the wife's income of the full amount of periodic payments received attributable to property in trust (whether or not out of trust income), while, if section 71 does not apply, section 682(a) requires amounts paid, credited, or required to be distributed to her to be included only to the extent they are includible in the taxable income of a trust beneficiary under subparts A through D (section 641 and following), part I, subchapter J, chapter 1 of the Code.

(3) Section 682(a) is designed to produce uniformity as between cases in which without section 682(a), the income of a so-called alimony trust would be taxable to the husband because of his continuing obligation to support his wife or former wife, and other cases in which the income of a so-called alimony trust is taxable to the wife or former wife because of the termination of the husband's obligation. Furthermore, section 682(a) taxes trust income to the wife in all cases in which the husband would otherwise be taxed not only because of the discharge of his alimony obligation but also because of his retention of control over the trust income or corpus. Section 682(a) applies whether the wife is the beneficiary under the terms of the trust instrument or is an assignee of a beneficiary.

(4) The application of section 682(a) may be illustrated by the following examples, in which it is assumed that both the husband and wife make their income tax returns on a calendar year basis:

Example (1). Upon the marriage of H and W, H irrevocably transfers property in trust to pay the income to W for her life for support, maintenance, and all other expenses. Some years later, W obtains a legal separation from H under an order of court. W, relying upon the income from the trust payable to her, does not ask for any provision for her support and the decree recites that since W is adequately provided for by the trust, no further provision is being made for her. Under these facts, section 682(a), rather than section 71, is applicable. Under the provisions of section 682(a), the income of the trust which becomes payable to W after the order of separation is includible in her income and is deductible by the trust. No part of the income is includible in H's income or deductible by him.

Example (2). H transfers property in trust for the benefit of W, retaining the power to revoke the trust at any time. H, however, promises that if he revokes the trust he will transfer to W property in the value of $100,000. The transfer in trust and the agreement were not incident to divorce, but some years later W divorces H. The court decree is silent as to alimony and the trust. After the divorce, income of the trust which becomes payable to W is taxable to her, and is not taxable to H or deductible by him. If H later terminates the trust and transfers $100,000 of property to W, the $100,000 is not income to W nor deductible by H.

(b) Alimony trust income designated for support of minor children. Section 682(a) does not require the inclusion in the wife's income of trust income which the terms of the divorce or separate maintenance decree, separation agreement, or trust instrument fix in terms of an amount of money or a portion of the income as a sum which is payable for the support of minor children of the husband. The portion of the income which is payable for the support of minor children is includible in the husband's income. If in such a case trust income fixed in terms of an amount of money is to be paid but a lesser amount becomes payable, the trust income is considered to be payable for the support of the husband's minor children to the extent of the sum which would be payable for their support out of the originally specified amount of trust income. This rule is similar to that provided in the case of periodic payments under section 71. See § 1.71-1.

T.D. 6269, 11/15/57.

§ 1.682(b)-1 Application of trust rules to alimony payments.

Caution: The Treasury has not yet amended Reg § 1.682(b)-1 to reflect changes made by P.L. 98-369.

(a) For the purpose of the application of subparts A through D (section 641 and following), part I, subchapter J, chapter 1 of the Code, the wife described in section 682 or section 71 who is entitled to receive payments attributable to property in trust is considered a beneficiary of the trust, whether or not the payments are made for the benefit of the husband in discharge of his obligations. A wife treated as a beneficiary of a trust under this section is also treated as the beneficiary of such trust for purposes of the tax imposed by section 56 (relating to the minimum tax for tax preferences). For rules relating to the treatment of items of tax preference with respect to a beneficiary of a trust, see § 1.58-3.

(b) A periodic payment includible in the wife's gross income under section 71 attributable to property in trust is included in full in her gross income in her taxable year in which any part is required to be included under section 652 or 662. Assume, for example, in a case in which both the wife and the trust file income tax returns on the calendar year basis, that an annuity of $5,000 is to be paid to the wife by the trustee every December 31 (out of trust income if possible and, if not, out of corpus) pursuant to the terms of a divorce decree. Of the $5,000 distributable on December 31, 1954, $4,000 is payable out of income and $1,000 out of corpus. The actual distribution is made in 1955. Although the periodic payment is received by the wife in 1955, since under section 662 the $4,000 income distributable on December 31, 1954, is to be included in the wife's income for 1954, the $1,000 payment out of corpus is also to be included in her income for 1954.

T.D. 6269, 11/15/57, amend T.D. 7564, 9/11/78.

§ 1.682(c)-1 Definitions.

For definitions of the terms "husband" and "wife" as used in section 682, see section 7701(a)(17) and the regulations thereunder.

T.D. 6269, 11/15/57.

§ 1.683-1 Applicability of provisions; general rule.

Caution: The Treasury has not yet amended Reg § 1.683-1 to reflect changes made by P.L. 94-455.

Part I (section 641 and following), subchapter J, chapter 1 of the Code, applies to estates and trusts and to beneficiaries only with respect to taxable years which begin after December 31, 1953, and end after August 16, 1954, the date of enactment of the Internal Revenue Code of 1954. In the case of an estate or trust, the date on which a trust is created or amended or on which an estate commences, and the taxable years of beneficiaries, grantors, or decedents concerned are immaterial. This provision applies equally to taxable years of normal and of abbreviated length.

T.D. 6217, 12/19/56.

§ 1.683-2 Exceptions.

Caution: The Treasury has not yet amended Reg § 1.683-2 to reflect changes made by P.L. 94-455.

(a) In the case of any beneficiary of an estate or trust, sections 641 through 682 do not apply to any amount paid, credited, or to be distributed by an estate or trust in any taxable year of the estate or trust which begins before January 1, 1954, or which ends before August 17, 1954. Whether an amount so paid, credited, or to be distributed is to be included in the gross income of a beneficiary is determined with reference to the Internal Revenue Code of 1939. Thus, if a trust in its fiscal year ending June 30, 1954, distributed its current income to a beneficiary on June 30, 1954, the extent to which the distribution is includible in the beneficiary's gross income for his taxable year (the calendar year 1954) and the character of such income will be determined under the Internal Revenue Code of 1939. The Internal Revenue Code of 1954, however, determines the beneficiary's tax liability for a taxable year of the beneficiary to which such Code applies, with respect even to gross income of the beneficiary determined under the Internal Revenue Code of 1939 in accordance with this paragraph. Accordingly, the beneficiary is allowed credits and deductions pursuant to the Internal Revenue Code of 1954 for a taxable year governed by the Internal Revenue Code of 1954. See subparagraph (ii) of example (1) in paragraph (c) of this section.

(b) For purposes of determining the time of receipt of dividends under sections 34 (for purposes of the credit for dividends received on or before December 31, 1964) and 116, the dividends paid, credited, or to be distributed to a beneficiary are deemed to have been received by the beneficiary ratably on the same dates that the dividends were received by the estate or trust.

(c) The application of this section may be illustrated by the following examples:

Example (1). (i) A trust, reporting on the fiscal year basis, receives in its taxable year ending November 30, 1954, dividends on December 3, 1953, and April 3, July 5, and October 4, 1954. It distributes the dividends to A, its sole beneficiary (who reports on the calendar year basis) on November 30, 1954. Since the trust has received dividends in a taxable year ending after July 31, 1954, it will receive a dividend credit under section 34 with respect to dividends received which otherwise qualify under that section, in this case dividends received on October 4, 1954 (i.e., received after July 31, 1954). See section 7851(a)(1)(C). This credit, however, is reduced to the extent the dividends are allocable to the beneficiary as a result of income being paid, credited, or required to be distributed to him. The trust will also be permitted the dividend exclusion under section 116, since it received its dividends in a taxable year ending after July 31, 1954.

(ii) A is entitled to the section 34 credit with respect to the portion of the October 4, 1954, dividends which is distributed to him even though the determination of whether the amount distributed to him is includible in his gross income is made under the Internal Revenue Code of 1939. The credit allowable to the trust is reduced proportionately to the extent A is deemed to have received the October 4 dividends. A is not entitled to a credit with respect to the dividends received by the trust on December 3, 1953, and April 3, and July 5, 1954, because, although he receives after July 31, 1954, the distribution resulting from the trust's receipt of dividends, he is deemed to have received the dividends ratably with the trust on dates prior to July 31, 1954. In determining the exclusion under section 116 to which he is entitled, all the dividends received by the trust in 1954 and distributed to him are aggregated with any other dividends received by him in 1954, since he is deemed to have received such dividends in 1954 and therefore within a taxable year ending after July 31, 1954. He is not, however, entitled to the exclusion for the dividends received by the trust in December 1953.

Example (2). (i) A simple trust reports on the basis of a fiscal year ending July 31. It receives dividends on October 3, 1953, and January 4, April 3, and July 5, 1954. It distributes the dividends to A, its sole beneficiary, on September 1, 1954. The trust, receiving dividends in a taxable year ending prior to August 17, 1954, is entitled neither to the dividend received credit under section 34 nor the dividend exclusion under section 116.

(ii) A (reporting on the calendar year basis) is not entitled to the section 34 credit, because, although he receives after July 31, 1954, the distribution resulting from the trust's receipt of dividends, he is deemed to have received the dividends ratably with the trust, that is, on October 3, 1953, and January 4, April 3, and July 5, 1954. He is, however, entitled to the section 116 exclusion with respect to the dividends received by the trust in 1954 (along with other dividends received by him in 1954) and distributed to him, since he is deemed to have received such dividends on January 4, April 3, and July 5, 1954, each a date in his taxable year ending after July 31, 1954. He is entitled to no exclusion for the dividends received by the trust on October 3, 1953, since he is deemed to receive the resulting distribution on the same date, which falls within a taxable year of his which ends before August 1, 1954, although he is required to include the October 1953 dividends in his 1954 income. See section 164 of the Internal Revenue Code of 1939.

Example (3). A simple trust on a fiscal year ending July 31, 1954, receives dividends August 5 and November 4, 1953. It distributes the dividends to A, its sole beneficiary (who is on a calendar year basis), on September 1, 1954. Neither the trust nor A is entitled to a credit under section 34 or an exclusion under section 116.

T.D. 6217, 12/19/56, amend T.D. 6777, 12/15/64.

---

§ 1.683-3 Application of the 65-day rule of the Internal Revenue Code of 1939.

Caution: The Treasury has not yet amended Reg § 1.683-3 to reflect changes made by P.L. 94-455.

If an amount is paid, credited, or to be distributed in the first 65 days of the first taxable year of an estate or trust (heretofore subject to the provisions of the Internal Revenue Code of 1939) to which the Internal Revenue Code of 1954 applies and the amount would be treated, if the Internal Revenue Code of 1939 were applicable, as if paid, credited, or to be distributed on the last day of the preceding taxable year, sections 641 through 682 do not apply to the amount. The amount so paid, credited, or to be distributed is taken into account as provided in the Internal Revenue Code of 1939. See 26 CFR (1939) 39.162-2(c) and (d) (Regulations 118).

T.D. 6217, 12/19/56.

---

§ 1.684-1 Recognition of gain on transfers to certain foreign trusts and estates.

(a) Immediate recognition of gain. *(1) In general.* Any U.S. person who transfers property to a foreign trust or foreign estate shall be required to recognize gain at the time of the transfer equal to the excess of the fair market value of the property transferred over the adjusted basis (for purposes of determining gain) of such property in the hands of the U.S. transferor unless an exception applies under the provisions of § 1.684-3. The amount of gain recognized is determined on an asset-by-asset basis.

(2) No recognition of loss. Under this section a U.S. person may not recognize loss on the transfer of an asset to a foreign trust or foreign estate. A U.S. person may not offset gain realized on the transfer of an appreciated asset to a foreign trust or foreign estate by a loss realized on the transfer of a depreciated asset to the foreign trust or foreign estate.

(b) Definitions. The following definitions apply for purposes of this section:

(1) U.S. person. The term U.S. person means a United States person as defined in section 7701(a)(30), and includes a nonresident alien individual who elects under section 6013(g) to be treated as a resident of the United States.

(2) U.S. transferor. The term U.S. transferor means any U.S. person who makes a transfer (as defined in § 1.684-2) of property to a foreign trust or foreign estate.

(3) Foreign trust. Section 7701(a)(31)(B) defines foreign trust. See also § 301.7701-7 of this chapter.

(4) Foreign estate. Section 7701(a)(31)(A) defines foreign estate.

(c) Reporting requirements. A U.S. person who transfers property to a foreign trust or foreign estate must comply with the reporting requirements under section 6048.

(d) Examples. The following examples illustrate the rules of this section. In all examples, A is a U.S. person and FT is a foreign trust. The examples are as follows:

Example (1). Transfer to foreign trust. A transfers property that has a fair market value of 1000X to FT. A's adjusted basis in the property is 400X. FT has no U.S. beneficiary within the meaning of § 1.679-2, and no person is treated as owning any portion of FT. Under paragraph (a)(1) of this section, A recognizes gain at the time of the transfer equal to 600X.

Example (2). Transfer of multiple properties. A transfers property Q, with a fair market value of 1000X, and property R, with a fair market value of 2000X, to FT. At the time of the transfer, A's adjusted basis in property Q is 700X, and A's adjusted basis in property R is 2200X. FT has no U.S. beneficiary within the meaning of § 1.679-2, and no person is treated as owning any portion of FT. Under paragraph (a)(1) of this section, A recognizes the 300X of gain attributable to property Q. Under paragraph (a)(2) of this section, A does not recognize the 200X of loss attributable to property R, and may not offset that loss against the gain attributable to property Q.

Example (3). Transfer for less than fair market value. A transfers property that has a fair market value of 1000X to FT in exchange for 400X of cash. A's adjusted basis in the property is 200X. FT has no U.S. beneficiary within the meaning of § 1.679-2, and no person is treated as owning any portion of FT. Under paragraph (a)(1) of this section, A recognizes gain at the time of the transfer equal to 800X.

Example (4). Exchange of property for private annuity. A transfers property that has a fair market value of 1000X to FT in exchange for FT's obligation to pay A 50X per year for the rest of A's life. A's adjusted basis in the property is 100X. FT has no U.S. beneficiary within the meaning of § 1.679-2, and no person is treated as owning any portion of FT. A is required to recognize gain equal to 900X immediately upon transfer of the property to the trust. This result applies even though A might otherwise have been allowed to defer recognition of gain under another provision of the Internal Revenue Code.

Example (5). Transfer of property to related foreign trust in exchange for qualified obligation. A transfers property that has a fair market value of 1000X to FT in exchange for FT's obligation to make payments to A during the next four years. FT is related to A as defined in § 1.679-1(c)(5). The obligation is treated as a qualified obligation within the meaning of § 1.679-4(d), and no person is treated as owning any portion of FT. A's adjusted basis in the property is 100X. A is required to recognize gain equal to 900X immediately upon transfer of the property to the trust. This result applies even though A might otherwise have been allowed to defer recognition of gain under another provision of the Internal Revenue Code. § 1.684-3(d) provides rules relating to transfers for fair market value to unrelated foreign trusts.

T.D. 8956, 7/19/2001.

§ 1.684-2 Transfers.

(a) In general. A transfer means a direct, indirect, or constructive transfer.

(b) Indirect transfers. *(1) In general.* § 1.679-3(c) shall apply to determine if a transfer to a foreign trust or foreign estate, by any person, is treated as an indirect transfer by a U.S. person to the foreign trust or foreign estate.

(2) Examples. The following examples illustrate the rules of this paragraph (b). In all examples, A is a U.S. citizen, FT is a foreign trust, and I is A's uncle, who is a nonresident alien. The examples are as follows:

Example (1). Principal purpose of tax avoidance. A creates and funds FT for the benefit of A's cousin, who is a nonresident alien. FT has no U.S. beneficiary within the meaning of § 1.679-2, and no person is treated as owning any portion of FT. In 2004, A decides to transfer additional property with a fair market value of 1000X and an adjusted basis of 600X to FT. Pursuant to a plan with a principal purpose of avoiding the application of section 684, A transfers the property to I. I subsequently transfers the property to FT. Under paragraph (b) of this section and § 1.679-3(c), A is treated as having transferred the property to FT.

Example (2). U.S. person unable to demonstrate that intermediary acted independently. A creates and funds FT for the benefit of A's cousin, who is a nonresident alien. FT has no U.S. beneficiary within the meaning of § 1.679-2, and no person is treated as owning any portion of FT. On July 1, 2004, A transfers property with a fair market value of 1000X and an adjusted basis of 300X to I, a foreign person. On January 1, 2007, at a time when the fair market value of the property is 1100X, I transfers the property to FT. A is unable to demonstrate to the satisfaction of the Commissioner, under § 1.679-3(c)(2)(ii), that I acted independently of A in making the transfer to FT. Under paragraph (b) of this section and § 1.679-3(c), A is treated as having transferred the property to FT. Under paragraph (b) of this section and § 1.679-3(c)(3), I is treated as an agent of A, and the transfer is deemed to have been made on January 1, 2007. Under § 1.684-1(a), A recognizes gain equal to 800X on that date.

(c) Constructive transfers. § 1.679-3(d) shall apply to determine if a transfer to a foreign trust or foreign estate is treated as a constructive transfer by a U.S. person to the foreign trust or foreign estate.

(d) Transfers by certain trusts. *(1) In general.* If any portion of a trust is treated as owned by a U.S. person, a transfer of property from that portion of the trust to a foreign trust is treated as a transfer from the owner of that portion to the foreign trust.

(2) Examples. The following examples illustrate the rules of this paragraph (d). In all examples, A is a U.S. person, DT is a domestic trust, and FT is a foreign trust. The examples are as follows:

Example (1). Transfer by a domestic trust. On January 1, 2001, A transfers property which has a fair market value of 1000X and an adjusted basis of 200X to DT. A retains the power to revoke DT. On January 1, 2003, DT transfers property which has a fair market value of 500X and an adjusted basis of 100X to FT. At the time of the transfer, FT has no U.S. beneficiary as defined in § 1.679-2 and no person is treated as owning any portion of FT. A is treated as having transferred the property to FT and is required to recognize gain of 400X, under § 1.684-1, at the time of the transfer by DT to FT.

Example (2). Transfer by a foreign trust. On January 1, 2001, A transfers property which has a fair market value of 1000X and an adjusted basis of 200X to FT1. At the time of the transfer, FT1 has a U.S. beneficiary as defined in § 1.679-2 and A is treated as the owner of FT1 under section 679. On January 1, 2003, FT1 transfers property which has a fair market value of 500X and an adjusted basis of 100X to FT2. At the time of the transfer, FT2 has no U.S. beneficiary as defined in § 1.679-2 and no person is treated as owning any portion of FT2. A is treated as having transferred the property to FT2 and is required to recognize gain of 400X, under § 1.684-1, at the time of the transfer by FT1 to FT2.

(e) Deemed transfers when foreign trust no longer treated as owned by a U.S. person. *(1) In general.* If any portion of a foreign trust is treated as owned by a U.S. person under subpart E of part I of subchapter J, chapter 1 of the Internal Revenue Code, and such portion ceases to be treated as owned by that person under such subpart (other than by reason of an actual transfer of property from the trust to which § 1.684-2(d) applies), the U.S. person shall be treated as having transferred, immediately before (but on the same date that) the trust is no longer treated as owned by that U.S. person, the assets of such portion to a foreign trust.

(2) Examples. The following examples illustrate the rules of this paragraph (e). In all examples, A is a U.S. citizen and FT is a foreign trust. The examples are as follows:

Example (1). Loss of U.S. beneficiary.

(i) On January 1, 2001, A transfers property, which has a fair market value of 1000X and an adjusted basis of 400X, to FT. At the time of the transfer, FT has a U.S. beneficiary within the meaning of § 1.679-2, and A is treated as owning FT under section 679. Under § 1.684-3(a), § 1.684-1 does not cause A to recognize gain at the time of the transfer.

(ii) On July 1, 2003, FT ceases to have a U.S. beneficiary as defined in § 1.679-2(c) and as of that date neither A nor any other person is treated as owning any portion of FT. Pursuant to § 1.679-2(c)(2), if FT ceases to be treated as having a U.S. beneficiary, A will cease to be treated as owner of FT beginning on the first day of the first taxable year following the last taxable year in which there was a U.S. beneficiary. Thus, on January 1, 2004, A ceases to be treated as owner of FT. On that date, the fair market value of the property is 1200X and the adjusted basis is 350X. Under paragraph (e)(1) of this section, A is treated as having transferred the property to FT on January 1, 2004, and must recognize 850X of gain at that time under § 1.684-1.

Example (2). Death of grantor.

(i) The initial facts are the same as in paragraph (i) of Example 1.

(ii) On July 1, 2003, A dies, and as of that date no other person is treated as the owner of FT. On that date, the fair market value of the property is 1200X, and its adjusted basis equals 350X. Under paragraph (e)(1) of this section, A is treated as having transferred the property to FT immediately before his death, and generally is required to recognize 850X of gain at that time under § 1.684-1. However, an exception may apply under § 1.684-3(c).

Example (3). Release of a power.

(i) On January 1, 2001, A transfers property that has a fair market value of 500X and an adjusted basis of 200X to FT. At the time of the transfer, FT does not have a U.S. beneficiary within the meaning of § 1.679-2. However, A retains the power to revoke the trust. A is treated as the owner of the trust under section 676 and, therefore, under § 1.684-3(a), A is not required to recognize gain under § 1.684-1 at the time of the transfer.

(ii) On January 1, 2007, A releases the power to revoke the trust and, as of that date, neither A nor any other person is treated as owning any portion of FT. On that date, the fair market value of the property is 900X, and its adjusted basis is 200X. Under paragraph (e)(1) of this section, A is treated as having transferred the property to FT on January 1, 2007, and must recognize 700X of gain at that time.

(f) Transfers to entities owned by a foreign trust. § 1.679-3(f) provides rules that apply with respect to transfers of property by a U.S. person to an entity in which a foreign trust holds an ownership interest.

T.D. 8956, 7/19/2001.

§ 1.684-3 Exceptions to general rule of gain recognition.

(a) Transfers to grantor trusts. The general rule of gain recognition under § 1.684-1 shall not apply to any transfer of property by a U.S. person to a foreign trust to the extent that any person is treated as the owner of the trust under section 671. § 1.684-2(e) provides rules regarding a subsequent change in the status of the trust.

(b) Transfers to charitable trusts. The general rule of gain recognition under § 1.684-1 shall not apply to any transfer of property to a foreign trust that is described in section 501(c)(3) (without regard to the requirements of section 508(a)).

(c) Certain transfers at death. The general rule of gain recognition under § 1.684-1 shall not apply to any transfer of property by reason of death of the U.S. transferor if the basis of the property in the hands of the foreign trust is determined under section 1014(a).

(d) Transfers for fair market value to unrelated trusts. The general rule of gain recognition under § 1.684-1 shall not apply to any transfer of property for fair market value to a foreign trust that is not a related foreign trust as defined in § 1.679-1(c)(5). § 1.671-2(e)(2)(ii) defines fair market value.

(e) Transfers to which section 1032 applies. The general rule of gain recognition under § 1.684-1 shall not apply to any transfer of stock (including treasury stock) by a domestic corporation to a foreign trust if the domestic corporation is not required to recognize gain on the transfer under section 1032.

(f) Certain distributions to trusts. For purposes of this section, a transfer does not include a distribution to a trust with respect to an interest held by such trust in an entity other than a trust or an interest in certain investment trusts described in § 301.7701-4(c) of this chapter, liquidating trusts described in § 301.7701-4(d) of this chapter, or environmental remediation trusts described in § 301.7701-4(e) of this chapter.

(g) Examples. The following examples illustrate the rules of this section. In all examples, A is a U.S. citizen and FT is a foreign trust. The examples are as follows:

Example (1). Transfer to owner trust. In 2001, A transfers property which has a fair market value of 1000X and an adjusted basis equal to 400X to FT. At the time of the transfer, FT has a U.S. beneficiary within the meaning of § 1.679-2, and A is treated as owning FT under section 679. Under paragraph (a) of this section, § 1.684-1 does not cause A to recognize gain at the time of the transfer. See § 1.684-2(e) for rules that may require A to recognize gain if the trust is no longer owned by A.

Example (2). Transfer of property at death: Basis determined under section 1014(a).

(i) The initial facts are the same as Example 1.

(ii) A dies on July 1, 2004. The fair market value at A's death of all property transferred to FT by A is 1500X. The basis in the property is 400X. A retained the power to revoke FT, thus, the value of all property owned by FT at A's death is includible in A's gross estate for U.S. estate tax purposes. Pursuant to paragraph (c) of this section, A is not required to recognize gain under § 1.684-1 because the basis of the property in the hands of the foreign trust is determined under section 1014(a).

Example (3). Transfer of property at death: Basis not determined under section 1014(a).

(i) The initial facts are the same as Example 1.

(ii) A dies on July 1, 2004. The fair market value at A's death of all property transferred to FT by A is 1500X. The basis in the property is 400X. A retains no power over FT, and FT's basis in the property transferred is not determined under section 1014(a). Under § 1.684-2(e)(1), A is treated as having transferred the property to FT immediately before his death, and must recognize 1100X of gain at that time under § 1.684-1.

Example (4). Transfer of property for fair market value to an unrelated foreign trust. A sells a house with a fair market value of 1000X to FT in exchange for a 30-year note issued by FT. A is not related to FT as defined in § 1.679-1(c)(5). FT is not treated as owned by any person. Pursuant to paragraph (d) of this section, A is not required to recognize gain under § 1.684-1.

T.D. 8956, 7/19/2001.

§ 1.684-4 Outbound migrations of domestic trusts.

(a) In general. If a U.S. person transfers property to a domestic trust, and such trust becomes a foreign trust, and neither trust is treated as owned by any person under subpart E of part I of subchapter J, chapter 1 of the Internal Revenue Code, the trust shall be treated for purposes of this section as having transferred all of its assets to a foreign trust and the trust is required to recognize gain on the transfer under § 1.684-1(a). The trust must also comply with the rules of section 6048.

(b) Date of transfer. The transfer described in this section shall be deemed to occur immediately before, but on the same date that, the trust meets the definition of a foreign trust set forth in section 7701(a)(31)(B).

(c) Inadvertent migrations. In the event of an inadvertent migration, as defined in § 301.7701-7(d)(2) of this chapter, a trust may avoid the application of this section by complying with the procedures set forth in § 301.7701-7(d)(2) of this chapter.

(d) Examples. The following examples illustrate the rules of this section. In all examples, A is a U.S. citizen, B is a U.S. citizen, C is a nonresident alien, and T is a trust. The examples are as follows:

Example (1). Migration of domestic trust with U.S. beneficiaries. A transfers property which has a fair market value of 1000X and an adjusted basis equal to 400X to T, a domestic trust, for the benefit of A's children who are also U.S. citizens. B is the trustee of T. On January 1, 2001, while A is still alive, B resigns as trustee and C becomes successor trustee under the terms of the trust. Pursuant to § 301.7701-7(d) of this chapter, T becomes a foreign trust. T has U.S. beneficiaries within the meaning of § 1.679-2 and A is, therefore, treated as owning FT under section 679. Pursuant to § 1.684-3(a), neither A nor T is required to recognize gain at the time of the migration. § 1.684-2(e) provides rules that may require A to recognize gain upon a subsequent change in the status of the trust.

Example (2). Migration of domestic trust with no U.S. beneficiaries. A transfers property which has a fair market value of 1000X and an adjusted basis equal to 400X to T, a domestic trust for the benefit of A's mother who is not a citizen or resident of the United States. T is not treated as owned by another person. B is the trustee of T. On January 1, 2001, while A is still alive, B resigns as trustee and C becomes successor trustee under the terms of the trust. Pursuant to § 301.7701-7(d) of this chapter, T becomes a foreign trust, FT. FT has no U.S. beneficiaries within the meaning of § 1.679-2 and no person is treated as owning any portion of FT. T is required to recognize gain of 600X on January 1, 2001. Paragraph (c) of this section provides rules with respect to an inadvertent migration of a domestic trust.

T.D. 8956, 7/19/2001.

§ 1.684-5 Effective date.

§§ 1.684-1 through 1.684-4 apply to transfers of property to foreign trusts and foreign estates after August 7, 2000.

T.D, 8956, 7/19/2001.

§ 1.691(a)-1 Income in respect of a decedent.

Caution: The Treasury has not yet amended Reg § 1.691(a)-1 to reflect changes made by P.L. 100-647, P.L. 100-203, P.L. 99-514, P.L. 96-471, P.L. 96-222, P.L. 95-600, P.L. 94-455.

(a) Scope of section 691. In general, the regulations under section 691 cover: (1) The provisions requiring that amounts which are not includible in gross income for the decedent's last taxable year or for a prior taxable year be included in the gross income of the estate or persons receiving such income to the extent that such amounts constitute "income in respect of a decedent"; (2) the taxable effect of a transfer of the right to such income; (3) the treatment of certain deductions and credit in respect of a decedent which are not allowable to the decedent for the taxable period ending with his death or for a prior taxable year; (4) the allowance to a recipient of income in respect of a decedent of a deduction for estate taxes attributable to the inclusion of the value of the right to such income in the decedent's estate; (5) special provisions with respect to installment obligations acquired from a decedent and with respect to the allowance of a deduction for estate taxes to a surviving annuitant under a joint and survivor annuity contract; and (6) special provisions relating to installment obligations transmitted at death when prior law applied to the transmission.

(b) General definition. In general, the term "income in respect of a decedent" refers to those amounts to which a decedent was entitled as gross income but which were not properly includible in computing his taxable income for the taxable year ending with the date of his death or for a previous taxable year under the method of accounting employed by the decedent. See the regulations under section 451. Thus, the term includes—

(1) All accrued income of a decedent who reported his income by use of the cash receipts and disbursements method;

(2) Income accrued solely by reason of the decedent's death in case of a decedent who reports his income by use of an accrual method of accounting; and

(3) Income to which the decedent had a contingent claim at the time of his death.

See sections 736 and 753 and the regulations thereunder for "income in respect of a decedent" in the case of a deceased partner.

(c) Prior decedent. The term "income in respect of a decedent" also includes the amount of all items of gross income in respect of a prior decedent, if (1) the right to receive such amount was acquired by the decedent by reason of the death of the prior decedent or by bequest, devise, or inheritance from the prior decedent and if (2) the amount of gross income in respect of the prior decedent was not properly includible in computing the decedent's taxable income for the taxable year ending with the date of his death or for a previous taxable year. See example (2) of paragraph (b) of § 1.691(a)-2.

(d) Items excluded from gross income. Section 691 applies only to the amount of items of gross income in respect of a decedent, and items which are excluded from gross income under subtitle A of the Code are not within the provisions of section 691.

(e) Cross reference. For items deemed to be income in respect of a decedent for purposes of the deduction for estate taxes provided by section 691(c), see paragraph (c) of § 1.691(c)-1.

T.D. 6257, 10/7/57, amend T.D. 6808, 3/15/65.

§ 1.691(a)-2 Inclusion in gross income by recipients.

Caution: The Treasury has not yet amended Reg § 1.691(a)-2 to reflect changes made by P.L. 100-647, P.L. 100-203, P.L. 99-514, P.L. 96-471, P.L. 96-222, P.L. 95-600, P.L. 94-455.

(a) Under section 691(a)(1), income in respect of a decedent shall be included in the gross income, for the taxable year when received, of—

(1) The estate of the decedent, if the right to receive the amount is acquired by the decedent's estate from the decedent;

(2) The person who, by reason of the death of the decedent, acquires the right to receive the amount, if the right to receive the amount is not acquired by the decedent's estate from the decedent; or

(3) The person who acquires from the decedent the right to receive the amount by bequest, devise, or inheritance, if the amount is received after a distribution by the decedent's estate of such right. These amounts are included in the income of the estate or of such persons when received by them whether or not they report income by use of the cash receipts and disbursements method.

(b) The application of paragraph (a) of this section may be illustrated by the following examples, in each of which it is assumed that the decedent kept his books by use of the cash receipts and disbursements method.

Example (1). The decedent was entitled at the date of his death to a large salary payment to be made in equal annual installments over five years. His estate, after collecting two installments, distributed the right to the remaining installment payments to the residuary legatee of the estate. The estate must include in its gross income the two installments received by it, and the legatee must include in his gross income each of the three installments received by him.

Example (2). A widow acquired, by bequest from her husband, the right to receive renewal commissions on life insurance sold by him in his lifetime, which commissions were payable over a period of years. The widow died before having received all of such commissions, and her son inherited the right to receive the rest of the commissions. The commissions received by the widow were includible in her gross income. The commissions received by the son were not includible in the widow's gross income but must be included in the gross income of the son.

Example (3). The decedent owned a Series E United States savings bond, with his wife as co-owner or beneficiary, but died before the payment of such bond. The entire amount of interest accruing on the bond and not includible in income by the decedent, not just the amount accruing after the death of the decedent, would be treated as income to his wife when the bond is paid.

Example (4). A, prior to his death, acquired 10,000 shares of the capital stock of the X Corporation at a cost of $100 per share. During his lifetime, A had entered into an agreement with X Corporation whereby X Corporation agreed to purchase and the decedent agreed that his executor would sell the 10,000 shares of X Corporation stock owned by him at the book value of the stock at the date of A's death. Upon A's death, the shares are sold by A's executor for $500 a share pursuant to the agreement. Since the sale of stock is consummated after A's death, there is no income in respect of a decedent with respect to the appreciation in value of A's stock to the date of his death. If, in this example, A had in fact sold the stock during his lifetime but payment had not been received before his death, any gain on the sale would constitute income in respect of a decedent when the proceeds were received.

Example (5). (i) A owned and operated an apple orchard. During his lifetime, A sold and delivered 1,000 bushels of apples to X, a canning factory, but did not receive payment before his death. A also entered into negotiations to sell 3,000 bushels of apples to Y, a canning factory, but did not complete the sale before his death. After A's death, the executor received payment from X. He also completed the sale to Y and transferred to Y 1,200 bushels of apples on hand at A's death and harvested and transferred an additional 1,800 bushels. The gain from the sale of apples by A to X constitutes income in respect of a decedent when received. On the other hand, the gain from the sale of apples by the executor to Y does not.

(ii) Assume that, instead of the transaction entered into with Y, A had disposed of the 1,200 bushels of harvested apples by delivering them to Z, a cooperative association, for processing and sale. Each year the association commingles the fruit received from all of its members into a pool and assigns to each member a percentage interest in the pool based on the fruit delivered by him. After the fruit is processed and the products are sold, the association distributes the net proceeds from the pool to its members in proportion to their interests in the pool. After A's death, the association made distributions to the executor with respect to A's share of the proceeds from the pool in which A had an interest. Under such circumstances, the proceeds from the disposition of the 1,200 bushels of apples constitute income in respect of a decedent.

T.D. 6257, 10/7/57.

§ 1.691(a)-3 Character of gross income.

Caution: The Treasury has not yet amended Reg § 1.691(a)-3 to reflect changes made by P.L. 100-647, P.L. 100-203, P.L. 99-514, P.L. 96-471, P.L. 96-222, P.L. 95-600, P.L. 94-455.

(a) The right to receive an amount of income in respect of a decedent shall be treated in the hands of the estate, or by the person entitled to receive such amount by bequest, devise, or inheritance from the decedent or by reason of his death, as if it had been acquired in the transaction by which the decedent (or a prior decedent) acquired such right, and shall be considered as having the same character it would have had if the decedent (or a prior decedent) had lived and received such amount. The provisions of section 1014(a), relating to the basis of property acquired from a decedent, do not apply to these amounts in the hands of the estate and such persons. See section 1014(c).

(b) The application of paragraph (a) of this section may be illustrated by the following:

(1) If the income would have been capital gain to the decedent, if he had lived and had received it, from the sale of property held for more than 1 year (6 months for taxable years beginning before 1977; 9 months for taxable years beginning in 1977), the income, when received, shall be treated in the hands of the estate or of such person as capital gain from the sale of the property, held for more than 1 year (6 months for taxable years beginning before 1977; 9 months for taxable years beginning in 1977), in the same manner as if such person had held the property for the period the decedent held it and had made the sale.

(2) If the income is interest on United States obligations which were owned by the decedent, such income shall be treated as interest on United States obligations in the hands of the person receiving it, for the purpose of determining the credit provided by section 35, as if such person had owned the obligations with respect to which such interest is paid.

(3) If the amounts received would be subject to special treatment under part I (section 1301 and following), subchapter Q, chapter 1 of the Code, relating to income attributable to several taxable years, as in effect for taxable years beginning before January 1, 1964, if the decedent had lived and included such amounts in his gross income, such sections apply with respect to the recipient of the income.

(4) The provisions of sections 632 and 1347, relating to the tax attributable to the sale of certain oil or gas property and to certain claims against the United States, apply to any amount included in gross income, the right to which was obtained by the decedent by a sale or claim within the provisions of those sections.

T.D. 6257, 10/7/57, amend T.D. 6885, 6/1/66, T.D. 7728, 10/31/80.

§ 1.691(a)-4 Transfer of right to income in respect of a decedent.

Caution: The Treasury has not yet amended Reg § 1.691(a)-4 to reflect changes made by P.L. 100-203, P.L. 99-514, P.L. 96-471, P.L. 96-222, P.L. 95-600, P.L. 94-455.

(a) Section 691(a)(2) provides the rules governing the treatment of income in respect of a decedent (or a prior decedent) in the event a right to receive such income is transferred by the estate or person entitled thereto by bequest, devise, or inheritance, or by reason of the death of the decedent. In general, the transferor must include in his gross income for the taxable period in which the transfer occurs the amount of the consideration, if any, received for the right or the fair market value of the right at the time of the transfer, whichever is greater. Thus, upon a sale of such right by the estate or person entitled to receive it, the fair market value of the right or the amount received upon the sale, whichever is greater, is included in the gross income of the vendor. Similarly, if such right is disposed of by gift, the fair market value of the right at the time of the gift must be included in the gross income of the donor. In the case of a satisfaction of an installment obligation at other than face value, which is likewise considered a transfer under section 691(a)(2), see § 1.691(a)-5.

(b) If the estate of a decedent or any person transmits the right to income in respect of a decedent to another who would be required by section 691(a)(1) to include such income when received in his gross income, only the transferee will include such income when received in his gross income. In this situation, a transfer within the meaning of section 691(a)(2) has not occurred. This paragraph may be illustrated by the following:

(1) If a person entitled to income in respect of a decedent dies before receiving such income, only his estate or other person entitled to such income by bequest, devise, or inheritance from the latter decedent, or by reason of the death of the latter decedent, must include such amount in gross income when received.

(2) If a right to income in respect of a decedent is transferred by an estate to a specific or residuary legatee, only the specific or residuary legatee must include such income in gross income when received.

(3) If a trust to which is bequeathed a right of a decedent to certain payments of income terminates and transfers the right to a beneficiary, only the beneficiary must include such income in gross income when received.

If the transferee described in subparagraphs (1), (2), and (3) of this paragraph transfers his right to receive the amounts in the manner described in paragraph (a) of this section, the principles contained in paragraph (a) are applied to such transfer. On the other hand, if the transferee transmits his right in the manner described in this paragraph, the principles of this paragraph are again applied to such transfer.

T.D. 6257, 10/7/57.

§ 1.691(a)-5 Installment obligations acquired from decedent.

Caution: The Treasury has not yet amended Reg § 1.691(a)-5 to reflect changes made by P.L. 100-203, P.L. 99-514, P.L. 96-471, P.L. 96-222, P.L. 95-600, P.L. 94-455.

(a) Section 691(a)(4) has reference to an installment obligation which remains uncollected by a decedent (or a prior decedent) and which was originally acquired in a transaction the income from which was properly reportable by the decedent on the installment method under section 453. Under the provisions of section 691(a)(4), an amount equal to the excess of the face value of the obligation over its basis in the hands of the decedent (determined under section 453(d)(2) and the regulations thereunder) shall be considered an amount of income in respect of a decedent and shall be treated as such. The decedent's estate (or the person entitled to receive such income by bequest or inheritance from the decedent or by reason of the decedent's death) shall include in its gross income when received the same proportion of any payment in satisfaction of such obligations as would be returnable as income by the decedent if he had lived and received such payment. No gain on account of the transmission of such obligations by the decedent's death is required to be reported as income in the return of the decedent for the year of his death. See § 1.691(e)-1 for special provisions relating to the filing of an election to have the provisions of section 691(a)(4) apply in the case of installment obligations in respect of which section 44(d) of the Internal Revenue Code of 1939 (or corresponding provisions of prior law) would have applied but for the filing of a bond referred to therein.

(b) If an installment obligation described in paragraph (a) of this section is transferred within the meaning of section 691(a)(2) and paragraph (a) of § 1.691(a)-4, the entire installment obligation transferred shall be considered a right to income in respect of a decedent but the amount includible in the gross income of the transferor shall be reduced by an amount equal to the basis of the obligation in the hands of the decedent (determined under section 453(d)(2) and the regulations thereunder) adjusted, however, to take into account the receipt of any installment payments after the decedent's death and before such transfer. Thus, the amount includible in the gross income of the transferor shall be the fair market value of such obligation at the time of the transfer or the consideration received for the transfer of the installment obligation, whichever is greater, reduced by the basis of the obligation as described in the preceding sentence. For purposes of this paragraph, the term "transfer" in section 691(a)(2) and paragraph (a) of § 1.691(a)-4 includes the satisfaction of an installment obligation at other than face value.

(c) The application of this section may be illustrated by the following example:

Example. An heir of a decedent is entitled to collect an installment obligation with a face value of $100, a fair market value of $80, and a basis in the hands of the decedent of $60. If the heir collects the obligation at face value, the excess of the amount collected over the basis is considered income in respect of a decedent and includible in the gross income of the heir under section 691(a)(1). In this case, the amount includible would be $40 ($100 less $60). If the heir collects the obligation at $90, an amount other than face value, the entire obligation is considered a right to receive income in respect of a decedent but the amount ordinarily required to be included in the heir's gross income under section 691(a)(2) (namely, the consideration received in satisfaction of the installment obligation or its fair market value, whichever is greater) shall be reduced by the amount of the basis of the obligation in the hands of the decedent. In this case, the amount includible would be $30 ($90 less $60).

T.D. 6257, 10/7/57, amend T.D. 6808, 3/15/65.

§ 1.691(b)-1 Allowance of deductions and credit in respect of decedents.

Caution: The Treasury has not yet amended Reg § 1.691(b)-1 to reflect changes made by P.L. 99-514, P.L. 98-369, P.L. 96-471, P.L. 96-222, P.L. 95-600, P.L. 94-455.

(a) Under section 691(b) the expenses, interest, and taxes described in sections 162, 163, 164, and 212 for which the decedent (or a prior decedent) was liable, which were not properly allowable as a deduction in his last taxable year or any prior taxable year, are allowed when paid—

(1) As a deduction by the estate; or

(2) If the estate was not liable to pay such obligation, as a deduction by the person who by bequest, devise, or inheritance from the decedent or by reason of the death of the decedent acquires, subject to such obligation, an interest in property of the decedent (or the prior decedent).

Similar treatment is given to the foreign tax credit provided by section 33. For the purposes of subparagraph (2) of this paragraph, the right to receive an amount of gross income in respect of a decedent is considered property of the decedent; on the other hand, it is not necessary for a person, otherwise within the provisions of subparagraph (2) of this paragraph, to receive the right to any income in respect of a decedent. Thus, an heir who receives a right to income in respect of a decedent (by reason of the death of the decedent) subject to an income tax imposed by a foreign country during the decedent's life, which tax must be satisfied out of such income, is entitled to the credit provided by section 33 when he pays the tax. If a decedent who reported income by use of the cash receipts and disbursements method owned real property on which accrued taxes had become a lien, and if such property passed directly to the heir of the decedent in a jurisdiction in which real property does not become a part of a decedent's estate, the heir, upon paying such taxes, may take the same deduction under section 164 that would be allowed to the decedent if, while alive, he had made such payment.

(b) The deduction for percentage depletion is allowable only to the person (described in section 691(a)(1)) who receives the income in respect of the decedent to which the deduction relates, whether or not such person receives the property from which such income is derived. Thus, an heir who (by reason of the decedent's death) receives income derived from sales of units of mineral by the decedent (who reported income by use of the cash receipts and disbursements method) shall be allowed the deduction for percentage depletion, computed on the gross income from such number of units as if the heir had the same economic interest in the property as the decedent. Such heir need not also receive any interest in the mineral property other than such income. If the decedent did not compute his deduction for depletion on the basis of percentage depletion, any deduction for depletion to which the decedent was entitled at the date of his death would be allowable in computing his taxable income for his last taxable year, and there can be no deduction in respect of the decedent by any other person for such depletion.

T.D. 6257, 10/7/57.

§ 1.691(c)-1 Deduction for estate tax attributable to income in respect of a decedent.

Caution: The Treasury has not yet amended Reg § 1.691(c)-1 to reflect changes made by P.L. 100-647, P.L. 100-203, P.L. 99-514, P.L. 96-471, P.L. 96-222, P.L. 95-600, P.L. 94-455.

(a) In general. A person who is required to include in gross income for any taxable year an amount of income in respect of a decedent may deduct for the same taxable year that portion of the estate tax imposed upon the decedent's estate which is attributable to the inclusion in the decedent's estate of the right to receive such amount. The deduction is determined as follows:

(1) Ascertain the net value in the decedent's estate of the items which are included under section 691 in computing gross income. This is the excess of the value included in the gross estate on account of the items of gross income in respect of the decedent (see § 1.691(a)-1 and paragraph (c) of this section) over the deductions from the gross estate for claims which represent the deductions and credit in respect of the decedent (see § 1.691(b)-1). But see section 691(d) and paragraph (b) of § 1.691(d)-1 for computation of the special value of a survivor's annuity to be used in computing the net value for estate tax purposes in cases involving joint and survivor annuities.

(2) Ascertain the portion of the estate tax attributable to the inclusion in the gross estate of such net value. This is the excess of the estate tax over the estate tax computed without including such net value in the gross estate. In computing the estate tax without including such net value in the gross estate, any estate tax deduction (such as the marital de-

duction) which may be based upon the gross estate shall be recomputed so as to take into account the exclusion of such net value from the gross estate. See example (2), paragraph (e) of § 1.691(d)-1.

For purposes of this section, the term "estate tax" means the tax imposed under section 2001 or 2101 (or the corresponding provisions of the Internal Revenue Code of 1939), reduced by the credits against such tax. Each person including in gross income an amount of income in respect of a decedent may deduct as his share of the portion of the estate tax (computed under subparagraph (2) of this paragraph) an amount which bears the same ratio to such portion as the value in the gross estate of the right to the income included by such person in gross income (or the amount included in gross income if lower) bears to the value in the gross estate of all the items of gross income in respect of the decedent.

(b) Prior decedent. If a person is required to include in gross income an amount of income in respect of a prior decedent, such person may deduct for the same taxable year that portion of the estate tax imposed upon the prior decedent's estate which is attributable to the inclusion in the prior decedent's estate of the value of the right to receive such amount. This deduction is computed in the same manner as provided in paragraph (a) of this section and is in addition to the deduction for estate tax imposed upon the decedent's estate which is attributable to the inclusion in the decedent's estate of the right to receive such amount.

(c) Amounts deemed to be income in respect of a decedent. For purposes of allowing the deduction under section 691(c), the following items are also considered to be income in respect of a decedent under section 691(a):

(1) The value for estate tax purposes of stock options in respect of which amounts are includible in gross income under section 421(b) (prior to amendment by section 221(a) of the Revenue Act of 1964), in the case of taxable years ending before January 1, 1964, or under section 422(c)(1), 423(c), or 424(c)(1), whichever is applicable, in the case of taxable years ending after December 31, 1963. See section 421(d)(6) (prior to amendment by sec. 221(a) of the Revenue Act of 1964), in the case of taxable years ending before January 1, 1964, and section 421(c)(2), in the case of taxable years ending after December 31, 1963.

(2) Amounts received by a surviving annuitant during his life expectancy period as an annuity under a joint and survivor annuity contract to the extent included in gross income under section 72. See section 691(d).

(d) Examples. Paragraphs (a) and (b) of this section may be illustrated by the following examples:

Example (1). X, an attorney who kept his books by use of the cash receipts and disbursements method, was entitled at the date of his death to a fee for services rendered in a case not completed at the time of his death, which fee was valued in his estate at $1,000, and to accrued bond interest, which was valued in his estate at $500. In all, $1,500 was included in his gross estate in respect of income described in section 691(a)(1). There were deducted as claims against his estate $150 for business expenses for which his estate was liable and $50 for taxes accrued on certain property which he owned. In all, $200 was deducted for claims which represent amounts described in section 691(b) which are allowable as deductions to his estate or to the beneficiaries of his estate. His gross estate was $185,000 and, considering deductions of $15,000 and an exemption of $60,000, his taxable estate amounted to $110,000. The estate tax on this amount is $23,700 from which is subtracted a $75 credit for State death taxes leaving an estate tax liability of $23,625. In the year following the closing of X's estate, the fee in the amount of $1,200 was collected by X's son, who was the sole beneficiary of the estate. This amount was included under section 691(a)(1)(C) in the son's gross income. The son may deduct, in computing his taxable income for such year, $260 on account of the estate tax attributable to such income, computed as follows:

(1)(i) Value of income described in section 691(a)(1) included in computing gross estate	$1,500
(ii) Deductions in computing gross estate for claims representing deductions described in section 691(b)	200
(iii) Net value of items described in section 691(a)(1)	1,300
(2)(i) Estate tax	23,625
(ii) Less: Estate tax computed without including $1,300 (item (1)(iii)) in gross estate	23,235
(iii) Portion of estate tax attributable to net value of items described in section 691(a)(1)	390
(3)(i) Value in gross estate of items described in section 691(a)(1) received in taxable year (fee) ..	1,000
(ii) Value in gross estate of all income items described in section 691(a)(1) (item (1)(i))	1,500
(iii) Part of estate tax deductible on account of receipt of $1,200 fee (1,000/1,500 of $390)	260

Although $1,200 was later collected as the fee, only the $1,000 actually included in the gross estate is used in the above computations. However, to avoid distortion, section 691(c) provides that if the value included in the gross estate is greater than the amount finally collected, only the amount collected shall be used in the above computations. Thus, if the amount collected as the fee were only $500, the estate tax deductible on the receipt of such amount would be 500/1,500 of $390, or $130. With respect to taxable years ending before January 1, 1964, see paragraph (d)(3) of § 1.421-5 for a similar example involving a restricted stock option. With respect to taxable years ending after December 31, 1963, see paragraph (c)(3) of § 1.421-8 for a similar example involving a stock option subject to the provisions of part II of subchapter D.

Example (2). Assume that in example (1) the fee valued at $1,000 had been earned by prior decedent Y and had been inherited by X who died before collecting it. With regard to the son, the fee would be considered income in respect of a prior decedent. Assume further that the fee was valued at $1,000 in Y's estate, that the net value in Y's estate of items described in section 691(a)(1) was $5,000 and that the estate tax imposed on Y's estate attributable to such net value was $550. In such case, the portion of such estate tax attributable to the fee would be 1,000/5,000 of $550, or $110. When the son collects the $1,200 fee, he will receive for the same taxable year a deduction of $110 with respect to the estate tax imposed on the estate of prior decedent Y as well as the deduction of $260 (as computed in example (1)) with respect to the estate tax imposed on the estate of decedent X.

T.D. 6257, 10/7/57, amend T.D. 6887, 6/23/66.

§ 1.691(c)-2 Estates and trusts.

Caution: The Treasury has not yet amended Reg § 1.691(c)-2 to reflect changes made by P.L. 100-647, P.L. 100-203, P.L. 99-514, P.L. 96-471, P.L. 96-222, P.L. 95-600, P.L. 94-455.

(a) In the case of an estate or trust, the deduction prescribed in section 691(c) is determined in the same manner as described in § 1.691(c)-1, with the following exceptions:

(1) If any amount properly paid, credited, or required to be distributed by an estate or trust to a beneficiary consists of income in respect of a decedent received by the estate or trust during the taxable year—

(i) Such income shall be excluded in determining the income in respect of the decedent with respect to which the estate or trust is entitled to a deduction under section 691(c), and

(ii) Such income shall be considered income in respect of a decedent to such beneficiary for purposes of allowing the deduction under section 691(c) to such beneficiary.

(2) For determination of the amount of income in respect of a decedent received by the beneficiary, see sections 652 and 662, and §§ 1.652(b)-2 and 1.662(b)-2. However, for this purpose, distributable net income as defined in section 643(a) and the regulations thereunder shall be computed without taking into account the estate tax deduction provided in section 691(c) and this section. Distributable net income as modified under the preceding sentence shall be applied for other relevant purposes of subchapter J, chapter 1 of the Code, such as the deduction provided by section 651 or 661, or subpart D, part I of subchapter J, relating to excess distributions by trusts.

(3) The rule stated in subparagraph (1) of this paragraph does not apply to income in respect of a decedent which is properly allocable to corpus by the fiduciary during the taxable year but which is distributed to a beneficiary in a subsequent year. The deduction provided by section 691(c) in such a case is allowable only to the estate or trust. If any amount properly paid, credited, or required to be distributed by a trust qualifies as a distribution under section 666, the fact that a portion thereof constitutes income in respect of a decedent shall be disregarded for the purposes of determining the deduction of the trust and of the beneficiaries under section 691(c) since the deduction for estate taxes was taken into consideration in computing the undistributed net income of the trust for the preceding taxable year.

(b) This section shall apply only to amounts properly paid, credited, or required to be distributed in taxable years of an estate or trust beginning after December 31, 1953, and ending after August 16, 1954, except as otherwise provided in paragraph (c) of this section.

(c) In the case of an estate or trust heretofore taxable under the provisions of the Internal Revenue Code of 1939, amounts paid, credited, or to be distributed during its first taxable year subject to the Internal Revenue Code of 1954 which would have been treated as paid, credited, or to be distributed on the last day of the preceding taxable year if the Internal Revenue Code of 1939 were still applicable shall not be subject to the provisions of section 691(c)(1)(B) or this section. See section 683 and the regulations thereunder.

(d) The provisions of this section may be illustrated by the following example, in which it is assumed that the estate and the beneficiary make their returns on the calendar year basis:

Example. (1) The fiduciary of an estate receives taxable interest of $5,500 and income in respect of a decedent of $4,500 during the taxable year. Neither the will of the decedent nor local law requires the allocation to corpus of income in respect of a decedent. The estate tax attributable to the income in respect of a decedent is $1,500. In his discretion, the fiduciary distributes $2,000 (falling within sections 661(a) and 662(a)) to a beneficiary during that year. On these facts the fiduciary and beneficiary are respectively entitled to estate tax deductions of $1,200 and $300, computed as follows:

(2) Distributable net income computed under section 643(a) without regard to the estate tax deduction under section 691(c) is $10,000, computed as follows:

Taxable interest	$5,500
Income in respect of a decedent	4,500
Total	10,000

(3) Inasmuch as the distributable net income of $10,000 exceeds the amount of $2,000 distributed to the beneficiary, the deduction allowable to the estate under section 661(a), and the amount taxable to the beneficiary under section 662(a) is $2,000.

(4) The character of the amounts distributed to the beneficiary under section 662(b) is shown in the following table:

	Taxable interest	Income in respect of a decedent	Total
Distributable net income	$5,500	$4,500	$10,000
Amount deemed distributed under section 622(b)	1,100	900	2,000

(5) Accordingly, the beneficiary will be entitled to an estate tax deduction of $300 (900/4,500 × $1,500) and the estate will be entitled to an estate tax deduction of $1,200 (3,600/4,500 × $1,500).

(6) The taxable income of the estate is $6,200, computed as follows:

Gross income		$10,000
Less:		
Distributions to the beneficiary	$2,000	
Estate tax deduction under section 691(c)	1,200	
Personal exemption	600	
		3,800
Taxable income		6,200

T.D. 6257, 10/7/57.

§ 1.691(d)-1 Amounts received by surviving annuitant under joint and survivor annuity contract.

Caution: The Treasury has not yet amended Reg § 1.691(d)-1 to reflect changes made by P.L. 99-514, P.L. 96-471, P.L. 96-222, P.L. 95-600, P.L. 94-455.

(a) In general. Under section 691(d), annuity payments received by a surviving annuitant under a joint and survivor annuity contract (to the extent indicated in paragraph (b) of this section) are treated as income in respect of a decedent under section 691(a) for the purpose of allowing the deduction for estate tax provided for in section 691(c)(1)(A). This section applies only if the deceased annuitant died after December 31, 1953, and after the annuity starting date as defined in section 72(c)(4).

(b) Special value for surviving annuitant's payments. Section 691(d) provides a special value for the surviving annuitant's payments to determine the amount of the estate tax deduction provided for in section 691(c)(1)(A). This special value is determined by multiplying—

(1) The excess of the value of the annuity at the date of death of the deceased annuitant over the total amount excludable from the gross income of the surviving annuitant under section 72 during his life expectancy period (see paragraph (d)(1)(i) of this section)

by

(2) A fraction consisting of the value of the annuity for estate tax purposes over the value of the annuity at the date of death of the deceased annuitant.

This special value is used for the purpose of determining the net value for estate tax purposes (see section 691(c)(2)(B) and paragraph (a)(1) of § 1.691(c)-1) and for the purpose of determining the portion of estate tax attributable to the survivor's annuity (see paragraph (a) of § 1.691(c)-1).

(c) Amount of deduction. The portion of estate tax attributable to the survivor's annuity (see paragraph (a) of § 1.691(c)-1) is allowable as a deduction to the surviving annuitant over his life expectancy period. If the surviving annuitant continues to receive annuity payments beyond this period, there is no further deduction under section 691(d). If the surviving annuitant dies before expiration of such period, there is no compensating adjustment for the unused deduction.

(d) Definitions. *(1)* For purposes of section 691(d) and this section—

(i) The term "life expectancy period" means the period beginning with the first day of the first period for which an amount is received by the surviving annuitant under the contract and ending with the close of the taxable year with or in which falls the termination of the life expectancy of the surviving annuitant.

(ii) The life expectancy of the surviving annuitant shall be determined as of the date of death of the deceased annuitant, with reference to actuarial Table I set forth in § 1.72-9 (but without making any adjustment under paragraph (a)(2) of § 1.72-5).

(iii) The value of the annuity at the date of death of the deceased annuitant shall be the entire value of the survivor's annuity determined by reference to the principles set forth in section 2031 and the regulations thereunder, relating to the valuation of annuities for estate tax purposes.

(iv) The value of the annuity for estate tax purposes shall be that portion of the value determined under subdivision (iii) of this subparagraph which was includible in the deceased annuitant's gross estate.

(2) The determination of the "life expectancy period" of the survivor for purposes of section 691(d) may be illustrated by the following example:

Example. H and W file their income tax returns on the calendar year basis. H dies on July 15, 1955, on which date W is 70 years of age. On August 1, 1955, W receives a monthly payment under a joint and survivor annuity contract. W's life expectancy determined as of the date of H's death is 15 years as determined from Table I in § 1.72-9; thus her life expectancy ends on July 14, 1970. Under the provisions of section 691(d), her life expectancy period begins as of July 1, 1955, and ends as of December 31, 1970, thus giving her a life expectancy period of 15½ years.

(e) Examples. The application of section 691(d) and this section may be illustrated by the following examples:

Example (1). (1) H and W, husband and wife, purchased a joint and survivor annuity contract for $203,800 providing for monthly payments of $1,000 starting January 28, 1954, and continuing for their joint lives and for the remaining life of the survivor. H contributed $152,850 and W contributed $50,950 to the cost of the annuity. As of the annuity starting date, January 1, 1954, H's age at his nearest birthday was 70 and W's age at her nearest birthday was 67. H dies on January 1, 1957, and beginning on January 28, 1957, W receives her monthly payments of $1,000. The value of the annuity at the date of H's death is $159,000 (see paragraph (d)(1)(iii) of this section), and the value of the annuity for estate tax purposes (see paragraph (d)(1)(iv) of this section) is $119,250 (152,850/203,800 of $159,000). As of the date of H's death, W's age is 70 and her life expectancy period is 15 years (see paragraph (d) of this section for method of computation). Both H and W reported income by use of the cash receipts and disbursements method and filed income tax returns on the calendar year basis.

(2) The following computations illustrate the application of section 72 in determining the excludable portions of the annuity payments to W during her life expectancy period:

Amount of annuity payments per year (12 × $1,000)	$ 12,000
Life expectancy of H and W as of the annuity starting date (see section 72(c)(3)(A) and Table II of § 1.72-9 (male, age 70; female, age 67))	19.7
Expected return as of the annuity starting date, January 1, 1954 ($12,000 × 19.7 as determined under section 72(c)(3)(A) and paragraph (b) of § 1.72-5)	$236,400
Investment in the contract as of the annuity starting date, Jan. 1, 1954 (see section 72(c)(1) and paragraph (a) of § 1.72-6)	203,800
Exclusion ratio (203,800/236,400 as determined under section 72(b) and § 1.72-4) (percent)	86.2
Exclusion per year under section 72 ($12,000 × 86.2 percent)	$ 10,344
Excludable during W's life expectancy period ($10,344 × 15)	$155,160

(3) For the purpose of computing the deduction for estate tax under section 691(c), the value for estate tax purposes of the amounts includible in W's gross income and considered income in respect of a decedent by virtue of section 691(d)(1) is $2,880. This amount is arrived at in accordance with the formula contained in section 691(d)(2), as follows:

Value of annuity at date of H's death	$159,000
Total amount excludable from W's gross income under section 72 during W's life expectancy period (see subparagraph (2) of this example)	$155,160
Excess	$ 3,840
Ratio which value of annuity for estate tax purposes bears to value of annuity at date of H's death (119,250/159,000) (percent)	75
Value for estate tax purposes (75 percent of $3,840)	$ 2,880

This amount ($2,880) is included in the items of income under section 691(a)(1) for the purpose of determining the estate tax attributable to each item under section 691(c)(1)(A). The estate tax determined to be attributable to the item of $2,880 is then allowed as a deduction to W over her 15-year life expectancy period (see example (2) of this paragraph).

Example (2). Assume, in addition to the facts contained in example (1) of this paragraph, that H was an attorney and was entitled at the date of his death to a fee for services rendered in a case not completed at the time of his death, which fee was valued at $1,000, and to accrued bond interest, which was valued at $500. Taking into consideration the annuity payments of example (1), valued at $2,880, a total of $4,380 was included in his gross estate in respect of income described in section 691(a)(1). There were deducted as claims against his estate $280 for business expenses for which his estate was liable and $100 for taxes accrued on certain property which he owned. In all, $380 was deducted for claims which represent amounts described in section 691(b) which are allowable as deductions to his estate or to the beneficiaries of his estate. His gross estate was $404,250 and considering deductions of $15,000, a marital deduction of $119,250 (assuming the annuity to be the only qualifying gift) and an exemption of $60,000, his taxable estate amounted to $210,000. The estate tax on this amount is $53,700 from which is subtracted a $175 credit for State death taxes, leaving an estate tax liability of $53,525. W may deduct, in computing her taxable income during each year of her 15-year life expectancy period, $14.73 on account of the estate tax attributable to the value for estate tax purposes of that portion of the annuity payments considered income in respect of a decedent, computed as follows:

(1)(i) Value of income described in section 691(a)(1) included in computing gross estate	$4,380.00
(ii) Deductions in computing gross estate for claims representing deductions described in section 691(b)	380.00
(iii) Net value of items described in section 691(a)(1)	4,000.00
(2)(i) Estate tax	53,525.00
(ii) Less: Estate tax computed without including $4,000 (item (1)(iii)) in gross estate and by reducing marital deduction by $2,880 (portion of item (1)(iii) allowed as a marital deduction)	53,189.00
(iii) Portion of estate tax attributable to net value of income items	336.00
(3)(i) Value in gross estate of income attributable to annuity payments	2,880.00
(ii) Value in gross estate of all income items described in section 691(a)(1) (item (1)(i))	4,380.00
(iii) Part of estate tax attributable to annuity income (2,880/4,380 of $336)	220.93
(iv) Deduction each year on account of estate tax attributable to annuity income ($220.93 ÷ 15 (life expectancy period))	14.73

T.D. 6257, 10/7/57.

§ 1.691(e)-1 Installment obligations transmitted at death when prior law applied.

Caution: The Treasury has not yet amended Reg § 1.691(e)-1 to reflect changes made by P.L. 99-514, P.L. 96-471, P.L. 96-222, P.L. 95-600, P.L. 94-455.

(a) In general. *(1) Application of prior law.* Under section 44(d) of the Internal Revenue Code of 1939 and corresponding provisions of prior law, gains and losses on account of the transmission of installment obligations at the death of a holder of such obligations were required to be reported in the return of the decedent for the year of his death. However, an exception to this rule was provided if there was filed with the Commissioner a bond assuring the return as income of any payment in satisfaction of these obligations in the same proportion as would have been returnable as income by the decedent had he lived and received such payments. Obligations in respect of which such bond was filed are referred to in this section as "obligations assured by bond".

(2) Application of present law. Section 691(a)(4) of the Internal Revenue Code of 1954 (effective for taxable years beginning after December 31, 1953, and ending after August 16, 1954) in effect makes the exception which under prior law applied to obligations assured by bond the general rule for obligations transmitted at death, but contains no requirement for a bond. Section 691(e)(1) provides that if the holder of the installment obligation makes a proper election, the provisions of section 691(a)(4) shall apply in the case of obligations assured by bond. Section 691(e)(1) further provides that the estate tax deduction provided by section 691(c)(1) is not allowable for any amount included in gross income by reason of filing such an election.

(b) Manner and scope of election. *(1) In general.* The election to have obligations assured by bond treated as obligations to which section 691(a)(4) applies shall be made by the filing of a statement with respect to each bond to be released, containing the following information:

(i) The name and address of the decedent from whom the obligations assured by bond were transmitted, the date of his death, and the internal revenue district in which the last income tax return of the decedent was filed.

(ii) A schedule of all obligations assured by the bond on which is listed—

(a) The name and address of the obligors, face amount, date of maturity, and manner of payment of each obligation,

(b) The name, identifying number (provided under section 6109 and the regulations thereunder), and address of each person holding the obligations, and

(c) The name, identifying number, and address, of each person who at the time of the election possesses an interest in each obligation, and a description of such interest.

(iii) The total amount of income in respect of the obligations which would have been reportable as income by the decedent if he had lived and received such payment.

(iv) The amount of income referred to in subdivision (iii) of this subparagraph which has previously been included in gross income.

(v) An unqualified statement, signed by all persons holding the obligations, that they elect to have the provisions of section 691(a)(4) apply to such obligations and that such election shall be binding upon them, all current beneficiaries, and any person to whom the obligations may be transmitted by gift, bequest, or inheritance.

(vi) A declaration that the election is made under the penalties of perjury.

(2) Filing of statement. This statement with respect to each bond to be released shall be filed in duplicate with the district director of internal revenue for the district in which the bond is maintained. The statement shall be filed not later than the time prescribed for filing the return for the first taxable year (including any extension of time for such filing) to which the election applies.

(3) Effect of election. The election referred to in subparagraph (1) of this paragraph shall be irrevocable. Once an election is made with respect to an obligation assured by bond, it shall apply to all payments made in satisfaction of such obligation which were received during the first taxable year to which the election applies and to all such payments received during each taxable year thereafter, whether the recipient is the person who made the election, a current beneficiary, or a person to whom the obligation may be transmit-

ted by gift, bequest, or inheritance. Therefore, all payments received to which the election applies shall be treated as payments made on installment obligations to which section 691(a)(4) applies. However, the estate tax deduction provided by section 691(c) is not allowable for any such payment. The application of this subparagraph may be illustrated by the following example:

Example. A, the holder of an installment obligation, died in 1952. The installment obligation was transmitted at A's death to B who filed a bond on Form 1132 pursuant to paragraph (c) of § 39.44-5 of Regulations 118 (26 CFR Part 39, 1939 ed.) for the necessary amount. On January 1, 1965, B, a calendar year taxpayer, filed an election under section 691(e) to treat the obligation assured by bond as an obligation to which section 691(a)(4) applies, and B's bond was released for 1964 and subsequent taxable years. B died on June 1, 1965, and the obligation was bequeathed to C. On January 1, 1966, C received an installment payment on the obligation which had been assured by the bond. Because B filed an election with respect to the obligation assured by bond, C is required to treat the proper proportion of the January 1, 1966, payment and all subsequent payments made in satisfaction of this obligation as income in respect of a decedent. However, no estate tax deduction is allowable to C under section 691(c)(1) for any estate tax attributable to the inclusion of the value of such obligation in the estate of either A or B.

(c) Release of bond. If an election according to the provisions of paragraph (b) of this section is filed, the liability under any bond filed under section 44(d) of the 1939 Code (or the corresponding provisions of prior law) shall be released with respect to each taxable year to which such election applies. However, the liability under any such bond for an earlier taxable year to which the election does not apply shall not be released until the district director of internal revenue for the district in which the bond is maintained is assured that the proper portion of each installment payment received in such taxable year has been reported and the tax thereon paid.

T.D. 6808, 3/15/65.

§ 1.691(f)-1 Cross reference.

See section 753 and the regulations thereunder for application of section 691 to income in respect of a deceased partner.

T.D. 6257, 10/7/57, amend T.D. 6808, 3/15/65.

§ 1.692-1 Abatement of income taxes of certain members of the Armed Forces of the United States upon death.

Caution: The Treasury has not yet amended Reg § 1.692-1 to reflect changes made by P.L. 104-117, P.L. 99-514, P.L. 98-369, P.L. 98-259.

(a) *(1)* This section applies if—

(i) An individual dies while in active service as a member of the Armed Forces of the United States, and

(ii) His death occurs while he is serving in a combat zone (as determined under section 112), or at any place as a result of wounds, disease, or injury incurred while he was serving in a combat zone.

(2) If an individual dies as described in paragraph (a)(1) of this section, the following liabilities for tax, under subtitle A of the Internal Revenue Code of 1954 or under chapter 1 of the Internal Revenue Code of 1939, are canceled:

(i) The liability of the deceased individual, for his last taxable year, ending on the date of his death, and for any prior taxable year ending on or after the first day he served in a combat zone in active service as a member of the U.S. Armed Forces after June 24, 1950, and

(ii) The liability of any other person to the extent the liability is attributable to an amount received after the individual's death (including income in respect of a decedent under section 691) which would have been includible in the individual's gross income for his taxable year in which the date of his death falls (determined as if he had survived).

If the tax (including interest, additions to the tax, and additional amounts) is assessed, the assessment will be abated. If the amount of the tax is collected (regardless of the date of collection), the amount so collected will be credited or refunded as an overpayment.

(3) If an individual dies as described in paragraph (a)(1) of this section, there will not be assessed any amount of tax of the individual for taxable years preceding the years specified in paragraph (a)(2) of this section, under subtitle A of the Internal Revenue Code of 1954, chapter 1 of the Internal Revenue Code of 1939, or corresponding provisions of prior revenue laws, remaining unpaid as of the date of death. If any such unpaid tax (including interest, additions to the tax, and additional amounts) has been assessed, the assessments will be abated. If the amount of any such unpaid tax is collected after the date of death, the amount so collected will be credited or refunded as an overpayment.

(4) As to what constitutes active service as a member of the Armed Forces, service in a combat zone, and wounds, disease, or injury incurred while serving in a combat zone, see section 112. As to who are members of the Armed Forces, see section 7701(a)(15). As to the period of time within which any claim for refund must be filed, see sections 6511(a) and 7508(a)(1)(E).

(b) If such an individual and his spouse have for any such year filed a joint return, the tax abated, credited, or refunded pursuant to the provisions of section 692 for such year shall be an amount equal to that portion of the joint tax liability which is the same percentage of such joint tax liability as a tax computed upon the separate income of such individual is of the sum of the taxes computed upon the separate income of such individual and his spouse, but with respect to taxable years ending before June 24, 1950, and with respect to taxable years ending before the first day such individual served in a combat zone, as determined under section 112, the amount so abated, credited, or refunded shall not exceed the amount unpaid at the date of death. For such purpose, the separate tax of each spouse—

(1) For taxable years beginning after December 31, 1953, and ending after August 16, 1954, shall be the tax computed under subtitle A of the Internal Revenue Code of 1954 before the application of sections 31, 32, 6401(b), and 6402, but after the application of section 33, as if such spouse were required to make a separate income tax return; and

(2) For taxable years beginning before January 1, 1954, and for taxable years beginning after December 31, 1953, and ending before August 17, 1954, shall be the tax computed under chapter 1 of the Internal Revenue Code of 1939 before the application of sections 32, 35, and 322(a), but after the application of section 31, as if such spouse were required to make a separate income tax return.

(c) If such an individual and his spouse filed a joint declaration of estimated tax for the taxable year ending with the date of his death, the estimated tax paid pursuant to such declaration may be treated as the estimated tax of either such individual or his spouse, or may be divided between them, in such manner as his legal representative and such spouse may agree. Should they agree to treat such estimated tax, or any portion thereof, as the estimated tax of such individual, the estimated tax so paid shall be credited or refunded as an overpayment for the taxable year ending with the date of his death.

(d) For the purpose of determining the tax which is unpaid at the date of death, amounts deducted and withheld under chapter 24, subtitle C of the Internal Revenue Code of 1954, or under subchapter D, chapter 9 of the Internal Revenue Code of 1939 (relating to income tax withheld at source on wages), constitute payment of tax imposed under subtitle A of the Internal Revenue Code of 1954 or under chapter 1 of the Internal Revenue Code of 1939, as the case may be.

(e) This section shall have no application whatsoever with respect to the liability of an individual as a transferee of property of a taxpayer where such liability relates to the tax imposed upon the taxpayer by subtitle A of the Internal Revenue Code of 1954 or by chapter 1 of the Internal Revenue Code of 1939.

T.D. 6257, 10/7/57, amend T.D. 7543, 5/4/78.

§ 1.701-1 Partners, not partnership, subject to tax.

Partners are liable for income tax only in their separate capacities. Partnerships as such are not subject to the income tax imposed by subtitle A but are required to make returns of income under the provisions of section 6031 and the regulations thereunder. For definition of the terms "partner" and "partnership", see sections 761 and 7701(a)(2), and the regulations thereunder. For provisions relating to the election of certain partnerships to be taxed as domestic corporations, see section 1361 and the regulations thereunder.

T.D. 6175, 5/23/56.

§ 1.701-2 Anti-abuse rule.

Caution: The Treasury has not yet amended Reg § 1.701-2 to reflect changes made by P.L. 105-34.

(a) Intent of subchapter K. Subchapter K is intended to permit taxpayers to conduct joint business (including investment) activities through a flexible economic arrangement without incurring an entity-level tax. Implicit in the intent of subchapter K are the following requirements—

(1) The partnership must be bona fide and each partnership transaction or series of related transactions (individually or collectively, the transaction) must be entered into for a substantial business purpose.

(2) The form of each partnership transaction must be respected under substance over form principles.

(3) Except as otherwise provided in this paragraph (a)(3), the tax consequences under subchapter K to each partner of partnership operations and of transactions between the partner and the partnership must accurately reflect the partners' economic agreement and clearly reflect the partner's income (collectively, proper reflection of income). However, certain provisions of subchapter K and the regulations thereunder were adopted to promote administrative convenience and other policy objectives, with the recognition that the application of those provisions to a transaction could, in some circumstances, produce tax results that do not properly reflect income. Thus, the proper reflection of income requirement of this paragraph (a)(3) is treated as satisfied with respect to a transaction that satisfies paragraphs (a)(1) and (2) of this section to the extent that the application of such a provision to the transaction and the ultimate tax results, taking into account all the relevant facts and circumstances, are clearly contemplated by that provision. See, for example, paragraph (d) Example 6 of this section (relating to the value-equals-basis rule in § 1.704-1(b)(2)(iii)(c)), paragraph (d) Example 9 of this section (relating to the election under section 754 to adjust basis in partnership property), and paragraph (d) Examples 10 and 11 of this section (relating to the basis in property distributed by a partnership under section 732). See also, for example, §§ 1.704-3(e)(1) and 1.752-2(e)(4) (providing certain de minimis exceptions).

(b) Application of subchapter K rules. The provisions of subchapter K and the regulations thereunder must be applied in a manner that is consistent with the intent of subchapter K as set forth in paragraph (a) of this section (intent of subchapter K). Accordingly, if a partnership is formed or availed of in connection with a transaction a principal purpose of which is to reduce substantially the present value of the partners' aggregate federal tax liability in a manner that is inconsistent with the intent of subchapter K, the Commissioner can recast the transaction for federal tax purposes, as appropriate to achieve tax results that are consistent with the intent of subchapter K, in light of the applicable statutory and regulatory provisions and the pertinent facts and circumstances. Thus, even though the transaction may fall within the literal words of a particular statutory or regulatory provision, the Commissioner can determine, based on the particular facts and circumstances, that to achieve tax results that are consistent with the intent of subchapter K—

(1) The purported partnership should be disregarded in whole or in part, and the partnership's assets and activities should be considered, in whole or in part, to be owned and conducted, respectively, by one or more of its purported partners;

(2) One or more of the purported partners of the partnership should not be treated as a partner;

(3) The methods of accounting used by the partnership or a partner should be adjusted to reflect clearly the partnership's or the partner's income;

(4) The partnership's items of income, gain, loss, deduction, or credit should be reallocated; or

(5) The claimed tax treatment should otherwise be adjusted or modified.

(c) Facts and circumstances analysis; factors. Whether a partnership was formed or availed of with a principal purpose to reduce substantially the present value of the partners' aggregate federal tax liability in a manner inconsistent with the intent of subchapter K is determined based on all of the facts and circumstances, including a comparison of the purported business purpose for a transaction and the claimed tax benefits resulting from the transaction. The factors set forth below may be indicative, but do not necessarily establish, that a partnership was used in such a manner. These factors are illustrative only, and therefore may not be the only factors taken into account in making the determination under this section. Moreover, the weight given to any factor (whether specified in this paragraph or otherwise) depends on all the facts and circumstances. The presence or absence of any factor described in this paragraph does not create a presumption that a partnership was (or was not) used in such a manner. Factors include:

(1) The present value of the partners' aggregate federal tax liability is substantially less than had the partners owned the partnership's assets and conducted the partnership's activities directly;

(2) The present value of the partners' aggregate federal tax liability is substantially less than would be the case if purportedly separate transactions that are designed to achieve a particular end result are integrated and treated as steps in a single transaction. For example, this analysis may indicate that it was contemplated that a partner who was necessary to achieve the intended tax results and whose interest in the partnership was liquidated or disposed of (in whole or in part) would be a partner only temporarily in order to provide the claimed tax benefits to the remaining partners;

(3) One or more partners who are necessary to achieve the claimed tax results either have a nominal interest in the partnership, are substantially protected from any risk of loss from the partnership's activities (through distribution preferences, indemnity or loss guaranty agreements, or other arrangements), or have little or no participation in the profits from the partnership's activities other than a preferred return that is in the nature of a payment for the use of capital;

(4) Substantially all of the partners (measured by number or interests in the partnership) are related (directly or indirectly) to one another;

(5) Partnership items are allocated in compliance with the literal language of §§ 1.704-1 and 1.704-2 but with results that are inconsistent with the purpose of section 704(b) and those regulations. In this regard, particular scrutiny will be paid to partnerships in which income or gain is specially allocated to one or more partners that may be legally or effectively exempt from federal taxation (for example, a foreign person, an exempt organization, an insolvent taxpayer, or a taxpayer with unused federal tax attributes such as net operating losses, capital losses, or foreign tax credits);

(6) The benefits and burdens of ownership of property nominally contributed to the partnership are in substantial part retained (directly or indirectly) by the contributing partner (or a related party); or

(7) The benefits and burdens of ownership of partnership property are in substantial part shifted (directly or indirectly) to the distributee partner before or after the property is actually distributed to the distributee partner (or a related party).

(d) Examples. The following examples illustrate the principles of paragraphs (a), (b), and (c) of this section. The examples set forth below do not delineate the boundaries of either permissible or impermissible types of transactions. Further, the addition of any facts or circumstances that are not specifically set forth in an example (or the deletion of any facts or circumstances) may alter the outcome of the transaction described in the example. Unless otherwise indicated, parties to the transactions are not related to one another.

Example (1). Choice of entity; avoidance of entity-level tax; use of partnership consistent with the intent of subchapter K.

(i) A and B form limited partnership PRS to conduct a bona fide business. A, the corporate general partner, has a 1% partnership interest. B, the individual limited partner, has a 99% interest. PRS is properly classified as a partnership under §§ 301.7701-2 and 301.7701-3. A and B chose limited partnership form as a means to provide B with limited liability without subjecting the income from the business operations to an entity-level tax.

(ii) Subchapter K is intended to permit taxpayers to conduct joint business activity through a flexible economic arrangement without incurring an entity-level tax. See paragraph (a) of this section. Although B has retained, indirectly, substantially all of the benefits and burdens of ownership of the money or property B contributed to PRS (see paragraph (c)(6) of this section), the decision to organize and conduct business through PRS under these circumstances is consistent with this intent. In addition, on these facts, the requirements of paragraphs (a)(1), (2), and (3) of this section have been satisfied. The Commissioner therefore cannot invoke paragraph (b) of this section to recast the transaction.

Example (2). Choice of entity; avoidance of subchapter S shareholder requirements; use of partnership consistent with the intent of subchapter K.

(i) A and B form partnership PRS to conduct a bona fide business. A is a corporation that has elected to be treated as an S corporation under subchapter S. B is a nonresident alien. PRS is properly classified as a partnership under §§ 301.7701-2 and 301.7701-3. Because section 1361(b) prohibits B from being a shareholder in A, A and B chose partnership form, rather than admit B as a shareholder in A, as a means to retain the benefits of subchapter S treatment for A and its shareholders.

(ii) Subchapter K is intended to permit taxpayers to conduct joint business activity through a flexible economic arrangement without incurring an entity-level tax. See paragraph (a) of this section. The decision to organize and conduct business through PRS is consistent with this intent. In addition, on these facts, the requirements of paragraphs (a)(1), (2), and (3) of this section have been satisfied. Although it may be argued that the form of the partnership transaction should not be respected because it does not reflect its substance (inasmuch as application of the substance over form doctrine arguably could result in B being treated as a shareholder of A, thereby invalidating A's subchapter S election), the facts indicate otherwise. The shareholders of A are subject to tax on their pro rata shares of A's income (see section 1361 et. seq.), and B is subject to tax on B's distributive share of partnership income (see sections 871 and 875). Thus, the form in which this arrangement is cast accurately reflects its substance as a separate partnership and S corporation. The Commissioner therefore cannot invoke paragraph (b) of this section to recast the transaction.

Example (3). Choice of entity; avoidance of more restrictive foreign tax credit limitation; use of partnership consistent with the intent of subchapter K.

(i) X, a domestic corporation, and Y, a foreign corporation, form partnership PRS under the laws of foreign Country A to conduct a bona fide joint business. X and Y each owns a 50% interest in PRS. PRS is properly classified as a partnership under §§ 301.7701-2 and 301.7701-3. PRS pays income taxes to Country A. X and Y chose partnership form to enable X to qualify for a direct foreign tax credit under section 901, with look-through treatment under § 1.904-5(h)(1). Conversely, if PRS were a foreign corporation for U.S. tax purposes, X would be entitled only to indirect foreign tax credits under section 902 with respect to dividend distributions from PRS. The look-through rules, however, would not apply, and pursuant to section 904(d)(1)(E) and § 1.904-4(g), the dividends and associated taxes would be subject to a separate foreign tax credit limitation for dividends from PRS, a noncontrolled section 902 corporation.

(ii) Subchapter K is intended to permit taxpayers to conduct joint business activity through a flexible economic arrangement without incurring an entity-level tax. See paragraph (a) of this section. The decision to organize and conduct business through PRS in order to take advantage of the look-through rules for foreign tax credit purposes, thereby maximizing X's use of its proper share of foreign taxes paid by PRS, is consistent with this intent. In addition, on these facts, the requirements of paragraphs (a)(1), (2), and (3) of this section have been satisfied. The Commissioner therefore cannot invoke paragraph (b) of this section to recast the transaction.

Example (4). Choice of entity; avoidance of gain recognition under sections 351(e) and 357(c); use of partnership consistent with the intent of subchapter K.

(i) X, ABC, and DEF form limited partnership PRS to conduct a bona fide real estate management business. PRS is properly classified as a partnership under §§ 301.7701-2 and 301.7701-3. X, the general partner, is a newly formed corporation that elects to be treated as a real estate investment trust as defined in section 856. X offers its stock to the public and contributes substantially all of the proceeds from the public offering to PRS. ABC and DEF, the limited partners, are existing partnerships with substantial real estate holdings. ABC and DEF contribute all of their real property assets to PRS, subject to liabilities that exceed their respective aggregate bases in the real property contributed, and terminate under section 708(b)(1)(A). In addition, some of the former partners of ABC and DEF each have the right, beginning two years after the formation of PRS, to require the redemption of their limited partnership interests in PRS in exchange for cash or X stock (at X's option) equal to the fair market value of their respective interests in PRS at the time of the redemption. These partners are not compelled, as a legal or practical matter, to exercise their exchange rights at any time. X, ABC, and DEF chose to form a partnership rather than have ABC and DEF invest directly in X to allow ABC and DEF to avoid recognition of gain under sections 351(e) and 357(c). Because PRS would not be treated as an investment company within the meaning of section 351(e) if PRS were incorporated (so long as it did not elect under section 856), section 721(a) applies to the contribution of the real property to PRS. See section 721(b).

(ii) Subchapter K is intended to permit taxpayers to conduct joint business activity through a flexible economic arrangement without incurring an entity-level tax. See paragraph (a) of this section. The decision to organize and conduct business through PRS, thereby avoiding the tax consequences that would have resulted from contributing the existing partnerships' real estate assets to X (by applying the rules of sections 721, 731, and 752 in lieu of the rules of sections 351(e) and 357(c)), is consistent with this intent. In addition, on these facts, the requirements of paragraphs (a)(1), (2), and (3) of this section have been satisfied. Although it may be argued that the form of the transaction should not be respected because it does not reflect its substance (inasmuch as the present value of the partners' aggregate federal tax liability is substantially less than would be the case if the transaction were integrated and treated as a contribution of the encumbered assets by ABC and DEF directly to X, see paragraph (c)(2) of this section), the facts indicate otherwise. For example, the right of some of the former ABC and DEF partners after two years to exchange their PRS interests for cash or X stock (at X's option) equal to the fair market value of their PRS interest at that time would not require that right to be considered as exercised prior to its actual exercise. Moreover, X may make other real estate investments and other business decisions, including the decision to raise additional capital for those purposes. Thus, although it may be likely that some or all of the partners with the right to do so will, at some point, exercise their exchange rights, and thereby receive either cash or X stock, the form of the transaction as a separate partnership and real estate investment trust is respected under substance over form principles (see paragraph (a)(2) of this section). The Commissioner therefore cannot invoke paragraph (b) of this section to recast the transaction.

Example (5). Special allocations; dividends received deductions; use of partnership consistent with the intent of subchapter K.

(i) Corporations X and Y contribute equal amounts to PRS, a bona fide partnership formed to make joint investments. PRS pays $100x for a share of common stock of Z, an unrelated corporation, which has historically paid an annual dividend of $6x. PRS specially allocates the dividend income on the Z stock to X to the extent of the London Inter-Bank Offered Rate (LIBOR) on the record date, applied to X's contribution of $50x, and allocates the remainder of the dividend income to Y. All other items of partnership income and loss are allocated equally between X and Y. The allocations under the partnership agreement have substantial economic effect within the meaning of § 1.704-1(b)(2). In addition to avoiding an entity-level tax, a principal purpose for the formation of the partnership was to invest in the Z common stock and to allocate the dividend income from the stock to provide X with a floating-rate return based on LIBOR, while permitting X and Y to claim the dividends received deduction under section 243 on the dividends allocated to each of them.

(ii) Subchapter K is intended to permit taxpayers to conduct joint business activity through a flexible economic arrangement without incurring an entity-level tax. See paragraph (a) of this section. The decision to organize and conduct business through PRS is consistent with this intent. In addition, on these facts, the requirements of paragraphs (a)(1), (2), and (3) of this section have been satisfied. Section 704(b) and § 1.704-1(b)(2) permit income realized by the partnership to be allocated validly to the partners separate from the partners' respective ownership of the capital to which the allocations relate, provided that the allocations satisfy both the literal requirements of the statute and regulations and the purpose of those provisions (see paragraph (c)(5) of this section). Section 704(e)(2) is not applicable to the facts of this example (otherwise, the allocations would be required to be proportionate to the partners' ownership of contributed capital). The Commissioner therefore cannot invoke paragraph (b) of this section to recast the transaction.

Example (6). Special allocations; nonrecourse financing; low-income housing credit; use of partnership consistent with the intent of subchapter K.

(i) A and B, high-bracket taxpayers, and X, a corporation with net operating loss carryforwards, form general partnership PRS to own and operate a building that qualifies for the low-income housing credit provided by section 42. The project is financed with both cash contributions from the partners and nonrecourse indebtedness. The partnership agreement provides for special allocations of income and deductions, including the allocation of all depreciation deductions attributable to the building to A and B equally in a manner that is reasonably consistent with allocations that have substantial economic effect of some other significant partnership item attributable to the building. The section 42 credits are allocated to A and B in accordance with the allocation of depreciation deductions. PRS's allocations comply with all applicable regulations, including the requirements of §§ 1.704-1(b)(2)(ii) (pertaining to economic effect) and 1.704-2(e) (requirements for allocations of nonrecourse deductions). The nonrecourse indebtedness is validly allocated to the partners under the rules of § 1.752-3, thereby increasing the basis of the partners' respective partnership interests. The basis increase created by the nonrecourse indebtedness enables A and B to deduct their distributive share of losses from the partnership (subject to all other applicable limitations under the Internal Revenue Code) against their nonpartnership income and to apply the credits against their tax liability.

(ii) At a time when the depreciation deductions attributable to the building are not treated as nonrecourse deductions under § 1.704-2(c) (because there is no net increase in partnership minimum gain during the year), the special allocation of depreciation deductions to A and B has substantial economic effect because of the value-equals-basis safe harbor contained in § 1.704-1(b)(2)(iii)(c) and the fact that A and B would bear the economic burden of any decline in the value of the building (to the extent of the partnership's investment in the building), notwithstanding that A and B believe it is unlikely that the building will decline in value (and, accordingly, they anticipate significant timing benefits through the special allocation). Moreover, in later years, when the depreciation deductions attributable to the building are treated as nonrecourse deductions under § 1.704-2(c), the special allocation of depreciation deductions to A and B is considered to be consistent with the partners' interests in the partnership under § 1.704-2(e).

(iii) Subchapter K is intended to permit taxpayers to conduct joint business activity through a flexible economic arrangement without incurring an entity-level tax. See paragraph (a) of this section. The decision to organize and conduct business through PRS is consistent with this intent. In addition, on these facts, the requirements of paragraphs (a)(1), (2), and (3) of this section have been satisfied. Section 704(b), § 1.704-1(b)(2), and § 1.704-2(e) allow partnership items of income, gain, loss, deduction, and credit to be allocated validly to the partners separate from the partners' respective ownership of the capital to which the allocations relate, provided that the allocations satisfy both the literal requirements of the statute and regulations and the purpose of those provisions (see paragraph (c)(5) of this section). Moreover, the application of the value-equals-basis safe harbor and the provisions of § 1.704-2(e) with respect to the allocations to A and B, and the tax results of the application of those provisions, taking into account all the facts and circumstances, are clearly contemplated. Accordingly, even if the allocations would not otherwise be considered to satisfy the proper reflection of income standard in paragraph (a)(3) of this section, that requirement will be treated as satisfied under these facts. Thus, even though the partners' aggregate federal tax liability may be substantially less than had the partners owned the partnership's assets directly (due to X's inability to use its allocable share of the partnership's losses and credits) (see paragraph (c)(1) of this section), the transaction is not inconsistent with the intent of subchapter K. The Commissioner therefore cannot invoke paragraph (b) of this section to recast the transaction.

Example (7). Partner with nominal interest; temporary partner; use of partnership not consistent with the intent of subchapter K.

(i) Pursuant to a plan a principal purpose of which is to generate artificial losses and thereby shelter from federal taxation a substantial amount of income, X (a foreign corporation), Y (a domestic corporation), and Z (a promoter) form partnership PRS by contributing $9,000x, $990x, and $10x, respectively, for proportionate interests (90.0%, 9.9%, and 0.1%, respectively) in the capital and profits of PRS. PRS purchases offshore equipment for $10,000x and validly leases the equipment offshore for a term representing most of its projected useful life. Shortly thereafter, PRS sells its rights to receive income under the lease to a third party for $9,000x, and allocates the resulting $9,000x of income $8,100x to X, $891x to Y, and $9x to Z. PRS thereafter makes a distribution of $9,000x to X in complete liquidation of its interest. Under § 1.704-1(b)(2)(iv)(f), PRS restates the partners' capital accounts immediately before making the liquidating distribution to X to reflect its assets consisting of the offshore equipment worth $1,000x and $9,000x in cash. Thus, because the capital accounts immediately before the distribution reflect assets of $19,000x (that is, the initial capital contributions of $10,000x plus the $9,000x of income realized from the sale of the lease), PRS allocates a $9,000x book loss among the partners (for capital account purposes only), resulting in restated capital accounts for X, Y, and Z of $9,000x, $990x, and $10x, respectively. Thereafter, PRS purchases real property by borrowing the $8,000x purchase price on a recourse basis, which increases Y's and Z's bases in their respective partnership interests from $1,881x and $19x, to $9,801x and $99x, respectively (reflecting Y's and Z's adjusted interests in the partnership of 99% and 1%, respectively). PRS subsequently sells the offshore equipment, subject to the lease, for $1,000x and allocates the $9,000x tax loss $8,910x to Y and $90x to Z. Y's and Z's bases in their partnership interests are therefore reduced to $891x and $9x, respectively.

(ii) On these facts, any purported business purpose for the transaction is insignificant in comparison to the tax benefits that would result if the transaction were respected for federal tax purposes (see paragraph (c) of this section). Accordingly, the transaction lacks a substantial business purpose (see paragraph (a)(1) of this section). In addition, factors (1), (2), (3), and (5) of paragraph (c) of this section indicate that PRS was used with a principal purpose to reduce substantially the partners' tax liability in a manner inconsistent with the intent of subchapter K. On these facts, PRS is not bona fide (see paragraph (a)(1) of this section), and the transaction is not respected under applicable substance over form principles (see paragraph (a)(2) of this section) and does not properly reflect the income of Y (see paragraph (a)(3) of this section). Thus, PRS has been formed and availed of with a principal purpose of reducing substantially the present value of the partners' aggregate federal tax liability in a manner inconsistent with the intent of subchapter K. Therefore (in addition to possibly challenging the transaction under judicial principles or the validity of the allocations under § 1.704-1(b)(2) (see paragraph (h) of this section)), the Commissioner can recast the transaction as appropriate under paragraph (b) of this section.

Example (8). Plan to duplicate losses through absence of section 754 election; use of partnership not consistent with the intent of subchapter K.

(i) A owns land with a basis of $100x and a fair market value of $60x. A would like to sell the land to B. A and B devise a plan a principal purpose of which is to permit the duplication, for a substantial period of time, of the tax benefit of A's built-in loss in the land. To effect this plan, A, C

(A's brother), and W (C's wife) form partnership PRS, to which A contributes the land, and C and W each contribute $30x. All partnership items are shared in proportion to the partners' respective contributions to PRS. PRS invests the cash in an investment asset (that is not a marketable security within the meaning of section 731(c)). PRS also leases the land to B under a three-year lease pursuant to which B has the option to purchase the land from PRS upon the expiration of the lease for an amount equal to its fair market value at that time. All lease proceeds received are immediately distributed to the partners. In year 3, at a time when the values of the partnership's assets have not materially changed, PRS agrees with A to liquidate A's interest in exchange for the investment asset held by PRS. Under section 732(b), A's basis in the asset distributed equals $100x, A's basis in A's partnership interest immediately before the distribution. Shortly thereafter, A sells the investment asset to X, an unrelated party, recognizing a $40x loss.

(ii) PRS does not make an election under section 754. Accordingly, PRS's basis in the land contributed by A remains $100x. At the end of year 3, pursuant to the lease option, PRS sells the land to B for $60x (its fair market value). Thus, PRS recognizes a $40x loss on the sale, which is allocated equally between C and W. C's and W's bases in their partnership interests are reduced to $10x each pursuant to section 705. Their respective interests are worth $30x each. Thus, upon liquidation of PRS (or their interests therein), each of C and W will recognize $20x of gain. However, PRS's continued existence defers recognition of that gain indefinitely. Thus, if this arrangement is respected, C and W duplicate for their benefit A's built-in loss in the land prior to its contribution to PRS.

(iii) On these facts, any purported business purpose for the transaction is insignificant in comparison to the tax benefits that would result if the transaction were respected for federal tax purposes (see paragraph (c) of this section). Accordingly, the transaction lacks a substantial business purpose (see paragraph (a)(1) of this section). In addition, factors (1), (2), and (4) of paragraph (c) of this section indicate that PRS was used with a principal purpose to reduce substantially the partners' tax liability in a manner inconsistent with the intent of subchapter K. On these facts, PRS is not bona fide (see paragraph (a)(1) of this section), and the transaction is not respected under applicable substance over form principles (see paragraph (a)(2) of this section). Further, the tax consequences to the partners do not properly reflect the partners' income; and Congress did not contemplate application of section 754 to partnerships such as PRS, which was formed for a principal purpose of producing a double tax benefit from a single economic loss (see paragraph (a)(3) of this section). Thus, PRS has been formed and availed of with a principal purpose of reducing substantially the present value of the partners' aggregate federal tax liability in a manner inconsistent with the intent of subchapter K. Therefore (in addition to possibly challenging the transaction under judicial principles or other statutory authorities, such as the substance over form doctrine or the disguised sale rules under section 707 (see paragraph (h) of this section)), the Commissioner can recast the transaction as appropriate under paragraph (b) of this section.

Example (9). Absence of section 754 election; use of partnership consistent with the intent of subchapter K.

(i) PRS is a bona fide partnership formed to engage in investment activities with contributions of cash from each partner. Several years after joining PRS, A, a partner with a capital account balance and basis in its partnership interest of $100x, wishes to withdraw from PRS. The partnership agreement entitles A to receive the balance of A's capital account in cash or securities owned by PRS at the time of withdrawal, as mutually agreed to by A and the managing general partner, P. P and A agree to distribute to A $100x worth of non-marketable securities (see section 731(c)) in which PRS has an aggregate basis of $20x. Upon distribution, A's aggregate basis in the securities is $100x under section 732(b). PRS does not make an election to adjust the basis in its remaining assets under section 754. Thus, PRS's basis in its remaining assets is unaffected by the distribution. In contrast, if a section 754 election had been in effect for the year of the distribution, under these facts section 734(b) would have required PRS to adjust the basis in its remaining assets downward by the amount of the untaxed appreciation in the distributed property, thus reflecting that gain in PRS's retained assets. In selecting the assets to be distributed, A and P had a principal purpose to take advantage of the facts that A's basis in the securities will be determined by reference to A's basis in its partnership interest under section 732(b), and because PRS will not make an election under section 754, the remaining partners of PRS will likely enjoy a federal tax timing advantage (i.e., from the $80x of additional basis in its assets that would have been eliminated if the section 754 election had been made) that is inconsistent with proper reflection of income under paragraph (a)(3) of this section.

(ii) Subchapter K is intended to permit taxpayers to conduct joint business activity through a flexible economic arrangement without incurring an entity-level tax. See paragraph (a) of this section. The decision to organize and conduct business through PRS is consistent with this intent. In addition, on these facts, the requirements of paragraphs (a)(1) and (2) of this section have been satisfied. The validity of the tax treatment of this transaction is therefore dependent upon whether the transaction satisfies (or is treated as satisfying) the proper reflection of income standard under paragraph (a)(3) of this section. A's basis in the distributed securities is properly determined under section 732(b). The benefit to the remaining partners is a result of PRS not having made an election under section 754. Subchapter K is generally intended to produce tax consequences that achieve proper reflection of income. However, paragraph (a)(3) of this section provides that if the application of a provision of subchapter K produces tax results that do not properly reflect income, but application of that provision to the transaction and the ultimate tax results, taking into account all the relevant facts and circumstances, are clearly contemplated by that provision (and the transaction satisfies the requirements of paragraphs (a)(1) and (2) of this section), then the application of that provision to the transaction will be treated as satisfying the proper reflection of income standard.

(iii) In general, the adjustments that would be made if an election under section 754 were in effect are necessary to minimize distortions between the partners' bases in their partnership interests and the partnership's basis in its assets following, for example, a distribution to a partner. The electivity of section 754 is intended to provide administrative convenience for bona fide partnerships that are engaged in transactions for a substantial business purpose, by providing those partnerships the option of not adjusting their bases in their remaining assets following a distribution to a partner. Congress clearly recognized that if the section 754 elections were not made, basis distortions may result. Taking into account all the facts and circumstances of the transaction, the electivity of section 754 in the context of the distribution from PRS to A, and the ultimate tax consequences that follow from the failure to make the election with respect to the transaction, are clearly contemplated by section 754. Thus, the tax consequences of this transaction will be treated as satisfying the proper reflection of income standard under paragraph (a)(3) of this section. The Commissioner therefore cannot invoke paragraph (b) of this section to recast the transaction.

Example (10). Basis adjustments under section 732; use of partnership consistent with the intent of subchapter K.

(i) A, B, and C are partners in partnership PRS, which has for several years been engaged in substantial bona fide business activities. For valid business reasons, the partners agree that A's interest in PRS, which has a value and basis of $100x, will be liquidated with the following assets of PRS: a nondepreciable asset with a value of $60x and a basis to PRS of $40x, and related equipment with two years of cost recovery remaining and a value and basis to PRS of $40x. Neither asset is described in section 751 and the transaction is not described in section 732(d). Under section 732(b) and (c), A's $100x basis in A's partnership interest will be allocated between the nondepreciable asset and the equipment received in the liquidating distribution in proportion to PRS's bases in those assets, or $50x to the nondepreciable asset and $50x to the equipment. Thus, A will have a $10x built-in gain in the nondepreciable asset ($60x value less $50x basis) and a $10x built-in loss in the equipment ($50x basis less $40x value), which it expects to recover rapidly through cost recovery deductions. In selecting the assets to be distributed to A, the partners had a principal purpose to take advantage of the fact that A's basis in the assets will be determined by reference to A's basis in A's partnership interest, thus, in effect, shifting a portion of A's basis from the nondepreciable asset to the equipment, which in turn would allow A to recover that portion of its basis more rapidly. This shift provides a federal tax timing advantage to A, with no offsetting detriment to B or C.

(ii) Subchapter K is intended to permit taxpayers to conduct joint business activity through a flexible economic arrangement without incurring an entity-level tax. See paragraph (a) of this section. The decision to organize and conduct business through PRS is consistent with this intent. In addition, on these facts, the requirements of paragraphs (a)(1) and (2) of this section have been satisfied. The validity of the tax treatment of this transaction is therefore dependent upon whether the transaction satisfies (or is treated as satisfying) the proper reflection of income standard under paragraph (a)(3) of this section. Subchapter K is generally intended to produce tax consequences that achieve proper reflection of income. However, paragraph (a)(3) of this section provides that if the application of a provision of subchapter K produces tax results that do not properly reflect income, but the application of that provision to the transaction and the ultimate tax results, taking into account all the relevant facts and circumstances, are clearly contemplated by that provision (and the transaction satisfies the requirements of paragraphs (a)(1) and (2) of this section), then the application of that provision to the transaction will be treated as satisfying the proper reflection of income standard.

(iii) A's basis in the assets distributed to it was determined under section 732(b) and (c). The transaction does not properly reflect A's income due to the basis distortions caused by the distribution and the shifting of basis from a nondepreciable to a depreciable asset. However, the basis rules under section 732, which in some situations can produce tax results that are inconsistent with the proper reflection of income standard (see paragraph (a)(3) of this section), are intended to provide simplifying administrative rules for bona fide partnerships that are engaged in transactions with a substantial business purpose. Taking into account all the facts and circumstances of the transaction, the application of the basis rules under section 732 to the distribution from PRS to A, and the ultimate tax consequences of the application of that provision of subchapter K, are clearly contemplated. Thus, the application of section 732 to this transaction will be treated as satisfying the proper reflection of income standard under paragraph (a)(3) of this section. The Commissioner therefore cannot invoke paragraph (b) of this section to recast the transaction.

Example (11). Basis adjustments under section 732; plan or arrangement to distort basis allocations artificially; use of partnership not consistent with the intent of subchapter K.

(i) Partnership PRS has for several years been engaged in the development and management of commercial real estate projects. X, an unrelated party, desires to acquire undeveloped land owned by PRS, which has a value of $95x and a basis of $5x. X expects to hold the land indefinitely after its acquisition. Pursuant to a plan a principal purpose of which is to permit X to acquire and hold the land but nevertheless to recover for tax purposes a substantial portion of the purchase price for the land, X contributes $100x to PRS for an interest therein. Subsequently (at a time when the value of the partnership's assets have not materially changed), PRS distributes to X in liquidation of its interest in PRS the land and another asset with a value and basis to PRS of $5x. The second asset is an insignificant part of the economic transaction but is important to achieve the desired tax results. Under section 732(b) and (c), X's $100x basis in its partnership interest is allocated between the assets distributed to it in proportion to their bases to PRS, or $50x each. Thereafter, X plans to sell the second asset for its value of $5x, recognizing a loss of $45x. In this manner, X will, in effect, recover a substantial portion of the purchase price of the land almost immediately. In selecting the assets to be distributed to X, the partners had a principal purpose to take advantage of the fact that X's basis in the assets will be determined under section 732(b) and (c), thus, in effect, shifting a portion of X's basis economically allocable to the land that X intends to retain to an inconsequential asset that X intends to dispose of quickly. This shift provides a federal tax timing advantage to X, with no offsetting detriment to any of PRS's other partners.

(ii) Although section 732 recognizes that basis distortions can occur in certain situations, which may produce tax results that do not satisfy the proper reflection of income standard of paragraph (a)(3) of this section, the provision is intended only to provide ancillary, simplifying tax results for bona fide partnership transactions that are engaged in for substantial business purposes. Section 732 is not intended to serve as the basis for plans or arrangements in which inconsequential or immaterial assets are included in the distribution with a principal purpose of obtaining substantially favorable tax results by virtue of the statute's simplifying rules. The transaction does not properly reflect X's income due to the basis distortions caused by the distribution that result in shifting a significant portion of X's basis to this inconsequential asset. Moreover, the proper reflection of income standard contained in paragraph (a)(3) of this section is not treated as satisfied, because, taking into account all the facts and circumstances, the application of section 732 to this arrangement, and the ultimate tax consequences that would thereby result, were not clearly contemplated by that provision of subchapter K. In addition, by using a partnership (if respected), the partners' aggregate federal tax liability would be substantially less than had they owned the partnership's assets directly (see paragraph (c)(1) of this section). On these facts, PRS has been formed and availed of with a principal purpose to reduce the taxpayers' aggregate federal tax liability in a manner that is inconsistent with the intent of subchapter K. Therefore (in addition to possibly challenging the transaction under applicable judicial principles and statutory authorities, such as the disguised sale rules under section 707, see paragraph (h) of this section), the Commissioner can recast the transaction as appropriate under paragraph (b) of this section.

(e) Abuse of entity treatment. *(1) General rule.* The Commissioner can treat a partnership as an aggregate of its partners in whole or in part as appropriate to carry out the purpose of any provision of the Internal Revenue Code or the regulations promulgated thereunder.

(2) Clearly contemplated entity treatment. Paragraph (e)(1) of this section does not apply to the extent that—

(i) A provision of the Internal Revenue Code or the regulations promulgated thereunder prescribes the treatment of a partnership as an entity, in whole or in part, and

(ii) That treatment and the ultimate tax results, taking into account all the relevant facts and circumstances, are clearly contemplated by that provision.

(f) Examples. The following examples illustrate the principles of paragraph (e) of this section. The examples set forth below do not delineate the boundaries of either permissible or impermissible types of transactions. Further, the addition of any facts or circumstances that are not specifically set forth in an example (or the deletion of any facts or circumstances) may alter the outcome of the transaction described in the example. Unless otherwise indicated, parties to the transactions are not related to one another.

Example (1). Aggregate treatment of partnership appropriate to carry out purpose of section 163(e)(5).

(i) Corporations X and Y are partners in partnership PRS, which for several years has engaged in substantial bona fide business activities. As part of these business activities, PRS issues certain high yield discount obligations to an unrelated third party. Section 163(e)(5) defers (and in certain circumstances disallows) the interest deductions on this type of obligation if issued by a corporation. PRS, X, and Y take the position that, because PRS is a partnership and not a corporation, section 163(e)(5) is not applicable.

(ii) Section 163(e)(5) does not prescribe the treatment of a partnership as an entity for purposes of that section. The purpose of section 163(e)(5) is to limit corporate-level interest deductions on certain obligations. The treatment of PRS as an entity could result in a partnership with corporate partners issuing those obligations and thereby circumventing the purpose of section 163(e)(5), because the corporate partner would deduct its distributive share of the interest on obligations that would have been deferred until paid or disallowed had the corporation issued its share of the obligation directly. Thus, under paragraph (e)(1) of this section, PRS is properly treated as an aggregate of its partners for purposes of applying section 163(e)(5) (regardless of whether any party had a tax avoidance purpose in having PRS issue the obligation). Each partner of PRS will therefore be treated as issuing its share of the obligations for purposes of determining the deductibility of its distributive share of any interest on the obligations. See also section 163(i)(5)(B).

Example (2). Aggregate treatment of partnership appropriate to carry out purpose of section 1059.

(i) Corporations X and Y are partners in partnership PRS, which for several years has engaged in substantial bona fide business activities. As part of these business activities, PRS purchases 50 shares of Corporation Z common stock. Six months later, Corporation Z announces an extraordinary dividend (within the meaning of section 1059). Section 1059(a) generally provides that if any corporation receives an extraordinary dividend with respect to any share of stock and the corporation has not held the stock for more than two years before the dividend announcement date, the basis in the stock held by the corporation is reduced by the nontaxed portion of the dividend. PRS, X, and Y take the position that section 1059(a) is not applicable because PRS is a partnership and not a corporation.

(ii) Section 1059(a) does not prescribe the treatment of a partnership as an entity for purposes of that section. The purpose of section 1059(a) is to limit the benefits of the dividends received deduction with respect to extraordinary dividends. The treatment of PRS as an entity could result in corporate partners in the partnership receiving dividends through partnerships in circumvention of the intent of section 1059. Thus, under paragraph (e)(1) of this section, PRS is properly treated as an aggregate of its partners for purposes of applying section 1059 (regardless of whether any party had a tax avoidance purpose in acquiring the Z stock through PRS). Each partner of PRS will therefore be treated as owning its share of the stock. Accordingly, PRS must make appropriate adjustments to the basis of the Corporation Z stock, and the partners must also make adjustments to the basis in their respective interests in PRS under section 705(a)(2)(B). See also section 1059(g)(1).

Example (3). Prescribed entity treatment of partnership; determination of CFC status clearly contemplated.

(i) X, a domestic corporation, and Y, a foreign corporation, intend to conduct a joint venture in foreign Country A. They form PRS, a bona fide domestic general partnership in which X owns a 40% interest and Y owns a 60% interest. PRS is properly classified as a partnership under §§ 301.7701-2 and 301.7701-3. PRS holds 100% of the voting stock of Z, a Country A entity that is classified as an association taxable as a corporation for federal tax purposes under § 301.7701-2. Z conducts its business operations in Country A. By investing in Z through a domestic partnership, X seeks to obtain the benefit of the look-through rules of section 904(d)(3) and, as a result, maximize its ability to claim credits for its proper share of Country A taxes expected to be incurred by Z.

(ii) Pursuant to sections 957(c) and 7701(a)(30), PRS is a United States person. Therefore, because it owns 10% or more of the voting stock of Z, PRS satisfies the definition of a U.S. shareholder under section 951(b). Under section 957(a), Z is a controlled foreign corporation (CFC) because more than 50% of the voting power or value of its stock is owned by PRS. Consequently, under section 904(d)(3), X qualifies for look-through treatment in computing its credit for foreign taxes paid or accrued by Z. In contrast, if X and Y owned their interests in Z directly, Z would not be a CFC because only 40% of its stock would be owned by U.S. shareholders. X's credit for foreign taxes paid or accrued by Z in that case would be subject to a separate foreign tax credit limitation for dividends from Z, a noncontrolled section 902 corporation. See section 904(d)(1)(E) and § 1.904-4(g).

(iii) Sections 957(c) and 7701(a)(30) prescribe the treatment of a domestic partnership as an entity for purposes of defining a U.S. shareholder, and thus, for purposes of determining whether a foreign corporation is a CFC. The CFC rules prevent the deferral by U.S. shareholders of U.S. taxation of certain earnings of the CFC and reduce disparities that otherwise might occur between the amount of income subject to a particular foreign tax credit limitation when a taxpayer earns income abroad directly rather than indirectly through a CFC. The application of the look-through rules for foreign tax credit purposes is appropriately tied to CFC status. See sections 904(d)(2)(E) and 904(d)(3). This analysis confirms that Congress clearly contemplated that taxpayers could use a bona fide domestic partnership to subject themselves to the CFC regime, and the resulting application of the look-through rules of section 904(d)(3). Accordingly, under paragraph (e) of this section, the Commissioner cannot treat PRS as an aggregate of its partners for purposes of determining X's foreign tax credit limitation.

(g) Effective date. Paragraphs (a), (b), (c), and (d) of this section are effective for all transactions involving a partnership that occur on or after May 12, 1994. Paragraphs (e) and (f) of this section are effective for all transactions involving a partnership that occur on or after December 29, 1994.

(h) Scope and application. This section applies solely with respect to taxes under subtitle A of the Internal Revenue Code, and for purposes of this section, any reference to a federal tax is limited to any tax imposed under subtitle A of the Internal Revenue Code.

(i) Application of nonstatutory principles and other statutory authorities. The Commissioner can continue to assert and to rely upon applicable nonstatutory principles and other statutory and regulatory authorities to challenge transactions. This section does not limit the applicability of those principles and authorities.

T.D. 8588, 12/29/94, amend T.D. 8592, 4/12/95.

---

§ 1.702-1 Income and credits of partner.

Caution: The Treasury has not yet amended Reg § 1.702-1 to reflect changes made by P.L. 108-27.

(a) General rule. Each partner is required to take into account separately in his return his distributive share, whether or not distributed, of each class or item of partnership income, gain, loss, deduction, or credit described in subparagraphs (1) through (9) of this paragraph. (For the taxable year in which a partner includes his distributive share of partnership taxable income, see section 706(a) and § 1.706-1(a). Such distributive share shall be determined as provided in section 704 and § 1.704-1.) Accordingly, in determining his income tax:

(1) Each partner shall take into account, as part of his gains and losses from sales or exchanges of capital assets held for not more than 1 year (6 months for taxable years beginning before 1977; 9 months for taxable years beginning in 1977), his distributive share of the combined net amount of such gains and losses of the partnership.

(2) Each partner shall take into account, as part of his gains and losses from sales or exchanges of capital assets held for more than 1 year (6 months for taxable years beginning before 1977; 9 months for taxable years beginning in 1977), his distributive share of the combined net amount of such gains and losses of the partnership.

(3) Each partner shall take into account, as part of his gains and losses from sales or exchanges of property described in section 1231 (relating to property used in the trade or business and involuntary conversions), his distributive share of the combined net amount of such gains and losses of the partnership. The partnership shall not combine such items with items set forth in subparagraph (1) or (2) of this paragraph.

(4) Each partner shall take into account, as part of the charitable contributions paid by him, his distributive share of each class of charitable contributions paid by the partnership within the partnership's taxable year. Section 170 determines the extent to which such amount may be allowed as a deduction to the partner. For the definition of the term "charitable contribution", see section 170(c).

(5) Each partner shall take into account, as part of the dividends received by him from domestic corporations, his distributive share of dividends received by the partnership, with respect to which the partner is entitled to a credit under section 34 (for dividends received on or before December 31, 1964), an exclusion under section 116, or a deduction under part VIII, subchapter B, chapter 1 of the Code.

(6) Each partner shall take into account, as part of his taxes described in section 901 which have been paid or accrued to foreign countries or to possessions of the United States, his distributive share of such taxes which have been paid or accrued by the partnership, according to its method of treating such taxes. A partner may elect to treat his total amount of such taxes, including his distributive share of such taxes of the partnership, as a deduction under section 164 or as a credit under section 901, subject to the provisions of sections 901 through 905.

(7) Each partner shall take into account, as part of the partially tax-exempt interest received by him on obligations of the United States or on obligations of instrumentalities of the United States, as described in section 35 or section 242, his distributive share of such partially tax-exempt interest received by the partnership. However, if the partnership elects to amortize premiums on bonds as provided in section 171, the amount received on such obligations by the partnership shall be reduced by the amortizable bond premium applicable to such obligations as provided in section 171(a)(3).

(8) (i) Each partner shall take into account separately, as part of any class of income, gain, loss, deduction, or credit, his distributive share of the following items: recoveries of bad debts, prior taxes, and delinquency amounts (section 111); gains and losses from wagering transactions (section 165(d)); soil and water conservation expenditures (section 175); nonbusiness expenses as described in section 212; medical, dental, etc., expenses (section 213); expenses for care of certain dependents (section 214); alimony, etc., payments (section 215); amounts representing taxes and interest paid to cooperative housing corporations (section 216); intangible drilling and developments costs (section 263(c)); exploration expenditures (section 615); certain mining exploration expenditures (section 617); income, gain, or loss to the partnership under section 751(b); and any items of income, gain, loss, deduction, or credit subject to a special allocation under the partnership agreement which differs from the allocation of partnership taxable income or loss generally.

(ii) Each partner must also take into account separately the partner's distributive share of any partnership item which, if separately taken into account by any partner, would result in an income tax liability for that partner, or for any other person, different from that which would result if that partner did not take the item into account separately. Thus, if any partner is a controlled foreign corporation, as defined in section 957, items of income that would be gross subpart F income if separately taken into account by the controlled foreign corporation must be separately stated for all partners. Under section 911(a), if any partner is a bona fide resident of a foreign country who may exclude from gross income the part of the partner's distributive share which qualifies as earned income, as defined in section 911(b), the earned income of the partnership for all partners must be separately stated. Similarly, all relevant items of income or deduction of the partnership must be separately stated for all partners in determining the applicability of section 183 (relating to activities not engaged in for profit) and the recomputation of tax thereunder for any partner. This paragraph (a)(8)(ii) applies to taxable years beginning on or after July 23, 2002.

(iii) Each partner shall aggregate the amount of his separate deductions or exclusions and his distributive share of partnership deductions or exclusions separately stated in determining the amount allowable to him of any deduction or exclusion under subtitle A of the Code as to which a limitation is imposed. For example, partner A has individual domestic exploration expenditures of $300,000. He is also a member of the AB partnership which in 1971 in its first year of operation has foreign exploration expenditures of $400,000. A's distributable share of this item is $200,000. However, the total amount of his distributable share that A can deduct as exploration expenditures under section 617(a) is limited to $100,000 in view of the limitation provided in section 617(h). Therefore, the excess of $100,000 ($200,000 minus $100,000) is not deductible by A.

(9) Each partner shall also take into account separately his distributive share of the taxable income or loss of the partnership, exclusive of items requiring separate computations under subparagraphs (1) through (8) of this paragraph. For limitation on allowance of a partner's distributive share of partnership losses, see section 704(d) and paragraph (d) of § 1.704-1.

(b) Character of items constituting distributive share. The character in the hands of a partner of any item of income, gain, loss, deduction, or credit described in section 702(a)(1) through (8) shall be determined as if such item were realized directly from the source from which realized by the partnership or incurred in the same manner as incurred by the partnership. For example, a partner's distributive share of gain from the sale of depreciable property used in the trade or business of the partnership shall be considered as gain from the sale of such depreciable property in the hands of the partner. Similarly, a partner's distributive share of partnership "hobby losses" (section 270) or his distributive share of partnership charitable contributions to organizations qualifying under section 170(b)(1)(A) retains such character in the hands of the partner.

(c) Gross income of a partner. *(1)* Where it is necessary to determine the amount or character of the gross income of a partner, his gross income shall include the partner's distributive share of the gross income of the partnership, that is, the amount of gross income of the partnership from which was derived the partner's distributive share of partnership taxable income or loss (including items described in section 702(a)(1) through (8)). For example, a partner is required to include his distributive share of partnership gross income:

(i) In computing his gross income for the purpose of determining the necessity of filing a return (section 6012(a));

(ii) In determining the application of the provisions permitting the spreading of income for services rendered over a 36-month period (section 1301, as in effect for taxable years beginning before January 1, 1964);

(iii) In computing the amount of gross income received from sources within possessions of the United States (section 937).

(iv) In determining a partner's "gross income from farming" (sections 175 and 6073); and

(v) In determining whether the de minimis or full inclusion rules of section 954(b)(3) apply.

(2) In determining the applicability of the 6-year period of limitation on assessment and collection provided in section 6501(e) (relating to omission of more than 25 percent of gross income), a partner's gross income includes his distributive share of partnership gross income (as described in section 6501(e)(1)(A)(i)). In this respect, the amount of partnership gross income from which was derived the partner's distributive share of any item of partnership income, gain, loss, deduction, or credit (as included or disclosed in the partner's return) is considered as an amount of gross income stated in the partner's return for the purposes of section 6501(e). For example, A, who is entitled to one-fourth of the profits of the ABCD partnership, which has $10,000 gross income and $2,000 taxable income, reports only $300 as his distributive share of partnership profits. A should have shown $500 as his distributive share of profits, which amount was derived from $2,500 of partnership gross income. However, since A included only $300 on his return without explaining in the return the difference of $200, he is regarded as having stated in his return only $1,500 ($300/$500 of $2,500) as gross income from the partnership.

(d) Partners in community property States. If separate returns are made by a husband and wife domiciled in a community property State, and only one spouse is a member of the partnership, the part of his or her distributive share of any item or items listed in paragraph (a)(1) through (9) of this section which is community property, or which is derived from community property, should be reported by the husband and wife in equal proportions.

(e) Special rules on requirements to separately state meal, travel, and entertainment expenses. Each partner shall take into account separately his or her distributive share of meal, travel, and entertainment expenses paid or incurred after December 31, 1986, by partnerships that have taxable years beginning before January 1, 1987, and ending with or within partner's taxable years beginning on or after January 1, 1987. In addition, with respect to skybox rentals under section 274(1)(2), each partner shall take into account separately his or her distributive share of rents paid or incurred after December 31, 1986, by partnerships that have taxable years beginning before January 1, 1989, and ending with or within partners' taxable years beginning on or after January 1, 1987.

(f) Cross references. For special rules in accordance with the principles of section 702 applicable solely for the purpose of the tax imposed by section 56 (relating to the minimum tax for tax preferences) see § 1.58-2(a). In the case of a disposition of an oil or gas property by the partnership, see the rules contained in section 613A(c)(7)(D) and § 1.613A-3(e).

T.D. 6175, 5/23/56, amend T.D. 6605, 8/14/62, T.D. 6777, 12/15/64, T.D. 7192, 6/29/72, T.D. 7564, 9/11/78, T.D. 7728, 10/31/80, T.D. 8247, 4/4/89, T.D. 8348, 5/10/91, T.D. 9008, 7/22/2002, T.D. 9194, 4/6/2005.

---

§ 1.702-2 Net operating loss deduction of partner.

For the purpose of determining a net operating loss deduction under section 172, a partner shall take into account his distributive share of items of income, gain, loss, deduction, or credit of the partnership. The character of any such item shall be determined as if such item were realized directly from the source from which realized by the partnership, or incurred in the same manner as incurred by the partnership. See section 702(b) and paragraph (b) of § 1.702-1. To the extent necessary to determine the allowance under section 172(d)(4) of the nonbusiness deductions of a partner arising from both partnership and nonpartnership sources), the partner shall separately take into account his distributive share of the deductions of the partnership which are not attributable to a trade or business and combine such amount with his nonbusiness deductions from nonpartnership sources, the partner shall separately take into account his distributive share of the gross income of the partnership not derived from a trade or business and combine such amount with his nonbusiness income from nonpartnership sources. See section 172 and the regulations thereunder.

T.D. 6175, 5/23/56.

---

§ 1.702-3T 4-year spread (temporary).

Caution: The Treasury has not yet amended Reg § 1.702-3T to reflect changes made by P.L. 100-647.

(a) Applicability. This section applies to a partner in a partnership if—

(1) The partnership is required by section 806 of the Tax Reform Act of 1986 (the 1986 Act), Pub. L. 99-514, 100 Stat. 2362, to change its taxable year for the first taxable year beginning after December 31, 1986 (partnership's year of change); and

(2) As a result of such change in taxable year, items from more than one taxable year of the partnership would, but for the provisions of this section, be included in the taxable year of the partner with or within which the partnership's year of change ends.

(b) Partner's treatment of items from the partnership's year of change. *(1) In general.* Except as provided in paragraph (c) of this section, if a partner's share of "income items" exceeds the partner's share of "expense items," the partner's share of each and every income and expense item shall be taken into account ratably (and retain its character) over the partner's first 4 taxable years beginning with the partner's taxable year with or within which the partnership's year of change ends.

(2) Definitions. (i) Income items. For purposes of this section, the term "income items" means the sum of—

(A) The partner's distributive share of taxable income (exclusive of separately stated items) from the partnership's year of change,

(B) The partner's distributive share of all separately stated income or gain items from the partnership's year of change, and

(C) Any amount includible in the partner's income under section 707(c) on account of payments during the partnership's year of change.

(ii) Expense items. For purposes of this section, the term "expense items" means the sum of—

(A) The partner's distributive share of taxable loss (exclusive of separately stated items) from the partnership's year of change, and

(B) The partner's distributive share of all separately stated items of loss or deduction from the partnership's year of change.

(c) Electing out of 4-year spread. A partner may elect out of the rules of paragraph (b) of this section by meeting the requirements of § 301.9100-7T of this chapter (temporary regulations relating to elections under the Tax Reform Act of 1986).

(d) Special rules for a partner that is a partnership or S corporation. *(1) In general.* Except as provided in paragraph (d)(2) of this section, a partner that is a partnership or S corporation may, if otherwise eligible, use the 4-year spread (with respect to partnership interests owned by the partner) described in this section.

(2) Certain partners prohibited from using 4-year spread. (i) In general. Except as provided in paragraph (d)(2)(ii) of this section, a partner that is a partnership or S corporation may not use the 4-year spread (with respect to partnership interests owned by the partner) if such partner is also changing its taxable year pursuant to section 806 of the 1986 Act.

(ii) Exception. If a partner's year of change does not include any income or expense items with respect to the partnership's year of change, such partner may, if otherwise eligible, use the 4-year spread (with respect to such partnership interest) described in this section even though the partner is a partnership or S corporation. See examples (13) and (14) in paragraph (h) of this section.

(e) Basis of partner's interest. The basis of a partner's interest in a partnership shall be determined as if the partner elected not to spread the partnership items over 4 years, regardless of whether such election was in fact made. Thus, for example, if a partner is eligible for the 4-year spread and does not elect out of the 4-year spread pursuant to paragraph (c) of this section, the partner's basis in the partnership interest will be increased in the first year of the 4-year spread period by an amount equal to the excess of the income items over the expense items. However, the partner's basis will not be increased again, with respect to the unamortized income and expense items, as they are amortized over the 4-year spread period.

(f) Effect on other provisions of the Code. Except as provided in paragraph (e) of this section, determinations with respect to a partner, for purposes of other provisions of the Code, must be made with regard to the manner in which partnership items are taken into account under the rules of this section. Thus, for example, a partner who does not elect out of the 4-year spread must take into account, for purposes of determining net earnings from self-employment under section 1402(a) for a taxable year, only the ratable portion of partnership items for that taxable year.

(g) Treatment of dispositions. *(1) In general.* If a partnership interest is disposed of before the last taxable year in the 4-year spread period, unamortized income and expense items that are attributable to the interest disposed of and that would be taken into account by the partner for subsequent taxable years in the 4-year spread period shall be taken into account by the partner as determined under paragraph (g)(2) of this section. For purposes of this section, the term "disposed of" means any transfer, including (but not limited to) transfers by sale, exchange, gift, and by reason of death.

(2) Year unamortized items taken into account. (i) In general. If, at the end of a partner's taxable year, the fraction determined under paragraph (g)(2)(ii) of this section is—

(A) Greater than ⅔, the partner must continue to take the unamortized income and expense items into account ratably over the 4-year spread period;

(B) Greater than ⅓ but less than or equal to ⅔, the partner must, in addition to its ratable amortization, take into account in such year 50 percent of the income and expense items that would otherwise be unamortized at the end of such year (however, this paragraph (g)(2)(i)(B) is only applied once with respect to a partner's interest in a particular partnership); or

(C) Less than or equal to ⅓, the partner must take into account the entire balance of unamortized income and expense items in such year.

(ii) Determination of fraction. For purposes of paragraph (g)(2)(i) of this section, the numerator of the fraction is the partner's proportionate interest in the partnership at the end of the partner's taxable year and the denominator is the partner's proportionate interest in the partnership as of the last day of the partnership's year of change.

(h) Examples. The provisions of this section may be illustrated by the following examples.

Example (1). Assume that P1, a partnership with a taxable year ending September 30, is required by the 1986 Act to change its taxable year to a calendar year. All of the partners of P1 are individual taxpayers reporting on a calendar year. P1 is required to change to a calendar year for its taxable year beginning October 1, 1987, and to file a return for the short taxable year ending December 31, 1987. Based on the above facts, the partners of P1 are required to include the items from more than one taxable year of P1 in income for their 1987 taxable year. Thus, under paragraph (b) of this section, if a partner's share of income items exceeds the partner's share of expense items, the partner's share of each and every income and expense item shall be taken into account ratably by such partner in each of the partner's first four taxable years' beginning with the partner's 1987 taxable year, unless such partner elects under paragraph (c) of this section to include all such amounts in his 1987 taxable year.

Example (2). Assume the same facts as in example (1), except P1 is a personal service corporation with all of its employee-owners reporting on a calendar year. Although P1 is required to change to a calendar year for its taxable year beginning October 1, 1987, neither P1 nor its employee-owners obtain the benefits of a 4-year spread. Pursuant to section 806(e)(2)(C) of the 1986 Act, the 4-year spread provision is only applicable to short taxable years of partnerships and S corporations required to change their taxable year under the 1986 Act.

Example (3). Assume the same facts as example (1) and that I is one of the individual partners of P1. Further assume that I's distributive share of P1's taxable income for the short taxable year ended December 31, 1987 (i.e., P1's year of change), is $10,000. In addition, I has $8,000 of separately stated expense from P1's year of change. Since I's income items (i.e., $10,000 of taxable income) exceed I's expense items (i.e., $8,000 of separately stated expense) attributable to P1's year of change, I is eligible for the 4-year spread provided by this section. If I does not elect out of the 4-year spread, I will recognize $2,500 of taxable income and $2,000 of separately stated expense in his 1987 calendar year return. Assuming I does not dispose of his partnership interest in P1 by December 31, 1989, the remaining $7,500 of taxable income and $6,000 of separately stated expense will be amortized (and retain its character) over I's next three taxable years (i.e., 1988, 1989 and 1990).

Example (4). Assume the same facts as example (3), except that I disposes of his entire interest in P1 during 1988. Pursuant to paragraph (g) of this section, I would recognize $7,500 of taxable income and $6,000 of separately stated expense in his 1988 calendar year return.

Example (5). Assume the same facts as in example (3), except that I disposes of 50 percent of his interest in P1 during 1989. Pursuant to paragraph (g) of this section, I would recognize $3,750 of taxable income in his 1989 calendar year return ($2,500 ratable portion for 1989 plus 50 percent of the $2,500 of income items that would otherwise be unamortized at the end of 1989). I would also recognize $3,000 of separately stated expense items in 1989 ($2,000 ratable portion for 1989 plus 50 percent of the $2,000 of separately stated expense items that would otherwise be unamortized at the end of 1989).

Example (6). Assume the same facts as in example (1), except that X, a personal service corporation as defined in section 441(i), is a partner of P1. X is a calendar year taxpayer, and thus is not required to change its taxable year under the 1986 Act. The same result occurs as in example 1 (i.e., unless X elects to the contrary, X is required to include one fourth of its share of income and expense items from P1's year of change in the first four taxable years of X beginning with the 1987 taxable year).

Example (7). Assume the same facts as in example (6), except that X is a fiscal year personal service corporation with a taxable year ending September 30. X is required under the 1986 Act to change to a calendar year for its taxable year beginning October 1, 1987, and to file a return for its short year ending December 31, 1987. Based on the above facts, X is not required to include the items from more than one taxable year of P1 in any one taxable year of X. Thus, the provisions of this section do not apply to X, and X is required to include the full amount of income and expense items from P1's year of change in X's taxable income for X's short year ending December 31. Under section 443 of the Code, X is required to annualize the taxable income for its short year ending December 31, 1987.

Example (8). Assume that P2 is a partnership with a taxable year ending September 30. Under the 1986 Act, P2 would have been required to change its taxable year to a calendar year, effective for the taxable year beginning October 1, 1987. However, P2 properly changed its taxable year to a calendar year for the year beginning October 1, 1986, and filed a return for the short period ending December 31, 1986. The provisions of the 1986 Act do not apply to P2 because the short year ending December 31, 1986, was not required by the amendments made by section 806 of the 1986 Act. Thus, the partners of P2 are required to take all items of income and expense for the short taxable year ending December 31, 1986, into account for the taxable year with or within which such short year ends.

Example (9). Assume that P3 is a partnership with a taxable year ending March 31 and I, a calendar year individual, is a partner in P3. Under the 1986 Act, P3 would have been required to change its taxable year to a calendar year. However, under Rev. Proc. 87-32, P3 establishes and changes to a natural business year beginning with the taxable year ending June 30, 1987. Thus, P3 is required to change its taxable year under section 806 of the 1986 Act, and I is required to include items from more than one taxable year of P3 in one of her taxable years. Furthermore, I's share of P3's income items exceeds her share of P3's expense items for the short period April 1, 1987 through June 30, 1987. Accordingly, under this section, unless I elects to the contrary, I is required to take one fourth of her share of items of income and expense from P3's short taxable year ending June 30, 1987 into account for her taxable year ending December 31, 1987.

Example (10). Assume that P4 is a partnership with a taxable year ending March 31. Y, a C corporation, owns a 51 percent interest in the profits and capital of P4. Y reports its income on the basis of a taxable year ending March 31. P4 establishes and changes to a natural business year beginning with the taxable year ending June 30, 1987, under Rev. Proc. 87-32. Under the above facts, P4 is not required to change its taxable year because its March 31 taxable year was the taxable year of Y, the partner owning a majority of the partnership's profits and capital. Therefore, the remaining partners of P4 owning 49 percent of the profits and capital are not permitted the 4-year spread of the items of income and expense with respect to the short year, even though they may be required to include their distributive share of P4's items from more than one taxable year in one of their years.

Example (11). Assume that X and Y are C corporations with taxable years ending June 30. Each owns a 50-percent interest in the profits and capital of partnership P5. P5 has a taxable year ending March 31. Assume that P5 cannot establish a business purpose in order to retain a taxable year ending March 31, and thus P5 must change to a June 30 taxable year, the taxable year of its partners. Furthermore, assume that X's share of P5's income items exceeds its share of P5's expense items for P5's short taxable year ending June 30, 1987. Unless X elects out of the 4-year spread, the taxable year ending June 30, 1987, is the first of the four taxable years in which X must take into account its share of the items of income and expense resulting from P5's short taxable year ending June 30, 1987.

Example (12). Assume that I, an individual who reports income on the basis of the calendar year, is a partner in two partnerships, P6 and P7. Both partnerships have a taxable year ending September 30. Neither partnership can establish a business purpose for retaining its taxable year. Consequently, each partnership will change its taxable year to December 31, for the taxable year beginning October 1, 1987. The election to avoid a 4-year spread is made at the partner level; in addition, a partner may make such elections on a partnership-by-partnership basis. Thus, assuming I is eligible to obtain the 4-year spread with respect to income and expense items from partnerships P6 and P7, I may use the 4-year spread with respect to items from P6, while not using the 4-year spread with respect to items from P7.

Example (13). I, an individual taxpayer using a calendar year, owns an interest in P8, a partnership using a taxable year ending June 30. Furthermore, P8 owns an interest in P9, a partnership with a taxable year ending March 31. Under section 806 of the 1986 Act, P8 will be required to change to a taxable year ending December 31, while P9 will be required to change to a taxable year ending June 30. As a result, P8's year of change will be July 1 through December 31, 1987, while P9's year of change will be from April 1 through June 30, 1987. Since P9's year of change does not end with or within P8's year of change, paragraph (d)(2) of this section does not prevent P8 from obtaining a 4-year spread with respect to its interest in P9.

Example (14). The facts are the same as in example (13), except that P9 has a taxable year ending September 30, and under the 1986 Act P9 is required to change to a taxable year ending December 31. Therefore, P9's year of change will be from October 1, 1987 through December 31, 1987. Although P8's year of change from July 1, 1987 through December 31, 1987 includes two taxable years of P9 *(i.e.,* October 1, 1986 through September 30, 1987 and October 1, 1987 through December 31, 1987), paragraph (d)(2) of this section prohibits P8 from using the 4-year spread with respect to its interest in P9, because P9's year of change ends with or within P8's year of change.

T.D. 8167, 12/18/87, amend T.D. 8435, 9/18/92.

---

§ 1.703-1 Partnership computations.

Caution: The Treasury has not yet amended Reg § 1.703-1 to reflect changes made by P.L. 103-66, P.L. 96-589, P.L. 95-30, P.L. 94-455, P.L. 94-12.

(a) Income and deductions. *(1)* The taxable income of a partnership shall be computed in the same manner as the taxable income of an individual, except as otherwise provided in this section. A partnership is required to state separately in its return the items described in section 702(a)(1) through (7) and, in addition, to attach to its return a statement setting forth separately those items described in section 702(a)(8) which the partner is required to take into account separately in determining his income tax. See paragraph (a)(8) of § 1.702-1. The partnership is further required to compute and to state separately in its return:

(i) As taxable income under section 702(a)(9), the total of all other items of gross income (not separately stated) over the total of all other allowable deductions (not separately stated), or

(ii) As loss under section 702(a)(9), the total of all other allowable deductions (not separately stated) over the total of all other items of gross income (not separately stated). The taxable income or loss so computed shall be accounted for by the partners in accordance with their partnership agreement.

(2) The partnership is not allowed the following deductions:

(i) The standard deduction provided in section 141.

(ii) The deduction for personal exemptions provided in section 151.

(iii) The deduction provided in section 164(a) for taxes, described in section 901, paid or accrued to foreign countries or possessions of the United States. Each partner's distributive share of such taxes shall be accounted for separately by him as provided in section 702(a)(6).

(iv) The deduction for charitable contributions provided in section 170. Each partner is considered as having paid within his taxable year his distributive share of any contribution or gift, payment of which was actually made by the partnership within its taxable year ending within or with the partner's taxable year. This item shall be accounted for separately by the partners as provided in section 702(a)(4). See also paragraph (b) of § 1.702-1.

(v) The net operating loss deduction provided in section 172. See § 1.702-2.

(vi) The additional itemized deductions for individuals provided in part VII, subchapter B, chapter 1 of the Code, as follows: expenses for production of income (section 212); medical, dental, etc., expenses (section 213); expenses for care of certain dependents (section 214); alimony, etc., payments (section 215); and amounts representing taxes and interest paid to cooperative housing corporation (section 216). However, see paragraph (a)(8) of § 1.702-1.

(vii) The deduction for depletion under section 611 with respect to domestic oil or gas which is produced after December 31, 1974, and to which gross income from the property is attributable after such year.

(viii) The deduction for capital gains provided by section 1202 and the deduction for capital loss carryover provided by section 1212.

(b) Elections of the partnership. *(1) General rule.* Any elections (other than those described in subparagraph (2) of this paragraph) affecting the computation of income derived from a partnership shall be made by the partnership. For example, elections of methods of accounting, of computing depreciation, of treating soil and water conservation expenditures, of treating exploration expenditures, and the option to deduct as expenses intangible drilling and development costs, shall be made by the partnership and not by the partners separately. All partnership elections are applicable to all partners equally, but any election made by a partnership shall not apply to any partner's nonpartnership interests.

(2) Exception. (i) Each partner shall add his distributive share of taxes described in section 901 paid or accrued by the partnership to foreign countries or possessions of the United States (according to its method of treating such taxes) to any such taxes paid or accrued by him (according to his method of treating such taxes), and may elect to use the total amount either as a credit against tax or as a deduction from income.

(ii) Each partner shall add his distributive share of expenses described in section 615 or section 617 paid or accrued by the partnership to any such expenses paid or accrued by him and shall treat the total amount according to his method of treating such expenses, notwithstanding the treatment of the expenses by the partnership.

(iii) Each partner who is a nonresident alien individual or a foreign corporation shall add his distributive share of income derived by the partnership from real property located in the United States, as described in section 871(d)(1) or 882(d)(1), to any such income derived by him and may elect under § 1.871-10 to treat all such income as income which is effectively connected for the taxable year with the conduct of a trade or business in the United States.

T.D. 6175, 5/23/56, amend T.D. 7192, 6/29/72, T.D. 7332, 12/20/74, T.D. 8348, 5/10/91.

§ 1.704-1 Partner's distributive share.

Caution: The Treasury has not yet amended Reg § 1.704-1 to reflect changes made by P.L. 101-239, P.L. 98-369.

(a) Effect of partnership agreement. A partner's distributive share of any item or class of items of income, gain, loss, deduction, or credit of the partnership shall be determined by the partnership agreement, unless otherwise provided by section 704 and paragraphs (b) through (e) of this section. For definition of partnership agreement see section 761(c).

(b) Determination of partner's distributive share. *(0) Cross-references.*

Heading	Section
Cross-references	1.704-1(b)(0)
In general	1.704-1(b)(1)
Basic principles	1.704-1(b)(1)(i)
Effective dates	1.704-1(b)(1)(ii)
Generally	1.704-1(b)(1)(ii)(a)
Foreign tax expenditures	1.704-1(b)(1)(ii)(b)
Effect of other sections	1.704-1(b)(1)(iii)
Other possible tax consequences	1.704-1(b)(1)(iv)
Purported allocations	1.704-1(b)(1)(v)
Section 704(c) determinations	1.704-1(b)(1)(vi)
Bottom line allocations	1.704-1(b)(1)(vii)
Substantial economic effect	1.704-1(b)(2)
Two-part analysis	1.704-1(b)(2)(i)
Economic effect	1.704-1(b)(2)(ii)
Fundamental principles	1.704-1(b)(2)(ii)(a)
Three requirements	1.704-1(b)(2)(ii)(b)
Obligation to restore deficit	1.704-1(b)(2)(ii)(c)
Alternate test for economic effect	1.704-1(b)(2)(ii)(d)
Partial economic effect	1.704-1(b)(2)(ii)(e)
Reduction of obligation to restore	1.704-1(b)(2)(ii)(f)
Liquidation defined	1.704-1(b)(2)(ii)(g)
Partnership agreement defined	1.704-1(b)(2)(ii)(h)
Economic effect equivalence	1.704-1(b)(2)(ii)(i)
Substantiality	1.704-1(b)(2)(iii)
General rules	1.704-1(b)(2)(iii)(a)
Shifting tax consequences	1.704-1(b)(2)(iii)(b)
Transitory allocations	1.704-1(b)(2)(iii)(c)
Maintenance of capital accounts	1.704-1(b)(2)(iv)
In general	1.704-1(b)(2)(iv)(a)
Basic rules	1.704-1(b)(2)(iv)(b)
Treatment of liabilities	1.704-1(b)(2)(iv)(c)
Contributed property	1.704-1(b)(2)(iv)(d)
In general	1.704-1(b)(2)(iv)(d)(1)
Contribution of promissory notes	1.704-1(b)(2)(iv)(d)(2)
Section 704(c) considerations	1.704-1(b)(2)(iv)(d)(3)
Distributed property	1.704-1(b)(2)(iv)(e)
In general	1.704-1(b)(2)(iv)(e)(1)
Distribution of promissory notes	1.704-1(b)(2)(iv)(e)(2)
Revaluations of property	1.704-1(b)(2)(iv)(f)
Adjustments to reflect book value	1.704-1(b)(2)(iv)(g)
In general	1.704-1(b)(2)(iv)(g)(1)
Payables and receivables	1.704-1(b)(2)(iv)(g)(2)
Determining amount of book items	1.704-1(b)(2)(iv)(g)(3)
Determinations of fair market value	1.704-1(b)(2)(iv)(h)
Section 705(a)(2)(B) expenditures	1.704-1(b)(2)(iv)(i)
In general	1.704-1(b)(2)(iv)(i)(1)
Expenses described in section 709	1.704-1(b)(2)(iv)(i)(2)
Disallowed losses	1.704-1(b)(2)(iv)(i)(3)
Basic adjustments to section 38 property	1.704-1(b)(2)(iv)(j)(1)
Depletion of oil and gas properties	1.704-1(b)(2)(iv)(k)
In general	1.704-1(b)(2)(iv)(k)(1)
Simulated depletion	1.704-1(b)(2)(iv)(k)(2)
Actual depletion	1.704-1(b)(2)(iv)(k)(3)
Effect of book values	1.704-1(b)(2)(iv)(k)(4)
Transfers of partnership interests	1.704-1(b)(2)(iv)(l)
Section 754 elections	1.704-1(b)(2)(iv)(m)

(1) In general. (i) Basic principles. Under section 704(b) if a partnership agreement does not provide for the allocation of income, gain, loss, deduction, or credit (or item thereof) to a partner, or if the partnership agreement provides for the allocation of income, gain, loss, deduction, or credit (or item thereof) to a partner but such allocation does not have substantial economic effect, then the partner's distributive share of such income, gain, loss, deduction, or credit (or item thereof) shall be determined in accordance with such partner's interest in the partnership (taking into account all facts and circumstances). If the partnership agreement provides for the allocation of income, gain, loss, deduction, or credit (or item thereof) to a partner, there are three ways in which such allocation will be respected under section 704(b) and this paragraph. First, the allocation can have substantial economic effect in accordance with paragraph (b)(2) of this section. Second, taking into account all facts and circumstances, the allocation can be in accordance with the partner's interest in the partnership. See paragraph (b)(3) of this section. Third, the allocation can be deemed to be in accordance with the partner's interest in the partnership pursuant to one of the special rules contained in paragraph (b)(4) of this section and § 1.704-2. To the extent an allocation under the partnership agreement of income, gain, loss, deduction, or credit (or item thereof) to a partner does not have substantial economic effect, is not in accordance with the partner's interest in the partnership, and is not deemed to be in accordance with the partner's interest in the partnership, such income, gain, loss, deduction, or credit (or item thereof) will be reallocated in accordance with the partner's interest in the partnership (determined under paragraph (b)(3) of this section).

(ii) Effective dates. (a) Generally. Except as otherwise provided in this section, the provisions of this paragraph are effective for partnership taxable years beginning after December 31, 1975. However, for partnership taxable years beginning after December 31, 1975, but before May 1, 1986, (January 1, 1987, in the case of allocations of nonrecourse deductions as defined in paragraph (b)(4)(iv)(a) of this section) an allocation of income, gain, loss, deduction, or credit (or item thereof) to a partner that is not respected under this paragraph nevertheless will be respected under section 704(b) if such allocation has substantial economic effect or is in accordance with the partners' interests in the partnership as those terms have been interpreted under the relevant case law, the legislative history of section 210(d) of the Tax Reform Act of 1976, and the provisions of this paragraph in effect for partnership taxable years beginning before May 1, 1986.

(b) Rules relating to foreign tax expenditures. (1) In general. The provisions of paragraphs (b)(3)(iv) and (b)(4)(viii) of this section (regarding the allocation of creditable foreign taxes) apply for partnership taxable years beginning on or after October 19, 2006. The rules that apply to allocations of creditable foreign taxes made in partnership taxable years beginning before October 19, 2006 are contained in §§ 1.704-1T(b)(1)(ii)(b)(1) and 1.704-1T(b)(4)(xi) as in effect prior to October 19, 2006 (see 26 CFR part 1 revised as of April 1, 2005). However, taxpayers may rely on the provisions of paragraphs (b)(3)(iv) and (b)(4)(viii) of this section for partnership taxable years beginning on or after April 21, 2004.

(2) Transition rule. Transition relief is provided herein to partnerships whose agreements were entered into prior to April 21, 2004. In such case, if there has been no material modification to the partnership agreement on or after April 21, 2004, then the partnership may apply the provisions of paragraph (b) of this section as if the amendments made by paragraphs (b)(3)(iv) and (b)(4)(viii) of this section had not occurred. If the partnership agreement was materially modified on or after April 21, 2004, then the rules provided in

paragraphs (b)(3)(iv) and (b)(4)(viii) of this section shall apply to the later of the taxable year beginning on or after October 19, 2006 or the taxable year within which the material modification occurred, and to all subsequent taxable years. If the partnership agreement was materially modified on or after April 21, 2004, and before a tax year beginning on or after October 19, 2006, see §§ 1.704-1T(b)(1)(ii)(b)(1) and 1.704-1T(b)(4)(xi) as in effect prior to October 19, 2006 (26 CFR part 1 revised as of April 1, 2005). For purposes of this paragraph (b)(1)(ii)(b)(2), any change in ownership constitutes a material modification to the partnership agreement. This transition rule does not apply to any taxable year (and all subsequent taxable years) in which persons that arc related to each other (within the meaning of section 267(b) and 707(b)) collectively have the power to amend the partnership agreement without the consent of any unrelated party.

(iii) Effect of other sections. The determination of a partner's distributive share of income, gain, loss, deduction, or credit (or item thereof) under section 704(b) and this paragraph is not conclusive as to the tax treatment of a partner with respect to such distributive share. For example, an allocation of loss or deduction to a partner that is respected under section 704(b) and this paragraph may not be deductible by such partner if the partner lacks the requisite motive for economic gain (see, *e.g.*, Goldstein v. Commissioner, 364 F.2d 734 (2d Cir. 1966)), or may be disallowed for that taxable year (and held in suspense) if the limitations of section 465 or section 704(d) are applicable. Similarly, an allocation that is respected under section 704(b) and this paragraph nevertheless may be reallocated under other provisions, such as section 482, section 704(e)(2), section 706(d) (and related assignment of income principles), and paragraph (b)(2)(ii) of § 1.751-1. If a partnership has a section 754 election in effect, a partner's distributive share of partnership income, gain, loss, or deduction may be affected as provided in § 1.743-1 (see paragraph (b)(2)(iv)(m)(2) of this section). A deduction that appears to be a nonrecourse deduction deemed to be in accordance with the partners' interests in the partnership may not be such because purported nonrecourse liabilities of the partnership in fact constitute equity rather than debt. The examples in paragraph (b)(5) of this section concern the validity of allocations under section 704(b) and this paragraph and, except as noted, do not address the effect of other sections or limitations on such allocations.

(iv) Other possible tax consequences. Allocations that are respected under section 704(b) and this paragraph may give rise to other tax consequences, such as those resulting from the application of section 61, section 83, section 751, section 2501, paragraph (f) of § 1.46-3, § 1.47-6, paragraph (b)(1) of § 1.721-1 (and related principles), and paragraph (e) of § 1.752-1. The examples in paragraph (b)(5) of this section concern the validity of allocations under section 704(b) and this paragraph and, except as noted, do not address other tax consequences that may result from such allocations.

(v) Purported allocations. Section 704(b) and this paragraph do not apply to a purported allocation if it is made to a person who is not a partner of the partnership (see section 7701(a)(2) and paragraph (d) of § 301.7701-3) or to a person who is not receiving the purported allocation in his capacity as a partner (see section 707(a) and paragraph (a) of § 1.707-1).

(vi) Section 704(c) determinations. Section 704(c) and § 1.704-3 generally require that if property is contributed by a partner to a partnership, the partners' distributive shares of income, gain, loss, and deduction, as computed for tax purposes, with respect to the property are determined so as to take account of the variation between the adjusted tax basis and fair market value of the property. Although section 704(b) does not directly determine the partners' distributive shares of tax items governed by section 704(c), the partners' distributive shares of tax items may be determined under section 704(c) and § 1.704-3 (depending on the allocation method chosen by the partnership under § 1.704-3) with reference to the partners' distributive shares of the corresponding book items, as determined under section 704(b) and this paragraph. (See paragraphs (b)(2)(iv)(d) and (b)(4)(i) of this section.) See § 1.704-3 for methods of making allocations under section 704(c), and § 1.704-3(d)(2) for a special rule in determining the amount of book items if the remedial allocation method is chosen by the partnership. See also paragraph (b)(5) Example (13)(i) of this section.

(vii) Bottom line allocations. Section 704(b) and this paragraph are applicable to allocations of income, gain, loss, deduction, and credit, allocations of specific items of income, gain, loss, deduction, and credit, and allocations of partnership net or "bottom line" taxable income and loss. An allocation to a partner of a share of partnership net or "bottom line" taxable income or loss shall be treated as an allocation to such partner of the same share of each item of income, gain, loss, and deduction that is taken into account in computing such net or "bottom line" taxable income or loss. See example (15)(i) of paragraph (b)(5) of this section.

(2) Substantial economic effect. (i) Two-part analysis. The determination of whether an allocation of income, gain, loss, or deduction (or item thereof) to a partner has substantial economic effect involves a two-part analysis that is made as of the end of the partnership taxable year to which the allocation relates. First, the allocation must have economic effect (within the meaning of paragraph (b)(2)(ii) of this section). Second, the economic effect of the allocation must be substantial (within the meaning of paragraph (b)(2)(iii) of this section).

(ii) Economic effect. (a) Fundamental principles. In order for an allocation to have economic effect, it must be consistent with the underlying economic arrangement of the partners. This means that in the event there is an economic benefit or economic burden that corresponds to an allocation, the partner to whom the allocation is made must receive such economic benefit or bear such economic burden.

(b) Three requirements. Based on the principles contained in paragraph (b)(2)(ii)(a) of this section, and except as otherwise provided in this paragraph, an allocation of income, gain, loss, or deduction (or item thereof) to a partner will have economic effect if, and only if, throughout the full term of the partnership, the partnership agreement provides—

(1) For the determination and maintenance of the partners' capital accounts in accordance with the rules of paragraph (b)(2)(iv) of this section,

(2) Upon liquidation of the partnership (or any partner's interest in the partnership), liquidating distributions are required in all cases to be made in accordance with the positive capital account balances of the partners, as determined after taking into account all capital account adjustments for the partnership taxable year during which such liquidation occurs (other than those made pursuant to this requirement (2) and requirement (3) of this paragraph (b)(2)(ii)(b)), by the end of such taxable year (or, if later, within 90 days after the date of such liquidation), and

(3) If such partner has a deficit balance in his capital account following the liquidation of his interest in the partnership, as determined after taking into account all capital account adjustments for the partnership taxable year during which such liquidation occurs (other than those made pursuant to this requirement (3)), he is unconditionally obligated to restore the amount of such deficit balance to the partnership by the end of such taxable year (or, if later, within 90 days after the date of such liquidation), which amount shall, upon liquidation of the partnership, be paid to creditors of the partnership or distributed to other partners in accordance with their positive capital account balances (in accordance with requirement (2) of this paragraph (b)(2)(ii)(b)).

For purposes of the preceding sentence, a partnership taxable year shall be determined without regard to section 706(c)(2)(A).

Requirements (2) and (3) of this paragraph (b)(2)(ii)(b) are not violated if all or part of the partnership interest of one or more partners is purchased (other than in connection with the liquidation of the partnership) by the partnership or by one or more partners (or one or more persons related, within the meaning of section 267(b) (without modification by section 267(e)(1)) or section 707(b)(1), to a partner) pursuant to an agreement negotiated at arm's length by persons who at the time such agreement is entered into have materially adverse interests and if a principal purpose of such purchase and sale is not to avoid the principles of the second sentence of paragraph (b)(2)(ii)(a) of this section. In addition, requirement (2) of this paragraph (b)(2)(ii)(b) is not violated if, upon the liquidation of the partnership, the capital accounts of the partners are increased or decreased pursuant to paragraph (b)(2)(iv)(f) of this section as of the date of such liquidation and the partnership makes liquidating distributions within the time set out in that requirement (2) in the ratios of the partners' positive capital accounts, except that it does not distribute reserves reasonably required to provide for liabilities (contingent or otherwise) of the partnership and installment obligations owed to the partnership, so long as such withheld amounts are distributed as soon as practicable and in the ratios of the partners' positive capital account balances. See examples (1)(i) and (ii), (4)(i), (8)(i), and (16)(i) of paragraph (b)(5) of this section.

(c) Obligation to restore deficit. If a partner is not expressly obligated to restore the deficit balance in his capital account, such partner nevertheless will be treated as obligated to restore the deficit balance in his capital account (in accordance with requirement (3) of paragraph (b)(2)(ii)(b) of this section) to the extent of—

(1) The outstanding principal balance of any promissory note (of which such partner is the maker) contributed to the partnership by such partner (other than a promissory note that is readily tradable on an established securities market), and

(2) The amount of any unconditional obligation of such partner (whether imposed by the partnership agreement or by State or local law) to make subsequent contributions to the partnership (other than pursuant to a promissory note of which such partner is the maker),

provided that such note or obligation is required to be satisfied at a time no later than the end of the partnership taxable year in which such partner's interest is liquidated (or, if later, within 90 days after the date of such liquidation). If a promissory note referred to in the previous sentence is negotiable, a partner will be considered required to satisfy such note within the time period specified in such sentence if the partnership agreement provides that, in lieu of actual satisfaction, the partnership will retain such note and such partner will contribute to the partnership the excess, if any, of the outstanding principal balance of such note over its fair market value at the time of liquidation. See paragraph (b)(2)(iv)(d)(2) of this section. See examples (1)(ix) and (x) of paragraph (b)(5) of this section. A partner in no event will be considered obligated to restore the deficit balance in his capital account to the partnership (in accordance with requirement (3) of paragraph (b)(2)(ii)(b) of this section) to the extent such partner's obligation is not legally enforceable, or the facts and circumstances otherwise indicate a plan to avoid or circumvent such obligation. See paragraphs (b)(2)(ii)(f), (b)(2)(ii)(h), and (b)(4)(vi) of this section for other rules regarding such obligation. For purposes of this paragraph (b)(2), if a partner contributes a promissory note to the partnership during a partnership taxable year beginning after December 29, 1988 and the maker of such note is a person related to such partner (within the meaning of § 1.752-1T(h), but without regard to subdivision (4) of that section), then such promissory note shall be treated as a promissory note of which such partner is the maker.

(d) Alternate test for economic effect. If—

(1) Requirements (1) and (2) of paragraph (b)(2)(ii)(b) of this section are satisfied, and

(2) The partner to whom an allocation is made is not obligated to restore the deficit balance in his capital account to the partnership (in accordance with requirement (3) of paragraph (b)(2)(ii)(b) of this section), or is obligated to restore only a limited dollar amount of such deficit balance, and

(3) The partnership agreement contains a "qualified income offset,"

such allocation will be considered to have economic effect under this paragraph (b)(2)(ii)(d) to the extent such allocation does not cause or increase a deficit balance in such partner's capital account (in excess of any limited dollar amount of such deficit balance that such partner is obligated to restore) as of the end of the partnership taxable year to which such allocation relates. In determining the extent to which the previous sentence is satisfied, such partner's capital account also shall be reduced for—

(4) Adjustments that, as of the end of such year, reasonably are expected to be made to such partner's capital account under paragraph (b)(2)(iv)(k) of this section for depletion allowances with respect to oil and gas properties of the partnership, and

(5) Allocations of loss and deduction that, as of the end of such year, reasonably are expected to be made to such partner pursuant to section 704(e)(2), section 706(d), and paragraph (b)(2)(ii) of § 1.751-1, and

(6) Distributions that, as of the end of such year, reasonably are expected to be made to such partner to the extent they exceed offsetting increases to such partner's capital account that reasonably are expected to occur during (or prior to) the partnership taxable years in which such distributions reasonably are expected to be made (other than increases pursuant to a minimum gain chargeback under paragraph (b)(4)(iv)(e) of this section or under § 1.704-2(f); however, increases to a partner's capital account pursuant to a minimum gain chargeback requirement are taken into account as an offset to distributions of nonrecourse liability proceeds that are reasonably expected to be made and that are allocable to an increase in partnership minimum gain.

For purposes of determining the amount of expected distributions and expected capital account increases described in (6) above, the rule set out in paragraph (b)(2)(iii)(c) of this section concerning the presumed value of partnership property shall apply. The partnership agreement contains a "qualified income offset" if, and only if, it provides that a partner who unexpectedly receives an adjustment, allocation, or distribution described in (4), (5), or (6) above, will be allocated items of income and gain (consisting of a pro rata portion of each item of partnership income, including gross income, and gain for such year) in an amount and manner sufficient to eliminate such deficit balance as quickly as possible. Allocations of items of income and gain made pursuant to the immediately preceding sentence shall be deemed to be made in accordance with the partners' interests in the partnership if requirements (1) and (2) of paragraph (b)(2)(ii)(b) of this section are satisfied. See examples (1)(iii), (iv), (v), (vi), (vii), (ix), and (x), (15), and (16)(ii) of paragraph (b)(5) of this section.

(e) Partial economic effect. If only a portion of an allocation made to a partner with respect to a partnership taxable year has economic effect, both the portion that has economic effect and the portion that is reallocated shall consist of a proportionate share of all items that made up the allocation to such partner for such year. See examples (15)(ii) and (iii) of paragraph (b)(5) of this section.

(f) Reduction of obligation to restore. If requirements (1) and (2) of paragraph (b)(2)(ii)(b) of this section are satisfied, a partner's obligation to restore the deficit balance in his capital account (or any limited dollar amount thereof) to the partnership may be eliminated or reduced as of the end of a partnership taxable year without affecting the validity of prior allocations (see paragraph (b)(4)(vi) of this section) to the extent the deficit balance (if any) in such partner's capital account, after reduction for the items described in (4), (5), and (6) of paragraph (b)(2)(ii)(d) of this section, will not exceed the partner's remaining obligation (if any) to restore the deficit balance in his capital account. See example (1)(viii) of paragraph (b)(5) of this section.

(g) Liquidation defined. For purposes of this paragraph, a liquidation of a partner's interest in the partnership occurs upon the earlier of (1) the date upon which there is a liquidation of the partnership, or (2) the date upon which there is a liquidation of the partner's interest in the partnership under paragraph (d) of § 1.761-1. For purposes of this paragraph, the liquidation of a partnership occurs upon the earlier of (3) the date upon which the partnership is terminated under section 708(b)(1), or (4) the date upon which the partnership ceases to be a going concern (even though it may continue in existence for the purpose of winding up its affairs, paying its debts, and distributing any remaining balance to its partners). Requirements (2) and (3) of paragraph (b)(2)(ii)(b) of this section will be considered unsatisfied if the liquidation of a partner's interest in the partnership is delayed after its primary business activities have been terminated (for example, by continuing to engage in a relatively minor amount of business activity, if such actions themselves do not cause the partnership to terminate pursuant to section 708(b)(1)) for a principal purpose of deferring any distribution pursuant to requirement (2) of paragraph (b)(2)(ii)(b) of this section or deferring any partner's obligations under requirement (3) of paragraph (b)(2)(ii)(b) of this section.

(h) Partnership agreement defined. For purposes of this paragraph, the partnership agreement includes all agreements among the partners, or between one or more partners and the partnership, concerning affairs of the partnership and responsibilities of partners, whether oral or written, and whether or not embodied in a document referred to by the partners as the partnership agreement. Thus, in determining whether distributions are required in all cases to be made in accordance with the partners' positive capital account balances (requirement (2) of paragraph (b)(2)(ii)(b) of this section), and in determining the extent to which a partner is obligated to restore a deficit balance in his capital account (requirement (3) of paragraph (b)(2)(ii)(b) of this section), all arrangements among partners, or between one or more partners and the partnership relating to the partnership, direct and indirect, including puts, options, and other buy-sell agreements, and any other "stop-loss" arrangement, are considered to be part of the partnership agreement. (Thus, for example, if one partner who assumes a liability of the partnership is indemnified by another partner for a portion of such liability, the indemnifying partner (depending upon the particular facts) may be viewed as in effect having a partial deficit makeup obligation as a result of such indemnity agreement.) In addition, the partnership agreement includes provisions of Federal, State, or local law that govern the affairs of the partnership or are considered under such law to be a part of the partnership agreement (see the last sentence of paragraph (c) of § 1.761-1). For purposes of this paragraph (b)(2)(ii)(h), an agreement with a partner or a partnership shall include an agreement with a person related, within the meaning of section 267(b) (without modification by section 267(e)(1)) or section 707(b)(1), to such partner or partnership. For purposes of the preceding sentence, sections 267(b) and 707(b)(1) shall be applied for partnership taxable years beginning after December 29, 1988 by (1) substituting "80 percent or more" for "more than 50 percent" each place it appears in such sections, (2) excluding brothers and sisters from the members of a person's family, and (3) disregarding section 267(f)(1)(A).

(i) Economic effect equivalence. Allocations made to a partner that do not otherwise have economic effect under this paragraph (b)(2)(ii) shall nevertheless be deemed to have economic effect, provided that as of the end of each partnership taxable year a liquidation of the partnership at the end of such year or at the end of any future year would produce the same economic results to the partners as would occur if requirements (1), (2), and (3) of paragraph (b)(2)(ii)(b) of this section had been satisfied, regardless of the economic performance of the partnership. See examples (4)(ii) and (iii) of paragraph (b)(5) of this section.

(iii) Substantiality. (a) General rules. Except as otherwise provided in this paragraph (b)(2)(iii), the economic effect of an allocation (or allocations) is substantial if there is a reasonable possibility that the allocation (or allocations) will affect substantially the dollar amounts to be received by the partners from the partnership, independent of tax consequences. Notwithstanding the preceding sentence, the economic effect of an allocation (or allocations) is not substantial if, at the time the allocation becomes part of the partnership agreement; (1) the after-tax economic consequences of at least one partner may, in present value terms, be enhanced compared to such consequences if the allocation (or allocations) were not contained in the partnership agreement, and (2) there is a strong likelihood that the after-tax economic consequences of no partner will, in present value terms, be substantially diminished compared to such consequences if the allocation (or allocations) were not contained in the partnership agreement. In determining the after-tax economic benefit or detriment to a partner, tax consequences that result from the interaction of the allocation with such partner's tax attributes that are unrelated to the partnership will be taken into account. See examples (5) and (9) of paragraph (b)(5) of this section. The economic effect of an allocation is not substantial in the two situations described in paragraphs (b)(2)(iii)(b) and (c) of this section. However, even if an allocation is not described therein, its economic effect may be insubstantial under the general rules stated in this paragraph (b)(2)(iii)(a). References in this paragraph (b)(2)(iii) to allocations includes capital account adjustments made pursuant to paragraph (b)(2)(iv)(k) of this section.

(b) Shifting tax consequences. The economic effect of an allocation (or allocations) in a partnership taxable year is not substantial if, at the time the allocation (or allocations) becomes part of the partnership agreement, there is a strong likelihood that—

(1) The net increases and decreases that will be recorded in the partners' respective capital accounts for such taxable year will not differ substantially from the net increases and decreases that would be recorded in such partners' respective capital accounts for such year if the allocations were not contained in the partnership agreement, and

(2) The total tax liability of the partners (for their respective taxable years in which the allocations will be taken into account) will be less than if the allocations were not contained in the partnership agreement (taking into account tax consequences that result from the interaction of the allocation (or allocations) with partner tax attributes that are unrelated to the partnership). If, at the end of a partnership taxable year to which an allocation (or allocations) relates, the net increases and decreases that are recorded in the partners' respective capital accounts do not differ substantially from the net increases and decreases that would have been recorded in such partners' respective capital accounts had the allocation (or allocations) not been contained in the partnership agreement, and the total tax liability of the partners is (as described in (2) above) less than it would have been had the allocation (or allocations) not been contained in the partnership agreement, it will be presumed that, at the time the allocation (or allocations) became part of such partnership agreement, there was a strong likelihood that these results would occur. This presumption may be overcome by a showing of facts and circumstances that prove otherwise. See examples (6), (7)(ii) and (iii), and (10)(ii) of paragraph (b)(5) of this section.

(c) Transitory allocations. If a partnership agreement provides for the possibility that one or more allocations (the "original allocation(s)") will be largely offset by one or more other allocations (the "offsetting allocation(s)"), and, at the time the allocations become part of the partnership agreement, there is a strong likelihood that—

(1) The net increases and decreases that will be recorded in the partners' respective capital accounts for the taxable years to which the allocations relate will not differ substantially from the net increases and decreases that would be recorded in such partners' respective capital accounts for such years if the original allocation(s) and offsetting allocation(s) were not contained in the partnership agreement, and

(2) The total tax liability of the partners (for their respective taxable years in which the allocations will be taken into account) will be less than if the allocations were not contained in the partnership agreement (taking into account tax consequences that result from the interaction of the allocation (or allocations) with partner tax attributes that are unrelated to the partnership)

the economic effect of the original allocation(s) and offsetting allocation(s) will not be substantial. If, at the end of a partnership taxable year to which an offsetting allocation(s) relates, the net increases and decreases recorded in the partners' respective capital accounts do not differ substantially from the net increases and decreases that would have been recorded in such partners' respective capital accounts had the original allocation(s) and the offsetting allocation(s) not been contained in the partnership agreement, and the total tax liability of the partners is (as described in (2) above) less than it would have been had such allocations not been contained in the partnership agreement, it will be presumed that, at the time the allocations became part of the partnership agreement, there was a strong likelihood that these results would occur. This presumption may be overcome by a showing of facts and circumstances that prove otherwise. See examples (1)(xi), (2), (3), (7), (8)(ii), and (17) of paragraph (b)(5) of this section. Notwithstanding the foregoing, the original allocation(s) and the offsetting allocation(s) will not be insubstantial (under this paragraph (b)(2)(iii)(c)) and, for purposes of paragraph (b)(2)(iii)(a), it will be presumed that there is a reasonable possibility that the allocations will affect substantially the dollar amounts to be received by the partners from the partnership if, at the time the allocations become part of the partnership agreement, there is a strong likelihood that the offsetting allocation(s) will not, in large part, be made within five years after the original allocation(s) is made (determined on a first-in, first-out basis). See example (2) of paragraph (b)(5) of this section. For purposes of applying the provisions of this paragraph (b)(2)(iii) (and paragraphs (b)(2)(ii)(d)(6) and (b)(3)(iii) of this section), the adjusted tax basis of partnership property (or, if partnership property is properly reflected on the books of the partnership at a book value that differs from its adjusted tax basis, the book value of such property) will be presumed to be the fair market value of such property, and adjustments to the adjusted tax basis (or book value) of such property will be presumed to be matched by corresponding changes in such property's fair market value. Thus, there cannot be a strong likelihood that the economic effect of an allocation (or allocations) will be largely offset by an allocation (or allocations) of gain or loss from the disposition of partnership property. See examples (1)(vi) and (xi) of paragraph (b)(5) of this section.

(iv) Maintenance of capital accounts. (a) In general. The economic effect test described in paragraph (b)(2)(ii) of this section requires an examination of the capital accounts of the partners of a partnership, as maintained under the partnership agreement. Except as otherwise provided in paragraph (b)(2)(ii)(i) of this section, an allocation of income, gain, loss, or deduction will not have economic effect under paragraph (b)(2)(ii) of this section, and will not be deemed to be in accordance with a partner's interest in the partnership under paragraph (b)(4) of this section, unless the capital accounts of the partners are determined and maintained throughout the full term of the partnership in accordance with the capital accounting rules of this paragraph (b)(2)(iv).

(b) Basic rules. Except as otherwise provided in this paragraph (b)(2)(iv), the partners' capital accounts will be considered to be determined and maintained in accordance with the rules of this paragraph (b)(2)(iv) if, and only if, each partner's capital account is increased by (1) the amount of money contributed by him to the partnership, (2) the fair market value of property contributed by him to the partnership (net of liabilities that the partnership is considered to assume or take subject to), and (3) allocations to him of partnership income and gain (or items thereof), including income and gain exempt from tax and income and gain described in paragraph (b)(2)(iv)(g) of this section, but excluding income and gain described in paragraph (b)(4)(i) of this section; and is decreased by (4) the amount of money distributed to him by the partnership, (5) the fair market value of property distributed to him by the partnership (net of liabilities that such partner is considered to assume or take subject to), (6) allocations to him of expenditures of the partnership described in section 705(a)(2)(B), and (7) allocations of partnership loss and deduction (or item thereof), including loss and deduction described in paragraph (b)(2)(iv)(g) of this section, but excluding items described in (6) above and loss or deduction described in paragraphs (b)(4)(i) or (b)(4)(iii) of this section; and is otherwise adjusted in accordance with the additional rules set forth in this paragraph (b)(2)(iv). For purposes of this paragraph, a partner who has more than one interest in a partnership shall have a single capital account that reflects all such interests, regardless of the class of interests owned by such partner (e.g., general or limited) and regardless of the time or manner in which such interests were acquired. For liabilities assumed before June 24, 2003, references to liabilities in this paragraph (b)(2)(iv)(b) shall include only liabilities secured by the contributed or distributed property that are taken into account under section 752(a) and (b).

(c) Treatment of liabilities. For purposes of this paragraph (b)(2)(iv), (1) money contributed by a partner to a partnership includes the amount of any partnership liabilities that are assumed by such partner (other than liabilities described in paragraph (b)(2)(iv)(b)(5) of this section that are assumed by a distributee partner) but does not include increases in such partner's share of partnership liabilities (see section 752(a)), and (2) money distributed to a partner by a partnership includes the amount of such partner's individual liabilities that are assumed by the partnership (other than liabilities described in paragraph (b)(2)(iv)(b)(2) of this section that are assumed by the partnership) but does not include decreases in such partner's share of partnership liabilities (see section 752(b)). For purposes of this paragraph (b)(2)(iv)(c), liabilities are considered assumed only to the extent the assuming party is thereby subjected to personal liability with respect to such obligation, the obligee is aware of the assumption and can directly enforce the assuming party's obligation, and, as between the assuming party and the party from whom the liability is assumed, the assuming party is ultimately liable.

(d) Contributed property. (1) In general. The basic capital accounting rules contained in paragraph (b)(2)(iv)(b) of this section require that a partner's capital account be increased by the fair market value of property contributed to the partnership by such partner on the date of contribution. See example (13)(i) of paragraph (b)(5) of this section. Consistent with section 752(c), section 7701(g) does not apply in determining such fair market value.

(2) Contribution of promissory notes. Notwithstanding the general rule of paragraph (b)(2)(iv)(b)(2) of this section, except as provided in this paragraph (b)(2)(iv)(d)(2), if a promissory note is contributed to a partnership by a partner who is the maker of such note, such partner's capital account will be increased with respect to such note only when there is a taxable disposition of such note by the partnership or when the partner makes principal payments on such note. See example (1)(ix) of paragraph (b)(5) of this section. The first sentence of this paragraph (b)(2)(iv)(d)(2) shall not apply if the note referred to therein is readily tradable on an established securities market. See also paragraph (b)(2)(ii)(c) of this section. Furthermore, a partner whose interest is liquidated will be considered as satisfying his obligation to restore the deficit balance in his capital account to the extent of (i) the fair market value, at the time of contribution, of any negotiable promissory note (of which such partner is the maker) that such partner contributes to the partnership on or after the date his interest is liquidated and within the time specified in paragraph (b)(2)(ii)(b)(3) of this section, and (ii) the fair market value, at the time of liquidation, of the unsatisfied portion of any negotiable promissory note (of which such partner is the maker) that such partner previously contributed to the partnership. For purposes of the preceding sentence, the fair market value of a note will be no less than the outstanding principal balance of such note, provided that such note bears interest at a rate no less than the applicable federal rate at the time of valuation.

(3) Section 704(c) considerations. Section 704(c) and § 1.704-3 govern the determination of the partners' distributive shares of income, gain, loss, and deduction, as computed for tax purposes, with respect to property contributed to a partnership (see paragraph (b)(1)(vi) of this section). In cases where section 704(c) and § 1.704-3 apply to partnership property, the capital accounts of the partners will not be considered to be determined and maintained in accordance with the rules of this paragraph (b)(2)(iv) unless the partnership agreement requires that the partners' capital accounts be adjusted in accordance with paragraph (b)(2)(iv)(g) of this section for allocations to them of income, gain, loss, and deduction (including depreciation, depletion, amortization, or other cost recovery) as computed for book purposes, with respect to the property. See, however, § 1.704-3(d)(2) for a special rule in determining the amount of book items if the partnership chooses the remedial allocation method. See also Example (13)(i) of paragraph (b)(5) of this section. Capital accounts are not adjusted to reflect allocations under section 704(c) and § 1.704-3 (e.g., tax allocations of precontribution gain or loss).

(e) Distributed property. (1) In general. The basic capital accounting rules contained in paragraph (b)(2)(iv)(b) of this section require that a partner's capital account be decreased by the fair market value of property distributed by the partnership (without regard to section 7701(g)) to such partner (whether in connection with a liquidation or otherwise). To satisfy this requirement, the capital accounts of the partners first must be adjusted to reflect the manner in which the unrealized income, gain, loss, and deduction inherent in such property (that has not been reflected in the capital accounts previously) would be allocated among the partners if there were a taxable disposition of such property for the fair market value of such property (taking section 7701(g) into account) on the date of distribution. See example (14)(v) of paragraph (b)(5) of this section.

(2) Distribution of promissory notes. Notwithstanding the general rule of paragraph (b)(2)(iv)(b)(5), except as provided in this paragraph (b)(2)(iv)(e)(2), if a promissory note is distributed to a partner by a partnership that is the maker of such note, such partner's capital account will be decreased with respect to such note only when there is a taxable disposition of such note by the partner or when the partnership makes principal payments on the note. The previous sentence shall not apply if a note distributed to a partner by a partnership who is the maker of such note is readily tradable on an established securities market. Furthermore, the capital account of a partner whose interest in a partnership is liquidated will be reduced to the extent of (i) the fair market value, at the time of distribution, of any negotiable promissory note (of which such partnership is the maker) that such partnership distributes to the partner on or after the date such partner's interest is liquidated and within the time specified in paragraph (b)(2)(ii)(b)(2) of this section, and (ii) the fair market value, at the time of liquidation, of the unsatisfied portion of any negotiable promissory note (of which such partnership is the maker) that such partnership previously

distributed to the partner. For purposes of the preceding sentence, the fair market value of a note will be no less than the outstanding principal balance of such note, provided that such note bears interest at a rate no less than the applicable federal rate at time of valuation.

(f) Revaluations of property. A partnership agreement may, upon the occurrence of certain events, increase or decrease the capital accounts of the partners to reflect a revaluation of partnership property (including intangible assets such as goodwill) on the partnership's books. Capital accounts so adjusted will not be considered to be determined and maintained in accordance with the rules of this paragraph (b)(2)(iv) unless—

(1) The adjustments are based on the fair market value of partnership property (taking section 7701(g) into account) on the date of adjustment, and

(2) The adjustments reflect the manner is which the unrealized income, gain, loss, or deduction inherent in such property (that has not been reflected in the capital accounts previously) would be allocated among the partners if there were a taxable disposition of such property for such fair market value on that date, and

(3) The partnership agreement requires that the partners' capital accounts be adjusted in accordance with paragraph (b)(2)(iv)(g) of this section for allocations to them of depreciation, depletion, amortization, and gain or loss, as computed for book purposes, with respect to such property, and

(4) The partnership agreement requires that the partners' distributive shares of depreciation, depletion, amortization, and gain or loss, as computed for tax purposes, with respect to such property be determined so as to take account of the variation between the adjusted tax basis and book value of such property in the same manner as under section 704(c) (see paragraph (b)(4)(i) of this section), and

(5) The adjustments are made principally for a substantial non-tax business purpose—

(i) In connection with a contribution of money or other property (other than a de minimis amount) to the partnership by a new or existing partner as consideration for an interest in the partnership, or

(ii) In connection with the liquidation of the partnership or a distribution of money or other property (other than a de minimis amount) by the partnership to a retiring or continuing partner as consideration for an interest in the partnership, or

(iii) In connection with the grant of an interest in the partnership (other than a de minimis interest) on or after May 6, 2004, as consideration for the provision of services to or for the benefit of the partnership by an existing partner acting in a partner capacity, or by a new partner acting in a partner capacity or in anticipation of being a partner.

(iv) Under generally accepted industry accounting practices, provided substantially all of the partnership's property (excluding money) consists of stock, securities, commodities, options, warrants, futures, or similar instruments that are readily tradable on an established securities market.

See example (14) and (18) of paragraph (b)(5) of this section. If the capital accounts of the partners are not adjusted to reflect the fair market value of partnership property when an interest in the partnership is acquired from or relinquished to the partnership, paragraphs (b)(1)(iii) and (b)(1)(iv) of this section should be consulted regarding the potential tax consequences that may arise if the principles of section 704(c) are not applied to determine the partners' distributive shares of depreciation, depletion, amortization, and gain or loss as computed for tax purposes, with respect to such property.

(g) Adjustments to reflect book value. (1) In general. Under paragraphs (b)(2)(iv)(d) and (b)(2)(iv)(f) of this section, property may be properly reflected on the books of the partnership at a book value that differs from the adjusted tax basis of such property. In these circumstances, paragraphs (b)(2)(iv)(d)(3) and (b)(2)(iv)(f)(3) of this section provide that the capital accounts of the partners will not be considered to be determined and maintained in accordance with the rules of this paragraph (b)(2)(iv) unless the partnership agreement requires the partners' capital accounts to be adjusted in accordance with this paragraph (b)(2)(iv)(g) for allocations to them of depreciation, depletion, amortization, and gain or loss, as computed for book purposes, with respect to such property. In determining whether the economic effect of an allocation of book items is substantial, consideration will be given to the effect of such allocation on the determination of the partners' distributive shares of corresponding tax items under section 704(c) and paragraph (b)(4)(i) of this section. See example (17) of paragraph (b)(5) of this section. If an allocation of book items under the partnership agreement does not have substantial economic effect (as determined under paragraphs (b)(2)(ii) and (b)(2)(iii) of this section), or is not otherwise respected under this paragraph, such items will be reallocated in accordance with the partners' interests in the partnership, and such reallocation will be the basis upon which the partners' distributive shares of the corresponding tax items are determined under section 704(c) and paragraph (b)(4)(i) of this section. See examples (13), (14), and (18) of paragraph (b)(5) of this section.

(2) Payables and receivables. References in this paragraph (b)(2)(iv) and paragraph (b)(4)(i) of this section to book and tax depreciation, depletion, amortization, and gain or loss with respect to property that has an adjusted tax basis that differs from book value include, under analogous rules and principles, the unrealized income or deduction with respect to accounts receivable, accounts payable, and other accrued but unpaid items.

(3) Determining amount of book items. The partners' capital accounts will not be considered adjusted in accordance with this paragraph (b)(2)(iv)(g) unless the amount of book depreciation, depletion, or amortization for a period with respect to an item of partnership property is the amount that bears the same relationship to the book value of such property as the depreciation (or cost recovery deduction), depletion, or amortization computed for tax purposes with respect to such property for such period bears to the adjusted tax basis of such property. If such property has a zero adjusted tax basis, the book depreciation, depletion, or amortization may be determined under any reasonable method selected by the partnership.

(h) Determinations of fair market value. For purposes of this paragraph (b)(2)(iv), the fair market value assigned to property contributed to a partnership, property distributed by a partnership, or property otherwise revalued by a partnership, will be regarded as correct, provided that (1) such value is reasonably agreed to among the partners in arm's-length negotiations, and (2) the partners have sufficiently adverse interests. If, however, these conditions are not satisfied and the value assigned to such property is overstated or understated (by more than an insignificant amount), the capital accounts of the partners will not be considered to be determined and maintained in accordance with the rules of this paragraph (b)(2)(iv). Valuation of property contributed to the partnership, distributed by the partnership, or otherwise revalued by the partnership shall be on a property-by-property basis, except to the extent the regulations under section 704(c) permit otherwise.

(i) Section 705(a)(2)(B) expenditures. (1) In general. The basic capital accounting rules contained in paragraph (b)(2)(iv)(b) of this section require that a partner's capital account be decreased by allocations made to such partner of expenditures described in section 705(a)(2)(B). See example (11) of paragraph (b)(5) of this section. If an allocation of these expenditures under the partnership agreement does not have substantial economic effect (as determined under paragraphs (b)(2)(ii) and (b)(2)(iii) of this section), or is not otherwise respected under this paragraph, such expenditures will be reallocated in accordance with the partners' interest in the partnership.

(2) Expenses described in section 709. Except for amounts with respect to which an election is properly made under section 709(b), amounts paid or incurred to organize a partnership or to promote the sale of (or to sell) an interest in such a partnership shall, solely for purposes of this paragraph, be treated as section 705(a)(2)(B) expenditures, and upon liquidation of the partnership no further capital account adjustments will be made in respect thereof.

(3) Disallowed losses. If a deduction for a loss incurred in connection with the sale or exchange of partnership property is disallowed to the partnership under section 267(a)(1) or section 707(b), that deduction shall, solely for purposes of this paragraph, be treated as a section 705(a)(2)(B) expenditure.

(j) Basis adjustments to section 38 property. The capital accounts of the partners will not be considered to be determined and maintained in accordance with the rules of this paragraph (b)(2)(iv) unless such capital accounts are adjusted by the partners' shares of any upward or downward basis adjustments allocated to them under this paragraph (b)(2)(iv)(j). When there is a reduction in the adjusted tax basis of partnership section 38 property under section 48(q)(1) or section 48(q)(3), section 48(q)(6) provides for an equivalent downward adjustment to the aggregate basis of partnership interests (and no additional adjustment is made under section 705(a)(2)(B)). These downward basis adjustments shall be shared among the partners in the same proportion as the adjusted tax basis or cost of (or the qualified investment in) such section 38 property is allocated among the partners under paragraph (f) of § 1.46-3 (or paragraph (a)(4)(iv) of § 1.48-8). Conversely, when there is an increase in the adjusted tax basis of partnership section 38 property under section 48(q)(2), section 48(q)(6) provides for an equivalent upward adjustment to the aggregate basis of partnership interests. These upward adjustments shall be allocated among the partners in the same proportion as the investment tax credit from such property is recaptured by the partners under § 1.47-6.

(k) Depletion of oil and gas properties. (1) In general. The capital accounts of the partners will not be considered to be determined and maintained in accordance with the rules of this paragraph (b)(2)(iv) unless such capital accounts are adjusted for depletion and gain or loss with respect to the oil or gas properties of the partnership in accordance with this paragraph (b)(2)(iv)(k).

(2) Simulated depletion. Except as provided in paragraph (b)(2)(iv)(k)(3) of this section, a partnership shall, solely for purposes of maintaining capital accounts under this paragraph, compute simulated depletion allowances with respect to its oil and gas properties at the partnership level. These allowances shall be computed on each depletable oil or gas property of the partnership by using either the cost depletion method or the percentage depletion method (computed in accordance with section 613 at the rates specified in section 613A(c)(5) without regard to the limitations of section 613A, which theoretically could apply to any partner) for each partnership taxable year that the property is owned by the partnership and subject to depletion. The choice between the simulated cost depletion method and the simulated percentage depletion method shall be made on a property-by-property basis in the first partnership taxable year beginning after April 30, 1986, for which it is relevant for the property, and shall be binding for all partnership taxable years during which the oil or gas property is held by the partnership. The partnership shall make downward adjustments to the capital accounts of the partners for the simulated depletion allowance with respect to each oil or gas property of the partnership, in the same proportion as such partners (or their predecessors in interest) were properly allocated the adjusted tax basis of each such property. The aggregate capital account adjustments for simulated percentage depletion allowances with respect to an oil or gas property of the partnership shall not exceed the aggregate adjusted tax basis allocated to the partners with respect to such property. Upon the taxable disposition of an oil or gas property by a partnership, such partnership's simulated gain or loss shall be determined by subtracting its simulated adjusted basis in such property from the amount realized upon such disposition. (The partnership's simulated adjusted basis in an oil or gas property is determined in the same manner as adjusted tax basis except that simulated depletion allowances are taken into account instead of actual depletion allowances.) The capital accounts of the partners shall be adjusted upward by the amount of any simulated gain in proportion to such partners' allocable shares of the portion of the total amount realized from the disposition of such property that exceeds the partnership's simulated adjusted basis in such property. The capital accounts of such partners shall be adjusted downward by the amount of any simulated loss in proportion to such partners' allocable shares of the total amount realized from the disposition of such property that represents recovery of the partnership's simulated adjusted basis in such property. See section 613A(c)(7)(D) and the regulations thereunder and paragraph (b)(4)(v) of this section. See example (19)(iv) of paragraph (b)(5) of this section.

(3) Actual depletion. Pursuant to section 613A(c)(7)(D) and the regulations thereunder, the depletion allowance under section 611 with respect to the oil and gas properties of a partnership is computed separately by the partners. Accordingly, in lieu of adjusting the partner's capital accounts as provided in paragraph (b)(2)(iv)(k)(2) of this section, the partnership may make downward adjustments to the capital account of each partner equal to such partner's depletion allowance with respect to each oil or gas property of the partnership (for the partner's taxable year that ends with or within the partnership's taxable year). The aggregate adjustments to the capital account of a partner for depletion allowances with respect to an oil or gas property of the partnership shall not exceed the adjusted tax basis allocated to such partner with respect to such property. Upon the taxable disposition of an oil or gas property by a partnership, the capital account of each partner shall be adjusted upward by the amount of any excess of such partner's allocable share of the total amount realized from the disposition of such property over such partner's remaining adjusted tax basis in such property. If there is no such excess, the capital account of such partner shall be adjusted downward by the amount of

any excess of such partner's remaining adjusted tax basis in such property over such partner's allocable share of the total amount realized from the disposition thereof. See section 613A(c)(7)(4)(D) and the regulations thereunder and paragraph (b)(4)(v) of this section.

(4) Effect of book values. If an oil or gas property of the partnership is, under paragraphs (b)(2)(iv)(d) or (b)(2)(iv)(f) of this section, properly reflected on the books of the partnership at a book value that differs from the adjusted tax basis of such property, the rules contained in this paragraph (b)(2)(iv)(k) and paragraph (b)(4)(v) of this section shall be applied with reference to such book value. A revaluation of a partnership oil or gas property under paragraph (b)(2)(iv)(f) of this section may give rise to a reallocation of the adjusted tax basis of such property, or a change in the partners' relative shares of simulated depletion from such property, only to the extent permitted by section 613A(c)(7)(D) and the regulations thereunder.

(l) Transfers of partnership interests. The capital accounts of the partners will not be considered to be determined and maintained in accordance with the rules of this paragraph (b)(2)(iv) unless, upon the transfer of all or a part of an interest in the partnership, the capital account of the transferor that is attributable to the transferred interest carries over to the transferee partner. (See paragraph (b)(2)(iv)(m) of this section for rules concerning the effect of a section 754 election on the capital accounts of the partners.) If the transfer of an interest in a partnership causes a termination of the partnership under section 708(b)(1)(B), the capital account of the transferee partner and the capital accounts of the other partners of the terminated partnership carry over to the new partnership that is formed as a result of the termination of the partnership under § 1.708-1(b)(1)(iv). Moreover, the deemed contribution of assets and liabilities by the terminated partnership to a new partnership and the deemed liquidation of the terminated partnership that occur under § 1.708-1(b)(1)(iv) are disregarded for purposes of paragraph (b)(2)(iv) of this section. See Example 13 of paragraph (b)(5) of this section and the example in § 1.708-1(b)(1)(iv). The previous three sentences apply to terminations of partnerships under section 708(b)(1)(B) occurring on or after May 9, 1997; however, the sentences may be applied to terminations occurring on or after May 9, 1996, provided that the partnership and its partners apply the sentences to the termination in a consistent manner.

(m) Section 754 elections. (1) In general. The capital accounts of the partners will not be considered to be determined and maintained in accordance with the rules of this paragraph (b)(2)(iv) unless, upon adjustment to the adjusted tax basis of partnership property under section 732, 734, or 743, the capital accounts of the partners are adjusted as provided in this paragraph (b)(2)(iv)(m).

(2) Section 743 adjustments. In the case of a transfer of all or a part of an interest in a partnership that has a section 754 election in effect for the partnership taxable year in which such transfer occurs, adjustments to the adjusted tax basis of partnership property under section 743 shall not be reflected in the capital account of the transferee partner or on the books of the partnership, and subsequent capital account adjustments for distributions (see paragraph (b)(2)(iv)(e)(1) of this section) and for depreciation, depletion, amortization, and gain or loss with respect to such property will disregard the effect of such basis adjustment. The preceding sentence shall not apply to the extent such basis adjustment is allocated to the common basis of partnership property under paragraph (b)(1) of § 1.734-2; in these cases, such basis adjustment shall, except as provided in paragraph (b)(2)(iv)(m)(5) of this section, give rise to adjustments to the capital accounts of the partners in accordance with their interests in the partnership under paragraph (b)(3) of this section. See examples (13)(iii) and (iv) of paragraph (b)(5) of this section.

(3) Section 732 adjustments. In the case of a transfer of all or a part of an interest in a partnership that does not have a section 754 election in effect for the partnership taxable year in which such transfer occurs, adjustments to the adjusted tax basis of partnership property under section 732(d) will be treated in the capital accounts of the partners in the same manner as section 743 basis adjustments are treated under paragraph (b)(2)(iv)(m)(2) of this section.

(4) Section 734 adjustments. Except as provided in paragraph (b)(2)(iv)(m)(5) of this section, in the case of a distribution of property in liquidation of a partner's interest in the partnership by a partnership that has a section 754 election in effect for the partnership taxable year in which the distribution occurs, the partner who receives the distribution that gives rise to the adjustment to the adjusted tax basis of partnership property under section 734 shall have a corresponding adjustment made to his capital account. If such distribution is made other than in liquidation of a partner's interest in the partnership, however, except as provided in paragraph (b)(2)(iv)(m)(5) of this section, the capital accounts of the partners shall be adjusted by the amount of the adjustment to the adjusted tax basis of partnership property under section 734, and such capital account adjustment shall be shared among the partners in the manner in which the unrealized income and gain that is displaced by such adjustment would have been shared if the property whose basis is adjusted were sold immediately prior to such adjustment for its recomputed adjusted tax basis.

(5) Limitations on adjustments. Adjustments may be made to the capital account of a partner (or his successor in interest) in respect of basis adjustments to partnership property under sections 732, 734, and 743 only to the extent that such basis adjustments (i) are permitted to be made to one or more items of partnership property under section 755, and (ii) result in an increase or a decrease in the amount at which such property is carried on the partnership's balance sheet, as computed for book purposes. For example, if the book value of partnership property exceeds the adjusted tax basis of such property, a basis adjustment to such property may be reflected in a partner's capital account only to the extent such adjustment exceeds the difference between the book value of such property and the adjusted tax basis of such property prior to such adjustment.

(n) Partnership level characterization. Except as otherwise provided in paragraph (b)(2)(iv)(k) of this section, the capital accounts of the partners will not be considered to be determined and maintained in accordance with the rules of this paragraph (b)(2)(iv) unless adjustments to such capital accounts in respect of partnership income, gain, loss, deduction, and section 705(a)(2)(B) expenditures (or item thereof) are made with reference to the Federal tax treatment of such items (and in the case of book items, with reference to the Federal tax treatment of the corresponding tax items) at the partnership level, without regard to any requisite or elective tax treatment of such items at the partner level (for example, under section 58(i)). However, a partnership that incurs mining exploration expenditures will determine the Federal tax treatment of income, gain, loss, and deduction with respect to the property to which such expenditures relate at the partnership level only after first taking into account the elections made by its partners under section 617 and section 703(b)(4).

(o) Guaranteed payments. Guaranteed payments to a partner under section 707(c) cause the capital account of the recipient partner to be adjusted only to the extent of such partner's distributive share of any partnership deduction, loss, or other downward capital account adjustment resulting from such payment.

(p) Minor discrepancies. Discrepancies between the balances in the respective capital accounts of the partners and the balances that would be in such respective capital accounts if they had been determined and maintained in accordance with this paragraph (b)(2)(iv) will not adversely affect the validity of an allocation, provided that such discrepancies are minor and are attributable to good faith error by the partnership.

(q) Adjustments where guidance is lacking. If the rules of this paragraph (b)(2)(iv) fail to provide guidance on how adjustments to the capital accounts of the partners should be made to reflect particular adjustments to partnership capital on the books of the partnership, such capital accounts will not be considered to be determined and maintained in accordance with those rules unless such capital account adjustments are made in a manner that (1) maintains equality between the aggregate governing capital accounts of the partners and the amount of partnership capital reflected on the partnership's balance sheet, as computed for book purposes, (2) is consistent with the underlying economic arrangement of the partners, and (3) is based, wherever practicable, on Federal tax accounting principles.

(r) Restatement of capital accounts. With respect to partnerships that began operating in a taxable year beginning before May 1, 1986, the capital accounts of the partners of which have not been determined and maintained in accordance with the rules of this paragraph (b)(2)(iv) since inception, such capital accounts shall not be considered to be determined and maintained in accordance with the rules of this paragraph (b)(2)(iv) for taxable years beginning after April 30, 1986, unless either—

(1) such capital accounts are adjusted, effective for the first partnership taxable year beginning after April 30, 1986, to reflect the fair market value of partnership property as of the first day of such taxable year, and in connection with such adjustment, the rules contained in paragraph (b)(2)(iv)(f)(2), (3), and (4) of this section are satisfied, or

(2) the differences between the balance in each partner's capital account and the balance that would be in such partner's capital account if capital accounts had been determined and maintained in accordance with this paragraph (b)(2)(iv) throughout the full term of the partnership are not significant (for example, such differences are solely attributable to a failure to provide for treatment of section 709 expenses in accordance with the rules of paragraph (b)(2)(iv)(i)(2) of this section or to a failure to follow the rules in paragraph (b)(2)(iv)(m) of this section), and capital accounts are adjusted to bring them into conformity with the rules of this paragraph (b)(2)(iv) no later than the end of the first partnership taxable year beginning after April 30, 1986.

With respect to a partnership that began operating in a taxable year beginning before May 1, 1986, modifications to the partnership agreement adopted on or before November 1, 1988, to make the capital account adjustments required to comply with this paragraph, and otherwise to satisfy the requirements of this paragraph, will be treated as if such modifications were included in the partnership agreement before the end of the first partnership taxable year beginning after April 30, 1986. However, compliance with the previous sentences will have no bearing on the validity of allocations that relate to partnership taxable years beginning before May 1, 1986.

(3) Partner's interest in the partnership. (i) In general. References in section 704(b) and this paragraph to a partner's interest in the partnership, or to the partners' interests in the partnership, signify the manner in which the partners have agreed to share the economic benefit or burden (if any) corresponding to the income, gain, loss, deduction, or credit (or item thereof) that is allocated. Except with respect to partnership items that cannot have economic effect (such as nonrecourse deductions of the partnership), this sharing arrangement may or may not correspond to the overall economic arrangement of the partners. Thus, a partner who has a 50 percent overall interest in the partnership may have a 90 percent interest in a particular item of income or deduction. (For example, in the case of an unexpected downward adjustment to the capital account of a partner who does not have a deficit make-up obligation that causes such partner to have a negative capital account, it may be necessary to allocate a disproportionate amount of gross income of the partnership to such partner for such year so as to bring that partner's capital account back up to zero.) The determination of a partner's interest in a partnership shall be made by taking into account all facts and circumstances relating to the economic arrangement of the partners. All partners' interests in the partnership are presumed to be equal (determined on a per capita basis). However, this presumption may be rebutted by the taxpayer or the Internal Revenue Service by establishing facts and circumstances that show that the partners' interests in the partnership are otherwise.

(ii) Factors considered. In determining a partner's interest in the partnership, the following factors are among those that will be considered:

(a) The partners' relative contributions to the partnership,

(b) The interests of the partners in economic profits and losses (if different than that in taxable income or loss),

(c) The interests of the partners in cash flow and other non-liquidating distributions, and

(d) The rights of the partners to distributions of capital upon liquidation.

The provisions of this subparagraph (b)(3) are illustrated by examples (1)(i) and (ii), (4)(i), (5)(i) and (ii), (6), (7), (8), (10)(ii), 16(i), and (19)(iii) of paragraph (b)(5) of this section. See paragraph (b)(4)(i) of this section concerning rules for determining the partners' interests in the partnership with respect to certain tax items.

(iii) Certain determinations. If—

(a) Requirements (1) and (2) of paragraph (b)(2)(ii)(b) of this section are satisfied, and

(b) All or a portion of an allocation of income, gain, loss, or deduction made to a partner for a partnership taxable year does not have economic effect under paragraph (b)(2)(ii) of this section. The partners' interests in the partnership with respect to the portion of the allocation that lacks economic effect will be determined by comparing the manner in which distributions (and contributions) would be made if all partnership property were sold at book value and the partnership were liquidated immediately following the end of the taxable year to which the allocation relates with the manner in which distributions (and contributions) would be made if all partnership property were sold at book value and the partnership were liquidated immediately following the end of the prior taxable year, and adjusting the result for the items described in (4), (5), and (6) of paragraph (b)(2)(ii)(d) of this section. A determination made under this paragraph (b)(3)(iii) will have no force if the economic effect of valid allocations made in the same manner is insubstantial under paragraph (b)(2)(iii) of this section. See examples (1)(iv), (v), and (vi), and (15)(ii) and (iii) of paragraph (b)(5) of this section.

(iv) Special rule for creditable foreign tax expenditures. In determining whether an allocation of a partnership item is in accordance with the partners' interests in the partnership, the allocation of the creditable foreign tax expenditure (CFTE) (as defined in paragraph (b)(4)(viii)(b) of this section) must be disregarded. This paragraph (b)(3)(iv) shall not apply to the extent the partners to whom such taxes are allocated reasonably expect to claim a deduction for such taxes in determining their U.S. tax liabilities.

(4) Special rules. (i) Allocations to reflect revaluations. If partnership property is, under paragraphs (b)(2)(iv)(d) or (b)(2)(iv)(f) of this section, properly reflected in the capital accounts of the partners and on the books of the partnership at a book value that differs from the adjusted tax basis of such property, then depreciation, depletion, amortization, and gain or loss, as computed for book purposes, with respect to such property will be greater or less than the depreciation, depletion, amortization, and gain or loss, as computed for tax purposes, with respect to such property. In these cases the capital accounts of the partners are required to be adjusted solely for allocations of the book items to such partners (see paragraph (b)(2)(iv)(g) of this section), and the partners' shares of the corresponding tax items are not independently reflected by further adjustments to the partners' capital accounts. Thus, separate allocations of these tax items cannot have economic effect under paragraph (b)(2)(ii)(b)(1) of this section, and the partners' distributive shares of such tax items must (unless governed by section 704(c)) be determined in accordance with the partners' interests in the partnership. These tax items must be shared among the partners in a manner that takes account of the variation between the adjusted tax basis of such property and its book value in the same manner as variations between the adjusted tax basis and fair market value of property contributed to the partnership are taken into account in determining the partners' shares of tax items under section 704(c). See examples (14) and (18) of paragraph (b)(5) of this section.

(ii) Credits. Allocations of tax credits and tax credit recapture are not reflected by adjustments to the partners' capital accounts (except to the extent that adjustments to the adjusted tax basis of partnership section 38 property in respect of tax credits and tax credit recapture give rise to capital account adjustments under paragraph (b)(2)(iv)(l) of this section). Thus, such allocations cannot have economic effect under paragraph (b)(2)(ii)(b)(1) of this section, and the tax credits and tax credit recapture must be allocated in accordance with the partners' interests in the partnership as of the time the tax credit or credit recapture arises. With respect to the investment tax credit provided by section 38, allocations of cost or qualified investment made in accordance with paragraph (f) of § 1.46-3 and paragraph (a)(4)(iv) of § 1.48-8 shall be deemed to be made in accordance with the partners' interests in the partnership. With respect to other tax credits, if a partnership expenditure (whether or not deductible) that gives rise to a tax credit in a partnership taxable year also gives rise to valid allocations of partnership loss or deduction (or other downward capital account adjustments) for such year, then the partners' interests in the partnership with respect to such credit (or the cost giving rise thereto) shall be in the same proportion as such partners' respective distributive shares of such loss or deduction (and adjustments). See example (11) of paragraph (b)(5) of this section. Identical principles shall apply in determining the partners' interests in the partnership with respect to tax credits that arise from receipts of the partnership (whether or not taxable).

(iii) Excess percentage depletion. To the extent the percentage depletion in respect of an item of depletable property of the partnership exceeds the adjusted tax basis of such property, allocations of such excess percentage depletion are not reflected by adjustments to the partners' capital accounts. Thus, such allocations cannot have economic effect under paragraph (b)(2)(ii)(b)(1) of this section, and such excess percentage depletion must be allocated in accordance with the partners' interests in the partnership. The partners' interests in the partnership for a partnership taxable year with respect to such excess percentage depletion shall be in the same proportion as such partners' respective distributive shares of gross income from the depletable property (as determined under section 613(c)) for such year. See example (12) of paragraph (b)(5) of this section. See paragraphs (b)(2)(iv)(k) and (b)(4)(v) of this section for special rules concerning oil and gas properties of the partnership.

(iv) Allocations attributable to nonrecourse liabilities. The rules for allocations attributable to nonrecourse liabilities are contained in § 1.704-2.

(v) Allocations under section 613A(c)(7)(D). Allocations of the adjusted tax basis of a partnership oil or gas property are controlled by section 613A(c)(7)(D) and the regulations thereunder. However, if the partnership agreement provides for an allocation of the adjusted tax basis of an oil or gas property among the partners, and such allocation is not otherwise governed under section 704(c) (or related principles under paragraph (b)(4)(i) of this section), that allocation will be recognized as being in accordance with the partners' interests in partnership capital under section 613A(c)(7)(D), provided (a) such allocation does not give rise to capital account adjustments under paragraph (b)(2)(iv)(k) of this section the economic effect of which is insubstantial (as determined under paragraph (b)(2)(iii) of this section), and (b) all other material allocations and capital account adjustments under the partnership agreement are recognized under this paragraph (b). Otherwise, such adjusted tax basis must be allocated among the partners pursuant to section 613A(c)(7)(D) in accordance with the partners' actual interests in partnership capital or income. For purposes of section 613A(c)(7)(D) the partners' allocable shares of the amount realized upon the partnership's taxable disposition of an oil or gas property will, except to the extent governed by section 704(c) (or related principles under paragraph (b)(4)(i) of this section), be determined under this paragraph (b)(4)(v). If, pursuant to paragraph (b)(2)(iv)(k)(2) of this section, the partners' capital accounts are adjusted to reflect the simulated depletion of an oil or gas property of the partnership, the portion of the total amount realized by the partnership upon the taxable disposition of such property that represents recovery of its simulated adjusted tax basis therein will be allocated to the partners in the same proportion as the aggregate adjusted tax basis of such property was allocated to such partners (or their predecessors in interest). If, pursuant to paragraph (b)(2)(iv)(k)(3) of this section, the partners' capital accounts are adjusted to reflect the actual depletion of an oil or gas property of the partnership, the portion of the total amount realized by the partnership upon the taxable disposition of such property that equals the partners' aggregate remaining adjusted basis therein will be allocated to the partners in proportion to their respective remaining adjusted tax bases in such property. An allocation provided by the partnership agreement of the portion of the total amount realized by the partnership on its taxable disposition of an oil or gas property that exceeds the portion of the total amount realized allocated under either of the previous two sentences (whichever is applicable) shall be deemed to be made in accordance with the partners' allocable shares of such amount realized, provided (c) such allocation does not give rise to capital account adjustments under paragraph (b)(2)(iv)(k) of this section the economic effect of which is insubstantial (as determined under paragraph (b)(2)(ii) of this section), and (d) all other allocations and capital account adjustments under the partnership agreement are recognized under this paragraph. Otherwise, the partners' allocable shares of the total amount realized by the partnership on its taxable disposition of an oil or gas property shall be determined in accordance with the partners' interests in the partnership under paragraph (b)(3) of this section. See example (19) of paragraph (b)(5) of this section. (See paragraph (b)(2)(iv)(k) of this section for the determination of appropriate adjustments to the partners' capital accounts relating to section 613A(c)(7)(D).)

(vi) Amendments to partnership agreement. If an allocation has substantial economic effect under paragraph (b)(2) of this section or is deemed to be made in accordance with the partners' interests in the partnership under paragraph (b)(4) of this section under the partnership agreement that is effective for the taxable year to which such allocation relates, and such partnership agreement thereafter is modified, both the tax consequences of the modification and the facts and circumstances surrounding the modification will be closely scrutinized to determine whether the purported modification was part of the original agreement. If it is determined that the purported modification was part of the original agreement, prior allocations may be reallocated in a manner consistent with the modified terms of the agreement, and subsequent allocations may be reallocated to take account of such modified terms. For example, if a partner is obligated by the partnership agreement to restore the deficit balance in his capital account (or any limited dollar amount thereof) in accordance with requirement (3) of paragraph (b)(2)(ii)(b) of this section and, thereafter, such obligation is eliminated or reduced (other than as provided in paragraph (b)(2)(ii)(f) of this section), or is not complied with in a timely manner, such elimination, reduction, or noncompliance may be treated as if it always were part of the partnership agreement for purposes of making any reallocations and determining the appropriate limitations period.

(vii) Recapture. For special rules applicable to the allocation of recapture income or credit, see paragraph (e) of § 1.1245-1, paragraph (f) of § 1.1250-1, paragraph (c) of § 1.1254-1, and paragraph (a) of § 1.47-6.

(viii) Allocation of creditable foreign taxes. (a) In general. Allocations of creditable foreign taxes do not have substantial economic effect within the meaning of paragraph (b)(2) of this section and, accordingly, such expenditures must be allocated in accordance with the partners' interests in the partnership. See paragraph (b)(3)(iv) of this section. An allocation of a creditable foreign tax expenditure (CFTE) will be deemed to be in accordance with the partners' interests in the partnership if—

(1) The CFTE is allocated (whether or not pursuant to an express provision in the partnership agreement) and reported on the partnership return in proportion to the distributive shares of income to which the CFTE relates; and

(2) Allocations of all other partnership items that, in the aggregate, have a material effect on the amount of CFTEs allocated to a partner pursuant to paragraph (b)(4)(viii)(a)(1) of this section are valid.

(b) Creditable foreign tax expenditures (CFTEs). For purposes of this section, a CFTE is a foreign tax paid or accrued by a partnership that is eligible for a credit under section 901(a) or an applicable U.S. income tax treaty. A foreign tax is a CFTE for these purposes without regard to whether a partner receiving an allocation of such foreign tax elects to claim a credit for such tax. Foreign taxes paid or accrued by a partner with respect to a distributive share of partnership income, and foreign taxes deemed paid under section 902 or 960 by a corporate partner with respect to stock owned, directly or indirectly, by or for a partnership, are not taxes paid or accrued by a partnership and, therefore, are not CFTEs subject to the rules of this section. See paragraphs (e) and (f) of § 1.901-2 for rules for determining when and by whom a foreign tax is paid or accrued.

(c) Income to which CFTEs relate. (1) In general. For purposes of paragraph (b)(4)(viii)(a) of this section, CFTEs are related to net income in the partnership's CFTE category or categories to which the CFTE is allocated and apportioned in accordance with the rules of paragraph (b)(4)(viii)(d) of this section. Paragraph (b)(4)(viii)(c)(2) of this section provides rules for determining a partnership's CFTE categories. Paragraph (b)(4)(viii)(c)(3) of this section provides rules for determining the net income in each CFTE category. Paragraph (b)(4)(viii)(c)(4) of this section provides guidance in determining a partner's distributive share of income in a CFTE category. Paragraph (b)(4)(viii)(c)(5) of this section provides a special rule for allocating CFTEs when a partnership has no net income in a CFTE category.

(2) CFTE category. (i) Income from activities. A CFTE category is a category of net income (or loss) attributable to one or more activities of the partnership. Net income (or loss) from all the partnership's activities shall be included in a single CFTE category unless the allocation of net income (or loss) from one or more activities differs from the allocation of net income (or loss) from other activities, in which case income from each activity or group of activities that is subject to a different allocation shall be treated as net income (or loss) in a separate CFTE category.

(ii) Different allocations. Different allocations of net income (or loss) generally will result from provisions of the partnership agreement providing for different sharing ratios for net income (or loss) from separate activities. Different allocations of net income (or loss) from separate activities generally will also result if any partnership item is shared in a different ratio than any other partnership item. A guaranteed payment described in paragraph (b)(4)(viii)(c)(3)(ii) of this section, gross income allocation, or other preferential allocation will result in different allocations of net income (or loss) from separate activities only if the amount of the payment or the allocation is determined by reference to income from less than all of the partnership's activities. For purposes of this paragraph (b)(4)(viii)(c)(2), a partnership item shall not include any item that is excluded from income attributable to an activity pursuant to the second sentence of paragraph (b)(4)(viii)(c)(3)(ii) of this section (relating to allocations or payments that result in a deduction under foreign law).

(iii) Activity. Whether a partnership has one or more activities, and the scope of each activity, shall be determined in a reasonable manner taking into account all the facts and circumstances. In evaluating whether aggregating or disaggregating income from particular business or investment operations constitutes a reasonable method of determining the scope of an activity, the principal consideration is whether the proposed determination has the effect of separating CFTEs from the related foreign income. Accordingly, relevant considerations include whether the partnership conducts business in more than one geographic location or through more than one entity or branch, and whether certain types of income are exempt from foreign tax or subject to preferential foreign tax treatment. In addition, income from a divisible part of a single activity shall be treated as income from a separate activity if necessary to prevent separating CFTEs from the related foreign income. The partnership's activities must be determined consistently from year to year absent a material change in facts and circumstances.

(3) Net income in a CFTE category. (i) In general. The net income in a CFTE category means the net income for U.S. Federal income tax purposes, determined by taking into account all partnership items attributable to the relevant activity or group of activities, including items of gross income, gain, loss, deduction, and expense and items allocated pursuant to section 704(c). The items of gross income attributable to an activity shall be determined in a consistent manner under any reasonable method taking into account all the facts and circumstances. Except as otherwise provided below, expenses, losses or other deductions shall be allocated and apportioned to gross income attributable to an activity in accordance with the rules of §§ 1.861-8 and 1.861-8T. Under these rules, if an expense, loss or other deduction is allocated to gross income from more than one activity, such expense, loss or deduction must be apportioned among each such activity using a reasonable method that reflects to a reasonably close extent the factual relationship between the deduction and the gross income from such activities. See § 1.861-8T(c). For purposes of determining net income in a CFTE category, the partnership's interest expense and research and experimental expenditures described in section 174 may be allocated and apportioned under any reasonable method, including but not limited to the methods prescribed in § 1.861-9 through § 1.861-13T (interest expense) and § 1.861-17 (research and experimental expenditures). For purposes of determining the net income attributable to any activity of a branch, the only items of gross income taken into account in applying this paragraph (b)(4)(viii)(c)(3) are those items of gross income recognized by the branch for U.S. income tax purposes. See paragraph (b)(5) Example 24 of this section (relating to inter-branch payments).

(ii) Special rules. Income attributable to an activity shall include the amount included in a partner's income as a guaranteed payment (within the meaning of section 707(c)) from the partnership to the extent that the guaranteed payment is not deductible by the partnership under foreign law. See paragraph (b)(5) Example 25 (iv) of this section. Except for an inter-branch payment described in paragraph (b)(4)(viii)(d)(3) of this section, income attributable to an activity shall not include an item of partnership income to the extent the allocation of such item of income (or payment thereof) results in a deduction under foreign law. See paragraph (b)(5) Example 25 (iii) and (iv) of this section. Similarly, income attributable to an activity shall not include net income that foreign law would exclude from the foreign tax base as a result of the status of a partner. See paragraph (b)(5) Example 27 of this section.

(4) Distributive shares of income. For purposes of paragraph (b)(4)(viii)(a)(1) of this section, distributive share of income means the net income from each CFTE category, determined in accordance with paragraph (b)(4)(viii)(c)(3) of this section, that is allocated to a partner. A guaranteed payment shall be treated as a distributive share of income for purposes of paragraph (b)(4)(viii)(a)(1) of this section to the extent that the guaranteed payment is treated as income attributable to an activity pursuant to paragraph (b)(4)(viii)(c)(3)(ii) of this section. See paragraph (b)(5) Example 25 (iv) of this section. If more than one partner receives positive income allocations (income in excess of expenses) from a CFTE category, which in the aggregate exceed the total net income in the CFTE category, then for purposes of paragraph (b)(4)(viii)(a)(1) of this section such partner's distributive share of income from the CFTE category shall equal the partner's positive income allocation from the CFTE category, divided by the aggregate positive income allocations from the CFTE category, multiplied by the net income in the CFTE category.

(5) No net income in a CFTE category. If a CFTE is allocated or apportioned to a CFTE category that does not have net income for the year in which the foreign tax is paid or accrued, the CFTE shall be deemed to relate to the aggregate of the net income (disregarding net losses) recognized by the partnership in that CFTE category in each of the three preceding taxable years. Accordingly, except as provided below, such CFTE must be allocated in the current taxable year in the same proportion as the allocation of the aggregate net income for the prior three-year period in order to satisfy the requirements of paragraph (b)(4)(viii)(a)(1) of this section. If the partnership does not have net income in the applicable CFTE category in either the current year or any of the previous three taxable years, the CFTE must be allocated in the same proportion that the partnership reasonably expects to allocate the aggregate net income (disregarding net losses) in the CFTE category for the succeeding three taxable years. If the partnership does not reasonably expect to have net income in the CFTE category for the succeeding three years and the partnership has net income in one or more other CFTE categories for the year in which the foreign tax is paid or accrued, the CFTE shall be deemed to relate to such other net income and must be allocated in proportion to the allocations of such other net income. If any CFTE is not allocated pursuant to the above provisions of this paragraph then the CFTE must be allocated in proportion to the partners' outstanding capital contributions.

(d) Allocation and apportionment of CFTEs to CFTE categories. (1) In general. CFTEs are allocated and apportioned to CFTE categories in accordance with the principles of § 1.904-6. Under these principles, a CFTE is related to income in a CFTE category if the income is included in the base upon which the foreign tax is imposed. In accordance with § 1.904-6(a)(1)(ii) as modified by this paragraph (b)(4)(viii)(d), if the foreign tax base includes income in more than one CFTE category, the CFTEs are apportioned among the CFTE categories based on the relative amounts of taxable income computed under foreign law in each CFTE category. For purposes of this paragraph (b)(4)(viii)(d), references in § 1.904-6 to a separate category or separate categories shall mean "CFTE category" or "CFTE categories" and the rules in § 1.904-6(a)(1)(ii) are modified as follows:

(i) The related party interest expense rule in § 1.904-6(a)(1)(ii) shall not apply in determining the amount of taxable income computed under foreign law in a CFTE category.

(ii) If foreign law does not provide for the direct allocation or apportionment of expenses, losses or other deductions allowed under foreign law to a CFTE category of income, then such expenses, losses or other deductions must be allocated and apportioned to gross income as determined under foreign law in a manner that is consistent with the allocation and apportionment of such items for purposes of determining the net income in the CFTE categories for U.S. tax purposes pursuant to paragraph (b)(4)(viii)(c)(3) of this section.

(2) Timing and base differences. A foreign tax imposed on an item that would be income under U.S. tax principles in another year (a timing difference) is allocated to the CFTE category that would include the income if the income were recognized for U.S. tax purposes in the year in which the foreign tax is imposed. A foreign tax imposed on an item that would not constitute income under U.S. tax principles in any year (a base difference) is allocated to the CFTE category that includes the partnership items attributable to the activity with respect to which the foreign tax is imposed. See paragraph (b)(5) Example 23 of this section.

(3) Special rules for inter-branch payments. Notwithstanding any other provision of this paragraph (d), the rules of this paragraph (b)(4)(viii)(d)(3) shall apply if a branch (including an entity described in § 301.7701-2(c)(2)(i) of this chapter) of the partnership is required to include in income under foreign law a payment it receives from another branch of the partnership. The foreign tax imposed on such payments ("inter-branch payments") is allocated to the CFTE category that includes the items attributable to the relevant activities of the recipient branch. In cases where the partnership agreement results in more than one CFTE category with respect to activities of the recipient branch, such tax is allocated to the CFTE category that includes the items attributable to the activity to which the inter-branch payment relates. The rules of this paragraph (b)(4)(viii)(d)(3) shall also apply to payments between a partnership and a branch of the partnership. See paragraph (b)(5) Example 24 of this section.

(ix) [Reserved].

(x) [Reserved].

(xi) [Reserved].

(5) Examples. The operation of the rules in this paragraph is illustrated by the following examples:

Example (1). (i) A and B form a general partnership with cash contributions of $40,000 each, which cash is used to purchase depreciable personal property at a cost of $80,000. The partnership elects under section 48(q)(4) to reduce the amount of investment tax credit in lieu of adjusting the tax basis of such property. The partnership agreement provides that A and B will have equal shares of taxable income and loss (computed without regard to cost recovery deductions) and cash flow and that all cost recovery deductions on the property will be allocated to A. The agreement further provides that the partners' capital accounts will be determined and maintained in accordance with paragraph (b)(2)(iv) of the section, but that upon liquidation of the partnership, distributions will be made equally between the partners (regardless of capital account balances) and no partner will be required to restore the deficit balance in his capital account for distribution to partners with positive capital accounts balances. In the partnership's first taxable year, it recognizes operating income equal to its operating expenses and has an additional $20,000 cost recovery deduction, which is allocated entirely to A. That A and B will be entitled to equal distributions on liquidation, even through A is allocated the entire $20,000 cost recovery deduction, indicates A will not bear the full risk of the economic loss corresponding to such deduction if such loss occurs. Under paragraph (b)(2)(ii) of this section, the allocation lacks economic effect and will be disregarded. The partners made equal contributions to the partnership, share equally in other taxable income and loss and in cash flow, and will share equally in liquidation proceeds, indicating that their actual economic arrangement is to bear the risk imposed by the potential decrease in the value of the property equally. Thus, under paragraph (b)(3) of this section the partners' interests in the partnership are equal, and the cost recovery deduction will be reallocated equally between A and B.

(ii) Assume the same facts as in (i) except that the partnership agreement provides that liquidation proceeds will be distributed in accordance with capital account balances if the partnership is liquidated during the first five years of its existence but that liquidation proceeds will be distributed equally if the partnership is liquidated thereafter. Since the partnership agreement does not provide for the requirement contained in paragraph (b)(2)(ii)(b)(2) of this section to be satisfied throughout the term of the partnership, the partnership allocations do not have economic effect. Even if the partnership agreement provided for the requirement contained in paragraph (b)(2)(ii)(b)(2) to be satisfied throughout the term of the partnership, such allocations would not have economic effect unless the requirement contained in paragraph (b)(2)(ii)(b)(3) of this section or the alternate economic effect test contained in paragraph (b)(2)(ii)(d) of this section were satisfied.

(iii) Assume the same facts as in (i) except that distributions in liquidation of the partnership (or any partner's interest) are to be made in accordance with the partners' positive capital account balances throughout the term of the partnership (as set forth in paragraph (b)(2)(ii)(b)(2) of this section). Assume further that the partnership agreement contains a qualified income offset (as defined in paragraph (b)(2)(ii)(d) of this section) and that, as of the end of each partnership taxable year, the items described in paragraphs (b)(2)(ii)(d)(4), (5), and (6) of this section are not reasonably expected to cause or increase a deficit balance in A's capital account.

	A	B
Capital account upon formation	$40,000	$40,000
Less: year 1 cost recovery deduction	(20,000)	0
Capital account at end of year 1	$20,000	$40,000

Under the alternate economic effect test contained in paragraph (b)(2)(ii)(d) of this section, the allocation of the $20,000 cost recovery deduction to A has economic effect.

(iv) Assume the same facts as in (iii) and that in the partnership's second taxable year it recognizes operating income equal to its operating expenses and has a $25,000 cost recovery deduction which, under the partnership agreement, is allocated entirely to A.

	A	B
Capital account at beginning of year 2 ..	$20,000	$40,000
Less: year 2 cost recovery deduction ...	(25,000)	0
Capital account at end of year 2	($5,000)	$40,000

The allocation of the $25,000 cost recovery deduction to A satisfies that alternate economic effect test contained in paragraph (b)(2)(ii)(d) of this section only to the extent of $20,000. Therefore, only $20,000 of such allocation has economic effect, and the remaining $5,000 must be reallocated in accordance with the partners' interests in the partnership. Under the partnership agreement, if the property were sold immediately following the end of the partnership's second taxable year for $35,000 (its adjusted tax basis), the $35,000 would be distributed to B. Thus, B, and not A, bears the economic burden corresponding to $5,000 of the $25,000 cost recovery deduction allocated to A. Under paragraph (b)(3)(iii) of this section, $5,000 of such cost recovery deduction will be reallocated to B.

(v) Assume the same facts as in (iv) except that the cost recovery deduction for the partnership's second taxable year is $20,000 instead of $25,000. The allocation of such cost recovery deduction to A has economic effect under the alternate economic effect test contained in paragraph (b)(2)(ii)(d) of this section. Assume further that the property is sold for $35,000 immediately following the end of the partnership's second taxable year, resulting in a $5,000 taxable loss ($40,000 adjusted tax basis less $35,000 sales price), and the partnership is liquidated.

	A	B
Capital account at beginning of year 2 . .	$20,000	$40,000
Less: year 2 cost recovery deduction . . .	(20,000)	0
Capital account at end of year 2	0	$40,000
Less: loss on sale	(2,500)	(2,500)
Capital account before liquidation	($2,500)	$37,500

Under the partnership agreement the $35,000 sales proceeds are distributed to B. Since B bears the entire economic burden corresponding to the $5,000 taxable loss from the sale of the property, the allocation of $2,500 of such loss to A does not have economic effect and must be reallocated in accordance with the partners' interests in the partnership. Under paragraph (b)(3)(iii) of this section, such $2,500 loss will be reallocated to B.

(vi) Assume the same facts as in (iv) except that the cost recovery deduction for the partnership's second taxable year is $20,000 instead of $25,000, and that as of the end of the partnership's second taxable year it is reasonably expected that during its third taxable year the partnership will (1) have operating income equal to its operating expenses (but will have no cost recovery deductions), (2) borrow $10,000 (recourse) and distribute such amount $5,000 to A and $5,000 to B, and (3) thereafter sell the partnership property, repay the $10,000 liability, and liquidate. In determining the extent to which the alternate economic effect test contained in paragraph (b)(2)(ii)(d) of this section is satisfied as of the end of the partnership's second taxable year, the fair market value of partnership property is presumed to be equal to its adjusted tax basis (in accordance with paragraph (b)(2)(iii)(c) of this section). Thus, it is presumed that the selling price of such property during the partnership's third taxable year will be its $40,000 adjusted tax basis. Accordingly, there can be no reasonable expectation that there will be increases to A's capital account in the partnership's third taxable year that will offset the expected $5,000 distribution to A. Therefore, the distribution of the loan proceeds must be taken into account in determining to what extent the alternate economic effect test contained in paragraph (b)(2)(ii)(d) is satisfied.

	A	B
Capital account at beginning of year 2	$20,000	$40,000
Less: expected future distribution	(5,000)	(5,000)
Less: year 2 cost recovery deduction . .	(20,000)	(0)
Hypothetical capital account at end of year 2	($5,000)	$35,000

Upon sale of the partnership property, the $40,000 presumed sales proceeds would be used to repay the $10,000 liability, and the remaining $30,000 would be distributed to B. Under these circumstances the allocation of the $20,000 cost recovery deduction to A in the partnership's second taxable year satisfies the alternate economic effect test contained in paragraph (b)(2)(ii)(d) of this section only to the extent of $15,000. Under paragraph (b)(3)(iii) of this section, the remaining $5,000 of such deduction will be reallocated to B. The results in this example would be the same even if the partnership agreement also provided that any gain (whether ordinary income or capital gain) upon the sale of the property would be allocated to A to the extent of the prior allocations of cost recovery deductions to him, and, at end of the partnership's second taxable year, the partners were confident that the gain on the sale of the property in the partnership's third taxable year would be sufficient to offset the expected $5,000 distribution to A.

(vii) Assume the same facts as in (iv) except that the partnership agreement also provides that any partner with a deficit balance in his capital account following the liquidation of his interest must restore that deficit to the partnership (as set forth in paragraph (b)(2)(ii)(b)(3) of this section). Thus, if the property were sold for $35,000 immediately after the end of the partnership's second taxable year, the $35,000 would be distributed to B, A would contribute $5,000 (the deficit balance in his capital account) to the partnership, and that $5,000 would be distributed to B. The allocation of the entire $25,000 cost recovery deduction to A in the partnership's second taxable year has economic effect.

(viii) Assume the same facts as in (vii) except that A's obligation to restore the deficit balance in his capital account is limited to a maximum of $5,000. The allocation of the $25,000 cost recovery deduction to A in the partnership's second taxable year has economic effect under the alternate economic effect test contained in paragraph (b)(2)(ii)(d) of this section. At the end of such year, A makes an additional $5,000 contribution to the partnership (thereby eliminating the $5,000 deficit balance in his capital account). Under paragraph (b)(2)(ii)(f) of this section, A's obligation to restore up to $5,000 of the deficit balance in his capital account may be eliminated after he contributes the additional $5,000 without affecting the validity of prior allocations.

(ix) Assume the same facts as in (iv) except that upon formation of the partnership A also contributes to the partnership his negotiable promissory note with a $5,000 principal balance. The note unconditionally obligates A to pay an additional $5,000 to the partnership at the earlier of (a) the beginning of the partnership's fourth taxable year, or (b) the end of the partnership taxable year in which A's interest is liquidated. Under paragraph (b)(2)(ii)(c) of this section, A is considered obligated to restore up to $5,000 of the deficit balance in his capital account to the partnership. Accordingly, under the alternate economic effect test contained in partnership (b)(2)(ii)(d) of this section, the allocation of the $25,000 cost recovery deduction to A in the partnership's second taxable year has economic effect. The results in this example would be the same if (1) the note A contributed to the partnership were payable only at the end of the partnership's fourth taxable year (so that A would not be required to satisfy the note upon liquidation of his interest in the partnership), and (2) the partnership agreement provided that upon liquidation of A's interest, the partnership would retain A's note, and A would contribute to the partnership the excess of the outstanding principal balance of the note over its then fair market value.

(x) Assume the same facts as in (ix) except that A's obligation to contribute an additional $5,000 to the partnership is not evidenced by a promissory note. Instead, the partnership agreement imposes upon A the obligation to make an additional $5,000 contribution to the partnership at the earlier of (a) the beginning of the partnership's fourth taxable year, or (b) the end of the partnership taxable year in which A's interest is liquidated. Under paragraph (b)(2)(ii)(c) of this section, as a result of A's deferred contribution requirement, A is considered obligated to restore up to $5,000 of the deficit balance in his capital account to the partnership. Accordingly, under the alternate economic effect test contained in paragraph (b)(2)(ii)(d) of this section, the allocation of the $25,000 cost recovery deduction to A in the partnership's second taxable year has economic effect.

(xi) Assume the same facts as in (vii) except that the partnership agreement also provides that any gain (whether ordinary income or capital gain) upon the sale of the property will be allocated to A to the extent of the prior allocations to A of cost recovery deductions from such property, and additional gain will be allocated equally between A and B. At the time the allocations of cost recovery deductions were made to A, the partners believed there would be gain on the sale of the property in an amount sufficient to offset the allocations of cost recovery deductions to A. Nevertheless, the existence of the gain chargeback provision will not cause the economic effect of the allocations to be insubstantial under paragraph (b)(2)(iii)(c) of this section, since in testing whether the economic effect of such allocations is substantial, the recovery property is presumed to decrease in value by the amount of such deductions.

Example (2). C and D form a general partnership solely to acquire and lease machinery that is 5-year recovery property under section 168. Each contributes $100,000, and the partnership obtains an $800,000 recourse loan to purchase the machinery. The partnership elects under section 48(q)(4) to reduce the amount of investment tax credit in lieu of adjusting the tax basis of such machinery. The partnership, C, and D have calendar taxable years. The partnership agreement provides that the partners' capital accounts will be determined and maintained in accordance with paragraph (b)(2)(iv) of this section, distributions in liquidation of the partnership (or any partner's interest) will be made in accordance with the partners' positive capital account balances, and any partner with a deficit balance in his capital account following the liquidation of his interest must restore that deficit to the partnership (as set forth in paragraphs (b)(2)(ii)(b)(2) and (3) of this section). The partnership agreement further provides that (a) partnership net taxable loss will be allocated 90 percent to C and 10 percent to D until such time as there is partnership net taxable income, and therefore C will be allocated 90 percent of such taxable income until he has been allocated partnership net taxable income equal to the partnership net taxable loss previously allocated to him, (b) all further partnership net taxable income or loss will be allocated equally between C and D, and (c) distributions of operating cash flow will be made equally between C and D. The partnership enters into a 12-year lease with a financially secure corporation under which the partnership expects to have a net taxable loss in each of its first 5 partnership taxable years due to cost recovery deductions with respect to the machinery and net taxable income in each of its following 7 partnership taxable years, in part due to the absence of such cost recovery deductions. There is a strong likelihood that the partnership's net taxable loss in partnership taxable years 1 through 5 will be $100,000, $90,000, $80,000, $70,000, and $60,000, respectively, and the partnership's net taxable income in partnership taxable years 6 through 12 will be $40,000, $50,000, $60,000, $70,000, $80,000, $90,000, and $100,000, respectively. Even though there is a strong likelihood that the allocations of net taxable loss in years 1 through 5 will be largely offset by other allocations in partnership taxable years 6 through 12, and even if it is assumed that the total tax liability of the partners in years 1 through 12 will be less than if the allocations had not been provided in the partnership agreement, the economic effect of the allocations will not be insubstantial under paragraph (b)(2)(iii)(c) of this section. This is because at the time such allocations became part of the partnership agreement, there was a strong likelihood that the allocations of net taxable loss in years 1 through 5 would not be largely offset by allocations of income within 5 years (determined on a first-in, first-out basis). The year 1 allocation will not be offset until years 6, 7, and 8, the year 2 allocation will not be offset until years 8 and 9, the year 3 allocation will not be offset until years 9 and 10, the year 4 allocation will not be offset until years 10 and 11, and the year 5 allocation will not be offset until years 11 and 12.

Example (3). E and F enter into a partnership agreement to develop and market experimental electronic devices. E contributes $2,500 cash and agrees to devote his full-time services to the partnership. F contributes $100,000 cash and agrees to obtain a loan for the partnership for any additional capital needs. The partnership agreement provides that all deductions for research and experimental expenditures and interest on partnership loans are to be allocated to F. In addition, F will be allocated 90 percent, and E 10 percent, of partnership taxable income or loss, computed net of the deductions for such research and experimental expenditures and interest, until F has received allocations of such taxable income equal to the sum of such research and experimental expenditures, such interest expense, and his share of such taxable loss. Thereafter, E and F will share all taxable income and loss equally. Operating cash flow will be distributed equally between E and F. The partnership agreement also provides that E's and F's capital accounts will be determined and maintained in accordance with paragraph (b)(2)(iv) of this section, distributions in liquidation of the partnership (or any partner's interest) will be made in accordance with the partners' positive capital account balances, and any partner with a deficit balance in his capital account following the liquidation of his interest must restore that deficit to the partnership (as set forth in paragraphs (b)(2)(ii)(b)(2) and (3) of this section). These allocations have economic effect. In addition, in view of the nature of the partnership's activities, there is not a strong likelihood at the time the allocations become part of the partnership agreement that the economic effect of the allocations to F of deductions for research and experimental expenditures and interest on partnership loans will be largely offset by allocations to F of partnership net taxable income. The economic effect of the allocations is substantial.

Example (4). (i) G and H contribute $75,000 and $25,000, respectively, in forming a general partnership. The partnership agreement provides that all income, gain, loss, and deduction will be allocated equally between the partners, that the partners' capital accounts will be determined and maintained in accordance with paragraph (b)(2)(iv) of this section, but that all partnership distributions will, regardless of capital account balances, be made 75 percent to G and 25 percent to H. Following the liquidation of the partnership, neither partner is required to restore the deficit balance in his capital account to the partnership for distribution to partners with positive capital account balances. The allocations in the partnership agreement do not have economic effect. Since contributions were made in a 75/25 ratio and the partnership agreement indicates that all economic profits and losses of the partnership are to be shared in a 75/25 ratio, under paragraph (b)(3) of this section, partnership income, gain, loss, and deduction will be reallocated 75 percent to G and 25 percent to H.

(ii) Assume the same facts as in (i) except that the partnership maintains no capital accounts and the partnership agreement provides that all income, gain, loss, deduction, and credit will be allocated 75 percent to G and 25 percent to H. G and H are ultimately liable (under a State law right of contribution) for 75 percent and 25 percent, respectively, of any debts of the partnership. Although the allocations do not satisfy the requirements of paragraph (b)(2)(ii)(b) of this section, the allocations have economic effect under the economic effect equivalence test of paragraph (b)(2)(ii)(i) of this section.

(iii) Assume the same facts as in (i) except that the partnership agreement provides that any partner with a deficit balance in his capital account must restore that deficit to the partnership (as set forth in paragraph (b)(2)(ii)(b)(2) of this section). Although the allocations do not satisfy the requirements of paragraph (b)(2)(ii)(b) of this section, the allocations have economic effect under the economic effect equivalence test of paragraph (b)(2)(ii)(i) of this section.

Example (5). (i) Individuals I and J are the only partners of an investment partnership. The partnership owns corporate stocks, corporate debt instruments, and tax-exempt debt instruments. Over the next several years, I expects to be in the 50 percent marginal tax bracket, and and J expects to be in the 15 percent marginal tax bracket. There is a strong likelihood that in each of the next several years the partnership will realize between $450 and $550 of tax-exempt interest and between $450 and $550 of a combination of taxable interest and dividends from its investments. I and J made equal capital contributions to the partnership, and they have agreed to share equally in gains and losses from the sale of the partnership's investment securities. I and J agree, however, that rather than share interest and dividends of the partnership equally, they will allocate the partnership's tax-exempt interest 80 percent to I and 20 percent to J and will distribute cash derived from interest received on the tax-exempt bonds in the same percentages. In addition, they agree to allocate 100 percent of the partnership's taxable interest and dividends to J and to distribute cash derived from interest and dividends received on the corporate stocks and debt instruments 100 percent to J. The partnership agreement further provides that the partners' capital accounts will be determined and maintained in accordance with paragraph (b)(2)(iv) of this section, distributions in liquidation of the partnership (or any partner's interest) will be made in accordance with the partner's positive capital account balances, and any partner with a deficit balance in his capital account following the liquidation of his interest must restore that deficit to the partnership (as set forth in paragraphs (b)(2)(ii)(b)(2) and (3) of this section). The allocation of taxable interest and dividends and tax-exempt interest has economic effect, but that economic effect is not substantial under the general rules set forth in paragraph (b)(2)(iii) of this section. Without the allocation I would be allocated between $225 and $275 of tax-exempt interest and between $225 and $275 of a combination of taxable interest and dividends, which (net of Federal income taxes he would owe on such income) would give I between $337.50 and $412.50 after tax. With the allocation, however, I will be allocated between $360 and $440 of tax-exempt interest and no taxable interest and dividends, which (net of Federal income taxes) will give I between $360 and $440 after tax. Thus, at the time the allocations became part of the partnership agreement, I is expected to enhance his after-tax economic consequences as a result of the allocations. On the other hand, there is a strong likelihood that neither I nor J will substantially diminish his after-tax economic consequences as a result of the allocations. Under the combination of likely investment outcomes least favorable for J, the partnership would realize $550 of tax-exempt interest and $450 of taxable interest and dividends, giving J $492.50 after tax (which is more than the $466.25 after tax J would have received if each of such amounts had been allocated equally between the partners). Under the combination of likely investment outcomes least favorable for I, the partnership would realize $450 of tax-exempt interest and $550 of taxable interest and dividends, giving I $360 after tax (which is not substantially less than the $362.50 he would have received if each of such amounts had been allocated equally between the partners). Accordingly, the allocations in the partnership agreement must be reallocated in accordance with the partners' interests in the partnership under paragraph (b)(3) of this section.

(ii) Assume the same facts as in (i). In addition, assume that in the first partnership taxable year in which the allocation arrangement described in (i) applies, the partnership realizes $450 of tax-exempt interest and $550 of taxable interest and dividends, so that, pursuant to the partnership agreement, I's capital account is credited with $360 (80 percent of the tax-exempt interest), and J's capital account is credited with $640 (20 percent of the tax-exempt interest and 100 percent of the taxable interest and dividends). The allocations of tax-exempt interest and taxable interest and dividends (which do not have substantial economic effect for the reasons stated in (i) will be disregarded and will be reallocated. Since under the partnership agreement I will receive 36 percent (360/1,000) and J will receive 64 percent (640/1,000) of the partnership's total investment income in such year, under paragraph (b)(3) of this section the partnership's tax-exempt interest and taxable interest and dividends each will be reallocated 36 percent to I and 64 percent to J.

Example (6). K and L are equal partners in a general partnership formed to acquire and operate property described in section 1231(b). The partnership, K, and L have calendar taxable years. The partnership agreement provides that the partners' capital accounts will be determined and maintained in accordance with paragraph (b)(2)(iv) of this section, that distributions in liquidation of the partnership (or any partner's interest) will be made in accordance with the partners' positive capital account balances, and that any partner with a deficit balance in his capital account following the liquidation of his interest must restore that deficit to the partnership (as set forth in paragraphs (b)(2)(ii)(b)(2) and (3) of this section). For a taxable year in which the partnership expects to incur a loss on the sale of a portion of such property, the partnership agreement is amended (at the beginning of the taxable year) to allocate such loss to K, who expects to have no gains from the sale of depreciable property described in section 1231(b) in that taxable year, and to allocate an equivalent amount of partnership loss and deduction for that year of a different character to L, who expects to have such gains. Any partnership loss and deduction in excess of these allocations will be allocated equally between K and L. The amendment is effective only for that taxable year. At the time the partnership agreement is amended, there is a strong likelihood that the partnership will incur deduction or loss in the taxable year other than loss from the sale of property described in section 1231(b) in an amount that will substantially equal or exceed the expected amount of the section 1231(b) loss. The allocations in such taxable year have economic effect. However, the economic effect of the allocations is insubstantial under the test described in paragraph (b)(2)(iii)(b) of this section because there is a strong likelihood, at the time the allocations become part of the partnership agreement, that the net increases and decreases to K's and L's capital accounts will be the same at the end of the taxable year to which they apply with such allocations in effect as they would have been in the absence of such allocations, and that the total taxes of K and L for such year will be reduced as a result of such allocations. If in fact the partnership incurs deduction or loss, other than loss from the sale of property described in section 1231(b), in an amount at least equal to the section 1231(b) loss, the loss and deduction in such taxable year will be reallocated equally between K and L under paragraph (b)(3) of this section. If not, the loss from the sale of property described in section 1231(b) and the items of deduction and other loss realized in such year will be reallocated between K and L in proportion to the net decreases in their capital accounts due to the allocation of such items under the partnership agreement.

Example (7). (i) M and N are partners in the MN general partnership, which is engaged in an active business. Income, gain, loss, and deduction from MN's business is allocated equally between M and N. The partnership, M, and N have calendar taxable years. Under the partnership agreement the partners' capital accounts will be determined and maintained in accordance with paragraph (b)(2)(iv) of this section, distributions in liquidation of the partnership (or any partner's interest) will be made in accordance with the partner's positive capital account balances, and any partner with a deficit balance in his capital account following the liquidation of his interest must restore that deficit to the partnership (as set forth in paragraphs (b)(2)(ii)(b)(2) and (3) of this section). In order to enhance the credit standing of the partnership, the partners contribute surplus funds to the partnership, which the partners agree to invest in equal dollar amounts of tax-exempt bonds and corporate stock for the partnership's first 3 taxable years. M is expected to be in a higher marginal tax bracket than N during those 3 years. At the time the decision to make these investments is made, it is agreed that, during the 3-year period of the investment, M will be allocated 90 percent and N 10 percent of the interest income from the tax-exempt bonds as well as any gain or loss from the sale thereof, and that M will be allocated 10 percent and N 90 percent of the dividend income from the corporate stock as well as any gain or loss from the sale thereof. At the time the allocations concerning the investments become part of the partnership agreement, there is not a strong likelihood that the gain or loss from the sale of the stock will be substantially equal to the gain or loss from the sale of the tax-exempt bonds, but there is a strong likelihood that the tax-exempt interest and the taxable dividends realized from these investments during the 3-year period will not differ substantially. These allocations have economic effect, and the economic effect of the allocations of the gain or loss on the sale of the tax-exempt bonds and corporate stock is substantial. The economic effect of the allocations of the tax-exempt interest and the taxable dividends, however, is not substantial under the test described in paragraph (b)(2)(iii)(c) of this section because there is a strong likelihood, at the time the allocations become part of the partnership agreement, that at the end of the 3-year period to which such allocations relate, the net increases and decreases to M's and N's capital accounts will be the same with such allocations as they would have been in the absence of such allocations, and that the total taxes of M and N for the taxable years to which such allocations relate will be reduced as a result of such allocations. If in fact the amounts of the tax-exempt interest and taxable dividends earned by the partnership during the 3-year period are equal, the tax-exempt interest and taxable dividends will be reallocated to the partners in equal shares under paragraph (b)(3) of this section. If not, the tax-exempt interest and taxable dividends will be reallocated between M and N in proportion to the net increases in their capital accounts during such 3-year period due to the allocation of such items under the partnership agreement.

(ii) Assume the same facts as in (i) except that gain or loss from the sale of the tax-exempt bonds and corporate stock will be allocated equally between M and N and the partnership agreement provides that the 90/10 allocation arrangement with respect to the investment income applies only to the first $10,000 of interest income from the tax-exempt bonds and the first $10,000 of dividend income from the corporate stock, and only to the first taxable year of the partnership. There is a strong likelihood at the time the 90/10 allocation of the investment income became part of the partnership agreement that in the first taxable year of the partnership, the partnership will earn more than $10,000 of tax-exempt interest and more than $10,000 of taxable dividends. The allocations of tax-exempt interest and taxable dividends provided in the partnership agreement have economic effect, but under the test contained in paragraph (b)(2)(iii)(b) of this section, such economic effect is not substantial for the same reasons stated in (i) (but applied to the 1 taxable year, rather than to a 3-year period). If in fact the partnership realizes at least $10,000 of tax-exempt interest and at least $10,000 of taxable dividends in such year, the allocations of such interest income and dividend income will be reallocated equally between M and N under paragraph (b)(3) of this section. If not, the tax-exempt interest and taxable dividends will be reallocated between M and N in proportion to the net increases in their capital accounts due to the allocations of such items under the partnership agreement.

(iii) Assume the same facts as in (ii) except that at the time the 90/10 allocation of investment income becomes part of the partnership agreement, there is not a strong likelihood that (1) the partnership will earn $10,000 or more of tax-exempt interest and $10,000 or more of taxable dividends in the partnership's first taxable year, and (2) the amount of tax-exempt interest and taxable dividends earned during such year will be substantially the same. Under these facts the economic effect of the allocations generally will be substantial. (Additional facts may exist in certain cases, however, so that the allocation is insubstantial under the second sentence of paragraph (b)(2)(iii). See example (5) above.)

Example (8). (i) O and P are equal partners in the OP general partnership. The partnership, O, and P have calendar taxable years. Partner O has a net operating loss carryover from another venture that is due to expire at the end of the partnership's second taxable year. Otherwise, both partners expect to be in the 50 percent marginal tax bracket in the next several taxable years. The partnership agreement provides that the partners' capital accounts will be determined and maintained in accordance with paragraph (b)(2)(iv) of this section, distributions in liquidation of the partnership (or any partner's interest) will be made in accordance with the partners' positive capital account balances, and any partner with a deficit balance in his capital account following the liquidation of his interest must restore that deficit to the partnership (as set forth in paragraphs (b)(2)(ii)(b)(2) and (3) of this section). The partnership agreement is amended (at the beginning of the partnership's second taxable year) to allocate all the partnership net taxable income for that year to O. Future partnership net taxable loss is to be allocated to O, and future partnership net taxable income to P, until the allocation of income to O in the partnership's second taxable year is offset. It is further agreed orally that in the event the partnership is liquidated prior to completion of such offset, O's capital account will be adjusted downward to the extent of one-half of the allocations of income to O in the partnership's second taxable year that have not been offset by other allocations, P's capital account will be adjusted upward by a like amount, and liquidation proceeds will be distributed in accordance with the partners' adjusted capital account balances. As a result of this oral amendment, all allocations of partnership net taxable income and net taxable loss made pursuant to the amendment executed at the beginning of the partnership's second taxable year lack economic effect and will be disregarded. Under the partnership agreement other allocations are made equally to O and P, and O and P will share equally in liquidation proceeds, indicating that the partners' interests in the partnership are equal. Thus, the disregarded allocations will be reallocated equally between the partners under paragraph (b)(3) of this section.

(ii) Assume the same facts as in (i) except that there is no agreement that O's and P's capital accounts will be adjusted downward and upward, respectively, to the extent of one-half of the partnership net taxable income allocated to O in the partnership's second taxable year that is not offset subsequently by other allocations. The income of the partnership is generated primarily by fixed interest payments received with respect to highly rated corporate bonds, which are expected to produce sufficient net taxable income prior to the end of the partnership's seventh taxable year to offset in large part the net taxable income to be allocated to O in the partnership's second taxable year. Thus, at the time the allocations are made part of the partnership agreement, there is a strong likelihood that the allocation of net taxable income to be made to O in the second taxable year will be offset in large part within 5 taxable years thereafter. These allocations have economic effect. However, the economic effect of the allocation of partnership net taxable income to O in the partnership's second taxable year, as well as the offsetting allocations to P, is not substantial under the test contained in paragraph (b)(2)(iii)(c) of this section because there is a strong likelihood that the net increases or decreases in O's and P's capital accounts will be the same at the end of the partnership's seventh taxable year with such allocations as they would have been in the absence of such allocations, and the total taxes of O and P for the taxable years to which such allocations relate will be reduced as a result of such allocations. If in fact the partnership, in its taxable years 3 through 7, realizes sufficient net taxable income to offset the amount allocated to O in the second taxable year, the allocations provided in the partnership agreement will be reallocated equally between the partners under paragraph (b)(3) of this section.

Example (9). Q and R form a limited partnership with contributions of $20,000 and $180,000, respectively. Q, the limited partner, is a corporation that has $2,000,000 of net operating loss carryforwards that will not expire for 8 years. Q does not expect to have sufficient income (apart from the income of the partnership) to absorb any of such net operating loss carryforwards. R, the general partner, is a corporation that expects to be in the 46 percent marginal tax bracket for several years. The partnership agreement provides that the partners' capital accounts will be determined and maintained in accordance with paragraph (b)(2)(iv) of this section, distributions in liquidation of the partnership (or any partner's interest) will be made in accordance with the partners' positive capital account balances, and any partner with a deficit balance in his capital account following the liquidation of his interest must restore that deficit to the partnership (as set forth in paragraphs (b)(2)(ii)(b)(2) and (3) of this section). The partnership's cash, together with the proceeds of an $800,000 loan, are invested in assets that are expected to produce taxable income and cash flow (before debt service) of approximately $150,000 a year for the first 8 years of the partnership's operations. In addition, it is expected that the partnership's total taxable income in its first 8 taxable years will not exceed $2,000,000. The partnership's $150,000 of cash flow in each of its first 8 years will be used to retire the $800,000 loan. The partnership agreement provides that partnership net taxable income will be allocated 90 percent to Q and 10 percent to R in the first through eighth partnership taxable years, and 90 percent to R and 10 percent to Q in all subsequent partnership taxable years. Net taxable loss will be allocated 90 percent to R and 10 percent to Q in all partnership taxable years. All distributions of cash from the partnership to partners (other than the priority distributions to Q described below) will be made 90 percent to R and 10 percent to Q. At the end of the partnership's eighth taxable year, the amount of Q's capital account in excess of one-ninth of R's capital account on such date will be designated as Q's "excess capital account." Beginning in the ninth taxable year of the partnership, the undistributed portion of Q's excess capital account will begin to bear interest (which will be paid and deducted under section 707(c) at a rate of interest below the rate that the partnership can borrow from commercial lenders, and over the next several years (following the eighth year) the partnership will make priority cash distributions to Q in prearranged percentages of Q's excess capital account designed to amortize Q's excess capital account and the interest thereon over a prearranged period. In addition, the partnership's agreement prevents Q from causing his interest in the partnership from being liquidated (and thereby receiving the balance in his capital account) without R's consent until Q's excess capital account has been eliminated. The below market rate of interest and the period over which the amortization will take place are prescribed such that, as of the end of the partnership's eighth taxable year, the present value of Q's right to receive such priority distributions is approximately 46 percent of the amount of Q's excess capital account as of such date. However, because the partnership's income for its first 8 taxable years will be realized approximately ratably over that period, the present value of Q's right to receive the priority distributions with respect to its excess capital account is, as of the date the partnership agreement is entered into, less than the present value of the additional Federal income taxes for which R would be liable if, during the partnership's first 8 taxable years, all partnership income were to be allocated 90 percent to R and 10 to Q. The allocations of partnership taxable income to Q and R in the first through eighth partnership taxable years have economic effect. However, such economic effect is not substantial under the general rules set forth in paragraph (b)(2)(iii) of this section. This is true because R may enhance his after-tax economic consequences, on a present value basis, as a result of the allocations to Q of 90 percent of partnership's income during taxable years 1 through

8, and there is a strong likelihood that neither R nor Q will substantially diminish its after-tax economic consequences, on a present value basis, as a result of such allocation. Accordingly, partnership taxable income for partnership taxable years 1 through 8 will be reallocated in accordance with the partners' interests in the partnership under paragraph (b)(3) of this section.

Example (10). (i) S and T form a general partnership to operate a travel agency. The partnership agreement provides that the partners' capital accounts will be determined and maintained in accordance with paragraph (b)(2)(iv) of this section, distributions in liquidation of the partnership (or any partner's interest) will be made in accordance with the partners' positive capital account balances, and any partner with a deficit balance in his capital account following the liquidation of his interest must restore that deficit to the partnership (as set forth in paragraphs (b)(2)(ii)(b)(2) and (3) of this section). The partnership agreement provides that T, a resident of a foreign country, will be allocated 90 percent, and S 10 percent, of the income, gain, loss, and deduction derived from operations conducted by T within his country, and all remaining income, gain, loss, and deduction will be allocated equally. The amount of such income, gain, loss, or deduction cannot be predicted with any reasonable certainty. The allocations provided by the partnership agreement have substantial economic effect.

(ii) Assume the same facts as in (i) except that the partnership agreement provides that all income, gain, loss, and deduction of the partnership will be shared equally, but that T will be allocated all income, gain, loss, and deduction derived from operations conducted by him within his country as a part of his equal share of partnership income, gain, loss, and deduction, upon to the amount of such share. Assume the total tax liability of S and T for each year to which these allocations relate will be reduced as a result of such allocation. These allocations have economic effect. However, such economic effect is not substantial under the test stated in paragraph (b)(2)(iii)(b) of this section because, at the time the allocations became part of the partnership agreement, there is a strong likelihood that the net increases and decreases to S's and T's capital accounts will be the same at the end of each partnership taxable year with such allocations as they would have been in the absence of such allocations, and that the total tax liability of S and T for each year to which such allocations relate will be reduced as a result of such allocations. Thus, all items of partnership income, gain, loss, and income, gain, loss, and deduction will be reallocated equally between S and T under paragraph (b)(3) of this section.

Example (11). (i) U and V share equally all income, gain, loss, and deduction of the UV general partnership, as well as all non-liquidating distributions made by the partnership. The partnership agreement provides that the partners' capital accounts will be determined and maintained in accordance with paragraph (b)(2)(iv) of this section, distributions in liquidation of the partnership (or any partner's interest) will be made in accordance with the partners' positive capital account balances, and any partner with a deficit balance in his capital account following the liquidation of his interest must restore such deficit to the partnership (as set forth in paragraphs (b)(2)(ii)(b)(2) and (3) of this section). The agreement further provides that the partners will be allocated equal shares of any section 705(a)(2)(B) expenditures of the partnership. In the partnership's first taxable year, it pays qualified first-year wages of $6,000 and is entitled to a $3,000 targeted jobs tax credit under sections 44B and 51 of the Code. Under section 280C the partnership must reduce its deduction for wages paid by the $3,000 credit claimed (which amount constitutes a section 705(a)(2)(B) expenditure). The partnership agreement allocates the credit to U. Although the allocations of wage deductions and section 705(a)(2)(B) expenditures have substantial economic effect, the allocation of tax credit cannot have economic effect since it cannot properly be reflected in the partners' capital accounts. Furthermore, the allocation is not in accordance with the special partners' interests in the partnership rule contained in paragraph (b)(4)(ii) of this section. Under that rule, since the expenses that gave rise to the credit are shared equally by the partners, the credit will be shared equally between U and V.

(ii) Assume the same facts as in (i) and that at the beginning of the partnership's second taxable year, the partnership agreement is amended to allocate to U all wage expenses incurred in that year (including wage expenses that constitute section 705(a)(2)(B) expenditures) whether or not such wages qualify for the credit. The partnership agreement contains no offsetting allocations. That taxable year the partnership pays $8,000 in total wages to its employees. Assume that the partnership has operating income equal to its operating expenses (exclusive of expenses for wages). Assume further that $6,000 of the $8,000 wage expense constitutes qualified first-year wages. U is allocated the $3,000 deduction and the $3,000 section 705(a)(2)(B) expenditure attributable to the $6,000 of qualified first-year wages, as well as the deduction for the other $2,000 in wage expenses. The allocations of wage deductions and section 705(a)(2)(B) expenditures have substantial economic effect. Furthermore, since the wage credit is allocated in the same proportion as the expenses that gave rise to the credit, and the allocation of those expenses has substantial economic effect, the allocation of such credit to U is in accordance with the special partners' interests in the partnership rule contained in paragraph (b)(4)(ii) of this section and is recognized thereunder.

Example (12). (i) W and X form a general partnership for the purpose of mining iron ore. W makes an initial contribution of $75,000, and X makes an initial contribution of $25,000. The partnership agreement provides that non-liquidating distributions will be made 75 percent to W and 25 percent to X, and that all items of income, gain, loss, and deduction will be allocated 75 percent to W and 25 percent to X, except that all percentage depletion deductions will be allocated to W. The agreement further provides that the partners' capital accounts will be determined and maintained in accordance with paragraphs (b)(2)(iv) of this section, distributions in liquidation of the partnership (or any partner's interest) will be made in accordance with the partners' positive capital account balances, and any partner with a deficit balance in his capital account following the liquidation of his interest must restore such deficit to the partnership (as set forth in paragraphs (b)(2)(ii)(b)(2) and (3) of this section). Assume that the adjusted tax basis of the partnership's only depletable iron ore property is $1,000 and that the percentage depletion deduction for the taxable year with respect to such property is $1,500. The allocation of partnership income, gain, loss, and deduction (excluding the percentage depletion deduction) as well as the allocation of $1,000 of the percentage depletion deduction have substantial economic effect. The allocation to W of the remaining $500 of the percentage depletion deduction, representing the excess of percentage depletion over adjusted tax basis of the iron ore property, cannot have economic effect since such amount cannot properly be reflected in the partners' capital accounts. Furthermore, the allocation to W of that $500 excess percentage depletion deduction is not in accordance with the special partners interests in the partnership rule contained in paragraph (b)(4)(iii) of this section, under which such $500 excess depletion deduction (and all further percentage depletion deductions from the mine) will be reallocated 75 percent to W and 25 percent to X.

(ii) Assume the same facts as in (i) except that the partnership agreement provides that all percentage depletion deductions of the partnership will be allocated 75 percent to W and 25 percent to X. Once again, the allocation of partnership income, gain, loss, and deduction (excluding the percentage depletion deduction) as well as the allocation of $1,000 of the percentage depletion deduction have substantial economic effect. Furthermore, since the $500 portion of the percentage depletion deduction that exceeds the adjusted basis of such iron ore property is allocated in the same manner as valid allocations of the gross income from such property during the taxable year (i.e., 75 percent to W and 25 percent to X), the allocation of the $500 excess percentage depletion contained in the partnership agreement is in accordance with the special partners' interests in the partnership rule contained in paragraph (b)(4)(iii) of this section.

Example (13). (i) Y and Z form a brokerage general partnership for the purpose of investing and trading in marketable securities. Y contributes cash of $10,000, and Z contributes securities of P corporation, which have an adjusted basis of $3,000 and a fair market value of $10,000. The partnership would not be an investment company under section 351(e) if it were incorporated. The partnership agreement provides that the partners' capital accounts will be determined and maintained in accordance with paragraph (b)(2)(iv) of this section, distributions in liquidation of the partnership (or any partner's interest) will be made in accordance with the partners' positive capital account balances, and any partner with a deficit balance in his capital account following the liquidation of his interest must restore that deficit to the partnership (as set forth in paragraphs (b)(2)(ii)(b)(2) and (3) of this section). The partnership uses the interim closing of the books method for purposes of section 706. The initial capital accounts of Y and Z are fixed at $10,000 each. The agreement further provides that all partnership distributions, income, gain, loss, deduction, and credit will be shared equally between Y and Z, except that the taxable gain attributable to the precontribution appreciation in the value of the securities of P corporation will be allocated to Z in accordance with section 704(c). During the partnership's first taxable year, it sells the securities of P corporation for $12,000, resulting in a $2,000 book gain ($12,000 less $10,000 book value) and a $9,000 taxable gain ($12,000 less $3,000 adjusted tax basis). The partnership has no other income, gain, loss, or deductions for the taxable year. The gain from the sale of the securities is allocated as follows:

	Y		Z	
	Tax	Book	Tax	Book
Capital account upon formation	$10,000	$10,000	$ 3,000	$10,000
Plus: gain	1,000	1,000	8,000	1,000
Capital account at end of year 1	$11,000	$11,000	$11,000	$11,000

The allocation of the $2,000 book gain, $1,000 each to Y and Z, has substantial economic effect. Furthermore, under section 704(c) the partners' distributive shares of the $9,000 taxable gain are $1,000 to Y and $8,000 to Z.

(ii) Assume the same facts as in (i) and that at the beginning of the partnership's second taxable year, it invests its $22,000 of cash in securities of G Corp. The G Corp. securities increase in value to $40,000, at which time Y sells 50 percent of his partnership interest (i.e., a 25 percent interest in the partnership) to LK for $10,000. The partnership does not have a section 754 election in effect for the partnership taxable year during which such sale occurs. In accordance with paragraph (b)(2)(iv)(l) of this section, the partnership agreement provides that LK inherits 50 percent of Y's $11,000 capital account balance. Thus, following the sale, LK and Y each have a capital account of $5,500, and Z's capital account remains at $11,000. Prior to the end of the partnership's second taxable year, the securities are sold for their $40,000 fair market value, resulting in an $18,000 taxable gain ($40,000 less $22,000 adjusted tax basis). The partnership has no other income, gain, loss, or deduction in such taxable year. Under the partnership agreement the $18,000 taxable gain is allocated as follows:

	Y	Z	LK
Capital account before sale of securities	$ 5,500	$11,000	$ 5,500
Plus gain	4,500	9,000	4,500
Capital account at end of year 2	$10,000	$20,000	$10,000

The allocation of the $18,000 taxable gain has substantial economic effect.

(iii) Assume the same facts as in (ii) except that the partnership has a section 754 election in effect for the partnership taxable year during which Y sells 50 percent of his interest to LK. Accordingly, under § 1.743-1 there is a $4,500 basis increase to the G Corp. securities with respect to LK. Notwithstanding this basis adjustment, as a result of the sale of the G Corp. securities, LK's capital account is, as in (ii), increased by $4,500. The fact that LK recognizes no taxable gain from such sale (due to his $4,500 section 743 basis adjustment) is irrelevant for capital accounting purposes since, in accordance with paragraph (b)(2)(iv)(m)(2) of this section, that basis adjustment is disregarded in the maintenance and computation of the partners' capital accounts.

(iv) Assume the same facts as in (iii) except that immediately following Y's sale of 50 percent of this interest to LK, the G Corp. securities decrease in value to $32,000 and are sold. The $10,000 taxable gain ($32,000 less $22,000 adjusted tax basis) is allocated as follows:

	Y	Z	LK
Capital account before sale of securities	$ 5,500	$11,000	$ 5,500
Plus: gain	2,500	5,000	2,500
Capital account at end of the year 2	$ 8,000	$16,000	$ 8,000

The fact that LK recognizes a $2,000 taxable loss from the sale of the G Corp. securities (due to his $4,500 section 743 basis adjustment) is irrelevant for capital accounting purposes since, in accordance with paragraph (b)(2)(iv)(m)(2) of this section, that basis adjustment is disregarded in the maintenance and computation of the partners' capital accounts.

(v) Assume the same facts as in (ii) except that Y sells 100 percent of his partnership interest (i.e., a 50 percent interest in the partnership) to LK for $20,000. Under section 708(b)(1)(B) the partnership terminates. Under paragraph (b)(1)(iv) of § 1.708-1, there is a constructive liquidation of the partnership. Immediately preceding the constructive liquidation, the capital accounts of Z and LK equal $11,000 each (LK having inherited Y's $11,000 capital account) and the book value of G Corp. securities is $22,000 (original purchase price of securities). Under paragraph (b)(2)(iv)(l) of this section, the deemed contribution of assets and liabilities by the terminated partnership to the new partnership and the deemed liquidation of the terminated partnership that occur under § 1.708-1(b)(1)(iv) in connection with the constructive liquidation of the terminated partnership are disregarded in the maintenance and computation of the partners' capital accounts. As a result, the capital accounts of Z and LK in the new partnership equal $11,000 each (their capital accounts in the terminated partnership immediately prior to the termination), and the book value of the G Corp. securities remains $22,000 (its book value immediately prior to the termination). This Example 13(v) may be applied to terminations occurring on or after May 9, 1996, provided that the partnership and its partners apply this Example 13(v) to the termination in a consistent manner.

Example (14). (i) MC and RW form a general partnership to which each contributes $10,000. The $20,000 is invested in securities of Ventureco (which are not readily tradable on an established securities market). In each of the partnership's taxable years, it recognizes operating income equal to its operating deductions (excluding gain or loss from the sale of securities). The partnership agreement provides that the partners' capital accounts will be determined and maintained in accordance with paragraph (b)(2)(iv) of this section, distributions in liquidation of the partnership (or any partner's interest) will be made in accordance with the partners' positive capital account balances, and any partner with a deficit balance in his capital account following the liquidation of his interest must restore that deficit to the partnership (as set forth in paragraphs (b)(2)(ii)(b)(2) and (3) of this section). The partnership uses the interim closing of the books method for purposes of section 706. Assume that the Ventureco securities subsequently appreciate in value to $50,000. At that time SK makes a $25,000 cash contribution to the partnership (thereby acquiring a one-third interest in the partnership), and the $25,000 is placed in a bank account. Upon SK's admission to the partnership, the capital accounts of MC and RW (which were $10,000 each prior to SK's admission) are, in accordance with paragraph (b)(2)(iv)(f) of this section, adjusted upward (to $25,000 each) to reflect their shares of the unrealized appreciation in the Ventureco securities that occurred before SK was admitted to the partnership. Immediately after SK's admission to the partnership, the securities are sold for their $50,000 fair market value, resulting in taxable gain of $30,000 ($50,000 less $20,000 adjusted tax basis) and no book gain or loss. An allocation of the $30,000 taxable gain cannot have economic effect since it cannot properly be reflected in the partners' book capital accounts. Under paragraph (b)(2)(iv)(f) of this section and the special partners' interests in the partnership rule contained in paragraph (b)(4)(i) of this section, unless the partnership agreement provides that the $30,000 taxable gain will, in accordance with section 704(c) principles, be shared $15,000 to MC and $15,000 to RW, the partners' capital accounts will not be considered maintained in accordance with paragraph (b)(2)(iv) of this section.

	MC		RW		SK	
	Tax	Book	Tax	Book	Tax	Book
Capital account following SK's admission	$10,000	$25,000	$10,000	$25,000	$25,000	$25,000
Plus: gain	15,000	0	15,000	0	0	0
Capital account following sale	$25,000	$25,000	$25,000	$25,000	$25,000	$25,000

(ii) Assume the same facts as (i), except that after SK's admission to the partnership, the Ventureco securities appreciate in value to $74,000 and are sold, resulting in taxable gain of $54,000 ($74,000 less $20,000 adjusted tax basis) and book gain of $24,000 ($74,000 less $50,000 book value). Under the partnership agreement the $24,000 book gain (the appreciation in value occurring after SK became a partner) is allocated equally among MC, RW, and SK, and such allocations have substantial economic effect. An allocation of the $54,000 taxable gain cannot have economic effect since it cannot properly be reflected in the partners' book capital accounts. Under paragraph (b)(2)(iv)(f) of this section and the special partners' interests in the partnership rule contained in paragraph (b)(4)(i) of this section, unless the partnership agreement provides that the taxable gain will, in accordance with section 704(c) principles, be shared $23,000 to MC $23,000 to RW, and $8,000 to SK, the partners' capital accounts will not be considered maintained in accordance with paragraph (b)(2)(iv) of this section.

	MC		RW		SK	
	Tax	Book	Tax	Book	Tax	Book
Capital account following SK's admission	$10,000	$25,000	$10,000	$25,000	$25,000	$25,000
Plus gain	23,000	8,000	23,000	8,000	8,000	8,000
Capital account following sale	$33,000	$33,000	$33,000	$33,000	$33,000	$33,000

(iii) Assume the same facts as (i) except that after SK's admission to the partnership, the Ventureco securities depreciate in value to $44,000 and are sold, resulting in taxable gain of $24,000 ($44,000 less $20,000 adjusted tax basis) and a book loss of $6,000 ($50,000 book value less $44,000). Under the partnership agreement the $6,000 book loss is allocated equally among MC, RW, and SK, and such allocations have substantial economic effect. An allocation of the $24,000 taxable gain cannot have economic effect since it cannot properly be reflected in the partners' book capital accounts. Under paragraph (b)(2)(iv)(f) of this section and the special partners' interests in the partnership rule contained in paragraph (b)(4)(i) of this section, unless the partnership agreement provides that the $24,000 taxable gain will, in accordance with section 704(c) principles, be shared equally between MC and RW, the partners' capital accounts will not be considered maintained in accordance with paragraph (b)(2)(iv) of this section.

	MC		RW		SK	
	Tax	Book	Tax	Book	Tax	Book
Capital account following SK's admission	$10,000	$25,000	$10,000	$25,000	$25,000	$25,000
Plus gain	12,000	0	12,000	0	0	0
Less loss	0	(2,000)	0	(2,000)	0	(2,000)
Capital account following sale	$22,000	$23,000	$22,000	$23,000	$25,000	$25,000

That SK bears an economic loss of $2,000 without a corresponding taxable loss is attributable entirely to the "ceiling rule." See paragraph (c)(2) of § 1.704-1.

(iv) Assume the same facts as in (ii) except that upon the admission of SK the capital accounts of MC and RW are not each adjusted upward from $10,000 to $25,000 to reflect the appreciation in the partnership's securities that occurred before SK was admitted to the partnership. Rather, upon SK's admission to the partnership, the partnership agreement is amended to provide that the first $30,000 of taxable gain upon the sale of such securities will be allocated equally between MC and RW, and that all other income, gain, loss, and deduction will be allocated equally between MC, RW, and SK. When the securities are sold for $74,000, the $54,000 of taxable gain is so allocated. These allocations of taxable gain have substantial economic effect. (If the agreement instead provides for all taxable gain (including the $30,000 taxable gain attributable to the appreciation in the securities prior to SK's admission to the partnership) to be allocated equally between MC, RW, and SK, the partners should consider whether, and to what extent, the provisions of paragraphs (b)(1)(iii) and (iv) of this section are applicable.)

(v) Assume the same facts as in (iv) except that instead of selling the securities, the partnership makes a distribution of the securities (which have a fair market value of $74,000). Assume the distribution does not give rise to a transaction described in section 707(a)(2)(B). In accordance with paragraph (b)(2)(iv)(e) of this section, the partners' capital accounts are adjusted immediately prior to the distribution to reflect how taxable gain ($54,000) would have been allocated had the securities been sold for their $74,000 fair market value, and capital account adjustments in respect of the distribution of the securities are made with reference to the $74,000 "booked-up" fair market value.

	MC	RW	SK
Capital account before adjustment	$10,000	$10,000	$25,000
Deemed sale adjustment	23,000	23,000	8,000
Less distribution	(24,667)	(24,667)	(24,667)
Capital account after distribution	$8,333	$8,333	$8,333

(vi) Assume the same facts as in (i) except that the partnership does not sell the Ventureco securities. During the next 3 years the fair market value of the Ventureco securities remains at $50,000, and the partnership engages in no other investment activities. Thus, at the end of that period the balance sheet of the partnership and the partners' capital accounts are the same as they were at the beginning of such period. At the end of the 3 years, MC's interest in the partnership is liquidated for the $25,000 cash held by the partnership. Assume the distributions does not give rise to a transaction described in section 707(a)(2)(B). Assume further that the partnership has a section 754 election in effect for the taxable year during which such liquidation occurs. Under sections 734(b) and 755 the partnership increases the basis of the Ventureco securities by the $15,000 basis adjustment (the excess of $25,000 over the $10,000 adjusted tax basis of MC's partnership interest).

	MC		RW		SK	
	Tax	Book	Tax	Book	Tax	Book
Capital account before distribution	$10,000	$25,000	$10,000	$25,000	$25,000	$25,000
Plus: basis adjustment	15,000	0	0	0	0	0
Less: distribution	(25,000)	(25,000)	0	0	0	0
Capital account after liquidation	0	0	$10,000	$25,000	$25,000	$25,000

(vii) Assume the same facts as in (vi) except that the partnership has no section 754 election in effect for the taxable year during which such liquidation occurs.

	MC		RW		SK	
	Tax	Book	Tax	Book	Tax	Book
Capital account before distribution	$10,000	$25,000	$10,000	$25,000	$25,000	$25,000
Less distribution	(25,000)	(25,000)	0	0	0	0
Capital account after liquidation	($15,000)	0	$10,000	$25,000	$25,000	$25,000

Following the liquidation of MC's interest in the partnership, the Ventureco securities are sold for their $50,000 fair market value, resulting in no book gain or loss but a $30,000 taxable gain. An allocation of this $30,000 taxable gain cannot have economic effect since it cannot properly be reflected in the partners' book capital accounts. Under paragraph (b)(2)(iv)(f) of this section and the special partners' interests in the partnership rule contained in paragraph (b)(4)(i) of this section, unless the partnership agreement provides that $15,000 of such taxable gain will, in accordance with section 704(c) principles, be included in RW's distributive share, the partners' capital accounts will not be considered maintained in accordance with paragraph (b)(2)(iv) of this section. The remaining $15,000 of such gain will, under paragraph (b)(3) of this section, be shared equally between RW and SK.

Example (15). (i) JB and DK form a limited partnership for the purpose of purchasing residential real estate to lease. JB, the limited partner, contributes $13,500, and DK, the general partner, contributes $1,500. The partnership, which uses the cash receipts and disbursements method of accounting, purchases a building for $100,000 (on leased land), incurring a recourse mortgage of $85,000 that requires the payment of interest only for a period of 3 years. The partnership agreement provides that partnership net taxable income and loss will be allocated 90 percent to JB and 10 percent to DK, the partners' capital accounts will be determined and maintained in accordance with paragraph (b)(2)(iv) of this section, distributions in liquidation of the partnership (or any partner's interest) will be made in accordance with the partners' positive capital account balances (as set forth in paragraph (b)(2)(ii)(b)(2) of this section), and JB is not required to restore any deficit balance in his capital account, but DK is so required. The partnership agreement contains a qualified income offset (as defined in paragraph (b)(2)(ii)(d) of this section). As of the end of each of the partnership's first 3 taxable years, the items described in paragraphs (b)(2)(ii)(d)(4), (5), and (6) of this section are not reasonably expected to cause or increase a deficit balance in JB's capital account: In the partnership's first taxable year, it has rental income of $10,000, operating expenses of $2,000, interest expense of $8,000, and cost recovery deductions of $12,000. Under the partnership agreement JB and DK are allocated $10,800 and $1,200, respectively, of the $12,000 net taxable loss incurred in the partnership's first taxable year.

	JB	DK
Capital account upon formation	$13,500	$1,500
Less year 1 net loss	(10,800)	(1,200)
Capital account at end of year 1	$2,700	$300

The alternate economic effect test contained in paragraph (b)(2)(ii)(d) of this section is satisfied as of the end of the partnership's first taxable year. Thus, the allocation made in the partnership's first taxable year has economic effect.

(ii) Assume the same facts as in (i) and that in the partnership's second taxable year it again has rental income of $10,000, operating expenses of $2,000, interest expense of $8,000, and cost recovery deductions of $12,000. Under the partnership agreement JB and DK are allocated $10,800 and $1,200, respectively, of the $12,000 net taxable loss incurred in the partnership's second taxable year.

	JB	DK
Capital account at beginning of year 1	$2,700	$300
Less: year 2 net loss	(10,800)	(1,200)
Capital account at end of year 2	($8,100)	($900)

Only $2,700 of the $10,800 net taxable loss allocated to JB satisfies the alternate economic effect test contained in paragraph (b)(2)(ii)(d) of this section as of the end of the partnership's second taxable year. The allocation of such $2,700 net taxable loss to JB (consisting of $2,250 of rental income, $450 of operating expenses, $1,800 of interest expense, and $2,700 of cost recovery deductions) has economic effect. The remaining $8,100 of net taxable loss allocated by the partnership agreement to JB must be reallocated in accordance with the partners' interests in the partnership. Under paragraph (b)(3)(iii) of this section, the determination of the partners' interests in the remaining $8,100 net taxable loss is made by comparing how distributions (and contributions) would be made if the partnership sold its property at its adjusted tax basis and liquidated immediately following the end of the partnership's first taxable year with the results of such a sale and liquidation immediately following the end of the partnership's second taxable year. If the partnership's real property were sold for its $88,000 adjusted tax basis and the partnership were liquidated immediately following the end of the partnership's first taxable year, the $88,000 sales proceeds would be used to repay the $85,000 note, and there would be $3,000 remaining in the partnership, which would be used to make liquidating distributions to DK and JB of $300 and $2,700, respectively. If such property were sold for its $76,000 adjusted tax basis and the partnership were liquidated immediately following the end of the partnership's second taxable year, DK would be required to contribute $9,000 to the partnership in order for the partnership to repay the $85,000 note, and there would be no assets remaining in the partnership to distribute. A comparison of these outcomes indicates that JB bore $2,700 and DK $9,300 of the economic burden that corresponds to the $12,000 net taxable loss. Thus, in addition to the $1,200 net taxable loss allocated to DK under the partnership agreement, $8,100 of net taxable loss will be reallocated to DK under paragraph (b)(3)(iii) of this section. Similarly, for subsequent taxable years, absent an increase in JB's capital account, all net taxable loss allocated to JB under the partnership agreement will be reallocated to DK.

(iii) Assume the same facts as in (ii) and that in the partnership's third taxable year there is rental income of $35,000, operating expenses of $2,000, interest expense of $8,000, and cost recovery deductions of $10,000. The capital accounts of the partners maintained on the books of the partnership do not take into account the reallocation to DK of the $8,100 net taxable loss in the partnership's second taxable year. Thus, an allocation of the $15,000 net taxable income $13,500 to JB and $1,500 to DK (as dictated by the partnership agreement and as reflected in the capital accounts of the partners) does not have economic effect. The partners' interests in the partnership with respect to such $15,000 taxable gain again is made in the manner described in paragraph (b)(3)(iii) of this section. If the partnership's real property were sold for its $76,000 adjusted tax basis and the partnership were liquidated immediately following the end of the partnership's second taxable year, DK would be required to contribute $9,000 to the partnership in order for the partnership to repay the $85,000 note, and there would be no assets remaining to distribute. If such property were sold for its $66,000 adjusted tax basis and the partnership were liquidated immediately following the end of the partnership's third taxable year, the $91,000 ($66,000 sales proceeds plus $25,000 cash on hand) would be used to repay the $85,000 note and there would be $6,000 remaining in the partnership, which would be used to make liquidating distributions to DK and JB of $600 and $5,400, respectively. Accordingly, under paragraph (b)(3)(iii) of this section the $15,000 net taxable income in the partnership's third taxable year will be reallocated $9,600 to DK (minus $9,000 at end of the second taxable year to positive $600 at end of the third taxable year) and $5,400 to JB (zero at end of the second taxable year to positive $5,400 at end of the third taxable year).

Example (16). (i) KG and WN form a limited partnership for the purpose of investing in improved real estate. KG, the general partner, contributes $10,000 to the partnership, and WN, the limited partner, contributes $990,000 to the partnership. The $1,000,000 is used to purchase an apartment building on leased land. The partnership agreement provides that (1) the partners' capital accounts will be determined and maintained in accordance with paragraph (b)(2)(iv) of this section; (2) cash will be distributed first to WN until such time as he has received the amount of his original capital contribution ($990,000), next to KG until such time as he has received the amount of his original capital contribution ($10,000), and thereafter equally between WN and KG; (3) partnership net taxable income will be allocated 99 percent to WN 1 percent to KG until the cumulative net taxable income allocated for all taxable years is equal to the cumulative net taxable loss previously allocated to the partners, and thereafter equally between WN and KG; (4) partnership net taxable loss will be allocated 99 percent to WN and 1 percent to KG, unless net taxable income has previously been allocated equally between WN and KG, in which case such net taxable loss first will be allocated equally until the cumulative net taxable loss allocated for all taxable years is equal to the cumulative net taxable income previously allocated to the partners; and (5) upon liquidation, WN is not required to restore any deficit balance in his capital account, but KG is so required. Since distributions in liquidation are not required to be made in accordance with the partners' positive capital account balances, and since WN is not required, upon the liquidation of his interest, to restore the deficit balance in his capital account to the partnership, the allocations provided by the partnership agreement do not have economic effect and will be reallocated in accordance with the partners' interests in the partnership under paragraph (b)(3) of this section.

(ii) Assume the same facts as in (i) except that the partnership agreement further provides that distributions in liquidation of the partnership (or any partner's interest) are to be made in accordance with the partners' positive capital account balances (as set forth in paragraph (b)(2)(ii)(b)(2) of this section).

Assume further that the partnership agreement contains a qualified income offset (as defined in paragraph (b)(2)(ii)(d) of this section) and that, as of the end of each partnership taxable year, the items described in paragraphs (b)(2)(iii)(d)(4), (5), and (6) of this section are not reasonably expected to cause or increase a deficit balance in WN's capital account. The allocations provided by the partnership agreement have economic effect.

Example (17). FG and RP form a partnership with FG contributing cash of $100 and RP contributing property, with 2 years of cost recovery deductions remaining, that has an adjusted tax basis of $80 and a fair market value of $100. The partnership, FG, and RP have calendar taxable years. The partnership agreement provides that the partners' capital accounts will be determined and maintained in accordance with paragraph (b)(2)(iv) of this section, liquidation proceeds will be made in accordance with capital account balances, and each partner is liable to restore the deficit balance in his capital account to the partnership upon liquidation of his interest (as set forth in paragraphs (b)(2)(ii)(b)(2) and (3) of this section). FG expects to be in a substantially higher tax bracket than RP in the partnership's first taxable year. In the partnership's second taxable year, and in subsequent taxable years, it is expected that both will be in approximately equivalent tax brackets. The partnership agreement allocates all items equally except that all $50 of book depreciation is allocated to FG in the partnership's first taxable year and all $50 of book depreciation is allocated to RP in the partnership's second taxable year. If the allocation to FG of all book depreciation in the partnership's first taxable year is respected, FG would be entitled under section 704(c) to the entire cost recovery deduction ($40) for such year. Likewise, if the allocation to RP of all the book depreciation in the partnership's second taxable year is respected, RP would be entitled under section 704(c) to the entire cost recovery deduction ($40) for such year. The allocation of book depreciation to FG and RP in the partnership's first 2 taxable years has economic effect within the meaning of paragraph (b)(2)(ii) of this section. However, the economic effect of these allocations is not substantial under the test described in paragraph (b)(2)(iii)(c) of this section since there is a strong likelihood at the time such allocations became part of the partnership agreement that at the end of the 2-year period to which such allocations relate, the net increases and decreases to FG's and RP's capital accounts will be the same with such allocations as they would have been in the absence of such allocation, and the total tax liability of FG and RP for the taxable years to which the section 704(c) determinations relate would be reduced as a result of the allocations of book depreciation. As a result the allocations of book depreciation in the partnership agreement will be disregarded. FG and RP will be allocated such book depreciation in accordance with the partners' interests in the partnership under paragraph (b)(3) of this section. Under these facts the book depreciation deductions will be reallocated equally between the partners, and section 704(c) will be applied with reference to such reallocation of book depreciation.

Example (18). (i) WM and JL form a general partnership by each contributing $300,000 thereto. The partnership uses the $600,000 to purchase an item of tangible personal property, which it leases out. The partnership elects under section 48(q)(4) to reduce the amount of investment tax credit in lieu of adjusting the tax basis of such property. The partnership agreement provides that (1) the partners' capital account will be determined and maintained in accordance with paragraph (b)(2)(iv) of this section, (2) distributions in liquidation of the partnership (or any partner's interest) will be made in accordance with the partners' positive capital account balances (as set forth in paragraph (b)(2)(ii)(b)(2) of this section), (3) any partner with a deficit balance in his capital account following the liquidation of his interest must restore that deficit to the partnership (as set forth in paragraph (b)(2)(ii)(b)(3) of this section), (4) all income, gain, loss, and deduction of the partnership will be allocated equally between the partners, and (5) all nonliquidating distributions of the partnership will be made equally between the partners. Assume that in each of the partnership's taxable years, it recognizes operating income equal to its operating deductions (excluding cost recovery and depreciation deductions and gain or loss on the sale of its property). During its first 2 taxable years, the partnership has an additional $200,000 cost recovery deduction in each year. Pursuant to the partnership agreement these items are allocated equally between WM and JL.

	WM	JL
Capital account upon formation . . .	$300,000	$300,000
Less: net loss for years 1 and 2 . .	(200,000)	(200,000)
Capital account at end of year 2 . .	$100,000	$100,000

The allocations made in the partnership's first 2 taxable years have substantial economic effect.

(ii) Assume the same facts as in (i) and that MK is admitted to the partnership at the beginning of the partnership's third taxable year. At the time of his admission, the fair market value of the partnership property is $600,000. MK contributes $300,000 to the partnership in exchange for an equal one-third interest in the partnership, and, as permitted under paragraph (b)(2)(iv)(g), the capital accounts of WM and JL are adjusted upward to $300,000 each to reflect the fair market value of partnership property. In addition, the partnership agreement is modified to provide that depreciation and gain or loss, as computed for tax purposes, with respect to the partnership property that appreciated prior to MK's admission will be shared among the partners in a manner that takes account of the variation between such property's $200,000 adjusted tax basis and its $600,000 book value in accordance with paragraph (b)(2)(iv)(f) and the special rule contained in paragraph (b)(4)(i) of this section. Depreciation and gain or loss, as computed for book purposes, with respect to such property will be allocated equally among the partners and, in accordance with paragraph (b)(2)(iv)(g) of this section, will be reflected in the partner's capital accounts, as will all other partnership income, gain, loss, and deduction. Since the requirements of (b)(2)(iv)(g) of this section are satisfied, the capital accounts of the partners (as adjusted) continue to be maintained in accordance with paragraph (B)(2)(iv) of this section.

(iii) Assume the same facts as in (ii) and that immediately after MK's admission to the partnership, the partnership property is sold for $600,000, resulting in a taxable gain of $400,000 ($600,000) less $200,000 adjusted tax basis) and no book gain or loss, and the partnership is liquidated. An allocation of the $400,000 taxable gain cannot have economic effect because such gain cannot properly be reflected in the partners' book capital accounts. Consistent with the special partners' interests in the partnership rule contained in paragraph (b)(4)(i) of this section, the partnership agreement provides that the $400,000 taxable gain will, in accordance with section 704(c) principles, be shared equally between WM and JL.

	WM		JL		MK	
	Tax	Book	Tax	Book	Tax	Book
Capital account at beginning of year 3	$00,000	$00,000	$00,000	$00,000	$00,000	$00,000
Plus: gain	200,000	0	200,000	0	0	0
Capital account before liquidation	$00,000	$00,000	$00,000	$00,000	$00,000	$00,000

The $900,000 of partnership cash ($600,000 sales proceeds plus $300,000 contributed by MK) is distributed equally among WM, JL, and MK in accordance with their adjusted positive capital account balances, each of which is $300,000.

(iv) Assume the same facts as in (iii) except that prior to liquidation the property appreciates and is sold for $900,000, resulting in a taxable gain of $700,000 ($900,000 less $200,000 adjusted tax basis) and a book gain of $300,000 ($900,000) less $600,000 book value). Under the partnership agreement the $300,000 of book gain is allocated equally among the partners, and such allocation has substantial economic effect.

	WM		JL		MK	
	Tax	Book	Tax	Book	Tax	Book
Capital account at beginning of year 3	$100,000	$300,000	$100,000	$300,000	$300,000	$300,000
Plus: gain	300,000	100,000	300,000	100,000	100,000	100,000
Capital account before liquidation	$400,000	$400,000	$400,000	$400,000	$400,000	$400,000

Consistent with the special partners' interests in the partnership rule contained in paragraph (b)(4)(i) of this section, the partnership agreement provides that the $700,000 taxable gain is, in accordance with section 704(c) principles, shared $300,000 to JL. $300,000 to WM, and $100,000 to MK. This ensures that (1) WM and JL share equally the $400,000 taxable gain that is attributable to appreciation in the property that occurred prior to MK's admission to the partnership in the same manner as it was reflected in their capital accounts upon MK's admission, and (2) WM, JL, and MK share equally the additional $300,000 taxable gain in the same manner as they shared the $300,000 book gain.

(v) Assume the same facts as in (ii) except that shortly after MK's admission the property depreciates and is sold for $450,000, resulting in a taxable gain of $250,000 ($450,000 less $200,000 adjusted tax basis) and a book loss of

$150,000 (450,000 less $600,000 book value). Under the partnership agreement these items are allocated as follow:

	WM		JL		MK	
	Tax	Book	Tax	Book	Tax	Book
Capital account at beginning of year 3	$100,000	$300,000	$100,000	$300,000	$300,000	$300,000
Plus: gain	125,000	0	125,000	0	0	0
Less: Loss	0	(50,000)	0	(50,000)	0	(50,000)
Capital account before liquidation	$225,000	$250,000	$225,000	$250,000	$300,000	$250,000

The $150,000 book loss is allocated equally among the partners, and such allocation has substantial economic effect. Consistent with the special partners' interests in the partnership rule contained in paragraph (b)(4)(i) of this section, the partnership agreement provides that the $250,000 taxable gain is, in accordance with section 704(c) principles, shared equally between WM and JL. The fact that MK bears an economic loss of $50,000 without a corresponding taxable loss is attributable entirely to the "ceiling rule." See paragraph (c)(2) of § 1.704-1.

(vi) Assume the same facts as in (ii) except that the property depreciates and is sold for $170,000, resulting in a $30,000 taxable loss ($200,000 adjusted tax basis less $170,000) and a book loss of $430,000 ($600,000 book value less $170,000). The book loss of $430,000 is allocated equally among the partners ($143,333 each) and has substantial economic effect. Consistent with the special partners' interests in the partnership rule contained in paragraph (b)(4)(i) of this section, the partnership agreement provides that the entire $30,000 taxable loss is, in accordance with section 704(c) principles, included in MK's distributive share.

	WM		JL		MK	
	Tax	Book	Tax	Book	Tax	Book
Capital account at beginning of year 3	$100,000	$300,000	$100,000	$300,000	$300,000	$300,000
Less Loss	0	(143,333)	0	(143,333)	(30,000)	(143,333)
Capital account before liquidation	$100,000	$156,667	$100,000	$156,667	$270,000	$156,667

(vii) Assume the same facts as in (ii) and that during the partnership's third taxable year, the partnership has an additional $100,000 cost recovery deduction and $300,000 book depreciation deduction attributable to the property purchased by the partnership in its first taxable year. The $300,000 book depreciation deduction is allocated equally among the partners, and that allocation has substantial economic effect. Consistent with the special partners' interests in the partnership rule contained in paragraph (b)(4)(i) of this section, the partnership agreement provides that the $100,000 cost recovery deduction for the partnership's third taxable year is, in accordance with section 704(c) principles, included in MK's distributive share. This is because under these facts those principles require MK to include the cost recovery deduction for such property in his distributive share up to the amount of the book depreciation deduction for such property properly allocated to him.

	WM		JL		MK	
	Tax	Book	Tax	Book	Tax	Book
Capital account at beginning of year 3	$100,000	$300,000	$100,000	$300,000	$300,000	$300,000
Less: recovery/depreciation deduction for year 3	0	(100,000)	0	(100,000)	(100,000)	(100,000)
Capital account at end of year 3	$100,000	$200,000	$100,000	$200,000	$200,000	$200,000

(viii) Assume the same facts as in (vii) except that upon MK's admission the partnership property has an adjusted tax basis of $220,000 (instead of $200,000), and thus the cost recovery deduction for the partnership's third taxable year is $110,000. Assume further that upon MK's admission WM and JL have adjusted capital account balances of $110,000 and $100,000, respectively. Consistent with the special partners' interests in the partnership rule contained in paragraph (b)(4)(i) of this section, the partnership agreement provides that the excess $10,000 cost recovery deduction ($110,000 less $100,000 included in MK's distributive share) is, in accordance with section 704 (c) principles, shared equally between WM and JL and is so included in their respective distributive shares for the partnership's third taxable year.

(ix) Assume the same facts as in (vii) except that upon MK's admission the partnership agreement is amended to allocate the first $400,000 of book depreciation and loss on partnership property equally between WM and JL and the last $200,000 of such book depreciation and loss to MK. Assume such allocations have substantial economic effect. Pursuant to this amendment the $300,000 book depreciation deduction in the partnership's third taxable year is allocated equally between WM and JL. Consistent with the special partners' interests in the partnership rule contained in paragraph (b)(4)(i) of this section, the partnership agreement provides that the $100,000 cost recovery deduction is, in accordance with section 704(c) principles, shared equally between WM and JL. In the partnership's fourth taxable year, it has a $60,000 cost recovery deduction and a $180,000 book depreciation deduction. Under the amendment described above, the $180,000 book depreciation deduction is allocated $50,000 to WM, $50,000 to JL, and $80,000 to MK. Consistent with the special partners' interests in the partnership rule contained in paragraph (b)(4)(i) of this section, the partnership agreement provides that the $60,000 cost recovery deduction is, in accordance with section 704(c) principles, included entirely in MK's distributive share.

	WM		JL		MK	
	Tax	Book	Tax	Book	Tax	Book
Capital account at beginning of year 3	$100,000	$300,000	$100,000	$300,000	$300,000	$300,000
Less:						
(a) recovery/depreciation deduction for year 3	(50,000)	(150,000)	(50,000)	(150,000)	0	0
(b) recovery/depreciation deduction for year 4	0	(50,000)	0	(50,000)	(60,000)	(80,000)
Capital account at end of year 4	$50,000	$100,000	$50,000	$100,000	$240,000	$220,000

(x) Assume the same facts as in (vii) and that at the beginning of the partnership's third taxable year, the partnership purchases a second item of tangible personal property for $300,000 and elects under section 48(q)(4) to reduce the amount of investment tax credit in lieu of adjusting the tax basis of such property. The partnership agreement is amended to allocate the first $150,000 of cost recovery deductions and loss from such property to WM and the next $150,000 of cost recovery deductions and loss from such property equally between JL and MK. Thus, in the partnership's third taxable year it has, in addition to the items specified in (vii), a cost recovery and book depreciation deduction of $100,000 attributable to the newly acquired property, which is allocated entirely to WM. As in (vii), the allocation of the $300,000 book depreciation attributable to the property purchased in the partnership's first taxable year equally among the partners has substantial economic effect, and consistent with the special partners' interests in the partnership rule contained in paragraph (b)(4)(i) of this section, the partnership agreement properly provides for the entire $100,000 cost recovery deduction attributable to such property to be included in MK's distributive share. Furthermore, the allocation to WM of the $100,000 cost recovery deduction attributable to the property purchased in the partnership's third taxable year has substantial economic effect.

	WM		JL		MK	
	Tax	Book	Tax	Book	Tax	Book
Capital account at beginning of year 3	$100,000	$300,000	$100,000	$300,000	$300,000	$300,000
Less:						
(a) recovery/depreciation deduction for property bought in year 1	0	(100,000)	0	(100,000)	(100,000)	(100,000)
(b) recovery/depreciation deduction for property bought in year 3	(100,000)	(100,000)	0	0	0	0
Capital account at end of year 3	0	$100,000	$100,000	$200,000	$200,000	$200,000

(xi) Assume the same facts as in (x) and that at the beginning of the partnership's fourth taxable year, the properties purchased in the partnership's first and third taxable years are disposed of for $90,000 and $180,000, respectively, and the partnership is liquidated. With respect to the property purchased in the first taxable year, there is a book loss of $210,000 ($300,000 book value less $90,000) and a taxable loss of $10,000 ($100,000 adjusted tax basis less $90,000). The book loss is allocated equally among the partners, and such allocation has substantial economic effect. Consistent with the special partners' interests in the partnership rule contained in paragraph (b)(4)(i) of this section, the partnership agreement provides that the taxable loss of $10,000 will, in accordance with section 704(c) principles, be included entirely in MK's distributive share. With respect to the property purchased in the partnership's third taxable year, there is a book and taxable loss of $20,000. Pursuant to the partnership agreement this loss is allocated entirely to WM, and such allocation has substantial economic effect.

	WM		JL		MK	
	Tax	Book	Tax	Book	Tax	Book
Capital account at beginning of year 4	0	$100,000	$100,000	$200,000	$200,000	$200,000
Less:						
(a) loss on property bought in year 1	0	(70,000)	0	(70,000)	(10,000)	(70,000)
(b) loss on property bought in year 3	(20,000)	(20,000)	0	0	0	0
Capital account before liquidation	($20,000)	$10,000	$100,000	$130,000	$190,000	$130,000

Partnership liquidation proceeds ($270,000) are properly distributed in accordance with the partners' adjusted positive book capital account balances ($10,000 to WM, $130,000 to JL and $130,000 to MK).

(xii) Assume the same facts as in (x) and that in the partnership's fourth taxable year it has a cost recovery deduction of $60,000 and book depreciation deduction of $180,000 attributable to the property purchased in the partnership's first taxable year, and a cost recovery and book depreciation deduction of $100,000 attributable to the property purchased in the partnership's third taxable year. The $180,000 book depreciation deduction attributable to the property purchased in the partnership's first taxable year is allocated equally among the partners, and such allocation has substantial economic effect. Consistent with the special partners' interests in the partnership rule contained in paragraph (b)(4)(i) of this section, the partnership agreement provides that the $60,000 cost recovery deduction attributable to the property purchased in the first taxable year is, in accordance with section 704(c) principles, included entirely in MK's distributive share. Furthermore, the $100,000 cost recovery deduction attributable to the property purchased in the third taxable year is allocated $50,000 to WM, $25,000 to JL, and $25,000 to MK, and such allocation has substantial economic effect

	WM		JL		MK	
	Tax	Book	Tax	Book	Tax	Book
Capital account at beginning of year 4	0	$100,000	$100,000	$200,000	$200,000	$200,000
Less:						
(a) recovery/depreciation deduction for property bought in year 1	0	(60,000)	0	(60,000)	(60,000)	(60,000)
(b) recovery/depreciation deduction for property bought in year 3	(50,000)	(50,000)	(25,000)	(25,000)	(25,000)	(25,000)
Capital account at end of year 4	($50,000)	($10,000)	$75,000	$115,000	$115,000	$115,000

At the end of the partnership's fourth taxable year the adjusted tax bases of the partnership properties acquired in its first and third taxable years are $40,000 and $100,000, respectively. If the properties are disposed of at the beginning of the partnership's fifth taxable year for their adjusted tax bases, there would be no taxable gain or loss, a book loss of $80,000 on the property purchased in the partnership's first taxable year ($120,000 book value less $40,000), and cash available for distribution of $140,000.

	WM		JL		MK	
	Tax	Book	Tax	Book	Tax	Book
Capital account at beginning of year 5	($50,000)	($10,000)	$ 75,000	$115,000	$115,000	$115,000
Less: loss	0	(26,667)	0	(26,667)	0	(26,667)
Capital account before liquidation	($50,000)	($36,667)	$ 75,000	$88,333	$115,000	$88,333

If the partnership is then liquidated, the $140,000 of cash on hand plus the $36,667 balance that WM would be required to contribute to the partnership (the deficit balance in his book capital account) would be distributed equally between JL and MK in accordance with their adjusted positive book capital account balances.

(xiii) Assume the same facts as in (i). Any tax preferences under section 57(a)(12) attributable to the partnership's cost recovery deductions in the first 2 taxable years will be taken into account equally by WM and JL. If the partnership agreement instead provides that the partnership's cost recovery deductions in its first 2 taxable years are allocated 25 percent to WM and 75 percent to JL (and such allocations have substantial economic effect), the tax preferences attributable to such cost recovery deductions would be taken into account 25 percent by WM and 75 percent by JL. The conclusion in the previous sentence is unchanged even if the partnership's operating expenses (exclusive of cost recovery and depreciation deductions) exceed its operating income in each of the partnership's first 2 taxable years, the resulting net loss is allocated entirely to WM, and the cost recovery deductions are allocated 25 percent to WM and 75 percent to JL (provided such allocations have substantial economic effect). If the partnership agreement instead provides that all income, gain, loss, and deduction (including cost recovery and depreciations) are allocated equally between JL and WM, the tax preferences attributable to the cost recovery deductions would be taken into account equally by JL and WM. In this case, if the partnership has a $100,000 cost recovery deduction in its first taxable year and an additional net loss of $100,000 in its first taxable year (i.e., its operating expenses exceed its operating income by $100,000) and purports to categorize JL's $100,000 distributive share of partnership loss as being attributable to the cost recovery deduction and WM's $100,000 distributive share of partnership loss as being attributable to the net loss, the economic effect of such allocations is not substantial, and each partner will be allocated one-half of all partnership income, gain, loss, and deduction and will take into account one-half of the tax preferences attributable to the cost recovery deductions.

Example (19). (i) DG and JC form a general partnership for the purpose of drilling oil wells. DG contributes an oil lease, which has a fair market value and adjusted tax basis of $100,000. JC contributes $100,000 in cash, which is used to finance the drilling operations. The partnership agreement provides that DG is credited with a capital account of $100,000, and JC is credited with a capital account of $100,000. The agreement further provides that the partners' capital accounts will be determined and maintained in accordance with paragraph (b)(2)(iv) of this section, distributions in liquidation of the partnership (or any partner's interest) will be made in accordance with the partners' positive capital account balances, and any partner with a deficit balance in his capital account following the liquidation of his interest must restore such deficit to the partnership (as set forth in paragraphs (b)(2)(ii)(b)(2) and (3) of this section. The partnership chooses to adjust capital accounts on a simulated cost depletion basis and elects under section 48(g)(4) to reduce the amount of investment tax credit in lieu of adjusting the basis of its section 38 property. The agreement further provides that (1) all additional cash requirements of the partnership will be borne equally by DG and JC, (2) the deductions attributable to the property (including money) contributed by each partner will be allocated to such partner, (3) all other income, gain, loss, and deductions (and item thereof) will be allocated equally between DG and JC, and (4) all cash from operations will be distributed equally between DG and JC. In the partnership's first taxable year $80,000 of partnership intangible drilling cost deductions and $20,000 of cost recovery deductions on partnership equipment are allocated to JC, and the $100,000 basis of the lease is, for purposes of the depletion allowance under sections 611 and 613A(c)(7)(D), allocated to DG. The allocations of income, gain, loss, and deduction provided in the partnership agreement have substantial economic effect. Furthermore, since the allocation of the entire basis of the lease to DG will not result in capital account adjustments (under paragraph (b)(2)(iv)(k) of this section) the economic effect of which is insubstantial, and since all other partnership allocations are recognized under this paragraph, the allocation of the $100,000 adjusted basis of the lease to DG is, under paragraph (b)(4)(v) of this section, recognized as being in accordance with the partners' interests in partnership capital for purposes of section 613A(c)(7)(D).

(ii) Assume the same facts as in (i) except that the partnership agreement provides that (1) all additional cash requirements of the partnership for additional expenses will be funded by additional contributions from JC, (2) all cash from operations will first be distributed to JC until the excess of such cash distributions over the amount of such additional expense equals his initial $100,000 contributions, (3) all deductions attributable to such additional operating expenses will be allocated to JC, and (4) all income will be allocated to JC until the aggregate amount of income allocated to him equals the amount of partnership operating expenses funded by his initial $100,000 contribution plus the amount of additional operating expenses paid from contributions made solely by him. The allocations of income, gain, loss, and deduction provided in partnership agreement have economic effect. In addition, the economic effect of the allocations provided in the agreement is substantial. Because the partnership's drilling activities are sufficiently speculative, there is not a strong likelihood at the time the disproportionate allocations of loss and deduction to JC are provided for by the partnership agreement that the economic effect of such allocations will be largely offset by allocations of income. In addition, since the allocation of the entire basis of the lease to DG will not result in capital account adjustments (under paragraph (b)(2)(iv)(k) of this section) the economic effect of which is insubstantial, and since all other partnership allocations are recognized under this paragraph, the allocation of the adjusted basis of the lease to DG is, under paragraph (b)(4)(v) of this section, recognized as being in accordance with the partners' interests in partnership capital under section 613A(c)(7)(D).

(iii) Assume the same facts as in (i) except that all distributions, including those made upon liquidation of the partnership, will be made equally between DG and JC, and no partner is obligated to restore the deficit balance in his capital account to the partnership following the liquidation of his interest for distribution to partners with positive capital account balances. Since liquidation proceeds will be distributed equally between DG and JC irrespective of their capital account balances, and since no partner is required to restore the deficit balance in his capital account to the partnership upon liquidation (in accordance with paragraph (b)(2)(ii)(b)(3) of this section), the allocations of income, gain, loss, and deduction provided in the partnership agreement do not have economic effect and must be reallocated in accordance with the partners' interests in the partnership under paragraph (b)(3) of this section. Under these facts all partnership income, gain, loss, and deduction (and item thereof) will be reallocated equally between JC and DG. Furthermore, the allocation of the $100,000 adjusted tax basis of the lease of DG is not, under paragraph (b)(4)(v) of this section, deemed to be in accordance with the partners' interests in partnership capital under section 613A(c)(7)(D), and such basis must be reallocated in accordance with the partners' interests in partnership capital or income as determined under section 613A(c)(7)(D). The results in this example would be the same if JC's initial cash contribution were $1,000,000 (instead of $100,000), but in such case the partners should consider whether, and to what extent, the provisions of paragraph (b)(1) of § 1.721-1, and principles related thereto, may be applicable.

(iv) Assume the same facts as in (i) and that for the partnership's first taxable year the simulated depletion deduction with respect to the lease is $10,000. Since DG properly was allocated the entire depletable basis of the lease (such allocation having been recognized as being in accordance with DG's interest in partnership capital with respect to such lease), under paragraph (b)(2)(iv)(k)(1) of this section the partnership's $10,000 simulated depletion deduction is allocated to DG and will reduce his capital account accordingly. If (prior to any additional simulated depletion deductions) the lease is sold for $100,000, paragraph (b)(4)(v) of this section requires that the first $90,000 (i.e., the partnership's simulated adjusted basis in the lease) out of the $100,000 amount realized on such sale be allocated to DG (but does not directly affect his capital account). The partnership agreement allocates the remaining $10,000 amount realized equally between JC and DG (but such allocation does not directly affect their capital accounts). This allocation of the $10,000 portion of amount realized that exceeds the partnership's simulated adjusted basis in the lease will be treated as being in accordance with the partners' allocable shares of such amount realized under section 613A(c)(7)(D) because such allocation will not result in capital account adjustments (under paragraph (b)(2)(iv)(k) of this section) the economic effect of which is insubstantial, and all other partnership allocations are recognized under this paragraph. Under paragraph (b)(2)(iv)(k) of this section, the partners' capital accounts are adjusted upward by the partnership's simulated gain of $10,000 ($100,000 sales price less $90,000 simulated adjusted basis) in proportion to such partners' allocable shares of the $10,000 portion of the total amount realized that exceeds the partnership's $90,000 simulated adjusted basis ($5,000 to JC and $5,000 to DG). If the lease is sold for $50,000, under paragraph (b)(4)(v) of this section the entire $50,000 amount realized on the sale of the lease will be allocated to DG (but will not directly affect his capital account). Under paragraph (b)(2)(iv)(k) of this section the partners' capital accounts will be adjusted downward by the partnership's $40,000 simulated loss ($50,000 sales price less $90,000 simulated adjusted basis) in proportion to the partners' allocable shares of the total amount realized from the property that represents recovery of the partnership's simulated adjusted basis therein. Accordingly, DG's capital account will be reduced by such $40,000.

Example (20). (i) A and B form AB, an eligible entity (as defined in § 301.7701-3(a) of this chapter), treated as a partnership for U.S. tax purposes. AB operates business M in country X and earns income from passive investments in country X. Country X imposes a 40 percent tax on business M income, which tax is a CFTE, but exempts from tax income from passive investments. In 2007, AB earns $100,000 of income from business M and $30,000 from passive investments and pays or accrues $40,000 of country X taxes. For purposes of section 904(d), the income from business M is general limitation income and the income from the passive investments is passive income. Pursuant to the partnership agreement, all partnership items, including CFTEs, from business M are allocated 60 percent to A and 40 percent to B, and all partnership items, including CFTEs, from passive investments are allocated 80 percent to A and 20 percent to B. Accordingly, A is allocated 60 percent of the business M income ($60,000) and 60 percent of the country X taxes ($24,000), and B is allocated 40 percent of the business M income ($40,000) and 40 percent of the country X taxes ($16,000). The income from the passive investments is allocated $24,000 to A and $6,000 to B. Assume that allocations of all items other than CFTEs are valid.

(ii) Because the partnership agreement provides for different allocations of the net income attributable to business M and the passive investments, the net income attributable to each is income in a separate CFTE category. See paragraph (b)(4)(viii)(c)(2) of this section. AB must determine the net income in each CFTE category and the CFTEs allocable to each CFTE category. Under paragraph (b)(4)(viii)(c)(3) of this section, the net income in the business M CFTE category is the $100,000 attributable to business M and the net income in the passive investments CFTE category is the $30,000 attributable to the passive investments. Under paragraph (b)(4)(viii)(d) of this section, the $40,000 of country X taxes is allocated to the business M CFTE category and no portion of the country X taxes is allocated to the passive investments CFTE category. Therefore, the $40,000 of country X taxes are related to the $100,000 of net income in the business M CFTE category. See paragraph (b)(4)(viii)(c)(1) of this section. Because AB's partnership agreement allocates the net income from the business M CFTE category 60 percent to A and 40 percent to B, and the country X taxes 60 percent to A and 40 percent to B, the allocations of the CFTEs are in proportion to the distributive shares of income to which the CFTEs relate. Because AB satisfies the requirement of paragraph (b)(4)(viii) of this section, the allocations of the country X taxes are deemed to be in accordance with the partners' interests in the partnership. Because the business M income is general limitation income, all $40,000 of taxes are attributable to the general limitation category. See § 1.904-6.

Example (21). (i) A and B form AB, an eligible entity (as defined in § 301.7701-3(a) of this chapter), treated as a partnership for U.S. tax purposes. AB operates business M in country X and business N in country Y. Country X imposes a 40 percent tax on business M income, country Y imposes a 20 percent tax on business N income, and the country X and country Y taxes are CFTEs. In 2007, AB has $100,000 of income from business M and $50,000 of income from business N. Country X imposes $40,000 of tax on the income from business M and country Y imposes $10,000 of tax on the income of business N. Pursuant to the partnership agreement, all partnership items, including CFTEs, from business M are allocated 75 percent to A and 25 percent to B, and all partnership items, including CFTEs, from business N are split evenly between A and B (50 percent each). Accordingly, A is allocated 75 percent of the income from business M ($75,000), 75 percent of the country X taxes ($30,000), 50 percent of the income from business N ($25,000), and 50 percent of the country Y taxes ($5,000). B is allocated 25 percent of the income from business M ($25,000), 25 percent of the country X taxes ($10,000), 50 percent of the income from business N ($25,000), and 50 percent of the country Y taxes ($5,000). Assume that allocations of all items other than CFTEs are valid. The income from business M and business N is general limitation income for purposes of section 904(d).

(ii) Because the partnership agreement provides for different allocations of the net income attributable to businesses M and N, the net income attributable to each business is income in a separate CFTE category even though all of the income is in the general limitation category for section 904(d) purposes. See paragraph (b)(4)(viii)(c)(2) of this section. Under paragraph (b)(4)(viii)(c)(3) of this section, the net income in the business M CFTE category is the $100,000 attributable to business M and the net income in the business N CFTE category is $50,000 attributable to business N. Under paragraph (b)(4)(viii)(d) of this section, the $40,000 of country X taxes is allocated to the business M CFTE category and the $10,000 of country Y taxes is allocated to the business N CFTE category. Therefore, the $40,000 of country X taxes are related to the $100,000 of net income in the business M CFTE category and the $10,000 of country Y taxes are related to the $50,000 of net income in the business N CFTE category. See paragraph (b)(4)(viii)(c)(1) of this section. Because AB's partnership agreement allocates the $40,000 of country X taxes in the same proportion as the net income in the business M CFTE category, and the $10,000 of country Y taxes in the same proportion as the net income in the business N CFTE category, the allocations of the country X taxes and the country Y taxes are in proportion to the distributive shares of income to which the foreign taxes relate. Because AB satisfies the requirements of paragraph (b)(4)(viii) of this section, the allocations of the country X and country Y taxes are deemed to be in accordance with the partners' interests in the partnership.

Example (22). (i) The facts are the same as in Example 21, except that the partnership agreement provides for the following allocations. Depreciation attributable to machine X, which is used in business M, is allocated 100 percent to A. B is allocated the first $20,000 of gross income attributable to business N, which allocation does not result in a deduction under foreign law. All remaining items, except CFTEs, are allocated 50 percent to A and 50 percent to B. For 2007, assume that business M generates $120,000 of income, before taking into account depreciation attributable to machine X. The total amount of depreciation attributable to machine X is $20,000, which results in $100,000 of net income attributable to business M for U.S. and country X tax purposes. Business N generates $70,000 of gross income and has $20,000 of expenses, resulting in $50,000 of net income for U.S. and country Y tax purposes. Pursuant to the partnership agreement, A is allocated $40,000 of the net income attributable to business M ($60,000 of business M income less $20,000 of depreciation attributable to machine X), and $15,000 of the net income attributable to business N. B is allocated $60,000 of the net income attributable to business M and $35,000 of the net income attributable to business N ($20,000 of gross income, plus $15,000 of net income).

(ii) As a result of the special allocations, the net income attributable to business M ($100,000) is allocated 40 percent to A and 60 percent to B. The net income attributable to business N ($50,000) is allocated 30 percent to A and 70 percent to B. Because the partnership agreement provides for different allocations of the net income attributable to businesses M and N, the net income from each of businesses M and N is income in a separate CFTE category. See paragraph (b)(4)(viii)(c)(2) of this section. Under paragraph (b)(4)(viii)(c)(3) of this section, the net income in the business M CFTE category is the $100,000 of net income attributable to business M and the net income in the business N CFTE category is the $50,000 of net income attributable to business N. Under paragraph (b)(4)(viii)(d)(1) of this section, the $40,000 of country X taxes is allocated to the business M CFTE category and the $10,000 of country Y taxes is allocated to the business N CFTE category. Therefore, the $40,000 of country X taxes relates to the $100,000 of net income in the business M CFTE and the $10,000 of country Y taxes relates to the $50,000 of net income in the business N CFTE category. See paragraph (b)(4)(viii)(c)(1) of this section. The allocations of the country X taxes will be in proportion to the distributive shares of income to which they relate and will be deemed to be in accordance with the partners' interests in the partnership if such taxes are allocated 40 percent to A and 60 percent to B. The allocations of the country Y taxes will be in proportion to the distributive shares of income to which they relate and will be deemed to be in accordance with the partners' interests in the partnership if such taxes are allocated 30 percent to A and 70 percent to B.

(iii) Assume that for 2008, all the facts are the same as in paragraph (i) of this Example 22, except that business M generates $60,000 of income before taking into account depreciation attributable to machine X and country X imposes $16,000 of tax on the $40,000 of net income attributable to business M. Pursuant to the partnership agreement, A is allocated 25 percent of the income from business M ($10,000), and B is allocated 75 percent of the income from business M ($30,000). Allocations of the country X taxes will be in proportion to the distributive shares of income to which they relate and will be deemed to be in accordance with the partners' interests in the partnership if such taxes are allocated 25 percent to A and 75 percent to B.

Example (23). (i) The facts are the same as in Example 21, except that AB does not actually receive the $50,000 of income accrued in 2007 with respect to business N until 2008 and AB accrues and receives an additional $100,000 with respect to business N in 2008. Also assume that A, B, and AB each report taxable income on an accrual basis for U.S. tax purposes and AB reports taxable income using the cash receipts and disbursements method of accounting for country X and country Y purposes. In 2007, AB pays or accrues country X taxes of $40,000. In 2008, AB pays or accrues country Y taxes of $30,000. Pursuant to the partnership agreement, in 2007, A is allocated 75 percent of business M income ($75,000) and country X taxes ($30,000) and 50 percent of business N income ($25,000). B is allocated 25 percent of business M income ($25,000) and country X taxes ($10,000) and 50 percent of business N income ($25,000). In 2008, A and B are each allocated 50 percent of the business N income ($50,000) and country Y taxes ($15,000).

(ii) For 2007, the $40,000 of country X taxes paid or accrued by AB relates to the $100,000 of net income in the business M CFTE category. No portion of the country X taxes paid or accrued in 2007 relates to the $50,000 of net income in the business N CFTE category. For 2008, the net income in the business N CFTE category is the $100,000 attributable to business N. See paragraph (b)(4)(viii)(c)(3) of this section. Under paragraph (b)(4)(viii)(d)(1) of this section, $20,000 of the country Y tax paid or accrued in 2008 is allocated to the business N CFTE category. The remaining $10,000 of country Y tax is allocated to the business N CFTE category under paragraph (b)(4)(viii)(d)(2) of this section (relating to timing differences). Therefore, the $30,000 of country Y taxes paid or accrued by AB in 2008 is related to the $100,000 of net income in the business N CFTE category for 2008. See paragraph (b)(4)(viii)(c)(1) of this section. Because AB's partnership agreement allocates the $40,000 of country X taxes and the $30,000 of country Y taxes in proportion to the distributive shares of income to which the taxes relate, the allocations of the country X and country Y taxes satisfy the requirements of paragraphs (b)(4)(viii)(a)(1) and (2) of this section and the allocations of the country X and Y taxes are deemed to be in accordance with the partners' interests in the partnership under paragraph (b)(4)(viii) of this section.

Example (24). (i) The facts are the same as in Example 21, except that businesses M and N are conducted by entities (DE1 and DE2, respectively) that are corporations for country X and Y tax purposes and disregarded entities for U.S. tax purposes. Also, assume that DE1 makes payments of $75,000 during 2007 to DE2 that are deductible by DE1 for country X tax purposes and includible in income of DE2 for country Y tax purposes. As a result of such payments, DE1 has taxable income of $25,000 for country X purposes on which $10,000 of taxes are imposed and DE2 has taxable income of $125,000 for country Y purposes on which $25,000 of taxes are imposed. For U.S. tax purposes, $100,000 of AB's income is attributable to the activities of DE1 and $50,000 of AB's income is attributable to the activities of DE2. Pursuant to the partnership agreement, all partnership items, including CFTEs, from business M are allocated 75 percent to A and 25 percent to B, and all partnership items, including CFTEs, from business N are split evenly between A and B (50 percent each). Accordingly, A is allocated 75 percent of the income from business M ($75,000), 75 percent of the country X taxes ($7,500), 50 percent of the income from business N ($25,000), and 50 percent of the country Y taxes ($12,500). B is allocated 25 percent of the income from business M ($25,000), 25 percent of the country X taxes ($2,500), 50 percent of the income from business N ($25,000), and 50 percent of the country Y taxes ($12,500).

(ii) Because the partnership agreement provides for different allocations of the net income attributable to businesses M and N, the net income attributable to each of business M and business N is income in separate CFTE categories. See paragraph (b)(4)(viii)(c)(2) of this section. Under paragraph (b)(4)(viii)(c)(3) of this section, the $100,000 of net income attributable to business M is in the business M CFTE category and the $50,000 of net income attributable to business N is in the business N CFTE category. Under paragraph (b)(4)(viii)(d)(1) of this section, the $10,000 of country X taxes is allocated to the business M CFTE category and $10,000 of the country Y taxes is allocated to the business N CFTE category. Under paragraph (b)(4)(viii)(d)(3) of this section, the additional $15,000 of country Y tax imposed with respect to the inter-branch payment is assigned to the business N CFTE category. Therefore, the $10,000 of country X taxes is related to the $100,000 of net income in the business M CFTE category and the $25,000 of country Y taxes is related to the $50,000 of net income in the business N CFTE category. See paragraph (b)(4)(viii)(c)(1) of this section. Because AB's partnership agreement allocates the $10,000 of country X taxes in the same proportion as the distributive shares of income to which the taxes relate and the $25,000 of country Y taxes in the same proportion as the distributive shares of income to which the taxes relate, AB satisfies the requirements of paragraph (b)(4)(viii) of this section and the allocations of the country X and country Y taxes are deemed to be in accordance with the partners' interests in the partnership. No inference is intended with respect to the application of other provisions to arrangements that involve disregarded payments. See paragraph (b)(1)(iii) of this section (relating to the effect of sections of the Internal Revenue Code other than section 704(b)).

(iii) Assume that the facts are the same as paragraph (i) of this Example 24, except that the partnership agreement provides that the $15,000 of country Y tax imposed with respect to the inter-branch payment is allocated 75 percent to A ($11,250) and 25 percent to B ($3,750) and that the remaining $10,000 of country Y tax is allocated 50 percent to A ($5,000) and 50 percent to B ($5,000). Thus, the country Y taxes are allocated 65 percent to A and 35 percent to B while the income in the business N CFTE category is allocated 50 percent to A and 50 percent to B. The allocations of the country Y tax are not deemed to be in accordance with the partners' interests because they are not in proportion to the allocations of the distributive shares of income from the business N CFTE category. However, upon sufficient substantiation that $15,000 of country Y tax paid by DE2 with respect to the $75,000 inter-branch payment relates to income that is recognized by DE1 for U.S. tax purposes, the allocations of the country Y taxes may be established to be actually in accordance with the partners' interests in the partnership. The allocations of the $10,000 of country X taxes are deemed to be in accordance with the partners' interests in the partnership because the country X taxes are allocated in the same proportion as the distributive shares of income to which they relate.

(iv) Assume that the facts are the same as in paragraph (i) of this Example 24, except that in order to reflect the $75,000 payment from DE1 to DE2, the partnership agreement allocates $75,000 of the income attributable to business M equally between A and B (50 percent each). Therefore, the total income attributable to business M is allocated 56.25 percent to A (75 percent of $25,000 plus 50 percent of $75,000) and 43.75 percent to B (25 percent of $25,000 and 50 percent of $75,000). The allocation of the country X taxes (75 percent to A and 25 percent to B) is not deemed to be in accordance with the partners' interests because it is not in proportion to the allocations of the distributive shares of income from the business M CFTE category. However, upon sufficient substantiation that all $10,000 of country X tax paid by DE1 relates to the $25,000 of DE1's income that is shared in the same 75-25 ratio, the allocations of the country X taxes may be established to be actually in accordance with the partners' interests in the partnership. The allocations of the $25,000 of country Y taxes are deemed to be in accordance with the partners' interests in the partnership because the country Y taxes are allocated in the same proportion as the distributive shares of income to which they relate.

Example (25). (i) A contributes $750,000 and B contributes $250,000 to form AB, an eligible entity (as defined in § 301.7701-3(a) of this chapter), treated as a partnership for U.S. tax purposes. AB operates business M in country X. Country X imposes a 20 percent tax on the net income from business M, which tax is a CFTE. In 2007, AB earns $300,000 of gross income, has deductible expenses of $100,000, and pays or accrues $40,000 of country X tax. Pursuant to the partnership agreement, the first $100,000 of gross income each year is allocated to A as a return on excess capital contributed by A. All remaining partnership items, including CFTEs, are split evenly between A and B (50 percent each). The gross income allocation is not deductible in determining AB's taxable income under country X law. Assume that allocations of all items other than CFTEs are valid.

(ii) AB has a single CFTE category because all of AB's net income is allocated in the same ratio. See paragraph (b)(4)(viii)(c)(2). Under paragraph (b)(4)(viii)(c)(3) of this section, the net income in the single CFTE category is $200,000. The $40,000 of taxes is allocated to the single CFTE category and, thus, related to the $200,000 of net income in the single CFTE category. In 2007, AB's partnership agreement allocates $150,000 or 75 percent of the net income to A ($100,000 attributable to the gross income allocation plus $50,000 of the remaining $100,000 of net income) and $50,000 or 25 percent of the net income to B. AB's partnership agreement allocates the country X taxes in accordance with the partners' shares of partnership items remaining after the $100,000 gross income allocation. Therefore, AB allocates the country X taxes 50 percent to A ($20,000) and 50 percent to B ($20,000). AB's allocations of country X taxes are not deemed to be in accordance with the partners' interests in the partnership under paragraph (b)(4)(viii) of this section, because they are not in proportion to the allocations of the distributive shares of income to which the country X taxes relate. Accordingly, the country X taxes will be reallocated according to the partners' interest in the partnership. Assuming that the partners do not reasonably expect to claim a deduction for the CFTE in determining their U.S. tax liabilities, a reallocation of the CFTEs under paragraph (b)(3) of this section would be 75 percent to A ($30,000) and 25 percent to B ($10,000). If the reallocation of the CFTEs causes the partners' capital accounts not to reflect their contemplated economic arrangement, the partners may need to reallocate other partnership items to ensure that the tax consequences of the partnership's allocations are consistent with their contemplated economic arrangement over the term of the partnership. The Commissioner will not reallocate other partnership items after the reallocation of the CFTEs.

(iii) The facts are the same as in paragraph (i) of this Example 25, except that the $100,000 allocation of gross income is deductible under country X law and that AB pays or accrues $20,000 of foreign tax. Under paragraph (b)(4)(viii)(c)(3) of this section, the net income in the single CFTE category is the $100,000 of net income, determined by disregarding the $100,000 of gross income that is allocated to A and deductible in determining AB's taxable income under the law of country X. See paragraph (b)(4)(viii)(c)(3)(ii) of this section. The $20,000 of country X tax is allocated to the single CFTE category, and, thus, related to the $100,000 of net income in the single CFTE category. See paragraphs (b)(4)(viii)(c)(1) and (d) of this section. No portion of the tax is related to the $100,000 of gross income allocated to A. Pursuant to the partnership agreement, AB allocates the country X taxes 50 percent to A ($10,000) and 50 percent to B ($10,000). AB's allocations of country X taxes are deemed to be in accordance with the partners' interests in the partnership under paragraph (b)(4)(viii) of this section.

(iv) The results in (ii) and (iii) of this Example 25 would be the same assuming all of the facts except that, rather than being a preferential gross income allocation, the $100,000 was a guaranteed payment to A within the meaning of section 707(c). See paragraph (b)(4)(viii)(c)(3) of this section.

Example (26). (i) A and B form AB, an eligible entity (as defined in § 301.7701-3(a) of this chapter), treated as a partnership for U.S. tax purposes. AB operates business M in country X and business N in country Y. A, a U.S. corporation, contributes a building with a fair market value of $200,000 and an adjusted basis of $50,000 for both U.S. and country X purposes. The building contributed by A is used in business M. B, a country X corporation, contributes $800,000 cash. The AB partnership agreement provides that AB will make allocations under section 704(c) using the traditional method under § 1.704-3(b) and that all other items, excluding creditable foreign taxes, will be allocated 20 percent to A and 80 percent to B. The partnership agreement provides that creditable foreign taxes will be allocated in proportion to the partners' distributive shares of net income in each CFTE category, which shall be determined by taking into accounts items allocated pursuant to section 704(c). Country X and Country Y impose tax at a rate of 20 percent and 40 percent, respectively, and such taxes are CFTEs. In 2007, AB sells the building contributed by A for $200,000, thereby recognizing taxable income of $150,000 for U.S. and country X purposes, and recognizes $250,000 of other income from the operation of business M. AB pays or accrues $80,000 of country X tax on such income. Also in 2007, business N recognizes $100,000 of taxable income for U.S. and country Y purposes and pays or accrues $40,000 of country Y tax. Pursuant to the partnership agreement, A is allocated $200,000 of business M income ($150,000 of taxable income in accordance with section 704(c) and $50,000 of other business M income) and $40,000 of country X tax, and 20 percent of both business N income ($20,000) and country Y tax ($8,000). B is allocated $200,000 of business M income and $40,000 of country X tax and 80 percent of both the business N income ($80,000) and country Y tax ($32,000). Assume that allocations of all items other than CFTEs are valid.

(ii) The net income attributable to business M ($400,000) is allocated 50 percent to A and 50 percent to B while the net income attributable to business N ($100,000) is allocated 20 percent to A and 80 percent to B. Because the partnership agreement provides for different allocations of the net income attributable to businesses M and N, the net income attributable to each activity is income in a separate CFTE category. See paragraph (b)(4)(viii)(c)(2) of this section. Under paragraph (b)(4)(viii)(c)(3) of this section, the net income in the business M CFTE category is the $400,000 of net income attributable to business M and the net income in the business N CFTE category is the $100,000 of net income attributable to business N. Under paragraph (b)(4)(viii)(d)(1) of this section, the $80,000 of country X tax is allocated to the business M CFTE category and the $40,000 of country Y tax is allocated to the business N CFTE category. Therefore, the $80,000 of country X tax relates to the $400,000 of net income in the business M CFTE category and the $40,000 of country Y tax relates to the $100,000 of net income in the business N CFTE category. See paragraph (b)(4)(viii)(c)(1) of this section. Because AB's partnership agreement allocates the $80,000 of country X taxes and $40,000 of country Y taxes in proportion to the distributive shares of income to which such taxes relate, the allocations are deemed to be in accordance with the partners' interests in the partnership under paragraph (b)(4)(viii) of this section.

Example (27). (i) A, a U.S. citizen, and B, a country X citizen, form AB, a country X eligible entity (as defined in § 301.7701-3(a) of this chapter), treated as a partnership for U.S. tax purposes. AB's only activity is business M, which it operates in country X. Country X imposes a 40 percent tax on the portion of AB's business M income that is the allocable share of AB's owners that are not citizens of country X, which tax is a CFTE. The partnership agreement provides that all partnership items, excluding CFTEs, from business M are allocated 40 percent to A and 60 percent to B. CFTEs are allocated 100 percent to A. In 2007, AB earns $100,000 of net income from business M and pays or accrues $16,000 of country X taxes on A's allocable share of AB's income ($40,000). Pursuant to the partnership agreement, A is allocated 40 percent of the business M income ($40,000) and 100 percent of the country X taxes ($16,000), and B is allocated 60 percent of the business M income ($60,000) and no country X taxes. Assume that allocations of all items other than CFTEs are valid.

(ii) AB has a single CFTE category because all of AB's net income is allocated in the same ratio. See paragraph (b)(4)(viii)(c)(2). Under paragraph (b)(4)(viii)(c)(3) of this section, the $40,000 of business M income that is allocated to A is included in the single CFTE category. Under paragraph (b)(4)(viii)(c)(3)(ii) of this section, no portion of the $60,000 allocated to B is included in the single CFTE category. Under paragraph (b)(4)(viii)(d) of this section, the $16,000 of taxes is allocated to the single CFTE category. Therefore, the $16,000 of country X taxes is related to the $40,000 of net income in the single CFTE category that is allocated to A. See paragraph (b)(4)(viii)(c)(1) of this section. Because AB's partnership agreement allocates the country X taxes in proportion to the distributive share of income to which the taxes relate, AB satisfies the requirement of paragraph (b)(4)(viii) of this section, and the allocation of the country X taxes is deemed to be in accordance with the partners' interests in the partnership.

(c) Contributed property; cross reference. See § 1.704-3 for methods of making allocations that take into account precontribution appreciation or diminution in value of property contributed by a partner to a partnership.

(d) Limitation on allowance of losses. *(1)* A partner's distributive share of partnership loss will be allowed only to the extent of the adjusted basis (before reduction by current year's losses) of such partner's interest in the partnership at the end of the partnership taxable year in which such loss occurred. A partner's share of loss in excess of his adjusted basis at the end of the partnership taxable year will not be allowed for that year. However, any loss so disallowed shall be allowed as a deduction at the end of the first succeeding partnership taxable year, and subsequent partnership taxable years, to the extent that the partner's adjusted basis for his partnership interest at the end of any such year exceeds zero (before reduction by such loss for such year).

(2) In computing the adjusted basis of a partner's interest for the purpose of ascertaining the extent to which a partner's distributive share of partnership loss shall be allowed as a deduction for the taxable year, the basis shall first be increased under section 705(a)(1) and decreased under section 705(a)(2), except for losses of the taxable year and losses previously disallowed. If the partner's distributive share of the aggregate of items of loss specified in section 702(a)(1), (2), (3), (8), and (9) exceeds the basis of the partner's interest computed under the preceding sentence, the limitation on losses under section 704(d) must be allocated to his distributive share of each such loss. This allocation shall be determined by taking the proportion that each loss bears to the total of all such losses. For purposes of the preceding sentence, the total losses for the taxable year shall be the sum of his distributive share of losses for the current year and his losses disallowed and carried forward from prior years.

(3) For the treatment of certain liabilities of the partner or partnership, see section 752 and § 1.752-1.

(4) The provisions of this paragraph may be illustrated by the following examples:

Example (1). At the end of the partnership taxable year 1955, partnership AB has a loss of $20,000. Partner A's distributive share of this loss is $10,000. At the end of such year, A's adjusted basis for his interest in the partnership (not taking into account his distributive share of the loss) is $6,000. Under section 704(d), A's distributive share of partnership loss is allowed to him (in his taxable year within or with which the partnership taxable year ends) only to the extent of his adjusted basis of $6,000. The $6,000 loss allowed for 1955 decreases the adjusted basis of A's interest to zero. Assume that, at the end of partnership taxable year 1956, A's share of partnership income has increased the adjusted basis of A's interest in the partnership to $3,000 (not taking into account the $4,000 loss disallowed in 1955). Of the $4,000 loss disallowed for the partnership taxable year 1955, $3,000 is allowed A for the partnership taxable year 1956, thus again decreasing the adjusted basis of his interest to zero. If, at the end of partnership taxable year 1957, A has an adjusted basis of his interest of at least $1,000 (not taking into account the disallowed loss of $1,000), he will be allowed the $1,000 loss previously disallowed.

Example (2). At the end of partnership taxable year 1955, partnership CD has a loss of $20,000. Partner C's distributive share of this loss is $10,000. The adjusted basis of his interest in the partnership (not taking into account his distributive share of such loss) is $6,000. Therefore, $4,000 of the loss is disallowed. At the end of partnership taxable year 1956, the partnership has no taxable income or loss, but owes $8,000 to a bank for money borrowed. Since C's share of this liability is $4,000, the basis of his partnership interest is increased from zero to $4,000. (See sections 752 and 722, and §§ 1.752-1 and 1.722-1.) C is allowed the $4,000 loss, disallowed for the preceding year under section 704(d), for his taxable year within or with which partnership taxable year 1956 ends.

Example (3). At the end of partnership taxable year 1955, partner C has the following distributive share of partnership items described in section 702(a): long-term capital loss, $4,000; short-term capital loss, $2,000; income as described in section 702(a)(9), $4,000. Partner C's adjusted basis for his partnership interest at the end of 1955, before adjustment for any of the above items, is $1,000. As adjusted under section 705(a)(1)(A), C's basis is increased from $1,000 to $5,000 at the end of the year. C's total distributive share of partnership loss is $6,000. Since without regard to losses, C has a basis of only $5,000, C is allowed only $5,000/$6,000 of each loss, that is, $3,333 of his long-term capital loss, and $1,667 of his short-term capital loss. C must carry forward to succeeding taxable years $667 as a long-term capital loss and $333 as a short-term capital loss.

(e) Family partnerships. *(1) In general.* (i) Introduction. The production of income by a partnership is attributable to the capital or services, or both, contributed by the partners. The provisions of subchapter K, chapter 1 of the Code, are to be read in the light of their relationship to section 61, which requires, inter alia, that income be taxed to the person who earns it through his own labor and skill and the utilization of his own capital.

(ii) Recognition of donee as partner. With respect to partnerships in which capital is a material income-producing factor, section 704(e)(1) provides that a person shall be recognized as a partner for income tax purposes if he owns a capital interest in such a partnership whether or not such interest is derived by purchase or gift from any other person. If a capital interest in a partnership in which capital is a material income-producing factor is created by gift, section 704(e)(2) provides that the distributive share of the donee under the partnership agreement shall be includible in his gross income, except to the extent that such distributive share is determined without allowance of reasonable compensation for services rendered to the partnership by the donor, and except to the extent that the portion of such distributive share attributable to donated capital is proportionately greater than the share of the donor attributable to the donor's capital. For rules of allocation in such cases, see subparagraph (3) of this paragraph.

(iii) Requirement of complete transfer to donee. A donee or purchaser of a capital interest in a partnership is not recognized as a partner under the principles of section 704(e)(1) unless such interest is acquired in a bona fide transaction, not a mere sham for tax avoidance or evasion purposes, and the donee or purchaser is the real owner of such interest. To be recognized, a transfer must vest dominion and control of the partnership interest in the transferee. The existence of such dominion and control in the donee is to be determined from all the facts and circumstances. A transfer is not recognized if the transferor retains such incidents of ownership that the transferee has not acquired full and complete ownership of the partnership interest. Transactions between members of a family will be closely scrutinized, and the circumstances, not only at the time of the purported transfer but also during the periods preceding and following it, will be taken into consideration in determining the bona fides or lack of bona fides of the purported gift or sale. A partnership may be recognized for income tax purposes as to some partners but not as to others.

(iv) Capital as a material income-producing factor. For purposes of section 704(e)(1), the determination as to whether capital is a material income-producing factor must be made by reference to all the facts of each case. Capital is a material income-producing factor if a substantial portion of the gross income of the business is attributable to the employment of capital in the business conducted by the partnership. In general, capital is not a material income-producing factor where the income of the business consists principally of fees, commissions, or other compensation for personal services performed by members or employees of the partnership. On the other hand, capital is ordinarily a material income-producing factor if the operation of the business requires substantial inventories or a substantial investment in plant, machinery, or other equipment.

(v) Capital interest in a partnership. For purposes of section 704(e), a capital interest in a partnership means an interest in the assets of the partnership, which is distributable to the owner of the capital interest upon his withdrawal from the partnership or upon liquidation of the partnership. The mere right to participate in the earnings and profits of a partnership is not a capital interest in the partnership.

(2) Basic tests as to ownership. (i) In general Whether an alleged partner who is a donee of a capital interest in a partnership is the real owner of such capital interest, and whether the donee has dominion and control over such interest, must be ascertained from all the facts and circumstances of the particular case. Isolated facts are not determinative; the reality of the donee's ownership is to be determined in the light of the transaction as a whole. The execution of legally sufficient and irrevocable deeds or other instruments of gift under State law is a factor to be taken into account but is not determinative of ownership by the donee for the purposes of section 704(e). The reality of the transfer and of the donee's ownership of the property attributed to him are to be ascertained from the conduct of the parties with respect to the alleged gift and not by any mechanical or formal test. Some of the more important factors to be considered in determining whether the donee has acquired ownership of the

capital interest in a partnership are indicated in subdivisions (ii) to (x), inclusive, of this subparagraph.

(ii) Retained controls. The donor may have retained such controls of the interest which he has purported to transfer to the donee that the donor should be treated as remaining the substantial owner of the interest. Controls of particular significance include, for example, the following:

(a) Retention of control of the distribution of amounts of income or restrictions on the distributions of amounts of income (other than amounts retained in the partnership annually with the consent of the partners, including the donee partner, for the reasonable needs of the business). If there is a partnership agreement providing for a managing partner or partners, then amounts of income may be retained in the partnership without the acquiescence of all the partners if such amounts are retained for the reasonable needs of the business.

(b) Limitation of the right of the donee to liquidate or sell his interest in the partnership at his discretion without financial detriment.

(c) Retention of control of assets essential to the business (for example, through retention of assets leased to the alleged partnership).

(d) Retention of management powers inconsistent with normal relationships among partners. Retention by the donor of control of business management or of voting control, such as is common in ordinary business relationships, is not by itself to be considered as inconsistent with normal relationships among partners, provided the donee is free to liquidate his interest at his discretion without financial detriment. The donee shall not be considered free to liquidate his interest unless, considering all the facts, it is evident that the donee is independent of the donor and has such maturity and understanding of his rights as to be capable of deciding to exercise, and capable of exercising, his right to withdraw his capital interest from the partnership.

The existence of some of the indicated controls, though amounting to less than substantial ownership retained by the donor, may be considered along with other facts and circumstances as tending to show the lack of reality of the partnership interest of the donee.

(iii) Indirect controls. Controls inconsistent with ownership by the donee may be exercised indirectly as well as directly, for example, through a separate business organization, estate, trust, individual, or other partnership. Where such indirect controls exist, the reality of the donee's interest will be determined as if such controls were exercisable directly.

(iv) Participation in management. Substantial participation by the donee in the control and management of the business (including participation in the major policy decisions affecting the business) is strong evidence of a donee partner's exercise of dominion and control over his interest. Such participation presupposes sufficient maturity and experience on the part of the donee to deal with the business problems of the partnership.

(v) Income distributions. The actual distribution to a donee partner of the entire amount or a major portion of his distributive share of the business income for the sole benefit and use of the donee is substantial evidence of the reality of the donee's interest, provided the donor has not retained controls inconsistent with real ownership by the donee. Amounts distributed are not considered to be used for the donee's sole benefit if, for example, they are deposited, loaned, or invested in such manner that the donor controls or can control the use or enjoyment of such funds.

(vi) Conduct of partnership business. In determining the reality of the donee's ownership of a capital interest in a partnership, consideration shall be given to whether the donee is actually treated as a partner in the operation of the business. Whether or not the donee has been held out publicly as a partner in the conduct of the business, in relations with customers, or with creditors or other sources of financing, is of primary significance. Other factors of significance in this connection include:

(a) Compliance with local partnership, fictitious names, and business registration statutes.

(b) Control of business bank accounts.

(c) Recognition of the donee's rights in distributions of partnership property and profits.

(d) Recognition of the donee's interest in insurance policies, leases, and other business contracts and in litigation affecting business.

(e) The existence of written agreements, records, or memoranda, contemporaneous with the taxable year or years concerned, establishing the nature of the partnership agreement and the rights and liabilities of the respective partners.

(f) Filing of partnership tax returns as required by law.

However, despite formal compliance with the above factors, other circumstances may indicate that the donor has retained substantial ownership of the interest purportedly transferred to the donee.

(vii) Trustees as partners. A trustee may be recognized as a partner for income tax purposes under the principles relating to family partnerships generally as applied to the particular facts of the trust-partnership arrangement. A trustee who is unrelated to and independent of the grantor, and who participates as a partner and receives distribution of the income distributable to the trust, will ordinarily be recognized as the legal owner of the partnership interest which he holds in trust unless the grantor has retained controls inconsistent with such ownership. However, if the grantor is the trustee, or if the trustee is amenable to the will of the grantor, the provisions of the trust instrument (particularly as to whether the trustee is subject to the responsibilities of a fiduciary), the provisions of the partnership agreement, and the conduct of the parties must all be taken into account in determining whether the trustee in a fiduciary capacity has become the real owner of the partnership interest. Where the grantor (or person amenable to his will) is the trustee, the trust may be recognized as a partner only if the grantor (or such other person) in his participation in the affairs of the partnership actively represents and protects the interests of the beneficiaries in accordance with the obligations of a fiduciary and does not subordinate such interests to the interests of the grantor. Furthermore, if the grantor (or person amenable to his will) is the trustee, the following factors will be given particular consideration:

(a) Whether the trust is recognized as a partner in business dealings with customers and creditors, and

(b) Whether, if any amount of the partnership income is not properly retained for the reasonable needs of the business, the trust's share of such amount is distributed to the trust annually and paid to the beneficiaries or reinvested with regard solely to the interests of the beneficiaries.

(viii) Interests (not held in trust) of minor children. Except where a minor child is shown to be competent to manage his own property and participate in the partnership activities in accordance with his interest in the property, a minor child generally will not be recognized as a member of a partnership unless control of the property is exercised by another person as fiduciary for the sole benefit of the child, and unless there is such judicial supervision of the conduct of the fiduciary as is required by law. The use of the child's property or income for support for which a parent is legally responsible will be considered a use for the parent's benefit. "Judicial supervision of the conduct of the fiduciary" includes filing of such accountings and reports as are required by law of the fiduciary who participates in the affairs of the partnership on behalf of the minor. A minor child will be considered as competent to manage his own property if he actually has sufficient maturity and experience to be treated by disinterested persons as competent to enter business dealings and otherwise to conduct his affairs on a basis of equality with adult persons, notwithstanding legal disabilities of the minor under State law.

(ix) Donees as limited partners. The recognition of a donee's interest in a limited partnership will depend, as in the case of other donated interests, on whether the transfer of property is real and on whether the donee has acquired dominion and control over the interest purportedly transferred to him. To be recognized for Federal income tax purposes, a limited partnership must be organized and conducted in accordance with the requirements of the applicable State limited-partnership law. The absence of services and participation in management by a donee in a limited partnership is immaterial if the limited partnership meets all the other requirements prescribed in this paragraph. If the limited partner's right to transfer or liquidate his interest is subject to substantial restrictions (for example, where the interest of the limited partner is not assignable in a real sense or where such interest may be required to be left in the business for a long term of years), or if the general partner retains any other control which substantially limits any of the rights which would ordinarily be exercisable by unrelated limited partners in normal business relationships, such restrictions on the right to transfer or liquidate, or retention of other control, will be considered strong evidence as to the lack of reality of ownership by the donee.

(x) Motive. If the reality of the transfer of interest is satisfactorily established, the motives for the transaction are generally immaterial. However, the presence or absence of a tax-avoidance motive is one of many factors to be considered in determining the reality of the ownership of a capital interest acquired by gift.

(3) Allocation of family partnership income. (i) In general. (a) Where a capital interest in a partnership in which capital is a material income-producing factor is created by gift, the donee's distributive share shall be includible in his gross income, except to the extent that such share is determined without allowance of reasonable compensation for services rendered to the partnership by the donor, and except to the extent that the portion of such distributive share attributable to donated capital is proportionately greater than the distributive share attributable to the donor's capital. For the purpose of section 704, a capital interest in a partnership purchased by one member of a family from another shall be considered to be created by gift from the seller, and the fair market value of the purchased interest shall be considered to be donated capital. The "family" of any individual, for the purpose of the preceding sentence, shall include only his spouse, ancestors, and lineal descendants, and any trust for the primary benefit of such persons.

(b) To the extent that the partnership agreement does not allocate the partnership income in accordance with (a) of this subdivision, the distributive shares of the partnership income of the donor and donee shall be reallocated by making a reasonable allowance for the services of the donor and by attributing the balance of such income (other than a reasonable allowance for the services, if any, rendered by the donee) to the partnership capital of the donor and donee. The portion of income, if any, thus attributable to partnership capital for the taxable year shall be allocated between the donor and donee in accordance with their respective interests in partnership capital.

(c) In determining a reasonable allowance for services rendered by the partners, consideration shall be given to all the facts and circumstances of the business, including the fact that some of the partners may have greater managerial responsibility than others. There shall also be considered the amount that would ordinarily be paid in order to obtain comparable services from a person not having an interest in the partnership.

(d) The distributive share of partnership income, as determined under (b) of this subdivision, of a partner who rendered services to the partnership before entering the Armed Forces of the United States shall not be diminished because of absence due to military service. Such distributive share shall be adjusted to reflect increases or decreases in the capital interest of the absent partner. However, the partners may by agreement allocate a smaller share to the absent partner due to his absence.

(ii) Special rules. (a) The provisions of subdivision (i) of this subparagraph, relating to allocation of family partnership income, are applicable where the interest in the partnership is created by gift, indirectly or directly. Where the partnership interest is created indirectly, the term "donor" may include persons other than the nominal transferor. This rule may be illustrated by the following examples:

Example (1). A father gives property to his son who shortly thereafter conveys the property to a partnership consisting of the father and the son. The partnership interest of the son may be considered created by gift and the father may be considered the donor of the son's partnership interest.

Example (2). A father, the owner of a business conducted as a sole proprietorship, transfers the business to a partnership consisting of his wife and himself. The wife subsequently conveys her interest to their son. In such case, the father, as well as the mother, may be considered the donor of the son's partnership interest.

Example (3). A father makes a gift to his son of stock in the family corporation. The corporation is subsequently liquidated. The son later contributes the property received in the liquidation of the corporation to a partnership consisting of his father and himself. In such case, for purposes of section 704, the son's partnership interest may be considered created by gift and the father may be considered the donor of his son's partnership interest.

(b) The allocation rules set forth in section 704(e) and subdivision (i) of this subparagraph apply in any case in which the transfer or creation of the partnership interest has any of the substantial characteristics of a gift. Thus, allocation may be required where transfer of a partnership interest is made between members of a family (including collaterals) under a purported purchase agreement, if the characteristics of a gift are ascertained from the terms of the purchase agreement, the terms of any loan or credit arrangements made to finance the purchase, or from other relevant data.

(c) In the case of a limited partnership, for the purpose of the allocation provisions of subdivision (i) of this subparagraph, consideration shall be given to the fact that a general partner, unlike a limited partner, risks his credit in the partnership business.

(4) Purchased interest. (i) In general. If a purported purchase of a capital interest in a partnership does not meet the requirements of subdivision (ii) of this subparagraph, the ownership by the transferee of such capital interest will be recognized only if it qualifies under the requirements applicable to a transfer of a partnership interest by gifts. In a case not qualifying under subdivision (ii) of this subparagraph, if payment of any part of the purchase price is made out of partnership earnings, the transaction may be regarded in the same light as a purported gift subject to deferred enjoyment of income. Such a transaction may be lacking in reality either as a gift or as a bona fide purchase.

(ii) Tests as to reality of purchased interests. A purchase of a capital interest in a partnership, either directly or by means of a loan or credit extended by a member of the family, will be recognized as bona fide if:

(a) It can be shown that the purchase has the usual characteristics of an arm's-length transaction, considering all relevant factors, including the terms of the purchase agreement (as to price, due date of payment, rate of interest, and security, if any) and the terms of any loan or credit arrangement collateral to the purchase agreement; the credit standing of the purchaser (apart from relationship to the seller) and the capacity of the purchaser to incur a legally binding obligation; or

(b) It can be shown, in the absence of characteristics of an arm's-length transaction, that the purchase was genuinely intended to promote the success of the business by securing participation of the purchaser in the business or by adding his credit to that of the other participants.

However, if the alleged purchase price or loan has not been paid or the obligation otherwise discharged, the factors indicated in (a) and (b) of this subdivision shall be taken into account only as an aid in determining whether a bona fide purchase or loan obligation existed.

T.D. 6175, 5/23/56, amend T.D. 6771, 11/19/64, T.D. 8065, 12/24/85, T.D. 8099, 9/8/86, T.D. 8237, 12/29/88, T.D. 8385, 12/26/91, T.D. 8500, 12/21/93, T.D. 8585, 12/27/94, T.D. 8717, 5/8/97, T.D. 9121, 4/20/2004, T.D. 9126, 5/5/2004, T.D. 9207, 5/23/2005, T.D. 9292, 10/18/2006.

PAR. 2. Section 1.704-1 is amended as follows:

1. Paragraph (b)(1)(ii)(a) is amended by adding a sentence at the end of the paragraph.

2. Paragraph (b)(1)(iii) is amended by revising the first three sentences and adding a new fourth sentence.

3. Paragraph (b)(2)(iii)(a) is redesignated as paragraph (b)(2)(iii)(a)(1) and revised.

4. A new paragraph (b)(2)(iii)(a)(2) is added.

5. The last two sentences of paragraph (b)(3)(i) are removed.

6. Paragraph (b)(5) Example 29 and Example 30 are added.

The additions and revisions read as follows:

Proposed § 1.704-1 Partner's distributive share. [*For Preamble, see ¶ 152,717*]

* * * * *

(b) * * *

(1) * * *

(ii) Effective dates. (a) * * * Paragraph (b)(2)(iii)(a)(2) and paragraph (b)(5) Example 30 of this section apply to taxable years beginning on or after the date on which final regulations are published in the Federal Register.

(iii) Effect of other sections. The determination of a partner's distributive share of income, gain, loss, deduction, or credit (or item thereof) under section 704(b) and this paragraph (b) is not conclusive as to the tax treatment of a partner with respect to such distributive share. For example, an allocation of loss or deduction to a partner that is respected under section 704(b) and this paragraph (b) may not be deductible by such partner if the partner lacks the requisite motive for economic gain (see, e.g., Goldstein v. Commissioner, 364 F.2d 734 (2d. Cir. 1966)), or may be disallowed for that taxable year (and held in suspense) if the limitations of section 465 or section 704(d) are applicable. Similarly, an allocation that is respected under section 704(b) and this paragraph (b) nevertheless may be reallocated under other provisions, such as section 482, section 704(e)(2), section 706(d) (and related assignment of income principles), and § 1.751-1(b)(2)(ii). See paragraph (b)(5) Example 29 of this section. * * *

(2) * * *

(iii) Substantiality. (a) In general. (1) Fundamental principles. Except as otherwise provided in this paragraph (b)(2)(iii), the economic effect of an allocation (or allocations) is substantial if there is a reasonable possibility that the allocation (or allocations) will affect substantially the dollar amounts to be received by the partners from the partnership, independent of tax consequences. Notwithstanding the preceding sentence, the economic effect of an allocation (or allocations) is not substantial if, at the time the allocation (or allocations) becomes part of the partnership agreement, the after-tax economic consequences of at least one partner may, in present value terms, be enhanced compared to such consequences if the allocation (or allocations) were not contained in the partnership agreement (and, thus, the allocation or allocations were allocated among the partners in accordance with the partners' interests in the partnership), and there is a strong likelihood that the after-tax economic consequences of no partner will, in present value terms, be substantially diminished compared to such consequences if the allocation (or allocations) were not contained in the partnership agreement (and, thus, the allocation or allocations were allocated among the partners in accordance with the partners' interests in the partnership). In determining the after-tax economic benefit or detriment to a partner, tax consequences that result from the interaction of the allocation with such partner's tax attributes that are unrelated to the partnership will be taken into account. See paragraph (b)(5) Examples 5 and 9 of this section. The economic effect of an allocation is not substantial in the two situations described in paragraphs (b)(2)(iii)(b) and (c) of this section. However, even if an allocation is not described therein, its economic effect may be insubstantial under the general rules stated in this paragraph (b)(2)(iii)(a). References in this paragraph (b)(2)(iii) to allocations include capital account adjustments made pursuant to paragraph (b)(2)(iv)(k) of this section.

(2) Partners that are look-through entities or members of a consolidated group. (i) Rule. For purposes of this paragraph (b)(2)(iii), in determining the after-tax economic benefit or detriment to any partner that is a look-through entity, the tax consequences that result from the interaction of the allocation with the tax attributes of any person that owns an interest in such a partner, whether directly or indirectly through one or more look-through entities, must be taken into ac-

count, and, in determining the after-tax economic benefit or detriment to any partner that is a member of a consolidated group (within the meaning of § 1.1502-1(h)), the tax consequences that result from the interaction of the allocation with the tax attributes of the consolidated group and with the tax attributes of another member with respect to a separate return year must be taken into account. See paragraph (b)(5) Example 30 of this section.

(ii) Definition. For purposes of this paragraph (b)(2)(iii)(a)(2), a look-through entity means—

(A) A partnership;

(B) A subchapter S corporation;

(C) A trust;

(D) An entity that is disregarded for Federal tax purposes, such as a qualified subchapter S subsidiary under section 1361(b)(3), an entity that is disregarded as an entity separate from its owner under §§ 301.7701-1 through 301.7701-3 of this chapter, or a qualified REIT subsidiary within the meaning of section 856(i)(2).

(E) A controlled foreign corporation, as defined in section 957(a), but only with respect to allocations of items of income, gain, loss, or deduction that enter into the corporation's computation of subpart F income or would enter into that computation if such items were allocated to the corporation (collectively, subpart F items). For purposes of this paragraph (b)(2)(iii)(a)(2)(ii)(E), the rule in paragraph (b)(2)(iii)(a)(2)(i) of this section shall apply only by taking into account the tax attributes of a person that is a United States shareholder of the controlled foreign corporation the amount of whose inclusions of gross income under section 951(a) are affected by the partnership's allocations of subpart F items (or would be affected if such items were allocated to the corporation).

* * * * *

(5) Examples. * * *

Example (29). (i) B, a domestic corporation, and C, a controlled foreign corporation, form BC, a partnership organized under the laws of country X. B and C each contribute 50 percent of the capital of BC. B and C are wholly-owned subsidiaries of A, a domestic corporation. Substantially all of BC's income would not be subpart F income if earned directly by C. The BC partnership agreement provides that, for the first fifteen years, BC's gross income will be allocated 10 percent to B and 90 percent to C, and BC's deductions and losses will be allocated 90 percent to B and 10 percent to C. The partnership agreement also provides that, after the initial fifteen year period, BC's gross income will be allocated 90 percent to B and 10 percent to C, and BC's deductions and losses will be allocated 10 percent to B and 90 percent to C.

(ii) Apart from the application of section 704(b), the Commissioner may reallocate or otherwise not respect the allocations under other sections. See paragraph (b)(1)(iii) of this section. For example, BC's allocations of gross income, deductions, and losses may be evaluated and reallocated (or not respected), as appropriate, if it is determined that the allocations result in the evasion of tax or do not clearly reflect income under section 482.

Example (30). PRS is a partnership with three partners, A, B, and C. A is a corporation that is a member of a consolidated group within the meaning of § 1.1502-1(h). B is a subchapter S corporation that is wholly-owned by D, an individual. C is a partnership with two partners, E, an individual, and F, a corporation that is member of a consolidated group within the meaning of § 1.1502-1(h). For purposes of paragraph (b)(2)(iii) of this section, in determining the after-tax economic benefit or detriment of an allocation to A, the tax consequences that result from the interaction of the allocation to A with the tax attributes of the consolidated group in which A is a member must be taken into account. In determining the after-tax economic benefit or detriment of an allocation to B, the tax consequences that result from the interaction of the allocation with the tax attributes of D must be taken into account. In determining the after-tax economic benefit or detriment of an allocation to C, the tax consequences that result from the interaction of the allocation with the tax attributes of E and the consolidated group in which F is a member must be taken into account.

PAR. 4. Section 1.704-1 is amended as follows:

1. In paragraph (b)(0), an entry is added to the table for § 1.704-1(b)(4)(xii).

2. In paragraph (b)(1)(ii)(a), a sentence is added at the end of the paragraph.

3. Paragraph (b)(2)(iv)(b)(1) is revised.

4. Paragraph (b)(2)(iv)(f)(5)(iii) is revised.

5. Paragraph (b)(4)(xii) is added.

6. Paragraph (b)(5) Example 29 is added.

The additions and revisions read as follows:

Proposed § 1.704-1 Partner's distributive share. [*For Preamble, see ¶ 152,663*]

* * * * *

(b) * * * (0) * * *

***** Substantially nonvested interests—1.704-1(b)(4)(xii)

* * * * *

(1) * * *

(ii) * * *

(a) * * * In addition, paragraph (b)(4)(xii) and paragraph (b)(5) Example 29 of this section apply to compensatory partnership interests (as defined in § 1.721-1(b)(3)) that are transferred on or after the date final regulations are published in the Federal Register.

* * * * *

(2) * * *

(iv) * * *

(b) * * *

(1) the amount of money contributed by that partner to the partnership and, in the case of a compensatory partnership interest (as defined in § 1.721-1(b)(3)) that is transferred on or after the date final regulations are published in the Federal Register, the amount included on or after that date in the partner's compensation income under section 83(a), (b), or (d)(2).

* * * * *

(f) * * *

(5) * * *

(iii) In connection with the transfer or vesting of a compensatory partnership interest (as defined in § 1.721-1(b)(3)) that is transferred on or after the date final regulations are published in the Federal Register, but only if the transfer or vesting results in the service provider recognizing income under section 83 (or would result in such recognition if the interest had a fair market value other than zero).

* * * * *

(4) * * *

(xii) Substantially nonvested interests. (a) In general. If a section 83(b) election has been made with respect to a substantially nonvested interest, the holder of the nonvested interest may be allocated partnership income, gain, loss, deduction, or credit (or items thereof) that will later be forfeited. For this reason, allocations of partnership items while the interest is substantially nonvested cannot have economic effect.

(b) Deemed Compliance with Partners' Interests in the Partnership. If a section 83(b) election has been made with respect to a substantially nonvested interest, allocations of partnership items while the interest is substantially nonvested will be deemed to be in accordance with the partners' interests in the partnership if—

(1) The partnership agreement requires that the partnership make forfeiture allocations if the interest for which the section 83(b) election is made is later forfeited; and

(2) All material allocations and capital account adjustments under the partnership agreement not pertaining to substantially nonvested partnership interests for which a section 83(b) election has been made are recognized under section 704(b).

(c) Forfeiture allocations. Forfeiture allocations are allocations to the service provider (consisting of a pro rata portion of each item) of gross income and gain or gross deduction and loss (to the extent such items are available) for the taxable year of the forfeiture in a positive or negative amount equal to—

(1) The excess (not less than zero) of the—

(i) Amount of distributions (including deemed distributions under section 752(b) and the adjusted tax basis of any property so distributed) to the partner with respect to the forfeited partnership interest (to the extent such distributions are not taxable under section 731); over

(ii) Amounts paid for the interest and the adjusted tax basis of property contributed by the partner (including deemed contributions under section 752(a)) to the partnership with respect to the forfeited partnership interest; minus

(2) The cumulative net income (or loss) allocated to the partner with respect to the forfeited partnership interest.

(d) Positive and negative amounts. For purposes of paragraph (b)(4)(xii)(c) of this section, items of income and gain are reflected as positive amounts, and items of deduction and loss are reflected as negative amounts.

(e) Exception. Paragraph (b)(4)(xii)(b) of this section shall not apply to allocations of partnership items made with respect to a substantially nonvested interest for which the holder has made a section 83(b) election if, at the time of the section 83(b) election, there is a plan that the interest will be forfeited. In such a case, the partners' distributive shares of partnership items shall be determined in accordance with the partners' interests in the partnership under paragraph (b)(3) of this section. In determining whether there is a plan that the interest will be forfeited, the Commissioner will consider all of the facts and circumstances (including the tax status of the holder of the forfeitable compensatory partnership interest).

(f) Cross references. Forfeiture allocations may be made out of the partnership's items for the entire taxable year of the forfeiture. See § 1.706-3(b) and paragraph (b)(5) Example 29 of this section.

* * * * *

(5) * * *

Example (29). (i) In Year 1, A and B each contribute cash to LLC, a newly formed limited liability company classified as a partnership for Federal tax purposes, in exchange for equal units in LLC. Under LLC's operating agreement, each unit is entitled to participate equally in the profits and losses of LLC. The operating agreement also provides that the partners' capital accounts will be determined and maintained in accordance with paragraph (b)(2)(iv) of this section, that liquidation proceeds will be distributed in accordance with the partners' positive capital account balances, and that any partner with a deficit balance in that partner's capital account following the liquidation of the partner's interest must restore that deficit to the partnership. At the beginning of Year 3, SP agrees to perform services for LLC. In connection with the performance of SP's services and a payment of $10 by SP to LLC, LLC transfers a 10% interest in LLC to SP. SP's interest in LLC is substantially nonvested (within the meaning of § 1.83-3(b)). At the time of the transfer of the LLC interest to SP, LLC's operating agreement is amended to provide that, if SP's interest is forfeited, then SP is entitled to a return of SP's $10 initial contribution, and SP's distributive share of all partnership items (other than forfeiture allocations under § 1.704-1(b)(4)(xii)) will be zero with respect to that interest for the taxable year of the partnership in which the interest was forfeited. The operating agreement is also amended to require that LLC make forfeiture allocations if SP's interest is forfeited. Additionally, the operating agreement is amended to provide that no part of LLC's compensation deduction is allocated to the service provider to whom the interest is transferred. SP makes an election under section 83(b) with respect to SP's interest in LLC. Upon receipt, the fair market value of SP's interest in LLC is $100. In each of Years 3, 4, 5, and 6, LLC has operating income of $100 (consisting of $200 of gross receipts and $100 of deductible expenses), and makes no distributions. SP forfeits SP's interest in LLC at the beginning of Year 6. At the time of the transfer of the interest to SP, there is no plan that SP will forfeit the interest in LLC.

(ii) Because a section 83(b) election is made, SP recognizes compensation income in the year of the transfer of the LLC interest. Therefore, SP recognizes $90 of compensation income in the year of the transfer of the LLC interest (the excess of the fair market value of SP's interest in LLC, $100, over the amount SP paid for the interest, $10). Under paragraph (b)(2)(iv)(b)(1) of this section, in Year 3, SP's capital account is initially credited with $100, the amount paid for the interest ($10) plus the amount included in SP's compensation income upon the transfer under section 83(b) ($90). Under §§ 1.83-6(b) and 1.721-1(b)(2), LLC does not recognize gain on the transfer of the interest to SP. LLC is entitled to a compensation deduction of $90 under section 83(h). Under the terms of the operating agreement, the deduction is allocated equally to A and B.

(iii) As a result of SP's election under section 83(b), SP is treated as a partner starting from the date of the transfer of the LLC interest to SP in Year 3. Section 1.761-1(b). In each of years 3, 4 and 5, SP's distributive share of partnership income is $10 (10% of $100), A's distributive share of partnership income is $45 (45% of $100), and B's distributive share of partnership income is $45 (45% of $100). In accordance with the operating agreement, SP's capital account is increased (to $130) by the end of Year 5 by the amounts allocated to SP, and A's and B's capital accounts are increased by the amounts allocated to A and B. Because LLC satisfies the requirements of paragraph (b)(4)(xii) of

	Basis	Value
Assets:		
Property A	$20,000	$35,000
Cash Premium	1,000	1,000
Exercise Price	15,000	15,000
Total	36,000	51,000
Liabilities and Capital:		
TM	10,000	17,000
PK	10,000	17,000
DH	16,000	17,000
Total	36,000	51,000

(ii) Under paragraphs (b)(2)(iv)(b)(2) and (b)(2)(iv)(d)(4) of this section, DH's capital account is credited with the amount paid for the option ($1,000) and the exercise price of the option ($15,000). Under the LLC agreement, however, DH is entitled to LLC capital corresponding to 100 units of LLC (1/3 of LLC's capital). Immediately after the exercise of the option, LLC's assets are cash of $16,000 ($1,000 premium and $15,000 exercise price contributed by DH) and Property A, which has a value of $35,000. Thus, the total value of LLC's assets is $51,000. DH is entitled to LLC capital equal to 1/3 of this value, or $17,000. As DH is entitled to $1,000 more LLC capital than DH's capital contributions to LLC, the provisions of paragraph (b)(2)(iv)(s) of this section apply.

(iii) Under paragraph (b)(2)(iv)(s) of this section, LLC must increase DH's capital account from $16,000 to $17,000 by, first, revaluing LLC property in accordance with the principles of paragraph (b)(2)(iv)(f) of this section and allocating the first $1,000 of book gain to DH. The net gain in LLC's assets (Property A) is $15,000 ($35,000 value less $20,000 basis). The first $1,000 of this gain must be allocated to DH, and the remaining $14,000 of this gain is allocated equally to TM and PK in accordance with the LLC agreement. Because the revaluation of LLC assets under paragraph (b)(2)(iv)(s)(2) of this section increases DH's capital account to the amount agreed on by the members, LLC is not required to make a capital account reallocation under paragraph (b)(2)(iv)(s)(3) of this section. Under paragraph (b)(2)(iv)(f)(4) of this section, the tax items from the revalued property must be allocated in accordance with section 704(c) principles.

	TM		PK		DH	
	Tax	Book	Tax	Book	Tax	Book
Capital account after exercise	$10,000	$10,000	$10,000	$10,000	$16,000	$16,000
Revaluation amount	—	$ 7,000	—	$ 7,000	—	$ 1,000
Capital account after revaluation	$10,000	$17,000	$10,000	$17,000	$16,000	$17,000

Example (21). (i) Assume the same facts as in Example 20, except that, in Year 1, LLC sells Property A for $40,000, recognizing gain of $20,000. LLC does not distribute the sale proceeds to its partners and it has no other earnings in Year 1. With the proceeds ($40,000), LLC purchases Property B, a nondepreciable property. Also assume that DH exercises the noncompensatory option at the beginning of Year 2 and that, at the time DH exercises the option, the value of Property B is $41,000. In Year 2, LLC has gross income of $3,000 and deductions of $1,500.

	Basis	Value
Assets:		
Property B	$40,000	$41,000
Cash	16,000	16,000
Total	56,000	57,000
Liabilities and Capital:		
TM	20,000	19,000
PK	20,000	19,000
DH	16,000	19,000
Total	56,000	57,000

(ii) Under paragraphs (b)(2)(iv)(b)(2) and (b)(2)(iv)(d)(4) of this section, DH's capital account is credited with the amount paid for the option ($1,000) and the exercise price of the option ($15,000). Under the LLC agreement, however, DH is entitled to LLC capital corresponding to 100 units of LLC (1/3 of LLC's capital). Immediately after the exercise of the option, LLC's assets are $16,000 cash ($1,000 option premium and $15,000 exercise price contributed by DH) and Property B, which has a value of $41,000. Thus, the total value of LLC's assets is $57,000. DH is entitled to LLC capital equal to 1/3 of this amount, or $19,000. As DH is entitled to $3,000 more LLC capital than DH's capital contributions to LLC, the provisions of paragraph (b)(2)(iv)(s) of this section apply.

(iii) Under paragraph (b)(2)(iv)(s) of this section, LLC must increase DH's capital account from $16,000 to $19,000 by, first, revaluing LLC property in accordance with the principles of paragraph (b)(2)(iv)(f) of this section, and allocating the $1,000 of book gain from the revaluation to DH. This brings DH's capital account to $17,000. Second, under paragraph (b)(2)(iv)(s)(3) of this section, LLC must reallocate $2,000 of capital from the existing partners (TM and PK) to DH to bring DH's capital account to $19,000 (the capital account reallocation). As TM and PK share equally in all items of income, gain, loss, and deduction of LLC, each member's capital account is reduced by ½ of the $2,000 reduction ($1,000).

(iv) Under paragraph (b)(2)(iv)(s)(4) of this section, beginning in the year in which the option is exercised, LLC must make corrective allocations so as to take into account the capital account reallocation. In Year 2, LLC has gross income of $3,000 and deductions of $1,500. The book gross income of $3,000 is shared equally by TM, PK, and DH. For tax purposes, however, LLC must allocate all of its gross income ($3,000) to DH. LLC's deductions ($1,500) must be allocated equally among TM, PK, and DH. Under paragraph (b)(2)(iv)(f)(4) of this section, the tax items from Property B must be allocated in accordance with section 704(c) principles.

	TM		PK		DH	
	Tax	Book	Tax	Book	Tax	Book
Capital account after exercise	$20,000	$20,000	$20,000	$20,000	$16,000	$16,000
Revaluation	—	—	—	—	—	$ 1,000
Capital account after revaluation	$20,000	$20,000	$20,000	$20,000	$16,000	$17,000
Capital account reallocation.	—	($ 1,000)	—	($ 1,000)	—	$ 2,000
Capital account after capital account reallocation	$20,000	$19,000	$20,000	$19,000	$16,000	$19,000
Income allocation (Yr. 2)	—	$ 1,000	—	$ 1,000	$ 3,000	$ 1,000
Deduction allocation (Yr. 2)	($ 500)	($ 500)	($ 500)	($ 500)	($ 500)	($ 500)
Capital account at end of year 2	$19,500	$19,500	$19,500	$19,500	$18,500	$19,500

Example (22). (i) In Year 1, AC and NE each contribute cash of $10,000 to LLC, a newly formed limited liability company classified as a partnership for Federal tax purposes, in exchange for 100 units in LLC. Under the LLC agreement, each unit is entitled to participate equally in the profits and losses of LLC. LLC uses the cash contributions to purchase two non-depreciable properties, Property A and Property B, for $10,000 each. Also in Year 1, at a time when Property A and Property B are still valued at $10,000 each, LLC issues an option to DR. The option allows DR to buy 100 units in LLC for an exercise price of $15,000 in Year 2. DR pays $1,000 to LLC for the issuance of the option. Assume that the LLC agreement requires that, on the exercise of a noncompensatory option, LLC comply with the rules of paragraph (b)(2)(iv)(s) of this section, and that all material allocations and capital account adjustments under the LLC agreement not pertaining to noncompensatory options are recognized under section 704(b). Also assume that DR's option is a noncompensatory option under § 1.721-2(d), and that DR is not treated as a partner with respect to the option.

(ii) Prior to the exercise of DR's option, ML contributes $17,000 to LLC for 100 units in LLC. At the time of ML's contribution, Property A has a value of $30,000 and a basis of $10,000, Property B has a value of $5,000 and a basis of $10,000, and the fair market value of DR's option is $2,000.

(iii) Upon ML's admission to the partnership, the capital accounts of AC and NE (which were $10,000 each prior to ML's admission) are, in accordance with paragraph (b)(2)(iv)(f) of this section, adjusted upward to reflect their shares of the unrealized appreciation in the partnership's assets. Under paragraph (b)(2)(iv)(f)(1) of this section, those adjustments must be based on the fair market value of LLC property (taking section 7701(g) into account) on the date of the adjustment. The fair market value of partnership property ($36,000) must be reduced by the consideration paid by DR to the partnership to acquire the option ($1,000) (under paragraph (b)(2)(iv)(f)(1) of this section), and the excess of the fair market value of the option as of the date of the adjustment over the consideration paid by DR to acquire the option ($1,000) (under paragraph (b)(2)(iv)(h)(2) of this section), but only to the extent of the unrealized appreciation in LLC property ($15,000). Therefore, the revaluation adjustments must be based on a value of $34,000. Accordingly, AC and NE's capital accounts must be increased to $17,000. This $1,000 reduction is allocated entirely to Property A, the only asset having unrealized appreciation. Therefore, the book value of Property A is $29,000. The $19,000 of built-in gain in Property A and the $5,000 of built-in loss in Property B must be allocated equally between AC and NE in accordance with section 704(c) principles.

	Assets basis	Value	Option Adjustment	704(c) Book
Property A	$10,000	$30,000	($ 1,000)	$29,000
Property B	$10,000	$ 5,000	0	$ 5,000
Cash	$ 1,000	$ 1,000	0	$ 1,000
Subtotal	$21,000	$36,000	($ 1,000)	$35,000
Cash contributed by ML	$17,000	$17,000	0	$17,000
Total	$38,000	$53,000	($ 1,000)	$52,000

Liabilities and Capital	Tax	Value
AC	$10,000	$17,000
NE	$10,000	$17,000
ML	$17,000	$17,000
Option	$ 1,000	$ 2,000
Total	$38,000	$53,000

(iv) After the admission of ML, when Property A still has a value of $30,000 and a basis of $10,000 and Property B still has a value of $5,000 and a basis of $10,000, DR exercises the option. On the exercise of the option, DR's capital account is credited with the amount paid for the option ($1,000) and the exercise price of the option ($15,000).

Under the LLC agreement, however, DR is entitled to LLC capital corresponding to 100 units of LLC (1/4 of LLC's capital). Immediately after the exercise of the option, LLC's assets are worth $68,000 ($15,000 contributed by DR, plus the value of LLC assets prior to the exercise of the option, $53,000). DR is entitled to LLC capital equal to 1/4 of this value, or $17,000. As DR is entitled to $1,000 more LLC capital than DR's capital contributions to LLC, the provisions of paragraph (b)(2)(iv)(s) of this section apply.

(v) Under paragraph (b)(2)(iv)(s) of this section, the LLC must increase DR's capital account from $16,000 to $17,000 by, first, revaluing LLC property in accordance with the principles of paragraph (b)(2)(iv)(f) of this section and allocating the first $1,000 of book gain to DR. The net increase in the value of LLC properties since the previous revaluation is $1,000 (the difference between the actual value of Property A, $30,000, and the book value of Property A, $29,000). The entire $1,000 of book gain is allocated to DR. Because the revaluation of LLC assets under paragraph (b)(2)(iv)(s)(2) of this section increases DR's capital account to the amount agreed on by the members, the LLC is not required to make a capital account reallocation under paragraph (b)(2)(iv)(s)(3) of this section. Under paragraph (b)(2)(iv)(f)(4) of this section, the tax items from Properties A and B must be allocated in accordance with section 704(c) principles.

	AC		NE		ML		DR	
	Book	Tax	Tax	Book	Tax	Book	Tax	Book
Capital account after admission of ML	$10,000	$17,000	$10,000	$17,000	$17,000	$17,000	—	—
Capital account after exercise of DH's option	$10,000	$17,000	$10,000	$17,000	$17,000	$17,000	$16,000	$16,000
Revaluation	—	—	—	—	—	—	—	$ 1,000
Capital account after revaluation	$10,000	$17,000	$10,000	$17,000	$17,000	$17,000	$16,000	$17,000

Example (23). (i) On the first day of Year 1, MS, VH, and SR form LLC, a limited liability company classified as a partnership for Federal tax purposes. MS and VH each contribute $10,000 cash to LLC for 100 units of common interest in LLC. SR contributes $10,000 cash for a convertible preferred interest in LLC. SR's convertible preferred interest entitles SR to receive an annual allocation and distribution of cumulative LLC net profits in an amount equal to 10 percent of SR's unreturned capital. SR's convertible preferred interest also entitles SR to convert, in year 3, SR's preferred interest into 100 units of common interest. If SR converts, SR has the right to the same share of LLC capital as SR would have had if SR had held the 100 units of common interest since the formation of LLC. Under the LLC agreement, each unit of common interest has an equal right to share in any LLC net profits that remains after payment of the preferred return. Assume that the LLC agreement requires that, on the exercise of a noncompensatory option, LLC comply with the rules of paragraph (b)(2)(iv)(s) of this section, and that all material allocations and capital account adjustments under the LLC agreement not pertaining to noncompensatory options are recognized under section 704(b). Also assume that SR's right to convert the preferred interest into a common interest qualifies as a noncompensatory option under § 1.721-2(d), and that, prior to the exercise of the conversion right, SR is not treated as a partner with respect to the conversion right.

(ii) LLC uses the $30,000 to purchase Property Z, a property that is depreciable on a straight-line basis over 15 years. In each of Years 1 and 2, LLC has net income of $2,500, comprised of $4,500 of gross receipts and $2,000 of depreciation. It allocates and distributes $1,000 of this net income to SR in each year. LLC allocates, but does not distribute, the remaining $1,500 of net income equally to MS and VH in each year.

	MS		VH		SR	
	Tax	Book	Tax	Book	Tax	Book
Capital account upon formation	$10,000	$10,000	$10,000	$10,000	$10,000	$10,000
Allocation of income Years 1 and 2	$ 1,500	$ 1,500	$ 1,500	$ 1,500	$ 2,000	$ 2,000
Distributions Years 1 and 2	—	—	—	—	($ 2,000)	($ 2,000)
Capital account end of Year 2	$11,500	$11,500	$11,500	$11,500	$10,000	$10,000

(iii) At the beginning of Year 3, when Property Z has a value of $38,000 and a basis of $26,000 ($30,000 original basis less $4,000 of depreciation) and LLC has accumulated undistributed cash of $7,000 ($9,000 gross receipts less $2,000 distributions), SR converts SR's preferred interest into a common interest. Under paragraphs (b)(2)(iv)(b)(2) and (b)(2)(iv)(d)(4) of this section, SR's capital account after the conversion equals SR's capital account before the conversion, $10,000. On the conversion of the preferred interest, however, SR is entitled to LLC capital corresponding to 100 units of common interest in LLC (1/3 of LLC's capital). At the time of the conversion, the total value of LLC assets is $45,000. SR is entitled to LLC capital equal to 1/3 of this value, or $15,000. As SR is entitled to $5,000 more LLC capital than SR's capital account immediately after the conversion, the provisions of paragraph (b)(2)(iv)(s) of this section apply.

	Basis	Value
Assets:		
Property Z	$26,000	$38,000
Undistributed Income	7,000	7,000
Total	33,000	45,000
Liabilities and Capital:		
MS	11,500	15,000
VH	11,500	15,000

SR	10,000	15,000
Total	33,000	45,000

(iv) Under paragraph (b)(2)(iv)(s) of this section, LLC must increase SR's capital account from $10,000 to $15,000 by, first, revaluing LLC property in accordance with the principles of paragraph (b)(2)(iv)(f) of this section, and allocating the first $5,000 of book gain from that revaluation to SR. The net unrealized gain in LLC's assets (Property Z) is $12,000 ($38,000 value less $26,000 basis). The first $5,000 of this gain must be allocated to SR. The remaining $7,000 of that gain must be allocated equally to MS and VH in accordance with the LLC agreement. Because the revaluation of LLC assets under paragraph (b)(2)(iv)(s)(2) of this section increases SR's capital account to the amount agreed on by the members, LLC is not required to make a capital account reallocation under paragraph (b)(2)(iv)(s)(3) of this section. Under paragraph (b)(2)(iv)(f)(4) of this section, the tax items from the revalued property must be allocated in accordance with section 704(c) principles.

	MS		VH		SR	
	Tax	Book	Tax	Book	Tax	Book
Capital account prior to conversion	$11,500	$11,500	$11,500	$11,500	$10,000	$10,000
Revaluation on conversion	—	$ 3,500	—	$ 3,500	—	$ 5,000
Capital account after conversion	$11,500	$15,000	$11,500	$15,000	$10,000	$15,000

Example (24). (i) On the first day of Year 1, AK and JP each contribute cash of $10,000 to LLC, a newly formed limited liability company classified as a partnership for Federal tax purposes, in exchange for 100 units in LLC. Immediately after its formation, LLC borrows $10,000 from JS. Under the terms of the debt instrument, interest of $1,000 is payable annually and principal is repayable in five years. Throughout the term of the indebtedness, JS has the right to convert the debt instrument into 100 units in LLC. If JS converts, JS has the right to the same share of LLC capital as JS would have had if JS had held 100 units in LLC since the formation of LLC. Under the LLC agreement, each unit participates equally in the profits and losses of LLC and has an equal right to share in LLC capital. Assume that the LLC agreement requires that, on the exercise of a noncompensatory option, LLC comply with the rules of paragraph (b)(2)(iv)(s) of this section, and that all material allocations and capital account adjustments not pertaining to noncompensatory options are recognized under section 704(b). Also assume that JS's right to convert the debt into an interest in LLC qualifies as a noncompensatory option under § 1.721-2(d), and that, prior to the exercise of the conversion right, JS is not treated as a partner with respect to the convertible debt.

(ii) LLC uses the $30,000 to purchase Property D, property that is depreciable on a straight-line basis over 15 years. In each of Years 1, 2, and 3, LLC has net income of $2,000, comprised of $5,000 of gross receipts, $2,000 of depreciation, and interest expense (representing payments of interest on the loan from JS) of $1,000. LLC allocates, but does not distribute, this income equally to AK and JP.

	AK		JP		JS	
	Tax	Book	Tax	Book	Tax	Book
Initial capital account	$10,000	$10,000	$10,000	$10,000	—	—
Year 1 net income	$ 1,000	$ 1,000	$ 1,000	$ 1,000	—	—
Years 2 net income	$ 1,000	$ 1,000	$ 1,000	$ 1,000	—	—
Years 3 net income	$ 1,000	$ 1,000	$ 1,000	$ 1,000	—	—
Year 4 initial capital account	$13,000	$13,000	$13,000	$13,000	0	0

(iii) At the beginning of year 4, at a time when Property D, the LLC's only asset, has a value of $33,000 and basis of $24,000 ($30,000 original basis less $6,000 depreciation in Years 1 through 3), and LLC has accumulated undistributed cash of $12,000 ($15,000 gross receipts less $3,000 of interest payments) in LLC, JS converts the debt into a 1/3 interest in LLC. Under paragraphs (b)(2)(iv)(b)(2) and (b)(2)(iv)(d)(4) of this section, JS's capital account after the conversion is the adjusted basis of the debt immediately before JS's conversion of the debt, $10,000, plus any accrued but unpaid qualified stated interest on the debt, $0. On the conversion of the debt, however, JS is entitled to receive LLC capital corresponding to 100 units of LLC (1/3 of LLC's capital). At the time of the conversion, the total value of LLC's assets is $45,000. JS is entitled to LLC capital equal to 1/3 of this value, or $15,000. As JS is entitled to $5,000 more LLC capital than JS's capital contribution to LLC ($10,000), the provisions of paragraph (b)(2)(iv)(s) of this section apply.

	Basis	Value
Assets:		
Property D	$24,000	$33,000
Cash	$12,000	$12,000
Total	$36,000	$45,000
Liabilities and Capital:		
AK	$13,000	$15,000
JP	$13,000	$15,000
JS	$10,000	$15,000
Total	$36,000	$45,000

(iv) Under paragraph (b)(2)(iv)(s) of this section, LLC must increase JS's capital account from $10,000 to $15,000 by, first, revaluing LLC property in accordance with the principles of paragraph (b)(2)(iv)(f) of this section, and allocating the first $5,000 of book gain from that revaluation to JS. The net unrealized gain in LLC's assets (Property D) is $9,000 ($33,000 value less $24,000 basis). The first $5,000 of this gain must be allocated to JS, and the remaining $4,000 of that gain must be allocated equally to AK and JP in accordance with the LLC agreement. Because the revaluation of LLC assets under paragraph (b)(2)(iv)(s)(2) of this section increases JS's capital account to the amount agreed upon by the members, LLC is not required to make a capital account reallocation under paragraph (b)(2)(iv)(s)(3) of this section. Under paragraph (b)(2)(iv)(f)(4) of this section, the tax items from the revalued property must be allocated in accordance with section 704(c) principles.

	AK		JP		JS	
	Tax	Book	Tax	Book	Tax	Book
Year 4 capital account prior to exercise	$13,000	$13,000	$13,000	$13,000	0	0
Capital account after exercise	$13,000	$13,000	$13,000	$13,000	$10,000	$10,000
Revaluation	—	$ 2,000	—	$ 2,000	—	$ 5,000
Capital account after revaluation	$13,000	$15,000	$13,000	$15,000	$10,000	$15,000

Proposed § 1.704-1 Partner's distributive share. [*For Preamble, see ¶ 150,829*]

* * * * *

(c) Special capital account adjustments. * * *

(4) Special rules. * * *

(iv) Nonrecourse debt. Allocations of loss or deduction (or item thereof) attributable to nonrecourse debt which is secured by partnership property do not have substantial economic effect since the creditor bears the economic burden of any losses attributable thereto. Thus, such allocations must be made in accordance with the partnersinterests in the partnership. A loss or deduction (or item thereof) is attributable to nonrecourse debt which is secured by partnership property to the extent of the excess of the outstanding principal balance of such debt (excluding any portion of such principal balance which would not be treated as an amount realized under section 1001 and paragraph (a) of § 1.1001-2 if such debt were foreclosed upon) over the adjusted basis of such property. This excess represents the minimum taxable gain (whether taxable as capital gain or as ordinary income) which would be recognized by the partnership if the nonrecourse debt were foreclosed upon and the partnership property securing such debt were transferred to the creditor in satisfaction thereof; it is hereinafter referred to as the "minimum gain." Allocations of loss or deduction (or item thereof) attributable to nonrecourse debt which is secured by partnership property shall be deemed to be made in accordance with the partnersinterests in the partnership if requirements (a), (b), and (c) of paragraph (b)(2)(ii) of this section are satisfied, or if the capital account equivalence test of paragraph (b)(2)(iv)(b) of this section is satisfied, or if requirements (a) and (b) of paragraph (b)(2)(ii) of this section are satisfied and:

(a) The allocation of loss or deduction (or item thereof) attributable to nonrecourse debt which is secured by partnership property does not cause the sum of the deficit capital account balances of the partner or partners receiving such allocations (excluding the portion of such deficit balances that must be restored to the partnership upon liquidation) to exceed the minimum gain (determined at the end of the partnership taxable year to which the allocations relate), and

(b) The partnership agreement provides that the partner or partners with deficit capital account balances resulting in whole or in part from allocations of loss or deduction (or item thereof) attributable to nonrecourse debt which is secured by partnership property shall, to the extent possible, be allocated income or gain (or item thereof) in an amount no less than the minimum gain and at a time no later than the time at which the minimum gain is reduced below the sum of such deficit capital account balances. See example (17) of paragraph (b)(5) of this section. If the partnersinterests in allocations of loss or deduction (or item thereof) attributable to nonrecourse debt which is secured by partnership property are varied among taxable years in order to reduce the overall tax liabilities of the partners (other than variations resulting solely from liabilities of the partner (other than variations resulting solely from the admission or retirement of a partner), allocations made pursuant to such variation shall not be deemed to be in accordance with the partnersinterests in the partnership under this subdivision. See example (17)(vi) of paragraph (b)(5) of this section. For purposes of computing the sum of the partnersdeficit capital account balances referred to in requirement (a) above, if any property (including cash) is held by the partnership at the end of the partnership taxable year and there is a reasonable expectation that such property will be distributed to a partner (other than in liquidation of the partnership) prior to a corresponding increase in such partner's capital account, such property shall be treated as having been distributed to such partner on the last day of such taxable year. Also, for purposes of requirement (a) above, the minimum gain shall be reduced by the cost of any capital improvements to be made to the subject property and the amount of any principal payments to be made with respect to the nonrecourse debt secured by such property to the extent there is a reasonable expectation that such improvements or payments will, without regard to this sentence, reduce the minimum gain below the sum of the deficit capital account balances referred to in requirement (a) above. If, after the application of the previous two sentences, an event nonetheless causes the sum of the partnersdeficit capital account balances referred to in requirements (a) above to exceed the minimum gain, requirements (a) and (b) above shall be deemed satisfied provided partnership income, gain, loss, and deduction (or item thereof) are thereafter allocated in a manner which reduces and eliminates the excess as rapidly as possible. For purposes of this paragraph, the term "nonrecourse debt" means a partnership liability with respect to which none of the partners has any personal liability as determined under paragraph (e) of § 1.752-1.

* * * * *

• ***Caution:*** Example (17) is reproduced below in connection with the segment of the proposed regs reproduced above on nonrecourse debt. To the extent other topics are covered in the example, the rules controlling them have been superseded by the final regs.]

Example (17). (i) JS and WN form a general partnership to acquire and operate an apartment building. JS and WN each contribute $100,000 to the partnership which obtains an $800,000 nonrecourse mortgage and purchases the apartment building (on leased land) for $1,000,000. No principal payments with respect to the nonrecourse obligation are required for 5 years. The partnership agreement provides that all income, gain, loss, and deduction will be allocated equally between JS and WN, with the exception of cost recovery deductions which will be allocated entirely to JS. The agreement also states that allocations will be reflected by appropriate adjustments to the partnerscapital accounts (maintained in accordance with paragraph (b)(2)(iv) of this section), and that liquidation proceeds are, throughout the term of the partnership, to be distributed in accordance with capital account balances, but that upon liquidation neither partner is required to restore to the partnership the deficit balance in his capital account for distribution to partners with positive capital account balances. In year 1, there is a $100,000 cost recovery deduction, all of which is charged to JScapital account, and the partnership has no other taxable income or loss for the year. In year 2 the partnership has another $100,000 cost recovery deduction and no other taxable income or loss. Since the principal balance of the nonrecourse mortgage does not exceed the adjusted basis of the property, neither the year 1 or year 2 cost recovery deduction is attributable to the nonrecourse obligation. The allocation for year 1 has substantial economic effect. The allocation in year 2 of the $100,000 cost recovery deduction to JS does not have substantial economic effect because the economic risk of loss associated with such cost recovery deduction is borne entirely by WN. Therefore, the $100,000 cost recovery deduction in year 2 is reallocated to WN pursuant to paragraph (b)(3) of this section.

(ii) Assume the same facts as in (i) except that the partnership agreement is amended to require any partner with a deficit capital account following the distribution of liquidation proceeds to restore the amount of such deficit to the partnership (as set forth in paragraph (b)(2)(ii)(c) of this section). In this case, the allocation of an additional $100,000 cost recovery deduction in year 2 to JS has substantial economic effect. The result in this example would be the same if the liability to restore capital account deficits is omitted from the partnership agreement but an identical liability is imposed under State law.

(iii) Assume the same facts as in (i). In year 3, the partnership has no taxable income or loss except for another $100,000 cost recovery deduction. The allocation of this deduction to JS (or to WN) has no economic effect since the risk of depreciation in excess of the partnersaggregate investment in the property is borne solely by the nonrecourse lender. Since the partnership agreement does not require JS to be allocated subsequent income and gain under the rule contained in paragraph (b)(4)(iv)(b) of this section, the allocation of the $100,000 cost recovery deduction to JS will not be deemed to be in accordance with his interest in the partnership, and must be reallocated in accordance with the partnersinterests in the partnership.

(iv) Assume the facts in (iii) except that the partnership agreement also provides that pursuant to paragraph (b)(4)(iv) of this section JS will be allocated partnership income and gain in an amount equal to the deficit balance in JScapital account and that such allocations will coincide, in amount and time, with any reduction of the principal balance of the nonrecourse debt. Since the principal balance of the nonrecourse obligation ($800,000) exceeds the adjusted basis ($700,000) by $100,000 and JS is bearing the burden of taxation of taxable income and gain in an amount at least equal to the deficit balance of his capital account, requirements (a) and (b) of paragraph (b)(4)(iv) of this section are satisfied and the allocation of the $100,000 cost recovery deduction to JS in year 3 is deemed to be in accordance with his interest in the partnership.

(v) Assume the same facts as in (iii) except that the partnership agreement is amended to require any partner with a deficit capital account following the distribution of liquidation proceeds to restore the amount of such deficit to the partnership (as set forth in paragraph (b)(2)(ii)(c) of this section). If the property were foreclosed upon at the end of year 3, there would be $100,000 gain ($800,000 nonrecourse debt less $700,000 adjusted basis), which would be allocated equally between JS and WN. JS would then have a deficit capital account of $50,000 which he would be required to contribute to the partnership to satisfy WN's positive $50,000 capital account. Accordingly, the allocation of the $100,000 cost recovery deduction to JS in year 3 will, under paragraph (b)(4)(iv) of this section, be deemed to be in accordance with the partnersinterests in the partnership.

(vi) Assume the same facts as in (iv) and that in year 4 the partnership has no taxable income or loss except for another $100,000 cost recovery deduction. In order to reduce the overall tax liabilities of the partners, the partnership agreement is amended at the beginning of year 4 to allocate the year 4 cost recovery deduction to WN. In addition, the agreement is amended to allocate partnership income or gain to WN in an amount equal to the deficit balance in his capital account and to require that such allocations coincide, in amount and time, with any principal reduction in the amount of nonrecourse debt. Since the allocations of loss or deduction attributable to nonrecourse debt are varied in year 4 in order to reduce the overall tax liabilities of the partners, the year 4 allocation will not be deemed to be in accordance with the partnersinterests in the partnership under paragraph (b)(4)(iv) of this section and the $100,000 cost recovery deduction must be reallocated in accordance with the partnersactual interests in the partnership.

(vii) Assume the same facts as in (iv) except that in a taxable year of the partnership after the cost recovery deductions have been taken by JS, but before the property is disposed of, the partnership agreement is amended by deleting the provisions which require gain and income to be charged back to JS. Thus, under the amended agreement, JS is no longer required to bear the burden of taxation of the taxable income and gain in an amount at least equal to his deficit capital account balance. Under these facts, any allocation of income, gain, loss, or deduction made after deletion of the chargeback provisions has no substantial economic effect. As a result, income, gain, loss, and deductions must be allocated in accordance with the partnersinterests in the partnership. Under the rule of paragraph (b)(4)(vi) of this section, the interest of JS in the partnership taxable gain and income is deemed to be that interest which is consistent with the original gain and income chargeback provisions, and, therefore, gain and income is allocated to JS and WN in accordance with those provisions.

(viii) Assume the same facts as in (ii). Any tax preference under section 57(a)(12) attributable to the partnership's year 1 and year 2 cost recovery deductions shall be taken into account solely by JS. If during year 1 and year 2 the partnership's cost recovery deductions are instead allocated 75 percent to JS and 25 percent to WN (and all other income, gain, loss, and deduction is allocated equally between JS and WN), the tax preference attributable to such cost recovery deductions shall be taken into account 75 percent by JS and 25 percent by WN. If the partnership agreement instead provides that all taxable income or loss is allocated equally between JS and WN, the tax preference attributable to the cost recovery deductions shall be taken into account equally between JS and WN. In this case, if the partnership has a $100,000 cost recovery deduction in year 1 and an additional operating loss of $100,000 in year 1, and purports to categorize the $100,000 loss allocated to JS as being attributable to the cost recovery deduction and the $100,000 loss allocated to WN as being attributable to the operating loss, such allocations will not be recognized and each partner will be allocated one-half of such operating loss and one-half of such cost recovery deduction, and each partner shall take into account one-half of the tax preference attributable to the cost recovery deduction.

* * * * *

§ 7.704-1 Partner's distributive share.

(a) [Reserved]

(b) [Reserved]

(c) [Reserved]

(d) Limitation on allowance of losses.

(1) [Reserved]

(2) [Reserved]

(3) (i) Section 213(e) of the Tax Reform Act of 1976 amended section 704(d) of the Internal Revenue Code relating to the deductions by partners of losses incurred by a partnership. A partner is entitled to deduct the share of partnership loss to the extent of the adjusted basis of the partner's interest in the partnership. As amended, section 704(d) provides, in general, that the adjusted basis of a partner's interest in the partnership for the purpose of deducting partnership losses shall not include any portion of a partnership liability for which the partner has no personal liability. This restriction, however, does not apply to any activity to the extent that section 465 of the Code applies nor to any partnership whose principal activity is investing in real property, other than mineral property. Section 465 does not apply to corporations other than a subchapter S corporation or a personal holding company.

(ii) The restrictions in the amendment to section 704(d) will not apply to any corporate partner with respect to liabilities incurred in an activity described in section 465(c)(1). In all other respects the restrictions in the amendment will apply to all corporate partners unless the partnership's principal activity is investment in real property, other than mineral property.

T.D. 7445, 12/17/76.

§ 1.704-2 Allocations attributable to nonrecourse liabilities.

(a) Table of contents. This paragraph contains a listing of the major headings of this § 1.704-2.

§ 1.704-2 Allocations attributable to nonrecourse liabilities.

(3) Nonrecourse debt proceeds distributed from the lower-tier partnership to the upper-tier partnership.

(4) Nonrecourse deductions of lower-tier partnership treated as depreciation by upper-tier partnership.

(5) Coordination with partner nonrecourse debt rules.

(l) Effective dates.

(1) In general.

(i) Prospective application.

(ii) Partnerships subject to temporary regulations.

(iii) Partnerships subject to former regulations.

(2) Special rule applicable to pre-January 30, 1989, related party nonrecourse debt.

(3) Transition rule for pre-March 1, 1984, partner nonrecourse debt.

(4) Election.

(m) Examples.

(b) General principles and definitions. *(1) Definition of and allocations of nonrecourse deductions.* Allocations of losses, deductions, or section 705(a)(2)(B) expenditures attributable to partnership nonrecourse liabilities ("nonrecourse deductions") cannot have economic effect because the creditor alone bears any economic burden that corresponds to those allocations. Thus, nonrecourse deductions must be allocated in accordance with the partners' interests in the partnership. Paragraph (e) of this section provides a test that deems allocations of nonrecourse deductions to be in accordance with the partners' interests in the partnership. If that test is not satisfied, the partners' distributive shares of nonrecourse deductions are determined under § 1.704-1(b)(3), according to the partners' overall economic interests in the partnership. See also paragraph (i) of this section for special rules regarding the allocation of deductions attributable to nonrecourse liabilities for which a partner bears the economic risk of loss (as described in paragraph (b)(4) of this section).

(2) Definition of and allocations pursuant to a minimum gain chargeback. To the extent a nonrecourse liability exceeds the adjusted tax basis of the partnership property it encumbers, a disposition of that property will generate gain that at least equals that excess ("partnership minimum gain"). An increase in partnership minimum gain is created by a decrease in the adjusted tax basis of property encumbered by a nonrecourse liability below the amount of that liability and by a partnership nonrecourse borrowing that exceeds the adjusted tax basis of the property encumbered by the borrowing. Partnership minimum gain decreases as reductions occur in the amount by which the nonrecourse liability exceeds the adjusted tax basis of the property encumbered by the liability. Allocations of gain attributable to a decrease in partnership minimum gain (a "minimum gain chargeback," as required under paragraph (f) of this section) cannot have economic effect because the gain merely offsets nonrecourse deductions previously claimed by the partnership. Thus, to avoid impairing the economic effect of other allocations, allocations pursuant to a minimum gain chargeback must be made to the partners that either were allocated nonrecourse deductions or received distributions of proceeds attributable to a nonrecourse borrowing. Paragraph (e) of this section provides a test that, if met, deems allocations of partnership income pursuant to a minimum gain chargeback to be in accordance with the partners' interests in the partnership if property encumbered by a nonrecourse liability is reflected on the partnership's books at a value that differs from its adjusted tax basis paragraph (d)(3) of this section provides that minimum gain is determined with reference to the property's book basis. See also paragraph (i)(4) of this section for special rules regarding the minimum gain chargeback requirement for partner nonrecourse debt.

(3) Definition of nonrecourse liability. "Nonrecourse liability" means a nonrecourse liability as defined in § 1.752-1(a)(2) or a § 1.752-7 liability (as defined in § 1.752-7(b)(3)(i)) assumed by the partnership from a partner on or after June 24, 2003.

(4) Definition of partner nonrecourse debt. "Partner nonrecourse debt" or "partner nonrecourse liability" means any partnership liability to the extent the liability is nonrecourse for purposes of § 1.1001-2, and a partner or related person (within the meaning of § 1.752-4(b)) bears the economic risk of loss under § 1.752-2 because, for example, the partner or related person is the creditor or a guarantor.

(c) Amount of nonrecourse deductions. The amount of nonrecourse deductions for a partnership taxable year equals the net increase in partnership minimum gain during the year (determined under paragraph (d) of this section), reduced (but not below zero) by the aggregate distributions made during the year of proceeds of a nonrecourse liability that are allocable to an increase in partnership minimum gain (determined under paragraph (h) of this section). See paragraph (m), Examples (1)(i) and (vi), (2), and (3) of this section. However, increases in partnership minimum gain resulting from conversions, refinancings, or other changes to a debt instrument (as described in paragraph (g)(3)) do not generate nonrecourse deductions. Generally, nonrecourse deductions consist first of certain depreciation or cost recovery deductions and then, if necessary, a pro rata portion of other partnership losses, deductions, and section 705(a)(2)(B) expenditures for that year; excess nonrecourse deductions are carried over. See paragraphs (j)(1)(ii) and (iii) of this section for more specific ordering rules. See also paragraph (m), Example (1)(iv) of this section.

(d) Partnership minimum gain. *(1) Amount of partnership minimum gain.* The amount of partnership minimum gain is determined by first computing for each partnership nonrecourse liability any gain the partnership would realize if it disposed of the property subject to that liability for no consideration other than full satisfaction of the liability, and then aggregating the separately computed gains. The amount of partnership minimum gain includes minimum gain arising from a conversion, refinancing, or other change to a debt instrument, as described in paragraph (g)(3) of this section, only to the extent a partner is allocated a share of that minimum gain. For any partnership taxable year, the net increase or decrease in partnership minimum gain is determined by comparing the partnership minimum gain on the last day of the immediately preceding taxable year with the partnership minimum gain on the last day of the current taxable year. See paragraph (m), Examples (1)(i) and (iv), (2), and (3) of this section.

(2) Property subject to more than one liability. (i) In general. If property is subject to more than one liability, only the portion of the property's adjusted tax basis that is allocated to a nonrecourse liability under paragraph (d)(2)(ii) of this section is used to compute minimum gain with respect to that liability.

(ii) Allocating liabilities. If property is subject to two or more liabilities of equal priority, the property's adjusted tax basis is allocated among the liabilities In proportion to their outstanding balances. If property is subject to two or more liabilities of unequal priority, the adjusted tax basis is allocated first to the liability of the highest priority to the extent of its outstanding balance and then to each liability in descending order of priority to the extent of its outstanding balance, until fully allocated. See paragraph (m), Example (1)(v) and (vii) of this section.

(3) Partnership minimum gain if there is a book/tax disparity. If partnership property subject to one or more nonrecourse liabilities is, under § 1.704-1(b)(2)(iv)(d), (f), or (r), reflected on the partnership's books at a value that differs from its adjusted tax basis, the determinations under this section are made with reference to the property's book value. See section 704(c) and § 1.704-1(b)(4)(i) for principles that govern the treatment of a partner's share of minimum gain that is eliminated by the revaluation. See also paragraph (m), Example (3) of this section.

(4) Special rule for year of revaluation. If the partners' capital accounts are increased pursuant to § 1.704-1(b)(2)(iv)(d), (f), or (r) to reflect a revaluation of partnership property subject to a nonrecourse liability, the net increase or decrease in partnership minimum gain for the partnership taxable year of the revaluation is determined by:

(i) First calculating the net decrease or increase in partnership minimum gain using the current year's book values and the prior year's partnership minimum gain amount; and

(ii) Then adding back any decrease in minimum gain arising solely from the revaluation.

See paragraph (m), Example (3)(iii) of this section. If the partners' capital accounts are decreased to reflect a revaluation, the net increases or decreases in partnership minimum gain are determined in the same manner as in the year before the revaluation, but by using book values rather than adjusted tax bases. See section 7701(g) and § 1.704-1(b)(2)(iv)(f)(1) (property being revalued cannot be booked down below the amount of any nonrecourse liability to which the property is subject).

(e) Requirements to be satisfied. Allocations of nonrecourse deductions are deemed to be in accordance with the partners' interests in the partnership only if—

(1) Throughout the full term of the partnership requirements (1) and (2) of § 1.704-1(b)(2)(ii)(b) are satisfied (i.e., capital accounts are maintained in accordance with § 1.704-1(b)(2)(iv) and liquidating distributions are required to be made in accordance with positive capital account balances), and requirement (3) of either § 1.704-1(b)(2)(ii)(b) or § 1.704-1(b)(2)(ii)(d) is satisfied (i.e., partners with deficit capital accounts have an unconditional deficit restoration obligation or agree to a qualified income offset);

(2) Beginning in the first taxable year of the partnership in which there are nonrecourse deductions and thereafter throughout the full term of the partnership, the partnership agreement provides for allocations of nonrecourse deductions in a manner that is reasonably consistent with allocations that have substantial economic effect of some other significant partnership item attributable to the property securing the nonrecourse liabilities;

(3) Beginning in the first taxable year of the partnership that it has nonrecourse deductions or makes a distribution of proceeds of a nonrecourse liability that are allocable to an increase in partnership minimum gain, and thereafter throughout the full term of the partnership, the partnership agreement contains a provision that complies with the minimum gain chargeback requirement of paragraph (f) of this section; and

(4) All other material allocations and capital account adjustments under the partnership agreement are recognized under § 1.704-1(b) (without regard to whether allocations of adjusted tax basis and amount realized under section 613A(c)(7)(D) are recognized under § 1.704-1(b)(4)(v)).

(f) Minimum gain chargeback requirement. *(1) In general.* If there is a net decrease in partnership minimum gain for a partnership taxable year, the minimum gain chargeback requirement applies and each partner must be allocated items of partnership income and gain for that year equal to that partner's share of the net decrease in partnership minimum gain (within the meaning of paragraph (g)(2)).

(2) Exception for certain conversions and refinancings. A partner is not subject to the minimum gain chargeback requirement to the extent the partner's share of the net decrease in partnership minimum gain is caused by a recharacterization of nonrecourse partnership debt as partially or wholly recourse debt or partner nonrecourse debt, and the partner bears the economic risk of loss (within the meaning of § 1.752-2) for the liability.

(3) Exception for certain capital contributions. A partner is not subject to the minimum gain chargeback requirement to the extent the partner contributes capital to the partnership that is used to repay the nonrecourse liability or is used to increase the basis of the property subject to the nonrecourse liability, and the partner's share of the net decrease in partnership minimum gain results from the repayment or the increase to the property's basis. See paragraph (m), Example (1)(iv) of this section.

(4) Waiver for certain income allocations that fail to meet minimum chargeback requirement if minimum gain chargeback distorts economic arrangement. In any taxable year that a partnership has a net decrease in partnership minimum gain, if the minimum gain chargeback requirement would cause a distortion in the economic arrangement among the partners and it is not expected that the partnership will have sufficient other income to correct that distortion, the Commissioner has the discretion, if requested by the partnership, to waive the minimum gain chargeback requirement. The following facts must be demonstrated in order for a request for a waiver to be considered:

(i) The partners have made capital contributions or received net income allocations that have restored the previous nonrecourse deductions and the distributions attributable to proceeds of a nonrecourse liability; and

(ii) The minimum gain chargeback requirement would distort the partners' economic arrangement as reflected in the partnership agreement and as evidenced over the term of the partnership by the partnership's allocations and distributions and the partners' contributions.

(5) Additional exceptions. The Commissioner may, by revenue ruling, provide additional exceptions to the minimum gain chargeback requirement.

(6) Partnership items subject to the minimum gain chargeback requirement. Any minimum gain chargeback required for a partnership taxable year consists first of certain gains recognized from the disposition of partnership property subject to one or more partnership nonrecourse liabilities and then if necessary consists of a pro rata portion of the partnership's other items of income and gain for that year. If the amount of the minimum gain chargeback requirement exceeds the partnership's income and gains for the taxable year, the excess carries over. See paragraphs (j)(2)(i) and (iii) of this section for more specific ordering rules.

(7) Examples. The following examples illustrate the provisions in § 1.704-2(f).

Example (1). Partnership AB consists of two partners, limited partner A and general partner B. Partner A contributes $90 and Partner B contributes $10 to the partnership. The partnership agreement has a minimum gain chargeback provision and provides that, except as otherwise required by section 704(c), all losses will be allocated 90 percent to A and 10 percent to B; and that all income will be allocated first to restore previous losses and thereafter 50 percent to A and 50 percent to B. Distributions are made first to return initial capital to the partners and then 50 percent to A and 50 percent to B. Final distributions are made in accordance with capital account balances. The partnership borrows $200 on a nonrecourse basis from an unrelated third party and purchases an asset for $300. The partnership's only tax item for each of the first three years is $100 of depreciation on the asset. A's and B's shares of minimum gain (under paragraph (g) of this section) and deficit capital account balances are $180 and $20 respectively at the end of the third year. In the fourth year, the partnership earns $400 of net operating income and allocates the first $300 to restore the previous losses (i.e., $270 to A and $30 to B); the last $100 is allocated $50 each. The partnership distributes $200 of the available cash that same year; the first $100 is distributed $90 to A and $10 to B to return their capital contributions; the last $100 is distributed $50 each to reflect their ratio for sharing profits.

	A	B
Capital account on formation	$90	$10
Less: net loss in years 1-3	($270)	($30)
Capital account at end of year 3	($180)	($20)
Allocation of operating income to restore nonrecourse deductions	$180	20
Allocation of operating income to restore capital contributions	$90	$10
Allocation of operating income to reflect profits	$50	$50

	A	B
Capital accounts after allocation of operating income	$140	$60
Distribution reflecting capital contribution	($90)	($10)
Distribution in profit-sharing ratio	($50)	($50)
Capital accounts following distribution	($0)	($0)

In the fifth year, the partnership sells the property for $300 and realizes $300 of gain. $200 of the proceeds are used to pay the nonrecourse lender. The partnership has $300 to distribute, and the partners expect to share that equally. Absent a waiver under paragraph (f)(4) of this section, the minimum gain chargeback would require the partnership to allocate the first $200 of the gain $180 to A and $20 to B, which would distort their economic arrangement. This allocation, together with the allocation of the $100 profit $50 to each partner, would result in A having a positive capital account balance of $230 and B having a positive capital account balance of $70. The allocation of income in year 4 in effect anticipated the minimum gain chargeback that did not occur until year 5. Assuming the partnership would not have sufficient other income to correct the distortion that would otherwise result, the partnership may request that the Commissioner exercise his or her discretion to waive the minimum gain chargeback requirement and recognize allocations that would allow A and B to share equally the gain on the sale of the property. These allocations would bring the partners' capital accounts to $150 each, allowing them to share the last $300 equally. The Commissioner may in his or her discretion, permit this allocation pursuant to paragraph (f)(4) of this section because the minimum gain chargeback would distort the partners' economic arrangement over the term of the partnership as reflected in the partnership agreement and as evidenced by the partners' contributions and the partnership's allocations and distributions.

Example (2). A and B form a partnership, contribute $25 each to the partnership's capital, and agree to share all losses and profits 50 percent each. Neither partner has an unconditional deficit restoration obligation and all the requirements in paragraph (e) of this section are met. The partnership obtains a nonrecourse loan from an unrelated third party of $100 and purchases two assets, stock for $50 and depreciable property for $100. The nonrecourse loan is secured by the partnership's depreciable property. The partnership generates $20 of depreciation in each of the first five years as its only tax item. These deductions are properly treated as nonrecourse deductions and the allocation of these deductions 50 percent to A and 50 percent to B is deemed to be in accordance with the partners' interests in the partnership. At the end of year five, A and B each have a $25 deficit capital account and a $50 share of partnership minimum gain. In the beginning of year six, (at the lender's request), A guarantees the entire nonrecourse liability. Pursuant to paragraph (d)(1) of this section, the partnership has a net decrease in minimum gain of $100 and under paragraph (g)(2) of this section. A's and B's shares of that net decrease are $50 each. Under paragraph (f)(1) of this section (the minimum gain chargeback requirement), B is subject to a $50 minimum gain chargeback. Because the partnership has no gross income in year six, the entire $50 carries over as a minimum gain chargeback requirement to succeeding taxable years until their is enough income to cover the minimum gain chargeback requirement. Under the exception to the minimum gain chargeback in paragraph (f)(2) of this section. A is not subject to a minimum gain chargeback for A's $50 share of the net decrease because A bears the economic risk of loss for the liability. Instead, A's share of partner nonrecourse debt minimum gain is $50 pursuant to paragraph (i)(3) of this section. In year seven, the partnership earns $100 of net operating income and uses the money to repay the entire $100 nonrecourse debt (that A has guaranteed). Under paragraph (i)(3) of this section, the partnership has a net decrease in partner nonrecourse debt minimum gain of $50. B must be allocated $50 of the operating income pursuant to the carried over minimum gain chargeback requirement: pursuant to paragraph (i)(4) of this section, the other $50 of operating income must be allocated to A as a partner nonrecourse debt minimum gain chargeback.

(g) Shares of partnership minimum gain. *(1) Partner's share of partnership minimum gain.* Except as increased in paragraph (g)(3) of this section, a partner's share of partnership minimum gain at the end of any partnership taxable year equals:

(i) The sum of nonrecourse deductions allocated to that partner (and to that partner's predecessors in interest) up to that time and the distributions made to that partner (and to that partner's predecessors in interest) up to that time of proceeds of a nonrecourse liability allocable to an increase in partnership minimum gain (see paragraph (h)(1) of this section); minus

(ii) The sum of that partner's (and that partner's predecessors in interest) aggregate share of the net decreases in partnership minimum gain plus their aggregate share of decreases resulting from revaluations of partnership property subject to one or more partnership nonrecourse liabilities.

For purposes of § 1.704-1(b)(2)(ii)(d), a partner's share of partnership minimum gain is added to the limited dollar amount, if any, of the deficit balance in the partner's capital account that the partner is obligated to restore. See paragraph (m), Examples (1)(i) and (3)(i) of this section.

(2) Partner's share of the net decrease in partnership minimum gain. A partner's share of the net decrease in partnership minimum gain is the amount of the total net decrease multiplied by the partner's percentage share of the partnership's minimum gain at the end of the immediately preceding taxable year. A partner's share of any decrease in partnership minimum gain resulting from a revaluation of partnership property equals the increase in the partner's capital account attributable to the revaluation to the extent the reduction in minimum gain is caused by the revaluation. See paragraph (m), Example (3)(ii) of this section.

(3) Conversions of recourse or partner nonrecourse debt into nonrecourse debt. A partner's share of partnership minimum gain is increased to the extent provided in this paragraph (g)(3) if a recourse or partner nonrecourse liability becomes partially or wholly nonrecourse. If a recourse, liability becomes a nonrecourse liability, a partner has a share of the partnership's minimum gain that results from the conversion equal to the partner's deficit capital account (determined under § 1.704-1(b)(2)(iv)) to the extent the partner no longer bears the economic burden for the entire deficit capital account as a result of the conversion. For purposes of the preceding sentence, the determination of the extent to which a partner bears the economic burden for a deficit capital account is made by determining the consequences to the partner in the case of a complete liquidation of the partnership immediately after the conversion applying the rules described in § 1.704-1(b)(2)(iii)(c) that deem the value of partnership property to equal its basis, taking into account section 7701(g) in the case of property that secures nonrecourse indebtedness. If a partner nonrecourse debt becomes a nonrecourse liability, the partner's share of partnership minimum gain is increased to the extent the partner is not subject to the minimum gain chargeback requirement under paragraph (i)(4) of this section.

(h) Distribution of nonrecourse liability proceeds allocable to an increase in partnership minimum gain. *(1) In general.* If during its taxable year a partnership makes a distribution to the partners allocable to the proceeds of a nonrecourse liability, the distribution is allocable to an increase in partnership minimum gain to the extent the increase results from encumbering partnership property with aggregate nonrecourse liabilities that exceed the property's adjusted tax basis. See paragraph (m), Example (1)(vi) of this section. If the net increase in partnership minimum gain for a partnership taxable year is allocable to more than one nonrecourse liability, the net increase is allocated among the liabilities in proportion to the amount each liability contributed to the increase in minimum gain.

(2) Distribution allocable to nonrecourse liability proceeds. A partnership may use any reasonable method to determine whether a distribution by the partnership to one or more partners is allocable to proceeds of a nonrecourse liability. The rules prescribed under § 1.163-8T for allocating debt proceeds among expenditures (applying those rules to the partnership as if it were an individual) constitute a reasonable method for determining whether the nonrecourse liability proceeds are distributed to the partners and the partners to whom the proceeds are distributed.

(3) Option when there is an obligation to restore. A partnership may treat any distribution to a partner of the proceeds of a nonrecourse liability (that would otherwise be allocable to an increase in partnership minimum gain) as a distribution that is not allocable to an increase in partnership minimum gain to the extent the distribution does not cause or increase a deficit balance in the partner's capital account that exceeds the amount the partner is otherwise obligated to restore (within the meaning of § 1.704-1(b)(2)(ii)(c)) as of the end of the partnership taxable year in which the distribution occurs.

(4) Carryover to immediately succeeding taxable year. The carryover rule of this paragraph applies if the net increase in partnership minimum gain for a partnership taxable year that is allocable to a nonrecourse liability under paragraph (h)(2) of this section exceeds the distributions allocable to the proceeds of the liability ("excess allocable amount"), and all or part of the net increase in partnership minimum gain for the year is carried over as an increase in partnership minimum gain for the immediately succeeding taxable year (pursuant to paragraph (j)(1)(iii) of this section). If the carryover rule of this paragraph applies, the excess allocable amount (or the amount carried over under paragraph (j)(1)(iii) of this section, if less) is treated in the succeeding taxable year as an increase in partnership minimum gain that arose in that year as a result of incurring the nonrecourse liability to which the excess allocable amount is attributable. See paragraph (m), Example (1)(vi) of this section. If for a partnership taxable year there is an excess allocable amount with respect to more than one partnership nonrecourse liability, the excess allocable amount is allocated to each liability in proportion to the amount each liability contributed to the increase in minimum gain.

(i) Partnership nonrecourse liabilities where a partner bears the economic risk of loss. *(1) In general.* Partnership losses, deductions, or section 705(a)(2)(B) expenditures that are attributable to a particular partner nonrecourse liability ("partner nonrecourse deductions." as defined in paragraph (i)(2) of this section) must be allocated to the partner that bears the economic risk of loss for the liability. If more than one partner bears the economic risk of loss for a partner nonrecourse liability, any partner nonrecourse deductions attributable to that liability must be allocated among the partners according to the ratio in which they bear the economic risk of loss. If partners bear the economic risk of loss for different portions of a liability, each portion is treated as a separate partner nonrecourse liability.

(2) Definition of and determination of partner nonrecourse deductions. For any partnership taxable year. the amount of partner nonrecourse deductions with respect to a partner nonrecourse debt equals the net increase during the year in minimum gain attributable to the partner nonrecourse debt ("partner nonrecourse debt minimum gain"), reduced (but not below zero) by proceeds of the liability distributed during the year to the partner bearing the economic risk of loss for the liability that are both attributable to the liability and allocable to an increase in the partner nonrecourse debt minimum gain. See paragraph (m), Example (1)(viii) and (ix) of this section The determination of which partnership items constitute the partner nonrecourse deductions with respect to a partner nonrecourse debt must be made in a manner consistent with the provisions of paragraphs (c) and (j)(1)(i) and (iii) of this section.

(3) Determination of partner nonrecourse debt minimum gain. For any partnership taxable year, the determination of partner nonrecourse debt minimum gain and the net increase or decrease in partner nonrecourse debt minimum gain must

be made in a manner consistent with the provisions of paragraphs (d) and (g)(3) of this section.

(4) Chargeback of partner nonrecourse debt minimum gain. If during a partnership taxable year there is a net decrease in partner nonrecourse debt minimum gain, any partner with a share of that partner nonrecourse debt minimum gain (determined under paragraph (i)(5) of this section) as of the beginning of the year must be allocated items of income and gain for the year (and, if necessary, for succeeding years) equal to that partner's share of the net decrease in the partner nonrecourse debt minimum gain. A partner's share of the net decrease in partner nonrecourse debt minimum gain is determined in a manner consistent with the provisions of paragraph (g)(2) of this section. A partner is not subject to this minimum gain chargeback, however, to the extent the net decrease in partner nonrecourse debt minimum gain arises because a partner nonrecourse liability becomes partially or wholly a nonrecourse liability. The amount that would otherwise be subject to the partner nonrecourse debt minimum gain chargeback is added to the partner's share of partnership minimum gain under paragraph (g)(3) of this section. In addition, rules consistent with the provisions of paragraphs (f)(2),(3),(4), and (5) of this section apply with respect to partner nonrecourse debt in appropriate circumstances. The determination of which items of partnership income and gain must be allocated pursuant to this paragraph (i)(4) is made in a manner that is consistent with the provisions of paragraph (f)(6) of this section. See paragraph (j)(2)(ii) and (iii) of this section for more specific rules.

(5) Partner's share of partner nonrecourse debt minimum gain. A partner's share of partner nonrecourse debt minimum gain at the end of any partnership taxable year is determined in a manner consistent with the provisions of paragraphs (g)(1) and (g)(3) of this section with respect to each particular partner nonrecourse debt for which the partner bears the economic risk of loss. For purposes of § 1.704-1(b)(2)(ii)(d), a partner's share of partner nonrecourse debt minimum gain is added to the limited dollar amount, if any, of the deficit balance in the partner's capital account that the partner is obligated to restore, and the partner is not otherwise considered to have a deficit restoration obligation as a result of bearing the economic risk of loss for any partner nonrecourse debt. See paragraph (m), Example (1)(viii) of this section.

(6) Distribution of partner nonrecourse debt proceeds allocable to an increase in partner nonrecourse debt minimum gain. Rules consistent with the provisions of paragraph (h) of this section apply to distributions of the proceeds of partner nonrecourse debt.

(j) Ordering Rules. For purposes of this section, the following ordering rules apply to partnership items. Notwithstanding any other provision in this section and § 1.704-1, allocations of partner nonrecourse deductions, nonrecourse deductions, and minimum gain chargebacks are made before any other allocations.

(1) Treatment of partnership losses and deductions. (i) Partner nonrecourse deductions. Partnership losses, deductions, and section 705(a)(2)(B) expenditures are treated as partner nonrecourse deductions in the amount determined under paragraph (i)(2) of this section (determining partner nonrecourse deductions) in the following order:

(A) First, depreciation or cost recovery deductions with respect to property that is subject to partner nonrecourse debt;

(B) Then, if necessary, a pro rata portion of the partnership's other deductions, losses, and section 705(a)(2)(B) items.

Depreciation or cost recovery deductions with respect to property that is subject to a partnership nonrecourse liability is first treated as a partnership nonrecourse deduction and any excess is treated as a partner nonrecourse deduction under this paragraph (j)(1)(i).

(ii) Partnership nonrecourse deductions. Partnership losses, deductions, and section 705(a)(2)(B) expenditures are treated as partnership nonrecourse deductions in the amount determined under paragraph (c) of this section (determining nonrecourse deductions) in the following order:

(A) First, depreciation or cost recovery deductions with respect to property that is subject to partnership nonrecourse liabilities;

(B) Then, if necessary, a pro rata portion of the partnership's other deductions, losses, and section 705(a)(2)(B) items.

Depreciation or cost recovery deductions with respect to property that is subject to partner nonrecourse debt is first treated as a partner nonrecourse deduction and any excess is treated as a partnership nonrecourse deduction under this paragraph (j)(1)(ii). Any other item that is treated as a partner nonrecourse deduction will in no event be treated as a partnership nonrecourse deduction.

(iii) Carryover to succeeding taxable year. If the amount of partner nonrecourse deductions or nonrecourse deductions exceeds the partnership's losses, deductions, and section 705(a)(2)(B) expenditures for the taxable year (determined under paragraphs (j)(1)(i) and (ii) of this section), the excess is treated as an increase in partner nonrecourse debt minimum gain or partnership minimum gain in the immediately succeeding partnership taxable year. See paragraph (m), Example (1)(vi) of this section.

(2) Treatment of partnership income and gains. (i) Minimum gain chargeback. Items of partnership income and gain equal to the minimum gain chargeback requirement (determined under paragraph (f) of this section) are allocated as a minimum gain chargeback in the following order:

(A) First, gain from the disposition of property subject to partnership nonrecourse liabilities;

(B) Then, if necessary, a pro rata portion of the partnership's other items of income and gain for that year.

Gain from the disposition of property subject to partner nonrecourse debt is allocated to satisfy a minimum gain chargeback requirement for partnership nonrecourse debt only to the extent not allocated under paragraph (j)(2)(ii) of this section.

(ii) Chargeback attributable to decrease in partner nonrecourse debt minimum gain. Items of partnership income and gain equal to the partner nonrecourse debt minimum gain chargeback (determined under paragraph (i)(4) of this section) are allocated to satisfy a partner nonrecourse debt minimum gain chargeback in the following order:

(A) First, gain from the disposition of property subject to partner nonrecourse debt;

(B) Then, if necessary, a pro rata portion of the partnership's other items of income and gain for that year.

Gain from the disposition of property subject to a partnership nonrecourse liability is allocated to satisfy a partner nonrecourse debt minimum gain chargeback only to the extent not allocated under paragraph (j)(2)(i) of this section. An item of partnership income and gain that is allocated to satisfy a minimum gain chargeback under paragraph (f) of this section is not allocated to satisfy a minimum gain chargeback under paragraph (i)(4).

(iii) Carryover to succeeding taxable year. If a minimum gain chargeback requirement (determined under paragraphs (f) and (i)(4) of this section) exceeds the partnership's income and gains for the taxable year, the excess is treated as a minimum gain chargeback requirement in the immediately succeeding partnership taxable years until fully charged back.

(k) Tiered partnerships. For purposes of this section, the following rules determine the effect on partnership minimum gain when a partnership ("upper-tier partnership") is a partner in another partnership ("lower-tier partnership").

(1) Increase in upper-tier partnership's minimum gain. The sum of the nonrecourse deductions that the lower-tier partnership allocates to the upper-tier partnership for any taxable year of the upper-tier partnership, and the distributions made during that taxable year from the lower-tier partnership to the upper-tier partnership of proceeds of nonrecourse debt that are allocable to an increase in the lower-tier partnership's minimum gain, is treated as an increase in the upper-tier partnership's minimum gain.

(2) Decrease in upper-tier partnership's minimum gain. The upper-tier partnership's share for its taxable year of the lower-tier partnership's net decrease in its minimum gain is treated as a decrease in the upper-tier partnership's minimum gain for that taxable year.

(3) Nonrecourse debt proceeds distributed from the lower-tier partnership to the upper-tier partnership. All distributions from the lower-tier partnership to the upper-tier partnership during the upper-tier partnership's taxable year of proceeds of a nonrecourse liability allocable to an increase in the lower-tier partnership's minimum gain are treated as proceeds of a nonrecourse liability of the upper-tier partnership. The increase in the upper-tier partnership's minimum gain (under paragraph (k)(1) of this section) attributable to the receipt of those distributions is, for purposes of paragraph (h) of this section, treated as an increase in the upper-tier partnership's minimum gain arising from encumbering property of the upper-tier partnership with a nonrecourse liability of the upper-tier partnership.

(4) Nonrecourse deductions of lower-tier partnership treated as depreciation by upper-tier partnership. For purposes of paragraph (c) of this section, all nonrecourse deductions allocated by the lower-tier partnership to the upper-tier partnership for the upper-tier partnership's taxable year are treated as depreciation or cost recovery deductions with respect to property owned by the upper-tier partnership and subject to a nonrecourse liability of the upper-tier partnership with respect to which minimum gain increased during the year by the amount of the nonrecourse deductions.

(5) Coordination with partner nonrecourse debt rules. The lower-tier partnership's liabilities that are treated as the upper-tier partnership's liabilities under § 1.752-4(a) are treated as the upper-tier partnership's liabilities for purposes of applying paragraph (i) of this section. Rules consistent with the provisions of paragraphs (k)(1) through (k)(4) of this section apply to determine the allocations that the upper-tier partnership must make with respect to any liability that constitutes a nonrecourse debt for which one or more partners of the upper-tier partnership bear the economic risk of loss.

(l) Effective dates. *(1) In general.* (i) Prospective application. Except as otherwise provided in this paragraph (l), this section applies for partnership taxable years beginning on or after December 28, 1991. For the rules applicable to taxable years beginning after December 29, 1988, and before December 28, 1991, see former § 1.704-1T(b)(4)(iv). For the rules applicable to taxable years beginning on or before December 29, 1988, see former § 1.704-1(b)(4)(iv).

(ii) Partnerships subject to temporary regulations. If a partnership agreement entered into after December 29, 1988, and before December 28, 1991, or a partnership agreement entered into on or before December 29, 1988, that elected to apply former § 1.704-1T(b)(4)(iv) (as contained in the CFR edition revised as of April 1, 1991), complied with the provisions of former § 1.704-1T(b)(4)(iv) before December 28, 1991—

(A) The Provisions of former § 1.704-1T(b)(4)(iv) continue to apply to the partnership for any taxable year beginning on or after December 28, 1991, (unless the partnership makes an election under paragraph (l)(4) of this section) and ending before any subsequent material modification to the partnership agreement; and

(B) The provisions of this section do not apply to the partnership for any of those taxable years.

(iii) Partnerships subject to former regulations. If a partnership agreement entered into on or before December 29, 1988, complied with the provisions of former § 1.704-1(b)(4)(iv)(d) on or before that date—

(A) The provisions of former § 1.704-1(b)(4)(iv)(a) through (f) continue to apply to the partnership for any taxable year beginning after that date (unless the partnership made an election under § 1.704-1T(b)(4)(iv)(m)(4) in a partnership taxable year ending before December 28, 1991, or makes an election under paragraph (l)(4) of this section) and ending before any subsequent material modification to the partnership agreement; and

(B) The provisions of this section do not apply to the partnership for any of those taxable years.

(iv) Paragraph (f)(2), the first sentence of paragraph (g)(3), and the third sentence of paragraph (i)(4) of this section apply to liabilities incurred or assumed by a partnership on or after October 11, 2006 other than liabilities incurred or assumed by a partnership pursuant to a written binding contract in effect prior to October 11, 2006. The rules applicable to liabilities incurred or assumed (or subject to a binding contract in effect) prior to October 11, 2006 are contained in this section in effect prior to October 11, 2006. (See 26 CFR part 1 revised as of April 1, 2006.)

(2) Special rule applicable to pre-January 30, 1989, related party of nonrecourse debt. For purposes of this section and former § 1.704-1T(b)(4)(iv), if—

(i) A partnership liability would, but for this paragraph (l)(2) of this section, constitute a partner nonrecourse debt; and

(ii) Sections 1.752-1 through -3 or former §§ 1.752-1T through -3T (whichever is applicable) do not apply to the liability;

the liability is, notwithstanding paragraphs (i) and (b)(4) of this section, treated as a nonrecourse liability of the partnership, and not as a partner nonrecourse debt, to the extent the liability would be so treated under this section (or § 1.704-1T(b)(4)(iv)) if the determination of the extent to which one or more partners bears the economic risk of loss for the liability under § 1.752-1 or former § 1.752-1T were made without regard to the economic risk of loss that any partner would otherwise be considered to bear for the liability by reason of any obligation undertaken or interest as a creditor acquired prior to January 30, 1989, by a person related to the partner (within the meaning of § 1.752-4(b) or former § 1.752-1T(h)). For purposes of the preceding sentence, if a related person undertakes an obligation or acquires an interest as a creditor on or after January 30, 1989, pursuant to a written binding contract in effect prior to January 30, 1989, and at all times thereafter, the obligation or interest as a creditor is treated as if it were undertaken or acquired prior to January 30, 1989. However, for partnership taxable years beginning on or after December 29, 1991, a pre-January 30, 1989, liability, other than a liability subject to paragraph (l)(3) of this section or former § 1.704-1T(b)(4)(iv)(m)(3) (whichever is applicable), that is treated as grandfathered under former §§ 1.752-1T through -3T (whichever is applicable) will be treated as a nonrecourse liability for purposes of this section provided that all partners in the partnership consistently treat the liability as nonrecourse for partnership taxable years beginning on or after December 29, 1988.

(3) Transition rule for pre-March 1, 1984, partner nonrecourse debt. If a partnership liability would, but for this paragraph (l)(3) or former § 1.704-1T(b)(4)(iv), constitute a partner nonrecourse debt and the liability constitutes grandfathered partner nonrecourse debt that is appropriately treated as a nonrecourse liability of the partnership under § 1.752-1 (as in effect prior to December 29, 1988)—

(i) The liability is, notwithstanding paragraphs (i) and (b)(4) of this section, former § 1.704-1T(b)(4)(iv), and former § 1.704-1(b)(4)(iv), treated as a nonrecourse liability of the partnership for purposes of this section and for purposes of former § 1.704-1T(b)(4)(iv) and former § 1.704-1(b)(4)(iv) to the extent of the amount, if any, by which the smallest outstanding balance of the liability during the period beginning at the end of the first partnership taxable year ending on or after December 31, 1986, and ending at the time of any determination under this paragraph (l)(3)(i) or former § 1.704-1T(b)(4)(iv)(m)(3)(i) exceeds the aggregate amount of the adjusted basis (or book value) of partnership property allocable to the liability (determined in accordance with former § 1.704-1(b)(4)(iv)(c)(1) and (2) at the end of the first partnership taxable year ending on or after December 31, 1986); and

(ii) In applying this section to the liability, former § 1.704-1(b)(4)(iv)(c)(1) and (2) is applied as if all of the adjusted basis of partnership property allocable to the liability is allocable to the portion of the liability that is treated as a partner nonrecourse debt and as if none of the adjusted basis of partnership property that is allocable to the liability is allocable to the portion of the liability that is treated as a nonrecourse liability under this paragraph (l)(3) and former § 1.704-1T(b)(4)(iv)(m)(3)(1).

For purposes of the preceding sentence, a grandfathered partner debt is any partnership liability that was not subject to former §§ 1.752-1T and -3T but that would have been subject to those sections under § 1.752-4T(b) if the liability had arisen (other than pursuant to a written binding contract) on or after March 1, 1984. A partnership liability is not considered to have been subject to §§ 1.752-2T and -3T solely because a portion of the liability was treated as a liability to which those sections apply under § 1.752-4(e).

(4) Election. A partnership may elect to apply the provisions of this section to the first taxable year of the partnership ending on or after December 28, 1991. An election under this paragraph (l)(4) is made by attaching a written statement to the partnership return for the first taxable year of the partnership ending on or after December 28, 1991. The written statement must include the name, address, and taxpayer identification number of the partnership making the statement and must declare that an election is made under this paragraph (l)(4).

(m) Examples. The principles of this section are illustrated by the following examples:

Example (1). Nonrecourse deductions and partnerships minimum gain. For Example 1, unless otherwise provided, the following facts are assumed. LP, the limited partner, and GP, the general partner, form a limited partnership to acquire and operate a commercial office building. LP contributes $180,000, and GP contributes $20,000. The partnership obtains an $800,000 nonrecourse loan and purchases the building (on leased land) for $1,000,000. The nonrecourse loan is secured only by the building, and no principal payments are due for 5 years. The partnership agreement provides that GP will be required to restore any deficit balance in GP's capital account following the liquidation of GP's interest (as set forth in § 1.704-1(b)(2)(ii)(b)(3)), and LP will not be required to restore any deficit balance in LP's capital account following the liquidation of LP's interest. The partnership agreement contains the following provisions required by paragraph (e) of this section: a qualified income offset (as defined in § 1.704-1(b)(2)(ii)(d)); a minimum gain chargeback (in accordance with paragraph (f) of this section); a provision that the partners' capital accounts will be determined and maintained in accordance with § 1.704-1(b)(2)(ii)(b)(1); and a provision that distributions will be made in accordance with partners' positive capital account balances (as set forth in § 1.704-1(b)(2)(ii)(b)(2)). In addition, as of the end of each partnership taxable year discussed herein, the items described in § 1.704-1(b)(2)(ii)(d)(4), (5), and (6) are not reasonably expected to cause or increase a deficit balance in LP's capital account. The partnership agreement provides that, except as otherwise required by its qualified income offset and minimum gain chargeback provisions, all partnership items will be allocated 90 percent to LP and 10 percent to GP until the first time when the partnership has recognized items of income and gain that exceed the items of loss and deduction it has recognized over its life, and all further partnership items will be allocated equally between LP and GP. Finally, the partnership agreement provides that all distributions, other than distributions in liquidation of the partnership or of a partner's interest in the partnership, will be made 90 percent to LP and 10 percent to GP until a total of $200,000 has been distributed, and thereafter all the distributions will be made equally to LP and GP. In each of the partnership's first 2 taxable years, it generates rental income of $95,000, operating expenses (including land lease payments) of $10,000, interest expense of $80,000, and a depreciation deduction of $90,000, resulting in a net taxable loss of $85,000 in each of those years. The allocations of these losses 90 percent to LP and 10 percent to GP have substantial economic effect.

	LP	GP
Capital account on formation	$180,000	$20,000
Less: net loss in years 1 and 2 . . .	(153,000)	(17,000)
Capital account at end of year 2	$27,000	$3,000

In the partnership's third taxable year, it again generates rental income of $95,000, operating expenses of $10,000, interest expense of $80,000, and a depreciation deduction of $90,000, resulting in net taxable loss of $85,000. The partnership makes no distributions.

(i) Calculation of nonrecourse deductions and partnership minimum gain. If the partnership were to dispose of the building in full satisfaction of the nonrecourse liability at the end of the third year, it would realize $70,000 of gain ($800,000 amount realized less $730,000 adjusted tax basis). Because the amount of partnership minimum gain at the end of the third year (and the net increase in partnership minimum gain during the year) is $70,000, there are partnership nonrecourse deductions for that year of $70,000, consisting of depreciation deductions allowable with respect to the building of $70,000. Pursuant to the partnership agreement, all partnership items comprising the net taxable loss of $85,000, including the $70,000 nonrecourse deduction, are allocated 90 percent to LP and 10 percent to GP. The allocation of these items, other than the nonrecourse deductions, has substantial economic effect.

	LP	GP
Capital account at end of year 2	$27,000	$3,000
Less: net loss in year 3 (without nonrecourse deductions)	(13,500)	(1,500)
Less nonrecourse deductions in year 3	(63,000)	(7,000)
Capital account at end of year 3	($49,500)	($5,500)

The allocation of the $70,000 nonrecourse deduction satisfies requirement (2) of paragraph (e) of this section because it is consistent with allocations having substantial economic effect of other significant partnership items attributable to the building. Because the remaining requirements of paragraph (e) of this section are satisfied, the allocation of nonrecourse deductions is deemed to be in accordance with the partners' interests in the partnership. At the end of the partnership's third taxable year, LP's and GP's shares of partnership minimum gain are $63,000 and $7,000, respectively. Therefore, pursuant to paragraph (g)(1) of this section, LP is treated as obligated to restore a deficit capital account balance of $63,000, so that in the succeeding year LP could be allocated up to an additional $13,500 of partnership deductions, losses, and section 705(a)(2)(B) items that are not nonrecourse deductions. Even though this allocation would increase a deficit capital account balance, it would be considered to have economic effect under the alternate economic effect test contained in § 1.704-1(b)(2)(ii)(d). If the partnership were to dispose of the building in full satisfaction of the nonrecourse liability at the beginning of the partnership's fourth taxable year (and had no other economic activity in that year), the partnership minimum gain would be decreased from $70,000 to zero, and the minimum gain chargeback would require that LP and GP be allocated $63,000 and $7,000, respectively, of the gain from that disposition.

(ii) Illustration of reasonable consistency requirement. Assume instead that the partnership agreement provides that all nonrecourse deductions of the partnership will be allocated equally between LP and GP. Furthermore, at the time the partnership agreement is entered into, there is a reasonable likelihood that over the partnership's life it will realize amounts of income and gain significantly in excess of amounts of loss and deduction (other than nonrecourse deductions). The equal allocation of excess income and gain has substantial economic effect.

	LP	GP
Capital account on formation........	$180,000	$20,000
Less: net loss in years 1 and 2 ...	(153,000)	(17,000)
Less: net loss in year (without nonrecourse deductions........	(13,500)	(1,500)
Less: nonrecourse deductions in year 3	(35,000)	(35,000)
Capital account at end of year 3	($21,500)	($33,500)

The allocation of the $70,000 nonrecourse deduction equally between LP and GP satisfies requirement (2) of paragraph (e) of his section because the allocation is consistent with allocations, which will have substantial economic effect, of other significant partnership items attributable to the building. Because the remaining requirements of paragraph (e) of this section are satisfied, the allocation of nonrecourse deductions is deemed to be in accordance with the partners' interests in the partnership. The allocation of the nonrecourse deductions 75 percent to LP and 25 percent to GP (or in any other ratio between 90 percent to LP/10 percent to GP and 50 percent to LP/50 percent to GP) also would satisfy requirement (2) of paragraph (e) of this section.

(iii) Allocation of nonrecourse deductions that fails reasonable consistency requirement. Assume instead that the partnership agreement provides that LP will be allocated 99 percent, and GP 1 percent, of all nonrecourse deductions of the partnership. Allocating nonrecourse deductions this way does not satisfy requirement (2) of paragraph (e) of this section because the allocations are not reasonably consistent with allocations, having substantial economic effect, of any other significant partnership item attributable to the building. Therefore, the allocation of nonrecourse deductions will be disregarded, and the nonrecourse deductions of the partnership will be reallocated according to the partners' overall economic interests in the partnership, determined under § 1.704-1(b)(3)(ii).

(iv) Capital contribution to pay down nonrecourse debt. At the beginning of the partnership's fourth taxable year. LP contributes $144,000 and GP contributes $16,000 of addition capital to the partnership, which the partnership immediately uses to reduce the amount of its nonrecourse liability from $800,000 to $640,000. In addition, in the partnership's fourth taxable year, it generates rental income of $95,000, operating expenses of $10,000, interest expense of $64,000 (consistent with the debt reduction), and a depreciation deduction of $90,000, resulting in e net taxable loss of $69,000. If the partnership were to dispose of the building in full satisfaction of the nonrecourse liability at the end of that year, it would realize no gain ($640,000 amount realized less $640,000 adjusted tax basis). Therefore, the amount of partnership minimum gain at the end of the year is zero, which represents a net decrease in partnership minimum gain of $70,000 during the year. LP's and GP's shares of this net decrease are $63,000 and $7,000 respectively, so that at the end of the partnership's fourth taxable year, LP's and GP's shares of partnership minimum gain are zero. Although there has been a net decrease in partnership minimum gain, pursuant to paragraph (f)(3) of this section LP and GP are not subject to a minimum gain chargeback.

	LP	GP
Capital account at end of year 3	($49,500)	($5,500)
Plus: contribution	144,000	16,000
Less: net loss in year 4	(62,100)	(6,900)
Capital account at end of year 4	32,400	(3,600)
Minimum gain chargeback carryforward	$0	$0

(v) Loans of unequal priority. Assume instead that the building acquired by the partnership is secured by a $700,000 nonrecourse loan and a $100,000 recourse loan, subordinate in priority to the nonrecourse loan. Under paragraph (d)(2) of this section, $700,000 of the adjusted basis of the building at the end of the partnership's third taxable year is allocated to the nonrecourse liability (with the remaining $30,000 allocated to the recourse liability) so that if the partnership disposed of the building in full satisfaction of the nonrecourse liability at the end of that year, it would realize no gain ($700,000 amount realized less $700,000 adjusted tax basis). Therefore, there is no minimum gain (or increase in minimum gain) at the end of the partnership's third taxable year. If, however, the $700,000 nonrecourse loan were subordinate in priority to the $100,000 recourse loan, under paragraph (d)(2) of this section, the first $100,000 of adjusted tax basis in the building would be allocated to the recourse liability, leaving only $630,000 of the adjusted basis of the building to be allocated to the $700,000 nonrecourse loan. In that case, the balance of the $700,000 nonrecourse liability would exceed the adjusted tax basis of the building by $70,000, so that there would be $70,000 of minimum gain (and a $70,000 increase in partnership minimum gain) in the partnership's third taxable year.

(vi) Nonrecourse borrowing; distribution of proceeds in subsequent year. The partnership obtains an additional nonrecourse loan of $200,000 at the end of its fourth taxable year, secured by a second mortgage on the building, and distributes $180,000 of this cash to its partners at the beginning of its fifth taxable year. In addition, in its fourth and fifth taxable years, the partnership again generates rental income of $95,000, operating expenses of $10,000, interest expense of $80,000 ($100,000 in the fifth taxable year reflecting the interest paid on both liabilities), and a depreciation deduction of $90,000, resulting in a net taxable loss of $85,000 ($105,000 in the fifth taxable year reflecting the interest paid on both liabilities), The partnership has distributed its $5,000 of operating cash flow in each year ($95,000 of rental income less $10,000 of operating expense and $80,000 of interest expense) to LP and GP at the end of each year. If the partnership were to dispose of the building in full satisfaction of both nonrecourse liabilities at the end of its fourth taxable year, the partnership would realize $360,000 of gain ($1,000,000 amount realized less $640,000 adjusted tax basis), Thus, the net increase in partnership minimum gain during the partnership's fourth taxable year is $290,000 ($360,000 of minimum gain at the end of the fourth year less $70,000 of minimum gain at the end of the third year). Because the partnership did not distribute any of the proceeds of the loan it obtained in its fourth year during that year, the potential amount of partnership nonrecourse deductions for that year is $290,000. Under paragraph (c) of this section, if the partnership had distributed the proceeds of that loan to its partners at the end of its fourth year, the partnership's nonrecourse deductions for that year would have been reduced by the amount of that distribution because the proceeds of that loan are allocable to an increase in partnership minimum gain under paragraph (h)(1) of this section. Because the nonrecourse deductions of $290,000 for the partnership's fourth taxable year exceed its total deductions for that year, all $180,000 of the partnership's deductions for that year are treated as nonrecourse deductions, and the $110,000 excess nonrecourse deductions are treated as an increase in partnership minimum gain in the partnership's fifth taxable year under paragraph (c) of this section.

	LP	GP
Capital account at end of year 3 (including cash flow distributions)	($63,000)	($7,000)
Plus: rental income in year 4	85,500	9,500
Less: nonrecourse deductions in year 4	(162,000)	(18,000)
Less: cash flow distribution in year 4	(4,500)	(500)
Capital account at end of year 4	($144,000)	($16,000)

At the end of the partnership's fourth taxable year, LP's and GP's shares of partnership minimum gain are $225,000 and $25,000, respectively (because the $110,000 excess of nonrecourse deductions is carried forward to the next year). If the partnership were to dispose of the building in full satisfaction of the nonrecourse liabilities at the end of its fifth taxable year, the partnership would realize $450,000 of gain ($1,000,000 amount realized less $550,000 adjusted tax basis). Therefore, the net increase in partnership minimum gain during the partnership's fifth taxable year is $200,000 ($110,000 deemed increase plus the $90,000 by which minimum gain at the end of the fifth year exceeds minimum gain at the end of the fourth year ($450,000 less $360,000)). At the beginning of its fifth year, the partnership distributes $180,000 of the loan proceeds (retaining $20,000 to pay the additional interest expense). Under paragraph (h) of this section, the first $110,000 of this distribution (an amount equal to the deemed increase in partnership minimum gain for the year) is considered allocable to an increase in partnership minimum gain for the year. As a result, the amount of nonrecourse deductions for the partnership's fifth taxable year is $90,000 ($200,000 net increase in minimum gain less $110,000 distribution of nonrecourse liability proceeds allocable to an increase in partnership minimum gain), and the nonrecourse deductions consist solely of the $90,000 depreciation deduction allowable with respect to the building. As a result of the distributions during the partnership's fifth taxable year, the total distributions to the partners over the partnership's life equal $205,000. Therefore, the last $5,000 distributed to the partners during the fifth year will be divided equally between them under the partnership agreement. Thus, out of the $185,000 total distribution during the partnership's fifth taxable year, the first $180,000 is distributed 90 percent to LP and 10 percent to GP, and the last $5,000 is divided equally between them.

	LP	GP
Capital account at end of year 4	($144,000)	($16,000)
Less: net loss in year 5 (without nonrecourse deductions)	(13,500)	(1,500)
Less: nonrecourse deductions in year 5	(81,000)	(9,000)
Less: distribution of loan proceeds	(162,000)	(18,000)
Less: cash flow distribution in year 5	(2,500)	(2,500)
Capital account at end of year 5	($403,000)	($47,000)

At the end of the partnership's fifth taxable year, LP's share of partnership minimum gain is $405,000 ($225,000 share of minimum gain at the end of the fourth year plus $81,000 of nonrecourse deductions for the fifth year and a $99,000 distribution of nonrecourse liability proceeds that are allocable to an increase in minimum gain) and GP's share of partnership minimum gain is $45,000 ($25,000 share of minimum gain at the end of the fourth year plus $9,000 of nonrecourse deductions for the fifth year and an $11,000 distribution of nonrecourse liability proceeds that are allocable to an increase in minimum gain).

(vii) Partner guarantee of nonrecourse debt. LP and GP personally guarantee the "first" $100,000 of the $800,000 nonrecourse loan (i.e., only if the building is worth less than $100,000 will they be called upon to make up any deficiency). Under paragraph (d)(2) of this section, only $630,000 of the adjusted tax basis of the building is allocated to the $700,000 nonrecourse portion of the loan because the collateral will be applied first to satisfy the $100,000 guaranteed portion, making it superior in priority to the remainder of the loan. On the other hand, if LP and GP were to guarantee the "last" $100,000 (i.e., if the building is worth less than $800,000, they will be called upon to make up the deficiency up to $100,000), $700,000 of the adjusted tax basis of the building would be allocated to the $700,000 nonrecourse portion of the loan because the guaranteed portion would be inferior in priority to it.

(viii) Partner nonrecourse debt. Assume instead that the $800,000 loan is made by LP, the limited partner. Under paragraph (b)(4) of this section, the $800,000 obligation does not constitute a nonrecourse liability of the partnership for purposes of this section because LP, a partner, bears the economic risk of loss for that loan within the meaning of § 1.752-2. Instead, the $800,000 loan constitutes a partner nonrecourse debt under paragraph (b)(4) of this section. In the partnership's third taxable year, partnership minimum gain would have increased by $70,000 if the debt were a nonrecourse liability of the partnership. Thus, under paragraph (i)(3) of this section, there is a net increase of $70,000 in the minimum gain attributable to the $800,000 partner nonrecourse debt for the partnership's third taxable year, and $70,000 of the $90,000 depreciation deduction from the building for the partnership's third taxable year constitutes a partner nonrecourse deduction with respect to the debt. See paragraph (i)(4) of this section. Under paragraph (i)(2,) of this section, this partner nonrecourse deduction must be allocated to LP, the partner that bears the economic risk of loss for that liability.

(ix) Nonrecourse debt and partner nonrecourse debt of differing priorities. As in Example 1 (viii) of this paragraph (m), the $800,000 loan is made to the partnership by LP, the limited partner, but the loan is a purchase money loan that "wraps around" a $700,000 underlying nonrecourse note (also secured by the building) issued by LP to an unrelated person in connection with LP's acquisition of the building. Under these circumstances, LP bears the economic risk of loss with respect to only $100,000 of the liability within the meaning of § 1.752-2. See § 1.752-2(f) (Example 6). Therefore, for purposes of paragraph (d) of this section, the $800,000 liability is treated as a $700,000 nonrecourse liability of the partnership and a $100,000 partner nonrecourse debt (inferior in priority to the $700,000 liability) of the partnership for which LP bears the economic risk of loss. Under paragraph (i)(2) of this section, $70,000 of the $90,000 depreciation deduction realized in the partnership's third taxable year constitutes a partner nonrecourse deduction that must be allocated to LP.

Example (2). Netting of increases and decreases in partnership minimum gain. For Example 2 unless otherwise provided. the following facts are assumed. X and Y form a general partnership to acquire and operate residential real properties. Each partner contributes $150,000 to the partnership. The partnership obtains a $1,500,000 nonrecourse loan and purchases 3 apartment buildings (on leased land) for $720,000 ("Property A"), $540,000 ("Property B"), and $540,000 ("Property C"). The nonrecourse loan is secured only by the 3 buildings, and no principal payments are due for 5 years. In each of the partnership's first 3 taxable years, it generates rental income of $225,000, operating expenses (including land lease payments) of $50,000, interest expense of $175,000, and depreciation deductions on the 3 properties of $150,000 ($60,000 on Property A and $45,000 on each of Property B end Property C), resulting in a net taxable loss of $150,000 in each of those years he partnership makes no distributions to X or Y.

(i) Calculation of net increases and decreases in partnership minimum gain. If the partnership were to dispose of the 3 apartment buildings in full satisfaction of its nonrecourse liability at the end of its third taxable year, it would realize $150,000 of gain ($1,500,000 amount realized less $1,350,000 adjusted tax basis), Because the amount of partnership minimum gain at the end of that year (and the net increase in partnership minimum gain during that year) is $150,000, the amount of partnership nonrecourse deductions for that year is $150,000, consisting of depreciation deductions allowable with respect to the 3 apartment buildings of $150,000. The result would be the same if the partnership obtained 3 separate nonrecourse loans that were "cross-collateralized" (i.e., if each separate loan were secured by all 3 of the apartment buildings).

(ii) Netting of increases and decreases in partnership minimum gain when there is a disposition. At the beginning of the partnership's fourth taxable year, the partnership (with the permission of the nonrecourse lender) disposes of Property A for $835,000 and uses a portion of the proceeds to repay $600,000 of the nonrecourse liability (the principal amount attributable to Property A), reducing the balance to $900,000. As a result of the disposition, the partnership realizes gain of $295,000 ($835,000 amount realized less $540,000 adjusted tax basis). If the disposition is viewed in isolation, the partnership has generated minimum gain of $60,000 on the sale of Property A ($600,000 of debt reduction less $540,000 adjusted tax basis). However, during the partnership's fourth taxable year it also generates rental income of $135,000, operating expenses of $30,000, interest expense of $105,000, and depreciation deductions of $90,000 ($45,000 on each remaining building). If the partnership were to dispose of the remaining two buildings in full satisfaction of its nonrecourse liability at the end of the partnership's fourth taxable year, it would realize gain of $180,000 ($900,000 amount realized less $720,000 aggregate adjusted tax basis), which is the amount of partnership minimum gain at the end of the year. Because the partnership minimum gain increased from $150,000 to $180,000 during the partnership's Fourth taxable year, the amount of partnership nonrecourse deductions for that year is $30,000, consisting of a ratable portion of depreciation deductions allowable with respect to the two remaining apartment buildings. No minimum gain chargeback is required for the taxable year, even through the partnership disposed of one of the properties subject to the nonrecourse liability during the year, because there is no net decrease in partnership minimum gain for the year. See paragraph (f)(1) of this section.

Example (3). Nonrecourse deductions and partnership minimum gain before third partner is admitted. For purposes of Example 3, unless otherwise provided, the following facts are assumed. Additional facts are given in each of Examples 3(ii), (iii), and (iv). A and B form a limited partnership to acquire and lease machinery that is 5-year recovery property. A, the limited partner, and B, the general partner, contribute $100,000 each to the partnership, which obtains an $800,000 nonrecourse loan and purchases the machinery for $1,000,000. The nonrecourse loan is secured only by the machinery. The principal amount of the loan is to be repaid $50,000 per year during each of the partnership's first 5 taxable years, with the remaining $550,000 of unpaid principal due on the first day of the partnership's sixth taxable year. The partnership agreement contains all of the provisions required by paragraph (e) of this section, and, as of the end of each partnership taxable year discussed herein, the items described in § 1.704-1(b)(2)(ii)(d)(4), (5), and (6) are not reasonably expected to cause or increase a deficit balance in A's or B's capital account. The partnership agreement provides that, except as otherwise required by its qualified income offset and minimum gain chargeback provisions, all partnership items will be allocated equally between A and B. Finally, the partnership agreement provides that all distributions, other than distributions in liquidation of the partnership or of a partner's interest in the partnership, will be made equally between A and B. In the partnership's first taxable year it generates rental income of $130,000, interest expense of $80,000, and a depreciation deduction of $150,000, resulting in a net taxable loss of $100,000. In addition, the partnership repays $50,000 of the nonrecourse liability, reducing that liability to $750,000. Allocations of these losses equally between A and B have substantial economic effect.

	A	B
Capital account on formation.......	$100,000	$100,000
Less: net loss in year 1	(50,000)	(50,000)
Capital account at end of year 1....	$50,000	$50,000

In the partnership's second taxable year, it generates rental income of $130,000, interest expense of $75,000, and a depreciation deduction of $220,000, resulting in a net taxable loss of $165,000. In addition, the partnership repays $50,000 of the nonrecourse liability, reducing that liability to $700,000, and distributes $2,500 of cash to each partner. If the partnership were to dispose of the machinery in full satisfaction of the nonrecourse liability at the end of that year, it would realize $70,000 of gain ($700,000 amount realized less $630,000 adjusted tax basis). Therefore, the amount of partnership minimum gain at the end of that year (and the net increase in partnership minimum gain during the year) is $70,000, and the amount of partnership nonrecourse deductions for the year is $70,000. The partnership nonrecourse deductions for its second taxable year consist of $70,000 of the depreciation deductions allowable with respect to the machinery. Pursuant to the partnership agreement, all partnership items comprising the net taxable loss of $165,000, including the $70,000 nonrecourse deduction, are allocated equally between A and B. The allocation of these items, other than the nonrecourse deductions, has substantial economic effect.

	A	B
Capital account at end of year 1......	$50,000	$50,000
Less: net loss in year 2 (without nonrecourse deductions)........	(47,500)	(47,500)
Less: nonrecourse deductions in year 2........................	($35,000)	($35,000)
Less: distribution................	(2,500)	(2,500)
Capital account at end of year 2......	($35,000)	($35,000)

(i) Calculation of nonrecourse deductions and partnership minimum gain. Because all of the requirements of paragraph (e) of this section are satisfied, the allocation of nonrecourse deductions is deemed to be made in accordance with the partners' interests in the partnership. At the end of the partnership's second taxable year, A's and B's shares of partnership minimum gain are $35,000 each. Therefore, pursuant to paragraph (g)(1) of this section, A and B are treated as obligated to restore deficit balances in their capital accounts of $35,000 each. If the partnership were to dispose of the machinery in full satisfaction of the nonrecourse liability at the beginning of the partnership's third taxable year (and had no other economic activity in that year), the partnership minimum gain would be decreased from $70,000 to zero. A's and B's shares of that net decrease would be $35,000 each. Upon that disposition, the minimum gain chargeback would require that A and B each be allocated $35,000 of that gain before any other allocation is made under section 704(b) with respect to partnership items for the partnership's third taxable year.

(ii) Nonrecourse deductions and restatement of capital accounts.

(a) Additional facts. C is admitted to the partnership at the beginning of the partnership's third taxable year. At the time of C's admission, the fair market value of the machinery is $900,000. C contributes $100,000 to the partnership (the partnership invests $95,000 of this in undeveloped land and holds the other $5,000 in cash) in exchange for an interest in the partnership. In connection with C's admission to the partnership, the partnership's machinery is revalued on the partnership's books to reflect its fair market value of $900,000. Pursuant to § 1.704-1(b)(2)(iv)(f), the capital accounts of A and B are adjusted upwards to $100,000 each to reflect the revaluation of the partnership's machinery. This adjustment reflects the manner in which the partnership gain of $270,000 ($900,000 fair market value minus $630,000 adjusted tax basis) would be shared if the machinery were sold for its fair market value immediately prior to C's admission to the partnership.

	A	B
Capital account before C's admission....................	($35,000)	($35,000)
Deemed sale adjustment........	135,000	135,000
Capital account adjusted for C's admission....................	$100,000	$100,000

The partnership agreement is modified to provide that, except as otherwise required by its qualified income offset and minimum gain chargeback provisions, partnership income, gain, loss, and deduction, as computed for book purposes, are allocated equally among the partners, and those allocations are reflected in the partners' capital accounts. The partnership agreement also is modified to provide that depreciation and gain or loss, as computed for tax purposes, with respect to the machinery will be shared among the partners in a manner that takes account of the variation between the property's $630,000 adjusted tax basis and its $900,000 book value, in accordance with § 1.704-1(b)(2)(iv)(f) and the special rule contained in § 1.704-1(b)(4)(i).

(b) Effect of revaluation. Because the requirements of § 1.704-1(b)(2)(iv)(g) are satisfied, the capital accounts of the partners (as adjusted) continue to be maintained in accordance with § 1.704-1(b)(2)(iv). If the partnership were to dispose of the machinery in full satisfaction of the nonrecourse liability immediately following the revaluation of the machinery, it would realize no book gain ($700,000 amount realized less $900,000 book value). As a result of the revaluation of the machinery upward by $270,000, under part of paragraph (d)(4) of this section, the partnership minimum gain is reduced from $70,000 immediately prior to the revaluation to zero; but under part (ii) of paragraph (d)(4) of this section, the partnership minimum gain is increased by the $70,000 decrease arising solely from the revaluation. Accordingly, there is no net increase or decrease solely on account of the revaluation, and so no minimum gain chargeback is triggered. All future nonrecourse deductions that occur will be the nonrecourse deductions as calculated for book purposes, and will be charged to all 3 partners in accordance with the partnership agreement. For purposes of determining the partners' shares of minimum gain under paragraph (g) of this section, A's and B's shares of the decrease resulting from the revaluation are $35,000 each. However, as illustrated below, under section 704(c) principles, the tax capital accounts of A and B will eventually be charged $35,000 each, reflecting their 50 percent shares of the decrease in partnership minimum gain that resulted from the revaluation.

(iii) Allocation of nonrecourse deductions following restatement of capital accounts.

(a) Additional facts. During the partnership's third taxable year, the partnership generates rental income of $130,000, interest expense of $70,000, a tax depreciation deduction of $210,000, and a book depreciation deduction (attributable to the machinery) of $300,000. As a result, the partnership has a net taxable loss of $150,000 and a net book loss of $240,000. In addition, the partnership repays $50,000 of the nonrecourse liability (after the data of C's admission), reducing the liability to $650,000 and distributes $5,000 of cash to each partner.

(b) Allocations. If the partnership were to dispose of the machinery in full satisfaction of the nonrecourse liability at the end of the year, $50,000 of book gain would result ($650,000 amount realized less $600,000 book basis). Therefore, the amount of partnership minimum gain at the end of the year is $50,000, which represents a net decrease in partnership minimum gain of $20,000 during the year. (This is so even though there would be an increase in partnership minimum gain in the partnership's third taxable year if minimum gain were computed with reference to the adjusted tax basis of the machinery.) Nevertheless, pursuant to paragraph (d)(4) of this section, the amount of nonrecourse deductions of the partnership for its third taxable year is $50,000 (the net increase in partnership minimum gain during the year determined by adding back the $70,000 decrease in partnership minimum gain attributable to the revaluation of the machinery to the $20,000 net decrease in partnership minimum gain during the year). The $50,000 of partnership nonrecourse deductions for the year consist of book depreciation deductions allowable with respect to the machinery of $50,000. Pursuant to the partnership agreement, all partnership items comprising the net book loss of $240,000, including the $50,000 nonrecourse deduction, are allocated equally among the partners. The allocation of these items, other than the nonrecourse deductions, has substantial economic effect. Consistent with the special partners' interests in the partnership rate contained in § 1.704-1(b)(4)(i), the partnership agreement provides that the depreciation deduction for tax purposes of $210,000 for the partnership's third taxable year is, in accordance with section 704(c) principles, shared $55,000 to A, $55,000 to B, and $100,000 to C.

	A		B		C	
	Tax	Book	Tax	Book	Tax	Book
Capital account at beginning of year 3 ...	($35,000)	$100,000	($35,000)	$100,000	$100,000	$100,000
Less: nonrecourse deductions	(9,166)	(16,666)	(9,166)	(16,666)	(16,666)	(16,666)
Less: items other than nonrecourse deductions in year 3	(25,834)	(63,334)	(25,834)	(63,334)	(63,334)	(63,334)
Less: distribution	(5,000)	(5,000)	(5,000)	(5,000)	(5,000)	(5,000)
Capital account at end of year 3	($75,000)	$15,000	($75,000)	$15,000	$15,000	$15,000

Because the requirements of paragraph (e) of this section are satisfied, the allocation of the nonrecourse deduction is deemed to be made in accordance with the partners' interests in the partnership. At the end of the partnership's third taxable year. A's, B's, and C's shares of partnership minimum gain are $16,666 each.

(iv) Subsequent allocation of nonrecourse deductions following restatement of capital accounts.

(a) Additional facts. The partners' capital accounts at the end of the second and third taxable years of the partnership are as stated in Example 3(iii) of this paragraph (m). In addition, during the partnership's fourth taxable year the partnership generates rental income of $130,000, interest expense of $65,000, a tax depreciation deduction of $210,000, and a book depreciation deduction (attributable to the machinery) of $300,000. As a result the partnership has a net taxable loss of $145,000 and a net book loss of $235,000. In addition, the partnership repays $50,000 of the nonrecourse liability, reducing that liability to $600,000, and distributes $5,000 of cash to each partner.

(b) Allocations. If the partnership were to dispose of the machinery in full satisfaction of the nonrecourse liability at the end of the fourth year, $300,000 of book gain would result ($600,000 amount realized less $300,000 book value). Therefore, the amount of partnership minimum gain as of the end of the year is $300,000, which represents a net increase in partnership minimum gain during the year of $250,000. Thus, the amount of partnership nonrecourse deductions for that year equals $250,000, consisting of book depreciation deductions of $250,000. Pursuant to the partnership agreement, all partnership items comprising the net book loss of $235,000, including the $250,000 nonrecourse deduction, are allocated equally among the partners. That allocation of all items, other than the nonrecourse deductions, has substantial economic effect. Consistent with the special partners' interests in the partnership rule contained in § 1.704-1(b)(4)(i), the partnership agreement provides that the depreciation deduction for tax purposes of $210,000 in the partnership's fourth taxable year is, in accordance with section 704(c) principles, allocated $55,000 to A, $55,000 to B, and $100,000 to C.

	A		B		C	
	Tax	Book	Tax	Book	Tax	Book
Capital account at end of year 3	($75,000)	$15,000	($75,000)	$15,000	$15,000	$15,000
Less: nonrecourse deductions	(45,833)	(83,333)	(45,833)	(83,333)	(83,333)	(83,333)
Plus: items other than nonrecourse deductions in year 4	12,499	5,000	12,499	5,000	5,000	5,000
Less: distribution	(5,000)	(5,000)	(5,000)	(5,000)	(5,000)	(5,000)
Capital account at end of year 4	($113,334)	($68,333)	($113,333)	($68,333)	($68,333)	($68,333)

The allocation of the $250,000 nonrecourse deduction equally among A, B, and C satisfies requirement (2) of paragraph (e) of this section. Because all of the requirements of paragraph (e) of this section are satisfied, the allocation is deemed to be in accordance with the partners' interests in the partnership. At the end of the partnership's fourth taxable year, A's, B's, and C's shares of partnership minimum gain are $100,000 each.

(v) Disposition of partnership property following restatement of capital accounts.

(a) Additional facts. The partners' capital accounts at the end of the fourth taxable year of the partnership are as stated above in (iv). In addition, at the beginning of the partnership's fifth taxable year it sells the machinery for $650,000 (using $600,000 of the proceeds to repay the nonrecourse liability), resulting in a taxable gain of $440,000 ($650,000 amount realized less $210,000 adjusted tax basis) and a book gain of $350,000 ($650,000 amount realized less $300,000 book basis). The partnership has no other items of income, gain, loss, or deduction for the year.

(b) Effect of disposition. As a result of the sale, partnership minimum gain is reduced from $300,000 to zero, reducing A's, B's, and C's shares of partnership minimum gain to zero from $100,000 each. The minimum gain chargeback requires that A, B. and C each be allocated $100,000 of that gain (an amount equal to each partner's share of the net decrease in partnership minimum gain resulting from the sale) before any allocation is made to them under section 704(b) with respect to partnership items for the partnership's fifth taxable year. Thus, the allocation of the first $300,000 of book gain $100,000 to each of the partners is deemed to be in accordance with the partners' interests in the partnership under paragraph (e) of this section. The allocation of the remaining $50,000 of book gain equally among the partners has substantial economic effect. Consistent with the special partners' interests in the partnership rule contained in § 1.704-1(b)(4)(i), the partnership agreement provides that the $440,000 taxable gain is, in accordance with section 704(c) principles, allocated $161,667 to A, $161,667 to B, and $116,666 to C.

	A		B		C	
	Tax	Book	Tax	Book	Tax	Book
Capital account at end of year 4	($113,334)	($68,333)	($113,334)	($68,333)	($68,333)	($68,333)
Plus: minimum gain chargeback	138,573	100,000	138,573	100,000	100,000	100,000
Plus: additional gain	23,094	16,666	23,094	16,666	16,666	16,666
Capital account before liquidation	$48,333	$48,333	$48,333	$48,333	$48,333	$48,333

Example (4). Allocations of increase in partnership minimum gain among partnership properties. For Example 4, unless otherwise provided, the following facts are assumed. A partnership owns 4 properties, each of which is subject to a nonrecourse liability of the partnership. During a taxable year of the partnership, the following events take place. First, the partnership generates a depreciation deduction (for both book and tax purposes) with respect to Property W of $10,000 and repays $5,000 of the nonrecourse liability secured only by that property, resulting in an increase in minimum gain with respect to that liability of $5,000. Second, the partnership generates a depreciation deduction (for both book and tax purposes) with respect to Property X of $10,000 and repays none of the nonrecourse liability secured by that property, resulting in an increase in minimum gain with respect to that liability of $10,000. Third, the partnership generates a depreciation deduction (for both book and tax purposes) of $2,000 with respect to Property Y and repays $11,000 of the nonrecourse liability secured only by that property, resulting in a decrease in minimum gain with respect to that liability of $9,000 (although at the end of that year, there remains minimum gain with respect to that liability). Finally, the partnership borrows $5,000 on a nonrecourse basis, giving as the only security for that liability Property Z, a parcel of undeveloped land with an adjusted tax basis (and book value) of $2,000, resulting in a net increase in minimum gain with respect to that liability of $3,000.

(i) Allocation of increase in partnership minimum gain. The net increase in partnership minimum gain during that partnership taxable year is $9,000, so that the amount of nonrecourse deductions of the partnership for that taxable year is $9,000. Those nonrecourse deductions consist of $3,000 of depreciation deductions with respect to Property W and $6,000 of depreciation deductions with respect to Property X. See paragraph (c) of this section. The amount of nonrecourse deductions consisting of depreciation deductions is determined as follows. With respect to the nonrecourse liability secured by Property Z, for which there is no depreciation deduction, the amount of depreciation deductions that constitutes nonrecourse deductions is zero. Similarly, with respect to the nonrecourse liability secured by Property Y, for which there is no increase in minimum gain, the amount of depreciation deductions that constitutes nonrecourse deductions is zero. With respect to each of the nonrecourse liabilities secured by Properties W and X, which are secured by property for which there are depreciation deductions and for which there is an increase in minimum gain, the amount of depreciation deductions that constitutes nonrecourse deductions is determined by the following formula:

net increase in the partnership minimum gain for that taxable year × total depreciation deductions for that taxable year on the specific property securing the nonrecourse liability to the extent minimum gain increased on that liability (divided by) total depreciation deductions for that taxable year on all properties securing nonrecourse liabilities to the extent of the aggregate increase in minimum gain on all those liabilities.

Thus, for the liability secured by Property W, the amount is $9,000 times $5,000/$15,000, or $3,000. For the liability secured by Property X, the amount is $9,000 times $10,000/$15,000, or $6,000. (If one depreciable property secured two partnership nonrecourse liabilities, the amount of depreciation or book depreciation with respect to that property would be allocated among those liabilities in accordance with the method by which adjusted basis is allocated under paragraph (d)(2) of this section).

(ii) Alternative allocation of increase in partnership minimum gain among partnership properties. Assume instead that the loan secured by Property Z is $15,000 (rather than $5,000), resulting in a net increase in minimum gain with respect to that liability of $13,000. Thus, the net increase in partnership minimum gain is $19,000, and the amount of nonrecourse deductions of the partnership for that taxable year is $19,000. Those nonrecourse deductions consist of $5,000 of depreciation deductions with respect to Property W, $10,000 of depreciation deductions with respect to Property X, and a pro rata portion of the partnership's other items of deduction, loss, and section 705(a)(2)(B) expenditure for that year. The method for computing the amounts of depreciation deductions that constitute nonrecourse deductions is the same as in (i) of this Example 4 for the liabilities secured by Properties Y and Z. With respect to each of the nonrecourse liabilities secured by Properties W and X, the amount of depreciation deductions that constitutes nonrecourse deductions equals the total depreciation deductions with respect to the partnership property securing that particular liability to the extent of the increase in minimum gain with respect to that liability.

T.D. 8385, 12/26/91, amend T.D. 9207, 5/23/2005, T.D. 9289, 10/10/2006.

---

§ 1.704-3 Contributed property.

Caution: The Treasury has not yet amended Reg § 1.704-3 to reflect changes made by P.L. 108-357.

(a) In general. *(1) General principles.* The purpose of section 704(c) is to prevent the shifting of tax consequences among partners with respect to precontribution gain or loss. Under section 704(c), a partnership must allocate income, gain, loss, and deduction with respect to property contributed by a partner to the partnership so as to take into account any variation between the adjusted tax basis of the property and its fair market value at the time of contribution. Notwithstanding any other provision of this section, the allocations must be made using a reasonable method that is consistent with the purpose of section 704(c). For this purpose, an allocation method includes the application of all of the rules of this section (e.g., aggregation rules). An allocation method is not necessarily unreasonable merely because another allocation method would result in a higher aggregate tax liability. Paragraphs (b), (c), and (d) of this section describe allocation methods that are generally reasonable. Other methods may be reasonable in appropriate circumstances. Nevertheless, in the absence of specific published guidance, it is not reasonable to use an allocation method in which the basis of property contributed to the partnership is increased (or decreased) to reflect built-in gain (or loss), or a method under which the partnership creates tax allocations of income, gain, loss, or deduction independent of allocations affecting book capital accounts. See § 1.704-3(d). Paragraph (e) of this section contains special rules and exceptions.

(2) Operating rules. Except as provided in paragraphs (e)(2) and (e)(3) of this section, section 704(c) and this section apply on a property-by-property basis. Therefore, in determining whether there is a disparity between adjusted tax basis and fair market value, the built-in gains and built-in losses on items of contributed property cannot be aggregated. A partnership may use different methods with respect to different items of contributed property, provided that the partnership and the partners consistently apply a single reasonable method for each item of contributed property and that the overall method or combination of methods are reasonable based on the facts and circumstances and consistent with the purpose of section 704(c). It may be unreasonable to use one method for appreciated property and another method for depreciated property. Similarly, it may be unreasonable to use the traditional method for built-in gain property contributed by a partner with a high marginal tax rate while using curative allocations for built-in gain property contributed by a partner with a low marginal tax rate. A new partnership formed as the result of the termination of a partnership under section 708(b)(1)(B) is not required to use the same method as the terminated partnership with respect to section 704(c) property deemed contributed to the new partnership by the terminated partnership under § 1.708-1(b)(1)(iv). The previous sentence applies to terminations of partnerships under section 708(b)(1)(B) occurring on or after May 9, 1997; however, the sentence may be applied to terminations occurring on or after May 9, 1996, provided that the partnership and its partners apply the sentence to the termination in a consistent manner.

(3) Definitions. (i) Section 704(c) Property. Property contributed to a partnership is section 704(c) property if at the time of contribution its book value differs from the contributing partner's adjusted tax basis. For purposes of this section, book value is determined as contemplated by § 1.704-1(b). Therefore, book value is equal to fair market value at the time of contribution and is subsequently adjusted for cost recovery and other events that affect the basis of the property. For a partnership that maintains capital accounts in accordance with § 1.704-1(b)(2)(iv), the book value of property is initially the value used in determining the contributing partner's capital account under § 1.704-1(b)(2)(iv)(d), and is appropriately adjusted thereafter (e.g., for book cost recovery under §§ 1.704-1(b)(2)(iv)(g)(3) and 1.704-3(d)(2) and other events that affect the basis of the property). A partnership that does not maintain capital accounts under § 1.704-1(b)(2)(iv) must comply with this section using a book capital account based on the same principles (i.e., a book capital account that reflects the fair market value of property at the time of contribution and that is subsequently adjusted for cost recovery and other events that affect the basis of the property). Property deemed contributed to a new partnership as the result of the termination of a partnership under section 708(b)(1)(B) is treated as section 704(c) property in the hands of the new partnership only to the extent that the property was section 704(c) property in the hands of the terminated partnership immediately prior to the termination. See § 1.708-1(b)(1)(iv) for an example of the application of this rule. The previous two sentences apply to terminations of partnerships under section 708(b)(1)(B) occurring on or after May 9, 1997; however, the sentences may be applied to terminations occurring on or after May 9, 1996, provided

that the partnership and its partners apply the sentences to the termination in a consistent manner.

(ii) Built-in gain and built-in loss. The built-in gain on section 704(c) property is the excess of the property's book value over the contributing partner's adjusted tax basis upon contribution. The built-in gain is thereafter reduced by decreases in the difference between the property's book value and adjusted tax basis. The built-in loss on section 704(c) property is the excess of the contributing partner's adjusted tax basis over the property's book value upon contribution. The built-in loss is thereafter reduced by decreases in the difference between the property's adjusted tax basis and book value. See § 1.460-4(k)(3)(v)(A) for a rule relating to the amount of built-in income or built-in loss attributable to a contract accounted for under a long-term contract method of accounting.

(4) Accounts payable and other accrued but unpaid items. Accounts payable and other accrued but unpaid items contributed by a partner using the cash receipts and disbursements method of accounting are treated as section 704(c) property for purposes of applying the rules of this section.

(5) Other provisions of the Internal Revenue Code. Section 704(c) and this section apply to a contribution of property to the partnership only if the contribution is governed by section 721, taking into account other provisions of the Internal Revenue Code. For example, to the extent that a transfer of property to a partnership is a sale under section 707, the transfer is not a contribution of property to which section 704(c) applies.

(6) Other applications of section 704(c) principles. (i) Revaluations under section 704(b). The principles of this section apply to allocations with respect to property for which differences between book value and adjusted tax basis are created when a partnership revalues partnership property pursuant to § 1.704-1(b)(2)(iv)(f) (reverse section 704(c) allocations). Partnerships are not required to use the same allocation method for reverse section 704(c) allocations as for contributed property, even if at the time of revaluation the property is already subject to section 704(c) and paragraph (a) of this section. In addition, partnerships are not required to use the same allocation method for reverse section 704(c) allocations each time the partnership revalues its property. A partnership that makes allocations with respect to revalued property must use a reasonable method that is consistent with the purposes of section 704(b) and (c).

(ii) Basis adjustments. A partnership making adjustments under § 1.743-1(b) or 1.751-1(a)(2) must account for built-in gain or loss under section 704(c) in accordance with the principles of this section.

(7) Transfer of a partnership interest. If a contributing partner transfers a partnership interest, built-in gain or loss must be allocated to the transferee partner as it would have been allocated to the transferor partner. If the contributing partner transfers a portion of the partnership interest, the share of built-in gain or loss proportionate to the interest transferred must be allocated to the transferee partner. This rule does not apply to any person who acquired a partnership interest from a § 1.752-7 liability partner in a transaction to which paragraph (e)(1) of § 1.752-7 applies. See § 1.752-7(c)(1).

(8) Special rules. (i) Disposition in a nonrecognition transaction. If a partnership disposes of section 704(c) property in a nonrecognition transaction the substituted basis property (within the meaning of section 7701(a)(42)) is treated as section 704(c) property with the same amount of built-in gain or loss as the section 704(c) property disposed of by the partnership. If gain or loss is recognized in such a transaction, appropriate adjustments must be made. The allocation method for the substituted basis property must be consistent with the allocation method chosen for the original property. If a partnership transfers an item of section 704(c) property together with other property to a corporation under section 351, in order to preserve that item's built-in gain or loss, the basis in the stock received in exchange for the section 704(c) property is determined as if each item of section 704(c) property had been the only property transferred to the corporation by the partnership.

(ii) Disposition in an installment sale. If a partnership disposes of section 704(c) property in an installment sale as defined in section 453(b), the installment obligation received by the partnership is treated as the section 704(c) property with the same amount of built-in gain as the section 704(c) property disposed of by the partnership (with appropriate adjustments for any gain recognized on the installment sale). The allocation method for the installment obligation must be consistent with the allocation method chosen for the original property.

(iii) Contributed contracts. If a partner contributes to a partnership a contract that is section 704(c) property, and the partnership subsequently acquires property pursuant to the contract in a transaction in which less than all of the gain or loss is recognized, then the acquired property is treated as the section 704(c) property with the same amount of built-in gain or loss as the contract (with appropriate adjustments for any gain or loss recognized on the acquisition). For this purpose, the term contract includes, but is not limited to, options, forward contracts, and futures contracts. The allocation method for the acquired property must be consistent with the allocation method chosen for the contributed contract.

(iv) Capitalized amounts. To the extent that a partnership properly capitalizes all or a portion of an item as described in paragraph (a)(12) of this section, then the item or items to which such cost is properly capitalized is treated as section 704(c) property with the same amount of built-in loss as corresponds to the amount capitalized.

(9) Tiered partnerships. If a partnership contributes section 704(c) property to a second partnership (the lower-tier partnership), or if a partner that has contributed section 704(c) property to a partnership contributes that partnership interest to a second partnership (the upper-tier partnership), the upper-tier partnership must allocate its distributive share of lower-tier partnership items with respect to that section 704(c) property in a manner that takes into account the contributing partner's remaining built-in gain or loss. Allocations made under this paragraph will be considered to be made in a manner that meets the requirements of § 1.704-1(b)(2)(iv)(q) (relating to capital account adjustments where guidance is lacking).

(10) Anti-abuse rule. An allocation method (or combination of methods) is not reasonable if the contribution of property (or event that results in reverse section 704(c) allocations) and the corresponding allocation of tax items with respect to the property are made with a view to shifting the tax consequences of built-in gain or loss among the partners in a manner that substantially reduces the present value of the partners' aggregate tax liability.

(11) Contributing and noncontributing partners' recapture shares. For special rules applicable to the allocation of depreciation recapture with respect to property contributed by a partner to a partnership, see §§ 1.1245-1(e)(2) and 1.1250-1(f).

(12) § 1.752-7 liabilities. Except as otherwise provided in § 1.752-7, § 1.752-7 liabilities (within the meaning of § 1.752-7(b)(2)) are section 704(c) property (built-in loss property that at the time of contribution has a book value that differs from the contributing partner's adjusted tax basis) for purposes of applying the rules of this section. See § 1.752-7(c). To the extent that the built-in loss associated with the § 1.752-7 liability exceeds the cost of satisfying the § 1.752-7 liability (as defined in § 1.752-7(b)(3)), the excess creates a ''ceiling rule'' limitation, within the meaning of § 1.704-3(b)(1), subject to the methods of allocation set forth in § 1.704-3(b), (c) and (d).

(b) Traditional method. *(1) In general.* This paragraph (b) describes the traditional method of making section 704(c) allocations. In general, the traditional method requires that when the partnership has income, gain, loss, or deduction attributable to section 704(c) property, it must make appropriate allocations to the partners to avoid shifting the tax consequences of the built-in gain or loss. Under this rule, if the partnership sells section 704(c) property and recognizes gain or loss, built-in gain or loss on the property is allocated to the contributing partner. If the partnership sells a portion of, or an interest in, section 704(c) property, a proportionate part of the built-in gain or loss is allocated to the contributing partner. For section 704(c) property subject to amortization, depletion, depreciation, or other cost recovery, the allocation of deductions attributable to these items takes into account built-in gain or loss on the property. For example, tax allocations to the noncontributing partners of cost recovery deductions with respect to section 704(c) property generally must, to the extent possible, equal book allocations to those partners. However, the total income, gain, loss, or deduction allocated to the partners for a taxable year with respect to a property cannot exceed the total partnership income, gain, loss, or deduction with respect to that property for the taxable year (the ceiling rule). If a partnership has no property the allocations from which are limited by the ceiling rule, the traditional method is reasonable when used for all contributed property.

(2) Examples. The following examples illustrate the principles of the traditional method.

Example (1). Operation of the traditional method.

(i) Calculation of built-in gain on contribution. A and B form partnership AB and agree that each will be allocated a 50 percent share of all partnership items and that AB will make allocations under section 704(c) using the traditional method under paragraph (b) of this section. A contributes depreciable property with an adjusted tax basis of $4,000 and a book value of $10,000, and B contributes $10,000 cash. Under paragraph (a)(3) of this section, A has built-in gain of $6,000, the excess of the partnership's book value for the property ($10,000) over A's adjusted tax basis in the property at the time of contribution ($4,000).

(ii) Allocation of tax depreciation. The property is depreciated using the straight-line method over a 10-year recovery period. Because the property depreciates at an annual rate of 10 percent, B would have been entitled to a depreciation deduction of $500 per year for both book and tax purposes if the adjusted tax basis of the property equalled its fair market value at the time of contribution. Although each partner is allocated $500 of book depreciation per year, the partnership is allowed a tax depreciation deduction of only $400 per year (10 percent of $4,000). The partnership can allocate only $400 of tax depreciation under the ceiling rule of paragraph (b)(1) of this section, and it must be allocated entirely to B. In AB's first year, the proceeds generated by the equipment exactly equal AB's operating expenses. At the end of that year, the book value of the property is $9,000 ($10,000 less the $1,000 book depreciation deduction), and the adjusted tax basis is $3,600 ($4,000 less the $400 tax depreciation deduction). A's built-in gain with respect to the property decreases to $5,400 ($9,000 book value less $3,600 adjusted tax basis). Also, at the end of AB's first year, A has a $9,500 book capital account and a $4,000 tax basis in A's partnership interest. B has a $9,500 book capital account and a $9,600 adjusted tax basis in B's partnership interest.

(iii) Sale of the property. If AB sells the property at the beginning of AB's second year for $9,000, AB realizes tax gain of $5,400 ($9,000, the amount realized, less the adjusted tax basis of $3,600). Under paragraph (b)(1) of this section, the entire $5,400 gain must be allocated to A because the property A contributed has that much built-in gain remaining. If AB sells the property at the beginning of AB's second year for $10,000, AB realizes tax gain of $6,400 ($10,000, the amount realized, less the adjusted tax basis of $3,600). Under paragraph (b)(1) of this section, only $5,400 of gain must be allocated to A to account for A's built-in gain. The remaining $1,000 of gain is allocated equally between A and B in accordance with the partnership agreement. If AB sells the property for less than the $9,000 book value, AB realizes tax gain of less than $5,400, and the entire gain must be allocated to A.

(iv) Termination and liquidation of partnership. If AB sells the property at the beginning of AB's second year for $9,000, and AB engages in no other transactions that year, A will recognize a gain of $5,400, and B will recognize no income or loss. A's adjusted tax basis for A's interest in AB will then be $9,400 ($4,000, A's original tax basis, increased by the gain of $5,400). B's adjusted tax basis for B's interest in AB will be $9,600 ($10,000, B's original tax basis, less the $400 depreciation deduction in the first partnership year). If the partnership then terminates and distributes its assets ($19,000 in cash) to A and B in proportion to their capital account balances, A will recognize a capital gain of $100 ($9,500, the amount distributed to A, less $9,400, the adjusted tax basis of A's interest). B will recognize a capital loss of $100 (the excess of B's adjusted tax basis, $9,600, over the amount received, $9,500).

Example (2). Unreasonable use of the traditional method.

(i) Facts. C and D form partnership CD and agree that each will be allocated a 50 percent share of all partnership items and that CD will make allocations under section 704(c) using the traditional method under paragraph (b) of this section. C contributes equipment with an adjusted tax basis of $1,000 and a book value of $10,000, with a view to taking advantage of the fact that the equipment has only one year remaining on its cost recovery schedule although its remaining economic life is significantly longer. At the time of contribution, C has a built-in gain of $9,000 and the equipment is section 704(c) property. D contributes $10,000 of cash, which CD uses to buy securities. D has substantial net operating loss carryforwards that D anticipates will otherwise expire unused. Under § 1.704-1(b)(2)(iv)(g)(3), the partnership must allocate the $10,000 of book depreciation to the partners in the first year of the partnership. Thus, there is $10,000 of book depreciation and $1,000 of tax depreciation in the partnership's first year. CD sells the equipment during the second year for $10,000 and recognizes a $10,000 gain ($10,000, the amount realized, less the adjusted tax basis of $0).

(ii) Unreasonable use of method.

(A) At the beginning of the second year, both the book value and adjusted tax basis of the equipment are $0. Therefore, there is no remaining built-in gain. The $10,000 gain on the sale of the equipment in the second year is allocated $5,000 each to C and D. The interaction of the partnership's one-year write-off of the entire book value of the equipment and the use of the traditional method results in a shift of $4,000 of the precontribution gain in the equipment from C to D (D's $5,000 share of CD's $10,000 gain, less the $1,000 tax depreciation deduction previously allocated to D).

(B) The traditional method is not reasonable under paragraph (a)(10) of this section because the contribution of property is made, and the traditional method is used, with a view to shifting a significant amount of taxable income to a partner with a low marginal tax rate and away from a partner with a high marginal tax rate.

(C) Under these facts, if the partnership agreement in effect for the year of contribution had provided that tax gain from the sale of the property (if any) would always be allocated first to C to offset the effect of the ceiling rule limitation, the allocation method would not violate the anti-abuse rule of paragraph (a)(10) of this section. See paragraph (c)(3) of this section. Under other facts, (for example, if the partnership holds multiple section 704(c) properties and either uses multiple allocation methods or uses a single allocation method where one or more of the properties are subject to the ceiling rule) the allocation to C may not be reasonable.

(c) Traditional method with curative allocations. *(1) In general.* To correct distortions created by the ceiling rule, a partnership using the traditional method under paragraph (b) of this section may make reasonable curative allocations to reduce or eliminate disparities between book and tax items of noncontributing partners. A curative allocation is an allocation of income, gain, loss, or deduction for tax purposes that differs from the partnership's allocation of the corresponding book item. For example, if a noncontributing partner is allocated less tax depreciation than book depreciation with respect to an item of section 704(c) property, the partnership may make a curative allocation to that partner of tax depreciation from another item of partnership property to make up the difference, notwithstanding that the corresponding book depreciation is allocated to the contributing partner. A partnership may limit its curative allocations to allocations of one or more particular tax items (e.g., only depreciation from a specific property or properties) even if the allocation of those available items does not offset fully the effect of the ceiling rule.

(2) Consistency. A partnership must be consistent in its application of curative allocations with respect to each item of section 704(c) property from year to year.

(3) Reasonable curative allocations. (i) Amount. A curative allocation is not reasonable to the extent it exceeds the amount necessary to offset the effect of the ceiling rule for the current taxable year or, in the case of a curative allocation upon disposition of the property, for prior taxable years.

(ii) Timing. The period of time over which the curative allocations are made is a factor in determining whether the allocations are reasonable. Notwithstanding paragraph (c)(3)(i) of this section, a partnership may make curative allocations in a taxable year to offset the effect of the ceiling rule for a prior taxable year if those allocations are made over a reasonable period of time, such as over the property's economic life, and are provided for under the partnership agreement in effect for the year of contribution. See paragraph (c)(4) Example 3(ii)(C) of this section.

(iii) Type. (A) In general. To be reasonable, a curative allocation of income, gain, loss, or deduction must be expected to have substantially the same effect on each partner's tax liability as the tax item limited by the ceiling rule. The expectation must exist at the time the section 704(c) property is obligated to be (or is) contributed to the partnership and the allocation with respect to that property becomes part of the partnership agreement. However, the expectation is tested at the time the allocation with respect to that property is actually made if the partnership agreement is not sufficiently specific as to the precise manner in which allocations are to be made with respect to that property. Under this paragraph (c), if the item limited by the ceiling rule is loss from the sale of property, a curative allocation of gain must be expected to have substantially the same effect as would an allocation to that partner of gain with respect to the sale of the property. If the item limited by the ceiling rule is depreciation or other cost recovery, a curative allocation of income to the contributing partner must be expected to have substantially the same effect as would an allocation to that partner of partnership income with respect to the contributed property. For example, if depreciation deductions with respect to leased equipment contributed by a tax-exempt partner are limited by the ceiling rule, a curative allocation of dividend or interest income to that partner generally is not reasonable, although a curative allocation of depreciation deductions from other leased equipment to the noncontributing partner is reasonable. Similarly, under this rule, if depreciation deductions apportioned to foreign source income in a particular statutory grouping under section 904(d) are limited by the ceiling rule, a curative allocation of income from another statutory grouping to the contributing partner generally is not reasonable, although a curative allocation of income from the same statutory grouping and of the same character is reasonable.

(B) Exception for allocation from disposition of contributed property. If cost recovery has been limited by the ceiling rule, the general limitation on character does not apply to income from the disposition of contributed property subject to the ceiling rule, but only if properly provided for in the partnership agreement in effect for the year of contribution or revaluation. For example, if allocations of depreciation deductions to a noncontributing partner have been limited by the ceiling rule, a curative allocation to the contributing partner of gain from the sale of that property, if properly provided for in the partnership agreement, is reasonable for purposes of paragraph (c)(3)(iii)(A) of this section even if not of the same character.

(4) Examples. The following examples illustrate the principles of this paragraph (c).

Example (1). Reasonable and unreasonable curative allocations.

(i) Facts. E and F form partnership EF and agree that each will be allocated a 50 percent share of all partnership items and that EF will make allocations under section 704(c) using the traditional method with curative allocations under paragraph (c) of this section. E contributes equipment with an adjusted tax basis of $4,000 and a book value of $10,000. The equipment has 10 years remaining on its cost recovery schedule and is depreciable using the straight-line method. At the time of contribution, E has a built-in gain of $6,000, and therefore, the equipment is section 704(c) property. F contributes $10,000 of cash, which EF uses to buy inventory for resale. In EF's first year, the revenue generated by the equipment equals EF's operating expenses. The equipment generates $1,000 of book depreciation and $400 of tax depreciation for each of 10 years. At the end of the first year EF sells all the inventory for $10,700, recognizing $700 of income. The partners anticipate that the inventory income will have substantially the same effect on their tax liabilities as income from E's contributed equipment. Under the traditional method of paragraph (b) of this section, E and F would each be allocated $350 of income from the sale of inventory for book and tax purposes and $500 of depreciation for book purposes. The $400 of tax depreciation would all be allocated to F. Thus, at the end of the first year, E and F's book and tax capital accounts would be as follows:

E		F		
Book	Tax	Book	Tax	
$10,000	$4,000	$10,000	$10,000	Initial contribution
<500>	<0>	<500>	<400>	Depreciation
350	350	350	350	Sales income
$ 9,850	$4,350	$ 9,850	$ 9,950	

(ii) Reasonable curative allocation. Because the ceiling rule would cause a disparity of $100 between F's book and tax capital accounts, EF may properly allocate to E under paragraph (c) of this section an additional $100 of income from the sale of inventory for tax purposes. This allocation results in capital accounts at the end of EF's first year as follows:

E		F		
Book	Tax	Book	Tax	
$10,000	$4,000	$10,000	$10,000	Initial contribution
<500>	<0>	<500>	<400>	Depreciation
350	450	350	250	Sales income
$ 9,850	$4,450	$ 9,850	$ 9,850	

(iii) Unreasonable curative allocation.

(A) The facts are the same as in paragraphs (i) and (ii) of this Example 1, except that E and F choose to allocate all the income from the sale of the inventory to E for tax purposes, although they share it equally for book purposes. This allocation results in capital accounts at the end of EF's first year as follows:

E		F		
Book	Tax	Book	Tax	
$10,000	$4,000	$10,000	$10,000	Initial contribution
<500>	<0>	<500>	<400>	Depreciation
350	700	350	0	Sales income
$ 9,850	$4,700	$ 9,850	$ 9,600	

(B) This curative allocation is not reasonable under paragraph (c)(3)(i) of this section because the allocation exceeds the amount necessary to offset the disparity caused by the ceiling rule.

Example (2). Curative allocations limited to depreciation.

(i) Facts. G and H form partnership GH and agree that each will be allocated a 50 percent share of all partnership items and that GH will make allocations under section 704(c) using the traditional method with curative allocations under paragraph (c) of this section, but only to the extent that the partnership has sufficient tax depreciation deductions. G contributes property G1, with an adjusted tax basis of $3,000 and a fair market value of $10,000, and H contributes property H1, with an adjusted tax basis of $6,000 and a fair market value of $10,000. Both properties have 5 years remaining on their cost recovery schedules and are depreciable using the straight-line method. At the time of contribution, G1 has a built-in gain of $7,000 and H1 has a built-in gain of $4,000, and therefore, both properties are section 704(c) property. G1 generates $600 of tax depreciation and $2,000 of book depreciation for each of five years. H1 generates $1,200 of tax depreciation and $2,000 of book depreciation for each of 5 years. In addition, the properties each generate $500 of operating income annually. G and H are each allocated $1,000 of book depreciation for each property. Under the traditional method of paragraph (b) of this section, G would be allocated $0 of tax depreciation for G1 and $1,000 for H1, and H would be allocated $600 of tax depreciation for G1 and $200 for H1. Thus, at the end of the first year, G and H's book and tax capital accounts would be as follows:

G		H		
Book	Tax	Book	Tax	
$ 10,000	$ 3,000	$ 10,000	$ 6,000	Initial contribution
<1,000>	<0>	<1,000>	<600>	G1 depreciation
<1,000>	<1,000>	<1,000>	<200>	H1 depreciation
500	500	500	500	Operating income
$ 8,500	$ 2,500	$ 8,500	$ 5,700	

(ii) Curative allocations. Under the traditional method, G is allocated more depreciation deductions than H, even though H contributed property with a smaller disparity reflected on GH's book and tax capital accounts. GH makes curative allocations to H of an additional $400 of tax depreciation each year, which reduces the disparities between G and H's book and tax capital accounts ratably each year. These allocations are reasonable provided the allocations meet the other requirements of this section. As a result of their agreement, at the end of the first year, G and H's capital accounts are as follows:

G		H		
Book	Tax	Book	Tax	
$ 10,000	$ 3,000	$ 10,000	$ 6,000	Initial contribution
<1,000>	<0>	<1,000>	<600>	G1 depreciation
<1,000>	<600>	<1,000>	<600>	H1 depreciation
500	500	500	500	Operating income
$ 8,500	$ 2,900	$ 8,500	$ 5,300	

Example (3). Unreasonable use of curative allocations.

(i) Facts. J and K form partnership JK and agree that each will receive a 50 percent share of all partnership items and that JK will make allocations under section 704(c) using the traditional method with curative allocations under paragraph (c) of this section. J contributes equipment with an adjusted tax basis of $1,000 and a book value of $10,000, with a view to taking advantage of the fact that the equipment has only one year remaining on its cost recovery schedule although it has an estimated remaining economic life of 10 years. J has substantial net operating loss carryforwards that J anticipates will otherwise expire unused. At the time of contribution, J has a built-in gain of $9,000, and therefore, the equipment is section 704(c) property. K contributes $10,000 of cash, which JK uses to buy inventory for resale. In JK's first year, the revenues generated by the equipment exactly equal JK's operating expenses. Under § 1.704-1(b)(2)(iv)(g)(3), the partnership must allocate the $10,000 of book depreciation to the partners in the first year of the partnership. Thus, there is $10,000 of book depreciation and $1,000 of tax depreciation in the partnership's first year. In addition, at the end of the first year JK sells all of the inventory for $18,000, recognizing $8,000 of income. The partners anticipate that the inventory income will have substantially the same effect on their tax liabilities as income from J's contributed equipment. Under the traditional method of paragraph (b) of this section, J and K's book and tax capital accounts at the end of the first year would be as follows:

J		K		
Book	Tax	Book	Tax	
$ 10,000	$ 1,000	$ 10,000	$ 10,000	Initial contribution
<5,000>	<0>	<5,000>	<1,000>	Depreciation
4,000	4,000	4,000	4,000	Sales income
$ 9,000	$ 5,000	$ 9,000	$ 13,000	

(ii) Unreasonable use of method.

(A) The use of curative allocations under these facts to offset immediately the full effect of the ceiling rule would result in the following book and tax capital accounts at the end of JK's first year:

J		K		
Book	Tax	Book	Tax	
$ 10,000	$ 1,000	$ 10,000	$ 10,000	Initial contribution
<5,000>	<0>	<5,000>	<1,000>	Depreciation
4,000	8,000	4,000	0	Sales income
$ 9,000	$ 9,000	$ 9,000	$ 9,000	

(B) This curative allocation is not reasonable under paragraph (a)(10) of this section because the contribution of property is made and the curative allocation method is used with a view to shifting a significant amount of partnership taxable income to a partner with a low marginal tax rate and away from a partner with a high marginal tax rate, within a period of time significantly shorter than the economic life of the property.

(C) The property has only one year remaining on its cost recovery schedule even though its economic life is considerably longer. Under these facts, if the partnership agreement had provided for curative allocations over a reasonable period of time, such as over the property's economic life, rather than over its remaining cost recovery period, the allocations would have been reasonable. See paragraph (c)(3)(ii) of this section. Thus, in this example, JK would make a curative allocation of $400 of sales income to J in the partnership's first year (10 percent of $4,000). J and K's book and tax capital accounts at the end of the first year would be as follows:

J		K		
Book	Tax	Book	Tax	
$ 10,000	$ 1,000	$ 10,000	$ 10,000	Initial contribution
<5,000>	<0>	<5,000>	<1,000>	Depreciation
4,000	4,400	4,000	3,600	Sales income
$ 9,000	$ 5,400	$ 9,000	$ 12,600	

(d) Remedial allocation method. *(1) In general.* A partnership may adopt the remedial allocation method described in this paragraph to eliminate distortions caused by the ceiling rule. A partnership adopting the remedial allocation method eliminates those distortions by creating remedial items and allocating those items to its partners. Under the remedial allocation method, the partnership first determines the amount of book items under paragraph (d)(2) of this section and the partners' distributive shares of these items under section 704(b). The partnership then allocates the corresponding tax items recognized by the partnership, if any, using the traditional method described in paragraph (b)(1) of this section. If the ceiling rule (as defined in paragraph (b)(1) of this section) causes the book allocation of an item to a noncontributing partner to differ from the tax allocation of the same item to the noncontributing partner, the partnership creates a remedial item of income, gain, loss, or deduction equal to the full amount of the difference and allocates it to the noncontributing partner. The partnership simultaneously creates an offsetting remedial item in an identical amount and allocates it to the contributing partner.

(2) Determining the amount of book items. Under the remedial allocation method, a partnership determines the amount of book items attributable to contributed property in the following manner rather than under the rules of § 1.704-1(b)(2)(iv)(g)(3). The portion of the partnership's book basis in the property equal to the adjusted tax basis in the property at the time of contribution is recovered in the same manner as the adjusted tax basis in the property is recovered (generally, over the property's remaining recovery period under section 168(i)(7) or other applicable Internal Revenue Code section). The remainder of the partnership's book basis in the property (the amount by which book basis exceeds adjusted tax basis) is recovered using any recovery period and depreciation (or other cost recovery) method (including first-year conventions) available to the partnership for newly purchased property (of the same type as the contributed property) that is placed in service at the time of contribution.

(3) Type. Remedial allocations of income, gain, loss, or deduction to the noncontributing partner have the same tax attributes as the tax item limited by the ceiling rule. The tax attributes of offsetting remedial allocations of income, gain, loss, or deduction to the contributing partner are determined by reference to the item limited by the ceiling rule. Thus, for example, if the ceiling rule limited item is loss from the sale of contributed property, the offsetting remedial allocation to the contributing partner must be gain from the sale of that property. Conversely, if the ceiling rule limited item is gain from the sale of contributed property, the offsetting remedial allocation to the contributing partner must be loss from the sale of that property. If the ceiling rule limited item is depreciation or other cost recovery from the contributed property, the offsetting remedial allocation to the contributing partner must be income of the type produced (directly or indirectly) by that property. Any partner level tax attributes are determined at the partner level. For example, if the ceiling rule limited item is depreciation from property used in a rental activity, the remedial allocation to the noncontributing partner is depreciation from property used in a rental activity and the offsetting remedial allocation to the contributing partner is ordinary income from that rental activity. Each partner then applies section 469 to the allocations as appropriate.

(4) Effect of remedial items. (i) Effect on partnership. Remedial items do not affect the partnership's computation of its taxable income under section 703 and do not affect the partnership's adjusted tax basis in partnership property.

(ii) Effect on partners. Remedial items are notional tax items created by the partnership solely for tax purposes and do not affect the partners' book capital accounts. Remedial items have the same effect as actual tax items on a partner's tax liability and on the partner's adjusted tax basis in the partnership interest.

(5) Limitations on use of methods involving remedial allocations. (i) Limitation on taxpayers. In the absence of published guidance, the remedial allocation method described in this paragraph (d) is the only reasonable section 704(c) method permitting the creation of notional tax items.

(ii) Limitation on internal revenue service. In exercising its authority under paragraph (a)(10) of this section to make adjustments if a partnership's allocation method is not reasonable, the Internal Revenue Service will not require a partnership to use the remedial allocation method described in this paragraph (d) or any other method involving the creation of notional tax items.

(6) Adjustments to application of method. The Commissioner may, by published guidance, prescribe adjustments to the remedial allocation method under this paragraph (d) as necessary or appropriate. This guidance may, for example, prescribe adjustments to the remedial allocation method to prevent the duplication or omission of items of income or deduction or to reflect more clearly the partners' income or the income of a transferee of a partner.

(7) Examples. The following examples illustrate the principles of this paragraph (d).

Example (1). Remedial allocation method.

(i) Facts. On January 1, L and M form partnership LM and agree that each will be allocated a 50 percent share of all partnership items. The partnership agreement provides that LM will make allocations under section 704(c) using the remedial allocation method under this paragraph (d) and that the straight-line method will be used to recover excess book basis. L contributes depreciable property with an adjusted tax basis of $4,000 and a fair market value of $10,000. The property is depreciated using the straight-line method with a 10-year recovery period and has 4 years remaining on its recovery period. M contributes $10,000, which the partnership uses to purchase land. Except for the depreciation deductions, LM's expenses equal its income in each year of the 10 years commencing with the year the partnership is formed.

(ii) Years 1 through 4. Under the remedial allocation method of this paragraph (d), LM has book depreciation for each of its first 4 years of $1,600 [$1,000 ($4,000 adjusted tax basis divided by the 4-year remaining recovery period) plus $600 ($6,000 excess of book value over tax basis, divided by the NEW 10-year recovery period)]. (For the purpose of simplifying the example, the partnership's book depreciation is determined without regard to any first-year depreciation conventions.) Under the partnership agreement, L and M are each allocated 50 percent ($800) of the book depreciation. M is allocated $800 of tax depreciation and L is allocated the remaining $200 of tax depreciation ($1,000 - $800). See paragraph (d)(1) of this section. No remedial allocations are made because the ceiling rule does not result in a book allocation of depreciation to M different from the tax allocation. The allocations result in capital accounts at the end of LM's first 4 years as follows:

L		M		
Book	Tax	Book	Tax	
$ 10,000	$ 4,000	$ 10,000	$ 10,000	Initial contribution
<3,200>	<800>	<3,200>	<3,200>	Depreciation
$ 6,800	$ 3,200	$ 6,800	$ 6,800	

(iii) Subsequent years.

(A) For each of years 5 through 10, LM has $600 of book depreciation ($6,000 excess of initial book value over adjusted tax basis divided by the 10-year recovery period that commenced in year 1), but no tax depreciation. Under the partnership agreement, the $600 of book depreciation is allocated equally to L and M. Because of the application of the ceiling rule in year 5, M would be allocated $300 of book depreciation, but no tax depreciation. Thus, at the end of LM's fifth year L's and M's book and tax capital accounts would be as follows:

L		M		
Book	Tax	Book	Tax	
$ 6,800	$ 3,200	$ 6,800	$ 6,800	End of year 4
<300>		<300>		Depreciation
$ 6,500	$ 3,200	$ 6,500	$ 6,800	

(B) Because the ceiling rule would cause an annual disparity of $300 between M's allocations of book and tax depreciation, LM must make remedial allocations of $300 of tax depreciation deductions to M under the remedial allocation method for each of years 5 through 10. LM must also make an offsetting remedial allocation to L of $300 of taxable income, which must be of the same type as income produced by the property. At the end of year 5, LM's capital accounts are as follows:

L		M		
Book	Tax	Book	Tax	
$ 6,800	$ 3,200	$ 6,800	$ 6,800	End of year 4
<300>		<300>		Depreciation
	300		<300>	Remedial allocations
$ 6,500	$ 3,500	$ 6,500	$ 6,500	

(C) At the end of year 10, LM's capital accounts are as follows:

L		M		
Book	Tax	Book	Tax	
$ 6,500	$ 3,500	$ 6,500	$ 6,500	End of year 5
<1,500>		<1,500>		Depreciation
	1,500		<1,500>	Remedial allocations
$ 5,000	$ 5,000	$ 5,000	$ 5,000	

Example (2). Remedial allocations on sale.

(i) Facts. N and P form partnership NP and agree that each will be allocated a 50 percent share of all partnership items. The partnership agreement provides that NP will make allocations under section 704(c) using the remedial allocation method under this paragraph (d). N contributes Blackacre (land) with an adjusted tax basis of $4,000 and a fair market value of $10,000. Because N has a built-in gain of $6,000, Blackacre is section 704(c) property. P contributes Whiteacre (land) with an adjusted tax basis and fair market value of $10,000. At the end of NP's first year, NP sells Blackacre to Q for $9,000 and recognizes a capital gain of $5,000 ($9,000 amount realized less $4,000 adjusted tax basis) and a book loss of $1,000 ($9,000 amount realized less $10,000 book basis). NP has no other items of income, gain, loss, or deduction. If the ceiling rule were applied, N would be allocated the entire $5,000 of tax gain and N and P would each be allocated $500 of book loss. Thus, at the end of NP's first year N's and P's book and tax capital accounts would be as follows:

N		P		
Book	Tax	Book	Tax	
$ 10,000	$ 4,000	$ 10,000	$ 10,000	Initial contribution
<500>	5,000	<500>		Sale of Blackacre
$ 9,500	$ 9,000	$ 9,500	$ 10,000	

(ii) Remedial allocation. Because the ceiling rule would cause a disparity of $500 between P's allocation of book and tax loss, NP must make a remedial allocation of $500 of capital loss to P and an offsetting remedial allocation to N of an additional $500 of capital gain. These allocations result in capital accounts at the end of NP's first year as follows:

N		P		
Book	Tax	Book	Tax	
$ 10,000	$ 4,000	$ 10,000	$ 10,000	Initial contribution
<500>	5,000	<500>		Sale of Blackacre
	500		<500>	Remedial allocations
$ 9,500	$ 9,500	$ 9,500	$ 9,500	

Example (3). Remedial allocation where built-in gain property sold for book and tax loss.

(i) Facts. The facts are the same as in Example 2, except that at the end of NP's first year, NP sells Blackacre to Q for $3,000 and recognizes a capital loss of $1,000 ($3,000 amount realized less $4,000 adjusted tax basis) and a book loss of $7,000 ($3,000 amount realized less $10,000 book basis). If the ceiling rule were applied, P would be allocated the entire $1,000 of tax loss and N and P would each be allocated $3,500 of book loss. Thus, at the end of NP's first year, N's and P's book and tax capital accounts would be as follows:

N		P		
Book	Tax	Book	Tax	
$ 10,000	$ 4,000	$ 10,000	$ 10,000	Initial contribution
<3,500>	0	<3,500>	<1,000>	Sale of Blackacre
$ 6,500	$ 4,000	$ 4,500	$ 10,000	

(ii) Remedial allocation. Because the ceiling rule would cause a disparity of $2,500 between P's allocation of book and tax loss on the sale of Blackacre, NP must make a remedial allocation of $2,500 of capital loss to P and an offsetting remedial allocation to N of $2,500 of capital gain. These allocations result in capital accounts at the end of NP's first year as follows:

N		P		
Book	Tax	Book	Tax	
$ 10,000	$ 4,000	$ 10,000	$ 10,000	Initial contribution
<3,500>	0	<3,500>	<1,000>	Sale of Blackacre
	2,500		<2,500>	Remedial allocations
$ 6,500	$ 6,500	$ 6,500	$ 6,500	

(e) Exceptions and special rules. *(1) Small disparities.* (i) General rule. If a partner contributes one or more items of property to a partnership within a single taxable year of the partnership, and the disparity between the book value of the property and the contributing partner's adjusted tax basis in the property is a small disparity, the partnership may—

(A) Use a reasonable section 704(c) method;

(B) Disregard the application of section 704(c) to the property; or

(C) Defer the application of section 704(c) to the property until the disposition of the property.

(ii) Definition of small disparity.

A disparity between book value and adjusted tax basis is a small disparity if the book value of all properties contributed by one partner during the partnership taxable year does not differ from the adjusted tax basis by more than 15 percent of the adjusted tax basis, and the total gross disparity does not exceed $20,000.

(2) Aggregation. Each of the following types of property may be aggregated for purposes of making allocations under section 704(c) and this section if contributed by one partner during the partnership taxable year.

(i) Depreciable property. All property, other than real property, that is included in the same general asset account of the contributing partner and the partnership under section 168.

(ii) Zero-basis property. All property with a basis equal to zero, other than real property.

(iii) Inventory. For partnerships that do not use a specific identification method of accounting, each item of inventory, other than qualified financial assets (as defined in paragraph (e)(3)(ii) of this section.).

(3) Special aggregation rule for securities partnerships. (i) General rule. For purposes of making reverse section 704(c) allocations, a securities partnership may aggregate gains and losses from qualified financial assets using any reasonable approach that is consistent with the purpose of section 704(c). Notwithstanding paragraphs (a)(2) and (a)(6)(i) of this section, once a partnership adopts an aggregate approach, that partnership must apply the same aggregate approach to all of its qualified financial assets for all taxable years in which the partnership qualifies as a securities partnership. Paragraphs (e)(3)(iv) and (e)(3)(v) of this section describe approaches for aggregating reverse section 704(c) gains and losses that are generally reasonable. Other approaches may be reasonable in appropriate circumstances. See, however, paragraph (a)(10) of this section, which describes the circumstances under which section 704(c) methods, including the aggregate approaches described in this paragraph (e)(3), are not reasonable. A partnership using an aggregate approach must separately account for any built-in gain or loss from contributed property.

(ii) Qualified financial assets. (A) In general. A qualified financial asset is any personal property (including stock) that is actively traded. Actively traded means actively traded as defined in § 1.1092(d)-1 (defining actively traded property for purposes of the straddle rules).

(B) Management companies. For a management company, qualified financial assets also include the following, even if not actively traded: shares of stock in a corporation; notes, bonds, debentures, or other evidences of indebtedness; interest rate, currency, or equity notional principal contracts; evidences of an interest in, or derivative financial instruments in, any security, currency, or commodity, including any option, forward or futures contract, or short position; or any similar financial instrument.

(C) Partnership interests. An interest in a partnership is not a qualified financial asset for purposes of this paragraph (e)(3)(ii). However, for purposes of this paragraph (e)(3), a partnership (upper-tier partnership) that holds an interest in a securities partnership (lower-tier partnership) must take into account the lower-tier partnership's assets and qualified financial assets as follows:

(1) In determining whether the upper-tier partnership qualifies as an investment partnership, the upper-tier partnership must treat its proportionate share of the lower-tier securities partnership's assets as assets of the upper-tier partnership; and

(2) If the upper-tier partnership adopts an aggregate approach under this paragraph (e)(3), the upper-tier partnership must aggregate the gains and losses from its directly held qualified financial assets with its distributive share of the gains and losses from the qualified financial assets of the lower-tier securities partnership.

(iii) Securities partnership. (A) In general. A partnership is a securities partnership if the partnership is either a management company or an investment partnership, and the partnership makes all of its book allocations in proportion to the partners' relative book capital accounts (except for reasonable special allocations to a partner that provides management services or investment advisory services to the partnership).

(B) Definitions. (1) Management company. A partnership is a management company if it is registered with the Securities and Exchange Commission as a management company under the Investment Company Act of 1940, as amended (15 U.S.C. 80a).

(2) Investment partnership. A partnership is an investment partnership if:

(i) On the date of each capital account restatement, the partnership holds qualified financial assets that constitute at least 90 percent of the fair market value of the partnership's non-cash assets; and

(ii) The partnership reasonably expects, as of the end of the first taxable year in which the partnership adopts an aggregate approach under this paragraph (e)(3), to make revaluations at least annually.

(iv) Partial netting approach. This paragraph (e)(3)(iv) describes the partial netting approach of making reverse section 704(c) allocations. See Example 1 of paragraph (e)(3)(ix) of this section for an illustration of the partial netting approach. To use the partial netting approach, the partnership must establish appropriate accounts for each partner for the purpose of taking into account each partner's share of the book gains and losses and determining each partner's share of the tax gains and losses. Under the partial netting approach, on the date of each capital account restatement, the partnership:

(A) Nets its book gains and book losses from qualified financial assets since the last capital account restatement and allocates the net amount to its partners;

(B) Separately aggregates all tax gains and all tax losses from qualified financial assets since the last capital account restatement; and

(C) Separately allocates the aggregate tax gain and aggregate tax loss to the partners in a manner that reduces the disparity between the book capital account balances and the tax capital account balances (book-tax disparities) of the individual partners.

(v) Full netting approach. This paragraph (e)(3)(v) describes the full netting approach of making reverse section 704(c) allocations on an aggregate basis. See Example 2 of paragraph (e)(3)(ix) of this section for an illustration of the full netting approach. To use the full netting approach, the partnership must establish appropriate accounts for each partner for the purpose of taking into account each partner's share of the book gains and losses and determining each partner's share of the tax gains and losses. Under the full netting approach, on the date of each capital account restatement, the partnership:

(A) Nets its book gains and book losses from qualified financial assets since the last capital account restatement and allocates the net amount to its partners;

(B) Nets tax gains and tax losses from qualified financial assets since the last capital account restatement; and

(C) Allocates the net tax gain (or net tax loss) to the partners in a manner that reduces the book-tax disparities of the individual partners.

(vi) Type of tax gain or loss. The character and other tax attributes of gain or loss allocated to the partners under this paragraph (e)(3) must:

(A) Preserve the tax attributes of each item of gain or loss realized by the partnership;

(B) Be determined under an approach that is consistently applied; and

(C) Not be determined with a view to reducing substantially the present value of the partners' aggregate tax liability.

(vii) Disqualified securities partnerships. A securities partnership that adopts an aggregate approach under this paragraph (e)(3) and subsequently fails to qualify as a securities partnership must make reverse section 704(c) allocations on an asset-by-asset basis after the date of disqualification. The partnership, however, is not required to disaggregate the book gain or book loss from qualified asset revaluations before the date of disqualification when making reverse section 704(c) allocations on or after the date of disqualification.

(viii) Transitional rule for qualified financial assets revalued after effective date. A securities partnership revaluing its qualified financial assets pursuant to § 1.704-1(b)(2)(iv)(f) on or after the effective date of this section may use any reasonable approach to coordinate with revaluations that occurred prior to the effective date of this section.

(ix) Examples. The following examples illustrate the principles of this paragraph (e)(3).

Example (1). Operation of the partial netting approach.

(i) Facts. Two regulated investment companies, X and Y, each contribute $150,000 in cash to form PRS, a partnership that registers as a management company. The partnership agreement provides that book items will be allocated in accordance with the partners' relative book capital accounts, that book capital accounts will be adjusted to reflect daily revaluations of property pursuant to § 1.704-1(b)(2)(iv)(f)(5)(iii), and that reverse section 704(c) allocations will be made using the partial netting approach described in paragraph (e)(3)(iv) of this section. X and Y each have an initial book capital account of $150,000. In addition, the partnership establishes for each of X and Y a revaluation account with a beginning balance of $0. On Day 1, PRS buys Stock 1, Stock 2, and Stock 3 for $100,000 each. On Day 2, Stock 1 increases in value from $100,000 to $102,000, Stock 2 increases in value from $100,000 to $105,000, and Stock 3 declines in value from $100,000 to $98,000. At the end of Day 2, Z, a regulated investment company, joins PRS by contributing $152,500 in cash for a one-third interest in the partnership [$152,500 divided by $300,000 (initial values of stock) + $5,000 (net gain at end of Day 2) + $152,500]. PRS uses this cash to purchase Stock 4. PRS establishes a revaluation account for Z with a $0 beginning balance. As of the close of Day 3, Stock 1 increases in value from $102,000 to $105,000, and Stocks 2, 3, and 4 decrease in value from $105,000 to $102,000, from $98,000 to $96,000, and from $152,500 to $151,500, respectively. At the end of Day 3, PRS sells Stocks 2 and 3.

(ii) Book allocations. Day 2. At the end of Day 2, PRS revalues the partnership's qualified financial assets and increases X's and Y's book capital accounts by each partner's 50 percent share of the $5,000 ($2,000 + $5,000 - $2,000) net increase in the value of the partnership's assets during Day 2. PRS increases X's and Y's respective revaluation account balances by $2,500 each to reflect the amount by which each partner's book capital account increased on Day 2. Z's capital account is not affected because Z did not join PRS until the end of Day 2. At the beginning of Day 3, the partnership's accounts are as follows:

	Stock 1	Stock 2	Stock 3	Stock 4
Opening Balance	$100,000	$100,000	$100,000	—
Day 2 Adjustment	2,000	5,000	(2,000)	—
Total	$102,000	$105,000	$ 98,000	$152,500

X

	Book	Tax	Revaluation Account
Opening Balance	$150,000	$150,000	$ 0
Day 2 Adjustment	2,500	0	2,500
Closing Balance	$152,500	$150,000	$ 2,500

Y

	Book	Tax	Revaluation Account
Opening Balance	$150,000	$150,000	$ 0
Day 2 Adjustment	2,500	0	2,500
Closing Balance	$152,500	$150,000	$ 2,500

Z

	Book	Tax	Revaluation Account
Opening Balance	—	—	—
Day 2 Adjustment	—	—	—
Closing Balance	$152,500	$152,500	$ 0

(iii) Book and tax allocations. Day 3. At the end of Day 3, PRS decreases the book capital accounts of X, Y, and Z by $1,000 to reflect each partner's share of the $3,000 ($3,000 − $3,000 − $2,000 − $1,000) net decrease in the value of the partnership's qualified financial assets. PRS also reduces each partner's revaluation account balance by $1,000. Accordingly, X's and Y's revaluation account balances are reduced to $1,500 each and Z's revaluation account balance is ($1,000). PRS then separately allocates the tax gain from the sale of Stock 2 and the tax loss from the sale of Stock 3. The $2,000 of tax gain recognized on the sale of Stock 2 ($102,000 − $100,000) is allocated among the partners with positive revaluation account balances in accordance with the relative balances of those revaluation accounts. X's and Y's revaluation accounts have equal positive balances; thus, PRS allocates $1,000 of the gain from the sale of Stock 2 to X and $1,000 of that gain to Y. PRS allocates none of the gain from the sale to Z because Z's revaluation account balance is negative. The $4,000 of tax loss recognized from the sale of Stock 3 ($96,000 − $100,000) is allocated first to the partners with negative revaluation account balances to the extent of those balances. Because Z is the only partner with a negative revaluation account balance, the tax loss is allocated first to Z to the extent of Z's ($1,000) balance. The remaining $3,000 of tax loss is allocated among the partners in accordance with their distributive shares of the loss. Accordingly, PRS allocates $1,000 of tax loss from the sale of Stock 3 to each of X and Y. PRS also allocates an additional $1,000 of the tax loss to Z, so that Z's total share of the tax loss from the sale of Stock 3 is $2,000. PRS then reduces each partner's revaluation account balance by the amount of any tax gain allocated to that partner and increases each partner's revaluation account balance by the amount of any tax loss allocated to that partner. At the beginning of Day 4, the partnership's accounts are as follows:

	Stock 1	Stock 2	Stock 3	Stock 4
Opening Balance	$100,000	$100,000	$100,000	$152,500
Day 2 Adjustment	2,000	5,000	(2,000)	—
Day 3 Adjustment	3,000	(3,000)	(2,000)	(1,000)
Total	$105,000	$102,000	$ 96,000	$151,500

	Book	X and Y Tax	Revaluation Account
Opening Balance	$150,000	$150,000	$ 0
Day 2 Adjustment	2,500	0	2,500
Day 3 Adjustment	(1,000)	0	(1,000)
Total	$151,500	$150,000	$ 1,500
Gain from Stock 2	0	1,000	(1,000)
Loss from Stock 3	0	(1,000)	1,000
Closing Balance	$151,500	$150,000	$ 1,500

	Book	Z Tax	Revaluation Account
Opening Balance	$152,500	$152,500	$ 0
Day 3 Adjustment	(1,000)	0	(1,000)
Total	$151,500	$152,500	($ 1,000)
Gain from Stock 2	0	0	0
Loss from Stock 3	0	(2,000)	2,000
Closing Balance	$151,500	$150,500	$ 1,000

Example (2). Operation of the full netting approach.

(i) Facts. The facts are the same as in Example 1, except that the partnership agreement provides that PRS will make reverse section 704(c) allocations using the full netting approach described in paragraph (e)(3)(v) of this section.

(ii) Book allocations. Days 2 and 3. PRS allocates its book gains and losses in the manner described in paragraphs (ii) and (iii) of Example 1 (the partial netting approach). Thus, at the end of Day 2, PRS increases the book capital accounts of X and Y by $2,500 to reflect the appreciation in the partnership's assets from the close of Day 1 to the close of Day 2 and records that increase in the revaluation account created for each partner. At the end of Day 3, PRS decreases the book capital accounts of X, Y, and Z by $1,000 to reflect each partner's share of the decline in value of the partnership's assets from Day 2 to Day 3 and reduces each partner's revaluation account by a corresponding amount.

(iii) Tax allocations. Day 3. After making the book adjustments described in the previous paragraph, PRS allocates its net tax gain (or net tax loss) from its sales of qualified financial assets during Day 3. To do so, PRS first determines its net tax gain (or net tax loss) recognized from its sales of qualified financial assets for the day. There is a $2,000 net tax loss ($2,000 gain from the sale of Stock 2 less $4,000 loss from the sale of Stock 3) on the sale of PRS's qualified financial assets. Because Z is the only partner with a negative revaluation account balance, the partnership's net tax loss is allocated first to Z to the extent of Z's ($1,000) revaluation account balance. The remaining net tax loss is allocated among the partners in accordance with their distributive shares of loss. Thus, PRS allocates $333.33 of the $2,000 net tax loss to each of X and Y. PRS also allocates an additional $333.33 of the net tax loss to Z, so that the total net tax loss allocation to Z is $1,333.33. PRS then increases each partner's revaluation account balance by the amount of net tax loss allocated to that partner. At the beginning of Day 4, the partnership's accounts are as follows:

	Stock 1	Stock 2	Stock 3	Stock 4
Opening Balance	$100,000	$100,000	$100,000	$152,500
Day 2 Adjustment	2,000	5,000	(2,000)	—
Day 3 Adjustment	3,000	(3,000)	(2,000)	(1,000)
Total	$105,000	$102,000	$ 96,000	$151,500

	Book	X and Y Tax	Revaluation Account
Opening Balance	$150,000	$150,000	$ 0
Day 2 Adjustment	2,500	0	2,500
Day 3 Adjustment	(1,000)	0	(1,000)
Total	$151,500	$150,000	$ 1,500
Net Tax Loss—Stocks 2&3	0	(333)	333
Closing Balance	$151,500	$149,667	$ 1,833

	Z		
	Book	Tax	Revaluation Account
Opening Balance	$152,500	$152,500	$ 0
Day 3 Adjustment	(1,000)	0	(1,000)
Total	$151,500	$152,500	($ 1,000)
Net Tax Loss—Stocks 2&3	0	(1,333)	1,333
Closing Balance	$151,500	$151,167	$ 333

(4) Aggregation as permitted by the commissioner. The Commissioner may, by published guidance or by letter ruling, permit:

(i) Aggregation of properties other than those described in paragraphs (e)(2) and (e)(3) of this section;

(ii) Partnerships and partners not described in paragraph (e)(3) of this section to aggregate gain and loss from qualified financial assets; and

(iii) Aggregation of qualified financial assets for purposes of making section 704(c) allocations in the same manner as that described in paragraph (e)(3) of this section.

(f) Effective dates. With the exception of paragraphs (a)(8)(ii), (a)(8)(iii) and (a)(11) of this section, this section applies to properties contributed to a partnership and to restatements pursuant to § 1.704-1(b)(2)(iv)(f) on or after December 21, 1993. Paragraph (a)(11) of this section applies to properties contributed by a partner to a partnership on or after August 20, 1997. However, partnerships may rely on paragraph (a)(11) of this section for properties contributed before August 20, 1997, and disposed of on or after August 20, 1997. Paragraph (a)(8)(ii) applies to installment obligations received by a partnership in exchange for section 704(c) property on or after November 24, 2003. Paragraph (a)(8)(iii) applies to property acquired on or after November 24, 2003, by a partnership pursuant to a contract that is section 704(c) property. Except as otherwise provided in § 1.752-7(k), paragraphs (a)(8)(iv) and (a)(12) apply to § 1.752-7 liability transfers, as defined in § 1.752-7(b)(4), occurring on or after June 24, 2003. See § 1.752-7(k).

T.D. 8500, 12/21/93, amend T.D. 8585, 12/27/94, T.D. 8717, 5/8/97, T.D. 8730, 8/19/97, T.D. 9137, 7/15/2004, T.D. 9193, 3/21/2005, T.D. 9207, 5/23/2005.

PAR. 3. Section 1.704-3 is amended by revising the first sentence of paragraph (a)(6)(i) to read as follows:

Proposed § 1.704-3 Contributed property. [*For Preamble, see ¶ 152,359*]

(a)

* * * * *

(6) Other applications of section 704(c) principles. (i) Revaluations under section 704(b). The principles of this section apply to allocations with respect to property for which differences between book value and adjusted tax basis are created when a partnership revalues partnership property pursuant to § 1.704-1(b)(2)(iv)(f) or 1.704-1(b)(2)(iv)(s) (reverse section 704(c) allocations). * * *

* * * * *

PAR. 2. Section 1.704-3 is amended as follows:

1. Paragraphs (a)(9) through (a)(12) are redesignated as paragraphs (a)(10) through (a)(13) respectively.

2. New paragraph (a)(9) is added.

3. Paragraph (f) is amended by revising the paragraph heading and adding one additional sentence at the end of the paragraph.

The revisions and additions read as follows:

Proposed § 1.704-3 Contributed Property. [*For Preamble, see ¶ 152,903*]

(a) * * *

(9) Section 704(c) property transferred in an assets-over merger. Assets transferred to a transferee partnership from the transferor partnership in an assets-over merger as defined in § 1.708-1(c)(3)(i) (the transferor partnership being the partnership considered to have been terminated under § 1.708-1(c)(1) and the transferee partnership being the partnership considered to be the resulting partnership under § 1.708-(1)(c)(1)) may have both original section 704(c) gain or loss (see § 1.704-4(c)(4)(ii)(A) for the definition of original section 704(c) gain or loss) and new section 704(c) gain or loss. The transferee partnership may continue to use the section 704(c) allocation method adopted by the transferor partnership with respect to section 704(c) property originally contributed to the transferor partnership or it may adopt another reasonable section 704(c) method. Also, the transferee partnership may continue to use the section 704(c) allocation method adopted by the transferor partnership with respect to new section 704(c) gain or loss to account for differences between book value and adjusted tax basis as a result of a prior revaluation. In addition, the transferee partnership may adopt any reasonable section 704(c) method with respect to new section 704(c) gain or loss in excess of the amount of new section 704(c) gain or loss described in the prior sentence. With respect to both original and new section 704(c) gain or loss, the transferee partnership must use a reasonable method that is consistent with the purpose of sections 704(b) and 704(c).

* * * * *

(f) Effective/applicability date. * * * Paragraph (a)(9) is effective for any distribution of property after January 19, 2005, if such property was contributed in a merger using the assets-over form after May 3, 2004.

§ 1.704-4 Distribution of contributed property.

Caution: The Treasury has not yet amended Reg § 1.704-4 to reflect changes made by P.L. 105-34.

(a) Determination of gain and loss. *(1) In general.* A partner that contributes section 704(c) property to a partnership must recognize gain or loss under section 704(c)(1)(B) and this section on the distribution of such property to another partner within five years of its contribution to the partnership in an amount equal to the gain or loss that would have been allocated to such partner under section 704(c)(1)(A) and § 1.704-3 if the distributed property had been sold by the partnership to the distributee partner for its fair market value at the time of the distribution. See § 1.704-3(a)(3)(i) for a definition of section 704(c) property.

(2) Transactions to which section 704(c)(1)(B) applies. Section 704(c)(1)(B) and this section apply only to the extent that a distribution by a partnership is a distribution to a partner acting in the capacity of a partner within the meaning of section 731.

(3) Fair market value of property. The fair market value of the distributed section 704(c) property is the price at which the property would change hands between a willing buyer and a willing seller at the time of the distribution, neither being under any compulsion to buy or sell and both having reasonable knowledge of the relevant facts. The fair market value that a partnership assigns to distributed section 704(c) property will be regarded as correct, provided that the value is reasonably agreed to among the partners in an arm's-length negotiation and the partners have sufficiently adverse interests.

(4) Determination of five-year period. (i) General rule. The five-year period specified in paragraph (a)(1) of this section begins on and includes the date of contribution.

(ii) Section 708(b)(1)(B) terminations. A termination of the partnership under section 708(b)(1)(B) does not begin a new five-year period for each partner with respect to the built-in gain and built-in loss property that the terminated partnership is deemed to contribute to the new partnership under § 1.708-1(b)(1)(iv). See § 1.704-3(a)(3)(ii) for the definitions of built-in gain and built-in loss on section 704(c) property. This paragraph (a)(4)(ii) applies to terminations of partnerships under section 708(b)(1)(B) occurring on or after May 9, 1997; however, this paragraph (a)(4)(ii) may be applied to terminations occurring on or after May 9, 1996, provided that the partnership and its partners apply this paragraph (a)(4)(ii) to the termination in a consistent manner.

(5) Examples. The following examples illustrate the rules of this paragraph (a). Unless otherwise specified, partnership income equals partnership expenses (other than depreciation deductions for contributed property) for each year of the partnership, the fair market value of partnership property does not change, all distributions by the partnership are subject to section 704(c)(1)(B), and all partners are unrelated.

Example (1). Recognition of gain.

(i) On January 1, 1995, A, B, and C form partnership ABC as equal partners. A contributes $10,000 cash and Property A, nondepreciable real property with a fair market value of $10,000 and an adjusted tax basis of $4,000. Thus, there is a built-in gain of $6,000 on Property A at the time of contribution. B contributes $10,000 cash and Property B, nondepreciable real property with a fair market value and adjusted tax basis of $10,000. C contributes $20,000 cash.

(ii) On December 31, 1998, Property A and Property B are distributed to C in complete liquidation of C's interest in the partnership.

(iii) A would have recognized $6,000 of gain under section 704(c)(1)(A) and § 1.704-3 on the sale of Property A at the time of the distribution ($10,000 fair market value less $4,000 adjusted tax basis). As a result, A must recognize $6,000 of gain on the distribution of Property A to C. B would not have recognized any gain or loss under section 704(c)(1)(A) and § 1.704-3 on the sale of Property B at the time of distribution because Property B was not section 704(c) property. As a result, B does not recognize any gain or loss on the distribution of Property B.

Example (2). Effect of post-contribution depreciation deductions.

(i) On January 1, 1995, A, B, and C form partnership ABC as equal partners. A contributes Property A, depreciable property with a fair market value of $30,000 and an adjusted tax basis of $20,000. Therefore, there is a built-in gain of $10,000 on Property A. B and C each contribute $30,000 cash. ABC uses the traditional method of making section 704(c) allocations described in § 1.704-3(b) with respect to Property A.

(ii) Property A is depreciated using the straight-line method over its remaining 10-year recovery period. The partnership has book depreciation of $3,000 per year (10 percent of the $30,000 book basis), and each partner is allocated $1,000 of book depreciation per year (one-third of the total annual book depreciation of $3,000). The partnership has a tax depreciation deduction of $2,000 per year (10 percent of the $20,000 tax basis in Property A). This $2,000 tax depreciation deduction is allocated equally between B and C, the noncontributing partners with respect to Property A.

(iii) At the end of the third year, the book value of Property A is $21,000 ($30,000 initial book value less $9,000 aggregate book depreciation) and the adjusted tax basis is $14,000 ($20,000 initial tax basis less $6,000 aggregate tax depreciation). A's remaining section 704(c)(1)(A) built-in gain with respect to Property A is $7,000 ($21,000 book value less $14,000 adjusted tax basis).

(iv) On December 31, 1997, Property A is distributed to B in complete liquidation of B's interest in the partnership. If Property A had been sold for its fair market value at the time of the distribution, A would have recognized $7,000 of gain under section 704(c)(1)(A) and § 1.704-3(b). Therefore, A recognizes $7,000 of gain on the distribution of Property A to B.

Example (3). Effect of remedial method.

(i) On January 1, 1995, A, B, and C form partnership ABC as equal partners. A contributes Property A1, nondepreciable real property with a fair market value of $10,000 and an adjusted tax basis of $5,000, and Property A2, nondepreciable real property with a fair market value and adjusted tax basis of $10,000. B and C each contribute $20,000 cash. ABC uses the remedial method of making section 704(c) allocations described in § 1.704-3(d) with respect to Property A1.

(ii) On December 31, 1998, when the fair market value of Property A1 has decreased to $7,000, Property A1 is distributed to C in a current distribution. If Property A1 had been sold by the partnership at the time of the distribution, ABC would have recognized the $2,000 of remaining built-in gain under section 704(c)(1)(A) on the sale (fair market value of $7,000 less $5,000 adjusted tax basis). All of this gain would have been allocated to A. ABC would also have recognized a book loss of $3,000 ($10,000 original book value less $7,000 current fair market value of the property). Book loss in the amount of $2,000 would have been allocated equally between B and C. Under the remedial method, $2,000 of tax loss would also have been allocated equally to B and C to match their share of the book loss. As a result, $2,000 of gain would also have been allocated to A as an offsetting remedial allocation. A would have recognized $4,000 of total gain under section 704(c)(1)(A) on the sale of Property A1 ($2,000 of section 704(c) recognized gain plus $2,000 remedial gain). Therefore, A recognizes $4,000 of gain on the distribution of Property A1 to C under this section.

(b) Character of gain or loss. *(1) General rule.* Gain or loss recognized by the contributing partner under section 704(c)(1)(B) and this section has the same character as the gain or loss that would have resulted if the distributed property had been sold by the partnership to the distributee partner at the time of the distribution.

(2) Example. The following example illustrates the rule of this paragraph (b). Unless otherwise specified, partnership income equals partnership expenses (other than depreciation deductions for contributed property) for each year of the partnership, the fair market value of partnership property does not change, all distributions by the partnership are subject to section 704(c)(1)(B), and all partners are unrelated.

Example. Character of gain.

(i) On January 1, 1995, A and B form partnership AB. A contributes $10,000 and Property A, nondepreciable real property with a fair market value of $10,000 and an adjusted tax basis of $4,000, in exchange for a 25 percent interest in partnership capital and profits. B contributes $60,000 cash for a 75 percent interest in partnership capital and profits.

(ii) On December 31, 1998, Property A is distributed to B in a current distribution. Property A is used in a trade or business of B.

(iii) A would have recognized $6,000 of gain under section 704(c)(1)(A) on a sale of Property A at the time of the distribution (the difference between the fair market value ($10,000) and the adjusted tax basis ($4,000) of the property at that time). Because Property A is not a capital asset in the hands of Partner B and B holds more than 50 percent of partnership capital and profits, the character of the gain on a sale of Property A to B would have been ordinary income under section 707(b)(2). Therefore, the character of the gain to A on the distribution of Property A to B is ordinary income.

(c) Exceptions. *(1) Property contributed on or before October 3, 1989.* Section 704(c)(1)(B) and this section do not apply to property contributed to the partnership on or before October 3, 1989.

(2) Certain liquidations. Section 704(c)(1)(B) and this section do not apply to a distribution of an interest in section 704(c) property to a partner other than the contributing partner in a liquidation of the partnership if—

(i) The contributing partner receives an interest in the section 704(c) property contributed by that partner (and no other property); and

(ii) The built-in gain or loss in the interest distributed to the contributing partner, determined immediately after the distribution, is equal to or greater than the built-in gain or loss on the property that would have been allocated to the contributing partner under section 704(c)(1)(A) and § 1.704-3 on a sale of the contributed property to an unrelated party immediately before the distribution.

(3) Section 708(b)(1)(B) terminations. Section 704(c)(1)(B) and this section do not apply to the deemed distribution of interests in a new partnership caused by the termination of a partnership under section 708(b)(1)(B). A subsequent distribution of section 704(c) property by the new partnership to a partner of the new partnership is subject to section 704(c)(1)(B) to the same extent that a distribution by the terminated partnership would have been subject to section 704(c)(1)(B). See also § 1.737-2(a) for a similar rule in the context of section 737. This paragraph (c)(3) applies to terminations of partnerships under section 708(b)(1)(B) occurring on or after May 9, 1997; however, this paragraph (c)(3) may be applied to terminations occurring on or after May 9, 1996, provided that the partnership and its partners apply this paragraph (c)(3) to the termination in a consistent manner.

(4) Complete transfer to another partnership. Section 704(c)(1)(B) and this section do not apply to a transfer by a partnership (transferor partnership) of all of its assets and liabilities to a second partnership (transferee partnership) in an exchange described in section 721, followed by a distribution of the interest in the transferee partnership in liquidation of the transferor partnership as part of the same plan or arrangement. A subsequent distribution of section 704(c) property by the transferee partnership to a partner of the transferee partnership is subject to section 704(c)(1)(B) to the same extent that a distribution by the transferor partnership would have been subject to section 704(c)(1)(B). See § 1.737-2(b) for a similar rule in the context of section 737.

(5) Incorporation of a partnership. Section 704(c)(1)(B) and this section do not apply to an incorporation of a partnership by any method of incorporation (other than a method involving an actual distribution of partnership property to the partners followed by a contribution of that property to a corporation), provided that the partnership is liquidated as part of the incorporation transaction. See § 1.737-2(c) for a similar rule in the context of section 737.

(6) Undivided interests. Section 704(c)(1)(B) and this section do not apply to a distribution of an undivided interest in property to the extent that the undivided interest does not exceed the undivided interest, if any, contributed by the distributee partner in the same property. See § 1.737-2(d)(4) for the application of section 737 in a similar context. The portion of the undivided interest in property retained by the partnership after the distribution, if any, that is treated as contributed by the distributee partner, is reduced to the extent of the undivided interest distributed to the distributee partner.

(7) Example. The following example illustrates the rule of paragraph (c)(2) of this section. Unless otherwise specified, partnership income equals partnership expenses (other than depreciation deductions for contributed property) for each year of the partnership, the fair market value of partnership property does not change, all distributions by the partnership are subject to section 704(c)(1)(B), and all partners are unrelated.

Example. (i) On January 1, 1995, A and B form partnership AB, as equal partners. A contributes Property A, nondepreciable real property with a fair market value and adjusted tax basis of $20,000. B contributes Property B, nondepreciable real property with a fair market value of $20,000 and an adjusted tax basis of $10,000. Property B therefore has a built-in gain of $10,000 at the time of contribution.

(ii) On December 31, 1998, the partnership liquidates when the fair market value of Property A has not changed, but the fair market value of Property B has increased to $40,000.

(iii) In the liquidation, A receives Property A and a 25 percent interest in Property B. This interest in Property B has a fair market value of $10,000 to A, reflecting the fact that A was entitled to 50 percent of the $20,000 post-contribution appreciation in Property B. The partnership distributes to B a 75 percent interest in Property B with a fair market value of $30,000. B's basis in this portion of Property B is $10,000 under section 732(b). As a result, B has a built-in gain of $20,000 in this portion of Property B immediately after the distribution ($30,000 fair market value less $10,000 adjusted tax basis). This built-in gain is greater than the $10,000 of built-in gain in Property B at the time of contribution to the partnership. B therefore does not recognize any gain on the distribution of a portion of Property B to A under this section.

(d) Special rules. *(1) Nonrecognition transactions, installment obligations, contributed contracts, and capitalized costs.* (i) Nonrecognition transactions. Property received by the partnership in exchange for section 704(c) property in a nonrecognition transaction is treated as the section 704(c) property for purposes of section 704(c)(1)(B) and this section to the extent that the property received is treated as section 704(c) property under § 1.704-3(a)(8). See § 1.737-2(d)(3) for a similar rule in the context of section 737.

(ii) [Reserved].

(iii) [Reserved].

(iv) Capitalized costs. Property to which the cost of section 704(c) property is properly capitalized is treated as section 704(c) property for purposes of section 704(c)(1)(B) and this section to the extent that such property is treated as section 704(c) property under § 1.704-3(a)(8)(iv). See § 1.737-2(d)(3) for a similar rule in the context of section 737.

(2) Transfers of a partnership interest. The transferee of all or a portion of the partnership interest of a contributing partner is treated as the contributing partner for purposes of section 704(c)(1)(B) and this section to the extent of the share of built-in gain or loss allocated to the transferee partner. See § 1.704-3(a)(7).

(3) Distributions of like-kind property. If section 704(c) property is distributed to a partner other than the contributing partner and like-kind property (within the meaning of section 1031) is distributed to the contributing partner no later than the earlier of (i) 180 days following the date of the distribution to the non-contributing partner, or (ii) the due date (determined with regard to extensions) of the contributing partner's income tax return for the taxable year of the distribution to the noncontributing partner, the amount of gain or loss, if any, that the contributing partner would otherwise have recognized under section 704(c)(1)(B) and this section is reduced by the amount of built-in gain or loss in the distributed like-kind property in the hands of the contributing partner immediately after the distribution. The contributing partner's basis in the distributed like-kind property is determined as if the like-kind property were distributed in an unrelated distribution prior to the distribution of any other property distributed as part of the same distribution and is determined without regard to the increase in the contributing partner's adjusted tax basis in the partnership interest under section 704(c)(1)(B) and this section. See § 1.707-3 for provisions treating the distribution of the like-kind property to the contributing partner as a disguised sale in certain situations.

(4) Example. The following example illustrates the rules of this paragraph (d). Unless otherwise specified, partnership income equals partnership expenses (other than depreciation deductions for contributed property) for each year of the partnership, the fair market value of partnership property does not change, all distributions by the partnership are subject to section 704(c)(1)(B), and all partners are unrelated.

Example. Distribution of like-kind property.

(i) On January 1, 1995, A, B, and C form partnership ABC as equal partners. A contributes Property A, nondepreciable real property with a fair market value of $20,000 and an adjusted tax basis of $10,000. B and C each contribute $20,000 cash. The partnership subsequently buys Property X, nondepreciable real property of a like-kind to Property A with a fair market value and adjusted tax basis of $8,000. The fair market value of Property X subsequently increases to $10,000.

(ii) On December 31, 1998, Property A is distributed to B in a current distribution. At the same time, Property X is distributed to A in a current distribution. The distribution of Property X does not result in the contribution of Property A being properly characterized as a disguised sale to the partnership under § 1.707-3. A's basis in Property X is $8,000 under section 732(a)(1). A therefore has $2,000 of built-in gain in Property X ($10,000 fair market value less $8,000 adjusted tax basis).

(iii) A would generally recognize $10,000 of gain under section 704(c)(1)(B) on the distribution of Property A, the difference between the fair market value ($20,000) of the property and its adjusted tax basis ($10,000). This gain is reduced, however, by the amount of the built-in gain of Property X in the hands of A. As a result, A recognizes only $8,000 of gain on the distribution of Property A to B under section 704(c)(1)(B) and this section.

(e) Basis adjustments. *(1) Contributing partner's basis in the partnership interest.* The basis of the contributing partner's interest in the partnership is increased by the amount of the gain, or decreased by the amount of the loss, recognized by the partner under section 704(c)(1)(B) and this section. This increase or decrease is taken into account in determining (i) the contributing partner's adjusted tax basis under section 732 for any property distributed to the partner in a distribution that is part of the same distribution as the distribution of the contributed property, other than like-kind property described in paragraph (d)(3) of this section (pertaining to the special rule for distributions of like-kind property), and (ii) the amount of the gain recognized by the contributing partner under section 731 or section 737, if any, on a distribution of money or property to the contributing partner that is part of the same distribution as the distribution of the contributed property. For a determination of basis in a distribution subject to section 737, see § 1.737-3(a).

(2) Partnership's basis in partnership property. The partnership's adjusted tax basis in the distributed section 704(c) property is increased or decreased immediately before the distribution by the amount of gain or loss recognized by the contributing partner under section 704(c)(1)(B) and this section. Any increase or decrease in basis is therefore taken into account in determining the distributee partner's adjusted tax basis in the distributed property under section 732. For a determination of basis in a distribution subject to section 737, see § 1.737- 3(b).

(3) Section 754 adjustments. The basis adjustments to partnership property made pursuant to paragraph (e)(2) of this section are not elective and must be made regardless of whether the partnership has an election in effect under section 754. Any adjustments to the bases of partnership property (including the distributed section 704(c) property) under section 734(b) pursuant to a section 754 election must be made after (and must take into account) the adjustments to basis made under paragraph (e)(2) of this section. See § 1.737-3(c)(4) for a similar rule in the context of section 737.

(4) Example. The following example illustrates the rules of this paragraph (e). Unless otherwise specified, partnership income equals partnership expenses (other than depreciation deductions for contributed property) for each year of the partnership, the fair market value of partnership property does not change, all distributions by the partnership are subject to section 704(c)(1)(B), and all partners are unrelated.

Example. Basis adjustment.

(i) On January 1, 1995, A, B, and C form partnership ABC as equal partners. A contributes $10,000 cash and Property A, nondepreciable real property with a fair market value of $10,000 and an adjusted tax basis of $4,000. B and C each contribute $20,000 cash.

(ii) On December 31, 1998, Property A is distributed to B in a current distribution.

(iii) Under paragraph (a) of this section, A recognizes $6,000 of gain on the distribution of Property A because that is the amount of gain that would have been allocated to A under section 704(c)(1)(A) and § 1.704-3 on a sale of Property A for its fair market value at the time of the distribution (fair market value of Property A ($10,000) less its adjusted tax basis at the time of distribution ($4,000)). The adjusted tax basis of A's partnership interest is increased from $14,000 to $20,000 to reflect this gain. The partnership's adjusted tax basis in Property A is increased from $4,000 to $10,000 immediately prior to its distribution to B. B's adjusted tax basis in Property A is therefore $10,000 under section 732(a)(1).

(f) Anti-abuse rule. *(1) In general.* The rules of section 704(c)(1)(B) and this section must be applied in a manner consistent with the purpose of section 704(c)(1)(B). Accordingly, if a principal purpose of a transaction is to achieve a tax result that is inconsistent with the purpose of section 704(c)(1)(B), the Commissioner can recast the transaction for federal tax purposes as appropriate to achieve tax results that are consistent with the purpose of section 704(c)(1)(B) and this section. Whether a tax result is inconsistent with the purpose of section 704(c)(1)(B) and this section must be determined based on all the facts and circumstances. See § 1.737-4 for an anti-abuse rule and examples in the context of section 737.

(2) Examples. The following examples illustrate the anti-abuse rule of this paragraph (f). The examples set forth below do not delineate the boundaries of either permissible or impermissible types of transactions. Further, the addition of any facts or circumstances that are not specifically set forth in an example (or the deletion of any facts or circumstances) may alter the outcome of the transaction described in the example. Unless otherwise specified, partnership income equals partnership expenses (other than depreciation deductions for contributed property) for each year of the partnership, the fair market value of partnership property does not change, all distributions by the partnership are subject to section 704(c)(1)(B), and all partners are unrelated.

Example (1). Distribution in substance made within five-year period; results inconsistent with the purpose of section 704(c)(1)(B).

(i) On January 1, 1995, A, B, and C form partnership ABC as equal partners. A contributes Property A, nondepreciable real property with a fair market value of $10,000 and an adjusted tax basis of $1,000. B and C each contributes $10,000 cash.

(ii) On December 31, 1998, the partners desire to distribute Property A to B in complete liquidation of B's interest in the partnership. If Property A were distributed at that time, however, A would recognize $9,000 of gain under section 704(c)(1)(B), the difference between the $10,000 fair market value and the $1,000 adjusted tax basis of Property A, because Property A was contributed to the partnership less than five years before December 31, 1998. On becoming aware of this potential gain recognition, and with a principal purpose of avoiding such gain, the partners amend the partnership agreement on December 31, 1998, and take any other steps necessary to provide that substantially all of the economic risks and benefits of Property A are borne by B as of December 31, 1998, and that substantially all of the economic risks and benefits of all other partnership property are borne by A and C. The partnership holds Property A until January 5, 2000, at which time it is distributed to B in complete liquidation of B's interest in the partnership.

(iii) The actual distribution of Property A occurred more than five years after the contribution of the property to the partnership. The steps taken by the partnership on December 31, 1998, however, are the functional equivalent of an actual distribution of Property A to B in complete liquidation of B's interest in the partnership as of that date. Section 704(c)(1)(B) requires recognition of gain when contributed section 704(c) property is in substance distributed to another partner within five years of its contribution to the partnership. Allowing a contributing partner to avoid section 704(c)(1)(B) through arrangements such as those in this Example 1 that have the effect of a distribution of property within five years of the date of its contribution to the partnership would effectively undermine the purpose of section 704(c)(1)(B) and this section. As a result, the steps taken by the partnership on December 31, 1998, are treated as causing a distribution of Property A to B for purposes of section 704(c)(1)(B) on that date, and A recognizes gain of $9,000 under section 704(c)(1)(B) and this section at that time.

(iv) Alternatively, if on becoming aware of the potential gain recognition to A on a distribution of Property A on December 31, 1998, the partners had instead agreed that B would continue as a partner with no changes to the partnership agreement or to B's economic interest in partnership operations, the distribution of Property A to B on January 5, 2000, would not have been inconsistent with the purpose of section 704(c)(1)(B) and this section. In that situation, Property A would not have been distributed until after the expiration of the five-year period specified in section 704(c)(1)(B) and this section. Deferring the distribution of Property A until the end of the five-year period for a principal purpose of avoiding the recognition of gain under section 704(c)(1)(B) and this section is not inconsistent with the purpose of section 704(c)(1)(B). Therefore, A would not have recognized gain on the distribution of Property A in that case.

Example (2). suspension of five-year period in manner consistent with the purpose of section 704(c)(1)(B).

(i) A, B, and C form partnership ABC on January 1, 1995, to conduct bona fide business activities. A contributes Property A, nondepreciable real property with a fair market value of $10,000 and an adjusted tax basis of $1,000, in exchange for a 49.5 percent interest in partnership capital and profits. B contributes $10,000 in cash for a 49.5 percent interest in partnership capital and profits. C contributes cash for a 1 percent interest in partnership capital and profits. A and B are wholly owned subsidiaries of the same affiliated group and continue to control the management of Property A by virtue of their controlling interests in the partnership. The partnership is formed pursuant to a plan a principal purpose of which is to minimize the period of time that A would have to remain a partner with a potential acquiror of Property A.

(ii) On December 31, 1997, D is admitted as a partner to the partnership in exchange for $10,000 cash.

(iii) On January 5, 2000, Property A is distributed to D in complete liquidation of D's interest in the partnership.

(iv) The distribution of Property A to D occurred more than five years after the contribution of the property to the partnership. On these facts, however, a principal purpose of the transaction was to minimize the period of time that A would have to remain partners with a potential acquiror of Property A, and treating the five-year period of section 704(c)(1)(B) as running during a time when Property A was still effectively owned through the partnership by members of the contributing affiliated group of which A is a member is inconsistent with the purpose of section 704(c)(1)(B). Prior to the admission of D as a partner, the pooling of assets between A and B, on the one hand, and C, on the other hand, although sufficient to constitute ABC as a valid partnership for federal income tax purposes, is not a sufficient pooling of assets for purposes of running the five-year period with respect to the distribution of Property A to D. Allowing a contributing partner to avoid section 704(c)(1)(B) through arrangements such as those in this Example 2 would have the effect of substantially nullifying the five-year requirement of section 704(c)(1)(B) and this section and elevating the form of the transaction over its substance. As a result, with respect to the distribution of Property A to D, the five-year period of section 704(c)(1)(B) is tolled until the admission of D as a partner on December 31, 1997. Therefore, the distribution of Property A occurred before the end of the five-year period of section 704(c)(1)(B), and A recognizes gain of $9,000 under section 704(c)(1)(B) on the distribution.

(g) Effective dates. This section applies to distributions by a partnership to a partner on or after January 9, 1995, except that paragraph (d)(1)(iv) applies to distributions by a partnership to a partner on or after June 24, 2003.

T.D. 8642, 12/22/95, amend T.D. 8717, 5/8/97, T.D. 9193, 3/21/2005, T.D. 9207, 5/23/2005.

PAR. 3. Section 1.704-4 is amended as follows:

1. Paragraph (a)(1) is amended by removing the phrase "five years" and adding in its place the phrase "seven years."

2. Paragraph (a)(4)(i) is amended by removing the phrase "five-year" and adding in its place "seven-year."

3. Paragraph (a)(4)(ii) is amended by removing the phrase "five-year" and adding in its place the phrase "seven-year."

4. Paragraphs (c)(4)(i) and (c)(4)(ii) are added.

5. Paragraph (c)(7) is redesignated as paragraph (c)(8).

6. A new paragraph (c)(7) is added.

7. Paragraphs (f)(2), Examples (1) and (2) are amended by removing the language "five-year" and replacing it with the language "seven-year" wherever it appears throughout both examples.

8. Paragraph (g) is amended by revising the paragraph heading and adding two sentences at the end of the paragraph.

The revisions and additions read as follows:

Proposed § 1.704-4 Distribution of contributed property.
[*For Preamble, see ¶ 152,903*]

* * * * *

(c) * * *

(4) Complete transfer to another partnership (Assets-Over Merger). (i) In general. Section 704(c)(1)(B) and this section do not apply to the transfer in an assets-over merger as defined in § 1.708-1(c)(3)(i) by a partnership (the transferor partnership, which is considered to be the terminated partnership as a result of the merger) of all of its assets and liabilities to another partnership (the transferee partnership, which is considered to be the resulting partnership after the merger), followed by a distribution of the interest in the transferee partnership in liquidation of the transferor partnership as part of the same plan or arrangement.

(ii) Subsequent distributions. Except as provided in paragraph (c)(4)(E) below, section 704(c)(1)(B) and this section apply to the subsequent distribution by the transferee partnership of section 704(c) property contributed by the transferor partnership to the transferee partnership in an assets-over merger, as provided in paragraphs (c)(4)(ii)(A) through (D) of this section.

(A) Original section 704(c) gain or loss. The seven-year period in section 704(c)(1)(B) does not restart with respect to original section 704(c) gain or loss as a result of the transfer of the section 704(c) property to the transferee partnership. For purposes of this paragraph (c)(4)(ii)(A), the amount of original section 704(c) gain or loss is the difference between the property's fair market value and the contributing partner's adjusted tax basis, at the time of contribution, to the extent such difference has not been eliminated by section 704(c) allocations, prior revaluations, or in connection with the merger. See §§ 1.704-4(a) and (b) for post-merger distributions of property contributed to the transferee partnership prior to the merger. A subsequent distribution by the transferee partnership of property with original section 704(c) gain or loss to a partner other than the partner that contributed such property to the transferor partnership is subject to section 704(c)(1)(B) if the distribution occurs within seven years of the contribution of the property to the transferor partnership. See § 1.704-4(c)(4)(ii)(B) for rules relating to the distribution of property with new section 704(c) gain or loss. See § 1.737-2(b)(1)(ii)(A) for a similar rule in the context of section 737.

(B) New section 704(c) gain or loss. A subsequent distribution of property with new section 704(c) gain or loss by the transferee partnership to a partner other than the contributing partner is subject to section 704(c)(1)(B) if the distribution occurs within seven years of the contribution of the property to the transferee partnership by the transferor partnership. For these purposes, a partner of the transferor partnership is deemed to have contributed to the transferee partnership an undivided interest in the property of the transferor partnership. The determination of the partners' undivided interest for this purpose shall be determined by the transferor partnership using any reasonable method. New section 704(c) gain or loss shall be allocated among the partners of the transferor partnership in a manner consistent with the principles of §§ 1.704-3(a)(7) and 1.704-3(a)(10). See § 1.737-2(b)(1)(ii)(B) for a similar rule in the context of section 737.

(C) Ordering Rule. (1) Post-merger partial recognition. For purposes of this section, if less than all of a section 704(c) property is distributed, then a proportionate amount of original and new section 704(c) gain or loss must be recognized.

(2) Post-merger revaluation. Revaluations after a merger that reflect a reduction in the amount of built-in gain or loss inherent in property will reduce new section 704(c) gain or loss prior to reducing original section 704(c) gain or loss.

(D) Subsequent Mergers. If the transferee partnership (first transferee partnership) is subsequently merged into another partnership (new transferee partnership) the new section 704(c) gain or loss that resulted from the merger of the transferor partnership into the first transferee partnership shall be subject to section 704(c)(1)(B) for seven years from the time of the contribution by the transferor partnership to the first transferee partnership (original merger) and new section 704(c) gain or loss that resulted from the merger of the first transferee into the new transferee (subsequent merger) shall be subject to section 704(c)(1)(B) for seven years from the time of the subsequent merger. See § 1.737-2(b)(1)(ii)(D) for a similar rule in the context of section 737.

(E) Identical Ownership or De Minimis Change in Ownership Exception. Section 704(c)(1)(B) and this section do not apply to new section 704(c) gain or loss in property transferred by the transferor partnership to the transferee partnership if both the transferor partnership and the transferee partnership are owned by the same owners in the same proportions or the difference in ownership is de minimis. The transferor partnership and the transferee partnership are owned by the same owners in the same proportions if each partner owns identical interests in book capital and in each item of income, gain, loss, deduction, and credit, and identical shares of distributions and liabilities in each of the transferor and transferee partnerships. A difference in ownership is de minimis if ninety seven percent of the interests in book capital and in each item of income, gain, loss, deduction and credit and shares of distributions, and liabilities of the transferor partnership and transferee partnership are owned by the same owners in the same proportions. See § 1.737-2(b)(1)(ii)(E) for a similar rule in the context of section 737.

(F) Examples. The following examples illustrate the rules of paragraph (c)(4)(ii) of this section.

Example (1). New section 704(c) gain. (i) Facts. On January 1, 2005, A contributes Asset 1, with a basis of $200x and a fair market value of $300x, to partnership PRS1 in exchange for a 50 percent interest. On the same date, B contributes $300x of cash to PRS1 in exchange for a 50 percent interest. Also on January 1, 2005, C contributes Asset 2, with a basis of $100x and a fair market value of $200x, to partnership PRS2 in exchange for a 50 percent interest. D contributes $200x of cash to PRS2 in exchange for a 50 percent interest. On January 1, 2008, PRS1 and PRS2 undertake an assets-over partnership merger in which PRS1 is the continuing partnership and PRS2 is the terminating partnership for both state law and federal tax purposes. At the time of the merger, PRS1's only assets are Asset 1, with a fair market value of $900x, and $300x in cash. PRS2's only assets are Asset 2, with a fair market value of $600x, and $200x in cash. After the merger, the partners have book capital and profits interests in PRS1 as follows: A, 30 percent; B, 30 percent; C, 20 percent; and D, 20 percent. PRS1 and PRS2 both have provisions in their respective partnership agreements requiring the revaluation of partnership property upon entry of a new partner. PRS1 would not be treated as an investment company (within the meaning of section 351) if it were incorporated. Neither partnership holds any unrealized receivables or inventory for purposes of section 751. In addition, neither partnership has a section 754 election in place. Asset 1 and Asset 2 are nondepreciable capital assets. On January 1, 2013, PRS1 has the same assets that it had after the merger. Each asset has the same value that it had at the time of the merger. On this date, PRS1 distributes Asset 2 to A in liquidation of A's interest.

(ii) Analysis. On the date of the merger of PRS2 into PRS1, the fair market value of Asset 2 ($600x) exceeded its adjusted tax basis ($100x). Thus, pursuant to § 1.704-4(c)(4)(ii)(A), when Asset 2 was contributed to PRS1 in the merger, it was section 704(c) gain property. The total amount of the section 704(c) gain was $500x ($600x (fair market value)-$100x (adjusted basis)). The amount of original section 704(c) gain attributable to Asset 2 equals $100x, the difference between its fair market value ($200x) and adjusted tax basis ($100x) upon contribution to PRS2 by C. The amount of new section 704(c) gain attributable to Asset 2 equals $400x, the total amount of section 704(c) gain ($500x) less the amount of the original section 704(c) gain ($100x). The distribution of Asset 2 to A occurs more than seven years after the contribution by C of Asset 2 to PRS2. Therefore, pursuant to § 1.704-4(c)(4)(ii)(A), section 704(c)(1)(B) does not apply to the $100x of original section 704(c) gain. The distribution of Asset 2 to A, however, occurs within seven years of the contribution in the merger of Asset 2 to PRS1 by PRS2. Pursuant to § 1.704-4(c)(4)(ii)(B), section 704(c)(1)(B) applies to the new section 704(c) gain. As the transferees of PRS2's partnership interest in PRS1, C and D succeed to one-half of the $400x of the new section 704(c) gain created by the merger. Thus, as a result of the distribution of Asset 2 to A within seven years of the merger, C and D are required to recognize $200x of gain each. See § 1.737-2(b)(1)(ii)(F), Example (1) for analysis of a similar example under section 737.

Example (2). Revaluation gain and merger gain. (i) Facts. The facts are the same as Example (1), except that during 2005, PRS2 admitted E as a new partner in PRS2 at a time when the fair market value of Asset 2 was $300x and PRS2's only other asset was cash of $200X. In exchange for a contribution of cash of $250x, E was admitted as a one-third partner in PRS2. In accordance with the terms of PRS2's partnership agreement, the partnership revalued its assets pursuant to § 1.704-1(b)(2)(iv)(f) upon admission of E so that the unrealized gain of $100X attributable to Asset 2 was allocated equally between C and D, or $50X each. On January 1, 2008, PRS2 merges into PRS1. At the time of the merger, PRS1's only assets are Asset 1, with a fair market value of $550x, and $300x in cash. PRS2's only assets are Asset 2, with a fair market value of $400x, and $400x in cash. After the merger, the partners have book capital and profits and loss interests in PRS1 as follows: A, 25.76 percent; B, 25.76 percent; C, 16.16 percent; D, 16.16 percent; and E, 16.16 percent. On January 1, 2011, Asset 2 is distributed to A when its value is still $400x.

(ii) Analysis. On the date of the merger of PRS2 into PRS1, the fair market value of Asset 2 ($400x) exceeded its adjusted tax basis ($100x). Thus, when Asset 2 was contributed to PRS1 in the merger, it was section 704(c) gain property. The total amount of the section 704(c) gain was $300x ($400x (fair market value)-$100x (adjusted basis)). The amount of the original section 704(c) gain attributable to Asset 2 equals $100x, the difference between its fair market value of $200x and adjusted tax basis $100x upon contribution to PRS2 by C. The amount of the new section 704(c) gain attributable to Asset 2 equals $200x, the total section 704(c) gain ($300x) less the amount of the original section 704(c) gain ($100x). The distribution of Asset 2 to A occurs within seven years after the contribution by C to PRS2. Therefore, pursuant to § 1.704-4(c)(4)(ii)(A), section 704(c)(1)(B) applies to the original section 704(c) gain. The distribution of Asset 2 to A also occurs within seven years of the contribution of Asset 2 to PRS1 by PRS2. Pursuant to § 1.704-4(c)(4)(ii)(B), section 704(c)(1)(B) applies to the new section 704(c) gain. As the transferees of PRS2's partnership interest in PRS1, C and D each succeed to $50x of new section 704(c) gain as a result of the revaluation of Asset 2 upon admission of E as a partner. Moreover, C, D and E each succeed to $33.33x of new section 704(c) gain as a result of the merger. C also has $100x of original section 704(c) gain as a result of the original contribution of Asset 2 to PRS2. Thus, as a result of the distribution of Asset 2 to A within seven years of the merger, C, D and E are each required to recognize gain. C will recognize a total of $183.33x of gain ($100x of original section 704(c) gain and $83.33x of new section 704(c) gain). D will recognize a total of $83.33x of gain (all new section 704(c) gain) and E will recognize $33.33x of gain (all new section 704(c) gain). See § 1.737-2(b)(1)(ii)(F), Example (2) for a similar example under section 737.

Example (3). Revaluation loss and merger gain. (i) Facts. The facts are the same as Example (1) except that during 2005, PRS2 admitted E as a new partner in PRS2 at a time when the fair market value of Asset 2 was $150x and PRS2's only other asset was cash of $200x. In exchange for a contribution of cash of $175x, E was admitted as a one-third partner in PRS2. In accordance with the terms of PRS2's partnership agreement, the partnership revalued its assets upon admission of E so that the unrealized loss of $50x attributable to Asset 2 was allocated equally between C and D, or $25x each. On January 1, 2008, PRS2 merges into PRS1. At the time of the merger, PRS1's only assets are Asset 1, with a fair market value of $900x, and $300x in cash. PRS2's only assets are Asset 2, with a fair market value of $600x, and $375x in cash. After the merger, the partners have book capital and profits and loss interests in PRS1 as follows: A, 27.5 percent; B, 27.5 percent; C, 15 percent; D, 15 percent; and E, 15 percent. On January 1, 2013, Asset 2 is distributed to A when its value is still $600x.

(ii) Analysis. On the date of the merger of PRS2 into PRS1, the fair market value of Asset 2 ($600x) exceeded its adjusted tax basis ($100x). Thus, when Asset 2 was contributed to PRS1 in the merger, it was section 704(c) gain property. The total amount of the section 704(c) gain was $500x ($600x (fair market value)--$100x (adjusted (adjusted basis)). The amount of the original section 704(c) gain attributable to Asset 2 equals $50x, the difference between its fair market value ($200x) and adjusted tax basis ($100x) upon contribution to PRS2 by C, less the unrealized loss ($50X) attributable to the revaluation of PRS2 on the admission of E as a partner in PRS2. The amount of the new section 704(c) gain attributable to Asset 2 equals $450x, the total section 704(c) gain ($500x) less the amount of the original section 704(c) gain ($50x). The distribution of Asset 2 to A occurs more than seven years after the contribution by C to PRS2. Therefore, pursuant to § 1.704-4(c)(4)(ii)(A), section 704(c)(1)(B) does not apply to the original section 704(c) gain. The distribution of Asset 2 to A, however, occurs within seven years of the contribution of Asset 2 to PRS1 and PRS2. Pursuant to § 1.704-4(c)(4)(ii)(B), section 704(c)(1)(B) applies to the new section 704(c) gain. As the transferees of PRS2's partnership interest in PRS1, C, D and E each succeed to $150x of new section 704(c) gain. Thus, as a result of the distribution of Asset 2 to A within seven years of the merger, C, D and E are each required to recognize $150x of gain.

Example (4). Reverse section 704(c) gain. (i) Facts. The facts are the same as Example (1), except that on January 1, 2013, PRS1 distributes Asset 1 to C in liquidation of C's interest in PRS1.

(ii) Analysis. The distribution of Asset 1 to C occurs more than seven years after the contribution of Asset 1 to PRS1. Thus, pursuant to § 1.704-4(c)(4)(ii)(A), section 704(c)(1)(B) does not apply to the original section 704(c) gain. Pursuant to § 1.704-4(c)(7), section 704(c)(1)(B) does not apply to reverse section 704(c) gain in Asset 1 resulting from a revaluation of PRS1's partnership property at the time of the merger. Accordingly, neither A nor B will recognize gain under section 704(c)(1)(B) as a result of the distribution of Asset 1 to C. See § 1.737-2(b)(1)(ii)(F), Example (4) for a similar example under section 737.

Example (5). Identical ownership exception. (i) Facts. In 1990, A, an individual, and B, a subchapter C corporation, formed PRS1, a partnership. A owned 75 percent of the interests in the book capital (as determined for purposes of § 1.704-1(b)(2)(iv)), profits, losses, distributions, and liabilities (under section 752) of PRS1. B owned the remaining 25 percent interest in the book capital, profits, losses, distributions, and liabilities of PRS1. In the same year, A and B also formed another partnership, PRS2, with A owning 75 percent of the interests in the book capital, profits, losses, distributions, and liabilities of PRS2 and B owning the remaining 25 percent of the book capital, profits, losses, distributions, and liabilities. Upon formation of the partnerships, A contributed Asset X to PRS1 and Asset Y to PRS2 and B contributed cash. Both Assets X and Y had section 704(c) built-in gain at the time of contribution to the partnerships.

(ii) In January 2005, PRS1 is merged into PRS2 in an assets-over merger in which PRS1 is the terminating partnership and PRS2 as the continuing partnership for both state law and federal income tax purposes. At the time of the merger, both Asset X and Y had increased in value from the time they were contributed to PRS1 and PRS2, respectively. As a result, a new layer of section 704(c) gain was created with respect to Asset X in PRS1, and reverse section 704(c) gain was created with respect to Asset Y in PRS2. After the merger, A had a 75 percent interest in PRS2's capital, profits, losses, distributions, liabilities, and all other items. B held the remaining 25 percent interest in PRS2's capital, profits, losses, distributions, liabilities, and all other items. In 2006, PRS2 distributes Asset X to A.

(iii) Analysis. The 2006 distribution of Asset X occurs more than seven years after the formation of the partnerships and the original contribution of both Assets X and Y to the partnerships. Therefore, the original layer of built-in gain created on the original contribution of Asset X to PRS1 is not taken into account in applying section 704(c)(1)(B) to the proposed distribution. In addition, paragraph (c)(4)(ii)(E) of this section provides that section 704(c)(1)(B) and paragraph (c)(4)(ii)(B) of this section do not apply to new section 704(c) gain or loss in property transferred by the transferor partnership to the transferee partnership if both the transferor partnership and the transferee partnership are owned by the same owners in the same proportions. The transferor partnership and the transferee partnership are owned by the same owners in the same proportions if each partner's percentage interest in the transferor partnership's book capital, profits, losses, distributions, and liabilities, is the same as the partner's percentage interest in those items of the transferee partnership. In this case, A owned 75 percent and B owned 25 percent of the interests in the book capital, and in each item of income, gain, loss and credit, and share of distributions and liabilities of PRS1 and PRS2 prior to the merger and 75 percent and 25 percent, respectively, of PRS2 after the merger. As a result, the requirements of the identical ownership exception of paragraph (c)(4)(ii)(E) of this section are satisfied. Thus, the new built-in gain created upon contribution of Asset X in connection with the partnership merger will not be taken into account in applying section 704(c)(1)(B) to the proposed distribution. See § 1.737-2(b)(1)(ii)(F), Example (5) for a similar example under section 737.

* * * * *

(7) Reverse section 704(c) gain or loss. Section 704(c)(1)(B) and this section do not apply to reverse section 704(c) gain or loss as described in § 1.704-3(a)(6)(i).

* * * * *

(g) Effective/applicability date. * * * Paragraphs (a)(1), (a)(4)(i), (a)(4)(ii), and (f)(2), Examples (1) and (2) are effective August 22, 2007. Paragraphs (c)(4)(i), (c)(4)(ii), (c)(4)(ii)(A), (c)(4)(ii)(B), (c)(4)(ii)(C), (c)(4)(ii)(D), (c)(4)(ii)(E), (c)(4)(ii)(F), and (c)(7) are effective for any distributions of property after January 19, 2005, if such property was contributed in a merger using the assets-over form after May 3, 2004.

§ 1.705-1 Determination of basis of partner's interest.

Caution: The Treasury has not yet amended Reg § 1.705-1 to reflect changes made by P.L. 94-455.

(a) General rule. *(1)* Section 705 and this section provides rules for determining the adjusted basis of a partner's interest in a partnership. A partner is required to determine the adjusted basis of his interest in a partnership only when necessary for the determination of his tax liability or that of any other person. The determination of the adjusted basis of a partnership interest is ordinarily made as of the end of a partnership taxable year. Thus, for example, such year-end determination is necessary in ascertaining the extent to which a partner's distributive share of partnership losses may be allowed. See section 704(d). However, where there has been a sale or exchange of all or a part of a partnership interest or a liquidation of a partner's entire interest in a partnership, the adjusted basis of the partner's interest should be determined as of the date of sale or exchange or liquidation. The adjusted basis of a partner's interest in a partnership is determined without regard to any amount shown in the partnership books as the partner's "capital", "equity", or similar account. For example, A contributes property with an adjusted basis to him of $400 (and a value of $1,000) to a partnership. B contributes $1,000 cash. While under their agreement each may have a "capital account" in the partnership of $1,000, the adjusted basis of A's interest is only $400 and B's interest $1,000.

(2) The original basis of a partner's interest in a partnership shall be determined under section 722 (relating to contributions to a partnership) or section 742 (relating to transfers of partnership interests). Such basis shall be increased under section 722 by any further contributions to the partnership and by the sum of the partner's distributive share for the taxable year and prior taxable years of—

(i) Taxable income of the partnership as determined under section 703(a),

(ii) Tax-exempt receipts of the partnership, and

(iii) The excess of the deductions for depletion over the basis of the depletable property, unless the property is an oil or gas property the basis of which has been allocated to partners under section 613A(c)(7)(D).

(3) The basis shall be decreased (but not below zero) by distributions from the partnership as provided in section 733 and by the sum of the partner's distributive share for the taxable year and prior taxable years of—

(i) Partnership losses (including capital losses), and

(ii) Partnership expenditures which are not deductible in computing partnership taxable income or loss and which are not capital expenditures.

(4) The basis shall be decreased (but not below zero) by the amount of the partner's deduction for depletion allowable under section 611 for any partnership oil and gas property to the extent the deduction does not exceed the proportionate share of the adjusted basis of the property allocated to the partner under section 613A(c)(7)(D).

(5) The basis shall be adjusted (but not below zero) to reflect any gain or loss to the partner resulting from a disposition by the partnership of a domestic oil or gas property after December 31, 1974.

(6) For the effect of liabilities in determining the amount of contributions made by a partner to a partnership or the amount of distributions made by a partnership to a partner, see section 752 and § 1.752-1, relating to the treatment of certain liabilities. In determining the basis of a partnership interest on the effective date of subchapter K, chapter 1 of the Code, or any of the sections thereof, the partner's share of partnership liabilities on that date shall be included.

(7) For basis adjustments necessary to coordinate sections 705 and 1032 in certain situations in which a partnership disposes of stock or any position in stock to which section 1032 applies of a corporation that holds a direct or indirect interest in the partnership, see § 1.705-2.

(8) For basis adjustments necessary to coordinate sections 705 and 358(h), see § 1.358-7(b). For certain basis adjustments with respect to a § 1.752-7 liability assumed by a partnership from a partner, see § 1.752-7.

(b) Alternative rule. In certain cases, the adjusted basis of a partner's interest in a partnership may be determined by reference to the partner's share of the adjusted basis of partnership property which would be distributable upon termination of the partnership. The alternative rule may be used to determine the adjusted basis of a partner's interest where circumstances are such that the partner cannot practicably apply the general rule set forth in section 705(a) and paragraph (a) of this section, or where, from a consideration of all the facts, it is, in the opinion of the Commissioner, reasonable to conclude that the result produced will not vary substantially from the result obtainable under the general rule. Where the alternative rule is used, adjustments may be necessary in determining the adjusted basis of a partner's interest in a partnership. Adjustments would be required, for example, in order to reflect in a partner's share of the adjusted basis of partnership property any significant discrepancies arising as a result of contributed property, transfers of partnership interests, or distributions of property to the partners. The operation of the alternative rules may be illustrated by the following examples:

Example (1). The ABC partnership, in which A, B, and C are equal partners, owns various properties with a total adjusted basis of $1,500 and has earned and retained an additional $1,500. The total adjusted basis of partnership property is thus $3,000. Each partner's share in the adjusted basis of partnership property is one-third of this amount, or $1,000. Under the alternative rule, this amount represents each partner's adjusted basis for his partnership interest.

Example (2). Assume that partner A in example (1) of this paragraph sells his partnership interest to D for $1,250 at a time when the partnership property with an adjusted basis of $1,500 had appreciated in value to $3,000, and when the partnership also had $750 in cash. The total adjusted basis of all partnership property is $2,250 and the value of such property is $3,750. D's basis for his partnership interest is his cost, $1,250. However, his one-third share of the adjusted basis of partnership property is only $750. Therefore, for the purposes of the alternative rule, D has an adjustment of $500 in determining the basis of his interest. This amount represents the difference between the cost of his partnership interest and his share of partnership basis at the time of his purchase. If the partnership subsequently earns and retains an additional $1,500, its property will have an adjusted basis of $3,750. D's adjusted basis for his interest under the alternative rule is $1,750, determined by adding $500, his basis adjustment to $1,250 (his one-third share of the $3,750 adjusted basis of partnership property). If the partnership distributes $250 to each partner in a current distribution, D's adjusted basis for his interest will be $1,500 ($1,000, his one-third share of the remaining basis of partnership property, $3,000, plus his basis adjustment of $500).

Example (3). Assume that BCD partnership in example (2) of this paragraph continues to operate. In 1960, D proposes to sell his partnership interest and wishes to evaluate the tax consequences of such sale. It is necessary, therefore, to determine the adjusted basis of his interest in the partnership. Assume further that D cannot determine the adjusted basis of his interest under the general rule. The balance sheet of the BCD partnership is as follows:

Assets	Adjusted basis per books	Market value
Cash	$ 3,000	$ 3,000
Receivables	4,000	4,000
Depreciable property	5,000	5,000
Land held for investment	18,000	30,000
Total	30,000	42,000

Liabilities and capital	Per books
Liabilities	$ 6,000
Capital accounts:	
B	4,500
C	4,500
D	15,000
Total	30,000

The $15,000 representing the amount of D's capital account does not reflect the $500 basis adjustment arising from D's purchase of his interest. See example (2) of this paragraph. The adjusted basis of D's partnership interest determined under the alternative rule is as follows:

D's share of the adjusted basis of partnership property (reduced by the amount of liabilities) at time of proposed sale	$15,000
D's share of partnership liabilities (under the partnership agreement liabilities are shared equally)	2,000
D's basis adjustment from example (2)	500
Adjusted basis of D's interest at the time of proposed sale, as determined under alternative rule	17,500

T.D. 6175, 5/23/56, amend T.D. 8437, 9/23/92, T.D. 8986, 3/28/2002, T.D. 9049, 3/17/2003, T.D. 9207, 5/23/2005.

Proposed § 1.705-1 Determination of basis of partner's interest. [*For Preamble, see ¶ 152,815*]

(a) * * *

(9) For basis adjustments necessary to coordinate sections 705 and 362(e)(2), see § 1.362-4(c)(6).

* * * * *

PAR. 6. Section 1.705-1(a)(3)(ii) is revised to read as follows:

Proposed § 1.705-1 Determination of basis of partner's interest. [*For Preamble, see ¶ 151,105*]

(a) * * *

(3) * * *

(ii) Partnership expenditures which are not deductible in computing partnership taxable income or loss and which are not capital expenditures (see § 1.48-7(c), § 1.48-7(f), and § 1.48-7(k)(3)(ii) with respect to the necessary adjustment to reflect the investment tax credit).

* * * * *

§ 1.705-2 Basis adjustments coordinating sections 705 and 1032.

(a) Purpose. This section coordinates the application of sections 705 and 1032 and is intended to prevent inappropriate increases or decreases in the adjusted basis of a corporate partner's interest in a partnership resulting from the partnership's disposition of the corporate partner's stock. The rules under section 705 generally are intended to preserve equality between the adjusted basis of a partner's interest in a partnership (outside basis) and such partner's share of the adjusted basis in partnership assets (inside basis). However, in situations where a section 754 election was not in effect for the year in which a partner acquired its interest, the partner's inside basis and outside basis may not be equal. Similarly, in situations where a section 754 election was not in effect for the year in which a partnership distributes money or other property to another partner and that partner recognizes gain or loss on the distribution or the basis of the property distributed to that partner is adjusted, the remaining partners' inside basis and outside basis may not be equal. In these situations, gain or loss allocated to the partner upon disposition of the partnership assets that is attributable to the difference between the adjusted basis of the partnership assets absent the section 754 election and the adjusted basis of the partnership assets had a section 754 election been in effect generally will result in an adjustment to the basis of the partner's interest in the partnership under section 705(a). Such gain (or loss) therefore generally will be offset by a corresponding decrease in the gain or increase in the loss (or increase in the gain or decrease in the loss) upon the subsequent disposition by the partner of its interest in the partnership. Where such a difference exists with respect to stock of a corporate partner that is held by the partnership, gain or loss from the disposition of corporate partner stock attributable to the difference is not recognized by the corporate partner under section 1032. To adjust the basis of the corporate partner's interest in the partnership for this unrecognized gain or loss would not be appropriate because it would create an opportunity for the recognition of taxable gain or loss on a subsequent disposition of the partnership interest where no economic gain or loss has been incurred by the corporate partner and no corresponding taxable gain or loss had previously been allocated to the corporate partner by the partnership.

(b) Single partnership. *(1) Required adjustments relating to acquisitions of partnership interest.* (i) This paragraph (b)(1) applies in situations where a corporation acquires an interest in a partnership that holds stock in that corporation (or the partnership subsequently acquires stock in that corporation in an exchanged basis transaction), the partnership does not have an election under section 754 in effect for the year in which the corporation acquires the interest, and the partnership later sells or exchanges the stock. In these situations, the increase (or decrease) in the corporation's adjusted basis in its partnership interest resulting from the sale or exchange of the stock equals the amount of gain (or loss) that the corporate partner would have recognized (absent the application of section 1032) if, for the year in which the corporation acquired the interest, a section 754 election had been in effect.

(ii) The provisions of this paragraph (b)(1) are illustrated by the following example:

Example. (i) A, B, and C form equal partnership PRS. Each partner contributes $30,000 in exchange for its partnership interest. PRS has no liabilities. PRS purchases stock in corporation X for $30,000, which appreciates in value to $120,000. PRS also purchases inventory for $60,000, which appreciates in value to $150,000. A sells its interest in PRS to corporation X for $90,000 in a year for which an election under section 754 is not in effect. PRS later sells the X stock for $150,000. PRS realizes a gain of $120,000 on the sale of the X stock. X's share of the gain is $40,000. Under section 1032, X does not recognize its share of the gain.

(ii) Normally, X would be entitled to a $40,000 increase in the basis of its PRS interest for its allocable share of PRS's gain from the sale of the X stock, but a special rule applies in this situation. If a section 754 election had been in effect for the year in which X acquired its interest in PRS, X would have been entitled to a basis adjustment under section 743(b) of $60,000 (the excess of X's basis for the transferred partnership interest over X's share of the adjusted basis to PRS of PRS's property). See § 1.743-1(b). Under § 1.755-1(b), the basis adjustment under section 743(b) would have been allocated $30,000 to the X stock (the amount of the gain that would have been allocated to X from the hypothetical sale of the stock), and $30,000 to the inventory (the amount of the gain that would have been allocated to X from the hypothetical sale of the inventory).

(iii) If a section 754 election had been in effect for the year in which X acquired its interest in PRS, the amount of gain that X would have recognized upon PRS's disposition of X stock (absent the application of section 1032) would be $10,000 (X's share of PRS's gain from the stock sale, $40,000, minus the amount of X's basis adjustment under section 743(b), $30,000). See § 1.743-1(j). Accordingly, the increase in the basis of X's interest in PRS is $10,000.

(2) Required adjustments relating to distributions. (i) This paragraph (b)(2) applies in situations where a corporation owns a direct or indirect interest in a partnership that owns stock in that corporation, the partnership distributes money or other property to another partner and that partner recognizes gain or loss on the distribution or the basis of the property distributed to that partner is adjusted during a year in which the partnership does not have an election under section 754 in effect, and the partnership subsequently sells or exchanges the stock. In these situations, the increase (or decrease) in the corporation's adjusted basis in its partnership interest resulting from the sale or exchange of the stock equals the amount of gain (or loss) that the corporate partner would have recognized (absent the application of section 1032) if, for the year in which the partnership made the distribution, a section 754 election had been in effect.

(ii) The provisions of this paragraph (b)(2) are illustrated by the following example:

Example. (i) A, B, and corporation C form partnership PRS. A and B each contribute $10,000 and C contributes $20,000 in exchange for a partnership interest. PRS has no liabilities. PRS purchases stock in corporation C for $10,000, which appreciates in value to $70,000. PRS distributes $25,000 to A in complete liquidation of A's interest in PRS in a year for which an election under section 754 is not in effect. PRS later sells the C stock for $70,000. PRS realizes a gain of $60,000 on the sale of the C stock. C's share of the gain is $40,000. Under section 1032, C does not recognize its share of the gain.

(ii) Normally, C would be entitled to a $40,000 increase in the basis of its PRS interest for its allocable share of PRS's gain from the sale of the C stock, but a special rule applies in this situation. If a section 754 election had been in effect for the year in which PRS made the distribution to A, PRS would have been entitled to adjust the basis of partnership property under section 734(b)(1)(A) by $15,000 (the amount of gain recognized by A with respect to the distribution to A under section 731(a)(1)). See § 1.734-1(b). Under § 1.755-1(c)(1)(ii), the basis adjustment under section 734(b) would have been allocated to the C stock, increasing its basis to $25,000 (where there is a distribution resulting in an adjustment under section 734(b)(1)(A) to the basis of undistributed partnership property, the adjustment is allocated only to capital gain property).

(iii) If a section 754 election had been in effect for the year in which PRS made the distribution to A, the amount of gain that PRS would have recognized upon PRS's disposition of C stock would be $45,000 ($70,000 minus $25,000 basis in the C stock), and the amount of gain C would have recognized upon PRS's disposition of the C stock (absent the application of section 1032) would be $30,000 (C's share of PRS's gain of $45,000 from the stock sale). Accordingly, upon PRS's sale of the C stock, the increase in the basis of C's interest in PRS is $30,000.

(c) Tiered partnerships and other arrangements. *(1) Required adjustments.* The purpose of these regulations as set forth in paragraph (a) of this section cannot be avoided through the use of tiered partnerships or other arrangements. For example, if a corporation acquires an indirect interest in its own stock through a chain of two or more partnerships (either where the corporation acquires a direct interest in a partnership or where one of the partnerships in the chain acquires an interest in another partnership), and gain or loss from the sale or exchange of the stock is subsequently allocated to the corporation, then the bases of the interests in the partnerships included in the chain shall be adjusted in a manner that is consistent with the purpose of this section. Similarly, if a corporation owns an indirect interest in its own stock through a chain of two or more partnerships, and a partnership in the chain distributes money or other property to another partner and that partner recognizes gain or loss on the distribution or the basis of the property distributed to that partner is adjusted during a year in which the partnership does not have an election under section 754 in effect, then upon any subsequent sale or exchange of the stock, the bases of the interests in the partnerships included in the chain shall be adjusted in a manner that is consistent with the purpose of this section.

(2) Examples. The provisions of this paragraph (c) are illustrated by the following examples:

Example (1). Acquisition of upper-tier partnership interest by corporation.

(i) A, B, and C form a partnership (UTP), with each partner contributing $25,000. UTP and D form a partnership (LTP). UTP contributes $75,000 in exchange for its interest in LTP, and D contributes $25,000 in exchange for D's interest in LTP. Neither UTP nor LTP has any liabilities. LTP purchases stock in corporation E for $100,000, which appreciates in value to $1,000,000. C sells its interest in UTP to corporation E for $250,000 in a year for which an election under section 754 is not in effect for UTP or LTP. LTP later sells the E stock for $2,000,000. LTP realizes a $1,900,000 gain on the sale of the E stock. UTP's share of the gain is $1,425,000, and E's share of the gain is $475,000. Under section 1032, E does not recognize its share of the gain.

(ii) With respect to the basis of UTP's interest in LTP, if all of the gain from the sale of the E stock (including E's share) were to increase the basis of UTP's interest in LTP, UTP's basis in such interest would be $1,500,000 ($75,000 + $1,425,000). The fair market value of UTP's interest in LTP is $1,500,000. Because UTP did not have a section 754 election in effect for the taxable year in which E acquired its interest in UTP, UTP's basis in the LTP interest does not reflect the purchase price paid by E for its interest. Increasing the basis of UTP's interest in LTP by the full amount of the gain that would be recognized (in the absence of section 1032) on the sale of the E stock preserves the conformity between UTP's inside basis and outside basis with respect to LTP (i.e., UTP's share of LTP's cash is equal to $1,500,000, and UTP's basis in the LTP interest is $1,500,000) and appropriately would cause UTP to recognize no gain or loss on the sale of UTP's interest in LTP immediately after the sale of the E stock. Accordingly, increasing the basis of UTP's interest in LTP by the entire amount of gain allocated to UTP (including E's share) from LTP's sale of the E stock is consistent with the purpose of this section. The $1,425,000 of gain allocated by LTP to UTP will increase the adjusted basis of UTP's interest in LTP under section 705(a)(1). The basis of UTP's interest in LTP immediately after the sale of the E stock is $1,500,000.

(iii) With respect to the basis of E's interest in UTP, if E's share of the gain allocated to UTP and then to E were to increase the basis of E's interest in UTP, E's basis in such interest would be $725,000 ($250,000 + $475,000) and the fair market value of such interest would be $500,000, so that E would recognize a loss of $225,000 if E sold its interest in UTP immediately after LTP's disposition of the E stock. It would be inappropriate for E to recognize a taxable loss of $225,000 upon a disposition of its interest in UTP because E would not incur an economic loss in the transaction, and E did not recognize a taxable gain upon LTP's disposition of the E stock that appropriately would be offset by a taxable loss on the disposition of its interest in UTP. Accordingly, increasing E's basis in its UTP interest by the entire amount of gain allocated to E from the sale of the E stock is not consistent with the purpose of this section. (Conversely, because A and B were allocated taxable gain on the disposition of the E stock, it would be appropriate to increase A's and B's bases in their respective interests in UTP by the full amount of the gain allocated to them.)

(iv) The appropriate basis adjustment for E's interest in UTP upon the disposition of the E stock by LTP can be determined as the amount of gain that E would have recognized (in the absence of section 1032) upon the sale by LTP of the E stock if both UTP and LTP had made section 754 elections for the taxable year in which E acquired the interest in UTP. If section 754 elections had been in effect for UTP and LTP for the year in which E acquired E's interest in UTP, the following would occur. E would be entitled to a $225,000 positive basis adjustment under section 743(b) with respect to the property of UTP. The entire basis adjustment would be allocated to UTP's only asset, its interest in LTP. In addition, the sale of C's interest in UTP would be treated as a deemed sale of E's share of UTP's interest in LTP for purposes of sections 754 and 743. The deemed selling price of E's share of UTP's interest in LTP would be $250,000 (E's share of UTP's adjusted basis in LTP, $25,000, plus E's basis adjustment under section 743(b) with respect to the assets of UTP, $225,000). The deemed sale of E's share of UTP's interest in LTP would trigger a basis adjustment under section 743(b) of $225,000 with respect to the assets of LTP (the excess of E's share of UTP's adjusted basis in LTP, including E's basis adjustment ($225,000), $250,000, over E's share of the adjusted basis of LTP's property, $25,000). This $225,000 adjustment by LTP would be allocated to LTP's only asset, the E stock, and would be segregated and allocated solely to E. The amount of LTP's gain from the sale of the E stock (before considering section 743(b)) would be $1,900,000. E's share of this gain, $475,000, would be offset in part by the $225,000 basis adjustment under section 743(b), so that E would recognize gain equal to $250,000 in the absence of section 1032.

(v) If the basis of E's interest in UTP were increased by $250,000, the total basis of E's interest would equal $500,000. This would conform to E's share of UTP's basis in the LTP interest ($1,500,000 x ⅓ = $500,000) as well as E's indirect share of the cash held by LTP ((⅓ x ¾) x $2,000,000 = $500,000). Such a basis adjustment does not create the opportunity for the recognition of an inappropriate loss by E on a subsequent disposition of E's interest in UTP and is consistent with the purpose of this section. Accordingly, under this paragraph (c), of the $475,000 gain allocated to E, only $250,000 will apply to increase the adjusted basis of E in UTP under section 705(a)(1). E's adjusted basis in its UTP interest following the sale of the E stock is $500,000.

Example (2). Acquisition of lower-tier partnership interest by upper-tier partnership.

(i) A, corporation B, and C form an equal partnership (UTP), with each partner contributing $100,000. D, E, and F also form an equal partnership (LTP), with each partner contributing $30,000. LTP purchases stock in corporation B for $90,000, which appreciates in value to $900,000. LTP has no liabilities. UTP purchases D's interest in LTP for $300,000. LTP does not have an election under section 754 in effect for the taxable year of UTP's purchase. LTP later sells the B stock for $900,000. UTP's share of the gain is $270,000, and B's share of that gain is $90,000. Under section 1032, B does not recognize its share of the gain.

(ii) With respect to the basis of UTP's interest in LTP, if all of the gain from the sale of the B stock (including B's share) were to increase the basis of UTP's interest in LTP, UTP's basis in the LTP interest would be $570,000 ($300,000 + $270,000), and the fair market value of such interest would be $300,000, so that B would be allocated a loss of $90,000 (($570,000 − $300,000) x ⅓) if UTP sold its interest in LTP immediately after LTP's disposition of the B stock. It would be inappropriate for B to recognize a taxable loss of $90,000 upon a disposition of UTP's interest in LTP. B would not incur an economic loss in the transaction, and B was not allocated a taxable gain upon LTP's disposition of the B stock that appropriately would be offset by a taxable loss on the disposition of UTP's interest in LTP. Accordingly, increasing UTP's basis in its LTP interest by the gain allocated to B from the sale of the B stock is not consistent with the purpose of this section. (Conversely, because E and F were allocated taxable gain on the disposition of the B stock, it would be appropriate to increase E's and F's bases in their respective interests in LTP by the full amount of such gain.)

(iii) The appropriate basis adjustment for UTP's interest in LTP upon the disposition of the B stock by LTP can be determined as the amount of gain that UTP would have recognized (in the absence of section 1032) upon the sale by LTP of the B stock if the portion of the gain allocated to UTP that subsequently is allocated to B were determined as if LTP had made an election under section 754 for the taxable year in which UTP acquired its interest in LTP. If a section 754 election had been in effect for LTP for the year in which UTP acquired its interest in LTP, then with respect to B, the following would occur. UTP would be entitled to a $90,000 positive basis adjustment under section 743(b), allocable to B, in the property of LTP. The entire basis adjustment would be allocated to LTP's only asset, its B stock. The amount of LTP's gain from the sale of the B stock (before considering section 743(b)) would be $810,000. UTP's share of this gain, $270,000, would be offset, in part, by the basis adjustment under section 743(b), so that UTP would recognize gain equal to $180,000.

(iv) If the basis of UTP's interest in LTP were increased by $180,000, the total basis of UTP's partnership interest would equal $480,000. This would conform to the sum of UTP's share of the cash held by LTP ((⅓ x $900,000 = $300,000) and the taxable gain recognized by A and C on the disposition of the B stock that appropriately may be offset on the disposition of their interests in UTP ($90,000 + $90,000 = $180,000). Such a basis adjustment does not inappropriately create the opportunity for the allocation of a loss to B on a subsequent disposition of UTP's interest in LTP and is consistent with the purpose of this section. Accordingly, of the $270,000 gain allocated to UTP, only $180,000 will apply to increase the adjusted basis of UTP in LTP under section 705(a)(1). Such $180,000 basis increase must be segregated and allocated $90,000 each to solely A and C. UTP's adjusted basis in its LTP interest following the sale of the B stock is $480,000.

(v) With respect to B's interest in UTP, if B's share of the gain allocated to UTP and then to B were to increase the basis of B's interest in UTP, B would have a UTP partnership interest with an adjusted basis of $190,000 ($100,000 + $90,000) and a value of $100,000, so that B would recognize a loss of $90,000 if B sold its interest in UTP immediately after LTP's disposition of the B stock. It would be inappropriate for B to recognize a taxable loss of $90,000 upon a disposition of its interest in UTP because B would not incur an economic loss in the transaction, and B did not recognize a taxable gain upon LTP's disposition of the B stock that appropriately would be offset by a taxable loss on the disposition of its interest in UTP. Accordingly, increasing B's basis in its UTP interest by the gain allocated to B from the sale of the B stock is not consistent with the purpose of this section. (Conversely, because A and C were allocated taxable gain on the disposition of the B stock that is a result of LTP not having a section 754 election in effect, it would be appropriate for A and C to recognize an offsetting taxable loss on the disposition of A's and C's interests in UTP. Accordingly, it would be appropriate to increase A's and C's bases in their respective interests in UTP by the amount of gain recognized by A and C.)

(vi) The appropriate basis adjustment for B's interest in UTP upon the disposition of the B stock by LTP can be determined as the amount of gain that B would have recognized (in the absence of section 1032) upon the sale by LTP of the B stock if the portion of the gain allocated to UTP that is subsequently allocated to B were determined as if LTP had made an election under section 754 for the taxable year in which UTP acquired its interest in LTP. If a section 754 election had been in effect for LTP for the year in which UTP acquired its interest in LTP, then with respect to B, the following would occur. UTP would be entitled to a basis adjustment under section 743(b) in the property of LTP of $90,000 with respect to B. The entire basis adjustment would be allocated to LTP's only asset, its B stock. The amount of LTP's gain from the sale of the B stock (before considering section 743(b)) would be $810,000. UTP's share of this gain, $270,000, would be offset, in part, by the $90,000 basis adjustment under section 743(b), so that UTP would recognize gain equal to $180,000. The $90,000 basis adjustment would completely offset the gain that otherwise would be allocated to B.

(vii) If no gain were allocated to B so that the basis of B's interest in UTP was not increased, the total basis of B's interest would equal $100,000. This would conform to B's share of UTP's basis in the LTP interest (($480,000 – $180,000 (i.e., A's and C's share of the basis that should offset taxable gain recognized as a result of LTP's failure to have a section 754 election)) x ⅓ = $100,000) as well as B's indirect share of the cash held by LTP ((⅓ x ⅓) x $900,000 = $100,000). Such a basis adjustment does not create the opportunity for the recognition of an inappropriate loss by B on a subsequent disposition of B's interest in UTP and is consistent with the purpose of this section. Accordingly, under this paragraph (c), of the $90,000 gain allocated to B, none will apply to increase the adjusted basis of B in UTP under section 705(a)(1). B's adjusted basis in its UTP interest following the sale of the B stock is $100,000.

(viii) Immediately after LTP's disposition of the B stock, UTP sells its interest in LTP for $300,000. UTP's adjusted basis in its LTP interest is $480,000, $180,000 of which must be allocated $90,000 each to A and C. Accordingly, upon UTP's sale of its interest in LTP, UTP realizes $180,000 of loss, and A and C in turn each realize $90,000 of loss.

(d) Positions in Stock. For purposes of this section, stock includes any position in stock to which section 1032 applies.

(e) Effective date. This section applies to gain or loss allocated with respect to sales or exchanges of stock occurring after December 6, 1999, except that paragraph (d) of this section is applicable with respect to sales or exchanges of stock occurring on or after March 29, 2002, and the fourth sentence of paragraph (a), paragraph (b)(2), and the third sentence of paragraph (c)(1) of this section are applicable with respect to sales or exchanges of stock occurring on or after March 18, 2003.

T.D. 8986, 3/28/2002, amend T.D. 9049, 3/17/2003.

---

§ 1.706-1 Taxable years of partner and partnership.

Caution: The Treasury has not yet amended Reg § 1.706-1 to reflect changes made by P.L. 108-357, P.L. 105-34, P.L. 100-647, P.L. 98-369, P.L. 94-455.

(a) Year in which partnership income is includible. *(1)* In computing taxable income for a taxable year, a partner is required to include the partner's distributive share of partnership items set forth in section 702 and the regulations thereunder for any partnership taxable year ending within or with the partner's taxable year. A partner must also include in taxable income for a taxable year guaranteed payments under section 707(c) that are deductible by the partnership under its method of accounting in the partnership taxable year ending within or with the partner's taxable year.

(2) The rules of this paragraph (a)(1) may be illustrated by the following example:

Example. Partner A reports income using a calendar year, while the partnership of which A is a member reports its income using a fiscal year ending May 31. The partnership reports its income and deductions under the cash method of accounting. During the partnership taxable year ending May 31, 2002, the partnership makes guaranteed payments of $120,000 to A for services and for the use of capital. Of this amount, $70,000 was paid to A between June 1 and December 31, 2001, and the remaining $50,000 was paid to A between January 1 and May 31, 2002. The entire $120,000 paid to A is includible in A's taxable income for the calendar year 2002 (together with A's distributive share of partnership items set forth in section 702 for the partnership taxable year ending May 31, 2002).

(3) If a partner receives distributions under section 731 or sells or exchanges all or part of a partnership interest, any gain or loss arising therefrom does not constitute partnership income.

(b) Taxable year. *(1) Partnership treated as a taxpayer.* The taxable year of a partnership must be determined as though the partnership were a taxpayer.

(2) Partnership's taxable year. (i) Required taxable year. Except as provided in paragraph (b)(2)(ii) of this section, the taxable year of a partnership must be—

(A) The majority interest taxable year, as defined in section 706(b)(4);

(B) If there is no majority interest taxable year, the taxable year of all of the principal partners of the partnership, as defined in 706(b)(3) (the principal partners' taxable year); or

(C) If there is no majority interest taxable year or principal partners' taxable year, the taxable year that produces the least aggregate deferral of income as determined under paragraph (b)(3) of this section.

(ii) Exceptions. A partnership may have a taxable year other than its required taxable year if it makes an election under section 444, elects to use a 52-53-week taxable year that ends with reference to its required taxable year or a taxable year elected under section 444, or establishes a business purpose for such taxable year and obtains approval of the Commissioner under section 442.

(3) Least aggregate deferral. (i) Taxable year that results in the least aggregate deferral of income. The taxable year that results in the least aggregate deferral of income will be the taxable year of one or more of the partners in the partnership which will result in the least aggregate deferral of income to the partners. The aggregate deferral for a particular year is equal to the sum of the products determined by multiplying the month(s) of deferral for each partner that would be generated by that year and each partner's interest in partnership profits for that year. The partner's taxable year that produces the lowest sum when compared to the other partner's taxable years is the taxable year that results in the least aggregate deferral of income to the partners. If the calculation results in more than one taxable year qualifying as the taxable year with the least aggregate deferral, the partnership may select any one of those taxable years as its taxable year. However, if one of the qualifying taxable years is also the partnership's existing taxable year, the partnership must maintain its existing taxable year. The determination of the taxable year that results in the least aggregate deferral of income generally must be made as of the beginning of the partnership's current taxable year. The director, however, may determine that the first day of the current taxable year is not the appropriate testing day and require the use of some other day or period that will more accurately reflect the ownership of the partnership and thereby the actual aggregate deferral to the partners where the partners engage in a transaction that has as its principal purpose the avoidance of the principles of this section. Thus, for example the preceding sentence would apply where there is a transfer of an interest in the partnership that results in a temporary transfer of that interest principally for purposes of qualifying for a specific taxable year under the principles of this section. For purposes of this section, deferral to each partner is measured in terms of months from the end of the partnership's taxable year forward to the end of the partner's taxable year.

(ii) Determination of the taxable year of a partner or partnership that uses a 52-53-week taxable year. For purposes of the calculation described in paragraph (b)(3)(i) of this section, the taxable year of a partner or partnership that uses a 52-53-week taxable year must be the same year determined under the rules of section 441(f) and the regulations thereunder with respect to the inclusion of income by the partner or partnership.

(iii) Special de minimis rule. If the taxable year that results in the least aggregate deferral produces an aggregate deferral that is less than .5 when compared to the aggregate deferral of the current taxable year, the partnership's current taxable year will be treated as the taxable year with the least aggregate deferral. Thus, the partnership will not be permitted to change its taxable year.

(iv) Examples. The principles of this section may be illustrated by the following examples:

Example (1). Partnership P is on a fiscal year ending June 30. Partner A reports income on the fiscal year ending June 30 and Partner B reports income on the fiscal year ending July 31. A and B each have a 50 percent interest in partnership profits. For its taxable year beginning July 1, 1987, the partnership will be required to retain its taxable year since the fiscal year ending June 30 results in the least aggregate deferral of income to the partners. This determination is made as follows:

Test 6/30	Year End	Interest in Partnership Profits	Months of Deferral for 6/30 Year End	Interest x Deferral
Partner A	6/30	.5	0	0
Partner B	7/31	.5	1	.5
Aggregate deferral				.5

Test 7/31	Year End	Interest in Partnership Profits	Months of Deferral for 7/31 Year End	Interest x Deferral

Partner A	6/30	.5	11	5.5
Partner B................	7/31	.5	0	0
Aggregate deferral				5.5

Example (2). The facts are the same as in Example 1 except that A reports income on the calendar year and B reports on the fiscal year ending November 30. For the partnership's taxable year beginning July 1, 1987, the partnership is required to change its taxable year to a fiscal year ending November 30 because such year results in the least aggregate deferral of income to the partners. This determination is made as follows:

Test 12/31	Year End	Interest in Partnership Profits	Months of Deferral for 12/31 Year End	Interest x Deferral
Partner A	12/31	.5	0	0
Partner B................	11/30	.5	11	5.5
Aggregate deferral				5.5

Test 11/30	Year End	Interest in Partnership Profits	Months of Deferral for 11/30 Year End	Interest x Deferral
Partner A	12/31	.5	1	.5
Partner B................	11/30	.5	0	0
Aggregate deferral				.5

Example (3). The facts are the same as in Example 2 except that B reports income on the fiscal year ending June 30. For the partnership's taxable year beginning July 1, 1987, each partner's taxable year will result in identical aggregate deferral of income. If the partnership's current taxable year was neither a fiscal year ending June 30 nor the calendar year, the partnership would select either the fiscal year ending June 30 or the calendar year as its taxable year. However, since the partnership's current taxable year ends June 30, it must retain its current taxable year. The determination is made as follows:

Test 12/31	Year End	Interest in Partnership Profits	Months of Deferral for 12/31 Year End	Interest x Deferral
Partner A	12/31	.5	0	0
Partner B................	6/30	.5	6	3.0
Aggregate deferral				3.0

Test 6/30	Year End	Interest in Partnership Profits	Months of Deferral for 6/30 Year End	Interest x Deferral
Partner A	12/31	.5	6	3.0
Partner B................	6/30	.5	0	0
Aggregate deferral				3.0

Example (4). The facts are the same as in Example 1 except that on December 31, 1987, partner A sells a 4 percent interest in the partnership to Partner C, who reports income on the fiscal year ending June 30, and a 40 percent interest in the partnership to Partner D, who also reports income on the fiscal year ending June 30. The taxable year beginning July 1, 1987, is unaffected by the sale. However, for the taxable year beginning July 31, 1988, the partnership must determine the taxable year resulting in the least aggregate deferral as of July 1, 1988. In this case, the partnership will be required to retain its taxable year since the fiscal year ending June 30 continues to be the taxable year that results in the least aggregate deferral of income to the partners.

Example (5). The facts are the same as in Example 4 except that Partner D reports income on the fiscal year ending April 30. As in Example 4, the taxable year during which the sale took place is unaffected by the shifts in interests. However, for its taxable year beginning July 1, 1988, the partnership will be required to change its taxable year to the fiscal year ending April 30. This determination is made as follows:

Test 7/31	Year End	Interest in Partnership Profits	Months of Deferral for 7/31 Year End	Interest x Deferral
Partner A	6/30	.06	11	.66
Partner B	7/31	.5	0	0
Partner C	6/30	.04	11	.44
Partner D	4/30	.4	9	3.60
Aggregate deferral				4.70

Test 6/30	Year End	Interest in Partnership Profits	Months of Deferral for 6/30 Year End	Interest x Deferral
Partner A	6/30	.06	0	0
Partner B	7/31	.5	1	.5
Partner C	6/30	.04	0	0
Partner D	4/30	.4	10	4.0
Aggregate deferral				4.5

Test 4/30	Year End	Interest in Partnership Profits	Months of Deferral for 4/30 Year End	Interest x Deferral
Partner A	6/30	.06	2	.12
Partner B	7/31	.5	3	1.50
Partner C	6/30	.04	2	.08
Partner D	4/30	.4	0	0
Aggregate deferral				1.70

§ 1.706-1(b)(3) Test:	
Current taxable year (June 30)	4.5
Less: Taxable year producing the least aggregate deferral (April 30)	1.7
Additional aggregate deferral (greater than .5)	2.8

Example (6). (i) Partnership P has two partners, A who reports income on the fiscal year ending March 31, and B who reports income on the fiscal year ending July 31. A and B share profits equally. P has determined its taxable year under paragraph (b)(3) of this section to be the fiscal year ending March 31 as follows:

Test 3/31	Year End	Interest in Partnership Profits	Deferral for 3/31 Year End	Interest x Deferral
Partner A	3/31	.5	0	0
Partner B	7/31	.5	4	2
Aggregate deferral				2

Test 7/31	Year End	Interest in Partnership Profits	Deferral for 7/31 Year End	Interest x Deferral
Partner A	3/31	.5	8	4
Partner B	7/31	.5	0	0
Aggregate deferral				4

(ii) In May 1988, Partner A sells a 45 percent interest in the partnership to C, who reports income on the fiscal year ending April 30. For the taxable period beginning April 1, 1989, the fiscal year ending April 30 is the taxable year that produces the least aggregate deferral of income to the partners. However, under paragraph (b)(3)(iii) of this section the partnership is required to retain its fiscal year ending March 31. This determination is made as follows:

Test 3/31	Year End	Interest in Partnership Profits	Deferral for 3/31 Year End	Interest x Deferral
Partner A	3/31	.05	0	0
Partner B	7/31	.5	4	2.0
Partner C	4/30	.45	1	.45
Aggregate deferral				2.45

Test 7/31	Year End	Interest in Partnership Profits	Deferral for 7/31 Year End	Interest x Deferral
Partner A	3/31	.05	8	.40
Partner B	7/31	.5	0	0
Partner C	4/30	.45	9	4.05
Aggregate deferral				4.45

Test 4/30	Year End	Interest in Partnership Profits	Deferral for 4/30 Year End	Interest x Deferral
Partner A	3/31	.05	11	.55
Partner B	7/31	.5	3	1.50
Partner C	4/30	.45	0	0
Aggregate deferral				2.05

§ 1.706-1(b)(3) Test:	
Current taxable year (3/31)	2.45
Less: Taxable year producing the least aggregate deferral (4/30)	2.05
Additional aggregate deferral (less than .5)	.40

(4) Measurement of partner's profits and capital interest. (i) In general. The rules of this paragraph (b)(4) apply in determining the majority interest taxable year, the principal partners' taxable year, and the least aggregate deferral taxable year.

(ii) Profits interest. (A) In general. For purposes of section 706(b), a partner's interest in partnership profits is generally the partner's percentage share of partnership profits for the current partnership taxable year. If the partnership does not expect to have net income for the current partnership taxable year, then a partner's interest in partnership profits instead must be the partner's percentage share of partnership net income for the first taxable year in which the partnership expects to have net income.

(B) Percentage share of partnership net income. The partner's percentage share of partnership net income for a partnership taxable year is the ratio of: the partner's distributive share of partnership net income for the taxable year, to the partnership's net income for the year. If a partner's percentage share of partnership net income for the taxable year depends on the amount or nature of partnership income for that year (due to, for example, preferred returns or special allocations of specific partnership items), then the partnership must make a reasonable estimate of the amount and nature of its income for the taxable year. This estimate must be based on all facts and circumstances known to the partnership as of the first day of the current partnership taxable year. The partnership must then use this estimate in determining the partners' interests in partnership profits for the taxable year.

(C) Distributive share. For purposes of this paragraph (b)(4)(ii), a partner's distributive share of partnership net income is determined by taking into account all rules and regulations affecting that determination, including, without limitation, sections 704(b), (c), and (e), 736, and 743.

(iii) Capital interest. Generally, a partner's interest in partnership capital is determined by reference to the assets of the partnership that the partner would be entitled to upon withdrawal from the partnership or upon liquidation of the partnership. If the partnership maintains capital accounts in accordance with § 1.704-1(b)(2)(iv), then for purposes of section 706(b), the partnership may assume that a partner's interest in partnership capital is the ratio of the partner's capital account to all partners' capital accounts as of the first day of the partnership taxable year.

(5) Taxable year of a partnership with tax-exempt partners. (i) Certain tax-exempt partners disregarded. In determining the taxable year (the current year) of a partnership under section 706(b) and the regulations thereunder, a partner that is tax-exempt under section 501(a) shall be disregarded if such partner was not subject to tax, under chapter 1 of the Internal Revenue Code, on any income attributable to its investment in the partnership during the partnership's taxable year immediately preceding the current year. However, if a partner that is tax-exempt under section 501(a) was not a partner during the partnership's immediately preceding taxable year, such partner will be disregarded for the current year if the partnership reasonably believes that the partner will not be subject to tax, under chapter 1 of the Internal Revenue Code, on any income attributable to such partner's investment in the partnership during the current year.

(ii) Example. The provisions of paragraph (b)(5)(i) of this section may be illustrated by the following example:

Example. Assume that partnership A has historically used the calendar year as its taxable year. In addition, assume that A is owned by 5 partners, 4 calendar year individuals (each owning 10 percent of A's profits and capital) and a tax-exempt organization (owning 60 percent of A's profits and capital). The tax-exempt organization has never had unrelated business taxable income with respect to A and has historically used a June 30 fiscal year. Finally, assume that A desires to retain the calendar year for its taxable year beginning January 1, 2003. Under these facts and but for the special rule in paragraph (b)(5)(i) of this section, A would be required under section 706(b)(1)(B)(i) to change to a year ending June 30, for its taxable year beginning January 1, 2003. However, under the special rule provided in paragraph (b)(5)(i) of this section the partner that is tax-exempt is disregarded, and A must retain the calendar year, under section 706(b)(1)(B)(i), for its taxable year beginning January 1.

(iii) Effective date. The provisions of this paragraph (b)(5) are applicable for taxable years beginning on or after July 23, 2002. For taxable years beginning before July 23, 2002, see § 1.706-3T as contained in 26 CFR part 1 revised April 1, 2002.

(6) Certain foreign partners disregarded. (i) Interests of disregarded foreign partners not taken into account. In determining the taxable year (the current taxable year) of a partnership under section 706(b) and the regulations thereunder, any interest held by a disregarded foreign partner is not taken into account. A foreign partner is a disregarded foreign partner unless such partner is allocated any gross income of the partnership that was effectively connected (or treated as effectively connected) with the conduct of a trade or business within the United States during the partnership's taxable year immediately preceding the current taxable year (or, if such partner was not a partner during the partnership's immediately preceding taxable year, the partnership reasonably believes that the partner will be allocated any such income during the current taxable year) and taxation of that income is not otherwise precluded under any U.S. income tax treaty.

(ii) Definition of foreign partner. For purposes of this paragraph (b)(6), a foreign partner is any partner that is not a U.S. person (as defined in section 7701(a)(30)), except that a partner that is a controlled foreign corporation (as defined in section 957(a)) or a foreign personal holding company (as defined in section 552) shall not be treated as a foreign partner.

(iii) Minority interest rule. If each partner that is not a disregarded foreign partner under paragraph (b)(6)(i) of this section (regarded partner) holds less than a 10-percent interest, and the regarded partners, in the aggregate, hold less than a 20-percent interest in the capital or profits of the partnership, then paragraph (b)(6)(i) of this section does not apply. In determining ownership in a partnership for purposes of this paragraph (b)(6)(iii), each regarded partner is treated as owning any interest in the partnership owned by a related partner. For this purpose, partners are treated as related if they are related within the meaning of sections 267(b) or 707(b) (using the language "10 percent" instead of "50 percent" each place it appears). However, for purposes of determining if partners hold less than a 20-percent interest in the aggregate, the same interests will not be considered as being owned by more than one regarded partner.

(iv) Example. The provisions of paragraph (b)(6) of this section may be illustrated by the following example:

Example. Partnership B is owned by two partners, F, a foreign corporation that owns a 95-percent interest in the capital and profits of partnership B, and D, a domestic corporation that owns the remaining 5-percent interest in the capital and profits of partnership B. Partnership B is not engaged in the conduct of a trade or business within the United States, and, accordingly, partnership B does not earn any income that is effectively connected with a U.S. trade or business. F uses a March 31 fiscal year, and causes partnership B to maintain its books and records on a March 31 fiscal year as well. D is a calendar year taxpayer. Under paragraph (b)(6)(i) of this section, F would be disregarded and partnership B's taxable year would be determined by reference to D. However, because D owns less than a 10-percent interest in the capital and profits of partnership B, the minority interest rule of paragraph (b)(6)(iii) of this section applies, and partnership B must adopt the March 31 fiscal year for Federal tax purposes.

(v) Effective date. (A) Generally. The provisions of this paragraph (b)(6) are applicable for the first taxable year of a partnership other than an existing partnership that begins on or after July 23, 2002. For this purpose, an existing partnership is a partnership that was formed prior to September 23, 2002.

(B) Voluntary change in taxable year. An existing partnership may change its taxable year to a year determined in accordance with this section. An existing partnership that makes such a change will cease to be exempted from the requirements of paragraph (b)(6) of this section.

(C) Subsequent sale or exchange of interests. If an existing partnership terminates under section 708(b)(1)(B), the resulting partnership is not an existing partnership for purposes of paragraph (b)(6)(v)(A) of this section.

(D) Transition rule. If, in the first taxable year beginning on or after July 23, 2002, an existing partnership voluntarily changes its taxable year to a year determined in accordance with this paragraph (b)(6), then the partners of that partnership may apply the provisions of § 1.702-3T to take into account all items of income, gain, loss, deduction, and credit attributable to the partnership year of change ratably over a four-year period.

(7) Adoption of taxable year. A newly-formed partnership may adopt, in accordance with § 1.441-1(c), its required taxable year, a taxable year elected under section 444, or a 52-53-week taxable year ending with reference to its required taxable year or a taxable year elected under section 444 without securing the approval of the Commissioner. If a newly-formed partnership wants to adopt any other taxable year, it must establish a business purpose and secure the approval of the Commissioner under section 442.

(8) Change in taxable year. (i) Partnerships. (A) Approval required. An existing partnership may change its taxable year only by securing the approval of the Commissioner under section 442 or making an election under section 444. However, a partnership may obtain automatic approval for certain changes, including a change to its required taxable year, pursuant to administrative procedures published by the Commissioner.

(B) Short period tax return. A partnership that changes its taxable year must make its return for a short period in accordance with section 443, but must not annualize the partnership taxable income.

(C) Change in required taxable year. If a partnership is required to change to its majority interest taxable year, then no further change in the partnership's required taxable year is required for either of the two years following the year of the change. This limitation against a second change within a three-year period applies only if the first change was to the majority interest taxable year and does not apply following a change in the partnership's taxable year to the principal partners' taxable year or the least aggregate deferral taxable year.

(ii) Partners. Except as otherwise provided in the Internal Revenue Code or the regulations thereunder (e.g., section 859 regarding real estate investment trusts or § 1.442-2(c) regarding a subsidiary changing to its consolidated parent's taxable year), a partner may not change its taxable year without securing the approval of the Commissioner under section 442. However, certain partners may be eligible to obtain automatic approval to change their taxable years pursuant to the regulations or administrative procedures published by the Commissioner. A partner that changes its taxable year must make its return for a short period in accordance with section 443.

(9) Retention of taxable year. In certain cases, a partnership will be required to change its taxable year unless it obtains the approval of the Commissioner under section 442, or makes an election under section 444, to retain its current taxable year. For example, a partnership using a taxable year that corresponds to its required taxable year must obtain the approval of the Commissioner to retain such taxable year if its required taxable year changes as a result of a change in ownership, unless the partnership previously obtained approval for its current taxable year or, if appropriate, makes an election under section 444.

(10) Procedures for obtaining approval or making a section 444 election. See § 1.442-1(b) for procedures to obtain the approval of the Commissioner (automatically or otherwise) to adopt, change, or retain a taxable year. See §§ 1.444-1T and 1.444-2T for qualifications, and § 1.444-3T for procedures, for making an election under section 444.

(11) Effect of partner elections under section 444. (i) Election taken into account. For purposes of section 706(b)(1)(B), any section 444 election by a partner in a partnership shall be taken into account in determining the taxable year of the partnership. See § 1.7519-1T(d), Example (4).

(ii) Effective date. The provisions of this paragraph (b)(11) are applicable for taxable years beginning on or after July 23, 2002. For taxable years beginning before July 23, 2002, see § 1.706-3T as contained in 26 CFR part 1 revised April 1, 2002.

(c) Closing of partnership year. *(1) General rule.* Section 706(c) and this paragraph provide rules governing the closing of partnership years. The closing of a partnership taxable year or a termination of a partnership for Federal income tax purposes is not necessarily governed by the "dissolution", "liquidation", etc., of a partnership under State or local law. The taxable year of a partnership shall not close as the result of the death of a partner, the entry of a new partner, the liquidation of a partner's entire interest in the partnership (as defined in section 761(d)), or the sale or exchange of a partner's interest in the partnership, except in the case of a termination of a partnership and except as provided in subparagraph (2) of this paragraph. In the case of termination, the partnership taxable year closes for all partners as of the date of termination. See section 708(b) and paragraph (b) of § 1.708-1.

(2) Partner who retires or sells interest in partnership. (i) Disposition of entire interest. A partnership taxable year shall close with respect to a partner who sells or exchanges his entire interest in a partnership, and with respect to a partner whose entire interest is liquidated. However, a partnership taxable year with respect to a partner who dies shall not close prior to the end of such partnership taxable year, or the time when such partner's interest (held by his estate or other successor) is liquidated or sold or exchanged, whichever is earlier. See subparagraph (3) of this paragraph.

(ii) Inclusions in taxable income. In the case of a sale, exchange, or liquidation of a partner's entire interest in a partnership, the partner shall include in his taxable income for his taxable year within or with which his membership in the partnership ends, his distributive share of items described in section 702(a), and any guaranteed payments under section 707(c), for his partnership taxable year ending with the date of such sale, exchange, or liquidation. In order to avoid an interim closing of the partnership books, such partner's distributive share of items described in section 702(a) may, by agreement among the partners, be estimated by taking his pro rata part of the amount of such items he would have included in his taxable income had he remained a partner until the end of the partnership taxable year. The proration may be based on the portion of the taxable year that has elapsed prior to the sale, exchange, or liquidation, or may be determined under any other method that is reasonable. Any partner who is the transferee of such partner's interest shall include in his taxable income, as his distributive share of items described in section 702(a) with respect to the acquired interest, the pro rata part (determined by the method used by the transferor partner) of the amount of such items he would have included had he been a partner from the beginning of the taxable year of the partnership. The application of this subdivision may be illustrated by the following example:

Example. Assume that a partner selling his partnership interest on June 30, 1955, has an adjusted basis for his interest of $5,000 on that date; that his pro rata share of partnership income up to June 30 is $15,000; and that he sells his interest for $20,000. Under the provisions of section 706(c)(2), the partnership year with respect to him closes at the time of the sale. The $15,000 is includible in his income as his distributive share and, under section 705, it increases the basis of his partnership interest to $20,000, which is also the selling price of his interest. Therefore, no gain is realized on the sale of his partnership interest. The purchaser of this partnership interest shall include in his income as his distributive share his pro rata part of partnership income for the remainder of the partnership taxable year.

(3) Partner who dies. (i) When a partner dies, the partnership taxable year shall not close with respect to such partner prior to the end of the partnership taxable year. The partnership taxable year shall continue both for the remaining partners and the decedent partner. Where the death of a partner results in the termination of the partnership, the partnership taxable year shall close for all partners on the date of such termination under section 708(b)(1)(A). See also paragraph (b)(1)(i)(b) of § 1.708-1 for the continuation of a 2-member partnership under certain circumstances after the death of a partner. However, if the decedent partner's estate or other successor sells or exchanges its entire interest in the partnership, or if its entire interest is liquidated, the partnership taxable year with respect to the estate or other successor in interest shall close on the date of such sale or exchange, or the date of completion of the liquidation.

(ii) The last return of a decedent partner shall include only his share of partnership taxable income for any partnership taxable year or years ending within or with the last taxable year for such decedent partner (i.e., the year ending with the date of his death). The distributive share of partnership taxable income for a partnership taxable year ending after the decedent's last taxable year is includible in the return of his estate or other successor in interest. If the estate or other successor in interest of a partner continues to share in the profits or losses of the partnership business, the distributive share thereof is includible in the taxable year of the estate or other successor in interest within or with which the taxable year of the partnership ends. See also paragraph (a)(1)(ii) of § 1.736-1. Where the estate or other successor in interest receives distributions, any gain or loss on such distributions is includible in its gross income for its taxable year in which the distribution is made.

(iii) If a partner (or a retiring partner), in accordance with the terms of the partnership agreement, designates a person to succeed to his interest in the partnership after his death, such designated person shall be regarded as a successor in interest of the deceased for purposes of this chapter. Thus, where a partner designates his widow as the successor in interest, her distributive share of income for the taxable year of the partnership ending within or with her taxable year may be included in a joint return in accordance with the provisions of sections 2 and 6013(a)(2) and (3).

(iv) If, under the terms of an agreement existing at the date of death of a partner, a sale or exchange of the decedent partner's interest in the partnership occurs upon that date, then the taxable year of the partnership with respect to such decedent partner shall close upon the date of death. See section 706(c)(2)(A)(i). The sale or exchange of a partnership interest does not, for the purpose of this rule, include any transfer of a partnership interest which occurs at death as a result of inheritance or any testamentary disposition.

(v) To the extent that any part of a distributive share of partnership income of the estate or other successor in interest of a deceased partner is attributable to the decedent for the period ending with the date of his death, such part of the distributive share is income in respect of the decedent under section 691. See section 691 and the regulations thereunder.

(vi) The provisions of this subparagraph may be illustrated by the following examples:

Example (1). B has a taxable year ending December 31 and is a member of partnership ABC, the taxable year of which ends on June 30. B dies on October 31, 1955. His estate (which as a new taxpayer may, under section 441 and the regulations thereunder, adopt any taxable year) adopts a taxable year ending October 31. The return of the decedent for the period January 1 to October 31, 1955, will include only his distributive share of taxable income of the partnership for its taxable year ending June 30, 1955. The distributive share of taxable income of the partnership for its taxable year ending June 30, 1956, arising from the interest of the decedent, will be includible in the return of the estate for its taxable year ending October 31, 1956. That part of the distributive share attributable to the decedent for the period ending with the date of his death (July 1 through October 31, 1955) is income in respect of a decedent under section 691.

Example (2). Assume the same facts as in example (1) of this subdivision, except that, prior to B's death, B and D had agreed that, upon B's death, D would purchase B's interest for $10,000. When B dies on October 31, 1955, the partnership taxable year beginning July 1, 1955, closes with respect to him. Therefore, the return for B's last taxable year (January 1 to October 31, 1955) will include his distributive share of taxable income of the partnership for its taxable year ending June 30, 1955, plus his distributive share of partnership taxable income for the period July 1 to October 31, 1955. See subdivision (iv) of this subparagraph.

Example (3). H is a member of a partnership having a taxable year ending December 31. Both H and his wife W are on a calendar year and file joint returns. H dies on March 31, 1955. Administration of the estate is completed and the estate, including the partnership interest, is distributed to W as legatee on November 30, 1955. Such distribution by the estate is not a sale or exchange of H's partnership interest. No part of the taxable income of the partnership for the taxable year ending December 31, 1955, which is allocable to H, will be included in H's taxable income for his last taxable year (January 1 through March 31, 1955) or in the taxable income of H's estate for the taxable year April 1 through November 30, 1955. The distributive share of partnership taxable income for the full calendar year that is allocable to H will be includible in the taxable income of W for her taxable year ending December 31, 1955, and she may file a joint return under sections 2 and 6013(a)(3). That part of the distributive share attributable to the decedent for the period ending with the date of his death (January 1 through March 31, 1955) is income in respect of a decedent under section 691.

Example (4). M is a member of partnership JKM which operates on a calendar year. M and his wife S file joint returns for calendar years. In accordance with the partnership agreement, M designated S to succeed to his interest in the partnership upon his death. M, who had withdrawn $10,000 from the partnership before his death, dies on October 20, 1955. S's distributive share of income for the taxable year 1955 is $15,000 ($10,000 of which represents the amount withdrawn by M). S shall include $15,000 in her income, even though M received $10,000 of this amount before his death. S may file a joint return with M for the year 1955 under sections 2 and 6013(a). That part of the $15,000 distributive share attributable to the decedent for the period ending with the date of his death (January 1 through October 20, 1955) is income in respect of a decedent under section 691.

(4) Disposition of less than entire interest. If a partner sells or exchanges a part of his interest in a partnership, or if the interest of a partner is reduced, the partnership taxable year shall continue to its normal end. In such case, the partner's distributive share of items which he is required to include in his taxable income under the provisions of section 702(a) shall be determined by taking into account his varying interests in the partnership during the partnership taxable year in which such sale, exchange, or reduction of interest occurred.

(5) Transfer of interest by gift. The transfer of a partnership interest by gift does not close the partnership taxable year with respect to the donor. However, the income up to the date of gift attributable to the donor's interest shall be allocated to him under section 704(e)(2).

(d) Effective date. The rules of this section are applicable for taxable years ending on or after May 17, 2002, except for paragraph (c), which applies for taxable years beginning after December 31, 1953.

T.D. 6175, 5/23/56, amend T.D. 7286, 9/26/73, T.D. 8123, 2/4/87, T.D. 8996, 5/16/2002, T.D. 9009, 7/22/2002.

PAR. 2. In § 1.706-1, paragraph (c)(6) is added to read as follows:

Proposed § 1.706-1 Taxable years of partner and partnership. [*For Preamble, see ¶ 152,781*]

* * * * *

(c) * * *

(6) Foreign taxes. For rules relating to the treatment of foreign taxes paid or accrued by a partnership, see § 1.901-2(f)(3)(i) and (ii).

* * * * *

§ 1.706-2T Temporary regulations; question and answer under the Tax Reform Act of 1984 (temporary).

Question 1: For purposes of section 706(d), how is an otherwise deductible amount that is deferred under section 267(a)(2) treated?

Answer 1: In the year the deduction is allowed, the deduction will constitute an allocable cash basis item under section 706(d)(2)(B)(iv).

T.D. 7991, 11/29/84.

Proposed § 1.706-3 Property transferred in connection with the performance of services. [*For Preamble, see ¶ 152,663*]

(a) Allocations of certain deductions under section 83(h). The transfer of property subject to section 83 in connection with the performance of services is not an allocable cash basis item within the meaning of section 706(d)(2)(B).

(b) Forfeiture allocations. If an election under section 83(b) is made with respect to a partnership interest that is substantially nonvested (within the meaning of § 1.83-3(b)), and that interest is later forfeited, the partnership must make forfeiture allocations to reverse prior allocations made with respect to the forfeited interest. See § 1.704-1(b)(4)(xii). Although the person forfeiting the interest may not have been a partner for the entire taxable year, forfeiture allocations may be made out of the partnership's items for the entire taxable year.

(c) Effective date. This section applies to transfers of property on or after the date final regulations are published in the Federal Register.

§ 1.707-0 Table of contents.

This section lists the captions that appear in §§ 1.707-1 through 1.707-9.

T.D. 8439, 9/25/92.

PAR. 2. Section 1.707-0 is amended as follows:

1. Adding an entry for § 1.707-5(a)(8).
2. Revising the entry for § 1.707-7.
3. Adding entries for §§ 1.707-7(a) through 1.707-7(l).
4. Revising the entry for § 1.707-8(c).
5. Revising the entries for §§ 1.707-9(a) and (a)(2).

The revisions and additions read as follows:

* * * * *

Proposed § 1.707-0 Table of contents. [*For Preamble, see ¶ 152,607*]

* * * * *

* * * * *

(c) Parties required to disclose.

* * * * *

§ 1.707-9 Effective dates and transitional rules.

(a) Sections 1.707-3 through 1.707-7.

(1) * * *

(2) Transfers occurring before effective dates.

* * * * *

§ 1.707-1 Transactions between partner and partnership.

Caution: The Treasury has not yet amended Reg § 1.707-1 to reflect changes made by P.L. 98-369.

(a) Partner not acting in capacity as partner. A partner who engages in a transaction with a partnership other than in his capacity as a partner shall be treated as if he were not a member of the partnership with respect to such transaction. Such transactions include, for example, loans of money or property by the partnership to the partner or by the partner to the partnership, the sale of property by the partner to the partnership, the purchase of property by the partner from the partnership, and the rendering of services by the partnership to the partner or by the partner to the partnership. Where a partner retains the ownership of property but allows the partnership to use such separately owned property for partnership purposes (for example, to obtain credit or to secure firm creditors by guaranty, pledge, or other agreement) the transaction is treated as one between a partnership and a partner not acting in his capacity as a partner. However, transfers of money or property by a partner to a partnership as contributions, or transfers of money or property by a partnership to a partner as distributions, are not transactions included within the provisions of this section. In all cases, the substance of the transaction will govern rather than its form. See paragraph (c)(3) of § 1.731-1.

(b) Certain sales or exchanges of property with respect to controlled partnerships. *(1) Losses disallowed.* (i) No deduction shall be allowed for a loss on a sale or exchange of property (other than an interest in the partnership), directly or indirectly, between a partnership and a partner who owns, directly or indirectly, more than 50 percent of the capital interest or profits interest in such partnership. A loss on a sale or exchange of property, directly or indirectly, between two partnerships in which the same persons own, directly or indirectly, more than 50 percent of the capital interest or profits interest in each partnership shall not be allowed.

(ii) If a gain is realized upon the subsequent sale or exchange by a transferee of property with respect to which a loss was disallowed under the provisions of subdivision (i) of this subparagraph, section 267(d) (relating to amount of gain where loss previously disallowed) shall apply as though the loss were disallowed under section 267(a)(1).

(2) Gains treated as ordinary income. Any gain recognized upon the sale or exchange, directly or indirectly, of property which, in the hands of the transferee immediately after the transfer, is property other than a capital asset, as defined in section 1221, shall be ordinary income if the transaction is between a partnership and a partner who owns, directly or indirectly, more than 80 percent of the capital interest or profits interest in the partnership. This rule also applies where such a transaction is between partnerships in which the same persons own, directly or indirectly, more than 80 percent of the capital interest or profits interest in each partnership. The term "property other than a capital asset" includes (but is not limited to) trade accounts receivable, inventory, stock in trade, and depreciable or real property used in the trade of business.

(3) Ownership of a capital or profits interest. In determining the extent of the ownership by a partner, as defined in section 761(b), of his capital interest or profits interest in a partnership, the rules for constructive ownership of stock provided in section 267(c)(1), (2), (4), and (5) shall be applied for the purpose of section 707(b) and this paragraph. Under these rules, ownership of a capital or profits interest in a partnership may be attributed to a person who is not a partner as defined in section 761(b) in order that another partner may be considered the constructive owner of such interest under section 267(c). However, section 707(b)(1)(A) does not apply to a constructive owner of a partnership interest since he is not a partner as defined in section 761(b). For example, where trust T is a partner in the partnership ABT, and AW, A's wife, is the sole beneficiary of the trust, the ownership of a capital and profits interest in the partnership by T will be attributed to AW only for the purpose of further attributing the ownership of such interest to A. See section 267(c)(1) and (5). If A, B, and T are equal partners, then A will be considered as owning more than 50 percent of the capital and profits interest in the partnership, and losses on transactions between him and the partnership will be disallowed by section 707(b)(1)(A). However, a loss sustained by AW on a sale or exchange of property with the partnership would not be disallowed by section 707, but will be disallowed to the extent provided in paragraph (b) of § 1.267(b)-1. See section 267(a) and (b), and the regulations thereunder.

(c) Guaranteed payments. Payments made by a partnership to a partner for services or for the use of capital are considered as made to a person who is not a partner, to the extent such payments are determined without regard to the income of the partnership. However, a partner must include such payments as ordinary income for his taxable year within or with which ends the partnership taxable year in which the partnership deducted such payments as paid or accrued under its method of accounting. See section 706(a) and paragraph (a) of § 1.706-1. Guaranteed payments are considered as made to one who is not a member of the partnership only for the purposes of section 61(a) (relating to gross income) and section 162(a) (relating to trade or business expenses). For a guaranteed payment to be a partnership deduction, it must meet the same tests under section 162(a) as it would if the payment had been to a person who is not a member of the partnership, and the rules of section 263 (relating to capital expenditures) must be taken into account. This rule does not affect the deductibility to the partnership of a payment described in section 736(a)(2) to a retiring partner or to a deceased partner's successor in interest. Guaranteed payments do not constitute an interest in partnership profits for purposes of sections 706(b)(3), 707(b), and 708(b). For the purposes of other provisions of the internal revenue laws, guaranteed payments are regarded as a partner's distributive share of ordinary income. Thus, a partner who receives guaranteed payments for a period during which he is absent from work because of personal injuries or sickness is not entitled to exclude such payments from his gross income under section 105(d). Similarly, a partner who receives guaranteed payments is not regarded as an employee of the partnership for the purposes of withholding of tax at source, deferred compensation plans, etc. The provisions of this paragraph may be illustrated by the following examples:

Example (1). Under the ABC partnership agreement, partner A is entitled to a fixed annual payment of $10,000 for services, without regard to the income of the partnership. His distributive share is 10 percent. After deducting the guaranteed payment, the partnership has $50,000 ordinary income. A must include $15,000 as ordinary income for his taxable year within or with which the partnership taxable year ends ($10,000 guaranteed payment plus $5,000 distributive share).

Example (2). Partner C in the CD partnership is to receive 30 percent of partnership income as determined before taking into account any guaranteed payments, but not less than $10,000. The income of the partnership is $60,000, and C is entitled to $18,000 (30 percent of $60,000) as his distributive share. No part of this amount is a guaranteed payment. However, if the partnership had income of $20,000 instead of $60,000, $6,000 (30 percent of $20,000) would be partner C's distributive share, and the remaining $4,000 payable to C would be a guaranteed payment.

Example (3). Partner X in the XY partnership is to receive a payment of $10,000 for services, plus 30 percent of the taxable income or loss of the partnership. After deducting the payment of $10,000 to partner X, the XY partnership has a loss of $9,000. Of this amount, $2,700 (30 percent of the loss) is X's distributive share of partnership loss and, subject to section 704(d), is to be taken into account by him in his return. In addition, he must report as ordinary income the guaranteed payment of $10,000 made to him by the partnership.

Example (4). Assume the same facts as in example (3) of this paragraph, except that, instead of a $9,000 loss, the partnership has $30,000 in capital gains and no other items of income or deduction except the $10,000 paid X as a guaranteed payment. Since the items of partnership income or loss must be segregated under section 702(a), the partnership has a $10,000 ordinary loss and $30,000 in capital gains. X's 30 percent distributive shares of these amounts are $3,000 ordinary loss and $9,000 capital gain. In addition, X has received a $10,000 guaranteed payment which is ordinary income to him.

T.D. 6175, 5/23/56, amend T.D. 6312, 9/10/58, T.D. 7891, 5/3/83.

PAR. 6. In § 1.707-1, paragraph (c) is amended by revising the second sentence to read as follows:

Proposed § 1.707-1 Transactions between partner and partnership. [*For Preamble, see ¶ 152,663*]

* * * * *

(c) Guaranteed payments. * * * However, except as otherwise provided in section 83 and the regulations thereunder, a partner must include such payments as ordinary income for that partner's taxable year within or with which ends the partnership taxable year in which the partnership deducted such payments as paid or accrued under its method of accounting. * * *

* * * * *

§ 1.707-2 Disguised payments for services. [Reserved]

§ 1.707-3 Disguised sales of property to partnership; general rules.

(a) Treatment of transfers as a sale. *(1) In general.* Except as otherwise provided in this section, if a transfer of property by a partner to a partnership and one or more transfers of money or other consideration by the partnership to that partner are described in paragraph (b)(1) of this section, the transfers are treated as a sale of property, in whole or in part, to the partnership.

(2) Definition and timing of sale. For purposes of §§ 1.707-3 through 1.707-5, the use of the term sale (or any variation of that word) to refer to a transfer of property by a partner to a partnership and a transfer of consideration by a partnership to a partner means a sale or exchange of that property, in whole or in part, to the partnership by the partner acting in a capacity other than as a member of the partnership, rather than a contribution and distribution to which sections 721 and 731, respectively, apply. A transfer that is treated as a sale under paragraph (a)(1) of this section is treated as a sale for all purposes of the Code (e.g., sections 453, 483, 1001, 1012, 1031 and 1274). The sale is considered to take place on the date that, under general principles of Federal tax law, the partnership is considered the owner of the property. If the transfer of money or other consideration from the partnership to the partner occurs after the transfer of property to the partnership, the partner and the partnership are treated as if, on the date of the sale, the partnership transferred to the partner an obligation to transfer to the partner money or other consideration.

(3) Application of disguised sale rules. If a person purports to transfer property to a partnership in a capacity as a partner, the rules of this section apply for purposes of determining whether the property was transferred in a disguised sale, even if it is determined after the application of the rules of this section that such person is not a partner. If after the application of the rules of this section to a purported transfer of property to a partnership, it is determined that no partnership exists because the property was actually sold, or it is otherwise determined that the contributed property is not owned by the partnership for tax purposes, the transferor of the property is treated as having sold the property to the person (or persons) that acquired ownership of the property for tax purposes.

(4) Deemed terminations under section 708. In applying the rules of this section, transfers resulting from a termination of a partnership under section 708(b)(1)(B) are disregarded.

(b) Transfers treated as a sale. *(1) In general.* A transfer of property (excluding money or an obligation to contribute money) by a partner to a partnership and a transfer of money or other consideration (including the assumption of or the taking subject to a liability) by the partnership to the partner constitute a sale of property, in whole or in part, by the partner to the partnership only if based on all the facts and circumstances—

(i) The transfer of money or other consideration would not have been made but for the transfer of property; and

(ii) In cases in which the transfers are not made simultaneously, the subsequent transfer is not dependent on the entrepreneurial risks of partnership operations.

(2) Facts and circumstances. The determination of whether a transfer of property by a partner to the partnership and a transfer of money or other consideration by the partnership to the partner constitute a sale, in whole or in part, under paragraph (b)(1) of this section is made based on all the facts and circumstances in each case. The weight to be given each of the facts and circumstances will depend on the particular case. Generally, the facts and circumstances existing on the date of the earliest of such transfers are the ones considered in determining whether a sale exists under paragraph (b)(1) of this section. Among the facts and circumstances that may tend to prove the existence of a sale under paragraph (b)(1) of this section are the following:

(i) That the timing and amount of a subsequent transfer are determinable with reasonable certainty at the time of an earlier transfer;

(ii) That the transferor has a legally enforceable right to the subsequent transfer;

(iii) That the partner's right to receive the transfer of money or other consideration is secured in any manner, taking into account the period during which it is secured;

(iv) That any person has made or is legally obligated to make contributions to the partnership in order to permit the partnership to make the transfer of money or other consideration;

(v) That any person has loaned or has agreed to loan the partnership the money or other consideration required to enable the partnership to make the transfer, taking into account whether any such lending obligation is subject to contingencies related to the results of partnership operations;

(vi) That the partnership has incurred or is obligated to incur debt to acquire the money or other consideration necessary to permit it to make the transfer, taking into account the likelihood that the partnership will be able to incur that debt (considering such factors as whether any person has agreed to guarantee or otherwise assume personal liability for that debt);

(vii) That the partnership holds money or other liquid assets, beyond the reasonable needs of the business, that are expected to be available to make the transfer (taking into account the income that will be earned from those assets);

(viii) That partnership distributions, allocations or control of partnership operations is designed to effect an exchange of the burdens and benefits of ownership of property;

(ix) That the transfer of money or other consideration by the partnership to the partner is disproportionately large in relationship to the partner's general and continuing interest in partnership profits; and

(x) That the partner has no obligation to return or repay the money or other consideration to the partnership, or has such an obligation but it is likely to become due at such a distant point in the future that the present value of that obligation is small in relation to the amount of money or other consideration transferred by the partnership to the partner.

(c) Transfers made within two years presumed to be a sale. *(1) In general.* For purposes of this section, if within a two-year period a partner transfers property to a partnership and the partnership transfers money or other consideration to the partner (without regard to the order of the transfers), the transfers are presumed to be a sale of the property to the partnership unless the facts and circumstances clearly establish that the transfers do not constitute a sale.

(2) Disclosure of transfers made within two years. Disclosure to the Internal Revenue Service in accordance with § 1.707-8 is required if—

(i) A partner transfers property to a partnership and the partnership transfers money or other consideration to the partner within a two-year period (without regard to the order of the transfers);

(ii) The partner treats the transfers other than as a sale for tax purposes; and

(iii) The transfer of money or other consideration to the partner is not presumed to be a guaranteed payment for capital under § 1.707-4(a)(1)(ii), is not a reasonable preferred return within the meaning of § 1.707-4(a)(3), and is not an operating cash flow distribution within the meaning of § 1.707-4(b)(2).

(d) Transfers made more than two years apart presumed not to be a sale. For purposes of this section, if a transfer of money or other consideration to a partner by a partnership and the transfer of property to the partnership by that partner are more than two years apart, the transfers are presumed not to be a sale of the property to the partnership unless the facts and circumstances clearly establish that the transfers constitute a sale.

(e) Scope. This section and §§ 1.707-4 through 1.707-9 apply to contributions and distributions of property described in section 707(a)(2)(A) and transfers described in section 707(a)(2)(B) of the Internal Revenue Code.

(f) Examples. The following examples illustrate the application of this section.

Example (1). Treatment of simultaneous transfers as a sale. A transfers property X to partnership AB on April 9, 1992, in exchange for an interest in the partnership. At the time of the transfer, property X has a fair market value of $4,000,000 and an adjusted tax basis of $1,200,000. Immediately after the transfer, the partnership transfers $3,000,000 in cash to A. Assume that, under this section, the partnership's transfer of cash to A is treated as part of a sale of property X to the partnership. Because the amount of cash A receives on April 9, 1992, does not equal the fair market value of the property, A is considered to have sold a portion of property X with a value of $3,000,000 to the partnership in exchange for the cash. Accordingly, A must recognize $2,100,000 of gain ($3,000,000 amount realized less $900,000 adjusted tax basis ($1,200,000 multiplied by $3,000,000/$4,000,000)). Assuming A receives no other transfers that are treated as consideration for the sale of the property under this section, A is considered to have contributed to the partnership, in A's capacity as a partner, $1,000,000 of the fair market value of the property with an adjusted tax basis of $300,000.

Example (2). Treatment of transfers at different times as a sale.

(i) The facts are the same as in Example 1, except that the $3,000,000 is transferred to A one year after A's transfer of property X to the partnership. Assume that under this section the partnership's transfer of cash to A is treated as part of a sale of property X to the partnership. Assume also that the applicable Federal short-term rate for April, 1992, is 10 percent, compounded semiannually.

(ii) Under paragraph (a)(2) of this section, A and the partnership are treated as if, on April 9, 1992, A sold a portion of property X to the partnership in exchange for an obligation to transfer $3,000,000 to A one year later. Section 1274 applies to this obligation because it does not bear interest and is payable more than six months after the date of the sale. As a result, A's amount realized from the receipt of the partnership's obligation will be the imputed principal amount of the partnership's obligation to transfer $3,000,000 to A, which equals $2,721,088 (the present value on April 9, 1992, of a $3,000,000 payment due one year later, determined using a discount rate of 10 percent, compounded semiannually). Therefore, A's amount realized from the receipt of the partnership's obligation is $2,721,088 (without regard to whether the sale is reported under the installment method). A is therefore considered to have sold only $2,721,088 of the fair market value of property X. The remainder of the $3,000,000 payment ($278,912) is characterized in accordance with the provisions of section 1272. Accordingly, A must recognize $1,904,761 of gain ($2,721,088 amount realized less $816,327 adjusted tax basis ($1,200,000 multiplied by $2,721,088/$4,000,000)) on the sale of property X to the partnership. The gain is reportable under the installment method of section 453 if the sale is otherwise eligible. Assuming A receives no other transfers that are treated as consideration for the sale of property under this section, A is considered to have contributed to the partnership, in A's capacity as a partner, $1,278,912 of the fair market value of property X with an adjusted tax basis of $383,673.

Example (3). Operation of presumption for transfers within two years.

(i) C transfers undeveloped land to the CD partnership in exchange for an interest in the partnership. The partnership intends to construct a building on the land. At the time the land is transferred to the partnership, it is unencumbered and has an adjusted tax basis of $500,000 and a fair market value of $1,000,000. The partnership agreement provides that upon completing construction of the building the partnership will distribute $900,000 to C.

(ii) If, within two years of C's transfer of land to the partnership, a transfer is made to C pursuant to the provision requiring a distribution upon completion of the building, the transfer is presumed to be, under paragraph (c) of this section, part of a sale of the land to the partnership. C may rebut the presumption that the transfer is part of a sale if the facts and circumstances clearly establish that—

(A) The transfer to C would have been made without regard to C's transfer of land to the partnership; or

(B) The partnership's obligation or ability to make this transfer to C depends, at the time of the transfer to the partnership, on the entrepreneurial risks of partnership operations.

(iii) For example, if the partnership will be able to fund the transfer of cash to C only to the extent that permanent loan proceeds exceed the cost of constructing the building, the fact that excess permanent loan proceeds will be available only if the cost to complete the building is significantly less than the amount projected by a reasonable budget would be evidence that the transfer to C is not part of a sale. Similarly, a condition that limits the amount of the permanent loan to the cost of constructing the building (and thereby limits the partnership's ability to make a transfer to C) unless all or a substantial portion of the building is leased would be evidence that the transfer to C is not part of a sale, if a significant risk exists that the partnership may not be able to lease the building to that extent. Another factor that may prove that the transfer of cash to C is not part of a sale would be that, at the time the land is transferred to the partnership, no lender has committed to make a permanent loan to fund the transfer of cash to C.

(iv) Facts indicating that the transfer of cash to C is not part of a sale, however, may be offset by other factors. An offsetting factor to restrictions on the permanent loan proceeds may be that the permanent loan is to be a recourse loan and certain conditions to the loan are likely to be waived by the lender because of the creditworthiness of the partners or the value of the partnership's other assets. Similarly, the factor that no lender has committed to fund the transfer of cash to C may be offset by facts establishing that the partnership is obligated to attempt to obtain such a loan and that its ability to obtain such a loan is not significantly dependent on the value that will be added by successful completion of the building, or that the partnership reasonably anticipates that it will have (and will utilize) an alternative source to fund the transfer of cash to C if the permanent loan proceeds are inadequate.

Example (4). Operation of presumption for transfers within two years. E is a partner in the equal EF partnership. The partnership owns two parcels of unimproved real property (parcels 1 and 2). Parcels 1 and 2 are unencumbered. Parcel 1 has a fair market value of $500,000, and parcel 2 has a fair market value of $1,500,000. E transfers additional unencumbered, unimproved real property (parcel 3) with a fair market value of $1,000,000 to the partnership in exchange for an increased interest in partnership profits of 66-⅔ percent. Immediately after this transfer, the partnership sells parcel 1 for $500,000 in a transaction not in the ordinary course of business. The partnership transfers the proceeds of the sale $333,333 to E and $166,667 to F in accordance with their respective partnership interests. The transfer of $333,333 to E is presumed to be, in accordance with paragraph (c) of this section, a sale, in part, of parcel 3 to the partnership. However, the facts of this example clearly establish that $250,000 of the transfer to E is not part of a sale of parcel 3 to the partnership because E would have been distributed $250,000 from the sale of parcel 1 whether or not E had transferred parcel 3 to the partnership. The transfer to E exceeds by $83,333 ($333,333 minus $250,000) the amount of the distribution that would have been made to E if E had not transferred parcel 3 to the partnership. Therefore, $83,333 of the transfer is presumed to be part of a sale of a portion of parcel 3 to the partnership by E.

Example (5). Operation of presumption for transfers more than two years apart.

(i) G transfers undeveloped land to the GH partnership in exchange for an interest in the partnership. At the time the land is transferred to the partnership, it is unencumbered and has an adjusted tax basis of $500,000 and a fair market value of $1,000,000. H contributes $1,000,000 in cash in exchange for an interest in the partnership. Under the partnership agreement, the partnership is obligated to construct a building on the land. The projected construction cost is $5,000,000, which the partnership plans to fund with its $1,000,000 in cash and the proceeds of a construction loan secured by the land and improvements.

(ii) Shortly before G's transfer of the land to the partnership, the partnership secures commitments from lending institutions for construction and permanent financing. To obtain the construction loan, H guarantees completion of the building for a cost of $5,000,000. The partnership is not obligated to reimburse or indemnify H if H must make payment on the completion guarantee. The permanent loan will be funded upon completion of the building, which is expected to occur two years after G's transfer of the land. The amount of the permanent loan is to equal the lesser of $5,000,000 or 80 percent of the appraised value of the improved property at the time the permanent loan is closed. Under the partnership agreement, the partnership is obligated to apply the proceeds of the permanent loan to retire the construction loan and to hold any excess proceeds for transfer to G 25 months after G's transfer of the land to the partnership. The appraised value of the improved property at the time the permanent loan is closed is expected to exceed $5,000,000 only if the partnership is able to lease a substantial portion of the improvements by that time, and there is a significant risk that the partnership will not be able to achieve a satisfactory occupancy level. The partnership completes construction of the building for the projected cost of $5,000,000 approximately two years after G's transfer of the land. Shortly thereafter, the permanent loan is funded in the amount of $5,000,000. At the time of funding the land and building have an appraised value of $7,000,000. The partnership transfers the $1,000,000 excess permanent loan proceeds to G 25 months after G's transfer of the land to the partnership.

(iii) G's transfer of the land to the partnership and the partnership's transfer of $1,000,000 to G occurred more than two years apart. In accordance with paragraph (d) of this section, those transfers are presumed not to be a sale unless the facts and circumstances clearly establish that the transfers constitute a sale of the property, in whole or part, to the partnership. The transfer of $1,000,000 to G would not have been made but for G's transfer of the land to the partnership. In addition, at the time G transferred the land to the partnership, G had a legally enforceable right to receive a transfer from the partnership at a specified time an amount that equals the excess of the permanent loan proceeds over $4,000,000. In this case, however, there was a significant risk that the appraised value of the property would be insufficient to support a permanent loan in excess of $4,000,000 because of the risk that the partnership would not be able to achieve a sufficient occupancy level. Therefore, the facts of this example indicate that at the time G transferred the land to the partnership the subsequent transfer of $1,000,000 to G depended on the entrepreneurial risks of partnership operations. Accordingly, G's transfer of the land to the partnership is not treated as part of a sale.

Example (6). Rebuttal of presumption for transfers more than two years apart. The facts are the same as in Example 5, except that the partnership is able to secure a commitment for a permanent loan in the amount of $5,000,000 without regard to the appraised value of the improved property at the time the permanent loan is funded. Under these facts, at the time that G transferred the land to the partnership the subsequent transfer of $1,000,000 to G was not dependent on the entrepreneurial risks of partnership operations, because during the period before the permanent loan is funded, the permanent lender's obligation to make a loan in the amount necessary to fund the transfer is not subject to contingencies related to the risks of partnership operations, and after the permanent loan is funded, the partnership holds liquid assets sufficient to make the transfer. Therefore, the facts and circumstances clearly establish that G's transfer of the land to the partnership is part of a sale.

Example (7). Operation of presumption for transfers more than two years apart. The facts are the same as in Example 6, except that H does not guarantee either that the improvements will be completed or that the cost to the partnership of completing the improvements will not exceed $5,000,000. Under these facts, if there is a significant risk that the improvements will not be completed, G's transfer of the land to the partnership will not be treated as part of a sale because the lender is not required to make the permanent loan if the improvements are not completed. Similarly, the transfers will not be treated as a sale to the extent that there is a significant risk that the cost of constructing the improvements will exceed $5,000,000, because, in the absence of a guarantee of the cost of the improvements by H, the $5,000,000 proceeds of the permanent loan might not be sufficient to retire the construction loan and fund the transfer to G. In either case, the transfer of cash to G would be dependent on the entrepreneurial risks of partnership operations.

Example (8). Rebuttal of presumption for transfers more than two years apart.

(i) On February 1, 1992, I, J, and K form partnership IJK. On formation of the partnership, I transfers an unencumbered office building with a fair market value of $50,000,000 and an adjusted tax basis of $20,000,000 to the partnership, and J and K each transfer United States government securities with a fair market value and an adjusted tax basis of $25,000,000 to the partnership. Substantially all of the rentable space in the office building is leased on a long-term basis. The partnership agreement provides that all items of income, gain, loss, and deduction from the office building are to be allocated 45 percent to J, 45 percent to K, and 10 percent to I. The partnership agreement also provides that all items of income, gain, loss, and deduction from the government securities are to be allocated 90 percent to I, 5 percent to J, and 5 percent to K. The partnership agreement requires that cash flow from the office building and government securities be allocated between partners in the same manner as the items of income, gain, loss, and deduction from those properties are allocated between them. The partnership agreement complies with the requirements of § 1.704-1(b)(2)(ii)(b). It is not expected that the partnership will need to resort to the government securities or the cash flow therefrom to operate the office building. At the time the partnership is formed, I, J, and K contemplated that I's interest in the partnership would be liquidated sometime after January 31, 1994, in exchange for a transfer of the government securities and cash (if necessary). On March 1, 1995, the partnership transfers cash and the government securities to I in liquidation of I's interest in the partnership. The cash transferred to I represents the excess of I's share of the appreciation in the office building since the formation of the partnership over J's and K's share of the appreciation in the government securities since they were acquired by the partnership.

(ii) I's transfer of the office building to the partnership and the partnership's transfer of the government securities and cash to I occurred more than two years apart. Therefore, those transfers are presumed not to be a sale unless the facts and circumstances clearly establish that the transfers constitute a sale. Absent I's transfer of the office building to the partnership, I would not have received the government securities from the partnership. The facts (including the amount and nature of partnership assets) indicate that, at the time that I transferred the office building to the partnership, the timing of the transfer of the government securities to I was anticipated and was not dependent on the entrepreneurial risks of partnership operations. Moreover, the facts indicate that the partnership allocations were designed to effect an exchange of the burdens and benefits of ownership of the government securities in anticipation of the transfer of those securities to I and those burdens and benefits were effectively shifted to I on formation of the partnership. Accordingly, the facts and circumstances clearly establish that I sold the office building to the partnership on February 1, 1992, in exchange for the partnership's obligation to transfer the government securities to I and to make certain other cash transfers to I.

T.D. 8439, 9/25/92.

PAR. 3. In § 1.707-3, the heading for paragraph (c)(2) and the text in paragraph (c)(2)(i) are amended by removing the language "two" and adding "seven" in its place.

Proposed § 1.707-3 [Amended]. [*For Preamble, see ¶ 152,607*]

§ 1.707-4 Disguised sales of property to partnership; special rules applicable to guaranteed payments, preferred returns, operating cash flow distributions, and reimbursements of preformation expenditures.

(a) Guaranteed payments and preferred returns. *(1) Guaranteed payment not treated as part of a sale.* (i) In general. A guaranteed payment for capital made to a partner is not treated as part of a sale of property under § 1.707-3(a) (relating to treatment of transfers as a sale). A party's characterization of a payment as a guaranteed payment for capital will not control in determining whether a payment is, in fact, a guaranteed payment for capital. The term guaranteed payment for capital means any payment to a partner by a partnership that is determined without regard to partnership income and is for the use of that partner's capital. See section 707(c). For this purpose, one or more payments are not made for the use of a partner's capital if the payments are designed to liquidate all or part of the partner's interest in property contributed to the partnership rather than to provide the partner with a return on an investment in the partnership.

(ii) Reasonable guaranteed payments. Notwithstanding the presumption set forth in § 1.707-3(c) (relating to transfers made within two years of each other), for purposes of section 707(a)(2) and the regulations thereunder a transfer of money to a partner that is characterized by the parties as a guaranteed payment for capital, is determined without regard to the income of the partnership and is reasonable (within the meaning of paragraph (a)(3) of this section) is presumed to be a guaranteed payment for capital unless the facts and circumstances clearly establish that the transfer is not a guaranteed payment for capital and is part of a sale.

(iii) Unreasonable guaranteed payments. A transfer of money to a partner that is characterized by the parties as a guaranteed payment for capital but that is not reasonable (within the meaning of paragraph (a)(3) of this section) is presumed not to be a guaranteed payment for capital unless the facts and circumstances clearly establish that the transfer is a guaranteed payment for capital. A transfer that is not a guaranteed payment for capital is subject to the rules of § 1.707-3.

(2) Presumption regarding reasonable preferred returns. Notwithstanding the presumption set forth in paragraph (c) of § 1.707-3 (relating to transfers made within two years of each other), a transfer of money to a partner that is characterized by the parties as a preferred return and that is reasonable (within the meaning of paragraph (a)(3) of this section) is presumed not to be part of a sale of property to the partnership unless the facts and circumstances (including the likelihood and expected timing of the subsequent allocation of income or gain to support the preferred return) clearly establish that the transfer is part of a sale. The term preferred return means a preferential distribution of partnership cash flow to a partner with respect to capital contributed to the partnership by the partner that will be matched, to the extent available, by an allocation of income or gain.

(3) Definition of reasonable preferred returns and guaranteed payments. (i) In general. A transfer of money to a partner that is characterized as a preferred return or guaranteed payment for capital is reasonable only to the extent that the transfer is made to the partner pursuant to a written provision of a partnership agreement that provides for payment for the use of capital in a reasonable amount, and only to the extent that the payment is made for the use of capital after the date on which that provision is added to the partnership agreement.

(ii) Reasonable amount. A transfer of money that is made to a partner during any partnership taxable year and is characterized as a preferred return or guaranteed payment for capital is reasonable in amount if the sum of any preferred return and any guaranteed payment for capital that is payable for that year does not exceed the amount determined by multiplying either the partner's unreturned capital at the beginning of the year or, at the partner's option, the partner's weighted average capital balance for the year (with either amount appropriately adjusted, taking into account the relevant compounding periods, to reflect any unpaid preferred return or guaranteed payment for capital that is payable to the partner) by the safe harbor interest rate for that year. The safe harbor interest rate for a partnership's taxable year equals 150 percent of the highest applicable federal rate, at the appropriate compounding period or periods, in effect at any time from the time that the right to the preferred return or guaranteed payment for capital is first established pursuant to a binding, written agreement among the partners through the end of the taxable year. A partner's unreturned capital equals the excess of the aggregate amount of money and the fair market value of other consideration (net of liabilities) contributed by the partner to the partnership over the aggregate amount of money and the fair market value of other consideration (net of liabilities) distributed by the partnership to the partner other than transfers of money that are presumed to be guaranteed payments for capital under paragraph (a)(1)(ii) of this section, transfers of money that are reasonable preferred returns within the meaning of this paragraph (a)(3), and operating cash flow distributions within the meaning of paragraph (b)(2) of this section.

(4) Examples. The following examples illustrate the application of paragraph (a) of this section:

Example (1). Transfer presumed to be a guaranteed payment.

(i) A transfers property with a fair market value of $100,000 to partnership AB. At the time of A's transfer, the partnership agreement is amended to provide that A is to receive a guaranteed payment for the use of A's capital of 10 percent (compounded annually) of the fair market value of the transferred property in each of the three years following the transfer. The partnership agreement provides that partnership net taxable income and loss will be allocated equally between partners A and B, and that partnership cash flow will be distributed in accordance with the allocation of partnership net taxable income and loss. The partnership would be allowed a deduction in the year paid if the transfers made to A are treated as guaranteed payments under section 707(c). Under the partnership agreement, that deduction would be allocated in the same manner as any other item of partnership deduction. The partnership agreement complies with the requirements of § 1.704-1(b)(2)(ii)(b). The partnership agreement does not provide for the payment of a preferred return and, other than the guaranteed payment to be paid to A, no transfer is expected to be made during the three year period following A's transfer that is not an operating cash flow distribution (within the meaning of paragraph (b)(2) of this section). Assume that the highest applicable federal rate in effect at the time of A's transfer is eight percent compounded annually.

(ii) The transfer of money to be made to A under the partnership agreement is characterized by the parties as a guaranteed payment for capital and is determined without regard to the income of the partnership. The transfer is also reasonable within the meaning of § 1.707-4(a)(3). The transfer, therefore, is presumed to be a guaranteed payment for capital. The presumption set forth in § 1.707-3(c) (relating to transfers made within two years of each other) thus does not apply to this transfer. The transfer will not be treated as part of a sale of property to the partnership unless the facts and circumstances clearly establish that the transfer is not a guaranteed payment for capital but is part of a sale.

(iii) The presumption that the transfer is a guaranteed payment for capital is not rebutted, because there are no facts indicating that the transfer is not a guaranteed payment for the use of capital.

Example (2). Transfers characterized as guaranteed payments treated as part of a sale. (i) C and D form partnership CD. C transfers property with a fair market value of $100,000 and an adjusted tax basis of $20,000 in exchange for a partnership interest. D is responsible for managing the day-to-day operations of the partnership and makes no capital contribution to the partnership upon its formation. The partnership agreement provides that C is to receive payments characterized as guaranteed payments and determined without regard to partnership income of $8,333 per year for the first four years of partnership operations for the use of C's capital. In addition, the partnership agreement provides that—

(1) Partnership net taxable income and loss will be allocated 75 percent to C and 25 percent to D; and

(2) All partnership cash flow (determined prior to consideration of the guaranteed payment) will be distributed 75 percent to C and 25 percent to D except that guaranteed payments that the partnership is obligated to make to C are payable solely out of D's share of the partnership's cash flow.

(ii) If D's share of the partnership's cash flow is not sufficient to make the guaranteed payment to C, then D is obligated to contribute any shortfall to the partnership, even in the event the partnership is liquidated. Thus, the effect of the guaranteed payment arrangement is that the guaranteed payment to C is funded entirely by D. The partnership agreement complies with the requirements of § 1.704-1(b)(2)(ii)(b). Assume that, at the time the partnership is formed, the partnership or D could borrow $25,000 pursuant to a loan requiring equal payments of principal and interest over a four-year term at the current market interest rate of approximately 12 percent (compounded annually). Assume that the highest applicable federal rate in effect at the time the partnership is formed is 10 percent compounded annually.

(iii) The transfer of money to be made to C under the partnership agreement is characterized by the parties as a guaranteed payment for capital and is determined without regard to the income of the partnership. The transfer is also reasonable within the meaning of § 1.707-4(a)(3). The transfer, therefore, is presumed to be a guaranteed payment for capital. The presumption set forth in § 1.707-3(c) (relating to transfers made within two years of each other) thus does not apply to this transfer. The transfer will not be treated as part of a sale of property to the partnership unless the facts and circumstances clearly establish that the transfer is not a guaranteed payment for capital and is part of a sale.

(iv) For the first four years of partnership operations, the total guaranteed payments made to C under the partnership agreement will equal $33,332. If the characterization of those payments as guaranteed payments for capital within the meaning of section 707(c) were respected, C would be allocated $24,999 of the deductions that would be claimed by the partnership for those payments, thereby leaving the balance in C's capital account approximately $25,000 less than it would have been if the guaranteed payments had not been made. The guaranteed payments thus have the effect of offsetting approximately $25,000 of the credit made to C's capital account for the property transferred to the partnership by C. C's resulting capital account is approximately equivalent to the capital account C would have had if C had only contributed 75 percent of the property to the partnership. Furthermore, the effect of D's funding the guaranteed payment to C (either through reduced distributions of cash flow to D or additional contributions) is that D's capital account is approximately equivalent to the capital account D would have had if D had contributed 25 percent of the property (or contributed cash so that the partnership could purchase the 25 percent). Moreover, a $25,000 loan requiring equal payments of principal and interest over a four-year term at the current market interest rate of 12 percent (compounded annually), would have resulted in annual payments of principal and interest of $8,230.86. Consequently, the guaranteed payments effectively place the partners in the same economic position that they would have been in had D purchased a one-quarter interest in the property from C financed at the current market rate of interest, and then C and D each contributed their share of the property to the partnership. In view of the burden the guaranteed payments place on D's right to transfers of partnership cash flow and D's legal obligation to make contributions to the partnership to the extent necessary to fund the guaranteed payments, D has effectively purchased through the partnership a one-quarter interest in the property from C.

(v) Under these facts, the presumption that the transfers to C are guaranteed payments for capital is rebutted, because the facts and circumstances clearly establish that the transfers are part of a sale and not guaranteed payments for capital. Under § 1.707-3(a), C and the partnership are treated as if C sold a one-quarter interest in the property to the partnership in exchange for a promissory note evidencing the partnership's obligation to make the guaranteed payments.

(b) Presumption regarding operating cash flow distributions. *(1) In general.* Notwithstanding the presumption set forth in § 1.707-3(c) (relating to transfers made within two years of each other), an operating cash flow distribution is presumed not to be part of a sale of property to the partnership unless the facts and circumstances clearly establish that the transfer is part of a sale.

(2) Operating cash flow distributions. (i) In general. One or more transfers of money by the partnership to a partner during a taxable year of the partnership are operating cash flow distributions for purposes of paragraph (b)(1) of this section to the extent that those transfers are not presumed to be guaranteed payments for capital under paragraph (a)(1)(ii) of this section, are not reasonable preferred returns within the meaning of paragraph (a)(3) of this section, are not characterized by the parties as distributions to the partner acting in a capacity other than as a partner, and to the extent they do not exceed the product of the net cash flow of the partnership from operations for the year multiplied by the lesser of the partner's percentage interest in overall partnership profits for that year or the partner's percentage interest in overall partnership profits for the life of the partnership. For purposes of the preceding sentence, the net cash flow of the partnership from operations for a taxable year is an amount equal to the taxable income or loss of the partnership arising in the ordinary course of the partnership's business and investment activities, increased by tax exempt interest, depreciation, amortization, cost recovery allowances and other noncash charges deducted in determining such taxable income and decreased by—

(A) Principal payments made on any partnership indebtedness;

(B) Property replacement or contingency reserves actually established by the partnership;

(C) Capital expenditures when made other than from reserves or from borrowings the proceeds of which are not included in operating cash flow; and

(D) Any other cash expenditures (including preferred returns) not deducted in determining such taxable income or loss.

(ii) Operating cash flow safe harbor. For any taxable year, in determining a partner's operating cash flow distributions for the year, the partner may use the partner's smallest percentage interest under the terms of the partnership agreement in any material item of partnership income or gain that may be realized by the partnership in the three-year period beginning with such taxable year. This provision is merely intended to provide taxpayers with a safe harbor and is not intended to preclude a taxpayer from using a different percentage under the rules of paragraph (b)(2)(i) of this section.

(iii) Tiered partnerships. In the case of tiered partnerships, the upper-tier partnership must take into account its share of the net cash flow from operations of the lower-tier partnership applying principles similar to those described in paragraph (b)(2)(i) of this section, so that the amount of the upper-tier partnership's operating cash flow distributions is neither overstated nor understated.

(c) Accumulation of guaranteed payments, preferred returns, and operating cash flow distributions. Guaranteed payments for capital, preferred returns, and operating cash flow distributions presumed not to be part of a sale under the rules of paragraphs (a) and (b) of this section do not lose the benefit of the presumption by reason of being retained for distribution in a later year.

(d) Exception for reimbursements of preformation expenditures. A transfer of money or other consideration by the partnership to a partner is not treated as part of a sale of property by the partner to the partnership under § 1.707-3(a) (relating to treatment of transfers as a sale) to the extent that the transfer to the partner by the partnership is made to reimburse the partner for, and does not exceed the amount of, capital expenditures that—

(1) Are incurred during the two-year period preceding the transfer by the partner to the partnership; and

(2) Are incurred by the partner with respect to—

(i) Partnership organization and syndication costs described in section 709; or

(ii) Property contributed to the partnership by the partner, but only to the extent the reimbursed capital expenditures do not exceed 20 percent of the fair market value of such property at the time of the contribution. However, the 20 percent of fair market value limitation of this paragraph (d)(2)(ii) does not apply if the fair market value of the contributed property does not exceed 120 percent of the partner's adjusted basis in the contributed property at the time of contribution.

(e) Other exceptions. The Commissioner may provide by guidance published in the Internal Revenue Bulletin that other payments or transfers to a partner are not treated as part of a sale for purposes of section 707(a)(2) and the regulations thereunder.

T.D. 8439, 9/25/92.

---

§ 1.707-5 Disguised sales of property to partnership; special rules relating to liabilities.

(a) Liability assumed or taken subject to by partnership. *(1) In general.* For purposes of this section and §§ 1.707-3 and 1.707-4, if a partnership assumes or takes property subject to a qualified liability (as defined in paragraph (a)(6) of this section) of a partner, the partnership is treated as transferring consideration to the partner only to the extent provided in paragraph (a)(5) of this section. By contrast, if the partnership assumes or takes property subject to a liability of the partner other than a qualified liability, the partnership is treated as transferring consideration to the partner to the extent that the amount of the liability exceeds the partner's share of that liability immediately after the partnership assumes or takes subject to the liability as provided in paragraphs (a)(2), (3) and (4) of this section.

(2) Partner's share of liability. A partner's share of any liability of the partnership is determined under the following rules:

(i) Recourse liability. A partner's share of a recourse liability of the partnership equals the partner's share of the liability under the rules of section 752 and the regulations thereunder. A partnership liability is a recourse liability to the extent that the obligation is a recourse liability under § 1.752-1(a)(1) or would be treated as a recourse liability under that section if it were treated as a partnership liability for purposes of that section.

(ii) Nonrecourse liability. A partner's share of a nonrecourse liability of the partnership is determined by applying the same percentage used to determine the partner's share of the excess nonrecourse liability under § 1.752-3(a)(3). A partnership liability is a nonrecourse liability of the partnership to the extent that the obligation is a nonrecourse liability under § 1.752-1(a)(2) or would be a nonrecourse liability of the partnership under § 1.752-1(a)(2) if it were treated as a partnership liability for purposes of that section.

(3) Reduction of partner's share of liability. For purposes of this section, a partner's share of a liability, immediately after a partnership assumes or takes subject to the liability, is determined by taking into account a subsequent reduction in the partner's share if—

(i) At the time that the partnership assumes or takes subject to a liability, it is anticipated that the transferring partner's share of the liability will be subsequently reduced; and

(ii) The reduction of the partner's share of the liability is part of a plan that has as one of its principal purposes minimizing the extent to which the assumption of or taking subject to the liability is treated as part of a sale under § 1.707-3.

(4) Special rule applicable to transfers of encumbered property to a partnership by more than one partner pursuant to a plan. For purposes of paragraph (a)(1) of this section, if the partnership assumes or takes property or properties subject to the liabilities of more than one partner pursuant to a plan, a partner's share of the liabilities assumed or taken subject to by the partnership pursuant to that plan immediately after the transfers equals the sum of that partner's shares of the liabilities (other than that partner's qualified liabilities, as defined in paragraph (a)(6) of this section) assumed or taken subject to by the partnership pursuant to the plan. This paragraph (a)(4) does not apply to any liability assumed or taken subject to by the partnership with a principal purpose of reducing the extent to which any other liability assumed or taken subject to by the partnership is treated as a

transfer of consideration under paragraph (a)(1) of this section.

(5) Special rule applicable to qualified liabilities. (i) If a transfer of property by a partner to a partnership is not otherwise treated as part of a sale, the partnership's assumption of or taking subject to a qualified liability in connection with a transfer of property is not treated as part of a sale. If a transfer of property by a partner to the partnership is treated as part of a sale without regard to the partnership's assumption of or taking subject to a qualified liability (as defined in paragraph (a)(6) of this section) in connection with the transfer of property, the partnership's assumption of or taking subject to that liability is treated as a transfer of consideration made pursuant to a sale of such property to the partnership only to the extent of the lesser of—

(A) The amount of consideration that the partnership would be treated as transferring to the partner under paragraph (a)(1) of this section if the liability were not a qualified liability; or

(B) The amount obtained by multiplying the amount of the qualified liability by the partner's net equity percentage with respect to that property.

(ii) A partner's net equity percentage with respect to an item of property equals the percentage determined by dividing—

(A) The aggregate transfers of money or other consideration to the partner by the partnership (other than any transfer described in this paragraph (a)(5)) that are treated as proceeds realized from the sale of the transferred property; by

(B) The excess of the fair market value of the property at the time it is transferred to the partnership over any qualified liability encumbering the property or, in the case of any qualified liability described in paragraph (a)(6)(i)(C) or (D) of this section, that is properly allocable to the property.

(6) Qualified liability of a partner defined. A liability assumed or taken subject to by a partnership in connection with a transfer of property to the partnership by a partner is a qualified liability of the partner only to the extent—

(i) The liability is—

(A) A liability that was incurred by the partner more than two years prior to the earlier of the date the partner agrees in writing to transfer the property or the date the partner transfers the property to the partnership and that has encumbered the transferred property throughout that two-year period;

(B) A liability that was not incurred in anticipation of the transfer of the property to a partnership, but that was incurred by the partner within the two-year period prior to the earlier of the date the partner agrees in writing to transfer the property or the date the partner transfers the property to the partnership and that has encumbered the transferred property since it was incurred (see paragraph (a)(7) of this section for further rules regarding a liability incurred within two years of a property transfer or of a written agreement to transfer);

(C) A liability that is allocable under the rules of § 1.163-8T to capital expenditures with respect to the property; or

(D) A liability that was incurred in the ordinary course of the trade or business in which property transferred to the partnership was used or held but only if all the assets related to that trade or business are transferred other than assets that are not material to a continuation of the trade or business; and

(ii) If the liability is a recourse liability, the amount of the liability does not exceed the fair market value of the transferred property (less the amount of any other liabilities that are senior in priority and that either encumber such property or are liabilities described in paragraph (a)(6)(i)(C) or (D) of this section) at the time of the transfer.

(7) Liability incurred within two years of transfer presumed to be in anticipation of the transfer. (i) In general. For purposes of this section, if within a two-year period a partner incurs a liability (other than a liability described in paragraph (a)(6)(i)(C) or (D) of this section) and transfers property to a partnership or agrees in writing to transfer the property, and in connection with the transfer the partnership assumes or takes the property subject to the liability, the liability is presumed to be incurred in anticipation of the transfer unless the facts and circumstances clearly establish that the liability was not incurred in anticipation of the transfer.

(ii) Disclosure of transfers of property subject to liabilities incurred within two years of the transfer. If a partner treats a liability assumed or taken subject to by a partnership as a qualified liability under paragraph (a)(6)(i)(B) of this section, such treatment is to be disclosed to the Internal Revenue Service in accordance with § 1.707-8.

(b) Treatment of debt-financed transfers of consideration by partnerships. *(1) In general.* For purposes of § 1.707-3, if a partner transfers property to a partnership, and the partnership incurs a liability and all or a portion of the proceeds of that liability are allocable under § 1.163-8T to a transfer of money or other consideration to the partner made within 90 days of incurring the liability, the transfer of money or other consideration to the partner is taken into account only to the extent that the amount of money or the fair market value of the other consideration transferred exceeds that partner's allocable share of the partnership liability.

(2) Partner's allocable share of liability. (i) In general. A partner's allocable share of a partnership liability for purposes of paragraph (b)(1) of this section equals the amount obtained by multiplying the partner's share of the liability as described in paragraph (a)(2) of this section by the fraction determined by dividing—

(A) The portion of the liability that is allocable under § 1.163-8T to the money or other property transferred to the partner; by

(B) The total amount of the liability.

(ii) Debt-financed transfers made pursuant to a plan.

(A) In general. Except as provided in paragraph (b)(2)(iii) of this section, if a partnership transfers to more than one partner pursuant to a plan all or a portion of the proceeds of one or more partnership liabilities, paragraph (b)(1) of this section is applied by treating all of the liabilities incurred pursuant to the plan as one liability, and each partner's allocable share of those liabilities equals the amount obtained by multiplying the sum of the partner's shares of each of the respective liabilities (as defined in paragraph (a)(2) of this section) by the fraction obtained by dividing—

(1) The portion of those liabilities that is allocable under § 1.163-8T to the money or other consideration transferred to the partners pursuant to the plan; by

(2) The total amount of those liabilities.

(B) Special rule. Paragraph (b)(2)(ii)(A) of this section does not apply to any transfer of money or other property to a partner that is made with a principal purpose of reducing the extent to which any transfer is taken into account under paragraph (b)(1) of this section.

(iii) Reduction of partner's share of liability. For purposes of paragraph (b)(2) of this section, a partner's share of a liability, immediately after the partnership assumes or takes subject to the liability, is determined by taking into account a subsequent reduction in the partner's share if—

(A) It is anticipated that the partner's share of the liability that is allocable to a transfer of money or other consideration to the partner will be reduced subsequent to the transfer; and

(B) The reduction of the partner's share of the liability is part of a plan that has as one of its principal purposes minimizing the extent to which the partnership's distribution of the proceeds of the borrowing is treated as part of a sale.

(c) Refinancings. To the extent that the proceeds of a partner or partnership liability (the refinancing debt) are allocable under the rules of § 1.163-8T to payments discharging all or part of any other liability of that partner or of the partnership, as the case may be, the refinancing debt is treated as the other liability for purposes of applying the rules of this section.

(d) Share of liability where assumption accompanied by transfer of money. For purposes of §§ 1.707-3 through 1.707-5, if pursuant to a plan a partner pays or contributes money to the partnership and the partnership assumes or takes subject to one or more liabilities (other than qualified liabilities) of the partner, the amount of those liabilities that the partnership is treated as assuming or taking subject to is reduced (but not below zero) by the money transferred.

(e) Tiered partnerships and other related persons. If a lower-tier partnership succeeds to a liability of an upper-tier partnership, the liability in the lower-tier partnership retains the characterization as qualified or nonqualified that it had under these rules in the upper-tier partnership. A similar rule applies to other related party transactions involving liabilities to the extent provided by guidance published in the Internal Revenue Bulletin.

(f) Examples. The following examples illustrate the application of this section.

Example (1). Partnership's assumption of nonrecourse liability encumbering transferred property.

(i) A and B form partnership AB, which will engage in renting office space. A transfers $500,000 in cash to the partnership, and B transfers an office building to the partnership. At the time it is transferred to the partnership, the office building has a fair market value of $1,000,000, an adjusted basis of $400,000, and is encumbered by a $500,000 liability, which B incurred 12 months earlier to finance the acquisition of other property. No facts rebut the presumption that the liability was incurred in anticipation of the transfer of the property to the partnership. Assume that this liability is a nonrecourse liability of the partnership within the meaning of section 752 and the regulations thereunder. The partnership agreement provides that partnership items will be allocated equally between A and B, including excess nonrecourse deductions under § 1.752-3(a)(3). The partnership agreement complies with the requirements of § 1.704-1(b)(2)(ii)(b).

(ii) The nonrecourse liability secured by the office building is not a qualified liability within the meaning of paragraph (a)(6) of this section. B would be allocated 50 percent of the excess nonrecourse liability under the partnership agreement. Accordingly, immediately after the partnership's assumption of that liability, B's share of the liability equals $250,000, which is equal to B's 50 percent share of the excess nonrecourse liability of the partnership as determined in accordance with B's share of partnership profits under § 1.752-3(a)(3).

(iii) The partnership's taking subject to the liability encumbering the office building is treated as a transfer of $250,000 of consideration to B (the amount by which the liability ($500,000) exceeds B's share of that liability immediately after taking subject to ($250,000)). B is treated as having sold $250,000 of the fair market value of the office building to the partnership in exchange for the partnership's taking subject to a $250,000 liability. This results in a gain of $150,000 ($250,000 minus ($250,000/$1,000,000 multiplied by $400,000)).

Example (2). Partnership's assumption of recourse liability encumbering transferred property.

(i) C transfers property Y to a partnership. At the time of its transfer to the partnership, property Y has a fair market value of $10,000,000 and is subject to an $8,000,000 liability that C incurred, immediately before transferring property Y to the partnership, in order to finance other expenditures. Upon the transfer of property Y to the partnership, the partnership assumed the liability encumbering that property. The partnership assumed this liability solely to acquire property Y. Under section 752 and the regulations thereunder, immediately after the partnership's assumption of the liability encumbering property Y, the liability is a recourse liability of the partnership and C's share of that liability is $7,000,000.

(ii) Under the facts of this example, the liability encumbering property Y is not a qualified liability. Accordingly, the partnership's assumption of the liability results in a transfer of consideration to C in connection with C's transfer of property Y to the partnership in the amount of $1,000,000 (the excess of the liability assumed by the partnership ($8,000,000) over C's share of the liability immediately after the assumption ($7,000,000)). See paragraphs (a)(1) and (2) of this section.

Example (3). Subsequent reduction of transferring partner's share of liability.

(i) The facts are the same as in Example 2. In addition, property Y is a fully leased office building, the rental income from property Y is sufficient to meet debt service, and the remaining term of the liability is ten years. It is anticipated that, three years after the partnership's assumption of the liability, C's share of the liability under section 752 will be reduced to zero because of a shift in the allocation of partnership losses pursuant to the terms of the partnership agreement. Under the partnership agreement, this shift in the allocation of partnership losses is dependent solely on the passage of time.

(ii) Under paragraph (a)(3) of this section, if the reduction in C's share of the liability was anticipated at the time of C's transfer, and the reduction was part of a plan that has as one of its principal purposes minimizing the extent of sale treatment under § 1.707-3 (i.e., a principal purpose of allocating a large percentage of losses to C in the first three years when losses were not likely to be realized was to minimize the extent to which C's transfer would be treated as part of a sale), C's share of the liability immediately after the assumption is treated as equal to C's reduced share.

Example (4). Trade payables as qualified liabilities.

(i) D and E form partnership DE which will engage in a consulting business that requires no overhead and minimal cash on hand for daily operating expenses. Previously, D and E, as individual sole proprietors, operated separate consulting businesses. D and E each transfer to the partnership sufficient cash to cover daily operating expenses together with the goodwill and trade payables related to each sole proprietorship. Due to uncertainty over the collection rate on the trade receivables related to their sole proprietorships, D and E agree that none of the trade receivables will be transferred to the partnership.

(ii) Under the facts of this example, all the assets related to the consulting business (other than the trade receivables) together with the trade payables were transferred to partnership DE. The trade receivables retained by D and E are not material to a continuation of the trade or business by the partnership because D and E contributed sufficient cash to cover daily operating expenses. Accordingly, the trade payables transferred to the partnership constitute qualified liabilities under paragraph (a)(6) of this section.

Example (5). Partnership's assumption of a qualified liability as sole consideration.

(i) F transfers property Z to a partnership. At the time of its transfer to the partnership, property Z has a fair market value of $165,000 and an adjusted tax basis of $75,000. Also, at the time of the transfer, property Z is subject to a $75,000 liability that F incurred more than two years before transferring property Z to the partnership. The liability has been secured by property Z since it was incurred by F. Upon the transfer of property Z to the partnership, the partnership assumed the liability encumbering that property. The partnership made no other transfers to F in consideration for the transfer of property Z to the partnership. Assume that, under section 752 and the regulations thereunder, immediately after the partnership's assumption of the liability encumbering property Z, the liability is a recourse liability of the partnership and F's share of that liability is $25,000.

(ii) The $75,000 liability secured by property Z is a qualified liability of F because F incurred the liability more than two years prior to the assumption of the liability by the partnership and the liability has encumbered property Z for more than two years prior to that assumption. See paragraph (a)(6) of this section. Therefore, since no other transfer to F was made as consideration for the transfer of property Z, under paragraph (a)(5) of this section, the partnership's assumption of the qualified liability of F encumbering property Z is not treated as part of a sale.

Example (6). Partnership's assumption of a qualified liability in addition to other consideration.

(i) The facts are the same as in Example 5, except that the partnership makes a transfer to D of $30,000 in money that is consideration for F's transfer of property Z to the partnership under § 1.707-3.

(ii) As in Example 5, the $75,000 liability secured by property Z is a qualified liability of F. Since the partnership transferred $30,000 to F in addition to assuming the qualified liability under paragraph (a)(5) of this section, the partnership's assumption of this qualified liability is treated as a transfer of additional consideration to F to the extent of the lesser of—

(A) The amount that the partnership would be treated as transferring to F if the liability were not a qualified liability ($50,000 (i.e., the excess of the $75,000 qualified liability over F's $25,000 share of that liability)); or

(B) The amount obtained by multiplying the qualified liability ($75,000) by F's net equity percentage with respect to property Z (one-third).

(iii) F's net equity percentage with respect to property Z equals the fraction determined by dividing—

(A) The aggregate amount of money or other consideration (other than the qualified liability) transferred to F and treated as part of a sale of property Z under § 1.707-3(a) ($30,000 transfer of money); by

(B) F's net equity in property Z ($90,000 (i.e., the excess of the $165,000 fair market value over the $75,000 qualified liability)).

(iv) Accordingly, the partnership's assumption of the qualified liability of F encumbering property Z is treated as a transfer of $25,000 (one-third of $75,000) of consideration to F pursuant to a sale. Therefore, F is treated as having sold $55,000 of the fair market value of property Z to the partnership in exchange for $30,000 in money and the partnership's assumption of $25,000 of the qualified liability. Accordingly, F must recognize $30,000 of gain on the sale (the excess of the $55,000 amount realized over $25,000 of F's adjusted basis for property Z (i.e., one-third of F's adjusted basis for the property, because F is treated as having sold one-third of the property to the partnership)).

Example (7). Partnership's assumptions of liabilities encumbering properties transferred pursuant to a plan.

(i) Pursuant to a plan, G and H transfer property 1 and property 2, respectively, to an existing partnership in exchange for interests in the partnership. At the time the properties are transferred to the partnership, property 1 has a fair market value of $10,000 and an adjusted tax basis of $6,000, and property 2 has a fair market value of $10,000 and an adjusted tax basis of $4,000. At the time properties 1 and 2 are transferred to the partnership, a $6,000 nonrecourse liability (liability 1) is secured by property 1 and a $7,000 recourse liability of F (liability 2) is secured by property 2. Properties 1 and 2 are transferred to the partnership, and the partnership takes subject to liability 1 and assumes liability 2. G and H incurred liabilities 1 and 2 immediately prior to transferring properties 1 and 2 to the partnership and used the proceeds for personal expenditures. The liabilities are not qualified liabilities. Assume that G and H are each allocated $2,000 of liability 1 in accordance with § 1.707-5(a)(2)(ii) (which determines a partner's share of a nonrecourse liability). Assume further that G's share of liability 2 is $3,500 and H's share is $0 in accordance with § 1.707-5(a)(2)(i) (which determines a partner's share of a recourse liability).

(ii) G and H transferred properties 1 and 2 to the partnership pursuant to a plan. Accordingly, the partnership's taking subject to liability 1 is treated as a transfer of only $500 of consideration to G (the amount by which liability 1 ($6,000) exceeds G's share of liabilities 1 and 2 ($5,500)), and the partnership's assumption of liability 2 is treated as a transfer of only $5,000 of consideration to H (the amount by which liability 2 ($7,000) exceeds H's share of liabilities 1 and 2 ($2,000)). G is treated under the rule in § 1.707-3 as having sold $500 of the fair market value of property 1 in exchange for the partnership's taking subject to liability 1 and H is treated as having sold $5,000 of the fair market value of property 2 in exchange for the assumption of liability 2.

Example (8). Partnership's assumption of liability pursuant to a plan to avoid sale treatment of partnership assumption of another liability. (i) The facts are the same as in Example 7, except that—

(A) H transferred the proceeds of liability 2 to the partnership; and

(B) H incurred liability 2 in an attempt to reduce the extent to which the partnership's taking subject to liability 1 would be treated as a transfer of consideration to G (and thereby reduce the portion of G's transfer of property 1 to the partnership that would be treated as part of a sale).

(ii) Because the partnership assumed liability 2 with a principal purpose of reducing the extent to which the partnership's taking subject to liability 1 would be treated as a transfer of consideration to G, liability 2 is ignored in applying paragraph (a)(3) of this section. Accordingly, the partnership's taking subject to liability 1 is treated as a transfer of $4,000 of consideration to G (the amount by which liability 1 ($6,000) exceeds G's share of liability 1 ($2,000)). On the other hand, the partnership's assumption of liability 2 is not treated as a transfer of any consideration to H because H's share of that liability equals $7,000 as a result of H's transfer of $7,000 in money to the partnership.

Example (9). Partnership's assumptions of qualified liabilities encumbering properties transferred pursuant to a plan in addition to other consideration.

(i) Pursuant to a plan, I transfers property 1 and J transfers property 2 plus $10,000 in cash to partnership IJ in exchange for equal interests in the partnership. At the time the properties are transferred to the partnership, property 1 has a fair market value of $100,000, an adjusted tax basis of $5,000, and is encumbered by a qualified liability of $50,000 (liability 1). Property 2 has a fair market value of $100,000, an adjusted tax basis of $5,000, and is encumbered by a qualified liability of $70,000 (liability 2). Pursuant to the plan, the partnership transferred to I $10,000 in cash. That amount is consideration for I's transfer of property 1 to the partnership under § 1.707-3. In accordance with § 1.707-5(a)(2), I and J are each allocated $25,000 of liability 1 and $35,000 of liability 2.

(ii) Because the partnership transferred $10,000 to I as consideration for the transfer of property, under § 1.707-5(a)(5), the partnership's assumption of liability 1 is treated as a transfer of additional consideration to I, even though liability 1 is a qualified liability, to the extent of the lesser of—

(A) The amount that the partnership would be treated as transferring to I if the liability were not a qualified liability; or

(B) The amount obtained by multiplying the qualified liability by I's net equity percentage with respect to property 1.

(iii) Because I and J transferred properties 1 and 2 to the partnership pursuant to a plan, treating I's qualified liability as a nonqualified liability under § 1.707-5(a)(5)(i)(A) enables I to apply the special rule applicable to transfers of encumbered property to a partnership by more than one partner pursuant to a plan under § 1.707-5(a)(4). Under this alternative test, the partnership's assumption of liability 1 encumbering property 1 is treated as a transfer of zero ($0) additional consideration to I pursuant to a sale. This is because the amount of liability 1 ($50,000) does not exceed the sum of I's share of liability 1 treated as a nonqualified liability ($25,000) and I's share of liability 2 ($35,000)).

(iv) The alternative under § 1.707-5(a)(5)(i)(B) is the amount obtained by multiplying the qualified liability ($50,000) by I's net equity percentage with respect to property 1. I's net equity percentage with respect to property 1 equals one-fifth, the fraction determined by dividing—

(1) The aggregate amount of money or other consideration (other than the qualified liability) transferred to I and treated as part of a sale of property 1 under § 1.707-3(a) (the $10,000 transfer of money); by

(2) I's net equity in property 1 ($50,000, i.e., the excess of the $100,000 fair market value over the $50,000 qualified liability).

(v) Under this alternative test, the partnership's assumption of the qualified liability encumbering property 1 is treated as a transfer of $10,000 (one-fifth of the $50,000 qualified liability) of additional consideration to I pursuant to a sale.

(vi) Applying § 1.707-5(a)(5) to these facts, the partnership's assumption of liability 1 is treated as a transfer of additional consideration to I to the extent of the lesser of—

(A) zero; or

(B) $10,000.

(vii) Therefore, the partnership's assumption of I's qualified liability encumbering property 1 is not treated as a transfer of any additional consideration to I pursuant to a sale, and I is treated as having only received $10,000 of the fair market value of property 1 to the partnership in exchange for $10,000 in cash. Accordingly, I must recognize $9,500 of gain on the sale, that is, the excess of the $10,000 amount realized over $500 of I's adjusted tax basis for property 1 (one-tenth of I's adjusted tax basis for the property, because I is treated as having sold one-tenth of the property to the partnership). Since no other transfer to J was made as consideration for the transfer of property 2, the partnership's assumption of the qualified liability of J encumbering property 2 is not treated as part of a sale.

Example (10). Treatment of debt-financed transfers of consideration by partnership.

(i) K transfers property Z to partnership KL in exchange for an interest therein on April 9, 1992. On September 13, 1992, the partnership incurs a liability of $20,000. On November 17, 1992, the partnership transfers $20,000 to K, and $10,000 of this transfer is allocable under the rules of § 1.163-8T to proceeds of the partnership liability incurred on September 13, 1992. The remaining $10,000 is paid from other partnership funds. Assume that, under section 752 and the corresponding regulations, the $20,000 liability incurred on September 13, 1992, is a recourse liability of the partnership and K's share of that liability is $10,000 on November 17, 1992.

(ii) Because a portion of the transfer made to K on November 17, 1992, is allocable under § 1.163-8T to proceeds of a partnership liability that was incurred by the partnership within 90 days of that transfer, K is required to take the transfer into account in applying the rules of this section and § 1.707-3 only to the extent that the amount of the transfer exceeds K's allocable share of the liability used to fund the transfer. K's allocable share of the $20,000 liability used to fund $10,000 of the transfer to K is $5,000 (K's share of the liability ($10,000) multiplied by the fraction obtained by dividing—

(A) The amount of the liability that is allocable to the distribution to K ($10,000); by

(B) The total amount of such liability ($20,000)).

(iii) Therefore, K is required to take into account only $15,000 of the $20,000 partnership transfer to K for purposes of this section and § 1.707-3. Under these facts, assuming the within-two-year presumption is not rebutted, this $15,000 transfer will be treated under the rule in § 1.707-3 as part of a sale by K of property Z to the partnership.

Example (11). Borrowing against pool of receivables.

(i) M generates receivables which have an adjusted basis of zero in the ordinary course of its business. For M to use receivables as security for a loan, a commercial lender requires M to transfer the receivables to a partnership in which M has a 90 percent interest. In January, 1992, M transfers to the partnership receivables with a face value of $100,000. N (who is not related to M) transfers $10,000 cash to the partnership in exchange for a 10 percent interest. The partnership borrows $80,000, secured by the receivables, and makes a distribution of $72,000 of the proceeds to M and $8,000 of the proceeds to N within 90 days of incurring the liability. M's share of the liability under § 1.707-5(a)(2) is $72,000 (90 percent × $80,000).

(ii) Because the transfer of the loan proceeds to M is allocable under § 1.163-8T to proceeds of a partnership loan that was incurred by the partnership within 90 days of that transfer, M is required to take the transfer into account in applying the rules of this section and § 1.707-3 only to the extent that the amount of the transfer ($72,000) exceeds M's allocable share of the liability used to fund the transfer. Because the distribution was a debt-financed transfer pursuant to a plan, M's allocable share of the liability is $72,000 ($72,000 × $80,000/80,000) under § 1.707-5(b)(2)(ii). Therefore, M is not required to take into account any of the loan proceeds for purposes of this section and § 1.707-3.

(iii) When the receivables are collected, M must be allocated the gain on the contributed receivables under section 704(c). However, the lender permits the partnership to distribute cash to the partners only to the extent of the value of new receivables contributed to the partnership. In 1993, M contributes additional receivables and receives a distribution of cash. The taxable income recognized by the partnership on the receivables is taxable income of the partnership arising in the ordinary course of the partnership's activities. To the extent the distribution does not exceed 90 percent (M's percentage interest in overall partnership profits) of the partnership's operating cash flow under § 1.707-4(b), the distribution to M is presumed not to be a part of a sale of receivables by M to the partnership, and the presumption is not rebutted under these facts.

T.D. 8439. 9/25/92.

PAR. 4. In § 1.707-5, new paragraph (a)(8) is added.

The addition reads as follows:

Proposed § 1.707-5 Disguised sales of property to partnership; special rules relating to liabilities. [*For Preamble, see ¶ 152,607*]

(a) * * *

(8) Disclosure of liabilities assumed or taken subject to within seven years of transfer. Disclosure to the Internal Revenue Service in accordance with § 1.707-8 is required if—

(i) A partner transfers property to a partnership and the partnership assumes or takes subject to a liability of the partner (whether or not the liability is qualified, as described in § 1.707-5(a)(6)) within a seven-year period (without regard to the order of the transactions);

(ii) The partner treats the transactions as other than as a sale for tax purposes; and

(iii) The transactions are not disclosed under paragraph (a)(7)(ii) of this section.

* * * * *

§ 1.707-6 Disguised sales of property by partnership to partner; general rules.

(a) In general. Rules similar to those provided in § 1.707-3 apply in determining whether a transfer of property by a partnership to a partner and one or more transfers of money or other consideration by that partner to the partnership are treated as a sale of property, in whole or in part, to the partner.

(b) Special rules relating to liabilities. *(1) In general.* Rules similar to those provided in § 1.707-5 apply to determine the extent to which an assumption of or taking subject to a liability by a partner, in connection with a transfer of property by a partnership, is considered part of a sale. Accordingly, if a partner assumes or takes property subject to a qualified liability (as defined in paragraph (b)(2) of this section) of a partnership, the partner is treated as transferring consideration to the partnership only to the extent provided in this paragraph (b). If the partner assumes or takes subject to a liability that is not a qualified liability, the amount treated as consideration transferred to the partnership is the amount that the liability assumed or taken subject to by the partner exceeds the partner's share of that liability (determined under the rules of § 1.707-5(a)(2)) immediately before the transfer. Similar to the rules provided in § 1.707-5(a)(4), if more than one partner assumes or takes subject to a liability pursuant to a plan, the amount that is treated as a transfer of consideration by each partner is the amount by which all of the liabilities (other than qualified liabilities) assumed or taken subject to by the partner pursuant to the plan exceed the partner's share of all of those liabilities immediately before the assumption or taking subject to. This paragraph (b)(1) does not apply to any liability assumed or taken subject to by a partner with a principal purpose of reducing the extent to which any other liability assumed or taken subject to by a partner is treated as a transfer of consideration under paragraph (b) of this section.

(2) Qualified liabilities. (i) If a transfer of property by a partnership to a partner is not otherwise treated as part of a sale, the partner's assumption of or taking subject to a qualified liability is not treated as part of a sale. If a transfer of property by a partnership to the partner is treated as part of a sale without regard to the partner's assumption of or taking subject to a qualified liability, the partner's assumption of or taking subject to that liability is treated as a transfer of consideration made pursuant to a sale of such property to the partner only to the extent of the lesser of—

(A) The amount of consideration that the partner would be treated as transferring to the partnership under paragraph (b) of this section if the liability were not a qualified liability; or

(B) The amount obtained by multiplying the amount of the liability at the time of its assumption or taking subject to by the partnership's net equity percentage with respect to that property.

(ii) A partnership's net equity percentage with respect to an item of property encumbered by a qualified liability equals the percentage determined by dividing—

(A) The aggregate transfers to the partnership from the partner (other than any transfer described in this paragraph (b)(2)) that are treated as the proceeds realized from the sale of the transferred property to the partner; by

(B) The excess of the fair market value of the property at the time it is transferred to the partner over any qualified liabilities of the partnership that are assumed or taken subject to by the partner at that time.

(iii) For purposes of this section, the definition of a qualified liability is that provided in § 1.707-5(a)(6) with the following exceptions—

(A) In applying the definition, the qualified liability is one that is originally an obligation of the partnership and is assumed or taken subject to by the partner in connection with a transfer of property to the partner; and

(B) If the liability was incurred by the partnership more than two years prior to the earlier of the date the partnership agrees in writing to transfer the property or the date the partnership transfers the property to the partner, that liability is a qualified liability whether or not it has encumbered the transferred property throughout the two-year period.

(c) Disclosure rules. Similar to the rules provided in §§ 1.707-3(c)(2) and 1.707-5(a)(7)(ii), a partnership is to disclose to the Internal Revenue Service, in accordance with § 1.707-8, the facts in the following circumstances:

(1) When a partnership transfers property to a partner and the partner transfers money or other consideration to the partnership within a two-year period (without regard to the order of the transfers) and the partnership treats the transfers as other than a sale for tax purposes; and

(2) When a partner assumes or takes subject to a liability of a partnership in connection with a transfer of property by the partnership to the partner, and the partnership incurred the liability within the two-year period prior to the earlier of the date the partnership agrees in writing to the transfer of property or the date the partnership transfers the property, and the partnership treats the liability as a qualified liability under rules similar to § 1.707-5(a)(6)(i)(B).

(d) Examples. The following examples illustrate the rules of this section.

Example (1). Sale of property by partnership to partner.

(i) A is a member of a partnership. The partnership transfers property X to A. At the time of the transfer, property X has a fair market value of $1,000,000. One year after the transfer, A transfers $1,100,000 to the partnership. Assume that under the rules of section 1274 the imputed principal amount of an obligation to transfer $1,100,000 one year after the transfer of property X is $1,000,000 on the date of the transfer.

(ii) Since the transfer of $1,100,000 to the partnership by A is made within two years of the transfer of property X to A, under rules similar to those provided in § 1.707-3(c), the transfers are presumed to be a sale unless the facts and circumstances clearly establish otherwise. If no facts exist that would rebut this presumption, on the date that the partnership transfers property X to A, the partnership is treated as having sold property X to A in exchange for A's obligation to transfer $1,100,000 to the partnership one year later.

Example (2). Assumption of liability by partner.

(i) B is a member of an existing partnership. The partnership transfers property Y to B. On the date of the transfer, property Y has a fair market value of $1,000,000 and is encumbered by a nonrecourse liability of $600,000. B takes the property subject to the liability. The partnership incurred the nonrecourse liability six months prior to the transfer of property Y to B and used the proceeds to purchase an unrelated asset. Assume that, under the rule of § 1.707-5(a)(2)(ii) (which determines a partner's share of a nonrecourse liability), B's share of the nonrecourse liability immediately before the transfer of property Y was $100,000.

(ii) The liability is not allocable under the rules of § 1.163-8T to capital expenditures with respect to the property transferred to B and was not incurred in the ordinary course of the trade or business in which the property transferred to the partner was used or held. Since the partnership incurred the nonrecourse liability within two years of the transfer to B, under rules similar to those provided in § 1.707-5(a)(5), the liability is presumed to be incurred in anticipation of the transfer unless the facts and circumstances clearly establish the contrary. Assuming no facts exist to rebut this presumption, the liability taken subject to by B is not a qualified liability. The partnership is treated as having received, on the date of the transfer of property Y to B, $500,000 ($600,000 liability assumed by B less B's share of the $100,000 liability immediately prior to the transfer) as consideration for the sale of one-half ($500,000/$1,000,000) of property Y to B. The partnership is also treated as having distributed to B, in B's capacity as a partner, the other one-half of property Y.

T.D. 8439, 9/25/92.

PAR. 5. In § 1.707-6 is amended as follows:

1. Revising paragraph (c) introductory text.

2. Amending paragraph (c)(1) by removing the language "two" and adding "seven" in its place.

3. Adding new paragraph (c)(3).

The revisions and addition read as follows:

Proposed § 1.707-6 Disguised sales of property by partnership to partners; general rule. [*For Preamble, see ¶ 152,607*]

* * * * *

(c) * * * Similar to the rules provided in §§ 1.707-3(c)(2), 1.707-5(a)(7)(ii), and 1.707-5(a)(8), a partnership is to disclose to the Internal Revenue Service, in accordance with § 1.707-8, the facts in the following circumstances:

* * * * *

(3) When a partnership transfers property to a partner and the partner assumes or takes subject to a liability of the partnership (whether or not the liability is qualified, as described in § 1.707-5(a)(6)) within a seven-year period (without regard to the order of the transactions), the partnership treats the transactions as other than as a sale for tax purposes, and the transactions are not disclosed under paragraph (c)(2) of this section.

* * * * *

§ 1.707-7 Disguised sales of partnership interests. [Reserved]

PAR. 6.

Section 1.707-7 is revised to read as follows:

Proposed § 1.707-7 Disguised sales of partnership interests. [*For Preamble, see ¶ 152,607*]

(a) Treatment of transfers as a sale. *(1) In general.* Except as otherwise provided in this section, if a transfer of money, property or other consideration (including the assumption of a liability) (consideration) by a partner (purchasing partner) to a partnership and a transfer of consideration by the partnership to another partner (selling partner) are described in paragraph (b)(1) of this section, the transfers are treated as a sale, in whole or in part, of the selling partner's interest in the partnership to the purchasing partner. For purposes of this section, the term transfer refers to a portion of a single transfer or to one or more transfers.

(2) Definition, timing and consequences of sale. (i) Definition of sale. For purposes of this section, the use of the term sale (or any variation of that word) to refer to a transfer of consideration by a purchasing partner to a partnership and a transfer of consideration by the partnership to a selling partner means a sale or exchange, in whole or in part, of the selling partner's interest in the partnership to the purchasing partner, rather than a contribution and distribution to which sections 721 and 731, respectively, apply. Transfers that are

treated as a sale under paragraph (a)(1) of this section are treated as a sale for all purposes of the Internal Revenue Code (e.g., sections 453, 483, 704, 708, 743, 751, 1001, 1012 and 1274).

(ii) Timing and consequences of sale. (A) In general. For purposes of this section, a transfer is treated as occurring on the date of the actual transfer, or if earlier, on the date that the transferor agrees in writing to make the transfer. The sale of the selling partner's partnership interest is considered to take place on the date of the earliest of the transfers described in paragraph (a)(1) of this section. On this date, the purchasing partner is treated as acquiring the partnership interest sold for all purposes of the Internal Revenue Code.

(B) Simultaneous transfers. If the transfer of consideration by the purchasing partner and the transfer of consideration to the selling partner are simultaneous and the consideration transferred is the same, the partners and the partnership are treated as if, on the date of the sale, the purchasing partner transferred that partner's consideration (purchasing partner's consideration) directly to the selling partner in exchange for all or a portion of the selling partner's interest in the partnership. If the transfer of consideration by the purchasing partner to the partnership and the transfer of consideration by the partnership to the selling partner are simultaneous and the consideration transferred is not the same, the partners and the partnership are treated as if, on the date of the sale, the purchasing partner transferred that partner's consideration to the partnership in exchange for the consideration to be transferred to the selling partner (selling partner's consideration) and then the purchasing partner transferred the selling partner's consideration to the selling partner in exchange for all or a portion of the selling partner's interest in the partnership.

(C) Transfer to selling partner first. If the transfer of consideration by the partnership to the selling partner occurs before the transfer of consideration by the purchasing partner to the partnership, the partners and the partnership are treated as if, on the date of the sale, the purchasing partner transferred an obligation to deliver the purchasing partner's consideration to the partnership in exchange for the selling partner's consideration and then the purchasing partner transferred the selling partner's consideration to the selling partner in exchange for all or a portion of the selling partner's interest in the partnership. On the date of the actual transfer of the purchasing partner's consideration, the purchasing partner and the partnership are treated as if the purchasing partner satisfied its obligation to deliver the purchasing partner's consideration to the partnership.

(D) Transfer by purchasing partner first. If the transfer of consideration by the partnership to the selling partner occurs after the transfer of consideration by the purchasing partner to the partnership, the partners and the partnership are treated as if, on the date of the sale, the purchasing partner transferred the purchasing partner's consideration to the partnership in exchange for an obligation of the partnership to deliver the selling partner's consideration and then the purchasing partner transferred that obligation to the selling partner in exchange for all or a portion of the selling partner's interest in the partnership. On the date of the actual transfer of the selling partner's consideration, the selling partner and the partnership are treated as if the partnership satisfied its obligation to deliver the selling partner's consideration to the selling partner.

(E) Consequences of deemed transactions. Transfers and exchanges that are deemed to occur under paragraphs (a)(2)(ii)(B), (a)(2)(ii)(C), and (a)(2)(ii)(D) of this section are treated as actual transfers or exchanges for all purposes of the Internal Revenue Code (e.g., sections 453, 483, 704, 708, 743, 751, 1001, 1012 and 1274).

(3) Amount of sale. (i) In general. If a transfer of consideration by a purchasing partner to a partnership and a transfer of consideration by the partnership to a selling partner are treated as a sale under paragraph (b)(1) of this section, the selling partner is treated as selling to the purchasing partner a partnership interest with a value equal to the lesser of the selling partner's consideration or the purchasing partner's consideration.

(ii) Aggregation of consideration. For purposes of paragraph (a)(3)(i) of this section, simultaneous transfers of consideration by more than one purchasing partner to a partnership or by a partnership to more than one selling partner are aggregated. In those cases—

(A) Each purchasing partner is presumed to have purchased that fraction of each partnership interest(s) sold equal to—

(1) The amount of consideration transferred by that partner to the partnership, divided; by

(2) The aggregate consideration transferred by all purchasing partners to the partnership; and

(B) Each selling partner is presumed to have sold that fraction of the total partnership interest(s) sold equal to—

(1) The amount of consideration transferred by the partnership to that partner, divided; by

(2) The aggregate consideration transferred by the partnership to all selling partners.

(4) Liability relief included in amount realized on sale. The amount realized by a selling partner on the sale of the selling partner's interest in the partnership includes any reduction in the selling partner's share of partnership liabilities that is treated as occurring as a result of the sale. If a sale of a partnership interest and either a distribution by the partnership to the selling partner under section 731 or a contribution by the purchasing partner to the partnership under section 721 occur on the same date, the reduction in the selling partner's share of partnership liabilities is computed immediately after the sale and before the distribution or the contribution, as the case may be. To the extent a reduction in a selling partner's share of partnership liabilities is included in the amount realized by the selling partner on the sale of an interest in a partnership because the amount is treated as consideration received by the selling partner in exchange for the selling partner's interest under paragraph (j)(2) of this section, the amount of the reduction shall not also be included in the amount realized by operation of this paragraph.

(5) Sale precedes excess distribution to selling partner. If a portion of a transfer of consideration by a partnership to a selling partner is not treated as part of a sale of the selling partner's interest in the partnership, but as a distribution to the selling partner under section 731, and the sale is treated as occurring on the same date as the distribution, then the distribution is treated as occurring immediately following the sale.

(6) Transfers first treated as a sale of property. To the extent that a transfer of consideration by a purchasing partner to a partnership or a transfer of consideration by a partnership to a selling partner may be treated as part of a sale of property under § 1.707-3(a), § 1.707-3(a) applies before this section, and to the extent the transfer is treated as part of a sale of property under § 1.707-3(a), such transfer is not taken into account in applying the rules of this section.

(7) Application of disguised sale rules. Except as otherwise provided in paragraph (a)(8) of this section, the rules of this section apply to transfers to and from a partnership even if, after the application of the rules of this section, it is determined that the partnership has terminated under section 708(b)(1)(A).

(8) Certain transfers disregarded. Section 707(a)(2)(B) and the rules of this section do not apply to deemed transfers resulting from a termination of a partnership under section 708(b)(1)(B) and transfers incident to the formation of a partnership. However, transfers incident to the formation of a partnership may be transfers to which § 1.707-3(a) applies.

(b) Transfers treated as sale. *(1) In general.* A transfer of consideration by a purchasing partner to a partnership and a transfer of consideration by the partnership to a selling partner constitute a sale, in whole or in part, of the selling partner's interest in the partnership to the purchasing partner only if, based on all the facts and circumstances—

(i) The transfer of consideration by the partnership to the selling partner would not have been made but for the transfer of consideration to the partnership by the purchasing partner; and

(ii) In cases in which the transfers are not made simultaneously, the subsequent transfer is not dependent on the entrepreneurial risks of partnership operations.

(2) Facts and circumstances. The determination of whether a transfer of consideration by a purchasing partner to a partnership and a transfer of consideration by the partnership to a selling partner constitute a sale under paragraph (b)(1) of this section is made based on all the facts and circumstances in each case. The weight to be given each of the facts and circumstances will depend on the particular case. Generally, the facts and circumstances existing on the date of the earliest of the transfers are the ones considered in determining if a sale exists under paragraph (b)(1) of this section. Among the facts and circumstances that may tend to prove the existence of a sale under paragraph (b)(1) of this section are the following:

(i) That the timing and amount of all or any portion of a subsequent transfer are determinable with reasonable certainty at the time of an earlier transfer;

(ii) That the person receiving the subsequent transfer has a legally enforceable right to the transfer or that the right to receive the transfer is secured in any manner, taking into account the period for which it is secured;

(iii) That the same property (other than money, including marketable securities that are treated as money under section 731(c)(1)) that is transferred to the partnership by the purchasing partner is transferred to the selling partner;

(iv) That partnership distributions, allocations or control of operations are designed to effect an exchange of the benefits and burdens of ownership of transferred property (other than money, including marketable securities that are treated as money under section 731(c)(1)), including a partnership interest;

(v) That the partnership holds transferred property (other than money, including marketable securities that are treated as money under section 731(c)(1)) for a limited period of time, or during the period of time the partnership holds transferred property (other than money, including marketable securities that are treated as money under section 731(c)(1)), the risk of gain or loss associated with the property is not significant;

(vi) That the transfer of consideration by the partnership to the selling partner is disproportionately large in relationship to the selling partner's general and continuing interest in partnership profits;

(vii) That the selling partner has no obligation to return or repay the consideration to the partnership, or has an obligation to return or repay the consideration due at such a distant point in the future that the present value of that obligation is small in relation to the amount of consideration transferred by the partnership to the selling partner;

(viii) That the transfer of consideration by the purchasing partner or the transfer of consideration to the selling partner is not made pro rata;

(ix) That there were negotiations between the purchasing partner and the selling partner (or between the partnership and each of the purchasing and selling partners with each partner being aware of the negotiations with the other partner) concerning any transfer of consideration; and

(x) That the selling partner and purchasing partner enter into one or more agreements, including an amendment to the partnership agreement (other than for admitting the purchasing partner) relating to the transfers.

(c) Transfers made within two years presumed to be a sale. For purposes of this section, if within a two-year period a purchasing partner transfers consideration to a partnership and the partnership transfers consideration to a selling partner (without regard to the order of the transfers), the transfers are presumed to be a sale, in whole or in part, of the selling partner's interest in the partnership to the purchasing partner unless the facts and circumstances clearly establish that the transfers do not constitute a sale.

(d) Transfers made more than two years apart presumed not to be a sale. For purposes of this section, if a transfer of consideration by a purchasing partner to a partnership and the transfer of consideration by the partnership to a selling partner (without regard to the order of the transfers) occur more than two years apart, the transfers are presumed not to be a sale, in whole or in part, of the selling partner's interest in the partnership to the purchasing partner unless the facts and circumstances clearly establish that the transfers constitute a sale.

(e) Transfers of money in liquidation of a partner's interest presumed not to be a sale. Notwithstanding the presumption set forth in paragraph (c) of this section, for purposes of this section, if a partnership transfers money, including marketable securities that are treated as money under section 731(c)(1), to a selling partner, or is treated as transferring consideration to the selling partner under paragraph (j)(2) of this section, in liquidation of the selling partner's interest in the partnership, the transfer is presumed not to be a sale, in whole or in part, of the selling partner's interest in the partnership to the purchasing partner unless the facts and circumstances clearly establish that the transfer is part of a sale. See § 1.761-1(d) for the definition of the term liquidation of a partner's interest.

(f) Application of § 1.707-4 (special rules applicable to guaranteed payments, preferred returns, operating cash flow distributions, and reimbursements of preformation expenditures). Notwithstanding the presumption set forth in paragraph (c) of this section, rules similar to those provided in § 1.707-4 apply to determine the extent to which a transfer to a selling partner is treated as part of a sale of the selling partner's interest in the partnership to the purchasing partner.

(g) Exception for certain transfers to and by service partnerships. Section 707(a)(2)(B) and the rules of this section do not apply to transfers of money, including marketable securities that are treated as money under section 731(c)(1), to and by a partnership that would be described in section 448(d)(2) if the partnership were a corporation. Solely for purposes of applying section 448(d)(2) to partnerships under this paragraph (g), partners are treated as employees of the partnership and "partnership interest" is substituted for "stock" in testing for ownership by the employees performing services.

(h) Other exceptions. The Commissioner may provide by guidance published in the Internal Revenue Bulletin that section 707(a)(2)(B) and the rules of this section do not apply to other transfers to and by a partnership.

(i) [Reserved.]

(j) Special rules relating to liabilities. *(1) In general.* For purposes of this section, deemed contributions to and distributions from a partnership under section 752 resulting from reallocations of partnership liabilities among partners are not treated as transfers of consideration. Under paragraph (a)(4) of this section, the preceding sentence does not apply if the transaction is otherwise treated as a sale of a partnership interest under the rules of this section.

(2) Partner liability assumed by partnership. For purposes of this section, if a partnership assumes a liability of a partner, the partnership is treated as transferring consideration to the partner to the extent that the amount of the liability exceeds the partner's share of that liability (determined under the rules of paragraphs (j)(4) and (5) of this section) immediately after the partnership assumes the liability. For purposes of this section, a partnership is treated as assuming a liability of a partner to the extent provided in §§ 1.752-1(d) and (e). For purposes of this paragraph (j)(2), if the partnership assumes the liabilities of more than one partner pursuant to a plan, a partner's share of the liabilities assumed by the partnership pursuant to that plan immediately after the assumptions equals the sum of that partner's shares of the liabilities assumed by the partnership pursuant to the plan. The preceding sentence does not apply to any liability assumed by the partnership with a principal purpose of reducing the extent to which any other liability assumed by the partnership is treated as a transfer of consideration to a partner under this paragraph (j)(2).

(3) Partnership liability assumed by partner. For purposes of this section, if a partner assumes a liability of a partnership, the partner is treated as transferring consideration to the partnership to the extent that the amount of the liability exceeds the partner's share of that liability (determined under the rules of paragraph (j)(4) of this section) immediately before the partner assumes the liability. For purposes of this section, a partner assumes a partnership liability to the extent provided in §§ 1.752-1(e) and 1.704-1(b)(2)(iv)(c). For purposes of this paragraph (j)(3), if more than one partner assumes a liability of the partnership pursuant to a plan, the amount that is treated as a transfer of consideration by each partner is the amount by which all of the liabilities assumed by the partner pursuant to the plan exceed the partner's share of all of those liabilities immediately before the assumption. The preceding sentence does not apply to any liability assumed by a partner with a principal purpose of reducing the extent to which any other liability assumed by a partner is treated as a transfer of consideration to a partnership under this paragraph (j)(3).

(4) Partner's share of liability. A partner's share of any liability of the partnership is determined under the following rules:

(i) Recourse liability. A partner's share of a recourse liability of the partnership equals the partner's share of the liability under the rules of section 752 and the regulations thereunder. A partnership liability is a recourse liability to the extent that the obligation is a recourse liability under § 1.752-1(a)(1) or would be treated as a recourse liability under that section if it were treated as a partnership liability for purposes of that section.

(ii) Nonrecourse liability. A partner's share of a nonrecourse liability of the partnership is determined by applying the same percentage used to determine the partner's share of the excess nonrecourse liability under § 1.752-3(a)(3). A partnership liability is a nonrecourse liability of the partnership to the extent that the obligation is a nonrecourse liability under § 1.752-1(a)(2) or would be treated as a nonrecourse liability under that section if it were treated as a partnership liability for purposes of that section.

(5) Reduction of partner's share of liability. For purposes of this section, a partner's share of a liability, immediately after a partnership assumes the liability, is determined by taking into account a subsequent reduction in the partner's share if—

(i) At the time that the partnership assumes a liability, it is anticipated that the transferring partner's share of the liability will be subsequently reduced; and

(ii) The reduction of the partner's share of the liability is part of a plan that has as one of its principal purposes minimizing the extent to which the assumption of the liability is treated as part of a sale under this section.

(6) Treatment of debt-financed transfers of consideration by partnerships.

(i) In general. For purposes of this section, if a partnership incurs a liability and all or a portion of the proceeds of that liability are allocable under § 1.163-8T to a transfer of consideration to a partner made within 90 days of incurring the liability, the transfer of consideration to the partner is taken into account only to the extent that the amount of consideration transferred exceeds that partner's allocable share of the partnership liability.

(ii) Partner's allocable share of liability. (A) In general. A partner's allocable share of a partnership liability for purposes of paragraph (j)(6)(i) of this section equals the amount obtained by multiplying the partner's share of the liability (as defined in paragraph (j)(4) of this section) by a fraction determined by dividing—

(1) The portion of the liability that is allocable under § 1.163-8T to the consideration transferred to the partner; by

(2) The total amount of the liability.

(B) Debt-financed transfers made pursuant to a plan. (1) In general. Except as provided in paragraph (j)(6)(ii)(C) of this section, if a partnership transfers to more than one partner pursuant to a plan all or a portion of the proceeds of one or more partnership liabilities, paragraph (j)(6)(i) of this section is applied by treating all of the liabilities incurred pursuant to the plan as one liability, and each partner's allocable share of those liabilities equals the amount obtained by multiplying the sum of the partner's shares of each of the respective liabilities (as defined in paragraph (j)(4) of this section) by the fraction obtained by dividing—

(i) The portion of those liabilities that is allocable under § 1.163-8T to the consideration transferred to the partners pursuant to the plan; by

(ii) The total amount of those liabilities.

(2) Special rule. Paragraph (j)(6)(ii)(B)(1) of this section does not apply to any transfer of consideration to a partner that is made with a principal purpose of reducing the extent to which any transfer is taken into account under paragraph (j)(6)(i) of this section.

(C) Reduction of partner's share of liability. For purposes of paragraph (j)(6)(ii) of this section, a partner's share of a liability is determined by taking into account a subsequent reduction in the partner's share if—

(1) It is anticipated that the partner's share of the liability that is allocable to a transfer of consideration to the partner will be reduced subsequent to the transfer; and

(2) The reduction of the partner's share of the liability is part of a plan that has as one of its principal purposes minimizing the extent to which the partnership's distribution of the proceeds of the borrowing is treated as part of a sale.

(7) Share of liability where assumption accompanied by transfer of money. For purposes of paragraph (j)(2) of this section, if pursuant to a plan a partner pays or contributes money to the partnership and the partnership assumes one or more liabilities of the partner, the amount of those liabilities that the partnership is treated as assuming is reduced (but not below zero) by the money transferred. Similarly, for purposes of paragraph (j)(3) of this section, if pursuant to a plan a partnership pays or distributes money to a partner and the partner assumes one or more liabilities of the partnership, the amount of those liabilities that the partner is treated as assuming is reduced (but not below zero) by the money transferred.

(8) Anti-abuse rule. For purposes of this section, an increase in a partner's share of a partnership liability may be treated as a transfer of consideration by the partner to the partnership, notwithstanding any other rule in this section, if—

(i) Within a short period of time after the partnership incurs or assumes the liability or another liability, one or more partners of the partnership, or related parties to a partner (within the meaning of section 267(b) or 707(b)), in substance bears an economic risk for the liability that is disproportionate to the partner's interest in partnership profits or capital; and

(ii) The transactions are undertaken pursuant to a plan that has as one of its principal purposes minimizing the extent to which the partner is treated as making a transfer of consideration to the partnership that may be treated as part of a sale under this section.

(k) Disclosure rules. Disclosure to the Internal Revenue Service in accordance with § 1.707-8 is required when a partner transfers consideration to a partnership and the partnership transfers consideration to another partner within a seven-year period (without regard to the order of the transfers), the partners treat the transfers other than as a sale for tax purposes, and the transfer of consideration by the partnership is not presumed to be a guaranteed payment for capital under § 1.707-4(a)(1)(ii), is not a reasonable preferred return within the meaning of § 1.707-4(a)(3), and is not an operating cash flow distribution within the meaning of § 1.707-4(b)(2). However, disclosure is not required under this paragraph if an exception provided in either paragraph (a)(8) (relating to transfers resulting from a termination of a partnership under section 708(b)(1)(B) and transfers incident to the formation of a partnership) or paragraph (g) (relating to transfers to and by service partnerships) applies to either of the transfers.

(l) Examples. The following examples illustrate the application of this section. For purposes of these examples, assume that the transfers would otherwise be respected as contributions and distributions and that, except as otherwise provided, sections 721(b), 751(b), 704(c)(1)(B), 737, and § 1.707-3 do not apply. All amounts and percentages in these examples are rounded to the nearest whole number.

Example (1). Treatment of simultaneous transfers as a sale by a selling partner to a purchasing partner. (i) A and B each owns a 50% interest in partnership AB. AB holds Blackacre, real property with a fair market value of $400x. AB has no liabilities. On May 25, 2008, C transfers $100x in cash to AB in exchange for an interest in AB. Simultaneously, AB transfers $100x in cash to A.

(ii) Because C's transfer of $100x to AB and AB's transfer of $100x to A occurred within two years, the transfers are presumed to be a sale of a portion of A's interest in AB to C under paragraph (c) of this section, unless the facts and circumstances clearly establish otherwise. There are no facts that rebut the presumption of sale treatment or that support the application of either of the presumptions against sale treatment provided in paragraphs (e) or (f) or the exception provided in paragraph (g) of this section. Thus, the transfers are treated as a sale of a portion of A's interest in AB to C. Under paragraph (a)(3)(i) of this section, the value of the partnership interest that A is treated as selling to C equals the lesser of the consideration transferred by AB to A or the consideration transferred by C to AB. C transferred $100x to AB, and A received $100x from AB. Thus, A is treated as having sold an interest in AB with a value of $100x to C.

Example (2). Treatment of non-simultaneous transfers as a sale by a selling partner to a purchasing partner. (i) The facts are the same as in Example 1, except that AB transfers $100x in cash to A on March 25, 2008, and C transfers $50x in cash to AB on May 25, 2008, in exchange for an interest in AB.

(ii) Because AB's transfer of $100x to A and C's transfer of $50x to AB occurred within two years, the transfers are presumed to be a sale of a portion of A's interest in AB to C under paragraph (c) of this section, unless the facts and circumstances clearly establish otherwise. There are no facts that rebut the presumption of sale treatment or that support the application of either of the presumptions against sale treatment provided in paragraphs (e) or (f) or the exception provided in paragraph (g) of this section. Thus, the transfers are treated as a sale of a portion of A's interest in AB to C. Under paragraph (a)(2)(ii)(A) of this section, the sale takes place on the date of the earliest of the transfers, March 25, 2008, upon AB's transfer of $100x to A. Under paragraph (a)(3)(i) of this section, the value of the partnership interest that A is treated as selling to C equals the lesser of the consideration transferred by AB to A or the consideration transferred by C to AB. C transferred $50x to AB, and A received $100x from AB. Thus, A is treated as having sold an interest in AB with a value of $50x to C. Under paragraph (a)(2)(ii)(C), because the transfer to A precedes the transfer by C, each of A, C, and AB is treated as if, on March 25, 2008, C transferred an obligation to deliver $50x to AB in exchange for $50x, and then C transferred $50x to A in exchange for a portion of A's interest in AB with a value of $50x. On May 25, 2008, when C actually transfers $50x to AB, C is treated as satisfying the obligation to deliver $50x to AB. A also is treated as receiving, in its capacity as a partner, a distribution from AB to which section 731 applies of $50x ($100x transfer–$50x amount of sale). Under paragraph (a)(5) of this section, the distribution is treated as occurring immediately following the sale.

Example (3). Treatment of deemed transfers and exchanges. (i) A and B each owns a 50% interest in partnership AB. AB holds Whiteacre, real property with a fair market value of $1,000x and a tax basis of $700x, along with other assets. AB has no liabilities. On January 1, 2008, C transfers Investment Property, with a fair market value of $1,500x and a tax basis of $300x, to AB. Simultaneously with that transfer, AB transfers Whiteacre to B.

(ii) Because C's transfer of Investment Property to AB and AB's transfer of Whiteacre to B occurred within two years, the transfers are presumed to be a sale of a portion of B's interest in AB to C under paragraph (c) of this section, unless the facts and circumstances clearly establish otherwise. There are no facts that rebut the presumption of sale treatment or that support the application of either of the presumptions against sale treatment provided in paragraphs (e) or (f) or the exception provided in paragraph (g) of this section. Thus, the transfers are treated as a sale of a portion of B's interest in AB to C. Under paragraph (a)(2)(ii)(A) of this section, the sale takes place on the date of the earliest of the transfers, January 1, 2008. Under paragraph (a)(3)(i) of this section, the value of the partnership interest that B is treated as selling to C equals the lesser of the consideration transferred by C to AB or the consideration transferred by AB to B. C transferred the Investment Property with a fair market value of $1,500x to AB, and B received Whiteacre with a fair market value of $1,000x from AB. Thus, B is treated as having sold an interest in AB with a value of $1,000x to C.

(iii) Under paragraph (a)(2)(ii)(B), because the transfers are simultaneous and the consideration transferred is not the same, each of B, C, and AB is treated as if, on January 1, 2008, C transferred $1,000x of the Investment Property to AB in exchange for Whiteacre and then C transferred Whiteacre to B in exchange for a portion of B's interest in AB with a value of $1,000x. In the deemed exchange of $1,000x worth of the Investment Property for Whiteacre, AB realizes and recognizes gain of $300x ($1,000x–$700x basis), and C realizes and recognizes gain of $800x ($1,000x–$200x allocable basis). In the deemed exchange of Whiteacre for B's interest in AB, B realizes and recognizes gain or loss under section 741 (and section 751(a), if applicable) based on an amount realized of $1,000x. C also is considered to have contributed to AB, in C's capacity as a partner, $500x of the Investment Property ($1,500x total value of transferred Investment Property–$1,000x amount treated as C's consideration) with an allocable basis of $100x in a transaction to which section 721 applies. Thus, the basis of the Investment Property in the hands of AB is $1,100x, C's basis in the partnership interest is $1,100x, and the basis of Whiteacre in the hands of B is $1,000x.

Example (4). Treatment of simultaneous transfers as a sale by a selling partner to more than one purchasing partner. (i) E and F each owns a 50% interest in partnership EF. EF holds a building with a fair market value of $500x. EF has no liabilities. On May 25, 2008, G and H each transfer $50x in cash to EF in exchange for an interest in EF. Simultaneously, EF distributes $100x in cash to E.

(ii) Because each of G's and H's transfers of $50x to EF and EF's transfer of $100x to E occurred within two years, G's transfer to EF and EF's transfer to E, and H's transfer to EF and EF's transfer to E, are presumed to be a sale of a portion of E's interest in EF to G and H, respectively, under paragraph (c) of this section, unless the facts and circumstances clearly establish otherwise. There are no facts that rebut the presumption of sale treatment or that support the application of either of the presumptions against sale treatment provided in paragraphs (e) or (f) or the exception provided in paragraph (g) of this section. Thus, the transfers are treated as a sale of a portion of E's partnership interest to G and H, respectively. Under paragraph (a)(3)(i) of this section, the value of the partnership interest that E is treated as selling to each of G and H equals the lesser of the consideration transferred by EF to E or the consideration transferred by G and H to EF. Because G and H made simultaneous transfers of consideration to EF, the transfers are aggregated under paragraph (a)(3)(ii) of this section. G and H together transferred $100x to EF, and E received $100x from EF. Thus, E is treated as having sold a partnership interest with a value of $100x to G and H. Under paragraph (a)(3)(ii) of this section, when transfers of multiple purchasing partners are aggregated, each purchasing partner is presumed to have purchased a pro rata portion of the selling partner's partnership interest. That is, G is presumed to have purchased the fraction of E's partnership interest sold that is equal to G's amount transferred ($50x) divided by the aggregate amount transferred by G and H ($100x), or one-half of the partnership interest that was sold. H also is presumed to have purchased the fraction of E's partnership interest equal to H's amount transferred ($50x) divided by the aggregate amount transferred by both G and H ($100x), or one-half of the partnership interest that was sold. Thus, each of G and H is treated as having purchased a fraction of E's partnership interest that is equal to $50x.

Example (5). Treatment of non-simultaneous transfers as a sale by a selling partner to more than one purchasing partner. (i) The facts are the same as in Example 4, except that partnership EF distributes $75x in cash to E on May 1, 2007. In addition, G transfers $50x in cash to EF on March 25, 2008, and H transfers $50x in cash to EF on May 25, 2008, each in exchange for a partnership interest in EF.

(ii) Because each of G's and H's transfers of $50x to EF and EF's transfer of $75x to E occurred within two years, G's transfer to EF and EF's transfer to E, and H's transfer to EF and EF's transfer to E, are presumed to be a sale of a portion of E's partnership interest to G and H, respectively, under paragraph (c) of this section, unless the facts and circumstances clearly establish otherwise. There are no facts that rebut the presumption of sale treatment or that support the application of either of the presumptions against sale treatment provided in paragraphs (e) or (f) or the exception provided in paragraph (g) of this section. Thus, the transfers are treated as a sale of a portion of E's interest in EF to each of G and H, respectively. Under paragraph (a)(2)(ii)(A) of this section, the sale takes place on the date of the earliest of the transfers, May 1, 2007, the date that EF transferred $75x to E. Under paragraph (a)(3)(i) of this section, the value of the partnership interest that E is treated as selling to each of G and H equals the lesser of the consideration transferred by G and H to EF, or the consideration transferred by EF to E. Because the transfers made by G and H were not simultaneous, the transfers are not aggregated. Rather, in accordance with paragraph (a)(2)(ii)(A) of this section, the transfers are considered in the order in which they were made. The value of the partnership interest that E is treated as selling to G equals $50x, the lesser of G's $50x transfer to EF and the $75x that E received from EF. The value of the partnership interest that E is treated as selling to H equals $25x, the lesser of the remaining amount of the transfer to E, $25x ($75x-$50x = $25x), and H's $50x transfer to

EF. H also is considered to have contributed to EF, in H's capacity as a partner, $25x ($50x transfer-$25x amount of sale), to which section 721 applies.

(iii) Under paragraph (a)(2)(ii)(C), each of E, G, and EF are treated as if, on May 1, 2007, G transferred an obligation to deliver $50x to EF in exchange for $50x, and, on that same date, G transferred $50x to E in exchange for a portion of E's interest in EF with a value of $50x. On March 25, 2008, when G actually transfers $50x to EF, G is treated as satisfying its obligation to deliver $50x to EF. Also, under paragraph (a)(2)(ii)(C), each of E, H, and EF are treated as if, on May 1, 2007, H transferred an obligation to deliver $25x to EF in exchange for $25x, and, on that same date, H transferred $25x to E in exchange for a portion of E's interest in EF with a value of $25x. On May 25, 2008, when H actually transfers $25x to EF, H is treated as satisfying its obligation to deliver $25x to EF.

Example (6). Operation of presumption for liquidation of a partner for money. (i) A and B each owns a 50% interest in partnership AB. AB holds marketable securities with a fair market value of $200x. AB has no liabilities. On April 1, 2008, C transfers $100x in cash to AB in exchange for an interest in AB. Simultaneously, AB distributes $100x of the marketable securities to A in liquidation of A's partnership interest in AB. Assume that the marketable securities transferred to A are treated, under section 731(c)(1), as money for purposes of section 731(a)(1).

(ii) Because C's transfer of $100x to AB and AB's transfer of $100x of marketable securities to A occurred within two years, the transfers are presumed to be a sale of a portion of A's interest in AB to C under paragraph (c) of this section. However, under paragraph (e) of this section, notwithstanding the presumption set forth in paragraph (c) of this section, AB's transfer of marketable securities to A in liquidation of A's interest in AB is presumed not to be a sale of A's partnership interest to C, unless the facts and circumstances clearly establish otherwise. If, however, one of the exceptions under section 731(c)(3) applies to the $100x of marketable securities distributed to A, the securities would not be treated as money for purposes of section 731(a)(1), and the presumption against sale treatment under paragraph (e) of this section would not apply.

Example (7). Transfers that would otherwise be treated as both a sale of property and a sale of a partnership interest. (i) C and D each owns a 50% interest in partnership CD. CD holds Greenacre, real property with a fair market value of $2,000x. CD has no liabilities. On June 1, 2008, E transfers $500x in cash to CD in exchange for a partnership interest in CD. Immediately after E's transfer, C transfers Redacre to CD, and CD distributes $500x in cash to C. At the time of the transfers, Redacre has a fair market value of $250x.

(ii) Because E's transfer of $500x to CD and CD's transfer of $500x to C occurred within two years, the transfers are presumed to be a sale of a portion of C's partnership interest in CD to E under paragraph (c) of this section, unless the facts and circumstances clearly establish otherwise. There are no facts that rebut the presumption of sale treatment or that support the application of either of the presumptions against sale treatment provided in paragraphs (e) or (f) or the exception provided in paragraph (g) of this section. Thus, the transfers are treated as a sale of a portion of C's partnership interest in CD to E. However, because C's transfer of Redacre to CD and CD's transfer of $500x to C occurred within two years, under § 1.707-3(c), the transfers are presumed to be a sale of Redacre by C to CD. There are no facts that rebut the presumption that the transfers are a sale of Redacre by C to CD. Under paragraph (a)(6) of this section, transfers that are in part a sale of a partnership interest and in part a sale of property are treated, first, as part of a sale of property.

Thus, C's transfer of Redacre to CD and $250x of CD's $500x transfer to C are treated, first, as a sale of Redacre by C to CD for $250x. Although the $250x distributed to C that is treated as part of a sale of Redacre is not treated as part of a sale of C's partnership interest in CD to E, the remaining $250x that is distributed to C is treated as part of a sale of C's partnership interest in CD to E. The value of the partnership interest that C is treated as selling to E equals $250x, the lesser of E's $500x transfer to CD, and the remaining $250x that C received from CD. E also is considered to have contributed to CD, in E's capacity as a partner, $250x ($500x contribution - $250x amount of sale), to which section 721 applies.

Example (8). Treatment of simultaneous transfers as a sale where partnership has nonrecourse liabilities. (i) A and B each owns a 50% interest in partnership AB. The partnership agreement states that the partners agree to share profits in proportion to the partners' booked-up capital accounts. AB holds $100x cash and Orangeacre, a parcel of raw land with a fair market value of $860x. Orangeacre is encumbered by a $360x nonrecourse liability incurred by AB in 1998 in connection with the purchase of Orangeacre. The liability, which has an issue price of $360x, has a term of 10 years and all principal is payable at maturity. The liability provides for adequate stated interest, all of which is qualified stated interest. On January 1, 2007, C contributes $100x to AB in exchange for an interest in AB. On the same date, A receives a transfer of $200x from AB.

(ii) For purposes of determining whether the transfers constitute a disguised sale of A's or B's interest in AB, the $360x liability is ignored because no partner assumes the liability. Because C's transfer of $100x to AB and AB's transfer of $200x to A occurred within two years, the transfers are presumed to be a sale of a portion of A's partnership interest in AB to C, under paragraph (c) of this section, unless the facts and circumstances clearly establish otherwise. There are no facts that rebut the presumption of sale treatment or that support the application of either of the presumptions against sale treatment provided in paragraphs (e) or (f) or the exception provided in paragraph (g) of this section. Thus, the transfers are treated as a sale of a portion of A's partnership interest in AB to C. Under paragraph (a)(3)(i) of this section, the value of the partnership interest that A is treated as selling to C equals the lesser of the consideration transferred by AB to A, or the consideration transferred by C to AB. C transferred $100x to AB, and A received $200x from AB. Thus, A is treated as having sold an interest in AB with a value of $100x to C. Under paragraph (a)(4) of this section, the amount realized by A on the sale of its partnership interest includes any reduction in A's share of the $360x partnership liability that is treated as occurring as a result of the sale. Before the sale, A's share of the nonrecourse liability under § 1.752-3(a)(3) was $180x (50% of the $360x liability). As a result of A's sale of its $100x partnership interest in AB to C, A's share of the nonrecourse liability under § 1.752-3(a)(3) was reduced to $120x (because A's partnership interest was 33% after the sale but immediately before the $100x distribution from AB that reduced A's interest in AB to 20%). Thus, A's amount realized on the sale of its partnership interest equals $100x plus the reduction in A's share of the $360x partnership liability of

$60x ($180x - $120x), or $160x. A also is treated as receiving, in its capacity as a partner, and without regard to any deemed distributions under section 752(b), a distribution from AB to which section 731 applies of $100x ($200x transfer - $100x amount of sale). Under paragraph (a)(5) of this section, the distribution is treated as occurring immediately following the sale.

Example (9). Treatment of simultaneous transfers as a sale where selling partner has recourse liabilities that are assumed by the partnership. (i) The facts are the same as those in Example 8, except that AB does not make a transfer to A but AB does assume a personal $80x recourse liability of A's, on January 1, 2007. Immediately after AB's assumption of A's personal $80x recourse liability, A is completely released from liability, and only B and C are ultimately liable on the $80x recourse debt.

(ii) As in Example 8, the $360x liability is ignored for purposes of determining whether the transfers constitute a sale of A's or B's interest in AB because no partner assumes the $360x liability. However, AB's assumption of A's $80x recourse liability is treated as a transfer of consideration to A to the extent that the amount of the liability exceeds A's share of that liability immediately after AB assumes the liability, determined as provided in paragraph (j)(4)(i) of this section. Under paragraph (j)(4)(i) of this section, A's share of the recourse liability immediately following the assumption is zero. Thus, the assumption is treated as a transfer of $80x to A by AB on January 1, 2007. Because C's transfer of $100x to AB, and AB's transfer of $80x to A, occurred within two years, the transfers are presumed to be a sale of a portion of A's partnership interest in AB to C, under paragraph (c) of this section, unless the facts and circumstances clearly establish otherwise. There are no facts that rebut the presumption of sale treatment or that support the application of either of the presumptions against sale treatment provided in paragraphs (e) or (f) or the exception provided in paragraph (g) of this section. Thus, the transfers are treated as a sale of a portion of A's partnership interest in AB to C. Under paragraph (a)(3)(i) of this section, the value of the partnership interest that A is treated as selling to C equals the lesser of the consideration transferred by AB to A, or the consideration transferred by C to AB. C transferred $100x to AB, and A received $80x from AB. Thus, A is treated as having sold a partnership interest in AB with a value of $80x to C. Under paragraph (a)(4) of this section, the amount realized by A on the sale of its partnership interest includes any reduction in A's share of the $360x partnership liability that is treated as occurring as a result of the sale. Before the sale, A's share of the nonrecourse liability under § 1.752-3(a)(3) was $180x (50% of the $360x liability). As a result of A's sale of its $80x partnership interest in AB to C, A's share of the nonrecourse liability under § 1.752-3(a)(3) was reduced to $133x (because A's partnership interest was 37% after the sale). Thus, A's amount realized on the sale of its partnership interest equals $80x plus the reduction in A's share of the $360x partnership liability of $47x ($180x - $133x), or $127x. C also is treated as making, in its capacity as a partner, and without regard to any deemed contributions under section 752(a), a contribution to AB to which section 721 applies of $20x ($100x contribution - $80x amount of sale).

§ 1.707-8 Disclosure of certain information.

(a) In general. The disclosure referred to in § 1.707-3(c)(2) (regarding certain transfers made within two years of each other), § 1.707-5(a)(7)(ii) (regarding a liability incurred within two years prior to a transfer of property), and § 1.707-6(c) (relating to transfers of property from a partnership to a partner in situations analogous to those listed above) is to be made in accordance with paragraph (b) of this section.

(b) Method of providing disclosure. Disclosure is to be made on a completed Form 8275 or on a statement attached to the return of the transferor of property for the taxable year of the transfer that includes the following:

(1) A caption identifying the statement as disclosure under section 707;

(2) An identification of the item (or group of items) with respect to which disclosure is made;

(3) The amount of each item; and

(4) The facts affecting the potential tax treatment of the item (or items) under section 707.

(c) Disclosure by certain partnerships. If more than one partner transfers property to a partnership pursuant to a plan, the disclosure required by this section may be made by the partnership on behalf of all the transferors rather than by each transferor separately.

T.D. 8439, 9/25/92.

PAR. 7. Section 1.707-8 is amended as follows:

1. Revising paragraph (a).

2. Revising paragraph (c).

The revisions read as follows:

Proposed § 1.707-8 Disclosure of certain information.
[*For Preamble, see ¶ 152,607*]

(a) In general. The disclosure referred to in § 1.707-3(c)(2) (regarding certain transfers made within seven years of each other), § 1.707-5(a)(7)(ii) (regarding a liability incurred within two years prior to a transfer of property), § 1.707-5(a)(8) (relating to liabilities assumed within seven years of the transfer), § 1.707-6(c) (relating to transfers of property from a partnership to a partner in situations analogous to those listed above), and § 1.707-7(k) (relating to certain transfers made within seven years of each other) is to be made in accordance with paragraphs (b) and (c) of this section.

* * * * *

(c) Parties required to disclose. The disclosure required by this section must be made by any person who makes a transfer that is required to be disclosed. The persons who are required to disclose may designate by written agreement a single person to make the disclosure. The designation of one person to make the disclosure does not relieve the other persons required to disclose from their obligation to make the disclosure if the designated person fails to make the disclosure in accordance with paragraph (b) of this section.

§ 1.707-9 Effective dates and transitional rules.

(a) Sections 1.707-3 through 1.707-6. *(1) In general.* Except as provided in paragraph (a)(3) of this section, §§ 1.707-3 through 1.707-6 apply to any transaction with respect to which all transfers that are part of a sale of an item of property occur after April 24, 1991.

(2) Transfers occurring on or before April 24, 1991. Except as otherwise provided in paragraph (a)(3) of this section, in the case of any transaction with respect to which one or more of the transfers occurs on or before April 24, 1991, the determination of whether the transaction is a disguised sale of property (including a partnership interest) under section 707(a)(2) is to be made on the basis of the statute and

the guidance provided regarding that provision in the legislative history of section 73 of the Tax Reform Act of 1984 (Pub. L. 98-369, 98 Stat. 494). See H.R. Rep. No. 861, 98th Cong., 2d Sess. 859-62 (1984); S. Prt. No. 169 (Vol. I), 98th Cong., 2d Sess. 223-32 (1984); H.R. Rep. No. 432 (Pt. 2), 98th Cong., 2d Sess. 1216-21 (1984).

(3) Effective date of section 73 of the Tax Reform Act of 1984. Sections 1.707-3 through 1.707-6 do not apply to any transfer of money or other consideration to which section 73(a) of the Tax Reform Act of 1984 (Pub. L. 98-369, 98 Stat. 494) does not apply pursuant to section 73(b) of that Act.

(b) Section 1.707-8 disclosure of certain information. The disclosure provisions described in § 1.707-8 apply to transactions with respect to which all transfers that are part of a sale of property occur after September 30, 1992.

T.D. 8439, 9/25/92.

PAR. 8. Section 1.707-9 is amended as follows:

1. Revising the heading for paragraph (a).

2. Revising paragraph (a)(1).

3. Revising the heading for paragraph (a)(2), and adding a sentence at the end of the paragraph.

4. Amending paragraph (a)(3) by removing the language "1.707-6" and adding "1.707-7" in its place.

5. Revising paragraph (b).

The revisions and addition read as follows:

Proposed § 1.707-9 Effective dates and transitional rules. [*For Preamble, see ¶ 152,607*]

(a) Sections 1.707-3 through 1.707-7. *(1) In general.* Except as provided in paragraph (a)(3) of this section, §§ 1.707-3 through 1.707-7 apply to any transaction with respect to which all transfers that are part of a sale of an item of property or of a partnership interest occur on or after the date these regulations are published as final regulations in the Federal Register. For any transaction with respect to which all transfers that are part of a sale of an item of property occur after April 24, 1991, but before the date these regulations are published as final regulations in the Federal Register, §§ 1.707-3 through 1.707-6 as contained in 26 CFR edition revised April 1, 2004, (TD 8439) apply, except as provided in paragraph (a)(3) of this section.

(2) Transfers occurring before effective dates. * * * In addition, except as provided in paragraph (a)(3) of this section, in the case of any transaction with respect to which one or more of the transfers occurs after April 24, 1991, but before the date these regulations are published as final regulations in the Federal Register, the determination of whether the transaction is a disguised sale of a partnership interest under section 707(a)(2)(B) is to be made on the same basis.

* * * * *

(b) * * * The disclosure provisions described in § 1.707-8 apply to transactions with respect to which all transfers that are part of a sale of property occur on and after the date these regulations are published as final regulations in the Federal Register. For transactions with respect to which all transfers that are part of a sale of property occur after September 30, 1992, but before the date these regulations are published as final regulations in the Federal Register, the disclosure provisions as described in § 1.707-8 as contained in the 26 CFR edition revised April 1, 2004, (TD 8439) apply.

* * * * *

§ 1.708-1 Continuation of partnership.

(a) General rule. For purposes of subchapter K, chapter 1 of the Code, an existing partnership shall be considered as continuing if it is not terminated.

(b) Termination. *(1) General rule.* A partnership shall terminate when the operations of the partnership are discontinued and no part of any business, financial operation, or venture of the partnership continues to be carried on by any of its partners in a partnership. For example, on November 20, 1956, A and B, each of whom is a 20-percent partner in partnership ABC, sell their interests to C, who is a 60-percent partner. Since the business is no longer carried on by any of its partners in a partnership, the ABC partnership is terminated as of November 20, 1956. However, where partners DEF agree on April 30, 1957, to dissolve their partnership, but carry on the business through a winding up period ending September 30, 1957, when all remaining assets, consisting only of cash, are distributed to the partners, the partnership does not terminate because of cessation of business until September 30, 1957.

(i) Upon the death of one partner in a 2-member partnership, the partnership shall not be considered as terminated if the estate or other successor in interest of the deceased partner continues to share in the profits or losses of the partnership business.

(ii) For the continuation of a partnership where payments are being made under section 736 (relating to payments to a retiring partner or a deceased partner's successor in interest, see paragraph (a)(6) of § 1.736-1.

(2) A partnership shall terminate when 50 percent or more of the total interest in partnership capital and profits is sold or exchanged within a period of 12 consecutive months. Such sale or exchange includes a sale or exchange to another member of the partnership. However, a disposition of a partnership interest by gift (including assignment to a successor in interest), bequest, or inheritance, or the liquidation of a partnership interest, is not a sale or exchange for purposes of this subparagraph. Moreover, if the sale or exchange of an interest in a partnership (upper-tier partnership) that holds an interest in another partnership (lower-tier partnership) results in a termination of the upper-tier partnership, the upper-tier partnership is treated as exchanging its entire interest in the capital and profits of the lower-tier partnership. If the sale or exchange of an interest in an upper-tier partnership does not terminate the upper-tier partnership, the sale or exchange of an interest in the upper-tier partnership is not treated as a sale or exchange of a proportionate share of the upper-tier partnership's interest in the capital and profits of the lower-tier partnership. The previous two sentences apply to terminations of partnerships under section 708(b)(1)(B) occurring on or after May 9, 1997; however, the sentences may be applied to terminations occurring on or after May 9, 1996, provided that the partnership and its partners apply the sentences to the termination in a consistent manner. Furthermore, the contribution of property to a partnership does not constitute such a sale or exchange. See, however, paragraph (c)(3) of § 1.731-1. Fifty percent or more of the total interest in partnership capital and profits means 50 percent or more of the total interest in partnership capital plus 50 percent or more of the total interest in partnership profits. Thus, the sale of a 30-percent interest in partnership capital and a 60-percent interest in partnership profits is not the sale or exchange of 50 percent or more of the total interest in partnership capital and profits. If one or more partners sell or exchange interests aggregating 50 percent or more of the total

interest in partnership capital and 50 percent or more of the total interest in partnership profits within a period of 12 consecutive months, such sale or exchange is considered as being within the provisions of this subparagraph. When interests are sold or exchanged on different dates, the percentages to be added are determined as of the date of each sale. For example, with respect to the ABC partnership, the sale by A on May 12, 1956, of a 30-percent interest in capital and profits to D, and the sale by B on March 27, 1957, of a 30-percent interest in capital and profits to E, is a sale of 50-percent or more interest. Accordingly, the partnership is terminated as of March 27, 1957. However, if, on March 27, 1957, D instead of B, sold his 30-percent interest in capital and profits to E, there would be no termination since only one 30-percent interest would have been sold or exchanged within a 12-month period.

(3) For purposes of subchapter K, chapter 1 of the Code, a partnership taxable year closes with respect to all partners on the date on which the partnership terminates. See section 706(c)(1) and paragraph (c)(1) of § 1.706-1. The date of termination is:

(ii) For purposes of section 708(b)(1)(A), the date on which the winding up of the partnership affairs is completed.

(ii) For purposes of section 708(b)(1)(B), the date of the sale or exchange of a partnership interest which, of itself or together with sales or exchanges in the preceding 12 months, transfers an interest of 50 percent or more in both partnership capital and profits.

(4) If a partnership is terminated by a sale or exchange of an interest, the following is deemed to occur: The partnership contributes all of its assets and liabilities to a new partnership in exchange for an interest in the new partnership; and, immediately thereafter, the terminated partnership distributes interests in the new partnership to the purchasing partner and the other remaining partners in proportion to their respective interests in the terminated partnership in liquidation of the terminated partnership, either for the continuation of the business by the new partnership or for its dissolution and winding up. In the latter case, the new partnership terminates in accordance with (b)(1) of this section. This paragraph (b)(4) applies to terminations of partnerships under section 708(b)(1)(B) occurring on or after May 9, 1997; however, this paragraph (b)(4) may be applied to terminations occurring on or after May 9, 1996, provided that the partnership and its partners apply this paragraph (b)(4) to the termination in a consistent manner. The provisions of this paragraph (b)(4) are illustrated by the following example:

Example. (i) A and B each contribute $10,000 cash to form AB, a general partnership, as equal partners. AB purchases depreciable Property X for $20,000. Property X increases in value to $30,000, at which time A sells its entire 50 percent interest to C for $15,000 in a transfer that terminates the partnership under section 708(b)(1)(B). At the time of the sale, Property X had an adjusted tax basis of $16,000 and a book value of $16,000 (original $20,000 tax basis and book value reduced by $4,000 of depreciation). In addition, A and B each had a capital account balance of $8,000 (original $10,000 capital account reduced by $2,000 of depreciation allocations with respect to Property X).

(ii) Following the deemed contribution of assets and liabilities by the terminated AB partnership to a new partnership (new AB) and the liquidation of the terminated AB partnership, the adjusted tax basis of Property X in the hands of new AB is $16,000. See Section 723. The book value of Property X in the hands of new partnership AB is also $16,000 (the book value of Property X immediately before the termination) and B and C each have a capital account of $8,000 in new AB (the balance of their capital accounts in AB prior to the termination). See § 1.704-1(b)(2)(iv)(l) (providing that the deemed contribution and liquidation with regard to the terminated partnership are disregarded in determining the capital accounts of the partners and the books of the new partnership). Additionally, under § 301.6109-1(d)(2)(iii) of this chapter, new AB retains the taxpayer identification number of the terminated AB partnership.

(iii) Property X was not section 704(c) property in the hands of terminated AB and is therefore not treated as section 704(c) property in the hands of new AB, even though Property X is deemed contributed to new AB at a time when the fair market value of Property X ($30,000) was different from its adjusted tax basis ($16,000). See § 1.704-3(a)(3)(i) (providing that property contributed to a new partnership under § 1.708-1(b)(4) is treated as section 704(c) property only to the extent that the property was section 704(c) property in the hands of the terminated partnership immediately prior to the termination).

(5) If a partnership is terminated by a sale or exchange of an interest in the partnership, a section 754 election (including a section 754 election made by the terminated partnership on its final return) that is in effect for the taxable year of the terminated partnership in which the sale occurs, applies with respect to the incoming partner. Therefore, the bases of partnership assets are adjusted pursuant to sections 743 and 755 prior to their deemed contribution to the new partnership. This paragraph (b)(5) applies to terminations of partnerships under section 708(b)(1)(B) occurring on or after May 9, 1997; however, this paragraph (b)(5) may be applied to terminations occurring on or after May 9, 1996, provided that the partnership and its partners apply this paragraph (b)(5) to the termination in a consistent manner.

(c) Merger or consolidation. *(1) General rule.* If two or more partnerships merge or consolidate into one partnership, the resulting partnership shall be considered a continuation of the merging or consolidating partnership the members of which own an interest of more than 50 percent in the capital and profits of the resulting partnership. If the resulting partnership can, under the preceding sentence, be considered a continuation of more than one of the merging or consolidating partnerships, it shall, unless the Commissioner permits otherwise, be considered the continuation solely of that partnership which is credited with the contribution of assets having the greatest fair market value (net of liabilities) to the resulting partnership. Any other merging or consolidating partnerships shall be considered as terminated. If the members of none of the merging or consolidating partnerships have an interest of more than 50 percent in the capital and profits of the resulting partnership, all of the merged or consolidated partnerships are terminated, and a new partnership results.

(2) Tax returns. The taxable years of any merging or consolidating partnerships which are considered terminated shall be closed in accordance with the provisions of section 706(c) and the regulations thereunder, and such partnerships shall file their returns for a taxable year ending upon the date of termination, i.e., the date of merger or consolidation. The resulting partnership shall file a return for the taxable year of the merging or consolidating partnership that is considered as continuing. The return shall state that the resulting partnership is a continuation of such merging or consolidating partnership, shall retain the employer identification number (EIN) of the partnership that is continuing, and shall include

the names, addresses, and EINs of the other merged or consolidated partnerships. The respective distributive shares of the partners for the periods prior to and including the date of the merger or consolidation and subsequent to the date of merger or consolidation shall be shown as a part of the return.

(3) Form of a merger or consolidation. (i) Assets-over form. When two or more partnerships merge or consolidate into one partnership under the applicable jurisdictional law without undertaking a form for the merger or consolidation, or undertake a form for the merger or consolidation that is not described in paragraph (c)(3)(ii) of this section, any merged or consolidated partnership that is considered terminated under paragraph (c)(1) of this section is treated as undertaking the assets-over form for Federal income tax purposes. Under the assets-over form, the merged or consolidated partnership that is considered terminated under paragraph (c)(1) of this section contributes all of its assets and liabilities to the resulting partnership in exchange for an interest in the resulting partnership, and immediately thereafter, the terminated partnership distributes interests in the resulting partnership to its partners in liquidation of the terminated partnership.

(ii) Assets-up form. Despite the partners' transitory ownership of the terminated partnership's assets, the form of a partnership merger or consolidation will be respected for Federal income tax purposes if the merged or consolidated partnership that is considered terminated under paragraph (c)(1) of this section distributes all of its assets to its partners (in a manner that causes the partners to be treated, under the laws of the applicable jurisdiction, as the owners of such assets) in liquidation of the partners' interests in the terminated partnership, and immediately thereafter, the partners in the terminated partnership contribute the distributed assets to the resulting partnership in exchange for interests in the resulting partnership.

(4) Sale of an interest in the merging or consolidating partnership. In a transaction characterized under the assets-over form, a sale of all or part of a partner's interest in the terminated partnership to the resulting partnership that occurs as part of a merger or consolidation under section 708(b)(2)(A), as described in paragraph (c)(3)(i) of this section, will be respected as a sale of a partnership interest if the merger agreement (or another document) specifies that the resulting partnership is purchasing interests from a particular partner in the merging or consolidating partnership and the consideration that is transferred for each interest sold, and if the selling partner in the terminated partnership, either prior to or contemporaneous with the transaction, consents to treat the transaction as a sale of the partnership interest. See section 741 and § 1.741-1 for determining the selling partner's gain or loss on the sale or exchange of the partnership interest.

(5) Examples. The following examples illustrate the rules in paragraphs (c)(1) through (4) of this section:

Example (1). Partnership AB, in whose capital and profits A and B each own a 50-percent interest, and partnership CD, in whose capital and profits C and D each own a 50-percent interest, merge on September 30, 1999, and form partnership ABCD. Partners A, B, C, and D are on a calendar year, and partnership AB and partnership CD also are on a calendar year. After the merger, the partners have capital and profits interests as follows: A, 30 percent; B, 30 percent; C, 20 percent; and D, 20 percent. Since A and B together own an interest of more than 50 percent in the capital and profits of partnership ABCD, such partnership shall be considered a continuation of partnership AB and shall continue to file returns on a calendar year basis. Since C and D own an interest of less than 50 percent in the capital and profits of partnership ABCD, the taxable year of partnership CD closes as of September 30, 1999, the date of the merger, and partnership CD is terminated as of that date. Partnership ABCD is required to file a return for the taxable year January 1 to December 31, 1999, indicating thereon that, until September 30, 1999, it was partnership AB. Partnership CD is required to file a return for its final taxable year, January 1 through September 30, 1999.

Example (2). (i) Partnership X, in whose capital and profits A owns a 40-percent interest and B owns a 60-percent interest, and partnership Y, in whose capital and profits B owns a 60-percent interest and C owns a 40-percent interest, merge on September 30, 1999. The fair market value of the partnership X assets (net of liabilities) is $100X, and the fair market value of the partnership Y assets (net of liabilities) is $200X. The merger is accomplished under state law by partnership Y contributing its assets and liabilities to partnership X in exchange for interests in partnership X, with partnership Y then liquidating, distributing interests in partnership X to B and C.

(ii) B, a partner in both partnerships prior to the merger, owns a greater than 50-percent interest in the resulting partnership following the merger. Accordingly, because the fair market value of partnership Y's assets (net of liabilities) was greater than that of partnership X's, under paragraph (c)(1) of this section, partnership X will be considered to terminate in the merger. As a result, even though, for state law purposes, the transaction was undertaken with partnership Y contributing its assets and liabilities to partnership X and distributing interests in partnership X to its partners, pursuant to paragraph (c)(3)(i) of this section, for Federal income tax purposes, the transaction will be treated as if partnership X contributed its assets to partnership Y in exchange for interests in partnership Y and then liquidated, distributing interests in partnership Y to A and B.

Example (3). (i) The facts are the same as in Example 2, except that partnership X is engaged in a trade or business and has, as one of its assets, goodwill. In addition, the merger is accomplished under state law by having partnership X convey an undivided 40-percent interest in each of its assets to A and an undivided 60-percent interest in each of its assets to B, with A and B then contributing their interests in such assets to partnership Y. Partnership Y also assumes all of the liabilities of partnership X.

(ii) Under paragraph (c)(3)(ii) of this section, the form of the partnership merger will be respected so that partnership X will be treated as following the assets-up form for Federal income tax purposes.

Example (4). (i) Partnership X and partnership Y merge when the partners of partnership X transfer their partnership X interests to partnership Y in exchange for partnership Y interests. Immediately thereafter, partnership X liquidates into partnership Y. The resulting partnership is considered a continuation of partnership Y, and partnership X is considered terminated.

(ii) The partnerships are treated as undertaking the assets-over form described in paragraph (c)(3)(i) of this section because the partnerships undertook a form that is not the assets-up form described in paragraph (c)(3)(ii) of this section. Accordingly, for Federal income tax purposes, partnership X is deemed to contribute its assets and liabilities to partnership Y in exchange for interests in partnership Y, and, immediately thereafter, partnership X is deemed to have distributed the interests in partnership Y to its partners in liquidation of their interests in partnership X.

Example (5). (i) A, B, and C are partners in partnership X. D, E, and F are partners in Partnership Y. Partnership X and partnership Y merge, and the resulting partnership is considered a continuation of partnership Y. Partnership X is considered terminated. Under state law, partnerships X and Y undertake the assets-over form of paragraph (c)(3)(i) of this section to accomplish the partnership merger. C does not want to become a partner in partnership Y, and partnership X does not have the resources to buy C's interest before the merger. C, partnership X, and partnership Y enter into an agreement specifying that partnership Y will purchase C's interest in partnership X for $150 before the merger, and as part of the agreement, C consents to treat the transaction in a manner that is consistent with the agreement. As part of the merger, partnership X receives from partnership Y $150 that will be distributed to C immediately before the merger, and interests in partnership Y in exchange for partnership X's assets and liabilities.

(ii) Because the merger agreement satisfies the requirements of paragraph (c)(4) of this section and C provides the necessary consent, C will be treated as selling its interest in partnership X to partnership Y for $150 before the merger. See section 741 and § 1.741-1 to determine the amount and character of C's gain or loss on the sale or exchange of its interest in partnership X.

(iii) Because the merger agreement satisfies the requirements of paragraph (c)(4) of this section, partnership Y is considered to have purchased C's interest in partnership X for $150 immediately before the merger. See § 1.704-1(b)(2)(iv)(l) for determining partnership Y's capital account in partnership X. Partnership Y's adjusted basis of its interest in partnership X is determined under section 742 and § 1.742-1. To the extent any built-in gain or loss on section 704(c) property in partnership X would have been allocated to C (including any allocations with respect to property revaluations under section 704(b) (reverse section 704(c) allocations)), see section 704 and § 1.704-3(a)(7) for determining the built-in gain or loss or reverse section 704(c) allocations apportionable to partnership Y. Similarly, after the merger is completed, the built-in gain or loss and reverse section 704(c) allocations attributable to C's interest are apportioned to D, E, and F under section 704(c) and § 1.704-3(a)(7).

(iv) Under paragraph (c)(3)(i) of this section, partnership X contributes its assets and liabilities attributable to the interests of A and B to partnership Y in exchange for interests in partnership Y; and, immediately thereafter, partnership X distributes the interests in partnership Y to A and B in liquidation of their interests in partnership X. At the same time, partnership X distributes assets to partnership Y in liquidation of partnership Y's interest in partnership X. Partnership Y's bases in the distributed assets are determined under section 732(b).

(6) Prescribed form not followed in certain circumstances. (i) If any transactions described in paragraph (c)(3) or (4) of this section are part of a larger series of transactions, and the substance of the larger series of transactions is inconsistent with following the form prescribed in such paragraph, the Commissioner may disregard such form, and may recast the larger series of transactions in accordance with their substance.

(ii) Example. The following example illustrates the rules in paragraph (c)(6) of this section:

Example. A, B, and C are equal partners in partnership ABC. ABC holds no section 704(c) property. D and E are equal partners in partnership DE. B and C want to exchange their interests in ABC for all of the interests in DE. However, rather than exchanging partnership interests, DE merges with ABC by undertaking the assets-up form described in paragraph (c)(3)(ii) of this section, with D and E receiving title to the DE assets and then contributing the assets to ABC in exchange for interests in ABC. As part of a prearranged transaction, the assets acquired from DE are contributed to a new partnership, and the interests in the new partnership are distributed to B and C in complete liquidation of their interests in ABC. The merger and division in this example represent a series of transactions that in substance are an exchange of interests in ABC for interests in DE. Even though paragraph (c)(3)(ii) of this section provides that the form of a merger will be respected for Federal income tax purposes if the steps prescribed under the assets-up form are followed, and paragraph (d)(3)(i) of this section provides a form that will be followed for Federal income tax purposes in the case of partnership divisions, these forms will not be respected for Federal income tax purposes under these facts, and the transactions will be recast in accordance with their substance as a taxable exchange of interests in ABC for interests in DE.

(7) Effective date. This paragraph (c) is applicable to partnership mergers occurring on or after January 4, 2001. However, a partnership may apply paragraph (c) of this section to partnership mergers occurring on or after January 11, 2000.

(d) Division of a partnership.

(1) General rule. Upon the division of a partnership into two or more partnerships, any resulting partnership (as defined in paragraph (d)(4)(iv) of this section) or resulting partnerships shall be considered a continuation of the prior partnership (as defined in paragraph (d)(4)(ii) of this section) if the members of the resulting partnership or partnerships had an interest of more than 50 percent in the capital and profits of the prior partnership. Any other resulting partnership will not be considered a continuation of the prior partnership but will be considered a new partnership. If the members of none of the resulting partnerships owned an interest of more than 50 percent in the capital and profits of the prior partnership, none of the resulting partnerships will be considered a continuation of the prior partnership, and the prior partnership will be considered to have terminated. Where members of a partnership which has been divided into two or more partnerships do not become members of a resulting partnership which is considered a continuation of the prior partnership, such members' interests shall be considered liquidated as of the date of the division.

(2) Tax consequences.

(i) Tax returns. The resulting partnership that is treated as the divided partnership (as defined in paragraph (d)(4)(i) of this section) shall file a return for the taxable year of the partnership that has been divided and retain the employer identification number (EIN) of the prior partnership. The return shall include the names, addresses, and EINs of all resulting partnerships that are regarded as continuing. The return shall also state that the partnership is a continuation of the prior partnership and shall set forth separately the respective distributive shares of the partners for the periods prior to and including the date of the division and subsequent to the date of division. All other resulting partnerships that are regarded as continuing and new partnerships shall file separate returns for the taxable year beginning on the day after the date of the division with new EINs for each partnership. The return for a resulting partnership that is regarded as continuing and that is not the divided partnership shall include the name, address, and EIN of the prior partnership.

(ii) Elections. All resulting partnerships that are regarded as continuing are subject to preexisting elections that were made by the prior partnership. A subsequent election that is made by a resulting partnership does not affect the other resulting partnerships.

(3) Form of a division (i) Assets-over form. When a partnership divides into two or more partnerships under applicable jurisdictional law without undertaking a form for the division, or undertakes a form that is not described in paragraph (d)(3)(ii) of this section, the transaction will be characterized under the assets-over form for Federal income tax purposes.

(A) Assets-over form where at least one resulting partnership is a continuation of the prior partnership. In a division under the assets-over form where at least one resulting partnership is a continuation of the prior partnership, the divided partnership (as defined in paragraph (d)(4)(i) of this section) contributes certain assets and liabilities to a recipient partnership (as defined in paragraph (d)(4)(iii) of this section) or recipient partnerships in exchange for interests in such recipient partnership or partnerships; and, immediately thereafter, the divided partnership distributes the interests in such recipient partnership or partnerships to some or all of its partners in partial or complete liquidation of the partners' interests in the divided partnership.

(B) Assets-over form where none of the resulting partnerships is a continuation of the prior partnership. In a division under the assets-over form where none of the resulting partnerships is a continuation of the prior partnership, the prior partnership will be treated as contributing all of its assets and liabilities to new resulting partnerships in exchange for interests in the resulting partnerships; and, immediately thereafter, the prior partnership will be treated as liquidating by distributing the interests in the new resulting partnerships to the prior partnership's partners.

(ii) Assets-up form. (A) Assets-up form where the partnership distributing assets is a continuation of the prior partnership. Despite the partners' transitory ownership of some of the prior partnership's assets, the form of a partnership division will be respected for Federal income tax purposes if the divided partnership (which, pursuant to § 1.708-1(d)(4)(i), must be a continuing partnership) distributes certain assets (in a manner that causes the partners to be treated, under the laws of the applicable jurisdiction, as the owners of such assets) to some or all of its partners in partial or complete liquidation of the partners' interests in the divided partnership, and immediately thereafter, such partners contribute the distributed assets to a recipient partnership or partnerships in exchange for interests in such recipient partnership or partnerships. In order for such form to be respected for transfers to a particular recipient partnership, all assets held by the prior partnership that are transferred to the recipient partnership must be distributed to, and then contributed by, the partners of the recipient partnership.

(B) Assets-up form where none of the resulting partnerships are a continuation of the prior partnership. If none of the resulting partnerships are a continuation of the prior partnership, then despite the partners' transitory ownership of some or all of the prior partnership's assets, the form of a partnership division will be respected for Federal income tax purposes if the prior partnership distributes certain assets (in a manner that causes the partners to be treated, under the laws of the applicable jurisdiction, as the owners of such assets) to some or all of its partners in partial or complete liquidation of the partners' interests in the prior partnership, and immediately thereafter, such partners contribute the distributed assets to a resulting partnership or partnerships in exchange for interests in such resulting partnership or partnerships. In order for such form to be respected for transfers to a particular resulting partnership, all assets held by the prior partnership that are transferred to the resulting partnership must be distributed to, and then contributed by, the partners of the resulting partnership. If the prior partnership does not liquidate under the applicable jurisdictional law, then with respect to the assets and liabilities that, in form, are not transferred to a new resulting partnership, the prior partnership will be treated as transferring these assets and liabilities to a new resulting partnership under the assets-over form described in paragraph (d)(3)(i)(B) of this section.

(4) Definitions.

(i) Divided partnership. For purposes of paragraph (d) of this section, the divided partnership is the continuing partnership which is treated, for Federal income tax purposes, as transferring the assets and liabilities to the recipient partnership or partnerships, either directly (under the assets-over form) or indirectly (under the assets-up form). If the resulting partnership that, in form, transferred the assets and liabilities in connection with the division is a continuation of the prior partnership, then such resulting partnership will be treated as the divided partnership. If a partnership divides into two or more partnerships and only one of the resulting partnerships is a continuation of the prior partnership, then the resulting partnership that is a continuation of the prior partnership will be treated as the divided partnership. If a partnership divides into two or more partnerships without undertaking a form for the division that is recognized under paragraph (d)(3) of this section, or if the resulting partnership that had, in form, transferred assets and liabilities is not considered a continuation of the prior partnership, and more than one resulting partnership is considered a continuation of the prior partnership, the continuing resulting partnership with the assets having the greatest fair market value (net of liabilities) will be treated as the divided partnership.

(ii) Prior partnership. For purposes of paragraph (d) of this section, the prior partnership is the partnership subject to division that exists under applicable jurisdictional law before the division.

(iii) Recipient partnership. For purposes of paragraph (d) of this section, a recipient partnership is a partnership that is treated as receiving, for Federal income tax purposes, assets and liabilities from a divided partnership, either directly (under the assets-over form) or indirectly (under the assets-up form).

(iv) Resulting partnership. For purposes of paragraph (d) of this section, a resulting partnership is a partnership resulting from the division that exists under applicable jurisdictional law after the division and that has at least two partners who were partners in the prior partnership. For example, where a prior partnership divides into two partnerships, both partnerships existing after the division are resulting partnerships.

(5) Examples. The following examples illustrate the rules in paragraphs (d)(1), (2), (3), and (4) of this section:

Example (1). Partnership ABCD is in the real estate and insurance businesses. A owns a 40-percent interest, and B, C, and D each owns a 20-percent interest, in the capital and profits of the partnership. The partnership and the partners report their income on a calendar year. On November 1,

1999, they separate the real estate and insurance businesses and form two partnerships. Partnership AB takes over the real estate business, and partnership CD takes over the insurance business. Because members of resulting partnership AB owned more than a 50-percent interest in the capital and profits of partnership ABCD (A, 40 percent, and B, 20 percent), partnership AB shall be considered a continuation of partnership ABCD. Partnership AB is required to file a return for the taxable year January 1 to December 31, 1999, indicating thereon that until November 1, 1999, it was partnership ABCD. Partnership CD is considered a new partnership formed at the beginning of the day on November 2, 1999, and is required to file a return for the taxable year it adopts pursuant to section 706(b) and the applicable regulations.

Example (2). (i) Partnership ABCD owns properties W, X, Y, and Z, and divides into partnership AB and partnership CD. Under paragraph (d)(1) of this section, partnership AB is considered a continuation of partnership ABCD and partnership CD is considered a new partnership. Partnership ABCD distributes property Y to C and titles property Y in C's name. Partnership ABCD distributes property Z to D and titles property Z in D's name. C and D then contribute properties Y and Z, respectively, to partnership CD in exchange for interests in partnership CD. Properties W and X remain in partnership AB.

(ii) Under paragraph (d)(3)(ii) of this section, partnership ABCD will be treated as following the assets-up form for Federal income tax purposes.

Example (3). (i) The facts are the same as in Example 2, except partnership ABCD distributes property Y to C and titles property Y in C's name. C then contributes property Y to partnership CD. Simultaneously, partnership ABCD contributes property Z to partnership CD in exchange for an interest in partnership CD. Immediately thereafter, partnership ABCD distributes the interest in partnership CD to D in liquidation of D's interest in partnership ABCD.

(ii) Under paragraph (d)(3)(i) of this section, because partnership ABCD did not undertake the assets-up form with respect to all of the assets transferred to partnership CD, partnership ABCD will be treated as undertaking the assets-over form in transferring the assets to partnership CD. Accordingly, for Federal income tax purposes, partnership ABCD is deemed to contribute property Y and property Z to partnership CD in exchange for interests in partnership CD, and immediately thereafter, partnership ABCD is deemed to distribute the interests in partnership CD to partner C and partner D in liquidation of their interests in partnership ABCD.

Example (4). (i) Partnership ABCD owns three parcels of property: property X, with a value of $500; property Y, with a value of $300; and property Z, with a value of $200. A and B each own a 40-percent interest in the capital and profits of partnership ABCD, and C and D each own a 10 percent interest in the capital and profits of partnership ABCD. On November 1, 1999, partnership ABCD divides into three partnerships (AB1, AB2, and CD) by contributing property X to a newly formed partnership (AB1) and distributing all interests in such partnership to A and B as equal partners, and by contributing property Z to a newly formed partnership (CD) and distributing all interests in such partnership to C and D as equal partners in exchange for all of their interests in partnership ABCD. While partnership ABCD does not transfer property Y, C and D cease to be partners in the partnership. Accordingly, after the division, the partnership holding property Y is referred to as partnership AB2.

(ii) Partnerships AB1 and AB2 both are considered a continuation of partnership ABCD, while partnership CD is considered a new partnership formed at the beginning of the day on November 2, 1999. Under paragraph (d)(3)(i)(A) of this section, partnership ABCD will be treated as following the assets-over form, with partnership ABCD contributing property X to partnership AB1 and property Z to partnership CD, and distributing the interests in such partnerships to the designated partners.

Example (5). (i) The facts are the same as in Example 4, except that partnership ABCD divides into three partnerships by operation of state law, without undertaking a form.

(ii) Under the last sentence of paragraph (d)(4)(i) of this section, partnership AB1 will be treated as the resulting partnership that is the divided partnership. Under paragraph (d)(3)(i)(A) of this section, partnership ABCD will be treated as following the assets-over form, with partnership ABCD contributing property Y to partnership AB2 and property Z to partnership CD, and distributing the interests in such partnerships to the designated partners.

Example (6). (i) The facts are the same as in Example 4, except that partnership ABCD divides into three partnerships by contributing property X to newly-formed partnership AB1 and property Y to newly-formed partnership AB2 and distributing all interests in each partnership to A and B in exchange for all of their interests in partnership ABCD.

(ii) Because resulting partnership CD is not a continuation of the prior partnership (partnership ABCD), partnership CD cannot be treated, for Federal income tax purposes, as the partnership that transferred assets (i.e., the divided partnership), but instead must be treated as a recipient partnership. Under the last sentence of paragraph (d)(4)(i) of this section, partnership AB1 will be treated as the resulting partnership that is the divided partnership. Under paragraph (d)(3)(i)(A) of this section, partnership ABCD will be treated as following the assets-over form, with partnership ABCD contributing property Y to partnership AB2 and property Z to partnership CD, and distributing the interests in such partnerships to the designated partners.

Example (7). (i) Partnership ABCDE owns Blackacre, Whiteacre, and Redacre, and divides into partnership AB, partnership CD, and partnership DE. Under paragraph (d)(1) of this section, partnership ABCDE is considered terminated (and, hence, none of the resulting partnerships are a continuation of the prior partnership) because none of the members of the new partnerships (partnership AB, partnership CD, and partnership DE) owned an interest of more than 50 percent in the capital and profits of partnership ABCDE.

(ii) Partnership ABCDE distributes Blackacre to A and B and titles Blackacre in the names of A and B. A and B then contribute Blackacre to partnership AB in exchange for interests in partnership AB. Partnership ABCDE will be treated as following the assets-up form described in paragraph (d)(3)(ii)(B) of this section for Federal income tax purposes.

(iii) Partnership ABCDE distributes Whiteacre to C and D and titles Whiteacre in the names of C and D. C and D then contribute Whiteacre to partnership CD in exchange for interests in partnership CD. Partnership ABCDE will be treated as following the assets-up form described in paragraph (d)(3)(ii)(B) of this section for Federal income tax purposes.

(iv) Partnership ABCDE does not liquidate under state law so that, in form, the assets in new partnership DE are not considered to have been transferred under state law.

Partnership ABCDE will be treated as undertaking the assets-over form described in paragraph (d)(3)(i)(B) of this section for Federal income tax purposes with respect to the assets of partnership DE. Thus, partnership ABCDE will be treated as contributing Redacre to partnership DE in exchange for interests in partnership DE; and, immediately thereafter, partnership ABCDE will be treated as distributing interests in partnership DE to D and E in liquidation of their interests in partnership ABCDE. Partnership ABCDE then terminates.

(6) Prescribed form not followed in certain circumstances. If any transactions described in paragraph (d)(3) of this section are part of a larger series of transactions, and the substance of the larger series of transactions is inconsistent with following the form prescribed in such paragraph, the Commissioner may disregard such form, and may recast the larger series of transactions in accordance with their substance.

(7) Effective date. This paragraph (d) is applicable to partnership divisions occurring on or after January 4, 2001. However, a partnership may apply paragraph (d) of this section to partnership divisions occurring on or after January 11, 2000.

T.D. 6175, 5/23/56, amend T.D. 8717, 5/8/97, T.D. 8925, 1/3/2001.

§ 1.709-1 Treatment of organization and syndication costs.

Caution: The Treasury has not yet amended Reg § 1.709-1 to reflect changes made by P.L. 108-357.

(a) General rule. Except as provided in paragraph (b) of this section, no deduction shall be allowed under chapter 1 of the Code to a partnership or to any partner for any amounts paid or incurred, directly or indirectly, in partnership taxable years beginning after December 31, 1975, to organize a partnership, or to promote the sale of, or to sell, an interest in the partnership.

(b) Amortization of organization expenses. *(1)* Under section 709(b) of the Code, a partnership may elect to treat its organizational expenses (as defined in section 709(b)(2) and in § 1.709-2(a)) paid or incurred in partnership taxable years beginning after December 31, 1976, as deferred expenses. If a partnership elects to amortize organizational expenses, it must select a period of not less than 60 months, over which the partnership will amortize all such expenses on a straight line basis. This period must begin with the month in which the partnership begins business (as determined under § 1.709-2(c)). However, in the case of a partnership on the cash receipts and disbursements method of accounting, no deduction shall be allowed for a taxable year with respect to any such expenses that have not been paid by the end of that taxable year. Portions of such expenses which would have been deductible under section 709(b) in a prior taxable year if the expenses had been paid are deductible in the year of payment. The election is irrevocable and the period selected by the partnership in making its election may not be subsequently changed.

(2) If there is a winding up and complete liquidation of the partnership prior to the end of the amortization period, the unamortized amount of organizational expenses is a partnership deduction in its final taxable year to the extent provided under section 165 (relating to losses). However, there is no partnership deduction with respect to its capitalized syndication expenses.

(c) Time and manner of making election. The election to amortize organizational expenses provided by section 709(b) shall be made by attaching a statement to the partnership's return of income for the taxable year in which the partnership begins business. The statement shall set forth a description of each organizational expense incurred (whether or not paid) with the amount of the expense, the date each expense was incurred, the month in which the partnership began business, and the number of months (not less than 60) over which the expenses are to be amortized. A taxpayer on the cash receipts and disbursements method of accounting shall also indicate the amount paid before the end of the taxable year with respect to each such expense. Expenses less than $10 need not be separately listed, provided the total amount of these expenses is listed with the dates on which the first and last of such expenses were incurred, and, in the case of a taxpayer on the cash receipts and disbursements method of accounting, the aggregate amount of such expenses that was paid by the end of the taxable year is stated. In the case of a partnership which begins business in a taxable year that ends after March 31, 1983, the original return and statement must be filed (and the election made) not later than the date prescribed by law for filing the return (including any extensions of time) for that taxable year. Once an election has been made, an amended return (or returns) and statement (or statements) may be filed to include any organizational expenses not included in the partnership's original return and statement.

T.D. 7891, 5/3/83.

§ 1.709-2 Definitions.

(a) Organizational expenses. Section 709(b)(2) of the Internal Revenue Code defines organizational expenses as expenses which:

(1) Are incident to the creation of the partnership;

(2) Are chargeable to capital account; and

(3) Are of a character which, if expended incident to the creation of a partnership having an ascertainable life, would (but for section 709(a)) be amortized over such life.

An expenditure which fails to meet one or more of these three tests does not qualify as an organizational expense for purposes of section 709(b) and this section. To satisfy the statutory requirement described in paragraph (a)(1) of this section, the expense must be incurred during the period beginning at a point which is a reasonable time before the partnership begins business and ending with the date prescribed by law for filing the partnership return (determined without regard to any extensions of time) for the taxable year the partnership begins business. In addition, the expenses must be for creation of the partnership and not for operation or starting operation of the partnership trade or business. To satisfy the statutory requirement described in paragraph (a)(3) of this section, the expense must be for an item of a nature normally expected to benefit the partnership throughout the entire life of the partnership. The following are examples of organizational expenses within the meaning of section 709 and this section: Legal fees for services incident to the organization of the partnership, such as negotiation and preparation of a partnership agreement; accounting fees for services incident to the organization of the partnership; and filing fees. The following are examples of expenses that are not organizational expenses within the meaning of section 709 and this section (regardless of how the partnership characterizes them): Expenses connected with acquiring assets for the partnership or transferring assets to the partnership; expenses connected with the admission or removal of partners other than at the time the partnership is first organized; expenses connected with a contract relating to the operation of the partnership trade or business (even where the contract is between the partnership and one of its members); and syndication expenses.

(b) Syndication expenses. Syndication expenses are expenses connected with the issuing and marketing of interests in the partnership. Examples of syndication expenses are brokerage fees; registration fees; legal fees of the underwriter or placement agent and the issuer (the general partner or the partnership) for securities advice and for advice pertaining to the adequacy of tax disclosures in the prospectus or placement memorandum for securities law purposes; accounting fees for preparation of representations to be included in the offering materials; and printing costs of the prospectus, placement memorandum, and other selling and promotional material. These expenses are not subject to the election under section 709(b) and must be capitalized.

(c) Beginning business. The determination of the date a partnership begins business for purposes of section 709 presents a question of fact that must be determined in each case in light of all the circumstances of the particular case. Ordinarily, a partnership begins business when it starts the business operations for which it was organized. The mere signing of a partnership agreement is not alone sufficient to show the beginning of business. If the activities of the partnership have advanced to the extent necessary to establish the nature of its business operations, it will be deemed to have begun business. Accordingly, the acquisition of operating assets which are necessary to the type of business contemplated may constitute beginning business for these purposes. The term "operating assets", as used herein, means assets that are in a state of readiness to be placed in service within a reasonable period following their acquisition.

T.D. 7891, 5/3/83.

§ 1.721-1 Nonrecognition of gain or loss on contribution.

Caution: The Treasury has not yet amended Reg § 1.721-1 to reflect changes made by P.L. 94-455.

(a) No gain or loss shall be recognized either to the partnership or to any of its partners upon a contribution of property, including installment obligations, to the partnership in exchange for a partnership interest. This rule applies whether the contribution is made to a partnership in the process of formation or to a partnership which is already formed and operating. Section 721 shall not apply to a transaction between a partnership and a partner not acting in his capacity as a partner since such a transaction is governed by section 707. Rather than contributing property to a partnership, a partner may sell property to the partnership or may retain the ownership of property and allow the partnership to use it. In all cases, the substance of the transaction will govern, rather than its form. See paragraph (c)(3) of § 1.731-1, Thus, if the transfer of property by the partner to the partnership results in the receipt by the partner of money or other consideration, including a promissory obligation fixed in amount and time for payment, the transaction will be treated as a sale or exchange under section 707 rather than as a contribution under section 721. For the rules governing the treatment of liabilities to which contributed property is subject, see section 752 and § 1.752-1.

(b) *(1)* Normally, under local law, each partner is entitled to be repaid his contributions of money or other property to the partnership (at the value placed upon such property by the partnership at the time of the contribution) whether made at the formation of the partnership or subsequent thereto. To the extent that any of the partners gives up any part of his right to be repaid his contributions (as distinguished from a share in partnership profits) in favor of another partner as compensation for services (or in satisfaction of an obligation), section 721 does not apply. The value of an interest in such partnership capital so transferred to a partner as compensation for services constitutes income to the partner under section 61. The amount of such income is the fair market value of the interest in capital so transferred, either at the time the transfer is made for past services, or at the time the services have been rendered where the transfer is conditioned on the completion of the transferee's future services. The time when such income is realized depends on all the facts and circumstances, including any substantial restrictions or conditions on the compensated partner's right to withdraw or otherwise dispose of such interest. To the extent that an interest in capital representing compensation for services rendered by the decedent prior to his death is transferred after his death to the decedent's successor in interest, the fair market value of such interest is income in respect of a decedent under section 691.

(2) To the extent that the value of such interest is: (i) compensation for services rendered to the partnership, it is a guaranteed payment for services under section 707(c); (ii) compensation for services rendered to a partner, it is not deductible by the partnership, but is deductible only by such partner to the extent allowable under this chapter.

(c) Underwritings of partnership interests. *(1) In general.* For the purpose of section 721, if a person acquires a partnership interest from an underwriter in exchange for cash in a qualified underwriting transaction, the person who acquires the partnership interest is treated as transferring cash directly to the partnership in exchange for the partnership interest and the underwriter is disregarded. A qualified underwriting transaction is a transaction in which a partnership issues partnership interests for cash in an underwriting in which either the underwriter is an agent of the partnership or the underwriter's ownership of the partnership is transitory.

(2) Effective date. This paragraph (c) is effective for qualified underwriting transactions occurring on or after May 1, 1996.

T.D. 6175, 5/23/56, amend T.D. 8665, 4/30/96.

PAR. 7. In § 1.721-1, paragraph (b) is revised to read as follows.

Proposed § 1.721-1 Nonrecognition of gain or loss on contribution. [*For Preamble, see ¶ 152,663*]

* * * * *

(b) *(1)* Except as otherwise provided in this section or § 1.721-2, section 721 does not apply to the transfer of a partnership interest in connection with the performance of services or in satisfaction of an obligation. The transfer of a partnership interest to a person in connection with the performance of services constitutes a transfer of property to which section 83 and the regulations thereunder apply. To the extent that a partnership interest transferred in connection with the performance of services rendered by a decedent prior to the decedent's death is transferred after the decedent's death to the decedent's successor in interest, the fair market value of such interest is an item of income in respect of a decedent under section 691.

(2) Except as provided in section 83(h) and 1.83-6(c), no gain or loss shall be recognized by a partnership upon—

(i) The transfer or substantial vesting of a compensatory partnership interest; or

(ii) The forfeiture of a compensatory partnership interest. See § 1.704-1(b)(4)(xii) for rules regarding forfeiture allocations of partnership items that may be required in the taxable year of a forfeiture.

(3) For purposes of this section, a compensatory partnership interest is an interest in the transferring partnership that is transferred in connection with the performance of services for that partnership (either before or after the formation of the partnership), including an interest that is transferred on the exercise of a compensatory partnership option. A compensatory partnership option is an option to acquire an interest in the issuing partnership that is granted in connection with the performance of services for that partnership (either before or after the formation of the partnership).

(4) To the extent that a partnership interest is—

(i) Transferred to a partner in connection with the performance of services rendered to the partnership, it is a guaranteed payment for services under section 707(c);

(ii) Transferred in connection with the performance of services rendered to a partner, it is not deductible by the partnership, but is deductible only by such partner to the extent allowable under Chapter 1 of the Code.

(5) This paragraph (b) applies to interests that are transferred on or after the date final regulations are published in the Federal Register.

* * * * *

Proposed § 1.721-2 Noncompensatory options. [*For Preamble, see ¶ 152,359*]

(a) Exercise of a noncompensatory option. Notwithstanding § 1.721-1(b)(1), section 721 applies to the exercise (as defined in paragraph (e)(4) of this section) of a noncompensatory option (as defined in paragraph (d) of this section). However, if the exercise price (as defined in paragraph (e)(5) of this section) of a noncompensatory option exceeds the capital account received by the option holder on the exercise of the noncompensatory option, the transaction will be given tax effect in accordance with its true nature.

(b) Transfer of property in exchange for a noncompensatory option. Section 721 does not apply to a transfer of property to a partnership in exchange for a noncompensatory option. For example, if a person purchases a noncompensatory option with appreciated property, the person recognizes income or gain to the extent that the fair market value of the noncompensatory option exceeds the person's basis in the surrendered property.

(c) Lapse of a noncompensatory option. Section 721 does not apply to the lapse of a noncompensatory option.

(d) Scope. The provisions of this section apply only to noncompensatory options and do not apply to any interest on convertible debt that has been accrued by the partnership (including accrued original issue discount). For purposes of this section, the term noncompensatory option means an option (as defined in paragraph (e)(1) of this section) issued by a partnership (the issuing partnership), other than an option issued in connection with the performance of services.

(e) Definitions. The following definitions apply for the purposes of this section.

(1) Option means a call option or warrant to acquire an interest in the issuing partnership, the conversion feature of convertible debt (as defined in paragraph (e)(2) of this section), or the conversion feature of convertible equity (as defined in paragraph (e)(3) of this section). A contract that otherwise constitutes an option shall not fail to be treated as such for purposes of this section merely because it may or must be settled in cash or property other than a partnership interest.

(2) Convertible debt is any indebtedness of a partnership that is convertible into an interest in that partnership.

(3) Convertible equity is preferred equity in a partnership that is convertible into common equity in that partnership. For this purpose, preferred equity is any interest in the issuing partnership that entitles the partner to a preferential return on capital and common equity is any interest in the issuing partnership that is not preferred equity.

(4) Exercise means the exercise of an option or warrant or the conversion of convertible debt or convertible equity.

(5) Exercise price means, in the case of a call option or warrant, the exercise price of the call option or warrant; in the case of convertible equity, the converting partner's capital account with respect to that convertible equity, increased by the fair market value of cash or other property contributed to the partnership in connection with the conversion; and, in the case of convertible debt, the adjusted issue price (within the meaning of § 1.1275-1(b)) of the debt converted, increased by accrued but unpaid qualified stated interest and by the fair market value of cash or other property contributed to the partnership in connection with the conversion.

(f) Example. The following example illustrates the provisions of this section:

Example. In Year 1, L and M form general partnership LM with cash contributions of $5,000 each, which are used to purchase land, Property D, for $10,000. In that same year, the partnership issues an option to N to buy a one-third interest in the partnership at any time before the end of Year 3. The exercise price of the option is $5,000, payable in either cash or property. N transfers Property E with a basis of $600 and a value of $1,000 to the partnership in exchange for the option. N provides no other consideration for the option. Assume that N's option is a noncompensatory option under paragraph (d) of this section and that N is not treated as a partner with respect to the option. Under paragraph (b) of this section, section 721(a) does not apply to N's transfer of Property E to LM in exchange for the option. In accordance with § 1.1001-2, upon N's transfer of Property E to the partnership in exchange for the option, N recognizes $400 of gain. Under open transaction principles applicable to noncompensatory options, the partnership does not recognize any gain upon receipt of appreciated property in exchange for the option. The partnership has a basis of $1,000 in Property E. In Year 3, when the partnership property is valued at $16,000, N exercises the option, contributing Property F with a basis of $3,000 and a fair market value of $5,000 to the partnership. Under paragraph (a) of this section, neither the partnership nor N recognizes gain upon N's contribution of property to the partnership upon the exercise of the option. Under section 723, the partnership has a basis of $3,000 in Property F. See § 1.704-1(b)(2)(iv)(d)(4) and (s) for special rules applicable to capital account adjustments on the exercise of a noncompensatory option.

(g) Effective date. This section applies to noncompensatory options that are issued on or after the date final regulations are published in the Federal Register.

§ 1.722-1 Basis of contributing partner's interest.

Caution: The Treasury has not yet amended Reg § 1.722-1 to reflect changes made by P.L. 94-455.

The basis to a partner of a partnership interest acquired by a contribution of property, including money, to the partnership shall be the amount of money contributed plus the adjusted basis at the time of contribution of any property contributed. If the acquisition of an interest in partnership capital results in taxable income to a partner, such income shall constitute an addition to the basis of the partner's interest. See paragraph (b) of § 1.721-1. If the contributed property is subject to indebtedness or if liabilities of the partner are assumed by the partnership, the basis of the contributing partner's interest shall be reduced by the portion of the indebtedness assumed by the other partners, since the partnership's assumption of his indebtedness is treated as a distribution of money to the partner. Conversely, the assumption by the other partners of a portion of the contributor's indebtedness is treated as a contribution of money by them. See section 752 and § 1.752-1. The provisions of this section may be illustrated by the following examples:

Example (1). A acquired a 20-percent interest in a partnership by contributing property. At the time of A's contribution, the property had a fair market value of $10,000, an adjusted basis to A of $4,000, and was subject to a mortgage of $2,000. Payment of the mortgage was assumed by the partnership. The basis of A's interest in the partnership is $2,400, computed as follows:

Adjusted basis to A of property contributed	$4,000
Less portion of mortgage assumed by other partners which must be treated as a distribution (80 percent of $2,000)	1,600
Basis of A's interest	2,400

Example (2). If, in example (1) of this section, the property contributed by A was subject to a mortgage of $6,000, the basis of A's interest would be zero, computed as follows:

Adjusted basis to A of property contributed	$4,000
Less portion of mortgage assumed by other partners which must be treated as a distribution (80 percent of $6,000)	4,800
	(800)

See § 1.460-4(k)(3)(iv)(A) for rules relating to basis adjustments required where a contract accounted for under a long-term contract method of accounting is transferred in a contribution to which section 721(a) applies. Since A's basis cannot be less than zero, the $800 in excess of basis, which is considered as a distribution of money under section 752(b), is treated as capital gain from the sale or exchange or a partnership interest. See section 731(a).

T.D. 6175, 5/23/56, amend T.D. 9137, 7/15/2004.

§ 1.723-1 Basis of property contributed to partnership.

Caution: The Treasury has not yet amended Reg § 1.723-1 to reflect changes made by P.L. 94-455.

The basis to the partnership of property contributed to it by a partner is the adjusted basis of such property to the contributing partner at the time of the contribution. Since such property has the same basis in the hands of the partnership as it had in the hands of the contributing partner, the holding period of such property for the partnership includes the period during which it was held by the partner. See section 1223(2). For elective adjustments to the basis of partnership property arising from distributions or transfers of partnership interests, see section 732(d), 734(b), and 743(b). See § 1.460-4(k)(3)(iv)(B)(2) for rules relating to adjustments to the basis of contracts accounted for using a long-term contract method of accounting that are acquired in certain contributions to which section 721(a) applies.

T.D. 6175, 5/23/56, amend T.D. 9137, 7/15/2004.

§ 1.731-1 Extent of recognition of gain or loss on distribution.

Caution: The Treasury has not yet amended Reg § 1.731-1 to reflect changes made by P.L. 103-465.

(a) Recognition of gain or loss to partner. *(1) Recognition of gain.* (i) Where money is distributed by a partnership to a partner, no gain shall be recognized to the partner except to the extent that the amount of money distributed exceeds the adjusted basis of the partner's interest in the partnership immediately before the distribution. This rule is applicable both to current distributions (i. e., distributions other than in liquidation of an entire interest) and to distributions in liquidation of a partner's entire interest in a partnership. Thus, if a partner with a basis for his interest of $10,000 receives a distribution of cash of $8,000 and property with a fair market value of $3,000, no gain is recognized to him. If $11,000 cash were distributed, gain would be recognized to the extent of $1,000. No gain shall be recognized to a distributee partner with respect to a distribution of property (other than money) until he sells or otherwise disposes of such property, except to the extent otherwise provided by section 736 (relating to payments to a retiring partner or a deceased partner's successor in interest) and section 751 (relating to unrealized receivables and inventory items). See section 731(c) and paragraph (c) of this section.

(ii) For the purposes of sections 731 and 705, advances or drawings of money or property against a partner's distributive share of income shall be treated as current distributions made on the last day of the partnership taxable year with respect to such partner.

(2) Recognition of loss. Loss is recognized to a partner only upon liquidation of his entire interest in the partnership, and only if the property distributed to him consists solely of money, unrealized receivables (as defined in section 751(c)), and inventory items (as defined in section 751(d)(2)). The term "liquidation of a partner's interest", as defined in section 761(d), is the termination of the partner's entire interest in the partnership by means of a distribution or a series of distributions. Loss is recognized to the distributee partner in such cases to the extent of the excess of the adjusted basis of such partner's interest in the partnership at the time of the distribution over the sum of—

(i) Any money distributed to him, and

(ii) The basis to the distributee, as determined under section 732, of any unrealized receivables and inventory items that are distributed to him. If the partner whose interest is liquidated receives any property other than money, unrealized receivables, or inventory items, then no loss will be recognized. Application of the provisions of this subparagraph may be illustrated by the following examples:

Example (1). Partner A has a partnership interest in partnership ABC with an adjusted basis to him of $10,000. He retires from the partnership and receives, as a distribution in liquidation of his entire interest, his share of partnership property. This share is $5,000 cash and inventory with a basis to him (under section 732) of $3,000. Partner A realizes a capital loss of $2,000, which is recognized under section 731(a)(2).

Example (2). Partner B has a partnership interest in partnership BCD with an adjusted basis to him of $10,000. He retires from the partnership and receives, as a distribution in liquidation of his entire interest, his share of partnership property. This share is $4,000 cash, real property (used in the trade or business) with an adjusted basis to the partnership of $2,000, and unrealized receivables having a basis to him (under section 732) of $3,000. No loss will be recognized to B on the transaction because he received property other than money, unrealized receivables, and inventory items. As determined under section 732, the basis to B for the real property received is $3,000.

(3) Character of gain or loss. Gain or loss recognized under section 731(a) on a distribution is considered gain or loss from the sale or exchange of the partnership interest of the distributee partner, that is, capital gain or loss.

(b) Gain or loss recognized by partnership. A distribution of property (including money) by a partnership to a partner does not result in recognized gain or loss to the partnership under section 731. However, recognized gain or loss may result to the partnership from certain distributions which, under section 751(b), must be treated as a sale or exchange of property between the distributee partner and the partnership.

(c) Exceptions. *(1)* Section 731 does not apply to the extent otherwise provided by—

(i) Section 736 (relating to payments to a retiring partner or to a deceased partner's successor in interest) and

(ii) Section 751 (relating to unrealized receivables and inventory items). For example, payments under section 736(a), which are considered as a distributive share or guaranteed payment, are taxable as such under that section.

(2) The receipt by a partner from the partnership of money or property under an obligation to repay the amount of such money or to return such property does not constitute a distribution subject to section 731 but is a loan governed by section 707(a). To the extent that such an obligation is canceled, the obligor partner will be considered to have received a distribution of money or property at the time of cancellation.

(3) If there is a contribution of property to a partnership and within a short period:

(i) Before or after such contribution other property is distributed to the contributing partner and the contributed property is retained by the partnership, or

(ii) After such contribution the contributed property is distributed to another partner, such distribution may not fall within the scope of section 731. Section 731 does not apply to a distribution of property, if, in fact, the distribution was made in order to effect an exchange of property between two or more of the partners or between the partnership and a partner. Such a transaction shall be treated as an exchange of property.

T.D. 6175, 5/23/56.

---

§ 1.731-2 Partnership distributions of marketable securities.

(a) Marketable securities treated as money. Except as otherwise provided in section 731(c) and this section, for purposes of sections 731(a)(1) and 737, the term money includes marketable securities and such securities are taken into account at their fair market value as of the date of the distribution.

(b) Reduction of amount treated as money. *(1) Aggregation of securities.* For purposes of section 731(c)(3)(B) and this paragraph (b), all marketable securities held by a partnership are treated as marketable securities of the same class and issuer as the distributed security.

(2) Amount of reduction. The amount of the distribution of marketable securities that is treated as a distribution of money under section 731(c) and paragraph (a) of this section is reduced (but not below zero) by the excess, if any, of—

(i) The distributee partner's distributive share of the net gain, if any, which would be recognized if all the marketable securities held by the partnership were sold (immediately before the transaction to which the distribution relates) by the partnership for fair market value; over

(ii) The distributee partner's distributive share of the net gain, if any, which is attributable to the marketable securities held by the partnership immediately after the transaction, determined by using the same fair market value as used under paragraph (b)(2)(i) of this section.

(3) Distributee partner's share of net gain. For purposes of section 731(c)(3)(B) and paragraph (b)(2) of this section, a partner's distributive share of net gain is determined—

(i) By taking into account any basis adjustments under section 743(b) with respect to that partner;

(ii) Without taking into account any special allocations adopted with a principal purpose of avoiding the effect of section 731(c) and this section; and

(iii) Without taking into account any gain or loss attributable to a distributed security to which paragraph (d)(1) of this section applies.

(c) Marketable securities. *(1) In general.* For purposes of section 731(c) and this section, the term marketable securities is defined in section 731(c)(2).

(2) Actively traded. For purposes of section 731(c) and this section, a financial instrument is actively traded (and thus is a marketable security) if it is of a type that is, as of the date of distribution, actively traded within the meaning of section 1092(d)(1). Thus, for example, if XYZ common stock is listed on a national securities exchange, particular shares of XYZ common stock that are distributed by a partnership are marketable securities even if those particular shares cannot be resold by the distributee partner for a designated period of time.

(3) Interests in an entity. (i) Substantially all. For purposes of section 731(c)(2)(B)(v) and this section, substantially all of the assets of an entity consist (directly or indirectly) of marketable securities, money, or both only if 90 percent or more of the assets of the entity (by value) at the time of the distribution of an interest in the entity consist (directly or indirectly) of marketable securities, money, or both.

(ii) Less than substantially all. For purposes of section 731(c)(2)(B)(vi) and this section, an interest in an entity is a marketable security to the extent that the value of the interest is attributable (directly or indirectly) to marketable securities, money, or both, if less than 90 percent but 20 percent or more of the assets of the entity (by value) at the time of the distribution of an interest in the entity consist (directly or indirectly) of marketable securities, money, or both.

(4) Value of assets. For purposes of section 731(c) and this section, the value of the assets of an entity is determined without regard to any debt that may encumber or otherwise

be allocable to those assets, other than debt that is incurred to acquire an asset with a principal purpose of avoiding or reducing the effect of section 731(c) and this section.

(d) Exceptions. *(1) In general.* Except as otherwise provided in paragraph (d)(2) of this section, section 731(c) and this section do not apply to the distribution of a marketable security if—

(i) The security was contributed to the partnership by the distributee partner;

(ii) The security was acquired by the partnership in a nonrecognition transaction, and the following conditions are satisfied—

(A) The value of any marketable securities and money exchanged by the partnership in the nonrecognition transaction is less than 20 percent of the value of all the assets exchanged by the partnership in the nonrecognition transaction; and

(B) The partnership distributed the security within five years of either the date the security was acquired by the partnership or, if later, the date the security became marketable; or

(iii) The security was not a marketable security on the date acquired by the partnership, and the following conditions are satisfied—

(A) The entity that issued the security had no outstanding marketable securities at the time the security was acquired by the partnership;

(B) The security was held by the partnership for at least six months before the date the security became marketable; and

(C) The partnership distributed the security within five years of the date the security became marketable.

(2) Anti-stuffing rule. Paragraph (d)(1) of this section does not apply to the extent that 20 percent or more of the value of the distributed security is attributable to marketable securities or money contributed (directly or indirectly) by the partnership to the entity to which the distributed security relates after the security was acquired by the partnership (other than marketable securities contributed by the partnership that were originally contributed to the partnership by the distributee partner). For purposes of this paragraph (d)(2), money contributed by the distributing partnership does not include any money deemed contributed by the partnership as a result of section 752.

(3) Successor security. Section 731(c) and this section apply to the distribution of a marketable security acquired by the partnership in a nonrecognition transaction in exchange for a security the distribution of which immediately prior to the exchange would have been excepted under this paragraph (d) only to the extent that section 731(c) and this section otherwise would have applied to the exchanged security.

(e) Investment partnerships. *(1) In general.* Section 731(c) and this section do not apply to the distribution of marketable securities by an investment partnership (as defined in section 731(c)(3)(C)(i)) to an eligible partner (as defined in section 731(c)(3)(C)(iii)).

(2) Eligible partner. (i) Contributed services. For purposes of section 731(c)(3)(C)(iii) and this section, a partner is not treated as a partner other than an eligible partner solely because the partner contributed services to the partnership.

(ii) Contributed partnership interests. For purposes of determining whether a partner is an eligible partner under section 731(c)(3)(C), if the partner has contributed to the investment partnership an interest in another partnership that meets the requirements of paragraph (e)(4)(i) of this section after the contribution, the contributed interest is treated as property specified in section 731(c)(3)(C)(i).

(3) Trade or business activities. For purposes of section 731(c)(3)(C) and this section, a partnership is not treated as engaged in a trade or business by reason of—

(i) Any activity undertaken as an investor, trader, or dealer in any asset described in section 731(c)(3)(C)(i), including the receipt of commitment fees, break-up fees, guarantee fees, director's fees, or similar fees that are customary in and incidental to any activities of the partnership as an investor, trader, or dealer in such assets;

(ii) Reasonable and customary management services (including the receipt of reasonable and customary fees in exchange for such management services) provided to an investment partnership (within the meaning of section 731(c)(3)(C)(i)) in which the partnership holds a partnership interest; or

(iii) Reasonable and customary services provided by the partnership in assisting the formation, capitalization, expansion, or offering of interests in a corporation (or other entity) in which the partnership holds or acquires a significant equity interest (including the provision of advice or consulting services, bridge loans, guarantees of obligations, or service on a company's board of directors), provided that the anticipated receipt of compensation for the services, if any, does not represent a significant purpose for the partnership's investment in the entity and is incidental to the investment in the entity.

(4) Partnership tiers. For purposes of section 731(c)(3)(C)(iv) and this section, a partnership (upper-tier partnership) is not treated as engaged in a trade or business engaged in by, or as holding (instead of a partnership interest) a proportionate share of the assets of, a partnership (lower-tier partnership) in which the partnership holds a partnership interest if—

(i) The upper-tier partnership does not actively and substantially participate in the management of the lower-tier partnership; and

(ii) The interest held by the upper-tier partnership is less than 20 percent of the total profits and capital interests in the lower-tier partnership.

(f) Basis rules. *(1) Partner's basis.* (i) Partner's basis in distributed securities. The distributee partner's basis in distributed marketable securities with respect to which gain is recognized by reason of section 731(c) and this section is the basis of the security determined under section 732, increased by the amount of such gain. Any increase in the basis of the marketable securities attributable to gain recognized by reason of section 731(c) and this section is allocated to marketable securities in proportion to their respective amounts of unrealized appreciation in the hands of the partner before such increase.

(ii) Partner's basis in partnership interest. The basis of the distributee partner's interest in the partnership is determined under section 733 as if no gain were recognized by the partner on the distribution by reason of section 731(c) and this section.

(2) Basis of partnership property. No adjustment is made to the basis of partnership property under section 734 as a result of any gain recognized by a partner, or any step-up in the basis in the distributed marketable securities in the hands of the distributee partner, by reason of section 731(c) and this section.

(g) Coordination with other sections. *(1) Sections 704(c)(1)(B) and 737.* (i) In general. If a distribution results in the application of sections 731(c) and one or both of sections 704(c)(1)(B) and 737, the effect of the distribution is determined by applying section 704(c)(1)(B) first, section 731(c) second, and finally section 737.

(ii) Section 704(c)(1)(B). The basis of the distributee partner's interest in the partnership for purposes of determining the amount of gain, if any, recognized by reason of section 731(c) (and for determining the basis of the marketable securities in the hands of the distributee partner) includes the increase or decrease, if any, in the partner's basis that occurs under section 704(c)(1)(B)(iii) as a result of a distribution to another partner of property contributed by the distributee partner in a distribution that is part of the same distribution as the marketable securities.

(iii) Section 737. (A) Marketable securities as other property. A distribution of marketable securities is treated as a distribution of property other than money for purposes of section 737 to the extent that the marketable securities are not treated as money under section 731(c). In addition, marketable securities contributed to the partnership are treated as property other than money in determining the contributing partner's net precontribution gain under section 737(b).

(B) Basis increase under section 737. The basis of the distributee partner's interest in the partnership for purposes of determining the amount of gain, if any, recognized by reason of section 731(c) (and for determining the basis of the marketable securities in the hands of the distributee partner) does not include the increase, if any, in the partner's basis that occurs under section 737(c)(1) as a result of a distribution of property to the distributee partner in a distribution that is part of the same distribution as the marketable securities.

(2) Section 708(b)(1)(B). If a partnership termination occurs under section 708(b)(1)(B), the successor partnership will be treated as if there had been no termination for purposes of section 731(c) and this section. Accordingly, a section 708(b)(1)(B) termination will not affect whether a partnership qualifies for any of the exceptions in paragraphs (d) and (e) of this section. In addition, a deemed distribution that may occur as a result of a section 708(b)(1)(B) termination will not be subject to section 731(c) and this section.

(h) Anti-abuse rule. The provisions of section 731(c) and this section must be applied in a manner consistent with the purpose of section 731(c) and the substance of the transaction. Accordingly, if a principal purpose of a transaction is to achieve a tax result that is inconsistent with the purpose of section 731(c) and this section, the Commissioner can recast the transaction for Federal tax purposes as appropriate to achieve tax results that are consistent with the purpose of section 731(c) and this section. Whether a tax result is inconsistent with the purpose of section 731(c) and this section must be determined based on all the facts and circumstances. For example, under the provisions of this paragraph (h)—

(1) A change in partnership allocations or distribution rights with respect to marketable securities may be treated as a distribution of the marketable securities subject to section 731(c) if the change in allocations or distribution rights is, in substance, a distribution of the securities;

(2) A distribution of substantially all of the assets of the partnership other than marketable securities and money to some partners may also be treated as a distribution of marketable securities to the remaining partners if the distribution of the other property and the withdrawal of the other partners is, in substance, equivalent to a distribution of the securities to the remaining partners; and

(3) The distribution of multiple properties to one or more partners at different times may also be treated as part of a single distribution if the distributions are part of a single plan of distribution.

(i) [Reserved]

(j) Examples. The following examples illustrate the rules of this section. Unless otherwise specified, all securities held by a partnership are marketable securities within the meaning of section 731(c); the partnership holds no marketable securities other than the securities described in the example; all distributions by the partnership are subject to section 731(a) and are not subject to sections 704(c)(1)(B), 707(a)(2)(B), 751(b), or 737; and no securities are eligible for an exception to section 731(c). The examples read as follows:

Example (1). Recognition of gain.

(i) A and B form partnership AB as equal partners. A contributes property with a fair market value of $1,000 and an adjusted tax basis of $250. B contributes $1,000 cash. AB subsequently purchases Security X for $500 and immediately distributes the security to A in a current distribution. The basis in A's interest in the partnership at the time of distribution is $250.

(ii) The distribution of Security X is treated as a distribution of money in an amount equal to the fair market value of Security X on the date of distribution ($500). (The amount of the distribution that is treated as money is not reduced under section 731(c)(3)(B) and paragraph (b) of this section because, if Security X had been sold immediately before the distribution, there would have been no gain recognized by AB and A's distributive share of the gain would therefore have been zero.) As a result, A recognizes $250 of gain under section 731(a)(1) on the distribution ($500 distribution of money less $250 adjusted tax basis in A's partnership interest).

Example (2). Reduction in amount treated as money—in general.

(i) A and B form partnership AB as equal partners. AB subsequently distributes Security X to A in a current distribution. Immediately before the distribution, AB held securities with the following fair market values, adjusted tax bases, and unrecognized gain or loss:

	Value	Basis	Gain (Loss)
Security X	100	70	30
Security Y	100	80	20
Security Z	100	110	(10)

(ii) If AB had sold the securities for fair market value immediately before the distribution to A, the partnership would have recognized $40 of net gain ($30 gain on Security X plus $20 gain on Security Y minus $10 loss on Security Z). A's distributive share of this gain would have been $20 (one-half of $40 net gain). If AB had sold the remaining securities immediately after the distribution of Security X to A, the partnership would have $10 of net gain ($20 of gain on Security Y minus $10 loss on Security Z). A's distributive share of this gain would have been $5 (one-half of $10 net gain). As a result, the distribution resulted in a decrease of $15 in A's distributive share of the net gain in AB's securities ($20 net gain before distribution minus $5 net gain after distribution).

(iii) Under paragraph (b) of this section, the amount of the distribution of Security X that is treated as a distribution of money is reduced by $15. The distribution of Security X is therefore treated as a distribution of $85 of money to A ($100 fair market value of Security X minus $15 reduction).

Example (3). Reduction in amount treated as money—carried interest.

(i) A and B form partnership AB. A contributes $1,000 and provides substantial services to the partnership in exchange for a 60 percent interest in partnership profits. B contributes $1,000 in exchange for a 40 percent interest in partnership profits. AB subsequently distributes Security X to A in a current distribution. Immediately before the distribution, AB held securities with the following fair market values, adjusted tax bases, and unrecognized gain:

	Value	Basis	Gain
Security X	100	80	20
Security Y	100	90	10

(ii) If AB had sold the securities for fair market value immediately before the distribution to A, the partnership would have recognized $30 of net gain ($20 gain on Security X plus $10 gain on Security Y). A's distributive share of this gain would have been $18 (60 percent of $30 net gain). If AB had sold the remaining securities immediately after the distribution of Security X to A, the partnership would have $10 of net gain ($10 gain on Security Y). A's distributive share of this gain would have been $6 (60 percent of $10 net gain). As a result, the distribution resulted in a decrease of $12 in A's distributive share of the net gain in AB's securities ($18 net gain before distribution minus $6 net gain after distribution).

(iii) Under paragraph (b) of this section, the amount of the distribution of Security X that is treated as a distribution of money is reduced by $12. The distribution of Security X is therefore treated as a distribution of $88 of money to A ($100 fair market value of Security X minus $12 reduction).

Example (4). Reduction in amount treated as money—change in partnership allocations.

(i) A is admitted to partnership ABC as a partner with a 1 percent interest in partnership profits. At the time of A's admission, ABC held no securities. ABC subsequently acquires Security X. A's interest in partnership profits is subsequently increased to 2 percent for securities acquired after the increase. A retains a 1 percent interest in all securities acquired before the increase. ABC then acquires Securities Y and Z and later distributes Security X to A in a current distribution. Immediately before the distribution, the securities held by ABC had the following fair market values, adjusted tax bases, and unrecognized gain or loss:

	Value	Basis	Gain (Loss)
Security X	1,000	500	500
Security Y	1,000	800	200
Security Z	1,000	1,100	(100)

(ii) If ABC had sold the securities for fair market value immediately before the distribution to A, the partnership would have recognized $600 of net gain ($500 gain on Security X plus $200 gain on Security Y minus $100 loss on Security Z). A's distributive share of this gain would have been $7 (1 percent of $500 gain on Security X plus 2 percent of $200 gain on Security Y minus 2 percent of $100 loss on Security Z).

(iii) If ABC had sold the remaining securities immediately after the distribution of Security X to A, the partnership would have $100 of net gain ($200 gain on Security Y minus $100 loss on Security Z). A's distributive share of this gain would have been $2 (2 percent of $200 gain on Security Y minus 2 percent of $100 loss on Security Z). As a result, the distribution resulted in a decrease of $5 in A's distributive share of the net gain in ABC's securities ($7 net gain before distribution minus $2 net gain after distribution).

(iv) Under paragraph (b) of this section, the amount of the distribution of Security X that is treated as a distribution of money is reduced by $5. The distribution of Security X is therefore treated as a distribution of $995 of money to A ($1000 fair market value of Security X minus $5 reduction).

Example (5). Basis consequences —distribution of marketable security.

(i) A and B form partnership AB as equal partners. A contributes nondepreciable real property with a fair market value and adjusted tax basis of $100.

(ii) AB subsequently distributes Security X with a fair market value of $120 and an adjusted tax basis of $90 to A in a current distribution. At the time of distribution, the basis in A's interest in the partnership is $100. The amount of the distribution that is treated as money is reduced under section 731(c)(3)(B) and paragraph (b)(2) of this section by $15 (one-half of $30 net gain in Security X). As a result, A recognizes $5 of gain under section 731(a) on the distribution (excess of $105 distribution of money over $100 adjusted tax basis in A's partnership interest).

(iii) A's adjusted tax basis in Security X is $95 ($90 adjusted basis of Security X determined under section 732(a)(1) plus $5 of gain recognized by A by reason of section 731(c)). The basis in A's interest in the partnership is $10 as determined under section 733 ($100 pre-distribution basis minus $90 basis allocated to Security X under section 732).

Example (6). Basis consequences—distribution of marketable security and other property.

(i) A and B form partnership AB as equal partners. A contributes nondepreciable real property, with a fair market value of $100 and an adjusted tax basis of $10.

(ii) AB subsequently distributes Security X with a fair market value and adjusted tax basis of $40 to A in a current distribution and, as part of the same distribution, AB distributes Property Z to A with an adjusted tax basis and fair market value of $40. At the time of distribution, the basis in A's interest in the partnership is $10. A recognizes $30 of gain under section 731(a) on the distribution (excess of $40 distribution of money over $10 adjusted tax basis in A's partnership interest).

(iii) A's adjusted tax basis in Security X is $35 ($5 adjusted basis determined under section 732(a)(2) plus $30 of gain recognized by A by reason of section 731(c)). A's basis in Property Z is $5, as determined under section 732(a)(2). The basis in A's interest in the partnership is $0 as determined under section 733 ($10 pre-distribution basis minus $10 basis allocated between Security X and Property Z under section 732).

(iv) AB's adjusted tax basis in the remaining partnership assets is unchanged unless the partnership has a section 754 election in effect. If AB made such an election, the aggregate basis of AB's assets would be increased by $70 (the difference between the $80 combined basis of Security X and Property Z in the hands of the partnership before the distribution and the $10 combined basis of the distributed property in the hands of A under section 732 after the distribution). Under section 731(c)(5), no adjustment is made to partnership property under section 734 as a result of any gain recognized by A by reason of section 731(c) or as a result of any step-up in basis in the distributed marketable securities in the hands of A by reason of section 731(c).

Example (7). Coordination with section 737.

(i) A and B form partnership AB. A contributes Property A, nondepreciable real property with a fair market value of $200 and an adjusted basis of $100 in exchange for a 25 percent interest in partnership capital and profits. AB owns marketable Security X.

(ii) Within five years of the contribution of Property A, AB subsequently distributes Security X, with a fair market value of $120 and an adjusted tax basis of $100, to A in a current distribution that is subject to section 737. As part of the same distribution, AB distributes Property Y to A with a fair market value of $20 and an adjusted tax basis of $0. At the time of distribution, there has been no change in the fair market value of Property A or the adjusted tax basis in A's interest in the partnership.

(iii) If AB had sold Security X for fair market value immediately before the distribution to A, the partnership would have recognized $20 of gain. A's distributive share of this gain would have been $5 (25 percent of $20 gain). Because AB has no other marketable securities, A's distributive share of gain in partnership securities after the distribution would have been $0. As a result, the distribution resulted in a decrease of $5 in A's share of the net gain in AB's securities ($5 net gain before distribution minus $0 net gain after distribution). Under paragraph (b)(2) of this section, the amount of the distribution of Security X that is treated as a distribution of money is reduced by $5. The distribution of Security X is therefore treated as a distribution of $115 of money to A ($120 fair market value of Security X minus $5 reduction). The portion of the distribution of the marketable security that is not treated as a distribution of money ($5) is treated as other property for purposes of section 737.

(iv) A recognizes total gain of $40 on the distribution. A recognizes $15 of gain under section 731(a)(1) on the distribution of the portion of Security X treated as money ($115 distribution of money less $100 adjusted tax basis in A's partnership interest). A recognizes $25 of gain under section 737 on the distribution of Property Y and the portion of Security X that is not treated as money. A's section 737 gain is equal to the lesser of (i) A's precontribution gain ($100) or (ii) the excess of the fair market value of property received ($20 fair market value of Property Y plus $5 portion of Security X not treated as money) over the adjusted basis in A's interest in the partnership immediately before the distribution ($100) reduced (but not below zero) by the amount of money received in the distribution ($115).

(v) A's adjusted tax basis in Security X is $115 ($100 basis of Security X determined under section 732(a) plus $15 of gain recognized by reason of section 731(c)). A's adjusted tax basis in Property Y is $0 under section 732(a). The basis in A's interest in the partnership is $25 ($100 basis before distribution minus $100 basis allocated to Security X under section 732(a) plus $25 gain recognized under section 737).

(k) Effective date. This section applies to distributions made on or after December 26, 1996. However, taxpayers may apply the rules of this section to distributions made after December 8, 1994, and before December 26, 1996.

T.D. 8707, 12/24/96.

---

§ 1.732-1 Basis of distributed property other than money.

Caution: The Treasury has not yet amended Reg § 1.732-1 to reflect changes made by P.L. 105-34, P.L. 103-465.

(a) Distributions other than in liquidation of a partner's interest. The basis of property (other than money) received by a partner in a distribution from a partnership, other than in liquidation of his entire interest, shall be its adjusted basis to the partnership immediately before such distribution. However, the basis of the property to the partner shall not exceed the adjusted basis of the partner's interest in the partnership, reduced by the amount of any money distributed to him in the same transaction. The provisions of this paragraph may be illustrated by the following examples:

Example (1). Partner A, with an adjusted basis of $15,000 for his partnership interest, receives in a current distribution property having an adjusted basis of $10,000 to the partnership immediately before distribution, and $2,000 cash. The basis of the property in A's hands will be $10,000. Under sections 733 and 705, the basis of A's partnership interest will be reduced by the distribution to $3,000 ($15,000, less $2,000 cash, less $10,000, the basis of the distributed property to A).

Example (2). Partner R has an adjusted basis of $10,000 for his partnership interest. He receives a current distribution of $4,000 cash and property with an adjusted basis to the partnership of $8,000. The basis of the distributed property to partner R is limited to $6,000 ($10,000, the adjusted basis of his interest, reduced by $4,000, the cash distributed).

(b) Distribution in liquidation. Where a partnership distributes property (other than money) in liquidation of a partner's entire interest in the partnership, the basis of such property to the partner shall be an amount equal to the adjusted basis of his interest in the partnership reduced by the amount of any money distributed to him in the same transaction. Application of this rule may be illustrated by the following example:

Example. Partner B, with a partnership interest having an adjusted basis to him of $12,000, retires from the partnership and receives cash of $2,000, and real property with an adjusted basis to the partnership of $6,000 and a fair market value of $14,000. The basis of the real property to B is $10,000 (B's basis for his partnership interest, $12,000, reduced by $2,000, the cash distributed).

(c) Allocation of basis among properties distributed to a partner. *(1) General rule.*

(i) Unrealized receivables and inventory items. The basis to be allocated to properties distributed to a partner under section 732(a)(2) or (b) is allocated first to any unrealized receivables (as defined in section 751(c)) and inventory items (as defined in section 751(d)(2)) in an amount equal to the adjusted basis of each such property to the partnership immediately before the distribution. If the basis to be allocated is less than the sum of the adjusted bases to the partnership of the distributed unrealized receivables and inventory items, the adjusted basis of the distributed property must be decreased in the manner provided in paragraph (c)(2)(i) of this section. See Sec. 1.460-4(k)(2)(iv)(D) for a rule determining the partnership's basis in a long-term contract accounted for under a long-term contract method of accounting.

(ii) Other distributed property. Any basis not allocated to unrealized receivables or inventory items under paragraph (c)(1)(i) of this section is allocated to any other property distributed to the partner in the same transaction by assigning to each distributed property an amount equal to the adjusted basis of the property to the partnership immediately before the distribution. However, if the sum of the adjusted bases to the partnership of such other distributed property does not equal the basis to be allocated among the distributed property, any increase or decrease required to make the amounts equal is allocated among the distributed property as provided in paragraph (c)(2) of this section.

(2) Adjustment to basis allocation. (i) Decrease in basis. Any decrease to the basis of distributed property required under paragraph (c)(1) of this section is allocated first to distributed property with unrealized depreciation in proportion to each property's respective amount of unrealized depreciation before any decrease (but only to the extent of each property's unrealized depreciation). If the required decrease exceeds the amount of unrealized depreciation in the distributed property, the excess is allocated to the distributed property in proportion to the adjusted bases of the distributed property, as adjusted pursuant to the immediately preceding sentence.

(ii) Increase in basis. Any increase to the basis of distributed property required under paragraph (c)(1)(ii) of this section is allocated first to distributed property (other than unrealized receivables and inventory items) with unrealized appreciation in proportion to each property's respective amount of unrealized appreciation before any increase (but only to the extent of each property's unrealized appreciation). If the required increase exceeds the amount of unrealized appreciation in the distributed property, the excess is allocated to the distributed property (other than unrealized receivables or inventory items) in proportion to the fair market value of the distributed property.

(3) Unrealized receivables and inventory items. If the basis to be allocated upon a distribution in liquidation of the partner's entire interest in the partnership is greater than the adjusted basis to the partnership of the unrealized receivables and inventory items distributed to the partner, and if there is no other property distributed to which the excess can be allocated, the distributee partner sustains a capital loss under section 731(a)(2) to the extent of the unallocated basis of the partnership interest.

(4) Examples. The provisions of this paragraph (c) are illustrated by the following examples:

Example (1). A is a one-fourth partner in partnership PRS and has an adjusted basis in its partnership interest of $650. PRS distributes inventory items and Assets X and Y to A in liquidation of A's entire partnership interest. The distributed inventory items have a basis to the partnership of $100 and a fair market value of $200. Asset X has an adjusted basis to the partnership of $50 and a fair market value of $400. Asset Y has an adjusted basis to the partnership and a fair market value of $100. Neither Asset X nor Asset Y consists of inventory items or unrealized receivables. Under this paragraph (c), A's basis in its partnership interest is allocated first to the inventory items in an amount equal to their adjusted basis to the partnership. A, therefore, has an adjusted basis in the inventory items of $100. The remaining basis, $550, is allocated to the distributed property first in an amount equal to the property's adjusted basis to the partnership. Thus, Asset X is allocated $50 and Asset Y is allocated $100. Asset X is then allocated $350, the amount of unrealized appreciation in Asset X. Finally, the remaining basis, $50, is allocated to Assets X and Y in proportion to their fair market values: $40 to Asset X (400/500 × $50), and $10 to Asset Y (100/500 × $50). Therefore, after the distribution, A has an adjusted basis of $440 in Asset X and $110 in Asset Y.

Example (2). B is a one-fourth partner in partnership PRS and has an adjusted basis in its partnership interest of $200. PRS distributes Asset X and Asset Y to B in liquidation of its entire partnership interest. Asset X has an adjusted basis to the partnership and fair market value of $150. Asset Y has an adjusted basis to the partnership of $150 and a fair market value of $50. Neither of the assets consists of inventory items or unrealized receivables. Under this paragraph (c), B's basis is first assigned to the distributed property to the extent of the partnership's basis in each distributed property. Thus, Asset X and Asset Y are each assigned $150. Because the aggregate adjusted basis of the distributed property, $300, exceeds the basis to be allocated, $200, a decrease of $100 in the basis of the distributed property is required. Assets X and Y have unrealized depreciation of zero and $100, respectively. Thus, the entire decrease is allocated to Asset Y. After the distribution, B has an adjusted basis of $150 in Asset X and $50 in Asset Y.

Example (3). C, a partner in partnership PRS, receives a distribution in liquidation of its entire partnership interest of $6,000 cash, inventory items having an adjusted basis to the partnership of $6,000, and real property having an adjusted basis to the partnership of $4,000. C's basis in its partnership interest is $9,000. The cash distribution reduces C's basis to $3,000, which is allocated entirely to the inventory items. The real property has a zero basis in C's hands. The partnership bases not carried over to C for the distributed properties are lost unless an election under section 754 is in effect requiring the partnership to adjust the bases of remaining partnership properties under section 734(b).

Example (4). Assume the same facts as in Example 3 of this paragraph except C receives a distribution in liquidation of its entire partnership interest of $1,000 cash and inventory items having a basis to the partnership of $6,000. The cash distribution reduces C's basis to $8,000, which can be allocated only to the extent of $6,000 to the inventory items. The remaining $2,000 basis, not allocable to the distributed property, constitutes a capital loss to partner C under section 731(a)(2). If the election under section 754 is in effect, see section 734(b) for adjustment of the basis of undistributed partnership property.

(5) Effective date. This paragraph (c) applies to distributions of property from a partnership that occur on or after December 15, 1999.

(d) Special partnership basis to transferee under section 732(d). *(1)* (i) A transfer of a partnership interest occurs upon a sale or exchange of an interest or upon the death of a partner. Section 732(d) provides a special rule for the determination of the basis of property distributed to a transferee partner who acquired any part of his partnership interest in a transfer with respect to which the election under section 754 (relating to the optional adjustment to basis of partnership property) was not in effect.

(ii) Where an election under section 754 is in effect, see section 743(b) and §§ 1.743-1 and 1.732-2.

(iii) If a transferee partner receives a distribution of property (other than money) from the partnership within 2 years after he acquired his interest or part thereof in the partnership by a transfer with respect to which the election under section 754 was not in effect, he may elect to treat as the adjusted partnership basis of such property the adjusted basis such property would have if the adjustment provided in section 743(b) were in effect.

(iv) If an election under section 732(d) is made upon a distribution of property to a transferee partner, the amount of the adjustment with respect to the transferee partner is not diminished by any depletion or depreciation of that portion of the basis of partnership property which arises from the special basis adjustment under section 732(d), since depletion or depreciation on such portion for the period prior to distribution is allowed or allowable only if the optional adjustment under section 743(b) is in effect.

(v) If property is distributed to a transferee partner who elects under section 732(d), and if such property is not the same property which would have had a special basis adjustment, then such special basis adjustment shall apply to any like property received in the distribution, provided that the transferee, in exchange for the property distributed, has relinquished his interest in the property with respect to which he would have had a special basis adjustment. This rule applies whether the property in which the transferee has relinquished his interest is retained or disposed of by the partnership. (For a shift of transferee's basis adjustment under section 743(b) to like property, see § 1.743-1(g).)

(vi) The provisions of this paragraph (d)(1) may be illustrated by the following example:

Example. (i) Transferee partner, T, purchased a one-fourth interest in partnership PRS for $17,000. At the time T purchased the partnership interest, the election under section 754 was not in effect and the partnership inventory had a basis to the partnership of $14,000 and a fair market value of $16,000. T's purchase price reflected $500 of this difference. Thus, $4,000 of the $17,000 paid by T for the partnership interest was attributable to T's share of partnership inventory with a basis of $3,500. Within 2 years after T acquired the partnership interest, T retired from the partnership and received in liquidation of its entire partnership interest the following property:

Assets

	Adjusted basis to PRS	Market value
Cash	$1,500	$1,500
Inventory	3,500	4,000
Asset X	2,000	4,000
Asset Y	4,000	5,000

(ii) The fair market value of the inventory received by T was one-fourth of the fair market value of all partnership inventory and was T's share of such property. It is immaterial whether the inventory T received was on hand when T acquired the interest. In accordance with T's election under section 732(d), the amount of T's share of partnership basis that is attributable to partnership inventory is increased by $500 (one-fourth of the $2,000 difference between the fair market value of the property, $16,000, and its $14,000 basis to the partnership at the time T purchased its interest). This adjustment under section 732(d) applies only for purposes of distributions to T, and not for purposes of partnership depreciation, depletion, or gain or loss on disposition. Thus, the amount to be allocated among the properties received by T in the liquidating distribution is $15,500 ($17,000, T's basis for the partnership interest, reduced by the amount of cash received, $1,500). This amount is allocated as follows: The basis of the inventory items received is $4,000, consisting of the $3,500 common partnership basis, plus the basis adjustment of $500 which T would have had under section 743(b). The remaining basis of $11,500 ($15,500 minus $4,000) is allocated among the remaining property distributed to T by assigning to each property the adjusted basis to the partnership of such property and adjusting that basis by any required increase or decrease. Thus, the adjusted basis to T of Asset X is $5,111 ($2,000, the adjusted basis of Asset X to the partnership, plus $2,000, the amount of unrealized appreciation in Asset X, plus $1,111 ($4,000/$9,000 multiplied by $2,500)). Similarly, the adjusted basis of Asset Y to T is $6,389 ($4,000, the adjusted basis of Asset Y to the partnership, plus $1,000, the amount of unrealized appreciation in Asset Y, plus, $1,389 ($5,000/$9,000 multiplied by $2,500)).

(2) A transferee partner who wishes to elect under section 732(d) shall make the election with his tax return—

(i) For the year of the distribution, if the distribution includes any property subject to the allowance for depreciation, depletion, or amortization, or

(ii) For any taxable year no later than the first taxable year in which the basis of any of the distributed property is pertinent in determining his income tax, if the distribution does not include any such property subject to the allowance for depreciation, depletion or amortization.

(3) A taxpayer making an election under section 732(d) shall submit with the return in which the election is made a schedule setting forth the following:

(i) That under section 732(d) he elects to adjust the basis of property received in a distribution; and

(ii) The computation of the special basis adjustment for the property distributed and the properties to which the adjustment has been allocated. For rules of allocation, see section 755.

(4) A partner who acquired any part of his partnership interest in a transfer to which the election provided in section 754 was not in effect, is required to apply the special basis rule contained in section 732(d) to a distribution to him, whether or not made within 2 years after the transfer, if at the time of his acquisition of the transferred interest—

(i) The fair market value of all partnership property (other than money) exceeded 110 percent of its adjusted basis to the partnership,

(ii) An allocation of basis under section 732(c) upon a liquidation of his interest immediately after the transfer of the interest would have resulted in a shift of basis from property not subject to an allowance for depreciation, depletion, or amortization, to property subject to such an allowance, and

(iii) A basis adjustment under section 743(b) would change the basis to the transferee partner of the property actually distributed.

(5) Required statements. If a transferee partner notifies a partnership that it plans to make the election under section 732(d) under paragraph (d)(3) of this section, or if a partnership makes a distribution to which paragraph (d)(4) of this section applies, the partnership must provide the transferee with such information as is necessary for the transferee properly to compute the transferee's basis adjustments under section 732(d).

(e) Exception. When a partnership distributes unrealized receivables (as defined in section 751(c)) or substantially appreciated inventory items (as defined in section 751(d)) in exchange for any part of a partner's interest in other partnership property (including money), or, conversely, partnership property (including money) other than unrealized receivables or substantially appreciated inventory items in exchange for any part of a partner's interest in the partnership's unrealized receivables or substantially appreciated inventory items, the distribution will be treated as a sale or exchange of property under the provisions of section 751(b). In such case, section 732 (including subsection (d) thereof) applies in determining the partner's basis of the property which he is treated as having sold to or exchanged with the partnership (as constituted after the distribution). The partner is considered as having received such property in a current distribution and, immediately thereafter, as having sold or exchanged it. See section 751(b) and paragraph (b) of § 1.751-1. However, section 732 does not apply in determining the basis of that part of property actually distributed to a partner which is treated as received by him in a sale or exchange under section 751(b). Consequently, the basis of such property shall be its cost to the partner.

T.D. 6175, 5/23/56, amend T.D. 8847, 12/14/99, T.D. 9137, 7/15/2004.

§ 1.732-2 Special partnership basis of distributed property.

(a) Adjustments under section 734(b). In the case of a distribution of property to a partner, the partnership bases of the distributed properties shall reflect any increases or decreases to the basis of partnership property which have been made previously under section 734(b) (relating to the optional adjustment to basis of undistributed partnership property) in connection with previous distributions.

(b) Adjustments under section 743(b). In the case of a distribution of property to a partner who acquired any part of his interest in a transfer as to which an election under section 754 was in effect, then, for the purposes of section 732 (other than subsection (d) thereof), the adjusted partnership bases of the distributed property shall take into account, in addition to any adjustments under section 734(b), the transferee's special basis adjustment for the distributed property under section 743(b). The application of this paragraph may be illustrated by the following example:

Example. Partner D acquired his interest in partnership ABD from a previous partner. Since the partnership had made an election under section 754, a special basis adjustment with respect to D is applicable to the basis of partnership property in accordance with section 743(b). One of the assets of the partnership at the time D acquired his interest was property X, which is later distributed to D in a current distribution. Property X has an adjusted basis to the partnership of $1,000 and with respect to D it has a special basis adjustment of $500. Therefore, for purposes of section 732(a)(1), the adjusted basis of such property to the partnership with respect to D immediately before its distribution is $1,500. However, if property X is distributed to partner A, a nontransferee partner, its adjusted basis to the partnership for purposes of section 732(a)(1) is only $1,000. In such case, D's $500 special basis adjustment may shift over to other property. See § 1.743-1(g).

(c) Adjustments to basis of distributed inventory and unrealized receivables. Under section 732, the basis to be allocated to distributed properties shall be allocated first to any unrealized receivables and inventory items. If the distributee partner is a transferee of a partnership interest and has a special basis adjustment for unrealized receivables or inventory items under either section 743(b) or section 732(d), then the partnership adjusted basis immediately prior to distribution of any unrealized receivables or inventory items distributed to such partner shall be determined as follows: If the distributee partner receives his entire share of the fair market value of the inventory items or unrealized receivables of the partnership, the adjusted basis of such distributed property to the partnership, for the purposes of section 732, shall take into account the entire amount of any special basis adjustment which the distributee partner may have for such assets. If the distributee partner receives less than his entire share of the fair market value of partnership inventory items or unrealized receivables, then, for purposes of section 732, the adjusted basis of such distributed property to the partnership shall take into account the same proportion of the distributee's special basis adjustment for unrealized receivables or inventory items as the value of such items distributed to him bears to his entire share of the total value of all such items of the partnership. The provisions of this paragraph may be illustrated by the following example:

Example. Partner C acquired his 40-percent interest in partnership AC from a previous partner. Since the partnership had made an election under section 754, C has a special basis adjustment to partnership property under section 743(b). C retires from the partnership when the adjusted basis of his partnership interest is $3,000. He receives from the partnership in liquidation of his entire interest, $1,000 cash, certain capital assets, depreciable property, and certain inventory items and unrealized receivables. C has a special basis adjustment of $800 with respect to partnership inventory items and of $200 with respect to unrealized receivables. The common partnership basis for the inventory items distributed to him is $500 and for the unrealized receivables is zero. If the value of inventory items and the unrealized receivables distributed to C in his 40 percent share of the total value of all partnership inventory items and unrealized receivables, then, for purposes of section 732, the adjusted basis of such property in C's hands will be $1,300 for the inventory items ($500 plus $800) and $200 for the unrealized receivables (zero plus $200). The remaining basis of $500, which constitutes the basis of the capital assets and depreciable property distributed to C, is determined as follows: $3,000 (total basis) less $1,000 cash, or $2,000 (the amount to be allocated to the basis of all distributed property), less $1,500 ($800 and $200 special basis adjustments, plus $500 common partnership basis, the amount allocated to inventory items and unrealized receivables). However, if the value of the inventory items and unrealized receivables distributed to C consisted of only 20 percent of the total fair market value of such property (i.e., only one-half of C's 40-percent share), then only only one-half of C's special basis adjustment of $800 for partnership inventory items and $200 for unrealized receivables would be taken into account. In that case, the basis of the inventory items in C's hands would be $650 ($250, the common partnership basis for inventory items distributed to him, plus $400, one-half of C's special basis adjustment for inventory items). The basis of the unrealized receivables in C's hands would be $100 (zero plus $100, one-half of C's special basis adjustment for unrealized receivables).

T.D. 6175, 5/23/56, amend T.D. 8847, 12/14/99.

§ 1.732-3 Corresponding adjustment to basis of assets of a distributed corporation controlled by a corporate partner.

The determination of whether a corporate partner has control of a distributed corporation for purposes of section

732(f) shall be made by applying the special aggregate stock ownership rules of § 1.1502-34.

T.D. 8949, 6/18/2001.

§ 1.733-1 Basis of distributee partner's interest.

In the case of a distribution by a partnership to a partner other than in liquidation of a partner's entire interest, the adjusted basis to such partner of his interest in the partnership shall be reduced (but not below zero) by the amount of any money distributed to such partner and by the amount of the basis to him of distributed property other than money as determined under section 732 and §§ 1.732-1 and 1.732-2.

T.D. 6175, 5/23/56.

§ 1.734-1 Optional adjustment to basis of undistributed partnership property.

Caution: The Treasury has not yet amended Reg § 1.734-1 to reflect changes made by P.L. 108-357, P.L. 98-369.

(a) General rule. A partnership shall not adjust the basis of partnership property as the result of a distribution of property to a partner, unless the election provided in section 754 (relating to optional adjustment to basis of partnership property) is in effect.

(b) Method of adjustment. *(1) Increase in basis.* Where an election under section 754 is in effect and a distribution of partnership property is made, whether or not in liquidation of the partner's entire interest in the partnership, the adjusted basis of the remaining partnership assets shall be increased by—

(i) The amount of any gain recognized under section 731(a)(1) to the distributee partner, or

(ii) The excess of the adjusted basis to the partnership immediately before the distribution of any property distributed (including adjustments under section 743(b) or section 732(d) when applied) over the basis under section 732 (including such special basis adjustments) of such property to the distributee partner.

See § 1.460-4(k)(2)(iv)(D) for a rule determining the partnership's basis in a long-term contract accounted for under a long-term contract method of accounting. The provisions of this paragraph (b)(1) are illustrated by the following examples:

Example (1). Partner A has a basis of $10,000 for his one-third interest in partnership ABC. The partnership has no liabilities and has assets consisting of cash of $11,000 and property with a partnership basis of $19,000 and a value of $22,000. A receives $11,000 in cash in liquidation of his entire interest in the partnership. He has a gain of $1,000 under section 731(a)(1). If the election under section 754 is in effect, the partnership basis for the property becomes $20,000 ($19,000 plus $1,000).

Example (2). Partner D has a basis of $10,000 for his one-third interest in partnership DEF. The partnership balance sheet before the distribution shows the following:

Assets

	Adjusted basis	Value
Cash	$4,000	$ 4,000
Property X	11,000	11,000
Property Y	15,000	18,000
Total	30,000	33,000

Liabilities and Capital

Liabilities	$0	$0
Capital:		
D	10,000	11,000
E	10,000	11,000
F	10,000	11,000
Total	30,000	33,000

In liquidation of his entire interest in the partnership, D received property X with a partnership basis of $11,000. D's basis for property X is $10,000 under section 732(b). Where the election under section 754 is in effect, the excess of $1,000 (the partnership basis before the distribution less D's basis for property X after distribution) is added to the basis of property Y. The basis of property Y becomes $16,000 ($15,000 plus $1,000). If the distribution is made to a transferee partner who elects under section 732(d), see § 1.734-2.

(2) Decrease in basis. Where the election provided in section 754 is in effect and a distribution is made in liquidation of a partner's entire interest, the partnership shall decrease the adjusted basis of the remaining partnership property by—

(i) The amount of loss, if any, recognized under section 731(a)(2) to the distributee partner, or

(ii) The excess of the basis of the distributed property to the distributee, as determined under section 732 (including adjustments under section 743(b) or section 732(d) when applied) over the adjusted basis of such property to the partnership (including such special basis adjustments) immediately before such distribution.

The provisions of this subparagraph may be illustrated by the following examples:

Example (1). Partner G has a basis of $11,000 for his one-third interest in partnership GHI. Partnership assets consist of cash of $10,000 and property with a basis of $23,000 and a value of $20,000. There are no partnership liabilities. In liquidation of his entire interest in the partnership, G receives $10,000 in cash. He has a loss of $1,000 under section 731(a)(2). If the election under section 754 is in effect, the partnership basis for the property becomes $22,000 ($23,000 less $1,000).

Example (2). Partner J has a basis of $11,000 for his one-third interest in partnership JKL. The partnership balance sheet before the distribution shows the following:

Assets

	Adjusted basis	Value
Cash	$5,000	$ 5,000
Property X	10,000	10,000
Property Y	18,000	15,000
Total	33,000	30,000

Liabilities and Capital

Liabilities	$0	$0
Capital:		
J	11,000	10,000
K	11,000	10,000

F	11,000	10,000
Total	33,000	30,000

In liquidation of his entire interest in the partnership, J receives property X with a partnership basis of $10,000. J's basis for property X under section 732(b) is $11,000. Where the election under section 754 is in effect, the excess of $1,000 ($11,000 basis of property X to J, the distributee, less its $10,000 adjusted basis to the partnership immediately before the distribution) decreases the basis of property Y in the partnership. Thus, the basis of property Y becomes $17,000 ($18,000 less $1,000). If the distribution is made to a transferee partner who elects under section 732(d), see § 1.734-2.

(c) Allocation of basis. For allocation among the partnership properties of basis adjustments under section 734(b) and paragraph (b) of this section, see section 755 and § 1.755-1.

(d) Returns. A partnership which must adjust the bases of partnership properties under section 734 shall attach a statement to the partnership return for the year of the distribution setting forth the computation of the adjustment and the partnership properties to which the adjustment has been allocated.

(e) Recovery of adjustments to basis of partnership property. *(1) Increases in basis.* For purposes of section 168, if the basis of a partnership's recovery property is increased as a result of the distribution of property to a partner, then the increased portion of the basis must be taken into account as if it were newly-purchased recovery property placed in service when the distribution occurs. Consequently, any applicable recovery period and method may be used to determine the recovery allowance with respect to the increased portion of the basis. However, no change is made for purposes of determining the recovery allowance under section 168 for the portion of the basis for which there is no increase.

(2) Decreases in basis. For purposes of section 168, if the basis of a partnership's recovery property is decreased as a result of the distribution of property to a partner, then the decrease in basis must be accounted for over the remaining recovery period of the property beginning with the recovery period in which the basis is decreased.

(3) Effective date. This paragraph (e) applies to distributions of property from a partnership that occur on or after December 15, 1999.

T.D. 6175, 5/23/56, amend T.D. 8847, 12/14/99, T.D. 9137, 7/15/2004.

§ 1.734-2 Adjustment after distribution to transferee partner.

(a) In the case of a distribution of property by the partnership to a partner who has obtained all or part of his partnership interest by transfer, the adjustments to basis provided in section 743(b) and section 732(d) shall be taken into account in applying the rules under section 734(b). For determining the adjusted basis of distributed property to the partnership immediately before the distribution where there has been a prior transfer of a partnership interest with respect to which the election provided in section 754 or section 732(d) is in effect, see §§ 1.732-1 and 1.732-2.

(b) *(1)* If a transferee partner, in liquidation of his entire partnership interest, receives a distribution of property (including money) with respect to which he has no special basis adjustment, in exchange for his interest in property with respect to which he has a special basis adjustment, and does not utilize his entire special basis adjustment in determining the basis of the distributed property to him under section 732, the unused special basis adjustment of the distributee shall be applied as an adjustment to the partnership basis of the property retained by the partnership and as to which the distributee did not use his special basis adjustment. The provisions of this subparagraph may be illustrated by the following example:

Example. Upon the death of his father, partner S acquires by inheritance a half-interest in partnership ACS. Partners A and C each have a one-quarter interest. The assets of the partnership consist of $10,000 cash and land used in farming worth $10,000 with a basis of $1,000 to the partnership. Since the partnership had made the election under section 754 at the time of transfer, partner S had a special basis adjustment of $4,500 under section 743(b) with respect to his undivided half-interest in the real estate. The basis of S's partnership interest, in accordance with section 742, is $10,000. S retires from the partnership and receives $10,000 in cash in exchange for his entire interest. Since S has received no part of the real estate, his special basis adjustment of $4,500 will be allocated to the real estate, the remaining partnership property, and will increase its basis to the partnership to $5,500.

(2) The provisions of this paragraph do not apply to the extent that certain distributions are treated as sales or exchanges under section 751(b) (relating to unrealized receivables and substantially appreciated inventory items). See section 751(b) and paragraph (b) of § 1.751-1.

T.D. 6175, 5/23/56.

§ 1.735-1 Character of gain or loss on disposition of distributed property.

Caution: The Treasury has not yet amended Reg § 1.735-1 to reflect changes made by P.L. 98-369.

(a) Sale or exchange of distributed property. *(1) Unrealized receivables.* Any gain realized or loss sustained by a partner on a sale or exchange or other disposition of unrealized receivables (as defined in paragraph (c)(1) of § 1.751-1) received by him in a distribution from a partnership shall be considered gain or loss from the sale or exchange of property other than a capital asset.

(2) Inventory items. Any gain realized or loss sustained by a partner on a sale or exchange of inventory items (as defined in section 751(d)(2)) received in a distribution from a partnership shall be considered gain or loss from the sale or exchange of property other than a capital asset if such inventory items are sold or exchanged within 5 years from the date of the distribution by the partnership. The character of any gain or loss from a sale or exchange by the distributee partner of such inventory items after 5 years from the date of distribution shall be determined as of the date of such sale or exchange by reference to the character of the assets in his hands at that date (inventory items, capital assets, property used in a trade or business, etc.)

(b) Holding period for distributed property. A partner's holding period for property distributed to him by a partnership shall include the period such property was held by the partnership. The provisions of this paragraph do not apply for the purpose of determining the 5-year period described in section 735(a)(2) and paragraph (a)(2) of this section. If the property has been contributed to the partnership by a partner, then the period that the property was held by such partner shall also be included. See section 1223(2). For a partnership's holding period for contributed property, see § 1.723-1.

(c) Effective date. Section 735(a) applies to any property distributed by a partnership to a partner after March 9, 1954. See section 771(b)(2) and paragraph (b)(2) of § 1.771-1. However, see section 771(c).

T.D. 6175, 5/23/56, amend T.D. 6832, 7/6/65.

§ 1.736-1 Payments to a retiring partner or a deceased partner's successor in interest.

Caution: The Treasury has not yet amended Reg § 1.736-1 to reflect changes made by 103-66.

(a) Payments considered as distributive share or guaranteed payment. *(1)* (i) Section 736 and this section apply only to payments made to a retiring partner or to a deceased partner's successor in interest in liquidation of such partner's entire interest in the partnership. See section 761(d). Section 736 and this section do not apply if the estate or other successor in interest of a deceased partner continues as a partner in its own right under local law. Section 736 and this section apply only to payments made by the partnership and not to transactions between the partners. Thus, a sale by partner A to partner B of his entire one-fourth interest in partnership ABCD would not come within the scope of section 736.

(ii) A partner retires when he ceases to be a partner under local law. However, for the purposes of subchapter K, chapter 1 of the Code, a retired partner or a deceased partner's successor will be treated as a partner until his interest in the partnership has been completely liquidated.

(2) When payments (including assumption of liabilities treated as a distribution of money under section 752) are made to a withdrawing partner, that is, a retiring partner or the estate or other successor in interest of a deceased partner, the amounts paid may represent several items. In part, they may represent the fair market value at the time of his death or retirement of the withdrawing partner's interest in all the assets of the partnership (including inventory) unreduced by partnership liabilities. Also, part of such payments may be attributable to his interest in unrealized receivables and part to an arrangement among the partners in the nature of mutual insurance. When a partnership makes such payments, whether or not related to partnership income, to retire the withdrawing partner's entire interest in the partnership, the payments must be allocated between (i) payments for the value of his interest in assets, except unrealized receivables and, under some circumstances, good will (section 736(b)), and (ii) other payments (section 736(a)). The amounts paid for his interest in assets are treated in the same manner as a distribution in complete liquidation under sections 731, 732, and, where applicable, 751. See paragraph (b)(4)(ii) of § 1.751-1. The remaining partners are allowed no deduction for these payments since they represent either a distribution or a purchase of the withdrawing partner's capital interest by the partnership (composed of the remaining partners).

(3) Under section 736(a), the portion of the payments made to a withdrawing partner for his share of unrealized receivables, good will (in the absence of an agreement to the contrary), or otherwise not in exchange for his interest in assets under the rules contained in paragraph (b) of this section will be considered either—

(i) A distributive share of partnership income, if the amount of payment is determined with regard to income of the partnership; or

(ii) A guaranteed payment under section 707(c), if the amount of the payment is determined without regard to income of the partnership.

(4) Payments, to the extent considered as a distributive share of partnership income under section 736(a)(1), are taken into account under section 702 in the income of the withdrawing partner and thus reduce the amount of the distributive shares of the remaining partners. Payments, to the extent considered as guaranteed payments under section 736(a)(2), are deductible by the partnership under section 162(a) and are taxable as ordinary income to the recipient under section 61(a). See section 707(c).

(5) The amount of any payments under section 736(a) shall be included in the income of the recipient for his taxable year with or within which ends the partnership taxable year for which the payment is a distributive share, or in which the partnership is entitled to deduct such amount as a guaranteed payment. On the other hand, payments under section 736(b) shall be taken into account by the recipient for his taxable year in which such payments are made. See paragraph (b)(4) of this section.

(6) A retiring partner or a deceased partner's successor in interest receiving payments under section 736 is regarded as a partner until the entire interest of the retiring or deceased partner is liquidated. Therefore, if one of the members of a 2-man partnership retires under a plan whereby he is to receive payments under section 736, the partnership will not be considered terminated, nor will the partnership year close with respect to either partner, until the retiring partner's entire interest is liquidated, since the retiring partner continues to hold a partnership interest in the partnership until that time. Similarly, if a partner in a 2-man partnership dies, and his estate or other successor in interest receives payments under section 736, the partnership shall not be considered to have terminated upon the death of the partner but shall terminate as to both partners only when the entire interest of the decedent is liquidated. See section 708(b).

(b) Payments for interest in partnership. *(1)* Payments made in liquidation of the entire interest of a retiring partner or deceased partner shall, to the extent made in exchange for such partner's interest in partnership property (except for unrealized receivables and good will as provided in subparagraphs (2) and (3) of this paragraph), be considered as a distribution by the partnership (and not as a distributive share or guaranteed payment under section 736(a)). Generally, the valuation placed by the partners upon a partner's interest in partnership property in an arm's length agreement will be regarded as correct. If such valuation reflects only the partner's net interest in the property (i.e., total assets less liabilities), it must be adjusted so that both the value of the partner's interest in property and the basis for his interest take into account the partner's share of partnership liabilities. Gain or loss with respect to distributions under section 736(b) and this paragraph will be recognized to the distributee to the extent provided in section 731 and, where applicable, section 751.

(2) Payments made to a retiring partner or to the successor in interest of a deceased partner for his interest in unrealized receivables of the partnership in excess of their partnership basis, including any special basis adjustment for them to which such partner is entitled, shall not be considered as made in exchange for such partner's interest in partnership property. Such payments shall be treated as payments under section 736(a) and paragraph (a) of this section. For definition of unrealized receivables, see section 751(c).

(3) For the purposes of section 736(b) and this paragraph, payments made to a retiring partner or to a successor in interest of a deceased partner in exchange for the interest of such partner in partnership property shall not include any amount paid for the partner's share of good will of the partnership in excess of its partnership basis, including any special basis adjustments for it to which such partner is entitled, except to the extent that the partnership agreement provides for a reasonable payment with respect to such good will. Such payments shall be considered as payments under section 736(a). To the extent that the partnership agreement provides for a reasonable payment with respect to good will, such payments shall be treated under section 736(b) and this paragraph. Generally, the valuation placed upon good will by an arm's length agreement of the partners, whether specific in amount or determined by a formula, shall be regarded as correct.

(4) Payments made to a retiring partner or to a successor in interest of a deceased partner for his interest in inventory shall be considered as made in exchange for such partner's interest in partnership property for the purposes of section 736(b) and this paragraph. However, payments for an interest in substantially appreciated inventory items, as defined in section 751(d), are subject to the rules provided in section 751(b) and paragraph (b) of § 1.751-1. The partnership basis in inventory items as to a deceased partner's successor in interest does not change because of the death of the partner unless the partnership has elected the optional basis adjustment under section 754. But see paragraph (b)(3)(iii) of § 1.751-1.

(5) Where payments made under section 736 are received during the taxable year, the recipient must segregate that portion of each such payment which is determined to be in exchange for the partner's interest in partnership property and treated as a distribution under section 736(b) from that portion treated as a distributive share or guaranteed payment under section 736(a). Such allocation shall be made as follows—

(i) If a fixed amount (whether or not supplemented by any additional amounts) is to be received over a fixed number of years, the portion of each payment to be treated as a distribution under section 736(b) for the taxable year shall bear the same ratio to the total fixed agreed payments for such year (as distinguished from the amount actually received) as the total fixed agreed payments under section 736(b) bear to the total fixed agreed payments under section 736(a) and (b). The balance, if any, of such amount received in the same taxable year shall be treated as a distributive share or a guaranteed payment under section 736(a)(1) or (2). However, if the total amount received in any one year is less than the amount considered as a distribution under section 736(b) for that year, then any unapplied portion shall be added to the portion of the payments for the following year or years which are to be treated as a distribution under section 736(b). For example, retiring partner W who is entitled to an annual payment of $6,000 for 10 years for his interest in partnership property, receives only $3,500 in 1955. In 1956, he receives $10,000. Of this amount $8,500 ($6,000 plus $2,500 from 1955) is treated as a distribution under section 736(b) for 1956; $1,500, as a payment under section 736(a).

(ii) If the retiring partner or deceased partner's successor in interest receives payments which are not fixed in amount, such payments shall first be treated as payments in exchange for his interest in partnership property under section 736(b) to the extent of the value of that interest and, thereafter, as payments under section 736(a).

(iii) In lieu of the rules provided in subdivisions (i) and (ii) of this subparagraph, the allocation of each annual payment between section 736(a) and (b) may be made in any manner to which all the remaining partners and the withdrawing partner or his successor in interest agree, provided that the total amount allocated to property under section 736(b) does not exceed the fair market value of such property at the date of death or retirement.

(6) Except to the extent section 751(b) applies, the amount of any gain or loss with respect to payments under section 736(b) for a retiring or deceased partner's interest in property for each year of payment shall be determined under section 731. However, where the total of section 736(b) payments is a fixed sum, a retiring partner or a deceased partner's successor in interest may elect (in his tax return for the first taxable year for which he receives such payments), to report and to measure the amount of any gain or loss by the difference between—

(i) The amount treated as a distribution under section 736(b) in that year, and

(ii) The portion of the adjusted basis of the partner for his partnership interest attributable to such distribution (i.e., the amount which bears the same proportion to the partner's total adjusted basis for his partnership interest as the amount distributed under section 736(b) in that year bears to the total amount to be distributed under section 736(b)).

A recipient who elects under this subparagraph shall attach a statement to his tax return for the first taxable year for which he receives such payments, indicating his election and showing the computation of the gain included in gross income.

(7) The provisions of this paragraph may be illustrated by the following examples:

Example (1). Partnership ABC is a personal service partnership and its balance sheet is as follows:

Assets

	Adjusted basis per books	Market value
Cash	$13,000	$13,000
Unrealized receivables	0	30,000
Capital and section 1231 assets	20,000	23,000
Total	33,000	66,000

Liabilities and Capital

	Per books	Value
Liabilities	$ 3,000	$ 3,000
Capital:		
A	10,000	21,000
B	10,000	21,000
C	10,000	21,000
Total	33,000	66,000

Partner A retires from the partnership in accordance with an agreement whereby his share of liabilities ($1,000) is assumed). In addition he is to receive $9,000 in the year of retirement plus $10,000 in each of the two succeeding years. Thus, the total that A receives for his partnership interest is $30,000 ($29,000 in cash and $1,000 in liabilities assumed). Under the agreement terminating A's interest, the value of A's interest in section 736(b) partnership property is $12,000 (one-third of $36,000, the sum of $13,000 cash and $23,000, the fair market value of capital and section 1231 assets). A's share in unrealized receivables is not included in his interest in partnership property described in section 736(b). Since the basis of A's interest is $11,000 ($10,000 plus $1,000, his share of partnership liabilities), he will realize a capital gain of $1,000 ($12,000 minus $11,000) from the disposition of his interest in partnership property. The remaining $18,000 ($30,000 minus $12,000) will constitute payments under section 736(a)(2) which are taxable to A as guaranteed payments under section 707(c). The payment for the first year is $10,000, consisting of $9,000 in cash, plus $1,000 in liability assumed (section 752(b)). Thus, unless the partners agree otherwise under subparagraph (5)(iii) of this paragraph, each annual payment of $10,000 will be allocated as follows: $6,000 (18,000/30,000 of $10,000) is a section 736(a)(2) payment and $4,000 (12,000/30,000 of $10,000) is a payment for an interest in section 736(b) partnership property. (The partnership may deduct the $6,000 guaranteed payment made to A in each of the 3 years.) The gain on the payments for partnership property will be determined under section 731, as provided in subparagraph (6) of this paragraph. A will treat only $4,000 of each payment as a distribution in a series in liquidation of his entire interest and, under section 731, will have a capital gain of $1,000 when the last payment is made. However, if A so elects, as provided in subparagraph (6) of this paragraph, he may treat such gain as follows: Of each $4,000 payment attributable to A's interest in partnership property, $333 is capital gain (one-third of the total capital gain of $1,000), and $3,667 is a return of capital.

Example (2). Assume the same facts as in example (1) of this subparagraph except that the agreement between the partners provides for payments to A for 3 years of a percentage of annual income instead of a fixed amount. Unless the partners agree otherwise under subparagraph (5)(iii) of this paragraph, all payments received by A up to $12,000 shall be treated under section 736(b) as payments for A's interest in partnership property. His gain of $1,000 will be taxed only after he has received his full basis under section 731. Since the payments are not fixed in amount, the election provided in subparagraph (6) of this paragraph is not available. Any payments in excess of $12,000 shall be treated as a distributive share of partnership income to A under section 736(a)(1).

Example (3). Assume the same facts as in example (1) of this subparagraph except that the partnership agreement provides that the payment for A's interest in partnership property shall include payment for his interest in the good will of the partnership. At the time of A's retirement, the partners determine the value of partnership good will to be $9,000. The value of A's interest in partnership property described in section 736(b) is thus $15,000 (one-third of $45,000, the sum of $13,000 cash, plus $23,000, the value of capital and section 1231 assets, plus $9,000 good will). From the disposition of his interest in partnership property, A will realize a capital gain of $4,000 ($15,000, minus $11,000) the basis of his interest. The remaining $15,000 ($30,000 minus $15,000) will constitute payments under section 736(a)(2) which are taxable to A as guaranteed payments under section 707(c).

Example (4). Assume the same facts as in example (1) of this subparagraph except that the capital and section 1231 assets consist of an item of section 1245 property (as defined in section 1245(a)(3)). Assume further that under paragraph (c)(4) of § 1.751-1 the section 1245 property is an unrealized receivable to the extent of $2,000. Therefore, the value of A's interest in section 736(b) partnership property is only $11,333 (one-third of $34,000, the sum of $13,000 cash and $21,000, the fair market value of section 1245 property to the extent not an unrealized receivable). From the disposition of his interest in partnership property, A will realize a capital gain of $333 ($11,333 minus $11,000, the basis of his interest). The remaining $18,667 ($30,000 minus $11,333) will constitute payments under section 736(a)(2) which are taxable to A as guaranteed payments under section 707(c).

(c) Cross reference. See section 753 for treatment of payments under section 736(a) as income in respect of a decedent under section 691.

T.D. 6175, 5/23/56, amend T.D. 6832, 7/6/65.

§ 1.737-1 Recognition of precontribution gain.

Caution: The Treasury has not yet amended Reg § 1.737-1 to reflect changes made by P.L. 105-34.

(a) Determination of gain. *(1) In general.* A partner that receives a distribution of property (other than money) must recognize gain under section 737 and this section in an amount equal to the lesser of the excess distribution (as defined in paragraph (b) of this section) or the partner's net precontribution gain (as defined in paragraph (c) of this section). Gain recognized under section 737 and this section is in addition to any gain recognized under section 731.

(2) Transactions to which section 737 applies. Section 737 and this section apply only to the extent that a distribution by a partnership is a distribution to a partner acting in the capacity of a partner within the meaning of section 731, except that section 737 and this section do not apply to the extent that section 751(b) applies to the distribution.

(b) Excess distribution. *(1) Definition.* The excess distribution is the amount (if any) by which the fair market value of the distributed property (other than money) exceeds the distributee partner's adjusted tax basis in the partner's partnership interest.

(2) Fair market value of property. The fair market value of the distributed property is the price at which the property would change hands between a willing buyer and a willing seller at the time of the distribution, neither being under any compulsion to buy or sell and both having reasonable knowledge of the relevant facts. The fair market value that a partnership assigns to distributed property will be regarded as correct, provided that the value is reasonably agreed to among the partners in an arm's-length negotiation and the partners have sufficiently adverse interests.

(3) Distributee partner's adjusted tax basis. (i) General rule. In determining the amount of the excess distribution, the distributee partner's adjusted tax basis in the partnership interest includes any basis adjustment resulting from the distribution that is subject to section 737 (for example, adjustments required under section 752) and from any other distribution or transaction that is part of the same distribution, except for—

(A) The increase required under section 737(c)(1) for the gain recognized by the partner under section 737; and

(B) The decrease required under section 733(2) for any property distributed to the partner other than property previously contributed to the partnership by the distributee partner. See § 1.704-4(e)(1) for a rule in the context of section 704(c)(1)(B). See also § 1.737-3(b)(2) for a special rule for determining a partner's adjusted tax basis in distributed property previously contributed by the partner to the partnership.

(ii) Advances or drawings. The distributee partner's adjusted tax basis in the partnership interest is determined as of the last day of the partnership's taxable year if the distribution to which section 737 applies is properly characterized as an advance or drawing against the partner's distributive share of income. See § 1.731-1(a)(1)(ii).

(c) Net precontribution gain. *(1) General rule.* The distributee partner's net precontribution gain is the net gain (if any) that would have been recognized by the distributee partner under section 704(c)(1)(B) and § 1.704-4 if all property that had been contributed to the partnership by the distributee partner within five years of the distribution and is held by the partnership immediately before the distribution had been distributed by the partnership to another partner other than a partner who owns, directly or indirectly, more than 50 percent of the capital or profits interest in the partnership. See § 1.704-4 for provisions determining a contributing partner's gain or loss under section 704(c)(1)(B) on an actual distribution of contributed section 704(c) property to another partner.

(2) Special rules. (i) Property contributed on or before October 3, 1989. Property contributed to the partnership on or before October 3, 1989, is not taken into account in determining a partner's net precontribution gain. See § 1.704-4(c)(1) for a similar rule in the context of section 704(c)(1)(B).

(ii) Section 734(b)(1)(A) adjustments. For distributions to a distributee partner of money by a partnership with a section 754 election in effect that are part of the same distribution as the distribution of property subject to section 737, for purposes of paragraph (a) and (c)(1) of this section the distributee partner's net precontribution gain is reduced by the basis adjustments (if any) made to section 704(c) property contributed by the distributee partner under section 734(b)(1)(A). See § 1.737-3(c)(4) for rules regarding basis adjustments for partnerships with a section 754 election in effect.

(iii) Transfers of a partnership interest. The transferee of all or a portion of a contributing partner's partnership interest succeeds to the transferor's net precontribution gain, if any, in an amount proportionate to the interest transferred. See § 1.704-3(a)(7) and § 1.704-4(d)(2) for similar provisions in the context of section 704(c)(1)(A) and section 704(c)(1)(B).

(iv) Section 704(c)(1)(B) gain recognized in related distribution. A distributee partner's net precontribution gain is determined after taking into account any gain or loss recognized by the partner under section 704(c)(1)(B) and § 1.704-4 (or that would have been recognized by the partner except for the like-kind exception in section 704(c)(2) and § 1.704-4(d)(3)) on an actual distribution to another partner of section 704(c) property contributed by the distributee partner that is part of the same distribution as the distribution to the distributee partner.

(v) Section 704(c)(2) disregarded. A distributee partner's net precontribution gain is determined without regard to the provisions of section 704(c)(2) and § 1.704-4(d)(3) in situations in which the property contributed by the distributee partner is not actually distributed to another partner in a distribution related to the section 737 distribution.

(d) Character of gain. The character of the gain recognized by the distributee partner under section 737 and this section is determined by, and is proportionate to, the character of the partner's net precontribution gain. For this purpose, all gains and losses on section 704(c) property taken into account in determining the partner's net precontribution gain are netted according to their character. Character is determined at the partnership level for this purpose, and any character with a net negative amount is disregarded. The character of the partner's gain under section 737 is the same as, and in proportion to, any character with a net positive amount. Character for this purpose is determined as if the section 704(c) property had been sold by the partnership to an unrelated third party at the time of the distribution and includes any item that would have been taken into account separately by the contributing partner under section 702(a) and § 1.702-1(a).

(e) Examples. The following examples illustrate the provisions of this section. Unless otherwise specified, partnership income equals partnership expenses (other than depreciation deductions for contributed property) for each year of the partnership, the fair market value of partnership property does not change, all distributions by the partnership are subject to section 737, and all partners are unrelated.

Example (1). Calculation of excess distribution and net precontribution gain.

(i) On January 1, 1995, A, B, and C form partnership ABC as equal partners. A contributes Property A, depreciable real property with a fair market value of $30,000 and an adjusted tax basis of $20,000. B contributes Property B, nondepreciable real property with a fair market value and adjusted tax basis of $30,000. C contributes $30,000 cash.

(ii) Property A has 10 years remaining on its cost recovery schedule and is depreciated using the straight-line method. The partnership uses the traditional method for allocating items under section 704(c) described in § 1.704-3(b)(1) for Property A. The partnership has book depreciation of $3,000 per year (10 percent of the $30,000 book basis in Property A) and each partner is allocated $1,000 of book depreciation per year (one-third of the total annual book depreciation of $3,000). The partnership also has tax depreciation of $2,000 per year (10 percent of the $20,000 adjusted tax basis in Property A). This $2,000 tax depreciation is allocated equally between B and C, the noncontributing partners with respect to Property A.

(iii) At the end of 1997, the book value of Property A is $21,000 ($30,000 initial book value less $9,000 aggregate book depreciation) and its adjusted tax basis is $14,000 ($20,000 initial tax basis less $6,000 aggregate tax depreciation).

(iv) On December 31, 1997, Property B is distributed to A in complete liquidation of A's partnership interest. The adjusted tax basis of A's partnership interest at that time is $20,000. The amount of the excess distribution is $10,000, the difference between the fair market value of the distributed Property B ($30,000) and A's adjusted tax basis in A's partnership interest ($20,000). A's net precontribution gain is $7,000, the difference between the book value of Property A ($21,000) and its adjusted tax basis at the time of the distribution ($14,000). A recognizes gain of $7,000 on the distribution, the lesser of the excess distribution and the net precontribution gain.

Example (2). Determination of distributee partner's basis.

(i) On January 1, 1995, A, B, and C form general partnership ABC as equal partners. A contributes Property A, nondepreciable real property with a fair market value of $10,000 and an adjusted tax basis of $4,000. B and C each contributes $10,000 cash.

(ii) The partnership purchases Property B, nondepreciable real property with a fair market value of $9,000, subject to a

$9,000 nonrecourse liability. This nonrecourse liability is allocated equally among the partners under section 752, increasing A's adjusted tax basis in A's partnership interest from $4,000 to $7,000.

(iii) On December 31, 1998, A receives $2,000 cash and Property B, subject to the $9,000 liability, in a current distribution.

(iv) In determining the amount of the excess distribution, the adjusted tax basis of A's partnership interest is adjusted to take into account the distribution of money and the shift in liabilities. A's adjusted tax basis is therefore increased to $11,000 for this purpose ($7,000 initial adjusted tax basis, less $2,000 distribution of money, less $3,000 (decrease in A's share of the $9,000 partnership liability), plus $9,000 (increase in A's individual liabilities)). As a result of this basis adjustment, the adjusted tax basis of A's partnership interest ($11,000) is greater than the fair market value of the distributed property ($9,000) and therefore, there is no excess distribution. A recognizes no gain under section 737.

Example (3). Net precontribution gain reduced for gain recognized under section 704(c)(1)(B).

(i) On January 1, 1995, A, B, and C form partnership ABC as equal partners. A contributes Properties A1 and A2, nondepreciable real properties located in the United States each with a fair market value of $10,000 and an adjusted tax basis of $6,000. B contributes Property B, nondepreciable real property located outside the United States, with a fair market value and adjusted tax basis of $20,000. C contributes $20,000 cash.

(ii) On December 31, 1998, Property B is distributed to A in complete liquidation of A's interest and, as part of the same distribution, Property A1 is distributed to B in a current distribution.

(iii) A's net precontribution gain before the distribution is $8,000 ($20,000 fair market value of Properties A1 and A2 less $12,000 adjusted tax basis of such properties). A recognizes $4,000 of gain under section 704(c)(1)(B) and § 1.704-4 on the distribution of Property A1 to B ($10,000 fair market value of Property A1 less $6,000 adjusted tax basis of Property A1). This gain is taken into account in determining A's excess distribution and net precontribution gain. As a result, A's net precontribution gain is reduced from $8,000 to $4,000, and the adjusted tax basis in A's partnership interest is increased by $4,000 to $16,000.

(iv) A recognizes gain of $4,000 on the receipt of Property B under section 737, an amount equal to the lesser of the excess distribution of $4,000 ($20,000 fair market value of Property B less $16,000 adjusted tax basis of A's interest in the partnership) and A's remaining net precontribution gain of $4,000.

Example (4). Character of gain.

(i) On January 1, 1995, A, B, and C form partnership ABC as equal partners. A contributes the following nondepreciable property to the partnership:

	Fair Market Value	Adjusted Tax Basis
Property A1	$30,000	$20,000
Property A2	30,000	38,000
Property A3	10,000	9,000

(ii) The character of gain or loss on Property A1 and Property A2 is long-term, U.S.-source capital gain or loss. The character of gain on Property A3 is long-term, foreign-source capital gain. B contributes Property B, nondepreciable real property with a fair market value and adjusted tax basis of $70,000. C contributes $70,000 cash.

(iii) On December 31, 1998, Property B is distributed to A in complete liquidation of A's interest in the partnership. A recognizes $3,000 of gain under section 737, an amount equal to the excess distribution of $3,000 ($70,000 fair market value of Property B less $67,000 adjusted tax basis in A's partnership interest) and A's net precontribution gain of $3,000 ($70,000 aggregate fair market value of properties contributed by A less $67,000 aggregate adjusted tax basis of such properties).

(iv) In determining the character of A's gain, all gains and losses on property taken into account in determining A's net precontribution gain are netted according to their character and allocated to A's recognized gain under section 737 based on the relative proportions of the net positive amounts. U.S.-source and foreign-source gains must be netted separately because A would have been required to take such gains into account separately under section 702. As a result, A's net precontribution gain of $3,000 consists of $2,000 of net long-term, U.S.-source capital gain ($10,000 gain on Property A1 and $8,000 loss on Property A2) and $1,000 of net long-term, foreign-source capital gain ($1,000 gain on Property A3).

(v) The character of A's gain under paragraph (d) of this section is therefore $2,000 long-term, U.S.-source capital gain ($3,000 gain recognized under section 737 × $2,000 net long-term, U.S.-source capital gain/$3,000 total net precontribution gain) and $1,000 long-term, foreign-source capital gain ($3,000 gain recognized under section 737 x $1,000 net long-term, foreign-source capital gain/$3,000 total net precontribution gain).

T.D. 8642, 12/22/95.

PAR. 4. Section 1.737-1(c)(1) is amended by removing the phrase "five years" and adding in its place the phrase "seven years".

Proposed § 1.737-1 [*For Preamble, see ¶ 152,903*]

§ 1.737-2 Exceptions and special rules.

Caution: The Treasury has not yet amended Reg § 1.737-2 to reflect changes made by P.L. 105-34.

(a) Section 708(b)(1)(B) terminations. Section 737 and this section do not apply to the deemed distribution of interests in a new partnership caused by the termination of a partnership under section 708(b)(1)(B). A subsequent distribution of property by the new partnership to a partner of the new partnership that was formerly a partner of the terminated partnership is subject to section 737 to the same extent that a distribution from the terminated partnership would have been subject to section 737. See also § 1.704-4(c)(3) for a similar rule in the context of section 704(c)(1)(B). This paragraph (a) applies to terminations of partnerships under section 708(b)(1)(B) occurring on or after May 9, 1997; however, this paragraph (a) may be applied to terminations occurring on or after May 9, 1996, provided that the partnership and its partners apply this paragraph (a) to the termination in a consistent manner.

(b) Transfers to another partnership. *(1) Complete transfer.* Section 737 and this section do not apply to a transfer by a partnership (transferor partnership) of all of its assets and liabilities to a second partnership (transferee partnership) in an exchange described in section 721, followed by a distribution of the interest in the transferee partnership in liquidation of the transferor partnership as part of the same plan or arrangement. See § 1.704-4(c)(4) for a similar rule in the context of section 704(c)(1)(B).

(2) Certain divisive transactions. Section 737 and this section do not apply to a transfer by a partnership (transferor partnership) of all of the section 704(c) property contributed by a partner to a second partnership (transferee partnership) in an exchange described in section 721, followed by a distribution as part of the same plan or arrangement of an interest in the transferee partnership (and no other property) in complete liquidation of the interest of the partner that originally contributed the section 704(c) property to the transferor partnership.

(3) Subsequent distributions. A subsequent distribution of property by the transferee partnership to a partner of the transferee partnership that was formerly a partner of the transferor partnership is subject to section 737 to the same extent that a distribution from the transferor partnership would have been subject to section 737.

(c) Incorporation of a partnership. Section 737 and this section do not apply to an incorporation of a partnership by any method of incorporation (other than a method involving an actual distribution of partnership property to the partners followed by a contribution of that property to a corporation), provided that the partnership is liquidated as part of the incorporation transaction. See § 1.704-4(c)(5) for a similar rule in the context of section 704(c)(1)(B).

(d) Distribution of previously contributed property. *(1) General rule.* Any portion of the distributed property that consists of property previously contributed by the distributee partner (previously contributed property) is not taken into account in determining the amount of the excess distribution or the partner's net precontribution gain. The previous sentence applies on or after May 9, 1997. See § 1.737-3(b)(2) for a special rule for determining the basis of previously contributed property in the hands of a distributee partner who contributed the property to the partnership.

(2) Limitation for distribution of previously contributed interest in an entity. An interest in an entity previously contributed to the partnership is not treated as previously contributed property to the extent that the value of the interest is attributable to property contributed to the entity after the interest was contributed to the partnership. The preceding sentence does not apply to the extent that the property contributed to the entity was contributed to the partnership by the partner that also contributed the interest in the entity to the partnership.

(3) Nonrecognition transactions, installment sales, contributed contracts, and capitalized costs. (i) Nonrecognition transactions. Property received by the partnership in exchange for contributed section 704(c) property in a nonrecognition transaction is treated as the contributed property with regard to the contributing partner for purposes of section 737 to the extent that the property received is treated as section 704(c) property under § 1.704-3(a)(8). See § 1.704-4(d)(1) for a similar rule in the context of section 704(c)(1)(B).

(ii) Installment sales. An installment obligation received by the partnership in an installment sale (as defined in section 453(b)) of section 704(c) property is treated as the contributed property with regard to the contributing partner for purposes of section 737 to the extent that the installment obligation received is treated as section 704(c) property under § 1.704-3(a)(8). See § 1.704-4(d)(1) for a similar rule in the context of section 704(c)(1)(B).

(iii) Contributed contracts. Property acquired by a partnership pursuant to a contract that is section 704(c) property is treated as the contributed property with regard to the contributing partner for purposes of section 737 to the extent that the acquired property is treated as section 704(c) property under § 1.704-3(a)(8). See § 1.704-4(d)(1) for a similar rule in the context of section 704(c)(1)(B).

(iv) Capitalized costs. Property to which the cost of section 704(c) property is properly capitalized is treated as section 704(c) property for purposes of section 737 to the extent that such property is treated as section 704(c) property under § 1.704-3(a)(8)(iv). See § 1.704-4(d)(1) for a similar rule in the context of section 704(c)(1)(B).

(4) Undivided interests. The distribution of an undivided interest in property is treated as the distribution of previously contributed property to the extent that the undivided interest does not exceed the undivided interest, if any, contributed by the distributee partner in the same property. See § 1.704-4(c)(6) for the application of section 704(c)(1)(B) in a similar context. The portion of the undivided interest in property retained by the partnership after the distribution, if any, that is treated as contributed by the distributee partner, is reduced to the extent of the undivided interest distributed to the distributee partner.

(e) Examples. The following examples illustrate the rules of this section. Unless otherwise specified, partnership income equals partnership expenses (other than depreciation deductions for contributed property) for each year of the partnership, the fair market value of partnership property does not change, all distributions by the partnership are subject to section 737, and all partners are unrelated.

Example (1). Distribution of previously contributed property.

(i) On January 1, 1995, A, B, and C form partnership ABC as equal partners. A contributes the following nondepreciable real property to the partnership:

	Fair Market Value	Adjusted Tax Basis
Property A1	$20,000	$10,000
Property A2	10,000	6,000

(ii) A's total net precontribution gain on the contributed property is $14,000 ($10,000 on Property A1 plus $4,000 on Property A2). B contributes $10,000 cash and Property B, nondepreciable real property with a fair market value and adjusted tax basis of $20,000. C contributes $30,000 cash.

(iii) On December 31, 1998, Property A2 and Property B are distributed to A in complete liquidation of A's interest in the partnership. Property A2 was previously contributed by A and is therefore not taken into account in determining the amount of the excess distribution or A's net precontribution gain. The adjusted tax basis of Property A2 in the hands of A is also determined under section 732 as if that property were the only property distributed to A.

(iv) As a result of excluding Property A2 from these determinations, the amount of the excess distribution is $10,000 ($20,000 fair market value of distributed Property B less $10,000 adjusted tax basis in A's partnership interest). A's net precontribution gain is also $10,000 ($14,000 total net precontribution gain less $4,000 gain with respect to previously contributed Property A2). A therefore recognizes $10,000 of gain on the distribution, the lesser of the excess distribution and the net precontribution gain.

Example (2). Distribution of a previously contributed interest in an entity.

(i) On January 1, 1995, A, B, and C form partnership ABC as equal partners. A contributes Property A, nondepreciable real property with a fair market value of $10,000 and an adjusted tax basis of $5,000, and all of the stock of Corporation X with a fair market value and adjusted tax basis of $500. B contributes $500 cash and Property B, nondepreciable real property with a fair market value and adjusted tax basis of $10,000. Partner C contributes $10,500 cash. On December 31, 1996, ABC contributes Property B to Corporation X in a nonrecognition transaction under section 351.

(ii) On December 31, 1998, all of the stock of Corporation X is distributed to A in complete liquidation of A's interest in the partnership. The stock is treated as previously contributed property with respect to A only to the extent of the $500 fair market value of the Corporation X stock contributed by A. The fair market value of the distributed stock for purposes of determining the amount of the excess distribution is therefore $10,000 ($10,500 total fair market value of Corporation X stock less $500 portion treated as previously contributed property). The $500 fair market value and adjusted tax basis of the Corporation X stock is also not taken into account in determining the amount of the excess distribution and the net precontribution gain.

(iii) A recognizes $5,000 of gain under section 737, the amount of the excess distribution ($10,000 fair market value of distributed property less $5,000 adjusted tax basis in A's partnership interest) and A's net precontribution gain ($10,000 fair market value of Property A less $5,000 adjusted tax basis in Property A).

Example (3). Distribution of undivided interest in property.

(i) On January 1, 1995, A and B form partnership AB as equal partners. A contributes $500 cash and an undivided one-half interest in Property X. B contributes $500 cash and an undivided one-half interest in Property X.

(ii) On December 31, 1998, an undivided one-half interest in Property X is distributed to A in a current distribution. The distribution of the undivided one-half interest in Property X is treated as a distribution of previously contributed property because A contributed an undivided one-half interest in Property X. As a result, A does not recognize any gain under section 737 on the distribution.

T.D. 8642, 12/22/95, amend T.D. 8717, 5/8/97, T.D. 9193, 3/21/2005, T.D. 9207, 5/23/2005.

PAR. 5. Section 1.737-2 is amended as follows:

1. Paragraph (b) is revised.
2. Paragraph (e) is redesignated as paragraph (f).
3. New paragraph (e) is added.

The addition and revision read as follows:

Proposed § 1.737-2 Exceptions and special rules. [*For Preamble, see ¶ 152,903*]

* * * * *

(b) Transfers to another partnership. *(1) Complete transfer to another partnership (Assets-over merger).* (i) In General. Section 737 and this section do not apply to a transfer in an assets-over merger as defined in § 1.708-1(c)(3) by a partnership (the transferor partnership, which is considered to be the terminated partnership as a result of the merger) of all of its assets and liabilities to another partnership (the transferee partnership, which is considered to be the resulting partnership after the merger) followed by a distribution of the interest in the transferee partnership in liquidation of the transferor partnership as part of the same plan or arrangement.

(ii) Subsequent distributions. (A) Original section 704(c) gain. If, immediately before the assets-over merger, the transferor partnership holds property that has original built-in gain (as defined in § 1.704-4(c)(4)(ii)(A)), the seven year period in section 737(b) does not restart with respect to such gain as a result of the transfer of such section 704(c) property to the transferee partnership. A subsequent distribution of other property by the transferee partnership to the partner who contributed the original section 704(c) gain property to the transferor partnership is only subject to section 737 with respect to the original section 704(c) gain if the distribution occurs within seven years of the time such property was contributed to the transferor partnership. See § 1.704-4(c)(4)(ii)(A) for a similar provision in the context of section 704. See § 1.737-1 for post-merger distribution of property contributed to the transferee partnership prior to the merger.

(B) New section 704(c) gain. Except as provided in paragraph (b)(1)(ii)(E) of this section, if new built-in gain is created upon the contribution of assets by the transferor partnership to the transferee partnership, a subsequent distribution by the transferee partnership of property to a partner of the transferee partnership (other than property deemed contributed by such partner) is subject to section 737, if such distribution occurs within seven years of the contribution by the transferor partnership to the transferee partnership. For these purposes, a partner of the transferor partnership is deemed to have contributed to the transferee partnership an undivided interest in the property of the transferor partnership. The determination of the partner's undivided interest for this purpose shall be determined by the transferor partnership using any reasonable method. See § 1.704-4(c)(4)(ii)(B) for a similar provision in the context of section 704.

(C) Ordering Rule. For purposes of this section, if a partner is required to recognize gain under this section, the partner shall recognize a proportionate amount of original and new section 704(c) gain.

(D) Subsequent Mergers. If the transferee partnership (first transferee partnership) is subsequently merged into another partnership (new transferee partnership) the section 704(c) gain that resulted from the merger of the transferor partnership into the first transferee partnership shall be subject to section 737 for seven years from the time of the contribution by the transferor partnership to the first transferee partnership (original merger) and section 704(c) gain that resulted from the merger of the first transferee partnership into the new transferee partnership shall be subject to section 737 for seven years from the time of the contribution by the first transferee partnership to the new transferee partnership (subsequent merger). See § 1.704-4(c)(4)(ii)(D) for a similar rule in the context of section 704.

(E) Identical Ownership or De Minimis Change in Ownership.

For purposes of section 737(b) and this section, net precontribution gain does not include new section 704(c) gain in property transferred by the transferor partnership to the transferee partnership if both the transferor partnership and the transferee partnership are owned by the same owners in the same proportions or if the difference in ownership is de minimis. The transferor partnership and the transferee partnership are owned by the same owners in the same proportions if each partner owns identical interests in book capital and each item of income, gain, loss, deduction, and credit, and identical shares of distributions and liabilities in each of the transferor and transferee partnerships. A difference in ownership is de minimis if ninety-seven percent of interests in book capital and each item of income, gain, loss, deduction and credit and shares in distributions and liabilities of the transferor partnership and transferee partnership are owned by the same owners in the same proportions. See § 1.704-4(c)(4)(ii)(E) for a similar provision in the context of section 704.

(F) Examples. The following examples illustrate the rules of paragraph (b)(3) of this section.

Example (1). No net precontribution gain. (i) Facts. On January 1, 2005, A contributes Asset 1, with a basis of $200x and a fair market value of $300x, to partnership PRS1 in exchange for a 50 percent interest. On the same date, B contributes $300x of cash to PRS1 in exchange for a 50 percent interest. Also on January 1, 2005, C contributes Asset 2, with a basis of $100x and a fair market value of $200x, to partnership PRS2 in exchange for a 50 percent interest. D contributes $200x of cash to PRS2 in exchange for a 50 percent interest. On January 1, 2008, PRS1 and PRS2 undertake an assets-over partnership merger in which PRS1 is the continuing partnership and PRS2 is the terminating partnership for both state law and federal tax purposes. At the time of the merger, PRS1's only assets are Asset 1, with a fair market value of $900x, and $300x in cash. PRS2's only assets are Asset 2, with a fair market value of $600x and $200x in cash. After the merger, the partners have capital and profits interests in PRS1 as follows: A, 30 percent; B, 30 percent; C, 20 percent; and D, 20 percent. PRS1 and PRS2 both have provisions in their respective partnership agreements requiring the revaluation of partnership property upon entry of a new partner. PRS1 would not be treated as an investment company (within the meaning of section 351) if it were incorporated. Neither partnership holds any unrealized receivables or inventory for purposes of section 751. In addition, neither partnership has a section 754 election in place. Asset 1 and Asset 2 are nondepreciable capital assets. On January 1, 2013, PRS1 has the same assets that it had after the merger. Each asset has the same value that it had at the time of the merger. On this date, PRS1 distributes Asset 2 to A in liquidation of A's interest.

(ii) Analysis. Section 737(a) requires A to recognize gain when it receives a distribution of property in an amount equal to the lesser of the excess distribution or the partner's net precontribution gain. The distribution of Asset 2 to A results in an excess distribution of $400x ($600x fair market value of Asset 2-$200x adjusted basis in A's partnership interest). However, the distribution of Asset 2 to A occurs more than seven years after the contribution by A of Asset 1 to PRS1 and A made no subsequent contributions to PRS1. Therefore, A's net precontribution gain for purposes of section 737(b) at the time of the distribution is zero. The $600x of reverse section 704(c) gain in Asset 1, resulting from a revaluation of PRS1's partnership property at the time of the merger, is not net precontribution gain (see § 1.737-2(e)). Accordingly, A will not recognize gain under section 737 as a result of the distribution of Asset 2. See § 1.704-4(c)(4)(ii)(F), Example (1) for a similar example under section 704.

Example (2). Revaluation gain and merger gain. (i) Facts. The facts are the same as Example (1), except that on January 1, 2007, E joins PRS2 as a one-third partner for $250x in cash. At the time E joins the partnership, Asset 2 has a fair market value of $300x. On January 1, 2008, PRS2 merges into PRS1. At the time of the merger, Asset 1 and Asset 2 both have a fair market value of $400x. On January 1, 2011, Asset 1 is distributed to C when its value is $275x.

(ii) Analysis. Section 737(a) requires A to recognize gain when it receives a distribution of property in an amount equal to the lesser of the excess distribution or the partner's net precontribution gain. The distribution of Asset 1 to C results in an excess distribution of $175x ($275x fair market value of Asset 1-$100x adjusted basis in C's partnership interest). The distribution of Asset 1 to C occurs within seven years of the original contribution of Asset 2 by C to PRS2. Therefore, C's net precontribution gain at the time of the distribution is $183.33x, which includes C's original section 704(c) gain from the contribution of Asset 2 to PRS2 of $100x plus C's share of new section 704(c) gain of $83.33x ($50x of reverse section 704(c) gain upon the admission of E, plus $33.33x of additional section 704(c) gain upon merger). C's excess distribution is less than C's net precontribution gain. Thus, C will recognize $175x of gain upon receipt of Asset 1 in accordance with section 737(a). See § 1.704-4(c)(4)(ii)(F), Example (2) for a similar example under section 704.

Example (3). Fluctuations in the value of an asset. (i) Facts. The facts are the same as Example (1), except that on January 1, 2011, Asset 1 is distributed to C when its fair market value is $300x. Immediately prior to the distribution, PRS1 revalues its property in accordance with § 1.704-1(b)(2)(iv)(f).

(ii) Analysis. The distribution of Asset 1 to C occurs within seven years of the original contribution of Asset 2 by C to PRS2 and within seven years of the date of the merger. Therefore, C's net precontribution gain at the time of the distribution equals $300x ($100x of original section 704(c) gain from the contribution of Asset 2 to PRS2 and $200x of new section 704(c) gain). The distribution of Asset 1 to C results in an excess distribution of $200x ($300x fair market value of Asset 1-$100x adjusted basis in C's partnership interest). Accordingly, in accordance with section 737(a), C will recognize gain of $200x upon receipt of Asset 1.

Example (4). Reverse section 704(c) gain. (i) Facts. The facts are the same as Example (1), except that on January 1, 2011, PRS1 distributes Asset 2 to A in liquidation of A's interest in PRS1. At the time of the distribution, Asset 2 has a value of $600x.

(ii) Analysis. Section 737(a) requires A to recognize gain when it receives a distribution of property in an amount equal to the lesser of the excess distribution or the partner's net precontribution gain. The distribution of Asset 2 to A results in an excess distribution of $400x ($600x fair market value - $200x adjusted basis in A's partnership interest). The distribution of Asset 2 to A occurs within seven years after the contribution of Asset 1 to PRS1 by A. Thus, A's net precontribution gain for purposes of section 737(b) at the time of the distribution is $100x (A's original section 704(c) gain from the contribution of Asset 1 to PRS1). Under § 1.737-2(e), A's net precontribution gain does not include A's reverse section 704(c) gain upon the revaluation of the Assets of PRS1 prior to the merger. Accordingly, A will recognize $100x of gain (the lesser of the excess distribution or net precontribution gain) under section 737 as a result of the distribution of Asset 2. See § 1.704-4(c)(4)(ii)(F), Example (4) for a similar example under section 704.

Example (5). Identical ownership exception. (i) Facts. In 1990, A, an individual, and B, a subchapter C corporation, formed PRS1, a partnership. A owned 75 percent of the interests in the book capital, profits, losses, distributions, and liabilities of PRS1. B owned the remaining 25 percent interest in the book capital, profits, losses, distributions, and liabilities of PRS1. In the same year, A and B also formed another partnership, PRS2, with A owning 75 percent of the interests in PRS2 and B owning the remaining 25 percent. Upon formation of the partnerships, A contributed Asset X to PRS1 and Asset Y to PRS2 and B contributed cash. Both Assets X and Y had section 704(c) built-in gain at the time of contribution to the partnerships.

(ii) In January 2005, PRS1 is merged into PRS2 in an assets-over merger in which PRS1 is the terminating partnership and PRS2 is the continuing partnership for both state law and federal income tax purposes. At the time of the merger, both Assets X and Y had increased in value from the time they were contributed to PRS1 and PRS2, respectively. As a result, a new layer of section 704(c) gain was created with respect to Asset X in PRS1. After the merger, A had a 75 percent interest in PRS2's book capital, profits, losses, distributions, and liabilities. B held the remaining 25 percent interest in PRS2's book capital, profits, losses, distributions, and liabilities. In 2006, PRS2 distributes Asset X to A.

(iii) Analysis. The 2006 distribution by PRS2 occurs more than seven years after the formation of the partnerships and the original contribution of Asset X to the partnerships. Therefore, the original layer of built-in gain created on the original contribution of Asset X to the partnerships should not be taken into account in applying section 737 to the proposed liquidation. In addition, paragraph (b)(1)(ii)(E) of this section provides that section 737(a) does not apply to newly created section 704(c) gain in property transferred by the transferor partnership to the transferee partnership if both the transferor partnership and the transferee partnership are owned by the same owners in the same proportions. The transferor partnership and the transferee partnership are owned by the same owners in the same proportions if each partner's percentage interest in the transferor partnership's book capital, profits, losses, distributions, and liabilities is the same as the partner's percentage interest in those items of the transferee partnership. In this case, A owned 75 percent and B owned 25 percent of the interests in the book capital, profits, losses, distributions, and liabilities of PRS1 and PRS2 prior to the merger and 75 percent and 25 percent, respectively, of PRS2 after the merger. As a result, the requirements of the identical ownership exception of paragraph (b)(1)(ii)(E) of this section are satisfied. Thus, the new built-in gain created upon contribution of Asset X in connection with the partnership merger will not be taken into account in applying section 737 to the proposed distribution. See § 1.704-4(c)(4)(ii)(F), Example (5) for a similar example under section 704.

(2) Certain divisive transactions. (i) In general. Section 737 and this section do not apply to a transfer by a partnership (transferor partnership) of all of the section 704(c) property contributed by a partner to a second partnership (transferee partnership) in an exchange described in section 721, followed by a distribution as part of the same plan or arrangement of an interest in the transferee partnership (and no other property) in complete liquidation of the interest of the partner that originally contributed the section 704(c) property to the transferor partnership (divisive transactions).

(ii) Subsequent distributions. After a divisive transaction referred to in paragraph (b)(2)(i) of this section, a subsequent distribution of property by the transferee partnership to a partner of the transferee partnership that was formerly a partner of the transferor partnership is subject to section 737 to the same extent that a distribution from the transferor partnership would have been subject to section 737.

* * * * *

(f) Reverse section 704(c) gain. For purposes of section 737(b), net precontribution gain does not include reverse section 704(c) gain as described in § 1.704-3(a)(6)(i).

§ 1.737-3 Basis adjustments; recovery rules.

Caution: The Treasury has not yet amended Reg § 1.737-3 to reflect changes made by P.L. 105-34.

(a) Distributee partner's adjusted tax basis in the partnership interest. The distributee partner's adjusted tax basis in the partnership interest is increased by the amount of gain recognized by the distributee partner under section 737 and this section. This increase is not taken into account in determining the amount of gain recognized by the partner under section 737(a)(1) and this section or in determining the amount of gain recognized by the partner under section 731(a) on the distribution of money in the same distribution or any related distribution. See § 1.704-4(e)(1) for a determination of the distributee partner's adjusted tax basis in a distribution subject to section 704(c)(1)(B).

(b) Distributee partner's adjusted tax basis in distributed property. *(1) In general.* The distributee partner's adjusted tax basis in the distributed property is determined under section 732(a) or (b) as applicable. The increase in the distributee partner's adjusted tax basis in the partnership interest under paragraph (a) of this section is taken into account in determining the distributee partner's adjusted tax basis in the distributed property other than property previously contributed by the partner. See § 1.704-4(e)(2) for a determination of basis in a distribution subject to section 704(c)(1)(B).

(2) Previously contributed property. The distributee partner's adjusted tax basis in distributed property that the partner previously contributed to the partnership is determined as if it were distributed in a separate and independent distribution prior to the distribution that is subject to section 737 and § 1.737-1.

(c) Partnership's adjusted tax basis in partnership property. *(1) Increase in basis.* The partnership's adjusted tax basis in eligible property is increased by the amount of gain recognized by the distributee partner under section 737.

(2) Eligible property. Eligible property is property that—

(i) Entered into the calculation of the distributee partner's net precontribution gain;

(ii) Has an adjusted tax basis to the partnership less than the property's fair market value at the time of the distribution;

(iii) Would have the same character of gain on a sale by the partnership to an unrelated party as the character of any of the gain recognized by the distributee partner under section 737; and

(iv) Was not distributed to another partner in a distribution subject to section 704(c)(1)(B) and § 1.704-4 that was part of the same distribution as the distribution subject to section 737.

(3) Method of adjustment. For the purpose of allocating the basis increase under paragraph (c)(2) of this section among the eligible property, all eligible property of the same character is treated as a single group. Character for this purpose is determined in the same manner as the character of the recognized gain is determined under § 1.737-1(d). The basis increase is allocated among the separate groups of eligible property in proportion to the character of the gain recognized under section 737. The basis increase is then allocated among property within each group in the order in which the property was contributed to the partnership by the

partner, starting with the property contributed first, in an amount equal to the difference between the property's fair market value and its adjusted tax basis to the partnership at the time of the distribution. For property that has the same character and was contributed in the same (or a related) transaction, the basis increase is allocated based on the respective amounts of unrealized appreciation in such properties at the time of the distribution.

(4) Section 754 adjustments. The basis adjustments to partnership property made pursuant to paragraph (c)(1) of this section are not elective and must be made regardless of whether the partnership has an election in effect under section 754. Any adjustments to the bases of partnership property (including eligible property as defined in paragraph (c)(2) of this section) under section 734(b) pursuant to a section 754 election (other than basis adjustments under section 734(b)(1)(A) described in the following sentence) must be made after (and must take into account) the adjustments to basis made under paragraph (a) and paragraph (c)(1) of this section. Basis adjustments under section 734(b)(1)(A) that are attributable to distributions of money to the distributee partner that are part of the same distribution as the distribution of property subject to section 737 are made before the adjustments to basis under paragraph (a) and paragraph (c)(1) of this section. See § 1.737-1(c)(2)(ii) for the effect, if any, of basis adjustments under section 734(b)(1)(A) on a partner's net precontribution gain. See also § 1.704-4(e)(3) for a similar rule regarding basis adjustments pursuant to a section 754 election in the context of section 704(c)(1)(B).

(d) Recovery of increase to adjusted tax basis. Any increase to the adjusted tax basis of partnership property under paragraph (c)(1) of this section is recovered using any applicable recovery period and depreciation (or other cost recovery) method (including first-year conventions) available to the partnership for newly purchased property (of the type adjusted) placed in service at the time of the distribution.

(e) Examples. The following examples illustrate the rules of this section. Unless otherwise specified, partnership income equals partnership expenses (other than depreciation deductions for contributed property) for each year of the partnership, the fair market value of partnership property does not change, all distributions by the partnership are subject to section 737, and all partners are unrelated.

Example (1). Partner's basis in distributed property.

(i) On January 1, 1995, A, B, and C form partnership ABC as equal partners. A contributes Property A, nondepreciable real property with a fair market value of $10,000 and an adjusted tax basis of $5,000. B contributes Property B, nondepreciable real property with a fair market value and adjusted tax basis of $10,000. C contributes $10,000 cash.

(ii) On December 31, 1998, Property B is distributed to A in complete liquidation of A's interest in the partnership. A recognizes $5,000 of gain under section 737, an amount equal to the excess distribution of $5,000 ($10,000 fair market value of Property B less $5,000 adjusted tax basis in A's partnership interest) and A's net precontribution gain of $5,000 ($10,000 fair market value of Property A less $5,000 adjusted tax basis of such property).

(iii) A's adjusted tax basis in A's partnership interest is increased by the $5,000 of gain recognized under section 737. This increase is taken into account in determining A's basis in the distributed property. Therefore, A's adjusted tax basis in distributed Property B is $10,000 under section 732(b).

Example (2). Partner's basis in distributed property in connection with gain recognized under section 704(c)(1)(B).

(i) On January 1, 1995, A, B, and C form partnership ABC as equal partners. A contributes the following nondepreciable real property located in the United States to the partnership:

	Fair Market Value	Adjusted Tax Basis
Property A1	$10,000	$5,000
Property A2	10,000	2,000

(ii) B contributes $10,000 cash and Property B, nondepreciable real property located outside the United States, with a fair market value and adjusted tax basis of $10,000. C contributes $20,000 cash.

(iii) On December 31, 1998, Property B is distributed to A in a current distribution and Property A1 is distributed to B in a current distribution. A recognizes $5,000 of gain under section 704(c)(1)(B) and § 1.704-4 on the distribution of Property A1 to B, the difference between the fair market value of such property ($10,000) and the adjusted tax basis in distributed Property A1 ($5,000). The adjusted tax basis of A's partnership interest is increased by this $5,000 of gain under section 704(c)(1)(B) and § 1.704-4(e)(1).

(iv) The increase in the adjusted tax basis of A's partnership interest is taken into account in determining the amount of the excess distribution. As a result, there is no excess distribution because the fair market value of Property B ($10,000) is less than the adjusted tax basis of A's interest in the partnership at the time of distribution ($12,000). A therefore recognizes no gain under section 737 on the receipt of Property B. A's adjusted tax basis in Property B is $10,000 under section 732(a)(1). The adjusted tax basis of A's partnership interest is reduced from $12,000 to $2,000 under section 733. See Example 3 of § 1.737-1(e).

Example (3). Partnership's basis in partnership property after a distribution with section 737 gain.

(i) On January 31, 1995, A, B, and C form partnership ABC as equal partners. A contributes the following nondepreciable property to the partnership:

	Fair Market Value	Adjusted Tax Basis
Property A1	$1,000	$500
Property A2	4,000	1,500
Property A3	4,000	6,000
Property A4	6,000	4,000

(ii) The character of gain or loss on Properties A1, A2, and A3 is long-term, U.S.-source capital gain or loss. The character of gain on Property A4 is long-term, foreign-source capital gain. B contributes Property B, nondepreciable real property with a fair market value and adjusted tax basis of $15,000. C contributes $15,000 cash.

(iii) On December 31, 1998, Property B is distributed to A in complete liquidation of A's interest in the partnership. A recognizes gain of $3,000 under section 737, an amount equal to the excess distribution of $3,000 ($15,000 fair market value of Property B less $12,000 adjusted tax basis in A's partnership interest) and A's net precontribution gain of $3,000 ($15,000 aggregate fair market value of the property contributed by A less $12,000 aggregate adjusted tax basis of such property).

(iv) $2,000 of A's gain is long-term, foreign-source capital gain ($3,000 total gain under section 737 x $2,000 net long-term, foreign-source capital gain/$3,000 total net precontribution gain). $1,000 of A's gain is long-term, U.S.-source capital gain ($3,000 total gain under section 737 × $1,000 net long-term, U.S.-source capital gain/$3,000 total net precontribution gain).

(v) The partnership must increase the adjusted tax basis of the property contributed by A by $3,000. All property contributed by A is eligible property. Properties A1, A2, and A3 have the same character and are grouped into a single group for purposes of allocating this basis increase. Property A4 is in a separate character group.

(vi) $2,000 of the basis increase must be allocated to long-term, foreign-source capital assets because $2,000 of the gain recognized by A was long-term, foreign-source capital gain. The adjusted tax basis of Property A4 is therefore increased from $4,000 to $6,000. $1,000 of the increase must be allocated to Properties A1 and A2 because $1,000 of the gain recognized by A is long-term, U.S.-source capital gain. No basis increase is allocated to Property A3 because its fair market value is less than its adjusted tax basis. The $1,000 basis increase is allocated between Properties A1 and A2 based on the unrealized appreciation in each asset before such basis adjustment. As a result, the adjusted tax basis of Property A1 is increased by $167 ($1,000 × $500/$3,000) and the adjusted tax basis of Property A2 is increased by $833 ($1,000 × $2,500/3,000).

T.D. 8642, 12/22/95.

§ 1.737-4 Anti-abuse rule.

Caution: The Treasury has not yet amended Reg § 1.737-4 to reflect changes made by P.L. 105-34.

(a) In general. The rules of section 737 and §§ 1.737-1, 1.737-2, and 1.737-3 must be applied in a manner consistent with the purpose of section 737. Accordingly, if a principal purpose of a transaction is to achieve a tax result that is inconsistent with the purpose of section 737, the Commissioner can recast the transaction for federal tax purposes as appropriate to achieve tax results that are consistent with the purpose of section 737. Whether a tax result is inconsistent with the purpose of section 737 must be determined based on all the facts and circumstances. See § 1.704-4(f) for an anti-abuse rule and examples in the context of section 704(c)(1)(B). The anti-abuse rule and examples under section 704(c)(1)(B) and § 1.704-4(f) are relevant to section 737 and §§ 1.737-1, 1.737-2, and 1.737-3 to the extent that the net precontribution gain for purposes of section 737 is determined by reference to section 704(c)(1)(B).

(b) Examples. The following examples illustrate the rules of this section. The examples set forth below do not delineate the boundaries of either permissible or impermissible types of transactions. Further, the addition of any facts or circumstances that are not specifically set forth in an example (or the deletion of any facts or circumstances) may alter the outcome of the transaction described in the example. Unless otherwise specified, partnership income equals partnership expenses (other than depreciation deductions for contributed property) for each year of the partnership, the fair market value of partnership property does not change, all distributions by the partnership are subject to section 737, and all partners are unrelated.

Example (1). Increase in distributee partner's basis by temporary contribution; results inconsistent with the purpose of section 737.

(i) On January 1, 1995, A, B, and C form partnership ABC as equal partners. A contributes Property A1, nondepreciable real property with a fair market value of $10,000 and an adjusted tax basis of $1,000. B contributes Property B, nondepreciable real property with a fair market value of $10,000 and an adjusted tax basis of $10,000. C contributes $10,000 cash.

(ii) On January 1, 1999, pursuant to a plan a principal purpose of which is to avoid gain under section 737, A transfers to the partnership Property A2, nondepreciable real property with a fair market value and adjusted tax basis of $9,000. A treats the transfer as a contribution to the partnership pursuant to section 721 and increases the adjusted tax basis of A's partnership interest from $1,000 to $10,000. On January 1, 1999, the partnership agreement is amended and all other necessary steps are taken so that substantially all of the economic risks and benefits of Property A2 are retained by A. On February 1, 1999, Property B is distributed to A in a current distribution. If the contribution of Property A2 is treated as a contribution to the partnership for purposes of section 737, there is no excess distribution because the fair market value of distributed Property B ($10,000) does not exceed the adjusted tax basis of A's interest in the partnership ($10,000), and therefore section 737 does not apply. A's adjusted tax basis in distributed Property B is $10,000 under section 732(a)(1) and the adjusted tax basis of A's partnership interest is reduced to zero under section 733.

(iii) On March 1, 2000, A receives Property A2 from the partnership in complete liquidation of A's interest in the partnership. A recognizes no gain on the distribution of Property A2 because the property was previously contributed property. See § 1.737-2(d).

(iv) Although A has treated the transfer of Property A2 as a contribution to the partnership that increased the adjusted tax basis of A's interest in the partnership, it would be inconsistent with the purpose of section 737 to recognize the transfer as a contribution to the partnership. Section 737 requires recognition of gain when the value of distributed property exceeds the distributee partner's adjusted tax basis in the partnership interest. Section 737 assumes that any contribution or other transaction that affects a partner's adjusted tax basis in the partnership interest is a contribution or transaction in substance and is not engaged in with a principal purpose of avoiding recognition of gain under section 737. Because the transfer of Property A2 to the partnership was not a contribution in substance and was made with a principal purpose of avoiding recognition of gain under section 737, the Commissioner can disregard the contribution of Property A2 for this purpose. As a result, A recognizes gain of $9,000 under section 737 on the receipt of Property B, an amount equal to the lesser of the excess distribution of $9,000 ($10,000 fair market value of distributed Property B less the $1,000 adjusted tax basis of A's partnership interest, determined without regard to the transitory contribution of Property A2) or A's net precontribution gain of $9,000 on Property A1.

Example (2). Increase in distributee partner's basis; Section 752 liability shift; results consistent with the purpose of section 737.

(i) On January 1, 1995, A and B form general partnership AB as equal partners. A contributes Property A, nondepreciable real property with a fair market value of $10,000 and an adjusted tax basis of $1,000. B contributes Property B, nondepreciable real property with a fair market value and adjusted tax basis of $10,000. The partnership also borrows $10,000 on a recourse basis and purchases Property C. The $10,000 liability is allocated equally between A and B under section 752, thereby increasing the adjusted tax basis in A's partnership interest to $6,000.

(ii) On December 31, 1998, the partners agree that A is to receive Property B in a current distribution. If A were to receive Property B at that time, A would recognize $4,000 of gain under section 737, an amount equal to the lesser of the excess distribution of $4,000 ($10,000 fair market value of Property B less $6,000 adjusted tax basis in A's partnership interest) or A's net precontribution gain of $9,000 ($10,000 fair market value of Property A less $1,000 adjusted tax basis of Property A).

(iii) With a principal purpose of avoiding such gain, A and B agree that A will be solely liable for the repayment of the $10,000 partnership liability and take the steps necessary so that the entire amount of the liability is allocated to A under section 752. The adjusted tax basis in A's partnership interest is thereby increased from $6,000 to $11,000 to reflect A's share of the $5,000 of liability previously allocated to B. As a result of this increase in A's adjusted tax basis, there is no excess distribution because the fair market value of distributed Property B ($10,000) is less than the adjusted tax basis of A's partnership interest. Recognizing A's increased adjusted tax basis as a result of the shift in liabilities is consistent with the purpose of section 737 and this section. Section 737 requires recognition of gain only when the value of the distributed property exceeds the distributee partner's adjusted tax basis in the partnership interest. The $10,000 recourse liability is a bona fide liability of the partnership that was undertaken for a substantial business purpose and A's and B's agreement that A will assume responsibility for repayment of that debt has substance. Therefore, the increase in A's adjusted tax basis in A's interest in the partnership due to the shift in partnership liabilities under section 752 is respected, and A recognizes no gain under section 737.

T.D. 8642, 12/22/95.

§ 1.737-5 Effective dates.

Caution: The Treasury has not yet amended Reg § 1.737-5 to reflect changes made by P.L. 105-34.

Sections 1.737-1, 1.737-2, 1.737-3, and 1.737-4 apply to distributions by a partnership to a partner on or after January 9, 1995, except that § 1.737-2(d)(3)(iv) applies to distributions by a partnership to a partner on or after June 24, 2003.

T.D. 8642, 12/22/95, amend T.D. 9193, 3/21/2005, T.D. 9207, 5/23/2005.

PAR. 6. Section 1.737-5 is amended by revising the section heading and adding two additional sentences at the end of the paragraph to read as follows:

Proposed § 1.737-5 Effective/applicability date. [*For Preamble, see ¶ 152,903*]

* * * Section 1.737-1(c) is effective as of August 22, 2007. Section 1.737-2(b)(1) is effective for any distribution of property after January 19, 2005, if such property was contributed in a merger using the assets-over form after May 3, 2004.

§ 1.741-1 Recognition and character of gain or loss on sale or exchange.

(a) The sale or exchange of an interest in a partnership shall, except to the extent section 751(a) applies, be treated as the sale or exchange of a capital asset, resulting in capital gain or loss measured by the difference between the amount realized and the adjusted basis of the partnership interest, as determined under section 705. For treatment of selling partner's distributive share up to date of sale, see section 706(c)(2). Where the provisions of section 751 require the recognition of ordinary income or loss with respect to a portion of the amount realized from such sale or exchange, the amount realized shall be reduced by the amount attributable under section 751 to unrealized receivables and substantially appreciated inventory items, and the adjusted basis of the transferor partner's interest in the partnership shall be reduced by the portion of such basis attributable to such unrealized receivables and substantially appreciated inventory items. See section 751 and § 1.751-1.

(b) Section 741 shall apply whether the partnership interest is sold to one or more members of the partnership or to one or more persons who are not members of the partnership. Section 741 shall also apply even though the sale of the partnership interest results in a termination of the partnership under section 708(b). Thus, the provisions of section 741 shall be applicable (1) to the transferor partner in a 2-man partnership when he sells his interest to the other partner, and (2) to all the members of a partnership when they sell their interests to one or more persons outside the partnership.

(c) See section 351 for nonrecognition of gain or loss upon transfer of a partnership interest to a corporation controlled by the transferor.

(d) For rules relating to the treatment of liabilities on the sale or exchange of interests in a partnership see §§ 1.752-1 and 1.1001-2.

(e) For rules relating to the capital gain or loss recognized when a partner sells or exchanges an interest in a partnership that holds appreciated collectibles or section 1250 property with section 1250 capital gain, see § 1.1(h)-1. This paragraph (e) applies to transfers of interests in partnerships that occur on or after September 21, 2000.

(f) For rules relating to dividing the holding period of an interest in a partnership, see § 1.1223-3. This paragraph (f) applies to transfers of partnership interests and distributions of property from a partnership that occur on or after September 21, 2000.

T.D. 6175, 5/23/56, amend T.D. 7741, 12/11/80, T.D. 8902, 9/20/2000.

§ 1.742-1 Basis of transferee partner's interest.

The basis to a transferee partner of an interest in a partnership shall be determined under the general basis rules for property provided by part II (section 1011 and following), subchapter O, chapter 1 of the Code. Thus, the basis of a purchased interest will be its cost. The basis of a partnership interest acquired from a decedent is the fair market value of the interest at the date of his death or at the alternate valuation date, increased by his estate's or other successor's share of partnership liabilities, if any, on that date, and reduced to the extent that such value is attributable to items constituting income in respect of a decedent (see section 753 and paragraph (c)(3)(v) of § 1.706-1 and paragraph (b) of § 1.753-1) under section 691. See section 1014(c). For basis of contributing partner's interest, see section 722. The basis so determined is then subject to the adjustments provided in section 705.

T.D. 6175, 5/23/56.

§ 1.743-1 Optional adjustment to basis of partnership property.

Caution: The Treasury has not yet amended Reg § 1.743-1 to reflect changes made by P.L. 108-357, P.L. 105-34, P.L. 98-369.

(a) Generally. The basis of partnership property is adjusted as a result of the transfer of an interest in a partnership by sale or exchange or on the death of a partner only if the election provided by section 754 (relating to optional adjustments to the basis of partnership property) is in effect with respect to the partnership. Whether or not the election provided in section 754 is in effect, the basis of partnership property is not adjusted as the result of a contribution of property, including money, to the partnership.

(b) Determination of adjustment. In the case of the transfer of an interest in a partnership, either by sale or exchange or as a result of the death of a partner, a partnership that has an election under section 754 in effect—

(1) Increases the adjusted basis of partnership property by the excess of the transferee's basis for the transferred partnership interest over the transferee's share of the adjusted basis to the partnership of the partnership's property; or

(2) Decreases the adjusted basis of partnership property by the excess of the transferee's share of the adjusted basis to the partnership of the partnership's property over the transferee's basis for the transferred partnership interest.

(c) Determination of transferee's basis in the transferred partnership interest. In the case of the transfer of a partnership interest by sale or exchange or as a result of the death of a partner, the transferee's basis in the transferred partnership interest is determined under section 742 and § 1.742-1. See also section 752 and §§ 1.752-1 through 1.752-5.

(d) Determination of transferee's share of the adjusted basis to the partnership of the partnership's property. *(1) Generally.* A transferee's share of the adjusted basis to the partnership of partnership property is equal to the sum of the transferee's interest as a partner in the partnership's previously taxed capital, plus the transferee's share of partnership liabilities. Generally, a transferee's interest as a partner in the partnership's previously taxed capital is equal to—

(i) The amount of cash that the transferee would receive on a liquidation of the partnership following the hypothetical transaction, as defined in paragraph (d)(2) of this section (to the extent attributable to the acquired partnership interest); increased by

(ii) The amount of tax loss (including any remedial allocations under § 1.704-3(d)), that would be allocated to the transferee from the hypothetical transaction (to the extent attributable to the acquired partnership interest); and decreased by

(iii) The amount of tax gain (including any remedial allocations under § 1.704-3(d)), that would be allocated to the transferee from the hypothetical transaction (to the extent attributable to the acquired partnership interest).

(2) Hypothetical transaction defined. For purposes of paragraph (d)(1) of this section, the hypothetical transaction means the disposition by the partnership of all of the partnership's assets, immediately after the transfer of the partnership interest, in a fully taxable transaction for cash equal to the fair market value of the assets. See § 1.460-4(k)(3)(v)(B) for a rule relating to the computation of income or loss that would be allocated to the transferee from a contract accounted for under a long-term contract method of accounting as a result of the hypothetical transaction.

(3) Examples. The provisions of this paragraph (d) are illustrated by the following examples:

Example (1). (i) A is a member of partnership PRS in which the partners have equal interests in capital and profits. The partnership has made an election under section 754, relating to the optional adjustment to the basis of partnership property. A sells its interest to T for $22,000. The balance sheet of the partnership at the date of sale shows the following:

Assets

	Adjusted basis	Fair Market value
Cash	$5,000	$5,000
Accounts receivable	10,000	10,000
Inventory	20,000	21,000
Depreciable assets	20,000	40,000
Total	55,000	76,000

Liabilities and Capital

	Adjusted per books	Fair Market value
Liabilities	$10,000	$10,000
Capital:		
A	15,000	22,000
B	15,000	22,000
C	15,000	22,000
Total	55,000	76,000

(ii) The amount of the basis adjustment under section 743(b) is the difference between the basis of T's interest in the partnership and T's share of the adjusted basis to the partnership of the partnership's property. Under section 742, the basis of T's interest is $25,333 (the cash paid for A's interest, $22,000, plus $3,333, T's share of partnership liabilities). T's interest in the partnership's previously taxed capital is $15,000 ($22,000, the amount of cash T would receive if PRS liquidated immediately after the hypothetical transaction, decreased by $7,000, the amount of tax gain allocated to T from the hypothetical transaction). T's share of the adjusted basis to the partnership of the partnership's property is $18,333 ($15,000 share of previously taxed capital, plus $3,333 share of the partnership's liabilities). The amount of the basis adjustment under section 743(b) to partnership property therefore, is $7,000, the difference between $25,333 and $18,333.

Example (2). A, B, and C form partnership PRS, to which A contributes land (Asset 1) with a fair market value of $1,000 and an adjusted basis to A of $400, and B and C each contribute $1,000 cash. Each partner has $1,000 credited to it on the books of the partnership as its capital contribution. The partners share in profits equally. During the partnership's first taxable year, Asset 1 appreciates in value to $1,300. A sells its one-third interest in the partnership to T for $1,100, when an election under section 754 is in effect. The amount of tax gain that would be allocated to T from the hypothetical transaction is $700 ($600 section 704(c) built-in gain, plus one-third of the additional gain). Thus, T's interest in the partnership's previously taxed capital is $400 ($1,100, the amount of cash T would receive if PRS liquidated immediately after the hypothetical transaction, decreased by $700, T's share of gain from the hypothetical transaction). The amount of T's basis adjustment under section 743(b) to partnership property is $700 (the excess of $1,100, T's cost basis for its interest, over $400, T's share of the adjusted basis to the partnership of partnership property).

(e) Allocation of basis adjustment. For the allocation of the basis adjustment under this section among the individual items of partnership property, see section 755 and the regulations thereunder.

(f) Subsequent transfers. Where there has been more than one transfer of a partnership interest, a transferee's basis adjustment is determined without regard to any prior transferee's basis adjustment. In the case of a gift of an interest in a partnership, the donor is treated as transferring, and the donee as receiving, that portion of the basis adjustment attributable to the gifted partnership interest. The provisions of this paragraph (f) are illustrated by the following example:

Example. (i) A, B, and C form partnership PRS. A and B each contribute $1,000 cash, and C contributes land with a basis and fair market value of $1,000. When the land has appreciated in value to $1,300, A sells its interest to T1 for $1,100 (one-third of $3,300, the fair market value of the partnership property). An election under section 754 is in effect; therefore, T1 has a basis adjustment under section 743(b) of $100.

(ii) After the land has further appreciated in value to $1,600, T1 sells its interest to T2 for $1,200 (one-third of $3,600, the fair market value of the partnership property). T2 has a basis adjustment under section 743(b) of $200. This amount is determined without regard to any basis adjustment under section 743(b) that T1 may have had in the partnership assets.

(iii) During the following year, T2 makes a gift to T3 of fifty percent of T2's interest in PRS. At the time of the transfer, T2 has a $200 basis adjustment under section 743(b). T2 is treated as transferring $100 of the basis adjustment to T3 with the gift of the partnership interest.

(g) Distributions. *(1) Distribution of adjusted property to the transferee.*

(i) Coordination with section 732. If a partnership distributes property to a transferee and the transferee has a basis adjustment for the property, the basis adjustment is taken into account under section 732. See § 1.732-2(b).

(ii) Coordination with section 734. For certain adjustments to the common basis of remaining partnership property after the distribution of adjusted property to a transferee, see § 1.734-2(b).

(2) Distribution of adjusted property to another partner.

(i) Coordination with section 732. If a partner receives a distribution of property with respect to which another partner has a basis adjustment, the distributee does not take the basis adjustment into account under section 732.

(ii) Reallocation of basis. A transferee with a basis adjustment in property that is distributed to another partner reallocates the basis adjustment among the remaining items of partnership property under § 1.755-1(c).

(3) Distributions in complete liquidation of a partner's interest. If a transferee receives a distribution of property (whether or not the transferee has a basis adjustment in such property) in liquidation of its interest in the partnership, the adjusted basis to the partnership of the distributed property immediately before the distribution includes the transferee's basis adjustment for the property in which the transferee relinquished an interest (either because it remained in the partnership or was distributed to another partner). Any basis adjustment for property in which the transferee is deemed to relinquish its interest is reallocated among the properties distributed to the transferee under § 1.755-1(c).

(4) Coordination with other provisions. The rules of sections 704(c)(1)(B), 731, 737, and 751 apply before the rules of this paragraph (g).

(5) Example. The provisions of this paragraph (g) are illustrated by the following example:

Example. (i) A, B, and C are equal partners in partnership PRS. Each partner originally contributed $10,000 in cash, and PRS used the contributions to purchase five nondepreciable capital assets. PRS has no liabilities. After five years, PRS's balance sheet appears as follows:

Assets

	Adjusted basis	Fair Market value
Asset 1	$10,000	$10,000
Asset 2	4,000	6,000
Asset 3	6,000	6,000
Asset 4	7,000	4,000
Asset 5	3,000	13,000
Total	30,000	39,000

Capital

	Adjusted per books	Fair Market value
Partner A	$10,000	$13,000
Partner B	10,000	13,000
Partner C	10,000	13,000
Total	30,000	39,000

(ii) A sells its interest to T for $13,000 when PRS has an election in effect under section 754. T receives a basis adjustment under section 743(b) in the partnership property that is equal to $3,000 (the excess of T's basis in the partnership interest, $13,000, over T's share of the adjusted basis to the partnership of partnership property, $10,000). The basis adjustment is allocated under section 755, and the partnership's balance sheet appears as follows:

Assets

	Adjusted basis	Fair Market value	Basis adjustment
Asset 1	$10,000	$10,000	0.00
Asset 2	4,000	6,000	666.67
Asset 3	6,000	6,000	0.00
Asset 4	7,000	4,000	(1,000.00)
Asset 5	3,000	13,000	3,333.33
Total	30,000	39,000	3,000.00

Capital

	Adjusted per books	Fair Market value	Special basis
Partner T	$10,000	$13,000	$3,000
Partner B	10,000	13,000	0

Partner C	10,000	13,000	0
Total	30,000	39,000	3,000

(iii) Assume that PRS distributes Asset 2 to T in partial liquidation of T's interest in the partnership. T has a basis adjustment under section 743(b) of $666.67 in Asset 2. Under paragraph (g)(1)(i) of this section, T takes the basis adjustment into account under section 732. Therefore, T will have a basis in Asset 2 of $4,666.67 following the distribution.

(iv) Assume instead that PRS distributes Asset 5 to C in complete liquidation of C's interest in PRS. T has a basis adjustment under section 743(b) of $3,333.33 in Asset 5. Under paragraph (g)(2)(i) of this section, C does not take T's basis adjustment into account under section 732. Therefore, the partnership's basis for purposes of sections 732 and 734 is $3,000. Under paragraph (g)(2)(ii) of this section, T's $3,333.33 basis adjustment is reallocated among the remaining partnership assets under § 1.755-1(c).

(v) Assume instead that PRS distributes Asset 5 to T in complete liquidation of its interest in PRS. Under paragraph (g)(3) of this section, immediately prior to the distribution of Asset 5 to T, PRS must adjust the basis of Asset 5. Therefore, immediately prior to the distribution, PRS's basis in Asset 5 is equal to $6,000, which is the sum of (A) $3,000, PRS's common basis in Asset 5, plus (B) $3,333.33, T's basis adjustment to Asset 5, plus (C) ($333.33), the sum of T's basis adjustments in Assets 2 and 4. For purposes of sections 732 and 734, therefore, PRS will be treated as having a basis in Asset 5 equal to $6,000.

(h) Contributions of adjusted property. *(1) Section 721(a) transactions.* If, in a transaction described in section 721(a), a partnership (the upper tier) contributes to another partnership (the lower tier) property with respect to which a basis adjustment has been made, the basis adjustment is treated as contributed to the lower-tier partnership, regardless of whether the lower-tier partnership makes a section 754 election. The lower tier's basis in the contributed assets and the upper tier's basis in the partnership interest received in the transaction are determined with reference to the basis adjustment. However, that portion of the basis of the upper tier's interest in the lower tier attributable to the basis adjustment must be segregated and allocated solely to the transferee partner for whom the basis adjustment was made. Similarly, that portion of the lower tier's basis in its assets attributable to the basis adjustment must be segregated and allocated solely to the upper tier and the transferee. A partner with a basis adjustment in property held by a partnership that terminates under section 708(b)(1)(B) will continue to have the same basis adjustment with respect to property deemed contributed by the terminated partnership to the new partnership under § 1.708-1(b)(1)(iv), regardless of whether the new partnership makes a section 754 election.

(2) Section 351 transactions. (i) Basis in transferred property. A corporation's adjusted tax basis in property transferred to the corporation by a partnership in a transaction described in section 351 is determined with reference to any basis adjustments to the property under section 743(b) (other than any basis adjustment that reduces a partner's gain under paragraph (h)(2)(ii) of this section).

(ii) Partnership gain. The amount of gain, if any, recognized by the partnership on a transfer of property by the partnership to a corporation in a transfer described in section 351 is determined without reference to any basis adjustment to the transferred property under section 743(b). The amount of gain, if any, recognized by the partnership on the transfer that is allocated to a partner with a basis adjustment in the transferred property is adjusted to reflect the partner's basis adjustment in the transferred property.

(iii) Basis in stock. The partnership's adjusted tax basis in stock received from a corporation in a transfer described in section 351 is determined without reference to the basis adjustment in property transferred to the corporation in the section 351 exchange. A partner with a basis adjustment in property transferred to the corporation, however, has a basis adjustment in the stock received by the partnership in the section 351 exchange in an amount equal to the partner's basis adjustment in the transferred property, reduced by any basis adjustment that reduced the partner's gain under paragraph (h)(2)(ii) of this section.

(iv) Example. The following example illustrates the principles of this paragraph (h)(2):

Example. (i) A, B, and C are equal partners in partnership PRS. The partnership's only asset, Asset 1, has an adjusted tax basis of $60 and a fair market value of $120. Asset 1 is a nondepreciable capital asset and is not section 704(c) property. A has a basis in its partnership interest of $40, and a positive section 743(b) adjustment of $20 in Asset 1. In a transaction to which section 351 applies, PRS contributes Asset 1 to X, a corporation, in exchange for $15 in cash and X stock with a fair market value of $105.

(ii) Under paragraph (h)(2)(ii) of this section, PRS realizes $60 of gain on the transfer of Asset 1 to X ($120, its amount realized, minus $60, its adjusted basis), but recognizes only $15 of that gain under section 351(b)(1). Of this amount, $5 is allocated to each partner. A must use $5 of its basis adjustment in Asset 1 to offset A's share of PRS's gain. Under paragraph (h)(2)(iii) of this section, PRS's basis in the stock received from X is $60. However, A has a basis adjustment in the stock received by PRS equal to $15 (its basis adjustment in Asset 1, $20, reduced by the portion of the adjustment which reduced A's gain, $5). Under paragraph (h)(2)(i) of this section, X's basis in Asset 1 equals $90 (PRS's common basis in the asset, $60, plus the gain recognized by PRS under section 351(b)(1), $15, plus A's basis adjustment under section 743(b), $20, less the portion of the adjustment which reduced A's gain, $5).

(i) [Reserved].

(j) Effect of basis adjustment. *(1) In general.* The basis adjustment constitutes an adjustment to the basis of partnership property with respect to the transferee only. No adjustment is made to the common basis of partnership property. Thus, for purposes of calculating income, deduction, gain, and loss, the transferee will have a special basis for those partnership properties the bases of which are adjusted under section 743(b) and this section. The adjustment to the basis of partnership property under section 743(b) has no effect on the partnership's computation of any item under section 703.

(2) Computation of partner's distributive share of partnership items. The partnership first computes its items of income, deduction, gain, or loss at the partnership level under section 703. The partnership then allocates the partnership items among the partners, including the transferee, in accordance with section 704, and adjusts the partners' capital accounts accordingly. The partnership then adjusts the transferee's distributive share of the items of partnership income, deduction, gain, or loss, in accordance with paragraphs (j)(3) and (4) of this section, to reflect the effects of the transferee's basis adjustment under section 743(b). These adjustments to the transferee's distributive shares must be reflected on Schedules K and K-1 of the partnership's return (Form

1065). These adjustments to the transferee's distributive shares do not affect the transferee's capital account. See § 1.460-4(k)(3)(v)(B) for rules relating to the effect of a basis adjustment under section 743(b) that is allocated to a contract accounted for under a long-term contract method of accounting in determining the transferee's distributive share of income or loss from the contract.

(3) Effect of basis adjustment in determining items of income, gain, or loss. (i) In general. The amount of a transferee's income, gain, or loss from the sale or exchange of a partnership asset in which the transferee has a basis adjustment is equal to the transferee's share of the partnership's gain or loss from the sale of the asset (including any remedial allocations under § 1.704-3(d)), minus the amount of the transferee's positive basis adjustment for the partnership asset (determined by taking into account the recovery of the basis adjustment under paragraph (j)(4)(i)(B) of this section) or plus the amount of the transferee's negative basis adjustment for the partnership asset (determined by taking into the account the recovery of the basis adjustment under paragraph (j)(4)(ii)(B) of this section).

(ii) Examples. The following examples illustrate the principles of this paragraph (j)(3):

Example (1). A and B form equal partnership PRS. A contributes nondepreciable property with a fair market value of $50 and an adjusted tax basis of $100. PRS will use the traditional allocation method under § 1.704-3(b). B contributes $50 cash. A sells its interest to T for $50. PRS has an election in effect to adjust the basis of partnership property under section 754. T receives a negative $50 basis adjustment under section 743(b) that, under section 755, is allocated to the nondepreciable property. PRS then sells the property for $60. PRS recognizes a book gain of $10 (allocated equally between T and B) and a tax loss of $40. T will receive an allocation of $40 of tax loss under the principles of section 704(c). However, because T has a negative $50 basis adjustment in the nondepreciable property, T recognizes a $10 gain from the partnership's sale of the property.

Example (2). A and B form equal partnership PRS. A contributes nondepreciable property with a fair market value of $100 and an adjusted tax basis of $50. B contributes $100 cash. PRS will use the traditional allocation method under § 1.704-3(b). A sells its interest to T for $100. PRS has an election in effect to adjust the basis of partnership property under section 754. Therefore, T receives a $50 basis adjustment under section 743(b) that, under section 755, is allocated to the nondepreciable property. PRS then sells the nondepreciable property for $90. PRS recognizes a book loss of $10 (allocated equally between T and B) and a tax gain of $40. T will receive an allocation of the entire $40 of tax gain under the principles of section 704(c). However, because T has a $50 basis adjustment in the property, T recognizes a $10 loss from the partnership's sale of the property.

Example (3). A and B form equal partnership PRS. PRS will make allocations under section 704(c) using the remedial allocation method described in § 1.704-3(d). A contributes nondepreciable property with a fair market value of $100 and an adjusted tax basis of $150. B contributes $100 cash. A sells its partnership interest to T for $100. PRS has an election in effect to adjust the basis of partnership property under section 754. T receives a negative $50 basis adjustment under section 743(b) that, under section 755, is allocated to the property. The partnership then sells the property for $120. The partnership recognizes a $20 book gain and a $30 tax loss. The book gain will be allocated equally between the partners. The entire $30 tax loss will be allocated to T under the principles of section 704(c). To match its $10 share of book gain, B will be allocated $10 of remedial gain, and T will be allocated an offsetting $10 of remedial loss. T was allocated a total of $40 of tax loss with respect to the property. However, because T has a negative $50 basis adjustment to the property, T recognizes a $10 gain from the partnership's sale of the property.

(4) Effect of basis adjustment in determining items of deduction. (i) Increases. (A) Additional deduction. The amount of any positive basis adjustment that is recovered by the transferee in any year is added to the transferee's distributive share of the partnership's depreciation or amortization deductions for the year. The basis adjustment is adjusted under section 1016(a)(2) to reflect the recovery of the basis adjustment.

(B) Recovery period. (1) In general. Except as provided in paragraph (j)(4)(i)(B)(2) of this section, for purposes of section 168, if the basis of a partnership's recovery property is increased as a result of the transfer of a partnership interest, then the increased portion of the basis is taken into account as if it were newly-purchased recovery property placed in service when the transfer occurs. Consequently, any applicable recovery period and method may be used to determine the recovery allowance with respect to the increased portion of the basis. However, no change is made for purposes of determining the recovery allowance under section 168 for the portion of the basis for which there is no increase.

(2) Remedial allocation method. If a partnership elects to use the remedial allocation method described in § 1.704-3(d) with respect to an item of the partnership's recovery property, then the portion of any increase in the basis of the item of the partnership's recovery property under section 743(b) that is attributable to section 704(c) built-in gain is recovered over the remaining recovery period for the partnership's excess book basis in the property as determined in the final sentence of § 1.704-3(d)(2). Any remaining portion of the basis increase is recovered under paragraph (j)(4)(i)(B)(1) of this section.

(C) Examples. The provisions of this paragraph (j)(4)(i) are illustrated by the following examples:

Example (1). (i) A, B, and C are equal partners in partnership PRS, which owns Asset 1, an item of depreciable property that has a fair market value in excess of its adjusted tax basis. C sells its interest in PRS to T while PRS has an election in effect under section 754. PRS, therefore, increases the basis of Asset 1 with respect to T.

(ii) Assume that in the year following the transfer of the partnership interest to T, T's distributive share of the partnership's common basis depreciation deductions from Asset 1 is $1,000. Also assume that, under paragraph (j)(4)(i)(B) of this section, the amount of the basis adjustment under section 743(b) that T recovers during the year is $500. The total amount of depreciation deductions from Asset 1 reported by T is equal to $1,500.

Example (2). (i) A and B form equal partnership PRS. A contributes property with an adjusted basis of $100,000 and a fair market value of $500,000. B contributes $500,000 cash. When PRS is formed, the property has five years remaining in its recovery period. The partnership's adjusted basis of $100,000 will, therefore, be recovered over the five years remaining in the property's recovery period. PRS elects to use the remedial allocation method under § 1.704-3(d) with respect to the property. If PRS had purchased the property at the time of the partnership's formation, the basis of the property would have been recovered over a 10-year period. The $400,000 of section 704(c) built-in gain will, therefore, be amortized under § 1.704-3(d) over a 10-year period beginning at the time of the partnership's formation.

(ii)

(A) Except for the depreciation deductions, PRS's expenses equal its income in each year of the first two years commencing with the year the partnership is formed. After two years, A's share of the adjusted basis of partnership property is $120,000, while B's is $440,000:

Capital Accounts

	A		B	
	Book	Tax	Book	Tax
Initial Contribution . . .	$500,000	$100,000	$500,000	$500,000
Depreciation Year 1	(30,000)		(30,000)	(20,000)
Remedial		10,000		(10,000)
	470,000	110,000	470,000	470,000
Depreciation Year 2	(30,000)		(30,000)	(20,000)
Remedial		10,000		(10,000)
	440,000	120,000	440,000	440,000

(B) A sells its interest in PRS to T for its fair market value of $440,000. A valid election under section 754 is in effect with respect to the sale of the partnership interest. Accordingly, PRS makes an adjustment, pursuant to section 743(b), to increase the basis of partnership property. Under section 743(b), the amount of the basis adjustment is equal to $320,000. Under section 755, the entire basis adjustment is allocated to the property.

(iii) At the time of the transfer, $320,000 of section 704(c) built-in gain from the property was still reflected on the partnership's books, and all of the basis adjustment is attributable to section 704(c) built-in gain. Therefore, the basis adjustment will be recovered over the remaining recovery period for the section 704(c) built-in gain under § 1.704-3(d).

(ii) Decreases.

(A) Reduced deduction. The amount of any negative basis adjustment allocated to an item of depreciable or amortizable property that is recovered in any year first decreases the transferee's distributive share of the partnership's depreciation or amortization deductions from that item of property for the year. If the amount of the basis adjustment recovered in any year exceeds the transferee's distributive share of the partnership's depreciation or amortization deductions from the item of property, then the transferee's distributive share of the partnership's depreciation or amortization deductions from other items of partnership property is decreased. The transferee then recognizes ordinary income to the extent of the excess, if any, of the amount of the basis adjustment recovered in any year over the transferee's distributive share of the partnership's depreciation or amortization deductions from all items of property.

(B) Recovery period. For purposes of section 168, if the basis of an item of a partnership's recovery property is decreased as the result of the transfer of an interest in the partnership, then the decrease is recovered over the remaining useful life of the item of the partnership's recovery property. The portion of the decrease that is recovered in any year during the recovery period is equal to the product of—

(1) The amount of the decrease to the item's adjusted basis (determined as of the date of the transfer); multiplied by

(2) A fraction, the numerator of which is the portion of the adjusted basis of the item recovered by the partnership in that year, and the denominator of which is the adjusted basis of the item on the date of the transfer (determined prior to any basis adjustments).

(C) Examples. The provisions of this paragraph (j)(4)(ii) are illustrated by the following examples:

Example (1). (i) A, B, and C are equal partners in partnership PRS, which owns Asset 2, an item of depreciable property that has a fair market value that is less than its adjusted tax basis. C sells its interest in PRS to T while PRS has an election in effect under section 754. PRS, therefore, decreases the basis of Asset 2 with respect to T.

(ii) Assume that in the year following the transfer of the partnership interest to T, T's distributive share of the partnership's common basis depreciation deductions from Asset 2 is $1,000. Also assume that, under paragraph (j)(4)(ii)(B) of this section, the amount of the basis adjustment under section 743(b) that T recovers during the year is $500. The total amount of depreciation deductions from Asset 2 reported by T is equal to $500.

Example (2). (i) A and B form equal partnership PRS. A contributes property with an adjusted basis of $100,000 and a fair market value of $50,000. B contributes $50,000 cash. When PRS is formed, the property has five years remaining in its recovery period. The partnership's adjusted basis of $100,000 will, therefore, be recovered over the five years remaining in the property's recovery period. PRS uses the traditional allocation method under § 1.704-3(b) with respect to the property. As a result, B will receive $5,000 of depreciation deductions from the property in each of years 1-5, and A, as the contributing partner, will receive $15,000 of depreciation deductions in each of these years.

(ii) Except for the depreciation deductions, PRS's expenses equal its income in each of the first two years commencing with the year the partnership is formed. After two years, A's share of the adjusted basis of partnership property is $70,000, while B's is $40,000. A sells its interest in PRS to T for its fair market value of $40,000. A valid election under section 754 is in effect with respect to the sale of the partnership interest. Accordingly, PRS makes an adjustment, pursuant to section 743(b), to decrease the basis of partnership property. Under section 743(b), the amount of the adjustment is equal to ($30,000). Under section 755, the entire adjustment is allocated to the property.

(iii) The basis of the property at the time of the transfer of the partnership interest was $60,000. In each of years 3 through 5, the partnership will realize depreciation deductions of $20,000 from the property. Thus, one third of the negative basis adjustment ($10,000) will be recovered in each of years 3 through 5. Consequently, T will be allocated, for tax purposes, depreciation of $15,000 each year from the partnership and will recover $10,000 of its negative basis adjustment. Thus, T's net depreciation deduction from the partnership in each year is $5,000.

Example (3). (i) A, B, and C are equal partners in partnership PRS, which owns Asset 2, an item of depreciable property that has a fair market value that is less than its adjusted tax basis. C sells its interest in PRS to T while PRS has an election in effect under section 754. PRS, therefore, decreases the basis of Asset 2 with respect to T.

(ii) Assume that in the year following the transfer of the partnership interest to T, T's distributive share of the partnership's common basis depreciation deductions from Asset 2 is $500. PRS allocates no other depreciation to T. Also assume that, under paragraph (j)(4)(ii)(B) of this section, the amount of the negative basis adjustment that T recovers during the year is $1,000. T will report $500 of ordinary income because the amount of the negative basis adjustment recovered during the year exceeds T's distributive share of the partnership's common basis depreciation deductions from Asset 2.

(5) Depletion. Where an adjustment is made under section 743(b) to the basis of partnership property subject to depletion, any depletion allowance is determined separately for each partner, including the transferee partner, based on the partner's interest in such property. See § 1.702-1(a)(8). For partnerships that hold oil and gas properties that are depleted at the partner level under section 613A(c)(7)(D), the transferee partner (and not the partnership) must make the basis adjustments, if any, required under section 743(b) with respect to such properties. See § 1.613A-3(e)(6)(iv).

(6) Example. The provisions of paragraph (j)(5) of this section are illustrated by the following example:

Example. A, B, and C each contributes $5,000 cash to form partnership PRS, which purchases a coal property for $15,000. A, B, and C have equal interests in capital and profits. C subsequently sells its partnership interest to T for $100,000 when the election under section 754 is in effect. T has a basis adjustment under section 743(b) for the coal property of $95,000 (the difference between T's basis, $100,000, and its share of the basis of partnership property, $5,000). Assume that the depletion allowance computed under the percentage method would be $21,000 for the taxable year so that each partner would be entitled to $7,000 as its share of the deduction for depletion. However, under the cost depletion method, at an assumed rate of 10 percent, the allowance with respect to T's one-third interest which has a basis to him of $100,000 ($5,000, plus its basis adjustment of $95,000) is $10,000, although the cost depletion allowance with respect to the one-third interest of A and B in the coal property, each of which has a basis of $5,000, is only $500. For partners A and B, the percentage depletion is greater than cost depletion and each will deduct $7,000 based on the percentage depletion method. However, as to T, the transferee partner, the cost depletion method results in a greater allowance and T will, therefore, deduct $10,000 based on cost depletion. See section 613(a).

(k) Returns. *(1) Statement of adjustments.* (i) In general. A partnership that must adjust the bases of partnership properties under section 743(b) must attach a statement to the partnership return for the year of the transfer setting forth the name and taxpayer identification number of the transferee as well as the computation of the adjustment and the partnership properties to which the adjustment has been allocated.

(ii) Special rule. Where an interest is transferred in a partnership which holds oil and gas properties that are depleted at the partner level under section 613A(c)(7)(D), the transferee must attach a statement to the transferee's return for the year of the transfer, setting forth the computation of the basis adjustment under section 743(b) which is allocable to such properties and the specific properties to which the adjustment has been allocated.

(iii) Example. The provisions of paragraph (k)(1)(ii) of this section are illustrated by the following example:

Example. (i) Partnership XYZ owns a single section 613A(c)(7)(D) domestic oil and gas property (Property) and other non-depletable assets. A, a partner in XYZ with an adjusted tax basis in Property of $100 (excluding any prior adjustments under section 743(b)), sells its partnership interest to B for $800 cash. Under § 1.613A-3(e)(6)(iv), A's adjusted basis of $100 in Property carries over to B.

(ii) Under section 755, XYZ determines that Property accounts for 50% of the fair market value of all partnership assets. The remaining 50% of B's purchase price ($400) is attributable to non-depletable property. XYZ must provide a statement to B containing the portion of B's adjusted basis attributable to non-depletable property ($400). Under this paragraph (k)(1), XYZ must report basis adjustments under section 743(b) to non-depletable property. B must report basis adjustments under section 743(b) to Property.

(2) Requirement that transferee notify partnership. (i) Sale or exchange. A transferee that acquires, by sale or exchange, an interest in a partnership with an election under section 754 in effect for the taxable year of the transfer, must notify the partnership, in writing, within 30 days of the sale or exchange. The written notice to the partnership must be signed under penalties of perjury and must include the names and addresses of the transferee and (if ascertainable) of the transferor, the taxpayer identification numbers of the transferee and (if ascertainable) of the transferor, the relationship (if any) between the transferee and the transferor, the date of the transfer, the amount of any liabilities assumed or taken subject to by the transferee, and the amount of any money, the fair market value of any other property delivered or to be delivered for the transferred interest in the partnership, and any other information necessary for the partnership to compute the transferee's basis.

(ii) Transfer on death. A transferee that acquires, on the death of a partner, an interest in a partnership with an election under section 754 in effect for the taxable year of the transfer, must notify the partnership, in writing, within one year of the death of the deceased partner. The written notice to the partnership must be signed under penalties of perjury and must include the names and addresses of the deceased partner and the transferee, the taxpayer identification numbers of the deceased partner and the transferee, the relationship (if any) between the transferee and the transferor, the deceased partner's date of death, the date on which the transferee became the owner of the partnership interest, the fair market value of the partnership interest on the applicable date of valuation set forth in section 1014, and the manner in which the fair market value of the partnership interest was determined.

(iii) Nominee reporting. If a partnership interest is transferred to a nominee which is required to furnish the statement under section 6031(c)(1) to the partnership, the nominee may satisfy the notice requirement contained in this paragraph (k)(2) by providing the statement required under § 1.6031(c)-1T, provided that the statement satisfies all requirements of § 1.6031(c)-1T and this paragraph (k)(2).

(3) Reliance. In making the adjustments under section 743(b) and any statement or return relating to such adjustments under this section, a partnership may rely on the written notice provided by a transferee pursuant to paragraph (k)(2) of this section to determine the transferee's basis in a partnership interest. The previous sentence shall not apply if any partner who has responsibility for federal income tax reporting by the partnership has knowledge of facts indicating that the statement is clearly erroneous.

(4) Partnership not required to make or report adjustments under section 743(b) until it has notice of the transfer. A partnership is not required to make the adjustments under

section 743(b) (or any statement or return relating to those adjustments) with respect to any transfer until it has been notified of the transfer. For purposes of this section, a partnership is notified of a transfer when either—

(i) The partnership receives the written notice from the transferee required under paragraph (k)(2) of this section; or

(ii) Any partner who has responsibility for federal income tax reporting by the partnership has knowledge that there has been a transfer of a partnership interest.

(5) Effect on partnership of the failure of the transferee to comply. If the transferee fails to provide the partnership with the written notice required by paragraph (k)(2) of this section, the partnership must attach a statement to its return in the year that the partnership is otherwise notified of the transfer. This statement must set forth the name and taxpayer identification number (if ascertainable) of the transferee. In addition, the following statement must be prominently displayed in capital letters on the first page of the partnership's return for such year, and on the first page of any schedule or information statement relating to such transferee's share of income, credits, deductions, etc.: "RETURN FILED PURSUANT TO § 1.743-1(k)(5)." The partnership will then be entitled to report the transferee's share of partnership items without adjustment to reflect the transferee's basis adjustment in partnership property. If, following the filing of a return pursuant to this paragraph (k)(5), the transferee provides the applicable written notice to the partnership, the partnership must make such adjustments as are necessary to adjust the basis of partnership property (as of the date of the transfer) in any amended return otherwise to be filed by the partnership or in the next annual partnership return of income to be regularly filedby the partnership. At such time, the partnership must also provide the transferee with such information as is necessary for the transferee to amend its prior returns to properly reflect the adjustment under section 743(b).

(l) Effective date. This section applies to transfers of partnership interests that occur on or after December 15, 1999.

T.D. 6175, 5/23/56, amend T.D. 8717, 5/8/97, T.D. 8847, 12/14/99, T.D. 9137, 7/15/2004.

§ 1.751-1 Unrealized receivables and inventory items.

> ***Caution:*** The Treasury has not yet amended Reg § 1.751-1 to reflect changes made by P.L. 105-34, P.L. 103-66, P.L. 98-369, P.L. 97-448, P.L. 95-618, P.L. 95-600, P.L. 94-455, P.L. 91-172, P.L. 89-570.

(a) Sale or exchange of interest in a partnership. *(1) Character of amount realized.* To the extent that money or property received by a partner in exchange for all or part of his partnership interest is attributable to his share of the value of partnership unrealized receivables or substantially appreciated inventory items, the money or fair market value of the property received shall be considered as an amount realized from the sale or exchange of property other than a capital asset. The remainder of the total amount realized on the sale or exchange of the partnership interest is realized from the sale or exchange of a capital asset under section 741. For definition of "unrealized receivables" and "inventory items which have appreciated substantially in value", see section 751(c) and (d). Unrealized receivables and substantially appreciated inventory items are hereafter in this section referred to as "section 751 property". See paragraph (e) of this section.

(2) Determination of gain or loss. The income or loss realized by a partner upon the sale or exchange of its interest in section 751 property is the amount of income or loss from section 751 property (including any remedial allocations under § 1.704-3(d)) that would have been allocated to the partner (to the extent attributable to the partnership interest sold or exchanged) if the partnership had sold all of its property in a fully taxable transaction for cash in an amount equal to the fair market value of such property (taking into account section 7701(g)) immediately prior to the partner's transfer of the interest in the partnership. Any gain or loss recognized that is attributable to section 751 property will be ordinary gain or loss. The difference between the amount of capital gain or loss that the partner would realize in the absence of section 751 and the amount of ordinary income or loss determined under this paragraph (a)(2) is the transferor's capital gain or loss on the sale of its partnership interest. See § 1.460-4(k)(2)(iv)(E) for rules relating to the amount of ordinary income or loss attributable to a contract accounted for under a long-term contract method of accounting.

(3) Statement required. A partner selling or exchanging any part of an interest in a partnership that has any section 751 property at the time of sale or exchange must submit with its income tax return for the taxable year in which the sale or exchange occurs a statement setting forth separately the following information--

(i) The date of the sale or exchange;

(ii) The amount of any gain or loss attributable to the section 751 property; and

(iii) The amount of any gain or loss attributable to capital gain or loss on the sale of the partnership interest.

(b) Certain distributions treated as sales or exchanges. *(1) In general.* (i) Certain distributions to which section 751(b) applies are treated in part as sales or exchanges of property between the partnership and the distributee partner, and not as distributions to which sections 731 through 736 apply. A distribution treated as a sale or exchange under section 751(b) is not subject to the provisions of section 707(b). Section 751(b) applies whether or not the distribution is in liquidation of the distributee partner's entire interest in the partnership. However, section 751(b) applies only to the extent that a partner either receives section 751 property in exchange for his relinquishing any part of his interest in other property, or receives other property in exchange for his relinquishing any part of his interest in section 751 property.

(ii) Section 751(b) does not apply to a distribution to a partner which is not in exchange for his interest in other partnership property. Thus, section 751(b) does not apply to the extent that a distribution consists of the distributee partner's share of section 751 property or his share of other property. Similarly, section 751(b) does not apply to current drawings or to advances against the partner's distributive share, or to a distribution which is, in fact, a gift or payment for services or for the use of capital. In determining whether a partner has received only his share of either section 751 property or of other property, his interest in such property remaining in the partnership immediately after a distribution must be taken into account. For example, the section 751 property in partnership ABC has a fair market value of $100,000 in which partner A has an interest of 30 percent, or $30,000. If A receives $20,000 of section 751 property in a distribution, and continues to have a 30-percent interest in the $80,000 of section 751 property remaining in the partnership after the distribution, only $6,000 ($30,000 minus $24,000 (30 percent of $80,000)) of the section 751 property received by him will be considered to be his share of such property. The remaining $14,000 ($20,000 minus $6,000) received is in excess of his share.

(iii) If a distribution is, in part, a distribution of the distributee partner's share of section 751 property, or of other property (including money) and, in part, a distribution in exchange of such properties, the distribution shall be divided for the purpose of applying section 751(b). The rules of section 751(b) shall first apply to the part of the distribution treated as a sale or exchange of such properties, and then the rules of sections 731 through 736 shall apply to the part of the distribution not treated as a sale or exchange. See paragraph (b)(4)(ii) of this section for treatment of payments under section 736(a).

(2) Distribution of section 751 property (unrealized receivables or substantially appreciated inventory items). (i) To the extent that a partner receives section 751 property in a distribution in exchange for any part of his interest in partnership property (including money) other than section 751 property, the transaction shall be treated as a sale or exchange of such properties between the distributee partner and the partnership (as constituted after the distribution).

(ii) At the time of the distribution, the partnership (as constituted after the distribution) realizes ordinary income or loss on the sale or exchange of the section 751 property. The amount of the income or loss to the partnership will be measured by the difference between the adjusted basis to the partnership of the section 751 property considered as sold to or exchanged with the partner, and the fair market value of the distributee partner's interest in other partnership property which he relinquished in the exchange. In computing the partners' distributive shares of such ordinary income or loss, the income or loss shall be allocated only to partners other than the distributee and separately taken into account under section 702(a)(8).

(iii) At the time of the distribution, the distributee partner realizes gain or loss measured by the difference between his adjusted basis for the property relinquished in the exchange (including any special basis adjustment which he may have) and the fair market value of the section 751 property received by him in exchange for his interest in other property which he has relinquished. The distributee's adjusted basis for the property relinquished is the basis such property would have had under section 732 (including subsection (d) thereof) if the distributee partner had received such property in a current distribution immediately before the actual distribution which is treated wholly or partly as a sale or exchange under section 751(b). The character of the gain or loss to the distributee partner shall be determined by the character of the property in which he relinquished his interest.

(3) Distribution of partnership property other than section 751 property. (i) To the extent that a partner receives a distribution of partnership property (including money) other than section 751 property in exchange for any part of his interest in section 751 property of the partnership, the distribution shall be treated as a sale or exchange of such properties between the distributee partner and the partnership (as constituted after the distribution).

(ii) At the time of the distribution, the partnership (as constituted after the distribution) realizes gain or loss on the sale or exchange of the property other than section 751 property. The amount of the gain to the partnership will be measured by the difference between the adjusted basis to the partnership of the distributed property considered as sold to or exchanged with the partner, and the fair market value of the distributee partner's interest in section 751 property which he relinquished in the exchange. The character of the gain or loss to the partnership is determined by the character of the distributed property treated as sold or exchanged by the partnership. In computing the partners' distributive shares of such gain or loss, the gain or loss shall be allocated only to partners other than the distributee and separately taken into account under section 702(a)(8).

(iii) At the time of the distribution, the distributee partner realizes ordinary income or loss on the sale or exchange of the section 751 property. The amount of the distributee partner's income or loss shall be measured by the difference between his adjusted basis for the section 751 property relinquished in the exchange (including any special basis adjustment which he may have), and the fair market value of other property including money) received by him in exchange for his interest in the section 751 property which he has relinquished. The distributee partner's adjusted basis for the section 751 property relinquished is the basis such property would have had under section 732 (including subsection (d) thereof) if the distributee partner had received such property in a current distribution immediately before the actual distribution which is treated wholly or partly as a sale or exchange under section 751(b).

(4) Exceptions. (i) Section 751(b) does not apply to the distribution to a partner of property which the distributee partner contributed to the partnership. The distribution of such property is governed by the rules set forth in sections 731 through 736, relating to distributions by a partnership.

(ii) Section 751(b) does not apply to payments made to a retiring partner or to a deceased partner's successor in interest to the extent that, under section 736(a), such payments constitute a distributive share of partnership income or guaranteed payments. Payments to a retiring partner or to a deceased partner's successor in interest for his interest in unrealized receivables of the partnership in excess of their partnership basis, including any special basis adjustment for them to which such partner is entitled, constitute payments under section 736(a) and, therefore, are not subject to section 751(b). However, payments under section 736(b) which are considered as made in exchange for an interest in partnership property are subject to section 751(b) to the extent that they involve an exchange of substantially appreciated inventory items for other property. Thus, payments to a retiring partner or to a deceased partner's successor in interest under section 736 must first be divided between payments under section 736(a) and section 736(b). The section 736(b) payments must then be divided, if there is an exchange of substantially appreciated inventory items for other property, between the payments treated as a sale or exchange under section 751(b) and payments treated as a distribution under sections 731 through 736. See subparagraph (1)(iii) of this paragraph, and section 736 and § 1.736-1.

(5) Statement required. A partnership which distributes section 751 property to a partner in exchange for his interest in other partnership property, or which distributes other property in exchange for any part of the partner's interest in section 751 property, shall submit with its return for the year of the distribution a statement showing the computation of any income, gain, or loss to the partnership under the provisions of section 751(b) and this paragraph. The distributee partner shall submit with his return a statement showing the computation of any income, gain, or loss to him. Such statement shall contain information similar to that required under paragraph (a)(3) of this section.

(c) Unrealized receivables. *(1)* The term "unrealized receivables," as used in subchapter K, chapter 1 of the Code, means any rights (contractual or otherwise) to payment for—

(i) Goods delivered or to be delivered (to the extent that such payment would be treated as received for property other than a capital asset), or

(ii) Services rendered or to be rendered,

to the extent that income arising from such rights to payment was not previously includible in income under the method of accounting employed by the partnership. Such rights must have arisen under contracts or agreements in existence at the time of sale or distribution, although the partnership may not be able to enforce payment until a later time. For example, the term includes trade accounts receivable of a cash method taxpayer, and rights to payment for work or goods begun but incomplete at the time of the sale or distribution.

(2) The basis for such unrealized receivables shall include all costs or expenses attributable thereto paid or accrued but not previously taken into account under the partnership method of accounting.

(3) In determining the amount of the sale price attributable to such unrealized receivables, or their value in a distribution treated as a sale or exchange, full account shall be taken not only of the estimated cost of completing performance of the contract or agreement, but also of the time between the sale or distribution and the time of payment.

(4) (i) With respect to any taxable year of a partnership ending after September 12, 1966 (but only in respect of expenditures paid or incurred after that date), the term *unrealized receivables,* for purposes of this section and sections 731, 736, 741, and 751, also includes potential gain from mining property defined in section 617(f)(2). With respect to each item of partnership mining property so defined, the potential gain is the amount that would be treated as gain to which section 617(d)(1) would apply if (at the time of the transaction described in section 731, 736, 741, or 751, as the case may be) the item were sold by the partnership at its fair market value.

(ii) With respect to sales, exchanges, or other dispositions after December 31, 1975, in any taxable year of a partnership ending after that date, the term *unrealized receivables,* for purposes of this section and sections 731, 736, 741, and 751, also includes potential gain from stock in a DISC as described in section 992(a). With respect to stock in such a DISC, the potential gain is the amount that would be treated as gain to which section 995(c) would apply if (at the time of the transaction described in section 731, 736, 741, or 751, as the case may be) the stock were sold by the partnership at its fair market value.

(iii) With respect to any taxable year of a partnership beginning after December 31, 1962, the term *unrealized receivables,* for purposes of this section and sections 731, 736, 741, and 751, also includes potential gain from section 1245 property. With respect to each item of partnership section 1245 property (as defined in section 1245(a)(3)), potential gain from section 1245 property is the amount that would be treated as gain to which section 1245(a)(1) would apply if (at the time of the transaction described in section 731, 736, 741, or 751, as the case may be) the item of section 1245 property were sold by the partnership at its fair market value. See § 1.1245-1(e)(1). For example, if a partnership would recognize under section 1245(a)(1) gain of $600 upon a sale of one item of section 1245 property and gain of $300 upon a sale of its only other item of such property, the potential section 1245 income of the partnership would be $900.

(iv) With respect to transfers after October 9, 1975, and to sales, exchanges, and distributions taking place after that date, the term *unrealized receivables,* for purposes of this section and sections 731, 736, 741, and 751, also includes potential gain from stock in certain foreign corporations as described in section 1248. With respect to stock in such a foreign corporation, the potential gain is the amount that would be treated as gain to which section 1248(a) would apply if (at the time of the transaction described in section 731, 736, 741, or 751, as the case may be) the stock were sold by the partnership at its fair market value.

(v) With respect to any taxable year of a partnership ending after December 31, 1963, the term *unrealized receivables,* for purposes of this section and sections 731, 736, 741, and 751, also includes potential gain from section 1250 property. With respect to each item of partnership section 1250 property (as defined in section 1250(c)), potential gain from section 1250 property is the amount that would be treated as gain to which section 1250(a) would apply if (at the time of the transaction described in section 731, 736, 741, or 751, as the case may be) the item of section 1250 property were sold by the partnership at its fair market value. See § 1.1250-1(f)(1).

(vi) With respect to any taxable year of a partnership beginning after December 31, 1969, the term *unrealized receivables,* for purposes of this section and sections 731, 736, 741, and 751, also includes potential gain from farm recapture property as defined in section 1251(e)(1) (as in effect before enactment of the Tax Reform Act of 1984). With respect to each item of partnership farm recapture property so defined, the potential gain is the amount which would be treated as gain to which section 1251(c) (as in effect before enactment of the Tax Reform Act of 1984) would apply if (at the time of the transaction described in section 731, 736, 741, or 751, as the case may be) the item were sold by the partnership at its fair market value.

(vii) With respect to any taxable year of a partnership beginning after December 31, 1969, the term *unrealized receivables,* for purposes of this section and sections 731, 736, 741, and 751, also includes potential gain from farm land as defined in section 1252(a)(2). With respect to each item of partnership farm land so defined, the potential gain is the amount that would be treated as gain to which section 1252(a) (1) would apply if (at the time of the transaction described in section 731, 736, 741, or 751, as the case may be) the item were sold by the partnership at its fair market value.

(viii) With respect to transactions which occur after December 31, 1976, in any taxable year of a partnership ending after that date, the term *unrealized receivables,* for purposes of this section and sections 731, 736, 741, and 751, also includes potential gain from franchises, trademarks, or trade names referred to in section 1253(a). With respect to each such item so referred to in section 1253(a), the potential gain is the amount that would be treated as gain to which section 1253(a) would apply if (at the time of the transaction described in section 731, 736, 741, or 751, as the case may be) the items were sold by the partnership at its fair market value.

(ix) With respect to any taxable year of a partnership ending after December 31, 1975, the term *unrealized receivables,* for purposes of this section and sections 731, 736, 741, and 751, also includes potential gain under section 1254(a) from natural resource recapture property as defined in § 1.1254-1(b)(2). With respect to each separate partnership natural resource recapture property so described, the potential gain is the amount that would be treated as gain to which section 1254(a) would apply if (at the time of the transaction described in section 731, 736, 741, or 751, as the case may be) the property were sold by the partnership at its fair market value.

(5) For purposes of subtitle A of the Internal Revenue Code, the basis of any potential gain described in paragraph (c)(4) of this section is zero.

(6) (i) If (at the time of any transaction referred to in paragraph (c)(4) of this section) a partnership holds property described in paragraph (c)(4) of this section and if—

(A) A partner had a special basis adjustment under section 743(b) in respect of the property;

(B) The basis under section 732 of the property if distributed to the partner would reflect a special basis adjustment under section 732(d); or

(C) On the date a partner acquired a partnership interest by way of a sale or exchange (or upon the death of another partner) the partnership owned the property and an election under section 754 was in effect with respect to the partnership, the partner's share of any potential gain described in paragraph (c)(4) of this section is determined under paragraph (c)(6)(ii) of this section.

(ii) The partner's share of the potential gain described in paragraph (c)(4) of this section in respect of the property to which this paragraph (c)(6)(ii) applies is that amount of gain that the partner would recognize under section 617(d)(1), 995(c), 1245(a), 1248(a), 1250(a), 1251(c) (as in effect before the Tax Reform Act of 1984), 1252(a), 1253(a), or 1254(a) (as the case may be) upon a sale of the property by the partnership, except that, for purposes of this paragraph (c)(6) the partner's share of such gain is determined in a manner that is consistent with the manner in which the partner's share of partnership property is determined; and the amount of a potential special basis adjustment under section 732(d) is treated as if it were the amount of a special basis adjustment under section 743(b). For example, in determining, for purposes of this paragraph (c) (6), the amount of gain that a partner would recognize under section 1245 upon a sale of partnership property, the items allocated under § 1245-1(e)(3)(ii) are allocated to the partner in the same manner as the partner's share of partnership property is determined. See § 1.1250-1(f) for rules similar to those contained in § 1.1245-1(e)(3)(ii).

(d) Inventory items which have substantially appreciated in value. *(1) Substantial appreciation.* Partnership inventory items shall be considered to have appreciated substantially in value if, at the time of the sale or distribution, the total fair market value of all the inventory items of the partnership exceeds 120 percent of the aggregate adjusted basis for such property in the hands of the partnership (without regard to any special basis adjustment of any partner) and, in addition, exceeds 10 percent of the fair market value of all partnership property other than money. The terms "inventory items which have appreciated substantially in value" or "substantially appreciated inventory items" refer to the aggregate of all partnership inventory items. These terms do not refer to specific partnership inventory items or to specific groups of such items. For example, any distribution of inventory items by a partnership the inventory items of which as a whole are substantially appreciated in value shall be a distribution of substantially appreciated inventory items for the purposes of section 751(b), even though the specific inventory items distributed may not be appreciated in value. Similarly, if the aggregate of partnership inventory items are not substantially appreciated in value, a distribution of specific inventory items, the value of which is more than 120 percent of their adjusted basis, will not constitute a distribution of substantially appreciated inventory items. For the purpose of this paragraph, the "fair market value" of inventory items has the same meaning as "market" value in the regulations under section 471, relating to general rule for inventories.

(2) Inventory items. The term "inventory items" as used in subchapter K, chapter 1 of the Code, includes the following types of property:

(i) Stock in trade of the partnership, or other property of a kind which would properly be included in the inventory of the partnership if on hand at the close of the taxable year, or property held by the partnership primarily for sale to customers in the ordinary course of its trade or business. See section 1221(1).

(ii) Any other property of the partnership which, on sale or exchange by the partnership, would be considered property other than a capital asset and other than property described in section 1231. Thus,. accounts receivable acquired in the ordinary course of business for services or from the sale of stock in trade constitute inventory items (see section 1221(4)), as do any unrealized receivables.

(iii) Any other property retained by the partnership which, if held by the partner selling his partnership interest or receiving a distribution described in section 751(b), would be considered property described in subdivisions (i) or (ii) of this subparagraph. Property actually distributed to the partner does not come within the provisions of section 751(d)(2)(C) and this subdivision.

(e) Section 751 property and other property. For the purposes of this section, "section 751 property means unrealized receivables or substantially appreciated inventory items, and "other property" means all property (including money) except section 751 property.

(f) Effective date. Section 751 applies to gain or loss to a seller, distributee, or partnership in the case of a sale, exchange, or distribution occurring after March 9, 1954. For the purpose of applying this paragraph in the case of a taxable year beginning before January 1, 1955, a partnership or a partner may elect to treat as applicable any other section of subchapter K, chapter 1 of the Code. Any such election shall be made by a statement submitted not later than the time prescribed by law for the filing of the return for such taxable year, or August 21, 1956, whichever date is later (but not later than 6 months after the time prescribed by law for the filing of the return for such year). See section 771(b)(3) and paragraph (b)(3) of § 1.771-1. See also section 771(c) and paragraph (c) of § 1.771-1. The rules contained in paragraphs (a)(2) and (a)(3) of this section apply to transfers of partnership interests that occur on or after December 15, 1999.

(g) Examples. Application of the provisions of section 751 may be illustrated by the following examples:

Example (1). (i)

(A) A and B are equal partners in personal service partnership PRS. B transfers its interest in PRS to T for $15,000 when PRS's balance sheet (reflecting a cash receipts and disbursements method of accounting) is as follows:

Assets

	Adjusted basis	Fair Market value
Cash	$3,000	$3,000
Loans Receivable	10,000	10,000
Capital Assets	7,000	5,000
Unrealized Receivables	0	14,000
Total	20,000	32,000

Liabilities and Capital

	Adjusted per books	Fair Market value
Liabilities	$2,000	$2,000
Capital:		
A	9,000	15,000
B	9,000	15,000
Total	20,000	32,000

(B) None of the assets owned by PRS is section 704(c) property, and the capital assets are nondepreciable. The total amount realized by B is $16,000, consisting of the cash received, $15,000, plus $1,000, B's share of the partnership liabilities assumed by T. See section 752. B's undivided half-interest in the partnership property includes a half-interest in the partnership's unrealized receivables items. B's basis for its partnership interest is $10,000 ($9,000, plus $1,000, B's share of partnership liabilities). If section 751(a) did not apply to the sale, B would recognize $6,000 of capital gain from the sale of the interest in PRS. However, section 751(a) does apply to the sale.

(ii) If PRS sold all of its section 751 property in a fully taxable transaction immediately prior to the transfer of B's partnership interest to T, B would have been allocated $7,000 of ordinary income from the sale of PRS's unrealized receivables. Therefore, B will recognize $7,000 of ordinary income with respect to the unrealized receivables. The difference between the amount of capital gain or loss that the partner would realize in the absence of section 751 ($6,000) and the amount of ordinary income or loss determined under paragraph (a)(2) of this section ($7,000) is the transferor's capital gain or loss on the sale of its partnership interest. In this case, B will recognize a $1,000 capital loss.

Example (2). (a) Facts. Partnership ABC makes a distribution to partner C in liquidation of his entire one-third interest in the partnership. At the time of the distribution, the balance sheet of the partnership, which uses the accrual method of accounting, is as follows:

Assets

	Adjusted basis per books	Market value
Cash	$15,000	$15,000
Accounts receivable	9,000	9,000
Inventory	21,000	30,000
Depreciable property	42,000	48,000
Land	9,000	9,000
Total	96,000	111,000

Liabilities and Capital

	Per books	Value
Current liabilities	$15,000	$15,000
Mortgage payable	$21,000	$21,000
Capital:		
A	20,000	25,000
B	20,000	25,000
C	20,000	25,000
Total	96,000	111,000

The distribution received by C consists of $10,000 cash and depreciable property with a fair market value of $15,000 and an adjusted basis to the partnership of $15,000.

(b) Presence of section 751 property. The partnership has no unrealized receivables, but the dual test provided in section 751(d)(1) must be applied to determine whether the inventory items of the partnership, in the aggregate, have appreciated substantially in value. The fair market value of all partnership inventory items, $39,000 (inventory $30,000, and accounts receivable $9,000), exceeds 120 percent of the $30,000 adjusted basis of such items to the partnership. The fair market value of the inventory items, $39,000, also exceeds 10 percent of the fair market value of all partnership property other than money (10 percent of $96,000 or $9,600). Therefore, the partnership inventory items have substantially appreciated in value.

(c) The properties exchanged. Since C's entire partnership interest is to be liquidated, the provisions of section 736 are applicable. No part of the payment, however, is considered as a distributive share or as a guaranteed payment under section 736(a) because the entire payment is made for C's interest in partnership property. Therefore, the entire payment is for an interest in partnership property under section 736(b), and, to the extent applicable, subject to the rules of section 751. In the distribution, C received his share of cash ($5,000) and $15,000 in depreciable property ($1,000 less than his $16,000 share). In addition, he received other partnership property ($5,000 cash and $12,000 liabilities assumed, treated as money distributed under section 752(b)) in exchange for his interest in accounts receivable ($3,000), inventory ($10,000), land ($3,000), and the balance of his interest in depreciable property ($1,000). Section 751(b) applies only to the extent of the exchange of other property for section 751 property (i.e., inventory items, which include trade accounts receivable). The section 751 property exchanged has a fair market value of $13,000 ($3,000 in accounts receivable and $10,000 in inventory). Thus, $13,000 of the total amount C received is considered as received for the sale of section 751 property.

(d) Distributee partner's tax consequences. C's tax consequences on the distribution are as follows:

(1) The section 751(b) sale or exchange. C's share of the inventory items is treated as if he received them in a current distribution, and his basis for such items is $10,000 ($7,000 for inventory and $3,000 for accounts receivable) as determined under paragraph (b)(3)(iii) of this section. Then C is considered as having sold his share of inventory items to the partnership for $13,000. Thus, on the sale of his share of inventory items, C realizes $3,000 of ordinary income.

(2) The part of the distribution not under section 751(b). Section 751(b) does not apply to the balance of the distribution. Before the distribution, C's basis for his partnership interest was $32,000 ($20,000 plus $12,000, his share of partnership liabilities). See section 752(a). This basis is reduced

by $10,000, the basis attributed to the section 751 property treated as distributed to C and sold by him to the partnership. Thus, C has a basis of $22,000 for the remainder of his partnership interest. The total distribution to C was $37,000 ($22,000 in cash and liabilities assumed, and $15,000 in depreciable property). Since C received no more than his share of the depreciable property, none of the depreciable property constitutes proceeds of the sale under section 751(b). C did receive more than his share of money. Therefore, the sale proceeds, treated separately in subparagraph (1) of this paragraph of this example, must consist of money and therefore must be deducted from the money distribution. Consequently, in liquidation of the balance of C's interest, he receives depreciable property and $9,000 in money ($22,000 less $13,000). Therefore, no gain or loss is recognized to C on the distribution. Under section 732(b), C's basis for the depreciable property is $13,000 (the remaining basis of his partnership interest, $22,000, reduced by $9,000, the money received in the distribution).

(e) Partnership's tax consequences. The tax consequences to the partnership on the distribution are as follows:

(1) The section 751(b) sale or exchange. The partnership consisting of the remaining members has no ordinary income on the distribution since it did not give up any section 751 property in the exchange. Of the $22,000 money distributed (in cash and the assumption of C's share of liabilities) $13,000 was paid to acquire C's interest in inventory ($10,000 fair market value) and in accounts receivable ($3,000). Since under section 751(b) the partnership is treated as buying these properties, it has a new cost basis for the inventory and accounts receivable acquired from C. Its basis for C's share of inventory and accounts receivable is $13,000, the amount which the partnership is considered as having paid C in the exchange. Since the partnership is treated as having distributed C's share of inventory and accounts receivable to him, the partnership must decrease its basis for inventory and accounts receivable ($30,000) by $10,000, the basis of C's share treated as distributed to him, and then increase the basis for inventory and accounts receivable by $13,000 to reflect the purchase prices of the items acquired. Thus, the basis of the partnership inventory is increased from $21,000 to $24,000 in the transaction. (Note that the basis of property acquired in a section 751(b) exchange is determined under section 1012 without regard to any elections of the partnership. See paragraph (e) of § 1.732-1.) Further, the partnership realizes no capital gain or loss on the portion of the distribution treated as a sale under section 751(b) since, to acquire C's interest in the inventory and accounts receivable, it gave up money and assumed C's share of liabilities.

(2) The part of the distribution not under section 751(b). In the remainder of the distribution to C which was not in exchange for C's interest in section 751 property, C received only other property as follows: $15,000 in depreciable property (with a basis to the partnership of $15,000) and $9,000 in money ($22,000 less $13,000 treated under subparagraph (1) of this paragraph of this example). Since this part of the distribution is not an exchange of section 751 property for other property, section 751(b) does not apply. Instead, the provisions which apply are sections 731 through 736, relating to distributions by a partnership. No gain or loss is recognized to the partnership on the distribution. (See section 731(b).) Further, the partnership makes no adjustment to the basis of remaining depreciable property unless an election under section 754 is in effect. (See section 734(a).) Thus, the basis of the depreciable property before the distribution, $42,000, is reduced by the basis of the depreciable property distributed, $15,000, leaving a basis for the depreciable property in the partnership of $27,000. However, if an election under section 754 is in effect, the partnership must make the adjustment required under section 734(b) as follows: Since the adjusted basis of the distributed property to the partnership had been $15,000, and is only $13,000 in C's hands (see paragraph (d)(2) of this example), the partnership will increase the basis of the depreciable property remaining in the partnership by $2,000 (the excess of the adjusted basis to the partnership of the distributed depreciable property immediately before the distribution over its basis to the distributee). Whether or not an election under section 754 is in effect, the basis for each of the remaining partner's partnership interests will be $38,000 ($20,000 original contribution, plus $12,000, each partner's original share of the liabilities, plus $6,000, the share of C's liabilities each assumed).

(f) Partnership trial balance. A trial balance of the AB partnership after the distribution in liquidation of C's entire interest would reflect the results set forth in the schedule below. Column I shows the amounts to be reflected in the records if an election is in effect under section 754 with respect to an optional adjustment under section 734(b) to the basis of undistributed partnership property. Column II shows the amounts to be reflected in the records where an election under section 754 is not in effect. Note that in column II, the total bases for the partnership assets do not equal the total of the bases for the partnership interests.

	I Sec. 754, Election in effect		II Sec. 754, Election not in effect	
	Basis	Fair market value	Basis	Fair market value
Cash	$ 5,000	$ 5,000	$ 5,000	$ 5,000
Accounts receivable	9,000	9,000	9,000	9,000
Inventory	24,000	30,000	24,000	30,000
Depreciable property	29,000	33,000	27,000	33,000
Land	9,000	9,000	9,000	9,000
	76,000	86,000	74,000	86,000
Current liabilities	15,000	15,000	15,000	15,000
Mortgage	21,000	21,000	21,000	21,000
Capital:				
A	20,000	25,000	20,000	25,000
B	20,000	25,000	20,000	25,000
	76,000	86,000	76,000	86,000

Example (3). (a) Facts. Assume that the distribution to partner C in example (2) of this paragraph in liquidation of his entire interest in partnership ABC consists of $5,000 in cash and $20,000 worth of partnership inventory with a basis of $14,000.

(b) Presence of section 751 property. For the same reason as stated in paragraph (b) of example (2), the partnership inventory items have substantially appreciated in value.

(c) The properties exchanged. In the distribution, C received his share of cash ($5,000) and his share of appreciated inventory items ($13,000). In addition, he received appreciated inventory with a fair market value of $7,000 (and with an adjusted basis to the partnership of $4,900) and $12,000 in money (liabilities assumed). C has relinquished his interest in $16,000 of depreciable property and $3,000 of land. Although C relinquished his interest in $3,000 of accounts receivable, such accounts receivable are inventory items and, therefore, that exchange was not an exchange of section 751 property for other property. Section 751(b) applies only to the extent of the exchange of other property for section 751 property (i.e., depreciable property or land for inventory items). Assume that the partners agree that the $7,000 of inventory in excess of C's share was received by him in exchange for $7,000 of depreciable property.

(d) Distributee partner's tax consequences. C's tax consequence on the distributions are as follows:

(1) The section 751(b) sale or exchange. C is treated as if he had received his 7/16ths share of the depreciable property in a current distribution. His basis for that share is $6,125 (42,000/48,000 of $7,000), as determined under paragraph (b)(2)(iii) of this section. Then C is considered as having sold his 7/16ths share of depreciable property to the partnership for $7,000, realizing a gain of $875.

(2) The part of the distribution not under section 751(b). Section 751(b) does not apply to the balance of the distribution. Before the distribution, C's basis for his partnership interest was $32,000 ($20,000, plus $12,000, his share of partnership liabilities). See section 752(a). This basis is reduced by $6,125, the basis of property treated as distributed to C and sold by him to the partnership. Thus, C will have a basis of $25,875 for the remainder of his partnership interest. Of the $37,000 total distribution to C, $30,000 ($17,000 in money, including liabilities assumed, and $13,000 in inventory) is not within section 751(b). Under section 732(b), C's basis for the inventory with a fair market value of $13,000 (which had an adjusted basis to the partnership of $9,100) is limited to $8,875, the amount of the remaining basis for his partnership interest, $25,875, reduced by $17,000, the money received. Thus, C's total aggregate basis for the inventory received is $15,875 ($7,000 plus $8,875), and not its $14,000 basis in the hands of the partnership.

(e) Partnership's tax consequences. The tax consequences to the partnership on the distribution are as follows:

(1) The section 751(b) sale or exchange. The partnership consisting of the remaining members has $2,100 of ordinary income on the sale of the $7,000 of inventory which had a basis to the partnership of $4,900 (21,000/30,000 of $7,000). This $7,000 of inventory was paid to acquire 7/16ths of C's interest in the depreciable property. Since, under section 751(b), the partnership is treated as buying this property from C, it has a new cost basis for such property. Its basis for the depreciable property is $42,875 ($42,000 less $6,125, the basis of the 7/16ths share considered as distributed to C, plus $7,000, the partnership purchase price for this share).

(2) The part of the distribution not under section 751(b). In the remainder of the distribution to C which was not a sale or exchange of section 751 property for other property, the partnership realizes no gain or loss. See section 731(b). Further, under section 734(a), the partnership makes no adjustment to the basis of the accounts receivable or the 7/16ths interest in depreciable property which C relinquished. However, if an election under section 754 is in effect, the partnership must make the adjustment required under section 734(b) since the adjusted basis to the partnership of the inventory distributed had been $9,100, and C's basis for such inventory after distribution is only $8,875. The basis of the inventory remaining in the partnership must be increased by $225. Whether or not an election under section 754 is in effect, the basis for each of the remaining partnership interests will be $39,050 ($20,000 original contribution, plus $12,000, each partner's original share of the liabilities, plus $6,000, the share of C's liabilities now assumed, plus $1,050, each partner's share of ordinary income realized by the partnership upon that part of the distribution treated as a sale or exchange).

Example (4). (a) Facts. Assume the same facts as in example (3) of this paragraph except that the partners did not identify the property which C relinquished in exchange for the $7,000 of inventory which he received in excess of his share.

(b) Presence of section 751 property. For the same reasons stated in paragraph (b) of example (2) of this paragraph, the partnership inventory items have substantially appreciated in value.

(c) The properties exchanged. The analysis stated in paragraph (c) of example (3) of this paragraph is the same in this example, except that, in the absence of a specific agreement among the partners as to the properties exchanged, C will be presumed to have sold to the partnership a proportionate amount of each property in which he relinquished an interest. Thus, in the absence of an agreement, C has received $7,000 of inventory in exchange for his release of 7/19ths of the depreciable property and 7/19ths of the land. ($7,000, fair market value of property released, over $19,000, the sum of the fair market values of C's interest in the land and C's interest in the depreciable property.

(d) Distributee partner's tax consequences. C's tax consequences on the distribution are as follows:

(1) The section 751(b) sale or exchange. C is treated as if he had received his 7/19ths shares of the depreciable property and land in a current distribution. His basis for those shares is $6,263 (51,000/57,000 of $7,000, their fair market value), as determined under paragraph (b)(2)(iii) of this section. Then C is considered as having sold his 7/19ths shares of depreciable property and land to the partnership for $7,000, realizing a gain of $737.

(2) The part of the distribution not under section 751(b). Section 751(b) does not apply to the balance of the distribution. Before the distribution C's basis for his partnership interest was $32,000 ($20,000 plus $12,000, his share of partnership liabilities). See section 752(a). This basis is reduced by $6,263, the bases of C's shares of depreciable property and land treated as distributed to him and sold by him to the partnership. Thus, C will have a basis of $25,737 for the remainder of his partnership interest. Of the total $37,000 distributed to C, $30,000 ($17,000 in money, including liabilities assumed, and $13,000 in inventory) is not within section 751(b). Under section 732(b), C's basis for the inventory (with a fair market value of $13,000 and an adjusted basis to the partnership of $9,100) is limited to $8,737, the amount of the remaining basis for his partnership interest ($25,737 less $17,000, money received). Thus, C's total aggregate basis for the inventory he received is $15,737 ($7,000 plus $8,737), and not the $14,000 basis it had in the hands of the partnership.

(e) Partnership's tax consequences. The tax consequences to the partnership on the distribution are as follows:

(1) The section 751(b) sale or exchange. The partnership consisting of the remaining members has $2,100 of ordinary income on the sale of $7,000 of inventory which had a basis to the partnership of $4,900 (21,000/30,000 of $7,000). This $7,000 of inventory was paid to acquire 7/19ths of C's interest in the depreciable property and land. Since, under section 751(b), the partnership is treated as buying this property from C, it has a new cost basis for such property. The bases of the depreciable property and land would be $42,737 and

$9,000, respectively. The basis for the depreciable property is computed as follows: The common partnership basis of $42,000 is reduced by the $5,158 basis (42,000/48,000 of $5,895) for C's 7/19ths interest constructively distributed and increased by $5,895 (16,000/19,000 of $7,000), the part of the purchase price allocated to the depreciable property. The basis of the land would be computed in the same way. The $9,000 original partnership basis is reduced by $1,105 basis ($9,000/9,000 of $1,105) of land constructively distributed to C, and increased by $1,105 (3,000/19,000 of $7,000), the portion of the purchase price allocated to the land.

(2) The part of the distribution not under section 751(b). In the remainder of the distribution to C which was not a sale or exchange of section 751 property for other property, the partnership realizes no gain or loss. See section 731(b). Further, under section 734(a), the partnership makes no adjustment to the basis of the accounts receivable or the 12/19ths interests in depreciable property and land which C relinquished. However, if an election under section 754 is in effect, the partnership must make the adjustment required under section 734(b) since the adjusted basis to the partnership of the inventory distributed had been $9,100 and C's basis for such inventory after the distribution is only $8,737. The basis of the inventory remaining in the partnership must be increased by the difference of $363. Whether or not an election under section 754 is in effect, the basis for each of the remaining partnership interests will be $39,050 ($20,000 original contribution plus $12,000, each partner's original share of the liabilities, plus $6,000, the share of C's liabilities assumed, plus $1,050, each partner's share of ordinary income realized by the partnership upon the part of the distribution treated as a sale or exchange).

Example (5). (a) Facts. Assume that partner C in example (2) of this paragraph agrees to reduce his interest in capital and profits from one-third to one-fifth for a current distribution consisting of $5,000 in cash, and $7,500 of accounts receivable with a basis to the partnership of $7,500. At the same time, the total liabilities of the partnership are not reduced. Therefore, after the distribution, C's share of the partnership liabilities has been reduced by $4,800 from $12,000 (⅓ of $36,000) to $7,200 (⅕ of $36,000).

(b) Presence of section 751 property. For the same reasons as stated in paragraph (b) of example (2) of this paragraph, the partnership inventory items have substantially appreciated in value.

(c) The properties exchanged. C's interest in the fair market value of the partnership properties before and after the distribution can be illustrated by the following table:

Item	C's interest Fair Market Value: One-third before	One-fifth after	C received: Distribution of share	In excess of share	C relinquished
Cash	$5,000	$2,000	$3,000	$2,000	
Liabilities assumed	(12,000)	(7,200)		4,800	
Inventory items:					
Accounts receivable	3,000	300	2,700	4,800	
Inventory	10,000	6,000			$ 4,000
Depreciable property	16,000	9,600			6,400
Land	3,000	1,800			1,200
Total	25,000	12,500	5,700	11,600	11,600

Although C relinquished his interest in $4,000 of inventory and received $4,800 of accounts receivable, both items constitute section 751 property and C has received only $800 of accounts receivable for $800 worth of depreciable property or for an $800 undivided interest in land. In the absence of an agreement identifying the properties exchanged, it is presumed C received $800 for proportionate shares of his interests in both depreciable property and land. To the extent that inventory was exchanged for accounts receivable, or to the extent cash was distributed for the release of C's interest in the balance of the depreciable property and land, the transaction does not fall within section 751(b) and is a current distribution under section 732(a). Thus, the remaining $6,700 of accounts receivable are received in a current distribution.

(d) Distributee partner's tax consequences. C's tax consequences on the distribution are as follows:

(1) The section 751(b) sale or exchange. Assuming that the partners paid $800 worth of accounts receivable for $800 worth of depreciable property, C is treated as if he received the depreciable property in a current distribution, and his basis for the $800 worth of depreciable property is $700 (42,000/48,000 of $800, its fair market value), as determined under paragraph (b)(2)(iii) of this section. Then C is considered as having sold his $800 share of depreciable property to the partnership for $800. On the sale of the depreciable property, C realizes a gain of $100. If, on the other hand, the partners had agreed that C exchanged an $800 interest in the land for $800 worth of accounts receivable, C would realize no gain or loss, because under paragraph (b)(2)(iii) of this section his basis for the land sold would be $800. In the absence of an agreement, the basis for the depreciable property and land (which C is considered as having received in a current distribution and then sold back to the partnership) would be $716 (51,000/57,000 of $800). In that case, on the sale of the balance of the $800 share of depreciable property and land, C would realize $84 of gain ($800 less $716).

(2) The part of the distribution not under section 751(b). Section 751(b) does not apply to the balance of the distribution. Under section 731, C does not realize either gain or loss on the balance of the distribution. The adjustments to the basis of C's interest are illustrated in the following table:

	If accounts receivable received for depreciable property	If accounts receivable received for land	If there is no agreement
Original basis for C's interest	$32,000	$32,000	$32,000

Less basis of property distributed prior to sec. 751 (b) sale or exchange	–700	–800	–716
	31,300	31,200	31,284
Less money received in distribution	–9,800	–9,800	–9,800
	21,500	21,400	21,484
Less basis of property received in a current distribution under sec. 732	–6,700	–6,700	–6,700
Resulting basis for C's interest	14,800	14,700	14,784

C's basis for the $7,500 worth of accounts receivable which he received in the distribution will be $7,500, composed of $800 for the portion purchased in the section 751(b) exchange, plus $6,700, the basis carried over under section 732(a) for the portion received in the current distribution.

(e) Partnership's tax consequences. The tax consequences to the partnership on the distribution are as follows:

(1) The section 751(b) sale or exchange. The partnership realizes no gain or loss in the section 751 sale or exchange because it had a basis of $800 for the accounts receivable for which it received $800 worth of other property. If the partnership agreed to purchase $800 worth of depreciable property, the partnership basis of depreciable property becomes $42,100 ($42,000 less $700 basis of property constructively distributed to C, plus $800, price of property purchased). If the partnership purchased land with the accounts receivable, there would be no change in the basis of the land to the partnership because the basis of land distributed was equal to its purchase price. If there were no agreement, the basis of the depreciable property and land would be $51,084 (depreciable property, $42,084 and land $9,000). The basis for the depreciable property is computed as follows: The common partnership basis of $42,000 is reduced by the $590 basis (42,000/48,000 of $674) for C's $674 interest constructively distributed, and increased by $674 (6,400/7,600 of $800), the part of the purchase price allocated to the depreciable property. The basis of the land would be computed in the same way. The $9,000 original partnership basis is reduced by $126 basis (9,000/9,000 of $126) of the land constructively distributed to C, and increased by $126 (1,200/7,600 of $800), the portion of the purchase price allocated to the land.

(2) The part of the distribution not under section 751(b). The partnership will realize no gain or loss in the balance of the distribution under section 731. Since the property in C's hands after the distribution will have the same basis it had in the partnership, the basis of partnership property remaining in the partnership after the distribution will not be adjusted (whether or not an election under 754 is in effect).

Example (6). (a) Facts. Partnership ABC distributes to partner C, in liquidation of his entire one-third interest in the partnership, a machine which is section 1245 property with a recomputed basis (as defined in section 1245(a)(2)) of $18,000. At the time of the distribution, the balance sheet of the partnership is as follows:

Assets

	Adjusted basis per books	Market value
Cash	$ 3,000	$ 3,000
Machine (section 1245 property)	9,000	15,000
Land	18,000	27,000
Total	30,000	45,000

Liabilities and Capital

	Per books	Value
Liabilities	$ 0	$ 0
Capital:		
A	10,000	15,000
B	10,000	15,000
C	10,000	15,000
Total	30,000	45,000

(b) Presence of section 751 property. The section 1245 property is an unrealized receivable of the partnership to the extent of the potential section 1245 income in respect of the property. Since the fair market value of the property ($15,000) is lower than its recomputed basis ($18,000), the excess of the fair market value over its adjusted basis ($9,000), or $6,000, is the potential section 1245 income of the partnership in respect of the property. The partnership has no other section 751 property.

(c) The properties exchanged. In the distribution C received his share of section 751 property (potential section 1245 income of $2,000, i.e., ⅓ of $6,000) and his share of section 1245 property (other than potential section 1245 income) with a fair market value of $3,000, i.e., ⅓ of ($15,000 minus $6,000), and an adjusted basis of $3,000, i.e., ⅓ of $9,000. In addition he received $4,000 of section 751 property (consisting of $4,000 ($6,000 minus $2,000) of potential section 1245 income) and section 1245 property (other than potential section 1245 income) with a fair market value of $6,000 ($9,000 minus $3,000). C relinquished his interest in $1,000 of cash and $9,000 of land. Assume that the partners agree that the $4,000 of section 751 property in excess of C's share was received by him in exchange for $4,000 of land.

(d) Distributee partner's tax consequences. C's tax consequences on the distributions are as follows:

(1) The section 751(b) sale or exchange. C is treated as if he received in a current distribution 4/9ths of his share of the land with a basis of $2,667 (18,000/27,000 × $4,000). Then C is considered as having sold his 4/9ths share of the land to the partnership for $4,000, realizing a gain of $1,333. C's basis for the remainder of his partnership interest after the current distribution is $7,333, i.e., the basis of his partnership interest before the current distribution ($10,000) minus the basis of the land treated as distributed to him ($2,667).

(2) The part of the distribution not under section 751(b). Of the $15,000 total distribution to C, $11,000 ($2,000 of potential section 1245 income and $9,000 section 1245 property other than potential section 1245 income) is not within section 751(b). Under section 732(b) and (c), C's basis for his share of potential section 1245 income is zero (see paragraph (c)(5) of this section) and his basis for $9,000 of section 1245 property (other than potential section 1245 income) is $7,333, i.e., the amount of the remaining basis for his partnership interest ($7,333) reduced by the basis for his share of potential section 1245 income (zero). Thus C's total aggregate basis for the section 1245 property (fair market value of $15,000) distributed to him is $11,333 ($4,000 plus $7,333). For an illustration of the computation of his recom-

puted basis for the section 1245 property immediately after the distribution, see example (2) of paragraph (f)(3) of § 1.1245-4.

(e) Partnership's tax consequences. The tax consequences to the partnership on the distribution are as follows:

(1) The section 751(b) sale or exchange. Upon the sale of $4,000 potential section 1245 income, with a basis of zero, for ⅘ths of C's interest in the land, the partnership consisting of the remaining members has $4,000 ordinary income under sections 751(b) and 1245(a)(1). See section 1245(b)(3) and (6)(A). The partnership's new basis for the land is $19,333, i.e., $18,000, less the basis of the ⅘ths share considered as distributed to C ($2,667), plus the partnership purchase price for this share ($4,000).

(2) The part of the distribution not under section 751(b). The analysis under this subparagraph should be made in accordance with the principles illustrated in paragraph (e)(2) of examples (3), (4), and (5) of this paragraph.

T.D. 6175, 5/23/56, amend T.D. 6832, 7/6/65, T.D. 7084, 1/7/71, T.D. 8586, 1/9/95, T.D. 8847, 12/14/99, T.D. 9137, 7/15/2004.

§ 1.752-0 Table of contents.

This section lists the major paragraphs that appear in §§ 1.752-1 through 1.752-7.

T.D. 8380, 12/20/91, amend T.D. 9207, 5/23/2005.

---

§ 1.752-1 Treatment of partnership liabilities.

(a) Definitions. For purposes of section 752, the following definitions apply:

(1) Recourse liability defined. A partnership liability is a recourse liability to the extent that any partner or related person bears the economic risk of loss set forth under § 1.752-2.

(2) Nonrecourse liability defined. A partnership liability is a nonrecourse liability to the extent that no partner or related person bears economic risk of loss for that liability under § 1.752-2.

(3) Related person. Related person means a person having a relationship to a partner that is described in § 1.752-4(b).

(4) Liability defined. (i) In general. An obligation is a liability for purposes of section 752 and the regulations thereunder (§ 1.752-1 liability), only if, when, and to the extent that incurring the obligation—

(A) Creates or increases the basis of any of the obligor's assets (including cash);

(B) Gives rise to an immediate deduction to the obligor; or

(C) Gives rise to an expense that is not deductible in computing the obligor's taxable income and is not properly chargeable to capital.

(ii) Obligation. For purposes of this paragraph and § 1.752-7, an obligation is any fixed or contingent obligation to make payment without regard to whether the obligation is otherwise taken into account for purposes of the Internal Revenue Code. Obligations include, but are not limited to, debt obligations, environmental obligations, tort obligations, contract obligations, pension obligations, obligations under a short sale, and obligations under derivative financial instruments such as options, forward contracts, futures contracts, and swaps.

(iii) Other liabilities. For obligations that are not § 1.752-1 liabilities, see §§ 1.752-6 and 1.752-7.

(iv) Effective date. Except as otherwise provided in § 1.752-7(k), this paragraph (a)(4) applies to liabilities that are incurred or assumed by a partnership on or after June 24, 2003.

(b) Increase in partner's share of liabilities. Any increase In a partners share of partnership liabilities, or any increase In a partner's Individual liabilities by reason of the partner's assumption of partnership liabilities, is treated as a contribution of money by that partner to the partnership.

(c) Decrease in partner's share of liabilities. Any decrease in a partner's share of partnership liabilities, or any decrease in a partner's individual liabilities by reason of the partnership's assumption of the individual liabilities of the partner, is treated as a distribution of money by the partnership to that partner.

(d) Assumption of liability. Except as otherwise provided In paragraph (e) of this section, a person is considered to assume a liability only to the extent that:

(1) The assuming person is personally obligated to pay the liability; and

(2) If a partner or related person assumes a partnership liability, the person to whom the liability is owed knows of the assumption and can directly enforce the partner's or related person's obligation for the liability, and no other partner or person that is a related person to another partner would bear the economic risk of loss for the liability immediately after the assumption.

(e) Property subject to a liability. If property is contributed by a partner to the partnership or distributed by the partnership to a partner and the property is subject to a liability of the transferor, the transferee is treated as having assumed the liability, to the extent that the amount of the liability does not exceed the fair market value of the property at the time of the contribution or distribution.

(f) Netting of increases and decreases in liabilities resulting from same transaction. If, as a result of a single transaction, a partner incurs both an increase in the partner's share of the partnership liabilities (or the partner's individual liabilities) and a decrease in the partner's share of the partnership liabilities (or the partner's individual liabilities), only the net decrease is treated as a distribution from the partnership and only the net increase is treated as a contribution of money to the partnership. Generally, the contribution to or distribution from a partnership of property subject to a liability or the termination of the partnership under section 708(b) will require that increases and decreases in liabilities associated with the transaction be netted to determine if a partner will be deemed to have made a contribution or received a distribution as a result of the transaction. When two or more partnerships merge or consolidate under section 708(b)(2)(A), as described in § 1.708-1(c)(3)(i), increases and decreases in partnership liabilities associated with the merger or consolidation are netted by the partners in the terminating partnership and the resulting partnership to determine the effect of the merger under section 752.

(g) Example. The following example illustrates the principles of paragraphs (b), (c), (e), and (f) of this section.

Example (1). Property contributed subject to a liability; netting of increase and decrease in partner's share of liability. B contributes property with an adjusted basis of $1,000 to a general partnership in exchange for a one-third interest in the partnership. At the time of the contribution, the partnership does not have liabilities outstanding and the property is subject to a recourse debt of $150 and has a fair market value in excess of $150. After the contribution, B remains personally liable to the creditor and none of the other partners bears any of the economic risk of loss for the liability under state law or otherwise. Under paragraph (e) of this section, the partnership is treated as having assumed the $150 liability. As a result, B's individual liabilities decrease by $150. At the same time, however, S's share of liabilities of the partnership increases by $150. Only the net increase or decrease in B's share of the liabilities of the partnership and B's individual liabilities is taken into account in applying section 752. Because there is no net change, B is not treated as having contributed money to the partnership or as having received a distribution of money from the partnership under paragraph (b) or (c) of this section. Therefore B's basis for B's partnership interest is $1,000 (B's basis for the contributed property).

Example (2). Merger or consolidation of partnerships holding property encumbered by liabilities.

(i) B owns a 70 percent interest in partnership T. Partnership T's sole asset is property X, which is encumbered by a $900 liability. Partnership T's adjusted basis in property X is $600, and the value of property X is $1,000. B's adjusted basis in its partnership T interest is $420. B also owns a 20 percent interest in partnership S. Partnership S's sole asset is property Y, which is encumbered by a $100 liability. Partnership S's adjusted basis in property Y is $200, the value of property Y is $1,000, and B's adjusted basis in its partnership S interest is $40.

(ii) Partnership T and partnership S merge under section 708(b)(2)(A). Under section 708(b)(2)(A) and § 1.708-1(c)(1), partnership T is considered terminated and the resulting partnership is considered a continuation of partnership S. Partnerships T and S undertake the form described in § 1.708-1(c)(3)(i) for the partnership merger. Under § 1.708-1(c)(3)(i), partnership T contributes property X and its $900 liability to partnership S in exchange for an interest in partnership S. Immediately thereafter, partnership T distributes the interests in partnership S to its partners in liquidation of their interests in partnership T. B owns a 25 percent interest in partnership S after partnership T distributes the interests in partnership S to B.

(iii) Under paragraph (f) of this section, B nets the increases and decreases in its share of partnership liabilities associated with the merger of partnership T and partnership S. Before the merger, B's share of partnership liabilities was $650 (B had a $630 share of partnership liabilities in partnership T and a $20 share of partnership liabilities in partnership S immediately before the merger). B's share of S's partnership liabilities after the merger is $250 (25 percent of S's total partnership liabilities of $1,000). Accordingly, B has a $400 net decrease in its share of S's partnership liabilities. Thus, B is treated as receiving a $400 distribution from partnership S under section 752(b). Because B's adjusted basis in its partnership S interest before the deemed distribution under section 752(b) is $460 ($420 + $40), B will not recognize gain under section 731. After the merger, B's adjusted basis in its partnership S interest is $60.

(h) Sale or exchange of a partnership interest. If a partnership interest is sold or exchanged, the reduction in the transferor partner's share of partnership liabilities is treated as an amount realized under section 1001 and the regulations thereunder. For example, if a partner sells an interest in a partnership for $750 cash and transfers to the purchaser the partner's share of partnership liabilities in the amount of $250, the seller realizes $1,000 on the transaction.

(i) Bifurcation of partnership liabilities. If one or more partners bears the economic risk of loss as to part, but not all, of a partnership liability represented by a single contractual obligation, that liability is treated as two or more separate liabilities for purposes of section 752. The portion of the liability as to which one or more partners bear the economic risk of loss is a recourse liability and the remainder of the liability, if any, is a nonrecourse liability.

T.D. 8380, 12/20/91, amend T.D. 8925, 1/3/2001, T.D. 9207, 5/23/2005.

§ 1.752-2 Partner's share of recourse liabilities.

(a) In general. A partner's share of a recourse partnership liability equals the portion of that liability, if any, for which the partner or related person bears the economic risk of loss. The determination of the extent to which a partner bears the economic risk of loss for a partnership liability is made under the rules in paragraphs (b) through (k) of this section.

(b) Obligation to make a payment. *(1) In general.* Except as otherwise provided in this section, a partner bears the economic risk of loss for a partnership liability to the extent that, if the partnership constructively liquidated, the partner or related person would be obligated to make a payment to any person (or a contribution to the partnership) because that liability becomes due and payable and the partner or related person would not be entitled to reimbursement from another partner or person that is a related person to another partner. Upon a constructive liquidation, all of the following events are deemed to occur simultaneously:

(i) All of the partnership's liabilities become payable in full;

(ii) With the exception of property contributed to secure a partnership liability (see § 1.752-2(h)(2)), all of the partnership's assets, including cash, have a value of zero;

(iii) The partnership disposes of all of its property in a fully taxable transaction for no consideration (except relief from liabilities for which the creditors' right to repayment is limited solely to one or more assets of the partnership);

(iv) All items of income, gain, loss, or deduction are allocated among the partners; and

(v) The partnership liquidates.

(2) Treatment upon deemed disposition. For purposes of paragraph (b)(1) of this section, gain or loss on the deemed disposition of the partnership's assets is computed in accordance with the following:

(i) If the creditor's right to repayment of a partnership liability is limited solely to one or more assets of the partnership, gain or loss is recognized in an amount equal to the difference between the amount of the liability that is extinguished by the deemed disposition and the tax basis (or book value to the extent section 704(c) or § 1.704-1(b)(4)(i) applies) in those assets.

(ii) A loss is recognized equal to the remaining tax basis (or book value to the extent section 704(c) or § 1.704-1(b)(4)(i) applies) of all the partnership's assets not taken into account in paragraph (b)(2)(i) of this section.

(3) Obligations recognized. The determination of the extent to which a partner or related person has an obligation to make a payment under paragraph (b)(1) of this section is based on the facts and circumstances at the time of the determination. All statutory and contractual obligations relating to the partnership liability are taken into account for purposes of applying this section, including:

(i) Contractual obligations outside the partnership agreement such as guarantees, indemnifications, reimbursement agreements, and other obligations running directly to creditors or to other partners, or to the partnership;

(ii) Obligations to the partnership that are imposed by the partnership agreement, including the obligation to make a capital contribution and to restore a deficit capital account upon liquidation of the partnership; and

(iii) Payment obligations (whether in the form of direct remittances to another partner or a contribution to the partnership) imposed by state law including the governing state partnership statute.

To the extent that the obligation of a partner to make a payment with respect to a partnership liability is not recognized under this paragraph (b)(3), paragraph (b) of this section is applied as if the obligation did not exist.

(4) Contingent obligations. A payment obligation is disregarded if, taking into account all the facts and circumstances, the obligation is subject to contingencies that make it unlikely that the obligation will ever be discharged. If a payment obligation would arise at a future time after the occurrence of an event that is not determinable with reasonable certainty, the obligation is ignored until the event occurs.

(5) Reimbursement rights. A partner's or related person's obligation to make a payment with respect to a partnership liability is reduced to the extent that the partner or related person is entitled to reimbursement from another partner or a person who is a related person to another partner.

(6) Deemed satisfaction of obligation. For purposes of determining the extent to which a partner or related person has a payment obligation and the economic risk of loss, it is assumed that all partners and related persons who have obligations to make payments actually perform those obligations, irrespective of their actual net worth, unless the facts and circumstances indicate a plan to circumvent or avoid the obligation. See paragraphs (j) and (k) of this section.

(c) Partner or related person as lender. *(1) In general.* A partner bears the economic risk of loss for a partnership liability to the extent that the partner or a related person makes (or acquires an interest in) a nonrecourse loan to the partnership and the economic risk of loss for the liability is not borne by another partner.

(2) Wrapped debt. If a partnership liability is owed to a partner or related person and that liability includes (*i.e.*, is "wrapped" around) a nonrecourse obligation encumbering partnership property that is owed to another person, the part-

nership liability will be treated as two separate liabilities. The portion of the partnership liability corresponding to the wrapped debt is treated as a liability owed to another person.

(d) De minimis exceptions. *(1) Partner as lender.* The general rule contained in paragraph (c)(1) of this section does not apply if a partner or related person whose interest (directly or indirectly through one or more partnerships including the interest of any related person) in each item of partnership income, gain, loss, deduction, or credit for every taxable year that the partner is a partner in the partnership is 10 percent or less, makes a loan to the partnership which constitutes qualified nonrecourse financing within the meaning of section 465(b)(6) (determined without regard to the type of activity financed).

(2) Partner as guarantor. The general rule contained in paragraph (b)(1) of this section does not apply if a partner or related person whose interest (directly or indirectly through one or more partnerships including the interest of any related person) in each item of partnership income, gain, loss, deduction, or credit for every taxable year that the partner is a partner in the partnership is 10 percent or less, guarantees a loan that would otherwise be a nonrecourse loan of the partnership and which would constitute qualified nonrecourse financing within the meaning of section 465(b)(6) (without regard to the type of activity financed) if the guarantor had made the loan to the partnership.

(e) Special rule for nonrecourse liability with interest guaranteed by a partner. *(1) In general.* For purposes of this section, if one or more partners or related persons have guaranteed the payment of more than 25 percent of the total interest that will accrue on a partnership nonrecourse liability over its remaining term, and it is reasonable to expect that the guarantor will be required to pay substantially all of the guaranteed future interest if the partnership fails to do so, then the liability is treated as two separate partnership liabilities. If this rule applies, the partner or related person that has guaranteed the payment of interest is treated as bearing the economic risk of loss for the partnership liability to the extent of the present value of the guaranteed future interest payments. The remainder of the stated principal amount of the partnership liability constitutes a nonrecourse liability. Generally, in applying this rule, it is reasonable to expect that the guarantor will be required to pay substantially all of the guaranteed future interest if, upon a default in payment by the partnership, the lender can enforce the interest guaranty without foreclosing on the property and thereby extinguishing the underlying debt. The guarantee of interest rule continues to apply even after the point at which the amount of guaranteed interest that will accrue is less than 25 percent of the total interest that will accrue on the liability.

(2) Computation of present value. The present value of the guaranteed future interest payments is computed using a discount rate equal to either the interest rate stated in the loan documents, or if interest is imputed under either section 483 or section 1274, the applicable federal rate, compounded semiannually. The computation takes into account any payment of interest that the partner or related person may be required to make only to the extent that the interest will accrue economically (determined in accordance with section 446 and the regulations thereunder) after the date of the interest guarantee. If the loan document contains a variable rate of interest that is an interest rate based on current values of an objective interest index, the present value is computed on the assumption that the interest determined under the objective interest index on the date of the computation will remain constant over the term of the loan. The term "objective interest index" has the meaning given to it in section 1275 and the regulations thereunder (relating to variable rate debt instruments). Examples of an objective interest index include the prime rate of a designated financial institution, LIBOR (London Interbank Offered Rate), and the applicable federal rate under section 1274(d).

(3) Safe harbor. The general rule contained in paragraph (e)(1) of this section does not apply to a partnership nonrecourse liability if the guarantee of interest by the partner or related person is for a period not in excess of the lesser of five years or one-third of the term of the liability.

(4) De minimis exception. The general rule contained in paragraph (e)(1) of this section does not apply if a partner or related person whose interest (directly or indirectly through one or more partnerships including the interest of any related person) in each item of partnership income, gain, loss, deduction, or credit for every taxable year that the partner is a partner in the partnership is 10 percent or less, guarantees the interest on a loan to that partnership which constitutes qualified nonrecourse financing within the meaning of section 465(b)(6) (determined without regard to the type of activity financed). An allocation of interest to the extent paid by the guarantor is not treated as a partnership item of deduction or loss subject to the 10 percent or less rule.

(f) Examples. The following examples illustrate the principles of paragraphs (a) through (e) of this section.

Example (1). Determining when a partner bears the economic risk of loss. A and B form a general partnership with each contributing $100 in cash. The partnership purchases an office building on leased land for $1,000 from an unrelated seller, paying $200 in cash and executing a note to the seller for the balance of $800. The note is a general obligation of the partnership, *i.e.*, no partner has been relieved from personal liability. The partnership agreement provides that all items are allocated equally except that tax losses are specially allocated 90% to A and 10% to B and that capital accounts will be maintained in accordance with the regulations under section 704(b), including a deficit capital account restoration obligation on liquidation. In a constructive liquidation, the $800 liability becomes due and payable. All of the partnership's assets, including the building, are deemed to be worthless. The building is deemed sold for a value of zero. Capital accounts are adjusted to reflect the loss on the hypothetical disposition, as follows:

	A	B
Initial contribution	$100	$100
Loss on hypothetical sale	(900)	(100)
	($800)	$0

Other than the partners' obligation to fund negative capital accounts on liquidation, there are no other contractual or statutory payment obligations existing between the partners, the partnership and the lender. Therefore, $800 of the partnership liability is classified as a recourse liability because one or more partners bears the economic risk of loss for non-payment. B has no share of the liability since the constructive liquidation produces no payment obligation for B. A's share of the partnership liability is $800 because A would have an obligation in that amount to make a contribution to the partnership.

Example (2). Recourse liability; deficit restoration obligation. C and D each contribute $500 in cash to the capital of a new general partnership, CD. CD purchases property from an unrelated seller for $1,000 in cash and a $9,000 mortgage note. The note is a general obligation of the partnership, *i.e.*, no partner has been relieved from personal liability. The partnership agreement provides that profits and losses are to be divided 40% to C and 60% to D. C and D are required to make up any deficit in their capital accounts. In a constructive liquidation, all partnership assets are deemed to become worthless and all partnership liabilities become due and payable in full. The partnership is deemed to dispose of all its assets in a fully taxable transaction for no consideration. Capital accounts are adjusted to reflect the loss on the hypothetical disposition, as follows:

	C	D
Initial contribution	$500	$500
Loss on hypothetical sale	(4,000)	(6,000)
	($3,500)	($5,500)

C's capital account reflects a deficit that C would have to make up to $3,500 and D's capital account reflects a deficit that D would have to make up of $5,500. Therefore, the $9,000 mortgage note is a recourse liability because one or more partners bear the economic risk of loss for the liability. C's share of the recourse liability is $3,500 and D's share is $5,500.

Example (3). Guarantee by limited partner; partner deemed to satisfy obligation. E and F form a limited partnership. E, the general partner, contributes $2,000 and F, the limited partner, contributes $8,000 in cash to the partnership. The partnership agreement allocates losses 20% to E and 80% to F until F's capital account is reduced to zero, after which all losses are allocated to E. The partnership purchases depreciable property for $25,000 using its $10,000 cash and a $15,000 recourse loan from a bank. F guarantee payment of the $15,000 loan to the extent the loan remains unpaid after the bank has exhausted its remedies against the partnership. In a constructive liquidation, the $15,000 liability becomes due and payable. All of the partnership's assets, including the depreciable property, are deemed to be worthless. The depreciable property is deemed sold for a value of zero. Capital accounts are adjusted to reflect the loss on the hypothetical disposition, as follows:

	E	F
Initial contribution	$2,000	$8,000
Loss on hypothetical sale	(17,000)	(8,000)
	($15,000)	$0

E, as a general partner, would be obligated by operation of law to make a net contribution to the partnership of $15,000. Because E is assumed to satisfy that obligation, it is also assumed that F would not have to satisfy F's guarantee. The $15,000 mortgage is treated as a recourse liability because one or more partners bear the economic risk of loss. E's share of the liability is $15,000, and F's share is zero. This would be so even if E's net worth at the time of the determination is less than $15,000, unless the facts and circumstances indicate a plan to circumvent or avoid E's obligation to contribute to the partnership.

Example (4). Partner guarantee with right of subrogation. G, a limited partner in the GH partnership, guarantees a portion of a partnership liability. The liability is a general obligation of the partnership, *i.e.*, no partner has been relieved from personal liability. If under state law G is subrogated to the rights of the lender, G would have the right to recover the amount G paid to the recourse lender from the general partner. Therefore, G does not bear the economic risk of loss for the partnership liability.

Example (5). Bifurcation of partnership liability; guarantee of part of nonrecourse liability. A partnership borrows $10,000, secured by a mortgage on real property. The mortgage note contains an exoneration clause which provides that in the event of default the holder's only remedy is to foreclose on the property. The holder may not look to any other partnership asset or to any partner to pay the liability. However, to induce the lender to make the loan, a partner guarantees payment of $200 of the loan principal. The exoneration clause does not apply to the partner's guarantee. If the partner paid pursuant to the guarantee, the partner would be subrogated to the rights of the lender with respect to $200 of the mortgage debt but the partner is not otherwise entitled to reimbursement from the partnership or any partner. For purposes of section 752, $200 of the $10,000 mortgage liability is treated as a recourse liability of the partnership and $9,800 is treated as a nonrecourse liability of the partnership. The partner's share of the recourse liability of the partnership is $200.

Example (6). Wrapped debt. I, an individual, purchases real estate from an unrelated seller for $10,000, paying $1,000 in cash and giving a $9,000 purchase mortgage note on which I has no personal liability and as to which the seller can look only to the property for satisfaction. At a time when the property is worth $15,000, I sells the property to a partnership in which I is a general partner. The partnership pays for the property with a partnership purchase money mortgage note of $15,000 on which neither the partnership nor any partner (or person related to a partner) has personal liability. The $15,000 mortgage note is a wrapped debt that includes the $9,000 obligation to the original seller. The liability is a recourse liability to the extent of $6,000 because I is the creditor with respect to the loan and I bears the economic risk of loss for $6,000. I's share of the recourse liability is $6,000. The remaining $9,000 is treated as a partnership nonrecourse liability that is owed to the unrelated seller.

Example (7). Guarantee of interest by partner treated as part recourse and part nonrecourse. On January 1, 1992, a partnership obtains a $4,000,000 loan secured by a shopping center owned by the partnership. Neither the partnership nor any partner has any personal liability under the loan documents for repayment of the stated principal amount. Interest accrues at a 15 percent annual rate and is payable on December 31 of each year. The principal is payable in a lump sum on December 31, 2006. A partner guarantees payment of 50 percent of each interest payment required by the loan. The guarantee can be enforced without first foreclosing on the property. When the partnership obtains the loan, the present value (discounted at 15 percent, compounded annually) of the future interest payments is $3,508,422, and of the future principal payment is $491,578. If tested on that date, the loan would be treated as a partnership liability of $1,754,211 ($3,508,422 × .5) for which the guaranteeing partner bears the economic risk of loss and a partnership nonrecourse liability of $2,245,789 ($1,754,211 + $491,578).

Example (8). Contingent obligation not recognized. J and K form a general partnership with cash contributions of $2,500 each. J and K share partnership profits and losses equally. The partnership purchases an apartment building for its $5,000 of cash and a $20,000 nonrecourse loan from a commercial bank. The nonrecourse loan is secured by a mortgage on the building. The loan documents provide that the partnership will be liable for the outstanding balance of the loan on a recourse basis to the extent of any decrease in the value of the apartment building resulting from the partnership's failure properly to maintain the property. There are no facts that establish with reasonable certainty the existence of any liability on the part of the partnership (and its partners) for damages resulting from the partnership's failure properly to maintain the building. Therefore, no partner bears the economic risk of loss, and the liability constitutes a nonrecourse liability. Under § 1.752-3, J and K share this nonrecourse liability equally because they share all profits and losses equally.

(g) Time-value-of-money considerations. *(1) In general.* The extent to which a partner or related person bears the economic risk of loss is determined by taking into account any delay in the time when a payment or contribution obligation with respect to a partnership liability is to be satisfied. If a payment obligation with respect to a partnership liability is not required to be satisfied within a reasonable time after the liability becomes due and payable, or if the obligation to make a contribution to the partnership is not required to be satisfied before the later of—

(i) The end of the year in which the partner's interest is liquidated, or

(ii) 90 days after the liquidation, the obligation is recognized only to the extent of the value of the obligation.

(2) Valuation of an obligation. The value of a payment or contribution obligation that is not required to be satisfied within the time period specified in paragraph (g)(1) of this section equals the entire principal balance of the obligation only if the obligation bears interest equal to or greater than the applicable federal rate under section 1274(d) at the time of valuation, commencing on—

(i) In the case of a payment obligation, the date that the partnership liability to a creditor or other person to whom the obligation relates becomes due and payable, or

(ii) In the case of a contribution obligation, the date of the liquidation of the partner's interest in the partnership. If the obligation does not bear interest at a rate at least equal to the applicable federal rate at the time of valuation, the value of the obligation is discounted to the present value of all payments due from the partner or related person *(i.e.,* the imputed principal amount computed under section 1274(b)). For purposes of making this present value determination, the partnership is deemed to have constructively liquidated as of the date on which the payment obligation is valued and the payment obligation is assumed to be a debt instrument subject to the rules of section 1274 *(i.e.,* the debt instrument is treated as if it were issued for property at the time of the valuation).

(3) Satisfaction of obligation with partner's promissory note. An obligation is not satisfied by the transfer to the obligee of a promissory note by a partner or related person unless the note is readily tradeable on an established securities market.

(4) Example. The following example illustrates the principle of paragraph (g) of this section.

Example. Value of obligation not required to be satisfied within specified time period. A, the general partner, and B, the limited partner, each contributes $10,000 to partnership AB. AB purchases property from an unrelated seller for $20,000 in cash and a $70,000 recourse purchase money note. The partnership agreement provides that profits and losses are to be divided equally. A and B are required to make up any deficit in their capital accounts. While A is required to restore any deficit balance in A's capital account within 90 days after the date of liquidation of the partnership, B is not required to restore any deficit for two years following the date of liquidation. The deficit in B's capital account will not bear interest during that two-year period. In a constructive liquidation, all partnership assets are deemed to become worthless and all partnership liabilities become due and payable in full. The partnership is deemed to dispose of all its assets in a fully taxable transaction for no consideration. Capital accounts are adjusted to reflect the loss on the hypothetical disposition, as follows:

	A	B
Initial contribution	$10,000	$10,000
Loss on hypothetical sale	(45,000)	(45,000)
	(35,000)	(35,000)

A's and B's capital accounts each reflect deficits of $35,000. B's obligation to make a contribution pursuant to B's deficit restoration obligation is recognized only to the extent of the fair market value of that obligation at the time of the constructive liquidation because B is not required to satisfy that obligation by the later of the end of the partnership taxable year in which B's interest is liquidated or within 90 days after the date of the liquidation. Because B's obligation does not bear interest, the fair market value is deemed to equal the imputed principal amount under section 1274(b). Under section 1274(b), the imputed principal amount of a debt instrument equals the present value of all payments due under the debt instrument. Assume the applicable federal rate with respect to B's obligation is 10 percent compounded semiannually. Using this discount rate, the present value of the $35,000 payment that B would be required to make two years after the constructive liquidation to restore the deficit balance in B's capital account equals $28,795 To the extent that B's deficit restoration obligation is not recognized, it is assumed that B's obligation does not exist. Therefore, A, as the sole general partner, would be obligated by operation of law to contribute an additional $6,205 of capital to the partnership. Accordingly, under paragraph (g) of this section, B bears the economic risk of loss for $28,795 and A bears the economic risk of loss for $41,205 ($35,000 + $6,205).

(h) Partner providing property as security for partnership liability. *(1) Direct pledge.* A partner is considered to bear the economic risk of loss for a partnership liability to the extent of the value of any the partner's or related person's separate property (other than a direct or indirect interest in the partnership) that is pledged as security for the partnership liability.

(2) Indirect pledge. A partner is considered to bear the economic risk of loss for a partnership liability to the extent of the value of any property that the partner contributes to the partnership solely for the purpose of securing a partnership liability. Contributed property is not treated as contributed solely for the purpose of securing a partnership liability unless substantially all of the items of income, gain, loss, and deduction attributable to the contributed property are allocated to the contributing partner, and this allocation is generally greater than the partner's share of other significant items of partnership income, gain, loss, or deduction.

(3) Valuation. The extent to which a partner bears the economic risk of loss for a partnership liability as a result of a direct pledge described in paragraph (h)(1) of this section or an indirect pledge described in paragraph (h)(2) of this section is limited to the net fair market value of the property (pledged property) at the time of the pledge or contribution.

If a partner provides additional pledged property, the addition is treated as a new pledge and the net fair market value of the pledged property (including but not limited to the additional property) must be determined at that time. For purposes of this paragraph (h), if pledged property is subject to one or more other obligations, those obligations must be taken into account in determining the net fair market value of pledged property at the time of the pledge or contribution.

(4) Partner's promissory note. For purposes of paragraph (h)(2) of this section, a promissory note of the partner or related person that is contributed to the partnership shall not be taken into account unless the note is readily tradeable on an established securities market.

(i) Treatment of recourse liabilities in tiered partnerships. If a partnership (the "upper-tier partnership") owns (directly or indirectly through one or more partnerships) an interest in another partnership (the "lower-tier partnership"), the liabilities of the lower-tier partnership are allocated to the upper-tier partnership in an amount equal to the sum of the following—

(1) The amount of the economic risk of loss that the upper-tier partnership bears with respect to the liabilities; and

(2) Any other amount of the liabilities with respect to which partners of the upper-tier partnership bear the economic risk of loss.

(j) Anti-abuse rules. *(1) In general.* An obligation of a partner or related person to make a payment may be disregarded or treated as an obligation of another person for purposes of this section if facts and circumstances indicate that a principal purpose of the arrangement between the parties is to eliminate the partner's economic risk of loss with respect to that obligation or create the appearance of the partner or related person bearing the economic risk of loss when, in fact, the substance of the arrangement is otherwise. Circumstances with respect to which a payment obligation may be disregarded include, but are not limited to, the situations described in paragraphs (j)(2) and (j)(3) of this section.

(2) Arrangements tantamount to a guarantee. Irrespective of the form of a contractual obligation, a partner is considered to bear the economic risk of loss with respect to a partnership liability, or a portion thereof, to the extent that:

(i) The partner or related person undertakes one or more contractual obligations so that the partnership may obtain a loan:

(ii) The contractual obligations of the partner or related person eliminate substantially all the risk to the lender that the partnership will not satisfy its obligations under the loan; and

(iii) One of the principal purposes of using the contractual obligations is to attempt to permit partners (other than those who are directly or indirectly liable for the obligation) to include a portion of the loan in the basis of their partnership interests.

The partners are considered to bear the economic risk of loss for the liability in accordance with their relative economic burdens for the liability pursuant to the contractual obligations. For example, a lease between a partner and a partnership which is not on commercially reasonable terms may be tantamount to a guarantee by the partner of a partnership liability.

(3) Plan to circumvent or avoid the obligation. An obligation of a partner to make a payment is not recognized if the facts and circumstances evidence a plan to circumvent or avoid the obligation.

(4) Example. The following example illustrates the principle of paragraph (j)(3) of this section.

Example. Plan to circumvent or avoid obligation. A and B form a general partnership. A, a corporation, contributes $20,000 and B contributes $90,000 to the partnership. A is obligated to restore any deficit in its partnership capital account. The partnership agreement allocates losses 20% to A and 80% to B until B's capital account is reduced to zero, after which all losses are allocated to A. The partnership purchases depreciable property for $250,000 using its $100,000 cash and a $150,000 recourse loan from a bank. B guarantees payment of the $150,000 loan to the extent the loan remains unpaid after the bank has exhausted its remedies against the partnership. A is a subsidiary, formed by a parent of a consolidated group, with capital limited to $20,000 to allow the consolidated group to enjoy the tax losses generated by the property while at the same time limiting its monetary exposure for such losses. These facts, when considered together with B's guarantee, indicate a plan to circumvent or avoid A's obligation to contribute to the partnership. The rules of section 752 must be applied as if A's obligation to contribute did not exist. Accordingly, the $150,000 liability is a recourse liability that is allocated entirely to B.

(k) Effect of a disregarded entity. *(1) In general.* In determining the extent to which a partner bears the economic risk of loss for a partnership liability, an obligation under paragraph (b)(1) of this section (§ 1.752-2(b)(1) payment obligation) of a business entity that is disregarded as an entity separate from its owner under sections 856(i) or 1361(b)(3) or §§ 301.7701-1 through 301.7701-3 of this chapter (disregarded entity) is taken into account only to the extent of the net value of the disregarded entity as of the allocation date (as defined in paragraph (k)(2)(iv) of this section) that is allocated to the partnership liability as determined under the rules of this paragraph (k). The rules of this paragraph (k) do not apply to a § 1.752-2(b)(1) payment obligation of a disregarded entity to the extent that the owner of the disregarded entity is otherwise required to make a payment (that satisfies the requirements of paragraph (b)(1) of this section) with respect to the obligation of the disregarded entity.

(2) Net value of a disregarded entity. (i) Definition. For purposes of this paragraph (k), the net value of a disregarded entity equals the following--

(A) The fair market value of all assets owned by the disregarded entity that may be subject to creditors' claims under local law (including the disregarded entity's enforceable rights to contributions from its owner and the fair market value of an interest in any partnership other than the partnership for which net value is being determined, but excluding the disregarded entity's interest in the partnership for which the net value is being determined and the net fair market value of property pledged to secure a liability of the partnership under paragraph (h)(1) of this section); less

(B) All obligations of the disregarded entity that do not constitute § 1.752-2(b)(1) payment obligations of the disregarded entity.

(ii) Timing of the net value determination. (A) Initial determination. If a partnership interest is held by a disregarded entity, and the partnership has or incurs a liability, all or a portion of which may be allocable to the owner of the disregarded entity under this paragraph (k), the disregarded entity's net value must be initially determined on the allocation date described in paragraph (k)(2)(iv) of this section.

(B) Other events. If a partnership interest is held by a disregarded entity, and the partnership has or incurs a liability, all or a portion of which may be allocable to the owner of the disregarded entity under this paragraph (k), then, if one or more valuation events (as defined in paragraph (k)(2)(iii) of this section) occur during the partnership taxable year, except as provided in paragraph (k)(2)(iii)(E) of this section, the net value of the disregarded entity is determined on the allocation date described in paragraph (k)(2)(iv) of this section.

(iii) Valuation events. The following are valuation events for purposes of this paragraph (k):

(A) A more than de minimis contribution to a disregarded entity of property other than property pledged to secure a partnership liability under paragraph (h)(1) of this section, unless the contribution is followed immediately by a contribution of equal net value by the disregarded entity to the partnership for which the net value of the disregarded entity otherwise would be determined, taking into account any obligations assumed or taken subject to in connection with such contributions.

(B) A more than de minimis distribution from a disregarded entity of property other than property pledged to secure a partnership liability under paragraph (h)(1) of this section, unless the distribution immediately follows a distribution of equal net value to the disregarded entity by the partnership for which the net value of the disregarded entity otherwise would be determined, taking into account any obligations assumed or taken subject to in connection with such distributions.

(C) A change in the legally enforceable obligation of the owner of the disregarded entity to make contributions to the disregarded entity.

(D) The incurrence, refinancing, or assumption of an obligation of the disregarded entity that does not constitute a § 1.752-2(b)(1) payment obligation of the disregarded entity.

(E) The sale or exchange of a non-de minimis asset of the disregarded entity (in a transaction that is not in the ordinary course of business). In this case, the net value of the disregarded entity may be adjusted only to reflect the difference, if any, between the fair market value of the asset at the time of the sale or exchange and the fair market value of the asset when the net value of the disregarded entity was last determined. The adjusted net value is taken into account for purposes of § 1.752-2(k)(1) as of the allocation date.

(iv) Allocation Date. For purposes of this paragraph (k), the allocation date is the earlier of--

(A) The first date occurring on or after the date on which the requirement to determine the net value of a disregarded entity arises under paragraph (k)(2)(ii)(A) or (B) of this section on which the partnership otherwise determines a partner's share of partnership liabilities under §§ 1.705-1(a) and 1.752-4(d); or

(B) The end of the partnership's taxable year in which the requirement to determine the net value of a disregarded entity arises under paragraph (k)(2)(ii)(A) or (B) of this section.

(3) Multiple liabilities. If one or more disregarded entities have § 1.752-2(b)(1) payment obligations with respect to one or more liabilities of a partnership, the partnership must allocate the net value of each disregarded entity among partnership liabilities in a reasonable and consistent manner, taking into account the relative priorities of those liabilities.

(4) Reduction in net value of a disregarded entity. For purposes of this paragraph (k), the net value of a disregarded entity is determined by taking into account a subsequent reduction in the net value of the disregarded entity if, at the time the net value of the disregarded entity is determined, it is anticipated that the net value of the disregarded entity will subsequently be reduced and the reduction is part of a plan that has as one of its principal purposes creating the appearance that a partner bears the economic risk of loss for a partnership liability.

(5) Information to be provided by the owner of a disregarded entity. A partner that may be treated as bearing the economic risk of loss for a partnership liability based upon a § 1.752-2(b)(1) payment obligation of a disregarded entity must provide information to the partnership as to the entity's tax classification and the net value of the disregarded entity that is appropriately allocable to the partnership's liabilities on a timely basis.

(6) Examples. The following examples illustrate the rules of this paragraph (k):

Example (1). Disregarded entity with net value of zero. (i) In 2007, A forms a wholly owned domestic limited liability company, LLC, with a contribution of $100,000. A has no liability for LLC's debts, and LLC has no enforceable right to contribution from A. Under § 301.7701-3(b)(1)(ii) of this chapter, LLC is a disregarded entity. Also in 2007, LLC contributes $100,000 to LP, a limited partnership with a calendar year taxable year, in exchange for a general partnership interest in LP, and B and C each contributes $100,000 to LP in exchange for a limited partnership interest in LP. The partnership agreement provides that only LLC is required to make up any deficit in its capital account. On January 1, 2008, LP borrows $300,000 from a bank and uses $600,000 to purchase nondepreciable property. The $300,000 debt is secured by the property and is also a general obligation of LP. LP makes payments of only interest on its $300,000 debt during 2008. LP has a net taxable loss in 2008, and under §§ 1.705-1(a) and 1.752-4(d), LP determines its partners' shares of the $300,000 debt at the end of its taxable year, December 31, 2008. As of that date, LLC holds no assets other than its interest in LP.

(ii) Because LLC is a disregarded entity, A is treated as the partner in LP for Federal tax purposes. Only LLC has an obligation to make a payment on account of the $300,000 debt if LP were to constructively liquidate as described in paragraph (b)(1) of this section. Therefore, under this paragraph (k), A is treated as bearing the economic risk of loss for LP's $300,000 debt only to the extent of LLC's net value. Because that net value is $0 on December 31, 2008, when LP determines its partners' shares of its $300,000 debt, A is not treated as bearing the economic risk of loss for any portion of LP's $300,000 debt. As a result, LP's $300,000 debt is characterized as nonrecourse under § 1.752-1(a) and is allocated as required by § 1.752-3.

Example (2). Disregarded entity with positive net value. (i) The facts are the same as in Example 1 except that on January 1, 2009, A contributes $250,000 to LLC. On January 5, 2009, LLC borrows $100,000 and LLC shortly thereafter uses the $350,000 to purchase unimproved land. LP makes payments of only interest on its $300,000 debt during 2009. As of December 31, 2009, LLC holds its interest in LP and the land, the value of which has declined to $275,000. LP has a net taxable loss in 2009, and under §§ 1.705-1(a) and 1.752-4(d), LP determines its partners' shares of the $300,000 debt at the end of its taxable year, December 31, 2009.

(ii) A's contribution of $250,000 to LLC on January 1, 2009, constitutes a more than de minimis contribution of property to LLC under paragraph (k)(2)(iii)(A) of this section and the debt incurred by LLC on January 5, 2009, is a valuation event under paragraph (k)(2)(iii)(D) of this section. Accordingly, under paragraph (k)(2)(ii) of this section, LLC's value must be redetermined as of the end of the partnership's taxable year. At that time LLC's net value is $175,000 ($275,000 land--$100,000 debt). Accordingly, $175,000 of LP's $300,000 debt will be recharacterized as recourse under § 1.752-1(a) and allocated to A under this section, and the remaining $125,000 of LP's $300,000 debt will remain characterized as nonrecourse under § 1.752-1(a) and is allocated as required by § 1.752-3.

Example (3). Multiple partnership liabilities. (i) The facts are the same as in Example 2 except that on January 1, 2010, A forms another wholly owned domestic limited liability company, LLC2, with a contribution of $120,000. Shortly thereafter, LLC2 uses the $120,000 to purchase stock in X corporation. A has no liability for LLC2's debts, and LLC2 has no enforceable right to contribution from A. Under § 301.7701-3(b)(1)(ii) of this chapter, LLC2 is a disregarded entity. On July 1, 2010, LP borrows $100,000 from a bank and uses the $100,000 to purchase nondepreciable property. The $100,000 debt is secured by the property and is also a general obligation of LP. The $100,000 debt is senior in priority to LP's existing $300,000 debt. Also, on July 1, 2010, LLC2 agrees to guarantee both LP's $100,000 and $300,000 debts. LP makes payments of only interest on both its $100,000 and $300,000 debts during 2010. LP has a net taxable loss in 2010 and, under §§ 1.705-1(a) and 1.752-4(d), must determine its partners' shares of its $100,000 and $300,000 debts at the end of its taxable year, December 31, 2010. As of that date, LLC holds its interest in LP and the land, and LLC2 holds the X corporation stock which has appreciated in value to $140,000.

(ii) Both LLC and LLC2 have obligations to make a payment on account of LP's debts if LP were to constructively liquidate as described in paragraph (b)(1) of this section. Therefore, under paragraph (k)(1) of this section, A is treated as bearing the economic risk of loss for LP's $100,000 and $300,000 debts only to the extent of the net values of LLC and LLC2, as allocated among those debts in a reasonable and consistent manner pursuant to paragraph (k)(3) of this section.

(iii) No events have occurred that would allow a valuation of LLC under paragraph (k)(2)(iii) of this section. Therefore, LLC's net value remains $175,000. LLC2's net value as of December 31, 2010, when LP determines its partners' shares of its liabilities, is $140,000. Under paragraph (k)(3) of this section, LP must allocate the net values of LLC and LLC2 between its $100,000 and $300,000 debts in a reasonable and consistent manner. Because the $100,000 debt is senior in priority to the $300,000 debt, LP first allocates the net values of LLC and LLC2, pro rata, to its $100,000 debt. Thus, LP allocates $56,000 of LLC's net value and $44,000 of LLC2's net value to its $100,000 debt, and A is treated as bearing the economic risk of loss for all of LP's $100,000 debt. As a result, all of LP's $100,000 debt is characterized as recourse under § 1.752-1(a) and is allocated to A under this section. LP then allocates the remaining $119,000 of LLC's net value and LLC2's $96,000 net value to its $300,000 debt, and A is treated as bearing the economic risk of loss for a total of $215,000 of the $300,000 debt. As a result, $215,000 of LP's $300,000 debt is characterized as recourse under § 1.752-1(a) and is allocated to A under this section, and the remaining $85,000 of LP's $300,000 debt is characterized as nonrecourse under § 1.752-1(a) and is allocated as required by § 1.752-3. This example illustrates one reasonable method of allocating net values of disregarded entities among multiple partnership liabilities.

Example (4). Disregarded entity with interests in two partnerships. (i) In 2007, B forms a wholly owned domestic limited liability company, LLC, with a contribution of $175,000. B has no liability for LLC's debts and LLC has no enforceable right to contribution from B. Under § 301.7701-3(b)(1)(ii) of this chapter, LLC is a disregarded entity. LLC contributes $50,000 to LP1 in exchange for a general partnership interest in LP1, and $25,000 to LP2 in exchange for a general partnership interest in LP2. LLC retains the $100,000 in cash. Both LP1 and LP2 have taxable years than end on December 31 and, under both LP1's and LP2's partnership agreements, only LLC is required to make up any deficit in its capital account. During 2007, LP1 and LP2 incur partnership liabilities that are general obligations of the partnership. LP1 borrows $300,000 (Debt 1), and LP2 borrows $60,000 (Debt 2) and $40,000 (Debt 3). Debt 2 is senior in priority to Debt 3. LP1 and LP2 make payments of only interest on Debts 1, 2, and 3 during 2007. As of the end of taxable year 2007, LP1 and LP2 each have a net taxable loss and must determine its partners' shares of partnership liabilities under §§ 1.705-1(a) and 1.752-4(d) as of December 31, 2007. As of that date, LLC's interest in LP1 has a fair market value of $45,000, and LLC's interest in LP2 has a fair market value of $15,000.

(ii) Because LLC is a disregarded entity, B is treated as the partner in LP1 and LP2 for federal tax purposes. Only LLC has an obligation to make a payment on account of Debts 1, 2, and 3 if LP1 and LP2 were to constructively liquidate as described in paragraph (b)(1) of this section. Therefore, under this paragraph (k), B is treated as bearing the economic risk of loss for LP1's and LP2's liabilities only to the extent of LLC's net value as of the allocation date, December 31, 2007.

(iii) LLC's net value with respect to LP1 is $115,000 ($100,000 cash + $15,000 interest in LP2). Therefore, under paragraph (k)(1) of this section, B is treated as bearing the economic risk of loss for $115,000 of Debt 1. Accordingly, $115,000 of LP1's $300,000 debt is characterized as recourse under § 1.752-1(a) and is allocated to B under this section. The balance of Debt 1 ($185,000) is characterized as nonrecourse under § 1.752-1(a) and is allocated as required by § 1.752-3.

(iv) LLC's net value with respect to LP2 is $145,000 ($100,000 cash + $45,000 interest in LP1). Therefore, under paragraph (k)(1) of this section, B is treated as bearing the economic risk of loss with respect to Debts 2 and 3 only to the extent of $145,000. Because Debt 2 is senior in priority to Debt 3, LP2 first allocates $60,000 of LLC's net value to Debt 2. LP2 then allocates $40,000 of LLC's net value to Debt 3. As a result, both Debts 2 and 3 are characterized as recourse under § 1.752-1(a) and allocated to B. This example illustrates one reasonable method of allocating the net value of a disregarded entity among multiple partnership liabilities.

(l) Effective dates. Paragraph (a), the last sentence of paragraph (b)(6), and paragraphs (h)(3) and (k) of this section apply to liabilities incurred or assumed by a partnership on or after October 11, 2006, other than liabilities incurred or assumed by a partnership pursuant to a written binding contract in effect prior to that date. The rules applicable to liabilities incurred or assumed (or subject to a binding contract in effect) prior to October 11, 2006 are contained in § 1.752-

2 in effect prior to October 11, 2006, (see 26 CFR part 1 revised as of April 1, 2006).

T.D. 8380, 12/20/91, amend T.D. 9289, 10/10/2006.

§ 1.752-3 Partner's share of nonrecourse liabilities.

(a) In general. A partner's share of the nonrecourse liabilities of a partnership equals the sum of paragraphs (a)(1) through (a)(3) of this section as follows—

(1) The partner's share of partnership minimum gain determined in accordance with the rules of section 704(b) and the regulations thereunder;

(2) The amount of any taxable gain that would be allocated to the partner under section 704(c) (or in the same manner as section 704(c) in connection with a revaluation of partnership property) if the partnership disposed of (in a taxable transaction) all partnership property subject to one or more nonrecourse liabilities of the partnership in full satisfaction of the liabilities and for no other consideration; and

(3) The partner's share of the excess nonrecourse liabilities (those not allocated under paragraphs (a)(1) and (a)(2) of this section) of the partnership as determined in accordance with the partner's share of partnership profits. The partner's interest in partnership profits is determined by taking into account all facts and circumstances relating to the economic arrangement of the partners. The partnership agreement may specify the partners' interests in partnership profits for purposes of allocating excess nonrecourse liabilities provided the interests so specified are reasonably consistent with allocations (that have substantial economic effect under the section 704(b) regulations) of some other significant item of partnership income or gain. Alternatively, excess nonrecourse liabilities may be allocated among the partners in accordance with the manner in which it is reasonably expected that the deductions attributable to those nonrecourse liabilities will be allocated. Additionally, the partnership may first allocate an excess nonrecourse liability to a partner up to the amount of built-in gain that is allocable to the partner on section 704(c) property (as defined under § 1.704-3(a)(3)(ii)) or property for which reverse section 704(c) allocations are applicable (as described in § 1.704-3(a)(6)(i)) where such property is subject to the nonrecourse liability to the extent that such built-in gain exceeds the gain described in paragraph (a)(2) of this section with respect to such property. This additional method does not apply for purposes of § 1.707-5(a)(2)(ii). To the extent that a partnership uses this additional method and the entire amount of the excess nonrecourse liability is not allocated to the contributing partner, the partnership must allocate the remaining amount of the excess nonrecourse liability under one of the other methods in this paragraph (a)(3). Excess nonrecourse liabilities are not required to be allocated under the same method each year.

(b) Allocation of a single nonrecourse liability among multiple properties. *(1) In general.* For purposes of determining the amount of taxable gain under paragraph (a)(2) of this section, if a partnership holds multiple properties subject to a single nonrecourse liability, the partnership may allocate the liability among the multiple properties under any reasonable method. A method is not reasonable if it allocates to any item of property an amount of the liability that, when combined with any other liabilities allocated to the property, is in excess of the fair market value of the property at the time the liability is incurred. The portion of the nonrecourse liability allocated to each item of partnership property is then treated as a separate loan under paragraph (a)(2) of this section. In general, a partnership may not change the method of allocating a single nonrecourse liability under this paragraph (b) while any portion of the liability is outstanding. However, if one or more of the multiple properties subject to the liability is no longer subject to the liability, the portion of the liability allocated to that property must be reallocated among the properties still subject to the liability so that the amount of the liability allocated to any property does not exceed the fair market value of such property at the time of reallocation.

(2) Reductions in principal. For purposes of this paragraph (b), when the outstanding principal of a partnership liability is reduced, the reduction of outstanding principal is allocated among the multiple properties in the same proportion that the partnership liability originally was allocated to the properties under paragraph (b)(1) of this section.

(c) Examples. The following examples illustrate the principles of this section:

Example (1). Partner's share of nonrecourse liabilities. The AB partnership purchases depreciable property for a $1,000 purchase money note that is nonrecourse liability under the rules of this section. Assume that this is the only nonrecourse liability of the partnership, and that no principal payments are due on the purchase money note for a year. The partnership agreement provides that all items of income, gain, loss, and deduction are allocated equally. Immediately after purchasing the depreciable property, the partners share the nonrecourse liability equally because they have equal interests in partnership profits. A and B are each treated as if they contributed $500 to the partnership to reflect each partner's increase in his or her share of partnership liabilities (from $0 to $500). The minimum gain with respect to an item of partnership property subject to a nonrecourse liability equals the amount of gain that would be recognized if the partnership disposed of the property in full satisfaction of the nonrecourse liability and for no other consideration. Therefore, if the partnership claims a depreciation deduction of $200 for the depreciable property for the year it acquires that property, partnership minimum gain for the year will increase by $200 (the excess of the $1,000 nonrecourse liability over the $800 adjusted tax basis of the property). See section 704(b) and the regulations thereunder. A and B each have a share of partnership minimum gain at the end of that year because the depreciation deduction is treated as a nonrecourse deduction. See section 704(b) and the regulation thereunder. Accordingly, at the end of that year, A and B are allocated $100 each of the nonrecourse liability to match their shares of partnership minimum gain. The remaining $800 of the nonrecourse liability will be allocated equally between A and B ($400 each).

Example (2). Excess nonrecourse liabilities allocated consistently with reasonably expected deductions. The facts are the same as in Example 1 except that the partnership agreement provides that depreciation deductions will be allocated to A. The partners agree to allocate excess nonrecourse liabilities in accordance with the manner in which it is reasonably expected that the deductions attributable to those nonrecourse liabilities will be allocated. Assuming that the allocation of all of the depreciation deductions to A is valid under section 704(b), immediately after purchasing the depreciable property, A's share of the nonrecourse liability is $1,000. Accordingly, A is treated as if A contributed $1,000 to the partnership.

Example (3). Allocation of liability among multiple properties.

(i) A and B are equal partners in a partnership (PRS). A contributes $70 of cash in exchange for a 50-percent interest in PRS. B contributes two items of property, X and Y, in exchange for a 50-percent interest in PRS. Property X has a fair market value (and book value) of $70 and an adjusted basis of $40, and is subject to a nonrecourse liability of $50. Property Y has a fair market value (and book value) of $120, an adjusted basis of $40, and is subject to a nonrecourse liability of $70. Immediately after the initial contributions, PRS refinances the two separate liabilities with a single $120 nonrecourse liability. All of the built-in gain attributable to Property X ($30) and Property Y ($80) is section 704(c) gain allocable to B.

(ii) The amount of the nonrecourse liability ($120) is less than the total book value of all of the properties that are subject to such liability ($70 + $120 = $190), so there is no partnership minimum gain. § 1.704-2(d). Accordingly, no portion of the liability is allocated pursuant to paragraph (a)(1) of this section.

(iii) Pursuant to paragraph (b)(1) of this section, PRS decides to allocate the nonrecourse liability evenly between the Properties X and Y. Accordingly, each of Properties X and Y are treated as being subject to a separate $60 nonrecourse liability for purposes of applying paragraph (a)(2) of this section. Under paragraph (a)(2) of this section, B will be allocated $20 of the liability for each of Properties X and Y (in each case, $60 liability minus $40 adjusted basis). As a result, a portion of the liability is allocated pursuant to paragraph (a)(2) of this section as follows:

Partner	Property	Tier 1	Tier 2
A	X	$0	$ 0
....	Y	0	0
B	X	0	20
....	Y	0	20

(iv) PRS has $80 of excess nonrecourse liability that it may allocate in any manner consistent with paragraph (a)(3) of this section. PRS determines to allocate the $80 of excess nonrecourse liabilities to the partners up to their share of the remaining section 704(c) gain on the properties, with any remaining amount of liabilities being allocated equally to A and B consistent with their equal interests in partnership profits. B has $70 of remaining section 704(c) gain ($10 on Property X and $60 on Property Y), and thus will be allocated $70 of the liability in accordance with this gain. The remaining $10 is divided equally between A and B. Accordingly, the overall allocation of the $120 nonrecourse liability is as follows:

Partner	Tier 1	Tier 2	Tier 3	Total
A	$0	$ 0	$ 5	$ 5
B	0	40	75	115

T.D. 8380, 12/20/91, amend T.D. 8906, 10/30/2000.

PAR. 9. § 1.752-3 [Amended]

Section 1.752-3 is amended in the sixth sentence of paragraph (a)(3) by revising the sentence "This additional method does not apply for purposes of § 1.707-5(a)(2)(ii)" to read "This additional method does not apply for purposes of §§ 1.707-5(a)(2)(ii) and 1.707-7(j)(4)(ii)."

Proposed § 1.752-3 [Amended] [*For Preamble, see ¶ 152,607*]

§ 1.752-4 Special rules.

(a) Tiered partnerships. An upper-tier partnership's share of the liabilities of a lower-tier partnership (other than any liability of the lower-tier partnership that is owed to the upper-tier partnership) is treated as a liability of the upper-tier partnership for purposes of applying section 752 and the regulations thereunder to the partners of the upper-tier partnership.

(b) Related person definition. *(1) In general.* A person is related to a partner if the person and the partner bear a relationship to each other that is specified in section 267(b) or 707(b)(1), subject to the following modifications:

(i) Substitute "80 percent or more" for "more than 50 percent" each place it appears in those sections;

(ii) A person's family is determined by excluding brothers and sisters; and

(iii) Disregard sections 267(e)(1) and 267(f)(1)(A).

(2) Person related to more than one partner. (i) In general. If, in applying the related person rules in paragraph (b)(1) of this section, a person is related to more than one partner, paragraph (b)(1) of this section is applied by treating the person as related only to the partner with whom there is the highest percentage of related ownership. If two or more partners have the same percentage of related ownership and no other partner has a greater percentage, the liability is allocated equally among the partners having the equal percentages of related ownership.

(ii) Natural persons. For purposes of determining the percentage of related ownership between a person and a partner, natural persons who are related by virtue of being members of the same family are treated as having a percentage relationship of 100 percent with respect to each other.

(iii) Related partner exception. Notwithstanding paragraph (b)(1) of this section (which defines related person), persons owning interests directly or indirectly in the same partnership are not treated as related persons for purposes of determining the economic risk of loss borne by each of them for the liabilities of the partnership. This paragraph (iii) does not apply when determining a partner's interest under the de minimis rules in §§ 1.752-2(d) and (e).

(iv) Special rule where entity structured to avoid related person status (A) In general. If—

(1) A partnership liability is owed to or guaranteed by another entity that is a partnership, an S corporation, a C corporation, or a trust;

(2) A partner or related person owns (directly or indirectly) a 20 percent or more ownership interest in the other entity; and

(3) A principal purpose of having the other entity act as a lender or guarantor of the liability was to avoid the determination that the partner that owns the interest bears the economic risk of loss for federal income tax purposes for all or part of the liability;

then the partner is treated as holding the other entity's interest as a creditor or guarantor to the extent of the partner's or related person's ownership interest in the entity.

(B) Ownership interest. For purposes of paragraph (b)(2)(iv)(A) of this section, a person's ownership interest in:

(1) A partnership equals the partner's highest percentage interest in any item of partnership loss or deduction for any taxable year;

(2) An S corporation equals the percentage of the outstanding stock in the S corporation owned by the shareholder;

(3) A C corporation equals the percentage of the fair market value of the issued and outstanding stock owned by the shareholder; and

(4) A trust equals the percentage of the actuarial interests owned by the beneficial owner of the trust.

(C) Example. Entity structured to avoid related person status. A, B, and C form a general partnership, ABC. A, B, and C are equal partners, each contributing $1,000 to the partnership. A and B want to loan money to ABC and have the loan treated as nonrecourse for purposes of section 752. A and B form partnership AB to which each contributes $50,000. A and B share losses equally in partnership AB. Partnership AB loans partnership ABC $100,000 on a nonrecourse basis secured by the property ABC buys with the loan. Under these facts and circumstances, A and B bear the economic risk of loss with respect to the partnership liability equally based on their percentage interest in losses of partnership AB

(c) Limitation. The amount of an indebtedness is taken into account only once, even though a partner (in addition to the Partner's liability for the indebtedness as a partner) may be separately liable therefor in a capacity other than as a partner.

(d) Time of determination. A partner's share of partnership liabilities must be determined whenever the determination is necessary in order to determine the tax liability of the partner or any other person. See § 1.705-1(a) for rules regarding when the adjusted basis of a partner's interest in the partnership must be determined.

T.D. 8380, 12/20/91.

§ 1.752-5 Effective dates and transition rules.

(a) In general. Except as otherwise provided in §§ 1.752-1 through 1.752-4, unless a partnership makes an election under paragraph (b)(1) of this section to apply the provisions of §§ 1.752-1 through 1.752-4 earlier, §§ 1.752-1 through 1.752-4 apply to any liability incurred or assumed by a partnership on or after December 28, 1991, other than a liability incurred or assumed by the partnership pursuant to a written binding contract in effect prior to December 28, 1991 and at all times thereafter. However, § 1.752-3(a)(3) fifth, sixth, and seventh sentences, (b), and (c) Example 3, do not apply to any liability incurred or assumed by a partnership prior to October 31, 2000. Nevertheless, § 1.752-3(a)(3) fifth, sixth, and seventh sentences, (b), and (c) Example 3, may be relied upon for any liability incurred or assumed by a partnership prior to October 31, 2000 for taxable years ending on or after October 31, 2000. In addition, § 1.752-1(f) last sentence and (g) Example 2, do not apply to any liability incurred or assumed by a partnership prior to January 4, 2001. Nevertheless, § 1.752-1(f) last sentence and (g) Example 2, may be relied on for any liability incurred or assumed by a partnership prior to January 4, 2001 and, unless the partnership makes an election under paragraph (b)(1) of this section, on or after December 28, 1991, other than a liability incurred or assumed by the partnership pursuant to a written binding contract in effect prior to December 28, 1991 and at all times thereafter. For liabilities incurred or assumed by a partnership prior to December 28, 1991 (or pursuant to a written binding contract in effect prior to December 28, 1991 and at all times thereafter), unless an election to apply these regulations has been made, see 1.752-0T to 1.752-4T, set forth in 26 CFR 1.752-0T through 1.752-4T as contained in 26 CFR edition revised April 1, 1991, (TD 8237, TD 8274, and TD 6355) and § 1.752-1, set forth in 26 CFR 1.752-1 as contained in 26 CFR edition revised April 1, 1991 (TD 6175 and TD 6500).

(b) Election. *(1) In general.* A partnership may elect to apply the provisions of §§ 1.752-1 through 1.752-4 to all of its liabilities to which the provisions of those sections do not otherwise apply as of the beginning of the first taxable year of the partnership ending on or after December 28, 1991.

(2) Time and manner of election. An election under this paragraph (b) is made by attaching a written statement to the partnership return for the first taxable year of the partnership ending on or after December 28, 1991. The written statement must include the name, address, and taxpayer identification number of the partnership making the statement and contain a declaration that an election is being made under this paragraph (b).

(c) Effect of section 708(b)(1)(B) termination on determining date liabilities are incurred or assumed. For purposes of applying this section, a termination of the partnership under section 708(b)(1)(B) will not cause partnership liabilities incurred or assumed prior to the termination to be treated as incurred or assumed on the date of the termination.

T.D. 8380, 12/20/91, amend T.D. 8906, 10/30/2000, T.D. 8925, 1/3/2001, T.D. 9207, 5/23/2005.

§ 1.752-6 Partnership assumption of partner's section 358(h)(3) liability after October 18, 1999, and before June 24, 2003.

(a) In general. If, in a transaction described in section 721(a), a partnership assumes a liability (defined in section 358(h)(3)) of a partner (other than a liability to which section 752(a) and (b) apply), then, after application of section 752(a) and (b), the partner's basis in the partnership is reduced (but not below the adjusted value of such interest) by the amount (determined as of the date of the exchange) of the liability. For purposes of this section, the adjusted value of a partner's interest in a partnership is the fair market value of that interest increased by the partner's share of partnership liabilities under §§ 1.752-1 through 1.752-5.

(b) Exceptions. *(1) In general.* Except as provided in paragraph (b)(2) of this section, the exceptions contained in section 358(h)(2)(A) and (B) apply to this section.

(2) Transactions described in Notice 2000-44. The exception contained in section 358(h)(2)(B) does not apply to an assumption of a liability (defined in section 358(h)(3)) by a partnership as part of a transaction described in, or a transaction that is substantially similar to the transactions described in, Notice 2000-44 (2000-2 C.B. 255). See § 601.601(d)(2) of this chapter.

(c) Example. The following example illustrates the principles of paragraph (a) of this section:

Example. In 1999, A and B form partnership PRS. A contributes property with a value and basis of $200, subject to a nonrecourse debt obligation of $50 and a fixed or contingent obligation of $100 that is not a liability to which section 752(a) and (b) applies, in exchange for a 50% interest in PRS. Assume that, after the contribution, A's share of partnership liabilities under §§ 1.752-1 through 1.752-5 is $25. Also assume that the $100 liability is not associated with a trade or business contributed by A to PRS or with assets contributed by A to PRS. After the contribution, A's basis in PRS is $175 (A's basis in the contributed land ($200) reduced by the nonrecourse debt assumed by PRS ($50), increased by A's share of partnership liabilities under §§ 1.752-1 through 1.752-5 ($25)). Because A's basis in the PRS interest is greater than the adjusted value of A's interest, $75 (the fair market value of A's interest ($50) increased by A's share of partnership liabilities ($25)), paragraph (a) of this section operates to reduce A's basis in the PRS interest (but not below the adjusted value of that interest) by the amount of liabilities described in section 358(h)(3) (other than liabilities to which section 752(a) and (b) apply) assumed by PRS. Therefore, A's basis in PRS is reduced to $75.

(d) Effective date. *(1) In general.* This section applies to assumptions of liabilities occurring after October 18, 1999, and before June 24, 2003.

(2) Election to apply § 1.752-7. The partnership may elect, under § 1.752-7(k)(2), to apply the provisions referenced in § 1.752-7(k)(2)(ii) to all assumptions of liabilities by the partnership occurring after October 18, 1999, and before June 24, 2003. Section 1.752-7(k)(2) describes the manner in which the election is made.

T.D. 9207, 5/23/2004.

§ 1.752-7 Partnership assumption of partner's § 1.752-7 liability on or after June 24, 2003.

(a) Purpose and structure. The purpose of this section is to prevent the acceleration or duplication of loss through the assumption of obligations not described in § 1.752-1(a)(4)(i) in transactions involving partnerships. Under paragraph (c) of this section, any such obligation that is assumed by a partnership from a partner in a transaction governed by section 721(a) is treated as section 704(c) property. Paragraphs (e), (f), and (g) of this section provide rules for situations where a partnership assumes such an obligation from a partner and, subsequently, that partner transfers all or part of the partnership interest, that partner receives a distribution in liquidation of the partnership interest, or another partner assumes part or all of that obligation from the partnership. These rules prevent the duplication of loss by prohibiting the partnership and any person other than the partner from whom the obligation was assumed from claiming a deduction, loss, or capital expense to the extent of the built-in loss associated with the obligation. These rules also prevent the acceleration of loss by deferring the partner's deduction or loss attributable to the obligation (if any) until the satisfaction of the § 1.752-7 liability (within the meaning of paragraph (b)(8) of this section). Paragraph (d) of this section provides a number of exceptions to paragraphs (e), (f), and (g) of this section, including a de minimis exception. Paragraph (i) provides a special rule for situations in which an amount paid to satisfy a § 1.752-7 liability is capitalized into other partnership property. Paragraph (j) of this section provides special rules for tiered partnership transactions.

(b) Definitions. For purposes of this section, the following definitions apply:

(1) Assumption. The principles of § 1.752-1(d) and (e) apply in determining if a § 1.752-7 liability has been assumed.

(2) Adjusted value. The adjusted value of a partner's interest in a partnership is the fair market value of that interest increased by the partner's share of partnership liabilities under §§ 1.752-1 through 1.752-5.

(3) § 1.752-7 liability. (i) In general. A § 1.752-7 liability is an obligation described in § 1.752-1(a)(4)(ii) to the extent that either—

(A) The obligation is not described in § 1.752-1(a)(4)(i); or

(B) The amount of the obligation (under paragraph (b)(3)(ii) of this section) exceeds the amount taken into account under § 1.752-1(a)(4)(i).

(ii) Amount and share of § 1.752-7 liability. The amount of a § 1.752-7 liability (or, for purposes of paragraph (b)(3)(i) of this section, the amount of an obligation) is the amount of cash that a willing assignor would pay to a willing assignee to assume the § 1.752-7 liability in an arm's-length transaction. If the obligation arose under a contract in exchange for rights granted to the obligor under that contract, and those contractual rights are contributed to the partnership in connection with the partnership's assumption of the contractual obligation, then the amount of the § 1.752-7 liability or obligation is the amount of cash, if any, that a willing assignor would pay to a willing assignee to assume the entire contract. A partner's share of a partnership's § 1.752-7 liability is the amount of deduction that would be allocated to the partner with respect to the § 1.752-7 liability if the partnership disposed of all of its assets, satisfied all of its liabilities (other than § 1.752-7 liabilities), and paid an unrelated person to assume all of its § 1.752-7 liabilities in a fully taxable arm's-length transaction (assuming such payment would give rise to an immediate deduction to the partnership).

(iii) Example. In 2005, A, B, and C form partnership PRS. A contributes $10,000,000 in exchange for a 25% interest in PRS and PRS's assumption of a debt obligation. The debt obligation was issued for cash and the issue price was equal to the stated redemption price at maturity ($5,000,000). The debt obligation bears interest, payable quarterly, at a fixed rate of interest, which was a market rate of interest when the debt obligation was issued. At the time of the assumption, all accrued interest has been paid. Prior to the partnership assuming the obligation, interest rates decrease, resulting in the debt obligation bearing an above-market interest rate. Assume that, as a result of the decline in interest rates, A would have had to pay a willing assignee $6,000,000 to assume the debt obligation. The assumption of the debt obligation by PRS from A is treated as an assumption of a § 1.752-1(a)(4)(i) liability in the amount of $5,000,000 (the portion of the total amount of the debt obligation that has created basis in A's assets, that is, the $5,000,000 that was issued in exchange for the debt obligation) and an assumption of a § 1.752-7 liability in the amount of $1,000,000 (the difference between the total obligation, $6,000,000, and the § 1.752-1(a)(4)(i)liability, $5,000,000).

(4) § 1.752-7 liability transfer. (i) In general. Except as provided in paragraph (b)(4)(ii) of this section, a § 1.752-7 liability transfer is any assumption of a § 1.752-7 liability by a partnership from a partner in a transaction governed by section 721(a).

(ii) Terminations under section 708(b)(1)(B). In determining if a deemed contribution of assets and assumption of liability as a result of a technical termination is treated as a § 1.752-7 liability transfer, only § 1.752-7 liabilities that were assumed by the terminating partnership as part of an earlier § 1.752-7 liability transfer are taken into account and, then, only to the extent of the remaining built-in loss associated with that § 1.752-7 liability.

(5) § 1.752-7 liability partner. (i) In general. A § 1.752-7 liability partner is a partner from whom a partnership assumes a § 1.752-7 liability as part of a § 1.752-7 liability transfer or any person who acquires a partnership interest

from the § 1.752-7 liability partner in a transaction to which paragraph (e)(3) of this section applies.

(ii) Tiered partnerships. (A) Assumption by a lower-tier partnership. If, in a § 1.752-7 liability transfer, a partnership (lower-tier partnership) assumes a § 1.752-7 liability from another partnership (upper-tier partnership), then both the upper-tier partnership and the partners of the upper-tier partnership are § 1.752-7 liability partners. Therefore, paragraphs (e) and (f) of this section apply on a sale or liquidation of any partner's interest in the upper-tier partnership and on a sale or liquidation of the upper-tier partnership's interest in the lower-tier partnership. See paragraph (j)(3) of this section. If, in a § 1.752-7 liability transfer, the upper-tier partnership assumes a § 1.752-7 liability from a partner, and, subsequently, in another § 1.752-7 liability transfer, a lower-tier partnership assumes that § 1.752-7 liability from the upper-tier partnership, then the partner from whom the upper-tier partnership assumed the § 1.752-7 liability continues to be the § 1.752-7 liability partner of the lower-tier partnership with respect to the remaining built-in loss associated with that § 1.752-7 liability. Any new built-in loss associated with the § 1.752-7 liability that is created on the assumption of the § 1.752-7 liability from the upper-tier partnership by the lower-tier partnership is shared by all the partners of the upper-tier partnership in accordance with their interests in the upper-tier partnership, and each partner of the upper-tier partnership is treated as a § 1.752-7 liability partner with respect to that new built-in loss. See paragraph (e)(3)(ii), Example 3 of this section.

(B) Distribution of partnership interest. If, in a transaction described in § 1.752-7(e)(3), an interest in a partnership (lower-tier partnership) that has assumed a § 1.752-7 liability is distributed by a partnership (upper-tier partnership) that is the § 1.752-7 liability partner with respect to that liability, then the persons receiving interests in the lower-tier partnership are § 1.752-7 liability partners with respect to the lower-tier partnership to the same extent that they were prior to the distribution.

(6) Remaining built-in loss associated with a § 1.752-7 liability. (i) In general. The remaining built-in loss associated with a § 1.752-7 liability equals the amount of the § 1.752-7 liability as of the time of the assumption of the § 1.752-7 liability by the partnership, reduced by the portion of the § 1.752-7 liability previously taken into account by the § 1.752-7 liability partner under paragraph (j)(3) of this section and adjusted as provided in paragraph (c) of this section and § 1.704-3 for—

(A) Any portion of that built-in loss associated with the § 1.752-7 liability that is satisfied by the partnership on or prior to the testing date (whether capitalized or deducted); and

(B) Any assumption of all or part of the § 1.752-7 liability by the § 1.752-7 liability partner (including any assumption that occurs on the testing date).

(ii) Partial dispositions and assumptions. In the case of a partial disposition of the § 1.752-7 liability partner's partnership interest or a partial assumption of the § 1.752-7 liability by another partner, the remaining built-in loss associated with § 1.752-7 liability is pro rated based on the portion of the interest sold or the portion of the § 1.752-7 liability assumed.

(7) § 1.752-7 liability reduction. (i) In general. The § 1.752-7 liability reduction is the amount by which the § 1.752-7 liability partner is required to reduce the basis in the partner's partnership interest by operation of paragraphs (e), (f), and (g) of this section. The § 1.752-7 liability reduction is the lesser of—

(A) The excess of the § 1.752-7 liability partner's basis in the partnership interest over the adjusted value of that interest (as defined in paragraph (b)(2) of this section); or

(B) The remaining built-in loss associated with the § 1.752-7 liability (as defined in paragraph (b)(6) of this section without regard to paragraph (b)(6)(ii) of this section).

(ii) Partial dispositions and assumptions. In the case of a partial disposition of the § 1.752-7 liability partner's partnership interest or a partial assumption of the § 1.752-7 liability by another partner, the § 1.752-7 liability reduction is pro rated based on the portion of the interest sold or the portion of the § 1.752-7 liability assumed.

(8) Satisfaction of § 1.752-7 liability—In general. A § 1.752-7 liability is treated as satisfied (in whole or in part) on the date on which the partnership (or the assuming partner) would have been allowed to take the § 1.752-7 liability into account for federal tax purposes but for this section. For example, a § 1.752-7 liability is treated as satisfied when, but for this section, the § 1.752-7 liability would give rise to—

(i) An increase in the basis of the partnership's or the assuming partner's assets (including cash);

(ii) An immediate deduction to the partnership or to the assuming partner;

(iii) An expense that is not deductible in computing the partnership's or the assuming partner's taxable income and not properly chargeable to capital account; or

(iv) An amount realized on the sale or other disposition of property subject to that liability if the property was disposed of by the partnership or the assuming partner at that time.

(9) Testing date. The testing date is—

(i) For purposes of paragraph (e) of this section, the date of the sale, exchange, or other disposition of part or all of the § 1.752-7 liability partner's partnership interest;

(ii) For purposes of paragraph (f) of this section, the date of the partnership's distribution in liquidation of the § 1.752-7 liability partner's partnership interest; and

(iii) For purposes of paragraph (g) of this section, the date of the assumption (or partial assumption) of the § 1.752-7 liability by a partner other than the § 1.752-7 liability partner.

(10) Trade or business. (i) In general. A trade or business is a specific group of activities carried on by a person for the purpose of earning income or profit, other than a group of activities consisting of acquiring, holding, dealing in, or disposing of financial instruments, if the activities included in that group include every operation that forms a part of, or a step in, the process of earning income or profit. Such group of activities ordinarily includes the collection of income and the payment of expenses. The group of activities must constitute the carrying on of a trade or business under section 162(a) (determined as though the activities were conducted by an individual).

(ii) Examples. The following examples illustrate the provisions of this paragraph (b)(10):

Example (1). Corporation Y owns, manages, and derives rental income from an office building and also owns vacant land that may be subject to environmental liabilities. Corporation Y contributes the land subject to the environmental liabilities to PRS in a transaction governed by section 721(a). PRS plans to develop the land as a landfill. The contribution of the vacant land does not constitute the contribution of a trade or business because Corporation Y did not conduct any significant business or development activities with respect to the land prior to the contribution.

Example (2). For the past 5 years, Corporation X has owned and operated gas stations in City A, City B, and City C. Corporation X transfers all of the assets associated with the operation of the gas station in City A to PRS for interests in PRS and the assumption by PRS of the § 1.752-7 liabilities associated with that gas station. PRS continues to operate the gas station in City A after the contribution. The contribution of the gas station to PRS constitutes the contribution of a trade or business.

Example (3). For the past 7 years, Corporation Z has engaged in the manufacture and sale of household products. Throughout this period, Corporation Z has maintained a research department for use in connection with its manufacturing activities. The research department has 10 employees actively engaged in the development of new products. Corporation Z contributes the research department to PRS in exchange for a PRS interest and the assumption by PRS of pension liabilities with respect to the employees of the research department. PRS continues the research operations on a contractual basis with several businesses, including Corporation Z. The contribution of the research operations to PRS constitutes a contribution of a trade or business.

(c) Application of section 704(b) and (c) to assumed § 1.752-7 liabilities. *(1) In general.* (i) Section 704(c). Except as otherwise provided in this section, sections 704(c)(1)(A) and (B), section 737, and the regulations thereunder, apply to § 1.752-7 liabilities. See § 1.704-3(a)(12). However, § 1.704-3(a)(7) does not apply to any person who acquired a partnership interest from a § 1.752-7 liability partner in a transaction to which paragraph (e)(1) of this section applies.

(ii) Section 704(b). Section 704(b) and § 1.704-1(b) apply to a post-contribution change in the value of a § 1.752-7 liability. If there is a decrease in the value of a § 1.752-7 liability that is reflected in the capital accounts of the partners under § 1.704-1(b)(2)(iv)(f), the amount of the decrease constitutes an item of income for purposes of section 704(b) and § 1.704-1(b). Conversely, if there is an increase in the value of a § 1.752-7 liability that is reflected in the capital accounts of the partners under § 1.704-1(b)(2)(iv)(f), the amount of the increase constitutes an item of loss for purposes of section 704(b) and § 1.704-1(b).

(2) Example. The following example illustrates the provisions of this paragraph (c):

Example. (i) Facts. In 2004, A, B, and C form partnership PRS. A contributes Property 1 with a fair market value and basis of $400X, subject to a § 1.752-7 liability of $100X, for a 25% interest in PRS. B contributes $300X cash for a 25% interest in PRS, and C contributes $600X cash for a 50% interest in PRS. Assume that the partnership complies with the substantial economic effect safe harbor of § 1.704-1(b)(2). Under § 1.704-1(b)(2)(iv)(b), A's capital account is credited with $300X (the fair market value of Property 1, $400X, less the § 1.752-7 liability assumed by PRS, $100X). In accordance with §§ 1.752-7(c)(1)(i) and 1.704-3, the partnership can use any reasonable method for section 704(c) purposes. In this case, the partnership elects the traditional method under § 1.704-3(b) and also elects to treat the deductions or losses attributable to the § 1.752-7 liability as coming first from the built-in loss. In 2005, PRS earns $200X of income and uses it to satisfy the § 1.752-7 liability which has increased in value to $200X. Assume that the cost to PRS of satisfying the § 1.752-7 liability is deductible by PRS. The $200X of partnership income is allocated according to the partnership agreement, $50X to A, $50X to B, and $100X to C.

A		B		C		
Book	Tax	Book	Tax	Book	Tax	
$300	$400	$300	$300	$600	$600	Initial Contribution
50	50	50	50	100	100	Income
(25)	(125)	(25)	(25)	(50)	(50)	Satisfaction of Liability
$325	$325	$325	$325	$650	$650	

(ii) Analysis. Pursuant to paragraph (c) of this section, $100X of the deduction attributable to the satisfaction of the § 1.752-7 liability is specially allocated to A, the § 1.752-7 liability partner, under section 704(c)(1)(A) and § 1.704-3. No book item corresponds to this tax allocation. The remaining $100X of deduction attributable to the satisfaction of the § 1.752-7 liability is allocated, for both book and tax purposes, according to the partnership agreement, $25X to A, $25X to B, and $50X to C. If the partnership, instead, satisfied the § 1.752-7 liability over a number of years, the first $100X of deduction with respect to the § 1.752-7 liability would be allocated to A, the § 1.752-7 liability partner, before any deduction with respect to the § 1.752-7 liability would be allocated to the other partners. For example, if PRS were to satisfy $50X of the § 1.752-7 liability, the $50X deduction with respect to the § 1.752-7 liability would be allocated to A for tax purposes only. No deduction would arise for book purposes. If PRS later paid a further $100X in satisfaction of the § 1.752-7 liability, $50X of the deduction with respect to the § 1.752-7 liability would be allocated, solely for tax purposes, to A and the remaining $50X would be allocated, for both book and tax purposes, according to the partnership agreement. Under these circumstances, the partnership's method of allocating the built-in loss associated with the § 1.752-7 liability is reasonable.

(d) Special rules for transfers of partnership interests, distributions of partnership assets, and assumptions of the § 1.752-7 liability after a § 1.752-7 liability transfer. *(1) In general.* Except as provided in paragraphs (d)(2) and (i) of this section, paragraphs (e), (f), and (g) of this section apply to certain partnership transactions occurring after a § 1.752-7 liability transfer.

(2) Exceptions. (i) In general. Paragraphs (e), (f), and (g) of this section do not apply—

(A) If the partnership assumes the § 1.752-7 liability as part of a contribution to the partnership of the trade or business with which the liability is associated, and the partnership continues to carry on that trade or business after the contribution (for the definition of a trade or business, see paragraph (b)(10) of this section); or

(B) If, immediately before the testing date, the amount of the remaining built-in loss with respect to all § 1.752-7 liabilities assumed by the partnership (other than § 1.752-7 liabilities assumed by the partnership with an associated trade or business) in one or more § 1.752-7 liability transfers is less than the lesser of 10% of the gross value of partnership assets or $1,000,000.

(ii) Examples. The following examples illustrate the principles of this paragraph (d)(2):

Example (1). For the past 5 years, Corporation X, a C corporation, has been engaged in Business A and Business B. In 2004, Corporation X contributes Business A, in a transaction governed by section 721(a), to PRS in exchange for a PRS interest and the assumption by PRS of pension liabilities with respect to the employees engaged in Business A. PRS plans to carry on Business A after the contribution. Because PRS has assumed the pension liabilities as part of a contribution to PRS of the trade or business with which the liabilities are associated, the treatment of the pension liabilities is not affected by paragraphs (e), (f), and (g) of this section with respect to any transaction occurring after the § 1.752-7 liability transfer of the pension liabilities.

Example (2). (i) Facts. The facts are the same as in Example 1, except that PRS also assumes from Corporation X certain pension liabilities with respect to the employees of Business B. At the time of the assumption, the amount of the pension liabilities with respect to the employees of Business A is $3,000,000 (the A liabilities) and the amount of the pension liabilities associated with the employees of Business B (the B liabilities) is $2,000,000. Two years later, Corporation X sells its interest in PRS to Y for $9,000,000. At the time of the sale, the remaining built-in loss associated with the A liabilities is $2,100,000, the remaining built-in loss associated with the B liabilities is $900,000, and the gross value of PRS's assets (excluding § 1.752-7 liabilities) is $20,000,000. Assume that PRS has no § 1.752-7 liabilities other than those assumed from Corporation X.

PRS Balance Sheet at Time of X's Sale of PRS Interest (in millions)

Assets	Liabilities	
$20		Gross Assets (including Business A)
	($2.1)	A Liabilities
	(0.9)	B Liabilities

(ii) Analysis. The only liabilities assumed by PRS from Corporation X that were not assumed as part of Corporation X's contribution of Business A were the B liabilities. Immediately before the testing date, the remaining built-in loss associated with the B liabilities ($900,000) was less than the lesser of 10% of the gross value of PRS's assets ($2,000,000) or $1,000,000. Therefore, paragraph (d)(2)(i)(B) of this section applies to exclude Corporation X's sale of the PRS interest to Y from the application of paragraph (e) of this section.

(e) Transfer of § 1.752-7 liability partner's partnership interest. *(1) In general.* Except as provided in paragraphs (d)(2), (e)(3), and (i) of this section, immediately before the sale, exchange, or other disposition of all or a part of a § 1.752-7 liability partner's partnership interest, the § 1.752-7 liability partner's basis in the partnership interest is reduced by the § 1.752-7 liability reduction (as defined in paragraph (b)(7) of this section). No deduction, loss, or capital expense is allowed to the partnership on the satisfaction of the § 1.752-7 liability (within the meaning of paragraph (b)(8) of this section) to the extent of the remaining built-in loss associated with the § 1.752-7 liability (as defined in paragraph (b)(6) of this section). For purposes of section 705(a)(2)(B) and § 1.704-1(b)(2)(ii)(b) only, the remaining built-in loss associated with the § 1.752-7 liability is not treated as a nondeductible, noncapital expenditure of the partnership. Therefore, the remaining partners' capital accounts and bases in their partnership interests are not reduced by the remaining built-in loss associated with the § 1.752-7 liability. If the partnership (or any successor) notifies the § 1.752-7 liability partner of the satisfaction of the § 1.752-7 liability, then the § 1.752-7 liability partner is entitled to a loss or deduction. The amount of that deduction or loss is, in the case of a partial satisfaction of the § 1.752-7 liability, the amount that the partnership would, but for this section, take into account on the partial satisfaction of the § 1.752-7 liability (but not, in total, more than the § 1.752-7 liability reduction) or, in the case of a complete satisfaction of the § 1.752-7 liability, the remaining § 1.752-7 liability reduction. To the extent of the amount that the partnership would, but for this section, take into account on the satisfaction of the § 1.752-7 liability, the character of that deduction or loss is determined as if the § 1.752-7 liability partner had satisfied the liability. To the extent that the § 1.752-7 liability reduction exceeds the amount that the partnership would, but for this section, take into account on the satisfaction of the § 1.752-7 liability, the character of the § 1.752-7 liability partner's loss is capital.

(2) Examples. The following examples illustrate the principles of paragraph (e)(1) of this section:

Example (1). (i) Facts. In 2004, A, B, and C form partnership PRS. A contributes Property 1 with a fair market value of $5,000,000 and basis of $4,000,000 subject to a § 1.752-7 liability of $2,000,000 in exchange for a 25% interest in PRS. B contributes $3,000,000 cash in exchange for a 25% interest in PRS, and C contributes $6,000,000 cash in exchange for a 50% interest in PRS. In 2006, when PRS has a section 754 election in effect, A sells A's interest in PRS to D for $3,000,000. At the time of the sale, the basis of A's PRS interest is $4,000,000, the remaining built-in loss associated with the § 1.752-7 liability is $2,000,000, and PRS has no liabilities (as defined in § 1.752-1(a)(4)). Assume that none of the exceptions of paragraph (d)(2) of this section apply and that the satisfaction of the § 1.752-7 liability would have given rise to a deductible expense to A. In 2007, PRS pays $3,000,000 to satisfy the liability.

PRS Balance Sheet (in millions)

Assets Value	Assets Basis		Liabilities/Equity Value	Liabilities/Equity Basis	
$5	$4	Property 1			
$9	$9	Cash	$2	–	§ 1.752-7 Liability
					Partner's Equity:
			$3	$4	A
			$3	$3	B
			$6	$6	C

(ii) Sale of A's PRS interest. Immediately before the sale of the PRS interest to D, A's basis in the PRS interest is reduced (to $3,000,000) by the § 1.752-7 liability reduction, i.e., the lesser of the excess of A's basis in the PRS interest ($4,000,000) over the adjusted value of that interest ($3,000,000), $1,000,000, or the remaining built-in loss associated with the § 1.752-7 liability, $2,000,000. Therefore, A neither realizes nor recognizes any gain or loss on the sale of the PRS interest to D. D's basis in the PRS interest is $3,000,000. D's share of the adjusted basis of partnership property, as determined under § 1.743-1(d), equals D's interest in the partnership's previously taxed capital of $2,000,000 (the amount of cash that D would receive on a liquidation of the partnership, $3,000,000, increased by the amount of tax loss that would be allocated to D in the hypothetical transaction, $0, and reduced by the amount of tax gain that would be allocated to D in the hypothetical transaction, $1,000,000). Therefore, the positive basis adjustment under section 743(b) is $1,000,000.

Computation of § 1.752-7 Liability Reduction (in millions)

1. Basis of A's PRS interest	$4
2. Less adjusted value of A's PRS interest	(3)
3. Difference	$1
4. Remaining built-in loss from § 1.752-7 liability	2
5. § 1.752-7 liability reduction (lesser of 3 or 4)	$1

Gain/Loss on Sale of A's PRS Interest (in millions)

1. Amount realized on sale	$3
2. Less basis of PRS interest	
Original	4
§ 1.752-7 liability reduction	1
Difference	($3)
3. Gain/Loss	0

(iii) Satisfaction of § 1.752-7 liability. Neither PRS nor any of its partners is entitled to a deduction, loss, or capital expense upon the satisfaction of the § 1.752-7 liability to the extent of the remaining built-in loss associated with the § 1.752-7 liability ($2,000,000). PRS is entitled to a deduction, however, for the amount by which the cost of satisfying the § 1.752-7 liability exceeds the remaining built-in loss associated with the § 1.752-7 liability. Therefore, in 2007, PRS may deduct $1,000,000 (cost to satisfy the § 1.752-7 liability, $3,000,000, less the remaining built-in loss associated with the § 1.752-7 liability, $2,000,000). If PRS notifies A of the satisfaction of the § 1.752-7 liability, then A is entitled to an ordinary deduction in 2007 of $1,000,000 (the § 1.752-7 liability reduction).

PRS's Deduction on Satisfaction of Liability (in millions)

1. Amount paid by PRS to satisfy § 1.752-7 liability	$3
2. Remaining built-in loss for § 1.752-7 liability	(2)
3. Difference	$1

Example (2). The facts are the same as in Example 1 except that, at the time of A's sale of the PRS interest to D, PRS has a nonrecourse liability of $4,000,000, of which A's share is $1,000,000. A's basis in PRS is $5,000,000. At the time of the sale of the PRS interest to D, the adjusted value of A's interest is $4,000,000 (the fair market value of the interest ($3,000,000), increased by A's share of partnership liabilities ($1,000,000)). The difference between the basis of A's interest ($5,000,000) and the adjusted value of that interest ($4,000,000) is $1,000,000. Therefore, the § 1.752-7 liability reduction is $1,000,000 (the lesser of this difference or the remaining built-in loss associated with the § 1.752-7 liability, $2,000,000). Immediately before the sale of the PRS interest to D, A's basis is reduced from $5,000,000 to $4,0000,000. A's amount realized on the sale of the PRS interest to D is $4,000,000 ($3,000,000 paid by D, increased under section 752(d) by A's share of partnership liabilities, or $1,000,000). Therefore, A neither realizes nor recognizes any gain or loss on the sale. D's basis in the PRS interest is $4,000,000. Because D's share of the adjusted basis of partnership property is $3,000,000 (D's share of the partnership's previously taxed capital, $2,000,000, plus D's share of partnership liabilities, $1,000,000), the basis adjustment under section 743(b) is $1,000,000.

PRS Balance Sheet (in millions)

Assets Value	Assets Basis		Liabilities/Equity Value	Liabilities/Equity Basis	
$5	$4	Property 1			
$3	$3	Cash			
			$4	–	Nonrecourse Debt
			$2	–	§ 1.752-7 Liability
					Partner's Equity:
			$3	$5	A
			$3	$4	B
			$6	$8	C

Computation of § 1.752-7 Liability Reduction (in millions)

1. Basis of A's PRS interest	$5
2. Less adjusted value of A's PRS interest	
Value of PRS interest	3
A's share of nonrecourse debt	1
Total	(4)
3. Difference between 1 and 2	1
4. Remaining built-in loss from § 1.752-7 liability	2
5. § 1.752-7 liability reduction (lesser of 3 or 4)	$1

Gain/Loss on Sale of A's PRS Interest (in millions)

1. Amount realized on sale	
Value of PRS interest	$3
A's share of nonrecourse debt	1
Total	$4
2. Less basis of PRS interest	
Original	$5
§ 1.752-7 liability reduction	$1
Difference	($4)
3. Gain/Loss	0

Example (3). The facts are the same as in Example 1, except that the satisfaction of the § 1.752-7 liability would have given rise to a capital expense to A or PRS. Neither PRS nor any of its partners are entitled to a capital expense upon the satisfaction of the § 1.752-7 liability to the extent of the remaining built-in loss associated with the § 1.752-7 liability ($2,000,000). PRS may, however, increase the basis of appropriate partnership assets by the amount by which the cost of satisfying the § 1.752-7 liability exceeds the remaining built-in loss associated with the § 1.752-7 liability. Therefore, in 2007, PRS may capitalize $1,000,000 (cost to satisfy the § 1.752-7 liability, $3,000,000, less the remaining built-in loss associated with the § 1.752-7 liability, $2,000,000) to the appropriate partnership assets. If A is notified by PRS that the § 1.752-7 liability has been satisfied, then A is entitled to a capital loss in 2007 as provided in paragraph (e)(1) of this section, the year of the satisfaction of the § 1.752-7 liability.

(3) Exception for nonrecognition transactions. (i) In general. Paragraph (e)(1) of this section does not apply where a § 1.752-7 liability partner transfers all or part of the partner's partnership interest in a transaction in which the transferee's basis in the partnership interest is determined in whole or in part by reference to the transferor's basis in the partnership interest. In addition, paragraph (e)(1) of this section does not apply to a distribution of an interest in the partnership (lower-tier partnership) that has assumed the § 1.752-7 liability by a partnership that is the § 1.752-7 liability partner (upper-tier partnership) if the partners of the upper-tier partnership that were § 1.752-7 liability partners with respect to the lower-tier partnership prior to the distribution continue to be § 1.752-7 liability partners with respect to the lower-tier partnership after the distribution. See paragraphs (b)(4)(ii) and (j)(3) of this section for rules on the application of this section to partners of the § 1.752-7 liability partner.

(ii) Examples. The following examples illustrate the provisions of this paragraph (e)(3):

Example (1). Transfer of partnership interest to lower-tier partnership. (i) Facts. In 2004, X contributes undeveloped land with a value and basis of $2,000,000 and subject to environmental liabilities of $1,500,000 to partnership LTP in exchange for a 50% interest in LTP. LTP develops the land as a landfill. In 2005, in a transaction governed by section 721(a), X contributes the LTP interest to UTP in exchange for a 50% interest in UTP. In 2008, X sells the UTP interest to A for $500,000. At the time of the sale, X's basis in UTP is $2,000,000, the remaining built-in loss associated with the environmental liability is $1,500,000, and the gross value of UTP's assets is $2,500,000. The environmental liabilities were not assumed by LTP as part of a contribution by X to LTP of a trade or business with which the liabilities were associated. (See paragraph (b)(10)(ii), Example 1 of this section.)

(ii) Analysis. Because UTP's basis in the LTP interest is determined by reference to X's basis in the LTP interest, X's contribution of the LTP interest to UTP is exempted from the rules of paragraph (e)(1) of this section. Under paragraph (j)(1) of this section, X's contribution of the LTP interest to UTP is treated as a contribution of X's share of the assets of LTP and UTP's assumption of X's share of the LTP liabilities (including § 1.752-7 liabilities). Therefore, X's transfer of the LTP interest to UTP is a § 1.752-7 liability transfer. The § 1.752-7 liabilities deemed transferred by X to UTP are not associated with a trade or business transferred to UTP for purposes of paragraph (d)(2)(i)(A) of this section, because they were not associated with a trade or business transferred by X to LTP as part of the original § 1.752-7 liability transfer. See paragraph (j)(2) of this section. Because none of the exceptions described in paragraph (d)(2) of this section apply to X's taxable sale of the UTP interest to A in 2008, paragraph (e)(1) of this section applies to that sale.

Example (2). Transfer of partnership interest to corporation. The facts are the same as in Example 1, except that, rather than transferring the LTP interest to UTP in 2005, X contributes the LTP interest to Corporation Y in an exchange to which section 351 applies. Because Corporation Y's basis in the LTP interest is determined by reference to X's basis in that interest, X's contribution of the LTP interest is exempted from the rules of paragraph (e)(1) of this section. But see section 358(h) and § 1.358-7 for appropriate basis adjustments.

Example (3). Partnership merger. (i) Facts. In 2004, A, B, C, and D form equal partnership PRS1. A contributes Blackacre with a value and basis of $2,000,000 to PRS1 and PRS1 assumes from A $1,500,000 of pension liabilities unrelated to Blackacre. B, C, and D each contribute $500,000 cash to PRS1. PRS1 uses the cash contributed by B, C, and D ($1,500,000) to purchase Whiteacre. In 2006, PRS1 merges into PRS2 in an assets-over merger under § 1.708-1(c)(3). Assume that, under § 1.708-1(c), PRS2 is the surviving partnership and PRS1 is the terminating partnership. At the time of the merger, the value of Blackacre is still $2,000,000, the remaining built-in loss with respect to the pension liabilities is still $1,500,000, but the value of Whiteacre has declined to $500,000.

(ii) Deemed assumption by PRS2 of PRS1 liabilities. Under § 1.708-1(c)(3), the merger is treated as a contribution of the assets and liabilities of PRS1 to PRS2, followed by a distribution of the PRS2 interests by PRS1 in liquidation of PRS1. Because PRS2 assumes a § 1.752-7 liability (the pension liabilities) of PRS1, PRS1 is a § 1.752-7 liability partner of PRS2. Under paragraph (b)(5)(ii)(A) of this section, A is also § 1.752-7 liability partner of PRS2 to the extent of the remaining $1,500,000 built-in loss associated with the pension liabilities. B, C, and D are not § 1.752-7 liability partners with respect to PRS1. If the amount of the pension liabilities had increased between the date of PRS1's assumption of those liabilities from A and the date of the merger of PRS1 into PRS2, then B, C, and D would be § 1.752-7 liability partners with respect to PRS2 to the extent of their respective shares of that increase. See paragraph (b)(5)(ii) of this section.

(iii) Deemed distribution of PRS2 interests. Paragraph (e)(1) does not apply to PRS1's deemed distribution of the PRS2 interests, because, under paragraph (b)(5)(ii)(B) of this section, all of the partners that were § 1.752-7 liability partners with respect to PRS2 before the distribution, i.e., A, continue to be § 1.752-7 liability partners after the distribution. After the distribution, A's share of the pension liabilities now held by PRS2 will continue to be $1,500,000.

Example (4). Partnership division; no shifting of § 1.752-7 liability. The facts are the same as in Example 3, except that PRS1 does not merge with PRS2, but instead contributes Blackacre to PRS2 in exchange for PRS2 interests and the assumption by PRS2 of the pension liabilities. Immediately thereafter, PRS1 distributes the PRS2 interests to A and B in liquidation of their interests in PRS1. The analysis is the same as in Example 3. After the assumption of the pension liabilities by PRS2, A is a § 1.752-7 liability partner with respect to PRS2. After the distribution of a PRS2 interest to A, A continues to be a § 1.752-7 liability partner with respect to PRS2, and the amount of A's built-in loss with respect to the § 1.752-7 liabilities continues to be $1,500,000. Therefore, paragraph (e)(1) of this section does not apply to the distribution of the PRS2 interests to A and B.

Example (5). Partnership division; shifting of § 1.752-7 liability. The facts are the same as in Example 4, except that PRS1 distributes the PRS2 interests not to A and B, but to C and D, in liquidation of their interests in PRS1. After this distribution, A does not continue to be a § 1.752-7 liability partner of PRS2, because A no longer has an interest in PRS2. Therefore, paragraph (e)(1) of this section applies to the distribution of the PRS2 interests to C and D.

(f) Distribution in liquidation of § 1.752-7 liability partner's partnership interest. *(1) In general.* Except as provided in paragraphs (d)(2) and (i) of this section, immediately before a distribution in liquidation of a § 1.752-7 liability partner's partnership interest, the § 1.752-7 liability partner's basis in the partnership interest is reduced by the § 1.752-7 liability reduction (as defined in paragraph (b)(7) of this section). This rule applies before section 737. No deduction, loss, or capital expense is allowed to the partnership on the satisfaction of the § 1.752-7 liability (within the meaning of paragraph (b)(8) of this section) to the extent of the remaining built-in loss associated with the § 1.752-7 liability (as defined in paragraph (b)(6) of this section). For purposes of section 705(a)(2)(B) and § 1.704-1(b)(2)(ii)(b) only, the remaining built-in loss associated with the § 1.752-7 liability is not treated as a nondeductible, noncapital expenditure of the partnership. Therefore, the remaining partners' capital accounts and bases in their partnership interests are not reduced by the remaining built-in loss associated with the § 1.752-7 liability. If the partnership (or any successor) notifies the § 1.752-7 liability partner of the satisfaction of the § 1.752-7 liability, then the § 1.752-7 liability partner is entitled to a loss or deduction. The amount of that deduction or loss is, in the case of a partial satisfaction of the § 1.752-7 liability, the amount that the partnership would, but for this section, take into account on the partial satisfaction of the § 1.752-7 liability (but not, in total, more than the § 1.752-7 liability reduction) or, in the case of a complete satisfaction of the § 1.752-7 liability, the remaining § 1.752-7 liability reduction. To the extent of the amount that the partnership would, but for this section, take into account on satisfaction of the § 1.752-7 liability, the character of that deduction or loss is determined as if the § 1.752-7 liability partner had satisfied the liability. To the extent that the § 1.752-7 liability reduction exceeds the amount that the partnership would, but for this section, take into account on satisfaction of the § 1.752-7 liability, the character of the § 1.752-7 liability partner's loss is capital.

(2) Example. The following example illustrates the provision of this paragraph (f):

Example. (i) Facts. In 2004, A, B, and C form partnership PRS. A contributes Property 1 with a fair market value and basis of $5,000,000 subject to a § 1.752-7 liability of $2,000,000 for a 25% interest in PRS. B contributes $3,000,000 cash for a 25% interest in PRS, and C contributes $6,000,000 cash for a 50% interest in PRS. In 2012, when PRS has a section 754 election in effect, PRS distributes Property 2, which has a basis and fair market value of $3,000,000, to A in liquidation of A's PRS interest. At the time of the distribution, the fair market value of A's PRS interest is still $3,000,000, the basis of that interest is still $5,000,000, and the remaining built-in loss associated with the § 1.752-7 liability is still $2,000,000. Assume that none of the exceptions of paragraph (d)(2) of this section apply to the distribution and that the satisfaction of the § 1.752-7 liability would have given rise to a deductible expense to A. In 2013, PRS pays $1,000,000 to satisfy the entire § 1.752-7 liability.

PRS Balance Sheet (in millions)

Assets			Liabilities/Equity		
Value	Basis		Value	Basis	
$5	$5	Property 1			
$9	$9	Cash			
			$2	–	§ 1.752-7 Liability
					Partner's Equity:
			$3	$5	A
			$3	$3	B
			$6	$6	C

(ii) Liquidation of A's PRS interest. Immediately before the distribution of Property 2 to A, A's basis in the PRS interest is reduced (to $3,000,000) by the § 1.752-7 liability reduction, i.e., the lesser of the excess of A's basis in the PRS interest ($5,000,000) over the adjusted value ($3,000,000) of that interest ($2,000,000) or the remaining built-in loss associated with the § 1.752-7 liability ($2,000,000). Therefore, A's basis in Property 2 under section 732(b) is $3,000,000. Because this is the same as the partnership's basis in Property 2 immediately before the distribution, the partnership's basis adjustment under section 734(b) is $0.

Computation of § 1.752-7 Liability Reduction (in millions)

1. Basis of A's PRS interest	$5
2. Less adjusted value of A's PRS interest	(3)
3. Difference	$2
4. Remaining built-in loss from § 1.752-7 liability	2
5. § 1.752-7 liability reduction (lesser of 3 or 4)	$2

(iii) Satisfaction of § 1.752-7 liability. PRS is not entitled to a deduction, loss, or capital expense on the satisfaction of the § 1.752-7 liability to the extent of the remaining built-in loss associated with the § 1.752-7 liability ($2,000,000). Because this amount exceeds the amount paid by PRS to satisfy the § 1.752-7 liability ($1,000,000), PRS is not entitled to any deduction for the § 1.752-7 liability in 2013. If, however, PRS notifies A of the satisfaction of the § 1.752-7 liability, A is entitled to an ordinary deduction in 2013 of $1,000,000 (the amount paid in satisfaction of the § 1.752-7 liability) and a capital loss of $1,000,000 (the remaining § 1.752-7 liability reduction).

PRS's Deduction on Satisfaction of Liability (in millions)

Amount paid by PRS to satisfy § 1.752-7 liability	$1
Remaining built-in loss for § 1.752-7 liability	(2)
Difference (but not below zero)	$0

(g) Assumption of § 1.752-7 liability by a partner other than § 1.752-7 liability partner. *(1) In general.* If this paragraph (g) applies, section 704(c)(1)(B) does not apply to an assumption of a § 1.752-7 liability from a partnership by a partner other than the § 1.752-7 liability partner. The rules of paragraph (g)(2) of this section apply only if the § 1.752-7 liability partner is a partner in the partnership at the time of the assumption of the § 1.752-7 liability from the partnership. The rules of paragraphs (g)(3) and (4) of this section apply to any assumption of the § 1.752-7 liability by a partner other than the § 1.752-7 liability partner, whether or not the § 1.752-7 liability partner is a partner in the partnership at the time of the assumption from the partnership.

(2) Consequences to § 1.752-7 liability partner. If, at the time of an assumption of a § 1.752-7 liability from a partnership by a partner other than the § 1.752-7 liability partner, the § 1.752-7 liability partner remains a partner in the partnership, then the § 1.752-7 liability partner's basis in the partnership interest is reduced by the § 1.752-7 liability reduction (as defined in paragraph (b)(7) of this section). If the assuming partner (or any successor) notifies the § 1.752-7 liability partner of the satisfaction of the § 1.752-7 liability (within the meaning of paragraph (b)(8) of this section), then the § 1.752-7 liability partner is entitled to a deduction or loss. The amount of that deduction or loss is, in the case of a partial satisfaction of the § 1.752-7 liability, the amount that the assuming partner would, but for this section, take into account on the satisfaction of the § 1.752-7 liability (but not, in total, more than the § 1.752-7 liability reduction) or, in the case of a complete satisfaction of the § 1.752-7 liability, the remaining § 1.752-7 liability reduction. To the extent of the amount that the assuming partner would, but for this section, take into account on the satisfaction of the § 1.752-7 liability, the character of that deduction or loss is determined as if the § 1.752-7 liability partner had satisfied the liability. To the extent that the § 1.752-7 liability reduction exceeds the amount that the assuming partner would, but for this section, take into account on the satisfaction of the § 1.752-7 liability, the character of the § 1.752-7 liability partner's loss is capital.

(3) Consequences to partnership. Immediately after the assumption of the § 1.752-7 liability from the partnership by a partner other than the § 1.752-7 liability partner, the partnership must reduce the basis of partnership assets by the remaining built-in loss associated with the § 1.752-7 liability (as defined in paragraph (b)(6) of this section). The reduction in the basis of partnership assets must be allocated among partnership assets as if that adjustment were a basis adjustment under section 734(b).

(4) Consequences to assuming partner. No deduction, loss, or capital expense is allowed to an assuming partner (other than the § 1.752-7 liability partner) on the satisfaction of the § 1.752-7 liability assumed from a partnership to the extent of the remaining built-in loss associated with the § 1.752-7 liability. Instead, upon the satisfaction of the § 1.752-7 liability, the assuming partner must adjust the basis of the partnership interest, any assets (other than cash, accounts receivable, or inventory) distributed by the partnership to the partner, or gain or loss on the disposition of the partnership interest, as the case may be. These adjustments are determined as if the assuming partner's basis in the partnership interest at the time of the assumption were increased by the lesser of the amount paid (or to be paid) to satisfy the § 1.752-7 liability or the remaining built-in loss associated with the § 1.752-7 liability. However, the assuming partner cannot take into account any adjustments to depreciable basis, reduction in gain, or increase in loss until the satisfaction of the § 1.752-7 liability.

(5) Example. The following example illustrates the provisions of this paragraph (g):

Example. (i) Facts. In 2004, A, B, and C form partnership PRS. A contributes Property 1, a nondepreciable capital asset with a fair market value and basis of $5,000,000, in exchange for a 25% interest in PRS and assumption by PRS of a § 1.752-7 liability of $2,000,000. B contributes $3,000,000 cash for a 25% interest in PRS, and C contributes $6,000,000 cash for a 50% interest in PRS. PRS uses the cash contributed to purchase Property 2. In 2007, PRS distributes Property 1, subject to the § 1.752-7 liability to B in liquidation of B's interest in PRS. At the time of the distribution, A's interest in PRS still has a value of $3,000,000 and a basis of $5,000,000, and B's interest in PRS still has a value and basis of $3,000,000. Also at that time, Property 1 still has a value and basis of $5,000,000, Property 2 still has a value and basis of $9,000,000, and the remaining built-in loss associated with the § 1.752-7 liability still is $2,000,000. Assume that none of the exceptions of paragraph (d)(2)(i) of this section apply to the assumption of the § 1.752-7 liability by B and that the satisfaction of the § 1.752-7 liability by A would have given rise to a deductible expense to A. In 2010, B pays $1,000,000 to satisfy the entire § 1.752-7 liability. At that time, B still owns Property 1, which has a basis of $3,000,000.

PRS Balance Sheet (in millions)

Assets			Liabilities/Equity		
Value	Basis		Value	Basis	
$5	$5	Property 1			
$9	$9	Property 2			
			$2	–	§ 1.752-7 Liability
					Partner's Equity:
			$3	$5	A
			$3	$3	B
			$6	$6	C

(ii) Assumption of § 1.752-7 liability by B. Section 704(c)(1)(B) does not apply to the assumption of the § 1.752-7 liability by B. Instead, A's basis in the PRS interest is reduced (to $3,000,000) by the § 1.752-7 liability reduction, i.e., the lesser of the excess of A's basis in the PRS interest ($5,000,000) over the adjusted value ($3,000,000) of that interest ($2,000,000), or the remaining built-in loss associated with the § 1.752-7 liability as of the time of the assumption ($2,000,000). PRS's basis in Property 2 is reduced (to $7,000,000) by the $2,000,000 remaining built-in loss associated with the § 1.752-7 liability. B's basis in Property 1 under section 732(b) is $3,000,000 (B's basis in the PRS interest). This is $2,000,000 less than PRS's basis in Property 1 before the distribution of Property 1 to B. If PRS has a section 754 election in effect for 2007, PRS may increase the basis of Property 2 under section 734(b) by $2,000,000.

§ 1.752-7 Liability Reduction (in millions)

1. Basis of A's PRS interest	$5
2. Less adjusted value of A's PRS interest	(3)
3. Difference	$2
4. Remaining built-in loss from § 1.752-7 liability	2
5. § 1.752-7 liability reduction (lesser of 3 or 4)	$2

A's Basis in PRS after Assumption by B (in millions)

1. Basis before assumption	$5
2. Less § 1.752-7 liability reduction	(2)
3. Basis after assumption	$3

PRS's Basis in Property 2 after Assumption by B (in millions)

1. Basis before assumption	$9
2. Less remaining built-in loss from § 1.752-7 liability	(2)
3. Plus section 734(b) adjustment (if partnership has a section 754 election)	2
4. Basis after assumption	$9

(iii) Satisfaction of § 1.752-7 liability. B is not entitled to a deduction on the satisfaction of the § 1.752-7 liability in 2010 to the extent of the remaining built-in loss associated with the § 1.752-7 liability ($2,000,000). As this amount exceeds the amount paid by B to satisfy the § 1.752-7 liability, B is not entitled to any deduction on the satisfaction of the § 1.752-7 liability in 2010. B may, however, increase the basis of Property 1 by the lesser of the remaining built-in loss associated with the § 1.752-7 liability ($2,000,000) or the amount paid to satisfy the § 1.752-7 liability ($1,000,000). Therefore, B's basis in Property 1 is increased to $4,000,000. If B notifies A of the satisfaction of the § 1.752-7 liability, then A is entitled to an ordinary deduction in 2010 of $1,000,000 (the amount paid in satisfaction of the § 1.752-7 liability) and a capital loss of $1,000,000 (the remaining § 1.752-7 liability reduction).

B's Basis in Property 1 After Satisfaction of Liability [In millions]

1. Basis in Property 1 after distribution	$3
2. Plus lesser of remaining built-in loss ($2) or amount paid to satisfy liability ($1)	1
3. Basis in Property 1 after satisfaction of liability	$4

(h) Notification by the partnership (or successor) of the satisfaction of the § 1.752-7 liability. For purposes of paragraphs (e), (f), and (g) of this section, notification by the partnership (or successor) of the satisfaction of the § 1.752-7 liability must be attached to the § 1.752-7 liability partner's return (whether an original or an amended return) for the year in which the loss is being claimed and must include—

(1) The amount paid in satisfaction of the § 1.752-7 liability, and whether the amounts paid were in partial or complete satisfaction of the § 1.752-7 liability;

(2) The name and address of the person satisfying the § 1.752-7 liability;

(3) The date of the payment on the § 1.752-7 liability; and

(4) The character of the loss to the § 1.752-7 liability partner with respect to the § 1.752-7 liability.

(i) Special rule for amounts that are capitalized prior to the occurrence of an event described in paragraphs (e), (f), or (g). *(1) In general.* If all or a portion of a § 1.752-7 liability is properly capitalized (capitalized basis) prior to an event described in paragraph (e), (f), or (g) of this section, then, before an event described in paragraph (e), (f), or (g) of this section, the partnership may take the capitalized basis into account for purposes of computing cost recovery and gain or loss on the sale of the asset to which the basis has been capitalized (and for any other purpose for which the basis of the asset is relevant), but after an event described in paragraph (e), (f), or (g) of this section, the partnership may not take any remaining capitalized basis into account for tax purposes.

(2) Example. The following example illustrates the provisions of this paragraph (i):

Example. (i) Facts. In 2004, A and B form partnership PRS. A contributes Property 1, a nondepreciable capital asset, with a fair market value and basis of 5,000,000, in exchange for a 25% interest in PRS and an assumption by PRS of a § 1.752-7 liability of $2,000,000. B contributes $9,000,000 in cash in exchange for a 75% interest in PRS. PRS uses $7,000,000 of the cash to purchase Property 2, also a nondepreciable capital asset. In 2007, when PRS's assets have not changed, PRS satisfies the § 1.752-7 liability by paying $2,000,000. Assume that PRS is required to capitalize the cost of satisfying the § 1.752-7 liability. In 2008, A sells his interest in PRS to C for $3,000,000. At the time of the sale, the basis of A's interest is still $5,000,000.

(ii) Analysis. On the sale of A's interest to C, A realizes a loss of $2,000,000 on the sale of the PRS interest (the excess of $5,000,000, the basis of the partnership interest, over

$3,000,000, the amount realized on sale). The remaining built-in loss associated with the § 1.752-7 liability at that time is zero because all of the § 1.752-7 liability as of the time of the assumption of the § 1.752-7 liability by the partnership was capitalized by the partnership. The partnership may not take any remaining capitalized basis into account for tax purposes.

Gain/Loss on Sale of A's PRS Interest (in millions)

1. Amount realized on sale	$3
2. Less basis of PRS interest	
Original Basis	$5
§ 1.752-7 liability reduction	$0
Difference	($5)
3.Gain/Loss	($2)

(iii) Partial Satisfaction. Assume that, prior to the sale of A's interest in PRS to C, PRS had paid $1,500,000 to satisfy a portion of the § 1.752-7 liability. Therefore, immediately before the sale of the PRS interest to C, A's basis in the PRS interest would be reduced (to $4,500,000) by the $500,000 remaining built-in loss associated with the § 1.752-7 liability ($2,000,000 less the 1,500,000 portion capitalized by the partnership as that time). On the sale of the PRS interest, A realizes a loss of $1,500,000 (the excess of $4,500,000, the basis of the PRS interest, over $3,000,000, the amount realized on the sale). Neither PRS nor any of its partners is entitled to a deduction, loss, or capital expense upon the satisfaction of the § 1.752-7 liability to the extent of the remaining built-in loss associated with the § 1.752-7 liability ($500,000). If PRS notifies A of the satisfaction of the remaining portion of the § 1.752-7 liability, then A is entitled to a deduction or loss of $500,000 (the remaining § 1.752-7 liability reduction). The partnership may not take any remaining capitalized basis into account for tax purposes.

Gain/Loss on Sale of A's PRS Interest (in millions)

1. Amount realized on sale	$3
2. Less basis of PRS interest	
Original Basis	$5
§ 1.752-7 liability reduction	($0.5)
Difference	($4.5)
3. Gain/Loss	($1.5)

(j) Tiered partnerships. *(1) Look-through treatment.* For purposes of this section, a contribution by a partner of an interest in a partnership (lower-tier partnership) to another partnership (upper-tier partnership) is treated as a contribution by the partner of the partner's share of each of the lower-tier partnership's assets and an assumption by the upper-tier partnership of the partner's share of the lower-tier partnership's liabilities (including § 1.752-7 liabilities). See paragraph (e)(3)(ii) Example 1 of this section. In addition, a partnership is treated as having its share of any § 1.752-7 liabilities of the partnerships in which it has an interest.

(2) Trade or business exception. If a partnership (upper-tier partnership) assumes a § 1.752-7 liability of a partner, and, subsequently, another partnership (lower-tier partnership) assumes that § 1.752-7 liability from the upper-tier partnership, then the § 1.752-7 liability is treated as associated only with any trade or business contributed to the upper-tier partnership by the § 1.752-7 liability partner. The same rule applies where a partnership assumes a § 1.752-7 liability of a partner, and, subsequently, the § 1.752-7 liability partner transfers that partnership interest to another partnership. See paragraph (e)(3)(ii) Example 1 of this section.

(3) Partnership as a § 1.752-7 liability partner. If a transaction described in paragraph (e), (f), or (g) of this section occurs with respect to a partnership (upper-tier partnership) that is a § 1.752-7 liability partner of another partnership (lower-tier partnership), then such transaction will also be treated as a transaction described in paragraph (e), (f), or (g) of this section, as appropriate, with respect to the partners of the upper-tier partnership, regardless of whether the upper-tier partnership assumed the § 1.752-7 liability from those partners. (See paragraph (b)(5) of this section for rules relating to the treatment of transactions by the partners of the upper-tier partnership). In such a case, each partner's share of the § 1.752-7 liability reduction in the upper-tier partnership is equal to that partner's share of the § 1.752-7 liability. The partners of the upper-tier partnership at the time of the transaction described in paragraph (e), (f), or (g) of this section, and not the upper-tier partnership, are entitled to the deduction or loss on the satisfaction of the § 1.752-7 liability. Similar principles apply where the upper-tier partnership is itself owned by one or a series of partnerships. This paragraph does not apply to the extent that § 1.752-7(j)(4) applied to the assumption of the § 1.752-7 liability by the lower-tier partnership.

(4) Transfer of § 1.752-7 liability by partnership to another partnership or corporation after a transaction described in paragraph (e), (f), or (g). (i) In general. If, after a transaction described in paragraph (e), (f), or (g) of this section with respect to a § 1.752-7 liability assumed by a partnership (the upper-tier partnership), another partnership or a corporation assumes the § 1.752-7 liability from the upper-tier partnership (or the assuming partner) in a transaction in which the basis of property is determined, in whole or in part, by reference to the basis of the property in the hands of the upper-tier partnership (or assuming partner), then—

(A) The upper-tier partnership (or assuming partner) must reduce its basis in any corporate stock or partnership interest received by the remaining built-in loss associated with the § 1.752-7 liability, at the time of the transaction described in paragraph (e), (f), or (g) of this section (but the partners of the upper-tier partnership do not reduce their bases or capital accounts in the upper-tier partnership); and

(B) No deduction, loss, or capital expense is allowed to the assuming partnership or corporation on the satisfaction of the § 1.752-7 liability to the extent of the remaining built-in loss associated with the § 1.752-7 liability.

(ii) Subsequent transfers. Similar rules apply to subsequent assumptions of the § 1.752-7 liability in transactions in which the basis of property is determined, in whole or in part, by reference to the basis of the property in the hands of the transferor. If, subsequent to an assumption of the § 1.752-7 liability by a partnership in a transaction to which paragraph (j)(4)(i) of this section applies, the § 1.752-7 liability is assumed from the partnership by a partner other than the partner from whom the partnership assumed the § 1.752-7 liability, then the rules of paragraph (g) of this section apply.

(5) Example. The following example illustrates the provisions of paragraphs (j)(3) and (4) of this section:

Example. (i) Assumption of § 1.752-7 liability by UTP and transfer of § 1.752-7 liability partner's interest in UTP. In 2004, A, B, and C form partnership UTP. A contributes Property 1 with a fair market value and basis of $5,000,000 subject to a § 1.752-7 liability of $2,000,000 in exchange for a 25% interest in UTP. B contributes $3,000,000 cash in exchange for a 25% interest in UTP, and C contributes $6,000,000 cash in exchange for a 50% interest in UTP.

UTP invests the $9,000,000 cash in Property 2. In 2006, A sells A's interest in UTP to D for $3,000,000. At the time of the sale, the basis of A's UTP interest is $5,000,000, the remaining built-in loss associated with the § 1.752-7 liability is $2,000,000, and UTP has no liabilities other than the § 1.752-7 liabilities assumed from A. Assume that none of the exceptions of paragraph (d)(2) of this section apply and that the satisfaction of the § 1.752-7 liability would give rise to a deductible expense to A and to UTP. Under paragraph (e) of this section, immediately before the sale of the UTP interest to D, A's basis in UTP is reduced to $3,000,000 by the $2,000,000 § 1.752-7 liability reduction. Therefore, A neither realizes nor recognizes any gain or loss on the sale of the UTP interest to D. D's basis in the UTP interest is $3,000,000.

UTP Balance Sheet Prior to A's Sale (in millions)

Assets			Liabilities/Equity		
Value	Basis		Value	Basis	
$5	$5	Property 1			
$9	$9	Property 2			
			$ 2		§ 1.752-7 Liability
					Partner's Equity:
			$ 3	$ 5	A (25%)
			$ 3	$ 3	B (25%)
			$ 6	$ 6	C (50%)
			$12	$14	Total Equity

Gain/Loss on Sale of A's PRS Interest to D (in millions)

1. Amount realized on sale	$3
2. Less basis of PRS interest	
Original	$5
§ 1.752-7 liability reduction	($2)
Difference	($3)
3. Gain/Loss	$0

(ii) Assumption of § 1.752-7 liability by LTP from UTP. In 2008, at a time when the estimated amount of the § 1.752-7 liability has increased to $3,500,000, UTP contributes Property 1 and Property 2, subject to the § 1.752-7 liability, to LTP in exchange for a 50% interest in LTP. At the time of the contribution, Property 1 still has a value and basis of $5,000,000 and Property 2 still has a value and basis of $9,000,000. UTP's basis in LTP under section 722 is $14,000,000. Under paragraph (j)(4)(i) of this section, UTP must reduce its basis in LTP by the $2,000,000 remaining built-in loss associated with the § 1.752-7 liability (as of the time of the sale of the UTP interest by A). The partners in UTP are not required to reduce their bases in UTP by this amount. UTP is a § 1.752-7 liability partner of LTP with respect to the entire $3,500,000 § 1.752-7 liability assumed by LTP. However, as A is no longer a partner of UTP, none of the partners of UTP (as of the time of the assumption of the § 1.752-7 liability by LTP) are § 1.752-7 liability partners of LTP with respect to the $2,000,000 remaining built-in loss associated with the § 1.752-7 liability (as of the time of the sale of the UTP interest by A). The UTP partners (as of the time of the assumption of the § 1.752-7 liability by LTP) are § 1.752-7 liability partners of LTP with respect to the $1,500,000 increase in the amount of the § 1.752-7 liability of UTP since the assumption of that § 1.752-7 liability by UTP from A.

UTP Balance Sheet Immediately Before Contribution to LTP (in millions)

Assets		Liabilities/Equity		
Value	Basis	Value	Basis	
$5	$5			Property 1
$9	$9			Property 2
				§ 1.752-7 Liability
		$ 2		Assumed from A
		$ 1.5		Additional
		$ 3.5		Total
				Partner's Equity:
		$ 2.625	$ 3	D (25%)
		$ 2.625	$ 3	B (25%)
		$ 5.25	$ 6	C (50%)
		$10.5	$12	Total Equity

UTP's Basis in LTP Immediately After Contribution (in millions)

1. Basis in assets	$14
2. Less remaining built-in loss at time of A's sale	($2)
3. UTP's basis in LTP	$12

(iii) Sale by UTP of LTP interest. In 2010, UTP sells its interest in LTP to E for $10,500,000. At the time of the sale, the LTP interest still has a value of $10,500,000 and a basis of $12,000,000, and the remaining built-in loss associated with the § 1.752-7 liability is $3,500,000. Under paragraph (e) of this section, immediately before the sale, UTP must reduce its basis in the LTP interest by the § 1.752-7 liability reduction. Under paragraph (a)(4) of this section, the remaining built-in loss associated with the § 1.752-7 liability is $1,500,000 (remaining built-in loss associated with the

§ 1.752-7 liability, $3,500,000, reduced by the amount of the § 1.752-7 liability taken into account under paragraph (j)(4) of this section, $2,000,000). The difference between the basis of the LTP interest held by UTP ($12,000,000) and the adjusted value of that interest ($10,500,000) is also $1,500,000. Therefore, the § 1.752-7 liability reduction is $1,500,000 and UTP's basis in the LTP interest must be reduced to $10,500,000. In addition, UTP's partners must reduce their bases in their UTP interests by their proportionate shares of the § 1.752-7 liability reduction. Thus, the basis of each of B's and D's interest in UTP must be reduced by $375,000 and the basis of C's interest in UTP must be reduced by $750,000. In 2011, D sells the UTP interest to F.

Computation of § 1.752-7 Liability Reduction (in millions)

1. Basis of UTP's LTP interest	$12
2. Less adjusted value of UTP's LTP interest	($10.5)
3. Difference between 1 and 2	$1.5
4. Remaining built-in loss from § 1.752-7 liability	$1.5
5. § 1.752-7 liability reduction (lesser of 3 or 4)	$1.5

Gain/Loss on Sale of UTP's PRS Interest to E (in millions)

1. Amount realized on sale	$10.5
2. Less basis of PRS interest	
Original	$12
§ 1.752-7 liability reduction	($1.5)
Difference	($10.5)
3. Gain/Loss	$0

Partner's Bases in UTP Interests after Sale of LTP Interest (in millions)

	B	C	D
Basis prior to sale	$3	$6	$3
Share of § 1.752-7 liability Reduction	($0.375)	($0.75)	($0.375)
Basis after sale	$2.625	$5.25	$2.625

(iv) Deduction, expense, or loss associated with the § 1.752-7 liability by LTP. In 2012, LTP pays $3,500,000 to satisfy the § 1.752-7 liability. Under paragraphs (e) and (j)(4) of this section, LTP is not entitled to any deduction with respect to the § 1.752-7 liability. Under paragraph (j)(3) of this section, UTP also is not entitled to any deduction with respect to the § 1.752-7 liability. If LTP notifies A, B, C and D of the satisfaction of the § 1.752-7 liability, then A is entitled to a deduction in 2012 of $2,000,000, B and D are each entitled to deductions in 2012 of $375,000, and C is entitled to a deduction in 2012 of $750,000.

(k) Effective dates. *(1) In general.* This section applies to § 1.752-7 liability transfers occurring on or after June 24, 2003. For assumptions occurring after October 18, 1999, and before June 24, 2003, see § 1.752-6. For § 1.752-7 liability transfers occurring on or after June 24, 2003 and before May 26, 2005, taxpayers may rely on the exception for trading and investment partnerships in paragraph (b)(8)(ii) of § 1.752.7 (2003-28 I.R.B. 46; 68 FR 37434).

(2) Election to apply this section to assumptions of liabilities occurring after October 18, 1999 and before June 24, 2003. (i) In general. A partnership may elect to apply this section to all assumptions of liabilities (including § 1.752-7 liabilities) occurring after October 18, 1999, and before June 24, 2003. Such an election is binding on the partnership and all of its partners. A partnership making such an election must apply all of the provisions of § 1.752-1 and § 1.752-7, including § 1.358-5T, § 1.358-7, § 1.704-1(b)(1)(ii) and (b)(2)(iv)(b), § 1.704-2(b)(3), § 1.704-3(a)(7), (a)(8)(iv), and (a)(12), § 1.704-4(d)(1)(iv), § 1.705-1(a)(8), § 1.732-2(d)(3)(iv), and § 1.737-5.

(ii) Manner of making election. A partnership makes an election under this paragraph (k)(2) by attaching the following statement to its timely filed return: [Insert name and employer identification number of electing partnership] elects under § 1.752-7 of the Income Tax Regulations to be subject to the rules of § 1.358-5T, § 1.358-7, § 1.704-1(b)(1)(ii) and (b)(2)(iv)(b), § 1.704-2(b)(3), § 1.704-3(a)(7), (a)(8)(iv), and (a)(12), § 1.704-4(d)(1)(iv), § 1.705-1(a)(8), § 1.732-2(d)(3)(iv), and § 1.737-5 with respect to all liabilities (including § 1.752-7 liabilities) assumed by the partnership after October 18, 1999 and before June 24, 2003. In the statement, the partnership must list, with respect to each liability (including each § 1.752-7 liability) assumed by the partnership after October 18, 1999 and before June 24, 2003—

(A) The name, address, and taxpayer identification number of the partner from whom the liability was assumed;

(B) The date on which the liability was assumed by the partnership;

(C) The amount of the liability as of the time of its assumption; and

(D) A description of the liability.

(iii) Filing of amended returns. An election under this paragraph (k)(2) will be valid only if the partnership and its partners promptly amend any returns for open taxable years that would be affected by the election.

(iv) Time for making election. An election under this paragraph (k)(2) must be filed with any timely filed Federal income tax return filed by the partnership on or after September 24, 2003 and on or before December 31, 2005.

T.D. 9207, 5/23/2005.

---

§ 1.753-1 Partner receiving income in respect of decedent.

(a) Income in respect of a decedent under section 736(a). All payments coming within the provisions of section 736(a) made by a partnership to the estate or other successor in interest of a deceased partner are considered income in respect of the decedent under section 691. The estate or other successor in interest of a deceased partner shall be considered to have received income in respect of a decedent to the extent that amounts are paid by a third person in exchange for rights to future payments from the partnership under section 736(a). When a partner who is receiving payments under section 736(a) dies, section 753 applies to any remaining payments under section 736(a) made to his estate or other successor in interest.

(b) Other income in respect of a decedent. When a partner dies, the entire portion of the distributive share which is attributable to the period ending with the date of his death and which is taxable to his estate or other successor constitutes income in respect of a decedent under section 691. This rule applies even though that part of the distributive share for the period before death which the decedent withdrew is not included in the value of the decedent's partnership interest for estate tax purposes. See paragraph (c)(3) of § 1.706-1.

(c) Example. The provisions of this section may be illustrated by the following example:

Example. A and the decedent B were equal partners in a business having assets (other than money) worth $40,000 with an adjusted basis of $10,000. Certain partnership business was well advanced towards completion before B's death and, after B's death but before the end of the partnership year, payment of $10,000 was made to the partnership for such work. The partnership agreement provided that, upon the death of one of the partners, all partnership property, including unfinished work, would pass to the surviving partner, and that the surviving partner would pay the estate of the decedent the undrawn balance of his share of partnership earnings to the date of death plus $10,000 in each of the three years after death. B's share of earnings to the date of his death was $4,000, of which he had withdrawn $3,000, B's distributive share of partnership income of $4,000 to the date of his death is income in respect of a decedent (although only the $1,000 undrawn at B's death will be reflected in the value of B's partnership interest on B's estate tax return). Assume that the value of B's interest in partnership property at the date of his death was $22,000, composed of the following items: B's one-half share of the assets of $40,000, plus $2,000, B's interest in partnership cash. It should be noted that B's $1,000 undrawn share of earnings to the date of his death is not a separate item but will be paid from partnership assets. Under the partnership agreement, A is to pay B's estate a total of $31,000. The difference of $9,000 between the amount to be paid by A ($31,000) and the value of B's interest in partnership property ($22,000) comes within section 736(a) and, thus, also constitutes income in respect of a decedent. (However, the $17,000 difference between the $5,000 basis for B's share of the partnership property and its $22,000 value at the date of his death does not constitute income in respect of a decedent.) If, before the close of the partnership taxable year, A pays B's estate $11,000, of which they agree to allocate $3,000 as the payment under section 736(a), B's estate will include $7,000 in its gross income (B's $4,000 distributive share plus $3,000 payment under section 736(a)). In computing the deduction under section 691(c), this $7,000 will be considered as the value for estate tax purposes of such income in respect of a decedent, even though only $4,000 ($1,000 of distributive share not withdrawn, plus $3,000, payment under section 736(a)) of this amount can be identified on the estate tax return as part of the partnership interest.

(d) Effective date. The provisions of section 753 apply only in the case of payments made with respect to decedents whose death occurred after December 31, 1954. See section 771(b)(4) and paragraph (b)(4) of § 1.771-1.

T.D. 6175, 5/23/56.

---

§ 1.754-1 Time and manner of making election to adjust basis of partnership property.

(a) In general. A partnership may adjust the basis of partnership property under sections 734(b) and 743(b) if it files an election in accordance with the rules set forth in paragraph (b) of this section. An election may not be filed to make the adjustments provided in either section 734(b) or section 743(b) alone, but such an election must apply to both sections. An election made under the provisions of this section shall apply to all property distributions and transfers of partnership interests taking place in the partnership taxable year for which the election is made and in all subsequent partnership taxable years unless the election is revoked pursuant to paragraph (c) of this section.

(b) Time and method of making election. *(1)* An election under section 754 and this section to adjust the basis of partnership property under sections 734(b) and 743(b), with respect to a distribution of property to a partner or a transfer of an interest in a partnership, shall be made in a written statement filed with the partnership return for the taxable year during which the distribution or transfer occurs. For the election to be valid, the return must be filed not later than the time prescribed by paragraph (e) of § 1.6031-1 (including extensions thereof) for filing the return for such taxable year (or before August 23, 1956, whichever is later). Notwithstanding the preceding two sentences, if a valid election has been made under section 754 and this section for a preceding taxable year and not revoked pursuant to paragraph (c) of this section, a new election is not required to be made. The statement required by this subparagraph shall (i) set forth the name and address of the partnership making the election, (ii) be signed by any one of the partners, and (iii) contain a declaration that the partnership elects under section 754 to apply the provisions of section 734(b) and section 743(b). For rules regarding extensions of time for filing elections see § 1.9100-1.

(2) The principles of this paragraph may be illustrated by the following example:

Example. A, a U.S. citizen, is a member of partnership ABC, which has not previously made an election under section 754 to adjust the basis of partnership property. The partnership and the partners use the calendar year as the taxable year. A sells his interest in the partnership to D on January 1, 1971. The partnership may elect under section 754 and this section to adjust the basis of partnership property under sections 734(b) and 743(b). Unless an extension of time to make the election is obtained under the provisions of § 1.9100-1, the election must be made in a written statement filed with the partnership return for 1971 and must contain the information specified in subparagraph (1) of this paragraph. Such return must be filed by April 17, 1972 (unless an extension of time for filing the return is obtained). The election will apply to all distributions of property to a partner and transfer of an interest in the partnership occurring in 1971 and subsequent years, unless revoked pursuant to paragraph (c) of this section.

(c) Revocation of election. *(1) In general.* A partnership having an election in effect under this section may revoke such election with the approval of the district director for the internal revenue district in which the partnership return is required to be filed. A partnership which wishes to revoke such an election shall file with the district director for the internal revenue district in which the partnership return is required to be filed an application setting forth the grounds on which the revocation is desired. The application shall be filed not later than 30 days after the close of the partnership taxable year with respect to which revocation is intended to take effect and shall be signed by any one of the partners. Examples of situations which may be considered sufficient reason for approving an application for revocation include a change in the nature of the partnership business, a substantial increase in the assets of the partnership, a change in the character of partnership assets, or an increased frequency of retirements or shifts of partnership interests, so that an increased administrative burden would result to the partnership from the election. However, no application for revocation of an election shall be approved when the purpose of the revocation is primarily to avoid stepping down the basis of partnership assets upon a transfer or distribution.

(2) Revocations effective on December 15, 1999. Notwithstanding paragraph (c)(1) of this section, any partnership having an election in effect under this section for its taxable year that includes December 15, 1999 may revoke such election effective for transfers or distributions occuring on or after December 15, 1999, by attaching a statement to the partnership's return for such year. For the revocation to be valid, the statement must be filed not later than the time prescribed by § 1.6031(a)-1(e) (including extensions thereof) for filing the return for such taxable year, and must set forth the name and address of the partnership revoking the election, be signed by any one of the partners who is authorized to sign the partnership's federal income tax return, and contain a declaration that the partnership revokes its election under section 754 to apply the provisions of section 734(b) and 743(b). In addition, the following statement must be prominently displayed in capital letters on the first page of the partnership's return for such year: "RETURN FILED PURSUANT TO 1.754-1(c)(2)".

T.D. 6175, 5/23/56, amend T.D. 7208, 10/2/72, T.D. 8847, 12/14/99.

§ 1.755-1 Rules for allocation of basis.

Caution: The Treasury has not yet amended Reg § 1.755-1 to reflect changes made by P.L. 108-357.

(a) In general. *(1) Scope.* This section provides rules for allocating basis adjustments under sections 743(b) and 734(b) among partnership property. If there is a basis adjustment to which this section applies, the basis adjustment is allocated among the partnership's assets as follows. First, the partnership must determine the value of each of its assets under paragraphs (a)(2) through (5) of this section. Second, the basis adjustment is allocated between the two classes of property described in section 755(b). These classes of property consist of capital assets and section 1231(b) property (capital gain property), and any other property of the partnership (ordinary income property). For purposes of this section, properties and potential gain treated as unrealized receivables under section 751(c) and the regulations thereunder shall be treated as separate assets that are ordinary income property. Third, the portion of the basis adjustment allocated to each class is allocated among the items within the class. Basis adjustments under section 743(b) are allocated among partnership assets under paragraph (b) of this section. Basis adjustments under section 734(b) are allocated among partnership assets under paragraph (c) of this section.

(2) Coordination of sections 755 and 1060. If there is a basis adjustment to which this section applies, and the assets of the partnership constitute a trade or business (as described in § 1.1060-1(b)(2)), then the partnership is required to use the residual method to assign values to the partnership's section 197 intangibles. To do so, the partnership must, first, determine the value of partnership assets other than section 197 intangibles under paragraph (a)(3) of this section. The partnership then must determine partnership gross value under paragraph (a)(4) of this section. Last, the partnership must assign values to the partnership's section 197 intangibles under paragraph (a)(5) of this section. For purposes of this section, the term section 197 intangibles includes all section 197 intangibles (as defined in section 197), as well as any goodwill or going concern value that would not qualify as a section 197 intangible under section 197.

(3) Values of properties other than section 197 intangibles. For purposes of this section, the fair market value of each item of partnership property other than section 197 intangibles shall be determined on the basis of all the facts and circumstances, taking into account section 7701(g).

(4) Partnership gross value. (i) Basis adjustments under section 743(b). (A) In general. Except as provided in paragraph (a)(4)(ii) of this section, in the case of a basis adjustment under section 743(b), partnership gross value generally is equal to the amount that, if assigned to all partnership property, would result in a liquidating distribution to the partner equal to the transferee's basis in the transferred partnership interest immediately following the relevant transfer (reduced by the amount, if any, of such basis that is attributable to partnership liabilities).

(B) Special situations. In certain circumstances, such as where income or loss with respect to particular section 197 intangibles are allocated differently among partners, partnership gross value may vary depending on the values of particular section 197 intangibles held by the partnership. In these special situations, the partnership must assign value, first, among section 197 intangibles (other than goodwill and going concern value) in a reasonable manner that is consistent with the ordering rule in paragraph (a)(5) of this section and would cause the appropriate liquidating distribution under paragraph (a)(4)(i)(A) of this section. If the actual fair market values, determined on the basis of all the facts and circumstances, of all section 197 intangibles (other than goodwill and going concern value) is not sufficient to cause the appropriate liquidating distribution, then the fair market value of goodwill and going concern value shall be presumed to equal an amount that if assigned to goodwill and going concern value would cause the appropriate liquidating distribution.

(C) Income in respect of a decedent. Solely for the purpose of determining partnership gross value under this paragraph (a)(4)(i), where a partnership interest is transferred as a result of the death of a partner, the transferee's basis in its partnership interest is determined without regard to section 1014(c), and is deemed to be adjusted for that portion of the interest, if any, that is attributable to items representing income in respect of a decedent under section 691.

(ii) Basis adjustments under section 743(b) resulting from substituted basis transactions. This paragraph (a)(4)(ii) applies to basis adjustments under section 743(b) that result from exchanges in which the transferee's basis in the partnership interest is determined in whole or in part by reference to the transferor's basis in the interest or to the basis of other property held at any time by the transferee (substituted basis transactions). In the case of a substituted basis transaction, partnership gross value equals the value of the entire partnership as a going concern, increased by the amount of partnership liabilities at the time of the exchange giving rise to the basis adjustment.

(iii) Basis adjustments under section 734(b). In the case of a basis adjustment under section 734(b), partnership gross value equals the value of the entire partnership as a going concern immediately following the distribution causing the adjustment, increased by the amount of partnership liabilities immediately following the distribution.

(5) Determining the values of section 197 intangibles. (i) Two classes. If the aggregate value of partnership property other than section 197 intangibles (as determined in paragraph (a)(3) of this section) is equal to or greater than partnership gross value (as determined in paragraph (a)(4) of this section), then all section 197 intangibles are deemed to have a value of zero for purposes of this section. In all other cases, the aggregate value of the partnership's section 197 intangibles (the residual section 197 intangibles value) is deemed to equal the excess of partnership gross value over the aggregate value of partnership property other than section 197 intangibles. The residual section 197 intangibles value must be allocated between two asset classes in the following order—

(A) Among section 197 intangibles other than goodwill and going concern value; and

(B) To goodwill and going concern value.

(ii) Values assigned to section 197 intangibles other than goodwill and going concern value. The fair market value assigned to a section 197 intangible (other than goodwill and going concern value) shall not exceed the actual fair market value (determined on the basis of all the facts and circumstances) of that asset on the date of the relevant transfer. If the residual section 197 intangibles value is less than the sum of the actual fair market values (determined on the basis of all the facts and circumstances) of all section 197 intangibles (other than goodwill and going concern value) held by the partnership, then the residual section 197 intangibles value must be allocated among the individual section 197 intangibles (other than goodwill and going concern value) as follows. The residual section 197 intangibles value is assigned first to any section 197 intangibles (other than goodwill and going concern value) having potential gain that would be treated as unrealized receivables under the flush language of section 751(c) (flush language receivables) to the extent of the basis of those section 197 intangibles and the amount of income arising from the flush language receivables that the partnership would recognize if the section 197 intangibles were sold for their actual fair market values (determined based on all the facts and circumstances) (collectively, the flush language receivables value). If the value assigned to section 197 intangibles (other than goodwill and going concern value) is less than the flush language receivables value, then the assigned value is allocated among the properties giving rise to the flush language receivables in proportion to the flush language receivables value in those properties. Any remaining residual section 197 intangibles value is allocated among the remaining portions of the section 197 intangibles (other than goodwill and going concern value) in proportion to the actual fair market values of such portions (determined based on all the facts and circumstances).

(iii) Value assigned to goodwill and going concern value. The fair market value of goodwill and going concern value is the amount, if any, by which the residual section 197 intangibles value exceeds the aggregate value of the partnership's section 197 intangibles (other than goodwill and going concern value).

(6) Examples. The provisions of paragraphs (a)(2) through (5) are illustrated by the following examples, which assume that the partnerships have an election in effect under section 754 at the time of the transfer and that the assets of each partnership constitute a trade or business (as described in § 1.1060-1(b)(2)). Except as provided, no partnership asset (other than inventory) is property described in section 751(a), and partnership liabilities are secured by all partnership assets. The examples are as follows:

Example (1). (i) A is the sole general partner in PRS, a limited partnership having three equal partners. PRS has goodwill and going concern value, two section 197 intangibles other than goodwill and going concern value (Intangible 1 and Intangible 2), and two other assets with fair market values (determined using all the facts and circumstances) as follows: inventory worth $1,000,000 and a building (a capital asset) worth $2,000,000. The fair market value of each of Intangible 1 and Intangible 2 is $50,000. PRS has one liability of $1,000,000, for which A bears the entire risk of loss under section 752 and the regulations thereunder. D purchases A's partnership interest for $650,000, resulting in a basis adjustment under section 743(b). After the purchase, D bears the entire risk of loss for PRS's liability under section 752 and the regulations thereunder. Therefore, D's basis in its interest in PRS is $1,650,000.

(ii) D's basis in the transferred partnership interest (reduced by the amount of such basis that is attributable to partnership liabilities) is $650,000 ($1,650,000--$1,000,000). Under paragraph (a)(4)(i) of this section, partnership gross value is $2,950,000 (the amount that, if assigned to all partnership property, would result in a liquidating distribution to D equal to $650,000).

(iii) Under paragraph (a)(3) of this section, the inventory has a fair market value of $1,000,000, and the building has a fair market value of $2,000,000. Thus, the aggregate value of partnership property other than section 197 intangibles, $3,000,000, is equal to or greater than partnership gross value, $2,950,000. Accordingly, under paragraphs (a)(3) and (5) of this section, the value assigned to each of the partnership's assets is as follows: inventory, $1,000,000; building, $2,000,000; Intangibles 1 and 2, $0; and goodwill and going concern value, $0. D's section 743(b) adjustment must be allocated under paragraph (b) of this section using these assigned fair market values.

Example (2). (i) Assume the same facts as in Example 1, except that the fair market values of Intangible 1 and Intangible 2 are each $300,000, and that D purchases A's interest in PRS for $1,000,000. After the purchase, D's basis in its interest in PRS is $2,000,000.

(ii) D's basis in the transferred partnership interest (reduced by the amount of such basis that is attributable to partnership liabilities) is $1,000,000 ($2,000,000--$1,000,000). Under paragraph (a)(4)(i) of this section, partnership gross value is $4,000,000 (the amount that, if assigned to all partnership property, would result in a liquidating distribution to D equal to $1,000,000).

(iii) Under paragraph (a)(5) of this section, the residual section 197 intangibles value is $1,000,000 (the excess of partnership gross value, $4,000,000, over the aggregate value of assets other than section 197 intangibles, $3,000,000 (the sum of the value of the inventory, $1,000,000, and the value of the building, $2,000,000)). The partnership must determine the values of section 197 assets by allocating the residual section 197 intangibles value among the partnership's assets. The residual section 197 intangibles value is assigned first to section 197 intangibles other than goodwill and going concern value, and then to goodwill and going concern value. Thus, $300,000 is assigned to each of Intangible 1 and Intangible 2, and $400,000 is assigned to goodwill and going concern value (the amount by which the residual section 197 intangibles value, $1,000,000, exceeds the fair market value of section 197 intangibles other than goodwill and going concern value, $600,000). D's section 743(b) adjustment must be allocated under paragraph (b) of this section using these assigned fair market values.

Example (3). (i) Assume the same facts as in Example 1, except that the fair market values of Intangible 1 and Intangible 2 are each $300,000, and that D purchases A's interest in PRS for $750,000. After the purchase, D's basis in its interest in PRS is $1,750,000. Also assume that Intangible 1 was originally purchased for $300,000, and that its adjusted basis has been decreased to $50,000 as a result of amortization. Assume that, if PRS were to sell Intangible 1 for $300,000, it would recognize $250,000 of gain that would be treated as an unrealized receivable under the flush language in section 751(c).

(ii) D's basis in the transferred partnership interest (reduced by the amount of such basis that is attributable to partnership liabilities) is $750,000 ($1,750,000--$1,000,000). Under paragraph (a)(4)(i) of this section, partnership gross value is $3,250,000 (the amount that, if assigned to all partnership property, would result in a liquidating distribution to D equal to $750,000).

(iii) Under paragraph (a)(5) of this section, the residual section 197 intangibles value is $250,000 (the amount by which partnership gross value, $3,250,000, exceeds the aggregate value of partnership property other than section 197 intangibles, $3,000,000). Intangible 1 has potential gain that would be treated as unrealized receivables under the flush language of section 751(c). The flush language receivables value in Intangible 1 is $300,000 (the sum of PRS's basis in Intangible 1, $50,000, and the amount of ordinary income, $250,000, that the partnership would recognize if Intangible 1 were sold for its actual fair market value). Because the residual section 197 intangibles value, $250,000, is less than the flush language receivables value of Intangible 1, Intangible 1 is assigned a value of $250,000, and Intangible 2 and goodwill and going concern value are assigned a value of zero. D's section 743(b) adjustment must be allocated under paragraph (b) of this section using these assigned fair market values.

Example (4). Assume the same facts as in Example 1, except that the fair market values of Intangible 1 and Intangible 2 are each $300,000, and that A does not sell its interest in PRS. Instead, A contributes its interest in PRS to E, a newly formed corporation wholly-owned by A, in a transaction described in section 351. Assume that the contribution results in a basis adjustment under section 743(b) (other than zero). PRS determines that its value as a going concern immediately following the contribution is $3,000,000. Under paragraph (a)(4)(ii) of this section, partnership gross value is $4,000,000 (the value of PRS as a going concern, $3,000,000, increased by the partnership's liability, $1,000,000, immediately after the contribution). Under paragraph (a)(5) of this section, the residual section 197 intangibles value is $1,000,000 (the amount by which partnership gross value, $4,000,000, exceeds the aggregate value of partnership property other than section 197 intangibles, $3,000,000). Of the residual section 197 intangibles value, $300,000 is assigned to each of Intangible 1 and Intangible 2, and $400,000 is assigned to goodwill and going concern value (the amount by which the residual section 197 intangibles value, $1,000,000, exceeds the fair market value of section 197 intangibles other than goodwill and going concern value, $600,000). E's section 743(b) adjustment must be allocated under paragraph (b)(5) of this section using these assigned fair market values.

Example (5). G is the sole general partner in PRS, a limited partnership having three equal partners (G, H, and I). PRS has goodwill and going concern value, two section 197 intangibles other than goodwill and going concern value (Intangible 1 and Intangible 2), and two capital assets with fair market values (determined using all the facts and circumstances) as follows: Vacant land worth $1,000,000, and a building worth $2,000,000. The fair market value of each of Intangible 1 and Intangible 2 is $300,000. PRS has one liability of $1,000,000, for which G bears the entire risk of loss under section 752 and the regulations thereunder. PRS distributes the land to H in liquidation of H's interest in PRS. Immediately prior to the distribution, PRS's basis in the land is $800,000, and H's basis in its interest in PRS is $750,000. The distribution causes the partnership to increase the basis of its remaining property by $50,000 under section 734(b)(1)(B). PRS determines that its value as a going concern immediately following the distribution is $2,000,000. Under paragraph (a)(4)(iii) of this section, partnership gross value is $3,000,000 (the value of PRS as a going concern, $2,000,000, increased by the partnership's liability, $1,000,000, immediately after the distribution). Under paragraph (a)(5) of this section, the residual section 197 intangibles value of PRS's section 197 intangibles is $1,000,000 (the amount by which partnership gross value, $3,000,000, exceeds the aggregate value of partnership property other than section 197 intangibles, $2,000,000). Of the residual section 197 intangibles value, $300,000 is assigned to each of Intangible 1 and Intangible 2, and $400,000 is assigned to goodwill and going concern value (the amount by which the residual section 197 intangibles value, $1,000,000, exceeds the fair market value of section 197 intangibles other than goodwill and going concern value, $600,000). PRS's section 734(b) adjustment must be allocated under paragraph (c) of this section using these assigned fair market values.

(b) Adjustments under section 743(b). *(1) Generally.* (i) Application. For basis adjustments under section 743(b) resulting from substituted basis transactions, paragraph (b)(5) of this section shall apply. For basis adjustments under section 743(b) resulting from all other transfers, paragraphs (b)(2) through (4) of this section shall apply. Except as provided in paragraph (b)(5) of this section, the portion of the basis adjustment allocated to one class of property may be an increase while the portion allocated to the other class is a decrease. This would be the case even though the total amount of the basis adjustment is zero. Except as provided in paragraph (b)(5) of this section, the portion of the basis adjustment allocated to one item of property within a class may be an increase while the portion allocated to another is a decrease. This would be the case even though the basis adjustment allocated to the class is zero.

(ii) Hypothetical transaction. For purposes of paragraphs (b)(2) through (b)(4) of this section, the allocation of the basis adjustment under section 743(b) between the classes of property and among the items of property within each class are made based on the allocations of income, gain, or loss (including remedial allocations under § 1.704-3(d)) that the transferee partner would receive (to the extent attributable to the acquired partnership interest) if, immediately after the transfer of the partnership interest, all of the partnership's property were disposed of in a fully taxable transaction for cash in an amount equal to the fair market value of such property (the hypothetical transaction). See § 1.460-

4(k)(3)(v)(B) for a rule relating to the computation of income or loss that would be allocated to the transferee from a contract accounted for under a long-term contract method of accounting as a result of the hypothetical transaction.

(2) Allocations between classes of property. (i) In general. The amount of the basis adjustment allocated to the class of ordinary income property is equal to the total amount of income, gain, or loss (including any remedial allocations under § 1.704-3(d)) that would be allocated to the transferee (to the extent attributable to the acquired partnership interest) from the sale of all ordinary income property in the hypothetical transaction. The amount of the basis adjustment to capital gain property is equal to—

(A) The total amount of the basis adjustment under section 743(b); less

(B) The amount of the basis adjustment allocated to ordinary income property under the preceding sentence; provided, however, that in no event may the amount of any decrease in basis allocated to capital gain property exceed the partnership's basis (or in the case of property subject to the remedial allocation method, the transferee's share of any remedial loss under § 1.704-3(d) from the hypothetical transaction) in capital gain property. In the event that a decrease in basis allocated to capital gain property would otherwise exceed the partnership's basis in capital gain property, the excess must be applied to reduce the basis of ordinary income property.

(ii) Examples. The provisions of this paragraph (b)(2) are illustrated by the following examples:

Example (1). (i) A and B form equal partnership PRS. A contributes $50,000 and Asset 1, a nondepreciable capital asset with a fair market value of $50,000 and an adjusted tax basis of $25,000. B contributes $100,000. PRS uses the cash to purchase Assets 2, 3, and 4. After a year, A sells its interest in PRS to T for $120,000. At the time of the transfer, A's share of the partnership's basis in partnership assets is $75,000. Therefore, T receives a $45,000 basis adjustment.

(ii) Immediately after the transfer of the partnership interest to T, the adjusted basis and fair market value of PRS's assets are as follows:

Assets

	Adjusted basis	Fair Market value
Capital Gain Property:		
Asset 1	$ 25,000	$ 75,000
Asset 2	100,000	117,500
Ordinary Income Property:		
Asset 3	40,000	45,000
Asset 4	10,000	2,500
Total	175,000	240,000

(iii) If PRS sold all of its assets in a fully taxable transaction at fair market value immediately after the transfer of the partnership interest to T, the total amount of capital gain that would be allocated to T is equal to $46,250 ($25,000 section 704(c) built-in gain from Asset 1, plus fifty percent of the $42,500 appreciation in capital gain property). T would also be allocated a $1,250 ordinary loss from the sale of the ordinary income property.

(iv) The amount of the basis adjustment that is allocated to ordinary income property is equal to ($1,250) (the amount of the loss allocated to T from the hypothetical sale of the ordinary income property).

(v) The amount of the basis adjustment that is allocated to capital gain property is equal to $46,250 (the amount of the basis adjustment, $45,000, less ($1,250), the amount of loss allocated to T from the hypothetical sale of the ordinary income property).

Example (2). (i) A and B form equal partnership PRS. A and B each contribute $1,000 cash which the partnership uses to purchase Assets 1, 2, 3, and 4. After a year, A sells its partnership interest to T for $1,000. T's basis adjustment under section 743(b) is zero.

(ii) Immediately after the transfer of the partnership interest to T, the adjusted basis and fair market value of PRS's assets are as follows:

Assets

	Adjusted basis	Fair Market value
Capital Gain Property:		
Asset 1	$ 500	$ 750
Asset 2	500	500
Ordinary Income Property:		
Asset 3	500	250
Asset 4	500	500
Total	2,000	2,000

(iii) If, immediately after the transfer of the partnership interest to T, PRS sold all of its assets in a fully taxable transaction at fair market value, T would be allocated a loss of $125 from the sale of the ordinary income property. Thus, the amount of the basis adjustment to ordinary income property is ($125). The amount of the basis adjustment to capital gain property is $125 (zero, the amount of the basis adjustment under section 743(b), less ($125), the amount of the basis adjustment allocated to ordinary income property).

(3) Allocation within the class. (i) Ordinary income property. The amount of the basis adjustment to each item of property within the class of ordinary income property is equal to—

(A) The amount of income, gain, or loss (including any remedial allocations under § 1.704-3(d)) that would be allocated to the transferee (to the extent attributable to the acquired partnership interest) from the hypothetical sale of the item; reduced by

(B) The product of—

(1) Any decrease to the amount of the basis adjustment to ordinary income property required pursuant to the last sentence of paragraph (b)(2)(i) of this section; multiplied by

(2) A fraction, the numerator of which is the fair market value of the item of property to the partnership and the denominator of which is the total fair market value of all of the partnership's items of ordinary income property.

(ii) Capital gain property. The amount of the basis adjustment to each item of property within the class of capital gain property is equal to—

(A) The amount of income, gain, or loss (including any remedial allocations under § 1.704-3(d)) that would be allocated to the transferee (to the extent attributable to the acquired partnership interest) from the hypothetical sale of the item; minus

(B) The product of—

(1) The total amount of gain or loss (including any remedial allocations under § 1.704-3(d)) that would be allocated to the transferee (to the extent attributable to the acquired

partnership interest) from the hypothetical sale of all items of capital gain property, minus the amount of the positive basis adjustment to all items of capital gain property or plus the amount of the negative basis adjustment to capital gain property; multiplied by

(2) A fraction, the numerator of which is the fair market value of the item of property to the partnership, and the denominator of which is the fair market value of all of the partnership's items of capital gain property.

(iii) Special rules. (A) Assets in which partner has no interest. An asset with respect to which the transferee partner has no interest in income, gain, losses, or deductions shall not be taken into account in applying paragraph (b)(3)(ii)(B) of this section.

(B) Limitation in decrease of basis. In no event may the amount of any decrease in basis allocated to an item of capital gain property under paragraph (b)(3)(ii)(B) of this section exceed the partnership's adjusted basis in that item (or in the case of property subject to the remedial allocation method, the transferee's share of any remedial loss under § 1.704-3(d) from the hypothetical transaction). In the event that a decrease in basis allocated under paragraph (b)(3)(ii)(B) of this section to an item of capital gain property would otherwise exceed the partnership's adjusted basis in that item, the excess must be applied to reduce the remaining basis, if any, of other capital gain assets pro rata in proportion to the bases of such assets (as adjusted under this paragraph (b)(3)).

(iv) Examples. The provisions of this paragraph (b)(3) are illustrated by the following examples:

Example (1). (i) Assume the same facts as Example 1 in paragraph (b)(2)(ii) of this section. Of the $45,000 basis adjustment, $46,250 was allocated to capital gain property. The amount allocated to ordinary income property was ($1,250).

(ii) Asset 1 is a capital gain asset, and T would be allocated $37,500 from the sale of Asset 1 in the hypothetical transaction. Therefore, the amount of the adjustment to Asset 1 is $37,500.

(iii) Asset 2 is a capital gain asset, and T would be allocated $8,750 from the sale of Asset 2 in the hypothetical transaction. Therefore, the amount of the adjustment to Asset 2 is $8,750.

(iv) Asset 3 is ordinary income property, and T would be allocated $2,500 from the sale of Asset 3 in the hypothetical transaction. Therefore, the amount of the adjustment to Asset 3 is $2,500.

(v) Asset 4 is ordinary income property, and T would be allocated ($3,750) from the sale of Asset 4 in the hypothetical transaction. Therefore, the amount of the adjustment to Asset 4 is ($3,750).

Example (2). (i) Assume the same facts as Example 1 in paragraph (b)(2)(ii) of this section, except that A sold its interest in PRS to T for $110,000 rather than $120,000. T, therefore, receives a basis adjustment under section 743(b) of $35,000. Of the $35,000 basis adjustment, ($1,250) is allocated to ordinary income property, and $36,250 is allocated to capital gain property.

(ii) Asset 3 is ordinary income property, and T would be allocated $2,500 from the sale of Asset 3 in the hypothetical transaction. Therefore, the amount of the adjustment to Asset 3 is $2,500.

(iii) Asset 4 is ordinary income property, and T would be allocated ($3,750) from the sale of Asset 4 in the hypothetical transaction. Therefore, the amount of the adjustment to Asset 4 is ($3,750).

(iv) Asset 1 is a capital gain asset, and T would be allocated $37,500 from the sale of Asset 1 in the hypothetical transaction. Asset 2 is a capital gain asset, and T would be allocated $8,750 from the sale of Asset 2 in the hypothetical transaction. The total amount of gain that would be allocated to T from the sale of the capital gain assets in the hypothetical transaction is $46,250, which exceeds the amount of the basis adjustment allocated to capital gain property by $10,000. The amount of the adjustment to Asset 1 is $33,604 ($37,500 minus $3,896 ($10,000 x $75,000/192,500)). The amount of the basis adjustment to Asset 2 is $2,646 ($8,750 minus $6,104 ($10,000 x $117,500/192,500)).

(4) Income in respect of a decedent. (i) In general. Where a partnership interest is transferred as a result of the death of a partner, under section 1014(c) the transferee's basis in its partnership interest is not adjusted for that portion of the interest, if any, which is attributable to items representing income in respect of a decedent under section 691. See § 1.742-1. Accordingly, if a partnership interest is transferred as a result of the death of a partner, and the partnership holds assets representing income in respect of a decedent, no part of the basis adjustment under section 743(b) is allocated to these assets. See § 1.743-1(b).

(ii) The provisions of this paragraph (b)(4) are illustrated by the following example:

Example. (i) A and B are equal partners in personal service partnership PRS. In 2004, as a result of B's death, B's partnership interest is transferred to T when PRS's balance sheet (reflecting a cash receipts and disbursements method of accounting) is as follows (based on all the facts and circumstances):

Assets

	Adjusted Basis	Fair Market Value
Section 197 Intangible	$2,000	$ 5,000
Unrealized Receivables	0	15,000
Total	$2,000	$20,000

Liabilities and Capital

	Adjusted Per Books	Fair Market Value
Capital:		
A	1,000	10,000
B	1,000	10,000
Total	$2,000	$20,000

(ii) None of the assets owned by PRS is section 704(c) property, and the section 197 intangible is not amortizable. The fair market value of T's partnership interest on the applicable date of valuation set forth in section 1014 is $10,000. Of this amount, $2,500 is attributable to T's 50% share of the partnership's section 197 intangible, and $7,500 is attributable to T's 50% share of the partnership's unrealized receivables. The partnership's unrealized receivables represent income in respect of a decedent. Accordingly, under section 1014(c), T's basis in its partnership interest is not adjusted for that portion of the interest which is attributable to the unrealized receivables. Therefore, T's basis in its partnership interest is $2,500.

(iii) Under paragraph (a)(4)(i)(C) of this section, solely for purposes of determining partnership gross value, T's basis in its partnership interest is deemed to be $10,000. Under paragraph (a)(4)(i) of this section, partnership gross value is $20,000 (the amount that, if assigned to all partnership property, would result in a liquidating distribution to T equal to $10,000).

(iv) Under paragraph (a)(5) of this section, the residual section 197 intangibles value is $5,000 (the excess of partnership gross value, $20,000, over the aggregate value of assets other than section 197 intangibles, $15,000). The residual section 197 intangibles value is assigned first to section 197 intangibles other than goodwill and going concern value, and then to goodwill and going concern value. Thus, $5,000 is assigned to the section 197 intangible, and $0 is assigned to goodwill and going concern value. T's section 743(b) adjustment must be allocated using these assigned fair market values.

(v) At the time of the transfer, B's share of the partnership's basis in partnership assets is $1,000. Accordingly, T receives a $1,500 basis adjustment under section 743(b). Under this paragraph (b)(4), the entire basis adjustment is allocated to the partnership's section 197 intangible.

(5) Substituted basis transactions. (i) In general. This paragraph (b)(5) applies to basis adjustments under section 743(b) that result from exchanges in which the transferee's basis in the partnership interest is determined in whole or in part by reference to the transferor's basis in that interest. For exchanges on or after June 9, 2003, this paragraph (b)(5) also applies to basis adjustments under section 743(b) that result from exchanges in which the transferee's basis in the partnership interest is determined by reference to other property held at any time by the transferee. For example, this paragraph (b)(5) applies if a partnership interest is contributed to a corporation in a transaction to which section 351 applies, if a partnership interest is contributed to a partnership in a transaction to which section 721(a) applies, or if a partnership interest is distributed by a partnership in a transaction to which section 731(a) applies.

(ii) Allocations between classes of property. If the total amount of the basis adjustment under section 743(b) is zero, then no adjustment to the basis of partnership property will be made under this paragraph (b)(5). If there is an increase in basis to be allocated to partnership assets, such increase must be allocated to capital gain property or ordinary income property, respectively, only if the total amount of gain or loss (including any remedial allocations under § 1.704-3(d)) that would be allocated to the transferee (to the extent attributable to the acquired partnership interest) from the hypothetical sale of all such property would result in a net gain or net income, as the case may be, to the transferee. Where, under the preceding sentence, an increase in basis may be allocated to both capital gain assets and ordinary income assets, the increase shall be allocated to each class in proportion to the net gain or net income, respectively, which would be allocated to the transferee from the sale of all assets in each class. If there is a decrease in basis to be allocated to partnership assets, such decrease must be allocated to capital gain property or ordinary income property, respectively, only if the total amount of gain or loss (including any remedial allocations under § 1.704-3(d)) that would be allocated to the transferee (to the extent attributable to the acquired partnership interest) from the hypothetical sale of all such property would result in a net loss to the transferee. Where, under the preceding sentence, a decrease in basis may be allocated to both capital gain assets and ordinary income assets, the decrease shall be allocated to each class in proportion to the net loss which would be allocated to the transferee from the sale of all assets in each class.

(iii) Allocations within the classes.

(A) Increases. If there is an increase in basis to be allocated within a class, the increase must be allocated first to properties with unrealized appreciation in proportion to the transferee's share of the respective amounts of unrealized appreciation before such increase (but only to the extent of the transferee's share of each property's unrealized appreciation). Any remaining increase must be allocated among the properties within the class in proportion to the transferee's share of the amount that would be realized by the partnership upon the hypothetical sale of each asset in the class.

(B) Decreases. If there is a decrease in basis to be allocated within a class, the decrease must be allocated first to properties with unrealized depreciation in proportion to the transferee's shares of the respective amounts of unrealized depreciation before such decrease (but only to the extent of the transferee's share of each property's unrealized depreciation). Any remaining decrease must be allocated among the properties within the class in proportion to the transferee's shares of their adjusted bases (as adjusted under the preceding sentence).

(C) Limitation in decrease of basis. Where, as the result of a transaction to which this paragraph (b)(5) applies, a decrease in basis must be allocated to capital gain assets, ordinary income assets, or both, and the amount of the decrease otherwise allocable to a particular class exceeds the transferee's share of the adjusted basis to the partnership of all depreciated assets in that class, the transferee's negative basis adjustment is limited to the transferee's share of the partnership's adjusted basis in all depreciated assets in that class.

(D) Carryover adjustment. Where a transferee's negative basis adjustment under section 743(b) cannot be allocated to any asset, because the adjustment exceeds the transferee's share of the adjusted basis to the partnership of all depreciated assets in a particular class, the adjustment is made when the partnership subsequently acquires property of a like character to which an adjustment can be made.

(iv) Examples. The provisions of this paragraph (b)(5) are illustrated by the following examples:

Example (1). A is a member of partnership LTP, which has made an election under section 754. The three partners in LTP have equal interests in capital and profits. Solely in exchange for a partnership interest in UTP, A contributes its interest in LTP to UTP in a transaction described in section 721. At the time of the transfer, A's basis in its partnership interest ($5,000) equals its share of inside basis (also $5,000). Under section 723, UTP's basis in its interest in LTP is $5,000. LTP's only two assets on the date of contribution are inventory with a basis of $5,000 and a fair market value of $7,500, and a nondepreciable capital asset with a basis of $10,000 and a fair market value of $7,500. The amount of the basis adjustment under section 743(b) to partnership property is $0 ($5,000, UTP's basis in its interest in LTP, minus $5,000, UTP's share of LTP's basis in partnership assets). Because UTP acquired its interest in LTP in a substituted basis transaction, and the total amount of the basis adjustment under section 743(b) is zero, UTP receives no special basis adjustments under section 743(b) with respect to the partnership property of LTP.

Example (2). (i) A purchases a partnership interest in LTP at a time when an election under section 754 is not in effect. The three partners in LTP have equal interests in capital and profits. During a later year for which LTP has an election under section 754 in effect, and in a transaction that is unrelated to A's purchase of the LTP interest, A contributes its interest in LTP to UTP in a transaction described in section 721 (solely in exchange for a partnership interest in UTP). At the time of the transfer, A's adjusted basis in its interest in LTP is $20,433. Under section 721, A recognizes no gain or loss as a result of the contribution of its partnership interest to UTP. Under section 723, UTP's basis in its partnership interest in LTP is $20,433. The balance sheet of LTP on the date of the contribution shows the following:

Assets

	Adjusted basis	Fair Market value
Cash	$ 5,000	$ 5,000
Accounts Receivable	10,000	10,000
Inventory	20,000	21,000
Nondepreciable capital asset	20,000	40,000
Total	55,000	76,000

Liabilities and Capital

	Adjusted per books	Fair Market value
Liabilities	$10,000	$10,000
Capital:		
A	15,000	22,000
B	15,000	22,000
C	15,000	22,000
Total	55,000	76,000

(ii) The amount of the basis adjustment under section 743(b) is the difference between the basis of UTP's interest in LTP and UTP's share of the adjusted basis to LTP of partnership property. UTP's interest in the previously taxed capital of LTP is $15,000 ($22,000, the amount of cash UTP would receive if LTP liquidated immediately after the hypothetical transaction, decreased by $7,000, the amount of tax gain allocated to UTP from the hypothetical transaction). UTP's share of the adjusted basis to LTP of partnership property is $18,333 ($15,000 share of previously taxed capital, plus $3,333 share of LTP's liabilities). The amount of the basis adjustment under section 743(b) to partnership property therefore, is $2,100 ($20,433 minus $18,333).

(iii) The total amount of gain that would be allocated to UTP from the hypothetical sale of capital gain property is $6,666.67 (one-third of the excess of the fair market value of LTP's nondepreciable capital asset, $40,000, over its basis, $20,000). The total amount of gain that would be allocated to UTP from the hypothetical sale of ordinary income property is $333.33 (one-third of the excess of the fair market value of LTP's inventory, $21,000, over its basis, $20,000). Under this paragraph (b)(5), LTP must allocate $2,000 ($6,666.67 divided by $7,000 times $2,100) of UTP's basis adjustment to the nondepreciable capital asset. LTP must allocate $100 ($333.33 divided by $7,000 times $2,100) of UTP's basis adjustment to the inventory.

(c) Adjustments under section 734(b). *(1) Allocations between classes of property.* (i) General rule. Where there is a distribution of partnership property resulting in an adjustment to the basis of undistributed partnership property under section 734(b)(1)(B) or (b)(2)(B), the adjustment must be allocated to remaining partnership property of a character similar to that of the distributed property with respect to which the adjustment arose. Thus, when the partnership's adjusted basis of distributed capital gain property immediately prior to distribution exceeds the basis of the property to the distributee partner (as determined under section 732), the basis of the undistributed capital gain property remaining in the partnership is increased by an amount equal to the excess. Conversely, when the basis to the distributee partner (as determined under section 732) of distributed capital gain property exceeds the partnership's adjusted basis of such property immediately prior to the distribution, the basis of the undistributed capital gain property remaining in the partnership is decreased by an amount equal to such excess. Similarly, where there is a distribution of ordinary income property, and the basis of the property to the distributee partner (as determined under section 732) is not the same as the partnership's adjusted basis of the property immediately prior to distribution, the adjustment is made only to undistributed property of the same class remaining in the partnership.

(ii) Special rule. Where there is a distribution resulting in an adjustment under section 734(b)(1)(A) or (b)(2)(A) to the basis of undistributed partnership property, the adjustment is allocated only to capital gain property.

(2) Allocations within the classes. (i) Increases. If there is an increase in basis to be allocated within a class, the increase must be allocated first to properties with unrealized appreciation in proportion to their respective amounts of unrealized appreciation before such increase (but only to the extent of each property's unrealized appreciation). Any remaining increase must be allocated among the properties within the class in proportion to their fair market values.

(ii) Decreases. If there is a decrease in basis to be allocated within a class, the decrease must be allocated first to properties with unrealized depreciation in proportion to their respective amounts of unrealized depreciation before such decrease (but only to the extent of each property's unrealized depreciation). Any remaining decrease must be allocated among the properties within the class in proportion to their adjusted bases (as adjusted under the preceding sentence).

(3) Limitation in decrease of basis. Where a decrease in the basis of partnership assets is required under section 734(b)(2) and the amount of the decrease exceeds the adjusted basis to the partnership of property of the required character, the basis of such property is reduced to zero (but not below zero).

(4) Carryover adjustment. Where, in the case of a distribution, an increase or a decrease in the basis of undistributed property cannot be made because the partnership owns no property of the character required to be adjusted, or because the basis of all the property of a like character has been reduced to zero, the adjustment is made when the partnership subsequently acquires property of a like character to which an adjustment can be made.

(5) Cross reference. See § 1.460-4(k)(3)(v)(B) for a rule relating to the computation of unrealized appreciation or depreciation in a contract accounted for under a long-term contract method of accounting.

(6) Example. The following example illustrates this paragraph (c):

Example. (i) A, B, and C form equal partnership PRS. A contributes $50,000 and Asset 1, nondepreciable capital gain property with a fair market value of $50,000 and an adjusted tax basis of $25,000. B and C each contributes $100,000.

PRS uses the cash to purchase Assets 2, 3, 4, 5, and 6. Assets 2 and 3 are nondepreciable capital assets, and Assets 4, 5, and 6 are inventory that has not appreciated substantially in value within the meaning of section 751(b)(3). Assets 4, 5, and 6 are the only assets held by the partnership that are subject to section 751. The partnership has an election in effect under section 754. After seven years, the adjusted basis and fair market value of PRS's assets are as follows:

Assets

	Adjusted basis	Fair Market value
Capital Gain Property:		
Asset 1	$ 25,000	$ 75,000
Asset 2	100,000	117,500
Asset 3	50,000	60,000
Ordinary Income Property:		
Asset 4	40,000	45,000
Asset 5	50,000	60,000
Asset 6	10,000	2,500
Total	275,000	360,000

(ii) Allocation between classes. Assume that PRS distributes Assets 3 and 5 to A in complete liquidation of A's interest in the partnership. A's basis in the partnership interest was $75,000. The partnership's basis in Assets 3 and 5 was $50,000 each. A's $75,000 basis in its partnership interest is allocated between Assets 3 and 5 under sections 732(b) and (c). A will, therefore, have a basis of $25,000 in Asset 3 (capital gain property), and a basis of $50,000 in Asset 5 (section 751 property). The distribution results in a $25,000 increase in the basis of capital gain property. There is no change in the basis of ordinary income property.

(iii) Allocation within class. The amount of the basis increase to capital gain property is $25,000 and must be allocated among the remaining capital gain assets in proportion to the difference between the fair market value and basis of each. The fair market value of Asset 1 exceeds its basis by $50,000. The fair market value of Asset 2 exceeds its basis by $17,500. Therefore, the basis of Asset 1 will be increased by $18,519 ($25,000, multiplied by $50,000, divided by $67,500), and the basis of Asset 2 will be increased by $6,481 ($25,000 multiplied by $17,500, divided by $67,500).

(d) Required statements. See § 1.743-1(k)(2) for provisions requiring the transferee of a partnership interest to provide information to the partnership relating to the transfer of an interest in the partnership. See § 1.743-1(k)(1) for a provision requiring the partnership to attach a statement to the partnership return showing the computation of a basis adjustment under section 743(b) and the partnership properties to which the adjustment is allocated under section 755. See § 1.732-1(d)(3) for a provision requiring a transferee partner to attach a statement to its return showing the computation of a basis adjustment under section 732(d) and the partnership properties to which the adjustment is allocated under section 755. See § 1.732-1(d)(5) for a provision requiring the partnership to provide information to a transferee partner reporting a basis adjustment under section 732(d).

(e) Effective date. *(1) Generally.* Except as provided in paragraphs (b)(5) and (e)(2) of this section, this section applies to transfers of partnership interests and distributions of property from a partnership that occur on or after December 15, 1999.

(2) Special rules. Paragraphs (a) and (b)(3)(iii) of this section apply to transfers of partnership interests and distributions of property from a partnership that occur on or after June 9, 2003.

T.D. 6175, 5/23/56, amend T.D. 8847, 12/14/99, T.D. 9059, 6/6/2003, T.D. 9137, 7/15/2004.

§ 1.761-1 Terms defined.

(a) Partnership. The term *partnership* means a partnership as determined under §§ 301.7701-1, 301.7701-2, and 301.7701-3 of this chapter.

(b) Partner. The term "partner" means a member of a partnership.

(c) Partnership agreement. For the purposes of subchapter K, a partnership agreement includes the original agreement and any modifications thereof agreed to by all the partners or adopted in any other manner provided by the partnership agreement. Such agreement or modifications can be oral or written. A partnership agreement may be modified with respect to a particular taxable year subsequent to the close of such taxable year, but not later than the date (not including any extension of time) prescribed by law for the filing of the partnership return. As to any matter on which the partnership agreement, or any modification thereof, is silent, the provisions of local law shall be considered to constitute a part of the agreement.

(d) Liquidation of partner's interest. The term "liquidation of a partner's interest" means the termination of a partner's entire interest in a partnership by means of a distribution, or a series of distributions, to the partner by the partnership. A series of distributions will come within the meaning of this term whether they are made in one year or in more than one year. Where a partner's interest is to be liquidated by a series of distributions, the interest will not be considered as liquidated until the final distribution has been made. For the basis of property distributed in one liquidating distribution, or in a series of distributions in liquidation, see section 732(b). A distribution which is not in liquidation of a partner's entire interest, as defined in this paragraph, is a current distribution. Current distributions, therefore, include distributions in partial liquidation of a partner's interest, interest, and distributions of the partner's distributive share. See paragraph (a)(1)(ii) of § 1.731-1.

(e) Distribution of partnership interest. For purposes of section 708(b)(1)(B) and § 1.708-1(b)(1)(iv), the deemed distribution of an interest in a new partnership by a partnership that terminates under section 708(b)(1)(B) is not a sale or exchange of an interest in the new partnership. However, the deemed distribution of an interest in a new partnership by a partnership that terminates under section 708(b)(1)(B) is treated as an exchange of the interest in the new partnership for purposes of section 743. This paragraph (e) applies to terminations of partnerships under section 708(b)(1)(B) occurring on or after May 9, 1997; however, this paragraph (e) may be applied to terminations occurring on or after May 9, 1996, provided that the partnership and its partners apply this paragraph (e) to the termination in a consistent manner.

T.D. 6175, 5/23/56, amend T.D. 6198, 8/15/56, T.D. 7012, 5/14/69, T.D. 7208, 10/2/72, T.D. 8697, 12/17/96, T.D. 8717, 5/8/97.

PAR. 8. Section 1.761-1(b) is amended by adding two sentences to the end of the paragraph to read as follows.

Proposed § 1.761-1 Terms defined. [*For Preamble, see ¶ 152,663*]

* * * * *

(b) * * * If a partnership interest is transferred in connection with the performance of services, and that partnership interest is substantially nonvested (within the meaning of § 1.83-3(b)), then the holder of the partnership interest is not treated as a partner solely by reason of holding the interest, unless the holder makes an election with respect to the interest under section 83(b). The previous sentence applies to partnership interests that are transferred on or after the date final regulations are published in the Federal Register.

§ 1.761-2 Exclusion of certain unincorporated organizations from the application of all or part of subchapter K of chapter 1 of the Internal Revenue Code.

Caution: The Treasury has not yet amended Reg § 1.761-2 to reflect changes made by P.L. 96-222.

(a) Exclusion of eligible unincorporated organizations. *(1) In general.* Under conditions set forth in this section, an unincorporated organization described in subparagraph (2) or (3) of this paragraph may be excluded from the application of all or a part of the provisions of subchapter K of chapter 1 of the Code. Such organization must be availed of (i) for investment purposes only and not for the active conduct of a business, or (ii) for the joint production, extraction, or use of property, but not for the purpose of selling services or property produced or extracted. The members of such organization must be able to compute their income without the necessity of computing partnership taxable income. Any syndicate, group, pool, or joint venture which is classifiable as an association, or any group operating under an agreement which creates an organization classifiable as an association, does not fall within these provisions.

(2) Investing partnership. Where the participants in the joint purchase, retention, sale, or exchange of investment property—

(i) Own the property as coowners,

(ii) Reserve the right separately to take or dispose of their shares of any property acquired or retained, and

(iii) Do not actively conduct business or irrevocably authorize some person or persons acting in a representative capacity to purchase, sell, or exchange such investment property, although each separate participant may delegate authority to purchase, sell, or exchange his share of any such investment property for the time being for his account, but not for a period of more than a year, then

such group may be excluded from the application of the provisions of subchapter K under the rules set forth in paragraph (b) of this section.

(3) Operating agreements. Where the participants in the joint production, extraction, or use of property—

(i) Own the property as coowners, either in fee or under lease or other form of contract granting exclusive operating rights, and

(ii) Reserve the right separately to take in kind or dispose of their shares of any property produced, extracted, or used, and

(iii) Do not jointly sell services or the property produced or extracted, although each separate participant may delegate authority to sell his share of the property produced or extracted for the time being for his account, but not for a period of time in excess of the minimum needs of the industry, and in no event for more than 1 year, then

such group may be excluded from the application of the provisions of subchapter K under the rules set forth in paragraph (b) of this section. However, the preceding sentence does not apply to any unincorporated organization one of whose principal purposes is cycling, manufacturing, or processing for persons who are not members of the organization. In addition, except as provided in paragraph (d)(2)(i) of this section, this paragraph (a)(3) does not apply to any unincorporated organization that produces natural gas under a joint operating agreement, unless all members of the unincorporated organization comply with paragraph (d) of this section.

(b) Complete exclusion from subchapter K. *(1) Time for making election for exclusion.* Any unincorporated organization described in subparagraph (1) and either (2) or (3) of paragraph (a) of this section which wishes to be excluded from all of subchapter K must make the election provided in section 761(a) not later than the time prescribed by paragraph (e) of § 1.6031-1 (including extensions thereof) for filing the partnership return for the first taxable year for which exclusion from subchapter K is desired. Notwithstanding the prior sentence such organization may be deemed to have made the election in the manner prescribed in subparagraph (2)(ii) of this paragraph.

(2) Method of making election. (i) Except as provided in subdivision (ii) of this subparagraph, any unincorporated organization described in subparagraphs (1) and either (2) or (3) of paragraph (a) of this section which wishes to be excluded from all of subchapter K must make the election provided in section 761(a) in a statement attached to, or incorporated in, a properly executed partnership return, Form 1065, which shall contain the information required in this subdivision. Such return shall be filed with the internal revenue officer with whom a partnership return, Form 1065, would be required to be filed if no election were made. Where, for the purpose of determining such officer, it is necessary to determine the internal revenue district (or service center serving such district) in which the electing organization has its principal office or place of business, the principal office or place of business of the person filing the return shall be considered the principal office or place of business of the organization. The partnership return must be filed not later than the time prescribed by paragraph (e) of § 1.6031-1 (including extensions thereof) for filing the partnership return with respect to the first taxable year for which exclusion from subchapter K is desired. Such partnership return shall contain, in lieu of the information required by Form 1065 and by the instructions relating thereto, only the name or other identification and the address of the organization together with information on the return, or in the statement attached to the return, showing the names, addresses, and identification numbers of all the members of the organization; a statement that the organization qualifies under subparagraphs (1) and either (2) or (3) of paragraph (a) of this section; a statement that all of the members of the organization elect that it be excluded from all of subchapter K; and a statement indicating where a copy of the agreement under which the organization operates is available (or if the agreement is oral, from whom the provisions of the agreement may be obtained).

(ii) If an unincorporated organization described in subparagraphs (1) and either (2) or (3) of paragraph (a) of this section does not make the election provided in section 761(a) in the manner prescribed by subdivision (i) of this subparagraph, it shall nevertheless be deemed to have made the election if it can be shown from all the surrounding facts and circumstances that it was the intention of the members of such organization at the time of its formation to secure exclusion from all of subchapter K beginning with the first taxable year of the organization. Although the following facts are not exclusive, either one of such facts may indicate the requisite intent:

(a) At the time of the formation of the organization there is an agreement among the members that the organization be excluded from subchapter K beginning with the first taxable year of the organization, or

(b) The members of the organization owning substantially all of the capital interests report their respective shares of the items of income, deductions, and credits of the organization on their respective returns (making such elections as to individual items as may be appropriate) in a manner consistent with the exclusion of the organization from subchapter K beginning with the first taxable year of the organization.

(3) Effect of election. (i) In general. An election under this section to be excluded will be effective unless within 90 days after the formation of the organization (or by October 15, 1956, whichever is later) any member of the organization notifies the Commissioner that the member desires subchapter K to apply to such organization, and also advises the Commissioner that he has so notified all other members of the organization by registered or certified mail. Such election is irrevocable as long as the organization remains qualified under subparagraphs (1) and either (2) or (3) of paragraph (a) of this section, or unless approval of revocation of the election is secured from the Commissioner. Application for permission to revoke the election must be submitted to the Commissioner of Internal Revenue, Attention: T:I, Washington, D.C. 20224, no later than 30 days after the beginning of the first taxable year to which the revocation is to apply.

(ii) Special rule. Notwithstanding subdivision (i) of this subparagraph, an election deemed made pursuant to subparagraph (2)(ii) of this paragraph will not be effective in the case of an organization which had a taxable year ending on or before November 30, 1972 if any member of the organization notifies the Commissioner that the member desires subchapter K to apply to such organization, and also advises the Commissioner that he has so notified all other members of the organization by registered or certified mail. Such notification to the Commissioner must be made on or before January 2, 1973 and must include the names and addresses of all of the members of the organization.

(c) Partial exclusion from subchapter K. An unincorporated organization which wishes to be excluded from only certain sections of subchapter K must submit to the Commissioner, no later than 90 days after the beginning of the first taxable year for which partial exclusion is desired, a request for permission to be excluded from certain provisions of subchapter K. The request shall set forth the sections of subchapter K from which exclusion is sought and shall state that such organization qualifies under subparagraphs (1) and either (2) or (3) of paragraph (a) of this section, and that the members of the organization elect to be excluded to the extent indicated. Such exclusion shall be effective only upon approval of the election by the Commissioner and subject to the conditions he may impose.

(d) Rules for gas producers that produce natural gas under joint operating agreements. *(1) Joint operating agreements and gas balancing.* Co-owners of a property producing natural gas enter into a joint operating agreement (JOA) to define the rights and obligations of each co-producer of the gas in place. The JOA determines, among other things, each co-producer's proportionate share of the natural gas as it is produced from the reservoir, together with the associated production expenses. A gas imbalance arises when a co-producer does not take its proportionate share of current gas production under the JOA (underproducer) and another co-producer takes more than its proportionate share of current production (overproducer). The co-producers often enter into a gas balancing agreement (GBA) as an addendum to their JOA to establish their rights and obligations when a gas imbalance arises. A GBA typically allows the overproducer to take the amount of the gas imbalance (overproduced gas) and entitles the underproducer to recoup the overproduced gas either from the volume of the gas remaining in the reservoir or by a cash balancing payment.

(2) Permissible gas balancing methods. (i) General requirement. All co-producers of natural gas operating under the same JOA must use the cumulative gas balancing method, as described in paragraph (d)(3) of this section, unless they use the annual gas balancing method described in paragraph (d)(4) of this section. A co-producer's failure to comply with the provisions of this paragraph (d)(2)(i) generally constitutes the use of an impermissible method of accounting, requiring a change to a permissible method under § 1.446-1(e)(3) with any terms and conditions as may be imposed by the Commissioner. The co-producers' election to be excluded from all or part of subchapter K will not be revoked, unless the Commissioner determines that there was willful failure to comply with the requirements of this paragraph (d)(2)(i).

(ii) Change in method of accounting; adoption of method of accounting. (A) In general. The annual gas balancing method and the cumulative gas balancing method are methods of accounting. Accordingly, a change to or from either of these methods is a change in method of accounting that requires the consent of the Commissioner. See section 446(e) and § 1.446-1(e). For purposes of this section, each JOA is treated as a separate trade or business. Paragraph (d)(2)(ii)(B) of this section provides rules for adopting either permissible method of accounting. Paragraph (d)(2)(ii)(C) of this section provides rules on the timing of required changes to either permissible method during the transitional period, and paragraph (d)(5) of this section contains the procedural provisions for making a change in method of accounting required in paragraph (d)(2)(ii)(C) of this section.

(B) Adoption of method of accounting. A co-producer must adopt a permissible method for each JOA entered into on or after the start of the co-producer's first taxable year beginning after December 31, 1994 (or, in the case of the use of the annual gas balancing method by co-producers not having the same taxable year, the start of the first taxable year beginning after December 31, 1994, of the co-producer whose taxable year begins latest in the calendar year). If a co-producer is adopting the cumulative method, the co-producer may adopt the method by using the method on its timely filed return for the taxable year of adoption. A co-producer may adopt the annual gas balancing method with the permission of the Commissioner under guidelines set forth in paragraph (d)(4)(ii) of this section.

(C) Required change in method of accounting for certain joint operating agreements. This paragraph (d)(2)(ii)(C) applies to certain JOAs entered into prior to 1996. Except in the case of a part-year change in method of accounting or in the case of the cessation of a JOA (both of which are described in this paragraph (d)(2)(ii)(C)), for each JOA entered into prior to a co-producer's first taxable year beginning after December 31, 1994, and in effect as of the beginning of that year, the co-producer must change its method of accounting for sales of gas and its treatment of certain related deductions and credits to a permissible method as of the start of its first taxable year beginning after December 31, 1994.

In the case of a JOA of co-producers that do not all have the same taxable year and that choose the annual gas balancing method, if the JOA is entered into prior to the first taxable year beginning after December 31, 1994 of the co-producer whose taxable year begins latest in the calendar year and the JOA is in effect as of January 1, 1996, a change to the annual gas balancing method by each co-producer under that JOA is made as of January 1, 1996 (part-year change in method of accounting). If the co-producers would have made a part-year change to the annual gas balancing method but for the fact that their JOA ceased to be in effect before January 1, 1996 (cessation of a JOA), the co-producers do not change their method of accounting with respect to the JOA. Rather, for their taxable years in which the JOA ceases to be in effect, the co-producers use their current method of accounting with respect to that JOA.

(3) Cumulative gas balancing method. (i) In general. The cumulative gas balancing method (cumulative method), solely for purposes of reporting income from gas sales and certain related deductions and credits, treats each co-producer under the same JOA as the sole owner of its percentage share of the total gas in the reservoir and disregards the ownership arrangement described in the JOA for gas as it is produced from the reservoir. Each co-producer is considered to be taking only its share of the total gas in the reservoir as long as the gas remaining in the reservoir is sufficient to satisfy the ownership rights of the co-producers in their percentage shares of the total gas in the reservoir. After a co-producer has taken its entire share of the total gas in the reservoir, any additional gas taken by that co-producer (taking co-producer) is treated as having been taken from its other co-producers' shares of the total gas in the reservoir. The effect of being treated as a taking co-producer under the cumulative method is that the taking co-producer generally may not claim an allowance for depletion and a production credit on its sales of its other co-producers' percentage shares of the total gas in the reservoir.

(ii) Requirements. (A) Reporting of income from sales of gas. Under the cumulative method, each co-producer must include in gross income under its overall method of accounting the amount of its sales from all gas produced from the reservoir, including sales of gas taken from another co-producer's share of the gas in the reservoir.

(B) Reporting of deduction of taking co-producer. A taking co-producer deducts the amount of a payment (in cash or property, other than gas produced under the JOA) made to another co-producer for sales of that co-producer's gas, but only for the taxable year in which the payment is made. Thus, an accrual method taking co-producer is not permitted a deduction for any obligation it has to pay another co-producer for sales of that co-producer's gas until a payment is made. See paragraph (d)(3)(iii)(B) of this section for a rule requiring a reduction of the amount of the deduction described in this paragraph (d)(3)(ii)(B) if the taking co-producer had mistakenly claimed a depletion deduction relating to those sales.

(C) Reporting of income by other co-producers. Any co-producer that is entitled to receive a payment from a taking co-producer must include the amount of the payment in gross income as proceeds from the sale of its gas only for the taxable year that the payment is actually received, regardless of its overall method of accounting.

(D) Reporting of production expenses. Each co-producer deducts its proportionate share of production expenses, as provided in the JOA, under its regular method of accounting for the expenses.

(iii) Special rules for production credits and depletion deductions under the cumulative method. (A) In general. Under the cumulative method, a co-producer's depletion allowance and production credit for a taxable year are based on its income from gas sales and production of gas from its percentage share of the total gas in the reservoir, and are not based on its current proportionate share of income and production as determined under the JOA. Thus, in general, a taking co-producer is not allowed a production credit or an allowance for depletion on its sales of gas in excess of its percentage share of the total gas in the reservoir. However, the Service will not disallow depletion deductions or production credits claimed by a taking co-producer on the gas of other co-producers if the taking co-producer had a reasonable but mistaken belief that the deductions or credits were claimed with respect to the taking co-producer's percentage share of total gas in the reservoir and the taking co-producer makes the appropriate reductions and additions to tax required in paragraphs (d)(3)(iii)(B) and (d)(3)(iii)(C) of this section. The reasonableness of the mistaken belief is determined at the time of filing the return claiming the deductions or credits. A co-producer receiving a payment for sales of its gas from a taking co-producer claims a production credit and an allowance for depletion relating to those sales only for the taxable year in which the amount of the payment is included in its gross income.

(B) Reduction of taking co-producer's payment deduction for depletion claimed on another co-producer's gas. If a taking co-producer claims an allowance for depletion on another co-producer's gas, the taking co-producer must reduce its deduction claimed in a later year for making a payment to the other co-producer for sales of that co-producer's gas by the amount of any percentage depletion deduction allowed on the gas sales to which the payment relates. If the percentage limitation of section 613A(d)(1) applied to disallow a depletion deduction for a previous year, the taking co-producer must reduce the amount of any carried over depletion deduction allowable in the year of the payment or in a future year by the portion of the carried over depletion deduction, if any, that relates to another co-producer's gas.

(C) Addition to tax of taking co-producer for production credit claimed on another co-producer's gas. If a taking co-producer claims a production credit on another co-producer's gas, the taking co-producer must add to its tax for the taxable year that it makes a payment to the other co-producer for sales of that co-producer's gas any production credit allowed in an earlier taxable year on the gas sales to which the payment relates, but only to the extent the credit allowed actually reduced the taking co-producer's tax in any earlier year. The taking co-producer also must reduce the amount of its minimum tax credit allowable by reason of section 53(d)(1)(B)(iii) in the year of the payment or in a future year by the portion of the credit, if any, that relates to another co-producer's gas.

(iv) Anti-abuse rule. If the Commissioner determines that co-producers using the cumulative method have arranged or altered their taking of production for a taxable year with a principal purpose of shifting the income, deductions, or credits relating to that production to avoid tax, the co-producers' election to be excluded from all or part of subchapter K will be revoked for that year and for subsequent years. In determining that a principal purpose was to avoid tax, the Commissioner will examine all the facts and circumstances surrounding the use of the cumulative method by the co-producers. See Examples 3 and 4 of paragraph (d)(6) of this section.

(4) Annual gas balancing method. (i) In general. The annual gas balancing method (annual method) takes into account each co-producer's ownership rights and obligations, as described in the JOA, with respect to the co-producer's current proportionate share of gas as it is produced from the reservoir. Under the annual method, gas imbalances relating to a JOA must be eliminated annually through a balancing payment, which may be in the form of cash, gas produced under the same JOA, or other property. If all the co-producers under a JOA have the same taxable year, any gas imbalance remaining at the end of a taxable year must be eliminated by a balancing payment from the overproducer to the underproducer by the due date of the overproducer's tax return for that taxable year (including extensions). If all the co-producers under a JOA do not have the same taxable year, any gas imbalance remaining at the end of a calendar year must be eliminated by a balancing payment from the overproducer to the underproducer by September 15 of the following calendar year. The annual method may be used only if the Commissioner's permission is obtained. Paragraph (d)(4)(ii) of this section provides guidelines for applying for this permission. The annual method is not available for a JOA with respect to which any co-producer made an election under paragraph (d)(5)(i)(B)(3) of this section (to take an aggregate section 481(a) adjustment for all JOAs of a co-producer into account in the year of change).

(ii) Obtaining the commissioner's permission to use the annual method. A request for the Commissioner's permission to adopt the annual method for a new JOA must be in writing and must set forth the names of all the co-producers under the JOA and the respective taxable year of adoption. See paragraphs (d)(2)(ii) and (d)(5)(ii) of this section for the rules for a change in method of accounting to the annual method. In addition, the request must contain an explanation of how the co-producers will report income from gas sales, the making or receiving of a balancing payment, production expenses, depletion deductions, and production credits. Permission will be granted under appropriate conditions, including, but not limited to, an agreement in writing by all co-producers to use the annual method and to eliminate any gas imbalances annually in accordance with paragraph (d)(4)(i) of this section.

(5) Transitional rules for making a change in method of accounting required in paragraph (d)(2)(ii)(C) of this section. (i) Change in method of accounting to the cumulative method. (A) Automatic consent to change in method of accounting to the cumulative method. A co-producer changing to the cumulative method for any JOA entered into prior to its first taxable year beginning after December 31, 1994, and in effect as of the beginning of that year is granted the consent of the Commissioner to change its method of accounting with respect to each JOA to the cumulative method, provided the co-producer—

(1) Makes the change on its timely filed return for its first taxable year beginning after December 31, 1994;

(2) Attaches a completed and signed Form 3115 to the co-producer's tax return for the year of change, stating that, pursuant to § 1.761-2(d)(2)(ii) of the regulations, the co-producer is changing its method of accounting for sales of gas and its treatment of certain related deductions and credits under each JOA to the cumulative method;

(3) In the case of a co-producer making an election under paragraph (d)(5)(i)(B)(3) of this section to take the aggregate section 481(a) adjustment into account in the year of change, attaches the statement described in paragraph (d)(5)(i)(B)(3)(ii) of this section; and

(4) In the case of a co-producer not making an election under paragraph (d)(5)(i)(B)(3) of this section, attaches a list of each JOA with respect to which there is a section 481(a) adjustment computed in accordance with paragraph (d)(5)(i)(B)(2)(i) of this section.

(B) Section 481(a) adjustment. (1) Application of section 481(a). A change in method of accounting to the cumulative method under the automatic consent procedure in paragraph (d)(5)(i)(A) of this section is a change in method of accounting to which the provisions of section 481(a) apply. Thus, a section 481(a) adjustment must be taken into account in the manner provided by this paragraph (d)(5)(i)(B) to prevent the omission or duplication of income. Paragraph (d)(5)(i)(B)(2) of this section provides the general rules for computing the amount of the section 481(a) adjustment of a co-producer relating to a particular JOA and for taking the section 481(a) adjustment into account. Paragraph (d)(5)(i)(B)(3) of this section provides rules for electing to take a co-producer's section 481(a) adjustment computed on an aggregate basis for all JOAs into account in the year of change. Paragraph (d)(5)(i)(C) of this section provides rules to coordinate the taking of a depletion deduction or a production credit with the inclusion of a section 481(a) adjustment arising from a change in method of accounting to the cumulative method under this paragraph (d)(5)(i).

(2) Computation of the section 481(a) adjustment relating to a joint operating agreement. (i) In general. The section 481(a) adjustment of a co-producer relating to a JOA is computed as of the first day of the co-producer's year of change and is equal to the difference between the amount of income reported under the co-producer's former method of accounting for all taxable years prior to the year of change and the amount of income that would have been reported if the co-producer's new method had been used in all those taxable years.

(ii) Section 481(a) adjustment period. Except to the extent that paragraph (d)(5)(i)(B)(3) of this section applies, a co-producer's section 481(a) adjustment relating to a JOA, whether positive or negative, is taken into account in computing taxable income ratably over the 6-taxable-year period beginning with the year of change (the section 481(a) adjustment period). If the co-producer has been in existence less than 6 taxable years, the adjustment is taken into account over the number of years the co-producer has been in existence. If the co-producer ceases to engage in the trade or business that gave rise to the section 481(a) adjustment at any time during the section 481(a) adjustment period, the entire remaining balance of the section 481(a) adjustment relating to that trade or business must be taken into account in the year of the cessation. For purposes of this paragraph (d)(5)(i)(B)(2)(ii), production under each JOA is treated as a separate trade or business. The determination as to whether the co-producer ceases to engage in its trade or business is to be made under the principles of § 1.446-1(e)(3)(ii) and its underlying administrative procedures. For example, the permanent cessation of production under a co-producer's JOA constitutes the cessation of a trade or business of the co-producer. Accordingly, for the year that production under a JOA permanently ceases, the remaining balance of the section 481(a) adjustment relating to the JOA must be taken into account.

(3) Election to take aggregate section 481(a) adjustment for all joint operating agreements into account in the year of change. (i) In general. A co-producer may elect to take into account its section 481(a) adjustment, computed on an aggregate basis for all of its JOAs, whether negative or posi-

tive, in the year of change, provided the co-producer uses the cumulative method for all of its JOAs entered into prior to its first taxable year beginning after December 31, 1994, and in effect as of the beginning of that year. The aggregate section 481(a) adjustment of a co-producer is equal to the difference between the amount of income reported under the co-producer's former method of accounting for all taxable years prior to the year of change and the amount of income that would have been reported if the co-producer's new method had been used in all of those taxable years for all JOAs for which the co-producer changes its method of accounting. An election made under this paragraph (d)(5)(i)(B)(3) is irrevocable. If any person who, together with another person, would be treated as a single taxpayer under section 41(f)(1)(A) or (B) makes an election under this paragraph (d)(5)(i)(B)(3), all persons within that single taxpayer group will be treated as if they had made an election under this paragraph (d)(5)(i)(B)(3) and, as such, will be irrevocably bound by that election. If a co-producer does not make an election under this paragraph, each JOA entered into prior to the start of its first taxable year beginning after December 31, 1994, and in effect as of the beginning of that year must be accounted for separately in computing the section 481(a) adjustment and taxable income of the co-producer for any year to which this paragraph (d) applies.

(ii) Time and manner for making the election. An election under this paragraph (d)(5)(i)(B)(3) is made by attaching a statement to the co-producer's timely filed return for its year of change indicating that the co-producer is electing under § 1.761-2(d)(5)(i)(B)(3) to take its aggregate section 481(a) adjustment into account in the year of change.

(C) Treatment of section 481(a) adjustment as a sale for purposes of computing a production credit and as gross income from the property for purposes of depletion deductions. Any positive section 481(a) adjustment arising as a result of a change in method of accounting for gas imbalances under this paragraph (d)(5)(i) and taken into account in computing taxable income under paragraph (d)(5)(i)(B) of this section is considered a sale by the taxpayer for purposes of computing any production credit in the year that the adjustment is taken into account. Similarly, the positive section 481(a) adjustment is considered gross income from the property and taxable income from the property for purposes of computing depletion deductions in the year the adjustment is taken into account. Sales amounts used in computing any production credit in any year in which a negative section 481(a) adjustment is taken into account in computing taxable income under paragraph (d)(5)(i)(B) of this section must be reduced by the amount of the negative section 481(a) adjustment taken into account in that year. Similarly, gross income from the property and taxable income from the property used in computing any depletion deduction in any year in which the negative section 481(a) adjustment is taken into account must be reduced by the amount of the negative adjustment. For these purposes, any taxpayer that makes an aggregate section 481(a) adjustment election under paragraph (d)(5)(i)(B)(3) of this section must allocate the adjustment among its properties in any reasonable manner that prevents a duplication or omission of depletion deductions.

(ii) Change in method of accounting to the annual method. (A) In general. A co-producer changing to the annual method in accordance with paragraph (d)(2)(ii) of this section must request a change under § 1.446-1(e)(3) and will be subject to any terms and conditions as may be imposed by the Commissioner.

(B) Section 481(a) adjustment. A change in method of accounting to the annual method is a change in method of accounting to which the provisions of section 481(a) apply. Thus, a section 481(a) adjustment must be taken into account to prevent the omission or duplication of income. If all the co-producers under a JOA have the same taxable year, the section 481(a) adjustment involved in a change to the annual method by a co-producer relating to the JOA is computed as of the first day of the co-producer's year of change. If the co-producers under a JOA do not all have the same taxable year (that is, in the case of a part-year change described in paragraph (d)(2)(ii)(C) of this section), the change in method of accounting occurs on January 1, 1996, and the section 481(a) adjustment is computed on that date.

(iii) Untimely change in method of accounting to comply with this section. Unless a co-producer required by this section to change its method of accounting complies with the provisions of this paragraph (d)(5) for its first applicable taxable year within the time prescribed by this paragraph (d)(5), the co-producer must take the section 481(a) adjustment into account under the provisions of any applicable administrative procedure that is prescribed by the Commissioner specifically for purposes of complying with this section. Absent such an administrative procedure, a co-producer must request a change under § 1.446-1(e)(3) and will be subject to any terms and conditions as may be imposed by the Commissioner.

(6) Examples. The following examples illustrate the application of the cumulative method described in paragraph (d)(3) of this section.

Example (1). Operation of the cumulative method.

(i) L, a corporation using the cash receipts and disbursements method of accounting, and M, a corporation using an accrual method, file returns on a calendar year basis. On January 1, 1995, L and M enter into a JOA to produce natural gas as an unincorporated organization from a reservoir located in State Y. The JOA allocates reservoir production 60 percent to L and 40 percent to M. L and M enter into a GBA as an addendum to the JOA. L and M agree to use the cumulative method to account for gas sales from the reservoir and elect under section 761(a) and this section to exclude the organization from the application of subchapter K. Production from the reservoir is eligible for the section 29 credit for producing fuel from a nonconventional source. L and M produce and sell the following amounts of natural gas (in mmcf) until 2000 during which year production from the reservoir ceases:

	1995	1996	1997	1998	1999	2000
L	720	480	600	-0-	-0-	-0-
M	240	60	120	160	80	40

(ii) By the end of 1996, neither L nor M has fully produced its percentage share of the total gas in the reservoir. In 1997, L produces a total of 600 mmcf of gas at the rate of 50 mmcf per month. Prior to filing its return for 1997, L determines that it fully produced its percentage share of gas in the reservoir as of June 30, 1997. Pursuant to the GBA executed by L and M, L pays M at the end of 2000 for the 300 mmcf of M's gas (as determined under the cumulative method) that L sold in the last half of 1997.

(iii) For 1995, L and M must include in their gross income the amounts relating to gas sales of 720 mmcf and 240 mmcf, respectively. For 1996, L and M must include the amounts relating to gas sales of 480 mmcf and 60 mmcf, respectively. For both 1995 and 1996, L and M compute an allowance for depletion and a section 29 credit based upon gas taken and sold by each from the reservoir for each taxable year.

(iv) For 1997, L and M must include in gross income the amounts relating to their gas sales of 600 mmcf and 120 mmcf, respectively. Under paragraph (d)(3)(iii)(A) of this section, L computes an allowance for depletion and the section 29 credit based only on production from L's proportionate share of gas in the reservoir (that is, based on L's production through June 30, 1997). Accordingly, for 1997, L claims depletion and the section 29 credit only with respect to 300 mmcf of gas (50 mmcf per month × 6 months). For 1997, because M has not fully produced from its percentage share of the total gas in the reservoir as of the end of 1997, M claims depletion and the section 29 credit on the 120 mmcf that M produced in 1997.

(v) In 1998 and 1999, M must include in gross income the amounts relating to M's sales of gas, that is, 160 mmcf for 1998 and 80 mmcf for 1999. For 2000, M must include in gross income the amount relating to sales of 340 mmcf of gas, which consists of its own sales of 40 mmcf plus the payment for 300 mmcf of gas that L made to M for having sold from M's share of the total gas in the reservoir during the last half of 1997. Because M produced from its percentage share of the total gas in the reservoir during 1998, 1999, and 2000, M claims a depletion deduction and a section 29 credit on its income and production for those years, that is, 160 mmcf for 1998, 80 mmcf for 1999, and 40 mmcf for 2000. Additionally, for 2000, M claims depletion and the section 29 credit relating to the payment that M received from L for the 300 mmcf of M's gas that L sold in the last half of 1997. Under paragraph (d)(3)(ii)(B) of this section, L's deduction for its payment to M for the 300 mmcf of M's gas that L sold in 1997 is allowable only for 2000.

Example (2). Adjustments under the cumulative method for depletion deductions and production credits that were claimed for sales in excess of a co-producer's percentage share of total gas in the reservoir.

(i) L, a corporation using the cash receipts and disbursements method of accounting, and M, a corporation using an accrual method, file returns on a calendar year basis. On January 1, 1995, L and M enter into a JOA to produce natural gas as an unincorporated organization from a reservoir located in State Y. The JOA allocates reservoir production 60 percent to L and 40 percent to M. L and M enter into a GBA as an addendum to the JOA. L and M agree to use the cumulative method to account for gas sales from the reservoir and elect under section 761(a) and this section to exclude the organization from the application of subchapter K. Production from the reservoir is eligible for the section 29 credit for producing fuel from a nonconventional source. L and M produce and sell the following amounts of natural gas (in mmcf) until 2000 during which year production from the reservoir ceases:

	1995	1996	1997	1998	1999	2000
L	720	480	600	60	60	-0-
M	240	60	120	60	60	40

(ii) In addition, L does not realize until December 31, 1999, that L fully produced its percentage share of the total gas in the reservoir as of June 30, 1997. At the time of filing its returns for 1997 and 1998, L reasonably believes that during 1997 and 1998, respectively, it did not fully produce its percentage share of the total gas in the reservoir. Thus, L claims depletion and the section 29 credit for its total sales of 600 mmcf in 1997 and 60 mmcf in 1998. Pursuant to the GBA executed by L and M, L pays M at the end of 2000 for the 420 mmcf of M's gas (as determined under the cumulative method) that L sold (300 mmcf in the last half of 1997 (assuming that production was at a rate of 50 mmcf per month), 60 mmcf in 1998, and 60 mmcf in 1999).

(iii) In 1997 and 1998, L and M include in gross income the amounts relating to their respective sales of gas, that is, for L 600 mmcf for 1997 and 60 mmcf for 1998, and for M 120 mmcf for 1997 and 60 mmcf for 1998.

(iv) For 1999, L must include in gross income the amount of its sales of 60 mmcf, but may not claim depletion or the section 29 credit on those sales. For 1999, M must include in gross income the amount of its sales of 60 mmcf and claims depletion and the section 29 credit with respect to those 60 mmcf.

(v) For 2000, M must include in gross income the amount relating to gas sales of 460 mmcf, that is, the amount of M's own gas sales of 40 mmcf and the amount of the payment received from L for the 420 mmcf of M's gas that L sold (consisting of 300 mmcf in 1997, 60 mmcf in 1998, and 60 mmcf in 1999). Under paragraph (d)(3)(iii)(A) of this section, M computes a depletion deduction and a production credit relating to the amount of M's actual gas sales for 2000 and the payment received from L, that is, relating to a total of 460 mmcf of gas (M's sales of 40 mmcf for 2000, plus L's payment for 420 mmcf of gas). Under paragraph (d)(3)(ii)(B) of this section, L's deduction for making its payment to M for 420 mmcf of gas is allowable only for 2000. Under paragraph (d)(3)(iii)(B) of this section, L must reduce its deduction by the amount of any percentage depletion deductions allowed on its sales of M's gas, that is, relating to 360 mmcf of gas (300 mmcf for 1997 and 60 mmcf for 1998). In addition, under paragraph (d)(3)(iii)(C) of this section, L must increase its tax for 2000 by the amount of any section 29 credit L claimed on its sales of M's gas, but only to the extent that the credit claimed actually reduced L's tax in any earlier year.

Example (3). Non-abusive altering of the taking of production for a taxable year.

(i) C and D enter into a JOA and a GBA on December 1, 1994, for gas production from a reservoir. The JOA allocates production at 50 percent to C and 50 percent to D. C and D agree in writing to use the cumulative method to account for gas sales. Additionally, C and D elect under section 761(a) and this section to exclude their organization from the application of subchapter K. C and D arrange to sell all their production under annually renewable contracts. In 1995, C and D each sell 480 mmcf of gas from the reservoir.

(ii) In November 1995, D is notified that its contract with its purchaser will not be renewed for 1996. D is unable to find a new purchaser for its gas for 1996. In December 1995, D notifies C that it will not be taking production from the reservoir in 1996. Pursuant to the GBA, C then contracts with its current gas purchaser to sell an additional 20 mmcf per month in 1996. Accordingly, C sells 720 mmcf in 1996 (60 mmcf per month × 12 months). Under the facts described in this example, a principal purpose of altering the taking of production is not to avoid tax. Accordingly, the co-producers' election under section 761(a) will not be revoked by reason of altering the taking of production.

Example (4). Abusive altering of the taking of production for a taxable year. The facts are the same as in Example 3(i). For 1996, C anticipates that C's regular tax (reduced by the credits allowable under sections 27 and 28) will not exceed C's tentative minimum tax. Accordingly, under section 29(b)(6), C's credit allowed under section 29(a) for sales of its gas will be zero. For 1997, C anticipates that its credit allowed under section 29(a) will not be limited by section 29(b)(6). On the other hand, D anticipates that any credit it may claim under section 29(a) for 1996, even including a credit based on sales of C's share of current production under the JOA, will not be limited by section 29(b)(6). However, for 1997, D anticipates that its credit under section 29(a) will be limited by section 29(b)(6). On January 1, 1996, C and D agree that D will contract with its purchaser to sell the entire 960 mmcf produced from the reservoir in 1996 and that C will contract with its purchaser to sell the entire 960 mmcf produced from the reservoir in 1997. Under these facts, a principal purpose of altering the taking of production is to avoid tax. Accordingly, the co-producers' election under section 761(a) will be revoked for 1996 and for subsequent years.

(7) Effective date. Except in the case of a part-year change to the annual method or the cessation of a JOA, both of which are described in paragraph (d)(2)(ii)(C) of this section, the provisions of this paragraph (d) apply to all taxable years beginning after December 31, 1994, of any producer that is a member of an unincorporated organization that produces natural gas under a JOA in effect on or after the start of the producer's first taxable year beginning after December 31, 1994. In the case of a part-year change, the provisions of this paragraph (d) apply on and after January 1, 1996. In the case of the cessation of a JOA, the co-producers use their current method of accounting with respect to that JOA until the JOA ceases to be in effect.

(e) Cross reference. For requirements with respect to the filing of a return on Form 1065 by a partnership, see § 1.6031-1.

T.D. 7208, 10/2/72, amend T.D. 8578, 12/22/94.

Proposed § 1.761-3 Certain option holders treated as partners. [*For Preamble, see ¶ 152,359*]

(a) In general. A noncompensatory option (as defined in paragraph (b) of this section) is treated as a partnership interest if the option (and any rights associated with it) provides the holder with rights that are substantially similar to the rights afforded to a partner. This paragraph applies only if, as of the date that the noncompensatory option is issued, transferred, or modified, there is a strong likelihood that the failure to treat the holder of the noncompensatory option as a partner would result in a substantial reduction in the present value of the partners' and the holder's aggregate tax liabilities. If the holder of a noncompensatory option is treated as a partner under this section, such partner's distributive share of the partnership's income, gain, loss, deduction or credit (or items thereof) is determined in accordance with that partner's interest in the partnership (taking into account all facts and circumstances) in accordance with § 1.704-1(b)(3).

(b) Definitions. *(1) Noncompensatory option.* For purposes of this section, a noncompensatory option means an option (as defined in paragraph (b)(2) of this section) issued by a partnership, other than an option issued in connection with the performance of services. A noncompensatory option issued by an eligible entity (as defined in § 301.7701-3(a)) that would become a partnership under § 301.7701-3(f)(2) of this chapter if the option holder were treated as a partner under this section is also a noncompensatory option for purposes of this section. If a noncompensatory option is issued by such an eligible entity, then the eligible entity is treated as a partnership for purposes of applying this section.

(2) Option. For purposes of this section, a call option or warrant to acquire an interest in the issuing partnership is an option. In addition, convertible debt (as defined in § 1.721-2(e)(2)) and convertible equity (as defined in § 1.721-2(e)(3)) are options for purposes of this section. A contract that otherwise constitutes an option shall not fail to be treated as such for purposes of this section merely because it may or must be settled in cash or property other than a partnership interest.

(c) Rights taken into account. *(1)* In determining whether a noncompensatory option provides the holder with rights that are substantially similar to the rights afforded to a partner, all facts and circumstances are considered, including whether the option is reasonably certain to be exercised (as of the time that the option is issued, transferred or modified) and whether the option holder possesses partner attributes. For purposes of this section, if a noncompensatory option is reasonably certain to be exercised, then the holder of the option ordinarily has rights that are substantially similar to the rights afforded to a partner.

(2) Reasonable certainty of exercise. The following factors are relevant in determining whether a noncompensatory option is reasonably certain to be exercised (as of the time that the noncompensatory option is issued, transferred, or modified)—

(i) The fair market value of the partnership interest that is the subject of the option;

(ii) The exercise price of the option;

(iii) The term of the option;

(iv) The volatility, or riskiness, of the partnership interest that is the subject of the option;

(v) The fact that the option premium and, if the option is exercised, the option exercise price, will become assets of the partnership;

(vi) Anticipated distributions by the partnership during the term of the option;

(vii) Any other special option features, such as an exercise price that declines over time or declines contingent on the happening of specific events;

(viii) The existence of related options, including reciprocal options; and

(ix) Any other arrangements (express or implied) affecting the likelihood that the option will be exercised.

(3) Partner attributes. Partner attributes include the extent to which the holder of the option will share in the economic benefit of partnership profits (including distributed profits) and in the economic detriment associated with partnership losses. Partner attributes also include the existence of any arrangement (either within the option agreement or in a related agreement) that, directly or indirectly, allows the holder of a noncompensatory option to control or restrict the activities of the partnership. For this purpose, rights in the partnership possessed by the option holder solely by virtue of owning a partnership interest and not by virtue of holding a noncompensatory option are not taken into account, provided that those rights are no greater than rights granted to other partners owning similar interests in the partnership.

(d) Examples. The following examples illustrate the provisions of this section. For the following examples, assume that:

(1) Each option agreement provides that the partnership cannot make distributions to its partners while the option remains outstanding; and

(2) The option holders do not have any significant rights to control or restrict the activities of the partnership (other than restricting distributions and dilutive issuances of partnership equity).

Example (1). Active trade or business. PRS is a partnership engaged in a telecommunications business. In exchange for a premium of $8x, PRS issues a noncompensatory option to A to acquire a 10 percent interest in PRS for $17x at any time during a 7-year period commencing on the date on which the option is issued. At the time of the issuance of the option, a 10 percent interest in PRS has a fair market value of $16x. Due to the riskiness of PRS's business, the value of a 10 percent PRS interest in 7 years is not reasonably predictable as of the time the option is issued. Therefore, it is not reasonably certain that A's option will be exercised. Furthermore, although the option provides A with substantially the same economic benefit of partnership profits as would a direct investment in PRS, A does not share in substantially the same economic detriment of partnership losses as would a partner in PRS. Given these facts, the option to acquire a PRS interest does not provide A with rights that are substantially similar to the rights afforded to a partner. Therefore, A is not treated as a partner under this section.

Example (2). Option issued by partnership with reasonably predictable earnings. PRS owns rental real property. The property is 95 percent rented to corporate tenants with a mid-investment grade bond rating or better and is expected to remain so for the next 20 years. The tenants of the building are responsible for paying all real estate taxes, insurance, and maintenance expenses relating to the property. Occupancy rates in properties of a similar character are high in the geographic area in which the property is located, and it is reasonably predictable that properties in that area will retain their value during the next 10 years. In exchange for a premium of $6.5x, PRS issues a noncompensatory option to B to acquire a 10 percent interest in PRS for $17x at the end of a 7-year period commencing on the date of the issuance of the option. At the time the option is issued, a 10 percent interest in PRS has a fair market value of $16.5x. Given the stability of PRS's rental property, PRS can reasonably predict that its net cash flow for each of the 7 years during which the option is outstanding will be $10x ($70x over the 7 years), and that there will be no decline in the value of the property during that time. In light of the reasonably predictable earnings of PRS and the fact that PRS will make no distributions to its partners during the 7 years that the option is outstanding, it is reasonably certain that the value of a 10 percent interest in PRS at the end of the option's 7-year term will significantly exceed the exercise price of the option. Therefore, the option is reasonably certain to be exercised. Because the option is reasonably certain to be exercised, under these facts, B has rights that are substantially similar to the rights afforded to a partner. Therefore, if there is a strong likelihood that failure to treat B as a partner would result in a substantial reduction in the partners' and B's aggregate tax liabilities, B will be treated as a partner. In such a case, B's distributive share of PRS's income, gain, loss, deduction, or credit (or items thereof) is determined in accordance with B's interest in the partnership (taking into account all facts and circumstances) in accordance with § 1.704-1(b)(3).

Example (3). Deep in the money options. (i) LP is a limited partnership engaged in an internet start-up venture. In exchange for a premium of $14x, LP issues a noncompensatory option to C to acquire a 5 percent interest in LP for $6x at any time during a 10-year period commencing on the date on which the option is issued. At the time of the issuance of the option, a 5 percent interest in LP has a fair market value of $15x. Because of the riskiness of LP's business, the option is not reasonably certain to be exercised. Nevertheless, because C has paid a $14x premium for a partnership interest that has a fair market value of $15x, C has substantially the same economic benefits and detriments as a result of purchasing the option as C would have had if C had purchased a partnership interest. Therefore, the option provides C with rights that are substantially similar to the rights afforded to a partner (partner attributes). See paragraph (c)(3) of this section. If there is a strong likelihood that failure to treat C as a partner would result in a substantial reduction in the partners' and C's aggregate tax liabilities, C will be treated as a partner. In such a case, C's distributive share of LP's income, gain, loss, deduction, or credit (or items thereof) is determined in accordance with C's interest in the partnership (taking into account all facts and circumstances) in accordance with § 1.704-1(b)(3).

(ii) The facts are the same as in paragraph (i) of this Example 3, except that C transfers $150x to LP in exchange for a note from LP that matures 10 years from the date of issuance and a warrant to acquire a 5 percent interest in LP for an exercise price of $6x. The warrant issued with the debt is exercisable at any time during the 10-year term of the debt. The debt instrument and the warrant comprise an investment unit within the meaning of section 1273(c)(2). Under § 1.1273-2(h), the issue price of the investment unit, $150x, is allocated $136x to the debt instrument and $14x to the warrant. As in paragraph (i), C has substantially the same economic benefits and detriments as a result of purchasing the warrant as C would have had if C had purchased a partnership interest. Therefore, the warrant provides C with rights that are substantially similar to the rights afforded to a partner. If there is a strong likelihood that failure to treat C as a partner would result in a substantial reduction in the partners' and C's aggregate tax liabilities, then C will be treated as a partner. In such a case, C's distributive share of LP's income, gain, loss, deduction, or credit (or items thereof) is determined in accordance with C's interest in the partnership (taking into account all facts and circumstances) in accordance with § 1.704-1(b)(3).

(e) Effective date. This section applies to noncompensatory options that are issued on or after the date final regulations are published in the Federal Register.

§ 1.801-2 Taxable years affected.

Caution: The Treasury has not yet amended Reg § 1.801-2 to reflect changes made by P.L. 98-369.

Section 1.801-1 is applicable only to taxable years beginning after December 31, 1953, and before January 1, 1955, and all references to sections of part I, subchapter L, chapter 1 of the Code are to the Internal Revenue Code of 1954, before amendments. Sections 1.801-3 through 1.801-7 are applicable only to taxable years beginning after December 31, 1957, and all references to sections of part I, subchapter L, chapter 1 of the Code are to the Internal Revenue Code of 1954, as amended by the Life Insurance Company Income Tax Act of 1959 (73 Stat. 112). Section 1.801-8 is applicable only to taxable years beginning after December 31, 1961, and all references to sections of part I, subchapter L, chapter 1 of the Code are to the Internal Revenue Code of 1954, as amended by the Life Insurance Company Income Tax Act of 1959 (73 Stat. 112) and section 3 of the Act of October 23, 1962 (76 Stat. 1134).

T.D. 6513, 12/9/60, amend T.D. 6886, 6/22/66.

§ 1.801-3 Definitions.

Caution: The Treasury has not yet amended Reg § 1.801-3 to reflect changes made by P.L. 98-369, P.L. 101-508.

For purposes of part I, subchapter L, chapter 1 of the Code, this section defines the following terms, which are to be used in determining if a taxpayer is a life insurance company (as defined in section 801(a) and paragraph (b) of this section):

(a) Insurance company. *(1)* The term "insurance company" means a company whose primary and predominant business activity during the taxable year is the issuing of insurance or annuity contracts or the reinsuring of risks underwritten by insurance companies. Thus, though its name, charter powers, and subjection to State insurance laws are significant in determining the business which a company is authorized and intends to carry on, it is the character of the business actually done in the taxable year which determines whether a company is taxable as an insurance company under the Internal Revenue Code.

(2) Insurance companies include both stock and mutual companies, as well as mutual benefit insurance companies. For taxable years beginning before January 1, 1970, a voluntary unincorporated association of employees, including an association fulfilling the requirements of section 801(b)(2)(B) (as in effect for such years), formed for the purpose of relieving sick and aged members and the dependents of deceased members, is an insurance company, whether the fund for such purpose is created wholly by membership dues or partly by contributions from the employer. A corporation which merely sets aside a fund for the insurance of its employees is not an insurance company, and the income from such fund shall be included in the return of the corporation.

(b) Life insurance company. *(1)* The term "life insurance company", as used in subtitle A of the Code, is defined in section 801(a). For the purpose of determining whether a company is a "life insurance company" within the meaning of that term as used in section 801(a), it must first be determined whether the company is taxable as an insurance company (as defined in paragraph (a) of this section). An insurance company shall be taxed as a life insurance company if it is engaged in the business of issuing life insurance and annuity contracts (either separately or combined with health and accident insurance), or noncancellable contracts of health and accident insurance, and its life insurance reserves (as defined in section 801(b) and § 1.801-4), plus unearned premiums, and unpaid losses (whether or not ascertained), on noncancellable life, health, or accident policies not included in life insurance reserves, comprise more than 50 percent of its total reserves (as defined in section 801(c) and § 1.801-5). For purposes of determining whether it satisfies the percentage requirements of the preceding sentence, a company shall first make any adjustments to life insurance reserves and total reserves required by section 806(a) (relating to adjustments for certain changes in reserves and assets) and then as required by section 801(d) (relating to adjustments in reserves for policy loans). For examples of the adjustments required under section 806(a), see paragraph (b)(4) of § 1.806-3. For an example of the adjustments required under section 801(d), see paragraph (c) of § 1.801-6. Furthermore, if an insurance company which computes its life insurance reserves on a preliminary term basis elects to revalue such reserves on a net level premium basis under section 818(c), such revalued basis shall be disregarded for purposes of section 801.

(2) An insurance company writing only noncancellable life, health, or accident policies and having no "life insurance reserves" may qualify as a life insurance company if its unearned premiums, and unpaid losses (whether or not ascertained), on such policies comprise more than 50 percent of its total reserves.

(3) Section 801(f) provides that a burial or funeral benefit insurance company engaged directly in the manufacture of funeral supplies or the performance of funeral services shall not be taxable under section 802 but shall be taxable under section 821 or section 831 as an insurance company other than life.

(c) Noncancellable life, health, or accident insurance policy. The term "noncancellable life, health, or accident insurance policy" means a health and accident contract, or a health and accident contract combined with a life insurance or annuity contract, which the insurance company is under an obligation to renew or continue at a specified premium and with respect to which a reserve in addition to the unearned premiums (as defined in paragraph (e) of this section) must be carried to cover that obligation. Such a health and accident contract shall be considered noncancellable even though it states a termination date at a stipulated age, if, with respect to the health and accident contract, such age termination date is 60 or over. Such a contract, however, shall not be considered to be noncancellable after the age termination date stipulated in the contract has passed. However, if the age termination date stipulated in the contract occurs during the period covered by a premium received by the life insurance company prior to such date, and the company cannot cancel or modify the contract during such period, the age termination date shall be deemed to occur at the expiration of the period for which the premium has been received.

(d) Guaranteed renewable life, health, and accident insurance policy. The term "guaranteed renewable life, health, and accident insurance policy" means a health and accident contract, or a health and accident contract combined with a life insurance or annuity contract, which is not cancellable by the company but under which the company reserves the right to adjust premium rates by classes in accordance with its experience under the type of policy involved, and with respect to which a reserve in addition to the unearned premiums (as defined in paragraph (e) of this section) must be carried to cover that obligation. Section 801(e) provides that such policies shall be treated in the same manner as noncancellable life, health, and accident insurance policies. For example, the age termination date requirements applicable to noncancellable health and accident insurance policies shall also apply to guaranteed renewable life, health, and accident insurance policies. See paragraph (c) of this section.

(e) Unearned premiums. The term "unearned premiums" means those amounts which shall cover the cost of carrying the insurance risk for the period for which the premiums have been paid in advance. Such term includes all unearned premiums, whether or not required by law.

(f) Life insurance reserves. For the definition of the term "life insurance reserves", see section 801(b) and § 1.801-4.

(g) Unpaid losses (whether or not ascertained). The term "unpaid losses (whether or not ascertained)" means a reasonable estimate of the amount of the losses (based upon the facts in each case and the company's experience with similar cases)—

(1) Reported and ascertained by the end of the taxable year but where the amount of the loss has not been paid by the end of the taxable year,

(2) Reported by the end of the taxable year but where the amount thereof has not been either ascertained or paid by the end of the taxable year, or

(3) Which have occurred by the end of the taxable year but which have not been reported or paid by the end of the taxable year.

(h) Total reserves. For the definition of the term "total reserves", see section 801(c) and § 1.801-5.

(i) Amount of reserves. For purposes of subsections (a), (b), and (c) of section 801 and this section, section 801(b)(5) provides that the amount of any reserve (or portion thereof) for any taxable year shall be the mean of such reserve (or portion thereof) at the beginning and end of the taxable year.

T.D. 6513, 12/9/60, amend T.D. 7172, 3/16/72.

§ 1.801-4 Life insurance reserves.

Caution: The Treasury has not yet amended Reg § 1.801-4 to reflect changes made by P.L. 98-369, P.L. 101-508.

(a) Life insurance reserves defined. For purposes of part I, subchapter L, chapter 1 of the Code, the term "life insurance reserves" (as defined in section 801(b)) means those amounts—

(1) Which are computed or estimated on the basis of recognized mortality or morbidity tables and assumed rates of interest;

(2) Which are set aside to mature or liquidate, either by payment or reinsurance, future unaccrued claims arising from life insurance, annuity, and noncancellable health and accident insurance contracts (including life insurance or annuity contracts combined with noncancellable health and accident insurance) involving, at the time with respect to which the reserve is computed, life, health, or accident contingencies; and

(3) Which, except as otherwise provided by section 801(b)(2) and paragraphs (b) and (c) of this section, are required by law. For the meaning of the term "reserves required by law", see paragraph (b) of § 1.801-5.

For purposes of determining life insurance reserves, only those amounts shall be taken into account which must be reserved either by express statutory provisions or by rules and regulations of the insurance department of a State, Territory, or the District of Columbia when promulgated in the exercise of a power conferred by statute. Moreover, such amounts must actually be held by the company during the taxable year for which the reserve is claimed. However, reserves held by the company with respect to the net value of risks reinsured in other solvent companies (whether or not authorized) shall be deducted from the company's life insurance reserves. For example, if an ordinary life policy with a reserve of $100 is reinsured in another solvent company on a yearly renewable term basis, and the reserve on such yearly renewable term policy is $10, the reinsured company shall include $90 ($100 minus $10) in determining its life insurance reserves. Generally, life insurance reserves, as in the case of level premium life insurance, are held to supplement the future premium receipts when the latter, alone, are insufficient to cover the increased risk in the later years. For examples of reserves which qualify as life insurance reserves, see paragraph (d) of this section. For examples of reserves which do not qualify as life insurance reserves, see paragraph (e) of this section.

(b) Certain reserves which need not be required by law. Section 801(b)(2) sets forth certain reserves which, though not required by law, may still qualify as life insurance reserves, provided, however, that they first satisfy the requirements of section 801(b)(1)(A) and (B) and paragraph (a)(1) and (2) of this section. Thus, reserves need not be required by law—

(1) In the case of policies covering life, health, and accident insurance combined in one policy issued on the weekly premium payment plan, continuing for life and not subject to cancellation, and

(2) For taxable years beginning before January 1, 1970, in the case of policies issued by an organization which met the requirements of section 501(c)(9) (as it existed prior to amendment by the Tax Reform Act of 1969) other than the requirement of subparagraph (B) thereof.

(c) Assessment companies. Section 801(b)(3) provides that in the case of an assessment life insurance company or association, the term "life insurance reserves" includes—

(1) Sums actually deposited by such company or association with officers of a State or Territory pursuant to law as guaranty or reserve funds, and

(2) Any funds maintained, under the charter or articles of incorporation or association of such company or association (or bylaws approved by the State insurance commissioner) of such company or association, exclusively for the payment of claims arising under certificates of membership or policies issued upon the assessment plan and not subject to any other use.

For purposes of part I, subchapter L, chapter 1 of the Code, the reserves described in this paragraph shall be included as life insurance reserves even though such reserves do not meet the requirements of section 801(b) and paragraph (a) of this section. However, for such reserves to be included as life insurance reserves, they must be deposited or maintained to liquidate future unaccrued claims arising from life insurance, annuity, or noncancellable health and accident insurance contracts (including life insurance or annuity contracts combined with noncancellable health and accident insurance) involving, at the time with respect to which the reserve is deposited or maintained, life, health, or accident contingencies. The rate of interest assumed in calculating the reserves described in this paragraph shall be 3 percent, regardless of the rate of interest (if any) specified in the contract in respect of such reserves.

(d) Reserves which qualify as life insurance reserves. The following reserves, provided they meet the requirements of section 801(b) and paragraph (a) of this section, are illustrative of reserves which shall be included as life insurance reserves:

(1) Reserves held under life insurance contracts.

(2) Reserves held under annuity contracts (including reserves held under variable annuity contracts as described in section 801(g)(1)).

(3) Reserves held under noncancellable health and accident insurance contracts (as defined in paragraph (c) of § 1.801-3) and reserves held under guaranteed renewable health and accident insurance contracts (as defined in paragraph (d) of § 1.801-3).

(4) Reserves held either separately or combined under contracts described in subparagraphs (1), (2), or (3) of this paragraph.

(5) Reserves held under deposit administration contracts. Generally, the reserves held by a life insurance company on both the active and retired lives under deposit administration contracts will meet the requirements of section 801(b) and paragraph (a) of this section.

However, reserves held by the company with respect to the net value of risks reinsured in other solvent companies (whether or not authorized) shall be deducted from the company's life insurance reserves. See paragraph (a) of this section.

(e) Reserves and liabilities which do not qualify as life insurance reserves. The following are illustrative of reserves and liabilities which do not meet the requirements of section 801(b) and paragraph (a) of this section and, accordingly, shall not be included as life insurance reserves:

(1) Liability for supplementary contracts not involving at the time with respect to which the liability is computed, life, health, or accident contingencies.

(2) In the case of cancellable health and accident policies and similar cancellable contracts, the unearned premiums and unpaid losses (whether or not ascertained).

(3) The unearned premiums, and unpaid losses (whether or not ascertained), on noncancellable life, health, or accident policies (and guaranteed renewable life, health, and accident policies) no included in life insurance reserves. (However, such amounts shall be taken into account under section 801(a)(2) for purposes of determining whether an insurance company is a life insurance company.)

(4) The deficiency reserve (as defined in section 801(b)(4)) for each individual contract, that is, that portion of the reserve for such contract equal to the amount (if any) by which—

(i) The present value of the future net premiums required for such contract, exceeds

(ii) The present value of the future actual premiums and consideration charged for such contract.

(5) Reserves required to be maintained to provide for the ordinary operating expenses of a business which must be currently paid by every company from its income if its business is to continue, such as taxes, salaries, and unpaid brokerage.

(6) Liability for premiums received in advance.

(7) Liability for premium deposit funds.

(8) Liability for annual and deferred dividends declared or apportioned.

(9) Liability for dividends left on deposit at interest.

(10) Liability for accrued but unsettled policy claims whether known or unreported.

(11) A mandatory securities valuation reserve.

(f) Adjustments to life insurance reserves. In the event it is determined on the basis of the facts of a particular case that premiums deferred and uncollected and premiums due and unpaid are not properly accruable for the taxable year under section 809 and, accordingly, are not properly includible under assets (as defined in section 805(b)(4)) for the taxable year, appropriate reduction shall be made in the life insurance reserves. This reduction shall be made when the insurance company has calculated life insurance reserves on the assumption that the premiums on all policies are paid annually or that all premiums due on or prior to the date of the annual statement have been paid.

T.D. 6513, 12/9/60, amend T.D. 7172, 3/16/72.

PAR. 2. Section 1.801-4 is amended by adding a new paragraph (g) to read as follows:

Proposed § 1.801-4 Life insurance reserves. [*For Preamble, see ¶ 151,777*]

* * * * *

(g) Recomputation of life insurance reserves. *(1) General.* If an insurance company does not compute or estimate its reserves for contracts involving, at the time with respect to which the reserves are computed, life, accident or health contingencies, on the basis of mortality or morbidity tables and assumed rates of interest, then the taxpayer or the Commissioner may recompute reserves for those contracts on the basis of mortality or morbidity tables and assumed rates of interest.

(2) Effect of recomputation. If reserves are recomputed pursuant to paragraph (g)(1) of this section, the recomputed reserves satisfy the requirements of section 816(b)(1)(A).

(3) Mean reserve. For purposes of section 816(b)(4) and § 1.801-3(i), if reserves are recomputed pursuant to paragraph (g)(1) of this section for a taxable year, the reserves must be recomputed for both the beginning and the end of the taxable year.

(4) Subsequently acquired information. No information acquired after the date as of which a reserve was initially computed or estimated may be taken into account in recomputing that reserve under paragraph (g)(1) of this section.

(5) Effective date. This section is applicable with respect to returns filed for taxable years beginning after the date final regulations are filed with the Office of the Federal Register.

§ 1.801-5 Total reserves.

Caution: The Treasury has not yet amended Reg § 1.801-5 to reflect changes made by P.L. 98-369.

(a) Total reserves defined. For purposes of section 801(a) and § 1.801-3, the term "total reserves" is defined in section 801(c) as the sum of—

(1) Life insurance reserves (as defined in section 801(b) and § 1.801-4),

(2) Unearned premiums (as defined in paragraph (e) of § 1.801-3), and unpaid losses (whether or not ascertained) (as defined in paragraph (g) of § 1.801-3), not included in life insurance reserves, and

(3) All other insurance reserves required by law.

The term "total reserves" does not, however, include deficiency reserves (within the meaning of section 801(b)(4) and paragraph (e)(4) of § 1.801-4), even though such deficiency reserves are required by State law. In determining total reserves, a company is permitted to make use of the highest aggregate reserve required by any State or Territory or the District of Columbia in which it transacts business, but the reserve must have been actually held during the taxable year for which the reserve is claimed. For example, during the taxable year 1958 a life insurance company sells life insurance and annuity contracts in States A and B. State A requires reserves of 10 against the life and 5 against the annuity business. State B requires reserves of 9 against the life and 7 against the annuity business. Assuming the company actually holds these reserves during the taxable year 1958, its highest aggregate reserve for such taxable year is the 16 required by State B. Thus, the company is not permitted to compute its highest aggregate reserve by taking State A's requirement of 10 against its life insurance business and adding it to State B's requirement of 7 against its annuity business.

(b) Reserves required by law defined. For purposes of part I, subchapter L, chapter 1 of the Code, the term "reserves required by law" means reserves which are required either by express statutory provisions or by rules and regulations of the insurance department of a State, Territory, or the District of Columbia when promulgated in the exercise of a power conferred by statute, and which are reported in the annual statement of the company and accepted by state regulatory authorities as held for the fulfillment of the claims of policyholders or beneficiaries.

(c) Information to be filed. In any case where reserves are claimed, sufficient information must be filed with the return to enable the district director to determine the validity of the claim. See section 6012 and paragraph (c) of § 1.6012-2. If the basis (for Federal income tax purposes) for determining the amount of any of the life insurance reserves as of the close of the taxable year differs from the basis for such determination as of the beginning of the taxable year then the following information must be filed with respect to all such changes in basis:

(1) The nature of the life insurance reserve (i.e., life, annuity, etc.);

(2) The mortality or morbidity table, assumed rate of interest, method used in computing or estimating such reserve on the old basis, and the amount of such reserve at the beginning and close of the taxable year computed on the old basis;

(3) The mortality or morbidity table, assumed rate of interest, method used in computing or estimating such reserve on the new basis, and the amount of such reserve at the close of the taxable year computed on the new basis;

(4) The deviation, if any, from recognized mortality or morbidity tables, or recognized methods of computation;

(5) The reasons for the change in basis of such reserve; and

(6) Whether such change in the reserve has been approved or accepted by the regulatory authorities of the State of domicile, and if so, a copy of the letter, certificate, or other evidence of such approval or acceptance.

(d) Illustration of principles. The provisions of section 801 relating to the percentage requirements for qualification as a life insurance company may be illustrated by the following example:

Example. The books of Y, an insurance company, selling life insurance, noncancellable health and accident insurance, and cancellable accident and health insurance, reflect (after adjustment under sections 806(a) and 801(d)) the following facts for the taxable year 1958:

	Jan. 1	Dec. 31	Mean of year
1. Life insurance reserves	$3,000	$5,000	$4,000
2. Unearned premiums, and unpaid losses (whether or not ascertained), on noncancellable accident and health insurance not included in life insurance reserves	400	600	500
3. Unearned premiums, and unpaid losses (whether or not ascertained), on cancellable accident and health insurance	1,800	2,200	2,000
4. All other insurance reserves required by law	900	1,100	1,000
5. Total reserves..............			7,500

The rules provided by section 801 require that the sum of the mean of the year figures in items 1 and 2 comprise more than 50 percent of the mean of the year figure in item 5 for an insurance company to qualify as a life insurance company. Thus, Y would qualify as a life insurance company for the taxable year 1958 as the sum of the mean of the year figures in items 1 and 2 ($4,500) comprise 60 percent of the mean of the year figure in item 5 ($7,500).

T.D. 6513, 12/9/60.

§ 1.801-6 Adjustments in reserves for policy loans.

Caution: The Treasury has not yet amended Reg § 1.801-6 to reflect changes made by P.L. 98-369.

(a) In general. Section 801(d) provides that for purposes only of determining whether or not an insurance company is a life insurance company (as defined in section 801(a) and paragraph (b) of § 1.801-3), the life insurance reserves (as defined in section 801(b) and § 1.801-4), and the total reserves (as defined in section 801(c) and paragraph (a) of § 1.801-5), shall each be reduced by an amount equal to the mean of the aggregates, at the beginning and end of the taxable year, of the policy loans outstanding with respect to contracts for which life insurance reserves are maintained. Such reduction shall be made after any adjustments required under section 806(a) and § 1.806-3 have been made.

(b) Policy loans defined. The term "policy loans" includes loans made by the insurance company, by whatever name called, for which the reserve on a contract is the collateral.

(c) Illustration of principles. The provisions of section 801(d) and this section may be illustrated by the following example:

Example. The books of T, an insurance company, selling only life insurance and cancellable accident and health insurance, reflect (after adjustment under section 806(a)) the following facts for the taxable year 1958:

	Jan. 1	Dec. 31	Mean of year
1. Life insurance reserves	$1,000	$2,000	$1,500
2. Policy loans	50	850	450
3. Life insurance reserves less policy loans			1,050

4. Unearned premiums, and unpaid losses (whether or not ascertained), on cancellable accident and health insurance	900	1,600	1,250
5. Total reserves adjusted for policy loans (item 3 plus item 4)			2,300

As the rules provided by section 801(a) and (d) require that the figure in item 3 ($1,050) be more than 50 percent of the mean of the year figure in item 5 ($2,300) for an insurance company to qualify as a life insurance company, T would not qualify as a life insurance company for the taxable year 1958.

T.D. 6513, 12/9/60.

§ 1.801-7 Variable annuities.

Caution: The Treasury has not yet amended Reg § 1.801-7 to reflect changes made by P.L. 98-369.

(a) In general. *(1)* Section 801(g)(1) provides that for purposes of part I, subchapter L, chapter 1 of the Code, an annuity contract includes a contract which provides for the payment of a variable annuity computed on the basis of recognized mortality tables and the investment experience of the company issuing such a contract. A variable annuity differs from the ordinary or fixed dollar annuity in that the annuity benefits payable under a variable annuity contract vary with the insurance company's investment experience with respect to such contracts while the annuity benefits paid under a fixed dollar annuity contract are guaranteed irrespective of the company's actual investment earnings.

(2) The reserves held with respect to the annuity contracts described in section 801(g)(1) and subparagraph (1) of this paragraph shall qualify as life insurance reserves within the meaning of section 801(b)(1) and paragraph (a) of § 1.801-4 provided such reserves are required by law (as defined in paragraph (b) of § 1.801-5) and are set aside to mature or liquidate, either by payment or reinsurance, future unaccrued claims arising from such contracts involving, at the time with respect to which the reserve is computed, life, health, or accident contingencies. Accordingly, a company issuing variable annuity contracts shall qualify as a life insurance company for Federal income tax purposes if it satisfies the requirements of section 801(a) (relating to the definition of life insurance company) and paragraph (b) of § 1.801-3.

(b) Special rules for variable annuities. *(1) Adjusted reserves rate; assumed rate.* The adjusted reserves rate for any taxable year with respect to the annuity contracts described in section 801(g)(1) and paragraph (a)(1) of this section, and the rate of interest assumed by the taxpayer for any taxable year in calculating the reserve on any such contract, shall be a rate equal to the current earnings rate determined under section 801(g)(3) and subparagraph (2) of this paragraph. However, any change in the rate of interest assumed by the taxpayer in calculating the reserve on a variable annuity contract for any taxable year which is attributable to an increase or decrease in the current earnings rate, shall not be treated as a change of basis in computing reserves for purposes of section 806(b) (relating to certain changes in reserves) or section 810(d)(1) (relating to adjustment for change in computing reserves).

(2) Current earnings rate. (i) The current earnings rate for any taxable year with respect to the annuity contracts described in section 801(g)(1) and paragraph (a)(1) of this section shall be the current earnings rate determined under section 805(b)(2) and paragraph (a)(2) of § 1.805-5 with respect to such contracts, reduced by the percentage obtained by dividing (a) the amount of the actuarial margin charge on all such variable annuity contracts issued by the taxpayer, by (b) the mean of the reserves for such contracts.

(ii) For purposes of section 801(g)(3) and subdivision (i) of this subparagraph, the term "actuarial margin charge" means any amount retained by the company from gross investment income pursuant to the terms of the variable annuity contract in excess of any portion of the investment expenses which is attributable to such contract and which is deductible under section 804(c) and paragraph (b) of § 1.804-4.

(3) Increases and decreases in reserves. (i) Section 801(g)(4) provides that for purposes of section 810(a) and (b) (relating to adjustments for increases or decreases in certain reserves), the sum of the items described in section 810(c) and paragraph (b) of § 1.810-2 taken into account as of the close of the taxable year shall be adjusted—

(a) By subtracting therefrom the sum of any amounts added from time to time (for the taxable year) to the reserves for variable annuity contracts described in section 801(g)(1) and paragraph (a)(1) of this section by reason of realized or unrealized appreciation in the value of the assets held in relation thereto, and

(b) By adding thereto the sum of any amounts subtracted from time to time (for the taxable year) from such reserves by reason of realized and unrealized depreciation in the value of such assets.

(ii) The application of section 801(g)(4) and subdivision (i) of this subparagraph may be illustrated by the following example:

Example. Company M, a life insurance company issuing only variable annuity contracts of the type described in section 801(g)(1) and paragraph (a)(1) of this section, increased its life insurance reserves held with respect to such contracts during the taxable year 1959 by $275,000. Of the total increase in the reserves, $100,000 was attributable to premium receipts, $50,000 to dividends and interest, $100,000 to unrealized appreciation in the value of the assets held in relation to such reserves, and $25,000 to realized capital gains on the sale of such assets. As of the close of the taxable year 1959, the reserves held by company M with respect to all variable annuity contracts amounted to $1,275,000. However, under section 801(g)(4) and subdivision (i) of this subparagraph, this amount must be reduced by the $100,000 unrealized asset value appreciation and the $25,000 of realized capital gains. Accordingly, for purposes of section 810(a) and (b), the amount of these reserves which is to be taken into account as of the close of the taxable year 1959 under section 810(c) is $1,150,000 ($1,275,000 less $125,000).

(c) Companies issuing variable annuities and other contracts. *(1)* In the case of a life insurance company which issues both annuity contracts described in section 801(g)(1) and paragraph (a)(1) of this section and other contracts, the policy and other contract liability requirements (as defined in section 805(a) and paragraph (b) of § 1.805-4) of such a company for any taxable year shall be considered to be the sum of—

(i) The policy and other contract liability requirements computed with respect to the items which relate to such variable annuity contracts, and

(ii) The policy and other contract liability requirements computed by excluding the items taken into account under subdivision (i) of this subparagraph.

(2) [Reserved for regulations to be issued under section 801(g)(5)(B).]

(d) Termination. Paragraphs (1), (2), (3), (4), and (5) of section 801(g) and paragraphs (a), (b), (c), and (d) of § 1.801-7 shall not apply with respect to any taxable year beginning after December 31, 1962.

T.D. 6610, 8/30/62.

---

§ 1.801-8 Contracts with reserves based on segregated asset accounts.

Caution: The Treasury has not yet amended Reg § 1.801-8 to reflect changes made by P.L. 104-188, P.L. 98-369.

(a) Definitions. *(1) Annuity contracts include variable annuity contracts.* Section 801(g)(1)(A) provides that for purposes of part I, subchapter L, chapter 1 of the Code, an annuity contract includes a contract which provides for the payment of a variable annuity computed on the basis of recognized mortality tables and the investment experience of the company issuing such a contract. A variable annuity differs from the ordinary or fixed dollar annuity in that the annuity benefits payable under a variable annuity contract vary with the insurance company's investment experience with respect to such contracts while the annuity benefits paid under a fixed dollar annuity contract are guaranteed irrespective of the company's actual investment earnings.

(2) Contracts with reserves based on a segregated asset account. (i) For purposes of part I, section 801(g)(1)(B) defines the term "contract with reserves based on a segregated asset account" as a contract (individual or group)—

(a) Which provides for the allocation of all or part of the amounts received under the contract to an account which, pursuant to State law or regulation, is segregated from the general asset accounts of the company,

(b) Which provides for the payment of annuities, and

(c) Under which the amounts paid in, or the amount paid as annuities, reflect the investment return and the market value of the segregated asset account.

(ii) The term "contract with reserves based on a segregated asset account" includes a contract such as a variable annuity contract, which reflects the investment return and the market value of the segregated asset account, even though such contract provides for the payment of an annuity computed on the basis of recognized mortality tables, but the term includes such contract only for the period during which it satisfies the requirements of section 801(g)(1)(B) and subdivision (1) of this subparagraph. However, such term does not include a pension contract written on the basis of the so-called new-money concept. Thus, for example, such term does not include a pension contract whereby reserves are credited on the basis of the company's new high yield investments. Furthermore, such term does not include a contract which during the taxable year contains a right to participate in the divisible surplus of the company where such right merely reflects the company's investment return. Nevertheless, the term does include a contract which meets the requirements of section 801(g)(1)(B) and of this subparagraph even if part of the amounts received are, for example, allocated to reserves under provisions of the contract which are written on the basis of the new-money concept. However, such reserves do not qualify as a segregated asset account referred to in section 801(g) and this section.

(iii) If at any time during taxable year a contract otherwise satisfying the requirements of section 801(g)(1)(B) and subdivision (i) of this subparagraph ceases to reflect current investment return and current market value, such contract shall not be considered as meeting the requirements of section 801(g)(1)(B)(iii) and subdivision (i)(c) of this subparagraph after such cessation. Thus, a contract which reserves based on a segregated asset account includes a contract under which the reflection of investment return and market value terminates at the beginning of the annuity payments, but only for the period prior to such termination. For example, if the purchaser of a variable annuity contract which meets such requirements elects an option which provides for the payment of a fixed dollar annuity, then such contract shall be considered as satisfying such requirements only for the period prior to the time such contract ceases to reflect current investment return and current market value. Furthermore, a group annuity contract which satisfies the requirements of section 801(g)(1)(B) and subdivision (i) of this subparagraph shall be considered as continuing to meet such requirements even though a certificate holder under the group contract elects an option which provides for the payment of a fixed dollar annuity. However, the annuity attributable to such certificate holder shall not be considered as satisfying such requirements as of the time such annuity ceases to reflect current investment return and current market value. On the other hand, a group annuity contract which does not reflect current market value shall not be considered as satisfying such requirements even though a certificate holder under the group contract elects an option which provides for the payment of a variable annuity. However, the variable annuity attributable to such certificate holder shall be considered as satisfying such requirements as of the time such variable annuity commences to reflect current investment return and current market value.

(b) Life insurance reserves. Section 801(g)(2) provides that for purposes of section 801(b)(1)(A), the reflection of the investment return and the market value of the segregated asset account shall be considered an assumed rate of interest. Thus, the reserves held with respect to contracts described in section 801(g)(1) and paragraph (a) of this section shall qualify as life insurance reserves within the meaning of section 801(b)(1) and paragraph (a) of § 1.801-4 provided such reserves are required by law (as defined in paragraph (b) of § 1.801-5) and are set aside to mature or liquidate, either by payment or reinsurance, future unaccrued claims arising from such contracts with reserves based on segregated asset accounts involving, at the time with respect to which the reserve is computed, life, health, or accident contingencies. Accordingly, a company issuing contracts with reserves based on segregated asset accounts shall qualify as a life insurance company for Federal income tax purposes if it satisfies the requirements of section 801(a) (relating to the definition of a life insurance company) and paragraph (b) of § 1.801-3.

(c) Separate accounting. *(1)* For purposes of part I, section 801(g)(3) provides that a life insurance company (as defined in section 801(a) and paragraph (b) of § 1.801-3) which issues contracts with reserves based on segregated asset accounts (as defined in section 801(g)(1)(B) and paragraph (a)(2) of this section) shall separately account for each and every income, exclusion, deduction, asset, reserve, and other liability item which is properly attributable to such segregated asset accounts. In those cases where such items are not directly accounted for, separate accounting shall be made—

(i) According to the method regularly employed by the company, if such method is reasonable, and

(ii) In all other cases in a manner which, in the opinion of the district director, is reasonable. A method of separate accounting for such items as are not accounted for directly will be deemed "regularly employed" by a life insurance company if the method was consistently followed in prior taxable years, or if, in the case of a company which has never before issued contracts with reserves based on segregated asset accounts, the company initiates in the first taxable year for which it issues such contracts a reasonable method of separate accounting for such items and consistently follows such method thereafter. Ordinarily, a company regularly employs a method of accounting in accordance with the statute of the State, Territory, or the District of Columbia, in which it operates.

(2) Every life insurance company issuing contracts with reserves based on segregated asset accounts shall keep such permanent records and other data relating to such contracts as is necessary to enable the district director to determine the correctness of the application of the rules prescribed in section 801(g) and this section and to ascertain the accuracy of the computations involved.

(d) Investment yield. *(1)* For purposes of part I, section 801(g)(4)(A) provides that the policy and other contract liability requirements (as determined under section 805) and the life insurance company's share of investment yield (as determined under sections 804(a) or 809(b)), shall be separately computed—

(i) With respect to the items separately accounted for in accordance with section 801(g)(3) and paragraph (c) of this section, and

(ii) Excluding the items taken into account under subdivision (i) of this subparagraph.

Thus, for purposes of determining both taxable investment income and gain or loss from operations, a life insurance company shall separately compute the life insurance company's share of the investment yield on the assets in its segregated asset account without regard to the policy and other contract liability requirements of, and the investment income attributable to, contracts with reserves that are not based on the segregated asset account. Such separate computations shall be made after any allocation required under section 801(g)(4)(B) and subparagraph (2) of this paragraph.

(2) (i) Section 801(g)(4)(B) provides that if the net short-term capital gain (as defined in section 1222(5)) exceeds the net long-term capital loss (as defined in section 1222(8)), determined without regard to any separate computations under section 801(g)(4)(A) and subparagraph (1) of this paragraph, then such excess shall be allocated between section 801(g)(4)(A)(i) and (ii) and subparagraph (1)(i) and (ii) of this paragraph. Such allocation shall be in proportion to the respective contributions to such excess of the items taken into account under each such section and subparagraph. The allocation under this subparagraph shall be made before the separate computations prescribed by section 801(g)(4)(A) and subparagraph (1) of this paragraph.

(ii) The operation of the allocation required under section 801(g)(4)(B) and subdivision (i) of this subparagraph may be illustrated by the following examples:

Example (1). For the taxable year 1962, T, a life insurance company which issues regular life insurance and annuity contracts and contracts with reserves based on segregated asset accounts, had (without regard to section 801(g)(4)(A)) realized short-term capital gains of $10,000 and short-term capital losses of $10,000 attributable to its general asset accounts and realized short-term capital gains of $12,000 attributable to its segregated asset accounts. For the taxable year 1962, the excess of the net short-term capital gain ($10,000 + $12,000 − $10,000, or $12,000) over the net long-term capital loss (0) was $12,000. Of the excess of $12,000, 100 percent was contributed by the segregated asset accounts. Applying the provisions of section 801(g)(4)(B), T would allocate the entire $12,000 to its segregated asset accounts for such taxable year.

Example (2). The facts are the same as in example (1), except that for the taxable year 1962, T had (without regard to section 801(g)(4)(A)) realized short-term capital losses of $8,000 attributable to its general asset accounts and realized long-term capital gains of $1,000 and long-term capital losses of $5,000 attributable to its segregated asset accounts. For the taxable year 1962, the excess of the net short-term capital gain ($10,000 + $12,000 − $8,000 or $14,000) over the net long-term capital loss ($5,000 − $1,000, or $4,000) was $10,000. Of the excess of $10,000, the general asset accounts contributed 20 percent ($2,000 ($10,000 − $8,000) ÷ $10,000) and the segregated asset accounts contributed 80 percent ($8,000 ($12,000 − $4,000) ÷ $10,000). Applying the provisions of section 801(g)(4)(B), T would allocate $2,000 ($10,000 × 20 percent) to its general asset accounts and $8,000 ($10,000 × 80 percent) to its segregated asset accounts for such taxable year.

Example (3). W is a life insurance company which issues regular life insurance and annuity contracts and contracts with reserves based on either of two segregated asset accounts, Separate Account C or Separate Account D. For the taxable year 1962, W had (without regard to section 801(g)(4)(A)) realized short-term capital gains of $16,000 and long-term capital losses of $15,000 attributable to its general asset accounts, long-term capital gains of $12,000 and short-term capital losses of $6,000 attributable to Separate Account C and long-term capital gains of $7,000 and short-term capital losses of $5,000 attributable to Separate Account D. For the taxable year 1962, the excess of the net short-term capital gain ($16,000 − $6,000 − $5,000) over the net long-term capital loss (0) was $5,000. Of the $5,000 excess, 20 percent ($16,000 − $15,000) ÷ ($5,000) was contributed by the general asset accounts, leaving 80 percent as the amount contributed by the segregated asset accounts. Applying the provisions of section 801(g)(4)(B) W would allocate $1,000 (20 percent of $5,000) to the general asset accounts, leaving $4,000 (80 percent of $5,000) to be allocated among the segregated asset accounts, Separate Account C and Separate Account D. W would allocate $3,000 of the $4,000 to Separate Account C computed as follows:

$$\$3{,}000 = \frac{(\$4{,}000) \times (\$12{,}000 - \$6{,}000)}{(\$12{,}000 - \$6{,}000) + (\$7{,}000 - \$5{,}000)}$$

W would allocate $1,000 of the $4,000 to Separate Account D computed as follows:

$$\$1{,}000 = \frac{(\$4{,}000) \times (\$7{,}000 - \$5{,}000)}{(\$12{,}000 - \$6{,}000) + (\$7{,}000 - \$5{,}000)}$$

(e) Policy and other contract liability requirements. *(1)* For purposes of part I, section 801(g)(5)(A) provides that with respect to life insurance reserves based on segregated asset accounts (as defined in section 801(g)(1)(B) and paragraph (a)(2) of this section), the adjusted reserves rate and the current earnings rate for purposes of section 805(b), and the rate of interest assumed by the taxpayer for purposes of sections 805(c) and 809(a)(2), shall be a rate equal to the current earnings rate determined under section 805(b)(2) and paragraph (a)(2) of § 1.805-5 with respect to the items separately accounted for in accordance with section 801(g)(3), reduced by the percentage obtained by dividing—

(i) Any amount retained with respect to all of the reserves based on a segregated asset account by the life insurance company from gross investment income (as defined in section 804(b) and paragraph (a) of § 1.804-3) on segregated assets, to the extent such retained amount exceeds the deductions allowable under section 804(c) which are attributable to such reserves, by

(ii) The means of such reserves.

(2) For purposes of part I, section 801(g)(5)(B) provides that with respect to reserves based on segregated asset accounts other than life insurance reserves, there shall be included as interest paid within the meaning of section 805(e)(1) and paragraph (b)(1) of § 1.805-8, an amount equal to the product of the means of such reserves multiplied by the rate of interest assumed as defined in section 801(g)(5)(A) and subparagraph (1) of this paragraph.

(3) For purposes of this paragraph, any change in the rate of interest assumed by the taxpayer in calculating the reserve on a contract with reserves based on a segregated asset account for any taxable year beginning after December 31, 1961, which is attributable to an increase or decrease in the current earnings rate, shall not be treated as a change of basis in computing reserves for purposes of section 806(b) (relating to certain changes in reserves) or section 810(d)(1) (relating to adjustment for change in computing reserves).

(4) The provisions of section 801(g)(3) through (5) may be illustrated by the following example. For purposes of this example, it is assumed that all computations have been carried out to a sufficient number of decimal places to insure substantial accuracy and to eliminate any significant error in the resulting tax liability.

Example. The books of R, a life insurance company, discloses the following facts with respect to items of investment yield, deductions, assets, and reserves for the taxable year 1962:

(a) Excerpts from Company Financial Statements.

(1) Investment yield	Company regular account	Separate account A	Separate account B
Interest wholly tax-exempt	$100,000	$3,000	$1,000
Interest—other	10,000,000	8,000	15,000
Dividends received	200,000	25,000	27,000
Other items of investment yield	100,000	2,000	1,000
Gross investment income	10,400,000	38,000	44,000
Less deductions (Sec. 804(c))	1,000,000	4,000	4,400
Investment yield	9,400,000	34,000	39,600
(2) Assets and reserves:			
(i) Assets:			
Jan. 1, 1962	190,000,000		
Dec. 31, 1962	210,000,000	1,600,000	1,800,000
Mean	200,000,000	800,000	900,000
(ii) Life insurance reserves:			
Jan. 1, 1962	152,000,000		
Dec. 31, 1962	168,000,000	1,600,000	1,640,000
Mean	160,000,000	800,000	820,000
(iii) Reserves based on segregated asset accounts other than life insurance reserves:			
Jan. 1, 1962			
Dec. 31, 1962			120,000
Mean			60,000

(b) Additional facts. In addition to the facts assumed in (a) above, assume the following: The company retained with respect to reserves based upon segregated asset accounts a total of $4,720 from gross investment income on Separate Account A and $5,720 from gross investment income on Separate Account B. With respect to the Company Regular Account computed without regard to the items in either of the separate accounts, the policy and other contract liability requirement is $6,580,000 and the required interest is $5,640,000. There are no items of interest paid with respect to the separate accounts other than those computed under section 801(g)(5)(B). Based on these facts, the current earnings rate (sec. 805(b)); adjusted reserves rate (sec. 805(b)); and rate of interest assumed (secs. 805(c) and 809(a)(2)); and the policy and other contract liability requirements are determined for each of the Separate Accounts A and B (and the policy and other contract liability requirements for the Company Regular Account) as set forth in items (c) through (1) below.

(c) Separate Account A. The current earnings rate determined under section 805(b)(2) with respect to the items separately accounted for under Separate Account A, prior to the reduction provided for under section 801(g)(5)(A), is 4.25 percent (the investment yield, $34,000, divided by the mean of the assets, $800,000). The company retained with respect to such reserves from gross investment income on Separate Account A a total of $4,720. The company had deductions allowable under section 804(c) with respect to such account of $4,000. Accordingly, for purposes of section 801(g)(5)(A)(i), the amount retained by the company was $720 (the total amount retained of $4,720 less the deductions allowable under section 804(c) of $4,000). The reduction percentage for purposes of section 801(g)(5)(A) is 0.09 percent (the amount retained of $720 divided by the mean of the life insurance reserves of $800,000). Therefore, the adjusted reserves rate and the current earnings rate for purposes of section 805(b), and the rate of interest assumed for purposes of sections 805(c) and 809(a)(2) is equal to 4.16 percent (the current earnings rate of 4.25 percent less the reduction percentage of 0.09 percent). The policy and other contract liability requirements with respect to Separate Account A is determined as follows: For purposes of section 805(a)(1) and (2), the amount is $33,280 (the mean of the life insurance reserves, $800,000, multiplied by the current earnings rate, as determined under section 801(g)(5)(A), 4.16 percent). Thus, the policy and other contract liability requirement for Separate Account A is $33,280.

(d) Separate Account B. The current earnings rate determined under section 805(b)(2) with respect to the items separately accounted for under Separate Account B, prior to the reduction provided for under section 801(g)(5)(A), is 4.40 percent (the investment yield, $39,600 divided by the mean of the assets, $900,000). The company retained with respect to such reserves from gross investment income on Separate Account B a total of $5,720. The company had deductions allowable under section 804(c) with respect to such account of $4,400. Accordingly, for purposes of section 801(g)(5)(A)(i) the amount retained by the company was

$1,320 (the total amount retained of $5,720 less the deductions allowable under section 804(c) of $4,400). The reduction percentage for purposes of section 801(g)(5)(A) is 0.15 percent (the amount retained of $1,320 divided by the mean of the reserves based on Separate Account B of $880,000 ($820,000 plus $60,000)). Therefore, the adjusted reserves rate and the current earnings rate for purposes of section 805(b), and the rate of interest assumed for purposes of section 805(c) and 809(a)(2) is equal to 4.25 percent (the current earnings rate of 4.40 percent less the reduction percentage of 0.15 percent).

With respect to reserves based on segregated asset accounts other than life insurance reserves, Separate Account B had such reserves at December 31, 1962, of $120,000. The mean of such reserves was $60,000. The rate of interest assumed with respect to such reserves is 4.25 percent, as computed above. Accordingly, there shall be included as interest paid within the meaning of section 805(e)(1) the amount of $2,550 (the mean of such reserves, $60,000 multiplied by the rate of interest assumed of 4.25 percent).

The policy and other contract liability requirements with respect to Separate Account B is determined as follows:

(1) For purposes of section 805(a)(1) and (2), the amount is $34,850 (the mean of the life insurance reserves, $820,000, multiplied by the current earnings rate, as determined under section 801(g)(5)(A), 4.25 percent).

(2) For purposes of section 805(a)(3), the amount is $2,550 (the mean of the reserves based on Separate Account B other than life insurance reserves, $60,000, multiplied by the rate of interest assumed, as determined under section 801(g)(5) (A), 4.25 percent). It has been assumed that there was no other interest paid on Separate Account B within the meaning of section 805(e). If there was other interest paid with respect to Separate Account B that met the requirements of section 805(e), however, then such interest would be included under section 805(a)(3). Thus, the policy and other contract liability requirement for Separate Account B is $37,400 ($34,850 + $2,550).

(e) Company Regular Account. The policy and other contract liability requirement with respect to the Company Regular Account is $6,580,000 (this amount is determined by the company in the manner provided by section 805 (and the regulations thereunder) without regard to either Separate Account A or Separate Account B).

(f) Policyholders' share and company's share of investment yield—section 804. The policyholders' and company's share of investment yield and taxable investment income are computed as follows:

(1) Company Regular Account:	
Policyholders' share of investment yield.	70% ($6,580,000 ÷ $9,400,000).
Company's share of investment yield (100% less 70%).	30%.
(2) Separate Account A:	
Policyholders' share of investment yield.	97.8824% ($33,280 ÷ $34,000).
Company's share of investment yield (100% less 97.8824%).	2.1176%.
(3) Separate Account B:	
Policyholders' share of investment yield.	94.444% ($37,400 ÷ $39,600).
Company's share of investment yield (100% less 94.444%).	5.556%.

(g) The company's share of investment yield under section 804 is determined as follows:

Investment yield (from item (a)(1)	Company regular account (30 percent times each amount in item (a)(1))	Separate account A(2.1176 percent times each amount in item (a)(1))	Separate account B (5.556 percent times each amount in item (a)(1))
Interest wholly tax-exempt	$30,000	$63.53	$55.56
Interest—other	3,000,000	169.41	833.40
Dividends received	60,000	529.40	1,500.12
Other items of gross investment income	30,000	42.35	55.56
	3,120,000	804.69	2,444.64
Less deductions	300,000	84.70	244.46
Investment yield	2,820,000	719.99	2,200.18

(h) Taxable investment income. The company's taxable investment income (without regard to any excess of net long-term capital gain over net short-term capital loss) is determined as follows:

Life insurance company's share of investment yield ($2,820,000 + $719.99 + $2,200.18)		$2,822,920.17
Less:		
Company's share of interest wholly tax-exempt ($30,000 + $63.53 + $55.56)	$30,119.09	
85 percent of company's share of dividends received (but not to exceed 85% of taxable investment income computed without regard to this deduction) (85% × $62,029.52) ($60,000 + $529.40 + $1,500.12)	52,725.09	
Small business deduction (10% of investment yield, $9,473,600, not to exceed $25,000)	25,000.00	107,844.18
Taxable investment income		2,715,075.99

(i) Required interest—section 809(a)(2)—

(1) Separate Account A. The rate of interest assumed by the company, with respect to Separate Account A is 4.16 percent (see (c) above). The required interest for purposes of section 809(a)(2) is determined as follows:

Life insurance reserves: 4.16% (rate assumed) times $800,000 (mean of life insurance reserves)	$33,280.00

(2) Separate Account B. The rate of interest assumed by the company with respect to Separate Account B is 4.25 percent (see (d) above). The required interest for purposes of section 809(a)(2) is determined as follows:

(i) Life insurance reserves: 4.25% (rate assumed) times $820,000 (mean of life insurance reserves) $34,850.00
(ii) Other section 810(c) reserves: 4.25% (rate assumed) times $60,000 (mean of reserves other than life insurance reserves) .... $ 2,550.00
$37,400.00

(3) Company Regular Account. The required interest with respect to the Company Regular Account is $5,640,000 (this amount is assumed for purposes of this example, but it would be determined by the company in the manner provided by section 809 without regard to either Separate Account A or Separate Account B).

(j) Policyholders' share and company's share of investment yield—section 809. The policyholders' share and the company's share of investment yield for purposes of section 809 is determined as follows:

(1) Company Regular Account:
Policyholders' share of investment yield .... 60% ($5,640,000 ÷ $9,400,000)
Company's share of investment yield (100 percent – 60%) 40%
(2) Separate Account A:
Policyholders' share of investment yield .... 97.8824% ($33,280 ÷ $34,000).
Company's share of investment yield (100% – 97.8824 percent) 2.1176%
(3) Separate Account B: ....
Policyholders' share of investment yield .... 94.444% ($37,400 ÷ $39,600)
Company's share of investment yield (100% – 94.444%) 5.556%

(k) The company's share of investment yield under section 809 is determined as follows:

Investment yield (from item (a)(1))	Company regular account (40 percent times each amount in item (a)(1))	Separate account A (2.1176 percent times each amount in item (a)(1))	Separate account B (5.556 percent times each amount in item (a)(1))
Interest wholly tax-exempt	$40,000	$63.53	$55.56
Interest—other	4,000,000	169.41	833.40
Dividends received	80,000	529.40	1,500.12
Other items of gross investment income	40,000	42.35	55.56
	4,160,000	804.69	2,444.64
Less deductions	400,000	84.70	244.46
Investment yield	3,760,000	719.99	2,200.18

(l) Deductions under section 809(d)(8). For purposes of section 809(d)(8), the life insurance company's share of each of such items is determined as follows:

(1) Wholly tax-exempt interest ($40,000 + $63.53 + $55.56) $40,119.09
(2) Dividends received 85% × $82,029.52 ($80,000 + $529.40 + $1,500.12) (it is assumed for purposes of this example that this amount does not exceed 85% of the gain from operations as computed under sec. 809(d)(8)(B)) 69,725.09

(f) Increases and decreases in reserves. *(1)* Section 801(g)(6) provides that for purposes of section 810(a) and (b) (relating to adjustments for increases or decreases in certain reserves), the sum of the items described in section 810(c) and paragraph (b) of § 1.810-2 taken into account as of the close of the taxable year shall be adjusted—

(i) By subtracting therefrom the sum of any amounts added from time to time (for the taxable year) to the reserves separately accounted for in accordance with section 801(g)(3) and paragraph (c) of this section by reason of realized or unrealized appreciation in value of the assets held in relation thereto, and

(ii) By adding thereto the sum of any amounts subtracted from time to time (for the taxable year) from such reserves by reason of realized or unrealized depreciation in the value of such assets.

(2) The provisions of subparagraph (1) of this paragraph may be illustrated by the following example:

Example. Company M, a life insurance company issuing only contracts with reserves based on segregated asset accounts as defined in section 801(g)(1)(B) and paragraph (a)(2) of this section (other than contracts described in section 805(d)(1) (A), (B), (C), or (D)), increased its life insurance reserves held with respect to such contracts during the taxable year 1962 by $275,000. Of the total increase in the reserves, $100,000 was attributable to premium receipts, $50,000 to dividends and interest, $100,000 to unrealized appreciation in the value of the assets held in relation to such reserves, and $25,000 to realized capital gains on the sale of such assets. As of the close of the taxable year 1962, the reserves held by company M with respect to all such contracts amounted to $1,275,000. However, under section 801(g)(6) and this subparagraph, this amount must be reduced by the $100,000 unrealized asset value appreciation and the $25,000 of realized capital gains. Accordingly, for purposes of section 810(a) and (b), the amount of these reserves which is to be taken into account as of the close of the taxable year 1962 under section 810(c) is $1,150,000 ($1,275,000 less $125,000). However, for purposes of section 810(a) and (b), the amount of these reserves which is to be taken into account as of the beginning of the taxable year 1963 under section 810(c) is $1,275,000 (the amount as of the close of the taxable year 1962 before reduction of $125,000 for unrealized appreciation and realized capital gains).

(3) (i) Under section 801(g)(6), the deduction allowable for items described in section 809(d)(1) and (7) (relating to death benefits and assumption reinsurance, respectively) with respect to segregated asset accounts shall be reduced to the extent that the amount of such items is increased for the taxable year by appreciation (or shall be increased to the extent that the amount of such items is decreased for the taxable year by depreciation) not reflected in adjustments required to be made under subparagraph (1) of this paragraph.

(ii) The provisions of this subparagraph may be illustrated by the following example:

Example. On June 30, 1962, X, a life insurance company, reinsured a portion of its insurance contracts with reserves based on segregated asset accounts with Y, a life insurance company, under an agreement whereby Y agreed to assume and become solely liable under the contracts reinsured. The reserves on the contracts reinsured by X were $90,000, of which $10,000 was attributable to unrealized appreciation in the value of the assets held in relation to such reserves. However, no amounts had been added to the reserves by reason of the unrealized appreciation of $10,000 and consequently, the $10,000 was not reflected in adjustments to reserves under section 809(g)(6) or subparagraph (1) of this paragraph. Under the reinsurance agreement, X made a payment of $90,000 in cash to Y for assuming such contracts. Applying the provisions of section 809(d)(7), and assuming no other such reinsurance transactions by X during the taxable year, X would have an allowable deduction of $90,000 as a result of this payment on June 30, 1962. However, applying the provisions of section 801(g)(6) and this subparagraph, the actual deduction allowed would be $80,000 ($90,000 less $10,000). See section 806(a) and § 1.806-3 for the adjustments in reserves and assets to be made by X and Y as a result of this transaction. For the treatment by Y of this $90,000 payment, see section 809(c)(1) and paragraph (a)(1)(i) of § 1.809-4.

(g) Basis of assets held for certain pension plan contracts. Section 801(g)(7) provides that in the case of contracts described in section 805(d)(1)(A), (B), (C), (D) or (E) (relating to the definition of pension plan reserves), the basis of each asset in a segregated asset account shall (in addition to all other adjustments to basis) be (i) increased by the amount of any appreciation in value, and (ii) decreased by the amount of any depreciation in value; but only to the extent that such appreciation and depreciation are reflected in the increases and decreases in reserves, or other items described in section 801(g)(6), with respect to such contracts. Thus, there shall be no capital gains tax payable by a life insurance company on appreciation realized on assets in a segregated asset account to the extent such appreciation has been reflected in reserves, or other items described in section 801(g)(6), for contracts described in section 805(d)(1)(A), (B), (C), (D) or (E), based on segregated asset accounts.

(h) Additional separate computation. *(1) Assets and total insurance liabilities.* A life insurance company which issues contracts with reserves based on segregated asset accounts (as defined in section 801(g)(1)(B) and paragraph (a)(2) of this section) shall separately compute and report with its return the assets and total insurance liabilities which are properly attributable to all of such segregated asset accounts. Each foreign corporation carrying on a life insurance business which issues such contracts shall separately compute and report with its return assets held in the United States and total insurance liabilities on United States business which are properly attributable to all of such segregated asset accounts.

(2) Foreign life insurance companies. For adjustment under section 819 in the case of a foreign life insurance company which issues contracts based on segregated asset accounts under section 801(g), see § 1.819-2(b)(4).

T.D. 6886, 6/22/66, amend T.D. 6970, 8/23/68, T.D. 7501, 8/22/77.

---

§ 1.804-3 Gross investment income of a life insurance company.

Caution: The Treasury has not yet amended Reg § 1.804-3 to reflect changes made by P.L. 98-369.

(a) Gross investment income defined. For purposes of part I, subchapter L, chapter 1 of the Code, section 804(b) defines the term "gross investment income" of a life insurance company as the sum of the following:

(1) The gross amount of income from—

(i) Interest (including tax-exempt interest and partially tax-exempt interest), as described in § 1.61-7. Interest shall be adjusted for amortization of premium and accrual of discount in accordance with the rules prescribed in section 818(b) and the regulations thereunder.

(ii) Dividends, as described in § 1.61-9.

(iii) Rents and royalties, as described in § 1.61-8.

(iv) The entering into of any lease, mortgage, or other instrument or agreement from which the life insurance company may derive interest, rents, or royalties.

(v) The alteration or termination of any instrument or agreement described in subdivision (iv) of this subparagraph.

For example, gross investment income includes amounts received as commitment fees, as a bonus for the entering into of a lease, or as a penalty for the early payment of a mortgage.

(2) In the case of a taxable year beginning after December 31, 1958, the amount (if any) by which the net short-term capital gain (as defined in section 1222(5)) exceeds the net long-term capital loss (as defined in section 1222(8)), and

(3) The gross income from any trade or business (other than an insurance business) carried on by the life insurance company, or by a partnership of which the life insurance company is a partner.

(b) No double inclusion of income. In computing the gross income from any trade or business (other than an insurance business) carried on by the life insurance company, or by a partnership of which the life insurance company is a partner, any item described in section 804(b)(1) and paragraph (a)(1) of this section shall not be considered as gross income arising from the conduct of such trade or business or partnership, but shall be taken into account under section 804(b)(1) and paragraph (a)(1) of this section.

(c) Exclusion of net long-term capital gains. Any net long-term capital gains from the sale or exchange of a capital asset (or any gain considered to be from the sale or exchange of a capital asset under applicable law) shall be excluded from the gross investment income of a life insurance company. However, section 804(b)(2) and paragraph (a)(2) of this section provide that the amount (if any) by which the net short-term capital gain exceeds the net long-term capital loss shall be included in the gross investment income of a life insurance company.

T.D. 6513, 12/9/60.

---

§ 1.804-4 Investment yield of a life insurance company.

Caution: The Treasury has not yet amended Reg § 1.804-4 to reflect changes made by P.L. 98-369.

(a) Investment yield defined. Section 804(c) defines the term "investment yield" of a life insurance company for purposes of part I, subchapter L, chapter 1 of the Code. Investment yield means gross investment income (as defined in section 804(b) and paragraph (a) of § 1.804-3), less the deductions provided in section 804(c) and paragraph (b) of this section for investment expenses, real estate expenses, depreciation, depletion, and trade or business (other than an insurance business) expenses. However, such expenses are deductible only to the extent that they relate to investment income and the deduction of such expenses is not disallowed by any other provision of subtitle A of the Code. For example, investment expenses are not allowable unless they are ordinary and necessary expenses within the meaning of section 162, and under section 265, no deduction is allowable for interest on indebtedness incurred or continued to purchase or carry obligations the interest on which is wholly exempt from taxation under chapter 1 of the Code. A deduction shall not be permitted with respect to the same item more than once.

(b) Deductions from gross investment income. *(1) Investment expenses.* (i) Section 804(c)(1) provides for the deduction of investment expenses by a life insurance company in determining investment yield. "Investment expenses" are those expenses of the taxable year which are fairly chargeable against gross investment income. For example, investment expenses include salaries and expenses paid exclusively for work in looking after investments, and amounts expended for printing, stationery, postage, and stenographic work incident to the collection of interest. An itemized schedule of such expenses shall be attached to the return.

(ii) Any assignment of general expenses to the investment department of a life insurance company for which a deduction is claimed under section 804(c)(1) subjects the entire deduction for investment expenses to the limitation provided in that section and subdivision (iii) of this subparagraph. As used in section 804(c)(1), the term "general expenses" means any expense paid or incurred for the benefit of more than one department of the company rather than for the benefit of a particular department thereof. For example, if real estate taxes, depreciation, or other expenses attributable to office space owned by the company and utilized by it in connection with its investment function are assigned to investment expenses, such items shall be deductible as general expenses assigned to or included in investment expenses and as such shall be subject to the limitation of section 804(c)(1) and subdivision (iii) of this subparagraph. Similarly, if an expense, such as a salary, is attributable to more than one department, including the investment department, such expense may be properly allocated among these departments. If such expenses are allocated, the amount properly allocable to the investment department shall be deductible as general expenses assigned to or included in investment expenses and as such shall be subject to the limitation of section 804(c)(1) and subdivision (iii) of this subparagraph. If general expenses are in part assigned to or included in investment expenses, the maximum allowance (as determined under section 804(c)(1)) shall not be granted unless it is shown to the satisfaction of the district director that such allowance is justified by a reasonable assignment of actual expenses. The accounting procedure employed is not conclusive as to whether any assignment has in fact been made. Investment expenses do not include Federal income and excess profits taxes, if any. In cases where the investment expenses allowable as deductions under section 804(c)(1) exceed the limitation contained therein, see section 809(d)(9).

(iii) If any general expenses are in part assigned to or included in investment expenses, the total deduction under section 804(c)(1) shall not exceed the sum of—

(a) One-fourth of one percent of the mean of the assets (as defined in section 805(b)(4) and paragraph (a)(4) of § 1.805-5) held at the beginning and end of the taxable year,

(b) The amount of the mortgage service fees for the taxable year, plus

(c) Whichever of the following is the greater:

(1) One-fourth of the amount by which the investment yield (computed without any deduction for investment expenses allowed by section 804(c)(1)) exceeds 3¾ percent of the mean of the assets (as defined in section 805((b)(4)) held at the beginning and end of the taxable year, reduced by the amount of the mortgage service fees for the taxable year, or

(2) One-fourth of one percent of the mean of the value of mortgages held at the beginning and end of the taxable year for which there are no mortgage service fees for the taxable year. For purposes of the preceding sentence, the term "mortgages held" refers to mortgages, and other similar liens, on real property which are held by the company as security for "mortgage loans". For purposes of section 804(c)(1)(B) and (C)(i) and (b) and (c)(1) of this subdivision, the term "mortgage service fees" includes mortgage origination fees. Such mortgage origination fees shall be amortized in accordance with the rules prescribed in section 818(b) and the regulations thereunder.

(iv) The operation of the limitation contained in section 804(c)(1) and subdivision (iii) of this subparagraph may be illustrated by the following example:

Example. The books of S, a life insurance company, reflect the following items for the taxable year 1958:

Investment expenses (including general expenses assigned to or included in investment expenses)	$ 125,000
Mean of the assets held at the beginning and end of the taxable year	20,000,000
Mortgage service fees	25,000
Investment yield computed without regard to investment expenses	1,200,000
Mean of the value of mortgages held at the beginning and end of the taxable year for which there are no mortgage service fees	6,000,000

In order to determine the limitation on investment expenses, S would make up the following schedule:

1. Mean of the assets held at the beginning and end of the taxable year		$20,000,000
2. One-fourth of 1 percent of item 1 (¼ of 1% of $20,000,000)		50,000
3. Mortgage service fees		$ 25,000
4. The greater of (a) or (b):		
(a)(i) Investment yield computed without regard to investment expenses	$1,200,000	
(ii) Three and three-fourths percent of item 1 (3¾% × $20,000,000)	750,000	
(iii) Excess of (i) over (ii) ($1,200,000 minus $750,000)	450,000	
(iv) One-fourth of (iii) (¼ × $450,000)	112,500	
(v) Less: Mortgage service fees (item 3)	25,000	
(vi) Excess of (iv) over (v) ($112,500 minus $25,000)	$ 87,500	

(b) One-fourth of 1 percent of the mean of the value of mortgages held at the beginning and end of the taxable year for which there are no mortgage service fees (¼ of 1% × $6,000,000)....	15,000	
5. The greater of item 4(a) or (b)		$ 87,500
6. Limitation on investment expenses (items 2, 3, and 4(a))		162,500

As the investment expenses (including general expenses assigned to or included in investment expenses) of S for the taxable year 1958 ($125,000) do not exceed the limitation on such expenses ($162,500), S would be entitled to deduct the entire $125,000, under section 804(c)(1).

(2) Real estate expenses and taxes. The deduction for expenses and taxes under section 804(c)(2) includes taxes (as defined in section 164) and other expenses for the taxable year exclusively on or with respect to real estate owned by the company. For example, no deduction shall be allowed under section 804(c)(2) for amounts allowed as a deduction under section 164(e) (relating to taxes of shareholders paid by a corporation). No deduction shall be allowed under section 804(c)(2) for any amount paid out for new buildings, or for permanent improvements or betterments made to increase the value of any property. An itemized schedule of such taxes and expenses shall be attached to the return. See subparagraph (4) of this paragraph for limitation of such deduction.

(3) Depreciation. The deduction allowed for depreciation is, except as provided in section 804(c)(3) and subparagraph (4) of this paragraph, identical to that allowed other corporations by section 167. Such amount allowed as a deduction from gross investment income in determining investment yield is limited to depreciation sustained on the property used, and to the extent used, for the purpose of producing the income specified in section 804(b). An election with respect to any of the methods of depreciation provided in section 167 shall not be affected in any way by the enactment of the Life Insurance Company Income Tax Act of 1959 (73 Stat 112). However, in appropriate cases, the method of depreciation may be changed with the consent of the Commissioner. See section 167(e) and § 1.167(e)-1. See subparagraph (4) of this paragraph for limitation of such deduction. See section 809(d)(12) and the regulations thereunder for the treatment of depreciable property used in the operation of a life insurance business.

(4) Limitation on deductions allowable under section 804(c)(2) and (c)(3). Section 804(c)(3) provides that the amount allowable as a deduction for taxes, expenses, and depreciation on or with respect to any real estate owned and occupied for insurance purposes in whole or in part by a life insurance company shall be limited to an amount which bears the same ratio to such deduction (computed without regard to this limitation) as the rental value of the space not so occupied bears to the rental value of the entire property. For example, T, a life insurance company, owns a twenty-story downtown home office building. The rental value of each floor of the building is identical. T rents nine floors to various tenants, one floor is utilized by it in operating its investment department, and the remaining ten floors are occupied by it in carrying on its insurance business. Since floor space equivalent to eleven-twentieths, or 55 percent, of the rental value of the entire property is owned and occupied for insurance purposes by the company, the deductions allowable under section 804(c)(2) and (3) for taxes, depreciation, and other real estate expenses shall be limited to nine-twentieths, or 45 percent, of the taxes, depreciation, and other real estate expenses on account of the entire property. However, the portion of such allowable deductions attributable to the operation of the investment department (one-twentieth, or 5 percent) may be deductible as general expenses assigned to or included in investment expenses and as such shall be subject to the limitations of section 804(c)(1). Where a deduction is claimed as provided in this section, the parts of the property occupied and the parts not occupied by the company in carrying on its insurance business, together with the respective rental values thereof, must be shown in a schedule accompanying the return.

(5) Depletion. The deduction for depletion (and depreciation) provided in section 804(c)(4) is identical to that allowed other corporations by section 611. The amount allowed by section 611 in the case of a life insurance company is limited to depletion (and depreciation) sustained on the property used, and to the extent used, for the purpose of producing the income specified in section 804(b). See section 611 and § 1.611-5 for special rules relating to the depreciation of improvements in the case of mines, oil and gas wells, other natural deposits, and timber.

(6) Trade or business deductions. (i) Under section 804(c)(5), the deductions allowed by subtitle A of the Code (without regard to this part) which are attributable to any trade or business (other than an insurance business) carried on by the life insurance company, or by a partnership of which the life insurance company is a partner are, subject to the limitations in subdivisions (ii), (iii), and (iv) of this subparagraph, allowable as deductions from the gross investment income of a life insurance company in determining its investment yield. Such deductions are allowable, however, only to the extent that they are attributable to the production of income which is included in the life insurance company's gross investment income by reason of section 804(b)(3). However, since any interest, dividends, rents, and royalties received by any trade or business (other than an insurance business) carried on by the life insurance company, or by a partnership of which the life insurance company is a partner, is included in the life insurance company's gross investment income by reason of section 804(b)(1) and paragraph (b) of § 1.804-3, any expenses fairly chargeable against the production of such income may be deductible under section 804(c)(1), (2), (3), or (4). The allowable deductions may exceed the gross income from such business.

(ii) In computing the deductions under section 804(c)(5), there shall be excluded losses—

(a) From (or considered as from) sales or exchanges of capital assets,

(b) From sales or exchanges of property used in the trade or business (as defined in section 1231(b)), and

(c) From the compulsory or involuntary conversion (as a result of destruction, in whole or in part, theft or seizure, or an exercise of the power of requisition or condemnation or the threat or imminence thereof) of property used in the trade or business (as so defined).

(iii) Any item, to the extent attributable to the carrying on of the insurance business, shall not be taken into account. For example, if a life insurance company operates a radio station primarily to advertise its own insurance services, a portion of the expenses of the radio station shall not be allowed as a deduction. The portion disallowed shall be an amount which bears the same ratio to the total expenses of the station as the value of advertising furnished to the insurance company bears to the total value of services rendered by the station.

(iv) The deduction for net operating losses provided in section 172, and the special deductions for corporations provided in part VIII, subchapter B, chapter 1 of the Code, shall not be allowed.

T.D. 6513, 12/9/60.

---

§ 1.806-1 Adjustment for certain reserves.

(a) For taxable years beginning after December 31, 1953, but before January 1, 1955, and ending after August 16, 1954, a life insurance company writing contracts other than life insurance or annuity contracts (either separately or combined with noncancellable health and accident insurance contracts) must add to its life insurance company taxable income (as a factor in determining 1954 adjusted taxable income) an amount equal to eight times the amount of the adjustment for certain reserves provided in paragraph (b) of this section.

(b) The adjustment for certain reserves referred to in paragraph (a) of this section shall be an amount equal to 3¼ percent of the mean of the unearned premiums and unpaid losses at the beginning and end of the taxable year on such other contracts as are not included in life insurance reserves. If such unearned premiums, however, are less than 25 percent of the net premiums written during the taxable year on such other contracts, then the adjustment shall be 3¼ percent of 25 percent of the net premiums written during the taxable year on such other contracts plus 3¼ percent of the mean of the unpaid losses at the beginning and end of the taxable year on such other contracts. As used in this section, the term "unearned premiums" has the same meaning as in section 832(b)(4) and § 1.832-1.

T.D. 6201, 9/4/56.

---

§ 1.806-2 Taxable years affected.

> ***Caution:*** The Treasury has not yet amended Reg § 1.806-2 to reflect changes made by P.L. 98-369.

Section 1.806-1 is applicable only to taxable years beginning after December 31, 1953, and before January 1, 1955, and all references to sections of part I, subchapter L, chapter 1 of the Code are to the Internal Revenue Code of 1954, before amendments. Sections 1.806-3 and 1.806-4 are applicable only to taxable years beginning after December 31, 1957, and all references to sections of part I, subchapter L, chapter 1 of the Code are to the Internal Revenue Code of 1954, as amended by the Life Insurance Company Income Tax Act of 1959 (73 Stat. 112).

T.D. 6513, 12/9/60.

§ 1.806-3 Certain changes in reserves and assets.

> ***Caution:*** The Treasury has not yet amended Reg § 1.806-3 to reflect changes made by P.L. 98-396, P.L. 101-508.

(a) In general. For purposes of part I, subchapter L, chapter 1 of the Code, section 806(a) provides that if there is a change in life insurance reserves (as defined in section 801(b)), during the taxable year, which is attributable to the transfer between the taxpayer and another person of liabilities under contracts taken into account in computing such life insurance reserves, then the means of such reserves, and the mean of the assets, shall be appropriately adjusted to reflect the amounts involved in such transfer. For example, the adjustments required under section 806(a) are applicable to transfers in which one life insurance company purchases or acquires a part or all of the business of another life insurance company under an arrangement whereby the purchaser or transferee becomes solely liable on the contracts transferred. This provision shall apply in the case of assumption reinsurance but not in the case of indemnity reinsurance or reinsurance ceded. Thus, no adjustments shall be required under section 806(a) when, in the ordinary course of business, an indemnity reinsurance contract is entered into with another company (on a yearly renewable term basis, on a coinsurance basis, or otherwise) whereby there is a sharing of risks under one or more individual contracts. It will be necessary for each life insurance company participating in a transfer described in section 806(a) to make the adjustments required by such section. Such adjustments shall be made without regard to whether or not the transferor of the liabilities was the original insurer.

(b) Manner in which adjustments shall be made. *(1) Daily basis.* The means of the life insurance reserves, and the mean of the assets, shall be appropriately adjusted, on a daily basis, to reflect the amounts involved in a transfer described in section 806(a) and paragraph (a) of this section. The transferor and the transferee shall be treated as having held such life insurance reserves and assets for a fraction of the year in which the transfer occurs.

(2) Determination of period held. In determining the fraction which represents the fractional year that such reserves and assets were held, the numerator shall be the number of days during the taxable year which such reserves and assets were actually held, and the denominator shall be the number of days in the calendar year of the transfer. In computing the period held for purposes of the numerator, the day on which such reserves and assets are transferred is included by the transferor and excluded by the transferee.

(3) Adjustments to the means of life insurance reserves and assets not transferred. All life insurance reserves and assets transferred during the taxable year, within the meaning of section 806(a), shall be excluded from the beginning and end of the taxable year balances of the transferor and transferee, respectively. The amount of assets to be excluded from the beginning of the taxable year balance of the transferor shall be an amount equal to the value of such reserves at the beginning of the taxable year. The amount of assets to be excluded from the end of the taxable year balance of the transferee shall be an amount equal to the value of such reserves at the end of the taxable year. The means of the life insurance reserves and assets not so transferred shall be determined in the ordinary manner, that is, the arithmetic means. There shall be added to these means an amount to appropriately adjust them, on a daily basis, for the life insurance reserves and assets that were transferred during the taxable year. This adjustment shall be determined by multiplying (i) the mean of the transferred life insurance reserves (or assets, as the case may be) at the beginning of the taxable year (or, if acquired later, at the beginning of the period held as defined in subparagraph (2) of this paragraph) and the end of the period held as defined in subparagraph (2) of this paragraph (or at the end of the taxable year, if held at such time) by (ii) the fraction determined under subparagraph (2) of this paragraph.

(4) Examples. The application of this paragraph may be illustrated by the following examples:

Example (1). On March 14, 1958, the M Company, a life insurance company transferred to the N Company, a life insurance company, pursuant to an assumption reinsurance agreement, all of its life insurance reserves, and related assets, on one block of policies. The reserves (and assets) for this block were held by the M Company on January 1, 1958, and totaled $60,000; on March 14, the reserves (and assets) totaled $64,000. The M Company had life insurance reserves of $1,000,000 at the beginning of 1958 (including those subsequently transferred) and $1,040,000 at the end of 1958. The M Company had assets of $1,300,000 at the beginning of 1958 (including those subsequently transferred) and $1,380,000 at the end of 1958. The mean of M's life insurance reserves for the taxable year 1958 is computed as follows:

Reserves at 1-1-58	$1,000,000	
Exclude reserves (at beginning of year) on contracts transferred to N	60,000	
Recomputed amount at 1-1-58		$ 940,000
Reserves at 12-31-58		1,040,000
Sum		1,980,000
Mean		990,000
Adjustment for reserves transferred on 3-14-58:		
Reserves at 1-1-58 on contracts transferred to N	$ 60,000	
Reserves at 3-14-58 on such contracts	64,000	
Sum	124,000	
Mean	62,000	
Fraction taken into account	73/365	
Adjustment (73/365 × $62,000)		$ 12,400
Mean of M's life insurance reserves after section 806(a) adjustment		1,002,400

Example (2). Assuming the facts to be the same as in example (1), the mean of M's assets for the taxable year 1958 is computed as follows:

Assets at 1-1-58	$1,300,000	
Exclude assets (at beginning of year) on contracts transferred to N	60,000	
Recomputed amount at 1-1-58		$1,240,000
Assets at 12-31-58		1,380,000
Sum		2,620,000
Mean		1,310,000
Adjustments for assets transferred on 3-14-58:		
Assets at 1-1-58 on contracts transferred to N	$ 60,000	
Assets at 3-14-58 on such contracts	64,000	
Sum	124,000	
Mean	62,000	
Fraction taken into account	73/365	
Adjustment (73/365 × $62,000)		12,400
Mean of M's assets after section 806(a) adjustment		1,322,400

Example (3). Assume the facts are the same as in example (1). At the end of 1958, N Company had life insurance reserves (and assets) of $80,000 on the contracts transferred on March 14, 1958. The N Company had life insurance reserves of $6,000,000 at the beginning of 1958 and $6,400,000 at the end of 1958 (including those transferred). The N Company had assets of $6,800,000 at the beginning of 1958 and $7,300,000 at the end of 1958 (including those on the contracts transferred). The mean of N's life insurance reserves for the taxable year 1958 is computed as follows:

Reserves at 1-1-58		$ 6,000,000
Reserves at 12-31-58	$6,400,000	
Exclude reserves (at end of year) on contracts transferred from M	80,000	
Recomputed amount at 12-31-58		6,320,000
Sum		12,320,000
Mean		6,160,000
Adjustment for reserves transferred on 3-14-58:		
Reserves at 3-14-58 on contracts transferred from M	$ 64,000	
Reserves at 12-31-58 on such contracts	80,000	
Sum	144,000	
Mean	72,000	
Fraction taken into account	292/365	
Adjustment (292/365 × $72,000)		$ 57,600
Mean of N's life insurance reserves after section 806(a) adjustment		6,217,600

Example (4). Assuming the facts to be the same as an example (3), the mean of N's assets for the taxable year 1958 is computed as follows:

Assets at 1-1-58		$ 6,800,000
Assets at 12-31-58	$7,300,000	
Exclude assets (at end of year) on contracts transferred from M	80,000	
Recomputed amount at 12-31-58		7,220,000
Sum		14,020,000
Mean		7,010,000
Adjustments for assets transferred on 3-14-58:		
Assets at 3-14-58 on contracts transferred from M	$ 64,000	
Assets at 12-31-58 on such contracts	80,000	
Sum	144,000	
Mean	72,000	
Fraction taken into account	292/365	
Adjustment (292/365 × $72,000)		$ 57,600
Mean of N's assets after section 806(a) adjustment		7,067,600

Example (5). The facts are the same as in example (1), except that on October 19, 1958, company N transfers to company P, a life insurance company, all of the life insurance reserves, and related assets, on the block of policies it had received from company M on March 14, 1958. The reserves (and assets) for this block totaled $76,000 on October 19, 1958. The means of company M's life insurance reserves and assets, as computed in examples (1) and (2), respectively, would be unchanged by the transfer of October 19, 1958. Since company N did not own this block of policies at either the beginning or end of the taxable year, it would not have to recompute its beginning or end of the taxable year reserves or assets. Company N will, however, have to adjust (or increase) the mean of its life insurance reserves and assets on account of the policies it received from company M. This adjustment will be $42,000, which is determined by multiplying the means of the life insurance reserves (or assets) on these policies as of March 15, 1958, and October 19, 1958, $70,000 ($64,000 + $76,000 = $140,000 ÷ 2) by the fraction 219/365 (the numerator of 219 is determined by excluding the day of the transfer to N, March 14, 1958, and including the day of the transfer from N to P, October 19, 1958). Company P will have to recompute its end of the year life insurance reserves and assets (in the same manner as illustrated in examples (3) and (4)). Assuming the end of the year reserves (and assets) on this block of policies is $80,000, company P will have an adjustment under section 806(a) of $15,600, which is determined by multiplying the means of the reserves on these policies as of October 20, 1958, and December 31, 1958, $78,000 ($76,000 + $80,000 = $156,000 ÷ 2) by the fraction 73/365.

T.D. 6513, 12/9/60.

§ 1.806-4 Change of basis in computing reserves.

Caution: The Treasury has not yet amended Reg § 1.806-4 to reflect changes made by P.L. 98-369.

(a) In general. For purposes of subpart B, part I subchapter L, chapter 1 of the Code, section 806(b) provides that if the basis for determining the amount of any item referred to in section 810(c) (relating to items taken into account) as of the close of the taxable year differs from the basis for such determination as of the beginning of the taxable year, then in determining taxable investment income the amount of the item as of the close of the taxable year shall be the amount computed on the old basis, and the amount of the item as of the beginning of the next taxable year shall be the amount computed on the new basis. For purposes of the preceding sentence, an election under section 818(c) shall not be treated as a change in basis for determining the amount of an item referred to in section 810(c). A change of basis in computing any of the items referred to in section 810(c) is not a change of accounting method requiring the consent of the Secretary or his delegate under section 446(e).

(b) Illustration of change of basis in computing reserves. The application of section 806(b) and paragraph (a) of this section may be illustrated by the following examples:

Example (1). Assume that the life insurance reserves of Y, a life insurance company, at the beginning of the taxable year 1959 are $100 and that during such taxable year a portion of the reserves is strengthened (by reason of a change in mortality or interest assumptions, or otherwise), so that at the end of the taxable year 1959 the reserves (computed on the new basis) are $130 but computed on the old basis would be $120. Assume further that at the close of the next taxable year, 1960, the reserves (computed on the new basis) are $142. Under the provisions of section 806(b) and paragraph (a) of this section, the mean of such reserves for the taxable year of the reserve strengthening, namely 1959, is $110 (the mean of $100, the balance at the beginning of the taxable year 1959, and $120, the balance at the end of the taxable year 1959 computed on the old basis). The mean of such reserves for the next taxable year, 1960, is $136 (the mean of $130, the balance at the beginning of the taxable year 1960 computed on the new basis, and $142, the balance at the end of the taxable year 1960 computed on the new basis).

Example (2). The life insurance reserves of S, a life insurance company, computed with respect to contracts for which such reserves are determined on a recognized preliminary term basis amount to $50 on January 1, 1959, and $80 on December 31, 1959. For the taxable year 1959, S elects to revalue such reserves on a net level premium basis under section 818(c). Such reserves computed under section 818(c) amount to $60 on January 1, 1959, and $96 on December 31, 1959. Under the provisions of paragraph (a) of this section, the mean of such reserves for the taxable year 1959 is $78 (the mean of $60, the balance at the beginning of the taxable year 1959 computed under section 818(c), and $96, the balance at the end of the taxable year 1959 computed under section 818(c)).

T.D. 6513, 12/9/60.

§ 1.807-1 Mortality and morbidity tables.

(a) Tables to be used. If there are no commissioners standard tables applicable to an insurance contract when the contract is issued, then the mortality and morbidity tables set forth in this subsection are used to compute reserves under section 807(d)(2) for the contract.

Type of Contract	Table
1. Group term life insurance (active life reserves).	1960 Commissioners' Standard Group Mortality Table.
2. Group life insurance (active life reserves); accidental death benefits.	1959 Accidental Death Benefits Table.
3. Permanent and paid-up group life insurance (active life reserves).	Same table as are applicable to males for ordinary life insurance.
4a. Group life insurance disability income benefits (active life reserves).	The tables of period 2 disablement rates and the 1930 to 1950 termination rates of the 1952 Disability Study of the Society of Actuaries.
4b. Group life insurance disability income benefits (disabled life reserves).	The 1930 to 1950 termination rates of the 1952 Disability study of the Society of Actuaries.
5. Group life insurance; survivor income benefits insurance.	Same tables as are applicable to group annuities.
6. Group life insurance; extended death benefits for disabled lives.	1970 Intercompany Group life Disability Valuation Table.
7. Credit life insurance	1958 Commissioners' Extended Term Table.
8. Supplementary contracts involving life contingencies.	Same tables as are applicable to individual immediate annuities.
9. Noncancellable accident and health insurance (active life reserves); benefits issued before 1984.	Tables used for NAIC annual statement reserves as of December 31, 1983.

10a. Noncancellable accident and health insurance (active life reserves); group disability benefits issued after 1983 and individual disability benefits issued after 1983 and before 1989.	1964 Commissioners' Disability Tables.
10b. Noncancellable accident and health insurance (active life reserves); individual disability benefits issued after 1988.	1985 Commissioners' Individual Disability Table A or Commissioners' Individual Disability Table B.
11. Noncancellable accident and health insurance (active life reserves); accidental death benefits issued after 1983.	1959 Accidental Death Benefits Tables.
12. Noncancellable accident and health insurance (active life reserves); all benefits issued after 1983 other than disability and accidental death.	Tables used for NAIC annual statement reserves.
13a. Noncancellable accident and health insurance (claim reserves); group disability benefits for all years of issue and individual disability benefits for years before 1989.	1964 Commissioners' Disability Tables.
13b. Noncancellable accident and health insurance (claim reserves); individual disability benefits for years after 1988.	1985 Commissioners' Individual Disability Table A or Commissioners' Individual Disability Table B.
14. Noncancellable accident and health insurance (claim reserves); all benefits other than disability for all years of issue	Tables used for annual statement reserves.

(b) Adjustments. An appropriate adjustment may be made to the tables in paragraph (a) of this section to reflect risks (such as substandard risks) incurred under the contract which are not otherwise taken into account.

(c) Special rule where more than 1 table or option applicable. If, with respect to any category of risks, there are 2 or more tables (or options under 1 or more tables) in paragraph (a) of this section, the table (and option thereunder) which generally yields the lowest reserves shall be used to compute reserves under section 807(d)(2) for the contract.

(d) Effective date. This section is effective for taxable years beginning after December 31, 1983 except that the 1985 Commissioners' Individual Disability Tables A and B shall be treated (for purposes of section 807(d)(5)(B) and for purposes of determining the issue dates of contracts for which they shall be used) as if the tables were new prevailing commissioners' standard tables adopted by the twenty-sixth State on December 26, 1989.

T.D. 6201, 9/4/56, amend T.D. 8278, 12/26/89.

§ 1.807-2 Cross-reference.

For special rules regarding the treatment of modified guaranteed contracts (as defined in section 817A and § 1.817A-1(a)(1)), see § 1.817A-1.

T.D. 9058, 5/6/2003.

§ 1.809-1 Taxable years affected.

Caution: The Treasury has not yet amended Reg § 1.809-1 to reflect changes made by P.L. 108-218, P.L. 107-147, P.L. 98-369.

Sections 1.809 through 1.809-8, except as otherwise provided therein, are applicable only to taxable years beginning after December 31, 1957, and all reference to sections of part I, subchapter L, chapter 1 of the Code are to the Internal Revenue Code of 1954, as amended by the Life Insurance Company Income Tax Act of 1959 (73 Stat. 112), the Act of June 27, 1961 (75 Stat. 120), the Act of October 10, 1962 (76 Stat. 808); the Act of October 23, 1962 (76 Stat. 1134), and section 214(b)(4) of the Revenue Act of 1964 (78 Stat. 55).

T.D. 6535, 1/19/61, amend T.D. 6886, 6/22/66, T.D. 6992, 1/17/69.

§ 1.809-2 Exclusion of share of investment yield set aside for policyholders.

Caution: The Treasury has not yet amended Reg § 1.809-2 to reflect changes made by P.L. 108-218, P.L. 98-369.

(a) In general. Section 809 provides the rules for determining the gain or loss from operations of a life insurance company, which amount is necessary to determine life insurance company taxable income. In order to determine gain or loss from operations, a life insurance company must first determine the share of each and every item of its investment yield (as defined in section 804(c) and paragraph (a) of § 1.804-4) set aside for policyholders (as computed under section 809(a)(1) and paragraph (b) of this section), as this share is excluded from gain or loss from operations (as defined in section 809(b)(1) and (2) and paragraphs (a) and (b) of § 1.809-3, respectively). The life insurance company shall then add its share of each and every item of its investment yield to the sum of the items comprising gross amount (as described in section 809(c) and paragraph (a) of § 1.809-4). In addition, the life insurance company shall, for taxable years beginning after December 31, 1961, add the amount (if any) by which its net long-term capital gain exceeds its net short-term loss. From the sum so computed (which includes the capital gains item only for taxable years beginning after December 31, 1961) there shall then be subtracted the deductions provided in section 809(d) and paragraph (a) of § 1.809-5. The amount thus obtained is the gain or loss from operations for the taxable year.

(b) Computation of share of investment yield set aside for policyholders. Section 809(a)(1) provides that the share of each and every item of investment yield (including tax-exempt interest, partially tax-exempt interest, and dividends received) of any life insurance company set aside for policyholders shall not be included in gain or loss from operations. For this purpose, the percentage used in determining the share of each of these items comprising the investment yield set aside for policyholders shall be determined by dividing the required interest (as defined in section 809(a)(2) and paragraph (d) of this section) by the investment yield (as defined in section 804(c) and paragraph (a) of § 1.804-4). The percentage thus obtained is then applied to each and every item of the investment yield so that the share of each and every item of investment yield set aside for policyholders shall be excluded from gain or loss from operations. However, if in any case the required interest exceeds the investment yield, then the share of any item set aside for policyholders shall be 100 percent.

(c) Computation of life insurance company's share of investment yield. For purposes of subpart C, part I, subchapter L, chapter 1 of the Code, section 809(b)(3) provides that the percentage used in determining the life insurance company's share of each and every item of investment yield (including tax-exempt interest, partially tax-exempt interest, and dividends received) shall be obtained by subtracting the percentage obtained under paragraph (b) of this section from 100 percent. For example, if the policyholders' percentage (as determined under section 809(a)(1) and paragraph (b) of this section) is 72.38 percent, then the life insurance company's share is 27.62 percent (100 percent minus 72.38 percent). In such a case, if the amount of a particular item is $200, then the life insurance company's share of such item included in determining gain or loss from operations is $55.24 ($200 multiplied by 27.62 percent) and the share of such item set aside for policyholders (which is excluded from gain or loss from operations) is $144.76 ($200 multiplied by 72.38 percent). For purposes of determining gain or loss from operations, the life insurance company's share of each and every item of investment yield (including tax-exempt interest, partially tax-exempt interest, and dividends received) shall be added to the sum of the items comprising gross amount (as described in section 809(c) and paragraph (a) of § 1.809-4).

(d) Required interest defined. *(1)* For purposes of part I, section 809(a)(2) defines the term "required interest" for any taxable year as the sum of the products obtained by multiplying (i) each rate of interest required, or assumed by the taxpayer, in calculating the reserves described in section 810(c), by (ii) the means of the amount of such reserves computed at that rate at the beginning and end of the taxable year. In the case of the reserves described in section 810(c)(1), such rate of interest shall be the same as that used by the taxpayer for purposes of paragraph (b) of § 1.801-5 (relating to the definition of reserves required by law) with respect to such reserves. In the case of the reserves described in section 810(c)(2) through (5), such rate of interest shall be the same as that actually paid, credited, or accrued by the taxpayer with respect to such reserves. Thus, the required interest for any taxable year includes the elements of interest paid (as defined in section 805(e)) with respect to the reserves described in section 810(c).

(2) For purposes of computing required interest under section 809(a)(2) and subparagraph (1) of this paragraph, the amount of life insurance reserves taken into account shall be adjusted first as required by section 818(c) (relating to an election with respect to life insurance reserves computed on a preliminary term basis) and then as required by section 806(a) (relating to adjustments for certain changes in reserves and assets) before applying the rate of interest required, or assumed by the taxpayer, thereto. However, in the case of the adjustments required by section 810(d) as a result of a change in the basis of computing reserves, the adjustments to any of the reserves described in section 810(c) shall be taken into account in accordance with the rules prescribed in section 810(d) and § 1.810-3.

T.D. 6535, 1/19/61, amend T.D. 6886, 6/22/66.

§ 1.809-3 Gain and loss from operations defined.

Caution: The Treasury has not yet amended Reg § 1.809-3 to reflect changes made by P.L. 108-218, P.L. 98-369, P.L. 101-508.

(a) Gain from operations. For purposes of part I, subchapter L, chapter 1 of the Code, section 809(b)(1) defines the term "gain from operations" as the excess of the sum of (1) the life insurance company's share of each and every item of investment yield (including tax-exempt interest, partially tax-exempt interest, and dividends received), (2) the items of gross amount taken into account under section 809(c) and paragraph (a) of § 1.809-4, and (3) for taxable years beginning after December 31, 1961, the amount (if any) by which the net long-term capital gain exceeds the net short-term capital loss, over the sum of the deductions provided by section 809(d) and § 1.809-5.

(b) Loss from operations. For purposes of part I, section 809(b)(2) defines the term "loss from operations" as the excess of the sum of the deductions provided by section 809(d) and § 1.809-5 over the sum of (1) the life insurance company's share of each and every item of investment yield (including tax-exempt interest, partially tax-exempt interest, and dividends received), (2) the items of gross amount taken into account under section 809(c) and paragraph (a) of § 1.809-4, and (3) for taxable years beginning after December 31, 1961, the amount (if any) by which the net long-term capital gain exceeds the net short-term capital loss.

(c) Illustration of principles. The provisions of section 809(b)(1) through (3) and paragraphs (a) and (b) of this section may be illustrated by the following example:

Example. For the taxable year 1958, T, a life insurance company, had investment yield of $900,000, including $150,000 of dividends received from domestic corporations subject to taxation under chapter 1 of the Code, $10,000 of wholly tax-exempt interest, and $78,000 of partially tax-exempt interest. T also had items of gross amount under section 809(c) in the amount of $12,000,000 and deductions under section 809(d) of $6,963,500 (exclusive of any deductions for wholly tax-exempt interest, partially tax-exempt interest, and dividends received). For such taxable year, the share of each and every item of investment yield set aside for policyholders was 80 percent and the company's share of each and every item of investment yield was 20 percent. Based upon these figures, T had a gain from operations of $5,180,000 for the taxable year 1958, computed as follows:

	Col. 1	Col.2 (80% × Col. 1) exclusion of policyholder's share	Col.3 (20% × Col. 1) company's share
Interest wholly tax-exempt	$10,000	$8,000	$2,000
Interest partially tax-exempt	78,000	62,400	15,600
Dividends received	150,000	120,000	30,000
Other items of investment yield	662,000	529,600	132,000
Investment yield	900,000	720,000	180,000

Gross amount (sum of items under sec. 809(c))		12,000,000
Total		12,180,000
Less:		
Deductions under sec. 809(d)(8):		
Company's share of interest wholly tax-exempt	$ 2,000	
30/52 of company's share of interest partially tax-exempt (30/52 × $15,600)	9,000	
85% of company's share of dividends received (but not to exceed 85% of gain from operations as computed under sec. 809(d)(8)(B)) (85% × $30,000)	25,500	
All other deductions under sec. 809(d)	6,963,500	
		7,000,000
Gain from operations		5,180,000

(d) Exception. *(1)* In accordance with section 809(b)(4), if it is established in any case to the satisfaction of the Commissioner, or by a determination of The Tax Court of the United States, or of any other court of competent jurisdiction, which has become final, that the application of the definition of gain from operations contained in section 809(b)(1) results in the imposition of tax on—

(i) Any interest which under section 103 is excluded from gross income,

(ii) Any amount of interest which under section 242 (as modified by section 804(a)(3)) is allowable as a deduction, or

(iii) Any amount of dividends received which under sections 243, 244, and 245 (as modified by section 809(d)(8)(B)) is allowable as a deduction, adjustment shall be made to the extent necessary to prevent such imposition.

(2) For the date upon which a decision by the Tax Court becomes final, see section 7481. For the date upon which a judgment of any other court becomes final, see paragraph (c) of § 1.313(a)-1.

T.D. 6535, 1/19/61, amend T.D. 6886, 6/22/66.

§ 1.809-4 Gross amount.

Caution: The Treasury has not yet amended Reg § 1.809-4 to reflect changes made by P.L. 108-218, P.L. 98-369, P.L. 101-508.

(a) Items taken into account. For purposes of determining gain or loss from operations under section 809(b)(1) and (2), respectively, section 809(c) specifies three categories of items which shall be taken into account. Such items are in addition to the life insurance company's share of the investment yield (as determined under section 809(a)(1) and paragraph (c) of § 1.809-2), and the amount (if any) by which the net long-term capital gain exceeds the net short-term capital loss (such capital gains item is included in determining gain or loss from operations only for taxable years beginning after December 31, 1961). The additional three categories of items taken into account are:

(1) Premiums. (i) The gross amount of all premiums and other consideration on insurance and annuity contracts (including contracts supplementary thereto); less return premiums and premiums and other consideration arising out of reinsurance ceded. The term "gross amount of all premiums" means the premiums and other consideration provided in the insurance or annuity contract. Thus, the amount to be taken into account shall be the total of the premiums and other consideration provided in the insurance or annuity contract. Thus, the amount to be taken into account shall be the total of the premiums and other consideration provided in the insurance or annuity contract without any deduction for commissions, return premiums, reinsurance, dividends to policyholders, dividends left on deposit with the company, discounts on premiums paid in advance, interest applied in reduction of premiums (whether or not required to be credited in reduction of premiums under the terms of the contract), or any other item of similar nature. Such term includes advance premiums, premiums deferred and uncollected and premiums due and unpaid, deposits, fees, assessments and consideration in respect of assuming liabilities under contracts not issued by the taxpayer (such as a payment or transfer of property in an assumption reinsurance transaction as defined in paragraph (a)(7)(ii) of § 1.809-5). The term also includes amounts a life insurance company charges itself representing premiums with respect to liability for insurance and annuity benefits for its employees (including full-time life insurance salesmen within the meaning of section 7701(a)(20)).

(ii) The term "return premiums" means amounts returned or credited which are fixed by contract and do not depend on the experience of the company or the discretion of the management. Thus, such term includes amounts refunded due to policy cancellations or erroneously computed premiums. Furthermore, amounts of premiums or other consideration returned to another life insurance company in respect of reinsurance ceded shall be included in return premiums. For the treatment of amounts which do not meet the requirements of return premiums, see section 811 (relating to dividends to policyholders).

(iii) For purposes of section 809(c)(1) and this subparagraph, the term "reinsurance ceded" means an arrangement whereby the taxpayer (the reinsured) remains solely liable to the policyholder, whether all or only a portion of the risk has been transferred to the reinsurer. Such term includes indemnity reinsurance transactions but does not include assumption reinsurance transactions. See paragraph (a)(7)(ii) of § 1.809-5 for the definition of assumption reinsurance.

(2) Decreases in certain reserves. Each net decrease in reserves which is required by section 810(a) and (d)(1) or 811(b)(2) to be taken into account for the taxable year as a net decrease for purposes of section 809(c)(2).

(3) Other amounts. All amounts, not included in computing investment yield and not otherwise taken into account under section 809(c)(1) or (2), shall be taken into account under section 809(c)(3) to the extent that such amounts are includible in gross income under subtitle A of the Code. See section 61 (relating to gross income defined) and the regulations thereunder.

(b) Treatment of net long-term capital gains. For taxable years beginning before January 1, 1962, any net long-term capital gains (as defined in section 1222(7)) from the sale or exchange of a capital asset (or any gain considered to be from the sale or exchange of a capital asset under applicable law) shall be excluded from the determination of gain or loss from operations of a life insurance company. On the other hand, with respect to taxable years beginning after December 31, 1961, the amount (if any) by which the net long-term capital gain exceeds the net short-term capital loss (as defined in section 1222(6)) shall be taken into account in determining gain or loss from operations under section 809.

However, for any taxable year beginning after December 31, 1958, the excess of net short-term capital gain (as defined in section 1222(5)) over net long-term capital loss (as defined in section 1222(8)) is included in computing investment yield (as defined in section 804(c)) and, to that extent, is taken into account in determining gain or loss from operations under section 809.

T.D. 6535, 1/19/61, amend T.D. 6610, 8/30/62, T.D. 6686, 6/22/66.

§ 1.809-5 Deductions.

Caution: The Treasury has not yet amended Reg § 1.809-5 to reflect changes made by P.L. 108-218, P.L. 98-369, P.L. 101-508.

(a) Deductions allowed. Section 809(d) provides the following deductions for purposes of determining gain or loss from operations under section 809(b)(1) and (2), respectively:

(1) Death benefits, etc. All claims and benefits accrued (less reinsurance recoverable), and all losses incurred (whether or not ascertained), during the taxable year on insurance and annuity contracts (including contracts supplementary thereto). The term "all claims and benefits accrued" includes, for example, matured endowments and amounts allowed on surrender. The term "losses incurred (whether or not ascertained)" includes a reasonable estimate of the amount of the losses (based upon the facts in each case and the company's experience with similar cases) incurred but not reported by the end of the taxable year as well as losses reported but where the amount thereof cannot be ascertained by the end of the taxable year.

(2) Increases in certain reserves. The net increase in reserves which is required by section 810(b) and (d)(1) to be taken into account for the taxable year as a net increase for purposes of section 809(d)(2).

(3) Dividends to policyholders. The deduction for dividends to policyholders as determined under section 811(b) and § 1.811-2. Except as provided in section 809(d)(3) and this subparagraph, no amount shall be allowed as a deduction in respect of dividends to policyholders under section 809(d). See section 809(f) and § 1.809-7 for limitation of such deduction.

(4) Operations loss deduction. The operations loss deduction as determined under section 812.

(5) Certain nonparticipating contracts. (i) An amount equal to the greater of:

(a) 10 percent of the increase for the taxable year in certain life insurance reserves for nonparticipating contracts (other than group contracts); or

(b) 3 percent of the premiums for the taxable year attributable to nonparticipating contracts (other than group contracts) which are issued or renewed for periods of 5 years or more.

(ii) For purposes of section 809(d)(5) and this subparagraph, the term "nonparticipating contracts" means those contracts which during the taxable year contain no right to participate in the divisible surplus of the company. For example, if at any time during the taxable year for which the deduction allowed under section 809(d)(5) and this subparagraph is claimed such contracts have rights to dividends or similar distributions (as defined in section 811(a) and paragraph (a) of § 1.811-2), such contracts shall no longer be deemed nonparticipating contracts and, therefore, no deduction shall be allowed. Thus, if a class of contracts having no right to participate in the divisible surplus of the company is in force for nine years and on March 10, 1958, it is announced that such contracts shall be accorded dividend rights as of August 1, 1958, no deduction shall be allowed under section 809(d)(5) and this subparagraph for the taxable year 1958 or any succeeding taxable year, whether or not dividends are actually paid on such contracts. However, if the announcement of March 10, 1958, states that such contracts shall be accorded dividend rights as of January 1, 1959, a deduction under section 809(d)(5) and this subparagraph shall be allowed for the taxable year 1958 but not for any succeeding taxable year.

(iii) For purposes of section 809(d)(5) and this subparagraph, the term "reserves for nonparticipating contracts" means such part of the life insurance reserves (as defined in section 801(b) and § 1.801-4), other than that portion of such reserves which is allocable to annuity features, as relates to nonparticipating contracts (as defined in subdivision (ii) of this subparagraph). The amount of life insurance reserves taken into account shall be adjusted first as required by section 818(c) (relating to an election with respect to life insurance reserves computed on a preliminary term basis) and then as required by section 806(a) (relating to adjustments for certain changes in reserves and assets). In the case of the adjustments required by section 810(d) (relating to adjustment for change in computing reserves), the increase in life insurance reserves attributable to reserve strengthening shall be taken into account in accordance with the rules prescribed in section 810(d) and § 1.810-3.

(iv) For purposes of section 809(d)(5) and this subparagraph, the term "premiums" means the net amount of the premiums and other consideration attributable to nonparticipating contracts (as defined in subdivision (ii) of this subparagraph) which are taken into account under section 809(c)(1). For this purpose, premiums include only such amounts attributable to such contracts which are issued or renewed for periods of 5 years or more, but does not include that portion of the premiums which is allocable to annuity features. No portion of a premium shall be deemed allocable to annuity features solely because a contract, such as an endowment contract, provides that at maturity the insured shall have an option to take an annuity. The determination of whether a contract meets the 5-year requirement shall be made as of the date the contract is issued, or as of the date it is renewed, whichever is applicable. Thus, a 20-year nonparticipating endowment policy shall qualify for the deduction under section 809(d)(5), even though the insured subsequently dies at the end of the second year, since the policy is issued for a period of 5 years or more. However, a 1-year renewable term contract shall not qualify, since as of the date it is issued (or of any renewal date) it is not issued (or renewed) for a period of 5 years or more. In like manner, a policy originally issued for a 3-year period and subsequently renewed for an additional 3-year period shall not qualify. However, if this policy is renewed for a period of 5 years or more, the policy shall qualify for the deduction under section 809(d)(5) from the date it is renewed.

(v) The provisions of section 809(d)(5) and this subparagraph may be illustrated by the following example:

Example. Assume the following facts with respect to X, a life insurance company, for the taxable year 1958:

Life insurance reserves on nonparticipating contracts without annuity features (other than group contracts) at 1-1-58	$150,000
Life insurance reserves on nonparticipating contracts without annuity features (other than group contracts) at 12-31-58	225,000
Annuity reserves on nonparticipating contracts (other than group contracts) at 1-1-58	48,000
Annuity reserves on nonparticipating contracts (other than group contracts) at 12-31-58	57,000
Premiums on nonparticipating contracts without annuity features (other than group contracts) issued or renewed for 5 years or more	85,000
Premiums on nonparticipating contracts allocable to annuity features (other than group contracts) issued or renewed for 5 years or more	14,000
Return premiums on nonparticipating contracts without annuity features (other than group contracts)	5,000

In order to determine the deduction under section 809(d)(5) (without regard to the limitation of section 809(f)), X would make up the following schedule:

(1) Life insurance reserves on nonparticipating contracts without annuity features (other than group contracts) at 12-31-58	$225,000	
(2) Life insurance reserves on nonparticipating contracts without annuity features (other than group contracts) at 1-1-58	150,000	
(3) Excess of item (1) over item (2) ($225,000 minus $150,000)	75,000	
(4) 10 percent of item (3) (10% × $75,000)		$7,500
(5) Net premiums on nonparticipating contracts without annuity features issued or renewed for 5 years or more (other than group contracts) (gross premiums on such contracts ($85,000) minus return premiums ($5,000) on such contracts)	80,000	
(6) 3 percent of item (5) (3% × $80,000)		2,400
(7) The greater of item (4) or item (6)		7,500
(8) Tentative deduction under sec. 809(d)(5) (computed without regard to the limitation of sec. 809(f))		7,500

(vi) See section 809(f) and § 1.809-7 for limitation of the deduction provided by this subparagraph.

(6) Certain accident and health insurance and group life insurance. (i) For taxable years beginning before January 1, 1963, an amount equal to two percent of the premiums for the taxable year attributable to group life insurance contracts, group accident and health insurance contracts, or group accident and health insurance contracts with a life feature. For taxable years beginning after December 31, 1962, the deduction shall be an amount equal to two percent of the premiums for the taxable year attributable to group life insurance contracts, accident and health insurance contracts (other than those to which section 809(d)(5) applies), or accident and health insurance contracts with a life feature (other than those to which section 809(d)(5) applies). For purposes of section 809(d)(6) and this subparagraph, the term "premiums" means the net amount of the premiums and other consideration attributable to such contracts taken into account under section 809(c)(1). The deduction allowed by section 809(d)(6) and this subparagraph for the taxable year and all preceding taxable years shall not exceed 50 percent of the net amount of the premiums attributable to such contracts for the taxable year. For example, assume that premiums attributable to group life insurance and group accident and health insurance contracts are $103,000 for the taxable year 1962. Assume further that there are $3,000 of return premiums attributable to such contracts for the taxable year. Under the provisions of section 809(d)(6) and this subparagraph, a deduction (determined without regard to section 809(f) of $2,000 (2 percent of $100,000 ($103,000 – $3,000)) is allowed. Assuming that the company continues to receive net premiums of $100,000 attributable to such contracts for 15 years, the cumulative amount of these deductions is $30,000 ($2,000 for 15 years). If, in the sixteenth year, net premiums attributable to such contracts amount to $60,000, no deduction shall be allowed under section 809(d)(6) and this subparagraph since the cumulative amount of these deductions ($30,000) equals 50 percent of the current year's premiums ($60,000) from such contracts.

(ii) In computing the deduction under section 809(d)(6), the determination as to when the 50 percent limitation on such deduction has been reached shall be based upon the amount allowed as a deduction for the taxable year and all preceding taxable years after the application of the limitation provided in section 809(f) and § 1.809-7. Thus, if in the example set forth in paragraph (c) of § 1.809-7 the application of the limitation provided by section 809(f) limited the deduction allowed for the taxable year under section 809(d)(6) to $3,250,000, then for purposes of determining the 50 percent limitation on such deduction, only $3,250,000 (the amount allowed) shall be taken into account.

(iii) For purposes of determining whether the 50 percent limitation applies to any taxable year, the deduction provided by section 809(d)(6) for all preceding taxable years shall be taken into account, irrespective of whether or not the life insurance company claimed a deduction for these amounts for such preceding taxable years.

(iv) See section 809(f) and § 1.809-7 for limitation of the deduction provided by this subparagraph.

(7) Assumption by another person of liabilities under insurance, etc., contracts. (i) The consideration (other than consideration arising out of reinsurance ceded as defined in paragraph (a)(1)(iii) of § 1.809-4) in respect of the assumption by another person of liabilities under insurance and annuity contracts (including contracts supplementary thereto) of the taxpayer.

(ii) For purposes of section 809(d)(7) and this subparagraph, the term "assumption reinsurance" means an arrangement whereby another person (the reinsurer) becomes solely liable to the policyholders on the contracts transferred by the taxpayer. Such term does not include indemnity reinsurance or reinsurance ceded (as defined in paragraph (a)(1)(iii) of § 1.809-4).

(iii) The provisions of section 809(d)(7) and this subparagraph may be illustrated by the following example:

Example. During the taxable year 1958, T, a life insurance company, transferred a block of insurance policies and made a payment of $50,000 to R, a life insurance company, under an arrangement whereby R became solely liable to the policyholders on the policies transferred by T. Under the provisions of section 809(d)(7) and this subparagraph, T is allowed a deduction of $50,000 for the taxable year 1958. For the treatment by R of this $50,000 payment, see section

809(c)(1) and paragraph (a)(1)(i) of § 1.809-4. See section 806(a) and § 1.806-3 for the adjustments in reserves and assets to be made by T and R as a result of this transaction.

(8) Tax-exempt interest, dividends, etc. (i) Each of the following items:

(a) The life insurance company's share of interest which under section 103 is excluded from gross income;

(b) The deduction for partially tax-exempt interest provided by section 242 (as modified by section 804(a)(3) and paragraph (d)(2)(i) of § 1.804-2) computed with respect to the life insurance company's share of such interest; and

(c) The deductions for dividends received provided by sections 243, 244, and 245 (as modified by section 809(d)(8)(B) and subdivision (ii) of this subparagraph) computed with respect to the life insurance company's share of the dividends received.

(ii) The modification contained in section 809(d)(8)(B) provides the method for applying section 246(b) (relating to limitation on aggregate amount of deductions for dividends received) for purposes of section 809(d)(8)(A)(iii) and subdivision (i)(c) of this subparagraph. Under this method, the sum of the deductions allowed by sections 243(a)(1) (relating to dividends received by corporations), 244(a) (relating to dividends received on certain preferred stock), and 245 (relating to dividends received from certain foreign corporations) shall be limited to 85 percent of the gain from operations computed without regard to:

(a) The deductions provided by section 809(d)(3), (5), and (6);

(b) The operations loss deductions provided by section 812; and

(c) The deductions allowed by sections 243(a)(1), 244(a), and 245.

If a life insurance company has a loss from operations (as determined under sec. 812) for the taxable year, the limitation provided in section 809(d)(8)(B) and this subdivision shall not be applicable for such taxable year. In that event, the deductions provided by sections 243(a)(1), 244(a), and 245 shall be allowable for all tax purposes to the life insurance company for such taxable year without regard to such limitation. If the life insurance company does not have a loss from operations for the taxable year, however, the limitation shall be applicable for all tax purposes for such taxable year. In determining whether a life insurance company has a loss from operations for the taxable year under section 812, the deductions allowed by sections 243(a)(1), 244(a), and 245 shall be computed without regard to the limitation provided in section 809(d)(8)(B) and this subdivision.

(9) Investment expenses, etc. (i) The amount of investment expenses to the extent not allowed as a deduction under section 804(c)(1) in computing investment yield. For example, if a deduction in the amount of $100,000 is claimed for investment expenses, which amount includes general expenses assigned to or included in investment expenses, and due to the operation of the limitation provided by section 804(c)(1) only $85,000 is allowed, then the excess ($15,000) shall be allowed as a deduction under section 809(d)(9) and this subparagraph.

(ii) The amount (if any) by which the sum of the deductions allowable under section 804(c) exceeds the gross investment income. For example, if gross investment income under section 804(b) equals $400,000, and the sum of the deductions allowable under section 804(c) equals $425,000, then the excess ($25,000) shall be allowed as a deduction under section 809(d)(9) and this subparagraph.

(iii) In determining the amount of the deductions allowed under subdivisions (i) and (ii) of this subparagraph, a life insurance company shall first take such deductions to the full extent allowable under section 804(c)(1), and any amount which is allowed as a deduction under section 804(c) shall not again be allowed as a deduction under section 809(d)(9).

(10) Small business deduction. The small business deduction as determined under section 804(a)(4).

(11) Certain mutualization distributions. The amount of distributions to shareholders actually made by the life insurance company in 1958, 1959, 1960, and 1961 in acquisition of stock pursuant to a plan of mutualization adopted by the company before January 1, 1958. If such deduction is claimed, there must be attached to the return of the company claiming such deduction a certified copy of the plan of mutualization and proof that such plan was adopted prior to January 1, 1958. See section 809(g) and § 1.809-8 for limitation of such deduction.

(12) Other deductions. Except as modified by section 809(e) and § 1.809-6, all other deductions allowed under subtitle A of the Code for purposes of computing taxable income to the extent not allowed as a deduction in computing investment yield. For example, a life insurance company shall be allowed a deduction under section 809(d)(12) and this subparagraph for amounts representing premiums charged itself with respect to liability for insurance and annuity benefits for its employees (including full-time life insurance salesmen within the meaning of section 7701(a)(20)) in accordance with the rules prescribed in sections 162 and 404 and the regulations thereunder, to the extent that a deduction for such amounts is not allowed under section 804(c)(1) and paragraph (b)(1) of § 1.804-4 or section 809(d)(9) and subparagraph (9) of this paragraph.

(b) Denial of double deduction. Nothing in section 809(d) shall permit the same item to be deducted more than once in determining gain or loss from operations. For example, if an item is allowed as a deduction for the taxable year by reason of its being a loss incurred within such taxable year (whether or not ascertained) under section 809(d)(1), such item, or any portion thereof, shall not also be allowed as a deduction for such taxable year under section 809(d)(2).

T.D. 6535, 1/19/61, amend T.D. 6610, 8/30/62, T.D. 6886, 6/22/66, T.D. 6992, 1/17/69.

§ 1.809-6 Modifications.

Caution: The Treasury has not yet amended Reg § 1.809-6 to reflect changes made by P.L. 108-218, P.L. 98-369, P.L. 101-508.

Under section 809(e), the deductions allowed under section 809(d)(12) and paragraph (a)(12) of § 1.809-5 (relating to other deductions) are subject to the following modifications—

(a) Interest. No deduction shall be allowed under section 163 for interest in respect of items described in section 810(c) since such interest is taken into account in the determination of required interest under section 809.

(b) Bad debts. No deduction shall be allowed for an addition to reserves for bad debts under section 166(c). However, a deduction for specific bad debts shall be allowed to the extent that such deduction is allowed under section 166 and the regulations thereunder. In the case of a loss incurred on the sale of mortgaged or pledged property, see § 1.166-6.

(c) Charitable, etc., contributions and gifts. *(1)* The deduction by a life insurance company in any taxable year for a charitable contribution (as defined in section 170(c) shall be limited to 5 percent of the gain from operations (as determined under section 809(b)(1)), computed without regard to any deductions for:

(i) Charitable contributions under section 170;

(ii) Dividends to policyholders under section 811(b);

(iii) Certain nonparticipating contracts under section 809(d)(5);

(iv) Group life insurance contracts and group accident and health insurance contracts under section 809(d)(6);

(v) Tax-exempt interest, dividends, etc., under section 809(d)(8); and

(vi) Any operations loss carryback to the taxable year under section 812.

(2) In applying the first sentence of section 170(b)(2) as contained in § 1.170 or, in the case of taxable years beginning after December 31, 1969, section 170(d)(2)(B) as contained in § 1.170A, any excess of the charitable contributions made by a life insurance company in a taxable year over the amount deductible in such year under the limitation contained in subparagraph (1) of this paragraph, shall be reduced to the extent that such excess:

(i) Reduces life insurance company taxable income (computed without regard to section 802(b)(3)) for the purpose of determining the offset referred to in section 812(b)(2); and

(ii) Increases an operations loss carryover under section 812 for a succeeding taxable year.

(3) The application of the rules provided in section 809(e)(3) and this paragraph may be illustrated by the following example:

Example. Assume that life insurance company P is organized on January 1, 1958, and has a loss from operations for that year in the amount of $100,000 which is an operations loss carryover to 1959. In 1959, company P has a gain from operations and tax base (computed without regard to section 802(b)(3) of $100,000 before the allowance of a deduction for a $5,000 charitable contribution made in 1959 and before the application of the operations loss carryover from 1958. Under section 170(b)(2), the operations loss carryover from 1958 is first applied to eliminate the $100,000 gain from operations and tax base in 1959 and the $5,000 charitable contribution carryover would (except for the limitation contained in this paragraph) become a charitable contribution carryover to 1960. However, for the purpose of computing the offset referred to in section 812(b)(2), the $5,000 charitable contribution is applied to reduce the gain from operations and tax base for 1959 to $95,000 before the application of the operations carryover from 1958. Since only $95,000 of the $100,000 loss from operations in 1958 is an offset for 1959, the remaining $5,000 becomes an operations loss carryover to 1960. Accordingly, under the limitation contained in this paragraph, the charitable contributions carryover provided under the second sentence of section 170(b)(2) is eliminated.

(d) Amortizable bond premium. No deduction shall be allowed under section 171 for the amortization of bond premiums since a special deduction for such premiums is specifically taken into account under section 818(b).

(e) Net operating loss deduction. No deduction shall be allowed under section 172 since section 812 allows an "operations loss deduction".

(f) Partially tax-exempt interest. No deduction shall be allowed under section 242 for partially tax-exempt interest since section 809(d)(8) allows a deduction for such interest.

(g) Dividends received. No deduction shall be allowed under sections 243, 244, and 245 for dividends received since section 809(d)(8) allows a deduction for such dividends.

T.D. 6535, 1/19/61, amend T.D. 7207, 10/3/72.

---

§ 1.809-7 Limitation on certain deductions.

Caution: The Treasury has not yet amended Reg § 1.809-7 to reflect changes made by P.L. 108-218, P.L. 98-369.

(a) In general. Section 809(f)(1) limits the deductions under section 809(d)(3), (5), and (6), relating to deductions for dividends to policyholders, certain nonparticipating contracts, and group life, accident, and health insurance contracts, respectively. This limitation provides that the amount of such deductions shall not exceed the sum of *(1)* the amount (if any) by which the gain from operations for the taxable year (determined without regard to such deductions) exceeds the taxpayer's taxable investment income for such year, plus *(2)* $250,000.

(b) Application of limitation. Section 809(f)(2) provides a priority system for applying the limitation contained in section 809(f)(1) and paragraph (a) of this section. Under this priority system, the limitation shall be applied in the following order—

(1) For taxable years beginning before January 1, 1962:

(i) First to the amount of the deduction under section 809(d)(6) (relating to group life, accident, and health insurance);

(ii) Then to the amount of the deduction under section 809(d)(5) (relating to certain nonparticipating contracts); and

(iii) Finally to the amount of the deduction under section 809(d)(3) (relating to dividends to policyholders).

(2) For taxable years beginning after December 31, 1961, the limitation shall be applied in the following order:

(i) First to the amount of the deduction under section 809(d)(3);

(ii) Then to the amount of the deduction under section 809(d)(6); and

(iii) Finally to the amount of the deduction under section 809(d)(5).

Thus, for taxable years beginning after December 31, 1961, the limitation and priority system would operate first to disallow a deduction under section 809(d)(5), then a deduction under section 809(d)(6), and finally a deduction under section 809(d)(3). For purposes of applying the 50 percent limitation contained in section 809(d)(6) with respect to a taxable year beginning after December 31, 1961, the amount of the deductions for taxable years beginning before January 1, 1962, shall be determined by applying the priority system contained in subparagraph (1) of this paragraph.

(c) Illustration of principles. The operation of the limitation and priority system provided by section 809(f) and this section may be illustrated by the following examples:

Example (1). Assume the following facts with respect to M, a life insurance company, for the taxable year 1958:

Gain from operations computed without regard to the deductions under sec. 809(d)(3), (5), and (6)	$100,000,000
Taxable investment income	83,000,000
Tentative deduction for group life, accident, and health insurance under sec. 809(d)(6)	4,000,000
Tentative deduction for certain nonparticipating contracts under sec. 809(d)(5)	6,000,000
Tentative deduction for dividends to policyholders under sec. 809(d)(3)	10,000,000

In order to determine the limitation on the deductions under section 809(d)(3), (5), and (6), M would make up the following schedule:

(1) Statutory amount provided under sec. 809(f)(1)		$ 250,000
(2) Gain from operations computed without regard to the deductions under sec. 809(d)(3), (5), and (6)	$100,000,000	
(3) Taxable investment income	83,000,000	
(4) Excess of item (2) over item (3)		17,000,000
(5) Limitation on deductions under sec. 809(d)(3), (5), and (6) (item (1) plus item (4))		17,250,000

Since the total tentative deductions under section 809(d)(3), (5), and (6) ($20,000,000) exceeds the limitation on such deductions ($17,250,000), M would make up the following schedule to determine the application of the priority system:

(6) Maximum possible deduction under sec. 809(d)(3), (5), and (6) (item (5))	$17,250,000
(7) Deduction for group life, accident, and health insurance under sec. 809(d)(6) (not in excess of item (6))	4,000,000
(8) Maximum possible deduction under sec. 809(d)(5) (item (6) less item (7))	13,250,000
(9) Deduction for certain nonparticipating contracts under sec. 809(d)(5) (not in excess of item (8))	6,000,000
(10) Maximum possible deduction under sec. 809(d)(3) (item (8) less item (9))	7,250,000
(11) Deduction for dividends to policyholders under sec. 809(d)(3) (not in excess of item (10))	7,250,000

Thus, as a result of the application of the limitation and priority system for the taxable year 1958, M shall be allowed a deduction of $4,000,000 under section 809(d)(6), $6,000,000 under section 809(d)(5), and only $7,250,000 of the $10,000,000 tentative deduction under section 809(d)(3).

Example (2). The facts are the same as in example (1), except that the taxable year is 1962. Since the total tentative deductions under section 809(d)(3), (5), and (6) ($20,000,000) exceeds the limitation on such deductions ($17,250,000), M would make up the following schedule to determine the application of the priority system:

(1) Maximum possible deductions under sec. 809(d)(3), (5), and (6) (item (5) in example (1))	$17,250,000
(2) Deduction for dividends to policyholders under sec. 809(d)(3) (not in excess of item (1))	10,000,000
(3) Maximum possible deduction under sec. 809(d)(6) (item (1) less item (2))	7,250,000
(4) Deduction for certain accident, health, and group life insurance under sec. 809(d)(6) (not in excess of item (3))	4,000,000
(5) Maximum possible deduction under sec. 809(d)(5) (item (4) less item (5))	3,250,000
(6) Deduction for certain nonparticipating contracts under sec. 809(d)(5) (not in excess of item (5))	3,250,000

Thus, as a result of the application of the limitation and priority system for the taxable year 1962, M shall be allowed a deduction of $10,000,000 under section 809(d)(3), $4,000,000 under section 809(d)(6), and only $3,250,000 of the $6,000,000 tentative deduction under section 809(d)(5).

T.D. 6535, 1/19/61, amend T.D. 6886, 6/22/66.

§ 1.809-8 Limitation on deductions for certain mutualization distributions.

Caution: The Treasury has not yet amended Reg § 1.809-8 to reflect changes made by P.L. 108-218, P.L. 98-369.

(a) Deduction not to reduce taxable investment income. Section 809(g)(1) limits the deduction under section 809(d)(11) for certain mutualization distributions. This limitation provides that such deduction shall not exceed the amount (if any) by which the gain from operations for the taxable year, computed without regard to such deduction (but after the application of the limitation contained in section 809(f) and § 1.809-7), exceeds the taxpayer's taxable investment income for such year.

(b) Deduction not to reduce tax below that imposed by 1957 law. Section 809(g)(2) further limits the deduction under section 809(d)(11). Under section 809(g)(2), such deduction shall be allowed only to the extent that it (after the application of all other deductions) does not reduce the tax imposed by section 802(a)(1) for the taxable year below the amount of tax which would have been imposed for such taxable year if the law in effect for 1957 applied for such taxable year. If such deduction is claimed for 1958 (or 1959), the company shall attach to its return a schedule showing what its tax for 1958 (or 1959) would have been had such tax been computed under the law in effect for 1957.

(c) Application of section 815. Section 809(g)(3) provides that any portion of a distribution which is allowed as a deduction under section 809(d)(11) shall not be treated as a distribution to shareholders for purposes of section 815; except that in the case of any distributions made in 1959, such portion shall be treated as a distribution with respect to which a reduction is required under section 815(e)(2)(B) (relating to adjustment in allocation ratio for certain distributions after December 31, 1958).

T.D. 6535, 1/19/61.

§ 1.809-9 Computation of the differential earnings rate and the recomputed differential earnings rate.

Caution: The Treasury has not yet amended Reg § 1.809-9 to reflect changes made by P.L. 108-218, P.L. 107-147.

(a) In general. Neither the differential earnings rate under section 809(c) nor the recomputed differential earnings rate that is used in computing the recomputed differential earnings amount under section 809(f)(3) may be less than zero.

(b) Definitions. *(1) Recomputed differential earnings amount.* The recomputed differential earnings amount, with respect to any taxable year, is the amount equal to the product of—

(i) The life insurance company's average equity base for the taxable year; multiplied by

(ii) The recomputed differential earnings rate for that taxable year.

(2) Recomputed differential earnings rate. The recomputed differential earnings rate for any taxable year equals the excess of—

(i) The imputed earnings rate for the taxable year; over

(ii) The average mutual earning rate for the calendar year in which the taxable year begins.

(c) Effective date. The regulations are effective for all taxable years beginning after December 31, 1986.

T.D. 8499, 12/7/93.

§ 1.809-10 Computation of equity base.

Caution: The Treasury has not yet amended Reg § 1.809-10 to reflect changes made by P.L. 108-218.

(a) In general. For purposes of section 809, the equity base of a life insurance company includes the amount of any asset valuation reserve and the amount of any interest maintenance reserve.

(b) Effective date. This section is effective for taxable years ending after December 31, 1991.

T.D. 8484, 9/3/93, amend T.D. 8564, 9/28/94.

§ 1.810-1 Taxable years affected.

Caution: The Treasury has not yet amended Reg § 1.810-1 to reflect changes made by P.L. 101-508, P.L. 98-369.

Sections 1.810-2 through 1.810-4 are applicable only to taxable years beginning after December 31, 1957, and all references to sections of part I, subchapter L, chapter 1 of the Code are to the Internal Revenue Code of 1954, as amended by the Life Insurance Company Income Tax Act of 1959 (73 Stat 112).

T.D. 6535, 1/19/61.

§ 1.810-2 Rules for certain reserves.

Caution: The Treasury has not yet amended Reg § 1.810-2 to reflect changes made by P.L. 101-508, P.L. 98-369.

(a) Adjustment for decrease or increase in certain reserve items. *(1) Adjustment for decrease.* Section 810(a) provides that if the sum of the items described in section 810(c) and paragraph (b) of this section at the beginning of the taxable year exceeds the sum of such items at the end of the taxable year (reduced by the amount of investment yield not included in gain or loss from operations for the taxable year by reason of section 809(a)(1)), the amount of such excess shall be taken into account as a net decrease referred to in section 809(c)(2) and paragraph (a)(2) of § 1.809-4 in determining gain or loss from operations.

(2) Adjustment for increase. Section 810(b) provides that if the sum of the items described in section 810(c) and paragraph (b) of this section at the end of the taxable year (reduced by the amount of investment yield not included in gain or loss from operations for the taxable year by reason of section 809(a)(1)) exceeds the sum of such items at the beginning of the taxable year, the amount of such excess shall be taken into account as a net increase referred to in section 809(d)(2) and paragraph (a)(2) of § 1.809-5 in determining gain or loss from operations.

(b) Items taken into account. The items described in section 810(c) and referred to in section 810(a) and (b) and paragraph (a) of this section are:

(1) The life insurance reserves (as defined in section 801(b) and § 1.801-4);

(2) The unearned premiums and unpaid losses included in total reserves under section 801(c)(2) and § 1.801-5;

(3) The amounts (discounted at the rates of interest assumed by the company) necessary to satisfy the obligations under insurance or annuity contracts (including contracts supplementary thereto), but only if such obligations do not involve (at the time with respect to which the computation is made under this subparagraph) life, health, or accident contingencies;

(4) Dividend accumulations, and other amounts, held at interest in connection with insurance or annuity contracts (including contracts supplementary thereto); and

(5) Premiums received in advance, and liabilities for premium deposit funds.

For purposes of this paragraph, the same item shall be counted only once and deficiency reserves (as defined in section 801(b)(4) and paragraph (e)(4) of § 1.801-4) shall not be taken into account.

(6) Special contingency reserves under contracts of group term life insurance or group health and accident insurance which are established and maintained for the provision of insurance on retired lives, for premium stabilization, or for a combination thereof.

(c) Special rules. For purposes of section 810(a) and (b) and paragraph (a) of this section, in determining whether there is a net increase or decrease in the sum of the items described in section 810(c) and paragraph (b) of this section for the taxable year, the following rules shall apply:

(1) Computation of net increase or decrease in reserves. The sum of the items described in section 810(c) and paragraph (b) of this section at the beginning of the taxable year shall be the aggregate of the sums of each of such items at the beginning of the taxable year. The sum of the items described in section 810(c) and paragraph (b) of this section at the end of the taxable year shall be the aggregate of the sums of each of such items at the end of the taxable year. However, in order to determine whether there is a net increase or decrease in such items for the taxable year, the aggregate of the sums of the items at the end of the taxable year must first be reduced by the amount of investment yield not included in gain or loss from operations for the taxable year by reason of section 809(a)(1).

(2) Effect of change in basis in computing reserves. Any increase or decrease in the sum of the items described in

section 810(c) and paragraph (d) of this section for the taxable year which is attributable to a change in the basis used in computing such items during the taxable year shall not be taken into account under section 810(a) or (b) and paragraph (a) of this section but shall be taken into account in the manner prescribed in section 810(d) and paragraph (a) of § 1.810-3.

(3) Effect of section 818(c) election. If a company which computes its life insurance reserves on a preliminary term basis elects to revalue such reserves on a net level premium basis under section 818(c), the sum of such reserves at the beginning and end of all taxable years (including the first taxable year) for which the election applies shall be the sum of such reserves computed on such net level premium basis.

(4) Cross references. For taxable years beginning before January 1, 1970, see section 810(e) (as in effect for such years) and § 1.810-4 for special rules for determining the net increase or decrease in the sum of the items described in section 810(c) and paragraph (b) of this section in the case of certain voluntary employees' beneficiary associations. For similar special rules in the case of life insurance companies issuing variable annuity contracts, see section 801(g)(4) and the regulations thereunder.

(d) Illustration of principles. The provisions of section 810(a) and (b) and this section may be illustrated by the following examples:

Example (1). Assume the following facts with respect to R, a life insurance company:

Sum of items described in sec. 810(c)(1) through (6) at beginning of taxable year	$940
Sum of items described in sec. 810(c)(1) through (6) at end of taxable year	1,060
Required interest (as defined in sec. 809(a)(2))	70
Investment yield (as defined in sec. 804(c))	100
Amount of investment yield not included in gain or loss from operations for the taxable year by reason of sec. 809(a)(1)	70

In order to determine the adjustment for decrease or increase in the sum of the items described in section 810(c) for the taxable year, R must first reduce the sum of such items at the end of the taxable year ($1,060) by the amount of investment yield ($70) not included in gain or loss from operations for the taxable year by reason of section 809(a)(1). Since the adjusted sum of such items at the end of the taxable year, $990 ($1,060 minus $70), exceeds the sum of such items at the beginning of the taxable year, $940, the excess of $50 ($990 minus $940) shall be taken into account as a net increase under section 809(d)(2) and paragraph (a)(2) of § 1.809-5 in determining gain or loss from operations.

Example (2). Assume the facts are the same as in example (1), except that the sum of the items described in section 810(c) at the beginning of the taxable year is $1000. Since the sum of the items described in section 810(c) at the beginning of taxable year, $1,000, exceeds the sum of such items at the end of the taxable year after adjustment for the amount of investment yield not included in gain or loss from operations for the taxable year by reason of section 809(a)(1), $990 ($1,060 minus $70), the excess of $10 ($1,000 minus $990) shall be taken into account as a net decrease under section 809(c)(2) and paragraph (a)(2) of § 1.809-4 in determining gain or loss from operations.

Example (3). Assume the following facts with respect to S, a life insurance company:

Sum of items described in sec. 810(c)(1) through (6) at beginning of taxable year	$1,970
Sum of items described in sec. 810(c)(1) through (6) at end of taxable year	2,040
Required interest (as defined in sec. 809(a)(2))	60
Investment yield (as defined in sec. 804(c))	40
Amount of investment yield not included in gain or loss from operations by reason of sec. 809(a)(1)	40

Under the provisions of section 809(a)(1), since the required interest ($60) exceeds the investment yield ($40), the share of each and every item of investment yield set aside for policyholders and not included in gain or loss from operations for the taxable year shall be 100 percent. Thus, applying the provisions of section 810(a) and (b), the sum of the items described in section 810(c) at the end of the taxable year ($2,040) must first be reduced by the entire amount of the investment yield ($40) in order to determine the net increase or decrease in the sum of such items for the taxable year. Since the adjusted sum of such items at the end of the taxable year, $2,000 ($2,040 minus $40), is greater than the sum of such items at the beginning of the taxable year, $1,970, the excess of $30 ($2,000 minus $1,970) shall be taken into account as a net increase under section 809(d)(2) and paragraph (a)(2) of § 1.809-5 in determining gain or loss from operations. No additional deduction is allowed under section 809(d) for the amount ($20) by which the required interest exceeds the investment yield for the taxable year.

Example (4). Assume the facts are the same as in example (1), except that as a result of a change in the basis used in computing an item described in section 810(c) during the taxable year, the sum of such items at the end of the taxable year is $1,200. Under the provisions of paragraph (c)(2) of this section, any increase or decrease in the sum of the section 810(c) items for the taxable year which is attributable to a change in the basis used in computing such items during the taxable year shall not be taken into account under section 810(a) and (b). Thus, for purposes of section 810(a) and (b), the sum of the items described in section 810(c) at the end of the taxable year shall be $1,060 (the amount computed without regard to the change in basis) and S shall treat the $50 computed in the manner described in example (1) as a net increase under section 809(d)(2) and paragraph (a)(2) of § 1.809-5 in determining its gain or loss from operations for the taxable year. The amount of the increase in the section 810(c) items which is attributable to the change in basis during the taxable year, $140 ($1,200 minus $1,060), shall be taken into account in the manner prescribed in section 810(d) and paragraph (a) of § 1.810-3.

Example (5). The life insurance reserves of M, a life insurance company, computed with respect to contracts for which such reserves are determined on a recognized preliminary term basis amount to $100 on January 1, 1960, and $110 on December 31, 1960. For the taxable year 1960, M elects to revalue such reserves on a net level premium basis under section 818(c). Such reserves computed under section 818(c) amount to $115 on January 1, 1960, and $127 on December 31, 1960. Under the provisions of paragraph (c)(3) of this section, a company which makes the section 818(c) election must use the net level premium basis in computing the sum of its life insurance reserves at the beginning and end of all taxable years for which the election applies. Thus, for purposes of section 810(a) and (b), in determining whether there is a net increase or decrease in the sum of the section 810(c) items for the taxable year 1960, M shall include $115 as its reserves with respect to such contracts under section 810(c)(1) at the beginning of the taxable year and $127 as its reserves with respect to such contracts under section 810(c)(1) at the end of the taxable year.

T.D. 6535, 1/19/61, amend T.D. 7163, 2/28/72, T.D. 7172, 3/16/72.

§ 1.810-3 Adjustment for change in computing reserves.

Caution: The Treasury has not yet amended Reg § 1.810-3 to reflect changes made by P.L. 98-369.

(a) Reserve strengthening or weakening. Section 810(d)(1) provides that if the basis for determining any item referred to in section 810(c) and paragraph (b) of § 1.810-2 at the end of any taxable year differs from the basis for such determination at the end of the preceding taxable year, then so much of the difference between—

(1) The amount of the item at the end of the taxable year, computed on the new basis, and

(2) The amount of the item at the end of the taxable year, computed on the old basis, as is attributable to contracts issued before the taxable year shall be taken into account as follows:

(i) If the amount of the item at the end of the taxable year computed on the new basis exceeds the amount of the item at the end of the taxable year computed on the old basis, 1/10 of such excess shall be taken into account, for each of the succeeding 10 taxable years, as a net increase to which section 809(d)(2) and paragraph (a)(2) of § 1.809-5 applies; or

(ii) If the amount of the item at the end of the taxable year computed on the old basis exceeds the amount of the item at the end of the taxable year computed on the new basis, 1/10 of such excess shall be taken into account, for each of the 10 succeeding taxable years, as a net decrease to which section 809(c)(2) and paragraph (a)(2) of § 1.809-4 applies.

(b) Illustration of principles. The provisions of section 810(d)(1) and paragraph (a) of this section may be illustrated by the following examples:

Example (1). Assume that the amount of an item described in section 810(c) of L, a life insurance company, at the beginning of the taxable year 1959 is $100. Assume that at the end of the taxable year 1959, as a result of a change in the basis used in computing such item during the taxable year, the amount of the item (computed on the new basis) is $200 but computed on the old basis would have been $150. Since the amount of the item at the end of the taxable year computed on the new basis, $200, exceeds the amount of the item at the end of the taxable year computed on the old basis, $150, by $50, 1/10 of the amount of such excess, or $5, shall be taken into account as a net increase referred to in section 809(d)(2) and paragraph (a)(2) of § 1.809-5 in determining gain or loss from operations for each of the 10 taxable years immediately following the taxable year 1959. Any increase (or decrease) in the sum of the section 810(c) items computed on the old basis at the end of the taxable year 1959 ($150) after adjustment for investment yield not included in gain or loss from operations for the taxable year by reason of section 809(a)(1), over the sum of such items computed on the old basis at the beginning of the taxable year 1959 ($100), shall be taken into account in the manner prescribed in section 810(a) or (b) and § 1.810-2 for purposes of determining L's gain or loss from operations for 1959.

Example (2). Assume the facts are the same as in example (1), and that the sum of the items described in section 810(c) (computed on the new basis) is $200 on January 1, 1960, and $260 on December 31, 1960. Under the provisions of section 810(d)(1), as a result of the reserve strengthening attributable to the change in basis which occurred in 1959, L would include $5 (computed in the manner described in example (1)) as a net increase under section 809(d)(2) and paragraph (a)(2) of § 1.809-5 in determining its gain or loss from operations for 1960. In addition to this amount, any increase (or decrease) in the sum of the items described in section 810(c) at the end of the taxable year 1960 ($260) after adjustment for investment yield not included in gain or loss from operations for the taxable year by reason of section 809(a)(1), over the sum of such items at the beginning of the taxable year 1960 ($200), shall be taken into account in the manner prescribed in section 810(a) or (b) and § 1.810-2 for purposes of determining L's gain or loss from operations for 1960.

(c) Termination as life insurance company. Section 810(d)(2) provides, subject to the provisions of section 381(c)(22) and the regulations thereunder (relating to carryovers in certain corporate readjustments), that if for any taxable year a company which previously was a life insurance company no longer meets the requirements of section 801(a) and paragraph (b) of § 1.801-3 (relating to the definition of a life insurance company), the balance of any adjustments remaining to be made under section 810(d)(1) and paragraph (a) of this section shall be taken into account for the preceding taxable year.

(d) Illustration of principles. The provisions of section 810(d)(2) and paragraph (c) of this section may be illustrated by the following example:

Example. Assume the facts are the same as in example (1) of paragraph (b) of this section, except that for the taxable year 1962, L no longer meets the requirements of section 801(a) (relating to the definition of a life insurance company) and that the provisions of section 381(c)(22) are not applicable. Under the provisions of section 810(d)(2), the entire balance of the adjustment remaining to be made with respect to the change in basis which occurred in 1959, 8/10 of $50, or $40, shall be taken into account for the taxable year 1961, the last year L was a life insurance company. Thus, for the taxable year 1961, the total amount to be taken into account by L as a net increase referred to in section 809(d)(2) and paragraph (a)(2) of § 1.809-5 in determining its gain or loss from operations shall be $45. Of this amount, $5 (1/10 of $50) represents the amount determined under the provisions of section 810(d)(1), and $40 represents the amount determined under the provisions of section 810(d)(2).

(e) Effect of preliminary term election. *(1)* Section 810(d)(3) provides that if a company which computes its life insurance reserves on a preliminary term basis elects to revalue such reserves on a net level premium basis under section 818(c), such election shall not be treated as a change in basis within the meaning of section 810(d)(1) and paragraph (a) of this section. Thus, any increase or decrease in reserves attributable to such election shall not be taken into account under section 810(d)(1) and paragraph (a) of this section but shall be taken into account in the manner prescribed in section 810(a) and (b) and paragraph (a) of § 1.810-2. See paragraph (c)(3) of § 1.810-2.

(2) Section 810(d)(3) further provides that where an election under section 818(c) would apply to an item referred to in section 810(c) but for the fact that the basis used in computing such item has actually been changed, any increase or decrease in such item attributable to such actual change in basis shall be subject to the adjustment required under section 810(d)(1) and paragraph (a) of this section. In such a

case, however, for purposes of section 810(d)(1)(B) and paragraph (a)(2) of this section, the amount of such item at the end of the taxable year computed on the old basis shall be the amount of such item at the end of the taxable year computed as if the election under section 818(c) applied in respect of such item for the taxable year.

(f) Illustration of principles. The provisions of section 810(d)(3) and paragraph (e) of this section may be illustrated by the following examples:

Example (1). Assume that S, a life insurance company which computes its life insurance reserves on a 3-percent assumed rate and the Commissioner's reserve valuation method (one of the recognized preliminary term reserve methods), elects to revalue such reserves on a net level premium method under section 818(c) and that the significant facts are as follows:

	Jan. 1, 1958	Dec. 31, 1958
Book reserves at 3-percent assumed rate, Commissioner's reserve valuation method	100	118
Reserves at 3-percent assumed rate, after restatement under section 818(c)	110	131

Under the provisions of section 810(d)(3), an election under section 818(c) is not treated as a change in basis for purposes of section 810(d)(1). Accordingly, the increase of $21 ($131 minus $110) attributable to such election shall not be subject to the adjustment provided by section 810(d)(1) but shall be taken into account in the manner prescribed in section 810(b). For purposes of determining the amount to be taken into account under section 810(b), the reserves with respect to the contracts subject to the section 818(c) election shall be $110 at the beginning of the taxable year 1958 and $131 at the end of the taxable year 1958. However, as a result of making the election under section 818(c), the difference ($10) between the reserves computed on the preliminary term basis on January 1, 1958 ($100) and the reserves restated on the net level premium basis on January 1, 1958 ($110) shall not be taken into account under section 809(d) for the year 1958, or for any subsequent taxable year.

Example (2). Assume the facts are the same as in example (1), except that during the taxable year 1959, S actually changed from the preliminary term basis to a net level premium basis which was identical with the net level premium basis used under the section 818(c) election and that the significant facts are as follows:

	Jan. 1, 1959	Dec. 31, 1959
Book reserves at 3-percent assumed rate, Commissioner's reserve valuation method	118	127
Reserves at 3-percent assumed rate, after restatement under section 818(c)	131	142
Strengthened reserves at 3-percent assumed rate and net level premium method		142

Under the provisions of section 810(d)(3), if a company which has made an election under section 818(c) which has not been revoked actually changes the basis used by it in computing the reserves subject to such election, any increase or decrease in reserves attributable to such change in basis shall be taken into account in the manner prescribed in section 810(d)(1). Since S actually changed to the same basis which it used in computing its reserves under section 818(c), the reserves at the end of the taxable year computed on the new basis ($142) are the same as the reserves at the end of the taxable year computed on the old basis ($142), i.e., the basis which would have applied under section 818(c) if the election applied for 1959. Accordingly, no adjustment under section 810(d)(1) is required.

Example (3). Assume the facts are the same as in example (1), except that during the taxable year 1960, S actually changed the basis used by it in computing its reserves on a certain block of contracts subject to the election under section 818(c) and that the significant facts with respect to this block of contracts are as follows:

	Jan. 1, 1960	Dec. 31, 1960
Book reserves at 3-percent assumed rate, Commissioner's reserve valuation method	50	63
Reserves at 3-percent assumed rate, after restatement under section 818(c)	60	75
Strengthened reserves at 2-percent assumed rate and net level premium method		95

Under the provisions of section 810(d)(3), the amount of the reserves subject to the section 818(c) election at the end of the taxable year computed on the old basis shall be the amount of such reserves at the end of the taxable year determined under section 818(c) ($75). Since the reserves at the end of the taxable year computed on the new basis, $95, exceed the reserves at the end of the taxable year computed on the old basis, $75, by $20, 1/10 of the excess of $20, or $2, shall be taken into account as a net increase referred to in section 809(d)(2) and paragraph (a)(2) of § 1.809-5 in determining gain or loss from operations for each of the 10 taxable years immediately following the taxable year 1960. For purposes of determining whether there is a net increase or decrease in the sum of the items described in section 810(c) for the taxable year 1960 under section 810(a) or (b), the sum of the reserves with respect to such block of contracts shall be $60 at the beginning of the taxable year and $75 at the end of the taxable year (the amount of such reserves computed under section 818(c) at the beginning and end of the taxable year). The difference ($10) between the reserves computed on the preliminary term basis on January 1, 1960 ($50) and the reserves restated on the net level premium basis on January 1, 1960 ($60) shall not be taken into account under section 809(d) for the year 1960, or for any subsequent taxable year.

T.D. 6535, 1/19/61.

§ 1.810-4 Certain decreases in reserves of voluntary employees' beneficiary associations.

Caution: The Treasury has not yet amended Reg § 1.810-4 to reflect changes made by P.L. 98-369.

(a) Decreases due to voluntary lapses of policies issued before January 1, 1958. *(1)* Section 810(e) provides that if for any taxable year a life insurance company which meets the requirements of section 501(c)(9), other than the requirement of subparagraph (B) thereof, makes an election in the manner provided in section 810(e)(3) and paragraph (b) of this section, only 11½ percent of any decrease in life insurance reserves (as defined in section 801(b) and § 1.801-4) attributable to the voluntary lapse on or after January 1, 1958, of any policy issued prior to that date shall be taken into account under section 810(a) or (b) and paragraph (a) of § 1.810-2 in determining the net increase or decrease in the sum of the items described in section 810(c) during the taxable year. In applying the preceding sentence, the decrease in the reserve for any policy shall be determined by reference to the amount of such reserve at the beginning of the taxable year, reduced by any amount allowable as a deduction under section 809(d)(1) and paragraph (a)(1) of § 1.809-5 in respect of such policy by reason of such lapse. The election under section 810(e) shall be adhered to in computing the company's gain or loss from operation for the taxable year for which the election is made and for all subsequent taxable years, unless consent to revoke such election is obtained from the Commissioner.

(2) The application of the election provided under section 810(e) and subparagraph (1) of this paragraph may be illustrated by the following example:

Example. For the taxable year 1960, M, a life insurance company which meets the requirements of section 501(c)(9), other than the requirement of subparagraph (B) thereof, makes the election under section 810(e). Assume the following facts with respect to a policy issued in 1955 which voluntarily lapsed during the taxable year:

(1) Life insurance reserve on January 1, 1960	$600
(2) Amount allowable as a deduction under sec. 809(d)(1)	200
(3) Decrease in life insurance reserves for sec. 810(e) purposes (item (1) minus item (2))	400
(4) Amount taken into account under sec. 810(a) and (b) by reason of sec. 810(e) election (11½× $400)	46

Under the provisions of section 810(e) and subparagraph (1) of this paragraph, M would include $46 as its life insurance reserve with respect to such policy under section 810(c)(1) at the beginning of the taxable year 1960 for purposes of determining the net increase or decrease in the sum of the items described in section 810(c) for the taxable year under section 810(a) or (b).

(b) Time and manner of making election. The election provided by section 810(e)(3) shall be made in a statement attached to the life insurance company's income tax return for the first taxable year for which the company desires the election to apply. The return and statement must be filed not later than the date prescribed by law (including extensions thereof) for filing the return for such taxable year. However, if the last day prescribed by law (including extensions thereof) for filing a return for the first taxable year for which the company desires the election to apply falls before January 20, 1961, the election provided by section 810(e)(3) may be made for such year by filing the statement and an amended return for such taxable year (and all subsequent taxable years for which returns have been filed) before April 21, 1961. The statement shall indicate that the company meets the requirements of section 501(c)(9), other than the requirement of subparagraph (B) thereof, and has made the election provided under section 810(e) and paragraph (a) of this section. The statement shall set forth the following information with respect to each policy described in paragraph (a) of this section which has voluntarily lapsed during such year:

(1) Type of policy.

(2) Date issued.

(3) Date lapsed.

(4) Reason for lapse.

(5) Policy reserve as of beginning of taxable year.

(6) Deduction allowable under section 809(d)(1) and paragraph (a)(1) of § 1.809-5 during taxable year by reason of lapse.

(7) Decrease in policy reserve for section 810(e) purposes (excess of (5) over (6)).

In addition, the statement shall set forth the total of the amounts referred to in subparagraph (7) of this paragraph with respect to all policies described in paragraph (a) of this section which have voluntarily lapsed during the taxable year.

(c) Scope of election. An election made under section 810(a)(3) and paragraph (a) of this section shall be effective for the taxable year for which made and for all succeeding taxable years, unless consent to revoke the election is obtained from the Commissioner. However, for taxable years beginning prior to January 20, 1961, a company make revoke the election provided by section 810(e)(3) without obtaining consent from the Commissioner by filing, before April 21, 1961, a statement that the company desires to revoke such election. An amended return reflecting such revocation must accompany the statement for all taxable years for which returns have been filed with respect to such election.

(d) Disallowance of carryovers from pre-1958 losses from operations. For any taxable year for which the election provided under section 810(e)(3) and paragraph (b) of this section is effective, the provisions of section 812(b)(1) and § 1.812-4 shall not apply with respect to any loss from operations for any taxable year beginning before January 1, 1958.

(e) Effective date; cross reference. The provisions of section 810(e) (as in effect for such years) and this section apply only with respect to taxable years beginning before January 1, 1970. For provisions relating to certain funded pension trusts applicable to taxable years beginning after December 31, 1969, see section 501(c)(18) and the regulations thereunder.

T.D. 6535, 1/19/61, amend T.D. 7172, 3/16/72.

§ 1.811-1 Taxable years affected.

Caution: The Treasury has not yet amended Reg § 1.811-1 to reflect changes made by P.L. 98-369.

Section 1.811-2, except as otherwise provided therein, is applicable only to taxable years beginning after December 31, 1957, and all references to sections of part I, subchapter L, chapter 1 of the Code are to the Internal Revenue Code of 1954, as amended by the Life Insurance Company Income Tax Act of 1959 (73 Stat 112).

T.D. 6535, 1/19/61.

§ 1.811-2 Dividends to policyholders.

Caution: The Treasury has not yet amended Reg § 1.811-2 to reflect changes made by P.L. 98-369.

(a) Dividends to policyholders defined. Section 811(a) defines the term "dividends to policyholders", for purposes of part I, subchapter L, chapter 1 of the Code, to mean dividends and similar distributions to policyholders in their capacity as such. The term includes amounts returned to policyholders where the amount is not fixed in the contract but depends on the experience of the company or the discretion of the management. In general, any payment not fixed in the contract which is made with respect to a participating contract (that is, a contract which during the taxable year contains a right to participate in the divisible surplus of the company) shall be treated as a dividend to policyholders. Similarly, any amount refunded or allowed as a rate credit with respect to either a participating or a nonparticipating contract shall be treated as a dividend to policyholders if such amount depends on the experience of the company. However, the term does not include interest paid (as defined in section 805(e) and paragraph (b) of § 1.805-8) or return premiums (as defined in section 809(c) and paragraph (a)(1)(ii) of § 1.809-4). Thus, so-called excess-interest dividends and amounts returned by one life insurance company to another in respect of reinsurance ceded shall not be treated as dividends to policyholders even though such amounts are not fixed in the contract but depend upon the experience of the company or the discretion of the management.

(b) Amount of deduction. *(1) In general.* Section 811(b)(1) provides, subject to the limitation of section 809(f), that the deduction for dividends to policyholders for any taxable year shall be an amount equal to the dividends to policyholders paid during the taxable year—

(i) Increased by the excess of the amounts held as reserves for dividends to policyholders at the end of the taxable year for payment during the year following the taxable year, over the amounts held as reserves for dividends to policyholders at the end of the preceding taxable year for payment during the taxable year, or

(ii) Decreased by the excess of the amounts held as reserves for dividends to policyholders at the end of the preceding taxable year for payment during the taxable year, over the amounts held as reserves for dividends to policyholders at the end of the taxable year for payment during the year following the taxable year.

For the rule as to when dividends are considered paid, see section 561 and the regulations thereunder. For the determination of the amounts held as reserves for dividends to policyholders, see paragraph (c) of this section. For special provisions relating to the treatment of dividends to policyholders paid with respect to policies reinsured under modified coinsurance contracts, see section 820(c)(5) and the regulations thereunder.

(2) Certain amounts to be treated as net decreases. Section 811(b)(2) provides that if the amount determined under subparagraph (1)(ii) of this paragraph exceeds the dividends to policyholders paid during the taxable year, the amount of such excess shall be a net decrease referred to in section 809(c)(2).

(c) Reserves for dividends to policyholders defined. *(1) In general.* The term "reserves for dividends to policyholders", as used in section 811(b)(1)(A) and (B) and paragraph (b)(1) of this section, means only those amounts—

(i) Actually held, or set aside as provided in subparagraph (2) of this paragraph and thus treated as actually held, by the company at the end of the taxable year, and

(ii) With respect to which, at the end of the taxable year or, if set aside, within the period prescribed in subparagraph (2) of this paragraph, the company is under an obligation, which is either fixed or determined according to a formula which is fixed and not subject to change by the company, to pay such amounts as dividends to policyholders (as defined in section 811(a) and paragraph (a) of this section) during the year following the taxable year.

(2) Amounts set aside. (i) In the case of a life insurance company (as defined in section 801(a) and paragraph (b) of § 1.801-3), all amounts set aside before the 16th day of the 3d month of the year following the taxable year for payment as dividends to policyholders (as defined in section 811(a) and paragraph (a) of this section) during the year following such taxable year shall be treated as amounts actually held at the end of the taxable year.

(ii) In the case of a mutual savings bank subject to the tax imposed by section 594, all amounts set aside before the 16th day of the 4th month of the year following the taxable year for payment as dividends to policyholders (as defined in section 811(a) and paragraph (a) of this section) during the year following such taxable year shall be treated as amounts actually held at the end of the taxable year.

(3) 1958 reserve for dividends to policyholders. For purposes of section 811(b) and paragraph (b) of this section, the amounts held at the end of 1957 as reserves for dividends to policyholders payable during 1958 shall be determined as if part I, subchapter L, chapter 1 of the Code (as in effect for 1958) applied for 1957. Any adjustment in the serves for dividends to policyholders at the beginning of 1957 required as a result of an understatement or overstatement of such reserves by the company shall be made to the balance of such reserves as of the beginning of 1957. For example, if at the beginning of 1957 the reserves for dividends to policyholders are stated to be $100 and it is subsequently determined that such reserves should have been $90, the reserves at the beginning of 1957 shall be reduced by $10. Under no circumstances shall an adjustment required with regard to the beginning 1957 reserves be made to the reserves at the end of 1957.

(4) Information to be filed. Every company claiming a deduction for dividends to policyholders shall keep such permanent records as are necessary to establish the amount of dividends actually paid during the taxable year. Such company shall also keep a copy of the dividend resolution and any necessary supporting data relating to the amounts of dividends declared and to the amounts held or set aside as reserves for dividends to policyholders during the taxable year. The company shall file with its return a concise statement of the pertinent facts relating to its dividend policy for the year, the amount of dividends actually paid during the taxable year, and the amounts held or set aside as reserves for dividends to policyholders during the taxable year.

(d) Illustration of principles. The provisions of section 811(b) and this section may be illustrated by the following examples:

Example (1). On December 31, 1959, M, a life insurance company, held $200 as reserves for dividends to policyholders due and payable in 1960. On March 10, 1960, M set aside an additional $50 as reserves for dividends to policyholders due and payable in 1960. During the taxable year 1960, M paid $240 as dividends to its policyholders and at the end of the taxable year 1960, held $175 as reserves for dividends to policyholders due and payable in 1961. No additional amount was set aside before March 16, 1961, as reserves for dividends to policyholders due and payable in 1961. For the taxable year 1960, subject to the limitation of section 809(f), M's deduction for dividends to policyholders is $165, computed as follows:

(1) Dividends paid to policyholders during the taxable year 1960		$240
(2) Decreased by the excess of item (a) over item (b):		
(a) Reserves for dividends to policyholders as of 12-31-59 (including amounts set aside as provided in paragraph (c)(2) of this section)	$250	
(b) Reserves for dividends to policyholders as of 12-31-60	175	
		75
(3) Deduction for dividends to policyholders under sec. 811(b) (computed without regard to the limitation of sec. 809(f))		165

Example (2). On December 31, 1960, S, a life insurance company, held $100 as reserves for dividends to policyholders due and payable in 1961. During the taxable year 1961, S paid $125 as dividends to its policyholders and at the end of the taxable year 1961, held $110 as reserves for dividends to policyholders due and payable in 1962. No additional amount was set aside for dividends to policyholders as provided in paragraph (c)(2) of this section before March 16, 1961, or March 16, 1962. For the taxable year 1961, subject to the limitation of section 809(f), S's deduction for dividends to policyholders is $135, computed as follows:

(1) Dividends paid to policyholders during the taxable year 1961		$125
(2) Increased by the excess of item (a) over item (b):		
(a) Reserves for dividends to policyholders as of 12-31-61	$110	
(b) Reserves for dividends to policyholders as of 12-31-60	100	
		10
(3) Deduction for dividends to policyholders under sec. 811(b) (computed without regard to the limitation of sec. 809(f))		135

Example (3). Assume the facts are the same as in example (2), except that on December 31, 1960, the amount held as reserves for dividends to policyholders due and payable in 1961 is $250. For the taxable year 1961, S's deduction for dividends to policyholders is zero, computed as follows:

(1) Dividends paid to policyholders during the taxable year 1961		$125
(2) Decreased by the excess of item (a) over item (b):(a) Reserves for dividends to policyholders as of 12-31-60	$250	
(b) Reserves for dividends to policyholders as of 12-31-61	110	
		140
(3) Deduction for dividends to policyholders under sec. 811(b) (computed without regard to the limitation of sec. 809(f))		0

Under the provisions of section 811(b)(2) and paragraph (b)(2) of this section, since the decrease in the reserves for dividends to policyholders during the taxable year, $140 ($250 minus $110), exceeds the dividends to policyholders paid during the taxable year 1961, $125, S shall include $15 (the amount of such excess) as a net decrease under section 809(c)(2) and paragraph (a)(2) of § 1.809-4 in determining its gain or loss from operations for 1961.

T.D. 6535, 1/19/61.

§ 1.811-3 Cross-reference.

For special rules regarding the treatment of modified guaranteed contracts (as defined in section 817A and § 1.817A-1(a)(1)), see § 1.817A-1.

T.D. 9058, 5/6/2003.

§ 1.812-1 Taxable years affected.

Caution: The Treasury has not yet amended Reg § 1.812-1 to reflect changes made by P.L. 98-369.

Sections 1.812-2 through 1.812-8, except as otherwise provided therein, are applicable only to taxable years beginning after December 31, 1957, and all references to sections of part I, subchapter L, chapter 1 of the Code are to the Internal Revenue Code of 1954, as amended by the Life Insurance Company Income Tax Act of 1959 (73 Stat. 112) and the Act of October 23, 1962 (76 Stat. 1134).

T.D. 6535, 1/19/61, amend T.D. 6886, 6/22/66.

§ 1.812-2 Operations loss deduction.

Caution: The Treasury has not yet amended Reg § 1.812-2 to reflect changes made by P.L. 98-369.

(a) Allowance of deduction. Section 812 provides that a life insurance company shall be allowed a deduction in computing gain or loss from operations for any taxable year beginning after December 31, 1957, in an amount equal to the aggregate of the operations loss carryovers and operations loss carrybacks to such taxable year. This deduction is referred to as the operations loss deduction. The loss from operations (computed under section 809), is the basis for the computation of the operations loss carryovers and operations loss carrybacks and ultimately for the operations loss deduction itself. Section 809(e)(5) provides that the net operating loss deduction provided in section 172 shall not be allowed a life insurance company since the operations loss deduction provided in section 812 and this paragraph shall be allowed in lieu thereof.

(b) Steps in computation of operations loss deduction. The three steps to be taken in the ascertainment of the operations loss deduction for any taxable year beginning after December 31, 1957, are as follows:

(1) Compute the loss from operations for any preceding or succeeding taxable year from which a loss from operations may be carried over or carried back to such taxable year.

(2) Compute the operations loss carryovers to such taxable year from such preceding taxable years and the operations loss carrybacks to such taxable year from such succeeding taxable years.

(3) Add such operations loss carryovers and carrybacks in order to determine the operations loss deduction for such taxable year.

(c) Statement with tax return. Every life insurance company claiming an operations loss deduction for any taxable year shall file with its return for such year a concise statement setting forth the amount of the operations loss deduction claimed and all material and pertinent facts relative thereto, including a detailed schedule showing the computation of the operations loss deduction.

(d) Ascertainment of deduction dependent upon operations loss carryback. If a life insurance company is entitled in computing its operations loss deduction to a carryback which it is not able to ascertain at the time its return is due, it shall compute the operations loss deduction on its return without regard to such operations loss carryback. When the life insurance company ascertains the operations loss carryback, it may within the applicable period of limitations file a claim for credit or refund of the overpayment, if any, resulting from the failure to compute the operations loss deduction for the taxable year with the inclusion of such carryback; or it may file an application under the provisions of section 6411 for a tentative carryback adjustment.

(e) Law applicable to computations. The following rules shall apply to all taxable years beginning after December 31, 1957—

(1) In determining the amount of any operations loss carryback or carryover to any taxable year, the necessary computations involving any other taxable year shall be made under the law applicable to such other taxable year.

(2) The loss from operations for any taxable year shall be determined under the law applicable to that year without regard to the year to which it is to be carried and in which, in effect, it is to be deducted as part of the operations loss deduction.

(3) The amount of the operations loss deduction which shall be allowed for any taxable year shall be determined under the law applicable for that year.

(f) Special rules. For purposes of taxable years beginning after December 31, 1954, and before January 1, 1958—

(1) The amount of any:

(i) Loss from operations;

(ii) Operations loss carryback; and

(iii) Operations loss carryover .

shall be computed as if part I, subchapter L, chapter 1 of the Code (as in effect for 1958) and section 381(c)(22) applied to such taxable years.

(2) A loss from operations (determined in accordance with the provisions of section 812(b)(1)(C) and this paragraph) for such taxable years shall in no way affect the tax liability of any life insurance company for such taxable years. However, such loss may, to the extent allowed as an operations loss carryover under section 812, affect the tax liability of a life insurance company for a taxable year beginning after December 31, 1957. For example, for the taxable year 1956, X, a life insurance company, has a loss from operations (determined in accordance with the provisions of section 812(b)(1)(C) and this paragraph). Such loss shall in no way affect X's tax liability for the taxable years 1956 (the year of the loss), 1955 (a year to which such loss shall be carried back), or 1957 (a year to which such loss shall be carried forward). However, to the extent allowed under section 812, any amount of the loss for 1956 remaining after such carryback and carryforward shall be taken into account in determining X's tax liability for taxable years beginning after December 31, 1957.

T.D. 6535, 1/19/61.

§ 1.812-3 Computation of loss from operations.

Caution: The Treasury has not yet amended Reg § 1.812-3 to reflect changes made by P.L. 98-369, P.L. 101-508.

(a) Modification of deductions. A loss from operations is sustained by a life insurance company in any taxable year, if and to the extent that, for such year, there is an excess of the sum of the deductions provided by section 809(d) over the sum of (1) the life insurance company's share of each and every item of investment yield (including tax-exempt interest, partially tax-exempt interest, and dividends received) as determined under section 809(b)(3), and (2) the sum of the items of gross amount taken into account under section 809(c). In determining the loss from operations for purposes of section 812—

(i) No deduction shall be allowed under section 812 for the operations loss deduction.

(ii) The 85 percent limitation on dividends received provided by section 246(b) as modified by section 809(d)(8)(B) shall not apply to the deductions otherwise allowed under—

(a) Section 243(a) in respect to dividends received by corporations,

(b) Section 244 in respect of dividends received on certain preferred stock of public utilities, and

(c) Section 245 in respect of dividends received from certain foreign corporations.

(b) Illustration of principles. The application of paragraph (a) of this section may be illustrated by the following example:

Example. For the taxable year 1960, X, a life insurance company, has items taken into account under section 809(c) amounting to $150,000, its share of the investment yield amounts to $250,000, and total deductions allowed by section 809(d) of $375,000, exclusive of any operations loss deduction and exclusive of any deduction for dividends received. In 1960, X received as its share of dividends entitled to the benefits of section 243(a) the amount of $100,000. These dividends are included in X's share of the investment yield. X has no other deductions to which section 812(c) applies. On the basis of these facts, X has a loss from operations for the taxable year 1960 of $60,000, computed as follows:

Deductions for 1960	$375,000
Plus: Deduction for dividends received computed without regard to the limitation provided by sec. 246(b), as modified by sec. 809(d)(8)(B) (85% of $100,000)	85,000
Total deductions as modified by sec. 812(c)	460,000
Less: Sum of sec. 809(c) items and X's share of investment yield (including $100,000 of dividends)	400,000
Loss from operations for 1960	(60,000)

T.D. 6535, 1/19/61.

§ 1.812-4 Operations loss carrybacks and operations loss carryovers.

Caution: The Treasury has not yet amended Reg § 1.812-4 to reflect changes made by P.L. 98-369, P.L. 101-508.

(a) In general. *(1) Years to which loss may be carried.* In order to compute the operations loss deduction of a life insurance company the company must first determine the part of any losses from operations for any preceding or succeeding taxable years which are carryovers or carrybacks to the taxable year in issue. Except as otherwise provided by this paragraph, a loss from operations for taxable years beginning after December 31, 1954, shall be carried back to each of the 3 taxable years preceding the loss year and shall be carried forward to each of the 5 taxable years succeeding the loss year. Except as limited by section 812(e)(2) and paragraph (b) of § 1.812-6, if the life insurance company is a new company (as defined in section 812(e)(1) for the loss year, the loss from operations shall be carried back to each of the 3 taxable years preceding the loss year and shall be carried forward to each of the 8 taxable years succeeding the loss year. In determining the span of years for which a loss from operations may be carried, taxable years in which a company does not qualify as a life insurance company (as defined in section 801(a)), or is not treated as a new company, shall be taken into account.

(2) Special transitional rules. (i) A loss from operations for any taxable year beginning before January 1, 1958, shall not be carried back to any taxable year beginning before January 1, 1955. Furthermore, a loss from operations for any taxable year beginning after December 31, 1957, shall not be carried back to any taxable year beginning before January 1, 1958.

(ii) If for any taxable year a life insurance company has made an election under section 810(e) (relating to certain decreases in reserves for voluntary employees' beneficiary associations) which is effective for such taxable year, the provisions of section 812(b)(1) and subparagraph (1) of this paragraph shall not apply with respect to any loss from operations for any taxable year beginning before January 1, 1958.

(3) Illustration of principles. The provisions of section 812(b)(1) and of this paragraph may be illustrated by the following examples:

Example (1). P, a life insurance company, organized in 1940, has a loss from operations of $1,000 in 1958. This loss cannot be carried back, but shall be carried forward to each of the 5 taxable years following 1958.

Example (2). Q, a life insurance company, organized in 1940, has a loss from operations of $1,200 in 1959. This loss shall be carried back to the taxable year 1958 and then shall be carried forward to each of the 5 taxable years following 1959.

Example (3). R, a life insurance company, organized in 1940, has a loss from operations of $1,300 for the taxable year 1956. This loss shall first be carried back to the taxable year 1955 and then shall be carried forward to each of the 5 taxable years following 1956. The loss for 1956, carryback to 1955, and carryover to 1957 shall each be computed as if part I, subchapter L, chapter 1 of the Code (as in effect for 1958) applied to such taxable years.

Example (4). S, a life insurance company, organized in 1958 and meeting the provisions of section 812(e) (rules relating to new companies), has a loss from operations of $1,400 for the taxable year 1958. This loss cannot be carried back, but shall be carried forward to each of the 8 taxable years following 1958, provided, however, S is not a nonqualified corporation at any time during the loss year (1958) or any taxable year thereafter.

Example (5). T, a life insurance company, organized in 1954 and meeting the provisions of section 812(e) (rules relating to new companies), has a loss from operations of $1,500 for the taxable year 1956. This loss shall first be carried back to the taxable year 1955 and then carried forward to each of the 8 taxable years following 1956, provided, however, T is not a nonqualified corporation at any time during the loss year (1956) or any taxable year thereafter. The loss for 1956, carryback to 1955, and carryover to 1957 shall each be computed as if part I of subchapter L (as in effect for 1958) applied to such taxable years.

(4) Periods of less than 12 months. A fractional part of a year which is a taxable year under sections 441(b) and 7701(a)(23) is a preceding or a succeeding taxable year for the purpose of determining under section 812 the first, second, etc., preceding or succeeding taxable year. For the determination of the loss from operations for periods of less than 12 months, see section 818(d) and the regulations thereunder.

(5) Amount of loss to be carried. The amount which is carried back or carried over to any taxable year is the loss from operations to the extent it was not absorbed in the computation of gain from operations for other taxable years, preceding such taxable year, to which it may be carried back or carried over. For the purpose of determining the gain from operations for any such preceding taxable year, the various operations loss carryovers and carrybacks to such taxable year are considered to be applied in reduction of the gain from operations in the order of the taxable years from which such losses are carried over or carried back, beginning with the loss for the earliest taxable year.

(6) Corporate acquisitions. For the computation of the operations loss carryovers in the case of certain acquisitions of the assets of a life insurance company by another life insurance company, see section 381(c)(22) and the regulations thereunder.

(b) Portion of loss from operations which is a carryback or a carryover to the taxable year in issue. *(1) Manner of computation.* (i) A loss from operations shall first be carried back to the earliest taxable year permissible under section 812(b) and paragraph (a) of this section for which such loss is allowable as a carryback or a carryover. The entire amount of the loss from operations shall be carried back to such earliest year.

(ii) Section 812(b)(2) provides that the portion of the loss from operations which shall be carried to each of the taxable years subsequent to the earliest taxable year shall be the excess (if any) of the amount of the loss from operations over the sum of the offsets (as defined in section 812(d) and paragraph (a) of § 1.812-5) for all prior taxable years to which the loss from operations may be carried.

(2) Illustration of principles. The application of this paragraph may be illustrated by the following example:

Example. T, a life insurance company (which is not a new company as defined in section 812(e)(1)), has a loss from operations for 1960. The entire amount of the loss from operations for 1960 shall first be carried back to 1958. The amount of the carryback to 1959 is the excess (if any) of the 1960 loss over the offset for 1958. The amount of the carryover to 1961 is the excess (if any) of the 1960 loss over the sum of the offsets for 1958 and 1959. The amount of the 1960 loss remaining (if any) to be carried over to 1962, 1963, or 1964 shall be computed in a like manner.

T.D. 6535, 1/19/61.

---

§ 1.812-5 Offset.

Caution: The Treasury has not yet amended Reg § 1.812-5 to reflect changes made by P.L. 98-369.

(a) Offset defined. Section 812(d) defines the term "offset" for purposes of section 812(b)(2) and paragraph (b)(1)(ii) of § 1.812-4. For any taxable year the offset is only that portion of the increase in the operations loss deduction for the taxable year which is necessary to reduce the life insurance company taxable income (computed without regard to section 802(b)(3)) for such year to zero. For purposes of the preceding sentence, the offset shall be determined with the modifications prescribed in paragraph (b) of this section. Such modifications shall be made independently of, and without reference to, the modifications required by paragraph (a) of § 1.812-3 for purposes of computing the loss from operations itself.

(b) Modifications. *(1) Operations loss deduction.* (i) In general. Section 812(d)(2) provides that for purposes of section 812(d)(1) (relating to the definition of offset), the operations loss deduction for any taxable year shall be computed by taking into account only such losses from operations otherwise allowable as carryovers or as carrybacks to such taxable year as were sustained in taxable years preceding the taxable year in which the life insurance company sustained the loss from operations from which the offset is to be deducted. Thus, for such purposes the loss from operations for the loss year or for any taxable year thereafter shall not be taken into account.

(ii) Illustration of principles. The provisions of this subparagraph may be illustrated by the following example:

Example. In computing the operations loss deduction for 1960, Y, a life insurance company, has a carryover from 1958 of $9,000, a carryover from 1959 of $6,000, a carryback from 1961 of $18,000, and a carryback from 1962 of $10,000, or an aggregate of $43,000 in carryovers and carrybacks. Thus, the operations loss deduction for 1960, for purposes of determining the tax liability for 1960, is $43,000. However, in computing the offset for 1960 which is subtracted from the loss from operations for 1961 for the purpose of determining the portion of such loss which may be carried over to subsequent taxable years, the operations loss deduction for 1960 is $15,000, that is, the aggregate of the $9,000 carryover from 1958 and the $6,000 carryover from 1959. In computing the operations loss deduction for such purpose, the $18,000 carryback from 1961 and the $10,000 carryback from 1962 are disregarded. In computing the offset for 1960, however, which is subtracted from the loss from operations for 1962 for the purpose of determining the portion of such 1962 loss which may be carried over for subsequent taxable years, the operations loss deduction for 1960 is $33,000, that is, the aggregate of the $9,000 carryover from 1958, the $6,000 carryover from 1959, and the $18,000 carryback from 1961. In computing the operations loss deduction for such purpose, the $10,000 carryback from 1962 is disregarded.

(2) Recomputation of deductions limited by section 809(f). (i) In general. If in any taxable year a life insurance company has deductions under section 809(d)(3), (5), and (6), as limited by section 809(f), and sustains a loss from operations in a succeeding taxable year which may be carried back as an operations loss deduction, such limitation and deductions shall be recomputed. This recomputation is required since the carryback must be taken into account for purposes of determining such limitation and deductions.

(ii) Illustration of principles. The provisions of this subparagraph may be illustrated by the following example:

(a) Facts. The books of P, a life insurance company, reveal the following facts:

Taxable year	Taxable investment income	Gain from operations	Loss from operations
1959	$9,000,000	$10,000,000	
1960			($9,800,000)

The gain from operations thus shown is computed without regard to any operations loss deduction or deductions under section 809(d)(3), (5), and (6), as limited by section 809(f). Assume that for the taxable year 1959, P has (without regard to the limitation of section 809(f) or the operations loss deduction for 1959) a deduction under section 809(d)(3) of $2,500,000 for dividends to policyholders and no deductions under section 809(d)(5) or (6).

(b) Determination of section 809(f) limitation and deduction for dividends to policyholders without regard to the operations loss deduction for 1959. In order to determine gain or loss from operations for 1959, P must determine the deduction for dividends to policyholders for such year. Under the provisions of section 809(f), the amount of such deduction shall not exceed the sum of (1) the amount (if any) by which the gain from operations for such year (determined without regard to such deduction) exceeds P's taxable investment income for such year, plus (2) $250,000. Since the gain from operations as thus determined ($10,000,000) exceeds the taxable investment income $9,000,000) by $1,000,000, the limitation on such deduction is $1,250,000 ($1,000,000 plus $250,000). Accordingly, only $1,250,000 of the $2,500,000 deduction for dividends to policyholders shall be allowed. The gain from operations for such year is $8,750,000 ($10,000,000 minus $1,250,000).

(c) Recomputation of section 809(f) limitation and deduction for dividends to policyholders after application of the operations loss deduction for 1959. Since P has sustained a loss from operations for 1960 which shall be carried back to 1959 as an operations loss deduction, it must recompute the section 809(f) limitation and deduction for dividends to policyholders. Taking into account the $9,800,000 operations loss deduction for 1959 reduces gain from operations for such year to $200,000 ($10,000,000 minus $9,800,000). Since the gain from operations as thus determined ($200,000) is less than the taxable investment income ($9,000,000), the limitation on the deduction for dividends to policyholders is $250,000. Thus, only $250,000 of the $2,500,000 deduction for dividends to policyholders shall be allowed. The gain from operations for such year as thus determined is $9,750,000 ($10,000,000 minus $250,000) since for purposes of this determination the operations loss deduction for 1959 is not taken into account (see section 812(c)(1)). Accordingly, the offset for 1959 is $9,750,000 (the increase in the operations loss deduction for 1959, computed without regard to the carryback for 1960, which reduces life insurance company taxable income for 1959 to zero); thus, the portion of the 1960 loss from operations which shall be carried forward to 1961 is $50,000 (the excess of the 1960 loss ($9,800,000) over the offset for 1959 ($9,750,000)).

(3) Minimum limitation. The life insurance company taxable income, as modified under this paragraph, shall in no case be considered less than zero.

T.D. 6535, 1/19/61.

§ 1.812-6 New company defined.

Caution: The Treasury has not yet amended Reg § 1.812-6 to reflect changes made by P.L. 98-369.

Section 812(e) provides that for purposes of part I, subchapter L, chapter 1 of the Code, a life insurance company is a "new company" for any taxable year only if such taxable year begins not more than 5 years after the first day on which it (or any predecessor if section 381(c)(22) applies or would have applied if in effect) was authorized to do business as an insurance company.

T.D. 6535, 1/19/61, amend T.D. 6886, 6/22/66, T.D. 7326, 9/30/74.

§ 1.812-7 Application of subtitle A and subtitle F.

Caution: The Treasury has not yet amended Reg § 1.812-7 to reflect changes made by P.L. 98-369.

Section 812(f) provides that except as modified by section 809(e) (relating to modifications of deduction items otherwise allowable under subtitle A of the Code) subtitles A and F of the Code shall apply to operations loss carrybacks and carryovers, and to the operations loss deduction, in the same manner and to the same extent that such subtitles apply in respect of net operation loss carrybacks, net operating loss carryovers, and the net operating loss deduction of corporations generally. For the computation of the operations loss carrybacks and carryovers, and of the operations loss deduction in the case of certain acquisitions of the assets of a life insurance company by another life insurance company, see section 381(c)(22) and the regulations thereunder.

T.D. 6535, 1/19/61.

§ 1.812-8 Illustration of operations loss carrybacks and carryovers.

Caution: The Treasury has not yet amended Reg § 1.812-8 to reflect changes made by P.L. 98-369.

The application of § 1.812-4 may be illustrated by the following example:

(a) Facts. The books of M, a life insurance company, organized in 1940, reveal the following facts:

Taxable year	Taxable investment income	Gain from operations	Loss from operations
1958	$11,000	$15,000	
1959	23,000	30,000	
1960			($75,000)
1961	25,000	20,000	
1962			(150,000)
1963	22,000	30,000	
1964	40,000	35,000	
1965	62,000	75,000	
1966	25,000	17,000	
1967	39,000	53,000	

The gain from operations thus shown is computed without regard to any operations loss deduction. The assumption is also made that none of the other modifications prescribed in paragraph (b) of § 1.812-5 apply. There are no losses from operations for 1955, 1956, 1957, 1968, 1969, 1970.

(b) Loss sustained in 1960. The portions of the $75,000 loss from operations for 1960 which shall be used as carrybacks to 1958 and 1959 and as carryovers to 1961, 1962, 1963, 1964, and 1965 are computed as follows:

(1) Carryback to 1958. The carryback to this year is $75,000, that is, the amount of the loss from operations.

(2) Carryback to 1959. The carryback to this year is $60,000 (the excess of the loss for 1960 over the offset for 1958), computed as follows:

Loss from operations	$75,000
Less:	
Offset for 1958 (the $15,000 gain from operations for such year computed without the deduction of the carryback from 1960)	15,000
Carryback	60,000

(3) Carryover to 1961. The carryover to this year is $30,000 (the excess, if any, of the loss for 1960 over the sum of the offsets for 1958 and 1959), computed as follows:

Loss from operations		$75,000
Less:		
Offset for 1958 (the $15,000 gain from operations for such year computed without the deduction of the carryback from 1960)	$15,000	
Offset for 1959 (the $30,000 gain from operations for such year computed without the deduction of the carryback from 1960 or the carryback from 1962)	30,000	
Sum of offsets		45,000
Carryover		30,000

(4) Carryover to 1962. The carryover to this year is $10,000 (the excess, if any, of the loss for 1960 over the sum of the offsets for 1958, 1959, and 1961), computed as follows:

Loss from operations		$75,000
Less:		
Offset for 1958 (the $15,000 gain from operations for such year computed without the deduction of the carryback from 1960)	$15,000	
Offset for 1959 (the $30,000 gain from operations for such year computed without the deduction of the carryback from 1960 or the carryback from 1962)	30,000	
Offset for 1961 (the $20,000 gain from operations for such year computed without the deduction of the carryover from 1960 or the carryback from 1962)	20,000	
Sum of offsets		65,000
Carryover		10,000

(5) Carryover to 1963. The carryover to this year is $10,000 (the excess, if any, of the loss for 1960 over the sum of the offsets for 1958, 1959, 1961, and 1962), computed as follows:

Loss from operations		$75,000
Less:		
Offset for 1958 (the $15,000 gain from operations for such year computed without the deduction of the carryback from 1960)	$15,000	
Offset for 1959 (the $30,000 gain from operations for such year computed without the deduction of the carryback from 1960 or the carryback from 1962)	30,000	
Offset for 1961 (the $20,000 gain from operations for such year computed without the deduction of the carryover from 1960 or the carryback from 1962)	20,000	

Offset for 1962 (a year in which a loss from operations was sustained)	0	
Sum of offsets		65,000
Carryover		10,000

(6) *Carryover to 1964.* The carryover to this year is $0 (the excess, if any, of the loss from 1960 over the sum of the offsets for 1958, 1959, 1961, 1962, and 1963), computed as follows:

Loss from operations		$75,000
Less:		
Offset for 1958 (the $15,000 gain from operations for such year computed without the deduction of the carryback from 1960)	$15,000	
Offset for 1959 (the $30,000 gain from operations for such year computed without the deduction of the carryback from 1960 or the carryback from 1962)	30,000	
Offset for 1961 (the $20,000 gain from operations for such year computed without the deduction of the carryover from 1960 or the carryback from 1962)	20,000	
Offset for 1962 (a year in which a loss from operations was sustained)	0	
Offset for 1963 (the $30,000 gain from operations for such year computed without the deduction of the carryover from 1960 or the carryover from 1962)	30,000	
Sum of offsets		95,000
Carryover		0

(7) *Carryover to 1965.* The carryover to this year is $0 (the excess, if any, of the loss from 1960 over the sum of the offsets for 1958, 1959, 1961, 1962, 1963, and 1964), computed as follows:

Loss from operations		$ 75,000
Less:		
Offset for 1958 (the $15,000 gain from operations for such year computed without the deduction of the carryback from 1960)	$15,000	
Offset for 1959 (the $30,000 gain from operations for such year computed without the deduction for the carryback from 1960 or the carryback from 1962)	30,000	
Offset for 1961 (the $20,000 gain from operations for such year computed without the deduction for the carryover from 1960 or the carryback from 1962)	20,000	
Offset for 1962 (a year in which a loss from operations was sustained)	0	
Offset for 1963 (the $30,000 gain from operations for such year computed without the deduction for the carryover from 1960 or the carryover from 1962)	30,000	
Offset for 1964 (the $35,000 gain from operations for such year computed without the deduction of the carryover from 1960 or the carryover from 1962)	35,000	
Sum of offsets		130,000
Carryover		0

(c) Loss sustained in 1962. The portions of the $150,000 loss from operations for 1962 which shall be used as carrybacks to 1959, 1960, and 1961 and as carryovers to 1963, 1964, 1965, 1966, and 1967 are computed as follows:

(1) *Carryback to 1959.* The carryback to this year is $150,000, that is, the amount of the loss from operations.

(2) *Carryback to 1960.* The carryback to this year is $150,000 (the excess, if any, of the loss from 1962 over the offset for 1959), computed as follows:

Loss from operations	$150,000
Less:	
Offset for 1959 (the $30,000 gain from operations for such year reduced by the carryback to such year of $60,000 from 1960, the carryback from 1962 to 1959 not being taken into account)	0
Carryback	150,000

(3) *Carryback to 1961.* The carryback to this year is $150,000 (the excess, if any, of the loss from 1962 over the sum of the offsets for 1959 and 1960), computed as follows:

Loss from operations		$150,000
Less:		
Offset for 1959 (the $30,000 gain from operations for such year reduced by the carryback to such year of $60,000 from 1960, the carryback from 1962 to 1959 not being taken into account)	$0	
Offset for 1960 (a year in which a loss from operations was sustained)	0	
Sum of offsets		0
Carryback		150,000

(4) *Carryover to 1963.* The carryover to this year is $150,000 (the excess, if any, of the loss from 1962 over the sum of the offsets for 1959, 1960, and 1961), computed as follows:

Loss from operations		$150,000
Less:		
Offset for 1959 (the $30,000 gain from operations for such year reduced by the carryback to such year of $60,000 from 1960, the carryback from 1962 to 1959 not being taken into account)	$0	
Offset for 1960 (a year in which a loss from operations was sustained)	0	
Offset for 1961 (the $20,000 gain from operations for such year reduced by the carryover to such year of $30,000 from 1960, the carryback from 1962 to 1961 not being taken into account)	0	
Sum of offsets		0
Carryover		150,000

(5) *Carryover to 1964.* The carryover to this year is $130,000 (the excess, if any, of the loss from 1962 over the

sum of the offsets for 1959, 1960, 1961, and 1963), computed as follows:

Loss from operations		$150,000
Less:		
Offset for 1959 (the $30,000 gain from operations for such year reduced by the carryback to such year of $60,000 from 1960, the carryback from 1962 to 1959 not being taken into account)	$ 0	
Offset for 1960 (a year in which a loss from operations was sustained)	0	
Offset for 1961 (the $20,000 gain from operations for such year reduced by the carryover to such year of $30,000 from 1960, the carryback from 1962 to 1961 not being taken into account)	0	
Offset for 1963 (the $30,000 gain from operations for such year reduced by the carryover to such year of $10,000 from 1960, the carryover from 1962 to 1963 not being taken into account)	20,000	
Sum of offsets		20,000
Carryover		130,000

(6) *Carryover to 1965.* The carryover to this year is $95,000 (the excess, if any, of the loss from 1962 over the sum of the offsets for 1959, 1960, 1961, 1963, and 1964), computed as follows:

Loss from operations		$150,000
Less:		
Offset for 1959 (the $30,000 gain from operations for such year reduced by the carryback to such year of $60,000 from 1960, the carryback from 1962 to 1959 not being taken into account)	$ 0	
Offset for 1960 (a year in which a loss from operations was sustained)	0	
Offset for 1961 (the $20,000 gain from operations for such year reduced by the carryover to such year of $30,000 from 1960, the carryback from 1962 to 1961 not being taken into account)	0	
Offset for 1963 (the $30,000 gain from operations for such year reduced by the carryover to such year of $10,000 from 1960, the carryover from 1962 to 1963 not being taken into account)	20,000	
Offset for 1964 (the $35,000 gain from operations for such year reduced by the carryover to such year of $0 from 1960, the carryover from 1962 to 1964 not being taken into account)	35,000	
Sum of offsets		55,000
Carryover		95,000

(7) *Carryover to 1966.* The carryover to this year is $20,000 (the excess, if any, of the loss from 1962 over the sum of the offsets for 1959, 1960, 1961, 1963, 1964, and 1965), computed as follows:

Loss from operations		$150,000
Less:		
Offset for 1959 (the $30,000 gain from operations for such year reduced by the carryback to such year of $60,000 from 1960, the carryback from 1962 to 1959 not being taken into account)	$ 0	
Offset for 1960 (a year in which a loss from operations was sustained)	0	
Offset for 1961 (the $20,000 gain from operations for such year reduced by the carryover to such year of $30,000 from 1960, the carryback from 1962 to 1961 not being taken into account)	0	
Offset for 1963 (the $30,000 gain from operations for such year reduced by the carryover for such year of $10,000 from 1960, the carryover from 1962 to 1963 not being taken into account)	20,000	
Offset for 1964 (the $35,000 gain from operations for such year reduced by the carryover to such year of $0 from 1960, the carryover from 1962 to 1964 not being taken into account)	35,000	
Offset for 1965 (the $75,000 gain from operations for such year reduced by the carryover to such year of $0 from 1960, the carryover from 1962 to 1965 not being taken into account)	75,000	
Sum of offsets		130,000
Carryover		20,000

(8) *Carryover to 1967.* The carryover to this year is $3,000 (the excess, if any, of the loss from 1962 over the sum of the offsets for 1959, 1960, 1961, 1963, 1964, 1965, and 1966), computed as follows:

Loss from operations		$150,000
Less:		
Offset for 1959 (the $30,000 gain from operations for such year reduced by the carryback to such year of $60,000 from 1960, the carryback from 1962 to 1959 not being taken into account)	$ 0	
Offset for 1960 (a year in which a loss from operations was sustained)	0	
Offset for 1961 (the $20,000 gain from operations for such year reduced by the carryover to such year of $30,000 from 1960, the carryback from 1962 to 1961 not being taken into account)	0	

Offset for 1963 (the $30,000 gain from operations for such year reduced by the carryover to such year of $10,000 from 1960, the carryover from 1962 to 1963 not being taken into account) 20,000
Offset for 1964 (the $35,000 gain from operations for such year reduced by the carryover to such year of $0 from 1960, the carryover from 1962 to 1964 not being taken into account) 35,000
Offset for 1965 (the $75,000 gain from operations for such year reduced by the carryover to such year of $0 from 1960, the carryover from 1962 to 1965 not being taken into account) 75,000
Offset for 1966 (the $17,000 gain from operations for such year computed without the deduction of the carryover from 1962) 17,000

Sum of offsets 147,000

Carryover.......................... 3,000

(d) Determination of operations loss deduction for each year. The carryovers and carrybacks computed under paragraphs (b) and (c) of this section are used as a basis for the computation of the operations loss deduction in the following manner:

	Carryover		Carryback		
Taxable year	From 1960	From 1962	From 1960	From 1962	Operations loss deductions
1958 ...			$75,000		$ 75,000
1959 ...			60,000	$150,000	210,000
1961 ...	$30,000			150,000	180,000
1963 ...	10,000	$150,000			160,000
1964 ...		130,000			130,000
1965 ...		95,000			95,000
1966 ...		20,000			20,000
1967 ...		3,000			3,000

T.D. 6535, 1/19/61.

§ 1.812-9 Cross-reference.

For special rules regarding the treatment of modified guaranteed contracts (as defined in section 817A and § 1.817A-1(a)(1)), see § 1.817A-1.

T.D. 9058, 5/6/2003.

§ 1.815-1 Taxable years affected.

Caution: The Treasury has not yet amended Reg § 1.815-1 to reflect changes made by P.L. 98-369.

Sections 1.815-2 through 1.815-6, except as otherwise provided therein, are applicable only to taxable years beginning after December 31, 1957, and all references to sections of part I, subchapter L, chapter 1 of the Code are to the Internal Revenue Code of 1954, as amended by the Life Insurance Company Income Tax Act of 1959 (73 Stat. 112), the Act of October 10, 1962 (76 Stat. 808), and the Act of October 23, 1962 (76 Stat. 1134).

T.D. 6535, 1/19/61, amend T.D. 6886, 6/22/66.

§ 1.815-2 Distributions to shareholders.

Caution: The Treasury has not yet amended Reg § 1.815-2 to reflect changes made by P.L. 108-357, P.L. 98-369.

(a) In general. Section 815 provides that every stock life insurance company subject to the tax imposed by section 802 shall establish and maintain two special surplus accounts for Federal income tax purposes. These special accounts are the shareholders surplus account (as defined in section 815(b) and § 1.815-3) and the policyholders surplus account (as defined in section 815(c) and § 1.815-4). To the extent that a distribution to shareholders (as defined in paragraph (c) of this section) is treated as being made out of the shareholders surplus account, no tax is imposed on the company with respect to such distribution. However, to the extent that a distribution to shareholders is treated as being made out of the policyholders surplus account, the amount subtracted from the policyholders surplus account by reason of such distribution shall be taken into account in determining life insurance company taxable income under section 802(b).

(b) Priority system for distributions to shareholders. *(1)* For purposes of section 815 (other than subsection (e) thereof relating to certain mutualizations) and section 802(b)(3) (relating to the determination of life insurance company taxable income), any distribution made to shareholders after December 31, 1958, shall be treated in the following manner:

(i) Distributions shall be treated as first being made out of the shareholders surplus account (as defined in section 815(b) and § 1.815-3);

(ii) Once the shareholders surplus account has been reduced to zero, distributions shall then be treated as being made out of the policyholders surplus account (as defined in section 815(c) and § 1.815-4) until that account has been reduced to zero; and

(iii) Finally, any distributions in excess of the amounts in the shareholders surplus account and the policyholders surplus account shall be treated as being made out of other accounts (as defined in § 1.815-5).

(2) For purposes of subparagraph (1) of this paragraph, in order to determine whether a distribution (or any portion thereof) shall be treated as being made out of the shareholders surplus account, policyholders surplus account, or other accounts, the amount in such accounts at the end of any taxable year shall be the cumulative balance in such accounts at the end of the taxable year, computed without diminution by reason of a distribution (or any portion thereof) during the taxable year which is treated as being made out of such accounts. For example, on January 1, 1960, S, a stock life insurance company, had $1,000 in its shareholders surplus account and $3,000 in its policyholders surplus account. On November 1, 1960, S distributed $4,000 to its shareholders. Under the provisions of section 815(b)(2) and paragraph (b) of § 1.815-3, S added $5,000 to its shareholders surplus account for the taxable year 1960. Since the distributions to shareholders during the taxable year 1960, $4,000, does not exceed the cumulative balance in the shareholders surplus account at the end of the taxable year, computed without diminution by reason of distributions treated as made out of such account during the taxable year, $6,000 ($1,000 plus $5,000), the entire distribution is treated as being made out of the shareholders surplus account.

(3) Except in the case of a distribution in cash and as otherwise provided herein, the amount to be charged to the special surplus accounts referred to in subparagraph (1) of this paragraph with respect to any distributions to shareholders (as defined in section 815(a) and paragraph (c) of this section) shall be the fair market value of the property distributed, determined as of the date of distribution. However, for the amount of the adjustment to earnings and profits reflecting such distributions, see section 312 and the regulations thereunder. For a special rule relating to the determination of the amount to be charged to such special surplus accounts in the case of a distribution by a foreign life insurance company carrying on a life insurance business within the United States, see section 819(c)(1) and the regulations thereunder.

(c) Distributions to shareholders defined. *(1)* Except as otherwise provided in section 815(f) and in subparagraph (2) of this paragraph, the term "distribution", as used in section 815(a) and paragraph (b) of this section, means any distribution of property made by a life insurance company to its shareholders. For purposes of the preceding sentence, the term "property" means any property (including money, securities, and indebtedness to the company) other than stock, or rights to acquire stock, in the company making the distribution. Thus, for example, the term includes a distribution which is considered a dividend under section 316, but is not limited to the extent that such distribution must be made out of the accumulated or current earnings and profits of the company making the distribution. For example, except as otherwise provided in section 815(f) and subparagraph (2) of this paragraph, there is a distribution within the meaning of this paragraph in any case in which a corporation acquires the stock of a shareholder in exchange for property in a redemption treated as a distribution in exchange for stock under section 302(a) or treated as a distribution of property under section 302(d). For special rules relating to distributions to shareholders in acquisition of stock pursuant to a plan of mutualization, see section 815(e) and paragraph (e) of § 1.815-6.

(2) The term "distribution", as used in section 815(a) and paragraph (b) of this section, does not (except for purposes of section 815(a)(3) and (e)(2)(B)) include any distribution in redemption of stock issued prior to January 1, 1958, where such stock was at all times on and after the date of its issuance and on and before the date of its redemption limited as to the amount of dividends payable and was callable, at the option of the issuer, at a price not in excess of 105 percent of the sum of its issue price plus the amount of contribution to surplus (if any) made by the original purchaser at the time of his purchase.

T.D. 6535, 1/19/61, amend T.D. 7189, 6/28/72.

§ 1.815-3 Shareholders surplus account.

Caution: The Treasury has not yet amended Reg § 1.815-3 to reflect changes made by P.L. 108-357, P.L. 98-369.

(a) In general. Every stock life insurance company subject to the tax imposed by section 802 shall establish and maintain a shareholders surplus account. This account shall be established as of January 1, 1958, and the beginning or opening balance of the shareholders surplus account on that date shall be zero.

(b) Additions to shareholders surplus account. *(1)* The amount added to the shareholders surplus account for any taxable year beginning after December 31, 1957, shall be the amount by which the sum of—

(i) The life insurance company taxable income (computed without regard to section 802(b)(3)),

(ii) In the case of a taxable year beginning after December 31, 1958, the amount (if any) by which the net long-term capital gain exceeds the net short-term capital loss, reduced (in the case of a taxable year beginning after December 31, 1961) by the amount referred to in subdivision (i) of this subparagraph.

(iii) The deduction for partially tax-exempt interest provided by section 242 (as modified by section 804(a)(3)), the deductions for dividends received provided by sections 243, 244, and 245 (as modified by section 809(d)(8)(B)), and the amount of interest excluded from gross income under section 103, and

(iv) The small business deduction provided by section 809(d)(10), exceeds the taxes imposed for the taxable year by section 802(a), computed without regard to section 802(b)(3).

(2) For amounts which are to be added to the shareholders surplus account at the beginning of the succeeding taxable year, see section 815(d)(1) and (4) and paragraphs (a) and (d) of § 1.815-6.

(c) Subtractions from shareholders surplus account. *(1) In general.* There shall be subtracted from the cumulative balance in the shareholders surplus account at the end of any taxable year, computed without diminution by reason of distributions made during the taxable year, the amount which is treated as being distributed out of such account under section 815(a) and paragraph (b) of § 1.815-2.

(2) Special rule; distributions in 1958. There shall be subtracted from the shareholders surplus account (to the extent thereof) for any taxable year beginning in 1958 the amount of the distributions to shareholders made by the company during 1958. For example, assume S, a stock life insurance company, had additions to its shareholders surplus account (as determined under section 815(b)(2) and paragraph (b) of this section) for the taxable year 1958 of $10,000, and actually distributed as dividends to its shareholders $8,000 during the year 1958. The balance in S's shareholders surplus account as of January 1, 1959, shall be $2,000. If S had distributed $12,000 as dividends in 1958, the balance in its shareholders surplus account as of January 1, 1959, would be zero and the other accounts referred to in section 815(a)(3) and paragraph (b)(1)(iii) of § 1.815-2 would be reduced by $2,000.

(d) Illustration of principles. The application of section 815(b) and this section may be illustrated by the following example:

Example. The books of S, a stock life insurance company, reflect the following items for the taxable year 1960:

Balance in shareholders surplus account as of 1-1-60	$5,000
Life insurance company taxable income computed without regard to sec. 802(b)(3)	4,000
Excess of net long-term capital gain over net short-term capital loss	1,700
Tax-exempt interest included in gross investment income under sec. 804(b)	100
Small business deduction (determined under sec. 809(d)(10))	200
Tax liability under sec. 802(a)(1) and (2) computed without regard to sec. 802(b)(3)	$1,625
Amount distributed to shareholders	9,000

For purposes of determining the amount to be subtracted from its shareholders surplus account for the taxable year, S would first make up the following schedule in order to determine the cumulative balance in the shareholders surplus account at the end of the taxable year, computed without diminution by reason of distributions made during the taxable year.

(1) Balance in shareholders surplus account as of 1-1-60		$5,000
(2) Additions to account:(a) Life insurance company taxable income computed without regard to sec. 802(b)(3)	$4,000	
(b) Excess of net long-term capital gain over net short-term capital loss	1,700	
(c) Tax-exempt interest included in gross investment income under sec. 804(b)	100	
(d) Small business deduction (determined under sec. 809(d)(10))	200	
Total	6,000	
Less:		
Tax liability under sec. 802(a)(1) and (2) computed without regard to sec. 802(b)(3)	1,625	
		4,375
(3) Cumulative balance in shareholders surplus account as of 12-31-60 (item (1) plus item (2))		9,375

Since the amount distributed to shareholders during the taxable year, $9,000, does not exceed the cumulative balance in the shareholders surplus account at the end of the taxable year, computed without diminution by reason of distributions made during the taxable year, $9,375, under the provisions of section 815(a), the entire distribution shall be treated as being made out of the shareholders surplus account. Thus, $9,000 shall be subtracted from the shareholders surplus account (leaving a balance of $375 in such account at the end of the taxable year) and S shall incur no additional tax liability by reason of the distribution to its shareholders during the taxable year 1960.

T.D. 6535, 1/19/61, amend T.D. 7189, 6/28/72.

§ 1.815-4 Policyholders surplus account.

Caution: The Treasury has not yet amended Reg § 1.815-4 to reflect changes made by P.L. 108-357, P.L. 98-369.

(a) In general. Every stock life insurance company subject to the tax imposed by section 802 shall establish and maintain a policyholders surplus account. This account shall be established as of January 1, 1959, and the beginning or opening balance of the policyholders surplus account on that date shall be zero.

(b) Additions to policyholders surplus account. The amount added to the policyholders surplus account for any taxable year beginning after December 31, 1958, shall be the sum of—

(1) An amount equal to 50 percent of the amount by which the gain from operations for the taxable year exceeds the taxable investment income,

(2) The deduction allowed or allowable under section 809(d)(5) (as limited by section 809(f)) for certain nonparticipating contracts, and

(3) The deduction allowed or allowable under section 809(d)(6) (as limited by section 809(f)) for taxable years beginning before January 1, 1963, for group life and group accident and health insurance contracts, and for taxable years beginning after December 31, 1962, for accident and health insurance and group life insurance contracts.

(c) Subtractions from policyholders surplus account. *(1) In general.* There shall be subtracted from the cumulative balance in the policyholders surplus account at the end of any taxable year, computed without diminution by reason of distributions made during the taxable year, an amount equal to the sum of—

(i) The amount which (without regard to subdivision (ii) of this subparagraph) is treated under section 815(a) as distributed out of the policyholders surplus account for the taxable year, plus

(ii) The amount (determined without regard to section 802(a)(3)) by which the tax imposed for taxable years beginning before January 1, 1962, by section 802(a)(1), and for taxable years beginning after December 31, 1961, by section 802(a), is increased by reason of section 802(b)(3).

In addition, there shall be subtracted from the policyholders surplus account for the taxable year those amounts which, at the close of the taxable year, are subtracted or treated as subtracted from the policyholders surplus account under section 815(d)(1) and (4) and paragraphs (a) and (d) of § 1.815-6. For purposes of this paragraph, the subtractions from the policyholders surplus account shall be treated as made in the following order:

(a) First the amount determined under section 815(c)(3) by reason of distributions to shareholders during the taxable year which are treated as being made out of the policyholders surplus account;

(b) Next the amount elected to be subtracted from the policyholders surplus account for the taxable year under section 815(d)(1);

(c) Then the amount which is treated as a subtraction from the policyholders surplus account for the taxable year by reason of the limitation provided in section 815(d)(4); and

(d) Finally the amount taken into account upon termination as a life insurance company as provided in section 815(d)(2).

(2) Method of computing amount subtracted from policyholders surplus account. (i) Where life insurance company taxable income, computed without regard to section 802(b)(3), exceeds $25,000. If the life insurance company taxable income for any taxable year computed under section 802(b), computed without regard to section 802(b)(3), exceeds $25,000, the amount subtracted from the policyholders surplus account shall be determined by multiplying the amount treated as distributed out of such account by a ratio, the numerator of which is 100 percent and the denominator of which is 100 percent minus the sum of the normal tax rate and the surtax rate for the taxable year.

(ii) Where life insurance company taxable income does not exceed $25,000. If the life insurance company taxable income for any taxable year, computed under section 802(b), does not exceed $25,000, the amount subtracted from the policyholders surplus account shall be determined by multiplying the amount treated as distributed out of such account by a ratio, the numerator of which is 100 percent and the denominator of which is 100 percent minus the normal tax rate for the taxable year.

(iii) Where life insurance company taxable income, computed without regard to section 802(b)(3) does not exceed $25,000, but computed with regard to section 802(b)(3) does exceed $25,000. If the life insurance company taxable income for any taxable year, computed without regard to section 802(b)(3) does not exceed $25,000, but computed with regard to section 802(b)(3) does exceed $25,000, the amount subtracted from the policy holders surplus account shall be determined in the following manner:

(a) First, determine the amount by which $25,000 exceeds the amount determined under section 802(b)(1) and (2);

(b) Then, multiply the amount determined under (a) by a ratio, the numerator of which is 100 percent minus the normal tax rate and the denominator of which is 100 percent;

(c) Next, determine the amount by which the amount treated as distributed out of the policyholders surplus account exceeds the amount determined under (b) and multiply such excess by a ratio, the numerator of which is 100 percent and the denominator of which is 100 percent minus the sum of the normal tax rate and the surtax rate; and

(d) Finally, add the amounts determined under (a) and (c).

(3) *Illustration of principles.* The application of section 815(c)(3) and subparagraph (2) of this paragraph may be illustrated by the following examples:

Example (1). The life insurance company taxable income of S, a stock life insurance company, computed without regard to section 802(b)(3), exceeds $25,000 for the taxable year 1959. Assume that of the amount distributed by S to its shareholders during the taxable year, $9,600 (as determined under section 815(a) and without regard to section 815(c)(3)(B)) is treated as distributed out of the policyholders surplus account. Since the sum of the normal tax rate (30%) and the surtax rate (22%) in effect for 1959 is 52 percent, S shall subtract $20,000 from its policyholders surplus account for the taxable year 1959, computed as follows:

$$\$9{,}600 \times \frac{100}{(100-52)} = \$9{,}600 \times \frac{100}{48} = \$20{,}000$$

Of this amount, $9,600 is due to the application of section 815(c)(3)(A) and $10,400 to the application of section 815(c)(3)(B).

Example (2). Assume that for the taxable year 1960, S, a stock life insurance company, has taxable investment income of $1,000 and a gain from operations of $2,000. Assume further that of the amount distributed by S to its shareholders during the taxable year, $3,500 (as determined under section 815(a) and without regard to section 815(c)(3)(B)) is treated as distributed out of the policyholders surplus account. Since S's life insurance company taxable income does not exceed $25,000 for the taxable year and the normal tax rate in effect for 1960 is 30 percent, S shall subtract $5,000 from its policyholders surplus account for the taxable year 1960, computed as follows:

$$\$3{,}500 \times \frac{100}{(100-30)} = \$3{,}500 \times \frac{100}{70} = \$5{,}000$$

Of this amount, $3,500 is due to the application of section 815(c)(3)(A), and $1,500 to the application of section 815(c)(3)(B).

Example (3). For the taxable year 1960, the life insurance company taxable income of S, a stock life insurance company, computed without regard to section 802(b)(3), is $10,000. Assume that of the amount distributed by S to its shareholders during the taxable year, $12,000 (as determined under section 815(a) and without regard to section 815(c)(3)(B)) is treated as distributed out of the policyholders surplus account. Since the life insurance company taxable income of S, computed with regard to section 802(b)(3), exceeds $25,000, in order to determine the amount to be subtracted from its policyholders surplus account, S would make up the following schedule:

(1) $25,000 minus life insurance company taxable income, computed without regard to sec. 802(b)(3) ($25,000 minus $10,000)	$15,000
(2) Item (1) multiplied by 100 percent minus the normal tax rate as in effect for 1960, over 100 percent $\$15{,}000 \times \frac{(100-30)}{100}$	10,500
(3) Amount by which the amount treated as distributed out of policyholders surplus account ($12,000) exceeds item (2) ($10,500), multiplied by 100 percent over 100 percent minus the sum of the normal tax rate and the surtax rate as in effect for 1960 $\$1{,}500 \times \frac{100}{(100-52)}$	3,125
(4) Item (1) plus item (3) ($15,000 plus $3,125)	18,125

For the taxable year 1960, S shall subtract $18,125 from its policyholders surplus account. Of this amount, $10,500 represents the distribution from the policyholders surplus account which is taxed at a 30 percent tax rate and $1,500 the distribution from the policyholders surplus account which is taxed at a 52 percent tax rate. Thus, of the amount subtracted from the policy holders surplus account for the taxable year 1960, $12,000 is due to the application of section 815(c)(3)(A), and $6,125 to the application of section 815(c)(3)(B).

(d) Illustration of principles. The application of section 815(c) and this section may be illustrated by the following example:

Example. The books of S, a stock life insurance company, reflect the following items for the taxable year 1960:

Taxable investment income	$25,000
Gain from operations	30,000
Tax base (sec. 802(b)(1) and (2))	27,500
Deduction for certain nonparticipating policies provided by sec. 809(d)(5) (as limited by sec. 809(f))	600
Deduction for group policies provided by sec. 809(d)(6) (as limited by sec. 809(f))	400
Amount distributed to shareholders	60,000
Cumulative balance in shareholders surplus account as of 12-31-60	36,000
Balance in policyholders surplus account of 1-1-60	48,000

For purposes of determining the amount to be subtracted from its policyholders surplus account for the taxable year, S would first make up the following schedule in order to determine the cumulative balance in the policyholders surplus account at the end of the taxable year, computed without diminution by reason of distributions made during the taxable year:

(1) Balance in policyholders surplus account as of 1-1-60 .... $48,000
(2) Additions to account:
  (a) 50 percent of the amount by which the gain from operations ($30,000) exceeds the taxable investment income ($25,000) (½× $5,000)........................... $2,500
  (b) The deduction for certain nonparticipating contracts provided by sec. 809(d)(5) (as limited by sec. 809(f) 600
  (c) The deduction for group contracts provided by sec. 809(d)(6) (as limited by sec. 809(f)) 400
  3,500
(3) Cumulative balance in policyholders account as of 12-31-60 (item (1) plus item (2))........... 51,500

Under the provisions of section 815(a), since the amount distributed to shareholders during the taxable year, $60,000, exceeds the cumulative balance in the shareholders surplus at the end of the taxable year, computed without diminution by reason of distributions during the taxable year, $86,000, the shareholders surplus account shall first be reduced to zero. The remaining $24,000 ($60,000 minus $36,000) of the distribution shall then be treated as made out of the policyholders surplus account. Thus, since the tax base under section 802(b)(1) and (2) is in excess of $25,000, the total amount to be subtracted from the policyholders surplus account at the end of the taxable year would be $50,000

$$\$24{,}000 \times \frac{100}{(100 - 52)}$$

Of this amount $26,000 ($50,000 minus $24,000) represents the tax on the portion of the distribution to shareholders which is treated as being out of the policyholders surplus account.

(e) Special rule for 1959 and 1960. For a special transitional rule applicable to any increase in tax liability under section 802(b)(3) for the taxable years 1959 and 1960 which is due solely to the operation of section 815(c)(3) and this section, see section 802(a)(3) and § 1.802-5.

T.D. 6535, 1/19/61, amend T.D. 6886, 6/22/66.

§ 1.815-5 Other accounts defined.

Caution: The Treasury has not yet amended Reg § 1.815-5 to reflect changes made by P.L. 108-357, P.L. 98-369.

The term "other accounts", as used in section 815(a)(3) and paragraph (b) of § 1.815-2, means all amounts which are not specifically included in the shareholders surplus account under section 815(b) and paragraph (b) of § 1.815-3, or in the policyholders surplus account under section 815(c) and paragraph (b) of § 1.815-4. Thus, for example, other accounts includes amounts representing the increase in tax due to the operation of section 802(b)(3) which is not taken into account for the taxable years 1959 and 1960 because of the special transitional rule provided in section 802(a)(3) and § 1.802-5, earnings and profits accumulated prior to January 1, 1958, paid-in surplus, capital, etc. To the extent that a distribution (or any portion thereof) is treated as being made out of other accounts, no tax is imposed on the company with respect to such distribution.

T.D. 6535, 1/19/61.

§ 1.815-6 Special rules.

Caution: The Treasury has not yet amended Reg § 1.815-6 to reflect changes made by P.L. 108-357, P.L. 98-369.

(a) Election to transfer amounts from policyholders surplus account to shareholders surplus account. *(1) In general.* Section 815(d)(1) permits a life insurance company to elect, after the close of any taxable year for which it is a life insurance company, to subtract any amount (or any portion thereof) in its policyholders surplus account as of the close of the taxable year. The effect of such election is to subject the company to tax on the amounts elected to be subtracted for the taxable year for which the election applies. The amount so subtracted, less the amount of tax imposed with respect to such amount by reason of section 802(b)(3), shall be added to the shareholders surplus account as of the beginning of the taxable year following the taxable year for which the election applies and no further tax shall be imposed upon the company if the amount elected to be transferred to the shareholders surplus account is subsequently distributed to shareholders.

(2) Manner and effect of election. (i) The election provided by section 815(d)(1) and this section shall be made in a statement attached to the life insurance company's income tax return for any taxable year for which the company desires the election to apply. The statement shall include the name and address of the taxpayer, shall be signed by the taxpayer (or his duly authorized representative), and shall be filed not later than the date prescribed by law (including extensions thereof) for filing the return for such taxable year. In addition, the statement shall indicate that the company has made the election provided under section 815(d)(1) for the taxable year and the amount elected to be subtracted from the policyholders surplus account.

(ii) An election made under section 815(d)(1)(B) and subdivision (i) of this subparagraph shall be effective only with respect to the taxable year for which the election is made. Thus, the company must make a new election for each taxable year for which it desires the election to apply. Once such an election has been made for any taxable year it may not be revoked.

(3) The application of subparagraph (1) of this paragraph may be illustrated by the following example:

Example. For the taxable year 1960, the life insurance company taxable income of S, a stock life insurance company, computed without regard to section 802(b)(3), exceeds $25,000. Assume that S elects to subtract $20,000 from its policyholders surplus account under section 815(d)(1) for the taxable year. Since S is subject to a 52 percent tax rate, the tax on the amount elected to be subtracted from the policyholders surplus account (as of the close of the taxable year 1960) is $10,400 ($20,000 × 52 percent). Thus, the amount to be added to the shareholders surplus account as of January 1, 1961, is $9,600 (the amount subtracted from the policyholders surplus account by virtue of the section 815(d)(1) election, less the tax imposed upon such amount by reason of section 802(b)(3), or $20,000 minus $10,400).

(b) Termination as life insurance company. *(1) Effect of termination.* Except as provided in section 381(c)(22) (relating to carryovers in certain corporate readjustments), section 815(d)(2)(A) provides that if for any taxable year the taxpayer is not an insurance company (as defined in paragraph (a) of § 1.801-3), or if for any two successive taxable years the taxpayer is not a life insurance company (as defined in section 801(a) and paragraph (b) of § 1.801-3), the amount taken into account under section 802(b)(3) for the last preceding year for which the company was a life insurance company shall be increased (after the application of section 815(d)(2)(B)) by the entire balance in the policyholders surplus account at the close of such last preceding taxable year.

(2) Effect of certain distributions. If for any taxable year the taxpayer is an insurance company (as defined in paragraph (a) of § 1.801-3) but is not a life insurance company (as defined in section 801(a) and paragraph (b) of § 1.801-3), section 815(d)(2)(B) provides that any distribution to shareholders during such taxable year shall be treated as having been made on the last day of the last preceding taxable year for which the company was a life insurance company.

(3) Examples. The application of section 815(d)(2) and this paragraph may be illustrated by the following examples:

Example (1). At the end of the taxable year 1959, the balance in the policyholders surplus account of S, a life insurance company within the meaning of section 801(a) and paragraph (b) of § 1.801-3, is $12,000. If S fails to qualify as an insurance company (as defined in paragraph (a) of § 1.801-3) for the taxable year 1960, and section 381(c)(22) does not apply, under the provisions of section 815(d)(2)(A), the entire balance of $12,000 in the policyholders surplus account at the end of 1959, the last year S was a life insurance company, shall be taken into account under section 802(b)(3) for purposes of determining S's tax liability for the taxable year 1959.

Example (2). Assume the facts are the same as in example (1), except that for the taxable years 1960 and 1961, S qualifies as an insurance company (as defined in paragraph (a) of § 1.801-3) but does not qualify as a life insurance company within the meaning of section 801(a) and paragraph (b) of § 1.801-3. Assume further that as a result of a distribution by S to its shareholders in 1960, $4,800 (as determined under section 815(a) and without regard to section 815(c)(3)(B)) is treated as distributed out of the policyholders surplus account. Under the provisions of section 815(d)(2)(B), if section 381(c)(22) does not apply, any distribution to shareholders during the taxable years 1960 and 1961 shall be treated as having been made on December 31, 1959 (the last day of the last preceding taxable year for which S was a life insurance company). Thus, assuming S is subject to a 52 percent tax rate on additions to life insurance company taxable income, $10,000 ($4,800 plus $5,200, the tax on the portion of the distribution treated as made out of the policyholders surplus account) shall be treated as being subtracted from the policyholders surplus account at the end of 1959 and shall be taken into account under section 802(b)(3) for purposes of determining S's tax liability for the taxable year 1959. Under the provisions of section 815(d)(2)(A), the entire balance of $2,000 ($12,000 minus $10,000) in the policyholders surplus account at the end of 1959 (after the application of section 815(d)(2)(B)), shall also be taken into account under section 802(b)(3) for purposes of determining S's tax liability for the taxable year 1959.

(c) Treatment of certain indebtedness. Section 815(d)(3) provides that if a taxpayer makes any payment in discharge of its indebtedness and such indebtedness is attributable to a distribution by the taxpayer to its shareholders after February 9, 1959, the amount of such payment shall be treated as a distribution in cash to shareholders both for purposes of section 802(b)(3) and section 815. However, this paragraph shall only apply to the extent that the distribution of such indebtedness to shareholders was treated as being out of accounts other than the shareholders and policyholders surplus accounts at the time of distribution.

(d) Limitation on amount in policyholders surplus account. *(1) In general.* Section 815(d)(4) provides a limitation on the amount that any life insurance company may accumulate in its policyholders surplus account. If the policyholders surplus account at the end of any taxable year (computed without regard to this paragraph) exceeds whichever of the following is the greatest—

(i) 15 percent of life insurance reserves (as defined in section 801(b) and paragraph (a) of § 1.801-4) at the end of the taxable year,

(ii) 25 percent of the amount by which the life insurance reserves at the end of the taxable year exceed the life insurance reserves at the end of 1958, or

(iii) 50 percent of the net amount of the premiums and other consideration taken into account for the taxable year under section 809(c)(1),

then such excess shall be treated as a subtraction from the policyholders surplus account as of the end of such taxable year. The amount so treated as subtracted, less the amount of tax imposed with respect to such amount by reason of section 802(b)(3), shall be added to the shareholders surplus account at the beginning of the succeeding taxable year.

(2) Example. The application of the limitation contained in subparagraph (1) of this paragraph may be illustrated by the following example:

Example. The books of S, a stock life insurance company, reflect the following items for the taxable year 1960:

Balance in policyholders surplus account, computed without regard to sec. 815(d)(4), as of 12-31-60	$ 175
Life insurance reserves (as defined in sec. 801(b)) as of 12-31-60	4,500
Life insurance reserves (as defined in sec. 801(b)) as of 12-31-58	3,900
Premiums and other consideration taken into account for the taxable year under sec. 809(c)(1)	310

In order to determine the limitations on the amount that it may accumulate in its policyholders surplus account at the end of the taxable year under section 815(d)(4), S would make up the following schedule:

(1) 15 percent of life insurance reserves at the end of the taxable year (15% × $4,500)	$675
(2) 25 percent of amount by which life insurance reserves at the end of the taxable year ($4,500) exceed life insurance reserves as of 12-31-58 ($3,900) (25% × $600)	$150
(3) 50 percent of premiums and other consideration taken into account under sec. 809(c)(1) for the taxable year (50% × $310)	155
(4) Limitation on policyholders surplus account (the greatest of items (1), (2), or (3))	675

Since the balance in the policyholders surplus account at the end of the taxable year 1960, $175, does not exceed the limitation provided by section 815(d)(4), $675, S is not required to make any further adjustment to its policyholders surplus account at the end of the taxable year.

(e) Special rule for certain mutualizations. *(1) In general.* Section 815(e) provides a rule for determining priorities which shall operate in place of section 815(a) and paragraph

(b) of § 1.815-2 where a life insurance company makes any distribution to its shareholders after December 31, 1958, in acquisition of stock pursuant to a plan of mutualization. Section 815(e)(1) provides that such a distribution shall first be treated as being made out of paid-in capital and paid-in surplus, and, to the extent thereof, no tax shall be imposed on the company with respect to such distribution. Thereafter, distributions made pursuant to such plan of mutualization shall be treated as made in two allocable parts. One part shall be treated as being made out of other accounts (as defined in § 1.815-5) and the company shall incur no tax with respect to such portion of the distribution. The other part shall be treated as a distribution to which section 815(a) and paragraph (b) of § 1.815-2 applies. Thus, such portion of the distribution shall be treated as first being made out of the shareholders surplus account (as defined in section 815(b) and § 1.815-3), to the extent thereof, and then out of the policyholders surplus account (as defined in section 815(c) and § 1.815-4), to the extent thereof. See paragraph (a) of § 1.815-2. For purposes of this paragraph, a distribution shall be considered as being made pursuant to a plan of mutualization only if the requirements of applicable State law for the adoption of such plan (as, for example, approval by the requisite majority of the board of directors, shareholders, and policyholders) have been fulfilled.

(2) Allocation ratio. Section 815(e)(2)(A) provides an allocation ratio which when applied to the amount distributed under a plan of mutualization in excess of the balance in the paid-in capital and paid-in surplus accounts determines the portion of such excess to be treated as distributed out of the shareholders surplus account, policyholders surplus account, or other accounts. The numerator of this ratio is the excess of the assets of the company (as defined in section 805(b)(4) and paragraph (a)(4) of § 1.805-5) over the total liabilities (including reserves), both determined as of December 31, 1958, and adjusted in the manner provided in subparagraph (3) of this paragraph. The denominator of this ratio is the amount included in the numerator plus the amounts in the shareholders surplus account and policyholders surplus account, all determined as of the beginning of the year of the distribution.

(3) Adjustment for certain distributions. Section 815(e)(2)(B) provides that if between 1958 and the year of distribution the taxpayer has been treated as having made a distribution (under a plan of mutualization or otherwise) which is treated as a return of paid-in capital and paid-in surplus or as out of other accounts (as defined in § 1.815-5), the aggregate amount of any such prior distributions must be subtracted from the numerator and denominator in all cases where the allocation ratio provided by subparagraph (2) of this paragraph applies.

(f) Recomputation required as a result of a subsequent loss from operations under section 812. *(1) In general.* Any amounts added to or subtracted from the special surplus accounts referred to in section 815(a) and paragraph (b) of § 1.815-2 for any taxable year shall be adjusted to the extent necessary to properly reflect a subsequent loss from operations which under section 812 is carried back to the taxable year for which such additions or subtractions were made.

(2) Example. The application of subparagraph (1) of this paragraph may be illustrated by the following example:

Example. Assume that for the taxable years 1959 through 1961, the books of S, a stock life insurance company subject to a 30 percent tax rate for all taxable years involved, reflect the following items:

	1959	1960	1961
Taxable investment income	$40.00	$40.00	$40.00
Gain from operations	60.00	60.00	60.00
Tax base (sec. 802(b)(1) and (2)	50.00	50.00	50.00
Tax (sec. 802(b)(1) and (2) base)	15.00	15.00	15.00
Shareholders surplus account—			
At beginning of year	0	35.00	37.00
Added at beginning of year by reason of election under sec. 815(d)(1)	0	7.00	0
Added for year (without regard to election under sec. 815(d)(1)	35.00	35.00	35.00
Subtracted (distributions)	0	40.00	40.00
Policyholders surplus account—			
At beginning of year	0	0	10.00
Added for year	10.00	10.00	10.00
Subtracted (distributions)	0	0	0
Subtracted (by reason of election under sec. 815(d)(1))	10.00	0	0
Tax base (sec. 802(b)(3))	10.00	0	0
Tax (sec. 802(b)(3) base)	3.00	0	0

Assume further that S has a loss from operations for the taxable year 1962 of $25. Under the provisions of section 812, the $25 loss from operations would be carried back to the taxable year 1959 and would reduce the 1959 tax base under section 802(b)(1) and (2) to $35 ($60 minus $25). After adjustments reflecting the 1962 loss from operations, the results for the taxable years 1959 through the beginning of 1962 would be as follows:

	1959	1960	1961	1962
Taxable investment income	$40.00	$40.00	$40.00	
Gain from operations	35.00	60.00	60.00	
Tax base (sec. 802(b)(1) and (2))	35.00	50.00	50.00	
Tax (sec. 802(b)(1) and (2) base)	10.50	15.00	15.00	
Shareholders surplus account—				
At beginning of year	0	24.50	19.50	$14.50
Added for year (without regard to election under sec. 815(d)(1))	24.50	35.00	35.00	
Added by reason of election under sec. 815(d)(1)	0	0	0	
Subtracted (distributions)	0	40.00	40.00	
Policyholders surplus account—				
At beginning of year	0	0	10.00	20.00
Added for year	0	10.00	10.00	
Subtracted (distributions)	0	0	0	
Subtracted (by reason of election under sec. 815(d)(1))	0	0	0	
Tax base (sec. 802(b)(3))	0	0	0	
Tax (sec. 802(b)(3) base)	0	0	0	

As a result of the loss from operations for 1962, the election under section 815(d)(1) for the taxable year 1959 has become inapplicable in its entirety since the balance in the policyholders surplus account at the end of 1959, as recomputed, is zero. Thus, S would be entitled to a total refund of $7.50 for the taxable year 1959. Of this amount, $4.50 is due to the recomputation of the section 802(b)(1) and (2) tax base and $3 to the amount of tax paid by reason of the election under section 815(d)(1).

T.D. 6535, 1/19/61.

§ 1.817-1 Taxable years affected.

Caution: The Treasury has not yet amended Reg § 1.817-1 to reflect changes made by P.L. 98-369.

Except as otherwise provided therein, §§ 1.817-2 through 1.817-4 are applicable only to taxable years beginning after December 31, 1957, and all references to sections of part I, subchapter L, chapter 1 of the Code are to the Internal Revenue Code of 1954, as amended by the Life Insurance Company Income Tax Act of 1959 (73 Stat. 112) and section 3 of the Act of October 23, 1962 (76 Stat. 1134).

T.D. 6558, 4/3/61.

§ 1.817-2 Treatment of capital gains and losses.

Caution: The Treasury has not yet amended Reg § 1.817-2 to reflect changes made by P.L. 98-369.

(a) In general. For taxable years beginning after December 31, 1958, and before January 1, 1962, if the net long-term capital gain (as defined in section 1222(7)) of any life insurance company exceeds its net short-term capital loss (as defined in section 1222(6)), section 802(a)(2) prior to its amendment by section 3 of the Act of October 23, 1962 (76 Stat. 1134), imposes a separate tax equal to 25 percent of such excess. For taxable years beginning after December 31, 1961, if the net long-term capital gain of any life insurance company exceeds its net short-term capital loss, section 802(a)(2) imposes an alternative tax in lieu of the tax imposed by section 802(a)(1), if and only if such alternative tax is less than the tax imposed by section 802(a)(1). Except as modified by section 817 (rules relating to certain gains and losses), the general rules of the Code relating to gains and losses, such as subchapter O (relating to gain or loss on disposition of property), subchapter P (relating to capital gains and losses), etc., shall apply with respect to life insurance companies.

(b) Modification of sections 1221 and 1231. *(1)* In the case of a life insurance company, section 817(a)(1) provides that for purposes of applying section 1231(a) (relating to property used in the trade or business and involuntary conversions), the term "property used in the trade or business" shall be treated as including only—

(i) Property used in carrying on an insurance business, of a character subject to the allowance for depreciation under section 167 (even though fully depreciated), held for more than 1 year (6 months for taxable years beginning before 1977; 9 months for taxable years beginning in 1977), and real property used in carrying on an insurance business, held for more than 1 year (6 months for taxable years beginning before 1977; 9 months for taxable years beginning in 1977), and which is not—

(a) Property of a kind which would properly be includible in the inventory of the taxpayer if on hand at the close of the taxable year;

(b) Property held by the taxpayer primarily for sale to customers in the ordinary course of business; or

(c) A copyright, a literary, musical, or artistic composition, a letter or memorandum, or similar property held by a taxpayer described in section 1221(3). In the case of a letter, memorandum, or property similar to a letter or memorandum, this subdivision *(c)* applies only to sales and other dispositions occurring after July 25, 1969.

(ii) The cutting or disposal of timber, or the disposal of coal or iron ore, to the extent considered arising from a sale or exchange by reason of the provisions of section 631 and the regulations thereunder.

(2) In the case of a life insurance company, section 817(a)(2) provides that for purposes of applying section 1221(2) (relating to the exclusion of certain property from the term capital asset), the reference to property used in trade or business shall be treated as including only property used in carrying on an insurance business.

(3) Section 1231(a), as modified by section 817(a)(1) and subparagraph (1) of this paragraph, shall apply to recognized gains and losses from the following:

(i) The sale, exchange, or involuntary conversion of the following property, if held for more than 1 year (6 months for taxable years beginning before 1977; 9 months for taxable years beginning in 1977)—

(a) The home office and branch office buildings (including land) owned and occupied by the life insurance company;

(b) Furniture and equipment owned by the life insurance company and used in the home office and branch office buildings occupied by the life insurance company; and

(c) Automobiles and other depreciable personal property used in connection with the operations conducted in the home office and branch office buildings occupied by the life insurance company.

(ii) The involuntary conversion of capital assets held for more than 1 year (6 months for taxable years beginning before 1977; 9 months for taxable years beginning in 1977).

(iii) The cutting or disposal of timber, or the disposal of coal or iron ore, to the extent considered arising from a sale or exchange by reason of the provisions of section 631 and the regulations thereunder.

(4) Section 1221(2), as modified by section 817(a)(2) and subparagraph (2) of this paragraph, shall include only the following property:

(i) The home office and branch office buildings (including land) owned and occupied by the life insurance company;

(ii) Furniture and equipment owned by the life insurance company and used in the home office and branch office buildings occupied by the life insurance company; and

(iii) Automobiles and other depreciable personal property used in connection with the operations conducted in the home office and branch office buildings occupied by the life insurance company.

(5) If an asset described in subparagraph (3)(i)(a), (b), or (c) or subparagraph (4) of this paragraph, or any portion thereof, is also an "investment asset" (an asset from which gross investment income, as defined in section 804(b), is derived), such asset, or portion thereof, shall not be treated as an asset used in carrying on an insurance business. Accordingly, the gains or losses from the sale or exchange (or considered as from the sale or exchange) of depreciable assets attributable to any trade or business, other than the insurance trade or business, carried on by the life insurance company, such as operating a radio station, housing development, or a farm, or renting various pieces of real estate shall be treated as gains or losses from the sale or exchange of a capital as-

set unless such asset is involuntarily converted (within the meaning of paragraph (e) of § 1.1231-1).

(c) Illustration of principles. The provisions of section 817(a) and this section may be illustrated by the following examples:

Example (1). L, a life insurance company, has recognized gains and losses for the taxable year 1959 from the sale or involuntary conversion of the following items:

	Gains	Losses
Stocks, held for more than 6 months...	$100,000	
Bonds, held for more than 6 months ..		$ 5,000
Housing development, held for more than 6 months		400,000
Branch office building owned and occupied by L, held for more than 6 months		115,000
Furniture and equipment used in the investment department, held for more than 6 months	30,000	
Radio station, held for more than 6 months	200,000	
Involuntary conversion of apartment building, held for more than 6 months	7,000	

The recognized gains and losses from the sale of the stocks, bonds, housing development, and radio station shall be treated as gains and losses from the sale of capital assets since such items are capital assets within the meaning of section 1221 (as modified by section 817(a)(2)). Accordingly, the provisions of section 1231 shall not apply to the sale of such capital assets. However, the provisions of section 1231 (as modified by section 817(a)(1)) shall apply to the sale of the branch office building and the furniture and equipment, and the apartment building involuntarily converted. Since the aggregate of the recognized losses ($115,000) exceeds the aggregate of the recognized gains ($37,000), the gains and losses are treated as ordinary gains and losses.

Example (2). Y, a life insurance company, owns a twenty-story home office building, having an adjusted basis of $15,000,000, ten floors of which it rents to various tenants, one floor of which is utilized by it in operating its investment department, and the remaining nine floors of which are occupied by it in carrying on its insurance business. If in 1960, Y sells the building for $10,000,000, Y must first apportion its basis between that portion of the building (one-half) used in carrying on an insurance business, and that portion of the building (one-half) classified as an "investment asset", before it can determine the character of the loss attributable to each portion of the building. For such purpose, the one floor utilized by Y in operating its investment department is treated as used in carrying on an insurance business. Assuming that each portion of the building bears an equal (one-half) relation to the basis of the entire building, Y (without regard to section 817(b)) would have a $2,500,000 ordinary loss on that portion used in carrying on an insurance business (assuming that Y had no gains subject to section 1231), and a $2,500,000 capital loss on that portion of the building classified as an investment asset.

T.D. 6558, 4/3/61, amend T.D. 6886, 6/22/66, T.D. 7369, 7/15/75, T.D. 7728, 10/31/80.

§ 1.817-3 Gain on property held on December 31, 1958, and certain substituted property acquired after 1958.

Caution: The Treasury has not yet amended Reg § 1.817-3 to reflect changes made by P.L. 98-369.

(a) Limitation on gain recognized on property held on December 31, 1958. *(1)* Section 817(b)(1) limits the amount of gain that shall be recognized on the sale or other disposition of property other than insurance and annuity contracts (and contracts supplementary thereto) and property described in section 1221(1) (relating to stock in trade or inventory-type property) if:

(i) The property was held (or treated as held within the meaning of paragraph (c)(1) of this section) by a life insurance company on December 31, 1958;

(ii) The taxpayer has been a life insurance company at all times on and after December 31, 1958, including the date of the sale or other disposition of the property; and

(iii) The fair market value of the property on December 31, 1958, exceeds the adjusted basis for determining gain as of such date.

The gain on the sale or other disposition of such property shall be limited to an amount (but not less than zero) equal to the amount by which the gain (determined without regard to section 817(b)(1)) exceeds the difference between fair market value of such property on December 31, 1958, and the adjusted basis for determining gain as of such date. Accordingly, the tax imposed under section 802(a) shall apply with respect to the amount of gain so limited. In addition, in the case of a stock life insurance company, the amount of such gain shall be taken into account under section 815(b)(2)(A)(ii) for purposes of determining the amount to be added to the shareholders surplus account (as defined in section 815(b) and § 1.815-3) for the taxable year. Furthermore, the amount of the gain (determined without regard to section 817(b)(1) and this paragraph) which is not taken into account under section 802(a) and under paragraph (f) of § 1.802-3 by reason of the application of section 817(b)(1) shall be included in other accounts (as defined in § 1.815-5) by such a company for the taxable year.

(2) Section 817(b)(1) and subparagraph (1) of this paragraph shall not apply for purposes of determining loss with respect to property held on December 31, 1958.

(b) Illustration of principles. The application of section 817(b)(1) and paragraph (a) of this section may be illustrated by the following examples:

Example (1). On December 31, 1958, J, a stock life insurance company, owned stock of Z Corporation and on such date the stock had an adjusted basis for determining gain of $5,000 and a fair market value of $6,000. On August 1, 1959, the company sells such stock for $8,000. Assuming J qualifies as a life insurance company for the taxable year 1959, and applying the provisions of section 817(b)(1) and paragraph (a) of this section, the gain recognized (assuming no adjustment to basis for the period since December 31, 1958) on the sale shall be limited to $2,000 (the amount by which the gain realized, $3,000, exceeds the difference, $1,000, between the fair market value, $6,000, and the adjusted basis, $5,000, for determining gain on December 31, 1958). Thus, J shall take into account $2,000 under section 815(b)(2)(A)(ii) for purposes of determining the amount to be added to its shareholders surplus account for the taxable year and shall include $1,000 in other accounts for the taxable year.

Example (2). The facts are the same as in example (1), except that the selling price is $5,800. In such case, no gain shall be recognized even though there is a realized gain of $800 since such realized gain does not exceed the difference ($1,000) between the fair market value ($6,000) and the adjusted basis ($5,000) for determining gain on December 31, 1958. Furthermore, no loss shall be realized or recognized as a result of this transaction. Thus, J shall include $800 in other accounts for the taxable year and shall not take into account any amount under section 815(b)(2)(A)(ii).

Example (3). The facts are the same as in example (1), except that the adjusted basis for determining loss is $5,000 and the selling price is $4,500. In such case, since J has sustained a loss, section 817(b)(1) does not apply.

(c) Certain substituted property acquired after December 31, 1958. Section 817(b)(2) provides that if a life insurance company acquires property after December 31, 1958, in exchange for property actually held by the company on December 31, 1958, and the property acquired has a substituted basis within the meaning of section 1016(b) and § 1.1016-10, the following rules shall apply:

(1) For purposes of section 817(b)(1), such acquired property shall be deemed as having been held continuously by the taxpayer since the beginning of the holding period thereof as determined under section 1223;

(2) The fair market value and adjusted basis referred to in section 817(b)(1) shall be that of that property for which the holding period taken into account includes December 31, 1958;

(3) Section 817(b)(1) shall apply only if the property or properties, the holding periods of which are taken into account, were held only by life insurance companies after December 31, 1958, during the holding periods so taken into account;

(4) The difference between the fair market value and adjusted basis referred to in section 817(b)(1) shall be reduced (but not below zero) by the excess of (i) the gain that would have been recognized but for section 817(b) on all prior sales or other dispositions after December 31, 1958, of properties referred to in section 817(b)(2)(C) over (ii) the gain that was recognized on such sales or other dispositions; and

(5) The basis of such acquired property shall be determined as if the gain which would have been recognized but for section 817(b) were recognized gain.

For purposes of section 817(b)(2) and this paragraph, the term "property" does not include insurance and annuity contracts (and contracts supplementary thereto) and property described in section 1221(1) (relating to stock in trade or inventory-type property). Furthermore, the provisions of section 817(b)(1) and paragraph (a)(1) of this section shall not apply for purposes of determining loss with respect to property described in section 817(b)(2) and this paragraph.

(d) Illustration of principles. The application of section 817(b)(2) and paragraph (c) of this section may be illustrated by the following example:

Example. Assume that W, a life insurance company, owns property B on December 31, 1958, at which time its adjusted basis was $1,000 and its fair market value was $1,800. On January 31, 1960, in a transaction to which section 1031 (relating to exchange of property held for productive use or investment) applies, W receives property H having a fair market value of $1,700 plus $300 in cash in exchange for property B. The gain realized on the transaction, without regard to section 817(b) is $1,000 (assuming no adjustments to basis for the period since December 31, 1958). Under the provisions of section 817(b)(1) the gain is limited to $200. The entire $200 shall be recognized since such amount is less than the amount of gain ($300) which would be recognized under section 1031. Applying the provisions of section 817(b)(2) and paragraph (c) of this section, the basis of property H shall be determined as if the entire $300 of cash received is recognized gain. Thus, the basis of property H under section 1031 is $1,000 ($1,000 (the basis of property B) minus $300 (the amount of money received) plus $300 (the recognized gain of $200 plus $100 which would have been recognized but for section 817(b)). If W later sells property H for $2,200 cash, and assuming no further adjustments to its basis of $1,000, the gain realized is $1,200, but due to the application of section 817(b)(2) the amount of gain recognized is $500, computed as follows:

Selling price		$2,200
Less: Adjusted basis as of date of sale		1,000
Gain realized		1,200
Fair market value as of 12-31-58	$1,800	
Adjusted basis as of 12-31-58	1,000	
Excess of fair market value over adjusted basis	800	
Less: Excess of gain which would have been recognized on all prior dispositions but for sec. 817(b) over gain recognized on all prior disposition ($300 minus $200)	100	
		700
Gain recognized		500

T.D. 6558, 4/3/61, amend T.D. 6886, 6/22/66.

§ 1.817-4 Special rules.

Caution: The Treasury has not yet amended Reg § 1.817-4 to reflect changes made by P.L. 98-369.

(a) Limitation on capital loss carryovers. Section 817(c) provides that a net capital loss (as defined in section 1222(10)) for any taxable year beginning before January 1, 1959, shall not be taken into account. For any taxable year beginning after December 31, 1958, the provisions of part II, subchapter P, chapter 1 of the Code (relating to the treatment of capital losses) shall be applicable to life insurance companies for purposes of determining the tax imposed by section 802(a) and § 1.802-3 (relating to the imposition of tax in case of capital gains).

(b) Gain on transactions occurring prior to January 1, 1959. For purposes of part I, subchapter L, chapter 1 of the Code, section 817(d) provides that—

(1) There shall be excluded from tax any gain from the sale or exchange of a capital asset, and any gain considered as gain from sale or exchange of a capital asset, which results from sales or other dispositions of property prior to January 1, 1959; and

(2) Any gain after December 31, 1958, resulting from the sale or other disposition of property prior to January 1, 1959, which, but for this subparagraph would be taken into account under section 1231, shall not be taken into account under section 1231.

For example, if a life insurance company makes an installment sale of a capital asset prior to January 1, 1959, and payments are received after such date, any capital gain attributable to such sale shall not be taken into account for purposes of section 802(a). Furthermore, any gain referred to in subparagraphs (1) and (2) and the preceding sentence shall not be taken into account in determining the excess of the net short-term capital gain over the net long-term capital loss (and for taxable years beginning after December 31, 1961, the excess of the net long-term capital gain over the net short-term capital loss) for purposes of computing taxable investment income under section 804(a)(2) or gain or loss from operations under section 809(b).

(c) Certain reinsurance transactions in 1958. For purposes of part I, section 817(e) provides that where a life insurance company reinsures (or sells) all of its insurance contracts of a particular type, such as an entire industrial department, in either a single transaction, or in a series of related transactions, all of which occurred during 1958, and the reinsuring (or purchasing) company or companies assume all liabilities under such contracts, such reinsurance (or sale) shall be treated as the sale of a capital asset. However, such transaction shall be subject to the provisions of section 806(a) and § 1.806-3 (relating to adjustments for certain changes in reserves and assets).

(d) Certain other reinsurance transactions. *(1)* For any taxable year beginning after December 31, 1958, the reinsurance of all or a part of the insurance contracts of a particular type by a life insurance company, in either a single transaction, or in a series of related transactions, occurring in any such taxable year, whereby the reinsuring company or companies assume all liabilities under such contracts, shall not be treated as the sale or exchange of a capital asset but shall be subject to the provisions of sections 806(a) and 809 and the regulations thereunder. However, if in connection with a transaction described in the preceding sentence the reinsured or reinsurer transfers an asset which is a capital asset within the meaning of section 1221 (as modified by section 817(a)(2)), such transfer shall be treated as the sale or exchange of a capital asset by the transferor.

(2) (i) The consideration paid by the reinsured to the reinsurer in connection with a transaction described in subparagraph (1) of this paragraph shall be treated as an item of deduction under section 809(d)(7). However, any amount received by the reinsured from the reinsurer shall be applied against and reduce (but not below zero) the amount of such consideration, and to the extent that it exceeds such consideration, shall be treated as an item of gross amount under section 809(c)(3).

(ii) In connection with an assumption reinsurance (as defined in paragraph (a)(7)(ii) of § 1.809-5) transaction, a reinsurer shall in any taxable year beginning after December 31, 1957—

(A) Treat the consideration received from the reinsured in any such taxable year as an item of gross amount under section 809(c)(1), and

(B) Treat any amount paid to the reinsured for the purchase of such contracts, to the extent such amount meets the requirements of section 162, as a deferred expense that may be amortized over the reasonably estimated life (as defined in paragraph (d)(2)(iv) of this section) of the contracts reinsured and treat the portion of the expense so amortized in each taxable year as a deduction under section 809(d)(12) irrespective of the taxable year in which such amount was paid to the reinsured.

(iii) For purposes of paragraph (d)(2)(ii) of this section where the reinsured transfers to the reinsurer in connection with the assumption reinsurance transaction a net amount which is less than the increase in the reinsurer's reserves resulting from the transaction, the reinsurer shall be treated as—

(A) Having received from the reinsured consideration in an amount equal to the net amount of the increase in the reinsurer's reserves resulting from the transaction, and

(B) Having paid the reinsured an amount for the purchase of the contracts equal to the excess of the amount of such increase in the reinsurer's reserves over the net amount received from the reinsured.

(iv) For purposes of this subparagraph, the term "reasonably estimated life" means the period during which the contract reinsured remains in force. Such period shall be based on the facts in each case (such as age, health, and sex of the insured, type of contract reinsured, etc.) and the assuming company's experience (such as mortality, lapse rate, etc.) with similar risks.

(3) The provisions of this paragraph may be illustrated by the following examples:

Example (1). On June 30, 1959, X, a life insurance company, reinsured a portion of its insurance contracts with Y, a life insurance company, under an agreement whereby Y agreed to assume and to become solely liable under the contracts reinsured. The reserves on the contracts reinsured by X were $100,000. Under the reinsurance agreement X agreed to pay Y $100,000 for assuming such contracts and Y agreed to pay X $17,000 for the right to receive future premium payments under this block of contracts. Rather than exchange payments of money, X agreed to pay Y a net amount of $83,000 in cash. Assuming that the reasonably estimated life of the contracts reinsured is 17 years, that there are no other insurance transactions by X or Y during the taxable year, and assuming that X and Y compute the reserves on the contracts reinsured on the same basis, X has income of $100,000 under section 809(c)(2) as a result of the net decrease in its reserves. X has a net deduction of $83,000 ($100,000 − $17,000) under section 809(d)(7). For the taxable year 1959, Y has income of $100,000 under section 809(c)(1) as a result of the consideration received from X and a deduction of $100,000 under section 809(d)(2) for the net increase in reserves and $1,000 ($17,000 divided by 17, the reasonably estimated life of the contracts reinsured), under section 809(d)(12). The remaining $16,000 shall be amortized over the next 16 succeeding taxable years (16 × $1,000 = $16,000) under section 809(d)(12) at the rate of $1,000 for each such taxable year.

Example (2). The facts are the same as in example (1), except X agreed to pay Y a consideration of $100,000 in cash for assuming these contracts and Y paid X a bonus of $17,000 in cash and that this bonus meets the requirements of section 162. Assuming that the reasonably estimated life of the contracts reinsured is 17 years, X has income of $100,000 under section 809(c)(2) as a result of this net decrease in its reserves and a deduction of $83,000 under section 809(d)(7) for the amount of the consideration ($100,000) paid to Y for assuming these contracts, reduced by the bonus ($17,000) received from Y. For the taxable year 1959, Y has income of $100,000 under section 809(c)(1) as a result of the consideration received from X and deductions of $100,000 under section 809(d)(2) for the net increase in reserves and $1,000 (the bonus of $17,000 divided by 17, the reasonably estimated life of the contracts reinsured), under section 809(d)(12). The remaining amount of the bonus ($16,000) shall be amortized over the next 16 succeeding taxable years (16 × $1,000 = $16,000) under section 809(d)(12) at the rate of $1,000 for each such taxable year.

Example (3). The facts are the same as in Example (1), except that the reinsurance agreement does not specifically provide that X agreed to pay Y $100,000 for assuming the contracts reinsured and Y agreed to pay X $17,000 for the right to receive future premium payments under such contracts. Instead, X agreed to pay Y a net amount of $83,000 in cash for assuming such contracts. Nevertheless, Y is treated as having received from X consideration equal to $100,000, the amount of the increase in Y's reserves, and as having paid $17,000 ($100,000 less $83,000) for the purchase of such contracts. Therefore, for the taxable year 1959, Y has income of $100,000 under section 809(c)(1). Y also has a deduction of $100,000 under section 809(d)(2) for the net increase in its reserves and an amortization deduction under section 809(d)(12) of $1,000 ($17,000 divided by 17, the reasonably estimated life of the contracts reinsured). The remaining $16,000 shall be amortized by Y over the next 16 succeeding years at the rate of $1,000 for each such year. For 1959, X has income of $100,000 under section 809(c)(2) as a result of the net decrease in its reserves and a deduction of $83,000 under section 809(d)(7) for the net amount of consideration paid to Y for assuming the contracts reinsured.

Example (4). The facts are the same as in example (1), except that X agreed to pay Y a consideration of $130,000 in cash for assuming such contracts. Based upon these facts, X has income of $100,000 under section 809(c)(2) as a result of this net decrease in its reserves and a deduction of $130,000 under section 809(d)(7) for the amount of the consideration paid to Y for assuming these contracts. Y has income of $130,000 under section 809(c)(1) as a result of the consideration received from X and a deduction of $100,000 under section 809(d)(2) for the net increase in its reserves.

Example (5). On August 1, 1960, R, a life insurance company, reinsured all of its insurance policies with S, a life insurance company, under an agreement whereby S agreed to assume and become solely liable under the contracts reinsured. The reserves on the contracts reinsured by R were $3,000,000. Under the reinsurance agreement, R agreed to pay S a consideration of $3,000,000 in stocks and bonds for assuming such contracts. Assuming no other insurance transactions by R or S during the taxable year, that R and S compute the reserves on the contracts reinsured on the same basis, and that R has a recognized gain (after the application of the limitation of section 817(b)(1)) of $20,000 due to appreciation in value of the assets transferred, the results to each company are as follows:

Company R (reinsured)		Company S (reinsurer)	
Income			
Net decrease in reserves (sec. 809(c)(2))	$3,000,000	Consideration received by S in respect of assuming liabilities under contracts issued by R(sec. 809(c)(1))	$3,000,000
Capital gain (as limited by sec. 817(b)(1)) to be taxed separately under sec. 802(a)(2)	20,000		
Deductions			
Consideration paid by R to S in respect of S's assuming liabilities under contracts issued by R (sec. 809(d)(7))	$3,000,000	Net increase in reserves (sec. 809(d)(2))	$3,000,000

T.D. 6558, 4/3/61, amend T.D. 6625, 12/18/62, T.D. 6886, 6/22/66, T.D. 7401, 2/3/76.

§ 1.817-5 Diversification requirements for variable annuity, endowment, and life insurance contracts.

(a) Consequences of nondiversification. *(1) In general.* Except as provided in paragraph (a)(2) of this section, for purposes of subchapter L, section 72, and section 7702(a), a variable contract (as defined in section 817(d)), other than a pension plan contract [as defined in section 818(a)), which is based on one or more segregated asset accounts shall not be treated as an annuity, endowment, or life insurance contract for any calendar quarter period for which the investments of any such account are not adequately diversified. For this purpose, a variable contract shall be treated as based on a segregated asset account for a calendar quarter period if amounts received under the contract (or earnings thereon) are allocated to the segregated asset account at any time during the period. In addition, a variable contract that is not treated as an annuity, endowment, or life insurance contract for any period by reason of this paragraph (a)(1) shall not be treated as an annuity, endowment, or life insurance contract for any subsequent period even if the investments are adequately diversified for such subsequent period. If a variable contract which is a life insurance or endowment contract under other applicable (e.g., State or foreign) law is not treated as a life insurance or endowment contract under section 7702(a), the income on the contract for any taxable year of the policyholder is treated as ordinary income received or accrued by the policyholder during such year in accordance with section 7702(g) and (h). Likewise, if a variable contract is not treated as an annuity contract under section 72, the income on the contract for any taxable year of the policyholder shall be treated as ordinary income received or accrued by the policyholder during such year in the same manner as a life insurance or endowment contract under section 7702(g) and (h).

(2) Inadvertent failure to diversify. The investments of a segregated asset account shall be treated as satisfying the requirements of paragraph (b) of this section for one or more periods, provided the following conditions are satisfied—

(i) The issuer or holder must show the Commissioner that the failure of the investments to satisfy the requirements of paragraph (b) of this section for such period or periods was inadvertent,

(ii) The investments of the account must satisfy the requirements of paragraph (b) of this section within a reasonable time after the discovery of such failure, and

(iii) The issuer or holder of the variable contract must agree to make such adjustments or pay such amounts as may be required by the Commissioner with respect to the period or periods during which the investments of the account did not satisfy the requirements of paragraph (b) of this section. The amount required by the Commissioner to be paid shall be an amount based upon the tax that would have been owed by the policyholders if they were treated as receiving the income on the contract (as defined in section 7702(g)(1)(B), without regard to section 7702(g)(1)(C)) for such period or periods.

(b) Diversification of investments. *(1) In general.* (i) Except as otherwise provided in this paragraph and paragraph (c) of this section, the investments of a segregated asset account shall be considered adequately diversified for purposes of this section and section 817(h) only if—

(A) No more than 55% of the value of the total assets of the account is represented by any one investment;

(B) No more than 70% of the value of the total assets of the account is represented by any two investments;

(C) No more than 80% of the value of the total assets of the account is represented by any three investments; and

(D) No more than 90% of the value of the total assets of the account is represented by any four investments.

(ii) For purposes of this section—

(A) All securities of the same issuer, all interests in the same real property project, and all interests in the same commodity are each treated as a single investment; and

(B) In the case of government securities, each government agency or instrumentality shall be treated as a separate issuer.

(iii) See paragraph (f) of this section for circumstances in which a segregated asset account is treated as the owner of assets held indirectly through certain pass-through entities and corporations taxed under subchapter M, chapter 1 of the Code.

(2) Safe harbor. A segregated asset account will be considered adequately diversified for purposes of this section and section 817(h) if—

(i) The account meets the requirements of section 851(b)(4) and the regulations thereunder; and

(ii) No more than 55% of the value of the total assets of the account is attributable to cash, cash items (including receivables), government securities, and securities of other regulated investment companies.

(3) Alternative diversification requirements for variable life insurance contracts. (i) A segregated asset account with respect to variable life insurance contracts will be considered adequately diversified for purposes of this section and section 817(h) if the requirements of paragraph (b)(1) or (b)(2) of this section are satisfied or if the assets of such account, other than Treasury securities, satisfy the percentage limitations prescribed in paragraph (b)(1) of this section increased by the Product of (A) .5 and (B) the percentage of the value of the total assets of the account that is represented by Treasury securities. In determining whether the assets of an account, other than Treasury securities, satisfy the increased percentage limitations, such limitations are applied as if the Treasury securities were not included in the account (i.e., the increased percentage limitations are not applied to Treasury securities and the value of the total assets of the account is reduced by the value of the Treasury securities).

(ii) The provisions of this paragraph (b)(3) may be illustrated by the following examples:

Example (1). On the last day of a quarter of a calendar year, a segregated asset account with respect to variable life insurance contracts holds assets having a total value of $100,000. The assets of the account are represented by Treasury securities having a total value of $90,000 and securities of Corporation A having a total value of $10,000. The 55% limit described in paragraph (b)(1)(i) of this section would be increased by 45% (0.5 × 90%) to 100%, and would then be applied to the assets of the account other than Treasury securities. Because no more than 100% of the value of the assets other than Treasury securities is represented by securities of Corporation A, the investments of the account will be considered adequately diversified.

Example (2). On the last day of a quarter of a calendar year, a segregated asset account with respect to variable life insurance contracts holds assets having a total value of $100,000. The assets of the account are represented by Treasury securities having a total value of $60,000, securities of Corporation A having a total value of $30,000, and securities of Corporation B having a total value of $10,000. The 55% and 70% limits described in paragraph (b)(1)(i) of this section would be increased by 30% (0.5 × 60%) to 85% and 100%, respectively, and would then be applied to the assets of the account other than Treasury securities. Securities of Corporation A represent 75%, and securities of Corporation B represent 25%, of the value of the assets of the account other than Treasury securities. Because no more than 85% of the value of the assets other than Treasury securities is represented by securities of Corporation A or B and no more than 100% of the value of the assets other than Treasury securities is represented by securities of Corporations A and B, the investments of the account will be considered adequately diversified.

(c) Periods for which an account is adequately diversified. *(1) In general.* A segregated asset account that satisfies the requirements of paragraph (b) of this section on the last day of a quarter of a calendar year (i.e., March 31, June 30, September 30, and December 31) or within 30 days after such last day shall be considered adequately diversified for such quarter.

(2) Start-up period. (i) Except as provided in paragraph (c)(2)(iv) of this section, a segregated asset account that is not a real property account on its first anniversary shall be considered adequately diversified until such first anniversary.

(ii) Except as provided in paragraph (c)(2)(iv) of this section, a segregated asset account that is a real property account on its first anniversary shall be considered adequately diversified until the earlier of its fifth anniversary or the anniversary on which the account ceases to be a real property account.

(iii) For purposes of paragraph (c)(2)(i) and (ii) of this section, the anniversary of a segregated asset account is the anniversary of the date on which any amount received under a life insurance or annuity contract, other than a pension plan contract (as defined in section 818(a)), is first allocated to the account.

(iv) If more than 30 percent of the amount allocated to a segregated asset account as of the last day of a calendar quarter is attributable to contracts entered into more than one year before such date, paragraph (c)(2)(i) of this section shall not apply to the segregated asset account for any period after such date. Similarly, if more than 30 percent or the amount allocated to a segregated asset account as of the last day of a calendar quarter is attributable to contracts entered into more than 5 years before such date, paragraph (c)(2)(ii) of this section shall not apply to the segregated asset account for any period after such date. For purposes of this paragraph (c)(2), amounts transferred to the account from a diversified account (determined without regard to this paragraph (c)(2)) or as a result of an exchange pursuant to section 1035 in which the issuer of the contract received in the exchange is not related in a manner specified in section

267(b) to the issuer of the contract transferred in the exchange are not treated as—

(A) Amounts attributable to contracts entered into more than one year before such date, in the case of accounts subject to paragraph (c)(2)(i) of this section, or

(B) Amounts attributable to contracts entered into more than five years before such date, in the case of accounts subject to paragraph (c)(2)(ii) of this section.

(3) Liquidation period. A segregated asset account that satisfies the requirements of paragraph (b) of this section on the date of a plan of liquidation is adopted shall be considered adequately diversified for—

(i) The one-year period beginning on the date the plan of liquidation is adopted if the account is not a real property account on such date; or

(ii) The two-year period beginning on the date the plan of liquidation is adopted if the account is a real property account on such date.

(d) Market fluctuations. A segregated asset account that satisfies the requirements of paragraph (b) of this section at the end of any calendar quarter (or within 30 days after the end of such calendar quarter) shall not be considered nondiversified in a subsequent quarter because of a discrepancy between the value of its assets and the diversification requirements unless such discrepancy exists immediately after the acquisition of any asset and such discrepancy is wholly or partly the result of such acquisition.

(e) Segregated asset account. For purposes of section 817(h) and this section, a segregated asset account shall consist of all assets the investment return and market value of each of which must be allocated in an identical manner to any variable contract invested in any of such assets. See paragraph (g) for examples illustrating the application of this paragraph (e).

(f) Look-through rule for assets held through certain investment companies, partnerships, or trusts. *(1) In general.* If this paragraph (f) applies, a beneficial interest in a regulated investment company, a real estate investment trust, a partnership, or a trust that is treated under sections 671 through 679 as owned by the grantor or another person ("investment company, partnership, or trust") shall not be treated as a single investment of a segregated asset account. Instead, a pro rata portion of each asset of the investment company, partnership, or trust shall be treated, for purposes of this section, as an asset of the segregated asset account. For purposes of this section, ratable interest of a partner in a partnership's assets shall be determined in accordance with the partner's capital interest in the partnership.

(2) Applicability. (i) Certain investment companies, partnerships, and trusts. This paragraph (f) shall apply to an investment company, partnership, or trust if—

(A) All the beneficial interests in the investment company, partnership, or trust (other than those described in paragraph (f)(3) of this section) are held by one or more segregated asset accounts of one or more insurance companies; and

(B) Public access to such investment company, partnership, or trust is available exclusively (except as otherwise permitted in paragraph (f)(3) of this section) through the purchase of a variable contract. Solely for this purpose, the status of a contract as a variable contract will be determined without regard to section 817(h) and this section.

(ii) Trusts holding Treasury securities. This paragraph (f) shall also apply to a trust that is treated under section 671 through 679 as owned by the grantor or another person if substantially all of the assets of the trust are represented by Treasury securities.

(3) Interests not held by segregated asset accounts. Satisfaction of the requirements of paragraph (f)(2)(i) of this section shall not be prevented by reason of beneficial interests in the investment company, partnership, or trust that are—

(i) Held by the general account of a life insurance company or a corporation related in a manner specified in section 267(b) to a life insurance company, but only if the return on such interests is computed in the same manner as the return on an interest held by a segregated asset account is computed (determined without regard to expenses attributable to variable contracts), there is no intent to sell such interests to the public, and a segregated asset account of such life insurance company also holds or will hold a beneficial interest in the investment company, partnership, or trust;

(ii) Held by the manager, or a corporation related in a manner specified in section 267(b) to the manager, of the investment company, partnership, or trust, but only if the holding of the interests is in connection with the creation or management of the investment company, partnership, or trust, the return on such interest is computed in the same manner as the return on an interest held by a segregated asset account is computed (determined without regard to expenses attributable to variable contracts), and there is no intent to sell such interests to the public;

(iii) Held by the trustee of a qualified pension or retirement plan; or

(iv) Held by the public, or treated as owned by policyholders pursuant to Rev. Rul. 81-225, 1981-2 C.B. 12, but only if (A) the investment company, partnership, or trust was closed to the public in accordance with Rev. Rul. 82-55, 1982-1 C.B. 12, or (B) all the assets of the segregated asset account are attributable to premium payments made by policyholders prior to September 26, 1981, to premium payments made in connection with a qualified pension or retirement plan, or to any combination of such premium payments.

(g) Examples. The provisions of paragraphs (e) and (f) of this section may be illustrated by the following examples.

Example (1). (i) The assets underlying variable contracts issued by a life insurance company consist of two groups of assets: (a) a diversified portfolio of debt securities and (b) interests in P, a partnership. All of the beneficial interests in P are held by one or more segregated asset accounts of one or more insurance companies and public access to P is available exclusively through the purchase of a variable contract. The variable contracts provide that policyholders may specify which portion of each premium is to be invested in the debt securities and which portion is to be invested in P interests. The portfolio of debt securities and the assets of P, considered separately, each satisfy the diversification requirements of paragraph (b) of this section.

(ii) As a result of the ability of policyholders to allocate premiums among the two groups of assets, the investment return and market value of the interests in P and the debt securities may be allocated to different variable contracts in a non-identical manner. Accordingly, under paragraph (e) of this section, the interests in P are treated as part of a single segregated asset account (" Account 1") and the debt securities are treated as part of a different segregated asset account ("Account 2").

(iii) Since P is described in paragraph (f)(2)(i) of this section, interests in P will not be treated as a single investment of Account 1. Rather, Account 1 is treated as owning a pro rata portion of the assets of P.

(iv) Since Account 1 and Account 2 each satisfy the requirements of paragraph (b) of this section, variable contracts that are based on either or both accounts are treated as annuity, endowment, or life insurance contracts.

Example (2). The facts are the same as in example (1) except that some of the beneficial interests in P are held by persons not described in paragraph (f)(3) of this section. Since P is not described in paragraph (f)(2) of this section, interests in P will be treated as a single investment of Account 1. As a result, Account 1 does not satisfy the requirements of paragraph (b) of this section. Variable contracts based in whole or in part on Account 1 are not treated as annuity, endowment, or life insurance contracts. Variable contracts that are not based on Account 1 at any time during the period in which such account fails to satisfy the requirements of paragraph (b) of this section (i.e., contracts based entirely on Account 2), are treated as annuity, endowment, or life insurance contracts. See paragraph (a)(1).

Example (3). The facts are the same as in example (2) except that the variable contracts do not permit policyholders to allocate premiums between or among the debt securities and interests in P. Thus, the investment return and market value of the interests in P and the debt securities must be allocated to the same variable contracts and in an identical manner. Under paragraph (e) of this section, the interests in P and the debt securities are treated as part of a single segregated asset account. If the interests in P and the debt securities, considered together, satisfy the requirements of paragraph (b) of this section, contracts based on this segregated asset account will be treated as annuity, endowment, or life insurance contracts.

(h) Definitions. The terms defined below shall, for purposes of this section, have the meanings set forth in such definitions:

(1) Government security. (i) General rule. The term "government security" shall mean any security issued or guaranteed or insured by the United States or an instrumentality of the United States; or any certificate of deposit for any of the foregoing. Any security or certificate or deposit insured or guaranteed only in part by the United States or an instrumentality thereof is treated as issued by the United States or its instrumentality only to the extent so insured or guaranteed, and as issued by the direct obligor to the extent not so insured or guaranteed. For purposes of this paragraph (h)(1), an instrumentality of the United States shall mean any person that is treated for purposes of 15 U.S.C. 80a-2 (16), as amended, as a person controlled or supervised by and acting as an instrumentality of the Government of the United States pursuant to authority granted by the Congress of the United States.

(ii) Example. A segregated asset account purchases a certificate of deposit in the amount of $150,000 from bank A. Deposits in bank A are insured by the Federal Deposit Insurance Corporation, an instrumentality of the United States, to the extent of $100,000 per depositor. The certificate of deposit is treated as a government security to the extent of the $100,000 insured amount and is treated as a security issued by bank A to the extent of the $50,000 excess of the value of the certificate of deposit over the insured amount.

(2) Treasury security. (i) General rule. For purposes of paragraph (b)(3) of this section and section 817(h)(3), the term "Treasury security" shall mean a security the direct obligor of which is the United States Treasury.

(ii) Example. A segregated asset account purchases put and call options on U.S. Treasury securities issued by the Options Clearing Corporation. The options are not Treasury securities for purposes of paragraph (b)(3) and section 817(h)(3) because the direct obligor of the options is not the United States Treasury.

(3) Real property. The term "real property" shall mean any property that is treated as real property under 1.856-3 (d) except that it shall not include interests in real property.

(4) Real property account. A segregated asset account is a real property account on an anniversary of the account (within the meaning of paragraph (c)(2)(iii) of this section) or on the date a plan of liquidation is adopted if not less than the applicable percentage of the total assets of the account is represented by real property or interests in real property on such anniversary or date. For this purpose, the applicable percentage is 40% for the period ending on the first anniversary of the date on which premium income is first received, 50% for the year ending on the second anniversary, 60% for the year ending on the third anniversary, 70% for the year ending on the fourth anniversary, and 80% thereafter. A segregated asset account will also be treated as a real property account on its first anniversary if on or before such first anniversary the issuer has stated in the contract or prospectus or in a submission to a regulatory agency, an intention that the assets of the account will be primarily invested in real property or interests in real property, provided that at least 40% of the total assets of the account are so invested within six months after such first anniversary.

(5) Commodity. The term "commodity" shall mean any type of personal property other than a security.

(6) Security. The term security shall include a cash item and any partnership interest, whether or not registered under a Federal or State law regulating the offering or sale of securities. The term shall not include any interest in real property, or any interest in a commodity.

(7) Interest in real property. The term "interest in real property" shall include the ownership and co-ownership of land or improvements thereon and leaseholds of land or improvements thereon. Such term shall not, however, include mineral, oil, or gas royalty interests, such as a retained economic interest in coal or iron ore with respect to which the special provisions of section 631(c) apply. The term "interest in real property" also shall include options to acquire land or improvements thereon, and options to acquire leaseholds of land or improvements thereon.

(8) Interest in a commodity. The term "interest in a commodity" shall include the ownership and co-ownership of any type of personal property other than a security, and any leaseholds thereof. Such term shall include mineral, oil, and gas royalty interests, including any fractional undivided interest therein. Such term also shall include any put, call, straddle, option, or privilege on any type of personal property other than a security.

(9) Value. The term "value" shall mean, with respect to investments for which market quotations are readily available, the market value of such investments; and with respect to other investments, fair value as determined in good faith by the managers of the segregated asset account.

(10) Terms used in section 851. To the extent not inconsistent with this paragraph (h) all terms used in this section shall have the same meaning as when used in section 851.

(i) Effective date. *(1) In general.* This section is effective for taxable years beginning after December 31, 1983.

(2) *Exceptions.* (i) If, at all times after December 31, 1983, an insurance company would be considered the owner of the assets of a segregated asset account under the principles of Rev. Rul. 81-225, 1981-2 C.B. 12, this section will not apply to such account until December 15, 1986.

(ii) This section will not apply to any variable contract to which Rev. Rul. 77-85, 1977-1 C.B. 12, or Rev. Rul. 81-225, 1981-2 C.B. 12, did not apply by reason of the limited retroactive effect of such rulings.

(iii) In determining whether a segregated asset account is adequately diversified for any calendar quarter ending before July 1, 1988, debt instruments that are issued, guaranteed, or insured by the United States or an instrumentality of the United States shall not be treated as government securities if such debt instruments are secured by a mortgage on real property (other than real property owned by the United States or an instrumentality of the United States) or represent an interest in a pool of debt instruments secured by such mortgages.

(iv) This section shall not apply until January 1, 1989, with respect to a variable contract (as defined in section 817(d)) that (1) provides for the payment of an immediate annuity (as defined in section 72(u)(4)); (2) was outstanding on September 12, 1986; and (3) the segregated asset account on which it was based was, on September 12, 1986, wholly invested in deposits insured by the Federal Deposit Insurance Corporation or the Federal Savings and Loan Insurance Corporation.

(v) A segregated asset account in existence before March 1, 2005, will be considered to be adequately diversified if—

(A) As of March 1, 2005, the account was adequately diversified within the meaning of section 817(h) and this regulation as in effect prior to that date; and

(B) By December 31, 2005, the account is adequately diversified within the meaning of section 817(h) and this regulation.

T.D. 8242, 3/2/89, amend T.D. 9185, 2/28/2005.

PAR. 2. Section 1.817-5 is amended as follows:

1. The last sentence of paragraph (a)(2)(iii) is removed.

2. Paragraph (f)(3)(iii) is revised.

3. Paragraph (f)(3)(iv) is redesignated as paragraph (f)(3)(vii).

4. New paragraphs (f)(3)(iv) through (vi) are added.

The revisions and additions read as follows:

Proposed § 1.817-5 Diversification requirements for variable annuity, endowment, and life insurance contracts. [*For Preamble, see ¶ 152,891*]

* * * * *

(f) * * *

(3) * * *

(iii) Held by the trustee of a qualified pension or retirement plan;

(iv) Held by a qualified tuition program as defined in section 529;

(v) Held by the trustee of a pension plan established and maintained outside of the United States, as defined in section 7701(a)(9), primarily for the benefit of individuals substantially all of whom are nonresident aliens, as defined in section 7701(b)(1)(B);

(vi) Held by an account which, pursuant to Puerto Rican law or regulation, is segregated from the general asset accounts of the life insurance company that owns the account, provided the requirements of section 817(d) and (h) are satisfied. Solely for purposes of this paragraph (f)(3)(vi), the requirement under section 817(d)(1) that the account be segregated pursuant to State law or regulation shall be disregarded; or

* * * * *

§ 1.817A-0 Table of contents.

This section lists the captions that appear in section 1.817A-1:

T.D. 9058, 5/6/2003.

§ 1.817A-1 Certain modified guaranteed contracts.

(a) Definitions. *(1) Modified guaranteed contract.* The term modified guaranteed contract (MGC) is defined in section 817A(d) as an annuity, life insurance, or pension plan contract (other than a variable contract described in section 817) under which all or parts of the amounts received under the contract are allocated to a segregated account. Assets and reserves in this segregated account must be valued from time to time with reference to market values for annual statement purposes. Further, an MGC must provide either for a net surrender value or for a policyholder's fund (as defined in section 807(e)(1)). If only a portion of a contract is not described in section 817, such portion is treated as a separate contract for purposes of applying section 817A.

(2) Temporary guarantee period. An MGC may temporarily guarantee a return other than the permanently guaranteed crediting rate for a period specified in the contract (the temporary guarantee period). During the temporary guarantee period, the amount paid to the policyholder upon surrender is usually increased or decreased by a market value adjustment, which is determined by a formula set forth under the terms of the MGC.

(3) Equity-indexed modified guaranteed contract. An equity-indexed MGC is an MGC, as defined in paragraph (a)(1) of this section, that provides a return during or at the end of the temporary guarantee period based on the perform-

ance of stocks, other equity instruments, or equity-based derivatives.

(4) Non-equity-indexed modified guaranteed contract. A non-equity-indexed MGC is an MGC, as defined in paragraph (a)(1) of this section, that provides a return during or at the end of the temporary guarantee period not based on the performance of stocks, other equity instruments, or equity-based derivatives.

(5) Current market rate for non-equity-indexed modified guaranteed contracts. The current market rate for a non-equity-indexed MGC issued by an insurer (whether issued in that tax year or a previous one) is the appropriate Treasury constant maturity interest rate published by the Board of Governors of the Federal Reserve System for the month containing the last day of the insurer's taxable year. The appropriate rate is that rate published for Treasury securities with the shortest published maturity that is greater than (or equal to) the remaining duration of the current temporary guarantee period under the MGC.

(6) Current market rate for equity-indexed modified guaranteed contracts. [Reserved]

(b) Applicable interest rates for non-equity-indexed modified guaranteed contracts. *(1) Tax reserves during temporary guarantee period.* An insurance company is required to determine the tax reserves for an MGC under sections 807(c)(3) or (d)(2). During a non-equity-indexed MGC's temporary guarantee period, the applicable interest rate to be used under sections 807(c)(3) and (d)(2)(B) is the current market rate, as defined in paragraph (a)(5) of this section.

(2) Required interest during temporary guarantee period. During the temporary guarantee period of a non-equity-indexed MGC, the applicable interest rate to be used to determine required interest under section 812(b)(2)(A) is the same current market rate, defined in paragraph (a)(5) of this section, that applies for that period for purposes of sections 807(c)(3) or (d)(2)(B).

(3) Application of section 811(d). An additional reserve computation rule applies under section 811(d) for contracts that guarantee certain interest payments beyond the end of the taxable year. Section 811(d) is waived for non-equity-indexed MGCs.

(4) Periods after the end of the temporary guarantee period. For periods after the end of the temporary guarantee period, sections 807(c)(3), 807(d)(2)(B), 811(d) and 812(b)(2)(A) are not modified when applied to non-equity-indexed MGCs. None of these sections are affected by the definition of current market rate contained in paragraph (a)(5) of this section once the temporary guarantee period has expired.

(5) Examples. The following examples illustrate this paragraph (b):

Example (1). (i) IC, a life insurance company as defined in section 816, issues a MGC (the Contract) on August 1 of 1996. The Contract is an annuity contract that gives rise to life insurance reserves, as defined in section 816(b). IC is a calendar year taxpayer. The Contract guarantees that interest will be credited at 8 percent per year for the first 8 contract years and 4 percent per year thereafter. During the 8-year temporary guarantee period, the Contract provides for a market value adjustment based on changes in a published bond index and not on the performance of stocks, other equity instruments or equity based derivatives. IC has chosen to avail itself of the provisions of these regulations for 1996 and taxable years thereafter. The 10-year Treasury constant maturity interest rate published for December of 1996 was 6.30 percent. The next shortest maturity published for Treasury constant maturity interest rates is 7 years. As of the end of 1996, the remaining duration of the temporary guarantee period for the Contract was 7 years and 7 months.

(ii) To determine under section 807(d)(2) the end of 1996 reserves for the Contract, IC must use a discount interest rate of 6.30 percent for the temporary guarantee period. The interest rate to be used in computing required interest under section 812(b)(2)(A) for 1996 reserves is also 6.30 percent.

(iii) The discount rate applicable to periods outside the 8-year temporary guarantee period is determined under sections 807(c)(3), 807(d)(2)(B), 811(d) and 812(b)(2)(A) without regard to the current market rate.

Example (2). Assume the same facts as in Example 1 except that it is now the last day of 1998. The remaining duration of the temporary guarantee period under the Contract is now 5 years and 7 months. The 7-year Treasury constant maturity interest rate published for December of 1998 was 4.65 percent. The next shortest duration published for Treasury constant maturity interest rates is 5 years. A discount rate of 4.65 percent is used for the remaining duration of the temporary guarantee period for the purpose of determining a reserve under section 807(d) and for the purpose of determining required interest under section 812(b)(2)(A).

Example (3). Assume the same facts as in Example 1 except that it is now the last day of 2001. The remaining duration of the temporary guarantee period under the Contract is now 2 years and 7 months. The 3-year Treasury constant maturity interest rate published for December of 2001 was 3.62 percent. The next shortest duration published for Treasury constant maturity interest rates is 2 years. A discount rate of 3.62 percent is used for the remaining duration of the temporary guarantee period for the purpose of determining a reserve under section 807(d) and for the purpose of determining required interest under section 812(b)(2)(A).

(c) Applicable interest rates for equity-indexed modified guaranteed contracts. [Reserved.]

(d) Effective date. Paragraphs (a), (b) and (d) of this section are effective on May 7, 2003. However, pursuant to section 7805(b)(7), taxpayers may elect to apply those paragraphs retroactively for all taxable years beginning after December 31, 1995, the effective date of section 817A.

T.D. 9058, 5/6/2003.

§ 1.818-1 Taxable years affected.

Caution: The Treasury has not yet amended Reg § 1.818-1 to reflect changes made by P.L. 98-369.

Sections 1.818-2 through 1.818-8, except as otherwise provided therein, are applicable only to taxable years beginning after December 31, 1957, and all references to sections of part I, subchapter L, chapter 1 of the Code are to the Internal Revenue Code of 1954, as amended by the Life Insurance Company Income Tax Act of 1959 (73 Stat. 112).

T.D. 6558, 4/3/61, amend T.D. 7469, 2/28/77.

§ 1.818-2 Accounting provisions.

Caution: The Treasury has not yet amended Reg § 1.818-2 to reflect changes made by P.L. 98-369.

(a) Method of accounting. *(1)* Section 818(a)(1) provides the general rule that all computations entering into the determination of taxes imposed by part I, subchapter L, chapter 1 of the Code, shall be made under an accrual method of accounting. Thus, the over-all method of accounting for life insurance companies shall be the accrual method. Except as otherwise provided in part I, the term "accrual method" shall have the same meaning and application in section 818 as it does under section 446 (relating to general rule for methods of accounting) and the regulations thereunder. For general rules relating to the taxable year for inclusion of income and deduction of expenses under an accrual method of accounting, see sections 451 and 461 and the regulations thereunder.

(2) Section 818(a)(2) provides that, to the extent permitted under this section, a life insurance company's method of accounting may be a combination of the accrual method with any other method of accounting permitted by chapter 1 of the Internal Revenue Code of 1954, other than the cash receipts and disbursements method. Thus, section 818(a)(2) specifically prohibits the use by a life insurance company of the cash receipts and disbursements method either separately or in combination with a permissible method of accounting. The term "method of accounting" includes not only the over-all method of accounting of the taxpayer but also the accounting treatment of any item. For purposes of section 818(a)(2), a life insurance company may elect to compute its taxable income under an over-all method of accounting consisting of the accrual method combined with the special methods of accounting for particular items of income and expense provided under other sections of chapter 1 of the Internal Revenue Code of 1954, other than the cash receipts and disbursements method. These methods of accounting for special items include the accounting treatment provided for depreciation (section 167), research and experimental expenditures (section 174), soil and water conservation expenditures (section 175), organizational expenditures (section 248), etc. In addition, a life insurance company may, where applicable, use the crop method of accounting (as provided in the regulations under sections 61 and 162), and the installment method of accounting for sales of realty and casual sales of personalty (as provided in section 453(b)). To the extent not inconsistent with the provisions of the Internal Revenue Code of 1954 or the regulations thereunder and the method of accounting adopted by the taxpayer pursuant to this section, all computations entering into the determination of taxes imposed by part I shall be made in a manner consistent with the manner required for purposes of the annual statement approved by the National Association of Insurance Commissioners.

(3) (i) An election to use any of the special methods of accounting referred to in subparagraph (2) of this paragraph which was made pursuant to any provisions of the Internal Revenue Code of 1954 or prior revenue laws for purposes of determining a company's tax liabilities for prior years, shall have the same force and effect in determining the items of gross investment income under section 804(b) and the items of deduction under section 804(c) of the Life Insurance Company Income Tax Act of 1959 (73 Stat. 112) as if such Act had not been enacted.

(ii) For purposes of determining gain or loss from operations under section 809(b), in computing the life insurance company's share of investment yield under section 809(b)(1)(A) and (2)(A), an election with respect to any of the special methods of accounting referred to in subparagraph (2) of this paragraph which was made pursuant to any provision of the Internal Revenue Code of 1954 or prior revenue laws, shall not be affected in any way by the enactment of the Life Insurance Company Income Tax Act of 1959 (73 Stat. 112).

(iii) For purposes of determining gain or loss from operations under section 809(b), in computing the items of gross amount under section 809(c) and the deduction items under section 809(d), an election to use any of the special methods of accounting referred to in subparagraph (2) of this paragraph must be made in accordance with the specific statutory provisions of the sections containing such elections and the regulations thereunder. However, where a particular election may be made only with the consent of the Commissioner (either because the time for making the election without the consent of the Commissioner has expired or because the particular section contained no provision for making an election without consent), and the time prescribed by the applicable regulations for submitting a request for permission to make such an election for the taxable year 1958 has expired, a life insurance company may make such an election for the year 1958 at the time of filing its return for that year (including extensions thereof). For example, a life insurance company may elect any of the methods of depreciation prescribed in section 167 (to the extent permitted under that section and the regulations thereunder) with respect to those assets, or any portion thereof, for which no depreciation was allowable under prior revenue laws, for example, furniture and fixtures used in the underwriting department. Similarly, a life insurance company shall be permitted to make an election under section 461(c) (relating to the accrual of real property taxes) with respect to real property for which no deduction was allowable under prior revenue laws. Any such election shall be made in the manner and form prescribed in the applicable regulations.

(iv) For purposes of subdivision (ii) of this subparagraph, the method used under section 1016(a)(3)(C) (relating to adjustments to basis) in determining the amount of exhaustion, wear and tear, obsolescence, and amortization actually sustained shall not preclude a taxpayer from electing any of the methods prescribed in section 167 in accordance with the provisions of that section and the regulations thereunder for determining the amount of such exhaustion, wear and tear, obsolescence, and amortization for the year 1958. For example, if the amount of depreciation actually sustained, under section 1016(a)(3)(C), on a life insurance company's home office building (other than that portion for which depreciation was allowable under prior revenue laws) is determined on the straight line method, the life insurance company may elect for the year 1958 to use any of the methods prescribed in section 167 for determining its depreciation allowance for 1958. However, such election shall be binding for 1958, and for all subsequent taxable years, unless consent to change such election, if required, is obtained from the Commissioner in accordance with the provisions of section 167 and the regulations thereunder.

(4) (i) For purposes of section 805(b)(3)(B)(i) (relating to the determination of the current earnings rate for any taxable year beginning before January 1, 1958), the determination for any year of the investment yield and the assets shall be made as though the taxpayer had been on the accrual method prescribed in subparagraph (1) of this paragraph for such year, or the accrual method in combination with the other methods of accounting prescribed in subparagraph (2) of this paragraph, if these other methods of accounting are used by the taxpayer in determining the investment yield and assets for the taxable year 1958. However, where the method used for determining the deduction under section 167 for the year 1958 differs from the method used in prior years, the amount of the deduction actually allowed or allowable for such prior years for purposes of section 1016(a)(2) (relating to adjustments to basis) shall be the amount to be taken into

account in determining the current earnings rate under section 805(b)(3)(B)(i).

(ii) For purposes of section 812(b)(1)(C) (relating to operations loss carrybacks and carryovers for years prior to 1958), the determination for those years of the gain or loss from operations shall be made as though the taxpayer had been on the accrual method of accounting prescribed in subparagraph (1) of this paragraph for such year, or the accrual method in combination with the other methods of accounting prescribed in subparagraph (2) of this paragraph, if these other methods of accounting are used by the taxpayer in the determination of gain or loss from operations for the taxable year 1958. However, where any adjustment to basis is required under section 1016(a)(3)(C) on account of exhaustion, wear and tear, obsolescence, amortization, and depletion sustained, the amount actually sustained as determined under section 1016(a)(3)(C) for each of the years involved shall be the amount allowed in the determination of gain or loss from operations for purposes of section 812(b)(1)(C).

(b) Adjustments required if accrual method of accounting was not used in 1957. The items of gross amount taken into account under section 809(c) and the items of deductions allowed under section 809(d) for the taxable year 1958 shall be determined as though the taxpayer had been on the accrual method of accounting prescribed in paragraph (a) of this section for all prior years. Thus, life insurance companies not on the accrual method for the year 1957 shall accrue, as of December 31, 1957, those items of gross amount which would have been properly taken into account for the year 1957 if the company had been on the accrual method described in section 818(a). Likewise, life insurance companies not on the accrual method for the year 1957 shall accrue, as of December 31, 1957, those items of deductions which would have been properly allowed for the year 1957 if the company had been on the accrual method described in section 818(a). For example, if certain premium amounts were received during the year 1958 but such amounts would have been properly taken into account for the year 1957 if the taxpayer had been on the accrual method for the year 1957, then the taxpayer will not be required to take such premium amounts into account for the year 1958. If, for example, certain claims, benefits, and losses were paid during the year 1958 but such items would have been properly taken into account for the year 1957 if the taxpayer had been on the accrual method for the year 1957, then the taxpayer will not be permitted to deduct such expense items for the year 1958. For a special transitional rule applicable with respect to changes in method of accounting required by section 818(a) and paragraph (a) of this section, see section 818(e) and § 1.818-6.

(c) Change of basis in computing reserves. *(1)* Section 806(b) provides that if the basis for determining the amount of any item referred to in section 810(c) as of the close of the taxable year differs from the basis for such determination as of the beginning of the taxable year, then for purposes of subpart B, part I, subchapter L, chapter 1 of the Code (relating to the determination of taxable investment income), the amount of such item shall be the amount computed on the old basis as of the close of the taxable year and the amount computed on the new basis as of the beginning of the next taxable year. Similarly, section 810(d)(1) provides rules for determining the amount of the adjustment to be made for purposes of subpart C, part I, subchapter L, chapter 1 of the Code (relating to the determination of gain or loss from operations), if the basis for determining any item referred to in section 810(c) as of the close of any taxable year differs from the basis for such determination as of the close of the preceding taxable year. Under an accrual method of accounting, a change in the basis or method of computing the amount of liability of any item referred to in section 810(c) occurs in the taxable year in which all the events have occurred which determine the change in the basis or method of computing the amount of such liability and, in which, the amount thereof (whether increased or decreased) can be determined with reasonable accuracy.

(2) The application of subparagraph (1) of this paragraph may be illustrated by the following examples:

Example (1). Assume that during the taxable year 1960, M, a life insurance company, determines that the amount of its life insurance reserves held with respect to a particular block of contracts is understated on the present basis being used in valuing such liability and that such liability can be more accurately reflected by changing from the present basis to a particular new basis. Assume that M uses such new basis in computing its reserves under such contracts at the end of the taxable year 1960. Under the provisions of section 818(a) and subparagraph (1) of this paragraph, the change in basis for purposes of sections 806(b) and 810(d) occurs during the taxable year 1960, the year in which all the events have occurred which determine the change in basis and the amount of any increase (or decrease) attributable to such change can be determined with reasonable accuracy. Such change shall be treated as having occurred during the taxable year 1960 whether M determines that its liability under such contracts was understated for the first time during 1960, or that its liability under such contracts has, in fact, been understated for a number of prior years.

Example (2). Assume the facts are the same as in example (1), except that during the taxable year 1960 the insurance department of State X issues a ruling, pursuant to authority conferred by statute, requiring M to use the particular new basis which more accurately reflects its liability with respect to such contracts and that as a result of such ruling, M uses the new basis in computing its reserves under such contracts for the taxable years 1958, 1959, and 1960. Under the provisions of section 818(a) and subparagraph (1) of this paragraph, the change in basis for purposes of sections 806(b) and 810(d) occurs during the taxable year 1960, the year in which all the events have occurred which determine that a change in basis should be made and the amount of any increase (or decrease) attributable to such change can be determined with reasonable accuracy.

T.D. 6558, 4/3/61.

§ 1.818-3 Amortization of premium and accrual of discount.

Caution: The Treasury has not yet amended Reg § 1.818-3 to reflect changes made by P.L. 98-369.

(a) In general. Section 818(b) provides that the appropriate items of income, deductions, and adjustments under part I, subchapter L, chapter 1 of the Code, shall be adjusted to reflect the appropriate amortization of premium and the appropriate accrual of discount on bonds, notes, debentures, or other evidences of indebtedness held by a life insurance company. Such adjustments are limited to the amount of appropriate amortization or accrual attributable to the taxable year with respect to such securities which are not in default as to principal or interest and which are amply secured. The question of ample security will be resolved according to the rules laid down from time to time by the National Association of Insurance Commissioners. The adjustment for amortization of premium decreases the gross investment income, the exclusion and reduction for wholly tax-exempt interest, the exclusion and deduction for partially tax-exempt interest, and the basis or adjusted basis of such securities. The adjustment for accrual of discount increases the gross investment income, the exclusion and reduction for wholly tax-exempt interest, the exclusion and deduction for partially tax-exempt interest, and the basis or adjusted basis of such securities. However, for taxable years beginning after May 31, 1960, only the accrual of discount relating to issue discount will increase the exclusion and reduction for wholly tax-exempt interest. See section 103.

(b) Acquisitions before January 1, 1958. *(1)* In the case of any such security acquired before January 1, 1958, the premium is the excess of its acquisition value over its maturity value and the discount is the excess of its maturity value over its acquisition value. The acquisition value of any such security is its cost (including buying commissions or brokerage but excluding any amounts paid for accrued interest) if purchased for cash, or if not purchased for cash, its then fair market value. The maturity value of any such security is the amount payable thereunder either at the maturity date or an earlier call date. The earlier call date of any such security may be the earliest interest payment date if it is callable or payable at such date, the earliest date at which it is callable at par, or such other call or payment date, prior to maturity, specified in the security as may be selected by the life insurance company. A life insurance company which adjusts amortization of premium or accrual of discount with reference to a particular call or payment date must make the adjustments with reference to the value on such date and may not, after selecting such date, use a different call or payment date, or value, in the calculation of such amortization or discount with respect to such security unless the security was not in fact called or paid on such selected date.

(2) The adjustments for amortization of premium and accrual of discount will be determined—

(i) According to the method regularly employed by the company, if such method is reasonable, or

(ii) According to the method prescribed by this section.

A method of amortization of premium or accrual of discount will be deemed "regularly employed" by a life insurance company if the method was consistently followed in prior taxable years, or if, in the case of a company which has never before made such adjustments, the company initiates in the first taxable year for which the adjustments are made a reasonable method of amortization of premium or accrual of discount and consistently follows such method thereafter. Ordinarily, a company regularly employs a method in accordance with the statute of some State, Territory, or the District of Columbia, in which it operates.

(3) The method of amortization and accrual prescribed by this section is as follows:

(i) The premium (or discount) shall be determined in accordance with this section; and

(ii) The appropriate amortization of premium (or accrual of discount) attributable to the taxable year shall be an amount which bears the same ratio to the premium (or discount) as the number of months in the taxable year during which the security was owned by the life insurance company bears to the number of months between the date of acquisition of the security and its maturity or earlier call date, determined in accordance with this section. For purposes of this section, a fractional part of a month shall be disregarded unless it amounts to more than half a month, in which case it shall be considered a month.

(c) Acquisitions after December 31, 1957. *(1)* In the case of—

(i) Any bond, as defined in section 171(d), acquired after December 31, 1957, the amount of the premium and the amortizable premium for the taxable year, shall be determined under section 171(b) and the regulations thereunder, as if the election set forth in section 171(c) had been made, and

(ii) Any bond, note, debenture, or other evidence of indebtedness not described in subdivision (i) of this subparagraph and acquired after December 31, 1957, the amount of the premium and the amortizable premium for the taxable year, shall be determined under paragraph (b) of this section.

(2) In the case of any bond, note, debenture, or other evidence of indebtedness acquired after December 31, 1957, the amount of the discount and the accrual of discount attributable to the taxable year shall be determined under paragraph (b) of this section.

(d) Convertible evidences of indebtedness. Section 818(b)(2)(B) provides that in no case shall the amount of premium on a convertible evidence of indebtedness (including any bond, note, or debenture) include any amount attributable to the conversion features of the evidence of indebtedness. This provision is the same as the one contained in section 171(b), and the rules prescribed in paragraph (c) of § 1.171-2 shall be applicable for purposes of section 818(b)(2)(B). This provision is to be applied without regard to the date upon which the evidence of indebtedness was acquired. Thus, where a convertible evidence of indebtedness was acquired before January 1, 1958, and a portion or all of the premium attributable to the conversion features of the evidence of indebtedness has been amortized for taxable years beginning before January 1, 1958, no adjustment for such amortization will be required by reason of section 818(b)(2)(B). Such amortization will, however, require an adjustment to the basis of the evidence of indebtedness under section 1016(a)(17). For taxable years beginning after December 31, 1957, no further amortization of the premium attributable to the conversion features of such an evidence of indebtedness will be taken into account.

(e) Adjustment to basis. Section 1016(a)(17) (relating to adjustments to basis) provides that in the case of any evidence of indebtedness referred to in section 818(b) and this section, the basis shall be adjusted to the extent of the adjustments required under section 818(b) (or the corresponding provisions of prior income tax laws) for the taxable year and all prior taxable years. The basis of any evidence of indebtedness shall be reduced by the amount of the adjustment required under section 818(b) (or the corresponding provision of prior income tax laws) on account of amortizable premium and shall be increased by the amount of the adjustment required under section 818(b) on account of accruable discounts.

(f) Denial of double inclusion. Any amount which is includible in gross investment income by reason of section 818(b) and paragraph (a) of this section shall not be includible in gross income under section 1232(a) (relating to the taxation of bonds and other evidences of indebtedness). See section 1232(a)(2)(C) and the regulations thereunder.

T.D. 6558, 4/3/61.

PAR. 16. In § 1.818-3, paragraph (f) is amended by removing the phrase "section 1232(a) (relating to the taxation of bonds and other evidences of indebtedness)" and adding in its place the phrase "section 1271 (relating to the treatment of amounts received on retirement or sale or exchange of debt instruments)", and by removing the phrase "section 1232(a)(2)(C)" and adding in its place the phrase "section 1271(d)".

Proposed § 1.818-3 [Amended] [*For Preamble, see ¶ 151,065*]

§ 1.818-4 Election with respect to life insurance reserves computed on preliminary term basis.

Caution: The Treasury has not yet amended Reg § 1.818-4 to reflect changes made by P.L. 98-369.

(a) In general. Section 818(c) permits a life insurance company issuing contracts with respect to which the life insurance reserves are computed on one of the recognized preliminary term bases to elect to revalue such reserves on a net level premium basis for the purpose of determining the amount which may be taken into account as life insurance reserves for purposes of part I, subchapter L, chapter 1 of the Code, other than section 801 (relating to the definition of a life insurance company). If such an election is made, the method to be used in making this revaluation of reserves shall be either the exact revaluation method (as described in section 818(c)(1) and paragraph (b)(1) of this section) or the approximate revaluation method (as described in section 818(c)(2) and paragraph (b)(2) of this section).

(b) Revaluation of reserves computed on preliminary term basis. If a life insurance company makes an election under section 818(c) in the manner provided in paragraph (e) of this section, the amount to be taken into account as life insurance reserves with respect to contract for which such reserves are computed on a preliminary term basis may be determined on either of the following bases:

(1) Exact revaluation method. As if the reserves for all such contracts had been computed on a net level premium basis (using the same mortality or morbidity assumptions and interest rates for both the preliminary term basis and the net level premium basis).

(2) Approximate revaluation method. The amount computed without regard to section 818(c)—

(i) Increased by $21 per $1,000 of insurance in force (other than term insurance) under such contracts, less 2.1 percent of reserves under such contracts, and

(ii) Increased by $5 per $1,000 of term insurance in force under such contracts which at the time of issuance cover a period of more than 15 years, less 0.5 percent of the reserves under such contracts.

(c) Exception. If a life insurance company which makes an election under section 818(c)(2) and paragraph (b)(2) of this section has life insurance reserves with respect to both life insurance and noncancellable accident and health contracts for which such reserves are computed on a preliminary term basis, it shall use the approximate revaluation method for all its life insurance reserves other than that portion of such reserves held with respect to its noncancellable accident and health contracts, and shall use the exact revaluation method for all its life insurance reserves held with respect to such noncancellable accident and health contracts.

(d) Reserves subject to recomputation. *(1)* For the first taxable year for which the election under section 818(c) and paragraph (b) of this section applies, a company making such election must revalue all its life insurance reserves held with respect to contracts for which such reserves are computed on a preliminary term basis at the end of such taxable year on the basis elected under section 818(c) and paragraph (b) of this section. However, for purposes of the preceding sentence, an election under section 818(c) shall not apply with respect to such reserves which would not be treated as being computed on the preliminary term basis at the end of such taxable year except for the provisions of section 810(a) or (b). See paragraph (c)(2) of § 1.810-2. For example, if S, a life insurance company which computes its life insurance reserves on a recognized preliminary term basis at the beginning of the taxable year 1958, strengthens a portion of such reserves during the taxable year by actually changing to a net level premium basis in computing such reserves, and then makes the election under section 818(c) and paragraph (b) of this section for 1958, such election shall not apply with respect to the strengthened contracts.

(2) For any taxable year other than the first taxable year for which the election under section 818(c) and paragraph (b) of this section applies, a company making such election must revalue all its life insurance reserves held with respect to contracts for which such reserves are computed on a preliminary term basis at the beginning or end of the taxable year on the basis elected under section 818(c) and paragraph (b) of this section. For example, if M, a life insurance company which made a valid outstanding election under section 818(c) in the manner provided in paragraph (e) of this section for the taxable year 1959, sells a block of contracts subject to such election on September 1, 1960, M would value such contracts on the basis elected under section 818(c) and paragraph (b) of this section on January 1, 1960, for purposes of determining the net decrease or increase in the sum of the items described in section 810(c) for the taxable year under section 810(a) or (b).

(3) For the effect of an election under section 818(c) and paragraph (b) of this section in determining gain or loss from operations for the taxable year, see paragraph (c)(3) of § 1.810-2 and paragraph (e) of § 1.810-3.

(e) Time and manner of making election. The election provided by section 818(c) shall be made in a statement attached to the life insurance company's income tax return for the first taxable year for which the company desires the election to apply. The return and statement must be filed not later than the date prescribed by law (including extensions thereof) for filing the return for such taxable year. However, if the last day prescribed by law (including extensions thereof) for filing a return for the first taxable year for which the company desires the election to apply falls before April 4, 1961, the election provided by section 818(c) may be made for such year by filing the statement and an amended return for such taxable year (and all subsequent taxable years for which returns have been filed) before July 4, 1961. The statement shall indicate whether the exact or the approximate method of revaluation has been adopted. The statement shall also set forth sufficient information as to mortality and morbidity assumptions; interest rates; the valuation method used; the amount of the reserves and the amount and type of insurance in force under all contracts for which reserves are computed on a preliminary term basis; and such other pertinent data as will enable the Commissioner to determine the correctness of the application of the revaluation method adopted and the accuracy of the computations involved in revaluing the reserves. The election to use either the exact revaluation method or the approximate revaluation method shall, except for the purposes of section 801, be adhered to in making the computations under part I for the taxable year for which such election is made and for all subsequent taxable years.

(f) Scope of election. An election made under section 818(c) and paragraph (b) of this section to use either the exact or the approximate method of revaluing the company's life insurance reserves shall be binding for the taxable year for which made, and, except as provided in paragraph (g) of this section, shall be binding for all succeeding taxable years, unless consent to revoke the election is obtained from the Commissioner. However, for taxable years beginning prior to April 4, 1961, a company may revoke the election provided by section 818(c) without obtaining consent from the Commissioner by filing, before July 4, 1961, a statement that the company desires to revoke such election. An amended return reflecting such revocation must accompany the statement for all taxable years for which returns have been filed with respect to such election.

(g) Special rule for 1958. If an election is made for a taxable year beginning in 1958 to use the approximate revaluation method described in section 818(c)(2) and paragraph (b)(2) of this section, the company may, for its first taxable year beginning after 1958, elect to change to the exact revaluation method described in section 818(c)(1) and paragraph (b)(1) of this section without obtaining the consent of the Commissioner. In such case, the election to change shall be made in a statement attached to the company's income tax return for such taxable year and filed not later than the date prescribed by law (including extensions thereof) for filing the return for such year. The statement shall indicate that the company has elected to change from the approximate to the exact revaluation method for such taxable year and shall include such information and data referred to in paragraph (e) of this section as will enable the Commissioner to determine the correctness and accuracy of the computations involved.

T.D. 6558, 4/3/61.

---

§ 1.818-5 Short taxable years.

Caution: The Treasury has not yet amended Reg § 1.818-5 to reflect changes made by P.L. 98-369.

(a) In general. Section 818(d) provides that if any return of a corporation made under part I, subchapter L, chapter 1 of the Code, is for a period of less than the entire calendar, then section 443 (relating to returns for a period of less than 12 months) shall not apply. This section further provides certain rules to be used in determining the life insurance company taxable income for a period of less than the entire calendar year.

(b) Returns for periods of less than the entire calendar year. A return for a short period, that is, for a taxable year consisting of a period of less than the entire calendar year, shall be made only under the following circumstances:

(1) If a company which qualifies as a life insurance company is not in existence for the entire taxable year, a return is required for the short period during which the taxpayer was in existence. For example, a life insurance company organized on August 1, is required to file a return for the short period from August 1 to December 31, and returns for each calendar year thereafter. Similarly, if a company which qualifies as a life insurance company completely dissolves during the taxable year it is required to file a return for the short period from January 1 to the date it goes out of existence. All items entering into the computation of taxable investment income and gain or loss from operations for the short period shall be determined on a consistent basis and in the manner provided in paragraph (c) of this section.

(2) A return must be filed for a short period resulting from the termination by the district director of a taxpayer's taxable year for jeopardy. See section 6851 and the regulations thereunder. A company which was an insurance company for the preceding taxable year (but not a life insurance company as defined in section 801(a) and paragraph (b) of § 1.801-3) and which for the current taxable year qualifies as a life insurance company shall not file a return for the short period from the time during the taxable year that it first qualifies as a life insurance company to the end of the taxable year. Similarly, an insurance company which was a life insurance company for the preceding taxable year but which for the current taxable year does not qualify as a life insurance company shall not file a return for the short period from the beginning of the taxable year to the time during the taxable year that it no longer qualifies as a life insurance company.

(c) Computation of life insurance company taxable income for short period. *(1)* If a return is made for a short period, section 818(d)(1) provides that the taxable investment income and the gain or loss from operations shall be determined on an annual basis by a ratable daily projection of the appropriate figures for the short period. The appropriate figures for the short period shall be determined on an annual basis by multiplying such figures by a fraction, the numerator of which is the number of days in the calendar year in which the short period occurs and the denominator of which is the number of days in the short period.

(2) (i) In computing taxable investment income for a short period, the investment yield, the policy and other contract liability requirements, the policyholders' share of each and every item of investment yield, and the company's share of any item of investment yield shall be determined on an annual basis.

(ii) For purposes of determining the investment yield on an annual basis, each item of gross investment income under section 804(b) and each item of deduction under section 804(c) shall be annualized in the manner provided in subparagraph (1) of this paragraph. In any case in which a limitation is placed on the amount of a deduction provided under section 804(c), the limitation shall apply to the item of deduction computed on an annual basis.

(iii) The policy and other contract liability requirements shall be determined on an annual basis in the following manner:

(a) The interest paid (as defined in section 805(e) and § 1.805-8) for the short period shall be annualized in the manner prescribed in subparagraph (1) of this paragraph.

(b) The current earnings rate for the taxable year in which the short period occurs shall be determined by dividing the taxpayer's investment yield, as determined on an annual basis under subdivision (ii) of this subparagraph, by the mean of the taxpayer's assets at the beginning and end of the short period. For purposes of section 805, any reference to the current earnings rate for the taxable year in which the short period occurs means the current earnings rate as determined under this subdivision.

(c) The adjusted life insurance reserves shall be determined as provided in section 805(c), and the pension plan reserves shall be determined as provided in section 805(d).

(iv) The policyholders' share of each and every item of investment yield (as defined in section 804(a)) shall be that percentage obtained by dividing the policy and other contract liability requirements, determined under subdivision

(iii) of this subparagraph, by the investment yield, determined under subdivision (ii) of this subparagraph.

(v) The taxable investment income for the short period shall be an amount (not less than zero) equal to the life insurance company's share of each and every item of investment yield, as determined under subdivision (ii) of this subparagraph, reduced by the items described in section 804(a)(2)(A) and (B). In determining these reductions under section 804(a)(2)(A) the amount of the respective items shall be the amount that is determined on an annual basis under subdivision (ii) of this subparagraph. The small business deduction, under section 804(a)(2)(B) shall be an amount (not to exceed $25,000) equal to 10 percent of the investment yield, determined under subdivision (ii) of this subparagraph, for the short period.

(vi) Except as provided in this paragraph, the determination of taxable investment income under subpart B, part I, subchapter L, chapter 1 of the Code, shall be made in accordance with all the provisions of that subpart.

(3) (i) In computing gain or loss from operations for a short period, the share of each and every item of investment yield set aside for policyholders, the life insurance company's share of each and every item of investment yield, the items of gross amount, and the items of deduction shall, except as modified by this subparagraph, be determined on an annual basis in the manner provided in subparagraph (1) of this paragraph. In any case in which a limitation is placed on the amount of a deduction provided under section 809, the limitation shall apply to the item of deduction computed on an annualized basis.

(ii) For purposes of section 809 and 810, the investment yield shall be determined in the manner provided in subparagraph (2)(ii) of this paragraph. The share of any item of investment yield set aside for policyholders shall be that percentage obtained by dividing the required interest as determined under section 809(a)(2), by the investment yield, as determined in this subparagraph, except that if the required interest exceeds the investment yield, then the share of any item of investment yield set aside for policyholders shall be 100 percent.

(iii) The items of gross amount and the items of deduction, other than the operations loss deduction under section 809(d)(4), shall be determined on an annual basis. See subdivision (iv) of this subparagraph for the manner in which the net decrease or net increase in reserves under section 810 shall be annualized.

(iv) For purposes of determining either a net decrease in reserves under section 810(a) or a net increase in reserves under section 810(b), the sum of the items described in section 810(c) as of the end of the short period shall be reduced by the amount of the investment yield not included in gain or loss from operations for the short period by reason of section 809(a)(1). The amount of investment yield excluded under section 809(a)(1) has been determined upon an annualized basis while the sum of the items described in section 810(c) at the end of the short period has been determined on an actual basis. In order to place these on the same basis, the amount of investment yield not included in gain or loss from operations by reason of section 809(a)(1), determined under subdivision (ii) shall, for purposes of section 810(a) and section 810(b), be reduced to an amount which bears the same ratio to the full amount as the number of days in the short period bears to the number of days in the entire calendar year. The net decrease or the net increase of the items referred to in section 810(c) for the short period shall then be determined, as provided in section 810(a) and section 810(b), respectively, and the result annualized.

(4) The portion of the life insurance company taxable income described in section 802(b)(1) and (2) (relating to taxable investment income and gain or loss from operations) shall be determined on an annual basis by treating the amounts ascertained under subparagraph (2) of this paragraph as the taxable investment income, and the amount ascertained under subparagraph (3) of this paragraph as the gain or loss from operations, for the taxable year.

(5) The portion of the life insurance company taxable income described in section 802(b)(1) and (2) for the short period shall be the amount which bears the same ratio to the amount ascertained under section 818(d)(2) and subparagraph (4) of this paragraph as the number of days in the short period bears to the number of days in the entire year.

(d) Special rules. *(1)* For purposes of determining the average earnings rate (as defined in section 805(b)(3)) for subsequent taxable years, the current earnings rate for the taxable year in which the short period occurs shall be the rate determined under paragraph (c)(2) of this section.

(2) For purposes of determining an operations loss deduction under section 812, the loss from operations for the short period shall be the loss from operations determined under paragraph (c)(5) of this section.

T.D. 6558, 4/3/61.

§ 1.818-7 Denial of double deductions.

Caution: The Treasury has not yet amended Reg § 1.818-7 to reflect changes made by P.L. 98-369.

Section 818(f) provides that the same item may not be deducted more than once under subpart B, part I, subchapter L, chapter 1 of the Code (relating to the determination of taxable investment income), and more than once under subpart C, part I, subchapter L, chapter 1 of the Code (relating to the determination of gain or loss from operations).

T.D. 6558, 4/3/61.

§ 1.818-8 Special rules relating to consolidated returns and certain capital losses.

Caution: The Treasury has not yet amended Reg § 1.818-8 to reflect changes made by P.L. 98-369.

Section 818(g) provides that, in the case of a life insurance company filing or required to file a consolidated return under section 1501 for a taxable year, the computations of the policyholders' share of investment yield under subparts B and C, part I, subchapter L, chapter 1 of the Code (including all determinations and computations incident thereto) shall be made as if such company were not filing a consolidated return. Thus, for example, if X and Y are life insurance companies which are entitled to file a consolidated return for 1975 and X has paid dividends to Y during such taxable year, Y must include such dividends in the computation of gross investment income under section 804(b). For other rules relating to the filing of consolidated returns, see sections 1501 through 1504 and the regulations thereunder.

T.D. 7469, 2/28/77.

§ 1.819-1 Taxable years affected.

Caution: The Treasury has not yet amended Reg § 1.819-1 to reflect changes made by P.L. 98-369.

Section 1.819-2 is applicable only to taxable years beginning after December 31, 1957, and all references to sections of part I, subchapter L, chapter 1 of the Code, are to the Internal Revenue Code of 1954, as amended by the Life Insurance Company Income Tax Act of 1959 (73 Stat. 112).

T.D. 6558, 4/3/61.

---

§ 1.819-2 Foreign life insurance companies.

Caution: The Treasury has not yet amended Reg § 1.819-2 to reflect changes made by P.L. 98-369.

(a) Carrying on United States insurance business. Section 819(a) provides that a foreign life insurance company carrying on a life insurance business within the United States, if with respect to its United States business it would qualify as a life insurance company under section 801, shall be taxable on its United States business under section 802 in the same manner as a domestic life insurance company. Thus, the life insurance company taxable income of such a foreign life insurance company shall not be determined in the manner provided by Part I, subchapter N, chapter 1 of the Code (relating to determination of sources of income), but shall be determined in the manner provided by part I, subchapter L, chapter 1 of the Code (relating to life insurance companies). See section 842. Accordingly, in determining its life insurance company taxable income from its United States business, such a foreign life insurance company shall take into account the appropriate items of income irrespective of whether such items of income are from sources within or without the United States. A foreign life insurance company shall take into account the appropriate items of expenses, losses, and other deductions properly allocable to such items of income from its United States business. To the extent not inconsistent with the provisions of this paragraph, section 818 (a), and section 819(b), all computations entering into the determination of taxes imposed by part I shall be made in a manner consistent with the manner required for purposes of the annual statement approved by the National Association of Insurance Commissioners.

(b) Adjustment where surplus held in the United States is less than specified minimum. *(1) In general.* Section 819(b)(1) provides that if the minimum figure for the taxable year determined under section 819(b)(2) and subparagraph (2)(i) of this paragraph exceeds the surplus held in the United States as of the end of the taxable year (as defined in section 819(b)(2)(B) and subparagraph (2)(ii) of this paragraph) by a foreign life insurance company carrying on a life insurance business within the United States and taxable under section 802, then—

(i) The amount of the policy and other contract liability requirements (determined under section 805 and § 1.805-4 without regard to this subparagraph), and

(ii) The amount of the required interest (determined under section 809(a)(2) and paragraph (d) of § 1.809-2 without regard to this subparagraph), shall each be reduced by an amount determined by multiplying such excess by the current earnings rate (as defined in section 805(b)(2) and paragraph (a)(2) of § 1.805-5) of such company. Such current earnings rate shall be determined by reference to the assets held by the company in the United States.

(2) Definitions. For purposes of section 819(b)(1) and subparagraph (1) of this paragraph—

(i) The term "minimum figure", in the case of a taxable year beginning after December 31, 1957, but before January 1, 1959, means the amount obtained by multiplying the company's total insurance liabilities on United States business by 9 percent. In the case of any taxable year beginning after December 31, 1958, such term means the amount obtained by multiplying the company's total insurance liabilities on United States business by the percentage determined and proclaimed by the Secretary as being applicable for such year.[1]

Year	Tax	%	T.D.
1959	Estimated Income	9	6413
1959	Income	12.5	6470
1960	Estimated Income	12.5	6491
1960	Income	14.3	6554
1961	Estimated Income	14.3	6567
1961	Income	13.4	6594
1962	Estimated Income	13.4	6594
1962	Income	14.5	6640
1963	Estimated Income	14.5	6640
1963	Income	15	6709
1964	Estimated Income	15	6709
1964	Income	15	6801
1965	Estimated Income	15	6801
1965	Income	15.8	6878
1966	Estimated Income	15.8	6878

(ii) The term "surplus held in the United States" means the excess of the assets held in the United States (as of the end of the taxable year) over the total insurance liabilities on United States business (as of the end of the taxable year).

(iii) The term "total insurance liabilities" means the sum of the total reserves (as defined in section 801(c) and paragraph (a) of § 1.801-5) as of the end of the taxable year plus (to the extent not included in total reserves) the items referred to in section 810(c)(3), (4), and (5) and paragraph (b)(3), (4), and (5) of § 1.801-2 as of the end of the taxable year; and

(iv) The term "assets" shall have the same meaning as that contained in section 805(b)(4) and paragraph (a)(4) of § 1.805-5.

(3) Illustration of principles. The provisions of section 819(b) and this paragraph may be illustrated by the following example:

Example. For the taxable year 1958, P, a foreign life insurance company carrying on a life insurance business within the United States and taxable under section 802, has total insurance liabilities on United States business (as of the end of the taxable year) of $940,000, assets held in the United States of $1,000,000 (as of the end of the taxable year), policy and other contract liability requirements in the amount of $30,000, required interest in the amount of $20,000, and a current earnings rate of 4 percent. In order to determine whether section 819(b) applies for the taxable year 1958, P must first compute its minimum figure, for if the minimum figure is less than the surplus held in the United States (as of the end of the taxable year), no section 819(b) adjustments need be made. Since the minimum figure, $84,600 ($940,000, the total insurance liabilities on United States business multiplied by 9 percent, the percentage applicable for 1958), exceeds the surplus held in the United States, $60,000 (the excess of the assets held in the United States, $1,000,000, over the total insurance liabilities on United States business, $940,000), by $24,600, section 819(b) applies for the taxable year 1958. Thus, the amount of the policy and other contract liability requirements, $30,000, and the amount of the required interest, $20,000, shall each be reduced by $984 ($24,600, the amount of such excess, multiplied by 4 percent, the current earnings rate).

(4) Segregated asset accounts. For taxable years beginning after December 31, 1967, pursuant to the provisions of section 801(g)—

(i) A foreign corporation carrying on a life insurance business which issues contracts based on segregated asset accounts shall separately compute in a manner consistent with this subparagraph the adjustment (if any) under section 819 to the amount of policy and other contract liability requirements and the amount of required interest properly attributable to each of such segregated asset accounts. The "minimum figure" used in section 819 in making the adjustment with respect to each of the segregated asset accounts shall be computed as provided in subdivision (ii) of this subparagraph in lieu of the manner provided in subparagraphs (1), (2), and (3) of this paragraph.

(ii) The minimum figure applicable to a segregated asset account referred to in subdivision (i) of this subparagraph is the amount determined by multiplying the total insurance liabilities on U.S. business attributable to such a segregated asset account, by 1 percent.

(iii) The minimum figure as computed under subdivision (ii) of this subparagraph shall be compared only with the surplus held in the United States attributable to each segregated asset account referred to in subdivision (i) of this subparagraph. Such surplus is the excess of assets held in the United States properly attributable to such segregated asset account over the total insurance liabilities on U.S. business properly attributable to such account.

(iv) If the minimum figure applicable to accounts other than segregated asset accounts exceed the surplus held in the United States attributable to such other accounts, for purposes of section 819 and this paragraph, the amount of such excess shall not exceed the company's overall excess, as defined in this subdivision. No adjustment under section 819 or this paragraph shall be made with respect to any account if there is no such overall excess. For purposes of this subdivision and of subdivision (v) of this subparagraph, the term "overall excess" means the amount, if any, by which the aggregate minimum figures applicable to segregated asset accounts plus the minimum figure applicable to accounts other than segregated asset accounts exceeds the surplus held in the United States with respect to the company's entire U.S. life insurance business, including segregated asset accounts as well as other accounts.

(v) In the case of a company which issues contracts based on one or more than one segregated asset account, if the minimum figure applicable to a segregated asset account exceeds the surplus held in the United States attributable to such account, then for purposes of section 819 and this paragraph, the amount of such excess shall not exceed the account limitation figure, as defined in this subdivision. Therefore, no adjustment under section 819 or under this subparagraph shall be made with respect to any segregated asset account if the aggregate of the account limitation figures is zero, but nothing in this subdivision shall preclude an adjustment under section 819 with respect to accounts other than segregated asset accounts. For purposes of this subdivision, the term "account limitation figure" is a segregated asset account's proportionate share of the aggregate of the account limitation figures. Such aggregate of the account limitation figures is equal to the lesser of either the company's overall excess as defined in subdivision (iv) of this subparagraph, or the amount, if any, by which the aggregate of the minimum figures applicable to segregated asset accounts exceeds the surplus held in the United States with respect to all such segregated asset accounts. For purposes of this subdivision, a segregated asset account's proportionate share of the aggregate of the account limitation figures is determined by multiplying the amount of such aggregate of account limitation figures by a percentage, the numerator of which is the amount by which the minimum figure applicable to such account exceeds the surplus held in the United States attributable to such account, and the denominator of which is the aggregate of the amounts by which the minimum figure applicable to each segregated asset account exceeds the surplus held in the United States attributable to such account.

(vi) Subdivisions (i), (ii), (iii), (iv), and (v) of this subparagraph may be illustrated by the following examples:

Example (1). (a) For the taxable year 1968, T, a foreign life insurance company carrying on a life insurance business within the United States and taxable under section 802, has the following assets and total insurance liabilities with respect to such U.S. business:

	Regular account	Separate account A	Separate account B
Assets	$9,300,000	$1,810,000	$515,000
Total insurance liabilities	8,000,000	1,800,000	500,000

It is further assumed that the percentage determined and proclaimed by the Secretary under section 819(a)(2)(A) for the taxable year 1968 is 15 percent.

(b) In order to determine whether any adjustment under section 819 must be made, T must compute the minimum figure applicable to its Regular Account as well as each of its Separate Accounts. The minimum figure for the Regular Account is $1,200,000 (15 percent of $8,000,000). The minimum figure applicable to Separate Account A is $18,000 (1 percent of $1,800,000). The minimum figure applicable to Separate Account B is $5,000 (1 percent of $500,000). The aggregate of the minimum figures is $1,223,000. ($1,200,000 + $18,000 + $5,000). The surplus held in the United States with respect to the Regular Account is $1,300,000 ($9,300,000 − $8,000,000), with respect to Separate Account A is $10,000 ($1,810,000 − $1,800,000) and with respect to Separate Account B is $15,000 ($515,000 − $500,000). The surplus held in the United States with respect to T's entire U.S. life insurance business is $1,325,000 ($1,300,000 + $10,000 + $15,000).

(c) Since the aggregate of the minimum figures ($1,223,000) does not exceed the surplus held in the United States attributable to T's entire U.S. life insurance business ($1,325,000), under subdivision (iv) of this subparagraph no adjustment under section 819 shall be made with respect to the Regular Account or either of the Separate Accounts.

Example (2). (a) The facts are the same as in example (1) except that the assets held in the United States with respect to the Regular Account is $8,300,000 instead of $9,300,000. Thus, the surplus held in the United States with respect to the Regular Account is $300,000 ($8,300,000 − $8,000,000), and the surplus held in the United States with respect to T's entire U.S. life insurance business is $325,000 ($300,000 + $10,000 + $15,000).

(b) Since the aggregate of the minimum figures with respect to the Separate Accounts, $23,000 ($18,000 + $5,000), does not exceed the surplus held in the United States with respect to both of such Separate Accounts, $25,000 ($10,000 + $15,000), under subdivision (v) of this subparagraph, no adjustment under section 819 must be made with respect to either of the Separate Accounts.

(c) The excess of the minimum figure for the Regular Account ($1,200,000) over the surplus held in the United States with respect to the Regular Account ($300,000) is equal to $900,000 ($1,200,000 – $300,000). However, the company's overall excess as defined in subdivision (iv) of this subparagraph, is $898,000 ($1,223,000 – $325,000). Under subdivision (iv) of this subparagraph the excess with respect to the Regular Account ($900,000) is limited to the amount of overall excess ($898,000). Thus, the amount of policy and other contract liability requirements with respect to T's Regular Account and the amount of required interest with respect to T's Regular Account (both computed without regard to section 819) shall each be reduced by an amount equal to the product of $898,000 and the current earnings rate computed only with respect to T's Regular Account.

(c) Distributions to shareholders. *(1) In general.* In the case of a foreign life insurance company carrying on a life insurance business within the United States and taxable under section 802, section 819(c)(1) provides alternative methods for determining the amount of distributions to shareholders for purposes of section 815 (relating to distributions to shareholders) and section 802(b)(3) (relating to life insurance company taxable income). Such a foreign life insurance company may elect (in the manner provided by subparagraph (4) of this paragraph) for each taxable year, whichever of the alternative methods provided by section 819(c)(1) and this subparagraph it desires, and the method elected for any one taxable year shall be effective only with respect to the taxable year for which the election is made. Such alternative methods are:

(i) The amount of the distributions to shareholders shall be the amount determined by multiplying the total amount of distributions to shareholders by the percentage which the minimum figure for the taxable year is of the excess of the assets of the company over the total insurance liabilities; or

(ii) The amount of the distributions for shareholders shall be the amount determined by multiplying the total amount of distributions for shareholders by the percentage which the total insurance liabilities on United States business for the taxable year is of the total insurance liabilities of the company.

(2) Definitions. For purposes of section 819(c)(1) and subparagraph (1) of this paragraph:

(i) The term "total amount of the distributions to shareholders" means all distributions (within the meaning of section 815 and § 1.815-2) by a foreign life insurance company to all of its shareholders whether or not in the United States;

(ii) The term "minimum figure for the taxable year" means the amount determined under section 819(b)(2)(A) and paragraph (b)(2) of this section;

(iii) The term "assets of the company" means all of the assets (as defined in section 805(b)(4) and paragraph (a)(4) of § 1.805-5) of the foreign life insurance company whether or not in the United States (as of the end of the taxable year); and

(iv) The term "total insurance liabilities of the company" means the total insurance liabilities (as defined in section 819(b)(2) and paragraph (b)(2) of this section on all of its business whether or not in the United States (as of the end of the taxable year).

(3) Illustration of principles. The provisions of section 819(c)(1) and subparagraphs (1) and (2) of this paragraph may be illustrated by the following examples:

Example (1). For the taxable year 1958, T, a foreign life insurance company carrying on a life insurance business within the United States and taxable under section 802, has a minimum figure of $40,000, total amount of distributions to all shareholders (within the meaning of section 815) of $5,000, assets (as of the end of the year) of $500,000, total insurance liabilities (as of the end of the year) of $450,000, and total insurance liabilities on United States business (as of the end of the year) of $180,000. Based upon these facts, if T elects the method provided in section 819 (c)(1)(A) and subparagraph (1)(i) of this paragraph, the amount of T's distributions to shareholders for the taxable year 1958 is $4,000, that is, $5,000 (the total amount of distributions to shareholders) multiplied by 80 percent (the percentage which the minimum figure for the taxable year, $40,000, is of $50,000, the excess of the assets of the company ($500,000) over the total insurance liabilities ($450,000)).

Example (2). The facts are the same as in example (1), except that for the taxable year 1958, T elects the method provided in section 819(c)(1)(B) and subparagraph (1)(ii) of this paragraph. Based upon these facts, the amount of T's distributions to shareholders for the taxable year 1958 is $2,000, that is, $5,000 (the total amount of distribution to shareholders) multiplied by 40 percent (the percentage which the total insurance liabilities on United States business ($180,000) is of the total insurance liabilities of the company ($450,000)).

(4) Manner and effect of election. (i) The election provided by section 819(c)(1) shall be made in a statement attached to the foreign life insurance company's income tax return for any taxable year for which the company desires the election to apply. The return and statement must be filed not later than the date prescribed by law (including extensions thereof) for filing the return for such taxable year. The statement shall indicate the method elected, the name and address of the taxpayer, and shall be signed by the taxpayer (or his duly authorized representative).

(ii) An election made under section 819(c)(1) and this paragraph shall be effective only with respect to the taxable year for which the election is made. Thus, the company must make a new election for each taxable year for which it desires the election to apply. Once such election has been made for any taxable year it may not be revoked. However, for taxable years beginning prior to April 4, 1961, a company may revoke the election provided by section 819(c)(1) without obtaining consent from the Commissioner by filing, before July 4, 1961, a statement that the company desires to revoke such election. An amended return reflecting such revocation and the selection of the other percentage must accompany the statement for all taxable years for which returns have been filed with respect to such election.

(5) Application of section 815. Once the amount of distributions to shareholders is determined under the provisions of section 819(c)(1) and this paragraph, the rules of section 815 (relating to distributions to shareholders) shall apply to the shareholders surplus account and the policyholders surplus account of a foreign stock life insurance company in the same manner as they would apply to a domestic stock life insurance company.

(d) Distributions pursuant to certain mutualizations. Section 819(c)(2) provides that for purposes of applying section 815(e) and paragraph (e) of § 1.815-6 (relating to a special rule for certain mutualizations) in the case of a foreign life insurance company subject to tax under section 802—

(1) The paid-in capital and paid-in surplus referred to in section 815(e)(1)(A) of a foreign life insurance company is the portion of such capital and surplus determined by multiplying such amounts by the percentage selected for the taxable year under section 819(C)(1) and paragraph (c)(1) of this section; and

(2) The excess referred to in section 815(e)(2)(A)(i) (without the adjustment provided by section 815(e)(2)(B)), is whichever of the following is the greater:

(i) The minimum figure for 1958 determined under section 819(b)(2)(A); or

(ii) The surplus held in the United States (as defined in section 819(b)(2)(B)) determined as of December 31, 1958.

(e) No United States insurance business. Foreign life insurance companies not carrying on an insurance business within the United States shall not be taxable under part I, subchapter L, chapter 1 of the Code, but shall be taxable as other foreign corporations. See section 881 and the regulations thereunder.

T.D. 6558, 4/3/61, amend T.D. 6970, 8/23/68.

§ 1.821-4 Tax on mutual insurance companies other than life insurance companies and other than fire, flood, or marine insurance companies subject to tax imposed by section 831.

Caution: The Treasury has not yet amended Reg § 1.821-4 to reflect changes made by P.L. 99-514.

(a) In general. *(1) Tax imposed.* (i) For taxable years beginning after December 31, 1962, all mutual insurance companies, including foreign insurance companies carrying on an insurance business within the United States, not taxable under section 802 or 831, and not specifically exempt under the provisions of section 501(c)(15), are subject either to the tax imposed by section 821(a) on mutual insurance company taxable income or, in the case of certain small companies, to the tax imposed by section 821(c) on taxable investment income. The determination of whether a mutual insurance company is taxable under section 821 (a) or (c) for the taxable year is dependent upon the gross amount received by the company during such taxable year from the items described in section 822(b) (other than paragraph (1)(D) thereof) and premiums (including deposits and assessments). If such gross amount received exceeds $150,000, but does not exceed $500,000 for the taxable year, the company is subject to the tax imposed by section 821(c) on taxable investment income, unless (a) the company elects under section 821(d) in the manner provided in paragraph (f) of this section to be subject to the tax imposed by section 821(a), or (b) there is a balance in its protection against loss account at the beginning of the taxable year. A company having a gross amount received in excess of $500,000 is subject to the tax imposed by section 821(a). For exemption from income tax of companies having a gross amount received not in excess of $150,000, see section 501(c)(15). For the alternative tax, in lieu of the tax imposed by section 821(a) or (c), where the net long-term capital gain for any taxable year exceeds the net short-term capital loss, see section 1201(a) and the regulations thereunder. For the definition of an insurance company, see § 1.801-3(a).

(ii) The term "premiums" as used in section 821 and this section has the same meaning as in section 501(c)(15) and § 1.501(c)(15)-1, and means the total amount of the premiums and other consideration provided in the insurance contract without any deduction for commissions, return premiums, reinsurance, dividends to policyholders, dividends left on deposit with the company, discounts on premiums paid in advance, interest applied in reduction of premiums (whether or not required to be credited in reduction of premiums under the terms of the contract), or any other item of similar nature. Such term includes advance premiums, premiums deferred and uncollected and premiums due and unpaid, deposits, fees, assessments, and consideration in respect of assuming liabilities under contracts not issued by the taxpayer (such as a payment or transfer of property in an assumption reinsurance transaction), but does not include amounts received from other insurance companies for losses paid under reinsurance contracts.

(2) Tax base. The taxable income of mutual insurance companies taxable under section 821 differs from the taxable income of other corporations. See sections 821(b) and 822. Mutual insurance companies have special items of income and special deductions not provided for other corporations. See, for example, sections 821(b)(1)(C), 822(d), 823(b), 824(a), and 825(a). Thus, the computation of mutual insurance company taxable income for a company taxable under section 821(a), and the computation of taxable investment income for a company taxable under section 821(c), must be made in strict accordance with the provisions of part II of subchapter L of the Code.

(3) Applicability of other provisions. All provisions of the Code and of the regulations in this part not inconsistent with the specific provisions of part II of subchapter L of the Code are applicable to the assessment and collection of the tax imposed by section 821(a) or (c), and mutual insurance companies subject to the tax imposed by section 821 are subject to the same penalties as are provided in the case of returns and payment of income tax by other corporations. The return shall be on Form 1120M.

(4) Certain foreign companies. Foreign mutual insurance companies (other than a life insurance company and other than a fire, flood, or marine insurance company subject to the tax imposed by section 831) not carrying on an insurance business within the United States are not taxable under section 821(a) or (c), but are taxable as other foreign corporations. See section 881.

(b) Rates of tax imposed by section 821(a). *(1) Normal tax.* For taxable years beginning before January 1, 1964, the normal tax imposed under section 821(a) is the lesser of 30 percent of mutual insurance company taxable income, or 60 percent of the amount by which mutual insurance company taxable income exceeds $6,000. In the case of taxable years beginning after December 31, 1963, the normal tax is imposed at the rate of 22 percent of mutual insurance company taxable income, or 44 percent of the amount by which mutual insurance company taxable income exceeds $6,000, whichever is the lesser. For example, a company subject to tax under section 821(a) will file a return but will pay no normal tax if mutual insurance company taxable income does not exceed $6,000. When mutual insurance company taxable income exceeds $6,000 but does not exceed $12,000, the company will pay a normal tax equal to 44 percent (60) percent in the case of taxable years beginning before Jan. 1, 1964) of the amount by which mutual insurance company taxable income exceeds $6,000. When mutual insurance company taxable income exceeds $12,000, the company will pay normal tax at the rate of 22 percent (30) percent in the case of taxable years beginning after Jan. 1, 1964) of such income.

(2) Surtax. (i) Taxable years beginning before January 1, 1964. For taxable years beginning before January 1, 1964, companies taxable under section 821(a) are subject to a surtax equal to 22 percent of so much of their mutual insurance company taxable income (computed without regard to the deduction provided in section 242 for partially tax-exempt interest) as exceeds $25,000. In the case of an interinsurer or reciprocal underwriter electing to be subject to the limitation provided in section 826(b), the surtax applies to any increase in mutual insurance company taxable income attributable to such election, without regard to the $25,000 surtax exemption otherwise provided by this subparagraph, and without regard to whether the company is liable for any normal tax under subparagraph (1) of this subparagraph. See section 826(f) and § 1.826-2.

(ii) Taxable years beginning after December 31, 1963. For taxable years beginning after December 31, 1963, companies taxable under section 821(a) are subject to a surtax at the rates and with the exemptions provided in section 11(c) on their mutual insurance company taxable income. In the case of an interinsurer or reciprocal underwriter electing to be subject to the limitation provided in section 826(b), the surtax applies to any increase in mutual insurance company taxable income attributable to such election, without regard to the surtax exemption otherwise provided by section 11(d), and without regard to whether the company is liable for any normal tax under section 821(a)(1) and subparagraph (1) of this paragraph. See section 826(f) and § 1.826-2.

(c) Mutual insurance company taxable income defined. The tax imposed by section 821(a) with respect to any taxable year is computed upon mutual insurance company taxable income for the taxable year. Section 821(b) provides that in the case of a mutual insurance company subject to the tax imposed by section 821(a), mutual insurance company taxable income means the amount by which—

(1) The sum of—

(i) The taxable investment income (as defined in section 822(a)(1) and paragraph (a)(1) of § 1.822-8),

(ii) The statutory underwriting income (as defined in section 823(a)(1) and paragraph (b)(1) of § 1.823-6), and

(iii) The amounts required by section 824(d) and paragraph (b)(3) of § 1.824-1 to be subtracted from the protection against loss account, exceeds

(2) The sum of—

(i) The investment loss (as defined in section 822(a)(2) and paragraph (a)(2) of § 1.822-8),

(ii) The statutory underwriting loss (as defined in section 823(a)(2) and paragraph (b)(2) of § 1.823-6), and

(iii) The unused loss deduction provided by section 825(a) and paragraph (a) of § 1.825-1.

If for any taxable year the amount determined under subparagraph (2) of this paragraph equals or exceeds the amount determined under subparagraph (1) of this paragraph, the mutual insurance company taxable income for such year shall be zero.

(d) Examples. The application of the tax imposed by section 821(a) may be illustrated by the following examples:

Example (1). (a) M, a mutual casualty insurance company, for the calendar year 1963 has gross receipts from the items described in section 822(b) (other than paragraph (1)(D) thereof) and premiums (including deposits and assessments) in excess of $500,000, and therefore is subject to the tax imposed by section 821(a). M's taxable investment income, computed under section 822, is $30,000 and its statutory underwriting income, computed under section 823, is $15,000. M subtracts $3,000 from its protection against loss account in accordance with the computation made under section 824(d). M has no unused loss deduction. If M is not subject to section 826, its mutual insurance company taxable income for the taxable year 1963 is $48,000, computed as follows:

(1) Taxable investment income	$30,000
(2) Statutory underwriting income	15,000
(3) Subtractions from protection against loss account	3,000
(4) Total income items	48,000
Less:	
(5) Investment loss	0
(6) Statutory underwriting loss	0
(7) Unused loss deduction	0
(8) Total loss items	0
(9) Mutual insurance company taxable income (item (4) minus item (8))	48,000

(b) Since M's mutual insurance company taxable income is in excess of $12,000, M will pay normal tax on its mutual insurance company taxable income at a rate of 30 percent. In addition, since M's mutual insurance company taxable income exceeds $25,000, M will pay surtax on such excess at a rate of 22 percent. M's total liability for the taxable year 1963 is $19,460, computed as follows:

(1) Mutual insurance company taxable income as computed in item (a)(9)	$48,000
(2) Normal tax; 30 percent of mutual insurance company taxable income	14,400
(3) Surtax exemption	25,000
(4) Mutual insurance company taxable income subject to the surtax (item (1) minus item (3))	23,000
(5) Surtax: 22 percent of mutual insurance company taxable income subject to the surtax	5,060
(6) Total tax (item (2) plus item (5))	19,460

Example (2). If in example (1), M's mutual insurance company taxable income for 1963 had been in excess of $6,000 but not in excess of $12,000, M would pay normal tax in an amount equal to 60 percent of the amount by which such income exceeded $6,000. Thus, if M had mutual insurance company taxable income of $11,000, M's total tax liability for the taxable year 1963 would be $3,000, computed as follows:

(1) Mutual insurance company taxable income	$11,000
(2) Mutual insurance company taxable income in excess of $6,000 ($11,000 minus $6,000)	5,000
(3) 30 percent of item (1)	3,300
(4) 60 percent of item (2)	3,000
(5) Normal tax (lesser of items (3) or (4))	3,000
(6) Surtax exemption	25,000

Since the surtax exemption exceeds the mutual insurance company taxable income for purposes of the surtax, there is no surtax liability. Since the normal tax under section 821(a) is the lesser of 30 percent of mutual insurance company taxable income or 60 percent of the amount by which such income exceeds $6,000, M's normal tax (and total income tax liability) is $3,000. If M's mutual insurance company taxable income was not in excess of $6,000, M would be required to file a return, but would not be liable for any normal tax, since, in such a case, 60 percent of M's mutual insurance company taxable income in excess of $6,000 would be zero.

Example (3). Assume the same income as in example (1) in the 1965 calendar year and that M is not a corporation to which section 1561 (with respect to certain controlled corporations) applies. Since M's mutual insurance company taxable income is in excess of $12,000, M will pay normal tax on its mutual insurance company taxable income at a rate of 22 percent. In addition, since M's mutual insurance company taxable income exceeds the surtax exemption provided in section 11(d) of $25,000, M will pay a surtax on such excess at the rate provided in section 11(c), 26 percent. M's total liability for the taxable year 1964 is $16,540, computed as follows:

(1) Mutual insurance company taxable income as computed in example (1)	$48,000
(2) Normal tax: 22 percent of mutual insurance company taxable income for normal tax purposes	10,560
(3) Surtax exemption provided by section 11(d)...	25,000
(4) Mutual insurance company taxable income subject to the surtax (item (1) minus item (3))	23,000
(5) Surtax: at rates provided in section 11(c): 26 percent of mutual insurance company taxable income subject to the surtax	5,980
(6) Total tax (item (2) plus item (5))............	16,540

(e) Alternative tax for certain small mutual insurance companies. *(1) In general.* (i) Section 821(c) provides an alternative tax for certain small mutual insurance companies. This alternative tax, which is in lieu of the tax imposed by section 821(a), is imposed on taxable investment income (as defined in section 822(a)(1) and paragraph (a)(1) of § 1.822-8) and consists of a normal tax and a surtax. The tax provided by section 821(c) is imposed on every mutual insurance company (other than a life insurance company and other than a fire, flood, or marine insurance company subject to the tax imposed by section 831) which received during the taxable year from the items described in section 822(b) (other than paragraph (1)(D) thereof) and premiums (including deposits and assessments) a gross amount in excess of $150,000 but not in excess of $500,000, except a company which has properly elected under section 821(d) and paragraph (f) of this section to be subject to the tax imposed by section 821(a), or a company which has a balance in its protection against loss account at the beginning of the taxable year.

(ii) Any company which would be taxable under section 821(c) but for the presence of an amount in its protection against loss account at the beginning of the taxable year may elect to subtract the balance from such account. See section 824(d)(5) and § 1.824-3. If such an election is made in such a case, the company shall not be subject to the tax imposed by section 821(a), but shall be subject to the tax imposed by section 821(c).

(2) Rates of tax imposed by section 821(c). (i) Normal tax. The normal tax for taxable years beginning before January 1, 1964, is the lesser of 30 percent of taxable investment income or 60 percent of the amount by which taxable investment income exceeds $3,000. For taxable years beginning after December 31, 1963, the normal tax is imposed at the rate of 22 percent of taxable investment income, or 44 percent of the amount by which taxable investment income exceeds $3,000, whichever is the lesser. Thus, a company subject to tax under section 821(c) will file a return but will pay no tax if for the taxable year its taxable investment income does not exceed $3,000; or will pay a normal tax equal to 44 percent (60 percent in the case of taxable years beginning before Jan. 1, 1964), of taxable investment income in excess of $3,000 when such income exceeds $3,000 but does not exceed $6,000. When taxable investment income exceeds $6,000, the normal tax is imposed at the rate of 22 percent (3 percent in the case of taxable years beginning before Jan. 1, 1964) of such income.

(ii) Surtax. For taxable years beginning before January 1, 1964, a surtax is imposed at the rate of 22 percent of taxable investment income (computed without regard to the deduction provided in section 242 for partially tax-exempt interest) in excess of $25,000. For taxable years beginning after December 31, 1963, a surtax is imposed at the rate provided in section 11(c) on taxable investment income in excess of the surtax exemption provided in section 11(d).

(f) Election to be taxed under section 821(a). *(1) In general.* Section 821(d) provides that any mutual insurance company taxable under section 821(c) may elect, in the manner provided by subparagraph (3) of this paragraph, to be taxed under section 821(a).

(2) Scope of election. Except as otherwise provided herein, an election made under section 821(d) and this paragraph to be taxable under section 821(a) shall be binding for the taxable year for which made and for all succeeding taxable years unless the Commissioner consents to a revocation of such election. If for any taxable year the gross amount received from the items described in section 822(b) (other than paragraph (1)(D) thereof) and premiums (including deposits and assessments) does not exceed $150,000, a company's prior election made under section 821(d) to be taxable under section 821(a) will automatically terminate and any balance in the protection against loss account will be taken into account for the preceding taxable year. (See section 824(d)(4) and § 1.824-2 for automatic termination of protection against loss account if company is not subject to the tax imposed by section 821(a).) If for any taxable year thereafter the gross amount received exceeds $150,000 but does not exceed $500,000, the company shall be taxable under section 821(c) unless it makes a new election to be taxable under section 821(a). If a company subject to tax under section 821(c) for a taxable year elects under section 821(d) and this section to be taxed under section 821(a) and, in a subsequent taxable year, the gross receipts of such company exceed $500,000, the election made for such earlier taxable year shall be considered as continuing in effect. Thus, such a company will continue to be taxable under section 821(a) notwithstanding that its gross receipts subsequently fall below $500,000 (so long as they do not fall below $150,000) unless the Commissioner consents to a revocation of the prior election. Whether revocation is permissible in any case will depend on the facts and circumstances of the particular case, but in no case will revocation be granted in the absence of a showing that the election creates an undue burden or material hardship on the company due to a substantial change in the character of its operations.

(3) Time and manner of making election. The election provided by section 821(d) shall be made in a statement attached to the company's income tax return for the first taxable year for which the election is to apply. The statement shall include the name and address of the taxpayer, shall be signed by the taxpayer (or its duly authorized representative), and shall be filed not later than the date prescribed by law (including extensions thereof) for filing the return for such taxable year.

(g) Examples. The application of the tax imposed by section 821(c) may be illustrated by the following examples:

Example (1). M, a mutual casualty insurance company, for the calendar year 1963 has a gross amount received from the items described in section 822(b) (other than paragraph (1)(D) thereof) and premiums (including deposits and assessments) of $400,000. Since M's gross amount received exceeds $150,000, but does not exceed $500,000, M is subject to the tax imposed by section 821(c) on taxable investment income unless it elects to be subject to the tax imposed on mutual insurance company taxable income by section 821(a). M computes its taxable investment income under section 822 to be $35,000. In computing taxable investment income, M deducted $2,000 of partially tax-exempt interest under section 242. If M does not make an election to be taxed under section 821(a), its total tax liability for the taxable year 1963 is $13,140 computed as follows:

(1) Taxable investment income as computed under section 822	$35,000
(2) 30 percent of taxable investment income	10,500
(3) 60 percent of taxable investment income in excess of $3,000	19,200
(4) Normal tax (lesser of items (2) or (3))	10,500
(5) Partially tax-exempt interest deducted in computing taxable investment income	2,000
(6) Taxable investment income for purposes of the surtax (item (1) plus item (5))	37,000
(7) Surtax exemption	25,000
(8) Taxable investment income subject to surtax (item (6) minus item (7))	12,000
(9) Surtax (22 percent of item (8))	2,640
(10) Total tax liability (item (4) plus item (9))	$13,140

Example (2). N, a mutual casualty insurance company, for the taxable year 1963 has a gross amount received from the items described in section 822(b) (other than paragraph (1)(D) thereof) and premiums (including deposits and assessments) of $210,000. Since N's gross amount received exceeds $150,000 but does not exceed $500,000, N is subject to the tax imposed by section 821(c) on taxable investment income unless it elects to be subject to the tax imposed by section 821(a). Furthermore, since the gross amount received by N does not exceed $250,000, N is entitled to the special tax reduction provided by section 821(c)(2). N computes its taxable investment income under section 822 to be $24,000. In computing taxable investment income, N deducted $2,000 of partially tax-exempt interest under section 242. If N does not make an election to be taxed under section 821(a), its total tax liability for the taxable year 1963 is $4,452 computed as follows:

(1) Taxable investment income as computed under section 822	$24,000
(2) 30 percent of taxable investment income	7,200
(3) 60 percent of taxable investment income in excess of $3,000	12,600
(4) Normal tax (lesser of items (2) or (3))	7,200
(5) Partially tax-exempt interest deducted in computing taxable investment income	2,000
(6) Taxable investment income for purposes of the surtax (item (1) plus item (5))	26,000
(7) Surtax exemption	25,000
(8) Taxable investment income subject to surtax (item (6) minus item (7))	1,000
(9) Surtax 22 percent of item (8)	220
(10) Tax liability computed without regard to special reduction (item (4) plus item (9))	7,420
(11) Amount by which gross receipts exceed $150,000 ($210,000, gross receipts minus $150,000)	60,000
(12) Percentage which item (1) bears to $100,000 ($60,000 over $100,000)	0.60
(13) Tax as adjusted (percentage determined in item (12) applied to item (10))	4,452

If N's taxable investment income for purposes of the surtax did not exceed $3,000, N would file a return but would pay no tax. Had N elected (under section 821(d) to be subject to tax under section 821(a), N would not be entitled to the special reduction afforded by section 821(c)(2), since that provision applies only to companies taxable under section 821(c).

T.D. 6681, 10/16/63, amend T.D. 7100, 3/19/71.

§ 1.823-1 Net premiums.

Caution: The Treasury has not yet amended Reg § 1.823-1 to reflect changes made by P.L. 99-514.

Net premiums are one of the items used, together with interest, dividends, and rents, less dividends to policyholders and wholly tax-exempt interest, in determining tax liability under section 821(a)(2). They are also used in section 822(c)(6) in determining the limitation on certain capital losses and in the application of section 1212. The term "net premiums" is defined in section 823(1) and includes deposits and assessments, but excludes amounts returned to policyholders which are treated as dividends under section 823(2).

T.D. 6201, 9/4/56.

§ 1.823-2 Dividends to policyholders.

Caution: The Treasury has not yet amended Reg § 1.823-2 to reflect changes made by P.L. 99-514.

(a) Dividends to policyholders is one of the deductions used, together with wholly tax-exempt interest, in determining tax liability under section 821(a)(2). They are also used in section 822(c)(6) in determining the limitation on certain capital losses and in the application of section 1212. The term "dividends to policyholders" is defined in section 823(2) as dividends and similar distributions paid or declared to policyholders. It includes amounts returned to policyholders where the amount is not fixed in the insurance contract but depends upon the experience of the company or the discretion of the management. Such amounts are not to be treated as return premiums under section 823(1). Similar distributions include such payments as the so-called unabsorbed premium deposits returned to policyholders by factory mutual fire insurance companies. The term "paid or declared" is to be construed according to the method of accounting regularly employed in keeping the books of the insurance company, and such method shall be consistently followed with respect to all deductions (including dividends and similar distributions to policyholders) and all items of income.

(b) If the method of accounting so employed is the cash receipts and disbursements method, the deduction is limited to the dividends and similar distributions actually paid to policyholders in the taxable year. If, on the other hand, the method of accounting so employed is the accrual method, the deduction, or a reasonably accurate estimate thereof, for dividends and similar distributions declared to policyholders for any taxable year will, in general, be computed as follows:

To dividends and similar distributions paid during the taxable year add the amount of dividends and similar distributions declared but unpaid at the end of the taxable year and deduct dividends and similar distributions declared but unpaid at the beginning of the taxable year.

If an insurance company using the accrual method does not compute the deduction for dividends and similar distributions declared to policyholders in the manner stated, it must submit with its return a full and complete explanation of the manner in which the deduction is computed. For the rule as to when dividends are considered paid, see the regulations under section 561.

T.D. 6201, 9/4/56.

§ 1.823-3 Taxable years affected.

Caution: The Treasury has not yet amended Reg § 1.823-3 to reflect changes made by P.L. 99-514.

Sections 1.823-1 and 1.823-2 are applicable only to taxable years beginning after December 31, 1953, but before January 1, 1955, and ending after August 16, 1954, and all references to sections of part II, subchapter L, chapter 1 of the Code are to the Internal Revenue Code of 1954, before amendments. Sections 1.823-4 and 1.823-5 are applicable only to taxable years beginning after December 31, 1954, but before January 1, 1963, and all references to sections of part II, subchapter L, chapter 1 of the Code are to the Internal Revenue Code of 1954, as amended by the Life Insurance Company Tax Act for 1955 (70 Stat. 36). Sections 1.823-6 through 1.823-8 are applicable only to taxable years beginning after December 31, 1962, and all references to sections of parts II and III, subchapter L, chapter 1 of the Code are to the Internal Revenue Code of 1954 as amended by section 8 of the Revenue Act of 1962 (76 Stat. 989).

T.D. 6610, 8/30/62, amend T.D. 6681, 10/16/63.

§ 1.823-4 Net premiums.

Caution: The Treasury has not yet amended Reg § 1.823-4 to reflect changes made by P.L. 99-514.

Net premiums are one of the items used, together with the gross amount of income during the taxable year from the items described in section 822(b) (other than paragraph (1)(D) thereof), less dividends to policyholders and wholly tax-exempt interest, in determining tax liability under section 821(a)(2). They are also used in section 822(c)(6) in determining the limitation on certain capital losses and in the application of section 1212. The term "net premiums" is defined in section 823(1) and includes deposits and assessments, but excludes amounts returned to policyholders which are treated as dividends under section 823(2).

T.D. 6610, 8/30/62.

§ 1.823-5 Dividends to policyholders.

Caution: The Treasury has not yet amended Reg § 1.823-5 to reflect changes made by P.L. 99-514.

(a) Dividends to policyholders is one of the deductions used, together with wholly tax-exempt interest, in determining tax liability under section 821(a)(2). They are also used in section 822(c)(6) in determining the limitation on certain capital losses and in the application of section 1212. The term "dividends to policyholders" is defined in section 823(2) as dividends and similar distributions paid or declared to policyholders. It includes amounts returned to policyholders where the amount is not fixed in the insurance contract but depends upon the experience of the company or the discretion of the management. Such amounts are not to be treated as return premiums under section 823(1). Similar distributions include such payments as the so-called unabsorbed premium deposits returned to policyholders by factory mutual fire insurance companies. The term "paid or declared" is to be construed according to the method of accounting regularly employed in keeping the books of the insurance company, and such method shall be consistently followed with respect to all deductions (including dividends with similar distributions to policyholders) and all items of income.

(b) If the method of accounting so employed is the cash receipts and disbursements method, the deduction is limited to the dividends and similar distributions actually paid to policyholders in the taxable year. If, on the other hand, the method of accounting so employed is the accrual method, the deduction, or a reasonably accurate estimate thereof, for dividends and similar distributions declared to policyholders for any taxable year will, in general, be computed as follows: To dividends and similar distributions paid during the taxable year add the amount of dividends and similar distributions declared but unpaid at the end of the taxable year and deduct dividends and similar distributions declared but unpaid at the beginning of the taxable year. If an insurance company using the accrual method does not compute the deduction for dividends and similar distributions declared to policyholders in the manner stated, it must submit with its return a full and complete explanation of the manner in which the deduction is computed. For the rule as to when dividends are considered paid, see the regulations under section 561.

T.D. 6610, 8/30/62.

§ 1.823-6 Determination of statutory underwriting income or loss.

Caution: The Treasury has not yet amended Reg § 1.823-6 to reflect changes made by P.L. 99-514.

(a) In general. Section 823(a) and this section provide that for purposes of determining statutory underwriting income or loss for the taxable year, a mutual insurance company subject to the tax imposed by section 821(a) must first take into account the same gross income and deduction items (except as modified by section 823(b) and paragraph (c) of this section) as a taxpayer subject to tax under section 831 would take into account for purposes of determining its taxable income under section 832. These items are then reduced to the extent that they include amounts which are included in determining taxable investment income or loss under section 822(a) and § 1.822-8. In addition, in computing its statutory underwriting income or loss for the taxable year, a company taxable under section 821(a) is allowed to deduct the amount determined under section 824(a) (relating to deduction to provide protection against losses) and, if its gross amount received is less than $1,100,000, is allowed to deduct the amount determined under section 823(c) and paragraph (d) of this section (relating to special deduction for certain small companies), subject to the limitations provided therein.

(b) Definitions. *(1) Statutory underwriting income defined.* Section 823(a)(1) defines the term "statutory underwriting income" for purposes of part II of subchapter L of the Code. Subject to the modifications provided by section 823(b) and paragraph (c) of this section, statutory underwriting income is defined as the amount by which—

(i) The gross income which would be taken into account in computing taxable income under section 832 if the taxpayer were subject to the tax imposed by section 831, reduced by the gross investment income (as determined under section 822(b)), exceeds

(ii) The sum of—

(a) The deductions which would be taken into account in computing taxable income if the taxpayer were subject to the tax imposed by section 831, reduced by the deductions provided in section 822(c) (relating to deductions allowed in computing taxable investment income), plus

(b) The deductions provided in section 823(c) (relating to special deduction for small company having gross amount of less than $1,100,000) and section 824(a) (relating to deduction to provide protection against losses).

For purposes of subdivision (ii)(a) of this subparagraph, the limitations on the amounts deductible under paragraphs (9) (relating to charitable, etc., contributions) and (12) (relating to partially tax-exempt interest and to dividends received) of section 832(c) shall be computed by reference to taxable income as defined by section 832(a), and as modified by section 823(b) and paragraph (c) of this section.

(2) Statutory underwriting loss defined. "Statutory underwriting loss" is defined in section 823(a)(2) as the amount by which the amount determined under section 823(a)(1)(B) and subparagraph (1)(ii) of this paragraph exceeds the amount determined under section 823(a)(1)(A) and subparagraph (1)(i) of this paragraph.

(c) Modifications. *(1) Net operating losses.* In applying section 832 for purposes of determining statutory underwriting income or loss under section 823(a) and paragraph (b) of this section, the deduction for net operating losses provided by section 172 is not allowed. However, see section 825(a) and § 1.825-1 for unused loss deduction allowed companies taxable under section 821(a) in computing mutual insurance company taxable income under section 821(b).

(2) Interinsurers and reciprocal underwriters. (i) In general. Section 823(b)(2) provides that in computing the statutory underwriting income or loss of a mutual insurance company which is an interinsurer or reciprocal underwriter, there shall be allowed as a deduction the increase for the taxable year in savings credited to subscriber accounts, or there shall be included as an item of gross income the decrease for the taxable year in savings credited to subscriber accounts. For purposes of this subparagraph, the term "savings credited to subscriber accounts" means such portion of the surplus for the taxable year as is credited to the individual accounts of subscribers before the 16th day of the third month following the close of the taxable year, but only if the company would be obligated to pay such amount promptly to such subscriber if he terminated his contract at the close of the company's taxable year, and only if the company mails notification to such subscriber of the amount credited to his individual account in the manner provided by subdivision (v) of this subparagraph.

(ii) Limitations. Amounts representing return premiums (as defined in paragraph (a)(1)(ii) of § 1.809-4) which the company would be obligated to pay to any subscriber terminating his contract at the close of the company's taxable year are not savings credited to subscriber accounts within the meaning of section 823(b)(2) and subdivision (i) of this subparagraph. The deduction for savings credited to individual subscriber accounts is allowed only in the case of reciprocal underwriters or interinsurers where the subscriber or policyholder has not only a legally enforceable right to receive the amount so credited if he withdraws from the exchange, but where the amounts credited, as a matter of actual practice, are paid to subscribers or policyholders who terminate their contracts. Thus, no deduction shall be allowed for savings credited to subscriber accounts if such savings are not in fact promptly returned to subscribers when they terminate their contracts.

(iii) Computation of increase or decrease in savings credited to subscriber accounts. For purposes of determining the increase or decrease for the taxable year in savings credited to subscriber accounts, every reciprocal underwriter or interinsurer claiming a deduction under section 823(b)(2) and this section shall establish and maintain an account for savings credited to subscriber accounts. The opening balance in such account for the first taxable year for which a deduction is claimed under section 823(b)(2) and this section shall be zero. In each taxable year there shall be added to such account the total amount of savings credited to subscriber accounts for the taxable year, and there shall be subtracted from such account the total amount of savings subtracted from subscriber accounts for the taxable year. However, in no case may the amount added to the account exceed the total amount of savings to subscribers for the taxable year, irrespective of the amount of savings credited to subscriber accounts for the taxable year. Credits made to subscriber accounts after the close of the taxable year and before the 16th day of the third month following the close of the taxable year will be taken into account as if such amounts had been credited on the last day of the taxable year to the extent such amounts would have become fixed and determinable legal obligations due subscribers if such subscribers had terminated their contracts on the last day of the company's taxable year unless, at the time the amounts are credited, the company specifically designates such amounts as being from surplus for the taxable year in which the amounts were actually credited. Such a designation, once made, shall be irrevocable: However, if a company credited savings to subscriber accounts after December 31, 1962, and before March 16, 1963, and failed to designate such credits as being from surplus for the taxable year 1963, such company may designate such credits as being from surplus for the taxable year 1963 for purposes of determining the total amount of credits to subscriber accounts for such year. In determining the total amount of savings subtracted from subscriber accounts for the taxable year, only amounts subtracted from savings credited for taxable years beginning with the first taxable year for which a deduction was claimed under section 823(b)(2) and this subparagraph will be taken into account. The method of accounting regularly employed by the taxpayer in keeping its books of account will be used for purposes of determining whether the amounts subtracted from the subscriber accounts are from savings for taxable years beginning before the first year for which a deduction is claimed under section 823(b)(2) and this subparagraph, or from savings for taxable years beginning with such first taxable years beginning with such first taxable year. Where the method of accounting regularly employed by the taxpayer in keeping its books of account does not clearly indicate whether an amount was subtracted from savings credited to subscriber accounts for taxable years beginning before the first taxable year for which a deduction is claimed under section 823(b)(2) and this subparagraph, or from savings credited for such first taxable year and subsequent taxable years, the amount subtracted will be deemed to have come from savings credited to subscriber accounts for all taxable years, on a pro rata basis. Where an amount is subtracted from a subscriber's account for record purposes, but such subtraction does not reflect the discharge of the company's legal obligation to pay the amount subtracted promptly to the subscriber if he terminates his contract, then such subtraction shall not be taken into account for purposes of section 823(b)(2) and this subparagraph. On the other hand, where the company ceases to be under a legal obligation to pay promptly to any subscriber the amount credited to his individual account, then such amount shall be considered as having been subtracted from such subscriber's account at the time such obligation ceased to exist. For purposes of section 823(b)(2) and this subparagraph, the increase (if any) for the taxable year in savings credited to subscriber accounts shall be the amount by which the balance in the account for savings credited to subscriber accounts as of the close of the taxable year exceeds the balance in such account as of the close of the preceding taxable year; and the decrease (if any) for the taxable year in savings credited to subscriber accounts shall be the amount by which the balance in the account for savings credited to subscriber accounts as of the close of the preceding taxable year exceeds the balance in such account as of the close of the taxable year.

(iv) Legal obligation. For purposes of this subparagraph, the existence of a legal obligation on the part of the company to pay to the subscriber the savings credited to him will be determined under the insurance contract pursuant to which the credits are made. Where it appears that the company is otherwise legally obligated to pay amounts credited to its subscribers, the requisite legal obligation will not be considered absent merely because a subscriber's credits remain subject to absorption by future losses incurred if left on deposit with the company.

(v) Notification to subscribers. Every reciprocal underwriter or interinsurer claiming a deduction under section 823(b)(2) and this subparagraph for amounts credited to the individual accounts of its subscribers must mail to each such subscriber written notification of the amount credited to the subscriber's account for the taxable year, the date on which such amount was credited, and the date on which the subscriber's right to such amount first would have become fixed if such subscriber had terminated his contract at the close of the company's taxable year. As an alternative to providing each subscriber with specific information relating to the amount of savings credited to his individual account, the notification required by this subdivision may be provided in the form of a table or formula mailed to the subscribers. However, a table or formula may not be used in lieu of the specific notification required by this subdivision unless such table or formula has been approved by the Commissioner. Generally, a table or formula will be approved if it enables the subscriber to simply and readily ascertain the amount of savings credited to his individual account for the taxable year, the date on which such amount was credited, and the date on which his right to such amount first would have become fixed if he had terminated his contract at the close of the company's taxable year. A reciprocal underwriter or interinsurer which desires to use such a table or formula should direct a written request for approval of such table or formula to the Commissioner of Internal Revenue, Attention: T:R, Washington, D.C., 20224. Such request must set forth a copy of the table or formula proposed to be used, together with sufficient information to permit the Commissioner to determine the basis upon which such table or formula was prepared and the manner in which the subscribers will use such table or formula in determining the amounts credited to their individual accounts. Once a table or formula has been approved, the use of such table or formula with respect to savings credited for subsequent taxable years will not require further approval unless the basis upon which such table or formula was prepared, or the manner in which such table or formula is to be applied, is substantially changed. The table or formula method of notification may be used with respect to all or less than all of the company's subscribers. For example, the company might provide the notification required by this subdivision to one class of subscribers in the form of a table or formula mailed to the individual subscribers, while providing another class of subscribers with specific statements of the amounts credited to their individual accounts. The notification required by this subdivision must be mailed before the 16th day of the third month following the close of the reciprocal's taxable year for which the account was credited. Where for any taxable year a reciprocal underwriter or interinsurer claims a deduction under section 823(b) and this subparagraph and fails to give notice as required by this subdivision, such deduction shall not be allowed unless the reciprocal establishes to the satisfaction of the district director that the failure to mail such notice within the prescribed period was due to reasonable cause.

(d) Special deduction for small company having gross amount of less than $1,100,000. *(1) In general.* In the case of a taxpayer subject to the tax imposed by section 821(a), section 823(c) provides that if the gross amount received during the taxable year from the items described in section 822(b) (other than paragraph (1)(D) thereof) and premiums (including deposits and assessments) is less than $1,100,000, then, subject to the limitation provided in section 823(c)(2) and subparagraph (2) of this paragraph, there shall be allowed an additional deduction for purposes of determining statutory underwriting income or loss under section 823(a) for the taxable year. The amount of the additional deduction is $6,000; except that if the gross amount received for the taxable year exceeds $500,000, the additional deduction is limited to an amount equal to 1 percent of the amount by which $1,100,000 exceeds such gross amount.

(2) Limitation. The amount of the deduction provided by section 823(c)(1) may not exceed the statutory underwriting income for the taxable year, computed without regard to the deduction allowed under section 823(c)(1) and subparagraph (1) of this paragraph, and the deduction allowed under section 824(a) (relating to deduction for protection against losses).

(3) Example. The application of section 823(c) and this paragraph may be illustrated by the following example:

M, a mutual insurance company subject to the tax imposed by section 821(a), has the following items for the taxable year 1963:

Gross amount for purposes of section 823(c)(1) . .	$800,000
Gross investment income (including capital gains)	150,000
Capital gains	100,000
Gross income under section 832	900,000
Deductions under section 822(c)	22,000
Deductions under section 832 (as modified by section 823(b)(2))	746,000

Under the provisions of section 823(c), M's special small company deduction for the taxable year 1963 would be $3,000, computed as follows:

(1) Gross amount for purposes of section 823(c)(1)	$800,000
(2) Amount by which $1,100,000 exceeds item (1) ($1,100,000 minus $800,000)	300,000
(3) 1 percent of item (2) (not to exceed $6,000)	3,000
(4) Gross income under section 832, reduced by gross investment income ($900,000 minus $150,000)	750,000
(5) Deductions under section 832 (as modified by section 823(b)), reduced by deductions under section 822(c) ($746,000 minus $22,000)	724,000

(6) Limitation on deduction under section 823(c)(1) (excess, if any, of item (4) over item (5))	26,000
(7) Deduction under section 823(c)(1) (item (3) or item (6), whichever is the lesser)	3,000

T.D. 6681, 10/16/63.

§ 1.823-7 Subscribers of reciprocal underwriters and interinsurers.

Caution: The Treasury has not yet amended Reg § 1.823-7 to reflect changes made by P.L. 99-514.

A subscriber or policyholder of a reciprocal underwriter or interinsurer entitled to the deduction allowed by section 823(b)(2) and paragraph (c)(2) of § 1.823-6 shall treat amounts representing savings credited to his individual account for the taxable year as a dividend paid or declared for purposes of computing his taxable income. If a reciprocal credits savings to subscriber accounts after the close of its taxable year, but before the 16th day of the third month following the close of the taxable year, and the reciprocal takes such credits into account as if they had been made on the last day of its taxable year, the subscribers of such reciprocal must take such savings into account as if they had in fact been credited on the last day of the company's taxable year. The subscriber shall take savings credited to his account without regard to whether the amounts credited are actually distributed to him in cash. To the extent the insurance premium constituted a deductible expense when paid or accrued, the subscriber's taxable income for the taxable year will be increased and any loss for the taxable year will be decreased, by the amount credited to his account. Amounts credited to a subscriber's account which are taken into income by him and which subsequently are used to absorb losses of the reciprocal shall be treated by the subscriber as an additional insurance expense for the taxable year in which the amounts are absorbed. Such amounts may be deducted in computing taxable income to the extent insurance constitutes an otherwise properly deductible expense for such taxable year.

T.D. 6681, 10/16/63.

§ 1.823-8 Special transitional underwriting loss; cross reference.

Caution: The Treasury has not yet amended Reg § 1.823-8 to reflect changes made by P.L. 99-514.

With respect to taxable years beginning after December 31, 1962, and before January 1, 1968, section 821(f) provides, for any company subject to the tax imposed by section 821(a), a special reduction in the statutory underwriting income if such company was subject to tax under section 821 for the five taxable years immediately preceding January 1, 1962, and incurred an underwriting loss in each of such five taxable years. For rules relating to the determination of the amount of such reduction, see section 821(f) and § 1.821-5.

T.D. 6681, 10/16/63.

§ 1.825-1 Unused loss deduction; in general.

Caution: The Treasury has not yet amended Reg § 1.825-1 to reflect changes made by P.L. 99-514.

(a) Amount of deduction. Section 825(a) provides that the unused loss deduction of a mutual insurance company subject to the tax imposed by section 821(a) shall be an amount equal to the sum of the unused loss carryovers and carrybacks to the taxable year. The amount so determined is used in the computation of mutual insurance company taxable income for the taxable year. See section 821(b) and § 1.821-4.

(b) Unused loss defined. Section 825(b) defines the term "unused loss" as the amount (if any) by which—

(1) The sum of the statutory underwriting loss (as defined in section 823(a)(2)) and the investment loss (as defined in section 822(a)(2)) exceeds

(2) The sum of—

(i) The taxable investment income (as defined in section 822(a)(1)),

(ii) The statutory underwriting income (as defined in section 823(a)(1)), and

(iii) The amounts required to be subtracted from the protection against loss account under section 824(d).

(c) Steps in computation of unused loss deduction. The three steps to be taken in the ascertainment of the unused loss deduction for any taxable year are as follows:

(1) Compute the unused loss for any preceding or succeeding taxable year from which an unused loss may be carried over or carried back to the taxable year.

(2) Compute the unused loss carryovers to the taxable year from such preceding taxable years and the unused loss carrybacks to the taxable year from such succeeding taxable years.

(3) Add such unused loss carryovers and carrybacks in order to determine the unused loss deduction for the taxable year.

(d) Statement with tax return. Every mutual insurance company taxable under section 821(a) claiming an unused loss deduction for any taxable year shall file with its return for such year a concise statement setting forth the amount of the unused loss deduction claimed and all material and pertinent facts relative thereto, including a detailed schedule showing the computation of the unused loss deduction.

(e) Ascertainment of deduction dependent upon unused loss carryback. If a mutual insurance company taxable under section 821(a) is entitled in computing its unused loss deduction to a carryback which it is not able to ascertain at the time its return is due, it shall compute the unused loss deduction on its return without regard to such unused loss carryback. When the company ascertains the unused loss carryback, it may within the applicable period of limitations file a claim for credit or refund of the overpayment, if any, resulting from the failure to compute the unused loss deduction for the taxable year with the inclusion of such carryback; or it may file an application under the provisions of section 6411 for a tentative carryback adjustment.

(f) Law applicable to computations. The following rules shall apply to taxable years for which the taxpayer is subject to the tax imposed by section 821(a)—

(1) In determining the amount of any unused loss carryback or carryover to any taxable year, the necessary computations involving any other taxable year shall be made under the law applicable to such other taxable year.

(2) The unused loss for any taxable year shall be determined under the law applicable to that year without regard to the year to which it is to be carried and in which, in effect, it is to be deducted as part of the unused loss deduction.

(3) The amount of the unused loss deduction which shall be allowed for any taxable year shall be determined under the law applicable for that year

T.D. 6681, 10/16/63.

§ 1.825-2 Unused loss carryovers and carrybacks.

Caution: The Treasury has not yet amended Reg § 1.825-2 to reflect changes made by P.L. 99-514.

(a) Years to which loss may be carried. *(1) In general.* In order to determine its unused loss deduction for any taxable year, a mutual insurance company taxable under section 821(a) must first determine the part of any unused losses for any preceding or succeeding taxable years which are carryovers or carrybacks to the taxable year in issue. An unused loss is to be an unused loss carryback to each of the 3 taxable years preceding the loss year, and an unused loss carryover to each of the 5 taxable years following the loss year, subject to the limitations provided in section 825(g) and subparagraph (2) of this paragraph.

(2) Limitations. An unused loss may not be carried—

(i) To or from any taxable year beginning before January 1, 1963,

(ii) To or from any taxable year for which the taxpayer is not subject to the tax imposed by section 821(a), nor

(iii) To any taxable year if, between the loss year and such taxable year, there is an intervening taxable year for which the taxpayer was not subject to the tax imposed by section 821(a).

(3) Periods of less than 12 months. A fractional part of a year which is a taxable year under sections 441(b) and 7701(a)(23) is a preceding or a succeeding taxable year for the purpose of determining under section 825 the first, second, etc., preceding or succeeding taxable year.

(b) Loss year defined. The term "loss year" as used in this section means any taxable year for which a company subject to the tax imposed by section 821(a) has an unused loss in excess of zero.

(c) Amount of carrybacks and carryovers. Section 825(e) provides that in the case of a loss year for a company taxable under section 821(a), the entire amount of the unused loss shall be carried to the earliest taxable year to which such loss may be carried under section 825(d) (subject to the limitations of section 825(g)). The amount of the unused loss carried to each of the other taxable years to which such loss may be carried under section 825(d) following such earliest taxable year shall be the excess (if any) of such loss over the sum of the offsets for each taxable year preceding the taxable year to which the unused loss is carried.

(d) Offset defined. *(1) In general.* Section 825(f) defines the term "offset" and provides that the taxable year to which an unused loss is carried shall be referred to as the "offset year". The definition of the term offset in the case of an unused loss carryback to an offset year, differs from the definition of such term in the case of an unused loss carryover to an offset year.

(2) Offset in case of carryback. In the case of an unused loss carryback from the loss year to the offset year, the offset is the mutual insurance company taxable income for the offset year, computed without regard to any unused loss carryback from the loss year or any taxable year thereafter.

(3) Offset in case of carryover. In the case of an unused loss carryover from the loss year to the offset year, the offset is equal to the sum of—

(i) The amount required to be subtracted from the protection against loss account under section 824(d)(1)(C) (relating to amounts equal to the unused loss carryovers to the offset year), plus

(ii) The mutual insurance company taxable income for the taxable year, computed without regard to any unused loss carryback or carryover from the loss year or any taxable year thereafter.

T.D. 6681, 10/16/63.

§ 1.825-3 Examples.

Caution: The Treasury has not yet amended Reg § 1.825-3 to reflect changes made by P.L. 99-514.

The application of section 825 may be illustrated by the following examples:

Example (1). For the taxable year 1967, F, a mutual insurance company subject to the tax imposed by section 821(a), has the following items:

Taxable investment income	1
Underwriting loss	59
Addition to protection against loss account	8
Statutory underwriting loss	67
The subtractions from the protection against loss account are as follows:	
Amount subtracted from amounts in account with respect to taxable years 1963 through 1966	18
Amount subtracted from amounts in account with respect to taxable year 1967	8
Total subtractions from protection against loss account under section 824(d)	26

The application of section 825 in this case may be illustrated by the facts and results shown in the following table and explained below:

Taxable Year

	1963	1964	1965	1966	1967	1968
Protection against loss account:						
Addition to account during taxable year	6	2	3	7	8	7
Subtraction from account during taxable year	0	0	0	0	8	7
Protection against loss account (at end of year)	6	2	3	7	0	0
Protection against loss account (at end of taxable year 1968)	0	0	0	0	0	0
Unused loss	0	0	0	0	40	0
Unused loss carryback	0	40	35	25	0	0
Unused loss carryover	0	0	0	0	0	18
Unused loss deduction	0	40	35	25	0	18
Mutual insurance company taxable income (computed without regard to unused loss)	13	5	10	7	0	2
Mutual insurance company taxable income (computed with regard to unused loss)	13	0	0	0	0	0
Offset for year	0	5	10	7	0	9
Offset total	0	5	15	22	22	31

1967. Under the provisions of section 825(b), F's unused loss for 1967 is 40, the amount by which the sum of the statutory underwriting loss and the investment loss, 67 (67 plus 0), exceeds the sum of the taxable investment income, the statutory underwriting income, and the amounts required to be subtracted from the protection against loss account under section 824(d) for the taxable year, 27 (the sum of 1, 0, and 26, respectively).

1967 carryback to 1964: Under the provisions of section 825(e), the entire unused loss for 1967 of 40 is carried back to 1964, the earliest year to which the loss may be carried under section 825(d). Since there are no other amounts carried to 1964, the unused loss deduction for 1964 is 40. Thus, after taking the unused loss deduction into account, the mutual insurance company taxable income for 1964 is zero, and the offset for 1964 is 5 (the mutual insurance company taxable income for 1964 determined without regard to the unused loss carryback from 1967 or any year thereafter).

1967 carryback to 1965: The portion of the unused loss for 1967 which is carried back to 1965 is 35 (40 minus 5, the offset for 1964). After taking the unused loss deduction into account, the mutual insurance company taxable income for 1965 is zero. The offset for 1965 is 10, the mutual insurance company taxable income for 1965 determined without regard to any unused loss carryback from 1967 or any year thereafter.

1967 carryback to 1966: The portion of the unused loss for 1967 which is carried back to 1966 is 25. This amount is the excess of the unused loss for 1967 of 40 over the sum of the offset for 1964 (5) and the offset for 1965 (10). As a result of the unused loss deduction the mutual insurance company taxable income for 1966 is reduced to zero. The offset for 1966 is 7.

1967 carryover to 1968: Under the provisions of section 825(d), the portion of the unused loss for 1967 which is carried forward to 1968 is 18 (40 minus the sum of 5, 10, and 7, the offsets for 1964, 1965, and 1966, respectively). Under section 825(f)(2), this amount is first applied against any amounts in the protection against loss account at the end of 1968, and is then applied against the mutual insurance company taxable income for 1968 (computed without regard to any unused loss carryovers or carrybacks from 1967 or any taxable year thereafter). Thus, assuming that there are no other subtractions from its protection against loss account under section 824(d) for 1968, F's protection against loss account of 7 is reduced to zero by reason of the subtraction under section 824(d)(1)(C). The remaining portion of the unused loss for 1967 which is carried to 1968, 11 (18 minus 7, the amount of the unused loss carryover to 1968 which is subtracted from the protection against loss account under section 824(d)(1)(C)), is then applied against the mutual insurance company taxable income for 1968 computed without regard to any unused carryback or carryover from the loss year (1967) or any taxable year thereafter. After the application of the unused loss deduction for 1968, the mutual insurance company taxable income for 1968 is zero. The offset for 1968 is 9, the sum of the amount required to be subtracted from the protection against loss account under section 824(d)(1)(C) for 1968 (7), plus the mutual insurance company taxable income for 1968, determined without regard to any unused loss carryover or carryback from 1967 or any year thereafter (2). The remaining 9 of the unused loss for 1967 (40 minus the sum of 5, 10, 7, and 9, the offsets for 1964, 1965, 1966, and 1968, respectively), is carried forward to 1969, and to the extent not used in that year or any year thereafter, may be carried forward to 1970, 1971, and 1972, in that order.

Example (2). If in example (1) F had an unused loss in 1966 of 22, then, with respect to F's 1967 unused loss of 40, the offset for 1964 would be zero; the offset for 1965 would be 6—the 1965 mutual insurance company taxable income of 10 less an unused loss carryback of 4 from 1966 (the 1966 unused loss of 22 minus the 1963 offset of 13 and the 1964 offset of 5); the offset for the loss year 1966 would be zero, and 34 (the 1967 unused loss of 40 minus the offset for 1965 of 6) would remain as an unused loss carryover to 1968, 1969, 1970, 1971, 1972, in that order. Thus, the unused loss carrybacks or carryovers to an offset year are applied against the mutual insurance company taxable income for such year in the order in which the losses occurred, with the earliest loss being offset first.

Example (3). For the taxable year 1963, M, a mutual insurance company subject to tax imposed by section 821(a), has an unused loss (as defined in section 825(b)) of $65,000. Under section 825(g), the loss may not be carried back to any taxable year beginning before 1963. However, the loss may be carried forward to each of the 5 taxable years following 1963 provided that for each of such succeeding taxable years M is subject to the tax imposed by section 821(a).

Example (4). Assume the facts are the same as in example (3), except that for the taxable year 1964, the gross amount received by M from the items described in section 822(b) (other than paragraph (1)(D) thereof) and premiums (including deposits and assessments) exceeds $150,000 but does not exceed $500,000. If M does not make the election under section 821(d) (relating to election to be taxed under section 821(a) for 1964, M's 1963 unused loss of $65,000 will not be allowed as an unused loss carryover or carryback since, by reason of section 825(g)(3), the unused loss may not be carried to any taxable year if, between the loss year and such taxable year, there is an intervening taxable year for which the insurance company was not subject to the tax imposed by section 821(a), and by reason of section 825(g)(1), the unused loss may not be carried to any taxable year beginning before 1963.

T.D. 6681, 10/16/63.

§ 1.826-1 Election by reciprocal underwriters and interinsurers.

Caution: The Treasury has not yet amended Reg § 1.826-1 to reflect changes made by P.L. 99-514.

(a) In general. Except as otherwise provided in section 826(c), any mutual insurance company which is an interinsurer or reciprocal underwriter taxable under section 821(a) may elect under section 826(a) to limit its deductions for amounts paid or incurred to its attorney-in-fact to the deductions of its attorney-in-fact which are allocable to income received by the attorney-in-fact from the reciprocal during the taxable year. See § 1.826-4 for rules relating to allocation of expenses. In no case may such an election increase the amount deductible by the reciprocal for amounts paid or due its attorney-in-fact for the taxable year. The election allowed by section 826(a) and this section in effect increases the income of the reciprocal by the net income of the attorney-in-fact attributable to its business with the reciprocal. A reciprocal making the election is allowed a credit for the amount of tax paid by the attorney-in-fact for the taxable year which is attributable to income received by the attorney-in-fact from the reciprocal. See section 826(e) and § 1.826-5.

(b) Companies eligible to elect under section 826(a). Any mutual insurance company which is a reciprocal underwriter or interinsurer subject to the tax imposed by section

821(a) may elect (in the manner prescribed by paragraph (c) of this section) to be subject to the limitation provided by section 826(b) and paragraph (a) of this section provided the attorney-in-fact of the electing reciprocal—

(1) Is subject to the taxes imposed by section 11(b) and (c) and the regulations thereunder;

(2) Consents (in the manner provided by paragraph (a) of § 1.826-3) to provide the information required under paragraph (b) of § 1.826-3 during the period in which the election made under section 826(a) and this section is in effect;

(3) Reports the income received from the reciprocal and the deductions allocable thereto under the same method of accounting used by the reciprocal in reporting its deductions for amounts paid or due its attorney-in-fact; and

(4) Files its income tax return on a calendar year basis.

(c) Manner of making election. The election provided by section 826(a) and this section shall be made in a statement attached to the taxpayer's income tax return for the first taxable year for which such election is to apply. The statement shall include the name and address of the taxpayer, shall be signed by the taxpayer (or its duly authorized representative), and shall be filed not later than the time prescribed by law for filing the income tax return (including extensions thereof) for the first taxable year for which such election is to apply. For information required of an electing reciprocal, see paragraph (e) of this section.

(d) Scope of election. The election allowed by section 826(a) is binding for the taxable year for which made and all succeeding taxable years unless the Commissioner consents to a revocation of such election. Whether revocation will be permitted will depend upon the facts and circumstances of each particular case.

(e) Information required of an electing company. Every reciprocal underwriter or interinsurer making the election provided by section 826(a) and this section shall, in the manner provided by paragraph (f) of this section, furnish the following information for each taxable year during which such election is in effect:

(1) The name and address of the attorney-in-fact with respect to which the election allowed by section 826(a) and this section is in effect; the district in which such attorney-in-fact filed its return for the taxable year; and a copy of the consent required by section 826 and § 1.826-3 and the date and district in which such consent was filed;

(2) The deductible amount paid or due to such attorney-in-fact from the reciprocal computed without regard to the limitation provided by section 826(b);

(3) The total amount claimed as a deduction by the reciprocal for amounts paid to its attorney-in-fact after giving effect to the limitation provided by section 826(b);

(4) The amount of the increase (if any) in underwriting gain (as defined in section 824(a)) attributable to the election allowed by section 826(a);

(5) The amount of the increase (if any) in the deduction allowed by section 824(a) (relating to deduction to provide protection against losses) attributable to the election allowed by section 826(a);

(6) The amount of any increase or decrease in the statutory underwriting income or loss for the taxable year (as computed under section 823) attributable to the election allowed by section 826(a);

(7) The amount of any increase or decrease in the mutual insurance company taxable income or unused loss for the taxable year attributable to the election allowed by section 826(a);

(8) The amount of the increase (if any) in the tax liability of the reciprocal for the taxable year attributable to the election allowed by section 826(a) before taking into account the credit provided by section 826(e);

(9) The amount of tax attributable to income received by the attorney-in-fact from the reciprocal during the taxable year (as determined under § 1.826-5) claimed (under section 826(e) and paragraph (a) of this section) by the reciprocal as a credit for the taxable year; and

(10) The information which the attorney-in-fact is required to submit to the reciprocal under paragraphs (b) and (c) of § 1.826-3.

(f) Manner in which information is to be provided. The information required by paragraph (e) of this section shall be set forth in a statement attached to the taxpayer's income tax return for each taxable year for which such information is required. Such statement shall include the name and address of the taxpayer; and shall be filed not later than the date prescribed by law (including extensions thereof) for filing the income tax return for the taxable year with respect to which such information is being provided.

T.D. 6681, 10/16/63.

§ 1.826-2 Special rules applicable to electing reciprocals.

Caution: The Treasury has not yet amended Reg § 1.826-2 to reflect changes made by P.L. 99-514.

(a) Protection against loss account. Section 826(d) provides that for purposes of determining the amount to be subtracted from the protection against loss account under section 824(d)(1)(D) and the regulations thereunder (relating to amounts added to the account for the fifth preceding taxable year) for any taxable year, any amount which was added to such account by reason of the election under section 826(a) and paragraph (a) of § 1.826-1 shall be treated as having been added by reason of section 824(a)(1)(A) and the regulations thereunder (relating to amounts equal to 1 percent of losses incurred during the taxable year). Thus, no amount added to the protection against loss account by reason of an election made under section 826(a) may remain in such account beyond the end of the fifth taxable year following the taxable year with respect to which such amount was added. See section 824(d)(1)(D) and paragraph (b)(3) of § 1.824-1. The amount added to the protection against loss account by reason of an election under section 826(a) is that amount which is equal to 25 percent (plus, in the case of a reciprocal which qualifies as a concentrated risk company under section 824(a), so much of the concentrated wind-storm, etc., premium percentage as exceeds 40 percent) of the amount by which—

(1) The underwriting gain (as defined by section 824(a)(1)) computed after taking into account the limitation provided by section 826(b) and § 1.826-1, exceeds

(2) The underwriting gain computed without regard to the limitation provided by section 826(b) and § 1.826-1.

(b) Denial of surtax exemption. Section 826(f) provides that the tax imposed upon any increase in the mutual insurance company taxable income of a reciprocal which is attributable to the limitation provided by section 826(b) shall be computed without regard to the surtax exemption provided by section 821(a)(2) and the regulations thereunder. Thus, a company making the election provided under section 826(a) will be subject to surtax, as well as normal tax, on the increase in its mutual insurance company taxable income for the taxable year which is attributable to such election. Similarly, any amount which was added to the protection against loss account by reason of an election under section 826(a) and § 1.826-1, and which is subtracted from such account in accordance with section 826(d) and paragraph (a) of this section, will be subject to surtax, as well as normal tax, to the extent such amount increases mutual insurance company taxable income in the year in which the subtraction is made. Furthermore, the company will be subject to surtax on such increases notwithstanding the fact that it may have no normal tax liability for the taxable year, because its mutual insurance company taxable income (after giving effect to the election provided by section 826(a)) does not exceed $6,000.

(c) Adjustment for refunds. Section 826(g) provides that if for any taxable year an attorney-in-fact is allowed a credit or refund for taxes paid with respect to which credit or refund to the reciprocal resulted under section 826(e), the taxes of such reciprocal for such taxable year shall be properly adjusted. The reciprocal shall make the adjustment required by section 826(g) by increasing its income tax liability for its taxable year in which the credit or refund is allowed to the attorney-in-fact by the amount of such credit or refund which is attributable to taxes paid by the attorney-in-fact on income received from the reciprocal, as determined under § 1.826-6, but only to the extent that the payment of such amount by the attorney-in-fact resulted in a credit or refund to the reciprocal. However, if the refund or credit to the attorney-in-fact is the result of an error in determining its items of income or deduction for the taxable year with respect to which the refund or credit is allowed, and such error affects the amount of deductions allocable to its reciprocal for such taxable year, then, if the reciprocal's period for filing an amended return has not otherwise expired, the preceding sentence shall not apply and the reciprocal shall make the adjustment required by section 826(g) by filing an amended return for such taxable year and all subsequent taxable years for which an adjustment is required. The reciprocal's amended return or returns shall give effect to the change in the deductions of the attorney-in-fact allocable to income received from the reciprocal and the tax paid by the attorney-in-fact attributable to such income. The amount of any adjustment required by section 826(g) and this section and the computation thereof shall be set forth in a statement attached to and filed with the taxpayer's income tax return for the taxable year for which the adjustment is made. Such statement shall include the name and address of the taxpayer, and a copy of the notification received by the attorney-in-fact indicating that it has been allowed the credit or refund requiring adjustment of the reciprocal's taxes.

T.D. 6681, 10/16/63, amend T.D. 7100, 3/19/71.

§ 1.826-3 Attorney-in-fact of electing reciprocals.

Caution: The Treasury has not yet amended Reg § 1.826-3 to reflect changes made by P.L. 99-514.

(a) Manner of making consent. Section 826(c)(2) provides that a reciprocal may not elect to be subject to the limitation provided by section 826(b) unless its attorney-in-fact consents to make certain information available. See paragraph (b) of this section. The attorney-in-fact of a reciprocal making the election provided by section 826(a) shall signify the consent required by section 826(c) in a statement attached to its income tax return for the first taxable year for which the reciprocal's election is to apply. Such statement shall include the name and address of the consenting taxpayer; the name and address of the reciprocal with respect to which such consent is to apply; shall be signed by the taxpayer (or its duly authorized representative); and shall be filed not later than the date prescribed by law (including extensions thereof) for filing the income tax return for the first taxable year for which such consent is to apply. In addition, such statement shall specify that the taxpayer is subject to the taxes imposed by section 11(b) and (c); the method of accounting used in reporting income received from its reciprocal and the deductions allocable thereto; and that its return is filed on the calendar year basis. Consent, once given, shall be irrevocable for the period during which the election provided for the reciprocal by section 826(a) is in effect. See paragraph (e) of § 1.826-1.

(b) Information required of consenting attorney-in-fact. Every attorney-in-fact making the consent provided by section 826(c)(2) and paragraph (a) of this section shall, in the manner prescribed by paragraph (c) of this section, furnish the following information for each taxable year during which the consent provided by section 826(c)(2) and paragraph (a) of this section is in effect:

(1) The name and address of the reciprocal with respect to which the consent required by section 826(c)(2) and paragraph (a) of this section is to apply;

(2) Gross income in total and by sources, adjusted for returns and allowances;

(3) Deductions (itemized to the same extent as on taxpayer's income tax return and accompanying schedules) allocable to each source of gross income and in total (see § 1.826-4);

(4) Method of allocation used in subparagraph (3) of this paragraph;

(5) Taxable income (if any) in total and by sources, as in subparagraph (2) of this paragraph (income by sources from subparagraph (2) of this paragraph minus expenses allocable thereto under subparagraph (3) of this paragraph);

(6) Total income tax liability (if any) for the taxable year;

(7) Taxes paid attributable (under § 1.826-5) to income earned by the taxpayer in dealing with the reciprocal;

(8) Such other information as may be required by the district director.

(c) Manner in which information is to be provided. *(1)* The information required by paragraph (b) of this section shall be set forth in a statement attached to the taxpayer's income tax return for each taxable year for which the consent provided by section 826(c)(2) and paragraph (a) of this section is in effect. Such statement shall include the name and address of the taxpayer, and shall be filed not later than the date prescribed by law (including extensions thereof) for filing the income tax return for each taxable year for which such information is required.

(2) A copy of the statement containing the information required by paragraph (b) of this section shall be submitted to the board of advisors (or other comparable body) of the reciprocal on whose behalf the consent provided under section 826(c)(2) is given. The copy shall be executed in the same manner as the original and shall be delivered to such board not later than 10 days before the last date prescribed by law (including extensions thereof) for filing the reciprocal's income tax return for the taxable year for which the information is required unless the attorney-in-fact establishes to the satisfaction of the district director that the failure to furnish such copy or the failure to furnish such copy within the prescribed 10 day period was due to circumstances beyond its control. In addition, there shall be attached to and made a

part of such copy, a copy of the income tax return of the attorney-in-fact (including accompanying schedules) for each taxable year for which such statement is required.

T.D. 6681, 10/16/63.

§ 1.826-4 Allocation of expenses.

Caution: The Treasury has not yet amended Reg § 1.826-4 to reflect changes made by P.L. 99-514.

An attorney-in-fact allocating expenses as required by section 826(b) and paragraph (b) of § 1.826-3 shall allocate each expense itemized in its income tax return (and accompanying schedules) for the taxable year to each source of gross income (as set forth pursuant to paragraph (b)(2) of § 1.826-3). However, no portion of the net operating loss deduction allowed by section 172 shall be allocated to income received or due from the reciprocal, and no expenses, other than those directly related thereto, shall be allocated to capital gains. Where the method of allocation used by the taxpayer does not reasonably reflect the expenses of the taxpayer allocable to income received or due from the reciprocal, the district director may require the taxpayer to use such other method of allocation as is reasonable under the circumstances.

T.D. 6681, 10/16/63.

§ 1.826-5 Attribution of tax.

Caution: The Treasury has not yet amended Reg § 1.826-5 to reflect changes made by P.L. 99-514.

(a) In general. Section 826(e) provides that a reciprocal making the election allowed by section 826(a) shall be credited with so much of the tax paid by the attorney-in-fact as is attributable to the income received by the attorney-in-fact from the reciprocal in such taxable year.

(b) Computation. For purposes of section 826(e) and paragraph (a) of this section, the amount of tax attributable to income received by the attorney-in-fact from the reciprocal in the taxable year shall be computed in the following manner:

(1) First, compute the taxable income (if any) from each source of gross income set forth in paragraph (b)(2) of § 1.826-3 by deducting from each such amount the expenses allocable thereto under § 1.826-4;

(2) Second, compute the normal tax on each amount of taxable income computed in subparagraph (1) of this paragraph at the rate provided by section 11(b) of the Code;

(3) Third, deduct from each amount determined in subparagraph (1) of this paragraph an amount which bears the same proportion to the surtax exemption provided by section 11(c) of the Code as each amount computed under subparagraph (1) of this paragraph bears to the total of the amounts computed under subparagraph (1) of this paragraph;

(4) Fourth, compute the surtax on each remainder computed in subparagraph (3) of this paragraph at the rate provided by section 11(c) of the Code;

(5) Fifth, add the normal tax computed under subparagraph (2) of this paragraph to the surtax computed under subparagraph (4) of this paragraph for each amount computed under subparagraph (1) of this paragraph;

(6) Sixth, deduct from each amount of tax computed under subparagraph (5) of this paragraph any tax credits (other than those arising from payments made with respect to the tax liability for the taxable year or other taxable years) allocable (in the same manner as provided for expenses under § 1.826-4) to such amount;

(7) Seventh, compute that amount which bears the same proportion to the tax actually paid with respect to the taxable year as each individual amount computed under subparagraph (6) of this paragraph bears to the total of the amounts computed under subparagraph (6) of this paragraph. The amount so determined with respect to each amount computed under subparagraph (6) of this paragraph is the tax paid which is attributable to the amount computed under subparagraph (1) of this paragraph.

To the extent the amounts determined under subparagraph (1) of this paragraph are attributable to amounts received from the reciprocal for the taxable year, the tax attributable to such amounts (as determined under subparagraph (7) of this paragraph) shall be the amount of tax attributable to income received by the attorney-in-fact from the reciprocal during the taxable year.

(c) Taxes of attorney-in-fact unaffected. Nothing in section 826 or the regulations thereunder shall increase or decrease the taxes imposed on the income of the attorney-in-fact.

T.D. 6681, 10/16/63.

§ 1.826-6 Credit or refund.

Caution: The Treasury has not yet amended Reg § 1.826-6 to reflect changes made by P.L. 99-514.

(a) Notification required. In any case where a taxpayer applies for a credit or refund of taxes paid by it in respect of a taxable year for which the taxpayer was the consenting attorney-in-fact of a reciprocal making the election provided by section 826(a), such taxpayer shall give written notice to its reciprocal for such taxable year, first, upon applying for the credit or refund; and again, within 10 days from the date on which a final determination is made that such credit or refund has been allowed or denied.

(b) Notice form. The notices required by this section shall include the name and address of the taxpayer and shall be signed by the taxpayer or its duly authorized representative. In addition, there shall be attached to and made a part of each first notice a concise statement of the claim upon which the application for refund or credit is based; and there shall be attached to and made a part of each second notice:

(1) A copy of the notification (if any) received by the taxpayer indicating that the credit or refund has been allowed; and

(2) A statement setting forth the amount of such credit or refund attributable to taxes paid by the taxpayer on income received from the reciprocal, and the computation by which such amount was determined.

(c) Manner of apportioning refund or credit. The taxpayer shall determine the amount of the refund or credit attributable to taxes paid on income received from its reciprocal by reallocating its income and expense items for the taxable year, with respect to which the refund or credit is allowed, in the manner provided by §§ 1.826-3 and 1.826-4 so as to reflect the adjustments (if any) in such items which resulted in the credit or refund of tax for the taxable year. The taxpayer shall then recompute the tax attributable to income received from its reciprocal for such taxable year in the manner provided by § 1.826-5. The district director may require such additional information as may be necessary in the circumstances to verify the computations required by this paragraph.

T.D. 6681, 10/16/63.

§ 1.826-7 Examples.

Caution: The Treasury has not yet amended Reg § 1.826-7 to reflect changes made by P.L. 99-514.

The application of section 826 may be illustrated by the following examples:

Example (1). For the taxable year 1963, R, a reciprocal underwriter subject to the taxes imposed by section 821(a), has the following items (determined before applying any election under section 826):

Gross income under sec. 832		578
Gross investment income		50
Deductions under sec. 832 (as modified by sec. 823(b)):		
Deduction for amounts paid by R to attorney-in-fact A	100	
All other deductions	500	
Total deductions under sec. 832	600	
Deductions under sec. 822(c)		40
Incurred losses		400
Protection against loss deduction		4
Underwriting gain		0
Mutual insurance company taxable income		0
Unused loss		22
Credit or refund for taxes paid		0

Assume that the deductions of attorney-in-fact A allocable to the income received by A from R are 60 and the tax paid by A allocable to the income received from R is 16. If R elects to be subject to the limitation provided in section 826(b), the results for 1963 would be as follows:

Gross income under sec. 832		578
Gross investment income		50
Deductions under sec. 832 (as modified by sec. 823(b)):		
Deduction for amounts paid by R to attorney-in-fact A	60	
All other deductions	500	
Total deduction under sec. 832	560	
Deductions under sec. 822(c)		40
Incurred losses		400
Underwriting gain		8
Protection against loss deduction		6
Mutual insurance company taxable income		12
Unused loss		0
Credit or refund for taxes paid		16

Under the provisions of section 826(b), R's deduction for amounts paid or incurred to the attorney-in-fact in the taxable year 1963 would be limited to the deductions of A allocable to the income received by A from R. Thus, R's deductions under section 832 (as modified by section 823(b)) for 1963 would be 60 (the deductions of A which are allocable to the income received by A from R). As a result of making the election under section 826(a) for the taxable year 1963, R's underwriting gain would be 8, and its statutory underwriting income would be 2 (the underwriting gain of 8 minus the protection against loss deduction of 6—of which 4 represents the amount determined under section 824(a)(1)(A)—and 2 represents the amount determined under section 824(a)(1)(B)—or 8 minus 6). R's mutual insurance company taxable income for 1963 would be 12, consisting of taxable investment income of 10 (gross investment income minus deductions under section 822(c), or 50 minus 40) plus statutory underwriting income of 2. Since all of R's mutual insurance company taxable income of 12 is attributable to the limitation under section 826(b), the entire amount is subject to the surtax under section 821(a)(2) without regard to the $25,000 surtax exemption. The credit of 16, representing that part of the tax paid by A which is allocable to the income received by A from R, may be applied by R against its taxes with respect to its mutual insurance company taxable income of 12 for 1963, and R would be entitled to a refund of any excess of the amount of such credit over its tax liability for 1963.

Under the provisions of section 826(d), no portion of the amount added to the protection against loss account in 1963 by reason of the election under section 826(a), 2 (25 percent of the amount by which the consolidated underwriting gain exceeds 25 percent of the underwriting gain determined without regard to the election under section 826(a), or the amount by which 25 percent of 8 exceeds 25 percent of 0), may remain in such account beyond the taxable year 1968.

Example (2). For the taxable year 1963, F is a corporate attorney-in-fact subject to the taxes imposed by section 11(b) and (c) of the Code. F files its return on the calendar year basis and reports income received from its reciprocal and the deductions allocable thereto under the same method of accounting used by its reciprocal in reporting its deductions for amounts paid to F. F properly consents to provide the information required by paragraph (b) of § 1.826-3. In addition to its attorney-in-fact business, F owns real estate for investment purposes, and operates a real estate management service. For the taxable year 1963, F has gross income from these various sources as follows:

Attorney-in-fact fees	$85,000
Real estate management fees	18,000
Rental income	25,000

F allocates its expenses for the taxable year on the basis of their direct relation to each source of income. During 1963, F acquired property for use in its attorney-in-fact operations which entitled

F to an investment credit of $800 under section 38. For 1963, F determines that the tax paid by it which is attributable to its reciprocal is $21,863, computed as follows:

	Attorney-in-fact fees	Real estate management	Rental income	Total
Gross income	$85,000	$18,000	$25,000	$128,000
Allocable expenses	25,000	3,000	35,000	63,000
Taxable income (loss)	60,000	15,000	(10,000)	65,000
Normal tax (30 percent)	18,000	4,500	0	19,500
Surtax exemption	20,000	5,000	0	25,000
Income subject to surtax	40,000	10,000	0	40,000
Surtax (22 percent)	8,800	2,200	0	8,800
Total tax	26,800	6,700	0	28,300
Investment credit	800	0	0	800
1963 tax liability	26,000	6,700	0	27,500
1963 tax paid				27,500
Allocation of tax paid	21,863	5,637	0	27,500

Under paragraph (b)(1) of § 1.826-5, F computes its taxable income from its attorney-in-fact fees to be $60,000 ($85,000 minus $25,000), and its taxable income from its real estate management to be $15,000 ($18,000 minus $3,000). Since F's rental operations resulted in a $10,000 loss for the taxable year ($25,000 minus $35,000), F's taxable income from its rental operations is zero. Using the 30 percent rate provided by section 11(b), F computes its normal tax to be $18,000 on its attorney-in-fact fees and $4,500 on its real estate management operations. F's normal tax on total income is $19,500. The $3,000 difference between the normal tax on F's total income and the normal taxes on F's profitable operations results from the loss on F's rental operations. Under paragraph (b)(3) of § 1.826-5, F allocates its surtax exemption as follows: $20,000 ($60,000/$75,000 × $25,000) to its attorney-in-fact fees; and $5,000 ($15,000/$75,000 × $25,000) to its real estate management operations. F computes its surtax on its profitable operations at the 22 percent rate provided by section 11(c) as follows: $8,800 (22 percent of $40,000) on attorney-in-fact fees; and $2,200 (22 percent of $10,000) on real estate management income. F adds its normal tax and surtax on its profitable operations and determines its total tax to be $26,800 on its attorney-in-fact operations; $6,700 on its real estate management operations; and $28,300 on its total income. F must allocate its investment credit on the same basis as it used to allocate its expenses. Thus, F's entire investment credit must be allocated to its attorney-in-fact operations. Accordingly, F's 1963 tax liability is $26,000 on its attorney-in-fact fees; $6,700 on its real estate management operations; $0 on its rental operations; and $27,500 on its total income. Under paragraph (b)(7) of § 1.826-5, F allocates $21,863 ($26,000/$32,700 × $27,500) of its 1963 tax paid to its attorney-in-facts fees; and $5,637 ($6,700/$32,700 × $27,500) of its 1963 tax paid to its real estate management business. F's reciprocal will be allowed a credit or refund of $21,863 for taxes paid by F which are attributable to F's income received from its reciprocal.

Example (3). Assume the same facts as in example (2), and assume further that in 1966 F sustains a net operating loss on its overall operations of $5,000. In carrying the loss back to 1963 as a net operating loss deduction under section 172, F must allocate the deduction under the same method it used in allocating its 1963 deductions. Thus, if the loss was entirely attributable to F's rental operations for the taxable year 1966, F would reduce its taxable income attributable to those operations by the entire amount of the loss and would recompute the tax attributable to those operations under paragraph (b) of § 1.826-5. As recomputed in the table below, F's 1963 tax liability from attorney-in-fact fees would be $19,800 and F's total tax liability would be $24,900.

	Attorney-in-fact fees	Real estate management	Rental income	Total
Gross income	$85,000	$18,000	$25,000	$128,000
Allocable expenses	25,000	3,000	35,000	63,000
Net operating loss deduction	0	0	5,000	5,000
Taxable income (loss)	60,000	15,000	(15,000)	60,000
Normal tax (30 percent)	18,000	4,500	0	18,000
Surtax exemption	20,000	5,000	0	25,000
Income subject to surtax	40,000	10,000	0	35,000
Surtax (22 percent)	8,800	2,200	0	7,700
Total tax	26,800	6,700	0	25,700
Investment credit	800	0	0	800
1963 tax liability	26,000	6,700	0	24,900
1963 tax paid				24,900
Allocation of tax paid	19,800	5,100	0	24,900

As a result of its 1966 net operating loss, F would be entitled to a refund of $2,600 (1963 taxes paid of $27,500 minus recomputed 1963 taxes of $24,900). Under paragraph (a) of § 1.826-6, F would be required to notify its reciprocal of its claim for refund and of the amount of the refund or credit attributable to taxes paid on income received from the reciprocal. Since the 1963 tax paid by F attributable to its reciprocal (as recomputed) is less than the amount claimed in 1963 by F's reciprocal as a credit, F's reciprocal would be required, under section 826(g), to add the difference—$2,063 ($21,863 minus $19,800), to its tax liability for 1966. Thus, F's reciprocal would first compute its tax liability for 1966 without regard to section 826(g) and then would increase such liability by $2,063.

T.D. 6681, 10/16/63.

§ 1.831-1 Tax on insurance companies (other than life or mutual), mutual marine insurance companies, and mutual fire insurance companies issuing perpetual policies.

(a) All insurance companies, other than life or mutual or foreign insurance companies not carrying on an insurance business within the United States, and all mutual marine insurance companies and mutual fire insurance companies exclusively issuing either perpetual policies, or policies for which the sole premium charged is a single deposit which, except for such deduction of underwriting costs as may be provided, is refundable upon cancellation or expiration of the policy, are subject to the tax imposed by section 831. As used in this section and §§ 1.832-1 and 1.832-2, the term "insurance companies" means only those companies which qualify as insurance companies under the definition provided by paragraph (b) of § 1.801-1 and which are subject to the tax imposed by section 831.

(b) All provisions of the Code and of the regulations in this part not inconsistent with the specific provisions of section 831 are applicable to the assessment and collection of the tax imposed by section 831(a), and insurance companies are subject to the same penalties as are provided in the case of returns and payment of income tax by other corporations.

(c) Since section 832 provides that the underwriting and investment exhibit of the annual statement approved by the National Convention of Insurance Commissioners shall be the basis for computing gross income and since the annual statement is rendered on the calendar year basis, the returns under section 831 shall be made on the basis of the calendar year and shall be on Form 1120. Insurance companies are entitled, in computing insurance company taxable income, to the deductions provided in part VIII (section 241 and following), subchapter B, chapter 1 of the Code.

(d) Foreign insurance companies not carrying on an insurance business within the United States are not taxable under section 831 but are taxable as other foreign corporations. See section 881.

(e) Insurance companies are subject to both normal tax and surtax. The normal tax shall be computed as provided in section 11(b) and the surtax shall be computed as provided in section 11(c). For the circumstances under which the $25,000 exemption from surtax for certain taxable years may be disallowed in whole or in part, see section 1551. For alternative tax where the net long-term capital gain for any taxable year exceeds the net short-term capital loss, see section 1201(a) and the regulations thereunder.

T.D. 6201, 9/4/56.

§ 1.831-2 Taxable years affected.

Section 1.831-1 is applicable only to taxable years beginning after December 31, 1953, but before January 1, 1963, and ending after August 16, 1954, and all references therein to sections of the Code and regulations are to sections of the Internal Revenue Code of 1954 and the regulations thereunder before amendments. Section 1.831-3 is applicable only to taxable years beginning after December 31, 1962, and all references therein to sections of the Code and regulations are to sections of the Internal Revenue Code of 1954 as amended. Section 1.831-4 is applicable only with respect to the companies described therein, and only with respect to taxable years beginning after December 31, 1961.

T.D. 6681, 10/16/63.

§ 1.831-3 Tax on insurance companies (other than life or mutual), mutual marine insurance companies, mutual fire insurance companies issuing perpetual policies, and mutual fire or flood insurance companies operating on the basis of premium deposits; taxable years beginning after December 31, 1962.

Caution: The Treasury has not yet amended Reg § 1.831-3 to reflect changes made by P.L. 99-514.

(a) All insurance companies, other than life or mutual or foreign insurance companies not carrying on an insurance business within the United States, and all mutual marine insurance companies and mutual fire or flood insurance companies exclusively issuing perpetual policies or whose principal business is the issuance of policies for which the premium deposits are the same regardless of the length of the term for which the policies are written, are subject to the tax imposed by section 831 if the unabsorbed portion of such premium deposits not required for losses, expenses or reserves is returned or credited to the policyholder on cancellation or expiration of the policy. For purposes of section 831 and this section, in the case of a mutual flood insurance company, the premium deposits will be considered to be the same if the payment of a premium increases the total insurance under the policy in an amount equal to the amount of such premium and the omission of any annual premium does not result in the reduction or suspension of coverage under the policy. As used in this section and section 832 and the regulations thereunder, the term "insurance companies" means only those companies which qualify as insurance companies under the definition provided by paragraph (b) of § 1.801-1 and which are subject to the tax imposed by section 831.

(b) All provisions of the Code and of the regulations in this part not inconsistent with the specific provisions of section 831 are applicable to the assessment and collection of the tax imposed by section 831(a), and insurance companies are subject to the same penalties as are provided in the case of returns and payment of income tax by other corporations.

(c) Since section 832 provides that the underwriting and investment exhibit of the annual statement approved by the National Convention of Insurance Commissioners shall be the basis for computing gross income and since the annual statement is rendered on the calendar year basis, the returns under section 831 shall be made on the basis of the calendar year and shall be on Form 1120. Insurance companies are entitled, in computing insurance company taxable income, to the deductions provided in part VIII (section 241 and following), subchapter B, chapter 1 of the Code.

(d) Foreign insurance companies not carrying on an insurance business within the United States are not taxable under section 831 but are taxable as other foreign corporations. See section 881.

(e) Insurance companies are subject to both normal tax and surtax. The normal tax shall be computed as provided in section 11(b) and the surtax shall be computed as provided in section 11(c). For the circumstances under which the $25,000 exemption from surtax for certain taxable years may be disallowed in whole or in part, see section 1551. For alternative tax where the net long-term capital gain for any taxable year exceeds the net short-term capital loss, see section 1201(a) and the regulations thereunder.

T.D. 6681, 10/16/63.

§ 1.831-4 Election of multiple line companies to be taxed on total income.

Caution: The Treasury has not yet amended Reg § 1.831-4 to reflect changes made by P.L. 99-514.

(a) In general. Section 831(c) provides that any mutual insurance company engaged in writing marine, fire, and casualty insurance which, for any 5-year period beginning after December 31, 1941, and ending before January 1, 1962, was subject to the tax imposed by section 831 (or the tax imposed by corresponding provisions of prior law) may elect, in the manner provided by paragraph (b) of this section, to be subject to the tax imposed by section 831, whether or not marine insurance is its predominant source of premium income. A company making an election under section 831(c) and this section will be subject to the tax imposed by section 831 for taxable years beginning after December 31, 1961, rather than subject to the tax imposed by section 821.

(b) Time and manner of making election. The election provided by section 831(c) and paragraph (a) of this section shall be made in a statement attached to the taxpayer's return for the taxable year 1962. The statement shall indicate that the taxpayer has made the election provided by section 831(c) and this section; shall include the name and address of the taxpayer, and shall be signed by the taxpayer or his duly authorized representative. In addition, the statement shall list the 5 consecutive taxable years prior to 1962 for which the taxpayer was subject to tax under section 831 (or the corresponding provisions of prior law); the types of insurance written by the company; and the percentage of marine insurance to total insurance written. The return and statement must be filed not later than the date prescribed by law (including extensions thereof) for filing the return for the taxable year 1962. However, if the last date prescribed by law (including extensions thereof) for filing the income tax return for the taxable year 1962 falls before October 17, 1963, the election provided by section 831(c) and this section may be made for such year by filing the statement and an amended return for such taxable year (and all subsequent taxable years for which returns have been filed) before January 16, 1964.

(c) Scope of election. An election made under section 831(c) and paragraph (b) of this section shall be binding for all taxable years beginning after December 31, 1961, unless consent to revoke the election is obtained from the Commissioner. However, if a taxpayer made the election provided by section 831(c) and this section for taxable years beginning prior to October 17, 1963, the taxpayer may revoke such election without obtaining consent from the Commissioner by filing, before January 16, 1964, a statement that the taxpayer desires to revoke such election. Such statement shall be signed by the taxpayer or its duly authorized representative. An amended return reflecting such revocation must accompany the statement for all taxable years for which returns have been filed with respect to such election.

(d) Limitation on certain net operating loss carryovers and carrybacks. In the case of a taxpayer making the election allowed under section 831(c) and this section, a net operating loss shall not be carried—

(1) To or from any taxable year for which the insurance company is not subject to the tax imposed by section 831(a) (or predecessor sections); or

(2) To any taxable year if, between the loss year and such taxable year, there is an intervening taxable year for which the insurance company was not subject to the tax imposed by section 831(a) (or predecessor sections).

T.D. 6681, 10/16/63.

§ 1.832-1 Gross income.

(a) Gross income as defined in section 832(b)(1) means the gross amount of income earned during the taxable year from interest, dividends, rents, and premium income, computed on the basis of the underwriting and investment exhibit of the annual statement approved by the National Convention of Insurance Commissioners, as well as the gain derived from the sale or other disposition of property, and all other items constituting gross income under section 61, except that in the case of a mutual fire insurance company described in § 1.831-1 the amount of single deposit premiums received, but not assessments, shall be excluded from gross income. Gross income does not include increase in liabilities during the year on account of reinsurance treaties, remittances from the home office of a foreign insurance company to the United States branch, borrowed money, or gross increase due to adjustments in book value of capital assets. The underwriting and investment exhibit is presumed to reflect the true net income of the company, and insofar as it is not inconsistent with the provisions of the Code will be recognized and used as a basis for that purpose. All items of the exhibit, however, do not reflect an insurance company's income as defined in the Code. By reason of the definition of investment income, miscellaneous items which are intended to reflect surplus but do not properly enter into the computation of income, such as dividends declared to shareholders in their capacity as such, home office remittances and receipts, and special deposits, are ignored. Gain or loss from agency balances and bills receivable not admitted as assets on the underwriting and investment exhibit will be ignored, excepting only such agency balances and bills receivable as have been allowed as deductions for worthless debts or, having been previously so allowed, are recovered during the taxable year. In computing "premiums earned on insurance contracts during the taxable year" the amount of the unearned premiums shall include (1) life insurance reserves as defined in section 803(b) and § 1.803-1 pertaining to the life, burial, or funeral insurance, or annuity business of an insurance company subject to the tax imposed by section 831 and not qualifying as a life insurance company under section 801, and (2) liability for return premiums under a rate credit or retrospective rating plan based on experience, such as the "War Department Insurance Rating Plan," and which return premiums are therefore not earned premiums. In computing "losses incurred" the determination of unpaid losses at the close of each year must represent actual unpaid losses as nearly as it is possible to ascertain them.

(b) Every insurance company to which this section applies must be prepared to establish to the satisfaction of the district director that the part of the deduction for "losses incurred" which represents unpaid losses at the close of the taxable year comprises only actual unpaid losses stated in amounts which, based upon the facts in each case and the company's experience with similar cases, can be said to represent a fair and reasonable estimate of the amount the company will be required to pay. Amounts included in, or added to, the estimates of such losses which, in the opinion of the district director are in excess of the actual liability determined as provided in the preceding sentence will be disallowed as a deduction. The district director may require any such insurance company to submit such detailed information with respect to its actual experience as is deemed necessary to establish the reasonableness of the deduction for "losses incurred."

(c) That part of the deduction for "losses incurred" which represents an adjustment to losses paid for salvage and reinsurance recoverable shall, except as hereinafter provided, include all salvage in course of liquidation, and all reinsurance in process of collection not otherwise taken into account as a reduction of losses paid, outstanding at the end of the taxable year. Salvage in course of liquidation includes all property (other than cash), real or personal, tangible or intangible, except that which may not be included by reason of express statutory provisions (or rules and regulations of an insurance department) of any State or Territory or the District of Columbia in which the company transacts business. Such salvage in course of liquidation shall be taken into account to the extent of the value thereof at the end of the taxable year as determined from a fair and reasonable estimate based upon either the facts in each case or the company's experience with similar cases. Cash received during the taxable year with respect to items of salvage or reinsurance shall be taken into account in computing losses paid during such taxable year.

T.D. 6201, 9/4/56.

§ 1.832-2 Deductions.

(a) The deductions allowable are specified in section 832(c) and by reason of the provisions of section 832(c)(10) and (12) include in addition certain deductions provided in sections 161, and 241 and following. The deductions, however, are subject to the limitation provided in section 265, relating to expenses and interest in respect of tax-exempt income. The net operating loss deduction is computed under section 172 and the regulations thereunder. For the purposes of section 172, relating to net operating loss deduction, "gross income" shall mean gross income as defined in section 832(b)(1) and the allowable deductions shall be those allowed by section 832(c) with the exceptions and limitations set forth in section 172(d). In addition to the deduction for capital losses provided in subchapter P (section 1201 and following), chapter 1 of the Code, insurance companies are allowed a deduction for losses from capital assets sold or exchanged in order to obtain funds to meet abnormal insurance losses and to provide for the payment of dividends and similar distributions to policyholders. A special rule is provided for the application of the capital loss carryover provisions of section 1212. The deduction is the same as that allowed mutual insurance companies subject to the tax imposed by section 821; see section 822(c)(6) and the regulations thereunder. Insurance companies, other than mutual fire insurance companies described in § 1.831-1, are also allowed a deduction for dividends and similar distributions paid or declared to policyholders in their capacity as such. The deduction is otherwise the same as that allowed mutual insurance companies subject to the tax imposed by section 821; see section 823(2) and the regulations thereunder.

(b) Among the items which may not be deducted are income and profits taxes imposed by the United States, income and profits taxes imposed by any foreign country or possession of the United States (in cases where the company chooses to claim to any extent a credit for such taxes), taxes assessed against local benefits, decrease during the year due to adjustments in the book value of capital assets, decrease in liabilities during the year on account of reinsurance treaties, dividends paid to shareholders in their capacity as such, remittances to the home office of a foreign insurance company by the United States branch, and borrowed money repaid.

(c) In computing taxable income of insurance companies, losses sustained during the taxable year from the sale or other disposition of property are deductible subject to the limitation contained in section 1211. Insurance companies are entitled to the alternative taxes provided in section 1201.

T.D. 6201, 9/4/56, amend T.D. 6867, 12/6/65.

§ 1.832-3 Taxable years affected.

Sections 1.832-1 and 1.832-2 are applicable only to taxable years beginning after December 31, 1953, and before January 1, 1963, and ending after August 16, 1954, and all references therein to sections of the Code and regulations are to sections of the Internal Revenue Code of 1954 and the regulations thereunder before amendments. Sections 1.832-4, 1.832-5, and 1.832-6 are applicable only to taxable years beginning after December 31, 1962, and all references therein to sections of the Code and regulations are to sections of the Internal Revenue Code of 1954 as amended.

T.D. 6681, 10/16/63.

§ 1.832-4 Gross income.

(a) *(1)* Gross income as defined in section 832(b)(1) means the gross amount of income earned during the taxable year from interest, dividends, rents, and premium income, computed on the basis of the underwriting and investment exhibit of the annual statement approved by the National Convention of Insurance Commissioners, as well as the gain derived from the sale or other disposition of property, and all other items constituting gross income under section 61, except that in the case of a mutual fire insurance company described in section 831(a)(3)(A) the amount of single deposit premiums received, but not assessments, shall be excluded from gross income. Section 832(b)(1)(D) provides that in the case of a mutual fire or flood insurance company described in section 831(a)(3)(B), there shall be included in gross income an amount equal to 2 percent of the premiums earned during the taxable year on contracts described in section 831(a)(3)(B) after deduction of premium deposits returned or credited during such taxable year with respect to such contracts. Gross income does not include increase in liabilities during the year on account of reinsurance treaties, remittances from the home office of a foreign insurance company to the United States branch, borrowed money, or gross increase due to adjustments in book value of capital assets.

(2) The underwriting and investment exhibit is presumed to reflect the true net income of the company, and insofar as it is not inconsistent with the provisions of the Code will be recognized and used as a basis for that purpose. All items of the exhibit, however, do not reflect an insurance company's income as defined in the Code. By reason of the definition of investment income, miscellaneous items which are intended to reflect surplus but do not properly enter into the computation of income, such as dividends declared to shareholders in their capacity as such, home office remittances and receipts, and special deposits, are ignored. Gain or loss from agency balances and bills receivable not admitted as assets on the underwriting and investment exhibit will be ignored, excepting only such agency balances and bills receivable as have been allowed as deductions for worthless debts or, having been previously so allowed, are recovered during the taxable year.

(3) Premiums earned. The determination of premiums earned on insurance contracts during the taxable year begins with the insurance company's gross premiums written on insurance contracts during the taxable year, reduced by return premiums and premiums paid for reinsurance. Subject to the exceptions in sections 832(b)(7), 832(b)(8), and 833(a)(3), this amount is increased by 80 percent of the unearned premiums on insurance contracts at the end of the preceding taxable year, and is decreased by 80 percent of the unearned premiums on insurance contracts at the end of the current taxable year.

(4) Gross premiums written. (1) In general. Gross premiums written are amounts payable for insurance coverage. The label placed on a payment in a contract does not determine whether an amount is a gross premium written. Gross premiums written do not include other items of income described in section 832(b)(1)(C) (for example, charges for providing loss adjustment or claims processing services under administrative services or cost-plus arrangements). Gross premiums written on an insurance contract include all amounts payable for the effective period of the insurance contract. To the extent that amounts paid or payable with respect to an arrangement are not gross premiums written, the insurance company may not treat amounts payable to customers under the applicable portion of such arrangements as losses incurred described in section 832(b)(5).

(ii) Items included. Gross premiums written include—

(A) Any additional premiums resulting from increases in risk exposure during the effective period of an insurance contract;

(B) Amounts subtracted from a premium stabilization reserve to pay for insurance coverage; and

(C) Consideration in respect of assuming insurance liabilities under insurance contracts not issued by the taxpayer (such as a payment or transfer of property in an assumption reinsurance transaction).

(5) Method of reporting gross premiums written. (i) In general. Except as otherwise provided under this paragraph (a)(5), an insurance company reports gross premiums written for the earlier of the taxable year that includes the effective date of the insurance contract or the year in which the company receives all or a portion of the gross premium for the insurance contract. The effective date of the insurance contract is the date on which the insurance coverage provided by the contract commences. The effective period of an insurance contract is the period over which one or more rates for insurance coverage are guaranteed in the contract. If a new rate for insurance coverage is guaranteed after the effective date of an insurance contract, the making of such a guarantee generally is treated as the issuance of a new insurance contract with an effective period equal to the duration of the new guaranteed rate for insurance coverage.

(ii) Special rule for additional premiums resulting from an increase in risk exposure. An insurance company reports additional premiums that result from an increase in risk exposure during the effective period of an insurance contract in gross premiums written for the taxable year in which the change in risk exposure occurs. Unless the increase in risk exposure is of temporary duration (for example, an increase in risk exposure under a workers' compensation policy due to seasonal variations in the policyholder's payroll), the company reports additional premiums resulting from an increase in risk exposure based on the remainder of the effective period of the insurance contract.

(iii) Exception for certain advance premiums. If an insurance company receives a portion of the gross premium for an insurance contract prior to the first day of the taxable year that includes the effective date of the contract, the company may report the advance premium (rather than the full amount of the gross premium for the contract) in gross premiums written for the taxable year in which the advance premium is received. An insurance company may adopt this method of reporting advance premiums only if the company's deduction for premium acquisition expenses for the taxable year in which the company receives the advance premium does not exceed the limitation of paragraph (a)(5)(vii) of this section. A company that reports an advance premium in gross premiums written under this paragraph (a)(5)(iii) takes into account the remainder of the gross premium written and premium acquisition expenses for the contract in the taxable year that includes the effective date of the contract. A company that adopts this method of reporting advance premiums must use the method for all contracts with advance premiums.

(iv) Exception for certain cancellable accident and health insurance contracts with installment premiums. If an insurance company issues or proportionally reinsures a cancellable accident and health insurance contract other than a contract with an effective period that exceeds 12 months) for which the gross premium is payable in installments over the effective period of the contract, the company may report the installment premiums (rather than the total gross premium for the contract) in gross premiums written for the earlier of the taxable year in which the installment premiums are due under the terms of the contract or the year in which the installment premiums are received. An insurance company may adopt this method of reporting installment premiums for a cancellable accident and health insurance contract only if the company's deduction for premium acquisition expenses for the first taxable year in which an installment premium is due or received under the contract does not exceed the limitation of paragraph (a)(5)(vii) of this section. A company that adopts this method of reporting installment premiums for a cancellable accident and health contract must use the method for all of its cancellable accident and health insurance contracts with installment premiums.

(v) Exception for certain multi-year insurance contracts. If an insurance company issues or proportionally reinsures an insurance contract, other than a contract described in paragraph (a)(5)(vi) of this section, with an effective period that exceeds 12 months, for which the gross premium is payable in installments over the effective period of the contract, the company may treat the insurance coverage provided under the multi-year contract as a series of separate insurance contracts. The first contract in the series is treated as having been written for an effective period of twelve months. Each subsequent contract in the series is treated as having been written for an effective period equal to the lesser of 12 months or the remainder of the period for which the rates for insurance coverage are guaranteed in the multi-year insurance contract. An insurance company may adopt this method of reporting premiums on a multi-year contract only if the company's deduction for premium acquisition expenses for each year of the multi-year contract does not exceed the limitation of paragraph (a)(5)(vii) of this section. A company that adopts this method of reporting premiums for a multi-year contract must use the method for all multi-year contracts with installment premiums.

(vi) Exception for insurance contracts described in section 832(b)(7). If an insurance company issues or reinsures the risks related to a contract described in section 832(b)(7), the company may report gross premiums written for the contract in the manner required by sections 803 and 811(a) for life insurance companies. An insurance company may adopt this method of reporting premiums on contracts described in section 832(b)(7) only if the company also determines the deduction for premium acquisition costs for the contract in accordance with section 811(a), as adjusted by the amount required to be taken into account under section 848 in connection with the net premiums of the contract. A company that adopts this method of reporting premiums for a contract described in section 832(b)(7) must use the method for all of its contracts described in that section.

(vii) Limitation on deduction of premium acquisition expenses. An insurance company's deduction for premium acquisition expenses (for example, commissions, state premium taxes, overhead reimbursements to agents or brokers, and other similar amounts) related to an insurance contract is within the limitation of this paragraph (a)(5)(vii) if--

(A) The ratio obtained by dividing the sum of the company's deduction for premium acquisition expenses related to the insurance contract for the taxable year and previous taxable years by the total premium acquisition expenses attributable to the insurance contract; does not exceed

(B) The ratio obtained by dividing the sum of the amounts included in gross premiums written with regard to the insurance contract for the taxable year and previous taxable years by the total gross premium written for the insurance contract.

(viii) Change in method of reporting gross premiums. An insurance company that adopts a method of accounting for gross premiums written and premium acquisition expenses described in paragraph (a)(5)(iii), (iv), (v), or (vi) of this section must continue to use the method to report gross premiums written and premium acquisition expenses unless the company obtains the consent of the Commissioner to change to a different method under section 446(e) and § 1.446-1(e).

(6) Return premiums. (i) In general. An insurance company's liability for return premiums includes amounts previously included in an insurance company's gross premiums written, which are refundable to a policyholder or ceding company, provided that the amounts are fixed by the insurance contract and do not depend on the experience of the insurance company or the discretion of its management.

(ii) Items included. Return premiums include amounts—

(A) Which were previously paid and become refundable due to policy cancellations or decreases in risk exposure during the effective period of an insurance contract;

(B) Which reflect the unearned portion of unpaid premiums for an insurance contract that is canceled or for which there is a decrease in risk exposure during its effective period; or

(C) Which are either previously paid and refundable or which reflect the unearned portion of unpaid premiums for an insurance contract, arising from the redetermination of a premium due to correction of posting or other similar errors.

(7) Method of reporting return premiums. An insurance company reports the liability for a return premium resulting from the cancellation of an insurance contract for the taxable year in which the contract is canceled. An insurance company reports the liability for a return premium attributable to a reduction in risk exposure under an insurance contract for the taxable year in which the reduction in risk exposure occurs.

(8) Unearned premiums. (i) In general. The unearned premium for a contract, other than a contract described in section 816(b)(1)(B), generally is the portion of the gross premium written that is attributable to future insurance coverage during the effective period of the insurance contract. However, unearned premiums held by an insurance company with regard to the net value of risks reinsured with other solvent companies (whether or not authorized to conduct business under state law) are subtracted from the company's unearned premiums. Unearned premiums also do not include any additional liability established by the insurance company on its annual statement to cover premium deficiencies. Unearned premiums do not include an insurance company's estimate of its liability for amounts to be paid or credited to a customer with regard to the expired portion of a retrospectively rated contract (retro credits). An insurance company's estimate of additional amounts payable by its customers with regard to the expired portion of a retrospectively rated contract (retro debits) cannot be subtracted from unearned premiums.

(ii) Special rules for unearned premiums. For purposes of computing "premiums earned on insurance contracts during the taxable year" under section 832(b)(4), the amount of unearned premiums includes—

(A) Life insurance reserves (as defined in section 816(b), but computed in accordance with section 807(d) and sections 811(c) and (d));

(B) In the case of a mutual flood or fire insurance company described in section 832(b)(1)(D) (with respect to contracts described in that section), the amount of unabsorbed premium deposits that the company would be obligated to return to its policyholders at the close of the taxable year if all its insurance contracts were terminated at that time;

(C) In the case of an interinsurer or reciprocal underwriter that reports unearned premiums on its annual statement net of premium acquisition expenses, the unearned premiums on the company's annual statement increased by the portion of premium acquisition expenses allocable to those unearned premiums; and

(D) In the case of a title insurance company, its discounted unearned premiums (computed in accordance with section 832(b)(8)).

(9) Method of determining unearned premiums. If the risk of loss under an insurance contract does not vary significantly over the effective period of the contract, the unearned premium attributable to the unexpired portion of the effective period of the contract is determined on a pro rata basis. If the risk of loss varies significantly over the effective period of the contract, the insurance company may consider the pattern and incidence of the risk in determining the portion of the gross premium that is attributable to the unexpired portion of the effective period of the contract. An insurance company that uses a method of computing unearned premiums other than the pro rata method must maintain sufficient information to demonstrate that its method of computing unearned premiums accurately reflects the pattern and incidence of the risk for the insurance contract.

(10) Examples. The provisions of paragraphs (a)(4) through (a)(9) of this section are illustrated by the following examples:

Example (1). (i) IC is a non-life insurance company which, pursuant to section 843, files its returns on a calendar year basis. IC writes a casualty insurance contract that provides insurance coverage for a one-year period beginning on July 1, 2000 and ending on June 30, 2001. IC charges a $500 premium for the insurance contract, which may be paid either in full by the effective date of the contract or in quarterly installments over the contract's one year term. The policyholder selects the installment payment option. As of December 31, 2000, IC collected $250 of installment premiums for the contract.

(ii) The effective period of the insurance contract begins on July 1, 2000 and ends on June 30, 2001. For the taxable year ending December 31, 2000, IC includes the $500 gross premium, based on the effective period of the contract, in gross premiums written under section 832(b)(4)(A). IC's unearned premium with respect to the contract was $250 as of December 31, 2000. Pursuant to section 832(b)(4)(B), to determine its premiums earned, IC deducts $200 ($250 x .8) for the insurance contract at the end of the taxable year.

Example (2). (i) The facts are the same as Example 1, except that the insurance contract has a stated term of 5 years. On each contract anniversary date, IC may adjust the rate charged for the insurance coverage for the succeeding 12 month period. The amount of the adjustment in the charge for insurance coverage is not substantially limited under the insurance contract.

(ii) Under paragraph (a)(5)(i) of this section, IC is required to report gross premiums written for the insurance contract based on the effective period for the contract. The effective period of the insurance contract is the period for which a rate for insurance coverage is guaranteed in the contract. Although the insurance contract issued by IC has a stated term of 5 years, a rate for insurance coverage is guaranteed only for a period of 12 months beginning with the contract's effective date and each anniversary date thereafter. Thus, for the taxable year ending December 31, 2000, IC includes the $500 gross premium for the 12 month period beginning with the contract's effective date in gross premiums written. IC's unearned premium with respect to the contract was $250 as of December 31, 2000. Pursuant to section 832(b)(4)(B), to determine its premiums earned, IC deducts $200 ($250 x .8) for the insurance contract at the end of the taxable year.

Example (3). (i) The facts are the same as Example 1, except that coverage under the insurance contract begins on January 1, 2001 and ends on December 31, 2001. On December 15, 2000, IC collects the first $125 premium installment on the insurance contract. For the taxable year ended December 31, 2000, IC deducts $20 of premium acquisition expenses related to the insurance contract. IC's total premium acquisition expenses, based on the insurance contract's $500 gross premium, are $80.

(ii) Under paragraph (a)(5)(iii) of this section, IC may elect to report only the $125 advance premium (rather than the contract's $500 gross premium) in gross premiums written for the taxable year ended December 31, 2000, provided that IC's deduction for the premium acquisition expenses related to the insurance contract does not exceed the limitation in paragraph (a)(5)(vii). IC's deduction for premium acquisition expenses is within this limitation only if the ratio of the insurance contract's premium acquisition expenses deducted for the taxable year and any previous taxable year to the insurance contract's total premium acquisition expenses does not exceed the ratio of the amounts included in gross premiums written for the taxable year and any previous taxable year for the contract to the total gross premium written for the contract.

(iii) For the taxable year ended December 31, 2000, IC deducts $20 of premium acquisition expenses related to the insurance contract. This deduction represents 25% of the total premium acquisition expenses for the insurance contract ($20/$80 = 25%). This ratio does not exceed the ratio of the $125 advance premium to the insurance contract's $500 gross premium ($125/$500 = 25%). Therefore, under paragraph (a)(5)(iii) of this section, IC may elect to report only the $125 advance premium (rather than the $500 gross premium) in gross premiums written for the taxable year ending December 31, 2000. IC reports the balance of the gross premium for the insurance contract ($375) and deducts the remaining premium acquisition expenses ($60) for the insurance contract in the taxable year ending December 31, 2001.

Example (4). (i) The facts are the same as Example 3, except that for the taxable year ending December 31, 2000, IC deducts $60 of premium acquisition expenses related to the insurance contract.

(ii) For the taxable year ended December 31, 2000, IC deducted 75% of total premium acquisition expenses for the insurance contract ($60/$80 = 75%). This ratio exceeds the ratio of the $125 advance premium to the $500 gross premium ($125/$500 = 25%). Because IC's deduction for premium acquisition expenses allocable to the contract exceeds the limitation in paragraph (a)(5)(vii) of this section, paragraph (a)(5)(i) of this section requires IC to report the $500 gross premium in gross premiums written for the taxable year ending December 31, 2000. IC's unearned premium with respect to the contract was $500 as of December 31, 2000. Pursuant to section 832(b)(4)(B), to determine its premiums earned, IC deducts $400 ($500 × .8) for the insurance contract at the end of the taxable year.

Example (5). (i) IC is a non-life insurance company which, pursuant to section 843, files its returns on a calendar year basis. On August 1, 2000, IC issues a one-year cancellable accident and health insurance policy to X, a corporation with 80 covered employees. The gross premium written for the insurance contract is $320,000. Premiums are payable in monthly installments. As of December 31, 2000, IC has collected $150,000 of installment premiums from X. For the taxable year ended December 31, 2000, IC has paid or incurred $21,000 of premium acquisition expenses related to the insurance contract. IC's total premium acquisition expenses for the insurance contract, based on the $320,000 gross premium, are $48,000.

(ii) Under paragraph (a)(5)(iv) of this section, IC may elect to report only the $150,000 of installment premiums (rather than the $320,000 estimated gross premium) in gross premiums written for the taxable year ended December 31, 2000, provided that its deduction for premium acquisition expenses allocable to the insurance contract does not exceed the limitation in paragraph (a)(5)(vii). For the taxable year ended December 31, 2000, IC deducts $21,000 of premium acquisition expenses related to the insurance contract, or 43.75% of total premium acquisition expenses for the insurance contract ($21,000/$48,000 = 43.75%). This ratio does not exceed the ratio of installment premiums to the gross premium for the contract ($150,000/$320,000 = 46.9%). Therefore, under paragraph (a)(5)(iv) of this section, IC may elect to report only $150,000 of installment premiums for the insurance contract (rather than $320,000 of gross premium) in gross premiums written for the taxable year ending December 31, 2000.

Example (6). (i) IC is a non-life insurance company which, pursuant to section 843, files its returns on a calendar year basis. On July 1, 2000, IC issues a one-year workers' compensation policy to X, an employer. The gross premium for the policy is determined by applying a monthly rate of $25 to each of X's employees. This rate is guaranteed for a period of 12 months, beginning with the effective date of the contract. On July 1, 2000, X has 1,050 employees. Based on the assumption that X's payroll would remain constant during the effective period of the contract, IC determines an estimated gross premium for the contract of $315,000 (1,050 × $25 × 12 = $315,000). The estimated gross premium is payable by X in equal monthly installments. At the end of each calendar quarter, the premiums payable under the contract are adjusted based on an audit of X's actual payroll during the preceding three months of coverage.

(ii) Due to an expansion of X's business in 2000, the actual number of employees covered under the contract during each month of the period between July 1, 2000 and December 31, 2000 is 1,050 (July), 1,050 (August), 1,050 (September), 1,200 (October), 1,200 (November), and 1,200 (December). The increase in the number of employees during the year is not attributable to a temporary or seasonal variation in X's business activities and is expected to continue for the remainder of the effective period of the contract.

(iii) Under paragraph (a)(5)(i) of this section, IC is required to report gross premiums written for the insurance contract based on the effective period of the contract. The effective period of X's contract is based on the 12 month period for which IC has guaranteed rates for insurance coverage. Under paragraph (a)(5)(ii), IC must also report the additional premiums resulting from the change in risk exposure under the contract for the taxable year in which the change in such exposure occurs. Unless the change in risk exposure is of temporary duration, the additional gross premiums are included in gross premiums written for the remainder of the effective period of the contract. Thus, for the taxable year ending December 31, 2000, IC reports gross premiums written of $348,750 with respect to the workers' compensation contract issued to X, consisting of the sum of the initial gross premium for the contract ($315,000) plus the additional gross premium attributable to the 150 employees added to X's payroll who will be covered during the last nine months of the contract's effective period (150 x $25 (monthly premium) × 9 = $33,750). IC's unearned premium with respect to the contract was $180,000 as of December 31, 2000, which consists of the sum of the remaining portion of the original gross premium ($315,000 × 6/12 = $157,500), plus the additional premiums resulting from the change in risk exposure ($33,750 × 6/9 = $22,500) that are allocable to the remaining six months of the contract's effective period. Pursuant to section 832(b)(4)(B), to determine its premiums earned, IC deducts $144,000 ($180,000 × .8) for the insurance contract at the end of the taxable year.

Example (7). (i) The facts are the same as Example 6, except that the increase in the number of X's employees for the period ending December 31, 2000 is attributable to a seasonal variation in X's business activity.

(ii) Under paragraph (a)(5)(ii) of this section, for the taxable year ending December 31, 2000, IC reports gross premiums written of $326,500, consisting of the sum of the initial gross premium for the contract ($315,000) plus the additional premium attributable to the temporary increase in risk exposure during the taxable year (150 × $25 × 3 = $11,250). The unearned premium that is allocable to the remaining six months of the effective period of the contract is $157,500. Pursuant to section 832(b)(4)(B), to determine its premiums earned, IC deducts $126,000 ($157,500 × .8) for the insurance contract at the end of the taxable year.

Example (8). (i) IC, a non-life insurance company, issues a noncancellable accident and health insurance contract (other than a qualified long-term care insurance contract, as defined in section 7702B(b)) to A, an individual, on July 1, 2000. The contract has an entry-age annual premium of $2,400, which is payable by A in equal monthly installments of $200 on the first day of each month of coverage. IC incurs agents' commissions, premium taxes, and other premium acquisition expenses equal to 10% of the gross premiums received for the contract. As of December 31, 2000, IC has collected $1,200 of installment premiums for the contract.

(ii) A noncancellable accident and health insurance contract is a contract described in section 832(b)(7). Thus, under paragraph (a)(5)(vi) of this section, IC may report gross premiums written in the manner required for life insurance companies under sections 803 and 811. Accordingly, for the taxable year ending December 31, 2000, IC may report gross premiums written of $1,200, based on the premiums actually received on the contract. Pursuant to section (a)(5)(vi) of this section, IC deducts a total of $28 of premium acquisition costs for the contract, based on the difference between the acquisition costs actually paid or incurred under section 811(a) ($1,200 × .10 = $120) and the amount required to be taken into account under section 848 in connection with the net premiums for the contract ($1,200 × .077 = $92).

(iii) Under paragraph (a)(8)(ii)(A) of this section, IC includes the amount of life insurance reserves (as defined in section 816(b), but computed in accordance with section 807(d) and sections 811(c) and (d)) in unearned premiums under section 832(b)(4)(B). Section 807(d)(3)(A)(iii) requires IC to use a two-year preliminary term method to compute the amount of life insurance reserves for a noncancellable accident and health insurance contract (other than a qualified long-term care contract). Under this tax reserve method, no portion of the $1,200 gross premium received by IC for A's contract is allocable to future insurance coverage. Accordingly, for the taxable year ending December 31, 2000, no life insurance reserves are included in IC's unearned premiums under section 832(b)(4)(B) with respect to the contract.

Example (9). (i) IC, a non-life insurance company, issues an insurance contract with a twelve month effective period for $1,200 on December 1, 2000. Immediately thereafter, IC reinsures 90% of its liability under the insurance contract for $900 with IC-2, an unrelated and solvent insurance company. On December 31, 2000, IC-2 has an $825 unearned premium with respect to the reinsurance contract it issued to IC. In computing its earned premiums, pursuant to section 832(b)(4)(B), IC-2 deducts $660 of unearned premiums ($825 × .8) with respect to the reinsurance contract.

(ii) Under paragraph (a)(8)(i) of this section, unearned premiums held by an insurance company with regard to the net value of the risks reinsured in other solvent companies are deducted from the ceding company's unearned premiums taken into account for purposes of section 832(b)(4)(B). If IC had not reinsured 90% of its risks, IC's unearned premium for the insurance contract would have been $1,100 ($1,200 × 11/12) and IC would have deducted $880 ($1,100 x .8) of unearned premiums with respect to such contract. However, because IC reinsured 90% of its risks under the contract with IC-2, as of December 31, 2000, the net value of the risks retained by IC for the remaining 11 months of the effective period of the contract is $110 ($1,100—$990). For the taxable year ending December 31, 2000, IC includes the $1,200 gross premium in its gross premiums written and deducts the $900 reinsurance premium paid to IC-2 under section 832(b)(4)(A). Pursuant to section 832(b)(4)(B), to determine its premiums earned, IC deducts $88 ($110 × .8) for the insurance contract at the end of the taxable year.

(11) Change in method of accounting.

(ii) In general. A change in the method of determining premiums earned to comply with the provisions of paragraphs (a)(3) through (a)(10) of this section is a change in method of accounting for which the consent of the Commissioner is required under section 446(e) and § 1.446-1(e).

(ii) Application. For the first taxable year beginning after December 31, 1999, a taxpayer is granted consent of the Commissioner to change its method of accounting for determining premiums earned to comply with the provisions of paragraphs (a)(3) through (a)(10) of this section. A taxpayer changing its method of accounting in accordance with this section must follow the automatic change in accounting provisions of Rev. Proc. 99-49, 1999-52 I.R.B. 725 (see § 601.601(d)(2) of this chapter), except that—

(A) The scope limitations in section 4.02 of Rev. Proc. 99-49 shall not apply;

(B) The timely duplicate filing requirement in section 6.02(2) of Rev. Proc. 99-49 shall not apply; and

(C) If the method of accounting for determining premiums earned is an issue under consideration within the meaning of section 3.09 of Rev. Proc. 99-49 as of January 5, 2000, then section 7.01 of Rev. Proc. 99-49 shall not apply.

(12) Effective date. Paragraphs (a)(3) through (a)(11) of this section are applicable with respect to the determination of premiums earned for taxable years beginning after December 31, 1999.

(13) In computing the amount of unabsorbed premium deposits which a mutual fire or flood insurance company described in section 831(a)(3)(B) would be obligated to return to its policyholders at the close of its taxable year, the company must use its own schedule of unabsorbed premium deposit returns then in effect. A copy of the applicable schedule must be filed with the company's income tax return for each taxable year for which a computation based upon such schedule is made. In addition, a taxpayer making such a computation must provide the following information for each taxable year for which the computation is made:

(i) The amount of gross premiums received during the taxable year, and the amount of premiums paid for reinsurance during the taxable year, on the policies described in section 831(a)(3)(B) and on other policies;

(ii) The amount of insurance written during the taxable year under the policies described in section 831(a)(3)(B) and under other policies, and the amount of such insurance written which was reinsured during the taxable year. The information required under this subdivision shall only be submitted upon the specific request of the district director for a statement setting forth such information, and, if required, such statement shall be filed in the manner provided by this subparagraph or in such other manner as is satisfactory to the district director;

(iii) The amount of premiums earned during the taxable year on the policies described in section 831(a)(3)(B) and on other policies and the computations by which such amounts were determined, including sufficient information to support the taxpayer's determination of the amount of unearned premiums on premium deposit plan and other policies at the beginning and end of the taxable year, and the amount of unabsorbed premium deposits at the beginning and end of the taxable year on policies described in section 831(a)(3)(B).

The information required by this subparagraph shall be set forth in a statement attached to the taxpayer's income tax return for the taxable year for which such information is being provided. Such statement shall include the name and address of the taxpayer, and shall be filed not later than the date prescribed by law (including extensions thereof) for filing the income tax return for the taxable year.

(14) In computing "losses incurred" the determination of unpaid losses at the close of each year must represent actual unpaid losses as nearly as it is possible to ascertain them.

(b) Losses incurred. Every insurance company to which this section applies must be prepared to establish to the satisfaction of the district director that the part of the deduction for "losses incurred" which represents unpaid losses at the close of the taxable year comprises only actual unpaid losses. See section 846 for rules relating to the determination of discounted unpaid losses. These losses must be stated in amounts which, based upon the facts in each case and the company's experience with similar cases, represent a fair and reasonable estimate of the amount the company will be required to pay. Amounts included in, or added to, the estimates of unpaid losses which, in the opinion of the district director, are in excess of a fair and reasonable estimate will be disallowed as a deduction. The district director may require any insurance company to submit such detailed information with respect to its actual experience as is deemed necessary to establish the reasonableness of the deduction for "losses incurred."

(c) Losses incurred are reduced by salvage. Under section 832(b)(5)(A), losses incurred are computed by taking into account losses paid reduced by salvage and reinsurance recovered, the change in discounted unpaid losses, and the change in estimated salvage and reinsurance recoverable. For purposes of section 832(b)(5)(A)(iii), estimated salvage recoverable includes all anticipated recoveries on account of salvage, whether or not the salvage is treated, or may be treated, as an asset for state statutory accounting purposes. Estimates of salvage recoverable must be based on the facts of each case and the company's experience with similar cases. Except as otherwise provided in guidance published by the Commissioner in the Internal Revenue Bulletin, estimated salvage recoverable must be discounted either—

(1) By using the applicable discount factors published by the Commissioner for estimated salvage recoverable; or

(2) By using the loss payment pattern for a line of business as the salvage recovery pattern for that line of business and by using the applicable interest rate for calculating unpaid losses under section 846(c).

For purposes of section 832(b)(5)(A) and the regulations thereunder, the term "salvage recoverable" includes anticipated recoveries on account of subrogation claims arising with respect to paid or unpaid losses.

(d) Increase in unpaid losses shown on annual statement in certain circumstances. *(1) In general.* An insurance company that takes estimated salvage recoverable into account in determining the amount of its unpaid losses shown on its annual statement is allowed to increase its unpaid losses by the amount of estimated salvage recoverable taken into account if the company complies with the disclosure requirement of paragraph (d)(2) of this section. This adjustment shall not be used in determining under section 846(d) the loss payment pattern for a line of business.

(2) Disclosure requirement. (i) In general. A company described in paragraph (d)(1) of this section is allowed to increase the unpaid losses shown on its annual statement only if the company either—

(a) Discloses on its annual statement, by line of business and accident year, the extent to which estimated salvage recoverable is taken into account in computing the unpaid losses shown on the annual statement filed by the company for the calendar year ending with or within the taxable year of the company; or

(b) Files a statement on or before the due date of its Federal income tax return (determined without regard to extensions) with the appropriate state regulatory authority of each state to which the company is required to submit an annual statement. The statement must be contained in a separate document captioned "DISCLOSURE CONCERNING LOSS RESERVES" and must disclose, by line of business and accident year, the extent to which estimated salvage recoverable is taken into account in computing the unpaid losses shown on the annual statement filed by the company for the calendar year ending with or within the taxable year of the company.

(ii) Transitional rule. For a taxable year ending before December 31, 1991, a taxpayer is deemed to satisfy the disclosure requirement of paragraph (d)(2)(i)(B) of this section if the taxpayer files the statement described in paragraph (d)(2)(i)(B) of this section before March 17, 1992.

(3) Failure to disclose in a subsequent year. If a company that claims the increase permitted by paragraph (d)(1) of this section fails in a subsequent taxable year to make the disclosure described in paragraph (d)(2) of this section, the company cannot claim an increase under paragraph (d)(1) of this section in any subsequent taxable year without the consent of the Commissioner.

(e) Treatment of estimated salvage recoverable. *(1) In general.* An insurance company is required to take estimated salvage recoverable (including that which cannot be treated as an asset for state statutory accounting purposes) into account in computing the deduction for losses incurred. Except as provided in paragraph (e)(2)(iii) of this section, an insurance company must apply this method of accounting to estimated salvage recoverable for all lines of business and for all accident years.

(2) Change in method of accounting. (i) If an insurance company did not take estimated salvage recoverable into account as required by paragraph (c) of this section for its last taxable year beginning before January 1, 1990, taking estimated salvage recoverable into account as required by paragraph (c) of this section is a change in method of accounting.

(ii) If a company does not claim the deduction under section 11305(c)(3) of the 1990 Act, the company must take into account 13 percent of the adjustment that would otherwise be required under section 481 for pre-1990 accident years as a result of the change in accounting method. This paragraph (e)(2)(ii) applies only to an insurance company subject to tax under section 831.

(iii) If a company claims the deduction under section 11305(c)(3) of the 1990 Act and paragraph (f) of this section, the company must implement the change in method of accounting for estimated salvage recoverable for post-1989 taxable years pursuant to a "cut-off" method.

(3) Rule for overestimates. An insurance company is required under section 11305(c)(4) of the 1990 Act to include in gross income 87 percent of any amount (adjusted for discounting) by which the section 481 adjustment is overestimated. The rule is applied by comparing the amount of the section 481 adjustment (determined without regard to paragraph (e)(2)(ii) of this section and any discounting) to the sum of the actual salvage recoveries and remaining undiscounted estimated salvage recoverable that are attributable to losses incurred in accident years beginning before 1990. For any taxable year beginning after December 31, 1989, any excess of the section 481 adjustment over this sum (reduced by amounts treated as overestimates in prior taxable years pursuant to this paragraph (e)(3)) is an overestimate. To determine the amount to be included in income, it is necessary to discount this excess and multiply the resulting amount by 87 percent.

(f) Special deduction. *(1) In general.* Under section 11305(c)(3) of the 1990 Act, an insurance company may deduct an amount equal to 87 percent of the discounted amount of estimated salvage recoverable that the company took into account in determining the deduction for losses incurred under section 832(b)(5) in the last taxable year beginning before January 1, 1990. A company that claims the special deduction must establish to the satisfaction of the district director that the deduction represents only the discounted amount of estimated salvage recoverable that was actually taken into account by the company in computing losses incurred for that taxable year.

(2) Safe harbor. The requirements of paragraph (f)(1) of this section are deemed satisfied and the amount that the company reports as bona fide estimated salvage recoverable is not subject to adjustment by the district director, if—

(i) The company files with the insurance regulatory authority of the company's state of domicile, on or before September 16, 1991, a statement disclosing the extent to which losses incurred for each line of business reported on its 1989 annual statement were reduced by estimated salvage recoverable,

(ii) The company attaches a statement to its Federal income tax return filed for the first taxable year beginning after December 31, 1989, agreeing to apply the special rule for overestimates under section 11305(c)(4) of the 1990 Act to the amount of estimated salvage recoverable for which it has taken the special deduction, and

(iii) In the case of a company that is a member of a consolidated group, each insurance company subject to tax under section 831 that is included in the consolidated group complies with paragraph (f)(2)(ii) of this section with respect to its special deduction, if any.

(3) Limitations on special deduction. (i) The special deduction under section 11305(c)(3) of the 1990 Act is available only to an insurance company subject to tax under section 831.

(ii) An insurance company that claimed the benefit of the "fresh start" with respect to estimated salvage recoverable under section 1023(e) of the Tax Reform Act of 1986 may not claim the special deduction allowed by section 11305(c)(3) of the 1990 Act to the extent of the estimated salvage recoverable for which a fresh start benefit was previously claimed.

(iii) A company that claims the special deduction is precluded from also claiming the section 481 adjustment provided in paragraph (e)(2)(ii) of this section for pre-1990 accident years.

(g) Effective date. Paragraphs (b) through (f) of this section are effective for taxable years beginning after December 31, 1989.

T.D. 6681, 10/16/63, amend T.D. 8171, 12/30/87, T.D. 8266, 9/21/89, T.D. 8293, 3/13/90, T.D. 8390, 1/27/92, T.D. 8857, 1/5/2000.

---

§ 1.832-5 Deductions.

Caution: The Treasury has not yet amended Reg § 1.832-5 to reflect changes made by P.L. 101-508, P.L. 99-514.

(a) The deductions allowable are specified in section 832(c) and by reason of the provisions of section 832(c)(10) and (12) include in addition certain deductions provided in sections 161, and 241 and following. The deductions, however, are subject to the limitation provided in section 265, relating to expenses and interest in respect of tax-exempt income. The net operating loss deduction is computed under section 172 and the regulations thereunder. For the purposes of section 172, relating to net operating loss deduction, "gross income" shall mean gross income as defined in section 832(b)(1) and the allowable deductions shall be those allowed by section 832(c) with the exceptions and limitations set forth in section 172(d). In addition to the deduction for capital losses provided in subchapter P (section 1201 and following), chapter 1 of the Code, insurance companies are allowed a deduction for losses from capital assets sold or exchanged in order to obtain funds to meet abnormal insurance losses and to provide for the payment of dividends and similar distributions to policyholders. A special rule is provided for the application of the capital loss carryover provisions of section 1212. The deduction is the same as that allowed mutual insurance companies subject to the tax imposed by section 821; see section 822(c)(6) and the regulations thereunder. Insurance companies, other than mutual fire insurance companies described in section 831(a)(3)(A) and the regulations thereunder, are also allowed a deduction for dividends and similar distributions paid or declared to policyholders in their capacity as such. Similar distributions include such payments as the so-called unabsorbed premium deposits returned to policyholders by factory mutual insurance companies. The deduction is otherwise the same as that allowed mutual insurance companies subject to the tax imposed by section 821; see section 822(f)(2) and the regulations thereunder.

(b) Among the items which may not be deducted are income and profits taxes imposed by the United States, income and profits taxes imposed by any foreign country or possession of the United States (in cases where the company chooses to claim to any extent a credit for such taxes), taxes assessed against local benefits, decrease during the year due to adjustments in the book value of capital assets, decrease in liabilities during the year on account of reinsurance treaties, dividends paid to shareholders in their capacity as such, remittances to the home office of a foreign insurance company by the United States branch, and borrowed money repaid.

(c) In computing taxable income of insurance companies, losses sustained during the taxable year from the sale or other disposition of property are deductible subject to the limitation contained in section 1211. Insurance companies are entitled to the alternative taxes provided in section 1201.

T.D. 6681, 10/16/63, amend T.D. 6867, 12/6/65.

§ 1.832-6 Policyholders of mutual fire or flood insurance companies operating on the basis of premium deposits.

For purposes of determining his taxable income for any taxable year, a taxpayer insured by a mutual fire or flood insurance company under a policy for which the premium deposit is the same regardless of the length of the term for which the policy is written, and who is entitled to have returned or credited to him on the cancellation or expiration of such policy the unabsorbed portion of the premium deposit not required for losses, expenses, or establishment of reserves, may, if such amount is otherwise deductible under this chapter, deduct so much of his premium deposit as was absorbed by the company during the taxpayer's taxable year. The amount of the premium deposit absorbed during the taxpayer's taxable year shall be determined in accordance with the schedule of unabsorbed premium deposit returns in effect for the company during such taxable year. If the taxpayer is unable to determine the applicable rate of absorption in effect during his taxable year, he shall compute his deduction on the basis of the rate of absorption in effect at the end of the company's taxable year which next preceded the end of the taxpayer's taxable year. In such a case, an appropriate adjustment will be made upon the final determination of the rate of absorption applicable to the taxable year.

T.D. 6681, 10/16/63.

§ 1.832-7T Treatment of salvage and reinsurance in computing "losses incurred" deduction, taxable years beginning before January 1, 1990 (temporary).

Caution: The Treasury has not yet amended Reg § 1.832-7T to reflect changes made by P.L. 101-508.

• ***Caution:*** Under Code Sec. 7805, temporary regulations expire within three years of the date of issuance. This temporary regulation was issued on 9/21/89.

(a) In computing "losses incurred" the determination of unpaid losses at the close of each year must represent actual unpaid losses as nearly as it is possible to ascertain them.

(b) Every insurance company to which this section applies must be prepared to establish to the satisfaction of the district director that the part of the deduction for "losses incurred" which represents unpaid losses at the close of the taxable year comprises only actual unpaid losses stated in amounts which, based upon the facts in each case and the company's experience with similar cases, can be said to represent a fair and reasonable estimate of the amount the company will be required to pay. Amounts included in, or added to, the estimates of such losses which in the opinion of the district director are in excess of the actual liability determined as provided in the preceding sentence will be disallowed as a deduction. The district director may require any such insurance company to submit such detailed information with respect to its actual experience as is deemed necessary to establish the reasonableness of the deduction for "losses incurred".

(c) That part of the deduction for "losses incurred" which represents an adjustment to losses paid for salvage and reinsurance recoverable shall, except as hereinafter provided, include all salvage in course of liquidation, and all reinsurance in process of collection not otherwise taken into account as a reduction of losses paid, outstanding at the end of the taxable year. Salvage in course of liquidation includes all property (other than cash), real or personal, tangible or intangible, except that which may not be included by reason of express statutory provisions (or rules and regulations of an insurance department) of any State or Territory or the District of Columbia in which the company transacts business. Such salvage in course of liquidation shall be taken into account to the extent of the value thereof at the end of the taxable year as determined from a fair and reasonable estimate based upon either the facts in each case or the company's experience with similar cases. Cash received during the taxable year with respect to items of salvage or reinsurance shall be taken into account in computing losses paid during such taxable year.

(d) This section is effective for taxable years beginning before January 1, 1990.

T.D. 8266, 9/21/89, amend T.D. 8293, 3/13/90.

§ 1.846-0 Outline of provisions.

The following is a list of the headings in §§ 1.846-1 through 1.846-4.

§ 1.846-1 Application of discount factors.

(a) In general.

(1) Rules.

(2) Examples.

(3) Increase in discounted unpaid losses shown on the annual statement.

(4) Increase in unpaid losses which take into account estimated salvage recoverable.

(b) Applicable discount factors.

(1) In general.

(i) Discount factors published by the Service.

(ii) Composite discount factors.

(iii) Annual statement changes.

(2) Title insurance company reserves.

(3) Reinsurance business.

(i) Proportional reinsurance for accident years after 1987.

(ii) Non-proportional reinsurance.

(A) Accident years after 1991.

(B) Accident years 1988 through 1991.

(iii) Reinsurance for accident years before 1988.

(iv) 90 percent exception.

(4) International business.

(5) Composite discount factors.

§ 1.846-2 Election by taxpayer to use its own historical loss payment pattern.

(a) In general.

(b) Eligible line of business.

(1) In general.

(2) Other published guidance.

(3) Special rule for 1987 determination year.

T.D. 8433, 9/4/92, amend T.D. 9257, 4/7/2006.

§ 1.846-1 Application of discount factors.

(a) In general. *(1) Rules.* A separate series of discount factors are computed for, and applied, to undiscounted unpaid losses attributable to each accident year of each line of business shown on the annual statement (as defined by section 846(f)(3)) filed by that taxpayer for the calendar year ending with or within the taxable year of the taxpayer. See § 1.832-4(b) relating to the determination of unpaid losses. Paragraph (b) of this section provides rules relating to applicable discount factors and § 1.846-3(b) contains guidance relating to discount factors applicable to accident years prior to the 1987 accident year. Once a taxpayer applies a series of discount factors to unpaid losses attributable to an accident year of a line of business, that series of discount factors must be applied to discount the unpaid losses for that accident year for that line of business for all future taxable years. The discount factors cannot be changed to reflect a change in the taxpayer's loss payment pattern during a subsequent year or to reflect a different interest rate assumption. However, discount factors may be changed for taxpayers who elect to use their own historical loss payment pattern, if information upon which the pattern is based is adjusted upon examination by the district director.

(2) Examples. The following examples illustrate the principles of paragraph (a)(1) of this section:

Example (1). A taxpayer discounts unpaid losses attributable to all accident years prior to 1992 using discount factors published by the Service. In 1992, the taxpayer elects, under § 1.846-2, to compute discount factors using its own historical loss payment pattern. The taxpayer must continue to discount unpaid losses attributable to pre-1992 accident years using the discount factors published for those accident years by the Service.

Example (2). On its annual statements through 1987, a taxpayer did not allocate unpaid losses attributable to proportional reinsurance to the line of business associated with the risks being reinsured. Beginning with the 1988 annual statement, the taxpayer allocated those losses for all accident years to the line of business being reinsured. The taxpayer must continue to discount the unpaid losses attributable to proportional reinsurance from pre-1988 accident years using the discount factors that were used in determining tax reserves for the 1987 tax year. (See paragraphs (b)(3) of this section for rules relating to the application of discount factors to reinsurance unpaid losses.)

(3) Increase in discounted unpaid losses shown on the annual statement. If the amount of unpaid losses shown on the annual statement is determined on a discounted basis, and the extent to which the unpaid losses were discounted can be determined on the basis of information disclosed on or with the annual statement, the amount of the unpaid losses to which the discount factors are applied shall be determined without regard to any reduction attributable to the discounting reflected on the annual statement.

(4) Increase in unpaid losses which take into account estimated salvage recoverable. If the amount of unpaid losses shown on the annual statement reflects a reduction for estimated salvage recoverable and the extent to which the unpaid losses were reduced by estimated salvage recoverable is appropriately disclosed as required by § 1.832-4(d)(2), the amount of unpaid losses shall be determined without regard to the reduction for salvage recoverable.

(b) Applicable discount factors. *(1) In general.* Except as otherwise provided in section 846(f)(6) (relating to certain accident and health lines of business), in § 1.846-2 (relating to a taxpayer's election to use its own historical loss payment pattern), in this paragraph (b), or in other guidance published in the Internal Revenue Bulletin, the following factors must be used—

(i) Discount factors published by the Service. If the Service has published discount factors for a line of business, a taxpayer must discount unpaid losses attributable to that line by applying those discount factors; and

(ii) Composite discount factors. If the Service has not published discount factors for a line of business, a taxpayer must discount unpaid losses attributable to that line by applying composite discount factors.

(iii) Annual statement changes. If the groupings of individual lines of business on the annual statement changes, taxpayers must discount the unpaid losses on the resulting lines of business with the discounting patterns that would have applied to those unpaid losses based on their annual statement classification prior to the change.

(2) Title insurance company reserves. A title insurance company may only take into account case reserves (relating to claims which have been reported to the insurance company). Unless the Service publishes other guidance, the reserves must be discounted using the "Miscellaneous Casu-

alty" discount factors published by the Service. Section 832(b)(8) provides rules for determining the discounted unearned premiums of a title insurance company.

(3) Reinsurance business. (i) Proportional reinsurance for accident years after 1987. For the 1988 accident year and subsequent accident years, unpaid losses for proportional reinsurance must be discounted using discount factors applicable to the line of business to which those unpaid losses are allocated as required on the annual statement.

(ii) Non-proportional reinsurance. (A) Accident years after 1991. For the 1992 accident year and subsequent accident years, unpaid losses for non-proportional reinsurance must be discounted using the applicable discount factors published by the Service for the appropriate reinsurance line of business.

(B) Accident years 1988 through 1991. For the 1988, 1989, 1990, and 1991 accident years unpaid losses for non-proportional reinsurance must be discounted using composite discount factors.

(iii) Reinsurance for accident years before 1988. If on its annual statement a taxpayer does not allocate unpaid losses to the applicable line of business for proportional or nonproportional reinsurance attributable to the 1987 accident year or a prior accident year, those losses must be discounted using composite discount factors. If on its annual statement a taxpayer allocates to the underlying line of business reinsurance unpaid losses that are attributable to the 1987 accident year or a prior accident year, those losses must be discounted using discount factors applicable to the underlying line of business.

(iv) 90 percent exception. For purposes of § 1.846-1(b)(3)(ii) and (iii), if more than 90 percent of all the unallocated losses of a taxpayer for an accident year relate to one underlying line of business, the taxpayer must discount all unallocable reinsurance unpaid losses attributable to that accident year using the discount factors published by the Service for the underlying line of business.

(4) International business. For any accident year, unpaid losses which are attributable to international business must be discounted using composite discount factors unless more than 90 percent of all losses for that accident year relate to one underlying line of business. If more than 90 percent of all losses for an accident year relate to one underlying line of business, the taxpayer must discount the losses attributable to that accident year using discount factors published by the Service for the underlying line of business.

(5) Composite discount factors. For purposes of the regulations under section 846, "composite discount factors" means the series of discount factors published annually by the Service determined on the basis of the appropriate composite loss payment pattern.

T.D. 8433, 9/4/92.

§ 1.846-2 Election by taxpayer to use its own historical loss payment pattern.

(a) In general. If a taxpayer has one or more eligible lines of business in a determination year, the taxpayer may elect on the taxpayer's timely filed Federal income tax return for the determination year to discount unpaid losses using its own historical loss payment pattern instead of the industry-wide pattern determined by the Secretary. A taxpayer making the election must use its own historical loss payment pattern in discounting unpaid losses for each line of business that is an eligible line of business in that determination year. The election applies to accident years ending with the determination year and to each of the four succeeding accident years. If a taxpayer makes the election for the 1987 determination year, the taxpayer must use its 1987 loss payment pattern (determined by reference to its 1985 annual statement) to discount unpaid losses attributable to all accident years prior to 1988.

(b) Eligible line of business. *(1) In general.* A line of business is an eligible line of business in a determination year if, on the most recent annual statement filed by the taxpayer before the beginning of that determination year, the taxpayer reports losses and loss expenses incurred (in Schedule P, part 1, column 24 of the 1990 annual statement or comparable location in an earlier or subsequently revised blank) for at least the number of accident years for which losses and loss expenses incurred for that line of business are required to be separately reported on that annual statement. For example, for the 1987 determination year, the 1985 annual statement is used. The annual statement to be used to determine eligibility in subsequent determination years is the annual statement for each fifth year after 1985 (e.g., 1990, 1995, etc.).

(2) Other published guidance. A line of business is also an eligible line of business for purposes of the election if the line is an eligible line under requirements published for this purpose in the Internal Revenue Bulletin.

(3) Special rule for 1987 determination year. A line of business is an eligible line of business in the 1987 determination year if it is eligible under paragraph (b)(1) or (2) of this section, or if on the most recent annual statement filed by the taxpayer before the beginning of the 1987 determination year; the taxpayer reports written premiums for the line of business for at least the number of accident years that unpaid losses for that line of business are required to be separately reported on that annual statement.

(c) Anti-abuse rule. To prevent avoidance of the requirement that the election to use historical loss payment patterns apply to all eligible lines of business of a taxpayer, the district director may—

(1) Nullify a taxpayer's election to compute discounted unpaid losses based on its historical loss payment pattern;

(2) Adjust a taxpayer's historical loss payment pattern; or

(3) Make other proper adjustments.

(d) Effect of section 338 election on section 846(e) election. [Reserved]. For further guidance, see § 1.846-2T(d).

T.D. 8433, 9/4/92, amend T.D. 9257, 4/7/2006.

PAR. 5. Section 1.846-2 is amended by adding new paragraph (d) to read as follows:

Proposed § 1.846-2 Election by taxpayer to use its own historical loss payment pattern. [*For Preamble, see ¶ 152,747*]

* * * * *

(d) Effect of section 338 election on section 846(e) election. [The text of the proposed § 1.846-2(d) is the same as the text for § 1.846-2T(d) published elsewhere in this issue of the Federal Register]. [See T.D. 9257, 04/07/2006, 71 Fed. Reg. 68.]

* * * * *

§ 1.846-2T Election by taxpayer to use its own historical loss payment pattern (temporary).

• *Caution:* Under Code Sec. 7805, temporary regulations expire within three years of the date of issuance. This temporary regulation was issued on 4/7/2006.

(a) through (c) [Reserved'. For further guidance, see § 1.846-2(a) through (c).

(d) Effect of section 338 election on section 846(e) election. For rules regarding qualified stock purchases occurring on or after April 10, 2006, see §§ 1.338-1(b)(2)(vii) and 1.338-11T(e).

T.D. 9257, 4/7/2006.

§ 1.846-3 Fresh start and reserve strengthening.

(a) In general. Section 1023(e) of the Tax Reform Act of 1986 ("the 1986 Act") provides rules relating to fresh start and reserve strengthening. For purposes of section 1023(e) of the 1986 Act, a taxpayer must discount its unpaid losses as of the end of the last taxable year beginning before January 1, 1987. The excess of undiscounted unpaid losses over discounted unpaid losses as of that time is not required to be included in income, except (as provided in paragraph (e) of this section) to the extent of any "reserve strengthening" in a taxable year beginning in 1986. The exclusion from income of this excess is known as "fresh start." The amount of fresh start is, however, included in earnings and profits for the first taxable year beginning after December 31, 1986.

(b) Applicable discount factors. *(1) Calculation of beginning balance.* For purposes of section 1023(e) of the 1986 Act, a taxpayer discounts unpaid losses as of the end of the last taxable year beginning before January 1, 1987—

(i) By using the same discount factors that are used in the succeeding taxable year to discount unpaid losses attributable to the 1987 accident year and prior accident years (see section 1023(e)(2) of the 1986 Act); and

(ii) By applying those discount factors as if the 1986 accident year were the 1987 accident year.

(2) Example. The following example illustrates the principles of this paragraph (b):

Example. X, a calendar year taxpayer, does not make an election in 1987 to use its own historical loss payment pattern. When X computes discounted unpaid losses for its last taxable year beginning before January 1, 1987, the discount factor for AY + 0 published in Rev. Rul. 87-34, 1987-1 C.B. 168, must be applied to unpaid losses attributable to the 1986 accident year; the discount factor for AY + 1 is applied to unpaid losses attributable to the 1985 accident year; etc.

(c) Rules for determining the amount of reserve strengthening (weakening). *(1) In general.* The amount of reserve strengthening (weakening) is the amount that is determined under paragraph (c)(2) or (3) or have been added to (subtracted from) an unpaid loss reserve in a taxable year beginning in 1986. For purposes of section 1023(e)(3)(B) of the 1986 Act, the amount of reserve strengthening (weakening) must be determined separately for each unpaid loss reserve by applying the rules of this paragraph (c). This determination is made without regard to the reasonableness of the amount of the unpaid loss reserve and without regard to the taxpayer's discretion, or lack thereof, in establishing the amount of the unpaid loss reserve. The amount of reserve strengthening for an unpaid loss reserve may not exceed the amount of the reserve, including any undiscounted strengthening amount, as of the end of the last taxable year beginning before January 1, 1987. For purposes of this section, an "unpaid loss reserve" is the aggregate of the unpaid loss estimate for losses (whether or not reported) incurred in an accident year of a line of business.

(2) Accident years after 1985. (i) In general. The amount of reserve strengthening (weakening) for an unpaid loss reserve for an accident year after 1985 is the amount by which that reserve at the end of the last taxable year beginning in 1986 exceeds (is less than) a hypothetical unpaid loss reserve.

(ii) Hypothetical unpaid loss reserve. For purposes of this paragraph (c)(2), the term "hypothetical unpaid loss reserve" means a reserve computed for losses the estimates of which were included, at the end of the last taxable year beginning in 1986, in the unpaid loss reserve for which reserve strengthening (weakening) is being determined. The hypothetical unpaid loss reserve must be computed using the same assumptions, other than the assumed interest rates in the case of reserves determined on a discounted basis for annual statement reporting purposes, that were used to determine the 1985 accident year reserve, if any, for the line of business for which the hypothetical reserve is being computed. If there was no 1985 accident year reserve for that line of business, the hypothetical unpaid loss reserve is the reserve, at the end of the last taxable year beginning in 1986, for which reserve strengthening (weakening) is being determined (and thus there is no reserve strengthening or weakening).

(3) Accident years before 1986. (i) In general. For each taxable year beginning in 1986, the amount of reserve strengthening (weakening) for an unpaid loss reserve for an accident year before 1986 is the amount by which the reserve at the end of that taxable year exceeds (is less than)—

(A) The reserve at the end of the immediately preceding taxable year; reduced by

(B) Claims paid and loss adjustment expenses paid ("loss payments") in the taxable year beginning in 1986 with respect to losses that are attributable to the reserve. The amount by which a reserve is reduced as a result of reinsurance ceded during a taxable year beginning in 1986 is treated as a loss payment made in that taxable year.

(ii) Exceptions. Notwithstanding paragraph (c)(3)(i) of this section, the amount of reserve strengthening (weakening) for an unpaid loss reserve for an accident year before 1986 does not include—

(A) An amount added to the reserve in a taxable year beginning in 1986 as a result of a loss reported to the taxpayer from a mandatory state or federal assigned risk pool if the amount of the loss reported is not discretionary with the taxpayer; or

(B) Payments made with respect to reinsurance assumed during a taxable year beginning in 1986 or amounts added to the reserve to take into account reinsurance assumed for a line of business during a taxable year beginning in 1986, but only to the extent that the amount does not exceed the amount of a hypothetical reserve for the reinsurance assumed. The amount of the hypothetical reserve is determined using the same assumptions (other than the assumed interest rates) that were used to determine a reserve for reinsurance assumed for the line of business in a taxable year beginning in 1985.

(iii) Certain transactions deemed to be reinsurance assumed (ceded) in 1986. For purposes of this paragraph (c)(3), reinsurance assumed (ceded) in a taxable year beginning in 1985 is treated as assumed (ceded) during the succeeding taxable year if the appropriate unpaid loss reserve is not adjusted to take into account the reinsurance transaction until that succeeding taxable year.

(d) Section 845. Any reinsurance transaction that has as one of its purposes the avoidance of the reserve strengthening limitation is subject to section 845.

(e) Treatment of reserve strengthening. The fresh start provision of section 1023(e)(3)(A) of the 1986 Act does not apply to the portion of the taxpayer's unpaid losses attributable to reserve strengthening. Thus, the difference between the undiscounted unpaid losses attributable to reserve strengthening and the discounted unpaid losses attributable to reserve strengthening must be included in income and, therefore, included in earnings and profits for the first taxable year beginning after December 31, 1986. The amount that a taxpayer must include in income for its first taxable year beginning after December 31, 1986, as a result of reserve strengthening is equal to the excess (if any) of—

(1) The sum of each amount of reserve strengthening multiplied by the difference between 100 percent and the discount factor that, under paragraph (b) of this section, is applicable to the unpaid loss reserve which was strengthened; over

(2) The sum of each reserve weakening multiplied by the difference between 100 percent and the discount factor that, under paragraph (b) of this section, is applicable to the unpaid loss reserve which was weakened.

(f) Examples. The following examples illustrate the principles of this section. For purposes of these examples, it is assumed that the taxpayers are property and casualty insurance companies that in 1987 did not elect to use their own historical loss payment patterns.

Example (1). (i) As of the end of 1985, X, a calendar year taxpayer, had undiscounted unpaid losses of $1,000,000 in the workers' compensation line of business for the 1984 accident year. The same reserve had undiscounted unpaid losses of $900,000 at the end of 1986. During 1986, X's loss payments for this reserve were $300,000. Accordingly, under paragraph (c)(3)(i) of this section, X has a reserve strengthening of $200,000 ($900,00 – ($1,000,000 – $300,000)).

(ii) This was X's only reserve strengthening or weakening. Thus, under paragraph (e) of this section, for 1987 X must include in income $54,361.40 ($200,000 × (100% – 72.8193%)). The factor of 72.8193% is the AY + 2 factor from the workers' compensation series of discount factors published in Rev. Rul. 87-34, 1987-1 C.B. 168.

Example (2). The facts are the same as in Example 1, except that X's 1986 loss payments for the reserve were $1,100,000. If only paragraph (c)(3)(i) of this section were applied, X would have a $1,000,000 reserve strengthening ($900,000 – ($1,000,000 – $1,100,000)). Under paragraph (c)(1) of this section, however, the amount of reserve strengthening for the reserve is limited to the amount of the reserve at the end of 1986. Accordingly, X has a reserve strengthening of $900,000 and for 1987 must include in income $244,626.30 ($900,000 × (100% – 72.1893%)).

Example (3). (i) As of the end of the 1985, Y, a calendar year taxpayer, had undiscounted unpaid losses of $1,000,000 in the auto physical damage line of business for the 1985 accident year. The same reserve included undiscounted unpaid losses of $600,000 at the end of 1986. During 1986, Y had loss payments of $300,000 for this line of business. Under paragraph (c)(3)(i) of this section Y has a $100,000 reserve weakening ($600,000 – ($1,000,000 – $300,000)).

(ii) Under paragraph (e) of this section, the only effect of the reserve weakening is to reduce the amount that Y is required to include in income as a result of any strengthening of another reserve.

Example (4). The facts are the same as in Example 1 except that X also has a $100,000 reserve weakening for the 1985 accident year in its auto physical damage line of business. Under paragraph (b) of this section, the reserve discount factor for the reserve is 93.3400, the AY + 1 factor from the auto physical damage series of discount factors published in Rev. Rul. 87-34. Thus, under paragraph (e) of this section, the amount that X is required to include in income in 1987 is reduced by $6,660 ($100,000 × (100% – 93.3400%)), resulting in an amount of $47,761.40 ($54,361.40 – $6,660).

Example (5). (i) At the end of 1985, Z, a calendar year taxpayer, had undiscounted unpaid losses of $1,000,000 in the workers' compensation line of business for the 1984 accident year. On May 1, 1986, Z ceded $130,000 of the reserve to an unrelated reinsurer. Z added $250,000 to the 1985 year end reserve to take into account workers' compensation risks for the 1984 accident year that Z assumed in a reinsurance transaction on September 1, 1986. Z had $230,000 of 1986 loss payments related to the 1984 accident year of its workers' compensation line, $60,000 of which was attributable to the reinsurance assumed by Z. At the end of 1986, Z's reserve for the workers' compensation line for the 1984 accident year was $1,100,000.

(ii) If only paragraph (c)(3)(i) of this section were applied, Z would have a $460,000 reserve strengthening ($1,100,000 – ($1,000,000 – $230,000 – $130,000)). Under paragraph (c)(3)(ii)(B) of this section, however, reserve strengthening does not include the $250,000 that Z added to the reserve to take into account the reinsurance assumed. Also, none of the $60,000 of loss payments attributable to the reinsurance assumed in 1986 are taken into account. Accordingly, Z has $150,000 of reserve strengthening ($460,000 – $250,000 – $60,000). If this is Z's only reserve strengthening or weakening, then the amount that Z must include in income for 1987 under paragraph (e) of this section is $40,771.05 ($150,000 × (100% – 72.8193%)). The factor of 72.8193% is the AY + 2 factor from the workers' compensation series of discount factors published in Rev. Rul. 87-34.

Example (6). (i) X was a calendar year taxpayer before July 1, 1986, the date on which X became a member of an affiliated group of corporations that files a consolidated return with a June 30 year end. Thus, X had two taxable years beginning in 1986: a short taxable year ending June 30, 1986, and a fiscal taxable year ending June 30, 1987.

(ii) As of the end of the 1985, X had undiscounted unpaid losses of $800,000 in the automobile liability line of business for the 1983 accident year. At the end of the short taxable year, X had reserves of $700,000 of undiscounted unpaid losses, and on June 30, 1987, had reserves of $600,000 of undiscounted unpaid losses. During the short taxable year, ending June 30, 1986, X's loss payments for this reserve were $120,000. During the taxable year ending June 30, 1987, X's loss payments for this reserve were $180,000. Under paragraph (c)(3)(i) of this section, X has a $100,000 reserve strengthening: of which $20,000 ($700,000 – ($800,000 – $120,000)) is attributable to the short taxable year ending June 30, 1986 and $80,000 ($600,000 − ($700,000 − $180,000)) is attributable to the taxable year ending June 30, 1987.

(iii) The amount of reserve strengthening for this line of business is determined pursuant to the principles of paragraph (c)(2) of this section.

T.D. 8433, 9/4/92.

§ 1.846-4 Effective dates.

(a) In general. Sections 1.846-1 through 1.846-3 apply to taxable years beginning after December 31, 1986.

(b) Section 338 election. [Reserved]. For further guidance, see § 1.846-2T(d).

T.D. 8433, 9/4/92, amend T.D. 9257, 4/7/2006.

PAR. 6. Section 1.846-4 is amended by:

1. The section heading is revised.
2. Redesignating the existing text as paragraph (a).
3. Adding new paragraph (b).

The revision and addition read as follows:

Proposed § 1.846-4 Effective dates. [*For Preamble, see ¶ 152,747*]

* * * * *

(b) Section 338 election. [The text of the proposed § 1.846-4(b) is the same as the text for § 1.846-4T(b) published elsewhere in this issue of the Federal Register]. [See T.D. 9257, 04/07/2006, 71 Fed. Reg. 68.]

* * * * *

§ 1.846-4T Effective dates (temporary).

• ***Caution:*** Under Code Sec. 7805, temporary regulations expire within three years of the date of issuance. This temporary regulation was issued on 4/7/2006.

(a) [Reserved]. For further guidance, see § 1.846-2(a).

(b) Section 338 election. Section 1.846-2(d) applies to section 846(e) elections made with regard to a qualified stock purchase made on or after April 10, 2006.

T.D. 9257, 4/7/2006.

§ 1.848-0 Outline of regulations under section 848.

This section lists the paragraphs in §§ 1.848-1 through 1.848-3.

§ 1.848-1 Definitions and special provisions.

(a) Scope and effective date.

(b) Specified insurance contract.

(1) In general.

(2) Exceptions.

(i) In general.

(ii) Reinsurance of qualified foreign contracts.

(c) Life insurance contract.

(d) Annuity contract.

(e) Noncancellable accident and health insurance contract.

(f) Guaranteed renewable accident and health insurance contract.

(g) Combination contract.

(1) Definition.

(2) Treatment of premiums on a combination contract.

(i) In general.

(ii) De minimis premiums.

(3) Example.

(h) Group life insurance contract.

(1) In general.

(2) Group affiliation requirement.

(i) In general.

(ii) Employee group.

(iii) Debtor group.

(iv) Labor union group.

(v) Association group.

(vi) Credit union group.

(vii) Multiple group.

(viii) Certain discretionary groups.

(ix) Employees treated as members.

(x) Class or classes of a group determined without regard to individual health characteristics.

(A) In general.

(B) Limitation of coverage based on certain work and age requirements permissible.

(3) Premiums determined on a group basis.

(i) In general.

(ii) Exception for substandard premium rates for certain high risk insureds.

(iii) Flexible premium contracts.

(iv) Determination of actual age.

(4) Underwriting practices used by company. [Reserved]

(5) Disqualification of group.

(i) In general.

(ii) Exception for de minimis failures.

(6) Supplemental life insurance coverage.

(7) Special rules relating to the payment of proceeds.

(i) Contracts issued to a welfare benefit fund.

(ii) Credit life insurance contracts.

(iii) "Organization or association" limited to the sponsor of the contract or the group policyholder.

(i) General deductions.

§ 1.848-2 Determination of net premiums.

(a) Net premiums.

(1) In general.

(2) Separate determination of net premiums for certain reinsurance agreements.

(b) Gross amount of premiums and other consideration.

(1) General rule.

(2) Items included.

(3) Treatment of premium deposits.

(i) In general.

(ii) Amounts irrevocably committed to the payment of premiums.

(iii) Retired lives reserves.

(4) Deferred and uncollected premiums.

(c) Policy exchanges.

(1) General rule.

(2) External exchanges.

(3) Internal exchanges resulting in fundamentally different contracts.

(i) In general.

(ii) Certain modifications treated as not changing the mortality, morbidity, interest, or expense guarantees.

(iii) Exception for contracts restructured by a court supervised rehabilitation or similar proceeding.

(4) Value of the contract.

(i) In general.

(ii) Special rule for group term life insurance contracts.

(iii) Special rule for certain policy enhancement and update programs.

(A) In general.

(B) Policy enhancement or update program defined.

(5) Example.

(d) Amounts excluded from the gross amount of premiums and other consideration.

(1) In general.

(2) Amounts received or accrued from a guaranty association.

(3) Exclusion not to apply to dividend accumulations.

(e) Return premiums.

(f) Net consideration for a reinsurance agreement.

(1) In general.

(2) Net consideration determined by a ceding company.

(i) In general.

(ii) Net negative and net positive consideration.

(3) Net consideration determined by the reinsurer.

(i) In general.

(ii) Net negative and net positive consideration.

(4) Timing consistency required.

(5) Modified coinsurance and funds-withheld reinsurance agreements.

(i) In general.

(ii) Special rule for certain funds-withheld reinsurance agreements.

(6) Treatment of retrocessions.

(7) Mixed reinsurance agreements.

(8) Treatment of policyholder loans.

(9) Examples.

(g) Reduction in the amount of net negative consideration to ensure consistency of capitalization for reinsurance agreements.

(1) In general.

(2) Application to reinsurance agreements subject to the interim rules.

(3) Amount of reduction.

(4) Capitalization shortfall.

(5) Required capitalization amount.

(i) In general.

(ii) Special rule with respect to net negative consideration.

(6) General deductions allocable to reinsurance agreements.

(7) Allocation of capitalization shortfall among reinsurance agreements.

(8) Election to determine specified policy acquisition expenses for an agreement without regard to general deductions limitation.

(i) In general.

(ii) Manner of making election.

(iii) Election statement.

(iv) Effect of election.

(9) Examples.

(h) Treatment of reinsurance agreements with parties not subject to U.S. taxation.

(1) In general.

(2) Agreements to which this paragraph (h) applies.

(i) In general.

(ii) Parties subject to U.S. taxation.

(A) In general.

(B) Effect of a closing agreement.

(3) Election to separately determine the amounts required to be capitalized for reinsurance agreements with parties not subject to U.S. taxation.

(i) In general.

(ii) Manner of making the election.

(4) Amount taken into account for purposes of determining specified policy acquisition expenses.

(5) Net foreign capitalization amount.

(i) In general.

(ii) Foreign capitalization amounts by category.

(6) Treatment of net negative foreign capitalization amount.

(i) Applied as a reduction to previously capitalized amounts.

(ii) Carryover of remaining net negative foreign capitalization amount.

(7) Reduction of net positive foreign capitalization amount by carryover amounts allowed.

(8) Examples.

(i) Carryover of excess negative capitalization amount.

(1) In general.

(2) Excess negative capitalization amount.

(3) Treatment of excess negative capitalization amount.

(4) Special rule for the treatment of an excess negative capitalization amount of an insolvent company.

(i) When applicable.

(ii) Election to forego carryover of excess negative capitalization amount.

(iii) Amount of reduction to the excess negative capitalization amount and specified policy acquisition expenses.

(iv) Manner of making election.

(v) Presumptions relating to the insolvency of an insurance company undergoing a court supervised rehabilitation or similar state proceeding.

(vi) Example.

(j) Ceding commissions with respect to reinsurance of contracts other than specified insurance contracts.

(k) Effective dates.

T.D. 8456, 12/28/92.

§ 1.848-1 Definitions and special provisions.

(a) Scope and effective date. The definitions and special provisions in this section apply solely for purposes of determining specified policy acquisition expenses under section 848 of the Internal Revenue Code, this section, and §§ 1.848-2 and 1.848-3. Unless otherwise specified, the rules of this section are effective for the taxable years of an insurance company beginning after November 14, 1991.

(b) Specified insurance contract. *(1) In general.* A "specified insurance contract" is any life insurance contract, annuity contract, noncancellable or guaranteed renewable accident and health insurance contract, or combination contract. A reinsurance agreement that reinsures the risks under a specified insurance contract is treated in the same manner as the reinsured contract.

(2) Exceptions. (i) In general. A "specified insurance contract" does not include any pension plan contract (as defined in section 818(a)), flight insurance or similar contract, or qualified foreign contract (as defined in section 807(e)(4)).

(ii) Reinsurance of qualified foreign contracts. The exception for qualified foreign contracts does not apply to reinsurance agreements that reinsure qualified foreign contracts.

(c) Life insurance contract. A "life insurance contract" is any contract—

(1) Issued after December 31, 1984, that qualifies as a life insurance contract under section 7702(a) (including an endowment contract as defined in 7702(h)); or

(2) Issued prior to January 1, 1985, if the premiums on the contract are reported as life insurance premiums on the insurance company's annual statement (or could be reported as life insurance premiums if the company were required to file the annual statement for life and accident and health companies).

(d) Annuity contract. An "annuity contract" is any contract (other than a life insurance contract as defined in paragraph (c) of this section) if amounts received under the contract are subject to the rules in section 72(b) or section 72(e) (determined without regard to section 72(u)). The term "annuity contract" also includes a contract that is a qualified funding asset under section 130(d).

(e) Noncancellable accident and health insurance contract. The term "noncancellable accident and health insurance contract" has the same meaning for purposes of section 848 as the term has for purposes of section 816(b).

(f) Guaranteed renewable accident and health insurance contract. The term "guaranteed renewable accident and health insurance contract" has the same meaning for purposes of section 848 as the term has for purposes of section 816(e).

(g) Combination contract. *(1) Definition.* A "combination contract" is a contract (other than a contract described in section 848(e)(3)) that provides two or more types of insurance coverage, at least one of which if offered separately would be a life insurance contract, an annuity contract, or a noncancellable or guaranteed renewable accident and health insurance contract.

(2) Treatment of premiums on a combination contract. (i) In general. If the premium allocable to each type of insurance coverage is separately stated on the insurance company's annual statement (or could be separately stated if the insurance company were required to file the annual statement for life and accident and health companies), the premium allocable to each type of insurance coverage in a combination contract is subject to the capitalization rate, if any, that would apply if that coverage was provided in a separate contract. If the premium allocable to each type of insurance coverage in a combination contract is not separately stated, the entire premium is subject to the highest capitalization percentage applicable to any of the coverages provided.

(ii) De minimis premiums. For purposes of this paragraph (g)(2)—

(A) A de minimis premium is not required to be separately stated;

(B) In determining the highest capitalization percentage applicable to a combination contract, the coverage to which a de minimis premium is allocable is disregarded;

(C) If the separate statement requirement of this paragraph (g)(2) is satisfied, a de minimis premium is treated in accordance with its characterization on the insurance company's annual statement; and

(D) Whether a premium for an insurance coverage is de minimis is determined by comparing that premium with the aggregate of the premiums for the combination contract. A premium that is not more than 2 percent of the premium for the entire contract is considered de minimis. Whether a premium that is more than 2 percent is de minimis is determined based on all the facts and circumstances.

(3) Example. The principles of this paragraph (g) are illustrated by the following example.

Example. A life insurance company (L1) issues a contract to an employer (X) which provides cancellable accident and health insurance coverage and group term life insurance coverage to X's employees. L1 charges a premium of $1,000 for the contract, $950 of which is attributable to the cancellable accident and health insurance coverage and $50 of which is attributable to the group term life insurance coverage. On its annual statement, L1 reports the premiums attributable to the accident and health insurance coverage separately from the premiums attributable to the group term life insurance coverage. The contract issued by L1 is a combination contract as defined in paragraph (g)(1) of this section. Pursuant to paragraph (g)(2)(i) of this section, only the premiums attributable to the group term life insurance coverage ($50) are subject to the provisions of section 848. The premiums attributable to the cancellable accident and health insurance coverage ($950) are not subject to the provisions of section 848.

(h) Group life insurance contract. *(1) In general.* A life insurance contract (as defined in paragraph (c) of this section) is a group life insurance contract if—

(i) The contract is a group life insurance contract under the applicable law;

(ii) The coverage is provided under a master contract issued to the group policyholder, which may be a trust, trustee, or agent;

(iii) The premiums on the contract are reported either as group life insurance premiums or credit life insurance premiums on the insurance company's annual statement (or could be reported as group life insurance premiums or credit life insurance premiums if the company were required to file the annual statement for life and accident and health companies);

(iv) The group affiliation requirement of paragraph (h)(2) of this section is satisfied;

(v) The premiums on the contract are determined on a group basis within the meaning of paragraph (h)(3) of this section; and

(vi) The proceeds of the contract are not payable to or for the benefit of the insured's employer, an organization or association to which the insured belongs, or other similar person. (See paragraph (h)(7) of this section for special rules that apply in determining if this requirement is satisfied.)

(2) Group affiliation requirement. (i) In general. The group affiliation requirement of section 848(e)(2)(A) and this paragraph (h)(2) is satisfied only if all of the individuals eligible for coverage under the contract constitute a group described in paragraphs (h)(2)(ii) through (viii) of this section.

(ii) Employee group. An employee group consists of all of the employees (including statutory employees within the meaning of section 3121(d)(3) and individuals who are treated as employed by a single employer under section 414(b), (c), or (m)), or any class or classes thereof within the meaning of paragraph (h)(2)(x) of this section, of an employer. For this purpose, the term "employee" includes—

(A) A retired or former employee;

(B) The sole proprietor, if the employer is a sole proprietorship;

(C) A partner of the partnership, if the employer is a partnership;

(D) A director of the corporation, if the employer is a corporation; and

(E) An elected or appointed official of the public body, if the employer is a public body.

(iii) Debtor group. A debtor group consists of all of the debtors, or any class or classes thereof within the meaning of paragraph (h)(2)(x) of this section, of a creditor. For this purpose, the term "debtor" includes a borrower of money or purchaser or lessee of goods, services, or property for which payment is arranged through a credit transaction.

(iv) Labor union group. A labor union group consists of all of the members, or any class or classes thereof within the meaning of paragraph (h)(2)(x) of this section, of a labor union or similar employee organization.

(v) Association group. An association group consists of all of the members, or any class or classes thereof within the meaning of paragraph (h)(2)(x) of this section, of an association that, at the time the master contract is issued—

(A) Is organized and maintained for purposes other than obtaining insurance;

(B) Has been in active existence for at least two years (including, in the case of a merged or successor association, the years of active existence of any predecessor association); and

(C) Has at least 100 members.

(vi) Credit union group. A credit union group consists of all of the members or borrowers, or any class or classes thereof within the meaning of paragraph (h)(2)(x) of this section, of a credit union.

(vii) Multiple group. A multiple group consists of two or more groups from any single category described in paragraphs (h)(2)(ii) through (vi) of this section. A multiple group may not include two or more groups from different categories described in paragraphs (h)(2)(ii) through (vi) of this section.

(viii) Certain discretionary groups. Provided that the contract otherwise satisfies the requirements of paragraph (h)(1) of this section, a contract issued to one of the following discretionary groups is treated as satisfying the group affiliation requirement of this paragraph (h)(2)—

(A) A contract issued to a group consisting of students of one or more universities or other educational institutions;

(B) A contract issued to a group consisting of members or former members of the U.S. Armed Forces;

(C) A contract issued to a group of individuals for the payment of future funeral expenses; and

(D) A contract issued to any other discretionary group as specified by the Commissioner in subsequent guidance published in the Internal Revenue Bulletin. (See § 601.601(d)(2)(ii)(b) of this chapter).

(ix) Employees treated as members. In determining whether the group affiliation requirement of paragraph (h)(2) of this section is satisfied, the employees of a labor union, credit union, or association may be treated as members of a labor union group, a credit union group, or an association group, respectively.

(x) Class or classes of a group determined without regard to individual health characteristics (A) In general. A class or classes of a group described in paragraphs (h)(2)(ii) through (viii) of this section may be determined using any reasonable characteristics (for example, amount of insurance, location, or occupation) other than individual health characteristics. The employees of a single employer covered under a policy issued to a multi-employer trust are considered a class of a group described in paragraph (h)(2)(ii) of this section.

(B) Limitation of coverage based on certain work and age requirements permissible. A limitation of coverage under a group contract to persons who are actively at work or of a preretirement age (for example, age 65 or younger) is not treated as based on individual health characteristics.

(3) Premiums determined on a group basis. (i) In general. Premiums for a contract are determined on a group basis for purposes of section 848(e)(2)(B) and this paragraph (h) only if the premium charged by the insurance company for each member of the group (or any class thereof) is determined on the basis of the same rates for the corresponding amount of coverage (for example, per $1,000 of insurance) or on the

basis of rates which differ only because of the gender, smoking habits, or age of the member.

(ii) Exception for substandard premium rates for certain high risk insureds. Any difference in premium rates is disregarded for purposes of this paragraph (h)(3) if the difference is charged for an individual who was accepted for coverage at a substandard rate prior to January 1, 1993.

(iii) Flexible premium contracts. In the case of a group universal life insurance contract, the identical premium requirement is satisfied if the premium rates used by the insurance company in determining the periodic mortality charges applied to the policy account value of any member insured by the contract differ from those of other members (within the same class) only because of the gender, smoking habits, or age of the member.

(iv) Determination of actual age. For purposes of this paragraph (h)(3), determinations of actual age may be made using any reasonable method, provided that this method is applied consistently for all members of the group.

(4) Underwriting practices used by company.[Reserved]

(5) Disqualification of group. (i) In general. Except as otherwise provided in this paragraph (h)(5), if the requirements of paragraph (h)(1), (2), and (3) of this section are not satisfied with respect to one or more members of the group, or of a class within a group (within the meaning of paragraph (h)(2)(x) of this section), the premiums for the entire group (or class) are treated as individual life insurance premiums.

(ii) Exception for de minimis failures. If the requirements of paragraphs (h)(1), (2), or (3) of this section are not satisfied with respect to one or more members of the group (or class), but the sum of the premiums charged by the insurance company for those individuals is no more than 5 percent of the aggregate premiums for the group (or class), only the premiums charged for those individuals are treated as premiums for an individual life insurance contract.

(6) Supplemental life insurance coverage. For purposes of determining whether the requirement in paragraph (h)(3)(i) of this section is satisfied, any supplemental life insurance coverage (including optional coverage for members of the group, their spouses, or their dependent children) is (or is treated as) a separate contract. In determining whether the group affiliation requirement of paragraph (h)(2) of this section is satisfied for the supplemental coverage, a member's spouse and dependent children are treated as members of the group if they are eligible for coverage.

(7) Special rules relating to the payment of proceeds. The following rules apply for purposes of section 848(e)(2) and paragraph (h)(1)(vi) of this section.

(i) Contracts issued to a welfare benefit fund. If a contract issued to a welfare benefit fund (as defined in section 419) provides for payment of proceeds to the welfare benefit fund, the proceeds of the contract are not considered payable to or for the benefit of the insured's employer, an organization or association to which the insured belongs, or other similar person, provided the proceeds are paid as benefits to the employee or the employee's beneficiary.

(ii) Credit life insurance contracts. If a credit life insurance contract provides for payment of proceeds to the insured's creditor, the proceeds of the contract are not treated as payable to or for the benefit of the insured's employer, an organization or association to which the insured belongs, or other similar person, provided the proceeds are applied against an outstanding indebtedness of the insured.

(iii) "Organization or association" limited to the sponsor of the contract or the group policyholder. The term "organization or association" means the organization or association that is either the sponsor of the contract or the group policyholder.

(i) General deductions. The term "general deductions" is defined in section 848(c)(2). An insurance company determines its general deductions for the taxable year without regard to amounts capitalized or amortized under section 848(a). The amount of a company's general deductions is also determined without regard to the rules of § 1.848-2(f), which apply only for purposes of determining net consideration for reinsurance agreements.

T.D. 8456, 12/28/92.

§ 1.848-2 Determination of net premiums.

(a) Net premiums. *(1) In general.* An insurance company must use the accrual method of accounting (as prescribed by section 811(a)(1)) to determine the net premiums with respect to each category of specified insurance contracts. With respect to any category of contracts, net premiums means—

(i) The gross amount of premiums and other consideration (see paragraph (b) of this section); reduced by

(ii) The sum of—

(A) The return premiums (see paragraph (e) of this section); and

(B) The net negative consideration for a reinsurance agreement (other than an agreement described in paragraph (h)(2) of this section). See paragraphs (f) and (g) of this section for rules relating to the determination of net negative consideration.

(2) Separate determination of net premiums for certain reinsurance agreements. Net premiums with respect to reinsurance agreements for which an election under paragraph (h)(3) of this section has been made (certain reinsurance agreements with parties not subject to United States taxation) are treated separately and are subject to the rules of paragraph (h) of this section.

(b) Gross amount of premiums and other consideration.

(1) General rule. The term "gross amount of premiums and other consideration" means the sum of—

(i) All premiums and other consideration (other than amounts on reinsurance agreements); and

(ii) The net positive consideration for any reinsurance agreement (other than an agreement for which an election under paragraph (h)(3) of this section has been made).

(2) Items included. The gross amount of premiums and other consideration includes—

(i) Advance premiums;

(ii) Amounts in a premium deposit fund or similar account, to the extent provided in paragraph (b)(3) of this section;

(iii) Fees;

(iv) Assessments;

(v) Amounts that the insurance company charges itself representing premiums with respect to benefits for its employees (including full-time life insurance salesmen treated as employees under section 7701(a)(20)); and

(vi) The value of a new contract issued in an exchange described in paragraph (c)(2) or (c)(3) of this section.

(3) Treatment of premium deposits. (i) In general. An amount in a premium deposit fund or similar account is taken into account in determining the gross amount of premiums and other consideration at the earlier of the time that the amount is applied to, or irrevocably committed to, the payment of a premium on a specified insurance contract. If an amount is irrevocably committed to the payment of a premium on a specified insurance contract, then neither that amount nor any earnings allocable to that amount are included in the gross amount of premiums and other consideration when applied to the payment of a premium on the same contract.

(ii) Amounts irrevocably committed to the payment of premiums. Except as provided in paragraph (b)(3)(iii) of this section, an amount in a premium deposit fund or similar account is irrevocably committed to the payment of premiums on a contract only if neither the amount nor any earnings allocable to that amount may be—

(A) Returned to the policyholder or any other person (other than on surrender of the contract); or

(B) Used by the policyholder to fund another contract.

(iii) Retired lives reserves. Premiums received by an insurance company under a retired lives reserve arrangement are treated as irrevocably committed to the payment of premiums on a specified insurance contract.

(4) Deferred and uncollected premiums. The gross amount of premiums and other consideration does not include deferred and uncollected premiums.

(c) Policy exchanges. *(1) General rule.* Except as otherwise provided in this paragraph (c), an exchange of insurance contracts (including a change in the terms of a specified insurance contract) does not result in any amount being included in the gross amount of premiums and other consideration.

(2) External exchanges. If a contract is exchanged for a specified insurance contract issued by another insurance company, the company that issues the new contract must include the value of the new contract in the gross amount of premiums and other consideration.

(3) Internal exchanges resulting in fundamentally different contracts. (i) In general. If a contract is exchanged for a specified insurance contract issued by the same insurance company that issued the original contract, the company must include the value of the new contract in the gross amount of premiums and other consideration if the new contract—

(A) Relates to a different category of specified insurance contract than the original contract;

(B) Does not cover the same insured as the original contract; or

(C) Changes the interest, mortality, morbidity, or expense guarantees with respect to the nonforfeiture benefits provided in the original contract.

(ii) Certain modifications treated as not changing the mortality, morbidity, interest, or expense guarantees. For purposes of paragraph (c)(3)(i)(C) of this section, the following items are not treated as changing the interest, mortality, morbidity, or expense guarantees with respect to the nonforfeiture benefits provided in the contract—

(A) A change in a temporary guarantee with respect to the amounts to be credited as interest to the policyholder's account, or charged as mortality, morbidity, or expense charges, if the new guarantee applies for a period of ten years or less;

(B) The determination of benefits on annuitization using rates which are more favorable to the policyholder than the permanently guaranteed rates; and

(C) Other items as specified by the Commissioner in subsequent guidance published in the Internal Revenue Bulletin.

(iii) Exception for contracts restructured by a court supervised rehabilitation or similar proceeding. No amount is included in the gross amount of premiums and other consideration with respect to any change made to the interest, mortality, morbidity, or expense guarantees with respect to the nonforfeiture benefits of contracts of an insurance company that is the subject of a rehabilitation, conservatorship, insolvency, or similar state proceeding. This treatment applies only if the change—

(A) Occurs as part of the rehabilitation, conservatorship, insolvency, or similar state proceeding; and

(B) Is approved by the state court, the state insurance department, or other state official with authority to act in the rehabilitation, conservatorship, insolvency, or similar state proceeding.

(4) Value of the contract. (i) In general. For purposes of paragraph (c)(2) or (c)(3) of this section, the value of the new contract is established through the most recent sale by the company of a comparable contract. If the value of the new contract is not readily ascertainable, the value may be approximated by using the interpolated terminal reserve of the original contract as of the date of the exchange.

(ii) Special rule for group term life insurance contracts. In the case of any exchange involving a group term life insurance contract without cash value, the value of the new contract is deemed to be zero.

(iii) Special rule for certain policy enhancement and update programs (A) In general. If the interest, mortality, morbidity, or expense guarantees with respect to the nonforfeiture benefits of a specified insurance contract are changed pursuant to a policy enhancement or update program, the value of the contract included in the gross amount of premiums and other consideration equals 30 percent of the value determined under paragraph (c)(4) of this section.

(B) Policy enhancement or update program defined. For purposes of paragraph (c)(4)(iii)(A) of this section, a policy enhancement or update program means any offer or commitment by the insurance company to all of the policyholders holding a particular policy form to change the interest, mortality, morbidity, or expense guarantees used to determine the contract's nonforfeiture benefits.

(5) Example. The principles of this paragraph (c) are illustrated by the following example.

Example. (i) An individual (A) owns a life insurance policy issued by a life insurance company (L1). On January 1, 1993, A purchases additional term insurance for $250, which is added as a rider to A's life insurance policy. The purchase of the additional term insurance does not change the interest, mortality, morbidity, or expense guarantees with respect to the nonforfeiture benefits provided by A's life insurance policy.

(ii) A's purchase of the term insurance rider is not considered to result in a fundamentally different contract under paragraph (c)(3) of this section because the addition of the rider did not change the interest, mortality, morbidity, or expense guarantees with respect to the nonforfeiture values of A's original life insurance policy. Therefore, L1 includes only the $250 received from A in the gross amount of premiums and other consideration.

(d) Amounts excluded from the gross amount of premiums and other consideration. *(1) In general.* The following items are not included in the gross amount of premiums and other consideration—

(i) Items treated by section 808(e) as policyholder dividends that are paid to the policyholder and immediately returned to the insurance company as a premium on the same contract that generated the dividends, including—

(A) A policyholder dividend applied to pay a premium under the contract that generated the dividend;

(B) Excess interest accumulated within the contract;

(C) A policyholder dividend applied for additional coverage (for example, a paid-up addition, extension of the period for which insurance protection is provided, or reduction of the period for which premiums are paid) on the contract that generated the dividend;

(D) A policyholder dividend applied to reduce premiums otherwise payable on the contract that generated the dividend;

(E) An experience-rated refund applied to pay a premium on the group contract that generated the refund; and

(F) An experience-rated refund applied to a premium stabilization reserve held with respect to the group contract that generated the refund;

(ii) Premiums waived as a result of the disability of an insured or the disability or death of a premium payor;

(iii) Premiums considered to be paid on a contract as the result of a partial surrender or withdrawal from the contract, or as a result of the surrender or withdrawal of a paid-up addition previously issued with respect to the same contract; and

(iv) Amounts treated as premiums upon the selection by a policyholder or by a beneficiary of a settlement option provided in a life insurance contract.

(2) Amounts received or accrued from a guaranty association. Amounts received or accrued from a guaranty association relating to an insurance company that is subject to an insolvency, delinquency, conservatorship, rehabilitation, or similar proceeding are not included in the gross amount of premiums and other consideration.

(3) Exclusion not to apply to dividend accumulations. For purposes of section 848(d)(3) and paragraph (d)(1) of this section, amounts applied from a dividend accumulation account to pay premiums on a specified insurance contract are not amounts treated as paid to, and immediately returned by, the policyholder.

(e) Return premiums. For purposes of section 848(d)(1)(B) and this section, return premiums do not include policyholder dividends (as defined in section 808), claims or benefits payments, or amounts returned to another insurance company under a reinsurance agreement. For the treatment of amounts returned to another insurance company under a reinsurance agreement, see paragraph (f) of this section.

(f) Net consideration for a reinsurance agreement. *(1) In general.* For purposes of section 848, the ceding company and the reinsurer must treat amounts arising from the reinsurance of a specified insurance contract consistently in determining their net premiums. See paragraph (g) of this section for restrictions on the amount of the net negative consideration for any reinsurance agreement that may be taken into account. See paragraph (h) of this section for special rules applicable to reinsurance agreements with parties not subject to United States taxation.

(2) Net consideration determined by a ceding company. (i) In general. The net consideration determined by a ceding company for a reinsurance agreement equals—

(A) The gross amount incurred by the reinsurer with respect to the reinsurance agreement, including any ceding commissions, annual allowances, reimbursements of claims and benefits, modified coinsurance reserve adjustments under paragraph (f)(5) of this section, experience-rated adjustments, and termination payments; less

(B) The gross amount of premiums and other consideration incurred by the ceding company with respect to the reinsurance agreement.

(ii) Net negative and net positive consideration. If the net consideration is less than zero, the ceding company has net negative consideration for the reinsurance agreement. If the net consideration is greater than zero, the ceding company has net positive consideration for the reinsurance agreement.

(3) Net consideration determined by the reinsurer. (i) In general. The net consideration determined by a reinsurer for a reinsurance agreement equals—

(A) The amount described in paragraph (f)(2)(i)(B) of this section; less

(B) The amount described in paragraph (f)(2)(i)(A) of this section.

(ii) Net negative and net positive consideration. If the net consideration is less than zero, the reinsurer has net negative consideration for the reinsurance agreement. If the net consideration is greater than zero, the reinsurer has net positive consideration for the reinsurance agreement.

(4) Timing consistency required. For purposes of determining the net consideration of a party for a reinsurance agreement, an income or expense item is taken into account for the first taxable year for which the item is required to be taken into account by either party. Thus, the ceding company and the reinsurer must take the item into account for the same taxable year (or for the same period if the parties have different taxable years).

(5) Modified coinsurance and funds-withheld reinsurance agreements. (i) In general. In the case of a modified coinsurance or funds-withheld reinsurance agreement, the net consideration for the agreement includes the amount of any payments or reserve adjustments, as well as any related loan transactions between the ceding company and the reinsurer. The amount of any investment income transferred between the parties as the result of a reserve adjustment or loan transaction is treated as an item of consideration under the reinsurance agreement.

(ii) Special rule for certain funds-withheld reinsurance agreements. In the case of a funds-withheld reinsurance agreement that is entered into after November 14, 1991, but before the first day of the first taxable year beginning after December 31, 1991, and is terminated before January 1, 1995, the parties' net consideration in the year of termination must include the amount of the original reserve for any reinsured specified insurance contract that, in applying the provisions of subchapter L, was treated as premiums and other consideration incurred for reinsurance for the taxable year in which the agreement became effective.

(6) Treatment of retrocessions. For purposes of this paragraph (f), a retrocession agreement is treated as a separate reinsurance agreement. The party that is relieved of liability under a retrocession agreement is treated as the ceding company.

(7) Mixed reinsurance agreements. If a reinsurance agreement includes more than one category of specified insurance contracts (or specified insurance contracts and contracts that are not specified insurance contracts), the portion of the agreement relating to each category of reinsured specified insurance contracts is treated as a separate agreement. The portion of the agreement relating to reinsured contracts that are not specified insurance contracts is similarly treated as a separate agreement.

(8) Treatment of policyholder loans. For purposes of determining the net consideration under a reinsurance agreement, the transfer of a policyholder loan receivable is treated as an item of consideration under the agreement. The interest credited with respect to a policyholder loan receivable is treated as investment income earned directly by the party holding the receivable. The amounts taken into account as claims and benefit reimbursements under the agreement must be determined without reduction for the policyholder loan.

(9) Examples. The principles of this paragraph (f) are illustrated by the following examples.

Example (1). On July 1, 1992, a life insurance company (L1) transfers a block of individual life insurance contracts to an unrelated life insurance company (L2) under an agreement whereby L2 becomes solely liable to the policyholders under the contracts reinsured. L1 and L2 are calendar year taxpayers. Under the assumption reinsurance agreement, L1 agrees to pay L2 $100,000 for assuming the life insurance contracts, and L2 agrees to pay L1 a $17,000 ceding commission. Under paragraph (f)(2) of this section, L1 has net negative consideration of ($83,000) ($17,000 ceding commission incurred by L2 - $100,000 incurred by L1 for reinsurance). Under paragraph (f)(3) of this section, L2 has net positive consideration of $83,000. Under paragraph (b)(1)(ii) of this section, L2 includes the net positive consideration in its gross amount of premiums and other consideration.

Example (2). (i) On July 1, 1992, a life insurance company (L1) transfers a block of individual life insurance contracts to an unrelated life insurance company (L2) under an agreement whereby L1 remains liable to the policyholders under the reinsured contracts. L1 and L2 are calendar year taxpayers. Under the indemnity reinsurance agreement, L1 agrees to pay L2 $100,000 for reinsuring the life insurance contracts, and L2 agrees to pay L1 a $17,000 ceding commission. L1 agrees to pay L2 an amount equal to the future premiums on the reinsured contracts. L2 agrees to indemnify L1 for claims and benefits and administrative expenses incurred by L1 while the reinsurance agreement is in effect.

(ii) For the period beginning July 1, 1992, and ending December 31, 1992, the following income and expense items are determined with respect to the reinsured contracts:

Item	Income	Expense
Premiums	$25,000	—
Death benefits	—	$10,000
Surrender benefits	—	8,000
Premium taxes and other expenses	—	2,000
Total	—	$20,000

(iii) Under paragraph (f)(2) of this section, L1's net negative consideration equals ($88,000), which is determined by subtracting the $125,000 ($100,000 + $25,000) incurred by L1 from the $37,000 incurred by L2 under the reinsurance agreement ($17,000 + $10,000 + $8,000 + $2,000). L2's net positive consideration is $88,000. Under paragraph (b)(1)(ii) of this section, L2 includes the $88,000 net positive consideration in its gross amount of premiums and other consideration.

Example (3). (i) Assume that the reinsurance agreement referred to in Example 2 is terminated on December 31, 1993. During the period from January 1, 1993 through December 31, 1993, the following income and expense items are determined with respect to the reinsured contracts:

Item	Income	Expense
Premiums	$45,000	—
Death benefits	—	$18,000
Surrender benefits	—	6,000
Premium taxes and other expenses	—	8,000
Total	—	$32,000

(ii) On the termination date of the reinsurance agreement, L1 receives a payment of $70,000 from L2 as consideration for releasing L2 from liability with respect to the reinsured contracts.

(iii) L1's net positive consideration equals $57,000, which is the excess of the $102,000 incurred by L2 for the year ($18,000 + $6,000 + $8,000 + $70,000) over the $45,000 incurred by L1. L2's net negative consideration is ($57,000). L1 includes the net positive consideration in its gross amount of premiums and other consideration.

Example (4). (i) On January 1, 1993, an insurance company (L1) enters into a modified coinsurance agreement with another insurance company (L2), covering a block of individual life insurance contracts. Both L1 and L2 are calendar year taxpayers. Under the agreement, L2 is credited with an initial reinsurance premium equal to L1's reserves on the reinsured contracts at the inception of the agreement, any new premiums received with respect to the reinsured contracts, any decrease in L1's reserves on the reinsured contracts, and an amount of investment income determined by reference to L1's reserves on the reinsured contracts. L2 is charged for all claims and expenses incurred with respect to the reinsured contracts plus an amount reflecting any increase in L1's reserves. The agreement further provides that cash settlements between the parties are made at the inception and termination of the agreement, as well as at the end of each calendar year while the agreement is in effect. The cash settlement is determined by netting the sum of the amounts credited to L2 against the sum of the amounts charged to L2 with respect to the reinsured policies. L1's reserves on the reinsured policies at the inception of the reinsurance agreement are $375,000.

(ii) Under the cash settlement formula, L2 is credited with an initial reinsurance premium equal to L1's reserves on the reinsured policies ($375,000), but is charged an amount reflecting L1's policy reserve requirements ($375,000).

(iii) For the period ending December 31, 1993, L2 is also credited and charged the following amounts with respect to the reinsured contracts.

Item	Income	Expense
Premiums	$100,000	—
Investment income	39,000	—
Death benefits	—	$65,000
Increase in reserves	—	75,000

(iv) Under paragraph (f)(5) of this section, L2's net negative consideration for the 1993 taxable year equals ($1,000) which is determined by subtracting the sum of the amounts charged to L2 ($375,000 + $65,000 + $75,000 = $515,000) from the sum of the amounts credited to L2 ($375,000 + $100,000 + $39,000 = $514,000). L1's net positive consideration for calendar year 1993 equals $1,000. Under paragraph (b)(1)(ii) of this section, L1 includes the $1,000 net positive consideration in its gross amount of premiums and other consideration.

Example (5). (i) On January 1, 1993, an insurance company (L1) enters into a coinsurance agreement with another insurance company (L2) covering a block of individual life insurance contracts. Both L1 and L2 are calendar year taxpayers. Under the agreement, L2 is credited with an initial reinsurance premium equal to L1's reserves on the effective date of the agreement, any new premiums received on the reinsured contracts, but must indemnify L1 for all claims and expenses incurred with respect to the contracts. As part of the agreement, L2 makes a loan to L1 equal to the amount of the reserves on the reinsured contracts. L1's reserves on the reinsured contracts on the effective date of the agreement are $375,000. Thus, on the inception date of the reinsurance agreement, L1 transfers to L2 its note for $375,000 as consideration for reinsurance.

(ii) The reinsurance agreement between L1 and L2 is a funds-withheld reinsurance agreement. Under paragraph (f)(5) of this section, the amount of any loan transaction is taken into account in determining the parties' net consideration. At the inception of the reinsurance agreement, L2 is credited with a reinsurance premium equal to L1's reserves on the reinsured contracts ($375,000). L2's $375,000 loan to L1 is treated as an amount returned to L1 under the agreement.

(iii) For the period ending December 31, 1993, L2 is credited and charged the following amounts with respect to the reinsured contracts and the loan transaction with L1.

Item	Income	Expense
Premiums	$100,000	—
Accrued Interest	39,000	—
Death benefits	—	$65,000
Increase in loan to L1	—	75,000

(iv) Under paragraph (f)(5) of this section, L2's net negative consideration for the 1993 taxable year equals ($1,000), which is determined by subtracting the sum of amounts incurred by L2 with respect to death benefits and the loan transaction ($375,000 + $65,000 + $75,000 = $515,000) from the sum of the amounts credited to L2 as reinsurance premiums and interest on the loan transaction ($375,000 + $100,000 + $39,000 = $514,000). L1's net positive consideration for calendar year 1993 equals $1,000. Under paragraph (b)(1)(ii) of this section, L1 includes the $1,000 net positive consideration in its gross amount of premiums and other consideration.

Example (6). (i) On December 31, 1993, an insurance company (L1) enters into a reinsurance agreement with another insurance company (L2) covering a block of individual life insurance contracts. Both L1 and L2 are calendar year taxpayers. Under the agreement, L2 is credited with L1's reserves on the reinsured contracts on the effective date of the agreement, plus any new premiums received on the reinsured contracts, but must indemnify L1 for all claims and expenses incurred with respect to the contracts. Under the agreement, L1 transfers cash of $325,000 to L2 plus rights to its policyholder loan receivables on the reinsured contracts ($50,000). L2 reports the reinsurance agreement by including the transferred policyholder loan receivables as an asset on its books.

(ii) For the period beginning January 1, 1994 and ending December 31, 1994, the following income and expense items are incurred with respect to the reinsured contracts.

Item	Income	Expense
Premiums	$100,000	—
Death benefits	—	$25,000
Surrender benefits	—	5,000
Premium taxes and other expenses	—	8,000
Total	—	38,000

(iii) These amounts are net of the outstanding policyholder loans held by L2 of $20,000 with respect to death benefits and $15,000 with respect to surrender benefits.

(iv) Under paragraph (f)(8) of this section, the transferred policyholder loan receivables are treated as an item of consideration under the reinsurance agreement. In determining the parties' net consideration for the agreement, the transferred policyholder loan receivables ($50,000) are treated as an item of consideration incurred by L1 under paragraph (f)(2)(i)(B) of this section. Therefore, for the 1993 taxable year, L1 has net negative consideration of ($375,000). L2 has net positive consideration of $375,000. Under paragraph (b)(1)(ii) of this section, L2 includes the $375,000 net positive consideration in its gross amount of premiums and other consideration.

(v) For the 1994 taxable year, L2 has net positive consideration for the reinsurance agreement of $62,000 before adjustment for the transferred policyholder loans. Under paragraph (f)(8) of this section, the amounts taken into account as claim and benefit payments must be adjusted by the amount of any transferred policyholder loan receivables which are netted against the reinsurer's claim and benefit reimbursements. Therefore, L2 takes into account $45,000 ($25,000 + $20,000 = $45,000) as reimbursements for death benefits, and $20,000 ($5,000 + $15,000 = $20,000) as reimbursements for surrender benefits. After adjustment for these items, L2 has net positive consideration of $27,000, which is determined by subtracting the sum of the amounts charged to L2 ($45,000 + $20,000 + $8,000 = $73,000) from the sum of the amounts credited to L2 ($100,000). L1 has net negative consideration of ($27,000) under the agreement. Under paragraph (b)(1)(ii) of this section, L2 includes the $27,000 net positive consideration in its gross amount of premiums and other consideration. The amount of any interest earned on the policyholder loan receivables after their transfer to L2 is treated as investment income earned directly by L2, and is not taken into account as an item of consideration under the agreement.

(g) Reduction in the amount of net negative consideration to ensure consistency of capitalization for reinsurance agreements. *(1) In general.* Paragraph (g)(3) of this section provides for a reduction in the amount of net negative consideration that a party to a reinsurance agreement (other than a reinsurance agreement described in paragraph (h)(2) of this section) may take into account in determining net premiums under paragraph (a)(2)(ii) of this section if the party with net positive consideration has a capitalization shortfall (as defined in paragraph (g)(4) of this section). Unless the party with net negative consideration demonstrates that the party with net positive consideration does not have a capitalization shortfall or demonstrates the amount of the other party's capitalization shortfall which is allocable to the reinsurance agreement, the net negative consideration that may be taken into account under paragraph (a)(2)(ii) of this section is zero. However, the reduction of paragraph (g)(3) of this section does not apply to a reinsurance agreement if the parties make a joint election under paragraph (g)(8) of this section. Under the election, the party with net positive consideration capitalizes specified policy acquisition expenses with respect to the agreement without regard to the general deductions limitation of section 848(c)(1).

(2) Application to reinsurance agreements subject to the interim rules. In applying this paragraph (g) to a reinsurance agreement that is subject to the interim rules of § 1.848-3, the term "premiums and other consideration incurred for reinsurance under section 848(d)(1)(B)" is substituted for "net negative consideration," and the term "gross amount of premiums and other consideration under section 848(d)(1)(A)" is substituted for "net positive consideration." If an insurance company has "premiums and other consideration incurred for reinsurance under section 848(d)(1)(B)" and a "gross amount of premiums and other consideration under section 848(d)(1)(A)" for the same agreement, the net of these amounts is taken into account for purposes of this paragraph (g).

(3) Amount of reduction. The reduction required by this paragraph (g)(3) equals the amount obtained by dividing—

(i) The portion of the capitalization shortfall (as defined in paragraph (g)(4) of this section) allocated to the reinsurance agreement under paragraph (g)(7) of this section; by

(ii) The applicable percentage set forth in section 848(c)(1) for the category of specified insurance contracts reinsured by the agreement.

(4) Capitalization shortfall. A "capitalization shortfall" equals the excess of—

(i) The sum of the required capitalization amounts (as defined in paragraph (g)(5) of this section) for all reinsurance agreements (other than reinsurance agreements for which an election has been made under paragraph (h)(3) of this section); over

(ii) The general deductions allocated to those reinsurance agreements, as determined under paragraph (g)(6) of this section.

(5) Required capitalization amount. (i) In general. The "required capitalization amount" for a reinsurance agreement (other than a reinsurance agreement for which an election has been made under paragraph (h)(3) of this section) equals the amount (either positive or negative) obtained by multiplying—

(A) The net positive or negative consideration for an agreement not described in paragraph (h)(2) of this section, and the net positive consideration for an agreement described in paragraph (h)(2) of this section, but for which an election under paragraph (h)(3) of this section has not been made; by

(B) The applicable percentage set forth in section 848(c)(1) for that category of specified insurance contracts.

(ii) Special rule with respect to net negative consideration. Solely for purposes of computing a party's required capitalization amount under this paragraph (g)(5)—

(A) If either party to the reinsurance agreement is the direct issuer of the reinsured contracts, the party computing its required capitalization amount takes into account the full amount of any net negative consideration without regard to any potential reduction under paragraph (g)(3) of this section; and

(B) If neither party to the reinsurance agreement is the direct issuer of the reinsured contracts, any net negative consideration is deemed to equal zero in computing a party's required capitalization amount except to the extent that the party with the net negative consideration establishes that the other party to that reinsurance agreement capitalizes the appropriate amount.

(6) General deductions allocable to reinsurance agreements. An insurance company's general deductions allocable to its reinsurance agreements equals the excess, if any, of—

(i) The company's general deductions (excluding additional amounts treated as general deductions under paragraph (g)(8) of this section); over

(ii) The amount determined under section 848(c)(1) on specified insurance contracts that the insurance company has issued directly (determined without regard to any reinsurance agreements).

(7) Allocation of capitalization shortfall among reinsurance agreements. The capitalization shortfall is allocated to each reinsurance agreement for which the required capitalization amount (as determined in paragraph (g)(5) of this section) is a positive amount. The portion of the capitalization shortfall allocable to each agreement equals the amount which bears the same ratio to the capitalization shortfall as the required capitalization amount for the reinsurance agreement bears to the sum of the positive required capitalization amounts.

(8) Election to determine specified policy acquisition expenses for an agreement without regard to general deductions limitation. (i) In general. The reduction specified by paragraph (g)(3) of this section does not apply if the parties to a reinsurance agreement make an election under this paragraph (g)(8). The election requires the party with net positive consideration to capitalize specified policy acquisition expenses with respect to the reinsurance agreement without regard to the general deductions limitation of section 848(c)(1). That party must reduce its deductions under section 805 or section 832(c) by the amount, if any, of the party's capitalization shortfall allocable to the reinsurance agreement. The additional capitalized amounts are treated as specified policy acquisition expenses attributable to premiums and other consideration on the reinsurance agreement, and are deductible in accordance with section 848(a)(2).

(ii) Manner of making election. To make an election under paragraph (g)(8) of this section, the ceding company and the reinsurer must include an election statement in the reinsurance agreement, either as part of the original terms of the agreement or by an addendum to the agreement. The parties must each attach a schedule to their federal income tax returns which identifies the reinsurance agreement for which the joint election under this paragraph (g)(8) has been made. The schedule must be attached to each of the parties' federal income tax returns filed for the later of—

(A) The first taxable year ending after the election becomes effective; or

(B) The first taxable year ending on or after December 29, 1992.

(iii) Election statement. The election statement in the reinsurance agreement must—

(A) Provide that the party with net positive consideration for the reinsurance agreement for each taxable year will capitalize specified policy acquisition expenses with respect to the reinsurance agreement without regard to the general deductions limitation of section 848(c)(1);

(B) Set forth the agreement of the parties to exchange information pertaining to the amount of net consideration under the reinsurance agreement each year to ensure consistency;

(C) Specify the first taxable year for which the election is effective; and

(D) Be signed by both parties.

(iv) Effect of election. An election under this paragraph (g)(8) is effective for the first taxable year specified in the election statement and for all subsequent taxable years for which the reinsurance agreement remains in effect. The election may not be revoked without the consent of the Commissioner.

(9) Examples. The principles of this paragraph (g) are illustrated by the following examples.

Example (1). (i) On December 31, 1992, a life insurance company (L1) transfers a block of individual life insurance contracts to an unrelated life insurance company (L2) under an agreement in which L2 becomes solely liable to the policyholders on the reinsured contracts. L1 transfers $105,000 to L2 as consideration for the reinsurance of the contracts.

(ii) L1 and L2 do not make an election under paragraph (g)(8) of this section to capitalize specified policy acquisition expenses with respect to the reinsurance agreement without regard to the general deductions limitation. L2 has no other insurance business, and its general deductions for the taxable year are $3,500.

(iii) Under paragraph (f)(2) of this section, L1's net negative consideration is ($105,000). Under paragraph (f)(3) of this section, L2's net positive consideration is $105,000. Pursuant to paragraph (b)(1)(ii) of this section, L2 includes the net positive consideration in its gross amount of premiums and other consideration.

(iv) The required capitalization amount under paragraph (g)(5) of this section for the reinsurance agreement is $8,085 ($105,000 × .077). L2's general deductions, all of which are allocable to the reinsurance agreement with L1, are $3,500. The $4,585 difference between the required capitalization amount ($8,085) and the general deductions allocable to the reinsurance agreement ($3,500) represents L2's capitalization shortfall under paragraph (g)(4) of this section.

(v) Since L2 has a capitalization shortfall allocable to the agreement, the rules of paragraph (g)(1) of this section apply for purposes of determining the amount by which L1 may reduce its net premiums. Under paragraph (g)(3) of this section, L1 must reduce the amount of net negative consideration that it takes into account under paragraph (a)(2)(ii) of this section by $59,545 ($4,585/.077). Thus, of the $105,000 net negative consideration under the reinsurance agreement, L1 may take into account only $45,455 as a reduction of its net premiums.

Example (2). The facts are the same as Example 1, except that L1 and L2 make the election under paragraph (g)(8) of this section to capitalize specified policy acquisition expenses with respect to the reinsurance agreement without regard to the general deductions limitation. Pursuant to this election, L2 must capitalize as specified policy acquisition expenses an amount equal to $8,085 ($105,000 × .077). L1 may reduce its net premiums by the $105,000 of net negative consideration.

Example (3). (i) A life insurance company (L1) is both a direct issuer and a reinsurer of life insurance and annuity contracts. For 1993, L1's net premiums under section 848 (d)(1) for directly issued individual life insurance and annuity contracts are as follows:

Category	Net Premiums
Life insurance contracts	$17,000,000
Annuity contracts	8,000,000

(ii) L1's general deductions for 1993 are $1,500,000.

(iii) For 1993, L1 is a reinsurer under four separate indemnity reinsurance agreements with unrelated insurance companies (L2, L3, L4, and L5). The agreements with L2, L3, and L4 cover life insurance contracts issued by those companies. The agreement with L5 covers annuity contracts issued by L5. The parties to the reinsurance agreements have not made the election under paragraph (g)(8) of this section to capitalize specified policy acquisition expenses with respect to these agreements without regard to the general deductions limitation.

(iv) L1's net consideration for 1993 with respect to its reinsurance agreements is as follows:

Agreement	Net consideration
L2	$1,200,000
L3	(350,000)
L4	300,000
L5	600,000

(v) To determine whether a reduction under paragraph (g)(3) of this section applies with respect to these reinsurance agreements, L1 must determine the required capitalization amounts for its reinsurance agreements and the amount of its general deductions allocable to these agreements.

(vi) Pursuant to paragraph (g)(5) of this section, the required capitalization amount for each reinsurance agreement is determined as follows:

L2	$1,200,000 × .077 = $92,400
L3	($350,000) × .077 = ($26,950)
L4	$300,000 × .077 = $23,100
L5	$600,000 × .0175 = $10,500

(vii) Thus, the sum of L1's required capitalization amounts on its reinsurance agreements equals $99,050.

(viii) Pursuant to paragraph (g)(6) of this section, L1 determines its general deductions allocable to its reinsurance agreements. The amount determined under section 848(c)(1) on its directly issued contracts is:

Category	
Annuity contracts	$8,000,000 × .0175 = $140,000
Life insurance contracts	$17,000,000 × .077 = 1,309,000
	$1,449,000

(ix) L1's general deductions allocable to its reinsurance agreements are $51,000 ($1,500,000 - $1,449,000).

(x) Pursuant to paragraph (g)(4) of this section, L1's capitalization shortfall equals $48,050, reflecting the excess of L1's required capitalization amounts for its reinsurance agreements ($99,050) over the general deductions allocable to its reinsurance agreements ($51,000).

(xi) Pursuant to paragraph (g)(7) of this section, the capitalization shortfall of $48,050 must be allocated between each of L1's reinsurance agreements with net positive consideration in proportion to their respective required capitalization amounts. The allocation of the shortfall between L1's reinsurance agreements is determined as follows:

L2 = $35,237 ($48,050 × 92,400/126,000)
L4 = $8,809 ($48,050 × 23,100/126,000)
L5 = $4,004 ($48,050 × 10,500/126,000)

(xii) Accordingly, the reduction under paragraph (g)(3) of this section that applies to the amount of net negative consideration that may be taken into account by L2, L4, and L5 under paragraph (a)(1)(ii)(B) of this section is determined as follows:

L2 = $457,623 ($35,237/.077)
L4 = $114,403 ($8,809/.077)
L5 = $228,800 ($4,004/.0175)

Example (4). The facts are the same as Example 3, except that L1 and L4 make a joint election under paragraph (g)(8) of this section to capitalize specified policy acquisition expenses with respect to the reinsurance agreement without regard to the general deductions limitation. Pursuant to this election, L1 must reduce its deductions under section 805 by an amount equal to the capitalization shortfall allocable to the reinsurance agreement with L4 ($8,809). L1 treats the additional capitalized amounts as specified policy acquisition expenses allocable to premiums and other consideration under the agreement. L4 may reduce its net premiums by the $300,000 net negative consideration. The election by L1 and L4 does not change the amount of the capitalization shortfall allocable under paragraph (g)(7) of this section to the reinsurance agreements with L2 and L5. Thus, the reduction required by paragraph (g)(3) of this section with respect to the amount of the net negative consideration that L2 and L5 may recognize under paragraph (a)(2)(ii) of this section is $457,623 and $228,800, respectively.

(h) Treatment of reinsurance agreements with parties not subject to U.S. taxation. (1) In general. Unless an election under paragraph (h)(3) of this section is made, an insurance company may not reduce its net premiums by the net negative consideration for the taxable year (or, with respect to a reinsurance agreement that is subject to the interim rules of § 1.848-3, by the premiums and other consideration incurred for reinsurance) under a reinsurance agreement to which this paragraph (h) applies.

(2) Agreements to which this paragraph (h) applies. (i) In general. This paragraph (h) applies to a reinsurance agreement if, with respect to the premiums and other consideration under the agreement, one party to that agreement is subject to United States taxation and the other party is not.

(ii) Parties subject to U.S. taxation (A) In general. A party is subject to United States taxation for this purpose if the party is subject to United States taxation either directly under the provisions of subchapter L of chapter 1 of the Internal Revenue Code (subchapter L), or indirectly under the provisions of subpart F of Part III of subchapter N of chapter 1 of the Internal Revenue Code (subpart F).

(B) Effect of a closing agreement. If a reinsurer agrees in a closing agreement with the Internal Revenue Service to be subject to tax under rules equivalent to the provisions of subchapter L on its premiums and other consideration from reinsurance agreements with parties subject to United States taxation, the reinsurer is treated as an insurance company subject to tax under subchapter L.

(3) Election to separately determine the amounts required to be capitalized for reinsurance agreements with parties not subject to U.S. taxation. (i) In general. This paragraph (h)(3) authorizes an insurance company to make an election to separately determine the amounts required to be capitalized for the taxable year with respect to reinsurance agreements with parties that are not subject to United States taxation. If this election is made, an insurance company separately determines a net foreign capitalization amount for the taxable year for all reinsurance agreements to which this paragraph (h) applies.

(ii) Manner of making the election. An insurance company makes the election authorized by this paragraph (h)(3) by attaching an election statement to the federal income tax return (including an amended return) for the taxable year for which the election becomes effective. The election applies to that taxable year and all subsequent taxable years unless permission to revoke the election is obtained from the Commissioner.

(4) Amount taken into account for purposes of determining specified policy acquisition expenses. If for a taxable year an insurance company has a net positive foreign capitalization amount (as defined in paragraph (h)(5)(i) of this section), any portion of that amount remaining after the reduction described in paragraph (h)(7) of this section is treated as additional specified policy acquisition expenses for the taxable year (determined without regard to amounts taken into account under this paragraph (h)). A net positive capitalization amount is treated as an amount otherwise required to be capitalized for the taxable year for purposes of the reduction under section 848(f)(1)(A).

(5) Net foreign capitalization amount. (i) In general. An insurance company's net foreign capitalization amount equals the sum of the foreign capitalization amounts (netting positive and negative amounts) determined under paragraph (h)(5)(ii) of this section for each category of specified insurance contracts reinsured by agreements described in paragraph (h)(2) of this section. If the amount is less than zero, the company has a net negative foreign capitalization amount. If the amount is greater than zero, the company has a net positive foreign capitalization amount.

(ii) Foreign capitalization amounts by category. The foreign capitalization amount for a category of specified insurance contracts is determined by—

(A) Combining the net positive consideration and the net negative consideration for the taxable year (or, with respect to a reinsurance agreement that is subject to the interim rules of § 1.848-3, by combining the gross amount of premiums and other consideration and the premiums and other consideration incurred for reinsurance) for all agreements described in paragraph (h)(2) of this section which reinsure specified insurance contracts in that category; and

(B) Multiplying the result (either positive or negative) by the percentage for that category specified in section 848(c)(1).

(6) Treatment of net negative foreign capitalization amount. (i) Applied as a reduction to previously capitalized amounts. If for a taxable year an insurance company has a net negative foreign capitalization amount, the negative amount reduces (but not below zero) the unamortized balances of the amounts previously capitalized (beginning with the amount capitalized for the most recent taxable year) to the extent attributable to prior years' net positive foreign capitalization amounts. The amount by which previously capitalized amounts is reduced is allowed as a deduction for the taxable year.

(ii) Carryover of remaining net negative foreign capitalization amount. The net negative foreign capitalization amount, if any, remaining after the reduction described in paragraph (h)(6)(i) of this section is carried over to reduce a future net positive capitalization amount. The remaining net negative foreign capitalization amount may only offset a net positive foreign capitalization amount in a future year, and may not be used to reduce the amounts otherwise required to be capitalized under section 848(a) for the taxable year, or to reduce the unamortized balances of specified policy acquisition expenses from preceding taxable years, with respect to directly written business or reinsurance agreements other than agreements for which the election under paragraph (h)(3) of this section has been made.

(7) Reduction of net positive foreign capitalization amount by carryover amounts allowed. If for a taxable year an insurance company has a net positive foreign capitalization amount, that amount is reduced (but not below zero) by any carryover of net negative foreign capitalization amounts from preceding taxable years. Any remaining net positive foreign capitalization amount is taken into account as provided in paragraph (h)(4) of this section.

(8) Examples. The principles of this paragraph (h) are illustrated by the following examples.

Example (1). (i) On January 1, 1993, a life insurance company (L1) enters into a reinsurance agreement with a foreign corporation (X) covering a block of annuity contracts issued to residents of the United States. X is not subject to taxation either directly under subchapter L or indirectly under subpart F on the premiums for the reinsurance agreement with L1. L1 makes the election under paragraph (h)(3) of this section to separately determine the amounts required to be capitalized for the taxable year with respect to parties not subject to United States taxation.

(ii) For the taxable year ended December 31, 1993, L1 has net negative consideration of ($25,000) under its reinsurance agreement with X. L1 has no other reinsurance agreements with parties not subject to United States taxation.

(iii) Under paragraph (h)(5) of this section, L1's net negative foreign capitalization amount for the 1993 taxable year equals ($437.50), which is determined by multiplying L1's net negative consideration on the agreement with X ($25,000) by the percentage in section 848(c)(1) for the reinsured specified insurance contracts (1.75%) Under paragraph (h)(6)(ii) of this section, L1 carries over the net negative foreign capitalization amount of ($437.50) to future taxable years. The net negative foreign capitalization amount may not be used to reduce the amounts which L1 is required to capitalize on directly written business or reinsurance agreements other than those agreements described in paragraph (h)(2) of this section.

Example (2). (i) The facts are the same as Example 1 except that L1 terminates its reinsurance agreement with X and receives $35,000 on December 31, 1994. For the 1994 taxable year, L1 has net positive consideration of $35,000 under its agreement with X. L1 has no other reinsurance agreements with parties not subject to United States taxation.

(ii) Under paragraph (h)(5) of this section, L1's net positive net foreign capitalization amount for the 1984 taxable year equals $612.50, which is determined by multiplying the net positive consideration on the agreement with X ($35,000) by the percentage in section 848(c)(1) for the reinsured specified insurance contracts (1.75%). Under paragraph (h)(4) of this section, L1 reduces the net positive foreign capitalization amount for the taxable year by the net negative foreign capitalization amount carried over from preceding taxable years ($437.50). After this reduction, L1 includes $175 ($612.50 – $437.50) as specified policy acquisition expenses for the 1994 taxable year.

(i) Carryover of excess negative capitalization amount. *(1) In general.* This paragraph (i) authorizes a carryover of an excess negative capitalization amount (as defined in paragraph (i)(2) of this section) to reduce amounts otherwise required to be capitalized under section 848. Paragraph (i)(4) provides special rules for the treatment of excess negative capitalization amounts of insolvent insurance companies.

(2) Excess negative capitalization amount. The excess negative capitalization amount with respect to a category of specified insurance contracts for a taxable year is equal to the excess of—

(A) The negative capitalization amount with respect to that category; over

(B) The amount that can be utilized under section 848(f)(1).

(3) Treatment of excess negative capitalization amount. The excess negative capitalization amount for a taxable year reduces the amounts that are otherwise required to be capitalized by an insurance company under section 848(c)(1) for future years.

(4) Special rule for the treatment of an excess negative capitalization amount of an insolvent company. (i) When applicable. This paragraph (i)(4) applies only for the taxable year in which an insolvent insurance company has an excess negative capitalization amount and has net negative consideration under a reinsurance agreement. See paragraph (i)(4)(v) of this section for the definition of "insolvent."

(ii) Election to forego carryover of excess negative capitalization amount. At the joint election of the insolvent insurance company and the other party to the reinsurance agreement—

(A) The insolvent insurance company reduces the excess negative capitalization amount which would otherwise be carried over under paragraph (i)(1) of this section by the amount determined under paragraph (i)(4)(iii) of this section; and

(B) The other party reduces the amount of its specified policy acquisition expenses for the taxable year by the amount determined under paragraph (i)(4)(iii) of this section.

(iii) Amount of reduction to the excess negative capitalization amount and specified policy acquisition expenses. To determine the reduction to the carryover of an insolvent insurance company's excess negative capitalization amount and the specified policy acquisition expenses of the other party with respect to a reinsurance agreement—

(A) Multiply the net negative consideration for each reinsurance agreement of the insolvent insurer for which there is net negative consideration for the taxable year by the appropriate percentage specified in section 848(c)(1) for the category of specified insurance contracts reinsured by the agreement;

(B) Sum the results for each agreement;

(C) Calculate the ratio between the results in paragraphs (i)(4)(iii)(A) and (B) of this section for each agreement; and

(D) Multiply that result by the increase in the excess negative capitalization amount of the insolvent insurer for the taxable year.

(iv) Manner of making election. To make an election under paragraph (i)(4) of this section, each party to the reinsurance agreement must attach an election statement to its federal income tax return (including an amended return) for the taxable year for which the election is effective. The election statement must identify the reinsurance agreement for which the joint election under this paragraph (i)(4) has been made, state the amount of the reduction to the insolvent insurance company's excess negative capitalization amount that is attributable to the agreement, and be signed by both parties. An election under this paragraph (i)(4) is effective for the taxable year specified in the election statement, and may not be revoked without the consent of the Commissioner.

(v) Presumptions relating to the insolvency of an insurance company undergoing a court supervised rehabilitation or similar state proceeding. For purposes of this paragraph (i)(4), an insurance company which is undergoing a rehabilitation, conservatorship, or similar state proceeding shall be presumed to be insolvent if the state proceeding results in—

(A) An order of the state court finding that the fair market value of the insurance company's assets is less than its liabilities;

(B) The use of funds, guarantees, or reinsurance from a guaranty association;

(C) A reduction of the policyholders' available account balances; or

(D) A substantial limitation on access to funds (for example, a partial or total moratorium on policyholder withdrawals or surrenders that applies for a period of 5 years).

(vi) Example. The principles of this paragraph (i)(4) are illustrated by the following example.

Example. (i) An insurance company (L1) is the subject of a rehabilitation proceeding under the supervision of a state court. The state court has made a finding that the fair market value of L1's assets is less than its liabilities. On December 31, 1993, L1 transfers a block of individual life insurance contracts to an unrelated insurance company (L2) under an assumption reinsurance agreement whereby L2 becomes solely liable to the policyholders under the contracts reinsured. Under the agreement, L1 agrees to pay L2 $2,000,000 for assuming the life insurance contracts. This negative net consideration causes L1 to incur an excess negative capitalization amount of $138,600 for the 1993 taxable year. L1 has no other reinsurance agreements for the taxable year.

(ii) As part of the reinsurance agreement, L1 and L2 agree to make an election under paragraph (i)(4) of this section. Under the election, L1 agrees to forego the carryover of the $138,600 excess negative capitalization amount for future taxable years. L2 must include the $2,000,000 net positive consideration for the reinsurance agreement in its gross amount of premiums and other consideration. L2 reduces its specified policy acquisition expenses for the 1993 taxable year by $138,600.

(j) Ceding commissions with respect to reinsurance of contracts other than specified insurance contracts. A ceding commission incurred with respect to the reinsurance of an insurance contract that is not a specified insurance contract is not subject to the provisions of section 848(g).

(k) Effective dates. *(1) In general.* Unless otherwise specified in this paragraph, the rules of this section are effective for the taxable years of an insurance company beginning after November 14, 1991.

(2) Reduction in the amount of net negative consideration to ensure consistency of capitalization for reinsurance agreements. Section 1.848-2(g) (which provides for an adjustment to ensure consistency) is effective for—

(i) All amounts arising under any reinsurance agreement entered into after November 14, 1991; and

(ii) All amounts arising under any reinsurance agreement for taxable years beginning after December 31, 1991, without regard to the date on which the reinsurance agreement was entered into.

(3) Net consideration rules. Section 1.848-2(f) (which provides rules for determining the net consideration for a reinsurance agreement) applies to—

(i) Amounts arising in taxable years beginning after December 31, 1991, under a reinsurance agreement entered into after November 14, 1991; and

(ii) Amounts arising in taxable years beginning after December 31, 1994, under a reinsurance agreement entered into before November 15, 1991.

(4) Determination of the date on which a reinsurance agreement is entered into. A reinsurance agreement is considered entered into at the earlier of—

(i) The date of the reinsurance agreement; or

(ii) The date of a binding written agreement to enter into a reinsurance transaction if the written agreement evidences the parties' agreement on substantially all material items relating to the reinsurance transaction.

(5) Special rule for certain reinsurance agreements with parties not subject to U.S. taxation. The election and special rules in paragraph (h) of this section relating to the determination of amounts required to be capitalized on reinsurance agreements with parties not subject to United States taxation apply to taxable years ending on or after September 30, 1990.

(6) Carryover of excess negative capitalization amount. The provisions of paragraph (i) of this section, including the special rule for the treatment of excess negative capitalization amounts of insolvent insurance companies, are effective with respect to amounts arising in taxable years ending on or after September 30, 1990.

T.D. 8456, 12/28/92.

§ 1.848-3 Interim rules for certain reinsurance agreements.

Caution: The Treasury has not yet amended Reg § 1.848-3 to reflect changes made by P.L. 103-66.

(a) Scope and effective dates. The rules of this section apply in determining net premiums for a reinsurance agreement with respect to—

(1) Amounts arising in taxable years beginning before January 1, 1992, under a reinsurance agreement entered into after November 14, 1991; and

(2) Amounts arising in taxable years beginning before January 1, 1995, under a reinsurance agreement entered into before November 15, 1991.

(b) Interim rules. In determining a company's gross amount of premiums and other consideration under section 848(d)(1)(A) and premiums and other consideration incurred for reinsurance under section 848(d)(1)(B), the general rules of subchapter L of the Internal Revenue Code apply with the adjustments and special rules set forth in paragraph (c) of this section. Except as provided in paragraph (c)(5) of this section (which applies to modified coinsurance transactions), the gross amount of premiums and other consideration is determined without any reduction for ceding commissions, annual allowances, reimbursements of claims and benefits, or other amounts incurred by a reinsurer with respect to reinsured contracts.

(c) Adjustments and special rules. This paragraph sets forth certain adjustments and special rules that apply for reinsurance agreements in determining the gross amount of premiums and other consideration under section

848(d)(1)(A) and premiums and other consideration incurred for reinsurance under section 848(d)(1)(B).

(1) Assumption reinsurance. The ceding company must treat the gross amount of consideration incurred with respect to an assumption reinsurance agreement as premiums and other consideration incurred for reinsurance under section 848(d)(1)(B). The reinsurer must include the same amount in the gross amount of premiums and other consideration under section 848(d)(1)(A). For rules relating to the determination and treatment of ceding commissions, see paragraph (c)(3) of this section.

(2) Reimbursable dividends. The reinsurer must treat the amount of policyholder dividends reimbursable to the ceding company (other than under a modified coinsurance agreement covered by paragraph (c)(5) of this section) as a return premium under section 848(d)(1)(B). The ceding company must include the same amount in the gross amount of premiums and other consideration under section 848(d)(1)(A). The amount of any experience-related refund due the ceding company is treated as a policyholder dividend reimbursable to the ceding company.

(3) Ceding commissions. (i) In general. The reinsurer must treat ceding commissions as a general deduction. The ceding company must treat ceding commissions as non-premium related income under section 803(a)(3). The ceding company may not reduce its general deductions by the amount of the ceding commission.

(ii) Amount of ceding commission. For purposes of this section, the amount of a ceding commission equals the excess, if any, of—

(A) The increase in the reinsurer's tax reserves resulting from the reinsurance agreement (computed in accordance with section 807(d)); over

(B) The gross consideration incurred by the ceding company for the reinsurance agreement, less any amount incurred by the reinsurer as part of the reinsurance agreement.

(4) Termination payments. The reinsurer must treat the gross amount of premiums and other consideration payable as a termination payment to the ceding company (including the tax reserves on the reinsured contracts) as premiums and other consideration incurred for reinsurance under section 848(d)(1)(B). The ceding company must include the same amount in the gross amount of premiums and other consideration under section 848(d)(1)(A). This paragraph does not apply to modified coinsurance agreements.

(5) Modified coinsurance agreements. In the case of a modified coinsurance agreement, the parties must determine their net premiums on a net consideration basis as described in § 1.848-2(f)(5).

(d) Examples. The principles of this section are illustrated by the following examples.

Example (1). On July 1, 1991, an insurance company (L1) transfers a block of individual life insurance contracts to an unrelated insurance company (L2) under an arrangement whereby L2 becomes solely liable to the policyholder under the contracts reinsured. The tax reserves on the reinsured contracts are $100,000. Under the assumption reinsurance agreement, L1 pays L2 $83,000 for assuming the life insurance contracts. Under paragraph (c)(3) of this section, since the increase in L2's tax reserves ($100,000) exceeds the net consideration transferred by L1 ($83,000), the reinsurance agreement provides for a ceding commission. The ceding commission equals $17,000 ($100,000 - $83,000). Under paragraph (c)(3) of this section, L1 reduces its gross amount of premiums and other consideration for the 1991 taxable year under section 848(d)(1)(B) by the $100,000 premium incurred for reinsurance, and L2 includes the $100,000 premium for reinsurance in its gross amount of premiums and other consideration under section 848(d)(1)(A). L1 treats the $17,000 ceding commission as non-premium related income under section 803(a)(3).

Example (2). On July 1, 1991, a life insurance company (L1) transfers a block of individual life insurance contracts to an unrelated insurance company (L2) under an arrangement whereby L2 becomes solely liable to the policyholder under the contracts reinsured. The tax reserves on the reinsured contracts are $100,000. Under the assumption reinsurance agreement, L1 pays L2 $100,000 for assuming the contracts, and L2 pays L1 a $17,000 ceding commission. Under paragraph (c)(1) of this section, L1 reduces its gross amount of premiums and other consideration under section 848(d)(1)(B) by $100,000. L2 includes $100,000 in its gross amount of premiums and other consideration under section 848(d)(1)(A). Under paragraph (c)(3) of this section, since the increase in L2's tax reserves ($100,000) exceeds the net consideration transferred by L1, the reinsurance agreement provides for a ceding commission. The ceding commission equals $17,000 ($100,000 increase in L2's tax reserves less $83,000 net consideration transferred by L1). L1 treats the $17,000 ceding commission as non-premium related income under section 803(a)(3).

Example (3). On July 1, 1991, a life insurance company (L1) transfers a block of individual life insurance contracts to an unrelated insurance company (L2) under an arrangement whereby L2 becomes solely liable to the policyholder under the contracts reinsured. Under the assumption reinsurance agreement, L1 transfers assets of $105,000 to L2. The tax reserves on the reinsured contracts are $100,000. Under paragraph (c)(1) of this section, L1 reduces its gross amount of premiums and other consideration under section 848(d)(1)(B) by $105,000, and L2 increases its gross amount of premiums and other consideration under section 848(d)(1)(A) by $105,000. Since the net consideration transferred by L1 exceeds the increase in L2's tax reserves, there is no ceding commission under paragraph (c)(3) of this section.

Example (4). (i) On June 30, 1991, a life insurance company (L1) reinsures 40% of certain individual life insurance contracts to be issued after that date with an unrelated insurance company (L2) under an agreement whereby L1 remains directly liable to the policyholders with respect to the contracts reinsured. The agreement provides that L2 is credited with 40% of any premiums received with respect to the reinsured contracts, but must indemnify L1 for 40% of any claims, expenses, and policyholder dividends. During the period from July 1 through December 31, 1991, L1 has the following income and expense items with respect to the reinsured policies:

Item	Income	Expense
Premiums	$8,000	—
Benefits paid	—	$1,000
Commissions	—	6,000
Policyholder dividends	—	500
Total	—	7,500

(ii) Under paragraphs (b) and (c)(2) of this section, L1 includes $8,200 in its gross amount of premiums and other consideration under section 848(d)(1)(A) ($8,000 gross premiums on the reinsured contracts plus $200 of policyholder dividends reimbursed by L2 ($500 × 40%)). L1 reduces its gross amount of premiums and other consideration by $3,200 (40% × $8,000) as premiums and other consideration incurred for reinsurance under section 848(d)(1)(B). The benefits and commissions incurred by L1 with respect to the reinsured contracts do not reduce L1's gross amount of premiums and other consideration under section 848(d)(1)(B). L2 includes $3,200 in its gross amount of premiums and other consideration (40% × $8,000) and is treated as having paid return premiums of $200 (the amount of reimbursable dividends paid to L1). L2 is also treated as having incurred the following expenses with respect to the reinsured contracts: $400 as benefits paid (40% × $1,000) and $2,400 as commissions expense (40% × $6,000). Under paragraph (b) of this section, these expenses do not reduce L2's gross amount of premiums and other consideration under section 848(d)(1)(A).

Example (5). On December 31, 1991, an insurance company (L1) terminates a reinsurance agreement with an unrelated insurance company (L2). The termination applies to a reinsurance agreement under which L1 had ceded 40% of its liability on a block of individual life insurance contracts to L2. Upon termination of the reinsurance agreement, L2 makes a final payment of $116,000 to L1 for assuming full liability under the contracts. The tax reserves attributable to L2's portion of the reinsured contracts are $120,000. Under paragraph (c)(4) of this section, L2 reduces its gross amount of premiums and other consideration under section 848(d)(1)(B) by $120,000. L1 includes $120,000 in its gross amount of premiums and other consideration under section 848(d)(1)(A).

Example (6). (i) On June 30, 1991, an insurance company (L1) reinsures 40% of its existing life insurance contracts with an unrelated life insurance company (L2) under a modified coinsurance agreement. For the period July 1, 1991 through December 31, 1991, L1 reports the following income and expense items with respect to L2's 40% share of the reinsured contracts:

Item	Income	Expense
Premiums	$10,000	
Benefits paid	—	$4,000
Policyholder dividends	—	500
Reserve adjustment	—	1,500
Total	—	6,000

(ii) Pursuant to paragraph (c)(5) of this section, L1 reduces its gross amount of premiums and other consideration under section 848(d)(1)(B) by the $4,000 net consideration for the modified coinsurance agreement ($10,000 - $6,000). L2 includes the $4,000 net consideration in its gross amount of premiums and other consideration under section 848(d)(1)(A).

T.D. 8456, 12/28/92.

§ 1.851-1 Definition of regulated investment company.

Caution: The Treasury has not yet amended Reg § 1.851-1 to reflect changes made by P.L. 99-514, P.L. 95-345, P.L. 94-12, P.L. 91-172.

(a) In general. The term "regulated investment company" is defined to mean any domestic corporation (other than a personal holding company as defined in section 542) which meets (1) the requirements of section 851(a) and paragraph (b) of this section, and (2) the limitations of section 851(b) and § 1.851-2. As to the definition of the term "corporation" , see section 7701(a)(3).

(b) Requirement. To qualify as a regulated investment company, a corporation must be:

(1) Registered at all times during the taxable year, under the Investment Company Act of 1940, as amended (15 U.S.C. 80 a-1 to 80 b-2), either as a management company or a unit investment trust, or

(2) A common trust fund or similar fund excluded by section 3(c)(3) of the Investment Company Act of 1940 (15 U.S.C. 80a-3(c)) from the definition of "investment company" and not included in the definition of "common trust fund" by section 584(a).

T.D. 6236, 6/3/57.

§ 1.851-2 Limitations.

Caution: The Treasury has not yet amended Reg § 1.851-2 to reflect changes made by P.L. 108-357, P.L. 105-34, P.L. 99-514, P.L. 95-600.

(a) Election to be a regulated investment company. Under the provisions of section 851(b)(1), a corporation, even though it satisfies the other requirements of part I, subchapter M, chapter 1 of the Code, for the taxable year, will not be considered a regulated investment company for such year, within the meaning of such part I, unless it elects to be a regulated investment company for such taxable year, or has made such an election for a previous taxable year which began after December 31, 1941. The election shall be made by the taxpayer by computing taxable income as a regulated investment company in its return for the first taxable year for which the election is applicable. No other method of making such election is permitted. An election once made is irrevocable for such taxable year and all succeeding taxable years.

(b) Gross income requirement. *(1) General rule.* Section 851(b)(2) and (3) provides that (i) at least 90 percent of the corporation's gross income for the taxable year must be derived from dividends, interest, and gains from the sale or other disposition of stocks or securities, and (ii) less than 30 percent of its gross income must have been derived from the sale or other disposition of stock or securities held for less than three months. In determining the gross income requirements under section 851(b)(2) and (3), a loss from the sale or other disposition of stock or securities does not enter into the computation. A determination of the period for which stock or securities have been held shall be governed by the provisions of section 1223 insofar as applicable.

(2) Special rules. (i) For purposes of section 851(b)(2), there shall be treated as dividends amounts which are included in gross income for the taxable year under section 951(a)(1)(A)(i) to the extent that (a) a distribution out of a foreign corporation's earnings and profits of the taxable year is not included in gross income by reason of section 959(a)(1), and (b) the earnings and profits are attributable to the amounts which were so included in gross income under section 951(a)(1)(A)(i). For allocation of distributions to earnings and profits of foreign corporations, see § 1.959-3. The provisions of this subparagraph shall apply with respect to taxable years of controlled foreign corporations beginning after December 31, 1975, and to taxable years of United States shareholders (within the meaning of section 951(b) within which or with which such taxable years of such controlled foreign corporations end.

(ii) For purposes of subdivision (i) of this subparagraph, if by reason of section 959(a)(1) a distribution of a foreign corporation's earnings and profits for a taxable year described in section 959(c)(2) is not included in a shareholder's gross income, then such distribution shall be allocated proportionately between amounts attributable to amounts included under each clause of section 951(a)(1)(A). Thus, for example, M is a United States shareholder in X Corporation, a controlled foreign corporation. M and X each use the calendar year as the taxable year. For 1977, M is required by section 951(a)(1)(a) to include $3,000 in its gross income, $1,000 of which is included under clause (i) thereof. In 1977, M received a distribution described in section 959(c)(2) of $2,700 out of X's earnings and profits for 1977, which is, by reason of section 959(a)(1), excluded from M's gross income. The amount of the distribution attributable to the amount included under section 951(a)(1)(A)(i) is $900, i.e., $2,700 multiplied by ($1,000/$3,000).

(c) Diversification of investments. *(1)* Subparagraph (A) of section 851(b)(4) requires that at the close of each quarter of the taxable year at least 50 percent of the value of the total assets of the taxpayer corporation be represented by one or more of the following:

(i) Cash and cash items, including receivables;

(ii) Government securities;

(iii) Securities of other regulated investment companies; or

(iv) Securities (other than those described in subdivisions (ii) and (iii) of this subparagraph) of any one or more issuers which meet the following limitations: (a) The entire amount of the securities of the issuer owned by the taxpayer corporation is not greater in value than 5 percent of the value of the total assets of the taxpayer corporation, and (b) the entire amount of the securities of such issuer owned by the taxpayer corporation does not represent more than 10 percent of the outstanding voting securities of such issuer. For the modification of the percentage limitations applicable in the case of certain venture capital investment companies, see section 851(e) and § 1.851-6.

Assuming that at least 50 percent of the value of the total assets of the corporation satisfies the requirements specified in this subparagraph, and that the limiting provisions of subparagraph (B) of section 851(b)(4) and subparagraph (2) of this paragraph are not violated, the corporation will satisfy the requirements of section 851(b)(4), notwithstanding that the remaining assets do not satisfy the diversification requirements of subparagraph (A) of section 851(b)(4). For example, a corporation may own all the stock of another corporation, provided it otherwise meets the requirements of subparagraphs (A) and (B) of section 851(b)(4).

(2) Subparagraph (B) of section 851(b)(4) prohibits the investment at the close of each quarter of the taxable year of more than 25 percent of the value of the total assets of the corporation (including the 50 percent or more mentioned in subparagraph (A) of section 851(b)(4)) in the securities (other than Government securities or the securities of other regulated investment companies) of any one issuer, or of two or more issuers which the taxpayer company controls and which are engaged in the same or similar trades or businesses or related trades or businesses, including such issuers as are merely a part of a unit contributing to the completion and sale of a product or the rendering of a particular service. Two or more issuers are not considered as being in the same or similar trades or businesses merely because they are engaged in the broad field of manufacturing or of any other general classification of industry, but issuers shall be construed to be engaged in the same or similar trades or businesses if they are engaged in a distinct branch of business, trade, or manufacture in which they render the same kind of service or produce or deal in the same kind of product, and such service or products fulfill the same economic need. If two or more issuers produce more than one product or render more than one type of service, then the chief product or service of each shall be the basis for determining whether they are in the same trade or business.

T.D. 6236, 6/3/57, amend T.D. 6598, 4/25/62, T.D. 7555, 7/25/78.

§ 1.851-3 Rules applicable to section 851(b)(4).

Caution: The Treasury has not yet amended Reg § 1.851-3 to reflect changes made by P.L. 105-34, P.L. 94-12, P.L. 91-172.

In determining the value of the taxpayer's investment in the securities of any one issuer, for the purposes of subparagraph (B) of section 851(b)(4), there shall be included its proper proportion of the investment of any other corporation, a member of a controlled group, in the securities of such issuer. See example (4) in § 1.851-5. For purposes of §§ 1.851-2, 1.851-4, 1.851-5, and 1.851-6, the terms "controls", "controlled group" , and "value" have the meaning assigned to them by section 851(c). All other terms used in such sections have the same meaning as when used in the Investment Company Act of 1940 (15 U.S.C., ch. 2D) or that act as amended.

T.D. 6236, 6/3/57.

§ 1.851-4 Determination of status.

Caution: The Treasury has not yet amended Reg § 1.851-4 to reflect changes made by P.L. 105-34, P.L. 94-12, P.L. 91-172.

With respect to the effect which certain discrepancies between the value of its various investments and the requirements of section 851(b)(4) and paragraph (c) of § 1.851-2, or the effect that the elimination of such discrepancies will have on the status of a company as a regulated investment company for purposes of part I, subchapter M, chapter 1 of the Code, see section 851(d). A company claiming to be a regulated investment company shall keep sufficient records as to investments so as to be able to show that it has complied with the provisions of section 851 during the taxable year. Such records shall be kept at all times available for inspection by any internal revenue officer or employee and shall be retained so long as the contents thereof may become material in the administration of any internal revenue law.

T.D. 6236, 6/3/57, amend T.D. 6598, 4/25/62.

§ 1.851-5 Examples.

Caution: The Treasury has not yet amended Reg § 1.851-5 to reflect changes made by P.L. 108-357, P.L. 105-34.

The provisions of section 851 may be illustrated by the following examples:

Example (1). Investment Company W at the close of its first quarter of the taxable year has its assets invested as follows:

	Percent
Cash	5
Government securities	10
Securities of regulated investment companies	20
Securities of Corporation A	10
Securities of Corporation B	15
Securities of Corporation C	20

Securities of various corporations (not exceeding 5 percent of its assets in any one company)	20
Total	100

Investment Company W owns all of the voting stock of Corporations A and B, 15 percent of the voting stock of Corporation C, and less than 10 percent of the voting stock of the other corporations. None of the corporations is a member of a controlled group. Investment Company W meets the requirements under section 851(b)(4) at the end of its first quarter. It complies with subparagraph (A) of section 851(b)(4) since it has 55 percent of its assets invested as provided in such subparagraph. It complies with subparagraph (B) of section 851(b)(4) since it does not have more than 25 percent of its assets invested in the securities of any one issuer, or of two or more issuers which it controls.

Example (2). Investment Company V at the close of a particular quarter of the taxable year has its assets invested as follows:

	Percent
Cash	10
Government securities	35
Securities of Corporation A	7
Securities of Corporation B	12
Securities of Corporation C	15
Securities of Corporation D	21
Total	100

Investment Company V fails to meet the requirements of subparagraph (A) of section 851(b)(4) since its assets invested in Corporation A, B, C, and D exceed in each case 5 percent of the value of the total assets of the company at the close of the particular quarter.

Example (3). Investment Company X at the close of the particular quarter of the taxable year has its assets invested as follows:

	Percent
Cash and Government securities	20
Securities of Corporation A	5
Securities of Corporation B	10
Securities of Corporation C	25
Securities of various corporations (not exceeding 5 percent of its assets in any one company)	40
Total	100

Investment Company X owns more than 20 percent of the voting power of Corporations B and C and less than 10 percent of the voting power of all of the other corporations. Corporation B manufactures radios and Corporation C acts as its distributor and also distributes radios for other companies. Investment Company X fails to meet the requirements of subparagraph (B) of section 851(b)(4) since it has 35 percent of its assets invested in the securities of two issuers which it controls and which are engaged in related trades or businesses.

Example (4). Investment Company Y at the close of a particular quarter of the taxable year has its assets invested as follows:

	Percent
Cash and Government securities	15
Securities of Corporation K (a regulated investment company)	30
Securities of Corporation A	10
Securities of Corporation B	20
Securities of various corporations (not exceeding 5 percent of its assets in any one company)	25
Total	100

Corporation K has 20 percent of its assets invested in Corporation L and Corporation L has 40 percent of its assets invested in Corporation B. Corporation A also has 30 percent of its assets invested in Corporation B, and owns more than 20 percent of the voting power in Corporation B. Investment Company Y owns more than 20 percent of the voting power of Corporations A and K. Corporation K owns more than 20 percent of the voting power of Corporation L, and Corporation L owns more than 20 percent of the voting power of Corporation L. Investment Company Y is disqualified under subparagraph (B) of section 851(b)(4) since more than 25 percent of its assets are considered invested in Corporation B as shown by the following calculation:

Percentage of assets invested directly in Corporation B	20.0
Percentage invested through the controlled group, Y-K-L-B (40 percent of 20 percent of 30 percent)	2.4
Percentage invested in the controlled group, Y-A-B (30 percent of 10 percent)	3.0
Total percentage of assets of Investment Company Y invested in Corporation B	25.4

Example (5). Investment Company Z, which keeps its books and makes its returns on the basis of the calendar year, at the close of the first quarter of 1955 meets the requirements of section 851(b)(4) and has 20 percent of its assets invested in Corporation A. Later during the taxable year it makes distributions to its shareholders and because of such distributions it finds at the close of the taxable year that it has more than 25 percent of its remaining assets invested in Corporation A. Investment Company Z does not lose its status as a regulated investment company for the taxable year 1955 because of such distributions, nor will it lose its status as a regulated investment company for 1956 or any subsequent year solely as a result of such distributions.

Example (6). Investment Company Q, which keeps its books and makes its returns on the basis of a calendar year, at the close of the first quarter of 1955, meets the requirements of section 851(b)(4) and has 20 percent of its assets invested in Corporation P. At the close of the taxable year 1955, it finds that it has more than 25 percent of its assets invested in Corporation P. This situation results entirely from fluctuations in the market values of the securities in Investment Company Q's portfolio and is not due in whole or in part to the acquisition of any security or other property. Corporation Q does not lose its status as a regulated investment company for the taxable year 1955 because of such fluctuations in the market values of the securities in its portfolio, nor will it lose its status as a regulated investment company for 1956 or any subsequent year solely as a result of such market value fluctuations.

T.D. 6236, 6/3/57.

§ 1.851-6 Investment companies furnishing capital to development corporations.

Caution: The Treasury has not yet amended Reg § 1.851-6 to reflect changes made by P.L. 105-34.

(a) Qualifying requirements. *(1)* In the case of a regulated investment company which furnishes capital to development corporations, section 851(e) provides an exception to the rule relating to the diversification of investments, made applicable to regulated investment companies by section 851(b)(4)(A). This exception (as provided in paragraph (b) of this section) is available only to registered management investment companies which the Securities and Exchange Commission determines, in accordance with regulations issued by it, and certifies to the Secretary or his delegate, not earlier than 60 days before the close of the taxable year of such investment company, to be principally engaged in the furnishing of capital to other corporations which are principally engaged in the development or exploitation of inventions, technological improvements, new processes, or products not previously generally available.

(2) For the purpose of the aforementioned determination and certification, unless the Securities and Exchange Commission determines otherwise, a corporation shall be considered to be principally engaged in the development or exploitation of inventions, technological improvements, new processes, or products not previously generally available, for at least 10 years after the date of the first acquisition of any security in such corporation or any predecessor thereof by such investment company if at the date of such acquisition the corporation or its predecessor was principally so engaged, and an investment company shall be considered at any date to be furnishing capital to any company whose securities it holds if within 10 years before such date it had acquired any of such securities, or any securities surrendered in exchange therefor, from such other company or its predecessor.

(b) Exception to general rule. *(1)* The registered management investment company, which for the taxable year meets the requirements of paragraph (a) of this section, may (subject to the limitations of section 851(e)(2) and paragraph (c) of this section) in the computation of 50 percent of the value of its assets under section 851(b)(4)(A) and paragraph (c)(1) of § 1.851-2 for any quarter of such taxable year, include the value of any securities of an issuer (whether or not the investment company owns more than 10 percent of the outstanding voting securities of such issuer) if at the time of the latest acquisition of any securities of such issuer the basis of all such securities in the hands of the investment company does not exceed 5 percent of the value of the total assets of the investment company at that time. The exception provided by section 851(e)(1) and this subparagraph is not applicable to the securities of an issuer if the investment company has continuously held any security of such issuer or of any predecessor company (as defined in paragraph (d) of this section) for 10 or more years preceding such quarter of the taxable year. The rule of section 851(e)(1) with respect to the relationship of the basis of the securities of an issuer to the value of the total assets of the investment company is, in substance, a qualification of the 5-percent limitation in section 851(b)(4)(A)(ii) and paragraph (c)(1)(iv) of § 1.851-2. All other provisions and requirements of section 851 and §§ 1.851-1 through 1.851-6 are applicable in determining whether such registered management investment company qualifies as a regulated investment company.

(2) The application of subparagraph (1) of this paragraph may be illustrated by the following examples:

Example (1). (i) The XYZ Corporation, a regulated investment company, qualified under section 851(e) as an investment company furnishing capital to development corporations. On June 30, 1954, the XYZ Corporation purchased 1,000 shares of the stock of the A Corporation at a cost of $30,000. On June 30, 1954, the value of the total assets of the XYZ Corporation was $1,000,000. Its investment in the stock of the A Corporation ($30,000) comprised 3 percent of the value of its total assets, and it therefore met the requirements prescribed by section 851(b)(4)(A)(ii) as modified by section 851(e)(1).

(ii) On June 30, 1955, the value of the total assets of the XYZ Corporation was $1,500,000 and the 1,000 shares of stock of the A Corporation which the XYZ Corporation owned appreciated in value so that they were then worth $60,000. On that date, the XYZ Investment Company increased its investment in the stock of the A Corporation by the purchase of an additional 500 shares of that stock at a total cost of $30,000. The securities of the A Corporation owned by the XYZ Corporation had a value of $90,000 (6 percent of the value of the total assets of the XYZ Corporation) which exceeded the limit provided by section 851(b)(4)(A)(ii). However, the investment of the XYZ Corporation in the A Corporation on June 30, 1955, qualified under section 851(b)(4)(A) as modified by section 851(e)(1), since the basis of those securities to the investment company did not exceed 5 percent of the value of its total assets as of June 30, 1955, illustrated as follows:

Basis to the XYZ Corporation of the A Corporation's stock acquired on June 30, 1954	$30,000
Basis of the 500 shares of the A Corporation's stock acquired by the XYZ Corporation on June 30, 1955	30,000
Basis of all stock of A Corporation	60,000

$$\frac{\text{Basis of stock of a Corporation}}{\text{Value of XYZ Corporation's total assets at June 30, 1955, time of the latest acquisition}} = \frac{\$\ 60{,}000}{\$\ 1{,}500{,}000} = 4 \text{ percent}$$

Example (2). The same facts existed as in example (1), except that on June 30, 1955, the XYZ Corporation increased its investment in the stock of the A Corporation by the purchase of an additional 1,000 shares of that stock (instead of 500 shares) at a total cost of $60,000. No part of the investment of the XYZ Corporation in the A Corporation qualified under the 5 percent limitation provided by section 851(b)(4)(A) as modified by section 851(e)(1), illustrated as follows:

Basis to the XYZ Corporation of the 1,000 shares of the A Corporation's stock acquired on June 30, 1954	$30,000
Basis of the 1,000 shares of the A Corporation's stock acquired on June 30, 1955	60,000
Total	90,000

$$\frac{\text{Basis of stock of a Corporation}}{\text{Value of XYZ Corporation's total assets at June 30, 1955, time of the latest acquisition}} = \frac{\$\ 90{,}000}{\$\ 1{,}500{,}000} = 6 \text{ percent}$$

Example (3). The same facts existed as in example (2) and on June 30, 1956, the XYZ Corporation increased its investment in the stock of the A Corporation by the purchase of an additional 100 shares of that stock at a total cost of $6,000. On June 30, 1956, the value of the total assets of the XYZ Corporation. was $2,000,000 and on that date the investment in the A Corporation qualified under section 851(b)(4)(A) as modified by section 851(e)(1) illustrated as follows:

Basis to the XYZ Corporation of investments in the A Corporation's stock:	
1,000 shares acquired June 30, 1954	$30,000
1,000 shares acquired June 30, 1955	60,000
100 shares acquired June 30, 1956	6,000
Total	96,000

$$\frac{\text{Basis of stock of a Corporation}}{\text{Value of XYZ Corporation's total assets at June 30, 1956, time of the latest acquisition}} = \frac{\$\ 96{,}000}{\$\ 2{,}000{,}000} = 4.8 \text{ percent}$$

(c) Limitation. Section 851(e) and this section do not apply in the quarterly computation of 50 percent of the value of the assets of an investment company under subparagraph (A) of section 851(b)(4) and paragraph (c)(1) of § 1.851-2 for any taxable year if at the close of any quarter of such taxable year more than 25 percent of the value of its total assets (including the 50 percent or more mentioned in such subparagraph (A)) is represented by securities (other than Government securities or the securities of other regulated investment companies) of issuers as to each of which such investment company (1) holds more than 10 percent of the outstanding voting securities of such issuer, and (2) has continuously held any security of such issuer (or any security of a predecessor of such issuer) for 10 or more years preceding such quarter, unless the value of its total assets so represented is reduced to 25 percent or less within 30 days after the close of such quarter.

(d) Definition of predecessor company. As used in section 851(e) and this section, the term "predecessor company" means any corporation the basis of whose securities in the hands of the investment company was, under the provisions of section 358 or corresponding provisions of prior law, the same in whole or in part as the basis of any of the securities of the issuer and any corporation with respect to whose securities any of the securities of the issuer were received directly or indirectly by the investment company in a transaction or series of transactions involving nonrecognition of gain or loss in whole or in part. The other terms used in this section have the same meaning as when used in section 851(b)(4). See paragraph (c) of § 1.851-2 and § 1.851-3.

T.D. 6236, 6/3/57, amend T.D. 6369, 3/16/59.

§ 1.851-7 Certain unit investment trusts.

(a) In general. For purposes of the Internal Revenue Code, a unit investment trust (as defined in paragraph (d) of this section) shall not be treated as a person (as defined in section 7701(a)(1)) except for years ending before January 1, 1969. A holder of an interest in such a trust will be treated as directly owning the assets of such trust for taxable years of such holder which end with or within any year of the trust to which section 851(f) and this section apply.

(b) Treatment of unit investment trust. A unit investment trust shall not be treated as an individual, a trust, estate, partnership, association, company, or corporation for purposes of the Internal Revenue Code. Accordingly, a unit investment trust is not a taxpayer subject to taxation under the Internal Revenue Code. No gain or loss will be recognized by the unit investment trust if such trust distributes a holder's proportionate share of the trust assets in exchange for his interest in the trust. Also, no gain or loss will be recognized by the unit investment trust if such trust sells the holder's proportionate share of the trust assets and distributes the proceeds from such share to the holder in exchange for his interest in the trust.

(c) Treatment of holder of interest in unit investment trust. *(1)* Each holder of an interest in a unit investment trust shall be treated (to the extent of such interest) as owning a proportionate share of the assets of the trust. Accordingly, if the trust distributes to the holder of an interest in such trust his proportionate share of the trust assets in exchange for his interest in the trust, no gain or loss shall be recognized by such holder (or by any other holder of an interest in such trust). For purposes of this paragraph, each purchase of an interest in the trust by the holder will be considered a separate interest in the trust. Items of income, gain, loss, deduction, or credit received by the trust or a custodian thereof shall be taxed to the holders of interests in the trust (and not to the trust) as though they had received their proportionate share of the items directly on the date such items were received by the trust or custodian.

(2) The basis of the assets of such trust which are treated under subparagraph (1) of this paragraph as being owned by the holder of an interest in such trust shall be the same as the basis of his interest in such trust. Accordingly, the amount of the gain or loss recognized by the holder upon the sale by the unit investment trust of the holder's pro rata share of the trust assets shall be determined with reference to the basis, of his interest in the trust. Also, the basis of the assets received by the holder, if the trust distributes a holder's pro rata share of the trust assets in exchange for his

interest in the trust, will be the same as the basis of his interest in the trust. If the unit investment trust sells less than all of the holder's pro rata share of the trust assets and the holder retains an interest in the trust, the amount of the gain or loss recognized by the holder upon the sale shall be determined with reference to the basis of his interest in the assets sold by the trust, and the basis of his interest in the trust shall be reduced accordingly. If the trust distributes a portion of the holder's pro rata share of the trust assets in exchange for a portion of his interest in the trust, the basis of the assets received by the holder shall be determined with reference to the basis of his interest in the assets distributed by the trust, and the basis of his interest in the trust shall be reduced accordingly.

(3) The period for which the holder of an interest in such trust has held the assets of the trust which are treated under subparagraph (1) of this paragraph as being owned by him is the same as the period for which such holder has held his interest in such trust. Accordingly, the character of the gain, loss, deduction, or credit recognized by the holder upon the sale by the unit investment trust of the holder's proportionate share of the trust assets shall be determined with reference to the period for which he has held his interest in the trust. Also, the holding period of the assets received by the holder if the trust distributes the holder's proportionate share of the trust assets in exchange for his interest in the trust will include the period for which the holder has held his interest in the trust.

(4) The application of the provisions of this paragraph may be illustrated by the following example:

Example. B entered a periodic payment plan of a unit investment trust (as defined in paragraph (d) of this section) with X Bank as custodian and Z as plan sponsor. Under this plan, upon B's demand, X must either redeem B's interest at a price substantially equal to the fair market value of the number of shares in Y, a management company, which are credited to B's account by X in connection with the unit investment trust, or at B's option distribute such shares of Y to B. B's plan provides for quarterly payments of $1,000. On October 1, 1969, B made his initial quarterly payment of $1,000 and X credited B's account with 110 shares of Y. On December 1, 1969, Y declared and paid a dividend of 25 cents per share, 5 cents of which was designated as a capital gain dividend pursuant to section 852(b)(3) and § 1.852-4. X credited B's account with $27.50 but did not distribute the money to B in 1969. On December 31, 1969, X charged B's account with $1 for custodial fees for calendar year 1969. On January 1, 1970, B paid X $1,000 and X credited B's account with 105 shares of Y. On April 1, 1970, B paid X $1,000 and X credited B's account with 100 shares of Y. B must include in his tax return for 1969 a dividend of $22 and a long-term capital gain of $5.50. In addition, B is entitled to deduct the annual custodial fee of $1 under section 212 of the Code.

(a) On April 4, 1970, at B's request, X sells the shares of Y credited to B's account (315 shares) for $10 per share and distributes the proceeds ($3,150) to B together with the remaining balance of $26.50 in B's account. The receipt of the $26.50 does not result in any tax consequences to B. B recognizes a long-term capital gain of $100 and a short-term capital gain of $50, computed as follows:

(1) B is treated as owning 110 shares of Y as of October 1, 1969. The basis of these shares is $1,000, and they were sold for $1,100 (110 shares at $10 per share). Therefore, B recognizes a gain from the sale or exchange of a capital asset held for more than 6 months in the amount of $100.

(2) B is treated as owning 105 shares of Y as of January 1, 1970, and 100 shares as of April 1, 1970. With respect to the shares acquired on April 1, 1970, there is no gain recognized as the shares were sold for $1,000, which is B's basis of the shares. The shares acquired on January 1, 1970, were sold for $1,050 (105 shares at $10 per share), and B's basis of these shares is $1,000. Therefore, B recognizes a gain of $50 from the sale or exchange of a capital asset held for not more than 6 months.

(b) On April 4, 1970, at B's request, X distributes to B the shares of Y credited to his account and $26.50 in cash. The receipt of the $26.50 does not result in any tax consequences to B. B does not recognize gain or loss on the distribution of the shares of Y to him. The bases and holding periods of B's interests in Y are as follows:

Number of shares	Date acquired	Basis
110	10-1-69	$ 9.09
105	1-1-70	9.52
100	4-1-70	10.00

(d) Definition. A unit investment trust to which this section refers is a business arrangement (other than a segregated asset account, whether or not it holds assets pursuant to a variable annuity contract, under the insurance laws or regulations of a State) which (except for taxable years ending before Jan. 1, 1969)—

(1) Is a unit investment trust (as defined in the Investment Company Act of 1940);

(2) Is registered under such Act;

(3) Issues periodic payment plan certificates (as defined in such Act) in one or more series;

(4) Possesses, as substantially all of its assets, as to all such series, securities issued by—

(i) A single management company (as defined in such Act), and securities acquired pursuant to subparagraph (5) of this paragraph, or

(ii) A single other corporation; and

(5) Has no power to invest in any other securities except securities issued by a single other management company, when permitted by such Act or the rules and regulations of the Securities and Exchange Commission.

(e) Investment in two single management companies. *(1)* A unit investment trust may possess securities issued by two or more separate single management companies (as defined in such Act) if—

(i) The trust issues a separate series of periodic payment plan certificates (as defined in such Act) with respect to the securities of each separate single management company which it possesses; and

(ii) None of the periodic payment plan certificates issued by the trust permits joint acquisition of an interest in each series nor the application of payments in whole or in part first to a series issued by one of the single management companies and then to any other series issued by any other single management company.

(2) If a unit investment trust possesses securities of two or more separate single management companies as described in subparagraph (1) of this paragraph and issues a separate series of periodic payment plan certificates with respect to the securities of each such management company, then the holder of an interest in a series shall be treated as the owner

of the securities in the single management company represented by such interest.

(i) A holder of an interest in a series of periodic payment plan certificates of a trust who transfers or sells his interest in the series in exchange for an interest in another series of periodic payment plan certificates of the trust shall recognize the gain or loss realized from the transfer or sale as if the trust had sold the shares credited to his interests in the series at fair market value and distributed the proceeds of the sale to him.

(ii) The basis of the interests in the series so acquired by the holder shall be the fair market value of his interests in the series transferred or sold.

(iii) The period for which the holder has held his interest in the series so acquired shall be measured from the date of his acquisition of his interest in that series.

(f) Cross references. *(1)* For reporting requirements imposed on custodians of unit investment trusts described in this section, see §§ 1.852-4, 1.852-9, 1.853-3, 1.854-2, and 1.6042-2.

(2) For rules relating to redemptions of certain unit investment trusts not described in this section, see § 1.852-10.

T.D. 7187, 7/5/72.

§ 1.852-1 Taxation of regulated investment companies.

Caution: The Treasury has not yet amended Reg § 1.852-1 to reflect changes made by P.L. 99-514.

(a) Requirements applicable thereto. *(1) In general.* Section 852(a) denies the application of the provisions of part I, subchapter M, chapter 1 of the Code (other than section 852(c), relating to earnings and profits), to a regulated investment company for a taxable year beginning after February 28, 1958, unless—

(i) The deduction for dividends paid for such taxable year as defined in section 561 (computed without regard to capital gain dividends) is equal to at least 90 percent of its investment company taxable income for such taxable year (determined without regard to the provisions of section 852(b)(2)(D) and paragraph (d) of § 1.852-3); and

(ii) The company complies for such taxable year with the provisions of § 1.852-6 (relating to records required to be maintained by a regulated investment company).

See section 853(b)(1)(B) and paragraph (a) of § 1.853-2 for amounts to be added to the dividends paid deduction, and section 855 and § 1.855-1, relating to dividends paid after the close of the taxable year.

(2) Special rule for taxable years of regulated investment companies beginning before March 1, 1958. The provisions of part I of subchapter M (including section 852(c) are not applicable to a regulated investment company for a taxable year beginning before March 1, 1958, unless such company meets the requirements of section 852(a) and subparagraph (1)(i) and (ii) of this paragraph.

(b) Failure to qualify. If a regulated investment company does not meet the requirements of section 852(a) and paragraph (a)(1)(i) and (ii) of this section for the taxable year, it will, even though it may otherwise be classified as a regulated investment company, be taxed in such year as an ordinary corporation and not as a regulated investment company. In such case, none of the provisions of part I of subchapter M (other than section 852(c) in the case of taxable years beginning after February 28, 1958) will be applicable to it. For the rules relating to the applicability of section 852(c), see § 1.852-5.

T.D. 6236, 6/3/57, amend T.D. 6369, 3/16/59, T.D. 6598, 4/25/62.

§ 1.852-2 Method of taxation of regulated investment companies.

Caution: The Treasury has not yet amended Reg § 1.852-2 to reflect changes made by P.L. 99-514, P.L. 95-600.

(a) Imposition of normal tax and surtax. Section 852(b)(1) imposes a normal tax and surtax, computed at the rates and in the manner prescribed in section 11, on the investment company taxable income, as defined in section 852(b)(2) and § 1.852-3, for each taxable year of a regulated investment company. The tax is imposed as if the investment company taxable income were the taxable income referred to in section 11. In computing the normal tax under section 11, the regulated investment company's taxable income and the dividends paid deduction (computed without regard to the capital gains dividends) shall both be reduced by the deduction for partially tax-exempt interest provided by section 242.

(b) Taxation of capital gains. *(1) In general.* Section 852(b)(3)(A) imposes (i) in the case of a taxable year beginning before January 1, 1970, a tax of 25 percent, or (ii) in the case of a taxable year beginning after December 31, 1969, a tax determined as provided in section 1201(a) and paragraph (a)(3) of § 1.1201-1, on the excess, if any, of the net long-term capital gain of a regulated investment company (subject to tax under part I, subchapter M, chapter 1 of the Code) over the sum of its net short-term capital loss and its deduction for dividends paid (as defined in section 561) determined with reference to capital gain dividends only. For the definition of capital gain dividend paid by a regulated investment company, see section 852(b)(3)(C) and paragraph (c) of § 1.852-4. In the case of a taxable year ending after December 31, 1969, and beginning before January 1, 1975, such deduction for dividends paid shall first be made from the amount subject to tax in accordance with section 1201(a)(1)(B), to the extent thereof, and then from the amount subject to tax in accordance with section 1201(a)(1)(A). See § 1.852-10, relating to certain distributions in redemption of interests in unit investment trusts which, for purposes of the deduction for dividends paid with reference to capital gain dividends only, are not considered preferential dividends under section 562(c). See section 855 and § 1.855-1, relating to dividends paid after the close of the taxable year.

(2) Undistributed capital gains. (i) In general. A regulated investment company (subject to tax under part I of subchapter M) may, for taxable years beginning after December 31, 1956, designate under section 852(b)(3)(D) an amount of undistributed capital gains to each shareholder of the company. For the definition of the term "undistributed capital gains" and for the treatment of such amounts by a shareholder, see paragraph (b)(2) of § 1.852-4. For the rules relating to the method of making such designation, the returns to be filed, and the payment of the tax in such cases, see paragraph (a) of § 1.852-9.

(ii) Effect on earnings and profits of a regulated investment company. If a regulated investment company designates an amount as undistributed capital gains for a taxable year, the earnings and profits of such regulated investment company for such taxable year shall be reduced by the total amount of the undistributed capital gains so designated. In such case, its capital account shall be increased—

(a) In the case of a taxable year ending before January 1, 1970, by 75 percent of the total amount designated,

(b) In the case of a taxable year ending after December 31, 1969, and beginning before January 1, 1975, by the total amount designated decreased by the amount of tax imposed by section 852(b)(3)(A) with respect to such amount, or

(c) In the case of a taxable year beginning after December 31, 1974, by 70 percent of the total amount designated. The earnings and profits of a regulated investment company shall not be reduced by the amount of tax which is imposed by section 852(b)(3)(A) on an amount designated as undistributed capital gains and which is paid by the corporation but deemed paid by the shareholder.

T.D. 6236, 6/3/57, amend T.D. 6369, 3/16/59, T.D. 6598, 4/25/62, T.D. 6921, 6/19/67, T.D. 7337, 12/26/74.

§ 1.852-3 Investment company taxable income.

Section 852(b)(2) requires certain adjustments to be made to convert taxable income of the investment company to investment company taxable income, as follows:

(a) The excess, if any, of the net long-term capital gain over the net short-term capital loss shall be excluded;

(b) The net operating loss deduction provided in section 172 shall not be allowed;

(c) The special deductions provided in part VIII (section 241 and following, except section 248), subchapter B, chapter 1 of the Code, shall not be allowed. Those not allowed are the deduction for partially tax-exempt interest provided by section 242, the deductions for dividends received provided by sections 243, 244, and 245, and the deduction for certain dividends paid provided by section 247. However, the deduction provided by section 248 (relating to organizational expenditures), otherwise allowable in computing taxable income, shall likewise be allowed in computing the investment company taxable income. See section 852(b)(1) and paragraph (a) of § 1.852-2 for treatment of the deduction for partially tax-exempt interest (provided by section 242) for purposes of computing the normal tax under section 11;

(d) The deduction for dividends paid (as defined in section 561) shall be allowed, but shall be computed without regard to capital gains dividends (as defined in section 852(b)(3)(C) and paragraph (c) of § 1.852-4; and

(e) The taxable income shall be computed without regard to section 443(b). Thus, the taxable income for a period of less than 12 months shall not be placed on an annual basis even though such short taxable year results from a change of accounting period.

T.D. 6236, 6/3/57, amend T.D. 6369, 3/16/59.

§ 1.852-4 Method of taxation of shareholders of regulated investment companies.

Caution: The Treasury has not yet amended Reg § 1.852-4 to reflect changes made by P.L. 110-172, P.L. 109-222, P.L. 103-66 P.L. 99-514, P.L. 98-369.

(a) Ordinary income. *(1)* Except as otherwise provided in paragraph (b) of this section (relating to capital gains), a shareholder receiving dividends from a regulated investment company shall include such dividends in gross income for the taxable year in which they are received.

(2) See section 853(b)(2) and (c) and paragraph (b) of § 1.853-2 and § 1.853-3 for the treatment by shareholders of dividends received from a regulated investment company which has made an election under section 853(a) with respect to the foreign tax credit. See section 854 and §§ 1.854-1 through 1.854-3 for limitations applicable to dividends received from regulated investment companies for the purpose of the credit under section 34 (for dividends received on or before December 31, 1964), the exclusion from gross income under section 116, and the deduction under section 243. See section 855(b) and (d) and paragraphs (c) and (f) of § 1.855-1 for treatment by shareholders of dividends paid by a regulated investment company after the close of the taxable year in the case of an election under section 855(a).

(b) Capital gains. *(1) In general.* Under section 852(b)(3)(B), shareholders of a regulated investment company who receive capital gain dividends (as defined in paragraph (c) of this section), in respect of the capital gains of an investment company for a taxable year for which it is taxable under part I, subchapter M, chapter 1 of the Code, as a regulated investment company, shall treat such capital gain dividends as gains from the sale or exchange of capital assets held for more than 1 year (6 months for taxable years beginning before 1977; 9 months for taxable years beginning in 1977) and realized in the taxable year of the shareholder in which the dividend was received. In the case of dividends with respect to any taxable year of a regulated investment company ending after December 31, 1969, and beginning before January 1, 1975, the portion of a shareholder's capital gain dividend to which section 1201(d)(1) or (2) applies is the portion so designated by the regulated investment company pursuant to paragraph (c)(2) of this section.

(2) Undistributed capital gains. (i) A person who is a shareholder of a regulated investment company at the close of a taxable year of such company for which it is taxable under part I of subchapter M shall include in his gross income as a gain from the sale or exchange of a capital asset held for more than 1 year (6 months for taxable years beginning before 1977; 9 months for taxable years beginning in 1977) any amount of undistributed capital gains. The term "undistributed capital gains" means the amount designated as undistributed capital gains in accordance with paragraph (a) of § 1.852-9, but the amount so designated shall not exceed the shareholder's proportionate part of the amount subject to tax under section 852(b)(3)(A). Such amount shall be included in gross income for the taxable year of the shareholder in which falls the last day of the taxable year of the regulated investment company in respect of which the undistributed capital gains were designated. The amount of such gains designated under paragraph (a) of § 1.852-9 as gain described in section 1201(d)(1) or (2) shall be included in the shareholder's gross income as gain described in section 1201(d)(1) or (2). For certain administrative provisions relating to undistributed capital gains, see § 1.852-9.

(ii) Any shareholder required to include an amount of undistributed capital gains in gross income under section 852(b)(3)(D)(i) and subdivision (i) of this subparagraph shall be deemed to have paid for his taxable year for which such amount is so includible—

(a) In the case of an amount designated with respect to a taxable year of the company ending before January 1, 1970, a tax equal to 25 percent of such amount.

(b) In the case of a taxable year of the company ending after December 31, 1969, and beginning before January 1, 1975, a tax equal to the tax designated under paragraph (a)(1) of § 1.852-9 by the regulated investment company as his proportionate share of the capital gains tax paid with respect to such amount, or

(c) In the case of an amount designated with respect to a taxable year of the company beginning after December 31, 1974, a tax equal to 30 percent of such amount. Such shareholder is entitled to a credit or refund of the tax so deemed paid in accordance with the rules provided in paragraph (c)(2) of § 1.852-9.

(iii) Any shareholder required to include an amount of undistributed capital gains in gross income under section 852(b)(3)(D)(i) and subdivision (i) of this subparagraph shall increase the adjusted basis of the shares of stock with respect to which such amount is so includible—

(a) In the case of an amount designated with respect to a taxable year of the company ending before January 1, 1970, by 75 percent of such amount.

(b) In the case of an amount designated with respect to a taxable year of the company ending after December 31, 1969, and beginning before January 1, 1975, by the amount designated under paragraph (a)(1)(iv) of § 1.852-9 by the regulated investment company, or

(c) In the case of an amount designated with respect to a taxable year of the company beginning after December 31, 1974, by 70 percent of such amount.

(iv) For purposes of determining whether the purchaser or seller of a share or regulated investment company stock is the shareholder at the close of such company's taxable year who is required to include an amount of undistributed capital gains in gross income, the amount of the undistributed capital gains shall be treated in the same manner as a cash dividend payable to shareholders of record at the close of the company's taxable year. Thus, if a cash dividend paid to shareholders of record as of the close of the regulated investment company's taxable year would be considered income to the purchaser, then the purchaser is also considered to be the shareholder of such company at the close of its taxable year for purposes of including an amount of undistributed capital gains in gross income. If, in such a case, notice on Form 2439 is, pursuant to paragraph (a)(1) of § 1.852-9, mailed by the regulated investment company to the seller, then the seller shall be considered the nominee of the purchaser and, as such, shall be subject to the provisions in paragraph (b) of § 1.852-9. For rules for determining whether a dividend is income to the purchaser or seller of a share of stock, see paragraph (c) of § 1.61-9.

(3) Partners and partnerships. If the shareholder required to include an amount of undistributed capital gains in gross income under section 852(b)(3)(D) and subparagraph (2) of this paragraph is a partnership, such amount shall be included in the gross income of the partnership for the taxable year of the partnership in which falls the last day of the taxable year of the regulated investment company in respect of which the undistributed capital gains were designated. The amount so includible by the partnership shall be taken into account by the partners as distributive shares of the partnership gains and losses from sales or exchanges of capital assets held for more than 1 year (6 months for taxable years beginning before 1977; 9 months for taxable years beginning in 1977) pursuant to section 702(a)(2) and paragraph (a)(2) of § 1.702-1. The tax with respect to the undistributed capital gains is deemed paid by the partnership (under section 852(b)(3)(D)(ii) and subparagraph (2)(ii) of this paragraph), and the credit or refund of such tax shall be taken into account by the partners in accordance with section 702(a)(8) and paragraph (a)(8)(ii) of § 1.702-1 and paragraph (c)(2) of § 1.852-9. In accordance with section 705(a), the partners shall increase the basis of their partnership interests under section 705(a)(1) by the distributive shares of such gains, and shall decrease the basis of their partnership interests by the distributive shares of the amount of the tax under section 705(a)(2)(B) (relating to certain nondeductible expenditures) and paragraph (a)(3) of § 1.705-1.

(4) Nonresident alien individuals. If the shareholder required to include an amount of undistributed capital gains in gross income under section 852(b)(3)(D) and subparagraph (2) of this paragraph is a nonresident alien individual, such shareholder shall be treated, for purposes of section 871 and the regulations thereunder, as having realized a long-term capital gain in such amount on the last day of the taxable year of the regulated investment company in respect of which the undistributed capital gains were designated.

(5) Effect on earnings and profits of corporate shareholders of a regulated investment company. If a shareholder required to include an amount of undistributed capital gains in gross income under section 852(b)(3)(D) and subparagraph (2) of this paragraph is a corporation, such corporation, in computing its earnings and profits for the taxable year for which such amount is so includible, shall treat such amount as if it had actually been received and the taxes paid shall include any amount of tax liability satisfied by a credit under section 852(b)(3)(D) and subparagraph (2) of this paragraph.

(c) Definition of capital gain dividend. *(1) General rule.* A capital gain dividend, as defined in section 852(b)(3)(C), is any dividend or part thereof which is designated by a regulated investment company as a capital gain dividend in a written notice mailed to its shareholders within the period specified in paragraph (c)(4) of this section If the aggregate amount so designated with respect to the taxable year (including capital gain dividends paid after the close of the taxable year pursuant to an election under section 855) is greater than the excess of the net long-term capital gain over the net short-term capital loss of the taxable year, the portion of each distribution which shall be a capital gain dividend shall be only that proportion of the amount so designated which such excess of the net long-term capital gain over the net short-term capital loss bears to the aggregate amount so designated. For example, a regulated investment company making its return on the calendar year basis advised its shareholders by written notice mailed December 30, 1955, that of a distribution of $500,000 made December 15, 1955, $200,000 constituted a capital gain dividend, amounting to $2 per share. It was later discovered that an error had been made in determining the excess of the net long-term capital gain over the net short-term capital loss of the taxable year, and that such excess was $100,000 instead of $200,000. In such case each shareholder would have received a capital gain dividend of $1 per share instead of $2 per share.

(2) Shareholder of record custodian of certain unit investment trusts. In any case where a notice is mailed pursuant to subparagraph (1) of this paragraph by a regulated investment company with respect to a taxable year of the regulated investment company ending after December 8, 1970, to a shareholder of record who is a nominee acting as a custodian of a unit investment trust described in section 851(f)(1) and paragraph (d) of § 1.851-7, the nominee shall furnish each holder of an interest in such trust with a written notice mailed on or before the 55th day following the close of the regulated investment company's taxable year. The notice shall designate the holder's proportionate share of the capital gain dividend shown on the notice received by the nominee pursuant to subparagraph (1) of this paragraph. The notice

shall include the name and address of the nominee identified as such. This subparagraph shall not apply if the regulated investment company agrees with the nominee to satisfy the notice requirements of subparagraph (1) of this paragraph with respect to each holder of an interest in the unit investment trust whose shares are being held by the nominee as custodian and, not later than 45 days following the close of the company's taxable year, files with the Internal Revenue Service office where the company's income tax return is to be filed for the taxable year, a statement that the holders of the unit investment trust with whom the agreement was made have been directly notified by the regulated investment company. Such statement shall include the name, sponsor, and custodian of each unit investment trust whose holders have been directly notified. The nominee's requirements under this paragraph shall be deemed met if the regulated investment company transmits a copy of such statement to the nominee within such 45-day period; provided however, if the regulated investment company fails or is unable to satisfy the requirements of this subparagraph with respect to the holders of interest in the unit investment trust, it shall so notify the Internal Revenue Service within 45 days following the close of its taxable year. The custodian shall, upon notice by the Internal Revenue Service that the regulated investment company has failed to comply with the agreement, satisfy the requirements of this subparagraph within 30 days of such notice.

If a notice under paragraph (c)(1) of this section is mailed within the 120-day period following the date of a determination pursuant to paragraph (c)(4)(ii) of this section, the 120-day period and the 130-day period following the date of the determination shall be substituted for the 45-day period and the 55-day period following the close of the regulated investment company's taxable year prescribed by this subparagraph (2).

(3) Subsection (d) gain for certain taxable years. In the case of capital gain dividends with respect to any taxable year of a regulated investment company ending after December 31, 1969, and beginning before January 1, 1975 (including capital gain dividends paid after the close of the taxable year pursuant to an election under section 855), the company must include in its written notice under paragraph (c)(1) of this section a statement showing the shareholder's proportionate share of the capital gain dividend which is gain described in section 1201(d)(1) and his proportionate share of such dividend which is gain described in section 1201(d)(2). In determining the portion of the capital gain dividend which, in the hands of a shareholder, is gain described in section 1201(d)(1) or (2), the regulated investment company shall consider that capital gain dividends for a taxable year are first made from its long-term capital gains for such year which are not described in section 1201(d)(1) or (2), to the extent thereof, and then from its long-term capital gains for such year which are described in section 1201(d)(1) or (2). A shareholder's proportionate share of gains which are described in section 1201(d)(1) is the amount which bears the same ratio to the amount paid to him as a capital gain dividend in respect of such year as (i) the aggregate amount of the company's gains which are described in section 1201(d)(1) and paid to all shareholders bears to (ii) the aggregate amount of the capital gain dividend paid to all shareholders in respect of such year. A shareholder's proportionate share of gains which are described in section 1201(d)(2) shall be determined in a similar manner. Every regulated investment company shall keep a record of the proportion of each capital gain dividend (to which this paragraph applies) which is gain described in section 1201(d)(1) or (2). If, for his taxable year, a shareholder must include in his gross income a capital gain dividend to which this paragraph applies, he shall attach to his income tax return for such taxable year a statement showing, with respect to the total of such dividends for such taxable year received from each regulated investment company, the name and address of the regulated investment company from which such dividends are received, the amount of such dividends, the portion of such dividends which was designated as gain described in section 1201(d)(1), and the portion of such dividends which was designated as gain described in section 1201(d)(2).

(4) Mailing of written notice to shareholders. (i) Except as provided in paragraph (c)(4)(ii) of this section, the written notice designating a dividend or part thereof as a capital gain dividend must be mailed to the shareholders not later than 45 days (30 days for a taxable year ending before February 26, 1964) after the close of the taxable year of the regulated investment company.

(ii) If a determination (as defined in section 860(e)) after November 6, 1978, increases the excess for the taxable year of the net capital gain over the deduction for capital gains dividends paid, then a regulated investment company may designate all or part of any dividend as a capital gain dividend in a written notice mailed to its shareholders at any time during the 120-day period immediately following the date of the determination. The aggregate amount designated during this period may not exceed this increase. A dividend may be designated if it is actually paid during the taxable year, is one paid after the close of the taxable year to which section 855 applies, or is a deficiency dividend as defined in section 860(f)), including a deficiency dividend paid by an acquiring corporation to which section 381(c)(25) applies. The date of a determination is established under § 1.860-2(b)(1).

(d) Special treatment loss on the sale or exchange of regulated investment company stock held less than 31 days. *(1) In general.* Under section 852(b)(4), if any person, with respect to a share of regulated investment company stock acquired by such person after December 31, 1957, and held for a period of less than 31 days, is required by section 852(b)(3)(B) or (D) to include in gross income as a gain from the sale or exchange of a capital asset held for more than 1 year (6 months for taxable years beginning before 1977; 9 months for taxable years beginning in 1977)

(i) The amount of a capital gain dividend, or

(ii) An amount of undistributed capital gains, then such person shall, to the extent of such amount, treat any loss on the sale or exchange of such share of stock as a loss from the sale or exchange of a capital asset held for more than 1 year (6 months for taxable years beginning before 1977; 9 months for taxable years beginning in 1977). Such special treatment with respect to the sale of regulated investment company stock held for a period of less than 31 days is applicable to losses for taxable years ending after December 31, 1957.

(2) Determination of holding period. The rules contained in section 246(c)(3) (relating to the determination of holding periods for purposes of the deduction for dividends received) shall be applied in determining whether, for purposes of section 852(b)(4) and this paragraph, a share of regulated investment company stock has been held for a period of less than 31 days. In applying those rules, however, "30 days" shall be substituted for the number of days specified in subparagraph (B) of section 246(c)(3).

(3) Example. The application of section 852(b)(4) and this paragraph may be illustrated by the following example:

Example. On December 15, 1958, A purchased a share of stock in the X regulated investment company for $20. The X regulated investment company declared a capital gain dividend of $2 per share to shareholders of record on December 31, 1958. A, therefore, received a capital gain dividend of $2 which, pursuant to section 852(b)(3)(B), he must treat as a gain from the sale or exchange of a capital asset held for more than 6 months. On January 5, 1959, A sold his share of stock in the X regulated investment company for $17.50, which sale resulted in a loss of $2.50. Under section 852(b)(4) and this paragraph, A must treat $2 of such loss (an amount equal to the capital gain dividend received with respect to such share of stock) as a loss from the sale or exchange of a capital asset held for more than 6 months.

T.D. 6236, 6/3/57, amend T.D. 6369, 3/16/59, T.D. 6531, 1/18/61, T.D. 6598, 4/25/62, T.D. 6777, 12/15/64, T.D. 6921, 6/19/67, T.D. 7187, 7/5/72, T.D. 7337, 12/26/74, T.D. 7728, 10/31/80, T.D. 7936, 1/17/84.

§ 1.852-5 Earnings and profits of a regulated investment company.

Caution: The Treasury has not yet amended Reg § 1.852-5 to reflect changes made by P.L. 99-514.

(a) Any regulated investment company, whether or not such company meets the requirements of section 852(a) and paragraph (a)(1)(i) and (ii) of § 1.852-1, shall apply paragraph (b) of this section in computing its earnings and profits for a taxable year beginning after February 28, 1958. However, for a taxable year of a regulated investment company beginning before March 1, 1958, paragraph (b) of this section shall apply only if the regulated investment company meets the requirements of section 852(a) and paragraph (a)(1)(i) and (ii) of § 1.852-1.

(b) In the determination of the earnings and profits of a regulated investment company, section 852(c) provides that such earnings and profits for any taxable year (but not the accumulated earnings and profits) shall not be reduced by any amount which is not allowable as a deduction in computing its taxable income for the taxable year. Thus, if a corporation would have had earnings and profits of $500,000 for the taxable year except for the fact that it had a net capital loss of $100,000, which amount was not deductible in determining its taxable income, its earnings and profits for that year if it is a regulated investment company would be $500,000. If the regulated investment company had no accumulated earnings and profits at the beginning of the taxable year, in determining its accumulated earnings and profits as of the beginning of the following taxable year, the earnings and profits for the taxable year to be considered in such computation would amount to $400,000 assuming that there had been no distribution from such earnings and profits. If distributions had been made in the taxable year in the amount of the earnings and profits then available for distribution, $500,000, the corporation would have as of the beginning of the following taxable year neither accumulated earnings and profits nor a deficit in accumulated earnings and profits, and would begin such year with its paid-in capital reduced by $100,000, an amount equal to the excess of the $500,000 distributed over the $400,000 accumulated earnings and profits which would otherwise have been carried into the following taxable year.

T.D. 6236, 6/3/57, amend T.D. 6369, 3/16/59.

§ 1.852-6 Records to be kept for purpose of determining whether a corporation claiming to be a regulated investment company is a personal holding company.

(a) Every regulated investment company shall maintain in the internal revenue district in which it is required to file its income tax return permanent records showing the information relative to the actual owners of its stock contained in the written statements required by this section to be demanded from the shareholders. The actual owner of stock includes the person who is required to include in gross income in his return the dividends received on the stock. Such records shall be kept at all times available for inspection by any internal revenue officer or employee, and shall be retained so long as the contents thereof may become material in the administration of any internal revenue law.

(b) For the purpose of determining whether a domestic corporation claiming to be a regulated investment company is a personal holding company as defined in section 542, the permanent records of the company shall show the maximum number of shares of the corporation (including the number and face value of securities convertible into stock of the corporation) to be considered as actually or constructively owned by each of the actual owners of any of its stock at any time during the last half of the corporation's taxable year, as provided in section 544.

(c) Statements setting forth the information (required by paragraph (b) of this section) shall be demanded not later than 30 days after the close of the corporation's taxable year as follows:

(1) In the case of a corporation having 2,000 or more record owners of its stock on any dividend record date, from each record holder of 5 percent or more of its stock; or

(2) In the case of a corporation having less than 2,000 and more than 200 record owners of its stock, on any dividend record date, from each record holder of 1 percent or more of its stock; or

(3) In the case of a corporation having 200 or less record owners of its stock, on any dividend record date, from each record holder of one-half of 1 percent or more of its stock.

When making demand for the written statements required of each shareholder by this paragraph, the company shall inform each of the shareholders of his duty to submit as a part of his income tax return the statements which are required by § 1.852-7 if he fails or refuses to comply with such demand. A list of the persons failing or refusing to comply in whole or in part with a company's demand shall be maintained as a part of its record required by this section. A company which fails to keep such records to show the actual ownership of its outstanding stock as are required by this section shall be taxable as an ordinary corporation and not as a regulated investment company.

T.D. 6236, 6/3/57.

§ 1.852-7 Additional information required in returns of shareholders.

Any person who fails or refuses to comply with the demand of a regulated investment company for the written statements which § 1.852-6 requires the company to demand from its shareholders shall submit as a part of its income tax return a statement showing, to the best of his knowledge and belief—

(a) The number of shares actually owned by him at any and all times during the period for which the return is filed in any company claiming to be a regulated investment company;

(b) The dates of acquisition of any such stock during such period and the names and addresses of persons from whom it was acquired;

(c) The dates of disposition of any such stock during such period and the names and addresses of the transferees thereof;

(d) The names and addresses of the members of his family (as defined in section 544(a)(2)); the names and addresses of his partners, if any, in any partnership; and the maximum number of shares, if any, actually owned by each in any corporation claiming to be a regulated investment company, at any time during the last half of the taxable year of such company;

(e) The names and addresses of any corporation, partnership, association, or trust in which he had a beneficial interest to the extent of at least 10 percent at any time during the period for which such return is made, and the number of shares of any corporation claiming to be a regulated investment company actually owned by each;

(f) The maximum number of shares (including the number and face value of securities convertible into stock of the corporation) in any domestic corporation claiming to be a regulated investment company to be considered as constructively owned by such individual at any time during the last half of the corporation's taxable year, as provided in section 544 and the regulations thereunder; and

(g) The amount and date of receipt of each dividend received during such period from every corporation claiming to be a regulated investment company.

T.D. 6236, 6/3/57.

§ 1.852-8 Information returns.

Nothing in §§ 1.852-6 and 1.852-7 shall be construed to relieve regulated investment companies or their shareholders from the duty of filing information returns required by regulations prescribed under the provisions of subchapter A, chapter 61 of the Code.

T.D. 6236, 6/3/57.

§ 1.852-9 Special procedural requirements applicable to designation under section 852(b)(3)(D).

Caution: The Treasury has not yet amended Reg § 1.852-9 to reflect changes made by P.L. 99-514.

(a) Regulated investment company. *(1) Notice to shareholders.* (i) A designation of undistributed capital gains under section 852(b)(3)(D) and paragraph (b)(2)(i) of § 1.852-2 shall be made by notice on Form 2439 mailed by the regulated investment company to each person who is a shareholder of record of the company at the close of the company's taxable year. The notice on Form 2439 shall show the name, address, and employer identification number of the regulated investment company; the taxable year of the company for which the designation is made; the name, address, and identifying number of the shareholder; the amount designated by the company for inclusion by the shareholder in computing his long-term capital gains; and the tax paid with respect thereto by the company which is deemed to have been paid by the shareholder.

(ii) In the case of a designation of undistributed capital gains with respect to a taxable year of the regulated investment company ending after December 31, 1969, and beginning before January 1, 1975, Form 2439 shall also show the shareholder's proportionate share of such gains which is gain described in section 1201(d)(1), his proportionate share of such gains which is gain described in section 1201(d)(2), and the amount (determined pursuant to subdivision (iv) of this subparagraph) by which the shareholder's adjusted basis in his shares shall be increased.

(iii) In determining under subdivision (ii) of this subparagraph the portion of the undistributed capital gains which, in the hands of the shareholder, is gain described in section 1201(d)(1) or (2), the company shall consider that capital gain dividends for a taxable year are made first from its long-term capital gains for such year which are not described in section 1201(d)(1) or (2), to the extent thereof, and then from its long-term capital gains for such year which are described in section 1201(d)(1) or (2). A shareholder's proportionate share of undistributed capital gains for a taxable year which is gain described in section 1201(d)(1) is the amount which bears the same ratio to the amount included in his income as designated undistributed capital gains for such year as (a) the aggregate amount of the company's gains for such year which are described in section 1201(d)(1) and designated as undistributed capital gains bears to (b) the aggregate amount of the company's gains for such year which are designated as undistributed capital gains. A shareholder's proportionate share of gains which are described in section 1201(d)(2) shall be determined in a similar manner. Every regulated investment company shall keep a record of the proportion of undistributed capital gains (to which this subdivision applies) which is gain described in section 1201(d)(1) or (2).

(iv) In the case of a designation of undistributed capital gains for any taxable year ending after December 31, 1969, and beginning before January 1, 1975, Form 2439 shall also show with respect to the undistributed capital gains of each shareholder the amount by which such shareholder's adjusted basis in his shares shall be increased under section 852(b)(3)(D)(iii). The amount by which each shareholders' adjusted basis in his shares shall be increased is the amount includible in his gross income with respect to such shares under section 852(b)(3)(D)(i) less the tax which the shareholder is deemed to have paid with respect to such shares. The tax which each shareholder is deemed to have paid with respect to such shares is the amount which bears the same ratio to the amount of the tax imposed by section 852(b)(3)(A) for such year with respect to the aggregate amount of the designated undistributed capital gains as the amount of such gains includible in the shareholder's gross income bears to the aggregate amount of such gains so designated.

(v) Form 2439 shall be prepared in triplicate, and copies B and C of the form shall be mailed to the shareholder on or before the 45th day (30th day for a taxable year ending before February 26, 1964) following the close of the company's taxable year. Copy A of each Form 2439 must be associated with the duplicate copy of the undistributed capital gains tax return of the company (Form 2438), as provided in subparagraph (2)(ii) of this paragraph.

(2) Return of undistributed capital gains tax. (i) Form 2438. Every regulated investment company which designates undistributed capital gains for any taxable year beginning after December 31, 1956, in accordance with subparagraph (1) of this paragraph, shall file for such taxable year an undistributed capital gains tax return on Form 2438 including on such return the total of its undistributed capital gains so designated and the tax with respect thereto. The return on Form

2438 shall be prepared in duplicate and shall set forth fully and clearly the information required to be included therein. The original of Form 2438 shall be filed on or before the 30th day after the close of the company's taxable year with the internal revenue officer designated in instructions applicable to Form 2438. The duplicate copy of Form 2438 for the taxable year shall be attached to and filed with the income tax return of the company on Form 1120 for such taxable year.

(ii) Copies A of Form 2439. For each taxable year which ends on or before December 31, 1965, there shall be submitted with the company's return on Form 2438 all copies A of Form 2439 furnished by the company to its shareholders in accordance with subparagraph (1) of this paragraph. For each taxable year which ends after December 31, 1965, there shall be submitted with the duplicate copy of the company's return on Form 2438, which is attached to and filed with the income tax return of the company on Form 1120 for the taxable year, all copies A of Form 2439 furnished by the company to its shareholders in accordance with subparagraph (1) of this paragraph. The copies A of Form 2439 shall be accompanied by lists (preferably in the form of adding machine tapes) of the amounts of undistributed capital gains and of the tax paid with respect thereto shown on such forms. The totals of the listed amounts of undistributed capital gains and of tax paid with respect thereto must agree with the corresponding entries on Form 2438.

(3) Payment of tax. The tax required to be returned on Form 2438 shall be paid by the regulated investment company on or before the 30th day after the close of the company's taxable year to the internal revenue officer with whom the return on Form 2438 is filed.

(b) Shareholder of record not actual owner. *(1) Notice to actual owner.* In any case in which a notice on Form 2439 is mailed pursuant to paragraph (a)(1) of this section by a regulated investment company to a shareholder of record who is a nominee of the actual owner or owners of the shares of stock to which the notice relates, the nominee shall furnish to each such actual owner notice of the owner's proportionate share of the amounts of undistributed capital gains and tax with respect thereto, shown on the Form 2439 received by the nominee from the regulated investment company. The nominee's notice to the actual owner shall be prepared in triplicate on Form 2439 and shall contain the information prescribed in paragraph (a)(1) of this section, except that the name and address of the nominee, identified as such, shall be entered on the form in addition to, and in the space provided for, the name and address of the regulated investment company, and the amounts of undistributed capital gains and tax with respect thereto entered on the form shall be the actual owner's proportionate share of the corresponding items shown on the nominee's notice from the regulated investment company. Copies B and C of the Form 2439 prepared by the nominee shall be mailed to the actual owner—

(i) For taxable years of regulated investment companies ending after February 25, 1964, on or before the 75th day (55th day in the case of a nominee who is acting as a custodian of a unit investment trust described in section 851(f)(1) and paragraph (d) of § 1.851-7 for taxable years of regulated investment companies ending after December 8, 1970, and 135th day if the nominee is a resident of a foreign country) following the close of the regulated investment company's taxable year, or

(ii) For taxable years of regulated investment companies ending before February 26, 1964, on or before the 60th day (120th day if the nominee is a resident of a foreign country) following the close of the regulated investment company's taxable year.

(2) Transmittal of Form 2439. The nominee shall enter the word "Nominee" in the upper right hand corner of copy B of the notice on Form 2439 received by him from the regulated investment company, and on or before the appropriate day specified in subdivision (i) or (ii) of subparagraph (1) of this paragraph shall transmit such copy B, together with all copies A of Form 2439 prepared by him pursuant to subparagraph (1) of this paragraph, to the internal revenue officer with whom his income tax return is required to be filed.

(3) Custodian of certain unit investment trusts. The requirements of this paragraph shall not apply to a nominee who is acting as a custodian of the unit investment trust described in section 851(f)(1) and paragraph (d) of § 1.851-7 provided that the regulated investment company agrees with the nominee to satisfy the notice requirements of paragraph (a) of this section with respect to each holder of an interest in the unit investment trust whose shares are being held by such nominee as custodian and on or before the 45th day following the close of the company's taxable year, files with the Internal Revenue Service office where the company's income tax return is to be filed for the taxable year, a statement that the holders of the unit investment trust with whom the agreement was made have been directly notified by the regulated investment company. Such statement shall include the name, sponsor, and custodian of each unit investment trust whose holders have been directly notified. The nominee's requirements under this paragraph shall be deemed met if the regulated investment company transmits a copy of such statement to the nominee within such 45-day period; provided however, if the regulated investment company fails or is unable to satisfy the requirements of this paragraph with respect to the holders of interest in the unit investment trust, it shall so notify the Internal Revenue Service within 45 days following the close of its taxable year. The custodian shall, upon notice by the Internal Revenue Service that the regulated investment company has failed to comply with the agreement, satisfy the requirements of this paragraph within 30 days of such notice.

(c) Shareholders. *(1) Return and Recordkeeping Requirements.* (i) Return requirements for taxable years beginning before January 1, 2002. For taxable years beginning before January 1, 2002, the copy B of Form 2439 furnished to a shareholder by the regulated investment company or by a nominee, as provided in Sec. 1.852-9(a) or (b) shall be attached to the income tax return of the shareholder for the taxable year in which the amount of undistributed capital gains is includible in gross income as provided in Sec. 1.852-4(b)(2).

(ii) Recordkeeping requirements for taxable years beginning after December 31, 2001. For taxable years beginning after December 31, 2001, the shareholder shall retain a copy of Form 2439 for as long as its contents may become material in the administration of any internal revenue law.

(2) Credit or refund. (i) In general. The amount of the tax paid by the regulated investment company with respect to the undistributed capital gains required under section 852(b)(3)(D) and paragraph (b)(2) of § 1.852-4 to be included by a shareholder in his computation of long-term capital gains for any taxable year is deemed paid by such shareholder under section 852(b)(3)(D)(ii) and such payment constitutes, for purposes of section 6513(a) (relating to time tax considered paid), an advance payment in like amount of the tax imposed under chapter 1 of the Code for such taxa-

ble year. In the case of an overpayment of tax within the meaning of section 6401, see section 6402 and the regulations in Part 301 of this chapter (Regulations on Procedure and Administration) for rules applicable to the treatment of an overpayment of tax and section 6511 and the regulations in Part 301 of this chapter (Regulations on Procedure and Administration) with respect to the limitations applicable to the credit or refund of an overpayment of tax.

(ii) Form to be used. Claim for refund or credit of the tax deemed to have been paid by a shareholder with respect to an amount of undistributed capital gains shall be made on the shareholder's income tax return for the taxable year in which such amount of undistributed capital gains is includable in gross income. In the case of a shareholder which is a partnership, claim shall be made by the partners on their income tax returns for refund or credit of their distributive shares of the tax deemed to have been paid by the partnership. In the case of a shareholder which is exempt from tax under section 501(a) and to which section 511 does not apply for the taxable year, claim for refund of the tax deemed to have been paid by such shareholder on an amount of undistributed capital gains for such year shall be made on Form 843 and copy B of Form 2439 furnished to such shareholder shall be attached to its claim. For other rules applicable to the filing of claims for credit or refund of an overpayment of tax, see § 301.6402-2 of this chapter (Regulations on Procedure and Administration), relating to claims for credit or refund, and § 301.6402-3 of this chapter, relating to special rules applicable to income tax.

(3) Records. The shareholder is required to keep copy C of the Form 2439 furnished for the regulated investment company's taxable years ending after December 31, 1969, and beginning before January 1, 1975, as part of his records to show increases in the adjusted basis of his shares in such company.

(d) Penalties. For criminal penalties for willful failure to file a return, supply information, or pay tax, and for filing a false or fraudulent return, statement, or other document, see sections 7203, 7206, and 7207.

T.D. 6369, 3/16/59, amend T.D. 6531, 1/18/61, T.D. 6921, 6/19/67, T.D. 7012, 5/14/69, T.D. 7187, 7/5/72, T.D. 7332, 12/20/74, T.D. 7337, 12/26/74, T.D. 8989, 4/23/2002, T.D. 9040, 1/30/2003.

§ 1.852-10 Distributions in redemption of interests in unit investment trusts.

(a) In general. In computing that part of the excess of its net long-term capital gain over net short-term capital loss on which it must pay a capital gains tax, a regulated investment company is allowed under section 852(b)(3)(A)(ii) a deduction for dividends paid (as defined in section 561) determined with reference to capital gains dividends only. Section 561(b) provides that in determining the deduction for dividends paid, the rules provided in section 562 are applicable. Section 562(c) (relating to preferential dividends) provides that the amount of any distribution shall not be considered as a dividend unless such distribution is pro-rata, with no preference to any share of stock as compared with other shares of the same class except to the extent that the former is entitled to such preference.

(b) Redemption distributions made by unit investment trust. *(1) In general.* Where a unit investment trust (as defined in paragraph (c) of this section) liquidates part of its portfolio represented by shares in a management company in order to make a distribution to a holder of an interest in the trust in redemption of part or all of such interest, and by so doing, the trust realizes net long-term capital gain, that portion of the distribution by the trust which is equal to the amount of the net long-term capital gain realized by the trust on the liquidation of the shares in the management company will not be considered a preferential dividend under section 562(c). For example, where the entire amount of net long-term capital gain realized by the trust on such a liquidation is distributed to the redeeming interest holder, the trust will be allowed the entire amount of net long-term capital gain so realized in determining the deduction under section 852(b)(3)(A)(ii) for dividends paid determined with reference to capital gains dividends only. This paragraph and section 852(d) shall apply only with respect to the capital gain net income (net capital gain for taxable years beginning before January 1, 1977) realized by the trust which is attributable to a redemption by a holder of an interest in such trust. Such dividend may be designated as a capital gain dividend by a written notice to the certificate holder. Such designation should clearly indicate to the holder that the holder's gain or loss on the redemption of the certificate may differ from such designated amount, depending upon the holder's basis for the redeemed certificate, and that the holder's own records are to be used in computing the holder's gain or loss on the redemption of the certificate.

(2) Example. The application of the provisions of this paragraph may be illustrated by the following example:

Example. B entered into a periodic payment plan contract with X as custodian and Z as plan sponsor under which he purchased a plan certificate of X. Under this contract, upon B's demand, X must redeem B's certificate at a price substantially equal to the value of the number of shares in Y, a management company, which are credited to B's account by X in connection with the unit investment trust. Except for a small amount of cash which X is holding to satisfy liabilities and to invest for other plan certificate holders, all of the assets held by X in connection with the trust consist of shares in Y. Pursuant to the terms of the periodic payment plan contract, 100 shares of Y are credited to B's account. Both X and Y have elected to be treated as regulated investment companies. On March 1, 1965, B notified X that he wished to have his entire interest in the unit investment trust redeemed. In order to redeem B's interest, X caused Y to redeem 100 shares of Y which X held. At the time of redemption, each share of Y had a value of $15. X then distributed the $1,500 to B. X's basis for each of the Y shares which was redeemed was $10. Therefore, X realized a long-term capital gain of $500 ($5 × 100 shares) which is attributable to the redemption by B of his interest in the trust. Under section 852(d), the $500 capital gain distributed to B will not be considered a preferential dividend. Therefore, X is allowed a deduction of $500 under section 852(b)(3)(A)(ii) for dividends paid determined with reference to capital gains dividends only, with the result that X will not pay a capital gains tax with respect to such amount.

(c) Definition of unit investment trust. A unit investment trust to which paragraph (a) of this section refers is a business arrangement which—

(1) Is registered under the Investment Company Act of 1940 as a unit investment trust;

(2) Issues periodic payment plan certificates (as defined in such Act);

(3) Possesses, as substantially all of its assets, securities issued by a management company (as defined in such Act);

(4) Qualifies as a regulated investment company under section 851; and

(5) Complies with the requirements provided for by section 852(a).

Paragraph (a) of this section does not apply to a unit investment trust described in section 851(f)(1) and paragraph (d) of § 1.851-7.

T.D. 6921, 6/20/67, amend T.D. 7187, 7/6/72, T.D. 7728, 10/31/80.

§ 1.852-11 Treatment of certain losses attributable to periods after October 31 of a taxable year.

(a) Outline of provisions. This paragraph lists the provisions of this section.

(a) Outline of provisions.

(b) Scope.

(1) In general.

(2) Limitation on application of section.

(c) Post-October capital loss defined.

(1) In general.

(2) Methodology.

(3) October 31 treated as last day of taxable year for purpose of determining taxable income under certain circumstances.

(i) In general.

(ii) Effect on gross income.

(d) Post-October currency loss defined.

(1) Post-October currency loss.

(2) Net foreign currency loss.

(3) Foreign currency gain or loss.

(e) Limitation on capital gain dividends.

(1) In general.

(2) Amount taken into account in current year.

(i) Net capital loss.

(ii) Net long-term capital loss.

(3) Amount taken into account in succeeding year.

(f) Regulated investment company may elect to defer certain losses for purposes of determining taxable income.

(1) In general.

(2) Effect of election in current year.

(3) Amount of loss taken into account in current year.

(i) If entire amount of net capital loss deferred.

(ii) If part of net capital loss deferred.

(A) In general.

(B) Character of capital loss not deferred.

(iii) If entire amount of net long-term capital loss deferred.

(iv) If part of net long-term capital loss deferred.

(v) If entire amount of post-October currency loss deferred.

(vi) If part of post-October currency loss deferred.

(4) Amount of loss taken into account in succeeding year and subsequent years.

(5) Effect on gross income.

(g) Earnings and profits.

(1) General rule.

(2) Special rule—treatment of losses that are deferred for purposes of determining taxable income.

(h) Examples.

(i) Procedure for making election.

(1) In general.

(2) When applicable instructions not available.

(j) Transition rules.

(1) In general.

(2) Retroactive election.

(i) In general.

(ii) Deadline for making election.

(3) Amended return required for succeeding year in certain circumstances.

(i) In general.

(ii) Time for filing amended return.

(4) Retroactive dividend

(i) In general.

(ii) Method of making election.

(iii) Deduction for dividends paid

(A) In general.

(B) Limitation on ordinary dividends.

(C) Limitation on capital gain dividends.

(D) Effect on other years.

(iv) Earnings and profits.

(v) Receipt by shareholders.

(vi) Foreign tax election.

(vii) Example.

(5) Certain distributions may be designated retroactively as capital gain dividends.

(k) Effective date.

(b) Scope. *(1) In general.* This section prescribes the manner in which a regulated investment company must treat a post-October capital loss (as defined in paragraph (c) of this section) or a post-October currency loss (as defined in paragraph (d)(1) of this section) for purposes of determining its taxable income, its earnings and profits, and the amount that it may designate as capital gain dividends for the taxable year in which the loss is incurred and the succeeding taxable year (the "succeeding year").

(2) Limitation on application of section. This section shall not apply to any post-October capital loss or post-October currency loss of a regulated investment company attributable to a taxable year for which an election is in effect under section 4982(e)(4) of the Code with respect to the company.

(c) Post-October capital loss defined. *(1) In general.* For purposes of this section, the term post-October capital loss means—

(i) Any net capital loss attributable to the portion of a regulated investment company's taxable year after October 31; or

(ii) If there is no such net capital loss, any net long-term capital loss attributable to the portion of a regulated investment company's taxable year after October 31.

(2) Methodology. The amount of any net capital loss or any net long-term capital loss attributable to the portion of the regulated investment company's taxable year after October 31 shall be determined in accordance with general tax law principles (other than section 1212) by treating the period beginning on November 1 of the taxable year of the regulated investment company and ending on the last day of such taxable year as though it were the taxable year of the regulated investment company. For purposes of this paragraph (c)(2), any item (other than a capital loss carryover)

that is required to be taken into account or any rule that must be applied, for purposes of section 4982 on October 31 as if it were the last day of the regulated investment company's taxable year must also be taken into account or applied in the same manner as required under section 4982, both on October 31 and again on the last day of the regulated investment company's taxable year.

(3) October 31 treated as last day of taxable year for purpose of determining taxable income under certain circumstances. (i) In general. If a regulated investment company has a post-October capital loss for a taxable year, any item that must be marked to market for purposes of section 4982 on October 31 as if it were the last day of the regulated investment company's taxable year must also be marked to market on October 31 and again on the last day of the regulated investment company's taxable year for purposes of determining its taxable income. If the regulated investment company does not have a post-October capital loss for a taxable year, the regulated investment company must treat items that must be marked to market for purposes of section 4982 on October 31 as if it were the last day of the regulated investment company's taxable year as marked to market only on the last day of its taxable year for purposes of determining its taxable income.

(ii) Effect on gross income. The marking to market of any item on October 31 of a regulated investment company's taxable year for purposes of determining its taxable income under paragraph (c)(3)(i) of this section shall not affect the amount of the gross income of such company for such taxable year for purposes of section 851(b) (2) or (3).

(d) Post-October currency loss defined. For purposes of this section—

(1) Post-October currency loss. The term post-October currency loss means any net foreign currency loss attributable to the portion of a regulated investment company's taxable year after October 31. For purposes of the preceding sentence, principles similar to those of paragraphs (c)(2) and (c)(3) of this section shall apply.

(2) Net foreign currency loss. The term "net foreign currency loss" means the excess of foreign currency losses over foreign currency gains.

(3) Foreign currency gain or loss. The terms "foreign currency gain" and "foreign currency loss" have the same meaning as provided in section 988(b).

(e) Limitation on capital gain dividends. *(1) In general.* For purposes of determining the amount a regulated investment company may designate as capital gain dividends for a taxable year, the amount of net capital gain for the taxable year shall be determined without regard to any post-October capital loss for such year.

(2) Amount taken into account in current year. (i) Net capital loss. If the post-October capital loss referred to in paragraph (e)(1) of this section is a post-October capital loss as defined in paragraph (c)(1)(i) of this section, the net capital gain of the company for the taxable year in which the loss arose shall be determined without regard to any capital gains or losses (both long-term and short-term) taken into account in computing the post-October capital loss for the taxable year.

(ii) Net long-term capital loss. If the post-October capital loss referred to in paragraph (e)(1) of this section is a post-October capital loss as defined in paragraph (c)(1)(ii) of this section, the net capital gain of the company for the taxable year in which the loss arose shall be determined without regard to any long-term capital gain or loss taken into account in computing the post-October capital loss for the taxable year.

(3) Amount taken into account in succeeding year. If a regulated investment company has a post-October capital loss (as defined in paragraph (c)(1)(i) or (c)(1)(ii) of this section) for any taxable year, then, for purposes of determining the amount the company may designate as capital gain dividends for the succeeding year, the net capital gain for the succeeding year shall be determined by treating all gains and losses taken into account in computing the post-October capital loss as arising on the first day of the succeeding year.

(f) Regulated investment company may elect to defer certain losses for purposes of determining taxable income. *(1) In general.* A regulated investment company may elect, in accordance with the procedures of paragraph (i) of this section, to compute its taxable income for a taxable year without regard to part or all of any post-October capital loss or post-October currency loss for that year.

(2) Effect of election in current year. The taxable income of a regulated investment company for a taxable year to which an election under paragraph (f)(1) of this section applies shall be computed without regard to that part of any post-October capital loss or post-October currency loss to which the election applies.

(3) Amount of loss taken into account in current year. (i) If entire amount of net capital loss deferred. If a regulated investment company elects, under paragraph (f)(1) of this section, to defer the entire amount of a post-October capital loss as defined in paragraph (c)(1)(i) of this section, the taxable income of the company for the taxable year in which the loss arose shall be determined without regard to any capital gains or losses (both long-term and short-term taken into account in computing the post-October capital loss for the taxable year.

(ii) If part of net capital loss deferred. (A) In general. If a regulated investment company elects, under paragraph (f)(1) of this section, to defer less than the entire amount of a post-October capital loss as defined in paragraph (c)(1)(i) of this section, the taxable income of the company for the taxable year in which the loss arose shall be determined by including an amount of capital loss taken into account in computing the post-October capital loss for the taxable year equal to the amount of the post-October capital loss that is not deferred. No amount of capital gain taken into account in computing the post-October capital loss for the taxable year shall be taken into account in the determination.

(B) Character of capital loss not deferred. The capital loss includible in the taxable income of the company under this paragraph (f)(3)(ii) for the taxable year in which the loss arose shall consist first of any short-term capital losses to the extent thereof, and then of any long-term capital losses, taken into account in computing the post-October capital loss for the taxable year.

(iii) If entire amount of net long-term capital loss deferred. If a regulated investment company elects, under paragraph (f)(1) of this section, to defer the entire amount of a post-October capital loss as defined in paragraph (c)(1)(ii) of this section, the taxable income of the company for the taxable year in which the loss arose shall be determined without regard to any long-term capital gains or losses taken into account in computing the post-October capital loss for the taxable year.

(iv) If part of net long-term capital loss deferred. If a regulated investment company elects, under paragraph (f)(1) of this section, to defer less than the entire amount of a post-

October capital loss as defined in paragraph (c)(1)(ii) of this section, the taxable income of the company for the taxable year in which the loss arose shall be determined by including an amount of long-term capital loss taken into account in computing the post-October capital loss for the taxable year equal to the amount of the post-October capital loss that is not deferred. No amount of long term capital gain taken into account in computing the post-October capital loss for the taxable year shall be taken into account in the determination.

(v) If entire amount of post-October currency loss deferred. If a regulated investment company elects, under paragraph (f)(1) of this section, to defer the entire amount of a post-October currency loss, the taxable income of the company for the taxable year in which the loss arose shall be determined without regard to any foreign currency gains or losses taken into account in computing the post-October currency loss for the taxable year.

(vi) If part of post-October currency loss deferred. If a regulated investment company elects, under paragraph (f)(1) of this section, to defer less than the entire amount of a post-October currency loss, the taxable income of the company for the taxable year in which the loss arose shall be determined by including an amount of foreign currency loss attributable to transactions after October 31 of the taxable year equal to the amount of the post-October currency loss that is not deferred. No amount of foreign currency gain taken into account in computing the post-October currency loss for the taxable year shall be taken into account in the determination.

(4) Amount of loss taken into account in succeeding year and subsequent years. If a regulated investment company has a post-October capital loss or a post-October currency loss for any taxable year and an election under paragraph (f)(1) is made for that year, then, for purposes of determining the taxable income of the company for the succeeding year and all subsequent years, all capital gains and losses taken into account in determining the post-October capital loss, and all foreign currency gains and losses taken into account in determining the post-October currency loss, that are not taken into account under the rules of paragraph (f)(3) of this section in determining the taxable income of the regulated investment company for the taxable year in which the loss arose shall be treated as arising on the first day of the succeeding year.

(5) Effect on gross income. An election by a regulated investment company to defer any post-October capital loss or any post-October currency loss for a taxable year under paragraph (f)(1) of this section shall not affect the amount of the gross income of such company for such taxable year (or the succeeding year) for purposes of section 851(b)(2) or (3).

(g) Earnings and profits. *(1) General rule.* The earnings and profits of a regulated investment company for a taxable year are determined without regard to any post-October capital loss or post-October currency loss for that year. If a regulated investment company distributes with respect to a calendar year amounts in excess of the limitation described in the succeeding sentence, then, with respect to those excess amounts, for the taxable year with respect to which the amounts are distributed, the earnings and profits of the company are computed without regard to the preceding sentence. The limitation described in this sentence is the amount that would be the required distribution for that calendar year under section 4982 if "100 percent" were substituted for each percentage set forth in section 4982(b)(1).

(2) Special Rule—Treatment of losses that are deferred for purposes of determining taxable income. If a regulated investment company elects to defer, under paragraph (f)(1) of this section, any part of a post-October capital loss or post-October currency loss arising in a taxable year, then, for both the taxable year in which the loss arose and the succeeding year, both the earnings and profits and the accumulated earnings and profits of the company are determined as if the part of the loss so deferred had arisen on the first day of the succeeding year.

(h) Examples. The provisions of paragraphs (e), (f), and (g) of this section may be illustrated by the following examples. For each example, assume that X is a regulated investment company that computes its income on a calendar year basis, and that no election is in effect under section 4982(e)(4).

Example (1). X has a $25 net foreign currency gain, a $50 net short-term capital loss, and a $75 net long-term capital gain for the post-October period of 1988. X has no post-October currency loss and no post-October capital loss for 1988, and this section does not apply.

Example (2). X has the following capital gains and losses for the periods indicated:

	Long-term	Short-term
01/01 to 10/31/88	115	80
	(15)	(20)
	100	60
11/01 to 12/31/88	75	150
	(150)	(50)
	(75)	100
01/01 to 10/31/89	30	40
	(5)	(20)
	25	20
11/01 to 12/31/89	35	100
	(0)	(50)
	35	50

X has a post-October capital loss of $75 for its 1988 taxable year due to a net long-term capital loss for the post-October period of 1988. X does not make an election under paragraph (f)(1) of this section.

(i) Capital gain dividends. X may designate up to $100 as a capital gain dividend for 1988 because X must disregard the $75 long-term capital gain and the $150 long-term capital loss for the post-October period of 1988 in computing its net capital gain for this purpose. In computing its net capital gain for 1989 for the purposes of determining the amount it may designate as a capital gain dividend for 1989, X must take into account the $75 long-term capital gain and the $150 long-term capital loss for the post-October period of 1988 in addition to the long-term and short-term capital gains and losses for 1989. Accordingly, X may not designate any amount as a capital gain dividend for 1989.

(ii) Taxable income. X must include the $75 long-term capital gain and the $150 long-term capital loss for its post-October period of 1988 in its taxable income for 1988 because it did not make an election under paragraph (f)(1) of this section for 1988. Accordingly, X's taxable income for 1988 will include a net capital gain of $25 and a net short-term capital gain of $160. X's taxable income for 1989 will include a net capital gain of $60 and a net short-term capital gain of $70.

(iii) Earnings and profits. X must determine its earnings and profits for 1988 without regard to the $75 long-term capital gain and the $150 long-term capital loss for the post-October period of 1988. X must, however, include the $75 long-term capital gain and $150 long-term capital loss for the post-October period of 1988 in determining its accumulated earnings and profits for 1988. Thus, X includes $260 of capital gain in its earnings and profits for 1988, includes $185 in its accumulated earnings and profits for 1988, and includes $130 of capital gain in its earnings and profits for 1989.

Example (3). Same facts as example (2), except that X elects to defer the entire $75 post-October capital loss for 1988 under paragraph (f)(1) of this section for purposes of determining its taxable income for 1988.

(i) Capital gain dividends. Same result as in example (2).

(ii) Taxable income. X must compute its taxable income for 1988 without regard to the $75 long-term capital gain and the $150 long-term capital loss for the post-October period of 1988 because it made an election to defer the entire $75 post-October capital loss for 1988 under paragraph (f)(1) of this section. Accordingly, X's taxable income for 1988 will include a net capital gain of $100 and a net short-term capital gain of $160. X must include the $75 long-term capital gain and the $150 long-term capital loss for the post-October period of 1988 in its taxable income for 1989 in addition to the long-term and short-term capital gains and losses for 1989. Accordingly, X's taxable income for 1989 will include a net long-term capital loss of $15 and a net short-term capital gain of $70.

(iii) Earnings and profits. For 1988, X must determine both its earnings and profits and its accumulated earnings and profits without regard to the $75 long-term capital gain and $150 long-term capital loss for the post-October period of 1988. In determining both its earnings and profits and its accumulated earnings and profits for 1989, X must include (in addition to the long-term and short-term capital gains and losses for 1989) the $75 long-term capital gain and $150 long-term capital loss for the post-October period of 1988 as if those deferred gains and losses arose on January 1, 1989. Thus, X will include $260 of capital gain in its earnings and profits for 1988 and $55 of capital gain in its earnings and profits for 1989.

Example (4). Same facts as example (2), except that X elects to defer only $50 of the post-October capital loss for 1988 under paragraph (f)(1) of this section for purposes of determining its taxable income for 1988.

(i) Capital gain dividends. Same results as in example (2).

(ii) Taxable income. X must compute its taxable income for 1988 without regard to the $75 long-term capital gain and $125 of the $150 long-term capital loss for the post-October period of 1988 because it made an election to defer $50 of the $75 post-October capital loss for 1988 under paragraph (f)(1) of this section. Accordingly, X's taxable income for 1988 will include a net capital gain of $75 and a net short-term capital gain of $160. X must include the $75 long-term capital gain and $125 of the $150 long-term capital loss for the post-October period of 1988 in its taxable income for 1989 in addition to the long-term and short-term capital gains and losses for 1989. Accordingly, X's taxable income for 1989 will include a net capital gain of $10 and a net short-term capital gain of $70.

(iii) Earnings and profits. X must determine its earnings and profits for 1988 without regard to the $75 long-term capital gain and the $150 long-term capital loss for the post-October period of 1988. X must include $25 of the $150 long-term capital loss for the post-October period of 1988 in determining its accumulated earnings and profits for 1988. In determining both its earnings and profits and its accumulated earnings and profits for 1989, X must include (in addition to the long-term and short-term capital gains and losses for 1989) and $75 long-term capital gain and $125 of the $150 long-term capital loss for the post-October period of 1988 as if those deferred gains and losses arose on January 1, 1989. Thus, X includes $260 of capital gain in its earnings and profits for 1988, includes $235 in its accumulated earnings and profits for 1988, and includes $80 of capital gain in its earnings and profits for 1989.

Example (5). X has the following capital gains and losses for the periods indicated:

	Long-term	Short-term
01/01 to 10/31/88	115	80
	(15)	(20)
	100	60
11/01 to 12/31/88	150	50
	(75)	(150)
	75	(100)
01/01 to 10/31/89	30	40
	(5)	(20)
	25	20
11/01 to 12/31/89	35	100
	(0)	(50)
	35	50

X has a post-October capital loss of $25 for its 1988 taxable year due to a net capital loss for the post-October period of 1988. X does not make an election under paragraph (f)(1) of this section.

(i) Capital gain dividends. X may designate up to $100 as a capital gain dividend for 1988 because X must disregard the $150 long-term capital gain, the $75 long-term capital loss, the $50 short-term capital gain, and the $150 short-term capital loss for the post-October period of 1988 in computing its net capital gain for this purpose. In computing its net capital gain for 1989 for purposes of determining the amount it may designate as a capital gain dividend for 1989, X must take into account the $150 long-term capital gain, the $75 long-term capital loss, the $50 short-term capital gain, and the $150 short-term capital loss for the post-October period of 1988 in addition to the long-term and short-term capital gains and losses for 1989. Accordingly, X may designate up to $105 as a capital gain dividend for 1989.

(ii) Taxable income. X must include the $150 long-term capital gain, the $75 long-term capital loss, the $50 short-term capital gain, and the $150 short-term capital loss for the post-October period of 1988 in its taxable income for 1988 because it did not make an election under paragraph (f)(1) of this section for 1988. Accordingly, X's taxable income for 1988 will include a net capital gain of $135 (consisting of a net long-term capital gain of $175 and a net short-term capital loss of $40). X's taxable income for 1989 will include a net capital gain of $60 and a net short-term capital gain of $70.

(iii) Earnings and profits. X must determine its earnings and profits for 1988 without regard to the $150 long-term capital gain, the $75 long-term capital loss, the $50 short-term capital gain, and the $150 short-term capital loss for the post-October period of 1988. X must, however, include the $150 long-term capital gain, the $75 long-term capital loss, the $50 short-term capital gain, and the $150 short-term capital loss for the post-October period of 1988 in determining its accumulated earnings and profits for 1988. Thus, X includes $160 of capital gain in its earnings and profits for 1988, includes $135 in its accumulated earnings and profits for 1988, and includes $130 of capital gain in its earnings and profits for 1989.

Example (6). Same facts as example (5), except that X elects to defer the entire $25 post-October capital loss for 1988 under paragraph (f)(1) of this section for purposes of determining its taxable income for 1988.

(i) Capital gain dividends. Same result as in example (5).

(ii) Taxable income. X must compute its taxable income for 1988 without regard to the $150 long-term capital gain, the $75 long-term capital loss, the $50 short-term capital gain, and the $150 short-term capital loss for the post-October period of 1988 because it made an election to defer the entire $25 post-October capital loss for 1988 under paragraph (f)(1) of this section. Accordingly, X's taxable income for 1988 will include a net capital gain of $100 and a net short-term capital gain of $60. X must include the $150 long-term capital gain, the $75 long-term capital loss, the $50 short-term capital gain, and the $150 short-term capital loss for the post-October period of 1988 in its taxable income for 1989 in addition to the long-term and short-term capital gains and losses for 1989. Accordingly, X's taxable income for 1989 will include a net capital gain of $105 (consisting of a net long-term capital gain of $135 and a net short-term capital loss of $30).

(iii) Earnings and profits. For 1988, X must determine both its earnings and profits and its accumulated earnings and profits without regard to the $150 long-term capital gain, the $75 long-term capital loss, the $50 short-term capital gain, and the $150 short-term capital loss for the post-October period of 1988. In determining both its earnings and profits and its accumulated earnings and profits for 1989, X must include (in addition to the long-term and short-term capital gains and losses for 1989) the $150 long-term capital gain, the $75 long-term capital loss, the $50 short-term capital gain, and the $150 short-term capital loss for the post-October period of 1988 as if those deferred gains and losses arose on January 1, 1989. Thus, X will include $160 of capital gain in its earnings and profits for 1988 and $105 of capital gain in its earnings and profits for 1989.

Example (7). Same facts as example (5), except that X elects to defer only $20 of the post-October capital loss for 1988 under paragraph (f)(1) of this section for purposes of determining its taxable income for 1988.

(i) Capital gain dividends. Same result as in example (5).

(ii) Taxable income. X must compute its taxable income for 1988 by including $5 of the $150 short-term capital loss for the post-October period of 1988, but without regard to the $150 long-term capital gain, the $75 long-term capital loss, the $50 short-term capital gain, and $145 of the $150 short-term capital loss for the post-October period of 1988 because it made an election to defer $20 of the $25 post-October capital loss for 1988 under paragraph (f)(1) of this section. Accordingly, X's taxable income for 1988 will include a net capital gain of $100 and a net short-term capital gain of $55. X must include the $150 long-term capital gain, the $75 long-term capital loss, the $50 short-term capital gain, and $145 of the $150 short-term capital loss for the post-October period of 1988 in its taxable income for 1989 in addition to the long-term and short-term capital gains and losses for 1989. Accordingly, X's taxable income for 1989 will include a net capital gain of $110 (consisting of a long-term capital gain of $135 and a net short-term capital loss of $25).

(iii) Earnings and profits. X must determine its earnings and profits for 1988 without regard to the $150 long-term capital gain, the $75 long-term capital loss, the $50 short-term capital gain, and the $150 short-term capital loss for the post-October period of 1988. In determining its accumulated earnings and profits for 1988, X must include $5 of the $150 short-term capital loss for the post-October period of 1988. In determining its accumulated earnings and profits for 1989, X must include (in addition to the long-term and short-term capital gains and losses for 1989) the $150 long-term capital gain, the $75 long-term capital loss, the $50 short-term capital gain, and $145 of the $150 short-term capital loss for the post-October period of 1988 as if those deferred gains and losses arose on January 1, 1989. Thus, X includes $160 of capital gain in its earnings and profits for 1988, includes $155 in its accumulated earnings and profits for 1988, and includes $110 of capital gain in its earnings and profits for 1989.

Example (8). X has the following capital gains and losses for the periods indicated:

	Long-term	Short-term
01/01 to 10/31/88	115	80
	(15)	(20)
	100	60
11/01 to 12/31/88	15	25
	(75)	(10)
	(60)	15
01/01 to 10/31/89	80	50
	(5)	(100)
	75	(50)
11/01 to 12/31/89	85	40
	(0)	(20)
	85	20

X has a post-October capital loss of $45 for its 1988 taxable year due to a net capital loss for the post-October period of 1988. X does not make an election under paragraph (f)(1) of this section.

(i) Capital gain dividends. X may designate up to $100 as a capital gain dividend for 1988 because X must disregard the $15 long-term capital gain, the $75 long-term capital loss, the $25 short-term capital gain, and the $10 short-term capital loss for the post-October period of 1988 in computing its net capital gain for this purpose. In computing its net capital gain for 1989 for purposes of determining the amount it may designate as a capital gain dividend for 1989, X must take into account the $15 long-term capital gain, the $75 long-term capital loss, the $25 short-term capital gain, and the $10 short-term capital loss for the post-October period of 1988 in addition to the long-term and short-term capital gains and losses for 1989. Accordingly, X may designate up to $85 as a capital gain dividend for 1989.

(ii) Taxable income. X must include the $15 long-term capital gain, the $75 long-term capital loss, the $25 short-term capital gain, and the $10 short-term capital loss for the post-October period of 1988 in its taxable income for 1988 because it did not make an election under paragraph (f)(1) of this section for 1988. Accordingly, X's taxable income for 1988 will include a net capital gain of $40 and a net short-term capital gain of $75. X's taxable income for 1989 will include a net capital gain of $130 for 1989 (consisting of a net long-term capital gain of $160 and a net short-term capital loss of $30).

(iii) Earnings and profits. X must determine its earnings and profits for 1988 without regard to the $15 long-term capital gain, the $75 long-term capital loss, the $25 short-term capital gain, and the $10 short-term capital loss for the post-October period of 1988. X must, however, include the $15 long-term capital gain, the $75 long-term capital loss, the $25 short-term capital gain, and the $10 short-term capital loss for the post-October period of 1988 in determining its accumulated earnings and profits for 1988. Thus, X includes $160 of capital gain in its earnings and profits for 1988, includes $115 in its accumulated earnings and profits for 1988, and includes $130 of capital gain in its earnings and profits for 1989.

Example (9). Same facts as example (8), except that X elects to defer the entire $45 post-October capital loss for 1988 under paragraph (f)(1) of this section for purposes of determining its taxable income for 1988.

(i) Capital gain dividends. Same result as in example (8).

(ii) Taxable income. X must compute its taxable income for 1988 without regard to the $15 long-term capital gain, the $75 long-term capital loss, the $25 short-term capital gain, and the $10 short-term capital loss for the post-October period of 1988 because it made an election to defer the entire $45 post-October capital loss for 1988 under paragraph (f)(1) of this section. Accordingly, X's taxable income for 1988 will include a net capital gain of $100 and a net short-term capital gain of $60. X must include the $15 long-term capital gain, the $75 long-term capital loss, the $25 short-term capital gain, and the $10 short-term capital loss for the post-October period of 1988 in its taxable income for 1989 in addition to the long-term and short-term capital gains and losses for 1989.

Accordingly, X's taxable income for 1989 will include a net capital gain of $85 (consisting of a net long-term capital gain of $100 and a net short-term capital loss of $15).

(iii) Earnings and profits. For 1988, X must determine both its earnings and profits and its accumulated earnings and profits without regard to the $15 long-term capital gain, the $75 long-term capital loss, the $25 short-term capital gain, and the $10 short-term capital loss for the post-October period of 1988. In determining both its earnings and profits and its accumulated earnings and profits for 1989, X must include (in addition to the long-term and short-term capital gains and losses for 1989) the $15 long-term capital gain, the $75 long-term capital loss, the $25 short-term capital gain, and the $10 short-term capital loss for the post-October period of 1988 as if those deferred gains and losses arose on January 1, 1989. Thus, X will include $160 of capital gain in its earnings and profits for 1988 and $85 of capital gain in its earnings and profits for 1989.

Example (10). Same facts as example (8), except that X elects to defer only $30 of the post-October capital loss for 1988 under paragraph (f)(1) of this section for purposes of determining its taxable income for 1988.

(i) Capital gain dividends. Same result as in example (8).

(ii) Taxable income. X must compute its taxable income for 1988 by including $5 of the $75 long-term capital loss and the $10 short-term capital loss for the post-October period of 1988, but without regard to the $15 long-term capital gain, $70 of the $75 long-term capital loss, and the $25 short-term capital gain for the post-October period of 1988 because it made an election to defer $30 of the $45 post-October capital loss for 1988 under paragraph (f)(1) of this section.

Accordingly, X's taxable income for 1988 will include a net capital gain of $95 and a net short-term capital gain of $50. X must include the $15 long-term capital gain, $70 of the $75 long-term capital loss, and the $25 short-term capital gain for the post-October period of 1988 in its taxable income for 1989 in addition to the long-term and short-term capital gains and losses for 1989. Accordingly, X's taxable income for 1989 will include a net capital gain of $100 (consisting of a net long-term capital gain of $105 and a net short-term capital loss of $5).

(iii) Earnings and profits. X must determine its earnings and profits for 1988 without regard to the $15 long-term capital gain, the $75 long-term capital loss, the $25 short-term capital gain, and the $10 short-term capital loss for the post-October period of 1988. In determining its accumulated earnings and profits for 1988, X must include $5 of the $75 long-term capital loss and the $10 short-term capital loss for the post-October period of 1988. In determining both its earnings and profits and its accumulated earnings and profits for 1989, X must include (in addition to the long-term and short-term capital gains and losses for 1989) the $15 long-term capital gain, $70 of the $75 long-term capital loss, and the $25 short-term capital gain for the post-October period of 1988 as if those deferred gains and losses arose on January 1, 1989. Thus, X includes $160 of capital gain in its earnings and profits for 1988, includes $145 in its accumulated earnings and profits for 1989, and includes $100 of capital gain in its earnings and profits for 1989 (consisting of a net long-term capital gain of $105 and a net short-term capital loss of $5).

Example (11). X has the following foreign currency gains and losses attributable to the periods indicated:

01/01 to 10/31/88	200
11/01 to 12/31/88	(100)
01/01 to 10/31/89	110
11/01 to 12/31/89	40

X has a $100 post-October currency loss for its 1988 taxable year due to a net foreign currency loss for the post-October period of 1988. X does not make an election under paragraph (f)(1) of this section.

(i) Taxable income. X must compute its taxable income for 1988 by including the $100 foreign currency loss for the post-October period of 1988 because it did not make an election under paragraph (f)(1) of this section. Accordingly, X's taxable income for 1988 will include a net foreign currency gain of $100. X's taxable income for 1989 will include a net foreign currency gain of $150.

(ii) Earnings and profits. X must determine its earnings and profits for 1988 without regard to the foreign currency loss for the post-October period of 1988. X must, however, include the $100 foreign currency loss for the post-October period 1988 in determining its accumulated earnings and profits for 1988. Thus, X includes $200 of foreign currency gain in its earnings and profits for 1988, includes $100 in its accumulated earnings and profits for 1988, and includes $150 of foreign currency gain in its earnings and profits for 1989.

Example (12). Same facts as example (11), except that X elects to defer the entire $100 post-October currency loss for 1988 under paragraph (f)(1) of this section for purposes of determining its taxable income for 1988.

(i) Taxable income. X must compute its taxable income for 1988 without regard to the $100 foreign currency loss for the post-October period of 1988 because it made an election to defer the entire $100 post-October currency loss for 1988 under paragraph (f)(1) of this section. Accordingly, X's taxable income for 1988 will include a net foreign currency gain of $200. X's taxable income for 1989 will include a net foreign currency gain of $50 because X must compute its taxable income for 1989 by including the $100 foreign currency loss for the post-October period of 1988 in addition to the foreign currency gains and losses for 1989.

(ii) Earnings and profits. For 1988, X must determine both its earnings and profits and its accumulated earnings and profits without regard to the $100 foreign currency loss for the post-October period of 1988. In determining both its earnings and profits and its accumulated earnings and profits for 1989, X must include (in addition to the foreign currency gains and losses for 1989) the $100 foreign currency loss for the post-October period 1988 as if that deferred loss arose on January 1, 1989. Thus, X will include $200 of foreign currency gain in its earnings and profits for 1988 and $50 of foreign currency gain in its earnings and profits for 1989.

Example (13). Same facts as example (11), except that X elects to defer only $75 of the post-October currency loss under paragraph (f)(1) of this section for purposes of determining its taxable income for 1988.

(i) Taxable income. X must compute its taxable income for 1988 by including $25 of the $100 foreign currency loss for the post-October period of 1988, but without regard to $75 of the $100 foreign currency loss for the post-October period of 1988 because it made an election to defer $75 of the $100 post-October currency loss for 1988 under paragraph (f)(1) of this section. Accordingly, X's taxable income for 1988 will include a net foreign currency gain of $175. X's taxable income will include a net foreign currency gain of $75 for 1989 because X must compute its taxable income for 1989 by including $75 of the $100 foreign currency loss for the post-October period of 1988 in addition to the foreign currency gains and losses for 1989.

(ii) Earnings and profits. X must determine its earnings and profits for 1988 without regard to the $100 foreign currency loss for the post-October period of 1988. X must, however, include $25 of the $100 foreign currency loss for the post-October period of 1988 in determining its accumulated earnings and profits for 1988. In determining both its earnings and profits and its accumulated earnings and profits for 1989, X must include (in addition to the foreign currency gains and losses for 1989) the $75 of the $100 foreign currency loss for the post-October period of 1988 as if that loss arose on January 1, 1989. Thus, X includes $200 of foreign currency gain in its earnings and profits for 1988, includes $175 in its accumulated earnings and profits for 1988, and includes $75 of foreign currency gain in its earnings and profits for 1989.

(i) Procedure for making election. *(1) In general.* Except as provided in paragraph (i)(2) of this section, a regulated investment company may make an election under paragraph (f)(1) of this section for a taxable year to which this section applies by completing its income tax return (including any necessary schedules) for that taxable year in accordance with the instructions for the form that are applicable to the election.

(2) When applicable instructions not available. If the instructions for the income tax returns of regulated investment companies for a taxable year to which this section applies do not reflect the provisions of this section, a regulated investment company may make an election under paragraph (f)(1) of this section for that year by entering the appropriate amounts on its income tax return (including any necessary schedules) for that year, and by attaching a written statement to the return that states—

(i) The taxable year for which the election under this section is made;

(ii) The fact that the regulated investment company elects to defer all or a part of its post-October capital loss or post-October currency loss for that taxable year for purposes of computing its taxable income under the terms of this section;

(iii) The amount of the post-October capital loss or post-October currency loss that the regulated investment company elects to defer for that taxable year; and

(iv) The name, address, and employer identification number of the regulated investment company.

(j) Transition rules. *(1) In general.* For a taxable year ending before March 2, 1990 in which a regulated investment company incurred a post-October capital loss or post-October currency loss, the company may use any method that is consistently applied and in accordance with reasonable business practice to determine the amounts taken into account in that taxable year for purposes of paragraphs (e)(2), (f)(3), and (g) of this section and to determine the amount taken into account in the succeeding year for purposes of paragraphs (e)(3), (f)(4), and (g) of this section. For example, for purposes of paragraph (e), a taxpayer may use a method that treats as incurred in a taxable year all capital gains taken into account in computing the post-October capital loss for that year and an amount of capital loss for such period equal to the amount of such gains and that treats the remaining amount of capital loss for such period as arising on the first day of the succeeding year.

Similarly, for purposes of paragraph (e)(3), a taxpayer may use a method that treats as arising on the first day of the succeeding year only the excess of the capital losses from sales or exchanges after October 31 over the capital gains for such period (that is, the net capital loss or net long-term capital loss for such period).

(2) Retroactive election. (i) In general. A regulated investment company may make an election (a "retroactive election") under paragraph (f)(1) for a taxable year with respect to which it has filed an income tax return on or before May 1, 1990 (a "retroactive election year") by filing an amended return (including any necessary schedules) for the retroactive election year reflecting the appropriate amounts and by attaching a written statement to the return that complies with the requirements of paragraph (i)(2) of this section.

(ii) Deadline for making election. A retroactive election may be made no later than December 31, 1990.

(3) Amended return required for succeeding year in certain circumstances. (i) In general. If, at the time a regulated investment company makes a retroactive election under this section, it has already filed an income tax return for the succeeding year, the company must file an amended return for such succeeding year reflecting the appropriate amounts.

(ii) Time for filing amended return. An amended return required under paragraph (j)(3)(i) of this section must be filed together with the amended return described in paragraph (j)(2)(i).

(4) Retroactive dividend. (i) In general. A regulated investment company that makes a retroactive election under this section for a retroactive election year may elect to treat any dividend (or portion thereof) declared and paid (or

treated as paid under section 852(b)(7)) by the regulated investment company after the retroactive election year and on or before December 31, 1990 as having been paid during the retroactive election year (a "retroactive dividend"). This election shall be irrevocable with respect to the retroactive dividend to which it applies.

(ii) Method of making election. The election under this paragraph (j)(4) must be made by the regulated investment company by treating the dividend (or portion thereof) to which the election applies as a dividend paid during the retroactive election year in computing its deduction for dividends paid in its tax returns for all applicable years (including the amended return(s) required to be filed under paragraphs (j)(2) and (3) of this section).

(iii) Deduction for dividends paid. (A) In general. Subject to the rules of sections 561 and 562, a regulated investment company shall include the amount of any retroactive dividend in computing its deduction for dividends paid for the retroactive election year. No deduction for dividends paid shall be allowed under this paragraph (j)(4)(iii)(A) for any amount not paid (or treated as paid under section 852(b)(7)) on or before December 31, 1990.

(B) Limitation on ordinary dividends. The amount of retroactive dividends (other than retroactive dividends qualifying as capital gain dividends) paid for a retroactive election year under this section shall not exceed the increase, if any, in the investment company taxable income of the regulated investment company (determined without regard to the deduction for dividends paid (as defined in section 561)) that is attributable solely to the regulated investment company having made the retroactive election.

(C) Limitation on capital gain dividends. The amount of retroactive dividends qualifying as capital gain dividends paid for a retroactive election year under this section shall not exceed the increase, if any, in the amount of the excess described in section 852(b)(3)(A) (relating to the excess of the net capital gain over the deduction for capital gain dividends paid) that is attributable solely to the regulated investment company having made the retroactive election.

(D) Effect on other years. A retroactive dividend shall not be includible in computing the deduction for dividends paid for—

(1) The taxable year in which such distribution is actually paid (or treated as paid under section 852(b)(7)); or

(2) Under section 855(a), the taxable year preceding the retroactive election year.

(iv) Earnings and profits. A retroactive dividend shall be considered as paid out of the earnings and profits of the retroactive election year (computed with the application of sections 852(c) and 855, § 1.852-5, § 1.855-1, and this section), and not out of the earnings and profits of the taxable year in which the distribution is actually paid (or treated as paid under section 852(b)(7)).

(v) Receipt by shareholders. Except as provided in section 852(b)(7), a retroactive dividend shall be included in the gross income of the shareholders of the regulated investment company for the taxable year in which the dividend is received by them.

(vi) Foreign tax election. If a regulated investment company to which section 853 (relating to foreign taxes) is applicable for a retroactive election year elects to treat a dividend paid (or treated as paid under section 852(b)(7)) during the taxable year as a retroactive dividend, the shareholders of the regulated investment company shall consider the amounts described in section 853(b)(2) allocable to such distribution as paid or received, as the case may be, in the shareholder's taxable year in which the distribution is made.

(vii) Example. The provisions of this paragraph (j)(4) may be illustrated by the following example:

Example. X is a regulated investment company that computes its income on a calendar year basis. No election is in effect under section 4982(e)(4). X has the following income for 1988:

Foreign Currency Gains and Losses

Gains and Losses

Jan. 1-Oct. 31-100

Nov. 1-Dec. 31-(75)

Capital Gains and Losses

Jan. 1-Oct. 31-short term, 100; long term, 100

Nov. 1-Dec. 31-short term, 50; long term, (100)

(A) X had investment company taxable income of $175 and no net capital gain for 1988 for taxable income purposes. X distributed $175 of investment company taxable income as an ordinary dividend for 1988.

(B) If X makes a retroactive election under this section to defer the entire $75 post-October currency loss and the entire $50 post-October capital loss for the post-October period of its 1988 taxable year for purposes of computing its taxable income, that deferral increases X's investment company taxable income for 1988 by $25 (due to an increase in foreign currency gain of $75 and a decrease in short-term capital gain of $50) to $200 and increases the excess described in section 852(b)(3)(A) for 1988 by $100 from $0 to $100. The amount that X may treat as a retroactive ordinary dividend is limited to $25, and the amount that X may treat as a retroactive capital gain dividend is limited to $100.

(5) Certain distributions may be designated retroactively as capital gain dividends. To the extent that a regulated investment company designated as capital gain dividends for a taxable year less than the maximum amount permitted under paragraph (e) of this section for that taxable year, the regulated investment company may designate an additional amount of dividends paid (or treated as paid under sections 852(b)(7) or 855, or paragraph (j)(4) of this section) for the taxable year as capital gain dividends, notwithstanding that a written notice was not mailed to its shareholders within 60 days after the close of the taxable year in which the distribution was paid (or treated as paid under section 852(b)(7)).

(k) Effective date. The provisions of this section shall apply to taxable years ending after October 31, 1987.

T.D. 8287, 1/30/90, amend T.D. 8320, 11/29/90.

§ 1.852-12 Non-RIC earnings and profits.

(a) Applicability of section 852(a)(2)(A). *(1) In general.* An investment company does not satisfy section 852(a)(2)(A) unless—

(i) Part I of subchapter M applied to the company for all its taxable years ending on or after November 8, 1983; and

(ii) For each corporation to whose earnings and profits the investment company succeeded by the operation of section 381, part I of subchapter M applied for all the corporation's taxable years ending on or after November 8, 1983.

(2) Special rule. See section 1071(a)(5)(D) of the Tax Reform Act of 1984, Pub. L. 98-369 (98 Stat. 1051), for a special rule which treats part I of subchapter M as having applied to an investment company's first taxable year ending after November 8, 1983.

(b) Applicability of section 852(a)(2)(B). *(1) In general.* An investment company does not satisfy section 852(a)(2)(B) unless, as of the close of the taxable year, it has no earnings and profits other than earnings and profits that—

(i) Were earned by a corporation in a year for which part I of subchapter M applied to the corporation and, at all times thereafter, were the earnings and profits of a corporation to which part I of subchapter M applied;

(ii) By the operation of section 381 pursuant to a transaction that occurred before December 22, 1992, became the earnings and profits of a corporation to which part I of subchapter M applied and, at all times thereafter, were the earnings and profits of a corporation to which part I of subchapter M applied;

(iii) Were accumulated in a taxable year ending before January 1, 1984, by a corporation to which part I of subchapter M applied for any taxable year ending before November 8, 1983; or

(iv) Were accumulated in the first taxable year of an investment company that began business in 1983 and that was not a successor corporation.

(2) Prior law. For purposes of paragraph (b) of this section, a reference to part I of subchapter M includes a reference to the corresponding provisions of prior law.

(c) Effective date. This regulation is effective for taxable years ending on or after December 22, 1992.

(d) For treatment of net built-in gain assets of a C corporation that become assets of a RIC, see § 1.337(d)-5T.

T.D. 8483, 8/17/93, amend T.D. 8872, 2/4/2000.

§ 1.853-1 Foreign tax credit allowed to shareholders.

(a) In general. Under section 853, a regulated investment company, meeting the requirements set forth in section 853(a) and paragraph (b) of this section, may make an election with respect to the income, war-profits, and excess profits taxes described in section 901(b)(1) which it pays to foreign countries or possessions of the United States during the taxable year, including such taxes as are deemed paid by it under the provisions of any income tax convention to which the United States is a party. If an election is made, the shareholders of the regulated investment company shall apply their proportionate share of such foreign taxes paid, or deemed to have been paid by it pursuant to any income tax convention, as either a credit (under section 901) or as a deduction (under section 164(a)) as provided by section 853(b)(2) and paragraph (b) of § 1.853-2. The election is not applicable with respect to taxes deemed to have been paid under section 902 (relating to the credit allowed to corporate stockholders of a foreign corporation for taxes paid by such foreign corporation). In addition, the election is not applicable to any tax with respect to which the regulated investment company is not allowed a credit by reason of any provision of the Internal Revenue Code other than section 853(b)(1), including, but not limited to, section 901(j), section 901(k), or section 901(l).

(b) Requirements. To qualify for the election provided in section 853(a), a regulated investment company (1) must have more than 60 percent of the value of its total assets, at the close of the taxable year for which the election is made, invested in stocks and securities of foreign corporations, and (2) must also, for that year, comply with the requirements prescribed in section 852(a) and paragraph (a) of § 1.852-1. The term "value", for purposes of the first requirement, is defined in section 851(c)(4). For the definition of foreign corporation, see section 7701(a).

(c) Effective/applicability date. The final sentence of paragraph (a) of this section is applicable for RIC taxable years ending on or after December 31, 2007.

T.D. 6236, 6/3/57, amend T.D. 9357, 8/23/2007.

§ 1.853-2 Effect of election.

(a) Regulated investment company. A regulated investment company making a valid election with respect to a taxable year under the provisions of section 853(a) is, for such year, denied both the deduction for foreign taxes provided by section 164(a) and the credit for foreign taxes provided by section 901 with respect to all income, war-profits, and excess profits taxes (described in section 901(b)(1)) which it has paid to any foreign country or possession of the United States. See section 853(b)(1)(A). However, under section 853(b)(1)(B), the regulated investment company is permitted to add the amount of such foreign taxes paid to its dividends paid deduction for that taxable year. See paragraph (a) of § 1.852-1.

(b) Shareholder. Under section 853(b)(2), a shareholder of an investment company, which has made the election under section 853, is, in effect, placed in the same position as a person directly owning stock in foreign corporations, in that he must include in his gross income (in addition to taxable dividends actually received) his proportionate share of such foreign taxes paid and must treat such amount as foreign taxes paid by him for the purposes of the deduction under section 164(a) and the credit under section 901. For such purposes he must treat as gross income from a foreign country or possession of the United States (1) his proportionate share of the taxes paid by the regulated investment company to such foreign country or possession and (2) the portion of any dividend paid by the investment company which represents income derived from such sources.

(c) Dividends paid after the close of the taxable year. For additional rules applicable to certain distributions made after the close of the taxable year which may be designated as income received from sources within and taxes paid to foreign countries or possessions of the United States, see section 855(d) and paragraph (f) of § 1.855-1.

(d) Example. This section is illustrated by the following example:

Example. (i) Facts. X Corporation, a regulated investment company with 250,000 shares of common stock outstanding, has total assets, at the close of the taxable year, of $10 million ($4 million invested in domestic corporations, $3.5 million in Foreign Country A corporations, and $2.5 million in Foreign Country B corporations). X Corporation received dividend income of $800,000 from the following sources: $300,000 from domestic corporations, $250,000 from Country A corporations, and $250,000 from Country B corporations. All dividends from Country A corporations and from Country B corporations were properly characterized as income from sources without the United States. The dividends from Country A corporations were subject to a 10 percent withholding tax ($25,000) and the dividends from Country B corporations were subject to a 20 percent withholding tax ($50,000). X Corporation's only expenses for the taxable year were $80,000 of operation and management expenses related to both its U.S. and foreign investments. In this case, Corporation X properly apportioned the $80,000 expense based on the relative amounts of its U.S. and foreign source gross income. Thus, $50,000 in expense was apportioned to foreign source income ($80,000 x $500,000/$800,000, total expense times the fraction of foreign dividend income over total dividend income) and $30,000 in expense was apportioned to U.S. source income ($80,000 x $300,000/$800,000, total expense times the fraction of U.S. source dividend income over total dividend income). During the taxable year, X Corporation distributed to its shareholders the entire $645,000 income that was available for distribution ($800,000, less $80,000 in expenses, less $75,000 in foreign taxes withheld).

(ii) Section 853 election. X Corporation meets the requirements of section 851 to be considered a RIC for the taxable year and the requirements of section 852(a) for part 1 of subchapter M to apply for the taxable year. X Corporation notifies each shareholder by mail, within the time prescribed by section 853(c), that by reason of the election the shareholders are to treat as foreign taxes paid $0.30 per share of stock ($75,000 of foreign taxes paid, divided by the 250,000 shares of stock outstanding). The shareholders must report as income $2.88 per share ($2.58 of dividends actually received plus the $0.30 representing foreign taxes paid). Of the $2.88 per share, $1.80 per share ($450,000 of foreign source taxable income divided by 250,000 shares) is to be considered as received from foreign sources. The $1.80 consists of $0.30, the foreign taxes treated as paid by the shareholder and $1.50, the portion of the dividends received by the shareholder from the RIC that represents income of the RIC treated as derived from foreign sources ($500,000 of foreign source income, less $50,000 of expense apportioned to foreign source income, less $75,000 of foreign tax withheld, which is $375,000, divided by 250,000 shares).

(e) Effective/applicability date. Paragraph (d) of this section is applicable for RIC taxable years ending on or after December 31, 2007. Notwithstanding the preceding sentence, for a taxable year that ends on or after December 31, 2007, and begins before August 24, 2007, a taxpayer may rely on this section as it was in effect on August 23, 2007.

T.D. 6236, 6/3/57, amend T.D. 9357, 8/23/2007.

§ 1.853-3 Notice to shareholders.

(a) General rule. If a regulated investment company makes an election under section 853(a), in the manner provided in § 1.853-4, the regulated investment company is required under section 853(c) to furnish its shareholders with a written notice mailed not later than 60 days after the close of its taxable year. The notice must designate the shareholder's portion of creditable foreign taxes paid to foreign countries or possessions of the United States and the portion of the dividend that represents income derived from sources within each country that is attributable to a period during which section 901(j) applies to such country, if any, and the portion of the dividend that represents income derived from other foreign countries and possessions of the United States. For purposes of section 853(b)(2) and § 1.853-2(b), the amount that a shareholder may treat as the shareholder's proportionate share of foreign taxes paid and the amount to be included as gross income derived from any foreign country that is attributable to a period during which section 901(j) applies to such country or gross income from sources within other foreign countries or possessions of the United States shall not exceed the amount so designated by the regulated investment company in such written notice. If, however, the amount designated by the regulated investment company in the notice exceeds the shareholder's proper proportionate share of foreign taxes or gross income from sources within foreign countries or possessions of the United States

(b) Shareholder of record custodian of certain unit investment trusts. In any case where a notice is mailed pursuant to paragraph (a) of this section by a regulated investment company with respect to a taxable year of the regulated investment company ending after December 8, 1970 to a shareholder of record who is a nominee acting as a custodian of a unit investment trust described in section 851(f)(1) and paragraph (b) of § 1.851-7, the nominee shall furnish each holder of an interest in such trust with a written notice mailed on or before the 70th day following the close of the regulated investment company's taxable year. The notice shall designate the holder's proportionate share of the amounts of creditable foreign taxes paid to foreign countries or possessions of the United States and the holder's proportionate share of the dividend that represents income derived from sources within each country that is attributable to a period during which section 901(j) applies to such country, if any, and the holder's proportionate share of the dividend that represents income derived from other foreign countries or possessions of the United States shown on the notice received by the nominee pursuant to paragraph (a) of this section. This paragraph shall not apply if the regulated investment company agrees with the nominee to satisfy the notice requirements of paragraph (a) of this section with respect to each holder of an interest in the unit investment trust whose shares are being held by the nominee as custodian and not later than 45 days following the close of the company's taxable year, files with the Internal Revenue Service office where such company's return for the taxable year is to be filed, a statement that the holders of the unit investment trust with whom the agreement was made have been directly notified by the regulated investment company. Such statement shall include the name, sponsor, and custodian of each unit investment trust whose holders have been directly notified. The nominee's requirements under this paragraph shall be deemed met if the regulated investment company transmits a copy of such statement to the nominee within such 60-day period; provided however, if the regulated investment company fails or is unable to satisfy the requirements of this paragraph with respect to the holders of interest in the unit investment trust, it shall so notify the Internal Revenue Service within 60 days following the close of its taxable year. The custodian shall, upon notice by the Internal Revenue Service that the regulated investment company has failed to comply with the agreement, satisfy the requirements of this paragraph within 30 days of such notice.

(c) Effective/applicability date. This section is applicable for RIC taxable years ending on or after December 31, 2007. Notwithstanding the preceding sentence, for a taxable year that ends on or after December 31, 2007, and begins before August 24, 2007, a taxpayer may rely on this section as it was in effect on August 23, 2007.

T.D. 6236, 6/3/57, amend T.D. 6369, 3/16/59, T.D. 6921, 6/19/67, T.D. 7187, 7/5/72, T.D. 9357, 8/23/2007.

§ 1.853-4 Manner of making election.

(a) General rule. To make an election under section 853 for a taxable year, a regulated investment company must file a statement of election as part of its Federal income tax return for the taxable year. The statement of election must state that the regulated investment company elects the application of section 853 for the taxable year and agrees to provide the information required by paragraph (c) of this section.

(b) Irrevocability of the election. The election shall be made with respect to all foreign taxes described in paragraph (c)(2) of this section, and must be made not later than the time prescribed for filing the return (including extensions). This election, if made, shall be irrevocable with respect to the dividend (or portion thereof), and the foreign taxes paid with respect thereto, to which the election applies.

(c) Required information. A regulated investment company making an election under section 853 must provide the following information:

(1) The total amount of taxable income received in the taxable year from sources within foreign countries and possessions of the United States and the amount of taxable income received in the taxable year from sources within each such foreign country or possession.

(2) The total amount of income, war profits, or excess profits taxes (described in section 901(b)(1)) to which the election applies that were paid in the taxable year to such foreign countries or possessions and the amount of such taxes paid to each such foreign country or possession.

(3) The amount of income, war profits, or excess profits taxes paid during the taxable year to which the election does not apply by reason of any provision of the Internal Revenue Code other than section 853(b), including, but not limited to, section 901(j), section 901(k), or section 901(l).

(4) The date, form, and contents of the notice to its shareholders.

(5) The proportionate share of creditable foreign taxes paid to each such foreign country or possession during the taxable year and foreign income received from sources within each such foreign country or possession during the taxable year attributable to one share of stock of the regulated investment company.

(d) Time and manner of providing information. The information specified in paragraph (c) of this section must be provided at the time and in the manner prescribed by the Commissioner and, unless otherwise prescribed, must be provided on or with a modified Form 1118 "Foreign Tax Credit--Corporations" filed as part of the RIC's timely filed Federal income tax return for the taxable year.

(e) Effective/applicability date. This section is applicable for RIC taxable years ending on or after December 31, 2007. Notwithstanding the preceding sentence, for a taxable year that ends on or after December 31, 2007, and begins before August 24, 2007, a taxpayer may rely on this section as it was in effect on August 23, 2007.

T.D. 6236, 6/3/57, amend T.D. 9357, 8/23/2007.

§ 1.854-1 Limitations applicable to dividends received from regulated investment company.

Caution: The Treasury has not yet amended Reg § 1.854-1 to reflect changes made by P.L. 108-311, P.L. 99-514, P.L. 98-369, P.L. 97-34.

(a) In general. Section 854 provides special limitations applicable to dividends received from a regulated investment company for purposes of the exclusion under section 116 for dividends received by individuals, the deduction under section 243 for dividends received by corporations, and, in the case of dividends received by individuals before January 1, 1965, the credit under section 34.

(b) Capital gain dividend. Under the provisions of section 854(a) a capital gain dividend as defined in section 852(b)(3) and paragraph (c) of § 1.852-4 shall not be considered a dividend for purposes of the exclusion under section 116, the deduction under section 243, and, in the case of taxable years ending before January 1, 1965, the credit under section 34.

(c) Rule for dividends other than capital gain dividends. *(1)* Section 854(b)(1) limits the amount that may be treated as a dividend (other than a capital gain dividend) by the shareholder of a regulated investment company, for the purposes of the credit, exclusion, and deduction specified in paragraph (b) of this section, where the investment company receives substantial amounts of income (such as interest, etc.) from sources other than dividends from domestic corporations, which dividends qualify for the exclusion under section 116.

(2) Where the "aggregate dividends received" (as defined in section 854(b)(3)(B) and paragraph (b) of § 1.854-3) during the taxable year by a regulated investment company (which meets the requirements of section 852(a) and paragraph (a) of § 1.852-1 for the taxable year during which it paid such dividend) are less than 75 percent of its gross income for such taxable year (as defined in section 854(b)(3)(A) and paragraph (a) of § 1.854-3), only that portion of the dividend paid by the regulated investment company which bears the same ratio to the amount of such dividend paid as the aggregate dividends received by the regulated investment company, during the taxable year, bears to its gross income for such taxable year (computed without regard to gains from the sale or other disposition of stocks or securities) may be treated as a dividend for purposes of such credit, exclusion, and deduction.

(3) Subparagraph (2) of this paragraph may be illustrated by the following example:

Example. The XYZ regulated investment company meets the requirements of section 852(a) for the taxable year and has received income from the following sources:

Capital gains (from the sale of stock or securities)	$100,000
Dividends (from domestic sources other than dividends described in section 116(b))	70,000
Dividend (from foreign corporations)	5,000
Interest	25,000
Total	200,000
Expenses	20,000
Taxable income	180,000

The regulated investment company decides to distribute the entire $180,000. It distributes a capital gain dividend of $100,000 and a dividend of ordinary income of $80,000. The aggregate dividends received by the regulated investment company from domestic corporations ($70,000) is less than 75 percent of its gross income ($100,000) computed without regard to capital gains from sales of securities. Therefore, an apportionment is required. Since $70,000 is 70 percent of $100,000, out of every $1 dividend of ordinary income paid by the regulated investment company only 70 cents would be available for the credit, exclusion, or deduction referred to in section 854(b)(1). The capital gains dividend and the dividend received from foreign corporations are excluded from the computation.

(d) Dividends received from a regulated investment company during taxable years of shareholders ending after July 31, 1954, and subject to the Internal Revenue Code of 1939. For the application of section 854 to taxable years of shareholders of a regulated investment company ending after July 31, 1954, and subject to the Internal Revenue Code of 1939, see § 1.34-5 and § 1.116-2.

T.D. 6236, 6/3/57, amend T.D. 6369, 3/16/59, T.D. 6921, 6/19/67.

§ 1.854-2 Notice to shareholders.

Caution: The Treasury has not yet amended Reg § 1.854-2 to reflect changes made by P.L. 99-514.

(a) General rule. Section 854(b)(2) provides that the amount that a shareholder may treat as a dividend for purposes of the exclusion under section 116 for dividends received by individuals, the deduction under section 243 for dividends received by corporations, and, in the case of dividends received by individuals before January 1, 1965, the credit under section 34, shall not exceed the amount so designated by the company in written notice to its shareholders mailed not later than 45 days (30 days for a taxable year ending before February 26, 1964) after the close of the company's taxable year. If, however, the amount so designated by the company in the notice exceeds the amount which may be treated by the shareholder as a dividend for such purposes, the shareholder is limited to the amount as correctly ascertained under section 854(b)(1) and paragraph (c) of § 1.854-1.

(b) Shareholder of record custodian of certain unit investment trusts. In any case where a notice is mailed pursuant to paragraph (a) of this section by a regulated investment company with respect to a taxable year of the regulated investment company ending after December 8, 1970 to a shareholder of record who is a nominee acting as a custodian of a unit investment trust described in section 851(f)(1) and paragraph (d) of § 1.851-7, the nominee shall furnish each holder of an interest in such trust with a written notice mailed on or before the 55th day following the close of the regulated investment company's taxable year. The notice shall designate the holder's proportionate share of the amounts that may be treated as a dividend for purposes of the exclusion under section 116 for dividends received by individuals and the deduction under section 243 for dividends received by corporations shown on the notice received by the nominee pursuant to paragraph (a) of this section. This notice shall include the name and address of the nominee identified as such. This paragraph shall not apply if the regulated investment company agrees with the nominee to satisfy the notice requirements of paragraph (a) of this section with respect to each holder of an interest in the unit investment trust whose shares are being held by the nominee as custodian and not later than 45 days following the close of the company's taxable year, files with the Internal Revenue Service office where such company's return is to be filed for the taxable year, a statement that the holders of the unit investment trust with whom the agreement was made have been directly notified by the regulated investment company. Such statement shall include the name, sponsor, and custodian of each unit investment trust whose holders have been directly notified. The nominee's requirement under this paragraph shall be deemed met if the regulated investment company transmits a copy of such statement to the nominee within such 45-day period; provided however, if the regulated investment company fails or is unable to satisfy the requirements of this paragraph with respect to the holders of interest in the unit investment trust, it shall so notify the Internal Revenue Service within 45 days following the close of its taxable year. The custodian shall, upon notice by the Internal Revenue Service that the regulated investment company has failed to comply with the agreement, satisfy the requirements of this paragraph within 30 days of such notice.

T.D. 6236, 6/3/57, amend T.D. 6921, 6/19/67, T.D. 7187, 7/5/72.

§ 1.854-3 Definitions.

Caution: The Treasury has not yet amended Reg § 1.854-3 to reflect changes made by P.L. 99-514.

(a) For the purpose of computing the limitation prescribed by section 854(b)(1)(B) and paragraph (c) of § 1.854-1, the term "gross income" does not include gain from the sale or other disposition of stock or securities. However, capital gains arising from the sale or other disposition of capital assets, other than stock or securities, shall not be excluded from gross income for this purpose.

(b) The term "aggregate dividends received" includes only dividends received from domestic corporations other than dividends described in section 116(b) (relating to dividends not eligible for exclusion from gross income). Accordingly, dividends received from foreign corporations will not be included in the computation of "aggregate dividends received". In determining the amount of any dividend for purposes of this section, the rules provided in section 116(c) (relating to certain distributions) shall apply.

T.D. 6236, 6/3/57.

§ 1.855-1 Dividends paid by regulated investment company after close of taxable year.

(a) General rule. In—

(1) Determining under section 852(a) and paragraph (a) of § 1.852-1 whether the deduction for dividends paid during the taxable year (without regard to capital gain dividends) by a regulated investment company equals or exceeds 90 percent of its investment company taxable income (determined without regard to the provisions of section 852(b)(2)(D)),

(2) Computing its investment company taxable income (under section 852(b)(2) and § 1.852-3), and

(3) Determining the amount of capital gain dividends (as defined in section 852(b)(3) and paragraph (c) of § 1.852-4 paid during the taxable year,

any dividend (or portion thereof) declared by the investment company either before or after the close of the taxable year but in any event before the time prescribed by law for the filing of its return for the taxable year (including the period of any extension of time granted for filing such return) shall, to the extent the company so elects in such return, be treated as having been paid during such taxable year. This rule is applicable only if the entire amount of such dividend is actually distributed to the shareholders in the 12-month period following the close of such taxable year and not later than the date of the first regular dividend payment made after such declaration.

(b) Election. *(1) Method of making election.* The election must be made in the return filed by the company for the taxable year. The election shall be made by the taxpayer (the regulated investment company) by treating the dividend (or portion thereof) to which such election applies as a dividend paid during the taxable year in computing its investment company taxable income, or if the dividend (or portion thereof) to which such election applies is to be designated by the company as a capital gain dividend, in computing the amount of capital gain dividends paid during such taxable year. The election provided in section 855(a) may be made only to the extent that the earnings and profits of the taxable year (computed with the application of section 852(c) and § 1.852-5) exceed the total amount of distributions out of such earnings and profits actually made during the taxable year (not including distributions with respect to which an election has been made for a prior year under section 855(a)). The dividend or portion thereof, with respect to which the regulated investment company has made a valid election under section 855(a), shall be considered as paid out of the earnings and profits of the taxable year for which such election is made, and not out of the earnings and profits of the taxable year in which the distribution is actually made.

(2) Irrevocability of the election. After the expiration of the time for filing the return for the taxable year for which an election is made under section 855(a), such election shall be irrevocable with respect to the dividend or portion thereof to which it applies.

(c) Receipt by shareholders. Under section 855(b), the dividend or portion thereof, with respect to which a valid election has been made, will be includible in the gross income of the shareholders of the regulated investment company for the taxable year in which the dividend is received by them.

(d) Examples. The application of paragraphs (a), (b), and (c) of this section may be illustrated by the following examples:

Example (1). The X Company, a regulated investment company, had taxable income (and earnings or profits) for the calendar year 1954 of $100,000. During that year the company distributed to shareholders taxable dividends aggregating $88,000. On March 10, 1955, the company declared a dividend of $37,000 payable to shareholders on March 20, 1955. Such dividend consisted of the first regular quarterly dividend for 1955 of $25,000 plus an additional $12,000 representing that part of the taxable income for 1954 which was not distributed in 1954. On March 15, 1955, the X Company filed its Federal income tax return and elected therein to treat $12,000 of the total dividend of $37,000 to be paid to shareholders on March 20, 1955, as having been paid during the taxable year 1954. Assuming that the X Company actually distributed the entire amount of the dividend of $37,000 on March 20, 1955, an amount equal to $12,000 thereof will be treated for the purposes of section 852(a) as having been paid during the taxable year 1954. Such amount ($12,000) will be considered by the X Company as a distribution out of the earnings and profits for the taxable year 1954, and will be treated by the shareholders as a taxable dividend for the taxable year in which such distribution is received by them.

Example (2). The Y Company, a regulated investment company, had taxable income (and earnings or profits) for the calendar year 1954 of $100,000, and for 1955 taxable income (and earnings or profits) of $125,000. On January 1, 1954, the company had a deficit in its earnings and profits accumulated since February 28, 1913, of $115,000. During the year 1954 the company distributed to shareholders taxable dividends aggregating $85,000. On March 5, 1955, the company declared a dividend of $65,000 payable to shareholders on March 31, 1955. On March 15, 1955, the Y Company filed its Federal income tax return in which it included $40,000 of the total dividend of $65,000 payable to shareholders on March 31, 1955, as a dividend paid by it during the taxable year 1954. On March 31, 1955, the Y Company distributed the entire amount of the dividend of $65,000 declared on March 5, 1955. The election under section 855(a) is valid only to the extent of $15,000, the amount of the undistributed earnings and profits for 1954 ($100,000 earnings and profits less $85,000 distributed during 1954). The remainder ($50,000) of the $65,000 dividend paid on March 31, 1955, could not be the subject of an election, and such amount will be regarded as a distribution by the Y Company out of earnings and profits for the taxable year 1955. Assuming that the only other distribution by the Y Company during 1955 was a distribution of $75,000 paid as a dividend on October 31, 1955, the total amount of the distribution of $65,000 paid on March 31, 1955, is to be treated by the shareholders as taxable dividends for the taxable year in which such dividend is received. The Y Company will treat the amount of $15,000 as a distribution of the earnings or profits of the company for the taxable year 1954, and the remaining $50,000 as a distribution of the earnings or profits for the year 1955. The distribution of $75,000 on October 31, 1955, is, of course, a taxable dividend out of the earnings and profits for the year 1955.

(e) Notice to shareholders. Section 855(c) provides that in the case of dividends, with respect to which a regulated investment company has made an election under section 855(a), any notice to shareholders required under subchapter M, chapter 1 of the Code, with respect to such amounts, shall be made not later than 45 days (30 days for a taxable year ending before February 26, 1964) after the close of the taxable year in which the distribution is made. Thus, the notice requirements of section 852(b)(3)(C) and paragraph (c) of § 1.852-4 with respect to capital gain dividends, section 853(c) and § 1.853-3 with respect to allowance to shareholder of foreign tax credit, and section 854(b)(2) and § 1.854-2 with respect to the amount of a distribution which may be treated as a dividend, may be satisfied with respect to amounts to which section 855(a) and this section apply if the notice relating to such amounts is mailed to the shareholders not later than 45 days (30 days for a taxable year ending before February 26, 1964) after the close of the taxable year in which the distribution is made. If the notice under section 855(c) relates to an election with respect to any capital gain dividends, such capital gain dividends shall be aggregated by the investment company with the designated capital gain dividends actually paid during the taxable year to which the election applies (not including such dividends with respect to which an election applies (not including such dividends with respect to which an election has been made for a prior year under section 855) for the purpose of determining whether the aggregate of the designated capital gain dividends with respect to such taxable year of the company is greater than the excess of the net long-term capital gain over the net short-term capital loss of the company. See section 852(b)(3)(C) and paragraph (c) of § 1.852-4.

(f) Foreign tax election. Section 855(d) provides that in the case of an election made under section 853 (relating to foreign taxes), the shareholder of the investment company shall consider the foreign income received, and the foreign tax paid, as received and paid, respectively, in the shareholder's taxable year in which distribution is made.

T.D. 6236, 6/3/57, amend T.D. 6369, 3/16/59, T.D. 6921, 6/19/67.

---

§ 1.856-0 Revenue Act of 1978 amendments not included.

The regulations under Part II of Subchapter M of the Code do not reflect the amendments made by the Revenue Act of 1978, other than the changes made by section 362 of the Act, relating to deficiency dividends.

T.D. 7767, 2/3/81, amend T.D. 7936, 1/17/84.

---

§ 1.856-1 Definition of real estate investment trust.

Caution: The Treasury has not yet amended Reg § 1.856-1 to reflect changes made by P.L. 108-27, P.L. 104-188.

(a) In general. The term "real estate investment trust" means a corporation trust, or association which (1) meets the status conditions in section 856(a) and paragraph (b) of this section, and (2) satisfies the gross income and asset diversification requirements under the limitations of section 856(c) and § 1.856-2.

(See, however, paragraph (f) of this section, relating to the requirement that, for taxable years beginning before October 5, 1976, a real estate investment trust must be an unincorporated trust or unincorporated association).

(b) Qualifying conditions. To qualify as a "real estate investment trust", an organization must be one—

(1) Which is managed by one or more trustees or directors,

(2) The beneficial ownership of which is evidenced by transferable shares or by transferable certificates of beneficial interest,

(3) Which would be taxable as a domestic corporation but for the provisions of part II, subchapter M, chapter 1 of the Code,

(4) Which, in the case of a taxable year beginning before October 5, 1976, does not hold any property (other than foreclosure property) primarily for sale to customers in the ordinary course of its trade or business,

(5) Which is neither (i) a financial institution to which section 585, 586, or 593 applies, nor (ii) an insurance company to which subchapter L applies,

(6) The beneficial ownership of which is held by 100 or more persons, and

(7) Which would not be a personal holding company (as defined in section 542) if all of its gross income constituted personal holding company income (as defined in section 543).

(c) Determination of status. The conditions described in subparagraphs (1) through (5) of paragraph (b) of this section must be met during the entire taxable year and the condition described in subparagraph (6) of paragraph (b) of this section must exist during at least 335 days of a taxable year of 12 months or during a proportionate part of a taxable year of less than 12 months. The days during which the latter condition must exit need not be consecutive. In determining the minimum number of days during which the condition described in paragraph (b)(6) of this section is required to exist in a taxable year of less than 12 months, fractional days shall be disregarded. For example, in a taxable year of 310 days, the actual number of days prescribed would be $284\frac{38}{73}$ days ($\frac{310}{365}$ of 335). The fractional day is disregarded so that the required condition in such taxable year need exist for only 284 days.

(d) Rules applicable to status requirements. For purposes of determining whether an organization meets the conditions and requirements in section 856(a), the following rules shall apply.

(1) Trustee. The term "trustee" means a person who holds legal title to the property of the real estate investment trust, and has such rights and powers as will meet the requirement of "centralization of management" under paragraph (c) of § 301.7701-2 of this chapter (Regulations on Procedure and Administration). Thus, the trustee must have continuing exclusive authority over the management of the trust, the conduct of its affairs, and (except as limited by section 856(d)(3) and § 1.856-4) the management and disposition of the trust property. For example, such authority will be considered to exist even though the trust instrument grants to the shareholders any or all of the following rights and powers: To elect or remove trustees; to terminate the trust, and to ratify amendments to the trust instrument proposed by the trustee. The existence of a mere fiduciary relationship does not, in itself, make one a trustee for purposes of section 856(a)(1). The trustee will be considered to hold legal title to the property of the trust, for purposes of this subparagraph, whether the title is held in the name of the trust itself, in the name of one or more of the trustees, or in the name of a nominee for the exclusive benefit of the trust.

(2) Beneficial ownership. Beneficial ownership shall be evidenced by transferable shares, or by transferable certificates of beneficial interest, and (subject to the provisions of paragraph (c) of this section) must be held by 100 or more persons, determined without reference to any rules of attribution. Provisions in the trust instrument or corporate charter or by laws which permit the trustee or directors to redeem shares or to refuse to transfer shares in any case where the trustee or directors, in good faith, believe that a failure to redeem shares or that a transfer of shares would result in the loss of status as a real estate investment trust will not render the shares "nontransferable." For purposes of the regulations under part II of subchapter M, the terms "stockholder," "stockholders," "shareholder," and "shareholders" include holders of beneficial interest in a real estate investment trust, the terms "stock," "shares," and "shares of stock" include certificates of beneficial interest, and the term "shares" includes shares of stock.

(3) Unincorporated organization taxable as a domestic corporation. The determination of whether an unincorporated organization would be taxable as a domestic corporation, in the absence of the provisions of part II of subchapter M, shall be made in accordance with the provisions of section 7701(a)(3) and (4) and the regulations thereunder and for such purposes an otherwise qualified real estate investment trust is deemed to satisfy the "objective to carry on business" requirement of paragraph (a) of § 301.7701-2 of this chapter (Regulations on Procedure and Administration).

(4) Property held for sale to customers. In the case of a taxable year beginning before October 5, 1976, a real estate investment trust may not hold any property (other than foreclosure property) primarily for sale to customers in the ordinary course of its trade or business. Whether property is held for sale to customers in the ordinary course of the trade or business of a real estate investment trust depends upon the facts and circumstances in each case.

(5) Personal holding company. A corporation, trust, or association even though it may otherwise meet the requirements of part II of subchapter M, will not be a real estate investment trust if, by considering all of its gross income as personal holding company income under section 543, it would be a personal holding company as defined in section 542. Thus, if at any time during the last half of the trust's taxable year more than 50 percent in value of its outstanding stock is owned (directly or indirectly under the provisions of section 544) by or for not more than 5 individuals, the stock ownership requirement in section 542(a)(2) will be met and the trust would be a personal holding company. See § 1.857-8, relating to record requirements for purposes of determining whether the trust is a personal holding company.

(e) Other rules applicable. To the extent that other provisions of chapter 1 of the Code are not inconsistent with those under part II of subchapter M thereof and the regulations thereunder, such provisions will apply with respect to both the real estate investment trust and its shareholders in the same manner that they would apply to any other organization which would be taxable as a domestic corporation. For example:

(1) Taxable income of a real estate investment trust is computed in the same manner as that of a domestic corporation;

(2) Section 301, relating to distributions of property, applies to distributions by a real estate investment trust in the same manner as it would apply to a domestic corporation;

(3) Sections 302, 303, 304, and 331 are applicable in determining whether distributions by a real estate investment trust are to be treated as in exchange for stock;

(4) Section 305 applies to distributions by a real estate investment trust of its own stock;

(5) Section 311 applies to distributions by a real estate investment trust;

(6) Except as provided in section 857(d), earnings and profits of a real estate investment trust are computed in the same manner as in the case of a domestic corporation;

(7) Section 316, relating to the definition of a dividend, applies to distributions by a real estate investment trust; and

(8) Section 341, relating to collapsible corporations, applies to gain on the sale or exchange of, or a distribution which is in exchange for, stock in a real estate investment trust in the same manner that it would apply to a domestic corporation.

(f) Unincorporated status required for certain taxable years. In the case of a taxable year beginning before October 5, 1976, a real estate investment trust must be an unincorporated trust or unincorporated association. Accordingly, in applying the regulations under part II of subchapter M of the Code with respect to such a taxable year, the term "an unincorporated trust or unincorporated association" is to be substituted for the term "a corporation, trust, or association" each place it appears, and the references to "directors" and "corporate charter or bylaws" are to be disregarded.

T.D. 6598, 4/25/62, amend T.D. 6928, 9/18/67, T.D. 7767, 2/3/81.

PARAGRAPH 1. Paragraph (d)(4) of § 1.856-1 is revised to read as follows:

Proposed § 1.856-1 Definition of real estate investment trust. [*For Preamble, see ¶ 150,099*]

* * * * *

(d) Rules applicable to status requirements. * * *

(4) Property held for sale to customers. A real estate investment trust may not hold any property primarily for sale to customers in the ordinary course of its trade or business. Whether property is held for sale to customers in the ordinary course of the trade or business of a real estate investment trust depends upon the facts and circumstances in each case. The application of the rules provided by this subparagraph may be illustrated by the following examples:

Example (1). Trust M, which otherwise qualifies as a real estate investment trust, has in its portfolio a construction loan for a condominium (a single multiunit dwelling). The loan originated with the trust and was made in accordance with prudent lending practices. The security for the loan is a mortgage on the condominium. After completion of the construction of the condominium, the debtor defaults on the loan and the trust becomes the owner of the condominium as a result of a foreclosure sale. The condominium is listed with a broker for sale as an undivided unit. The condominium is sold to an unrelated party within a reasonable period of time after foreclosure of the mortgage. Assuming that in all other respects the condominium would not be considered as held primarily for sale to customers in the ordinary course of the trust's trade or business, solely for purposes of section 856(a)(4) and this section, the trust is not considered to have held the condominium primarily for sale to customers in the ordinary course of its trade or business merely because of the circumstances under which the foreclosure was made and the property was sold.

Example (2). The facts are the same as in Example (1), except that, at the time the trust obtains ownership of the condominium, the construction of the condominium is 80 percent completed (determined on the basis of a comparison of actual construction costs at such time with expected total construction costs) and that the trust employs an unrelated contractor to complete construction of the condominium. Solely for purposes of section 856(a)(4) and this section, the trust is not considered to have held the condominium primarily for sale to customers in the ordinary course of its trade or business merely because of the circumstances under which the foreclosure was made and the property was sold.

* * * * *

§ 5.856-1 Extensions of the grace period for foreclosure property by a real estate investment trust.

(a) In general. Under section 856(e), a real estate investment trust (" REIT") may elect to treat as foreclosure property certain real property (including interests in real property), and any personal property incident to such real property, that the REIT acquires after December 31, 1973. In general, the REIT must acquire the property as the result of having bid in the property at foreclosure, or having otherwise reduced the property to ownership or possession by agreement or process of law, after there was default (or default was imminent) on a lease of such property (where the REIT was the lessor) or on an indebtedness owed to the REIT which such property secured. Property that a REIT elects to treat as foreclosure property ceases to be foreclosure property with respect to such REIT at the end of a grace period. The grace period ends on the date which is 2 years after the date on which the REIT acquired the property, unless the REIT has been granted an extension or extensions of the grace period. If the grace period is extended, the property ceases to be foreclosure property on the day immediately following the last day of the grace period, as extended.

(b) Rules for extensions of the grace period. In general, § 1.856-6(g) prescribes rules regarding extensions of the grace period. However, in order to reflect the amendment of section 856(e)(3) of the Code by section 363(c) of the Revenue Act of 1978, the following rules also apply:

(1) In the case of extensions granted after November 6, 1978, with respect to extension periods beginning after December 31, 1977, the district director may grant one or more extensions of the grace period for the property, subject to the limitation that no extension shall extend the grace period beyond the date which is 6 years after the date the REIT acquired the property. In any other case, an extension shall be for a period of not more than 1 year, and not more than two extensions can be granted with respect to the property.

(2) In the case of an extension period beginning after December 31, 1977, a request for an extension filed on or

before March 28, 1980, will be considered to be timely if the limitation on the number and length of extensions in section 856(e)(3), as in effect before the amendment made by section 363(c) of the Revenue Act of 1978, would have barred the extension.

T.D. 7767, 2/3/81.

§ 1.856-2 Limitations.

Caution: The Treasury has not yet amended Reg § 1.856-2 to reflect changes made by P.L. 108-357, P.L. 105-34, P.L. 99-514.

(a) Effective date. The provisions of part II, subchapter M, chapter 1 of the Code, and the regulations thereunder apply only to taxable years of a real estate investment trust beginning after December 31, 1960.

(b) Election. Under the provisions of section 856(c)(1), a trust, even though it satisfies the other requirements of part II of subchapter M for the taxable year, will not be considered a "real estate investment trust" for such year, within the meaning of such part II, unless it elects to be a real estate investment trust for such taxable year, or has made such an election for a previous taxable year which has not been terminated or revoked under section 856(g)(1) or (2). The election shall be made by the trust by computing taxable income as a real estate investment trust in its return for the first taxable year for which it desires the election to apply, even though it may have otherwise qualified as a real estate investment trust for a prior year. No other method of making such election is permitted. An election cannot be revoked with respect to a taxable year beginning before October 5, 1976. Thus, the failure of an organization to be a qualified real estate investment trust for a taxable year beginning before October 5, 1976, does not have the effect of revoking a prior election by the organization to be a real estate investment trust, even though the organization is not taxable under part II of subchapter M for such taxable year. See section 856(g) and § 1.856-8 for rules under which an election may be revoked with respect to taxable years beginning after October 4, 1976.

(c) Gross income requirements. Section 856(c)(2), (3), and (4), provides that a corporation, trust, or association is not a "real estate investment trust" for a taxable year unless it meets certain requirements with respect to the sources of its gross income for the taxable year. In determining whether the gross income of real estate investment trust satisfies the percentage requirements of section 856(c)(2), (3), and (4), the following rules shall apply:

(1) Gross income. For purposes of both the numerator and denominator in the computation of the specified percentages, the term "gross income" has the same meaning as that term has under section 61 and the regulations thereunder. Thus, in determining the gross income requirements under section 856(c)(2), (3), and (4), a loss from the sale or other disposition of stock, securities, real property, etc. does not enter into the computation.

(2) Lapse of options. Under section 856(c)(6)(C), the term "interests in real property" includes options to acquire land or improvements thereon, and options to acquire leaseholds of land and improvements thereon. However, where a corporation, trust, or association writes an option giving the holder the right to acquire land or improvements thereon, or writes an option giving the holder the right to acquire a leasehold of land or improvements thereon, any income that the corporation, trust, or association recognizes because the option expires unexercised is not considered to be gain from the sale or other dispositions of real property (including interests in real property) for purposes of section 856(c)(2)(D) and (3)(C). The rule in the preceding sentence also applies for purposes of section 856(c)(4)(C) in determining gain from the sale or other disposition of real property for the 30-percent-of-gross-income limitation.

(3) Commitment fees. For purposes of section 856(c)(2)(G) and (3)(G), if consideration is received or accrued for an agreement to make a loan secured by a mortgage covering both real property and other property, or for an agreement to purchase or lease both real property and other property an apportionment of the consideration is required. The apportionment of consideration received or accrued for an agreement to make a loan secured by a mortgage covering both real property and other property shall be made under the principles of § 1.856-5(c), relating to the apportionment of interest income.

(4) Holding period of property. For purposes of the 30-percent limitation of section 856(c)(4), the determination of the period for which property described in such section has been held is governed by the provisions of section 1223 and the regulations thereunder.

(5) Rents from real property and interest. See §§ 1.856-4 and 1.856-5 for rules relating to rents from real property and interest.

(d) Diversification of investment requirements. *(1) 75-percent test.* Section 856(c)(5)(A) requires that at the close of each quarter of the taxable year at least 75 percent of the value of the total assets of the trust be represented by one or more of the following:

(i) Real estate assets;

(ii) Government securities; and

(iii) Cash and cash items (including receivables). For purposes of this subparagraph the term "receivables" means only those receivables which arise in the ordinary course of the trust's operation and does not include receivables purchased from another person. Subject to the limitations in section 856(c)(5)(B) and subparagraph (2) of this paragraph, the character of the remaining 25 percent (or less) of the value of the total assets is not restricted.

(2) Limitations on certain securities. Under section 856(c)(5)(B), not more than 25 percent of the value of the total assets of the trust may be represented by securities other than those described in section 856(c)(5)(A). The ownership of securities under the 25-percent limitation in section 856(c)(5)(B) is further limited in respect of any one issuer to an amount not greater in value than 5 percent of the value of the total assets of the trust and to not more than 10 percent of the outstanding voting securities of such issuer. Thus, if the real estate investment trust meets the 75-percent asset diversification requirement in section 856(c)(5)(A), it will also meet the first test under section 856(c)(5)(B) since it will, of necessity, have not more than 25 percent of its total assets represented by securities other than those described in section 856(c)(5)(A). However, the trust must also meet two additional tests under section 856(c)(5)(B), i.e. it cannot own the securities of any one issuer in an amount (i) greater in value than 5 percent of the value of the trust's total assets, or (ii) representing more than 10 percent of the outstanding voting securities of such issuer.

(3) Determination of investment status. The term "total assets" means the gross assets of the trust determined in accordance with generally accepted accounting principles. In order to determine the effect, if any, which an acquisition of any security or other property may have with respect to the

status of a trust as a real estate investment trust, section 856(c)(5) requires a revaluation of the trust's assets at the end of the quarter in which such acquisition was made. A revaluation of assets is not required at the end of any quarter during which there has been no acquisition of a security or other property since the mere change in market value of property held by the trust does not, of itself, affect the status of the trust as a real estate investment trust. A change in the nature of "cash items", for example, the prepayment of insurance or taxes, does not constitute the acquisition of "other property" for purposes of this subparagraph. A real estate investment trust shall keep sufficient records as to investments so as to be able to show that it has complied with the provisions of section 856(c)(5) during the taxable year. Such records shall be kept at all times available for inspection by any internal revenue officer or employee and shall be retained so long as the contents thereof may become material in the administration of any internal revenue law.

(4) Illustrations. The application of section 856(c)(5) and this paragraph may be illustrated by the following examples:

Example (1). Real Estate Investment Trust M, at the close of the first quarter of its taxable year, has its assets invested as follows:

	Percent
Cash	6
Government securities	7
Real estate assets	63
Securities of various corporations (not exceeding, with respect to any one issuer, 5 percent of the value of the total assets of the trust nor 10 percent of the outstanding voting securities of such issuer)	24
Total	100

Example (2). Real Estate Investment Trust P, at the close of the first quarter of its taxable year, has its assets invested as follows:

	Percent
Cash	6
Government securities	7
Real estate assets	63
Securities of Corporation Z	20
Securities of Corporation X	4
Total	100

Trust P meets the requirement of section 856(c)(5)(A) since at least 75 percent of the value of the total assets is represented by cash, Government securities, and real estate assets. However, Trust P does not meet the diversification requirements of section 856(c)(5)(B) because its investment in the voting securities of Corporation Z exceeds 5 percent of the value of the trust's total assets.

Example (3). Real Estate Investment Trust G, at the close of the first quarter of its taxable year, has its assets invested as follows:

	Percent
Cash	4
Government securities	9
Real estate assets	70
Securities of Corporation S	5
Securities of Corporation L	4
Securities of Corporation U	4
Securities of Corporation M (which equals 25 percent of Corporation M's outstanding voting securities)	4
Total	100

Trust G meets the 75-percent requirement of section 856(c)(5)(A), but does not meet the requirements of section 856(c)(5)(B) because its investment in the voting securities of Corporation M exceeds 10 percent of Corporation M's outstanding voting securities.

Example (4). Real Estate Investment Trust R, at the close of the first quarter of its taxable year (i.e. calendar year), is a qualified real estate investment trust and has its assets invested as follows:

Cash	$ 5,000
Government securities	4,000
Receivables	4,000
Real estate assets	68,000
Securities of Corporation P	4,000
Securities of Corporation O	5,000
Securities of Corporation U	5,000
Securities of Corporation T	5,000
Total assets	100,000

During the second calendar quarter the stock in Corporation P increases in value to $50,000 while the value of the remaining assets has not changed. If Real Estate Investment Trust R has made no acquisition of stock or other property during such second quarter it will not lose its status as a real estate investment trust merely by reason of the appreciation in the value of P's stock. If, during the third quarter, Trust R acquires stock of Corporation S worth $2,000, such acquisition will necessitate a revaluation of all of the assets of Trust R as follows:

Cash	$ 3,000
Government securities	4,000
Receivables	4,000
Real estate assets	68,000
Securities in Corporation P	50,000
Securities in Corporation O	5,000
Securities in Corporation U	5,000
Securities in Corporation T	5,000
Securities in Corporation S	2,000
Total assets	146,000

Because of the discrepancy between the value of its various investments and the 25-percent limitation in section 856(c)(5), resulting in part from the acquisition of the stock of Corporation S, Trust R, at the end of the third quarter, loses its status as a real estate investment trust. However, if Trust R, within 30 days after the close of such quarter, eliminates the discrepancy so that it meets the 25-percent limitation, the trust will be considered to have met the requirements of section 856(c)(5) at the close of the third quarter, even though the discrepancy between the value of its investment in Corporation P and the 5-percent limitation in section 856(c)(5) (resulting solely from appreciation) may still exist. If instead of acquiring stock of Corporation S, Trust R had acquired additional stock of Corporation P, then because of the discrepancy between the value of its investments and both the 5-percent and the 25-percent limitations in section 856(c)(5) resulting in part from this acquisition, Trust R, at the end of the third quarter, would lose its status as a real estate investment trust, unless within 30 days after the close of such quarter both of the discrepancies are eliminated.

Example (5). If, in the previous example, the stock of Corporation P appreciates only to $10,000 during the second quarter and, in the third quarter, Trust R acquires stock of Corporation S worth $1,000, the assets as of the end of the third quarter would be as follows:

Cash	$ 4,000
Government securities	4,000
Receivables	4,000
Real estate assets	68,000
Securities in Corporation P	10,000
Securities in Corporation O	5,000
Securities in Corporation U	5,000
Securities in Corporation T	5,000
Securities in Corporation S	1,000
Total assets	106,000

Because the discrepancy between the value of its investment in Corporation P and the 5-percent limitation in section 856(c)(5) results solely from appreciation, and because there is no discrepancy between the value of its various investments and the 25-percent limitation, Trust R, at the end of the third quarter, does not lose its status as a real estate investment trust. If, instead of acquiring stock of Corporation S, Trust R had acquired additional stock of Corporation P worth $1,000, then, because of the discrepancy between the value of its investment in Corporation P and the 5-percent limitation resulting in part from this acquisition, Trust R, at the end of the third quarter, would lose its status as a real estate investment trust, unless within 30 days after the close of such quarter this discrepancy is eliminated.

T.D. 6598, 4/25/62, amend T.D. 7728, 10/31/80, T.D. 7767, 2/3/81.

PAR. 2. Paragraph (c)(2)(ii) of § 1.856-2 is revised to read as follows:

Proposed § 1.856-2 Limitations. [*For Preamble, see ¶ 150,099*]

* * * * *

(c) Gross income requirements. * * *

(2) * * *

(ii) Interest. In computing the percentage requirements in section 856(c)(2)(B) and (3)(B) there shall be included as interest only the amount which constitutes interest for the loan or forbearance of money. Thus, for example, a fee imposed upon a borrower which is in fact a charge for a service in addition to the charge for the use of borrowed money shall not be included as interest. In the case of loans made after December 7, 1972, an amount received or accrued with respect to an obligation shall not be included as interest for purposes of section 856(c)(2)(B) or (3)(B) if the determination of such amount depends in whole or in part on the income or profits of any person. For purposes of the preceding sentence, a loan is considered to be made if there is a binding commitment to make a loan, but not if the transaction is merely in the negotiation stage. To the extent limited by this subdivision, the 90-percent requirement in section 856(c)(2)(B) permits the inclusion of interest generally, while the 75-percent requirement in section 856(c)(3)(B) includes interest only to the extent that it relates to obligations secured by mortgages on real property. Where a mortgage covers both real and other property an apportionment of the interest income must be made for purposes of the 75-percent requirement. For purposes of such requirement, the apportionment is made as follows:

(a) If the loan value of the real property is equal to or exceeds the amount of the loan and is equal to or exceeds the loan value of the other property, then the entire interest income shall be apportioned to the real property.

(b) If the loan value of the other property exceeds both the amount of the loan and the loan value of the real property, then the entire interest income shall be apportioned to the other property.

(c) If the amount of the loan exceeds either the loan value of the real property or the total loan value of the other property, or both such values, then the interest income shall be apportioned between the real property and other property on the basis of their respective loan values.

For purposes of this subdivision, the term "other property" does not include property to the extent that its value is determined by reference to the value of property which is security for the obligation. For example, where a real estate investment trust makes a loan to a corporation which is secured by a mortgage on real property owned by the corporation and a pledge of the stock of such corporation, for purposes of this subdivision, the term "other property" does not include the stock of the corporation to the extent of the loan value of such real property.

* * * * *

§ 1.856-3 Definitions.

Caution: The Treasury has not yet amended Reg § 1.856-3 to reflect changes made by P.L. 108-357, P.L. 105-34, P.L. 104-188, P.L. 99-514.

For purposes of the regulations under part II, subchapter M, chapter 1 of the Code, the following definitions shall apply.

(a) Value. The term "value" means, with respect to securities for which market quotations are readily available, the market value of such securities; and with respect to other securities and assets, fair value as determined in good faith by the trustees of the real estate investment trust. In the case of securities of other qualified real estate investment trusts, fair value shall not exceed market value or asset value, whichever is higher.

(b) Real estate assets. *(1) In general.* The term "real estate assets" means real property, interests in mortgages on real property (including interests in mortgages on leaseholds of land or improvements thereon), and shares in other qualified real estate investment trusts. The term "mortgages on real property" includes deeds of trust on real property.

(2) Treatment of REMIC interests as real estate assets. (i) In general. If, for any calendar quarter, at least 95 percent of a REMIC's assets (as determined in accordance with § 1.860F-4(e)(1)(ii) or § 1.6049-7(f)(3)) are real estate assets (as defined in paragraph (b)(1) of this section), then, for that calendar quarter, all the regular and residual interests in that REMIC are treated as real estate assets and, except as provided in paragraph (b)(2)(iii) of this section, any amount includible in gross income with respect to those interests is treated as interest on obligations secured by mortgages on real property. If less than 95 percent of a REMIC's assets are real estate assets, then the real estate investment trust is treated as holding directly its proportionate share of the assets and as receiving directly its proportionate share of the income of the REMIC. See §§ 1.860F-4(e)(1)(ii)(B) and 1.6049-7(f)(3) for information required to be provided to regular and residual interest holders if the 95-percent test is not met.

(ii) Treatment of REMIC assets for section 856 purposes (A) Manufactured housing treated as real estate asset. For purposes of paragraphs (b)(1) and (2) of this section, the term "real estate asset" includes manufactured housing treated as a single family residence under section 25(e)(10).

(B) Status of cash flow investments. For purposes of this paragraph (b)(2), cash flow investments (as defined in section 860G(a)(6) and § 1.860G-2(g)(1)) are real estate assets.

(iii) Certain contingent interest payment obligations held by a REIT. If a REIT holds a residual interest in a REMIC for a principal purpose of avoiding the limitation set out in section 856(f) (concerning interest based on mortgagor net profits) or section 856(j) (concerning shared appreciation provisions), then, even if the REMIC satisfies the 95-percent test of paragraph (b)(i) of this section, the REIT is treated as receiving directly the REMIC's items of income for purposes of section 856.

(c) Interests in real property. The term "interests in real property" includes fee ownership and co-ownership of land or improvements thereon, leaseholds of land or improvements thereon, options to acquire land or improvements thereon, and options to acquire leaseholds of land or improvements thereon. The term also includes timeshare interests that represent an undivided fractional fee interest, or undivided leasehold interest, in real property, and that entitle the holders of the interests to the use and enjoyment of the property for a specified period of time each year. The term also includes stock held by a person as a tenant-stockholder in a cooperative housing corporation (as those terms are defined in section 216). Such term does not, however, include mineral, oil, or gas royalty interests, such as a retained economic interest in coal or iron ore with respect to which the special provisions of section 631(c) apply.

(d) Real property. The term "real property" means land or improvements thereon, such as buildings or other inherently permanent structures thereon (including items which are structural components of such buildings or structures). In addition, the term "real property" includes interests in real property. Local law definitions will not be controlling for purposes of determining the meaning of the term "real property" as used in section 856 and the regulations thereunder. The term includes, for example, the wiring in a building, plumbing systems, central heating or central air-conditioning machinery, pipes or ducts, elevators or escalators installed in the building, or other items which are structural components of a building or other permanent structure. The term does not include assets accessory to the operation of a business, such as machinery, printing press, transportation equipment which is not a structural component of the building, office equipment, refrigerators, individual air-conditioning units, grocery counters, furnishings of a motel, hotel, or office building, etc., even though such items may be termed fixtures under local law.

(e) Securities. The term "securities" does not include "interests in real property" or "real estate assets" as those terms are defined in section 856 and this section.

(f) Qualified real estate investment trusts. The term "qualified real estate investment trust" means a real estate investment trust within the meaning of part II of subchapter M which is taxable under such part as a real estate investment trust. For purposes of the 75-percent requirement in section 856(c)(5)(A), the trust whose stock has been included by another trust as "real estate assets" must be a "qualified real estate investment trust" for its full taxable year in which falls the close of each quarter of the trust's taxable year for which the computation is made. For example, Real Estate Investment Trust Z for its taxable year ending December 31, 1963, holds as "real estate assets" stock in Real Estate investment Trust Y, which is also on a calendar year. If Trust Y is not a qualified real estate investment trust for its full taxable year ending December 31, 1963, Trust Z may not include the stock of Trust Y as "real estate assets" in computing the 75-percent requirement as of the close of any quarter of its taxable year ending December 31, 1963.

(g) Partnership interest. In the case of a real estate investment trust which is a partner in a partnership, as defined in section 7701(a)(2) and the regulations thereunder, the trust will be deemed to own its proportionate share of each of the assets of the partnership and will be deemed to be entitled to the income of the partnership attributable to such share. For purposes of section 856, the interest of a partner in the partnership's assets shall be determined in accordance with his capital interest in the partnership. The character of the various assets in the hands of the partnership and items of gross income of the partnership shall retain the same character in the hands of the partners for all purposes of section 856. Thus, for example, if the trust owns a 30-percent capital interest in a partnership which owns a piece of rental property the trust will be treated as owning 30 percent of such property and as being entitled to 30 percent of the rent derived from the property by the partnership. Similarly, if the partnership holds any property primarily for sale to customers in the ordinary course of its trade or business, the trust will be treated as holding its proportionate share of such property primarily for such purpose. Also, for example, where a partnership sells real property or a trust sells its interest in a partnership which owns real property, any gross income realized from such sale, to the extent that it is attributable to the real property, shall be deemed gross income from the sale or disposition of real property held for either the period that the partnership has held the real property or the period that the trust was a member of the partnership, whichever is the shorter.

(h) Net capital gain. The term "net capital gain" means the excess of the net long-term capital gain for the taxable year over the net short-term capital loss for the taxable year.

T.D. 6598, 4/25/62, amend T.D. 6841, 7/26/65, T.D. 7767, 2/3/81, T.D. 8458, 12/23/92.

PAR. 3. Paragraph (d) of § 1.856-3 is revised to read as follows:

Proposed § 1.856-3 Definitions. [*For Preamble, see ¶ 150,099*]

* * * * *

(d) Real property. The term "real property" means land or improvements thereon, such as buildings or other inherently permanent structures thereon (including items which are structural components of such buildings or structures). In addition, the term "real property" includes interests in real property. Local law definitions will not be controlling for purposes of determining the meaning of the term "real property" as used in section 856 and the regulations thereunder. The term includes, for example, the wiring in a building, plumbing systems, central heating or central air-conditioning machinery, built-in air-conditioning units, built-in stoves, built-in refrigerators, permanently installed carpeting, pipes or ducts, elevators or escalators installed in the building, or other items which are structural components of a building or other permanent structure. The term does not includes assets accessory to the operation of a business, such as machinery, printing presses, transportation equipment which is not a structural component of the building, office equipment, refrigerators and other appliances which are not built-in, "window" air-conditioning units, grocery counters, furnishings of a motel, hotel, or office building, etc., even though such items may be termed fixtures under local law.

* * * * *

§ 1.856-4 Rents from real property.

Caution: The Treasury has not yet amended Reg § 1.856-4 to reflect changes made by P.L. 108-357, P.L. 105-34, P.L. 99-514.

(a) In general. Subject to the exceptions of section 856(d) and paragraph (b) of this section, the term "rents from real property" means, generally, the gross amounts received for the use of, or the right to use, real property of the real estate investment trust.

(b) Amounts specifically included or excluded. *(1) Charges for customary services.* For taxable years beginning after October 4, 1976, the term "rents from real property", for purposes of paragraphs (2) and (3) of section 856(c), includes charges for services customarily furnished or rendered in connection with the rental of real property, whether or not the charges are separately stated. Services furnished to the tenants of a particular building will be considered as customary if, in the geographic market in which the building is located, tenants in buildings which are of a similar class (such as luxury apartment buildings) are customarily provided with the service. The furnishing of water, heat, light, and air-conditioning, the cleaning of windows, public entrances, exits, and lobbies, the performance of general maintenance and of janitorial and cleaning services, the collection of trash, and the furnishing of elevator services, telephone answering services, incidental storage space, laundry equipment, watchman or guard services, parking facilities, and swimming pool facilities are examples of services which are customarily furnished to the tenants of a particular class of buildings in many geographic marketing areas. Where it is customary, in a particular geographic marketing area, to furnish electricity or other utilities to tenants in buildings of a particular class, the submetering of such utilities to tenants in such buildings will be considered a customary service. To qualify as a service customarily furnished, the service must be furnished or rendered to the tenants of the real estate investment trust or, primarily for the convenience or benefit of the tenant, to the guests, customers, or subtenants of the tenant. The service must be furnished through an independent contractor from whom the trust does not derive or receive any income. See paragraph (b)(5) of this section. For taxable years beginning before October 5, 1976, the rules in paragraph (b)(3) of 26 CFR 1.856-4 (revised as of April 1, 1977), relating to the furnishing of services, shall continue to apply.

(2) Amounts received with respect to certain personal property. (i) In general. In the case of taxable years beginning after October 4, 1976, rent attributable to personal property that is leased under, or in connection with, the lease of real property is treated under section 856(d)(1)(C) as "rents from real property" (and thus qualified for purposes of the income source requirements) if the rent attributable to the personal property is not more than 15 percent of the total rent received or accrued under the lease for the taxable year. If, however, the rent attributable to personal property is greater than 15 percent of the total rent received or accrued under the lease for the taxable year, then the portion of the rent from the lease that is attributable to personal property will not qualify as "rents from real property".

(ii) Application. In general, the 15-percent test in section 856(d)(1)(C) is applied separately to each lease of real property. However, where the real estate investment trust rents all (or a portion of all) the units in a multiple unit project under substantially similar leases (such as the leasing of apartments in an apartment building or complex to individual tenants), the 15-percent test may be applied with respect to the aggregate rent received or accrued for the taxable year under the similar leases of the property, by using the average of the trust's aggregate adjusted bases of all of the personal property subject to such leases, and the average of the trust's aggregate adjusted bases of all real and personal property subject to such leases. A lease of a furnished apartment is not considered to be substantially similar to a lease of an unfurnished apartment (including an apartment where the trust provides only personal property, such as major appliances, that is commonly provided by a landlord in connection with the rental of unfurnished living quarters).

(iii) Taxable years beginning before October 5, 1976. In the case of taxable years beginning before October 5, 1976, any amount of rent that is attributable to personal property does not qualify as rent from real property.

(3) Disqualification of rent which depends on income or profits of any person. Except as provided in paragraph (b)(6)(ii) of this section, no amount received or accrued, directly or indirectly, with respect to any real property (or personal property leased under, or in connection with, real property) qualifies as "rents from real property" where the determination of the amount depends in whole or in part on the income or profits derived by any person from the property. However, any amount so accrued or received shall not be excluded from the term "rents from real property" solely by reason of being based on a fixed percentage or percentages of receipts or sales (whether or not receipts or sales are adjusted for returned merchandise, or Federal, State, or local sales taxes). Thus, for example, "rents from real property" would include rents where the lease) provides for differing percentages or receipts or sales from different departments or from separate floors of a retail store so long as each percentage is fixed at the time of entering into the lease and a change in such percentage is not renegotiated during the term of the lease (including any renewal periods of the lease in a manner which has the effect of basing the rent on income of profits. See paragraph (b)(6) of this section for rules relating to certain amounts received or accrued by a trust which are considered to be based on the income or profits of a sublessee of the prime tenant. The amount received or accrued as rent for the taxable year which is based on a fixed percentage or percentages of the lessee's receipts or sales reduced by escalation receipts (including those determined under a formula clause) will qualify as "rents from real property". Escalation receipts include amounts received by a prime tenant from subtenants by reason of an agreement that rent shall be increased to reflect all or a portion of an increase in real estate taxes, property insurance, operating costs of the prime tenant, or similar items customarily included in lease escalation clauses. Where in accordance with the terms of an agreement an amount received or accrued as rent for the taxable year includes both a fixed rental and a percentage of all or a portion of the lessee's income or profits, neither the fixed rental nor the additional amount will qualify as "rents from real property". However, where the amount received or accrued for the taxable year under such an agreement includes only the fixed rental, the determination of which does not depend in whole or in part on the income or profits derived by the lessee, such amount may qualify as "rents from real property". An amount received

or accrued as rent for the taxable year which consists, in whole or in part, of one or more percentages of the lessee's receipts or sales in excess of determinable dollar amounts may qualify as "rents from real property", but only if two conditions exist. First, the determinable amounts must not depend in whole or in part on the income or profits of the lessee. Second, the percentages and, in the case of leases entered into after July 7, 1978, the determinable amounts, must be fixed at the time the lease is entered into and a change in percentages and determinable amounts is not renegotiated during the term of the lease (including any renewal periods of the lease) in a manner which has the effect of basing rent on income or profits. In any event, an amount will not qualify as "rents from real property" if, considering the lease and all the surrounding circumstances, the arrangement does not conform with normal business practice but is in reality used as a means of basing the rent on income or profits. The provisions of this subparagraph may be illustrated by the following example:

Example. A real estate investment trust owns land underlying an office building. On January 1, 1975, the trust leases the land for 50 years to a prime tenant for an annual rental of \$100 *x* plus 20 percent of the prime tenant's annual gross receipts from the office building in excess of a fixed base amount of \$5,000 *x* and 10 percent of such gross receipts in excess of \$10,000 *x*. For this purpose the lease defines gross receipts as all amounts received by the prime tenant from occupancy tenants pursuant to leases of space in the office building reduced by the amount by which real estate taxes, property insurance, and operating costs related to the office building for a particular year exceed the amount of such items for 1974. The exclusion from gross receipts of increases since 1974 in real estate taxes, property insurance, and other expenses relating to the office building reflects the fact that the prime tenant passes on to occupancy tenants by way of a customary lease escalation provision the risk that such expenses might increase during the term of an occupancy lease. The exclusion from gross receipts of these expense escalation items will not cause the rental received by the real estate investment trust from the prime tenant to fail to qualify as "rents from real property" for purposes of section 856(c).

(4) Disqualification of amounts received from persons owned in whole or in part by the trust. "Rents from real property" does not include any amount received or accrued, directly or indirectly, from any person in which the real estate investment trust owns, at any time during the taxable year, the specified percentage or number of shares of stock (or interest in the assets or net profits) of that person. Any amount received from such person will not qualify as "rents from real property" if such person is a corporation and the trust owns 10 percent or more of the total combined voting power of all classes of its stock entitled to vote or 10 percent or more of the total number of shares of all classes of its outstanding stock, or if such person is not a corporation and the trust owns a 10-percent-or-more interest in its assets or net profits. For example, a trust leases an office building to a tenant for which it receives rent of \$100,000 for the taxable year 1962. The lessee of the building subleases space to various subtenants for which it receives gross rent of \$500,000 for the year 1962. The trust owns 15 percent of the total assets of an unincorporated subtenant. The rent paid by this subtenant for the taxable year is \$50,000. Therefore, \$10,000 (50,000/500,000 × \$100,000) of the rent paid to the trust does not qualify as "rents from real property". Where the real estate investment trust receives, directly or indirectly, any amount of rent from any person in which it owns any proprietary interest, the trust shall submit, at the time it files its return for the taxable year (or before June 1, 1962, whichever is later), a schedule setting forth—

(i) The name and address of such person and the amount received as rent from such person; and

(ii) If such person is a corporation, the highest percentage of the total combined voting power of all classes of its stock entitled to vote, and the highest percentage of the total number of shares of all classes of its outstanding stock, owned by the trust at any time during the trust's taxable year; or

(iii) If such person is not a corporation, the highest percentage of the trust's interest in the assets or net profits of such person, owned by the trust at any time during its taxable year.

(5) Furnishing of services or management of property must be through an independent contractor. (i) In general. No amount received or accrued, directly or indirectly, with respect to any real property (or any personal property leased under, or in connection with, the real property) qualifies as "rents from real property" if the real estate investment trust furnishes or renders services to the tenants of the property or manages or operates the property, other than through an independent contractor from whom the trust itself does not derive or receive any income. The prohibition against the trust deriving or receiving any income from the independent contractor applies regardless of the source from which the income was derived by the independent contractor. Thus, for example, the trust may not receive any dividends from the independent contractor. The requirement that the trust not receive any income from an independent contractor requires that the relationship between the two be an arm's-length relationship. The independent contractor must be adequately compensated for any services which are performed for the trust. Compensation to an independent contractor determined by reference to an unadjusted percentage of gross rents will generally be considered to be adequate where the percentage is reasonable taking into account the going rate of compensation for managing similar property in the same locality, the services rendered, and other relevant factors. The independent contractor must not be an employee of the trust (i.e., the manner in which he carries out his duties as independent contractor must not be subject to the control of the trust). Although the cost of services which are customarily rendered or furnished in connection with the rental of real property may be borne by the trust, the services must be furnished or rendered through an independent contractor. Furthermore, the facilities through which the services are furnished must be maintained and operated by an independent contractor. For example, if a heating plant is located in the building, it must be maintained and operated by an independent contractor. To the extent that services (other than those customarily furnished or rendered in connection with the rental of real property) are rendered to the tenants of the property by the independent contractor, the cost of the services must be borne by the independent contractor, a separate charge must be made for the services, the amount of the separate charge must be received and retained by the independent contractor, and the independent contractor must be adequately compensated for the services.

(ii) Trustee or director functions. The trustees or directors of the real estate investment trust are not required to delegate or contract out their fiduciary duty to manage the trust itself, as distinguished from rendering or furnishing services to the tenants of its property of managing or operating the property. Thus, the trustees or directors may do all those things necessary, in their fiduciary capacities, to manage and conduct the affairs of the trust itself. For example, the trustees or directors may establish rental terms, choose tenants, enter into and renew leases, and deal with taxes, interest, and insurance, relating to the trust's property. The trustees or directors may also make capital expenditures with respect to the trust's property (as defined in section 263) and may make decisions as to repairs of the trust's property (of the type which would be deductible under section 162), the cost of which may be borne by the trust.

(iii) Independent contractor defined. The term "independent contractor" means—

(a) A person who does not own, directly or indirectly, at any time during the trust's taxable year more than 35 percent of the shares in the real estate investment trust, or

(b) A person—

(1) If a corporation, not more than 35 percent of the total combined voting power of whose stock (or 35 percent of the total shares of all classes of whose stock), or 2.7

(2) If not a corporation, not more than 35 percent of the interest in whose assets or net profits is owned, directly or indirectly, at any time during the trust's taxable year by one or more persons owning at any time during such taxable year 35 percent or more of the shares in the trust.

(iv) Information required. The real estate investment trust shall submit with its return for the taxable year (or before June 1, 1962, whichever is later) a statement setting forth the name and address of each independent contractor; and

(a) The highest percentage of the outstanding shares in the trust owned at any time during its taxable year by such independent contractor and by any person owning at any time during such taxable year any shares of stock or interest in the independent contractor.

(b) If the independent contractor is a corporation such statement shall set forth the highest percentage of the total combined voting power of its stock and the highest percentage of the total number of shares of all classes of its stock owned at any time during its taxable year by any person owning shares in the trust at any time during such taxable year.

(c) If the independent contractor is not a corporation such statement shall set forth the highest percentage of any interest in its assets or net profits owned at any time during its taxable year by any person owning shares in the trust at any time during such taxable year.

(6) Amounts based on income or profits of subtenants. (i) Except as provided in paragraph (b)(6)(ii) of this section, if a trust leases real property to a tenant under terms other than solely on a fixed sum rental (for example, a percentage of the tenant's gross receipts), and the tenant subleases all or a part of such property under an agreement which provides for a rental based in whole or in part on the income or profits of the sublessee, the entire amount of the rent received by the trust from the prime tenant with respect to such property is disqualified as "rents from real property".

(ii) Exception. For taxable years beginning after October 4, 1976, section 856(d)(4) provides an exception to the general rule that amounts received or accrued, directly or indirectly, by a real estate investment trust do not qualify as rents from real property if the determination of the amount depends in whole or in part on the income or profits derived by any person from the property. This exception applies where the trust rents property to a tenant (the prime tenant) for a rental which is based, in whole or in part, on a fixed percentage or percentages of the receipts or sales of the prime tenant, and the rent which the trust receives or accrues from the prime tenant pursuant to the lease would not qualify as "rents from real property" solely because the prime tenant receives or accrues from subtenants (including concessionaires) rents or other amounts based on the income or profits derived by a person from the property. Under the exception, only a proportionate part of the rent received or accrued by the trust does not qualify as "rents from real property". The proportionate part of the rent received or accrued by the trust which in non-qualified is the lesser of the following two amounts:

(A) The rent received or accrued by the trust from the prime tenant pursuant to the lease, that is based on a fixed percentage or percentages of receipts or sales, or

(B) The product determined by multiplying the total rent which the trust receives or accrues from the prime tenant pursuant to the lease by a fraction, the numerator of which is the rent or other amount received by the prime tenant that is based, in whole or in part, on the income or profits derived by any person from the property, and the denominator of which is the total rent or other amount received by the prime tenant from the property. For example, assume that a real estate investment trust owns land underlying a shopping center. The trust rents the land to the owner of the shopping center for an annual rent of $10x plus 2 percent of the gross receipts which the prime tenant receives from subtenants who lease space in the shopping center. Assume further that, for the year in question, the prime tenant derives total rent from the shopping center of $100x and, of that amount, $25x is received from subtenants whose rent is based, in whole or in part, on the income or profits derived from the property. Accordingly, the trust will receive a total rent of $12x, of which $2x is based on a percentage of the gross receipts of the prime tenant. The portion of the rent which is disqualified is the lesser of $2x (the rent received by the trust which is based on a percentage of gross receipts), or $3x, ($12x multiplied by $25x/$100x). Accordingly, $10x of the rent received by the trust qualifies as "rents from real property" and $2x does not qualify.

(7) Attribution rules. Paragraphs (2) and (3) of section 856(d) relate to direct or indirect ownership of stock, assets, or net profits by the persons described therein. For purposes of determining such direct or indirect ownership, the rules prescribed by section 318(a) (for determining the ownership of stock) shall apply except that "10 percent" shall be substituted for "50 percent" in section 318(a)(2)(C) and (3)(C).

T.D. 6598, 4/25/62, amend T.D. 6969, 8/22/68, T.D. 7767, 2/3/81.

PAR. 4. Paragraphs (b)(1), (b)(3)(i)(b), and (b)(3)(i)(c) of § 1.856-4 are revised to read as follows:

Proposed § 1.856-4 Rents from real property. [*For Preamble, see ¶ 150,099*]

Caution: The Treasury has not yet amended Reg § 1.856-4 to reflect changes made by P.L. 105-34.

* * * * *

(b) Amounts not includible as rent. * * *

(1) Where amount of rent depends on income or profits of any person. Any amount received or accrued, directly or indirectly, with respect to any real property if the determination of such amount depends in whole or in part on the income or profits derived by any person from such property. However, any amount so accrued or received shall not be excluded from the term "rents from real property" solely by

reason of being based on a fixed percentage or percentages of receipts or sales (whether or not receipts or sales are adjusted for returned merchandise, or Federal, State, or local sales taxes). Thus, for example, "rents from real property" would include rents where the lease provides for differing percentages of receipts or sales from different departments or from separate floors of a retail store so long as each percentage is fixed at the time of entering into the lease. However, where a trust leases real property to a tenant under terms other than solely on a fixed sum rental (i.e., for example, a percentage of the tenant's gross receipts), and the tenant subleases all or a part of such property under an agreement which provides for a rental based in whole or in part on the income or profits of the sublessee, the entire amount of the rent received by the trust from the prime tenant with respect to such property is disqualified as "rents from real property." "Rents from real property" are not based in whole or in part on the income or profits derived by any person from such property if the amount of the rent is based on a fixed percentage or percentages of receipts or sales reduced by permissible escalation receipts. For purposes for this subparagraph, the term "permissible escalation receipts" means amounts received by reason of an agreement that rent shall be increased to reflect all or a portion of an increase in those costs which relate to the rental property and, in the case of a cost incurred for services, increases in costs for services which the real estate investment trust is permitted to directly furnish or render to the tenants of the property under subparagraph (3)(i) *(b)* of this paragraph. For purposes of the preceding sentence, costs which relate to the property include (but are not limited to) real estate taxes, personal property taxes, property insurance, and maintenance expenses, and costs which do not relate to the property) include (but are not limited to) compensation to managerial and clerical personnel, office supplies, and income taxes. Where in accordance with the terms of an agreement an amount received or accrued as rent for the taxable year includes both a fixed rental and a percentage of the lessee's income or profits in excess of a specific amount (usually determined before deducting the fixed rental and sometimes called "overage rents"), neither the fixed rental nor the additional amount will qualify as "rents from real property." However, where the amount received or accrued for the taxable year under such an agreement includes only the fixed rental, the determination of which does not depend in whole or in part on the income or profits derived by the lessee, such amount may qualify as "rents from real property." Similarly, where the amount received or accrued as rent for the taxable year consists, in whole or in part, of a percentage of the lessee's receipts or sales in excess of a specific amount which amount does not depend in whole or in part on the income or profits derived by the lessee, such amount may qualify as "rents from real property." Thus, an amount received or accrued as rent which consists of a fixed rental plus a percentage of the lessee's receipts or sales in excess of a specific amount may qualify as "rents from real property." In any event, an amount will not qualify as "rents from real property" if, considering the lease and all the surrounding circumstances, the arrangement does not conform with normal business practices but is in reality used as a means of basing the rent on income or profits. The application of the rules provided in this subparagraph may be illustrated by the following example:

Example. Trust R, which otherwise qualifies as a real estate investment trust, leases real property to PT, a prime tenant. PT subleases the real property to ST, a subtenant. The lease between PT and ST provides for rent equal to a fixed dollar amount plus an additional amount equal to any increase in property taxes, property insurance, and clerical salaries of PT above specified dollar amounts. The lease between R and PT excluding all gross for a rent equal to a fixed percentage of gross receipts of PT excluding all gross receipts attributable to rents measured by increased costs of PT. The rent received by R from PT does not qualify as "rents from real property" because the amounts excluded from gross receipts of PT include amounts which are not "permissible escalation receipts" .

* * * * *

(3) Trust furnishing services or managing property through an independent contractor. (i) In general. * * *

(b) Customary services for which no separate charge is made. Under section 856(d)(3), the trust (through its trustees or its own employees) may not directly furnish or render any services to the tenants of its property and may not directly manage or operate the property. However, for purposes of part II, subchapter M, chapter 1 of the Code, an amount will not be disqualified as "rent" if services, such as are usually or customarily furnished or rendered in connection with the mere rental of real property, are furnished or rendered to tenants of the property through an independent contractor. The independent contractor must not, however, be an employee of the trust (i.e., the manner in which he carries out his duties as independent contractor must not be subject to the control of the trust). The supplying of water, heat, air conditioning, and light; the cleaning of windows, public entrances, exits, and lobbies; the performance of general maintenance and other janitorial services; the collection of trash; and the furnishing of elevator service, telephone answering service, incidental storage space, laundry equipment, swimming facilities and other recreation facilities which are integral parts of multiple occupancy real property provided primarily to the tenants of such real property where no services are performed other than providing a lifeguard and sanitation (but only to the extent that such recreation facilities are actually used by such tenants or their guests), a parking facility which is an integral part of multiple occupancy real property provided primarily for the convenience of the tenants of such real property where attendants perform no services other than the parking of vehicles (but only to the extent that such parking facility is actually used by such tenants or their guests or their customers), and watchman or guard services, are examples of services which are customary or incidental to the mere rental of multiple-occupancy real estate. Although the cost of such incidental services may be borne by the trust, the services must, nevertheless, be furnished or rendered through an independent contractor. Furthermore, the facilities through which such services are furnished must be maintained and operated by an independent contractor. For example, if a heating plant is located in the building, it must be maintained and operated by an independent contractor. Where no separate charge is made for such services, no apportionment is required to be made between rents from real property and compensation for these services.

(c) Services for which a separate charge is made. Under section 856(d)(3), the trust may not derive or receive any income from an independent contractor who furnishes or renders services to the tenants of the trust property or who manages or operates such property, regardless of the source from which such income was derived by the independent contractor. To the extent that services, other than those usually or customarily rendered in connection with the mere rental of real property, are rendered to the tenants of the property by the independent contractor, the cost of such services must be borne by the independent contractor, a separate charge must be made therefor, and the amount thereof must be received and retained by the independent contractor; no amount attributable to such services shall be included in the gross income of the trust. In any event, the independent contractor must be adequately compensated for such services. Also, if a separate charge is made for the customary services described in (b) of this subdivision (i), such charge must be made and the amount thereof must be received and retained, by the independent contractor rather than by the trust. The furnishing of hotel, maid, boarding house, motel, laundry, or warehouse services are examples of services which are not usually or customarily furnished or rendered in connection with the mere rental of real estate, and the trust must not receive any income which is attributable to the furnishing or rendering of such services to tenants of the trust property. Furthermore, where electric current is purchased and then sold to the tenants at a price in excess of the purchase price (for example, submetered), such purchase and sale must be made by the independent contractor and no income therefrom may inure, directly or indirectly, to the trust.

* * * * *

§ 1.856-5 Interest.

Caution: The Treasury has not yet amended Reg § 1.856-5 to reflect changes made by P.L. 99-514.

(a) In general. In computing the percentage requirements in section 856(c)(2)(B) and (3)(B), the term "interest" includes only an amount which constitutes compensation for the use or forbearance of money. For example, a fee received or accrued by a lender which is in fact a charge for services performed for a borrower rather than a charge for the use of borrowed money is not includable as interest.

(b) Where amount depends on income or profits of any person. Except as provided in paragraph (d) of this section, any amount received or accrued, directly or indirectly, with respect to an obligation is not includable as interest for purposes of section 856(c)(2)(B) and (3)(B) if, under the principles set forth in paragraph (b)(3) and (6)(i) of § 1.856-4, the determination of the amount depends in whole or in part on the income or profits of any person (whether or not derived from property secured by the obligation). Thus, for example, if in accordance with a loan agreement an amount is received or accrued by the trust with respect to an obligation which includes both a fixed amount of interest and a percentage of the borrower's income or profits, neither the fixed interest nor the amount based upon the percentage will qualify as interest for purposes of section 856(c)(2)(B) and (3)(B). This paragraph and paragraph (d) of this section apply only to amounts received or accrued in taxable years beginning after October 4, 1976, pursuant to loans made after May 27, 1976. For purposes of the preceding sentence, a loan is considered to be made before May 28, 1976, if it is made pursuant to a binding commitment entered into before May 28, 1976.

(c) Apportionment of interest. *(1) In general.* Where a mortgage covers both real property and other property, an apportionment of the interest income must be made for purposes of the 75-percent requirement of section 856(c)(3). For purposes of the 75-percent requirement, the apportionment shall be made as follows:

(i) If the loan value of the real property is equal to or exceeds the amount of the loan, then the entire interest income shall be apportioned to the real property.

(ii) If the amount of the loan exceeds the loan value of the real property, then the interest income apportioned to the real property is an amount equal to the interest income multiplied by a fraction, the numerator of which is the loan value of the real property, and the denominator of which is the amount of the loan. The interest income apportioned to the other property is an amount equal to the excess of the total interest income over the interest income apportioned to the real property.

(2) Loan value. For purposes of this paragraph, the loan value of the real property is the fair market value of the property, determined as of the date on which the commitment by the trust to make the loan becomes binding on the trust. In the case of a loan purchased by the trust, the loan value of the real property is the fair market value of the property, determined as of the date on which the commitment by the trust to purchase the loan becomes binding on the trust. However, in the case of a construction loan or other loan made for purposes of improving or developing real property, the loan value of the real property is the fair market value of the land plus the reasonably estimated cost of the improvements or developments (other than personal property) which will secure the loan and which are to be constructed from the proceeds of the loan. The fair market value of the land and the reasonably estimated cost of improvements or developments shall be determined as of the date on which a commitment to make the loan becomes binding on the trust. If the trust does not make the construction loan but commits itself to provide long-term financing following completion of construction, the loan value of the real property is determined by using the principles for determining the loan value for a construction loan. Moreover, if the mortgage on the real property is given as additional security (or as a substitute for other security) for the loan after the trust's commitment is binding, the real property loan value is its fair market value when it becomes security for the loan (or, if earlier, when the borrower makes a binding commitment to add or substitute the property as security).

(3) Amount of loan. For purposes of this paragraph, the amount of the loan means the highest principal amount of the loan outstanding during the taxable year.

(d) Exception. Section 856(f)(2) provides an exception to the general rule that amounts received, directly or indirectly, with respect to an obligation do not qualify as "interest" where the determination of the amounts depends in whole or in part on the income or profits of any person. The exception applies where the trust receives or accrues, with respect to the obligation of its debtor, an amount that is based in whole or in part on a fixed percentage or percentages of receipts or sales of the debtor, and the amount would not qualify as interest solely because the debtor has receipts or sale proceeds that are based on the income of profits of any person. Under this exception only a proportionate part of the amount received or accrued by the trust fails to qualify as interest for purposes of the percentage-of-income requirements of section 856(c)(2) and (3). The proportionate part of the amount received or accrued by the trust that is non-qualified is the lesser of the following two amounts:

(1) The amount received or accrued by the trust from the debtor with respect to the obligation that is based on a fixed percentage or percentages of receipts or sales, or

(2) The product determined by multiplying by a fraction the total amount received or accrued by the trust from the debtor with respect to the obligation. The numerator of the fraction is the amount of receipts or sales of the debtor that is based, in whole or in part, on the income or profits of any person and the denominator is the total amount of the receipts or sales of the debtor. For purposes of the preceding

sentence, the only receipts or sales to be taken into account are those taken into account in determining the payment to the trust pursuant to the loan agreement.

T.D. 7767, 2/3/81.

§ 1.856-6 Foreclosure property.

Caution: The Treasury has not yet amended Reg § 1.856-6 to reflect changes made by P.L. 105-34.

(a) In general. Under section 856(e) a real estate investment trust may make an irrevocable election to treat as "foreclosure property" certain real property (including interests in real property), and any personal property incident to the real property, acquired by the trust after December 31, 1973. This section prescribes rules relating to the election, including rules relating to property eligible for the election. This section also prescribes rules relating to extensions of the general two-year period (hereinafter the "grace period") during which property retains its status as foreclosure property, as well as rules relating to early termination of the grace period under section 856(e)(4). The election to treat property as foreclosure property does not alter the character of the income derived therefrom (other than for purposes of section 856(c)(2)(F) and (3)(F)). For example, if foreclosure property is sold, the determination of whether it is property described in section 1221(1) will not be affected by the fact that it is foreclosure property.

(b) Property eligible for the election. *(1) Rules relating to acquisitions.* In general, the trust must acquire the property after December 31, 1973, as the result of having bid in the property at foreclosure, or having otherwise reduced the property to ownership or possession by agreement or process of law, after there was default (or default was imminent) on a lease of the property (where the trust was the lessor) or on an indebtedness owed to the trust which the property secured. Foreclosure property which secured an indebtedness owed to the trust is acquired for purposes of section 856(e) on the date on which the trust acquires ownership of the property for Federal income tax purposes. Foreclosure property which a trust owned and leased to another is acquired for purposes of section 856(e) on the date on which the trust acquires possession of the property from its lessee. A trust will not be considered to have acquired ownership of property for purposes of section 856(e) where it takes control of the property as a mortgagee-in-possession and cannot receive any profit or sustain any loss with respect to the property except as a creditor of the mortgagor. A trust may be considered to have acquired ownership of property for purposes of section 856(e) even through legal title to the property is held by another person. For example, where, upon foreclosure of a mortgage held by the trust, legal title to the property is acquired in the name of a nominee for the exclusive benefit of the trust and the trust is the equitable owner of the property, the trust will be considered to have acquired ownership of the property for purposes of section 856(e). Generally, the fact that under local law the mortgagor has a right of redemption after foreclosure is not relevant in determining whether the trust has acquired ownership of the property for purposes of section 856(e). Property is not ineligible for the election solely because the property, in addition to securing an indebtedness owed to the trust, also secures debts owed to other creditors. Property eligible for the election includes a building or other improvement which has been constructed on land owned by the trust and which is acquired by the trust upon default of a lease of the land.

(2) Personal property. Personal property (including personal property not subject to a mortgage or lease of the real property) will be considered incident to a particular item of real property if the personal property is used in a trade or business conducted on the property or the use of the personal property is otherwise an ordinary and necessary corollary of the use to which the real property is put. In the case of a hotel, such items as furniture, appliances, linens, china, food, etc. would be examples of incidental personal property. Personal property incident to the real property is eligible for the election even though it is acquired after the real property is acquired or is placed in the building or other improvement in the course of the completion of construction.

(3) Property with respect to which default is anticipated. Property is not eligible for the election to be treated as foreclosure property if the loan or lease with respect to which the default occurs (or is imminent) was made or entered into (or the lease or indebtedness was acquired) by the trust with an intent to evict or foreclose, or when the trust knew or had reason to know that default would occur ("improper knowledge"). For purposes of the preceding sentence, a trust will not be considered to have improper knowledge with respect to a particular lease or loan, if the lease or loan was made pursuant to a binding commitment entered into by the trust at a time when it did not have improper knowledge. Moreover, if the trust, in an attempt to avoid default or foreclosure, advances additional amounts to the borrower in excess of amounts contemplated in the original loan commitment or modifies the lease or loan, such advance or modification will be considered not to have been made with an intent to evict or foreclose, or with improper knowledge, unless the original loan or lease was entered into with that intent or knowledge.

(c) Election. *(1) In general.* (i) An election to treat property as foreclosure property applies to all of the eligible real property acquired in the same taxable year by the trust upon the default (or as a result of the imminence of default) on a particular lease (where the trust is the lessor) or on a particular indebtedness owed to the trust. For example, if a loan made by a trust is secured by two separate tracts of land located in different cities, and in the same taxable year the trust acquires both tracts on foreclosure upon the default (or imminence of default) of the loan, the trust must include both tracts in the election. For a further example, the trust may choose to make a separate election for only one of the tracts if they are acquired in different taxable years or were not security for the same loan. If real property subject to the same election is acquired at different times in the same taxable year, the grace period for a particular property begins when that property is acquired.

(ii) If the trust acquires separate pieces of real property that secure the same indebtedness (or are under the same lease) in different taxable years because the trust delays acquiring one of them until a later taxable year, and the primary purpose for the delay is to include only one of them in an election, then if the trust makes an election for one piece it must also make an election for the other piece. A trust will not be considered to have delayed the acquisition of property for this purpose if there is a legitimate business reason for the delay (such as an attempt to avoid foreclosure by further negotiations with the debtor or lessee).

(iii) All of the eligible personal property incident to the real property must also be included in the election.

(2) Time for making election. The election to treat property as foreclosure property must be made on or before the due date (including extensions of time) for filing the trust's income tax return for the taxable year in which the trust ac-

quires the property with respect to which the election is being made, or April 3, 1975, whichever is later.

(3) Manner of making the election. An election made after February 6, 1981, shall be made by a statement attached to the income tax return for the taxable year in which the trust acquired the property with respect to which the election is being made. The statement shall indicate that the election is made under section 856(e) and shall identify the property to which the election applies. The statement shall also set forth—

(i) The name, address, and taxpayer identification number of the trust,

(ii) The date the property was acquired by the trust, and

(iii) A brief description of how the real property was acquired, including the name of the person or persons from whom the real property was acquired and a description of the lease or indebtedness with respect to which default occurred or was imminent.

An election made on or before February 6, 1981 shall be filed in the manner prescribed in 26 CFR 10.1(f) (revised as of April 1, 1977) (temporary regulations relating to the election to treat property as foreclosure property) as in effect when the election is made.

(4) Status of taxpayer. In general, a taxpayer may make an election with respect to an acquisition of property only if the taxpayer is a qualified real estate investment trust for the taxable year in which the acquisition occurs. If, however, the taxpayer establishes, to the satisfaction of the district director for the internal revenue district in which the taxpayer maintains its principal place of business or principal office or agency, that its failure to be a qualified real estate investment trust for a taxable year was to due to reasonable cause and not due to willful neglect, the taxpayer may make the election with respect to property acquired in such taxable year. The principles of §§ 1.856.7(c) and 1.856.8(d) (including the principles relating to expert advice will apply in determining whether, for purposes of this subparagraph, the failure of the taxpayer to be a qualified real estate investment trust for the taxable year in which the property is acquired was due to reasonable cause and not due to willful neglect. If a taxpayer makes a valid election to treat property as foreclosure property, the property will not lose its status as foreclosure property solely because the taxpayer is not a qualified real estate investment trust for a subsequent taxable year (including a taxable year which encompasses an extension of the grace period). However, the rules relating to the termination of foreclosure property status in section 856(e)(4) (but not the tax on income from foreclosure property imposed by section 857(b)(4)) apply to the year in which the property is acquired and all subsequent years, even though the taxpayer is not a qualified real estate investment trust for such year.

(d) Termination of 2-year grace period; subsequent leases. *(1) In general.* Under section 856(e)(4)(A), all real property (and any incidental personal property) for which a particular election has been made (see paragraph (c)(1) of this section) shall cease to be foreclosure property on the first day (occurring on or after the day on which the trust acquired the property) on which the trust either—

(i) Enters into a lease with respect to any of the property which, by its terms, will give rise to income of the trust which is not described in section 856(c)(3) (other than section 856(c)(3)(F)), or

(ii) Receives or accrues, directly or indirectly, any amount which is not described in section 856(c)(3) (other than section 856(c)(3)(F)) pursuant to a lease with respect to any of the real property entered into by the trust on or after the day the trust acquired the property.

For example, assume the trust acquires, in a particular taxable year, a shopping center upon the default of an indebtedness owed to the trust. Also assume that the trust subsequently enters into a lease with respect to one of several stores in the shopping center that requires the lessee to pay rent to the trust which is not income described in section 856(c)(3) (other than section 856(c)(3)(F)). In such case, the entire shopping center will cease to be foreclosure property on the day the trust enters into the lease.

(2) Extensions or renewals of leases. Generally, the extension or renewal of a lease of foreclosure property will be treated as the entering into of a new lease only if the trust has a right to renegotiate the terms of the lease. If, however, by operation of law or by contract, the acquisition of the foreclosure property by the trust terminates a preexisting lease of the property, or gives the trust a right to terminate the lease, then for purposes of section 856(e)(4)(A), a trust, in such circumstances, will not be considered to have entered into a lease with respect to the property solely because the terms of the preexisting lease are continued in effect after foreclosure without substantial modification. The letting of rooms in a hotel or motel does not constitute the entering into a lease for purposes of section 856(e)(4)(A).

(3) Rent attributable to personal property. Solely for the purposes of section 856(e)(4)(A), if a trust enters into a lease with respect to real property on or after the day upon which the trust acquires such real property by foreclosure, and a portion of the rent from such lease is attributable to personal property which is foreclosure property incident to such real property, such rent attributable to the incidental personal property will not be considered to terminate the status of such real property (or such incidental personal property) as foreclosure property.

(e) Termination of 2-year grace period; completion of construction. *(1) In general.* Under section 856(e)(4)(B), all real property (and any incidental personal property) for which a particular election has been made (see paragraph (c)(1) of this section) shall cease to be foreclosure property on the first day (occurring on or after the day on which the trust acquired the property) on which any construction takes place on the property, other than completion of a building (or completion of any other improvement) where more than 10 percent of the construction of the building (or other improvement) was completed before default became imminent. If more than one default occurred with respect to an indebtedness or lease in respect of which there is an acquisition, the more-than-10-percent test (including the rule prescribed in this paragraph relating to the test) will not be applied at the time a particular default became imminent if it is clear that the acquisition did not occur as the result of such default. For example, if the debtor fails to make four consecutive payments of principal and interest on the due dates, and the trust takes action to acquire the property securing the debt only after the fourth default becomes imminent, the 10-percent test is applied at the time the fourth default became imminent (even though the trust would not have foreclosed on the property had not all four defaults occurred).

(2) Determination of percentage of completion. The determination of whether the construction of a building or other improvement was more than 10 percent complete when default became imminent shall be made by comparing the total direct costs of construction incurred with respect to the building or other improvement as of the date default became

imminent with the estimated total direct costs of construction as of such date. If the building or other improvement qualifies as more than 10 percent complete under this method, the building or other improvement shall be considered to be more than 10 percent complete. For purposes of this subparagraph, direct costs of construction include the cost of labor and materials which are directly connected with the construction of the building or improvement.

Thus, for example, direct costs of construction incurred as of the date default became imminent would include amounts paid, or for which liability has been incurred, for labor which has been performed as of such date that is directly connected with the construction of the building or other improvement and for building materials and supplies used or consumed in connection with the construction as of such date. For purposes of applying the 10-percent test the trust may also take into account the cost of building materials and supplies which have been delivered to the construction site as of the date default became imminent and which are to be used or consumed in connection with the construction. On the other hand, architect's fees, administrative costs of the developer or builder, lawyers' fees, and expenses incurred in connection with obtaining zoning approval or building permits are not considered to be direct costs of construction. Any construction by the trust as mortgagee-in-possession is considered to have taken place after default resulting in acquisition of the property became imminent. Generally, the trust's estimate of the total direct costs of completing construction as of the date the default became imminent will be accepted, provided that the estimate is reasonable, in good faith, and is based on all of the data reasonably available to the trust when the trust undertakes completion of construction of the building or other improvement. Appropriate documentation which shows that construction was more than 10 percent complete when default became imminent must be available at the principal place of business of the trust for inspection in connection with an examination of the income tax return. Construction includes the renovation of a building, such as the remodeling of apartments, or the renovation of an apartment building to convert rental units to a condominium. The renovation must be more than 10 percent complete (determined by comparing the total direct cost of the physical renovation which has been incurred when default became imminent with the estimated total direct cost of renovation as of such date) when default became imminent in order for the property not to lose its status as foreclosure property if the trust undertakes the renovation.

(3) Modification of a building or improvement. Generally, the terms "building" and "improvement" in section 856(e)(4)(B) mean the building or improvement (including any integral part thereof) as planned by the mortgagor or lessee (or other person in possession of the property, if appropriate) as of the date default became imminent. The trust, however, may estimate the total direct costs of construction and complete the construction of the building or other improvement by modifying the building or other improvement as planned as of the date default became imminent so as to reduce the estimated direct cost of construction of the building or improvement. If the trust does so modify the planned construction of the building or improvement, the 10-percent test is to be applied by comparing the direct costs of construction incurred as of the date default became imminent that are attributable to the building or improvement as modified, with the estimated total direct costs (as of such date) of construction of the building or other improvement as modified. The trust, in order to meet the 10-percent test, may not, however, modify the planned building or improvement by reducing the estimated direct cost of construction to such an extent that the building or improvement is not functional.

Also, the trust may make subsequent modifications which increase the direct cost of construction of the building or improvement if such modifications—

(i) Are required by a Federal, State, or local agency, or

(ii) Are alterations that are either required by a prospective lessee or purchaser as a condition of leasing or buying the property or are necessary for the property to be used for the purpose planned at the time default became imminent.

Subdivision (ii) of the preceding sentence applies, however, only if the building or improvement, as modified, was more than 10 percent complete when default became imminent. A building completed by the trust will not cease to be foreclosure property solely because the building is used in a manner other than that planed by the defaulting mortgagor or lessee. Thus, for example, assume a trust acquired on foreclosure a planned apartment building which was 20 percent complete when default became imminent and that the trust completes the building without modifications which increase the direct cost of construction. The property will not cease to be foreclosure property by reason of section 856(e)(4)(B) solely because the trust sells the dwelling units in the building as condominium units, rather than holding them for rent as planned by the defaulting mortgagor. (See, however, section 856(e)(4)(C) and paragraph (f)(2) of this section for rules relating to the requirement that where foreclosure property is used in a trade or business (including a trade or business of selling the foreclosure property), the trade or business must be conducted through an independent contractor after 90 days after the property is acquired.)

(4) Application on building-by-building basis. Generally the more than 10 percent test is to be applied on a building-by-building basis. Thus, for example, if a trust has foreclosed on land held by a developer building a housing subdivision, the trust may complete construction of the houses which were more than 10 percent complete when default became imminent. The trust, however, may not complete construction of houses which were only 10 percent (or less) complete, nor may the trust begin construction of other houses planned for the subdivision on which construction has not begun. The trust, however, may construct an additional building or improvement (whether or not the construction thereof has begun) which is an integral part of another building or other improvement that was more than 10 percent complete when default became imminent if the additional building or improvement and the other building or improvement, taken together as a unit, meet the more than 10 percent test. For purposes of this paragraph, an additional building or other improvement will be considered to be an integral part of another building or improvement if—

(i) It is ancillary to the other building or improvement and its principal intended use is to furnish services or facilities which either supplement the use of such other building or improvement or are necessary for such other building or improvement to be utilized in the manner or for the purpose for which it is intended, or

(ii) The buildings or improvements are intended to comprise constituent parts of an interdependent group of buildings or other improvements.

However, a building or other improvement will not be considered to be an integral part of another building or improvement unless the buildings or improvements were planned as part of the same overall construction plan or project before default became imminent. An additional building or other improvement (such as, for example, an outdoor swimming pool or a parking garage) may be considered to be an integral part of another building or improvement, even though the additional building or improvement was also intended to be used to provide facilities or services for use in connection with several other buildings or improvements which will not be completed. If the trust chooses not to undertake the construction of an additional building or other improvement which qualifies as an integral part of another building or improvement, so much of the costs of construction (including both the direct costs of construction incurred before the default became imminent and the estimated costs of completion) as are attributable to that "integral part" shall not be taken into account in determining whether any other building or improvement was more than 10 percent complete when default became imminent. For example, assume the trust acquires on foreclosure a property on which the defaulting mortgagor has begun construction of a motel. The motel, as planned by the mortgagor, was to consist of a two-story building containing 30 units, and two detached one-story wings, each of which was to contain 20 units. At the time default became imminent, the defaulting mortgagor had completed more than 10 percent of the construction of the two-story structure but the two wings, an access road, a parking lot, and an outdoor swimming pool planned for the motel were each less than 10 percent complete. The trust may construct the two wings of the motel, the access road, the parking lot, and the swimming pool: Provided, That the motel and the other improvements which the trust undertakes to construct, taken together as a unit, were more than 10 percent complete when default became imminent. If, however, the trust chooses not to undertake construction of the swimming pool, the cost of construction attributable to the swimming pool, whether incurred before default became imminent or estimated as the cost of completion, shall not be taken into account in determining whether the trust can complete construction of the other buildings and improvements. For another example, assume that the trust acquires a planned shopping center on foreclosure. At the time default became imminent several large buildings intended to house shops and stores in the shopping center were more than 10 percent complete. Less than 10 percent of the construction, however, had been completed on a separate structure intended to house a bank. The bank was planned as a component of the shopping center in order to provide, in conjunction with the other shops and stores, a specific range and variety of goods and services with which to attract customers to the shopping center. The trust may complete construction of the bank: Provided, That the bank and the other buildings and improvements which the trust undertakes to complete, taken together as a unit, were more than 10 percent complete when default became imminent. If the trust chooses not to construct the bank, no actual or estimated construction costs attributable to the bank are to be taken into account in applying the 10-percent test with respect to the other buildings and improvements in the shopping center. For a third example, assume that a defaulting mortgagor had planned to construct two identical apartment buildings, A and B, on the same tract of land, that neither building is to provide substantial facilities or services to be used in connection with the other, and that only building A was more than 10 percent complete when default became imminent. The trust, in this case, may not complete building B. On the other hand, if the facts are the same except that pursuant to the plans of the defaulting mortgagor, one of the buildings is to contain the furnace and central air conditioning machinery for both buildings A and B, the trust may complete both buildings A and B: Provided, That, taken together as a unit, the two buildings meet the more-than-10-percent test.

(5) Repair and maintenance. Under this paragraph (e), "construction" does not include—

(i) The repair or maintenance of a building or other improvement (such as the replacement of worn or obsolete furniture and appliances) to offset normal wear and tear or obsolescence, and the restoration of property required because of damage from fire, storm, vandalism or other casualty,

(ii) The preparation of leased space for a new tenant which does not substantially extend the useful life of the building or other improvement or significantly increase its value, even though, in the case of commercial space, this preparation includes adapting the property to the conduct of a different business, or

(iii) The performing of repair or maintenance described in paragraph (e)(5)(i) of this section after property is acquired that was deferred by the defaulting party and that does not constitute renovation under paragraph (e)(2) of this section.

(6) Independent contractor required. If any construction takes place on the foreclosure property more than 90 days after the day on which such property was acquired by the trust, such construction must be performed by an independent contractor (as defined in section 856(d)(3) and § 1.856-4(b)(5)(iii)) from whom the trust does not derive or receive any income. Otherwise, the property will cease to be foreclosure property.

(7) Failure to complete construction. Property will not cease to be foreclosure property solely because a trust which undertakes the completion of construction of a building or other improvement on the property that was more than 10 percent complete when default became imminent does not complete the construction. Thus, for example, if a trust continues construction of a building that was 20 percent complete when default became imminent, and the trust constructs an additional 40 percent of the building and then sells the property, the property will not lose its status as foreclosure property solely because the trust fails to complete construction of the building.

(f) Termination of 2-year grace period; use of foreclosure property in a trade or business *(1) In general.* Under section 856(e)(4)(C), all real property (and any incidental personal property) for which a particular election has been made (see paragraph (c)(1) of this section) shall cease to be foreclosure property on the first day (occurring more than 90 days after the day on which the trust acquired the property) on which the property is used in a trade or business conducted by the trust, other than a trade or business conducted by the trust through an independent contractor from whom the trust itself does not derive or receive any income. (See section 856(d)(3) for the definition of independent contractor.)

(2) Property held primarily for sale to customers. For the purposes of section 856(e)(4)(C), foreclosure property held by the trust primarily for sale to customers in the ordinary course of a trade or business in considered to be property used in a trade or business conducted by the trust. Thus, if a trust holds foreclosure property (whether real property or personal property incident to real property) for sale to customers in the ordinary course of a trade or business more than 90 days after the day on which the trust acquired the real property, the trade or business of selling the property must be conducted by the trust through an independent contractor from whom the trust does not derive or receive any

income. Otherwise, after such 90th day the property will cease to be foreclosure property.

(3) Change in use. Foreclosure property will not cease to be foreclosure property solely because the use of the property in a trade or business by the trust differs from the use to which the property was put by the person from whom it was acquired. Thus, for example, if a trust acquires a rental apartment building on foreclosure, the property will not cease to be foreclosure property solely because the trust converts the building to a condominium apartment building and, through an independent contractor from whom the trust derives no income, engages in the trade or business of selling the individual condominium units.

(g) Extension of 2-year grace period. *(1) In general.* A real estate investment trust may apply to the district director of the internal revenue district in which is located the principal place of business (or principal office or agency) of the trust for an extension of the 2-year grace period. If the trust establishes to the satisfaction of the district director that an extension of the grace period is necessary for the orderly liquidation of the trust's interest in foreclosure property, or for an orderly renegotiation of a lease or leases of the property, the district director may extend the 2-year grace period. See section 856(e)(3) (as in effect with respect to the particular extension) for rules relating to the maximum length of an extension, and the number of extensions which may be granted. An extension of the grace period may be granted by the district director either before or after the date on which the grace period, but for the extension, would expire. The extension shall be effective as of the date on which the grace period, but for the extension, would expire.

(2) Showing required. Generally, in order to establish the necessity of an extension, the trust must demonstrate that it has made good faith efforts to renegotiate leases with respect to, or dispose of, the foreclosure property. In certain cases, however, the trust may establish the necessity of an extension even though it has not made such efforts. For example, if the trust demonstrates that, for valid business reasons, construction of the foreclosure property could not be completed before the expiration of the grace period, the necessity of the extension could be established even though the trust had made no effort to sell the property. For another example, if the trust demonstrates that due to a depressed real estate market, it could not sell the foreclosure property before the expiration of the grace period except at a distress price, the necessity of an extension could be established even though the trust had made no effort to sell the property. The fact that property was acquired as foreclosure property prior to January 3, 1975 (the date of enactment of section 856(e)), generally will be considered as a factor (but not a controlling factor) which tends to establish that an extension of the grace period is necessary.

(3) Time for requesting an extension of the grace period. A request for an extension of the grace period must be filed with the appropriate district director more than 60 days before the day on which the grace period would otherwise expire. In the case of a grace period which would otherwise expire before August 6, 1976, a request for an extension will be considered to be timely filed if filed on or before June 7, 1976.

(4) Information required. The request for an extension of the grace period shall identify the property with respect to which the request is being made and shall also include the following information:

(i) The name, address, and taxpayer identification number of the trust,

(ii) The date the property was acquired as foreclosure property by the trust,

(iii) The taxable year of the trust in which the property was acquired,

(iv) If the trust has been previously granted an extension of the grace period with respect to the property, a statement to that effect (which shall include the date on which the grace period, as extended, expires) and a copy of the information which accompanied the request for the previous extension,

(v) A statement of the reasons why the grace period should be extended,

(vi) A description of any efforts made by the trust after the acquisition of the property to dispose of the property or to renegotiate any lease with respect to the property, and

(vii) A description of any other factors which tend to establish that an extension of the grace period is necessary for the orderly liquidation of the trust's interest in the property, or for an orderly renegotiation of a lease or leases of the property.

The trust shall also furnish any additional information requested by the district director after the request for extension is filed.

(5) Automatic extension. If a real estate investment trust files a request for an extension with the district director more than 60 days before the expiration of the grace period, the grace period shall be considered to be extended until the end of the 30th day after the date on which the district director notifies the trust by certified mail sent to its last known address that the period of extension requested by the trust is not granted. For further guidance regarding the definition of last known address, see § 301.6212-2 of this chapter. In no event, however, shall the rule in the preceding sentence extend the grace period beyond the expiration of (i) the period of extension requested by the trust, or (ii) the 1-year period following the date that the grace period (but for the automatic extension) would expire. The date of the postmark on the sender's receipt is considered to be the date of the certified mail for purposes of this subparagraph. This subparagraph does not apply, however, if the date of the notification by certified mail described in the first sentence is more than 30 days before the date that the grace period (determined without regard to this subparagraph) expires. Moreover, this subparagraph shall not operate to allow any period of extension that is prohibited by the last sentence of section 856(e)(3) (as in effect with respect to the particular extension).

(6) Extension of time for filing. If a real estate investment trust fails to file the request for an extension of the grace period within the time provided in paragraph (g)(3) of this section, then the district director shall grant a reasonable extension of time for filing such request, provided (i) it is established to the satisfaction of the district director that there was reasonable cause for failure to file the request within the prescribed time and (ii) a request for such extension is filed within such time as the district director considers reasonable under the circumstances.

(7) Status of taxpayer. The reference to "real estate investment trust" or "trust" in this paragraph (g) shall be considered to include a taxpayer that is not a qualified real estate investment trust, if the taxpayer establishes to the satisfaction of the district director that its failure to be a qualified real estate investment trust for the taxable year was due to reasonable cause and not due to willful neglect. The principles of § 1.856-7(c) and § 1.856-8(d) (including the

principles relating to expert advice) shall apply for determining reasonable cause (and absence of willful neglect) for this purpose.

T.D. 7767, 2/3/81, amend T.D. 8939, 1/11/2001.

§ 1.856-7 Certain corporations, etc., that are considered to meet the gross income requirements.

Caution: The Treasury has not yet amended Reg § 1.856-7 to reflect changes made by P.L. 108-357, P.L. 105-34.

(a) In general. A corporation, trust, or association which fails to meet the requirements of paragraph (2) or (3) of section 856(c), or of both such paragraphs, for any taxable year nevertheless is considered to have satisfied these requirements if the corporation, trust, or association meets the requirements of subparagraphs (A), (B), and (C) of section 856(c)(7) (relating to a schedule attached to the return, the absence of fraud, and reasonable cause).

(b) Contents of the schedule. The schedule required by subparagraph (A) of section 856(c)(7) must contain a breakdown, or listing, of the total amount of gross income falling under each of the separate subparagraphs of section 856(c)(2) and (3). Thus, for example, the real estate investment trust, for purposes of listing its income from the sources described in section 856(c)(2), would list separately the total amount of dividends, the total amount of interest, the total amount of rents from real property, etc. The listing is not required to be on a lease-by-lease, loan-by-loan, or project-by-project basis, but the real estate investment trust must maintain adequate records on such a basis with which to substantiate each total amount listed in the schedule.

(c) Reasonable cause *(1) In general.* The failure to meet the requirements of paragraph (2) or (3) of section 856(c) (or of both paragraphs) will be considered due to reasonable cause and not due to willful neglect if the real estate investment trust exercised ordinary business care and prudence in attempting to satisfy the requirements. Such care and prudence must be exercised at the time each transaction is entered into by the trust. However, even if the trust exercised ordinary business care and prudence in entering into a transaction, if the trust later determines that the transaction results in the receipt or accrual of nonqualified income and that the amounts of such nonqualified income, in the context of the trust's overall portfolio, reasonably can be expected to cause a source-of-income requirement to be failed, the trust must use ordinary business care and prudence in an effort to renegotiate the terms of the transaction, dispose of property acquired or leased in the transaction, or alter other elements of its portfolio. In any case, failure to meet an income source requirement will be considered due to willful neglect and not due to reasonable cause if the failure is willful and the trust could have avoided such failure by taking actions not inconsistent with ordinary business care and prudence. For example, if the trust enters into a lease knowing that it will produce nonqualified income which reasonably can be expected to cause a source-of-income requirement to be failed, the failure is due to willful neglect even if the trust has a legitimate business purpose for entering into the lease.

(2) Expert advice. (i) In general. The reasonable reliance on a reasoned, written opinion as to the characterization for purposes of section 856 of gross income to be derived (or being derived) from a transaction generally constitutes "reasonable cause" if income from that transaction causes the trust to fail to meet the requirements of paragraph (2) or (3) of section 856(c) (or of both paragraphs). The absence of such a reasoned, written opinion with respect to a transaction does not, by itself, give rise to any inference that the failure to meet a percentage of income requirement was without reasonable cause. An opinion as to the character of income from a transaction includes an opinion pertaining to the use of a standard form of transaction or standard operating procedure in a case where such standard form or procedure is in fact used or followed.

(ii) If the opinion indicates that a portion of the income from a transaction will be nonqualified income, the trust must still exercise ordinary business care and prudence with respect to the nonqualified income and determine that the amount of that income, in the context of its overall portfolio, reasonably cannot be expected to cause a source-of-income requirement to be failed. Reliance on an opinion is not reasonable if the trust has reason to believe that the opinion is incorrect (for example, because the trust withholds facts from the person rendering the opinion).

(iii) Reasoned written opinion. For purposes of this subparagraph (2), a written opinion means an opinion, in writing, rendered by a tax advisor (including house counsel) whose opinion would be relied on by a person exercising ordinary business care and prudence in the circumstances of the particular transaction. A written opinion is considered "reasoned" even if it reaches a conclusion which is subsequently determined to be incorrect, so long as the opinion is based on a full disclosure of the factual situation by the real estate investment trust and is addressed to the facts and law which the person rendering the opinion believes to be applicable. However, an opinion is not considered "reasoned" if it does nothing more than recite the facts and express a conclusion.

(d) Application of section 856(c)(7) to taxable years beginning before October 5, 1976. Pursuant to section 1608(b) of the Tax Reform Act of 1976, paragraph (7) of section 856(c) and this section apply to a taxable year of a real estate investment trust which begins before October 5, 1976, only if as the result of a determination occurring after October 4, 1976, the trust does not meet the requirements of paragraph (2) or (3) of section 856(c), or both paragraphs, as in effect for the taxable year. The requirement that the schedule described in subparagraph (A) of section 856(c)(7) be attached to the income tax return of a real estate investment trust in order for section 856(c)(7) to apply is not applicable to taxable years beginning before October 5, 1976. For purposes of section 1608(b) of the Tax Reform Act of 1976 and this paragraph, the rules relating to determinations prescribed in section 860(e) and § 1.860-2(b)(1) (other than the second, third, and last sentences of § 1.860-2(b)(1)(ii)) shall apply. However, a determination consisting of an agreement between the taxpayer and the district director (or other official to whom authority to sign the agreement is delegated) shall set forth the amount of gross income for the taxable year to which the determination applies, the amount of the 90 percent and 75 percent source-of-income requirements for the taxable year to which the determination applies, and the amount by which the real estate investment trust failed to meet either or both of the requirements. The agreement shall also set forth the amount of tax for which the trust is liable pursuant to section 857(b)(5). The agreement shall also contain a finding as to whether the failure to meet the requirements of paragraph (2) or (3) of section 856(c) (or of both paragraphs) was due to reasonable cause and not due to willful neglect.

T.D. 7767, 2/3/81, amend T.D. 7936, 1/17/84.

§ 1.856-8 Revocation or termination of election.

Caution: The Treasury has not yet amended Reg § 1.856-8 to reflect changes made by P.L. 108-357.

(a) Revocation of an election to be a real estate investment trust. A corporation, trust, or association that has made an election under section 856(c)(1) to be a real estate investment trust may revoke the election for any taxable year after the first taxable year for which the election is effective. The revocation must be made by filing a statement with the district director for the internal revenue district in which the taxpayer maintains its principal place of business or principal office or agency. The statement must be filed on or before the 90th day after the first day of the first taxable year for which the revocation is to be effective. The statement must be signed by an official authorized to sign the income tax return of the taxpayer and must—

(1) Contain the name, address, and taxpayer identification number of the taxpayer,

(2) Specify the taxable year for which the election was made, and

(3) Include a statement that the taxpayer, pursuant to section 856(g)(2), revokes its election under section 856(c)(1) to be a real estate investment trust.

The revocation may be made only with respect to a taxable year beginning after October 4, 1976, and is effective for the taxable year in which made and for all succeeding taxable years. A revocation with respect to a taxable year beginning after October 4, 1976, that is filed before February 6, 1981, in the time and manner prescribed in § 7.856(g)-1 of this chapter (as in effect when the revocation was filed) is considered to meet the requirements of this paragraph.

(b) Termination of election to be a real estate investment trust. An election of a corporation, trust, or association under section 856(c)(1) to be a real estate investment trust shall terminate if the corporation, trust, or association is not a qualified real estate investment trust for any taxable year (including the taxable year with respect to which the election is made) beginning after October 4, 1976. (This election terminates whether the failure to be a qualified real estate investment trust is intentional or inadvertent.) The term "taxable year" includes a taxable year of less than 12 months for which a return is made under section 443. The termination of the election is effective for the first taxable year beginning after October 4, 1976, for which the corporation, trust, or association is not a qualified real estate investment trust and for all succeeding taxable years.

(c) Restrictions on election after termination or revocation. *(1) General rule.* Except as provided in paragraph (d) of this section, if a corporation, trust, or association has made an election under section 856(c)(1) to be a real estate investment trust and the election has been terminated or revoked under section 856(g)(1) or (2), the corporation, trust, or association (and any successor corporation, trust, or association) is not eligible to make a new election under section 856(c)(1) for any taxable year prior to the fifth taxable year which begins after the first taxable year for which the termination or revocation is effective.

(2) Successor corporation. The term "successor corporation, trust, or association", as used in section 856(g)(3), means a corporation, trust, or association which meets both a continuity of ownership requirement and a continuity of assets requirement with respect to the corporation, trust, or association whose election has been terminated under section 856(g)(1) or revoked under section 856(g)(2). A corporation, trust, or association meets the continuity of ownership requirement only if at any time during the taxable year the persons who own, directly or indirectly, 50 percent or more in value of its outstanding shares owned, at any time during the first taxable year for which the termination or revocation was effective, 50 percent or more in value of the outstanding shares of the corporation, trust, or association whose election has been terminated or revoked. A corporation, trust, or association meets the continuity of assets requirement only if either (i) a substantial portion of its assets were assets of the corporation, trust, or association whose election has been revoked or terminated, or (ii) it acquires a substantial portion of the assets of the corporation, trust, or association whose election has been terminated or revoked.

(3) Effective date. Section 856(g)(3) does not apply to the termination of an election that was made by a taxpayer pursuant to section 856(c)(1) on or before October 4, 1976, unless the taxpayer is a qualified real estate investment trust for a taxable year ending after October 4, 1976, for which the pre-October 5, 1976, election is in effect. For example, assume that Trust X, a calendar year taxpayer, files a timely election under section 856(c)(1) with respect to its taxable year 1974, and is a qualified real estate investment trust for calendar years 1974 and 1975. Assume further that Trust X is not a qualified real estate investment trust for 1976 and 1977 because it willfully fails to meet the asset diversification requirements of section 856(c)(5) for both years. The failure (whether or not willful) to meet these requirements in 1977 terminates the election to be a real estate investment trust made with respect to 1974. (See paragraph (b) of this section.) The termination is effective for 1977 and all succeeding taxable years. However, under section 1608(d)(3) of the Tax Reform Act of 1976, Trust X is not prohibited by section 856(g)(3) from making a new election under section 856(c)(1) with respect to 1978.

(d) Exceptions. Section 856(g)(4) provides an exception to the general rule of section 856(g)(3) that the termination of an election to be a real estate investment trust disqualifies the corporation, trust, or association from making a new election for the 4 taxable years following the first taxable year for which the termination is effective. This exception applies where the corporation, trust, or association meets the requirements of section 856(g)(4)(A), (B) and (C) (relating to the timely filing of a return, the absence of fraud, and reasonable cause, respectively) for the taxable year with respect to which the termination of election occurs. In order to meet the requirements of section 856(g)(4)(C), the corporation, trust, or association must establish, to the satisfaction of the district director for the internal revenue district in which the corporation, trust, or association maintains its principal place of business or principal office or agency, that its failure to be a qualified real estate investment trust for the taxable year in question was due to reasonable cause and not due to willful neglect. The principles of § 1.856-7(c) (including the principles relating to expert advice will apply in determining whether, for purposes of section 856(g)(4), the failure of a corporation, trust, or association to be a qualified real estate investment trust for a taxable year was due to reasonable cause and not due to willful neglect. Thus, for example, the corporation, trust, or association must exercise ordinary business care and prudence in attempting to meet the status conditions of section 856(a) and the distribution and recordkeeping requirements of section 857(a), as well as the gross income requirements of section 856(c). The provisions of section 856(g)(4) do not apply to a taxable year in which the corporation, trust, or association makes a valid revocation, under section 856(g)(2), of an election to be a real estate investment trust.

T.D. 7767, 2/3/81.

§ 1.856-9 Treatment of certain qualified REIT subsidiaries.

(a) In general. A qualified REIT subsidiary, even though it is otherwise not treated as a corporation separate from the REIT, is treated as a separate corporation for purposes of:

(1) Federal tax liabilities of the qualified REIT subsidiary with respect to any taxable period for which the qualified REIT subsidiary was treated as a separate corporation.

(2) Federal tax liabilities of any other entity for which the qualified REIT subsidiary is liable.

(3) Refunds or credits of Federal tax.

(b) Examples. The following examples illustrate the application of paragraph (a) of this section:

Example (1). X, a calendar year taxpayer, is a domestic corporation 100 percent of the stock of which is acquired by Y, a real estate investment trust, in 2002. X was not a member of a consolidated group at any time during its taxable year ending in December 2001. Consequently, X is treated as a qualified REIT subsidiary under the provisions of section 856(i) for 2002 and later periods. In 2004, the Internal Revenue Service (IRS) seeks to extend the period of limitations on assessment for X's 2001 taxable year. Because X was treated as a separate corporation for its 2001 taxable year, X is the proper party to sign the consent to extend the period of limitations.

Example (2). The facts are the same as in Example 1, except that upon Y's acquisition of X, Y and X jointly elect under section 856(l) to treat X as a taxable REIT subsidiary of Y. In 2003, Y and X jointly revoke that election. Consequently, X is treated as a qualified REIT subsidiary under the provisions of section 856(i) for 2003 and later periods. In 2004, the IRS determines that X miscalculated and underreported its income tax liability for 2001. Because X was treated as a separate corporation for its 2001 taxable year, the deficiency may be assessed against X and, in the event that X fails to pay the liability after notice and demand, a general tax lien will arise against all of X's property and rights to property.

Example (3). X is a qualified REIT subsidiary of Y under the provisions of section 856(i). In 2001, Z, a domestic corporation that reports its taxes on a calendar year basis, merges into X in a state law merger. Z was not a member of a consolidated group at any time during its taxable year ending in December 2000. Under the applicable state law, X is the successor to Z and is liable for all of Z's debts. In 2004, the IRS seeks to extend the period of limitations on assessment for Z's 2000 taxable year. Because X is the successor to Z and is liable for Z's 2000 taxes that remain unpaid, X is the proper party to sign the consent to extend the period of limitations.

(c) Effective date. This section applies on or after April 1, 2004.

T.D. 9183, 2/24/2005.

§ 1.857-1 Taxation of real estate investment trusts.

Caution: The Treasury has not yet amended Reg § 1.857-1 to reflect changes made by P.L. 105-34.

(a) Requirements applicable thereto. Section 857(a) denies the application of the provisions of part II, subchapter M, chapter 1 of the Code (other than sections 856(g), relating to the revocation or termination of an election, and 857(d), relating to earnings and profits) to a real estate investment trust for a taxable year unless—

(1) The deduction for dividends paid for the taxable year as defined in section 561 (computed without regard to capital gain dividends) equals or exceeds the amount specified in section 857(a)(1), as in effect for the taxable year; and

(2) The trust complies for such taxable year with the provisions of § 1.857-8 (relating to records required to be maintained by a real estate investment trust).

See section 858 and § 1.858-1, relating to dividends paid after the close of the taxable year.

(b) Failure to qualify. If a real estate investment trust does not meet the requirements of section 857(a) and paragraph (a) of this section for the taxable year, it will, even though it may otherwise be classified as a real estate investment trust, be taxed in such year as an ordinary corporation and not as a real estate investment trust. In such case, none of the provisions of part II of subchapter M (other than sections 856(g) and 857(d)) will be applicable to it. For the rules relating to the applicability of sections 856(g) and 857(d), see § 1.857-7.

T.D. 6598, 4/25/62, amend T.D. 7767, 2/3/81.

§ 1.857-2 Real estate investment trust taxable income and net capital gain.

Caution: The Treasury has not yet amended Reg § 1.857-2 to reflect changes made by P.L. 108-357, P.L. 108-311, P.L. 105-34.

(a) Real estate investment trust taxable income. Section 857(b)(1) imposes a normal tax and surtax, computed at the rates and in the manner prescribed in section 11, on the "real estate investment trust taxable income", as defined in section 857(b)(2). Section 857(b)(2) requires certain adjustments to be made to convert taxable income of the real estate investment trust to "real estate investment trust taxable income". The adjustments are as follows:

(1) Net capital gain. In the case of taxable years ending before October 5, 1976, the net capital gain, if any, is excluded.

(2) Special deductions disallowed. The special deductions provided in part VIII, subchapter B, chapter 1 of the Code (except the deduction under section 248) are not allowed.

(3) Deduction for dividends paid. (i) General rule. The deduction for dividends paid (as defined in section 561) is allowed. In the case of taxable years ending before October 5, 1976, the deduction for dividends paid is computed without regard to capital gains dividends.

(ii) Deduction for dividends paid if there is net income from foreclosure property. If for any taxable year the trust has net income from foreclosure property (as defined in section 857(b)(4)(B) and § 1.857-3), the deduction for dividends paid is an amount equal to the amount which bears the same proportion to the total dividends paid or considered as paid during the taxable year that otherwise meet the requirements for the deduction for dividends paid (as defined in section 561) as the real estate investment trust taxable income (determined without regard to the deduction for dividends paid) bears to the sum of—

(A) The real estate investment trust taxable income (determined without regard to the deduction for dividends paid), and

(B) The amount by which the net income from foreclosure property exceeds the tax imposed on such income by section 857(b)(4)(A).

For purposes of the preceding sentence, the term "total dividends paid or considered as paid during the taxable year" includes deficiency dividends paid with respect to the taxable year that are not otherwise excluded under this subdivision or section 857(b)(3)(A). The term, however, does not include either deficiency dividends paid during the taxable year with respect to a preceding taxable year or, in the case of taxable years ending before October 5, 1976, capital gains dividends.

(iii) Deduction for dividends paid for purposes of the alternative tax. The rules in section 857(b)(3)(A) apply in determining the amount of the deduction for dividends paid that is taken into account in computing the alternative tax. Thus, for example, if a real estate investment trust has net income from foreclosure property for a taxable year ending after October 4, 1976, then for purposes of determining the partial tax described in section 857(b)(3)(A)(i), the amount of the deduction for dividends paid is computed pursuant to paragraph (a)(3)(ii) of this section, except that capital gains dividends are excluded from the dividends paid or considered as paid during the taxable year, and the net capital gain is excluded in computing real estate investment trust taxable income.

(4) Section 443(b) disregarded. The taxable income is computed without regard to section 443(b). Thus, the taxable income for a period of less than 12 months is not placed on an annual basis even though the short taxable year results from a change of accounting period.

(5) Net operating loss deduction. In the case of a taxable year ending before October 5, 1976, the net operating loss deduction provided in section 172 is not allowed.

(6) Net income from foreclosure property. An amount equal to the net income from foreclosure property (as defined in section 857(b)(4)(B) and paragraph (a) of § 1.857-3), if any, is excluded.

(7) Tax imposed by section 857(b)(5). An amount equal to the tax (if any) imposed on the trust by section 857(b)(5) for the taxable year is excluded.

(8) Net income or loss from prohibited transactions. An amount equal to the amount of any net income derived from prohibited transactions (as defined in section 857(b)(6)(B)(i)) is excluded. On the other hand, an amount equal to the amount of any net loss derived from prohibited transactions (as defined in section 857(b)(6)(B)(ii)) is included. Because the amount of the net loss derived from prohibited transactions is taken into account in computing taxable income before the adjustments required by section 857(b)(2) and this section are made, the effect of including an amount equal to the amount of the loss is to disallow a deduction for the loss.

(b) Net capital gain in taxable years ending before October 5, 1976. The rules relating to the taxation of capital gains in 26 CFR 1.857-2(b) (revised as of April 1, 1977) apply to taxable years ending before October 5, 1976.

T.D. 6598, 4/25/62, amend T.D. 7767, 2/3/81.

§ 1.857-3 Net income from foreclosure property.

Caution: The Treasury has not yet amended Reg § 1.857-3 to reflect changes made by P.L. 99-514.

(a) In general. For purposes of section 857(b)(4)(B), net income from foreclosure property means the aggregate of—

(1) All gains and losses from sales or other dispositions of foreclosure property described in section 1221(1), and

(2) The difference (hereinafter called "net gain or loss from operations") between (1) the gross income derived from foreclosure property (as defined in section 856(e)) to the extent such gross income is not described in subparagraph (A), (B), (C), (D), (E), or (G) of section 856(c)(3), and (ii) the deductions allowed by chapter 1 of the Code which are directly connected with the production of such gross income.

Thus, the sum of the gains and losses from sales or other dispositions of foreclosure property described in section 1221(1) is aggregated with the net gain or loss from operations in arriving at net income from foreclosure property. For example, if for a taxable year a real estate investment trust has gain of $100 from the sale of an item of foreclosure property described in section 1221(1), a loss of $50 from the sale of an item of foreclosure property described in section 1221(1), gross income of $25 from the rental of foreclosure property that is not gross income described in subparagraph (A), (B), (C), (D), or (G) of section 856(c)(3), and deductions of $35 allowed by chapter 1 of the Code which are directly connected with the production of the rental income, the net income from foreclosure property for the taxable years is $40 (($100 − $50) + ($25 − $35)).

(b) Directly connected deductions. A deduction which is otherwise allowed by chapter 1 of the Code is "directly connected" with the production of gross income from foreclosure property if it has a proximate and primary relationship to the earning of the income. Thus, in the case of gross income from real property that is foreclosure property, "directly connected" deductions would include depreciation on the property, interest paid or accrued on the indebtedness of the trust (whether or not secured by the property) to the extent attributable to the carrying of the property, real estate taxes, and fees paid to an independent contractor hired to manage the property. On the other hand, general overhead and administrative expenses of the trust are not "directly connected" deductions. Thus, salaries of officers and other administrative employees of the trust are not "directly connected" deductions. The net operating loss deduction provided by section 172 is not allowed in computing net income from foreclosure property.

(c) Net loss from foreclosure property. The tax imposed by section 857(b)(4) applies only if there is net income from foreclosure property. If there is a net loss from foreclosure property (that is, if the aggregate computed under paragraph (a) of this section results in a negative amount) the loss is taken into account in computing real estate investment trust taxable income under section 857(b)(2).

(d) Gross income not subject to tax on foreclosure property. If the gross income derived from foreclosure property consists of two classes, a deduction directly connected with the production of both classes (including interest attributable to the carrying of the property) must be apportioned between them. The two classes are:

(1) Gross income which is taken into account in computing net income from foreclosure property and

(2) Other income (such as income described in subparagraph (A), (B), (C), (D), or (G) of section 856(c)(3)).

The apportionment may be made on any reasonable basis.

(e) Allocation and apportionment of interest. For purposes of determining the amount of interest attributable to the carrying of foreclosure property under paragraph (b) of this section, the following rules apply:

(1) Deductible interest. Interest is taken into account under this paragraph (e) only if it is otherwise deductible under chapter 1 of the Code.

(2) Interest specifically allocated to property. Interest that is specifically allocated to an item of property is attributable only to the carrying of that property. Interest is specifically allocated to an item of property if (i) the indebtedness on which the interest is paid or accrued is secured only by that property, (ii) such indebtedness was specifically incurred for the purpose of purchasing, constructing, maintaining, or improving that property, and (iii) the proceeds of the borrowing were applied for that purpose.

(3) Other interest. Interest which is not specifically allocated to property is apportioned between foreclosure property and other property under the principles of § 1.861-8(e)(2)(v).

(4) Effective date. The rules in this paragraph (e) are mandatory for all taxable years ending after February 6, 1981.

T.D. 7767, 2/3/81.

---

§ 1.857-4 Tax imposed by reason of the failure to meet certain source-of-income requirements.

Section 857(b)(5) imposes a tax on a real estate investment trust that is considered, by reason of section 856(c)(7), as meeting the source-of-income requirements of paragraph (2) or (3) of section 856(c) (or both such paragraphs). The amount of the tax is determined in the manner prescribed in section 857(b)(5).

T.D. 7767, 2/3/81.

---

§ 1.857-5 Net income and loss from prohibited transactions.

Caution: The Treasury has not yet amended Reg § 1.857-5 to reflect changes made by P.L. 105-34, P.L. 99-514.

(a) In general. Section 857(b)(6) imposes, for each taxable year, a tax equal to 100 percent of the net income derived from prohibited transactions. A prohibited transaction is a sale or other disposition of property described in section 1221(1) that is not foreclosure property. The 100-percent tax is imposed to preclude a real estate investment trust from retaining any profit from ordinary retailing activities such as sales to customers of condominium units or subdivided lots in a development tract. In order to prevent a trust from receiving any tax benefit from such activities, a net loss from prohibited transactions effectively is disallowed in computing real estate investment trust taxable income. See § 1.857-2(a)(8). Such loss, however, does reduce the amount which a trust is required to distribute as dividends. For purposes of applying the provisions of the Code, other than those provisions of part II of subchapter M which relate to prohibited transactions, no inference is to be drawn from the fact that a type of transaction does not constitute a prohibited transaction.

(b) Special rules. In determining whether a particular transaction constitutes a prohibited transaction, the activities of a real estate investment trust with respect to foreclosure property and its sales of such property are disregarded. Also, if a real estate investment trust enters into a purchase and leaseback of real property with an option in the seller-lessee to repurchase the property at the end of the lease period, and the seller exercises the option pursuant to its terms, income from the sale generally will not be considered to be income from a prohibited transaction solely because the purchase and leaseback was entered into with an option in the seller to repurchase and because the option was exercised pursuant to its terms. Other facts and circumstances, however, may require a conclusion that the property is held primarily for sale to customers in the ordinary course of a trade or business. Gain from the sale or other disposition of property described in section 1221(1) (other than foreclosure property) that is included in gross income for a taxable year of a qualified real estate investment trust constitutes income from a prohibited transaction, even though the sale or other disposition from which the gain is derived occurred in a prior taxable year. For example, if a corporation that is a qualified real estate investment trust for the current taxable year elected to report the income from the sale of an item of section 1221(1) property (other than foreclosure property) on the installment method of reporting income, the gain from the sale that is taken into income by the real estate investment trust for the current taxable year is income from a prohibited transaction. This result follows even though the sale occurred in a prior taxable year for which the corporation did not qualify as a real estate investment trust. On the other hand, if the gain is taken into income in a taxable year for which the taxpayer is not a qualified real estate investment trust, the 100-percent tax does not apply.

(c) Net income or loss from prohibited transactions. Net income or net loss from prohibited transactions is determined by aggregating all gains from the sale or other disposition of property (other than foreclosure property) described in section 1221(1) with all losses from the sale or other disposition of such property. Thus, for example, if a real estate investment trust sells two items of property described in section 1221(1) (other than foreclosure property) and recognizes a gain of $100 on the sale of one item and a loss of $40 on the sale of the second item, the net income from prohibited transactions will be $60.

T.D. 7767, 2/3/81.

---

§ 1.857-6 Method of taxation of shareholders of real estate investment trusts.

Caution: The Treasury has not yet amended Reg § 1.857-6 to reflect changes made by P.L. 110-172, P.L. 108-27, P.L. 105-34.

(a) Ordinary income. Except as otherwise provided in paragraph (b) of this section (relating to capital gains), a shareholder receiving dividends from a real estate investment trust shall include such dividends in gross income for the taxable year in which they are received. See section 858(b) and paragraph (c) of § 1.858-1 for treatment by shareholders of dividends paid by a real estate investment trust after the close of its taxable year in the case of an election under section 858(a).

(b) Capital gains. Under section 857(b)(3)(B), shareholders of a real estate investment trust who receive capital gain dividends (as defined in paragraph (e) of this section), in respect of the capital gains of a corporation, trust, or association for a taxable year for which it is taxable under part II of subchapter M as a real estate investment trust, shall treat such capital gain dividends as gains from the sale or exchange of capital assets held for more than 1 year (6 months for taxable years beginning before 1977; 9 months for taxable years beginning in 1977) and realized in the taxable year of the shareholder in which the dividend was received. In the case of dividends with respect to any taxable year of a real estate investment trust ending after December 31, 1969, and beginning before January 1, 1975, the portion of a shareholder's capital gain dividend which in his hands is gain to which section 1201(d)(1) or (2) applies is the portion so designated by the real estate investment trust pursuant to paragraph (e)(2) of this section.

(c) Special treatment of loss on the sale or exchange of real estate investment trust stock held less than 31 days. *(1) In general.* Under section 857(b)(7), if any person with respect to a share of real estate investment trust stock held for a period of less than 31 days, is required by section 857(b)(3)(B) to include in gross income as a gain from the sale or exchange of a capital asset held for more than 1 year (6 months for taxable years beginning before 1977; 9 months for taxable years beginning in 1977) the amount of a capital gains dividend, then such person shall, to the extent of such amount, treat any loss on the sale or exchange of such share as a loss from the sale or exchange of a capital asset held for more than 1 year (6 months for taxable years beginning before 1977; 9 months for taxable years beginning in 1977).

(2) Determination of holding period. The rules contained in section 246(c)(3) (relating to the determination of holding periods for purposes of the deduction for dividends received) shall be applied in determining whether, for purposes of section 857(b)(7)(B) and this paragraph, a share of real estate investment trust stock has been held for a period of less than 31 days. In applying those rules, however, "30 days" shall be substituted for the number of days specified in subparagraph (B) of such section.

(3) Illustration. The application of section 857(b)(7) and this paragraph may be illustrated by the following example:

Example. On December 15, 1961, A purchased a share of stock in the S Real Estate Investment Trust for $20. The S trust declared a capital gains dividend of $2 per share to shareholders of record on December 31, 1961. A, therefore, received a capital gain dividend of $2 which, pursuant to section 857(b)(3)(B), he must treat as a gain from the sale or exchange of a capital asset held for more than six months. On January 5, 1962, A sold his share of stock in the S trust for $17.50, which sale resulted in a loss of $2.50. Under section 857(b)(7) and this paragraph, A must treat $2 of such loss (an amount equal to the capital gain dividend received with respect to such share of stock) as a loss from the sale or exchange of a capital asset held for more than six months.

(d) Dividend received credit, exclusion, and deduction not allowed. Any dividend received from a real estate investment trust which, for the taxable year to which the dividend relates, is a qualified real estate investment trust, shall not be eligible for the dividend received credit (for dividends received on or before December 31, 1964) under section 34(a), the dividend received exclusion under section 116, or the dividend received deduction under section 243.

(e) Definition of capital gain dividend. *(1)* (i) A capital gain dividend, as defined in section 857(b)(3)(C), is any dividend or part thereof which is designated by a real estate investment trust as a capital gain dividend in a written notice mailed to its shareholders within the period specified in section 857(b)(3)(C) and paragraph (f) of this section. If the aggregate amount so designated with respect to the taxable year (including capital gain dividends paid after the close of the taxable year pursuant to an election under section 858) is greater than the excess of the net long-term capital gain over the net short-term capital loss of the taxable year, the portion of each distribution which shall be a capital gain dividend shall be only that proportion of the amount so designated which such excess of the net long-term capital gain over the net short-term capital loss bears to the aggregate of the amount so designated. For example, a real estate investment trust making its return on the calendar year basis advised its shareholders by written notice mailed December 30, 1961, that $200,000 of a distribution of $500,000 made December 15, 1961, constituted a capital gain dividend, amounting to $2 per share. It was later discovered that an error had been made in determining the excess of the net long-term capital gain over the net short-term capital loss of the taxable year and the net capital gain was $100,000 instead of $200,000. In such case, each shareholder would have received a capital gain dividend of $1 per share instead of $2 per share.

(ii) For purposes of section 857(b)(3)(C) and this paragraph, the net capital gain for a taxable year ending after October 4, 1976, is deemed not to exceed the real estate investment trust taxable income determined by taking into account the net operating loss deduction for the taxable year but not the deduction for dividends paid. See example (2) in § 1.172-5(a)(4).

(2) In the case of capital gain dividends designated with respect to any taxable year of a real estate investment trust ending after December 31, 1969, and beginning before January 1, 1975 (including capital gain dividends paid after the close of the taxable year pursuant to an election under section 858), the real estate investment trust must include in its written notice designating the capital gain dividend a statement showing the shareholder's proportionate share of such dividend which is gain described in section 1201(d)(1) and his proportionate share of such dividend which is gain described in section 1201(d)(2). In determining the portion of the capital gain dividend which, in the hands of a shareholder, is gain described in section 1201(d)(1) or (2), the real estate investment trust shall consider that capital gain dividends for a taxable year are first made from its long-term capital gains which are not described in section 1201(d)(1) or (2), to the extent thereof, and then from its long-term capital gains for such year which are described in section 1201(d)(1) or (2). A shareholder's proportionate share of gains which are described in section 1201(d)(1) is the amount which bears the same ratio to the amount paid to him as a capital gain dividend in respect of such year as (i) the aggregate amount of the trust's gains which are described in section 1201(d)(1) and paid to all shareholders bears to (ii) the aggregate amount of the capital gain dividend paid to all shareholders in respect of such year. A shareholder's proportionate share of gains which are described in section 1201(d)(2) shall be determined in a similar manner. Every real estate investment trust shall keep a record of the proportion of each capital dividend (to which this subparagraph applies) which is gain described in section 1201(d)(1) or (2).

(f) Mailing of written notice to shareholders. *(1) General rule.* Except as provided in paragraph (f)(2) of this section, the written notice designating a dividend or part thereof as a capital gain dividend must be mailed to the shareholders not later than 30 days after the close of the taxable year of the real estate investment trust.

(2) Net capital gain resulting from a determination. If, as a result of a determination (as defined in section 860(e)), occurring after October 4, 1976, there is an increase in the amount by which the net capital gain exceeds the deduction for dividends paid (determined with reference to capital gains dividends only) for the taxable year, then a real estate investment trust may designate a dividend (or part thereof) as a capital gain dividend in a written notice mailed to its shareholders at any time during the 120-day period immediately following the date of the determination. The designa-

tion may be made with respect to a dividend (or part thereof) paid during the taxable year to which the determination applies (including a dividend considered as paid during the taxable year pursuant to section 858). A deficiency dividend (as defined in section 860(f)), or a part thereof, that is paid with respect to the taxable year also may be designated as a capital gain dividend by the real estate investment trust (or by the acquiring corporation to which section 381(c)(25) applies) before the expiration of the 120-day period immediately following the determination. However, the aggregate amount of the dividends (or parts thereof) that may be designated as capital gain dividends after the date of the determination shall not exceed the amount of the increase in the excess of the net capital gain over the deduction for dividends paid (determined with reference to capital gains dividends only) that results from the determination. The date of a determination shall be established in accordance with § 1.860-2(b)(1).

T.D. 6598, 4/25/62, amend T.D. 6777, 12/15/64, T.D. 7337, 12/26/74, T.D. 7728, 10/31/80, T.D. 7767, 2/3/81, T.D. 7936, 1/17/84, T.D. 8107, 12/1/86.

§ 1.857-7 Earnings and profits of a real estate investment trust.

Caution: The Treasury has not yet amended Reg § 1.857-7 to reflect changes made by P.L. 99-514.

(a) Any real estate investment trust, whether or not such trust meets the requirements of section 857(a) and paragraph (a) of § 1.857-1 for any taxable year beginning after December 31, 1960, shall apply paragraph (b) of this section in computing its earnings and profits for such taxable year.

(b) In the determination of the earnings and profits of a real estate investment trust, section 857(d) provides that such earnings and profits for any taxable year (but not the accumulated earnings and profits) shall not be reduced by any amount which is not allowable as a deduction in computing its taxable income for the taxable year. Thus, if a trust would have had earnings and profits of $500,000 for the taxable year except for the fact that it had a net capital loss of $100,000, which amount was not deductible in determining its taxable income, its earnings and profits for that year if it is a real estate investment trust would be $500,000. If the real estate investment trust had no accumulated earnings and profits at the beginning of the taxable year, in determining its accumulated earnings and profits as of the beginning of the following taxable year, the earnings and profits for the taxable year to be considered in such computation would amount to $400,000 assuming that there had been no distribution from such earnings and profits. If distributions had been made in the taxable year in the amount of the earnings and profits then available for distribution, $500,000, the trust would have as of the beginning of the following taxable year neither accumulated earnings and profits nor a deficit in accumulated earnings and profits, and would begin such year with its paid-in capital reduced by $100,000, an amount equal to the excess of the $500,000 distributed over the $400,000 accumulated earnings and profits which would otherwise have been carried into the following taxable year. For purposes of section 857(d) and this section, if an amount equal to any net loss derived from prohibited transactions is included in real estate investment trust taxable income pursuant to section 857(b)(2)(F), that amount shall be considered to be an amount which is not allowable as a deduction in computing taxable income for the taxable year. The earnings and profits for the taxable year (but not the accumulated earnings and profits) shall not be considered to be less than (i) in the case of a taxable year ending before October 5, 1976, the amount (if any) of the net capital gain for the taxable year, or (ii) in the case of a taxable year ending after December 31, 1973, the amount (if any), of the excess of the net income from foreclosure property for the taxable year over the tax imposed thereon by section 857(b)(4)(A).

T.D. 6598, 4/25/62, amend T.D. 7767, 2/3/81.

§ 1.857-8 Records to be kept by a real estate investment trust.

(a) In general. Under section 857 (a)(2) a real estate investment trust is required to keep such records as will disclose the actual ownership of its outstanding stock. Thus, every real estate investment trust shall maintain in the internal revenue district in which it is required to file its income tax return permanent records showing the information relative to the actual owners of its stock contained in the written statements required by this section to be demanded from its shareholders. Such records shall be kept at all times available for inspection by any internal revenue officer or employee, and shall be retained so long as the contents thereof may become material in the administration of any internal revenue law.

(b) Actual owner of stock. The actual owner of stock of a real estate investment trust is the person who is required to include in gross income in his return the dividend received on the stock. Generally, such person is the shareholder of record of the real estate investment trust. However, where the shareholder of record is not the actual owner of the stock, the stockholding record of the real estate investment trust may not disclose the actual ownership of such stock. Accordingly, the real estate investment trust shall demand written statement from shareholders of record disclosing the actual owners of stock as required in paragraph (d) of this section.

(c) Stock ownership for personal holding company determination. For the purpose of determining under section 856(a)(6) whether a trust, claiming to be a real estate investment trust, is a personal holding company, the permanent records of the trust shall show the maximum number of shares of the trust (including the number and face value of securities convertible into stock of the trust) to be considered as actually or constructively owned by each of the actual owners of any of its stock at any time during the last half of the trust's taxable year, as provided in section 544.

(d) Statements to be demanded from shareholders. The information required by paragraphs (b) and (c) of this section shall be set forth in written statements which shall be demanded from shareholders of record as follows:

(1) In the case of a trust having 2,000 or more shareholders of record of its stock on any dividend record date, from each record holder of 5 percent or more of its stock; or

(2) In the case of a trust having less than 2,000 and more than 200 shareholders of record of its stock on any dividend record date, from each record holder of 1 percent or more of its stock; or

(3) In the case of a trust having 200 or less shareholders of record of its stock on any dividend record date, from each record holder of one-half of 1 percent or more of its stock.

(e) Demands for statements. The written statements from shareholders of record shall be demanded by the real estate investment trust in accordance with paragraph (d) of this section within 30 days after the close of the real estate investment trust's taxable year (or before June 1, 1962, whichever is later). When making demand for such written statements, the trust shall inform each such shareholder of his duty to submit at the time he files his income tax return (or before July 1, 1962, whichever is later) the statements which are required by § 1.857-9 if he fails or refuses to comply with such demand. A list of the persons failing or refusing to comply in whole or in part with the trust's demand for statements under this section shall be maintained as a part of the trust's records required by this section. A trust which fails to keep such records to show, to the extent required by this section, the actual ownership of its outstanding stock shall be taxable as an ordinary corporation and not as a real estate investment trust.

T.D. 6598, 4/25/62, amend T.D. 7767, 2/3/81.

§ 1.857-9 Information required in returns of shareholders.

(a) In general. Any person who fails or refuses to submit to a real estate investment trust the written statements required under § 1.857-8 to be demanded by such trust from its shareholders of record shall submit at the time he files his income tax return for his taxable year which ends with, or includes, the last day of the trust's taxable year (or before July 1, 1962, whichever is later) a statement setting forth the information required by this section.

(b) Information required. *(1) Shareholder of record not actual owner.* In the case of any person holding shares of stock in any trust claiming to be a real estate investment trust who is not the actual owner of such stock, the name and address of each actual owner, the number of shares owned by each actual owner at any time during such person's taxable year, and the amount of dividends belonging to each actual owner.

(2) Actual owner of shares. In the case of an actual owner of shares of stock in any trust claiming to be a real estate investment trust—

(i) The name and address of each such trust, the number of shares actually owned by him at any and all times during his taxable year, and the amount of dividends from each such trust received during his taxable year;

(ii) If shares of any such trust were acquired or disposed of during such person's taxable year, the name and address of the trust, the number of shares acquired or disposed of, the dates of acquisition or disposition, and the names and addresses of the persons from whom such shares were acquired or to whom they were transferred;

(iii) If any shares of stock (including securities convertible into stock) of any such trust are also owned by any member of such person's family (as defined in section 544(a)(2)), or by any of his partners, the name and address of the trust, the names and addresses of such members of his family and his partners, and the number of shares owned by each such member of his family or partner at any and all times during such person's taxable year; and

(iv) The names and addresses of any corporation, partnership, association, or trust, in which such person had a beneficial interest of 10 percent or more at any time during his taxable year.

T.D. 6598, 4/25/62, amend T.D. 6628, 12/27/62, T.D. 7767, 2/3/81.

§ 1.857-10 Information returns.

Nothing in §§ 1.857-8 and 1.857-9 shall be construed to relieve a real estate investment trust or its shareholders from the duty of filing information returns required by regulations prescribed under the provisions of subchapter A, chapter 61 of the Code.

T.D. 6598, 4/25/62, amend T.D. 7767, 2/3/81.

§ 1.857-11 Non-REIT earnings and profits.

Caution: The Treasury has not yet amended Reg § 1.857-11 to reflect changes made by P.L. 105-34.

(a) Applicability of section 857(a)(3)(A). A real estate investment trust does not satisfy section 857(a)(3)(A) unless—

(1) Part II of subchapter M applied to the trust for all its taxable years beginning after February 28, 1986; and

(2) For each corporation to whose earnings and profits the trust succeeded by the operation of section 381, part II of subchapter M applied for all the corporation's taxable years beginning after February 28, 1986.

(b) Applicability of section 857(a)(3)(B); In general. A real estate investment trust does not satisfy section 857(a)(3)(B) unless, as of the close of the taxable year, it has no earnings and profits other than earnings and profits that—

(1) Were earned by a corporation in a year for which part II of subchapter M applied to the corporation and, at all times thereafter, were the earnings and profits of a corporation to which part II of subchapter M applied; or

(2) By the operation of section 381 pursuant to a transaction that occurred before December 22, 1992, became the earnings and profits of a corporation to which part II of subchapter M applied and, at all times thereafter, were the earnings and profits of a corporation to which part II of subchapter M applied.

(c) Distribution procedures similar to those for regulated investment companies to apply. Distribution procedures similar to those in section 852(e) for regulated investment companies apply to non-REIT earnings and profits of real estate investment trusts.

(d) Effective date. This regulation is effective for taxable years ending on or after December 22, 1992.

(e) For treatment of net built-in gain assets of a C corporation that become assets of a REIT, see § 1.337(d)-5T.

T.D. 8483, 8/17/93, amend T.D. 8872, 2/4/2000.

§ 1.858-1 Dividends paid by a real estate investment trust after close of taxable year.

(a) General rule. Under section 858, a real estate investment trust may elect to treat certain dividends that are distributed within a specified period after the close of a taxable year as having been paid during the taxable year. The dividend is taken into account in determining the deduction for dividends paid for the taxable year in which it is treated as paid. The dividend may be an ordinary dividend or, subject to the requirements of sections 857(b)(3)(C) and 858(c), a capital gain dividend. The trust may make the dividend declaration required by section 858(a)(1) either before or after the close of the taxable year as long as the declaration is made before the time prescribed by law for filing its return for the taxable year (including the period of any extension of time granted for filing the return).

(b) Election. *(1) Method of making election.* The election must be made in the return filed by the trust for the taxable year. The election shall be made by treating the dividend (or portion thereof) to which the election applies as a dividend paid during the taxable year of the trust in computing its real estate investment trust taxable income and, if applicable, the alternative tax imposed by section 857(b)(3)(A). (In the case of an election with respect to a taxable year ending before October 5, 1976, if the dividend (or portion thereof) to which the election is to apply is a capital gain dividend, the trust shall treat the dividend as paid during such taxable year in computing the amount of capital gains dividends paid during the taxable year.) In the case of an election with respect to a taxable year beginning after October 4, 1976, the trust must also specify in its return (or in a statement attached to its return) the exact dollar amount that is to be treated as having been paid during the taxable year.

(2) Limitation based on earnings and profits. The election provided in section 858(a) may be made only to the extent that the earnings and profits of the taxable year (computed with the application of sections 857(d) and 1.857-7) exceed the total amount of distributions out of such earnings and profits actually made during the taxable year. For purposes of the preceding sentence, deficiency dividends and distributions with respect to which an election has been made for a prior year under section 858(a) are disregarded in determining the total amount of distributions out of earnings and profits actually made during the taxable year. The dividend or portion thereof, with respect to which the real estate investment trust has made a valid election under section 858(a), shall be considered as paid out of the earnings and profits of the taxable year for which such election is made, and not out of the earnings and profits of the taxable year in which the distribution is actually made.

(3) Additional limitation based on amount specified. The amount treated under section 858(a) as having been paid in a taxable year beginning after October 4, 1976, cannot exceed the lesser of (i) the dollar amount specified by the trust in its return (or a statement attached thereto) in making the election or (ii) the amount allowable under the limitation prescribed in paragraph (b)(2) of this section.

(4) Irrevocability of the election. After the expiration of the time for filing the return for the taxable year for which an election is made under section 858(a), such election shall be irrevocable with respect to the dividend or portion thereof to which it applies.

(c) Receipt by shareholders. Under section 858(b), the dividend or portion thereof, with respect to which a valid election has been made, will be includible in the gross income of the shareholders of the real estate investment trust for the taxable year in which the dividend is received by them.

(d) Illustrations. The application of paragraphs (a), (b), and (c) of this section may be illustrated by the following examples:

Example (1). The X Trust, a real estate investment trust, had taxable income (and earnings and profits) for the calendar year 1961 of $100,000. During that year the trust distributed to shareholders taxable dividends aggregating $88,000. On March 10, 1962, the trust declared a dividend of $37,000 payable to shareholders on March 20, 1962. Such dividend consisted of the first regular quarterly dividend for 1962 of $25,000 plus an additional $12,000 representing that part of the taxable income for 1961 which was not distributed in 1961. On March 15, 1962, the X Trust filed its Federal income tax return and elected therein to treat $12,000 of the total dividend of $37,000 to be paid to shareholders on March 20, 1962, as having been paid during the taxable year 1961. Assuming that the X Trust actually distributed the entire amount of the dividend of $37,000 on March 20, 1962, an amount equal to $12,000 thereof will be treated for the purposes of section 857(a) as having been paid during the taxable year 1961. Upon distribution of such dividend the trust becomes a qualified real estate investment trust for the taxable year 1961. Such amount ($12,000) will be considered by the X Trust as a distribution out of the earnings and profits for the taxable year 1961, and will be treated by the shareholders as a taxable dividend for the taxable year in which such distribution is received by them. However, assuming that the X Trust is not a qualified real estate investment trust for the calendar year 1962, nevertheless, the $12,000 portion of the dividend (paid on March 20, 1962) which the trust elected to relate to the calendar year 1961, will not qualify as a dividend for purposes of section 34, 116, or 243.

Example (2). The Y Trust, a real estate investment trust, had taxable income (and earnings and profits) for the calendar year 1964 of $100,000, and for 1965 taxable income (and earnings and profits) of $125,000. On January 1, 1964, the trust had a deficit in its earnings and profits accumulated since February 28, 1913, of $115,000. During the year 1964 the trust distributed to shareholders taxable dividends aggregating $85,000. On March 5, 1965, the trust declared a dividend of $65,000 payable to shareholders on March 31, 1965. On March 15, 1965, the Y Trust filed its Federal income tax return in which it included $40,000 of the total dividend of $65,000 payable to shareholders on March 31, 1965, as a dividend paid by it during the taxable year 1964. On March 31, 1965, the Y Trust distributed the entire amount of the dividend of $65,000 declared on March 5, 1965. The election under section 858(a) is valid only to the extent of $15,000, the amount of the undistributed earnings and profits for 1964 ($100,000 earnings and profits less $85,000 distributed during 1964). The remainder ($50,000) of the $65,000 dividend paid on March 31, 1965, could not be the subject of an election, and such amount will be regarded as a distribution by the Y Trust out of earnings and profits for the taxable year 1965. Assuming that the only other distribution by the Y Trust during 1965 was a distribution of $75,000 paid as a dividend on October 31, 1965, the total amount of the distribution of $65,000 paid on March 31, 1965, is to be treated by the shareholders as taxable dividends for the taxable year in which such dividend is received. The Y Trust will treat the amount of $15,000 as a distribution of the earnings or profits of the trust for the taxable year 1964, and the remaining $50,000 as a distribution of the earnings or profits for the year 1965. The distribution of $75,000 on October 31, 1965, is, of course, a taxable dividend out of the earnings and profits for the year 1965.

Example (3). Assume the facts are the same as in example (2), except that the taxable years involved are calendar years 1977 and 1978, and Y Trust specified in its Federal income tax return for 1977 that the dollar amount of $40,000 of the $65,000 distribution payable to shareholders on March 31, 1978, is to be treated as having been paid in 1977. The result will be the same as in example (2), since the amount of the undistributed earnings and profits for 1977 is less than the $40,000 amount specified by Y Trust in making its election. Accordingly, the election is valid only to the extent of $15,000. Y Trust will treat the amount of $15,000 as a distribution, in 1977, of earnings and profits of the trust for the taxable year 1977 and the remaining $50,000 as a distribution, in 1978, of the earnings and profits for 1978.

(e) Notice to shareholders. Section 858(c) provides that, in the case of dividends with respect to which a real estate investment trust has made an election under section 858(a), any notice to shareholders required under part II, subchapter M, chapter 1 of the Code, with respect to such amounts, shall be made not later than 30 days after the close of the taxable year in which the distribution is made. Thus, the notice requirement of section 857(b)(3)(C) and paragraph (f) of § 1.857-6 with respect to capital gains dividends may be satisfied with respect to amounts to which section 858(a) and this section apply if the notice relating to such amounts is mailed to the shareholders not later than 30 days after the close of the taxable year in which the distribution is made. If the notice under section 858(c) relates to an election with respect to any capital gains dividends, such capital gains dividends shall be aggregated by the real estate investment trust with the designated capital gains dividends actually paid during the taxable year to which the election applies (not including deficiency dividends or dividends with respect to which an election has been made for a prior taxable year under section 858) to determine whether the aggregate of the designated capital gains dividends with respect to such taxable year exceeds the net capital gain of the trust. See section 857(b)(3)(C) and paragraph (f) of § 1.857-6.

T.D. 6598, 4/25/62, amend T.D. 7767, 2/3/81.

§ 1.860-1 Deficiency dividends.

Section 860 allows a qualified investment entity to be relieved from the payment of a deficiency in (or to be allowed a credit or refund of) certain taxes. "Qualified investment entity" is defined in section 860(b). The taxes referred to are those imposed by sections 852(b)(1) and (3), 857(b)(1) or (3), the minimum tax on tax preferences imposed by section 56 and, if the entity fails the distribution requirements of section 852(a)(1)(A) or 857(a)(1) (as applicable), the corporate income tax imposed by section 11(a) or 1201(a). The method provided by section 860 is to allow an additional deduction for a dividend distribution (that meets the requirements of section 860 and § 1.860-2) in computing the deduction for dividends paid for the taxable year for which the deficiency is determined. A deficiency divided may be an ordinary dividend or, subject to the limitations of sections 852(b)(3)(C), 857(b)(3)(C), and 860(f)(2)(B), may be a capital gain dividend.

T.D. 7767, 2/3/81, amend T.D. 7936, 1/17/84.

§ 1.860-2 Requirements for deficiency dividends.

(a) In general. *(1) Determination, etc.* A qualified investment entity is allowed a deduction for a deficiency dividend only if there is a determination (as defined in section 860(e) and paragraph (b)(1) of this section) that results in an adjustment (as defined in section 860(d)(1) or (2)) for the taxable year for which the deficiency dividend is paid. An adjustment does not include an increase in the excess of (i) the taxpayer's interest income excludable from gross income under section 103(a) over (ii) its deductions disallowed under section 265 and 171(a)(2).

(2) Payment date and claim. The deficiency dividend must be paid on, or within 90 days after, the date of the determination and before the filing of a claim under section 860(g) and paragraph (b)(2) of this section. This claim must be filed within 120 days after the date of the determination.

(3) Nature and amount of distribution. (i) The deficiency dividend must be a distribution of property (including money) that would have been properly taken into account in computing the dividends paid deduction under section 561 for the taxable year for which tax liability resulting from the determination exists if the property had been distributed during that year. Thus, if the distribution would have been a divided under section 316(a) if it had been made during the taxable year for which the determination applies, and the distribution may qualify under sections 316(b)(3), 562(a), and 860(f)(1), even though the distributing corporation, trust, or association has no current or accumulated earnings and profits for the taxable year in which the distribution is actually made. The amount of the distribution is determined under section 301 as of the date of the distribution.

The amount of the deduction is subject to the applicable limitations under sections 562 and 860(f)(2). Thus, if the entity distributes to an individual shareholder property (other than money) which on the date of the distribution has a fair market value in excess of its adjusted basis in the hands of the entity, the amount of the deficiency dividend in the individual's hands for purposes of section 316(b)(3) is determined by using the property's fair market value on that date. Nevertheless, the amount of the deficiency dividend the entity may deduct is limited, under § 1.562-1(a), to the adjusted basis of the property and the amount taxable to the individual as a dividend is determined by reference to the current and accumulated earnings and profits for the year to which the determination applies.

(ii) The qualified investment entity does not have to distribute the full amount of the adjustment in order to pay a deficiency dividend. For example, assume that in 1983 a determination with respect to a calendar year regulated investment company results in an increase of $100 in investment company taxable income (computed without the dividends paid deduction) for 1981 and no other change. The regulated investment company may choose to pay a deficiency dividend of $100 or of any lesser amount and be allowed a dividends paid deduction for 1981 for the amount of that deficiency dividend.

(4) Status of distributor. The corporation, trust, or association that pays the deficiency dividend does not have to be a qualified investment entity at the time of payment.

(5) Certain definitions to apply. For purposes of sections 860(d) (defining adjustment) and (f)(2) (limitations) the definitions of the terms "investment company taxable income," "real estate investment trust taxable income," and "capital gains dividends" in sections 852(b)(2), 857(b)(2), 852(b)(3)(C), and 857(b)(3)(C) apply, as appropriate to the particular entity.

(b) Determination and claim for deduction. *(1) Determination.* For purposes of applying section 860(e), the following rules apply:

(i) The date of determination by a decision of the United States Tax Court, the date upon which a judgment of a court becomes final, and the date of determination by a closing agreement shall be determined under the rules in § 1.547-2(b)(1)(ii), (iii), and (iv).

(ii) A determination under section 860(e)(3) may be made by an agreement signed by the district director or another official to whom authority to sign the agreement is delegated, and by or on behalf of the taxpayer. The agreement shall set forth the amount, if any, of each adjustment described in subparagraphs (A), (B), and (C) of section 860(d)(1) or (2) (as appropriate) for the taxable year and the amount of the liability for any tax imposed by section 11(a), 56(a), 852(b)(1), 852(b)(3)(A), 857(b)(1), 857(b)(3)(A), or 1201(a) for the taxable year. The agreement shall also set forth the amount of the limitation (determined under section 860(f)(2)) on the amount of deficiency dividends that can qualify as capital gain dividends and ordinary dividends, respectively, for the taxable year. An agreement under this subdivision (ii) which is signed by the district director (or other delegate) shall be sent to the taxpayer at its last known address by either registered or certified mail. For further guidance regarding the definition of last known address, see § 301.6212-2 of this chapter. If registered mail is used, the date of registration is the date of determination. If certified mail is used, the date of the postmark on the sender's receipt is the date of determination. However, if a dividend is paid by the taxpayer before the registration or postmark date, but on or after the date the agreement is signed by the district director (or other delegate), the date of determination is the date of signing.

(2) Claim for deduction. A claim for deduction for a deficiency dividend shall be made, with the requisite declaration, on Form 976 and shall contain the following information and have the following attachments:

(i) The name, address, and taxpayer identification number of the corporation, trust, or association;

(ii) The amount of the deficiency and the taxable year or years involved;

(iii) The amount of the unpaid deficiency or, if the deficiency has been paid in whole or in part, the date of payment and the amount thereof;

(iv) A statement as to how the deficiency was established (i.e., by an agreement under section 860(e)(3), by a closing agreement under section 7121, or by a decision of the Tax Court or court judgment);

(v) Any date or other information with respect to the determination that is required by Form 976;

(vi) The amount and date of payment of the dividend with respect to which the claim for the deduction for deficiency dividends is filed;

(vii) The amount claimed as a deduction for deficiency dividends;

(viii) If the amount claimed as a deduction for deficiency dividends includes any amount designated (or to be designated) as capital gain dividends, the amount of capital gain dividends for which a deficiency dividend deduction is claimed;

(ix) Any other information required by the claim form;

(x) A certified copy of the resolution of the trustees, directors, or other authority authorizing the payment of the dividend with respect to which the claim is filed; and

(xi) A copy of any court decision, judgment, agreement, or other document required by Form 976.

(3) Filing claim. The claim, together with the accompanying documents, shall be filed with the district director, or director of the internal revenue service center, with whom the income tax return for the taxable year for which the determination applies was filed. In the event that the determination is an agreement with the district director (or other delegate) described in section 860(e)(3) and paragraph (b)(1)(ii) of this section, the claim may be filed with the district director with whom (or pursuant to whose delegation) the agreement was made.

(The reporting requirements of this section have been assigned OMB Control Number 1545-0045.)

T.D. 7767, 2/3/81, amend T.D. 7936, 1/17/84, T.D. 8939, 1/11/2001.

§ 1.860-3 Interest and additions to tax.

(a) In general. If a qualified investment entity is allowed a deduction for deficiency dividends with respect to a taxable year, under section 860(c)(1) the tax imposed on the entity by chapter 1 of the Code (computed by taking into account the deduction) for that year is deemed to be increased by the amount of the deduction. This deemed increase in tax, however, applies solely for purposes of determining the liability of the entity for interest under subchapter A of chapter 67 of the Code and for additions to tax and additional amounts under chapter 68 of the Code. For purposes of applying subchapter A of chapter 67 and chapter 68, the last date prescribed for payment of the deemed increase in tax is considered to be the last date prescribed for the payment of tax (determined in the manner provided in section 6601(b)) for the taxable year for which the deduction for deficiency dividends is allowed. The deemed increase in tax is considered to be paid as of the date that the claim for the deficiency dividend deduction described in section 860(g) is filed.

(b) Overpayments of tax. If a qualified investment entity is entitled to a credit or refund of an overpayment of the tax imposed by chapter 1 of the Code for the taxable year for which the deficiency dividend deduction is allowed, then, for purposes of computing interest, additions to tax, and additional amounts, the payment (or payments) that result in the overpayment and that precede the filing of the claim described in section 860(g) will be applied against and reduce the increase in tax that is deemed to occur under section 860(c)(1).

(c) Examples. This section is illustrated by the following examples:

Example (1). Corporation X is a real estate investment trust that files its income tax return on a calendar year basis. X receives an extension of time until June 15, 1978, to file its 1977 income tax return and files the return on May 15, 1978. X does not elect to pay any tax due in installments. For 1977, X reports real estate investment trust taxable income (computed without the dividends paid deduction) of $100, a dividends paid deduction of $100, and no tax liability. Following an examination of X's 1977 return, the district director and X enter into an agreement which is a determination under section 860(e)(3). The determination is dated November 1, 1979, and increases X's real estate investment trust taxable income (computed without the dividends paid deduction) by $20 to $120. Thus, taking into account the $100 of dividends paid in 1977, X has undistributed real estate investment trust taxable income of $20 as a result of the determination. X pays a dividend of $20 on November 10, 1979, files a claim for a deficiency dividend deduction of this $20 pursuant to section 860(g) on November 15, 1979, and is allowed a deficiency dividend deduction of $20 for 1977. After taking into account this deduction, X has no real estate investment trust taxable income and meets the distribution requirements of section 857(a)(1). However, for purposes of section 6601 (relating to interest on underpayment of tax), the tax imposed by chapter 1 of the Code on X for 1977 is deemed increased by this $20, and the last date prescribed for payment of the tax is March 15, 1978 (the due date of the 1977 return determined without any extension of time). The tax of $20 is deemed paid on November 15, 1979, the date the claim for the deficiency dividend deduction is filed. Thus, X is liable for interest on $20, at the rate established under section 6621, for the period from March 15, 1978, to November 15, 1979. Also, for purposes of determining whether X is liable for any addition to tax or additional amount imposed by chapter 68 of the Code (including the penalty prescribed by section 6697), the amount of tax imposed on X by chapter 1 of the Code is deemed to be increased by $20 (the amount of the deficiency dividend deduction allowed), the last date prescribed for payment of such tax is March 15, 1978, and the tax of $20 is deemed to be paid on November 15, 1979. X, however, is not subject to interest and penalties for the amount of any tax for which it would have been liable under section 11(a), 56(a), 1201(a), or 857(b) had it not been allowed the $20 deduction for deficiency dividends.

Example (2). Assume the facts are the same as in example (1) except that the district director, upon examining X's income tax return, asserts an income tax deficiency of $4, based on an asserted increase of $10 in real estate investment trust taxable income, and no agreement is entered into between the parties. X pays the $4 on June 1, 1979, and files suit for refund in the United States District Court. The District Court, in a decision which becomes final on November 1, 1980, holds that X did fail to report $10 of real estate investment trust taxable income and is not entitled to any refund. (No other item of income or deduction is in issue.) X pays a dividend of $10 on November 10, 1980, files a claim for a deficiency dividend deduction of this $10 on November 15, 1980, and is allowed a deficiency dividend deduction of $10 for 1977. Assume further that $4 is refunded to X on December 31, 1980, as the result of the $10 deficiency dividend deduction being allowed. Also assume that any assessable penalties, additional amounts, and additions to tax (including the penalty imposed by section 6697) for which X is liable are paid within 10 days of notice and demand, so that no interest is imposed on such penalties, etc. X's liability for interest for the period March 15, 1978, to June 1, 1979, is determined with respect to $10 (the amount of the deficiency dividend deduction allowed). X's liability for interest for the period June 1, 1979, to November 15, 1980, is determined with respect to $6, *i.e.,* $10 minus the $4 payment. X is entitled to interest on the $4 overpayment for the period described in section 6611(b)(2), beginning on November 15, 1980.

T.D. 7767, 2/3/81, amend T.D. 7936, 1/17/84.

§ 1.860-4 Claim for credit or refund.

If the allowance of a deduction for a deficiency dividend results in an overpayment of tax, the taxpayer, in order to secure credit or refund of the overpayment, must file a claim on Form 1120X in addition to the claim for the deficiency dividend deduction required under section 860(g). The credit or refund will be allowed as if on the date of the determination (as defined in section 860(e)) two years remained before the expiration of the period of limitations on the filing of claim for refund for the taxable year to which the overpayment relates.

(The reporting requirements of this section have been assigned OMB Control Number 1545-0045)

T.D. 7767, 2/3/81, amend T.D. 7936, 1/17/84.

§ 1.860-5 Effective date.

(a) In general. Section 860 and §§ 1.860-1 through 1.860-4 apply with respect to determinations after November 6, 1978.

(b) Prior determination of real estate investments trusts. Section 859 (as in effect before the enactment of the Revenue Act of 1978) applies to determinations with respect to real estate investment trusts occurring after October 4, 1976, and before November 7, 1978. In the case of such a determination, the rules in §§ 1.860-1 through 1.860-4 apply, a reference in this chapter 1 to section 860 (or to a particular provision of section 860) shall be considered to be a reference to section 859 (or to the corresponding substantive provision of section 859), as in effect before enactment of the Revenue Act of 1978, and "qualified investment entity" in §§ 1.381(c)25-1(a) and 1.860-1 through 1.860-3 means a real estate investment trust.

T.D. 7936, 1/17/84.

§ 1.860A-0 Outline of REMIC provisions.

This section lists the paragraphs contained in §§ 1.860A-1 through 1.860G-3.

§ 1.860A-1 Effective dates and transition rules.

(a) In general.

(b) Exceptions.

(1) Reporting regulations.

(2) Tax avoidance rules.

(i) Transfers of certain residual interests.

(ii) Transfers to foreign holders.

(iii) Residual interests that lack significant value.

(3) Excise taxes.

(4) Rate based on current interest rate.

(i) In general.

(ii) Rate based on index.

(iii) Transition obligations.

(5) [Reserved].

§ 1.860A-1T Effective dates and transition rules (temporary).

(a) through (b)(4) [Reserved].

(5) Accounting for REMIC net income of foreign persons.

§ 1.860C-1 Taxation of holders of residual interests.

(a) Pass-thru of income or loss.

(b) Adjustments to basis of residual interests.

(1) Increase in basis.

(2) Decrease in basis.

(3) Adjustments made before disposition.

(c) Counting conventions.

(d) Treatment of REMIC inducement fees.

§ 1.860C-2 Determination of REMIC taxable income or net loss.

(a) Treatment of gain or loss.

(b) Deductions allowable to a REMIC.

(1) In general.

(2) Deduction allowable under section 163.

(3) Deduction allowable under section 166.

(4) Deduction allowable under section 212.

(5) Expenses and interest relating to tax-exempt income.

§ 1.860D-1 Definition of a REMIC.

(a) In general.

(b) Specific requirements.

(1) Interests in a REMIC.

(i) In general.

(ii) De minimis interests.

(2) Certain rights not treated as interests.

(i) Payments for services.

(ii) Stripped interests.

(iii) Reimbursement rights under credit enhancement contracts.

(iv) Rights to acquire mortgages.

(3) Asset test.

(i) In general.

(ii) Safe harbor.

(4) Arrangements test.

(5) Reasonable arrangements.

(i) Arrangements to prevent disqualified organizations from holding residual interests.

(ii) Arrangements to ensure that information will be provided.

(6) Calendar year requirement.

(c) Segregated pool of assets.

(1) Formation of REMIC.

(2) Identification of assets.

(3) Qualified entity defined.

(d) Election to be treated as a real estate mortgage investment conduit.

(1) In general.

(2) Information required to be reported in the REMIC's first taxable year.

(3) Requirement to keep sufficient records.

§ 1.860E-1 Treatment of taxable income of a residual interest holder in excess of daily accruals.

(a) Excess inclusion cannot be offset by otherwise allowable deductions.

(1) In general.

(2) Affiliated groups.

(3) Special rule for certain financial institutions.

(i) In general.

(ii) Ordering rule.

(A) In general.

(B) Example.

(iii) Significant value.

(iv) Determining anticipated weighted average life.

(A) Anticipated weighted average life of the REMIC.

(B) Regular interests that have a specified principal amount.

(C) Regular interests that have no specified principal amount or that have only a nominal principal amount, and all residual interests.

(D) Anticipated payments.

(b) Treatment of a residual interest held by REITs, RICs, common trust funds, and subchapter T cooperatives. [Reserved]

(c) Transfers of noneconomic residual interests.

(1) In general.

(2) Noneconomic residual interest.

(3) Computations.

(4) Safe harbor for establishing lack of improper knowledge.

(5) Asset test.

(6) Definitions for asset test.

(7) Formula test.

(8) Conditions and limitations on formula test.

(9) Examples.

(10) Effective dates.

(d) Transfers to foreign persons.

§ 1.860E-2 Tax on transfers of residual interest to certain organizations.

(a) Transfers to disqualified organizations.

(1) Payment of tax.

(2) Transitory ownership.

(3) Anticipated excess inclusions.

(4) Present value computation.

(5) Obligation of REMIC to furnish information.

(6) Agent.

(7) Relief from liability.

(i) Transferee furnishes information under penalties of perjury.

(ii) Amount required to be paid.

(b) Tax on pass-thru entities.

(1) Tax on excess inclusions.

(2) Record holder furnishes information under penalties of perjury.

(3) Deductibility of tax.

(4) Allocation of tax.

§ 1.860F-1 Qualified liquidations.

§ 1.860F-2 Transfers to a REMIC.

(a) Formation of a REMIC.

(1) In general.

(2) Tiered arrangements.

(i) Two or more REMICs formed pursuant to a single set of organizational documents.

(ii) A REMIC and one or more investment trusts formed pursuant to a single set of documents.

(b) Treatment of sponsor.

(1) Sponsor defined.

(2) Nonrecognition of gain or loss.

(3) Basis of contributed assets allocated among interests.

(i) In general.

(ii) Organizational expenses.

(A) Organizational expense defined.

(B) Syndication expenses.

(iii) Pricing date.

(4) Treatment of unrecognized gain or loss.

(i) Unrecognized gain on regular interests.

(ii) Unrecognized loss on regular interests.

(iii) Unrecognized gain on residual interests.

(iv) Unrecognized loss on residual interests.

(5) Additions to or reductions of the sponsor's basis.

(6) Transferred basis property.

(c) REMIC's basis in contributed assets.

§ 1.860F-4 REMIC reporting requirements and other administrative rules.

(a) In general.

(b) REMIC tax return.

(1) In general.

(2) Income tax return.

(c) Signing of REMIC return.

(1) In general.

(2) REMIC whose startup day is before November 10, 1988.

(i) In general.

(ii) Startup day.

(iii) Exception.

(d) Designation of tax matters person.

(e) Notice to holders of residual interests.

(1) Information required.

(i) In general.

(ii) Information with respect to REMIC assets.

(A) 95 percent asset test.

(B) Additional information required if the 95 percent test not met.

(C) For calendar quarters in 1987.

(D) For calendar quarters in 1988 and 1989.

(iii) Special provisions.

(2) Quarterly notice required.

(i) In general.

(ii) Special rule for 1987.

(3) Nominee reporting.

(i) In general.

(ii) Time for furnishing statement.

(4) Reports to the Internal Revenue Service.

(f) Information returns for persons engaged in a trade or business.

§ 1.860G-1 Definition of regular and residual interests.

(a) Regular interest.

(1) Designation as a regular interest.

(2) Specified portion of the interest payments on qualified mortgages.

(i) In general.

(ii) Specified portion cannot vary.

(iii) Defaulted or delinquent mortgages.

(iv) No minimum specified principal amount is required.

(v) Specified portion includes portion of interest payable on regular interest.

(vi) Examples.

(3) Variable rate.

(i) Rate based on current interest rate.

(ii) Weighted average rate.

(A) In general.

(B) Reduction in underlying rate.

(iii) Additions, subtractions, and multiplications.

(iv) Caps and floors.

(v) Funds-available caps.

(A) In general.

(B) Facts and circumstances test.

(C) Examples.

(vi) Combination of rates.

(4) Fixed terms on the startup day.

(5) Contingencies prohibited.

(b) Special rules for regular interests.

(1) Call premium.

(2) Customary prepayment penalties received with respect to qualified mortgages.

(3) Certain contingencies disregarded.

(i) Prepayments, income, and expenses.

(ii) Credit losses.

(iii) Subordinated interests.

(iv) Deferral of interest.

(v) Prepayment interest shortfalls.

(vi) Remote and incidental contingencies.

(4) Form of regular interest.

(5) Interest disproportionate to principal.

(i) In general.

(ii) Exception.

(6) Regular interest treated as a debt instrument for all Federal income tax purposes.

(c) Residual interest.

(d) Issue price of regular and residual interests.

(1) In general.

(2) The public.

§ 1.860G-2 Other rules.

(a) Obligations principally secured by an interest in real property.

(1) Tests for determining whether an obligation is principally secured.

(i) The 80-percent test.

(ii) Alternative test.

(2) Treatment of liens.

(3) Safe harbor.

(i) Reasonable belief that an obligation is principally secured.

(ii) Basis for reasonable belief.

(iii) Later discovery that an obligation is not principally secured.

(4) Interests in real property; real property.

(5) Obligations secured by an interest in real property.

(6) Obligations secured by other obligations; residual interests.

(7) Certain instruments that call for contingent payments are obligations.

(8) Defeasance.

(9) Stripped bonds and coupons.

(b) Assumptions and modifications.

(1) Significant modifications are treated as exchanges of obligations.

(2) Significant modification defined.

(3) Exceptions.

(4) Modifications that are not significant modifications.

(5) Assumption defined.

(6) Pass-thru certificates.

(c) Treatment of certain credit enhancement contracts.

(1) In general.

(2) Credit enhancement contracts.

(3) Arrangements to make certain advances.

(i) Advances of delinquent principal and interest.

(ii) Advances of taxes, insurance payments, and expenses.

(iii) Advances to ease REMIC administration.

(4) Deferred payment under a guarantee arrangement.

(d) Treatment of certain purchase agreements with respect to convertible mortgages.

(1) In general.

(2) Treatment of amounts received under purchase agreements.

(3) Purchase agreement.

(4) Default by the person obligated to purchase a convertible mortgage.

(5) Convertible mortgage.

(e) Prepayment interest shortfalls.

(f) Defective obligations.

(1) Defective obligation defined.

(2) Effect of discovery of defect.

(g) Permitted investments.

(1) Cash flow investment.

(i) In general.

(ii) Payments received on qualified mortgages.

(iii) Temporary period.

(2) Qualified reserve funds.

(3) Qualified reserve asset.

(i) In general.

(ii) Reasonably required reserve.

(A) In general.

(B) Presumption that a reserve is reasonably required.

(C) Presumption may be rebutted.

(h) Outside reserve funds.

(i) Contractual rights coupled with regular interests in tiered arrangements.

(1) In general.

(2) Example.

(j) Clean-up call.

(1) In general.

(2) Interest rate changes.

(3) Safe harbor.

(k) Startup day.

§ 1.860G-3 Treatment of foreign persons.

(a) Transfer of a residual interest with tax avoidance potential.

(1) In general.

(2) Tax avoidance potential.

(i) Defined.

(ii) Safe harbor.

(3) Effectively connected income.

(4) Transfer by a foreign holder.

(b) Accounting for REMIC net income. [Reserved].

§ 1.860G-3T Treatment of foreign persons (temporary).

(a) [Reserved].

(b) Accounting for REMIC net income.

(1) Allocation of partnership income to a foreign partner.

(2) Excess inclusion income allocated by certain pass-through entities to a foreign person.

T.D. 8458, 12/23/92, amend T.D. 8614, 8/16/95, T.D. 9004, 7/18/2002, T.D. 9128, 5/7/2004, T.D. 9272, 7/31/2006.

PAR. 2. Section 1.860A-0 is amended by adding an entry for § 1.860G-2(b)(7) to read as follows:

Proposed § 1.860A-0 Outline of REMIC provisions. [*For Preamble, see ¶ 152,929*]

* * * * *

§ 1.860G-2 Other rules.

* * * * *

(b) * * *

(7) Principally secured test; appraisal requirement.

* * * * *

§ 1.860A-1 Effective dates and transition rules.

Caution: The Treasury has not yet amended Reg § 1.860A-1 to reflect changes made by P.L. 104-188.

(a) In general. Except as otherwise provided in paragraph (b) of this section, the regulations under sections 860A through 860G are effective only for a qualified entity (as defined in § 1.860D-1(c)(3)) whose startup day (as defined in section 860G(a)(9) and § 1.860G-2(k)) is on or after November 12, 1991.

(b) Exceptions. *(1) Reporting regulations.* (i) Sections 1.860D-1(c)(1) and (3), and § 1.860D-1(d)(1) through (3) are effective after December 31, 1986.

(ii) Sections 1.860F-4(a) through (e) are effective after December 31, 1986 and are applicable after that date except as follows:

(A) Section 1.860F-4(c)(1) is effective for REMICs with a startup day on or after November 10, 1988.

(B) Sections 1.860F-4(e)(1)(ii)(A) and (B) are effective for calendar quarters and calendar years beginning after December 31, 1988.

(C) Section 1.860F-4(e)(1)(ii)(C) is effective for calendar quarters and calendar years beginning after December 31, 1986 and ending before January 1, 1988.

(D) Section 1.860F-4(e)(1)(ii)(D) is effective for calendar quarters and calendar years beginning after December 31, 1987 and ending before January 1, 1990.

(2) Tax avoidance rules. (i) Transfers of certain residual interests. Section 1.860E-1(c) (concerning transfers of noneconomic residual interests) and § 1.860G-3(a)(4) (concerning transfers by a foreign holder to a United States person) are effective for transfers of residual interests on or after September 27, 1991.

(ii) Transfers to foreign holders. Generally, § 1.860G-3(a) (concerning transfers of residual interests to foreign holders) is effective for transfers of residual interests after April 20, 1992. However, § 1.860G-3(a) does not apply to a transfer of a residual interest in a REMIC by the REMIC's sponsor (or by another transferor contemporaneously with formation of the REMIC) on or before June 30, 1992 if—

(A) The terms of the regular interests and the prices at which regular interests were offered had been fixed on or before April 20, 1992;

(B) On or before June 30, 1992, a substantial portion of the regular interests in the REMIC were transferred, with the terms and at the prices that were fixed on or before April 20, 1992, to investors who were unrelated to the REMIC's sponsor at the time of the transfer; and

(C) At the time of the transfer of the residual interest, the expected future distributions on the residual interest were equal to at least 30 percent of the anticipated excess inclusions (as defined in § 1.860E-2(a)(3)), and the transferor reasonably expected that the transferee would receive sufficient distributions from the REMIC at or after the time at which the excess inclusions accrue in an amount sufficient to satisfy the taxes on the excess inclusions.

(iii) Residual interests that lack significant value. The significant value requirement in § 1.860E-1(a)(1) and (3) (concerning excess inclusions accruing to organizations to which section 593 applies) generally is effective for residual interests acquired on or after September 27, 1991. The significant value requirement in § 1.860E-1(a)(1) and (3) does not apply, however, to residual interests acquired by an organization to which section 593 applies as a sponsor at formation of a REMIC in a transaction described in § 1.860F-2(a)(1) if more than 50 percent of the interests in the REMIC (determined by reference to issue price) were sold to unrelated investors before November 12, 1991. The exception from the significant value requirement provided by the preceding sentence applies only so long as the sponsor owns the residual interests.

(3) Excise taxes. Section 1.860E-2(a)(1) is effective for transfers of residual interests to disqualified organizations after March 31, 1988. Section 1.860E-2(b)(1) is effective for excess inclusions accruing to pass-thru entities after March 31, 1988.

(4) Rate based on current interest rate. (i) In general. Section 1.860G-1(a)(3)(i) applies to obligations (other than transition obligations described in paragraph (b)(4)(iii) of this section) intended to qualify as regular interests that are issued on or after April 4, 1994.

(ii) Rate based on index. Section 1.860G-1(a)(3)(i) (as contained in 26 CFR part 1 revised as of April 1, 1994) applies to obligations intended to qualify as regular interests that—

(A) Are issued by a qualified entity (as defined in § 1.860D-1(c)(3)) whose startup date (as defined in section 860G(a)(9) and § 1.860G-2(k)) is on or after November 12, 1991; and

(B) Are either—

(1) Issued before April 4, 1994; or

(2) Transition obligations described in paragraph (b)(4)(iii) of this section.

(iii) Transition obligations. Obligations are described in this paragraph (b)(4)(iii) if—

(A) The terms of the obligations and the prices at which the obligations are offered are fixed before April 4, 1994; and

(B) On or before June 1, 1994, a substantial portion of the obligations are transferred, with the terms and at the prices that are fixed before April 4, 1994, to investors who are unrelated to the REMIC's sponsor at the time of the transfer.

(5) [Reserved]. For further guidance, see § 1.860A-1T(b)(5).

T.D. 8458, 12/23/92, amend T.D. 8614, 8/16/95, T.D. 9272, 7/31/2006.

PAR. 3. Section 1.860A-1 is amended by adding paragraph (b)(6) to read as follows:

Proposed § 1.860A-1 Effective dates and transition rules. [*For Preamble, see ¶ 152,929*]

* * * * *

(b) * * *

(6) Exceptions for certain modified obligations. Paragraphs (b)(3)(v), (b)(3)(vi) and (b)(7) of § 1.860G-2 apply to modifications made to the terms of an obligation on or after the date of publication of this document in the Federal Register as a Treasury decision.

PAR. 2. In § 1.860A-1, paragraph (b)(5) is added to read as follows:

Proposed § 1.860A-1 Effective dates and transition rules. [*For Preamble, see ¶ 152,777*]

* * * * *

(b) * * *

(5) [The text of the proposed amendment to § 1.860A-1(b)(5) is the same as the text of § 1.860A-1T(b)(5) published elsewhere in this issue of the Federal Register].

§ 1.860A-1T Effective dates and transition rules (temporary).

(a) through (b)(4) [Reserved]. For further guidance, see § 1.860A-1(a) through (b)(4).

(b) *(5) Accounting for REMIC net income of foreign persons.* Section 1.860G-3T(b) is applicable to REMIC net income (including excess inclusions) of a foreign person with respect to a REMIC residual interest if the first net income allocation under section 860C(a)(1) to the foreign person with respect to that interest occurs on or after August 1, 2006. This section will expire July 31, 2009.

T.D. 9272, 7/31/2006.

§ 1.860C-1 Taxation of holders of residual interest.

Caution: The Treasury has not yet amended Reg § 1.860C-1 to reflect changes made by P.L. 104-188.

(a) Pass-thru of income or loss. Any holder of a residual interest in a REMIC must take into account the holder's daily portion of the taxable income or net loss of the REMIC for each day during the taxable year on which the holder owned the residual interest.

(b) Adjustments to basis of residual interests. *(1) Increase in basis.* A holder's basis in a residual interest is increased by—

(i) The daily portions of taxable income taken into account by that holder under section 860C(a) with respect to that interest; and

(ii) The amount of any contribution described in section 860G(d)(2) made by that holder.

(2) Decrease in basis. A holder's basis in a residual interest is reduced (but not below zero) by—

(i) First, the amount of any cash or the fair market value of any property distributed to that holder with respect to that interest; and

(ii) Second, the daily portions of net loss of the REMIC taken into account under section 860C(a) by that holder with respect to that interest.

(3) Adjustments made before disposition. If any person disposes of a residual interest, the adjustments to basis prescribed in paragraph (b)(1) and (2) of this section are deemed to occur immediately before the disposition.

(c) Counting conventions. For purposes of determining the daily portion of REMIC taxable income or net loss under section 860C(a)(2), any reasonable convention may be used.

An example of a reasonable convention is "30 days per month/90 days per quarter/360 days per year."

(d) For rules on the proper accounting for income from inducement fees, see § 1.446-6.

T.D. 8458, 12/23/92, amend T.D. 9128, 5/7/2004.

§ 1.860C-2 Determination of REMIC taxable income or net loss.

Caution: The Treasury has not yet amended Reg § 1.860C-2 to reflect changes made by P.L. 104-188.

(a) Treatment of gain or loss. For purposes of determining the taxable income or net loss of a REMIC under section 860C(b), any gain or loss from the disposition of any asset, including a qualified mortgage (as defined in section 860G(a)(3)) or a permitted investment (as defined in section 860G(a)(5) and § 1.860G-2(g)), is treated as gain or loss from the sale or exchange of property that is not a capital asset.

(b) Deductions allowable to a REMIC. *(1) In general.* Except as otherwise provided in section 860C(b) and in paragraph (b)(2) through (5) of this section, the deductions allowable to a REMIC for purposes of determining its taxable income or net loss are those deductions that would be allowable to an individual, determined by taking into account the same limitations that apply to an individual.

(2) Deduction allowable under section 163. A REMIC is allowed a deduction, determined without regard to section 163(d), for any interest expense accrued during the taxable year.

(3) Deduction allowable under section 166. For purposes of determining a REMIC's bad debt deduction under section 166, debt owed to the REMIC is not treated as nonbusiness debt under section 166(d).

(4) Deduction allowable under section 212. A REMIC is not treated as carrying on a trade or business for purposes of section 162. Ordinary and necessary operating expenses paid or incurred by the REMIC during the taxable year are deductible under section 212, without regard to section 67. Any expenses that are incurred in connection with the formation of the REMIC and that relate to the organization of the REMIC and the issuance of regular and residual interests are not treated as expenses of the REMIC for which a deduction is allowable under section 212. See § 1.860F-2(b)(3)(ii) for treatment of those expenses.

(5) Expenses and interest relating to tax-exempt income. Pursuant to section 265(a), a REMIC is not allowed a deduction for expenses and interest allocable to tax-exempt income. The portion of a REMIC's interest expense that is allocable to tax-exempt interest is determined in the manner prescribed in section 265(b)(2), without regard to section 265(b)(3).

T.D. 8458, 12/23/92.

§ 1.860D-1 Definition of a REMIC.

(a) In general. A real estate mortgage investment conduit (or REMIC) is a qualified entity, as defined in paragraph (c)(3) of this section, that satisfies the requirements of section 860D(a). See paragraph (d)(1) of this section for the manner of electing REMIC status.

(b) Specific requirements. *(1) Interests in a REMIC.* (i) In general. A REMIC must have one class, and only one class, of residual interests. Except as provided in paragraph (b)(1)(ii) of this section, every interest in a REMIC must be either a regular interest (as defined in section 860G(a)(1) and § 1.860G-1(a)) or a residual interest (as defined in section 860G(a)(2) and § 1.860G-1(c)).

(ii) De minimis interests. If, to facilitate the creation of an entity that elects REMIC status, an interest in the entity is created and, as of the startup day (as defined in section 860G(a)(9) and § 1.860G-2(k)), the fair market value of that interest is less than the lesser of $1,000 or 1/1,000 of one percent of the aggregate fair market value of all the regular and residual interests in the REMIC, then, unless that interest is specifically designated as an interest in the REMIC, the interest is not treated as an interest in the REMIC for purposes of section 860D(a)(2) and (3) and paragraph (b)(1)(i) of this section.

(2) Certain rights not treated as interests. Certain rights are not treated as interests in a REMIC. Although not an exclusive list, the following rights are not interests in a REMIC.

(i) Payments for services. The right to receive from the REMIC payments that represent reasonable compensation for services provided to the REMIC in the ordinary course of its operation is not an interest in the REMIC. Payments made by the REMIC in exchange for services may be expressed as a specified percentage of interest payments due on qualified mortgages or as a specified percentage of earnings from permitted investments. For example, a mortgage servicer's right to receive reasonable compensation for servicing the mortgages owned by the REMIC is not an interest in the REMIC.

(ii) Stripped interests. Stripped bonds or stripped coupons not held by the REMIC are not interests in the REMIC even if, in a transaction preceding or contemporaneous with the formation of the REMIC, they and the REMIC's qualified mortgages were created from the same mortgage obligation. For example, the right of a mortgage servicer to receive a servicing fee in excess of reasonable compensation from payments it receives on mortgages held by a REMIC is not an interest in the REMIC. Further, if an obligation with a fixed principal amount provides for interest at a fixed or variable rate and for certain contingent payment rights (e.g., a shared appreciation provision or a percentage of mortgagor profits provision), and the owner of the obligation contributes the fixed payment rights to a REMIC and retains the contingent payment rights, the retained contingent payment rights are not an interest in the REMIC.

(iii) Reimbursement rights under credit enhancement contracts. A credit enhancer's right to be reimbursed for amounts advanced to a REMIC pursuant to the terms of a credit enhancement contract (as defined in § 1.860G-2(c)(2)) is not an interest in the REMIC even if the credit enhancer is entitled to receive interest on the amounts advanced.

(iv) Rights to acquire mortgages. The right to acquire or the obligation to purchase mortgages and other assets from a REMIC pursuant to a clean-up call (as defined in § 1.860G-2(j)) or a qualified liquidation (as defined in section 860F(a)(4)), or on conversion of a convertible mortgage (as defined in § 1.860G-2(d)(5)), is not an interest in the REMIC.

(3) Asset test. (i) In general. For purposes of the asset test of section 860D(a)(4), substantially all of a qualified entity's assets are qualified mortgages and permitted investments if the qualified entity owns no more than a de minimis amount of other assets.

(ii) Safe harbor. The amount of assets other than qualified mortgages and permitted investments is de minimis if the aggregate of the adjusted bases of those assets is less than one percent of the aggregate of the adjusted bases of all of the REMIC's assets. Nonetheless, a qualified entity that does not meet this safe harbor may demonstrate that it owns no more than a de minimis amount of other assets.

(4) Arrangements test. Generally, a qualified entity must adopt reasonable arrangements designed to ensure that—

(i) Disqualified organizations (as defined in section 860E(e)(5)) do not hold residual interests in the qualified entity; and

(ii) If a residual interest is acquired by a disqualified organization, the qualified entity will provide to the Internal Revenue Service, and to the persons specified in section 860E(a)(3), information needed to compute the tax imposed under section 860E(e) on transfers of residual interests to disqualified organizations.

(5) Reasonable arrangements. (i) Arrangements to prevent disqualified organizations from holding residual interests. A qualified entity is considered to have adopted reasonable arrangements to ensure that a disqualified organization (as defined in section 860E(e)(5)) will not hold a residual interest if—

(A) The residual interest is in registered form (as defined in § 5f.103-1(c) of this chapter); and

(B) The qualified entity's organizational documents clearly and expressly prohibit a disqualified organization from acquiring beneficial ownership of a residual interest, and notice of the prohibition is provided through a legend on the document that evidences ownership of the residual interest or through a conspicuous statement in a prospectus or private offering document used to offer the residual interest for sale.

(ii) Arrangements to ensure that information will be provided. A qualified entity is considered to have made reasonable arrangements to ensure that the Internal Revenue Service and persons specified in section 860E(e)(3) as liable for the tax imposed under section 860E(e) receive the information needed to compute the tax if the qualified entity's organizational documents require that it provide to the Internal Revenue Service and those persons a computation showing the present value of the total anticipated excess inclusions with respect to the residual interest for periods after the transfer. See § 1.860E-2(a)(5) for the obligation to furnish information on request.

(6) Calendar year requirement. A REMIC's taxable year is the calendar year. The first taxable year of a REMIC begins on the startup day and ends on December 31 of the same year. If the startup day is other than January 1, the REMIC has a short first taxable year.

(c) Segregated pool of assets. *(1) Formation of REMIC.* A REMIC may be formed as a segregated pool of assets rather than as a separate entity. To constitute a REMIC, the assets identified as part of the segregated pool must be treated for all Federal income tax purposes as assets of the REMIC and interests in the REMIC must be based solely on assets of the REMIC.

(2) Identification of assets. Formation of the REMIC does not occur until—

(i) The sponsor identifies the assets of the REMIC, such as through execution of an indenture with respect to the assets; and

(ii) The REMIC issues the regular and residual interests in the REMIC.

(3) Qualified entity defined. For purposes of this section, the term "qualified entity" includes an entity or a segregated pool of assets within an entity.

(d) Election to be treated as a real estate mortgage investment conduit. *(1) In general.* A qualified entity, as defined in paragraph (c)(3) of this section, elects to be treated as a REMIC by timely filing, for the first taxable year of its existence, a Form 1066, U.S. Real Estate Mortgage Investment Conduit Income Tax Return, signed by a person authorized to sign that return under § 1.860F-4(c). See § 1.9100-1 for rules regarding extensions of time for making elections. Once made, this election is irrevocable for that taxable year and all succeeding taxable years.

(2) Information required to be reported in the REMIC's first taxable year. For the first taxable year of the REMIC's existence, the qualified entity, as defined in paragraph (c)(3) of this section, must provide either on its return or in a separate statement attached to its return—

(i) The REMIC's employer identification number, which must not be the same as the identification number of any other entity,

(ii) Information concerning the terms and conditions of the regular interests and the residual interest of the REMIC, or a copy of the offering circular or prospectus containing such information,

(iii) A description of the prepayment and reinvestment assumptions that are made pursuant to section 1272(a)(6) and the regulations thereunder, including a statement supporting the selection of the prepayment assumption,

(iv) The form of the electing qualified entity under State law or, if an election is being made with respect to a segregated pool of assets within an entity, the form of the entity that holds the segregated pool of assets, and

(v) Any other information required by the form.

(3) Requirement to keep sufficient records. A qualified entity, as defined in paragraph (c)(3) of this section, that elects to be a REMIC must keep sufficient records concerning its investments to show that it has complied with the provisions of sections 860A through 860G and the regulations thereunder during each taxable year.

T.D. 8366, 9/27/91, amend T.D. 8458, 12/23/92.

---

§ 1.860E-1 Treatment of taxable income of a residual interest holder in excess of daily accruals.

Caution: The Treasury has not yet amended Reg § 1.860E-1 to reflect changes made by P.L. 104-188.

(a) Excess inclusion cannot be offset by otherwise allowable deductions. *(1) In general.* Except as provided in paragraph (a)(3) of this section, the taxable income of any holder of a residual interest for any taxable year is in no event less than the sum of the excess inclusions attributable to that holder's residual interests for that taxable year. In computing the amount of a net operating loss (as defined in section 172(c)) or the amount of any net operating loss carryover (as defined in section 172(b)(2)), the amount of any excess inclusion is not included in gross income or taxable income. Thus, for example, if a residual interest holder has $100 of gross income, $25 of which is an excess inclusion, and $90 of business deductions, the holder has taxable income of $25, the amount of the excess inclusion, and a net operating loss of $15 ($75 of other income – $90 of business deductions).

(2) Affiliated groups. If a holder of a REMIC residual interest is a member of an affiliated group filing a consolidated income tax return, the taxable income of the affiliated group cannot be less than the sum of the excess inclusions attributable to all residual interests held by members of the affiliated group.

(3) Special rule for certain financial institutions. (i) In general. If an organization to which section 593 applies holds a residual interest that has significant value (as defined in paragraph (a)(3)(iii) of this section), section 860E(a)(1) and paragraph (a)(1) of this section do not apply to that organization with respect to that interest. Consequently, an organization to which section 593 applies may use its allowable deductions to offset an excess inclusion attributable to a residual interest that has significant value, but, except as provided in section 860E(a)(4)(A), may not use its allowable deductions to offset an excess inclusion attributable to a residual interest held by any other member of an affiliated group, if any, of which the organization is a member. Further, a net operating loss of any other member of an affiliated group of which the organization is a member may not be used to offset an excess inclusion attributable to a residual interest held by that organization.

(ii) Ordering rule. (A) In general. In computing taxable income for any year, an organization to which section 593 applies is treated as having applied its allowable deductions for the year first to offset that portion of its gross income that is not an excess inclusion and then to offset that portion of its income that is an excess inclusion.

(B) Example. The following example illustrates the provisions of paragraph (a)(3)(ii) of this section:

Example. Corp. X, a corporation to which section 593 applies, is a member of an affiliated group that files a consolidated return. For a particular taxable year, Corp. X has gross income of $1,000, and of this amount, $150 is an excess inclusion attributable to a residual interest that has significant value. Corp. X has $975 of allowable deductions for the taxable year. Corp. X must apply its allowable deductions first to offset the $850 of gross income that is not an excess inclusion, and then to offset the portion of its gross income that is an excess inclusion. Thus, Corp. X has $25 of taxable income ($1,000 – $975), and that $25 is an excess inclusion that may not be offset by losses sustained by other members of the affiliated group.

(iii) Significant value. A residual interest has significant value if—

(A) The aggregate of the issue prices of the residual interests in the REMIC is at least 2 percent of the aggregate of the issue prices of all residual and regular interests in the REMIC; and

(B) The anticipated weighted average life of the residual interests is at least 20 percent of the anticipated weighted average life of the REMIC.

(iv) Determining anticipated weighted average life (A) Anticipated weighted average life of the REMIC. The anticipated weighted average life of a REMIC is the weighted average of the anticipated weighted average lives of all classes of interests in the REMIC. This weighted average is determined under the formula in paragraph (a)(3)(iv)(B) of this section, applied by treating all payments taken into account in computing the anticipated weighted average lives of regular and residual interests in the REMIC as principal payments on a single regular interest.

(B) Regular interests that have a specified principal amount. Generally, the anticipated weighted average life of a regular interest is determined by—

(1) Multiplying the amount of each anticipated principal payment to be made on the interest by the number of years (including fractions thereof) from the startup day (as defined in section 860G(a)(9) and § 1.860G-2(k)) to the related principal payment date;

(2) Adding the results; and

(3) Dividing the sum by the total principal paid on the regular interest.

(C) Regular interests that have no specified principal amount or that have only a nominal principal amount, and all residual interests. If a regular interest has no specified principal amount, or if the interest payments to be made on a regular interest are disproportionately high relative to its specified principal amount (as determined by reference to § 1.860G-1(b)(5)(i)), then, for purposes of computing the anticipated weighted average life of the interest, all anticipated payments on that interest, regardless of their designation as principal or interest, must be taken into account in applying the formula set out in paragraph (a)(3)(iv)(B) of this section. Moreover, for purposes of computing the weighted average life of a residual interest, all anticipated payments on that interest, regardless of their designation as principal or interest, must be taken into account in applying the formula set out in paragraph (a)(3)(iv)(B) of this section.

(D) Anticipated payments. The anticipated principal payments to be made on a regular interest subject to paragraph (a)(3)(iv)(B) of this section, and the anticipated payments to be made on a regular interest subject to paragraph (a)(3)(iv)(C) of this section or on a residual interest, must be determined based on—

(1) The prepayment and reinvestment assumptions adopted under section 1272(a)(6), or that would have been adopted had the REMIC's regular interests been issued with original issue discount; and

(2) Any required or permitted clean up calls or any required qualified liquidation provided for in the REMIC's organizational documents.

(b) Treatment of residual interests held by REITs, RICs, common trust funds, and subchapter T cooperatives. [Reserved]

(c) Transfers of noneconomic residual interests. *(1) In general.* A transfer of a noneconomic residual interest is disregarded for all Federal tax purposes if a significant purpose of the transfer was to enable the transferor to impede the assessment or collection of tax. A significant purpose to impede the assessment or collection of tax exists if the transferor, at the time of the transfer, either knew or should have known (had "improper knowledge") that the transferee would be unwilling or unable to pay taxes due on its share of the taxable income of the REMIC.

(2) Noneconomic residual interest. A residual interest is a noneconomic residual interest unless, at the time of the transfer—

(i) The present value of the expected future distributions on the residual interest at least equals the product of the present value of the anticipated excess inclusions and the highest rate of tax specified in section 11(b)(1) for the year in which the transfer occurs; and

(ii) The transferor reasonably expects that, for each anticipated excess inclusion, the transferee will receive distributions from the REMIC at or after the time at which the taxes accrue on the anticipated excess inclusion in an amount sufficient to satisfy the accrued taxes.

(3) Computations. The present value of the expected future distributions and the present value of the anticipated excess inclusions must be computed under the procedure specified in § 1.860E-2(a)(4) for determining the present value of anticipated excess inclusions in connection with the transfer of a residual interest to a disqualified organization.

(4) Safe harbor for establishing lack of improper knowledge. A transferor is presumed not to have improper knowledge if—

(i) The transferor conducted, at the time of the transfer, a reasonable investigation of the financial condition of the transferee and, as a result of the investigation, the transferor found that the transferee had historically paid its debts as they came due and found no significant evidence to indicate that the transferee will not continue to pay its debts as they come due in the future;

(ii) The transferee represents to the transferor that it understands that, as the holder of the noneconomic residual interest, the transferee may incur tax liabilities in excess of any cash flows generated by the interest and that the transferee intends to pay taxes associated with holding the residual interest as they become due;

(iii) The transferee represents that it will not cause income from the noneconomic residual interest to be attributable to a foreign permanent establishment or fixed base (within the meaning of an applicable income tax treaty) of the transferee or another U.S. taxpayer; and

(iv) The transfer satisfies either the asset test in paragraph (c)(5) of this section or the formula test in paragraph (c)(7) of this section.

(5) Asset test. The transfer satisfies the asset test if it meets the requirements of paragraphs (c)(5)(i), (ii) and (iii) of this section. (i) At the time of the transfer, and at the close of each of the transferee's two fiscal years preceding the transferee's fiscal year of transfer, the transferee's gross assets for financial reporting purposes exceed $100 million and its net assets for financial reporting purposes exceed $10 million. For purposes of the preceding sentence, the gross assets and net assets of a transferee do not include any obligation of any related person (as defined in paragraph (c)(6)(ii) of this section) or any other asset if a principal purpose for holding or acquiring the other asset is to permit the transferee to satisfy the conditions of this paragraph (c)(5)(i).

(ii) The transferee must be an eligible corporation (defined in paragraph (c)(6)(i) of this section) and must agree in writing that any subsequent transfer of the interest will be to another eligible corporation in a transaction that satisfies paragraphs (c)(4)(i), (ii), and (iii) and this paragraph (c)(5). The direct or indirect transfer of the residual interest to a foreign permanent establishment (within the meaning of an applicable income tax treaty) of a domestic corporation is a transfer that is not a transfer to an eligible corporation. A transfer also fails to meet the requirements of this paragraph (c)(5)(ii) if the transferor knows, or has reason to know, that the transferee will not honor the restrictions on subsequent transfers of the residual interest.

(iii) A reasonable person would not conclude, based on the facts and circumstances known to the transferor on or before the date of the transfer, that the taxes associated with the residual interest will not be paid. The consideration given to the transferee to acquire the noneconomic residual interest in the REMIC is only one factor to be considered, but the transferor will be deemed to know that the transferee cannot or will not pay if the amount of consideration is so low compared to the liabilities assumed that a reasonable person would conclude that the taxes associated with holding the residual interest will not be paid. In determining whether the amount of consideration is too low, the specific terms of the formula test in paragraph (c)(7) of this section need not be used.

(6) Definitions for asset test. The following definitions apply for purposes of paragraph (c)(5) of this section:

(i) Eligible corporation means any domestic C corporation (as defined in section 1361(a)(2)) other than—

(A) A corporation which is exempt from, or is not subject to, tax under section 11;

(B) An entity described in section 851(a) or 856(a);

(C) A REMIC; or

(D) An organization to which part I of subchapter T of chapter 1 of subtitle A of the Internal Revenue Code applies.

(ii) Related person is any person that—

(A) Bears a relationship to the transferee enumerated in section 267(b) or 707(b)(1), using "20 percent" instead of "50 percent" where it appears under the provisions; or

(B) Is under common control (within the meaning of section 52(a) and (b)) with the transferee.

(7) Formula test. The transfer satisfies the formula test if the present value of the anticipated tax liabilities associated with holding the residual interest does not exceed the sum of—

(i) The present value of any consideration given to the transferee to acquire the interest;

(ii) The present value of the expected future distributions on the interest; and

(iii) The present value of the anticipated tax savings associated with holding the interest as the REMIC generates losses.

(8) Conditions and limitations on formula test. The following rules apply for purposes of the formula test in paragraph (c)(7) of this section.

(i) The transferee is assumed to pay tax at a rate equal to the highest rate of tax specified in section 11(b)(1). If the transferee has been subject to the alternative minimum tax under section 55 in the preceding two years and will compute its taxable income in the current taxable year using the alternative minimum tax rate, then the tax rate specified in section 55(b)(1)(B) may be used in lieu of the highest rate specified in section 11(b)(1).

(ii) The direct or indirect transfer of the residual interest to a foreign permanent establishment or fixed base (within the meaning of an applicable income tax treaty) of a domestic transferee is not eligible for the formula test.

(iii) Present values are computed using a discount rate equal to the Federal short-term rate prescribed by section 1274(d) for the month of the transfer and the compounding period used by the taxpayer.

(9) Examples. The following examples illustrate the rules of this section:

Example (1). Transfer to partnership. X transfers a noneconomic residual interest in a REMIC to Partnership P in a transaction that does not satisfy the formula test of paragraph (c)(7) of this section. Y and Z are the partners of P. Even if Y and Z are eligible corporations that satisfy the requirements of paragraph (c)(5)(i) of this section, the transfer fails to satisfy the asset test requirements found in paragraph (c)(5)(ii) of this section because P is a partnership rather than an eligible corporation within the meaning of (c)(6)(i) of this section.

Example (2). Transfer to a corporation without capacity to carry additional residual interests. During the first ten months of a year, Bank transfers five residual interests to Corporation U under circumstances meeting the requirements of the asset test in paragraph (c)(5) of this section. Bank is the major creditor of U and consequently has access to U's financial records and has knowledge of U's financial circumstances. During the last month of the year, Bank transfers three additional residual interests to U in a transaction that does not meet the formula test of paragraph (c)(7) of this section. At the time of this transfer, U's financial records indicate it has retained the previously transferred residual interests. U's financial circumstances, including the aggregate tax liabilities it has assumed with respect to REMIC residual interests, would cause a reasonable person to conclude that U will be unable to meet its tax liabilities when due. The transfers in the last month of the year fail to satisfy the investigation requirement in paragraph (c)(4)(i) of this section and the asset test requirement of paragraph (c)(5)(iii) of this section because Bank has reason to know that U will not be able to pay the tax due on those interests.

Example (3). Transfer to a foreign permanent establishment of an eligible corporation. R transfers a noneconomic residual interest in a REMIC to the foreign permanent establishment of Corporation T. Solely because of paragraph (c)(8)(ii) of this section, the transfer does not satisfy the formula test of paragraph (c)(7) of this section. In addition, even if T is an eligible corporation, the transfer does not satisfy the asset test because the transfer fails the requirements of paragraph (c)(5)(ii) of this section.

(10) Effective dates. Paragraphs (c)(4) through (c)(9) of this section are applicable to transfers occurring on or after February 4, 2000, except for paragraphs (c)(4)(iii) and (c)(8)(iii) of this section, which are applicable for transfers occurring on or after August 19, 2002. For the dates of applicability of paragraphs (a) through (c)(3) and (d) of this section, see § 1.860A-1.

(d) Transfers to foreign persons. Paragraph (c) of this section does not apply to transfers of residual interests to which § 1.860G-3(a)(1), concerning transfers to certain foreign persons, applies.

T.D. 8458, 12/23/92, amend T.D. 9004, 7/18/2002.

PAR. 2. Section 1.860E-1 is amended by:

1. Revising paragraph (c)(4).

2. Adding paragraphs (c)(5) and (c)(6).

The addition and revision read as follows:

Proposed § 1.860E-1 Treatment of taxable income of a residual interest holder in excess of daily accruals.
[*For Preamble, see ¶ 152,047*]

* * * * *

(c) * * *

(4) Safe harbor for establishing lack of improper knowledge. A transferor is presumed not to have improper knowledge if—

(i) The transferor conducted, at the time of the transfer, a reasonable investigation of the financial condition of the transferee and, as a result of the investigation, the transferor found that the transferee had historically paid its debts as they came due and found no significant evidence to indicate that the transferee will not continue to pay its debts as they come due in the future;

(ii) The transferee represents to the transferor that it understands that, as the holder of the noneconomic residual interest, the transferee may incur tax liabilities in excess of any cash flows generated by the interest and that the transferee intends to pay taxes associated with holding residual interest as they become due; and

(iii) The present value of the anticipated tax liabilities associated with holding the residual interest does not exceed the sum of—

(A) The present value of any consideration given to the transferee to acquire the interest;

(B) The present value of the expected future distributions on the interest; and

(C) The present value of the anticipated tax savings associated with holding the interest as the REMIC generates losses.

(5) Computational assumptions. The following rules apply for purposes of paragraph (c)(4)(iii) of this section:

(i) The transferee is assumed to pay tax at a rate equal to the highest rate of tax specified in section 11(b)(1); and

(ii) Present values are computed using a discount rate equal to the applicable Federal rate prescribed by section 1274(d) compounded semiannually (a lower discount rate may be used if the transferee can demonstrate that it regularly borrows, in the course of its trade or business, substantial funds at such lower rate from unrelated third parties).

(6) Effective date. Paragraphs (c)(4) and (5) of this section are applicable on February 4, 2000.

§ 1.860E-2 Tax on transfers of residual interests to certain organizations.

Caution: The Treasury has not yet amended Reg § 1.860E-2 to reflect changes made by P.L. 104-188.

(a) Transfers to disqualified organizations. *(1) Payment of tax.* Any excise tax due under section 860E(e)(1) must be paid by the later of March 24, 1993, or April 15th of the year following the calendar year in which the residual interest is transferred to a disqualified organization. The Commissioner may prescribe rules for the manner and method of collecting the tax.

(2) Transitory ownership. For purposes of section 860E(e) and this section, a transfer of a residual interest to a disqualified organization in connection with the formation of a REMIC is disregarded if the disqualified organization has a binding contract to sell the interest and the sale occurs within 7 days of the startup day (as defined in section 860G(a)(9) and § 1.860G-2(k)).

(3) Anticipated excess inclusions. The anticipated excess inclusions are the excess inclusions that are expected to accrue in each calendar quarter (or portion thereof) following the transfer of the residual interest. The anticipated excess inclusions must be determined as of the date the residual interest is transferred and must be based on—

(i) Events that have occurred up to the time of the transfer;

(ii) The prepayment and reinvestment assumptions adopted under section 1272(a)(6), or that would have been adopted had the REMIC's regular interests been issued with original issue discount; and

(iii) Any required or permitted clean up calls, or required qualified liquidation provided for in the REMIC's organizational documents.

(4) Present value computation. The present value of the anticipated excess inclusions is determined by discounting the anticipated excess inclusions from the end of each remaining calendar quarter in which those excess inclusions are expected to accrue to the date the disqualified organization acquires the residual interest. The discount rate to be used for this present value computation is the applicable Federal rate (as specified in section 1274(d)(1)) that would apply to a debt instrument that was issued on the date the disqualified organization acquired the residual interest and whose term ended on the close of the last quarter in which excess inclusions were expected to accrue with respect to the residual interest.

(5) Obligation of REMIC to furnish information. A REMIC is not obligated to determine if its residual interests have been transferred to a disqualified organization. However, upon request of a person designated in section 860E(e)(3), the REMIC must furnish information sufficient to compute the present value of the anticipated excess inclusions. The information must be furnished to the requesting party and to the Internal Revenue Service within 60 days of the request. A reasonable fee charged to the requestor is not income derived from a prohibited transaction within the meaning of section 860F(a).

(6) Agent. For purposes of section 860E(e)(3), the term "agent" includes a broker (as defined in section 6045(c) and § 1.6045-1(a)(1)), nominee, or other middleman.

(7) Relief from liability. (i) Transferee furnishes information under penalties of perjury. For purposes of section 860E(e)(4), a transferee is treated as having furnished an affidavit if the transferee furnishes—

(A) A social security number, and states under penalties of perjury that the social security number is that of the transferee; or

(B) A statement under penalties of perjury that it is not a disqualified organization.

(ii) Amount required to be paid. The amount required to be paid under section 860E(e)(7)(B) is equal to the product of the highest rate specified in section 11(b)(1) for the taxable year in which the transfer described in section 860E(e)(1) occurs and the amount of excess inclusions that accrued and were allocable to the residual interest during the period that the disqualified organization held the interest.

(b) Tax on pass-thru entities. *(1) Tax on excess inclusions.* Any tax due under section 860E(e)(6) must be paid by the later of March 24, 1993, or by the fifteenth day of the fourth month following the close of the taxable year of the pass-thru entity in which the disqualified person is a record holder. The Commissioner may prescribe rules for the manner and method of collecting the tax.

(2) Record holder furnishes information under penalties of perjury. For purposes of section 860E(e)(6)(D), a record holder is treated as having furnished an affidavit if the record holder furnishes—

(i) A social security number and states, under penalties of perjury, that the social security number is that of the record holder; or

(ii) A statement under penalties of perjury that it is not a disqualified organization.

(3) Deductibility of tax. Any tax imposed on a pass-thru entity pursuant to section 860E(e)(6)(A) is deductible against the gross amount of ordinary income of the pass-thru entity. For example, in the case of a REIT, the tax is deductible in determining real estate investment trust taxable income under section 857(b)(2).

(4) Allocation of tax. Dividends paid by a RIC or by a REIT are not preferential dividends within the meaning of section 562(c) solely because the tax expense incurred by the RIC or REIT under section 860E(e)(6) is allocated solely to the shares held by disqualified organizations.

T.D. 8458, 12/23/92.

§ 1.860F-1 Qualified liquidations.

A plan of liquidation need not be in any special form. If a REMIC specifies the first day in the 90-day liquidation period in a statement attached to its final return, then the REMIC will be considered to have adopted a plan of liquidation on the specified date.

T.D. 8458, 12/23/92.

§ 1.860F-2 Transfers to a REMIC.

(a) Formation of a REMIC. *(1) In general.* For Federal income tax purposes, a REMIC formation is characterized as the contribution of assets by a sponsor (as defined in paragraph (b)(1) of this section) to a REMIC in exchange for REMIC regular and residual interests. If, instead of exchanging its interest in mortgages and related assets for regular and residual interests, the sponsor arranges to have the REMIC issue some or all of the regular and residual interests for cash, after which the sponsor sells its interests in mortgages and related assets to the REMIC, the transaction is, nevertheless, viewed for Federal income tax purposes as the sponsor's exchange of mortgages and related assets for regular and residual interests, followed by a sale of some or all of those interests. The purpose of this rule is to ensure that the tax consequences associated with the formation of a REMIC are not affected by the actual sequence of steps taken by the sponsor.

(2) Tiered arrangements. (i) Two or more REMICs formed pursuant to a single set of organizational documents. Two or more REMICs can be created pursuant to a single set of organizational documents even if for state law purposes or for Federal securities law purposes those documents create only one organization. The organizational documents must, however, clearly and expressly identify the assets of, and the interests in, each REMIC, and each REMIC must satisfy all of the requirements of section 860D and the related regulations.

(ii) A REMIC and one or more investment trusts formed pursuant to a single set of documents. A REMIC (or two or more REMICs) and one or more investment trusts can be created pursuant to a single set of organizational documents and the separate existence of the REMIC(s) and the investment trust(s) will be respected for Federal income tax purposes even if for state law purposes or for Federal securities law purposes those documents create only one organization. The organizational documents for the REMIC(s) and the investment trust(s) must, however, require both the REMIC(s) and the investment trust(s) to account for items of income and ownership of assets for Federal tax purposes in a manner that respects the separate existence of the multiple entities. See § 1.860G-2(i) concerning issuance of regular interests coupled with other contractual rights for an illustration of the provisions of this paragraph.

(b) Treatment of sponsor. *(1) Sponsor defined.* A sponsor is a person who directly or indirectly exchanges qualified mortgages and related assets for regular and residual interests in a REMIC. A person indirectly exchanges interests in qualified mortgages and related assets for regular and residual interests in a REMIC if the person transfers, other than in a nonrecognition transaction, the mortgages and related assets to another person who acquires a transitory ownership interest in those assets before exchanging them for interests in the REMIC, after which the transitory owner then transfers some or all of the interests in the REMIC to the first person.

(2) Nonrecognition of gain or loss. The sponsor does not recognize gain or loss on the direct or indirect transfer of any property to a REMIC in exchange for regular or residual interests in the REMIC. However, the sponsor, upon a subsequent sale of the REMIC regular or residual interests, may recognize gain or loss with respect to those interests.

(3) Basis of contributed assets allocated among interests. (i) In general. The aggregate of the adjusted bases of the regular and residual interests received by the sponsor in the exchange described in paragraph (a) of this section is equal to the aggregate of the adjusted bases of the property transferred by the sponsor in the exchange, increased by the amount of organizational expenses (as described in paragraph (b)(3)(ii) of this section). That total is allocated among all the interests received in proportion to their fair market values on the pricing date (as defined in paragraph (b)(3)(iii) of this section) if any, or, if none, the startup day (as defined in section 860G(a)(9) and § 1.860G-2(k)).

(ii) Organizational expenses (A) Organizational expense defined. An organizational expense is an expense that is incurred by the sponsor or by the REMIC and that is directly related to the creation of the REMIC. Further, the organizational expense must be incurred during a period beginning a reasonable time before the startup day and ending before the date prescribed by law for filing the first REMIC tax return (determined without regard to any extensions of time to file). The following are examples of organizational expenses: legal fees for services related to the formation of the REMIC, such as preparation of a pooling and servicing agreement and trust indenture; accounting fees related to the formation of the REMIC; and other administrative costs related to the formation of the REMIC.

(B) Syndication expenses. Syndication expenses are not organizational expenses. Syndication expenses are those expenses incurred by the sponsor or other person to market the interests in a REMIC, and, thus, are applied to reduce the amount realized on the sale of the interests. Examples of syndication expenses are brokerage fees, registration fees, fees of an underwriter or placement agent, and printing costs of the prospectus or placement memorandum and other selling or promotional material.

(iii) Pricing date. The term "pricing date" means the date on which the terms of the regular and residual interests are fixed and the prices at which a substantial portion of the regular interests will be sold are fixed.

(4) Treatment of unrecognized gain or loss. (i) Unrecognized gain on regular interests. For purposes of section 860F(b)(1)(C)(i), the sponsor must include in gross income the excess of the issue price of a regular interest over the sponsor's basis in the interest as if the excess were market discount (as defined in section 1278(a)(2)) on a bond and the sponsor had made an election under section 1278(b) to include this market discount currently in gross income. The sponsor is not, however, by reason of this paragraph (b)(4)(i), deemed to have made an election under section 1278(b) with respect to any other bonds.

(ii) Unrecognized loss on regular interests. For purposes of section 860F(b)(1)(D)(i), the sponsor treats the excess of the sponsor's basis in a regular interest over the issue price of the interest as if that excess were amortizable bond premium (as defined in section 171(b)) on a taxable bond and the sponsor had made an election under section 171(c). The sponsor is not, however, by reason of this paragraph (b)(4)(ii), deemed to have made an election under section 171(c) with respect to any other bonds.

(iii) Unrecognized gain on residual interests. For purposes of section 860F(b)(1)(C)(ii), the sponsor must include in gross income the excess of the issue price of a residual interest over the sponsor's basis in the interest ratably over the anticipated weighted average life of the REMIC (as defined in § 1.860E-1(a)(3)(iv)).

(iv) Unrecognized loss on residual interests. For purposes of section 860F(b)(1)(D)(ii), the sponsor deducts the excess of the sponsor's basis in a residual interest over the issue price of the interest ratably over the anticipated weighted average life of the REMIC.

(5) Additions to or reductions of the sponsor's basis. The sponsor's basis in a regular or residual interest is increased by any amount included in the sponsor's gross income under paragraph (b)(4) of this section. The sponsor's basis in a regular or residual interest is decreased by any amount allowed as a deduction and by any amount applied to reduce interest payments to the sponsor under paragraph (b)(4)(ii) of this section.

(6) Transferred basis property. For purposes of paragraph (b)(4) of this section, a transferee of a regular or residual interest is treated in the same manner as the sponsor to the extent that the basis of the transferee in the interest is determined in whole or in part by reference to the basis of the interest in the hands of the sponsor.

(c) REMIC's basis in contributed assets. For purposes of section 860F(b)(2), the aggregate of the REMIC's bases in the assets contributed by the sponsor to the REMIC in a transaction described in paragraph (a) of this section is equal to the aggregate of the issue prices (determined under section 860G(a)(10) and § 1.860G-1(d)) of all regular and residual interests in the REMIC.

T.D. 8458, 12/23/92.

§ 1.860F-4 REMIC reporting requirements and other administrative rules.

Caution: The Treasury has not yet amended Reg § 1.860F-4 to reflect changes made by P.L. 104-188.

(a) In general. Except as provided in paragraph (c) of this section, for purposes of subtitle F of the Internal Revenue Code, a REMIC is treated as a partnership and any holder of a residual interest in the REMIC is treated as a partner. A REMIC is not subject, however, to the rules of subchapter C of chapter 63 of the Internal Revenue Code, relating to the treatment of partnership items, for a taxable year if there is at no time during the taxable year more than one holder of a residual interest in the REMIC. The identity of a holder of a residual interest in a REMIC is not treated as a partnership item with respect to the REMIC for purposes of subchapter C of chapter 63.

(b) REMIC tax return. *(1) In general.* To satisfy the requirement under section 6031 to make a return of income for each taxable year, a REMIC must file the return required by paragraph (b)(2) of this section. The due date and any extensions for filing the REMIC's annual return are determined as if the REMIC were a partnership.

(2) Income tax return. The REMIC must make a return, as required by section 6011(a), for each taxable year on Form 1066, U.S. Real Estate Mortgage Investment Conduit Income Tax Return. The return must include—

(i) The amount of principal outstanding on each class of regular interests as of the close of the taxable year,

(ii) The amount of the daily accruals determined under section 860E(c), and

(iii) The information specified in § 1.860D-1(d)(2) (i), (iv), and (v).

(c) Signing of REMIC return. *(1) In general.* Although a REMIC is generally treated as a partnership for purposes of subtitle F, for purposes of determining who is authorized to sign a REMIC's income tax return for any taxable year, the REMIC is not treated as a partnership and the holders of residual interests in the REMIC are not treated as partners. Rather, the REMIC return must be signed by a person who could sign the return of the entity absent the REMIC election. Thus, the return of a REMIC that is a corporation or trust under applicable State law must be signed by a corporate officer or a trustee, respectively. The return of a REMIC that consists of a segregated pool of assets must be signed by a person who could sign the return of the entity that owns the assets of the REMIC under applicable State law.

(2) REMIC whose startup day is before November 10, 1988. (i) In general. The income tax return of a REMIC whose startup day is before November 10, 1988, may be signed by any person who held a residual interest during the taxable year to which the return relates, or, as provided in section 6903, by a fiduciary, as defined in section 7701(a)(6), who is acting for the REMIC and who has furnished adequate notice in the manner prescribed in § 301.6903-1(b) of this chapter.

(ii) Startup day. For purposes of paragraph (c)(2) of this section, startup day means any day selected by a REMIC that is on or before the first day on which interests in such REMIC are issued.

(iii) Exception. A REMIC whose startup day is before November 10, 1988, may elect to have paragraph (c)(1) of this section apply, instead of paragraph (c)(2) of this section, in determining who is authorized to sign the REMIC return. See section 1006(t)(18)(B) of the Technical and Miscellaneous Revenue Act of 1988 (102 Stat. 3426) and § 5h.6(a)(1) of this chapter for the time and manner for making this election.

(d) Designation of tax matters person. A REMIC may designate a tax matters person in the same manner in which a partnership may designate a tax matters partner under § 301.6231(a)(7)-1T of this chapter. For purposes of applying that section, all holders of residual interests in the REMIC are treated as general partners.

(e) Notice to holders of residual interests. *(1) Information required.* As of the close of each calendar quarter, a REMIC must provide to each person who held a residual interest in the REMIC during that quarter notice on Schedule Q (Form 1066) of information specified in paragraphs (e)(1) (i) and (ii) of this section.

(i) In general. Each REMIC must provide to each of its residual interest holders the following information—

(A) That person's share of the taxable income or net loss of the REMIC for the calendar quarter;

(B) The amount of the excess inclusion (as defined in section 860E and the regulations thereunder), if any, with respect to that person's residual interest for the calendar quarter;

(C) If the holder of a residual interest is also a pass-through interest holder (as defined in § 1.67-3T(a)(2)), the allocable investment expenses (as defined in § 1.67-3T(a)(4)) for the calendar quarter, and

(D) Any other information required by Schedule Q (Form 1066).

(ii) Information with respect to REMIC assets (A) 95 percent asset test. For calendar quarters after 1988, each REMIC must provide to each of its residual interest holders the following information—

(1) The percentage of REMIC assets that are qualifying real property loans under section 593,

(2) The percentage of REMIC assets that are assets described in section 7701(a)(19), and

(3) The percentage of REMIC assets that are real estate assets defined in section 856(c)(6)(B), computed by reference to the average adjusted basis (as defined in section 1011) of the REMIC assets during the calendar quarter (as described in paragraph (e)(1)(iii) of this section). If the percentage of REMIC assets represented by a category is at least 95 percent, then the REMIC need only specify that the percentage for that category was at least 95 percent.

(B) Additional information required if the 95 percent test not met. If, for any calendar quarter after 1988, less than 95 percent of the assets of the REMIC are real estate assets defined in section 856(c)(6)(B), then, for that calendar quarter, the REMIC must also provide to any real estate investment trust (REIT) that holds a residual interest the following information—

(1) The percentage of REMIC assets described in section 856(c)(5)(A), computed by reference to the average adjusted basis of the REMIC assets during the calendar quarter (as described in paragraph (e)(1)(iii) of this section),

(2) The percentage of REMIC gross income (other than gross income from prohibited transactions defined in section 860F(a)(2)) described in section 856(c)(3)(A) through (E), computed as of the close of the calendar quarter, and

(3) The percentage of REMIC gross income (other than gross income from prohibited transactions defined in section 860F(a)(2)) described in section 856(c)(3)(F), computed as of the close of the calendar quarter. For purposes of this paragraph (e)(1)(ii)(B)(3), the term "foreclosure property" contained in section 856(c)(3)(F) has the meaning specified in section 860G(a)(8). In determining whether a REIT satisfies the limitations of section 856(c)(2), all REMIC gross income is deemed to be derived from a source specified in section 856(c)(2).

(C) For calendar quarters in 1987. For calendar quarters in 1987, the percentages of assets required in paragraphs (e)(1)(ii) (A) and (B) of this section may be computed by reference to the fair market value of the assets of the REMIC as of the close of the calendar quarter (as described in paragraph (e)(1)(iii) of this section), instead of by reference to the average adjusted basis during the calendar quarter.

(D) For calendar quarters in 1988 and 1989. For calendar quarters in 1988 and 1989, the percentages of assets required in paragraphs (e)(1)(ii) (A) and (B) of this section may be computed by reference to the average fair market value of the assets of the REMIC during the calendar quarter (as described in paragraph (e)(1)(iii) of this section), instead of by reference to the average adjusted basis of the assets of the REMIC during the calendar quarter.

(iii) Special provisions. For purposes of paragraph (e)(1)(ii) of this section, the percentage of REMIC assets represented by a specified category computed by reference to average adjusted basis (or fair market value) of the assets during a calendar quarter is determined by dividing the average adjusted bases (or for calendar quarters before 1990, fair market value) of the assets in the specified category by the average adjusted basis (or, for calendar quarters before 1990, fair market value) of all the assets of the REMIC as of the close of each month, week, or day during that calendar quarter. The monthly, weekly, or daily computation period must be applied uniformly during the calendar quarter to all categories of assets and may not be changed in succeeding calendar quarters without the consent of the Commissioner.

(2) Quarterly notice required. (i) In general. Schedule Q must be mailed (or otherwise delivered) to each holder of a residual interest during a calendar quarter no later than the last day of the month following the close of the calendar quarter.

(ii) Special rule for 1987. Notice to any holder of a REMIC residual interest of the information required in paragraph (e)(1) of this section for any of the four calendar quarters of 1987 must be mailed (or otherwise delivered) to each holder no later than March 28, 1988.

(3) Nominee reporting. (i) In general. If a REMIC is required under paragraphs (e)(1) and (2) of this section to provide notice to an interest holder who is a nominee of another person with respect to an interest in the REMIC, the nominee must furnish that notice to the person for whom it is a nominee.

(ii) Time for furnishing statement. The nominee must furnish the notice required under paragraph (e)(3)(i) of this section to the person for whom it is a nominee no later than 30 days after receiving this information.

(4) Reports to the Internal Revenue Service. For each person who was a residual interest holder at any time during a REMIC's taxable year, the REMIC must attach a copy of Schedule Q to its income tax return for that year for each quarter in which that person was a residual interest holder. Quarterly notice to the Internal Revenue Service is not required.

(f) Information returns for persons engaged in a trade or business. See § 1.6041-1(b)(2) for the treatment of a REMIC under sections 6041 and 6041A.

T.D. 8366, 9/27/91, amend T.D. 8458, 12/23/92, T.D. 9184, 2/24/2005.

PAR. 2. In § 1.860F-4, paragraph (a) is amended by adding a sentence at the end to read as follows:

Proposed § 1.860F-4 REMIC reporting requirements and other administrative rules. [*For Preamble, see ¶ 152,563*]

(a) * * * The identity of a holder of a residual interest in a REMIC is not treated as a partnership item with respect to the REMIC for purposes of subchapter C of chapter 63.

* * * * *

PAR. 3. Section 1.860F-4 is amended by revising paragraph (e)(2)(i) to read as follows:

Proposed § 1.860F-4 REMIC reporting requirements and other administrative rules. [*For Preamble, see ¶ 151,317*]

* * * * *

(e) * * *

(2) * * *

(i) In general. Schedule Q must be mailed (or otherwise delivered) to each holder of a residual interest during a calendar quarter no later than the 41st day following the close of the calendar quarter.

* * * * *

§ 1.860G-1 Definition of regular and residual interests.

(a) Regular interest. *(1) Designation as a regular interest.* For purposes of section 860G(a)(1), a REMIC designates an interest as a regular interest by providing to the Internal Revenue Service the information specified in § 1.860D-1(d)(2)(ii) in the time and manner specified in § 1.860D-1(d)(2).

(2) Specified portion of the interest payments on qualified mortgages. (i) In general. For purposes of section 860G(a)(1)(B)(ii), a specified portion of the interest payments on qualified mortgages means a portion of the interest payable on qualified mortgages, but only if the portion can be expressed as—

(A) A fixed percentage of the interest that is payable at either a fixed rate or at a variable rate described in paragraph (a)(3) of this section on some or all of the qualified mortgages;

(B) A fixed number of basis points of the interest payable on some or all of the qualified mortgages; or

(C) The interest payable at either a fixed rate or at a variable rate described in paragraph (a)(3) of this section on some or all of the qualified mortgages in excess of a fixed number of basis points or in excess of a variable rate described in paragraph (a)(3) of this section.

(ii) Specified portion cannot vary. The portion must be established as of the startup day (as defined in section 860G(a)(9) and § 1.860G-2(k)) and, except as provided in paragraph (a)(2)(iii) of this section, it cannot vary over the period that begins on the startup day and ends on the day that the interest holder is no longer entitled to receive payments.

(iii) Defaulted or delinquent mortgages. A portion is not treated as varying over time if an interest holder's entitlement to a portion of the interest on some or all of the qualified mortgages is dependent on the absence of defaults or delinquencies on those mortgages.

(iv) No minimum specified principal amount is required. If an interest in a REMIC consists of a specified portion of the interest payments on the REMIC's qualified mortgages, no minimum specified principal amount need be assigned to that interest. The specified principal amount can be zero.

(v) Specified portion includes portion of interest payable on regular interest. (A) The specified portions that meet the requirements of paragraph (a)(2)(i) of this section include a specified portion that can be expressed as a fixed percentage of the interest that is payable on some or all of the qualified mortgages where—

(1) Each of those qualified mortgages is a regular interest issued by another REMIC; and

(2) With respect to that REMIC in which it is a regular interest, each of those regular interests bears interest that can

be expressed as a specified portion as described in paragraph (a)(2)(i)(A), (B), or (C) of this section.

(B) See § 1.860A-1(a) for the effective date of this paragraph (a)(2)(v).

(vi) Examples. The following examples, each of which describes a pass-through trust that is intended to qualify as a REMIC, illustrate the provisions of this paragraph (a)(2).

Example (1). (i) A sponsor transferred a pool of fixed rate mortgages to a trustee in exchange for two classes of certificates. The Class A certificate holders are entitled to all principal payments on the mortgages and to interest on outstanding principal at a variable rate based on the current value of One-Month LIBOR, subject to a lifetime cap equal to the weighted average rate payable on the mortgages. The Class B certificate holders are entitled to all interest payable on the mortgages in excess of the interest paid on the Class A certificates. The Class B certificates are subordinate to the Class A certificates so that cash flow shortfalls due to defaults or delinquencies on the mortgages will be borne first by the Class B certificate holders.

(ii) The Class B certificate holders are entitled to all interest payable on the pooled mortgages in excess of a variable rate described in paragraph (a)(3)(vi) of this section. Moreover, the portion of the interest payable to the Class B certificate holders is not treated as varying over time solely because payments on the Class B certificates may be reduced as a result of defaults or delinquencies on the pooled mortgages. Thus, the Class B certificates provide for interest payments that consist of a specified portion of the interest payable on the pooled mortgages under paragraph (a)(2)(i)(C) of this section.

Example (2). (i) A sponsor transferred a pool of variable rate mortgages to a trustee in exchange for two classes of certificates. The mortgages call for interest payments at a variable rate based on the current value of the One-Year Constant Maturity Treasury Index (hereinafter "CMTI") plus 200 basis points, subject to a lifetime cap of 12 percent. Class C certificate holders are entitled to all principal payments on the mortgages and interest on the outstanding principal at a variable rate based on the One-Year CMTI plus 100 basis points, subject to a lifetime cap of 12 percent. The interest rate on the Class C certificates is reset at the same time the rate is reset on the pooled mortgages.

(ii) The Class D certificate holders are entitled to all interest payments on the mortgages in excess of the interest paid on the Class C certificates. So long as the One-Year CMTI is at 10 percent or lower, the Class D certificate holders are entitled to 100 basis points of interest on the pooled mortgages. If, however, the index exceeds 10 percent on a reset date, the Class D certificate holders' entitlement shrinks, and it disappears if the index is at 11 percent or higher.

(iii) The Class D certificate holders are entitled to all interest payable on the pooled mortgages in excess of a qualified variable rate described in paragraph (a)(3) of this section. Thus, the Class D certificates provide for interest payments that consist of a specified portion of the interest payable on the qualified mortgages under paragraph (a)(2)(i)(C) of this section.

Example (3). (i) A sponsor transferred a pool of fixed rate mortgages to a trustee in exchange for two classes of certificates. The fixed interest rate payable on the mortgages varies from mortgage to mortgage, but all rates are between 8 and 10 percent. The Class E certificate holders are entitled to receive all principal payments on the mortgages and interest on outstanding principal at 7 percent. The Class F certificate holders are entitled to receive all interest on the mortgages in excess of the interest paid on the Class E certificates.

(ii) The Class F certificates provide for interest payments that consist of a specified portion of the interest payable on the mortgages under paragraph (a)(2)(i) of this section. Although the portion of the interest payable to the Class F certificate holders varies from mortgage to mortgage, the interest payable can be expressed as a fixed percentage of the interest payable on each particular mortgage.

(3) Variable rate. A regular interest may bear interest at a variable rate. For purposes of section 860G(a)(1)(B)(i), a variable rate of interest is a rate described in this paragraph (a)(3).

(i) Rate based on current interest rate. A qualified floating rate as defined in § 1.1275-5(b)(1) (but without the application of paragraph (b)(2) or (3) of that section) set at a current value, as defined in § 1.1275-5(a)(4), is a variable rate. In addition, a rate equal to the highest, lowest, or average of two or more qualified floating rates is a variable rate. For example, a rate based on the average cost of funds of one or more financial institutions is a variable rate.

(ii) Weighted average rate. (A) In general. A rate based on a weighted average of the interest rates on some or all of the qualified mortgages held by a REMIC is a variable rate. The qualified mortgages taken into account must, however, bear interest at a fixed rate or at a rate described in this paragraph (a)(3). Generally, a weighted average interest rate is a rate that, if applied to the aggregate outstanding principal balance of a pool of mortgage loans for an accrual period, produces an amount of interest that equals the sum of the interest payable on the pooled loans for that accrual period. Thus, for an accrual period in which a pool of mortgage loans comprises $300,000 of loans bearing a 7 percent interest rate and $700,000 of loans bearing a 9.5 percent interest rate, the weighted average rate for the pool of loans is 8.75 percent.

(B) Reduction in underlying rate. For purposes of paragraph (a)(3)(ii)(A) of this section, an interest rate is considered to be based on a weighted average rate even if, in determining that rate, the interest rate on some or all of the qualified mortgages is first subject to a cap or a floor, or is first reduced by a number of basis points or a fixed percentage. A rate determined by taking a weighted average of the interest rates on the qualified mortgage loans net of any servicing spread, credit enhancement fees, or other expenses of the REMIC is a rate based on a weighted average rate for the qualified mortgages. Further, the amount of any rate reduction described above may vary from mortgage to mortgage.

(iii) Additions, subtractions, and multiplications. A rate is a variable rate if it is—

(A) Expressed as the product of a rate described in paragraph (a)(3)(i) or (ii) of this section and a fixed multiplier;

(B) Expressed as a constant number of basis points more or less than a rate described in paragraph (a)(3)(i) or (ii) of this section; or

(C) Expressed as the product, plus or minus a constant number of basis points, of a rate described in paragraph (a)(3)(i) or (ii) of this section and a fixed multiplier (which may be either a positive or a negative number).

(iv) Caps and floors. A rate is a variable rate if it is a rate that would be described in paragraph (a)(3)(i) through (iii) of this section except that it is—

(A) Limited by a cap or ceiling that establishes either a maximum rate or a maximum number of basis points by which the rate may increase from one accrual or payment period to another or over the term of the interest; or

(B) Limited by a floor that establishes either a minimum rate or a maximum number of basis points by which the rate may decrease from one accrual or payment period to another or over the term of the interest.

(v) Funds-available caps. (A) In general. A rate is a variable rate if it is a rate that would be described in paragraph (a)(3)(i) through (iv) of this section except that it is subject to a "funds-available" cap. A funds-available cap is a limit on the amount of interest to be paid on an instrument in any accrual or payment period that is based on the total amount available for the distribution, including both principal and interest received by an issuing entity on some or all of its qualified mortgages as well as amounts held in a reserve fund. The term "funds-available cap" does not, however, include any cap or limit on interest payments used as a device to avoid the standards of paragraph (a)(3)(i) through (iv) of this section.

(B) Facts and circumstances test. In determining whether a cap or limit on interest payments is a funds-available cap within the meaning of this section and not a device used to avoid the standards of paragraph (a)(3)(i) through (iv) of this section, one must consider all of the facts and circumstances. Facts and circumstances that must be taken into consideration are—

(1) Whether the rate of the interest payable to the regular interest holders is below the rate payable on the REMIC's qualified mortgages on the start-up day; and

(2) Whether, historically, the rate of interest payable to the regular interest holders has been consistently below that payable on the qualified mortgages.

(C) Examples. The following examples, both of which describe a pass-through trust that is intended to qualify as a REMIC, illustrate the provisions of this paragraph (a)(3)(v).

Example (1). (i) A sponsor transferred a pool of mortgages to a trustee in exchange for two classes of certificates. The pool of mortgages has an aggregate principal balance of $100x. Each mortgage in the pool provides for interest payments based on the eleventh district cost of funds index (hereinafter COFI) plus a margin. The initial weighted average rate for the pool is COFI plus 200 basis points. The trust issued a Class X certificate that has a principal amount of $100x and that provides for interest payments at a rate equal to One-Year LIBOR plus 100 basis points, subject to a cap described below. The Class R certificate, which the sponsor designated as the residual interest, entitles its holder to all funds left in the trust after the Class X certificates have been retired. The Class R certificate holder is not entitled to current distributions.

(ii) At the time the certificates were issued, COFI equalled 4.874 percent and One-Year LIBOR equalled 3.375 percent. Thus, the initial weighted average pool rate was 6.874 percent and the Class X certificate rate was 4.375 percent. Based on historical data, the sponsor does not expect the rate paid on the Class X certificate to exceed the weighted average rate on the pool.

(iii) Initially, under the terms of the trust instrument, the excess of COFI plus 200 over One-Year LIBOR plus 100 (excess interest) will be applied to pay expenses of the trust, to fund any required reserves, and then to reduce the principal balance on the Class X certificate. Consequently, although the aggregate principal balance of the mortgages initially matched the principal balance of the Class X certificate, the principal balance on the Class X certificate will pay down faster than the principal balance on the mortgages as long as the weighted average rate on the mortgages is greater than One-Year LIBOR plus 100. If, however, the rate on the Class X certificate (One-Year LIBOR plus 100) ever exceeds the weighted average rate on the mortgages, then the Class X certificate holders will receive One-Year LIBOR plus 100 subject to a cap based on the current funds that are available for distribution.

(iv) The funds available cap here is not a device used to avoid the standards of paragraph (a)(3)(i) through (iv) of this section. First, on the date the Class X certificates were issued, a significant spread existed between the weighted average rate payable on the mortgages and the rate payable on the Class X certificate. Second, historical data suggest that the weighted average rate payable on the mortgages will continue to exceed the rate payable on the Class X certificate. Finally, because the excess interest will be applied to reduce the outstanding principal balance of the Class X certificate more rapidly than the outstanding principal balance on the mortgages is reduced, One-Year LIBOR plus 100 basis points would have to exceed the weighted average rate on the mortgages by an increasingly larger amount before the funds available cap would be triggered. Accordingly, the rate paid on the Class X certificates is a variable rate.

Example (2). (i) The facts are the same as those in Example 1, except that the pooled mortgages are commercial mortgages that provide for interest payments based on the gross profits of the mortgagors, and the rate on the Class X certificates is 400 percent of One-Year LIBOR (a variable rate under paragraph (a)(3)(iii) of this section), subject to a cap equal to current funds available to the trustee for distribution.

(ii) Initially, 400 percent of One-Year LIBOR exceeds the weighted average rate payable on the mortgages. Furthermore, historical data suggest that there is a significant possibility that, in the future, 400 percent of One-Year LIBOR will exceed the weighted average rate on the mortgages.

(iii) The facts and circumstances here indicate that the use of 400 percent of One-Year LIBOR with the above-described cap is a device to pass through to the Class X certificate holder contingent interest based on mortgagor profits. Consequently, the rate paid on the Class X certificate here is not a variable rate.

(vi) Combination of rates. A rate is a variable rate if it is based on—

(A) One fixed rate during one or more accrual or payment periods and a different fixed rate or rates, or a rate or rates described in paragraph (a)(3)(i) through (v) of this section, during other accrual or payment periods; or

(B) A rate described in paragraph (a)(3)(i) through (v) of this section during one or more accrual or payment periods and a fixed rate or rates, or a different rate or rates described in paragraph (a)(3)(i) through (v) of this section in other periods.

(4) Fixed terms on the startup day. For purposes of section 860G(a)(1), a regular interest in a REMIC has fixed terms on the startup day if, on the startup day, the REMIC's organizational documents irrevocably specify—

(i) The principal amount (or other similar amount) of the regular interest;

(ii) The interest rate or rates used to compute any interest payments (or other similar amounts) on the regular interest; and

(iii) The latest possible maturity date of the interest.

(5) Contingencies prohibited. Except for the contingencies specified in paragraph (b)(3) of this section, the principal amount (or other similar amount) and the latest possible maturity date of the interest must not be contingent.

(b) Special rules for regular interests. *(1) Call premium.* An interest in a REMIC does not qualify as a regular interest if the terms of the interest entitle the holder of that interest to the payment of any premium that is determined with reference to the length of time that the regular interest is outstanding and is not described in paragraph (b)(2) of this section.

(2) Customary prepayment penalties received with respect to qualified mortgages. An interest in a REMIC does not fail to qualify as a regular interest solely because the REMIC's organizational documents provide that the REMIC must allocate among and pay to its regular interest holders any customary prepayment penalties that the REMIC receives with respect to its qualified mortgages. Moreover, a REMIC may allocate prepayment penalties among its classes of interests in any manner specified in the REMIC's organizational documents. For example, a REMIC could allocate all or substantially all of a prepayment penalty that it receives to holders of an interest-only class of interests because that class would be most significantly affected by prepayments.

(3) Certain contingencies disregarded. An interest in a REMIC does not fail to qualify as a regular interest solely because it is issued subject to some or all of the contingencies described in paragraph (b)(3)(i) through (vi) of this section.

(i) Prepayments, income, and expenses. An interest does not fail to qualify as a regular interest solely because—

(A) The timing of (but not the right to or amount of) principal payments (or other similar amounts) is affected by the extent of prepayments on some or all of the qualified mortgages held by the REMIC or the amount of income from permitted investments (as defined in § 1.860G-2(g)); or

(B) The timing of interest and principal payments is affected by the payment of expenses incurred by the REMIC.

(ii) Credit losses. An interest does not fail to qualify as a regular interest solely because the amount or the timing of payments of principal or interest (or other similar amounts) with respect to a regular interest is affected by defaults on qualified mortgages and permitted investments, unanticipated expenses incurred by the REMIC, or lower than expected returns on permitted investments.

(iii) Subordinated interests. An interest does not fail to qualify as a regular interest solely because that interest bears all, or a disproportionate share, of the losses stemming from cash flow shortfalls due to defaults or delinquencies on qualified mortgages or permitted investments, unanticipated expenses incurred by the REMIC, lower than expected returns on permitted investments, or prepayment interest shortfalls before other regular interests or the residual interest bear losses occasioned by those shortfalls.

(iv) Deferral of interest. An interest does not fail to qualify as a regular interest solely because that interest, by its terms, provides for deferral of interest payments.

(v) Prepayment interest shortfalls. An interest does not fail to qualify as a regular interest solely because the amount of interest payments is affected by prepayments of the underlying mortgages.

(vi) Remote and incidental contingencies. An interest does not fail to qualify as a regular interest solely because the amount or timing of payments of principal or interest (or other similar amounts) with respect to the interest is subject to a contingency if there is only a remote likelihood that the contingency will occur. For example, an interest could qualify as a regular interest even though full payment of principal and interest on that interest is contingent upon the absence of significant cash flow shortfalls due to the operation of the Soldiers and Sailors Civil Relief Act, 50 U.S.C. app. § 526 (1988).

(4) Form of regular interest. A regular interest in a REMIC may be issued in the form of debt, stock, an interest in a partnership or trust, or any other form permitted by state law. If a regular interest in a REMIC is not in the form of debt, it must, except as provided in paragraph (a)(2)(iv) of this section, entitle the holder to a specified amount that would, were the interest issued in debt form, be identified as the principal amount of the debt.

(5) Interest disproportionate to principal. (i) In general. An interest in a REMIC does not qualify as a regular interest if the amount of interest (or other similar amount) payable to the holder is disproportionately high relative to the principal amount or other specified amount described in paragraph (b)(4) of this section (specified principal amount). Interest payments (or other similar amounts) are considered disproportionately high if the issue price (as determined under paragraph (d) of this section) of the interest in the REMIC exceeds 125 percent of its specified principal amount.

(ii) Exception. A regular interest in a REMIC that entitles the holder to interest payments consisting of a specified portion of interest payments on qualified mortgages qualifies as a regular interest even if the amount of interest is disproportionately high relative to the specified principal amount.

(6) Regular interest treated as a debt instrument for all Federal income tax purposes. In determining the tax under chapter 1 of the Internal Revenue Code, a REMIC regular interest (as defined in section 860G(a)(1)) is treated as a debt instrument that is an obligation of the REMIC. Thus, sections 1271 through 1288, relating to bonds and other debt instruments, apply to a regular interest. For special rules relating to the accrual of original issue discount on regular interests, see section 1272(a)(6).

(c) Residual interest. A residual interest is an interest in a REMIC that is issued on the startup day and that is designated as a residual interest by providing the information specified in § 1.860D-1(d)(2)(ii) at the time and in the manner provided in § 1.860D-1(d)(2). A residual interest need not entitle the holder to any distributions from the REMIC.

(d) Issue price of regular and residual interests. *(1) In general.* The issue price of any REMIC regular or residual interest is determined under section 1273(b) as if the interest were a debt instrument and, if issued for property, as if the requirements of section 1273(b)(3) were met. Thus, if a class of interests is publicly offered, then the issue price of an interest in that class is the initial offering price to the public at which a substantial amount of the class is sold. If the interest is in a class that is not publicly offered, the issue price is the price paid by the first buyer of that interest regardless of the price paid for the remainder of the class. If the interest is in a class that is retained by the sponsor, the issue price is its fair market value on the pricing date (as defined in § 1.860F-2(b)(3)(iii)), if any, or, if none, the startup day, regardless of whether the property exchanged therefor is publicly traded.

(2) The public. The term "the public" for purposes of this section does not include brokers or other middlemen, nor

does it include the sponsor who acquires all of the regular and residual interests from the REMIC on the startup day in a transaction described in § 1.860F-2(a).

T.D. 8458, 12/23/92, amend T.D. 8614, 8/16/95.

§ 1.860G-2 Other rules.

(a) Obligations principally secured by an interest in real property. *(1) Tests for determining whether an obligation is principally secured.* For purposes of section 860G(a)(3)(A), an obligation is principally secured by an interest in real property only if it satisfies either the test set out in paragraph (a)(1)(i) or the test set out in paragraph (a)(1)(ii) of this section.

(i) The 80-percent test. An obligation is principally secured by an interest in real property if the fair market value of the interest in real property securing the obligation—

(A) Was at least equal to 80 percent of the adjusted issue price of the obligation at the time the obligation was originated (see paragraph (b)(1) of this section concerning the origination date for obligations that have been significantly modified); or

(B) Is at least equal to 80 percent of the adjusted issue price of the obligation at the time the sponsor contributes the obligation to the REMIC.

(ii) Alternative test. For purposes of section 860G(a)(3)(A), an obligation is principally secured by an interest in real property if substantially all of the proceeds of the obligation were used to acquire or to improve or protect an interest in real property that, at the origination date, is the only security for the obligation. For purposes of this test, loan guarantees made by the United States or any state (or any political subdivision, agency, or instrumentality of the United States or of any state), or other third party credit enhancement are not viewed as additional security for a loan. An obligation is not considered to be secured by property other than real property solely because the obligor is personally liable on the obligation.

(2) Treatment of liens. For purposes of paragraph (a)(1)(i) of this section, the fair market value of the real property interest must be first reduced by the amount of any lien on the real property interest that is senior to the obligation being tested, and must be further reduced by a proportionate amount of any lien that is in parity with the obligation being tested.

(3) Safe harbor. (i) Reasonable belief that an obligation is principally secured. If, at the time the sponsor contributes an obligation to a REMIC, the sponsor reasonably believes that the obligation is principally secured by an interest in real property within the meaning of paragraph (a)(1) of this section, then the obligation is deemed to be so secured for purposes of section 860G(a)(3). A sponsor cannot avail itself of this safe harbor with respect to an obligation if the sponsor actually knows or has reason to know that the obligation fails both of the tests set out in paragraph (a)(1) of this section.

(ii) Basis for reasonable belief. For purposes of paragraph (a)(3)(i) of this section, a sponsor may base a reasonable belief concerning any obligation on—

(A) Representations and warranties made by the originator of the obligation; or

(B) Evidence indicating that the originator of the obligation typically made mortgage loans in accordance with an established set of parameters, and that any mortgage loan originated in accordance with those parameters would satisfy at least one of the tests set out in paragraph (a)(1) of this section.

(iii) Later discovery that an obligation is not principally secured. If, despite the sponsor's reasonable belief concerning an obligation at the time it contributed the obligation to the REMIC, the REMIC later discovers that the obligation is not principally secured by an interest in real property, the obligation is a defective obligation and loses its status as a qualified mortgage 90 days after the date of discovery. See paragraph (f) of this section, relating to defective obligations.

(4) Interests in real property; real property. The definition of "interests in real property" set out in § 1.856-3(c), and the definition of "real property" set out in § 1.856-3(d), apply to define those terms for purposes of section 860G(a)(3) and paragraph (a) of this section.

(5) Obligations secured by an interest in real property. Obligations secured by interests in real property include the following: mortgages, deeds of trust, and installment land contracts; mortgage pass-thru certificates guaranteed by GNMA, FNMA, FHLMC, or CMHC (Canada Mortgage and Housing Corporation); other investment trust interests that represent undivided beneficial ownership in a pool of obligations principally secured by interests in real property and related assets that would be considered to be permitted investments if the investment trust were a REMIC, and provided the investment trust is classified as a trust under § 301.7701-4(c) of this chapter; and obligations secured by manufactured housing treated as single family residences under section 25(e)(10) (without regard to the treatment of the obligations or the properties under state law).

(6) Obligations secured by other obligations; residual interests. Obligations (other than regular interests in a REMIC) that are secured by other obligations are not principally secured by interests in real property even if the underlying obligations are secured by interests in real property. Thus, for example, a collateralized mortgage obligation issued by an issuer that is not a REMIC is not an obligation principally secured by an interest in real property. A residual interest (as defined in section 860G(a)(2)) is not an obligation principally secured by an interest in real property.

(7) Certain instruments that call for contingent payments are obligations. For purposes of section 860G(a)(3) and (4), the term "obligation" includes any instrument that provides for total noncontingent principal payments that at least equal the instrument's issue price even if that instrument also provides for contingent payments. Thus, for example, an instrument that was issued for $100x and that provides for noncontingent principal payments of $100x, interest payments at a fixed rate, and contingent payments based on a percentage of the mortgagor's gross receipts, is an obligation.

(8) Defeasance. If a REMIC releases its lien on real property that secures a qualified mortgage, that mortgage ceases to be a qualified mortgage on the date the lien is released unless—

(i) The mortgagor pledges substitute collateral that consists solely of government securities (as defined in section 2(a)(16) of the Investment Company Act of 1940 as amended (15 U.S.C. 80a-1));

(ii) The mortgage documents allow such a substitution;

(iii) The lien is released to facilitate the disposition of the property or any other customary commercial transaction, and not as part of an arrangement to collateralize a REMIC offering with obligations that are not real estate mortgages; and

(iv) The release is not within 2 years of the startup day.

(9) Stripped bonds and coupons. The term "qualified mortgage" includes stripped bonds and stripped coupons (as defined in section 1286(e)(2) and (3)) if the bonds (as defined in section 1286(e)(1)) from which such stripped bonds or stripped coupons arose would have been qualified mortgages.

(b) Assumptions and modifications. *(1) Significant modifications are treated as exchanges of obligations.* If an obligation is significantly modified in a manner or under circumstances other than those described in paragraph (b)(3) of this section, then the modified obligation is treated as one that was newly issued in exchange for the unmodified obligation that it replaced. Consequently—

(i) If such a significant modification occurs after the obligation has been contributed to the REMIC and the modified obligation is not a qualified replacement mortgage, the modified obligation will not be a qualified mortgage and the deemed disposition of the unmodified obligation will be a prohibited transaction under section 860F(a)(2); and

(ii) If such a significant modification occurs before the obligation is contributed to the REMIC, the modified obligation will be viewed as having been originated on the date the modification occurs for purposes of the tests set out in paragraph (a)(1) of this section.

(2) Significant modification defined. For purposes of paragraph (b)(1) of this section, a "significant modification" is any change in the terms of an obligation that would be treated as an exchange of obligations under section 1001 and the related regulations.

(3) Exceptions. For purposes of paragraph (b)(1) of this section, the following changes in the terms of an obligation are not significant modifications regardless of whether they would be significant modifications under paragraph (b)(2) of this section—

(i) Changes in the terms of the obligation occasioned by default or a reasonably foreseeable default;

(ii) Assumption of the obligation;

(iii) Waiver of a due-on-sale clause or a due on encumbrance clause; and

(iv) Conversion of an interest rate by a mortgagor pursuant to the terms of a convertible mortgage.

(4) Modifications that are not significant modifications. If an obligation is modified and the modification is not a significant modification for purposes of paragraph (b)(1) of this section, then the modified obligation is not treated as one that was newly originated on the date of modification.

(5) Assumption defined. For purposes of paragraph (b)(3) of this section, a mortgage has been assumed if—

(i) The buyer of the mortgaged property acquires the property subject to the mortgage, without assuming any personal liability;

(ii) The buyer becomes liable for the debt but the seller also remains liable; or

(iii) The buyer becomes liable for the debt and the seller is released by the lender.

(6) Pass-thru certificates. If a REMIC holds as a qualified mortgage a pass-thru certificate or other investment trust interest of the type described in paragraph (a)(5) of this section, the modification of a mortgage loan that backs the pass-thru certificate or other interest is not a modification of the pass-thru certificate or other interest unless the investment trust structure was created to avoid the prohibited transaction rules of section 860F(a).

(c) Treatment of certain credit enhancement contracts. *(1) In general.* A credit enhancement contract (as defined in paragraph (c)(2) and (3) of this section) is not treated as a separate asset of the REMIC for purposes of the asset test set out in section 860D(a)(4) and § 1.860D-1(b)(3), but instead is treated as part of the mortgage or pool of mortgages to which it relates. Furthermore, any collateral supporting a credit enhancement contract is not treated as an asset of the REMIC solely because it supports the guarantee represented by that contract. See paragraph (g)(1)(ii) of this section for the treatment of payments made pursuant to credit enhancement contracts as payments received under a qualified mortgage.

(2) Credit enhancement contracts. For purposes of this section, a credit enhancement contract is any arrangement whereby a person agrees to guarantee full or partial payment of the principal or interest payable on a qualified mortgage or on a pool of such mortgages, or full or partial payment on one or more classes of regular interests or on the class of residual interests, in the event of defaults or delinquencies on qualified mortgages, unanticipated losses or expenses incurred by the REMIC, or lower than expected returns on cash flow investments. Types of credit enhancement contracts may include, but are not limited to, pool insurance contracts, certificate guarantee insurance contracts, letters of credit, guarantees, or agreements whereby the REMIC sponsor, a mortgage servicer, or other third party agrees to make advances described in paragraph (c)(3) of this section.

(3) Arrangements to make certain advances. The arrangements described in this paragraph (c)(3) are credit enhancement contracts regardless of whether, under the terms of the arrangement, the payor is obligated, or merely permitted, to advance funds to the REMIC.

(i) Advances of delinquent principal and interest. An arrangement by a REMIC sponsor, mortgage servicer, or other third party to advance to the REMIC out of its own funds an amount to make up for delinquent payments on qualified mortgages is a credit enhancement contract.

(ii) Advances of taxes, insurance payments, and expenses. An arrangement by a REMIC sponsor, mortgage servicer, or other third party to pay taxes and hazard insurance premiums on, or other expenses incurred to protect the REMIC's security interest in, property securing a qualified mortgage in the event that the mortgagor fails to pay such taxes, insurance premiums, or other expenses is a credit enhancement contract.

(iii) Advances to ease REMIC administration. An agreement by a REMIC sponsor, mortgage servicer, or other third party to advance temporarily to a REMIC amounts payable on qualified mortgages before such amounts are actually due to level out the stream of cash flows to the REMIC or to provide for orderly administration of the REMIC is a credit enhancement contract. For example, if two mortgages in a pool have payment due dates on the twentieth of the month, and all the other mortgages have payment due dates on the first of each month, an agreement by the mortgage servicer to advance to the REMIC on the fifteenth of each month the payments not yet received on the two mortgages together with the amounts received on the other mortgages is a credit enhancement contract.

(4) Deferred payment under a guarantee arrangement. A guarantee arrangement does not fail to qualify as a credit enhancement contract solely because the guarantor, in the

event of a default on a qualified mortgage, has the option of immediately paying to the REMIC the full amount of mortgage principal due on acceleration of the defaulted mortgage, or paying principal and interest to the REMIC according to the original payment schedule for the defaulted mortgage, or according to some other deferred payment schedule. Any deferred payments are payments pursuant to a credit enhancement contract even if the mortgage is foreclosed upon and the guarantor, pursuant to subrogation rights set out in the guarantee arrangement, is entitled to receive immediately the proceeds of foreclosure.

(d) Treatment of certain purchase agreements with respect to convertible mortgages. *(1) In general.* For purposes of sections 860D(a)(4) and 860G(a)(3), a purchase agreement (as described in paragraph (d)(3) of this section) with respect to a convertible mortgage (as described in paragraph (d)(5) of this section) is treated as incidental to the convertible mortgage to which it relates. Consequently, the purchase agreement is part of the mortgage or pool of mortgages and is not a separate asset of the REMIC.

(2) Treatment of amounts received under purchase agreements. For purposes of sections 860A through 860G and for purposes of determining the accrual of original issue discount and market discount under sections 1272(a)(6) and 1276, respectively, a payment under a purchase agreement described in paragraph (d)(3) of this section is treated as a prepayment in full of the mortgage to which it relates. Thus, for example, a payment under a purchase agreement with respect to a qualified mortgage is considered a payment received under a qualified mortgage within the meaning of section 860G(a)(6) and the transfer of the mortgage is not a disposition of the mortgage within the meaning of section 860F(a)(2)(A).

(3) Purchase agreement. A purchase agreement is a contract between the holder of a convertible mortgage and a third party under which the holder agrees to sell and the third party agrees to buy the mortgage for an amount equal to its current principal balance plus accrued but unpaid interest if and when the mortgagor elects to convert the terms of the mortgage.

(4) Default by the person obligated to purchase a convertible mortgage. If the person required to purchase a convertible mortgage defaults on its obligation to purchase the mortgage upon conversion, the REMIC may sell the mortgage in a market transaction and the proceeds of the sale will be treated as amounts paid pursuant to a purchase agreement.

(5) Convertible mortgage. A convertible mortgage is a mortgage that gives the obligor the right at one or more times during the term of the mortgage to elect to convert from one interest rate to another. The new rate of interest must be determined pursuant to the terms of the instrument and must be intended to approximate a market rate of interest for newly originated mortgages at the time of the conversion.

(e) Prepayment interest shortfalls. An agreement by a mortgage servicer or other third party to make payments to the REMIC to make up prepayment interest shortfalls is not treated as a separate asset of the REMIC and payments made pursuant to such an agreement are treated as payments on the qualified mortgages. With respect to any mortgage that prepays, the prepayment interest shortfall for the accrual period in which the mortgage prepays is an amount equal to the excess of the interest that would have accrued on the mortgage during that accrual period had it not prepaid, over the interest that accrued from the beginning of that accrual period up to the date of the prepayment.

(f) Defective obligations. *(1) Defective obligation defined.* For purposes of sections 860G(a)(4)(B)(ii) and 860F(a)(2), a defective obligation is a mortgage subject to any of the following defects.

(i) The mortgage is in default, or a default with respect to the mortgage is reasonably foreseeable.

(ii) The mortgage was fraudulently procured by the mortgagor.

(iii) The mortgage was not in fact principally secured by an interest in real property within the meaning of paragraph (a)(1) of this section.

(iv) The mortgage does not conform to a customary representation or warranty given by the sponsor or prior owner of the mortgage regarding the characteristics of the mortgage, or the characteristics of the pool of mortgages of which the mortgage is a part. A representation that payments on a qualified mortgage will be received at a rate no less than a specified minimum or no greater than a specified maximum is not customary for this purpose.

(2) Effect of discovery of defect. If a REMIC discovers that an obligation is a defective obligation, and if the defect is one that, had it been discovered before the startup day, would have prevented the obligation from being a qualified mortgage, then, unless the REMIC either causes the defect to be cured or disposes of the defective obligation within 90 days of discovering the defect, the obligation ceases to be a qualified mortgage at the end of that 90 day period. Even if the defect is not cured, the defective obligation is, nevertheless, a qualified mortgage from the startup day through the end of the 90 day period. Moreover, even if the REMIC holds the defective obligation beyond the 90 day period, the REMIC may, nevertheless, exchange the defective obligation for a qualified replacement mortgage so long as the requirements of section 860G(a)(4)(B) are satisfied. If the defect is one that does not affect the status of an obligation as a qualified mortgage, then the obligation is always a qualified mortgage regardless of whether the defect is or can be cured. For example, if a sponsor represented that all mortgages transferred to a REMIC had a 10 percent interest rate, but it was later discovered that one mortgage had a 9 percent interest rate, the 9 percent mortgage is defective, but the defect does not affect the status of that obligation as a qualified mortgage.

(g) Permitted investments. *(1) Cash flow investment.* (i) In general. For purposes of section 860G(a)(6) and this section, a cash flow investment is an investment of payments received on qualified mortgages for a temporary period between receipt of those payments and the regularly scheduled date for distribution of those payments to REMIC interest holders. Cash flow investments must be passive investments earning a return in the nature of interest.

(ii) Payments received on qualified mortgages. For purposes of paragraph (g)(1) of this section, the term "payments received on qualified mortgages" includes—

(A) Payments of interest and principal on qualified mortgages, including prepayments of principal and payments under credit enhancement contracts described in paragraph (c)(2) of this section;

(B) Proceeds from the disposition of qualified mortgages;

(C) Cash flows from foreclosure property and proceeds from the disposition of such property;

(D) A payment by a sponsor or prior owner in lieu of the sponsor's or prior owner's repurchase of a defective obligation, as defined in paragraph (f) of this section, that was transferred to the REMIC in breach of a customary warranty; and

(E) Prepayment penalties required to be paid under the terms of a qualified mortgage when the mortgagor prepays the obligation.

(iii) Temporary period. For purposes of section 860G(a)(6) and this paragraph (g)(1), a temporary period generally is that period from the time a REMIC receives payments on qualified mortgages and permitted investments to the time the REMIC distributes the payments to interest holders. A temporary period may not exceed 13 months. Thus, an investment held by a REMIC for more than 13 months is not a cash flow investment. In determining the length of time that a REMIC has held an investment that is part of a commingled fund or account, the REMIC may employ any reasonable method of accounting. For example, if a REMIC holds mortgage cash flows in a commingled account pending distribution, the first-in, first-out method of accounting is a reasonable method for determining whether all or part of the account satisfies the 13 month limitation.

(2) Qualified reserve funds. The term qualified reserve fund means any reasonably required reserve to provide for full payment of expenses of the REMIC or amounts due on regular or residual interests in the event of defaults on qualified mortgages, prepayment interest shortfalls (as defined in paragraph (e) of this section), lower than expected returns on cash flow investments, or any other contingency that could be provided for under a credit enhancement contract (as defined in paragraph (c)(2) and (3) of this section).

(3) Qualified reserve asset. (i) In general. The term "qualified reserve asset" means any intangible property (other than a REMIC residual interest) that is held both for investment and as part of a qualified reserve fund. An asset need not generate any income to be a qualified reserve asset.

(ii) Reasonably required reserve. (A) In general. In determining whether the amount of a reserve is reasonable, it is appropriate to consider the credit quality of the qualified mortgages, the extent and nature of any guarantees relating to either the qualified mortgages or the regular and residual interests, the expected amount of expenses of the REMIC, and the expected availability of proceeds from qualified mortgages to pay the expenses. To the extent that a reserve exceeds a reasonably required amount, the amount of the reserve must be promptly and appropriately reduced. If at any time, however, the amount of the reserve fund is less than is reasonably required, the amount of the reserve fund may be increased by the addition of payments received on qualified mortgages or by contributions from holders of residual interests.

(B) Presumption that a reserve is reasonably required. The amount of a reserve fund is presumed to be reasonable (and an excessive reserve is presumed to have been promptly and appropriately reduced) if it does not exceed—

(1) The amount required by a nationally recognized independent rating agency as a condition of providing the rating for REMIC interests desired by the sponsor; or

(2) The amount required by a third party insurer or guarantor, who does not own directly or indirectly (within the meaning of section 267(c)) an interest in the REMIC (as defined in § 1.860D-1(b)(1)), as a condition of providing credit enhancement.

(C) Presumption may be rebutted. The presumption in paragraph (g)(3)(ii)(B) of this section may be rebutted if the amounts required by the rating agency or by the third party insurer are not commercially reasonable considering the factors described in paragraph (g)(3)(ii)(A) of this section.

(h) Outside reserve funds. A reserve fund that is maintained to pay expenses of the REMIC, or to make payments to REMIC interest holders is an outside reserve fund and not an asset of the REMIC only if the REMIC's organizational documents clearly and expressly—

(1) Provide that the reserve fund is an outside reserve fund and not an asset of the REMIC;

(2) Identify the owner(s) of the reserve fund, either by name, or by description of the class (e.g., subordinated regular interest holders) whose membership comprises the owners of the fund; and

(3) Provide that, for all Federal tax purposes, amounts transferred by the REMIC to the fund are treated as amounts distributed by the REMIC to the designated owner(s) or transferees of the designated owner(s).

(i) Contractual rights coupled with regular interests in tiered arrangements. *(1) In general.* If a REMIC issues a regular interest to a trustee of an investment trust for the benefit of the trust certificate holders and the trustee also holds for the benefit of those certificate holders certain other contractual rights, those other rights are not treated as assets of the REMIC even if the investment trust and the REMIC were created contemporaneously pursuant to a single set of organizational documents. The organizational documents must, however, require that the trustee account for the contractual rights as property that the trustee holds separate and apart from the regular interest.

(2) Example. The following example, which describes a tiered arrangement involving a pass-thru trust that is intended to qualify as a REMIC and a pass-thru trust that is intended to be classified as a trust under § 301.7701-4(c) of this chapter, illustrates the provisions of paragraph (i)(1) of this section.

Example. (i) A sponsor transferred a pool of mortgages to a trustee in exchange for two classes of certificates. The pool of mortgages has an aggregate principal balance of $100x. Each mortgage in the pool provides for interest payments based on the eleventh district cost of funds index (hereinafter COFI) plus a margin. The trust (hereinafter REMIC trust) issued a Class N bond, which the sponsor designates as a regular interest, that has a principal amount of $100x and that provides for interest payments at a rate equal to One-Year LIBOR plus 100 basis points, subject to a cap equal to the weighted average pool rate. The Class R interest, which the sponsor designated as the residual interest, entitles its holder to all funds left in the trust after the Class N bond has been retired. The Class R interest holder is not entitled to current distributions.

(ii) On the same day, and under the same set of documents, the sponsor also created an investment trust. The sponsor contributed to the investment trust the Class N bond together with an interest rate cap contract. Under the interest rate cap contract, the issuer of the cap contract agrees to pay to the trustee for the benefit of the investment trust certificate holders the excess of One-Year LIBOR plus 100 basis points over the weighted average pool rate (COFI plus a margin) times the outstanding principal balance of the Class N bond in the event One-Year LIBOR plus 100 basis points ever exceeds the weighted average pool rate. The trustee (the same institution that serves as REMIC trust trustee), in exchange for the contributed assets, gave the sponsor certificates representing undivided beneficial ownership interests in the Class N bond and the interest rate cap contract. The organizational documents require the trustee to account for the regular interest and the cap contract as discrete property rights.

(iii) The separate existence of the REMIC trust and the investment trust are respected for all Federal income tax purposes. Thus, the interest rate cap contract is an asset beneficially owned by the several certificate holders and is not an asset of the REMIC trust. Consequently, each certificate holder must allocate its purchase price for the certificate between its undivided interest in the Class N bond and its undivided interest in the interest rate cap contract in accordance with the relative fair market values of those two property rights.

(j) Clean-up call. *(1) In general.* For purposes of section 860F(a)(5)(B), a clean-up call is the redemption of a class of regular interests when, by reason of prior payments with respect to those interests, the administrative costs associated with servicing that class outweigh the benefits of maintaining the class. Factors to consider in making this determination include—

(i) The number of holders of that class of regular interests;

(ii) The frequency of payments to holders of that class;

(iii) The effect the redemption will have on the yield of that class of regular interests;

(iv) The outstanding principal balance of that class; and

(v) The percentage of the original principal balance of that class still outstanding.

(2) Interest rate changes. The redemption of a class of regular interests undertaken to profit from a change in interest rates is not a clean-up call.

(3) Safe harbor. Although the outstanding principal balance is only one factor to consider, the redemption of a class of regular interests with an outstanding principal balance of no more than 10 percent of its original principal balance is always a clean-up call.

(k) Startup day. The term "startup day" means the day on which the REMIC issues all of its regular and residual interests. A sponsor may, however, contribute property to a REMIC in exchange for regular and residual interests over any period of 10 consecutive days and the REMIC may designate any one of those 10 days as its startup day. The day so designated is then the startup day, and all interests are treated as issued on that day.

T.D. 8458, 12/23/92.

PAR. 4. Section 1.860G-2 is amended by:

1. Revising paragraphs (a)(8), (b)(3)(iii) and (b)(3)(iv).

2. Adding paragraphs (b)(3)(v), (b)(3)(vi) and (b)(7).

The additions and revisions read as follows:

Proposed § 1.860G-2 Other rules. [*For Preamble, see ¶ 152,929*]

(a) * * *

(8) Release of interest in real property securing a qualified mortgage; defeasance. If a REMIC releases its lien on real property that secures a qualified mortgage, that mortgage ceases to be a qualified mortgage on the date the lien is released unless—

(i) The REMIC releases its lien pursuant to a modification described in paragraph (b)(3)(v) of this section addressing changes to the collateral for, guarantees on, or other form of credit enhancement on a mortgage; or

(ii) The mortgage is defeased in the following manner—

(A) The mortgagor pledges substitute collateral that consists solely of government securities (as defined in section 2(a)(16) of the Investment Company Act of 1940 as amended (15 U.S.C. 80a-1));

(B) The mortgage documents allow such a substitution;

(C) The lien is released to facilitate the disposition of the property or any other customary commercial transaction, and not as part of an arrangement to collateralize a REMIC offering with obligations that are not real estate mortgages; and

(D) The release is not within 2 years of the startup day.

* * * * *

(b) * * *

(3) * * *

(iii) Waiver of a due-on-sale clause or a due on encumbrance clause;

(iv) Conversion of an interest rate by a mortgagor pursuant to the terms of a convertible mortgage;

(v) A modification that releases, substitutes, adds or otherwise alters a substantial amount of the collateral for, a guarantee on, or other form of credit enhancement for a recourse or nonrecourse obligation, so long as the obligation continues to be principally secured by an interest in real property following such release, substitution, addition or other alteration; and

(vi) A change in the nature of the obligation from recourse (or substantially all recourse) to nonrecourse (or substantially all nonrecourse), so long as the obligation continues to be principally secured by an interest in real property following such a change.

* * * * *

(7) Principally secured test; appraisal requirement. For purposes of paragraph (b)(3)(v) and (vi) of this section, in determining whether an obligation continues to be principally secured by an interest in real property, the fair market value of the interest in real property securing the obligation, determined as of the date of the modification, must be equal to at least 80 percent of the adjusted issue price of the modified obligation, determined as of the date of the modification. For purposes of this test, the fair market value of the interest in real property securing the obligation must be determined by an appraisal performed by an independent appraiser.

* * * * *

§ 1.860G-3 Treatment of foreign persons.

(a) Transfer of a residual interest with tax avoidance potential. *(1) In general.* A transfer of a residual interest that has tax avoidance potential is disregarded for all Federal tax purposes if the transferee is a foreign person. Thus, if a residual interest with tax avoidance potential is transferred to a foreign holder at formation of the REMIC, the sponsor is liable for the tax on any excess inclusion that accrues with respect to that residual interest.

(2) Tax avoidance potential. (i) Defined. A residual interest has tax avoidance potential for purposes of this section unless, at the time of the transfer, the transferor reasonably expects that, for each excess inclusion, the REMIC will distribute to the transferee residual interest holder an amount that will equal at least 30 percent of the excess inclusion, and that each such amount will be distributed at or after the time at which the excess inclusion accrues and not later than

the close of the calendar year following the calendar year of accrual.

(ii) Safe harbor. For purposes of paragraph (a)(2)(i) of this section, a transferor has a reasonable expectation if the 30-percent test would be satisfied were the REMIC's qualified mortgages to prepay at each rate within a range of rates from 50 percent to 200 percent of the rate assumed under section 1272(a)(6) with respect to the qualified mortgages (or the rate that would have been assumed had the mortgages been issued with original issue discount).

(3) Effectively connected income. Paragraph (a)(1) of this section will not apply if the transferee's income from the residual interest is subject to tax under section 871(b) or section 882.

(4) Transfer by a foreign holder. If a foreign person transfers a residual interest to a United States person or a foreign holder in whose hands the income from a residual interest would be effectively connected income, and if the transfer has the effect of allowing the transferor to avoid tax on accrued excess inclusions, then the transfer is disregarded and the transferor continues to be treated as the owner of the residual interest for purposes of section 871(a), 881, 1441, or 1442.

(b) Accounting for REMIC net income. [Reserved]. For further guidance, see § 1.860G-3T(b).

T.D. 8458, 12/23/92, amend T.D. 9272, 7/31/2006.

PAR. 3: In § 1.860G-3, paragraph (b) is added to read as follows:

Proposed § 1.860G-3 Treatment of foreign persons. [*For Preamble, see ¶ 152,777*]

* * * * *

(b) [The text of the proposed amendment to § 1.860G-3(b) is the same as the text of § 1.860G-3T(b) published elsewhere in this issue of the Federal Register].

§ 1.860G-3T Treatment of foreign persons (temporary).

(a) [Reserved]. For further guidance, see § 1.860G-3(a).

(b) Accounting for REMIC net income. *(1) Allocation of partnership income to a foreign partner.* A domestic partnership shall separately state its allocable share of REMIC taxable income or net loss in accordance with § 1.702-1(a)(8). If a domestic partnership allocates all or some portion of its allocable share of REMIC taxable income to a partner that is a foreign person, the amount allocated to the foreign partner shall be taken into account by the foreign partner for purposes of sections 871(a), 881, 1441, and 1442 as if that amount were received on the last day of the partnership's taxable year, except to the extent that some or all of the amount is required to be taken into account by the foreign partner at an earlier time under section 860G(b) as a result of a distribution by the partnership to the foreign partner or a disposition of the foreign partner's indirect interest in the REMIC residual interest. A disposition in whole or in part of the foreign partner's indirect interest in the REMIC residual interest may occur as a result of a termination of the REMIC, a disposition of the partnership's residual interest in the REMIC, a disposition of the foreign partner's interest in the partnership, or any other reduction in the foreign partner's allocable share of the portion of the REMIC net income or deduction allocated to the partnership. See § 1.871-14(d)(2) for the treatment of interest received on a regular or residual interest in a REMIC. For a partnership's withholding obligations with respect to excess inclusion amounts described in this paragraph (b)(1), see § 1.1441-2T(b)(5), § 1.1441-2T(d)(4), § 1.1441-5(b)(2)(i)(A) and §§ 1.1446-1 through 1.1446-7.

(2) Excess inclusion income allocated by certain pass-through entities to a foreign person. If an amount is allocated under section 860E(d)(1) to a foreign person that is a shareholder of a real estate investment trust or a regulated investment company, a participant in a common trust fund, or a patron of an organization to which part I of subchapter T applies and if the amount so allocated is governed by section 860E(d)(2) (treating it "as an excess inclusion with respect to a residual interest held by" the taxpayer), the amount shall be taken into account for purposes of sections 871(a), 881, 1441, and 1442 at the same time as the time prescribed for other income of the shareholder, participant, or patron from the trust, company, fund, or organization.

T.D. 9272, 7/31/2006.

Proposed § 1.860H-0 Table of contents. [*For Preamble, see ¶ 152,047*]

This section lists captions that appear in §§ 1.860H-1 through 1.860L-4.

§ 1.860H-1 FASIT defined, FASIT election, other definitions.

(a) FASIT defined.

(b) FASIT election.

(1) Person that makes the election.

(2) Form of election.

(3) Time for filing election.

(4) Contents of election.

(5) Required signatures.

(6) Special rules regarding startup day.

(c) General definitions.

(1) Owner.

(2) Transfer.

§ 1.860H-2 Assets permitted to be held by a FASIT.

(a) Substantially all.

(b) Permitted debt instrument.

(1) In general.

(2) Special rules for short-term debt instruments issued by the Owner or related person.

(3) Exceptions.

(c) Cash and cash equivalents.

(d) Hedges and guarantees.

(1) In general.

(2) Referencing other than permitted assets.

(3) Association with particular assets or regular interests.

(4) Creating an investment prohibited.

(e) Hedges and guarantees issued by Owner (or related person).

(1) Hedges.

(2) Guarantees.

(f) Foreclosure property.

(g) Special rule for contracts or agreements in the nature of a line of credit.

(h) Contracts to acquire hedges or debt instruments.

§ 1.860H-3 Cessation of a FASIT.

Proposed § 1.860H-1 FASIT defined, FASIT election, other definitions. [*For Preamble, see ¶ 152,047*]

(a) FASIT defined. *(1)* A FASIT is a qualified arrangement (as defined in paragraph (a)(2) of this section) that meets the requirements of section 860L(a)(1) and the FASIT regulations (as defined in paragraph (c) of this section). A qualified arrangement fails to meet the requirements of section 860L(a)(1) unless it has one and only one ownership interest and that ownership interest is held by one and only one eligible corporation (as defined in section 860L(a)(2)).

(2) Except as provided in paragraph (a)(3) of this section, a qualified arrangement is an arrangement that is either—

(i) An entity (other than a regulated investment company as defined in section 851(a)); or

(ii) A segregated pool of assets if—

(A) The initial assets of the pool are clearly identified, such as through an indenture; and

(B) Changes in the assets of the pool are clearly identified, such as through instruments of conveyance or release.

(3) Notwithstanding paragraph (a)(2) of this section, a qualified arrangement does not include—

(i) An entity created or organized under the law of a foreign country or a possession of the United States;

(ii) An entity any of the income of which is or ever has been subject to net tax by a foreign country or a possession of the United States; or

(iii) A segregated pool of assets any of the income of which at any time is subject to net tax by a foreign country or a possession of the United States.

(b) FASIT election. *(1) Person that makes the election.* For a qualified arrangement to be a FASIT an eligible corporation (as defined in section 860L(a)(2)) must make the election required under section 860L(a)(1)(A).

(i) If the qualified arrangement is an entity described in paragraph (a)(2)(i) of this section, the eligible corporation making the election must hold one or more interests in the entity, and one of those interests must be the interest designated as the FASIT's ownership interest.

(ii) If the qualified arrangement is a segregated pool of assets described in paragraph (a)(2)(ii) of this section, the eligible corporation making the election must be the first taxpayer to be treated as the Owner of the resulting FASIT.

(2) Form of election. Unless the Commissioner prescribes otherwise, a FASIT election is made by means of a statement attached to the Federal income tax return of the eligible corporation making the election.

(3) Time for filing election. The statement referred to in paragraph (b)(2) of this section must be attached to a timely filed (including extensions) original Federal income tax return for the eligible corporation's taxable year in which the FASIT's startup day occurs. An election may not be made on an amended return.

(4) Contents of election. The statement referred to in paragraph (b)(2) of this section must include—

(i) For other than a segregated pool of assets, the name, address, and taxpayer identification number of the arrangement (if one was issued prior to the making of the election);

(ii) For a segregated pool of assets, the following information—

(A) The name, address, and taxpayer identification number of the person or persons holding legal title to the pool of assets;

(B) The name, address, and taxpayer identification number of the person or persons that, immediately before the startup day, are considered to own the pool for Federal income tax purposes; and

(C) Information describing the origin of the pool (including the caption and date of execution of any instruments of indenture or similar documents that govern the pool);

(iii) The startup day; and

(iv) The name and title of all persons signing the statement.

(5) Required signatures. The statement referred to in paragraph (b)(2) of this section must be signed by the authorized person, described in this paragraph (b)(5).

(i) For other than a segregated pool of assets, the authorized person is any person authorized to sign the qualified arrangement's Federal income tax return in the absence of a FASIT election. For example, if a qualified arrangement is a corporation or trust under applicable state law, an authorized person is a corporate officer or trustee, respectively.

(ii) For a segregated pool of assets, the authorized person is each person who, for Federal income tax purposes, owns the assets of the pool immediately before the earlier of the date on which—

(A) An outstanding interest in the pool is designated as a regular or ownership interest in a FASIT; or

(B) The pool issues an interest designated at the time of issuance as a regular or ownership interest in a FASIT.

(6) Special rule regarding startup day. The startup day must be a day on which the eligible corporation making the election is described in paragraph (b)(1)(i) or (ii) of this section.

(c) General definitions. For purposes of the regulations issued under part V of subchapter M of chapter 1 of subtitle A of the Internal Revenue Code (the FASIT regulations)—

(1) Owner means the eligible corporation that holds the interest described in section 860L(b)(2);

(2) Transfer includes a sale, contribution, endorsement, or other conveyance of a legal or beneficial interest in property.

Proposed § 1.860H-2 Assets permitted to be held by a FASIT. [*For Preamble, see ¶ 152,047*]

(a) Substantially all. For purposes of section 860L(a)(1)(D), substantially all of the assets held by a FASIT consist of permitted assets if the total adjusted bases of the permitted assets is more than 99 percent of the total adjusted bases of all the assets held by the FASIT, including those assets deemed to be held under section 860I(b)(2).

(b) Permitted debt instrument. *(1) In general.* Except as otherwise provided, a debt instrument is described in section 860L(c)(1)(B) only if it is a permitted debt instrument. For purposes of the FASIT regulations, a permitted debt instrument is—

(i) A fixed rate debt instrument, including a debt instrument having more than one payment schedule for which a single yield can be determined under § 1.1272-1(c) or (d);

(ii) A variable rate debt instrument within the meaning of § 1.1275-5 if the debt instrument provides for interest at a qualified floating rate within the meaning of § 1.1275-5(b);

(iii) A REMIC regular interest;

(iv) A FASIT regular interest (including a FASIT regular interest issued by anotherFASIT in which the Owner (or a related person) holds an ownership interest);

(v) An inflation-indexed debt instrument as defined in § 1.1275-7;

(vi) Any receivable generated through an extension of credit under a revolving credit agreement (such as a credit card account);

(vii) A stripped bond or stripped coupon (as defined in section 1286(e)(2) and (3)), if the debt instrument from which the stripped bond or stripped coupon is created is described in paragraphs (b)(1)(i) through (vi) of this section; and

(viii) A certificate of trust representing a beneficial ownership interest in a debt instrument described in paragraphs (b)(1)(i) through (vii) of this section.

(2) Special rules for short-term debt instruments issued by the Owner or related person. Notwithstanding section 860L(c)(2) and paragraph (b)(3)(iii) of this section, a debt instrument issued by the Owner (or a related person) is a permitted debt instrument if it—

(i) Is described in paragraph (b)(1)(i) or (ii) of this section;

(ii) Has an original stated maturity of 270 days or less;

(iii) Is rated at least investment quality by a nationally recognized statistical rating organization that is not a related person of the issuer; and

(iv) Is acquired to temporarily invest cash awaiting either reinvestment in permitted assets not described in this paragraph (b)(2), or distribution to the Owner or holders of one or more FASIT regular interests.

(3) Exceptions. Notwithstanding paragraph (b)(1) of this section, the following debt instruments are not permitted assets.

(i) Equity-linked debt instrument. A debt instrument is not a permitted asset if the debt instrument contains a provision that permits the instrument to be converted into, or exchanged for, any legal or beneficial ownership interest in any asset other than a permitted debt instrument (such as a debt instrument that is exchangeable for an interest in a partnership). Similarly, a debt instrument is not a permitted asset if the debt instrument contains a provision under which one or more payments on the instrument are determined by reference to, or are contingent upon, the value of any asset other than a permitted debt instrument (such as a debt instrument containing a provision under which one or more payments on the instrument are determined by reference to, or are contingent upon, the value of stock).

(ii) Defaulted debt instrument. A debt instrument is not a permitted asset if, on the date the debt instrument is acquired by the FASIT, the debt instrument is in default due to the debtor's failure to have timely made one or more of the payments owed on the debt instrument and the Owner has no reasonable expectation that all delinquent payments on the debt instrument, including any interest and penalties thereon, will be fully paid on or before the date that is 90 days after the date the instrument is first held by the FASIT.

(iii) Owner debt. A debt instrument is not a permitted asset if the debt instrument is issued by the Owner (or a related person) and the debt instrument does not qualify as a permitted debt instrument under paragraphs (b)(1)(iv) or (2) of this section.

(iv) Certain Owner-guaranteed debt. A debt instrument is not a permitted asset if the debt instrument is guaranteed by the Owner (or a related person) and, based on all of the facts and circumstances existing at the time the guarantee is given, or at the time the FASIT acquires the guaranteed debt instrument the Owner (or a related person) is, in substance, the primary obligor on the debt instrument. For this purpose, a guarantee includes any promise to pay in the case of the default or imminent default of any debt instrument.

(v) Debt instrument linked to the Owner's credit. A debt instrument that is issued by a person other than the Owner (or a related person) is not a permitted asset if the timing or amount of payments on the instrument are determined by reference to, or are contingent on, the timing or amount of payments made on a debt instrument issued by the Owner (or a related person).

(vi) Partial interests in non-permitted debt instruments. A debt instrument is not a permitted asset if the debt instrument is a partial interest such a stripped bond or stripped coupon (as defined in section 1286(e)) in a debt instrument described in paragraphs (b)(3)(i) through (v) of this section.

(vii) Certain Foreign Debt Subject to Withholding Tax. A debt instrument is not a permitted asset if the debt instrument is traded on an established securities market (within the meaning of § 1.860I-2) and interest on the debt instrument is subject to any tax determined on a gross basis (such as a withholding tax) other than a tax which is in the nature of a prepayment of a tax imposed on a net basis.

(c) Cash and cash equivalents. For purposes of section 860L(c)(1)(A) and the FASIT regulations, the term cash and cash equivalents means—

(1) The United States dollar;

(2) A currency other than the United States dollar if the currency is received as payment on a permitted asset described in § 1.860H-2, or the currency is required by the FASIT to make a payment on a regular interest issued by the FASIT according to the terms of the regular interest;

(3) A debt instrument if it—

(i) Is described—

(A) In paragraphs (b)(1)(i), (ii), or (v) of this section, or

(B) In paragraph (b)(vii) of this section if it is created from an instrument described in paragraphs (b)(1)(i), (ii), or (v) of this section;

(ii) Has a remaining maturity of 270 days or less; and

(iii) Is rated at least investment quality by a nationally recognized statistical rating organization that is not a related person to the issuer; and

(4) Shares in a U.S.-dollar-denominated money market fund (as defined in 17 CFR 270.2a-7).

(d) Hedges and guarantees. *(1) In general.* Subject to the rules in paragraphs (d)(2) through (4) of this section, a hedge or guarantee contract is described in section 860L(c)(1)(D) (a permitted hedge) only if the hedge or guarantee contract is reasonably required to offset any differences that any risk factor may cause between the amount or timing of the receipts on assets the FASIT holds (or expects to hold) and the amount or timing of the payments on the regular interests the FASIT has issued (or expects to issue). For purposes of this paragraph (d), the risk factors are—

(i) Fluctuations in market interest rates;

(ii) Fluctuations in currency exchange rates;

(iii) The credit quality of, or default on, the FASIT's assets or debt instruments underlying the FASIT's assets; and

(iv) The receipt of payments on the FASIT's assets earlier or later than originally anticipated.

(2) Referencing other than permitted assets. A hedge or guarantee contract is not a permitted hedge if it references an asset other than a permitted asset or if it references an index, economic indicator, or financial average, that is not both widely disseminated and designed to correlate closely with changes in one or more of the risk factors described in paragraphs (d)(1)(i) through (iv) of this section.

(3) Association with particular assets or regular interests. A hedge or guarantee contract need not be associated with any of the FASIT's assets or regular interests, or any group of its assets or regular interests, if the hedge or guarantee contract offsets the differences described in paragraph (d)(1) of this section.

(4) Creating an investment prohibited. A hedge or guarantee contract is not a permitted hedge if at the time the hedge or guarantee is entered into, it in substance creates an investment in the FASIT.

(e) Hedges and guarantees issued by Owner (or related person). *(1) Hedges.* A hedge contract issued by the Owner (or a related person) is a permitted asset only if—

(i) The contract is a permitted hedge other than a guarantee contract;

(ii) The Owner (or the related person) regularly provides, offers, or sells substantially similar contracts in the ordinary course of its trade or business;

(iii) On the date the contract is acquired by the FASIT (and on any later date that it is substantially modified) its terms are consistent with the terms that would apply in the case of an arm's length transaction between unrelated parties; and

(iv) The Owner maintains records that—

(A) Show the terms of the contract are consistent with the terms that would apply in the case of an arm's length transaction between unrelated parties; and

(B) Explain how the Owner (or related person) determined the consideration for the contract.

(2) Guarantees. A guarantee contract issued by the Owner (or a related person) is a permitted asset only if—

(i) The contract is a permitted hedge and satisfies paragraphs (e)(1)(iii) and (iv) of this section;

(ii) The contract is a credit enhancement contract under § 1.860G-2(c); and

(iii) Immediately after the contract is acquired by the FASIT (and on any later date that it is substantially modified), the value (determined under section 860I and § 1.860I-2) of all the FASIT's guarantee contracts issued by the Owner (and related persons) is less than 3 percent of the value (determined under section 860I and § 1.860I-2) of all the FASIT's assets.

(f) Foreclosure property. Property acquired in connection with the default or imminent default of a debt instrument held by a FASIT may qualify both as foreclosure property under section 860L(c)(1)(C) and as another type of permitted asset under section 860L(c)(1). If foreclosure property qualifies as another type of permitted asset, the FASIT may hold the property beyond the grace period prescribed for foreclosure property under section 860L(c)(3). In this case, immediately after the grace period ends, the taxpayer must recognize gain, if any, as if the property had been contributed by the Owner to the FASIT on that date. See § 1.860I-1(a)(1)(iii). In addition, after the close of the grace period, disposition of the property is subject to the prohibited transactions tax imposed under section 860L(e) without the benefit of the exception for foreclosure property.

(g) Special rule for contracts or agreements in the nature of a line of credit. For purposes of section 860L(c)(1), the term permitted asset includes a lender's position in a contract or agreement in the nature of a line of credit (other than a contract or agreement that is originated by the FASIT). Such a contract or agreement is not subject to the rules of section 860I(a) at the time the contract or agreement is transferred to the FASIT. Extensions of credit under the contract or agreement are subject to the rules of section 860I(a) at the time the extension is made. See section 860I(d)(2). To determine whether a contract or agreement is originated by a FASIT, see § 1.860L-1.

(h) Contracts to acquire hedges or debt instruments. A contract is not described in section 860L(c)(1)(E) if it is an agreement under which the Owner (or a related person) agrees to transfer permitted hedges or permitted debt instruments to a FASIT for less than—

(1) Fair market value, in the case of hedges or debt instruments traded on an established securities market (as defined in § 1.860I-2); or

(2) Ninety percent of their value, as determined under section 860I(d)(1)(A) and the FASIT regulations, in the case of debt instruments not traded on an established securities market.

Proposed § 1.860H-3 Cessation of a FASIT. [*For Preamble, see ¶ 152,047*]

(a) In general. An arrangement ceases to be a FASIT if it revokes its election with the consent of the Commissioner or if it fails to qualify as a FASIT and the Commissioner does not determine the failure to be inadvertent.

(b) Time of cessation. An arrangement ceases to be a FASIT at the close of the day designated by the Commissioner in the consent to revoke, or if there is no consent to revoke or determination of inadvertence, at the close of the day on which the arrangement initially fails to qualify as a FASIT.

(c) Consequences of cessation. Except as otherwise determined by the Commissioner, the consequences of cessation are as follows:

(1) The FASIT and the underlying arrangement. The arrangement that made the FASIT election (the underlying arrangement) is no longer a FASIT and cannot re-elect FASIT treatment without the Commissioner's approval. Immediately after the cessation, the arrangement's classification (for example, as a partnership or corporation) is determined under general principles of Federal income tax law. Immediately after the cessation, the arrangement holds the FASIT's assets with a fair market value basis. Any election the Owner made (other than the FASIT election), and any method of accounting the Owner adopted with respect to those assets, binds the underlying arrangement as if the underlying arrangement itself had made the election or adopted the method of accounting. If the underlying arrangement is a segregated pool of assets, the person holding legal title to the pool is responsible for complying with any tax filing or reporting requirements arising from the pool's operation.

(2) The Owner. (i) The Owner is treated as exchanging the assets of the FASIT for an amount equal to their value (as determined under § 1.860I-2). Gain realized on the exchange is treated as gain from a prohibited transaction and the Owner is subject to the tax imposed by 860L without exception. Loss, if any, is disallowed. The determination of gain or loss on assets for purposes of this paragraph is made on an asset-by-asset basis.

(ii) The Owner must recognize cancellation of indebtedness income in an amount equal to the adjusted issue price of the regular interests outstanding immediately before the cessation over the fair market value of those interests immediately before the cessation. This determination is made on a regular interest by regular interest basis. The Owner cannot take any deduction for acquisition premium.

(iii) If, after the cessation, the Owner has a continuing economic interest in the assets, the characterization of this economic interest (for example, as stock or a partnership interest) is determined under general principles of Federal income tax law. If the Owner has a continuing economic interest in the assets immediately after cessation, the Owner holds the interest with a fair market value basis.

(3) The regular interest holders. Holders of the regular interests are treated as exchanging their regular interests for interests in the underlying arrangement. Interests in the underlying arrangement are classified (for example, as debt or equity) under general principles of Federal income tax law. Gain must be recognized if a regular interest is exchanged

either for an interest not classified as debt or for an interest classified as debt that differs materially either in kind or extent. No loss may be recognized on the exchange. The basis of an interest in the underlying arrangement equals the basis in the regular interest exchanged for it, increased by any gain recognized on the exchange under this paragraph (c)(3).

(d) Disregarding inadvertent failures to remain qualified. *(1)* If a qualified arrangement that ceases to be a FASIT meets the requirements of paragraph (d)(2) of this section, then the Commissioner may either—

(i) Deem the qualified arrangement as continuing to be a FASIT notwithstanding the cessation; or

(ii) Allow the qualified arrangement to re-elect FASIT status after cessation notwithstanding the prohibition in section 860L(a)(4).

(2) The requirements of this paragraph are satisfied if—

(i) The Commissioner determines that the cessation was inadvertent;

(ii) No later than a reasonable time after the discovery of the event resulting in the cessation, steps are taken so that all of the requirements for a FASIT are satisfied; and

(iii) The qualified arrangement and each person holding an interest in the qualified arrangement at any time during the period the qualified arrangement failed to qualify as a FASIT agree to make such adjustments (consistent with the treatment of the qualified arrangement as a FASIT or the treatment of the Owner as a C corporation) as the Commissioner may require with respect to such period.

Proposed § 1.860H-4 Regular interests in general. [*For Preamble, see ¶ 152,047*]

(a) Issue price of regular interests. *(1) Regular interests not issued for property.* The issue price of a FASIT regular interest not issued for property is determined under section 1273(b).

(2) Regular interests issued for property. Notwithstanding sections 1273 and 1274 and the regulations thereunder, the issue price of a FASIT regular interest issued for property is the fair market value of the regular interest determined as of the issue date.

(b) Special rules for high-yield regular interests. *(1) High-yield interests held by a securities dealer.* (i) Due date of tax imposed on securities dealer under section 860K(d). The excise tax imposed under section 860K(d) (treatment of high-yield interest held by a securities dealer that is not an eligible corporation) must be paid on or before the due date of the securities dealer's Federal income tax return for the earlier of the taxable year in which the securities dealer—

(A) Ceases to be a dealer in securities; or

(B) Commences holding the high-yield interest for investment.

(ii) [Reserved]

(2) High-yield interests held by a pass-thru. (i) Nature and due date of tax imposed under section 860K(e). The tax imposed under section 860K(e) (treatment of high-yield interest held by a pass-thru entity) is an excise tax which must be paid on or before the due date of the pass-thru entity's Federal income tax return for the taxable year in which the pass-thru entity issues the debt or equity interest described in section 860K(e).

(ii) Pass-thru entity includes REMIC. For purposes of section 860K(e), a pass-thru entity includes a real estate mortgage investment conduit (REMIC) as defined in section 860D.

Proposed § 1.860H-5 Foreign resident holders of regular interests. [*For Preamble, see ¶ 152,047*]

(a) Look-through to underlying FASIT debt. If, during the same period, a foreign resident holds (either directly or through a vehicle which itself is not subject to the Federal income tax such as a partnership or trust) a regular interest in a FASIT and a conduit debtor (as defined in paragraph (b) of this section) pays or accrues interest on a debt instrument held by the FASIT, then any interest received or accrued by the foreign resident with respect to the regular interest during that period is treated as received or accrued from the conduit debtor. This rule applies to both the foreign resident holder of the FASIT regular interest and the conduit debtor for all purposes of subtitle A and the regulations thereunder.

(b) Conduit debtor. A debtor is a conduit debtor if the debtor is a U.S. resident taxpayer or a foreign resident taxpayer to which interest expense paid or accrued with respect to the debt held by the FASIT is treated as paid or accrued by a U.S. trade or business of the foreign taxpayer under section 884(f)(1)(A), and the foreign resident holder described in paragraph (a) of this section—

(1) Is a 10-percent shareholder of the debtor (within the meaning of section 871(h)(3)(B));

(2) Is a controlled foreign corporation, but only if the debtor is a related person (within the meaning of section 864(d)(4)) with respect to the controlled foreign corporation; or

(3) Is related to the debtor (within the meaning of section 267(b) or 707(b)(1)).

(c) Limitation. The amount of income treated under paragraph (a) of this section as received from a conduit debtor is the lesser of—

(1) The income received or accrued by the foreign resident holder with respect to the FASIT regular interest; or

(2) The amount paid or accrued by the conduit debtor with respect to the debt instrument held by the FASIT.

(d) Cross references. For the treatment of related-party interest accrued to foreign related persons, see sections 163(e)(3), 163(j), 871(h)(3), 881(c)(3)(B), and 881(c)(3)(C).

Proposed § 1.860H-6 Taxation of owner, owner's reporting requirements, transfers of ownership interest. [*For Preamble, see ¶ 152,047*]

(a) In general. For purposes of determining an Owner's credits and taxable income, all assets, liabilities, and items of income, gain, deduction, loss, and credit of the FASIT are treated as assets, liabilities, and such items of the Owner.

(b) Constant yield method to apply. The income from each debt instrument a FASIT holds is determined by applying the constant yield method (including the rules of section 1272(a)(6)) described in § 1.1272-3(c).

(c) Method of accounting for, and character of, hedges. The method of accounting used for a permitted hedge (as described in § 1.860H-2(e)) must clearly reflect income and otherwise comply with the rules of § 1.446-4 (whether or not the permitted hedge instrument is part of a hedging transaction as defined in § 1.1221-2(b)). The character of any gain or loss realized on a permitted hedge (as described in § 1.860H-2(e)) is ordinary.

(d) Coordination with mark-to market provisions. *(1) No mark to market accounting.* Mark to market accounting does not apply to any asset (other than a non-permitted asset) while it is held, or deemed held, by a FASIT.

(2) Transfer of a mark to market asset to a FASIT. If an Owner transfers a permitted asset to a FASIT and the asset would have been marked to market if the taxable year had ended immediately before the transfer (for example, an asset accounted for under section 475(a)), then immediately before the transfer, the Owner must mark the asset to market and take gain or loss into account as if the taxable year had ended at that point. See § 1.475(b)-1(b)(4). If the asset is a debt instrument that is valued under the special valuation rule of § 1.860I-2(a), then immediately after the asset is marked to market under this paragraph (d)(2), the asset is also valued under § 1.860I-2(a), and any additional gain is taken into account under section 860I. The latter gain, but not any mark to market gain, is subject to section 860J.

(e) Owner's annual reporting requirements. Unless the Commissioner otherwise prescribes, specified information regarding the FASIT must be reported by means of a separate statement, attached by the Owner to its income tax return for the taxable year that includes the reporting period. The reporting period is the period in the Owner's taxable year during which the Owner holds the ownership interest in the FASIT. Unless the Commissioner otherwise requires, the statement must set forth—

(1) The name, address, and taxpayer identification number (if any) of the FASIT and any other information necessary to establish the identity of the FASIT for which the statement is being filed;

(2) If the ownership interest was acquired from another person during the Owner's taxable year, the date on which it was acquired, and the name and address of the person from which it was acquired;

(3) If the ownership interest was transferred by the Owner during the Owner's taxable year, the date on which it was transferred, the name and address of the person to which it was transferred, and whether such person is described in section 860L(a)(2);

(4) If any regular interests are issued during the reporting period, a description of the prepayment and reinvestment assumptions that are made pursuant to section 1272(a)(6) and any regulations thereunder, including a statement supporting the selection of the prepayment assumption;

(5) The FASIT's items (taken into account during the reporting period) of income, gain, loss, deduction and credit from permitted transactions, and separately stated, the FASIT's items (taken into account during the reporting period) of income, gain, loss, deduction and credit from prohibited transactions;

(6) Information detailing the extent to which the items described in paragraph (f)(5) of this section consist of interest accrued that, but for section 860H(b)(4), is exempt from the taxes imposed under subtitle A of 26 U.S.C.; and

(7) If a qualified arrangement ceases to be a FASIT during a reporting period (including at the close of a reporting period), information disclosing—

(i) The effective date of the cessation;

(ii) A description of how the cessation occurred; and

(iii) A statement regarding whether the arrangement will continue after cessation and, if so, the continuing arrangement's name, address, and taxpayer identification number.

(f) Treatment of FASIT under subtitle F of Title 26 U.S.C. For purposes of subtitle F (Procedure and Administration)—

(1) A FASIT is treated as a branch or division of the Owner;

(2) The Owner is treated as the issuer of the regular interests; and

(3) The regular interests are treated as collateralized debt obligations as defined in § 1.6049-7(d)(2).

(g) Transfer of ownership interest. *(1) In general.* If, at the time of any transfer of the ownership interest, the Owner knew or should have known that the transferee would be unwilling or unable to pay some or all of the tax arising from the application of section 860H(b), then the transfer is disregarded for all Federal tax purposes.

(2) Safe harbor for establishing lack of improper knowledge. A transfer will not be disregarded under paragraph (g)(1) of this section if the rules of § 1.860E-1(c)(4) (safe harbor for establishing lack of improper knowledge on the transfer of a non-economic REMIC residual interest) are satisfied with respect to the FASIT ownership interest.

Proposed § 1.860I-1 Gain recognition on property transferred to FASIT or supporting FASIT regular interests. [*For Preamble, see ¶ 152,047*]

(a) In general. *(1)* Except as provided in paragraphs (a)(2) and (d) of this section, the Owner of a FASIT (or a related person) must recognize gain (if any) on—

(i) Property the Owner (or the related person) transfers either to the FASIT or its regular interest holders;

(ii) Support property; and

(iii) Property acquired by the FASIT as foreclosure property and held beyond the grace period allowed for foreclosure property.

(2) An Owner (or a related person) does not have to recognize gain under section 860I or paragraph (a)(1) of this section on a transfer or pledge of property to a regular interest holder, if the Owner (or the related person) makes the transfer or pledge in a capacity other than as Owner (or related person), and the regular interest holder receives the transfer or pledge in a capacity other than regular interest holder.

(b) Support property defined. Property is support property if the Owner (or a related person)—

(1) Pledges the property, directly or indirectly, to pay a FASIT regular interest, or otherwise identifies the property as providing security for the payment of a FASIT regular interest;

(2) Sets aside the property for transfer to a FASIT under any agreement or understanding; or

(3) Holds an interest in the property that is subordinate to the FASIT's interest in the property (for example, the Owner holds subordinate interests in a pool of mortgages and the FASIT holds senior interests in the same pool).

(c) Timing of gain determination and recognition. Gain is determined and recognized under paragraph (a)(1) of this section immediately before the property is transferred to the FASIT or becomes support property, or in the case of foreclosure property, on the day immediately following the termination of the grace period allowed for foreclosure property.

(d) Gain deferral election. [Reserved]

(e) Amount of gain. Except as provided in paragraph (f) of this section, the amount of gain recognized under paragraph (a)(1) of this section is the same as if the Owner (or the related person) had sold the property for its value as determined under § 1.860I-2.

(f) Recordkeeping requirements. The Owner is required to maintain such books and records as may be necessary or appropriate to demonstrate that the requirements of this section are satisfied.

(g) Special rule applicable to property of related persons. Except in the case of property traded on an established securities market (as defined in § 1.860I-2(b)), if a related person holds property that becomes support property, or if a related person transfers property to a FASIT or its regular interest holders, then for purposes of applying the gain recognition provisions of this section—

(1) The related person is treated as transferring the property to the Owner for the property's fair market value as determined under general tax principles; and

(2) The Owner is treated as transferring the property to the FASIT for the property's value as determined under § 1.860I-2.

Proposed § 1.860I-2 Value of property. [*For Preamble, see ¶ 152,047*]

(a) Special valuation rule. For purposes of section 860I(d)(1)(A), except as provided in paragraph (c) of this section, the value of a debt instrument not traded on an established securities market is the present value of the reasonably expected payments on the instrument determined—

(1) As of the date the instrument is to be valued (as described in § 1.860I-1(c)); and

(2) By using a discount rate equal to 120 percent of the applicable federal rate, compounded semi-annually, for instruments having the same term as the weighted average maturity of the reasonably expected payments on the instrument. For this purpose, the applicable federal rate is the rate prescribed under section 1274(d) for the period that includes the date the instrument is valued (as described in § 1.860I-1(c)).

(b) Traded on an established securities market. For purposes of section 860I(d)(1)(A), a debt instrument is traded on an established securities market if it is traded on a market described in § 1.1273-2(f)(2), (3), or (4).

(c) Reasonably expected payments. *(1) In general.* Reasonably expected payments on an instrument must be determined in a commercially reasonable manner and, except as otherwise provided in this section (c), may take into account reasonable assumptions concerning early repayments, late payments, non-payments, and loan servicing costs. No other assumptions may be considered.

(2) Consistency requirements. Except as provided in paragraph (c)(3) of this section, any assumption used in determining the reasonably expected payments on an instrument must be consistent with (and no less favorable than) the first of the following categories that applies—

(i) Representations made in connection with the offering of a regular interest in the FASIT;

(ii) Representations made to any nationally recognized statistical rating organizations;

(iii) Representations made in any filings or registrations with any governmental agency with respect to the FASIT; and

(iv) Industry customs or standards (as defined in paragraph (e) of this section).

(3) Servicing costs. Notwithstanding paragraph (c)(2) of this section, the amount of loan servicing costs assumed may not exceed the lesser of—

(i) The amount the FASIT agrees to pay the Owner for servicing the loans held by the FASIT if the Owner is providing the servicing; or

(ii) The amount a third party would reasonably pay for servicing identical loans.

(4) Nonconforming or unreasonable assumptions. If a taxpayer, in determining the expected payments on an instrument, takes into account an assumption that either fails to meet the requirements of paragraph (c)(2) or (3) of this section or is unreasonable, the Commissioner may determine the reasonably expected payments on the instrument without the assumption. Thus, for example, if a taxpayer makes an unreasonable assumption concerning non-payments, the Commissioner may compute expected payments without any adjustment for non-payments.

(d) Special rules. *(1) Beneficial ownership interests.* A certificate representing beneficial ownership of a debt instrument, is deemed to represent beneficial ownership of a debt instrument traded on an established securities market, if either—

(i) The certificate is traded on an established securities market; or

(ii) The certificate represents ownership in a pool of assets composed solely of debt instruments all of which are traded on established securities markets.

(2) Stripped interests. A stripped bond or stripped coupon (as defined in section 1286(e)) not otherwise traded on an established securities market is considered as being traded on an established securities market, if—

(i) The underlying bond (the bond from which the stripped bond or stripped coupon is created) is traded on an established securities market; and

(ii) The stripped bond or stripped coupon is valued using a commercially reasonable method based on the market value of the underlying bond.

(3) Contemporaneous purchase and transfer of debt instruments. (i) Notwithstanding paragraph (a) of this section, the value of a debt instrument not traded on an established securities market is its cost to the Owner (or a related person) if—

(A) The debt instrument is purchased from an unrelated person in an arm's length transaction in which no other property is transferred or services provided;

(B) The debt instrument is acquired solely for cash;

(C) The price of the debt instrument is fixed no more than 15 days before the date of purchase; and

(D) The debt instrument is transferred to the FASIT no more than 15 days after the date of purchase.

(ii) For purposes of paragraph (d)(3)(i) of this section, the date of purchase is the earliest date on which the burdens and benefits of ownership of the debt instrument irrevocably pass to the Owner (or a related person).

(4) Guarantees. Notwithstanding paragraph (c)(1) of this section, if a guarantee qualifying as a permitted hedge under this paragraph (d) relates solely to a debt instrument not traded on an established securities market and the taxpayer determines the reasonably expected payments on the debt instrument by including the reasonably expected payments on the guarantee, then the guarantee and the property need not be valued separately.

(e) Definitions. For purposes of § 1.860I-2—

(1) An industry custom is any long-standing practice in use by entities that engage in asset securitization as part of their ordinary business activities; and

(2) An industry standard is any standard that is both—

(i) Commonly used in evaluating the expected payments on securitized debt instruments (or debt instruments pending securitization) in similar transactions; and

(ii) Disseminated through written or electronic means by any independent, nationally recognized trade association or other authority that is recognized as competent to issue the standard.

Proposed § 1.860J-1 Non-FASIT losses not to offset certain FASIT inclusions. [*For Preamble, see ¶ 152,047*]

(a) In general. For purposes of applying section 860J(a)(1), an Owner's taxable income from a FASIT includes any gains recognized by the Owner under § 1.860I-1(a).

(b) Special rule for holders of multiple ownership interests. For purposes of applying section 860J and the rules of § 1.860J-1, a person may aggregate the net income (or loss) from all FASITs in which the person holds the ownership interest.

(c) Related persons. *(1) Taxable income.* The taxable income of a related person for any taxable year is no less than the sum of—

(i) The amounts specified in section 860J(a); plus

(ii) Any gains recognized under § 1.860I-1(a).

(2) Effect on net operating loss. Any increase in a related person's taxable income attributable to paragraph (c)(1) of this section is disregarded—

(i) In determining under section 172 the amount of the related person's net operating loss for the taxable year; and

(ii) In determining the related person's taxable income for such taxable year for purposes of the second sentence of section 172(b)(2).

(3) Coordination with minimum tax. For purposes of part VI of subchapter A of chapter 1 of subtitle A of Title 26 U.S.C., the alternative minimum taxable income of any related person is in no event less than the related person's taxable income as computed under paragraph (c)(1) of this section.

Proposed § 1.860L-1 Prohibited transactions. [*For Preamble, see ¶ 152,047*]

(a) Loan origination. *(1) In general.* Section 860L(e) imposes a prohibited transactions tax on the receipt of any income derived from any loan originated by a FASIT. Except as provided in paragraphs (a)(2) and (3) of this section, whether a FASIT originates a loan for purposes of section 860L(e) depends on all the facts and circumstances.

(2) Acquisitions presumed not to be loan origination. Except as provided in paragraph (a)(3) of this section, a FASIT is considered not to have originated a loan if the FASIT acquires the loan—

(i) From an established securities market described in § 1.1273-2(f)(2), (3), or (4);

(ii) On a date more than 12 months after the loan was issued; or

(iii) From a person (including the Owner or a related person) that regularly originates similar loans (such as through a standardized contract) in the ordinary course of its business.

(3) Activities presumed to be loan origination. (i) Notwithstanding paragraph (a)(2) of this section, a FASIT is considered to originate a loan if the FASIT either engages in or facilitates (other than through a person from whom the FASIT acquires the loan and who is described in paragraph (a)(2)(iii) of this section)—

(A) Soliciting the loan, including advertising to solicit borrowers, accepting the loan application, or generally making any offer to lend funds to any person;

(B) Evaluating an applicant's financial condition;

(C) Negotiating or establishing any terms of the loan;

(D) Preparing or processing any document related to negotiating or entering into the loan; or

(E) Closing the loan transaction.

(ii) For purposes of paragraph (a)(3)(i) of this section, if a FASIT enters into a contract to engage in purchases described in paragraph (a)(2)(iii) of this section, the FASIT is not treated as originating the loans it acquires solely because it was a party to the contract.

(4) Loan workouts. If a FASIT holds a loan, the FASIT is not treated as originating a new loan that it receives from the same obligor in exchange for the old loan in the context of a workout.

(b) Origination of a contract or agreement in the nature of a line of credit. *(1) In general.* A FASIT is presumed not to have originated a contract or agreement in the nature of a line of credit if the FASIT acquires the contract or agreement from a person (including the Owner or a related person) that regularly originates similar contracts or agreements in the ordinary course of its business.

(2) Activities presumed to be origination. If a FASIT assumes the role of a lender under a contract or agreement in the nature of a line of credit from a person that does not regularly originate similar contracts or agreements in the ordinary course of its business, the FASIT is considered to originate the contract or agreement if, with respect to the contract or agreement, the FASIT engages in any of the activities described in paragraphs (A) through (E) of § 1.860L-1(a)(3)(i) of this section.

(3) Debt instruments issued under contracts or agreements in the nature of a line of credit. If a FASIT acquires a debt instrument as a result of the FASIT's position as a lender under a contract or agreement in the nature of a line of credit, the FASIT is presumed to have originated the debt instrument if and only if the FASIT originated the related contract or agreement.

(c) Disposition of debt instruments. Notwithstanding sections 860L(e)(3)(B)(i) and (ii) (certain exceptions from the prohibited transactions tax), the distribution to the Owner of a debt instrument contributed by the Owner, and the transfer to the Owner of one debt instrument in exchange for another, are prohibited transactions, if within 180 days of receiving the debt instrument the Owner realizes a gain on the disposition of the instrument to any person, regardless of whether the realized gain is recognized.

(d) Exclusion of prohibited transactions tax to dispositions of hedges. The rules of section 860L(e) and paragraph (b) of this section do not apply to the disposition of any asset described in section 860L(c)(1)(D).

Proposed § 1.860L-2 Anti-abuse rule. [*For Preamble, see ¶ 152,047*]

(a) Intent of FASIT provisions. Part V of subchapter M of the Internal Revenue Code (the FASIT provisions) is intended to promote the spreading of credit risk on debt instruments by facilitating the securitization of those debt instruments. Implicit in the intent of the FASIT provisions are the following requirements—

(1) Assets to be securitized through a FASIT consist primarily of permitted debt instruments;

(2) The source of principal and interest payments on a FASIT's regular interests is primarily the principal and interest payments on permitted debt instruments held by the FASIT (as opposed to receipts on other assets or deposits of cash); and

(3) No FASIT provision may be used to achieve a Federal tax result that cannot be achieved without the provision unless the provision clearly contemplates that result.

(b) Application of FASIT provisions. The FASIT provisions and the FASIT regulations must be applied in a manner consistent with the intent of the FASIT provisions as set forth in paragraph (a) of this section. Therefore, if a principal purpose of forming or using a FASIT is to achieve results inconsistent with the intent of the FASIT provisions and the FASIT regulations, the Commissioner may make any appropriate adjustments with regard to the FASIT and any arrangement or transaction (or series of transactions) involving the FASIT. The Commissioner's authority includes—

(1) Disregarding a FASIT election;

(2) Treating one or more assets of a FASIT as held by a person or persons other than the Owner;

(3) Allocating FASIT income, loss, deductions and credits to a person or persons other than the Owner;

(4) Disallowing any item of FASIT income, loss, deduction, or credit;

(5) Treating the ownership interest in a FASIT as held by a person other than the nominal holder;

(6) Treating a FASIT regular interest as other than a debt instrument; and

(7) Treating a regular interest held by any person as having the same tax characteristics as one or more of the assets held by the FASIT.

(c) Facts and circumstances analysis. Whether a FASIT is created or used for a principal purpose of achieving a result inconsistent with the intent of the FASIT provisions is determined based on all of the facts and circumstances, including a comparison of the purported business purpose for a transaction and the claimed tax benefits resulting from the transaction.

(d) Effective date. This section is applicable on February 4, 2000.

Proposed § 1.860L-3 Transition rule for pre-effective date FASITs. [*For Preamble, see ¶ 152,047*]

(a) Scope. This section applies if a pre-effective date FASIT has one or more pre-FASIT interests outstanding on the startup day of the FASIT.

(1) Pre-effective date FASIT defined. A pre-effective date FASIT is a FASIT whose underlying qualifying arrangement was in existence on August 31, 1997.

(2) Pre-FASIT interest defined. A pre-FASIT interest is an interest in a pre-effective date FASIT that—

(i) Was issued before February 4, 2000;

(ii) Was outstanding on the date the FASIT election for the underlying qualifying arrangement goes into effect; and

(iii) Is considered debt of the Owner under general principles of Federal income tax law.

(3) FASIT gain defined. For purposes of this section, the term FASIT gain means any gain that the Owner of a pre-effective date FASIT must recognize under the rules of this section.

(b) Election to defer gain. The Owner of a pre-effective date FASIT may elect to defer the recognition of FASIT gain on assets that are held by the FASIT but that are allocable to pre-FASIT interests. An Owner that elects under this section must establish a method of accounting for its FASIT gain. To clearly reflect income, this method must periodically determine the aggregate amount of FASIT gain on all of the assets in the FASIT and exclude the portion of the FASIT gain attributable to the pre-FASIT interests.

(c) Safe-harbor method. This paragraph (c) provides a safe-harbor method for determining the amount of FASIT gain that can be deferred under this section. The method has the following steps:

(1) Step one: Establish pools. (i) Group assets into pools. The Owner must group the assets of the FASIT into one or more pools. No pool may contain assets of more than one of the following three types—

(A) Assets that are valued under the special valuation rule of § 1.860I-2(a) and that have FASIT gain on the first day held by the FASIT;

(B) Assets that are valued for FASIT gain purposes under a standard other than the special valuation rule of § 1.860I-2(a) and that have FASIT gain on the first day held by the FASIT; and

(C) Assets that do not have FASIT gain on the first day held by the FASIT.

(ii) Treatment of pools. If a pool contains assets described in paragraph (c)(1)(i)(A) or (B) of this section, the Owner must apply paragraphs (c)(2) through (5) of this section to the pool. If a pool contains assets described in paragraph (c)(1)(i)(C) of this section, the pool is ignored for FASIT gain purposes.

(2) Step two: Determine the FASIT gain (or loss) at the pool level. (i) In general. For each taxable year, the FASIT gain (or loss) at the pool level is equal to the net increase (or decrease) in the value of the pool minus the income that is included with respect to the pool under general income tax principles (without regard to the FASIT rules). For purposes of the preceding sentence, the net increase (or decrease) in the value of the pool is equal to—

(A) The sum of the value of the pool (as determined under § 1.860I-2) at the end of the taxable year and the amount of any cash distributed (even if reinvested) from the pool during the taxable year; minus

(B) The sum of the value of the pool (as determined under § 1.860I-2) at the end of the previous taxable year and the Owner's adjusted basis in the assets contributed to the pool during the taxable year.

(ii) Limitation. This paragraph applies if the calculation in paragraph (c)(2)(i) of this section produces a loss for the taxable year and the amount of the loss exceeds the net amount of the FASIT gain from the pool in all prior years. In this case, the amount of the loss for the current year is limited to the amount of net FASIT gain for all previous years.

(3) Step three: Determine the percentage of total FASIT gain that must be recognized by the end of the current taxable year. The percentage of FASIT gain that must be recognized by the end of the current taxable year is equal to 100 percent minus the percentage of FASIT gain that may be deferred at the end of the current taxable year. The percentage

of FASIT gain that may be deferred at the end of the taxable year is equal to the lesser of 100 percent and the ratio of—

(i) The product of 107 percent and aggregate adjusted issue prices of all pre-FASIT interests outstanding on the last day of the taxable year; over

(ii) The total value of all assets held by the FASIT on the last day of the taxable year.

(4) Step four: Determine the total amount of FASIT gain that is not attributed to pre-effective date FASIT interests. The total amount of FASIT gain that is not attributed to pre-effective date FASIT interests is equal to the product of—

(i) The sum of the amount of FASIT gain (as determined under paragraph (c)(2) of this section) for the current taxable year and all previous taxable years; and

(ii) The percentage of FASIT gain that must be recognized in the current taxable year (as determined under paragraph (c)(3) of this section).

(5) Step five: Determine the amount of FASIT gain (or loss) to be recognized in the taxable year. For the taxable year that includes the startup date, the amount of FASIT gain to be recognized is equal to the total amount of FASIT gain not attributable to pre-effective date FASIT interests (as determined under paragraph (c)(4) of this section). Thereafter, the amount of FASIT gain (or loss) to be recognized in a given taxable year is equal to the total amount of FASIT gain not attributable to pre-effective date FASIT interests for that taxable year (as determined under paragraph (c)(4) of this section) less the amount of FASIT gain not attributable to pre-effective date FASIT interests for the immediately preceding taxable year (as determined under paragraph (c)(4) of this section).

(d) Example. The rules of this section are illustrated by the following example:

Example. (i) Facts. O is an eligible corporation within the meaning of section 860(a)(2) that uses the calendar year as its taxable year. On July 1, 1996, O forms TR, a trust. Shortly thereafter, O contributes credit card receivables to TR and TR issues certificates that, for Federal income tax purposes, are characterized as debt of O. Effective March 31, 1999, O elects FASIT status for TR. On March 31, 1999, TR holds credit card receivables that have an outstanding principal balance of $20,000,000 and TR has outstanding certificates (that are characterized for Federal income tax purposes as debt of O) that have an aggregate adjusted issue price of $10,000,000.

(ii) Status as a pre-effective date FASIT. TR is a pre-effective date FASIT because TR was a trust that was in existence on August 31, 1997. The certificates outstanding on March 1, 1999, are pre-FASIT interests because they were outstanding on March 31, 1999, and they were considered debt of O under general principles of Federal income tax law.

(iii) Facts: 1999. From April 1, 1999, through December 31, 1999, the credit card receivables held by TR generated $800,000 of taxable income and $4,000,000 of total cash flow. TR distributed $2,500,000 of the cash flow to O in exchange for new receivables having an outstanding principal balance of $2,500,000. TR used the remaining $1,500,000 of cash flow to make payments on its outstanding debt instruments. On December 31, 1999, TR contributed additional credit card receivables with an outstanding principal balance of $10,700,000 and an aggregate adjusted basis of $10,700,000. On December 31, 1999, TR held credit card receivables that had an outstanding principal balance of $30,000,000, an aggregate adjusted basis of $30,000,000, and a value (as determined under § 1.860I-2(a)) of $30,300,000. In addition, on December 31, 1999, the outstanding adjusted issue price of the pre-FASIT interests was $9,000,000.

(iv) FASIT gain recognition for 1999. (A) Establish pools. TR elects to defer gain recognition under the safe harbor method. Consistent with paragraph (c)(1) of this section, TR groups the assets of the FASIT into a single pool because all of the assets of the FASIT are credit card receivables subject to the special valuation rule of § 1.860I-1(a) and the assets have FASIT gain on the date they are acquired by the FASIT.

(B) Determination of FASIT gain for 1999. The sum of the value of the pool at the end of 1999 ($30,300,000) and the cash distributed during 1999 ($4,000,000) is $34,300,000. There are three contributions of assets by O during 1999: one of $20,000,000 on March 31, 1999; one of $2,500,000 over the course of 1999; and an additional contribution of $10,700,000 on December 31, 1999. Thus, O's basis in assets contributed to the pool during 1999 is $33,200,000. The net increase in the value of the pool is $1,100,000 ($34,300,000 minus $33,200,000). Under paragraph (c)(2) of this section, the FASIT gain for 1999 is $300,000 ($1,100,000 net increase in value minus $800,000 taxable income).

(C) Determination of percentage of total FASIT gain that must be recognized by the end of 1999. Under paragraph (c)(3) of this section, the percentage of FASIT gain that may be deferred for the taxable year is 31.78 percent (107 percent × $9,000,000 adjusted issue price of pre-FASIT interests divided by $30,300,000 value of the assets). The percentage of the FASIT gain that must be recognized is for the taxable year, therefore, 68.22 percent (1– 31.78 percent).

(D) Determination of total amount of FASIT gain not attributed to pre-effective date FASIT interests in 1999. Under paragraph (c)(4) of this section, the total amount of FASIT gain not attributed to pre-effective date FASIT interests in 1999 is $204,660 ($300,000 FASIT gain × 68.22 percent).

(E) Determine the amount of FASIT gain to be recognized in 1999. Under paragraph (c)(5) of this section, because 1999 includes the startup date, TR must include in income the entire $204,660 of FASIT gain not attributed to pre-effective date FASIT interests.

(v) Facts: 2000. In 2000, the credit card receivables held by TR generated $1,500,000 of taxable income and $5,000,000 of cash flow. TR distributed $4,000,000 of the cash flow to O in exchange for new receivables having an outstanding principal balance of $4,000,000. TR used the remaining $1,000,000 of cash flow to make payments on its outstanding debt instruments. On December 31, 2000, TR contributed additional credit card receivables with an outstanding principal balance of $9,500,000 and an aggregate adjusted basis of $9,500,000. On December 31, 2000, TR held credit card receivables that had an outstanding principal balance of $40,000,000, an aggregate adjusted basis of $40,000,000, and a value (as determined under § 1.860I-2(a)) of $40,800,000. In addition, on December 31, 2000, the outstanding adjusted issue price of the pre-FASIT interests was $8,500,000.

(vi) FASIT gain recognition for 2000. (A) Determination of FASIT gain for 2000. The sum of the value of the pool on December 31, 2000 ($40,800,000) and the cash distributed during 2000 ($5,000,000) is $45,800,000. The value of the pool on December 31, 1999, was $30,300,000. During 2000, O contributed receivables in which O had a basis of

$13,500,000 ($4,000,000 over the course of the year and $9,500,000 on December 31, 2000). The net increase in the value of the pool during 2000 is $2,000,000 ($45,800,000 minus $43,800,000). Under paragraph (c)(2), the FASIT gain for 2000 is $500,000 ($2,000,000 net increase in value minus $1,500,000 taxable income).

(B) Determination of percentage of total FASIT gain that must be recognized by the end of 2000. Under paragraph (c)(3), the percentage of FASIT gain that may be deferred for the taxable year is 22.29 percent (107 percent times $8,500,000 adjusted issue price of pre-FASIT interests divided by $40,800,000 value of the assets). The percentage of the FASIT gain that must be recognized is, therefore, 77.71 percent (1– 22.29 percent).

(C) Determination of total amount of FASIT gain not attributed to pre-effective date FASIT interests in 2000. Under paragraph (c)(4) of this section, the total amount of FASIT gain not attributed to pre-effective date FASIT interests in 2000 is $388,500 ($500,000 FASIT gain multiplied by 77.71 percent).

(D) Determine the amount of FASIT gain to be recognized in 2000. Under paragraph (c)(5) of this section, the FASIT gain to be recognized for 2000 is equal to the FASIT gain that not attributable to pre-effective date FASIT interests in 2000 ($388,500) minus the FASIT gain not attributable to pre-effective date FASIT interests in 1999 ($204,660). Thus, in 2000, TR must include $183,840.

(e) Election to apply gain deferral retroactively. The Owner of a pre-effective date FASIT, including a pre-effective date FASIT having a startup date before February 4, 2000, may apply the rules of paragraph (a) of this section for the period beginning on the startup date by making an election in the manner prescribed by the Commissioner.

(f) Effective date. This section is applicable on February 4, 2000.

Proposed § 1.860L-4 Effective date. [*For Preamble, see ¶ 152,047*]

Except as otherwise provided in § 1.860L-2(e) (relating to the rules on anti-abuse) and § 1.860L-3(f) (relating to the rules governing transition entities) this section is applicable on the date final regulations are filed with the Federal Register.

§ 1.861-1 Income from sources within the United States.

Caution: The Treasury has not yet amended Reg § 1.861-1 to reflect changes made by P.L. 100-647, P.L. 99-514.

(a) Categories of income. Part I (section 861 and following), subchapter N, chapter 1 of the Code, and the regulations thereunder determine the sources of income for purposes of the income tax. These sections explicitly allocate certain important sources of income to the United States or to areas outside the United States, as the case may be; and, with respect to the remaining income (particularly that derived partly from sources within and partly from sources without the United States), authorize the Secretary or his delegate to determine the income derived from sources within the United States, either by rules of separate allocation or by processes or formulas of general apportionment. The statute provides for the following three categories of income:

(1) Within the United States. The gross income from sources within the United States, consisting of the items of gross income specified in section 861(a) plus the items of gross income allocated or apportioned to such sources in accordance with section 863(a). See §§ 1.861-2 to 1.861-7, inclusive, and § 1.863-1. The taxable income from sources within the United States, in the case of such income, shall be determined by deducting therefrom, in accordance with sections 861(b) and 863(a), the expenses, losses, and other deductions properly apportioned or allocated thereto and a ratable part of any other expenses, losses, or deductions which cannot definitely be allocated to some item or class of gross income. See §§ 1.861-8 and 1.863-1.

(2) Without the United States. The gross income from sources without the United States, consisting of the items of gross income specified in section 862(a) plus the items of gross income allocated or apportioned to such sources in accordance with section 863(a). See §§ 1.862-1 and 1.863-1. The taxable income from sources without the United States, in the case of such income, shall be determined by deducting therefrom, in accordance with sections 862(b) and 863(a), the expenses, losses, and other deductions properly apportioned or allocated thereto and a ratable part of any other expenses, losses, or deductions which cannot definitely be allocated to some item or class of gross income. See §§ 1.862-1 and 1.863-1.

(3) Partly within and partly without the United States. The gross income derived from sources partly within and partly without the United States, consisting of the items specified in section 863(b)(1), (2), and (3). The taxable income allocated or apportioned to sources within the United States, in the case of such income, shall be determined in accordance with section 863(a) or (b). See §§ 1.863-2 to 1.863-5, inclusive.

(4) Exceptions. An owner of certain aircraft or vessels first leased on or before December 28, 1980, may elect to treat income in respect of these aircraft or vessels as income from sources within the United States for purposes of sections 861(a) and 862(a). See § 1.861-9. An owner of certain aircraft, vessels, or spacecraft first leased after December 28, 1980, must treat income in respect of these craft as income from sources within the United States for purposes of sections 861(a) and 862(a). See § 1.861-9A.

(b) Taxable income from sources within the United States. The taxable income from sources within the United States shall consist of the taxable income described in paragraph (a)(1) of this section plus the taxable income allocated or apportioned to such sources, as indicated in paragraph (a)(3) of this section.

(c) Computation of income. If a taxpayer has gross income from sources within or without the United States, together with gross income derived partly from sources within and partly from sources without the United States, the amounts thereof, together with the expenses and investment applicable thereto, shall be segregated; and the taxable income from sources within the United States shall be separately computed therefrom.

T.D. 6258, 10/23/57, amend T.D. 7635, 8/7/79, T.D. 7928, 12/15/83.

§ 1.861-2 Interest.

Caution: The Treasury has not yet amended Reg § 1.861-2 to reflect changes made by P.L. 108-357.

(a) In general. *(1)* Gross income consisting of interest from the United States or any agency of instrumentality thereof (other than a possession of the United States or an agency or instrumentality of a possession), a State or any political subdivision thereof, or the District of Columbia, and interest from a resident of the United States on a bond, note, or other interest-bearing obligation issued, assumed or incurred by such person shall be treated as income from sources within the United States. Thus, for example, income from sources within the United States includes interest received on any refund of income tax imposed by the United States, a State of any political subdivision thereof, or the District of Columbia. Interest other than that described in this paragraph is not to be treated as income from sources within the United States. See paragraph (a)(7) of this section for special rules concerning substitute interest paid or accrued pursuant to a securities lending transaction.

(2) The term "resident of the United States", as used in this paragraph, includes (i) an individual who at the time of payment of the interest is a resident of the United States, (ii) a domestic corporation, (iii) a domestic partnership which at any time during its taxable year is engaged in trade or business in the United States, or (iv) a foreign corporation or a foreign partnership, which at any time during its taxable year is engaged in trade or business in the United States.

(3) The method by which, or the place where, payment of the interest is made is immaterial in determining whether interest is derived from sources within the United States.

(4) For purposes of this section, the term "interest" includes all amounts treated as interest under section 483, and the regulations thereunder. It also includes original issue discount, as defined in section 1232(b)(1), whether or not the underlying bond, debenture, note, certificate, or other evidence of indebtedness is a capital asset in the hands of the taxpayer within the meaning of section 1221.

(5) If interest is paid on an obligation of a resident of the United States by a nonresident of the United States acting in the nonresident's capacity as a guarantor of the obligation of the resident, the interest will be treated as income from sources within the United States.

(6) In the case of interest received by a nonresident alien individual or foreign corporation this paragraph (a) applies whether or not the interest is effectively connected for the taxable year with the conduct of a trade or business in the United States by such individual or corporation.

(7) A substitute interest payment is a payment, made to the transferor of a security in a securities lending transaction or a sale-repurchase transaction, of an amount equivalent to an interest payment which the owner of the transferred security is entitled to receive during the term of the transaction. A securities lending transaction is a transfer of one or more securities that is described in section 1058(a) or a substantially similar transaction. A sale-repurchase transaction is an agreement under which a person transfers a security in exchange for cash and simultaneously agrees to receive substantially identical securities from the transferee in the future in exchange for cash. A substitute interest payment shall be sourced in the same manner as the interest accruing on the transferred security for purposes of this section and § 1.862-1. See also §§ 1.864-5(b)(2)(iii), 1.871-7(b)(2), 1.881-2(b)(2) and for the character of such payments and § 1.894-1(c) for the application tax treaties to these transactions.

(b) Interest not derived from U.S. sources. Notwithstanding paragraph (a) of this section, interest shall be treated as income from sources without the United States to the extent provided by subparagraphs (A) through (H), of section 861(a)(1) and by the following subparagraphs of this paragraph.

(1) Interest on bank deposits and on similar amounts. (i) Interest paid or credited before January 1, 1977, to a nonresident alien individual or foreign corporation on—

(a) Deposits with persons, including citizens of the United States or alien individuals and foreign or domestic partnerships or corporations, carrying on the banking business in the United States,

(b) Deposits or withdrawable accounts with savings institutions chartered and supervised as savings and loan or similar associations under Federal or State law, or

(c) Amounts held by an insurance company under an agreement to pay interest thereon,

shall be treated as income from sources without the United States if such interest is not effectively connected for the taxable year with the conduct of a trade or business in the United States by such nonresident alien individual or foreign corporation. If such interest is effectively connected for the taxable year with the conduct of a trade or business in the United States by such nonresident alien individual or foreign corporation, it shall be treated as income from sources within the United States under paragraph (a) of this section unless it is treated as income from sources without the United States under another subparagraph of this paragraph. For a special rule for determining whether such interest is effectively connected for the taxable year with the conduct of a trade or business in the United States, see paragraph (c)(1)(ii) or § 1.864-4.

(ii) Subdivision (i)(b) of this subparagraph applies to interest on deposits or withdrawable accounts described therein only to the extent that the interest paid or credited by the savings institution described therein is deductible under section 591 in determining the taxable income of such institution; and, for this purpose, whether an amount is deductible under section 591 shall be determined without regard to section 265, relating to deductions allocable to tax-exempt income. Thus, for example, such subdivision does not apply to amounts paid by a savings and loan or similar association on or with respect to its nonwithdrawable capital stock or on or with respect to funds held in restricted accounts which represent a proprietary interest in such association. Subdivision (i)(b) of this subparagraph also applies to so-called dividends paid or credited on deposits or withdrawable accounts if such dividends are deductible under section 591 without reference to section 265.

(iii) For purposes of subdivision (i)(c) of this subparagraph, amounts held by an insurance company under an agreement to pay interest thereon include policyholder dividends left with the company to accumulate, prepaid insurance premiums, proceeds of policies left on deposit with the company, and overcharges of premiums. Such subdivision does not apply to (a) the so-called "interest element" in the case of annuity or installment payments under life insurance or endowment contracts or (b) interest paid by an insurance company to its creditors on notes, bonds, or similar evidences of indebtedness, if the debtor-creditor relationship does not arise by virtue of a contract of insurance with the insurance company.

(iv) For purposes of subdivision (i) of this subparagraph, interest received by a partnership shall be treated as received by each partner of such partnership to the extent of his distributive share of such item.

(2) Interest from a resident alien individual or domestic corporation deriving substantial income from sources without the United States. Interest received from a resident alien individual or a domestic corporation shall be treated as income

from sources without the United States when it is shown to the satisfaction of the district director (or, if applicable, the Director of International Operations) that less than 20 percent of the gross income from all sources of such individual or corporation has been derived from sources within the United States, as determined under the provisions of sections 861 to 863, inclusive, and the regulations thereunder, for the 3-year period ending with the close of the taxable year of such individual or corporation preceding its taxable year in which such interest is paid or credited, or for such part of such period as may be applicable. If 20 percent or more of the gross income from all sources of such individual or corporation has been derived from sources within the United States, as so determined, for such 3-year period (or part thereof), the entire amount of the interest from such individual or corporation shall be treated as income from sources within the United States.

(3) Interest from a foreign corporation not deriving major portion of its income from a U.S. business. (i) Interest from a foreign corporation which, at any time during the taxable year, is engaged in trade or business in the United States shall be treated as income from sources without the United States when it is shown to the satisfaction of the district director (or, if applicable, the Director of International Operations) that (a) less than 50 percent of the gross income from all sources of such foreign corporation for the 3-year period ending with the close of its taxable year preceding its taxable year in which such interest is paid or credited (or for such part of such period as the corporation has been in existence) was effectively connected with the conduct by such corporation of a trade or business in the United States, as determined under section 864(c) and § 1.864-3, or (b) such foreign corporation had gross income for such 3-year period (or part thereof) but none was effectively connected with the conduct of a trade or business in the United States.

(ii) If 50 percent or more of the gross income from all sources of such foreign corporation for such 3-year period (or part thereof) was effectively connected with the conduct by such corporation of a trade or business in the United States, see section 861(a)(1)(D) and paragraph (c)(1) of this section for determining the portion of interest from such corporation which is treated as income from sources within the United States.

(iii) For purposes of this subparagraph the gross income which is effectively connected with the conduct of a trade or business in the United States includes the gross income which, pursuant to section 882(d) or (e) and the regulations thereunder, is treated as income which is effectively connected with the conduct of a trade or business in the United States.

(iv) This subparagraph does not apply to interest paid or credited after December 31, 1969, by a branch in the United States of a foreign corporation if, at the time of payment or crediting, such branch is engaged in the commercial banking business in the United States; furthermore, such interest is treated under paragraph (a) of this section as income from sources within the United States unless it is treated as income from sources without the United States under subparagraph (1) or (4) of this paragraph.

(4) Bankers' acceptances. Interest derived by a foreign central bank of issue from bankers' acceptances shall be treated as income from sources without the United States. For this purpose, a foreign central bank of issue is a bank which is by law or government sanction the principal authority, other than the government itself, issuing instruments intended to circulate as currency. Such a bank is generally the custodian of the banking reserves of the country under whose laws it is organized.

(5) Foreign banking branch of a domestic corporation or partnership. Interest paid or credited on deposits with a branch outside the United States (as defined in section 7701(a)(9)) of a domestic corporation or of a domestic partnership shall be treated as income from sources without the United States if, at the time of payment or crediting, such branch is engaged in the commercial banking business. For purposes of applying this subparagraph, it is immaterial (i) whether the domestic corporation or domestic partnership is carrying on a banking business in the United States, (ii) whether the recipient of the interest is a citizen or resident of the United States, a foreign corporation, or a foreign partnership, (iii) whether the interest is effectively connected with the conduct of a trade or business in the United States by the recipient, or (iv) whether the deposits with the branch located outside the United States are payable in the currency of a foreign country. Notwithstanding the provisions of § 1.863-6, interest to which this subparagraph applies shall be treated as income from sources within the foreign country, possession of the United States, or other territory in which the branch is located.

(6) Section 4912(c) debt obligations. (i) In general.

Under section 861(a)(1) (G), interest on a debt obligation shall not be treated as income from sources within the United States if—

(a) The debt obligation was part of an issue of debt obligations with respect to which an election has been made under section 4912(c) (relating to the treatment of such debt obligations as debt obligations of a foreign obligor for purposes of the interest equalization tax),

(b) The debt obligation had a maturity not exceeding 15 years (within the meaning of subdivision (ii) of this subparagraph) on the date it is originally issued or on the date it is treated under section 4912(c)(2) as issued by reason of being assumed by a certain domestic corporation,

(c) The debt obligation, when originally issued, was purchased by one or more underwriters (within the meaning of subdivision (iii) of this subparagraph) with a view to distribution through resale (within the meaning of subdivision (iv) of this subparagraph), and

(d) The interest on the debt obligation is attributable to periods after the effective date of an election under section 4912(c) to treat such debt obligations as debt obligations of a foreign obligor for purposes of the interest equalization tax.

(ii) Maturity not exceeding 15 years.

The date the debt obligation is issued or treated as issued is not included in the 15 year computation, but the date of maturity of the debt obligation is included in such computation.

(iii) Purchased by one or more underwriters.

For purposes of this subparagraph, the debt obligation when originally issued will not be treated as purchased by one or more underwriters unless the underwriter purchases the debt obligation for his own account and bears the risk of gain or loss on resale. Thus, for example, a debt obligation, when originally issued, will not be treated as purchased by one or more underwriters if the underwriter acts only in the capacity of an agent of the issuer. Neither will a debt obligation, when originally issued, be treated as purchased by one or more underwriters if the agreement between the underwriter and issuer is merely for a "best efforts" underwriting, for the purchase by the underwriter of all or a portion of the debt obligations remaining unsold at the expiration of a fixed period of time, or for any other arrangement under the terms of which the debt obligations are not purchased by the underwriter with a view to distribution through resale. The fact that an underwriter is related to the issuer will not prevent the underwriter from meeting the requirements of this subparagraph. In determining whether a related underwriter meets the requirements of this subparagraph consideration shall be given to whether the purchase by the underwriter of the debt obligation from the issuer for resale was effected by a transaction subject to conditions similar to those which would have been imposed between independent persons.

(iv) With a view to distribution through resale. (a) An underwriter who purchased a debt obligation shall be deemed to have purchased it with a view to distribution through resale if the requirements of (b) or (c) of this subdivision (iv) are met.

(b) The requirement of this subdivision (b) is that—

(1) The debt obligation is registered, approved, or listed for trading on one or more foreign securities exchanges or foreign established securities markets within 4 months after the date on which the underwriter purchases the debt obligation, or by the date of the first interest payment on the debt obligation, whichever is later, or

(2) The debt obligation, or any substantial portion of the issue of which the debt obligation is a part, is actually traded on one or more foreign securities markets on or within 15 calendar days after the date on which the underwriter purchases the debt obligation.

For purposes of this subdivision (iv), a foreign established securities market includes any foreign over-the-counter market as reflected by the existence of an interdealer quotation system for regularly disseminating to brokers and dealers quotations of obligations by identified brokers or dealers, other than quotations prepared and distributed by a broker or dealer in the regular course of his business and containing only quotations of such broker or dealer.

(c) The requirements of this subdivision (c) are that, except as provided in (d) of this subdivision, the underwriter is under no written or implied restriction imposed by the issuer with respect to whom he may resell the debt obligation and either—

(1) Within 30 calendar days after he purchased the debt obligation the underwriter or underwriters either (i) sold it or (ii) sold at least 95 percent of the face amount of the issue of which the debt obligation is a part, or

(2) (i) The debt obligation is evidenced by an instrument which, under the laws of the jurisdiction in which it is issued, is either negotiable or transferable by assignment (whether or not it is registered for trading), and (ii) it appears from all the relevant facts and circumstances, including any written statements or assurances made by the purchasing underwriter or underwriters, that such debt obligation was purchased with a view to distribution through resale.

(d) The requirements of (c) of this subdivision may be met whether or not the underwriter is restricted from reselling the debt obligations—

(1) To a United States person (as defined in section 7701(a)(30)) or

(2) To any particular person or persons pursuant to a restriction imposed by, or required to be met in order to comply with, United States or foreign securities or other law.

(v) Statement with return. Any taxpayer who is required to file a tax return and who excludes from gross income interest of the type specified in this subparagraph must comply with the requirements of paragraph (d) of this section.

(vi) Effect of termination of IET. If the interest equalization tax expires, the provisions of section 861(a)(1)(G) and this subparagraph shall apply to interest paid on debt obligations only with respect to which a section 4912(c) election was made.

(vii) Definition of term underwriter. For purposes of section 861(a)(1)(G) and this subparagraph, the term "underwriter" shall mean any underwriter as defined in section 4919(c)(1).

(c) Special rules. *(1) Proration of interest from a foreign corporation deriving major portion of its income from U.S. business.* If, after applying the first sentence of paragraph (b)(3) of this section to interest to which that paragraph applies, it is determined that the interest may not be treated as income from sources without the United States, the amount of the interest from the foreign corporation which at some time during the taxable year is engaged in trade or business in the United States which is to be treated as income from sources within the United States shall be the amount that bears the same ratio to such interest as the gross income of such foreign corporation for the 3-year period ending with the close of its taxable year preceding its taxable year in which such interest is paid or credited (or for such part of such period as the corporation has been in existence) which was effectively connected with the conduct by such corporation of a trade or business in the United States bears to its gross income from all sources for such period.

(2) Payors having no gross income for period preceding taxable year of payment. If the resident alien individual, domestic corporation, or foreign corporation, as the case may be, paying interest has no gross income from any source for the 3-year period (or part thereof) specified in subparagraph (2) or (3) of paragraph (b) of this section, or subparagraph (1) of this paragraph, the 20-percent test or the 50-percent test, or the apportionment formula, as the case may be, described in such subparagraph shall be applied solely with respect to the taxable year or the payor in which the interest is paid or credited. This subparagraph applies whether the lack of gross income for the 3-year period (or part thereof) stems from the business inactivity of the payor, from the fact that the payor is a corporation which is newly created or organized, or from any other cause.

(3) Transitional rule. For purposes of applying paragraph (b)(3) of this section, and subparagraph (1) of this paragraph, the gross income of the foreign corporation for any period before the first taxable year beginning after December 31, 1966, which is from sources within the United States (determined as provided by sections 861 through 863, and the regulations thereunder, as in effect immediately before amendment by section 102 of the Foreign Investors Tax Act of 1966 (Pub. L. 89-809, 80 Stat. 1541)) shall be treated as gross income for such period which is effectively connected with the conduct of a trade or business in the United States by such foreign corporation.

(4) Gross income determinations. In making determinations under subparagraph (2) or (3) of paragraph (b) of this section, or subparagraph (1) or (3) of this paragraph—

(i) The gross income of a domestic corporation or a resident alien individual is to be determined by excluding any items specifically excluded from gross income under chapter 1 of the Code, and

(ii) The gross income of a foreign corporation which is effectively connected with the conduct of a trade or business in the United States is to be determined under section 882(b)(2) and by excluding any items specifically excluded from gross income under chapter 1 of the Code, and

(iii) The gross income from all sources of a foreign corporation is to be determined without regard to section 882(b) and without excluding any items otherwise specifically excluded from gross income under chapter 1 of the Code.

(d) Statement with return. Any taxpayer who is required to file a return and applies any provision of this section to exclude an amount of interest from his gross income must file with his return a statement setting forth the amount so excluded, the date of its receipt, the name and address of the obligor of the interest, and, if known, the location of the records which substantiate the amount of the exclusion. A statement from the obligor setting forth such information and indicating the amount of interest to be treated as income from sources without the United States may be used for this purpose. See §§ 1.6012-1(b)(1)(i) and 1.6012-2(g)(1)(i).

(e) Effective dates. Except as otherwise provided, this section applies with respect to taxable years beginning after December 31, 1966. For corresponding rules applicable to taxable years beginning before January 1, 1967, (see 26 CFR part 1 revised April 1, 1971). Paragraph (a)(7) of this section is applicable to payments made after November 13, 1997.

T.D. 6258, 10/23/57, amend T.D. 6873, 1/24/66, T.D. 7314, 5/22/74, T.D. 7378, 9/29/75, T.D. 8257, 8/1/89, T.D. 8735, 10/6/97.

PAR. 17. In § 1.861-2, paragraph (a)(4) is amended by removing the phrase "section 1232(b)(1)" and adding in its place the phrase "section 1273(a)(1)".

Proposed § 1.861-2 [Amended] [*For Preamble, see ¶ 151,065*]

§ 1.861-3 Dividends.

Caution: The Treasury has not yet amended Reg § 1.861-3 to reflect changes made by P.L. 100-647, P.L. 100-203.

(a) General. *(1) Dividends included in gross income.* Gross income from sources within the United States includes a dividend described in subparagraph (2), (3), (4), or (5) of this paragraph. For purposes of subparagraphs (2), (3), and (4) of this paragraph, the term "dividend" shall have the same meaning as set forth in section 316 and the regulations thereunder. See subparagraph (5) of this paragraph for special rules with respect to certain dividends from a DISC or former DISC. See also paragraph (a)(6) of this section for special rules concerning substitute dividend payments received pursuant to a securities lending transaction.

(2) [Reserved]. For further guidance, see § 1.861-3T(a)(2).

(3) Dividend from a foreign corporation. (i) In general. (a) A dividend described in this subparagraph is a dividend from a foreign corporation (other than a dividend to which subparagraph (4) of this paragraph applies) unless less than 50 percent of the gross income from all sources of such foreign corporation for the 3-year period ending with the close of its taxable year preceding the taxable year in which occurs the declaration of such dividend (or for such part of such period as the corporation has been in existence) was effectively connected with the conduct by such corporation of a trade or business in the United States, as determined under section 864(c) and § 1.864-3. Thus, no portion of a dividend from a foreign corporation shall be treated as income from sources within the United States under section 861(a)(2)(B) if less than 50 percent of the gross income of such foreign corporation from all sources for such 3-year period (or part thereof) was effectively connected with the conduct by such corporation of a trade or business in the United States or if such foreign corporation had gross income for such 3-year period (or part thereof) but none was effectively connected with the conduct by such corporation of a trade or business in the United States.

(b) If 50 percent or more of the gross income from all sources of such foreign corporation for such 3-year period (or part thereof) was effectively connected with the conduct by such corporation of a trade or business in the United States, the amount of the dividend which is to be treated as income from sources within the United States under section 861(a)(2)(B) shall be the amount that bears the same ratio to such dividend as the gross income of such foreign corporation for such 3-year period (or part thereof) which was effectively connected with the conduct by such corporation of a trade or business in the United States bears to its gross income from all sources for such period.

(c) For purposes of this subdivision (i), the gross income which is effectively connected with the conduct of a trade or business in the United States includes the gross income which, pursuant to section 882(d) or (e), is treated as income which is effectively connected with the conduct of a trade or business in the United States.

(ii) Rule applicable in applying limitation on amount of foreign tax credit. For purposes of determining under section 904 the limitation upon the amount of the foreign tax credit—

(a) So much of a dividend from a foreign corporation as exceeds (and only to the extent it so exceeds) the amount which is 100/85ths of the amount of the deduction allowable under section 245(a) in respect of such dividend, plus

(b) An amount which bears the same proportion to any section 78 dividend to which the dividend from the foreign corporation gives rise as the amount of the excess determined under (a) of this subdivision bears to the total amount of the dividend from the foreign corporation,

shall, notwithstanding subdivision (i) of this subparagraph, be treated as income from sources without the United States. This subdivision applies to a dividend for which no dividends-received deduction is allowed under section 245 or for which the 85 percent dividends-received deduction is allowed under section 245(a) but does not apply to a dividend for which a deduction is allowable under section 245(b). All of a dividend for which the 100 percent dividends-received deduction is allowed under section 245(b) shall be treated as income from sources within the United States for purposes of determining under section 904 the limitation upon the amount of the foreign tax credit. If the amount of a distribution of property other than money (constituting a dividend under section 316) is determined by applying section 301(b)(1)(C), such amount must be used as the dividend for purposes of applying (a) of this subdivision even though the amount used for purposes of section 245(a) is determined by applying section 301(b)(1)(D). In making determinations under this subdivision, a dividend (other than a section 78 dividend referred to in (b) of this subdivision) shall be determined without regard to section 78.

(iii) Illustrations. The application of this subparagraph may be illustrated by the following examples:

Example (1). D, a domestic corporation, owns 80 percent of the outstanding stock of M, a foreign manufacturing corporation. M, which makes its returns on the basis of the calendar year, has earnings and profits of $200,000 for 1971 and 60 percent of its gross income for that year is effectively connected for 1971 with the conduct of a trade or business in the United States. For an uninterrupted period of 36 months ending on December 31, 1970, M has been engaged in trade or business in the United States and has received gross income effectively connected with the conduct of a trade or business in the United States amounting to 60 percent of its gross income from all sources for such period. The only distribution by M to D for 1971 is a cash dividend of $100,000; of this amount, $60,000 ($100,000 × 60%) is treated under subdivision (i) of this subparagraph as income from sources within the United States, and $40,000 ($100,000 – $60,000) is treated under § 1.862-1(a)(2) as income from sources without the United States. Accordingly, under section 245(a), D is entitled to a dividends-received deduction of $51,000 ($60,000 × 85%), and under subdivision (ii) of this subparagraph $40,000 ($100,000 – [$51,000 × 100/85]) is treated as income from sources without the United States for purposes of determining under section 904(a)(1) or (2) the limitation upon the amount of the foreign tax credit.

Example (2). (a) The facts are the same as in example (1) except that the distribution for 1971 consists of property which has a fair market value of $100,000 and an adjusted basis of $30,000 in M's hands immediately before the distribution. The amount of the dividend under section 316 is $58,000, determined by applying section 301(b)(1)(c) as follows:

Portion of adjusted basis of property attributable to gross income of M effectively connected for 1971 with conduct of trade or business in United States ($30,000 × 60%)	$18,000
Portion of fair market value of property attributable to gross income of M not effectively connected for 1971 with conduct of trade or business in United States ($100,000 × 40%)	40,000
Total dividend	58,000

(b) Of the total dividend, $34,800 ($58,000 × 60% (percentage applicable to 3-year period)) is treated under subdivision (i) of this subparagraph as income from sources within the United States, and $28,200 ($58,000 × 40%) is treated under § 1.862-1(a)(2) as income from sources without the United States. However, by reason of section 245(c) the adjusted basis of the property ($30,000) is used under section 245(a) in determining the dividends-received deduction. Thus, under section 245(a), D is entitled to a dividends-received deduction of $15,300 ($30,000 × 60% × 85%).

(c) Under subdivision (ii) of this subparagraph, the amount of the dividend for purposes of applying *(a)* of that subdivision is the amount ($58,000) determined by applying section 301(b)(1)(C) rather than the amount ($30,000) determined by applying section 301(b)(1)(B). Accordingly, under subdivision (ii) of this subparagraph $40,000 ($58,000 – [$15,300 × 100/85]) is treated as income from sources without the United States for purposes of determining under section 904(a)(1) or (2) the limitation upon the amount of the foreign tax credit.

Example (3). (a) D, a domestic corporation which makes its returns on the basis of the calendar year, owns 100 percent of the outstanding stock of N, a foreign corporation which is not a less developed country corporation under section 902(d). N, which makes its returns on the basis of the calendar year, has total gross income for 1971 of $100,000, of which $80,000 (including $60,000 from sources within foreign country X) is effectively connected for that year with the conduct of a trade or business in the United States. For 1971 N is assumed to have paid $27,000 of income taxes to country X and to have accumulated profits of $81,000 for purposes of section 902(c)(1)(A). N's accumulated profits in excess of foreign income taxes amount to $54,000. For 1971 D receives a cash dividend of $42,000 from N, which is D's only income for that year.

(b) For 1971 D chooses the benefits of the foreign tax credit under section 901, and as a result is required under section 78 to include in gross income an amount equal to the foreign income taxes of $21,000 ($27,000 × $42,000/$54,000) it is deemed to have paid under section 902(a)(1). Thus, assuming no other deductions for the taxable year, D has gross income of $63,000 ($42,000 + $21,000) for 1971 less a dividends-received deduction under section 245(a) of $28,560 ([$42,000 × $80,000/$100,000] × 85%), or taxable income for 1971 of $34,440.

(c) Under subdivision (ii) of this subparagraph, for purposes of determining under section 904(a)(1) or (2) the limitation upon the amount of the foreign tax credit, $12,600 is treated as income from sources without the United States, determined as follows:

Excess of dividend from N over amount which is 100/85ths of amount of section 245(a) deduction ($42,000 – [$28,560 × 100/85])	$ 8,400
Proportionate part of section 78 dividend ($21,000 × $8,400/$42,000)	4,200
Taxable income from sources without the United States	12,600

Example (4). A, an individual citizen of the United States who makes his return on the basis of the calendar year, receives in 1971 a cash dividend of $10,000 from M, a foreign corporation, which makes its return on the basis of the calendar year. For the 3-year period ending with 1970 M has been engaged in trade or business in the United States and has received gross income effectively connected with the conduct of a trade or business in the United States amounting to 80 percent of its gross income from all sources for such period. Of the total dividend, $8,000 ($10,000 × 80%) is treated under subdivision (i) of this subparagraph as income from sources within the United States and $2,000 ($10,000 – $8,000) is treated under § 1.862-1(a)(2) as income from sources without the United States. Since under section 245 no dividends received-deduction is allowable to an individual, A is entitled under subdivision (ii) of this subparagraph to treat the entire dividend of $10,000 ($10,000 – [$0 × 100/85]) as income from sources without the United States for purposes of determining under section 904(a) (1) or (2) the limitation upon the amount of the foreign tax credit.

(4) Dividend from a foreign corporation succeeding to earnings of a domestic corporation. A dividend described in this subparagraph is a dividend from a foreign corporation, if such dividend is received by a corporation after December 31, 1959, but only to the extent that such dividend is treated by such recipient corporation under the provisions of § 1.243-3 as a dividend from a domestic corporation subject to taxation under chapter 1 of the Code. To the extent that this subparagraph applies to a dividend received from a foreign corporation, subparagraph (3) of this paragraph shall not apply to such dividend.

(5) Certain dividends from a DISC or former DISC. (i) General rule. A dividend described in this subparagraph is a

dividend from a corporation that is a DISC or former DISC (as defined in section 992(a)) other than a dividend that—

(a) Is deemed paid by a DISC, for taxable years beginning before January 1, 1976, under section 995(b)(1)(D) as in effect for taxable years beginning before January 1, 1976, and for taxable years beginning after December 31, 1975, under section 995(b)(1)(D), (E), and (F) to the extent provided in subdivision (iii) of this subparagraph or

(b) Reduces under § 1.996-3(b)(3) accumulated DISC income (as defined in subdivision (ii)(b) of this subparagraph) to the extent provided in subdivision (iv) of this subparagraph.

Thus, a dividend deemed paid under section 995(b)(1)(A), (B), or (C) (relating to certain deemed distributions in qualified years) will be treated in full as gross income from sources within the United States. To the extent that a dividend from a DISC or former DISC is paid out of other earnings and profits (as defined in § 1.996-3(d)), subparagraph (2) of this paragraph shall apply. To the extent that a dividend from a DISC or former DISC is paid out of previously taxed income (as defined in § 1.996-3(c)), see section 996(a)(3) (relating to the exclusion from gross income of amounts distributed out of previously taxed income). In determining the source of income of certain dividends from a DISC or former DISC, the source of income from any transaction which gives rise to gross receipts (as defined in § 1.993-6), in the hands of the DISC or former DISC, is immaterial.

(ii) Definitions. For purposes of this subparagraph, the term—

(a) "Dividend from" means any amount actually distributed which is a dividend within the meaning of section 316 (including distributions to meet qualification requirements under section 992(c)) and any amount treated as a distribution taxable as a dividend pursuant to section 995(b) (relating to deemed distributions in qualified years or upon disqualification) or included in gross income as a dividend pursuant to section 995(c) (relating to gain on certain dispositions of stock in a DISC or former DISC), and

(b) "Accumulated DISC income" means the amount of accumulated DISC income as of the close of the taxable year immediately preceding the taxable year in which the dividend was made increased by the amount of DISC income for the taxable year in which the dividend was made (as determined under § 1.996-3(b)(2)).

(c) "Nonqualified export taxable income" means the taxable income of a DISC from any transaction which gives rise to gross receipts (as defined in § 1.993-6) which are not qualified export receipts (as defined in § 1.993-1) other than a transaction giving rise to gain described in section 995(b)(1)(B) or (C).

For purposes of subdivisions (i)(b) and (iv) of this subparagraph, if by reason of section 995(c), gain is included in the shareholder's gross income as a dividend, accumulated DISC income shall be treated as if it were reduced under § 1.996-3(b)(3).

(iii) Determination of source of income for deemed distributions, for taxable years beginning before January 1, 1976, under section 995(b)(1)(D) as in effect for taxable years beginning before January 1, 1976, and for taxable years beginning after December 31, 1975, under section 995(b)(1)(D), (E), and (F).

(a) If for its taxable year a DISC does not have any nonqualified export taxable income, then for such year the entire amount treated, for taxable years beginning before January 1, 1976, under section 995(b)(1)(D) as in effect for taxable years beginning before January 1, 1976, and for taxable years beginning after December 31, 1975, under section 995(b)(1)(D), (E), an (F) as a deemed distribution taxable as a dividend will be treated as gross income from sources without the United States.

(b) If for its taxable year a DISC has any nonqualified export taxable income, then for such year the portion of the amount treated, for taxable years beginning before January 1, 1976, under section 995(b)(1)(D) as in effect for taxable years beginning before January 1, 1976, and for taxable years beginning after December 31, 1975, under section 995(b)(1)(D), (E), and (F) as a deemed distribution taxable as a dividend that will be treated as income from sources within the United States shall be equal to the amount of such nonqualified export taxable income multiplied by the following fraction. The numerator of the fraction is the sum of the amounts treated, for taxable years beginning before January 1, 1976, under section 995(b)(1)(D) as in effect for taxable years beginning before January 1, 1976, and for taxable years beginning after December 31, 1975, under section 995(b)(1)(D), (E), and (F) as deemed distributions taxable as dividends. The denominator of the fraction is the taxable income of the DISC for the taxable year, reduced by the amounts treated under section 995(b)(1)(A), (B), and (C) as deemed distributions taxable as dividends. However, in no event shall the numerator exceed the denominator. The remainder of such dividend will be treated as gross income from sources without the United States.

(iv) Determination of source of income for dividends that reduce accumulated DISC income (a) If no portion of the accumulated DISC income of a DISC or former DISC is attributable to nonqualified export taxable income from any transaction during a year for which it is (or is treated as) a DISC, then the entire amount of any dividend that reduces under § 1.996-3(b)(3) accumulated DISC income will be treated as income from sources without the United States.

(b) If any portion of the accumulated DISC income of a DISC or former DISC is attributable to nonqualified export taxable income from any transaction during a year for which it is (or is treated as) a DISC, then the portion of any dividend during its taxable year that reduces under § 1.996-3(b)(3) accumulated DISC income that will be treated as income from sources within the United States shall be equal to the amount of such dividend multiplied by a fraction (determined as of the close of such year) the numerator of which is the amount of accumulated DISC income attributable to nonqualified export taxable income, and the denominator of which is the total amount of accumulated DISC income. The remainder of such dividend will be treated as gross income from sources without the United States.

(v) Special rules. For purposes of subdivisions (iii) and (iv) of this subparagraph—

(a) Taxable income shall be determined under § 1.992-3(b)(2)(i) (relating to the computation of deficiency distribution), and

(b) The proration of any deemed distribution taxable as a dividend, for taxable years beginning before January 1, 1976, under section 995(b)(1)(D) as in effect for taxable years beginning before January 1, 1976, and for taxable years beginning after December 31, 1975, under section 995(b)(1)(D), (E), and (F) or amount under § 1.996-3(b)(3)(i) through (iv) that is treated as gross income from sources within the United States during the taxable year shall be considered to reduce the amount of nonqualified export taxable income as of the close of such year.

(vi) Illustrations. This subparagraph may be illustrated by the following examples:

Example (1). (a) Y is a corporation which uses the calendar year as its taxable year and which elects to be treated as a DISC beginning with 1972. X is its sole shareholder. In 1973, Y has $18,000 of taxable income from qualified export receipts (none of which are interest and gains described in section 995(b)(1)(A), (B), and (C)) and $1,000 of nonqualified export taxable income. Under these facts, X is deemed to have received a distribution under section 995(b)(1)(D) as in effect for taxable years beginning before January 1, 1976, of $9,500, i.e., $19,000 X ½. X is treated under subdivision (iii)(b) of this subparagraph as having $500, i.e., $1,000 X $9,500/$19,000, from sources within the United States and $9,000 from sources without the United States.

(b) For 1972, assume that Y did not have any nonqualified export taxable income. Pursuant to subdivision (v)(b) of this subparagraph, at the beginning of 1974, $500 of Y's accumulated DISC income is attributable to nonqualified export taxable income, i.e., $1,000 – $500.

Example (2). The facts are the same as in example (1) except that in 1973, in addition to the taxable income described in such example, Y has $450 of taxable income from gross interest from producer's loans described in section 995(b)(1)(A). Under these facts, the deemed distribution of $450 under section 995(b)(1)(A) is treated in full under subdivision (i) of this subparagraph as gross income from sources within the United States. The deemed distribution under section 995(b)(1)(D) as in effect for taxable years beginning before January 1, 1976, of $9,500 will be treated in the same manner as in example (1), i.e., $1,000 X $9,500/($19,450 – $450).

Example (3). (a) The facts are the same as in example (1) except that in 1973, in addition to the distribution described in such example, Y makes a deemed distribution taxable as a dividend to $100 under section 995(b)(1)(G) (relating to foreign investment attributable to producer's loans) and actual distributions of all of its previously taxed income and of $2,000 taxable as a dividend which reduces accumulated DISC income (as defined in subdivision (ii)(b) of this subparagraph). Under § 1.996-3(b)(3), accumulated DISC income is first reduced by the deemed distribution of $100 and then by the actual distribution taxable as a dividend of $2,000. As indicated in example (1), for 1972 Y did not have any nonqualified export taxable income. Assume that Y had accumulated DISC income of $12,000 at the end of 1973, $500 of which under example (1) is attributable to nonqualified export taxable income.

Example (4). (a) Z is a corporation which uses the calendar year as its taxable year and which elects to be treated as a DISC beginning with 1972. W is its sole shareholder. At the end of the 1976 Z has previously taxed income of $12,000 and accumulated DISC income of $4,000, $900 of which is attributable to nonqualified export taxable income. In 1977, Z has $20,050 of taxable income from qualified export receipts, of which $550 is from gross income from producer's loans described in section 995(b)(1)(A); Z has $950 of taxable income giving rise to gross receipts which are not qualified export receipts, of which $450 is gain described in section 995(b)(1)(B). Of its total taxable income of $21,000 (which is equal to its earnings and profits for 1977), $1,000 is attributable to sales of military property. Z has an international boycott factor (determined under section 999) of 0.10, and made an illegal bribe (within the meaning of section 162(c)) of $1,265. The proportion which the amount of Z's adjusted base period export receipts bears to Z's export gross receipts for 1977 is 0.40 (see section 995(e)(1)). Z makes a deemed distribution taxable as a dividend of $1,000 under section 995(b)(1)(G) (relating to foreign investment attributable to producer's loans) and actual distributions of $32,000.

(b) The deemed distributions of $550 under section 995(b)(1)(A) and $450 under section 995(b)(1)(B) are treated in full under subdivision (i) of this subparagraph as gross income from sources within the United States.

(c) Under these facts, Z has also made the following deemed distributions taxable as dividends to W under the following subdivisions of section 995(b)(1):

(D)	$ 500,	i.e., ½ × $1,000
(E)	7,800,	i.e., 0.40 × [$21,000 – $(550 + 450 + 550)].
(F)(i)	5,850,	i.e., ½ × [$21,000 $(550 + 450 + 500 + 7,800)].
(ii)	585,	i.e., $5,850 × 0.10.
(iii)	1,265	
Total	16,000	

(d) The portion of the total amount of these deemed distributions ($16,000) that is treated under subdivision (iii)(b) as gross income from sources within the United States is computed as follows:

(1) The amount of nonqualified export taxable income is $500, i.e., taxable income giving rise to gross receipts which are not qualified export receipts ($950) minus gain described in section 995(b)(1)(B) or (C) ($450).

(2) $500 × $16,000/$[21,000 – (550 + 450)] = $400.

The remainder of these distributions, $15,600 ($16,000 minus $400), is treated under subdivision (iii)(b) of this subparagraph as gross income from sources without the United States.

(e) The sum of the amounts deemed and actually distributed as dividends for 1973 that are treated as gross income from sources within the United States is as follows:

	Total dividend	Amount of dividend from sources within the United States
Deemed distribution under section 995(b)(1)(D) as in effect for taxable years beginning before Jan. 1, 1976	$ 9,500	$500.00
Deemed distribution under section 995(b)(1)(G)	100	4.17
Actual distribution that reduces accumulated DISC income	2,000	83.33
Totals	11,600	587.50

Thus, pursuant to subdivision (v)(b) of this subparagraph, at the beginning of 1974 Y has $412.50, i.e., $1,000—$587.50, of nonqualified export taxable income.

(b) The distribution from previously taxed income is excluded from gross income pursuant to section 996(a)(3).

(c) Of the deemed distribution of $100, X is treated under subdivision (iv)(b) as having $4.17, i.e., $100 × 500/12,000, from sources within the United States and $95.83, i.e., $100 – $4.17, from sources without the United States.

(d) Of the actual distribution taxable as a dividend of $2,000, X is treated under subdivision (iv)(b) as having $83.33, i.e., $2,000 × 500/12,000, from sources within the United States and $1,916,67, i.e., $2,000 − $83.33, from sources without the United States.

(e) The sum of the amounts deemed and actually distributed as dividends for 1973 that are treated as gross income from sources within the United States is as follows:

	Total dividend	Amount of dividend from sources within the United States
Deemed distribution under section 995(b)(1)(D)	$ 9,500	$500.00
Deemed distribution under section 995(b)(1)(E)	100	4.17
Actual distribution that reduces accumulated DISC income	2,000	83.33
Totals	11,600	587.50

Thus, pursuant to subdivision (v)(b) of this subparagraph, at the beginning of 1974 Y has $412.50, i.e., $1,000 − $587.50, nonqualified export of taxable income.

(f) The result would be the same if Y made an actual distribution taxable as a dividend of $1,500 on March 30, 1973, and another distribution of $500 on December 31, 1973.

(6) Substitute dividend payments. A substitute dividend payment is a payment, made to the transferor of a security in a securities lending transaction or a sale-repurchase transaction, of an amount equivalent to a dividend distribution which the owner of the transferred security is entitled to receive during the term of the transaction. A securities lending transaction is a transfer of one or more securities that is described in section 1058(a) or a substantially similar transaction. A sale-repurchase transaction is an agreement under which a person transfers a security in exchange for cash and simultaneously agrees to receive substantially identical securities from the transferee in the future in exchange for cash. A substitute dividend payment shall be sourced in the same manner as the distributions with respect to the transferred security for purposes of this section and § 1.862-1. See also §§ 1.864-5(b)(2)(iii), 1.871-7(b)(2) and 1.881-2(b)(2) for the character of such payments and § 1.894-1(c) for the application of tax treaties to these transactions.

(b) Special rules. *(1) Foreign corporation having no gross income for period preceding declaration of dividend.* If the foreign corporation has no gross income from any source for the 3-year period (or part thereof) specified in paragraph (a)(3)(i) of this section, the 50-percent test, or the apportionment formula, as the case may be, described in such paragraph shall be applied solely with respect to the taxable year of such corporation in which the declaration of the dividend occurs. This subparagraph applies whether the lack of gross income for the 3-year period (or part thereof) stems from the business inactivity of the foreign corporation, from the fact that such corporation is newly created or organized, or from any other cause.

(2) Transitional rule. For purposes of applying paragraph (a)(3)(i) of this section, the gross income of the foreign corporation for any period before the first taxable year beginning after December 31, 1966, which is from sources within the United States (determined as provided by sections 861 through 863, and the regulations thereunder, as in effect immediately before amendment by section 102 of the Foreign Investors Tax Act of 1966 (Pub. L. 89-809, 80 Stat. 1541)) shall be treated as gross income for such period which is effectively connected with the conduct of a trade or business within the United States by such foreign corporation.

(3) Gross income determinations. In making determinations under subparagraph (2) or (3) of paragraph (a) of this section or subparagraph (2) of this paragraph—

(i) The gross income of a domestic corporation is to be determined by excluding any items specifically excluded from gross income under chapter 1 of the Code.

(ii) The gross income of a foreign corporation which is effectively connected with the conduct of a trade or business in the United States is to be determined under section 882(b)(2) and by excluding any items specifically excluded from gross income under chapter 1 of the Code, and

(iii) The gross income from all sources of a foreign corporation is to be determined without regard to section 882(b) and without excluding any items otherwise specifically excluded from gross income under chapter 1 of the Code.

(c) Statement with return. Any taxpayer who is required to file a return and applies any provision of this section to exclude any dividend from his gross income must file with his return a statement setting forth the amount so excluded, the date of its receipt, the name and address of the corporation paying the dividend, and, if known, the location of the records which substantiate the amount of the exclusion. A statement from the paying corporation setting forth such information and indicating the amount of the dividend to be treated as income from sources within the United States may be used for this purpose. See §§ 1.6012-1(b)(1)(i) and 1.6012-2(g)(1)(i).

(d) Effective date. Except as otherwise provided in this paragraph this section applies with respect to dividends received or accrued after December 31, 1966. Paragraph (a)(5) of this section applies to certain dividends from a DISC or former DISC in taxable years ending after December 31, 1971. Paragraph (a)(6) of this section is applicable to payments made after November 13, 1997. For corresponding rules applicable with respect to dividends received or accrued before January 1, 1967, see 26 CFR 1.861-3 (Rev. as of Jan. 1, 1972). For purposes of paragraph (a)(5) of this section, any reference to a distribution taxable as a dividend under section 995(b)(1)(F) (ii) and (iii) for taxable years beginning after December 31, 1975, shall also constitute a reference to any distribution taxable as a dividend under section 995(b)(1)(F) (ii) and (iii) for taxable years beginning after November 30, 1975, but before January 1, 1976.

T.D. 6258, 10/23/57, amend T.D. 6830, 6/22/65, T.D. 7378, 9/29/75, T.D. 7472, 3/1/77, T.D. 7591, 1/24/79, T.D. 7854, 11/16/82, T.D. 8735, 10/6/97, T.D. 9194, 4/6/2005.

PAR. 4. In § 1.861-3, paragraph (a)(2) is revised to read as follows:

Proposed § 1.861-3 Dividends. [*For Preamble, see ¶ 152,645*]

• ***Caution:*** This Notice of Proposed Rulemaking was partially finalized by TD 9248, 01/30/2006. Regs. §§ 1.1-1, 1.170A-1, 1.861-3, 1.861-8, 1.871-1, 1.876-1, 1.881-5, 1.884-0, 1.901-1, 1.931-1, 1.932-1, 1.933-1, 1.934-1, 1.935-1, 1.937-2, 1.937-3, 1.957-3, 1.1402(a)-12, 1.6038-2, 1.6046-1,

301.6688-1, 301.7701-3, and 301.7701(b)-1 remain proposed.

* * * * *

(a) * * *

(2) [The text of the proposed amendment to § 1.861-3 is the same as the text of § 1.861-3T(a)(2) published elsewhere in this issue of the Federal Register]. [*See T.D. 9194, 4/11/2005, 70 Fed. Reg. 68.*]

§ 1.861-3T Dividends (temporary).

• ***Caution:*** Under Code Sec. 7805, temporary regulations expire within three years of the date of issuance. This temporary regulation was issued on 4/6/2005.

(a) *(1)* [Reserved]. For further guidance, see § 1.861-3(a)(1).

(2) Dividend from a domestic corporation. A dividend described in this paragraph (a)(2) is a dividend from a domestic corporation other than a corporation which has an election in effect under section 936. See paragraph (a)(5) of this section for the treatment of certain dividends from a DISC or former DISC.

(3) through (c) [Reserved]. For further guidance, see § 1.861-3(a)(3) through (c).

(d) Effective date. This section shall apply for taxable years ending after October 22, 2004.

T.D. 9194, 4/6/2005.

§ 1.861-4 Compensation for labor or personal services.

Caution: The Treasury has not yet amended Reg § 1.861-4 to reflect changes made by P.L. 107-16, P.L. 105-34.

(a) Compensation for labor or personal services performed wholly within the United States. *(1)* Generally, compensation for labor or personal services, including fees, commissions, fringe benefits, and similar items, performed wholly within the United States is gross income from sources within the United States. Gross income from sources within the United States includes compensation for labor or personal services performed in the United States irrespective of the residence of the payer, the place in which the contract for service was made, or the place or time of payment; except that such compensation shall be deemed not to be income from sources within the United States, if—

(i) The labor or services are performed by a nonresident alien individual temporarily present in the United States for a period or periods not exceeding a total of 90 days during his taxable year.

(ii) The compensation for such labor or services does not exceed in the aggregate a gross amount of $3,000, and

(iii) The compensation is for labor or services performed as an employee of, or under any form of contract with—

(a) A nonresident alien individual, foreign partnership, or foreign corporation, not engaged in trade or business within the United States, or

(b) An individual who is a citizen or resident of the United States, a domestic partnership, or a domestic corporation, if such labor or services are performed for an office or place of business maintained in a foreign country or in a possession of the United States by such individual, partnership, or corporation.

(2) As a general rule, the term "day", as used in subparagraph (1)(i) of this paragraph, means a calendar day during any portion of which the nonresident alien individual is physically present in the United States.

(3) Solely for purposes of applying this paragraph, the nonresident alien individual, foreign partnership, or foreign corporation for which the nonresident alien individual is performing personal services in the United States shall not be considered to be engaged in trade or business in the United States by reason of the performance of such services by such individual.

(4) In determining for purposes of subparagraph (1)(ii) of this paragraph whether compensation received by the nonresident alien individual exceeds in the aggregate a gross amount of $3,000, any amounts received by the individual from an employer as advances or reimbursements for travel expenses incurred on behalf of the employer shall be omitted from the compensation received by the individual, to the extent of expenses incurred, where he was required to account and did account to his employer for such expenses and has met the tests for such accounting provided in § 1.162-17 and paragraph (e)(4) of § 1.274-5. If advances or reimbursements exceed such expenses, the amount of the excess shall be included as compensation for personal services for purposes of such subparagraph. Pensions and retirement pay attributable to labor or personal services performed in the United States are not to be taken into account for purposes of subparagraph (1)(ii) of this paragraph.

(5) For definition of the term "United States", when used in a geographical sense, see sections 638 and 7701(a)(9).

(b) Compensation for labor or personal services performed partly within and partly without the United States. *(1) Compensation for labor or personal services performed by persons other than individuals* (i) In general. In the case of compensation for labor or personal services performed partly within and partly without the United States by a person other than an individual, the part of that compensation that is attributable to the labor or personal services performed within the United States, and that is therefore included in gross income as income from sources within the United States, is determined on the basis that most correctly reflects the proper source of the income under the facts and circumstances of the particular case. In many cases, the facts and circumstances will be such that an apportionment on the time basis, as defined in paragraph (b)(2)(ii)(E) of this section, will be acceptable.

(ii) Example. The application of paragraph (b)(1)(i) is illustrated by the following example.

Example. Corp X, a domestic corporation, receives compensation of $150,000 under a contract for services to be performed concurrently in the United States and in several foreign countries by numerous Corp X employees. Each Corp X employee performing services under this contract performs his or her services exclusively in one jurisdiction. Although the number of employees (and hours spent by employees) performing services under the contract within the United States equals the number of employees (and hours spent by employees) performing services under the contract without the United States, the compensation paid to employees performing services under the contract within the United States is higher because of the more sophisticated nature of the services performed by the employees within the United States. Accordingly, the payroll cost for employees performing services under the contract within the United States is $20,000 out of a total contract payroll cost of $30,000. Under these facts and circumstances, a determination based upon relative payroll costs would be the basis that most correctly reflects the proper source of the income received under the contract. Thus, of the $150,000 of compensation included in Corp X's gross income, $100,000 ($150,000 x $20,000/$30,000) is attributable to the labor or personal services performed within the United States and $50,000 ($150,000 x $10,000/ $30,000) is attributable to the labor or personal services performed without the United States.

(2) Compensation for labor or personal services performed by an individual. (i) In general. Except as provided in paragraph (b)(2)(ii) of this section, in the case of compensation for labor or personal services performed partly within and partly without the United States by an individual, the part of such compensation that is attributable to the labor or personal services performed within the United States, and that is therefore included in gross income as income from sources within the United States, is determined on the basis that most correctly reflects the proper source of that income under the facts and circumstances of the particular case. In many cases, the facts and circumstances will be such that an apportionment on a time basis, as defined in paragraph (b)(2)(ii)(E) of this section, will be acceptable.

(ii) Employee compensation. (A) In general. Except as provided in paragraph (b)(2)(ii)(B) or (C) of this section, in the case of compensation for labor or personal services performed partly within and partly without the United States by an individual as an employee, the part of such compensation that is attributable to the labor or personal services performed within the United States, and that is therefore included in gross income as income from sources within the United States, is determined on a time basis, as defined in paragraph (b)(2)(ii)(E) of this section.

(B) Certain fringe benefits sourced on a geographical basis. Except as provided in paragraph (b)(2)(ii)(C) of this section, items of compensation of an individual as an employee for labor or personal services performed partly within and partly without the United States that are described in paragraphs (b)(2)(ii)(D)(1) through (6) of this section are sourced on a geographical basis in accordance with those paragraphs.

(C) Exceptions and special rules. (1) Alternative basis. (i) Individual as an employee generally. An individual may determine the source of his or her compensation as an employee for labor or personal services performed partly within and partly without the United States under an alternative basis if the individual establishes to the satisfaction of the Commissioner that, under the facts and circumstances of the particular case, the alternative basis more properly determines the source of the compensation than a basis described in paragraph (b)(2)(ii)(A) or (B), whichever is applicable, of this section. An individual that uses an alternative basis must retain in his or her records documentation setting forth why the alternative basis more properly determines the source of the compensation. In addition, the individual must provide the information related to the alternative basis required by applicable Federal tax forms and accompanying instructions.

(ii) Determination by Commissioner. The Commissioner may, under the facts and circumstances of the particular case, determine the source of compensation that is received by an individual as an employee for labor or personal services performed partly within and partly without the United States under an alternative basis other than a basis described in paragraph (b)(2)(ii)(A) or (B) of this section if such compensation either is not for a specific time period or constitutes in substance a fringe benefit described in paragraph (b)(2)(ii)(D) of this section notwithstanding a failure to meet any requirement of paragraph (b)(2)(ii)(D) of this section. The Commissioner may make this determination only if such alternative basis determines the source of compensation in a more reasonable manner than the basis used by the individual pursuant to paragraph (b)(2)(ii)(A) or (B) of this section.

(2) Ruling or other administrative pronouncement with respect to groups of taxpayers. The Commissioner may, by ruling or other administrative pronouncement applying to similarly situated taxpayers generally, permit individuals to determine the source of their compensation as an employee for labor or personal services performed partly within and partly without the United States under an alternative basis. Any such individual shall be treated as having met the requirement to establish such alternative basis to the satisfaction of the Commissioner under the facts and circumstances of the particular case, provided that the individual meets the other requirements of paragraph (b)(2)(ii)(C)(1)(i) of this section. The Commissioner also may, by ruling or other administrative pronouncement, indicate the circumstances in which he will require individuals to determine the source of certain compensation as an employee for labor or personal services performed partly within and partly without the United States under an alternative basis pursuant to the authority under paragraph (b)(2)(ii)(C)(1)(ii) of this section.

(3) Artists and athletes. [Reserved.]

(D) Fringe benefits sourced on a geographical basis. Except as provided in paragraph (b)(2)(ii)(C) of this section, compensation of an individual as an employee for labor or personal services performed partly within and partly without the United States in the form of the following fringe benefits is sourced on a geographical basis as indicated in this paragraph (b)(2)(ii)(D). The amount of the compensation in the form of the fringe benefit must be reasonable, and the individual must substantiate such amounts by adequate records or by sufficient evidence under rules similar to those set forth in § 1.274-5T(c) or (h) or § 1.132-5. For purposes of this paragraph (b)(2)(ii)(D), the term principal place of work has the same meaning that it has for purposes of section 217 and § 1.217-2(c)(3).

(1) Housing fringe benefit. The source of compensation in the form of a housing fringe benefit is determined based on the location of the individual's principal place of work. For purposes of this paragraph (b)(2)(ii)(D)(1), a housing fringe benefit includes payments to or on behalf of an individual (and the individual's family if the family resides with the individual) only for rent, utilities (other than telephone charges), real and personal property insurance, occupancy taxes not deductible under section 164 or 216(a), nonrefundable fees paid for securing a leasehold, rental of furniture and accessories, household repairs, residential parking, and the fair rental value of housing provided in kind by the individual's employer. A housing fringe benefit does not include payments for expenses or items set forth in § 1.911-4(b)(2).

(2) Education fringe benefit. The source of compensation in the form of an education fringe benefit for the education expenses of the individual's dependents is determined based on the location of the individual's principal place of work. For purposes of this paragraph (b)(2)(ii)(D)(2), an education fringe benefit includes payments only for qualified tuition

and expenses of the type described in section 530(b)(4)(A)(i) (regardless of whether incurred in connection with enrollment or attendance at a school) and expenditures for room and board and uniforms as described in section 530(b)(4)(A)(ii) with respect to education at an elementary or secondary educational institution.

(3) Local transportation fringe benefit. The source of compensation in the form of a local transportation fringe benefit is determined based on the location of the individual's principal place of work. For purposes of this paragraph (b)(2)(ii)(D)(3), an individual's local transportation fringe benefit is the amount that the individual receives as compensation for local transportation of the individual or the individual's spouse or dependents at the location of the individual's principal place of work. The amount treated as a local transportation fringe benefit is limited to the actual expenses incurred for local transportation and the fair rental value of any vehicle provided by the employer and used predominantly by the individual or the individual's spouse or dependents for local transportation. For this purpose, actual expenses incurred for local transportation do not include the cost (including interest) of the purchase by the individual, or on behalf of the individual, of an automobile or other vehicle.

(4) Tax reimbursement fringe benefit. The source of compensation in the form of a foreign tax reimbursement fringe benefit is determined based on the location of the jurisdiction that imposed the tax for which the individual is reimbursed.

(5) Hazardous or hardship duty pay fringe benefit. The source of compensation in the form of a hazardous or hardship duty pay fringe benefit is determined based on the location of the hazardous or hardship duty zone for which the hazardous or hardship duty pay fringe benefit is paid. For purposes of this paragraph (b)(2)(ii)(D)(5), a hazardous or hardship duty zone is any place in a foreign country which is either designated by the Secretary of State as a place where living conditions are extraordinarily difficult, notably unhealthy, or where excessive physical hardships exist, and for which a post differential of 15 percent or more would be provided under section 5925(b) of Title 5 of the U.S. Code to any officer or employee of the U.S. Government present at that place, or where a civil insurrection, civil war, terrorism, or wartime conditions threatens physical harm or imminent danger to the health and well-being of the individual. Compensation provided an employee during the period that the employee performs labor or personal services in a hazardous or hardship duty zone may be treated as a hazardous or hardship duty pay fringe benefit only if the employer provides the hazardous or hardship duty pay fringe benefit only to employees performing labor or personal services in a hazardous or hardship duty zone. The amount of compensation treated as a hazardous or hardship duty pay fringe benefit may not exceed the maximum amount that the U.S. government would allow its officers or employees present at that location.

(6) Moving expense reimbursement fringe benefit. Except as otherwise provided in this paragraph (b)(2)(ii)(D)(6), the source of compensation in the form of a moving expense reimbursement is determined based on the location of the employee's new principal place of work. The source of such compensation is determined based on the location of the employee's former principal place of work, however, if the individual provides sufficient evidence that such determination of source is more appropriate under the facts and circumstances of the particular case. For purposes of this paragraph (b)(2)(ii)(D)(6), sufficient evidence generally requires an agreement, between the employer and the employee, or a written statement of company policy, which is reduced to writing before the move and which is entered into or established to induce the employee or employees to move to another country. Such written statement or agreement must state that the employer will reimburse the employee for moving expenses that the employee incurs to return to the employee's former principal place of work regardless of whether he or she continues to work for the employer after returning to that location. The writing may contain certain conditions upon which the right to reimbursement is determined as long as those conditions set forth standards that are definitely ascertainable and can only be fulfilled prior to, or through completion of, the employee's return move to the employee's former principal place of work.

(E) Time basis. The amount of compensation for labor or personal services performed within the United States determined on a time basis is the amount that bears the same relation to the individual's total compensation as the number of days of performance of the labor or personal services by the individual within the United States bears to his or her total number of days of performance of labor or personal services. A unit of time less than a day may be appropriate for purposes of this calculation. The time period for which the compensation for labor or personal services is made is presumed to be the calendar year in which the labor or personal services are performed, unless the taxpayer establishes to the satisfaction of the Commissioner, or the Commissioner determines, that another distinct, separate, and continuous period of time is more appropriate. For example, a transfer during a year from a position in the United States to a foreign posting that lasted through the end of that year would generally establish two separate time periods within that taxable year. The first of these time periods would be the portion of the year preceding the start of the foreign posting, and the second of these time periods would be the portion of the year following the start of the foreign posting. However, in the case of a foreign posting that requires short-term returns to the United States to perform services for the employer, such short-term returns would not be sufficient to establish distinct, separate, and continuous time periods within the foreign posting time period but would be relevant to the allocation of compensation relating to the overall time period. In each case, the source of the compensation on a time basis is based upon the number of days (or unit of time less than a day, if appropriate) in that separate time period.

(F) Multi-year compensation arrangements. The source of multi-year compensation is determined generally on a time basis, as defined in paragraph (b)(2)(ii)(E) of this section, over the period to which such compensation is attributable. For purposes of this paragraph (b)(2)(ii)(F), multi-year compensation means compensation that is included in the income of an individual in one taxable year but that is attributable to a period that includes two or more taxable years. The determination of the period to which such compensation is attributable, for purposes of determining its source, is based upon the facts and circumstances of the particular case. For example, an amount of compensation that specifically relates to a period of time that includes several calendar years is attributable to the entirety of that multi-year period. The amount of such compensation that is treated as from sources within the United States is the amount that bears the same relationship to the total multi-year compensation as the number of days (or unit of time less than a day, if appropriate) that labor or personal services were performed within the United States in connection with the project bears to the total number of days (or unit of time less than a day, if appropriate) that labor or personal services were performed in connection with the project. In the case of stock options, the facts and circumstances generally will be such that the applicable period to which the compensation is attributable is the period between the grant of an option and the date on which all employment-related conditions for its exercise have been satisfied (the vesting of the option).

(G) Examples. The following examples illustrate the application of this paragraph (b)(2)(ii):

Example (1). B, a nonresident alien individual, was employed by Corp M, a domestic corporation, from March 1 to December 25 of the taxable year, a total of 300 days, for which B received compensation in the amount of $80,000. Under B's employment contract with Corp M, B was subject to call at all times by Corp M and was in a payment status on a 7-day week basis. Pursuant to that contract, B performed services (or was available to perform services) within the United States for 180 days and performed services (or was available to perform services) without the United States for 120 days. None of B's $80,000 compensation was for fringe benefits as identified in paragraph (b)(2)(ii)(D) of this section. B determined the amount of compensation that is attributable to his labor or personal services performed within the United States on a time basis under paragraph (b)(2)(ii)(A) and (E) of this section. B did not assert, pursuant to paragraph (b)(2)(ii)(C)(1)(i) of this section, that, under the particular facts and circumstances, an alternative basis more properly determines the source of that compensation than the time basis. Therefore, B must include in income from sources within the United States $48,000 ($80,000 x 180/300) of his compensation from Corporation M.

Example (2). (i) Same facts as in Example 1 except that Corp M had a company-wide arrangement with its employees, including B, that they would receive an education fringe benefit, as described in paragraph (b)(2)(ii)(D)(2) of this section, while working in the United States. During the taxable year, B incurred education expenses for his dependent daughter that qualified for the education fringe benefit in the amount of $10,000, for which B received a reimbursement from Corp M. B did not maintain adequate records or sufficient evidence of this fringe benefit as required by paragraph (b)(2)(ii)(D) of this section. When B filed his Federal income tax return for the taxable year, B did not apply paragraphs (b)(2)(ii)(B) and (D)(2) of this section to treat the compensation in the form of the education fringe benefit as income from sources within the United States, the location of his principal place of work during the 300-day period. Rather, B combined the $10,000 reimbursement with his base compensation of $80,000 and applied the time basis of paragraph (b)(2)(ii)(A) of this section to determine the source of his gross income.

(ii) On audit, B argues that because he failed to substantiate the education fringe benefit in accordance with paragraph (b)(2)(ii)(D) of this section, his entire employment compensation from Corp M is sourced on a time basis pursuant to paragraph (b)(2)(ii)(A) of this section. The Commissioner, after reviewing Corp M's fringe benefit arrangement, determines, pursuant to paragraph (b)(2)(ii)(C)(1)(ii) of this section, that the $10,000 educational expense reimbursement constitutes in substance a fringe benefit described in paragraph (b)(2)(ii)(D)(2) of this section, notwithstanding a failure to meet all of the requirements of paragraph (b)(2)(ii)(D) of this section, and that an alternative geographic source basis, under the facts and circumstances of this particular case, is a more reasonable manner to determine the source of the compensation than the time basis used by B.

Example (3). (i) A, a United States citizen, is employed by Corp N, a domestic corporation. A's principal place of work is in the United States. A earns an annual salary of $100,000. During the first quarter of the calendar year (which is also A's taxable year), A performed services entirely within the United States. At the beginning of the second quarter of the calendar year, A was transferred to Country X for the remainder of the year and received, in addition to her annual salary, $30,000 in fringe benefits that are attributable to her new principal place of work in Country X. Corp N paid these fringe benefits separately from A's annual salary. Corp N supplied A with a statement detailing that $25,000 of the fringe benefit was paid for housing, as defined in paragraph (b)(2)(ii)(D)(1) of this section, and $5,000 of the fringe benefit was paid for local transportation, as defined in paragraph (b)(2)(ii)(D)(3) of this section. None of the local transportation fringe benefit is excluded from the employee's gross income as a qualified transportation fringe benefit under section 132(a)(5). Under A's employment contract, A was required to work on a 5-day week basis, Monday through Friday. During the last three quarters of the year, A performed services 30 days in the United States and 150 days in Country X and other foreign countries.

(ii) A determined the source of all of her compensation from Corp N pursuant to paragraphs (b)(2)(ii)(A), (B), and (D)(1) and (3) of this section. A did not assert, pursuant to paragraph (b)(2)(ii)(C)(1)(i) of this section, that, under the particular facts and circumstances, an alternative basis more properly determines the source of that compensation than the bases set forth in paragraphs (b)(2)(ii)(A), (B), and (D)(1) and (3) of this section. However, in applying the time basis set forth in paragraph (b)(2)(ii)(E) of this section, A establishes to the satisfaction of the Commissioner that the first quarter of the calendar year and the last three quarters of the calendar year are two separate, distinct, and continuous periods of time. Accordingly, $25,000 of A's annual salary is attributable to the first quarter of the year (25 percent of $100,000). This amount is entirely compensation that was attributable to the labor or personal services performed within the United States and is, therefore, included in gross income as income from sources within the United States. The balance of A's compensation as an employee of Corp N, $105,000 (which includes the $30,000 in fringe benefits that are attributable to the location of A's principal place of work in Country X), is compensation attributable to the final three quarters of her taxable year. During those three quarters, A's periodic performance of services in the United States does not result in distinct, separate, and continuous periods of time. Of the $75,000 paid for annual salary, $12,500 (30/180 x $75,000) is compensation that was attributable to the labor or personal services performed within the United States and $62,500 (150/180 x $75,000) is compensation that was attributable to the labor or personal services performed outside the United States. Pursuant to paragraphs (b)(2)(ii)(B) and (D)(1) and (3) of this section, A sourced the $25,000 received for the housing fringe benefit and the $5,000 received for the local transportation fringe benefit based on the location of her principal place of work, Country X. Accordingly, A included the $30,000 in fringe benefits in her gross income as income from sources without the United States.

Example (4). Same facts as in Example 3. Of the 150 days during which A performed services in Country X and in other foreign countries (during the final three quarters of

A's taxable year), she performed 30 days of those services in Country Y. Country Y is a country designated by the Secretary of State as a place where living conditions are extremely difficult, notably unhealthy, or where excessive physical hardships exist and for which a post differential of 15 percent or more would be provided under section 5925(b) of Title 5 of the U.S. Code to any officer or employee of the U.S. government present at that place. Corp N has a policy of paying its employees a $65 premium per day for each day worked in countries so designated. The $65 premium per day does not exceed the maximum amount that the U. S. government would pay its officers or employees stationed in Country Y. Because A performed services in Country Y for 30 days, she earned additional compensation of $1,950. The $1,950 is considered a hazardous duty or hardship pay fringe benefit and is sourced under paragraphs (b)(2)(ii)(B) and (D)(5) of this section based on the location of the hazardous or hardship duty zone, Country Y. Accordingly, A included the amount of the hazardous duty or hardship pay fringe benefit ($1,950) in her gross income as income from sources without the United States.

Example (5). (i) During 2006 and 2007, Corp P, a domestic corporation, employed four United States citizens, E, F, G, and H to work in its manufacturing plant in Country V. As part of his or her compensation package, each employee arranged for local transportation unrelated to Corp P's business needs. None of the local transportation fringe benefit is excluded from the employee's gross income as a qualified transportation fringe benefit under section 132(a)(5) and (f).

(ii) Under the terms of the compensation package that E negotiated with Corp P, Corp P permitted E to use an automobile owned by Corp P. In addition, Corp P agreed to reimburse E for all expenses incurred by E in maintaining and operating the automobile, including gas and parking. Provided that the local transportation fringe benefit meets the requirements of paragraph (b)(2)(ii)(D)(3) of this section, E's compensation with respect to the fair rental value of the automobile and reimbursement for the expenses E incurred is sourced under paragraphs (b)(2)(ii)(B) and (D)(3) of this section based on E's principal place of work in Country V. Thus, the local transportation fringe benefit will be included in E's gross income as income from sources without the United States.

(iii) Under the terms of the compensation package that F negotiated with Corp P, Corp P let F use an automobile owned by Corp P. However, Corp P did not agree to reimburse F for any expenses incurred by F in maintaining and operating the automobile. Provided that the local transportation fringe benefit meets the requirements of paragraph (b)(2)(ii)(D)(3) of this section, F's compensation with respect to the fair rental value of the automobile is sourced under paragraphs (b)(2)(ii)(B) and (D)(3) of this section based on F's principal place of work in Country V. Thus, the local transportation fringe benefit will be included in F's gross income as income from sources without the United States.

(iv) Under the terms of the compensation package that G negotiated with Corp P, Corp P agreed to reimburse G for the purchase price of an automobile that G purchased in Country V. Corp P did not agree to reimburse G for any expenses incurred by G in maintaining and operating the automobile. Because the cost to purchase an automobile is not a local transportation fringe benefit as defined in paragraph (b)(2)(ii)(D)(3) of this section, the source of the compensation to G will be determined pursuant to paragraph (b)(2)(ii)(A) or (C) of this section.

(v) Under the terms of the compensation package that H negotiated with Corp P, Corp P agreed to reimburse H for the expenses that H incurred in maintaining and operating an automobile, including gas and parking, which H purchased in Country V. Provided that the local transportation fringe benefit meets the requirements of paragraph (b)(2)(ii)(D)(3) of this section, H's compensation with respect to the reimbursement for the expenses H incurred is sourced under paragraphs (b)(2)(ii)(B) and (D)(3) of this section based on H's principal place of work in Country V. Thus, the local transportation fringe benefit will be included in H's gross income as income from sources without the United States.

Example (6). (i) On January 1, 2006, Company Q compensates employee J with a grant of options to which section 421 does not apply that do not have a readily ascertainable fair market value when granted. The stock options permit J to purchase 100 shares of Company Q stock for $5 per share. The stock options do not become exercisable unless and until J performs services for Company Q (or a related company) for 5 years. J works for Company Q for the 5 years required by the stock option grant. In years 2006-08, J performs all of his services for Company Q within the United States. In 2009, J performs ½ of his services for Company Q within the United States and ½ of his services for Company Q without the United States. In year 2010, J performs his services entirely without the United States. On December 31, 2012, J exercises the options when the stock is worth $10 per share. J recognizes $500 in taxable compensation (($10-$5) x 100) in 2012.

(ii) Under the facts and circumstances, the applicable period is the 5-year period between the date of grant (January 1, 2006) and the date the stock options become exercisable (December 31, 2010). On the date the stock options become exercisable, J performs all services necessary to obtain the compensation from Company Q. Accordingly, the services performed after the date the stock options become exercisable are not taken into account in sourcing the compensation from the stock options. Therefore, pursuant to paragraph (b)(2)(ii)(A), since J performs 3½ years of services for Company Q within the United States and 1½ years of services for Company Q without the United States during the 5-year period, 7/10 of the $500 of compensation (or $350) recognized in 2012 is income from sources within the United States and the remaining 3/10 of the compensation (or $150) is income from sources without the United States.

(c) Coastwise travel. Except as to income excluded by paragraph (a) of this section, wages received for services rendered inside the territorial limits of the United States and wages of an alien seaman earned on a coastwise vessel are to be regarded as from sources within the United States.

(d) Effective date. This section applies with respect to taxable years beginning after December 31, 1966. For corresponding rules applicable to taxable years beginning before January 1, 1967, see 26 CFR 1.861-4 (Rev. as of Jan. 1, 1972). Paragraph (b) and the first sentence of paragraph (a)(1) of this section apply to taxable years beginning on or after July 14, 2005.

T.D. 6258, 10/23/57, amend T.D. 7378, 9/29/75, T.D. 9212, 7/13/2005.

PAR. 2. Section 1.861-4 is amended by:

1. Removing the heading for paragraph (b)(1)(i).

2. Redesignating paragraph (b)(1)(i) as paragraph (b)(1).

3. In the last sentence of newly designated paragraph (b)(1), adding the language "or on the event basis as defined

in paragraph (b)(2)(ii)(G) of this section," after the language "paragraph (b)(2)(ii)(E) of this section,".

4. In the last sentence of paragraph (b)(2)(i), adding the language "or on the event basis as defined in paragraph (b)(2)(ii)(G) of this section," after the language "paragraph (b)(2)(ii)(E) of this section,".

5. In the first sentence of paragraph (b)(2)(ii)(C)(1)(i), adding the language ", including an event basis as defined in paragraph (b)(2)(ii)(G) of this section," after the language "alternative basis" wherever the language "alternative basis" appears in the sentence.

6. In the first sentence of paragraph (b)(2)(ii)(C)(1)(ii), adding the language "event basis as defined in paragraph (b)(2)(ii)(G) of this section or other" after the language "partly without the United States under an".

7. Removing paragraph (b)(2)(ii)(C)(3).

8. In the first sentence of paragraph (b)(2)(ii)(E), removing the language "individual's" and adding the language "person's" in its place, removing the language "individual" and adding the language "person" in its place, and removing the language "his or hers" and adding the language "such person's" in its place.

9. In the second sentence of paragraph (b)(2)(ii)(F), removing the language "an individual" and adding the language "a person" in its place.

10. Redesignating paragraphs (c) and (d) as new paragraphs (d) and (e), respectively.

11. Redesignating paragraph (b)(2)(ii)(G) as new paragraph (c).

12. Adding a new paragraph (b)(2)(ii)(G).

13. In the introductory language of newly-designated paragraph (c), removing the language "paragraph (b)(2)(ii)" and adding the language "section" in its place.

14. Adding new Examples 7, 8, 9, and 10 to newly-designated paragraph (c).

15. Redesignating paragraph (b)(1)(ii) Example, as new Example 11 in newly-designated paragraph (c), revising the paragraph heading and removing paragraph (b)(1)(ii).

16. Adding a new sentence at the end of newly-designated paragraph (e) and revising the paragraph heading.

The additions read as follows:

Proposed § 1.861-4 Compensation for labor or personal services. [*For Preamble, see ¶ 152,921*]

* * * * *

(b) * * *

(2) * * *

(ii) * * *

(G) Event basis. The amount of compensation for labor or personal services determined on an event basis is the amount of the person's compensation which, based on the facts and circumstances, is attributable to the labor or personal services performed at the location of a specific event. The source of compensation for labor or personal services determined on an event basis is the location of the specific event. A basis that purports to determine the source of compensation from the performance of labor or personal services at a specific event, whether on a time basis or otherwise, by taking into account the location of labor or personal services performed in preparation for the performance of labor or personal services at the specific event will generally not be the basis that most correctly determines the source of the compensation.

(c) Examples. * * *

Example (7). P, a citizen and resident of Country A, is paid by Company Z to make a presentation in the United States in 2009. In 2010, Company Z pays P to make 10 presentations, four of which are in the United States and six of which are outside the United States. P is compensated separately by Company Z for each presentation. For some presentations P receives a flat fee from Company Z. For the remaining presentations P receives compensation that is based on a formula. Under the facts and circumstances of the particular case, the source of the compensation for each presentation is most correctly reflected on an event basis, as defined in paragraph (b)(2)(ii)(G) of this section. Because P is compensated separately for each presentation, the source of P's compensation from Company Z for the 2009 presentation within the United States and the four 2010 presentations in the United States will be from sources in the United States. The amounts will be determined based on the flat fee or the formula as contractually determined.

Example (8). (i) Facts. Group B, a Country N corporation, is a musical group. All of the members of Group B are citizens and residents of Country N. Group B has an employment arrangement with Corp Y, a Country N corporation, to perform as directed by Corp Y. Corp Y and a tour promoter enter into a contract to provide the services of Group B to perform in musical concerts in the United States and Country M during a 45-day period. Under the contract, Group B performs concerts in 15 cities, 10 of which are in the United States. Prior to entering the United States, Group B spends 60 days rehearsing and preparing in Country N. Under the contract with Corp Y, Group B receives a flat fee of $10,000,000 for performing in all 15 cities. The fee is based on expected revenues from the musical concerts. Each concert is expected to require a similar amount and type of labor or personal services by Group B. At the end of the tour, an analysis of the revenues from all of the concerts shows that 80% of the total revenues from the tour were from the performances within the United States.

(ii) Analysis. Under the facts and circumstances basis of paragraph (b)(1) of this section, the source of the compensation received under the contract is most correctly reflected on an event basis, as defined in paragraph (b)(2)(ii)(G) of this section, with amounts determined based on the relative gross receipts attributable to the performances within and without the United States. Thus, of the $10,000,000 of compensation included in Group B's gross income, $8,000,000 ($10,000,000 x .80) is attributable to labor or personal services performed by Group B within the United States and $2,000,000 ($10,000,000 x .20) is attributable to the labor or personal services performed by Group B without the United States.

Example (9). (i) Facts. A, a citizen and resident of Country M, is an employee of Corp X, a Country M corporation. During 2008, Corp X is contractually obligated to provide A's services to perform in a specific athletic event in the United States. Under A's employment contract with Corp X, A is required to perform at a professional level that requires training and other preparation prior to the event. A undertakes all of this preparation in Country M. Solely as a result of A's performance at the athletic event in the United States, A receives $2,000,000 from Corp X.

(ii) Analysis. The entire $2,000,000 received by A for performing labor or personal services at the athletic event in the United States is income from sources within the United States on an event basis as defined in paragraph (b)(2)(ii)(G) of this section. A's compensation is attributable entirely to labor or personal services performed within the United States at the athletic event. It is inappropriate to conclude that the source of A's compensation for labor or personal services is performed partly within and partly without the United States simply because A's preparation for the athletic event involved activities in Country M.

Example (10). (i) Facts. X, a citizen and resident of Country M, is employed under a standard player's contract by a professional sports team (Team) that plays its games both within and without the United States during its season. The term of the contract is for twelve months beginning on October 1. Under the contract, X's salary could be paid in semimonthly installments beginning with the first game of the regular season and ending with the final game played by the Team. Alternatively, because the regular playing season was shorter than the one-year period covered by the contract, X had the option to receive his salary over a twelve-month period. X elected this option. In addition, during the period of this employment contract, X, as an employee of Team, was required to practice at the direction of the Team as well as to participate in games. During 2008, X participated in all practices and games of Team and received a salary. Team qualified for postseason games in 2008. X also received in 2008 additional amounts for playing in preseason and postseason games for the Team.

(ii) Analysis. The salary paid to X by the Team is considered to be personal services compensation of X that X received as an employee of the Team. The source of this compensation within the United States is determined under the time basis method described in paragraph (b)(2)(ii)(A) of this section and accordingly is determined based upon the number of days X performed services for the Team within the United States during 2008 over the total number of days that X performed services for the Team during 2008. The source of the additional amounts X received for playing in preseason and postseason games is determined under the event basis method described in paragraph (b)(2)(ii)(G) of this section and accordingly is determined based on the location where each such preseason or postseason game was played.

Example (11). * * *

* * * * *

(e) Effective/applicability date. * * * The revisions in paragraphs (b)(1), (b)(2)(i), and (b)(2)(ii)(C)(1)(i) and (ii) of this section which refer to the event basis; the revisions of paragraphs (b)(2)(ii)(C)(3), (b)(2)(ii)(E), (b)(2)(ii)(F), (b)(2)(ii)(G), and (c) of this section; and Examples 7 through 11 of paragraph (c) of this section apply to taxable years beginning after the date final regulations are published in the Federal Register.

§ 1.861-5 Rentals and royalties.

Gross income from sources within the United States includes rentals or royalties from property located in the United States or from any interest in such property, including rentals or royalties for the use of, or for the privilege of using, in the United States, patents, copyrights, secret processes and formulas, good will, trademarks, trade brands, franchises, and other like property. The income arising from the rental of property, whether tangible or intangible, located within the United States, or from the use of property, whether tangible or intangible, within the United States, is from sources within the United States. For taxable years beginning after December 31, 1966, gains described in section 871(a)(1)(D) and section 881(a)(4) from the sale or exchange after October 4, 1966, of patents, copyrights, and other like property shall be treated, as provided in section 871(e)(2), as rentals or royalties for the use of, or privilege of using, property or an interest in property. See paragraph (e) of § 1.871-11.

T.D. 6258, 10/23/57, amend T.D. 7378, 9/29/75.

§ 1.861-6 Sale of real property.

Gross income from sources within the United States includes gain, computed under the provisions of section 1001 and the regulations thereunder, derived from the sale or other disposition of real property located in the United States. For the treatment of capital gains and losses, see subchapter P (section 1201 and following), chapter 1 of the Code, and the regulations thereunder.

T.D. 6258, 10/23/57.

§ 1.861-7 Sale of personal property.

(a) General. Gains, profits, and income derived from the purchase and sale of personal property shall be treated as derived entirely from the country in which the property is sold. Thus, gross income from sources within the United States includes gains, profits, and income derived from the purchase of personal property without the United States on its sale within the United States.

(b) Purchase within a possession. Notwithstanding paragraph (a) of this section, income derived from the purchase of personal property within a possession of the United States and its sale within the United States shall be treated as derived partly from sources within and partly from sources without the United States. See section 863(b)(3) and § 1.863-2.

(c) Country in which sold. For the purposes of part I (section 861 and following), subchapter N, chapter 1 of the Code, and the regulations thereunder, a sale of personal property is consummated at the time when, and the place where, the rights, title, and interest of the seller in the property are transferred to the buyer. Where bare legal title is retained by the seller, the sale shall be deemed to have occurred at the time and place of passage to the buyer of beneficial ownership and the risk of loss. However, in any case in which the sales transaction is arranged in a particular manner for the primary purpose of tax avoidance, the foregoing rules will not be applied. In such cases, all factors of the transaction, such as negotiations, the execution of the agreement, the location of the property, and the place of payment, will be considered, and the sale will be treated as having been consummated at the place where the substance of the sale occurred.

(d) Production and sale. For provisions respecting the source of income derived from the sale of personal property produced by the taxpayer, see section 863(b)(2) and paragraphs (b) of §§ 1.863-1 and 1.863-2.

(e) Section 306 stock. For determining the source of gain on the disposition of section 306 stock, see section 306(f) and the regulations thereunder.

T.D. 6258, 10/23/57.

§ 1.861-8 Computation of taxable income from sources within the United States and from other sources and activities.

Caution: The Treasury has not yet amended Reg § 1.861-8 to reflect changes made by P.L. 104-188, P.L. 103-66, P.L. 101-508, P.L. 100-647.

(a) In general. *(1) Scope.* Sections 861(b) and 863(a) state in general terms how to determine taxable income of a taxpayer from sources within the United States after gross income from sources within the United States has been determined. Sections 862(b) and 863(a) state in general terms how to determine taxable income of a taxpayer from sources without the United States after gross income from sources without the United States has been determined. This section provides specific guidance for applying the cited Code sections by prescribing rules for the allocation and apportionment of expenses, losses, and other deductions (referred to collectively in this section as "deductions") of the taxpayer. The rules contained in this section apply in determining taxable income of the taxpayer from specific sources and activities under other sections of the Code, referred to in this section as operative sections. See paragraph (f)(1) of this section for a list and description of operative sections. The operative sections include, among others, sections 871(b) and 882 (relating to taxable income of a nonresident alien individual or a foreign corporation which is effectively connected with the conduct of a trade or business in the United States), section 904(a)(1) (as in effect before enactment of the Tax Reform Act of 1976, relating to taxable income from sources within specific foreign countries), and section 904(a)(2) (as in effect before enactment of the Tax Reform Act of 1976, or section 904(a) after such enactment, relating to taxable income from all sources without the United States).

(2) Allocation and apportionment of deductions in general. A taxpayer to which this section applies is required to allocate deductions to a class of gross income and, then, if necessary to make the determination required by the operative section of the Code, to apportion deductions within the class of gross income between the statutory grouping of gross income (or among the statutory groupings) and the residual grouping of gross income. Except for deductions, if any, which are not definitely related to gross income (see paragraphs (c)(3) and (e)(9) of this section) and which, therefore, are ratably apportioned to all gross income, all deductions of the taxpayer (except the deductions for personal exemptions enumerated in paragraph (e)(11) of this section) must be so allocated and apportioned. As further detailed below, allocations and apportionments are made on the basis of the factual relationship of deductions to gross income.

(3) Class of gross income. For purposes of this section, the gross income to which a specific deduction is definitely related is referred to as a "class of gross income" and may consist of one or more items (or subdivisions of these items) of gross income enumerated in section 61, namely:

(i) Compensation for services, including fees, commissions, and similar items;

(ii) Gross income derived from business;

(iii) Gains derived from dealings in property;

(iv) Interest;

(v) Rents;

(vi) Royalties;

(vii) Dividends;

(viii) Alimony and separate maintenance payments;

(ix) Annuities;

(x) Income from life insurance and endowment contracts;

(xi) Pensions;

(xii) Income from discharge of indebtedness;

(xiii) Distributive share of partnership gross income;

(xiv) Income in respect of a decedent;

(xv) Income from an interest in an estate or trust.

(4) Statutory grouping of gross income and residual grouping of gross income. For purposes of this section, the term "statutory grouping of gross income" or "statutory grouping" means the gross income from a specific source or activity which must first be determined in order to arrive at taxable income from such specific source or activity under an operative section. (See paragraph (f)(1) of this section.) Gross income from other sources or activities is referred to as the "residual grouping of gross income" or "residual grouping". For example, for purposes of determining taxable income from sources within specific foreign countries and possessions of the United States, in order to apply the per-country limitation to the foreign tax credit (as in effect before enactment of the Tax Reform Act of 1976), the statutory groupings are the separate gross incomes from sources within each country and possession. Moreover, if the taxpayer has income subject to section 904(d) (as in effect after enactment of the Tax Reform Act of 1976), such income constitutes one or more separate statutory groupings. In the case of the per-country limitation, the residual grouping is the aggregate of gross income from sources within the United States. In some instances, where the operative section so requires, the statutory grouping or the residual grouping may include, or consist entirely of, excluded income. See paragraph (d)(2) of this section with respect to the allocation and apportionment of deductions to excluded income.

(5) Effective date. (i) Taxable years beginning after December 31, 1976. The provisions of this section apply to taxable years beginning after December 31, 1976.

(ii) [Reserved]. For further guidance, see § 1.861-8T(a)(5)(ii).

(iii) Taxable years beginning before January 1, 1977. For taxable years beginning before January 1, 1977, § 1.861-8 applies as in effect on October 23, 1957 (T.D. 6258), as amended on August 22, 1966 (T.D. 6892) and on September 29, 1975 (T.D. 7378). The specific rules for allocation and apportionment of deductions set forth in this section may, at the option of the taxpayer, apply to those taxable years on a deduction-by-deduction basis if the rules are applied consistently to all taxable years with respect to which action by the Internal Revenue Service is not barred by any statute of limitations. Thus, for example, a calendar year taxpayer may choose to have the rules of paragraph (e)(2) of this section apply for the allocation and apportionment of all interest expenses for the two taxable years ending December 31, 1975 and 1976, which are open years under examination, and may justify the allocation and apportionment of all research and development expenses for those years on a basis supportable under § 1.861-8 as in effect for 1975 and 1976 without regard to the rules of paragraph (e)(3) of this section.

(b) Allocation. *(1) In general.* For purposes of this section, the gross income to which a specific deduction is definitely related is referred to as a "class of gross income" and may consist of one or more items of gross income. The rules emphasize the factual relationship between the deduction and a class of gross income. See paragraph (d)(1) of this section which provides that in a taxable year there may be no item of gross income in a class or less gross income than deductions allocated to the class, and paragraph (d)(2) of this section which provides that a class of gross income may include excluded income. Allocation is accomplished by determining, with respect to each deduction, the class of gross income to which the deduction is definitely related and then allocating the deduction to such class of gross income (without regard to the taxable year in which such gross income is received or accrued or is expected to be received or accrued). The classes of gross income are not predetermined but must be determined on the basis of the deductions to be allocated. Although most deductions will be definitely related to some class of a taxpayer's total gross income, some deductions are related to all gross income. In addition, some deductions are treated as not definitely related to any gross income and are ratably apportioned to all gross income. (See paragraph (e)(9) of this section.) In allocating deductions it is not necessary to differentiate between deductions related to one item of gross income and deductions related to another item of gross income where both items of gross income are exclusively within the same statutory grouping or exclusively within the residual grouping.

(2) Relationship to activity or property. A deduction shall be considered definitely related to a class of gross income and therefore allocable to such class if it is incurred as a result of, or incident to, an activity or in connection with property from which such class of gross income is derived. Where a deduction is incurred as a result of, or incident to, an activity or in connection with property, which activity or property generates, has generated, or could reasonably have been expected to generate gross income, such deduction shall be considered definitely related to such gross income as a class whether or not there is any item of gross income in such class which is received or accrued during the taxable year and whether or not the amount of deductions exceeds the amount of the gross income in such class. See paragraph (d)(1) of this section and example (17) of paragraph (g) of this section with respect to cases in which there is an excess of deductions. In some cases, it will be found that this subparagraph can most readily be applied by determining, with respect to a deduction, the categories of gross income to which it is not related and concluding that it is definitely related to a class consisting of all other gross income.

(3) Supportive functions.[Reserved] For guidance, see § 1.861-8T(b)(3).

(4) Deductions related to a class of gross income. See paragraph (e) of this section for rules relating to the allocation and apportionment of certain specific deductions definitely related to a class of gross income. See paragraph (c)(1) of this section for rules relating to the apportionment of deductions.

(5) Deductions related to all gross income. If a deduction does not bear a definite relationship to a class of gross income constituting less than all of gross income, it shall ordinarily be treated as definitely related and allocable to all of the taxpayer's gross income except where provided to the contrary under paragraph (e) of this section. Paragraph (e)(9) of this section lists various deductions which generally are not definitely related to any gross income and are ratably apportioned to all gross income.

(c) Apportionment of deductions. *(1) Deductions definitely related to a class of gross income. [Reserved]* For guidance, see § 1.861-8T(c)(1).

(2) Allocation and apportionment of deductions in general. [Reserved] For guidance, see § 1.861-8T(c)(2).

(3) Deductions not definitely related to any gross income. If a deduction is not definitely related to any gross income (see paragraph (e)(9) of this section), the deduction must be apportioned ratably between the statutory grouping (or among the statutory groupings) of gross income and the residual grouping. Thus, the amount apportioned to each statutory grouping shall be equal to the same proportion of the deduction which the amount of gross income in the statutory grouping bears to the total amount of gross income. The amount apportioned to the residual grouping shall be equal to the same proportion of the deduction which the amount of the gross income in the residual grouping bears to the total amount of gross income.

(d) Excess of deductions and excluded and eliminated income. *(1) Excess of deductions.* Each deduction which bears a definite relationship to a class of gross income shall be allocated to that class in accordance with paragraph (b)(1) of this section even though, for the taxable year, no gross income in such class is received or accrued or the amount of the deduction exceeds the amount of such class of gross income. In apportioning deductions, it may be that, for the taxable year, there is no gross income in the statutory grouping (or residual grouping), or that deductions exceed the amount of gross income in the statutory grouping (or residual grouping). If there is no gross income in a statutory grouping or the amount of deductions allocated and apportioned to a statutory grouping exceeds the amount of gross income in the statutory grouping, the effects are determined under the operative section. If the taxpayer is a member of a group filing a consolidated return, such excess of deductions allocated or apportioned to a statutory grouping of income of such member is taken into account in determining the consolidated taxable income from such statutory grouping, and such excess of deductions allocated or apportioned to the residual grouping of income is taken into account in determining the consolidated taxable income from the residual grouping. See § 1.1502-4(d)(1) and the last sentence of § 1.1502-12. For an illustration of the principles of this paragraph (d)(1), see example (17) of paragraph (g) of this section.

(2) Allocation and apportionment to exempt, excluded or eliminated income. [Reserved] For guidance, see § 1.861-8T(d)(2).

(e) Allocation and apportionment of certain deductions. *(1) In general.* Paragraphs (e)(2) and (e)(3) of this section contain rules with respect to the allocation and apportionment of interest expense and research and development expenditures, respectively. Paragraphs (e)(4) through (e)(8) of this section contain rules with respect to the allocation of certain other deductions. Paragraph (e)(9) of this section lists those deductions which are ordinarily considered as not being definitely related to any class of gross income. Paragraph (e)(10) of this section lists special deductions of corporations which must be allocated and apportioned. Paragraph (e)(11) of this section lists personal exemptions which are neither allocated nor apportioned. Paragraph (e)(12) of this section contains rules with respect to the allocation and apportionment of deductions for charitable contributions. Examples of allocation and apportionment are contained in paragraph (g) of this section.

(2) Interest. [Reserved] For guidance, see § 1.861-8T(e)(2).

(3) Research and experimental expenditures. For rules regarding the allocation and apportionment of research and experimental expenditures, see § 1.861-17.

(4) [Reserved]. For further guidance, see § 1.861-8T(e)(4).

(5) Legal and accounting fees and expenses. Fees and other expenses for legal and accounting services are ordinarily definitely related and allocable to specific classes of gross income or to all the taxpayer's gross income, depending on the nature of the services rendered (and are apportioned as provided in paragraph (c)(1) of this section). For example, accounting fees for the preparation of a study of

the costs involved in manufacturing a specific product will ordinarily be definitely related to the class of gross income derived from (or which could reasonably have been expected to be derived from) that specific product. The taxpayer is not relieved from his responsibility to make a proper allocation and apportionment of fees on the grounds that the statement of services rendered does not identify the services performed beyond a generalized designation such as "professional," or does not provide any type of allocation, or does not properly allocate the fees involved.

(6) Income taxes. (i) In general. The deduction for state, local, and foreign income, war profits and excess profits taxes ("state income taxes") allowed by section 164 shall be considered definitely related and allocable to the gross income with respect to which such state income taxes are imposed. For example, if a domestic corporation is subject to state income taxation and the state income tax is imposed in part on an amount of foreign source income, then that part of the taxpayer's deduction for state income tax that is attributable to foreign source income is definitely related and allocable to foreign source income. In allocating and apportioning the deduction for state income tax for purposes including (but not limited to) the computation of the foreign tax credit limitation under section 904 of the Code and the consolidated foreign tax credit under § 1.1502-4 of the regulations, the income upon which the state income tax is imposed is determined by reference to the law of the jurisdiction imposing the tax. Thus, if a state attributes taxable income to a corporate taxpayer by applying an apportionment formula that takes into consideration the income and factors of one or more corporations related by ownership to the corporate taxpayer and engaging in activities related to the business of the corporate taxpayer, then the income so attributed is the income upon which the state income tax is imposed. If the income so attributed to the corporate taxpayer includes foreign source income, then, in computing the taxpayer's foreign tax credit limitation under section 904, for example, the taxpayer's deduction for state income tax will be considered definitely related and allocable to a class of gross income that includes the statutory grouping of foreign source income. When the law of the state includes dividends that are treated under section 862(a)(2) as income from sources without the United States in taxable income apportionable to the state, but does not include factors of the corporation paying such dividends in the apportionment formula used to determine state taxable income, an appropriate portion of the deduction for state income tax will be considered definitely related and allocable to a class of gross income consisting solely of foreign source dividend income. A deduction for state income tax will not be considered definitely related to a hypothetical amount of income calculated under federal tax principles when the jurisdiction imposing the tax computes taxable income under different principles. A corporate taxpayer's deduction for a state franchise tax that is computed on the basis of income attributable to business activities conducted within the state must be allocated and apportioned in the same manner as the deduction for state income taxes. In determining, for example, both the foreign tax credit under section 904 of the Code and the consolidated foreign tax credit limitation under § 1.1502-4 of the regulations, the deduction for state income tax may be allocable and apportionable to foreign source income in a statutory grouping described in section 904(d) in a taxable year in which the taxpayer has no foreign source income in such statutory grouping. Alternatively, such an allocation or apportionment may be appropriate if a taxpayer corporation has no foreign source income in a statutory grouping, but its deduction is attributable to foreign source income in such grouping that is attributed to the taxpayer corporation under the law of a state which attributes taxable income to a corporation by applying an apportionment formula that takes into consideration the income and factors of one or more corporations related by ownership to the taxpayer corporation and engaging in activities related to the business of the taxpayer corporation. Example 30 of paragraph (g) of this section illustrates the application of this last rule.

(ii) Methods of allocation and apportionment. (A) In general. A taxpayer's deduction for a state income tax is to be allocated (and then apportioned, if necessary, subject to the rules of § 1.861-8(d)) by reference to the taxable income that the law of the taxing jurisdiction attributes to the taxpayer ("state taxable income").

(B) Effect of subsequent recomputations of state income tax. [Reserved]

(C) Illustrations. (1) In general. Examples 25 through 32 of paragraph (g) of § 1.861-8 illustrate, in the given factual situations, the application of this paragraph (e)(6) and the general rule of paragraph (b)(1) of this section that a deduction must be allocated to the class of gross income to which the deduction is factually related. In general, these examples employ a presumption that state income taxes are allocable to a class of gross income that includes the statutory grouping of income from sources without the United States when the total amount of taxable income determined under state law exceeds the amount of taxable income determined under the Code (without taking into account the deduction for state income taxes) in the residual grouping of income from sources within the United States. A taxpayer that allocates and apportions the deduction for state income tax in accordance with the methodology of Example 25 of paragraph (g) of this section must also apply the modifications illustrated in Examples 26 and 27 of paragraph (g) of this section, when applicable. The modification illustrated in Example 26 is applicable when the deduction for state income tax is attributable in part to taxes imposed by a state which factually excludes foreign source income (as determined for federal income tax purposes) from state taxable income. The modification illustrated in Example 27 is applicable when the taxpayer has income-producing activities in a state which does not impose a corporate income tax. The specific allocation of state income tax illustrated in Example 28 follows the rule in paragraph (e)(6)(i) of this section, and must be applied whenever a taxpayer's state taxable income includes dividends apportioned to the state under a formula that does not take into account the factors of the corporations paying those dividends, regardless of whether the taxpayer uses the methodology of Example 25 with respect to the remainder of the deduction for state income taxes.

(2) Modifications. Before applying a method of allocation and apportionment illustrated in the examples, the computation of state taxable income under state law may be modified, subject to the approval of the District Director, to reflect more accurately the income with respect to which the state income tax is imposed. Any modification to the state law computation of state taxable income must yield an allocation and apportionment of the deduction for state income taxes that is consistent with the rules contained in this paragraph (e)(6), and that accurately reflects the factual relationship between the state income tax and the income on which that tax is imposed. For example, a modification to the computation of taxable income under state law might be appropriate to compensate for differences between the state law definition of taxable income and the federal definition of

taxable income, due to a difference in the rate of allowable depreciation or the amount of another deduction that is allowable under both systems. This rule is illustrated in Example 31 of paragraph (g) of this section. However, a modification to the computation of taxable income under state law will not be appropriate, and will not more accurately reflect the factual relationship between the state tax and the income on which the tax is imposed, to the extent such modification reflects the fact that the state does not follow federal tax principles in attributing income to the taxpayer's activities in the state. This rule is illustrated in Example 32 of paragraph (g) of this section. A taxpayer may not modify the methods illustrated in the examples, or use an alternative method of allocation and apportionment of the deduction for state income taxes, if the modification or alternative method would be inconsistent with the rules of paragraph (e)(6)(i) of this section. A taxpayer that uses a method of allocation and apportionment other than one illustrated in Example 25 (as modified by Examples 26 and 27), or 29 with respect to a factual situation similar to those of the examples, must describe the alternative method on an attachment to its federal income tax return and establish to the satisfaction of the District Director, upon examination, that the result of the alternative method more accurately reflects the factual relationship between the state income tax and the income on which the tax is imposed.

(D) Elective safe harbor methods. (1) In general. In lieu of applying the rules set forth in paragraphs (e)(6)(ii)(A) through (C) of this section, a taxpayer may elect to allocate and apportion the deduction for state income tax in accordance with one of the two safe harbor methods described in paragraph (e)(6)(ii)(D)(2) and (3) of this section. A taxpayer shall make this election for a taxable year by filing a timely tax return for that year that reflects an allocation and apportionment of the deduction for state income tax under one of the safe harbor methods and attaching to such return a statement that the taxpayer has elected to use the safe harbor method provided in either paragraph (e)(6)(ii)(D)(2) or (3) of this section, as appropriate. Once made, this election is effective for the taxable year for which made and all subsequent taxable years, and may be revoked only with the consent of the Commissioner. Example 33 of paragraph (g) of this section illustrates the application of these safe harbor methods.

(2) Method One. (i) Step One—Specific allocation to foreign source portfolio dividends and other income. If any portion of the deduction for state income tax is attributable to tax imposed by a state which includes in a corporate taxpayer's taxable income apportionable to the state, portfolio dividends (as defined in paragraph (i) of Example 28 of paragraph (g) of this section) that are treated under section 862(a)(2) as income from sources without the United States, but does not include factors of the corporations paying the portfolio dividends in the apportionment formula used to determine state taxable income, the taxpayer shall allocate an appropriate portion of the deduction to a class of gross income consisting solely of foreign source portfolio dividends. The portion of the deduction so allocated, and the amount of foreign source portfolio dividends included in such class, shall be determined in accordance with the methodology illustrated in paragraph (ii) of Example 28 of paragraph (g). If a state income tax is determined based upon formulary apportionment of the total taxable income attributable to the taxpayer's unitary business, the taxpayer must also apply the methodology illustrated in paragraph (ii)(C) through (G) of Example 29 of paragraph (g) of this section to make specific allocations of appropriate portions of the deduction for state income tax on the basis of income that, under separate accounting, would have been attributed to other members of the unitary group. The taxpayer shall reduce its aggregate state taxable income by the amount of foreign source portfolio dividends and other income to which a specific allocation is made (the reduced amount being referred to hereinafter as "adjusted state taxable income").

(ii) Step Two—Adjustment of U.S. source federal taxable income. If the taxpayer has significant income-producing activities in a state which does not impose a corporate income tax or other state tax measured by income derived from business activities in the state, the taxpayer shall reduce its U.S. source federal taxable income (solely for purposes of this safe harbor method) by the amount of federal taxable income attributable to its activities in such state. This amount shall be determined in accordance with the methodology illustrated in paragraph (ii) of Example 27 of paragraph (g) of this section, provided that the taxpayer shall be required to use the rules of the Uniform Division of Income for Tax Purposes Act to attribute income to the relevant state. The taxpayer's U.S. source federal taxable income, as so reduced, is referred to hereinafter as "adjusted U.S. source federal taxable income."

(iii) Step Three—Allocation. The taxpayer shall allocate the remainder of the deduction for state income tax (after reduction by the portion allocated to foreign source portfolio dividends and other income under Step One) in accordance with the methodology illustrated in paragraph (ii) of Example 25 of paragraph (g) of this section. However, the taxpayer shall substitute for the comparison of aggregate state taxable income to U.S. source federal taxable income, illustrated in paragraph (ii) of Example 25 of paragraph (g) of this section, a comparison of its adjusted state taxable income to an amount equal to 110% of its adjusted U.S. source federal taxable income.

(iv) Step Four—Apportionment. In the event that apportionment of the remainder of the deduction for state income tax is required, the taxpayer shall apportion that remaining deduction to U.S. source income in accordance with the methodology illustrated in paragraph (iii) of Example 25 of paragraph (g) of this section, substituting for domestic source income in that paragraph an amount equal to 110% of the taxpayer's adjusted U.S. source federal taxable income. The remaining portion of the deduction shall be apportioned to the statutory groupings of foreign source income described in section 904(d) of the Code in accordance with the proportion of the income in each statutory grouping of foreign source income described in section 904(d) to the taxpayer's total foreign source federal taxable income (after reduction by the amount of foreign source portfolio dividends to which tax has been specifically allocated under Step One, above). (i) (3) Method Two. (i) Step One—Specific allocation to foreign source portfolio dividends and other income. Step One of this method is the same as Step One of Method One (as described in paragraph (e)(6)(ii)(D)(2)(i) of this section).

(ii) Step Two—Adjustment of U.S. source federal taxable income. Step Two of this method is the same as Step Two of Method One (as described in paragraph (e)(6)(ii)(D)(2)(ii) of this section).

(iii) Step Three—Allocation. The taxpayer shall allocate the remainder of the deduction for state income tax (after reduction by the portion allocated to foreign source portfolio dividends and other income under Step One) in accordance with the methodology illustrated in paragraph (ii) of Example 25 of paragraph (g) of this section. However, the taxpayer shall substitute for the comparison of aggregate state taxable income to U.S. source federal taxable income, illustrated in paragraph (ii) of Example 25 of paragraph (g) of this section, a comparison of its adjusted state taxable income to its adjusted U.S. source federal taxable income.

(iv) Step Four—Apportionment. In the event that apportionment of the deduction is required, the taxpayer shall apportion to U.S. source income that portion of the deduction that is attributable to state income taxes imposed upon an amount of state taxable income equal to adjusted U.S. source federal taxable income. The taxpayer shall apportion the remaining amount of the deduction to U.S. and foreign source income in the same proportions that the taxpayer's adjusted U.S. source federal taxable income and foreign source federal taxable income (after reduction by the amount of foreign source portfolio dividends to which tax has been specifically allocated under Step One, above) bear to its total federal taxable income (taking into account the adjustment of U.S. source federal taxable income under Step Two and after reduction by the amount of foreign source portfolio dividends to which tax has been specifically allocated under Step One). The portion of the deduction apportioned to foreign source income shall be apportioned among the statutory groupings described in section 904(d) of the Code in accordance with the proportions of the taxpayer's total foreign source federal taxable income (after reduction by the amount of foreign source portfolio dividends to which tax has been specifically allocated under Step One, above) in each grouping.

(iii) Effective dates. The rules of § 1.861-8(e)(6)(i) and the language preceding the examples in § 1.861-8(g) are effective for taxable years beginning after December 31, 1976. The rules of § 1.861-8(e)(6)(ii) (other than § 1.861-8(e)(6)(ii)(D)) and Examples 25 through 32 of § 1.861-8(g) are effective for taxable years beginning on or after January 1, 1988. The rules of § 1.861-8(e)(6)(ii)(D) and Example 33 of § 1.861-8(g) are effective for taxable years ending after March 12, 1991. At the option of the taxpayer, however, the rules of § 1.861-8(e)(6)(ii) (other than § 1.861-8(e)(6)(ii)(D)) and Examples 25 through 32 of § 1.861-8(g) may be applied with respect to deductions for state taxes incurred in taxable years beginning before January 1, 1988.

(7) Losses on the sale, exchange, or other disposition of property. (i) Allocation. The deduction allowed for loss recognized on the sale, exchange, or other disposition of a capital asset or property described in section 1231(b) shall be considered a deduction which is definitely related and allocable to the class of gross income to which such asset or property ordinarily gives rise in the hands of the taxpayer. Where the nature of gross income generated from the asset or property has varied significantly over several taxable years of the taxpayer, such class of gross income shall generally be determined by reference to gross income generated from the asset or property during the taxable year or years immediately preceding the sale, exchange, or other disposition of such asset or property. Thus, for example, where an asset generates primarily sales income from domestic sources in the early years of its operation and then is leased by the taxpayer to a foreign subsidiary in later years, the class of gross income to which the asset gives rise will be considered to be the rental income derived from the lease and will not include sales income from domestic sources.

(ii) Apportionment of losses. Where in the unusual circumstances that an apportionment of a deduction for losses on the sale, exchange, or other disposition of a capital asset or property described in section 1231(b) is necessary, the amount of such deduction shall be apportioned between the statutory grouping (or among the statutory groupings) of gross income (within the class of gross income) and the residual grouping (within the class of gross income) in the same proportion that the amount of gross income within such statutory grouping (or statutory groupings) and such residual grouping bear, respectively, to the total amount of gross income within the class of gross income. Apportionment will be necessary where, for example, the class of gross income to which the deduction is allocated consists of gross income (such as royalties) attributable to an intangible asset used both within and without the United States, or gross income (such as from sales or services) attributable to a tangible asset used both within and without the United States.

(iii) Allocation of loss recognized in taxable years after 1986. See §§ 1.865-1 and 1.865-2 for rules regarding the allocation of certain loss recognized in taxable years beginning after December 31, 1986.

(8) Net operating loss deduction. A net operating loss deduction allowed under section 172 shall be allocated and apportioned in the same manner as the deductions giving rise to the net operating loss deduction.

(9) Deductions which are not definitely related. Deductions which shall generally be considered as not definitely related to any gross income, and therefore are ratably apportioned as provided in paragraph (c)(3) of this section, are—

(i) The deduction allowed by section 163 for interest described in subparagraph (2)(iii) of this paragraph (e);

(ii) The deduction allowed by section 164 for real estate taxes on a personal residence or for sales tax on the purchase of items for personal use;

(iii) The deduction for medical expenses allowed by section 213; and

(iv) The deduction for alimony payments allowed by section 215.

(10) Special deductions. The special deductions allowed in the case of a corporation by section 241 (relating to the deductions for partially tax exempt interest, dividends received, etc.), section 922 (relating to Western Hemisphere trade corporations), and section 941 (relating to China Trade Act corporations) shall be allocated and apportioned consistent with the principles of this section.

(11) Personal exemptions. The deductions for the personal exemptions allowed by section 151, 642(b), or 873(b)(3) shall not be taken into account for purposes of allocation and apportionment under this section.

(12) Deductions for certain charitable contributions. (i) In general. The deduction for charitable contributions that is allowed under sections 170, 873(b)(2), and 882(c)(1)(B) is definitely related and allocable to all of the taxpayer's gross income. The deduction allocated under this paragraph (e)(12)(i) shall be apportioned between the statutory grouping (or among the statutory groupings) of gross income and the residual grouping on the basis of the relative amounts of gross income from sources in the United States in each grouping.

(ii) Treaty provisions. If a deduction for charitable contributions not otherwise permitted by sections 170, 873(b)(2), and 882(c)(1)(B) is allowed under a U.S. income tax treaty, and such treaty limits the amount of the deduction based on a percentage of income arising from sources within the treaty partner, the deduction is definitely related and allocable to all of the taxpayer's gross income. The deduction allocated under this paragraph (e)(12)(ii) shall be apportioned between the statutory grouping (or among the statutory groupings) of gross income and the residual grouping on the basis of the relative amounts of gross income from sources within the treaty partner within each grouping.

(iii) Coordination with §§ 1.861-14 and 1.861-14T. A deduction for a charitable contribution by a member of an affiliated group shall be allocated and apportioned under the rules of this section, § 1.861-14(e)(6), and § 1.861-14T(c)(1).

(iv) Effective date. (A) The rules of paragraphs (e)(12)(i) and (iii) of this section shall apply to charitable contributions made on or after July 28, 2004. Taxpayers may apply the provisions of paragraphs (e)(12)(i) and (iii) of this section to charitable contributions made before July 28, 2004, but during the taxable year ending on or after July 28, 2004.

(B) The rules of paragraphs (e)(12)(ii) of this section shall apply to charitable contributions made on or after July 14, 2005. Taxpayers may apply the provisions of paragraph (e)(12)(ii) of this section to charitable contributions made before July 14, 2005, but during the taxable year ending on or after July 14, 2005.

(f) Miscellaneous matters. *(1) Operative sections.* The operative sections of the Code which require the determination of taxable income of the taxpayer from specific sources or activities and which give rise to statutory groupings to which this section is applicable include the sections described below.

(i) Overall limitation to the foreign tax credit. Under the overall limitation to the foreign tax credit, as provided in section 904(a)(2) (as in effect before enactment of the Tax Reform Act of 1976, or section 904(a) after such enactment), the amount of the foreign tax credit may not exceed the tentative U.S. tax (i.e., the U.S. tax before application of the foreign tax credit) multiplied by a fraction, the numerator of which is the taxable income from sources without the United States and the denominator of which is the entire taxable income. Accordingly, in this case, the statutory grouping is foreign source income (including, for example, interest received from a domestic corporation which meets the tests of section 861(a)(1)(B), dividends received from a domestic corporation which has an election in effect under section 936, and other types of income specified in section 862). Pursuant to sections 862(b) and 863(a) and §§ 1.862-1 and 1.863-1, this section provides rules for identifying the deductions to be taken into account in determining taxable income from sources without the United States. See section 904(d) (as in effect after enactment of the Tax Reform Act of 1976) and the regulations thereunder which require separate treatment of certain types of income. See example (3) of paragraph (g) of this section for one example of the application of this section to the overall limitation.

(ii) Reserved

(iii) DISC and FSC taxable income. Sections 925 and 994 provide rules for determining the taxable income of a FSC and DISC, respectively, with respect to qualified sales and leases of export property and qualified services. The combined taxable income method available for determining a DISC's taxable income provides, without consideration of export promotion expenses, that the taxable income of the DISC shall be 50 percent of the combined taxable income of the DISC and the related supplier derived from sales and leases of export property and from services. In the FSC context, the taxable income of the FSC equals 23 percent of the combined taxable income of the FSC and the related supplier. Pursuant to regulations under section 925 and 994, this section provides rules for determining the deductions to be taken into account in determining combined taxable income, except to the extent modified by the marginal costing rules set forth in the regulations under sections 925(b)(2) and 994(b)(2) if used by the taxpayer. See *Examples* (22) and (23) of paragraph (g) of this section. In addition, the computation of combined taxable income is necessary to determine the applicability of the section 925(d) limitation and the "no loss" rules of the regulations under sections 925 and 994.

(iv) Effectively connected taxable income. Nonresident alien individuals and foreign corporations engaged in trade or business within the United States are taxed, as provided under sections 871(b)(1) and 882(a)(1), on taxable income which is effectively connected with the conduct of a trade or business within the United States. Such taxable income is determined in most instances by initially determining, under section 864(c), the amount of gross income which is effectively connected with the conduct of a trade or business within the United States. Pursuant to sections 873 and 882(c), this section is applicable for purposes of determining the deductions from such gross income (other than the deduction for interest expense allowed to foreign corporations (see § 1.882-5)) which are to be taken into account in determining taxable income. See example (21) of paragraph (g) of this section.

(v) Foreign base company income. Section 954 defines the term "foreign base company income" with respect to controlled foreign corporations. Section 954(b)(5) provides that in determining foreign base company income the gross income shall be reduced by the deductions of the controlled foreign corporation "properly allocable to such income". This section provides rules for identifying which deductions are properly allocable to foreign base company income.

(vi) Other operative sections. The rules provided in this section also apply in determining—

(A) The amount of foreign source items of tax preference under section 58(g) determined for purposes of the minimum tax;

(B) The amount of foreign mineral income under section 901(e);

(C) Reserved

(D) The amount of foreign oil and gas extraction income and the amount of foreign oil related income under section 907;

(E) [Reserved].

(F) [Reserved].

(G) The limitation under section 934 on the maximum reduction in income tax liability incurred to the Virgin Islands;

(H) [Reserved].

(I) The special deduction granted to China Trade Act corporations under section 941;

(J) The amount of certain U.S. source income excluded from the subpart F income of a controlled foreign corporation under section 952(b);

(K) The amount of income from the insurance of U.S. risks under section 953(b)(5);

(L) The international boycott factor and the specifically attributable taxes and income under section 999; and

(M) The taxable income attributable to the operation of an agreement vessel under section 607 of the Merchant Marine Act of 1936, as amended, and the Capital Construction Fund Regulations thereunder (26 CFR, pt. 3). See 26 CFR 3.2(b)(3).

(2) (i) Application to more than one operative section. Where more than one operative section applies, it may be necessary for the taxpayer to apply this section separately for each applicable operative section. In such a case, the taxpayer is required to use the same method of allocation and the same principles of apportionment for all operative sections.

(ii) When expenses, losses, and other deductions that have been properly allocated and apportioned between combined gross income of a related supplier and a DISC or former DISC and residual gross income, regardless of which of the administrative pricing methods of section 994 has been applied, such deductions are no also allocated and apportioned to gross income consisting of distributions from the DISC or former DISC attributable to income of the DISC or former DISC as determined under the administrative pricing methods with respect to DISC or former DISC taxable years beginning after December 31, 1986. Accordingly, *Example* (22) of paragraph (g) of this section does not apply to distributions from a DISC or former DISC with respect to DISC or former DISC taxable years beginning after December 31, 1986. This rule does not apply to the extent that the taxable income of the DISC or former DISC is determined under the section 994(a)(3) transfer pricing method. In addition, for taxable years beginning after December 31, 1986, in the case of expenses, losses, and other deductions that have been properly allocated and apportioned between combined gross income of a related supplier and a FSC and residual gross income, regardless of which of the administrative pricing methods of section 925 has been applied, such deductions are not also allocated and apportioned to gross income consisting of distributions from the FSC or former FSC which are attributable to the foreign trade income of the FSC or former FSC as determined under the administrative pricing methods. This rule does not apply to the extent that the foreign trade income of the FSC or former FSC is determined under the section 925(a)(3) transfer pricing method. See *Example* (23) of paragraph (g) of this section.

(3) Special rules of section 863(b). (i) In general. Special rules under section 863(b) provide for the application of rules of general apportionment provided in §§ 1.863-3 to 1.863-5, to worldwide taxable income in order to attribute part of such worldwide taxable income to U.S. sources and the remainder of such worldwide taxable income to foreign sources. The activities specified in section 863(b) are—

(A) Transportation or other services rendered partly within and partly without the United States,

(B) Sales of personal property produced by the taxpayer within and sold without the United States, or produced by the taxpayer without and sold within the United States, and

(C) Sales within the United States of personal property purchased within a possession of the United States.

In the instances provided in §§ 1.863-3 and 1.863-4 with respect to the activities described in (A), (B), and (C) of this subdivision, this section is applicable only in determining worldwide taxable income attributable to these activities.

(ii) Relationship of sections 861, 862, 863(a), and 863(b). Sections 861, 862, 863(a), and 863(b) are the four provisions applicable in determining taxable income from specific sources. Each of these four provisions applies independently. Where a deduction has been allocated and apportioned to income under one of these four provisions, the deduction shall not again be allocated and apportioned to gross income under any of the other three provisions. However, two or more of these provisions may have to be applied at the same time to determine the proper allocation and apportionment of a deduction. The special rules under section 863(b) take precedence over the general rules of Code sections 861, 862 and 863(a). For example, where a deduction is allocable in whole or in part to gross income to which section 863(b) applies, such deduction or part thereof shall not otherwise be allocated under section 861, 862, or 863(a). However, where the gross income to which the deduction is allocable includes both gross income to which section 863(b) applies and gross income to which section 861, 862, or 863(a) applies, more than one section must be applied at the same time in order to determine the proper allocation and apportionment of the deduction.

(4) Adjustments made under other provisions of the Code. (i) [Reserved]. For further guidance, see § 1.861-8T(f)(4)(i).

(ii) Example. X, a domestic corporation, purchases and sells consumer items in the United States and foreign markets. Its sales in foreign markets are made to related foreign subsidiaries. X reported $1,500,000 as sales during the taxable year of which $1,000,000 was domestic sales and $500,000 was foreign sales. X took a deduction for expenses incurred by its marketing department during the taxable year in the amount of $150,000. These expenses were determined to be allocable to both domestic and foreign sales and are apportionable between such sales. Thus, X allocated and apportioned the marketing department deduction as follows:

To gross income from domestic sales:

$\$150{,}000 \times \frac{\$1{,}000{,}000}{1{,}500{,}000}$ $100,000

To gross income from foreign sales:

$\$150{,}000 \times \frac{\$500{,}000}{1{,}500{,}000}$ 50,000

Total 150,000

On audit of X's return for the taxable year, the District Director adjusted, under section 482, X's sales to related foreign subsidiaries by increasing the sales price by a total of $100,000, thereby increasing X's foreign sales and total sales by the same amount. As a result of the section 482 adjustment, the apportionment of the deduction for the marketing department expenses is redetermined as follows:

To gross income from domestic sales:

$\$150{,}000 \times \frac{\$1{,}000{,}000}{1{,}6000{,}000}$ .... $ 93,750

To gross income from foreign sales:

$\$150{,}000 \times \frac{\$600{,}000}{1{,}600{,}000}$ 56,250

Total 150,000

(5) Verification of allocations and apportionments. Since, under this section, allocations and apportionments are made on the basis of the factual relationship between deductions and gross income, the taxpayer is required to furnish, at the request of the District Director, information from which such factual relationships can be determined. In reviewing the overall limitation to the foreign tax credit of a domestic corporation, for example, the District Director should consider information which would enable him to determine the extent to which deductions attributable to functions performed in

the United States are related to earning foreign source income, United States source income, or income from both sources. In addition to functions with a specific international purpose, consideration should be given to the functions of management, the direction and results of an acquisition program, the functions of operating units and personnel located at the head office, the functions of support units (including but not limited to engineering, legal, budget, accounting, and industrial relations), the functions of selling and advertising units and personnel, the direction and uses of research and development, and the direction and uses of services furnished by independent contractors. Thus, for example when requested by the District Director, the taxpayer shall make available any of its organization charts, manuals, and other writings which relate to the manner in which its gross income arises and to the functions of organizational units, employees, and assets of the taxpayer and arrange for the interview of such of its employees as the District Director deems desirable in order to determine the gross income to which deductions relate. See section 7602 and the regulations thereunder which generally provide for the examination of books and witnesses. See also section 905(b) and the regulations thereunder which require proof of foreign tax credits to the satisfaction of the Secretary or his delegate.

(g) General examples. The following examples illustrate the principles of this section. In each example, unless otherwise specified, the operative section which is applied and gives rise to the statutory grouping of gross income is the overall limitation to the foreign tax credit under section 904(a). In addition, in each example, where a method of allocation or apportionment is illustrated as an acceptable method, it is assumed that such method is used by the taxpayer on a consistent basis from year to year (except in the case of the optional method for apportioning research and development expense under paragraph (e)(3)(iii) of § 1.861-8). Further, it is assumed that each party named in each example operates on a calendar year accounting basis and, where the party is a U.S. taxpayer, files returns on a calendar year basis.

Example (1). [Reserved]

Example (2). [Reserved]

Example (3). [Reserved]

Example (4). [Reserved]

Example (5). [Reserved]

Example (6). [Reserved]

Example (7). [Reserved]

Example (8). [Reserved]

Example (9). [Reserved]

Example (10). [Reserved]

Example (11). [Reserved]

Example (12). [Reserved]

Example (13). [Reserved]

Example (14). [Reserved]

Example (15). [Reserved]

Example (16). [Reserved]

Example (17). [Reserved]. For further guidance, see § 1.861-8T(g), Example 17.

Example (18). [Reserved]. For further guidance, see § 1.861-8T(g), Example 18.

Example (19). Supportive expense.

(i) Facts. X, a domestic corporation, purchases and sells products both in the United States and in foreign countries. X has no foreign subsidiary and no international department. During the taxable year, X incurs the following expenses with respect to its worldwide activities:

Personnel department expenses	$ 50,000
Training department expenses	35,000
General and administrative expenses	55,000
President's salary	40,000
Sales manager's salary	20,000
Total	200,000

X has domestic gross receipts from sales of $750,000 and foreign gross receipts from sales of $500,000 and has gross income from such sales in the same ratio, namely $300,000 from domestic sources and $200,000 from foreign sources.

(ii) Allocation. The above expenses are definitely related and allocable to all of X's gross income derived from both domestic and foreign markets.

(iii) Apportionment. For purposes of applying the overall limitation, the statutory grouping is gross income from sources outside the United States and the residual grouping is gross income from sources within the United States. X's deductions for its worldwide sales activities must be apportioned between these groupings. Company X in this example (unlike Company X in example (18)) does not have a separate international division which performs essentially all of the functions required to manage and oversee its foreign activities. The president and sales manager do not maintain time records. The division of their time between domestic and foreign activities varies from day to day and cannot be estimated on an annual basis with any reasonable degree of accuracy. Similarly, there are no facts which would justify a method of apportionment of their salaries or of one of the other listed deductions based on more specific factors than gross receipts or gross income. An acceptable method of apportionment would be on the basis of gross receipts. The apportionment of the $200,000 deduction is as follows:

Apportionment of the $200,000 expense to the statutory grouping of gross income:

$$\$200{,}000 \times \frac{\$500{,}000}{(\$500{,}000 + \$750{,}000)} \quad \$80{,}000$$

Apportionment of the $200,000 expense the residual grouping of gross income:

$$\$200{,}000 \times \frac{\$750{,}000}{(\$500{,}000 + \$750{,}000)} \quad 120{,}000$$

Total apportioned general and administrative expense	200,000

Example (20). Supportive Expense.

(i) Facts. Assume the same facts as above except that X's president devotes only 5 percent of his time to the foreign operations and 95 percent of his time to the domestic operations and that X's sales manager devotes approximately 10 percent of his time to foreign sales and 90 percent of his time to domestic sales.

(ii) Allocation. The expenses incurred by X with respect to its worldwide activities are definitely related, and therefore allocable to X's gross income from both its foreign and domestic markets.

(iii) Apportionment. On the basis of the additional facts it is not acceptable to apportion the salaries of the president and the sales manager on the basis of gross receipts. It is acceptable to apportion such salaries between the statutory grouping (gross income from sources without the United States) and residual grouping (gross income from sources within the United States) on the basis of time devoted to each sales activity. Remaining expenses may still be apportioned on the basis of gross receipts. The apportionment is as follows:

Apportionment of the $200,000 expense to the statutory grouping of gross income:

President's salary: $40,000 × 95%	$2,000
Sales manager's salary: $20,000 × 10%	2,000
Remaining expenses:	
$\$140{,}000 \times \frac{\$500{,}000}{(\$500{,}000 + \$750{,}000)}$	56,000
Subtotal: Apportionment of expense to statutory grouping	60,000

Apportionment of the $200,000 expense to the residual grouping of gross income:

President's salary: $40,000 × 95%	38,000
Sales manager's salary: $20,000 × 90%	18,000
Remaining expenses:	
$\$140{,}000 \times \frac{\$750{,}000}{(\$500{,}000 + \$750{,}000)}$	84,000
Subtotal: Apportionment of expense to residual grouping	140,000
Total: Apportioned general and administrative expense	200,000

Example (21). Supportive Expense.

(i) Facts. X, a foreign corporation doing business in the United States, is a manufacturer of metal stamping machines. X has no United States subsidiaries and no separate division to manage and oversee its business in the United States. X manufactures and sells these machines in the United States and in foreign countries A and B and has a separate manufacturing facility in each country. Sales of these machines are X's only source of income. In 1977, X incurs general and administrative expenses related to both its U.S. and foreign operations of $100,000. It has machine sales of $500,000, $1,000,000 and $1,000,000 on which it earns gross income of $200,000, $400,000 and $400,000 in the United States, country A, and country B, respectively. The income from the manufacture and sale of the machines in countries A and B is not effectively connected with X's business in the United States.

(ii) Allocation. The $100,000 of general and administrative expense is definitely related to the income to which it gives rise, namely a part of the gross income from sales of machines in the United States, in country A, and in country B. The expenses are allocable to this class of income, even though X's gross income from sources outside the United States is excluded income since it is not effectively connected with a U.S. trade or business.

(iii) Apportionment. Since X is a foreign corporation, the statutory grouping is gross income effectively connected with X's trade or business in the United States, namely gross income from sources within the United States, and the residual grouping is gross income not effectively connected with a trade or business in the United States, namely gross income from countries A and B. Since there are no facts which would require a method of apportionment other than on the basis of sales or gross income, the amount may be apportioned between the two groupings on the basis of amounts of gross income as follows:

Apportionment of general and administrative expense to the statutory grouping, gross income from sources within the United States:	
$\$100{,}000 \times \frac{\$200{,}000}{(\$200{,}000 + \$400{,}000 + \$400{,}000)}$	$ 20,000
Apportionment of general and administrative expense to the residual grouping, gross income from sources without the United States:	
$\$100{,}000 \times \frac{(\$400{,}000 + \$400{,}000)}{(\$200{,}000 + \$400{,}000 + \$400{,}000)}$	$ 80,000
Total apportioned general and administrative expense	100,000

Example (22). Domestic International Sales Corporations.

(i) Facts. X, a domestic corporation, manufactures a line of kitchenware and sells it to retailers in the United States, France, and the United Kingdom. After the Domestic International Sales Corporation (DISC) legislation was passed in 1971, X established, as of January 1, 1972, a DISC and thereafter did all its foreign marketing through sales by the DISC. In 1977 the DISC has total sales of $7,700,000 for which X's cost of goods sold is $6,000,000. Thus, the gross income attributable to exports through the DISC is $1,700,000 ($7,700,000 − $6,000,000). Moreover, X has U.S. domestic sales of kitchenware of $12,000,000 on which it earned gross income of $900,000, and X receives royalty income from the foreign license of its kitchenware technology in the amount of $800,000. The DISC's expenses attributable to the resale of export property are $400,000 of which $300,000 qualify as export promotion expenses. X also incurs $125,000 of general and administrative expenses in connection with its domestic and foreign sales activities, and its foreign licensing activities. X and the DISC determine transfer prices charged on the basis of a single product grouping and the "50-50" combined taxable income method (without marginal costing) which permits the DISC to have a taxable income equal to 50 percent of the combined taxable income attributable to the production and sales of the export property, plus 10 percent of the DISC's export promotion expenses.

(ii) Allocation. For purposes of determining combined taxable income of X and the DISC from export sales, general and administrative expenses of $125,000 must be allocated to and apportioned between gross income resulting from the production and sale of kitchenware for export, and from the production and sale of kitchenware for the domestic market. The deduction of $400,000 for expenses attributable to the resale of export property is allocated solely to gross income from the production and sale of kitchenware in foreign markets.

(iii) Apportionment. Apportionment of expense takes place in two stages. In the first stage, for computing combined taxable income from the production and sale of export property, the general and administrative expense should be apportioned between the statutory grouping of gross income from the export of kitchenware and the residual grouping of gross income from domestic sales and foreign licenses. In the second stage, since the limitation on the foreign tax credit requires the use of a separate limitation with respect to dividends from a DISC (section 904(d)), the general and administrative expense should be apportioned between two statutory groupings, DISC dividends and foreign royalty income (for which the overall limitation is used), and the residual grouping of gross income from sales within the United States. In the first stage, in the absence of more specific or contrary information, the general and administrative expense may be apportioned on the basis of gross income in the respective groupings, as follows:

Apportionment of general and administrative expense to the statutory grouping, gross income from exports of kitchenware:

$$\$125{,}000 \times \frac{\$1{,}700{,}000}{(\$1{,}700{,}000 + \$900{,}000 + \$800{,}000)} \ldots\ldots \$62{,}500$$

Apportionment of general administrative expense the residual grouping, gross income from domestic sales of kitchenware and foreign royalty income from licensing kitchenware technology:

$$\$125{,}000 \times \frac{(\$900{,}000 + \$800{,}000)}{(\$1{,}700{,}000 + \$900{,}000 + \$800{,}000)} \ldots\ldots \$\ 62{,}500$$

Total apportionment of general and administrative expense 125,000

On the basis of this apportionment, the combined taxable income, and the DISC portion of taxable income may be calculated as follows:

Gross income from exports		$1,700,000
Less:		
DISC expense for resale of export property..............	$400,000	
Apportioned general and administrative expense........	62,500	
		462,500
Combined taxable income from production and export of kitchenware................		1,237,500
DISC income:		
50% of combined taxable income		618,750
10% of export expense of $300,000		30,000
Total DISC income		648,750
DISC income as a percentage of combined taxable income..........................		52.4

In the second stage, in the absence of more specific or contrary information, the general and administrative expense may also be apportioned on the basis of gross income in the respective groupings. Since DISC taxable income is 52.4 percent of combined taxable income, DISC gross income is treated as 52.4 percent of the gross income from exports, $1,700,000. The apportionment follows:

Apportionment of general and administrative expense to the statutory grouping, DISC dividends:

$$\$125{,}000 \times \frac{(0.524 \times \$1{,}700{,}000)}{(\$1{,}700{,}000 + \$900{,}000 + \$800{,}000)} \ldots\ldots \$32{,}750$$

Apportionment of general and administrative expense to the statutory grouping, foreign royalty income:

$$\$125{,}000 \times \frac{\$800{,}000}{(\$1{,}700{,}000 + \$900{,}000 + \$800{,}000)} \ldots\ldots 29{,}412$$

Apportionment of general and administrative expense to the residual grouping, gross income from sources within the United States:

$$\$125{,}000 \times \frac{(\$900{,}000 + (0.476 \times \$1{,}700{,}000))}{(\$1{,}700{,}000 + \$900{,}000 + \$800{,}000)} \ldots\ldots 62{,}838$$

Total apportioned general and administrative expense 125,000

(iv) This *Example* (22) applies only to DISC taxable years ending before January 1, 1987, and to distributions from a DISC or former DISC with respect to DISC or former DISC taxable years ending before January 1, 1987.

Example (23). [Reserved]

Example (24). [Reserved] For guidance, see § 1.861-8T(g) *Example* 24.

Example (25). Income Taxes.

(i) Facts. X, a domestic corporation, is a manufacturer and distributor of electronic equipment with operations in states A, B, and C. X also has a branch in country Y which manufactures and distributes the same type of electronic equipment. In 1988, X has taxable income from these activities, as described under the Code (without taking into account the deduction for state income taxes), of $1,000,000, of which $200,000 is foreign source general limitation income subject to a separate limitation under section 904(d)(1)(I) ("general limitation income") and $800,000 is domestic source income. States A, B, and C each determine X's income subject to tax within their state by making adjustments to X's taxable income as determined under the Code, and then apportioning the adjusted taxable income on the basis of the relative amounts of X's payroll, property, and sales within each state as compared to X's worldwide payroll, property, and sales. The adjustments made by states A, B, and C all involve adding and subtracting enumerated items from taxable income as determined under the Code. However, in making these adjustments to taxable income, none of the states specifically exempts foreign source income as determined under the Code. On this basis, it is determined that X has taxable income of $550,000, $200,000, and $200,000 in states A, B, and C, respectively. The corporate tax rates in states A, B, and C are 10 percent, 5 percent, and 2 percent, respectively, and X has total state income tax liabilities of $69,000 ($55,000 + $10,000 + $4,000), which it deducts as an expense for federal income tax purposes.

(ii) Allocation. X's deduction of $69,000 for state income taxes is definitely related and thus allocable to the gross income with respect to which the taxes are imposed. Since the statutes of states A, B, and C do not specifically exempt foreign source income (as determined under the Code) from taxation and since, in the aggregate, states A, B, and C tax $950,000 of X's income while only $800,000 is domestic source income under the Code, it is presumed that state income taxes are imposed on $150,000 of foreign source income. The deduction for state income taxes is therefore related and allocable to both X's foreign source and domestic source income.

(iii) Apportionment. For purposes of computing the foreign tax credit limitation, X's income is comprised of one statutory grouping, foreign source general limitation gross income, and one residual grouping, gross income from sources within the United States. The state income tax deduction of $69,000 must be apportioned between these two groupings. Corporation X calculates the apportionment on the basis of the relative amounts of foreign source general limitation taxable income and U.S. source taxable income subject to state taxation. In this case, state income taxes are presumed to be imposed on $800,000 of domestic source income and $150,000 of foreign source general limitation income.

State income tax deduction apportioned to foreign source general limitation income (statutory grouping): $69,000 × ($150,000/$950,000)	$10,895
State income tax deduction apportioned to income from sources within the United States (residual grouping): $69,000 ×X ($800,000/$950,000)	58,105
Total apportioned state income tax deduction ..	$69,000

Example (26). Income Taxes.

(i) Facts. Assume the same facts as in Example 25 except that the language of state A's statute and the statute's operation exempt from taxation all foreign source income, as determined under the Code, so that foreign source income is not included in adjusted taxable income subject to apportionment in state A (and factors relating to X's country Y branch are not taken into account in computing the state A apportionment fraction).

(ii) Allocation. X's deduction of $69,000 for state income taxes is definitely related and thus allocable to the gross income with respect to which the taxes are imposed. Since state A exempts all foreign source income by statute, state A is presumed to impose tax on $550,000 of X's $800,000 of domestic source income. X's state A tax of $55,000 is allocable, therefore, solely to domestic source income. Since the statutes of states B and C do not specifically exclude all foreign source income as determined under the Code, and since states B and C impose tax on $400,000 ($200,000 + $200,000) of X's income of which only $250,000 ($800,000 – $550,000) is presumed to be domestic source, the deduction for the $14,000 of income taxes imposed by states B and C is related and allocable to both foreign source and domestic source income.

(iii) Apportionment.

(A) For purposes of computing the foreign tax credit limitation, X's income is comprised of one statutory grouping, foreign source general limitation gross income, and one residual grouping, gross income from sources within the United States. The deduction of $14,000 for income taxes of states B and C must be apportioned between these two groupings.

(B) Corporation X calculates the apportionment on the basis of the relative amounts of foreign source general limitation income and U.S. source income subject to state taxation.

States B and C income tax deduction apportioned to foreign source general limitation income (statutory grouping): $14,000 × ($150,000/$400,000)	$ 5,250
States B and C income tax deduction apportioned to income from sources within the United States (residual grouping): $14,000 × ($250,000/$400,000)	8,750
Total apportioned state income tax deduction ..	$14,000

(C) Of X's total income taxes of $69,000, the amount allocated and apportioned to foreign source general limitation income equals $5,250. The total amount of state income taxes allocated and apportioned to U.S. source income equals $63,750 ($55,000 + $8,750).

Example (27). Income Tax.

(i) Facts. Assume the same facts as in Example 25 except that state A, in which X has significant income-producing activities, does not impose a corporate income tax or other state tax computed on the basis of income derived from business activities conducted in state A. X therefore has a total state income tax liability in 1988 of $14,000 ($10,000 paid to state B plus $4,000 paid to state C), all of which is subject to allocation and apportionment under paragraph (b) of this section.

(ii) Allocation.

(A) X's deduction of $14,000 for state income taxes is definitely related and allocable to the gross income with respect to which the taxes are imposed. However, in these facts, an adjustment is necessary before the aggregate state taxable incomes can be compared with U.S. source income on the federal income tax return in the manner described in Examples 25 and 26. Unlike the facts in Examples 25 and 26, state A imposes no income tax and does not define taxable income attributable to activities in state A. The total amount of X's income subject to state taxation is, therefore, $400,000 ($200,000 in state B and $200,000 in state C). This total presumptively does not include any income attributable to activities performed in state A and therefore can not properly be compared to total U.S. source taxable income reported by X for federal income tax purposes, which does include income attributable to state A activities.

(B)

(1) Accordingly, before applying the method used in Examples 25 and 26 to the facts of this example, it is necessary first to estimate the amount of taxable income that state A could reasonably attribute to X's activities in state A, and then to reduce federal taxable income by that amount.

(2) Any reasonable method may be used to attribute taxable income to X's activities in state A. For example, the rules of the Uniform Division of Income for Tax Purposes Act ("UDITPA") attribute income to a state on the basis of the average of three ratios that are based upon the taxpayer's facts—property within the state over total property, payroll within the state over total payroll, and sales within the state over total sales—and, with adjustments, provide a reasonable method for this purpose. When applying the rules of UDITPA to estimate U.S. source income derived from state A activities, the taxpayer's UDITPA factors must be adjusted to eliminate both taxable income and factors attributable to a foreign branch. Therefore, in this example all taxable income as well as UDITPA apportionment factors (property, payroll, and sales) attributable to X's country Y branch must be eliminated.

(C)

(1) Since it is presumed that, if state A had had an income tax, state A would not attempt to tax the income derived by X's country Y branch, any reasonable estimate of the income that would be taxed by state A must exclude any foreign source income.

(2) When using the rules of UDITPA to estimate the income that would have been taxable by state A in these facts, foreign source income is excluded by starting with federally defined taxable income (before deduction for state income taxes) and subtracting any income derived by X's country Y branch. The hypothetical state A taxable income is then determined by multiplying the resulting difference by the average of X's state A property, payroll, and sales ratios, determined using the principles of UDITPA (after adjustment by eliminating the country Y branch factors). The resulting product is presumed to be exclusively U.S. source income,

and the allocation and apportionment method described in Example 26 must then be applied.

(3) If, for example, state A taxable income were determined to equal $550,000, then $550,000 of U.S. source income for federal income tax purposes would be presumed to constitute state A taxable income. Under Example 26, the remaining $250,000 ($800,000 – $550,000) of U.S. source income for federal income tax purposes would be presumed to be subject to tax in states B and C. Since states B and C impose tax on $400,000, the application of Example 25 would result in a presumption that $150,000 is foreign source income and $250,000 is domestic source income. The deduction for the $14,000 of income taxes of states B and C would therefore be related and allocable to both foreign source and domestic source income and would be subject to apportionment.

(iii) Apportionment. The deduction of $14,000 for income taxes of states B and C is apportioned in the same manner as in Example 26. As a result, $5,250 of the $14,000 of state B and state C income taxes is apportioned to foreign source general limitation income ($14,000 × $150,000/$400,000), and $8,750 ($14,000 × $250,000/$400,000) of the $14,000 of state B and state C income taxes is apportioned to U.S. source income.

Example (28). Income Tax.

(i) Facts.

(A) Assume the same facts as in Example 25 (X has $1,000,000 of taxable income for federal income tax purposes, $800,000 of which is U.S. source income and $200,000 of which is foreign source general limitation income), except that $100,000 of X's $200,000 of foreign source general limitation income consists of dividends from first-tier controlled foreign corporations ("CFCs") (as defined in section 957(a) of the Code) which derive exclusively foreign source general limitation income. X owns stock representing 10 to 50 percent of the vote and value in such CFCs.

(B) State A taxable income is computed by first making adjustments to X's federal taxable income. These adjustments result in X having a total of $1,100,000 of apportionable taxable income for state A tax purposes. None of the $100,000 of adjustments made by state A relate to the dividends paid by the CFCs. As in Example 25, the amount of apportionable taxable income attributable to business activities conducted in state A is determined by multiplying apportionable taxable income by a fraction (the "state apportionment fraction") that compares the relative amounts of X's payroll, property, and sales within state A with X's worldwide payroll, property and sales. An analysis of state A law indicates that state A law includes in its definition of the taxable business income of X which is apportionable to X's state A activities, dividends paid to X by its subsidiaries that are in the same business as X, but are less than 50 percent owned by X ("portfolio dividends"). The dividends received by X from the 10 to 50 percent owned first-tier CFCs, therefore, are considered to be portfolio dividends includable in apportionable business income for state A tax purposes. However, the factors of these CFCs are not included in the state A apportionment fraction for purposes of apportioning income to X's activities in the state. The comparison of X's state A factors with X's worldwide factors results in a state apportionment fraction of 50 percent. Applying this fraction to apportionable taxable income of $1,100,000, as determined under state law, results in attributing 50 percent of apportionable taxable income to state A, and produces total state A taxable income of $550,000. State A imposes an income tax at a rate of 10 percent on the amount of income that is attributed to state A, which results in $55,000 of tax imposed by state A.

(ii) Allocation.

(A) States A, B, and C impose income taxes of $69,000 which must be allocated to the classes of gross income upon which the taxes are imposed. A portion of X's federal income tax deduction of $55,000 for state A income tax is definitely related and thus allocable to the class of gross income consisting of foreign source portfolio dividends. A definite relationship exists between a deduction for state income tax and portfolio dividends when a state includes portfolio dividends in state taxable income apportionable to the state, but determines state taxable income by applying an apportionment fraction that excludes the factors of the corporations paying those dividends. By applying a state apportionment fraction that excludes factors of the corporations paying portfolio dividends to apportionable taxable income that includes the $100,000 of foreign source portfolio dividends, $50,000 (50 percent of the $100,000) of the portfolio dividends is attributed to X's activities in state A and subjected to state A income tax. Applying the state A income tax rate of 10 percent to the $50,000 of foreign source portfolio dividends subjected to state A income tax, $5,000 of X's $55,000 total state A income tax liability is definitely related and allocable to a class of gross income consisting of the foreign source portfolio dividends. Since under the look-through rules of section 904(d)(3) the foreign source portfolio dividends from the first-tier CFCs are included within the general limitation described in section 904(d)(1)(I), the $5,000 of state A tax on foreign source portfolio dividends is allocated entirely to foreign source general limitation income and, therefore, is not apportioned. (If the total amount of state A tax imposed on foreign source portfolio dividends were to exceed the actual amount of X's state A income tax liability (for example, due to net operating losses), the actual amount of state A tax would be allocated entirely to those foreign source portfolio dividends.) After allocation of a portion of the state A tax to portfolio dividends, $50,000 ($55,000 – $5,000) of state A tax remains to be allocated.

(B) A total of $64,000 (the aggregate of the $50,000 remaining state A tax, and the $10,000 and $4,000 of taxes imposed by states B and C, respectively) is to be allocated (as provided in Example 25) by comparing U.S. source taxable income (as determined under the Code) with the aggregate of the state taxable incomes determined by states A, B, and C (after reducing state apportionable taxable incomes by the amount of any portfolio dividends included in apportionable taxable income to which tax has been specifically allocated). X's state A taxable income, after reduction by the $50,000 of portfolio dividends taxed by state A, equals $500,000. X also has taxable income of $200,000 and $200,000 in states B and C, respectively. In the aggregate, therefore, states A, B, and C tax $900,000 of X's income, after excluding state taxable income attributable to portfolio dividends. Since X has only $800,000 of U.S. source taxable income for federal income tax purposes, it is presumed that state income taxes are imposed on $100,000 of foreign source income. The remaining deduction of $64,000 for state income taxes is therefore related and allocable to both foreign source and domestic source income and is subject to apportionment.

(iii) Apportionment. For purposes of computing the foreign tax credit limitation, X's income is comprised of one statutory grouping, foreign source general limitation income, and one residual grouping, gross income from sources within the United States. The remaining state income tax deduction of $64,000 must be apportioned between these two groupings on the basis of relative amounts of foreign source general limitation taxable income and U.S. source taxable income subject to state taxation. In this case, the $64,000 of state income taxes is considered to be imposed on $800,000 of domestic source income and $100,000 of foreign source general limitation income and is apportioned as follows:

State income tax deduction apportioned to foreign source general limitation income (statutory grouping): $64,000 × ($100,000/$900,000)	$ 7,111
State income tax deduction apportioned to income from sources within the United States (residual grouping): $64,000 × ($800,000/$900,000)	56,889
Total apportioned state income tax deduction ..	$64,000

Of the total state income taxes of $69,000, the amount allocated and apportioned to foreign source general limitation income equals $12,111 ($5,000 + $7,111). The total amount of state income taxes allocated and apportioned to U.S. source income equals $56,889.

Example (29). Income Taxes. (i) Facts.

(A) P, a domestic corporation, is a manufacturer and distributor of electronic equipment with operations in states F, G, and H. P also has a branch in country Y which manufactures and distributes the same type of electronic equipment. In addition, P has three wholly owned subsidiaries, US1, US2, and FS, the latter a controlled foreign corporation ("CFC") as defined in section 957(a) of the Code. P also owns stock representing 10 to 50 percent of the vote and value of various other first-tier CFCs that derive exclusively foreign source general limitation income.

(B) In 1988, P derives $1,000,000 of federal taxable income (without taking into account the deduction for state income taxes), which consists of $250,000 of foreign source general limitation income and $750,000 of U.S. source income. The foreign source general limitation income consists of a $25,000 subpart F inclusion with respect to FS, $150,000 of dividends from the other first-tier CFCs deriving exclusively foreign source general limitation income, in which P owns stock representing 10 to 50 percent of the vote and value, and $75,000 of manufacturing and sales income derived by P's U.S. operations and country Y branch. The $750,000 of U.S. source income consists of manufacturing and sales income derived by P's U.S. operations.

(C) For federal income tax purposes, US1 derives $75,000 of taxable income, before deduction for state income taxes, which consists entirely of U.S. source income. US2, a so-called "80/20" corporation described in section 861(c)(1), derives $250,000 of federal taxable income before deduction for state or foreign income taxes, all of which is derived from foreign operations and consists entirely of foreign source general limitation income. FS is not engaged in a U.S. trade or business and derives $550,000 of foreign source general limitation income before deduction for foreign income taxes.

(D) State F imposes a corporate income tax of 10 percent of P's state F taxable income, which is determined by formulary apportionment of the total taxable income attributable to P's worldwide unitary business. State F determines P's taxable income for state F tax purposes by first making adjustments to the taxable income, as determined for federal income tax purposes, of the members of the unitary business group to determine the total taxable income of the group. State F then computes P's state taxable income by attributing a portion of that unitary business taxable income to activities of P that are conducted in state F. State F does this by multiplying the unitary business taxable income (federal taxable income with state adjustments) by a fraction (the "state apportionment fraction") that compares the relative amounts of the unitary business group's payroll, property, and sales (the "factors") in state F with the payroll, property, and sales of the unitary business group. P is the only member of its unitary business group that has state F factors and that is thereby subject to state F income tax and filing requirements. State F defines the unitary business group to include any corporation more than 50 percent of which is directly or indirectly owned by a state F taxpayer and is engaged in the same unitary business. P's unitary business group, therefore, includes P, US1, US2, and FS, but does not include the 10 to 50 percent owned CFCs. The income of the unitary business group excludes intercompany dividends between members of the unitary business group and subpart F inclusions with respect to a member of the unitary business group. Dividends paid from nonmembers of the unitary group (the 10 to 50 percent owned CFCs) for state F tax purposes are referred to as "portfolio dividends" and are included in taxable income of the unitary business. None of the factors (in state F or worldwide) of the corporations paying portfolio dividends are included in the state F apportionment fraction for purposes of apportioning total taxable income of the unitary business to P's state F activities.

(E) After state adjustments to the taxable income of the unitary business group, as determined under federal tax principles, the total taxable income of P's unitary business group equals $2,000,000, consisting of $1,050,000 of P's income ($100,000 of foreign source manufacturing and sales income, $150,000 of foreign source portfolio dividends, and $800,000 of U.S. source manufacturing and sales income, but excluding the $25,000 subpart F inclusion attributable to FS since FS is a member of the unitary business group), $100,000 of US1's income (from sales made in the United States), $275,000 of US2's income (from an active business outside the United States), and $575,000 of FS's income. The differences between taxable income under federal tax principles and state F apportionable taxable income for P, US1, US2, and FS represent adjustments to taxable income under federal tax principles that are made pursuant to the tax laws of state F.

(F) The taxable income for each member of the unitary business group under federal tax principles and state law principles is summarized in the following table. (The items of income listed in the "Federal" column of the table refer to taxable income before deduction for state income tax.)

	Federal	State F
P		
U.S. source income	$750,000	$800,000
Foreign source general limitation income:		
Portfolio dividends	150,000	150,000
Subpart F income	25,000	0
Manufacturing and sales income ..	75,000	100,000
Total taxable income	1,000,000	1,050,000
US1		
U.S. source income	75,000	100,000
US2		
Foreign source general limitation income	250,000	275,000
FS		

Foreign source general limitation income	550,000	575,000
Taxable income of the unitary business group		2,000,000

(G) State F deems P to have state F taxable income of $500,000, which is determined by multiplying the total taxable income of the unitary business group ($2,000,000) by the group's state F apportionment fraction, which is assumed to be 25 percent in these facts. P's state F taxable income is then multiplied by the state F tax rate of 10 percent, resulting in a state F tax liability of $50,000. State G and state H, unlike state F, do not tax portfolio dividends. Although state G and state H apportion taxable income, respectively, on the basis of an apportionment fraction that compares state factors to total factors, state G and state H, unlike state F, do not apply a unitary business theory and consider only P's taxable income and factors in computing P's taxable income. P's taxable income under state G law equals $300,000, which is subject to a 5 percent tax rate resulting in a state G tax liability of $15,000. P's taxable income under state H law is $300,000, which is subject to a tax rate of 2 percent resulting in a state H tax liability of $6,000. P has a total federal income tax deduction for state income taxes of $71,000 ($50,000 + 15,000 + 6,000).

(ii) Allocation. (A) P's deduction of $71,000 for state income taxes is definitely related and allocable to the gross income with respect to which the taxes are imposed. Adjustments may be necessary, however, before aggregate state taxable incomes can be compared with U.S. source taxable income on the federal income tax return in the manner described in Examples 25 and 26. In allocating P's deduction for state income taxes, it is necessary first to determine the portion, if any, of the deduction that is definitely related and allocable to a particular class of gross income. A definite relationship exists between a deduction for state income tax and dividend income when a state includes portfolio dividends in state taxable income apportionable to the taxpayer's activities in the state, but determines state taxable income by applying an apportionment formula that excludes the factors of the corporations paying portfolio dividends.

(B) In this case, $150,000 of foreign source portfolio dividends are subject to a state F apportionment fraction of 25 percent, which results in a total of $37,500 of state F taxable income attributable to such dividends. As illustrated in Example 28, $3,750 ($150,000 × 25 percent state F apportionment percentage × 10 percent state F tax rate) of P's state F income tax is definitely related and allocable to a class of gross income consisting entirely of the foreign source portfolio dividends. Since under the look-through rules of section 904(d)(3) the foreign source portfolio dividends paid by first-tier CFCs are included within the general limitation described in section 904(d)(1)(I), the $3,750 of state F tax on foreign source portfolio dividends is allocated entirely to foreign source general limitation income and, therefore, is not apportioned.

(C) After reducing state F taxable income of the unitary business group by the taxable income attributable to portfolio dividends, P's remaining state F taxable income equals $462,500 ($500,000 − $37,500), the portion of the taxable income of the unitary business that state F attributes to P's activities in state F. Accordingly, in order to allocate and apportion the remaining $46,250 of state F tax ($50,000 of state F tax minus the $3,750 of state F tax allocated to foreign source portfolio dividends), it is necessary first to determine if state F is taxing only P's non-unitary taxable income (as defined below) or is imposing its tax partly on other unitary business income that is attributed under state F law to P's activities in state F. P's state F non-unitary taxable income is computed by applying the state F apportionment formula, solely on the basis of P's income (excluding portfolio dividends) and state F apportionment factors. If the state F taxable income (after reduction by the portfolio dividends attributed to state F) attributed to P under state F law exceeds P's non-unitary taxable income, a portion of the state F tax must be allocated and apportioned on the basis of the other unitary business income that is attributed to and taxable to P under state F law. If P's non-unitary taxable income equals or exceeds the $462,500 of remaining state F taxable income, it is presumed that state F is only taxing P's non-unitary taxable income, so that the entire amount of the remaining state F tax should be allocated and apportioned in the manner described in Example 25.

(D) If P's non-unitary taxable income is less than the $462,500 of remaining state F taxable income (after reduction for the $37,500 of state F taxable income attributable to portfolio dividends), it is presumed that state F is attributing to P, and taxing P upon, other unitary business income. In such a case, it is necessary to determine if state F is attributing to P, and imposing its income tax on, a part of the foreign source income that would be generally presumed under separate accounting to be the income of foreign affiliates and 80/20 companies included in the unitary group, or whether state F is limiting the income it attributes to P, and its taxation of P, to the U.S. source income that would be generally presumed under separate accounting to be the income of domestic members of the unitary group.

(E) Assume for purposes of this example that the non-unitary taxable income attributable to P equals $396,000, computed by multiplying P's state F taxable income of $900,000 (P's state F taxable income (before state F apportionment) of $1,050,000 less the $150,000 of foreign source portfolio dividends) by P's non-unitary state F apportionment fraction, which is assumed to be 44 percent. Because P's non-unitary taxable income of $396,000 is less than the $462,500 of remaining state F taxable income, state F is presumed to be attributing to P and taxing the income that would have been generally attributed under separate accounting to P's affiliates in the unitary group. To determine if state F tax is being imposed on members of the unitary group (other than P) that produce foreign source income, it is necessary to compute a hypothetical state F taxable income for all companies in the unitary group with significant U.S. operations. (For this purpose, the hypothetical group of companies with significant domestic operations is referred to as the "water's edge group.") State F is presumed to be attributing to P and taxing income that would have been generally attributable under separate accounting to foreign corporations and 80/20 companies to the extent that the remaining state F taxable income ($462,500) of P exceeds the hypothetical state F taxable income that would have been attributed under state F law to P if state F had defined the unitary group to be the water's edge group.

(F) The members of the water's edge group would have been P and US1. The unitary business income of this water's edge group is $1,000,000, the sum of $900,000 (P's state F taxable income (before state F apportionment) of $1,050,000 less the $150,000 of foreign source portfolio dividends) and $100,000 (US1's state F taxable income). For purposes of this example, the state F apportionment fraction determined on a unitary basis for this water's edge group is assumed to equal 40 percent, the average of P and US1's state F payroll, property, and sales factor ratios (the water's edge group's state F factors over its worldwide factors). Applying this apportionment fraction to the $1,000,000 of unitary business income of the water's edge group yields state F water's edge taxable income of $400,000. The excess of the remaining $462,500 of P's state F taxable income over the $400,000 of P's state F water's edge taxable income equals $62,500, and is attributable to the inclusion of US2 and FS in the unitary group. The state F tax attributable to the $62,500 of taxable income attributed to P under state F law, and that would have generally been attributed to US2 and FS under non-unitary accounting, equals $6,250 and is allocated entirely to a class of gross income consisting of foreign source general limitation income, because the income of FS and US2 consists entirely of such income. After the $6,250 of state F tax attributable to US2 and FS is subtracted from the remaining $46,250 of net state F tax, P has $40,000 of state F tax remaining to be allocated and apportioned.

(G) To the extent that the remainder of P's state F taxable income ($400,000) exceeds P's non-unitary state F taxable income ($396,000), it is presumed that state F is attributing to and imposing on P a tax on U.S. source income that would have been attributed under separate accounting to members of the water's edge group other than P. In these facts, the $4,000 difference in P's state F taxable income results from the inclusion of US1 in the unitary group. The $400 of P's state F tax attributable to this $4,000 is allocated entirely to P's U.S. source income. P's remaining $39,600 of state F tax ($40,000 of P's state F tax resulting from the attribution of P of income that would have been attributed under non-unitary accounting to other members of the water's edge group, minus $400 of state F tax attributable to US1 and allocated to P's U.S. source income) is the state F tax attributable to P's non-unitary state F taxable income that is to be allocated and apportioned together with P's state G tax of $15,000 and state H tax of $6,000 as illustrated in Example 25.

(H) In allocating the $60,600 of state tax liabilities ($39,600 state F tax attributable to P's non-unitary state F income + $15,000 state G tax + $6,000 state H tax) under Example 25, P's state taxable income in state G and state H ($300,000 + $300,000) must be added to P's non-unitary state F taxable income ($396,000). The resulting $996,000 of combined state taxable incomes is compared with $750,000 of U.S. source income on P's federal income tax return. Because P's combined state taxable incomes exceeds P's federal U.S. source taxable income, it is presumed that the remaining $60,600 of P's total state income taxes is imposed in part on foreign source income. Accordingly, P's remaining deduction of $60,600 ($39,600 + $15,000 + $6,000) for state income taxes is related and allocable to both P's foreign source and domestic source income and is subject to apportionment.

(iii) Apportionment. The $60,600 of state taxes (the remaining $39,600 of state F tax + $15,000 of state G tax + $6,000 of state H tax) must be apportioned between foreign source general limitation income and U.S. source income for federal income tax purposes. This apportionment is based upon the relative amounts of foreign source general limitation taxable income and U.S. source taxable income comprising the $996,000 of income subject to tax by the states, after reducing the total amount of income subject to tax by the portfolio dividends and the income attributed to P under state F law that would have been attributed under arm's length principles to other members of P's state F unitary business group. The deduction for the $60,600 of state income taxes is apportioned as follows:

State income tax deduction apportioned to foreign source general limitation income (statutory grouping): $60,600 × ($246,000/$996,000)	$14,967
State income tax deduction apportioned to income from sources within the United States (residual grouping): $60,600 × ($750,000/$996,000)	45,633
Total apportioned state income tax deduction . .	60,600

Of the total state income taxes of $71,000, the amount allocated and apportioned to foreign source general limitation income is $24,967—the sum of $14,967 of state F, state G, and state H taxes apportioned to foreign source general limitation income, $3,750 of state F tax allocated to foreign source apportionable dividend income, and the $6,250 of state F tax allocated to foreign source general limitation income as the result of state F's worldwide unitary business theory of taxation. The total amount of state income taxes allocated and apportioned to U.S. source income equals $46,033—the sum of the $400 of state F tax attributable to the inclusion of US1 in the state F unitary business group and $45,633 of combined state F, G, and H tax apportioned under the method provided in Example 25.

Example (30). [Reserved]. For further guidance, see § 1.861-8T(g), Example 30.

Example (31). Income Taxes.

(i) Facts. Assume that the facts are the same as in Example 29, except that state G requires P to adjust its federal taxable income by depreciating an asset at a different rate than is allowed P under the Internal Revenue Code for the same asset. Before using the methodology of Example 25 to determine whether a portion of its deduction for state income taxes is allocable to a class of gross income that includes foreign source income, P recomputes its taxable income under state G law by using the rate of depreciation that it is entitled to use under the Code, and uses this recomputed amount in applying the methodology of Example 25.

(ii) Allocation. P's modification of its state G taxable income is permissible. Under the methodology of Example 25, this modification of state G taxable income will produce a reasonable determination of the portion (if any) of P's state income taxes that is allocable to a class of gross income that includes foreign sources income.

Example (32). Income Taxes.

(i) Facts. Assume the facts are the same as Example 29, except that P's state F taxable income differs from the amount of its U.S. source income under federal income tax principles solely because state F determines P's state taxable income under a worldwide unitary business theory instead of the arm's length principles applied in the Code. Before using the methodology of Example 25 to determine whether a portion of its deduction for state income taxes is allocable to a class of gross income that includes foreign source income, P recomputes state F taxable income under the arm's length principles applied in the Code. P substitutes that recomputed amount for the amount of taxable income actually determined under state F law in applying the methodology of Example 25.

(ii) Allocation. P's modification of state F taxable income does not accurately reflect the factual relationship between the deduction for state F income tax and the income on which the tax is imposed, because there is no factual relationship between the state F income tax and the state F taxable income as recomputed under Code principles. State F does not impose its income tax upon P's income as it might have been defined under the Internal Revenue Code. Consequently, P's modification of state F taxable income is impermissible because it will not produce a reasonable determination of the portion (if any) of P's state income taxes that is allocable to a class of gross income that includes foreign source income.

Example (33). Income Taxes.

(i) Facts. Assume the same facts as in Example 29, except that state G does not impose an income tax on corporations, and P's non-unitary state F taxable income equals $462,500. Thus only $56,000 of state income taxes ($50,000 of state F income tax and $6,000 of state H income tax) are deductible and required to be allocated and (if necessary) apportioned. As in Example 29, P has $800,000 of aggregate state taxable income ($500,000 of state F taxable income and $300,000 of state H taxable income).

(ii) Method One. Assume that P has elected to allocate and apportion its deduction for state income tax under the safe harbor method provided in § 1.861-8(e)(6)(ii)(D)(2) ("Method One").

(A) Step One—Specific allocation to foreign source portfolio dividends. P applies the methodology of paragraph (ii) of Example 28 to determine the portion of the deduction that must be allocated to a class of gross income consisting solely of foreign source portfolio dividends. As illustrated in paragraphs (ii)(A) and (B) of Example 29, $3,750 of the deduction for state F income tax is attributable to the $37,500 of foreign source portfolio dividends attributed under state F law to P's activities in state F. Thus $3,750 of P's deduction for state income tax must be specifically allocated to a class of gross income consisting solely of $37,500 of foreign source portfolio dividends. No apportionment of the $3,750 is necessary. P's adjusted state taxable income is $762,500 (aggregate state taxable income of $800,000 reduced by $37,500 of foreign source portfolio dividends). Because the remaining amount of state F taxable income ($462,500) equals P's non-unitary state F taxable income, no further specific allocation of state tax is required.

(B) Step Two—Adjustment of U.S. source federal taxable income. P applies the methodology illustrated in paragraph (ii) of Example 27 (including the rules of UDITPA described therein) to determine the amount of its federal taxable income attributable to its activities in state G. Assume that P determines under this methodology that $300,000 of its federal taxable income is attributable to activities in state G. P's adjusted U.S. source federal taxable income equals $450,000 ($750,000 minus the $300,000 attributed to P's activities in state G).

(C) Step Three—Allocation. The portion of P's deduction for state income tax remaining to be allocated equals $52,250 ($56,000 minus the $3,750 specifically allocated to foreign source portfolio dividends). P allocates this portion by applying the methodology illustrated in paragraph (ii) of Example 25, as modified by paragraph (e)(6)(ii)(D)(2)(iii) of this section. Thus, P compares its adjusted state taxable income (as determined under Step One in paragraph (A) above) with an amount equal to 110% of its adjusted U.S. source federal taxable income (as determined under Step Two in paragraph (B) above). Because P's adjusted state taxable income ($762,500) exceeds 110% of P's adjusted U.S. source federal taxable income ($495,000, or 110% of $450,000), the remaining portion of P's deduction for state income tax ($52,500) must be allocated to a class of gross income that includes both U.S. and foreign source income.

(D) Step Four—Apportionment. P must apportion to U.S. source income the portion of the deduction that is attributable to state income tax imposed upon state taxable income in an amount equal to 110% of P's adjusted U.S. source federal taxable income. The remainder of the deduction must be apportioned to foreign source general limitation income.

Amount of deduction to be apportioned	$52,250.00
Less portion of deduction to be apportioned to income from sources within the United States (residual grouping); ($52,250 × ($495,000/$762,500)	$33,919.67
Equals Portion of deduction to be apportioned to foreign source general limitation income (statutory grouping)	$18,330.33

(iii) Method Two. Assume that P has elected to allocate and apportion its deduction for state income tax under the safe harbor method provided in § 1.861-8(e)(6)(ii)(D)(3) ("Method Two").

(A) Step One—Specific allocation. Step One of Method Two is the same as Step One of Method One. Therefore, as described in paragraph (A) of paragraph (ii) above, $3,750 of P's deduction for state income tax must be specifically allocated to a class of gross income consisting solely of $37,500 of foreign source portfolio dividends. No apportionment of the $3,750 is necessary. P's adjusted state taxable income is $762,500 (aggregate state taxable income of $800,000 reduced by $37,500 of foreign source portfolio dividends).

(B) Step Two—Adjustment of U.S. source federal taxable income. Step Two of Method Two is the same as Step Two of Method One. Therefore, as described in paragraph (B) of paragraph (ii) above, assume that P determines that $300,000 of its federal taxable income is attributable to activities in state G. P's adjusted U.S. source federal taxable income equals $450,000 ($750,000 minus the $300,000 attributed to P's activities in state G).

(C) Step Three—Allocation. The portion of P's deduction for state income tax remaining to be allocated equals $52,250 ($56,000 minus the $3,750 of state F income tax specifically allocated to foreign source portfolio dividends). P allocates this portion by applying the methodology illustrated in paragraph (ii) of Example 25, as modified by paragraph (e)(6)(ii)(D)(3)(iii) of this section. Thus, P compares its adjusted state taxable income (as determined under Step One in paragraph (A) above) with its adjusted U.S. source federal taxable income (as determined under Step Two in paragraph (B) above). Because P's adjusted state taxable income ($762,500) exceeds P's adjusted U.S. source federal taxable income ($450,000), the remaining portion of P's deduction for state income tax ($52,500) must be allocated to a class of gross income that includes both U.S. and foreign source income.

(D) Step Four—Apportionment. P must apportion to U.S. source income the portion of the deduction that is attributable to state income tax imposed upon state taxable income in an amount equal to P's adjusted U.S. source federal taxable income.

Amount of deduction to be apportioned	$52,250.00
Less portion of deduction initially apportioned to income from sources within the United States (residual grouping): $52,250 × ($450,000/$762,500)	30,836.07

Remainder requiring further apportionment:
$52,250 × ($312,500/$762,500) 21,413.93

The remainder of $21,413.93 must be further apportioned between foreign source general limitation income and U.S. source federal taxable income in the same proportions that P's adjusted U.S. source federal taxable income and foreign source general limitation income bear to P's total federal taxable income (taking into account the adjustment of U.S. source federal taxable income and reduced by the amount of foreign source portfolio dividends to which the tax has been specifically allocated).

Portion of remainder apportioned to foreign source general limitation income (statutory grouping): $21,413.93 × ($212,500/$662,500) $ 6,868.62
Remaining state income tax deduction to be apportioned to income from sources within the United States (residual grouping): $21,413.93 × ($450,000/$662,500) $14,545.31

Of P's total deduction of $56,000 for state income tax, the portion allocated and apportioned to foreign source general limitation income equals $10,618.62—the sum of $6,868.62 apportioned under Step Four and the $3,750.00 specifically allocated to foreign source portfolio dividend income under Step One. The portion of the deduction allocated and apportioned to U.S. source income equals $45,381.38—the sum of the $30,836.07 and the $14,545.31 apportioned under Step Four.

T.D. 6258, 10/23/57, amend T.D. 6892, 8/22/66, T.D. 7378, 9/29/75, T.D. 7456, 1/3/77, T.D. 7749, 12/30/80, T.D. 7939, 2/3/84, T.D. 8228, 9/9/88, T.D. 8236, 12/7/88, T.D. 8286, 1/29/90, T.D. 8337, 3/11/91, T.D. 8646, 12/21/95, T.D. 8805, 1/8/99, T.D. 8973, 12/27/2001, T.D. 9143, 7/27/2004, T.D. 9194, 4/6/2005, T.D. 9211, 7/13/2005, T.D. 9278, 7/31/2006.

PAR. 9. Section 1.861-8 is amended by revising paragraphs (a)(5), the fifth and sixth sentences in paragraph (b)(3), (e)(4), (f)(4)(i), (g) Examples 17, 18, and 30, and the first sentence in paragraph (h) introductory text to read as follows:

Proposed § 1.861-8 Computation of taxable income from sources within the United States and from other sources and activities. [*For Preamble, see ¶ 152,783*]

(a) * * *

(5) [The text of the proposed amendment to § 1.861-8(a)(5) is the same as the text of § 1.861-8T(a)(5) published elsewhere in this issue of the Federal Register] [See T.D. 9278, 07/31/2006, 71 Fed. Reg. 150.]

(b) * * *

(3) * * * [The text of the proposed amendment to § 1.861-8(b)(3) is the same as the text in § 1.861-8T(b)(3) published elsewhere in this issue of the Federal Register]. [See T.D. 9278, 07/31/2006, 71 Fed. Reg. 150.] * * *

* * * * *

(e) * * *

(4) [The text of the proposed amendment to § 1.861-8(e)(4) is the same as the text of § 1.861-8T(e)(4) published elsewhere in this issue of the Federal Register]. [See T.D. 9278, 07/31/2006, 71 Fed. Reg. 150.]

(f) * * *

(4) * * * (i) [The text of the proposed amendment to § 1.861-8(f)(4)(i) is the same as the text of § 1.861-8T(f)(4)(i) published elsewhere in this issue of the Federal Register]. [See T.D. 9278, 07/31/2006, 71 Fed. Reg. 150.]

(g) * * *

Example (17). [The text of the proposed amendment to § 1.861-8(g) Example 17 is the same as the text of § 1.861-8T(g) Example 17, published elsewhere in this issue of the Federal Register]. [See T.D. 9278, 07/31/2006, 71 Fed. Reg. 150.]

Example (18). [The text of the proposed amendment to § 1.861-8(g) Example 18 is the same as the text of § 1.861-8T(g) Example 18, published elsewhere in this issue of the Federal Register]. [See T.D. 9278, 07/31/2006, 71 Fed. Reg. 150.]

* * * * *

Example (30). [The text of the proposed amendment to § 1.861-8(g) Example 30 is the same as the text of § 1.861-8T(g) Example 30, published elsewhere in this issue of the Federal Register]. [See T.D. 9278, 07/31/2006, 71 Fed. Reg. 150.]

(h) [The text of the proposed amendment to § 1.861-8(h) is the same as the text of § 1.861-8T(h) published elsewhere in this issue of the Federal Register]. [See T.D. 9278, 07/31/2006, 71 Fed. Reg. 150.] * * *

* * * * *

PAR. 5. In § 1.861-8, paragraphs (f)(1)(vi)(E), (F) and (H) are revised to read as follows:

Proposed § 1.861-8 Computation of taxable income from sources within the United States and from other sources and activities. [*For Preamble, see ¶ 152,645*]

• ***Caution:*** This Notice of Proposed Rulemaking was partially finalized by TD 9248, 01/30/2006. Regs. §§ 1.1-1, 1.170A-1, 1.861-3, 1.861-8, 1.871-1, 1.876-1, 1.881-5, 1.884-0, 1.901-1, 1.931-1, 1.932-1, 1.933-1, 1.934-1, 1.935-1, 1.937-2, 1.937-3, 1.957-3, 1.1402(a)-12, 1.6038-2, 1.6046-1, 301.6688-1, 301.7701-3, and 301.7701(b)-1 remain proposed.

* * * * *

(f) * * *

(1) * * *

(vi) * * *

(E) The tax base for individuals entitled to the benefits of section 931 and the section 936 tax credit of a domestic corporation which has an election in effect under section 936;

(F) The exclusion for income from Puerto Rico for bona fide residents of Puerto Rico under section 933;

* * * * *

(H) The income derived from the U.S. Virgin Islands or from a section 935 possession (as defined in § 1.935-1T(a)(3)(i)).

* * * * *

§ 1.861-8T Computation of taxable income from sources within the United States and from other sources and activities (temporary).

(a) In general.

(1) [Reserved]

(2) Allocation and apportionment of deductions in general. If an affiliated group of corporations joins in filing a consol-

idated return under section 1501, the provisions of this section are to be applied separately to each member in that affiliated group for purposes of determining such member's taxable income, except to the extent that expenses, losses, and other deductions are allocated and apportioned as if all domestic members of an affiliated group were a single corporation under section 864(e) and the regulations thereunder. See § 1.861-9T through § 1.861-11T for rules regarding the affiliated group allocation and apportionment of interest expense, and § 1.861-14T for rules regarding the affiliated group allocation and apportionment of expenses other than interest.

(3) through (4) [Reserved]

(5)

* * * * *

(ii) Paragraph (e)(4), the last sentence of paragraph (f)(4)(i), and paragraph (g), Example 17, Example 18, and Example 30 of this section are generally applicable for taxable years beginning after December 31, 2006. In addition, a person may elect to apply the provisions of paragraph (e)(4) of this section to earlier years. Such election shall be made in accordance with the rules set forth in § 1.482-9T(n)(2).

(b) Allocation.

(1) and (2) [Reserved]

(3) Supportive functions. Deductions which are supportive in nature (such as overhead, general and administrative, and supervisory expenses) may relate to other deductions which can more readily be allocated to gross income. In such instance, such supportive deductions may be allocated and apportioned along with the deductions to which they relate. On the other hand, it would be equally acceptable to attribute supportive deductions on some reasonable basis directly to activities or property which generate, have generated or could reasonably be expected to generate gross income. This would ordinarily be accomplished by allocating the supportive expenses to all gross income or to another broad class of gross income and apportioning the expenses in accordance with paragraph (c)(1) of this section. For this purpose, reasonable departmental overhead rates may be utilized. For examples of the application of the principles of this paragraph (b)(3) to expenses other than expenses attributable to stewardship activities, see Examples 19 through 21 of paragraph (g) of this section. See paragraph (e)(4)(ii) of this section for the allocation and apportionment of deductions attributable to stewardship expenses. However, supportive deductions that are described in § 1.861-14T(e)(3) shall be allocated and apportioned in accordance with the rules of § 1.861-14T and shall not be allocated and apportioned by reference only to the gross income of a single member of an affiliated group of corporations as defined in § 1.861-14T(d).

(4) and (5) [Reserved]

(c) Apportionment of deductions. *(1) Deductions definitely related to a class of gross income.* Where a deduction has been allocated in accordance with paragraph (b) of this section to a class of gross income which is included in one statutory grouping and the residual grouping, the deduction must be apportioned between the statutory grouping and the residual grouping. Where a deduction has been allocated to a class of gross income which is included in more than one statutory grouping, such deduction must be apportioned among the statutory groupings and, where necessary, the residual grouping. Thus, in determining the separate limitations on the foreign tax credit imposed by section 904(d)(1) or by section 907, the income within a separate limitation category constitutes a statutory grouping of income and all other income not within that separate limitation category (whether domestic or within a different separate limitation category) constitutes the residual grouping. In this regard, the same method of apportionment must be used in apportioning a deduction to each separate limitation category. Also, see paragraph (f)(1)(iii) of this section with respect to the apportionment of deductions among the statutory groupings designated in section 904(d)(1). If the class of gross income to which a deduction has been allocated consists entirely of a single statutory grouping or the residual grouping, there is no need to apportion that deduction. If a deduction is not definitely related to any gross income, it must be apportioned ratably as provided in paragraph (c)(3) of this section. A deduction is apportioned by attributing the deduction to gross income (within the class to which the deduction has been allocated) which is in one or more statutory groupings and to gross income (within the class) which is in the residual grouping. Such attribution must be accomplished in a manner which reflects to a reasonably close extent the factual relationship between the deduction and the grouping of gross income. In apportioning deductions, it may be that for the taxable year there is no gross income in the statutory grouping or that deductions will exceed the amount of gross income in the statutory grouping. See paragraph (d)(1) of this section with respect to cases in which deductions exceed gross income. In determining the method of apportionment for a specific deduction, examples of bases and factors which should be considered include, but are not limited to—

(i) Comparison of units sold,

(ii) Comparison of the amount of gross sales or receipts,

(iii) Comparison of costs of goods sold,

(iv) Comparison of profit contribution,

(v) Comparison of expenses incurred, assets used, salaries paid, space utilized, and time spent which are attributable to the activities or properties giving rise to the class of gross income, and

(vi) Comparison of the amount of gross income.

Paragraph (e)(2) through (8) of this section provides the applicable rules for allocation and apportionment of deductions for interest, research and development expenses, and certain other deductions. The effects on tax liability of the apportionment of deductions and the burden of maintaining records not otherwise maintained and making computations not otherwise made shall be taken into consideration in determining whether a method of apportionment and its application are sufficiently precise. A method of apportionment described in this paragraph (c)(1) may not be used when it does not reflect, to a reasonably close extent, the factual relationship between the deduction and the groupings of income. Furthermore, certain methods of apportionment described in this paragraph (c)(1) may not be used in connection with any deduction for which another method is prescribed. The principles set forth above are applicable in apportioning both deductions definitely related to a class which constitutes less than all of the taxpayer's gross income and to deductions related to all of the taxpayer's gross income. If a deduction is not related to any class of gross income, it must be apportioned ratably as provided in paragraph (c)(3) of this section.

(2) Apportionment based on assets. Certain taxpayers are required by paragraph (e)(2) of this section and § 1.861-9T to apportion interest expense on the basis of assets. A taxpayer may apportion other deductions based on the comparative value of assets that generate income within each grouping, provided that such method reflects the factual

relationship between the deduction and the groupings of income and is applied in accordance with the rules of § 1.861-9T(g). In general, such apportionments must be made either on the basis of the tax book value of those assets or on their fair market value. However, once the taxpayer uses fair market value, the taxpayer and all related persons must continue to use such method unless expressly authorized by the Commissioner to change methods. For purposes of this paragraph (c)(2) the term "related persons" means two or more persons in a relationship described in section 267(b). In determining whether two or more corporations are members of same controlled group under section 267(b)(3), a person is considered to own stock owned directly by such person, stock owned with the application of section 1563(e)(1), and stock owned by the application of section 267(c). In determining whether a corporation is related to a partnership under section 267(b)(10), a person is considered to own the partnership interest owned directly by such person and the partnership interest owned with the application of section 267(e)(3). In the case of any corporate taxpayer that—

(i) Uses tax book value, and

(ii) Owns directly or indirectly (within the meaning of § 1.861-12T(c)(2)(ii)) 10 percent or more of the total combined voting power of all classes of stock entitled to vote in any other corporation (domestic or foreign) that is not a member of the affiliated group (as defined in section 864(e)(5)), such taxpayer shall adjust its basis in that stock in the manner described in § 1.861-12T(c).

(3) [Reserved]

(d) Excess of deductions and excluded and eliminated items of income.

(1) [Reserved]

(2) Allocation and apportionment to exempt, excluded or eliminated income. (i) In general. In the case of taxable years beginning after December 31, 1986, except to the extent otherwise permitted by § 1.861-13T, the following rules shall apply to take account of income that is exempt of excluded, or assets generating such income, with respect to allocation and apportionment of deductions.

(A) Allocation of deductions. In allocating deductions that are definitely related to one or more classes of gross income, exempt income (as defined in paragraph (d)(2)(ii) of this section) shall be taken into account.

(B) Apportionment of deductions. In apportioning deductions that are definitely related either to a class of gross income consisting of multiple groupings of income (whether statutory or residual) or to all gross income, exempt income and exempt assets (as defined in paragraph (d)(2)(ii) of this section) shall not be taken into account.

For purposes of apportioning deductions which are not taken into account under § 1.1502-13 in determining gain or loss from intercompany transactions, as defined in § 1.1502-13, income from such transactions shall be taken into account in the year such income is ultimately included in gross income.

(ii) Exempt income and exempt asset defined. (A) In general. For purposes of this section, the term "exempt income" means any income that is, in whole or in part, exempt, excluded, or eliminated for federal income tax purposes. The term "exempt asset" means any asset the income from which is, in whole or in part, exempt, excluded, or eliminated for federal tax purposes.

(B) Certain stock and dividends. The term "exempt income" includes the portion of the dividends that are deductible under—

(1) Section 243(a)(1) or (2) (relating to the dividends received deduction),

(2) Section 245(a) (relating to the dividends received deduction for dividends from certain foreign corporations).

Thus, for purposes of apportioning deductions using a gross income method, gross income would not include a dividend to the extent that it gives rise to a dividend received deduction under either section 243(a)(1), section 243(a)(2), or section 245(a). In the case of a life insurance company taxable under section 801, the amount of such stock that is treated as tax exempt shall not be reduced because a portion of the dividends received deduction is disallowed as attributable to the policyholder's share of such dividends. See § 1.861-14T(h) for a special rule concerning the allocation of reserve expenses of a life insurance company. In addition, for purposes of apportioning deductions using an asset method, assets would not include that portion of stock equal to the portion of dividends paid thereon that would be deductible under either section 243(a)(1), section 243(a)(2), or section 245(a). In the case of stock which generates, has generated, or can reasonably be expected to generate qualifying dividends deductible under section 243(a)(3), such stock shall not constitute a tax exempt asset. Such stock and the dividends thereon will, however, be eliminated from consideration in the apportionment of interest expense under the consolidation rule set forth in § 1.861-10T(c), and in the apportionment of other expenses under the consolidation rules set forth in § 1.861-14T.

(iii) Income that is not considered tax exempt. The following items are not considered to be exempt, eliminated, or excluded income and, thus, may have expenses, losses, or other deductions allocated and apportioned to them:

(A) In the case of a foreign taxpayer (including a foreign sales corporation (FSC)) computing its effectively connected income, gross income (whether domestic or foreign source) which is not effectively connected to the conduct of a United States trade or business;

(B) In computing the combined taxable income of a DISC or FSC and its related supplier, the gross income of a DISC or a FSC;

(C) For all purposes under subchapter N of the Code, Including the computation of combined taxable income of a possessions corporation and its affiliates under section 936(h), the gross income of a possessions corporation for which a credit is allowed under section 936(a); and

(D) Foreign earned income as defined in section 911 and the regulations thereunder (however, the rules of § 1.911-6 do not require the allocation and apportionment of certain deductions, including home mortgage interest, to foreign earned income for purposes of determining the deductions disallowed under section 911(d)(6)).

(iv) Prior years. For expense allocation and apportionment rules applicable to taxable years beginning before January 1, 1987, and for later years to the extent permitted by § 1.861-13T, see § 1.861-8(d)(2) (Revised as of April 1, 1986).

(e) Allocation and apportionment of certain deductions.

(1) [Reserved] For further guidance, see § 1.861-8(e)(1).

(2) Interest. The rules concerning the allocation and apportionment of interest expense and certain interest equivalents are set forth in §§ 1.861-9T through 1.861-13T.

(3) through (11) [Reserved] For further guidance, see § 1.861-8(e)(3) thorugh (e)(11).

(4) Stewardship and controlled services. (i) Expenses attributable to controlled services. If a corporation performs a

controlled services transaction (as defined in § 1.482-9T(l)(3)), which includes any activity by one member of a group of controlled taxpayers that results in a benefit to a related corporation, and the rendering corporation charges the related corporation for such services, section 482 and these regulations provide for an allocation where the charge is not consistent with an arm's length result as determined. The deductions for expenses of the corporation attributable to the controlled services transaction are considered definitely related to the amounts so charged and are to be allocated to such amounts.

(ii) Stewardship expenses attributable to dividends received. Stewardship expenses, which result from "overseeing" functions undertaken for a corporation's own benefit as an investor in a related corporation, shall be considered definitely related and allocable to dividends received, or to be received, from the related corporation. For purposes of this section, stewardship expenses of a corporation are those expenses resulting from "duplicative activities" (as defined in § 1.482-9T(l)(3)(iii)) or "shareholder activities" (as defined in § 1.482-9T(l)(3)(iv)) of the corporation with respect to the related corporation. Thus, for example, stewardship expenses include expenses of an activity the sole effect of which is either to protect the corporation's capital investment in the related corporation or to facilitate compliance by the corporation with reporting, legal, or regulatory requirements applicable specifically to the corporation, or both. If a corporation has a foreign or international department which exercises overseeing functions with respect to related foreign corporations and, in addition, the department performs other functions that generate other foreign-source income (such as fees for services rendered outside of the United States for the benefit of foreign related corporations, foreign-source royalties, and gross income of foreign branches), some part of the deductions with respect to that department are considered definitely related to the other foreign-source income. In some instances, the operations of a foreign or international department will also generate United States source income (such as fees for services performed in the United States). Permissible methods of apportionment with respect to stewardship expenses include comparisons of time spent by employees weighted to take into account differences in compensation, or comparisons of each related corporation's gross receipts, gross income, or unit sales volume, assuming that stewardship activities are not substantially disproportionate to such factors. See paragraph (f)(5) of this section for the type of verification that may be required in this respect. See § 1.482-9T(l)(5) for examples that illustrate the principles of § 1.482-9T(l)(3). See Example 17 and Example 18 of paragraph (g) of this section for the allocation and apportionment of stewardship expenses. See paragraph (b)(3) of this section for the allocation and apportionment of deductions attributable to supportive functions other than stewardship expenses, such as expenses in the nature of day-to-day management, and paragraph (e)(5) of this section generally for the allocation and apportionment of deductions attributable to legal and accounting fees and expenses.

(6) [Reserved]

(7) through (11) [Reserved]

(f) Miscellaneous matters. *(1) Operative sections.*

(i) [Reserved]

(ii) Separate limitations to the foreign tax credit. Section 904(d)(1) requires that the foreign tax credit limitation be determined separately in the case of the types of income specified therein. Accordingly, the income within each separate limitation category constitutes a statutory grouping of income and all other income not within that separate limitation category (whether domestic or within a different separate limitation category) constitutes the residual groups.

(iii) [Reserved]

(2) to (3) [Reserved]

(4) Adjustments made under other provisions of the Code. (i) In general. If an adjustment which affects the taxpayer is made under section 482 or any other provision of the Code, it may be necessary to recompute the allocations and apportionments required by this section in order to reflect changes resulting from the adjustment. The recomputation made by the Commissioner shall be made using the same method of allocation and apportionment as was originally used by the taxpayer, provided such method as originally used conformed with paragraph (a)(5) of this section and, in light of the adjustment, such method does not result in a material distortion. In addition to adjustments which would be made aside from this section, adjustments to the taxpayer's income and deductions which would not otherwise be made may be required before applying this section in order to prevent a distortion in determining taxable income from a particular source of activity. For example, if an item included as a part of the cost of goods sold has been improperly attributed to specific sales, and, as a result, gross income under one of the operative sections referred to in paragraph (f)(1) of this section is improperly determined, it may be necessary for the Commissioner to make an adjustment to the cost of goods sold, consistent with the principles of this section, before applying this section. Similarly, if a domestic corporation transfers the stock in its foreign subsidiaries to a domestic subsidiary and the parent corporation continues to incur expenses in connection with protecting its capital investment in the foreign subsidiaries (see paragraph (e)(4) of this section), it may be necessary for the Commissioner to make an allocation under section 482 with respect to such expenses before making allocations and apportionments required by this section, even though the section 482 allocation might not otherwise be made.

(ii) to (5) [Reserved]

(g) [Reserved]

Example (1). through (16). [Reserved]

Example (17). Stewardship Expenses (Consolidation). (i) (A) Facts. X, a domestic corporation, wholly owns M, N, and O, also domestic corporations. X, M, N, and O file a consolidated income tax return. All the income of X and O is from sources within the United States, all of M's income is general limitation income from sources within South America, and all of N's income is general limitation income from sources within Africa. X receives no dividends from M, N, or O. During the taxable year, the consolidated group of corporations earned consolidated gross income of $550,000 and incurred total deductions of $370,000 as follows:

	Gross income	Deductions
Corporations:		
X	$100,000	$50,000
M	250,000	100,000
N	150,000	200,000
O	50,000	20,000
Total	550,000	370,000

(B) Of the $50,000 of deductions incurred by X, $15,000 relates to X's ownership of M; $10,000 relates to X's ownership of N; $5,000 relates to X's ownership of O; and the sole effect of the entire $30,000 of deductions is to protect X's capital investment in M, N, and O. X properly categorizes the $30,000 of deductions as stewardship expenses. The remainder of X's deductions ($20,000) relates to production of United States source income from its plant in the United States.

(ii) (A) Allocation. X's deductions of $50,000 are definitely related and thus allocable to the types of gross income to which they give rise, namely $25,000 wholly to general limitation income from sources outside the United States ($15,000 for stewardship of M and $10,000 for stewardship of N) and the remainder ($25,000) wholly to gross income from sources within the United States. Expenses incurred by M and N are entirely related and thus wholly allocable to general limitation income earned from sources without the United States, and expenses incurred by O are entirely related and thus wholly allocable to income earned within the United States. Hence, no apportionment of expenses of X, M, N, or O is necessary. For purposes of applying the foreign tax credit limitation; the statutory grouping is general limitation gross income from sources without the United States and the residual grouping is gross income from sources within the United States. As a result of the allocation of deductions, the X consolidated group has taxable income from sources without the United States in the amount of $75,000, computed as follows:

Foreign source general limitation gross income:	
($250,000 from M + $150,000 from N)	$400,000
Less: Deductions allocable to foreign source general limitation gross income:	
($25,000 from X, $100,000 from M, and $200,000 from N)	325,000
Total foreign-source taxable income	75,000

(B) Thus, in the combined computation of the general limitation, the numerator of the limiting fraction (taxable income from sources outside the United States) is $75,000.

Example (18). Stewardship and Supportive Expenses. (i) (A) Facts. X, a domestic corporation, manufactures and sells pharmaceuticals in the United States. X's domestic subsidiary S, and X's foreign subsidiaries T, U, and V perform similar functions in the United States and foreign countries T, U, and V, respectively. Each corporation derives substantial net income during the taxable year that is general limitation income described in section 904(d)(1). X's gross income for the taxable year consists of:

Domestic sales income	$32,000,000
Dividends from S (before dividends received deduction)	3,000,000
Dividends from T	2,000,000
Dividends from U	1,000,000
Dividends from V	0
Royalties from T and U	1,000,000
Fees from U for services performed by X	1,000,000
Total gross income	40,000,000

(B) In addition, X incurs expenses of its supervision department of $1,500,000.

(C) X's supervision department (the Department) is responsible for the supervision of its four subsidiaries and for rendering certain services to the subsidiaries, and this Department provides all the supportive functions necessary for X's foreign activities. The Department performs three principal types of activities. The first type consists of services for the direct benefit of U for which a fee is paid by U to X. The cost of the services for U is $900,000 (which results in a total charge to U of $1,000,000). The second type consists of activities described in § 1.482-9(l)(3)(iii) that are in the nature of shareholder oversight that duplicate functions performed by the subsidiaries' own employees and that do not provide an additional benefit to the subsidiaries. For example, a team of auditors from X's accounting department periodically audits the subsidiaries' books and prepares internal reports for use by X's management. Similarly, X's treasurer periodically reviews for the board of directors of X the subsidiaries' financial policies. These activities do not provide an additional benefit to the related corporations. The cost of the duplicative services and related supportive expenses is $540,000. The third type of activity consists of providing services which are ancillary to the license agreements which X maintains with subsidiaries T and U. The cost of the ancillary services is $60,000.

(ii) Allocation. The Department's outlay of $900,000 for services rendered for the benefit of U is allocated to the $1,000,000 in fees paid by U. The remaining $600,000 in the Department's deductions are definitely related to the types of gross income to which they give rise, namely dividends from subsidiaries S, T, U, and V and royalties from T and U. However, $60,000 of the $600,000 in deductions are found to be attributable to the ancillary services and are definitely related (and therefore allocable) solely to royalties received from T and U, while the remaining $540,000 in deductions are definitely related (and therefore allocable) to dividends received from all the subsidiaries.

(iii) (A) Apportionment. For purposes of applying the foreign tax credit limitation, the statutory grouping is general limitation gross income from sources outside the United States and the residual grouping is gross income from sources within the United States. X's deduction of $540,000 for the Department's expenses and related supportive expenses which are allocable to dividends received from the subsidiaries must be apportioned between the statutory and residual groupings before the foreign tax credit limitation may be applied. In determining an appropriate method for apportioning the $540,000, a basis other than X's gross income must be used since the dividend payment policies of the subsidiaries bear no relationship either to the activities of the Department or to the amount of income earned by each subsidiary. This is evidenced by the fact that V paid no dividends during the year, whereas S, T, and U paid dividends of $1 million or more each. In the absence of facts that would indicate a material distortion resulting from the use of such method, the stewardship expenses ($540,000) may be apportioned on the basis of the gross receipts of each subsidiary.

(B) The gross receipts of the subsidiaries were as follows:

S	$4,000,000
T	3,000,000
U	500,000
V	1,500,000
Total	9,000,000

(C) Thus, the expenses of the Department are apportioned for purposes of the foreign tax credit limitation as follows:

Apportionment of stewardship expenses to the statutory grouping of gross income: $540,000 × [($3,000,000 + $500,000 + $1,500,000)/$9,000,000]	$300,000
Apportionment of supervisory expenses to the residual grouping of gross income: $540,000 × [$4,000,000/9,000,000]	240,000
Total: Apportioned stewardship expense	540,000

Example (19). to (23). [Reserved]

Example (24). Exempt, excluded, or eliminated income. (i) Income method. (A) Facts. X, a domestic corporation organized on January 1, 1987, is engaged in a number of businesses worldwide. X owns a 25-percent voting interest in each of five corporations engaged in the business A, two of which are domestic and three of which are foreign. X incurs stewardship expenses in connection with these five stock investments in the amount of $100. X apportions its stewardship expenses using a gross income method. Each of the five companies pays a dividend in the amount of $100. X is entitled to claim the 80-percent dividends received deduction on dividends paid by the two domestic companies. Because tax exempt income is considered in the allocation of deductions, X's $100 stewardship expense is allocated to the class of income consisting of dividends from business A companies. However, because tax exempt income is not considered in the apportionment of deductions within a class of gross income, the gross income of the two domestic companies must be reduced to reflect the availability of the dividends received deduction. Thus, for purposes of apportionment, the gross income paid by the three foreign companies is considered to be $100 each, while the gross income paid by the domestic companies is considered to be $20 each. Accordingly, X has total gross income from business A companies, for purposes of apportionment, of $340. As a result, $29.41 of X's stewardship expense is apportioned to each of the foreign companies and $5.88 of X's stewardship expense is apportioned to each of the domestic companies.

(ii) Asset method. (A) Facts. X, a domestic corporation organized on January 1, 1987, carries on a trade or business in the United States. X has deductible interest expense incurred in 1987 of $60,000. X owns all the stock of Y, a foreign corporation. X also owns 49 percent of the voting stock of Z, a domestic corporation. Neither Y nor Z has retained earnings and profits at the end of 1987. X apportions its interest expense on the basis of the fair market value of its assets. X has assets worth $1,500,000 that generate domestic source income, among which are tax exempt municipal bonds worth $100,000, and the stock of Z, which has a value of $500,000. The Y stock owned by X has a fair market value of $2,000,000 and generates solely foreign source general limitation income.

(B) Allocation. No portion of X's interest expense is directly allocable solely to identified property within the meaning of § 1.861-10T. Thus, X's deduction for interest is definitely related to all its gross income as a class.

(C) Apportionment. For purposes of apportioning expenses, assets that generate exempt, eliminated, or excluded income are not taken into account. Because X's municipal bonds are tax exempt, they are not taken into account in apportioning interest expense. Since X is entitled to claim under section 243 to 80-percent dividends received deduction with respect to the dividend it received from Z, 80 percent of the value of that stock is not taken into account as an asset for purposes of apportionment under the asset method. X apportions its interest deduction between the statutory grouping of foreign source general limitation income and the residual grouping of domestic source income as follows:

To foreign source general limitation income:

$$\text{Interest expense} \times \frac{\text{General limitation assets that are not tax exempt}}{\text{Worldwide assets that are not tax exempt}}$$

$$\$60{,}000 \times \frac{\$2{,}000{,}000}{(\$100{,}000 + \$900{,}000 + \$2{,}000{,}000)} = \$40{,}000$$

$$\frac{\text{Nonexempt foreign assets}}{\text{20 percent of Z stock value} + \text{Nonexempt domestic assets} + \text{Nonexempt foreign assets}}$$

To domestic source income:

$$\text{Interest expense} \times \frac{\text{Domestic assets that are not tax exempt}}{\text{Worldwide assets that are not tax exempt}}$$

$$\$60{,}000 \times \frac{\$100{,}000 + \$900{,}000}{(\$100{,}000 + \$900{,}000 + \$2{,}000{,}000)} = \$20{,}000$$

$$\frac{\text{20 percent of Z stock value} + \text{nonexempt domestic assets}}{\text{20 percent of Z stock value} + \text{Nonexempt domestic assets} + \text{Nonexempt foreign assets}}$$

Example (30). Income Taxes. (i) (A) Facts. As in Example 17 of this paragraph, X is a domestic corporation that wholly owns M, N, and O, also domestic corporations. X, M, N, and O file a consolidated income tax return. All the income of X and O is from sources within the United States, all of M's income is general limitation income from sources within South America, and all of N's income is general limitation income from sources within Africa. X receives no dividends from M, N, or O. During the taxable year, the consolidated group of corporations earned consolidated gross income of $550,000 and incurred total deductions of $370,000. X has gross income of $100,000 and deductions of $50,000, without regard to its deduction for state income tax. Of the $50,000 of deductions incurred by X, $15,000 relates to X's ownership of M; $10,000 relates to X's ownership of N; $5,000 relates to X's ownership of O; and the entire $30,000 constitutes stewardship expenses. The remainder of X's $20,000 of deductions (which is assumed not to include state income tax) relates to production of U.S. source income from its plant in the United States. M has gross income of $250,000 and deductions of $100,000, which yield foreign-source general limitation taxable income of $150,000. N has gross income of $150,000 and deductions of $200,000, which yield a foreign-source general limitation loss of $50,000. O has gross income of $50,000 and deductions of $20,000, which yield U.S. source taxable income of $30,000.

(B) Unlike Example 17 of this paragraph (g), however, X also has a deduction of $1,800 for state A income taxes. X's state A taxable income is computed by first making adjustments to the Federal taxable income of X to derive apportionable taxable income for state A tax purposes. An analysis of state A law indicates that state A law also includes in its definition of the taxable business income of X which is apportionable to X's state A activities, the taxable income of M, N, and O, which is related to X's business. As in Example 25, the amount of apportionable taxable income attributable to business activities conducted in state A is determined by multiplying apportionable taxable income by a fraction (the "state apportionment fraction") that compares the relative amounts of payroll, property, and sales within state A with worldwide payroll, property, and sales. Assuming that X's apportionable taxable income equals $180,000, $100,000 of which is from sources without the United States, and $80,000 is from sources within the United States, and that the state apportionment fraction is equal to 10 percent, X has state A taxable income of $18,000. The state A income tax of $1,800 is then derived by applying the state A income tax rate of 10 percent to the $18,000 of state A taxable income.

(i) Allocation and apportionment. Assume that under Example 29, it is determined that X's deduction for state A income tax is definitely related to a class of gross income consisting of income from sources both within and without the United States, and that the state A tax is apportioned $1,000 to sources without the United States, and $800 to sources within the United States. Under Example 17, without regard to the deduction for X's state A income tax, X has a separate loss of ($25,000) from sources without the United States. After taking into account the deduction for state A income tax, X's separate loss from sources without the United States is increased by the $1,000 state A tax apportioned to sources without the United States, and equals a loss of ($26,000), for purposes of computing the numerator of the consolidated general limitation foreign tax credit limitation.

(h) Effective dates. *(1) In general.* In general, the rules of this section, as well as the rules of §§ 1.861-9T, 1.861-10T, 1.861-11T, 1.861-12T, and 1.861-14T apply for taxable years beginning after December 31, 1986, except for paragraphs (a)(5)(ii), (b)(3), (e)(4), (f)(4)(i), and paragraph (g) Example 17, Example 18, and Example 30 of this section, which are generally applicable for taxable years beginning after December 31, 2006. Also, see §§ 1.861-8(e)(12)(iv) and 1.861-14(e)(6) for rules concerning the allocation and apportionment of deductions for charitable contributions. In the case of corporate taxpayers, transition rules set forth in § 1.861-13T provide for the gradual phase-in of certain provisions of this and the foregoing sections. However, the following rules are effective for taxable years commencing after December 31, 1988:

(i) Section 1.861-9T(b)(2) (concerning the treatment of certain foreign currency).

(ii) Section 1.861-9T(d)(2) (concerning the treatment of interest incurred by nonresident aliens).

(iii) Section 1.861-10T(b)(3)(ii) (providing an operating costs test for purposes of the nonrecourse indebtedness exception).

(iv) Section 1.861-10T(b)(6) (concerning excess collaterilzation of nonrecourse borrowings).

(2) In addition, 1.861-10T(e) (concerning the treatment of related controlled foreign corporation indebtedness) is applicable for taxable years commencing after December 31, 1987. For rules for taxable years beginning before January 1, 1987, and for later years to the extent permitted by 1.861-13T, see 1.861-8 (revised as of April 1, 1986).

(3) Expiration date. The applicability of the paragraphs (a)(5)(ii), (b)(3), (e)(4), (f)(4)(i), and paragraph (g) Example 17, Example 18, and Example 30 of this section, expires on or before July 31, 2009.

T.D. 8228, 9/9/88, amend T.D. 8236, 12/7/88, T.D. 8286, 1/29/90, T.D. 8337, 3/11/91, T.D. 8597, 7/12/95, T.D. 8805, 1/8/99, T.D. 8973, 12/27/2001, T.D. 9143, 7/27/2004, T.D. 9211, 7/13/2005, T.D. 9278, 7/31/2006.

§ 1.861-9 Allocation and apportionment of interest expense.

(a) through (g)(1)(i) [Reserved]. For further guidance, see § 1.861-9T(a) through (g)(1)(i).

(g) *(1)* (ii) [Reserved]. For further guidance, see the second sentence in § 1.861-9T(g)(1)(ii).

(iii) through (h)(4) [Reserved]. For further guidance, see § 1.861-9T(g)(1)(iii) through (h)(4).

(h) *(5) Characterizing stock in related persons.* (i) General rule. Stock in a related person held by the taxpayer or by another related person shall be characterized on the basis of the fair market value of the taxpayer's pro rata share of assets held by the related person attributed to each statutory grouping and the residual grouping under the stock characterization rules of § 1.861-12T(c)(3)(ii), except that the portion of the value of intangible assets of the taxpayer and related persons that is apportioned to the related person under § 1.861-9T(h)(2) shall be characterized on the basis of the net income before interest expense of the related person within each statutory grouping or residual grouping (excluding income that is passive under § 1.904-4(b)).

(ii) Special rule for section 936 corporations regarding alternative minimum tax. For purposes of characterizing stock in a related section 936 corporation in determining foreign source alternative minimum taxable income within each separate category and the alternative minimum tax foreign tax credit pursuant to section 59(a), the rules of § 1861-9T(g)(3) shall apply and § 1.861-9(h)(5)(i) shall not apply. Thus, for taxable years beginning after December 31, 1989, and before January 1, 1994, stock in a related section 936 corporation is characterized for alternative minimum tax purposes as a foreign source passive asset because the stock produces foreign source passive dividend income under sections 861(a)(2)(A), 862(a)(2), and 904(d)(2)(A) and the regulations under those sections. For taxable years beginning after December 31, 1993, stock in a related section 936 corporation would be characterized for alternative minimum tax purposes as an asset subject to the separate limitation for section 936 corporation dividends because the stock produces foreign source dividend income that, for alternative minimum tax purposes, is subject to a separate foreign tax credit limitation under section 56(g)(4)(C)(iii)(IV). However, stock in a section 936 corporation is characterized as a U.S. source asset to the extent required by section 904(g). For the definition of the term section 936 corporation see § 1.861-11(d)(2)(ii).

(iii) Effective date. This paragraph (h)(5) applies to taxable years beginning after December 31, 1989.

(6) [Reserved]. For further guidance, see § 1.861-9T(h)(6).

(i) Alternative tax book value method. *(1) Alternative value for certain tangible property.* A taxpayer may elect to determine the tax book value of its tangible property that is depreciated under section 168 (section 168 property) using the rules provided in this paragraph (i)(1) (the alternative tax book value method). The alternative tax book value method applies solely for purposes of apportioning expenses (including the calculation of the alternative minimum tax foreign tax credit pursuant to section 59(a)) under the asset method described in paragraph (g) of this section.

(i) The tax book value of section 168 property placed in service during or after the first taxable year to which the election to use the alternative tax book value method applies shall be determined as though such property were subject to the alternative depreciation system set forth in section 168(g) (or a successor provision) for the entire period that such property has been in service.

(ii) In the case of section 168 property placed in service prior to the first taxable year to which the election to use the alternative tax book value method applies, the tax book value of such property shall be determined under the depreciation method, convention, and recovery period provided for under section 168(g) for the first taxable year to which the election applies.

(iii) If a taxpayer revokes an election to use the alternative tax book value method (the prior election) and later makes another election to use the alternative tax book value method (the subsequent election) that is effective for a taxable year that begins within 3 years of the end of the last taxable year to which the prior election applied, the taxpayer shall determine the tax book value of its section 168 property as though the prior election has remained in effect.

(iv) The tax book value of section 168 property shall be determined without regard to the election to expense certain depreciable assets under section 179.

(v) Examples. The provisions of this paragraph (i)(1) are illustrated in the following examples:

Example (1). In 2000, a taxpayer purchases and places in service section 168 property used solely in the United States. In 2005, the taxpayer elects to use the alternative tax book value method, effective for the current taxable year. For purposes of determining the tax book value of its section 168 property, the taxpayer's depreciation deduction is determined by applying the method, convention, and recovery period rules of the alternative depreciation system under section 168(g)(2) as in effect in 2005 to the taxpayer's original cost basis in such property. In 2006, the taxpayer acquires and places in service in the United States new section 168 property. The tax book value of this section 168 property is determined under the rules of section 168(g)(2) applicable to property placed in service in 2006.

Example (2). Assume the same facts as in Example 1, except that the taxpayer revokes the alternative tax book value method election effective for taxable year 2010. Additionally, in 2011, the taxpayer acquires new section 168 property and places it in service in the United States. If the taxpayer elects to use the alternative tax book value method effective for taxable year 2012, the taxpayer must determine the tax book value of its section 168 property as though the prior election still applied. Thus, the tax book value of property placed in service prior to 2005 would be determined by applying the method, convention, and recovery period rules of the alternative depreciation system under section 168(g)(2) applicable to property placed in service in 2005. The tax book value of section 168 property placed in service during any taxable year after 2004 would be determined by applying the method, convention, and recovery period rules of the alternative depreciation system under section 168(g)(2) applicable to property placed in service in such taxable year.

(2) Timing and scope of election. (i) Except as provided in this paragraph (i)(2), a taxpayer may elect to use the alternative tax book value method with respect to any taxable year beginning on or after March 26, 2004. However, pursuant to § 1.861-8T(c)(2), a taxpayer that has elected the fair market value method must obtain the consent of the Commissioner prior to electing the alternative tax book value method. Any election made pursuant to this paragraph (i)(2) shall apply to all members of an affiliated group of corporations as defined in §§ 1.861-11(d) and 1.861-11T(d). Any election made pursuant to this paragraph (i)(2) shall apply to all subsequent taxable years of the taxpayer unless revoked by the taxpayer. Revocation of such an election, other than in conjunction with an election to use the fair market value method, for a taxable year prior to the sixth taxable year for which the election applies requires the consent of the Commissioner.

(ii) Example. The provisions of this paragraph (i)(2) are illustrated in the following example:

Example. Corporation X, a calendar year taxpayer, elects on its original, timely filed tax return for the taxable year ending December 31, 2007, to use the alternative tax book value method for its 2007 year. The alternative tax book value method applies to Corporation X's 2007 year and all subsequent taxable years. Corporation X may not, without the consent of the Commissioner, revoke its election and determine tax book value using a method other than the alternative tax book value method with respect to any taxable year beginning before January 1, 2012. However, Corporation X may automatically elect to change from the alternative tax book value method to the fair market value method for any open year.

(3) Certain other adjustments. [Reserved.]

(4) Effective date. This paragraph (i) applies to taxable years beginning on or after March 26, 2004.

(j) [Reserved]. For further guidance, see § 1.861-9T(j).

T.D. 8916, 12/27/2000, amend T.D. 9120, 3/25/2004, T.D. 9247, 1/27/2006.

PAR. 2. In § 1.861-9, paragraph (f) is revised to read as follows:

Proposed § 1.861-9 Allocation and apportionment of interest expense. [*For Preamble, see ¶ 152,753*]

* * * * *

(f) The text of proposed § 1.861-9(f) is the same as the text of § 1.861-9T(f) published elsewhere in this issue of the Federal Register.] [*See T.D. 9260, 04/24/2006, 71 Fed. Reg. 79.*]

* * * * *

§ 1.861-9T Allocation and apportionment of interest expense (temporary).

(a) In general. Any expense that is deductible under section 163 (including original issue discount) constitutes interest expense for purposes of this section, as well as for purposes of §§ 1.861-10T, 1.861-11T, 1.861-12T, and 1.861-13T. The term interest refers to the gross amount of interest expense incurred by a taxpayer in a given tax year. The method of allocation and apportionment for interest set forth in this section is based on the approach that, in general, money is fungible and that interest expense is attributable to all activities and property regardless of any specific purpose for incurring an obligation on which interest is paid. Exceptions to the fungibility rule are set forth in § 1.861-10T. The fungibility approach recognizes that all activities and property require funds and that management has a great deal of flexibility as to the source and use of funds. When money is borrowed for a specific purpose, such borrowing will generally free other funds for other purposes, and it is reasonable under this approach to attribute part of the cost of borrowing to such other purposes. Consistent with the principles of fungibility, except as otherwise provided, the aggregate of deductions for interest in all cases shall be considered related to all income producing activities and assets of the taxpayer and, thus, allocable to all the gross income which the assets of the taxpayer generate, have generated, or could reasonably have been expected to generate. In the case of the interest expense of members of an affiliated group, interest expense shall be considered to be allocable to all gross income of the members of the group under § 1.861-11T. That section requires the members of an affiliated group to allocate and apportion the interest expense of each member of the group as if all members of such group were a single corporation. For the method of determining the interest deduction allowed to foreign corporations under section 882(c), see § 1.882-5.

(b) Interest equivalent. *(1) Certain expenses and losses.* (i) General rule. Any expense or loss (to the extent deductible) incurred in a transaction or series of integrated or related transactions in which the taxpayer secures the use of funds for a period of time shall be subject to allocation and apportionment under the rules of this section if such expense or loss is substantially incurred in consideration of the time value of money. However, the allocation and apportionment of a loss under this paragraph (b) shall not affect the characterization of such loss as capital or ordinary for other purposes of the Code and the regulations thereunder.

(ii) Examples. The rule of this paragraph (b)(1) may be illustrated by the following examples.

Example (1). W, a domestic corporation, borrows from X two ounces of gold at a time when the spot price for gold is $500 per ounce. W agrees to return the two ounces of gold in six months. W sells the two ounces of gold to Y for $1000. W then enters into a contract with Z to purchase two ounces of gold six months in the future for $1,050. In exchange for the use of $1,000 in cash, W has sustained a loss of $50 on related transactions. This loss is subject to allocation and apportionment under the rules of this section in the same manner as interest expense.

Example (2). X, a domestic corporation with a dollar functional currency, borrows 100 pounds on January 1, 1987 for a three-year term at an interest rate greater than the applicable federal rate for dollar loans. At this time, the interest rate on the pound was approximately equal to the interest rate on dollar borrowings and the forward price on the pound, vis-a-vis the dollar, was approximately equal to the spot price. On January 1, 1987, X converted 100 pounds into dollars and entered into a currency swap that substantially hedged X's foreign currency exposure on the pound borrowing, both with respect to interest and principal. The borrowing, coupled with the swap, represents a series of related transactions in which the taxpayer secures the use of funds in its functional currency. Any net foreign currency loss on this series of transactions constitutes a loss incurred substantially in consideration of the time value of money and shall be apportioned in the same manner as interest expense. Thus, if the pound depreciates against the dollar, such that when the first payment on the pound borrowing is due the taxpayer has a currency loss on the swap payment hedging its first interest payment, such loss shall, even if the transaction is not integrated under section 988(d), be allocated and apportioned in the same manner as interest expense under the authority of this paragraph (b)(1).

Example (3). On January 1, 1987, X, a domestic corporation with a dollar functional currency, enters into a dollar interest rate swap contract with Y, a domestic counterparty. Under the terms of this agreement, X agrees to pay Y floating rate interest with respect to a notional principal amount of $100 for five years. In return, Y agrees to pay X fixed rate interest at 10 percent with respect to a notional principal amount of $100 for five years. On the same day, Y prepays the fixed leg of the swap by making a lump sum payment of $37 to X. This lump sum payment represents the present value of five $10 swap payments. Because X secures the use of $37 in this transaction, any net swap expense arising from the transaction represents an expense incurred substantially in consideration of the time value of money. Assuming this lump sum payment is not otherwise characterized as a loan from Y to X, and that X must amortize the $37 lump sum payment under the principles of Notice 89-21, any net swap expense incurred by X with respect to this transaction (*i.e.*, the excess, if any, of X's annual swap payment to Y over the annual amortization of the $37 lump sum payment that is taken into income by X) represents an expense equivalent to interest expense. The result would be the same if X sold the fixed leg to a third party for $37. While this example presents the case of a lump sum payment, the rules of paragraph (b)(1) would also apply to any transaction in which the swap payments are not substantially contemporaneous if the pricing of the transaction is materially affected by the time value of money. Thus, expenses and losses will be subject to apportionment under the rules of this section to the extent that such expenses or losses were incurred in consideration of the time value of money.

(2) Certain foreign currency borrowings. (i) Rule. If a taxpayer borrows in a nonfunctional currency at a rate of interest that is less than the applicable federal rate (or its equivalent in functional currency if the functional currency is not the dollar), any swap, forward, future, option, or similar financial arrangement (or any combination thereof) entered into by the taxpayer or by a related person (as defined in § 1.861-8T(c)(2)) that exists during the term of the borrowing and that substantially diminishes currency risk with respect to the borrowing or interest expense thereon will be presumed to constitute a hedge of such borrowing, unless the taxpayer can demonstrate on the basis of facts and circumstances that the two transactions are in fact unrelated. Under this presumption, the currency loss incurred on the borrowing during taxable years beginning after December 31, 1988, in connection with hedged nonfunctional currency borrowings, reduced or increased by the gain or loss on the hedge, will be apportioned in the same manner as interest expense. This presumption can be rebutted by a showing that the financial arrangement was entered into in connection with hedging currency exposure arising in the ordinary course of a trade or business (other than with respect to the borrowing).

(ii) Examples. The principles of this paragraph (b)(2) may be illustrated by the following examples.

Example (1). Taxpayer has a dollar functional currency and does not have any qualified business units with a functional currency other than the dollar. On January 1, 1989, when the unit of foreign currency is worth $1, taxpayer borrows 100 units of foreign currency for a three-year period bearing interest at the annual rate of 3 percent and immediately converts the proceeds of the borrowing into dollars for use in its business. In the ordinary course of its business, taxpayer has no foreign currency exposure in this currency. In March 1989, taxpayer enters into a three-year swap agreement that covers most, but not all, of the payment of interest and principal. Because the swap substantially diminishes currency risk with respect to the borrowing, it is presumed to hedge the loan. Since taxpayer cannot demonstrate that it was hedging currency exposure arising in the ordinary course of its business (other than currency exposure with respect to the borrowing), the net currency loss on the borrowing adjusted for any gain or loss on the swap must be apportioned in the same manner as interest expense.

Example (2). Assume the same facts as in Example 1, except that the taxpayer borrows in two separate foreign currencies on terms described in Example 1 and enters into a swap agreement in a single currency that substantially diminishes the taxpayer's aggregate foreign currency risk. The net currency loss on the borrowings adjusted for any gain or loss on the swap must be apportioned in the same manner as interest expense.

(3) Losses on sale of certain receivables. (i) General rule. Any loss on the sale of a trade receivable (as defined in § 1.954-2(h)) shall be allocated and apportioned, solely for purposes of this section and §§ 1.861-10T, 1.861-11T, 1.861-12T, and 1.861-13T, in the same manner as interest expense, unless at the time of sale of the receivable, it bears interest at a rate which is at least 120 percent of the short term applicable federal rate (as determined under section 1274(d) of the Code), or its equivalent in foreign currency in the case of receivables denominated in foreign currency, determined at the time the receivable arises. This treatment shall not affect the characterization of such expense as interest for other purposes of the Internal Revenue Code.

(ii) Exceptions. To the extent that a loss on the sale of a trade receivable exceeds the discount on the receivable that would be computed applying to the amount received on the sale of the receivable 120 percent of the applicable federal rate (or its equivalent in foreign currency in the case of receivables denominated in foreign currency) for the period commencing with the date on which the receivable is sold and ending with the earlier of the date on which the receivable begins to bear interest at such rate or the anticipated payment date of the receivable, such excess shall not be allocated and apportioned in the same manner as interest expense but rather shall be allocated and apportioned to the gross income generated by the receivable. In cases of transfers of receivables to a domestic international sales corporation described § 1.994-1(c)(6)(v), the rule of this paragraph (b)(3) shall not apply for purposes of computing combined taxable income. In computing the combined taxable income of a foreign sales corporation and its related supplier, loss on the sale of receivables to a third party incurred either by the foreign sales corporation or its related supplier shall offset combined taxable income, notwithstanding the provisions of this paragraph (b)(3). See § 1.924(a)-1T(g)(7).

Example. On October 1, X sells a widget to Y for $100 payable in 30 days, after which the receivable will bear stated interest at 13 percent. On October 4, X sells Y's obligation to Z for $98. Assume that the applicable federal rate for the month of October is 10 percent. Applying 120 percent of the applicable federal rate to the $98 received on the sale of the receivable, the obligation is discounted at a 12 percent rate for a period of 27 days. At this discount rate, the obligation would have sold for $99.22. Thus, 78 cents of the $2 loss on the sale is apportioned in the same manner as interest expense, and $1.22 of the $2 loss on the sale is directly allocated to the income generated on the widget sale.

(4) Rent in certain leasing transactions. [Reserved]

(5) Treatment of bond premium. (i) Treatment by the issuer. If a bond or other debt obligation is issued at a premium, an amount of interest expense incurred by the issuer on that bond or other debt obligation equal to the amortized portion of that premium that is included in gross income for the year shall be allocated and apportioned solely to the amortized portion of premium derived by the issuer for the year.

(ii) Treatment by the holder. If a bond or debt obligation is purchased at a premium, the portion of that premium amortized during the year by the holder under section 171 and the regulations thereunder shall be allocated and apportioned solely to interest income derived from the bond by the holder for the year.

(6) Financial products that alter effective cost of borrowing. (i) In general. Various derivative financial products can be part of transactions or series of transactions described in paragraph (b)(1) of this section. Such derivative financial products, including interest rate swaps, options, forwards, caps, and collars, potentially alter a taxpayer's effective cost of borrowing with respect to an actual liability of the taxpayer. For example, a taxpayer that is obligated to pay interest at a fixed rate may, in effect, pay interest at a floating rate by entering into an interest rate swap. Similarly, a taxpayer that is obligated to pay interest at a floating rate may, in effect, limit its exposure to rising interest rates by purchasing a cap. Such a taxpayer may have gains or losses associated with such derivative financial products. This paragraph (b)(6) provides rules for the treatment of gains and losses from such derivative financial products ("financial products") that are part of transactions described in paragraph (b)(1) of this section and that are used by the taxpayer to alter its effective cost of borrowing with respect to an actual liability. This paragraph (b)(6) shall only apply where the hedge and the borrowing are in the same currency and shall not apply to the extent otherwise provided in section 988 and the regulations thereunder. The allocation and apportionment of a loss under this paragraph (b) shall not affect the characterization of such loss as capital or ordinary for other purposes of the Code and the regulations thereunder.

(ii) Definition of gain and loss. For purposes of this paragraph (b)(6), the term "gain" refers to the excess of the amounts properly taken into income under a financial product that alters the effective cost of borrowing over the amounts properly allowed as a deduction thereunder within a given taxable year. See, *e.g.*, Notice 89-21. The term "loss" refers to the excess of the amounts properly allowed as a deduction under such a financial product over the amounts properly taken into income thereunder within a given taxable year.

(iii) Treatment of gain or loss on the disposition of a financial product. [Reserved.]

(iv) Entities that are not financial services entities. An entity that does not constitute a financial services entity within the meaning of § 1.904-4(e)(3) shall treat gains and losses on financial products described in paragraph (b)(6)(i) of this section as follows.

(A) Losses. Losses on any financial product described in paragraph (b)(6)(i) of this section shall be apportioned in the same manner as interest expense whether or not such financial product is identified by the taxpayer under paragraph (b)(6)(iv)(C) of this section as a liability hedge.

(B) Gains, Gains on any financial product described in paragraph (b)(6)(i) of this section shall reduce the taxpayer's total interest expense that is subject to apportionment, but only if such financial product is identified by the taxpayer under paragraph (b)(6)(iv)(C) of this section as a liability hedge. Such reduction is accomplished by directly allocating interest expense to the income derived from such a financial product.

(C) Identification of financial products. A taxpayer can identify a financial product described in paragraph (b)(6)(i) of this section as hedging a particular interest-bearing liability (or any group of such liabilities) by clearly identifying on its books and records on the same day that it becomes a party to such arrangement that such arrangement hedges a given liability (or group of liabilities). In the case of a partial hedge, such identification shall apply to only that part of the liability that is hedged. If the taxpayer clearly identifies on its books and records a financial product as a hedge of an interest-bearing asset (or any group of such assets), it will create a rebuttable presumption that such financial product is not described in paragraph (b)(6)(i) of this section. A taxpayer may identify a hedge as relating to an anticipated liability, provided that such liability is in fact incurred within 120 days following the date of such identification. Gains and losses on such an anticipatory arrangement accruing prior to the time at which the liability is incurred shall constitute an adjustment to interest expense.

(v) Financial services entities. [Reserved]

(vi) Dealers. The rule of paragraph (b)(6)(iv) of this section shall not apply to a person acting in its capacity as a regular dealer in the financial products described in paragraph (b)(6)(i) of this section. Instead, losses sustained by a regular dealer in connection with such financial products shall be allocated to the class of gross income from such arrangements. Gains of a regular dealer in notional principal contracts are governed by the rules of § 1.863-7T(b). Amounts received or accrued by any person from any financial product that is integrated as specified in Notice 89-90 with an asset shall not be treated as amounts received or accrued by a person acting in its capacity as a regular dealer in financial products.

(vii) Examples. The principles of this paragraph (b)(6) may be illustrated by the following examples.

Example (1). X is not a financial services entity or regular dealer in the financial products described in paragraph (b)(6)(i) of this section and has a dollar functional currency. In 1990, X incurred a total of $200 of interest expense. On January 1, 1990, X entered into an interest rate swap agreement with Y, in order to hedge its interest rate exposure with respect to a pre-existing floating rate liability. On the same day, X properly identified the agreement as a hedge of such liability. Under the agreement, X is required to pay Y an amount equal to a fixed rate of 10 percent on a notional principal amount of $1,000. Y is required to pay X an amount equal to a floating rate of interest on the same notional principal amount. Under the agreement, X received from Y during 1990 a net payment of $25. Because X identified the swap agreement as a liability hedge under the rules of paragraph (b)(6)(iv)(C), X may effectively reduce its total allocable interest expense for 1990 to $175 by directly allocating $25 of interest expense to the swap income. Had X not properly identified the swap as a liability hedge, this swap payment would have been treated as domestic source income in accordance with the rule of § 1.863-7T(b).

Example (2). Assume the same facts as Example (1), except that X did not properly identify the agreement as a liability hedge on January 1, 1990. In 1990, X made a net payment of $25 to Y under the swap agreement. This swap payment is allocated and apportioned in the same manner as interest expense under the rules of paragraph (b)(6)(iv)(A).

(viii) Effective dates. (A) Losses. The rules of this paragraph (b)(6) shall apply to losses on any transaction described in paragraph (b)(6)(i) of this section that was entered into after September 14, 1988.

(B) Gains. Except as provided in paragraph (b)(6)(viii)(C) of this section, the rules of this paragraph (b)(6) shall apply to any gain that was realized on any transaction described in paragraph (b)(6)(i) of this section that was entered into after August 14, 1989.

(C) Exception for interim gains. Taxpayers shall be permitted to apply the rules of this paragraph (b)(6) to any gain that was realized on any transaction described in paragraph (b)(6)(i) of this section that was entered into after September 14, 1988 and on or before August 14, 1989, if the taxpayer can demonstrate to the satisfaction of the Commissioner that substantially all of the arrangements described in paragraph (b)(6)(i) of this section to which the taxpayer became a party during the interim period were identified on the taxpayer's books and records with the liabilities of the taxpayer in a substantially contemporaneous manner and that all losses and expenses that are subject to the rules of this paragraph (b)(6) were treated in the same manner as interest expense. For this purpose, arrangements that were identified in a substantially contemporaneous manner with the taxpayer's assets shall be ignored.

(7) Foreign currency gain or loss. In addition to the rules of paragraph (b)(1), (b)(2), and (b)(6) of this section, any foreign currency loss that is treated as an adjustment to interest expense under regulations issued under section 988 shall be allocated and apportioned in the same manner as interest expense. Any foreign currency gain that is treated as an adjustment to interest expense under regulations issued under section 988 shall offset apportionable interest expense.

(c) Allowable deductions. In order for an interest expense to be allocated and apportioned, it must first be determined that the interest expense is currently deductible. A number of provisions in the Code disallow or suspend deductions of interest expense or require the capitalization thereof.

(1) Disallowed deductions. A taxpayer does not allocate and apportion interest expense under this section that is permanently disallowed as a deduction by operation of section 163(h), section 265, or any other provision or rule that permanently disallows the deduction of interest expense.

(2) Section 263A. Section 263A requires the capitalization of interest expense that is allocable to designated types of property. Any interest expense that is capitalized under section 263A does not constitute deductible interest expense for purposes of this section. Furthermore, interest expense capitalized in inventory or depreciable property is not separately allocated and apportioned when the inventory is sold or depreciation is allowed. Capitalized interest expense is effectively allocated and apportioned as part of, and in the same manner as, the cost of goods sold, amortization, or depreciation deduction.

(3) Section 163(d). Section 163(d) suspends the deduction for interest expense to the extent that it exceeds net investment income. In the year that suspended investment interest expense becomes allowable under the rules of section 163(d), that interest expense is apportioned under rules set forth in paragraph (d)(1) of this section as though it were incurred in the taxable year in which the expense is deducted.

(4) Section 469. (i) General rule. Section 469 suspends the deduction of passive activity losses to the extent that they exceed passive activity income for the year. Passive activity losses may consist in part of interest expense properly allocable to passive activity. In the year that suspended interest expense becomes allowable as a deduction under the rules of section 469, that interest expense is apportioned under rules set forth in paragraph (d)(1) of this section as though it were incurred in the taxable year in which the expense is deducted.

(ii) Identification of the interest component of a suspended passive loss. A suspended passive loss may consist of a variety of items of expense other than interest expense. Suspended interest expense for any taxable year is computed by multiplying the total suspended passive loss for the year by a fraction, the numerator of which is passive interest expense for the year (determined under regulations issued under section 163) and the denominator of which is total passive expenses for the year. The amount of the suspended interest expense that is considered to be deductible in a subsequent taxable year is computed by multiplying the amount of any cumulative suspended interest expense (reduced by suspended interest expense allowed as a deduction in prior taxable years) times a fraction, the numerator of which is the portion of cumulative suspended passive losses that become deductible in the taxable year and the denominator of which is the cumulative suspended passive losses for prior taxable years (reduced by suspended passive losses allowed as deductions in prior taxable years).

(iii) Example. The rules of this paragraph (c)(4) may be illustrated by the following example.

Example. On January 1, 1987, A, a United States citizen, invested in a passive activity. In 1987, the passive activity generated no passive income and $100 in passive losses, all of which were suspended by operation of section 469. The suspended loss included $10 of suspended interest expense. In 1988, the passive activity generated $50 in passive income and $150 in passive expenses which included $30 of interest expense. The entire $100 passive loss was suspended in 1988 and included $20 of interest expense ($100 suspended passive loss × $30 passive interest expense/$150 total passive expenses). Thus, at the end of 1988, A had total suspended passive losses of $200, including $30 of suspended interest expense. In 1989, the passive activity generated $100 in passive income and no passive expenses. Thus, $100 of A's cumulative suspended passive loss was therefore allowed in 1989. The $100 of deductible passive loss includes $15 of suspended interest expense ($30 cumulative suspended interest expense × $100 of cumulative suspended passive losses allowable in 1989/$200 of total cumulative suspended passive losses). The $15 of interest expense is apportioned under the rules of paragraph (d) of this section as though it were incurred in 1989.

(d) Apportionment rules for individuals, estates, and certain trusts. *(1) United States individuals.* In the case of taxable years beginning after December 31, 1986, individuals generally shall apportion interest expense under different rules according to the type of interest expense incurred. The interest expense of individuals shall be characterized under the regulations issued under section 163. However, in the case of an individual whose foreign source income (including income that is excluded under section 911) does not exceed a gross amount of $5,000, the apportionment of interest expense under this section is not required. Such an individual's interest expense may be allocated entirely to domestic source income.

(i) Interest incurred in the conduct of a trade or business. An individual who incurs business interest described in section 163(h)(2)(A) shall apportion such interest expense using an asset method by reference to the individual's business assets.

(ii) Investment interest. An individual who incurs investment interest described in section 163(h)(2)(B) shall apportion that interest expense on the basis of the individual's investment assets.

(iii) Interest incurred in a passive activity. An individual who incurs passive activity interest described in section 163(h)(2)(C) shall apportion that interest expense on the basis of the individual's passive activity assets. Individuals who receive a distributive share of interest expense incurred in a partnership are subject to special rules set forth in paragraph (e) of this section.

(iv) Qualified residence and deductible personal interest. Individuals who incur qualified residence interest described in section 163(h)(2)(D) shall apportion that interest expense under a gross income method, taking into account all income (including business, passive activity, and investment income) but excluding income that is exempt under section 911. For purposes of this section, any qualified residence that is rented shall be considered to be a business asset for the period in which it is rented, with the result that the interest on such a residence is not apportioned under this subdivision (iv) but instead under subdivisions (i) or (iii) of this paragraph (d)(1). To the extent that personal interest described in section 163(h)(2) remains deductible under transitional rules, individuals shall apportion such interest expense in the same manner as qualified residence interest.

(v) Example. The following example illustrates the principles of this section.

Example. (i) Facts. A is a resident individual taxpayer engaged in the active conduct of a trade or business, which A operates as a sole proprietor. A's business generates only domestic source income. A's investment portfolio consists of several less than 10 percent stock investments. Certain stocks in which A's adjusted basis is $40,000 generate domestic source income and other stocks in which A's adjusted basis is $60,000 generate foreign source passive income. In addition, A owns his personal residence, which is subject to a mortgage in the amount of $100,000. All interest expense incurred with respect to A's mortgage is qualified residence interest for purposes of section 163(h)(2)(D). A's other indebtedness consists of a bank loan in the amount of $40,000. Under the regulations issued under section 163(h), it is determined that the proceeds of the $40,000 loan were divided equally between A's business and his investment portfolio. In 1987, the gross income of A's business, before the apportionment of interest expense, was $50,000. A's investment portfolio generated $4,000 in domestic source income and $6,000 in foreign source passive income. All of A's debt obligations bear interest at the annual rate of 10 percent.

(ii) Analysis of business interest. Under section 163(h) of the Code, $2,000 of A's interest expense is attributable to his business. Under the rules of paragraph (d)(1)(i), such interest must be apportioned on the basis of the business assets. Applying the asset method described in paragraph (g) of this section, it is determined that all of A's business assets generate domestic income and, therefore, constitute domestic assets. Thus, the $2,000 in interest expense on the business loan is allocable to domestic source income.

(iii) Analysis of investment interest. Under section 163(h) of the Code, $2,000 of A's interest expense is investment interest. Under the rules of paragraph (d)(1)(ii) of this section, such interest must be apportioned on the basis of investment assets. Applying the asset method, A's investment assets consist of stock generating domestic source income with an adjusted basis of $40,000 and stock generating foreign source passive income with an adjusted basis of $60,000. Thus, 40 percent ($800) of A's investment interest is apportioned to domestic source income and 60 percent ($1,200) of A's investment interest is apportioned to foreign source passive income for purposes of section 904.

(iv) Analysis of qualified residence interest. The $10,000 of qualified residence interest expense is apportioned under the rules of paragraph (d)(1)(iv) of this section on the basis of all of A's gross income. A's gross income consists of $60,000, $54,000 of which is domestic source and $6,000 of which is foreign source passive income. Thus, $9,000 of A's qualified residence interest is apportioned to domestic source income and $1,000 of A's qualified residence interest is apportioned to foreign source passive income.

(2) Nonresident aliens. (i) General rule. For taxable years beginning on or after January 1, 1989, interest expense incurred by a nonresident alien shall be considered to be connected with income effectively connected with a United States trade or business only to the extent that interest expense is incurred with respect to liabilities that—

(A) Are entered on the books and records of the United States trade or business when incurred, or

(B) Are secured by assets that generate such effectively connected income.

(ii) Limitations. (A) Maximum debt capitalization. Interest expense incurred by a nonresident alien is not considered to be connected with effectively connected income to the extent that it is incurred with respect to liabilities that exceed 80 percent of the gross assets of the United States trade or business.

(B) Collateralization by other assets. Interest expense on indebtedness that is secured by specific assets (not including the general credit of the nonresident alien) other than the assets of the United States trade or business shall not be considered to be connected with effectively connected income.

(3) Estates and trusts. Estates shall be treated in the same manner as individuals. In the case of a trust that is beneficially owned by individuals and is a complex trust, the trust shall be treated in the same manner as individuals under the rules of paragraph (d) of this section, except that no de minimis amount shall apply. In the case of a trust that is beneficially owned by one or more corporations, the trust shall be treated either as a partnership or as a corporation depending on how the trust is characterized under the rules of section 7701 and the regulations thereunder.

(e) Partnerships. *(1) In general—aggregate rule.* A partner's distributive share of the interest expense of a partnership that is directly allocable under § 1.861-10T to income from specific partnership property shall be treated as directly allocable to the income generated by such partnership property. Subject to the exceptions set forth in paragraph (e)(4), a partner's distributive share of the interest expense of a partnership that is not directly allocable under § 1.861-10T generally is considered related to all income producing activities and assets of the partner and shall be subject to apportionment under the rules described in this paragraph. For purposes of this section, a partner's percentage interest in a partnership shall be determined by reference to the partner's interest in partnership income for the year. Similarly, a partner's pro rata share of partnership assets shall be determined by reference to the partner's interest in partnership income for the year.

(2) Corporate partners whose interest in the partnership is 10 percent or more. A corporate partner shall apportion its distributive share of partnership interest expense by reference to the partner's assets, including the partner's pro rata share of partnership assets, under the rules of paragraph (f) of this section if the corporate partner's direct and indirect interest in the partnership (as determined under the attribution rules of section 318) is 10 percent or more. A corporation using the tax book value method of apportionment shall use the partnership's inside basis in its assets, adjusted to the extent required under § 1.861-10T(d)(2). A corporation using the fair market value method of apportionment shall use the fair market value of the partnership's assets, adjusted to the extent required under § 1.861-10T(d)(2).

(3) Individual partners who are general partners or who are limited partners with an interest in the partnership of 10 percent or more. An individual partner is subject to the rules of this paragraph (e)(3) if either the individual is a general partner or the individual's direct and indirect interest (as determined under the attribution rules of section 318) in the partnership is 10 percent or more. The individual shall first classify his or her distributive share of partnership interest expense as interest incurred in the active conduct of a trade or business, as passive activity interest, or as investment interest under regulations issued under section 163 and 469. The individual must then apportion his or her interest expense (including the partner's distributive share of partnership interest expense) under the rules of paragraph (d) of this section. Each such individual partner shall take into account his or her distributive share of partnership gross income or pro rata share of the partnership assets in applying such rules. An individual using the tax book value method of apportionment shall use the partnership's inside basis in its assets, adjusted to the extent required under § 1.861-10T(d)(2). An individual using the fair market value method of apportionment shall use the fair market value of the partnership's assets, adjusted to the extent required under § 1.861-10T(d)(2).

(4) Less than 10 percent limited partners and less than 10 percent corporate general partners—entity rule. (i) Partnership interest expense. A limited partner (whether individual or corporate) or corporate general partner whose direct and indirect interest (as determined under the attribution rules of section 318) in the partnership is less than 10 percent shall directly allocate its distributive share of partnership interest expense to its distributive share of partnership gross income. Under § 1.904-5(h)(2)(i) of the regulations, such a partner's distributive share of foreign source income of the partnership is treated as passive income (subject to the high taxed income exception of section 904(d)(2)(F)), except in the case of high withholding tax interest or income from a partnership interest held in the ordinary course of the partner's active trade or business, as defined in § 1.904-5(h)(2)(i). A partner's distributive share of partnership interest expense (other than partnership interest expense that is directly allocated to identified property under § 1.861-10T) shall be apportioned in accordance with the partner's relative distributive share of gross foreign source income in each limitation category and of domestic source income from the partnership. To the extent that partnership interest expense is directly allocated under § 1.861-10T, a comparable portion of the income to which such interest expense is allocated shall be disregarded in determining the partner's relative distributive share of gross foreign source income in each limitation category and domestic source income. The partner's distributive share of the interest expense of the partnership that is directly allocable under § 1.861-10T shall be allocated according to the treatment, after application of § 1.904-5(h)(2)(i), of the partner's distributive share of the income to which the expense is allocated.

(ii) Other interest expense of the partner. For purposes of apportioning other interest expense of the partner on an asset basis, the partner's interest in the partnership, and not the partner's pro rata share of partnership assets, is considered to be the relevant asset. The value of this asset for apportionment purposes is either the tax book value or fair market value of the partner's partnership interest, depending on the method of apportionment used by the taxpayer. This amount of a partner's interest in the partnership is allocated among various limitation categories in the same manner as partnership interest expense (that is not directly allocable under § 1.861-10T) is apportioned in subdivision (i) of this paragraph (e)(4). If the partner uses the tax book value method of apportionment, the partner's interest in the partnership must be reduced, for this purpose, to the extent that the partner's basis consists of liabilities that are taken into account under section 752. Under either the tax book value or fair market value method of apportionment, for purposes of this section only, the value of the partner's interest in the partnership must be reduced by the principal amount of any indebtedness of the partner the interest on which is directly allocated to its partnership interest under § 1.861-10T.

(5) Tiered partnerships. If a partnership is a partner in another partnership, the distributive share of interest expense of a lower-tier partnership that is subject to the rules of paragraph (e)(4) shall not be reapportioned in the hands of any higher-tier partner. However, the distributive share of interest expense of lower-tier partnership that is subject to the rules of paragraph (e)(2) or (3) shall be apportioned by the partner of the higher-tier partnership or by any higher-tier partnership to which the rules of paragraph (e)(4) apply, taking into account the partner's indirect pro rata share of the lower-tier partnership's income or assets.

(6) Example. (i) Facts. A, B, and C are partners in a limited partnership. A is a corporate general partner, owns a 5 percent interest in the partnership, and has an adjusted basis in its partnership interest, determined without regard to section 752 of the Code, of $5. A's investment in the partnership is not held in the ordinary course of the taxpayer's active trade or business, as defined in § 1.904-7(i)(2). B, a corporate limited partner, owns a 70 percent interest in the partnership, and has an adjusted basis in its partnership interest, determined without regard to section 752 of the Code, of $70. C is an individual limited partner, owns a 25 percent interest in the partnership, and has an adjusted basis in the partnership interest, determined without regard to section 752 of the Code, of $25. The partners' interests in the profits and losses of the partnership conform to their respective interests. None of the interest expense incurred directly by any of the partners is directly allocable to their partnership interest under § 1.861-10T. The ABC partnership's sole assets are two apartment buildings, one domestic and the other foreign. The domestic building has an adjusted inside basis of $600 and the foreign building has an adjusted inside basis of $500. Each of the buildings is subject to a nonrecourse liability in the amount of $500. The ABC partnership's total interest expense for the taxable year is $120, both nonrecourse liabilities bearing interest at the rate of 12 percent. The indebtedness on the domestic building qualifies for direct allocation under the rules of § 1.861-10T. The indebtedness on the foreign building does not so qualify. The partnership incurred no foreign taxes. The partnership's gross income for the taxable year is $360, consisting of $100 in foreign source income and $260 in domestic source income. Under § 1.752-1(e), the nonrecourse liabilities of the partnership are allocated among the partners according to their share of the partnership profits. Accordingly, the adjusted basis of A, B, and C in their respective partnership interests (for other than apportionment purposes) is, respectively, $55, $770, and $275.

(ii) Determination of the amount of partnership interest expense that is subject to allocation and apportionment. Interest on the nonrecourse loan on the domestic building is, under § 1.861-10T, directly allocable to income from that investment. The interest expense is therefore directly allocable to domestic income. Interest on the nonrecourse loan on the foreign building is not directly allocable. The interest expense is therefore subject to allocation and apportionment. Thus, $60 of interest expense is directly allocable to domestic income and $60 of interest expense is subject to allocation and apportionment.

(iii) Analysis for Partner A. A's distributive share of the partnership's gross income is $18, which consists of $5 in foreign source income and $13 in domestic source income. A's distributive share of the ABC interest expense is $6, $3 of which is directly allocable to domestic income and $3 of which is subject to apportionment. After direct allocation of qualifying interest expense, A's distributive share of the partnership's gross income consists of $5 in foreign source income and $10 in domestic source income. Because A is a less than 10 percent corporate partner, A's distributive share of any foreign source partnership income is considered to be passive income. Accordingly, in apportioning the $3 of partnership interest expense that is subject to apportionment on a gross income method, one-third ($1) is apportioned to foreign source passive income and two-thirds ($2) is apportioned to domestic source income. In apportioning its other interest expense, A uses the tax book value method. A's adjusted basis in A's partnership interest ($55) includes A's share of the partnership's liabilities ($50), which are included in basis under section 752. For purposes of apportioning other interest expense, A's adjusted basis in the partnership must be reduced to the extent of such liabilities. Thus, A's adjusted basis in the partnership, for purposes of apportionment, is $5. For the purpose of apportioning A's other interest expense, this $5 in basis is characterized one-third as a foreign passive asset and two-thirds as a domestic asset, which is the ratio determined in paragraph (e)(4)(i).

(iv) Analysis for Partner B. B's distributive share of the ABC interest expense is $84, $42 of which is directly allocable to domestic income and $42 of which is subject to apportionment. As a corporate limited partner whose interest in the partnership is 10 percent or more, B is subject to the rules of paragraph (e)(2) and paragraph (f) of this section. These rules require that a corporate partner apportion its distributive share of partnership interest expense at the partner level on the asset method described in paragraph (g) of this section by reference to its corporate assets, which include, for this purpose, 70 percent of the partnership's assets, adjusted in the manner described in § 1.861-10T(e) to reflect directly allocable interest expense.

(v) Analysis for Partner C. C's distributive share of the ABC interest expense is $30, $15 of which is directly allocable to domestic income and $15 of which is subject to apportionment. As an individual limited partner whose interest in the partnership is 10 percent or more, C is subject to the rules of paragraph (e)(3) of this section. These rules require that an individual's share of partnership interest expense be classified under regulations issued under section 163(h) and then apportioned under the rules applicable to individuals, which are set forth in paragraph (d) of this section.

(7) Foreign partners. The distributive share of partnership interest expense of a nonresident alien who is a partner in a partnership shall be considered to be connected with effectively connected income based on the percentage of the assets of the partnership that generate effectively connected income. No interest expense directly incurred by the partner may be allocated and apportioned to effectively connected income derived by the partnership.

(f) Corporations. *(1) Domestic corporations.* Domestic corporations shall apportion interest expense using the asset method described in paragraph (g) of this section and the applicable rules of §§ 1.861-10T through 1.861-13T.

(2) Foreign branches of domestic corporations. In the application of the asset method described in paragraph (g) of this section, a domestic corporation shall—

(i) Take into account the assets of any foreign branch, translated according to the rules set forth in paragraph (g) of this section, and

(ii) Combine with its own interest expense any deductible interest expense incurred by a branch, translated according to the rules of section 987 and the regulations thereunder.

For purposes of computing currency gain or loss on any remittance from a branch or other qualified business unit (as defined in § 1.989(a)-1T) under section 987, the rules of this paragraph (f) shall not apply. The branch shall compute its currency gain or loss on remittances by taking into account only its separate expenses and its separate income.

Example. (i) Facts. X is a domestic corporation which operates B, a branch doing business in a foreign country. In 1988, without regard to branch B, X has gross domestic source income of $1,000 and gross foreign source general limitation income of $500 and incurs $200 of interest expense. Using the tax book value method of apportionment, X, without regard to branch B, determines the value of its assets that generate domestic source income to be $6,000 and the value of its assets that generate foreign source general limitation income to be $1,000. B constitutes a qualified business unit within the meaning of section 989 with a functional currency other than the U.S. dollar and uses the profit and loss method prescribed by section 987. Applying the translation rules of section 987, B earned $500 of gross foreign general limitation income and incurred $100 of interest expense. B incurred no other expenses. For 1988, the average functional currency book value of B's assets that generate foreign general limitation income translated at the year-end rate for 1988 is $3,000.

(ii) Computation of net income. The combined assets of X and B for 1988 (averaged under the rules of § 1.861-9T(g)(3)) consist 60 percent of assets generating domestic source income and 40 percent of assets generating foreign source general limitation income. The combined interest expense of both X and B is $300. Thus, $180 of the combined interest expense is apportioned to domestic source income and $120 is apportioned to the foreign source income, yielding net domestic source income of $820 and net foreign source general limitation income of $880.

(iii) Computation of currency gain or loss. For purposes of computing currency gain or loss on branch remittances, B takes into account only its gross income and its separate expenses. In 1988, B therefore has a net amount of income in foreign currency units equal in value to $400. Gain or loss on remittances shall be computed by reference to this amount.

(3) Controlled foreign corporations. (i) In general. For purposes of computing subpart F income and computing earnings and profits for all other federal tax purposes, the interest expense of a controlled foreign corporation may be apportioned either using the asset method described in paragraph (g) of this section or using the modified gross income method described in paragraph (j) of this section, subject to the rules of subdivisions (ii) and (iii) of this paragraph (f)(3). However, the gross income method described in paragraph (j) of this section is not available to any controlled foreign corporation if a United States shareholder and the members of its affiliated group (as defined in § 1.861-11T(d)) constitute controlling shareholders of such controlled foreign corporation and such affiliated group elects the fair market

value method of apportionment under paragraph (g) of this section.

(ii) Manner of election. The election to use the asset method described in paragraph (g) of this section or the modified gross income method described in paragraph (j) of this section may be made either by the controlled foreign corporation or by the controlling United States shareholders on behalf of the controlled foreign corporation. The term "controlling United States shareholders" means those United States shareholders (as defined in section 951(b)) who, in aggregate, own (within the meaning of section 958(a)) greater than 50 percent of the total combined voting power of all classes of stock of the foreign corporation entitled to vote. In the case of a controlled foreign corporation in which the United States shareholders own stock representing more than 50 percent of the value of the stock in such corporation, but less than 50 percent of the combined voting power of all classes of stock in such corporation, the term "controlling United States shareholders" means all the United States shareholders (as defined in section 951(b)) who own (within the meaning of section 958(a)) stock of the controlled foreign corporation. All United States shareholders are bound by the election of either the controlled foreign corporation or the controlling United States shareholders. The election shall be made by filing a statement described in § 1.964-1T(c)(3)(ii) at the time and in the manner described therein and providing a written notice described in § 1.964-1T(c)(3)(iii), except that no such statement or notice is required to be filed or sent before July 24, 2006.

(iii) Consistency requirement. The same method of apportionment must be employed by all controlled foreign corporations in which a United States taxpayer and the members of its affiliated group (as defined in § 1.861-11T(d)) constitute controlling United States shareholders. A controlled foreign corporation that is required by this paragraph (f)(3)(iii) to utilize a particular method of apportionment must do so with respect to all United States shareholders.

(iv) Stock characterization. Pursuant to § 1.861-12T(c)(2), the stock of a controlled foreign corporation shall be characterized in the hands of any United States shareholder using the same method that the controlled foreign corporation uses to apportion its interest expense.

(4) Noncontrolled section 902 corporations. (i) In general. For purposes of computing earnings and profits of a noncontrolled section 902 corporation (as defined in section 904(d)(2)(E)) for federal tax purposes, the interest expense of a noncontrolled section 902 corporation may be apportioned using either the asset method described in paragraph (g) of this section or the modified gross income method described in paragraph (j) of this section. A noncontrolled section 902 corporation that is not a controlled foreign corporation may elect to use a different method of apportionment than that elected by one or more of its shareholders. A noncontrolled section 902 corporation must use the same method of apportionment with respect to all its domestic corporate shareholders.

(ii) Manner of election. The election to use the asset method described in paragraph (g) of this section or the modified gross income method described in paragraph (j) of this section may be made either by the noncontrolled section 902 corporation or by the majority domestic corporate shareholders (as defined in § 1.964-1T(c)(5)(ii)) on behalf of the noncontrolled section 902 corporation. The election shall be made by filing a statement described in § 1.964-1T(c)(3)(ii) at the time and in the manner described therein and providing a written notice described in § 1.964-1T(c)(3)(iii), except that no such statement or notice is required to be filed or sent before July 24, 2006.

(iii) Stock characterization. In general, the stock of a noncontrolled section 902 corporation shall be characterized in the hands of any domestic corporation that meets the ownership requirements of section 902(a) with respect to the noncontrolled section 902 corporation, or in the hands of any member of the same qualified group as defined in section 902(b)(2), using the same method that the noncontrolled section 902 corporation uses to apportion its interest expense. Stock in a noncontrolled section 902 corporation shall be characterized as a passive category asset in the hands of any such shareholder that fails to meet the substantiation requirements of § 1.904-5T(c)(4)(iii), or in the hands of any shareholder that is not eligible to compute an amount of foreign taxes deemed paid with respect to a dividend from the noncontrolled section 902 corporation for the taxable year. See § 1.861-12T(c)(4).

(iv) Effective date. This paragraph (f)(4) applies for taxable years of shareholders ending after the first day of the first taxable year of the noncontrolled section 902 corporation beginning after December 31, 2002.

(5) Other relevant provisions. Affiliated groups of corporations are subject to special rules set forth in § 1.861-11T. Section 1.861-12T sets forth rules relating to basis adjustments for stock in nonaffiliated 10 percent owned corporations, special rules relating to the consideration and characterization of certain assets in the apportionment of interest expense, and to other special rules pertaining to the apportionment of interest expense. Section 1.861-13T contains transition rules limiting the application of the rules of §§ 1.861-8T through 1.861-12T, which are otherwise applicable to taxable years beginning after 1986. In the case of an affiliated group of corporations as defined in § 1.861-11T(d), any reference in §§ 1.861-8T through 1.861-13T to the "taxpayer" with respect to the allocation and apportionment of interest expense generally denotes the entire affiliated group of corporations and not the separate members thereof, unless the context otherwise requires.

(g) Asset method. *(1) In general.* (i) Under the asset method, the taxpayer apportions interest expense to the various statutory groupings based on the average total value of assets within each such grouping for the taxable year, as determined under the asset valuation rules of this paragraph (g)(1) and paragraph (g)(2) of this section and the asset characterization rules of paragraph (g)(3) of this section and § 1.861-12T. Except to the extent otherwise provided (see, e.g., paragraph (d)(1)(iv) of this section); taxpayers must apportion interest expense only on the basis of asset values and may not apportion any interest deduction on the basis of gross income.

(ii) A taxpayer may elect to determine the value of its assets on the basis of either the tax book value or the fair market value of its assets. For rules concerning the application of an alternative method of valuing assets for purposes of the tax book value method, see § 1.861-9(i). For rules concerning the application of an alternative method of valuing assets for purposes of the tax book value method, see paragraph (i) of this section. In the case of an affiliated group—

(A) The parent of which used the fair market value method prior to 1987, or

(B) A substantial portion of which used the fair market value method prior to 1987,

such a taxpayer may use either the fair market value method or the tax book value method for its tax year commencing in

1987 and may use either such method in its tax year commencing in 1988 without regard to which method was used in its tax year commencing in 1987 and without securing the Commissioner's consent. The use of the fair market value method in 1988, however, shall operate as a binding election as described in § 1.861-8T(c)(2). For rules requiring consistency in the use of the tax book value or fair market value method, see § 1.861-8T(c)(2).

(iii) A taxpayer electing to apportion its interest expense on the basis of the fair market value of its assets must establish the fair market value to the satisfaction of the Commissioner. If a taxpayer fails to establish the fair market value of an asset to the satisfaction of the Commissioner, the Commissioner may determine the appropriate asset value. If a taxpayer fails to establish the value of a substantial portion of its assets to the satisfaction of the Commissioner, the Commissioner may require the taxpayer to use the tax book value method of apportionment.

(iv) For rules relating to earnings and profits adjustments by taxpayers using the tax book value method for the stock in certain nonaffiliated 10 percent owned corporations, see § 1.861-12T(b).

(v) The provisions of this paragraph (g)(1) may be illustrated by the following examples.

Example (1). (i) Facts. X, a domestic corporation organized on January 1, 1987, has deductible interest expense in 1987 in the amount of $150,000. X apportions its expenses according to the tax book value method. The adjusted basis of X's assets is $3,600,000, $3,000,000 of which generate domestic source income and $600,000 of which generate foreign source general limitation income.

(ii) Allocation. No portion of the $150,000 deduction is directly allocable solely to identified property within the meaning of $1.861-10T. Thus, X's deduction for interest is related to all its activities and assets.

(iii) Apportionment. X apportions its interest expense as follows: To foreign source general limitation income:

$$\$150{,}000 \times \frac{\$\ 600{,}000}{\$3{,}600{,}000} \cdots\cdots\cdots \$\ 25{,}000$$

To domestic source income:

$$\$150{,}000 \times \frac{\$3{,}000{,}000}{\$3{,}600{,}000} \cdots\cdots\cdots \$125{,}000$$

Example (2). (i) Facts. Assume the same facts as in Example (1), except that X apportions its interest expense on the basis of the fair market value of its assets. X's total assets have a fair market value of $4,000,000, $3,200,000 of which generate domestic source income and $800,000 of which generate foreign source general limitation income.

(ii) Allocation. No portion of the $150,000 deduction is directly allocable solely to identified property within the meaning of § 1.861-10T. Thus, X's deduction for interest is related to all its activities and properties.

(iii) Apportionment. If it establishes the fair market value of its assets to the satisfaction of the Commissioner, X may apportion its interest expense as follows: To foreign source general limitation income:

$$\$150{,}000 \times \frac{\$\ 800{,}000}{\$4{,}000{,}000} \cdots\cdots\cdots \$30{,}000$$

To domestic source income:

$$\$150{,}000 \times \frac{\$3{,}200{,}000}{\$4{,}000{,}000} \cdots\cdots\cdots \$120{,}000$$

(2) Asset values. (i) General rule. For purposes of determining the value of assets under this section, an average of values (book or market) within each statutory grouping and the residual grouping shall be computed for the year on the basis of values of assets at the beginning and end of the year. For the first taxable year beginning after 1986, a taxpayer may choose to determine asset values solely by reference to the year-end value of its assets, provided that all the members of an affiliated group as defined in § 1.861-11T(d) make the same choice. Thus, no averaging is required for the first taxable year beginning after 1986. Where a substantial distortion of asset values would result from averaging beginning-of-year and year-end values, as might be the case in the event of a major corporate acquisition or disposition, the taxpayer must use a different method of asset valuation that more clearly reflects the average value of assets weighted to reflect the time such assets are held by the taxpayer during the taxable year.

(ii) Special rule for qualified business units of domestic corporations with functional currency other than the U.S. dollar. (A) Tax book value method. In the case of taxpayers using the tax book value method of apportionment, the following rules shall apply to determine the value of the assets of a qualified business unit (as defined in section 989(a)) of a domestic corporation with a functional currency other than the dollar.

(1) Profit and loss branch. In the case of a branch for which an election is not effective under § 1.985-2T to use the dollar approximate separate transactions method of computing currency gain or loss, the tax book value shall be determined by applying the rules of paragraph (g)(2)(i) and (3) of this section with respect to beginning-of-year and end-of-year tax book value in units of functional currency that are translated into dollars at the end-of-year exchange rate between the functional currency and the U.S. dollar.

Example. At the end of 1987, a profit and loss branch has assets that generate foreign source general limitation income with a tax book value in units of functional currency of 100. At the end of 1987, the unit is worth $1. At the end of 1988, the branch has assets that generate foreign source general limitation income with a tax book value in units of functional currency of 80. At the end of 1988, the unit is worth $2. The average value of foreign source general limitation assets for 1988 is 90 units, which is worth $180.

(2) Approximate separate transactions method. In the case of a branch for which an election is effective under § 1.985-2T to use the dollar approximate separate transactions method to compute currency gain or loss, the beginning-of-year dollar amount of the assets shall be determined by reference to the end-of-year balance sheet of the branch for the immediately preceding taxable year, adjusted for United States generally accepted accounting principles and United States tax accounting principles, and translated into U.S. dollars as provided in § 1.985-3T. The year-end dollar amount of the assets of the branch shall be determined in the same manner by reference to the end-of-year balance sheet for the current taxable year. The beginning-of-year and end-of-year dollar tax book value of assets, as so determined, within each grouping must then be averaged as provided in paragraph (g)(2)(i) of this section.

(B) Fair market value method. In the case of taxpayers using the fair market value method of apportionment, the beginning-of-year and end-of-year fair market values of branch assets within each grouping shall be computed in dollars and averaged as provided in this paragraph (g)(2).

(iii) Adjustment for directly allocated interest. Prior to averaging, the year-end value of any asset to which interest expense is directly allocated during the current taxable year under the rules of § 1.861-10T (b) or (c) shall be reduced (but not below zero) by the percentage of the principal amount of indebtedness outstanding at year-end equal to the percentage of all interest on the debt for the taxable year that is directly allocated.

(iv) Assets in intercompany transactions. In the application of the asset method described in this paragraph (g), the tax book value of assets transferred between affiliated corporations in intercompany transactions shall be determined without regard to the gain or loss that is deferred under the regulations issued under section 1502.

(v) Example. X is a domestic corporation that uses the fair market value method of apportionment. X is a calendar year taxpayer. X owns 25 percent of the stock of A, a noncontrolled section 902 corporation. At the end of 1987, the fair market value of X's assets by income grouping are as follows:

Domestic	$1,000,000
Foreign general limitation	500,000
Foreign passive	500,000
Noncontrolled section 902 corporation	50,000

For its 1987 tax year, X apportions its interest expense by reference to the 1987 year-end values. In July of 1988, X sells a portion of its investment in A and in an asset acquisition purchases a shipping business, the assets of which generate exclusively foreign shipping income. At the end of 1988, the fair market values of X's assets by income grouping are as follows:

Domestic	$800,000
Foreign general limitation	900,000
Foreign passive	300,000
Noncontrolled section 902 corporation	40,000
Foreign shipping	100,000

For its 1988 tax year, X shall apportion its interest expense by reference to the average of the 1988 beginning-of-year values (the 1987 year-end values) and the 1988 year-end values, assuming that the averaging of beginning-of-year and end-of-year values does not cause a substantial distortion of asset values. These averages are as follows:

Domestic	$900,000
Foreign general limitation	700,000
Foreign passive	400,000
Foreign shipping	50,000
Noncontrolled section 902 corporation	45,000

(3) Characterization of assets. Assets are characterized for purposes of this section according to the source and type of the income that they generate, have generated, or may reasonably be expected to generate. The physical location of assets is not relevant to this determination. Subject to the special rules of paragraph (h) concerning the application of the fair market value method of apportionment, the value of assets within each statutory grouping and the residual grouping at the beginning and end of each year shall be determined by dividing the taxpayer's assets into three types—

(i) Single category assets. Assets that generate income that is exclusively within a single statutory grouping or the residual grouping;

(ii) Multiple category assets. Assets that generate income within more than one grouping of income (statutory or residual); and

(iii) Assets without directly identifiable yield. Assets that produce no directly identifiable income yield or that contribute equally to the generation of all the income of the taxpayer (such as assets used in general and administrative functions).

Single category assets are directly attributable to the relevant statutory or residual grouping of income. In order to attribute multiple category assets to the relevant groupings of income, the income yield of each such asset for the taxable year must be analyzed to determine the proportion of gross income generated by it within each relevant grouping. The value of each asset is then prorated among the relevant groupings of income according to their respective proportions of gross income. The value of each asset without directly identifiable income yield must be identified. However, because prorating the value of such assets cannot alter the ratio of assets within the various groupings of income (as determined by reference to the single and multiple category assets), they are not taken into account in determining that ratio. Special asset characterization rules that are set forth in § 1.861-12T. An example demonstrating the application of the asset method is set forth in § 1.861-12T(d).

(h) The fair market value method. An affiliated group (as defined in § 1.861-11T(d)) or other taxpayer (the "taxpayer") that elects to use the fair market value method of apportionment shall value its assets according to the following methodology.

(1) Determination of values. (i) Valuation of group assets. The taxpayer shall first determine the aggregate value of the assets of the taxpayer on the last day of its taxable year without excluding the value of stock in foreign subsidiaries or any other asset. In the case of a publicly traded corporation, this determination shall be equal to the aggregate trading value of the taxpayer's stock traded on established securities markets at year-end increased by the taxpayer's year-end liabilities to unrelated persons and its pro rata share of year-end liabilities of all related persons owed to unrelated persons. In determining whether persons are related, § 1.861-8T(c)(2) shall apply. In the case of a corporation that is not publicly traded, this determination shall be made by reference to the capitalization of corporate earnings, in accordance with the rules of Rev. Rul. 68-609. In either case, control premium shall not be taken into account.

(ii) Valuation of tangible assets. The taxpayer shall determine the value of all assets held by the taxpayer and its pro rata share of assets held by other related persons on the last day of its taxable year, excluding stock or indebtedness in such persons, any intangible property as defined in section 936(h)(3)(B), or goodwill or going concern value intangibles. Such valuations shall be made using generally accepted valuation techniques. For this purpose, assets may be combined into reasonable groupings. Statistical methods of valuation may only be used in connection with fungible property, such as commodities. The value of stock in any corporation that is not a related person shall be determined under the rules of paragraph (h)(1)(i) of this section, except that no liabilities shall be taken into account.

(iii) Computation of intangible asset value. The value of the intangible assets of the taxpayer and of intangible assets of all related persons attributable to the taxpayer's ownership in related persons is equal to the amount obtained by subtracting the amount determined under paragraph (h)(1)(ii) of this section from the amount determined under paragraph (h)(1)(i) of this section.

(2) Apportionment of intangible asset value. The value of the intangible assets determined under paragraph (h)(1)(iii) of this section is apportioned among the taxpayer and all related persons in proportion to the net income before interest expense of the taxpayer and the taxpayer's pro rata share of the net income before interest expense of each related person held by the taxpayer, excluding income that is passive under § 1.904-4(b). For this purpose, net income is determined before reduction for income taxes. Net income of the taxpayer and of related persons shall be computed without regard to dividends or interest received from any person that is related to the taxpayer.

(3) Characterization of affiliated group's portion of intangible asset value. The portion of the value of intangible assets of the taxpayer and related persons that is apportioned to the taxpayer under paragraph (h)(2) of this section is characterized on the basis of net income before interest expense, as determined under paragraph (h)(2) of this section, of the taxpayer within each statutory or residual grouping of income.

(4) Valuing stock in related persons held by the taxpayer. The value of stock in a related person held by the taxpayer equals the sum of the following amounts reduced by the taxpayer's pro rata share of liabilities of such related person:

(i) The portion of the value of intangible assets of the taxpayer and related persons that is apportioned to such related person under paragraph (h)(2) of this section;

(ii) The taxpayer's pro rata share of tangible assets held by the related person (as determined under paragraph (h)(1)(ii) of this section); and

(iii) The total value of stock in all related person held by the related person as determined under this paragraph (h)(4).

(5) [Reserved]. For further guidance, see § 1.861-9(h)(5).

(6) Adjustments for apportioning related person expenses. For purposes of apportioning expenses of a related person, the value of stock in a second related person as otherwise determined under paragraph (h)(4) of this section (which is determined on the basis of the taxpayer's percentage ownership interest in the second related person) shall be increased to reflect the first related person's percentage ownership interest in the second related person to the extent it is larger.

Example. Assume that a taxpayer owns 80 percent of CFC1, which owns 100 percent of CFC2. The value of CFC1 is determined generally under paragraph (h)(4) on the basis of the taxpayer's 80 percent indirect interest in CFC2. For purposes of apportioning expenses of CFC1, 100 percent of the stock of CFC1 must be taken into account. Therefore, the value of CFC2 stock in the hands of CFC1 shall equal the value of CFC2 stock in the hands of CFC1 as determined under paragraph (h)(4) of this section, increased by 25 percent of such amount to reflect the fact that CFC1 owns 100 percent and not 80 percent of CFC2.

(i) [Reserved]. For further guidance, see § 1.861-9(i).

(j) Modified gross income method. Subject to rules set forth in paragraph (f)(3) of this section, the interest expense of a controlled foreign corporation may be allocated according to the following rules.

(1) Single-tier controlled foreign corporation. In the case of a controlled foreign corporation that does not hold stock in any lower-tier controlled foreign corporation, the interest expense of the controlled foreign corporation shall be apportioned based on its gross income.

(2) Multiple vertically owned controlled foreign corporations. In the case of a controlled foreign corporation that holds stock in any lower-tier controlled foreign corporation, the interest expense of that controlled foreign corporation and such upper-tier controlled foreign corporation shall be apportioned based on the following methodology:

(i) Step 1. Commencing with the lowest-tier controlled foreign corporation in the chain, allocate and apportion its interest expense based on its gross income as provided in paragraph (j)(1) of this section, yielding gross income in each grouping net of interest expense.

(ii) Step 2. Moving to the next higher-tier controlled foreign corporation, combine the gross income of such corporation within each grouping with its pro rata share of the gross income net of interest expense of all lower-tier controlled foreign corporations held by such higher-tier corporation within the same grouping adjusted as follows:

(A) Exclude from the gross income of the upper-tier corporation any dividends or other payments received from the lower-tier corporation other than interest subject to look-through under section 904(d)(3); and

(B) Exclude from the gross income net of interest expense of any lower-tier corporation any subpart F income (net of interest expense apportioned to such income).

Then apportion the interest expense of the higher-tier controlled foreign corporation based on the adjusted combined gross income amounts. Repeat this step 2 for each next higher-tier controlled foreign corporation in the chain. For purposes of this paragraph (j)(2)(ii), pro rata share shall be determined under principles similar to section 951(a)(2).

T.D. 8228, 9/9/88, amend T.D. 8257, 8/1/89, T.D. 8597, 7/12/95, T.D. 8658, 3/5/96, T.D. 8916, 12/27/2000, T.D. 9120, 3/25/2004, T.D. 9247, 1/27/2006, T.D. 9260, 4/24/2006.

PAR. 2. Section 1.861-9T is amended as follows:

1. Paragraph (g)(2)(ii)(A)(1) is revised.

2. Paragraph (g)(2)(vi) is added.

The revisions read as follows:

Proposed § 1.861-9T Allocation and apportionment of interest expense (temporary). [*For Preamble, see ¶ 152,801*]

* * * * *

(g) * * *

(2) * * *

(ii) * * * (A) * * *

(1) Section 987 QBU. In the case of a section 987 QBU, the tax book value shall be determined by applying the rules of paragraphs (g)(2)(i) and (3) of this section to the beginning of year and end of year functional currency amount of assets. The beginning of year functional currency amount of assets shall be determined by reference to the functional currency amount of assets computed under § 1.987-4(d)(1)(i)(B) and (e) on the last day of the preceding taxable year. The end of year functional currency amount of assets shall be determined by reference to the functional currency amount of assets computed under § 1.987-4(d)(1)(i)(A) and (e) on the last day of the current taxable year. The beginning of year and end of year functional currency amount of assets, as so determined within each grouping must then be averaged as provided in paragraph (g)(2)(i) of this section.

* * * * *

(vi) Effective date. Generally, paragraph (g)(2)(ii)(A)(1) of this section shall apply to taxable years beginning one year after the first day of the first taxable year following the date of publication of a Treasury decision adopting this rule as a final regulation in the Federal Register. If a taxpayer makes an election under § 1.987-11(b), then the effective date of paragraph (g)(2)(ii)(A)(1) of this section with respect to the taxpayer shall be consistent with such election.

* * * * *

PAR. 4. Section 1.861-9T is amended by redesignating the text of paragraph (g)(2)(iii) as paragraph (g)(2)(iii)(A) and adding a heading to new paragraph (g)(2)(iii)(A), and adding paragraph (g)(2)(iii)(B):

Proposed § 1.861-9T Allocation and apportionment of interest expense (temporary regulations). [*For Preamble, see ¶ 152,047*]

* * * * *

(g) * * *

(2) * * *

(iii) Adjustment for directly allocated interest. (A) Nonrecourse indebtedness and integrated financial transactions. * * *

(B) FASIT interest expense. The rules of paragraph (g)(2)(iii)(A) of this section shall also apply to all assets to which FASIT interest expense is directly allocated during the current taxable year under the rules of § 1.861-10T(f). This paragraph (g)(2)(iii)(B) applies on the date final regulations are filed with the Federal Register.

§ 1.861-10 Special allocations of interest expense.

(a) through(d). [Reserved]

(e) Treatment of certain related group indebtedness. *(1) In general.* If, for any taxable year beginning after December 31, 1991, a U.S. shareholder (as defined in paragraph (e)(5)(i) of this section) has both—

(i) Excess related group indebtedness (as determined under Step One in paragraph (e)(2) of this section) and

(ii) Excess U.S. shareholder indebtedness (as determined under Step Two in paragraph (e)(3) of this section), the U.S. shareholder shall allocate, to its gross income in the various separate limitation categories described in section 904(d)(1), a portion of its interest expense paid or accrued to any obligee who is not a member of the affiliated group (as defined in § 1.861-11T(d)) of the U.S. shareholder (" third party interest expense"), excluding amounts allocated under paragraphs (b) and (c) of § 1.861-10T. The amount of third party interest expense so allocated shall equal the total amount of interest income derived by the U.S. shareholder during the year from related group indebtedness, multiplied by the ratio of the lesser of the foregoing two amounts of excess indebtedness for the year to related group indebtedness for the year. This amount of third party interest expense is allocated as described in Step Three in paragraph (e)(4) of this section.

(2) Step One: Excess related group indebtedness. (i) The excess related group indebtedness of a U.S. shareholder for the year equals the amount by which its related group indebtedness for the year exceeds its allowable related group indebtedness for the year.

(ii) The "related group indebtedness" of the U.S. shareholder is the average of the aggregate amounts at the beginning and end of the year of indebtedness owed to the U.S. shareholder by each controlled foreign corporation which is a related person (as defined in paragraph (e)(5)(ii) of this section) with respect to the U.S. shareholder.

(iii) The "allowable related group indebtedness" of a U.S. shareholder for the year equals—

(A) The average of the aggregate values at the beginning and end of the year of the assets (including stock holdings in and obligations of related persons, other than related controlled foreign corporations) of each related controlled foreign corporation, multiplied by

(B) The foreign base period ratio of the U.S. shareholder for the year.

(iv) The "foreign base period ratio" of the U.S. shareholder for the year is the average of the related group debt-to-asset ratios of the U.S. shareholder for each taxable year comprising the foreign base period for the current year (each a "base year"). For this purpose, however, the related group debt-to-asset ratio of the U.S. shareholder for any base year may not exceed 110 percent of the foreign base period ratio for that base year. This limitation shall not apply with respect to any of the five taxable years chosen as initial base years by the U.S. shareholder under paragraph (e)(2)(v) of this section or with respect to any base year for which the related group debt-to-asset ratio does not exceed 0.10.

(v) (A) The foreign base period for any current taxable year (except as described in paragraphs (e)(2)(v)(B) and (C) of this section) shall consist of the five taxable years immediately preceding the current year.

(B) The U.S. shareholder may choose as foreign base periods for all of its first five taxable years for which this paragraph (e) is effective the following alternative base periods:

(1) For the first effective taxable year, the 1982, 1983, 1984, 1985 and 1986 taxable years;

(2) For the second effective taxable year, the 1983, 1984, 1985 and 1986 taxable years and the first effective taxable year;

(3) For the third effective taxable year, the 1984, 1985 and 1986 taxable years and the first and second effective taxable years;

(4) For the fourth effective taxable year, the 1985 and 1986 taxable years and the first, second and third effective taxable years; and

(5) For the fifth effective taxable year, the 1986 taxable year and the first, second, third and fourth effective taxable years.

(C) If, however, the U.S. shareholder does not choose, under paragraph (e)(10)(ii) of this section, to apply this paragraph (e) to one or more taxable years beginning before January 1, 1992, the U.S. shareholder may not include within any foreign base period the taxable year immediately preceding the first effective taxable year. Thus, for example, a U.S. shareholder for which the first effective taxable year is the taxable year beginning on October 1, 1992, may not include the taxable year beginning on October 1, 1991, in any foreign base period. Assuming that the U.S. shareholder does not elect the alternative base periods described in paragraph (e)(2)(v)(B) of this section, the initial foreign base period for the U.S. shareholder will consist of the taxable years beginning on October 1 of 1986, 1987, 1988, 1989, and 1990. The foreign base period for the U.S. shareholder for the following taxable year, beginning on October 1, 1993, will consist of the taxable years beginning on October 1 of 1987, 1988, 1989, 1990, and 1992.

(D) If the U.S. shareholder chooses the base periods described in paragraph (e)(2)(v)(B) of this section as foreign base periods, it must make a similar election under paragraph (e)(3)(v)(B) of this section with respect to its U.S. base periods.

(vi) The "related group debt-to-asset ratio" of a U.S. shareholder for a year is the ratio between—

(A) The related group indebtedness of the U.S. shareholder for the year (as determined under paragraph (e)(2)(ii) of this section); and

(B) The average of the aggregate values at the beginning and end of the year of the assets (including stock holdings in and obligations of related persons, other than related controlled foreign corporations) of each related controlled foreign corporation.

(vii) Notwithstanding paragraph (e)(2)(i) of this section, a U.S. shareholder is considered to have no excess related group indebtedness for the year if—

(A) Its related group indebtedness for the year does not exceed its allowable related group indebtedness for the immediately preceding year (as determined under paragraph (e)(2)(iii) of this section); or

(B) Its related group debt-to-asset ratio (as determined under paragraph (e)(2)(vi) of this section) for the year does not exceed 0.10.

(3) Step Two: Excess U.S. shareholder indebtedness. (i) The excess indebtedness of a U.S. shareholder for the year equals the amount by which its unaffiliated indebtedness for the year exceeds its allowable indebtedness for the year.

(ii) The "unaffiliated indebtedness" of the U.S. shareholder is the average of the aggregate amounts at the beginning and end of the year of indebtedness owed by the U.S. shareholder to any obligee, other than a member of the affiliated group (as defined in § 1.861-11T(d)) of the U.S shareholder.

(iii) The "allowable indebtedness" of a U.S. shareholder for the year equals—

(A) The average of the aggregate values at the beginning and end of the year of the assets of the U.S. shareholder (including stock holdings in and obligations of related controlled foreign corporations, but excluding stock holdings in and obligations of members of the affiliated group (as defined in § 1.861-11T(d)) of the U.S. shareholder), reduced by the amount of the excess related group indebtedness of the U.S. shareholder for the year (as determined under Step One in paragraph (e)(2) of this section), multiplied by

(B) The U.S. base period ratio of the U.S. shareholder for the year.

(iv) The "U.S. base period ratio" of the U.S. shareholder for the year is the average of the debt-to-asset ratios of the U.S. shareholder for each taxable year comprising the U.S. base period for the current year (each a "base year"). For this purpose, however, the debt-to-asset ratio of the U.S. shareholder for any base year may not exceed 110 percent of the U.S. base period ratio for that base year. This limitation shall not apply with respect to any of the five taxable years chosen as initial base years by the U.S. shareholder under paragraph (e)(3)(v) of this section or with respect to any base year for which of the debt-to-asset ratio does not exceed 0.10.

(v) (A) The U.S. base period for any current taxable year (except as described in paragraphs (e)(3)(v)(B) and (C) of this section) shall consist of the five taxable years immediately preceding the current year.

(B) The U.S. shareholder may choose as U.S. base periods for all of its first five taxable years for which this paragraph (e) is effective the following alternative base periods:

(1) For the first effective taxable year, the 1982, 1983, 1984, 1985 and 1986 taxable years;

(2) For the second effective taxable year, the 1983, 1984, 1985 and 1986 taxable years and the first effective taxable year;

(3) For the third effective taxable year, the 1984, 1985 and 1986 taxable years and the first and second effective taxable years;

(4) For the fourth effective taxable year, the 1985 and 1986 taxable years and the first, second and third effective taxable years; and

(5) For the fifth effective taxable year, the 1986 taxable year and the first, second, third and fourth effective taxable years.

(C) If, however, the U.S. shareholder does not choose, under paragraph (e)(10)(ii) of this section, to apply this paragraph (e) to one or more taxable years beginning before January 1, 1992, the U.S. shareholder may not include within any U.S. base period the taxable year immediately preceding the first effective taxable year. Thus, for example, a U.S. shareholder for which the first effective taxable year is the taxable year beginning on October 1, 1992, may not include the taxable year beginning on October 1, 1991, in any U.S. base period. Assuming that the U.S. shareholder does not elect the alternative base periods described in paragraph (e)(3)(v)(B) of this section, the initial U.S. base period for the U.S. shareholder will consist of the taxable years beginning on October 1, of 1986, 1987, 1988, 1989, and 1990. The U.S. base period for the U.S. shareholder for the following taxable year, beginning on October 1, 1993, will consist of the taxable years beginning on October 1, 1987, 1988, 1989, 1990, and 1992.

(D) If the U.S. shareholder chooses the base periods described in paragraph (e)(3)(v)(B) of this section as U.S. base periods, it must make a similar election under paragraph (e)(2)(v)(B) of this section with respect to its foreign base periods.

(vi) The "debt-to-asset ratio" of a U.S. shareholder for a year is the ratio between—

(A) The unaffiliated indebtedness of the U.S. shareholder for the year (as determined under paragraph (e)(3)(ii) of this section): and

(B) The average of the aggregate values at the beginning and end of the year of the assets of the U.S. shareholder. For this purpose, the assets of the U.S. shareholder include stock holdings in and obligations of related controlled foreign corporations but do not include stock holdings in and obligations of members of the affiliated group (as defined in § 1.861-11T(d)).

(vii) A U.S. shareholder is considered to have no excess indebtedness for the year if its debt-to-asset ratio (as determined under paragraph (e)(3)(vi) of this section) for the year does not exceed 0.10.

(4) Step Three: Allocation of third party interest expense. (i) A U.S. shareholder shall allocate to its gross income in the various separate limitation categories described in section 904(d)(1) a portion of its third party interest expense incurred during the year equal in amount to the interest income derived by the U.S. shareholder during the year from allocable related group indebtedness.

(ii) The "allocable related group indebtedness" of a U.S. shareholder for any year is an amount of related group indebtedness equal to the lesser of—

(A) The excess related group indebtedness of the U.S. shareholder for the year (determined under Step One in paragraph (e)(2) of this section); or

(B) The excess U.S. shareholder indebtedness for the year (determined under Step Two in paragraph (e)(3) of this section).

(iii) The amount of interest income derived by a U.S. shareholder from allocable related group indebtedness during the year equals the total amount of interest income derived by the U.S. shareholder during the year with respect to related group indebtedness, multiplied by the ratio of allocable related group indebtedness for the year to the aggregate amount of related group indebtedness for the year.

(iv) The portion of third party interest expense described in paragraph (e)(4)(i) of this section shall be allocated in proportion to the relative average amounts of related group indebtedness held by the U.S. shareholder in each separate limitation category during the year. The remaining portion of third party interest expense of the U.S. shareholder for the year shall be apportioned as provided in §§ 1.861-8T through 1.861-13T, excluding paragraph (e) of § 1.861-10T and this paragraph (e).

(v) The average amount of related group indebtedness held by the U.S. shareholder in each separate limitation category during the year equals the average of the aggregate amounts of such indebtedness in each separate limitation category at the beginning and end of the year. Solely for purposes of this paragraph (e)(4) each debt obligation of a related controlled foreign corporation held by the U.S. shareholder at the beginning or end of the year is attributed to separate limitation categories in the same manner as the stock of the obligor would be attributed under the rules of § 1.861-12T(c)(3), whether or not such stock is held directly by the U.S. shareholder.

(vi) The amount of third party interest expense of a U.S. shareholder allocated pursuant to this paragraph (e)(4) shall not exceed the total amount of the third party interest expense of the U.S. shareholder for the year (excluding any third party interest expense allocated under paragraphs (b) and (c) of § 1.861-10T).

(5) Definitions. For purposes of this paragraph (e), the following terms shall have the following meanings.

(i) U.S. shareholder. The term "U.S. shareholder" has the same meaning as the term "United States shareholder" when used in section 957, except that in the case of a United States shareholder that is a member of an affiliated group (as defined in § 1.861-11T(d)), the entire affiliated group is considered to constitute a single U.S. shareholder.

(ii) Related person. For the definition of the term "related person" , see § 1.861-8T(c)(2). A controlled foreign corporation is considered "related" to a U.S. shareholder if it is a related person with respect to the U.S. shareholder.

(6) Determination of asset values. A U.S. shareholder shall determine the values of the assets of each related controlled foreign corporation (for purposes of Step One in paragraph (e)(2) of this section) and the assets of the U.S. shareholder (for purposes of Step Two in paragraph (e)(3) of this section) for any year in accordance with the valuation method (tax book value or fair market value) elected for that year pursuant to § 1.861-9T(g). However, solely for purposes of this paragraph (e), a U.S. shareholder may instead choose to determine the values of the assets of all related controlled foreign corporations by reference to their values as reflected on Forms 5471 (the annual information return with respect to each related controlled foreign corporation), subject to the translation rules of paragraph (e)(8)(i) of this section. This method of valuation may be used only if the taxable years of each of the related controlled foreign corporations begin with, or no more than one month earlier than, the taxable year of the U.S. shareholder. Once chosen for a taxable year, this method of valuation must be used in each subsequent taxable year and may be changed only with the consent of the Commissioner.

(7) Adjustments to asset value. For purposes of apportioning remaining interest expense under § 1.861-9T, a U.S. shareholder shall reduce (but not below zero) the value of its assets for the year (as determined under § 1.861-9T (g)(3) or (h)) by an amount equal to the allocable related group indebtedness of the U.S. shareholder for the year (as determined under Step Three in paragraph (e)(4)(ii) of this section). This reduction is allocated among assets in each separate limitation category in proportion to the average amount of related group indebtedness held by the U.S. shareholder in each separate limitation category during the year (as determined under Step Three in paragraph (e)(4)(v) of this section).

(8) Special rules. (i) Exchange rates. All indebtedness amounts and asset values (including current year and base year amounts and values) denominated in a foreign currency shall be translated into U.S. dollars at the exchange rate for the current year. The exchange rate for the current year may be determined under any reasonable method (e.g., average of month-end exchange rates for each month in the current year) if it is consistently applied to the current year and all base years. Once chosen for a taxable year, a method for determining an exchange rate must be used in each subsequent taxable year and will be treated as a method of accounting for purposes of section 446. A taxpayer may apply a different translation rule only with the prior consent of the Commissioner. In this regard, the Commissioner will be guided by the extent to which a different rule would reduce the comparability of dollar amounts of indebtedness and dollar asset values for the base years and the current year.

(ii) Exempt assets. Solely for purposes of this paragraph (e), any exempt assets otherwise excluded under section 864(e)(3) and § 1.861-8T(d) shall be included as assets of the U.S. shareholder or related controlled foreign corporation.

(iii) Exclusion of certain directly allocated indebtedness and assets. Qualified nonrecourse indebtedness (as defined in § 1.861-10T(b)(2)) and indebtedness incurred in connection with an integrated financial transaction (as defined in § 1.861-10T(c)(2)) shall be excluded from U.S. shareholder indebtedness and related group indebtedness. In addition, assets which are the subject of qualified nonrecourse indebtedness or integrated financial transactions shall be excluded from the assets of the U.S. shareholder and each related controlled foreign corporation.

(iv) Exclusion of certain receivables. Receivables between related controlled foreign corporations (or between members of the affiliated group constituting the U.S. shareholder) shall be excluded from the assets of the related controlled foreign corporation (or affiliated group member) holding such receivables. See also § 1.861-11T(e)(1).

(v) Classification of certain loans as related group indebtedness. If—

(A) A U.S. shareholder owns stock in a related controlled foreign corporation which is a resident of a country that—

(1) Does not impose a withholding tax of 5 percent or more upon payments of dividends to a U.S. shareholder; and

(2) Does not, for the taxable year of the controlled foreign corporation, subject the income of the controlled foreign corporation to an income tax which is greater than that percentage specified under § 1.954-1T(d)(1)(i) of the maximum rate of tax specified under section 11 of the Code, and

(B) The controlled foreign corporation has outstanding a loan or loans to one or more other related controlled foreign corporations, or the controlled foreign corporation has made a direct or indirect capital contribution to one or more other related controlled foreign corporations which have outstanding a loan or loans to one or more other related controlled foreign corporations, then, to the extent of the aggregate amount of its capital contributions in taxable years beginning after December 31, 1986, to the related controlled foreign corporation that made such loans or additional contributions, the U.S. shareholder itself shall be treated as having made the loans described in paragraph (e)(8)(v)(B) of this section and, thus, such loan amounts shall be considered related group indebtedness. However, for purposes of paragraph (e)(4) of this section, interest income derived by the U.S. shareholder during the year from related group indebtedness shall not include any income derived with respect to the U.S. shareholder's ownership of stock in the related controlled foreign corporation that made such loans or additional contributions.

(vi) Classification of certain stock as related person indebtedness. In determining the amount of its related group indebtedness for any taxable year, a U.S. shareholder must treat as related group indebtedness its holding of stock in a related controlled foreign corporation if, during such taxable year, such related controlled foreign corporation claims a deduction for interest under foreign law for distributions on such stock. However, for purposes of paragraph (e)(4) of this section, interest income derived by the U.S. shareholder during the year from related group indebtedness shall not include any income derived with respect to the U.S. shareholder's ownership of stock in the related controlled foreign corporation.

(9) Corporate events. (i) Initial acquisition of a controlled foreign corporation. If the foreign base period of the U.S. shareholder for any year includes a base year in which the U.S. shareholder did not hold stock in any related controlled foreign corporation, then, in computing the foreign base period ratio, the related group debt-to-asset ratio of the U.S. shareholder for any such base year shall be deemed to be 0.10.

(ii) Incorporation of U.S. shareholder. (A) Nonapplication. This paragraph (e) does not apply to the first taxable year of the U.S. shareholder. However, this paragraph (e) does apply to all following years, including years in which later members of the affiliated group may be incorporated.

(B) Foreign and U.S. base period ratios. In computing the foreign and U.S. base period ratios, the foreign and U.S. base periods of the U.S. shareholder shall be considered to be only the period prior to the current year that the U.S. shareholder was in existence if this prior period is less than five taxable years.

(iii) Acquisition of additional corporations. (A) If a U.S. shareholder acquires (directly or indirectly) stock of a foreign or domestic corporation which, by reason of the acquisition, then becomes a related controlled foreign corporation or a member of the affiliated group, then in determining excess related group indebtedness or excess U.S. shareholder indebtedness, the indebtedness and assets of the acquired corporation shall be taken into account only at the end of the acquisition year and in following years. Thus, amounts of indebtedness and assets and the various debt-to-asset ratios of the U.S. shareholder existing at the beginning of the acquisition year or relating to preceding years are not recalculated to take account of indebtedness and assets of the acquired corporation existing as of dates before the end of the year. If, however, a major acquisition is made within the last three months of the year and a substantial distortion of values for the year would otherwise result, the taxpayer must take into account the average values of the acquired indebtedness and assets weighted to reflect the time such indebtedness is owed and such assets are held by the taxpayer during the year.

(B) In the case of a reverse acquisition subject to this paragraph (e)(9), the rules of § 1.1502-75(d)(3) apply in determining which corporations are the acquiring and acquired corporations. For this purpose, whether corporations are affiliated is determined under § 1.861-11T(d).

(C) If the stock of a U.S. shareholder is acquired by (and, by reason of such acquisition, the U.S. shareholder becomes affiliated with) a corporation described below, then such U.S. shareholder shall be considered to have acquired such corporation for purposes of the application of the rules of this paragraph (e). A corporation to which this paragraph (e)(9)(iii)(C) applies is—

(1) A corporation which is not affiliated with any other corporation (other than other similarly described corporation); and

(2) Substantially all of the assets of which consist of cash, securities and stock.

(iv) Election to compute base period ratios by including acquired corporations. A U.S. shareholder may choose, solely for purposes of paragraph (e)(9)(i) and (iii) of this section, to compute its foreign and U.S. base period ratios for the acquisition year and all subsequent years by taking into account the indebtedness and asset values of the acquired corporation or corporations (including related group indebtedness owed to a former U.S. shareholder) at the beginning of the acquisition year and in each of the five base years preceding the acquisition year. This election, if made for an acquisition, must be made for all other acquisitions occurring during the same taxable year or initiated in that year and concluded in the following year.

(v) Dispositions. If a U.S. shareholder disposes of stock of a foreign or domestic corporation which. by reason of the disposition, then ceases to be a related controlled foreign corporation or a member of the affiliated group (unless liquidated or merged into a related corporation), in determining excess related group indebtedness or excess U.S. shareholder indebtedness, the indebtedness and assets of the divested corporation shall be taken into account only at the beginning of the disposition year and for the relevant preceding years. Thus, amounts of indebtedness and assets and the various debt-to-asset ratios of the U.S. shareholder existing at the end of the year or relating to following years are not affected by indebtedness and assets of the divested corporation existing as of dates after the beginning of the year. If, however, a major disposition is made within the first three months of the year and a substantial distortion of values for the year would otherwise result, the taxpayer must take into account the average values of the divested indebtedness and assets weighted to reflect the time such indebtedness is owed and such assets are held by the taxpayer during the year.

(vi) Election to compute base period ratios by excluding divested corporations. A U.S. shareholder may choose, solely for purposes of paragraph (e)(9)(v) and (vii) of this section, to compute its foreign and U.S. base period ratios for the disposition year and all subsequent years without taking into account the indebtedness and asset values of the divested corporation or corporations at the beginning of the disposition year and in each of the five base years preceding the disposition year. This election, if made for a disposition, must be made for all other dispositions occurring during the same taxable year or initiated in that year and concluded in the following year.

(vii) Section 355 transactions. A U.S. corporation which becomes a separate U.S. shareholder as a result of a distribution of its stock to which section 355 applies shall be considered—

(A) As disposed of by the U.S. shareholder of the affiliated group of which the distributing corporation is a member, with this disposition subject to the rules of paragraphs (e)(9)(v) and (vi) of this section; and

(B) As having the same related group debt-to-asset ratio and debt-to-asset ratio as the distributing U.S. shareholder in each year preceding the year of distribution for purposes of applying this paragraph (e) to the year of distribution and subsequent years of the distributed corporation.

(10) Effective date. (i) Taxable years beginning after December 31, 1991. The provisions of this paragraph (e) apply to all taxable years beginning after December 31, 1991.

(ii) Taxable years beginning after December 31, 1987 and before January 1, 1992. The provisions of § 1.861-10T(e) apply to taxable years beginning after December 31, 1987 and before January 1, 1992. The taxpayer may elect to apply the provisions of this paragraph (e) (in lieu of the provisions of § 1.861-10T (e)) for any taxable year beginning after December 31, 1987, but this paragraph (e) must then be applied to all subsequent taxable years.

(11) The following example illustrates the provisions of this paragraph (e):

Example. (i) Facts. X, a domestic corporation elects to apply this paragraph (e) to its 1990 tax year. X has a calendar taxable year and apportions its interest expense on the basis of the tax book value of its assets. In 1990, X incurred deductible third-party interest expense of $24,960 on an average amount of indebtedness (determined on the basis of beginning-of-year and end-of-year amounts) of $249,600. X manufactures widgets, all of which are sold in the United States. X owns all of the stock of Y, a controlled foreign corporation that also has a calendar taxable year and is also engaged in the manufacture and sale of widgets. Y has no earnings and profits or deficit of earnings and profits attributable to taxable years prior to 1987. X's total assets and their average tax book values (determined on the basis of beginning-of-year and end-of-year tax book values) for 1990 are:

Asset	Average tax book value
Plant and equipment	$315,000
Corporate headquarters	60,000
Y stock	75,000
Y note	50,000
Total	500,000

Y had $25,000 of income before the deduction of any interest expense. Of this total, $5,000 is high withholding tax interest income. The remaining $20,000 is derived from widget sales, and constitutes foreign source general limitation income. Assume that Y has no deductions from gross income other than interest expense. During 1990, Y paid $5,000 of interest expense to X on the Y note and $10,000 of interest expense to third parties, giving Y total interest expense of $15,000. X elects pursuant to § 1.861-9T to apportion Y's interest expense under the gross income method prescribed in section 1.861-9T(j).

(ii) Step 1: Using a beginning and end of year average, X (the U.S. shareholder) held the following average amounts of indebtedness of Y and Y had the following average asset values:

	1985	1986-88	1989	1990
(A) Related group indebtedness	$ 11,000	24,000	26,000	50,000
(B) Average Value of Assets of Related CFC	100,000	200,000	200,000	250,000
(C) Related Group Debt-to-Asset Ratio	.11	.12	.13	.20

(1) X's "foreign base period ratio" for 1990, an average of its ratios of related group indebtedness to related group assets for 1985 through 1989, is:

(.11 + .12 + .12 + .12 + .13)/5 = .12

(2) X's "allowable related group indebtedness" for 1990 is:

$250,000 × .12 = $30,000.

(3) X's "excess related group indebtedness" for 1990 is:

$50,000 − $30,000 = $20,000

X's related group indebtedness of $50,000 for 1990 is greater than its allowable related group indebtedness of $24,000 for 1989 (assuming a foreign base period ratio in 1989 of .12), and X's related group debt-to-asset ratio for 1990 is .20, which is greater than the ratio of .10 described in paragraph (e)(2)(vii)(B) of this section. Therefore, X's excess related group indebtedness for 1990 remains at $20,000.

(iii) Step 2: Using a beginning and end of year average, X has the following average amounts of U.S. and foreign indebtedness and average asset values:

	1985	1986	1987	1988	1989	1990
(1)	$231,400	225,000	225,000	225,000	220,800	249,600
(2)	445,000	450,000	450,000	450,000	460,000	480,000
(3)	.52	.50	.50	.50	.48	(a) .52

(1) U.S. and foreign indebtedness

(2) Average value of assets of U.S. shareholder

(3) Debt-to-Asset ratio of U.S. shareholder

(a) [500,000 − 20,000 (excess related group indebtedness determined in Step 1)] X's "U.S. base period ratio" for 1990 is:

(.52 + .50 + .50 + .50 + .48)/5 = .50

X's "allowable indebtedness" for 1990 is:

$480,000 × .50 = $240,000

X's "excess U.S. shareholder indebtedness" for 1990 is:

$249,000 − $240,000 = $9,600

X's debt-to-asset ratio for 1990 is .52, which is greater than the ratio of .10 described in paragraph (e)(3)(vii) of this section. Therefore, X's excess U.S. shareholder indebtedness for 1990 remains at $9,600.

(iv) Step 3: (a) Since X's excess U.S. shareholder indebtedness of $9,600 is less than its excess related group indebtedness of $20,000, X's allocable related group indebtedness for 1990 is $9,600. The amount of interest received by X during 1990 on allocable related group indebtedness is: $5,000 × $9,600/$50,000 = $960

(b) Therefore, $960 of X's third party interest expense ($24,960) shall be allocated among various separate limitation categories in proportion to the relative average amounts of Y obligations held by X in each such category. The amount of Y obligations in each limitation category is determined in the same manner as the stock of Y would be attributed under the rules of § 1.861-12T(c)(3). Since Y's interest expense is apportioned under the gross income method prescribed in § 1.861-9T(j), the Y stock must be characterized under the gross income method described in § 1.861-12T(c)(3)(iii). Y's gross income net of interest expense is determined as follows:

Foreign source high withholding tax interest income
= $5,000 − [($15,000) multiplied by ($5,000)/($5,000 + $20,000)]
= $2,000
and
Foreign source general limitation income
= $20,000 − [($15,000) multiplied by ($20,000)/($5,000 + $20,000)]
= $8,000.

(c) Therefore, $192 [($960 × $2,000/($2,000 + $8,000)] of X's third party interest expense is allocated to foreign source high withholding tax interest income and $768 ($960 × $8,000/($2,000 + $8,000)] is, allocated to foreign source general limitation income.

(v) As a result of these direct allocations, for purposes of apportioning X's remaining interest expense under § 1.861-9T, the value of X's assets generating foreign source general limitation income is reduced by the principal amount of indebtedness the interest on which is directly allocated to foreign source general limitation income ($7,680), and the value of X's assets generating foreign source high withholding tax interest income is reduced by the principal amount of indebtedness the interest on which is directly allocated to foreign source high withholding tax interest income ($1,920), determined as follows: Reduction of X's assets generating foreign source general limitation income:

X's allocable related group indebtedness	×	Y's foreign source general limitation income / Y's Foreign source income
$9,600	+	$8,000/($8,000 + $2,000) = $7,680

Reduction of X's assets generating foreign source high withholding tax interest income:

X's allocable related group indebtedness	×	Y's Foreign source high withholding tax interest income / Y's Foreign source income
$9,600	×	$2,000/($8,000 + $2,000) = $1,920

T.D. 8410, 4/14/92.

§ 1.861-10T Special allocations of interest expense (temporary).

(a) In general. This section applies to all taxpayers and provides three exceptions to the rules of § 1.861-9T that require the allocation and apportionment of interest expense on the basis of all assets of all members of the affiliated group. Paragraph (b) of this section describes the direct allocation of interest expense to the income generated by certain assets that are subject to qualified nonrecourse indebtedness. Paragraph (c) of this section describes the direct allocation of interest expense to income generated by certain assets that are acquired in integrated financial transaction. Paragraph (d) of this section provides special rules that are applicable to all transactions described in paragraphs (b) and (c) of this section. Paragraph (e) of this section requires the direct allocation of third party interest of an affiliated group to such group's investment in related controlled foreign corporations in cases involving excess related person indebtedness (as defined therein). See also § 1.861-9T(b)(5), which requires direct allocation of amortizable bond premium.

(b) Qualified nonrecourse indebtedness. *(1) In general.* In the case of qualified nonrecourse indebtedness (as defined in paragraph (b)(2) of this section), the deduction for interest shall be considered directly allocable solely to the gross income which the property acquired, constructed, or improved with the proceeds of the indebtedness generates, has generated, or could reasonably be expected to generate.

(2) Qualified nonrecourse indebtedness defined. The term "qualified nonrecourse indebtedness" means any borrowing that is not excluded by paragraph (b)(4) of this section if:

(i) The borrowing is specifically incurred for the purpose of purchasing, constructing, or improving identified property that is either depreciable tangible personal property or real property with a useful life of more than one year or for the purpose of purchasing amortizable intangible personal property with a useful life of more than one year;

(ii) The proceeds are actually applied to purchase, construct, or improve the identified property;

(iii) Except as provided in paragraph (b)(7)(ii) (relating to certain third party guarantees in leveraged lease transactions), the creditor can look only to the identified property (or any lease or other interest therein) as security for payment of the principal and interest on the loan and, thus, cannot look to any other property, the borrower, or any third party with respect to repayment of principal or interest on the loan;

(iv) The cash flow from the property, as defined in paragraph (b)(3) of this section, is reasonably expected to be sufficient in the first year of ownership as well as in each subsequent year of ownership to fulfill the terms and conditions of the loan agreement with respect to the amount and timing of payments of interest and original issue discount and periodic payments of principal in each such year; and

(v) There are restrictions in the loan agreement on the disposal or use of the property consistent with the assumptions described in subdivisions (iii) and (iv) of this paragraph (b)(2).

(3) Cash flow defined. (i) In general. The term "cash flow from the property" as used in paragraph (b)(2)(iv) of this section means a stream of revenue (as computed under paragraph (b)(3)(iii) of this section) substantially all of which derives directly from the property. The phrase "cash flow from the property" does not include revenue if a significant portion thereof is derived from activities such as sales, labor, services, or the use of other property. Thus, revenue derived from the sale or lease of inventory or of similar property does not constitute cash flow from the property, including plant or equipment used in the manufacture and sale or lease, or purchase and sale or lease, of such inventory or similar property. In addition, revenue derived in part from the performance of services that are not ancillary and subsidiary to the use of property does not constitute cash flow from the property.

(ii) Self-constructed assets. The activities associated with self-construction of assets shall be considered to constitute labor or services for purposes of paragraph (b)(3)(i) only if the self-constructed asset—

(A) Is constructed for the purpose of resale, or

(B) Without regard to purpose, is sold to an unrelated person within one year from the date that the property is placed in service for purposes of section 167.

(iii) Computation of cash flow. Cash flow is computed by subtracting cash disbursements excluding debt service from cash receipts.

(iv) Analysis of operating costs. [Reserved]

(v) Examples. The principles of this paragraph may be demonstrated by the following examples.

Example (1). In 1987, X borrows $100,000 in order to purchase an apartment building, which X then purchases. The loan is secured only by the building and the leases thereon. Annual debt service on the loan is $12,000. Annual gross rents from the building are $20,000. Annual taxes on the building are $2,000. Other expenses deductible under section 162 are $2,000. Rents are reasonably expected to remain stable or increase in subsequent years, and taxes and expenses are reasonably expected to remain proportional to gross rents in subsequent years. X provides security, maintenance, and utilities to the tenants of the building. Based on facts and circumstances, it is determined that, although services are provided to tenants, these services are ancillary and subsidiary to the occupancy of the apartments. Accordingly, the case flow of $16,000 is considered to constitute a return from the property. Furthermore, such cash flow is sufficient to fulfill the terms and conditions of the loan agreement as required by paragraph (b)(2)(iv).

Example (2). In 1987, X borrows funds in order to purchase a hotel, which X then purchases and operates. The loan is secured only by the hotel. Based on facts and circumstances, it is determined that the operation of the hotel involves services the value of which is significant in relation to amounts paid to occupy the rooms. Thus, a significant portion of the cash flow is derived from the performance of services not incidental to the occupancy of hotel rooms. Accordingly, the cash flow from the hotel is considered not to constitute a return on or from the property.

Example (3). In 1987, X borrows funds in order to build a factory which X then builds and operates. The loan is secured only by the factory and the equipment therein. Based on the facts and circumstances, it is determined that the operation of the factory involves significant expenditures for labor and raw materials. Thus, a significant portion of the cash flow is derived from labor and the processing of raw materials. Accordingly, the cash flow from the factory is considered not to constitute a return on or from the property.

(4) Exclusions. The term "qualified nonrecourse indebtedness" shall not include any transaction that—

(i) Lacks economic significance within the meaning of paragraph (b)(5) of this section;

(ii) Involves cross collateralization within the meaning of paragraph (b)(6) of this section;

(iii) Except in the case of a leveraged lease described in paragraph (b)(7)(ii) of this section, involves credit enhancement within the meaning of paragraph (b)(7) of this section or, with respect to loans made on or after October 14, 1988, does not under the terms of the loan documents, prohibit the acquisition by the holder of bond insurance or similar forms of credit enhancement;

(iv) Involves the purchase of inventory;

(v) Involves the purchase of any financial asset, including stock in a corporation, an interest in a partnership or a trust, or the debt obligation of any obligor (although interest incurred in order to purchase certain financial instruments may qualify for direct allocation under paragraph (c) of this section);

(vi) Involves interest expense that constitutes qualified residence interest as defined in section 163(h)(3); or

(vii) [Reserved].

(5) Economic significance. Indebtedness that otherwise qualifies under paragraph (b)(2) shall nonetheless be subject to apportionment under § 1.861-9T if, taking into account all the facts and circumstances, the transaction (including the security arrangement) lacks economic significance.

(6) Cross collateralization. The term "cross collateralization" refers to the pledge as security for a loan of—

(i) Any asset of the borrower other than the identified property described in paragraph (b)(2) of this section, or

(ii) Any asset belonging to any related person, as defined in § 1.861-8T(c)(2).

(7) Credit enhancement. (i) In general. Except as provided in paragraph (b)(7)(ii) of this section, the term "credit enhancement" refers to any device, including a contract, letter of credit, or guaranty, that expands the creditor's rights, directly or indirectly, beyond the identified property purchased, constructed, or improved with the funds advanced and, thus effectively provides as security for a loan the assets of any person other than the borrower. The acquisition of bond insurance or any other contract of suretyship by an initial or subsequent holder of an obligation shall constitute credit enhancement.

(ii) Special rule for leveraged leases. For purposes of this paragraph (b), the term "credit enhancement" shall not include any device under which any person that is not a related person within the meaning of § 1.861-8T(c)(2) agrees to guarantee, without recourse to the lessor or any person related to the lessor, a lessor's payment of principal and interest on indebtedness that was incurred in order to purchase or improve an asset that is depreciable tangible personal property or depreciable tangible real property (and the land on which such real property is situated) that is leased to a lessee that is not a related person in a transaction that constitutes a lease for federal income tax purposes.

(iii) Syndication of credit risk and sale of loan participations. The term "syndication of credit risk" refers to an arrangement in which one primary lender secures the promise of a secondary lender to bear a portion of the primary lender's credit risk on a loan. The term "sale of loan participations" refers to an arrangement in which one primary lender divides a loan into several portions, sells and assigns all rights with respect to one or more portions to participating secondary lenders, and does not remain at risk in any manner with respect to the portion assigned. For purposes of this paragraph (b), the syndication of credit risk shall constitute credit enhancement because the primary lender can look to secondary lenders for payment of the loan, notwithstanding limitations on the amount of the secondary lender's liability. Conversely, the sale of loan participations does not constitute credit enhancement, because the holder of each portion of the loan can look solely to the asset securing the loan and not to the credit or other assets of any person.

(8) Other arrangements that do not constitute cross collateralization or credit enhancement. For purposes of paragraphs (b)(6) and (7) of this section, the following arrangements do not constitute cross collateralization or credit enhancement:

(i) Integrated projects. A taxpayer's pledge of multiple assets of an integrated project. An integrated project consists of functionally related and geographically contiguous assets that, as to the taxpayer, are used in the same trade or business.

(ii) Insurance. A taxpayer's purchase of third-party casualty and liability insurance on the collateral or, by contract, bearing the risk of loss associated with destruction of the collateral or with respect to the attachment of third party liability claims.

(iii) After-acquired property. Extension of a creditor's security interest to improvements made to the collateral, provided that the extension does not constitute excess collateralization under paragraph (b)(12), determined by taking into account the value of improvements at the time the improvements are made and the value of the original property at the time the loan was made.

(iv) Warranties of completion and maintenance. A taxpayer's warranty to a creditor that it will complete construction or manufacture of the collateral or that it will maintain the collateral in good condition.

(v) Substitution of collateral. A taxpayer's right to substitute collateral under any loan contract. However, after the right is exercised, the loan shall no longer constitute qualified nonrecourse indebtedness.

(9) Refinancings. If a taxpayer refinances qualified nonrecourse indebtedness (as defined in paragraph (b)(2) of this section) with new indebtedness, such new indebtedness shall continue to qualify only if—

(i) The principal amount of the new indebtedness does not exceed by more than five percent the remaining principal amount of the original indebtedness,

(ii) The term of the new indebtedness does not exceed by more than six months the remaining term of the original indebtedness, and

(iii) The requirements of this paragraph (other than those of paragraph (b)(2)(i) and (ii) of this section) are satisfied at the time of the refinancing, and the exclusions contained in this paragraph (b)(4) do not apply.

(10) Post-construction permanent financing. Financing that is obtained after the completion of constructed property will be deemed to satisfy the requirements of paragraph (b)(2)(i) and (ii) of this section if—

(i) The financing is obtained within one year after the constructed property or substantially all of a constructed integrated project (as defined in paragraph (b)(8)(i) of this section) is placed in service for purposes of section 167; and

(ii) The financing does not exceed the cost of construction (including construction period interest).

(11) Assumptions of pre-existing qualified nonrecourse indebtedness. If a transferee of property that is subject to qualified nonrecourse indebtedness assumes such indebtedness, the indebtedness shall continue to constitute qualified nonrecourse indebtedness, provided that the assumption in no way alters the qualified status of the debt.

(12) Excess collateralization.[Reserved]

(c) Direct allocations in the case of certain integrated financial transactions. *(1) General rule.* Interest expense incurred on funds borrowed in connection with an integrated financial transaction (as defined in paragraph (c)(2) of this section) shall be directly allocated to the income generated by the investment funded with the borrowed amounts.

(2) Definition. The term "integrated financial transaction" refers to any transaction in which—

(i) The taxpayer—

(A) Incurs indebtedness for the purpose of making an identified term investment,

(B) Identifies the indebtedness as incurred for such purpose at the time the indebtedness is incurred, and

(C) Makes the identified term investment within ten business days after incurring the indebtedness;

(ii) The return on the investment is reasonably expected to be sufficient throughout the term of the investment to fulfill the terms and conditions of the loan agreement with respect to the amount and timing of payments of principal and interest or original issue discount;

(iii) The income constitutes interest or original issue discount or would constitute income equivalent to interest if earned by a controlled foreign corporation (as described in § 1.954-2T(h));

(iv) The debt incurred and the investment mature within ten business days of each other;

(v) The investment does not relate in any way to the operation of, and is not made in the normal course of, the trade or business of the taxpayer or any related person, including the financing of the sale of goods or the performance of services by the taxpayer or any related person, or the compensation of the taxpayer's employees (including any contribution or loan to an employee stock ownership plan (as defined in section 4975(e)(7)) or other plan that is qualified under section 401(a)); and

(vi) The borrower does not constitute a financial services entity (as defined in section 904 and the regulations thereunder).

(3) Rollovers. In the event that a taxpayer sells of otherwise liquidates an investment described in paragraph (c)(2) of this section, the interest expense incurred on the borrowing shall, subsequent to that liquidation, no longer qualify for direct allocation under this paragraph (c).

(4) Examples. The principles of this paragraph (c) may be demonstrated by the following examples.

Example (1). X is a manufacturer and does not constitute a financial services entity as defined in the regulations under section 904. On January 1, 1988, X borrows $100 for 6 months at an annual interest rate of 10 percent. X identifies on its books and records by the close of that day that the indebtedness is being incurred for the purpose of making an investment that is intended to qualify as an integrated financial transaction. On January 5, 1988, X uses the proceeds to purchase a portfolio of stock that approximates the composition of the Standard & Poor's 500 Index. On that day, X also enters into a forward sale contract that requires X to sell the stock on June 1, 1988 for $110. X identifies on its books and records by the close of January 5, 1988, that the portfolio stock purchases and the forward sale contract constitute part of the integrated financial transaction with respect to which the identified borrowing was incurred. Under § 1.954-2T(h), the income derived from the transaction would constitute income equivalent to interest. Assuming that the return on the investment to be derived on June 1, 1988, will be sufficient to pay the interest due on June 1, 1988, the interest on the borrowing is directly allocated to the gain from the investment.

Example (2). X does not constitute a financial services entity as defined in the regulations under section 904. X is in the business of, among other things, issuing credit cards to consumers and purchasing from merchants who accept the X card the receivables of consumers who make purchases with the X card. X borrows from Y in order to purchase X credit card receivables from Z, a merchant. Assuming that the Y borrowing satisfies the other requirements of paragraph (c)(2) of this section, the transaction nonetheless cannot constitute an integrated financial transaction because the purchase relates to the operation of X's trade or business.

Example (3). Assume the same facts as in Example 2, except that X borrows in order to purchase the receivables of A, a merchant who does not accept the X card and is not otherwise engaged directly or indirectly in any business transaction with X. Because the borrowing is not related to the operation of X's trade or business, the borrowing may qualify as an integrated financial transaction if the other requirements of paragraph (c)(2) of this section are satisfied.

(d) Special rules. In applying paragraphs (b) and (c) of this section, the following special rules shall apply.

(1) Related person transactions. The rules of this section shall not apply to the extent that any transaction—

(i) Involves either indebtedness between related persons (as defined in section § 1.861-8T(c)(2)) or indebtedness incurred from unrelated persons for the purpose of purchasing property from a related person; or

(ii) Involves the purchase of property that is leased to a related person (as defined in § 1.861-8T(c)(2)) in a transaction described in paragraph (b) of this section. If a taxpayer purchases property and leases such property in whole or in part to a related person, a portion of the interest incurred in connection with such an acquisition, based on the ratio that the value of the property leased to the related person bears to the total value of the property, shall not qualify for direct allocation under this section.

(2) Consideration of assets or income to which interest is directly allocated in apportioning other interest expense. In apportioning interest expense under § 1.861-9T, the year-end value of any asset to which interest expense is directly allocated under this section during the current taxable year shall be reduced to the extent provided in § 1.861-9T(g)(2)(iii) to reflect the portion of the principal amount of the indebtedness outstanding at year-end relating to the interest which is directly allocated. A similar adjustment shall be made to the end-of-year value of assets for the prior year for purposes of determining the beginning-of-year value of assets for the current year. These adjustments shall be made prior to averaging beginning-of-year and end-of-year values pursuant to § 1.861-9T(g)(2). In apportioning interest expense under the modified gross income method, gross income shall be reduced by the amount of income to which interest expense is directly allocated under this section.

(e) Treatment of certain related controlled foreign corporation indebtedness. *(1) In general.* In taxable years beginning after 1987, if a United States shareholder has incurred substantially disproportionate indebtedness in relation to the indebtedness of its related controlled foreign corporations so that such corporations have excess related person indebtedness (as determined under step 4 in subdivision (iv) of this paragraph (e)(1), the third party interest expense of the related United States shareholder (excluding amounts allocated under paragraphs (b) and (c)) in an amount equal to the interest income received on such excess related person indebtedness shall be allocated to gross income in the various separate limitation categories described in section 904(d)(1) in the manner prescribed in step 6 in subdivision (vi) of this paragraph (e)(1). This computation shall be performed as follows.

(i) Step 1: Compute the debt-to-asset ratio of the related United States shareholder. The debt-to-asset ratio of the related United States shareholder is the ratio between—

(A) The average month-end debt level of the related United States shareholder taking into account debt owing to any obligee who is not a related person as defined in section § 1.861-8T(c)(2), and

(B) The value of assets (tax book or fair market) of the related United States shareholder including stockholdings and obligations of related controlled foreign corporations but excluding stockholdings and obligations of members of the affiliated group (as defined in § 1.861-11T(d)).

(ii) Step 2: Compute aggregate debt-to-asset ratio of all related controlled foreign corporations. The aggregate debt-to-asset ratio of all related controlled foreign corporations is the ratio between—

(A) The average aggregate month-end debt level of all related controlled foreign corporations for their taxable years ending during the related United States shareholder's taxable year taking into account only indebtedness owing to persons other than the related United States shareholder or the related United States shareholder's other related controlled foreign corporations ("third party indebtedness"), and

(B) The aggregate value (tax book or fair market) of the assets of all related controlled foreign corporations for their taxable years ending during the related United States shareholder's taxable year excluding stockholdings in and obligations of the related United States shareholder or the related United States shareholder's other related controlled foreign corporations.

(iii) Step 3: Compute aggregate related person debt of all related controlled foreign corporations. This amount equals the average aggregate month-end debt level of all related controlled foreign corporations for their taxable years ending with or within the related United States shareholder's taxable year, taking into account only debt which is owned to the related United States shareholder (" related person indebtedness").

(iv) Step 4: Computation of excess related person indebtedness and computation of the income therefrom. (A) General rule. If the ratio computed under step 2 is less than applicable percentage of the ratio computed under step 1, the taxpayer shall add to the aggregate third party indebtedness of all related controlled foreign corporations determined under paragraph (e)(1)(ii)(A) of this section that portion of the related person indebtedness computed under step 3 that, when combined with the aggregate third party indebtedness of all controlled foreign corporations, makes the ratio computed under step 2 equal to applicable percentage of the ratio computed under step 1. The amount of aggregate related person debt that is so added to the aggregate third party debt of related controlled foreign corporations is considered to constitute excess related person indebtedness. For purposes of this paragraph (e)(1)(iv)(A), the term "applicable percentage" means the designated percentages for taxable years beginning during the following calendar years:

Taxable years beginning in	Applicable percentage
1988	50
1989	65
1990 and thereafter	80

(B) Elective quadratic formula. In calculating the amount of excess related party indebtedness of related controlled foreign corporations, the United States shareholder's debt-to-asset ratio may be adjusted to reflect the amount by which its debt and assets would be reduced had the related controlled foreign corporations incurred the excess related party indebtedness directly to third parties. In such case, the ratio computed in Step 1 is adjusted to reflect a reduction of both portions of the ratio by the amount of excess related person indebtedness as computed under this paragraph (e)(1)(ii)(A). Excess related person indebtedness may be computed under the following formula, under which excess related person indebtedness equals the smallest positive amount (not exceeding the aggregate amount of related controlled foreign corporation indebtedness) that is a solution to the following formula (with X equalling the amount of excess related person indebtedness):

$$\frac{\text{Aggregate third party debt of related US shareholder} - X}{\text{US shareholder assets} - X} \times \text{Applicable percentage for year} = \frac{\text{Aggregate third party debt of related CFCs} + X}{\text{Related CFC assets}}$$

Guidance concerning the solution of this equation is set forth in Example (2) of § 1.861-12(k).

(C) Computation of interest income received on excess related party indebtedness. The amount of interest income received on excess related person indebtedness equals the total interest income on related person indebtedness derived by the related United States shareholder during the taxable year multiplied by the ratio of excess related person indebtedness over the aggregate related person indebtedness for the taxable year.

(v) Step 5: Determine the aggregate amount of related controlled foreign corporation obligations held by the related United States shareholder in each limitation category. The aggregate amount of related controlled foreign corporation obligations held by the related United States shareholder in each limitation category equals the sum of the value of all such obligations in each limitation category. Solely for purposes of this paragraph (e)(1)(v), each debt obligation in a related controlled foreign corporation held by a related United States shareholder shall be attributed to separate limitation categories in the same manner as the stock of the obligor would be attributed under the rules of § 1.861-12T(c)(3), whether or nor such stock is held directly by such related United States shareholder.

(vi) 6: Direct allocation of United States shareholder third party interest expense. Third party interest expense of the related United States shareholder equal to the amount of interest income received on excess related person indebtedness as determined in step 4 shall be allocated among the various separate limitation categories in proportion to the relative aggregate amount of related controlled foreign corporation obligations held by the related United States shareholder in each such category, as determined under step 5. The remaining portion of third party interest expense will be apportioned as provided in §§ 1.861-8T through 1.861-13T, excluding this paragraph.

(2) Definitions. (i) United States shareholder. For purposes of this paragraph, the term "United States shareholder" has the same meaning as defined by section 957, except that, in the case of a United States shareholder that is a member an affiliated group (as defined in § 1.861-11T(d)), the entire affiliated group shall be considered to constitute a single United States shareholder. The term "related United States shareholder" is the United States shareholder (as defined in this paragraph (e)(2)(i)) with respect to which related controlled foreign corporations (as defined in paragraph (e)(2)(ii) of this section) are related within the meaning of that paragraph.

(ii) Related controlled foreign corporation. For purposes of this section, the term "related controlled foreign corporation" means any controlled foreign corporation which is a related person (as defined in § 1.861-8T(c)(2)) to a United States shareholder (as defined paragraph (e)(2)(i) of this section).

(iii) Value of assets and amount of liabilities. For purposes of this section, the value of assets is determined under § 1.861-9T(g). Thus, in the case of assets that are denominated in foreign currency, the average of the beginning-of-year and end-of-year values is determined in foreign currency and translated into dollars using exchange rates on the last day of the related United States shareholder's taxable year. In the case of liabilities that are denominated in foreign currency, the average month-end debt level of such liabilities is determined in foreign currency and then translated into dollars using exchange rates on the last day of the related United States shareholder's taxable year.

(3) Treatment of certain stock. To the extent that there is insufficient related person indebtedness of all related controlled foreign corporations under step 3 in paragraph (e)(1)(iii) of this section to achieve as equal ratio in step 4 of paragraph (e)(1)(iv) of this section, certain stock held by the related United States shareholder will be treated as related person indebtedness. Such stock includes—

(i) Any stock in the related controlled foreign corporation that is treated in the same manner as debt under the law of any foreign country that grants a deduction for interest or original issue discount relating to such stock, and

(ii) Any stock in a related controlled foreign corporation that has made loans to, or held stock described in this paragraph (e)(3) in, another related controlled foreign corporation. However, such stock shall be treated as related person indebtedness only to the extent of the principal amount of such loans.

For purposes of computing income from excess related person indebtedness in step 4 of paragraph (e)(1)(iv) of this section, stock that is treated under this paragraph as related person indebtedness shall be considered to yield interest in an amount equal to the interest that would be computed on an equal amount of indebtedness under section 1274. Only dividends actually paid thereon shall be included in gross income for other purposes.

(4) Adjustments to assets in apportioning other interest expense. In apportioning interest expense under § 1.861-9T, the value of assets in each separate limitation category for the taxable year as determined under § 1.861-9T(g)(3) shall be reduced (but not below zero) by the principal amount of third party indebtedness of the related United States shareholder the interest expense on which is allocated to each such category under paragraph (e)(1) of this section.

(5) Exceptions. (i) Per company rule. If—

(A) A related controlled foreign corporation with obligations owing to a related United States shareholder has a greater proportion of passive assets than the proportion of passive assets held by the related United States shareholder,

(B) Such passive assets are held in liquid or short term investments, and

(C) There are frequent cash transfers between the related controlled foreign corporation and the related United States shareholder, the Commissioner, in his discretion, may choose to exclude such a corporation from other related controlled foreign corporations in the application of the rules of this paragraph (e).

(ii) Aggregate rule. If it is determined that, in aggregate, the application of the rules of this paragraph (e) increases a taxpayer's foreign tax credit as determined under section 901(a), the Commissioner, in his discretion, may choose not to apply the rules of this paragraph. If the Commissioner exercises discretion under this paragraph (e)(5)(ii), then paragraph (e) shall not apply to any extent to any interest expense of the taxpayer.

T.D. 8228, 9/9/88.

PAR. 5. Section 1.861-10T is amended by—

1. Revising paragraph (a); and
2. Adding paragraph (f).

Proposed § 1.861-10T Special allocations of interest expense (temporary regulations). [*For Preamble, see ¶ 152,047*]

(a) In general. This section applies to all taxpayers and provides four exceptions to the rules of § 1.861-9T that require the allocation and apportionment of interest expense on the basis of all assets of all members of the affiliated group. Paragraph (b) of this section describes the direct allocation of interest expense to the income generated by certain assets that are subject to qualified nonrecourse indebtedness. Paragraph (c) of this section describes the direct allocation of interest expense to income generated by certain assets that are acquired in integrated financial transactions. Paragraph (d) of this section provides special rules that are applicable to all transactions described in paragraphs (b) and (c) of this section. Paragraph (e) of this section requires the direct allocation of third party interest of an affiliated group to such group's investment in related controlled foreign corporations in cases involving excess related person indebtedness (as defined therein). Paragraph (f) of this section provides rules for the direct allocation and apportionment of all FASIT interest expense to all FASIT gross income, on the basis of all FASIT assets. See also § 1.861-9T(b)(5), which requires direct allocation of amortizable bond premium.

* * * * *

(f) FASIT interest expense. *(1) In general.* All FASIT interest expense of the taxpayer's affiliated group (or the taxpayer, if the taxpayer is not a member of an affiliated group) shall be directly allocated solely to the FASIT gross income of the affiliated group (or the taxpayer, if the taxpayer is not a member of an affiliated group).

(2) Asset method. Interest expense that is directly allocated under this paragraph (f) shall be treated as directly related to all the activities and assets of all FASITs in which the taxpayer or any member of the taxpayer's affiliated group holds the ownership interest. The directly allocated interest expense shall be apportioned among all of the FASIT gross income of the affiliated group (or the taxpayer, if the taxpayer is not a member of an affiliated group) under the asset method described in § 1.861-9T(g).

(3) FASIT period. After a FASIT's startup day (as defined in section 860L(d)(1)), the taxpayer must allocate the interest expense of the FASIT according to the rules of this paragraph (f) during the entire period that the arrangement continues to be a FASIT. If an arrangement ceases to be a FASIT, interest expense with respect to the ceased FASIT arrangement shall no longer be allocated and apportioned under the rules of this paragraph (f) as of the time the arrangement is treated as having ceased in accordance with § 1.860H-3(b). The Commissioner may continue to allocate

interest expense with respect to a ceased FASIT arrangement under this paragraph (f) if the Commissioner determines that the principal purpose of ending the arrangement's qualification as a FASIT was to affect the taxpayer's interest expense allocation.

(4) Application of special rules. In applying this paragraph (f), the rules of paragraph (d)(2) of this section shall apply.

(5) Definitions. For purposes of this paragraph (f):

(i) FASIT defined. *FASIT* has the meaning given such term in § 1.860H-1(a).

(ii) FASIT interest expense defined. (A) In general. *FASIT interest expense* means any amount paid or accrued by or on behalf of a FASIT to a holder of a regular interest in such FASIT, if such amount is—

(1) treated as incurred by the taxpayer or any member of the taxpayer's affiliated group by reason of § 1.860H-6(a), because the taxpayer or such member holds the ownership interest in a FASIT; and

(2) treated as interest by reason of section 860H(c).

(B) Interest equivalents. FASIT interest expense includes any expense or loss from a hedge that is a permitted asset (as described in § 1.860H-2 (d) and (e)), but only to the extent such expense or loss is an interest equivalent as described in § 1.861-9T(b).

(iii) FASIT gross income defined. *FASIT gross income* means gross income of the taxpayer's affiliated group (or the taxpayer, if the taxpayer is not a member of an affiliated group) treated as received or accrued by the taxpayer, or any member of the taxpayer's affiliated group, by reason of § 1.860H-6(a).

(iv) Affiliated group defined. *Affiliated group* has the meaning given such term by § 1.861-11T(d).

(6) Coordination with other provisions. If any FASIT interest expense is directly allocable under both this paragraph (f) and paragraph (b) or (c) (determined without regard to this paragraph (f)(6)), only the rules of this paragraph (f) shall apply.

(7) Effective date. The rules of this section apply for taxable years beginning after December 31, 1986. However, paragraphs (a) and (f) apply as of the date final regulations are filed with the Federal Register, and paragraph (e) applies to all taxable years beginning after December 31, 1991.

§ 1.861-11 Special rules for allocating and apportioning interest expense of an affiliated group of corporations.

(a) through (c) [Reserved]. For further guidance, see § 1.861-11T(a) through (c).

(d) Definition of affiliated group. *(1) General rule.* For purposes of this section, in general, the term affiliated group has the same meaning as is given that term by section 1504, except that section 936 corporations are also included within the affiliated group to the extent provided in paragraph (d)(2) of this section. Section 1504(a) defines an affiliated group as one or more chains of includible corporations connected through 80-percent stock ownership with a common parent corporation which is an includible corporation (as defined in section 1504(b)). In the case of a corporation that either becomes or ceases to be a member of the group during the course of the corporation's taxable year, only the interest expense incurred by the group member during the period of membership shall be allocated and apportioned as if all members of the group were a single corporation. In this regard, assets held during the period of membership shall be taken into account. Other interest expense incurred by the group member during its taxable year but not during the period of membership shall be allocated and apportioned without regard to the other members of the group.

(2) Inclusion of section 936 corporations. (i) Rule. (A) In general. Except as otherwise provided in paragraph (d)(2)(i)(B) of this section, the exclusion of section 936 corporations from the affiliated group under section 1504(b)(4) does not apply for purposes of this section. Thus, a section 936 corporation that meets the ownership requirements of section 1504(a) is a member of the affiliated group.

(B) Exception for purposes of alternative minimum tax. The exclusion from the affiliated group of section 936 corporations under section 1504(b)(4) shall be operative for purposes of the application of this section solely in determining the amount of foreign source alternative minimum taxable income within each separate category and the alternative minimum tax foreign tax credit pursuant to section 59(a). Thus, a section 936 corporation that meets the ownership requirements of section 1504(a) is not a member of the affiliated group for purposes of determining the amount of foreign source alternative minimum taxable income within each separate category and the alternative minimum tax foreign tax credit pursuant to section 59(a).

(ii) Section 936 corporation defined. For purposes of this section, § 1.861-9, and § 1.861-14, the term section 936 corporation means, for any taxable year, a corporation with an election in effect to be eligible for the credit provided under section 936(a)(1) or section 30A for the taxable year.

(iii) Example. This example illustrates the provisions of paragraph (d)(2)(i) of this section:

Example. (A) Facts. X owns all of the stock of Y. XY constitutes an affiliated group of corporations within the meaning of section 1504(a) and uses the tax book value method of apportionment. In 2000, Y owns all of the stock of Z, a section 936 corporation. Z manufactures widgets in Puerto Rico. Y purchases these widgets and markets them exclusively in the United States. Of the three corporations, only Z has foreign source income, which includes both qualified possessions source investment income and general limitation income. For purposes of section 904, Z's qualified possessions source investment income constitutes foreign source passive income. In computing the section 30A benefit, Y and Z have elected the cost sharing method. Of the three corporations, only X has debt and, thus, only X incurs interest expense.

(B) Analysis for regular tax. Assume first that X has no alternative minimum tax liability. Under paragraph (d)(2) of this section, Z is treated as a member of the XY affiliated group for purposes of allocating and apportioning interest expense for regular tax purposes. As provided in § 1.861-11T(b)(2), section 864(e)(1) and (5) do not apply in computing the combined taxable income of Y and Z under section 936, but these rules do apply in computing the foreign source taxable income of the XY affiliated group. The effect of including Z in the affiliated group is that X, the only debtor corporation in the group, must, under the asset method described in § 1.861-9T(g), apportion a part of its interest expense to foreign source passive income and foreign source general limitation income. This is because the assets of Z that generate qualified possessions source investment income and general limitation income are included in computing the group apportionment fractions. The result is that, under section 904(f), X has an overall foreign loss in both the passive and general limitation categories, which currently offsets domestic income and must be recaptured against any subsequent years' foreign passive income and general limitation income, respectively, under the rules of that section.

(C) Analysis for alternative minimum tax. Assume, alternatively, that X is liable to pay the alternative minimum tax. Pursuant to section 59(a), X must compute its alternative minimum tax foreign tax credit as if section 904 were applied on the basis of alternative minimum taxable income instead of taxable income. Under paragraph (d)(2)(i)(B) of this section, for purposes of the apportionment of interest expense in determining alternative minimum taxable income within each limitation category, Z is not considered a member of the XY affiliated group. Thus, the stock (and not the assets) of Z are included in computing the group apportionment fractions. Pursuant to sections 59(g)(4)(C)(iii)(IV), 861(a)(2)(A), and 862(a)(2), dividends paid by a section 936 corporation are foreign source income subject to a separate foreign tax credit limitation for alternative minimum tax purposes. Thus, under § 1.861-9T(g)(3), the stock of Z must be considered attributable solely to the statutory grouping consisting of foreign source dividends from Z. The effect of excluding Z from the affiliated group is that X must apportion a part of its interest expense to the separate category for foreign source dividends from Z in computing alternative minimum taxable income within each separate category. If, as a result, under section 904(f), X has a separate limitation loss or an overall foreign loss in the category for dividends from Z for alternative minimum tax purposes, then that loss must be allocated against X's other income (separate limitation or United States source, as the case may be). The loss must be recaptured in subsequent years under the rules of section 904(f) for purposes of the alternative minimum tax foreign tax credit. * * *

(iv) Effective date. This paragraph (d)(2) applies to taxable years beginning after December 31, 1989.

(3) through (6) [Reserved]. For further guidance see § 1.861-11T(d)(3) through (6).

(7) Special rules for the application of § 1.861-11T(d)(6). The attribution rules of section 1563(e) and the regulations under that section shall apply in determining indirect ownership under § 1.861-11T(d)(6). The Commissioner shall have the authority to disregard trusts, partnerships, and pass-through entities that break affiliated status. Corporations described in § 1.861-11T(d)(6) shall be considered to constitute members of an affiliated group that does not file a consolidated return and shall therefore be subject to the limitations imposed under § 1.861-11T(g). The affiliated group filing a consolidated return shall be considered to constitute a single corporation for purposes of applying the rules of § 1.861-11T(g). For taxable years beginning after December 31, 1989, § 1.861-11T(d)(6)(i) shall not apply in determining foreign source alternative minimum taxable income within each separate category and the alternative minimum tax foreign tax credit pursuant to section 59(a) to the extent that such application would result in the inclusion of a section 936 corporation within the affiliated group. This paragraph (d)(7) applies to taxable years beginning after December 31, 1986.

(e) through (g) [Reserved]. For further guidance, see § 1.861-11T(e) through (g).

T.D. 8916, 12/27/2000.

§ 1.861-11T Special rules for allocating and apportioning interest expense of an affiliated group of corporations (temporary).

(a) In general. Sections 1.861-9T, 1.861-10T, 1.861-12T, and 1.861-13T provide rules that are generally applicable in apportioning interest expense. The rules of this section relate to affiliated groups of corporations and implement section 864(e)(1) and (5), which requires affiliated group allocation and apportionment of interest expense. The rules of this section apply to taxable years beginning after December 31, 1986, except as otherwise provided in § 1.861-13T. Paragraph (b) of this section describes the scope of the application of the rule for the allocation and apportionment of interest expense of affiliated groups of corporations, which is contained in paragraph (c) of this section. Paragraph (d) of this section sets forth the definition of the term "affiliated group" for purposes of this section. Paragraph (e) describes the treatment of loans between members of an affiliated group. Paragraph (f) of this section provides rules concerning the affiliated group allocation and apportionment of interest expense in computing the combined taxable income of a FSC or DISC and its related supplier. Paragraph (g) of this section describes the treatment of losses caused by apportionment of interest expense in the case of an affiliated group that does not file a consolidated return.

(b) Scope of application. *(1) Application of section 864(e)(1) and (5) (concerning the definition and treatment of affiliated groups).* Section 864(e)(1) and (5) and the portions of this section implementing section 864(e)(1) and (5) apply to the computation of foreign source taxable income for purposes of section 904 (relating to various limitations on the foreign tax credit). Section 904 imposes separate foreign tax credit limitations on passive income, high withholding interest income, financial services income, shipping income, income consisting of dividends from each noncontrolled section 902 corporation, income consisting of dividends from a DISC or former DISC, taxable income attributable to foreign trade income within the meaning of section 923(b), distributions from a FSC or former FSC, and all other forms of foreign source income not enumerated above ("general limitation income"). Section 864(e)(1) and (5) and the portions of this section implementing section 864(e)(1) and (5) also apply in connection with section 907 to determine reductions in the amount allowed as a foreign tax credit under section 901. Section 864(e)(1) and (5) and the portions of this section implementing section 864(e)(1) and (5) also apply to the computation of the combined taxable income of the related supplier and a foreign sales corporation (FSC) (under sections 921 through 927) as well as the combined taxable income of the related supplier and a domestic international sales corporation (DISC) (under sections 991 through 997).

(2) Nonapplication of section 864(e)(1) and (5) (concerning the definition and treatment of affiliated groups). Section 864(e)(1) and (5) and the portions of this section implementing section 864(e)(1) and (5) do not apply to the computation of subpart F income of controlled foreign corporations (under sections 951 through 964), the computation of combined taxable income of a possessions corporation and its affiliates (under section 936), or the computation of effectively connected taxable income of foreign corporations. For the rules with respect to the allocation and apportionment of interest expenses of foreign corporations other than controlled foreign corporations, see §§ 1.882-4 and 1.882-5.

(c) General rule for affiliated corporations. Except as otherwise provided in this section, the taxable income of each member of an affiliated group within each statutory grouping shall be determined by allocating and apportioning the interest expense of each member according to apportionment fractions which are computed as if all members of such group were a single corporation. For purposes of determining these apportionment fractions, stock in corporations within the affiliated group (as defined in section 864(e)(5) and the rules of this section) shall not be taken into account. In the case of an affiliated group of corporations that files a consolidated return, consolidated foreign tax credit limitations are computed for the group in accordance with the rules of § 1.1502-4. Except as otherwise provided, all the interest expense of all members of the group will be treated as definitely related and therefore allocable to all the gross income of the members of the group and all the assets of all the members of the group shall be taken into account in apportioning this interest expense. For purposes of this section, the term "taxpayer" refers to the affiliated group (regardless of whether the group files a consolidated return), rather than to the separate members thereof.

(d) Definition of affiliated group. *(1) and (2) [Reserved].* For further guidance, see § 1.861-11(d)(1) and (2).

(3) Treatment of life insurance companies subject to taxation under section 801. (i) General rule. A life insurance company that is subject to taxation under section 801 shall be considered to constitute a member of the affiliated group composed of companies not taxable under section 801 only if a parent corporation so elects under section 1504(c)(2)(A) of the Code. If a parent does not so elect, no adjustments shall be required with respect to such an insurance company under paragraph (g) of this section.

(ii) Treatment of stock. Stock of a life insurance company that is subject to taxation under section 801 that is not included in an affiliated group shall be disregarded in the allocation and apportionment of the interest expense of such affiliated group.

(4) Treatment of certain financial corporations. (i) In general. In the case of an affiliated group (as defined in paragraph (d)(1) of this section), any member that constitutes financial corporations as defined in paragraph (d)(4)(ii) of this section shall be treated as a separate affiliated group consisting of financial corporations (the "financial group"). The members of the group that do not constitute financial corporations shall be treated as members of a separate affiliated group consisting of nonfinancial corporations ("the nonfinancial group").

(ii) Financial corporation defined. The term "financial corporation" means any corporation which meets all of the following conditions:

(A) It is described in section 581 (relating to the definition of a bank) or section 591 (relating to the deduction for dividends paid on deposits by mutual savings banks, cooperative banks, domestic building and loan associations, and other savings institutions chartered and supervised as savings and loan or similar associations);

(B) Its business is predominantly with persons other than related persons (within the meaning of section 864(d)(4) and the regulations thereunder) or their customers; and

(C) It is required by state or Federal law to be operated separately from any other entity which is not such an institution.

(iii) Treatment of bank holding companies. The total aggregate interest expense of any member of an affiliated group that constitutes a bank holding company subject to regulation under the Bank Holding Company Act of 1956 shall be prorated between the financial group and the nonfinancial group on the basis of the assets in the financial and nonfinancial groups. For purposes of making this proration, the assets of each member of each group, and not the stock basis in each member, shall be taken into account. Any direct or indirect subsidiary of a bank holding company that is predominantly engaged in the active conduct of a banking, financing, or similar business shall be considered to be a financial corporation for purposes of this paragraph (d)(4). The interest expense of the bank holding company must be further apportioned in accordance with § 1.861-9T(f) to the various section 904(d) categories of income contained in both the financial group and the nonfinancial group on the basis of the assets owned by each group. For purposes of computing the apportionment fractions for each group, the assets owned directly by a bank holding company within each limitation category described in section 904(d)(1) (other than stock in affiliates or assets described in § 1.861-9T(f)) shall be treated as owned pro rata by the nonfinancial group and the financial group based on the relative amounts of investments of the bank holding company in the nonfinancial group and financial group.

(iv) Consideration of stock of the members of one group held by members of the other group. In apportioning interest expense, the nonfinancial group shall not take into account the stock of any lower-tier corporation that is treated as a member of the financial group under paragraph (d)(4)(i) of this section. Conversely, in apportioning interest expense, the financial group shall not take into account the stock of any lower-tier corporation that is treated as a member of the nonfinancial group under paragraph (d)(4)(i) of this section. For the treatment of loans between members of the financial group and members of the nonfinancial group, see paragraph (e)(1) of this section.

(5) Example. (i) Facts. X, a domestic corporation which is not a bank holding company, is the parent of domestic corporations Y and Z. Z owns 100 percent of the stock Z1, which is also a domestic corporation. X, Y, Z, and Z1 were organized after January 1, 1987, and constitute an affiliated group within the meaning of paragraph (d)(1) of this section. Y and Z are financial corporations described in paragraph (d)(4) of this section. X also owns 25 percent of the stock of A, a domestic corporation. Y owns 25 percent of the voting stock of B, a foreign corporation that is not a controlled foreign corporation. Z owns less than 10 percent of the voting stock of C, another foreign corporation. The foreign source income generated by Y's or Z's direct assets is exclusively financial services income. The foreign source income generated by X's or Z1's direct assets is exclusively general limitation income. X and Z1 are not financial corporations described in paragraph (d)(4)(ii) of this section. Y and Z, therefore, constitute a separate affiliated group apart from X and Z1 for purposes of section 864(e). The combined interest expense of Y and Z of $100,000 ($50,000 each) is apportioned separately on the basis of their assets. The combined interest expense of X and Z1 of $50,000 ($25,000 each) is allocated on the basis of the assets of the XZ1 group.

Analysis of the YZ group assets

Adjusted basis of assets of the YZ group that generate foreign source financial services income (excluding stock of foreign subsidiaries not included in the YZ affiliated group)	$ 200,000

Z's basis in the C stock (not adjusted by the allocable amount of C's earnings and profits because Z owns less than 10 percent of the stock) which would be considered to generate passive income in the hands of a nonfinancial services entity but is considered to generate financial services income when in the hands of Z, a financial services entity ...	$ 100,000
Y's basis in the B stock (adjusted by the allocable amount of B's earnings and profits) which generates dividends subject to a separate limitation for B dividends	$ 100,000
Adjusted basis of assets of the YZ group that generate U.S. source income	$ 600,000
Total assets	$1,000,000

Analysis of the XZ1 group assets

Adjusted basis of assets of the XZ1 group that generate foreign source general limitation income	$ 500,000
Adjusted basis of assets of the XZ1 group other than A stock that generate domestic source income	$1,900,000
X's basis in the A stock adjusted by the allocable amount of A's earnings and profits	$ 100,000
Total domestic assets	$2,000,000
Total assets	$2,500,000

(ii) Allocation. No portion of the $50,000 deduction of the YZ group is definitely related solely to specific property within the meaning of § 1.861-10T. Thus, the YZ group's deduction for interest is related to all its activities and properties. Similarly, no portion of the $50,000 deduction of the XZ1 group is definitely related solely to specific property within the meaning of § 1.861-10T. Thus, the XZ1 group's deduction for interest is related to all its activities and properties.

(iii) Apportionment. The YZ group would apportion its interest expense as follows:

To gross financial services income from sources outside the United States:

$$\$50{,}000 \times \frac{\$\ 300{,}000}{\$1{,}000{,}000} \quad \ldots\ldots\ldots\ \$15{,}000$$

To gross income subject to a separate limitation for dividends from B:

$$\$50{,}000 \times \frac{\$\ 100{,}000}{\$1{,}000{,}000} \quad \ldots\ldots\ \$5{,}000$$

To gross income from sources inside the United States:

$$\$50{,}000 \times \frac{\$\ 600{,}000}{\$1{,}000{,}000} \quad \ldots\ldots\ \$30{,}000$$

The XZ1 group would apportion its interest expense as follows:

To gross general limitation income from sources outside the United States:

$$\$50{,}000 \times \frac{\$\ 500{,}000}{\$2{,}500{,}000} \quad \ldots\ldots\ \$10{,}000$$

To gross income from sources inside the United States:

$$\$50{,}000 \times \frac{\$2{,}000{,}000}{\$2{,}500{,}000} \quad \ldots\ldots\ \$40{,}000$$

(6) Certain unaffiliated corporations. Certain corporations that are not described in paragraph (d)(1) of this section will nonetheless be considered to constitute affiliated corporations for purposes of §§ 1.861-9T through 1.861-13T. These corporations include:

(i) Any includible corporation (as defined in section 1504(b) without regard to section 1504(b)(4)) if 80 percent of either the vote or value of all outstanding stock of such corporation is owned directly or indirectly by an includible corporation or by members of an affiliated group, and

(ii) Any foreign corporation if 80 percent of either the vote or value of all outstanding stock of such corporation is owned directly or indirectly by members of an affiliated group, and if more than 50 percent of the gross income of such corporation for the taxable year is effectively connected with the conduct of a United States trade or business. If 80 percent or more of the gross income of such corporation is effectively connected income, then all the assets of such corporation and all of its interest expense shall be taken into account. If between 50 and 80 percent of the gross income of such corporation is effectively connected income, then only the assets of such corporation that generate effectively connected income and a percentage of its interest expense equal to the percentage of its assets that generate effectively connected income shall be taken into account.

(7) Special rules for the application of § 1.861-11T(d)(6). [Reserved]. Special rules for the application of § 1.861-11T(d)(6), see § 1.861-11(d)(7).

(e) Loans between members of an affiliated group. *(1) General rule.* In the case of loans (including any receivable) between members of an affiliated group, as defined in paragraph (d) of this section, for purposes of apportioning interest expense, the indebtedness of the member borrower shall not be considered an asset of the member lender. However, in the case of members of separate financial and nonfinancial groups under paragraph (d)(4) of this section, the indebtedness of the member borrower shall be considered an asset of the member lender and such asset shall be characterized by reference to the member lender's income from the asset as determined under paragraph (e)(2)(ii) of this section. For purposes of this paragraph (e), the terms "related person interest income" and "related person interest payment" refer to interest paid and received by members of the same affiliated group as defined in paragraph (d) of this section.

(2) Treatment of interest expense within the affiliated group. (i) General rule. A member borrower shall deduct related person interest payments in the same manner as unrelated person interest expense using group apportionment fractions computed under § 1.861-9T(f). A member lender shall include related person interest income in the same class of gross income as the class of gross income from which the member borrower deducts the related person interest payment.

(ii) Special rule for loans between financial and nonfinancial affiliated corporations. In the case of a loan between two affiliated corporations only one of which constitutes a financial corporation under paragraph (d)(4) of this section, the member borrower shall allocate and apportion related person interest payments in the same manner as unrelated person interest expense using group apportionment fractions computed under § 1.861-9T(f). The source of the related person interest income to the member lender shall be determined under section 861(a)(1).

(iii) Special rule for high withholding tax interest. In the case of an affiliated corporation that pays interest that is high withholding tax interest under § 1.904-5(f)(1) to another affiliated corporation, the interest expense of the payor shall be allocated to high withholding tax interest.

(3) Back-to-back loans. If a member of the affiliated group makes a loan to a nonmember who makes a loan to a member borrower, the rule of paragraphs (e)(1) and (2) of this section shall apply, in the Commissioner's discretion, as if the member lender made the loan directly to the member borrower, provided that the loans constitute a back-to-back loan transaction. Such loans will constitute a back-to-back loan for purposes of this paragraph (e) if the loan by the nonmember would not have been made or maintained on substantially the same terms irrespective of the loan of funds by the lending member to the nonmember or other intermediary party.

(4) Examples. The rules of this paragraph (e) may be illustrated by the following examples.

Example (1). X, a domestic corporation, is the parent of Y, a domestic corporation. X and Y were organized after January 1, 1987, and constitute an affiliated group within the meaning of paragraph (d)(1) of this section. Among X's assets is the note of Y for the amount of $100,000. Because X and Y are members of an affiliated group, Y's note does not constitute an asset for purposes of apportionment. The apportionment fractions for the relevant tax year of the XY group are 50 percent domestic, 40 percent foreign general, and 10 percent foreign passive. Y deducts its related person interest payment using those apportionment fractions. Of the $10,000 in related person interest income received by X, $5,000 consists of domestic source income, $4,000 consists of foreign general limitation income, and $1,000 consists of foreign passive income.

Example (2). X is a domestic corporation organized after January 1, 1987. X owns all the stock of Y, a domestic corporation. On June 1, 1987, X loans $100,000 to Z, an unrelated person. On June 2, 1987, Z makes a loan to Y with terms substantially similar to those of the loan from X to Z. Based on the facts and circumstances of the transaction, it is determined that Z would not have made the loan to Y on the same terms if X had not made the loan to Z. Because the transaction constitutes a back-to-back loan, as defined in paragraph (e)(3) of this section, the Commissioner may require, in his discretion, that neither the note of Y nor the note of Z may be considered an asset of X for purposes of this section.

(f) Computations of combined taxable income. In the computation of the combined taxable income of any FSC or DISC and its related supplier which is a member of an affiliated group under the pricing rules of sections 925 or 994, the combined taxable income of such FSC or DISC and its related supplier shall be reduced by the portion of the total interest expense of the affiliated group that is incurred in connection with those assets of the group used in connection with export sales involving that FSC or DISC. This amount shall be computed by multiplying the total interest expense of the affiliated group and interest expense of the FSC or DISC by a fraction the numerator of which is the assets of the affiliated group and of the FSC or DISC generating foreign trade income or gross income attributable to qualified export receipts, as the case may be, and the denominator of which is the total assets of the affiliated group and the FSC or DISC. Under this rule, interest of other group members may be attributed to the combined taxable income of a FSC or DISC and its related supplier without affecting the amount of interest otherwise deductible by the FSC or DISC, the related supplier or other member of the affiliated group. The FSC or DISC is entitled to only the statutory portion of the combined taxable income, net of any deemed interest expense, which determines the commission paid to the FSC or DISC or the transfer price of qualifying export property sold to the FSC or DISC.

(g) Losses created through apportionment. *(1) General rules.* In the case of an affiliated group that is eligible to file, but does not file, a consolidated return and in the case of any corporation described in paragraph (d)(6) of this section, the foreign tax credits in any separate limitation category are limited to the credits computed under the rules of this paragraph (g). As a consequence of the affiliated group allocation and apportionment of interest expense required by section 864(e)(1) and this section, interest expense of a group member may be apportioned for section 904 purposes to a limitation category in which that member has no gross income, resulting in a loss in that limitation category. The same is true in connection with any expense other than interest that is subject to apportionment under the rules of section 864(e)(6) of the Code. Any reference to "interest expense" in this paragraph (g) shall be treated as including such expenses. For purposes of this paragraph, the term "limitation category" includes domestic source income, as well as the types of income described in section 904(d)(1)(A) through (I). A loss of one affiliate in a limitation category will reduce the income of another member in the same limitation category if a consolidated return is filed. (See § 1.1502-4.) If a consolidated return is not filed, this netting does not occur. Accordingly, in such a case, the following adjustments among members are required in order to give effect to the group allocation of interest expense:

(i) Losses created through group apportionment of interest expense in one or more limitation categories within a given member must be eliminated; and

(ii) A corresponding amount of income of other members in the same limitation category must be recharacterized. Such adjustments shall be accomplished, in accordance with paragraph (g)(2) of this section, without changing the total taxable income of any member and before the application of section 904(f). Section 904(f) (including section 904(f)(5)) does not apply to a loss created through the apportionment of interest expense to the extent that the loss is eliminated pursuant to paragraph (g)(2)(ii) of this section. For purposes of this section, the terms "limitation adjustment" and "recharacterization" mean the recharacterization of income in one limitation category as income in another limitation category.

(2) Mechanics of computation. (i) Step 1: Computation of consolidated taxable income. The members of an affiliated group must first allocate and apportion all other deductible expenses other than interest. The members must then deduct from their respective gross incomes within each limitation category interest expense apportioned under the rules of § 1.861-9T(f). The taxable income of the entire affiliated group within each limitation category is then totalled.

(ii) Step 2: Loss offset adjustments. If, after step 1, a member has losses in a given limitation category or limitation categories created through apportionment of interest expense, any such loss (i.e., the portion of such loss equal to interest expense) shall be eliminated by offsetting that loss against taxable income in other limitation categories of that member to the extent of the taxable income of other members within the same limitation category as the loss. If the member has taxable income in more than one limitation category, then the loss shall offset taxable income in all such limitation categories on a pro rata basis. If there is insufficient domestic income of the member to offset the net losses in all foreign limitation categories caused by the apportionment of interest expense, the losses in each limitation category shall be recharacterized as domestic losses to the extent of the taxable income of other members in the same respective limitation categories. After these adjustments are made, the income of the entire affiliated group within each limitation category is totalled again.

(iii) Step 3: Determination of amount subject to recharacterization. In order to determine the amount of income to be recharacterized in step 4, the income totals computed under step 1 in each limitation category shall be subtracted from the income totals computed under step 2 in each limitation category.

(iv) Step 4: Recharacterization. Because any differences determined under step 3 represent deviations from the consolidated totals computed under Step 1, such differences (in any limitation category) must be eliminated.

(A) Limitation categories to be reduced. In the case of any limitation category in which there is a positive change, the income of group members with income in that limitation category must be reduced on a pro rata basis (by reference to net income figures as determined under Step 2) to the extent of such positive change ("limitation reductions"). Each member shall separately compute the sum of the limitation reductions.

(B) Limitation categories to be increased. In any case in which only one limitation category has a negative change in Step 3, the sum of the limitation reductions within each member is added to that limitation category. In the case in which multiple limitation categories have negative changes in Step 3, the sum of the limitation reductions within each member is prorated among the negative change limitation categories based on the ratio that the negative change for the entire group in each limitation category bears to the total of all negative changes for the entire group in all limitation categories.

(3) Examples. The following examples illustrate the principles of this paragraph.

Example (1). (i) Facts. X, a domestic corporation, is the parent of domestic corporations Y and Z. X, Y, and Z were organized after January 1, 1987, constitute an affiliated group within the meaning of paragraph (d)(1) of this section, but do not file a consolidated return. The XYZ group apportions its interest expense on the basis of the fair market value of its assets. X, Y, and Z have the following assets, interest expense, and taxable income before apportioning interest expense:

Assets	X	Y	Z	Total
Domestic	2,000.00	0	1,000.00	3,000.00
Foreign Passive	0	50.00	50.00	100.00
Foreign General	0	700.00	200.00	900.00
Interest expense	48.00	12.00	80.00	140.00
Taxable income (pre-interest):				
Domestic	100.00	0	63.00	163.00
Foreign Passive	0	5.00	5.00	10.00
Foreign General	0	60.00	35.00	95.00

(ii) Step 1: Computation of consolidated taxable income. Each member of the XYZ group apportions its interest expense according to group apportionment ratios determined under the asset method described in § 1.861-9T(f), yielding the following results:

Apportioned interest expense	X	Y	Z	Total
Domestic	36.00	9.00	60.00	105.00
Foreign Passive	1.20	0.30	2.00	3.50
Foreign General	10.80	2.70	18.00	31.50
Total	48.00	12.00	80.00	140.00

The members of the group then compute taxable income within each category by deducting the apportioned interest expense from the amounts of pre-interest taxable income specified in the facts in paragraph (i), yielding the following results:

Taxable income	X	Y	Z	Total
Domestic	64.00	– 9.00	3.00	58.00
Foreign Passive	– 1.20	4.70	3.00	6.50
Foreign General	– 10.80	57.30	17.00	63.50
Total	52.00	53.00	23.00	128.00

(iii) Step 2: Loss offset adjustments. Because X and Y have losses created through apportionment, these losses must be eliminated by reducing taxable income of the member in other limitation categories. Because X has a total of $12 in apportionment losses and because it has only one limitation category with income (i.e., domestic), domestic income must be reduced by $12, thus eliminating its apportionment losses. Because Y has a total of $9 in apportionment losses and because it has two limitation categories with income (i.e., foreign passive and foreign general limitation), the income in these two limitation categories must be reduced on a pro rata basis in order to eliminate its apportionment losses. In summary, the following adjustments are required:

Loss offset Adjustments	X	Y	Z	Total
Domestic	– 12.00	+ 9.00	0	– 3.00
Foreign Passive	+ 1.20	– 0.68	0	+ 0.52
Foreign General	+ 10.80	– 8.32	0	+ 2.48

These adjustments yield the following adjusted taxable income figures:

Adjusted taxable income	X	Y	Z	Total
Domestic	52.00	0	3.00	55.00
Foreign Passive	0	4.02	3.00	7.02
Foreign General	0	48.96	17.00	65.98
Total	52.00	53.00	23.00	128.00

(iv) Step 3: Determination of amount subject to recharacterization. The adjustments performed under Step 2 led to a change in the group's taxable income within each limitation category. The total loss offset adjustments column shown in paragraph (iii) above shows the net deviations between Step 1 and 2.

(v) Step 4: Recharacterization. The loss offset adjustments yield a positive change in the foreign passive and the foreign general limitation categories. Y and Z both have income in these limitation categories. Accordingly, the income of Y and Z in each of these limitation categories must be reduced on a pro rata basis (by reference to the adjusted taxable income figures) to the extent of the positive change in each limitation category. The total positive change in the foreign passive limitation category is $0.52. The adjusted taxable income of Y in the foreign passive limitation category is $4.02 and the adjusted taxable income of Z in the foreign passive limitation category is $3. Therefore, $0.30 is drawn from Y and $0.22 is drawn from Z. The total positive change in the foreign general limitation category is $2.48. The adjusted taxable income of Y in the foreign general limitation category is $48.98, and the adjusted taxable income of Z in the foreign general limitation category is $17. Therefore, $1.84 is drawn from Y and $.64 is drawn from Z. The members must then separately compute the sum of the limitation reductions. Y has limitation reductions of $0.30 in the foreign passive limitation category and $1.84 in the foreign general limitation category, yielding total limitation reduction of $2.14. Under these facts, domestic income is the only limitation category requiring a positive adjustment. Accordingly, Y's domestic income is increased by $2.14. Z has limitation reductions of $0.22 in the foreign passive limitation category and $0.64 in the foreign general limitation category, yielding total limitation reductions of $0.86. Under these facts, domestic income is the only limitation category of Z requiring a positive adjustment. Accordingly, Z's domestic income is increased by $0.86.

Recharacterization adjustments	X	Y	Z	Total
Domestic	0	+ 2.14	+ 0.86	+ 3.00
Foreign Passive	0	− 0.30	− 0.22	− 0.52
Foreign General	0	− 1.84	− 0.64	− 2.48

These recharacterization adjustments yield the following final taxable income figures:

Final Taxable income	X	Y	Z	Total
Domestic	52.00	2.14	3.86	58.00
Foreign Passive	0	3.72	2.78	6.50
Foreign General	0	47.14	16.36	63.50
Total	52.00	53.00	23.00	128.00

Example (2). (i) Facts. X, a domestic corporation, is the parent of domestic corporations Y and Z. X, Y, and Z were organized after January 1, 1987, constitute an affiliated group within the meaning of paragraph (d)(1) of this section, but do not file a consolidated return. Moreover, X has served as the sole borrower in the group and, as a result, has sustained an overall loss. The XYZ group apportions its interest expense on the basis of the fair market value of its assets. X, Y, and Z have the following assets, interest expense, and taxable income before interest expense:

Assets	X	Y	Z	Total
Domestic	2,000	0	1,000	3,000
Foreign Passive	0	50	50	100
Foreign General	0	700	200	900
Interest Expense	140	0	0	140
Taxable Income (pre-interest):				
Domestic	100	0	100	200
Foreign Passive	0	5	5	10
Foreign General	0	70	35	105

(ii) Step 1: Computation of consolidated taxable income. Each member of the XYZ group apportions its interest expense according to group apportionment ratios determined under the asset method described in § 1.861-9T(g), yielding the following results:

Apportioned interest expense	X	Y	Z	Total
Domestic	105.00	0	0	105.00
Foreign Passive	3.50	0	0	3.50
Foreign General	31.50	0	0	31.50
Total	140.00	0	0	140.00

The members of the group then compute taxable income within each category by deducting the apportioned interest expense from the amounts of pre-interest taxable income specified in the facts in paragraph (i), yielding the following results:

Taxable income	X	Y	Z	Total
Domestic	− 5.00	0	100.00	95.00
Foreign Passive	− 3.50	5.00	5.00	6.50
Foreign General	− 31.50	70.00	35.00	73.50
Total	− 40.00	75.00	140.00	175.00

(iii) Step 2: Loss offset adjustment. Because X has insufficient domestic income to offset the sum of the losses in the foreign limitation categories caused by apportionment, the amount of apportionment losses in each limitation category shall be recharacterized as domestic losses to the extent of taxable income of other members in the same limitation category. This is accomplished by adding to each foreign limitation categories an amount equal to the loss therein and by subtracting the sum of such foreign losses from domestic income, as follows:

Loss offset adjustments	X	Y	Z	Total
Domestic	− 35.00	0	0	− 35.00
Foreign Passive	+3.50	0	0	+3.50
Foreign General	+31.50	0	0	+31.50

These adjustments yield the following adjusted taxable income figures:

Adjusted taxable income	X	Y	Z	Total
Domestic	− 40	0	100	60
Foreign Passive	0	5	5	10
Foreign General	0	70	35	105
Total	− 40	75	140	175

(iv) Step 3: Determination of amount subject to recharacterization. The adjustments performed under Step 2 led to a change in the group's taxable income within each limitation category. The total loss offset adjustment column shown in paragraph (iii) above shows the net deviations between Steps 1 and 2.

(v) Step 4: Recharacterization. The loss offset adjustments yield a positive change in the foreign passive and the foreign general limitation categories. Y and Z both have income in these limitation categories. Accordingly, the income of Y and Z in each of these limitation categories must be reduced on a pro rata basis (by reference to the adjusted taxable income figures) to the extent of the positive change in each limitation category. The total positive change in the foreign passive limitation category is $3.50. The adjusted taxable income of Y in the foreign passive limitation category is $5, and the adjusted taxable income of Z in the foreign passive limitation category is $5. Therefore, $1.75 is drawn from Y and $1.75 is drawn from Z. The total positive change in the foreign general limitation category is $70, and the adjusted taxable income of Z in the foreign general limitation category is $35. Therefore, $21 is drawn from Y and $10.50 is drawn from Z. The members must then separately compute the sum of the limitation reductions. Y has limitation reductions of $1.75 in the foreign passive limitation category and $21 in the foreign general limitation category, yielding total limitation reductions of $22.75. Under these facts, domestic income is the only limitation category requiring a positive adjustment. Accordingly, Y's domestic income is increased by $22.75. Z has limitation reductions of $1.75 in the foreign passive limitation category and $10.50 in the foreign general limitation category, yielding total limitation reductions of $12.25. Under these facts, domestic income is the only limitation category requiring a positive adjustment. Accordingly, Z's domestic income is increased by $12.25.

Recharacterization adjustments	X	Y	Z	Total
Domestic	0	+ 22.75	+ 12.25	+ 35.00
Foreign Passive	0	− 1.75	− 1.75	− 3.50
Foreign General	0	− 21.00	− 10.50	− 31.50

These recharacterization adjustments yield the following final taxable income figures:

Final taxable income	X	Y	Z	Total
Domestic	− 40.00	22.75	112.25	95.00
Foreign Passive	0	3.25	3.25	6.50
Foreign General	0	49.00	24.50	73.50
Total	− 40.00	75.00	140.00	175.00

T.D. 8228, 9/9/88, amend T.D. 8916, 12/17/2000.

PAR. 3. In § 1.861-12, paragraph (c) is revised to read as follows:

Proposed § 1.861-12 Characterization rules and adjustments for certain assets. [*For Preamble, see ¶ 152,753*]

* * * * *

(c) [The text of proposed § 1.861-12(c) is the same as the text of § 1.861-12T(c) published elsewhere in this issue of the Federal Register.] [*See T.D. 9260, 04/24/2006, 71 Fed. Reg. 79.*]

* * * * *

§ 1.861-12T Characterization rules and adjustments for certain assets (Temporary regulations.)

(a) In general. These rules are applicable to taxpayers in apportioning expenses under an asset method to income in various separate limitation categories under section 904(d), and supplement other rules provided in §§ 1.861-9T, 1.861-10T, and 1.861-11T. The rules of this section apply to taxable years beginning after December 31, 1986, except as otherwise provided in § 1.861-13T. Paragraph (b) of this section describes the treatment of inventories. Paragraph (c)(1) of this section concerns the treatment of various stock assets. Paragraph (c)(2) of this section describes a basis adjustment for stock in nonaffiliated 10 percent owned corporations. Paragraph (c)(3) of this section sets forth rules for characterizing the stock in controlled foreign corporations. Paragraph (c)(4) of this section describes the treatment of stock of noncontrolled section 902 corporations. Paragraph (d)(1) of this section concerns the treatment of notes. Paragraph (d)(2) of this section concerns the treatment of the notes of controlled foreign corporations. Paragraph (e) of this section describes the treatment of certain portfolio securities that constitute inventory or generate income primarily in the form of gains. Paragraph (f) of this section describes the treatment of assets that are subject to the capitalization rules of section 263A. Paragraph (g) of this section concerns the treatment of FSC stock and of assets of the related supplier generating foreign trade income. Paragraph (h) of this section concerns the treatment of DISC stock and of assets of the related supplier generating qualified export receipts. Paragraph (i) of this section is reserved. Paragraph (j) of this section sets forth an example illustrating the rules of this section, as well as the rules of § 1.861-9T(g).

(b) Inventories. Inventory must be characterized by reference to the source and character of sales income, or sales receipts in the case of LIFO inventory, from that inventory during the taxable year. If a taxpayer maintains separate inventories for any federal tax purpose, including the rules for establishing pools of inventory items under sections 472 and 474 of the Code, each separate inventory shall be separately characterized in accordance with the previous sentence.

(c) Treatment of stock. *(1) In general.* Subject to the adjustment and special rules of paragraphs (c) and (e) of this section, stock in a corporation is taken into account in the application of the asset method described in § 1.861-9T(g). However, an affiliated group (as defined in § 1.861-11T(d)) does not take into account the stock of any member in the application of the asset method.

(2) Basis adjustment for stock in nonaffiliated 10 percent owned corporations. (i) Taxpayers using the tax book value method. For purposes of apportioning expenses on the basis of the tax book value of assets, the adjusted basis of any stock in a 10 percent owned corporation owned by the taxpayer either directly or, for taxable years beginning after April 25, 2006, indirectly through a partnership or other pass-through entity shall be—

(A) Increased by the amount of the earnings and profits of such corporation (and of lower-tier 10 percent owned corporations) attributable to such stock and accumulated during the period the taxpayer or other members of its affiliated group held 10 percent or more of such stock, or

(B) Reduced (but not below zero) by any deficit in earnings and profits of such corporation (and of lower-tier 10 percent owned corporations) attributable to such stock for such period.

Solely for purposes of this section, a taxpayer's basis in the stock of a controlled foreign corporation shall not include any amount included in basis under section 961 or 1293(d) of the Code. For purposes of this paragraph (c)(2), earnings and profits and deficits are computed under the rules of section 312 and, in the case of a foreign corporation, section 902 and the regulations thereunder for taxable years of the 10 percent owned corporation ending on or before the close of the taxable year of the taxpayer. The rules of section 1248 and the regulations thereunder shall apply to determine the amount of earnings and profits that is attributable to stock without regard to whether earned and profits (or deficits) were derived (or incurred) during taxable years beginning before or after December 31, 1962. This adjustment is to be made annually and is noncumulative. Thus, the adjusted basis of the stock (determined without prior years' adjustments under this section) is to be adjusted annually by the amount of accumulated earnings and profits (or any deficit) attributable to such stock as of the end of each year. Earnings and profits or deficits of a qualified business unit that has a functional currency other than the dollar must be computed under this paragraph (c)(2) in functional currency and translated into dollars using the exchange rate at the end of the taxpayer's current taxable year with respect to which interest is being allocated (and not the exchange rates for the years in which the earnings and profits or deficits were derived or incurred).

(ii) 10 percent owned corporation defined. (A) In general. The term "10 percent owned corporation" means any corporation (domestic or foreign)—

(1) Which is not included within the taxpayer's affiliated group as defined in § 1.861-11T(d)(1) or (6).

(2) In which the members of the taxpayer's affiliated group own directly or indirectly 10 percent or more of the total combined voting power of all classes of the stock entitled to vote, and

(3) Which is taken into account for purposes of apportionment.

(B) Rule of attribution. Stock that is owned by a corporation, partnership, or trust shall be treated as being indirectly owned proportionately by its shareholders, partners, or beneficiaries. For this purpose, a partner's interest in stock held by a partnership shall be determined by reference to the partner's distributive share of partnership income.

(iii) Earnings and profits of lower-tier corporations taken into account. For purposes of the adjustment to the basis of the stock of the 10 percent owned corporation owned by the taxpayer under paragraph (c)(2)(i) of this section, the earnings and profits of that corporation shall include its pro rata share of the earnings and profits (or any deficit therein) of each succeeding lower-tier 10 percent owned corporation. Thus, a first-tier 10 percent owned corporation shall combine with its own earnings and profits its pro rata share of the earnings and profits of all such lower-tier corporations. The affiliated group shall then adjust its basis in the stock of the first-tier corporation by its pro rata share of the total combined earnings and profits of the first-tier and the lower-tier corporations. In the case of a 10 percent owned corporation whose tax year does not conform to that of the taxpayer, the taxpayer shall include the annual earnings and profits of such 10 percent owned corporation for the tax year ending within the tax year of the taxpayer, whether or not such 10 percent owned corporation is owned directly by the taxpayer.

(iv) Special rules for foreign corporations in pre-effective date tax years. Solely for purposes of determining the adjustment required under paragraph (c)(2)(i) of this section, for tax years beginning after 1912 and before 1987, financial earnings (or losses) of a foreign corporation computed using United States generally accepted accounting principles may be substituted for earnings and profits in making the adjustment required by paragraph (c)(2)(i) of this section. A taxpayer is not required to isolate the financial earnings of a foreign corporation derived or incurred during its period of 10 percent ownership or during the post-1912 taxable years and determine earnings and profits (or deficits) attributable under section 1248 principles to the taxpayer's stock in a 10 percent owned corporation. Instead, the taxpayer may include all historic financial earnings for purposes of this adjustment. If the affiliated group elects to use financial earnings with respect to any foreign corporation, financial earnings must be used by that group with respect to all foreign corporations, except that earnings and profits may in any event be used for controlled foreign corporations for taxable years beginning after 1962 and before 1987. However, if the affiliated group elects to use earnings and profits with respect to any single controlled foreign corporation for the 1963 through 1986 period, such election shall apply with respect to all its controlled foreign corporations.

(v) Taxpayers using the fair market value method. Because the fair market value of any asset which is stock will reflect retained earnings and profits, taxpayers who use the fair market value method shall not adjust stock basis by the amount of retained earnings and profits, as otherwise required by paragraph (c)(2)(i) of this section.

(vi) Examples. Certain of the rules of this paragraph (c)(2) may be illustrated by the following examples.

Example (1). X, an affiliated group that uses the tax book value method of apportionment, owns 20 percent of the stock of Y, which owns 50 percent of the stock of Z. X's basis in the Y stock is $1,000. X, Y, and Z have calendar taxable years. The undistributed earnings and profits of Y and Z at year-end attributable to X's period of ownership are $80 and $40, respectively. Because Y owns half of the Z stock, X's pro rata share of Z's earnings attributable to X's Y stock is $16. For purposes of apportionment, the tax book value of the Y stock is, therefore, considered $16. For purposes of apportionment, the tax book value of the Y stock is, therefore, considered to be $1,020.

Example (2). X, an unaffiliated domestic corporation that was organized on January 1, 1987, has owned all the stock of Y, a foreign corporation with a functional currency other than the U.S. dollar, since January 1, 1987. Both X and Y have calendar taxable years. All of Y's assets generate general limitation income. X has a deductible interest expense incurred in 1987 of $160,000. X apportions its interest expense using the tax book value method. The adjusted basis of its assets that generate domestic income is $7,500,000. The adjusted basis of its assets that generate foreign source general limitation income (other than the stock of Y) is $400,000. X's adjusted basis in the Y stock is $2,000,000. Y has undistributed earnings and profits for 1987 of $100,000, translated into dollars from Y's functional currency at the exchange rate on the last day of X's taxable year. Because X is required under paragraph (b)(1) of this § 1.861-10T to increase its basis in the Y stock by the computed amount of earnings and profits, X's adjusted basis in the Y stock is considered to be $2,100,000, and its adjusted basis of assets that generate foreign source general limitation income is, thus, considered to be $2,500,000. X would apportion its interest expense as follows:

To foreign source general limitation income:

$$\text{Interest expense} \times \frac{\text{Adjusted basis of foreign general limitation assets}}{\text{Adjusted basis of foreign general limitation assets} + \text{Adjusted basis of domestic assets}}$$

$$\$160{,}000 \times \frac{\$2{,}500{,}000}{\$2{,}500{,}000 + \$7{,}500{,}000} = \$40{,}000$$

To domestic source income:

$$\text{Interest expense} \times \frac{\text{Adjusted basis of domestic assets}}{\text{Adjusted basis of foreign general limitation assets} + \text{Adjusted basis of domestic assets}}$$

$$\$160{,}000 \times \frac{\$7{,}500{,}000}{\$2{,}500{,}000 + \$7{,}500{,}000} = \$120{,}000$$

(3) Characterization of stock of controlled foreign corporations. (i) In general. Stock in a controlled foreign corporation (as defined in section 957) shall be characterized as an asset in the various separate limitation categories either on the basis of:

(A) The asset method described in paragraph (c)(3)(ii) of this section, or

(B) The modified gross income method described in paragraph (c)(3)(iii) of this section.

Stock in a controlled foreign corporation whose interest expense is apportioned on the basis of assets shall be characterized in the hands of its United States shareholders under the asset method described in paragraph (c)(3)(ii). Stock in a controlled foreign corporation whose interest expense is apportioned on the basis of gross income shall be characterized in the hands of its United States shareholders under the gross income method described in paragraph (c)(3)(iii).

(ii) Asset method. Under the asset method, the taxpayer characterizes the tax book value or fair market value of the stock of a controlled foreign corporation based on an analysis of the assets owned by the controlled foreign corporation during the foreign corporation's taxable year that ends with or within the taxpayer's taxable year. This process is based on the application of § 1.861-9T(g) at the level of the controlled foreign corporation. In the case of a controlled foreign corporation that owns stock in one or more lower-tier controlled foreign corporations in which the United States taxpayer is a United States shareholder, the characterization of the tax book value of the fair market value of the stock of the first-tier controlled foreign corporation to the various separate limitation categories of the affiliated group must take into account the stock in lower-tier corporations. For this purpose, the stock of each such lower-tier corporation shall be characterized by reference to the assets owned during the lower-tier corporation's taxable year that ends during the taxpayer's taxable year. The analysis of assets within a chain of controlled foreign corporations must begin at the lowest-tier controlled foreign corporation and proceed up the chain to the first-tier controlled foreign corporation. For purposes of this paragraph (c), the value of any passive asset to which related person interest is allocated under § 1.904-5(c)(2)(ii) must be reduced by the principal amount of indebtedness on which such interest is incurred. Furthermore, the value of any asset to which interest expense is directly allocated under § 1.861-10T must be reduced as provided in § 1.861-9T(g)(2)(iii). See § 1.861-9T(h)(5) for further guidance concerning characterization of stock in a related person under the fair market value method.

(iii) Modified gross income method. Under the gross income method, the taxpayer characterizes the tax book value of the stock of the first-tier controlled foreign corporation based on the gross income net of interest expense of the controlled foreign corporation (as computed under § 1.861-9T(j)) within each relevant category for the taxable year of the controlled foreign corporation ending with or within the taxable year of the taxpayer. For this purpose, however, the gross income of the first-tier controlled foreign corporation shall include the total amount of net subpart F income of any lower-tier controlled foreign corporation that was excluded under the rules of § 1.861-9T(j)(2)(ii)(B).

(4) Characterization of stock of noncontrolled section 902 corporations. (i) General rule. The principles of paragraph (c)(3) of this section shall apply to stock in a noncontrolled section 902 corporation (as defined in section 904(d)(2)(E)). Accordingly, stock in a noncontrolled section 902 corporation shall be characterized as an asset in the various separate limitation categories on the basis of either the asset method described in (c)(3)(ii) of this section or the modified gross income method described in (c)(3)(iii) of this section. Stock in a noncontrolled section 902 corporation the interest expense of which is apportioned on the basis of assets shall be characterized in the hands of its domestic shareholders (as defined in § 1.902-1(a)(1)) under the asset method described in paragraph (c)(3)(ii). Stock in a noncontrolled section 902 corporation the interest expense of which is apportioned on the basis of gross income shall be characterized in the hands of its domestic shareholders under the gross income method described in paragraph (c)(3)(iii).

(ii) Nonqualifying shareholders. Stock in a noncontrolled section 902 corporation shall be characterized as a passive category asset in the hands of a shareholder that is not eligible to compute an amount of foreign taxes deemed paid with respect to a dividend from the noncontrolled section 902 corporation for the taxable year, and in the hands of any shareholder with respect to whom look-through treatment is not substantiated. See § 1.904-5T(c)(4)(iii).

(iii) Effective date. This paragraph (c)(4) applies for taxable years of shareholders ending after the first day of the first taxable year of the noncontrolled section 902 corporation beginning after December 31, 2002.

(d) Treatment of notes. *(1) General rule.* Subject to the adjustments and special rules of this paragraph (d) and paragraph (e) of this section, all notes held by a taxpayer are taken into account in the application of the asset method described in § 1.861-9T(g). However, the notes of an affiliated corporation are subject to special rules set forth in § 1.861-11T(e). For purposes of this section, the term "notes" means all interest bearing debt, including debt bearing original issue discount.

(2) Characterization of related controlled foreign corporation notes. The debt of a controlled foreign corporation shall be characterized according to the taxpayer's treatment of the interest income derived from that debt obligation after application of the look-through rule of section 904(d)(3)(C). Thus, a United States shareholder includes interest income from a controlled foreign corporation in the same category of income as the category of income from which the controlled foreign corporation deducts the interest expense. See

section 954(b)(5) and § 1.904-5(c)(2) for rules concerning the allocation of related person interest payments to the foreign personal holding company income of a controlled foreign corporation.

(e) Portfolio securities that constitute inventory or generate primarily gains. Because gain on the sale of securities is sourced by reference to the residence of the seller, a resident of the United States will generally receive domestic source income (and a foreign resident will generally receive foreign source income) upon sale or disposition of securities that otherwise generate foreign source dividends and interest (or domestic source dividends and interest in the case of a foreign resident). Although under paragraphs (c) and (d) of this section securities are characterized by reference to the source and character of dividends and interest, the source and character of income on gain or disposition must also be taken into account for purposes of characterizing portfolio securities if:

(1) The securities constitute inventory in the hands of the holder, or

(2) 80 percent or more of the gross income generated by a taxpayer's entire portfolio of such securities during a taxable year consists of gains. For this purpose, a portfolio security is a security in any entity other than a controlled foreign corporation with respect to which the taxpayer is a United States shareholder under section 957, a noncontrolled section 902 corporation with respect to the taxpayer, or a 10 percent owned corporation as defined in § 1.861-12(c)(2)(ii). In taking gains into account, a taxpayer must treat all portfolio securities generating foreign source dividends and interest as a single asset and all portfolio securities generating domestic source dividends as a single asset and shall characterize the total value of that asset based on the source of all income and gain generated by those securities in the taxable year.

(f) Assets funded by disallowed interest. *(1) Rule.* In the case of any asset in connection with which interest expense accruing at the end of the taxable year is capitalized, deferred, or disallowed under any provision of the Code, the adjusted basis or fair market value (depending on the taxpayer's choice of apportionment methods) of such an asset shall be reduced by the principal amount of indebtedness the interest on which is so capitalized, deferred, or disallowed.

(2) Example. The rules of this paragraph (f) may be illustrated by the following example.

Example. X is a domestic corporation which uses the tax book value method of apportionment. X has $1000 of indebtedness and $100 of interest expense. X constructs an asset with an adjusted basis of $800 before interest capitalization and is required under the rules of section 263A to capitalize $80 in interest expense. Because interest on $800 of debt is capitalized and because the production period is in progress at the end of X's taxable year, $800 of the principal amount of X's debt is allocable to the building. The $800 of debt allocable to the building. The $800 of debt allocable to the building reduces its adjusted basis for purposes of apportioning the balance of X's interest expense ($20).

(g) Special rules for FSCs. *(1) Treatment of FSC stock.* No interest expense shall be allocated or apportioned to stock of a foreign sales corporation (" FSC") to the extent that the FSC stock is attributable to the separate limitation for certain FSC distributions described in section 904(d)(1)(H). FSC stock is considered to be attributable solely to the separate limitation category described in section 904(d)(1)(H) unless the taxpayer can demonstrate that more than 20 percent of the FSC's gross income for the taxable year consists of income other than foreign trading income.

(2) Treatment of assets that generate foreign trade income. Assets of the related supplier that generate foreign trade income must be prorated between assets attributable to foreign source general limitation income and assets attributable to domestic source income in proportion to foreign source general limitation income and domestic source income derived from transactions generating foreign trade income.

(i) Value of assets attributable to foreign source income. The value of assets attributable to foreign source general limitation income is computed by multiplying the value of assets for the taxable year generating foreign trading gross receipts by a fraction:

(A) The numerator of which is foreign source general limitation income for the taxable year derived from transactions giving rise to foreign trading gross receipts, after the application of the limitation provided in section 927(e)(1), and

(B) The denominator of which is total income for the taxable year derived from the transaction giving rise to foreign trading gross receipts.

(ii) Value of assets attributable to domestic source income. The value of assets attributable to domestic source income is computed by subtracting from the total value of assets for the taxable year generating foreign trading gross receipts the value of assets attributable to foreign source general limitation income as computed under paragraph (g)(2)(i) of this section.

(h) Special rules for DISCs. *(1) Treatment of DISC stock.* No interest shall be allocated or apportioned to stock in a DISC (or stock in a former DISC to the extent that the stock in the former DISC is attributable to the separate limitation category described in section 904(d)(1)(F)).

(2) Treatment of assets that generate qualified export receipts. Assets of the related supplier that generate qualified export receipts must be prorated between assets attributable to foreign source general limitation income and assets attributable to domestic source income in proportion to foreign source general limitation income and domestic source income derived from transactions during the taxable year from transactions generating qualified export receipts.

(i) [Reserved.]

(j) Examples. Certain of the rules in this section and §§ 1.861-9T(g) and 1.861-10(e) are illustrated by the following example.

Example (1). (1) Facts. X, a domestic corporation organized on January 1, 1987, has a calendar taxable year and apportions its interest expense on the basis of the tax book value of its assets. In 1987, X incurred a deductible third-party interest expense of $100,000 on an average month-end debt amount of $1 million. The total tax book value of X's assets (adjusted as required under paragraph (b) of this section for retained earnings and profits) is $2 million. X manufactures widgets. One-half of the widgets are sold in the United States and one-half are exported and sold through a foreign branch with title passing outside the United States. X owns all the stock of Y, a controlled foreign corporation that also has a calendar taxable year and is also engaged in the manufacture and sale of widgets. Y has no earnings and profits or deficits in earnings and profits prior to 1987. For 1987, Y has taxable income and earnings and profits of $50,000 before the deductible for related person interest expense. Half of the $50,000 is foreign source personal holding company income and the other half is derived from widget sales and constitutes foreign source general limitation income. Assume that Y has no deductibles from gross income other than interest expense. Y's foreign personal holding company taxable income is included in X's gross income under section 951. Y paid no dividends in 1987. Prior to 1987, Y did not borrow any funds from X. The average month-end level of borrowings by Y from X in 1987 is $100,000, on which Y paid a total of $10,000 in interest. The total tax book value of Y's assets in 1987 is $500,000. Y has no liabilities to third parties. X elects pursuant to § 1.861-9T for Y to apportion Y's interest expense under the gross income method prescribed in § 1.861-9T(g).

In addition to its stock in Y, X owns 20 percent of the stock of Z, a noncontrolled section 902 corporation.

X's total assets and their tax book values are:

Asset	Tax book value
Plant & equipment	$1,000,000
Corporate headquarters	500,000
Inventory	200,000
Automobiles	20,000
Patents	50,000
Trademarks	10,000
Y stock (including paragraph (c)(2) adjustment)	80,000
Y note	100,000
Z stock	40,000

(2) Categorization of Assets. Single Category Assets

1. Automobiles: X's automobiles are used exclusively by its domestic sales force in the generation of United States source income. Thus, these assets are attributable solely to the grouping of domestic income.

2. Y Note: Under paragraph (d)(2) of this section, the Y note in the hands of X is characterized according to X's treatment of the interest income received on the Y note. In determining the source and character of the interest income on the Y note, the look-through rules of sections 904(d)(3)(C) and 904(g) apply. Under section 954(b)(5) and § 1.904-5(c)(2)(ii), Y's $10,000 interest payment to X is allocated directly to, and thus reduces, Y's foreign personal holding company income of $25,000 (yielding foreign personal holding company taxable income of $15,000). Therefore, the Y note is attributable solely to the statutory grouping of foreign source passive income.

3. Z stock: Because Z is a noncontrolled section 902 corporation, the dividends paid by Z are subject to a separate limitation under section 904(d)(1)(E). Thus, this asset is attributable solely to the statutory grouping consisting of Z dividends.

Multiple Category Assets

1. Plant & equipment, inventory, patents, and trademarks: In 1987, X sold half its widgets in the United States and exported half outside the United States. A portion of the taxable income from export sales will be foreign source income, since the export sales were accomplished through a foreign branch and title passed outside the United States. Thus, these assets are attributable both to the statutory grouping of foreign general limitation and the grouping of domestic income.

2. Y Stock: Since Y's interest expense is apportioned under the gross income method prescribed in § 1.861-9T(j), the Y stock must be characterized under the gross income method described in paragraph (c)(3)(iii) of this section.

Assets without Directly Identifiable Yield

1. Corporate headquarters: This asset generates no directly identifiable income yield. The value of the asset is disregarded.

(3) Analysis of Income Yield for Multiple Category Assets.

1. Plant & Equipment, inventory, patents, and trademarks: As noted above, X's 1987 widget sales were half domestic and half foreign. Assume that Example 2 of § 1.863-3(b)(2) applies in sourcing the export income from the export sales. Under Example 2, the income generated by the export sales is sourced half domestic and half foreign. The income generated by the domestic sales is entirely domestic source. Accordingly, three-quarters of the income generated on all sales is domestic source and one-quarter of the income is foreign source. Thus, three-quarters of the fair market value of these assets are attributed to the grouping of domestic source income and one-quarter of the fair market value of these assets is attributed to the statutory grouping of foreign source general limitation income.

2. Y Stock: Under the gross income method described in paragraph (c)(3)(iii) of this section, Y's gross income net of interest expenses in each limitation category must be determined— $25,000 foreign source general limitatión income and $15,000 of foreign source passive income. Of X's adjusted basis of $80,000 in Y stock, $50,000 is attributable to foreign source general limitation income and $30,000 is attributable to foreign source passive income.

(4) Application of the Special Allocation Rule of § 1.861-10T(e). Assume that the taxable year in question is 1990 and that the applicable percentage prescribed by § 1.861-10T(e)(1)(iv)(A) is 80 percent. Assume that X has elected to use the quadratic formula provided in § 1.861-10T(e)(1)(iv)(B).

Step 1. X's average month-end level of debt owning to unrelated persons is $1 million. The tax book value of X's assets is $2 million. Thus, X's debt-to-asset ratio computed under § 1.861-10T(e)(1)(i) is 1 to 2.

Step 2. The tax book value of Y's assets is $500,000. Because Y has no debt to persons other than X, Y's debt-to-asset ratio computed under § 1.861-10T(e)(1)(ii) is $0 to $500,000.

Step 3. Y's average month-end liabilities to X, as computed under § 1.861-10T(e)(1)(iii) for 1987 are $100,000.

Step 4. Adding the $100,000 of Y's liabilities owed to X as computed under Step 3 to Y's third party liabilities ($0) would be insufficient to make Y's debt-to-asset ratio computed in Step 2 ($100,000-to-$500,000, or 1:5) equal to at least 80 percent of X's debt-to-asset ratio computed under Step 1, as adjusted to reflect a reduction in X's debt and assets by the $100,000 of excess related person indebtedness (.80 × $900,000/$1,900,000 or 1:2.6). Therefore, the entire amount of Y's liabilities to X ($100,000) constitute excess related person indebtedness under § 1.861-10T(e)(1)(ii). Thus, the entire $10,000 of interest received by X from Y during 1987 constitutes interest received on excess related person indebtedness.

Step 5. The Y note held by X has a tax book value of $100,000. Solely for purposes of § 1.861-10(e)(1)(v), the Y note is attributed to separate limitation categories in the same manner as the Y stock. Under paragraph (c)(3)(iii) of this section, of the $80,000 of Y stock held by X, $50,000 is attributable to foreign source general limitation income, and $30,000 is attributable to foreign source passive income. Thus, for purposes of $1.861-10T(e)(1)(v), $62,500 of the $100,000 Y note is considered to be a foreign source general limitation asset and $37,500 of the $100,000 Y note is considered to be a foreign source passive asset.

Step 6. Since $10,000 of related person interest income received by X constitutes interest received on excessive related person indebtedness, $10,000 of X's third party interest expense is allocated to X's debt investment in Y. Under § 1.861-10T(e)(1)(vi), 62.5 percent of the $10,000 of X's third party interest expense ($6,250) is allocated to foreign source general limitation income and 37.5 percent of the $10,000 of X's third party interest expense ($3,750) is allocated to foreign source passive income. As a result of this direct allocation, the value of X's assets generating foreign source general limitation income are reduced by the principal amount of indebtedness the interest on which is directly allocated to foreign source general limitation income ($62,500), and X's assets generating foreign source passive limitation income are reduced by the principal amount of indebtedness the interest on which is directly allocated to foreign passive income ($37,500).

(5) Totals.

Having allocated $10,000 of its third party interest expense to its debt investment in Y, X would apportion the $90,000 balance of its interest according to the following apportionment fractions:

Asset	Domestic source	Foreign general	Foreign passive	Noncontrolled section 902
Plant and equipment	$750,000	$250,000		
Inventory	$150,000	$50,000		
Automobiles	$20,000			
Patents	$37,500	$12,500		
Trademarks	$7,500	$2,500		
Y stock		$50,000	$30,000	
Y note			$100,000	
Z stock				$40,000
Totals	$965,000	$365,000	$130,000	$40,000
Adjustments for directly allocable interest		($62,500)	($37,500)	
Adjusted totals	$965,000	$302,500	$92,500	$40,000
Percentage	69	22	6	3

Example (2). Assume the same facts as in Example 1, except that Y has $100,000 of third party indebtedness. Further, assume for purposes of the application of the special allocation rule of § 1.861-10T(e) that the taxable year is 1990 and that the applicable percentage prescribed by § 1.861-10T(e)(1)(iv)(A) is 80 percent. The application of the § 1.861-10(e) would be modified as follows.

Step 1. X's debt-to-asset ratio computed under § 1.861-10T(e)(1)(i) remains 1 to 2 (or 0.5).

Step 2. The tax book value of Y's assets is $500,000. Y has $100,000 of indebtedness to third parties. Y's debt-to-asset ratio computed under § 1.861-10T(e)(1)(ii) is $100,000 to $500,000 (1:5 or 0.2).

Step 3. Y's average month-end liabilities to X, as computed under § 1.861-10T(e)(1)(iii) remain $100,000.

Step 4. X's debt-to-asset ratio is 0.5 and 80 percent of 0.5 is 0.4. Because Y's debt-to-asset ratio is 0.2, there is excess related person indebtedness, the amount of which can be computed based on the following formula:

$$\frac{\text{Aggregate third party debt of related U.S. shareholder} - X}{\text{U.S. shareholder assets} - X} \times \text{Applicable percentage for year (0.8)} = \frac{\text{Aggregate third party debt of related CFCs} + X}{\text{Related CFC assets}}$$

Supplying the facts as given, this equation is as follows:

$$\frac{1{,}000{,}000 - X}{2{,}000{,}000 - X} \times .8 = \frac{100{,}000 + X}{500{,}000}$$

Multiplying both sides by 500,000 and (2,000,000 − X), yielding:

$$4 \times 10^{11} - 400{,}000X = 2 \times 10^{11} + 2{,}000{,}000X - 100{,}000X - X^2$$

$$X^2 + (-2{,}300{,}000)X + (2 \times 10^{11}) = 0$$

Apply the quadratic formula:

$$X = \frac{-b \pm \sqrt{b^2 - 4(a)(c)}}{2(a)}$$

Since there is an X^2 in this equation, a quadratic formula must be utilized to solve for X. Group the components in this equation, segregating the X and the X^2.

a = 1 (coefficient of X^2)

b = − 2,300,000 (coefficient of X)

c = 2×10^{11} (remaining element of equation)

Therefore, X equals either 90,519 or (2.21×10^{11}). For purposes of computing excess related person indebtedness, X is the lowest positive amount derived from this equation, which is 90,519.

Steps 5 and 6 are unchanged from Example 1, except that the total amount of interest on excess related party indebtedness is $9,051.

T.D. 8228, 9/9/88, amend T.D. 9260, 4/24/2006.

§ 1.861-13T Transition rules for interest expenses (temporary regulations).

• *Caution:* Under Code Sec. 7805, temporary regulations expire within three years of the date of issuance. This temporary regulation was issued on 8/1/89.

(a) In general. *(1) Optional application.* The rules of this section may be applied at the choice of a corporate taxpayer. In the case of an affiliated group, however, the choice must be made on a consistent basis for all members. Therefore, a corporate taxpayer (or affiliated group) may allocate and apportion its interest expense entirely on the basis of the rules contained in §§ 1.861-8T through 1.861-12T and without regard to the rules of this section. The choice is made on an annual basis and, thus, is not binding with respect to subsequent tax years.

(2) Transition relief. This section contains transitional rules that limit the application of the rules for allocating and apportioning interest expense of corporate taxpayers contained in §§ 1.861-8T through 1.861-12T, which are applicable in allocating and apportioning the interest expense of corporate taxpayers generally for taxable years beginning after 1986. Sections 1.861-9(d) (relating to individuals, estates, and certain trusts) and 1.861-9(e) (relating to partnerships) are effective for taxable years beginning after 1986. Thus, the taxpayers to whom those sections apply do not qualify for transition relief under this section.

(3) Indebtedness defined. For purposes of this section, the term "indebtedness" means any obligation or other evidence of indebtedness that generates an expense that constitutes interest expense within the meaning of § 1.861-9T(a). In the case of an obligation that does not bear interest initially, but becomes interest bearing with the lapse of time or upon the occurrence of an event, such obligation shall only be considered to constitute indebtedness when it first bears interest. Obligations that are outstanding as of November 16, 1985 shall only qualify for transition relief under this section if they bear interest-bearing as of that date. For this purpose, any obligation that has original issue discount within the meaning of section 1273(a)(1) of the Code shall be considered to be interest-bearing.

(4) Exceptions. The term "indebtedness" shall not include any obligation existing between affiliated corporations, as defined in § 1.861-11T(d). Moreover, the term "indebtedness" shall not include any obligation the interest on which is directly allocable under §§ 1.861-10T(b) and 1.861-10T(c). Under § 1.861-9T(b)(6)(iv)(B), certain interest expense is directly allocated to the gain derived from an appropriately identified financial product. When interest expense on a liability is reduced by such gain, the principal amount of such liability shall be reduced pro rata by the relative amount of interest expense that is directly allocated.

(b) General phase-in. *(1) In general.* In the case of each of the first three taxable years of the taxpayer beginning after December 31, 1986, the rules of §§ 1.861-8T through 1.861-12T shall not apply to interest expenses paid or accrued by the taxpayer during the taxable year with respect to an aggregate amount of indebtedness which does not exceed the general phase-in amount, as defined in paragraph (b)(2) of this section.

(2) General phase-in amount defined. Subject to the limitation imposed by paragraph (b)(3) of this section, the general phase-in amount means the amount which is the applicable percentage (determined under the following table) of the aggregate amount of indebtedness of the taxpayer outstanding on November 16, 1985:

Taxable year beginning after December 31, 1986	Percentage
First	75
Second	50
Third	25

(3) Reductions in indebtedness. The general phase-in amount shall not exceed the taxpayer's historic lowest month-end debt level taking into account all months after October 1985. However, for the taxable year in which a taxpayer attains a new historic lowest month-end debt level (but not for subsequent taxable years), the general phase-in amount shall not exceed the average of month-end debt levels within that taxable year (without taking into account any increase in month-end debt levels occurring in such taxable Year after the new historic lowest month-end debt level is attained).

Example. X is a calendar year taxpayer that had $100 of indebtedness outstanding on November 16, 1985. X's month-end debt level remained $100 for all subsequent months until July 1987, when X's month-end debt level fell to $50. In computing transition relief for 1987, X's general phase-in amount cannot exceed $75 (900 divided by 12), which is the average of month-end debt levels in 1987. Assuming that X's month-end debt level for any subsequent month does not fall below $50, the limitation on its general phase-in amount for all taxable years after 1987 will be $50, its historic lowest month-end debt level after October 1985.

(c) Nonapplication of the consolidation rule. *(1) General rule.* In the case of each of the first five taxable years of the taxpayer beginning after December 31, 1986, the consolidation rule contained in § 1.861-11T(c) shall not apply to interest expenses paid or accrued by the taxpayer during the taxable year with respect to an aggregate amount of indebtedness which does not exceed the special phase-in amount, as defined in paragraph (c)(2) of this section.

(2) Special phase-in amount. The special phase-in amount is the sum of—

(i) The general phase-in amount,

(ii) The five-year phase-in amount, and

(iii) The four-year phase-in amount.

(3) Five-year phase-in amount. The five-year phase-in amount is the lesser of—

(i) The applicable percentage (the "unreduced percentage" in the following table) of the five-year debt amount, or

(ii) The applicable percentage (the "reduced percentage" in the following table) of the five-year debt amount reduced by paydowns (if any):

Transition year	Unreduced percentage	Reduced percentage
Year 1	8⅓	10
Year 2	16⅔	25
Year 3	25	50
Year 4	33⅓	100
Year 5	16⅔	100

(4) Four-year phase-in amount. The four-year phase-in amount is the lesser of—

(i) The applicable percentage (the "unreduced percentage" in the following table) of the four-year debt amount, or

(ii) The applicable percentage (the "reduced percentage" in the following table) of the four-year debt amount reduced by paydowns (if any) to the extent that such paydowns exceed the five-year debt amount:

Transition year	Unreduced percentage	Reduced percentage
Year 1	5	6¼
Year 2	10	16⅔
Year 3	15	37½
Year 4	20	100

(5) Five-year debt amount. The "five-year debt amount" means the excess (if any) of—

(i) The amount of the outstanding indebtedness of the taxpayer on May 29, 1985, over

(ii) The amount of the outstanding indebtedness of the taxpayer on December 31, 1983. The five-year debt amount shall not exceed the aggregate amount of indebtedness of the taxpayer outstanding on November 16, 1985.

(6) Four-year debt amount. The "four-year debt amount" means the excess (if any) of—

(i) The amount of the outstanding indebtedness of the taxpayer on December 31, 1983, over

(ii) The amount of the outstanding indebtedness of the taxpayer on December 31, 1982. The four-year debt amount shall not exceed the aggregate amount of indebtedness of the taxpayer outstanding on November 16, 1985, reduced by the five-year debt amount.

(7) Paydowns. The term "paydowns" means the excess (if any) of—

(i) The aggregate amount of indebtedness of the taxpayer outstanding on November 16, 1985, over

(ii) The limitation on the general phase-in amount described in paragraph (b)(3) of this section.

Paydowns are first applied to the five-year debt amount to the extent thereof and then to the four-year debt amount for purposes of computing the five-year and the four-year phase-in amounts.

(d) Treatment of affiliated group. For purposes of this section, all members of the same affiliated group of corporations (as defined in § 1.861-11(d)) shall be treated as one taxpayer whether or not such members filed a consolidated return. Interaffiliate debt is not taken into account in computing transition relief. Moreover, any reduction in the amount of interaffiliate debt is not taken into account in determining the amount of paydowns.

(e) Mechanics of computation. *(1) Step 1: Determination of the amounts within the various categories of debt.* Each separate member of an affiliated group must determine each of its following amounts:

(i) November 16, 1985 amount. The amount of its debt outstanding on November 16, 1985 (after the elimination of interaffiliate indebtedness),

(ii) Unreduced five-year debt. The amount of any net increase in the amount of its indebtedness on May 29, 1985 (after elimination of interaffiliate indebtedness) over the amount of its indebtedness on December 31, 1983 (after elimination of interaffiliate indebtedness),

(iii) Unreduced four-year debt. The amount of any net increase in the amount of its indebtedness on December 31, 1983 (after elimination of interaffiliate indebtedness) over the amount of its indebtedness on December 31, 1982 (after elimination of interaffiliate indebtedness), and

(iv) Month-end debt. The amount of its month-end debt level for all months after October 1985 (after elimination of interaffiliate indebtedness).

(2) Step 2: Aggregation of the separate company amounts. Each of the designated amounts for the separate companies identified in Step 1 must be aggregated in order to compute consolidated transition relief. Paragraph (e)(10)(iv) of this section (Step 10) requires the use of the taxpayer's current year average debt level for the purpose of computing the percentages of debt that are subject to the three sets of rules that are identified in Step 10. For use in that computation, the taxpayer should compute the current year average debt level by aggregating separate company month-end debt levels and then by averaging those aggregate amounts.

(3) Step 3: Calculation of the lowest historic month-end debt level of the taxpayer. In order to calculate the lowest historic month-end debt level of the taxpayer, determine the month-end debt level of each separate company for each month ending after October 1985 and aggregate these amounts on a month-by-month basis. On such aggregate basis, in any taxable year in which the taxpayer attains an aggregate new lowest historic month-end debt level, add together all the aggregate month-end debt levels within the taxable year (without taking into account any increase in aggregate debt level subsequent to the attainment of such lowest historic month-end debt level) and divide by the number of months in that taxable year, yielding the average of month-end debt levels for such year. Such average shall constitute the taxpayer's lowest historic month-end debt level for that taxable year in which the aggregate new lowest historic month-end debt level was attained. Unless otherwise specified, all subsequent references to any amount refer to the aggregate amount for all members of the same affiliated group of corporations.

(4) Step 4: Computation of paydowns. Paydowns equal the amount by which the November 16, 1985 amount exceeds the taxpayer's lowest historic month-end debt level, determined under Step 3.

(5) Step 5: Computation of limitations on unreduced five-year debt and unreduced four-year debt. (i) The unreduced five-year debt cannot exceed the November 16, 1985 amount.

(ii) The unreduced four-year debt cannot exceed the November 16, 1985 amount less the unreduced five-year debt.

(6) Step 6: Computation of reduced five-year and reduced four-year debt. (i) Reduced five-year debt. Compute the amount of reduced five-year debt by subtracting from the unreduced five-year debt (see Step 5) the amount of paydowns (see Step 4).

(ii) Reduced four-year debt. To the extent that the amount of paydowns (see step 4) exceeds the amount of unreduced five-year debt (see Step 5), compute the amount of reduced four-year debt by subtracting such excess from the unreduced four-year debt (see Step 1).

(iii) To the extent that paydowns do not offset either the unreduced five-year amount or the unreduced four-year amount, the reduced and the unreduced amounts are the same.

(7) Step 7: Computation of the general phase-in amount. The general phase-in amount is the lesser of—

(i) The percentage of the November 16, 1985 amount designated for the relevant transition year in the table below, or

(ii) The lowest group month-end debt level (see Step 3).

General Phase-in Table

Transition year	Percentage
Year 1	75
Year 2	50
Year 3	25

(8) Step 8: Computation of Five-Year Phase-in Amount. The five-year phase-in amount is the lesser of—

(i) The percentage of the unreduced five-year debt designated for the relevant transition year in the table below, or

(ii) The percentage of the reduced five-year debt designated for the relevant transition year in the table below.

Five-Year Phase-In Table

Transition year	Unreduced percentage	Reduced percentage
Year 1	8⅓	10
Year 2	16⅔	25
Year 3	25	50
Year 4	33⅓	100
Year 5	16⅔	100

(9) Step 9: Computation of Four-year Phase-in Amount. The Four-year phase-in amount is the lesser of—

(i) The percentage of the unreduced four-year debt designated for the relevant transition year in the table below, or

(ii) The percentage of the reduced four-year debt designated for the relevant transition year in the table below.

Four-Year Phase-In Table

Transition year	Unreduced percentage	Reduced percentage
Year 1	5	6¼
Year 2	10	16⅔
Year 3	15	37½
Year 4	20	100

(10) Step 10: Determination of group debt ratio and application of transition relief to separate company interest expense. (i) The general phase-in amount consists of the amount computed under Step 7. Interest expense on this amount is subject to pre-1987 rules of allocation and apportionment.

(ii) The post-1986 separate company amount consists of the sum of the amounts determined under Steps 8 and 9. Interest expense on this amount is subject to post-1986 rules of allocation and apportionment as applied on a separate company basis. Thus, § 1.861-11T(c) does not apply with respect to this amount of indebtedness. Because the consolidation rule does not apply, stock in affiliated corporations shall be taken into account in computing the apportionment fractions for each separate company in the same manner as under pre-1987 rules.

(iii) The post-1986 one-taxpayer amount consists of any indebtedness that does not qualify for transition relief under Steps 7, 8, and 9. Interest expense on this amount is subject to post-1986 rules as applied on a consolidated basis.

(iv) To determine the extent to which the interest expense of each separate company is subject to any of these sets of allocation and apportionment rules, each company shall prorate its own interest expense using two fractions. The general phase-in fraction is the general phase-in amount over the current year average debt level of the affiliated group (see Step 2). The post-1986 separate company fraction is the post-1986 separate company amount over the current year average debt level of the affiliated group. The balance of each separate company's interest expense is subject to post-1986 one-taxpayer rules.

(f) Example. XYZ form an affiliate group.

(1) Step 1: Determination of the amounts within the various debt categories.

	Historic 3rd party debt	Increase
Company X:		
Nov. 16, 1985	$100,000	
May 29, 1983 (5-year)	90,000	$ 10,000
Dec. 31, 1983 (4-year)	80,000	10,000
Dec. 31, 1982	70,000	
Current Interest Expense	10,000	
Company Y:		
Nov. 18, 1985	200,000	
May 29, 1985 (5-year)	170,000	120,000
Dec. 31, 1983 (4-year)	50,000	10,000
Dec. 31, 1982	40,000	
Current Interest Expense	30,000	
Company Z:		
Nov. 16, 1985	300,000	
May 29, 1985 (5-year)	300,000	50,000
Dec. 31, 1983 (4-year)	250,000	100,000
Dec. 31, 1982	150,000	
Current Interest Expense	30,000	

(2) Step 2: Aggregation of the separate company amounts.

Aggregate Nov. 16, 1985	$600,000
Aggregate 5-year debt	180,000
Aggregate 4-year debt	120,000
Current year average debt level	700,000

(3) Step 3: Calculation of lowest historic month-end debt level.

An analysis of historic month-end debt levels indicates that in 1986, XYZ's aggregate month-end debt level fell to $500,000, which represents the lowest sum for all years under consideration. Because this historic low occurred in a prior tax year, there is no averaging of month-end debt levels in the current taxable year.

(4) Step 4: Computation of paydowns.

The aggregate November 16, 1985 amount ($600,000), less the lowest historic month-end debt level ($500,000), yields a total paydown in the amount of $100,000.

(5) Step 5: Computation of limitations on aggregate unreduced five-year debt and aggregate unreduced four-year debt.

Aggregate Nov. 16, 1985 amount	$600,000
Aggregate unreduced 5-year debt	180,000
Aggregate unreduced 4-year debt	120,000

Because the November 16, 1985 amount exceeds the unreduced 4- and 5-year debt, the full amount of the 4- and 5-year debt qualify for transition relief. In cases where the November 16, 1985 amount is less than the 4- or 5-year debt (or the sum of both), the latter amounts are limited to the November 16, 1985 amount. See the limitations on the 4-year and 5-year debt amounts in paragraphs (c)(6) and (c)(5), respectively, of this section.

(6) Step 6: Computation of reduced five-year and four-year debt. The paydowns computed under Step 4 are deemed to first offset the aggregate unreduced five-year debt. Accordingly, the reduced amount of five-year debt is $80,000. Since the paydowns are less than the aggregate unreduced five-year debt, there is no paydown in connection with aggregate unreduced four-year debt. Accordingly, the unreduced four-year debt and the reduced four year debt are both considered to be $120,000.

(7) Step 7: Computation of the general phase-in amount. In transition year 1, the general transition amount is the lesser of:

(i) 75 percent of the aggregate November 16, 1985 amount (75% of $600,000 = $450,000); or

(ii) the lowest month-end debt level since November 16, 1985 ($500,000). Therefore, the general transition amount is $450,000.

(8) Step 8: Computation of the five-year phase-in amount. In transition year 1, the five-year phase-in amount is the lesser of:

(i) 8⅓ percent of the unreduced five-year amount (8⅓% of $180,000 = $15,000); or

(ii) 10 percent of the reduced five-year amount (10% of $80,000 = $8,000). Therefore, the five-year phase-in amount is $8,000.

(9) Step 9: Computation of the four-year phase-in amount. In transition year 1, the four-year phase-in amount is the lesser of:

(i) 5 percent of the unreduced four-year amount (5% of $120,000 = $6,000); or

(ii) 6¼ percent of the reduced four-year amount (6¼% of $120,000 = $7,500).

Therefore, the four-year phase-in amount is $6,000.

(10) Step 10: Determination of group debt ratio and application of relief to separate company interest expense.

(i) As determined under Step 7, interest expense on a total of $450,000 of the XYZ debt in the first transition year is computed under pre-1987 rules of allocation and apportionment.

(ii) The sum of Steps 8 ($8,000) and 9 ($6,000) is $14,000. Interest expense on a total of $14,000 of XYZ debt is computed under post-1986 rules of allocation and apportionment as applied on a separate company basis.

(iii) The balance of XYZ's current year interest expense is computed under post-1986 rules of allocation and apportionment as applied on a consolidated basis. X, Y, and Z, respectively, have current interest expense of $10,000, $30,000, and $30,000. Thus, 64.3 percent (450,000/700,000) of the interest expense of each separate company is subject to pre-1987 rules. Two percent (14,000/700,000) of the interest expense of each separate company is subject to post-1986 rules applied on a separate company basis. Finally, the balance of each separate company's current year interest expense (33.7 percent) is subject to post-1986 rules applied on a consolidated basis.

(g) Corporate transfers. *(1) Effect on transferee.* (i) General rule. Except as provided in paragraph (g)(1)(ii) of this section, if a domestic corporation or an affiliated group acquires stock in a domestic corporation that was not a member of the transferee's affiliated group before the acquisition, but becomes a member of the transferee's affiliated group after the acquisition, the transferee group shall take into account the following transition attributes of the acquired corporation in computing its transition relief:

(A) November 16, 1985 amount;

(B) Unreduced five-year amount;

(C) Unreduced four-year amount; and

(D) The amount of any transferor paydowns attributed to the acquired corporation under the rules of paragraph (h)(1) of this section.

(ii) Special rule for year of acquisition. To compute the amount of the transition attributes described in paragraph (g)(1)(i) of this section that a transferee takes into account in the transferee's taxable year of the acquisition, such transition attributes shall be multiplied by a fraction, the numerator of which is the number of months within the taxable year that the transferee held the acquired corporation and the denominator of which is the number of months in such taxable year. In order for the transferee to assert ownership of a subsidiary for a given month, the transferee and the acquired corporation must be affiliated corporations as of the last day of the month. In addition, the transferor and the transferee shall take account of the month-end debt level of the transferred corporation only for those months at the end of which the transferred corporation was a member of the transferor's or the transferee's respective affiliated group.

(iii) Aggregation of transition attributes. The transition attributes of the acquired corporation shall be aggregated with the respective amounts of the transferee group.

(iv) Conveyance of transferor paydowns. The total paydowns of the transferee group shall include the amount of any paydown of the transferor group that was attributed to the acquired corporation under the rules of paragraph (h)(1) of this section.

(v) Effect of certain elections. If an election—

(A) Is made under section 338(g) (whether or not an election under 338(h)(10) is made),

(B) Is deemed to be made under section 338(e) (other than (e)(2)), or section 338(f), or,

(C) Is made under section 336(e), no indebtedness of the acquired corporation shall qualify for transition relief for the year such election first becomes effective and for subsequent taxable years, and no other transition attributes of the acquired corporation shall be taken into account by the transferee group.

(2) Effect on transferor. (i) General rule. Except as provided in paragraph (g)(2)(ii) of this section, in the case of an acquisition of a member of an affiliated group by a nonmember of the group, the transferor shall not take into account the transition attributes of the acquired corporation in computing the transition relief of the transferor group in subsequent taxable years. Thus, the November 16, 1985 amount, the unreduced five-year and four-year debt amounts, and the end-of-month debt levels of the transferor group shall be computed without regard to the acquired corporation's respective amounts for purposes of computing transition relief of the transferor group for years thereafter.

(ii) Special rule for the year of disposition. To compute the amount of the transition attributes described in paragraph (g)(2)(i) of this section that a transferor shall take into account in the transferor's taxable year of the disposition, such transition attributes shall be multiplied by a fraction, the numerator of which is the number of months within the taxable year that the transferor held the acquired corporation and the denominator of which is the number of months in such taxable year. In order for the transferor to assert ownership of a subsidiary for a given month, the transferor and the acquired corporation must be affiliated corporations as of the last day of the month.

(iii) Effect of prior paydowns. Any paydowns of the acquired corporation that are considered to reduce the debt of other members of the transferor group under the rules of paragraph (h)(1) of this section (whether incurred in a prior taxable year or in that portion of a year of disposition that is taken into account by the transferor) shall continue to be taken into account by the transferor group after the disposition.

(3) Special rule for assumptions of indebtedness. In connection with the transfer of a corporation, if the indebtedness of an acquired corporation is assumed by any party other than the transferee or another member of the transferee's affiliated group, the transition attributes of the acquired corporation shall not be taken into account in computing the transition relief of the transferee group. See paragraph (g)(2) of this section concerning the treatment of the transferor group. Also in connection with the transfer of a corporation, if the transferee or another member of the transferee's affiliated group assumes the indebtedness of an acquired corporation, such assumed indebtedness shall only qualify for transition relief during the period in which the acquired corporation remains a member of the transferee group. Further, if the transferee group subsequently disposes of the acquired corporation, the indebtedness of the acquired corporation will continue to qualify for transition relief only if the indebtedness is assumed by the new purchaser as of the time such corporation is acquired.

(4) Effect of asset sales. If substantially all of the assets of a corporation are sold, the indebtedness of such corporation shall cease to be qualified for transition relief. Thus, the transition attributes of such corporation shall not be taken into account in computing transition relief.

(h) Rules for attributing paydowns among separate companies. *(1) General rule.* In the case of a corporate transfer under paragraph (g) of this section, it is necessary to determine the amount of paydowns attributable to the acquired corporation. Under paragraph (c)(7) of this section, paydowns are deemed to reduce first the five-year phase-in amount, then the four-year phase-in amount, and then the general phase-in amount. Thus, for example, a reduction in indebtedness of the group caused by a reduction in the debt of a group member that has no five-year debt will nevertheless be deemed under this ordering rule to reduce the indebtedness of those group members that do have five-year debt. In order to preserve the effect of paydowns caused by a reduction, each member must determine on a separate company basis at the time of any transfer of any member of the affiliated group the impact of paydowns (including those paydowns occurring in the year of transfer prior to the time of the transfer) on the various categories of indebtedness.

(2) Mechanics of computation. Separate company accounts of paydowns are determined by prorating any paydown among all group members with five-year debt to the extent thereof on the basis of the relative amounts of five-year debt. Paydowns in excess of five-year debt are prorated on a similar basis among all group members with four-year debt to the extent thereof on the basis of the relative amounts of four-year debt. Paydowns in excess of four-year and five-year debt are prorated among all group members with general phase-in debt to the extent thereof on the basis of the relative amounts of general phase-in debt. After an initial paydown has been prorated among the members of an affiliated group, any further reduction in the amount of aggregate month-end debt level as compared to the November 16, 1985 amount is prorated among all members of the affiliated group based on the remaining net amounts of four-year and five-year debt.

(3) Examples. The rules of paragraphs (g) and (h) of this section may be illustrated by the following examples.

Example (1). Computing separate company accounts of reductions.

(i) Facts. XYZ constitutes an affiliated group of corporations that has a calendar taxable year and the following transition attributes:

	Historic 3rd party debt	Increase
Company X:		
Nov. 16, 1985	$100,000	
May 29, 1985 (5-year)	80,000	$ 0
Dec. 31, 1983 (4-year)	80,000	10,000
Dec. 31, 1982	70,000	
Company Y:		
Nov. 16, 1985	200,000	
May 29, 1985 (5-year)	170,000	120,000
Dec. 31, 1983 (4-year)	50,000	10,000
Dec. 31, 1982	40,000	
Company Z:		
Nov. 16, 1985	300,000	
May 29, 1985 (5-year)	290,000	40,000
Dec. 31, 1983 (4-year)	250,000	100,000
Dec. 31, 1982	150,000	

In 1986, the XYZ group attained its lowest historic month-end debt level of $500,000. Because the November 16, 1985 amount is $600,000 the XYZ group therefore has a paydown in the amount of $100,000. This paydown partially offsets the $160,000 of five-year debt in the XYZ group.

(ii) Analysis. Applying the rule of paragraph (h)(1) of this section, separate company accounts of paydowns are computed by prorating the $100,000 paydown among those members of the group that have five-year debt. Accordingly, the paydown is prorated between Y and Z as follows:

To Y:

$$\$100{,}000 \times \frac{\$120{,}000}{\$160{,}000} = \$75{,}000$$

To Z:

$$\$100{,}000 \times \frac{\$40{,}000}{\$160{,}000} = \$25{,}000$$

Example (2). Corporate acquisitions.

(i) Facts. The facts are the same as in example (1). On July 15, 1987, the XYZ group sells all the stock of Y to A. Having held the stock of Y for six months in 1987, the XZ group computes its transition relief for that year taking into account half of the transition attributes of Y. AY constitutes an affiliated group of corporations after the acquisition. Having held the stock of Y for six months in 1987, the AY group computes its transition relief for that year taking into account half of the transition attributes of Y. In 1987, the AY group attained a new lowest month-end debt level that yields an average lowest month-end debt level for 1987 of $150,000.

(ii) Transferee group. The following analysis applies in determining transition relief for purposes of apportioning the interest expense of the transferee group for 1987. The AY group has the following transition attributes for 1987:

	Historic 3rd party debt	Increase
Company A:		
Nov. 16, 1985	$100,000	
May 29, 1985 (5-year)	250,000	$ 5,000
Dec. 31, 1983 (4-year)	245,000	10,000
Dec. 31, 1982	235,000	
Company Y (half-year amounts):		
Nov. 16, 1985	100,000	
May 29, 1985 (5-year)	85,000	60,000
Dec. 31, 1983 (4-year)	25,000	5,000
Dec. 31, 1982	20,000	
Pre-acquisition year paydown by another member of the transferor group that reduced Y's five-year debt (one half of $75,000)	37,500	

Because the November 16, 1985 amount of the AY group in 1987 is $200,000 and because the 1987 average of historic month-end debt levels was $150,000, the AY group has a paydown in the amount of $50,000. In addition, the 1986 paydown by the XYZ group that was deemed to reduce Y debt is added to the paydown computed above, yielding a total paydown of $87,500. This amount is prorated between members, eliminating the four and five year debt of the AY group. Note that Y is only a member of the AY group for half of the 1987 taxable year. In 1988, Y's entire transition indebtedness and a $75,000 paydown must be taken into account in computing the amount of interest expense eligible for transition relief.

(iii) Transferor group. The following analysis applies in determining transition relief for purposes of apportioning the interest expense of the transferor group for 1987. The XZ group has the transition attributes stated below for 1987. In 1987, the XZ group attained a new lowest month-end debt level that yields an average lowest month-end debt level for 1987 of $250,000.

	Historic 3rd party debt	Increase
Company X:		
Nov. 16, 1985	$100,000	
May 29, 1985 (5-year)	80,000	$ 0
Dec. 31, 1983 (4-year)	80,000	10,000
Dec. 31, 1982	70,000	
Pre-disposition paydown that reduced X's debt	0	
Company Y (half-year amounts):		
Nov. 16, 1985	100,000	
May 29, 1985 (5-year)	85,000	60,000
Dec. 31, 1983 (4-year)	25,000	5,000
Dec. 31, 1982	20,000	
Pre-disposition paydown that reduced Y's debt	37,500	
Company Z:		
Nov. 16, 1985	300,000	
May 29, 1985 (5-year)	290,000	40,000
Dec. 31, 1983 (4-year)	250,000	100,000
Dec. 31, 1982	150,000	
Pre-disposition paydown that reduced Z's debt	25,000	

Because the revised November 16, 1985 amount of the XZ group is $500,000 and because the 1987 average of lowest historic month-end debt levels of the XZ group was $250,000, the XZ group has a paydown in the amount of $250,000. This paydown offsets the total five and four year debt of the XZ group. Had the 1987 paydown of the XZ group been an amount less than the five-year amount, the paydown would have been prorated based on Y's adjusted 5-year amount of $22,500 and Z's adjusted 5-year amount of $15,000.

T.D. 8257, 8/1/89.

§ 1.861-14 Special rules for allocating and apportioning certain expenses (other than interest expense) of an affiliated group of corporations.

(a) through (c) [Reserved]. For further guidance, see § 1.861-14T(a) through (c).

(d) Definition of affiliated group. *(1) General rule.* For purposes of this section, the term affiliated group has the same meaning as is given that term by section 1504, except that section 936 corporations (as defined in § 1.861-11(d)(2)(ii)) are also included within the affiliated group to the extent provided in paragraph (d)(2) of this section. Section 1504(a) defines an affiliated group as one or more chains of includible corporations connected through 80% stock ownership with a common parent corporation which is an includible corporation (as defined in section 1504(b)). In the case of a corporation that either becomes or ceases to be a member of the group during the course of the corporation's taxable year, only the expenses incurred by the group member during the period of membership shall be allocated and apportioned as if all members of the group were a single corporation. In this regard, the apportionment factor chosen shall relate only to the period of membership. For example, if apportionment on the basis of assets is chosen, the average amount of assets (tax book value or fair market value) for the taxable year shall be multiplied by a fraction, the numerator of which is the number of months of the corporation's taxable year during which the corporation was a member of the affiliated group, and the denominator of which is the number of months within the corporation's taxable year. If apportionment on the basis of gross income is chosen, only gross income generated during the period of membership shall be taken into account. If apportionment on the basis of units sold or sales receipts is chosen, only units sold or sales receipts during the period of membership shall be taken into account. Expenses incurred by the group member during its taxable year, but not during the period of membership, shall be allocated and apportioned without regard to other members of the group. This paragraph (d)(1) applies to taxable years beginning after December 31, 1989.

(2) Inclusion of section 936 corporations. (i) General rule. Except as otherwise provided in paragraph (d)(2)(ii) of this section, the exclusion from the affiliated group of section 936 corporations under section 1504(b)(4) does not apply for purposes of this section. Thus, a section 936 corporation that meets the ownership requirements of section 1504(a) is a member of the affiliated group.

(ii) Exception for purposes of alternative minimum tax. The exclusion from the affiliated group of section 936 corporations under section 1504(b)(4) shall be operative for purposes of the application of this section solely in determining the amount of foreign source alternative minimum taxable income within each separate category and the alternative minimum tax foreign tax credit pursuant to section

59(a). Thus, a section 936 corporation that meets the ownership requirements of section 1504(a) is not a member of the affiliated group for purposes of determining the amount of foreign source alternative minimum taxable income within each separate category and the alternative minimum tax foreign tax credit pursuant to section 59(a).

(iii) Effective date. This paragraph (d)(2) applies to taxable years beginning after December 31, 1989.

(3) through (e)(5) [Reserved]. For further guidance, see § 1.861-14T(d)(3) through (e)(5).

(6) Charitable contribution expenses. (i) In general. A deduction for a charitable contribution by a member of an affiliated group shall be allocated and apportioned under the rules of Sec. § 1.861-8(e)(12) and 1.861-14T(c)(1).

(ii) Effective date. (A) The rules of this paragraph shall apply to charitable contributions subject to § 1.861-8(e)(12)(i) that are made on or after July 28, 2004, and, for taxpayers applying the second sentence of § 1.861-8(e)(12)(iv)(A), to charitable contributions made during the taxable year ending on or after July 28, 2004.

(B) The rules of this paragraph shall apply to charitable contributions subject to § 1.861-8(e)(12)(ii) that are made on or after July 14, 2005, and, for taxpayers applying the second sentence of § 1.861-8(e)(12)(iv)(B), to charitable contributions made during the taxable year ending on or after July 14, 2005.

(f) through (j) [Reserved]. For further guidance, see § 1.861-14T(f) through (j).

T.D. 8916, 12/27/2000, amend T.D. 9211, 7/12/2005.

§ 1.861-14T Special rules for allocating and apportioning certain expenses (other than interest expense) of an affiliated group of corporations (temporary).

(a) In general. Section 1.861-11T provides special rules for allocating and apportioning interest expense of an affiliated group of corporations. The rules of this § 1.861-14T also relate to affiliated groups of corporations and implement section 864(e)(6), which requires affiliated group allocation and apportionment of expenses other than interest which are not directly allocable and apportionable to any specific income producing activity or property. In general, the rules of this section apply to taxable years beginning after December 31, 1986. Paragraph (b) of this section describes the scope of the application of the rule for the allocation and apportionment of such expenses of affiliated groups of corporations. Such rules is then set forth in paragraph (c) of this section. Paragraph (d) of this section contains the definition of the term "affiliated group" for purposes of this section. Paragraph (e) of this section describes the expenses subject to allocation and apportionment under the rules of this section. Paragraph (f) of this section provides rules concerning the affiliated group allocation and apportionment of such expenses in computing the combined taxable income of a FSC or DISC and its related supplier. Paragraph (g) of this section describes the treatment of losses caused by apportionment of such expenses in the case of an affiliated group that does not file a consolidated return. Paragraph (h) of this section provides rules concerning the treatment of the reserve expenses of a life insurance company. Paragraph (j) of this section provides examples illustrating the application of this section.

(b) Scope. *(1) Application of section 864(e)(6).* Section 864(e)(6) and this section apply to the computation of taxable income for purposes of computing separate limitations on the foreign tax credit under section 904. Section 864(e)(6) and this section also apply in connection with section 907 to determine reductions in the amount allowed as a foreign tax credit under section 901. Section 864(e)(6) and this section also apply to the computation of the combined taxable income of the related supplier and a foreign sales corporation (FSC) (under sections 921 through 927) as well as the combined taxable income of the related supplier and a domestic international sales corporation (DISC) (under sections 991 through 997).

(2) Nonapplication of section 864(e)(6). Section 864(e)(6) and this section do not apply to the computation of Subpart F income of controlled foreign corporations (under sections 951 through 964) or the computation of effectively connected taxable income of foreign corporations.

(3) Application of section 864(e)(6) to the computation of combined taxable income of a possessions corporation and its affiliates.[Reserved.]

(c) General rule for affiliated corporations. *(1) General rule.* (i) Except as otherwise provided in paragraph (c)(2) of this section, the taxable income of each member of an affiliated group within each statutory grouping shall be determined by allocating and apportioning the expenses described in paragraph (e) of this section of each member according to apportionment fractions which are computed as if all members of such group were a single corporation. For purposes of determining these apportionment fractions, any interaffiliate transactions or property that are duplicative with respect to the measure of apportionment chosen shall be eliminated. For example, in the application of an asset method of apportionment, stock in affiliated corporations shall not be taken into account, and loans between members of an affiliated group shall be treated in accordance with the rules of § 1.861-11T(e). Similarly, in the application of a gross income method of apportionment, interaffiliate dividends and interest, gross income from sales or services, and other interaffiliate gross income shall be eliminated. Likewise, in the application of a method of apportionment based on units sold or sales receipts, interaffiliate sales shall be eliminated.

(ii) Except as otherwise provided in this section, the rules of § 1.861-8T apply to the allocation and apportionment of the expenses described in paragraph (e) of this section. Thus, allocation under this paragraph (c) is accomplished by determining, with respect to each expense described in paragraph (e), the class of gross income to which the expense is definitely related and then allocating the deduction to such class of gross income. For this purpose, the gross income of all members of the affiliated group must be taken in account. Then, the expense is apportioned by attributing the expense to gross income (within the class to which the expense has been allocated) which is in the statutory grouping and to gross income (within the class) which is in the residual grouping. Section 1.861-8T(c)(1) identifies a number of factors upon which apportionment may be based, such as comparison of units sold, gross sales or receipts, assets used, or gross income. The apportionment method chosen must be applied consistently by each member of the affiliated group in apportioning the expense when more than one member incurred the expense or when members incurred separate portions of the expense. The apportionment fraction must take into account the apportionment factors contributed by all members of the affiliated group. In the case of an affiliated group of corporations that files a consolidated return, consolidated foreign tax credit limitations are computed for the group in accordance with the rules of § 1.1502-4. For purposes of this section the term "taxpayer" refers to the affiliated group (regardless of whether the group files a consolidated return), rather than to the separate members thereof.

(2) Expenses relating to fewer than all members. An expense relates to fewer than all members of an affiliated group if the expense is allocable under paragraph (e)(1) of this section to gross income of at least one member other than the member that incurred the expense but fewer than all members of the affiliated group. The taxable income of the member that incurred the expense shall be determined by apportioning that expense under the rules of paragraph (c)(1) of this section as if the members of the affiliated group that derive gross income to which such expense is allocable under paragraph (e)(1) were treated as a single corporation.

(3) Prior application of section 482. The rules of this section do not supersede the application of section 482 and the regulations thereunder. Section 482 may be applied effectively to deny a deduction for an expense to one member of an affiliated group and to allow a deduction for that expense to another member of the affiliated group. In cases to which section 482 is applied, expenses shall be reallocated and reapportioned under section 864(e)(6) and this section after taking into account the application of section 482.

(d) and (2) [Reserved]. For further guidance, see § 1.861-14(d)(1) and (2).

(e) Expenses to be allocated and apportioned under this section. *(1) Expenses not directly traceable to specific income producing activities or property.* (i) The expenses that are required to be allocated and apportioned under the rules of this section are expenses related to certain supportive functions, research and experimental expenses, stewardship expenses, and legal and accounting expenses, to the extent that such expenses are not directly allocable to specific income producing activities or property solely of the member of the affiliated group that incurred the expense. Interest expense of members of an affiliated group of corporations is allocated and apportioned under § 1.861-11T and not under the rules of this section. Expenses that are included in inventory costs or that are capitalized are not subject to allocation and apportionment under the rules of this section.

(ii) An item of expense is not considered to be directly allocable to specific income producing activities or property solely of the member incurring the expense if, were all members of the affiliated group treated as a single corporation, the expense would not be considered definitely related, within the meaning of § 1.861-8(b)(2), only to a class of gross income derived solely by the member which actually incurred the expense. Furthermore, the expense is presumed not to be definitely related only to a class of gross income derived solely by the member incurring the expense (and is, therefore, presumed not to be directly allocable to specific income producing activities or property of that member) unless the taxpayer is able affirmatively to establish otherwise. As provided in paragraph (c)(1) of this section, expenses described in this paragraph (e)(1) generally shall be apportioned by the member incurring the expense according to apportionment fractions computed as if all members of the affiliated group were a single corporation. Under paragraph (c)(2) of this section, however, an expense shall be apportioned according to apportionment fractions computed as if only some (but fewer than all) members of the affiliated group were a single corporation, if the expense is considered allocable to gross income of at least one member other than the member incurring the expense but fewer than all members of the affiliated group. An item of expense shall be considered to be allocable to gross income of fewer than all members of the group if, were all members of the affiliated group treated as a single corporation, the expense would not be considered definitely related within the meaning of § 1.861-8(b)(2) to gross income derived by all members of the group. In such case, the expense shall be considered allocable, for purposes of paragraph (c)(2) of this section, to gross income of those members of the group that generated (or could reasonably be expected to generate) the gross income to which the expense would be considered definitely related if the group were treated as a single corporation.

(2) Research and experimental expenses. (i) In general. The allocation and apportionment of research and experimental expenses is governed by the rules of § 1.861-8(e)(3). In the case of research and experimental expenses incurred by a member of an affiliated group, the rules of § 1.861-8(e)(3) shall be applied as if all members of the affiliated group were a single taxpayer. Thus, research and experimental expenses shall be allocated to all income of all members of the affiliated group reasonably connected with the relevant broad product category to which such expenses are definitely related under § 1.861-8(e)(3)(i). If fewer than all members of the affiliated group derive gross income reasonably connected with that relevant broad product category, then such expenses shall be apportioned under the rules of this paragraph (c)(2) only among those members, as if those members were a single corporation. See Example (1) of paragraph (j) of this section. Such expenses shall then be apportioned, if the sales method is used, in accordance with the rules of § 1.861-8(e)(3)(ii) between the statutory grouping (within the class of gross income) and the residual grouping (within the class of gross income) taking into account the amount of sales of all members of the affiliated group from the product category which resulted in such gross income. Section 1.861-8(e)(3)(ii)(D), relating to sales of controlled parties, shall be applied as if all members of the affiliated group were the "taxpayer" referred to therein. If either of the optional gross income methods of apportionment is used, gross income of all members of the affiliated group that generate, have generated, or could reasonably have been expected to generate gross income within the relevant class of gross income must be taken into account.

(ii) Expenses subject to the statutory moratorium. The rules of this section do not apply to research and experimental expenses allocated under section 1216 of Pub. L. 99-514.

(3) Expenses related to supportive functions. Expenses which are supportive in nature (such as overhead, general and administrative, supervisory expenses, advertising, marketing, and other sales expenses) are to be allocated and apportioned in accordance with the rules of § 1.861-8T(b)(3). To the extent that such expenses are not directly allocable under paragraph (e)(1)(ii) of this section to specific income producing activities or property of the member of the affiliated group that incurred the expense, such expenses must be allocated and apportioned as if all members of the affiliated group were a single corporation in accordance with the rules of paragraph (c) of this section. Specifically, such expenses must be allocated to a class of gross income that take into account gross income that is generated, has been generated, or could reasonably have been expected to have been generated by the members of the affiliated group. If the expenses relate to the gross income of fewer than all members of the affiliated group as determined under paragraph (c)(2) of this section, then those expenses must be apportioned under the rules of paragraph (c)(2) of this section, as if those fewer members were a single corporation. See Example (3) of paragraph (j) of this section. Such expenses must be apportioned between statutory and residual groupings of income

within the appropriate class of gross income by reference to the apportionment factors contributed by the members of the affiliated group that are treated as a single corporation.

(4) Stewardship expenses. Stewardship expenses are to be allocated and apportioned in accordance with the rules of § 1.861-8T(e)(4). In general, stewardship expenses are considered definitely related and allocable to dividends received or to be received from a related corporation. If members of the affiliated group, other than the member that incurred the stewardship expense, receive or may receive dividends from the related corporation, such expense must be allocated and apportioned in accordance with the rules of paragraph (c) of this section as if all such members of the affiliated group that receive or may receive dividends were a single corporation. See Example (4) of paragraph (j) of this section. Such expenses must be apportioned between statutory and residual groupings of income within the appropriate class of gross income by reference to the apportionment factors contributed by the members of the affiliated group treated as a single corporation.

(5) Legal and accounting fees and expenses. Legal and accounting fees and expenses are to be allocated and apportioned under the rules of § 1.861-8T(e)(5). To the extent that such expenses are not directly allocable under paragraph (e)(1)(ii) of this section to specific income producing activities or property of the member of the affiliated group that incurred the expense, such expenses must be allocated and apportioned as if all members of the affiliated group were a single corporation. Specifically, such expenses must be allocated to a class of gross income that takes into account the gross income which is generated, has been generated, or could reasonably have been expected to have been generated by the other members of the affiliated group. If the expenses relate to the gross income of fewer than all members of the affiliated group as determined under paragraph (c)(2) of this section, then those expenses must be apportioned under the rules of paragraph (c)(2) of this section, as if those fewer members were a single corporation. See Example (5) of paragraph (j) of this section. Such expenses must be apportioned taking into account the apportionment factors contributed by the members of the group that are treated as a single corporation.

(f) Computation of FSC or DISC combined taxable income. In the computation under the pricing rules of sections 925 and 994 of the combined taxable income of any FSC or DISC and its related supplier which are members of an affiliated group, the combined taxable income of such FSC or DISC and its related supplier shall be reduced by the portion of the expenses of the affiliated group described in paragraph (e) of this section that is incurred in connection with export sales involving that FSC or DISC. In order to determine the portion of the expenses of the affiliated group that is incurred in connection with export sales by or through a FSC or DISC, the portion of the total of the apportionment factor chosen that relates to the generation of that export income must be determined. Thus, if gross income is the apportionment factor chosen, the portion of total gross income of the affiliated group that consists of combined gross income derived from transactions involving the FSC or DISC and related supplier must be determined. Similarly, if units sold or sales receipts is the apportionment factor chosen, the portion of total units sold or sales receipts that generated export income of the FSC or DISC and related supplier must be determined. The amount of the expense shall then be multiplied by a fraction, the numerator of which is the export related apportionment factor as determined above, and the denominator of which is the total apportionment factor. Thus, if gross income is the apportionment factor chosen, apportionment is based on a fraction, the numerator of which is export related combined gross income of the FSC or DISC and related supplier and the denominator of which is the total gross income of the affiliated group. Similarly, if units sold or sales receipts is the apportionment factor chosen, the fraction is the units sold or sales receipts that generated export income of the FSC or DISC and related supplier over the total units sold or sales receipts of the affiliated group. Under this rule, expenses of other group members may be attributed to the combined gross income of a FSC of DISC and its related supplier without affecting the amount of expenses (other than any commission payable by the related supplier to the FSC or DISC) otherwise deductible by the FSC or DISC, the related supplier, or other members of the affiliated group. The FSC or DISC must calculate combined taxable income, taking into account any reduction by expenses attributed from other members of the affiliated group to determine the commission derived by the FSC or DISC or the transfer price of qualifying export property sold to the FSC or DISC.

(g) Losses created through apportionment. In the case of an affiliated group that does not file a consolidated return, the taxable income in any separate limitation category must be adjusted under this paragraph (g) for purposes of computing the separate foreign tax credit limitations under section 904(d). As a consequence of the affiliated group allocation and apportionment of expenses required by section 864(e)(6) and this section, expenses of a group member may be apportioned for section 904 purposes to a limitation category with a consequent loss in that limitation category. For purposes of this paragraph, the term "limitation category" includes domestic source income, as well as the types of income described in section 904(d)(1)(A) through (I). A loss of one affiliate in a limitation category will reduce the income of another member in the same limitation category if a consolidated return is filed. (See § 1.1502-4.) If a consolidated return is not filed, this netting does not occur. Accordingly, in such a case, the following adjustments among members are required, in order to give effect to the group allocation of expense:

(1) Losses created through group apportionment of expense in one or more limitation categories within a given member must be eliminated; and

(2) A corresponding amount of income of other members in the same limitation category must be recharacterized. Such adjustments shall be accomplished in accordance with the rules of § 1.861-11T(g).

(h) Special rule for the allocation of reserve expenses of a life insurance company. An amount of reserve expenses of a life insurance company equal to the dividends received deduction that is disallowed because it is attributable to the policyholders' share of dividends received shall be treated as definitely related to such dividends. The remaining reserve expenses of such company shall be allocated and apportioned under the rules of § 1.861-8 and this section.

(i) [Reserved.]

(j) Examples. The rules of this section may be illustrated by the following examples. All of these examples assume that section 482 has not been applied by the Commissioner.

Example (1). (i) Facts. P owns all of the stock of X and all of the stock of Y. P, X and Y are domestic corporations. P is a holding company for the stock of X and Y. Both X and Y manufacture and sell a product which is included in a broad product category listed in § 1.861-8(e)(3)(i). During 1988, X incurred $100,000 on research connected with that product. All of the research was performed in the United States. In 1988, the domestic sales by X of the product totalled $400,000 and the foreign sales of the product totalled $200,000; Y's domestic sales of the product totalled $200,000 and Y's foreign sales of the product totalled $200,000. In 1988, X's gross income is $300,000, of which $200,000 is from domestic sales and $100,000 is from foreign sales; Y's gross income is $200,000 of which $100,000 is from domestic sales and $100,000 is from foreign sales.

(ii) P, X and Y are affiliated corporations within the meaning of section 864(e)(5) and this section. There search expenses incurred by X are allocable to all income connected with the relevant broad category listed in § 1.861-8T(e)(3)(i). Both X and Y have gross income includible within the class of gross income related to that product category. Accordingly, the research and experimental expenses incurred by X are to be allocated and apportioned as if X and Y were a single corporation. The apportionment for 1988 is as follows:

Tentative Apportionment on the Basis of Sales

Research expenses to be apportioned	$100,000
Exclusive apportionment to United States source gross income	$ 30,000
Research expense to be apportioned on the basis of sales	$ 70,000

Apportionment of research expense to foreign source general limitation income:

$$\$70{,}000 \times \frac{\$200{,}000 + \$200{,}000}{\$600{,}000 + \$400{,}000} = \$28{,}000$$

Apportionment of research expense to United States source gross income:

$$\$70{,}000 \times \frac{\$400{,}000 + \$200{,}000}{\$600{,}000 + \$400{,}000} = \$42{,}000$$

Total apportioned deduction for research	$100,000
Of which—	
Apportioned to foreign source gross income	$ 28,000
Apportioned to U.S. source gross income ($30,000 + $42,000)	$ 72,000

Tentative Apportionment on the Basis of Gross Income

Research expense apportioned to foreign source gross income:

$$\$100{,}000 \times \frac{\$100{,}000 + \$100{,}000}{\$300{,}000 + \$200{,}000} = \$40{,}000$$

Research expense apportioned to United States income:

$$\$100{,}000 \times \frac{\$200{,}000 + \$100{,}000}{\$300{,}000 + \$200{,}000} = \$60{,}000$$

Example (2). (i) Facts. P owns all of the stock of X, which owns all of the stock of Y. P, X and Y are all domestic corporations. P has incurred general training program expenses of $100,000 in 1987. Employees of P, X and Y participate in the training program. In 1987, P had United States source gross income of $200,000 and foreign source general limitation income of $200,000; X had U.S. source gross income of $100,000 and foreign source general limitation income of $100,000; and Y had U.S. source gross income of $300,000 and foreign source general limitation income of $100,000.

(ii) Analysis. P, X and Y are an affiliated group of corporations within the meaning of section 864(e)(5). The training expenses incurred by P are not definitely related solely to specific income producing activities or property of P. The employees of X and Y also participate in the training program. Thus, this expense relates to gross income generated by P, X and Y. This expense is definitely related and allocable to all of the gross income from foreign and domestic sources of P, X and Y. It is assumed that apportionment on the basis of gross income is reasonable. The apportionment of the expense is as follows: Apportionment of $100,000 expense to foreign source general limitation income:

$$\$100{,}000 \times \frac{\$200{,}000 + \$100{,}000 + \$100{,}000}{\$400{,}000 + \$200{,}000 + \$400{,}000} = \$40{,}000$$

Apportionment of $100,000 expense to United States source gross income:

$$\$100{,}000 \times \frac{\$200{,}000 + \$100{,}000 + \$300{,}000}{\$400{,}000 + \$200{,}000 + \$400{,}000} = \$60{,}000$$

Total apportioned expense	$100,000

Example (3). (i) Facts. The facts are the same as in Example (2) above, except that only employees of P and X participate in the training program.

(ii) Analysis. Because only the employees of P and X participate in the training program and they perform no services for Y, the expense relates only to gross income generated by P and X. Accordingly, the $100,000 expense must be allocated and apportioned as if P and X were a single corporation. The apportionment of the $100,000 expense is as follows: Apportionment of $100,000 expense to foreign source general limitation income:

$$\$100{,}000 \times \frac{\$200{,}000 + \$100{,}000}{\$400{,}000 + \$200{,}000} = \$50{,}000$$

Apportionment of $100,000 expense to U.S. source gross income:

$$\$100{,}000 \times \frac{\$200{,}000 + \$100{,}000}{\$400{,}000 + \$200{,}000} = \$50{,}000$$

Example (4). (i) Facts. P owns all of the stock of X which owns all of the stock of Y. P and X are domestic corporations; Y is a foreign corporation. In 1987 P incurred $10,000 of stewardship expenses relating to an audit of Y.

(ii) Analysis. The stewardship expenses incurred by P are not directly allocable to specific income producing activities or property of P. The expense is definitely related and allocable to dividends received or to be received by X. Accordingly, the expense of P is allocated and apportioned as if P and X were a single corporation. The expense is definitely related to dividends received or to be received by X from Y, a foreign corporation. Such dividends are foreign source general limitation income. Thus, the entire amount of the expense must be allocated to foreign source dividend income.

Example (5). (i) Facts. P owns all of the stock of X which owns all of the stock of Y P, X and Y are all domestic corporations. In 1987, P incurred $10,000 legal expense relating to the testimony of certain employees of P in connection with litigation to which Y is a party. This expense is not allocable to specific income of Y. In 1987, Y had $100,000 foreign source general limitation income and $300,000 U.S. source gross income.

(ii) Analysis. The legal expenses incurred by P are not definitely related solely to specific income producing activities or property of P. The expense is definitely related and allocable to the class of gross income which includes only gross income generated by Y. Accordingly, the expense of P is allocated and apportioned as if Y were the only member of the affiliated group, as follows: Apportionment of legal expenses to foreign source general limitation income:

$$\$10{,}000 \times \frac{\$100{,}000}{\$400{,}000} \quad \ldots\ldots\ldots \quad \$2{,}500$$

Apportionment of legal expenses to U.S. source gross income:

$$\$10{,}000 \times \frac{\$300{,}000}{\$400{,}000} \quad \ldots\ldots\ldots \quad \$7{,}500$$

Example (6). (i) Facts. P owns all of the stock of R, which owns all of the stock of F. P and R are domestic corporations, and F is a foreign sales corporation under section 922 of the Code. R and F have entered into an agreement whereby F is paid a commission with respect to sales of product A. In 1987, P had gross receipts of $1,000,000 from domestic sales of product A, and gross receipts of $1,000,000 from foreign sales of product A. R had gross receipts of $1,000,000 from domestic sales of product A, and $1,000,000 from export sales of product A. R's cost of goods sold attributable to export sales is $500,000. R has deductible expenses of $100,000 directly related to its export sales and F has such deductible expenses of $100,000. During 1987, P incurred an expense of $100,000 for marketing studies involving the worldwide market for product A.

(ii) Analysis. P and R are an affiliated group of corporations within the meaning of section 864(e)(5) and this section. The expense incurred by P for marketing studies regarding the worldwide market for product A is an expense that is not directly related solely to the activities of P, but also to the activities of R. This expense must be allocated and apportioned under the rules of paragraph (c)(1) of this section, as if P and R were a single corporation. The expense is allocable to the class of gross income that includes all gross income generated by sales of product A. Apportionment on the basis of gross receipts is reasonable under these facts. F, a foreign corporation, is not a member of the affiliated group. However, for purposes of determining F's commission on its sales, the combined gross income of F and R must be reduced by the portion of the marketing studies expense of P that is incurred in connection with export sales involving F under the rules of paragraph (f) of this section. The computation of the combined taxable income of R and F is as follows:

Combined Income of R and F

R's gross receipts from export sales	$1,000,000
R's cost of goods sold	$ 500,000
Combined Gross Income	$ 500,000
Less:	
R's other deductible expenses	$ 100,000
F's other deductible expenses	100,000
Apportionment of P's expense:	
$\$100{,}000 \times \frac{\$1{,}000{,}000}{\$200{,}000 + \$2{,}000{,}000}$	$ 25,000
Total	$ 225,000
Combined Taxable Income	$ 275,000

T.D. 8228, 9/9/88, amend T.D. 8916, 12/27/2000, T.D. 9143, 7/27/2004, T.D. 9211, 7/13/2005.

§ 1.861-15 Income from certain aircraft or vessels first leased by the taxpayer on or before December 28, 1980.

(a) General rule. A taxpayer who owns an aircraft or vessel described in paragraph (b) of this section and who leases the aircraft or vessel to a United States person (other than a member of the same controlled group of corporations (as defined in section 1563) as the taxpayer) may elect under paragraph (f) of this section to treat all amounts includible in gross income with respect to the aircraft or vessel as income from sources within the United States for any taxable year ending after the commencement of the lease. This paragraph (a) applies only with respect to taxable years ending after August 15, 1971, and only with respect to leases entered into after that date of aircraft or vessels first leased by the taxpayer on or before December 28, 1980. An election once made applies to the taxable year for which made and to all subsequent taxable years unless it is revoked or terminated in accordance with paragraph (g) of this section. A taxpayer need not be a United States person to be eligible to make the election under this section, unless otherwise required by a provision of law not contained in the Internal Revenue Code of 1954. In addition, the taxpayer need not be a bank or other financial institution to be eligible to make this election. The term "United States person" as used in this section has the meaning assigned to it by section 7701(a)(30).

(b) Property to which the election applies. *(1) section 38 property.* An election made under this section may be made only if the aircraft or vessel is section 38 property, or property which would be section 38 property but for section 48(a)(5) (relating to property used by governmental units), at the time the election is made and for all taxable years to which the election applies. The aircraft or vessel must be property which qualifies for the investment credit under section 38 unless the property does not qualify because it is described in section 48(a)(5). If an aircraft is used predominantly outside the United States (determined under § 1.48-1(g)(1)), it must qualify under the provisions of section 48(a)(2)(B)(i) and § 1.48-1(g)(2)(i). If a vessel is used predominantly outside the United States, it must qualify under the provisions of section 48(a)(2)(B)(iii) and § 1.48-1(g)(2)(iii). The aircraft or vessel may not be suspension or termination period property described in section 48(h) or section 49(a) (as in effect before the enactment of the Revenue Act of 1978). See paragraph (g)(3) and (4) of this section for rules which apply if the property ceases to be section 38 property.

(2) United States manufacture or construction. An election under this section may be made only if the aircraft or vessel is manufactured or constructed in the United States. The aircraft or vessel will be considered to be manufactured or constructed in the United States if 50 percent or more of the basis of the aircraft or vessel is attributable to value added within the United States.

(3) Exclusion of certain property used outside the United States. The term "aircraft or vessel" as used in this paragraph (b) does not include any property which is used predominantly outside the United States and which qualifies as section 38 property under—

(i) Section 48(a)(2)(B)(v), relating to containers used in the transportation of property to and from the United States.

(ii) Section 48(a)(2)(B)(vi), relating to certain property used for the purpose of exploring for, developing, removing, or transporting resources from the Outer Continental Shelf, or

(iii) Section 48(a)(2)(B)(x), relating to certain property used in international or territorial waters.

(c) Leases or subleases to which the election applies. At the time the election under this section is made and for all taxable years for which the election applies, the lessee of the aircraft or vessel must be a United States person. In addition, the aircraft or vessel may not be subleased to a person who is not a United States person unless the sublease is a short-term sublease. For purposes of this section, a short-term sublease is a sublease for a period of time (including any period for which the sublease may be renewed or extended) which is less than 30 percent of the asset guideline period of the aircraft or vessel leased (determined under section 167(m)). See paragraph (g)(3) and (4) of this section for rules which apply if the requirements of this paragraph (c) are not met.

(d) Income to which the election applies. An election under this section applies to all amounts derived by the taxpayer with respect to the aircraft or vessel which is subject to the election. The election applies to all amounts which are includible in the taxpayer's gross income whether or not includible during or after the period of a lease to which the election applies. Amounts derived by the taxpayer with respect to the aircraft or vessel include any gain from the sale, exchange, or other disposition of the aircraft or vessel. If by reason of the allowance of expenses and other deductions, there is a loss with respect to an aircraft or vessel, the election applies to treat the loss as having a source within the United States. Similarly, if the sale, exchange or other disposition of the aircraft or vessel which is subject to an election results in a loss, it is treated as having a source within the United States. See paragraph (e)(2) of this section for the application of an election under this section to the income of certain transferees or distributees.

(e) Effect of election. *(1) In general.* An election under this section applies to the taxable year for which it is made and to all subsequent taxable years for which amounts in respect of the aircraft or vessel to which the election relates are includible in gross income. However, the election may be revoked under paragraph (g)(1) or (2) of this section or terminated under paragraph (g)(3) of this section.

(2) Certain transfers involving carryover of basis. (i) If an electing taxpayer transfers or distributes an aircraft or vessel which is subject to the election under this section, the transferee or distributee will be treated as having made an election under this section with respect to the aircraft or vessel if the basis of the aircraft or vessel in the hands of the transferee or distributee is determined by reference to its basis in the hands of the transferor or distributor. This paragraph (e)(2)(i) applies even though the transferor or distributor recognizes an amount of gain which increases basis in the hands of the transferee or distributee and even though the transferee of distributee is a nonresident alien individual or foreign corporation. For example, if a corporation distributes a vessel which is subject to an election under this section to its parent corporation in a complete liquidation described in section 332(b), the parent corporation will be required to treat all amounts includible in its gross income with respect to the vessel as income from source within the United States, if, unless the election is revoked or terminated under paragraph (g) of this section, the basis of the property in the hands of the parent is determined under section 334(b)(1) (relating to the general rule on carryover of basis). In further illustration, if a corporation distributes a vessel (subject to an election) in a distribution to which section 301(a) applies, the distributee will be treated as having made the election with respect to the vessel if its basis is determined under section 301(d)(2) (relating to basis of corporate distributees) even though the basis is the fair market value of the vessel under section 301(d)(2)(A).

(ii) If a member of an affiliated group which files a consolidated return transfers an aircraft or vessel subject to an election to another member of that group, the transferee will be treated as having made the election with respect to the aircraft or vessel. In addition, if a partnership distributes an aircraft or vessel subject to an election to a partner, the partner will be treated as having made the election with respect to the aircraft or vessel.

(iii) If paragraph (e)(2)(i) and (ii) of this section do not apply, the election under this section with respect to an aircraft or vessel will not be considered as made by a transferee or distributee.

(f) Election. *(1) Time for making the election.* The election under this section must be made before the expiration of the period prescribed by section 6511(a) (or section 6511(c) if the period is extended by agreement) for making a claim for credit or refund of the tax imposed by chapter 1 for the first taxable year for which the election is to apply. The period for that first taxable year is determined without regard to the special periods prescribed by section 6511(d).

(2) Manner of making the election. An election under this section must be made by filing with the income tax return (or an amended return) for the first taxable year for which the election is to apply a statement, signed by the taxpayer, to the effect that the election under section 861(e) is being made. The statement must—

(i) Set forth sufficient facts to identify the aircraft or vessel which is the subject of the election.

(ii) State that the aircraft or vessel was manufactured or constructed in the United States.

(iii) State that the aircraft or vessel is section 38 property described in § 1.861-9(b) which was leased to a United States person (as defined in section 7701(a)(30) of the Code) pursuant to a lease entered into after August 15, 1971.

(iv) State that the electing taxpayer is the owner of the aircraft or vessel.

(v) State the lessee of the aircraft or vessel is not a member of a controlled group of corporations (as defined in section 1563) of which the taxpayer is a member.

(vi) Give the name and taxpayer identification number of the lessee of the aircraft or vessel, and

(vii) State that the aircraft or vessel is not subject to a sublease (other than a short-term sublease) to any person who is not a United States person.

(3) Election by partnership Any election under this section with respect to an aircraft or vessel owned by a partnership shall be made by the partnership. Any partnership election is applicable to each partner's partnership interest in the aircraft or vessel. However, an election made by a partner before August 8, 1979 will be recognized where the partnership made no election and the election can no longer be revoked without the consent of the Commissioner under paragraph (g)(1) of this section.

(g) Termination of election. *(1) Revocation without consent.* A taxpayer may revoke an election within the time prescribed in paragraph (f)(1) of this section without the consent of the Commissioner. In such a case, the taxpayer must file an amended income tax return for any taxable year to which the election applied.

(2) Revocation with consent. Except as provided in paragraph (g)(1) or (3) of this section, an election made under this section is binding unless consent to revoke is obtained from the Commissioner. A request to revoke the election must be made in writing and addressed to the Assistant Commissioner of Internal Revenue (Technical), Attention: T:C:C:3, Washington, D.C. 20224. The request must include the name and address of the taxpayer and be signed by the taxpayer or his duly authorized representative. It must specify the taxable year or years for which the revocation is to be effective and must be filed at least 90 days prior to the time (not including extensions) prescribed by law for filing the income tax return for the first taxable year for which the revocation of the election is to be effective or by November 6, 1979 whichever is later. The request must specify the grounds which are considered to justify the revocation. The Commissioner may require such additional information as may be necessary in order to determine whether the proposed revocation will be permitted. Consent will generally not be given to revoke an election where the revocation would result in treating gross income with respect to the aircraft or vessel (including any gain from the sale, exchange, or other disposition of such aircraft or vessel) as income from sources without the United States where, during the period the election was in effect, there were losses from sources within the United States. A copy of the consent of the Commissioner to revoke must be attached to the taxpayer's income tax return (or amended return) for each taxable year affected by the revocation.

(3) Automatic termination. If an aircraft or vessel subject to an election under section 861(e) ceases to be section 38 property, ceases to be leased by its owner directly to a United States person, or is subleased (other than a short-term sublease) to a person who is not a United States person, within the period set forth in section 6511(a) (or section 6511(c) if the period is extended by agreement) for making a claim for credit or refund of the tax imposed by chapter 1 for the first taxable year for which the election applied, then the election with respect to such aircraft or vessel will automatically terminate. If the election terminates, the taxpayer who made the election must file an amended tax return or claim for credit or refund, as the case may be, for any taxable year to which the election applied.

(4) Factors not causing revocation or termination. The fact that an aircraft or vessel ceases to be section 38 property, ceases to be leased by its owner directly to a United States person, or is leased or subleased for any period of time to a person who is not a United States person, after expiration of the period set forth in section 6511(a) (or section 6511(c) if the period is extended by agreement) for making a claim for credit or refund of the tax imposed by chapter 1 for the first taxable year for which the election applied, will not cause a termination of the election made under this section with respect to the aircraft or vessel. For example, the electing taxpayer is not relieved from any of the consequences of making the election merely because the aircraft or vessel is subleased to a person who is not a United States person for a period in excess of that allowed for short-term subleases under paragraph (c) of this section after expiration of the later of 3 years from the time the return was filed for the first taxable year to which the election applied or 2 years from the time the tax was paid for that year where the period set forth in section 6511(a) has not been extended by agreement.

(5) Effect of revocation or termination. If an election is revoked or terminated under this paragraph (g), the taxpayer is required to recompute the tax for the appropriate taxable years without reference to section 861(e)(1).

T.D. 7635, 8/7/79, amend T.D. 7928, 12/15/83, T.D. 8228, 9/9/88.

§ 1.861-16 Income from certain craft first leased after December 28, 1980.

(a) General rule. If a taxpayer—

(1) Owns a qualified craft (as defined in paragraph (b) of this section).

(2) Leases such qualified craft after December 28, 1980, to a United States person that is not a member of the same controlled group of corporations as the taxpayer, and

(3) The lease is the taxpayer's first lease of the craft and the taxpayer is not considered to have made an election with respect to the craft under § 1.861-9(e)(2),

then the taxpayer shall treat all amounts includible in gross income with respect to the qualified craft as income from sources within the United States for each taxable year ending after commencement of the lease. If this section applies to income with respect to a craft, it applies to all such amounts that are includible in the taxpayer's gross income, whether or not includible during or after the period of a lease to a United States person. Amounts derived by the taxpayer with respect to the qualified craft include any gain from the sale, exchange, or other disposition of the qualified craft. If this section applies to income with respect to a craft and there is a loss with respect to that craft (either due to the allowance of expenses and other deductions or due to a sale, exchange, or other disposition of the qualified craft), such loss is treated as allocable or apportionable to sources within the United States. The fact that a craft ceases to be section 38 property, ceases to be leased by the taxpayer to a United States person, or is leased or subleased for any period of time to a person who is not a United States person will not terminate the application of this section.

(b) Qualified craft. *(1) In general.* A qualified craft is a vessel, aircraft, or spacecraft that—

(i) Is section 38 property (or would be section 38 property but for section 48(a)(5), relating to use by governmental units, and

(ii) Is manufactured or constructed in the United States.

(2) Vessel. The term "vessel" includes every type of watercraft capable of being used as a means of transportation on water, and any items of property that are affixed in a permanent fashion or are integral to the vessel. A vessel that is used predominately outside the United States must be described in section 48(a)(2)(B)(iii) and § 1.48-1(g)(2)(iii), relating to vessels documented for use in the foreign or domestic commerce of the United States, to be a qualified craft.

(3) Aircraft. An aircraft used predominantly outside the United States must be described in section 48(a)(2)(B)(i) and § 1.48-1(g)(2)(i), relating to aircraft registered by the Administrator of the Federal Aviation Agency, and operated to and from the United States or operated under contract with the United States, to be a qualified craft.

(4) Spacecraft. A spacecraft must be described in section 48(a)(2)(B)(viii) and § 1.48-1(g)(2)(viii), relating to commu-

nications satellites, or any interest therein, of a United States person, to be a qualified craft.

(5) United States manufacture or construction. A craft will be considered to be manufactured or constructed in the United States if 50 percent or more of the basis of the craft on the date of the lease to a United States person is attributable to value added within the United States.

(c) United States person. For purposes of this section, the term "United States person" includes those persons described in section 7701(a)(30) and individuals with respect to whom an election under section 6013(g) or (h) (relating to nonresident alien individuals married to United States citizens or residents) is in effect.

(d) Controlled group. For purposes of paragraph (a)(2) of this section, whether a taxpayer and a United States person are members of the same controlled group of corporations is determined under section 1563. Solely for purposes of this section, if at least 80% of the capital interest, or the profits interest, in a partnership is owned, directly or indirectly, by a member or members of a controlled group of corporations, then the partnership shall be considered a member of that controlled group of corporations. In addition, if at least 80% of the capital interest, or the profits interest, in a partnership is owned, directly or indirectly, by a corporation, then the partnership and that corporation shall be considered members of a controlled group of corporations.

(e) Certain transfers and distributions. *(1) Transfers and distributions involving carryover of basis. If—*

(i) The income with respect to a craft is subject to this section.

(ii) The taxpayer transfers or distributes such craft, and

(iii) The basis of such craft in the hands of the transferee or distributee is determined by reference to its basis in the hands of the transferor or distributor,

then this section will apply to the income with respect to the craft includible in the gross income of the transferee or distributee. This paragraph (e)(1) applies even though the transferor or distributor recognizes an amount of gain that increases basis in the hands of the transferee or distributee and even though the transferee or distributee is a nonresident alien or foreign corporation. For example, if a corporation distributes a craft the income of which is subject to this section to its parent corporation in a complete liquidation described in section 332(b), the parent corporation will be treated as if it satisfied the requirements of paragraph (a) of this section with respect to such craft if the basis of the property in the hands of the parent corporation is determined under section 334(b) (relating to the general rule on carryover of basis in liquidations). In further illustration, if a corporation distributes a craft the income of which is subject to this section, in a distribution to which section 301(a) applies, the distributee will be treated as if it satisfied the requirements of paragraph (a) of this section with respect to such craft if its basis is determined under section 301(d)(2) (relating to basis of corporate distributees) even though the basis may be the fair market value of the craft under section 301(d)(2)(A).

(2) Partnerships. If a partnership satisfies the requirements of paragraph (a)(1), (2), and (3) of this section, each partner shall treat all amounts includible in gross income with respect to the craft as income from sources within the United States for any taxable year of the partnership ending after commencement of the lease. In addition, if a partnership distributes a craft the income of which is subject to this section, to a partner, the partner will be treated as if he or she satisfied the requirements of paragraph (a) of this section with respect to such craft.

(3) Affiliated groups. If a member of a group of corporations that files a consolidated return transfers a craft, the income of which is subject to this section, to another member of that same group, the transferee will be treated as if it satisfied the requirements of paragraph (a) of this section with respect to the craft.

T.D. 7928, 12/15/83, amend T.D. 8228, 9/9/88.

---

§ 1.861-17 Allocation and apportionment of research and experimental expenditures.

(a) Allocation.

(1) In general. The methods of allocation and apportionment of research and experimental expenditures set forth in this section recognize that research and experimentation is an inherently speculative activity, that findings may contribute unexpected benefits, and that the gross income derived from successful research and experimentation must bear the cost of unsuccessful research and experimentation. Expenditures for research and experimentation that a taxpayer deducts under section 174 ordinarily shall be considered deductions that are definitely related to all income reasonably connected with the relevant broad product category (or categories) of the taxpayer and therefore allocable to all items of gross income as a class (including income from sales, royalties, and dividends) related to such product category (or categories). For purposes of this allocation, the product category (or categories) that a taxpayer may be considered to have shall be determined in accordance with the provisions of paragraph (a)(2) of this section.

(2) Product categories. (i) Allocation based on product categories. Ordinarily, a taxpayer's research and experimental expenditures may be divided between the relevant product categories. Where research and experimentation is conducted with respect to more than one product category, the taxpayer may aggregate the categories for purposes of allocation and apportionment; however, the taxpayer may not subdivide the categories. Where research and experimentation is not clearly identified with any product category (or categories), it will be considered conducted with respect to all the taxpayer's product categories.

(ii) Use of three digit standard industrial classification codes. A taxpayer shall determine the relevant product categories by reference to the three digit classification of the Standard Industrial Classification Manual (SIC code). A copy may be purchased from the Superintendent of Documents, United States Government Printing Office, Washington, DC 20402. The individual products included within each category are enumerated in Executive Office of the President, Office of Management and Budget, Standard Industrial Classification Manual, 1987 (or later edition, as available).

(iii) Consistency. Once a taxpayer selects a product category for the first taxable year for which this section is effective with respect to the taxpayer, it must continue to use that product category in following years, unless the taxpayer establishes to the satisfaction of the Commissioner that, due to changes in the relevant facts, a change in the product category is appropriate. For this purpose, a change in the taxpayer's selection of a product category shall include a change from a three digit SIC code category to a two digit SIC code category, a change from a two digit SIC code category to a three digit SIC code category, or any other aggregation, disaggregation or change of a previously selected SIC code category.

(iv) Wholesale trade category. The two digit SIC code category "Wholesale trade" is not applicable with respect to sales by the taxpayer of goods and services from any other of the taxpayer's product categories and is not applicable with respect to a domestic international sales corporation (DISC) or foreign sales corporation (FSC) for which the taxpayer is a related supplier of goods and services from any of the taxpayer's product categories.

(v) Retail trade category. The two digit SIC code category "Retail trade" is not applicable with respect to sales by the taxpayer of goods and services from any other of the taxpayer's product categories, except wholesale trade, and is not applicable with respect to a DISC or FSC for which the taxpayer is a related supplier of goods and services from any other of the taxpayer's product categories, except wholesale trade.

(3) Affiliated groups. (i) In general. Except as provided in paragraph (a)(3)(ii) of this section, the allocation and apportionment required by this section shall be determined as if all members of the affiliated group (as defined in § 1.861-14T(d)) were a single corporation. See § 1.861-14T.

(ii) Possessions corporations. (A) For purposes of the allocation and apportionment required by this section, sales and gross income from products produced in whole or in part in a possession by an electing corporation (within the meaning of section 936(h)(5)(E)), and dividends from an electing corporation, shall not be taken into account, except that this paragraph (a)(3)(ii) shall not apply to sales of (and gross income and dividends attributable to sales of) products with respect to which an election under section 936(h)(5)(F) is not in effect.

(B) The research and experimental expenditures taken into account for purposes of this section shall be reduced by the amount of such expenditures included in computing the cost-sharing amount (determined under section 936(h)(5)(C)(i)).

(4) Legally mandated research and experimentation. Where research and experimentation is undertaken solely to meet legal requirements imposed by a political entity with respect to improvement or marketing of specific products or processes, and the results cannot reasonably be expected to generate amounts of gross income (beyond de minimis amounts) outside a single geographic source, the deduction for such research and experimentation shall be considered definitely related and therefore allocable only to the grouping (or groupings) of gross income within that geographic source as a class (and apportioned, if necessary, between such groupings as set forth in paragraphs (c) and (d) of this section). For example, where a taxpayer performs tests on a product in response to a requirement imposed by the U.S. Food and Drug Administration, and the test results cannot reasonably be expected to generate amounts of gross income (beyond de minimis amounts) outside the United States, the costs of testing shall be allocated solely to gross income from sources within the United States.

(b) Exclusive apportionment. *(1) In general.* An exclusive apportionment shall be made under this paragraph (b), where an apportionment based upon geographic sources of income of a deduction for research and experimentation is necessary (after applying the exception in paragraph (a)(4) of this section).

(i) Exclusive apportionment under the sales method. If the taxpayer apportions on the sales method under paragraph (c) of this section, an amount equal to fifty percent of such deduction for research and experimentation shall be apportioned exclusively to the statutory grouping of gross income or the residual grouping of gross income, as the case may be, arising from the geographic source where the research and experimental activities which account for more than fifty percent of the amount of such deduction were performed.

(ii) Exclusive apportionment under the optional gross income methods. If the taxpayer apportions on the optional gross income methods under paragraph (d) of this section, an amount equal to twenty-five percent of such deduction for research and experimentation shall be apportioned exclusively to the statutory grouping or the residual grouping of gross income, as the case may be, arising from the geographic source where the research and experimental activities which account for more than fifty percent of the amount of such deduction were performed.

(iii) Exception. If the applicable fifty percent geographic source test of the preceding paragraph (b)(1)(i) or (ii) is not met, then no part of the deduction shall be apportioned under this paragraph (b)(1).

(2) Facts and circumstances supporting an increased exclusive apportionment. (i) In general. The exclusive apportionment provided for in paragraph (b)(1) of this section reflects the view that research and experimentation is often most valuable in the country where it is performed, for two reasons. First, research and experimentation often benefits a broad product category, consisting of many individual products, all of which may be sold in the nearest market but only some of which may be sold in foreign markets. Second, research and experimentation often is utilized in the nearest market before it is used in other markets, and in such cases, has a lower value per unit of sales when used in foreign markets. The taxpayer may establish to the satisfaction of the Commissioner that, in its case, one or both of the conditions mentioned in the preceding sentences warrant a significantly greater exclusive allocation percentage than allowed by paragraph (b)(1) of this section because the research and experimentation is reasonably expected to have very limited or long delayed application outside the geographic source where it was performed. Past experience with research and experimentation may be considered in determining reasonable expectations.

(ii) Not all products sold in foreign markets. For purposes of establishing that only some products within the product category (or categories) are sold in foreign markets, the taxpayer shall compare the commercial production of individual products in domestic and foreign markets made by itself, by uncontrolled parties (as defined under paragraph (c)(2)(i) of this section) of products involving intangible property which was licensed or sold by the taxpayer, and by those controlled corporations (as defined under paragraph (c)(3)(ii) of this section) that can reasonably be expected to benefit directly or indirectly from any of the taxpayer's research expense connected with the product category (or categories). The individual products compared for this purpose shall be limited, for nonmanufactured categories, solely to those enumerated in Executive Office of the President, Office of Management and Budget Standard Industrial Classification Manual, 1987 (or later edition, as available), and, for manufactured categories, solely to those enumerated at a 7-digit level in the U.S. Bureau of the Census, Census of Manufacturers: 1992, Numerical List of Manufactured Products, 1993, (or later edition, as available). Copies of both of these documents may be purchased from the Superintendent of Documents, United States Government Printing Office, Washington, DC 20402.

(iii) Delayed application of research findings abroad. For purposes of establishing the delayed application of research findings abroad, the taxpayer shall compare the commercial introduction of its own particular products and processes (not limited by those listed in the Standard Industrial Classification Manual or the Numerical List of Manufactured Products) in the United States and foreign markets, made by itself, by uncontrolled parties (as defined under paragraph (c)(2)(i) of this section) of products involving intangible property that was licensed or sold by the taxpayer, and by those controlled corporations (as defined under paragraph (c)(3)(i) of this section) that can reasonably be expected to benefit, directly or indirectly, from the taxpayer's research expense. For purposes of evaluating the delay in the application of research findings in foreign markets, the taxpayer shall use a safe haven discount rate of 10 percent per year of delay unless he is able to establish to the satisfaction of the Commissioner, by reference to the cost of money and the number of years during which economic benefit can be directly attributable to the results of the taxpayer's research, that another discount rate is more appropriate.

(c) Sales method. *(1) In general.* The amount equal to the remaining portion of such deduction for research and experimentation, not apportioned under paragraph (a)(4) or (b)(1)(i) of this section, shall be apportioned between the statutory grouping (or among the statutory groupings) within the class of gross income and the residual grouping within such class in the same proportions that the amount of sales from the product category (or categories) that resulted in such gross income within the statutory grouping (or statutory groupings) and in the residual grouping bear, respectively, to the total amount of sales from the product category (or categories).

(i) Apportionment in excess of gross income. Amounts apportioned under this section may exceed the amount of gross income related to the product category within the statutory grouping. In such case, the excess shall be applied against other gross income within the statutory grouping. See § 1.861-8(d)(1) for instances where the apportionment leads to an excess of deductions over gross income within the statutory grouping.

(ii) Leased property. For purposes of this paragraph (c), amounts received from the lease of equipment during a taxable year shall be regarded as sales receipts for such taxable year.

(2) Sales of uncontrolled parties. For purposes of the apportionment under paragraph (c)(1) of this section, the sales from the product category (or categories) by each party uncontrolled by the taxpayer, of particular products involving intangible property that was licensed or sold by the taxpayer to such uncontrolled party shall be taken fully into account both for determining the taxpayer's apportionment and for determining the apportionment of any other member of a controlled group of corporations to which the taxpayer belongs if the uncontrolled party can reasonably be expected to benefit directly or indirectly (through any member of the controlled group of corporations to which the taxpayer belongs) from the research expense connected with the product category (or categories) of such other member. An uncontrolled party can reasonably be expected to benefit from the research expense of a member of a controlled group of corporations to which the taxpayer belongs if such member can reasonably be expected to license, sell, or transfer intangible property to that uncontrolled party or transfer secret processes to that uncontrolled party, directly or indirectly through a member of the controlled group of corporations to which the taxpayer belongs. Past experience with research and experimentation shall be considered in determining reasonable expectations.

(i) Definition of uncontrolled party. For purposes of this paragraph (c)(2) the term uncontrolled party means a party that is not a person with a relationship to the taxpayer specified in section 267(b), or is not a member of a controlled group of corporations to which the taxpayer belongs (within the meaning of section 993(a)(3) or 927(d)(4)).

(ii) Licensed products. In the case of licensed products, if the amount of sales of such products is unknown (for example, where the licensed product is a component of a large machine), a reasonable estimate based on the principles of section 482 should be made.

(iii) Sales of intangible property. In the case of sales of intangible property, regardless of whether the consideration received in exchange for the intangible is a fixed amount or is contingent on the productivity, use, or disposition of the intangible, if the amount of sales of products utilizing the intangible property is unknown, a reasonable estimate of sales shall be made annually. If necessary, appropriate economic analyses shall be used to estimate sales.

(3) Sales of controlled parties. For purposes of the apportionment under paragraph (c)(1) of this section, the sales from the product category (or categories) of the taxpayer shall be taken fully into account and the sales from the product category (or categories) of a corporation controlled by the taxpayer shall be taken into account to the extent provided in this paragraph (c)(3) for determining the taxpayer's apportionment, if such corporation can reasonably be expected to benefit directly or indirectly (through another member of the controlled group of corporations to which the taxpayer belongs) from the taxpayer's research expense connected with the product category (or categories). A corporation controlled by the taxpayer can reasonably be expected to benefit from the taxpayer's research expense if the taxpayer can be expected to license, sell, or transfer intangible property to that corporation or transfer secret processes to that corporation, either directly or indirectly through a member of the controlled group of corporations to which the taxpayer belongs. Past experience with research and experimentation shall be considered in determining reasonable expectations.

(i) Definition of a corporation controlled by the taxpayer. For purposes of this paragraph (c)(3), the term a corporation controlled by the taxpayer means any corporation that has a relationship to the taxpayer specified in section 267(b) or is a member of a controlled group of corporations to which the taxpayer belongs (within the meaning of section 993(a)(3) or 927(d)(4).

(ii) Sales to be taken into account. The sales from the product category (or categories) of a corporation controlled by the taxpayer taken into account shall be equal to the amount of sales that bear the same proportion to the total sales of the controlled corporation as the total value of all classes of the stock of such corporation owned directly or indirectly by the taxpayer, within the meaning of section 1563, bears to the total value of all classes of stock of such corporation.

(iii) Sales not to be taken into account more than once. Sales from the product category (or categories) between or among such controlled corporations or the taxpayer shall not be taken into account more than once; in such a situation, the amount sold by the selling corporation to the buying corporation shall be subtracted from the sales of the buying corporation.

(iv) Effect of cost-sharing arrangements. If the corporation controlled by the taxpayer has entered into a bona fide cost-sharing arrangement, in accordance with the provisions of § 1.482-7, with the taxpayer for the purpose of developing intangible property, then that corporation shall not reasonably be expected to benefit from the taxpayer's share of the research expense.

(d) Gross income methods. *(1)* (i) In general. In lieu of applying the sales method of paragraph (c) of this section, the remaining amount of the deduction for research and experimentation, not apportioned under paragraph (a)(4) or (b)(1)(ii) of this section, shall be apportioned as prescribed in paragraphs (d)(2) and (3) of this section, between the statutory grouping (or among the statutory groupings) of gross income and the residual grouping of gross income.

(ii) Optional methods to be applied to all research and experimental expenditures. These optional methods must be applied to the taxpayer's entire deduction for research and experimental expense remaining after applying the exception in paragraph (a)(4) of this section, and may not be applied on a product category basis. Thus, after the allocation of the taxpayer's entire deduction for research and experimental expense under paragraph (a)(2) of this section (by attribution to SIC code categories), the taxpayer must then apportion as necessary the entire deduction as allocated by separate amounts to various product categories, using only the sales method under paragraph (c) of this section or only the optional gross income methods under this paragraph (d). The taxpayer may not use the sales method for a portion of the deduction and optional gross income methods for the remainder of the deduction separately allocated.

(2) Option one. The taxpayer may apportion its research and experimental expenditures ratably on the basis of gross income between the statutory grouping (or among the statutory groupings) of gross income and the residual grouping of gross income in the same proportions that the amount of gross income in the statutory grouping (or groupings) and the amount of gross income in the residual grouping bear, respectively, to the total amount of gross income, if the conditions described in paragraph (d)(2)(i) and (ii) of this section are both met.

(i) The amount of research and experimental expense ratably apportioned to the statutory grouping (or groupings in the aggregate) is not less than fifty percent of the amount that would have been so apportioned if the taxpayer had used the method described in paragraph (c) of this section; and

(ii) The amount of research and experimental expense ratably apportioned to the residual grouping is not less than fifty percent of the amount that would have been so apportioned if the taxpayer had used the method described in paragraph (c) of this section.

(3) Option two. If, when the amount of research and experimental expense is apportioned ratably on the basis of gross income, either of the conditions described in paragraph (d)(2)(i) or (ii) of this section is not met, the taxpayer may either—

(i) Where the condition of paragraph (d)(2)(i) of this section is not met, apportion fifty percent of the amount of research and experimental expense that would have been apportioned to the statutory grouping (or groupings in the aggregate) under paragraph (c) of this section to such statutory grouping (or to such statutory groupings in the aggregate and then among such groupings on the basis of gross income within each grouping), and apportion the balance of the amount of research and experimental expenses to the residual grouping; or

(ii) Where the condition of paragraph (d)(2)(ii) of this section is not met, apportion fifty percent of the amount of research and experimental expense that would have been apportioned to the residual grouping under paragraph (c) of this section to such residual grouping, and apportion the balance of the amount of research and experimental expenses to the statutory grouping (or to the statutory groupings in the aggregate and then among such groupings ratably on the basis of gross income within each grouping).

(e) Binding election. *(1) In general.* A taxpayer may choose to use either the sales method under paragraph (c) of this section or the optional gross income methods under paragraph (d) of this section for its original return for its first taxable year to which this section applies. The taxpayer's use of either the sales method or the optional gross income methods for its return filed for its first taxable year to which this section applies shall constitute a binding election to use the method chosen for that year and for four taxable years thereafter.

(2) Change of method. The taxpayer's election of a method may not be revoked during the period referred to in paragraph (e)(1) of this section without the prior consent of the Commissioner. After the expiration of that period, the taxpayer may change methods without the prior consent of the Commissioner. However, the taxpayer's use of the new method shall constitute a binding election to use the new method for its return filed for the first year for which the taxpayer uses the new method and for four taxable years thereafter. The taxpayer's election of the new method may not be revoked during that period without the prior consent of the Commissioner.

(i) Short taxable years. For purposes of this paragraph (e), the term *taxable year* includes a taxable year of less than twelve months.

(ii) Affiliated groups. In the case of an affiliated group, the period referred to in paragraph (e)(1) of this section shall commence as of the latest taxable year in which any member of the group has changed methods.

(f) Special rules for partnerships. *(1) Research and experimental expenditures.* For purposes of applying this section, if research and experimental expenditures are incurred by a partnership in which the taxpayer is a partner, the taxpayer's research and experimental expenditures shall include the taxpayer's distributive share of the partnership's research and experimental expenditures.

(2) Purpose and location of expenditures. In applying the exception for expenditures undertaken to meet legal requirements under paragraph (a)(4) of this section and the exclusive apportionment for the sales method and the optional gross income methods under paragraph (b) of this section, a partner's distributive share of research and experimental expenditures incurred by a partnership shall be treated as incurred by the partner for the same purpose and in the same location as incurred by the partnership.

(3) Apportionment under the sales method. In applying the remaining apportionment for the sales method under paragraph (c) of this section, a taxpayer's sales from a product category shall include the taxpayer's share of any sales from the product category of any partnership in which the taxpayer is a partner. For purposes of the preceding sentence, a taxpayer's share of sales shall be proportionate to the tax-

payer's distributive share of the partnership's gross income in the product category.

(g) Effective date. This section applies to taxable years beginning after December 31, 1995. However, a taxpayer may at its option, apply this section in its entirety to all taxable years beginning after August 1, 1994.

(h) Examples. The following examples illustrate the application of this section:

Example (1). (i) Facts. X, a domestic corporation, is a manufacturer and distributor of small gasoline engines for lawn mowers. Gasoline engines are a product within the category, Engines and Turbines (SIC Industry Group 351). Y, a wholly owned foreign subsidiary of X, also manufactures and sells these engines abroad. During 1996, X incurred expenditures of $60,000 on research and experimentation, which it deducts as a current expense, to invent and patent a new and improved gasoline engine. All of the research and experimentation was performed in the United States. In 1996, the domestic sales by X of the new engine total $500,000 and foreign sales by Y total $300,000. X provides technology for the manufacture of engines to Y via a license that requires the payment of an arm's length royalty. In 1996, X's gross income is $160,000, of which $140,000 is U.S. source income from domestic sales of gasoline engines and $10,000 is foreign source royalties from Y, and $10,000 is U.S. source interest income.

(ii) Allocation. The research and experimental expenditures were incurred in connection with small gasoline engines and they are definitely related to the items of gross income to which the research gives rise, namely gross income from the sale of small gasoline engines in the United States and royalties received from subsidiary Y, a foreign manufacturer of gasoline engines. Accordingly, the expenses are allocable to this class of gross income. The U.S. source interest income is not within this class of gross income and, therefore, is not taken into account.

(iii) Apportionment. (A) For purposes of applying the foreign tax credit limitation, the statutory grouping is general limitation gross income from sources without the United States and the residual grouping is gross income from sources within the United States. Since the related class of gross income derived from the use of engine technology consists of both gross income from sources without the United States (royalties from Y) and gross income from sources within the United States (gross income from engine sales), X's deduction of $60,000 for its research and experimental expenditure must be apportioned between the statutory and residual grouping before the foreign tax credit limitation may be determined. Because more than 50 percent of X's research and experimental activity was performed in the United States, 50 percent of that deduction can be apportioned exclusively to the residual grouping of gross income, gross income from sources within the United States. The remaining 50 percent of the deduction can then be apportioned between the residual and statutory groupings on the basis of sales of small gasoline engines by X and Y. Alternatively, X's deduction for research and experimentation can be apportioned under the optional gross income method. The apportionment for 1996 is as follows: Tentative Apportionment on the Basis of Sales.

(i) Research and experimental expense to be apportioned between residual and statutory groupings of gross income:	$60,000
(ii) Less: Exclusive apportionment of research and experimental expense to the residual grouping of gross income ($60,000 × 50 percent):	$30,000
(iii) Research and experimental expense to be apportioned between residual and statutory groupings of gross income on the basis of sales:	$30,000
(iv) Apportionment of research and experimental expense to the residual grouping of gross income ($30,000 × $500,000/($500,000 + $300,000)):	$18,750
(v) Apportionment of research and experimental expense to the statutory grouping of gross income ($30,000 × $300,000/($500,000 + $300,000)):	$11,250
(vi) Total apportioned deduction for research and experimentation:	$60,000
(vii) Amount apportioned to the residual grouping ($30,000 + $18,750):	$48,750
(viii) Amount apportioned to the statutory grouping:	$11,250

(2) Tentative Apportionment on the Basis of Gross Income.

(i) Exclusive apportionment of research and experimental expense to the residual grouping of gross income ($60,000 × 25 percent):	$15,000
(ii) Research and experimental expense apportioned to sources within the United States (residual grouping) ($45,000 × $140,000/($140,000 + $10,000)):	$42,000
(iii) Research and experimental expense apportioned to sources within country Y (statutory grouping) ($45,000 × $10,000/($140,000 + $10,000)):	$ 3,000
(iv) Amount apportioned to the residual grouping:	$57,000
(v) Amount apportioned to the statutory grouping:	$ 3,000

(B) The total research and experimental expense apportioned to the statutory grouping ($3,000) under the gross income method is approximately 26 percent of the amount apportioned to the statutory grouping under the sales method. Thus, X may use option two of the gross income method (paragraph (d)(3) of this section) and apportion to the statutory grouping fifty percent (50%) of the $11,250 apportioned to that grouping under the sales method. Thus, X apportions $5,625 of research and experimental expense to the statutory grouping. X's use of the optional gross income methods will constitute a binding election to use the optional gross income methods for 1996 and four taxable years thereafter.

Example (2). (i) Facts. Assume the same facts as in Example 1 except that X also spends $30,000 in 1996 for research on steam turbines, all of which is performed in the United States, and X has steam turbine sales in the United States of $400,000. X's foreign subsidiary Y neither manufactures nor sells steam turbines. The steam turbine research is in addition to the $60,000 in research which X does on gasoline engines for lawnmowers. X thus has a deduction of $90,000 for its research activity. X's gross income is $200,000, of which $140,000 is U.S. source income from domestic sales of gasoline engines, $50,000 is U.S. source income from domestic sales of steam turbines, and $10,000 is foreign source royalties from Y.

(ii) Allocation. X's research expenses generate income from sales of small gasoline engines and steam turbines. Both of these products are in the same three digit SIC code category, Engines and Turbines (SIC Industry Group 351). Therefore, the deduction is definitely related to this product category and allocable to all items of income attributable to it. These items of X's income are gross income from the sale of small gasoline engines and steam turbines in the United States and royalties from foreign subsidiary Y, a foreign manufacturer and seller of small gasoline engines.

(iii) Apportionment. (A) For purposes of applying the foreign tax credit limitation, the statutory grouping is general limitation gross income from sources outside the United States and the residual grouping is gross income from sources within the United States. X's deduction of $90,000 must be apportioned between the statutory and residual groupings. Because more than 50 percent of X's research and experimental activity was performed in the United States, 50 percent of that deduction can be apportioned exclusively to the residual grouping, gross income from sources within the United States. The remaining 50 percent of the deduction can then be apportioned between the residual and statutory groupings on the basis of total sales of small gasoline engines and steam turbines by X and Y. Alternatively, X's deduction for research and experimentation can be apportioned under the optional gross income methods. The apportionment for 1996 is as follows: Tentative Apportionment on the Basis of Sales.

(i) Research and experimental expense to be apportioned between residual and statutory groupings of gross income:	$90,000
(ii) Less: Exclusive apportionment of the research and experimental expense to the residual grouping of gross income ($90,000 × 50 percent):	$45,000
(iii) Research and experimental expense to be apportioned between the residual and statutory groupings of gross income on the basis of sales:	$45,000
(iv) Apportionment of research and experimental expense to the residual grouping of gross income ($45,000 × ($500,000 + 400,000)/($500,000 + $400,000 + $300,000)):	$33,750
(v) Apportionment of research and experimental expense to the statutory grouping of gross income ($45,000 × $300,000/($500,000 + $400,000 + $300,000)):	$11,250
(vi) Total apportioned deduction for research and experimentation:	$90,000
(vii) Amount apportioned to the residual grouping ($45,000 + $33,750):	$78,750
(viii) Amount apportioned to the statutory grouping:	$11,250

(2) Tentative Apportionment on the Basis of Gross Income.

(i) Exclusive apportionment of research and experimental expense to the residual grouping of gross income ($90,000 × 25 percent):	$22,500
(ii) Research and experimental expense apportioned to sources within the United States (residual grouping) ($67,500 × $190,000/($140,000 + $50,000 + $10,000)):	$64,125
(iii) Research and experimental expense apportioned to sources within country Y (statutory grouping) ($67,500 × $10,000/($140,000 + $50,000 + $10,000)):	$ 3,375
(iv) Amount apportioned to the residual grouping:	$86,625
(v) Amount apportioned to the statutory grouping:	$ 3,375

(B) The total research and experimental expense apportioned to the statutory grouping ($3,375) under the gross income method is 30 percent of the amount apportioned to the statutory grouping under the sales method. Thus, X may use option two of the gross income method (paragraph (d)(3) of this section) and apportion to the statutory grouping fifty percent (50%) of the $11,250 apportioned to that grouping under the sales method. Thus, X apportions $5,625 of research and experimental expense to the statutory grouping. X's use of the optional gross income methods will constitute a binding election to use the optional gross income methods for 1996 and four taxable years thereafter.

Example (3). (i) Facts. Assume the same facts as in Example 1 except that in 1997 X continues its sales of the new engines, with sales of $600,000 in the United States and $400,000 abroad by subsidiary Y. X also acquires a 60 percent (by value) ownership interest in foreign corporation Z and a 100 percent ownership interest in foreign corporation C. X transfers its engine technology to Z for a royalty equal to 5 percent of sales, and X enters into an arm's length cost-sharing arrangement with C to share the funding of all of X's research activity. In 1997, corporation Z has sales in country Z equal to $1,000,000. X incurs expense of $80,000 on research and experimentation in 1997, and in addition, X performs $15,000 of research on gasoline engines which was funded by the cost-sharing arrangement with C. All of Z's sales are from the product category, Engines and Turbines (SIC Industry Group 351). X performs all of its research in the United States and $20,000 of its expenditure of $80,000 is made solely to meet pollution standards mandated by law. X establishes, to the satisfaction of the Commissioner, that the expenditure in response to pollution standards is not expected to generate gross income (beyond de minimis amounts) outside the United States.

(ii) Allocation. The $20,000 of research expense which X incurred in connection with pollution standards is definitely related and thus allocable to the residual grouping, gross income from sources within the United States. The remaining $60,000 in research and experimental expenditure incurred by X is definitely related to all gasoline engines and is therefore allocable to the class of gross income to which the engines give rise, gross income from sales of gasoline engines in the United States, royalties from country Y, and royalties from country Z. No part of the $60,000 research expense is allocable to dividends from country C, because corporation C has already paid, through its cost-sharing arrangement, for research activity performed by X which may benefit C.

(iii) Apportionment. For purposes of applying the foreign tax credit limitation, the statutory grouping is general limitation gross income from sources without the United States, and the residual grouping is gross income from sources within the United States. X's deduction of $60,000 for its research and experimental expenditure must be apportioned between these groupings. Because more than 50 percent of the research and experimentation was performed in the United States, 50 percent of the $60,000 deduction can be apportioned exclusively to the residual grouping. The remaining 50 percent of the deduction can then be apportioned between the residual and the statutory grouping on the basis of sales of gasoline engines by X, Y, and Z. (If X utilized the optional gross income methods in 1996, then its use of such methods constituted a binding election to use the optional gross income methods in 1996 and for four taxable years thereafter. If X utilized the sales method in 1996, then its use of such method constituted a binding election to use the sales method in 1996 and for four taxable years thereafter.) The optional gross income methods are not illustrated in this Example 3 (see instead Examples 1 and 2). Since X has only a 60 percent ownership interest in corporation Z, only

60 percent of Z's sales (60% of $1,000,000, or $600,000) are included for purposes of apportionment. The allocation and apportionment for 1997 is as follows:

(A) X's total research expense:	$80,000
(B) Less: Legally mandated research directly allocated to the residual grouping of gross income:	$20,000
(C) Tentative apportionment on the basis of sales.	
(1) Research and experimental expense to be apportioned between residual and statutory groupings of gross income:	$60,000
(2) Less: Exclusive apportionment of research and experimental expense to the residual grouping of gross income ($60,000 × 50 percent):	$30,000
(3) Research and experimental expense to be apportioned between the residual and the statutory groupings on the basis of sales:	$30,000
(4) Apportionment of research and experimental expense to gross income from sources within the United States (residual grouping) ($30,000 × $600,000 / ($600,000 + $400,000 + $600,000)):	$11,250
(5) Apportionment of research and experimental expense to general limitation gross income from countries Y and Z (statutory grouping) ($30,000 × $400,000 + $600,000/($600,000 + $400,000 + $600,000)):	$18,750
(6) Total apportioned deduction for research and experimentation ($30,000 + $30,000):	$60,000
(7) Amount apportioned to the residual grouping ($30,000 + $11,250):	$41,250
(8) Amount apportioned to the statutory grouping of gross income from sources within countries Y and Z:	$18,750

Example (4). Research and experimentation.

(i) Facts. X, a domestic corporation, manufactures and sells forklift trucks and other types of materials handling equipment in the United States. The manufacture and sale of forklift trucks and other materials handling equipment belongs to the product category, Construction, Mining, and Materials Handling Machinery and Equipment (SIC Industry Group 353). X also sells its forklift trucks to a wholesaling subsidiary located in foreign country Y (but title passes in the United States), and X manufactures forklift trucks in foreign country Z. The wholesaling of forklift trucks to country Y also belongs to X's product category Transportation equipment and, therefore, may not belong to the product category, Wholesale trade (SIC Major Group 50 and 51). In 1997, X sold $7,000,000 of forklift trucks to purchasers in the United States, $3,000,000 of forklift trucks to the wholesaling subsidiary in Y, and transferred forklift truck components with an FOB export value of $2,000,000 to its branch in Z. The branch's sales of finished forklift trucks were $5,000,000. In response to legally mandated emission control requirements, X's United States research department has been engaged in a research project to improve the performance and quality of engine exhaust systems used on its products in the United States. It incurs expenses of $100,000 for this purpose in 1997. In the past, X has customarily adapted the product improvements developed originally for the domestic market to its forklift trucks manufactured abroad. During the taxable year 1997, development of an improved engine exhaust system is completed and X begins installing the new system during the latter part of the taxable year in products manufactured and sold in the United States. X continues to manufacture and sell forklift trucks in foreign countries without the improved engine exhaust systems.

(ii) Allocation. X's deduction for its research expense is definitely related to the income to which it gives rise, namely income from the manufacture and sale of forklift trucks within the United States and in country Z. Although the research is undertaken in response to a legal mandate, it can reasonably be expected to generate gross income from the manufacture and sale of trucks by the branch in Z. Therefore, the deduction is not allocable solely to income from X's domestic sales of forklift trucks. It is allocable to income from such sales and income from the sales of X's branch in Z.

(iii) Apportionment. For the method of apportionment on the basis of either sales or gross income, see Example 3. However, in determining the amount of research apportioned to income from foreign and domestic sources, the net sales of the branch in Z are $3,000,000 ($5,000,000 less $2,000,000) and the sales within the United States are $12,000,000 ($7,000,000 plus $3,000,000 plus $2,000,000). See § 1.861-17(c)(3)(iii).

Example (5). (i) Facts. X, a domestic corporation, is a drug company that manufactures a wide variety of pharmaceutical products for sale in the United States. Pharmaceutical products belong to the product category, Drugs (SIC Industry Group 283). X exports its pharmaceutical products through a foreign sales corporation (FSC). X's wholly owned foreign subsidiary Y also manufactures pharmaceutical products. In 1997, X has domestic sales of pharmaceutical products of $10,000,000, the FSC has sales of pharmaceutical products of $3,000,000, and Y has sales of pharmaceutical products of $5,000,000. In that same year, 1997, X incurs expense of $200,000 on research to test a product in response to requirements imposed by the United States Food and Drug Administration (FDA). X is able to show that, even though country Y imposes certain testing requirements on pharmaceutical products, the research performed in the United States is not accepted by country Y for purposes of its own licensing requirements, and the research has minimal use abroad. X is further able to show that FSC sells goods to countries that do not accept or do not require research performed in the United States for purposes of their own licensing standards.

(ii) Allocation. Since X's research expense of $200,000 is undertaken to meet the requirements of the United States Food and Drug Administration, and since it is reasonable to expect that the expenditure will not generate gross income (beyond de minimis amounts) outside the United States, the deduction is definitely related and thus allocable to the residual grouping.

(iii) Apportionment. No apportionment is necessary since the entire expense is allocated to the residual grouping, gross income from sales within the United States.

Example (6). (i) Facts. X, a domestic corporation, is engaged in continuous research and experimentation to improve the quality of the products that it manufactures and sells, which are floodlights, flashlights, fuse boxes, and solderless connectors. X incurs and deducts $100,000 of expenditure for research and experimentation in 1997 that was performed exclusively in the United States. As a result of this research activity, X acquires patents that it uses in its own manufacturing activity. X licenses its floodlight patent to Y and Z, uncontrolled foreign corporations, for use in their own territories, countries Y and Z, respectively. Corporation Y pays X an arm's length royalty of $3,000 plus $0.20 for each floodlight sold. Sales of floodlights by Y for the taxable year are $135,000 (at $4.50 per unit) or 30,000 units, and the royalty is $9,000 ($3,000 + $0.20 × 30,000).

Y has sales of other products of $500,000. Z pays X an arm's length royalty of $3,000 plus $0.30 for each unit sold. Z manufactures 30,000 floodlights in the taxable year, and the royalty is $12,000 ($3,000 + $0.30 × 30,000). The dollar value of Z's floodlight sales is not known and cannot be reasonably estimated because, in this case, the floodlights are not sold separately by Z but are instead used as a component in Z's manufacture of lighting equipment for theaters. The sales of all Z's products, including the lighting equipment for theaters, are $1,000,000. Y and Z each sell the floodlights exclusively within their respective countries. X's sales of floodlights for the taxable year are $500,000 and its sales of its other products, flashlights, fuse boxes, and solderless connectors, are $400,000. X has gross income of $500,000, consisting of gross income from domestic sources from sales of floodlights, flashlights, fuse boxes, and solderless connectors of $479,000, and royalty income of $9,000 and $12,000 from foreign corporations Y and Z respectively. X utilized the optional gross income methods of apportionment for its return filed for its first taxable year to which this section applies.

(ii) Allocation. X's research and experimental expenses are definitely related to all of the products that it produces, which are floodlights, flashlights, fuse boxes, and solderless connectors. All of these products are in the same three digit SIC Code category, Electric Lighting and Wiring Equipment (SIC Industry Group 364). Thus, X's research and experimental expenses are allocable to all items of income attributable to this product category, domestic sales income and royalty income from the foreign countries in which corporations Y and Z operate.

(iii) Apportionment. (A) The statutory grouping of gross income is general limitation income from sources without the United States. The residual grouping is gross income from sources within the United States. X's deduction of $100,000 for its research expenditures must be apportioned between the groupings. For apportionment on the basis of sales in accordance with paragraph (c) of this section, X is entitled to an exclusive apportionment of 50 percent of its research and experimental expense to the residual grouping, gross income from sources within the United States, since more than 50 percent of the research activity was performed in the United States. The remaining 50 percent of the deduction can then be apportioned between the residual and statutory groupings on the basis of sales. Since Y and Z are unrelated licensees of X, only their sales of the licensed product, floodlights, are included for purposes of apportionment. Floodlight sales of Z are unknown, but are estimated at ten times royalties from Z, or $120,000. All of X's sales from the entire product category are included for purposes of apportionment on the basis of sales. Alternatively, X may apportion its deduction on the basis of gross income, in accordance with paragraph (d) of this section. The apportionment is as follows: Tentative Apportionment on the Basis of Sales.

(i) Research and experimental expense to be apportioned between statutory and residual groupings of gross income:	$100,000
(ii) Less: Exclusive apportionment of research and experimental expense to the residual groupings of gross income ($100,000 × 50 percent):	$ 50,000
(iii) Research and experimental expense to be apportioned between the statutory and residual groupings of gross income on the basis of sales:	$ 50,000
(iv) Apportionment of research and experimental expense to the residual groupings of gross income ($50,000 × $900,000/($900,000 + $135,000 + $120,000)):	$ 38,961
(v) Apportionment of research and experimental expense to the statutory grouping, royalty income from countries Y and Z ($50,000 × $135,000 + $120,000/($900,000 + $135,000 + $120,000)):	$ 11,039
(vi) Total apportioned deduction for research and experimentation:	$100,000
(vii) Amount apportioned to the residual grouping ($50,000 + $38,961):	$ 88,961
(viii) Amount apportioned to the statutory grouping of sources within countries Y and Z:	$ 11,039

(2) Tentative Apportionment on Gross Income Basis.

(i) Exclusive apportionment of research and experimental expense to the residual grouping of gross income ($100,000 × 25 percent)	$25,000
(ii) Apportionment of research and experimental expense to the residual grouping of gross income ($75,000 × $479,000/$500,000):	$71,850
(iii) Apportionment of research and experimental expense to the statutory grouping of gross income ($75,000 × $9,000 + $12,000/$500,000):	$ 3,150
(iv) Amount apportioned to the residual grouping:	$96,850
(v) Amount apportioned to the statutory grouping of general limitation income from sources without the United States:	$ 3,150

(B) Since X has elected to use the optional gross income methods of apportionment and its apportionment on the basis of gross income to the statutory grouping, $3,150, is less than 50 percent of its apportionment on the basis of sales to the statutory grouping, $11,039, it must use Option two of paragraph (d)(3) of this section and apportion $5,520 (50 percent of $11,039) to the statutory grouping.

T.D. 8646, 12/21/95.

PAR. 10. Section 1.861-17 is amended by revising paragraph (c)(3)(iv) to read as follows:

Proposed § 1.861-17 Allocation and apportionment of research and experimental expenditures. [*For Preamble, see ¶ 152,697*]

* * * * *

(c) * * *

(3) * * *

(iv) Effect of cost sharing arrangements. If the corporation controlled by the taxpayer has entered into a cost sharing arrangement, in accordance with the provisions of § 1.482-7, with the taxpayer for the purpose of developing intangible property, then that corporation shall not reasonably be expected to benefit from the taxpayer's share of the research expense.

* * * * *

§ 1.861-18 Classification of transactions involving computer programs.

Caution: The Treasury has not yet amended Reg § 1.861-18 to reflect changes made by P.L. 108-357.

(a) General. *(1) Scope.* This section provides rules for classifying transactions relating to computer programs for purposes of subchapter N of chapter 1 of the Internal Revenue Code, sections 367, 404A, 482, 551, 679, 1059A, chapter 3, chapter 5, sections 842 and 845 (to the extent involving a foreign person), and transfers to foreign trusts not covered by section 679.

(2) Categories of transactions. This section generally requires that such transactions be treated as being solely within one of four categories (described in paragraph (b)(1) of this section) and provides certain rules for categorizing such transactions. In the case of a transfer of a copyright right, this section provides rules for determining whether the transaction should be classified as either a sale or exchange, or a license generating royalty income. In the case of a transfer of a copyrighted article, this section provides rules for determining whether the transaction should be classified as either a sale or exchange, or a lease generating rental income.

(3) Computer program. For purposes of this section, a computer program is a set of statements or instructions to be used directly or indirectly in a computer in order to bring about a certain result. For purposes of this paragraph (a)(3), a computer program includes any media, user manuals, documentation, data base or similar item if the media, user manuals, documentation, data base or similar item is incidental to the operation of the computer program.

(b) Categories of transactions. *(1) General.* Except as provided in paragraph (b)(2) of this section, a transaction involving the transfer of a computer program, or the provision of services or of know-how with respect to a computer program (collectively, a transfer of a computer program) is treated as being solely one of the following—

(i) A transfer of a copyright right in the computer program;

(ii) A transfer of a copy of the computer program (a copyrighted article);

(iii) The provision of services for the development or modification of the computer program; or

(iv) The provision of know-how relating to computer programming techniques.

(2) Transactions consisting of more than one category. Any transaction involving computer programs which consists of more than one of the transactions described in paragraph (b)(1) of this section shall be treated as separate transactions, with the appropriate provisions of this section being applied to each such transaction. However, any transaction that is de minimis, taking into account the overall transaction and the surrounding facts and circumstances, shall not be treated as a separate transaction, but as part of another transaction.

(c) Transfers involving copyright rights and copyrighted articles. *(1) Classification.* (i) Transfers treated as transfers of copyright rights. A transfer of a computer program is classified as a transfer of a copyright right if, as a result of the transaction, a person acquires any one or more of the rights described in paragraphs (c)(2)(i) through (iv) of this section. Whether the transaction is treated as being solely the transfer of a copyright right or is treated as separate transactions is determined pursuant to paragraph (b)(1) and (b)(2) of this section. For example, if a person receives a disk containing a copy of a computer program which enables it to exercise, in relation to that program, a non-de minimis right described in paragraphs (c)(2)(i) through (iv) of this section (and the transaction does not involve, or involves only a de minimis provision of services as described in paragraph (d) of this section or of know-how as described in paragraph (e) of this section), then, under paragraph (b)(2) of this section, the transfer is classified solely as a transfer of a copyright right.

(ii) Transfers treated solely as transfers of copyrighted articles. If a person acquires a copy of a computer program but does not acquire any of the rights described in paragraphs (c)(2)(i) through (iv) of this section (or only acquires a de minimis grant of such rights), and the transaction does not involve, or involves only a de minimis, provision of services as described in paragraph (d) of this section or of know-how as described in paragraph (e) of this section, the transfer of the copy of the computer program is classified solely as a transfer of a copyrighted article.

(2) Copyright rights. The copyright rights referred to in paragraph (c)(1) of this section are as follows—

(i) The right to make copies of the computer program for purposes of distribution to the public by sale or other transfer of ownership, or by rental, lease or lending;

(ii) The right to prepare derivative computer programs based upon the copyrighted computer program;

(iii) The right to make a public performance of the computer program; or

(iv) The right to publicly display the computer program.

(3) Copyrighted article. A copyrighted article includes a copy of a computer program from which the work can be perceived, reproduced, or otherwise communicated, either directly or with the aid of a machine or device. The copy of the program may be fixed in the magnetic medium of a floppy disk, or in the main memory or hard drive of a computer, or in any other medium.

(d) Provision of services. The determination of whether a transaction involving a newly developed or modified computer program is treated as either the provision of services or another transaction described in paragraph (b)(1) of this section is based on all the facts and circumstances of the transaction, including, as appropriate, the intent of the parties (as evidenced by their agreement and conduct) as to which party is to own the copyright rights in the computer program and how the risks of loss are allocated between the parties.

(e) Provision of know-how. The provision of information with respect to a computer program will be treated as the provision of know-how for purposes of this section only if the information is—

(1) Information relating to computer programming techniques;

(2) Furnished under conditions preventing unauthorized disclosure, specifically contracted for between the parties; and

(3) Considered property subject to trade secret protection.

(f) Further classification of transfers involving copyright rights and copyrighted articles. *(1) Transfers of copyright rights.* The determination of whether a transfer of a copyright right is a sale or exchange of property is made on the basis of whether, taking into account all facts and circumstances, there has been a transfer of all substantial rights in the copyright. A transaction that does not constitute a sale or exchange because not all substantial rights have been transferred will be classified as a license generating royalty income. For this purpose, the principles of sections 1222 and 1235 may be applied. Income derived from the sale or exchange of a copyright right will be sourced under section 865(a), (c), (d), (e), or (h), as appropriate. Income derived from the licensing of a copyright right will be sourced under section 861(a)(4) or 862(a)(4), as appropriate.

(2) Transfers of copyrighted articles. The determination of whether a transfer of a copyrighted article is a sale or exchange is made on the basis of whether, taking into account all facts and circumstances, the benefits and burdens of ownership have been transferred. A transaction that does not constitute a sale or exchange because insufficient benefits and burdens of ownership of the copyrighted article have been transferred, such that a person other than the transferee is properly treated as the owner of the copyrighted article, will be classified as a lease generating rental income. Income from transactions that are classified as sales or exchanges of copyrighted articles will be sourced under sections 861(a)(6), 862(a)(6), 863, 865(a), (b), (c), or (e), as appropriate. Income derived from the leasing of a copyrighted article will be sourced under section 861(a)(4) or section 862(a)(4), as appropriate.

(3) Special circumstances of computer programs. In connection with determinations under this paragraph (f), consideration must be given as appropriate to the special characteristics of computer programs in transactions that take advantage of these characteristics (such as the ability to make perfect copies at minimal cost). For example, a transaction in which a person acquires a copy of a computer program on disk subject to a requirement that the disk be destroyed after a specified period is generally the equivalent of a transaction subject to a requirement that the disk be returned after such period. Similarly, a transaction in which the program deactivates itself after a specified period is generally the equivalent of returning the copy.

(g) Rules of operation. *(1) Term applied to transaction by parties.* Neither the form adopted by the parties to a transaction, nor the classification of the transaction under copyright law, shall be determinative. Therefore, for example, if there is a transfer of a computer program on a single disk for a one-time payment with restrictions on transfer and reverse engineering, which the parties characterize as a license (including, but not limited to, agreements commonly referred to as shrink-wrap licenses), application of the rules of paragraphs (c) and (f) of this section may nevertheless result in the transaction being classified as the sale of a copyrighted article.

(2) Means of transfer not to be taken into account. The rules of this section shall be applied irrespective of the physical or electronic or other medium used to effectuate a transfer of a computer program.

(3) To the public. (i) In general. For purposes of paragraph (c)(2)(i) of this section, a transferee of a computer program shall not be considered to have the right to distribute copies of the program to the public if it is permitted to distribute copies of the software to only either a related person, or to identified persons who may be identified by either name or by legal relationship to the original transferee. For purposes of this subparagraph, a related person is a person who bears a relationship to the transferee specified in section 267(b)(3), (10), (11), or (12), or section 707(b)(1)(B). In applying section 267(b), 267(f), 707(b)(1)(B), or 1563(a), "10 percent" shall be substituted for "50 percent."

(ii) Use by individuals. The number of employees of a transferee of a computer program who are permitted to use the program in connection with their employment is not relevant for purposes of this paragraph (g)(3). In addition, the number of individuals with a contractual agreement to provide services to the transferee of a computer program who are permitted to use the program in connection with the performance of those services is not relevant for purposes of this paragraph (g)(3).

(h) Examples. The provisions of this section may be illustrated by the following examples:

Example (1). (i) Facts. Corp A, a U.S. corporation, owns the copyright in a computer program, Program X. It copies Program X onto disks. The disks are placed in boxes covered with a wrapper on which is printed what is generally referred to as a shrink-wrap license. The license is stated to be perpetual. Under the license no reverse engineering, decompilation, or disassembly of the computer program is permitted. The transferee receives, first, the right to use the program on two of its own computers (for example, a laptop and a desktop) provided that only one copy is in use at any one time, and, second, the right to make one copy of the program on each machine as an essential step in the utilization of the program. The transferee is permitted by the shrink-wrap license to sell the copy so long as it destroys any other copies it has made and imposes the same terms and conditions of the license on the purchaser of its copy. These disks are made available for sale to the general public in Country Z. In return for valuable consideration, P, a Country Z resident, receives one such disk.

(ii) Analysis. (A) Under paragraph (g)(1) of this section, the label license is not determinative. None of the copyright rights described in paragraph (c)(2) of this section have been transferred in this transaction. P has received a copy of the program, however, and, therefore, under paragraph (c)(1)(ii) of this section, P has acquired solely a copyrighted article.

(B) Taking into account all of the facts and circumstances, P is properly treated as the owner of a copyrighted article. Therefore, under paragraph (f)(2) of this section, there has been a sale of a copyrighted article rather than the grant of a lease.

Example (2). (i) Facts. The facts are the same as those in Example 1, except that instead of selling disks, Corp A, the U.S. corporation, decides to make Program X available, for a fee, on a World Wide Web home page on the Internet. P, the Country Z resident, in return for payment made to Corp A, downloads Program X (via modem) onto the hard drive of his computer. As part of the electronic communication, P signifies his assent to a license agreement with terms identical to those in Example 1, except that in this case P may make a back-up copy of the program on to a disk.

(ii) Analysis. (A) None of the copyright rights described in paragraph (c)(2) of this section have passed to P. Although P did not buy a physical copy of the disk with the program on it, paragraph (g)(2) of this section provides that the means of transferring the program is irrelevant. Therefore, P has acquired a copyrighted article.

(B) As in Example 1, P is properly treated as the owner of a copyrighted article. Therefore, under paragraph (f)(2) of this section, there has been a sale of a copyrighted article rather than the grant of a lease.

Example (3). (i) Facts. The facts are the same as those in Example 1, except that Corp A only allows P, the Country Z resident, to use Program X for one week. At the end of that week, P must return the disk with Program X on it to Corp A. P must also destroy any copies made of Program X. If P wishes to use Program X for a further period he must enter into a new agreement to use the program for an additional charge.

(ii) Analysis. (A) Under paragraph (c)(2) of this section, P has received no copyright rights. Because P has received a copy of the program under paragraph (c)(1)(ii) of this section, he has, therefore, received a copyrighted article.

(B) Taking into account all of the facts and circumstances, P is not properly treated as the owner of a copyrighted article. Therefore, under paragraph (f)(2) of this section, there has been a lease of a copyrighted article rather than a sale. Taking into account the special characteristics of computer programs as provided in paragraph (f)(3) of this section, the result would be the same if P were required to destroy the disk at the end of the one week period instead of returning it since Corp A can make additional copies of the program at minimal cost.

Example (4). (i) Facts. The facts are the same as those in Example 2, where P, the Country Z resident, receives Program X from Corp A's home page on the Internet, except that P may only use Program X for a period of one week at the end of which an electronic lock is activated and the program can no longer be accessed. Thereafter, if P wishes to use Program X, it must return to the home page and pay Corp A to send an electronic key to reactivate the program for another week.

(ii) Analysis. (A) As in Example 3, under paragraph (c)(2) of this section, P has not received any copyright rights. P has received a copy of the program, and under paragraph (g)(2) of this section, the means of transmission is irrelevant. P has, therefore, under paragraph (c)(1)(ii) of this section, received a copyrighted article.

(B) As in Example 3, P is not properly treated as the owner of a copyrighted article. Therefore, under paragraph (f)(2) of this section, there has been a lease of a copyrighted article rather than a sale. While P does retain Program X on its computer at the end of the one week period, as a legal matter P no longer has the right to use the program (without further payment) and, indeed, cannot use the program without the electronic key. Functionally, Program X is no longer on the hard drive of P's computer. Instead, the hard drive contains only a series of numbers which no longer perform the function of Program X. Although in Example 3, P was required to physically return the disk, taking into account the special characteristics of computer programs as provided in paragraph (f)(3) of this section, the result in this Example 4 is the same as in Example 3.

Example (5). (i) Facts. Corp A, a U.S. corporation, transfers a disk containing Program X to Corp B, a Country Z corporation, and grants Corp B an exclusive license for the remaining term of the copyright to copy and distribute an unlimited number of copies of Program X in the geographic area of Country Z, prepare derivative works based upon Program X, make public performances of Program X, and publicly display Program X. Corp B will pay Corp A a royalty of $y a year for three years, which is the expected period during which Program X will have commercially exploitable value.

(ii) Analysis. (A) Although Corp A has transferred a disk with a copy of Program X on it to Corp B, under paragraph (c)(1)(i) of this section because this transfer is accompanied by a copyright right identified in paragraph (c)(2)(i) of this section, this transaction is a transfer solely of copyright rights, not of copyrighted articles. For purposes of paragraph (b)(2) of this section, the disk containing a copy of Program X is a de minimis component of the transaction.

(B) Applying the all substantial rights test under paragraph (f)(1) of this section, Corp A will be treated as having sold copyright rights to Corp B. Corp B has acquired all of the copyright rights in Program X, has received the right to use them exclusively within Country Z, and has received the rights for the remaining life of the copyright in Program X. The fact the payments cease before the copyright term expires is not controlling. Under paragraph (g)(1) of this section, the fact that the agreement is labelled a license is not controlling (nor is the fact that Corp A receives a sum labelled a royalty). (The result in this case would be the same if the copy of Program X to be used for the purposes of reproduction were transmitted electronically to Corp B, as a result of the application of the rule of paragraph (g)(2) of this section.)

Example (6). Example 6. (i) Facts. Corp A, a U.S. corporation, transfers a disk containing Program X to Corp B, a Country Z corporation, and grants Corp B the non exclusive right to reproduce (either directly or by contracting with either Corp A or another person to do so) and distribute for sale to the public an unlimited number of disks at its factory in Country Z in return for a payment related to the number of disks copied and sold. The term of the agreement is two years, which is less than the remaining life of the copyright.

(ii) Analysis. (A) As in Example 5, the transfer of the disk containing the copy of the program does not constitute the transfer of a copyrighted article under paragraph (c)(1) of this section because Corp B has also acquired a copyright right under paragraph (c)(2)(i) of this section, the right to reproduce and distribute to the public. For purposes of paragraph (b)(2) of this section, the disk containing Program X is a de minimis component of the transaction.

(B) Taking into account all of the facts and circumstances, there has been a license of Program X to Corp B, and the payments made by Corp B are royalties. Under paragraph (f)(1) of this section, there has not been a transfer of all substantial rights in the copyright to Program X because Corp A has the right to enter into other licenses with respect to the copyright of Program X, including licenses in Country Z (or even to sell that copyright, subject to Corp B's interest). Corp B has acquired no right itself to license the copyright rights in Program X. Finally, the term of the license is for less than the remaining life of the copyright in Program X.

Example (7). (i) Facts. Corp C, a distributor in Country Z, enters into an agreement with Corp A, a U.S. corporation, to purchase as many copies of Program X on disk as it may from time-to-time request. Corp C will then sell these disks to retailers. The disks are shipped in boxes covered by shrink-wrap licenses (identical to the license described in Example 1).

(ii) Analysis. (A) Corp C has not acquired any copyright rights under paragraph (c)(2) of this section with respect to Program X. It has acquired individual copies of Program X, which it may sell to others. The use of the term license is not dispositive under paragraph (g)(1) of this section. Under paragraph (c)(1)(ii) of this section, Corp C has acquired copyrighted articles.

(B) Taking into account all of the facts and circumstances, Corp C is properly treated as the owner of copyrighted articles. Therefore, under paragraph (f)(2) of this section, there has been a sale of copyrighted articles.

Example (8). (i) Facts. Corp A, a U.S. corporation, transfers a disk containing Program X to Corp D, a foreign corporation engaged in the manufacture and sale of personal computers in Country Z. Corp A grants Corp D the non-exclusive right to copy Program X onto the hard drive of an unlimited number of computers, which Corp D manufactures, and to distribute those copies (on the hard drive) to the public. The term of the agreement is two years, which is less than the remaining life of the copyright in Program X. Corp D pays Corp A an amount based on the number of copies of Program X it loads on to computers.

(ii) Analysis. The analysis is the same as in Example 6. Under paragraph (c)(2)(i) of this section, Corp D has acquired a copyright right enabling it to exploit Program X by copying it on to the hard drives of the computers that it manufactures and then sells. For purposes of paragraph (b)(2) of this section, the disk containing Program X is a de minimis component of the transaction. Taking into account all of the facts and circumstances, Corp D has not, however, acquired all substantial rights in the copyright to Program X (for example, the term of the agreement is less than the remaining life of the copyright). Under paragraph (f)(1) of this section, this transaction is, therefore, a license of Program X to Corp D rather than a sale and the payments made by Corp D are royalties. (The result would be the same if Corp D included with the computers it sells an archival copy of Program X on a floppy disk.)

Example (9). (i) Facts. The facts are the same as in Example 8, except that Corp D, the Country Z corporation, receives physical disks. The disks are shipped in boxes covered by shrink-wrap licenses (identical to the licenses described in Example 1). The terms of these licenses do not permit Corp D to make additional copies of Program X. Corp D uses each individual disk only once to load a single copy of Program X onto each separate computer. Corp D transfers the disk with the computer when it is sold.

(ii) Analysis. (A) As in Example 7 (unlike Example 8) no copyright right identified in paragraph (c)(2) of this section has been transferred. Corp D acquires the disks without the right to reproduce and distribute publicly further copies of Program X. This is therefore the transfer of copyrighted articles under paragraph (c)(1)(ii) of this section.

(B) Taking into account all of the facts and circumstances, Corp D is properly treated as the owner of copyrighted articles. Therefore, under paragraph (f)(2) of this section, the transaction is classified as the sale of a copyrighted article. (The result would be the same if Corp D used a single physical disk to copy Program X onto each computer, and transferred an unopened box containing Program X with each computer, if Corp D were not permitted to copy Program X onto more computers than the number of individual copies purchased.)

Example (10). (i) Facts. Corp A, a U.S. corporation, transfers a disk containing Program X to Corp E, a Country Z corporation, and grants Corp E the right to load Program X onto 50 individual workstations for use only by Corp E employees at one location in return for a one-time per-user fee (generally referred to as a site license or enterprise license). If additional workstations are subsequently introduced, Program X may be loaded onto those machines for additional one-time per-user fees. The license which grants the rights to operate Program X on 50 workstations also prohibits Corp E from selling the disk (or any of the 50 copies) or reverse engineering the program. The term of the license is stated to be perpetual.

(ii) Analysis. (A) The grant of a right to copy, unaccompanied by the right to distribute those copies to the public, is not the transfer of a copyright right under paragraph (c)(2) of this section. Therefore, under paragraph (c)(1)(ii) of this section, this transaction is a transfer of copyrighted articles (50 copies of Program X).

(B) Taking into account all of the facts and circumstances, P is properly treated as the owner of copyrighted articles. Therefore, under paragraph (f)(2) of this section, there has been a sale of copyrighted articles rather than the grant of a lease. Notwithstanding the restriction on sale, other factors such as, for example, the risk of loss and the right to use the copies in perpetuity outweigh, in this case, the restrictions placed on the right of alienation.

(C) The result would be the same if Corp E were permitted to copy Program X onto an unlimited number of workstations used by employees of either Corp E or corporations that had a relationship to Corp E specified in paragraph (g)(3) of this section.

Example (11). (i) Facts. The facts are the same as in Example 10, except that Corp E, the Country Z corporation, acquires the right to make Program X available to workstation users who are Corp E employees by way of a local area network (LAN). The number of users that can use Program X on the LAN at any one time is limited to 50. Corp E pays a one-time fee for the right to have up to 50 employees use the program at the same time.

(ii) Analysis. Under paragraph (g)(2) of this section the mode of utilization is irrelevant. Therefore, as in Example 10, under paragraph (c)(2) of this section, no copyright right has been transferred, and, thus, under paragraph (c)(1)(ii) of this section, this transaction will be classified as the transfer of a copyrighted article. Under the benefits and burdens test of paragraph (f)(2) of this section, this transaction is a sale of copyrighted articles. The result would be the same if an unlimited number of Corp E employees were permitted to use Program X on the LAN or if Corp E were permitted to copy Program X onto LANs maintained by corporations that had a relationship to Corp E specified in paragraph (g)(3) of this section.

Example (12). (i) Facts. The facts are the same as in Example 11, except that Corp E pays a monthly fee to Corp A, the U.S. corporation, calculated with reference to the permitted maximum number of users (which can be changed) and the computing power of Corp E's server. In return for this monthly fee, Corp E receives the right to receive upgrades of Program X when they become available. The agreement may be terminated by either party at the end of any month. When the disk containing the upgrade is received, Corp E must return the disk containing the earlier version of Program X to Corp A. If the contract is terminated, Corp E must delete (or otherwise destroy) all copies made of the current version of Program X. The agreement also requires Corp A to provide technical support to Corp E but the agreement does not allocate the monthly fee between the right to receive upgrades of Program X and the technical support services. The amount of technical support that Corp A will provide to Corp E is not foreseeable at the time the contract is entered into but is expected to be de minimis. The agreement specifically provides that Corp E has not thereby been granted an option to purchase Program X.

(ii) Analysis. (A) Corp E has received no copyright rights under paragraph (c)(2) of this section. Corp A has not provided any services described in paragraph (d) of this section. Based on all the facts and circumstances of the transaction, Corp A has provided de minimis technical services to Corp E. Therefore, under paragraph (c)(1)(ii) of this section, the transaction is a transfer of a copyrighted article.

(B) Taking into account all facts and circumstances, under the benefits and burdens test Corp E is not properly treated as the owner of the copyrighted article. Corp E does not receive the right to use Program X in perpetuity, but only for so long as it continues to make payments. Corp E does not have the right to purchase Program X on advantageous (or, indeed, any) terms once a certain amount of money has been paid to Corp A or a certain period of time has elapsed (which might indicate a sale). Once the agreement is terminated, Corp E will no longer possess any copies of Program X, current or superseded. Therefore under paragraph (f)(2) of this section there has been a lease of a copyrighted article.

Example (13). (i) Facts. The facts are the same as in Example 12, except that, while Corp E must return copies of Program X as new upgrades are received, if the agreement terminates, Corp E may keep the latest version of Program X (although Corp E is still prohibited from selling or otherwise transferring any copy of Program X).

(ii) Analysis. For the reasons stated in Example 10, paragraph (ii)(B), the transfer of the program will be treated as a sale of a copyrighted article rather than as a lease.

Example (14). (i) Facts. Corp G, a Country Z corporation, enters into a contract with Corp A, a U.S. corporation, for Corp A to modify Program X so that it can be used at Corp G's facility in Country Z. Under the contract, Corp G is to acquire one copy of the program on a disk and the right to use the program on 5,000 workstations. The contract requires Corp A to rewrite elements of Program X so that it will conform to Country Z accounting standards and states that Corp A retains all copyright rights in the modified Program X. The agreement between Corp A and Corp G is otherwise identical as to rights and payment terms as the agreement described in Example 10.

(ii) Analysis. (A) As in Example 10, no copyright rights are being transferred under paragraph (c)(2) of this section. In addition, since no copyright rights are being transferred to Corp G, this transaction does not involve the provision of services by Corp A under paragraph (d) of this section. This transaction will be classified, therefore, as a transfer of copyrighted articles under paragraph (c)(1)(ii) of this section.

(B) Taking into account all facts and circumstances, Corp G is properly treated as the owner of copyrighted articles. Therefore, under paragraph (f)(2) of this section, there has been the sale of a copyrighted article rather than the grant of a lease.

Example (15). (i) Facts. Corp H, a Country Z corporation, enters into a license agreement for a new computer program. Program Q is to be written by Corp A, a U.S. corporation. Corp A and Corp H agree that Corp A is writing Program Q for Corp H and that, when Program Q is completed, the copyright in Program Q will belong to Corp H. Corp H gives instructions to Corp A programmers regarding program specifications. Corp H agrees to pay Corp A a fixed monthly sum during development of the program. If Corp H is dissatisfied with the development of the program, it may cancel the contract at the end of any month. In the event of termination, Corp A will retain all payments, while any procedures, techniques or copyrightable interests will be the property of Corp H. All of the payments are labelled royalties. There is no provision in the agreement for any continuing relationship between Corp A and Corp H, such as the furnishing of updates of the program, after completion of the modification work.

(ii) Analysis. Taking into account all of the facts and circumstances, Corp A is treated as providing services to Corp H. Under paragraph (d) of this section, Corp A is treated as providing services to Corp H because Corp H bears all of the risks of loss associated with the development of Program Q and is the owner of all copyright rights in Program Q. Under paragraph (g)(1) of this section, the fact that the agreement is labelled a license is not controlling (nor is the fact that Corp A receives a sum labelled a royalty).

Example (16). (i) Facts. Corp A, a U.S. corporation, and Corp I, a Country Z corporation, agree that a development engineer employed by Corp A will travel to Country Z to provide know-how relating to certain techniques not generally known to computer programmers, which will enable Corp I to more efficiently create computer programs. These techniques represent the product of experience gained by Corp A from working on many computer programming projects, and are furnished to Corp I under nondisclosure conditions. Such information is property subject to trade secret protection.

(ii) Analysis. This transaction contains the elements of know-how specified in paragraph (e) of this section. Therefore, this transaction will be treated as the provision of know-how.

Example (17). (i) Facts. Corp A, a U.S. corporation, transfers a disk containing Program Y to Corp E, a Country Z corporation, in exchange for a single fixed payment. Program Y is a computer program development program, which is used to create other computer programs, consisting of several components, including libraries of reusable software components that serve as general building blocks in new software applications. No element of these libraries is a significant component of any overall new program. Because a computer program created with the use of Program Y will not operate unless the libraries are also present, the license agreement between Corp A and Corp E grants Corp E the right to distribute copies of the libraries with any program developed using Program Y. The license agreement is otherwise identical to the license agreement in Example 1.

(ii) Analysis. (A) No non-de minimis copyright rights described in paragraph (c)(2) of this section have passed to Corp E. For purposes of paragraph (b)(2) of this section, the right to distribute the libraries in conjunction with the programs created using Program Y is a de minimis component of the transaction. Because Corp E has received a copy of the program under paragraph (c)(1)(ii) of this section, it has received a copyrighted article.

(B) Taking into account all the facts and circumstances, Corp E is properly treated as the owner of a copyrighted article. Therefore, under paragraph (f)(2) of this section, there has been the sale of a copyrighted article rather than the grant of a lease.

Example (18). (i) Facts.(A) Corp A, a U.S. corporation, transfers a disk containing Program X to Corp E, a country Z Corporation. The disk contains both the object code and the source code to Program X and the license agreement grants Corp E the right to—

(1) Modify the source code in order to correct minor errors and make minor adaptations to Program X so it will function on Corp E's computer; and

(2) Recompile the modified source code.

(B) The license does not grant Corp E the right to distribute the modified Program X to the public. The license is otherwise identical to the license agreement in Example 1.

(ii) Analysis. (A) No non-de minimis copyright rights described in paragraph (c)(2) of this section have passed to Corp E. For purposes of paragraph (b)(2) of this section, the right to modify the source code and recompile the source code in order to create new code to correct minor errors and make minor adaptations is a de minimis component of the transaction. Because Corp E has received a copy of the program under paragraph (c)(1)(ii) of this section, it has received a copyrighted article.

(B) Taking into account all the facts and circumstances, Corp E is properly treated as the owner of a copyrighted article. Therefore, under paragraph (f)(2) of this section, there has been the sale of a copyrighted article rather than the grant of a lease.

(i) Effective date. *(1) General.* This section applies to transactions occurring pursuant to contracts entered into on or after December 1, 1998.

(2) Elective transition rules. (i) Contracts entered into in taxable years ending on or after October 2, 1998. A taxpayer may elect to apply this section to transactions occurring pursuant to contracts entered into in taxable years ending on or after October 2, 1998. A taxpayer that makes an election under this paragraph (i)(2)(i) must apply this section to all contracts entered into in taxable years ending on or after October 2, 1998.

(ii) Contracts entered into before October 2, 1998. A taxpayer may elect to apply this section to transactions occurring in taxable years ending on or after October 2, 1998 pursuant to contracts entered into before October 2, 1998 provided the taxpayer would not be required under this section to change its method of accounting as a result of such election, or the taxpayer would be required to change its method of accounting but the resulting section 481(a) adjustment would be zero. A taxpayer that makes an election under this paragraph (i)(2)(ii) must apply this section to all transactions occurring in taxable years ending on or after October 2, 1998 pursuant to contracts entered into before October 2, 1998.

(3) Manner of making election. Taxpayers may elect, under paragraph (i)(2)(i) or (i)(2)(ii) of this section, to apply this section, by treating the transactions in accordance with these regulations on their original tax return.

(4) Examples. The following examples illustrate application of the transition rule of paragraph (i)(2)(ii) of this section:

Example (1). Corp A develops computer programs for sale to third parties. Corp A uses an overall accrual method of accounting and files its tax return on a calendar-year basis. In year 1, Corp A enters into a contract to deliver a computer program in that year, and to provide updates for each of the following four years. Under the contract, the computer program and the updates are priced separately, and Corp A is entitled to receive payments for the computer program and each of the updates upon delivery. Assume Corp A properly accounts for the contract as a contract for the provision of services. Corp A properly includes the payments under the contract in gross income in the taxable year the payments are received and the computer program or updates are delivered. Corp A properly deducts the cost of developing the computer program and updates when the costs are incurred. Year 3 includes October 2, 1998. Assume under the rules of this section, the provision of updates would properly be accounted for as the transfer of copyrighted articles. If Corp A made an election under paragraph (i)(2)(ii) of this section, Corp A would not be required to change its method of accounting for income under the contract as a result of the election. Corp A would also not be required to change its method of accounting for the cost of developing the computer program and the updates under the contract as a result of the election. Therefore, under paragraph (i)(2)(ii) of this section, Corp A may elect to apply the provisions of this section to the updates provided in years 3, 4, and 5, because Corp A is not required to change from its method of accounting for the contract as a result of the election.

Example (2). Corp A develops computer programs for sale to third parties. Corp A uses an overall accrual method of accounting and files its tax return on a calendar-year basis. In year 1, Corp A enters into a contract to deliver a computer program and to provide one update the following year. Under the contract, the computer program and the update are priced separately, and Corp A is entitled to receive payment for the computer program and the update upon delivery of the computer program. Assume Corp A properly accounts for the contract as a contract for the provision of services. Corp A properly includes the portion of the payment relating to the computer program in gross income in year 1, the taxable year the payment is received and the program delivered. Corp A properly includes the portion of the payment relating to the update in gross income in year 2, the taxable year the update is provided, under Rev. Proc. 71-21, 1971-2 CB 549 (see § 601.601 (d)(2) of this chapter). Corp A properly deducts the cost of developing the computer program and update when the costs are incurred. Year 2 includes October 2, 1998. Assume under the rules of this section, provision of the update would properly be accounted for as the transfer of a copyrighted article. If Corp A made an election under paragraph (i)(2)(ii) of this section, Corp A would be required to change its method of accounting for deferring income under its contract as a result of the election. However, the section 481(a) adjustment would be zero because the portion of the payment relating to the update would be includible in gross income in year 2, the taxable year the update is provided, under both Rev. Proc. 71-21 and § 1.451-5. Corp A would not be required to change its method of accounting for the cost of developing the computer program and the update under the contract as a result of the election. Therefore, under paragraph (i)(2)(ii) of this section, Corp A may elect to apply the provisions of this section to the update in year 2, because the section 481(a) adjustment resulting from the change in method of accounting for deferring advance payments under the contract is zero, and because Corp A is not required to change from its method of accounting for the cost of developing the computer program and updates under the contract as a result of the election.

Example (3). Assume the same facts as in Example 1 except that Corp A is entitled to receive payments for the computer program and each of the updates 30 days after delivery. Corp A properly includes the amounts due under the contract in gross income in the taxable year the computer program or updates are provided. Assume that Corp A properly uses the nonaccrual-experience method described in section 448(d)(5) and § 1.448-2T to account for income on its contracts. If Corp A made an election under paragraph (i)(2)(ii) of this section, Corp A would be required to change from the nonaccrual-experience method for income as a result of the election, because the method is only available with respect to amounts to be received for the performance of services. Therefore, Corp A may not elect to apply the provisions of this section to the updates provided in years 3, 4, and 5, under paragraph (i)(2)(ii) of this section, because Corp A would be required to change from the nonaccrual-experience method of accounting for income on the contract as a result of the election.

(j) Change in method of accounting required by this section. *(1) Consent.* A taxpayer is granted consent to change its method of accounting for contracts involving computer programs, to conform with the classification prescribed in this section. The consent is granted for contracts entered into on or after December 1, 1998, or in the case of a taxpayer making an election under paragraph (i)(2)(i) of this section, the consent is granted for contracts entered into in taxable years ending on or after October 2, 1998. In addition, a taxpayer that makes an election under paragraph (i)(2)(ii) of this section is granted consent to change its method of accounting for any contract with transactions subject to the election, if the taxpayer is required to change its method of accounting as a result of the election.

(2) Year of change. The year of change is the taxable year that includes December 1, 1998, or in the case of a taxpayer making an election under paragraph (i)(2)(i) or (i)(2)(ii) of this section, the taxable year that includes October 2, 1998.

(k) Time and manner of making change in method of accounting.

(1) General. A taxpayer changing its method of accounting in accordance with this section must file a Form 3115, Application for Change in Method of Accounting, in duplicate. The taxpayer must type or print the following statement at the top of page 1 of the Form 3115: "FILED UNDER TREASURY REGULATION § 1.861-18." The original Form 3115 must be attached to the taxpayers original return for the year of change. A copy of the Form 3115 must be filed with the National Office no later than when the original Form 3115 is filed for the year of change.

(2) Copy of Form 3115. The copy required by this paragraph (k)(l) to be sent to the national office should be sent to the Commissioner of Internal Revenue, Attention: CC:DOM:IT&A, P.O. Box 7604, Benjamin Franklin Station, Washington DC 20044 (or in the case of a designated private delivery service: Commissioner of Internal Revenue, Attention: CC:DOM:IT&A, 1111 Constitution Avenue, NW., Washington, DC 20224).

(3) Effect of consent and Internal Revenue Service review. A change in method of accounting granted under this section is subject to review by the district director and the national office and may be modified or revoked in accordance with the provisions of Rev. Proc. 97-37 (1997-33 IRB 18) (or its successors) (see § 601.601(d)(2) of this chapter).

T.D. 8785, 9/30/98.

§ 1.862-1 Income specifically from sources without the United States.

Caution: The Treasury has not yet amended Reg § 1.862-1 to reflect changes made by P.L. 99-514.

(a) Gross income. *(1)* The following items of gross income shall be treated as income from sources without the United States:

(i) Interest other than that specified in section 861(a)(1) and § 1.861-2 as being derived from sources within the United States;

(ii) Dividends other than those derived from sources within the United States as provided in section 861(a)(2) and § 1.861-3;

(iii) Compensation for labor or personal services performed without the United States;

(iv) Rentals or royalties from property located without the United States or from any interest in such property, including rentals or royalties for the use of, or for the privilege of using, without the United States, patents, copyrights, secret processes and formulas, good-will, trademarks, trade brands, franchises, and other like property;

(v) Gains, profits, and income from the sale of real property located without the United States; and

(vi) Gains, profits, and income derived from the purchase of personal property within the United States and its sale without the United States.

(2) In applying subparagraph (1)(iv) of this paragraph for taxable years beginning after December 31, 1966, gains described in section 871(a)(1)(D) and section 881(a)(4) from the sale or exchange after October 4, 1966, of patents, copyrights, and other like property shall be treated, as provided in section 871(e)(2), as rentals or royalties for the use of, or privilege of using, property or an interest in property. See paragraph (e) of § 1.871-11.

(3) For determining the time and place of sale of personal property for purposes of subparagraph (1)(vi) of this paragraph, see paragraph (c) of § 1.861-7.

(4) Income derived from the purchase of personal property within the United States and its sale within a possession of the United States shall be treated as derived entirely from within that possession.

(5) If interest is paid on an obligation of a nonresident of the United States by a resident of the United States acting in the resident's capacity as a guarantor of the obligation of the nonresident, the interest will be treated as income from sources without the United States.

(6) For rules treating certain interest as income from sources without the United States, see paragraph (b) of § 1.861-2.

(7) For the treatment of compensation for labor or personal services performed partly within the United States and partly without the United States, see paragraph (b) of § 1.861-4.

(b) Taxable income. The taxable income from sources without the United States, in the case of the items of gross income specified in paragraph (a) of this section, shall be determined on the same basis as that used in § 1.861-8 for determining the taxable income from sources within the United States.

(c) Income from certain property. For provisions permitting a taxpayer to elect to treat amounts of gross income attributable to certain aircraft or vessels first leased on or before December 28, 1980, as income from sources within the United States which would otherwise be treated as income from sources without the United States under paragraph (a) of this section, see § 1.861-9. For provisions requiring amounts of gross income attributable to certain aircraft, vessels, or spacecraft first leased by the taxpayer after December 28, 1980, to be treated as income from sources within the United States which would otherwise be treated as income from sources without the United States under paragraph (a) of this section, see § 1.861-9A.

T.D. 6258, 10/23/57, amend T.D. 7378, 9/29/75, T.D. 7635, 8/7/79, T.D. 7928, 12/15/83.

§ 1.863-0 Table of contents.

This section lists captions contained in §§ 1.863-1, 1.863-2, and 1.863-3.

T.D. 8687, 11/27/96, amend T.D. 9128, 5/7/2004, T.D. 9272, 7/31/2006.

§ 1.863-1 Allocation of gross income under section 863(a).

Caution: The Treasury has not yet amended Reg § 1.863-1 to reflect changes made by P.L. 104-188.

(a) In general. Items of gross income other than those specified in section 861(a) and section 862(a) will generally be separately allocated to sources within or without the United States. See § 1.863-2 for alternate methods to determine the income from sources within or without the United States in the case of items specified in § 1.863-2(a). See also sections 865(b) and (e)(2). In the case of sales of property involving partners and partnerships, the rules of § 1.863-3(g) apply.

(b) Natural resources. *(1) In general.* Notwithstanding any other provision, except to the extent provided in paragraph (b)(2) of this section, gross receipts from the sale outside the United States of products derived from the ownership or operation of any farm, mine, oil or gas well, other natural deposit, or timber within the United States, must be allocated between sources within and without the United States based on the fair market value of the product at the export terminal (as defined in paragraph (b)(3)(iii) of this section). Notwithstanding any other provision, except to the extent provided in paragraph (b)(2) of this section, gross receipts from the sale within the United States of products derived from the ownership or operation of any farm, mine, oil or gas well, other natural deposit, or timber outside the United States must be allocated between sources within and without the United States based on the fair market value of the product at the export terminal. For place of sale, see §§ 1.861-7(c) and 1.863-3(c)(2). The source of gross receipts equal to the fair market value of the product at the export terminal will be from sources where the farm, mine, well, deposit, or uncut timber is located. The source of gross receipts from the sale of the product in excess of its fair market value at the export terminal (excess gross receipts) will be determined as follows—

(i) If the taxpayer engages in additional production activities subsequent to shipment from the export terminal and outside the country of sale, the source of excess gross receipts must be determined under § 1.863-3. For purposes of applying § 1.863-3, only production assets used in additional production activity subsequent to the export terminal are taken into account.

(ii) In all other cases, excess gross receipts will be from sources within the country of sale. This paragraph (b)(1)(ii) applies to a taxpayer that engages in additional production activities in the country of sale, as well as to a taxpayer that does not engage in additional production activities at all.

(2) Additional production prior to export terminal. Notwithstanding any other provision of this section, gross receipts from the sale of products derived by a taxpayer who performs additional production activities as defined in paragraph (b)(3)(ii) of this section before the relevant product is shipped from the export terminal are allocated between sources within and without the United States based on the fair market value of the product immediately prior to the additional production activities. The source of gross receipts equal to the fair market value of the product immediately prior to the additional production activities will be from sources where the farm, mine, well, deposit, or uncut timber is located. The source of gross receipts from the sale of the product in excess of the fair market value immediately prior to the additional production activities must be determined under § 1.863-3. For purposes of applying § 1.863-3, only production assets used in the additional production activities are taken into account.

(3) Definitions. (i) Production activity. For purposes of this section, production activity means an activity that creates, fabricates, manufactures, extracts, processes, cures, or ages inventory. See § 1.864-1. Except as otherwise provided in § 1.1502-13 or 1.863-3(g)(2), only production activities conducted directly by the taxpayer are taken into account.

(ii) Additional production activities. For purposes of this section, additional production activities are substantial production activities performed directly by the taxpayer in addition to activities from the ownership or operation of any farm, mine, oil or gas well, other natural deposit, or timber. Whether a taxpayer's activities constitute additional production activities will be determined under the principles of § 1.954-3(a)(4). However, in no case will activities that prepare the natural resource itself for export, including those that are designed to facilitate the transportation of the natural resource to or from the export terminal, be considered additional production activities for purposes of this section.

(iii) Export terminal. Where the farm, mine, well, deposit, or uncut timber is located without the United States, the export terminal will be the final point in a foreign country from which goods are shipped to the United States. If there is no such final point in a foreign country (e.g., the property is extracted and produced on the high seas), the export terminal will be the place of production. Where the farm, mine, well, deposit, or uncut timber is located within the United States, the export terminal will be the final point in the United States from which goods are shipped from the United States to a foreign country. The location of the export terminal is determined without regard to any contractual terms agreed to by the taxpayer and without regard to whether there is an actual sale of the products at the export terminal.

(4) Determination of fair market value. For purposes of this section, fair market value depends on all of the facts and circumstances as they exist relative to a party in any particular case. Where the products are sold to a related party in a transaction subject to section 482, the determination of fair market value under this section must be consistent with the arm's length price determined under section 482.

(5) Determination of gross income. To determine the amount of a taxpayer's gross income from sources within or without the United States, the taxpayer's gross receipts from sources within or without the United States determined under this paragraph (b) must be reduced by the cost of goods sold properly attributable to gross receipts from sources within or without the United States.

(6) Tax return disclosure. A taxpayer that determines the source of its income under this paragraph (b) shall attach a statement to its return explaining the methodology used to determine fair market value under paragraph (b)(4) of this section, and explaining any additional production activities (as defined in paragraph (b)(3)(ii) of this section) performed by the taxpayer. In addition, the taxpayer must provide such other information as is required by § 1.863-3.

(7) Examples. The following examples illustrate the rules of this paragraph (b):

Example (1). No additional production. U.S. Mines, a U.S. corporation, operates a copper mine and mill in country X. U.S. Mines extracts copper-bearing rocks from the ground and transports the rocks to the mill where the rocks are ground and processed to produce copper-bearing concentrate. The concentrate is transported to a port where it is dried in preparation for export, stored and then shipped to purchasers in the United States. Because title to the property is passed in the United States and, under the facts and circumstances, none of U.S. Mine's activities constitutes additional production prior to the export terminal within the meaning of paragraph (b)(3)(ii) of this section, under paragraph (b)(1) and (b)(1)(ii) of this section, gross receipts equal to the fair market value of the concentrate at the export terminal will be from sources without the United States, and excess gross receipts will be from sources within the United States.

Example (2). No additional production. US Gas, a U.S. corporation, extracts natural gas within the United States, and transports the natural gas to a U.S. port where it is liquified in preparation for shipment. The liquified natural gas is then transported via freighter and sold without additional production activities in a foreign country. Liquefaction of natural gas is not an additional production activity because liquefaction prepares the natural gas for transportation from the export terminal. Therefore, under paragraph (b)(1) and (b)(1)(ii) of this section, gross receipts equal to the fair market value of the liquefied natural gas at the export terminal will be from sources within the United States, and excess gross receipts will be from sources without the United States.

Example (3). Sale in third country. US Gold, a U.S. corporation, mines gold in country X, produces gold jewelry in the United States, and sells the jewelry in country Y. Assume that the fair market value of the gold at the export terminal in country X is $40, and that US Gold ultimately sells the gold jewelry in country Y for $100. Under section 1.863-1(b), $40 of US Gold's gross receipts will be allocated to sources without the United States. Under paragraph (b)(1)(i) of this section, the source of the remaining $60 of gross receipts will be determined under § 1.863-3. If US Gold applies the 50/50 method described in § 1.863-3, $20 of cost of goods sold is properly attributable to activities subsequent to the export terminal, and all of US Gold's production assets subsequent to the export terminal are located in the United States, then $20 of gross income will be allocated to sources within the United States and $20 of gross income will be allocated to sources without the United States.

Example (4). Production in country of sale. US Oil, a U.S. corporation, extracts oil in country X, transports the oil via pipeline to the export terminal in country Y, refines the oil in the United States, and sells the refined product in the United States to unrelated persons. Assume that the fair market value of the oil at the export terminal in country Y is $80, and that US Oil ultimately sells the refined product for $100. Under paragraph (b)(1) of this section, $80 of US Oil's gross receipts will be allocated to sources without the United States, and under paragraph (b)(1)(ii) of this section the remaining $20 of gross receipts will be allocated to sources within the United States.

Example (5). Additional production prior to export. The facts are the same as in Example 1, except that U.S. Mines also operates a smelter in country X. The concentrate output from the mill is transported to the smelter where it is transformed into smelted copper. The smelted copper is exported to purchasers in the United States. Under the facts and circumstances, all of the processes applied to make copper concentrate are considered mining. Therefore, under paragraph (b)(2) of this section, gross receipts equal to the fair market value of the concentrate at the smelter will be from sources without the United States. Under the facts and circumstances, the conversion of the concentrate into smelted copper is an additional production activity in a foreign country within the meaning of paragraph (b)(3)(ii) of this section. Therefore, the source of U.S. Mine's excess gross receipts will be determined pursuant to paragraph (b)(2) of this section.

(c) Determination of taxable income. The taxpayer's taxable income from sources within or without the United States will be determined under the rules of §§ 1.861-8 through 1.861-14T for determining taxable income from sources within the United States.

(d) Scholarships, fellowship grants, grants, prizes and awards. *(1) In general.* This paragraph (d) applies to scholarships, fellowship grants, grants, prizes and awards. The provisions of this paragraph (d) do not apply to amounts paid as salary or other compensation for services.

(2) Source of income. The source of income from scholarships, fellowship grants, grants, prizes and awards is determined as follows:

(i) United States source income. Except as provided in paragraph (d)(2)(iii) of this section, scholarships, fellowship grants, grants, prizes and awards made by a U.S. citizen or resident, a domestic partnership, a domestic corporation, an estate or trust (other than a foreign estate or trust within the meaning of section 7701(a)(31)), the United States (or an instrumentality or agency thereof), a State (or any political subdivision thereof), or the District of Columbia shall be treated as income from sources within the United States.

(ii) Foreign source income. Scholarships, fellowship grants, grants, prizes and awards made by a foreign government (or an instrumentality, agency, or any political subdivision thereof), an international organization (as defined in section 7701 (a)(18)), or a person other than a U.S. person (as defined in section 7701(a)(30)) shall be treated as income from sources without the United States.

(iii) Certain activities conducted outside the United States. Scholarships, fellowship grants, targeted grants, and achievement awards received by a person other than a U.S. person (as defined in section 7701(a)(30)) with respect to activities previously conducted (in the case of achievement awards) or to be conducted (in the case of scholarships, fellowships grants, and targeted grants) outside the United States shall be treated as income from sources without the United States.

(3) Definitions. The following definitions apply for purposes of this paragraph (d):

(i) Scholarships are defined in section 117 and the regulations thereunder.

(ii) Fellowship grants are defined in section 117 and the regulations thereunder.

(iii) Prizes and awards are defined in section 74 and the regulations thereunder.

(iv) Grants are amounts described in subparagraph (3) of section 4945(g) and the regulations thereunder, and are not amounts otherwise described in paragraphs (d)(3)(i), (ii), or (iii) of this section. For purposes of this paragraph (d), the reference to section 4945(g)(3) is applied without regard to the identity of the payor or recipient and without the application of the objective and nondiscriminatory basis test and the requirement of a procedure approved in advance.

(v) Targeted grants are grants—

(A) Issued by an organization described in section 501(c)(3), the United States (or an instrumentality or agency thereof), a State (or any political subdivision thereof), or the District of Columbia; and

(B) For an activity undertaken in the public interest and not primarily for the private financial benefit of a specific person or persons or organization.

(vi) Achievement awards are awards—

(A) Issued by an organization described in section 501(c)(3), the United States (or an instrumentality or agency thereof), a State (or political subdivision thereof), or the District of Columbia; and

(B) For a past activity undertaken in the public interest and not primarily for the private financial benefit of a specific person or persons or organization.

(4) Effective dates. The following are the effective dates concerning this paragraph (d):

(i) Scholarships and fellowship grants. This paragraph (d) is effective for scholarship and fellowship grant payments made after December 31, 1986. However, for scholarship and fellowship grant payments made after May 14, 1989, and before June 16, 1993, the residence of the payor rule of paragraph (d)(2)(i) and (ii) of this section may be applied without applying paragraph (d)(2)(iii) of this section.

(ii) Grants, prizes and awards. This paragraph (d) is effective for payments made for grants, prizes and awards, targeted grants, and achievement awards after September 25, 1995. However, the taxpayer may elect to apply the provisions of this paragraph (d) to payments made for grants, prizes and awards, targeted grants, and achievement awards after December 31, 1986, and before September 26, 1995.

(e) Residual interest in a REMIC. *(1) REMIC inducement fees.* An inducement fee (as defined in § 1.446-6(b)(2)) shall be treated as income from sources within the United States.

(2) Excess inclusion income and net losses. [Reserved]. For further guidance, see § 1.863-1T(e)(2).

(f) Effective dates. The rules of paragraphs (a), (b), and (c) of this section apply to taxable years beginning after December 30, 1996. However, taxpayers may apply the rules of paragraphs (a), (b), and (c) of this section for taxable years beginning after July 11, 1995, and on or before December 30, 1996. For years beginning before December 30, 1996, see § 1.863-1 (as contained in 26 CFR part 1 revised as of April 1, 1996). See paragraph (d)(4) of this section for rules regarding the applicability date of paragraph (d) of this section. Paragraph (e)(1) of this section is applicable for taxable years ending on or after May 11, 2004. For further guidance, see § 1.863-1T(f).

T.D. 6258, 10/23/57, amend T.D. 6348, 1/10/59, T.D. 8615, 8/24/95, T.D. 8687, 11/27/96, T.D. 9128, 5/7/2004, T.D. 9272, 7/31/2006.

PAR. 4. Section 1.863-1 is amended as follows:

1. The paragraph heading for paragraph (e) is revised.

2. The text of paragraph (e) is redesignated as (e)(1).

3. A new paragraph heading for paragraph (e)(1) is added.

4. A new paragraph (e)(2) is added.

5. The last sentence of paragraph (f) is revised and a new sentence is added to the end.

The revisions and additions read as follows:

Proposed § 1.863-1 Allocation of gross income under section 863(a). [*For Preamble, see ¶ 152,777*]

* * * * *

(e) Residual interest in a REMIC. *(1) REMIC inducement fees.* * * *

(2) [The text of the proposed amendment to § 1.863-1(e)(2) is the same as the text of § 1.863-1T(e)(2) published elsewhere in this issue of the Federal Register].

(f) [The text of proposed amendment to § 1.863-1(f) is the same as the text of § 1.863-1T(f) published elsewhere in this issue of the Federal Register].

§ 1.863-1T Allocation of gross income under section 863(a) (temporary).

(a) through (d) [Reserved]. For further guidance, see § 1.863-1(a) through (d).

(e) Residual interest in a REMIC. *(1) REMIC inducement fees.* [Reserved]. For further guidance, see § 1.863-1(e)(1).

(2) Excess inclusion income and net losses. An excess inclusion (as defined in section 860E(c)) shall be treated as income from sources within the United States. To the extent of excess inclusion income previously taken into account with respect to a residual interest (reduced by net losses previously taken into account under this paragraph), a net loss (described in section 860C(b)(2)) with respect to the residual interest shall be allocated to the class of gross income and apportioned to the statutory grouping(s) or residual grouping of gross income to which the excess inclusion income was assigned.

(f) Effective date. Paragraph (e)(2) of this section applies for taxable years ending after August 1, 2006. For further guidance, see § 1.863-1(f). This section will expire July 31, 2009.

T.D. 9272, 7/31/2006.

§ 1.863-2 Allocation and apportionment of taxable income.

Caution: The Treasury has not yet amended Reg § 1.863-2 to reflect changes made by P.L. 104-188, P.L. 98-369.

(a) Determination of taxable income. Section 863(b) provides an alternate method for determining taxable income from sources within the United States in the case of gross income derived from sources partly within and partly without the United States. Under this method, taxable income is determined by deducting from such gross income the expenses, losses, or other deductions properly apportioned or allocated thereto and a ratable part of any other expenses, losses, or deductions that cannot definitely be allocated to some item or class of gross income. The income to which this section applies (and that is treated as derived partly from sources within and partly from sources without the United States) will consist of gains, profits, and income

(1) From certain transportation or other services rendered partly within and partly without the United States to the extent not within the scope of section 863(c) or other specific provisions of this title;

(2) From the sale of inventory property (within the meaning of section 865(i)) produced (in whole or in part) by the taxpayer in the United States and sold outside the United States or produced (in whole or in part) by the taxpayer outside the United States and sold in the United States; or

(3) Derived from the purchase of personal property within a possession of the United States and its sale within the United States, to the extent not excluded from the scope of these regulations under § 1.936-6(a)(5), Q&A 7.

(b) Determination of source of taxable income. Income treated as derived from sources partly within and partly without the United States under paragraph (a) of this section may be allocated to sources within and without the United States pursuant to § 1.863-1 or apportioned to such sources in accordance with the methods described in other regulations under section 863. To determine the source of certain types of income described in paragraph (a)(1) of this section, see § 1.863-4. To determine the source of gross income described in paragraph (a)(2) of this section, see § 1.863-1 for natural resources and see § 1.863-3 for other inventory. Taxpayers, at their election, may apply the principles of § 1.863-3(b)(1) and (c) to determine the source of taxable income (rather than gross income) from sales of inventory property (other than natural resources). To determine the source of income partly from sources within a possession of the United States, including income described in paragraph (a)(3) of this section, see § 1.863-3(f).

(c) Effective dates. This section will apply to taxable years beginning after December 30, 1996. However, taxpayers may apply the rules of this section for taxable years beginning after July 11, 1995, and on or before December 30, 1996. For years beginning before December 30, 1996, see § 1.863-2 (as contained in 26 CFR part 1 revised as of April 1, 1996).

T.D. 6258, 10/23/57, amend T.D. 8687, 11/27/96.

§ 1.863-3A Income from the sale of personal property derived partly from within and partly from without the United States.

Caution: The Treasury has not yet amended Reg § 1.863-3A to reflect changes made by P.L. 104-188.

(a) General. *(1) Classes of income.* Income from the sale of property to which paragraph (b)(2) and (3) of § 1.863-2 applies is divided into two classes for purposes of this section, namely, income which is treated as derived partly from sources within the United States and partly from sources within a foreign country, and income which is treated as derived partly from sources within the United States and partly from sources within a possession of the United States.

(2) Definition. For purposes of this section, the word "produced" includes created, fabricated, manufactured, extracted, processed, cured, or aged. For determining the time and place of sale of personal property for purposes of this section, see paragraph (c) of § 1.861-7.

(b) Income partly from sources within a foreign country. *(1) General.* This paragraph relates to gains, profits, and income derived from the sale of personal property produced (in whole or in part) by the taxpayer within the United States and sold within a foreign country, or produced (in whole or in part) by the taxpayer within a foreign country and sold within the United States. Pursuant to section 863(b) such items shall be treated as derived partly from sources within the United States and partly from sources within a foreign country.

(2) Allocation or apportionment. The taxable income from sources within the United States, in the case of the items to which this paragraph applies, shall be determined according to the examples set forth in this subparagraph. For such purposes, the deductions for the personal exemptions shall not be taken into account, but the special deductions described in paragraph (c) of § 1.861-8 shall be taken into account.

Example (1). Where the manufacturer or producer regularly sells part of his output to wholly independent distributors or other selling concerns in such a way as to establish fairly an independent factory or production price—or shows to the satisfaction of the district director (or, if applicable, the Director of International Operations) that such an independent factory or production price has been otherwise established—unaffected by considerations of tax liability, and the selling or distributing branch or department of the business is located in a different country from that in which the factory is located or the production carried on, the taxable income attributable to sources within the United States shall be computed by an accounting which treats the products as sold by the factory or productive department of the business to the distributing or selling department at the independent factory price so established. In all such cases the basis of the accounting shall be fully explained in a statement attached to the return for the taxable year.

Example (2). (i) and (ii) [Reserved] For guidance, see § 1.863-3T(b)(2) *Example* (2)(i) and (ii).

(iii) The term "gross sales", as used in this example, refers only to the sales of personal property produced (in whole or in part) by the taxpayer within the United States and sold within a foreign country or produced (in whole or in part) by the taxpayer within a foreign country and sold within the United States.

(iv) The term "property", as used in this example, includes only the property held or used to produce income which is derived from such sales. Such property should be taken at its actual value, which in the case of property valued or appraised for purposes of inventory, depreciation, depletion, or other purposes of taxation shall be the highest amount at which so valued or appraised, and which in other cases shall be deemed to be its book value in the absence of affirmative evidence showing such value to be greater or less than the actual value. The average value during the taxable year or period shall be employed. The average value of property as above prescribed at the beginning and end of the taxable year or period ordinarily may be used, unless by reason of material changes during the taxable year or period such average does not fairly represent the average for such year or period, in which event the average shall be determined upon a monthly or daily basis.

(v) Bills and accounts receivable shall (unless satisfactory reason for a different treatment is shown) be assigned or allocated to the United States when the debtor resides in the United States, unless the taxpayer has no office, branch, or agent in the United States.

Example (3). Application for permission to base the return upon the taxpayer's books of account will be considered by the district director (or, if applicable, the Director of International Operations) in the case of any taxpayer who, in good faith and unaffected by considerations of tax liability, regularly employs in his books of account a detailed allocation of receipts and expenditures which reflects more clearly than the processes or formulas herein prescribed the taxable income derived from sources within the United States.

(c) Income partly from sources within a possession of the United States. *(1) General.* This paragraph relates to gains, profits, and income which, pursuant to section 863(b), are treated as derived partly from sources within the United States and partly from sources within a possession of the United States. The items so treated are described in subparagraphs (3) and (4) of this paragraph.

(2) Allocation or apportionment. The taxable income from sources within the United States, in the case of the items to which this paragraph applies, shall be determined according to the examples set forth in subparagraphs (3) and (4) of this paragraph. For such purposes, the deductions for the personal exemptions shall not be taken into account, but the special deductions described in paragraph (c) of § 1.861-8 shall be taken into account.

(3) Personal property produced and sold. This subparagraph relates to gross income derived from the sale of personal property produced (in whole or in part) by the taxpayer within the United States and sold within a possession of the United States, or produced (in whole or in part) by the taxpayer within a possession of the United States and sold within the United States.

Example (1). Same as example (1) under paragraph (b)(2) of this section.

Example (2). (i) Where an independent factory or production price has not been established as provided under example (1), the taxable income shall first be computed by deducting from the gross income derived from the sale of personal property produced (in whole or in part) by the taxpayer within the United States and sold within a possession of the United States, or produced (in whole or in part) by the taxpayer within a possession of the United States and sold within the United States, the expenses, losses, or other deductions properly allocated and apportioned thereto in accordance with the rules set forth in § 1.861-8.

(ii) Of the amount of taxable income so determined, one-half shall be apportioned in accordance with the value of the taxpayer's property within the United States and within the possession of the United States, the portion attributable to sources within the United States being determined by multiplying such one-half by a fraction the numerator of which consists of the value of the taxpayer's property within the United States, and the denominator of which consists of the value of the taxpayer's property both within the United States and within the possession of the United States. The remaining one-half of such taxable income shall be apportioned in accordance with the total business of the taxpayer within the United States and within the possession of the United States, the portion attributable to sources within the United States being determined by multiplying such one-half by a fraction the numerator of which consists of the amount of the taxpayer's business for the taxable year or period within the United States, and the denominator of which consists of the amount of the taxpayer's business for the taxable year or period both within the United States and within the possession of the United States.

(iii) The "business of the taxpayer", as used in this example, shall be measured by the amounts which the taxpayer paid out during the taxable year or period for wages, salaries, and other compensation of employees and for the purchase of goods, materials, and supplies consumed in the regular course of business, plus the amounts received during the taxable year or period from gross sales, such expenses, purchases, and gross sales being limited to those attributable to the production (in whole or in part) of personal property within the United States and its sale within a possession of the United States or to the production (in whole or in part) of personal property within a possession of the United States and its sale within the United States. The term "property", as used in this example, includes only the property held or used to produce income which is derived from such sales.

Example (3). Same as example (3) under paragraph (b)(2) of this section.

(4) Personal property purchased and sold. This subparagraph relates to gross income derived from the purchase of personal property within a possession of the United States and its sale within the United States.

Example (1). (i) The taxable income shall first be computed by deducting from such gross income the expenses, losses, or other deductions properly allocated or apportioned thereto in accordance with the rules set forth in § 1.861-8.

(ii) The amount of taxable income so determined shall be apportioned in accordance with the total business of the taxpayer within the United States and within the possession of the United States, the portion attributable to sources within the United States being that percentage of such taxable income which the amount of the taxpayer's business for the taxable year or period within the United States bears to the amount of the taxpayer's business for the taxable year or period both within the United States and within the possession of the United States.

(iii) The "business of the taxpayer", as that term is used in this example, shall be measured by the amounts which the taxpayer paid out during the taxable year or period for wages, salaries, and other compensation of employees and for the purchase of goods, materials, and supplies sold or consumed in the regular course of business, plus the amount received during the taxable year or period from gross sales, such expenses, purchases, and gross sales being limited to those attributable to the purchase of personal property within a possession of the United States and its sale within the United States.

Example (2). Same as example (3) under paragraph (b)(2) of this section.

T.D. 6258, 10/23/57, amend T.D. 7456, 1/3/77, T.D. 8228, 9/9/88, T.D. 8687, 11/27/96.

§ 1.863-3AT Income from the sale of personal property derived partly from within and partly from without the United States (temporary).

(a) [Reserved]

(b) Income partly from sources within a foreign country.

(1) [Reserved]

(2) Allocation or apportionment.

Example (1). [Reserved]

Example (2). (i) Where an independent factory or production price has not been established as provided under Example (1), the gross income derived from the sale of personal property produced (in whole or in part) by the taxpayer within the United States and sold within a foreign country or produced (in whole or in part) by the taxpayer within a foreign country and sold within the United States shall be computed.

(ii) Of this gross amount, one-half shall be apportioned in accordance with the value of the taxpayer's property within the United States and within the foreign country, the portion attributable to sources within the United States being determined by multiplying such one-half by a fraction, the numerator of which consists of the value of the taxpayer's property within the United States and the denominator of which consists of the value of the taxpayer's property both within the United States and within the foreign country. The remaining one-half of such gross income shall be apportioned in accordance with the gross sales of the taxpayer within the United States and within the foreign country, the portion attributable to sources within the United States being determined by multiplying such one-half by a fraction the numerator of which consists of the taxpayer's gross sales for the taxable year or period within the United States, and the denominator of which consists of the taxpayer's gross sales for the taxable year or period both within the United States and within the foreign country. Deductions from gross income that are allocable and apportionable to gross income described in paragraph (i) of this Example 2 shall be apportioned between the United States and foreign source portions of such income, as determined under this paragraph (ii), on a pro rata basis, without regard to whether the deduction relates primarily or exclusively to the production of property or to the sale of property.

(iii) through (c)(4) [Reserved]

T.D. 8228, 9/9/88, amend T.D. 8687, 11/27/96.

§ 1.863-4 Certain transportation services.

Caution: The Treasury has not yet amended Reg § 1.863-4 to reflect changes made by P.L. 105-34.

(a) General. A taxpayer carrying on the business of transportation service (other than an activity giving rise to transportation income described in section 863(c) or to income subject to other specific provisions of this title) between points in the United States and points outside the United States derives income partly from sources within and partly from sources without the United States.

(b) Gross income. The gross income from sources within the United States derived from such services shall be determined by taking such a portion of the total gross revenues therefrom as (1) the sum of the costs or expenses of such transportation business carried on by the taxpayer within the United States and a reasonable return upon the property used in its transportation business while within the United States bears to (2) the sum of the total costs or expenses of such transportation business carried on by the taxpayer and a reasonable return upon the total property used in such transportation business. Revenues from operations incidental to transportation services, such as the sale of money orders, shall be apportioned on the same basis as direct revenues from transportation services.

(c) Allocation of costs or expenses. In allocating the total costs or expenses incurred in such transportation business, costs or expenses incurred in connection with that part of the services which was wholly rendered in the United States shall be assigned to the cost of transportation business within the United States. For example, expenses of loading and unloading in the United States, rentals, office expenses, salaries, and wages wholly incurred for services rendered to the taxpayer in the United States belong to this class. Costs and expenses incurred in connection with services rendered partly within and partly without the United States may be prorated on a reasonable basis between such services. For example, ship wages, charter money, insurance, and supplies chargeable to voyage expenses shall ordinarily be prorated for each voyage on the basis of the proportion which the number of days the ship was within the territorial limits of the United States bears to the total number of days on the voyage; and fuel consumed on each voyage may be prorated on the basis of the proportion which the number of miles sailed within the territorial limits of the United States bears to the total number of miles sailed on the voyage. For other expenses entering into the cost of services, only such expenses as are allowable deductions under the internal revenue laws shall be taken into account.

(d) Items not included as costs or expenses. *(1) Taxes and interest.* Income, war profits, and excess profits taxes shall not be regarded as costs or expenses for the purpose of determining the proportion of gross income from sources within the United States; and, for such purpose, interest and other expenses for the use of borrowed capital shall not be taken into the cost of services rendered, for the reason that the return upon the property used measures the extent to which such borrowed capital is the source of the income. See paragraph (f)(2) of this section.

(2) Other business activity and general expenses. If a taxpayer subject to this section is also engaged in a business other than that of providing transportation service between points in the United States and points outside the United States, the costs and expenses, including taxes, properly apportioned or allocated to such other business shall be excluded both from the deductions and from the apportionment process prescribed in paragraph (c) of this section; but, for the purpose of determining taxable income, a ratable part of any general expenses, losses, or deductions, which cannot definitely be allocated to some item or class of gross income, may be deducted from the gross income from sources within the United States after the amount of such gross income has been determined. Such ratable part shall ordinarily be based upon the ratio of gross income from sources within the United States to the total gross income. See paragraph (f)(3) of this section.

(3) Personal exemptions and special deductions. The deductions for the personal exemptions, and the special deductions described in paragraph (c) of § 1.861-8, shall not be taken into account for purposes of paragraph (c) of this section.

(e) Property used while within the United States. *(1) General.* The value of the property used shall be determined upon the basis of cost less depreciation. Eight percent may ordinarily be taken as a reasonable rate of return to apply to such property. The property taken shall be the average property employed in the transportation service between points in the United States and points outside the United States during the taxable year.

(2) Average property. For ships, the average shall be determined upon a daily basis for each ship, and the amount to be apportioned for each ship as assets employed within the United States shall be computed upon the proportion which the number of days the ship was within the territorial limits of the United States bears to the total number of days the ship was in service during the taxable period. For other assets employed in the transportation business, the average of the assets at the beginning and end of the taxable period ordinarily may be taken, but if the average so obtained does not, by reason of material changes during the taxable year, fairly represent the average for such year either for the assets employed in the transportation business in the United States or in total, the average must be determined upon a monthly or daily basis.

(3) Current assets. Current assets shall be decreased by current liabilities and allocated to services between the United States and foreign countries and to other services. The part allocated to services between the United States and foreign countries shall be based on the proportion which the gross receipts from such services bear to services between the United States and foreign countries shall be further allocated to services rendered within the United States and to services rendered without the United States. The portion allocable to services rendered within the United States shall be based on the proportion which the expenses incurred within the territorial limits of the United States bear to the total expenses incurred in services between the United States and foreign countries.

(f) Taxable income. *(1) General.* In computing taxable income from sources within the United States there shall be allowed as deductions from the gross income from such sources, determined in accordance with paragraph (b) of this section, (i) the expenses of the transportation business carried on within the United States (as determined under paragraphs (c) and (d) of this section) and (ii) the expenses and deductions determined in accordance with this paragraph.

(2) Interest and taxes. Interest and income, war-profits, and excess profits taxes shall be excluded from the apportionment process, as indicated in paragraph (d) of this section; but, for the purpose of computing taxable income there may be deducted from the gross income from sources within the United States, after the amount of such gross income has been determined, a ratable part of all interest deductible under section 163 and of all income, war-profits, and excess profits taxes deductible under section 164, paid or accrued in respect of the business of transportation service between points in the United States and points outside the United States. The ratable part shall ordinarily be based upon the ratio of gross income from sources within the United States to the total gross income, from such transportation service.

(3) General expenses. General expenses, losses, or deductions shall be deducted under this paragraph to the extent indicated in paragraph (d)(2) of this section.

(4) Personal exemptions. The deductions for the personal exemptions shall be allowed under this paragraph to the same extent as provided by paragraph (b) of § 1.861-8.

(5) Special deductions. The special deductions allowed in the case of a corporation by sections 241, 922, and 941 shall be allowed under this paragraph to the same extent as provided by paragraph (c) of § 1.861-8.

(g) Allocation based on books of account. Application for permission to base the return upon the taxpayer's books of account will be considered by the district director (or, if applicable, the Director of International Operations) in the case of any taxpayer subject to this section, who, in good faith and unaffected by considerations of tax liability, regularly employs in his books of account a detailed allocation of receipts and expenditures which more clearly reflects the income derived from sources within the United States than does the process prescribed by paragraphs (b) to (f), inclusive, of this section.

T.D. 6258, 10/23/57, amend T.D. 8687, 11/27/96.

---

§ 1.863-6 Income from sources within a foreign country.

The principles applied in sections 861 through 863 and section 865 and the regulations thereunder for determining the gross and the taxable income from sources within and without the United States shall generally be applied in determining the gross and the taxable income from sources within and without a particular foreign country when such a determination must be made under any provision of Subtitle A of the Internal Revenue Code, including section 952(a)(5). This section shall not apply, however, to the extent it is determined by applying § 1.863-3 that a portion of the taxable income is from sources within the United States and the balance of the taxable income is from sources within a foreign country. In the application of this section, the name of the particular foreign country shall be used instead of the term United States, and the term domestic shall be construed to mean created or organized in such foreign country. In applying section 861 and the regulations thereunder for purposes of this section, references to sections 243 and 245 shall be excluded, and the exception in section 861(a)(3) shall not apply. In the case of any item of income, the income from sources within a foreign country shall not exceed the amount which, by applying any provision of sections 861 through 863 and section 865 and the regulations thereunder without reference to this section, is treated as income from sources without the United States. See § 1.937-2T for rules for determining income from sources within a possession of the United States.

T.D. 6258, 10/23/57, amend T.D. 7378, 9/29/75, T.D. 9194, 4/6/2005.

PAR. 8.

Section 1.863-7(a)(1) is amended by revising the second sentence to read as follows:

Proposed § 1.863-7 Allocation of income attributable to certain notional principal contracts under section 863(a). [*For Preamble, see ¶ 151,855*]

(a) Scope. *(1) Introduction.* * * * This section does not apply to income from a section 988 transaction (as defined in section 988(c) and § 1.988-1(a)), or to income from a global dealing operation (as defined in § 1.482-8(a)(2)(i)) that is sourced under the rules of § 1.863-3(h). * * *

* * * * *

§ 1.863-7 Allocation of income attributable to certain notional principal contracts under section 863(a).

(a) Scope. *(1) Introduction* This section provides rules relating to the source and, in certain cases, the character of notional principal contract income. However, this section does not apply to income from a section 988 transaction within the meaning of section 988 and the regulations thereunder, relating to the treatment of certain nonfunctional currency transactions. Notional principal contract income is income attributable to a notional principal contract. A notional principal contract is a financial instrument that provides for the payment of amounts by one party to another at specified intervals calculated by reference to a specified index upon a notional principal amount in exchange for specified consideration or a promise to pay similar amounts. An agreement between a taxpayer and a qualified business unit (as defined in section 989(a)) of the taxpayer, or among qualified business units of the same taxpayer, is not a notional principal contract, because a taxpayer cannot enter into a contract with itself.

(2) Effective date. This section applies to notional principal contract income includible in income on or after February 13, 1991. However, any taxpayer desiring to apply paragraph (b)(2)(iv) of this section to notional principal contract income includible in income prior to February 13, 1991, in lieu of temporary Income Tax Regulations § 1.863-7T(b)(2)(iv) may (on a consistent basis) so choose. See paragraph (c) of this section for an election to apply the rules of this section to notional principal contract income includible in income before December 24, 1986.

(b) Source of notional principal contract income. *(1) General rule.* Unless paragraph (b)(2) or (3) of this section applies, the source of notional principal contract income shall be determined by reference to the residence of the taxpayer as determined under section 988(a)(3)(B)(i).

(2) Qualified business unit exception. The source of notional principal contract income shall be determined by reference to the residence of a qualified business unit of a taxpayer if—

(i) The taxpayer's residence, determined under section 988(a)(3)(B)(i), is the United States;

(ii) The qualified business unit's residence, determined under section 988(a)(3)(B)(ii), is outside the United States;

(iii) The qualified business unit is engaged in the conduct of a trade or business where it is a resident as determined under section 988(a)(3)(B)(ii); and

(iv) The notional principal contract is properly reflected on the books of the qualified business unit. Whether a notional principal contract is properly reflected on the books of such qualified business unit is a question of fact. The degree of participation in the negotiation and acquisition of a notional principal contract shall be considered in this determination. Participation in connection with the negotiation or acquisition of a notional principal contract may be disregarded if the district director determines that a purpose for such participation was to affect the source of notional principal contract income.

(3) Effectively connected notional principal contract income. Notional principal contract income that under principles similar to those set forth in § 1.864-4(c) arises from the conduct of a United States trade or business shall be sourced in the United States and such income shall be treated as effectively connected to the conduct of a United States trade or business for purposes of sections 871(b) and 882(a)(1).

(c) Election. *(1) Eligibility and effect.* A taxpayer described in paragraph (b)(2)(i) of this section may make an election to apply the rules of this section to all, but not part, of the taxpayer's income attributable to notional principal contracts for all taxable years (or portion thereof) beginning before December 24, 1986, for which the period of limitations for filing a claim for refund under section 6511(a) has not expired. A taxpayer not described in paragraph (b)(2)(i) of this section that is engaged in trade or business within the United States may make an election to apply the rules of this section to all, but not part, of the taxpayer's income described in paragraph (b)(3) of this section for all taxable years (or portion thereof) beginning before December 24, 1986, for which the period of limitations for filing a claim for refund under section 6511(a) has not expired. If a taxpayer makes an election pursuant to this paragraph (c)(1) in the time and manner provided in paragraph (c)(2) and (3) of this section, then, with respect to such taxable years (or portion thereof), no tax shall be deducted or withheld under sections 1441 and 1442 with respect to payments made by the taxpayer pursuant to a notional principal contract the income attributable to which is subject to such election. The election may be revoked only with the consent of the Commissioner.

(2) Time for making election. The election specified in paragraph (c)(1) of this section shall be made by May 14, 1991

(3) Manner of making election. The election described in paragraph (c)(1) of this section shall be made by attaching a statement to the tax return or an amended tax return for each taxable year beginning before December 24, 1986, in which the taxpayer accrued or received notional principal contract income. The statement shall—

(i) Contain the name, address, and taxpayer identifying number of the electing taxpayer;

(ii) Identify the election as a "Notional Principal Contract Election under § 1.863-7"; and

(iii) Specify each taxable year described in paragraph (c)(1) of this section in which payments were made.

(d) Example. The operation of this section is illustrated by the following example:

(1) On January 1, 1990, X, a calendar year domestic corporation, entered into an interest rate swap contract with FZ, an unrelated foreign corporation. X does not have a qualified business unit outside the United States. Under the contract, X is required to pay FZ fixed rate dollar amounts, and FZ is required to pay X floating rate dollar amounts, each determined solely by reference to a notional dollar denominated principal amount specified under the contract. The contract is a notional principal contract under § 1.863-7(a) because the contract provides for the payment of amounts at specified intervals calculated by reference to a specified index upon a notional principal amount in exchange for a promise to pay similar amounts.

(2) Assume that during 1990 X had notional principal contract income of $100 in connection with the notional principal contract described in (1) above. Also assume that the contract provides that payments more than 30 days late give rise to a $5 fee, and that X receives such a fee in 1990. Under paragraph (b)(1) of this section, the source of X's $100 of income attributable to the swap agreement is domestic. The $5 fee is not notional principal contract income.

(e) Cross references. See § 1.861-9T(b) for the allocation of expense to certain notional principal contracts. For rules relating to the source of income from nonfunctional currency notional principal contracts, see § 1.988-4T. For rules relating to the taxable amount of notional principal contract income allocable under this section to sources inside or outside the United States, see § 1.863-1(c).

T.D. 8330, 1/11/91.

§ 1.863-8 Source of income derived from space and ocean activity under section 863(d).

(a) In general. Income of a United States or a foreign person derived from space and ocean activity (space and ocean income) is sourced under the rules of this section, notwithstanding any other provision, including sections 861, 862, 863, and 865. A taxpayer will not be considered to derive income from space or ocean activity, as defined in paragraph (d) of this section, if such activity is performed by another person, subject to the rules for the treatment of consolidated groups in § 1.1502-13.

(b) Source of gross income from space and ocean activity. *(1) Space and ocean income derived by a United States person.* Space and ocean income derived by a United States person is income from sources within the United States. However, space and ocean income derived by a United States person is income from sources without the United States to the extent the income, based on all the facts and circumstances, is attributable to functions performed, resources employed, or risks assumed in a foreign country or countries.

(2) Space and ocean income derived by a foreign person. (i) In general. Space and ocean income derived by a person other than a United States person is income from sources without the United States, except as otherwise provided in this paragraph (b)(2).

(ii) Space and ocean income derived by a controlled foreign corporation. Space and ocean income derived by a controlled foreign corporation within the meaning of section 957 (CFC) is income from sources within the United States. However, space and ocean income derived by a CFC is income from sources without the United States to the extent the income, based on all the facts and circumstances, is attributable to functions performed, resources employed, or risks assumed in a foreign country or countries.

(iii) Space and ocean income derived by foreign persons engaged in a trade or business within the United States. Space and ocean income derived by a foreign person (other than a CFC) engaged in a trade or business within the United States is income from sources within the United States to the extent the income, based on all the facts and circumstances, is attributable to functions performed, resources employed, or risks assumed within the United States.

(3) Source rules for income from certain sales of property. (i) Sales of purchased property. When a taxpayer sells purchased property in space or international water, the source of gross income from the sale generally will be determined under paragraph (b)(1) or (2) of this section, as applicable. However, if such property is inventory property within the meaning of section 1221(a)(1) (inventory property) and is sold for use, consumption, or disposition outside space and international water, the source of income from the sale will be determined under § 1.861-7(c).

(ii) Sales of property produced by the taxpayer. (A) General. If the taxpayer both produces property and sells such property, the taxpayer must allocate gross income from such sales between production activity and sales activity under the 50/50 method. Under the 50/50 method, one-half of the taxpayer's gross income will be considered income allocable to production activity, and the source of that income will be determined under paragraph (b)(3)(ii)(B) or (C) of this section. The remaining one-half of such gross income will be considered income allocable to sales activity, and the source of that income will be determined under paragraph (b)(3)(ii)(D) of this section.

(B) Production only in space or international water, or only outside space and international water. When production occurs only in space or international water, income allocable to production activity is sourced under paragraph (b)(1) or (2) of this section, as applicable. When production occurs only outside space and international water, income allocable to production activity is sourced under § 1.863-3(c)(1).

(C) Production both in space or international water and outside space and international water. When property is produced both in space or international water and outside space and international water, gross income allocable to production activity must be allocated to production occurring in space or international water and production occurring outside space and international water. Such gross income is allocated to production activity occurring in space or international water to the extent the income, based on all the facts and circumstances, is attributable to functions performed, resources employed, or risks assumed in space or international water. The balance of such gross income is allocated to production activity occurring outside space and international water. The source of gross income allocable to production activity in space or international water is determined under paragraph (b)(1) or (2) of this section, as applicable. The source of gross income allocated to production activity occurring outside space and international water is determined under § 1.863-3(c)(1).

(D) Source of income allocable to sales activity. When property produced by the taxpayer is sold outside space and international water, the source of gross income allocable to sales activity will be determined under §§ 1.861-7(c) and 1.863-3(c)(2). When property produced by the taxpayer is sold in space or international water, the source of gross income allocable to sales activity generally will be determined under paragraph (b)(1) or (2) of this section, as applicable. However, if such property is inventory property within the meaning of section 1221(a)(1) and is sold in space or international water for use, consumption, or disposition outside space, international water, and the United States, the source of gross income allocable to sales activity will be determined under §§ 1.861-7(c) and 1.863-3(c)(2).

(4) Special rule for determining the source of gross income from services. To the extent a transaction characterized as the performance of a service constitutes a space or ocean activity, as determined under paragraph (d)(2)(ii) of this section, the source of gross income derived from such transaction is determined under paragraph (b)(1) or (2) of this section.

(5) Special rule for determining source of income from communications activity (other than income from international communications activity). Space and ocean activity, as defined in paragraph (d) of this section, includes activity that occurs in space or international water that is characterized as a communications activity as defined in § 1.863-9(h)(1) (other than international communications activity). The source of space and ocean income that is also communications income as defined in § 1.863-9(h)(2) (but not space/ocean communications income as defined in § 1.863-9(h)(3)(v)) is determined under the rules of § 1.863-9(c), (d), and (f), as applicable, rather than under paragraph (b) of this section. The source of space and ocean income that is also space/ocean communications income as defined in § 1.863-9(h)(3)(v) is determined under the rules of paragraph (b) of this section. See § 1.863-9(e).

(c) Taxable income. When a taxpayer allocates gross income under paragraph (b)(1), (b)(2), (b)(3)(ii)(C), or (b)(4) of this section, the taxpayer must allocate expenses, losses, and other deductions as prescribed in §§ 1.861-8 through 1.861-14T to the class or classes of gross income that include the income so allocated in each case. A taxpayer must then apply the rules of §§ 1.861-8 through 1.861-14T to apportion properly amounts of expenses, losses, and other deductions so allocated to such gross income between gross income from sources within the United States and gross income from sources without the United States.

(d) Space and ocean activity. *(1) Definition.* (i) Space activity. In general, space activity is any activity conducted in space. For purposes of this section, space means any area not within the jurisdiction (as recognized by the United States) of a foreign country, possession of the United States, or the United States, and not in international water. For purposes of determining space activity, the Commissioner may separate parts of a single transaction into separate transactions or combine separate transactions as part of a single transaction. Paragraph (d)(3) of this section lists specific exceptions to the general definition of space activity. Activities that constitute space activity include but are not limited to—

(A) Performance and provision of services in space, as defined in paragraph (d)(2)(ii) of this section;

(B) Leasing of equipment located in space, including spacecraft (for example, satellites) or transponders located in space;

(C) Licensing of technology or other intangibles for use in space;

(D) Production, processing, or creation of property in space, as defined in paragraph (d)(2)(i) of this section;

(E) Activity occurring in space that is characterized as communications activity (other than international communications activity) under § 1.863-9(h)(1);

(F) Underwriting income from the insurance of risks on activities that produce space income; and

(G) Sales of property in space (see § 1.861-7(c)).

(ii) Ocean activity. In general, ocean activity is any activity conducted on or under water not within the jurisdiction (as recognized by the United States) of a foreign country, possession of the United States, or the United States (collectively, in international water). For purposes of determining ocean activity, the Commissioner may separate parts of a single transaction into separate transactions or combine separate transactions as part of a single transaction. Paragraph (d)(3) of this section lists specific exceptions to the general definition of ocean activity. Activities that constitute ocean activity include but are not limited to—

(A) Performance and provision of services in international water, as defined in paragraph (d)(2)(ii) of this section;

(B) Leasing of equipment located in international water, including underwater cables;

(C) Licensing of technology or other intangibles for use in international water;

(D) Production, processing, or creation of property in international water, as defined in paragraph (d)(2)(i) of this section;

(E) Activity occurring in international water that is characterized as communications activity (other than international communications activity) under § 1.863-9(h)(1);

(F) Underwriting income from the insurance of risks on activities that produce ocean income;

(G) Sales of property in international water (see § 1.861-7(c));

(H) Any activity performed in Antarctica;

(I) The leasing of a vessel that does not transport cargo or persons for hire between ports-of-call (for example, the leasing of a vessel to engage in research activities in international water); and

(J) The leasing of drilling rigs, extraction of minerals, and performance and provision of services related thereto, except as provided in paragraph (d)(3)(ii) of this section.

(2) Determining a space or ocean activity. (i) Production of property in space or international water. For purposes of this section, production activity means an activity that creates, fabricates, manufactures, extracts, processes, cures, or ages property within the meaning of section 864(a) and § 1.864-1.

(ii) Special rule for performance of services. (A) General. Except as provided in paragraph (d)(2)(ii)(B) of this section, if a transaction is characterized as the performance of a service, then such service will be treated as a space or ocean activity in its entirety when any part of the service is performed in space or international water. Services are performed in space or international water if functions are performed, resources are employed, or risks are assumed in space or international water, regardless of whether performed by personnel, equipment, or otherwise.

(B) Exception to the general rule. If the taxpayer can demonstrate the value of the service attributable to performance occurring in space or international water, and the value of the service attributable to performance occurring outside space and international water, then such service will be treated as space or ocean activity only to the extent of the activity performed in space or international water. The value of the service is attributable to performance occurring in space or international water to the extent the performance of the service, based on all the facts and circumstances, is attributable to functions performed, resources employed, or risks assumed in space or international water. In addition, if the taxpayer can demonstrate, based on all the facts and circumstances, that the value of the service attributable to performance in space and international water is de minimis, such service will not be treated as space or ocean activity.

(3) Exceptions to space or ocean activity. Space or ocean activity does not include the following types of activities:

(i) Any activity giving rise to transportation income as defined in section 863(c).

(ii) Any activity with respect to mines, oil and gas wells, or other natural deposits, to the extent the mines, wells, or natural deposits are located within the jurisdiction (as recognized by the United States) of any country, including the United States and its possessions.

(iii) Any activity giving rise to international communications income as defined in § 1.863-9(h)(3)(ii).

(e) Treatment of partnerships. This section is applied at the partner level.

(f) Examples. The following examples illustrate the rules of this section:

Example (1). Space activity—activity occurring on land and in space. (i) Facts. S, a United States person, owns satellites in orbit. S leases one of its satellites to A. S, as lessor, will not operate the satellite. Part of S's performance as lessor in this transaction occurs on land. Assume that the combination of S's activities is characterized as the lease of equipment.

(ii) Analysis. Because the leased equipment is located in space, the transaction is defined in its entirety as space activity under paragraph (d)(1)(i) of this section. Income derived from the lease will be sourced under paragraph (b)(1) of this section. Under paragraph (b)(1) of this section, S's space income is sourced outside the United States to the extent the income, based on all the facts and circumstances, is attributable to functions performed, resources employed, or risks assumed in a foreign country or countries.

Example (2). Space activity. (i) Facts. X is an Internet service provider. X offers a service that permits a customer (C) to connect to the Internet via a telephone call, initiated by the modem of C's personal computer, to a control center. X transmits information requested by C to C's personal computer, in part using satellite capacity leased by X from S. X performs the uplink and downlink functions. X charges its customers a flat monthly fee. Assume that neither X nor S derive international communications income within the meaning of § 1.863-9(h)(3)(ii). In addition, assume that X is able to demonstrate, pursuant to paragraph (d)(2)(ii)(B) of this section, the extent to which the value of the service is attributable to functions performed, resources employed, and risks assumed in space.

(ii) Analysis. Under paragraph (d)(2)(ii) of this section, the service performed by X constitutes space activity to the extent the value of the service is attributable to functions performed, resources employed, and risks assumed in space. To the extent the service performed by X constitutes space activity, the source of X's income from the service transaction is determined under paragraph (b) of this section. To the extent the service performed by X does not constitute space or ocean activity, the source of X's income from the service is determined under sections 861, 862, and 863, as applicable. To the extent that X derives space and ocean income that is also communications income within the meaning of § 1.863-9(h)(2), the source of X's income is determined under paragraph (b) of this section and § 1.863-9(c), (d), and (f), as applicable, as provided in paragraph (b)(5) of this section. S derives space and ocean income that is also communications income within the meaning of § 1.863-9(h)(2), and the source of S's income is therefore determined under paragraph (b) of this section and § 1.863-9(c), (d), and (f), as applicable, as provided in paragraph (b)(5) of this section.

Example (3). Services as space activity—de minimis value attributable to performance occurring in space. (i) Facts. R owns a retail outlet in the United States. R engages S to provide a security system for R's premises. S operates its security system by transmitting images from R's premises directly to a satellite, and from the satellite to a group of S employees located in Country B, who monitor the premises by viewing the transmitted images. The satellite is used as a medium of delivery and not as a method of surveillance. O provides S with transponder capacity on O's satellite, which S uses to transmit those images. Assume that S's transaction with R is characterized as the performance of a service. Assume that O's provision of transponder capacity is also viewed as the provision of a service. Assume also that S is able to demonstrate, pursuant to § 1.863-9(h)(1), that the value of the transaction with R attributable to communications activities is de minimis.

(ii) Analysis. S derives income from providing monitoring services. S can demonstrate, pursuant to paragraph (d)(2)(ii) of this section, that based on all the facts and circumstances, the value of S's service transaction attributable to performance in space is de minimis. Thus, S is not treated as engaged in a space activity, and none of S's income from the service transaction is space income. In addition, because S demonstrates that the value of the transaction with R attributable to communications activities is de minimis, S is not required under § 1.863-9(h)(1)(ii) to treat the transaction as separate communications and non-communications transactions, and none of S's gross income from the transaction is treated as communications income within the meaning of § 1.863-9(h)(2). O's provision of transponder capacity is viewed as the provision of a service. Based on all the facts and circumstances, the value of O's service transaction attributable to performance in space is not de minimis. Thus, O's activity will be considered space activity, pursuant to paragraph (d)(2)(ii) of this section, to the extent the value of the services transaction is attributable to performance in space (unless O's activity in space is international communications activity). To the extent that O derives communications income, the source of such income is determined under paragraph (b) of this section and § 1.863-9(b), (c), (d), and (f), as applicable, as provided in paragraph (b)(5) of this section. R does not derive any income from space activity.

Example (4). Space activity. (i) Facts. L, a domestic corporation, offers programming and certain other services to customers located both in the United States and in foreign countries. Assume that L's provision of programming and other services in this Example 4 is characterized as the provision of a service, and that no part of the service transaction occurs in space or international water. Assume that the delivery of the programming constitutes a separate transaction also characterized as the performance of a service. L uses satellite capacity acquired from S to deliver the programming service directly to customers' television sets. L performs the uplink and downlink functions, so that part of the value of the delivery transaction derives from functions performed and resources employed in space. Assume that these contributions to the value of the delivery transaction occurring in space are not considered de minimis under paragraph (d)(2)(ii)(B) of this section. Customer C pays L to provide and deliver programming to C's residence in the United States. Assume S's provision of satellite capacity in this Example 4 is viewed as the provision of a service, and also that S does not derive international communications income within the meaning of § 1.863-9(h)(3)(ii).

(ii) Analysis. S's activity will be considered space activity. To the extent that S derives space and ocean income that is also communications income under § 1.863-9(h)(2), the source of S's income is determined under paragraph (b) of this section and § 1.863-9(c), (d), and (f), as applicable, as provided in paragraph (b)(5) of this section. On these facts, L's activities are treated as two separate service transactions: the provision of programming (and other services), and the delivery of programming. L's income derived from provision of programming and other services is not income derived from space activity. L's delivery of programming and other services is considered space activity, pursuant to paragraph (d)(2)(ii) of this section, to the extent the value of the delivery transaction is attributable to performance in space. To the extent that the delivery of programming is treated as a space activity, the source of L's income derived from the delivery transaction is determined under paragraph (b)(1) of this section, as provided in paragraph (b)(4) of this section. To the extent that L derives space and ocean income that is also communications income within the meaning of § 1.863-9(h)(2), the source of such income is determined under paragraph (b) of this section and § 1.863-9(b), (c), (d), (e), and (f), as applicable, as provided in paragraph (b)(5) of this section.

Example (5). Space activity. (i) Facts. The facts are the same as in Example 4, except that L does not deliver the programming service directly but instead engages R, a domestic corporation specializing in content delivery, to deliver by transmission its programming. For all portions of a transmission which require satellite capacity, R, in turn, contracts out such functions to S. S performs the uplink and downlink functions, so that part of the value of the delivery transaction derives from functions performed and resources employed in space.

(ii) Analysis. L's activity will not be considered space activity because none of L's activity occurs in space. Thus, L does not derive any space and ocean income. L does, however, derive communications income within the meaning of § 1.863-9(h)(2). This is the case even though L does not perform the transmission function because L is paid by Customer C to transmit, and bears the risk of transmitting, the communications or data. To the extent that L's activity consists in part of non-de minimis communications and non-de minimis non-communications activity, each part of the transaction must be treated as a separate transaction and gross income is allocated accordingly under § 1.863-9(h)(1)(ii). In addition, L must also allocate expenses, losses, and other deductions, for example, payments to R, to the class or classes of gross income that include the income so allocated. R's activity will not be considered space activity. Since R contracts out all of the functions involving satellite capacity to S, no part of R's activity occurs in space. Thus, R does not derive any space and ocean income. R does, however, derive communications income within the meaning of § 1.863-9(h)(2). This is the case even though R does not perform the transmission function because R is paid by L to transmit, and bears the risk of transmitting, the communications or data. S's activity will be considered space activity. To the extent that S derives space and ocean income that is also communications income within the meaning of § 1.863-9(h)(2), the source of such income is determined under paragraph (b) of this section and § 1.863-9(b), (c), (d), (e), and (f), as applicable, as provided in paragraph (b)(5) of this section.

Example (6). Space activity—treatment of land activity. (i) Facts. S, a United States person, offers remote imaging products and services to its customers. In year 1, S uses its satellite's remote sensors to gather data on certain geographical terrain. In year 3, C, a construction development company, contracts with S to obtain a satellite image of an area for site development work. S pulls data from its archives and transfers to C the images gathered in year 1, in a transaction that is characterized as a sale of the data. S's rights, title, and interest in the data pass to C in the United States. Before transferring the images to C, S uses computer software in its land-based office to enhance the images so that the images can be used.

(ii) Analysis. The collection of data and creation of images in space is characterized as the creation of property in space. Because S both produces and sells the data, S must allocate gross income from the sale of the data between production activity and sales activity under the 50/50 method of paragraph (b)(3)(ii)(A). The source of S's income allocable to production activity is determined under paragraph (b)(3)(ii)(C) of this section because production activities occur both in space and on land. The source of S's income attributable to sales activity is determined under paragraph (b)(3)(ii)(D) of this section (by reference to § 1.863-3(c)(2)) as U.S. source income because S's rights, title, and interest in the data pass to C in the United States.

Example (7). Use of intangible property in space. (i) Facts. X acquires a license to use a particular satellite slot or orbit, which X sublicenses to C. C pays X a royalty.

(ii) Analysis. Because the royalty is paid for the right to use intangible property in space, the source of the royalty paid by C to X is determined under paragraph (b) of this section.

Example (8). Performance of services. (i) Facts. E, a domestic corporation, operates satellites with sensing equipment that can determine how much heat and light particular plants emit and reflect. Based on the data, E will provide F, a U.S. farmer, a report analyzing the data, which F will use in growing crops. E analyzes the data from offices located in the United States. Assume that E's combined activities are characterized as the performance of services.

(ii) Analysis. Based on all the facts and circumstances, the value of E's service transaction attributable to performance in space is not de minimis. Thus, E's activities will be considered space activities, pursuant to paragraph (d)(2)(ii) of this section, to the extent the value of E's service transaction is attributable to performance in space. To the extent E's service transaction constitutes a space activity, the source of E's income derived from the service transaction will be determined under paragraph (b)(4) of this section, by reference to paragraph (b)(1) of this section. To the extent that E's service transaction does not constitute a space or ocean activity, the source of E's income derived from the service transaction is determined under sections 861, 862, and 863, as applicable.

Example (9). Separate transactions. (i) Facts. The same facts as Example 8, except that E provides the raw data to F in a transaction characterized as a sale of a copyrighted article. In addition, E provides an analysis in the form of a report to F. The price F pays E for the raw data is separately stated.

(ii) Analysis. To the extent that the provision of raw data and the analysis of the data are each treated as separate transactions, the source of income from the production and sale of data is determined under paragraph (b)(3)(ii) of this section. The provision of services would be analyzed in the same manner as in Example 8.

Example (10). Sale of property in international water. (i) Facts. T purchased and owns transatlantic cable that lies in international water. T sells the cable to B, with T's rights, title, and interest in the cable passing to B in international water. Assume that the transatlantic cable is not inventory property within the meaning of section 1221(a)(1).

(ii) Analysis. Because T's rights, title, and interest in the property pass to B in international water, the sale takes place in international water under § 1.861-7(c), and the sale transaction is ocean activity under paragraph (d)(1)(ii) of this section. The source of T's sales income is determined under paragraph (b)(3)(i) of this section, by reference to paragraph (b)(1) or (2) of this section.

Example (11). Sale of property in space. (i) Facts. S, a United States person, manufactures a satellite in the United States and sells it to a customer who is not a United States person. S's rights, title, and interest in the satellite pass to the customer in space.

(ii) Analysis. Because S's rights, title, and interest in the satellite pass to the customer in space, the sale takes place in space under § 1.861-7(c), and the sale transaction is space activity under paragraph (d)(1)(i) of this section. The source of income derived from the sale of the satellite in space is determined under paragraph (b)(3)(ii) of this section, with the source of income allocable to production activity determined under paragraphs (b)(3)(ii)(A) and (B) of this section, and the source of income allocable to sales activity determined under paragraphs (b)(3)(ii)(A) and (D) of this section. Under paragraph (b)(1) of this section, S's space income is sourced outside the United States to the extent the income, based on all the facts and circumstances, is attributable to functions performed, resources employed, or risks assumed in a foreign country or countries.

Example (12). Sale of property in space. (i) Facts. S has a right to operate from a particular position (satellite slot or orbit) in space. S sells the right to operate from that position to P. Assume that the sale of the satellite slot is characterized as a sale of property and that S's rights, title, and interest in the satellite slot pass to P in space.

(ii) Analysis. The sale of the satellite slot takes place in space under § 1.861-7(c) because S's rights, title, and interest in the satellite slot pass to P in space. The sale of the satellite slot is space activity under paragraph (d)(1)(i) of this section, and income or gain from the sale is sourced under paragraph (b)(3)(i) of this section, by reference to paragraph (b)(1) or (2) of this section.

Example (13). Source of income of a foreign person. (i) Facts. FP, a foreign corporation that is not a CFC, derives income from the operation of satellites. FP operates ground stations in the United States and in foreign Country FC. Assume that FP is considered engaged in a trade or business within the United States based on FP's operation of the ground station in the United States.

(ii) Analysis. Under paragraph (b)(2)(iii) of this section, FP's space income is sourced in the United States to the extent the income, based on all the facts and circumstances, is attributable to functions performed, resources employed, or risks assumed within the United States.

Example (14). Source of income of a foreign person. (i) Facts. FP, a foreign corporation that is not a CFC, operates remote sensing satellites in space to collect data and images for its customers. FP uses an independent agent, A, in the United States who provides marketing, order-taking, and other customer service functions. Assume that FP is considered engaged in a trade or business within the United States based on A's activities on FP's behalf in the United States.

(ii) Analysis. Under paragraph (b)(2)(iii) of this section, FP's space income is sourced in the United States to the extent the income, based on all the facts and circumstances, is attributable to functions performed, resources employed, or risks assumed within the United States.

(g) Reporting and documentation requirements. *(1) In general.* A taxpayer making an allocation of gross income under paragraph (b)(1), (b)(2), (b)(3)(ii)(C), or (b)(4) of this section must satisfy the requirements in paragraphs (g)(2), (3), and (4) of this section.

(2) Required documentation. In all cases, a taxpayer must prepare and maintain documentation in existence when its return is filed regarding the allocation of gross income and allocation and apportionment of expenses, losses, and other deductions, the methodologies used, and the circumstances justifying use of those methodologies. The taxpayer must make available such documentation within 30 days upon request.

(3) Access to software. If the taxpayer or any third party used any computer software, within the meaning of section 7612(d), to allocate gross income, or to allocate or apportion expenses, losses, and other deductions, the taxpayer must make available upon request—

(i) Any computer software executable code, within the meaning of section 7612(d), used for such purposes, including an executable copy of the version of the software used in the preparation of the taxpayer's return (including any plug-ins, supplements, etc.) and a copy of all related electronic data files. Thus, if software subsequently is upgraded or supplemented, a separate executable copy of the version used in preparing the taxpayer's return must be retained;

(ii) Any related computer software source code, within the meaning of section 7612(d), acquired or developed by the taxpayer or a related person, or primarily for internal use by the taxpayer or such person rather than for commercial distribution; and

(iii) In the case of any spreadsheet software or similar software, any formulae or links to supporting worksheets.

(4) Use of allocation methodology. In general, when a taxpayer allocates gross income under paragraph (b)(1), (b)(2),

(b)(3)(ii)(C), or (b)(4) of this section, it does so by making the allocation on a timely filed original return (including extensions). However, a taxpayer will be permitted to make changes to such allocations made on its original return with respect to any taxable year for which the statute of limitations has not closed as follows:

(i) In the case of a taxpayer that has made a change to such allocations prior to the opening conference for the audit of the taxable year to which the allocation relates or who makes such a change within 90 days of such opening conference, if the IRS issues a written information document request asking the taxpayer to provide the documents and such other information described in paragraphs (g)(2) and (3) of this section with respect to the changed allocations and the taxpayer complies with such request within 30 days of the request, then the IRS will complete its examination, if any, with respect to the allocations for that year as part of the current examination cycle. If the taxpayer does not provide the documents and information described in paragraphs (g)(2) and (3) of this section within 30 days of the request, then the procedures described in paragraph (g)(4)(ii) of this section shall apply.

(ii) If the taxpayer changes such allocations more than 90 days after the opening conference for the audit of the taxable year to which the allocations relate or the taxpayer does not provide the documents and information with respect to the changed allocations as requested in accordance with paragraphs (g)(2) and (3) of this section, then the IRS will, in a separate cycle, determine whether an examination of the taxpayer's allocations is warranted and complete any such examination. The separate cycle will be worked as resources are available and may not have the same estimated completion date as the other issues under examination for the taxable year. The IRS may ask the taxpayer to extend the statute of limitations on assessment and collection for the taxable year to permit examination of the taxpayer's method of allocation, including an extension limited, where appropriate, to the taxpayer's method of allocation.

(h) Effective date. This section applies to taxable years beginning on or after December 27, 2006.

T.D. 9305, 12/26/2006.

§ 1.863-9 Source of income derived from communications activity under section 863(a), (d), and (e).

(a) In general. Income of a United States or a foreign person derived from each type of communications activity, as defined in paragraph (h)(3) of this section, is sourced under the rules of this section, notwithstanding any other provision including sections 861, 862, 863, and 865. Notwithstanding that a communications activity would qualify as space or ocean activity under section 863(d) and the regulations thereunder, the source of income derived from such communications activity is determined under this section, and not under section 863(d) and the regulations thereunder, except to the extent provided in § 1.863-8(b)(5).

(b) Source of international communications income. *(1) International communications income derived by a United States person.* Income derived from international communications activity (international communications income) by a United States person is one-half from sources within the United States and one-half from sources without the United States.

(2) International communications income derived by foreign persons. (i) In general. International communications income derived by a person other than a United States person is, except as otherwise provided in this paragraph (b)(2), wholly from sources without the United States.

(ii) International communications income derived by a controlled foreign corporation. International communications income derived by a controlled foreign corporation within the meaning of section 957 (CFC) is one-half from sources within the United States and one-half from sources without the United States.

(iii) International communications income derived by foreign persons with a fixed place of business in the United States. International communications income derived by a foreign person, other than a CFC, that is attributable to an office or other fixed place of business of the foreign person in the United States is from sources within the United States. The principles of section 864(c)(5) apply in determining whether a foreign person has an office or fixed place of business in the United States. See § 1.864-7. International communications income is attributable to an office or other fixed place of business to the extent of functions performed, resources employed, or risks assumed by the office or other fixed place of business.

(iv) International communications income derived by foreign persons engaged in a trade or business within the United States. International communications income derived by a foreign person (other than a CFC) engaged in a trade or business within the United States is income from sources within the United States to the extent the income, based on all the facts and circumstances, is attributable to functions performed, resources employed, or risks assumed within the United States.

(c) Source of U.S. communications income. Income derived by a United States or foreign person from U.S. communications activity is from sources within the United States.

(d) Source of foreign communications income. Income derived by a United States or foreign person from foreign communications activity is from sources without the United States.

(e) Source of space/ocean communications income. The source of income derived by a United States or foreign person from space/ocean communications activity is determined under section 863(d) and the regulations thereunder.

(f) Source of communications income when taxpayer cannot establish the two points between which the taxpayer is paid to transmit the communication. Income derived by a United States or foreign person from communications activity, when the taxpayer cannot establish the two points between which the taxpayer is paid to transmit the communication as required in paragraph (h)(3)(i) of this section, is from sources within the United States.

(g) Taxable income. When a taxpayer allocates gross income under paragraph (b)(2)(iii), (b)(2)(iv), or (h)(1)(ii) of this section, the taxpayer must allocate expenses, losses, and other deductions as prescribed in §§ 1.861-8 through 1.861-14T to the class or classes of gross income that include the income so allocated in each case. A taxpayer must then apply the rules of §§ 1.861-8 through 1.861-14T properly to apportion amounts of expenses, losses, and other deductions so allocated to such gross income between gross income from sources within the United States and gross income from sources without the United States. For amounts of expenses, losses, and other deductions allocated to gross income derived from international communications activity, when the source of income is determined under the 50/50 method of paragraph (b)(1) or (b)(2)(ii) of this section, taxpayers generally must apportion expenses, losses, and other deductions between sources within the United States and sources without the United States pro rata based on the relative amounts of gross income from sources within the United States and gross income from sources without the United States. However, the preceding sentence shall not apply to research and experimental expenditures qualifying under § 1.861-17, which are to be allocated and apportioned under the rules of that section.

(h) Communications activity and income derived from communications activity. *(1) Communications activity.* (i) General rule. For purposes of this part, communications activity consists solely of the delivery by transmission of communications or data (communications). Delivery of communications other than by transmission (for example, by delivery of physical packages and letters) is not communications activity within the meaning of this section. Communications activity also includes the provision of capacity to transmit communications. Provision of content or any other additional service provided along with, or in connection with, a non-de minimis communications activity must be treated as a separate non-communications activity unless de minimis. Communications activity or non-communications activity will be treated as de minimis to the extent, based on the facts and circumstances, the value attributable to such activity is de minimis.

(ii) Separate transaction. To the extent that a taxpayer's transaction consists in part of non-de minimis communications activity and in part of non-de minimis non-communications activity, each such part of the transaction must be treated as a separate transaction. Gross income is allocated to each such communications activity transaction and non-communications activity transaction to the extent the income, based on all the facts and circumstances, is attributable to functions performed, resources employed, or risks assumed in each such activity.

(2) Income derived from communications activity. Income derived from communications activity (communications income) is income derived from the delivery by transmission of communications, including income derived from the provision of capacity to transmit communications. Income may be considered derived from a communications activity even if the taxpayer itself does not perform the transmission function, but in all cases, the taxpayer derives communications income only if the taxpayer is paid to transmit, and bears the risk of transmitting, the communications.

(3) Determining the type of communications activity. (i) In general. Whether income is derived from international communications activity, U.S. communications activity, foreign communications activity, or space/ ocean communications activity is determined by identifying the two points between which the taxpayer is paid to transmit the communication. The taxpayer must establish the two points between which the taxpayer is paid to transmit, and bears the risk of transmitting, the communication. Whether the taxpayer contracts out part or all of the transmission function is not relevant. A taxpayer may satisfy the requirement that the taxpayer establish the two points between which the taxpayer is paid to transmit, and bears the risk of transmitting, the communication by using any consistently applied reasonable method to establish one or both endpoints. In evaluating the reasonableness of such method, consideration will be given to all the facts and circumstances, including whether the endpoints would otherwise be identifiable absent this reasonable method provision and the reliability of the data. Depending on the facts and circumstances, methods based on, for example, records of port or transport charges, customer billing records, a satellite footprint, or records of termination fees made pursuant to an international settlement agreement may be reasonable. In addition, practices used by taxpayers to classify or categorize certain communications activity in connection with preparation of statements and analyses for the use of management, creditors, minority shareholders, joint ventures, or other parties or governmental agencies in interest may be reliable indicators of the reasonableness of the method chosen, but need not be accorded conclusive weight by the Commissioner. In all cases, the method chosen to establish the two points between which the taxpayer is paid to transmit, and bears the risk of transmitting, the communication must be supported by sufficient documentation to permit verification by the Commissioner.

(ii) Income derived from international communications activity. Income derived by a taxpayer from international communications activity (international communications income) is income derived from communications activity, as defined in paragraph (h)(2) of this section, when the taxpayer is paid to transmit—

(A) Between a point in the United States and a point in a foreign country (or a possession of the United States); or

(B) Foreign-originating communications (communications with a beginning point in a foreign country or a possession of the United States) from a point in space or international water to a point in the United States.

(iii) Income derived from U.S. communications activity. Income derived by a taxpayer from U.S. communications activity (U.S. communications income) is income derived from communications activity, as defined in paragraph (h)(2) of this section, when the taxpayer is paid to transmit—

(A) Between two points in the United States; or

(B) Between the United States and a point in space or international water, except as provided in paragraph (h)(3)(ii)(B) of this section.

(iv) Income derived from foreign communications activity. Income derived by a taxpayer from foreign communications activity (foreign communications income) is income derived from communications activity, as defined in paragraph (h)(2) of this section, when the taxpayer is paid to transmit—

(A) Between two points in a foreign country or countries (or a possession or possessions of the United States);

(B) Between a foreign country and a possession of the United States; or

(C) Between a foreign country (or a possession of the United States) and a point in space or international water.

(v) Income derived from space/ocean communications activity. Income derived by a taxpayer from space/ocean communications activity (space/ ocean communications income) is income derived from communications activity, as defined in paragraph (h)(2) of this section, when the taxpayer is paid to transmit between a point in space or international water and another point in space or international water.

(i) Treatment of partnerships. This section is applied at the partner level.

(j) Examples. The following examples illustrate the rules of this section:

Example (1). Income derived from non-communications activity— remote data base access. (i) Facts. D provides its customers in various foreign countries with access to its data base, which contains information on certain individuals' health care insurance coverage. Customer C obtains access to D's data base by placing a call to D's telephone number.

Assume that C's telephone service, used to access D's data base, is provided by a third party, and that D assumes no responsibility for the transmission of the information via telephone.

(ii) Analysis. D is not paid to transmit communications and does not derive income from communications activity within the meaning of paragraph (h)(2) of this section. Rather, D derives income from provision of content or provision of services to its customers. Therefore, the rules of this section do not apply to determine the source of D's income.

Example (2). Income derived from U.S. communications activity— U.S. portion of international communication. (i) Facts. TC, a local telephone company, receives an access fee from an international carrier for picking up a call from a local telephone customer and delivering the call to a U.S. point of presence (POP) of the international carrier. The international carrier picks up the call from its U.S. POP and delivers the call to a foreign country.

(ii) Analysis. TC is not paid to carry the transmission between the United States and a foreign country. TC is paid to transmit a communication between two points in the United States. TC derives U.S. communications income as defined in paragraph (h)(3)(iii) of this section, which is sourced under paragraph (c) of this section as U.S. source income.

Example (3). Income derived from international communications activity—underwater cable. (i) Facts. TC, a domestic corporation, owns an underwater fiber optic cable. Pursuant to contracts, TC makes available to its customers capacity to transmit communications via the cable. TC's customers then solicit telephone customers and arrange to transmit the telephone customers' calls. The cable runs in part through U.S. waters, in part through international waters, and in part through foreign country waters.

(ii) Analysis. TC derives international communications income as defined in paragraph (h)(3)(ii) of this section because TC is paid to make available capacity to transmit communications between the United States and a foreign country. Because TC is a United States person, TC's international communications income is sourced under paragraph (b)(1) of this section as one-half from sources within the United States and one-half from sources without the United States.

Example (4). Income derived from international communications activity—satellite. (i) Facts. S, a United States person, owns satellites in orbit and uplink facilities in Country X, a foreign country. B, a resident of Country X, pays S to deliver B's programming from S's uplink facility, located in Country X, to a downlink facility in the United States owned by C, a customer of B.

(ii) Analysis. S derives international communications income under paragraph (h)(3)(ii) of this section because S is paid to transmit the communications between a beginning point in a foreign country and an endpoint in the United States. Because S is a United States person, the source of S's international communications income is determined under paragraph (b)(1) of this section as one-half from sources within the United States and one-half from sources without the United States.

Example (5). The paid-to-do rule—foreign communications via domestic route. (i) Facts. TC is paid to transmit communications from Toronto, Canada, to Paris, France. TC transmits the communications from Toronto to New York. TC pays another communications company, IC, to transmit the communications from New York to Paris.

(ii) Analysis. Under the paid-to-do rule of paragraph (h)(3)(i) of this section, TC derives foreign communications income under paragraph (h)(3)(iv) of this section because TC is paid to transmit communications between two points in foreign countries, Toronto and Paris. Under paragraph (h)(3)(i) of this section, the character of TC's communications activity is determined without regard to the fact that TC pays IC to transmit the communications for some portion of the delivery path. IC has international communications income under paragraph (h)(3)(ii) of this section because IC is paid to transmit the communications between a point in the United States and a point in a foreign country.

Example (6). The paid-to-do rule—domestic communication via foreign route. (i) Facts. TC is paid to transmit a call between two points in the United States, but routes the call through Canada.

(ii) Analysis. Under paragraph (h)(3)(i) of this section, the character of income derived from communications activity is determined by the two points between which the taxpayer is paid to transmit, and bears the risk of transmitting, the communications, without regard to the path of the transmission between those two points. Thus, under paragraph (h)(3)(iii) of this section, TC derives income from U.S. communications activity because it is paid to transmit the communications between two U.S. points.

Example (7). The paid-to-do rule—foreign-originating communications. (i) Facts. Under an international settlement agreement, G, a Country X international carrier, pays T to receive all calls originating in Country X that are bound for the United States and to terminate such calls in the United States. Due to Country X legal restrictions, the international settlement agreement specifies that G carries the transmission to a point outside the territory of Country X and that T carries the foreign-originating transmission from such point to the destined point in the United States. T, in turn, contracts out with another communications company, S, to transmit the U.S. portion of the communications. Tracing and identifying the endpoints of each transmission is not possible or practical. T does, however, keep records of termination fees received from G for terminating the foreign-originating calls.

(ii) Analysis. T derives communications income as defined in paragraph (h)(2) of this section. Based on all the facts and circumstances, T can establish that T is paid to transmit, and bears the risk of transmitting, foreign-originating calls from a point in space or international water to a point in the United States using a reasonable method to establish the endpoints, assuming that this method is consistently applied. In this case, T can reasonably establish that T is paid to receive foreign-originating calls and terminate such calls in the United States based on the records of termination fees pursuant to an international settlement agreement. Under paragraph (h)(3)(ii)(B) of this section, a taxpayer derives income from international communications activity when the taxpayer is paid to transmit foreign-originating communications from space or international water to the United States. Thus, under paragraph (h)(3)(ii)(B) of this section, T derives income from international communications. If, based on all the facts and circumstances, T could reasonably trace and identify the endpoints, then T would have to directly establish that each call originated in a foreign country. Assuming T is able to do so, the rest of the analysis in this Example 7 remains the same. Under paragraph (h)(3)(iii) of this section, S derives income from U.S. communications activity because S is paid to transmit the communications between two U.S. points.

Example (8). Indeterminate endpoints—prepaid telephone calling cards. (i) Facts. S purchases capacity from TC to transmit telephone calls. S sells prepaid telephone calling cards that give customers access to TC's telephone lines for a certain number of minutes. Assume that S cannot establish the endpoints of its customers' telephone calls, even under the reasonable method rule of paragraph (h)(3) of this section.

(ii) Analysis. S derives communications income as defined in paragraph (h)(2) of this section because S makes capacity to transmit communications available to its customers. In this case, S cannot establish the two points between which the communications are transmitted. Therefore, S's communications income is U.S. source income, as provided by paragraph (f) of this section.

Example (9). Reasonable methods—minutes of use data on long distance calling plans. (i) Facts. B provides both domestic and international long distance services in a calling plan for a limited number of minutes for a set amount each month. Tracing and identifying the endpoints of each transmission is not possible or practical. B is, however, able to establish that the calling plan generated $10,000 of revenue for 25,000 minutes based on reports derived from customer billing records. Based on minutes of use data in these reports, B is able to establish that of the total 25,000 minutes, 60 percent or 15,000 minutes were for U.S. long distance calls and 40 percent or 10,000 minutes were for international calls.

(ii) Analysis. B derives communications income as defined in paragraph (h)(2) of this section. Based on all the facts and circumstances, B can establish the two points between which B is paid to transmit, and bears the risk of transmitting, the communications using a reasonable method to establish the endpoints, assuming that this method is consistently applied. In this case, B can reasonably establish that 60 percent of the income derived from the long distance calling plan is U.S. communications income and 40 percent is international communications income based on the minutes of use data derived from customer billing records to establish the endpoints of the communications. If, based on all the facts and circumstances, B could reasonably trace and identify the endpoints, then B would have to directly identify the endpoints between which B is paid to transmit the communications.

Example (10). Reasonable methods—system design. (i) Facts. D operates satellites which are designed to transmit signals through two separate ranges of signal frequencies (bands). Due to technological limitations, requirements, and practicalities, one band is designed to only transmit signals within the United States. The other band is designed to transmit signals between foreign countries and the United States. D cannot trace and identify the endpoints of each individual transmission. D does, however, track the total transmission through each band and the total income derived from transmitting signals through each band.

(ii) Analysis. D derives communications income as defined in paragraph (h)(2) of this section. Based on all the facts and circumstances, D can establish the two points between which D is paid to transmit, and bears the risk of transmitting, the communications using a reasonable method to establish endpoints, assuming that this method is consistently applied. In this case, D can reasonably establish that income derived from transmissions through the first band is U.S. communications income and income derived from transmissions through the second band is international communications income based on the design of the bands to establish the endpoints of the communications.

Example (11). Reasonable methods—port locations. (i) Facts. X provides its customer, C, with a virtual private network (VPN) so that C's U.S. headquarter office can connect and communicate with offices in the United States, Country X, Country Y, and Country Z. Assume that the VPN is only for communications with the U.S. headquarter office. X cannot trace and identify the endpoints of each transmission. C pays X a set amount each month for the entire service, regardless of the magnitude of the usage or the geographic points between which C uses the service.

(ii) Analysis. X derives communications income as defined in paragraph (h)(2) of this section. Based on the facts and circumstances, X can establish the two points between which X is paid to transmit, and bears the risk of transmitting, the communications using a reasonable method to establish endpoints, assuming that this method is consistently applied. In this case, X can reasonably establish that one-fourth of the income derived from the VPN service is U.S. communications income and three-fourths is international communications income based on the location of the VPN ports to establish the endpoints of the communications.

Example (12). Indeterminate endpoints—Internet access. (i) Facts. B, a domestic corporation, is an Internet service provider. B charges its customer, C, a monthly lump sum for Internet access. C accesses the Internet via a telephone call, initiated by the modem of C's personal computer, to one of B's control centers, which serves as C's portal to the Internet. B transmits data sent by C from B's control center in France to a recipient in England, over the Internet. B does not maintain records as to the beginning and endpoints of the transmission.

(ii) Analysis. B derives communications income as defined in paragraph (h)(2) of this section. The source of B's communications income is determined under paragraph (f) of this section as income from sources within the United States because B cannot establish the two points between which it is paid to transmit the communications.

Example (13). De minimis non-communications activity. (i) Facts. The same facts as in Example 12. Assume in addition that B replicates frequently requested sites on B's own servers, solely to speed up response time. Assume that B's replication of frequently requested sites would be considered a de minimis non-communications activity under this section.

(ii) Analysis. On these facts, because B's replication of frequently requested sites would be considered a de minimis non-communications activity, B is not required to treat the replication activity as a separate non-communications activity transaction under paragraph (h)(1) of this section. B derives communications income under paragraph (h)(2) of this section. The character and source of B's communications income are determined by demonstrating the points between which B is paid to transmit the communications, under paragraph (h)(3)(i) of this section.

Example (14). Income derived from communications and non-communications activity—bundled services. (i) Facts. A, a domestic corporation, offers customers local and long distance phone service, video, and Internet services. Customers pay a flat monthly fee plus 10 cents a minute for all long-distance calls, including international calls.

(ii) Analysis. Under paragraph (h)(1)(ii) of this section, to the extent that A's transaction with its customer consists in part of non-de minimis communications activity and in part of non-de minimis non-communications activity, each such part of the transaction must be treated as a separate transaction. A's gross income from the transaction is allocated to each such communications activity transaction and non-communications activity transaction in accordance with paragraph (h)(1)(ii) of this section. To the extent A can establish that it derives international communications income as defined in paragraph (h)(3)(ii) of this section, A would determine the source of such income under paragraph (b)(1) of this section. If A cannot establish the points between which it is paid to transmit communications, as required by paragraph (h)(3)(i) of this section, A's communications income is from sources within the United States, as provided by paragraph (f) of this section.

Example (15). Income derived from communications and non-communications activity. (i) Facts. B, a domestic corporation, is paid by D, a cable system operator in Foreign Country, to provide television programs and to transmit the television programs to Foreign Country. Using its own satellite transponder, B transmits the television programs from the United States to downlink facilities owned by D in Foreign Country. D receives the transmission, unscrambles the signals, and distributes the broadcast to D's customers in Foreign Country. Assume that B's provision of television programs is a non-de minimis non-communications activity, and that B's transmission of television programs is a non-de minimis communications activity.

(ii) Analysis. Under paragraph (h)(1)(ii) of this section, B must treat its communications and non-communications activities as separate transactions. B's gross income is allocated to each such separate communications and non-communications activity transaction in accordance with paragraph (h)(1)(ii) of this section. Income derived by B from the transmission of television programs to D's Foreign Country downlink facility is international communications income as defined in paragraph (h)(3)(ii) of this section because B is paid to transmit communications from the United States to a foreign country.

Example (16). Income derived from foreign communications activity. (i) Facts. STS provides satellite capacity to B, a broadcaster located in Australia. B beams programming from Australia to the satellite. S's satellite picks the communications up in space and beams the programming over a footprint covering Southeast Asia.

(ii) Analysis. S derives communications income as defined in paragraph (h)(2) of this section. S's income is characterized as foreign communications income under paragraph (h)(3)(iv) of this section because S picks up the communication in space, and beams it to a footprint entirely covering a foreign area. Under paragraph (d) of this section, S's foreign communications income is from sources without the United States. If S were beaming the programming over a satellite footprint that covered area both in the United States and outside the United States, S would be required to allocate the income derived from the different types of communications activity.

(k) Reporting and documentation requirements. *(1) In general.* A taxpayer making an allocation of gross income under paragraph (b)(2)(iii), (b)(2)(iv), or (h)(1)(ii) of this section must satisfy the requirements in paragraphs (k)(2), (3), and (4) of this section.

(2) Required documentation. In all cases, a taxpayer must prepare and maintain documentation in existence when its return is filed regarding the allocation of gross income, and allocation and apportionment of expenses, losses, and other deductions, the methodologies used, and the circumstances justifying use of those methodologies. The taxpayer must make available such documentation within 30 days upon request.

(3) Access to software. If the taxpayer or any third party used any computer software, within the meaning of section 7612(d), to allocate gross income, or to allocate or apportion expenses, losses, and other deductions, the taxpayer must make available upon request—

(i) Any computer software executable code, within the meaning of section 7612(d), used for such purposes, including an executable copy of the version of the software used in the preparation of the taxpayer's return (including any plug-ins, supplements, etc.) and a copy of all related electronic data files. Thus, if software subsequently is upgraded or supplemented, a separate executable copy of the version used in preparing the taxpayer's return must be retained;

(ii) Any related computer software source code, within the meaning of section 7612(d), acquired or developed by the taxpayer or a related person, or primarily for internal use by the taxpayer or such person rather than for commercial distribution; and

(iii) In the case of any spreadsheet software or similar software, any formulae or links to supporting worksheets.

(4) Use of allocation methodology. In general, when a taxpayer allocates gross income under paragraph (b)(2)(iii), (b)(2)(iv), or (h)(1)(ii) of this section, it does so by making the allocation on a timely filed original return (including extensions). However, a taxpayer will be permitted to make changes to such allocations made on its original return with respect to any taxable year for which the statute of limitations has not closed as follows:

(i) In the case of a taxpayer that has made a change to such allocations prior to the opening conference for the audit of the taxable year to which the allocation relates or who makes such a change within 90 days of such opening conference, if the IRS issues a written information document request asking the taxpayer to provide the documents and such other information described in paragraphs (k)(2) and (3) of this section with respect to the changed allocations and the taxpayer complies with such request within 30 days of the request, then the IRS will complete its examination, if any, with respect to the allocations for that year as part of the current examination cycle. If the taxpayer does not provide the documents and information described in paragraphs (k)(2) and (3) of this section within 30 days of the request, then the procedures described in paragraph (k)(4)(ii) of this section shall apply.

(ii) If the taxpayer changes such allocations more than 90 days after the opening conference for the audit of the taxable year to which the allocations relate or the taxpayer does not provide the documents and information with respect to the changed allocations as requested in accordance with paragraphs (k)(2) and (3) of this section, then the IRS will, in a separate cycle, determine whether an examination of the taxpayer's allocations is warranted and complete any such examination. The separate cycle will be worked as resources are available and may not have the same estimated completion date as the other issues under examination for the taxable year. The IRS may ask the taxpayer to extend the statute of limitations on assessment and collection for the taxable year to permit examination of the taxpayer's method of allocation, including an extension limited, where appropriate, to the taxpayer's method of allocation.

(l) Effective date. This section applies to taxable years beginning on or after December 27, 2006.

T.D. 9305, 12/26/2006.

§ 1.864-1 Meaning of sale, etc.

For purposes of §§ 1.861 through 1.864-7, the word "sale" includes "exchange"; the word "sold" includes "exchanged"; the word "produced" includes "created", "fabricated", "manufactured", "extracted", "processed", "cured", and "aged".

T.D. 6948, 3/27/68.

§ 1.864-2 Trade or business within the United States.

Caution: The Treasury has not yet amended Reg § 1.864-2 to reflect changes made by P.L. 105-34.

(a) In general. As used in part I (section 861 and following) and part II (section 871 and following), subchapter N, chapter 1 of the Code, and chapter 3 (section 1441 and following) of the Code, and the regulations thereunder, the term "engaged in trade or business within the United States" does not include the activities described in paragraphs (c) and (d) of this section, but includes the performance of personal services within the United States at any time within the taxable year except to the extent otherwise provided in this section.

(b) Performance of personal services for foreign employer. *(1) Expected services.* For purposes of paragraph (a) of this section, the term "engaged in trade or business within the United States" does not include the performance of personal services. (i) For a nonresident alien individual, foreign partnership, or foreign corporation, not engaged in trade or business within the United States at any time during the taxable year, or

(ii) For an office or place of business maintained in a foreign country or in a possession of the United States by an individual who is a citizen or resident of the United States or by a domestic partnership or a domestic corporation, by a nonresident alien individual who is temporarily present in the United States for a period or periods not exceeding a total of 90 days during the taxable year and whose compensation for such services does not exceed in the aggregate a gross amount of $3,000.

(2) Rules of application. (i) As a general rule, the term "day", as used in subparagraph (1) of this paragraph, means a calendar day during any portion of which the nonresident alien individual is physically present in the United States.

(ii) Solely for purposes of applying this paragraph, the nonresident alien individual, foreign partnership, or foreign corporation for which the nonresident alien individual is performing personal services in the United States shall not be considered to be engaged in trade or business in the United States by reason of the performance of such services by such individual.

(iii) In applying subparagraph (1) of this paragraph it is immaterial whether the services performed by the nonresident alien individual are performed as an employee for his employer or under any form of contract with the person for whom the services are performed.

(iv) In determining for purposes of subparagraph (1) of this paragraph whether compensation received by the nonresident alien individual exceeds in the aggregate a gross amount of $3,000, any amounts received by the individual from an employer as advances or reimbursements for travel expenses incurred on behalf of the employer shall be omitted from the compensation received by the individual, to the extent of expenses incurred, where he was required to account and did account to his employer for such expenses and has met the tests for such accounting provided in § 1.162-17 and paragraph (e)(4) of § 1.274-5. If advances or reimbursements exceed such expenses, the amount of the excess shall be included as compensation for personal services for purposes of such subparagraph. Pensions and retirement pay attributable to personal services performed in the United States are not to be taken into account for purposes of subparagraph (1) of this paragraph.

(v) See section 7701(a)(5) and § 301.7701-5 of this chapter (Procedure and Administration Regulations) for the meaning of "foreign" when applied to a corporation or partnership.

(vi) As to the source of compensation for personal services, see §§ 1.861-4 and 1.862-1.

(3) Illustrations. The application of this paragraph may be illustrated by the following examples:

Example (1). During 1967, A, a nonresident alien individual, is employed by the London office of a domestic partnership. A, who uses the calendar year as his taxable year, is temporarily present in the United States during 1967 for 60 days performing personal services in the United States for the London office of the partnership and is paid by that office a total gross salary of $2,600 for such services. During 1967, A is not engaged in trade or business in the United States solely by reason of his performing such personal services for the London office of the domestic partnership.

Example (2). The facts are the same as in example (1), except that A's total gross salary for the services performed in the United States during 1967 amounts to $3,500, of which $2,625 is received in 1967 and $875 is received in 1968. During 1967, A is engaged in trade or business in the United States by reason of his performance of personal services in the United States.

(c) Trading in stocks or securities. For purposes of paragraph (a) of this section—

(1) In general. The term "engaged in trade or business within the United States" does not include the effecting of transactions in the United States in stocks or securities through a resident broker, commission agent, custodian, or other independent agent. This subparagraph shall apply to any taxpayer, including a broker or dealer in stocks or securities, except that it shall not apply if at any time during the taxable year the taxpayer has an office or other fixed place of business in the United States through which, or by the direction of which, the transactions in stocks or securities are effected. The volume of stock or security transactions effected during the taxable year shall not be taken into account in determining under this subparagraph whether the taxpayer is engaged in trade or business within the United States.

(2) Trading for taxpayer's own account. (i) In general. The term "engaged in trade or business within the United States" does not include the effecting of transactions in the United States in stocks or securities for the taxpayer's own account, irrespective of whether such transactions are effected by or through—

(a) The taxpayer himself while present in the United States,

(b) Employees of the taxpayer, whether or not such employees are present in the United States while effecting the transactions, or

(c) A broker, commission agent, custodian, or other agent of the taxpayer, whether or not such agent while effecting the transactions is (1) dependent or independent, or (2) resident, nonresident, or present, in the United States,

and irrespective of whether any such employee or agent has discretionary authority to make decisions in effecting such transactions. For purposes of this paragraph, the term "securities" means any note, bond, debenture, or other evidence of indebtedness, or any evidence of an interest in or right to subscribe to or purchase any of the foregoing; and the effecting of transactions in stocks or securities includes buying, selling (whether or not by entering into short sales), or trading in stocks, securities, or contracts or options to buy or sell stocks or securities, on margin or otherwise, for the account and risk of the taxpayer, and any other activity closely related thereto (such as obtaining credit for the purpose of effectuating such buying, selling, or trading). The volume of stock of security transactions effected during the taxable year shall not be taken into account in determining under this subparagraph whether the taxpayer is engaged in trade or business within the United States. The application of this subdivision may be illustrated by the following example:

Example. A, a nonresident alien individual who is not a dealer in stocks or securities, authorizes B, an individual resident of the United States, as his agent to effect transactions in the United States in stocks and securities for the account of A. B is empowered with complete authority to trade in stocks and securities for the account of A and to use his own discretion as to when to buy or sell for A's account. This grant of discretionary authority from A to B is also communicated in writing by A to various domestic brokerage firms through which A ordinarily effects transactions in the United States in stocks or securities. Under the agency arrangement B has the authority to place orders with the brokers, and all confirmations are to be made by the brokers to B, subject to his approval. The brokers are authorized by A to make payments to B and to charge such payments to the account of A. In addition, B is authorized to obtain and advance the necessary funds, if any, to maintain credits with the brokerage firms. Pursuant to his authority B carries on extensive trading transactions in the United States during the taxable year through the various brokerage firms for the account of A. During the taxable year A makes several visits to the United States in order to discuss with B various aspects of his trading activities and to make necessary changes in his trading policy. A is not engaged in trade or business within the United States during the taxable year solely because of the effecting by B of transactions in the United States in stocks or securities during such year for the account of A.

(ii) Partnerships. A nonresident alien individual, foreign partnership, foreign estate, foreign trust, or foreign corporation shall not be considered to be engaged in trade or business within the United States solely because such person is a member of a partnership (whether domestic or foreign) which, pursuant to discretionary authority granted to such partnership by such person, effects transactions in the United States in stocks or securities for the partnership's own account or solely because an employee of such partnership, or a broker, commission agent, custodian, or other agent, pursuant to discretionary authority granted by such partnership, effects transactions in the United States in stocks or securities for the account of such partnership. This subdivision shall not apply, however, to any member of (a) a partnership which is a dealer in stocks or securities or (b) a partnership (other than a partnership in which, at any time during the last half of its taxable year, more than 50 percent of either the capital interest or the profits interest is owned, directly or indirectly, by five or fewer partners who are individuals) the principal business of which is trading in stocks or securities for its own account, if the principal office of such partnership is in the United States at any time during the taxable year. The principles of subdivision (iii) of this subparagraph for determining whether a foreign corporation has its principal office in the United States shall apply in determining under this subdivision whether a partnership has its principal office in the United States. See section 707(b)(3) and paragraph (b)(3) of § 1.707-1 for rules for determining the extent of the ownership by a partner of a capital interest or profits interest in a partnership. The application of this subdivision may be illustrated by the following examples:

Example (1). B, a nonresident alien individual, is a member of partnership X, the members of which are U.S. citizens, nonresident alien individuals, and foreign corporations. The principal business of partnership X is trading in stocks or securities for its own account. Pursuant to discretionary authority granted by B, partnership X effects transactions in the United States in stocks or securities for its own account. Partnership X is not a dealer in stocks or securities, and more than 50 percent of either the capital interest or the profits interest in partnership X is owned throughout its taxable year by five or fewer partners who are individuals. B is not engaged in trade or business within the United States solely by reason of such effecting of transactions in the United States in stocks or securities by partnership X for its own account.

Example (2). The facts are the same as in example (1), except that not more than 50 percent of either the capital interest or the profits interest in partnership X is owned throughout the taxable year by five or fewer partners who are individuals. However, partnership X does not maintain its principal office in the United States at any time during the taxable year. B is not engaged in trade or business within the United States solely by reason of the trading in stocks or securities by partnership X for its own account.

Example (3). The facts are the same as in example (1), except that, pursuant to discretionary authority granted by partnership X, domestic broker D effects transactions in the United States in stocks or securities for the account of partnership X. B is not engaged in trade or business in the United States solely by reason of such trading in stocks or securities for the account of partnership X.

(iii) Dealers in stocks or securities and certain foreign corporations. This subparagraph shall not apply to the effecting of transactions in the United States for the account of (a) a dealer in stocks or securities or (b) a foreign corporation (other than a corporation which is, or but for section 542(c)(7) or 543(b)(1)(C) would be, a personal holding company) the principal business of which is trading in stocks or securities for its own account, if the principal office of such corporation is in the United States at any time during the taxable year. Whether a foreign corporation's principal office is in the United States for this purpose is to be determined by comparing the activities (other than trading in stocks or securities) which the corporation conducts from its office or other fixed place of business located in the United States with the activities it conducts from its offices or other fixed places of business located outside the United States. For purposes of this subdivision, a foreign corporation is considered to have only one principal office, and an office of such corporation will not be considered to be its principal office merely because it is a statutory office of such corporation. For example, a foreign corporation which carries on most or all of its investment activities in the United States but maintains a general business office or offices outside the United

States in which its management is located will not be considered as having its principal office in the United States if all or a substantial portion of the following functions is carried on at or from an office or offices located outside the United States:

(1) Communicating with its shareholders (including the furnishing of financial reports),

(2) Communicating with the general public,

(3) Soliciting sales of its own stock,

(4) Accepting the subscriptions of new stockholders,

(5) Maintaining its principal corporate records and books of account,

(6) Auditing its books of account,

(7) Disbursing payments of dividends, legal fees, accounting fees, and officers' and directors' salaries,

(8) Publishing or furnishing the offering and redemption price of the shares of stock issued by it,

(9) Conducting meetings of its shareholders and board of directors, and

(10) Making redemptions of its own stock.

The application of this subdivision may be illustrated by the following examples:

Example (1). (a) Foreign corporation X (not a corporation which is, or but for section 542(c)(7) or 543(b)(1)(C) would be, a personal holding company) was organized to sell its shares to nonresident alien individuals and foreign corporations and to invest the proceeds from the sale of such shares in stocks or securities in the United States. Foreign corporation X is engaged primarily in the business of investing, reinvesting, and trading in stocks or securities for its own account.

(b) For a period of three years, foreign corporation X irrevocably authorizes domestic corporation Y to exercise its discretion in effecting transactions in the United States in stocks or securities for the account and risk of foreign corporation X. Foreign corporation X issues a prospectus in which it is stated that its funds will be invested pursuant to an investment advisory contract with domestic corporation Y and otherwise advertises its services. Shares of foreign corporation X are sold to nonresident aliens and foreign corporations who are customers of the United States brokerage firms unrelated to domestic corporation Y or foreign corporation X. The principal functions performed for foreign corporation X by domestic corporation Y are the rendering of investment advice and the effecting of transactions in the United States in stocks or securities for the account of foreign corporation X. Moreover, domestic corporation Y occasionally communicates with prospective foreign investors in foreign corporation X (through speaking engagements abroad by management of domestic corporation Y, and otherwise) for the purpose of explaining the investment techniques and policies used by domestic corporation Y in investing the funds of foreign corporation X. However, domestic corporation Y does not participate in the day-to-day conduct of other business activities of foreign corporation X.

(c) Foreign corporation X maintains a general business office or offices outside the United States in which its management is permanently located and from which it carries on, except to the extent noted heretofore, the functions enumerated in (b)(1) through (10) of this subdivision. The management of foreign corporation X at all times retains the independent power to cancel the investment advisory contract with domestic corporation Y subject to the contractual limitations contained therein and is in all other respects independent of the management of domestic corporation Y. The managing personnel of foreign corporation X communicate on a regular basis with domestic corporation Y, and periodically visit the offices of domestic corporation Y, in connection with the business activities of foreign corporation X.

(d) The principal office of foreign corporation X will not be considered to be in the United States; and, therefore, foreign corporation X is not engaged in trade or business within the United States solely by reason of its relationship with domestic corporation Y.

Example (2). The facts are the same as in example (1) except that, in lieu of having the investment advisory contract with domestic corporation Y, foreign corporation X has an office in the United States in which its employees perform the same functions as are performed by domestic corporation Y in example (1). Foreign corporation X is not engaged in trade or business within the United States during the taxable year solely because the employees located in its United States office effect transactions in the United States in stocks or securities for the account of that corporation.

(iv) Definition of dealer in stocks or securities. (a) In general. For purposes of this subparagraph, a dealer in stocks or securities is a merchant of stocks or securities, with an established place of business, regularly engaged as a merchant in purchasing stocks or securities and selling them to customers with a view to the gains and profits that may be derived therefrom. Persons who buy and sell, or hold, stocks or securities for investment or speculation, irrespective of whether such buying or selling constitutes the carrying on of a trade or business, and officers of corporations, members of partnerships, or fiduciaries, who in their individual capacities buy and sell, or hold, stocks or securities for investment or speculation are not dealers in stocks or securities within the meaning of this subparagraph solely by reason of that activity. In determining under this subdivision whether a person is a dealer in stocks or securities such person's transactions in stocks or securities effected both in and outside the United States shall be taken into account.

(b) Underwriting syndicates and dealers trading for others. A foreign person who otherwise may be considered a dealer in stocks or securities under *(a)* of this subdivision shall not be considered a dealer in stocks or securities for purposes of this subparagraph—

(1) Solely because he acts as an underwriter, or as a selling group member, for the purpose of making a distribution of stocks or securities of a domestic issuer to foreign purchasers of such stocks or securities, irrespective of whether other members of the selling group distribute the stocks or securities of the domestic issuer to domestic purchasers, or

(2) Solely because of transactions effected in the United States in stocks or securities pursuant to his grant of discretionary authority to make decisions in effecting those transactions, if he can demonstrate to the satisfaction of the Commissioner that the broker, commission agent, custodian, or other agent through whom the transactions were effected acted pursuant to his written representation that the funds in respect of which such discretion was granted were the funds of a customer who is neither a dealer in stocks or securities, a partnership described in subdivision (ii)(b) of this subparagraph, nor a foreign corporation described in subdivision (iii)(b) of this subparagraph.

For purposes of this (b), a foreign person includes a nonresident alien individual, a foreign corporation, or a partnership any member of which is a nonresident alien individual or a foreign corporation. This (b) shall apply only if the foreign person at no time during the taxable year has an office or other fixed place of business in the United States through which, or by the direction of which, the transactions in stocks or securities are effected.

(c) Illustrations. The application of this subdivision may be illustrated by the following examples:

Example (1). Foreign corporation X is a member of an underwriting syndicate organized to distribute stock issued by domestic corporation Y. Foreign corporation X distributes the stock of domestic corporation Y to foreign purchasers only. Domestic corporation M is syndicate manager of the underwriting syndicate and, pursuant to the terms of the underwriting agreement, reserves the right to sell certain quantities of the underwritten stock on behalf of all the members of the syndicate so as to engage in stabilizing transactions and to take certain other actions which may result in the realization of profit by all members of the underwriting syndicate. Foreign corporation X is not engaged in trade or business within the United States solely by reason of its participation as a member of such underwriting syndicate for the purpose of distributing the stock of domestic corporation Y to foreign purchasers or by reason of the exercise by M corporation of its discretionary authority as manager of such syndicate.

Example (2). Foreign corporation Y, a calendar year taxpayer, is a bank which trades in stocks or securities both for its own account and for the account of others. During 1967 foreign corporation Y authorizes domestic corporation M, a broker, to exercise its discretion in effecting transactions in the United States in stocks or securities for the account of B, a nonresident alien individual who has a trading account with foreign corporation Y. Foreign corporation Y furnishes a written representation to domestic corporation M to the effect that the funds in respect of which foreign corporation Y has authorized domestic corporation M to use its discretion in trading in the United States in stocks or securities are not funds in respect of which foreign corporation Y is trading for its own account but are the funds of one of its customers who is neither a dealer in stocks or securities, a partnership described in subdivision (ii)(b) of this subparagraph, or a foreign corporation described in subdivision (iii)(b) of this subparagraph. Pursuant to the discretionary authority so granted, domestic corporation M effects transactions in the United States during 1967 in stocks or securities for the account of the customer of foreign corporation Y. At no time during 1967 does foreign corporation Y have an office or other fixed place of business in the United States through which, or by the direction of which, such transactions in stocks or securities are effected by domestic corporation M. During 1967 foreign corporation Y is not engaged in trade or business within the United States solely by reason of such trading in stocks or securities during such year by domestic corporation M for the account of the customer of foreign corporation Y. Copies of the written representations furnished to domestic corporation M should be retained by foreign corporation Y for inspection by the Commissioner, if inspection is requested.

(d) Trading in commodities. For purposes of paragraph (a) of this section—

(1) In general. The term "engaged in trade or business within the United States" does not include the effecting of transactions in the United States in commodities (including hedging transactions) through a resident broker, commission agent, custodian, or other independent agent if (i) the commodities are of a kind customarily dealt in on an organized commodity exchange, such as a grain futures or a cotton futures market, (ii) the transaction is of a kind customarily consummated at such place, and (iii) the taxpayer at no time during the taxable year has an office or other fixed place of business in the United States through which, or by the direction of which, the transactions in commodities are effected. The volume of commodity transactions effected during the taxable year shall not be taken into account in determining under this subparagraph whether the taxpayer is engaged in trade or business in the United States.

(2) Trading for taxpayer's own account. (i) In general. The term "engaged in trade or business within the United States" does not include the effecting of transactions in the United States in commodities (including hedging transactions) for the taxpayer's own account if the commodities are of a kind customarily dealt in on an organized commodity exchange and if the transaction is of a kind customarily consummated at such place. This rule shall apply irrespective of whether such transactions are effected by or through—

(a) The taxpayer himself while present in the United States,

(b) Employees of the taxpayer, whether or not such employees are present in the United States while effecting the transactions, or

(c) A broker, commission agent, custodian, or other agent of the taxpayer, whether or not such agent while effecting the transactions is (1) dependent or independent, or (2) resident, nonresident, or present, in the United States,

and irrespective of whether any such employee or agent has discretionary authority to make decisions in effecting such transactions. The volume of commodity transactions effected during the taxable year shall not be taken into account in determining under this subparagraph whether the taxpayer is engaged in trade or business within the United States. This subparagraph shall not apply to the effecting of transactions in the United States for the account of a dealer in commodities.

(ii) Partnerships. A nonresident alien individual, foreign partnership, foreign estate, foreign trust, or foreign corporation shall not be considered to be engaged in trade or business within the United States solely because such person is a member of a partnership (whether domestic or foreign) which, pursuant to discretionary authority granted to such partnership by such person, effects transactions in the United States in commodities for the partnership's account or solely because an employee of such partnership, or a broker, commission agent, custodian, or other agent, pursuant to discretionary authority granted by such partnership, effects transactions in the United States in commodities for the account of such partnership. This subdivision shall not apply to any member of a partnership which is a dealer in commodities.

(iii) Illustration. The application of this subparagraph may be illustrated by the following example:

Example. Foreign corporation X, a calendar year taxpayer, is engaged as a merchant in the business of purchasing grain in South America and selling such cash grain outside the United States under long-term contracts for delivery in foreign countries. Foreign corporation X consummates a sale of 100,000 bushels of cash grain in February 1967 for July delivery to Sweden. Because foreign corporation X does not actually own such grain at the time of the sales transaction, such corporation buys as a hedge a July "futures contract" for delivery of 100,000 bushels of grain, in order to protect itself from loss by reason of a possible rise in the price of grain between February and July. The "futures contract" is ordered through domestic corporation Y, a futures commission merchant registered under the Commodity Exchange Act. Foreign corporation X is not engaged in trade or business within the United States during 1967 solely by reason of its effecting of such futures contract for its own account through domestic corporation Y.

(3) Definition of commodity. For purposes of section 864(b)(2)(B) and this paragraph the term "commodities" does not include goods or merchandise in the ordinary channels of commerce.

(e) Other rules. The fact that a person is not determined by reason of this section to be not engaged in trade or business with the United States is not to be considered a determination that such person is engaged in trade or business within the United States. Whether or not such person is engaged in trade or business within the United States shall be determined on the basis of the facts and circumstances in each case. For other rules relating to the determination of whether a taxpayer is engaged in trade or business in the United States see section 875 and the regulations thereunder.

(f) Effective date. The provisions of this section shall apply only in the case of taxable years beginning after December 31, 1966.

T.D. 6948, 3/27/68, amend T.D. 7378, 9/29/75.

§ 1.864-3 Rules for determining income effectively connected with U.S. business of nonresident aliens or foreign corporations.

(a) In general. For purposes of the Internal Revenue Code, in the case of a nonresident alien individual or a foreign corporation that is engaged in a trade or business in the United States at any time during the taxable year, the rules set forth in §§ 1.864-4 through 1.864-7 and this section shall apply in determining whether income, gain, or loss shall be treated as effectively connected for a taxable year beginning after December 31, 1966, with the conduct of a trade or business in the United States. Except as provided in sections 871(c) and (d) and 882(d) and (e), and the regulations thereunder, in the case of a nonresident alien individual or a foreign corporation that is at no time during the taxable year engaged in a trade or business in the United States, no income, gain, or loss shall be treated as effectively connected for the taxable year with the contact of a trade or business in the United States. The general rule prescribed by the preceding sentence shall apply even though the income, gain, or loss would have been treated as effectively connected with the conduct of a trade or business in the United States if such income or gain had been received or accrued, or such loss had been sustained, in an earlier taxable year when the taxpayer was engaged in a trade or business in the United States. In applying §§ 1.864-4 through 1.864-7 and this section, the determination whether an item of income, gain, or loss is effectively connected with the conduct of a trade or business in the United States shall not be controlled by any administrative, judicial, or other interpretation made under the laws of any foreign country.

(b) Illustrations. The application of this section may be illustrated by the following examples:

Example (1). During 1967 foreign corporation N, which uses the calendar year as the taxable year, is engaged in the business of purchasing and selling household equipment on the installment plan. During 1967 N is engaged in business in the United States by reason of the sales activities it carries on in the United States for the purpose of selling therein some of the equipment which it has purchased. During 1967 N receives installment payments of $800,000 on sales it makes that year in the United States, and the income from sources within the United States for 1967 attributable to such payments is $200,000. By reason of section 864(c)(3) and paragraph (b) of § 1.864-4 this income of $200,000 is effectively connected for 1967 with the conduct of a trade or business in the United States by N. In December of 1967, N discontinues its efforts to make any further sales of household equipment in the United States, and at no time during 1968 is N engaged in a trade or business in the United States. During 1968 N receives installment payments of $500,000 on the sales it made in the United States during 1967, and the income from sources within the United States for 1968 attributable to such payments is $125,000. By reason of section 864(c)(1)(B) and this section, this income of $125,000 is not effectively connected for 1968 with the conduct of a trade or business in the United States by N, even though such amount, if it had been received by N during 1967, would have been effectively connected for 1967 with the conduct of a trade or business in the United States by that corporation.

Example (2). R, a foreign holding company, owns all of the voting stock in five corporations, two of which are domestic corporations. All of the subsidiary corporations are engaged in the active conduct of a trade or business. R has an office in the United States where its chief executive officer, who is also the chief executive officer of one of the domestic corporations, spends a substantial portion of the taxable year supervising R's investment in its operating subsidiaries and performing his function as chief executive officer of the domestic operating subsidiary. R is not considered to be engaged in a trade or business in the United States during the taxable year by reason of the activities carried on in the United States by its chief executive officer in the supervision of its investment in its operating subsidiary corporations. Accordingly, the dividends from sources within the United States received by R during the taxable year from its domestic subsidiary corporations are not effectively connected for that year with the conduct of a trade or business in the United States by R.

Example (3). During the months of June through December 1971, B, a nonresident alien individual who uses the calendar year as the taxable year and the cash receipts and disbursements method of accounting, is employed in the United States by domestic corporation M for a salary of $2,000 per month, payable semimonthly. During 1971, B receives from M salary payments totaling $13,000, all of which income by reason of section 864(c)(2) and paragraph (c)(6)(ii) of § 1.864-4, is effectively connected for 1971 with the conduct of a trade or business in the United States by B. On December 31, 1971, B terminates his employment with M and departs from the United States. At no time during 1972 is B engaged in a trade or business in the United States. In January of 1972, B receives from M salary of $1,000 for the last half of December 1971, and a bonus of $1,000 in consideration of the services B performed in the United States during 1971 for that corporation. By reason of section 864(c)(1)(B) and this section, the $2,000 received by B during 1972 from sources within the United States is not effectively connected for that year with the conduct of a trade or business in the United States, even though such amount, if it had been received by B during 1971, would have been effectively connected for 1971 with the conduct of a trade or business in the United States by B.

T.D. 7216, 11/2/72.

PAR. 9. Section 1.864-4 is amended as follows:

1. Paragraphs (c)(2)(iv), (c)(2)(v), (c)(3)(ii), and (c)(5)(vi)(a) and (b) are redesignated as (c)(2)(v), (c)(2)(vi), (c)(3)(iii), and (c)(5)(vi) (b) and (c), respectively.

2. New paragraphs (c)(2)(iv), (c)(3)(ii), and (c)(5)(vi)(a) are added.

The additions read as follows:

Proposed § 1.864-4 U.S. source income effectively connected with U.S. business. [*For Preamble, see ¶ 151,855*]

* * * * *

(c) * * *

(2) * * *

(iv) Special rule relating to a global dealing operation. An asset used in a global dealing operation, as defined in § 1.482-8(a)(2)(i), will be treated as an asset used in a U.S. trade or business only if and to the extent that the U.S. trade or business is a participant in the global dealing operation under § 1.863-3(h)(3), and income, gain or loss produced by the asset is U.S. source under § 1.863-3(h) or would be treated as U.S. source if § 1.863-3(h) were to apply to such amounts.

* * * * *

(3) * * *

(ii) Special rule relating to a global dealing operation. A U.S. trade or business shall be treated as a material factor in the realization of income, gain or loss derived in a global dealing operation, as defined in § 1.482-8(a)(2)(i), only if and to the extent that the U.S. trade or business is a participant in the global dealing operation under § 1.863-3(h)(3), and income, gain or loss realized by the U.S. trade or business is U.S. source under § 1.863-3(h) or would be treated as U.S. source if § 1.863-3(h) were to apply to such amounts.

* * * * *

(5) * * *

(vi) * * *

(a) Certain income earned by a global dealing operation. Notwithstanding paragraph (c)(5)(ii) of this section, U.S. source interest, including substitute interest as defined in § 1.861-2(a)(7), and dividend income, including substitute dividends as defined in § 1.861-3(a)(6), derived by a participant in a global dealing operation, as defined in § 1.482-8(a)(2)(i), shall be treated as attributable to the foreign corporation's U.S. trade or business, only if and to the extent that the income would be treated as U.S. source if § 1.863-3(h) were to apply to such amounts.

§ 1.864-4 U.S. source income effectively connected with U.S. business.

Caution: The Treasury has not yet amended Reg § 1.864-4 to reflect changes made by P.L. 100-647, P.L. 99-514, P.L. 98-369.

(a) In general. This section applies only to a nonresident alien individual or a foreign corporation that is engaged in a trade or business in the United States at some time during a taxable year beginning after December 31, 1966, and to the income, gain, or loss of such person form sources within the United States. If the income, gain, or loss of such person for the taxable year from sources within the United States consists of (1) gain or loss from the sale or exchange of capital assets or (2) fixed or determinable annual or periodical gains, profits, and income or certain other gains described in section 871(a)(1) or 881(a), certain factors must be taken into account, as prescribed by section 864(c)(2) and paragraph (c) of this section, in order to determine whether the income, gain, or loss is effectively connected for the taxable year with the conduct of a trade or business in the United States by that person. All other income, gain, or loss of such person for the taxable year from sources within the United States shall be treated as effectively connected for the taxable year with conduct of a trade or business in the United States by that person, as prescribed by section 864(c)(3) and paragraph (b) of this section.

(b) Income other than fixed or determinable income and capital gains. All income, gain, or loss for the taxable year derived by a nonresident alien individual or foreign corporation engaged in a trade or business in the United States from sources within the United States which does not consist of income, gain, or loss described in section 871(a)(1) or 881(a), or of gain or loss from the sale or exchange of capital assets, shall, for purposes of paragraph (a) of this section, be treated as effectively connected for the taxable year with the conduct of a trade or business in the United States. This income, gain, or loss shall be treated as effectively connected for the taxable year with the conduct of a trade or business in the United States, whether or not the income, gain, or loss is derived from the trade or business being carried on in the United States during the taxable year. The application of this paragraph may be illustrated by the following examples:

Example (1). M, a foreign corporation which uses the calendar year as the taxable year, is engaged in the business of manufacturing machine tools in a foreign country. It establishes a branch office in the United States during 1968 which solicits orders from customers in the United States for the machine tools manufactured by that corporation. All negotiations with respect to such sales are carried on in the United States. By reason of its activity in the United States M is engaged in business in the United States during 1968. The income or loss from sources within the United States from such sales during 1968 is treated as effectively connected for that year with the conduct of a business in the United States by M. Occasionally, during 1968 the customers in the United States write directly to the home office of M, and the home office makes sales directly to such customers without routing the transactions through it branch office in the United States. The income or loss from sources within the United States for 1968 from these occasional direct sales by the home office is also treated as effectively connected for that year with the conduct of a business in the United States by M.

Example (2). The facts are the same as in example (1) except that during 1967 M was also engaged in the business of purchasing and selling office machines and that it used the installment method of accounting for the sales made in this separate business. During 1967 M was engaged in business in the United States by reason of the sales activities it carried on in the United States for the purpose of selling therein a number of the office machines which it had purchased. Although M discontinued this business activity in the United States in December of 1967, it received in 1968 some installment payments on the sales which it had made in the United States during 1967. The income of M for 1968 from sources within the United States which is attributable to such installment payments is effectively connected for 1968 with the conduct of a business in the United States, even though such income is not connected with the business carried on in the United States during 1968 through its sales office located in the United States for the solicitation of orders for the machine tools it manufacturers.

Example (3). Foreign corporation S, which uses the calendar year as the taxable year, is engaged in the business of purchasing and selling electronic equipment. The home office of such corporation is also engaged in the business of purchasing and selling vintage wines. During 1968, S establishes a branch office in the United States to sell electronic equipment to customers, some of whom are located in the United States and the balance, in foreign countries. This branch office is not equipped to sell, and does not participate in sales of, wine purchased by the home office. Negotiations for the sales of the electronic equipment take place in the United States. By reason of the activity of its branch office in the United States, S is engaged in business in the United States during 1968. As a result of advertisements which the home office of S places in periodicals sold in the United States, customers in the United States frequently place orders for the purchase of wines with the home office in the foreign country, and the home office makes sales of wine in 1968 directly to such customers without routing the transactions through its branch office in the United States. The income or loss from sources within the United States for 1968 from sales of electronic equipment by the branch office, together with the income or loss from sources within the United States for that year from sales of wine by the home office, is treated as effectively connected for that year with the conduct of a business in the United States by S.

(c) Fixed or determinable income and capital gains. *(1) Principal factors to be taken into account.* (i) In general. In determining for purposes of paragraph (a) of this section whether any income for the taxable year from sources within the United States which is described in section 871(a)(1) or 881(a), relating to fixed or determinable annual or periodical gains, profits, and income and certain other gains, or whether gain or loss from sources within the United States for the taxable year from the sale or exchange of capital assets, is effectively connected for the taxable year with the conduct of a trade or business in the United States, the principal tests to be applied are (a) the asset-use test, that is, whether the income, gain, or loss is derived from assets used in, or held for use in, the conduct of the trade or business in the United States, and (b) the business-activities test, that is, whether the activities of the trade or business conducted in the United States were a material factor in the realization of the income, gain, or loss.

(ii) Special rule relating to interest on certain deposits. For purposes of determining under section 861(a)(1)(A) (relating to interest on deposits with banks, savings and loan associations, and insurance companies paid or credited before Jan. 1, 1976) whether the interest described therein is effectively connected for the taxable year with the conduct of a trade or business in the United States, such interest shall be treated as income from sources within the United States for purposes of applying this paragraph and § 1.864-5. If by reason of the application of this paragraph such interest is determined to be income which is not effectively connected for the taxable year with the conduct of a trade or business in the United States, it shall then be treated as interest from sources without the United States which is not subject to the application of § 1.864-5.

(2) Application of the asset-use test. (i) In general. For purposes of subparagraph (1) of this paragraph, the asset-use test ordinarily shall apply in making a determination with respect to income, gain, or loss of a passive type where the trade or business activities as such do not give rise directly to the realization of the income, gain, or loss. However, even in the case of such income, gain, or loss, any activities of the trade or business which materially contribute to the realization of such income, gain, or loss shall also be taken into account as a factor in determining whether the income, gain, or loss is effectively connected with the conduct of a trade or business in the United States. The asset-use test is of primary significance where, for example, interest income is derived from sources within the United States by a nonresident alien individual or foreign corporation that is engaged in the business of manufacturing or selling goods in the United States. See also subparagraph (5) of this paragraph for rules applicable to taxpayers conducting a banking, financing, or similar business in the United States.

(ii) Cases where applicable. Ordinarily, an asset shall be treated as used in, or held for use in, the conduct of a trade or business in the United States if the asset is—

(a) Held for the principal purpose of promoting the present conduct of the trade or business in the United States; or

(b) Acquired and held in the ordinary course of the trade or business conducted in the United States, as, for example, in the case of an account or note receivable arising from that trade or business; or

(c) Otherwise held in a direct relationship to the trade or business conducted in the United States, as determined under paragraph (c)(2)(iv) of this section.

(iii) Application of asset-use test to stock. (a) In general. Except as provided in paragraph (c)(2)(iii)(b) of this section, stock of a corporation (whether domestic or foreign) shall not be treated as an asset used in, or held for use in, the conduct of a trade or business in the United States.

(b) Stock held by foreign insurance companies. This paragraph (c)(2)(iii) shall not apply to stock of a corporation (whether domestic or foreign) held by a foreign insurance company unless the foreign insurance company owns 10 percent or more of the total voting power or value of all classes of stock of such corporation. For purposes of this section, section 318(a) shall be applied in determining ownership, except that in applying section 318(a)(2)(C), the phrase "10 percent" is used instead of the phrase "50 percent."

(iv) Direct relationship between holding of asset and trade or business. (a) In general. In determining whether an asset is held in a direct relationship to the trade or business conducted in the United States, principal consideration shall be given to whether the asset is needed in that trade or business. An asset shall be considered needed in a trade or business, for this purpose, only if the asset is held to meet the present needs of that trade or business and not its anticipated future needs. An asset shall be considered as needed in the trade or business conducted in the United States if, for example, the asset is held to meet the operating expenses of that trade or business. Conversely, an asset shall be considered as not needed in the trade or business conducted in the United States if, for example, the asset is held for the purpose of providing for (1) future diversification into a new trade or business, (2) expansion of trade or business activities conducted outside of the United States, (3) future plant replacement, or (4) future business contingencies.

(b) Presumption of direct relationship. Generally, an asset will be treated as held in a direct relationship to the trade or business if (1) the asset was acquired with funds generated by that trade or business, (2) the income from the asset is retained or reinvested in that trade or business, and (3) personnel who are present in the United States and actively involved in the conduct of that trade or business exercise significant management and control over the investment of such asset.

(v) Illustration. The application of paragraph (iv) may be illustrated by the following examples:

Example (1). M, a foreign corporation which uses the calendar year as the taxable year, is engaged in industrial manufacturing in a foreign country. M maintains a branch in the United States which acts as importer and distributor of the merchandise it manufactures abroad; by reason of these branch activities, M is engaged in business in the United States during 1968. The branch in the United States is required to hold a large current cash balance for business purposes, but the amount of the cash balance so required varies because of the fluctuating seasonal nature of the branch's business. During 1968 at a time when large cash balances are not required the branch invests the surplus amount in U.S. Treasury bills. Since these Treasury bills are held to meet the present needs of the business conducted in the United States they are held in a direct relationship to that business, and the interest for 1968 on these bills is effectively connected for that year with the conduct of the business in the United States by M.

Example (2). Foreign corporation M, which uses the calendar year as the taxable year, has a branch office in the United States where it sells to customers located in the United States various products which are manufactured by that corporation in a foreign country. By reason of this activity M is engaged in business in the United States during 1997. The U.S. branch establishes in 1997 a fund to which are periodically credited various amounts which are derived from the business carried on at such branch. The amounts in this fund are invested in various securities issued by domestic corporations by the managing officers of the U.S. branch, who have the responsibility for maintaining proper investment diversification and investment of the fund. During 1997, the branch office derives from sources within the United States interest on these securities, and gains and losses resulting from the sale or exchange of such securities. Since the securities were acquired with amounts generated by the business conducted in the United States, the interest is retained in that business, and the portfolio is managed by personnel actively involved in the conduct of that business, the securities are presumed under paragraph (c)(2)(iv)(b) of this section to be held in a direct relationship to that business.

(3) Application of the business-activities test. (i) In general. For purposes of subparagraph (1) of this paragraph, the business-activities test shall ordinarily apply in making a determination with respect to income, gain, or loss which, even though generally of the passive type, arises directly from the active conduct of the taxpayer's trade or business in the United States. The business-activities test is of primary significance, for example, where (a) dividends or interest are derived by a dealer in stocks or securities, (b) gain or loss is derived from the sale or exchange of capital assets in the active conduct of a trade or business by an investment company, (c) royalties are derived in the active conduct of a business consisting of the licensing of patents or similar intangible property, or (d) service fees are derived in the active conduct of a servicing business. In applying the business-activities test, activities relating to the management of investment portfolios shall not be treated as activities of the trade or business conducted in the United States unless the maintenance of the investments constitutes the principal activity of that trade or business. See also subparagraph (5) of this paragraph for rules applicable to taxpayers conducting a banking, financing, or similar business in the United States.

(ii) Illustrations. The application of this subparagraph may be illustrated by the following examples:

Example (1). Foreign corporation S is a foreign investment company organized for the purpose of investing in stocks and securities. S is not a personal holding company or a corporation which would be a personal holding company but for section 542(c)(7) or 543(b)(1)(C). Its investment portfolios consist of common stocks issued by both foreign and domestic corporations and a substantial amount of high grade bonds. The business activity of S consists of the management of its portfolios for the purpose of investing, reinvesting, or trading in stocks and securities. During the taxable year 1968, S has its principal office in the United States within the meaning of paragraph (c)(2)(iii) of § 1.864-2, and, by reason of its trading in the United States in stocks and securities, is engaged in business in the United States. The dividends and interest derived by S during 1968 from sources within the United States, and the gains and losses from sources within the United States for such year from the sale of stocks and securities from its investment portfolios, are effectively connected for 1968 with the conduct of the business in the United States by that corporation, since its activities in connection with the management of its investment portfolios are activities of that business and such activities are a material factor in the realization of such income, gains, or losses.

Example (2). N, a foreign corporation which uses the calendar year as the taxable year, has a branch in the United States which acts as an importer and distributor of merchandise; by reason of the activities of that branch, N is engaged in business in the United States during 1968. N also carries on a business in which it licenses patents to unrelated persons in the United States for use in the United States. The businesses of the licensees in which these patents are used have no direct relationship to the business carried on in N's branch in the United States, although the merchandise marketed by the branch is similar in type to that manufactured under the patents. The negotiations and other activities leading up to the consummation of these licenses are conducted by employees of N who are not connected with the U.S. branch of that corporation, and the U.S. branch does not otherwise participate in arranging for the licenses. Royalties received by N during 1968 from these licenses are not effectively connected for that year with the conduct of its business in the United States because the activities of that business are not a material factor in the realization of such income.

(4) Method of accounting as a factor. In apply-the asset-use test or the business-activities test described in subparagraph (1) of this paragraph, due regard shall be given to whether or not the asset, or the income, gain, or loss is accounted for through the trade or business conducted in the United States, that is, whether or not the asset, or the income, gain or loss, is carried on books of account separately kept for that trade or business, but this accounting test shall not by itself be controlling. In applying this subparagraph, consideration shall be given to whether the accounting treatment of an item reflects the consistent application of generally accepted accounting principles in a particular trade or business in accordance with accepted condition or practices in that trade or business and whether there is a consistent accounting treatment of that item from year to year by the taxpayer.

(5) Special rules relating to banking, financing, similar business activity. (i) Definition of banking, financing, or similar business. A nonresident alien individual or a foreign

corporation shall be considered for purposes of this section and paragraph (b)(2) of § 1.864-5 to be engaged in the active conduct of a banking, financing, or similar business in the United States if at some time during the taxable year the taxpayer is engaged in business in the United States and the activities of such business consist of any one or more of the following activities carried on, in whole or in part, in the United States in transactions with persons situated within or without the United States:

(a) Receiving deposits of funds from the public,

(b) Making personal, mortgage, industrial, or other loans to the public,

(c) Purchasing, selling, discounting, or negotiating for the public on a regular basis, notes, drafts, checks, bills of exchange, acceptances, or other evidences of indebtedness,

(d) Issuing letter of credit to the public and negotiating drafts drawn thereunder,

(e) Providing trust services for the public, or

(f) Financing foreign exchange transactions for the public.

Although the fact that the taxpayer is subjected to the banking and credit laws of a foreign country shall be taken into account in determining whether he is engaged in the active conduct of a banking, financing, or similar business, the character of the business actually carried on during the taxable year in the United States shall determine whether the taxpayer is actively conducting a banking, financing, or similar business in the United States. A foreign corporation which acts merely as a financing vehicle for borrowing funds for its parent corporation or any other person who would be a related person within the meaning of section 954(d)(3) if such foreign corporation were a controlled foreign corporation shall not be considered to be engaged in the active conduct of a banking, financing, or similar business in the United States.

(ii) Effective connection of income from stocks or securities with active conduct of a banking, financing, or similar business. Notwithstanding the rules in subparagraphs (2) and (3) of this paragraph with respect to the asset-use test and the business-activities test, any dividends or interest from stocks or securities, or any gain or loss from the sale or exchange of stocks or securities which are capital assets, which is from sources within the United States and derived by a nonresident alien individual or a foreign corporation in the active conduct during the taxable year of a banking, financing, or similar business in the United States shall be treated as effectively connected for such year with the conduct of that business only if the stocks or securities giving rise to such income, gain, or loss are attributable to the U.S. office through which such business is carried on and—

(a) Were acquired—

(1) As a result of, or in the course of making loans to the public,

(2) In the course of distributing such stocks or securities to the public, or

(3) For the purpose of being used to satisfy the reserve requirements, or other requirements similar to reserve requirements, established by a duly constituted banking authority in the United States, or

(b) Consist of securities (as defined in subdivision (v) of this subparagraph) which are—

(1) Payable on demand or at a fixed maturity date not exceeding 1 year from the date of acquisition.

(2) Issued by the United States, or any agency or instrumentality thereof, or

(3) Not described in (a) or (1) or (2) of this (b).

However, the amount of interest from securities described in (b)(3) of this subdivision (ii) which shall be treated as effectively connected for the taxable year with the active conduct of a banking, financing, or similar business in the United States shall be an amount (but not in excess of the entire interest for the taxable year from sources within the United States from such securities) determined by multiplying the entire interest for the taxable year from sources within the United States from such securities by a fraction the numerator of which is 10 percent and the denominator of which is the same percentage, determined on the basis of a monthly average for the taxable year, as the book value of the total of such securities held by the U.S. office through which such business is carried on bears to the book value of the total assets of such office. The amount of gain or loss, if any, for the taxable year from the sale or exchange of such securities which shall be treated as effectively connected for the taxable year with the active conduct of a banking, financing, or similar business in the United States shall be an amount (but not in excess of the entire gain or loss for the taxable year from sources within the United States from the sale or exchange of such securities) determined by multiplying the entire gain or loss for the taxable year from sources within the United States from the sale or exchange of such securities by the fraction described in the immediately preceding sentence. The percentage of the denominator of the limiting fraction for such purposes shall be the percentage obtained by separately adding the book value of such securities and such total assets held at the close of each month in the taxable year, dividing each such sum by 12, and then dividing the amount of securities so obtained by the amount of assets so obtained. This subdivision does not apply to dividends from stock owned by a foreign corporation in a domestic corporation of which more than 50 percent of the total combined voting power of all classes of stock entitled to vote is owned by such foreign corporation and which is engaged in the active conduct of a banking business in the United States. The application of this subdivision may be illustrated by the following example:

Example. Foreign corporation M, created under the laws of foreign country Y, has in the United States a branch, B, which during the taxable year is engaged in the active conduct of the banking business in the United States within the meaning of subdivision (i) of this subparagraph. During the taxable year M derives from sources within the United States through the activities carried on through B, $7,500,000 interest from securities described in subdivision (b)(3) of this subdivision (ii) and $7,500,000 gain from the sale or exchange of such securities. The monthly average, determined as of the last day of each month in the taxable year, of such securities held by B divided by the monthly average, as so determined, of the total assets held by B equals 15 percent. Under this subdivision, the amount of interest income from such securities that shall be treated as effectively connected for the taxable year with the active conduct by M of a banking business in the United States is $5 million ($7,500,000 interest × 10%/15%), and the amount of gain from the sale or exchange of such securities that shall be treated as effectively connected for such year with the active conduct of such business is $5 million ($7,500,000 gain × 10%/15%).

(iii) Stocks or securities attributable to U.S. office. (a) In general. For purposes of paragraph (c)(5)(ii) of this section, a stock or security shall be deemed to be attributable to a

U.S. office only if such office actively and materially participated in soliciting, negotiating, or performing other activities required to arrange the acquisition of the stock or security. The U.S. office need not have been the only active participant in arranging the acquisition of the stock or security.

(b) Exceptions. A stock or security shall not be deemed to be attributable to a U.S. office merely because such office conducts one or more of the following activities:

(1) Collects or accounts for the dividends, interest, gain, or loss from such stock or security,

(2) Exercises general supervision over the activities of the persons directly responsible for carrying on the activities described in paragraph (c)(5)(iii)(a) of this section,

(3) Performs merely clerical functions incident to the acquisition of such stock or security,

(4) Exercises final approval over the execution of the acquisition of such stock or security, or

(5) Holds such stock or security in the United States or records such stock or security on its books or records as having been acquired by such office or for its account.

(c) Effective date. This paragraph (c)(5)(iii) shall be effective for income includible in taxable years beginning on or after June 18, 1984, except that 26 CFR 1.864-4(c)(5)(iii) as it appeared in the Code of Federal Regulations revised as of April 1, 1983, shall apply to income received or accrued under a loan made by the taxpayer on or before May 18, 1984, or pursuant to a written binding commitment entered into on or before May 18, 1984.

(iv) Acquisitions in course of making loans to the public. For purposes of subdivision (ii) of this subparagraph—

(a) A stock or security shall be considered to have been acquired in the course of making a loan to the public where, for example, such stock or security was acquired as additional consideration for the making of the loan,

(b) A stock or security shall be considered to have been acquired as a result of making a loan to the public if, for example, such stock or security was acquired by foreclosure upon a bona fide default of the loan and is held as an ordinary and necessary incident to the active conduct of the banking, financing, or similar business in the United States, and

(c) A stock or security acquired on a stock exchange or organized over-the-counter market shall be considered not to have been acquired as a result of, or in the course of, making loans to the public.

(v) Security defined. For purposes of this subparagraph, a security is any bill, note, bond, debenture, or other evidence of indebtedness, or any evidence of an interest in, or right to subscribe to or purchase, any of the foregoing items.

(vi) Limitations on application of subparagraph. (a) Other business activity. This subparagraph provides rules for determining when certain income from stocks or securities is effectively connected with the active conduct of a banking, financing, or similar business in the United States. Any dividends, interest, gain, or loss from sources within the United States which by reason of the application of subdivision (ii) of this subparagraph is not effectively connected with the active conduct by a non-resident alien individual or a foreign corporation of a banking, financing, or similar business in the United States may be effectively connected for the taxable year, under subparagraph (2) or (3) of this paragraph with the conduct by such taxpayer of another trade or business in the United States, such as, for example, the business of selling or manufacturing goods or merchandise or of trading in stocks or securities for the taxpayer's own account.

(b) Other income. For rules relating to income, gain, or loss from sources within the United States (other than dividends or interest from, or gain or loss from the sale or exchange of, stocks or securities referred to in subdivision (ii) of this subparagraph) derived in the active conduct of a banking, financing, or similar business in the United States, see subparagraphs (2) and (3) of this paragraph and paragraph (b) of this section.

(vii) Illustrations. The application of this subparagraph may be illustrated by the following examples:

Example (1). Foreign corporation F, which is created under the laws of foreign country X and engaged in the active conduct of the banking business in country X and a number of other foreign countries, has in the United States a branch, B, which during the taxable year is engaged in the active conduct of the banking business in the United States within the meaning of subdivision (i) of this subparagraph. In the course of its banking business in foreign countries, F receives at its branches located in country X and other foreign countries substantial deposits in U.S. dollars which are transferred to the accounts of B in the United States. During the taxable year, B actively participates in negotiating loans to residents of the United States, such as call loans to U.S. brokers, which are financed from the U.S. dollar deposits transferred to B by F. In addition, B actively participates in purchasing on the New York Stock Exchange and over-the-counter markets long-term bonds and notes issued by the U.S. Government, U.S. Treasury bills, and long-term interest-bearing bonds issued by domestic corporations and having a maturity date of less than 1 year from the date of acquisition, all of which are purchased from the deposits transferred to B by F. All of the securities so acquired are held by B and recorded on its books in the United States. Pursuant to subdivision (ii) of this subparagraph, the interest received by F during the taxable year on these loans, bonds, notes, and bills is effectively connected for such year with the active conduct by F on a banking business in the United States.

Example (2). The facts are the same as in example (1) except that B also actively participates in using part of the U.S. dollar deposits, which are transferred to it by F, to purchase on the New York Stock Exchange shares of common stock issued by various domestic corporations. All of the shares so purchased are considered to be capital assets within the meaning of section 1221 and are recorded on B's books in the United States. None of the shares so purchased were acquired for the purpose of meeting reserve or other similar requirements. During the taxable year some of the shares are sold by B on the stock exchange. Pursuant to subdivision (ii) of this subparagraph, the dividends and gains received by F during the taxable year on these shares of stock are not effectively connected with the active conduct by F of a banking, financing, or similar business in the United States.

Example (3). The facts are the same as in example (1) except that B also uses part of the U.S. dollar deposits, which are transferred to it by F, to make a loan to domestic corporation M. As part of the consideration for the loan, M gives to B a number of shares of common stock issued by M. All of these shares of stock are considered to be capital assets within the meaning of section 1221 and are recorded on B's books in the United States. During the taxable year one-half of these shares of stock is sold by B on the New York Stock Exchange. Pursuant to subdivision (ii) of this subparagraph, the dividends and gains received by F during the taxable year on these shares of stock are effectively connected for such year with the active conduct by F of a banking business in the United States.

Example (4). The facts are the same as in example (1) except that during the taxable year the home office of F in country X actively participates in negotiating loans to residents of the United States, such as call loans to U.S. brokers, which are financed by the U.S. dollar deposits received at the home office and are recorded on the books of the home office. B does not participate in negotiating these loans. Pursuant to subdivision (ii) of this subparagraph the interest received by F during the taxable year on these loans made by the home office in country X is not effectively connected with the active conduct by F on a banking, financing, or similar business in the United States.

Example (5). Foreign corporation Y, which is created under the laws of foreign country X and is engaged in the active conduct of a banking business in country X and other foreign countries, has a branch, C, in the United States that is engaged in the active conduct of a banking business in the United States, within the meaning of paragraph (c)(5)(i) of this section, during the taxable year. C handles the negotiation and acquisition of securities involved in loans made by Y to U.S. persons. C also presents interest coupons with respect to such securities for payment, presents all such securities for payment at maturity, and maintains compete photocopy files with respect to such securities. The activities of the office of Y in country X with respect to these securities consist of giving pro forma approval of the loans, storing the original securities, and recording the securities on the books of the country X office. Pursuant to paragraphs (c)(5)(ii) and (c)(5)(iii) of this section, the U.S. source interest income received by Y during the taxable year on these securities is effectively connected for such year with the active conduct by Y of a banking business in the United States.

(6) Income related to personal services of an individual. (i) Income, gain, or loss from assets. Income or gains from sources within the United States described in section 871(a)(1) and derived from an asset, and gain or loss from sources within the United States from the sale of exchange of capital assets, realized by a nonresident alien individual engaged in a trade or business in the United States during the taxable year solely by reason of his performing personal services in the United States shall not be treated as income, gain, or loss which is effectively connected for the taxable year with the conduct of a trade or business in the United States, unless there is a direct economic relationship between his holding of the asset from which the income, gain, or loss results and his trade or business or performing the personal services.

(ii) Wages, salaries, and pensions. Wages, salaries, fees, compensations, emoluments, or other remunerations, including bonuses, received by a nonresident alien individual for performing personal services in the United States which, under paragraph (a) of § 1.864-2, constitute engaging in a trade or business in the United States, and pensions and retirement pay attributable to such personal services, constitute income which is effectively connected for the taxable year with the conduct of a trade or business in the United States by that individual if he is engaged in a trade or business in the United States at some time during the taxable year in which such income is received.

(7) Effective date. Paragraphs (c)(2) and (c)(6)(i) of this section are effective for taxable years beginning on or after June 6, 1996.

T.D. 7216, 11/2/72, amend T.D. 7332, 12/20/74, T.D. 7958, 5/17/84, T.D. 8657, 3/5/96, T.D. 9226, 9/30/2005.

§ 1.864-5 Foreign source income effectively connected with U.S. business.

(a) In general. This section applies only to a nonresident alien individual or a foreign corporation that is engaged in a trade or business in the United States at some time during a taxable year beginning after December 31, 1966, and to the income, gain, or loss of such person from sources without the United States. The income, gain, or loss of such person for the taxable year, from sources without the United States which is specified in paragraph (b) of this section shall be treated as effectively connected for the taxable year with the conduct of a trade or business in the United States, only if he also has in the United States at some time during the taxable year, but not necessarily at the time the income, gain, or loss is realized, an office or other fixed place of business, as defined in § 1.864-7, to which such income, gain, or loss is attributable in accordance with § 1.864-6. The income of such person for the taxable year from sources without the United States which is specified in paragraph (c) of this section shall be treated as effectively connected for the taxable year with the conduct of a trade or business in the United States when derived by a foreign corporation carrying on a life insurance business in the United States. Except as provided in paragraphs (b) and (c) of this section, no income, gain, or loss of a nonresident alien individual or a foreign corporation for the taxable year from sources without the United States shall be treated as effectively connected for the taxable year with the conduct of a trade or business in the United States by that person. Any income, gain, or loss described in paragraph (b) or (c) of this section which, if it were derived by the taxpayer from sources within the United States for the taxable year, would not be treated under § 1.864-4 as effectively connected for the taxable year with the conduct of a trade or business in the United States shall not be treated under this section as effectively connected for the taxable year with the conduct of a trade or business in the United States.

(b) Income other than income attributable to U.S. life insurance business. Income, gain, or loss from sources without the United States other than income described in paragraph (c) of this section shall be taken into account pursuant to paragraph (a) of this section in applying §§ 1.864-6 and 1.864-7 only if it consists of—

(1) Rents, royalties, or gains on sales of intangible property. (i) Rents or royalties for the use of, or for the privilege of using, intangible personal property located outside the United States or from any interest in such property, including rents or royalties for the use, or for the privilege of using, outside the United States, patents, copyrights, secret processes and formulas, good will, trademarks, trade brands, franchises, and other like properties, if such rents or royalties are derived in the active conduct of the trade or business in the United States.

(ii) Gains or losses on the sale or exchange of intangible personal property located outside the United States or from any interest in such property, including gains or losses on the sale or exchange of the privilege of using, outside the United States, patents, copyrights, secret processes and formulas, good will, trademarks, trade brands, franchises, and other like properties, if such gains or losses are derived in the active conduct of the trade or business in the United States.

(iii) Whether or not such an item of income, gain, or loss is derived in the active conduct of a trade or business in the United States shall be determined from the facts and circumstances of each case. The frequency with which a nonresident alien individual or a foreign corporation enters into transactions of the type from which the income, gain, or loss is derived shall not of itself determine that the income, gain, or loss is derived in the active conduct of a trade or business.

(iv) This subparagraph shall not apply to rents or royalties for the use of, or for the privilege of using, real property or tangible personal property, or to gain or loss form the sale or exchange of such property.

(2) Dividends or interest, or gains or loss from sales of stocks or securities. (i) In general. Dividends or interest from any transaction, or gains or losses on the sale or exchange of stocks or securities, realized by (a) a nonresident alien individual or a foreign corporation in the active conduct of a banking, financing, or similar business in the United States or (b) a foreign corporation engaged in business in the United States whose principal business is trading in stocks or securities for its own account. Whether the taxpayer is engaged in the active conduct of a banking, financing, or similar business in the United States for purposes of this subparagraph shall be determined in accordance with the principles of paragraph (c)(5)(i) of § 1.864-4.

(ii) Substitute payments. For purposes of this paragraph (b)(2), a substitute interest payment (as defined in § 1.861-2(a)(7)) received by a foreign person subject to tax under this paragraph (b) pursuant to a securities lending transaction or a sale-repurchase transaction (as defined in § 1.861-2(a)(7)) with respect to a security (as defined in § 1.864-6(b)(2)(ii)(c)) shall have the same character as interest income paid or accrued with respect to the terms of the transferred security. Similarly, for purposes of this paragraph (b)(2), a substitute dividend payment (as defined in § 1.861-3(a)(6)) received by a foreign person pursuant to a securities lending transaction or a sale-repurchase transaction (as defined in § 1.861-3(a)(6)) with respect to a stock shall have the same character as a distribution received with respect to the transferred security. This paragraph (b)(2)(ii) is applicable to payments made after November 13, 1997.

(iii) Incidental investment activity. This subparagraph shall not apply to income, gain, or loss realized by a nonresident alien individual or foreign corporation on stocks or securities held, sold, or exchanged in connection with incidental investment activities carried on by that person. Thus, a foreign corporation which is primarily a holding company owning significant percentages of the stocks or securities issued by other corporations shall not be treated under this subparagraph as a corporation the principal business of which is trading in stocks or securities for its own account, solely because it engages in sporadic purchases or sales of stocks or securities to adjust its portfolio. The application of this subdivision may be illustrated by the following example:

Example. F, a foreign corporation, owns voting stock in foreign corporations M, N, and P, its holdings in such corporations constituting 15, 20, and 100 percent, respectively, of all classes of their outstanding voting stock. Each of such stock holdings by F represents approximately 20 percent of its total assets. The remaining 40 percent of F's assets consist of other investments, 20 percent being invested in securities issued by foreign governments and in stocks and bonds issued by other corporations in which F does not own a significant percentage of their outstanding voting stock, and 20 percent being invested in bonds issued by N. None of the assets of F are held primarily for sale; but, if the officers of that corporation were to decide that other investments would be preferable to its holding of such assets, F would sell the stocks and securities and reinvest the proceeds therefrom in other holdings. Any income, gain, or loss which F may derive from this investment activity is not considered to be realized by a foreign corporation described in subdivision (i) of this subparagraph.

(3) Sale of goods or merchandise through U.S. office. (i) Income, gain, or loss from the sale of inventory items or of property held primarily for sale to customers in the ordinary course of business, as described in section 1221(1), where the sale is outside the United States but through the office or other fixed place of business which the non-resident alien or foreign corporation has in the United States, irrespective of the destination to which such property is sent for use, consumption, or disposition.

(ii) This subparagraph shall not apply to income, gain, or loss resulting from a sales contract entered into on or before February 24, 1966. See section 102(e)(1) of the Foreign Investors Tax Act of 1966 (80 Stat. 1547). Thus, for example, the sales office in the United States of a foreign corporation enters into negotiations for the sale of 500,000 industrial bearings which the corporation produces in a foreign country for consumption in the Western Hemisphere. These negotiations culminate in a binding agreement entered into on January 1, 1966. By its terms delivery under the contract is to be made over a period of 3 years beginning in March of 1966. Payment is due upon delivery. The income from sources without the United States resulting from this sale negotiated by the U.S. sales office of the foreign corporation shall not be taken into account under this subparagraph for any taxable year.

(iii) This subparagraph shall not apply to gains or losses on the sale or exchange of intangible personal property to which subparagraph (1) of this paragraph applies or of stocks or securities to which subparagraph (2) of this paragraph applies.

(c) Income attributable to U.S. life insurance business. *(1)* All of the income for the taxable year of a foreign corporation described in subparagraph (2) of this paragraph from sources without the United States, which is attributable to its U.S. life insurance business, shall be treated as effectively connected for the taxable year with the conduct of a trade or business in the United States by that corporation. Thus, in determining its life insurance company taxable income from its U.S. business for purposes of section 802, the foreign corporation shall include all of its items of income from sources without the United States which would appropriately be taken into account in determining the life insurance company taxable income of a domestic corporation. The income to which this subparagraph applies shall be taken into account for purposes of paragraph (a) of this section without reference to §§ 1.864-6 and 1.864-7.

(2) A foreign corporation to which subparagraph (1) of this paragraph applies is a foreign corporation carrying on an insurance business in the United States during the taxable year which—

(i) Without taking into account its income not effectively connected for that year with the conduct of any trade or business in the United States, would qualify as a life insurance company under part I (section 801 and following) of subchapter L, chapter 1 of the Code, if it were a domestic corporation, and

(ii) By reason of section 842 is taxable under that part on its income which is effectively connected for that year with its conduct of any trade or business in the United States.

(d) Excluded foreign source income. Notwithstanding paragraphs (b) and (c) of this section, no income from sources without the United States shall be treated as effectively connected for any taxable year with the conduct of a trade or business in the United States by a non-resident alien individual or a foreign corporation if the income consists of—

(1) Dividends, interest, or royalties paid by a related foreign corporation. Dividends, interest, or royalties paid by a foreign corporation in which the non-resident alien individual or the foreign corporation described in paragraph (a) of this section owns, within the meaning of section 958(a), or is considered as owning, by applying the ownership rules of section 958(b), at the time such items are paid more than 50 percent of the total combined voting power of all classes of stock entitled to vote.

(2) Subpart F income of a controlled foreign corporation. Any income of the foreign corporation described in paragraph (a) of this section which is subpart F income for the taxable year, as determined under section 952(a), even though part of the income is attributable to amounts which, if distributed by the foreign corporation, would be distributed with respect to its stock which is owned by shareholders who are not U.S. shareholders within the meaning of section 951(b). This subparagraph shall not apply to any income of the foreign corporation which is excluded in determining its subpart F income for the taxable year for purposes of section 952(a). Thus, for example, this subparagraph shall not apply to—

(i) Foreign base company shipping income which is excluded under section 954(b)(2),

(ii) Foreign base company income amounting to less than 10 percent (30 percent in the case of taxable years of foreign corporations ending before January 1, 1976) of gross income which by reason of section 954(b)(3)(A) does not become subpart F income for the taxable year,

(iii) Any income excluded from foreign base company income under section 954(b)(4), relating to exception for foreign corporations not availed of to reduce taxes,

(iv) Any income derived in the active conduct of a trade or business which is excluded under section 954(c)(3), or

(v) Any income received from related persons which is excluded under section 954(c)(4).

This subparagraph shall apply to the foreign corporation's entire subpart F income for the taxable year determined under section 952(a), even though no amount is included in the gross income of a U.S. shareholder under section 951(a) with respect to that subpart F income because of the minimum distribution provisions of section 963(a) or because of the reduction under section 970(a) with respect to an export trade corporation. This subparagraph shall apply only to a foreign corporation which is a controlled foreign corporation within the meaning of section 957 and the regulations thereunder. The application of this subparagraph may be illustrated by the following examples:

Example (1). Controlled foreign corporation M, incorporated under the laws of foreign country X, is engaged in the business of purchasing and selling merchandise manufactured in foreign country Y by an unrelated person. M negotiates sales, through its sales office in the United States, of its merchandise for use outside of country X. These sales are made outside the United States, and the merchandise is sold for use outside the United States. No office maintained by M outside the United States participates materially in the sales made through its U.S. sales office. These activities constitute the only activities of M. During the taxable year M derives $100,000 income from these sales made through its U.S. sales office, and all of such income is foreign base company sales income by reason of section 954(d)(2) and paragraph (b) of § 1.954-3. The entire $100,000 is also subpart F income, determined under section 952(a). In addition, all of this income would, without reference to section 864(c)(4)(D)(ii) and this subparagraph, be treated as effectively connected for the taxable year with the conduct of a trade or business in the United States by M. Through its entire taxable year 60 percent of the one class of stock of M is owned within the meaning of section 958(a) by U.S. shareholders, as defined in section 951(b), and 40 percent of its one class of stock is owned within the meaning of section 958(a) by persons who are not U.S. shareholders, as defined in section 951(b). Although only $60,000 of the subpart F income of M for the taxable year is includible in the income of the U.S. shareholders under section 951(a), the entire subpart F income of $100,000 constitutes income which, by reason of section 864(c)(4)(D)(ii) and this subparagraph, is not effectively connected for the taxable year with the conduct of a trade or business in the United States by M.

Example (2). The facts are the same as in example (1) except that the foreign base company sales income amounts to $150,000 determined in accordance with paragraph (d)(3)(i) of § 1.954-1, and that M also has gross income from sources without the United States of $50,000 from sales, through its sales office in the United States, of merchandise for use in country X. These sales are made outside the United States. All of this income would, without reference to section 864(c)(4)(D)(ii) and this subparagraph, be treated as effectively connected for the taxable year with the conduct of a trade or business in the United States by M. Since the foreign base company income of $150,000 amounts to 75 percent of the entire gross income of $200,000, determined as provided in paragraph (d)(3)(ii) of § 1.954-1, the entire $200,000 constitutes foreign base company income under section 954(a)(3)(B). Assuming that M has no amounts to be taken into account under paragraphs (1), (2), (4), and (5) of section 954(b), the $200,000 is also subpart F income, determined under section 952(a). This subpart F income of $200,000 constitutes income which, by reason of section 864(c)(4)(D)(ii) and this subparagraph, is not effectively connected for the taxable year with the conduct of a trade or business in the United States by M.

(3) Interest on certain deposits. Interest which, by reason of section 861(a)(1)(A) (relating to interest on deposits with banks, savings and loan associations, and insurance companies paid or credited before January 1, 1976) and paragraph (c) of § 1.864-4, is determined to be income from sources without the United States because it is not effectively connected for the taxable year with the conduct of a trade or business in the United States by the non-resident alien individual or foreign corporation.

T.D. 7216. 11/2/72, amend T.D. 7893, 5/11/83, T.D. 8735, 10/6/97.

§ 1.864-6 Income, gain, or loss attributable to an office or other fixed place of business in the United States.

Caution: The Treasury has not yet amended Reg § 1.864-6 to reflect changes made by P.L. 100-647, P.L. 99-514, P.L. 98-369.

(a) In general. Income, gain, or loss from sources without the United States which is specified in paragraph (b) of § 1.864-5 and received by a nonresident alien individual or a foreign corporation engaged in a trade or business in the United States at some time during a taxable year beginning after December 31, 1966, shall be treated as efficiently connected for the taxable year with the conduct of a trade or business in the United States only if the income, gain, or loss is attributable under paragraphs (b) and (c) of this section to an office or other fixed place of business, as defined in § 1.864-7, which the taxpayer has in the United States at some time during the taxable year.

(b) Material factor test. *(1) In general.* For purposes of paragraph (a) of this section, income, gain, or loss is attributable to an office or other fixed place of business which a nonresident alien individual or a foreign corporation has in the United States only if such office or other fixed place of business is a material factor in the realization of the income, gain, or loss, and if the income, gain, or loss is realized in the ordinary course of the trade or business carried on through that office or other fixed place of business. For this purpose, the activities of the office or other fixed place of business shall not be considered to be a material factor in the realization of the income, gain, or loss unless they provide a significant contribution to, by being an essential economic element in, the realization of the income, gain, or loss. Thus, for example, meetings in the United States of the board of directors of a foreign corporation do not of themselves constitute a material factor in the realization of income, gain, or loss. It is not necessary that the activities of the office or other fixed place of business in the United States be a major factor in the realization of the income, gain, or loss. An office or other fixed place of business located in the United States at some time during a taxable year may be a material factor in the realization of an item of income, gain, or loss for that year even though the office or other fixed place of business is not present in the United States when the income, gain, or loss is realized.

(2) Application of material factor test to specific classes of income. For purposes of paragraph (a) of this section, an office or other fixed place of business which a nonresident alien individual or a foreign corporation, engaged in a trade or business in the United States at some time during the taxable year, had in the United States, shall be considered a material factor in the realization of income, gain, or loss consisting of—

(i) Rents, royalties, or gains on sales of intangible property. Rents, royalties, or gains or losses, from intangible personal property specified in paragraph (b)(1) of § 1.864-5, if the office or other fixed place of business either actively participates in soliciting, negotiating, or performing other activities required to arrange, the lease, license, sale, or exchange from which such income, gain, or loss is derived or performs significant services incident to such lease, license, sale, or exchange. An office or other fixed place of business in the United States shall not be considered to be a material factor in the realization of income, gain, or loss for purposes of this subdivision merely because the office or other fixed place of business conducts one or more of the following activities: (a) develops, creates, produces, or acquires and adds substantial value to, the property which is leased, licensed, or sold, or exchanged, (b) collects or accounts for the rents, royalties, gains, or losses, (c) exercises general supervision over the activities of the persons directly responsible for carrying on the activities or services described in the immediately preceding sentence, (d) performs merely clerical functions incident to the lease, license, sale, or exchange or (e) exercises final approval over the execution of the lease, license, sale, or exchange. The application of this subdivision may be illustrated by the following examples:

Example (1). F, a foreign corporation, is engaged in the active conduct of the business of licensing patents which it has either purchased or developed in the United States. F has a business office in the United States. Licenses for the use of such patents outside the United States are negotiated by offices of F located outside the United States, subject to approval by an officer of such corporation located in the U.S. office. All services which are rendered to F's foreign licenses are performed by employees of F's offices located outside the United States. None of the income, gain, or loss resulting from the foreign licenses so negotiated by F is attributable to its business office in the United States.

Example (2). N, a foreign corporation, is engaged in the active conduct of the business of distributing motion picture films and television programs. N does not distribute such films or programs in the United States. The foreign distribution rights to these films and programs are acquired by N's U.S. business office from the U.S. owners of these films and programs. Employees of N's offices located in various foreign countries carry on in such countries all the solicitations and negotiations for the licensing of these films and programs to licensees located in such countries and provide the necessary incidental services to the licensees. N's U.S. office collects the rentals from the foreign licensees and maintains the necessary records of income and expense. Officers of N located in the United States also maintain general supervision over the employees of the foreign offices, but the foreign employees conduct the day to day business of N outside the United States of soliciting, negotiating, or performing other activities required to arrange the foreign licenses. None of the income, gain, or loss resulting from the foreign licenses so negotiated by N is attributable to N's U.S. office.

(ii) Dividends or interest, or gains or losses from sales of stock or securities. (a) In general. Dividends, or interest from any transaction, or gains or losses on the sale or exchange of stocks or securities, specified in paragraph (b)(2) of § 1.864-5, if the office or other fixed place of business either activity participates in soliciting, negotiating, or performing other activities required to arrange, the issue, acquisition, sale, or exchange, of the asset from which such income, gain, or loss is derived or performs significant services incident to such issue, acquisition, sale or exchange. An office or other fixed place of business in the United States shall not be considered to be a material factor in the realization of income, gain, or loss for purposes of this subdivision merely because the office or other fixed place of business conducts one or more of the following activities: (1) collects or accounts for the dividends, interest, gains, or losses, (2) exercises general supervision over the activities of the persons directly responsible for carrying on the activities or services described in the immediately preceding sentence, (3) performs merely clerical functions incident to the issue, acquisition, sale, or exchange, or (4) exercises final approval over the execution of the issue, acquisition, sale, or exchange.

(b) Effective connection of income from stocks or securities with active conduct of a banking, financing, or similar business. Notwithstanding (a) of this subdivision (ii), the determination as to whether any dividends or interest from stocks or securities, or gain or loss from the sale or exchange of stocks or securities which are capital assets, which is from sources without the United States and derived by a nonresident alien individual or a foreign corporation in the active conduct during the taxable year of a banking, financing, or similar business in the United States, shall be treated as effectively connected for such year with the active conduct of that business shall be made by applying the principles of paragraph (c)(5)(ii) of § 1.864-4 for determining whether income, gain, or loss of such type from sources within the United States is effectively connected for such year with the active conduct of that business.

(c) Security defined. For purposes of this subdivision (ii), a security is any bill, note, bond, debenture, or other evidence of indebtedness, or any evidence of an interest in, or right to subscribe to or purchase, any of the foregoing items.

(d) Limitations on application of rules on banking, financing, or similar business. (1) Trading for taxpayer's own account. The provisions of (b) of this subdivision (ii) apply for purposes of determining when certain income, gain, or loss from stocks or securities is effectively connected with the active conduct of a banking, financing, or similar business in the United States. Any dividends, interest, gain, or loss from sources without the United States which by reason of the application of (b) of this subdivision (ii) is not effectively connected with the active conduct by a foreign corporation of a banking, financing, or similar business in the United States may be effectively connected for the taxable year, under (a) of this subdivision (ii), with the conduct by such taxpayer of a trade or business in the United States which consists of trading in stocks or securities for the taxpayer's own account.

(2) Other income. For rules relating to dividends or interest from sources without the United States (other than dividends or interest from, or gain or loss from the sale or exchange of, stocks or securities referred to in (b) of this subdivision (ii)) derived in the active conduct of a banking, financing, or similar business in the United States, see (a) of this subdivision (ii).

(iii) Sale of goods or merchandise through U.S. office. Income, gain, or loss from sales of goods or merchandise specified in paragraph (b)(3) of § 1.864-5, if the office or other fixed place of business actively participates in soliciting the order, negotiating the contract of sale, or performing other significant services necessary for the consummation of the sale which are not the subject of a separate agreement between the seller and the buyer. The office or other fixed place of business in the United States shall be considered a material factor in the realization of income, gain, or loss from a sale made as a result of a sales order received in such office or other fixed place of business except where the sales order is received unsolicited and that office or other fixed place of business is not held out of potential customers as the place to which such sales should be sent. The income, gain, or loss must be realized in the ordinary course of the trade or business carried on through the office or other fixed place of business in the United States. Thus, if a foreign corporation is engaged solely in a manufacturing business in the United States, the income derived by its office in the United States as a result of an occasional sale outside the United States is not attributable to the U.S. office if the sales office of the manufacturing business is located outside the United States. On the other hand, if a foreign corporation establishes a sales office in the United States to sell for consumption in the Western Hemisphere merchandise which the corporation produces in Africa, the income derived by the sales office in the United States as a result of an occasional sale made by it in Europe shall be attributable to the U.S. sales office. An office or other fixed place of business in the United States shall not be considered to be a material factor in the realization of income, gain, or loss for purposes of this subdivision merely because of one or more of the following activities: (a) the sale is made subject to the final approval of such office or other fixed place of business, (b) the property sold is held in, and distributed from, such office or other fixed place of business, (c) samples of the property sold are displayed (but not otherwise promoted or sold) in such office or other fixed place of business, or (d) such office or other fixed place of business performs merely clerical functions incident to the sale. Activities carried on by employees of an office or other fixed place of business constitute activities of that office or other fixed place of business.

(3) Limitation where foreign office is a material factor in realization of income. (i) Goods or merchandise destined for foreign use, consumption, or disposition. Notwithstanding subparagraphs (1) and (2) of this paragraph, an office or other fixed place of business which a nonresident alien individual or a foreign corporation has in the United States shall not be considered, for purposes of paragraph (a) of this section, to be a material factor in the realization of income, gain, or loss from sales of goods or merchandise specified in paragraph (b)(3) of § 1.864-5 if the property is sold for use, consumption, or disposition outside the United States and an office or other fixed place of business, as defined in § 1.864-7, which such nonresident alien individual or foreign corporation has outside the United States participates materially in the sale. For this purpose an office or other fixed place of business which the taxpayer has outside the United States shall be considered to have participated materially in a sale made through the office or other fixed place of business in the United States if the office or other fixed place of business outside the United States actively participates in soliciting the order resulting in the sale, negotiating the contract of sale, or performing other significant services necessary for the consummation of the sale which are not the subject of a separate agreement between the seller and buyer. An office or other fixed place of business which the taxpayer has outside the United States shall not be considered to have participated materially in a sale merely because of one or more of the following activities: (a) The sale is made subject to the final approval of such office or other fixed place of business, (b) the property sold is held in, and distributed from, such office or other fixed place of business, (c) samples of the property sold are displayed (but not otherwise promoted or sold) in such office or other fixed place of business, (d) such office or other fixed place of business is used for purposes of having title to the property pass outside the United States, or (e) such office or other fixed place of business performs merely clerical functions incident to the sale.

(ii) Rules for determining country of use, consumption, or disposition. (a) In general. As a general rule, personal property which is sold to an unrelated person shall be presumed for purposes of that subparagraph to have been sold for use, consumption, or disposition in the country of destination of the property sold; for such purpose, the occurrence in a country of a temporary interruption in shipment of property shall not cause that country to be considered the country of destination. However, if at the time of a sale of personal property to an unrelated person the taxpayer knew, or should have known form the facts and circumstances surrounding the transaction, that the property probably would not be used, consumed, or disposed of in the country of destination, the taxpayer must determine the country of ultimate use, consumption, or disposition of the property or the property shall be presumed to have been sold for use, consumption, or disposition in the United States. A taxpayer who sells personal property to a related person shall be presumed to have sold the property for use, consumption, or disposition in the United States unless the taxpayer establishes the use made of the property by the related person; once he has established that the related person has disposed of the property, the rules in the two immediately preceding sentences relating to sales to an unrelated person shall apply at the first stage in the chain of distribution at which a sale is made by a related person to an unrelated person. Notwithstanding the preceding provisions of this subdivision (a), a taxpayer who sells personal property to any person whose principal business consists of selling from inventory to retail customers at retail outlets outside the United States may assume at the time of the sale to that person that the property will be used, consumed, or disposed of outside the United States. For purposes of this (a), a person is related to another person if either person owns or controls directly or indirectly the other, or if any third person or persons own or control directly or indirectly both. For this purpose, the term "control" includes any kind of control, whether or not legally enforceable, and however exercised or exercisable. For illustrations of the principles of this subdivision, see paragraph (a)(3)(iv) of § 1.954-3.

(b) Fungible goods. For purposes of this subparagraph, a taxpayer who sells to a purchaser personal property which because of its fungible nature cannot reasonably be specifically traced to other purchasers and to the countries of ultimate use, consumption, or disposition shall, unless the taxpayer establishes a different disposition as being proper, treat that property as being sold, for ultimate use, consumption, or disposition in those countries, and to those other purchasers, in the same proportions in which property from the fungible mass of the first purchaser is sold in the ordinary course of business by such first purchaser. No apportionment is required to be made, however, on the basis of sporadic sales by the first purchaser. This (b) shall apply only in a case where the taxpayer knew, or should have known from the facts and circumstances surrounding the transaction, the manner in which the first purchaser disposes of property from the fungible mass.

(iii) Illustration. The application of this subparagraph may be illustrated by the following example:

Example. Foreign corporation M has a sales office in the United States during the taxable year through which it sells outside the United States for use in foreign countries industrial electrical generators which such corporation manufactures in a foreign country. M is not a controlled foreign corporation within the meaning of section 957 and the regulations thereunder, and, by reason of its activities in the United States, is engaged in business in the United States during the taxable year. The generators require specialized installation and continuous adjustment and maintenance services. M has an office in foreign country X which is the only organization qualified to perform these installation, adjustment, and maintenance services. During the taxable year M sells several generators through its U.S. office for use in foreign country Y under sales contracts which also provide for installation, adjustment, and maintenance by its office in country X. The generators are installed in country Y by employees of M's office in country X, who also are responsible for the servicing of the equipment. Since the office of M in country X performs significant services incident to these sales which are necessary for their consummation and are not the subject of a separate agreement between M and the purchaser, the U.S. office of M is not considered to be a material factor in the realization of the income from the sales and, for purposes of paragraph (a) of this section, such income is not attributable to the U.S. office of that corporation.

(c) Amount of income, gain, or loss allocable to U.S. office. *(1) In general.* If, in accordance with paragraph (b) of this section, an office or other fixed place of business which a nonresident alien individual or a foreign corporation has in the United States at some time during the taxable year is a material factor in the realization for that year of an item of income, gain, or loss specified in paragraph (b) of § 1.864-5, such item of income, gain, or loss shall be considered to be allocable in its entirety to that office or other fixed place of business. In no case may any income, gain, or loss for the taxable year from sources without the United States, or part thereof, be allocable under this paragraph to an office or other fixed place of business which a nonresident alien individual or a foreign corporation has in the United States if the taxpayer is at no time during the taxable year engaged in a trade or business in the United States.

(2) Special limitation in case of sales of goods or merchandise through U.S. office. Notwithstanding subparagraph (1) of this paragraph, in the case of a sale of goods or merchandise specified in paragraph (b)(3) of § 1.864-5, which is not a sale to which paragraph (b)(3)(i) of this section applies, the amount of income which shall be considered to be allocable to the officer or other fixed place of business which the nonresident alien individual or foreign corporation has in the United States shall not exceed the amount which would be treated as income from sources within the United States if the taxpayer had sold the goods or merchandise in the United States. See, for example, section 863(b)(2) and paragraph (b) of § 1.863-3, which prescribes, as available methods for determining the income from sources within the United States, the independent factory or production price method, the gross sales and property apportionment method, and any other method regularly employed by the taxpayer which more clearly reflects taxable income from such sources than those specifically authorized.

(3) Illustrations. The application of this paragraph may be illustrated by the following examples:

Example (1). Foreign corporation M, which is not a controlled foreign corporation within the meaning of section 957 and the regulations thereunder, manufactures machinery in a foreign country and sells the machinery outside the United States through its sales office in the United States for use in foreign countries. Title to the property which is sold is transferred to the foreign purchaser outside the United States, but no office or other fixed place of business of M in a foreign country participates materially in the sale made through its U.S. office. During the taxable year M derives a total taxable income (determined as though M were a domestic corporation) of $250,000 from these sales. If the sales made through the U.S. office for the taxable year had been made in the United States and the property had been sold for use in the United States, the taxable income from sources within the United States from such sales would have been $100,000, determined as provided in section 863 and 882(c) and the regulations thereunder. The taxable income which is allocable to M's U.S. sales office pursuant to this paragraph and which is effectively connected for the taxable year with the conduct of a trade or business within the United States by that corporation is $100,000.

Example (2). Foreign corporation N, which is not a controlled foreign corporation within the meaning of section 957 and the regulations thereunder, has an office in a foreign country which purchases merchandise and sells it through its sales offices in the United States for use in various foreign countries, such sales being made outside the United States and title to the property passing outside the United States. No other office of N participates materially in these sales made through its U.S. office. By reason of its sales activities in the United States, N is engaged in business in the United States during the taxable year. During the taxable year N derives taxable income (determined as though N were a domestic corporation) of $300,000 from these sales made through its U.S. sales office. If the sales made through the U.S. office for the taxable year had been made in the United States and the property had been sold for use in the United States, the taxable income from sources within the United States from such sales would also have been $300,000, determined as provided in sections 861 and 882(c) and the regulations thereunder. The taxable income which is allocable to N's U.S. sales office pursuant to this paragraph and which is effectively connected for the taxable year with the conduct of a trade or business in the United States by that corporation is $300,000.

Example (3). The facts are the same as in example (2), except that N has an office in a foreign country which participates materially in the sales which are made through its U.S. office. The taxable income which is allocable to N's U.S. sales office is not effectively connected for the taxable year with the conduct of a trade or business in the United States by that corporation.

T.D. 7216, 11/2/72.

PAR. 10. Section 1.864-6 is amended as follows:

1. Paragraph (b)(2)(ii)(d)(3) and (b)(3)(ii)(c) are added.

2. Paragraph (b)(3)(i) is revised by adding a new sentence after the last sentence.

The additions and revision read as follows:

Proposed § 1.864-6 Income, gain or loss attributable to an office or other fixed place of business in the United States. [*For Preamble, see ¶ 151,855*]

* * * * *

(b) * * *

(2) * * *

(ii) * * *

(d) * * *

(3) Certain income earned by a global dealing operation. Notwithstanding paragraphs (b)(2)(ii) (a) or (b) of this section, foreign source interest, including substitute interest as defined in § 1.861-2(a)(7), or dividend income, including substitute dividends as defined in § 1.861-3(a)(6), derived by a participant in a global dealing operation, as defined in § 1.482-8(a)(2)(i) shall be treated as attributable to the foreign corporation's U.S. trade or business only if and to the extent that the income would be treated as U.S. source if § 1.863-3(h) were to apply to such amounts. * * *

(3) * * *

(i) * * * Notwithstanding paragraphs (b)(3)(i)(1) and (2) of this section, an office or other fixed place of business of a nonresident alien individual or a foreign corporation which is located in the United States and which is a participant in a global dealing operation, as defined in § 1.482-8(a)(2)(i), shall be considered to be a material factor in the realization of foreign source income, gain or loss, only if and to the extent that such income, gain or loss would be treated as U.S. source if § 1.863-3(h) were to apply to such amounts.

(ii) * * *

(c) Property sales in a global dealing operation. Notwithstanding paragraphs (b)(3)(ii)(a) or (b) of this section, personal property described in section 1221(1) and sold in the active conduct of a taxpayer's global dealing operation, as defined in § 1.482-8(a)(2)(i), shall be presumed to have been sold for use, consumption, or disposition outside of the United States only if and to the extent that the income, gain or loss to which the sale gives rise would be sourced outside of the United States if § 1.863-3(h) were to apply to such amounts.

§ 1.864-7 Definition of office or other fixed place of business.

Caution: The Treasury has not yet amended Reg § 1.864-7 to reflect changes made by P.L. 100-647, P.L. 99-514, P.L. 98-369.

(a) In general. *(1)* This section applies for purposes of determining whether a nonresident alien individual or a foreign corporation that is engaged in a trade or business in the United States at some time during a taxable year beginning after December 31, 1966, has an office or other fixed place of business in the United States for purposes of applying section 864(c)(4)(B) and § 1.864-6 to income, gain, or loss specified in paragraph (b) of § 1.864-5 from sources without the United States or has an office or other fixed place of business outside the United States for purposes of applying section 864(c)(4)(B)(iii) and paragraph (b)(3)(i) of § 1.864-6 to sales of goods or merchandise for use, consumption, or disposition outside the United States.

(2) In making a determination under this section due regard shall be given to the facts and circumstances of each case, particularly to the nature of the taxpayer's trade or business and the physical facilities actually required by the taxpayer in the ordinary course of the conduct of his trade or business.

(3) The law of a foreign country shall not be controlling in determining whether a nonresident alien individual or a foreign corporation has an office or other fixed place of business.

(b) Fixed facilities. *(1) In general.* As a general rule, an office or other fixed place of business is a fixed facility, that is, a place, site, structure, or other similar facility, through which a nonresident alien individual or a foreign corporation engages in a trade or business. For this purpose an office or other fixed place of business shall include, but shall not be limited to, a factory; a store or other sales outlet; a workshop; or a mine, quarry, or other place of extraction of natural resources. A fixed facility may be considered an office or other fixed place of business whether or not the facility is continuously used by a nonresident alien individual or foreign corporation.

(2) Use of another person's office or other fixed place of business. A nonresident alien individual or a foreign corporation shall not be considered to have an office or other fixed place of business merely because such alien individual or foreign corporation uses another person's office or other fixed place of business, whether or not the office or place of business of a related person, through which to transact a trade or business, if the trade or business activities of the alien individual or foreign corporation in that office or other fixed place of business are relatively sporadic or infrequent, taking into account the overall needs and conduct of that trade or business.

(c) Management activity. A foreign corporation shall not be considered to have an office or other fixed place of business merely because a person controlling that corporation has an office or other fixed place of business from which general supervision and control over the policies of the foreign corporation are exercised. The fact that top management decisions affecting the foreign corporation are made in a country shall not of itself mean that the foreign corporation has an office or other fixed place of business in that country. For example, a foreign sales corporation which is a wholly owned subsidiary of a domestic corporation shall not be considered to have an office or other fixed place of business in the United States merely because of the presence in the United States of officers of the domestic parent corporation who are generally responsible only for the policy decisions affecting the foreign sales corporation, provided that the foreign corporation has a chief executive officer, whether or not he is also an officer of the domestic parent corporation, who conducts the day-to-day trade or business of the foreign corporation from a foreign office. The result in this example would be the same even if the executive officer should (1) regularly confer with the officers of the domestic parent corporation, (2) occasionally visit the U.S. office of the domestic parent corporation, and (3) during such visits to the United States temporarily conduct the business of the foreign subsidiary corporation out of the domestic parent corporation's office in the United States.

(d) Agent activity. *(1) Dependent agents.* (i) In general. In determining whether a nonresident alien individual or a foreign corporation has an office or other fixed place of business, the office or other fixed place of business of an agent who is not an independent agent, as defined in subparagraph (3) of this paragraph, shall be disregarded unless such agent (a) has the authority to negotiate and conclude contracts in the name of the nonresident alien individual or foreign corporation, and regularly exercises that authority, or (b) has a stock of merchandise belonging to the nonresident alien individual or foreign corporation from which orders are regularly filed on behalf of such alien individual or foreign corporation. A person who purchases goods from a nonresident alien individual or a foreign corporation shall not be considered to be an agent for such alien individual or foreign corporation for purposes of this paragraph where such person is carrying on such purchasing activities in the ordinary course of its own business, even though such person is related in some manner to the nonresident alien individual or foreign corporation. For example, a wholly owned domestic subsidiary corporation of a foreign corporation shall not be treated as an agent of the foreign parent corporation merely because the subsidiary corporation purchases goods from the foreign parent corporation and resells them in its own name. However, if the domestic subsidiary corporation regularly negotiates and concludes contracts in the name of its foreign parent corporation or maintains a stock of merchandise from which it regularly fills orders on behalf of the foreign parent corporation, the office or other fixed place of business of the domestic subsidiary corporation shall be treated as the office or other fixed place of business of the foreign parent corporation unless the domestic subsidiary corporation is an independent agent within the meaning of subparagraph (3) of this paragraph.

(ii) Authority to conclude contracts or fill orders. For purposes of subdivision (i) of this subparagraph, an agent shall be considered regularly to exercise authority to negotiate and conclude contracts or regularly to fill orders on behalf of his foreign principal only if the authority is exercised, or the orders are filled, with some frequency over a continuous period of time. This determination shall be made on the basis of the facts and circumstances in each case, taking into account the nature of the business of the principal; but, in all cases, the frequency and continuity tests are to be applied conjunctively. Regularity shall not be evidenced by occasional or incidental activity. An agent shall not be considered regularly to negotiate and conclude contracts on behalf of his foreign principal if the agent's authority to negotiate and conclude contracts is limited only to unusual cases or such authority must be separately secured by the agent from his principal with respect to each transaction effected.

(2) Independent agents. The office or other fixed place of business of an independent agent, as defined in subparagraph (3) of this paragraph, shall not be treated as the office or other fixed place of business of his principal who is a nonresident alien individual or a foreign corporation, irrespective of whether such agent has authority to negotiate and conclude contracts in the name of his principal, and regularly exercises that authority, or maintains a stock of goods from which he regularly fills orders on behalf of his principal.

(3) Definition of independent agent. (i) In general. For purposes of this paragraph, the term "independent agent" means a general commission agent, broker, or other agent of an independent status acting in the ordinary course of his business in that capacity. Thus, for example, an agent who, in pursuance of his usual trade or business, and for compensation, sells goods or merchandise consigned or entrusted to his possession, management, and control for that purpose by or for the owner of such goods or merchandise is an independent agent;

(ii) Related persons. The determination of whether an agent is an independent agent for purposes of this paragraph shall be made without regard to facts indicating that either the agent or the principal own or control directly or indirectly both. For example, a wholly owned domestic subsidiary corporation of a foreign corporation which acts as an agent for the foreign parent corporation may be treated as acting in the capacity of independent agent for the foreign parent corporation. The facts and circumstances of a specific case shall determine whether the agent, while acting for his principal, is acting in pursuance of his usual trade or business and in such manner as to constitute him an independent agent in his relations with the nonresident alien individual or foreign corporation.

(iii) Exclusive agents. Where an agent who is otherwise an independent agent within the meaning of subdivision (i) of this subparagraph acts in such capacity exclusively, or almost exclusively, for one principal who is a nonresident alien individual or a foreign corporation, the facts and circumstances of a particular case shall be taken into account in determining whether the agent, while acting in that capacity, may be classified as an independent agent.

(e) Employee activity. Ordinarily, an employee of a nonresident alien individual or a foreign corporation shall be treated as a dependent agent to whom the rules of paragraph (d)(1) of this section apply if such employer does not in and of itself have a fixed facility (as defined in paragraph (b) of this section) in the United States or outside the United States, as the case may be. However, where the employee, in the ordinary course of his duties, carries on the trade or business of his employer in or through a fixed facility of such employer which is regularly used by the employee in the course of carrying out such duties, such fixed facility shall be considered the office or other fixed place of business of the employer, irrespective of the rules of paragraph (d)(1) of this section. The application of this paragraph may be illustrated by the following example:

Example. M, a foreign corporation, opens a showroom office in the United States for the purpose of promoting its sales of merchandise which it purchases in foreign country X. The employees of the U.S. office, consisting of salesmen and general clerks, are empowered only to run the office, to arrange for the appointment of distributing agents for the merchandise offered by M, and to solicit orders generally. These employees do not have the authority to negotiate and conclude contracts in the name of M, nor do they have a stock of merchandise from which to fill orders on behalf of M. Any negotiations entered into by these employees are under M's instructions and subject to its approval as to any decision reached. The only independent authority which the employees have is in the appointment of distributors to whom M is to sell merchandise, but even this authority is subject to the right of M to approve or disapprove these buyers on receipt of information as to their business standing. Under the circumstances this office used by a group of salesmen for sales promotion is a fixed place of business which M has in the United States.

(f) Office or other fixed place of business of a related person. The fact that a nonresident alien individual or a foreign corporation is related in some manner to another person who has an office or other fixed place of business shall not of itself mean that such office or other fixed place of business of the other person is the office or other fixed place of business of the nonresident alien individual or foreign corporation. Thus, for example, the U.S. office of foreign corporation M, a wholly owned subsidiary corporation of foreign corporation N, shall not be considered the office or other fixed place of business of N unless the facts and circumstances show that N is engaged in trade or business in the United States through that office or other fixed place of business. However, see paragraph (b)(2) of this section.

(g) Illustrations. The application of this section may be illustrated by the following examples:

Example (1). S, a foreign corporation, is engaged in the business of buying and selling tangible personal property. S is a wholly owned subsidiary of P, a domestic corporation engaged in the business of buying and selling similar property, which has an office in the United States. Officers of P are generally responsible for the policies followed by S and are directors of S, but S has an independent group of officers, none of whom are regularly employed in the United States. In addition to this group of officers, S has a chief executive officer, D, who is also an officer of P but who is permanently stationed outside the United States. The day-to-day conduct of S's business is handled by D and the other officers of such corporation, but they regularly confer with the officers of P and on occasion temporarily visit P's offices in the United States, at which time they continue to conduct the business of S. S does not have an office or other fixed place of business in the United States for purposes of this section.

Example (2). The facts are the same as in example (1) except that, on rare occasions, an employee of P receives an order which he, after consultation with officials of S and because P cannot fill the order, accepts on behalf of S rather than on behalf of P. P does not hold itself out as a person which those wishing to do business with S should contact. Assuming that orders for S are seldom handled in this manner and that they do not constitute a significant part of that corporation's business, S shall not be considered to have an office or other fixed place of business in the United States because of these activities of an employee of P.

Example (3). The facts are the same as in example (1) except that all orders received by S are subject to review by an officer of P before acceptance. S has a business office in the United States.

Example (4). S, a foreign corporation organized under the laws of Puerto Rico, is engaged in the business of manufacturing dresses in Puerto Rico and is entitled to an income tax exemption under the Puerto Rico Industrial Incentive Act of 1963. S is a wholly owned subsidiary of P, a domestic corporation engaged in the business of buying and selling dresses to customers in the United States. S sells most of the dresses it produces to P, the assumption being made that the income from these sales is derived from sources without the United States. P in turn sells these dresses in the United States in its name and through the efforts of its own employees and of distributors appointed by it. S does not have a fixed facility in the United States, and none of its employees are stationed in the United States. On occasion, employees of S visit the office of P in the United States, and executives of P visit the office of S in Puerto Rico, to discuss with one another matters of mutual business interest involving both corporations, including the strategy for marketing the dresses produced by S. These matters are also regularly discussed by such persons by telephone calls between the United States and Puerto Rico. S's employees do not otherwise participate in P's marketing activities. Officers of P are generally responsible for the policies followed by S and are directors of S, but S has a chief executive officer in Puerto Rico who, from its office therein, handles the day-to-day conduct of S's business. Based upon the facts presented, and assuming there are no other facts which would lead to a different determination, S shall not be considered to have an office or other fixed place of business in the United States for purposes of this section.

Example (5). The facts are the same as in example (4) except that the dresses are manufactured by S in styles and designs furnished by P and out of goods and raw materials purchased by P and sold to S. Based upon the facts presented, and assuming there are no other facts which would lead to a different determination, S shall not be considered to have an office or other fixed place of business in the United States for purposes of this section.

Example (6). The facts are the same as in example (5) except that, pursuant to the instructions of P, the dresses sold by P are shipped by S directly to P's customers in the United States. Based upon the facts presented, and assuming there are no other facts which would lead to a different determination, S shall not be considered to have an office or other fixed place of business in the United States for purposes of this section.

T.D. 7216, 11/2/72.

---

§ 1.864-8T Treatment of related person factoring income (temporary).

(a) Applicability. *(1) General rule.* This section applies for purposes of determining the treatment of income derived by a person from a trade or service receivable acquired from a related person. Except as provided in paragraph (d) of this section, if a person acquires (directly or indirectly) a trade or service receivable from a related person, any income (including any stated interest, discount or service fee) derived from the trade or service receivable shall be treated as if it were interest received on a loan to the obligor under the receivable. The characterization of income as interest pursuant to this section shall apply only for purposes of sections 551-

558 (relating to foreign personal holding companies), sections 951-964 (relating to controlled foreign corporations), and section 904 (relating to the limitation on the foreign tax credit) of the Code and the regulations thereunder. The principles of sections 861 through 863 and the regulations thereunder shall be applied to determine the source of such interest income for purposes of section 904.

(2) Override. With respect to income characterized as interest under this section, the special rules of section 864(d) and this section override any conflicting provisions of the Code and regulations relating to foreign personal holding companies, controlled foreign corporations, and the foreign tax credit limitation. Thus, for example, pursuant to section 864(d)(5) and paragraph (e) of this section, stated interest derived from a factored trade or service receivable is not eligible for the Subpart F de minimis rule of section 954(b)(3), the same country exception of section 954(c)(3)(A)(i), or the special rules for export financing interest of sections 904(d)(2) and 954(c)(2)(B), even if in the absence of this section the treatment of such stated interest would be governed by those sections.

(3) Limitation. Section 864(d) and this section apply only with respect to the tax treatment of income derived from a trade or service receivable acquired from a related person. Therefore, neither section 864(d) nor this section affects the characterization of an expense or loss of either the seller of a receivable or the obligor under a receivable. Accordingly, the obligor under a trade or service receivable shall not be allowed to treat any part of the purchase price of property or services as interest (other than amounts treated as interest under provisions other than section 864(d)).

(b) Definitions. The following definitions apply for purposes of this section and § 1.956-3T.

(1) Trade or service receivable. The term "trade or service receivable" means any account receivable or evidence of indebtedness, whether or not issued at a discount and whether or not bearing stated interest, arising out of the disposition by a related person of property described in section 1221(l) (hereinafter referred to as "inventory property") or the performance of services by a related person.

(2) Related person. A "related person" is:

(i) A person who is a related person within the meaning of section 267(b) and the regulations thereunder;

(ii) A United States shareholder (as defined in section 951(b)); or

(iii) A person who is related (within the meaning of section 267(b) and the regulations thereunder) to a United States shareholder.

(c) Acquisition of a trade or service receivable. *(1) General rule.* A trade or service receivable is considered to be acquired by a person at the time when that person is entitled to receive all or a portion of the income from the trade or service receivable. A person who acquires a trade or service receivable (hereinafter referred to as the "factor") is considered to have acquired a trade or service receivable regardless of whether:

(i) The acquisition is characterized for federal income tax purposes as a sale, a pledge of collateral for a loan, an assignment, a capital contribution, or otherwise;

(ii) The factor takes title to or obtains physical possession of the trade or service receivable;

(iii) The related person assigns the trade or service receivable with or without recourse;

(iv) The factor or some other person is obligated to collect the payments due under the trade or service receivable;

(v) The factor is liable for all property, excise, sales, or similar taxes due upon collection of the receivable;

(vi) The factor advances the entire face amount of the trade or service receivable transferred;

(vii) All trade or service receivables assigned by the related person are assigned to one factor; and

(viii) The obligor under the trade or service receivable is notified of the assignment.

(2) Example. The following example illustrates the application of paragraphs (a), (b), and (c)(1) of this section.

Example. P, a domestic corporation, owns all of the outstanding stock of FS, a controlled foreign corporation. P manufactures and sells paper products to customers, including X, an unrelated domestic corporation. As part of a sales transaction, P takes back a trade receivable from X and sells the receivable to FS. Because FS has acquired a trade or service receivable from a related person, the income derived by FS from P's receivable is interest income described in paragraph (a)(1) of this section.

(3) Indirect acquisitions. (i) Acquisition through unrelated person. A trade or service receivable will be considered to be acquired from a related person if it is acquired from an unrelated person who acquired (directly or indirectly) such receivable from a person who is a related person to the factor. The following example illustrates the application of this paragraph (c)(3)(i).

Example. A, a United States citizen, owns all of the outstanding stock of FPHC, a foreign personal holding company. A performs engineering services within and without the United States for customers, including X, an unrelated corporation. A performs engineering services for X and takes back a service receivable. A sells the receivable to Y, an unrelated corporation engaged in the factoring business. Y resells the receivable to FPHC. Because FPHC has indirectly acquired a service receivable from a related person, the income derived by FPHC from A's receivable is interest income described in paragraph (a)(1) of this section.

(ii) Acquisition by nominee or passthrough entity. A factor will be considered to have acquired a trade or service receivable held on its behalf by a nominee or by a partnership, simple trust, S corporation or other pass-through entity to the extent the factor owns (directly or indirectly) a beneficial interest in such partnership or other pass-through entity. The rule of this paragraph (c)(3)(ii) does not limit the application of paragraph (c)(3)(iii) of this section regarding the characterization of trade or service receivables of unrelated persons acquired pursuant to certain swap or pooling arrangements. The following example illustrates the application of this paragraph (c)(3)(ii).

Example. FS1, a controlled foreign corporation, acquires a 20 percent limited partnership interest in PS, a partnership. PS purchases trade or service receivables resulting from the sale of inventory property by FS1's domestic parent, P. PS does not purchase receivables of any person who is related to any other partner in PS. FS1 is considered to have acquired a 20 percent interest in the receivables acquired by PS. Thus, FS1's distributive share of the income derived by PS from the receivables of P is considered to be interest income described in paragraph (a)(1) of this section.

(iii) Swap or pooling arrangements. A trade or service receivable of a person unrelated to the factor will be considered to be a trade or service receivable acquired from a related person and subject to the rules of this section if it is acquired in accordance with an arrangement that involves two or more groups of related persons that are unrelated to each other and the effect of the arrangement is that one or more related persons in each group acquire (directly or indirectly) trade or service receivables of one or more unrelated persons who are also parties to the arrangement, in exchange for reciprocal purchases of the first group's receivables. The following example illustrates the application of this paragraph (c)(3)(iii).

Example. Controlled foreign corporations A, B, C, and D are wholly-owned subsidiaries of domestic corporations M, N, O, and P, respectively. M, N, O, and P are not related persons. According to a prearranged plan, A, B, C, and D each acquire trade or service receivables of M, N, O, and/or P, except that neither A, B, C nor D acquires receivables of its own parent corporation. Because the effect of this arrangement is that the unrelated groups acquire each other's trade or service receivables pursuant to the arrangement, income derived by A, B, C, and D from the receivables acquired from M, N, O, and P is interest income described in paragraph (a)(1) of this section.

(iv) Financing arrangements. If a controlled foreign corporation (as defined in section 957(a)) participates (directly or indirectly) in a lending transaction that results in a loan to the purchaser of inventory property, services, or trade or service receivables of a related person (or a loan to a person who is related to the purchaser), and if the loan would not have been made or maintained on the same terms but for the corresponding purchase, then the controlled foreign corporation shall be considered to have indirectly acquired a trade or service receivable, and income derived by the controlled foreign corporation from such a loan shall be considered to be income described in paragraph (a)(1) of this section. For purposes of this paragraph (c)(3)(iv), it is immaterial that the sums lent are not, in fact, the sums used to finance the purchase of a related person's inventory property, services, or trade or service receivables. The amount of income derived by the controlled foreign corporation to be taken into account shall be the total amount of income derived from a lending transaction described in this paragraph (c)(3)(iv), if the amount lent is less than or equal to the purchase price of the inventory property, services, or trade or service receivables. If the amount lent is greater than the purchase price of the inventory property, services or receivables, the amount to be taken into account shall be the proportion of the interest charge (including original issue discount) that the purchase price bears to the total amount lent pursuant to the lending transaction. The following examples illustrate the application of this paragraph (c)(3)(iv).

Example (1). P, a domestic corporation, owns all of the outstanding stock of FS1, a controlled foreign corporation engaged in the financing business in Country X. P manufactures and sells toys, including sales to C, an unrelated corporation. Prior to P's sale of toys to C for $2,000, D, a wholly-owned Country X subsidiary of C, borrows $3,000 from FS1. The loan from FS1 to D would not have been made or maintained on the same terms but for C's purchase of toys from P. Two-thirds of the income derived by FS1 from the loan to D is interest income described in paragraph (a)(1) of this section.

Example (2). P, a domestic corporation, owns all of the outstanding stock of FS1, a controlled foreign corporation organized under the laws of Country X. FS1 has accumulated cash reserves. P has uncollected trade and service receivables of foreign obligors. FS1 makes a $1,000 loan to U, a foreign corporation that is unrelated to P or FS1. U purchases P's trade and service receivables for $2,000. The loan would not have been made or maintained on the same terms but for U's purchase of P's receivables. The income derived by U from the receivables is not interest income within the meaning of paragraph (a) of this section. However, the interest paid by U to FS1 is interest income described in paragraph (a)(1) of this section.

Example (3). The facts are the same as in Example (2), except that U is a wholly-owned Country Y subsidiary of FS1. Because U is related to P within the meaning of paragraph (b)(2) of this section, under paragraph (c)(1) of this section, income derived by U from P's receivables is interest income described in paragraph (a)(1) of this section. In addition, the income derived by FS1 from the loan to U is interest income described in paragraph (a)(1) of this section.

(d) Same country exception. *(1) Income from trade or service receivables.* Income derived from a trade or service receivable acquired from a related person shall not be treated as interest income described in paragraph (a)(1) of this section if:

(i) The person acquiring the trade or service receivable and the related person are created or organized under the laws of the same foreign country;

(ii) The related person has a substantial part of its assets used in its trade or business located in such foreign country; and

(iii) The related person would not have derived foreign base company income, as defined in section 954(a) and the regulations thereunder, or income effectively connected with a United States trade or business from such receivable if the related person had collected the receivable.

For purposes of paragraph (d)(1)(ii) of this section, the standards contained in § 1.954-2(e) shall apply in determining the location of a substantial part of the assets of a related person. For purposes of paragraph (d)(1)(iii) of this section, a determination of whether the related person would have derived foreign base company income shall be made without regard to the de minimis test described in section 954(b)(3)(A). The following examples illustrate the application of this paragraph (d)(1).

Example (1). FS1, a controlled foreign corporation incorporated under the laws of Country X, owns all of the outstanding stock of FS2, which is also incorporated under the laws of Country X. FS1 has a substantial part of its assets used in its business in Country X. FS1 manufactures and sells toys for use in Country Y. The toys sold are considered to be manufactured in Country X under § 1.954-3(a)(2). FS1 is not considered to have a branch or similar establishment in Country Y that is treated as a separate corporation under section 954(d)(2) and § 1.954-3(b). Thus, gross income derived by FS1 from the toy sales is not foreign base company sales income. FS1 takes back receivables without stated interest from its customers. FS1 assigns those receivables to FS2. The income derived by FS2 from the receivables of FS1 is not interest income described in paragraph (a)(1) of this section, because it satisfies the same country exception under paragraph (d)(1) of this section.

Example (2). The facts are the same as in Example (1), except that the toys sold by FS1 are purchased from FS1's U.S. parent and are sold for use outside of Country X. Thus, any income derived by FS1 from the sale of the toys would be foreign base company sales income. Therefore, income derived by FS2 from the receivables of FS1 is interest income described in paragraph (a)(1) of this section. FS2 is considered to derive interest income from the receivable even if, solely by reason of the de minimis rule of section 954(b)(3)(A), FS1 would not have derived foreign base company income if FS1 had collected the receivable.

(2) Income from financing arrangements. Income derived by a controlled foreign corporation from a loan to a person that purchases inventory property or services of a person that is related to the controlled foreign corporation, or from other loans described in paragraph (c)(3)(iv) of this section, shall not be treated as interest income described in paragraph (a)(1) of this section if:

(i) The person providing the financing and the related person are created or organized under the laws of the same foreign country;

(ii) The related person has a substantial part of its assets used in its trade or business located in such foreign country; and

(iii) The related person would not have derived foreign base company income or income effectively connected with a United States trade or business:

(A) From the sale of inventory property or services to the borrower or from financing the borrower's purchase of inventory property or services, in the case of a loan to the purchaser of inventory property or services of a related person; or

(B) From collecting amounts due under the receivable or from financing the purchase of the receivable, in the case of a loan to the purchaser of a trade or service receivable of a related person.

For purposes of paragraph (d)(2)(ii) of this section, the standards contained in § 1.954-2(e) shall apply in determining the location of a substantial part of the assets of a related person. For purposes of paragraph (d)(2)(iii) of this section, a determination of whether the related person would have derived foreign base company income shall be made without regard to the de minimis test described in section 954(b)(3)(A). The following examples illustrate the application of this paragraph (d)(2).

Example (1). FS1, a controlled foreign corporation incorporated under the laws of Country X, owns all of the outstanding stock of FS2, which is also incorporated under the laws of Country X. FS1, which has a substantial part of its assets used in its business located in Country X, manufactures and sells toys for use in Country Y. The toys sold are considered to be manufactured in Country X under § 1.954-3(a)(2). FS1 is not considered to have a branch or similar establishment in Country Y that is treated as a separate corporation under section 954(d)(2) and § 1.954-3(b). Thus, the gross income derived by FS1 from the toy sales is not foreign base company sales income. FS2 makes a loan to FS3, a wholly-owned subsidiary of FS1 which is also incorporated under the laws of Country X, in connection with FS3's purchase of toys from FS1. FS3 does not earn any subpart F gross income. Thus, FS1 would not have derived foreign personal holding company interest income if FS1 had made the loan to FS3, because the interest would be covered by the same country exception of section 954(c)(3). Therefore, the income derived by FS2 from its loan to FS3 is not treated as interest income described in paragraph (a)(1) of this section, because it satisfies the same country exception under paragraph (d)(2) of this section. Such income is also not treated as foreign personal holding company income described in section 954(c)(1)(A) because the same country exception of section 954(c)(3) also applies to the interest actually derived by FS2 from its loan to FS3.

Example (2). FS1, a controlled foreign corporation incorporated under the laws of Country X, owns all of the outstanding stock of FS2, which is also incorporated under the laws of Country X. FS1 purchases toys from its U.S. parent and resells them for use outside of Country X. As part of a sales transaction, FS1 takes back trade receivables. FS2 makes a loan to U, an unrelated corporation, to finance U's purchase of FS1's trade receivables. Because FS1 would have derived foreign base company income if FS1 had collected the receivables or made the loan itself, the same country exception of paragraph (d)(2) of this section does not apply. Accordingly, under paragraph (c)(3)(iv) of this section, the income derived by FS2 from its loan to U is treated as interest income described in paragraph (a)(1) of this section.

(e) Special rules. *(1) Foreign personal holding companies and controlled foreign corporations.* For purposes of sections 551-558 (relating to foreign personal holding companies), the exclusion provided by section 552(c) for interest described in section 954(c)(3)(A) shall not apply to income described in paragraph (a)(1) of this section. For purposes of the sections 951-964 (relating to controlled foreign corporations), income described in paragraph (a)(1) of this section shall be included in a United States shareholder's pro rata share of a controlled foreign corporation's Subpart F income without regard to the de minimis rule under section 954(b)(3)(A). However, income described in paragraph (a)(1) of this section shall be included in the computation of a controlled foreign corporation's foreign base company income for purposes of applying the de minimis rule under section 954(b)(3)(A) and the more than 70 percent of gross income test under section 954(b)(3)(B). In addition, income described in paragraph (a)(1) of this section shall be considered to be Subpart F income without regard to the exclusions from foreign base company income provided by section 954(c)(2)(B) (relating to export financing interest derived in the conduct of a banking business) and section 954(c)(3)(A)(i) (relating to certain interest income received from related persons).

(2) Foreign tax credit. Income described in paragraph (a)(1) of this section shall be considered to be interest income for purposes of the section 904 foreign tax credit limitation and is not eligible for the exceptions for export financing interest provided in section 904(d)(2)(A)(iii)(II), (B)(ii), and (C)(iii). In addition, such income will be subject to the look-through rule for Subpart F income set forth in section 904(d)(3) without regard to the de minimis exception provided in section 904(d)(3)(E).

(3) Possessions corporations. (i) Limitation on credit. Income described in paragraph (a)(1) of this section shall not be treated as income described in section 936(a)(1)(A) or (B) unless the income is considered under the principles of § 1.863-6 to be derived from sources within the possessions. Thus, the credit provided by section 936 is not available for income described in paragraph (a)(1) of this section unless the obligor under the receivable is a resident of a possession. In the case of a loan described in section 864(d)(6), the credit provided by section 936 is not available for income described in paragraph (a)(1) of this section unless the purchaser of the inventory property or services is a resident of a possession.

(ii) Eligibility determination. Notwithstanding the limitation on the availability of the section 936 credit for income described in paragraph (a)(1) of this section, if income treated as interest income under paragraph (a)(1) of this section is derived from sources within a possession (determined without regard to this section), such income shall be eligible for inclusion in a corporation's gross income for purposes of section 936(a)(2)(A). If such income is derived from the active conduct of a trade or business within a possession (determined without regard to this section), such income shall be eligible for inclusion in a corporation's gross income for purposes of section 936(a)(2)(B). (These rules apply for purposes of determining whether a corporation is eligible to elect the credit provided under section 936(a).)

(iii) Example. The following example illustrates the application of paragraph (e)(3) of this section.

Example. Corporation X is operating in a possession as a possessions corporation. In 1985, X earned $50,000 from the active conduct of a business in the possession, including $5,000 from trade or service receivables acquired from a related party. Obligors under the receivables acquired by X are not residents of the possession. Corporation X also earned $20,000 from activities other than its active conduct of business in the possession. The $5,000 derived by X from the receivables is not eligible for the section 936 credit. However, the $5,000 may be used by X to meet the percentage tests under section 936(a)(2) to the extent that such income is considered to be derived from sources within the possession (for purposes of section 936(a)(2)(A)) or is considered to be derived from the active conduct of a trade or business in the possession (for purposes of section 936(a)(2)(B)), in either case determined without regard to the characterization of such income under this section.

(f) Effective date. The provisions of this section shall apply with respect to accounts receivable and evidences of indebtedness transferred after March 1, 1984 and are effective June 14, 1988.

T.D. 8209, 6/13/88.

Proposed § 1.864(b)-1 Trading in derivatives. [*For Preamble, see ¶ 151,863*]

(a) Trading for taxpayer's own account. As used in part I (section 861 and following) and part II (section 871 and following), subchapter N, chapter 1 of the Internal Revenue Code (Code), and chapter 3 (section 1441 and following) of the Code, and the regulations thereunder, if a taxpayer is an eligible nondealer, the term engaged in trade or business within the United States does not include effecting transactions in derivatives for the taxpayer's own account, including hedging transactions within the meaning of § 1.1221-2.

(b) Definitions. *(1) Eligible nondealer.* For purposes of this section, an *eligible nondealer* is a foreign corporation or a person that is not a resident of the United States and either of which is not, at any place (domestic or foreign), nor at any time during that person's taxable year, any of the following—

(i) A dealer in stocks or securities as defined in § 1.864-2(c)(2)(iv)(a);

(ii) A dealer in commodities as that term is used in § 1.864-2(d); or

(iii) A person that regularly offers to enter into, assume, offset, assign or otherwise terminate positions in derivatives with customers in the ordinary course of a trade or business, including regularly holding oneself out, in the ordinary course of one's trade or business, as being willing and able to enter into either side of a derivative transaction.

(2) Derivative. For purposes of this section, the term *derivative* includes—

(i) An interest rate, currency (as defined in paragraph (b)(3) of this section), equity, or commodity (as the term is used in section 864(b)(2)(B) and § 1.864-2(d)) notional principal contract (as the term is used in section 475(c)(2)); or

(ii) An evidence of an interest, or a derivative financial instrument (including any option, forward contract, short position and any similar financial instrument), in any—

(A) Commodity (as the term is used in section 864(b)(2)(B) and § 1.864-2(d));

(B) Currency (as defined in paragraph (b)(3) of this section);

(C) Share of stock (as the term is used in § 1.864-2(c)(2));

(D) Partnership or beneficial ownership interest in a widely held or publicly traded partnership or trust;

(E) Note, bond, debenture, or other evidence of indebtedness; or

(F) Notional principal contract described in paragraph (b)(2)(i) of this section.

(3) Limitation. For purposes of this section, the term *currency* is limited to currencies of a kind customarily dealt in on an organized commodity exchange.

§ 1.865-1 Loss with respect to personal property other than stock.

(a) General rules for allocation of loss. *(1) Allocation against gain.* Except as otherwise provided in § 1.865-2 and paragraph (c) of this section, loss recognized with respect to personal property shall be allocated to the class of gross income and, if necessary, apportioned between the statutory grouping of gross income (or among the statutory groupings) and the residual grouping of gross income, with respect to which gain from a sale of such property would give rise in the hands of the seller. For purposes of this section, loss includes bad debt deductions under section 166 and loss on property that is marked-to-market (such as under section 475) and subject to the rules of this section. Thus, for example, loss recognized by a United States resident on the sale or worthlessness of a bond generally is allocated to reduce United States source income.

(2) Loss attributable to foreign office. Except as otherwise provided in § 1.865-2 and paragraph (c) of this section, and except with respect to loss subject to paragraph (b) of this section, in the case of loss recognized by a United States resident with respect to property that is attributable to an office or other fixed place of business in a foreign country within the meaning of section 865(e)(3), the loss shall be allocated to reduce foreign source income if a gain on the sale of the property would have been taxable by the foreign country and the highest marginal rate of tax imposed on such gains in the foreign country is at least 10 percent. However, paragraph (a)(1) of this section and not this paragraph (a)(2) will apply if gain on the sale of such property would be sourced under section 865(c), (d)(1)(B), or (d)(3).

(3) Loss recognized by United States citizen or resident alien with foreign tax home. Except as otherwise provided in § 1.865-2 and paragraph (c) of this section, and except with respect to loss subject to paragraph (b) of this section, in the case of loss with respect to property recognized by a United States citizen or resident alien that has a tax home (as defined in section 911(d)(3)) in a foreign country, the loss shall be allocated to reduce foreign source income if a gain on the sale of such property would have been taxable by a foreign country and the highest marginal rate of tax imposed on such gains in the foreign country is at least 10 percent.

(4) Allocation for purposes of section 904. For purposes of section 904, loss recognized with respect to property that is allocated to foreign source income under this paragraph (a) shall be allocated to the separate category under section 904(d) to which gain on the sale of the property would have been assigned (without regard to section 904(d)(2)(A)(iii)(III)). For purposes of § 1.904-4(c)(2)(ii)(A), any such loss allocated to passive income shall be allocated (prior to the application of § 1.904-4(c)(2)(ii)(B)) to the group of passive income to which gain on a sale of the property would have been assigned had a sale of the property resulted in the recognition of a gain under the law of the relevant foreign jurisdiction or jurisdictions.

(5) Loss recognized by partnership. A partner's distributive share of loss recognized by a partnership with respect to personal property shall be allocated and apportioned in accordance with this section as if the partner had recognized the loss. If loss is attributable to an office or other fixed place of business of the partnership within the meaning of section 865(e)(3), such office or fixed place of business shall be considered to be an office of the partner for purposes of this section.

(b) Special rules of application. *(1) Depreciable property.* In the case of a loss recognized with respect to depreciable personal property, the gain referred to in paragraph (a)(1) of this section is the gain that would be sourced under section 865(c)(1) (depreciation recapture).

(2) Contingent payment debt instrument. Loss described in the last sentence of § 1.1275-4(b)(9)(iv)(A) that is recognized with respect to a contingent payment debt instrument to which § 1.1275-4(b) applies (instruments issued for money or publicly traded property) shall be allocated to the class of gross income and, if necessary, apportioned between the statutory grouping of gross income (or among the statutory groupings) and the residual grouping of gross income, with respect to which interest income from the instrument (in the amount of the loss subject to this paragraph (b)(2)) would give rise.

(c) Exceptions. *(1) Foreign currency and certain financial instruments.* This section does not apply to loss governed by section 988 and loss recognized with respect to options contracts or derivative financial instruments, including futures contracts, forward contracts, notional principal contracts, or evidence of an interest in any of the foregoing.

(2) Inventory. This section does not apply to loss recognized with respect to property described in section 1221(a)(1).

(3) Interest equivalents and trade receivables. Loss subject to § 1.861-9T(b) (loss equivalent to interest expense and loss on trade receivables) shall be allocated and apportioned under the rules of § 1.861-9T and not under the rules of this section.

(4) Unamortized bond premium. If a taxpayer recognizing loss with respect to a bond (within the meaning of § 1.171-1(b)) did not amortize bond premium to the full extent permitted by section 171 and the regulations thereunder, then, to the extent of the amount of bond premium that could have been, but was not, amortized by the taxpayer, loss recognized with respect to the bond shall be allocated to the class of gross income and, if necessary, apportioned between the statutory grouping of gross income (or among the statutory groupings) and the residual grouping of gross income, with respect to which interest income from the bond was assigned.

(5) Accrued interest. Loss attributable to accrued but unpaid interest on a debt obligation shall be allocated to the class of gross income and, if necessary, apportioned between the statutory grouping of gross income (or among the statutory groupings) and the residual grouping of gross income, with respect to which interest income from the obligation was assigned. For purposes of this section, whether loss is attributable to accrued but unpaid interest (rather than to principal) shall be determined under the principles of §§ 1.61-7(d) and 1.446-2(e).

(6) Anti-abuse rules. (i) Transactions involving built-in losses. If one of the principal purposes of a transaction is to change the allocation of a built-in loss with respect to personal property by transferring the property to another person, qualified business unit, office or other fixed place of business, or branch that subsequently recognizes the loss, the loss shall be allocated by the transferee as if it were recognized by the transferor immediately prior to the transaction. If one of the principal purposes of a change of residence is to change the allocation of a built-in loss with respect to personal property, the loss shall be allocated as if the change of residence had not occurred. If one of the principal purposes of a transaction is to change the allocation of a built-in loss on the disposition of personal property by converting the original property into other property and subsequently recognizing loss with respect to such other property, the loss shall be allocated as if it were recognized with respect to the original property immediately prior to the transaction. Transactions subject to this paragraph shall include, without limitation, reorganizations within the meaning of section 368(a), liquidations under section 332, transfers to a corporation under section 351, transfers to a partnership under section 721, transfers to a trust, distributions by a partnership, distributions by a trust, transfers to or from a qualified business unit, office or other fixed place of business, or branch, or exchanges under section 1031. A person may have a principal purpose of affecting loss allocation even though this purpose is outweighed by other purposes (taken together or separately).

(ii) Offsetting positions. If a taxpayer recognizes loss with respect to personal property and the taxpayer (or any person described in section 267(b) (after application of section 267(c)), 267(e), 318 or 482 with respect to the taxpayer) holds (or held) offsetting positions with respect to such property with a principal purpose of recognizing foreign source income and United States source loss, the loss shall be allocated and apportioned against such foreign source income. For purposes of this paragraph (c)(6)(ii), positions are offsetting if the risk of loss of holding one or more positions is substantially diminished by holding one or more other positions.

(iii) Matching rule. If a taxpayer (or a person described in section 1059(c)(3)(C) with respect to the taxpayer) engages in a transaction or series of transactions with a principal purpose of recognizing foreign source income that results in the creation of a corresponding loss with respect to personal property (as a consequence of the rules regarding the timing of recognition of income, for example), the loss shall be allocated and apportioned against such income to the extent of the recognized foreign source income. For an example illustrating a similar rule with respect to stock loss, see § 1.865-2(b)(4)(iv) Example 3.

(d) Definitions. *(1) Contingent payment debt instrument.* A contingent payment debt instrument is any debt instrument that is subject to § 1.1275-4.

(2) Depreciable personal property. Depreciable personal property is any property described in section 865(c)(4)(A).

(3) Terms defined in § 1.861-8. See § 1.861-8 for the meaning of class of gross income, statutory grouping of gross income, and residual grouping of gross income.

(e) Examples. The application of this section may be illustrated by the following examples:

Example (1). On January 1, 2000, A, a domestic corporation, purchases for $1,000 a machine that produces widgets, which A sells in the United States and throughout the world. Throughout A's holding period, the machine is located and used in Country X. During A's holding period, A incurs depreciation deductions of $400 with respect to the machine. Under § 1.861-8, A allocates and apportions depreciation deductions of $250 against foreign source general limitation income and $150 against U.S. source income. On December 12, 2002, A sells the machine for $100 and recognizes a loss of $500. Because the machine was used predominantly outside the United States, under sections 865(c)(1)(B) and 865(c)(3)(B)(ii) gain on the disposition of the machine would be foreign source general limitation income to the extent of the depreciation adjustments. Therefore, under paragraph (b)(1) of this section, the entire $500 loss is allocated against foreign source general limitation income.

Example (2). On January 1, 2002, A, a domestic corporation, loans $2,000 to N, its wholly-owned controlled foreign corporation, in exchange for a contingent payment debt instrument subject to § 1.1275-4(b). During 2002 through 2004, A accrues and receives interest income of $630, $150 of which is foreign source general limitation income and $480 of which is foreign source passive income under section 904(d)(3). Assume there are no positive or negative adjustments pursuant to § 1.1275-4(b)(6) in 2002 through 2004. On January 1, 2005, A disposes of the debt instrument and recognizes a $770 loss. Under § 1.1275-4(b)(8)(ii), $630 of the loss is treated as ordinary loss and $140 is treated as capital loss. Assume that $140 of interest income earned in 2005 with respect to the debt instrument would be foreign source passive income under section 904(d)(3). Under § 1.1275-4(b)(9)(iv), $150 of the ordinary loss is allocated against foreign source general limitation income and $480 of the ordinary loss is allocated against foreign source passive income. Under paragraph (b)(2) of this section, the $140 capital loss is allocated against foreign source passive income.

Example (3). (i) On January 1, 2003, A, a domestic corporation, purchases for $1,200 a taxable bond maturing on December 31, 2008, with a stated principal amount of $1,000, payable at maturity. The bond provides for unconditional payments of interest of $100, payable December 31 of each year. The issuer of the bond is a foreign corporation and interest on the bond is thus foreign source. Interest payments for 2003 and 2004 are timely made. A does not elect to amortize its bond premium under section 171 and the regulations thereunder, which would have permitted A to offset the $100 of interest income by $28.72 of bond premium in 2003, and by $30.42 in 2004. On January 1, 2005, A sells the bond and recognizes a $100 loss. Under paragraph (c)(4) of this section, $59.14 of the loss is allocated against foreign source income. Under paragraph (a)(1) of this section, the remaining $40.86 of the loss is allocated against U.S. source income.

(ii) The facts are the same as in paragraph (i) of this Example 3, except that A made the election to amortize its bond premium effective for taxable year 2004 (see § 1.171-4(c)). Under paragraph (c)(4) of this section, $28.72 of the loss is allocated against foreign source income. Under paragraph (a)(1) of this section, the remaining $71.28 of the loss is allocated against U.S. source income.

Example (4). On January 1, 2002, A, a domestic corporation, purchases for $1,000 a bond maturing December 31, 2014, with a stated principal amount of $1,000, payable at maturity. The bond provides for unconditional payments of interest of $100, payable December 31 of each year. The issuer of the bond is a foreign corporation and interest on the bond is thus foreign source. Between 2002 and 2006, A accrues and receives foreign source interest income of $500 with respect to the bond. On January 1, 2007, A sells the bond and recognizes a $500 loss. Under paragraph (a)(1) of this section, the $500 loss is allocated against U.S. source income.

Example (5). On January 1, 2002, A, a domestic corporation on the accrual method of accounting, purchases for $1,000 a bond maturing December 31, 2012, with a stated principal amount of $1,000, payable at maturity. The bond provides for unconditional payments of interest of $100, payable December 31 of each year. The issuer of the bond is a foreign corporation and interest on the bond is thus foreign source. On June 10, 2002, after A has accrued $44 of interest income, but before any interest has been paid, the issuer suddenly becomes insolvent and declares bankruptcy. A sells the bond (including the accrued interest) for $20. Assuming that A properly accrued $44 of interest income, A treats the $20 proceeds from the sale of the bond as payment of interest previously accrued and recognizes a $1,000 loss with respect to the bond principal and a $24 loss with respect to the accrued interest. See § 1.61-7(d). Under paragraph (a)(1) of this section, the $1,000 loss with respect to the principal is allocated against U.S. source income. Under paragraph (c)(5) of this section, the $24 loss with respect to accrued but unpaid interest is allocated against foreign source interest income.

(f) Effective date. *(1) In general.* Except as provided in paragraph (f)(2) of this section, this section is applicable to loss recognized on or after January 8, 2002. For purposes of this paragraph (f), loss that is recognized but deferred (for example, under section 267 or 1092) shall be treated as recognized at the time the loss is taken into account.

(2) Application to prior periods. A taxpayer may apply the rules of this section to losses recognized in any taxable year beginning on or after January 1, 1987, and all subsequent years, provided that—

(i) The taxpayer's tax liability as shown on an original or amended tax return is consistent with the rules of this section for each such year for which the statute of limitations does not preclude the filing of an amended return on June 30, 2002; and

(ii) The taxpayer makes appropriate adjustments to eliminate any double benefit arising from the application of this section to years that are not open for assessment.

(3) Examples. See § 1.865-2(e)(3) for examples illustrating an applicability date provision similar to the applicability date provided in this paragraph (f).

T.D. 8973, 12/27/2001.

§ 1.865-2 Loss with respect to stock.

(a) General rules for allocation of loss with respect to stock. *(1) Allocation against gain.* Except as otherwise provided in paragraph (b) of this section, loss recognized with respect to stock shall be allocated to the class of gross income and, if necessary, apportioned between the statutory grouping of gross income (or among the statutory groupings) and the residual grouping of gross income, with respect to which gain (other than gain treated as a dividend under section 964(e)(1) or 1248) from a sale of such stock would give rise in the hands of the seller (without regard to section 865(f)). For purposes of this section, loss includes loss on property that is marked-to-market (such as under section 475) and subject to the rules of this section. Thus, for example, loss recognized by a United States resident on the sale of stock generally is allocated to reduce United States source income.

(2) Stock attributable to foreign office. Except as otherwise provided in paragraph (b) of this section, in the case of loss recognized by a United States resident with respect to stock that is attributable to an office or other fixed place of business in a foreign country within the meaning of section 865(e)(3), the loss shall be allocated to reduce foreign source income if a gain on the sale of the stock would have been taxable by the foreign country and the highest marginal rate of tax imposed on such gains in the foreign country is at least 10 percent.

(3) Loss recognized by United States citizen or resident alien with foreign tax home. (i) In general. Except as otherwise provided in paragraph (b) of this section, in the case of loss with respect to stock that is recognized by a United States citizen or resident alien that has a tax home (as defined in section 911(d)(3)) in a foreign country, the loss shall be allocated to reduce foreign source income if a gain on the sale of the stock would have been taxable by a foreign country and the highest marginal rate of tax imposed on such gains in the foreign country is at least 10 percent.

(ii) Bona fide residents of Puerto Rico. Except as otherwise provided in paragraph (b) of this section, in the case of loss with respect to stock in a corporation described in section 865(g)(3) recognized by a United States citizen or resident alien that is a bona fide resident of Puerto Rico during the entire taxable year, the loss shall be allocated to reduce foreign source income. If gain from a sale of such stock would give rise to income exempt from tax under section 933, the loss with respect to such stock shall be allocated to amounts that are excluded from gross income under section 933(1) and therefore shall not be allowed as a deduction from gross income. See section 933(1) and § 1.933-1(c).

(4) Stock constituting a United States real property interest. Loss recognized by a nonresident alien individual or a foreign corporation with respect to stock that constitutes a United States real property interest shall be allocated to reduce United States source income. For additional rules governing the treatment of such loss, see section 897 and the regulations thereunder.

(5) Allocation for purposes of section 904. For purposes of section 904, loss recognized with respect to stock that is allocated to foreign source income under this paragraph (a) shall be allocated to the separate category under section 904(d) to which gain on a sale of the stock would have been assigned (without regard to section 904(d)(2)(A)(iii)(III)). For purposes of § 1.904-4(c)(2)(ii)(A), any such loss allocated to passive income shall be allocated (prior to the application of § 1.904-4(c)(2)(ii)(B)) to the group of passive income to which gain on a sale of the stock would have been assigned had a sale of the stock resulted in the recognition of a gain under the law of the relevant foreign jurisdiction or jurisdictions.

(b) Exceptions. *(1) Dividend recapture exception.* (i) In general. If a taxpayer recognizes a loss with respect to shares of stock, and the taxpayer (or a person described in section 1059(c)(3)(C) with respect to such shares) included in income a dividend recapture amount (or amounts) with respect to such shares at any time during the recapture period, then, to the extent of the dividend recapture amount (or amounts), the loss shall be allocated and apportioned on a proportionate basis to the class or classes of gross income or the statutory or residual grouping or groupings of gross income to which the dividend recapture amount was assigned.

(ii) Exception for de minimis amounts. Paragraph (b)(1)(i) of this section shall not apply to a loss recognized by a taxpayer on the disposition of stock if the sum of all dividend recapture amounts (other than dividend recapture amounts eligible for the exception described in paragraph (b)(1)(iii) of this section (passive limitation dividends)) included in income by the taxpayer (or a person described in section 1059(c)(3)(C)) with respect to such stock during the recapture period is less than 10 percent of the recognized loss.

(iii) Exception for passive limitation dividends. Paragraph (b)(1)(i) of this section shall not apply to the extent of a dividend recapture amount that is treated as income in the separate category for passive income described in section 904(d)(2)(A) (without regard to section 904(d)(2)(A)(iii)(III)). The exception provided for in this paragraph (b)(1)(iii) shall not apply to any dividend recapture amount that is treated as income in the separate category for financial services income described in section 904(d)(2)(C).

(iv) Examples. The application of this paragraph (b)(1) may be illustrated by the following examples:

Example (1). (i) P, a domestic corporation, is a United States shareholder of N, a controlled foreign corporation. N has never had any subpart F income and all of its earnings and profits are described in section 959(c)(3). On May 5, 1998, N distributes a dividend to P in the amount of $100. The dividend gives rise to a $5 foreign withholding tax, and P is deemed to have paid an additional $45 of foreign income tax with respect to the dividend under section 902. Under the look-through rules of section 904(d)(3) the dividend is general limitation income described in section 904(d)(1)(I).

(ii) On February 6, 2000, P sells its shares of N and recognizes a $110 loss. In 2000, P has the following taxable income, excluding the loss on the sale of N:

(A) $1,000 of foreign source income that is general limitation income described in section 904(d)(1)(I);

(B) $1,000 of foreign source capital gain from the sale of stock in a foreign affiliate that is sourced under section 865(f) and is passive income described in section 904(d)(1)(A); and

(C) $1,000 of U.S. source income.

(iii) The $100 dividend paid in 1998 is a dividend recapture amount that was included in P's income within the recapture period preceding the disposition of the N stock. The de minimis exception of paragraph (b)(1)(ii) of this section does not apply because the $100 dividend recapture amount exceeds 10 percent of the $110 loss. Therefore, to the extent of the $100 dividend recapture amount, the loss must be allocated under paragraph (b)(1)(i) of this section to the separate limitation category to which the dividend was assigned (general limitation income).

(iv) P's remaining $10 loss on the disposition of the N stock is allocated to U.S. source income under paragraph (a)(1) of this section.

(v) After allocation of the stock loss, P's foreign source taxable income in 2000 consists of $900 of foreign source general limitation income and $1,000 of foreign source passive income.

Example (2). (i) P, a domestic corporation, owns all of the stock of N1, which owns all of the stock of N2, which owns all of the stock of N3. N1, N2, and N3 are controlled foreign corporations. All of the corporations use the calendar year as their taxable year. On February 5, 1997, N3 distributes a dividend to N2. The dividend is foreign personal holding company income of N2 under section 954(c)(1)(A) that results in an inclusion of $100 in P's income under section 951(a)(1)(A)(i) as of December 31, 1997. Under section 904(d)(3)(B) the inclusion is general limitation income described in section 904(d)(1)(I). The income inclusion to P results in a corresponding increase in P's basis in the stock of N1 under section 961(a).

(ii) On March 5, 1999, P sells its shares of N1 and recognizes a $110 loss. The $100 1997 subpart F inclusion is a dividend recapture amount that was included in P's income within the recapture period preceding the disposition of the N1 stock. The de minimis exception of paragraph (b)(1)(ii) of this section does not apply because the $100 dividend recapture amount exceeds 10 percent of the $110 loss. Therefore, to the extent of the $100 dividend recapture amount, the loss must be allocated under paragraph (b)(1)(i) of this section to the separate limitation category to which the dividend recapture amount was assigned (general limitation income). The remaining $10 loss is allocated to U.S. source income under paragraph (a)(1) of this section.

Example (3). (i) P, a domestic corporation, owns all of the stock of N1, which owns all of the stock of N2. N1 and N2 are controlled foreign corporations. All the corporations use the calendar year as their taxable year and the U.S. dollar as their functional currency. On May 5, 1998, N2 pays a dividend of $100 to N1 out of general limitation earnings and profits.

(ii) On February 5, 2000, N1 sells its N2 stock to an unrelated purchaser. The sale results in a loss to N1 of $110 for U.S. tax purposes. In 2000, N1 has the following current earnings and profits, excluding the loss on the sale of N2:

(A) $1,000 of non-subpart F foreign source general limitation earnings and profits described in section 904(d)(1)(I);

(B) $1,000 of foreign source gain from the sale of stock that is taken into account in determining foreign personal holding company income under section 954(c)(1)(B)(i) and which is passive limitation earnings and profits described in section 904(d)(1)(A);

(C) $1,000 of foreign source interest income received from an unrelated person that is foreign personal holding company income under section 954(c)(1)(A) and which is passive limitation earnings and profits described in section 904(d)(1)(A).

(iii) The $100 dividend paid in 1998 is a dividend recapture amount that was included in N1's income within the recapture period preceding the disposition of the N2 stock. The de minimis exception of paragraph (b)(1)(ii) of this section does not apply because the $100 dividend recapture amount exceeds 10 percent of the $110 loss. Therefore, to the extent of the $100 dividend recapture amount, the loss must be allocated under paragraph (b)(1)(i) of this section to the separate limitation category to which the dividend was assigned (general limitation earnings and profits).

(iv) N1's remaining $10 loss on the disposition of the N2 stock is allocated to foreign source passive limitation earnings and profits under paragraph (a)(1) of this section.

(v) After allocation of the stock loss, N1's current earnings and profits for 1998 consist of $900 of foreign source general limitation earnings and profits and $1,990 of foreign source passive limitation earnings and profits.

(vi) After allocation of the stock loss, N1's subpart F income for 2000 consists of $1,000 of foreign source interest income that is foreign personal holding company income under section 954(c)(1)(A) and $890 of foreign source net gain that is foreign personal holding company income under section 954(c)(1)(B)(i). P includes $1,890 in income under section 951(a)(1)(A)(i) as passive income under sections 904(d)(1)(A) and 904(d)(3)(B).

Example (4). P, a foreign corporation, has two wholly-owned subsidiaries, S, a domestic corporation, and B, a foreign corporation. On January 1, 2000, S purchases a one-percent interest in N, a foreign corporation, for $100. On January 2, 2000, N distributes a $20 dividend to S. The $20 dividend is foreign source financial services income. On January 3, 2000, S sells its N stock to B for $80 and recognizes a $20 loss that is deferred under section 267(f). On June 10, 2008, B sells its N stock to an unrelated person for $55. Under section 267(f) and § 1.267(f)-1(c)(1), S's $20 loss is deferred until 2008. Under this paragraph (b)(1), the $20 loss is allocated to reduce foreign source financial services income in 2008 because the loss was recognized (albeit deferred) within the 24-month recapture period following the receipt of the dividend. See §§ 1.267(f)-1(a)(2)(i)(B) and 1.267(f)-1(c)(2).

Example (5). The facts are the same as in Example 4, except P, S, and B are domestic corporations and members of the P consolidated group. Under the matching rule of § 1.1502-13(c)(1), the separate entity attributes of S's intercompany items and B's corresponding items are redetermined to the extent necessary to produce the same effect on consolidated taxable income as if S and B were divisions of a single corporation and the intercompany transaction was a transaction between divisions. If S and B were divisions of a single corporation, the transfer of N stock on January 3, 2000 would be ignored for tax purposes, and the corporation would be treated as selling that stock only in 2008. Thus, the corporation's entire $45 loss would have been allocated against U.S. source income under paragraph (a)(1) of this section because a dividend recapture amount was not received during the corporation's recapture period. Accordingly, S's $20 loss and B's $25 loss are allocated to reduce U.S. source income.

Example (6). (i) On January 1, 1998, P, a domestic corporation, purchases N, a foreign corporation, for $1,000. On March 1, 1998, P causes N to sell its operating assets, distribute a $400 general limitation dividend to P, and invest its remaining $600 in short-term government securities. P converted the N assets into low-risk investments with a principal purpose of holding the N stock without significant risk of loss until the recapture period expired. N earns interest income from the securities. The income constitutes subpart F income that is included in P's income under section 951, increasing P's basis in the N stock under section 961(a). On March 1, 2002, P sells N and recognizes a $400 loss.

(ii) Pursuant to paragraph (d)(3) of this section, the recapture period is increased by the period in which N's assets were held as low-risk investments because P caused N's assets to be converted into and held as low-risk investments with a principal purpose of enabling P to hold the N stock without significant risk of loss. Accordingly, under paragraph (b)(1)(i) of this section the $400 loss is allocated against foreign source general limitation income.

(2) Exception for inventory. This section does not apply to loss recognized with respect to stock described in section 1221(1).

(3) Exception for stock in an S corporation. This section does not apply to loss recognized with respect to stock in an S corporation (as defined in section 1361).

(4) Anti-abuse rules. (i) Transactions involving built-in losses. If one of the principal purposes of a transaction is to change the allocation of a built-in loss with respect to stock by transferring the stock to another person, qualified business unit (within the meaning of section 989(a)), office or other fixed place of business, or branch that subsequently recognizes the loss, the loss shall be allocated by the transferee as if it were recognized with respect to the stock by the transferor immediately prior to the transaction. If one of the principal purposes of a change of residence is to change the allocation of a built-in loss with respect to stock, the loss shall be allocated as if the change of residence had not occurred. If one of the principal purposes of a transaction is to change the allocation of a built-in loss with respect to stock (or other personal property) by converting the original property into other property and subsequently recognizing loss with respect to such other property, the loss shall be allocated as if it were recognized with respect to the original property immediately prior to the transaction. Transactions subject to this paragraph shall include, without limitation, reorganizations within the meaning of section 368(a), liquidations under section 332, transfers to a corporation under section 351, transfers to a partnership under section 721, transfers to a trust, distributions by a partnership, distributions by a trust, or transfers to or from a qualified business unit, office or other fixed place of business. A person may have a principal purpose of affecting loss allocation even though this purpose is outweighed by other purposes (taken together or separately).

(ii) Offsetting positions. If a taxpayer recognizes loss with respect to stock and the taxpayer (or any person described in section 267(b) (after application of section 267(c)), 267(e), 318 or 482 with respect to the taxpayer) holds (or held) offsetting positions with respect to such stock with a principal purpose of recognizing foreign source income and United States source loss, the loss will be allocated and apportioned against such foreign source income. For purposes of this paragraph (b)(4)(ii), positions are offsetting if the risk of loss of holding one or more positions is substantially diminished by holding one or more other positions.

(iii) Matching rule. If a taxpayer (or a person described in section 1059(c)(3)(C) with respect to the taxpayer) engages in a transaction or series of transactions with a principal purpose of recognizing foreign source income that results in the creation of a corresponding loss with respect to stock (as a consequence of the rules regarding the timing of recognition of income, for example), the loss shall be allocated and apportioned against such income to the extent of the recognized foreign source income. This paragraph (b)(4)(iii) applies to any portion of a loss that is not allocated under paragraph (b)(1)(i) of this section (dividend recapture rule), including a loss in excess of the dividend recapture amount and a loss that is related to a dividend recapture amount described in paragraph (b)(1)(ii) (de minimis exception) or (b)(1)(iii) (passive dividend exception) of this section.

(iv) Examples. The application of this paragraph (b)(4) may be illustrated by the following examples. No inference is intended regarding the application of any other Internal Revenue Code section or judicial doctrine that may apply to disallow or defer the recognition of loss. The examples are as follows:

Example (1). (i) Facts. On January 1, 2000, P, a domestic corporation, owns all of the stock of N1, a controlled foreign corporation, which owns all of the stock of N2, a controlled foreign corporation. N1's basis in the stock of N2 exceeds its fair market value, and any loss recognized by N1 on the sale of N2 would be allocated under paragraph (a)(1) of this section to reduce foreign source passive limitation earnings and profits of N1. In contemplation of the sale of N2 to an unrelated purchaser, P causes N1 to liquidate with principal purposes of recognizing the loss on the N2 stock and allocating the loss against U.S. source income. P sells the N2 stock and P recognizes a loss.

(ii) Loss allocation. Because one of the principal purposes of the liquidation was to transfer the stock to P in order to change the allocation of the built-in loss on the N2 stock, under paragraph (b)(4)(i) of this section the loss is allocated against P's foreign source passive limitation income.

Example (2). (i) Facts. On January 1, 2000, P, a domestic corporation, forms N and F, foreign corporations, and contributes $1,000 to the capital of each. N and F enter into offsetting positions in financial instruments that produce financial services income. Holding the N stock substantially diminishes P's risk of loss with respect to the F stock (and vice versa). P holds N and F with a principal purpose of recognizing foreign source income and U.S. source loss. On March 31, 2000, when the financial instrument held by N is worth $1,200 and the financial instrument held by F is worth $800, P sells its F stock and recognizes a $200 loss.

(ii) Loss allocation. Because P held an offsetting position with respect to the F stock with a principal purpose of recognizing foreign source income and U.S. source loss, the $200 loss is allocated against foreign source financial services income under paragraph (b)(4)(ii) of this section.

Example (3). (i) Facts. On January 1, 2002, P and Q, domestic corporations, form R, a domestic partnership. The corporations and partnership use the calendar year as their taxable year. P contributes $900 to R in exchange for a 90-percent partnership interest and Q contributes $100 to R in exchange for a 10-percent partnership interest. R purchases a dance studio in country X for $1,000. On January 2, 2002, R enters into contracts to provide dance lessons in Country X for a 5-year period beginning January 1, 2003. These contracts are prepaid by the dance studio customers on December 31, 2002, and R recognizes foreign source taxable income of $500 from the prepayments (R's only income in 2002). P takes into income its $450 distributive share of partnership taxable income. On January 1, 2003, P's basis in its partnership interest is $1,350 ($900 from its contribution under section 722, increased by its $450 distributive share of partnership income under section 705). On September 22, 2003, P contributes its R partnership interest to S, a newly-formed domestic corporation, in exchange for all the stock of S. Under section 358, P's basis in S is $1,350. On December 1, 2003, P sells S to an unrelated party for $1050 and recognizes a $300 loss.

(ii) Loss allocation. P recognized foreign source income for tax purposes before the income had economically accrued, and the accelerated recognition of income increased P's basis in R without increasing its value by a corresponding amount, which resulted in the creation of a built-in loss with respect to the S stock. Under paragraph (b)(4)(iii) of this section the $300 loss is allocated against foreign source income if P had a principal purpose of recognizing foreign source income and corresponding loss.

(c) Loss recognized by partnership. A partner's distributive share of loss recognized by a partnership shall be allocated and apportioned in accordance with this section as if the partner had recognized the loss. If loss is attributable to an office or other fixed place of business of the partnership within the meaning of section 865(e)(3), such office or fixed place of business shall be considered to be an office of the partner for purposes of this section.

(d) Definitions. *(1) Terms defined in § 1.861-8.* See § 1.861-8 for the meaning of *class of gross income, statutory grouping of gross income,* and *residual grouping of gross income.*

(2) Dividend recapture amount. A dividend recapture amount is a dividend (except for an amount treated as a dividend under section 78), an inclusion described in section 951(a)(1)(A)(i) (but only to the extent attributable to a dividend (including a dividend under section 964(e)(1)) included in the earnings of a controlled foreign corporation (held directly or indirectly by the person recognizing the loss) that is included in foreign personal holding company income under section 954(c)(1)(A)) and an inclusion described in section 951(a)(1)(B).

(3) Recapture period. A recapture period is the 24-month period ending on the date on which a taxpayer recognized a loss with respect to stock. For example, if a taxpayer recognizes a loss on March 15, 2002, the recapture period begins on and includes March 16, 2000, and ends on and includes March 15, 2002. A recapture period is increased by any period of time in which the taxpayer has diminished its risk of loss in a manner described in section 246(c)(4) and the regulations thereunder and by any period in which the assets of the corporation are hedged against risk of loss (or are converted into and held as low-risk investments) with a principal purpose of enabling the taxpayer to hold the stock without significant risk of loss until the recapture period has expired. In the case of a loss recognized after a dividend is declared but before such dividend is paid, the recapture period is extended through the date on which the dividend is paid.

(4) United States resident. See section 865(g) and the regulations thereunder for the definition of United States resident.

(e) Effective date. *(1) In general.* This section is applicable to loss recognized on or after January 11, 1999, except that paragraphs (a)(3)(ii), (b)(1)(iv) Example 6, (b)(4)(iii), (b)(4)(iv) Example 3, and (d)(3) of this section are applicable to loss recognized on or after January 8, 2002. For purposes of this paragraph (e), loss that is recognized but deferred (for example, under section 267 or 1092) shall be treated as recognized at the time the loss is taken into account.

(2) Application to prior periods. A taxpayer may apply the rules of this section to losses recognized in any taxable year beginning on or after January 1, 1987, and all subsequent years, provided that—

(i) The taxpayer's tax liability as shown on an original or amended tax return is consistent with the rules of this section for each such year for which the statute of limitations does not preclude the filing of an amended return on June 30, 2002; and

(ii) The taxpayer makes appropriate adjustments to eliminate any double benefit arising from the application of this section to years that are not open for assessment.

(3) Examples. The rules of this paragraph (e) may be illustrated by the following examples:

Example (1). (i) P, a domestic corporation, has a calendar taxable year. On March 10, 1985, P recognizes a $100 capital loss on the sale of N, a foreign corporation. Pursuant to sections 1211(a) and 1212(a), the loss is not allowed in 1985 and is carried over to the 1990 taxable year. The loss is allocated against foreign source income under § 1.861-8(e)(7). In 1999, P chooses to apply this section to all losses recognized in its 1987 taxable year and in all subsequent years.

(ii) Allocation of the loss on the sale of N is not affected by the rules of this section because the loss was recognized in a taxable year that did not begin after December 31, 1986.

Example (2). (i) P, a domestic corporation, has a calendar taxable year. On March 10, 1988, P recognizes a $100 capital loss on the sale of N, a foreign corporation. Pursuant to sections 1211(a) and 1212(a), the loss is not allowed in 1988 and is carried back to the 1985 taxable year. The loss is allocated against foreign source income under § 1.861-8(e)(7) on P's federal income tax return for 1985 and increases an overall foreign loss account under sect;1.904(f)-1.

(ii) In 1999, P chooses to apply this section to all losses recognized in its 1987 taxable year and in all subsequent years. Consequently, the loss on the sale of N is allocated against U.S. source income under paragraph (a)(1) of this section. Allocation of the loss against U.S. source income reduces P's overall foreign loss account and increases P's tax liability in 2 years: 1990, a year that will not be open for assessment on June 30, 1999, and 1997, a year that will be open for assessment on June 30, 1999. Pursuant to paragraph (e)(2)(i) of this section, P must file an amended federal income tax return that reflects the rules of this section for 1997, but not for 1990.

Example (3). (i) P, a domestic corporation, has a calendar taxable year. On March 10, 1989, P recognizes a $100 capital loss on the sale of N, a foreign corporation. The loss is allocated against foreign source income under § 1.861-8(e)(7) on P's federal income tax return for 1989 and results in excess foreign tax credits for that year. The excess credit is carried back to 1988, pursuant to section 904(c). In 1999, P chooses to apply this section to all losses recognized in its 1989 taxable year and in all subsequent years. On June 30, 1999, P's 1988 taxable year is closed for assessment, but P's 1989 taxable year is open with respect to claims for refund.

(ii) Because P chooses to apply this section to its 1989 taxable year, the loss on the sale of N is allocated against U.S. source income under paragraph (a)(1) of this section. Allocation of the loss against U.S. source income would have permitted the foreign tax credit to be used in 1989, reducing P's tax liability in 1989. Nevertheless, under paragraph (e)(2)(ii) of this section, because the credit was carried back to 1988, P may not claim the foreign tax credit in 1989.

T.D. 8805, 1/8/99, amend T.D. 8973, 12/27/2001.

§ 1.871-1 Classification and manner of taxing alien individuals.

(a) Classes of aliens. For purposes of the income tax, alien individuals are divided generally into two classes, namely, resident aliens and nonresident aliens. Resident alien individuals are, in general, taxable the same as citizens of the United States; that is, a resident alien is taxable on income derived from all sources, including sources without the United States. See § 1.1-1(b). Nonresident alien individuals are taxable only on certain income from sources within the

United States and on the income described in section 864(c)(4) from sources without the United States which is effectively connected for the taxable year with the conduct of a trade or business in the United States. However, nonresident alien individuals may elect, under section 6013(g) or (h), to be treated as U.S. residents for purposes of determining their income tax liability under chapters 1, 5, and 24 of the Code. Accordingly, any reference in §§ 1.1-1 through 1.1388-1 and §§ 1.1491-1 through 1.1494-1 of this part to nonresident alien individuals does not include those with respect to whom an election under section 6013(g) or (h) is in effect, unless otherwise specifically provided. Similarly, any reference to resident aliens or U.S. residents includes those with respect to whom an election is in effect, unless otherwise specifically provided.

(b) Classes of nonresident aliens. *(1) In general.* For purposes of the income tax, nonresident alien individuals are divided into the following three classes:

(i) Nonresident alien individuals who at no time during the taxable year are engaged in a trade or business in the United States,

(ii) Nonresident alien individuals who at any time during the taxable year are, or are deemed under § 1.871-9 to be, engaged in a trade or business in the United States, and

(iii) Nonresident alien individuals who are bona fide residents of Puerto Rico during the entire taxable year.

An individual described in subdivision (i) or (ii) of this subparagraph is subject to tax pursuant to the provisions of subpart A (section 871 and following), part II, subchapter N, chapter 1 of the Code, and the regulations thereunder. See §§ 1.871-7 and 1.871-8. The provisions of subpart A do not apply to individuals described in subdivision (iii) of this subparagraph, but such individuals, except as provided in section 933 with respect to Puerto Rican source income, are subject to the tax imposed by section 1 or section 1201(b). See § 1.876-1.

(2) Treaty income. If the gross income of a nonresident alien individual described in subparagraph (1)(i) or (ii) of this paragraph includes income on which the tax is limited by tax convention, see § 1.871-12.

(3) Exclusions from gross income. For rules relating to the exclusion of certain items from the gross income of a nonresident alien individual, including annuities excluded under section 871(f), see §§ 1.872-2 and 1.894-1.

(4) Expatriation to avoid tax. For special rules applicable in determining the tax of a nonresident alien individual who has lost United States citizenship with a principal purpose of avoiding certain taxes, see section 877.

(5) Adjustment of tax of certain nonresident aliens. For the application of pre-1967 income tax provisions to residents of a foreign country which imposes a more burdensome income tax than the United States, and for the adjustment of the income tax of a national or resident of a foreign country which imposes a discriminatory income tax on the income of citizens of the United States or domestic corporations, see section 896.

(6) Conduit financing arrangements. For rules regarding conduit financing arrangements, see §§ 1.881-3 and 1.881-4.

(d [sic (c)]) Effective date. This section shall apply for taxable years beginning after December 31, 1966. For corresponding rules applicable to taxable years beginning before January 1, 1967, see 26 CFR 1.871-1 and 1.871-7(a) (Rev. as of Jan. 1, 1971).

T.D. 6258, 10/23/57, amend T.D. 7332, 12/20/74, T.D. 7670, 1/30/80, T.D. 8611, 8/10/95, T.D. 9194, 4/6/2005.

PAR. 6. Section 1.871-1 is amended as follows:

1. Revise paragraph (b)(1)(iii).

2. Revise the last two sentences of the undesignated paragraph following paragraph (b)(1)(iii).

The revisions are as follows:

Proposed § 1.871-1 Classification and manner of taxing alien individuals. [*For Preamble, see ¶ 152,645*]

• ***Caution:*** This Notice of Proposed Rulemaking was partially finalized by TD 9248, 01/30/2006. Regs. §§ 1.1-1, 1.170A-1, 1.861-3, 1.861-8, 1.871-1, 1.876-1, 1.881-5, 1.884-0, 1.901-1, 1.931-1, 1.932-1, 1.933-1, 1.934-1, 1.935-1, 1.937-2, 1.937-3, 1.957-3, 1.1402(a)-12, 1.6038-2, 1.6046-1, 301.6688-1, 301.7701-3, and 301.7701(b)-1 remain proposed.

* * * * *

(b) * * *

(1) * * *

(iii) Nonresident alien individuals who are bona fide residents of a section 931 possession (as defined in § 1.931-1T(c)(1) of this chapter) or Puerto Rico during the entire taxable year.

* * * The provisions of subpart A do not apply to individuals described in paragraph (b)(1)(iii) of this section, but such individuals, except as provided in section 931 or 933, are subject to the tax imposed by section 1 or 55. See § 1.876-1.

§ 1.871-2 Determining residence of alien individuals.

Caution: The Treasury has not yet amended Reg § 1.871-2 to reflect changes made by P.L. 108-357.

(a) General. The term "nonresident alien individual" means an individual whose residence is not within the United States, and who is not a citizen of the United States. The term includes a nonresident alien fiduciary. For such purpose the term "fiduciary" shall have the meaning assigned to it by section 7701(a)(6) and the regulations in Part 301 of this chapter (Regulations on Procedure and Administration). For presumption as to an alien's nonresidence, see paragraph (b) of § 1.871-4.

(b) Residence defined. An alien actually present in the United States who is not a mere transient or sojourner is a resident of the United States for purposes of the income tax. Whether he is a transient is determined by his intentions with regard to the length and nature of his stay. A mere floating intention, indefinite as to time, to return to another country is not sufficient to constitute him a transient. If he lives in the United States and has no definite intention as to his stay, he is a resident. One who comes to the United States for a definite purpose which in its nature may be promptly accomplished is a transient; but, if his purpose is of such a nature that an extended stay may be necessary for its accomplishment, and to that end the alien make his home temporarily in the United States, he becomes a resident, though it may be his intention at all times to return to his domicile abroad when the purpose for which he came has been consummated or abandoned. An alien whose stay in the United States is limited to a definite period by the immigration laws is not a resident of the United States within the meaning of this section, in the absence of exceptional circumstances.

(c) Application and effective dates. Unless the context indicates otherwise, §§ 1.871-2 through 1.871-5 apply to determine the residence of aliens for taxable years beginning before January 1, 1985. To determine the residence of aliens for taxable years beginning after December 31, 1984, see section 7701(b) and §§ 301.7701(b)-1 through 301.7701(b)-9 of this chapter. However, for purposes of determining whether an individual is a qualified individual under section 911(d)(1)(A), the rules of §§ 1.871-2 and 1.871-5 shall continue to apply for taxable years beginning after December 31, 1984. For purposes of determining whether an individual is a resident of the United States for estate and gift tax purposes, see § 20.0-1(b)(1) and (2) and § 25.2501-1(b) of this chapter, respectively.

T.D. 6258, 10/23/57, amend T.D. 8411, 4/24/92.

§ 1.871-3 Residence of alien seamen.

In order to determine whether an alien seaman is a resident of the United States for purposes of the income tax, it is necessary to decide whether the presumption of nonresidence (as prescribed by paragraph (b) of § 1.871-4) is overcome by facts showing that he has established a residence in the United States. Residence may be established on a vessel regularly engaged in coastwide trade, but the mere fact that a sailor makes his home on a vessel which is flying the United States flag and is engaged in foreign trade is not sufficient to establish residence in the United States, even though the vessel, while carrying on foreign trade, touches at American ports. An alien seaman may acquire an actual residence in the United States within the rules laid down in § 1.871-4, although the nature of his calling requires him to be absent for a long period from the place where his residence is established. An alien seaman may acquire such a residence at a sailors' boarding house or hotel, but such a claim should be carefully scrutinized in order to make sure that such residence is bona fide. The filing of Form 1078 or taking out first citizenship papers is proof of residence in the United States from the time the form is filed or the papers taken out, unless rebutted by other evidence showing an intention to be a transient.

T.D. 6258, 10/23/57.

§ 1.871-4 Proof of residence of aliens.

(a) Rules of evidence. The following rules of evidence shall govern in determining whether or not an alien within the United States has acquired residence therein for purposes of the income tax.

(b) Nonresidence presumed. An alien, by reason of his alienage, is presumed to be a nonresident alien.

(c) Presumption rebutted. *(1) Departing alien.* In the case of an alien who presents himself for determination of tax liability before departure from the United States, the presumption as to the alien's nonresidence may be overcome by proof—

(i) That the alien, at least six months before the date he so presents himself, has filed a declaration of his intention to become a citizen of the United States under the naturalization laws; or

(ii) That the alien, at least six months before the date he so presents himself, has filed Form 1078 or its equivalent; or

(iii) Of acts and statements of the alien showing a definite intention to acquire residence in the United States or showing that his stay in the United States has been of such an extended nature as to constitute him a resident.

(2) Other aliens. In the case of other aliens, the presumption as to the alien's nonresidence may be overcome by proof—

(i) That the alien has filed a declaration of his intention to become a citizen of the United States under the naturalization laws; or

(ii) That the alien has filed Form 1078 or its equivalent; or

(iii) Of acts and statements of the alien showing a definite intention to acquire residence in the United States or showing that his stay in the United States has been of such an extended nature as to constitute him a resident.

(d) Certificate. If, in the application of paragraphs (c)(1)(iii) or (2)(iii) of this section, the internal revenue officer or employee who examines the alien is in doubt as to the facts, such officer or employee may, to assist him in determining the facts, require a certificate or certificates setting forth the facts relied upon by the alien seeking to overcome the presumption. Each such certificate, which shall contain, or be verified by, a written declaration that it is made under the penalties of perjury, shall be executed by some credible person or persons, other than the alien and members of his family, who have known the alien at least six months before the date of execution of the certificate or certificates.

T.D. 6258, 10/23/57.

§ 1.871-5 Loss of residence by an alien.

An alien who has acquired residence in the United States retains his status as a resident until he abandons the same and actually departs from the United States. An intention to change his residence does not change his status as a resident alien to that of a nonresident alien. Thus, an alien who has acquired a residence in the United States is taxable as a resident for the remainder of his stay in the United States.

T.D. 6258, 10/23/57.

§ 1.871-6 Duty of withholding agent to determine status of alien payees.

For the obligation of a withholding agent to withhold the tax imposed by this section, see chapter 3 of the Internal Revenue Code and the regulations thereunder.

T.D. 6258, 10/23/57, amend T.D. 7332, 12/20/74, T.D. 7977, 9/19/84, T.D. 8734, 10/6/97.

§ 1.871-7 Taxation of nonresident alien individuals not engaged in U.S. business.

Caution: The Treasury has not yet amended Reg § 1.871-7 to reflect changes made by P.L. 103-465, P.L. 103-66, P.L. 102-318, P.L. 100-647, P.L. 99-514, P.L. 98-369.

(a) Imposition of tax. *(1)* This section applies for purposes of determining the tax of a nonresident alien individual who at no time during the taxable year is engaged in trade or business in the United States. However, see also § 1.871-8 where such individual is a student or trainee deemed to be engaged in trade or business in the United

States or where he has an election in effect for the taxable year in respect to real property income. Except as otherwise provided in § 1.871-12, a nonresident alien individual to whom this section applies is not subject to the tax imposed by section 1 or section 1201(b) but pursuant to the provision of section 871(a), is liable to a flat tax of 30 percent upon the aggregate of the amounts determined under paragraphs (b), (c), and (d) of this section which are received during the taxable year from sources within the United States. Except as specifically provided in such paragraphs, such amounts do not include gains from the sale or exchange of property. To determine the source of such amounts, see sections 861 through 863, and the regulations thereunder.

(2) The tax of 30 percent is imposed by section 871(a) upon an amount only to the extent the amount constitutes gross income. Thus, for example, the amount of an annuity which is subject to such tax shall be determined in accordance with section 72.

(3) Deductions shall not be allowed in determining the amount subject to tax under this section except that losses from sales or exchanges of capital assets shall be allowed to the extent provided in section 871(a)(2) and paragraph (d) of this section.

(4) Except as provided in §§ 1.871-9 and 1.871-10, a nonresident alien individual not engaged in trade or business in the United States during the taxable year has no income, gain, or loss for the taxable year which is effectively connected for the taxable year with the conduct of a trade or business in the United States. See section 864(c)(1)(B) and § 1.864-3.

(5) Gains and losses which, by reason of section 871(d) and § 1.871-10, are treated as gains or losses which are effectively connected for the taxable year with the conduct of a trade or business in the United States by the nonresident alien individually shall not be taken into account in determining the tax under this section. See, for example, paragraph (c)(2) of § 1.871-10.

(6) For special rules applicable in determining the tax of certain nonresident alien individuals, see paragraph (b) of § 1.871-1.

(b) Fixed or determinable annual or periodical income. *(1) General rule.* The tax of 30 percent imposed by section 871(a)(1) applies to the gross amount received from sources within the United States as fixed or determinable annual or periodical gains, profits, or income. Specific items of fixed or determinable annual or periodical income are enumerated in section 871(a)(1)(A) as interest, dividends, rents, salaries, wages, premiums, annuities, compensations, remunerations, and emoluments, but other items of fixed or determinable annual or periodical gains, profits, or income are also subject to the tax, as, for instance, royalties, including royalties for the use of patents, copyrights, secret processes and formulas, and other like property. As to the determination of fixed or determinable annual or periodical income, see § 1.1441-2(b). For special rules treating gain on the disposition of section 306 stock as fixed or determinable annual or periodical income for purposes of section 871(a), see section 306(f) and paragraph (h) of § 1.306-3.

(2) Substitute payments. For purposes of this section, a substitute interest payment (as defined in § 1.861-2(a)(7)) received by a foreign person pursuant to a securities lending transaction or a sale-repurchase transaction (as defined in § 1.861-2(a)(7)) shall have the same character as interest income paid or accrued with respect to the terms of the transferred security. Similarly, for purposes of this section, a substitute dividend payment (as defined in § 1.861-3(a)(6)) received by a foreign person pursuant to a securities lending transaction or a sale-repurchase transaction (as defined in § 1.861-3(a)(6)) shall have the same character as a distribution received with respect to the transferred security. Where, pursuant to a securities lending transaction or a sale-repurchase transaction, a foreign person transfers to another person a security the interest on which would qualify as portfolio interest under section 871(h) in the hands of the lender, substitute interest payments made with respect to the transferred security will be treated as portfolio interest, provided that in the case of interest on an obligation in registered form (as defined in § 1.871-14(c)(1)(i)), the transferor complies with the documentation requirement described in § 1.871-14(c)(1)(ii)(C) with respect to the payment of the substitute interest and none of the exceptions to the portfolio interest exemption in sections 871(h)(3) and (4) apply. See also §§ 1.861-2(b)(2) and 1.894-1(c).

(c) Other income and gains. *(1) Items subject to tax.* The tax of 30 percent imposed by section 871(a)(1) also applies to the following gains received during the taxable year from sources within the United States:

(i) Gains described in section 402(a)(2), relating to the treatment of total distributions from certain employees' trusts; section 403(a)(2), relating to treatment of certain payments under certain employee annuity plans; and section 631(b) or (c), relating to treatment of gain on the disposal of timber, coal, or iron ore with a retained economic interest;

(ii) [Reserved]

(iii) Gains on transfers described in section 1235, relating to certain transfers of patent rights, made on or before October 4, 1966; and

(iv) Gains from the sale or exchange after October 4, 1966, of patents, copyrights, secret processes and formulas, goodwill, trademarks, trade brands, franchises, or other like property, or of any interest in any such property, to the extent the gains are from payments (whether in a lump sum or in installments) which are contingent on the productivity, use or disposition of the property or interest sold or exchanged, or from payments which are treated under section 871(e) and § 1.871-11 as being so contingent.

(2) Nonapplication of 183-day rule. The provisions of section 871(a)(2), relating to gains from the sale or exchange of capital assets, and paragraph (d)(2) of this section do not apply to the gains described in this paragraph; as a consequence, the taxpayer receiving gains described in subparagraph (1) of this paragraph during a taxable year is subject to the tax of 30 percent thereon without regard to the 183-day rule contained in such provisions.

(3) Determination of amount of gain. The tax of 30 percent imposed upon the gains described in subparagraph (1) of this paragraph applies to the full amount of the gains and is determined (i) without regard to the alternative tax imposed by section 1201(b) upon the excess of the net long-term capital gain over the net short-term capital loss; (ii) without regard to the deduction allowed by section 1202 in respect of capital gains; (iii) without regard to section 1231, relating to property used in the trade or business and involuntary conversions; and (iv), except in the case of gains described in subparagraph (1)(ii) of this paragraph, whether or not the gains are considered to be gains from the sale or exchange of property which is a capital asset.

(d) Gains from sale or exchange of capital assets. *(1) Gains subject to tax.* The tax of 30 percent imposed by section 871(a)(2) applies to the excess of gains derived from sources within the United States over losses allocable to sources within the United States, which are derived from the sale or exchange of capital assets, determined in accordance with the provisions of subparagraphs (2) through (4) of this paragraph.

(2) *Presence in the United States 183 days or more.* (i) If the nonresident alien individual has been present in the United States for a period or periods aggregating 183 days or more during the taxable year, he is liable to a tax of 30 percent upon the amount by which his gains, derived from sources within the United States, from sales or exchanges of capital assets effected at any time during the year exceed his losses, allocable to sources within the United States, from sales or exchanges of capital assets effected at any time during that year. Gains and losses from sales or exchanges effected at any time during such taxable year are to be taken into account for this purpose even though the nonresident alien individual is not present in the United States at the time the sales or exchanges are effected. In addition, if the nonresident alien individual has been present in the United States for a period or periods aggregating 183 days or more during the taxable year, gains and losses for such taxable year from sales or exchanges of capital assets effected during a previous taxable year beginning after December 31, 1966, are to be taken into account, but only if he was also present in the United States during such previous taxable year for a period or periods aggregating 183 days or more.

(ii) If the nonresident alien individual has not been present in the United States during the taxable year, or if he has been present in the United States for a period or periods aggregating less than 183 days during the taxable year, gains and losses from sales or exchanges of capital assets effected during the year are not to be taken into account, except as required by paragraph (c) of this section, in determining the tax of such individual even though the sales or exchanges are effected during his presence in the United States. Moreover, gains and losses for such taxable year from sales or exchanges of capital assets effected during a previous taxable year beginning after December 31, 1966, are not to be taken into account, even though the nonresident alien individual was present in the United States during such previous year for a period or periods aggregating 183 days or more.

(iii) For purposes of this subparagraph, a nonresident alien individual is not considered to be present in the United States by reason of the presence in the United States of a person who is an agent or partner of such individual or who is a fiduciary of an estate or trust of which such individual is a beneficiary or a grantor-owner to whom section 671 applies.

(iv) The application of this subparagraph may be illustrated by the following examples:

Example (1). B, a nonresident alien individual not engaged in trade or business in the United States and using the calendar year as the taxable year, is present in the United States from May 1, 1971, to November 15, 1971, a period of more than 182 days. While present in the United States, B effects for his own account on various dates a number of transactions in stocks and securities on the stock exchange, as a result of which he has recognized capital gains of $10,000. During the period from January 1, 1971, to April 30, 1971, he carries out similar transactions through an agent in the United States, as a result of which B has recognized capital gains of $5,000. On December 15, 1971, through an agent in the United States B sells a capital asset on the installment plan, no payments being made by the purchaser in 1971. During 1972, B receives installment payments of $50,000 on the installment sale made in 1971, and the capital gain from sources within the United States for 1972 attributable to such payments is $12,500. In addition, during the period from January 1, 1972, to May 31, 1972, B effects for his own account, through an agent in the United States, a number of transactions in stocks and securities on the stock exchange, as a result of which B has recognized capital gains of $20,000. At no time during 1972 is B present in the United States or engaged in trade or business in the United States. Accordingly, for 1971, B is subject to tax under section 871(a)(2) on his capital gains of $15,000 from the transactions in that year on the stock exchange. For 1972, B is not subject to tax on the capital gain of $12,500 from the installment sale in 1971 or on the capital gains of $20,000 from the transactions in 1972 on the stock exchange.

Example (2). The facts are the same as in example (1) except that B is present in the United States from June 15, 1972, to December 31, 1972, a period of more than 182 days. Accordingly, B is subject to tax under section 871(a)(2) for 1971 on his capital gains of $15,000 from the transactions in that year on the stock exchange. He is also subject to tax under section 871(a)(2) for 1972 on his capital gains of $32,500 ($12,500 from the installment sale in 1971 plus $20,000 from the transactions in 1972 on the stock exchange).

Example (3). D, a nonresident alien individual not engaged in trade or business in the United States and using the calendar year as the taxable year, is present in the United States from April 1, 1971, to August 31, 1971, a period of less than 183 days. While present in the United States, D effects for his own account on various dates a number of transactions in stocks and securities on the stock exchange, as a result of which he has recognized capital gains of $15,000. During the period from January 1, 1971, to March 31, 1971, he carries out similar transactions through an agent in the United States, as a result of which D has recognized capital gains of $8,000. On December 20, 1971, through an agent in the United States D sells a capital asset on the installment plan, no payments being made by the purchaser in 1971. During 1972, D receives installment payments of $200,000 on the installment sale made in 1971, and the capital gain from sources within the United States for 1972 attributable to such payments is $50,000. In addition, during the period from February 1, 1972, to August 15, 1972, a period of more than 182 days. D effects for his own account, through an agent in the United States, a number of transactions in stocks and securities on the stock exchange, as a result of which D has recognized capital gains of $25,000. At no time during 1972 is D present in the United States or engaged in trade or business in the United States. Accordingly, D is not subject to tax for 1971 or 1972 on any of his recognized capital gains.

Example (4). The facts are the same as in example (3) except that D is present in the United States from February 1, 1972, to August 15, 1972, a period of more than 182 days. Accordingly, D is not subject to tax for 1971 on his capital gains of $23,000 from the transactions in that year on the stock exchange. For 1972 he is subject to tax under section 871(a)(2) on his capital gains of $25,000 from the transactions in that year on the stock exchange, but he is not subject to the tax on the capital gain of $50,000 from the installment sale in 1971.

(3) *Determination of 183-day period.* (i) In general. In determining the total period of presence in the United States for a taxable year for purposes of subparagraph (2) of this paragraph, all separate periods of presence in the United

States during the taxable year are to be aggregated. If the nonresident alien individual has not previously established a taxable year, as defined in section 441(b), he shall be treated as having a taxable year which is the calendar year as defined in section 441(d). Subsequent adoption by such individual of a fiscal year as the taxable year will be treated as a change in the taxpayer's annual accounting period to which section 442 applies, and the change must be authorized under this part (Income Tax Regulations) or prior approval must be obtained by filing an application on Form 1128 in accordance with paragraph (b) of § 1.442-1. If in the course of his taxable year the nonresident alien individual changes his status from that of a citizen or resident of the United States to that of a nonresident alien individual, or vice versa, the determination of whether the individual has been present in the United States for 183 days or more during the taxable year shall be made by taking into account the entire taxable year, and not just that part of the taxable year during which he has the status of a nonresident alien individual.

(ii) Definition of "day". The term "day", as used in subparagraph (2) of this paragraph, means a calendar day during any portion of which the nonresident alien individual is physically present in the United States (within the meaning of sections 7701(a)(9) and 638) except that, in the case of an individual who is a resident of Canada or Mexico and, in the normal course of his employment in transportation service touching points within both Canada or Mexico and the United States, performs personal services in both the foreign country and the United States, the following rules shall apply:

(a) The performance of labor or personal services during 8 hours or more in any 1 day within the United States shall be considered as 1 day in the United States, except that if a period of more or less than 8 hours is considered a full workday in the transportation job involved, such period shall be considered as 1 day within the United States.

(b) The performance of labor or personal services during less than 8 hours in any day in the United States shall, except as provided in (a) of this subdivision, be considered as a fractional part of a day in the United States. The total number of hours during which such services are performed in the United States during the taxable year, when divided by eight, shall be the number of days during which such individual shall be considered present in the United States during the taxable year.

(c) The aggregate number of days determined under (a) and (b) of this subdivision shall be considered the total number of days during which such individual is present in the United States during the taxable year.

(4) Determination of amount of excess gains. (i) In general. For the purpose of determining the excess of gains over losses subject to tax under this paragraph, gains and losses shall be taken into account only if, and to the extent that, they would be recognized and taken into account if the nonresident alien individual were engaged in trade or business in the United States during the taxable year and such gains and losses were effectively connected for such year with the conduct of a trade or business in the United States by such individual. However, in determining such excess of gains over losses no deduction may be taken under section 1202, relating to the deduction for capital gains, or section 1212, relating to the capital loss carryover. Thus, for example, in determining such excess gains all amounts considered under chapter 1 of the Code as gains or losses from the sale or exchange of capital assets shall be taken into account, except those gains which are described in section 871(a)(1)(B) or (D) and taken into account under paragraph (c) of this section and are considered to be gains from the sale or exchange of capital assets. Also, for example, a loss described in section 631(b) or (c) which is considered to be a loss from the sale of a capital asset shall be taken into account in determining the excess gains which are subject to tax under this paragraph. In further illustration, in determining such excess gains no deduction shall be allowed, pursuant to the provisions of section 267, for losses from sales or exchanges of property between related taxpayers. Any gains which are taken into account under section 871(a)(1) and paragraph (c) of this section shall not be taken into account in applying section 1231 for purposes of this paragraph. Gains and losses are to be taken into account under this paragraph whether they are short-term or long-term capital gains or losses within the meaning of section 1222.

(ii) Gains not included. The provisions of this paragraph do not apply to any gains described in section 871(a)(1)(B) or (D), and in subdivision (i), (iii), or (iv) of paragraph (c)(1) of this section, which are considered to be gains from the sale or exchange of capital assets.

(iii) Allowance of losses. In determining the excess of gains over losses subject to tax under this paragraph losses shall be allowed only to the extent provided by section 165(c). Losses from sales or exchanges of capital assets in excess of gains from sales or exchanges of capital assets shall not be taken into account.

(e) Credits against tax. The credits allowed by section 31 (relating to tax withheld on wages), by section 32 (relating to tax withheld at source on nonresident aliens), by section 39 (relating to certain uses of gasoline and lubricating oil), and by section 6402 (relating to overpayments of tax) shall be allowed against the tax of a nonresident alien individual determined in accordance with this section.

(f) Effective date. Except as otherwise provided in this paragraph, this section shall apply for taxable years beginning after December 31, 1966. Paragraph (b)(2) of this section is applicable to payments made after November 13, 1997. For corresponding rules applicable to taxable years beginning before January 1, 1967, see 26 CFR 1.871-7(b) and (c) (Rev. as of Jan. 1, 1971).

T.D. 6258, 10/23/57, amend T.D. 6464, 5/11/60, T.D. 6782, 12/23/64, T.D. 6823, 5/5/65, T.D. 6841, 7/26/65, T.D. 7332, 12/20/74, T.D. 8734, 10/6/97, T.D. 8735, 10/6/97.

§ 1.871-8 Taxation of nonresident alien individuals engaged in U.S. business or treated as having effectively connected income.

Caution: The Treasury has not yet amended Reg § 1.871-8 to reflect changes made by P.L. 94-455.

(a) Segregation of income. This section applies for purposes of determining the tax of a nonresident alien individual who at any time during the taxable year is engaged in trade or business in the United States. It also applies for purposes of determining the tax of a nonresident alien student or trainee who is deemed under section 871(c) and § 1.871-9 to be engaged in trade or business in the United States or of a nonresident alien individual who at no time during the taxable year is engaged in trade or business in the United States but has an election in effect for the taxable year under section 871(d) and § 1.871-10 in respect to real property income. A nonresident alien individual to whom this section applies must segregate his gross income for the taxable year into two categories, namely (1) the income which is effectively connected for the taxable year with the conduct of a trade or business in the United States by that individual, and (2) the income which is not effectively connected for the taxable year with the conduct of a trade or business in the United States by that individual. A separate tax shall then be determined upon each such category of income, as provided in paragraph (b) of this section. The determination of whether income or gain is or is not effectively connected for the taxable year with the conduct of a trade or business in the United States by the nonresident alien individual shall be made in accordance with section 864(c) and §§ 1.864-3 through 1.864-7. For purposes of this section income which is effectively connected for the taxable year with the conduct of a trade or business in the United States includes all income which is treated under section 871(c) or (d) and § 1.871-9 or § 1.871-10 as income which is effectively connected such year with the conduct of a trade or business in the United States by the nonresident alien individual.

(b) Imposition of tax. *(1) Income not effectively connected with the conduct of a trade or business in the United States.* If a nonresident alien individual who is engaged in trade or business in the United States at any time during the taxable year derives during such year from sources within the United States income or gains described in section 871(a)(1), and paragraph (b) or (c) of § 1.871-7 or gains from the sale or exchange of capital assets determined as provided in section 871(a)(2) and paragraph (d) of § 1.871-7, which are not effectively connected for the taxable year with the conduct of a trade or business in the United States by that individual, such income or gains shall be subject to a flat tax of 30 percent of the aggregate amount of such items. This tax shall be determined in the manner, and subject to the same conditions, set forth in § 1.871-7 as though the income or gains were derived by a nonresident alien individual not engaged in trade or business in the United States during the taxable year, except that (i) the rule in paragraph (d)(3) of such section for treating the calendar year as the taxable year shall not apply and (ii) in applying paragraph (c) and (d)(4) of such section, there shall not be taken into account any gains or losses which are taken into account in determining the tax under section 871(b) and subparagraph (2) of this paragraph. A nonresident alien individual who has an election in effect for the taxable year under section 871(d) and § 1.871-10 and who at no time during the taxable year is engaged in trade or business in the United States must determine his tax under § 1.871-7 on his income which is not treated as effectively connected with the conduct of a trade or business in the United States, subject to the exception contained in subdivision (ii) of this subparagraph.

(2) Income effectively connected with the conduct of a trade or business in the United States. (i) In general. If a nonresident alien to whom this section applies derives income or gains which are effectively connected for the taxable year with the conduct of a trade or business in the United States by that individual, the taxable income or gains shall, except as provided in § 1.871-12, be taxed in accordance with section 1 or, in the alternative, section 1201(b). See section 871(b)(1). Any income of the nonresident alien individual which is not effectively connected for the taxable year with the conduct of a trade or business in the United States by that individual shall not be taken into account in determining either the rate or amount of such tax. See paragraph (b) of § 1.872-1.

(ii) Determination of taxable income. The taxable income for any taxable year for purposes of this subparagraph consists only of the nonresident alien individual's taxable income which is effectively connected for the taxable year with the conduct of a trade or business in the United States by that individual; and, for this purpose, it is immaterial that the trade or business with which that income is effectively connected is not the same as the trade or business carried on in the United States by that individual during the taxable year. See example (2) in § 1.864-4(b). In determining such taxable income all amounts constituting, or considered to be, gains or losses for the taxable year from the sale or exchange of capital assets shall be taken into account if such gains or losses are effectively connected for the taxable year with the conduct of a trade or business in the United States by that individual, and, for such purpose, the 183-day rule set forth in section 871(a)(2) and paragraph (d)(2) of § 1.871-7 shall not apply. Losses which are not effectively connected for the taxable year with the conduct of a trade or business in the United States by that individual shall not be taken into account in determining taxable income under this subdivision, except as provided in section 873(b)(1).

(iii) Cross references. For rules for determining the gross income and deductions for the taxable year, see sections 872 and 873, and the regulations thereunder.

(c) Change in trade or business status. *(1) In general.* The determination as to whether a nonresident alien individual is engaged in trade or business within the United States during the taxable year is to be made for each taxable year. If at any time during the taxable year he is engaged in a trade or business in the United States, he is considered to be engaged in trade or business within the United States during the taxable year for purposes of sections 864(c)(1) and 871(b), and the regulations thereunder. Income, gain, or loss of a nonresident alien individual is not treated as being effectively connected for the taxable year with the conduct of a trade or business in the United States if he is not engaged in trade or business within the United States during such year, even though such income, gain, or loss may have been effectively connected for a previous taxable year with the conduct of a trade or business in the United States. See § 1.864-3. However, income, gain, or loss which is treated as effectively connected for the taxable year with the conduct of a trade or business in the United States by a nonresident alien individual will generally be treated as effectively connected for a subsequent taxable year if he is engaged in a trade or business in the United States during such subsequent year, even though such income, gain, or loss is not effectively connected with the conduct of the trade or business carried on in the United States during such subsequent year. This subparagraph does not apply to income described in section 871(c) or (d). It may not apply to a nonresident alien individual who for the taxable year uses an accrual method of accounting or to income which is constructively received in the taxable year within the meaning of § 1.451-2.

(2) Illustrations. The application of this paragraph may be illustrated by the following examples:

Example (1). B, a nonresident alien individual using the calendar year as the taxable year and the cash receipts and disbursements method of accounting, is engaged in business (business R) in the United States from January 1, 1971, to August 31, 1971. During the period of September 1, 1971, to December 31, 1971, B receives installment payments of $30,000 on sales made in the United States by business R during that year, and the income from sources within the United States for that year attributable to such payments is $7,509. On September 15, 1971, another business (business S), which is carried on by B only in a foreign country sells to U.S. customers on the installment plan several pieces of equipment from inventory. During the period of September

16, 1971, to December 31, 1971, B receives installment payments of $50,000 on these sales by business S, and the income from sources within the United States for that year attributable to such payments is $10,000. Under section 864(c)(3) and paragraph (b) of § 1.864-4 the entire income of $17,500 is effectively connected for 1971 with the conduct of a business in the United States by B. Accordingly, such income is taxable to B under paragraph (b)(2) of this section.

Example (2). Assume the same facts as in example (1), except that during 1972 B receives installment payments of $20,000 from the sales made during 1971 in the United States by business R, and of $80,000 from the sales made in 1971 to U.S. customers by business S, the total income from sources within the United States for 1972 attributable to such payments being $13,000. At no time during 1972 is B engaged in a trade or business in the United States. Under section 864(c)(1)(B) the income of $13,000 for 1972 is not effectively connected with the conduct of a trade or business in the United States by B. Moreover, such income is not fixed or determinable annual or periodical income. Accordingly, no amount of such income is taxable to B under section 871.

Example (3). Assume the same facts as in example (2), except that during 1972 B is engaged in a new business (business T) in the United States from July 1, 1972, to December 31, 1972. Under section 864(c)(3) and paragraph (b) of § 1.864-4, the income of $13,000 is effectively connected for 1972 with the conduct of a business in the United States by B. Accordingly, such income is taxable to B under paragraph (b)(2) of this section.

Example (4). Assume the same facts as in example (2), except that the installment payments of $20,000 from the sales made during 1971 in the United States by business R and not received by B until 1972 could have been received by B in 1971 if he had so desired. Under § 1.451-2, B is deemed to have constructively received the payments of $20,000 in 1971. Accordingly, the income attributable to such payments is effectively connected for 1971 with the conduct of a business in the United States by B and is taxable to B in 1971 under paragraph (b)(2) of this section.

(d) Credits against tax. The credits allowed by section 31 (relating to tax withheld on wages), section 32 (relating to tax withheld at source on nonresident aliens), section 33 (relating to the foreign tax credit), section 35 (relating to partially tax-exempt interest), section 38 (relating to investment in certain depreciable property), section 39 (relating to certain uses of gasoline and lubricating oil), section 40 (relating to expenses of work incentive programs), and section 6402 (relating to overpayments of tax) shall be allowed against the tax determined in accordance with this section. However, the credits allowed by sections 33, 38, and 40 shall not be allowed against the flat tax of 30 percent imposed by section 871(a) and paragraph (b)(1) of this section. Moreover, no credit shall be allowed under section 35 to a nonresident alien individual with respect to whom a tax is imposed for the taxable year under section 871(a) and paragraph (b)(1) of this section, even though such individual has income for such year upon which tax is imposed under section 871(b) and paragraph (b)(2) of this section. For special rules applicable in determining the foreign tax credit, see section 906(b) and the regulations thereunder. For the disallowance of certain credits where a return is not filed for the taxable year, see section 874 and § 1.874-1.

(e) Effective date. This section shall apply for taxable years beginning after December 31, 1966. For corresponding rules applicable to taxable years beginning before January 1, 1967, see 26 CFR 1.871-7(d) (Rev. as of Jan. 1, 1971).

T.D. 6258, 10/23/57, amend T.D. 6782, 12/23/64, T.D. 7332, 12/20/74.

§ 1.871-9 Nonresident alien students or trainees deemed to be engaged in U.S. business.

(a) Participants in certain exchange or training programs. For purposes of §§ 1.871-7 and 1.871-8 a nonresident alien individual who is temporarily present in the United States during the taxable year as a nonimmigrant under subparagraph (F) (relating to the admission of students into the United States) or subparagraph (J) (relating to the admission of teachers, trainees, specialists, etc., into the United States) of section 101(a)(15) of the Immigration and Nationality Act (8 U.S.C. 1101(a)(15) (F) or (J)), and who without regard to this paragraph is not engaged in trade or business in the United States during such year, shall be deemed to be engaged in trade or business in the United States during the taxable year. For purposes of determining whether an alien who is present in the United States on an F visa or a J visa is a resident of the United States, see §§ 301.7701(b)-1 through 301.7701(b)-9 of this chapter.

(b) Income treated as effectively connected with U.S. business. Any income described in paragraph (1) relating to the nonexcluded portion of certain scholarship or fellowship grants) or paragraph (2) (relating to certain nonexcluded expenses incident to such grants) of section 144(b) which is received during the taxable year from sources within the United States by a nonresident alien individual described in paragraph (a) of this section is to be treated for purposes of §§ 1.871-7, 1.871-8, 1.872-1, and 1.873-1 as income which is effectively connected for the taxable year with the conduct of a trade or business in the United States by that individual. However, such income is not to be treated as effectively connected for the taxable year with the conduct of a trade or business in the United States for purposes of section 1441(c)(1) and paragraph (a) of § 1.1441-4. For exclusion relating to compensation paid to such individual by a foreign employer, see paragraph (b) of § 1.872-2.

(c) Exchange visitors. For purposes of paragraph (a) of this section a nonresident alien individual who is temporarily present in the United States during the taxable year as a nonimmigrant under subparagraph (J) of section 101(a)(15) of the Immigration and Nationality Act includes a nonresident alien individual admitted to the United States as an "exchange visitor" under section 201 of the U.S. Information and Educational Exchange Act of 1948 (22 U.S.C. 1446), which section was repealed by section 111 of the Mutual Educational and Cultural Exchange Act of 1961 (75 Stat. 538).

(d) Mandatory application of rule. The application of this section is mandatory and not subject to an election by the taxpayer.

(e) Effective date. This section shall apply for taxable years beginning after December 31, 1966. For corresponding rules applicable to taxable years beginning before January 1, 1967, see 26 CFR 1.871-7(a)(3) (Rev. as of Jan. 1, 1971).

T.D. 7332, 12/20/74, amend T.D. 8411, 4/24/92.

§ 1.871-10 Election to treat real property income as effectively connected with U.S. business.

(a) When election may be made. A nonresident alien individual or foreign corporation which during the taxable year derives any income from real property which is located in the United States and, in the case of a nonresident alien individual, held for the production of income, or derives income from any interest in any such property, may elect, pursuant to section 871(d) or 882(d) and this section, to treat all such income as income which is effectively connected for the taxable year with the conduct of a trade or business in the United States by that taxpayer. The election may be made whether or not the taxpayer is engaged in trade or business in the United States during the taxable year for which the election is made or whether or not the taxpayer has income from real property which for the taxable year is effectively connected with the conduct of a trade or business in the United States, but it may be made only with respect to that income from sources within the United States which, without regard to this section, is not effectively connected for the taxable year with the conduct of a trade or business in the United States by the taxpayer. If for the taxable year the taxpayer has no income from real property located in the United States, or from any interest in such property, which is subject to the tax imposed by section 871(a) or 881(a), the election may not be made. But if an election has been properly made under this section for a taxable year, the election remains in effect, unless properly revoked, for subsequent taxable years even though during any such subsequent taxable year there is no income from the real property, or interest therein, in respect of which the election applies.

(b) Income to which the election applies. *(1) Included income.* An election under this section shall apply to all income from real property which is located in the United States and, in the case of a nonresident alien individual, held for the production of income, and to all income derived from any interest in such property, including (i) gains from the sale or exchange of such property or an interest therein, (ii) rents or royalties from mines, oil or gas wells, or other natural resources, and (iii) gains described in section 631 (b) or (c), relating to treatment of gain on the disposal of timber, coal, or iron ore with a retained economic interest. The election may not be made with respect to only one class of such income. For purposes of the election, income from real property, or from any interest in real property, includes any amount included under section 652 or 662 in the gross income of a nonresident alien individual or foreign corporation that is the beneficiary of an estate or trust if, by reason of the application of section 652(b) or 662(b), and the regulations thereunder, such amount has the character in the hands of that beneficiary of income from real property, or from any interest in real property. It is immaterial that no tax would be imposed on the income by section 871(a) and paragraph (a) of § 1.871-7, or by section 881(a) and paragraph (a) of § 1.881-2, if the election were not in effect. Thus, for example, if an election under this section has been made by a nonresident alien individual not engaged in trade or business in the United States during the taxable year, the tax imposed by section 871(b)(1) and paragraph (b)(2) of § 1.871-8 applies to his gains derived from the sale of real property located in the United States and held for the production of income, even though such income would not be subject to tax under section 871(a) if the election had not been made. In further illustration, assume that a nonresident alien individual not engaged in trade or business, or present, in the United States during the taxable year has income from sources within the United States consisting of oil royalties, rentals from a former personal residence, and capital gain from the sale of another residence held for the production of income. If he makes an election under this section, it will apply with respect to his royalties, rentals, and capital gain, even though such capital gain would not be subject to tax under section 871(a) if the election had not been made.

(2) Income not included. For purposes of subparagraph (1) of this paragraph, income from real property, or from any interest in real property, does not include (i) interest on a debt obligation secured by a mortgage of real property, (ii) any portion of a dividend, within the meaning of section 316, which is paid by a corporation or a trust, such as a real estate investment trust described in section 857, which derives income from real property, (iii) in the case of a nonresident alien individual, income from real property, such as a personal residence, which is not held for the production of income or from any transaction in such property which was not entered into for profit, (iv) rentals from personal property, or royalties from intangible personal property, within the meaning of subparagraph (3) of this paragraph, or (v) income which, without regard to section 871(d) or 882(d) and this section, is treated as income which is effectively connected for the taxable year with the conduct of a trade or business in the United States.

(3) Rules applicable to personal property. For purposes of subparagraph (2) of this paragraph, in the case of a sales agreement, or rental or royalty agreement, affecting both real and personal property, the income from the transaction is to be allocated between the real property and the personal property in proportion to their respective fair market values unless the agreement specifically provides otherwise. In the case of such a rental or royalty agreement, the respective fair market values are to be determined as of the time the agreement is signed. In making determinations of this subparagraph, the principles of paragraph (c) of § 1.48-1, relating to the definition of "section 38 property," apply for purposes of determining whether property is tangible or intangible personal property and of paragraph (a)(5) of § 1.1245-1 apply for purposes of making the allocation of income between real and personal property.

(c) Effect of the election. *(1) Determination of tax.* The income to which, in accordance with paragraph (b) of this section, an election under this section applies shall be subject to tax in the manner, and subject to the same conditions, provided by section 871(b)(1) and paragraph (b)(2) of § 1.871-8, or by section 882(a)(1) and paragraph (b)(2) of § 1.882-1. For purposes of determining such tax for the taxable year, income to which the election applies shall be aggregated with all other income of the nonresident alien individual or foreign corporation which is effectively connected for the taxable year with the conduct of a trade or business in the United States by that taxpayer. To the extent that deductions are connected with income from real property to which the election applies, they shall be treated for purposes of section 873(a) or section 882(c)(1) as connected with income which is effectively connected for the taxable year with the conduct of a trade or business in the United States by the nonresident alien individual or foreign corporation. An election under this section does not cause a nonresident alien individual or foreign corporation, which is not engaged in trade or business in the United States during the taxable year, to be treated as though such taxpayer were engaged in trade or business in the United States during the taxable year. Thus, for example, the compensation received during the taxable year for services performed in the United States in a previous taxable year by a nonresident alien individual, who has an election in effect for the taxable year under this section but is engaged in trade or business in the United States at no time during the taxable year, is not effectively connected for the taxable year with the conduct of a trade or business in the United States. In further illustration, gain for the taxable year from the casual sale of personal property described in section 1221(1) derived by a nonresident alien individual who is not engaged in trade or business in the United States during the taxable year but has an election in effect for such year under this section is not effectively connected with the conduct of a trade or business in the United States. See § 1.864-3. If an election under this section is in effect for the taxable year, the income to which the election applies shall be treated, for purposes of section 871(b)(1) or section 882(a)(1), section 1441(c)(1), and paragraph (a) of § 1.1441-4, as income which is effectively connected for the taxable year with the conduct of a trade or business in the United States by the taxpayer.

(2) Treatment of property to which election applies. Any real property, or interest in real property, with respect to which an election under this section applies shall be treated as a capital asset which, if depreciable, is subject to the allowance for depreciation provided in section 167 and the regulations thereunder. Such property, or interest in property, shall be treated as property not used in a trade or business for purposes of applying any provisions of the Code, such as section 172(d)(4)(A), relating to gain or loss attributable to a trade or business for purposes of determining a net operating loss; section 1221(2), relating to property not constituting a capital asset; or section 1231(b), relating to special rules for treatment of gains and losses. For example, if a nonresident alien individual makes the election under this section and, while the election is in effect, sells unimproved land which is located in the United States and held for investment purposes, any gain or loss from the sale shall be considered gain or loss from the sale of a capital asset and shall be treated, for purposes of determining the tax under section 871(b)(1) and paragraph (b)(2) of § 1.871-8, as a gain or loss which is effectively connected for the taxable year with the conduct of a trade or business in the United States.

(d) Manner of making or revoking an election. *(1) Election, or revocation, without consent of Commissioner.* (i) In general. A nonresident alien individual or foreign corporation may, for the first taxable year for which the election under this section is to apply, make the initial election at any time before the expiration of the period prescribed by section 6511(a), or by section 6511(c) if the period for assessment is extended by agreement, for filing a claim for credit or refund of the tax imposed by chapter 1 of the Code for such taxable year. This election may be made without the consent of the Commissioner. Having made the initial election, the taxpayer may, within the time prescribed for making the election for such taxable year, revoke the election without the consent of the Commissioner. If the revocation is timely and properly made, the taxpayer may make his initial election under this section for a later taxable year without the consent of the Commissioner. If the taxpayer revokes the initial election without the consent of the Commissioner he must file amended income tax returns, or claims for credit or refund, where applicable, for the taxable years to which the revocation applies.

(ii) Statement to be filed with return. An election made under this section without the consent of the Commissioner shall be made for a taxable year by filing with the income tax return required under section 6012 and the regulations thereunder for such taxable year a statement to the effect that the election is being made. This statement shall include (a) a complete schedule of all real property, or any interest in real property, of which the taxpayer is titular or beneficial owner, which is located in the United States, (b) an indication of the extent to which the taxpayer has direct or beneficial ownership in each such item of real property, or interest in real property, (c) the location of the real property or interest therein, (d) a description of any substantial improvements on any such property, and (e) an identification of any taxable year or years in respect of which a revocation or new election under this section has previously occurred. This statement may not be filed with any return under section 6851 and the regulations thereunder.

(iii) Exemption from withholding of tax. For statement to be filed with a withholding agent at the beginning of a taxable year in respect of which an election under this section is to be made, see paragraph (a) of § 1.1441-4.

(2) Revocation, or election, with consent of Commissioner. (i) In general. If the nonresident alien individual or foreign corporation makes the initial election under this section for any taxable year and the period prescribed by subparagraph (1)(i) of this paragraph for making the election for such taxable year has expired, the election shall remain in effect for all subsequent taxable years, including taxable years for which the taxpayer realizes no income from real property, or from any interest therein, or for which he is not required under section 6012 and the regulations thereunder to file an income tax return. However, the election may be revoked in accordance with subdivision (iii) of this subparagraph for any subsequent taxable year with the consent of the Commissioner. If the election for any such taxable year is revoked with the consent of the Commissioner, the taxpayer may not make a new election before his fifth taxable year which begins after the first taxable year for which the revocation is effective unless consent is given to such new election by the Commissioner in accordance with subdivision (iii) of this subparagraph.

(ii) Effect of new election. A new election made for the fifth taxable year, or taxable year thereafter, without the consent of the Commissioner, and a new election made with the consent of the Commissioner, shall be treated as an initial election to which subparagraph (1) of this paragraph applies.

(iii) Written request required. A request to revoke an election made under this section when such revocation requires the consent of the Commissioner, or to make a new election when such election requires the consent of the Commissioner, shall be made in writing and shall be addressed to the Director of International Operations, Internal Revenue Service, Washington, D.C. 20225. The request shall include the name and address of the taxpayer and shall be signed by the taxpayer or his duly authorized representative. It must specify the taxable year for which the revocation or new election is to be effective and shall be filed within 75 days after the close of the first taxable year for which it is desired to make the change. The request must specify the grounds which are considered to justify the revocation or new election. The Director of International Operations may require such other information as may be necessary in order to determine whether the proposed change will be permitted. A copy of the consent by the Director of International Operations shall be attached to the taxpayer's return required under section 6012 and the regulations thereunder for the taxable year for which the revocation or new election is effective. A copy of such consent may not be filed with any return under section 6851 and the regulations thereunder.

(3) Election by partnership. If a nonresident alien individual or foreign corporation is a member of a partnership which has income described in paragraph (b)(1) of this section from real property, any election to be made under this section in respect of such income shall be made by the part-

ners and not by the partnership. A nonresident alien or foreign corporation that makes an election generally must provide the partnership a Form W-8ECI, "Certificate of Foreign Person's Claim for Exemption from Withholding on Income Effectively Connected with the Conduct of a Trade or Business in the United States," and attach to such form a copy of the election (or a statement that indicates that the nonresident alien or foreign corporation will make the election). However, if the nonresident alien or foreign corporation has already submitted a valid form to the partnership that establishes such partner's foreign status, the partner shall furnish the partnership a copy of the election (or a statement that indicates that the nonresident alien or foreign corporation will make the election). To the extent the partnership has income to which the election pertains, the partnership shall treat such income as effectively connected income subject to withholding under section 1446. See also § 1.1446-2.

(e) Effective dates. This section shall apply for taxable years beginning after December 31, 1966, except the last four sentences of paragraph (d)(3) of this section shall apply to partnership taxable years beginning after May 18, 2005, or such earlier time as the regulations under §§ 1.1446-1 through 1.1446-5 apply by reason of an election under § 1.1446-7. There are no corresponding rules in this part for taxable years beginning before January 1, 1967.

T.D. 7332, 12/20/74, amend T.D. 9200, 5/13/2005.

§ 1.871-11 Gains from sale or exchange of patents, copyrights, or similar property.

(a) Contingent payment defined. For purposes of section 871(a)(1)(D), section 881(a)(4), § 1.871-7(c)(1)(iv), § 1.881-2(c)(1)(iii), and this section, payments which are contingent on the productivity, use, or disposition of property or of an interest therein include continuing payments measured by a percentage of the selling price of the products marketed, or based on the number of units manufactured or sold, or based in a similar manner upon production, sale or use, or disposition of the property or interest transferred. A payment which is certain as to the amount to be received, but contingent as to the time of payment, or an installment payment of a principal sum agreed upon in a transfer agreement, shall not be treated as a contingent payment for purposes of this paragraph. For the inapplication of section 1253 to certain amounts described in this paragraph, see paragraph (a) of § 1.1253-1.

(b) Payments treated as contingent on use. Pursuant to section 871(e), if more than 50 percent of the gain of a nonresident alien individual or foreign corporation for any taxable year from the sale or exchange after October 4, 1966, of any patent, copyright, secret process or formula, goodwill, trademark, trade brand, franchise, or other like property, or of any interest in any such property, is from payments which are contingent on the productivity, use, or disposition of such property or interest, all of the gain of such individual or corporation for the taxable year from the sale or exchange of such property or interest are, for purposes of section 871(a)(1)(D), section 881(a)(4), section 1441(b), or section 1442(a), and the regulations thereunder, to be treated as being from payments which are contingent on the productivity, use, or disposition of such property or interest. This paragraph does not apply for purposes of determining under section 871(b)(1) or 882(a)(1) the tax of a nonresident alien individual or foreign corporation on income which is effectively connected for the taxable year with the conduct of a trade or business in the United States.

(c) Sale or exchange. A sale or exchange for purposes of this section includes, but is not limited to, a transfer by an individual which by reason of section 1235, relating to the sale or exchange of patents, is considered the sale or exchange of a capital asset. The provisions of section 1253, relating to transfers of franchises, trademarks, and trade names, do not apply in determining whether a transfer is a sale or exchange for purposes of this section.

(d) Recovery of adjusted basis. For purposes of determining for any taxable year the amount of gains which are subject to tax under section 871(a)(1)(D) or 881(a)(4), payments received by the nonresident alien individual or foreign corporation during such year must be reduced by amounts representing recovery of the taxpayer's adjusted basis of the property or interest which is sold or exchanged. Where the taxpayer receives in the same taxable year payments which, without reference to section 871(e) and this section, are not contingent on the productivity, use, or disposition of the property or interest which is sold or exchanged and payments which are contingent on the productivity, use, or disposition of the property or interest which is sold or exchanged, the taxpayer's unrecovered adjusted basis in the property or interest which is sold or exchanged must be allocated for the taxable year between such payments on the basis of the gross amount of each such type of payments. Where the taxpayer receives in the taxable year only payments which are not so contingent or only payments which are so contingent, the taxpayer's unrecovered basis must be allocated in its entirety to such payments for the taxable year.

(e) Source rule. In determining whether gains described in section 871(a)(1)(D) or 881(a)(4) and paragraph (b) of this section are received from sources within the United States, such gains shall be treated, for purposes of section 871(a)(1)(D), section 881(a)(4), section 1441(b), and section 1442(a), as rentals or royalties for the use of, or privilege of using, property or an interest in property. See section 861(a)(4), § 1.861-5, and paragraph (a) of § 1.862-1.

(f) Illustrations. The application of this section may be illustrated by the following examples:

Example (1). (a) A, a nonresident alien individual who uses the cash receipts and disbursements method of accounting and the calendar year as the taxable year, holds a U.S. patent which he developed through his own effort. On December 15, 1967, A enters into an agreement of sale with M Corporation, a domestic corporation, whereby A assigns to M Corporation all of his U.S. rights in the patent. In consideration of the sale, M Corporation is obligated to pay a fixed sum of $60,000, $20,000 being payable on execution of the contract and the balance payable in four annual installments of $10,000 each. As additional consideration, M Corporation agrees to pay to A a royalty in the amount of 2 percent of the gross sales of the products manufactured by M Corporation under the patent. A is not engaged in trade or business in the United States at any time during 1967 and 1968. His adjusted basis in the patent at the time of sale is $28,800.

(b) In 1967, A receives only the $20,000 paid by M Corporation on the execution of the contract of sale. No gain is realized by A upon receipt of this amount, and his unrecovered adjusted basis in the patent is reduced to $8,800 ($28,800 less $20,000).

(c) In 1968, M Corporation has gross sales of $600,000 from products manufactured under the patent. Consequently, for 1968, M Corporation pays $22,000 to A, $10,000 being the annual installment on the fixed payment and $12,000 being payments under the terms of the royalty provision. A's recognized gain for 1968 is $13,200 ($22,000 reduced by the unrecovered adjusted basis of $8,800). Of the total gain of $13,200, gain in the amount of $6,000 ($10,000 – [$8,800 × $10,000/$22,000]) is considered to be from the fixed installment payment and of $7,200 ($12,000 – [$8,800 × $12,000/$22,000]) is considered to be from the royalty payment. Since 54.5 percent ($7,200/$13,200) of the gain recognized in 1968 from the sale of the patent is from payments which are contingent on the productivity, use, or disposition of the patent, all of the $13,200 gain recognized in 1968 is treated, for purposes of section 871(a)(1)(D) and section 1441(b), as being from payments which are contingent on the productivity, use, or disposition of the patent.

Example (2). (a) F, a foreign corporation using the calendar year as the taxable year and not engaged in trade or business in the United States, holds a U.S. patent on certain property which it developed through its own efforts. Corporation F uses the cash receipts and disbursements method of accounting. On December 1, 1966, F Corporation enters into an agreement of sale with D Corporation, a domestic corporation, whereby D Corporation purchases the exclusive right and license, and the right to sublicense to others, to manufacture, use, and/or sell certain devices under the patent in the United States during the term of the patent. The agreement grants D Corporation the right to dispose, anywhere in the world, of machinery manufactured in the United States and equipped with such devices. Corporation D is granted the right, at its own expense, to prosecute infringers in its own name or in the name of F Corporation, or both, and to retain any damages recovered.

(b) Corporation D agrees to pay to F Corporation annually $5 for each device manufactured under the patent during the year but in no case less than $5,000 per year. In 1967, D Corporation manufactures 2,500 devices under the patent; and, in 1968, 1,500 devices. Under the terms of the contract D Corporation pays to F Corporation in 1967 $12,500 with respect to production in that year and $7,500 in 1968 with respect to production in that year. F Corporation's basis in the patent at the time of the sale is $17,000.

(c) With respect to the payments received by F Corporation in 1967, no gain is realized by that corporation and its unrecovered adjusted basis in the patent is reduced to $4,500 ($17,000 less $12,500).

(d) With respect to the payments received by F Corporation in 1968, such corporation has recognized gain of $3,000 ($7,500 reduced by unrecovered adjusted basis of $4,500). Of the total gain of $3,000, gain in the amount of $2,000 ($5,000 – [$4,500 × $5,000/$7,500]) is considered to be from the fixed installment payment and of $1,000 ($2,500 – [$4,500 × $2,500/$7,500]) is considered to be from payments which are contingent on the productivity, use, or disposition of the patent. Since 33.3 percent ($1,000/$3,000) of the gain recognized in 1968 from the sale of the patent is from payments which are contingent on the productivity, use, or disposition of the patent, only $1,000 of the $3,000 gain for that year constitutes gains which, for purposes of section 881(a)(4) and section 1442(a), are from payments which are contingent on the productivity, use, or disposition of the patent. The balance of $2,000 is gain from the sale of property and is not subject to tax under section 881(a).

(g) Effective date. This section shall apply for taxable years beginning after December 31, 1966, but only in respect of gains from sales or exchanges occurring after October 4, 1966. There are no corresponding rules in this part for taxable years beginning before January 1, 1967.

T.D. 7332, 12/20/74.

---

§ 1.871-12 Determination of tax on treaty income.

(a) In general. This section applies for purposes of determining under § 1.871-7 or § 1.871-8 the tax of a nonresident alien individual, or under § 1.881-2 or § 1.882-1 the tax of a foreign corporation, which for the taxable year has income described in section 872(a) or 882(b) upon which the tax is limited by an income tax convention to which the United States is a party. Income for such purposes does not include income of any kind which is exempt from tax under the provisions of an income tax convention to which the United States is a party. See §§ 1.872-2(c) and 1.883-1(b). This section shall not apply to a nonresident alien individual who is a bona fide resident of Puerto Rico during the entire taxable year.

(b) Definition of treaty and nontreaty income. *(1) In general.* (i) For purposes of this section the term "treaty income" shall be construed to mean the gross income of a nonresident alien individual or foreign corporation, as the case may be, the tax on which is limited by a tax convention. The term "nontreaty income" shall be construed, for such purposes, to mean the gross income of the nonresident alien individual or foreign corporation other than the treaty income. Neither term includes income of any kind which is exempt from the tax imposed by chapter 1 of the Code.

(ii) In determining either the treaty or non-treaty income the gross income shall be determined in accordance with §§ 1.872-1 and 1.872-2, or with §§ 1.882-3 and 1.883-1, except that in determining the treaty income the exclusion granted by section 116(a) for dividends shall not be taken into account. Thus, for example, treaty income includes the total amount of dividends paid by a domestic corporation not disqualified by section 116(b) and received from sources within the United States if, in accordance with a tax convention, the dividends are subject to the income tax at a rate not to exceed 15 percent but does not include interest which, in accordance with a tax convention, is exempt from the income tax. In further illustration, neither the treaty nor the nontreaty income includes interest on certain governmental obligations which by reason of section 103 is excluded from gross income, or interest which by reason of a tax convention is exempt from the tax imposed by chapter 1 of the Code.

(iii) For purposes of applying any income tax convention to which the United States is a party, original issue discount which is subject to tax under section 871(a)(1)(C) or 881(a)(3) is to be treated as interest, and gains which are subject to tax under section 871(a)(1)(D) or 881(a)(4) are to be treated as royalty income. This subdivision shall not apply, however, where its application would be contrary to any treaty obligation of the United States.

(2) Application of permanent establishment rule of treaties. In applying this section with respect to income which is not effectively connected for the taxable year with the conduct of a trade or business in the United States by a nonresident alien individual or foreign corporation, see section 894(b), which provides that with respect to such income the nonresident alien individual or foreign corporation shall be deemed not to have a permanent establishment in the United States at any time during the taxable year for purposes of applying any exemption from, or reduction in rate of, tax provided by any tax convention.

(c) Determination of tax. *(1) In general.* If the gross income of a nonresident alien individual or foreign corporation, as the case may be, consists of both treaty and nontreaty income, the tax liability for the taxable year shall be the sum of the amounts determined in accordance with subparagraphs (2) and (3) of this paragraph. In no case, however, may the tax liability so determined exceed the tax liability (tax reduced by allowable credits) with respect to the taxpayer's entire income, determined in accordance with § 1.871-7 or § 1.871-8, or with § 1.881-2 or § 1.882-1, as though the tax convention had not come into effect and without reference to the provisions of this section. Determinations under this paragraph shall be made without taking into account any credits allowed by sections 31, 32, 39, and 6402, but such credits shall be allowed against the tax liability determined in accordance with this subparagraph.

(2) Tax on nontreaty income. For purposes of subparagraph (1) of this paragraph, compute a partial tax (determined without the allowance of any credit) upon only the nontreaty income in accordance with § 1.187-1 or § 1.871-8, or with § 1.881-2 or § 1.882-1, whichever applies, as though the tax convention had not come into effect. To the extent allowed by paragraph (d) of § 1.871-8, or paragraph (c) of § 1.882-1, the credits allowed by sections 33, 35, 38, and 40 shall then be allowed, without taking into account any item included in the treaty income, against the tax determined under this subparagraph.

(3) Tax on treaty income. For purposes of subparagraph (1) of this paragraph, compute a tax upon the gross amount, determined without the allowance of any deduction, of each separate item of treaty income at the reduced rate applicable to that item under the tax convention. No credits shall be allowed against the tax determined under this subparagraph.

(d) Illustration. The application of this section may be illustrated by the following example:

Example. (a) A nonresident alien individual who is a resident of a foreign country with which the United States has entered into a tax convention receives during the taxable year 1967 from sources within the United States total gross income of $22,000, consisting of the following items:

Compensation for personal services the tax on which is not limited by the tax convention (effectively connected income under Sec. 1.864-4(c)(6)(ii))	$20,000
Oil royalties the tax on which is limited by the tax convention to 15 percent of the gross amount thereof (effectively connected income by reason of election under Sec. 1.871-10)	2,000
Total gross income	$22,000

(b) The taxpayer is engaged in business in the United States during the taxable year but does not have a permanent establishment therein. There are no allowable deductions, other than the deductions allowed by sections 613 and 873(b)(3).

(c) The tax liability for the taxable year is $6,100, determined as follows:

Nontreaty gross income	$20,000
Less: Deduction for personal exemption	600
Nontreaty taxable income	19,400
Tax under section 1 of the Code on nontreaty taxable income ($5,170 plus 45 percent of $1,400)	5,800
Plus: Tax on treaty income (Gross oil royalties) ($2,000 × 15 percent)	300
Total tax (determined as provided in paragraph (c)(2) and (3) of this section)	6,100

(d) If the tax had been determined under paragraph (b)(2) of § 1.871-8 as though the tax liability would have been $6,478, determined as follows and by taking into account the election under § 1.871-10:

Total gross income		$22,000
Less: Deduction under section 613 for percentage depletion ($2000 × 27½ percent)	$550	
Deduction for personal exemption	600	1,150
Taxable income		20,850
Tax under section 1 of the Code on taxable income ($6,070 plus 48 percent of $850)		6,478

(e) Effective date. This section shall apply for taxable years beginning after December 31, 1966. For corresponding rules applicable to taxable years beginning before January 1, 1967, see 26 CFR 1.871-7(e) (Rev. as of Jan. 1, 1971).

T.D. 7332, 12/20/74, amend T.D. 8657, 3/5/96.

§ 1.871-13 Taxation of individuals for taxable year of change of U.S. citizenship or residence.

(a) In general. *(1)* An individual who is a citizen or resident of the United States at the beginning of the taxable year but a nonresident alien at the end of the taxable year, or a nonresident alien at the beginning of the taxable year but a citizen or resident of the United States at the end of the taxable year, is taxable for such year as though his taxable year were comprised of two separate periods, one consisting of the time during which he is a citizen or resident of the United States and the other consisting of the time during which he is not a citizen or resident of the United States. Thus, for example, the income tax liability of an alien individual under chapter 1 of the Code for the taxable year in which he changes his residence will be computed under two different sets of rules, one relating to resident aliens for the period of residence and the other relating to nonresident aliens for the period of nonresidence. However, in determining the taxable income for such year which is subject to the graduated rate of tax imposed by section 1 or 1201 of the Code, all income for the period of U.S. citizenship or residence must be aggregated with the income for the period of nonresidence which is effectively connected for such year with the conduct of a trade or business in the United States. This section does not apply to alien individuals treated as residents for the entire taxable year under section 6013(g) or (h). These individuals are taxed under the rules in § 1.1-1(b).

(2) For purposes of this section, an individual is deemed to be a citizen or resident of the United States for the day on which he becomes a citizen or resident of the United States, a nonresident of the United States for the day on which he abandons his U.S. residence, and an alien for the day on which he gives up his U.S. citizenship.

(b) Acquisition of U.S. citizenship or residence. Income from sources without the United States which is not effectively connected with the conduct by the taxpayer of a trade or business in the United States is not taxable if received by an alien individual while he is not a resident of the United States, even though he becomes a citizen or resident of the United States after its receipt and before the close of the taxable year. However, income from sources without the United States which is not effectively connected with the conduct by the taxpayer of a trade or business in the United States is taxable if received by an individual while he is a citizen or resident of the United States, even though he earns the income earlier in the taxable year while he is neither a citizen nor resident of the United States.

(c) Abandonment of U.S. citizenship or residence. Income from sources without the United States which is not effectively connected with the conduct by the taxpayer of a trade or business in the United States is not taxable if received by an alien individual while he is not a resident of the United States, even though he earns the income earlier in the taxable year while he is a citizen or resident of the United States. However, income from sources without the United States which is not effectively connected with the conduct by the taxpayer of a trade or business in the United States is taxable if received by an individual while he is a citizen or resident of the United States, even though he abandons his U.S. citizenship or residence after its receipt and before the close of the taxable year.

(d) Special rules. *(1) Method of accounting.* Paragraphs (b) and (c) of this section may not apply to an individual who for the taxable year uses an accrual method of accounting.

(2) Deductions for personal exemptions. An alien individual to whom this section applies is entitled to deduct one personal exemption for the taxable year under section 151. In addition, he is entitled to such additional exemptions as are allowed as a deduction under section 151 but only to the extent the amount of such additional exemptions do not exceed his taxable income (determined without regard to any deduction for personal exemptions) for the period in the taxable year during which he is a citizen or resident of the United States. This subparagraph does not apply to the extent it is inconsistent with section 873, and the regulations thereunder, or with the provisions of an income tax convention to which the United States is a party.

(3) Exclusion of dividends received. In determining the $100 exclusion for the taxable year provided by section 116 in respect of certain dividends, only those dividends for the period during which the individual is neither a citizen nor resident of the United States may be taken into account as are effectively connected for the taxable year with the conduct of a trade or business in the United States. See § 1.116-1(e)(1).

(e) Illustrations. The application of this section may be illustrated by the following examples:

Example (1). A, a married alien individual who uses the calendar year as the taxable year and the cash receipts and disbursements method of accounting, becomes a resident of the United States on June 1, 1971. During the period of nonresidence from January 1, 1971, to May 31, 1971, inclusive, A receives $15,000 income from sources without the United States which is not effectively connected with the conduct of a trade or business in the United States. During the period of residence from June 1, 1971, to December 31, 1971, A receives wages of $10,000, dividends of $200 from a foreign corporation, and dividends of $75 from a domestic corporation qualifying under section 116(a). Of the amount of wages so received, $2,000 is for services performed by A outside the United States during the period of nonresidence. Total allowable deductions (other than for personal exemptions) amount to $700, none of which are deductible under section 62 in computing adjusted gross income. For 1971 A's spouse has no gross income and is not the dependent of another taxpayer. For 1971, A's taxable income is $8,200, all of which is subject to tax under section 1, as follows:

Wages		$10,000
Dividends from foreign corporation		200
Dividends from domestic corporation ($75 less $75 exclusion)		0
Adjusted gross income		10,200
Less deductions:		
Personal exemptions (2 × $650)	$1,300	
Other allowable deductions	700	2,000
Taxable income		8,200

Example (2). The facts are the same as in example (1) except that during the period of nonresidence from January 1, 1971, to May 31, 1971, A receives from sources within the United States income of $1,850 which is effectively connected with the conduct by A of a business in the United States and $350 in dividends from domestic corporations qualifying under section 116(a). Only $50 of these dividends are effectively connected with the conduct by A of a business in the United States. The assumption is made that there are no allowable deductions connected with such effectively connected income. For 1971, A has taxable income of $10,075 subject to tax under section 1 and $300 income subject to tax under section 871(a)(1)(A), as follows:

Wages		$10,000
Business income		1,850
Dividends from foreign corporation		200
Dividends from domestic corporation ($125 less $100 exclusion)		25
Adjusted gross income		12,075
Less deductions:		
Personal exemptions (2 × $650)	$1,300	
Other allowable deductions	700	2,000
Taxable income subject to tax under section 1		10,075
Income subject to tax under section 871(a)(1)(A)		300

Example (3). A, a married alien individual with three children, uses the calendar year as the taxable year and the cash receipts and disbursements method of accounting. On October 1, 1971, A and his family become residents of the United States. During the period of nonresidence from January 1, 1971, to September 30, 1971, A receives income of $18,000 from sources without the United States which is not effectively connected with the conduct of a trade or business in the United States and of $2,500 from sources within the United States which is effectively connected with the conduct of a business in the United States. It is assumed there are no allowable deductions connected with such effectively connected income. During the period of residence from October 1, 1971, to December 31, 1971, A receives wages of $2,000, of which $400 is for services performed outside the United States during the period of nonresidence. Total allowable deductions (other than for personal exemptions) amount to $250, none of which are deductible under section 62 in computing adjusted gross income. Neither the spouse nor any of the children has any gross income for 1971, and the spouse is not the dependent of another taxpayer for such year. For 1971, A's taxable income is $1,850, all of which is subject to tax under section 1, as follows:

Wages (residence period)	$2,000	
Less: Allowable deductions	250	
Taxable income (without deduction for personal exemptions) (residence period)		$1,750
Business income (nonresidence period)		2,500
Total taxable income (without deduction for personal exemptions)		4,250
Less deduction for personal exemptions:		
Taxpayer	650	
Wife and 3 children (4 × $650, but not to exceed $1,750)	1,750	
		2,400
Taxable income		1,850

(f) Effective date. This section shall apply for taxable years beginning after December 31, 1966. There are no corresponding rules in this part for taxable years beginning before January 1, 1967.

T.D. 7332, 12/20/74, amend T.D. 7670, 1/30/80.

§ 1.871-14 Rules relating to repeal of tax on interest of nonresident alien individuals and foreign corporations received from certain portfolio debt investments.

(a) General rule. No tax shall be imposed under section 871(a)(1)(A), 871(a)(1)(C), 881(a)(1) or 881(a)(3) on any portfolio interest as defined in sections 871(h)(2) and 881(c)(2) received by a foreign person. But see section 871(b) or 882(a) if such interest is effectively connected with the conduct of a trade or business within the United States.

(b) Rules concerning obligations in bearer form. *(1) In general.* Interest (including original issue discount) with respect to an obligation in bearer form is portfolio interest within the meaning of section 871(h)(2)(A) or 881(c)(2)(A) only if it is paid with respect to an obligation issued after July 18, 1984, that is described in section 163(f)(2)(B) and the regulations under that section and an exception under section 871(h) or 881(c) does not apply. Any obligation that is not in registered form as defined in paragraph (c)(1)(i) of this section is an obligation in bearer form.

(2) Coordination with withholding and reporting rules. For an exemption from withholding under section 1441 with respect to obligations described in this paragraph (b), see § 1.1441-1(b)(4)(i). For rules relating to an exemption from Form 1099 reporting and backup withholding under section 3406, see section 6049 and § 1.6049-5(b)(8) for the payment of interest and § 1.6045-1(g)(1)(ii) for the redemption, retirement, or sale of an obligation in bearer form.

(c) Rules concerning obligations in registered form. *(1) In general.* (i) Obligation in registered form. For purposes of this section, an obligation is in registered form only as provided in this paragraph (c)(1)(i). The conditions for an obligation to be considered in registered form are identical to the conditions described in § 5f.103-1 of this chapter. Therefore, an obligation that would be an obligation in registered form except for the fact that it can be converted at any time in the future into an obligation that is not in registered form shall not be an obligation in registered form. An obligation that is not in registered form by reason of the preceding sentence may nevertheless be in registered form, but only after the possibility of conversion is terminated. An obligation that is not in registered form and can be converted into an obligation that would meet the requirements of this paragraph (c)(1)(i) for being in registered form shall be considered in registered form only after the conversion is effected. For purposes of this section, an obligation is convertible if the obligation can be transferred by any means not described in § 5f.103-1(c) of this chapter. An obligation is treated as an obligation in registered form if—

(A) The obligation is registered as to both principal and any stated interest with the issuer (or its agent) and transfer of the obligation may be effected only by surrender of the old instrument, and either the reissuance by the issuer of the old instrument to the new holder or the issuance by the issuer of a new instrument to the new holder;

(B) The right to the principal of, and stated interest on, the obligation may be transferred only through a book entry system maintained by the issuer (or its agent) described in this paragraph (c)(1)(i)(B). An obligation shall be considered transferable through a book entry system if the ownership of an interest in the obligation, is required to be reflected in a book entry, whether or not physical securities are issued. A book entry is a record of ownership that identifies the owner of an in interest in the obligation; or

(C) It is registered as to both principal and any stated interest with the issuer (or its agent) and may be transferred by way of either of the methods described in paragraph (c)(1)(i)(A) or (B) of this section.

(ii) Requirements for portfolio interest qualification in the case of an obligation in registered form. Interest (including original issue discount) received on an obligation that is in registered form qualifies as portfolio interest only if—

(A) The interest is paid on an obligation issued after July 18, 1984;

(B) The interest would be subject to tax under section 871(a)(1)(A), 871(a)(1)(C), 881(a)(1) or 881(a)(3) but for section 871(h) or 881(c);

(C) A United States (U.S.) person otherwise required to deduct and withhold tax under chapter 3 of the Internal Revenue Code (Code) receives a statement that meets the requirements of section 871(h)(5) that the beneficial owner of the obligation is not a U.S. person; and

(D) An exception under section 871(h) or 881(c) does not apply.

(2) Required statement. For purposes of paragraph (c)(1)(ii)(C) of this section, a U.S. person will be considered to have received a statement that meets the requirements of section 871(h)(5) if either it complies with one of the procedures described in this paragraph (c)(2) and does not have actual knowledge or reason to know that the beneficial owner is a U.S. person or it complies with the procedures described in paragraph (d) or (e) of this section.

(i) The U.S. person (or its authorized foreign agent described in § 1.1441-7(c)(2)) can reliably associate the payment with documentation upon which it can rely to treat the payment as made to a foreign beneficial owner in accordance with § 1.1441-1(e)(1)(ii). See § 1.1441-1(b)(2)(vii) for rules regarding reliable association with documentation.

(ii) The U.S. person (or its authorized foreign agent described in § 1.1441-7(c)(2)) can reliably associate the payment with a withholding certificate described in § 1.1441-5(c)(2)(iv) from a person claiming to be withholding foreign partnership and the foreign partnership can reliably associate the payment with documentation upon which it can rely to treat the payment as made to a foreign beneficial owner in accordance with § 1.1441-1(e)(1)(ii).

(iii) The U.S. person (or its authorized foreign agent described in § 1.1441-7(c)(2)) can reliably associate the payment with a withholding certificate described in § 1.1441-1(e)(3)(ii) from a person representing to be a qualified intermediary that has assumed primary withholding responsibility in accordance with § 1.1441-1(e)(5)(iv) and the qualified intermediary can reliably associate the payment with documentation upon which it can rely to treat the payment as made to a foreign beneficial owner in accordance with its agreement with the Internal Revenue Service (IRS).

(iv) The U.S. person (or its authorized foreign agent described in § 1.1441-7(c)(2)) can reliably associate the payment with a withholding certificate described in § 1.1441-1(e)(3)(v) from a person claiming to be a U.S. branch of a foreign bank or of a foreign insurance company that is described in § 1.1441-1(b)(2)(iv)(A) or a U.S. branch designated in accordance with § 1.1441-1(b)(2)(iv)(E) and the U.S. branch can reliably associate the payment with documentation upon which it can rely to treat the payment as made to a foreign beneficial owner in accordance with § 1.1441-1(e)(1)(ii).

(v) The U.S. person receives a statement from a securities clearing organization, a bank, or another financial institution that holds customers' securities in the ordinary course of its trade or business. In such case the statement must be signed under penalties of perjury by an authorized representative of the financial institution and must state that the institution has received from the beneficial owner a withholding certificate described in § 1.1441-1(e)(2)(i) (a Form W-8 or an acceptable substitute form as defined § 1.1441-1(e)(4)(vi)) or that it has received from another financial institution a similar statement that it, or another financial institution acting on behalf of the beneficial owner, has received the Form W-8 from the beneficial owner. In the case of multiple financial institutions between the beneficial owner and the U.S. person, this statement must be given by each financial institution to the one above it in the chain. No particular form is required for the statement provided by the financial institutions. However, the statement must provide the name and address of the beneficial owner, and a copy of the Form W-8 provided by the beneficial owner must be attached. The statement is subject to the same rules described in § 1.1441-1(e)(4) that apply to intermediary Forms W-8 described in § 1.1441-1(e)(3)(iii). If the information on the Form W-8 changes, the beneficial owner must so notify the financial institution acting on its behalf within 30 days of such changes, and the financial institution must promptly so inform the U.S. person. This notice also must be given if the financial institution has actual knowledge that the information has changed but has not been so informed by the beneficial owner. In the case of multiple financial institutions between the beneficial owner and the U.S. person, this notice must be given by each financial institution to the institution above it in the chain.

(vi) The U.S. person complies with procedures that the U.S. competent authority may agree to with the competent authority of a country with which the United States has an income tax treaty in effect.

(3). Time for providing certificate or documentary evidence. (i) General rule. Interest on a registered obligation shall qualify as portfolio interest if the withholding certificate or documentary evidence that must be provided is furnished before expiration of the beneficial owner's period of limitation for claiming a refund of tax with respect to such interest. See, however, § 1.1441-1(b)(7) for consequences to a withholding agent that makes a payment without withholding even though it cannot reliably associate the payment with the documentation prior to the payment. If a withholding agent withholds an amount under chapter 3 of the Code because it cannot reliably associate the payment with the documentation for the beneficial owner on the date of payment, the beneficial owner may nevertheless claim the benefit of an exemption from tax under this section by claiming a refund or credit for the amount withheld based upon the procedures described in §§ 1.1464-1 and 301.6402-3(e) of this chapter. For this purpose, the taxpayer must attach a withholding certificate described in § 1.1441-1(e)(2)(i) to the income tax filed for claiming a refund of tax. In the alternative, adjustments to any amount of overwithheld tax may be made under the procedures described in § 1.1461-2(a) (for example, if the beneficial owner furnishes documentation to the withholding agent before the due date for filing the return required under § 1.1461-1(b) with respect to that payment).

(ii) Example. The following example illustrates the rules of this paragraph (c)(3) and their coordination with § 1.1441-1(b)(7):

Example. A is a withholding agent who, on October 12, 2001, pays interest on a registered obligation to B, a foreign corporation. B is a calendar year taxpayer, engaged in the conduct of a trade or business in the United States, and is, therefore, required to file an annual income tax return on Form 1120F. The interest, however, is not effectively connected with B's U.S. trade or business. On the date of payment, B has not furnished, and A cannot associate the payment with documentation for B. However, A does not withhold under section 1442, even though, under § 1.1441-1(b)(3)(iii)(A), A should presume that B is a foreign person, because A's communications with B are mailed to an address in a foreign country. Assuming that B files a return for its taxable year ending December 31, 2001, and that its statute of limitations period with regard to that year expires on June 15, 2003, the interest paid on October 12, 2001, may qualify as portfolio interest only if B provides appropriate documentation to A on or before June 15, 2003. If B does not provide the documentation on or before June 15, 2005, and does not pay the tax, A is liable for the tax under section 1463, even if B provides the documentation to A after June 15, 2005. Therefore, the provisions in § 1.1441-1(b)(7), regarding late-received documentation would not help A avoid liability for tax under section 1463 even if the documentation is furnished within the statute of limitations period of A. This is because, in a case involving interest, the documentation received within the limitations period of the beneficial owner serves as a condition for the interest to qualify as portfolio interest. When documentation is received after the expiration of the beneficial owner's limitations period, the interest can no longer qualify as portfolio interest. On the other hand, A could rely on documentation that it receives after the expiration of B's limitations period to establish B's right to a reduced rate of withholding under an applicable income tax treaty (since, in such a case, a claim of treaty benefits is not conditioned upon providing documentation prior to the expiration of the beneficial owner's limitations period).

(4) Coordination with withholding and reporting rules. For an exemption from withholding under section 1441 with respect to obligations described in this paragraph (c), see § 1.1441-1(b)(4)(i). For rules applicable to withholding certificates, see § 1.1441-1(e)(4). For rules regarding documentary evidence, see § 1.6049-5(c)(1). For application of presumptions when the U.S. person cannot reliably associate the

payment with documentation, see § 1.1441-1(b)(3). For standards of knowledge applicable to withholding agents, see § 1.1441-7(b). For rules relating to an exemption from Form 1099 reporting and backup withholding under section 3406, see section 6049 and § 1.6049-5(b)(8) for the payment of interest and § 1.6045-1(g)(1)(i) for the redemption, retirement, or sale of an obligation in registered form. For rules relating to reporting on Forms 1042 and 1042-S, see § 1.1461-1(b) and (c).

(d) Application of repeal of 30-percent withholding to pass-through certificates. *(1) In general.* Interest received on a pass-through certificate qualifies as portfolio interest under section 871(h)(2) or 881(c)(2) if the interest satisfies the conditions described in paragraph (b)(1), (c)(1), or (e) of this section without regard to whether any obligation held by the fund or trust to which the pass-through certificate relates is described in paragraph (b)(1), (c)(1)(ii), or (e) of this section. This paragraph (d)(1) applies only to payments made to the holder of the pass-through certificate from the trustee of the pass-through trust and does not apply to payments made to the trustee of the pass-through trust. For example, a mortgage pass-through certificate in bearer form must meet the requirements set forth in paragraph (b)(1) of this section, but the obligations held by the fund or trust to which the mortgage pass-through certificate relates need not meet the requirements set forth in paragraph (b)(1), (c)(1)(ii), or (e) of this section. However, for purposes of paragraphs (b)(1), (c)(1)(ii), and (e) of this section and section 127 of the Tax Reform Act of 1984, a pass-through certificate will be considered as issued after July 18, 1984, only to the extent that the obligations held by the fund or trust to which the pass-through certificate relates are issued after July 18, 1984.

(2) Interest in REMICs. Interest received on a regular or residual interest in a REMIC qualifies as portfolio interest under section 871(h)(2) or 881(c)(2) if the interest satisfies the conditions described in paragraph (b)(1), (c)(1)(ii), or (e) of this section. For purposes of paragraph (b)(1), (c)(1)(ii), or (e) of this section, interest on a regular interest in a REMIC is not considered interest on any mortgage obligations held by the REMIC. The foregoing rule, however, applies only to payments made to the holder of the regular interest from the REMIC and does not apply to payments made to the REMIC. For purposes of paragraph (b)(1), (c)(1)(ii), or (e) of this section, interest on a residual interest in a REMIC is considered to be interest on or with respect to the obligations held by the REMIC, and not on or with respect to the residual interest. For purposes of paragraphs (b)(1), (c)(1)(ii), and (e) of this section and section 127 of the Tax Reform Act of 1984, a residual interest in a REMIC will be considered as issued after July 18, 1984, only to the extent that the obligations held by the REMIC are issued after July 18, 1984, but a regular interest in a REMIC will be considered as issued after July 18, 1984, if the regular interest was issued after July 18, 1984, without regard to the date on which the mortgage obligations held by the REMIC were issued.

(3) Date of issuance. In general, a mortgage pass-through certificate will be considered to have been issued after July 18, 1984, if all of the mortgages held by the fund or trust were issued after July 18, 1984. If some of the mortgages held by the fund or trust were issued before July 19, 1984, then the portion of any interest payment which represents interest on those mortgages shall not be considered to be portfolio interest. The preceding sentence shall not apply, however, if all of the following conditions are satisfied:

(i) The mortgage pass-through certificate is issued after December 31, 1986;

(ii) Payment of the mortgage pass-through certificate is guaranteed by, and a guarantee commitment has been issued by, an entity that is independent from the issuer of the underlying obligation;

(iii) The guarantee commitment with respect to the mortgage pass-through certificate cannot have been issued more than 14 months prior to the date on which the mortgage pass-through certificate is issued; and

(iv) The fund or trust to which the mortgage pass-through certificate relates cannot contain mortgage obligations on which the first scheduled monthly payment of principal and interest was made more than twelve months before the date on which the guarantee commitment was made.

(e) Foreign-targeted registered obligations. *(1) General rule.* The statement described in paragraph (c)(1)(ii)(C) of this section is not required with respect to interest paid on a registered obligation that is targeted to foreign markets in accordance with the provisions of paragraph (e)(2) of this section if the interest is paid by a U.S. person, a withholding foreign partnership, or a U.S. branch described in § 1.1441-1(b)(2)(iv)(A) or (E) to a registered owner at an address outside the United States, provided that the registered owner is a financial institution described in section 871(h)(5)(B). In that case, the U.S. person otherwise required to deduct and withhold tax may treat the interest as portfolio interest if it does not have actual knowledge that the beneficial owner is a United States person and if it receives the certificate described in paragraph (e)(3)(i) of this section from a financial institution or member of a clearing organization, which member is the beneficial owner of the obligation, or the documentary evidence or statement described in paragraph (e)(3)(ii) of this section from the beneficial owner, in accordance with the procedures described in paragraph (e)(4) of this section.

(2) Definition of a foreign-targeted registered obligation. An obligation is considered to be targeted to foreign markets for purposes of paragraph (e)(1) of this section if it is sold (or resold in connection with its original issuance) only to foreign persons (or to foreign branches of United States financial institutions described in section 871(h)(5)(B)) in accordance with procedures similar to those prescribed in § 1.163-5(c)(2)(i)(A), (B), or (D). However, the provisions of that section that require an obligation to be offered for sale or resale in connection with its original issuance only outside the United States do not apply with respect to registered obligations offered for sale through a public auction. Similarly, the provisions of that section that require delivery to be made outside the United States do not apply to registered obligations offered for sale through a public auction if the obligations are considered to be in registered form by virtue of the fact that they may be transferred only through a book entry system. The obligation, if evidenced by a physical document other than a confirmation receipt, must contain on its face a legend indicating that it has been sold (or resold in connection with its original issuance) in accordance with those procedures.

(3) Documentation. A certificate described in paragraph (e)(3)(i) of this section is required if the United States person otherwise required to deduct and withhold tax (the withholding agent) pays interest to a financial institution described in section 871(h)(5)(B) or to a member of a clearing organization, which member is the beneficial owner of the obligation. The documentation described in paragraph (e)(3)(ii) of this section is required if a withholding agent

pays interest to a beneficial owner that is neither a financial institution described in section 871(h)(5)(B) nor a member of a clearing organization.

(i) Interest paid to a financial institution or a member of a clearing organization. (A) Requirement of a certificate. (1) If the withholding agent pays interest to a financial institution described in section 871(h)(5)(B) or to a member of a clearing organization, which member is the beneficial owner of the obligation, the withholding agent must receive a certificate which states that, beginning at the time the last preceding certificate under this paragraph (e)(3)(i) was provided and while the financial institution or clearing organization member has held the obligation, with respect to each foreign-targeted registered obligation which has been held by the person providing the certificate at any time since the provision of such last preceding certificate, either—

(i) The beneficial owner of the obligation has not been a United States person on each interest payment date; or

(ii) If the person providing the certificate is a financial institution which is holding or has held an obligation on behalf of the beneficial owner, the beneficial owner of the obligation has been a United States person on one or more interest payment dates (identifying such date or dates), and the person making the certification has forwarded or will forward the appropriate United States beneficial ownership notification to the withholding agent in accordance with the provisions of paragraph (e)(4) of this section.

(2) The person providing the certificate need not state the foregoing where no previous certificate has been required to be provided by the payee to the withholding agent under this paragraph (e)(3)(i).

(B) Additional representations. Whether or not a previous certificate has been required to be provided with respect to the obligation, each certificate furnished pursuant to the provisions in this paragraph (e)(3)(i) must further state that, for each foreign-targeted registered obligation held and every other such obligation to be acquired and held by the person providing the certificate during the period beginning on the date of the certificate and ending on the date the next certificate is required to be provided, the beneficial owner of the obligation will not be a United States person on each interest payment date while the financial institution or clearing organization member holds the obligation and that, if the person providing the certificate is a financial institution which is holding or will be holding the obligation on behalf of a beneficial owner, such person will provide a United States beneficial ownership notification to the withholding agent (and a clearing organization that is not a withholding agent where a member organization is required by this paragraph (e)(3) to furnish the clearing organization with a statement) in accordance with paragraph (e)(4) of this section in the event such certificate (or statement in the case of a statement provided by a member organization to a clearing organization that is not a withholding agent) is or becomes untrue with respect to any obligation. A clearing organization is an entity which is in the business of holding obligations for member organizations and transferring obligations among such members by credit or debit to the account of a member without the necessity of physical delivery of the obligation.

(C) Obligation must be identified. The certificate described in paragraph (e)(3)(ii)(A) of this section must identify the obligation or obligations with respect to which it is given, except where the certification is given with respect to an obligation that has not been acquired at the time the certification is made. An obligation is identified if it or the larger issuance of which it is a part is described on a list (e.g., $5 million principal amount of 12% debentures of ABC Savings and Loan Association due February 25, 1995, $3 million principal amount of 10% U.S. Treasury notes due May 28, 1990) of all registered obligations targeted to foreign markets held by or on behalf of the person providing the certificate and the list is attached to, and incorporated by reference into, the certificate. The certificate must identify and provide the address of the person furnishing the certificate.

(D) Payment to a depository of a clearing organization. If the withholding agent pays interest to a depository of a clearing organization, then the clearing organization must provide the certificate described in this paragraph (e)(3)(i) to the withholding agent. Any certificate that is provided by a clearing organization must state that the clearing organization has received a statement from each member which complies with the provisions of this paragraph (e)(3)(i) and of paragraph (e)(4) of this section (as if the clearing organization were the withholding agent and regardless of whether the member is a financial institution described in section 871(h)(5)(B)).

(E) Statement in lieu of Form W-8. Subject to the requirements set out in paragraph (e)(4) of this section, a certificate or statement in the form described in this paragraph (e)(3)(i), in conjunction with the next annual certificate or statement, will serve as the certificate that may be provided in lieu of a Form W-8 with respect to interest on all foreign-targeted registered obligations held by the person making the certification or statement and which is paid to such person within the period beginning on the date of the certificate and ending on the date the next certificate is required to be provided.

(F) Electronic transmission. The certificate described in this paragraph (e)(3)(i) may be provided electronically under the terms and conditions of § 1.163-5(c)(2)(i)(D)(3)(ii).

(ii) Payment to a person other than a financial institution or member of a clearing organization. If the withholding agent pays interest to the beneficial owner of an obligation that is neither a financial institution described in section 871(h)(5)(B) nor a member of a clearing organization, then such owner must provide the withholding agent a statement described in paragraph (c)(1)(ii)(C) of this section.

(4) Applicable procedures regarding documentation. (i) Procedures applicable to certificates required under paragraph (e)(3)(i) of this section. (A) Time for providing certificate. Where no previous certificate for foreign-targeted registered obligations has been provided to the withholding agent by the person providing the certificate under paragraph (e)(3)(i) of this section, such certificate must be provided within the period beginning 90 days prior to the first interest payment date on which the person holds a foreign-targeted registered obligation. The withholding agent may, in its discretion, withhold under section 1441(a), 1442(a), or 1443 if the certificate is not received by the date 30 days prior to the interest payment. Thereafter the certificate must be filed within the period beginning on January 15 and ending January 31 of each year. If a certificate provided pursuant to the first sentence of this paragraph (e)(4)(i)(A) is provided during the period beginning on January 15 and ending on January 31 of any year, then no other certificate need be provided during such period in such year.

(B) Change of status notification on Form W-9. If, on any interest payment date after the obligation was acquired by the person making the certification, the beneficial owner of the obligation is a U.S. person, then the person to whom the withholding agent pays interest must furnish the withholding agent with a U.S. beneficial ownership notification within 30 days after such interest payment date. A U.S. beneficial ownership notification must include a statement that the beneficial owner of the obligation has been a U.S. person on an interest payment date (identifying such date), that such owner has provided to the person providing the notification a Form W-9 (or a substitute form that is substantially similar to Form W-9 and completed under penalties of perjury), and that the person providing the notification has been and will be complying with the information reporting requirements of section 6049, if applicable.

(C) Alternative notification statement. Where the person providing the notification described in paragraph (e)(4)(i)(B) of this section is neither a controlled foreign corporation within the meaning of section 957(a), nor a foreign corporation 50-percent or more of the gross income of which from all sources for the three-year period ending with the close of the taxable year preceding the date of the statement was effectively connected with the conduct of trade or business in the United States, such person must attach to the notification a copy of the Form W-9 (or substitute form that is substantially similar to Form W-9 and completed under penalties of perjury) provided by the beneficial owner. When a person that provides the U.S. beneficial ownership notification does not attach to it a copy of such Form W-9 (or substitute form that is substantially similar to Form W-9 and completed under penalties of perjury), such person must state that it is either a controlled foreign corporation within the meaning of section 957(a), or a foreign corporation 50-percent or more of the gross income of which from all sources for the three-year period ending with the close of its taxable year preceding the date of the statement was effectively connected with the conduct of a trade or business in the United States. A withholding agent that receives a Form W-9 (or a substitute form that is substantially similar to Form W-9 and completed under penalties of perjury) must send a copy of such form to the IRS, at such address as the IRS shall indicate, within 30 days after receiving it and must attach a statement that the Form W-9 or substitute form was provided pursuant to this paragraph (e)(4) with respect to a U.S. person that has owned a foreign-targeted registered obligation on one or more interest payment dates.

(D) Failure to provide notification. If either a Form W-9 (or a substitute form that is substantially similar to a Form W-9 and completed under penalties of perjury) or the statement described in paragraph (e)(4)(i)(C) of this section is not attached to the U.S. beneficial ownership notification provided pursuant to paragraph (e)(4)(i)(B) of this section, the withholding agent is required to withhold under section 1441, 1442, or 1443 on a payment of interest made after the withholding agent has received the notification unless such form or statement (or a statement that the beneficial owner of the obligation is no longer a U.S. person) is received before the interest payment date from the person who provided the notification (or transferee). If, during the period beginning on the next January 15 and ending on the next January 31, such person certifies as set out in paragraph (e)(3)(i) of this section (subject to paragraph (e)(3)(i)(A)(2) of this section) then the withholding agent is not required to withhold during the year following such certification (unless such person again provides a U.S. beneficial ownership notification without attaching a Form W-9 or substitute form that is substantially similar to Form W-9 and completed under penalties of perjury or the statement described in paragraph (e)(4)(i)(C) of this section).

(E) Procedures for clearing organizations. Within the period beginning 10 days before the end of the calendar quarter and ending on the last day of each calendar quarter, any clearing organization (including a clearing organization that is a withholding agent) relying on annual certificates or statements from its member organizations, as set forth in paragraph (e)(3)(i) of this section, must send each member organization having submitted such certificate or statement a reminder that the member organization must give the clearing organization a U.S. beneficial ownership notification in the circumstances described in paragraph (e)(4)(i)(B) of this section.

(F) Retention of certificates. The certificate described in paragraph (e)(3)(i) of this section must be retained in the records of the withholding agent for four years from the end of the calendar year in which it was received. The statement described in paragraph (e)(3)(i) of this section that is received by a clearing organization from a member organization must be retained in the records of the clearing organization for four years from the end of the calendar year in which it was received.

(G) No reporting requirement. The withholding agent who receives the certificate described in paragraph (e)(3)(i) of this section is not required to file Form 1042S to report payments under § 1.1461-1(b) or (c) of interest that are made with respect to foreign-targeted registered obligations held by the person providing the certificate and are made within the period beginning with the certificate date and ending on the last date for filing the next certificate.

(ii) Procedures regarding certificates required under paragraph (e)(3)(ii) of this section. (A) Time for providing certificate. The statement described in paragraph (e)(3)(ii) of this section must be provided to the withholding agent within the period beginning 90 days prior to and ending on the first interest payment date on which the withholding agent pays interest to the beneficial owner. The withholding agent may, in its discretion, withhold under section 1441(a), 1442(a), or 1443 if the statement is not received by the date 30 days prior to the interest payment. The beneficial owner must confirm to the withholding agent the continuing validity of the documentary evidence within the period beginning 90 days prior to the first day of the third calendar year following the provision of such evidence and during the same period every three years thereafter while the owner still owns the obligation. The withholding agent who receives the statement described in paragraph (e)(3)(ii) of this section is not required to report payments of interest under § 1.1461-1(b) or (c) if the payments are made with respect to foreign-targeted registered obligations held by the person who provides the statement and are made within the period beginning with the date on which the statement is provided and ending on the last date for confirming the validity of the statement. The statement received for purposes of paragraph (e)(3)(ii) of this section is subject to the applicable procedures set forth in § 1.1441-1(e)(4).

(B) Change of status notification on Form W-9. If on any interest payment date after the obligation was acquired by the person providing the statement described in paragraph (e)(3)(ii) of this section, the beneficial owner of the obligation is a U.S. person, then the beneficial owner must so inform the withholding agent within 30 days after such interest payment date and must provide a Form W-9 (or substitute form that is substantially similar completed under penalties of perjury) to the withholding agent. However, the beneficial owner is not required to provide another Form W-9 (or substitute form that is substantially similar and completed under penalties of perjury) if such person has already provided it to the withholding agent within the same calendar year.

(iii) Disqualification of documentation. In accordance with the provisions of section 871(h)(4), the Secretary may make a determination in appropriate cases that a certificate or statement by any person, or class of persons, does not satisfy the requirements of that section. Should that determination be made, all payments of interest that otherwise qualify as portfolio interest to that person would become subject to 30-percent withholding under section 1441(a), 1442(a), or 1443.

(iv) Special effective date. Notwithstanding the foregoing requirements of this section—

(A) Any certificate that is required to be filed with the withholding agent during the period beginning on January 15 and ending on January 31, 1986, is not required to state that the beneficial owner of an obligation, prior to the date of the certificate, either was not a United States person or was a United States person if the obligation was acquired by the person providing the certificate on or before September 19, 1985; and

(B) All of the requirements of this paragraph (e), as in effect prior to the effective date of these amendments, shall remain effective with respect to each interest payment prior to the filing of the certificate described in paragraph (e)(4)(iv)(A) of this section, except that the provisions of paragraph (e)(3) of this section relating to which persons are required to receive certificates or statements and paragraph (e)(3)(ii) or (4)(ii) of this section shall become effective with respect to each interest payment after September 20, 1985.

(5) Information reporting. See § 1.6049-5(b)(7) for special information reporting rules applicable to interest on foreign-targeted registered obligations. See § 1.6045-1(g)(1)(ii) for information reporting rules applicable to the redemption, retirement, or sale of foreign-targeted registered obligations.

(f) Securities lending transactions. For applicable rules regarding substitute interest payments received pursuant to a securities lending transaction or a sale-repurchase transaction, see §§ 1.871-7(b)(2) and 1.881-2(b)(2).

(g) Portfolio interest not to include interest received by 10-percent shareholders. *(1) In general.* For purposes of section 871(h), the term portfolio interest shall not include any interest received by a 10-percent shareholder.

(2) Ten-percent shareholder. (i) In general. The term 10-percent shareholder means—

(A) In the case of an obligation issued by a corporation, any person who owns 10-percent or more of the total combined voting power of all classes of stock of such corporation entitled to vote; or

(B) In the case of an obligation issued by a partnership, any person who owns 10-percent or more of the capital or profits interest in such partnership.

(ii) Ownership. (A) Stock ownership. For purposes of paragraph (g)(2)(i)(A) of this section, stock owned means stock directly or indirectly owned and stock owned by reason of the attribution rules of section 318(a), as modified by section 871(h)(3)(C).

(B) Ownership of partnership interest. For purposes of paragraph (g)(2)(i)(B) of this section, rules similar to the rules in paragraph (g)(2)(ii)(A) of this section shall be applied in determining the ownership of a capital or profits interest in a partnership.

(3) Application of 10-percent shareholder test to partners receiving interest through a partnership. (i) Partner level test. Whether interest paid to a partnership and included in the distributive share of a partner that is a nonresident alien individual or foreign corporation is received by a 10 percent shareholder shall be determined by applying the rules of this paragraph (g) only at the partner level.

(ii) Time at which 10-percent shareholder test is applied. The determination of whether a nonresident alien individual or foreign corporation that is a partner in a partnership is a 10-percent shareholder under the rules of section 871(h)(3), section 881(c)(3), and this paragraph (g) with respect to interest paid to such partnership shall be made at the time that the withholding agent, absent the provisions of section 871(h), 881(c) and the rules of this paragraph, would otherwise be required to withhold under sections 1441 and 1442 with respect to such interest. For example, in the case of U.S. source interest paid by a domestic corporation to a domestic partnership or withholding foreign partnership (as defined in § 1.1441-5(c)(2)), the 10-percent shareholder test is applied when any distributions that include the interest are made to a foreign partner and, to the extent that a foreign partner's distributive share of the interest has not actually been distributed, on the earlier of the date that the statement required under section 6031(b) is mailed or otherwise provided to such partner, or the due date for furnishing such statement. See § 1.1441-5(b)(2) and (c)(2)(iii).

(4) Application of 10-percent shareholder test to interest paid to a simple trust or grantor trust. Whether interest paid to a simple trust or grantor trust and distributed to or included in the gross income of a nonresident alien individual or foreign corporation that is a beneficiary or owner of such trust, as the case may be, is received by a 10-percent shareholder shall be determined by applying the rules of this paragraph (g) only at the beneficiary or owner level. The 10-percent shareholder test is applied with respect to a nonresident alien individual or foreign corporation that is a beneficiary of a simple trust or an owner of a grantor trust at the time that a withholding agent, absent any exceptions, would otherwise be required to withhold under sections 1441 and 1442 with respect to such interest.

(h) Definitions. For purposes of this section, the terms *U.S. person* and *foreign person* have the meaning set forth in § 1.1441-1(c)(2), the term *beneficial owner* has the meaning set forth in § 1.1441-1(c)(6), the term *withholding agent* has the meaning set forth in § 1.1441-7(a); the term *payee* has the meaning set forth in § 1.1441-1(b)(2); and the term *payment* has the meaning set forth in § 1.1441-2(e).

(i) Effective date. *(1) In general.* This section shall apply to payments of interest made after December 31, 2000. The rules of paragraph (g) apply to interest paid after April 12, 2007. Taxpayers may choose to apply the rules of paragraph (g) to interest paid in any taxable year not closed by the period of limitations as of April 12, 2007, provided they do so consistently for all relevant partnerships during such years.

(2) Transition rule. For purposes of this section, the validity of a Form W-8 that was valid on January 1, 1998, under the regulations in effect prior to January 1, 2001 (see 26 CFR parts 1 and 35a, revised April 1, 1999) and expired, or will expire, at any time during 1998, is extended until December 31, 1998. The validity of a Form W-8 that is valid on or after January 1, 1999 remains valid until its validity expires under the regulations in effect prior to January 1, 2001 (see 26 CFR parts 1 and 35a, revised April 1, 1999) but in no event will such a form remain valid after December 31, 2000. The rule in this paragraph (h)(2), however, does not apply to extend the validity period of a Form W-8 that expired solely by reason of changes in the circumstances of the person whose name is on the certificate. Notwithstanding the first three sentences of this paragraph (h)(2), a withholding agent or payor may choose to not take advan-

tage of the transition rule in this paragraph (h)(2) with respect to one or more withholding certificates valid under the regulations in effect prior to January 1, 2001 (see 26 CFR parts 1 and 35a, revised April 1, 1999) and, therefore, may choose to obtain withholding certificates conforming to the requirements described in this section (new withholding certificates). For purposes of this section, a new withholding certificate is deemed to satisfy the documentation requirement under the regulations in effect prior to January 1, 2001 (see 26 CFR parts 1 and 35a, revised April 1, 1999). Further, a new withholding certificate remains valid for the period specified in § 1.1441-1(e)(4)(ii), regardless of when the certificate is obtained.

T.D. 8734, 10/6/97, amend T.D. 8804, 12/30/98, T.D. 8856, 12/29/99, T.D. 9323, 4/11/2007.

§ 1.872-1 Gross income of nonresident alien individuals.

(a) In general. *(1) Inclusions.* The gross income of a nonresident alien individual for any taxable year includes only (i) the gross income which is derived from sources within the United States and which is not effectively connected for the taxable year with the conduct of a trade or business in the United States by that individual and (ii) the gross income, irrespective of whether such income is derived from sources within or without the United States, which is effectively connected for the taxable year with the conduct of a trade or business in the United States by that individual. For the determination of the sources of income, see sections 861 through 863 and the regulations thereunder. For the determination of whether income from sources within or without the United States is effectively connected for the taxable year with the conduct of a trade or business in the United States, see sections 864(c) and 871(c) and (d), §§ 1.864-3 through 1.864-7, and §§ 1.871-9 and 1.871-10. For special rules for determining the income of an alien individual who changes his residence during the taxable year, see § 1.871-13.

(2) Exchange transactions. Even though a nonresident alien individual who effects certain transactions in the United States in stocks, securities, or commodities during the taxable year may not, by reason of section 864(b)(2) and paragraph (c) or (d) of § 1.864-2, be engaged in trade or business in the United States during the taxable year through the effecting of such transactions, nevertheless he shall be required to include in gross income for the taxable year the gains and profits from those transactions to the extent required by § 1.871-7 or § 1.871-8.

(3) Exclusions. For exclusions from gross income, see § 1.872-2.

(b) Individuals not engaged in U.S. business. In the case of a nonresident alien individual who at no time during the taxable year is engaged in trade or business in the United States, the gross income shall include only (1) the gross income from sources within the United States which is described in section 871(a) and paragraphs (b), (c), and (d) of § 1.871-7, and (2) the gross income from sources within the United States which, by reason of section 871 (c) or (d) and § 1.871-9 or § 1.871-10, is treated as effectively connected for the taxable year with the conduct of a trade or business in the United States by that individual.

(c) Individuals engaged in U.S. business. In the case of a nonresident alien individual who is engaged in trade or business in the United States at any time during the taxable year, the gross income shall include (1) the gross income from sources within and without the United States which is effectively connected for the taxable year with the conduct of a trade or business in the United States by that individual, (2) the gross income from sources within the United States which, by reason of the election provided in section 871(d) and § 1.871-10, is treated as effectively connected for the taxable year with the conduct of a trade or business in the United States by that individual, and (3) the gross income from sources within the United States which is described in section 871(a) and paragraphs (b), (c), and (d) of § 1.871-7 and is not effectively connected for the taxable year with the conduct of a trade or business in the United States by that individual.

(d) Special rules applicable to certain expatriates. For special rules for determining the gross income of a nonresident alien individual who has lost U.S. citizenship with a principal purpose of avoiding certain taxes, see section 877(b)(1).

(e) Alien resident of Puerto Rico. This section shall not apply in the case of a nonresident alien individual who is a bona fide resident of Puerto Rico during the entire taxable year. See section 876 and § 1.876-1.

(f) Effective date. This section shall apply for taxable years beginning after December 31, 1966. For corresponding rules applicable to taxable years beginning before January 1, 1967, see 26 CFR 1.872-1 (Rev. as of Jan. 1, 1971).

T.D. 6258, 10/23/57, amend T.D. 7332, 12/20/74.

§ 1.872-2 Exclusions from gross income of nonresident alien individuals.

Caution: The Treasury has not yet amended Reg § 1.872-2 to reflect changes made by P.L. 108-357, P.L. 104-188, P.L. 100-647, P.L. 99-514.

(a) Earnings of foreign ships or aircraft. *(1) Basic rule.* So much of the income from sources within the United States of a nonresident alien individual as consists of earnings derived from the operation of a ship or ships documented, or of aircraft registered, under the laws of a foreign country which grants an equivalent exemption to citizens of the United States nonresident in that foreign country and to corporations organized in the United States shall not be included in gross income.

(2) Equivalent exemption. (i) Ships. A foreign country which either imposes no income tax, or, in imposing an income tax, exempts from taxation so much of the income of a citizen of the U.S. nonresident in that foreign country and of a corporation organized in the United States as consists of earnings derived from the operation of a ship or ships documented under the laws of the United States is considered as granting an equivalent exemption for purposes of the exclusion from gross income of the earnings of a foreign ship or ships.

(ii) Aircraft. A foreign country which either imposes no income tax, or, in imposing an income tax, exempts from taxation so much of the income of a citizen of the U.S. nonresident in that foreign country and of a corporation organized in the United States as consists of earnings derived from the operation of aircraft registered under the laws of the United States is considered as granting an equivalent exemption for purposes of the exclusion from gross income of the earnings of foreign aircraft.

(3) Definition of earnings. For purposes of subparagraphs (1) and (2) of this paragraph, compensation for personal services performed by an individual aboard a ship or aircraft does not constitute earnings derived by such individual from the operation of ships or aircraft.

(b) Compensation paid by foreign employer to participants in certain exchange or training programs. *(1) Exclusion from income.* Compensation paid to a nonresident alien individual for the period that the nonresident alien individual is temporarily present in the United States as a nonimmigrant under subparagraph (F) (relating to the admission of students into the United States) or subparagraph (J) (relating to the admission of teachers, trainees, specialists, etc., into the United States) of section 101(a)(15) of the Immigration and Nationality Act (8 U.S.C. 1101(a)(15)(F) or (J)) shall be excluded from gross income if the compensation is paid to such alien by his foreign employer. Compensation paid to a nonresident alien individual by the U.S. office of a domestic bank which is acting as paymaster on behalf of a foreign employer constitutes compensation paid by a foreign employer for purposes of this paragraph if the domestic bank is reimbursed by the foreign employer for such payment. A nonresident alien individual who is temporarily present in the United States as a nonimmigrant under such subparagraph (J) includes a nonresident alien individual admitted to the United States as an "exchange visitor" under section 201 of the U.S. Information and Educational Exchange Act of 1948 (22 U.S.C. 1446), which section was repealed by section 111 of the Mutual Education and Cultural Exchange Act of 1961 (75 Stat. 538).

(2) Definition of foreign employer. For purposes of this paragraph, the term "foreign employer" means a nonresident alien individual, a foreign partnership, a foreign corporation, or an office or place of business maintained in a foreign country or in a possession of the United States by a domestic corporation, a domestic partnership, or an individual who is a citizen or resident of the United States. The term does not include a foreign government. However, see section 893 and § 1.893-1. Thus, if a French citizen employed in the Paris branch of a banking company incorporated in the State of New York were admitted to the United States under section 101(a)(15)(J) of the Immigration and Nationality Act to study monetary theory and continued to receive a salary from such foreign branch while studying in the United States, such salary would not be includable in his gross income.

(c) Tax convention. Income of any kind which is exempt from tax under the provisions of a tax convention or treaty to which the United States is a party shall not be included in the gross income of a nonresident alien individual. Income on which the tax is limited by tax convention shall be included in the gross income of a nonresident alien individual if it is not otherwise excluded from gross income. See §§ 1.871-12 and 1.894-1.

(d) Certain bond income of residents of the Ryukyu Islands or the Trust Territory of the Pacific Islands. Income derived by a nonresident alien individual from a series E or series H U.S. savings bond shall not be included in gross income if such individual acquired the bond while he was a resident of the Ryukyu Islands or the Trust Territory of the Pacific Islands. It is not necessary that the individual continue to be a resident of such Islands or Trust Territory for the period when, without regard to section 872(b)(4) and this paragraph, the income from the bond would otherwise be includible in his gross income under the provisions of section 446 or 454.

(e) Certain annuities received under qualified plans. Pursuant to section 871(f), income received by a nonresident alien individual as an annuity under a qualified annuity plan described in section 403(a)(1) (relating to taxation of employee annuities), or from a qualified trust described in section 401(a) (relating to qualified pension, profitsharing, and stock bonus plans) which is exempt from tax under section 501(a) (relating to exemption from tax on corporations, certain trusts, etc.), shall not be included in gross income, and shall be exempt from tax, for purposes of section 871 and §§ 1.871-7 and 1.871-8, if—

(1) All of the personal services by reason of which the annuity is payable were either—

(i) Personal services performed outside the United States by an individual (whether or not the annuitant) who, at the time of performance of the services, was a nonresident alien individual, or

(ii) Personal services performed in the United States by a nonresident alien individual (whether or not the annuitant) which, by reason of section 864(b)(1) (or corresponding provision of any prior law), were not personal services causing such individual to be engaged in trade or business in the United States during the taxable year, and

(2) At the time the first amount is paid (even though paid in a taxable year beginning before January 1, 1967) as such annuity under such annuity plan, or by such trust, to (i) the individual described in subparagraph (1) of this paragraph, or (ii) his nonresident alien beneficiary if such beneficiary is entitled to receive such first amount, 90 percent or more of the employees or annuitants for whom contributions or benefits are provided under the annuity plan, or under the plan or plans of which the trust is a part, are citizens or residents of the United States.

This paragraph shall apply whether or not the taxpayer is engaged in trade or business in the United States at any time during the taxable year in which the annuity is received. This paragraph shall not apply to distributions by an employees' trust or from an annuity plan which give rise to gains described in section 402(a)(2) or 403(a)(2), whichever applies. See section 871(a)(1)(B) and paragraph (c)(1)(i) of § 1.871-7. For exemption from withholding of tax at source on an annuity which is exempt from tax under section 871(f) and this paragraph, see paragraph (g) of § 1.1441-4.

(f) Other exclusions. Income which is from sources without the United States, as determined under the provisions of sections 861 through 863, and the regulations thereunder, is not included in the gross income of a nonresident alien individual unless such income is effectively connected for the taxable year with the conduct of a trade or business in the United States by that individual. To determine specific exclusions in the case of other items which are from sources within the United States, see the applicable sections of the Code. For special rules under a tax convention for determining the sources of income and for excluding, from gross income, income from sources without the United States which is effectively connected with the conduct of a trade or business in the United States, see the applicable tax convention. For determining which income from sources without the United States is effectively connected with the conduct of a trade or business in the United States, see section 864(c)(4) and § 1.864-5.

(g) Effective date. This section shall apply for taxable years beginning after December 31, 1966. For corresponding rules applicable to taxable years beginning before January 4, 1967 see 26 CFR 1.872-2 (Rev. as of Jan. 1, 1971).

---

* T.D. 6258, 10/23/57, amend T.D. 6782, 12/23/64, T.D. 7332, 12/20/74.

---

§ 1.873-1 Deductions allowed nonresident alien individuals.

Caution: The Treasury has not yet amended Reg § 1.873-1 to reflect changes made by P.L 105-277, P.L. 98-369, P.L. 95-30, P.L. 92-580, P.L. 89-809.

(a) General provisions. *(1) Allocation of deductions.* In computing the taxable income of a nonresident alien individual the deductions otherwise allowable shall be allowed only if, and to the extent that, they are connected with income from sources within the United States. No deduction shall be allowed in respect of any item, or portion thereof, which is not connected with income from such sources. For this purpose, the proper apportionment and allocation of the deductions with respect to sources of income within and without the United States shall be determined as provided in part I (section 861 and following), subchapter N, chapter 1 of the Code, and the regulations thereunder, except as may otherwise be provided by tax convention. Thus, from the items of gross income specifically from sources within the United States and from the items allocated thereto under the provisions of section 863(a), there shall be deducted (i) the expenses, losses, and other deductions which are connected with those items of income and are properly apportioned or allocated thereto, and (ii) a ratable part of any other expenses, losses, or deductions which are connected with those items of income but cannot definitely be allocated to some item or class of gross income. The ratable part shall be based upon the ratio of gross income from sources within the United States to the total gross income. See §§ 1.861-8 and 1.863-1. In the case of income partly from within and partly from without the United States the expenses, losses, and other deductions connected with income from sources within the United States shall also be deducted in the manner prescribed by §§ 1.863-2 through 1.863-5 in order to ascertain under section 863 the portion of the taxable income attributable to sources within the United States.

(2) Personal exemptions. The deductions for the personal exemptions allowed by section 151 or 642(b) shall not be taken into account for purposes of subparagraph (1) of this paragraph but shall be allowed to the extent provided by paragraphs (b) and (c) of this section.

(3) Adjusted gross income. The adjusted gross income of a nonresident alien individual shall be the gross income from sources within the United States, determined in accordance with § 1.871-7, minus the deductions prescribed by section 62 to the extent such deductions are allowed under this section in computing taxable income.

(4) Standard deduction. The standard deduction shall not be allowed in computing the taxable income of a nonresident alien individual. See section 142(b)(1) and the regulations thereunder.

(5) Exempt income. No deduction shall be allowed under this section for the amount of any item or part thereof allocable to a class or classes of exempt income, including income exempt by tax convention. See section 265 and the regulations thereunder.

(b) No United States business. *(1) Income of not more than $15,400.* (i) Deduction for losses only. A nonresident alien individual within class 1 shall not be allowed any deductions other than the deduction for losses from sales or exchanges of capital assets determined in the manner prescribed by paragraph (b)(4)(vii) of § 1.871-7. Thus, an individual within this class shall not be allowed any deductions for the personal exemptions otherwise allowed by section 151 or 642(b).

(ii) Source of losses. Notwithstanding the provisions of section 873(b)(1), losses from sales or exchanges of capital assets shall be allowed under this subparagraph only if allocable to sources within the United States. See paragraph (b)(4)(i) of § 1.871-7.

(2) Aggregate more than $15,400. (i) Deductions allowed. In computing the income subject to tax under section 1 or section 1201(b), a nonresident alien individual within class 2 shall be allowed deductions to the extent prescribed by paragraph (c)(3) of § 1.871-7, but subject to the limitations of this section. For this purpose, the deduction for the personal exemptions shall be allowed in accordance with subdivision (iii) of this subparagraph.

(ii) Deductions disallowed. In computing the minimum tax prescribed by section 871(b)(3), that individual shall not be allowed any deductions other than the deduction for losses from sales or exchanges of capital assets determined in the manner prescribed by paragraph (b)(4)(vii) of § 1.871-7. For this purpose, the deductions for the personal exemptions shall not be allowed. See paragraph (c)(4) of § 1.871-7.

(iii) Personal exemptions. When the deductions for personal exemptions are allowed under this subparagraph, only one exemption under section 151 shall be allowed in the case of an individual who is not a resident of Canada or Mexico. A resident of either of those countries shall be allowed all the exemptions granted by section 151 to the extent prescribed therein. An estate or trust, whether or not a resident of Canada or Mexico, shall determine its deduction for the personal exemption in accordance with section 642(b) and the regulations thereunder.

(iv) Source of losses. Notwithstanding the provisions of section 873(b), losses from sales or exchanges of capital assets shall be allowed under this subparagraph only if allocable to sources within the United States. See paragraph (c)(3)(i) of § 1.871-7.

(3) Election to be taxed on a net basis. Notwithstanding the other provisions of this paragraph, a nonresident alien individual within class 1 or 2 shall be allowed the deductions allowed by paragraph (c) of this section, if pursuant to a tax convention he is entitled, and does elect, to be subject to United States tax on a net basis as though he were engaged in trade or business within the United States through a permanent establishment situated therein.

(c) United States business. *(1) Deductions in general.* For purposes of computing the income subject to tax, a nonresident alien individual within class 3 shall be allowed deductions to the extent prescribed by paragraph (d) of § 1.871-7, but subject to the limitations of this section. For this purpose, the deductions for the personal exemptions shall be allowed in accordance with subparagraph (3) of this paragraph.

(2) Special deductions. Notwithstanding the rule of source prescribed in paragraph (a) of this section, an individual within class 3 shall be allowed the following deductions whether or not they are connected with income from sources within the United States:

(i) Losses on transactions for profit. Any loss sustained during the taxable year and not compensated for by insurance or otherwise, if incurred in any transaction entered into for profit, though not connected with a trade or business, shall be allowed to the extent allowed by section 165(c)(2), but only if and to the extent that the profit, if the transaction had resulted in a profit, would be taxable to such individual. Losses allowed under this subdivision shall be deducted in full, as provided subdivision shall be deducted in full, as provided in §§ 1.861-8 and 1.863-1, when the profit from the transaction, if it had resulted in a profit, would, under the provisions of section 861(a) or 863(a), have been taxable in full as income from sources within the United States; but shall be deducted under the provisions of § 1.863-3 when the profit from the transaction, if it had resulted in profit, would have been taxable only in part.

(ii) Casualty losses. Any loss of property not connected with a trade or business, sustained during the taxable year and not compensated for by insurance or otherwise, if the loss arises from fire, storm, shipwreck, or other casualty, or from theft, shall be allowed to the extent allowed by section 165(c)(3), but only if the loss is of property within the United States. Losses allowed under this subdivision shall be deducted in full, as provided in §§ 1.861-8 and 1.863-1, from the items of gross income specified under sections 861(a) and 863(a) as being derived in full from sources within the United States; but, if greater than the sum of those items, the unabsorbed loss shall be deducted from the income apportioned under the provisions of § 1.863-3 to sources within the United States.

(iii) Charitable contributions. The deduction for charitable contributions and gifts, to the extent allowed by section 170, shall be allowed under this subparagraph, but only as to contributions or gifts made to domestic corporations, or to community chests, funds, or foundations, created in the United States.

(3) Personal exemptions. Only one exemption under section 151 shall be allowed in the case of an individual who is not a resident of Canada or Mexico. A resident of either of those countries shall be allowed all the exemptions granted by section 151 to the extent prescribed therein. An estate or trust, whether or not a resident of Canada or Mexico, shall determine its deduction for the personal exemption in accordance with section 642(b) and the regulations thereunder.

T.D. 6258, 10/23/57.

§ 1.874-1 Allowance of deductions and credits to nonresident alien individuals.

Caution: The Treasury has not yet amended Reg § 1.874-1 to reflect changes made by P.L. 98-369, P.L. 97-424, P.L. 89-809.

(a) Return required. A nonresident alien individual shall receive the benefit of the deductions and credits otherwise allowable with respect to the income tax, only if the nonresident alien individual timely files or causes to be filed with the Philadelphia Service Center, in the manner prescribed in subtitle F, a true and accurate return of the income which is effectively connected, or treated as effectively connected, with the conduct of a trade or business within the United States by the nonresident alien individual. No provision of this section (other than paragraph (c)(2)) shall be construed, however, to deny the credits provided by sections 31, 32, 33, 34 and 852(b)(3)(D)(ii). In addition, notwithstanding the requirement that a nonresident alien must file a timely return in order to receive the benefit of the deductions and credits otherwise allowable with respect to the income tax, the nonresident alien individual may, for purposes of determining the amount of tax to be withheld under section 1441 from remuneration paid for labor or personal services performed within the United States, receive the benefit of the deduction for personal exemptions provided in section 151, to the extent allowable under section 873(b)(3) and paragraph (c)(3) of § 1.873-1, or in any applicable tax convention, by filing a claim therefore with the withholding agent. The amount of the deduction for the personal exemptions and the amount of the tax to be withheld under those circumstances shall be determined in accordance with paragraph (e)(2) of § 1.1441-3. The deductions and credits allowed such a nonresident alien individual electing under a tax convention to be subject to tax on a net basis may be obtained by filing a return of income in the manner prescribed in the regulations (if any) under the tax convention or under any other guidance issued by the Commissioner.

(b) Filing deadline for return. *(1) General rule.* As provided in paragraph (a) of this section, for purposes of computing the nonresident alien individual's taxable income for any taxable year, otherwise allowable deductions and credits will be allowed only if a true and accurate return for that taxable year is filed by the nonresident alien individual on a timely basis. For taxable years of a nonresident alien individual ending after July 31, 1990, whether a return for the current taxable year has been filed on a timely basis is dependent upon whether the nonresident alien individual filed a return for the taxable year immediately preceding the current taxable year. If a return was filed for that immediately preceding taxable year, or if the current taxable year is the first taxable year of the nonresident alien individual for which a return is required to be filed, the required return for the current taxable year must be filed within 16 months of the due date, as set forth in section 6072 and the regulations under that section, for filing the return for the current taxable year. If no return for the taxable year immediately preceding the current taxable year has been filed, the required return for the current taxable year (other than the first taxable year of the nonresident alien individual for which a return is required to be filed) must have been filed no later than the earlier of the date which is 16 months after the due date, as set forth in section 6072, for filing the return for the current taxable year or the date the Internal Revenue Service mails a notice to the nonresident alien individual advising the nonresident alien individual that the current year tax return has not been filed and that no deductions or credits (other than those provided in sections 31, 32, 33, 34 and 852(b)(3)(D)(ii)) may be claimed by the nonresident alien individual.

(2) Waiver. The filing deadlines set forth in paragraph (b)(1) of this section may be waived if the nonresident alien individual establishes to the satisfaction of the Commissioner or his or her delegate that the individual, based on the facts and circumstances, acted reasonably and in good faith in failing to file a U.S. income tax return (including a protective return (as described in paragraph (b)(6) of this section)). For this purpose, a nonresident alien individual shall not be considered to have acted reasonably and in good faith if the individual knew that he or she was required to file the return and chose not to do so. In addition, a nonresident alien individual shall not be granted a waiver unless the individual cooperates in determining his or her U.S. income tax liability for the taxable year for which the return was not filed. The Commissioner or his or her delegate shall consider the following factors in determining whether the nonresident alien individual, based on the facts and circumstances, acted reasonably and in good faith in failing to file a U.S. income tax return—

(i) Whether the individual voluntarily identifies himself or herself to the Internal Revenue Service as having failed to file a U.S. income tax return before the Internal Revenue Service discovers the failure to file;

(ii) Whether the individual did not become aware of his or her ability to file a protective return (as described in paragraph (b)(6) of this section) by the deadline for filing the protective return;

(iii) Whether the individual had not previously filed a U.S. income tax return;

(iv) Whether the individual failed to file a U.S. income tax return because, after exercising reasonable diligence (taking into account his or her relevant experience and level of sophistication), the individual was unaware of the necessity for filing the return;

(v) Whether the individual failed to file a U.S. income tax return because of intervening events beyond the individual's control; and

(vi) Whether other mitigating or exacerbating factors existed.

(3) Examples. The following examples illustrate the provisions of paragraph (b). In all examples, A is a nonresident alien individual and uses the calendar year as A's taxable year. The examples are as follows:

Example (1). Nonresident alien individual discloses own failure to file. In Year 1, A became a limited partner with a passive investment in a U.S. limited partnership that was engaged in a U.S. trade or business. During Year 1 through Year 4, A incurred losses with respect to A's U.S. partnership interest. A's foreign tax advisor incorrectly concluded that because A was a limited partner and had only losses from A's partnership interest, A was not required to file a U.S. income tax return. A was aware neither of A's obligation to file a U.S. income tax return for those years nor of A's ability to file a protective return for those years. A had never filed a U.S. income tax return before. In Year 5, A began realizing a profit rather than a loss with respect to the partnership interest and, for this reason, engaged a U.S. tax advisor to handle A's responsibility to file U.S. income tax returns. In preparing A's U.S. income tax return for Year 5, A's U.S. tax advisor discovered that returns were not filed for Year 1 through Year 4. Therefore, with respect to those years for which applicable filing deadlines in paragraph (b)(1) of this section were not met, A would be barred by paragraph (a) of this section from claiming any deductions that otherwise would have given rise to net operating losses on returns for these years, and that would have been available as loss carryforwards in subsequent years. At A's direction, A's U.S. tax advisor promptly contacted the appropriate examining personnel and cooperated with the Internal Revenue Service in determining A's income tax liability, for example, by preparing and filing the appropriate income tax returns for Year 1 through Year 4 and by making A's books and records available to an Internal Revenue Service examiner. A has met the standard described in paragraph (b)(2) of this section for waiver of any applicable filing deadlines in paragraph (b)(1) of this section.

Example (2). Nonresident alien individual refuses to cooperate. Same facts as in Example 1, except that while A's U.S. tax advisor contacted the appropriate examining personnel and filed the appropriate income tax returns for Year 1 through Year 4, A refused all requests by the Internal Revenue Service to provide supporting information (for example, books and records) with respect to those returns. Because A did not cooperate in determining A's U.S. tax liability for the taxable years for which an income tax return was not timely filed, A is not granted a waiver as described in paragraph (b)(2) of this section of any applicable filing deadlines in paragraph (b)(1) of this section.

Example (3). Nonresident alien individual fails to file a protective return. Same facts as in Example 1, except that in Year 1 through Year 4, A also consulted a U.S. tax advisor, who advised A that it was uncertain whether U.S. income tax returns were necessary for those years and that A could protect A's right subsequently to claim the loss carryforwards by filing protective returns under paragraph (b)(6) of this section. A did not file U.S. income tax returns or protective returns for those years. A did not present evidence that intervening events beyond A's control prevented A from filing an income tax return, and there were no other mitigating factors. A has not met the standard described in paragraph (b)(2) of this section for waiver of any applicable filing deadlines in paragraph (b)(1) of this section.

Example (4). Nonresident alien with effectively connected income. In Year 1, A, a computer programmer, opened an office in the United States to market and sell a software program that A had developed outside the United States. A had minimal business or tax experience internationally, and no such experience in the United States. Through A's personal efforts, U.S. sales of the software produced income effectively connected with a U.S. trade or business. A, however, did not file U.S. income tax returns for Year 1 or Year 2. A was aware neither of A's obligation to file a U.S. income tax return for those years, nor of A's ability to file a protective return for those years. A had never filed a U.S. income tax return before. In November of Year 3, A engaged U.S. counsel in connection with licensing software to an unrelated U.S. company. U.S. counsel reviewed A's U.S. activities and advised A that A should have filed U.S. income tax returns for Year 1 and Year 2. A immediately engaged a U.S. tax advisor who, at A's direction, promptly contacted the appropriate examining personnel and cooperated with the Internal Revenue Service in determining A's income tax liability, for example, by preparing and filing the appropriate income tax returns for Year 1 and Year 2 and by making A's books and records available to an Internal Revenue Service examiner. A has met the standard described in paragraph (b)(2) of this section for waiver of any applicable filing deadlines in paragraph (b)(1) of this section.

Example (5). IRS discovers nonresident alien's failure to file. In Year 1, A, a computer programmer, opened an office in the United States to market and sell a software program that A had developed outside the United States. Through A's personal efforts, U.S. sales of the software produced income effectively connected with a U.S. trade or business. A had extensive experience conducting similar business activities in other countries, including making the appropriate tax filings. A, however, was aware neither of A's obligation to file a U.S. income tax return for those years, nor of A's ability to file a protective return for those years. A had never filed a U.S. income tax return before. Despite A's extensive experience conducting similar business activities in other countries, A made no effort to seek advice in connection with A's U.S. tax obligations. A failed to file either U.S. income tax returns or protective returns for Year 1 and Year 2. In November of Year 3, an Internal Revenue Service examiner asked A for an explanation of A's failure to file U.S. income tax returns. A immediately engaged a U.S. tax advisor, and cooperated with the Internal Revenue Service in determining A's income tax liability, for example, by preparing and filing the appropriate income tax returns for Year 1 and Year 2 and by making A's books and records available to the examiner. A did not present evidence that intervening events beyond A's control prevented A from filing a return, and there were no other mitigating factors. A has not met the standard described in paragraph (b)(2) of this section for waiver of any applicable filing deadlines in paragraph (b)(1) of this section.

Example (6). Nonresident alien with prior filing history. A began a U.S. trade or business in Year 1 as a sole proprietorship. A's tax advisor filed the appropriate U.S. income tax returns for Year 1 through Year 6, reporting income effectively connected with A's U.S. trade or business. In Year 7, A replaced this tax advisor with a tax advisor unfamiliar with U.S. tax law. A did not file a U.S. income tax return for any year from Year 7 through Year 10, although A had effectively connected income for those years. A was aware of A's ability to file a protective return for those years. In Year 11, an Internal Revenue Service examiner contacted A and asked for an explanation of A's failure to file income tax returns after Year 6. A immediately engaged a U.S. tax advisor and cooperated with the Internal Revenue Service in determining A's income tax liability, for example, by preparing and filing the appropriate income tax returns for Year 7 through Year 10 and by making A's books and records available to the examiner. A did not present evidence that intervening events beyond A's control prevented A from filing a return, and there were no other mitigating factors. A has not met the standard described in paragraph (b)(2) of this section for waiver of any applicable filing deadlines in paragraph (b)(1) of this section.

(4) Effective date. Paragraphs (b)(2) and (3) of this section are applicable to open years for which a request for a waiver is filed on or after January 29, 2002.

(5) Income tax treaties. A nonresident alien individual who has a permanent establishment or fixed base, as defined in an income tax treaty between the United States and the country of residence of the nonresident alien individual, in the United States is subject to the filing deadlines as set forth in paragraph (b)(1) of this section.

(6) Protective return. If a nonresident alien individual conducts limited activities in the United States in a taxable year which the nonresident alien individual determines does not give rise to gross income which is effectively connected with the conduct of a trade or business within the United States as defined in sections 871(b) and 864(b) and (c) and the regulations under those sections, the nonresident alien individual may nonetheless file a return for that taxable year on a timely basis under paragraph (b)(1) of this section and thereby protect the right to receive the benefit of the deductions and credits attributable to that gross income if it is later determined, after the return was filed, that the original determination was incorrect. On that timely filed return, the nonresident alien individual is not required to report any gross income as effectively connected with a United States trade or business or any deductions or credits but should attach a statement indicating that the return is being filed for the reason set forth in this paragraph (b)(4). If the nonresident alien individual determines that part of the activities which he or she conducts in the United States in a taxable year gives rise to gross income which is effectively connected with the conduct of a trade or business and part does not, the nonresident alien individual must timely file a return for that taxable year to report the gross income determined to be effectively connected, or treated as effectively connected, with the conduct of that trade or business within the United States and the deductions and credits attributable to the gross income. In addition, the nonresident alien individual should attach to that return the statement described in this paragraph (b)(4) with regard to the other activities. The nonresident alien individual may follow the same procedure if the nonresident alien individual determines initially that he or she has no United States tax liability under the provisions of an applicable income tax treaty. In the event the nonresident alien individual relies on the provisions of an income tax treaty to reduce or eliminate the income subject to taxation, or to reduce the rate of tax to which that income is subject, disclosure may be required pursuant to section 6114.

(c) Allowed deductions and credits. *(1) In general.* Except for losses of property located within the United States, charitable contributions and personal exemptions (see section 873(b)), deductions are allowed to a nonresident alien individual only to the extent they are connected with gross income which is effectively connected, or treated as effectively connected, with the conduct of the nonresident alien individual's trade or business in the United States. Other than credits allowed by sections 31, 32, 33, 34, and 852(b)(3)(D)(ii), the nonresident alien individual is entitled to credits only if they are attributable to effectively connected income. See paragraph (a) of this section for the requirement that a return be timely filed. Except as provided by section 906, a nonresident alien individual shall not be allowed the credit against the tax for taxes of foreign countries and possessions of the United States allowed by section 901.

(2) Verification. At the request of the Internal Revenue Service, a nonresident alien individual claiming deductions from gross income which is effectively connected or treated as effectively connected, with the conduct of a trade or business in the United States and credits attributable to that income must furnish at the place designated pursuant to § 301.7605-1(a) information sufficient to establish that the nonresident alien individual is entitled to the deductions and credits in the amounts claimed. All information must be furnished in a form suitable to permit verification of the claimed deductions and credits. The Internal Revenue Service may require, as appropriate, that an English translation be provided with any information in a foreign language. If a nonresident alien individual fails to furnish sufficient information, the Internal Revenue Service may in its discretion disallow any claimed deductions and credits in full or in part.

(d) Return by Internal Revenue Service. If a nonresident alien individual has various sources of income within the United States, so that from any one source, or from all sources combined, the amount of income shall call for the assessment of a tax greater than that withheld at the source in the case of that individual, and a return of income has not been filed in the manner prescribed by subtitle F, including the filing deadlines set forth in paragraph (b)(1) of this section, the Internal Revenue Service shall:

(1) Cause a return of income to be made,

(2) Include on the return the income described in § 1.871-7 or § 1.871-8 of that individual from all sources concerning which it has information, and

(3) Assess the tax. If the nonresident alien individual is not engaged in, or does not receive income that is treated as being effectively connected with, a United States trade or business and § 1.871-7 is applicable, the tax shall be assessed on the basis of gross income without allowance for deductions or credits (other than the credits provided by sections 31, 32, 33, 34 and 852(b)(3)(D)(ii)) and collected from one or more sources of income within the United States. If the nonresident alien individual is engaged in a United States trade or business or is treated as having effectively connected income and § 1.871-8 applies, the tax on the income of the nonresident alien individual that is not effectively connected, or treated as effectively connected with the conduct of a United States trade or business shall be assessed on the basis of gross income, determined in accordance with the rules of § 1.871-7, without allowance for de-

ductions or credits (other than the credits provided by sections 31, 32, 33, 34 and 852(b)(3)(D)(ii)) and collected from one or more of the sources of income within the United States. Tax on income that is effectively connected, or treated as effectively connected, with the conduct of a United States trade or business shall be assessed in accordance with either section 1, 55 or 402(e)(1) without allowance for deductions or credits (other than the credits provided by sections 31, 32, 33, 34 and 852(b)(3)(D)(ii)) and collected from one or more of the sources of income within the United States.

(e) Alien resident of Puerto Rico, Guam, American Samoa, or the Commonwealth of the Northern Mariana Islands. This section shall not apply to a nonresident alien individual who is a bona fide resident of Puerto Rico, Guam, American Samoa, or the Commonwealth of the Northern Mariana Islands during the entire taxable year. See section 876 and § 1.876-1.

T.D. 6258, 10/23/57, amend T.D. 6462, 5/5/60, T.D. 6669, 8/26/63, T.D. 8322, 12/10/90, T.D. 8981, 1/28/2002, T.D. 9043, 3/7/2003.

§ 1.875-1 Partnerships.

Caution: The Treasury has not yet amended Reg § 1.875-1 to reflect changes made by P.L. 89-809.

Whether a nonresident alien individual who is a member of a partnership is taxable in accordance with subsection (a), (b), or (c) of section 871 may depend on the status of the partnership. A nonresident alien individual who is a member of a partnership which is not engaged in trade or business within the United States is subject to the provisions of section 871(a) or (b), as the case may be, depending on whether or not he receives during the taxable year an aggregate of more than $15,400 gross income described in section 871(a), if he is not otherwise engaged in trade or business within the United States. A nonresident alien individual who is a member of a partnership which at any time within the taxable year is engaged in trade or business within the United States is considered as being engaged in trade or business within the United States and is therefore taxable under section 871(c). For definition of what the term "partnership" includes, see section 7701(a)(2) and the regulations in Part 301 of this chapter (Regulations on Procedure and Administration). The test of whether a partnership is engaged in trade or business within the United States is the same as in the case of a nonresident alien individual. See § 1.871-8.

T.D. 6258, 10/23/57.

§ 1.875-2 Beneficiaries of estates or trusts.

(a) [Reserved]

(b) Exception for certain taxable years. Notwithstanding paragraph (a) of this section, for any taxable year beginning before January 1, 1975, the grantor of a trust, whether revocable or irrevocable, is not deemed to be engaged in trade or business within the United States merely because the trustee is engaged in trade or business within the United States.

(c) [Reserved]

T.D. 7332, 12/20/74.

§ 1.876-1 Alien residents of Puerto Rico, Guam, American Samoa, or the Northern Mariana Islands.

[Reserved]. For further guidance, see § 1.876-1T.

T.D. 6258, 10/23/57, amend T.D. 6777, 12/15/64, T.D. 7332, 12/20/74, T.D. 9194, 4/6/2005.

PAR. 7.

Section 1.876-1 is revised to read as follows:

Proposed § 1.876-1 Alien residents of Puerto Rico, Guam, American Samoa, or the Northern Mariana Islands. [*For Preamble, see ¶ 152,645*]

• ***Caution:*** This Notice of Proposed Rulemaking was partially finalized by TD 9248, 01/30/2006. Regs. §§ 1.1-1, 1.170A-1, 1.861-3, 1.861-8, 1.871-1, 1.876-1, 1.881-5, 1.884-0, 1.901-1, 1.931-1, 1.932-1, 1.933-1, 1.934-1, 1.935-1, 1.937-2, 1.937-3, 1.957-3, 1.1402(a)-12, 1.6038-2, 1.6046-1, 301.6688-1, 301.7701-3, and 301.7701(b)-1 remain proposed.

[The text of the proposed amendment to § 1.876-1 is the same as the text of § 1.876-1T published elsewhere in this issue of the Federal Register]. [*See T.D. 9194, 4/11/2005, 70 Fed. Reg. 68.*]

§ 1.876-1T Alien residents of Puerto Rico, Guam, American Samoa, or the Northern Mariana Islands (temporary).

• ***Caution:*** Under Code Sec. 7805, temporary regulations expire within three years of the date of issuance. This temporary regulation was issued on 4/6/2005.

(a) Scope. Section 876 and this section apply to any nonresident alien individual who is a bona fide resident of Puerto Rico or of a section 931 possession during the entire taxable year.

(b) In general. An individual to whom this section applies is, in accordance with the provisions of section 876, subject to tax under sections 1 and 55 in generally the same manner as an alien resident of the United States. See §§ 1.1-1(b) and 1.871-1. The tax generally is imposed upon the taxable income of such individual, determined in accordance with section 63(a) and the regulations thereunder, from sources both within and without the United States, except for amounts excluded from gross income under the provisions of section 931 or 933. For determining the form of return to be used by such an individual, see section 6012 and the regulations thereunder.

(c) Exceptions. Though subject to the tax imposed by section 1, an individual to whom this section applies shall nevertheless be treated as a nonresident alien individual for the purpose of many provisions of the Internal Revenue Code relating to nonresident alien individuals. Thus, for example, such an individual is not allowed the standard deduction (section 63(c)(6)); is subject to withholding of tax at source under chapter 3 of the Internal Revenue Code (e.g., section 1441(e)); is generally excepted from the collection of income tax at source on wages for services performed in the possession (section 3401(a)(6)); is not allowed to make a joint return (section 6013(a)(1)); and, if described in section 6072(c), must pay his first installment of estimated income tax on or before the 15th day of the 6th month of the taxable year (section 6654(j) and (k)) and must pay his income tax on or before the 15th day of the 6th month following the close of the taxable year (sections 6072(c) and 6151(a)). In addition, under section 152(b)(3), an individual is not allowed a deduction for a dependent who is a resident of the relevant possession unless the dependent is a citizen or national of the United States.

(d) Credits against tax. *(1)* Certain credits under the Internal Revenue Code are available to any taxpayer subject to the tax imposed by section 1, including individuals to whom this section applies. For example, except as otherwise provided under section 931 or 933, the credits provided by the following sections are allowable to the extent provided under such sections against the tax determined in accordance with this section—

(i) Section 23 (relating to the credit for adoption expenses);

(ii) Section 31 (relating to the credit for tax withheld on wages);

(iii) Section 33 (relating to the credit for tax withheld at source on nonresident aliens); and

(iv) Section 34 (relating to the credit for certain uses of gasoline and special fuels).

(2) Certain credits under the Internal Revenue Code are not available to nonresident aliens or are subject to limitations based on such factors as principal place of abode in the United States. For example, the credits provided by the following sections are not allowable against the tax determined in accordance with this section except to the extent otherwise provided under such sections--

(i) Section 22 (relating to the credit for the elderly and disabled);

(ii) Section 25A (relating to the Hope Scholarship and Lifetime Learning Credits); and

(iii) Section 32 (relating to the earned income credit).

(e) Definitions. For purposes of this section:

(1) Bona fide resident is defined in § 1.937-1T.

(2) Section 931 possession is defined in § 1.931-1T(c)(1).

(f) Effective date. This section shall apply for taxable years ending after October 22, 2004.

T.D. 9194, 4/6/2005.

§ 1.879-1 Treatment of community income.

Caution: The Treasury has not yet amended Reg § 1.879-1 to reflect changes made by P.L. 98-369.

(a) Treatment of community income. *(1) In general.* For taxable years beginning after December 31, 1976, community income of a citizen or resident of the United States who is married to a nonresident alien individual, and the deductions properly allocable to that income, shall be divided between the U.S. citizen or resident spouse in accordance with the rules in section 879 and paragraph (a)(2) through (a)(6) of this section. This section does not apply for any taxable year with respect to which an election under section 6013(g) or (h) is in effect. Community income for this purpose includes all gross income, whether derived from sources within or without the United States, which is treated as community income of the spouses under the community property laws of the State, foreign country, or possession of the United States in which the recipient of the income is domiciled. Income from real property also may be community income if so treated under the laws of the jurisdiction in which the real property is located.

(2) Earned income. Wages, salaries, or professional fees, and other amounts received as compensation for personal services actually performed, which are community income for the taxable year, shall be treated as the income of the spouse who actually performed the personal services. This paragraph (a)(2) does not apply, however, to the following items of community income:

(i) Community income derived from any trade or business carried on by the husband or the wife.

(ii) Community income attributable to a spouse's distributive share of income of a partnership to which paragraph (a)(4) of this section applies.

(iii) Community income consisting of compensation for personal services rendered to a corporation which represents a distribution of the earnings and profits of the corporation rather than a reasonable allowance as compensation for the personal services actually performed, but not including any income that would be treated as earned income under the second sentence of section 911(b).

(iv) Community income derived from property which is acquired as consideration for personal services performed.

These items of community income are divided in accordance with the rules in paragraph (a)(3) through (a)(6) of this section.

(3) Trade or business income. If any income derived from a trade or business carried on by the husband or wife is community income for the taxable year, all of the gross income, and the deductions attributable to that income, shall be treated as the gross income and deductions of the husband. However, if the wife exercises substantially all of the management and control of the trade or business, all of the gross income and deductions shall be treated as the gross income and deductions of the wife. This paragraph (a)(3) does not apply to any income derived from a trade or business carried on by a partnership of which both or one of the spouses is a member (see paragraph (a)(4) of this section). For purposes of this paragraph (a)(3), income derived from a trade or business includes any income derived from a trade or business in which both personal services and capital are material income producing factors. The term "management and control" means management and control in fact, not the management and control imputed to the husband under the community property laws of a State, foreign country or possession of the United States. For example, a wife who operates a pharmacy without any appreciable collaboration on the part of a husband is considered as having substantially all of the management and control of the business despite the provisions of any community property laws of a State, foreign country, or possession of the United States, vesting in the husband the right of management and control of community property. The income and deductions attributable to the operation of the pharmacy are considered the income and deductions of the wife.

(4) Partnership income. If any portion of a spouse's distributive share of the income of a partnership, of which the spouse is a member, is community income for the taxable year, all of that distributive share shall be treated as the income of that spouse and shall not be taken into account in determining the income of the other spouse. If both spouses are members of the same partnership, the distributive share

of the income of each spouse which is community income shall be treated as the income of that spouse. A spouse's distributive share of the income of a partnership that is community income shall be determined as provided in section 704 and the regulations thereunder.

(5) Income from separate property. Any community income for the taxable year, other than income described in section 879(a)(1) or (2) and paragraph (a)(2), (3), or (4) of this section, which is derived from the separate property of one of the spouses shall be treated as the income of that spouse. The determination of what property is separate property for this purpose shall be made in accordance with the laws of the State, foreign country, or possession of the United States in which, in accordance with paragraph (a)(1) of this section, the recipient of the income is domiciled or, in the case of income from real property, in which the real property is located.

(6) Other community income. Any community income for the taxable year, other than income described in section 879(a)(1), (2), or (3), and paragraph (a)(2), (3), (4), or (5) of this section, shall be treated as income of that spouse who has a proprietary vested interest in that income under the laws of the state, foreign country, or possession of the United States in which, in accordance with paragraph (a)(1) of this section, the recipient of the income is domiciled or, in the case of income from real property, in which the real property is located. Thus, for example, this paragraph (a)(6) applies to community income not described in paragraph (a)(2), (3), (4), or (5) of this section which consists of dividends, interest, rents, royalties, or gains, from community property or of the earnings of unemancipated minor children.

(7) Illustrations. The application of this paragraph may be illustrated by the following examples:

Example (1). H, a U.S. citizen, and W, a nonresident alien individual, each of whose taxable years is the calendar year, were married throughout 1977. H and W were residents of, and domiciled in, foreign country Z during the entire taxable year. No election under section 6013 (g) or (h) is in effect for 1977. During 1977, H earned $10,000 from the performance of personal services as an employee. H also received $500 in dividend income from stock which under the community property laws of country Z is considered to be the separate property of H. W had no separate income for 1977. Under the community property laws of country Z all income earned by either spouse is considered to be community income, and one-half of this income is considered to belong to the other spouse. In addition, the laws of country Z provide that all income derived from property held separately by either spouse is to be treated as community income and treated as belonging one-half to each spouse. Thus, under the community property laws of country Z, H and W are both considered to have realized income of $5,250 during 1977, even though Z's laws recognize the stock as the separate property of H. Under the rules of paragraph (a)(2) and (5) of this section all of the income of $10,500 derived during 1977 is treated, for U.S. income tax purposes, as the income of H.

Example (2). (a) The facts are the same as in example (1), except that H is the sole proprietor of a retail merchandising company, which has a $10,000 profit during 1977. W exercises no management and control over the business. In addition. H is a partner in a wholesale distributing company, and his distributive share of the partnership profit is $5,000. Both of these amounts of income are treated as community income under the community property laws of country Z, and under these laws both H and W are treated as realizing $7,500 of the income. Under the rule of paragraph (a)(3) and (4) of this section all $15,000 of the income is treated as the income of H for U.S. income tax purposes.

(b) If W exercises substantially all of the management and control over the retail merchandising company, then for U.S. income tax purposes the $10,000 profit is treated as the income of W.

Example (3). The facts are the same as in example (1), except that H also received $1,000 in dividends on stock held separately in his name. Under the community property laws of country Z the stock is considered to be community property, the dividends to be community income, and one-half of the income to be the income of each spouse. Under the rule of paragraph (a)(6) of this section, $500 of the dividend income is treated, for U.S. income tax purposes, as the income of each spouse.

(b) Definitions and other special rules. *(1) Spouses with different taxable years.* A special rule applies if the nonresident alien and the United States citizen or resident spouse of the alien do not have the same taxable years, as defined in section 441(b) and the regulations thereunder. The special rule is as follows. With respect to the U.S. citizen or resident spouse, section 879 and this section shall apply to each taxable year of the U.S. citizen or resident spouse for which no election under section 6013(g) or (h) is in effect. With respect to the nonresident alien spouse, section 879 and this section apply to each period falling within the consecutive taxable years of the nonresident alien spouse which coincides with a taxable year of the U.S. citizen or resident spouse to which section 879 and this section apply.

(2) Determination of marital status. For purposes of this section, marital status shall be determined under section 143(a).

T.D. 7670, 1/30/80.

§ 1.881-0 Table of contents.

This section lists the major headings for §§ 1.881-1 through 1.881-4.

T.D. 8611, 8/10/95.

§ 1.881-1 Manner of taxing foreign corporations.

Caution: The Treasury has not yet amended Reg § 1.881-1 to reflect changes made by P.L. 98-369.

(a) Classes of foreign corporations. For purposes of the income tax, foreign corporations are divided into two classes, namely, foreign corporations which at no time during the taxable year are engaged in trade or business in the United States and foreign corporations which, at any time during the taxable year, are engaged in trade or business in the United States.

(b) Manner of taxing. *(1) Foreign corporations not engaged in U.S. business.* A foreign corporation which at no time during the taxable year is engaged in trade or business in the United States is taxable, as provided in § 1.881-2, on all income received from sources within the United States which is fixed or determinable annual or periodical income and on other items of income enumerated under section 881(a). Such a foreign corporation is also taxable on certain income from sources within the United States which, pursuant to § 1.882-2, is treated as effectively connected for the taxable year with the conduct of a trade or business in the United States.

(2) Foreign corporations engaged in U.S. business. A foreign corporation which at any time during the taxable year is engaged in trade or business in the United States is taxable, as provided in § 1.882-1, on all income from whatever source derived, whether or not fixed or determinable annual or periodical income, which is effectively connected for the taxable year with the conduct of a trade or business in the United States. Such a foreign corporation is also taxable, as provided in § 1.882-1, on income received from sources within the United States which is not effectively connected for the taxable year with the conduct of a trade or business

in the United States and consists of (i) fixed or determinable annual or periodical income, or (ii) other items of income enumerated in section 881(a). A foreign corporation which at any time during the taxable year is engaged in trade or business in the United States is also taxable on certain income from sources within the United States which, pursuant to § 1.882-2, is treated as effectively connected for the taxable year with the conduct of a trade or business in the United States.

(c) Meaning of terms. For the meaning of the term "engaged in trade or business within the United States", as used in section 881 and this section, see section 864(b) and the regulations thereunder. For determining when income, gain, or loss of a foreign corporation for a taxable year is effectively connected for that year with the conduct of a trade or business in the United States, see section 864(c), the regulations thereunder, and § 1.882-2. The term foreign corporation has the meaning assigned to it by section 7701(a)(3) and (5) and the regulations thereunder. However, for special rules relating to possessions of the United States, see § 1.881-5T.

(d) Rules applicable to foreign insurance companies. *(1) Corporations qualifying under subchapter L.* A foreign corporation carrying on an insurance business in the United States at any time during the taxable year, which, without taking into account its income not effectively connected for the taxable year with the conduct of a trade or business in the United States, would qualify for the taxable year under part I, II, or III of subchapter L if it were a domestic corporation, shall be taxable for such year under that part on its entire taxable income (whether derived from sources within or without the United States) which is, or which pursuant to section 882(d) or (e) and § 1.882-2 is treated as, effectively connected for the taxable year with the conduct of a trade or business (whether or not its insurance business) in the United States. Any income derived by that foreign corporation from sources within the United States which is not effectively connected for the taxable year with the conduct of a trade or business in the United States is taxable as provided in section 881(a) and § 1.882-1. See sections 842 and 861 through 864, and the regulations thereunder.

(2) Corporations not qualifying under subchapter L. A foreign corporation which carries on an insurance business in the United States at any time during the taxable year, and which, without taking into account its income not effectively connected for the taxable year with the conduct of a trade or business in the United States, would not qualify for the taxable year under part I, II, or III of subchapter L if it were a domestic corporation, and a foreign insurance company which does not carry on an insurance business in the United States at any time during the taxable year, shall be taxable—

(i) Under section 881(a) and § 1.881-2 or § 1.882-1 on its income from sources within the United States which is not effectively connected for the taxable year with the conduct of a trade or business in the United States,

(ii) Under section 882(a)(1) and § 1.882-1 on its income (whether derived from sources within or without the United States) which is effectively connected for the taxable year with the conduct of a trade or business in the United States, and

(iii) Under section 882(a)(1) and § 1.882-1 on its income from sources within the United States which pursuant to section 882(d) or (e) and § 1.882-2, is treated as effectively connected for the taxable year with the conduct of a trade or business in the United States.

(e) Other provisions applicable to foreign corporations. *(1) Accumulated earnings tax.* For the imposition of the accumulated earnings tax upon the accumulated taxable income of a foreign corporation formed or availed of for tax avoidance purposes, whether or not such corporation is engaged in trade or business in the United States, see section 532 and the regulations thereunder.

(2) Personal holding company tax. For the imposition of the personal holding company tax upon the undistributed personal holding company income of a foreign corporation which is a personal holding company, whether or not such corporation is engaged in trade or business in the United States, see sections 541 through 547, and the regulations thereunder. Except in the case of a foreign corporation having personal service contract income to which section 543(a)(7) applies, a foreign corporation is not a personal holding company if all of its stock outstanding during the last half of the taxable year is owned by non-resident alien individuals, whether directly or indirectly through foreign estates, foreign trusts, foreign partnerships, or other foreign corporations. See section 542(c)(7).

(3) Foreign personal holding companies. For the mandatory inclusion in the gross income of the United States shareholders of the undistributed foreign personal holding company income of a foreign personal holding company, see section 551 and the regulations thereunder.

(4) Controlled foreign corporations. (i) Subpart F income and increase of earnings invested in U.S. Property. For the mandatory inclusion in the gross income of the U.S. shareholders of the subpart F income, of the previously excluded subpart F income withdrawn from investment in less developed countries, of the previously excluded subpart F income withdrawn from investment in foreign base company shipping operations, and of the increase in earnings invested in U.S. property, of a controlled foreign corporation, see sections 951 through 964, and the regulations thereunder.

(ii) Certain accumulations of earnings and profits. For the inclusion in the gross income of U.S. persons as a dividend of the gain recognized on certain sales or exchanges of stock in a foreign corporation, to the extent of certain earnings and profits attributable to the stock which were accumulated while the corporation was a controlled foreign corporation, see section 1248 and the regulations thereunder.

(5) Changes in tax rate. For provisions respecting the effect of any change in rate of tax during the taxable year on the income of a foreign corporation, see section 21 and the regulations thereunder.

(6) Consolidated returns. Except in the case of certain corporations organized under the laws of Canada or Mexico and maintained solely for the purpose of complying with the laws of that country as to title and operation of property, a foreign corporation is not an includible corporation for purposes of the privilege of making a consolidated return by an affiliated group of corporations. See section 1504 and the regulations thereunder.

(7) Adjustment of tax of certain foreign corporations. For the application of pre-1967 income tax provisions to corporations of a foreign country which imposes a more burdensome income tax than the United States, and for the adjustment of the income tax of a corporation of a foreign country which imposes a discriminatory income tax on the income of citizens of the United States or domestic corporations, see section 896.

(f) Effective date. This section applies for taxable years beginning after December 31, 1966. For corresponding rules applicable to taxable years beginning before January 1, 1967, see 26 CFR 1.881-1 (Rev. as of Jan. 1, 1971).

T.D. 6258, 10/23/57, amend T.D. 7293, 11/27/73, T.D. 7385, 10/28/75, T.D. 7893, 5/11/83, T.D. 9194, 4/6/2005.

§ 1.881-2 Taxation of foreign corporations not engaged in U.S. business.

Caution: The Treasury has not yet amended Reg § 1.881-2 to reflect changes made by P.L. 99-514, P.L. 98-369.

(a) Imposition of tax. *(1)* This section applies for purposes of determining the tax of a foreign corporation which at no time during the taxable year is engaged in trade or business in the United States. However, see also § 1.882-2 where such corporation has an election in effect for the taxable year in respect to real property income or receives interest on obligations of the United States. Except as otherwise provided in § 1.871-12, a foreign corporation to which this section applies is not subject to the tax imposed by section 11 or section 1201(a) but, pursuant to the provisions of section 881(a), is liable to a flat tax of 30 percent upon the aggregate of the amounts determined under paragraphs (b) and (c) of this section which are received during the taxable year from sources within the United States. Except as specifically provided in such paragraphs, such amounts do not include gains from the sale or exchange of property. To determine the source of such amounts, see sections 861 through 863, and the regulations thereunder.

(2) The tax of 30 percent is imposed by section 881(a) upon an amount only to the extent the amount constitutes gross income.

(3) Deductions shall not be allowed in determining the amount subject to tax under this section.

(4) Except as provided in § 1.882-2, a foreign corporation which at no time during the taxable year is engaged in trade or business in the United States has no income, gain, or loss for the taxable year which is effectively connected for the taxable year with the conduct of a trade or business in the United States. See section 864(c)(1)(B) and § 1.864-3.

(5) Gains and losses which, by reason of section 882(d) and § 1.882-2, are treated as gains or losses which are effectively connected for the taxable year with the conduct of a trade or business in the United States by such a foreign corporation shall not be taken into account in determining the tax under this section. See, for example, paragraph (c)(2) of § 1.871-10.

(6) Interest received by a foreign corporation pursuant to certain portfolio debt instruments is not subject to the flat tax of 30 percent described in paragraph (a)(1) of this section. For rules applicable to a foreign corporation's receipt of interest on certain portfolio debt instruments, see sections 871(h), 881(c), and § 1.871-14.

(b) Fixed or determinable annual or periodical income. *(1) General rule.* The tax of 30 percent imposed by section 881(a) applies to the gross amount received from sources within the United States as fixed or determinable annual or periodical gains, profits, or income. Specific items of fixed or determinable annual or periodical income are enumerated in section 881(a)(1) as interest, dividends, rents, salaries, wages, premiums, annuities, compensations, remunerations, and emoluments, but other items of fixed or determinable annual or periodical gains, profits, or income are also subject to the tax as, for instance, royalties, including royalties for the use of patents, copyrights, secret processes and formulas, and other like property. As to the determination of fixed or determinable annual or periodical income, see paragraph (a) of § 1.1441-2. For special rules treating gain on the disposition of section 306 stock as fixed or determinable annual or periodical income for purposes of section 881(a), see section 306(f) and paragraph (h) of § 1.306-3.

(2) Substitute payments. For purposes of this section, a substitute interest payment (as defined in § 1.861-2(a)(7)) received by a foreign person pursuant to a securities lending transaction or a sale-repurchase transaction (as defined in § 1.861-2(a)(7)) shall have the same character as interest income received pursuant to the terms of the transferred security. Similarly, for purposes of this section, a substitute dividend payment (as defined in § 1.861-3(a)(6)) received by a foreign person pursuant to a securities lending transaction or a sale-repurchase transaction (as defined in § 1.861-2(a)(7)) shall have the same character as a distribution received with respect to the transferred security. Where, pursuant to a securities lending transaction or a sale-repurchase transaction, a foreign person transfers to another person a security the interest on which would qualify as portfolio interest under section 881(c) in the hands of the lender, substitute interest payments made with respect to the transferred security will be treated as portfolio interest, provided that in the case of interest on an obligation in registered form (as defined in § 1.871-14(c)(1)(i)), the transferor complies with the documentation requirement described in § 1.871-14(c)(1)(ii)(C) with respect to the payment of substitute interest and none of the exceptions to the portfolio interest exemption in sections 881(c)(3) and (4) apply. See also §§ 1.871-7(b)(2) and 1.894-1(c).

(c) Other income and gains. *(1) Items subject to tax.* The tax of 30 percent imposed by section 881(a) also applies to the following gains received during the taxable year from sources within the United States:

(i) Gains described in section 631(b) or (c), relating to the treatment of gain on the disposal of timber, coal, or iron ore with a retained economic interest;

(ii) [Reserved]

(iii) Gains from the sale or exchange after October 4, 1966, of patents, copyrights, secret processes and formulas, goodwill, trademarks, trade brands, franchises, or other like property, or of any interest in any such property, to the extent the gains are from payments (whether in a lump sum or in installments) which are contingent on the productivity, use, or disposition of the property or interest sold or exchanged, or from payments which are treated under section 871(e) and § 1.871-11 as being so contingent.

(2) Determination of amount of gain. The tax of 30 percent imposed upon the gains described in subparagraph (1) of this paragraph applies to the full amount of the gains and is determined (i) without regard to the alternative tax imposed by section 1201(a) upon the excess of net long-term capital gain over the net short-term capital loss; (ii) without regard to section 1231, relating to property used in the trade or business and involuntary conversions; and (iii) except in the case of gains described in subparagraph (1)(ii) of this paragraph, whether or not the gains are considered to be gains from the sale or exchange of property which is a capital asset.

(d) Credits against tax. The credits allowed by section 32 (relating to tax withheld at source on foreign corporations), by section 39 (relating to certain uses of gasoline and lubricating oil), and by section 6402 (relating to overpayments of tax) shall be allowed against the tax of a foreign corporation determined in accordance with this section.

(e) Effective date. Except as otherwise provide in this paragraph, this section applies for taxable years beginning after December 31, 1966. Paragraph (b)(2) of this section is applicable to payments made after November 13, 1997. For corresponding rules applicable to taxable years beginning before January 1, 1967, see 26 CFR 1.881-2 (Rev. as of Jan. 1, 1971).

T.D. 6258, 10/23/57, amend T.D. 6841, 7/26/65, T.D. 7293, 11/27/73, T.D. 8735, 10/6/97, T.D. 9323, 4/11/2007.

§ 1.881-3 Conduit financing arrangements.

(a) General rules and definitions. *(1) Purpose and scope.* Pursuant to the authority of section 7701(1), this section provides rules that permit the district director to disregard, for purposes of section 881, the participation of one or more intermediate entities in a financing arrangement where such entities are acting as conduit entities. For purposes of this section, any reference to tax imposed under section 881 includes, except as otherwise provided and as the context may require, a reference to tax imposed under sections 871 or 884(f)(1)(A) or required to be withheld under section 1441 or 1442. See § 1.881-4 for recordkeeping requirements concerning financing arrangements. See §§ 1.1441-3(j) and 1.1441-7(d) for withholding rules applicable to conduit financing arrangements.

(2) Definitions. The following definitions apply for purposes of this section and §§ 1.881-4, 1.1441-3(j) and 1.1441-7(d).

(i) Financing arrangement. (A) In general. Financing arrangement means a series of transactions by which one person (the financing entity) advances money or other property, or grants rights to use property, and another person (the financed entity) receives money or other property, or rights to use property, if the advance and receipt are effected through one or more other persons (intermediate entities) and, except in cases to which paragraph (a)(2)(i)(B) of this section applies, there are financing transactions linking the financing entity, each of the intermediate entities, and the financed entity. A transfer of money or other property in satisfaction of a repayment obligation is not an advance of money or other property. A financing arrangement exists regardless of the order in which the transactions are entered into, but only for the period during which all of the financing transactions coexist. See Examples 1, 2, and 3 of paragraph (e) of this section for illustrations of the term financing arrangement.

(B) Special rule for related parties. If two (or more) financing transactions involving two (or more) related persons would form part of a financing arrangement but for the absence of a financing transaction between the related persons, the district director may treat the related persons as a single intermediate entity if he determines that one of the principal purposes for the structure of the financing transactions is to prevent the characterization of such arrangement as a financing arrangement. This determination shall be based upon all of the facts and circumstances, including, without limitation, the factors set forth in paragraph (b)(2) of this section. See Examples 4 and 5 of paragraph (e) of this section for illustrations of this paragraph (a)(2)(i)(B).

(ii) Financing transaction. (A) In general. Financing transaction means—

(1) Debt;

(2) Stock in a corporation (or a similar interest in a partnership or trust) that meets the requirements of paragraph (a)(2)(ii)(B) of this section;

(3) Any lease or license; or

(4) Any other transaction (including an interest in a trust described in sections 671 through 679) pursuant to which a person makes an advance of money or other property or grants rights to use property to a transferee who is obligated to repay or return a substantial portion of the money or other property advanced, or the equivalent in value. This paragraph (a)(2)(ii)(A)(4) shall not apply to the posting of collateral unless the collateral consists of cash or the person holding the collateral is permitted to reduce the collateral to cash (through a transfer, grant of a security interest or similar transaction) prior to default on the financing transaction secured by the collateral.

(B) Limitation on inclusion of stock or similar interests. (1) In general. Stock in a corporation (or a similar interest in a partnership or trust) will constitute a financing transaction only if one of the following conditions is satisfied—

(i) The issuer is required to redeem the stock or similar interest at a specified time or the holder has the right to require the issuer to redeem the stock or similar interest or to make any other payment with respect to the stock or similar interest;

(ii) The issuer has the right to redeem the stock or similar interest, but only if, based on all of the facts and circumstances as of the issue date, redemption pursuant to that right is more likely than not to occur; or

(iii) The owner of the stock or similar interest has the right to require a person related to the issuer (or any other person who is acting pursuant to a plan or arrangement with the issuer) to acquire the stock or similar interest or make a payment with respect to the stock or similar interest.

(2) Rules of special application. (i) Existence of a right. For purposes of this paragraph (a)(2)(ii)(B), a person will be considered to have a right to cause a redemption or payment if the person has the right (other than rights arising, in the ordinary course, between the date that a payment is declared and the date that a payment is made) to enforce the payment through a legal proceeding or to cause the issuer to be liquidated if it fails to redeem the interest or to make a payment. A person will not be considered to have a right to force a redemption or a payment if the right is derived solely from ownership of a controlling interest in the issuer in cases where the control does not arise from a default or similar contingency under the instrument. The person is considered to have such a right if the person has the right as of the issue date or, as of the issue date, it is more likely than not that the person will receive such a right, whether through the occurrence of a contingency or otherwise.

(ii) Restrictions on payment. The fact that the issuer does not have the legally available funds to redeem the stock or similar interest, or that the payments are to be made in a blocked currency, will not affect the determinations made pursuant to this paragraph (a)(2)(ii)(B).

(iii) *Conduit entity* means an intermediate entity whose participation in the financing arrangement may be disregarded in whole or in part pursuant to this section, whether or not the district director has made a determination that the intermediate entity should be disregarded under paragraph (a)(3)(i) of this section.

(iv) *Conduit financing arrangement* means a financing arrangement that is effected through one or more conduit entities.

(v) *Related* means related within the meaning of sections 267(b) or 707(b)(1), or controlled within the meaning of section 482, and the regulations under those sections. For purposes of determining whether a person is related to another person, the constructive ownership rules of section 318 shall apply, and the attribution rules of section 267(c) also shall apply to the extent they attribute ownership to persons to whom section 318 does not attribute ownership.

(3) Disregard of participation of conduit entity. (i) Authority of district director. The district director may determine that the participation of a conduit entity in a conduit financing arrangement should be disregarded for purposes of section 881. For this purpose, an intermediate entity will constitute a conduit entity if it meets the standards of paragraph (a)(4) of this section. The district director has discretion to determine the manner in which the standards of paragraph (a)(4) of this section apply, including the financing transactions and parties composing the financing arrangement.

(ii) Effect of disregarding conduit entity. (A) In general. If the district director determines that the participation of a conduit entity in a financing arrangement should be disregarded, the financing arrangement is recharacterized as a transaction directly between the remaining parties to the financing arrangement (in most cases, the financed entity and the financing entity) for purposes of section 881. To the extent that a disregarded conduit entity actually receives or makes payments pursuant to a conduit financing arrangement, it is treated as an agent of the financing entity. Except as otherwise provided, the recharacterization of the conduit financing arrangement also applies for purposes of sections 871, 884(f)(1)(A), 1441, and 1442 and other procedural provisions relating to those sections. This recharacterization will not otherwise affect a taxpayer's Federal income tax liability under any substantive provisions of the Internal Revenue Code. Thus, for example, the recharacterization generally applies for purposes of section 1461, in order to impose liability on a withholding agent who fails to withhold as required under § 1.1441-3(j), but not for purposes of § 1.882-5.

(B) Character of payments made by the financed entity. If the participation of a conduit financing arrangement is disregarded under this paragraph (a)(3), payments made by the financed entity generally shall be characterized by reference to the character (e.g., interest or rent) of the payments made to the financing entity. However, if the financing transaction to which the financing entity is a party is a transaction described in paragraph (a)(2)(ii)(A)(2) or (4) of this section that gives rise to payments that would not be deductible if paid by the financed entity, the character of the payments made by the financed entity will not be affected by the disregard of the participation of a conduit entity. The characterization provided by this paragraph (a)(3)(ii)(B) does not, however, extend to qualification of a payment for any exemption from withholding tax under the Internal Revenue Code or a provision of any applicable tax treaty if such qualification depends on the terms of, or other similar facts or circumstances relating to, the financing transaction to which the financing entity is a party that do not apply to the financing transaction to which the financed entity is a party. Thus, for example, payments made by a financed entity that is not a bank cannot qualify for the exemption provided by section 881(i) of the Code even if the loan between the financed entity and the conduit entity is a bank deposit.

(C) Effect of income tax treaties. Where the participation of a conduit entity in a conduit financing arrangement is disregarded pursuant to this section, it is disregarded for all purposes of section 881, including for purposes of applying any relevant income tax treaties. Accordingly, the conduit entity may not claim the benefits of a tax treaty between its country of residence and the United States to reduce the amount of tax due under section 881 with respect to payments made pursuant to the conduit financing arrangement. The financing entity may, however, claim the benefits of any income tax treaty under which it is entitled to benefits in order to reduce the rate of tax on payments made pursuant to the conduit financing arrangement that are recharacterized in accordance with paragraph (a)(3)(ii)(B) of this section.

(D) Effect on withholding tax. For the effect of recharacterization on withholding obligations, see §§ 1.1441-3(j) and 1.1441-7(d).

(E) Special rule for a financing entity that is unrelated to both intermediate entity and financed entity. (1) Liability of financing entity. Notwithstanding the fact that a financing arrangement is a conduit financing arrangement, a financing entity that is unrelated to the financed entity and the conduit entity (or entities) shall not itself be liable for tax under section 881 unless the financing entity knows or has reason to know that the financing arrangement is a conduit financing arrangement. But see § 1.1441-3(j) for the withholding agent's withholding obligations.

(2) Financing entity's knowledge. (i) In general. A financing entity knows or has reason to know that the financing arrangement is a conduit financing arrangement only if the financing entity knows or has reason to know of facts sufficient to establish that the financing arrangement is a conduit financing arrangement, including facts sufficient to establish that the participation of the intermediate entity in the financing arrangement is pursuant to a tax avoidance plan. A person that knows only of the financing transactions that comprise the financing arrangement will not be considered to know or have reason to know of facts sufficient to establish that the financing arrangement is a conduit financing arrangement.

(ii) Presumption regarding financing entity's knowledge. It shall be presumed that the financing entity does not know or have reason to know that the financing arrangement is a conduit financing arrangement if the financing entity is unrelated to all other parties to the financing arrangement and the financing entity establishes that the intermediate entity who is a party to the financing transaction with the financing entity is actively engaged in a substantial trade or business. An intermediate entity will not be considered to be engaged in a trade or business if its business is making or managing investments, unless the intermediate entity is actively engaged in a banking, insurance, financing or similar trade or business and such business consists predominantly of transactions with customers who are not related persons. An intermediate entity's trade or business is substantial if it is reasonable for the financing entity to expect that the intermediate entity will be able to make payments under the financing transaction out of the cash flow of that trade or business. This presumption may be rebutted if the district director establishes that the financing entity knew or had reason to know that the financing arrangement is a conduit financing arrangement. See Example 6 of paragraph (e) of this section for an illustration of the rules of this paragraph (a)(3)(ii)(E).

(iii) Limitation on taxpayer's use of this section. A taxpayer may not apply this section to reduce the amount of its Federal income tax liability by disregarding the form of its financing transactions for Federal income tax purposes or by compelling the district director to do so. See, however, paragraph (b)(2)(i) of this section for rules regarding the taxpayer's ability to show that the participation of one or more intermediate entities results in no significant reduction in tax.

(4) Standard for treatment as a conduit entity. (i) In general. An intermediate entity is a conduit entity with respect to a financing arrangement if—

(A) The participation of the intermediate entity (or entities) in the financing arrangement reduces the tax imposed by section 881 (determined by comparing the aggregate tax imposed under section 881 on payments made on financing transactions making up the financing arrangement with the tax that would have been imposed under paragraph (d) of this section);

(B) The participation of the intermediate entity in the financing arrangement is pursuant to a tax avoidance plan; and

(C) Either—

(1) The intermediate entity is related to the financing entity or the financed entity; or

(2) The intermediate entity would not have participated in the financing arrangement on substantially the same terms but for the fact that the financing entity engaged in the financing transaction with the intermediate entity.

(ii) Multiple intermediate entities. (A) In general. If a financing arrangement involves multiple intermediate entities, the district director will determine whether each of the intermediate entities is a conduit entity. The district director will make the determination by applying the special rules for multiple intermediate entities provided in this section or, if no special rules are provided, applying principles consistent with those of paragraph (a)(4)(i) of this section to each of the intermediate entities in the financing arrangement.

(B) Special rule for related persons. The district director may treat related intermediate entities as a single intermediate entity if he determines that one of the principal purposes for the involvement of multiple intermediate entities in the financing arrangement is to prevent the characterization of an intermediate entity as a conduit entity, to reduce the portion of a payment that is subject to withholding tax or otherwise to circumvent the provisions of this section. This determination shall be based upon all of the facts and circumstances, including, but not limited to, the factors set forth in paragraph (b)(2) of this section. If a district director determines that related persons are to be treated as a single intermediate entity, financing transactions between such related parties that are part of the conduit financing arrangement shall be disregarded for purposes of applying this section. See Examples 7 and 8 of paragraph (e) of this section for illustrations of the rules of this paragraph (a)(4)(ii).

(b) Determination of whether participation of intermediate entity is pursuant to a tax avoidance plan. *(1) In general.* A tax avoidance plan is a plan one of the principal purposes of which is the avoidance of tax imposed by section 881. Avoidance of the tax imposed by section 881 may be one of the principal purposes for such a plan even though it is outweighed by other purposes (taken together or separately). In this regard, the only relevant purposes are those pertaining to the participation of the intermediate entity in the financing arrangement and not those pertaining to the existence of a financing arrangement as a whole. The plan may be formal or informal, written or oral, and may involve any one or more of the parties to the financing arrangement. The plan must be in existence no later than the last date that any of the financing transactions comprising the financing arrangement is entered into. The district director may infer the existence of a tax avoidance plan from the facts and circumstances. In determining whether there is a tax avoidance plan, the district director will weigh all relevant evidence regarding the purposes for the intermediate entity's participation in the financing arrangement. See Examples 11 and 12 of paragraph (e) of this section for illustrations of the rule of this paragraph (b)(1).

(2) Factors taken into account in determining the presence or absence of a tax avoidance purpose. The factors described in paragraphs (b)(2)(i) through (iv) of this section are among the facts and circumstances taken into account in determining whether the participation of an intermediate entity in a financing arrangement has as one of its principal purposes the avoidance of tax imposed by section 881.

(i) Significant reduction in tax. The district director will consider whether the participation of the intermediate entity (or entities) in the financing arrangement significantly reduces the tax that otherwise would have been imposed under section 881. The fact that an intermediate entity is a resident of a country that has an income tax treaty with the United States that significantly reduces the tax that otherwise would have been imposed under section 881 is not sufficient, by itself, to establish the existence of a tax avoidance plan. The determination of whether the participation of an intermediate entity significantly reduces the tax generally is made by comparing the aggregate tax imposed under section 881 on payments made on financing transactions making up the financing arrangement with the tax that would be imposed under paragraph (d) of this section. However, the taxpayer is not barred from presenting evidence that the financing entity, as determined by the district director, was itself an intermediate entity and another entity should be treated as the financing entity for purposes of applying this test. A reduction in the absolute amount of tax may be significant even if the reduction in rate is not. A reduction in the amount of tax may be significant if the reduction is large in absolute terms or in relative terms. See Examples 13, 14 and 15 of paragraph (e) of this section for illustrations of this factor.

(ii) Ability to make the advance. The district director will consider whether the intermediate entity had sufficient available money or other property of its own to have made the advance to the financed entity without the advance of money or other property to it by the financing entity (or in the case of multiple intermediate entities, whether each of the intermediate entities had sufficient available money or other property of its own to have made the advance to either the financed entity or another intermediate entity without the advance of money or other property to it by either the financing entity or another intermediate entity).

(iii) Time period between financing transactions. The district director will consider the length of the period of time that separates the advances of money or other property, or the grants of rights to use property, by the financing entity to the intermediate entity (in the case of multiple intermediate entities, from one intermediate entity to another), and ultimately by the intermediate entity to the financed entity. A short period of time is evidence of the existence of a tax avoidance plan while a long period of time is evidence that there is not a tax avoidance plan. See Example 16 of paragraph (e) of this section for an illustration of this factor.

(iv) Financing transactions in the ordinary course of business. If the parties to the financing transaction are related, the district director will consider whether the financing transaction occurs in the ordinary course of the active conduct of complementary or integrated trades or businesses engaged in by these entities. The fact that a financing transaction is described in this paragraph (b)(2)(iv) is evidence that the participation of the parties to that transaction in the financing arrangement is not pursuant to a tax avoidance plan. A loan will not be considered to occur in the ordinary course of the active conduct of complementary or integrated trades or businesses unless the loan is a trade receivable or the parties to the transaction are actively engaged in a banking, insurance, financing or similar trade or business and such business consists predominantly of transactions with customers who are not related persons. See Example 17 of paragraph (e) of this section for an illustration of this factor.

(3) Presumption if significant financing activities performed by a related intermediate entity. (i) General rule. It shall be presumed that the participation of an intermediate entity (or entities) in a financing arrangement is not pursuant to a tax avoidance plan if the intermediate entity is related to either or both the financing entity or the financed entity and the intermediate entity performs significant financing activities with respect to the financing transactions forming part of the financing arrangement to which it is a party. This presumption may be rebutted if the district director establishes that the participation of the intermediate entity in the financing arrangement is pursuant to a tax avoidance plan. See Examples 21, 22 and 23 of paragraph (e) of this section for illustrations of this presumption.

(ii) Significant financing activities. For purposes of this paragraph (b)(3), an intermediate entity performs significant financing activities with respect to such financing transactions only if the financing transactions satisfy the requirements of either paragraph (b)(3)(ii)(A) or (B) of this section.

(A) Active rents or royalties. An intermediate entity performs significant financing activities with respect to leases or licenses if rents or royalties earned with respect to such leases or licenses are derived in the active conduct of a trade or business within the meaning of section 954(c)(2)(A), to be applied by substituting the term *intermediate* entity for the term *controlled foreign corporation.*

(B) Active risk management. (1) In general. An intermediate entity is considered to perform significant financing activities with respect to financing transactions only if officers and employees of the intermediate entity participate actively and materially in arranging the intermediate entity's participation in such financing transactions (other than financing transactions described in paragraph (b)(3)(ii)(B)(3) of this section) and perform the business activity and risk management activities described in paragraph (b)(3)(ii)(B)(2) of this section with respect to such financing transactions, and the participation of the intermediate entity in the financing transactions produces (or reasonably can be expected to produce) efficiency savings by reducing transaction costs and overhead and other fixed costs.

(2) Business activity and risk management requirements. An intermediate entity will be considered to perform significant financing activities only if, within the country in which the intermediate entity is organized (or, if different, within the country with respect to which the intermediate entity is claiming the benefits of a tax treaty), its officers and employees—

(i) Exercise management over, and actively conduct, the day-to-day operations of the intermediate entity. Such operations must consist of a substantial trade or business or the supervision, administration and financing for a substantial group of related persons; and

(ii) Actively manage, on an ongoing basis, material market risks arising from such financing transactions as an integral part of the management of the intermediate entity's financial and capital requirements (including management of risks of currency and interest rate fluctuations) and management of the intermediate entity's short-term investments of working capital by entering into transactions with unrelated persons.

(3) Special rule for trade receivables and payables entered into in the ordinary course of business. If the activities of the intermediate entity consist in whole or in part of cash management for a controlled group of which the intermediate entity is a member, then employees of the intermediate entity need not have participated in arranging any such financing transactions that arise in the ordinary course of a substantial trade or business of either the financed entity or the financing entity. Officers or employees of the financing entity or financed entity, however, must have participated actively and materially in arranging the transaction that gave rise to the trade receivable or trade payable. Cash management includes the operation of a sweep account whereby the intermediate entity nets intercompany trade payables and receivables arising from transactions among the other members of the controlled group and between members of the controlled group and unrelated persons.

(4) Activities of officers and employees of related persons. Except as provided in paragraph (b)(3)(ii)(B)(3) of this section, in applying this paragraph (b)(3)(ii)(B), the activities of an officer or employee of an intermediate entity will not constitute significant financing activities if any officer or employee of a related person participated materially in any of the activities described in this paragraph, other than to approve any guarantee of a financing transaction or to exercise general supervision and control over the policies of the intermediate entity.

(c) Determination of whether an unrelated intermediate entity would not have participated in financing arrangement on substantially the same terms. *(1) In general.* The determination of whether an intermediate entity would not have participated in a financing arrangement on substantially the same terms but for the financing transaction between the financing entity and the intermediate entity shall be based upon all of the facts and circumstances.

(2) Effect of guarantee. (i) In general. The district director may presume that the intermediate entity would not have participated in the financing arrangement on substantially the same terms if there is a guarantee of the financed entity's liability to the intermediate entity (or in the case of multiple intermediate entities, a guarantee of the intermediate entity's liability to the intermediate entity that advanced money or property, or granted rights to use other property). However, a guarantee that was neither in existence nor contemplated on the last date that any of the financing transactions comprising the financing arrangement is entered into does not give rise to this presumption. A taxpayer may rebut this presumption by producing clear and convincing evidence that the intermediate entity would have participated in the financing transaction with the financed entity on substantially the same terms even if the financing entity had not entered into a financing transaction with the intermediate entity.

(ii) Definition of guarantee. For the purposes of this paragraph (c)(2), a guarantee is any arrangement under which a person, directly or indirectly, assures, on a conditional or unconditional basis, the payment of another person's obligation with respect to a financing transaction. The term shall be interpreted in accordance with the definition of the term in section 163(j)(6)(D)(iii).

(d) Determination of amount of tax liability. *(1) Amount of payment subject to recharacterization.* (i) In general. If a financing arrangement is a conduit financing arrangement, a portion of each payment made by the financed entity with respect to the financing transactions that comprise the conduit financing arrangement shall be recharacterized as a transaction directly between the financed entity and the financing entity. If the aggregate principal amount of the financing transaction(s) to which the financed entity is a party is less than or equal to the aggregate principal amount of the financing transaction(s) linking any of the parties to the financing arrangement, the entire amount of the payment shall be so recharacterized. If the aggregate principal amount of the financing transaction(s) to which the financed entity is a party is greater than the aggregate principal amount of the financing transaction(s) linking any of the parties to the financing arrangement, then the recharacterized portion shall be determined by multiplying the payment by a fraction the numerator of which is equal to the lowest aggregate principal amount of the financing transaction(s) linking any of the parties to the financing arrangement (other than financing transactions that are disregarded pursuant to paragraphs (a)(2)(i)(B) and (a)(4)(ii)(B) of this section) and the denominator of which is the aggregate principal amount of the financing transaction(s) to which the financed entity is a party. In the case of financing transactions the principal amount of which is subject to adjustment, the fraction shall be determined using the average outstanding principal amounts for the period to which the payment relates. The average principal amount may be computed using any method applied consistently that reflects with reasonable accuracy the amount outstanding for the period. See Example 24 of paragraph (e) of this section for an illustration of the calculation of the amount of tax liability.

(ii) Determination of principal amount. (A) In general. Unless otherwise provided in this paragraph (d)(1)(ii), the principal amount equals the amount of money advanced, or the fair market value of other property advanced or subject to a lease or license, in the financing transaction. In general, fair market value is calculated in U.S. dollars as of the close of business on the day on which the financing transaction is entered into. However, if the property advanced, or the right to use property granted, by the financing entity is the same as the property or rights received by the financed entity, the fair market value of the property or right shall be determined as of the close of business on the last date that any of the financing transactions comprising the financing arrangement is entered into. In the case of fungible property, property of the same type shall be considered to be the same property. See Example 25 of paragraph (e) for an illustration of the calculation of the principal amount in the case of financing transactions involving fungible property. The principal amount of a financing transaction shall be subject to adjustments, as set forth in this paragraph (d)(1)(ii).

(B) Debt instruments and certain stock. In the case of a debt instrument or of stock that is subject to the current inclusion rules of sections 305(c)(3) or (e), the principal amount generally will be equal to the issue price. However, if the fair market value on the issue date differs materially from the issue price, the fair market value of the debt instrument shall be used in lieu of the instrument's issue price. Appropriate adjustments will be made for accruals of original issue discount and repayments of principal (including accrued original issue discount).

(C) Partnership and trust interests. In the case of a partnership interest or an interest in a trust, the principal amount is equal to the fair market value of the money or property contributed to the partnership or trust in return for that partnership or trust interest.

(D) Leases or licenses. In the case of a lease or license, the principal amount is equal to the fair market value of the property subject to the lease or license on the date on which the lease or license is entered into. The principal amount shall be adjusted for depreciation or amortization, calculated on a basis that accurately reflects the anticipated decline in the value of the property over its life.

(2) Rate of tax. The rate at which tax is imposed under section 881 on the portion of the payment that is recharacterized pursuant to paragraph (d)(1) of this section is determined by reference to the nature of the recharacterized transaction, as determined under paragraphs (a)(3)(ii)(B) and (C) of this section.

(e) Examples. The following examples illustrate this section. For purposes of these examples, unless otherwise indicated, it is assumed that FP, a corporation organized in country N, owns all of the stock of FS, a corporation organized in country T, and DS, a corporation organized in the United States. Country T, but not country N, has an income tax treaty with the United States. The treaty exempts interest, rents and royalties paid by a resident of one state (the source state) to a resident of the other state from tax in the source state.

Example (1). Financing arrangement. (i) On January 1, 1996, BK, a bank organized in country T, lends $1,000,000 to DS in exchange for a note issued by DS. FP guarantees to BK that DS will satisfy its repayment obligation on the loan. There are no other transactions between FP and BK.

(ii) BK's loan to DS is a financing transaction within the meaning of paragraph (a)(2)(ii)(A)(1) of this section. FP's guarantee of DS's repayment obligation is not a financing transaction as described in paragraphs (a)(2)(ii)(A)(1) through (4) of this section. Therefore, these transactions do not constitute a financing arrangement as defined in paragraph (a)(2)(i) of this section.

Example (2). Financing arrangement. (i) On January 1, 1996, FP lends $1,000,000 to DS in exchange for a note issued by DS. On January 1, 1997, FP assigns the DS note to FS in exchange for a note issued by FS. After receiving notice of the assignment, DS remits payments due under its note to FS.

(ii) The DS note held by FS and the FS note held by FP are financing transactions within the meaning of paragraph (a)(2)(ii)(A)(1) of this section, and together constitute a financing arrangement within the meaning of paragraph (a)(2)(i) of this section.

Example (3). Financing arrangement. (i) On December 1, 1994 FP creates a special purposes subsidiary, FS. On that date FP capitalizes FS with $1,000,000 in cash and $10,000,000 in debt from BK, a Country N bank. On January 1, 1995, C, a U.S. person, purchases an automobile from DS in return for an installment note. On August 1, 1995, DS sells a number of installment notes, including C's, to FS in exchange for $10,000,000. DS continues to service the installment notes for FS.

(ii) The C installment note now held by FS (as well as all of the other installment notes now held by FS) and the FS note held by BK are financing transactions within the meaning of paragraph (a)(2)(ii)(A)(1) of this section, and together constitute a financing arrangement within the meaning of paragraph (a)(2)(i) of this section.

Example (4). Related persons treated as a single intermediate entity. (i) On January 1, 1996, FP deposits $1,000,000 with BK, a bank that is organized in country N and is unrelated to FP and its subsidiaries. M, a corporation also organized in country N, is wholly-owned by the sole shareholder of BK but is not a bank within the meaning of section 881(c)(3)(A). On July 1, 1996, M lends $1,000,000 to DS in exchange for a note maturing on July 1, 2006. The note is in registered form within the meaning of section 881(c)(2)(B)(i) and DS has received from M the statement required by section 881(c)(2)(B)(ii). One of the principal purposes for the absence of a financing transaction between BK and M is the avoidance of the application of this section.

(ii) The transactions described above would form a financing arrangement but for the absence of a financing transaction between BK and M. However, because one of the principal purposes for the structuring of these financing transactions is to prevent characterization of such arrangement as a financing arrangement, the district director may treat the financing transactions between FP and BK, and between M and DS as a financing arrangement under paragraphs (a)(2)(i)(B) of this section. In such a case, BK and M would be considered a single intermediate entity for purposes of this section. See also paragraph (a)(4)(ii)(B) of this section for the authority to treat BK and M as a single intermediate entity.

Example (5). Related persons treated as a single intermediate entity. (i) On January 1, 1995, FP lends $10,000,000 to FS in exchange for a 10-year note that pays interest annually at a rate of 8 percent per annum. On January 2, 1995, FS contributes $10,000,000 to FS2, a wholly-owned subsidiary of FS organized in country T, in exchange for common stock of FS2. On January 1, 1996, FS2 lends $10,000,000 to DS in exchange for an 8-year note that pays interest annually at a rate of 10 percent per annum. FS is a holding company whose most significant asset is the stock of FS2. Throughout the period that the FP-FS loan is outstanding, FS causes FS2 to make distributions to FS, most of which are used to make interest and principal payments on the FP-FS loan. Without the distributions from FS2, FS would not have had the funds with which to make payments on the FP-FS loan. One of the principal purposes for the absence of a financing transaction between FS and FS2 is the avoidance of the application of this section.

(ii) The conditions of paragraph (a)(4)(i)(A) of this section would be satisfied with respect to the financing transactions between FP, FS, FS2 and DS but for the absence of a financing transaction between FS and FS2. However, because one of the principal purposes for the structuring of these financing transactions is to prevent characterization of an entity as a conduit, the district director may treat the financing transactions between FP and FS, and between FS2 and DS as a financing arrangement. See paragraph (a)(4)(ii)(B) of this section. In such a case, FS and FS2 would be considered a single intermediate entity for purposes of this section. See also paragraph (a)(2)(i)(B) of this section for the authority to treat FS and FS2 as a single intermediate entity.

Example (6). Presumption with respect to unrelated financing entity. (i) FP is a corporation organized in country T that is actively engaged in a substantial manufacturing business. FP has a revolving credit facility with a syndicate of banks, none of which is related to FP and FP's subsidiaries, which provides that FP may borrow up to a maximum of $100,000,000 at a time. The revolving credit facility provides that DS and certain other subsidiaries of FP may borrow directly from the syndicate at the same interest rates as FP, but each subsidiary is required to indemnify the syndicate banks for any withholding taxes imposed on interest payments by the country in which the subsidiary is organized. BK, a bank that is organized in country N, is the agent for the syndicate. Some of the syndicate banks are organized in country N, but others are residents of country O, a country that has an income tax treaty with the United States which allows the United States to impose a tax on interest at a maximum rate of 10 percent. It is reasonable for BK and the syndicate banks to have determined that FP will be able to meet its payment obligations on a maximum principal amount of $100,000,000 out of the cash flow of its manufacturing business. At various times throughout 1995, FP borrows under the revolving credit facility until the outstanding principal amount reaches the maximum amount of $100,000,000. On December 31, 1995, FP receives $100,000,000 from a public offering of its equity. On January 1, 1996, FP pays BK $90,000,000 to reduce the outstanding principal amount under the revolving credit facility and lends $10,000,000 to DS. FP would have repaid the entire principal amount, and DS would have borrowed directly from the syndicate, but for the fact that DS did not want to incur the U.S. withholding tax that would have applied to payments made directly by DS to the syndicate banks.

(ii) Pursuant to paragraph (a)(3)(ii)(E)(1) of this section, even though the financing arrangement is a conduit financing arrangement (because the financing arrangement meets the standards for recharacterization in paragraph (a)(4)(i)), BK and the other syndicate banks have no section 881 liability unless they know or have reason to know that the financing arrangement is a conduit financing arrangement. Moreover, pursuant to paragraph (a)(3)(ii)(E)(2)(ii) of this section, BK and the syndicate banks are presumed not to know that the financing arrangement is a conduit financing arrangement. The syndicate banks are unrelated to both FP and DS, and FP is actively engaged in a substantial trade or business—that is, the cash flow from FP's manufacturing business is sufficient for the banks to expect that FP will be able to make the payments required under the financing transaction. See § 1.1441-3(j) for the withholding obligations of the withholding agents.

Example (7). Multiple intermediate entities—special rule for related persons. (i) On January 1, 1995, FP lends $10,000,000 to FS in exchange for a 10-year note that pays interest annually at a rate of 8 percent per annum. On January 2, 1995, FS contributes $9,900,000 to FS2, a wholly-owned subsidiary of FS organized in country T, in exchange for common stock and lends $100,000 to FS2. On January 1, 1996, F52 lends $10,000,000 to DS in exchange for an 8-year note that pays interest annually at a rate of 10 percent per annum. FS is a holding company that has no significant assets other than the stock of FS2. Throughout the period that the FP-FS loan is outstanding, FS causes FS2 to make distributions to FS, most of which are used to make interest and principal payments on the FP-FS loan. Without the distributions from FS2, FS would not have had the funds with which to make payments on the FP-FS loan. One of the principal purposes for structuring the transactions between FS and FS2 as primarily a contribution of capital is to reduce-the amount of the payment that would be recharacterized under paragraph (d) of this section.

(ii) Pursuant to paragraph (a)(4)(ii)(B) of this section, the district director may treat FS and FS2 as a single intermediate entity for purposes of this section since one of the principal purposes for the participation of multiple intermediate entities is to reduce the amount of the tax liability on any recharacterized payment by inserting a financing transaction with a low principal amount.

Example (8). Multiple intermediate entities. (i) On January 1, 1995, FP deposits $1,000,000 with BK, a bank that is organized in country T and is unrelated to FP and its subsidiaries, FS and DS. On January 1, 1996, at a time when the FP-BK deposit is still outstanding, BK lends $500,000 to BK2, a bank that is wholly-owned by BK and is organized in country T. On the same date, BK2 lends $500,000 to FS. On July 1, 1996, FS lends $500,000 to DS. FP pledges its deposit with BK to BK2 in support of FS' obligation to repay the BK2 loan. FS', BK's and BK2's participation in the financing arrangement is pursuant to a tax avoidance plan.

(ii) The conditions of paragraphs (a)(4)(i)(A) and (B) of this section are satisfied because the participation of BK, BK2 and FS in the financing arrangement reduces the tax imposed by section 881, and FS', BK's and BK2's participation in the financing arrangement is pursuant to a tax avoidance plan. However, since BK and BK2 are unrelated to FP and DS, under paragraph (a)(4)(i)(C)(2) of this section, BK and BK2 will be treated as conduit entities only if BK and BK2 would not have participated in the financing arrangement on substantially the same terms but for the financing transaction between FP and BK.

(iii) It is presumed that BK2 would not have participated in the financing arrangement on substantially the same terms but for the BK-BK2 financing transaction because FP's pledge of an asset in support of FS' obligation to repay the BK2 loan is a guarantee within the meaning of paragraph (c)(2)(ii) of this section. If the taxpayer does not rebut this presumption by clear and convincing evidence, then BK2 will be a conduit entity.

(iv) Because BK and BK2 are related intermediate entities, the district director must determine whether one of the principal purposes for the involvement of multiple intermediate entities was to prevent characterization of an entity as a conduit entity. In making this determination, the district director may consider the fact that the involvement of two related intermediate entities prevents the presumption regarding guarantees from applying to BK. In the absence of evidence showing a business purpose for the involvement of both BK and BK2, the district director may treat BK and BK2 as a single intermediate entity for purposes of determining whether they would have participated in the financing arrangement on substantially the same terms but for the financing transaction between FP and BK. The presumption that applies to BK2 therefore will apply to BK. If the taxpayer does not rebut this presumption by clear and convincing evidence, then BK will be a conduit entity.

Example (9). Reduction of tax. (i) On February 1, 1995, FP issues debt to the public that would satisfy the requirements of section 871(h)(2)(A)(relating to obligations that are not in registered form) if issued by a U.S. person. FP lends the proceeds of the debt offering to DS in exchange for a note.

(ii) The debt issued by FP and the DS note are financing transactions within the meaning of paragraph (a)(2)(ii)(A)(1) of this section and together constitute a financing arrangement within the meaning of paragraph (a)(2)(i) of this section. The holders of the FP debt are the financing entities, FP is the intermediate entity and DS is the financed entity. Because interest payments on the debt issued by FP would not have been subject to withholding tax if the debt had been issued by DS, there is no reduction in tax under paragraph (a)(4)(i)(A) of this section. Accordingly, FP is not a conduit entity.

Example (10). Reduction of tax. (i) On January 1, 1995, FP licenses to FS the rights to use a patent in the United States to manufacture product A. FS agrees to pay FP a fixed amount in royalties each year under the license. On January 1, 1996, FS sublicenses to DS the rights to use the patent in the United States. Under the sublicense, DS agrees to pay FS royalties based upon the units of product A manufactured by DS each year. Although the formula for computing the amount of royalties paid by DS to FS differs from the formula for computing the amount of royalties paid by FS to FP, each represents an arm's length rate.

(ii) Although the royalties paid by DS to FS are exempt from U.S. withholding tax, the royalty payments between FS and FP are income from U.S. sources under section 861(a)(4) subject to the 30 percent gross tax imposed by § 1.881-2(b) and subject to withholding under § 1.1441-2(a). Because the rate of tax imposed on royalties paid by FS to FP is the same as the rate that would have been imposed on royalties paid by DS to FP, the participation of FS in the FP-FS-DS financing arrangement does not reduce the tax imposed by section 881 within the meaning of paragraph (a)(4)(i)(A) of this section. Accordingly, FP is not a conduit entity.

Example (11). A principal purpose. (i) On January 1, 1995, FS lends $10,000,000 to DS in exchange for a 10-year note that pays interest annually at a rate of 8 percent per annum. As was intended at the time of the loan from FS to DS, on July 1, 1995, FP makes an interest-free demand loan of $10,000,000 to FS. A principal purpose for FS' participation in the FP-FS-DS financing arrangement is that FS generally coordinates the financing for all of FP's subsidiaries (although FS does not engage in significant financing activities with respect to such financing transactions). However, another principal purpose for FS' participation is to allow the parties to benefit from the lower withholding tax rate provided under the income tax treaty between country T and the United States.

(ii) The financing arrangement satisfies the tax avoidance purpose requirement of paragraph (a)(4)(i)(B) of this section because FS participated in the financing arrangement pursuant to a plan one of the principal purposes of which is to allow the parties to benefit from the country T-U.S. treaty.

Example (12). A principal purpose. (i) DX is a U.S. corporation that intends to purchase property to use in its manufacturing business. FX is a partnership organized in country N that is owned in equal parts by LC1 and LC2, leasing companies that are unrelated to DX. BK, a bank organized in country N and unrelated to DX, LC1 and LC2, lends $100,000,000 to FX to enable FX to purchase the property. On the same day, FX purchases the property and engages in a transaction with DX which is treated as a lease of the property for country N tax purposes but a loan for U.S. tax purposes. Accordingly, DX is treated as the owner of the property for U.S. tax purposes. The parties comply with the requirements of section 881(c) with respect to the debt obligation of DX to FX. FX and DX structured these transactions in this manner so that LC1 and LC2 would be entitled to accelerated depreciation deductions with respect to the property in country N and DX would be entitled to accelerated depreciation deductions in the United States. None of the parties would have participated in the transaction if the payments made by DX were subject to U.S. withholding tax.

(ii) The loan from BK to FX and from FX to DX are financing transactions and, together constitute a financing arrangement. The participation of FX in the financing arrangement reduces the tax imposed by section 881 because payments made to FX, but not BK, qualify for the portfolio interest exemption of section 881(c) because BK is a bank making an extension of credit in the ordinary course of its trade or business within the meaning of section 881(c)(3)(A). Moreover, because DX borrowed the money from FX instead of borrowing the money directly from BK to avoid the tax imposed by section 881, one of the principal purposes of the participation of FX was to avoid that tax (even though another principal purpose of the participation of FX was to allow LC1 and LC2 to take advantage of accelerated depreciation deductions in country N). Assuming that FX would not have participated in the financing arrangement on substantially the same terms but for the fact that BK loaned it $100,000,000, FX is a conduit entity and the financing arrangement is a conduit financing arrangement.

Example (13). Significant reduction of tax. (i) FS owns all of the stock of FS1, which also is a resident of country T. FS1 owns all of the stock of DS. On January 1, 1995, FP contributes $10,000,000 to the capital of FS in return for perpetual preferred stock. On July 1, 1995, FS lends $10,000,000 to FS1. On January 1, 1996, FS1 lends $10,000,000 to DS. Under the terms of the country T-U.S. income tax treaty, a country T resident is not entitled to the reduced withholding rate on interest income provided by the treaty if the resident is entitled to specified tax benefits under country T law. Although FS1 may deduct interest paid on the loan from FS, these deductions are not pursuant to any special tax benefits provided by country T law. However, FS qualifies for one of the enumerated tax benefits pursuant to which it may deduct dividends paid with respect to the stock held by FP. Therefore, if FS had made a loan directly to DS, FS would not have been entitled to the benefits of the country T-U.S. tax treaty with respect to payments it received from DS, and such payments would have been subject to tax under section 881 at a 30 percent rate.

(ii) The FS-FS1 loan and the FS1-DS loan are financing transactions within the meaning of paragraph (a)(2)(ii)(A)(1) of this section and together constitute a financing arrangement within the meaning of paragraph (a)(2)(i) of this section. Pursuant to paragraph (b)(2)(i) of this section, the significant reduction in tax resulting from the participation of FS1 in the financing arrangement is evidence that the participation of FS1 in the financing arrangement is pursuant to a tax avoidance plan. However, other facts relevant to the presence of such a plan must also be taken into account.

Example (14). Significant reduction of tax. (i) FP owns 90 percent of the voting stock of FX, an unlimited liability company organized in country T. The other 10 percent of the common stock of FX is owned by FP1, a subsidiary of FP that is organized in country N. Although FX is a partnership for U.S. tax purposes, FX is entitled to the benefits of the U.S.-country T income tax treaty because FX is subject to tax in country T as a resident corporation. On January 1, 1996, FP contributes $10,000,000 to FX in exchange for an instrument denominated as preferred stock that pays a dividend of 7 percent and that must be redeemed by FX in seven years. For U.S. tax purposes, the preferred stock is a partnership interest. On July 1, 1996, FX makes a loan of $10,000,000 to DS in exchange for a 7-year note paying interest at 6 percent.

(ii) Because FX is required to redeem the partnership interest at a specified time, the partnership interest constitutes a financing transaction within the meaning of paragraph (a)(2)(ii)(A)(2) of this section. Moreover, because the FX-DS note is a financing transaction within the meaning of paragraph (a)(2)(ii)(A)(1) of this section, together the transactions constitute a financing arrangement within the meaning of (a)(2)(i) of this section. Payments of interest made directly by DS to FP and FP1 would not be eligible for the portfolio interest exemption and would not be entitled to a reduction in withholding tax pursuant to a tax treaty. Therefore, there is a significant reduction in tax resulting from the participation of FX in the financing arrangement, which is evidence that the participation of FX in the financing arrangement is pursuant to a tax avoidance plan. However, other facts relevant to the existence of such a plan must also be taken into account.

Example (15). Significant reduction of tax. (i) FP owns a 10 percent interest in the profits and capital of FX, a partnership organized in country N. The other 90 percent interest in FX is owned by G, an unrelated corporation that is organized in country T. FX is not engaged in business in the United States. On January 1, 1996, FP contributes $10,000,000 to FX in exchange for an instrument documented as perpetual subordinated debt that provides for quarterly interest payments at 9 percent per annum. Under the terms of the instrument, payments on the perpetual subordinated debt do not otherwise affect the allocation of income between the partners. FP has the right to require the liquidation of FX if FX fails to make an interest payment. For U.S. tax purposes, the perpetual subordinated debt is treated as a partnership interest in FX and the payments on the perpetual subordinated debt constitute guaranteed payments within the meaning of section 707(c). On July 1, 1996, FX makes a loan of $10,000,000 to DS in exchange for a 7-year note paying interest at 8 percent per annum.

(ii) Because FP has the effective right to force payment of the interest on the perpetual subordinated debt, the instrument constitutes a financing transaction within the meaning of paragraph (a)(2)(ii)(A)(2) of this section. Moreover, because the note between FX and DS is a financing transaction within the meaning of paragraph (a)(2)(ii)(A)(1) of this section, together the transactions are a financing arrangement within the meaning of (a)(2)(i) of this section. Without regard to this section, 90 percent of each interest payment received by FX would be treated as exempt from U.S. withholding tax because it is beneficially owned by G, while 10 percent would be subject to a 30 percent withholding tax because beneficially owned by FP. If FP held directly the note issued by DS, 100 percent of the interest payments on the note would have been subject to the 30 percent withholding tax. The significant reduction in the tax imposed by section 881 resulting from the participation of FX in the financing arrangement is evidence that the participation of FX in the financing arrangement is pursuant to a tax avoidance plan. However, other facts relevant to the presence of such a plan must also be taken into account.

Example (16). Time period between transactions. (i) On January 1, 1995, FP lends $10,000,000 to FS in exchange for a 10-year note that pays no interest annually. When the note matures, FS is obligated to pay $24,000,000 to FP. On January 1, 1996, FS lends $10,000,000 to DS in exchange for a 10-year note that pays interest annually at a rate of 10 percent per annum.

(ii) The FS note held by FP and the DS note held by FS are financing transactions within the meaning of paragraph (a)(2)(ii)(A)(1) of this section and together constitute a financing arrangement within the meaning of (a)(2)(i) of this section. Pursuant to paragraph (b)(2)(iii) of this section, the short period of time (twelve months) between the loan by FP to FS and the loan by FS to DS is evidence that the participation of FS in the financing arrangement is pursuant to a tax avoidance plan. However, other facts relevant to the presence of such a plan must also be taken into account.

Example (17). Financing transactions in the ordinary course of business. (i) FP is a holding company. FS is actively engaged in country T in the business of manufacturing and selling product A. DS manufactures product B, a principal component in which is product A. FS' business activity is substantial. On January 1, 1995, FP lends $100,000,000 to

FS to finance FS' business operations. On January 1, 1996, FS ships $30,000,000 of product A to DS. In return, FS creates an interest-bearing account receivable on its books. FS' shipment is in the ordinary course of the active conduct of its trade or business (which is complementary to DS' trade or business.)

(ii) The loan from FP to FS and the accounts receivable opened by FS for a payment owed by DS are financing transactions within the meaning of paragraph (a)(2)(ii)(A)(1) of this section and together constitute a financing arrangement within the meaning of paragraph (a)(2)(i) of this section. Pursuant to paragraph (b)(2)(iv) of this section, the fact that DS' liability to FS is created in the ordinary course of the active conduct of DS' trade or business that is complementary to a business actively engaged in by DS is evidence that the participation of FS in the financing arrangement is not pursuant to a tax avoidance plan. However, other facts relevant to the presence of such a plan must also be taken into account.

Example (18). Tax avoidance plan—other factors. (i) On February 1, 1995, FP issues debt in Country N that is in registered form within the meaning of section 881(c)(3)(A). The FP debt would satisfy the requirements of section 881(c) if the debt were issued by a U.S. person and the withholding agent received the certification required by section 871(h)(2)(B)(ii). The purchasers of the debt are financial institutions and there is no reason to believe that they would not furnish Forms W-8. On March 1, 1995, FP lends a portion of the proceeds of the offering to DS.

(ii) The FP debt and the loan to DS are financing transactions within the meaning of paragraph (a)(2)(ii)(A)(l) of this section and together constitute a financing arrangement within the meaning of paragraph (a)(2)(i) of this section. The owners of the FP debt are the financing entities, FP is the intermediate entity and DS is the financed entity. Interest payments on the debt issued by FP would be subject to withholding tax if the debt were issued by DS, unless DS received all necessary Forms W-8. Therefore, the participation of FP in the financing arrangement potentially reduces the tax imposed by section 881(a). However, because it is reasonable to assume that the purchasers of the FP debt would have provided certifications in order to avoid the withholding tax imposed by section 881, there is not a tax avoidance plan. Accordingly, FP is not a conduit entity.

Example (19). Tax avoidance plan—other factors. (i) Over a period of years, FP has maintained a deposit with BK, a bank organized in the United States, that is unrelated to FP and its subsidiaries. FP often sells goods and purchases raw materials in the United States. FP opened the bank account with BK in order to facilitate this business and the amounts it maintains in the account are reasonably related to its dollar-denominated working capital needs. On January 1, 1995, BK lends $5,000,000 to DS. After the loan is made, the balance in FP's bank account remains within a range appropriate to meet FP's working capital needs.

(ii) FP's deposit with BK and BK's loan to DS are financing transactions within the meaning of paragraph (a)(2)(ii)(A)(1) of this section and together constitute a financing arrangement within the meaning of paragraph (a)(2)(i) of this section. Pursuant to section 881(i), interest paid by BK to FP with respect to the bank deposit is exempt from withholding tax. Interest paid directly by DS to FP would not be exempt from withholding tax under section 881(i) and therefore would be subject to a 30% withholding tax. Accordingly, there is a significant reduction in the tax imposed by section 881, which is evidence of the existence of a tax avoidance plan. See paragraph (b)(2)(i) of this section. However, the district director also will consider the fact that FP historically has maintained an account with BK to meet its working capital needs and that, prior to and after BK's loan to DS, the balance within the account remains within a range appropriate to meet those business needs as evidence that the participation of BK in the FP-BK-DS financing arrangement is not pursuant to a tax avoidance plan. In determining the presence or absence of a tax avoidance plan, all relevant facts will be taken into account.

Example (20). Tax avoidance plan—other factors. (i) Assume the same facts as in Example 19, except that on January 1, 2000, FP's deposit with BK substantially exceeds FP's expected working capital needs and on January 2, 2000, BK lends additional funds to DS. Assume also that BK's loan to DS provides BK with a right of offset against FP's deposit. Finally, assume that FP would have lent the funds to DS directly but for the imposition of the withholding tax on payments made directly to FP by DS.

(ii) As in Example 19, the transactions in paragraph (i) of this Example 20 are a financing arrangement within the meaning of paragraph (a)(2)(i) and the participation of the BK reduces the section 881 tax. In this case, the presence of funds substantially in excess of FP's working capital needs and the fact that FP would have been willing to lend funds directly to DS if not for the withholding tax are evidence that the participation of BK in the FP-BK-FS financing arrangement is pursuant to a tax avoidance plan. However, other facts relevant to the presence of such a plan must also be taken into account. Even if the district director determines that the participation of BK in the financing arrangement is pursuant to a tax avoidance plan, BK may not be treated as a conduit entity unless BK would not have participated in the financing arrangement on substantially the same terms in the absence of FP's deposit with BK. BK's right of offset against FP's deposit (a form of guarantee of BK's loan to DS) creates a presumption that BK would not have made the loan to DS on substantially the same terms in the absence of FP's deposit with BK. If the taxpayer overcomes the presumption by clear and convincing evidence, BK will not be a conduit entity.

Example (21). Significant financing activities. (i) FS is responsible for coordinating the financing of all of the subsidiaries of FP, which are engaged in substantial trades or businesses and are located in country T, country N, and the United States. FS maintains a centralized cash management accounting system for FP and its subsidiaries in which it records all intercompany payables and receivables; these payables and receivables ultimately are reduced to a single balance either due from or owing to FS and each of FP's subsidiaries. FS is responsible for disbursing or receiving any cash payments required by transactions between its affiliates and unrelated parties. FS must borrow any cash necessary to meet those external obligations and invests any excess cash for the benefit of the FP group. FS enters into interest rate and foreign exchange contracts as necessary to manage the risks arising from mismatches in incoming and outgoing cash flows. The activities of FS are intended (and reasonably can be expected) to reduce transaction costs and overhead and other fixed costs. FS has 50 employees, including clerical and other back office personnel, located in country T. At the request of DS, on January 1, 1995, FS pays a supplier $1,000,000 for materials delivered to DS and charges DS an open account receivable for this amount. On February 3, 1995, FS reverses the account receivable from

DS to FS when DS delivers to FP goods with a value of $1,000,000.

(ii) The accounts payable from DS to FS and from FS to other subsidiaries of FP constitute financing transactions within the meaning of paragraph (a)(2)(ii)(A)(1) of this section, and the transactions together constitute a financing arrangement within the meaning of paragraph (a)(2)(i) of this section. FS's activities constitute significant financing activities with respect to the financing transactions even though FS did not actively and materially participate in arranging the financing transactions because the financing transactions consisted of trade receivables and trade payables that were ordinary and necessary to carry on the trades or businesses of DS and the other subsidiaries of FP. Accordingly, pursuant to paragraph (b)(3)(i) of this section, FS' participation in the financing arrangement is presumed not to be pursuant to a tax avoidance plan.

Example (22). Significant financing activities—active risk management. (i) The facts are the same as in Example 21, except that, in addition to its short-term funding needs, DS needs long-term financing to fund an acquisition of another U.S. company; the acquisition is scheduled to close on January 15, 1995. FS has a revolving credit agreement with a syndicate of banks located in Country N. On January 14, 1995, FS borrows ¥10 billion for 10 years under the revolving credit agreement, paying yen LIBOR plus 50 basis points on a quarterly basis. FS enters into a currency swap with BK, an unrelated bank that is not a member of the syndicate, under which FS will pay BK ¥10 billion and will receive $100 million on January 15, 1995; these payments will be reversed on January 15, 2004. FS will pay BK U.S. dollar LIBOR plus 50 basis points on a notional principal amount of $100 million semi-annually and will receive yen LIBOR plus 50 basis points on a notional principal amount of ¥10 billion quarterly. Upon the closing of the acquisition on January 15, 1995, DS borrows $100 million from FS for 10 years, paying U.S. dollar LIBOR plus 50 basis points semi-annually.

(ii) Although FS performs significant financing activities with respect to certain financing transactions to which it is a party, FS does not perform significant financing activities with respect to the financing transactions between FS and the syndicate of banks and between FS and DS because FS has eliminated all material market risks arising from those financing transactions through its currency swap with BK. Accordingly, the financing arrangement does not benefit from the presumption of paragraph (b)(3)(i) of this section and the district director must determine whether the participation of FS in the financing arrangement is pursuant to a tax avoidance plan on the basis of all the facts and circumstances. However, if additional facts indicated that FS reviews its currency swaps daily to determine whether they are the most cost efficient way of managing their currency risk and, as a result, frequently terminates swaps in favor of entering into more cost efficient hedging arrangements with unrelated parties, FS would be considered to perform significant financing activities and FS' participation in the financing arrangements would not be pursuant to a tax avoidance plan.

Example (23). Significant financing activities—presumption rebutted. (i) The facts are the same as in Example 21, except that, on January 1, 1995, FP lends to FS DM 15,000,000 (worth $10,000,000) in exchange for a 10 year note that pays interest annually at a rate of 5 percent per annum. Also, on March 15, 1995, FS lends $10,000,000 to DS in exchange for a 10-year note that pays interest annually at a rate of 8 percent per annum. FS would not have had sufficient funds to make the loan to DS without the loan from FP. FS does not enter into any long-term hedging transaction with respect to these financing transactions, but manages the interest rate and currency risk arising from the transactions on a daily, weekly or quarterly basis by entering into forward currency contracts.

(ii) Because FS performs significant financing activities with respect to the financing transactions between FS, DS and FP, the participation of FS in the financing arrangement is presumed not to be pursuant to a tax avoidance plan. The district director may rebut this presumption by establishing that the participation of FS is pursuant to a tax avoidance plan, based on all the facts and circumstances. The mere fact that FS is a resident of country T is not sufficient to establish the existence of a tax avoidance plan. However, the existence of a plan can be inferred from other factors in addition to the fact that FS is a resident of country T. For example, the loans are made within a short time period and FS would not have been able to make the loan to DS without the loan from FP.

Example (24). Determination of amount of tax liability. (i) On January 1, 1996, FP makes two three-year installment loans of $250,000 each to FS that pay interest at a rate of 9 percent per annum. The loans are self-amortizing with payments on each loan of $7,950 per month. On the same date, FS lends $1,000,000 to DS in exchange for a two-year note that pays interest semi-annually at a rate of 10 percent per annum, beginning on June 30, 1996. The FS-DS loan is not self-amortizing. Assume that for the period of January 1, 1996 through June 30, 1996, the average principal amount of the financing transactions between FP and FS that comprise the financing arrangement is $469,319. Further, assume that for the period of July 1, 1996 through December 31, 1996, the average principal amount of the financing transactions between FP and FS is $393,632. The average principal amount of the financing transaction between FS and DS for the same periods is $1,000,000. The district director determines that the financing transactions between FP and FS, and FS and DS, are a conduit financing arrangement.

(ii) Pursuant to paragraph (d)(1)(i) of this section, the portion of the $50,000 interest payment made by DS to FS on June 30, 1996, that is recharacterized as a payment to FP is $23,450 computed as follows: ($50,000 × $469,319/$1,000,000) = $23,450. The portion of the interest payment made on December 31, 1996 that is recharacterized as a payment to FP is $19,650, computed as follows: ($50,000 × $393,632/$1,000,000) = $19,650. Furthermore, under § 1.1441-3(j), DS is liable for withholding tax at a 30 percent rate on the portion of the $50,000 payment to FS that is recharacterized as a payment to FP, i.e., $7,035 with respect to the June 30, 1996 payment and $5,895 with respect to the December 31, 1996 payment.

Example (25). Determination of principal amount. (i) FP lends DM 5,000,000 to FS in exchange for a ten year note that pays interest semi-annually at a rate of 8 percent per annum. Six months later, pursuant to a tax avoidance plan, FS lends DM 10,000,000 to DS in exchange for a 10 year note that pays interest semi-annually at a rate of 10 percent per annum. At the time FP make its loan to FS, the exchange rate is DM 1.5/$1. At the time FS makes its loan to DS the exchange rate is DM 1.4/$1.

(ii) FP's loan to FS and FS' loan to DS are financing transactions and together constitute a financing arrangement. Furthermore, because the participation of FS reduces the tax imposed under section 881 and FS' participation is pursuant to a tax avoidance plan, the financing arrangement is a conduit financing arrangement.

(iii) Pursuant to paragraph (d)(1)(i) of this section, the amount subject to recharacterization is a fraction the numerator of which is the lowest aggregate principal amount advanced and the denominator of which is the principal amount advanced from FS to DS. Because the property advanced in these financing transactions is the same type of fungible property, under paragraph (d)(1)(ii)(A) of this section, both are valued on the date of the last financing transaction. Accordingly, the portion of the payments of interest that is recharacterized is ((DM 5,000,000 × DM 1.4/$1)/(DM 10,000,000 × DM 1.4/$1) or 0.5.

(f) Effective date. This section is effective for payments made by financed entities on or after September 11, 1995. This section shall not apply to interest payments covered by section 127(g)(3) of the Tax Reform Act of 1984, and to interest payments with respect to other debt obligations issued prior to October 15, 1984 (whether or not such debt was issued by a Netherlands Antilles corporation).

T.D. 8611, 8/10/95.

§ 1.881-4 Recordkeeping requirements concerning conduit financing arrangements.

(a) Scope. This section provides rules for the maintenance of records concerning certain financing arrangements to which the provisions of § 1.881-3 apply.

(b) Recordkeeping requirements *(1) In general.* Any person subject to the general recordkeeping requirements of section 6001 must keep the permanent books of account or records, as required by section 6001, that may be relevant to determining whether that person is a party to a financing arrangement and whether that financing arrangement is a conduit financing arrangement.

(2) Application of sections 6038 and 6038A. A financed entity that is a reporting corporation within the meaning of section 6038A(a) and the regulations under that section, and any other person that is subject to the recordkeeping requirements of § 1.6038A-3, must comply with those recordkeeping requirements with respect to records that may be relevant to determining whether the financed entity is a party to a financing arrangement and whether that financing arrangement is a conduit financing arrangement. Such records, including records that a person is required to maintain pursuant to paragraph (c) of this section, shall be considered records that are required to be maintained pursuant to section 6038 or 6038A. Accordingly, the provisions of sections 6038 and 6038A (including, without limitation, the penalty provisions thereof), and the regulations under those sections, shall apply to any records required to be maintained pursuant to this section.

(c) Records to be maintained *(1) In general.* An entity described in paragraph (b) of this section shall be required to retain any records containing the following information concerning each financing transaction that the entity knows or has reason to know comprises the financing arrangement—

(i) The nature (e.g., loan, stock, lease, license) of each financing transaction;

(ii) The name, address, taxpayer identification number (if any) and country of residence of—

(A) Each person that advanced money or other property, or granted rights to use property;

(B) Each person that was the recipient of the advance or rights; and

(C) Each person to whom a payment was made pursuant to the financing transaction (to the extent that person is a different person than the person who made the advance or granted the rights);

(iii) The date and amount of—

(A) Each advance of money or other property or grant of rights; and

(B) Each payment made in return for the advance or grant of rights;

(iv) The terms of any guarantee provided in conjunction with a financing transaction, including the name of the guarantor; and

(v) In cases where one or both-of the parties to a financing transaction are related to each other or another entity in the financing arrangement, the manner in which these persons are related.

(2) Additional documents. An entity described in paragraph (b) of this section must also retain all records relating to the circumstances surrounding its participation in the financing transactions and financing arrangements. Such documents may include, but are not limited to—

(i) Minutes of board of directors meetings;

(ii) Board resolutions or other authorizations for the financing transactions;

(iii) Private letter rulings;

(iv) Financial reports (audited or unaudited);

(v) Notes to financial statements;

(vi) Bank statements;

(vii) Copies of wire transfers;

(viii) Offering documents;

(ix) Materials from investment advisors, bankers and tax advisors; and

(x) Evidences of indebtedness.

(3) Effect of record maintenance requirement. Record maintenance in accordance with paragraph (b) of this section generally does not require the original creation of records that are ordinarily not created by affected entities. If, however, a document that is actually created is described in this paragraph (c), it is to be retained even if the document is not of a type ordinarily created by the affected entity.

(d) Effective date. This section is effective September 11, 1995. This section shall not apply to interest payments covered by section 127(g)(3) of the Tax Reform Act of 1984, and to interest payments with respect to other debt obligations issued prior to October 15, 1984 (whether or not such debt was issued by a Netherlands Antilles corporation).

T.D. 8611, 8/10/95.

§ 1.881-5 Exception for certain possessions corporations.

(a) through (f)(3) [Reserved]. For more information, see § 1.881-5T(a) through (f)(3).

(f) *(4) Bona fide resident.*

(i) With respect to a particular possession, means[

(A) An individual who is a bona fide resident of the possession as defined in § 1.937-1; or

(B) A business entity organized under the laws of the possession and taxable as a corporation in the possession; and

(ii) With respect to the United States, means[

(A) An individual who is a citizen or resident of the United States (as defined under section 7701(b)(1)(A)); or

(B) A business entity organized under the laws of the United States or any State that is classified as a corporation for Federal tax purposes under § 301.7701-2(b) of this chapter.

(5) through (7) [Reserved]. For more information, see § 1.881-5T(f)(5) through (7).

(8) Effective date. This section applies to payments made after January 31, 2006. However, taxpayers may choose to apply this section to all payments made after October 22, 2004 for which the statute of limitations under section 6511 is open.

(g) through (i) [Reserved]. For more information, see § 1.881-5T(g) through (i).

T.D. 9248, 1/30/2006.

Proposed § 1.881-5 Exception for certain possessions corporations. [*For Preamble, see ¶ 152,645*]

• ***Caution:*** This Notice of Proposed Rulemaking was partially finalized by TD 9248, 01/30/2006. Regs. §§ 1.1-1, 1.170A-1, 1.861-3, 1.861-8, 1.871-1, 1.876-1, 1.881-5, 1.884-0, 1.901-1, 1.931-1, 1.932-1, 1.933-1, 1.934-1, 1.935-1, 1.937-2, 1.937-3, 1.957-3, 1.1402(a)-12, 1.6038-2, 1.6046-1, 301.6688-1, 301.7701-3, and 301.7701(b)-1 remain proposed.

[The text of the proposed § 1.881-5 is the same as the text of § 1.881-5T published elsewhere in this issue of the Federal Register]. [*See T.D. 9194, 4/11/2005, 70 Fed. Reg. 68.*]

§ 1.881-5T Exception for certain possessions corporations (temporary).

• ***Caution:*** Under Code Sec. 7805, temporary regulations expire within three years of the date of issuance. This temporary regulation was issued on 4/6/2005.

(a) Scope. Section 881(b) and this section provide special rules for the application of sections 881 and 884 to certain corporations created or organized in possessions of the United States. Paragraph (g) of this section provides special rules for the application of sections 881 and 884 to corporations created or organized in the United States for purposes of determining tax liability incurred to certain possessions that administer income tax laws that are identical (except for the substitution of the name of the possession for the term United States where appropriate) to those in force in the United States. See § 1.884-0T(b) for special rules relating to the application of section 884 with respect to possessions of the United States.

(b) Operative rules. *(1)* Corporations described in paragraphs (c) and (d) of this section are not treated as foreign corporations for purposes of section 881. Accordingly, they are exempt from the tax imposed by section 881(a).

(2) For corporations described in paragraph (e) of this section, the rate of tax imposed by section 881(a) on U.S. source dividends received is 10 percent (rather than the generally applicable 30 percent).

(c) U.S.V.I. and section 931 possessions. A corporation created or organized in, or under the law of, the United States Virgin Islands or a section 931 possession is described in this paragraph (c) for a taxable year when the following conditions are satisfied—

(1) At all times during such taxable year, less than 25 percent in value of the stock of such corporation is beneficially owned (directly or indirectly) by foreign persons;

(2) At least 65 percent of the gross income of such corporation is shown to the satisfaction of the Commissioner upon examination to be effectively connected with the conduct of a trade or business in such a possession or the United States for the 3-year period ending with the close of the taxable year of such corporation (or for such part of such period as the corporation or any predecessor has been in existence); and

(3) No substantial part of the income of such corporation for the taxable year is used (directly or indirectly) to satisfy obligations to persons who are not bona fide residents of such a possession or the United States.

(d) Section 935 possessions. A corporation created or organized in, or under the law of, a section 935 possession is described in this paragraph (d) for a taxable year when the following conditions are satisfied—

(1) At all times during such taxable year, less than 25 percent in value of the stock of such corporation is owned (directly or indirectly) by foreign persons; and

(2) At least 20 percent of the gross income of such corporation is shown to the satisfaction of the Commissioner upon examination to have been derived from sources within such possession for the 3-year period ending with the close of the preceding taxable year of such corporation(or for such part of such period as the corporation has been in existence).

(e) Puerto Rico. A corporation created or organized in, or under the law of, Puerto Rico is described in this paragraph (e) for a taxable year when the conditions of paragraphs (c)(1) through (3) are satisfied(using the language ''Puerto Rico'' instead of ''such a possession'').

(f) Definitions and other rules. For purposes of this section:

(1) Section 931 possession is defined in § 1.931-1T(c)(1).

(2) Section 935 possession is defined in § 1.935-1T(a)(3)(i).

(3) Foreign person means any person other than—

(i) A United States person (as defined in section 7701(a)(30) and the regulations thereunder); or

(ii) A person who would be a United States person if references to the United States in section 7701 included references to a possession of the United States.

(4) [Reserved]. For more information, see § 1.881-5(f)(4).

(5) Source. The rules of § 1.937-2T shall apply for determining whether income is from sources within a possession.

(6) Effectively connected income. The rules of § 1.937-3T (other than paragraph (c) of that section) shall apply for determining whether income is effectively connected with the conduct of a trade or business in a possession.

(7) Indirect ownership. The rules of section 318(a)(2) shall apply except that the language ''5 percent'' shall be used instead of ''50 percent'' in section 318(a)(2)(C).

(g) Mirror code jurisdictions. For purposes of applying mirrored section 881 to determine tax liability incurred to a section 935 possession or the United States Virgin Islands—

(1) The rules of paragraphs (b) through (d) of this section shall not apply; and

(2) A corporation created or organized in, or under the law of, such possession or the United States shall not be considered a foreign corporation.

(h) Example. The principles of this section are illustrated by the following example:

Example (1). X is a corporation organized under the law of the United States Virgin Islands (USVI) with a branch located in State F. At least 65 percent of the gross income of X is effectively connected with the conduct of a trade or business in the USVI and no substantial part of the income of X for the taxable year is used to satisfy obligations to persons who are not bona fide residents of the United States or the USVI. Seventy-four percent of the stock of X is owned by unrelated individuals who are residents of the United States or the USVI. Y, a corporation organized under the law of State D, and Z, a partnership organized under the law of State F, each own 13 percent of the stock of X. A, an unrelated foreign individual, owns 100 percent of the stock of corporation Y. B and C, unrelated foreign individuals, each own a 50 percent interest in partnership Z. Thus, the condition of paragraph (c)(1) of this section is not satisfied, because 26 percent of X is owned indirectly by foreign persons (A, B, and C). Accordingly, X is treated as a foreign corporation for purposes of section 881.

(i) Effective dates. Except as provided in this paragraph (i), this section applies to payments made after April 11, 2005. The rules of paragraphs (b)(2) and (e) apply to dividends paid after October 22, 2004. However, if, on or after October 22, 2004, an increase in the rate of the Commonwealth of Puerto Rico's withholding tax which is generally applicable to dividends paid to United States corporations not engaged in a trade or business in the Commonwealth to a rate greater than 10 percent takes effect, the rules of paragraphs (b)(2) and (e) shall not apply to dividends received on or after the effective date of the increase.

T.D. 9194, 4/6/2005, amend T.D. 9248, 1/30/2006.

§ 1.882-0 Table of contents.

This section lists captions contained in §§ 1.882-1, 1.882-2, 1.882-3, 1.882-4 and 1.882-5.

(iii) Determination of amount of worldwide liabilities.

(iv) [Reserved].

(v) Hedging transactions.

(vi) Treatment of partnership interests and liabilities.

(vii) Computation of actual ratio of insurance companies.

(viii) Interbranch transactions.

(ix) Amounts must be expressed in a single currency.

(3) Adjustments.

(4) [Reserved].

(5) Examples.

(d) Step 3: Determination of amount of interest expense allocable to ECI under the adjusted U.S. booked liabilities method.

(1) General rule.

(2) U.S. booked liabilities.

(i) In general.

(ii) Properly reflected on the books of the U.S. trade or business of a foreign corporation that is not a bank.

(A)

(2) through (3) [Reserved]. For further guidance, see § 1.882-5T(d)(2)(ii)(A)(2) through (3).

(B) Identified liabilities not properly reflected.

(iii) Properly reflected on the books of the U.S. trade or business of a foreign corporation that is a bank.

(A) [Reserved].

(B) Inadvertent error.

(iv) Liabilities of insurance companies.

(v) Liabilities used to increase artificially interest expense on U.S. booked liabilities.

(vi) Hedging transactions.

(vii) Amount of U.S. booked liabilities of a partner.

(viii) Interbranch transactions.

(3) Average total amount of U.S. booked liabilities.

(4) Interest expense where U.S. booked liabilities equal or exceed U.S. liabilities.

(i) In general.

(ii) Scaling ratio.

(iii) Special rules for insurance companies.

(5) U.S.-connected interest rate where U.S. booked liabilities are less than U.S.-connected liabilities.

(i) In general.

(ii) [Reserved].

(6) Examples.

(e) Separate currency pools method.

(1) General rule.

(i) Determine the value of U.S. assets in each currency pool.

(ii) Determine the U.S.-connected liabilities in each currency pool.

(iii) Determine the interest expense attributable to each currency pool.

(2) Prescribed interest rate.

(3) Hedging transactions.

(4) Election not available if excessive hyperinflationary assets.

(5) Examples.

(f) Effective date.

(1) General rule.

(2) Special rules for financial products.

§ 1.882-5T Determination of interest deduction (temporary).

(a) [Reserved].

(1) Overview.

(i) In general.

(ii) Direct allocations.

(A) In general.

(B) Partnership interests.

(2) Coordination with tax treaties.

(3) through (6) [Reserved].

(7) Elections under § 1.882-5.

(i) In general.

(ii) Failure to make the proper election.

(iii) Step 2 special election for banks.

(8) through (b)(2)(ii) [Reserved].

(b)(2)(ii)(A) In general.

(B) through (b)(2)(iii)(B) [Reserved].

(3) Computation of total value of U.S. assets.

(i) General rule.

(ii) Adjustment to basis of financial instruments.

(c) through (c)(2)(iii) [Reserved].(2)(iv) Determination of value of worldwide assets.

(v) through (c)(3) [Reserved].

(4) Elective fixed ratio method of determining U.S. liabilities.

(5) through (d)(2)(iii) [Reserved].

(d)(2)(iii)(A) In general.

(B) through (d)(5)(i) [Reserved].

(ii) Interest rate on excess U.S.-connected liabilities.

(A) General rule.

(B) Annual published rate election.

(6) through (f)(2) [Reserved].

T.D. 8658, 3/5/96, amend T.D. 9281, 8/16/2006.

§ 1.882-1 Taxation of foreign corporations engaged in U.S. business or of foreign corporations treated as having effectively connected income.

Caution: The Treasury has not yet amended Reg § 1.882-1 to reflect changes made by P.L. 100-647, P.L. 99-514.

(a) Segregation of income. This section applies for purposes of determining the tax of a foreign corporation which at any time during the taxable year is engaged in trade or business in the United States. It also applies for purposes of determining the tax of a foreign corporation which at no time during the taxable year is engaged in trade or business in the United States but has for the taxable year real property income or interest on obligations of the United States which, by reason of section 882(d) or (e) and § 1.882-2, is treated as effectively connected for the taxable year with the conduct of a trade or business in the United States by that corporation. A foreign corporation to which this section applies must segregate its gross income for the taxable year into two categories, namely, the income which is effectively connected for the taxable year with the conduct of a trade or business in the United States by that corporation and the income which is not effectively connected for the taxable year with the conduct of a trade or business in the United States by that corporation. A separate tax shall then be determined upon each such category of income, as provided in paragraph (b) of this section. The determination of whether income or gain is or is not effectively connected for the taxable year with the conduct of a trade or business in the United States by the foreign corporation shall be made in accordance with section 864(c) and §§ 1.864-3 through 1.864-7. For purposes of this section income which is effectively connected for the taxable year with the conduct of a trade or business in the United States includes all income which is treated under section 882(d) or (e) and § 1.882-2 as income which is effectively connected for the taxable year with the conduct of a trade or business in the United States by the foreign corporation.

(b) Imposition of tax. *(1) Income not effectively connected with the conduct of a trade or business in the United States.* If a foreign corporation to which this section applies derives during the taxable year from sources within the United States income or gains described in section 881(a) and paragraph (b) or (c) of § 1.881-2 which are not effectively connected for the taxable year with the conduct of a trade or business in the United States by that corporation, such income or gains shall be subject to a flat tax of 30 percent of the aggregate amount of such items. This tax shall be determined in the manner, and subject to the same conditions, set forth in § 1.881-2 as though the income or gains were derived by a foreign corporation not engaged in trade or business in the United States during the taxable year, except that in applying paragraph (c) of such section there shall not be taken into account any gains which are taken into account in determining the tax under section 882(a)(1) and subparagraph (2) of this paragraph.

(2) Income effectively connected with the conduct of a trade or business in the United States. (i) In general. If a foreign corporation to which this section applies derives income or gains which are effectively connected for the taxable year with the conduct of a trade or business in the United States by that corporation, the taxable income or gains shall, except as provided in § 1.871-12, be taxed in accordance with section 11 or, in the alternative, section 1201(a). See sections 11(f) and 882(a)(1). Any income of the foreign corporation which is not effectively connected for the taxable year with the conduct of a trade or business in the United States by that corporation shall not be taken into account in determining either the rate or amount of such tax.

(ii) Determination of taxable income. The taxable income for any taxable year for purposes of this subparagraph consists only of the foreign corporation's taxable income which is effectively connected for the taxable year with the conduct of a trade or business in the United States by that corporation; and, for this purpose, it is immaterial that the trade or business with which that income is effectively connected is not the same as the trade or business carried on in the United States by that corporation during the taxable year. See example (2) in § 1.864-4(b). In determining such taxable income all amounts constituting, or considered to be, gains or losses for the taxable year from the sale or exchange of capital assets shall be taken into account if such gains or losses are effectively connected for the taxable year with the conduct of a trade or business in the United States by that corporation.

(iii) Cross references. For rules for determining the gross income and deductions for the taxable year, see section 882(b) and (c)(1) and the regulations thereunder.

(c) Change in trade or business status. The principles of paragraph (c) of § 1.871-8 shall apply to cases where there has been a change in the trade or business status of a foreign corporation.

(d) Credits against tax. The credits allowed by section 32 (relating to tax withheld at source on foreign corporations), section 33 (relating to the foreign tax credit), section 38 (relating to investment in certain depreciable property), section 39 (relating to certain uses of gasoline and lubricating oil), section 40 (relating to expenses of work incentive programs), and section 6042 (relating to overpayments of a tax) shall be allowed against the tax determined in accordance with this section. However, the credits allowed by sections 33, 38, and 40 shall not be allowed against the flat tax of 30 percent imposed by section 881(a) and paragraph (b)(1) of this section. For special rules applicable in determining the foreign tax credit, see section 906(b) and the regulations thereunder. For the disallowance of certain credits where a return is not filed for the taxable year see section 882(c)(2) and the regulations thereunder.

(e) Payment of estimated tax. Every foreign corporation which for the taxable year is subject to tax under section 11 or 1201(a) and this section in accordance with section 6154 and the regulations thereunder. In determining the amount of the estimated tax the foreign corporation must treat the tax imposed by section 881(a) and paragraph (b)(1) of this section as though it were a tax imposed by section 11.

(f) Effective date. This section applies for taxable years beginning after December 31, 1966. For corresponding rules applicable to taxable years beginning before January 1, 1967, see 26 CFR 1.882-1 (Rev. as of Jan. 1, 1971).

T.D. 6258, 10/23/57, amend T.D. 7244, 12/29/72, T.D. 7293, 11/27/73.

§ 1.882-2 Income of foreign corporation treated as effectively connected with U.S. business.

Caution: The Treasury has not yet amended Reg § 1.882-2 to reflect changes made by P.L. 100-647.

(a) Election as to real property income. A foreign corporation which during the taxable year derives any income from real property which is located in the United States, or derives income from any interest in any such real property, may elect, pursuant to section 882(d) and § 1.871-10, to treat all such income as income which is effectively connected for the taxable year with the conduct of a trade or business in the United States by that corporation. The election may be made whether or not the foreign corporation is engaged in trade or business in the United States during the taxable year for which the election is made or whether or not the corporation has income from real property which for the taxable year is effectively connected with the conduct of a trade or business in the United States, but it may be made only with respect to income from sources within the United States which, without regard to section 882(d) and § 1.871-10, is not effectively connected for the taxable year with the conduct of a trade or business in the United States by that corporation. The income to which the election applies shall be determined as provided in paragraph (b) of § 1.871-10 and shall be subject to tax in the manner, and subject to the same conditions, provided by section 882(a)(1) and paragraph (b)(2) of § 1.882-1. Section 871(d)(2) and (3) and the provisions of § 1.871-10 there under shall apply in respect of an election under section 882(d) in the same manner and to the same extent as they apply in respect of elections under section 871(d).

(b) Interest on U.S. obligations received by banks organized in possessions. Interest received from sources within the United States during the taxable year on obligations of the United States by a foreign corporation created or organized in, or, under the law of, a possession of the United States and carrying on the banking business in a possession of the United States during the taxable year shall be treated, pursuant to section 882(e) and this paragraph, as income which is effectively connected for the taxable year with the conduct of a trade or business in the United States by that corporation. This paragraph applies whether or not the foreign corporation is engaged in trade or business in the United States at any time during the taxable year but only with respect to income which, without regard to this paragraph, is not effectively connected for the taxable year with the conduct of a trade or business in the United States by that corporation. Any interest to which this paragraph applies shall be subject to tax in the manner, and subject to the same conditions, provided by section 882(a)(1) and paragraph (b)(2) of § 1.882-1. To the extent that deductions are connected with interest to which this paragraph applies, they shall be treated for purposes of section 882(c)(1) and the regulations thereunder as connected with income which is effectively connected for the taxable year with the conduct of a trade or business in the United States by the foreign corporation. An election by the taxpayer is not required in respect of the income to which this paragraph applies. For purposes of this paragraph the term "possession of the United States" includes Guam, the Midway Islands, the Panama Canal Zone, the Commonwealth of Puerto Rico, American Samoa, the Virgin Islands, and Wake Island.

(c) Treatment of income. Any income in respect of which an election described in paragraph (a) of this section is in effect, and any interest to which paragraph (b) of this section applies, shall be treated, for purposes of paragraph (b)(2) of § 1.882-1 and paragraph (a) of § 1.1441-4, as income which is effectively connected for the taxable year with the conduct of a trade or business in the United States by the foreign corporation. A foreign corporation shall not be treated as being engaged in trade or business in the United States merely by reason of having such income for the taxable year.

(d) Effective date. This section applies for taxable years beginning after December 31, 1966. There are no corresponding rules in this part for taxable years beginning before January 1, 1967.

T.D. 6258, 10/23/57, amend T.D. 7293, 11/27/73.

§ 1.882-3 Gross income of a foreign corporation.

(a) In general. *(1) Inclusions.* The gross income of a foreign corporation for any taxable year includes only (i) the gross income which is derived from sources within the United States and which is not effectively connected for the taxable year with the conduct of a trade or business in the United States by that corporation, and (ii) the gross income, irrespective of whether such income is derived from sources within or without the United States, which is effectively connected for the taxable year with the conduct of a trade or business in the United States by that corporation. For the determination of the sources of income, see sections 861 through 863, and the regulations thereunder. For the determination of whether income from sources within or without the United States is effectively connected for the taxable year with the conduct of a trade or business in the United States, see sections 864(c) and 882(d) and (e), §§ 1.864-3 through 1.864-7, and § 1.882-2.

(2) Exchange transactions. Even though a foreign corporation which effects certain transactions in the United States in stocks, securities, or commodities during the taxable year may not, by reason of section 864(b)(2) and paragraph (c) or (d) of § 1.364-2, be engaged in trade or business in the United States during the taxable year through the effecting of such transactions, nevertheless it shall be required to include in gross income for the taxable year the gains and profits from those transactions to the extent required by paragraph (c) of § 1.881-2 or by paragraph (a) of § 1.882-1.

(3) Exclusions. For exclusions from gross income of a foreign corporation, see § 1.883-1.

(b) Foreign corporations not engaged in U.S. business. In the case of a foreign corporation which at no time during the taxable year is engaged in trade or business in the United States the gross income shall include only (1) the gross income from sources within the United States which is described in section 881(a) and paragraphs (b) and (c) of § 1.881-2, and (2) the gross income from sources within the United States which, by reason of section 882(d) or (e) and § 1.882-2, is treated as effectively connected for the taxable year with the conduct of a trade or business in the United States by that corporation.

(c) Foreign corporations engaged in U.S. business. In the case of a foreign corporation which is engaged in trade or business in the United States at any time during the taxable year, the gross income shall include (1) the gross income from sources within and without the United States which is effectively connected for the taxable year with the conduct of a trade or business in the United States by that corporation, (2) the gross income from sources within the United States which, by reason of section 882(d) or (e) and § 1.882-2, is treated as effectively connected for the taxable year with the conduct of a trade or business in the United States by that corporation, and (3) the gross income from sources within the United States which is described in section 881(a) and paragraphs (b) and (c) of § 1.881-2 and is not effectively connected for the taxable year with the conduct of a trade or business in the United States by that corporation.

(d) Effective date. This section applies for taxable years beginning after December 31, 1966. For corresponding rules applicable to taxable years beginning before January 1, 1967, see 26 CFR 1.882-2 (Rev. as of Jan. 1, 1971).

T.D. 6258, 10/23/57, amend T.D. 7293, 11/27/73.

§ 1.882-4 Allowance of deductions and credits to foreign corporations.

(a) Foreign corporations. *(1) In general.* A foreign corporation that is engaged in, or receives income treated as effectively connected with, a trade or business within the United States is allowed the deductions which are properly allocated and apportioned to the foreign corporation's gross income which is effectively connected, or treated as effectively connected, with its conduct of a trade or business within the United States. The foreign corporation is entitled to credits which are attributable to that effectively connected income. No provision of this section (other than paragraph (b)(2)) shall be construed to deny the credits provided by sections 33, 34 and 852(b)(3)(D)(ii) or the deduction allowed by section 170.

(2) Return necessary. A foreign corporation shall receive the benefit of the deductions and credits otherwise allowed to it with respect to the income tax, only if it timely files or causes to be filed with the Philadelphia Service Center, in the manner prescribed in subtitle F, a true and accurate return of its taxable income which is effectively connected, or treated as effectively connected, for the taxable year with the conduct of a trade or business in the United States by that corporation. The deductions and credits allowed such a corporation electing under a tax convention to be subject to tax on a net basis may be obtained by filing a return of income in the manner prescribed in the regulations (if any) under the tax convention or under any other guidance issued by the Commissioner.

(3) Filing deadline for return. (i) As provided in paragraph (a)(2) of this section, for purposes of computing the foreign corporation's taxable income for any taxable year, otherwise allowable deductions (other than that allowed by section 170) and credits (other than those allowed by sections 33, 34 and 852(b)(3)(D)(ii)) will be allowed only if a return for that taxable year is filed by the foreign corporation on a timely basis. For taxable years of a foreign corporation ending after July 31, 1990, whether a return for the current taxable year has been filed on a timely basis is dependent upon whether the foreign corporation filed a return for the taxable year immediately preceding the current taxable year. If a return was filed for that immediately preceding taxable year, or if the current taxable year is the first taxable year of the foreign corporation for which a return is required to be filed, the required return for the current taxable year must be filed within 18 months of the due date as set forth in section 6072 and the regulations under that section, for filing the return for the current taxable year. If no return for the taxable year immediately preceding the current taxable year has been field, the required return for the current taxable year (other than the first taxable year of the foreign corporation for which a return is required to be filed) must have been filed no later than the earlier of the date which is 18 months after the due date, as set forth in section 6072, for filing the return for the current taxable year or the date the Internal Revenue Service mails a notice to the foreign corporation advising the corporation that the current year tax return has not been filed and that no deductions (other than that allowed under section 170) or credits (other than those allowed under sections 33, 34 and 852(b)(3)(D)(ii)) may be claimed by the taxpayer.

(ii) The filing deadlines set forth in paragraph (a)(3)(i) of this section may be waived if the foreign corporation establishes to the satisfaction of the Commissioner or his or her delegate that the corporation, based on the facts and circumstances, acted reasonably and in good faith in failing to file a U.S. income tax return (including a protective return (as described in paragraph (a)(3)(vi) of this section)). For this purpose, a foreign corporation shall not be considered to have acted reasonably and in good faith if it knew that it was required to file the return and chose not to do so. In addition, a foreign corporation shall not be granted a waiver unless it cooperates in the process of determining its income tax liability for the taxable year for which the return was not filed. The Commissioner or his or her delegate shall consider the following factors in determining whether the foreign corporation, based on the facts and circumstances, acted reasonably and in good faith in failing to file a U.S. income tax return—

(A) Whether the corporation voluntarily identifies itself to the Internal Revenue Service as having failed to file a U.S. income tax return before the Internal Revenue Service discovers the failure to file;

(B) Whether the corporation did not become aware of its ability to file a protective return (as described in paragraph (a)(3)(vi) of this section) by the deadline for filing a protective return;

(C) Whether the corporation had not previously filed a U.S. income tax return;

(D) Whether the corporation failed to file a U.S. income tax return because, after exercising reasonable diligence (taking into account its relevant experience and level of sophistication), the corporation was unaware of the necessity for filing the return;

(E) Whether the corporation failed to file a U.S. income tax return because of intervening events beyond its control; and

(F) Whether other mitigating or exacerbating factors existed.

(iii) The following examples illustrate the provisions of this section. In all examples, FC is a foreign corporation and uses the calendar year as its taxable year. The examples are as follows:

Example (1). Foreign corporation discloses own failure to file. In Year 1, FC became a limited partner with a passive investment in a U.S. limited partnership that was engaged in a U.S. trade or business. During Year 1 through Year 4, FC incurred losses with respect to its U.S. partnership interest. FC's foreign tax director incorrectly concluded that because it was a limited partner and had only losses from its partnership interest, FC was not required to file a U.S. income tax return. FC's management was aware neither of FC's obligation to file a U.S. income tax return for those years, nor of its ability to file a protective return for those years. FC had never filed a U.S. income tax return before. In Year 5, FC began realizing a profit rather than a loss with respect to its partnership interest and, for this reason, engaged a U.S. tax advisor to handle its responsibility to file U.S. income tax returns. In preparing FC's income tax return for Year 5, FC's U.S. tax advisor discovered that returns were not filed for Year 1 through Year 4. Therefore, with respect to those years for which applicable filing deadlines in paragraph (a)(3)(i) of this section were not met, FC would be barred by paragraph (a)(2) of this section from claiming any deductions that otherwise would have given rise to net operating losses on returns for those years, and that would have been available as loss carryforwards in subsequent years. At FC's direction, its U.S. tax advisor promptly contacted the appropriate examining personnel and cooperated with the Internal Revenue Service in determining FC's income tax liability, for example, by preparing and filing the appropriate income tax returns for Year 1 through Year 4 and by making FC's books and records available to an Internal Revenue Service examiner. FC has met the standard described in paragraph (a)(3)(ii) of this section for waiver of any applicable filing deadlines in paragraph (a)(3)(i) of this section.

Example (2). Foreign corporation refuses to cooperate. Same facts as in Example 1, except that while FC's U.S. tax advisor contacted the appropriate examining personnel and filed the appropriate income tax returns for Year 1 through Year 4, FC refused all requests by the Internal Revenue Service to provide supporting information (for example, books and records) with respect to those returns. Because FC did not cooperate in determining its U.S. tax liability for the taxable years for which an income tax return was not timely filed, FC is not granted a waiver as described in paragraph (a)(3)(ii) of this section of any applicable filing deadlines in paragraph (a)(3)(i) of this section.

Example (3). Foreign corporation fails to file a protective return. Same facts as in Example 1, except that in Year 1 through Year 4, FC's tax director also consulted a U.S. tax advisor, who advised FC's tax director that it was uncertain whether U.S. income tax returns were necessary for those years and that FC could protect its right subsequently to claim the loss carryforwards by filing protective returns under paragraph (a)(3)(vi) of this section. FC did not file U.S. income tax returns or protective returns for those years. FC did not present evidence that intervening events beyond FC's control prevented it from filing an income tax return, and there were no other mitigating factors. FC has not met the standard described in paragraph (a)(3)(ii) of this section for waiver of any applicable filing deadlines in paragraph (a)(3)(i) of this section.

Example (4). Foreign corporation with effectively connected income. In Year 1, FC, a technology company, opened an office in the United States to market and sell a software program that FC had developed outside the United States. FC had minimal business or tax experience internationally, and no such experience in the United States. Through FC's direct efforts, U.S. sales of the software produced income effectively connected with a U.S. trade or business. FC, however, did not file U.S. income tax returns for Year 1 or Year 2. FC's management was aware neither of FC's obligation to file a U.S. income tax return for those years, nor of its ability to file a protective return for those years. FC had never filed a U.S. income tax return before. In January of Year 4, FC engaged U.S. counsel in connection with licensing software to an unrelated U.S. company. U.S. counsel reviewed FC's U.S. activities and advised FC that it should have filed U.S. income tax returns for Year 1 and Year 2. FC immediately engaged a U.S. tax advisor who, at FC's direction, promptly contacted the appropriate examining personnel and cooperated with the Internal Revenue Service in determining FC's income tax liability, for example, by preparing and filing the appropriate income tax returns for Year 1 and Year 2 and by making FC's books and records available to an Internal Revenue Service examiner. FC has met the standard described in paragraph (a)(3)(ii) of this section for waiver of any applicable filing deadlines in paragraph (a)(3)(i) of this section.

Example (5). IRS discovers foreign corporation's failure to file. In Year 1, FC, a technology company, opened an office in the United States to market and sell a software program that FC had developed outside the United States. Through FC's direct efforts, U.S. sales of the software produced income effectively connected with a U.S. trade or business. FC had extensive experience conducting similar business activities in other countries, including making the appropriate tax filings. However, FC's management was aware neither of FC's obligation to file a U.S. income tax return for those years, nor of its ability to file a protective return for those years. FC had never filed a U.S. income tax return before. Despite FC's extensive experience conducting similar business activities in other countries, it made no effort to seek advice in connection with its U.S. tax obligations. FC failed to file either U.S. income tax returns or protective returns for Year 1 and Year 2. In January of Year 4, an Internal Revenue Service examiner asked FC for an explanation of FC's failure to file U.S. income tax returns. FC immediately engaged a U.S. tax advisor, and cooperated with the Internal Revenue Service in determining FC's income tax liability, for example, by preparing and filing the appropriate income tax returns for Year 1 and Year 2 and by making FC's books and records available to the examiner. FC did not present evidence that intervening events beyond its control prevented it from filing a return, and there were no other mitigating factors. FC has not met the standard described in paragraph (a)(3)(ii) of this section for waiver of any applicable filing deadlines in paragraph (a)(3)(i) of this section.

Example (6). Foreign corporation with prior filing history. FC began a U.S. trade or business in Year 1. FC's tax advisor filed the appropriate U.S. income tax returns for Year 1 through Year 6, reporting income effectively connected with FC's U.S. trade or business. In Year 7, FC replaced its tax advisor with a tax advisor unfamiliar with U.S. tax law. FC did not file a U.S. income tax return for any year from Year 7 through Year 10, although it had effectively connected income for those years. FC's management was aware of FC's ability to file a protective return for those years. In Year 11, an Internal Revenue Service examiner contacted FC and asked its chief financial officer for an explanation of FC's failure to file U.S. income tax returns after Year 6. FC immediately engaged a U.S. tax advisor and cooperated with the Internal Revenue Service in determining FC's income tax liability, for example, by preparing and filing the appropriate income tax returns for Year 7 through Year 10 and by making FC's books and records available to the examiner. FC did not present evidence that intervening events beyond its control prevented it from filing a return, and there were no other mitigating factors. FC has not met the standard described in paragraph (a)(3)(ii) of this section for waiver of any applicable filing deadlines in paragraph (a)(3)(i) of this section.

(iv) Paragraphs (a)(3)(ii) and (iii) of this section are applicable to open years for which a request for a waiver is filed on or after January 29, 2002.

(v) A foreign corporation which has a permanent establishment, as defined in an income tax treaty between the United States and the foreign corporation's country of residence, in the United States is subject to the filing deadlines set forth in paragraph (a)(3)(i) of this section.

(vi) If a foreign corporation conducts limited activities in the United States in a taxable year which the foreign corporation determines does not give rise to gross income which is effectively connected with the conduct of a trade or business within the United States as defined in sections 882(b) and 864(b) and (c) and the regulations under those sections, the foreign corporation may nonetheless file a return for that taxable year on a timely basis under paragraph (a)(3)(i) of this section and thereby protect the right to receive the benefit of the deductions and credits attributable to that gross income if it is later determined, after the return was filed, that the original determination was incorrect. On that timely filed return, the foreign corporation is not required to report any gross income as effectively connected with a United States trade or business or any deductions or credits but should attach a statement indicating that the return is being filed for the reason set forth in this paragraph (a)(3). If the foreign corporation determines that part of the activities which it conducts in the United States in a taxable year gives rise to gross income which is effectively connected with the conduct of a trade or business and part does not, the foreign corporation must timely file a return for that taxable year to report the gross income determined to be effectively connected, or treated as effectively connected, with the conduct of the trade or business within the United States and the deductions and credits attributable to the gross income. In addition, the foreign corporation should attach to that return the statement described in this paragraph (b)(3) with regard to the other activities. The foreign corporation may follow the same procedure if it determines initially that it has no United States tax liability under the provisions of an applicable income tax treaty. In the event the foreign corporation relies on the provisions of an income tax treaty to reduce or eliminate the income subject to taxation, or to reduce the rate of tax, disclosure may be required pursuant to section 6114.

(vii) In order to be eligible for any deductions and credits for purposes of computing the accumulated earnings tax of section 531, a foreign corporation must file a true and accurate return; on a timely basis, in the manner as set forth in paragraph (a)(2) and (3) of this section.

(4) Return by Internal Revenue Service. If a foreign corporation has various sources of income within the United States and a return of income has not been filed, in the manner prescribed by subtitle F, including the filing deadlines set forth in paragraph (a)(3) of this section, the Internal Revenue Service shall:

(i) Cause a return of income to be made,

(ii) Include on the return the income described in § 1.882-1 of that corporation from all sources concerning which it has information, and

(iii) Assess the tax and collect it from one or more of those sources of income within the United States, without allowance for any deductions (other than that allowed by section 170) or credits (other than those allowed by sections 33, 34 and 852(b)(3)(D)(ii)).

If the income of the corporation is not effectively connected with, or if the corporation did not receive income that is treated as being effectively connected with, the conduct of a United States trade or business, the tax will be assessed under § 1.882-1(b)(1) on a gross basis, without allowance for any deduction (other than that allowed by section 170) or credit (other than the credits allowed by sections 33, 34 and 852(b)(3)(D)(ii)). If the income is effectively connected, or treated as effectively connected, with the conduct of a United States trade on business, tax will be assessed in accordance with either section 11, 55 or 1201(a) without allowance for any deduction (other than that allowed by section 170) or credit (other than the credits allowed by sections 33, 34 and 852(b)(3)(D)(ii)).

(b) Allowed deductions and credits. *(1) In general.* Except for the deduction allowed under section 170 for charitable contributions and gifts (see section 882(c)(1)(B)), deductions are allowed to a foreign corporation only to the extent they are connected with gross income which is effectively connected, or treated as effectively connected, with the conduct of a trade or business in the United States. Deductible expenses (other than interest expense) are properly allocated and apportioned to effectively connected gross income in accordance with the rules of § 1.861-8. For the method of determining the interest deduction allowed to a foreign corporation, see § 1.882-5. Other than the credits allowed by sections 33, 34 and 852(b)(3)(D)(ii), the foreign corporation is entitled to credits only if they are attributable to effectively connected income. See paragraph (a)(2) of this section for the requirement that a return be filed. Except as provided by section 906, a foreign corporation shall not be allowed the credit against the tax for taxes of foreign countries and possessions of the United States allowed by section 901.

(2) Verification. At the request of the Internal Revenue Service, a foreign corporation claiming deductions from gross income which is effectively connected, or treated as effectively connected, with the conduct of a trade or business in the United States or credits which are attributable to that income must furnish at the place designated pursuant to § 301.7605-1(a) information sufficient to establish that the corporation is entitled to the deductions and credits in the amounts claimed. All information must be furnished in a form suitable to permit verification of claimed deductions and credits. The Internal Revenue Service may require, as appropriate, that an English translation be provided with any information in a foreign language. If a foreign corporation fails to furnish sufficient information, the Internal Revenue Service may in its discretion disallow any claimed deductions and credits in full or in part. For additional filing requirements and for penalties for failure to provide information, see also section 6038A.

T.D. 6258, 10/23/57, amend T.D. 7749, 12/30/80, T.D. 8322, 12/10/90, T.D. 8981, 1/28/2002, T.D. 9043, 3/7/2003.

§ 1.882-5 Determination of interest deduction.

(a) Rules of general application. *(1)* through (a)(2) [Reserved]. For further guidance, see entry in § 1.882-5T(a)(1) through (a)(2).

(3) Limitation on interest expense. In no event may the amount of interest expense computed under this section exceed the amount of interest on indebtedness paid or accrued by the taxpayer within the taxable year (translated into U.S. dollars at the weighted average exchange rate for each currency prescribed by § 1.989(b)-1 for the taxable year).

(4) Translation convention for foreign currency. For each computation required by this section, the taxpayer shall translate values and amounts into the relevant currency at a spot rate or a weighted average exchange rate consistent with the method such taxpayer uses for financial reporting purposes, provided such method is applied consistently from year to year. Interest expense paid or accrued, however, shall be translated under the rules of § 1.988-2. The district director or the Assistant Commissioner (International) may require that any or all computations required by this section be made in U.S. dollars if the functional currency of the taxpayer's home office is a hyperinflationary currency, as defined in § 1.985-1, and the computation in U.S. dollars is necessary to prevent distortions.

(5) Coordination with other sections. Any provision that disallows, defers, or capitalizes interest expense applies after determining the amount of interest expense allocated to ECI under this section. For example, in determining the amount of interest expense that is disallowed as a deduction under section 265 or 163(j), deferred under section 163(e)(3) or 267(a)(3), or capitalized under section 263A with respect to a United States trade or business, a taxpayer takes into account only the amount of interest expense allocable to ECI under this section.

(6) Special rule for foreign governments. The amount of interest expense of a foreign government, as defined in § 1.892-2T(a), that is allocable to ECI is the total amount of interest paid or accrued within the taxable year by the United States trade or business on U.S. booked liabilities (as defined in paragraph (d)(2) of this section). Interest expense of a foreign government, however, is not allocable to ECI to the extent that it is incurred with respect to U.S. booked liabilities that exceed 80 percent of the total value of U.S. assets for the taxable year (determined under paragraph (b) of this section). This paragraph (a)(6) does not apply to con-

trolled commercial entities within the meaning of § 1.892-5T.

(7) through (a)(7)(iii) [Reserved]. For further guidance, see entry in § 1.882-5T(a)(7) through (a)(7)(iii).

(8) Examples. The following examples illustrate the application of paragraph (a) of this section:

Example (1). Direct allocations.

(i) Facts: FC is a foreign corporation that conducts business through a branch, B, in the United States. Among B's U.S. assets is an interest in a partnership, P, that is engaged in airplane leasing solely in the U.S. FC contributes 200x to P in exchange for its partnership interest. P incurs qualified nonrecourse indebtedness within the meaning of § 1.861-10T to purchase an airplane. FC's share of the liability of P, as determined under section 752, is 800x.

(ii) Analysis: Pursuant to paragraph (a)(1)(ii)(B) of this section, FC is permitted to directly allocate its distributive share of the interest incurred with respect to the qualified nonrecourse indebtedness to FC's distributive share of the rental income generated by the airplane. A liability the interest on which is allocated directly to the income from a particular asset under paragraph (a)(1)(ii)(B) of this section is disregarded for purposes of paragraphs (b)(1), (c)(2)(vi), and (d)(2)(vii) or (e)(1)(ii) of this section. Consequently, for purposes of determining the value of FC's assets under paragraphs (b)(1) and (c)(2)(vi) of this section, FC's basis in P is reduced by the 800x liability as determined under section 752, but is not increased by the 800x liability that is directly allocated under paragraph (a)(1)(ii)(B) of this section. Similarly, pursuant to paragraph (a)(1)(ii)(B) of this section, the 800x liability is disregarded for purposes of determining FC's liabilities under paragraphs (c)(2)(vi) and (d)(2)(vii) of this section.

Example (2). Limitation on interest expense.

(i) FC is a foreign corporation that conducts a real estate business in the United States. In its 1997 tax year, FC has no outstanding indebtedness, and therefore incurs no interest expense. FC elects to use the 50% fixed ratio under paragraph (c)(4) of this section.

(ii) Under paragraph (a)(3) of this section, FC is not allowed to deduct any interest expense that exceeds the amount of interest on indebtedness paid or accrued in that taxable year. Since FC incurred no interest expense in taxable year 1997, FC will not be entitled to any interest deduction for that year under § 1.882-5, notwithstanding the fact that FC has elected to use the 50% fixed ratio.

Example (3). Coordination with other sections.

(i) FC is a foreign corporation that is a bank under section 585(a)(2) and a financial institution under section 265(b)(5). FC is a calendar year taxpayer, and operates a U.S. branch, B. Throughout its taxable year 1997, B holds only two assets that are U.S. assets within the meaning of paragraph (b)(1) of this section. FC does not make a fair-market value election under paragraph (b)(2)(ii) of this section, and, therefore, values its U.S. assets according to their bases under paragraph (b)(2)(i) of this section. The first asset is a taxable security with an adjusted basis of $100. The second asset is an obligation the interest on which is exempt from federal taxation under section 103, with an adjusted basis of $50. The tax-exempt obligation is not a qualified tax-exempt obligation as defined by section 265(b)(3)(B).

(ii) FC calculates its interest expense under § 1.882-5 to be $12. Under paragraph (a)(5) of this section, however, a portion of the interest expense that is allocated to FC's effectively connected income under § 1.882-5 is disallowed in accordance with the provisions of section 265(b). Using the methodology prescribed under section 265, the amount of disallowed interest expense is $4, calculated as follows:

$$\$12 \times \frac{\$50 \text{ Tax-exempt U.S. assets}}{\$150 \text{ Total U.S. assets}} = \$4$$

(iii) Therefore, FC deducts a total of $8 ($12 − $4) of interest expense attributable to its effectively connected income in 1997.

Example (4). Treaty exempt asset.

(i) FC is a foreign corporation, resident in Country X, that is actively engaged in the banking business in the United States through a permanent establishment, B. The income tax treaty in effect between Country X and the United States provides that FC is not taxable on foreign source income earned by its U.S. permanent establishment. In its 1997 tax year, B earns $90 of U.S. source income from U.S. assets with an adjusted tax basis of $900, and $12 of foreign source interest income from U.S. assets with an adjusted tax basis of $100. FC's U.S. interest expense deduction, computed in accordance with § 1.882-5, is $500.

(ii) Under paragraph (a)(5) of this section, FC is required to apply any provision that disallows, defers, or capitalizes interest expense after determining the interest expense allocated to ECI under § 1.882-5. Section 265(a)(2) disallows interest expense that is allocable to one or more classes of income that are wholly exempt from taxation under subtitle A of the Internal Revenue Code. Section 1.265-1(b) provides that income wholly exempt from taxes includes both income excluded from tax under any provision of subtitle A and income wholly exempt from taxes under any other law. Section 894 specifies that the provisions of subtitle A are applied with due regard to any relevant treaty obligation of the United States. Because the treaty between the United States and Country X exempts foreign source income earned by B from U.S. tax, FC has assets that produce income wholly exempt from taxes under subtitle A, and must therefore allocate a portion of its § 1.882-5 interest expense to its exempt income. Using the methodology prescribed under section 265, the amount of disallowed interest expense is $50, calculated as follows:

$$\$500 \times \frac{\$100 \text{ Treaty-exempt U.S. assets}}{\$1000 \text{ Total U.S. assets}} = \$50$$

(iii) Therefore, FC deducts a total of $450 ($500 − $50) of interest expense attributable to its effectively connected income in 1997.

(b) Step 1: Determination of total value of U.S. assets for the taxable year. *(1) Classification of an asset as a U.S. asset.* (i) General rule. Except as otherwise provided in this paragraph (b)(1), an asset is a U.S. asset for purposes of this section to the extent that it is a U.S. asset under § 1.884-1(d). For purposes of this section, the term *determination date,* as used in § 1.884-1(d), means each day for which the total value of U.S. assets is computed under paragraph (b)(3) of this section.

(ii) Items excluded from the definition of U.S. asset. For purposes of this section, the term *U.S. asset* excludes an asset to the extent it produces income or gain described in sections 883(a)(3) and (b).

(iii) Items included in the definition of U.S. asset. For purposes of this section, the term *U.S. asset* includes—

(A) U.S. real property held in a wholly-owned domestic subsidiary of a foreign corporation that qualifies as a bank under section 585(a)(2)(B) (without regard to the second sentence thereof), provided that the real property would qualify as used in the foreign corporation's trade or business within the meaning of § 1.864-4(c)(2) or (3) if held directly by the foreign corporation and either was initially acquired through foreclosure or similar proceedings or is U.S. real property occupied by the foreign corporation (the value of which shall be adjusted by the amount of any indebtedness that is reflected in the value of the property);

(B) An asset that produces income treated as ECI under section 921(d) or 926(b) (relating to certain income of a FSC and certain dividends paid by a FSC to a foreign corporation);

(C) An asset that produces income treated as ECI under section 953(c)(3)(C) (relating to certain income of a captive insurance company that a corporation elects to treat as ECI) that is not otherwise ECI; and

(D) An asset that produces income treated as ECI under section 882(e) (relating to certain interest income of possessions banks).

(iv) Interbranch transactions. A transaction of any type between separate offices or branches of the same taxpayer does not create a U.S. asset.

(v) Assets acquired to increase U.S. assets artificially. An asset shall not be treated as a U.S. asset if one of the principal purposes for acquiring or using that asset is to increase artificially the U.S. assets of a foreign corporation on the determination date. Whether an asset is acquired or used for such purpose will depend upon all the facts and circumstances of each case. Factors to be considered in determining whether one of the principal purposes in acquiring or using an asset is to increase artificially the U.S. assets of a foreign corporation include the length of time during which the asset was used in a U.S. trade or business, whether the asset was acquired from a related person, and whether the aggregate value of the U.S. assets of the foreign corporation increased temporarily on or around the determination date. A purpose may be a principal purpose even though it is outweighed by other purposes (taken together or separately).

(2) Determination of the value of a U.S. asset. (i) General rule. The value of a U.S. asset is the adjusted basis of the asset for determining gain or loss from the sale or other disposition of that item, further adjusted as provided in paragraph (b)(2)(iii) of this section.

(ii) Fair-market value election. (A) [Reserved]. For further guidance, see § 1.882-5T(b)(2)(ii)(A).

(B) Adjustment to partnership basis. If a partner makes a fair market value election under paragraph (b)(2)(ii) of this section, the value of the partner's interest in a partnership that is treated as an asset shall be the fair market value of his partnership interest, increased by the fair market value of the partner's share of the liabilities determined under paragraph (c)(2)(vi) of this section. See § 1.884-1(d)(3).

(iii) Reduction of total value of U.S. assets by amount of bad debt reserves under section 585. (A) In general. The total value of loans that qualify as U.S. assets shall be reduced by the amount of any reserve for bad debts additions to which are allowed as deductions under section 585.

(B) Example. The following example illustrates the provisions of paragraph (b)(2)(iii)(A) of this section:

Example. Foreign banks; bad debt reserves. FC is a foreign corporation that qualifies as a bank under section 585(a)(2)(B) (without regard to the second sentence thereof), but is not a large bank as defined in section 585(c)(2). FC conducts business through a branch, B, in the United States. Among B's U.S. assets are a portfolio of loans with an adjusted basis of $500. FC accounts for its bad debts for U.S. federal income tax purposes under the reserve method, and B maintains a deductible reserve for bad debts of $50. Under paragraph (b)(2)(iii) of this section, the total value of FC's portfolio of loans is $450 ($500 – $50).

(3) [Reserved]. For further guidance, see § 1.882-5T(b)(3).

(c) Step 2: Determination of total amount of U.S.-connected liabilities for the taxable year. *(1) General rule.* The amount of U.S.-connected liabilities for the taxable year equals the total value of U.S. assets for the taxable year (as determined under paragraph (b)(3) of this section) multiplied by the actual ratio for the taxable year (as determined under paragraph (c)(2) of this section) or, if the taxpayer has made an election in accordance with paragraph (c)(4) of this section, by the fixed ratio.

(2) Computation of the actual ratio. (i) In general. A taxpayer's actual ratio for the taxable year is the total amount of its worldwide liabilities for the taxable year divided by the total value of its worldwide assets for the taxable year. The total amount of worldwide liabilities and the total value of worldwide assets for the taxable year is the average of the sums of the amounts of the taxpayer's worldwide liabilities and the values of its worldwide assets (determined under paragraphs (c)(2)(iii) and (iv) of this section). In each case, the sums must be computed semi-annually (beginning, middle and end of taxable year) by a large bank (as defined in section 585(c)(2)) and annually (beginning and end of taxable year) by any other taxpayer.

(ii) Classification of items. The classification of an item as a liability or an asset must be consistent from year to year and in accordance with U.S. tax principles.

(iii) Determination of amount of worldwide liabilities. The amount of a liability must be determined consistently from year to year and must be substantially in accordance with U.S. tax principles. To be substantially in accordance with U.S. tax principles, the principles used to determine the amount of a liability must not differ from U.S. tax principles to a degree that will materially affect the value of taxpayer's worldwide liabilities or the taxpayer's actual ratio.

(iv) [Reserved]. For further guidance, see § 1.882-5T(c)(2)(iv).

(v) Hedging transactions. [Reserved]

(vi) Treatment of partnership interests and liabilities. For purposes of computing the actual ratio, the value of a partner's interest in a partnership that will be treated as an asset is the partner's adjusted basis in its partnership interest, reduced by the partner's share of liabilities of the partnership as determined under section 752 and increased by the partner's share of liabilities determined under this paragraph (c)(2)(vi). If the partner has made a fair market value election under paragraph (b)(2)(ii) of this section, the value of its interest in the partnership shall be increased by the fair market value of the partner's share of the liabilities determined under this paragraph (c)(2)(vi). For purposes of this section a partner shares in any liability of a partnership in the same proportion that it shares, for income tax purposes, in the expense attributable to that liability for the taxable year. A partner's adjusted basis in a partnership interest cannot be less than zero.

(vii) Computation of actual ratio of insurance companies. [Reserved]

(viii) Interbranch transactions. A transaction of any type between separate offices or branches of the same taxpayer does not create an asset or a liability.

(ix) Amounts must be expressed in a single currency. The actual ratio must be computed in either U.S. dollars or the functional currency of the home office of the taxpayer, and that currency must be used consistently from year to year. For example, a taxpayer that determines the actual ratio annually using British pounds converted at the spot rate for financial reporting purposes must translate the U.S. dollar values of assets and amounts of liabilities of the U.S. trade or business into pounds using the spot rate on the last day of its taxable year. The district director or the Assistant Commissioner (International) may require that the actual ratio be computed in dollars if the functional currency of the taxpayer's home office is a hyperinflationary currency, as defined in § 1.985-1, that materially distorts the actual ratio.

(3) Adjustments. The district director or the Assistant Commissioner (International) may make appropriate adjustments to prevent a foreign corporation from intentionally and artificially increasing its actual ratio. For example, the district director or the Assistant Commissioner (International) may offset a loan made from or to one person with a loan made to or from another person if any of the parties to the loans are related persons, within the meaning of section 267(b) or 707(b)(1), and one of the principal purposes for entering into the loans was to increase artificially the actual ratio of a foreign corporation. A purpose may be a principal purpose even though it is outweighed by other purposes (taken together or separately).

(4) [Reserved]. For further guidance, see § 1.882-5T(c)(4).

(5) Examples. The following examples illustrate the application of paragraph (c) of this section:

Example (1). Classification of item not in accordance with U.S. tax principles. Bank Z, a resident of country X, has a branch in the United States through which it conducts its banking business. In preparing its financial statements in country X, Z treats an instrument documented as perpetual subordinated debt as a liability. Under U.S. tax principles, however, this instrument is treated as equity. Consequently, the classification of this instrument as a liability for purposes of paragraph (c)(2)(iii) of this section is not in accordance with U.S. tax principles.

Example (2). Valuation of item not substantially in accordance with U.S. tax principles. Bank Z, a resident of country X, has a branch in the United States through which it conducts its banking business. Bank Z is a large bank as defined in section 585(c)(2). The tax rules of country X allow Bank Z to take deductions for additions to certain reserves. Bank Z decreases the value of the assets on its financial statements by the amounts of the reserves. The additions to the reserves under country X tax rules cause the value of Bank Z's assets to differ from the value of those assets determined under U.S. tax principles to a degree that materially affects the value of taxpayer's worldwide assets. Consequently, the valuation of Bank Z's worldwide assets under country X tax principles is not substantially in accordance with U.S. tax principles. Bank Z must increase the value of its worldwide assets under paragraph (c)(2)(iii) of this section by the amount of its country X reserves.

Example (3). Valuation of item substantially in accordance with U.S. tax principles. Bank Z, a resident of country X, has a branch in the United States through which it conducts its banking business. In determining the value of its worldwide assets, Bank Z computes the adjusted basis of certain non-U.S. assets according to the depreciation methodology provided under country X tax laws, which is different than the depreciation methodology provided under U.S. tax law. If the depreciation methodology provided under country X tax laws does not differ from U.S. tax principles to a degree that materially affects the value of Bank Z's worldwide assets or Bank Z's actual ratio as computed under paragraph (c)(2) of this section, then the valuation of Bank Z's worldwide assets under paragraph (c)(2)(iv) of this section is substantially in accordance with U.S. tax principles.

Example (4). [Reserved]

Example (5). Adjustments. FC is a foreign corporation engaged in the active conduct of a banking business through a branch, B, in the United States. P, an unrelated foreign corporation, deposits $100,000 in the home office of FC. Shortly thereafter, in a transaction arranged by the home office of FC, B lends $80,000 bearing interest at an arm's length rate to S, a wholly owned U.S. subsidiary of P. The district director or the Assistant Commissioner (International) determines that one of the principal purposes for making and incurring such loans is to increase FC's actual ratio. For purposes of this section, therefore, P is treated as having directly lent $80,000 to S. Thus, for purposes of paragraph (c) of this section (Step 2), the district director or the Assistant Commissioner (International) may offset FC's liability and asset arising from this transaction, resulting in a net liability of $20,000 that is not a booked liability of B. Because the loan to S from B was initiated and arranged by the home office of FC, with no material participation by B, the loan to S will not be treated as a U.S. asset.

(d) Step 3: Determination of amount of interest expense allocable to ECI under the adjusted U.S. booked liabilities method. *(1) General rule.* The adjustment to the amount of interest expense paid or accrued on U.S. booked liabilities is determined by comparing the amount of U.S.-connected liabilities for the taxable year, as determined under paragraph (c) of this section, with the average total amount of U.S. booked liabilities, as determined under paragraphs (d)(2) and (3) of this section. If the average total amount of U.S. booked liabilities equals or exceeds the amount of U.S.-connected liabilities, the adjustment to the interest expense on U.S. booked liabilities is determined under paragraph (d)(4) of this section. If the amount of U.S.-connected liabilities exceeds the average total amount of U.S. booked liabilities, the adjustment to the amount of interest expense paid or accrued on U.S. booked liabilities is determined under paragraph (d)(5) of this section.

(2) U.S. booked liabilities. (i) In general. A liability is a *U.S. booked liability* if it is properly reflected on the books of the U.S. trade or business, within the meaning of paragraph (d)(2)(ii) or (iii) of this section.

(ii) Properly reflected on the books of the U.S. trade or business of a foreign corporation that is not a bank. (A) In general. A liability, whether interest bearing or non-interest bearing, is properly reflected on the books of the U.S. trade or business of a foreign corporation that is not a bank as described in section 585(a)(2)(B) (without regard to the second sentence thereof) if—

(1) The liability is secured predominantly by a U.S. asset of the foreign corporation;

(2) through (3) [Reserved]. For further guidance, see § 1.882-5T(d)(2)(ii)(A)(2) through (3).

(B) Identified liabilities not properly reflected. A liability is not properly reflected on the books of the U.S. trade or business merely because a foreign corporation identifies the liability pursuant to § 1.884-4(b)(1)(ii) and (b)(3).

(iii) Properly reflected on the books of the U.S. trade or business of a foreign corporation that is a bank. (A) [Reserved]. For further guidance, see § 1.882-5T(d)(2)(iii)(A).

(B) Inadvertent error. If a bank fails to enter a liability in the books of the activity that produces ECI before the close of the day on which the liability was incurred, the liability may be treated as a U.S. booked liability only if, under the facts and circumstances, the taxpayer demonstrates a direct connection or relationship between the liability and the activity that produces ECI and the failure to enter the liability in those books was due to inadvertent error.

(iv) Liabilities of insurance companies. [Reserved]

(v) Liabilities used to increase artificially interest expense on U.S. booked liabilities. U.S. booked liabilities shall not include a liability if one of the principal purposes for incurring or holding the liability is to increase artificially the interest expense on the U.S. booked liabilities of a foreign corporation. Whether a liability is incurred or held for the purpose of artificially increasing interest expense will depend upon all the facts and circumstances of each case. Factors to be considered in determining whether one of the principal purposes for incurring or holding a liability is to increase artificially the interest expense on U.S. booked liabilities of a foreign corporation include whether the interest expense on the liability is excessive when compared to other liabilities of the foreign corporation denominated in the same currency and whether the currency denomination of the liabilities of the U.S. branch substantially matches the currency denomination of the U.S. branch's assets. A purpose may be a principal purpose even though it is outweighed by other purposes (taken together or separately).

(vi) Hedging transactions. [Reserved]

(vii) Amount of U.S. booked liabilities of a partner. A partner's share of liabilities of a partnership is considered a booked liability of the partner provided that it is properly reflected on the books (within the meaning of paragraph (d)(2)(ii) of this section) of the U.S. trade or business of the partnership.

(viii) Interbranch transactions. A transaction of any type between separate offices or branches of the same taxpayer does not result in the creation of a liability.

(3) Average total amount of U.S. booked liabilities. The *average total amount* of U.S. booked liabilities for the taxable year is the average of the sums of the amounts (determined under paragraph (d)(2) of this section) of U.S. booked liabilities. The amount of U.S. booked liabilities shall be computed at the most frequent, regular intervals for which data are reasonably available. In no event shall the amount of U.S. booked liabilities be computed less frequently than monthly by a large bank (as defined in section 585(c)(2)) and semi-annually by any other taxpayer.

(4) Interest expense where U.S. booked liabilities equal or exceed U.S. liabilities. (i) In general. If the average total amount of U.S. booked liabilities (as determined in paragraphs (d)(2) and (3) of this section) exceeds the amount of U.S.-connected liabilities (as determined under paragraph (c) of this section (Step 2)), the interest expense allocable to ECI is the product of the total amount of interest paid or accrued within the taxable year by the U.S. trade or business on U.S. booked liabilities and the scaling ratio set out in paragraph (d)(4)(ii) of this section. For purposes of this section, the reduction resulting from the application of the scaling ratio is applied pro-rata to all interest expense paid or accrued by the foreign corporation. A similar reduction in income, expense, gain, or loss from a hedging transaction (as described in paragraph (d)(2)(vi) of this section) must also be determined by multiplying such income, expense, gain, or loss by the scaling ratio. If the average total amount of U.S. booked liabilities (as determined in paragraph (d)(3) of this section) equals the amount of U.S.-connected liabilities (as determined under Step 2), the interest expense allocable to ECI is the total amount of interest paid or accrued within the taxable year by the U.S. trade or business on U.S. booked liabilities.

(ii) Scaling ratio. For purposes of this section, the scaling ratio is a fraction the numerator of which is the amount of U.S.-connected liabilities and the denominator of which is the average total amount of U.S. booked liabilities.

(iii) Special rules for insurance companies. [Reserved]

(5) U.S.-connected interest rate where U.S. booked liabilities are less than U.S.-connected liabilities. (i) In general. If the amount of U.S.-connected liabilities (as determined under paragraph (c) of this section (Step 2)) exceeds the average total amount of U.S. booked liabilities, the interest expense allocable to ECI is the total amount of interest paid or accrued within the taxable year by the U.S. trade or business on U.S. booked liabilities, plus the excess of the amount of U.S.-connected liabilities over the average total amount of U.S. booked liabilities multiplied by the interest rate determined under paragraph (d)(5)(ii) of this section.

(ii) [Reserved]. For further guidance, see § 1.882-5T(d)(5)(ii).

(6) Examples. The following examples illustrate the rules of this section:

Example (1). Computation of interest expense; actual ratio. (i) Facts.

(A) FC is a foreign corporation that is not a bank and that actively conducts a real estate business through a branch, B, in the United States. For the taxable year, FC's balance sheet and income statement is as follows (assume amounts are in U.S. dollars and computed in accordance with paragraphs (b)(2) and (b)(3) of this section):

	Value
Asset 1	$2,000
Asset 2	$2,500
Asset 3	$5,500

	Amount	Interest Expense
Liability 1	$ 800	56
Liability 2	$3,200	256
Capital	$6,000	0

(B) Asset 1 is the stock of FC's wholly-owned domestic subsidiary that is also actively engaged in the real estate business. Asset 2 is a building in the United States producing rental income that is entirely ECI to FC. Asset 3 is a building in the home country of FC that produces rental income. Liabilities 1 and 2 are loans that bear interest at the rates of 7% and 8%, respectively. Liability 1 is a booked liability of B, and Liability 2 is booked in FC's home country. Assume that FC has not elected to use the fixed ratio in Step 2.

(ii) Step 1. Under paragraph (b)(1) of this section, Assets 1 and 3 are not U.S. assets, while Asset 2 qualifies as a U.S. asset. Thus, under paragraph (b)(3) of this section, the total value of U.S. assets for the taxable year is $2,500, the value of Asset 2.

(iii) Step 2. Under paragraph (c)(1) of this section, the amount of FC's U.S.-connected liabilities for the taxable year is determined by multiplying $2,500 (the value of U.S. assets determined under Step 1) by the actual ratio for the taxable year. The actual ratio is the average amount of FC's worldwide liabilities divided by the average value of FC's worldwide assets. The amount of Liability 1 is $800, and the amount of Liability 2 is $3,200. Thus, the numerator of the actual ratio is $4,000. The average value of worldwide assets is $10,000 (Asset 1 + Asset 2 + Asset 3). The actual ratio, therefore, is 40% ($4,000/$10,000), and the amount of U.S.-connected liabilities for the taxable year is $1,000 ($2,500 U.S. assets × 40%).

(iv) Step 3. Because the amount of FC's U.S.-connected liabilities ($1,000) exceeds the average total amount of U.S. booked liabilities of B ($800), FC determines its interest expense in accordance with paragraph (d)(5) of this section by adding the interest paid or accrued on U.S. booked liabilities, and the interest expense associated with the excess of its U.S.-connected liabilities over its average total amount of U.S. booked liabilities. Under paragraph (d)(5)(ii) of this section, FC determines the interest rate attributable to its excess U.S.-connected liabilities by dividing the interest expense paid or accrued by the average amount of U.S.-dollar denominated liabilities, which produces an interest rate of 8% ($256/$3200). Therefore, FC's allocable interest expense is $72 ($56 of interest expense from U.S. booked liabilities plus $16 ($200 × 8%) of interest expense attributable to its excess U.S.-connected liabilities).

Example (2). Computation of interest expense; fixed ratio.

(i) The facts are the same as in Example 1, except that FC makes a fixed ratio election under paragraph (c)(4) of this section. The conclusions under Step 1 are the same as in Example 1.

(ii) Step 2. Under paragraph (c)(1) of this section, the amount of U.S.-connected liabilities for the taxable year is determined by multiplying $2,500 (the value of U.S. assets determined under Step 1) by the fixed ratio for the taxable year, which, under paragraph (c)(4) of this section is 50 percent. Thus, the amount of U.S.-connected liabilities for the taxable year is $1,250 ($2,500 U.S. assets × 50%).

(iii) Step 3. As in Example 1, the amount of FC's U.S.-connected liabilities exceed the average total amount of U.S. booked liabilities of B, requiring FC to determine its interest expense under paragraph (d)(5) of this section. In this case, however, FC has excess U.S.-connected liabilities of $450 ($1,250 of U.S.-connected liabilities − $800 U.S. booked liabilities). FC therefore has allocable interest expense of $92 ($56 of interest expense from U.S. booked liabilities plus $36 ($450 × 8%) of interest expense attributable to its excess U.S.-connected liabilities).

Example (3). Scaling ratio.

(i) Facts. Bank Z, a resident of country X, has a branch in the United States through which it conducts its banking business. For the taxable year, Z has U.S.-connected liabilities, determined under paragraph (c) of this section, equal to $300. Z, however, has U.S. booked liabilities of $300 and U500. Therefore, assuming an exchange rate of the U to the U.S. dollar of 5:1, Z has U.S. booked liabilities of $400 ($300 + (U500 ÷ 5)).

(ii) U.S.-connected liabilities. Because Z's U.S. booked liabilities of $400 exceed its U.S.-connected liabilities by $100, all of Z's interest expense allocable to its U.S. trade or business must be scaled back pro-rata. To determine the scaling ratio, Z divides its U.S.-connected liabilities by its U.S. booked liabilities, as required by paragraph (d)(4) of this section. Z's interest expense is scaled back pro rata by the resulting ratio of ¾ ($300 ÷ $400). Z's income, expense, gain or loss from hedging transactions described in paragraph (d)(2)(vi) of this section must be similarly reduced.

Example (4). [Reserved]

Example (5). [Reserved]. For further guidance, see § 1.882-5T(d)(6) Example 5.

(e) Separate currency pools method. *(1) General rule.* If a foreign corporation elects to use the method in this paragraph, its total interest expense allocable to ECI is the sum of the separate interest deductions for each of the currencies in which the foreign corporation has U.S. assets. The separate interest deductions are determined under the following three-step process.

(i) Determine the value of U.S. assets in each currency pool. First, the foreign corporation must determine the amount of its U.S. assets, using the methodology in paragraph (b) of this section, in each currency pool. The foreign corporation may convert into U.S. dollars any currency pool in which the foreign corporation holds less than 3% of its U.S. assets. A transaction (or transactions) that hedges a U.S. asset shall be taken into account for purposes of determining the currency denomination and the value of the U.S. asset.

(ii) Determine the U.S.-connected liabilities in each currency pool. Second, the foreign corporation must determine the amount of its U.S.-connected liabilities in each currency pool by multiplying the amount of U.S. assets (as determined under paragraph (b)(3) of this section) in the currency pool by the foreign corporation's actual ratio (as determined under paragraph (c)(2) of this section) for the taxable year or, if the taxpayer has made an election in accordance with paragraph (c)(4) of this section, by the fixed ratio.

(iii) Determine the interest expense attributable to each currency pool. Third, the foreign corporation must determine the interest expense attributable to each currency pool by multiplying the U.S.-connected liabilities in each currency pool by the prescribed interest rate as defined in paragraph (e)(2) of this section.

(2) Prescribed interest rate. For each currency pool, the prescribed interest rate is determined by dividing the total interest expense that is paid or accrued for the taxable year with respect to the foreign corporation's worldwide liabilities denominated in that currency, by the foreign corporation's average worldwide liabilities (whether interest bearing or not) denominated in that currency. The interest expense and liabilities are to be stated in that currency.

(3) Hedging transactions. [Reserved]

(4) Election not available if excessive hyperinflationary assets. The election to use the separate currency pools method of this paragraph (e) is not available if the value of the foreign corporation's U.S. assets denominated in a hyperinflationary currency, as defined in § 1.985-1, exceeds ten percent of the value of the foreign corporation's total U.S. assets. If a foreign corporation made a valid election to use the separate currency pools method in a prior year but no longer qualifies to use such method pursuant to this paragraph (e)(4), the taxpayer must use the method provided by paragraphs (b) through (d) of this section.

(5) Examples. The separate currency pools method of this paragraph (e) is illustrated by the following examples:

Example (1). Separate currency pools method. (i) Facts.

(A) Bank Z, a resident of country X, has a branch in the United States through which it conducts its banking business. For its 1997 taxable year, Z has U.S. assets, as defined in paragraph (b) of this section, that are denominated in U.S.

dollars and in U, the country X currency. Accordingly, Z's U.S. assets are as follows:

	Average Value
U.S. Dollar Assets	$ 20,000
U Assets	U 5,000

(B) Z's worldwide liabilities are also denominated in U.S. Dollars and in U. The average interest rates on Z's worldwide liabilities, including those in the United States, are 6% on its U.S. dollar liabilities, and 12% on its liabilities denominated in U. Assume that Z has properly elected to use its actual ratio of 95% to determine its U.S.-connected liabilities in Step 2, and has also properly elected to use the separate currency pools method provided in paragraph (e) of this section.

(ii) Determination of interest expense. Z determines the interest expense attributable to its U.S.-connected liabilities according to the steps described below.

(A) First, Z separates its U.S. assets into two currency pools, one denominated in U.S. dollars ($20,000) and the other denominated in U (U5,000).

(B) Second, Z multiplies each pool of assets by the applicable ratio of worldwide liabilities to assets, which in this case is 95%. Thus, Z has U.S.-connected liabilities of $19,000 ($20,000 × 95%), and U4750 (U5000 × 95%).

(C) Third, Z calculates its interest expense by multiplying each pool of its U.S.-connected liabilities by the relevant interest rates. Accordingly, Z's allocable interest expense for the year is $1140 ($19,000 × 6%), the sum of the expense associated with its U.S. dollar liabilities, plus U570 (U4750 × 12%), the interest expense associated with its liabilities denominated in U. Z must translate its interest expense denominated in U in accordance with the rules provided in section 988, and then must determine whether it is subject to any other provision of the Code that would disallow or defer any portion of its interest expense so determined.

Example (2). [Reserved]

(f) Effective date. *(1) General rule.* This section is effective for taxable years beginning on or after June 6, 1996.

(2) Special rules for financial products. [Reserved]

T.D. 7749, 12/30/80, amend T.D. 7939, 2/2/84, T.D. 8658, 3/5/96, T.D. 9281, 8/16/2006.

PAR. 2. Section 1.882-5 is amended to read as follows:

1. Paragraphs (a)(1) through (a)(2), (a)(7), (a)(7)(i) through (a)(7)(ii), (b)(2)(ii)(A), (b)(3), (c)(2)(iv), (c)(4), (d)(2)(ii)(A)(2), (d)(2)(ii)(A)(3), (d)(2)(iii)(A), and (d)(5)(ii) are revised.

2. Paragraph (d)(6) Example 5 is added.

The revisions and addition read as follows:

Proposed § 1.882-5 Determination of interest deduction. *[For Preamble, see ¶ 152,789]*

(a) * * *

(1) through (a)(2) [The text of this proposed amendment is the same as the text of § 1.882-5T(a)(1) through (a)(2) published elsewhere in this issue of the Federal Register]. [See T.D. 9281, 08/17/2006, 71 Fed. Reg. 159.]

* * * * *

(7) [The text of this proposed amendment is the same as the text of § 1.882-5T(a)(7) published elsewhere in this issue of the Federal Register]. [See T.D. 9281, 08/17/2006, 71 Fed. Reg. 159.]

* * * * *

(b) *(2)* (ii) (A) [The text of this proposed amendment is the same as the text of § 1.882-5T(b)(2)(ii)(A) published elsewhere in this issue of the Federal Register]. [See T.D. 9281, 08/17/2006, 71 Fed. Reg. 159.]

* * * * *

(iv) [The text of this proposed amendment is the same as the text of § 1.882-5T(b)(2)(iv) published elsewhere in this issue of the Federal Register]. [See T.D. 9281, 08/17/2006, 71 Fed. Reg. 159.]

* * * * *

(3) [The text of this proposed amendment is the same as the text of § 1.882-5T(b)(3) published elsewhere in this issue of the Federal Register]. [See T.D. 9281, 08/17/2006, 71 Fed. Reg. 159.]

* * * * *

(c) *(2)* (iv) [The text of this proposed amendment is the same as the text of § 1.882-5T(c)(2)(iv) published elsewhere in this issue of the Federal Register]. [See T.D. 9281, 08/17/2006, 71 Fed. Reg. 159.]

* * * * *

(4) [The text of this proposed amendment is the same as the text of § 1.882-5T(c)(4) published elsewhere in this issue of the Federal Register]. [See T.D. 9281, 08/17/2006, 71 Fed. Reg. 159.]

* * * * *

(d) *(2)* (ii) (A) (2) through (3) [The text of these proposed amendments are the same as the text of § 1.882-5T(d)(2)(ii)(A)(2) through (3) published elsewhere in this issue of the Federal Register]. [See T.D. 9281, 08/17/2006, 71 Fed. Reg. 159.]

* * * * *

(iii) (A) [The text of this proposed amendment is the same as the text of § 1.882-5T(d)(2)(iii)(A) published elsewhere in this issue of the Federal Register]. [See T.D. 9281, 08/17/2006, 71 Fed. Reg. 159.]

* * * * *

(5) (ii) [The text of this proposed amendment is the same as the text of § 1.882-5T(d)(5)(ii) published elsewhere in this issue of the Federal Register]. [See T.D. 9281, 08/17/2006, 71 Fed. Reg. 159.]

* * * * *

(6)

Example (5). [The text of this proposed amendment is the same as the text of § 1.882-5T(d)(6) Example 5 published elsewhere in this issue of the Federal Register]. [See T.D. 9281, 08/17/2006, 71 Fed. Reg. 159.]

* * * * *

PAR. 2. Section 1.882-5 is amended as follows:

1. The text of paragraph (b)(2)(iv) is added.

2. The text of paragraph (c)(2)(v) is added.

3. In paragraph (c)(5), Example 4, Example 6, and Example 7 are added.

4. The text of paragraph (d)(2)(vi) is added.

5. In paragraph (d)(6), Example 4 is added.

6. The text of paragraph (e)(3) is added.

7. In paragraph (e)(5), Example 2 is added.

8. The text of paragraph (f)(2) is added.

The added provisions read as follows:

Proposed § 1.882-5 Determination of interest deduction.
[*For Preamble, see ¶ 151,713*]

* * * * *

(b) * * *

(2) * * *

(iv) Adjustment to basis of financial instruments. The basis of a security or contract that is marked to market pursuant to section 475 or section 1256 will be determined as if each determination date were the last business day of the taxpayer's taxable year. A financial instrument with a fair market value of less than zero is a liability, not an asset, for purposes of this section.

* * * * *

(c) * * *

(2) * * *

(v) Hedging transactions. A transaction (or transactions) that hedges an asset or liability, or a pool of assets or a pool of liabilities, will be taken into account in determining the value, amount and currency denomination of the asset or liability that it hedges. A transaction will be considered to hedge an asset or liability only if the transaction meets the requirements of § 1.1221-2.

* * * * *

(5) * * *

Example (4). Partnership liabilities. X and Y are each foreign corporations engaged in the active conduct of a trade or business within the United States through a partnership, P. Under the partnership agreement, X and Y each have a 50% interest in the capital and profits of P, and X is also entitled to a return of 6% per annum on its capital account that is a guaranteed payment under section 707(c). In addition, P has incurred a liability of $100x to an unrelated bank, B. Under paragraph (c)(2)(vi) of this section, X and Y each share equally in P's liability to B. In accordance with U.S. tax principles, P's obligation to make guaranteed payments to X does not constitute a liability of P, and therefore neither X nor Y take into account that obligation of the partnership in computing their actual ratio.

* * * * *

Example (6). Securities in ratio as assets. FC is a foreign corporation engaged in a trade or business in the United States through a U.S. branch. FC is a dealer in securities within the meaning of section 475(c)(1)(B) because it regularly offers to enter into positions in currency spot and forward contracts with customers in the ordinary course of its trade or business. FC has not elected to use the fixed ratio. On December 31, 1996, the end of FC's taxable year, the mark-to-market value of the spot and forward contracts entered into by FC worldwide is 1000x, which includes a mark-to-market gain of 500x with respect to the spot and forward contracts that are shown on the books of its U.S. branch and that produce effectively connected income. On its December 31, 1996, determination date, FC includes 500x in its U.S. assets, and 1000x in its worldwide assets.

Example (7). Securities in ratio as assets and liabilities. The facts are the same as in Example 4, except that on December 31, 1996, the mark-to-market value of the spot and forward contracts entered into by FC worldwide is 1000x, and FC has a mark-to-market loss of 500x with respect to the spot and forward contracts that are shown on the books of its U.S. branch and that would produce effectively connected income. On its December 31, 1996, determination date, FC includes the 1000x in its worldwide assets for purposes of determining its ratio of worldwide liabilities to worldwide assets. For purposes of Step 3, however, FC has U.S-booked liabilities in the United States equal to the 500x U.S. loss position.

(d) * * *

(2) * * *

(vi) Hedging transactions. A transaction (or transactions) that hedges a U.S. booked liability, or a pool of U.S. booked liabilities, will be taken into account in determining the currency denomination, amount of, and interest rate associated with, that liability. A transaction will be considered to hedge a U.S. booked liability only if the transaction meets the requirements of § 1.1221-2(a), (b), and (c), and is identified in accordance with the requirements of § 1.1221-2(e).

* * * * *

(6) * * *

Example (4). Liability hedge. (i) Facts. FC is a foreign corporation that meets the definition of a bank, as defined in section 585(a)(2)(B) (without regard to the second sentence thereof), and that is engaged in a banking business in the United States through its branch, B. FC's corporate policy is to match the currency denomination of its assets and liabilities, thereby minimizing potential gains and losses from currency fluctuations. Thus, at the close of each business day, FC enters into one or more hedging transactions as needed to maintain a balanced currency position, and instructs each branch to do the same. At the close of business on December 31, 1998, B has 100x of U.S. dollar assets, and U.S. booked liabilities of 90x U.S. dollars and 1000x Japanese yen (exchange rate: $1 = ¥100). To eliminate the currency mismatch in this situation, B enters into a forward contract with an unrelated third party that requires FC to pay 10x dollars in return for 1000x yen. Through this hedging transaction, FC has effectively converted its 1000x Japanese yen liability into a U.S. dollar liability. FC uses its actual ratio of 90% in 1998 for Step 2, the adjusted U.S. booked liabilities method for purposes of Step 3, and is a calendar year taxpayer.

(ii) Analysis. Under paragraph 1.882-5(d)(2)(vi), FC is required to take into account hedges of U.S. booked liabilities in determining the currency denomination, amount, and interest rate associated with those liabilities. Accordingly, FC must treat the Japanese yen liabilities booked in the United States on December 31, 1998, as U.S. dollar liabilities to determine both the amount of the liabilities and the interest paid or accrued on U.S. booked liabilities for purposes of this section. Moreover, in applying the scaling ratio prescribed in paragraph (d)(4)(i) of this section, FC must scale back both the U.S. booked liabilities and the hedge(s) of those liabilities. Assuming that FC's average U.S. booked liabilities for the year ending December 31, 1998, exceed its U.S.-connected liabilities determined under paragraphs (a)(1) through (c)(5) of this section by 10%, FC must scale back by 10% both its interest expense associated with U.S. booked liabilities, and any income or loss from the forward contract to purchase Japanese yen that hedges its U.S. booked liabilities.

(e) * * *

(3) Hedging transactions. A transaction (or transactions) that hedges a liability, or a pool of liabilities, will be taken into account in determining the amount of, or interest rate associated with, that liability. A transaction will be considered to hedge a liability only if the transaction meets the requirements of § 1.1221-2(a), (b), and (c).

* * * * *

(5) * * *

Example (2). Asset hedge. (i) Facts. FC is a foreign corporation that meets the definition of a bank, as defined in section 585(a)(2)(B) (without regard to the second sentence thereof), and that is engaged in the banking business in the United States through its branch, B. FC's corporate policy is to match the currency denomination of its assets and liabilities, thereby minimizing potential gains and losses from currency fluctuations. Thus, at the close of each business day, FC enters into one or more hedging transactions as needed to maintain a balanced currency position, and instructs each branch to do the same. At the close of business on December 31, 1998, B has two U.S. assets, a loan of 90x U.S. dollars and a loan of 1000x Japanese yen (exchange rate: $1 = ¥100). B has U.S. booked liabilities, however, of 100x U.S. dollars. To eliminate the currency mismatch, B enters into a forward contract with an unrelated third party that requires FC to pay 1000x yen in return for 10x dollars. Through this hedging transaction, FC has effectively converted its 1000x Japanese yen asset into a U.S. dollar asset. FC uses its actual ratio of 90% in 1998 for Step 2, has elected the separate currency pools method in paragraph (e) of this section, and is a calendar year taxpayer.

(ii) Analysis. Under paragraph (e)(1)(i) of this section, FC must take into account any transaction that hedges a U.S. asset in determining the currency denomination and value of that asset. FC's Japanese yen asset will therefore be treated as a U.S. dollar asset in determining its U.S. assets in each currency. Accordingly, FC will be treated as having only U.S. dollar assets in making its separate currency pools computation.

(f) * * *

(2) Special rules for financial products. Paragraphs (b)(2)(iv), (c)(2)(v), (d)(2)(vi), and (e)(3) of this section will be effective for taxable years beginning on or after the date these regulations are published as final regulations in the Federal Register.

§ 1.882-5T Determination of interest deduction (temporary).

(a) [Reserved]. For further guidance, see § 1.882-5(a).

(1) Overview. (i) In general. The amount of interest expense of a foreign corporation that is allocable under section 882(c) to income which is (or is treated as) effectively connected with the conduct of a trade or business within the United States (ECI) is the sum of the interest allocable by the foreign corporation under the three-step process set forth in paragraphs (b), (c), and (d) of this section and the specially allocated interest expense determined under paragraph (a)(1)(ii) of this section. The provisions of this section provide the exclusive rules for allocating interest expense to the ECI of a foreign corporation under section 882(c). Under the three-step process, the total value of the U.S. assets of a foreign corporation is first determined under paragraph (b) of this section (Step 1). Next, the amount of U.S.-connected liabilities is determined under paragraph (c) of this section (Step 2). Finally, the amount of interest paid or accrued on U.S.-booked liabilities, as determined under paragraph (d)(2) of this section, is adjusted for interest expense attributable to the difference between U.S.-connected liabilities and U.S.-booked liabilities (Step 3). Alternatively, a foreign corporation may elect to determine its interest rate on U.S.-connected liabilities by reference to its U.S. assets, using the separate currency pools method described in paragraph (e) of this section.

(ii) Direct allocations. (A) In general. A foreign corporation that has a U.S. asset and indebtedness that meet the requirements of § 1.861-10T(b) or (c), as limited by § 1.861-10T(d)(1), shall directly allocate interest expense from such indebtedness to income from such asset in the manner and to the extent provided in § 1.861-10T. For purposes of paragraph (b)(1) or (c)(2) of this section, a foreign corporation that allocates its interest expense under the direct allocation rule of this paragraph (a)(1)(ii)(A) shall reduce the basis of the asset that meets the requirements of § 1.861-10T (b) or (c) by the principal amount of the indebtedness that meets the requirements of § 1.861-10T(b) or (c). The foreign corporation shall also disregard any indebtedness that meets the requirements of § 1.861-10T(b) or (c) in determining the amount of the foreign corporation's liabilities under paragraphs (c)(2) and (d)(2) of this section and shall not take into account any interest expense paid or accrued with respect to such a liability for purposes of paragraph (d) or (e) of this section.

(B) Partnership interest. A foreign corporation that is a partner in a partnership that has a U.S. asset and indebtedness that meet the requirements of § 1.861-10T(b) or (c), as limited by § 1.861-10T(d)(1), shall directly allocate its distributive share of interest expense from that indebtedness to its distributive share of income from that asset in the manner and to the extent provided in § 1.861-10T. A foreign corporation that allocates its distributive share of interest expense under the direct allocation rule of this paragraph (a)(1)(ii)(B) shall disregard any partnership indebtedness that meets the requirements of § 1.861-10T(b) or (c) in determining the amount of its distributive share of partnership liabilities for purposes of paragraphs (b)(1), (c)(2)(vi), and (d)(2)(vii) or (e)(1)(ii) of this section, and shall not take into account any partnership interest expense paid or accrued with respect to such a liability for purposes of paragraph (d) or (e) of this section. For purposes of paragraph (b)(1) of this section, a foreign corporation that directly allocates its distributive share of interest expense under this paragraph (a)(1)(ii)(B) shall—

(1) Reduce the partnership's basis in such asset by the amount of such indebtedness in allocating its basis in the partnership under § 1.884-1(d)(3)(ii); or

(2) Reduce the partnership's income from such asset by the partnership's interest expense from such indebtedness under § 1.884-1(d)(3)(iii).

(2) Coordination with tax treaties. Except as expressly provided by or pursuant to a U.S. income tax treaty or accompanying documents (such as an exchange of notes), the provisions of this section provide the exclusive rules for determining the interest expense attributable to the business profits of a permanent establishment under a U.S. income tax treaty.

(3) through (a)(6) [Reserved]. For further guidance, see § 1.882-5(a)(3) through (a)(6).

(7) Elections under § 1.882-5. (i) In general. A corporation must make each election provided in this section on the corporation's original timely filed Federal income tax return for the first taxable year it is subject to the rules of this section. An amended return does not qualify for this purpose,

nor shall the provisions of § 301.9100-1 of this chapter and any guidance promulgated thereunder apply. Except as provided elsewhere in this section, each election under this section, whether an election for the first taxable year or a subsequent change of election, shall be made by the corporation calculating its interest expense deduction in accordance with the methods elected. An elected method (other than the fair market value method under § 1.882-5(b)(2)(ii), or the annual 30-day London Interbank Offered Rate (LIBOR) election in paragraph (d)(5)(ii) of this section) must be used for a minimum period of five years before the taxpayer may elect a different method. To change an election before the end of the requisite five-year period, a taxpayer must obtain the consent of the Commissioner or his delegate. The Commissioner or his delegate will generally consent to a taxpayer's request to change its election only in rare and unusual circumstances. After the five-year minimum period, an elected method may be changed for any subsequent year on the foreign corporation's original timely filed tax return for the first year to which the changed election applies.

(ii) Failure to make the proper election. If a taxpayer, for any reason, fails to make an election provided in this section in a timely fashion, the Director of Field Operations may make any or all of the elections provided in this section on behalf of the taxpayer, and such elections shall be binding as if made by the taxpayer.

(iii) Step 2 special election for banks. For the first tax year for which an original income tax return is due (including extensions) after August 17, 2006 and not later than December 31, 2006, in which a taxpayer that is a bank as described in § 1.882-5(c)(4) is subject to the requirements of this section, a taxpayer may make a new election to use the fixed ratio on either an original timely filed return, or on an amended return filed within 180 days after the original due date (including extensions). A new fixed ratio election may be made in any subsequent year subject to the timely filing and five-year minimum period requirements of paragraph (a)(7)(i) of this section. A new fixed ratio election under this paragraph (a)(7)(iii) is subject to the adjusted basis or fair market value conforming election requirements of paragraph (b)(2)(ii)(A)(2) of this section and may not be made if a taxpayer elects or maintains a fair market value election for purposes of § 1.882-5(b). Taxpayers that already use the fixed ratio method under an existing election may continue to use the new fixed ratio at the higher percentage without having to make a new five-year election in the first year that the higher percentage is effective.

(8) through (b)(2)(ii) [Reserved]. For further guidance, see § 1.882-5(a)(8) through (b)(2)(ii) .

(b) *(2)* (ii) (A) In general. (1) Fair market value conformity requirement. A taxpayer may elect to value all of its U.S. assets on the basis of fair market value, subject to the requirements of § 1.861-9T(g)(1)(iii), and provided the taxpayer is eligible and uses the actual ratio method under § 1.882-5(c)(2) and the methodology prescribed in § 1.861-9T(h). Once elected, the fair market value must be used by the taxpayer for both Step 1 and Step 2 described in Sec. § 1.882-5(b) and (c), and must be used in all subsequent taxable years unless the Commissioner or his delegate consents to a change.

(2) Conforming election requirement. Taxpayers that as of the effective date of this paragraph (b)(2)(ii)(A)(2) have elected and currently use both the fair market value method for purposes of § 1.882-5(b) and a fixed ratio for purposes of paragraph (c)(4) of this section must conform either the adjusted basis or fair market value methods in Step 1 and Step 2 of the allocation formula by making an adjusted basis election for § 1.882-5(b) purposes while continuing the fixed ratio for Step 2, or by making an actual ratio election under § 1.882-5(c)(2) while remaining on the fair market value method under § 1.882-5(b). Taxpayers who elect to conform Step 1 and Step 2 of the formula to the adjusted basis method must remain on both methods for the minimum five-year period in accordance with the provisions of paragraph (a)(7) of this section. Taxpayers that elect to conform Step 1 and Step 2 of the formula to the fair market value method must remain on the actual ratio method until the consent of the Commissioner or his delegate is obtained to switch to the adjusted basis method. If consent to use the adjusted basis method in Step 1 is granted in a later year, the taxpayer must remain on the actual ratio method for the minimum five-year period unless consent to use the fixed ratio is independently obtained under the requirements of paragraph (a)(7) of this section. For the first tax year for which an original income tax return is due (including extensions) after August 17, 2006 and not later than December 31, 2006, taxpayers that are required to make a conforming election under this paragraph (b)(2)(ii)(A)(2), may do so either on a timely filed original return or on an amended return within 180 days after the original due date (including extensions). If a conforming election is not made within the timeframe provided in this paragraph, the Director of Field Operations or his delegate may make the conforming elections in accordance with the provisions of paragraph (a)(7)(ii) of this section.

(B) through (b)(2)(iii)(B) [Reserved]. For further guidance, see § 1.882-5(b)(2)(ii)(B) through (b)(2)(iii)(B).

(3) Computation of total value of U.S. assets. (i) General rule. The total value of U.S. assets for the taxable year is the average of the sums of the values (determined under paragraph (b)(2) of this section) of U.S. assets. For each U.S. asset, value shall be computed at the most frequent regular intervals for which data are reasonably available. In no event shall the value of any U.S. asset be computed less frequently than monthly (beginning of taxable year and monthly thereafter) by a large bank (as defined in section 585(c)(2)) or a dealer in securities (within the meaning of section 475) and semi-annually (beginning, middle and end of taxable year) by any other taxpayer.

(ii) Adjustment to basis of financial instruments. For purposes of determining the total average value of U.S. assets in this paragraph (b)(3), the value of a security or contract that is marked to market pursuant to section 475 or section 1256 will be determined as if each determination date is the most frequent regular interval for which data are reasonably available that reflects the taxpayer's consistent business practices for reflecting mark-to-market valuations on its books and records.

(c) through (c)(2)(iii) [Reserved]. For further guidance, see § 1.882-5(c) through (c)(2)(iii).

(2) (iv) The rules of § 1.882-5(b)(3) apply in determining the total value of applicable worldwide assets for the taxable year, except that the minimum number of determination dates are those stated in § 1.882-5(c)(2)(i).

(v) through (c)(3) [Reserved]. For further guidance, see § 1.882-5(c)(2)(v) through (c)(3).

(4) Elective fixed ratio method of determining U.S. liabilities. A taxpayer that is a bank as defined in section 585(a)(2)(B) (without regard to the second sentence thereof or whether any such activities are effectively connected with a trade or business within the United States) may elect to

use a fixed ratio of 95 percent in lieu of the actual ratio. A taxpayer that is neither a bank nor an insurance company may elect to use a fixed ratio of 50 percent in lieu of the actual ratio.

(5) through (d)(2)(ii)(A)(1) [Reserved]. For further guidance, see § 1.882-5(c)(5) through (d)(2)(ii)(A)(1).

(d) *(2)* (ii) (A) (2) The foreign corporation enters the liability on a set of books reasonably contemporaneous with the time at which the liability is incurred and the liability relates to an activity that produces ECI.

(3) The foreign corporation maintains a set of books and records relating to an activity that produces ECI and the Director of Field Operations determines that there is a direct connection or relationship between the liability and that activity. Whether there is a direct connection between the liability and an activity that produces ECI depends on the facts and circumstances of each case.

(B) through (d)(2)(iii) [Reserved]. For further guidance, see § 1.882-5(d)(2)(ii)(B) through (d)(2)(iii).

(iii) (A) In general. A liability, whether interest-bearing or non-interest-bearing, is properly reflected on the books of the U.S. trade or business of a foreign corporation that is a bank as described in section 585(a)(2)(B) (without regard to the second sentence thereof) if—

(1) The bank enters the liability on a set of books before the close of the day on which the liability is incurred, and the liability relates to an activity that produces ECI; and

(2) There is a direct connection or relationship between the liability and that activity. Whether there is a direct connection between the liability and an activity that produces ECI depends on the facts and circumstances of each case. For example, a liability that is used to fund an interbranch or other asset that produces non-ECI may have a direct connection to an ECI producing activity and may constitute a U.S.-booked liability if both the interbranch or non-ECI activity is the same type of activity in which ECI assets are also reflected on the set of books (for example, lending or money market interbank placements), and such ECI activities are not de minimis. Such U.S. booked liabilities may still be subject to § 1.882-5(d)(2)(v).

(B) through (d)(5)(i) [Reserved]. For further guidance, see § 1.882-5(d)(2)(iii)(B) through (d)(5)(i).

(5) (ii) Interest rate on excess U.S.-connected liabilities. (A) General rule. The applicable interest rate on excess U.S.-connected liabilities is determined by dividing the total interest expense paid or accrued for the taxable year on U.S.-dollar liabilities that are not U.S.-booked liabilities (as defined in § 1.882-5(d)(2)) and that are shown on the books of the offices or branches of the foreign corporation outside the United States by the average U.S.-dollar denominated liabilities (whether interest-bearing or not) that are not U.S.-booked liabilities and that are shown on the books of the offices or branches of the foreign corporation outside the United States for the taxable year.

(B) Annual published rate election. For each taxable year beginning with the first year end for which the original tax return due date (including extensions) is after August 17, 2006, in which a taxpayer is a bank within the meaning of section 585(a)(2)(B) (without regard to the second sentence thereof or whether any such activities are effectively connected with a trade or business within the United States), such taxpayer may elect to compute its excess interest by reference to a published average 30-day London Interbank Offering Rate (LIBOR) for the year. The election may be made for any eligible year by attaching a statement to a timely filed tax return (including extensions) that shows the 3-step components of the taxpayer's interest expense allocation under the adjusted U.S.-booked liabilities method and identifies the provider (for example, International Monetary Fund statistics) of the 30-day LIBOR rate selected. Once selected, the provider and the rate may not be changed by the taxpayer. If a taxpayer that is eligible to make the 30-day LIBOR election either does not file a timely return or files a calculation that allocates interest expense under the scaling ratio in § 1.882-5(d)(4) and it is determined by the Director of Field Operations that the taxpayer's U.S.-connected liabilities exceed its U.S.-booked liabilities, then the Director of Field Operations, and not the taxpayer, may choose whether to determine the taxpayer's excess interest rate under paragraph (d)(5)(ii)(A) or (B) of this section and may select the published 30-day LIBOR rate. For the first taxable year for which an original tax return due date (including extensions) is after August 17, 2006 and not later than December 31, 2006, an eligible taxpayer may make the 30-day LIBOR election one time for the taxable year on an amended return within 180 days after the original due date (including extensions).

(6) through (d)(6) Example 4 [Reserved]. For further guidance, see § 1.882-5(d)(6) through (d)(6) Example 4.

Example (5). U.S. booked liabilities—direct relationship. (i) Facts. Bank A, a resident of Country X, maintains a banking office in the U.S. that records transactions on three sets of books for State A, an International Banking Facility (IBF) for its bank regulatory approved international transactions, and a shell branch licensed operation in Country C. Bank A records substantial ECI assets from its bank lending and placement activities and a mix of interbranch and non-ECI producing assets from the same or similar activities on the books of State A branch and on its IBF. Bank A's Country C branch borrows substantially from third parties, as well as from its home office, and lends all of its funding to its State A branch and IBF to fund the mix of ECI, interbranch and non-ECI activities on those two books. The consolidated books of State A branch and IBF indicate that a substantial amount of the total book assets constitute U.S. assets under § 1.882-5(b). Some of the third-party borrowings on the books of the State A branch are used to lend directly to Bank A's home office in Country X. These borrowings reflect the average borrowing rate of the State A branch, IBF and Country C branches as a whole. All third-party borrowings reflected on the books of State A branch, the IBF and Country C branch were recorded on such books before the close of business on the day the liabilities were acquired by Bank A.

(ii) U.S. booked liabilities. The facts demonstrate that the separate State A branch, IBF and Country C branch books taken together, constitute a set of books within the meaning of (d)(2)(iii)(A)(1) of this section. Such set of books as a whole has a direct relationship to an ECI activity under (d)(2)(iii)(A)(2) of this section even though the Country C branch books standing alone would not. The third-party liabilities recorded on the books of Country C constitute U.S. booked liabilities because they were timely recorded and the overall set of books on which they were reflected has a direct relationship to a bank lending and interbank placement ECI producing activity. The third-party liabilities that were recorded on the books of State A branch that were used to lend funds to Bank A's home office also constitute U.S. booked liabilities because the interbranch activity the funds were used for is a lending activity of a type that also gives rise to a substantial amount of ECI that is properly reflected on the same set of books as the interbranch loans. Accordingly, the liabilities are not traced to their specific interbranch use but to the overall activity of bank lending and interbank placements which gives rise to substantial ECI. The facts show that the liabilities were not acquired to increase artificially the interest expense of Bank A's U.S. booked liabilities as a whole under § 1.882-5(d)(2)(v). The third-party liabilities also constitute U.S. booked liabilities for purposes of determining Bank A's branch interest under § 1.884-4(b)(1)(i)(A) regardless of whether Bank A uses the Adjusted U.S. booked liability method, or the Separate Currency Pool method to allocate its interest expense under § 1.882-5(e).

(e) through (f)(2) [Reserved]. For further guidance, see § 1.882-5(e) through (f)(2).

(g) Effective date. *(1)* This section is applicable for the first tax year in which an original tax return due date (including extensions) is after August 17, 2006.

(2) The applicability of this section expires on or before August 15, 2009.

T.D. 9281, 8/16/2006.

§ 1.883-0 Outline of major topics.

This section lists the major paragraphs contained in §§ 1.883-1 through 1.883-5.

§ 1.883-1 Exclusion of income from the international operation of ships or aircraft.

(a) General rule.

(b) Qualified income.

(c) Qualified foreign corporation.

(1) General rule.

(2) Stock ownership test.

(3) Substantiation and reporting requirements.

(i) General rule.

(ii) Further documentation.

(4) Commissioner's discretion to cure defects in documentation.

(d) Qualified foreign country.

(e) Operation of ships or aircraft.

(1) General rule.

(2) Pool, partnership, strategic alliance, joint operating agreement, code-sharing arrangement or other joint venture.

(3) Activities not considered operation of ships or aircraft.

(4) Examples.

(5) Definitions.

(i) Bareboat charter.

(ii) Code-sharing arrangement.

(iii) Dry lease.

(iv) Entity.

(v) Fiscally transparent entity under the income tax laws of the United States.

(vi) Full charter.

(vii) Nonvessel operating common carrier.

(viii) Space or slot charter.

(ix) Time charter.

(x) Voyage charter.

(xi) Wet lease.

(f) International operation of ships or aircraft.

(1) General rule.

(2) Determining whether income is derived from international operation of ships or aircraft.

(i) International carriage of passengers.

(A) General rule.

(B) Round trip travel on ships.

(ii) International carriage of cargo.

(iii) Bareboat charter of ships or dry lease of aircraft used in international operation of ships or aircraft.

(iv) Charter of ships or aircraft for hire.

(g) Activities incidental to the international operation of ships or aircraft.

(1) General rule.

(2) Activities not considered incidental to the international operation of ships or aircraft.

(3) [Reserved]. For further guidance, see the entry for § 1.883-1T(g)(3).

(4) Activities involved in a pool, partnership, strategic alliance, joint operating agreement, code-sharing arrangement or other joint venture.

(h) Equivalent exemption.

(1) General rule.

(2) Determining equivalent exemptions for each category of income.

(3) [Reserved]. For further guidance, see the entry for § 1.883-1T(g)(3).

(4) Exemptions not qualifying as equivalent exemptions.

(i) General rule.

(ii) Reduced tax rate or time limited exemption.

(iii) Inbound or outbound freight tax.

(iv) Exemptions for limited types of cargo.

(v) Territorial tax systems.

(vi) Countries that tax on a residence basis.

(vii) Exemptions within categories of income.

(i) Treatment of possessions.

(j) Expenses related to qualified income.

§ 1.883-2 Treatment of publicly-traded corporations.

(a) General rule.

(b) Established securities market.

(1) General rule.

(2) Exchanges with multiple tiers.

(3) Computation of dollar value of stock traded.

(4) Over-the-counter market.

(5) Discretion to determine that an exchange does not qualify as an established securities market.

(c) Primarily traded.

(d) Regularly traded.

(1) General rule.

(2) Classes of stock traded on a domestic established securities market treated as meeting trading requirements.

(3) Closely-held classes of stock not treated as meeting trading requirements.

(i) General rule.

(ii) Exception.

(iii) Five-percent shareholders.

(A) Related persons.

(B) Investment companies.

(4) Anti-abuse rule.

(5) Example.

(e) Substantiation that a foreign corporation is publicly traded.

(1) General rule.

(2) [Reserved]. For further guidance, see the entry for § 1.883-2T(e)(2).

(f) Reporting requirements.

§ 1.883-3 Treatment of controlled foreign corporations. [Reserved]. For further guidance, see the entry for § 1.883-3T.

§ 1.883-4 Qualified shareholder stock ownership test.

(a) General rule.

(b) Qualified shareholder.

(1) General rule.

(2) Residence of individual shareholders.

(i) General rule.

(ii) Tax home.

(3) Certain income tax convention restrictions applied to shareholders.

(4) Not-for-profit organizations.

(5) Pension funds.

(i) Pension fund defined.

(ii) Government pension funds.

(iii) Nongovernment pension funds.

(iv) Beneficiary of a pension fund.

(c) Rules for determining constructive ownership.

(1) General rules for attribution.

(2) Partnerships.

(i) General rule.

(ii) Partners resident in the same country.

(iii) Examples.

(3) Trusts and estates.

(i) Beneficiaries.

(ii) Grantor trusts.

(4) Corporations that issue stock.

(5) Taxable nonstock corporations.

(6) Mutual insurance companies and similar entities.

(7) Computation of beneficial interests in nongovernment pension funds.

(d) Substantiation of stock ownership.

(1) General rule.

(2) Application of general rule.

(i) Ownership statements.

(ii) Three-year period of validity.

(3) Special rules.

(i) Substantiating residence of certain shareholders.

(ii) Special rule for registered shareholders owning less than one percent of widely-held corporations.

(iii) Special rule for beneficiaries of pension funds.

(A) Government pension fund.

(B) Nongovernment pension fund.

(iv) Special rule for stock owned by publicly-traded corporations.

(v) Special rule for not-for-profit organizations.

(vi) Special rule for a foreign airline covered by an air services agreement.

(vii) Special rule for taxable nonstock corporations.

(viii) Special rule for closely-held corporations traded in the United States.

(4) Ownership statements from shareholders.

(i) Ownership statements from individuals.

(ii) Ownership statements from foreign governments.

(iii) Ownership statements from publicly-traded corporate shareholders.

(iv) Ownership statements from not-for-profit organizations.

(v) Ownership statements from intermediaries.

(A) General rule.

(B) Ownership statements from widely-held intermediaries with registered shareholders owning less than one percent of such widely-held intermediary.

(C) Ownership statements from pension funds.

(1) Ownership statements from government pension funds.

(2) Ownership statements from nongovernment pension funds.

(3) Time for making determinations.

(D) Ownership statements from taxable nonstock corporations.

(5) Availability and retention of documents for inspection.

(e) Reporting requirements.

§ 1.883-5 Effective dates.

(a) General rule.

(b) Election for retroactive application.

(c) Transitional information reporting rule.

(d) [Reserved]. For further guidance, see the entry for § 1.883-5T(d).

(e) [Reserved]. For further guidance, see the entry for § 1.883-5T(e).

T.D. 9087, 8/25/2003, amend T.D. 9332, 6/22/2003.

PAR. 2. Section 1.883-0 is amended by revising the entries for §§ 1.883-1(g)(3) and (h)(3), 1.883-2(e)(2), 1.883-3, and 1.883-5(d) and (e) to read as follows:

Proposed § 1.883-0 Outline of major topics. *[For Preamble, see ¶ 152,877]*

* * * * *

* * * * *

§ 1.883-1 Exclusion of income from the international operation of ships or aircraft.

* * * * *

(g) * * *

(3) [The text of the proposed entry for § 1.883-1(g)(3) is the same as the text of the entry for § 1.883-1T(g)(3) published elsewhere in this issue of the Federal Register]. [See T.D. 9332, 06/25/2007].

* * * * *

(h) * * *

(3) * * *

(i) through (iv) [The text of the proposed entries for § 1.883-1(h)(3)(i) through (iv) is the same as the text of the entries for § 1.883-1T(h)(3)(i) through (iv) published elsewhere in this issue of the Federal Register]. [See T.D. 9332, 06/25/2007].

* * * * *

§ 1.883-2 Treatment of publicly traded corporations.

* * * * *

(e) * * *

(2) The text of the proposed entry for § 1.883-2(e)(2) is the same as the text of the entry for § 1.883-2T(e)(2) published elsewhere in this issue of the Federal Register]. [See T.D. 9332, 06/25/2007].

* * * * *

§ 1.883-3 Treatment of controlled foreign corporations.

***** [The text of the proposed entry for § 1.883-3 is the same as the entry for § 1.883-3T published elsewhere in this issue of the Federal Register]. [See T.D. 9332, 06/25/2007].

§ 1.883-5 Effective/applicability dates.

* * * * *

(d) and (e) [The text of the proposed entries for § 1.883-5(d) and (e) is the same as the text of the entries for § 1.883-5T(d) and (e) published elsewhere in this issue of the Federal Register]. [See T.D. 9332, 06/25/2007].

§ 1.883-0T Outline of major topics (temporary).

This section lists the major paragraphs contained in §§ 1.883-1T through 1.883-5T.

§ 1.883-1T Exclusion of income from the international operation of ships or aircraft (temporary).

(a) through (c)(3)(i) [Reserved]. For further guidance, see entries for § 1.883-1(a) through (c)(3)(i).

(3)(ii) Further documentation.

(A) General rule.

(A) Names and addresses of certain shareholders.

(c)(4) through (g)(2) [Reserved]. For further guidance, see entries for § 1.883-1(c)(4) through (g)(2).

(g)(3) Other services. [Reserved].

(4) through (h)(2) [Reserved]. For further guidance, see entries for § 1.883-1(g)(4) through (h)(2).

(h)(3) Special rules with respect to income tax conventions.

(i) Countries with only an income tax convention.

(ii) Countries with both an income tax convention and an equivalent exemption.

(A) General rule.

(B) Special rule for simultaneous benefits under section 883 and an income tax convention.

(iii) Participation in certain joint ventures.

(iv) Independent interpretation of income tax conventions.

(4) through (j) [Reserved]. For further guidance, see entries for § 1.883-1(h)(4) through (j).

§ 1.883-2T Treatment of publicly-traded corporations (temporary).

(a) through (e)(1) [Reserved]. For further guidance, see entries for § 1.883-2(a) through (e)(1).

(2) Availability and retention of documents for inspection.

(f) [Reserved]. For further guidance, see entry for § 1.883-2(f).

§ 1.883-3T Treatment of controlled foreign corporations (temporary).

(a) General rule.

(b) Qualified U.S. person ownership test.

(1) General rule.

(2) Qualified U.S. person.

(3) Treatment of bearer shares.

(4) Attribution of ownership through certain domestic entities.

(5) Examples.

(c) Substantiation of CFC stock ownership.

(1) In general.

(2) Ownership statements from qualified U.S. persons.

(3) Ownership statements from intermediaries.

(4) Three-year period of validity.

(5) Availability and retention of documents for inspection.

(d) Reporting requirements.

§ 1.883-5T Effective/applicability dates (temporary).

(a) through (c) [Reserved]. For further guidance, see entries for § 1.883-5(a) through (c).

(d) Effective date.

(e) Applicability dates.

(f) Expiration date.

T.D. 9087, 8/25/2003, amend T.D. 9332, 6/22/2003.

§ 1.883-1 Exclusion of income from the international operation of ships or aircraft.

Caution: The Treasury has not yet amended Reg § 1.883-1 to reflect changes made by P.L. 100-647, P.L. 94-164.

(a) General rule. Qualified income derived by a qualified foreign corporation from its international operation of ships or aircraft is excluded from gross income and exempt from United States Federal income tax. Paragraph (b) of this section defines the term qualified income. Paragraph (c) of this section defines the term qualified foreign corporation. Paragraph (f) of this section defines the term international operation of ships or aircraft.

(b) Qualified income. Qualified income is income derived from the international operation of ships or aircraft that—

(1) Is properly includible in any of the income categories described in paragraph (h)(2) of this section; and

(2) Is the subject of an equivalent exemption, as defined in paragraph (h) of this section, granted by the qualified foreign country, as defined in paragraph (d) of this section, in which the foreign corporation seeking qualified foreign corporation status is organized.

(c) Qualified foreign corporation. *(1) General rule.* A qualified foreign corporation is a corporation that is organized in a qualified foreign country and considered engaged in the international operation of ships or aircraft. The term corporation is defined in section 7701(a)(3) and the regulations thereunder. Paragraph (d) of this section defines the term qualified foreign country. Paragraph (e) of this section defines the term operation of ships or aircraft, and paragraph (f) of this section defines the term international operation of ships or aircraft. To be a qualified foreign corporation, the corporation must satisfy the stock ownership test of paragraph (c)(2) of this section and satisfy the substantiation and reporting requirements described in paragraph (c)(3) of this section. A corporation may be a qualified foreign corporation with respect to one category of qualified income but not with respect to another such category. See paragraph (h)(2) of this section for a discussion of the categories of qualified income.

(2) Stock ownership test. To be a qualified foreign corporation, a foreign corporation must satisfy the publicly-traded test of § 1.883-2(a), the CFC stock ownership test of § 1.883-3(a), or the qualified shareholder stock ownership test of § 1.883-4(a).

(3) Substantiation and reporting requirements. (i) General rule. To be a qualified foreign corporation, a foreign corporation must include the following information in its Form 1120-F, "U.S. Income Tax Return of a Foreign Corporation," in the manner prescribed by such form and its accompanying instructions—

(A) The corporation's name and address (including mailing code);

(B) The corporation's U.S. taxpayer identification number;

(C) The foreign country in which the corporation is organized;

(D) [Reserved]. For further guidance, see § 1.883-1T(c)(3)(i)(D).

(E) The category or categories of qualified income for which an exemption is being claimed;

(F) A reasonable estimate of the gross amount of income in each category of qualified income for which the exemption is claimed, to the extent such amounts are readily determinable;

(G) through (I) [Reserved]. For further guidance, see § 1.883-1T(c)(3)(i)(G) through (I).

(ii) [Reserved]. For further guidance, see § 1.883-1T(c)(3)(ii).

(4) Commissioner's discretion to cure defects in documentation. The Commissioner retains the discretion to cure any defects in the documentation where the Commissioner is satisfied that the foreign corporation would otherwise be a qualified foreign corporation.

(d) Qualified foreign country. A qualified foreign country is a foreign country that grants to corporations organized in the United States an equivalent exemption, as described in paragraph (h) of this section, for the category of qualified income, as described in paragraph (h)(2) of this section, derived by the foreign corporation seeking qualified foreign corporation status. A foreign country may be a qualified foreign country with respect to one category of qualified income but not with respect to another such category.

(e) Operation of ships or aircraft. *(1) General rule.* Except as provided in paragraph (e)(2) of this section, a foreign corporation is considered engaged in the operation of ships or aircraft only during the time it is an owner or lessee of one or more entire ships or aircraft and uses such ships or aircraft in one or more of the following activities—

(i) Carriage of passengers or cargo for hire;

(ii) In the case of a ship, the leasing out of the ship under a time or voyage charter (full charter), space or slot charter, or bareboat charter, as those terms are defined in paragraph (e)(5) of this section, provided the ship is used to carry passengers or cargo for hire; and

(iii) In the case of aircraft, the leasing out of the aircraft under a wet lease (full charter), space, slot, or block-seat charter, or dry lease, as those terms are defined in paragraph (e)(5) of this section, provided the aircraft is used to carry passengers or cargo for hire.

(2) Pool, partnership, strategic alliance, joint operating agreement, code-sharing arrangement or other joint venture. A foreign corporation is considered engaged in the operation of ships or aircraft within the meaning of paragraph (e)(1) of this section with respect to its participation in a pool, partnership, strategic alliance, joint operating agreement, code-sharing arrangement or other joint venture if it directly, or indirectly through one or more fiscally transparent entities under the income tax laws of the United States, as defined in paragraph (e)(5)(v) of this section—

(i) Owns an interest in a partnership, disregarded entity, or other fiscally transparent entity under the income tax laws of the United States that itself would be considered engaged in the operation of ships or aircraft under paragraph (e)(1) of this section if it were a foreign corporation; or

(ii) Participates in a pool, strategic alliance, joint operating agreement, code-sharing arrangement, or other joint venture that is not an entity, as defined in paragraph (e)(5)(iv) of this section, involving one or more activities described in paragraphs (e)(1)(i) through (iii) of this section, but only if—

(A) In the case of a direct interest, the foreign corporation is otherwise engaged in the operation of ships or aircraft under paragraph (e)(1) of this section; or

(B) In the case of an indirect interest, either the foreign corporation is otherwise engaged, or one of the fiscally transparent entities would be considered engaged if it were a foreign corporation, in the operation of ships or aircraft under paragraph (e)(1) of this section.

(3) Activities not considered operation of ships or aircraft. Activities that do not constitute operation of ships or aircraft include, but are not limited to—

(i) The activities of a nonvessel operating common carrier, as defined in paragraph (e)(5)(vii) of this section;

(ii) Ship or aircraft management;

(iii) Obtaining crews for ships or aircraft operated by another party;

(iv) Acting as a ship's agent;

(v) Ship or aircraft brokering;

(vi) Freight forwarding;

(vii) The activities of travel agents and tour operators;

(viii) Rental by a container leasing company of containers and related equipment; and

(ix) The activities of a concessionaire.

(4) Examples. The rules of paragraphs (e)(1) through (3) of this section are illustrated by the following examples:

Example (1). Three tiers of charters.

(i) Facts. A, B, and C are foreign corporations. A purchases a ship. A and B enter into a bareboat charter of the ship for a term of 20 years, and B, in turn, enters into a time charter of the ship with C for a term of 5 years. Under the time charter, B is responsible for the complete operation of the ship, including providing the crew and maintenance. C uses the ship during the term of the time charter to carry its customers' freight between U.S. and foreign ports. C owns no ships.

(ii) Analysis. Because A is the owner of the entire ship and leases out the ship under a bareboat charter to B, and because the sublessor, C, uses the ship to carry cargo for hire, A is considered engaged in the operation of a ship under paragraph (e)(1) of this section during the term of the time charter. B leases in the entire ship from A and leases out the ship under a time charter to C, who uses the ship to carry cargo for hire. Therefore, B is considered engaged in the operation of a ship under paragraph (e)(1) of this section during the term of the time charter. C time charters the entire ship from B and uses the ship to carry its customers' freight during the term of the charter. Therefore, C is also engaged in the operation of a ship under paragraph (e)(1) of this section during the term of the time charter.

Example (2). Partnership with contributed shipping assets.

(i) Facts. X, Y, and Z, each a foreign corporation, enter into a partnership, P. P is a fiscally transparent entity under the income tax laws of the United States, as defined in paragraph (e)(5)(v) of this section. Under the terms of the partnership agreement, each partner contributes all of the ships in its fleet to P in exchange for interests in the partnership and shares in the P profits from the international carriage of cargo. The partners share in the overall management of P, but each partner, acting in its capacity as partner, continues to crew and manage all ships previously in its fleet.

(ii) Analysis. P owns the ships contributed by the partners and uses these ships to carry cargo for hire. Therefore, if P were a foreign corporation, it would be considered engaged in the operation of ships within the meaning of paragraph (e)(1) of this section. Accordingly, because P is a fiscally transparent entity under the income tax laws of the United States, as defined in paragraph (e)(5)(v) of this section, X, Y, and Z are each considered engaged in the operation of ships through P, within the meaning of paragraph (e)(2)(i) of this section, with respect to their distributive share of income from P's international carriage of cargo.

Example (3). Joint venture with chartered in ships.

(i) Facts. Foreign corporation A owns a number of foreign subsidiaries involved in various aspects of the shipping business, including S1, S2, S3, and S4. S4 is a foreign corporation that provides cruises but does not own any ships. S1, S2, and S3 are foreign corporations that own cruise ships. S1, S2, S3, and S4 form joint venture JV, in which they are all interest holders, to conduct cruises. JV is a fiscally transparent entity under the income tax laws of the United States, as defined in paragraph (e)(5)(v) of this section. Under the terms of the joint venture, S1, S2, and S3 each enter into time charter agreements with JV, pursuant to which S1, S2, and S3 retain control of the navigation and management of the individual ships, and JV will use the ships to carry passengers for hire. The overall management of the cruise line will be provided by S4.

(ii) Analysis. S1, S2, and S3 each owns ships and time charters those ships to JV, which uses the ships to carry passengers for hire. Accordingly, S1, S2, and S3 are each considered engaged in the operation of ships under paragraph (e)(1) of this section. JV leases in entire ships by means of the time charters, and JV uses those ships to carry passengers on cruises. Thus, JV would be engaged in the operation of ships within the meaning of paragraph (e)(1) of this section if it were a foreign corporation. Therefore, although S4 does not directly own or lease in a ship, S4 also is engaged in the operation of ships, within the meaning of paragraph (e)(2)(i) of this section, with respect to its participation in JV.

Example (4). Tiered partnerships.

(i) Facts. Foreign corporations A, B, and C enter into a partnership, P1. P1 is one of several shareholders of Poolco, a foreign limited liability company that makes an election pursuant to § 301.7701-3 of this chapter to be treated as a partnership for U.S. tax purposes. P1 acquires several ships and time charters them out to Poolco. Poolco slot or voyage charters such ships out to third parties for use in the carriage of cargo for hire. P1 and Poolco are fiscally transparent entities under the income tax laws of the United States, as defined in paragraph (e)(5)(v) of this section.

(ii) Analysis. A, B, and C are considered engaged in the operation of ships under paragraph (e)(2)(i) of this section with respect to their direct interest in P1 and with respect to their indirect interest in Poolco because both P1 and Poolco are fiscally transparent entities under the income tax laws of the United States and would be considered engaged in the operation of ships under paragraph (e)(1) of this section if they were foreign corporations. The result would be the same if Poolco were a single-member disregarded entity owned solely by P1.

(5) Definitions. (i) Bareboat charter. A bareboat charter is a contract for the use of a ship or aircraft whereby the lessee is in complete possession, control, and command of the ship or aircraft. For example, in a bareboat charter, the lessee is responsible for the navigation and management of the ship or aircraft, the crew, supplies, repairs and maintenance, fees, insurance, charges, commissions and other expenses connected with the use of the ship or aircraft. The lessor of the ship bears none of the expense or responsibility of operation of the ship or aircraft.

(ii) Code-sharing arrangement. A code-sharing arrangement is an arrangement in which one air carrier puts its identification code on the flight of another carrier. This arrangement allows the first carrier to hold itself out as providing service in markets where it does not otherwise operate or where it operates infrequently. Code-sharing arrangements can range from a very limited agreement between two carriers involving only one market to agreements involving multiple markets and alliances between or among international carriers which also include joint marketing, baggage handling, one-stop check-in service, sharing of frequent flyer awards, and other services. For rules involving the sale of code-sharing tickets, see paragraph (g)(1)(vi) of this section.

(iii) Dry lease. A dry lease is the bareboat charter of an aircraft.

(iv) Entity. For purposes of this paragraph (e), an entity is any person that is treated by the United States as other than an individual for U.S. Federal income tax purposes. The term includes disregarded entities.

(v) Fiscally transparent entity under the income tax laws of the United States. For purposes of this paragraph (e), an entity is fiscally transparent under the income tax laws of the United States if the entity would be considered fiscally transparent under the income tax laws of the United States under the principles of § 1.894-1(d)(3).

(vi) Full charter. Full charter (or full rental) means a time charter or a voyage charter of a ship or a wet lease of an aircraft but during which the full crew and management are provided by the lessor.

(vii) Nonvessel operating common carrier. A nonvessel operating common carrier is an entity that does not exercise control over any part of a vessel, but holds itself out to the public as providing transportation for hire, issues bills of lading, assumes responsibility or is liable by law as a common carrier for safe transportation of shipments, and arranges in its own name with other common carriers, including those engaged in the operation of ships, for the performance of such transportation.

(viii) Space or slot charter. A space or slot charter is a contract for use of a certain amount of space (but less than all of the space) on a ship or aircraft, and may be on a time or voyage basis. When used in connection with passenger aircraft this sort of charter may be referred to as the sale of block seats.

(ix) Time charter. A time charter is a contract for the use of a ship or aircraft for a specific period of time, during which the lessor of the ship or aircraft retains control of the navigation and management of the ship or aircraft (i.e., the lessor continues to be responsible for the crew, supplies, repairs and maintenance, fees and insurance, charges, commissions and other expenses connected with the use of the ship or aircraft).

(x) Voyage charter. A voyage charter is a contract similar to a time charter except that the ship or aircraft is chartered for a specific voyage or flight rather than for a specific period of time.

(xi) Wet lease. A wet lease is the time or voyage charter of an aircraft.

(f) International operation of ships or aircraft. *(1) General rule.* The term international operation of ships or aircraft means the operation of ships or aircraft, as defined in paragraph (e) of this section, with respect to the carriage of passengers or cargo on voyages or flights that begin or end in the United States, as determined under paragraph (f)(2) of this section. The term does not include the carriage of passengers or cargo on a voyage or flight that begins and ends in the United States, even if the voyage or flight contains a segment extending beyond the territorial limits of the United States, unless the passenger disembarks or the cargo is unloaded outside the United States. Operation of ships or aircraft beyond the territorial limits of the United States does not constitute in itself international operation of ships or aircraft.

(2) Determining whether income is derived from international operation of ships or aircraft. Whether income is derived from international operation of ships or aircraft is determined on a passenger by passenger basis (as provided in paragraph (f)(2)(i) of this section) and on an item-of-cargo by item-of-cargo basis (as provided in paragraph (f)(2)(ii) of this section). In the case of the bareboat charter of a ship or the dry lease of an aircraft, whether the charter income for a particular period is derived from international operation of ships or aircraft is determined by reference to how the ship or aircraft is used by the lowest-tier lessee in the chain of lessees (as provided in paragraph (f)(2)(iii) of this section).

(i) International carriage of passengers. (A) General rule. Except in the case of a round trip described in paragraph (f)(2)(i)(B) of this section, income derived from the carriage of a passenger will be income from international operation of ships or aircraft if the passenger is carried between a beginning point in the United States and an ending point outside the United States, or vice versa. Carriage of a passenger will be treated as ending at the passenger's final destination even if, en route to the passenger's final destination, a stop is made at an intermediate point for refueling, maintenance, or other business reasons, provided the passenger does not change ships or aircraft at the intermediate point. Similarly, carriage of a passenger will be treated as beginning at the passenger's point of origin even if, en route to the passenger's final destination, a stop is made at an intermediate point, provided the passenger does not change ships or aircraft at the intermediate point. Carriage of a passenger will be treated as beginning or ending at a U.S. or foreign intermediate point if the passenger changes ships or aircraft at that intermediate point. Income derived from the sale of a ticket for international carriage of a passenger will be treated as income derived from international operation of ships or aircraft even if the passenger does not begin or complete an international journey because of unanticipated circumstances.

(B) Round trip travel on ships. In the case of income from the carriage of a passenger on a ship that begins its voyage in the United States, calls on one or more foreign intermediate ports, and returns to the same or another U.S. port, such income from carriage of a passenger on the entire voyage will be treated as income derived from international operation of ships or aircraft under paragraph (f)(2)(i)(A) of this section. This result obtains even if such carriage includes one or more intermediate stops at a U.S. port or ports and even if the passenger does not disembark at the foreign intermediate point.

(ii) International carriage of cargo. Income from the carriage of cargo will be income derived from international operation of ships or aircraft if the cargo is carried between a beginning point in the United States and an ending point outside the United States, or vice versa. Carriage of cargo will be treated as ending at the final destination of the cargo even if, en route to that final destination, a stop is made at a U.S. intermediate point, provided the cargo is transported to its ultimate destination on the same ship or aircraft. If the cargo is transferred to another ship or aircraft, the carriage of the cargo may nevertheless be treated as ending at its final destination, if the same taxpayer transports the cargo to and from the U.S. intermediate point and the cargo does not pass through customs at the U.S. intermediate point. Similarly, carriage of cargo will be treated as beginning at the cargo's point of origin, even if en route to its final destination a stop is made at a U.S. intermediate point, provided the cargo is transported to its ultimate destination on the same ship or aircraft. If the cargo is transferred to another ship or aircraft at the U.S. intermediate point, the carriage of the cargo may nevertheless be treated as beginning at the point of origin, if the same taxpayer transports the cargo to and from the U.S. intermediate point and the cargo does not pass through customs at the U.S. intermediate point. Repackaging, recontainerization, or any other activity involving the unloading of the cargo at the U.S. intermediate point does not change these results, provided the same taxpayer transports the cargo to and from the U.S. intermediate point and the cargo does not pass through customs at the U.S. intermediate point. A lighter vessel that carries cargo to, or picks up cargo from, a vessel located beyond the territorial limits of the United States and correspondingly loads or unloads that cargo at a U.S. port, carries cargo between a point in the United States and a point outside the United States. However, a lighter vessel that carries cargo to, or picks up cargo from, a vessel located within the territorial limits of the United States, and correspondingly loads or unloads that cargo at a U.S. port, is not engaged in international operation of ships or aircraft. Income from the carriage of military cargo on a voyage that begins in the United States, stops at a foreign intermediate port or a military prepositioning location, and returns to the same or another U.S. port without unloading its cargo at the foreign intermediate point, will nevertheless be treated as derived from international operation of ships or aircraft.

(iii) Bareboat charter of ships or dry lease of aircraft used in international operation of ships or aircraft. If a qualified foreign corporation bareboat charters a ship or dry leases an aircraft to a lessee, and the lowest tier lessee in the chain of ownership uses such ship or aircraft for the international carriage of passengers or cargo for hire, as described in paragraphs (f)(2)(i) and (ii) of this section, then the amount of charter income attributable to the period the ship or aircraft is used by the lowest tier lessee is income from international operation of ships or aircraft. The foreign corporation generally must determine the amount of the charter income that is attributable to such international operation of ships or aircraft by multiplying the amount of charter income by a fraction, the numerator of which is the total number of days of uninterrupted travel on voyages or flights of such ship or aircraft between the United States and the farthest point or points where cargo or passengers are loaded en route to, or discharged en route from, the United States during the smaller of the taxable year or the particular charter period, and the denominator of which is the total number of days in the smaller of the taxable year or the particular charter period. For this purpose, the number of days during which the ship or aircraft is not generating transportation income, within the meaning of section 863(c)(2), are not included in the numerator or denominator of the fraction. However, the foreign corporation may adopt an alternative method for determining the amount of the charter income that is attributable to the international operation of ships or aircraft if it can establish that the alternative method more accurately reflects the amount of such income.

(iv) Charter of ships or aircraft for hire. For purposes of this section, if a foreign corporation time, voyage, or bareboat charters out a ship or aircraft, and the lowest-tier lessee uses the ship or aircraft to carry passengers or cargo on a fee basis, the ship or aircraft is considered used to carry passengers or cargo for hire, regardless of whether the ship or aircraft may be empty during a portion of the charter period due to a backhaul voyage or flight or for purposes of repositioning. If a foreign corporation time, voyage, or bareboat charters out a ship or aircraft, and the lowest-tier lessee uses the ship or aircraft for the carriage of proprietary goods, including an empty backhaul voyage or flight or repositioning related to such carriage of proprietary goods, the ship or aircraft similarly will be treated as used to carry cargo for hire.

(g) Activities incidental to the international operation of ships or aircraft. *(1) General rule.* Certain activities of a foreign corporation engaged in the international operation of ships or aircraft are so closely related to the international operation of ships or aircraft that they are considered incidental to such operation, and income derived by the foreign corporation from its performance of these incidental activities is deemed to be income derived from the international operation of ships or aircraft. Examples of such activities include—

(i) Temporary investment of working capital funds to be used in the international operation of ships or aircraft by the foreign corporation;

(ii) Sale of tickets by the foreign corporation engaged in the international operation of ships for the international carriage of passengers by ship on behalf of another corporation engaged in the international operation of ships;

(iii) Sale of tickets by the foreign corporation engaged in the international operation of aircraft for the international carriage of passengers by air on behalf of another corporation engaged in the international operation of aircraft;

(iv) Contracting with concessionaires for performance of services onboard during the international operation of the foreign corporation's ships or aircraft;

(v) Providing (either by subcontracting or otherwise) for the carriage of cargo preceding or following the international carriage of cargo under a through bill of lading, airway bill or similar document through a related corporation or through an unrelated person (and the rules of section 267(b) shall apply for purposes of determining whether a corporation or other person is related to the foreign corporation);

(vi) To the extent not described in paragraph (g)(1)(iii) of this section, the sale or issuance by the foreign corporation engaged in the international operation of aircraft of intraline, interline, or code-sharing tickets for the carriage of persons by air between a U.S. gateway and another U.S. city preceding or following international carriage of passengers, provided that all such flight segments are provided pursuant to the passenger's original invoice, ticket or itinerary and in the case of intraline tickets are a part of uninterrupted international air transportation (within the meaning of section 4262(c)(3));

(vii) Arranging for port city hotel accommodations within the United States for a passenger for the one night before or after the international carriage of that passenger by the foreign corporation engaged in the international operation of ships;

(viii) Bareboat charter of ships or dry lease of aircraft normally used by the foreign corporation in international operation of ships or aircraft but currently not needed, if the ship or aircraft is used by the lessee for international carriage of cargo or passengers;

(ix) through (xi) [Reserved]. For further guidance, see § 1.883-1T(g)(1)(ix) through (xi).

(2) Activities not considered incidental to the international operation of ships or aircraft. Examples of activities that are not considered incidental to the international operation of ships or aircraft include—

(i) The sale of or arranging for train travel, bus transfers, single day shore excursions, or land tour packages;

(ii) Arranging for hotel accommodations within the United States other than as provided in paragraph (g)(1)(vii) of this section;

(iii) The sale of airline tickets or cruise tickets other than as provided in paragraph (g)(1)(ii), (iii), or (vi) of this section;

(iv) The sale or rental of real property;

(v) Treasury activities involving the investment of excess funds or funds awaiting repatriation, even if derived from the international operation of ships or aircraft;

(vi) The carriage of passengers or cargo on ships or aircraft on domestic legs of transportation not treated as either international operation of ships or aircraft under paragraph (f) of this section or as an activity that is incidental to such operation under paragraph (g)(1) of this section;

(vii) The carriage of cargo by bus, truck or rail by a foreign corporation between a U.S. inland point and a U.S. gateway port or airport preceding or following the international carriage of such cargo by the foreign corporation; and

(viii) The provision of containers or other related equipment by the foreign corporation within the United States other than as provided in paragraph (g)(1)(x) of this section, including warehousing.

(3) [Reserved]. For further guidance, see § 1.883-1T(g)(3).

(4) Activities involved in a pool, partnership, strategic alliance, joint operating agreement, code-sharing arrangement or other joint venture. Notwithstanding paragraph (g)(1) of this section, an activity is considered incidental to the international operation of ships or aircraft by a foreign corporation, and income derived by the foreign corporation with respect to such activity is deemed to be income derived from

the international operation of ships or aircraft, if the activity is performed by or pursuant to a pool, partnership, strategic alliance, joint operating agreement, code-sharing arrangement or other joint venture in which such foreign corporation participates directly, or indirectly through a fiscally transparent entity under the income tax laws of the United States, provided that—

(i) Such activity is incidental to the international operation of ships or aircraft by the pool, partnership, strategic alliance, joint operating agreement, code-sharing arrangement or other joint venture, and provided that it is described in paragraph (e)(2)(i) of this section; or

(ii) Such activity would be incidental to the international operation of ships or aircraft by the foreign corporation, or fiscally transparent entity if it performed such activity itself, and provided the foreign corporation is engaged or the fiscally transparent entity would be considered engaged if it were a foreign corporation in the operation of ships or aircraft under paragraph (e)(1) of this section.

(h) Equivalent exemption. *(i) General rule.* A foreign country grants an equivalent exemption when it exempts from taxation income from the international operation of ships or aircraft derived by corporations organized in the United States. Whether a foreign country provides an equivalent exemption must be determined separately with respect to each category of income, as provided in paragraph (h)(2) of this section. An equivalent exemption may be available for income derived from the international operation of ships even though income derived from the international operation of aircraft may not be exempt, and vice versa. For rules regarding foreign corporations organized in countries that provide exemptions only through an income tax convention, see paragraph (h)(3) of this section. An equivalent exemption may exist where the foreign country—

(i) Generally imposes no tax on income, including income from the international operation of ships or aircraft;

(ii) [Reserved]. For further guidance, see § 1.883-1T(h)(1)(ii).

(iii) Exchanges diplomatic notes with the United States, or enters into an agreement with the United States, that provides for a reciprocal exemption for purposes of section 883.

(2) Determining equivalent exemptions for each category of income. Whether a foreign country grants an equivalent exemption must be determined separately with respect to income from the international operation of ships and income from the international operation of aircraft for each category of income listed in paragraphs (h)(2)(i) through (v), (vii), and (viii) of this section. If an exemption is unavailable in the foreign country for a particular category of income, the foreign country is not considered to grant an equivalent exemption with respect to that category of income. Income in that category is not considered to be the subject of an equivalent exemption and, thus, is not eligible for exemption from income tax in the United States, even though the foreign country may grant an equivalent exemption for other categories of income. With respect to paragraph (h)(2)(vi) of this section, a foreign country may be considered to grant an equivalent exemption for one or more types of income described in paragraph (g)(1) of this section. The following categories of income derived from the international operation of ships or aircraft may be exempt from United States income tax if an equivalent exemption is available—

(i) Income from the carriage of passengers and cargo;

(ii) Time or voyage (full) charter income of a ship or wet lease income of an aircraft;

(iii) Bareboat charter income of a ship or dry charter income of an aircraft;

(iv) Incidental bareboat charter income or incidental dry lease income;

(v) Incidental container-related income;

(vi) Income incidental to the international operation of ships or aircraft other than incidental income described in paragraphs (h)(2)(iv) and (v) of this section;

(vii) Capital gains derived by a qualified foreign corporation engaged in the international operation of ships or aircraft from the sale, exchange or other disposition of a ship, aircraft, container or related equipment or other moveable property used by that qualified foreign corporation in the international operation of ships or aircraft; and

(viii) Income from participation in a pool, partnership, strategic alliance, joint operating agreement, code-sharing arrangement, international operating agency, or other joint venture described in paragraph (e)(2) of this section.

(3) For further guidance, see the entry for § 1.883-1T(h)(3).

(4) Exemptions not qualifying as equivalent exemptions. (i) General rule. Certain types of exemptions provided to corporations organized in the United States by foreign countries do not satisfy the equivalent exemption requirements of this section. Paragraphs (h)(4)(ii) through (vii) of this section provide descriptions of some of the types of exemptions that do not qualify as equivalent exemptions for purposes of this section.

(ii) Reduced tax rate or time limited exemption. The exemption granted by the foreign country's law or income tax convention must be a complete exemption. The exemption may not constitute merely a reduction to a nonzero rate of tax levied against the income of corporations organized in the United States derived from the international operation of ships or aircraft or a temporary reduction to a zero rate of tax, such as in the case of a tax holiday.

(iii) Inbound or outbound freight tax. With respect to the carriage of cargo, the foreign country must provide an exemption from tax for income from transporting freight both inbound and outbound. For example, a foreign country that imposes tax only on outbound freight will not be treated as granting an equivalent exemption for income from transporting freight inbound into that country.

(iv) Exemptions for limited types of cargo. A foreign country must provide an exemption from tax for income from transporting all types of cargo. For example, if a foreign country were generally to impose tax on income from the international carriage of cargo but were to provide a statutory exemption for income from transporting agricultural products, the foreign country would not be considered to grant an equivalent exemption with respect to income from the international carriage of cargo, including agricultural products.

(v) Territorial tax systems. A foreign country with a territorial tax system will be treated as granting an equivalent exemption if it treats all income derived from the international operation of ships or aircraft derived by a U.S. corporation as entirely foreign source and therefore not subject to tax, including income derived from a voyage or flight that begins or ends in that foreign country.

(vi) Countries that tax on a residence basis. A foreign country that provides an equivalent exemption to corporations organized in the United States but also imposes a residence-based tax on certain corporations organized in the

United States may nevertheless be considered to grant an equivalent exemption if the residence-based tax is imposed only on a corporation organized in the United States that maintains its center of management and control or other comparable attributes in that foreign country. If the residence-based tax is imposed on corporations organized in the United States and engaged in the international operation of ships or aircraft that are not managed and controlled in that foreign country, the foreign country shall not be treated as a qualified foreign country and shall not be considered to grant an equivalent exemption for purposes of this section.

(vii) Exemptions within categories of income. With respect to paragraphs (h)(2)(i) through (v), (vii), and (viii) of this section, a foreign country must provide an exemption from tax for all income in a category of income, as defined in paragraph (h)(2) of this section. For example, a country that exempts income from the bareboat charter of passenger aircraft but not the bareboat charter of cargo aircraft does not provide an equivalent exemption. However, an equivalent exemption may be available for income derived from the international operation of ships even though income derived from the international operation of aircraft may not be exempt, and vice versa. With respect to paragraph (h)(2)(vi) of this section, a foreign country may be considered to grant an equivalent exemption for one or more types of income described in paragraph (g)(1) of this section.

(i) Treatment of possessions. For purposes of this section, a possession of the United States will be treated as a foreign country. A possession of the United States will be considered to grant an equivalent exemption and will be treated as a qualified foreign country if it applies a mirror system of taxation. If a possession does not apply a mirror system of taxation, the possession may nevertheless be a qualified foreign country if, for example, it provides for an equivalent exemption through its internal law. A possession applies the mirror system of taxation if the U.S. Internal Revenue Code of 1986, as amended, applies in the possession with the name of the possession used instead of "United States" where appropriate.

(j) Expenses related to qualified income. If a qualified foreign corporation derives qualified income from the international operation of ships or aircraft as well as income that is not qualified income, and the nonqualified income is effectively connected with the conduct of a trade or business within the United States, the foreign corporation may not deduct from such nonqualified income any amount otherwise allowable as a deduction from qualified income, if that qualified income is excluded under this section. See section 265(a)(1).

T.D. 6258, 10/23/57, amend T.D. 7293, 11/27/73, T.D. 9087, 8/25/2003, T.D. 9332, 6/22/2007.

PAR. 3. Section 1.883-1 is amended by revising paragraphs (c)(3)(i)(D), (c)(3)(i)(G), (c)(3)(i)(H), (c)(3)(i)(I), (c)(3)(ii), (g)(1)(ix), (g)(1)(x), (g)(1)(xi), (g)(3), (h)(1)(ii), and (h)(3) to read as follows:

Proposed § 1.883-1 Exclusion of income from the international operation of ships or aircraft. [*For Preamble, see ¶ 152,877*]

* * * * *

(c) * * *

(3) * * *

(i) * * *

(D) [The text of the proposed amendment to § 1.883-1(c)(3)(i)(D) is the same as the text of § 1.883-1T(c)(3)(i)(D) published elsewhere in this issue of the Federal Register]. [See T.D. 9332, 06/25/2007].

* * * * *

(G) through (I) [The text of the proposed amendments to § 1.883-1(c)(3)(i)(G) through (I) is the same as the text of § 1.883-1T(c)(3)(i)(G) through (I) published elsewhere in this issue of the Federal Register]. [See T.D. 9332, 06/25/2007].

(ii) [The text of the proposed amendment to § 1.883-1(c)(3)(ii) is the same as the text of § 1.883-1T(c)(3)(ii) published elsewhere in this issue of the Federal Register]. [See T.D. 9332, 06/25/2007].

* * * * *

(g) * * *

(1) * * *

(ix) through (xi) [The text of the proposed amendments to § 1.883-1(g)(1)(ix) through (xi) is the same as the text of § 1.883-1T(g)(1)(ix) through (xi) published elsewhere in this issue of the Federal Register]. [See T.D. 9332, 06/25/2007].

* * * * *

(3) [The text of the proposed amendment to § 1.883-1(g)(3) is the same as the text of § 1.883-1T(g)(3) published elsewhere in this issue of the Federal Register]. [See T.D. 9332, 06/25/2007].

* * * * *

(h) * * *

(1) * * *

(ii) [The text of the proposed amendment to § 1.883-1(h)(1)(ii) is the same as the text of § 1.883-1T(h)(1)(ii) published elsewhere in this issue of the Federal Register]. [See T.D. 9332, 06/25/2007].

(2) * * *

(3) [The text of the proposed amendment to § 1.883-1(h)(3) is the same as the text of § 1.883-1T(h)(3) published elsewhere in this issue of the Federal Register]. [See T.D. 9332, 06/25/2007].

* * * * *

§ 1.883-1T Exclusion of income from the international operation of ships or aircraft (temporary).

(a) through (c)(3)(i)(C) [Reserved]. For further guidance, see § 1.883-1(a) through (c)(3)(i)(C).

(c) *(3)* (i) (D) The applicable authority for an equivalent exemption, for example, the citation of a statute in the country where the corporation is organized, a diplomatic note between the United States and such country, or an income tax convention between the United States and such country in the case of a corporation described in paragraphs (h)(3)(i) through (iii) of this section;

(E) through (F) [Reserved]. For further guidance, see § 1.883-1(c)(3)(i)(E) through (F).

(G) A statement that none of the foreign corporation's shares or shares of any intermediary entity, if any, that are held by qualified shareholders and relied on to satisfy any of the stock ownership tests described in § 1.883-1(c)(2) are issued in bearer form;

(H) Any other information required under § 1.883-2(f), § 1.883-2T(f), § 1.883-3T(d), § 1.883-4(e), or § 1.883-4T(e), as applicable; and

(I) Any other relevant information specified in Form 1120-F, "U.S. Income Tax Return of a Foreign Corporation," and its accompanying instructions.

(ii) Further documentation. (A) General rule. Except as provided in this paragraph (c)(3)(ii)(B), if the Commissioner requests in writing that the foreign corporation document or substantiate representations made under paragraph (c)(3)(i) of this section, or under § 1.883-2(f), § 1.883-2T(f), § 1.883-3T(d), § 1.883-4(e), or § 1.883-4T(e), as applicable, the foreign corporation must provide the documentation or substantiation within 60 days following the written request. If the foreign corporation does not provide the documentation and substantiation requested within the 60-day period, but demonstrates that the failure was due to reasonable cause and not willful neglect, the Commissioner may grant the foreign corporation a 30-day extension. Whether a failure to obtain the documentation or substantiation in a timely manner was due to reasonable cause and not willful neglect shall be determined by the Commissioner after considering all the facts and circumstances.

(B) Names and addresses of certain shareholders. If the Commissioner requests the names and permanent addresses of individual qualified shareholders of a foreign corporation, as represented on each such individual's ownership statement, to substantiate the requirements of the exception to the closely-held test in the publicly-traded test in § 1.883-2(e), the qualified shareholder stock ownership test in § 1.883-4(a), or the qualified U.S. person ownership test in § 1.883-3T(b), the foreign corporation must provide the documentation and substantiation within 30 days following the written request. If the foreign corporation does not provide the documentation and substantiation within the 30-day period, but demonstrates that the failure was due to reasonable cause and not willful neglect, the Commissioner may grant the foreign corporation a 30-day extension. Whether a failure to obtain the documentation or substantiation in a timely manner was due to reasonable cause and not willful neglect shall be determined by the Commissioner after considering all the facts and circumstances.

(4) through (g)(1)(viii) [Reserved]. For further guidance see § 1.883-1(c)(4) through (g)(1)(viii).

(g) *(1)* (ix) Arranging by means of a space or slot charter for the carriage of cargo listed on a bill of lading or airway bill or similar document issued by the foreign corporation on the ship or aircraft of another corporation engaged in the international operation of ships or aircraft;

(x) The provision of containers and related equipment by the foreign corporation in connection with the international carriage of cargo for use by its customers, including short-term use within the United States immediately preceding or following the international carriage of cargo (and for this purpose, a period of five days or less shall be presumed to be short-term); and

(xi) The provision of goods and services by engineers, ground and equipment maintenance staff, cargo handlers, catering staff, and customer services personnel, and the provision of facilities such as passenger lounges, counter space, ground handling equipment, and hanger facilities.

(2) [Reserved]. For further guidance, see § 1.883-1(g)(2).

(3) Other services. [Reserved].

(4) through (h)(1)(i) [Reserved]. For further guidance, see § 1.883-1(g)(4) through (h)(1)(i).

(h) *(1)* (ii) Specifically provides a domestic law tax exemption for income derived from the international operation of ships or aircraft, either by statute, decree, income tax convention, or otherwise; or

(iii) and (h)(2) [Reserved]. For further guidance, see § 1.883-1(h)(1)(iii) and (h)(2).

(3) Special rules with respect to income tax conventions. (i) Countries with only an income tax convention. If a foreign country only provides an exemption from tax for profits from the operation of ships or aircraft in international transport or international traffic under the shipping and air transport or gains article of an income tax convention with the United States, a foreign corporation organized in that country may treat that exemption as an equivalent exemption for purposes of section 883, but only if—

(A) The foreign corporation meets all the conditions for claiming benefits with respect to such profits under the income tax convention; and

(B) The profits that are exempt pursuant to the income tax convention also fall within a category of income described in paragraphs (h)(2)(i) through (viii) of this section.

(ii) Countries with both an income tax convention and an equivalent exemption. (A) General rule. If a foreign country provides an exemption from tax for profits from the operation of ships or aircraft in international transport or international traffic under the shipping and air transport or gains article of an income tax convention, and that foreign country also provides an equivalent exemption under section 883 by some other means for one or more categories of income under paragraph (h)(2) of this section, the foreign corporation may choose annually whether to claim an exemption under section 883 or the income tax convention. Except as provided in this paragraph (h)(3)(ii)(B), any such choice will apply with respect to all categories of qualified income of the foreign corporation and cannot be made separately with respect to different categories of income. If a foreign corporation bases its claim for an exemption on section 883, it must satisfy all of the requirements of this section to qualify for an exemption from U.S. income tax. If the foreign corporation bases its claim for an exemption on an income tax convention, it must satisfy all of the requirements for claiming benefits under the income tax convention. See § 1.883-4(b)(3) for rules about satisfying the stock ownership test of § 1.883-1(c)(2) using shareholders resident in a foreign country that offers an exemption under an income tax convention.

(B) Special rule for simultaneous benefits under section 883 and an income tax convention. If a foreign corporation is organized in a foreign country that offers an exemption from tax under an income tax convention and also by some other means, such as by diplomatic note or domestic statutory law, with respect to the same category of income, and the foreign corporation chooses to claim an exemption under an income tax convention under paragraph (h)(3)(ii)(A) of this section, it may simultaneously claim an exemption under section 883 with respect to a category of income exempt from tax by such other means if it satisfies the requirements of paragraphs (h)(3)(i)(A) and (B) of this section for each category of income, satisfies one of the stock ownership tests of paragraph (c)(2) of this section, and complies with the substantiation and reporting requirements in paragraph (c)(3) of this section.

(iii) Participation in certain joint ventures. A foreign corporation resident in a foreign country that provides an exemption only through an income tax convention will not be precluded from treating that exemption as an equivalent exemption if it derives income through a participation, directly or indirectly, in a pool, partnership, strategic alliance, joint operating agreement, code-sharing arrangement, or other joint venture described in § 1.883-1(e)(2), and the foreign corporation would be ineligible to claim benefits under the convention for that category of income solely because the joint venture was not fiscally transparent, within the meaning of § 1.894-1(d)(3)(iii)(A), with respect to that category of income under the income tax laws of the foreign corporation's country of residence.

(iv) Independent interpretation of income tax conventions. Nothing in §§ 1.883-1 through 1.883-5, or in this section and §§ 1.883-2T through 1.883-5T, affects the rights or obligations under any income tax convention. The definitions provided in §§ 1.883-1 through 1.883-5, or in this section and §§ 1.883-2T through 1.883-5T, shall not give meaning to similar terms used in any income tax convention, or provide guidance regarding the scope of any exemption provided by such convention, unless the income tax convention entered into force after August 26, 2003, and it, or its legislative history, explicitly refers to section 883 and guidance promulgated under that section for its meaning.

T.D. 9332, 6/22/2007.

§ 1.883-2 Treatment of publicly-traded corporations.

(a) General rule. A foreign corporation satisfies the stock ownership test of § 1.883-1(c)(2) if it is considered a publicly-traded corporation and satisfies the substantiation and reporting requirements of paragraphs (e) and (f) of this section. To be considered a publicly-traded corporation, the stock of the foreign corporation must be primarily traded and regularly traded, as defined in paragraphs (c) and (d) of this section, respectively, on one or more established securities markets, as defined in paragraph (b) of this section, in either the United States or any qualified foreign country.

(b) Established securities market. *(1) General rule.* For purposes of this section, the term established securities market means, for any taxable year—

(i) A foreign securities exchange that is officially recognized, sanctioned, or supervised by a governmental authority of the qualified foreign country in which the market is located, and has an annual value of shares traded on the exchange exceeding $1 billion during each of the three calendar years immediately preceding the beginning of the taxable year;

(ii) A national securities exchange that is registered under section 6 of the Securities Act of 1934 (15 U.S.C. 78f);

(iii) A United States over-the-counter market, as defined in paragraph (b)(4) of this section;

(iv) Any exchange designated under a Limitation on Benefits article in a United States income tax convention; and

(v) Any other exchange that the Secretary may designate by regulation or otherwise.

(2) Exchanges with multiple tiers. If an exchange in a foreign country has more than one tier or market level on which stock may be separately listed or traded, each such tier shall be treated as a separate exchange.

(3) Computation of dollar value of stock traded. For purposes of paragraph (b)(1)(i) of this section, the value in U.S. dollars of shares traded during a calendar year shall be determined on the basis of the dollar value of such shares traded as reported by the International Federation of Stock Exchanges located in Paris, or, if not so reported, then by converting into U.S. dollars the aggregate value in local currency of the shares traded using an exchange rate equal to the average of the spot rates on the last day of each month of the calendar year.

(4) Over-the-counter market. An over-the-counter market is any market reflected by the existence of an interdealer quotation system. An interdealer quotation system is any system of general circulation to brokers and dealers that regularly disseminates quotations of stocks and securities by identified brokers or dealers, other than by quotation sheets that are prepared and distributed by a broker or dealer in the regular course of business and that contain only quotations of such broker or dealer.

(5) Discretion to determine that an exchange does not qualify as an established securities market. The Commissioner may determine that a securities exchange that otherwise meets the requirements of paragraph (b) of this section does not qualify as an established securities market, if—

(i) The exchange does not have adequate listing, financial disclosure, or trading requirements (or does not adequately enforce such requirements); or

(ii) There is not clear and convincing evidence that the exchange ensures the active trading of listed stocks.

(c) Primarily traded. For purposes of this section, stock of a corporation is primarily traded in a country on one or more established securities markets, as defined in paragraph (b) of this section, if, with respect to each class of stock described in paragraph (d)(1)(i) of this section (relating to classes of stock relied on to meet the regularly traded test)—

(1) The number of shares in each such class that are traded during the taxable year on all established securities markets in that country exceeds.

(2) The number of shares in each such class that are traded during that year on established securities markets in any other single country.

(d) Regularly traded.

(1) General rule. For purposes of this section, stock of a corporation is regularly traded on one or more established securities markets, as defined in paragraph (b) of this section, if—

(i) One or more classes of stock of the corporation that, in the aggregate, represent more than 50 percent of the total combined voting power of all classes of stock of such corporation entitled to vote and of the total value of the stock of such corporation are listed on such market or markets during the taxable year; and

(ii) With respect to each class relied on to meet the more than 50 percent requirement of paragraph (d)(1)(i) of this section—

(A) Trades in each such class are effected, other than in de minimis quantities, on such market or markets on at least 60 days during the taxable year (or ⅙ of the number of days in a short taxable year); and

(B) The aggregate number of shares in each such class that are traded on such market or markets during the taxable year are at least 10 percent of the average number of shares outstanding in that class during the taxable year (or, in the case of a short taxable year, a percentage that equals at least 10 percent of the average number of shares outstanding in that class during the taxable year multiplied by the number of days in the short taxable year, divided by 365).

(2) Classes of stock traded on a domestic established securities market treated as meeting trading requirements. A class of stock that is traded during the taxable year on an established securities market located in the United States shall be considered to meet the trading requirements of paragraph

(d)(1)(ii) of this section if the stock is regularly quoted by dealers making a market in the stock. A dealer makes a market in a stock only if the dealer regularly and actively offers to, and in fact does, purchase the stock from, and sell the stock to, customers who are not related persons (as defined in section 954(d)(3)) with respect to the dealer in the ordinary course of a trade or business.

(3) Closely-held classes of stock not treated as meeting trading requirements. (i) General rule. Except as provided in paragraph (d)(3)(ii) of this section, a class of stock of a foreign corporation that otherwise meets the requirements of paragraph (d)(1) or (2) of this section shall not be treated as meeting such requirements for a taxable year if, for more than half the number of days during the taxable year, one or more persons who own at least 5 percent of the vote and value of the outstanding shares of the class of stock, as determined under paragraph (d)(3)(iii) of this section (each a 5-percent shareholder), own, in the aggregate, 50 percent or more of the vote and value of the outstanding shares of the class of stock. If one or more 5-percent shareholders own, in the aggregate, 50 percent or more of the vote and value of the outstanding shares of the class of stock, such shares held by the 5-percent shareholders will constitute a closely-held block of stock.

(ii) Exception. Paragraph (d)(3)(i) of this section shall not apply to a class of stock if the foreign corporation can establish that qualified shareholders, as defined in § 1.883-4(b), applying the attribution rules of § 1.883-4(c), own sufficient shares in the closely-held block of stock to preclude nonqualified shareholders in the closely-held block of stock from owning 50 percent or more of the total value of the class of stock of which the closely-held block is a part for more than half the number of days during the taxable year. Any shares that are owned, after application of the attribution rules in § 1.883-4(c), by a qualified shareholder shall not also be treated as owned by a nonqualified shareholder in the chain of ownership for purposes of the preceding sentence. A foreign corporation must obtain the documentation described in § 1.883-4(d) from the qualified shareholders relied upon to satisfy this exception. However, no person shall be treated for purposes of this paragraph (d)(3) as a qualified shareholder if such person holds an interest in the class of stock directly or indirectly through bearer shares.

(iii) Five-percent shareholders. (A) Related persons. Solely for purposes of determining whether a person is a 5-percent shareholder, persons related within the meaning of section 267(b) shall be treated as one person. In determining whether two or more corporations are members of the same controlled group under section 267(b)(3), a person is considered to own stock owned directly by such person, stock owned through the application of section 1563(e)(1), and stock owned through the application of section 267(c). In determining whether a corporation is related to a partnership under section 267(b)(10), a person is considered to own the partnership interest owned directly by such person and the partnership interest owned through the application of section 267(e)(3).

(B) Investment companies. For purposes of this paragraph (d)(3), an investment company registered under the Investment Company Act of 1940, as amended (54 Stat. 789), shall not be treated as a 5-percent shareholder.

(4) Anti-abuse rule. Trades between or among related persons described in section 267(b), as modified by paragraph (d)(3)(iii) of this section, and trades conducted in order to meet the requirements of paragraph (d)(1) of this section shall be disregarded. A class of stock shall not be treated as meeting the trading requirements of paragraph (d)(1) of this section if there is a pattern of trades conducted to meet the requirements of that paragraph. For example, trades between two persons that occur several times during the taxable year may be treated as an arrangement or a pattern of trades conducted to meet the trading requirements of paragraph (d)(1)(ii) of this section.

(5) Example. The closely-held test in paragraph (d)(3) of this section is illustrated by the following example:

Example. Closely-held exception.

(i) Facts. X is a foreign corporation organized in a qualified foreign country and engaged in the international operation of ships. X has one class of stock, which is primarily traded on an established securities market in the qualified foreign country. The stock of X meets the regularly traded requirements of paragraph (d)(1)(ii) of this section without regard to paragraph (d)(3)(i) of this section. A, B, C and D are four members of the corporation's founding family who each own, during the entire taxable year, 25 percent of the stock of Hold Co., a company that issues registered shares. Hold Co., in turn, owns 60 percent of the stock of X during the entire taxable year. The remaining 40 percent of the stock of X is not owned by any 5-percent shareholder, as determined under paragraph (d)(3)(iii) of this section. A, B, and C are not residents of a qualified foreign country, but D is a resident of a qualified foreign country.

(ii) Analysis. Because Hold Co. owns 60 percent of the stock of X for more than half the number of days during the taxable year, Hold Co. is a 5-percent shareholder that owns 50 percent or more of the value of the stock of X. Thus, the shares owned by Hold Co. constitute a closely-held block of stock. Under paragraph (d)(3)(i) of this section, the stock of X will not be regularly traded within the meaning of paragraph (d)(1) of this section unless X can establish, under paragraph (d)(3)(ii) of this section, that qualified shareholders within the closely-held block of stock own sufficient shares in the closely-held block of stock to preclude nonqualified shareholders in the closely-held block of stock from owning 50 percent or more of the value of the outstanding shares in the class of stock for more than half the number of days during the taxable year. A, B, and C are not qualified shareholders within the meaning of § 1.883-4(b) because they are not residents of a qualified foreign country, but D is a resident of a qualified foreign country and therefore is a qualified shareholder. D owns 15 percent of the outstanding shares of X through Hold Co. (25 percent x 60 percent = 15 percent) while A, B, and C in the aggregate own 45 percent of the outstanding shares of X through Hold Co.. D, therefore, owns sufficient shares in the closely-held block of stock to preclude the nonqualified shareholders in the closely-held block of stock, A, B and C, from owning 50 percent or more of the value of the class of stock (60 percent-15 percent = 45 percent) of which the closely-held block is a part. Provided that X obtains from D the documentation described in § 1.883-4(d), X's sole class of stock meets the exception in paragraph (d)(3)(ii) of this section and will not be disqualified from the regularly traded test by virtue of paragraph (d)(3)(i) of this section.

(e) Substantiation that a foreign corporation is publicly traded. *(1) General rule.* A foreign corporation that relies on the publicly traded test of this section to meet the stock ownership test of § 1.883-1(c)(2) must substantiate that the stock of the foreign corporation is primarily and regularly traded on one or more established securities markets, as that term is defined in paragraph (b) of this section. If one of the classes of stock on which the foreign corporation relies to meet this test is closely-held within the meaning of paragraph (d)(3)(i) of this section, the foreign corporation must obtain an ownership statement described in § 1.883-4(d) from each qualified shareholder and intermediary that it relies upon to satisfy the exception to the closely-held test, but only to the extent such statement would be required if the foreign corporation were relying on the qualified shareholder stock ownership test of § 1.883-4 with respect to those shares of stock. The foreign corporation must also maintain and provide to the Commissioner upon request a list of its shareholders of record and any other relevant information known to the foreign corporation supporting its entitlement to an exemption under this section.

(2) [Reserved]. For further guidance, see § 1.883-2T(e)(2).

(f) Reporting requirements. A foreign corporation relying on this section to satisfy the stock ownership test of § 1.883-1(c)(2) must provide the following information in addition to the information required in § 1.883-1(c)(3) to be included in its Form 1120-F, "U.S. Income Tax Return of a Foreign Corporation," for the taxable year. The information must be current as of the end of the corporation's taxable year and must include the following—

(1) The name of the country in which the stock is primarily traded;

(2) The name of the established securities market or markets on which the stock is listed;

(3) [Reserved]. For further guidance, see § 1.883-2T(f)(3).

(4) For each class of stock relied upon to meet the requirements of paragraph (d) of this section, if one or more 5-percent shareholders, as defined in paragraph (d)(3)(i) of this section, own in the aggregate 50 percent or more of the vote and value of the outstanding shares of that class of stock for more than half the number of days during the taxable year—

(i) The days during the taxable year of the corporation in which the stock was closely-held without regard to the exception in paragraph (d)(3)(ii) of this section and the percentage of the vote and value of the class of stock that is owned by 5-percent shareholders during such days;

(ii) [Reserved]. For further guidance, see § 1.883-2T(f)(4)(ii).

(5) Any other relevant information specified by Form 1120-F and its accompanying instructions.

T.D. 9087, 8/25/2003, amend T.D. 9332, 6/22/2007.

PAR. 4. Section 1.883-2 is amended by revising paragraphs (e)(2), (f)(3), and (f)(4)(ii) to read as follows:

Proposed § 1.883-2 Treatment of publicly-traded corporations. [*For Preamble, see ¶ 152,877*]

* * * * *

(e) * * *

(2) [The text of the proposed amendment to § 1.883-2(e)(2) is the same as the text of § 1.883-2T(e)(2) published elsewhere in this issue of the Federal Register]. [See T.D. 9332, 06/25/2007].

(f) * * *

(3) [The text of the proposed amendment to § 1.883-2(f)(3) is the same as the text of § 1.883-2T(f)(3) published elsewhere in this issue of the Federal Register]. [See T.D. 9332, 06/25/2007].

(4) * * *

(ii) [The text of the proposed amendment to § 1.883-2(f)(4)(ii) is the same as the text of § 1.883-2T(f)(4)(ii) published elsewhere in this issue of the Federal Register]. [See T.D. 9332, 06/25/2007].

* * * * *

§ 1.883-2T Treatment of publicly-traded corporations (temporary).

(a) through (e)(1) [Reserved]. For further guidance, see § 1.883-2(a) through (e)(1).

(e) *(2) Availability and retention of documents for inspection.* The documentation described in § 1.883-2(e)(1) must be retained by the corporation seeking qualified foreign corporation status until the expiration of the statute of limitations for the taxable year of the foreign corporation to which the documentation relates. Such documentation must be made available for inspection by the Commissioner at such time and such place as the Commissioner may request in writing in accordance with § 1.883-1T(c)(3)(ii)(A) or (B), as applicable.

(f) through (f)(2) [Reserved]. For further guidance, see § 1.883-2(f) through (f)(2).

(3) A description of each class of stock relied upon to meet the requirements of § 1.883-2(d), including whether the class of stock is issued in registered or bearer form, the number of issued and outstanding shares in that class of stock as of the close of the taxable year, and the value of each class of stock in relation to the total value of all the corporation's shares outstanding as of the close of the taxable year;

(4) and (4)(i) [Reserved]. For further guidance, see § 1.883-2(f)(4) and (f)(4)(i).

(ii) With respect to all qualified shareholders who own directly, or by application of the attribution rules in § 1.883-4(c), stock in the closely-held block of stock upon which the corporation intends to rely to satisfy the exception to the closely-held test of § 1.883-2(d)(3)(ii)--

(A) The total number of qualified shareholders, as defined in § 1.883-4(b)(1);

(B) The total percentage of the value of the shares owned, directly or indirectly, by such qualified shareholders by country of residence, determined under § 1.883-4(b)(2) (residence of individual shareholders) or § 1.883-4(d)(3) (special rules for residence of certain shareholders); and

(C) The days during the taxable year of the corporation that such qualified shareholders owned, directly or indirectly, their shares in the closely held block of stock.

(5) [Reserved]. For further guidance, see § 1.883-2(f)(5).

T.D. 9332, 6/22/2007.

§ 1.883-3 Treatment of controlled foreign corporations.

[Reserved]. For further guidance, see § 1.883-3T.

T.D. 9087, 8/25/2003, amend T.D. 9332, 6/22/2007.

PAR. 5.

Section 1.883-3 is revised to read as follows:

Proposed § 1.883-3 Treatment of controlled foreign corporations. [*For Preamble, see ¶ 152,877*]

[The text of this proposed section is the same as the text of § 1.883-3T published elsewhere in this issue of the Federal Register]. [See T.D. 9332, 06/25/2007].

§ 1.883-3T Treatment of controlled foreign corporations (temporary).

(a) General rule. A foreign corporation satisfies the stock ownership test of § 1.883-1(c)(2) if it is a controlled foreign corporation (as defined in section 957(a)), satisfies the qualified U.S. person ownership test in paragraph (b) of this section, and satisfies the substantiation and reporting requirements of paragraphs (c) and (d) of this section, respectively. A CFC that fails the qualified U.S. person ownership test of paragraph (b) of this section will not satisfy the stock ownership test of § 1.883-1(c)(2) unless it meets either the publicly-traded test of § 1.883-2(a) or the qualified shareholder stock ownership test of § 1.883-4(a).

(b) Qualified U.S. person ownership test. *(1) General rule.* A foreign corporation will satisfy the requirements of the qualified U.S. person ownership test only if it—

(i) Is a CFC for more than half the days in the corporation's taxable year; and

(ii) More than 50 percent of the total value of its outstanding stock is owned (within the meaning of section 958(a) and paragraph (b)(4) of this section) by one or more qualified U.S. persons for more than half the days of the CFC's taxable year, provided such days of ownership are concurrent with the time period during which the foreign corporation satisfies the requirement in paragraph (b)(1)(i) of this section.

(2) Qualified U.S. person. For purposes of this section, the term qualified U.S. person means a U.S. citizen, resident alien, domestic corporation, or domestic trust described in section 501(a), but only if the person provides the CFC with an ownership statement as described in paragraph (c)(2) of this section, and the CFC meets the reporting requirements of paragraph (d) of this section with respect to that person.

(3) Treatment of bearer shares. For purposes of applying the qualified U.S. person ownership test, the value of the stock of a CFC that is owned (directly or indirectly) through bearer shares by qualified U.S. persons is not taken into account in the numerator of the fraction, but is taken into account in the denominator to determine the portion of the value of stock owned by qualified U.S. persons.

(4) Attribution of ownership through certain domestic entities. For purposes of applying the qualified U.S. person ownership test of paragraph (b)(1) of this section, stock owned, directly or indirectly, by or for a domestic partnership, domestic trust not described in section 501(a), or domestic estate, shall be treated as owned proportionately by its partners, beneficiaries, grantors, or other interest holders, respectively, applying the rules of section 958(a) as if such domestic entity were a foreign entity. Stock considered to be owned by a person by reason of the preceding sentence shall, for purposes of applying such sentence, be treated as actually owned by such person.

(5) Examples. The qualified U.S. person ownership test of paragraph (b)(1) of this section is illustrated in the following examples:

Example (1). Ship Co is a CFC for more than half the days of Ship Co's taxable year. Ship Co is organized in a qualified foreign country. All of its shares are owned by a domestic partnership for the entire taxable year. All of the partners in the domestic partnership are citizens and residents of foreign countries. Ship Co fails the qualified U.S. person ownership test of paragraph (b)(1) of this section because none of the value of Ship Co's stock is owned, applying the attribution rules of paragraph (b)(4) of this section, for at least half the number of days of Ship Co's taxable year, by one or more qualified U.S. persons. Therefore, Ship Co must satisfy the qualified shareholder stock ownership test of § 1.883-4(a) in order to satisfy the stock ownership test of § 1.883-1(c)(2), and be considered a qualified foreign corporation.

Example (2). Ship Co is a CFC for more than half the days of its taxable year. Ship Co is organized in a qualified foreign country. Corp A, a foreign corporation whose stock is owned by a citizen and resident of a foreign country, owns 40 percent of the value of the stock of Ship Co for the entire taxable year. X, a domestic partnership, owns the remaining 60 percent of the value of the stock of Ship Co for Ship Co's entire taxable year. X is owned by 20 partners, all of whom are U.S. citizens and each of whom has owned a 5-percent interest in X for the entire taxable year of Ship Co. Ship Co satisfies the qualified U.S. person ownership test of paragraph (b)(1) of this section because 60 percent of the value of the stock of Ship Co is owned, applying the attribution of ownership rules of paragraph (b)(4) of this section, for at least half the number of days of Ship Co's taxable year by the partners of X, who are all qualified U.S. persons as defined in paragraph (b)(2) of this section. If Ship Co satisfies the substantiation and reporting requirements of paragraphs (c) and (d) of this section, it will meet the stock ownership test of § 1.883-1(c)(2).

Example (3). Ship Co is a foreign corporation organized in a qualified foreign country. Ship Co has two classes of stock, Class A representing 60 percent of the vote and value of all the shares outstanding of Ship Co, and Class B representing the remaining 40 percent of the vote and value of Ship Co. A, a U.S. citizen, holds for the entire taxable year all of the Class A stock, which is issued in bearer form, and B, a nonresident alien, owns all the Class B stock, which is in registered form. Ship Co cannot satisfy the qualified U.S. person ownership test of paragraph (b)(1) of this section because A's bearer shares cannot be taken into account as being owned by a qualified U.S. person in determining if the qualified U.S. person ownership test has been met; the shares are, however, taken into account in determining the total value of Ship Co's outstanding shares.

(c) Substantiation of CFC stock ownership. *(1) In general.* A foreign corporation that relies on this CFC test to satisfy the stock ownership test of § 1.883-1(c)(2) must establish all the facts necessary to demonstrate to the Commissioner that it satisfies the qualified U.S. person ownership test of paragraph (b)(1) of this section. Specifically, the CFC must obtain a written ownership statement, signed under penalties of perjury by an individual authorized to sign that person's Federal tax or information return, from—

(i) Each qualified U.S. person upon whose stock ownership it relies to meet this test; and

(ii) Each domestic intermediary described in paragraph (b)(4) of this section, each foreign intermediary (including a foreign corporation, partnership, trust, or estate), and mere legal owners or record holders acting as nominees standing in the chain of ownership between each such qualified U.S. person and the CFC, if any.

(2) Ownership statements from qualified U.S. persons. A qualified U.S. person ownership statement must contain the following information:

(i) The qualified U.S. person's name, permanent address, and taxpayer identification number.

(ii) If the qualified U.S. person owns shares directly in the CFC, the number of shares of each class of stock of the CFC owned by the qualified person, the period of time during the taxable year of the CFC when the person owned the stock, and a representation that its interest in the CFC is not held through bearer shares.

(iii) If the qualified person owns an indirect interest in the CFC through an intermediary described in paragraph (c)(1)(ii) of this section, the name of that intermediary, the amount and nature of the interest in the intermediary, the period of time during the taxable year of the CFC when the person held such interest, and, in the case of an interest in a foreign corporate intermediary, a representation that such interest is not held through bearer shares.

(iv) Any other information as specified in guidance published by the Internal Revenue Service (see § 601.601(d)(2) of this chapter).

(3) Ownership statements from intermediaries. An intermediary ownership statement required of an intermediary described in paragraph (c)(1)(ii) of this section must contain the following information:

(i) The intermediary's name, permanent address, and taxpayer identification number, if any.

(ii) If the intermediary directly owns stock in the CFC, the number of shares of each class of stock of the CFC owned by the intermediary, the period of time during the taxable year of the CFC when the intermediary owned the stock, and a representation that such interest is not held through bearer shares.

(iii) If the intermediary indirectly owns the stock of the CFC, the name and address of each intermediary standing in the chain of ownership between it and the CFC, the period of time during the taxable year of the CFC when the intermediary owned the interest, the percentage of interest it holds indirectly in the CFC, and, in the case of a foreign corporate intermediary, a representation that its interest is not held through bearer shares.

(iv) Any other information as specified in guidance published by the Internal Revenue Service (see § 601.601(d)(2) of this chapter).

(4) Three-year period of validity. The rules of § 1.883-4(d)(2)(ii) apply for purposes of determining the validity of the ownership statements required under paragraph (c)(2) of this section.

(5) Availability and retention of documents for inspection. The documentation described in this paragraph (c) must be retained by the corporation seeking qualified foreign corporation status (the CFC) until the expiration of the statute of limitations for the taxable year of the CFC to which the documentation relates. Such documentation must be made available for inspection by the Commissioner at such place as the Commissioner may request in writing in accordance with § 1.883-1T(c)(3)(ii).

(d) Reporting requirements. Foreign corporation that relies on the CFC test of this section to satisfy the stock ownership test of § 1.883-1(c)(2) must provide the following information in addition to the information required by § 1.883-1(c)(3) to be included in its Form 1120-F, "U.S. Income Tax Return of a Foreign Corporation," for the taxable year. The information must be based upon the documentation received by the foreign corporation pursuant to paragraph (c) of this section and must be current as of the end of the corporation's taxable year—

(1) The percentage of the value of the shares of the CFC that is owned by all qualified U.S. persons identified in paragraph (c)(2) of this section, applying the attribution of ownership rules of paragraph (b)(4) of this section;

(2) The period during which such qualified U.S. persons held such stock;

(3) The period during which the foreign corporation was a CFC;

(4) A statement that the CFC is directly held by qualified U.S. persons and does not have any bearer shares outstanding or, in the alternative, that it is not relying on direct or indirect ownership of such shares to meet the qualified U.S. person ownership test; and

(5) Any other relevant information specified by Form 1120-F, and its accompanying instructions, or in guidance published by the Internal Revenue Service (see § 601.601(d)(2) of this chapter).

T.D. 9332, 6/22/2007.

§ 1.883-4 Qualified shareholder stock ownership test.

(a) General rule. A foreign corporation satisfies the stock ownership test of § 1.883-1(c)(2) if more than 50 percent of the value of its outstanding shares is owned, or treated as owned by applying the attribution rules of paragraph (c) of this section, for at least half of the number of days in the foreign corporation's taxable year by one or more qualified shareholders, as defined in paragraph (b) of this section. A shareholder may be a qualified shareholder with respect to one category of income while not being a qualified shareholder with respect to another. A foreign corporation will not be considered to satisfy the stock ownership test of § 1.883-1(c)(2) pursuant to this section unless the foreign corporation meets the substantiation and reporting requirements of paragraphs (d) and (e) of this section.

(b) Qualified shareholder. *(1) General rule.* A shareholder is a qualified shareholder only if the shareholder—

(i) With respect to the category of income for which the foreign corporation is seeking an exemption, is—

(A) An individual who is a resident, as described in paragraph (b)(2) of this section, of a qualified foreign country;

(B) The government of a qualified foreign country (or a political subdivision or local authority of such country);

(C) A foreign corporation that is organized in a qualified foreign country and meets the publicly traded test of § 1.883-2(a);

(D) A not-for-profit organization described in paragraph (b)(4) of this section that is not a pension fund as defined in paragraph (b)(5) of this section and that is organized in a qualified foreign country;

(E) An individual beneficiary of a pension fund (as defined in paragraph (b)(5)(iv) of this section) that is administered in or by a qualified foreign country, who is treated as a resident under paragraph (d)(3)(iii) of this section, of a qualified foreign country; or

(F) A shareholder of a foreign corporation that is an airline covered by a bilateral Air Services Agreement in force between the United States and the qualified foreign country in which the airline is organized, provided the United States has not waived the ownership requirement in the Air Services Agreement, or that the ownership requirement has not otherwise been made ineffective;

(ii) Does not own its interest in the foreign corporation through bearer shares, either directly or by applying the attribution rules of paragraph (c) of this section; and

(iii) Provides to the foreign corporation the documentation required in paragraph (d) of this section and the foreign corporation meets the reporting requirements of paragraph (e) of this section with respect to such shareholder.

(2) Residence of individual shareholders. (i) General rule. An individual described in paragraph (b)(1)(i)(A) of this section is a resident of a qualified foreign country only if the individual is fully liable to tax as a resident in such country (e.g., an individual who is liable to tax on a remittance basis in a foreign country will not be treated as a resident of that country unless all residents of that country are taxed on a remittance basis only) and, in addition—

(A) The individual has a tax home, within the meaning of paragraph (b)(2)(ii) of this section, in that qualified foreign country for 183 days or more of the taxable year; or

(B) The individual is treated as a resident of a qualified foreign country based on special rules pursuant to paragraph (d)(3) of this section.

(ii) Tax home. For purposes of this section, an individual's tax home is considered to be located at the individual's regular or principal (if more than one regular) place of business. If the individual has no regular or principal place of business because of the nature of his business (or lack of a business), then the individual's tax home is located at his regular place of abode in a real and substantial sense. If an individual has no regular or principal place of business and no regular place of abode in a real and substantial sense in a qualified foreign country for 183 days or more of the taxable year, that individual does not have a tax home for purposes of this section. A foreign estate or trust, as defined in section 7701(a)(31), does not have a tax home for purposes of this section. See paragraph (c)(3) of this section for alternative rules in the case of trusts or estates.

(3) Certain income tax convention restrictions applied to shareholders. For purposes of paragraph (b)(1) of this section, a shareholder described in paragraph (b)(1) of this section may be considered a resident of, or organized in, a qualified foreign country if that foreign country provides an exemption by means of an income tax convention with the United States, but only if the shareholder demonstrates that it is treated as a resident of that country under the convention and qualifies for benefits under any Limitation on Benefits article, and that the convention provides an exemption for the relevant category of income. If the convention has a requirement in the shipping and air transport article other than residence, such as place of registration or documentation of the ship or aircraft, the shareholder is not required to demonstrate that the corporation seeking qualified foreign corporation status could satisfy any such additional requirement.

(4) Not-for-profit organizations. The term not-for-profit organization means an organization that meets the following requirements—

(i) It is a corporation, association taxable as a corporation, trust, fund, foundation, league or other entity operated exclusively for religious, charitable, educational, or recreational purposes, and not organized for profit;

(ii) It is generally exempt from tax in its country of organization by virtue of its not-for-profit status; and

(iii) Either—

(A) More than 50 percent of its annual support is expended on behalf of individuals described in paragraph (b)(1)(i)(A) of this section (see paragraph (d)(3)(v) of this section for special rules to substantiate the residence of individual beneficiaries of not-for-profit organizations) and on behalf of U.S. exempt organizations that have received determination letters under section 501(c)(3); or

(B) More than 50 percent of its annual support is derived from individuals described in paragraph (b)(1)(i)(A) of this section (see paragraph (d)(3)(v) of this section for special rules to substantiate the residence of individual supporters of not-for-profit organizations).

(5) Pension funds. (i) Pension fund defined. The term pension fund shall mean a government pension fund or a nongovernment pension fund, as those terms are defined, respectively, in paragraphs (b)(5)(ii) and (iii) of this section, that is a trust, fund, foundation, or other entity that is established exclusively for the benefit of employees or former employees of one or more employers, the principal purpose of which is to provide retirement, disability, and death benefits to beneficiaries of such entity and persons designated by such beneficiaries in consideration for prior services rendered.

(ii) Government pension funds. A government pension fund is a pension fund that is a controlled entity of a foreign sovereign within the principles of § 1.892-2T(c)(1) (relating to pension funds established for the benefit of employees or former employees of a foreign government).

(iii) Nongovernment pension funds. A nongovernment pension fund is a pension fund that—

(A) Is administered in a foreign country and is subject to supervision or regulation by a governmental authority (or other authority delegated to perform such supervision or regulation by a governmental authority) in such country;

(B) Is generally exempt from income taxation in its country of administration;

(C) Has 100 or more beneficiaries; and

(D) The trustees, directors or other administrators of which pension fund provide the documentation required in paragraph (d) of this section.

(iv) Beneficiary of a pension fund. The term beneficiary of a pension fund shall mean any person who has made contributions to a pension fund, as that term is defined in paragraph (b)(5)(i) of this section, or on whose behalf contributions have been made, and who is currently receiving retirement, disability, or death benefits from the pension fund or can reasonably be expected to receive such benefits in the future, whether or not the person's right to receive benefits from the fund has vested. See paragraph (c)(7) of this section for rules regarding the computation of stock ownership through nongovernment pension funds.

(c) Rules for determining constructive ownership. *(1) General rules for attribution.* For purposes of applying paragraph (a) of this section and the exception to the closely-held test in § 1.883-2(d)(3)(ii), stock owned by or for a corporation, partnership, trust, estate, or mutual insurance company or similar entity shall be treated as owned proportionately by its shareholders, partners, beneficiaries, grantors, or other interest holders, as provided in paragraphs (c)(2) through (7) of this section. The proportionate interest rules of this paragraph (c) shall apply successively upward through a chain of ownership, and a person's proportionate interest shall be computed for the relevant days or period taken into account in determining whether a foreign corporation satisfies the requirements of paragraph (a) of this section. Stock treated as owned by a person by reason of this paragraph (c) shall be treated as actually owned by such person for purposes of this section. An owner of an interest in an association taxable as a corporation shall be treated as a shareholder of such association for purposes of this paragraph (c). No attribution will apply to an interest held directly or indirectly through bearer shares.

(2) Partnerships. (i) General rule. A partner shall be treated as having an interest in stock of a foreign corporation owned by a partnership in proportion to the least of—

(A) The partner's percentage distributive share of the partnership's dividend income from the stock;

(B) The partner's percentage distributive share of gain from disposition of the stock by the partnership; or

(C) The partner's percentage distributive share of the stock (or proceeds from the disposition of the stock) upon liquidation of the partnership.

(ii) Partners resident in the same country. For purposes of this paragraph, all qualified shareholders that are partners in a partnership and that are residents of, or organized in, the same qualified foreign country shall be treated as one partner. Thus, the percentage distributive shares of dividend income, gain and liquidation rights of all qualified shareholders that are partners in a partnership and that are residents of, or organized in, the same qualified foreign country are aggregated prior to determining the least of the three percentages set out in paragraph (c)(2)(i) of this section. For the meaning of the term resident, see paragraph (b)(2) of this section.

(iii) Examples. The rules of paragraph (c)(2)(ii) of this section are illustrated by the following examples:

Example (1). Stock held solely by qualified shareholders through a partnership. Country X grants an equivalent exemption. A and B are individual residents of Country X and are qualified shareholders within the meaning of paragraph (b)(1) of this section. A and B are the sole partners of Partnership P. P's only asset is the stock of Corporation Z, a Country X corporation seeking a reciprocal exemption under this section. A's distributive share of P's income and gain on the disposition of P's assets is 80 percent, but A's distributive share of P's assets (or the proceeds therefrom) on P's liquidation is 20 percent. B's distributive share of P's income and gain is 20 percent and B is entitled to 80 percent of the assets (or proceeds therefrom) on P's liquidation. Under the attribution rules of paragraph (c)(2)(ii) of this section, A and B will be treated as a single partner owning in the aggregate 100 percent of the stock of Z owned by P.

Example (2). Stock held by both qualified and nonqualified shareholders through a partnership. Assume the same facts as in Example 1 except that C, an individual who is not a resident of a qualified foreign country, is also a partner in P and that C's distributive share of P's income is 60 percent. The distributive shares of A and B are the same as in Example 1, except that A's distributive share of income is 20 percent. Under the attribution rules of paragraph (c)(2)(ii) of this section, qualified shareholders A and B will be treated as a single partner owning in the aggregate 40 percent of the stock of Z owned by P (i.e., the lowest aggregate percentage of A and B's distributive shares of dividend income (40 percent), gain (100 percent), and liquidation rights (100 percent) with respect to the Z stock). Thus, only 40 percent of the Z stock is treated as owned by qualified shareholders.

Example (3). Stock held through tiered partnerships. Country X grants an equivalent exemption. A and B are individual residents of Country X and are qualified shareholders within the meaning of paragraph (b)(1) of this section. A and B are the sole partners of Partnership P. P is a partner in Partnership P1, which owns the stock of Corporation Z, a Country X corporation seeking a reciprocal exemption under this section. Assume that P's distributive share of the dividend income, gain and liquidation rights with respect to the Z stock held by P1 is 40 percent. Assume that of the remaining partners of P1 only D is a qualified shareholder. D's distributive share of P1's dividend income and gain is 15 percent; D's distributive share of P1's assets on liquidation is 25 percent. Under the attribution rules of paragraph (c)(2)(ii) of this section, A and B, treated as a single partner, will own 40 percent of the Z stock owned by P1 (100 percent x 40 percent) and D will be treated as owning 15 percent of the Z stock owned by P1 (the least of D's dividend income (15 percent), gain (15 percent), and liquidation rights (25 percent) with respect to the Z stock). Thus, 55 percent of the Z stock owned by P1 is treated as owned by qualified shareholders.

(3) Trusts and estates. (i) Beneficiaries. In general, an individual shall be treated as having an interest in stock of a foreign corporation owned by a trust or estate in proportion to the individual's actuarial interest in the trust or estate, as provided in section 318(a)(2)(B)(i), except that an income beneficiary's actuarial interest in the trust will be determined as if the trust's only asset were the stock. The interest of a remainder beneficiary in stock will be equal to 100 percent minus the sum of the percentages of any interest in the stock held by income beneficiaries. The ownership of an interest in stock owned by a trust shall not be attributed to any beneficiary whose interest cannot be determined under the preceding sentence, and any such interest, to the extent not attributed by reason of this paragraph (c)(3)(i), shall not be considered owned by a beneficiary unless all potential beneficiaries with respect to the stock are qualified shareholders. In addition, a beneficiary's actuarial interest will be treated as zero to the extent that someone other than the beneficiary is treated as owning the stock under paragraph (c)(3)(ii) of this section. A substantially separate and independent share of a trust, within the meaning of section 663(c), shall be treated as a separate trust for purposes of this paragraph (c)(3)(i), provided that payment of income, accumulated income or corpus of a share of one beneficiary (or group of beneficiaries) cannot affect the proportionate share of income, accumulated income or corpus of another beneficiary (or group of beneficiaries).

(ii) Grantor trusts. A person is treated as the owner of stock of a foreign corporation owned by a trust to the extent that the stock is included in the portion of the trust that is treated as owned by the person under sections 671 through 679 (relating to grantors and others treated as substantial owners).

(4) Corporations that issue stock. A shareholder of a corporation that issues stock shall be treated as owning stock of a foreign corporation that is owned by such corporation on any day in a proportion that equals the value of the stock owned by such shareholder to the value of all stock of such corporation. If, however, there is an agreement, express or implied, that a shareholder of a corporation will not receive distributions from the earnings of stock owned by the corporation, the shareholder will not be treated as owning that stock owned by the corporation.

(5) Taxable nonstock corporations. A taxable nonstock corporation that is entitled in its country of organization to deduct from its taxable income amounts distributed for charitable purposes may deem a recipient of such charitable distributions to be a shareholder of such taxable nonstock corporation in the same proportion as the amount that such beneficiary receives in the taxable year bears to the total income of such taxable nonstock corporation in the taxable year. Whether each such recipient is a qualified shareholder may then be determined under paragraph (b) of this section

or under the special rules of paragraph (d)(3)(vii) of this section.

(6) Mutual insurance companies and similar entities. Stock held by a mutual insurance company, mutual savings bank, or similar entity (including an association taxable as a corporation that does not issue stock interests) shall be considered owned proportionately by the policyholders, depositors, or other owners in the same proportion that such persons share in the surplus of such entity upon liquidation or dissolution.

(7) Computation of beneficial interests in nongovernment pension funds. Stock held by a pension fund shall be considered owned by the beneficiaries of the fund equally on a pro-rata basis if—

(i) The pension fund meets the requirements of paragraph (b)(5)(iii) of this section;

(ii) The trustees, directors or other administrators of the pension fund have no knowledge, and no reason to know, that a pro-rata allocation of interests of the fund to all beneficiaries would differ significantly from an actuarial allocation of interests in the fund (or, if the beneficiaries' actuarial interest in the stock held directly or indirectly by the pension fund differs from the beneficiaries' actuarial interest in the pension fund, the actuarial interests computed by reference to the beneficiaries' actuarial interest in the stock);

(iii) Either—

(A) Any overfunding of the pension fund would be payable, pursuant to the governing instrument or the laws of the foreign country in which the pension fund is administered, only to, or for the benefit of, one or more corporations that are organized in the country in which the pension fund is administered, individual beneficiaries of the pension fund or their designated beneficiaries, or social or charitable causes (the reduction of the obligation of the sponsoring company or companies to make future contributions to the pension fund by reason of overfunding shall not itself result in such overfunding being deemed to be payable to or for the benefit of such company or companies); or

(B) The foreign country in which the pension fund is administered has laws that are designed to prevent overfunding of a pension fund and the funding of the pension fund is within the guidelines of such laws; or

(C) The pension fund is maintained to provide benefits to employees in a particular industry, profession, or group of industries or professions and employees of at least 10 companies (other than companies that are owned or controlled, directly or indirectly, by the same interests) contribute to the pension fund or receive benefits from the pension fund; and

(iv) The trustees, directors or other administrators provide the relevant documentation as required in paragraph (d) of this section.

(d) Substantiation of stock ownership. *(1) General rule.* A foreign corporation that relies on this section to satisfy the stock ownership test of § 1.883-1(c)(2), must establish all the facts necessary to satisfy the Commissioner that more than 50 percent of the value of its shares is owned, or treated as owned applying paragraph (c) of this section, by qualified shareholders. A foreign corporation cannot meet this requirement with respect to any stock that is issued in bearer form. A shareholder that holds shares in the foreign corporation either directly or indirectly in bearer form cannot be a qualified shareholder.

(2) Application of general rule. (i) Ownership statements. Except as provided in paragraph (d)(3) of this section, a person shall only be treated as a qualified shareholder of a foreign corporation if—

(A) For the relevant period, the person completes an ownership statement described in paragraph (d)(4) of this section or has a valid ownership statement in effect under paragraph (d)(2)(ii) of this section;

(B) In the case of a person owning stock in the foreign corporation indirectly through one or more intermediaries (including mere legal owners or recordholders acting as nominees), each intermediary in the chain of ownership between that person and the foreign corporation seeking qualified foreign corporation status completes an intermediary ownership statement described in paragraph (d)(4)(v) of this section or has a valid intermediary ownership statement in effect under paragraph (d)(2)(ii) of this section; and

(C) The foreign corporation seeking qualified foreign corporation status obtains the statements described in paragraphs (d)(2)(i)(A) and (B) of this section.

(ii) Three-year period of validity. The ownership statements required in paragraph (d)(2)(i) of this section shall remain valid until the earlier of the last day of the third calendar year following the year in which the ownership statement is signed, or the day that a change of circumstance occurs that makes any information on the ownership statement incorrect. For example, an ownership statement signed on September 30, 2000, remains valid through December 31, 2003, unless a change of circumstance occurs that makes any information on the ownership statement incorrect.

(3) Special rules. (i) Substantiating residence of certain shareholders. A foreign corporation seeking qualified foreign corporation status or an intermediary that is a direct or indirect shareholder of such foreign corporation may substantiate the residence of certain shareholders, for purposes of paragraph (b)(2)(i)(B) of this section, under one of the following special rules in paragraphs (d)(3)(ii) through (viii) of this section, in lieu of obtaining the ownership statements required in paragraph (d)(2)(i) of this section from such shareholders.

(ii) Special rule for registered shareholders owning less than one percent of widely-held corporations. A foreign corporation with at least 250 registered shareholders, that is not a publicly-traded corporation, as described in § 1.883-2 (a widely-held corporation), is not required to obtain an ownership statement from an individual shareholder owning less than one percent of the widely-held corporation at all times during the taxable year if the requirements of paragraphs (d)(3)(ii)(A) and (B) of this section are satisfied. If the widely-held foreign corporation is the foreign corporation seeking qualified foreign corporation status, or an intermediary that meets the documentation requirements of paragraphs (d)(4)(v)(A) and (B) of this section, the widely-held foreign corporation may treat the address of record in its ownership records as the residence of any less than one percent individual shareholder if—

(A) The individual's address of record is a specific street address and not a nonresidential address, such as a post office box or in care of a financial intermediary or stock transfer agent; and

(B) The officers and directors of the widely-held corporation neither know nor have reason to know that the individual does not reside at that address.

(iii) Special rule for beneficiaries of pension funds. (A) Government pension fund. An individual who is a beneficiary of a government pension fund, as defined in paragraph (b)(5)(ii) of this section, may be treated as a resident of the country in which the pension fund is administered if the pension fund satisfies the documentation requirements of paragraphs (d)(4)(v)(A) and (C)(1) of this section.

(B) Nongovernment pension fund. An individual who is a beneficiary of a nongovernment pension fund, as described in paragraph (b)(5)(iii) of this section, may be treated as a resident of the country of the beneficiary's address as it appears on the records of the fund, provided it is not a nonresidential address, such as a post office box or an address in care of a financial intermediary, and provided none of the trustees, directors or other administrators of the pension fund know, or have reason to know, that the beneficiary is not an individual resident of such foreign country. The rules of this paragraph (d)(3)(iii)(B) shall apply only if the nongovernment pension fund satisfies the documentation requirements of paragraphs (d)(4)(v)(A) and (C)(2) of this section.

(iv) Special rule for stock owned by publicly-traded corporations. Any stock in a foreign corporation seeking qualified foreign corporation status that is owned by a publicly-traded corporation will be treated as owned by an individual resident in the country where the publicly-traded corporation is organized if the foreign corporation receives the statement described in paragraph (d)(4)(iii) of this section from the publicly-traded corporation and copies of any relevant ownership statements from shareholders of the publicly-traded corporation relied on to satisfy the exception to the closely-held test of § 1.883-2(d)(3)(ii), as required in paragraph (d)(2)(i) of this section.

(v) Special rule for not-for-profit organizations. For purposes of meeting the ownership requirements of paragraph (a) of this section, a not-for-profit organization may rely on the addresses of record of its individual beneficiaries and supporters to determine the residence of an individual beneficiary or supporter, within the meaning of paragraph (b)(2)(i)(B) of this section, to the extent required under paragraph (b)(4) of this section, provided that—

(A) The addresses of record are not nonresidential addresses such as a post office box or in care of a financial intermediary;

(B) The officers, directors or administrators of the organization do not know or have reason to know that the individual beneficiaries or supporters do not reside at that address; and

(C) The foreign corporation seeking qualified foreign corporation status receives the statement required in paragraph (d)(4)(iv) of this section from the not-for-profit organization.

(vi) Special rule for a foreign airline covered by an air services agreement. A foreign airline that is covered by a bilateral Air Services Agreement in force between the United States and the qualified foreign country in which the airline is organized may rely exclusively on the Air Services Agreement currently in effect and will not have to otherwise substantiate its ownership under this section, provided that the United States has not waived the ownership requirements in the agreement or that the ownership requirements have not otherwise been made ineffective. Such an airline will be treated as owned by qualified shareholders resident in the country where the foreign airline is organized.

(vii) Special rule for taxable nonstock corporations. Any stock in a foreign corporation seeking qualified foreign corporation status that is owned by a taxable nonstock corporation will be treated as owned, in any taxable year, by the recipients of distributions made during that taxable year, as set out in paragraph (c)(5) of this section. The taxable nonstock corporation may treat the address of record in its distribution records as the residence of any recipient if—

(A) An individual recipient's address is in a qualified foreign country and is a specific street address and not a nonresidential address, such as a post office box or in care of a financial intermediary or stock transfer agent;

(B) The address of a nonindividual recipient's principal place of business is in a qualified foreign country;

(C) The officers and directors of the taxable nonstock corporation neither know nor have reason to know that the recipients do not reside or have their principal place of business at such addresses; and

(D) The foreign corporation receives the statement described in paragraph (d)(4)(v)(D) of this section from the taxable nonstock corporation intermediary.

(viii) Special rule for closely-held corporations traded in the United States. To demonstrate that a class of stock is not closely-held for purposes of § 1.883-2(d)(3)(i), a foreign corporation whose stock is traded on an established securities market in the United States may rely on current Schedule 13D and Schedule 13G filings with the Securities and Exchange Commission to identify its 5-percent shareholders in each class of stock relied upon to meet the regularly traded test, without having to make any independent investigation to determine the identity of the 5-percent shareholder. However, if any class of stock is determined to be closely-held within the meaning of § 1.883-2(d)(3)(i), the publicly traded corporation cannot satisfy the requirements of § 1.883-2(e) unless it obtains sufficient documentation described in this paragraph (d) to demonstrate that the requirements of § 1.883-2(d)(3)(ii) are met with respect to the 5-percent shareholders.

(4) Ownership statements from shareholders. (i) Ownership statements from individuals. An ownership statement from an individual is a written statement signed by the individual under penalties of perjury stating—

(A) The individual's name, permanent address, and country where the individual is fully liable to tax as a resident, if any;

(B) If the individual was not a resident of the country for the entire taxable year of the foreign corporation seeking qualified foreign corporation status, each of the foreign countries in which the individual resided and the dates of such residence during the taxable year of such foreign corporation;

(C) and (D) [Reserved]. For further guidance, see § 1.883-4T(d)(4)(i)(C) and (D).

(E) To the extent known by the individual, a description of the chain of ownership through which the individual owns stock in the corporation seeking qualified foreign corporation status, including the name and address of each intermediary standing between the intermediary described in paragraph (d)(4)(i)(D) of this section and the foreign corporation and whether this interest is owned either directly or indirectly through bearer shares; and

(F) Any other information as specified in guidance published by the Internal Revenue Service (see § 601.601(d)(2) of this chapter).

(ii) Ownership statements from foreign governments. An ownership statement from a foreign government that is a qualified shareholder is a written statement—

(A) Signed by any one of the following—

(1) An official of the governmental authority, agency or office who has supervisory authority with respect to the gov-

ernment's ownership interest and who is authorized to sign such a statement on behalf of the authority, agency or office; or

(2) The competent authority of the foreign country (as defined in the income tax convention between the United States and the foreign country); or

(3) An income tax return preparer that, for purposes of this paragraph (d)(4)(ii) only, shall mean a firm of licensed or certified public accountants, a law firm whose principals or members are admitted to practice in one or more states, territories or possessions of the United States or the country of such government, or a bank or other financial institution licensed to do business in such foreign country and having assets at least equivalent to 50 million U.S. dollars and who is authorized to represent the government or governmental authority; and

(B) That provides—

(1) The title of the official or other person signing the statement;

(2) The name and address of the government authority, agency or office that has supervisory authority and, if applicable, the income tax preparer which has prepared such ownership statement;

(3) The information described in paragraphs (d)(4)(i)(C) through (E) of this section (as if the language applied "government" instead of "individual") with respect to the government's direct or indirect ownership of stock in the corporation seeking qualified resident status;

(4) In the case of an ownership statement prepared by an income tax return preparer, a statement under penalties of perjury identifying the documentation relied upon in the conduct of due diligence for the taxable year to determine the aggregate government investment in the stock of the shipping or aircraft company in preparation of such ownership statement attached to a valid power of attorney to represent the taxpayer for the taxable year; and

(5) Any other information as specified in guidance published by the Internal Revenue Service (see § 601.601(d)(2) of this chapter).

(iii) Ownership statements from publicly-traded corporate shareholders. An ownership statement from a publicly-traded corporation that is a direct or indirect owner of the corporation seeking qualified foreign corporation status is a written statement, signed under penalties of perjury by a person that would be authorized to sign a tax return on behalf of the shareholder corporation containing the following information—

(A) The name of the country in which the stock is primarily traded;

(B) The name of the established securities market or markets on which the stock is listed;

(C) A description of each class of stock relied upon to meet the requirements of § 1.883-2(d)(1), including the number of shares issued and outstanding as of the close of the taxable year;

(D) For each class of stock relied upon to meet the requirements of § 1.883-2(d)(1), if one or more 5-percent shareholders, as defined in § 1.883-2(d)(3)(i), own in the aggregate 50 percent or more of the vote and value of the outstanding shares of that class of stock for more than half the number of days during the taxable year—

(1) The days during the taxable year of the corporation in which the stock was closely-held without regard to the exception in paragraph (d)(3)(ii) of this section and the percentage of the vote and value of the class of stock that is owned by 5-percent shareholders during such days;

(2) For each qualified shareholder who owns or is treated as owning stock in the closely-held block upon whom the corporation intends to rely to satisfy the exception to the closely-held test of § 1.883-2(d)(3)(ii)—

(i) The name of each such shareholder;

(ii) The percentage of the total value of the class of stock held by each such shareholder and the days during which the stock was held;

(iii) The address of record of each such shareholder; and

(iv) The country of residence of each such shareholder, determined under paragraph (b)(2) or (d)(3) of this section;

(E) The information described in paragraphs (d)(4)(i)(C) through (E) of this section (as if the language applied "publicly-traded corporation" instead of "individual") with respect to the publicly-traded corporation's direct or indirect ownership of stock in the corporation seeking qualified resident status; and

(F) Any other information as specified in guidance published by the Internal Revenue Service (see § 601.601(d)(2) of this chapter).

(iv) Ownership statements from not-for-profit organizations. An ownership statement from a not-for-profit organization (other than a pension fund as defined in paragraph (b)(5) of this section) is a written statement signed by a person authorized to sign a tax return on behalf of the organization under penalties of perjury stating—

(A) The name, permanent address, and principal location of the activities of the organization (if different from its permanent address);

(B) The information described in paragraphs (d)(4)(i)(C) through (E) of this section (as if the language applied "not-for-profit organization" instead of "individual");

(C) A representation that the not-for-profit organization satisfies the requirements of paragraph (b)(4) of this section; and

(D) Any other information as specified in guidance published by the Internal Revenue Service (see § 601.601(d)(2) of this chapter).

(v) Ownership statements from intermediaries. (A) General rule. The foreign corporation seeking qualified foreign corporation status under the shareholder stock ownership test must obtain an intermediary ownership statement from each intermediary standing in the chain of ownership between it and the qualified shareholders on whom it relies to meet this test. An intermediary ownership statement is a written statement signed under penalties of perjury by the intermediary (if the intermediary is an individual) or a person who would be authorized to sign a tax return on behalf of the intermediary (if the intermediary is not an individual) containing the following information—

(1) The name, address, country of residence, and principal place of business (in the case of a corporation or partnership) of the intermediary, and, if the intermediary is a trust or estate, the name and permanent address of all trustees or executors (or equivalent under foreign law), or if the intermediary is a pension fund, the name and permanent address of place of administration of the intermediary;

(2) The information described in paragraphs (d)(4)(i)(C) through (E) of this section (as if the language applied "intermediary" instead of "individual");

(3) If the intermediary is a nominee for a shareholder or another intermediary, the name and permanent address of the shareholder, or the name and principal place of business of such other intermediary;

(4) If the intermediary is not a nominee for a shareholder or another intermediary, the name and country of residence (within the meaning of paragraph (b)(2) of this section) and the proportionate interest in the intermediary of each direct shareholder, partner, beneficiary, grantor, or other interest holder (or if the direct holder is a nominee, of its beneficial shareholder, partner, beneficiary, grantor, or other interest holder), on which the foreign corporation seeking qualified foreign corporation status intends to rely to satisfy the requirements of paragraph (a) of this section. In addition, such intermediary must obtain from all such persons an ownership statement that includes the period of time during the taxable year for which the interest in the intermediary was owned by the shareholder, partner, beneficiary, grantor or other interest holder. For purposes of this paragraph (d)(4)(v)(A), the proportionate interest of a person in an intermediary is the percentage interest (by value) held by such person, determined using the principles for attributing ownership in paragraph (c) of this section;

(5) If the intermediary is a widely-held corporation with registered shareholders owning less than one percent of the stock of such widely-held corporation, the statement set out in paragraph (d)(4)(v)(B) of this section, relating to ownership statements from widely-held intermediaries with registered shareholders owning less than one percent of such widely-held intermediaries;

(6) If the intermediary is a pension fund, within the meaning of paragraph (b)(5) of this section, the statement set out in paragraph (d)(4)(v)(C) of this section, relating to ownership statements from pension funds;

(7) If the intermediary is a taxable nonstock corporation, within the meaning of paragraph (c)(5) of this section, the statement set out in paragraph (d)(4)(v)(D) of this section, relating to ownership statements from intermediaries that are taxable nonstock corporations; and

(8) Any other information as specified in guidance published by the Internal Revenue Service (see § 601.601(d)(2) of this chapter).

(B) Ownership statements from widely-held intermediaries with registered shareholders owning less than one percent of such widely-held intermediary. An ownership statement from an intermediary that is a corporation with at least 250 registered shareholders, but that is not a publicly-traded corporation within the meaning of § 1.883-2, and that relies on paragraph (d)(3)(ii) of this section, relating to the special rule for registered shareholders owning less than one percent of widely-held corporations, must provide the following information in addition to the information required in paragraph (d)(4)(v)(A) of this section—

(1) The aggregate proportionate interest by country of residence in the widely-held corporation of such registered shareholders or other interest holders whose address of record is a specific street address and not a nonresidential address, such as a post office box or in care of a financial intermediary or stock transfer agent; and

(2) A representation that the officers and directors of the widely-held intermediary neither know nor have reason to know that the individual shareholder does not reside at his or her address of record in the corporate records; and

(3) Any other information as specified in guidance published by the Internal Revenue Service (see § 601.601(d)(2) of this chapter).

(C) Ownership statements from pension funds. (1) Ownership statements from government pension funds. A government pension fund (as defined in paragraph (b)(5)(ii) of this section) that relies on paragraph (d)(3)(iii) of this section (relating to the special rules for pension funds) generally must provide the documentation required in paragraph (d)(4)(v)(A) of this section, and, in addition, the government pension fund must also provide the following information—

(i) The name of the country in which the plan is administered;

(ii) A representation that the fund is established exclusively for the benefit of employees or former employees of a foreign government, or employees or former employees of a foreign government and nongovernmental employees or former employees that perform or performed governmental or social services;

(iii) A representation that the funds that comprise the trust are managed by trustees who are employees of, or persons appointed by, the foreign government;

(vi) A representation that the trust forming part of the pension plan provides for retirement, disability, or death benefits in consideration for prior services rendered;

(v) A representation that the income of the trust satisfies the obligations of the foreign government to the participants under the plan, rather than inuring to the benefit of a private person; and

(vi) Any other information as specified in guidance published by the Internal Revenue Service (see § 601.601(d)(2) of this chapter).

(2) Ownership statements from nongovernment pension funds. The trustees, directors, or other administrators of the nongovernment pension fund, as defined in paragraph (b)(5)(iii) of this section, that rely on paragraph (d)(3)(iii) of this section, relating to the special rules for pension funds, generally must provide the pension fund's intermediary ownership statement described in paragraph (d)(4)(v)(A) of this section. In addition, the nongovernment pension fund must also provide the following information—

(i) The name of the country in which the pension fund is administered;

(ii) A representation that the pension fund is subject to supervision or regulation by a governmental authority (or other authority delegated to perform such supervision or regulation by a governmental authority) in such country, and, if so, the name of the governmental authority (or other authority delegated to perform such supervision or regulation);

(iii) A representation that the pension fund is generally exempt from income taxation in its country of administration;

(iv) The number of beneficiaries in the pension plan;

(v) The aggregate percentage interest of beneficiaries by country of residence based on addresses shown on the books and records of the fund, provided the addresses are not nonresidential addresses, such as a post office box or an address in care of a financial intermediary, and provided none of the trustees, directors or other administrators of the pension fund know, or have reason to know, that the beneficiary is not a resident of such foreign country;

(vi) A representation that the pension fund meets the requirements of paragraph (b)(5)(iii) of this section;

(vii) A representation that the trustees, directors or other administrators of the pension fund have no knowledge, and no reason to know, that a pro-rata allocation of interests of the fund to all beneficiaries would differ significantly from an actuarial allocation of interests in the fund (or, if the beneficiaries' actuarial interest in the stock held directly or indirectly by the pension fund differs from the beneficiaries' actuarial interest in the pension fund, the actuarial interests computed by reference to the beneficiaries' actuarial interest in the stock);

(viii) A representation that any overfunding of the pension fund would be payable, pursuant to the governing instrument or the laws of the foreign country in which the pension fund is administered, only to, or for the benefit of, one or more corporations that are organized in the country in which the pension fund is administered, individual beneficiaries of the pension fund or their designated beneficiaries, or social or charitable causes (the reduction of the obligation of the sponsoring company or companies to make future contributions to the pension fund by reason of overfunding shall not itself result in such overfunding being deemed to be payable to or for the benefit of such company or companies); or that the foreign country in which the pension fund is administered has laws that are designed to prevent overfunding of a pension fund and the funding of the pension fund is within the guidelines of such laws; or that the pension fund is maintained to provide benefits to employees in a particular industry, profession, or group of industries or professions, and that employees of at least 10 companies (other than companies that are owned or controlled, directly or indirectly, by the same interests) contribute to the pension fund or receive benefits from the pension fund; and

(ix) Any other information as specified in guidance published by the Internal Revenue Service (see § 601.601(d)(2) of this chapter).

(3) Time for making determinations. The determinations required to be made under this paragraph (d)(4)(v)(C) shall be made using information shown on the records of the pension fund for a date during the foreign corporation's taxable year to which the determination is relevant.

(D) Ownership statements from taxable nonstock corporations. An ownership statement from an intermediary that is a taxable nonstock corporation must provide the following information in addition to the information required in paragraph (d)(4)(v)(A) of this section—

(1) With respect to paragraph (d)(4)(v)(A)(7) of this section, for each beneficiary that is treated as a qualified shareholder, the name, address of residence (in the case of an individual beneficiary, the address must be a specific street address and not a nonresidential address, such as a post office box or in care of a financial intermediary; in the case of a nonindividual beneficiary, the address of the principal place of business) and percentage that is the same proportion as the amount that the beneficiary receives in the tax year bears to the total net income of the taxable nonstock corporation in the tax year;

(2) A representation that the officers and directors of the taxable nonstock corporation neither know nor have reason to know that the individual beneficiaries do not reside at the address listed in paragraph (d)(4)(v)(D)(1) of this section or that any other nonindividual beneficiary does not conduct its primary activities at such address or in such country of residence; and

(3) Any other information as specified in guidance published by the Internal Revenue Service (see § 601.601(d)(2) of this chapter).

(5) Availability and retention of documents for inspection. The documentation described in paragraphs (d)(3) and (4) of this section must be retained by the corporation seeking qualified foreign corporation status (the foreign corporation) until the expiration of the statute of limitations for the taxable year of the foreign corporation to which the documentation relates. Such documentation must be made available for inspection by the Commissioner at such time and place as the Commissioner may request in writing.

(e) Reporting requirements. A foreign corporation relying on the qualified shareholder stock ownership test of this section to meet the stock ownership test of § 1.883-1(c)(2) must provide the following information in addition to the information required in § 1.883-1(c)(3) to be included in its Form 1120-F, "U.S. Income Tax Return of a Foreign Corporation," for each taxable year. The information should be current as of the end of the corporation's taxable year. The information must include the following—

(1) A representation that more than 50 percent of the value of the outstanding shares of the corporation is owned (or treated as owned by reason of paragraph (c) of this section) by qualified shareholders for each category of income for which the exemption is claimed;

(2) and (3) [Reserved]. For further guidance, see § 1.883-4T(e)(2) and (3).

T.D. 9087, 8/25/2003, amend T.D. 9332, 6/22/2007.

PAR. 6. Section 1.883-4 is amended by revising paragraphs (d)(4)(i)(C), (d)(4)(i)(D), (e)(2), and (e)(3) to read as follows:

Proposed § 1.883-4 Qualified shareholder stock ownership test. [*For Preamble, see ¶ 152,877*]

* * * * *

(d) * * *

(4) * * *

(i) * * *

(C) and (D) [The text of the proposed amendments to § 1.883-4(d)(4)(i)(C) and (D) is the same as the text of § 1.883-4T(d)(4)(i)(C) and (D) published elsewhere in this issue of the Federal Register]. [See T.D. 9332, 06/25/2007].

* * * * *

(e) * * *

(2) and (3) [The text of the proposed amendments to § 1.883-4(e)(2) and (3) is the same as the text of § 1.883-4T(e)(2) and (3) published elsewhere in this issue of the Federal Register]. [See T.D. 9332, 06/25/2007].

§ 1.883-4T Qualified shareholder stock ownership test (temporary).

(a) through (d)(4)(i)(B) [Reserved]. For further guidance see § 1.883-4(a) through (d)(4)(i)(B).

(d) *(4)* (i) (C) If the individual directly owns stock in the corporation seeking qualified foreign corporation status, the name of the corporation, the number of shares in each class of stock of the corporation that are so owned, with a statement that such shares are not issued in bearer form, and the period of time during the taxable year of the foreign corporation when the individual owned the stock;

(D) If the individual directly owns an interest in a corporation, partnership, trust, estate, or other intermediary that directly or indirectly owns stock in the corporation seeking qualified foreign corporation status, the name of the intermediary, the number and class of shares or the amount and nature of the interest of the individual in such intermediary, and, in the case of a corporate intermediary, a statement that such shares are not held in bearer form, and the period of time during the taxable year of the foreign corporation seeking qualified foreign corporation status when the individual held such interest;

(E) through (e)(1) [Reserved]. For further guidance see § 1.883-4(d)(4)(i)(E) through (e)(1).

(e) *(2)* With respect to all qualified shareholders relied upon to satisfy the 50 percent ownership test of § 1.883-4(a), the total number of such qualified shareholders as defined in § 1.883-4(b)(1); the total percentage of the value of the outstanding shares owned, applying the attribution rules of § 1.883-4(c), by such qualified shareholders by country of residence or organization, whichever is applicable; and the period during the taxable year of the foreign corporation that such stock was held by qualified shareholders; and

(3) Any other relevant information specified by the Form 1120-F, "U.S. Income Tax Return of a Foreign Corporation," and its accompanying instructions, or in guidance published by the Internal Revenue Service (see § 601.601(d)(2) of this chapter).

T.D. 9332, 6/22/2007.

§ 1.883-5 Effective/applicability dates.

(a) General rule. Sections 1.883-1 through 1.883-4 apply to taxable years of a foreign corporation seeking qualified foreign corporation status beginning after September 24, 2004.

(b) Election for retroactive application. Taxpayers may elect to apply §§ 1.883-1 through 1.883-4 for any open taxable year of the foreign corporation beginning after December 31, 1986, except that the substantiation and reporting requirements of § 1.883-1(c)(3) (relating to the substantiation and reporting required to be treated as a qualified foreign corporation) or §§ 1.883-2(f), 1.883-3(d) and 1.883-4(e) (relating to additional information to be included in the return to demonstrate whether the foreign corporation satisfies the stock ownership test) will not apply to any year beginning before September 25, 2004. Such election shall apply to the taxable year of the election and to all subsequent taxable years beginning before September 25, 2004.

(c) Transitional information reporting rule. For taxable years of the foreign corporation beginning after September 24, 2004, and until such time as the Form 1120-F, "U.S. Income Tax Return of a Foreign Corporation," or its instructions are revised to provide otherwise, the information required in § 1.883-1(c)(3) and § 1.883-2(f), § 1.883-3(d) or § 1.883-4(e), as applicable, must be included on a wirtten statement attached to the Form 1120-F and file with the return.

(d) through (e) [Reserved]. For further guidance, see § 1.883-5T(d) through (e).

T.D. 9087, 8/25/2003, amend T.D. 9218, 8/5/2005, T.D. 9332, 6/22/2007.

PAR. 7. Section 1.883-5 is amended by revising paragraphs (d) and (e) to read as follows:

Proposed § 1.883-5 Effective/applicability dates.

* * * * *

(d) [The text of the proposed amendment to § 1.883-5(d) is the same as the text of § 1.883-5T(d) published elsewhere in this issue of the Federal Register]. [See T.D. 9332, 06/25/2007].

(e) [The text of the proposed amendment to § 1.883-5(e) is the same as the text of § 1.883-5T(e) published elsewhere in this issue of the Federal Register]. [See T.D. 9332, 06/25/2007].

§ 1.883-5T Effective/applicability dates (temporary).

(a) through (c) [Reserved]. For further guidance, see § 1.883-5(a) through (c).

(d) Effective date. These regulations are effective on June 25, 2007.

(e) Applicability dates. Sections 1.883-1T, 1.883-2T, 1.883-3T, and 1.883-4T are applicable to taxable years of the foreign corporation beginning after June 25, 2007. Taxpayers may elect to apply § 1.883-3T to any open taxable years of the foreign corporation beginning on or after December 31, 2004.

(f) Expiration date. The applicability of §§ 1.883-1T, 1.883-2T, 1.883-3T, and 1.883-4T expires on or before June 22, 2010.

T.D. 9332, 6/22/2007.

§ 1.884-0 Overview of regulation provisions for section 884.

(a) Introduction. Section 884 consists of three main parts: a branch profits tax on certain earnings of a foreign corporation's U.S. trade or business; a branch-level interest tax on interest paid, or deemed paid, by a foreign corporation's U.S. trade or business; and an anti-treaty shopping rule. A foreign corporation is subject to section 884 by virtue of owning an interest in a partnership, trust, or estate that is engaged in a U.S. trade or business or has income treated as effectively connected with the conduct of a trade or business in the United States. An international organization (as defined in section 7701(a)(18)) is not subject to the branch profits tax by reason of section 884(e)(5). A foreign government treated as a corporate resident of its country of residence under section 892(a)(3) shall be treated as a corporation for purposes of section 884. The preceding sentence shall be effective for taxable years ending on or after September 11, 1992, except that, for the first taxable year ending on or after that date, the branch profits tax shall not apply to effectively connected earnings and profits of the foreign government earned prior to that date nor to decreases in the U.S. net equity of a foreign government occurring after the close of the preceding taxable year and before that date. Similarly, § 1.884-4 shall apply, in the case of branch interest, only with respect to amounts of interest accrued and paid by a foreign government on or after that date, or, in the case of excess interest, only with respect to amounts attributable to interest accrued by a foreign government on or after that date and apportioned to ECI, as defined in § 1.884-1(d)(1)(iii). Except as otherwise provided, for purposes of the regulations under section 884, the term "U.S. trade or business" includes all the U.S. trades or businesses of a foreign corporation.

(1) The branch profits tax. Section 1.884-1 provides rules for computing the branch profits tax and defines various terms that affect the computation of the tax. In general, section 884(a) imposes a 30-percent branch profits tax on the

after-tax earnings of a foreign corporation's U.S. trade or business that are not reinvested in a U.S. trade or business by the close of the taxable year, or are disinvested in a later taxable year. Changes in the value of the equity of the foreign corporation's U.S. trade or business are used as the measure of whether earnings have been reinvested in, or disinvested from, a U.S. trade or business. An increase in the equity during the taxable year is generally treated as a reinvestment of the earnings for the current taxable year; a decrease in the equity during the taxable year is generally treated as a disinvestment of prior years' earnings that have not previously been subject to the branch profits tax. The amount subject to the branch profits tax for the taxable year is the dividend equivalent amount. Section 1.884-2T contains special rules relating to the effect on the branch profits tax of the termination or incorporation of a U.S. trade or business or the liquidation or reorganization of a foreign corporation or its domestic subsidiary.

(2) The branch-level interest tax. Section 1.884-4 provides rules for computing the branch-level interest tax. In general, interest paid by a U.S. trade or business of a foreign corporation ("branch interest", as defined in § 1.884-4(b)) is treated as if it were paid by a domestic corporation and may be subject to tax under section 871(a) or 881, and to withholding under section 1441 or 1442. In addition, if the interest apportioned to ECI exceeds branch interest, the excess is treated as interest paid to the foreign corporation by a wholly-owned domestic corporation and is subject to tax under section 881(a).

(3) Qualified resident. Section 1.884-5 provides rules for determining whether a foreign corporation is a qualified resident of a foreign country. In general, a foreign corporation must be a qualified resident of a foreign country with which the United States has an income tax treaty in order to claim an exemption or rate reduction with respect to the branch profits tax, the branch-level interest tax, and the tax on dividends paid by the foreign corporation.

(b) Special rules for U.S. possessions. [Reserved]. For further guidance, see § 1.884-0T(b).

(c) Outline of major topics in §§ 1.884-1 through 1.884-5. *§ 1.884-1 Branch profits tax.*

(a) General rule.

(b) Dividend equivalent amount.

(1) Definition.

(2) Adjustment for increase in U.S. net equity.

(3) Adjustment for decrease in U.S. net equity.

(4) Examples.

(c) U.S. net equity.

(1) Definition.

(2) Definition of amount of a U.S. asset.

(3) Definition of determination date.

(d) U.S. assets.

(1) Definition of a U.S. asset.

(2) Special rules for certain assets.

(3) Interest in a partnership.

(4) Interest in a trust or estate.

(5) Property that is not a U.S. asset.

(6) E&P basis of a U.S. asset.

(e) U.S. liabilities.

(1) Liabilities based on § 1.882-5.

(2) Insurance reserves.

(3) Election to reduce liabilities.

(4) Artificial decrease in U.S. liabilities.

(5) Examples.

(f) Effectively connected earnings and profits.

(1) In general.

(2) Income that does not produce ECEP.

(3) Allocation of deductions attributable to income that does not produce ECEP.

(4) Examples.

(g) Corporations resident in countries with which the United States has an income tax treaty.

(1) General rule.

(2) Special rules for foreign corporations that are qualified residents on the basis of their ownership.

(3) Exemptions for foreign corporations resident in certain countries with income tax treaties in effect on January 1, 1987.

(4) Modifications with respect to other income tax treaties.

(5) Benefits under treaties other than income tax treaties.

(h) Stapled entities.

(i) Effective date.

(1) General rule.

(2) Election to reduce liabilities.

(3) Separate election for installment obligations.

(4) Special rule for certain U.S. assets and liabilities.

(j) Transition rules.

(1) General rule.

(2) Installment obligations.

§ 1.884-2T Special rules for termination or incorporation of a U.S. trade or business or liquidation or reorganization of a foreign corporation or its domestic subsidiary (temporary).

(a) Complete termination of a U.S. trade or business.

(1) General rule.

(2) Operating rules.

(3) Complete termination in the case of a section 338 election.

(4) Complete termination in the case of a foreign corporation with income under section 864(c)(6) or 864(c)(7).

(5) Special rule if a foreign corporation terminates an interest in a trust. [Reserved]

(6) Coordination with second-level withholding tax.

(b) Election to remain engaged in a U.S. trade or business.

(1) General rule.

(2) Marketable security.

(3) Identification requirements.

(4) Treatment of income from deemed U.S. assets.

(5) Method of election.

(6) Effective date.

(c) Liquidation, reorganization, etc. of a foreign corporation.

(1) Inapplicability of paragraph (a)(1) to section 381(a) transactions.

(2) Transferor's dividend equivalent amount for the taxable year in which a section 381(a) transaction occurs.

(3) Transferor's dividend equivalent amount for any taxable year succeeding the taxable year in which the section 381(a) transaction occurs.

(4) Earnings and profits of the transferor carried over to the transferee pursuant to the section 381(a) transaction.

(5) Determination of U.S. net equity of a transferee that is a foreign corporation.

(6) Special rules in the case of the disposition of stock or securities in a domestic transferee or in the transferor.

(d) Incorporation under section 351.

(1) In general.

(2) Inapplicability of paragraph (a)(1) of this section to section 351 transactions.

(3) Transferor's dividend equivalent amount for the taxable year in which a section 351 transaction occurs.

(4) Election to increase earnings and profits.

(5) Dispositions of stock or securities of the transferee by the transferor.

(6) Example.

(e) Certain transactions with respect to a domestic subsidiary.

(f) Effective date.

§ 1.884-3T Coordination of branch profits tax with second-tier withholding (temporary). [Reserved]

§ 1.884-4 Branch-level interest tax.

(a) General rule.

(1) Tax on branch interest.

(2) Tax on excess interest.

(3) Original issue discount.

(4) Examples.

(b) Branch interest.

(1) Definition of branch interest.

(2) [Reserved]

(3) Requirements relating to specifically identified liabilities.

(4) [Reserved]

(5) Increase in branch interest where U.S. assets constitute 80 percent or more of a foreign corporation's assets.

(6) Special rule where branch interest exceeds interest apportioned to ECI of a foreign corporation.

(7) Effect of election under paragraph (c)(1) of this section to treat interest as if paid in year of accrual.

(8) Effect of treaties.

(c) Rules relating to excess interest.

(1) Election to compute excess interest by treating branch interest that is paid and accrued in different years as if paid in year of accrual.

(2) Interest paid by a partnership.

(3) Effect of treaties.

(4) Example.

(d) Stapled entities.

(e) Effective dates.

(1) General rule.

(2) Special rule.

(f) Transition rules.

(1) Election under paragraph (c)(1) of this section.

(2) Waiver of notification requirement for non-banks under Notice 89-80.

(3) Waiver of legending requirement for certain debt issued prior to January 3, 1989.

§ 1.884-5 Qualified resident.

(a) Definition of qualified resident.

(b) Stock ownership requirement.

(1) General rule.

(2) Rules for determining constructive ownership.

(3) Required documentation.

(4) Ownership statements from qualifying shareholders.

(5) Certificate of residency.

(6) Intermediary ownership statement.

(7) Intermediary verification statement.

(8) Special rules for pension funds.

(9) Availability of documents for inspection.

(10) Examples.

(c) Base erosion.

(d) Publicly-traded corporations.

(1) General rule.

(2) Established securities market.

(3) Primarily traded.

(4) Regularly traded.

(5) Burden of proof for publicly-traded corporations.

(e) Active trade or business.

(1) General rule.

(2) Active conduct of a trade or business.

(3) Substantial presence test.

(4) Integral part of an active trade or business in the foreign corporation's country of residence.

(f) Qualified resident ruling.

(1) Basis for ruling.

(2) Factors.

(3) Procedural requirements.

(g) Effective dates.

(h) Transition rule.

T.D. 8432, 9/10/92, amend T.D. 8657, 3/5/96, T.D. 9194, 4/6/2005.

PAR. 9. In § 1.884-0, paragraph (b) is redesignated as paragraph (c), and a new paragraph (b) is added to read as follows:

Proposed § 1.884-0 Overview of regulation provisions for section 884. [*For Preamble, see ¶ 152,645*]

• ***Caution:*** This Notice of Proposed Rulemaking was partially finalized by TD 9248, 01/30/2006. Regs. §§ 1.1-1, 1.170A-1, 1.861-3, 1.861-8, 1.871-1, 1.876-1, 1.881-5, 1.884-0, 1.901-1, 1.931-1, 1.932-1, 1.933-1, 1.934-1, 1.935-1, 1.937-2, 1.937-3, 1.957-3, 1.1402(a)-12, 1.6038-2, 1.6046-1, 301.6688-1, 301.7701-3, and 301.7701(b)-1 remain proposed.

* * * * *

(b) [The text of the proposed amendment to § 1.884-0 is the same as the text of § 1.884-0T published elsewhere in this issue of the Federal Register]. [*See T.D. 9194, 4/11/2005, 70 Fed. Reg. 68.*]

§ 1.884-0T Overview of regulation provisions for section 884 (temporary).

• *Caution:* Under Code Sec. 7805, temporary regulations expire within three years of the date of issuance. This temporary regulation was issued on 4/6/2005.

(a) [Reserved]. For further guidance, see § 1.884-0(a).

(b) Special rules for U.S. possessions. *(1)* Section 884 does not apply to a corporation created or organized in, or under the law of, American Samoa, Guam, the Northern Mariana Islands, or the United States Virgin Islands, provided that the conditions of § 1.881-5T(c)(1) through (3) are satisfied with respect to such corporation. The preceding sentence applies for taxable years ending after April 11, 2005.

(2) Section 884 does not apply for purposes of determining tax liability incurred to a section 935 possession or the United States Virgin Islands by a corporation created or organized in, or under the law of, such possession or the United States. The preceding sentence applies for taxable years ending after April 11, 2005.

(c) [Reserved]. For further guidance, see § 1.884-0(c).

T.D. 9194, 4/6/2005.

§ 1.884-1 Branch profits tax.

(a) General rule. A foreign corporation shall be liable for a branch profits tax in an amount equal to 30 percent of the foreign corporation's dividend equivalent amount for the taxable year. The branch profits tax shall be in addition to the tax imposed by section 882 and shall be reported on a foreign corporation's income tax return for the taxable year. The tax shall be due and payable as provided in section 6151 and such other provisions of Subtitle F of the Internal Revenue Code as apply to the income tax liability of corporations. However, no estimated tax payments shall be due with respect to a foreign corporation's liability for the branch profits tax. See paragraph (g) of this section for the application of the branch profits tax to corporations that are residents of countries with which the United States has an income tax treaty, and § 1.884-2T for the effect on the branch profits tax of the termination or incorporation of a U.S. trade or business, or the liquidation or reorganization of a foreign corporation or its domestic subsidiary.

(b) Dividend equivalent amount. *(1) Definition.* The term "dividend equivalent amount" means a foreign corporation's effectively connected earnings and profits ("ECEP", as defined in paragraph (f)(1) of this section) for the taxable year, adjusted pursuant to paragraph (b)(2) or (3) of this section, as applicable. The dividend equivalent amount cannot be less than zero.

(2) Adjustment for increase in U.S. net equity. If a foreign corporation's U.S. net equity (as defined in paragraph (c) of this section) as of the close of the taxable year exceeds the foreign corporation's U.S. net equity as of the close of the preceding taxable year, then, for purposes of computing the foreign corporation's dividend equivalent amount for the taxable year, the foreign corporation's ECEP for the taxable year shall be reduced (but not below zero) by the amount of such excess.

(3) Adjustment for decrease in U.S. net equity. (i) In general. Except as provided in paragraph (b)(3)(ii) of this section, if a foreign corporation's U.S. net equity as of the close of the taxable year is less than the foreign corporation's U.S. net equity as of the close of the preceding taxable year, then, for purposes of computing the foreign corporation's dividend equivalent amount for the taxable year, the foreign corporation's ECEP for the taxable year shall be increased by the amount of such difference.

(ii) Limitation based on accumulated ECEP. The increase of a foreign corporation's ECEP under paragraph (b)(3)(i) of this section shall not exceed the accumulated ECEP of the foreign corporation as of the beginning of the taxable year. The term "accumulated ECEP" means the aggregate amount of ECEP of a foreign corporation for preceding taxable years beginning after December 31, 1986, minus the aggregate dividend equivalent amounts for such preceding taxable years. Accumulated ECEP may be less than zero.

(4) Examples. The principles of paragraph (b)(2) and (3) of this section are illustrated by the following examples.

Example (1). Reinvestment of all ECEP. Foreign corporation A, a calendar year taxpayer, had $1,000 U.S. net equity as of the close of 1986 and $100 of ECEP for 1987. A acquires $100 of additional U.S. assets during 1987 and its U.S. net equity as of the close of 1987 is $1,100. In computing A's dividend equivalent amount for 1987, A's ECEP of $100 is reduced under paragraph (b)(2) of this section by the $100 increase in U.S. net equity between the close of 1986 and the close of 1987. A has no dividend equivalent amount for 1987.

Example (2). Partial reinvestment of ECEP. Assume the same facts as in Example 1 except that A acquires $40 (rather than $100) of U.S. assets during 1987 and its U.S. net equity as of the close of 1987 is $1,040. In computing A's dividend equivalent amount for 1987, A's ECEP of $100 is reduced under paragraph (b)(2) of this section by the $40 increase in U.S. net equity between the close of 1986 and the close of 1987. A has a dividend equivalent amount of $60 for 1987.

Example (3). Disinvestment of prior year's ECEP. Assume the same facts as in Example 1 for 1987. A has no ECEP for 1988. A's U.S. net equity decreases by $40 (to $1,060) as of the close of 1988. A has a dividend equivalent amount of $40 for 1988, even though it has no ECEP for 1988. A's ECEP of $0 for 1988 is increased under paragraph (b)(3)(i) of this section by the $40 reduction in U.S. net equity (subject to the limitation in paragraph (b)(3)(ii) of this section of $100 of accumulated ECEP).

Example (4). Accumulated ECEP limitation. Assume the same facts as in Example 2 for 1987. For 1988, A has $125 of ECEP and its U.S. net equity decreases by $50. A's U.S. net equity as of the close of 1988 is $990 ($1,040-$50). In computing A's dividend equivalent amount for 1988, the $125 of ECEP for 1988 is not increased under paragraph (b)(3)(i) of this section by the full amount of the $50 decrease in U.S. net equity during 1988. Rather, the increase in ECEP resulting from the decrease in U.S. net equity is limited to A's accumulated ECEP as of the beginning of 1988. A had $100 of ECEP for 1987 and a dividend equivalent amount of $60 for that year, so A had $40 of accumulated ECEP as of the beginning of 1988. The increase in ECEP resulting from a decrease in U.S. net equity is thus limited to $40, and the dividend equivalent amount for 1988 is $165 ($125 ECEP + $40 decrease in U.S. net equity).

Example (5). Effect of deficits in ECEP. Foreign corporation A, a calendar year taxpayer, has $150 of accumulated ECEP as of the beginning of 1991 ($200 aggregate ECEP less $50 aggregate dividend equivalent amounts for years preceding 1991). A has U.S. net equity of $450 as of the close of 1990, U.S. net equity of $350 as of the close of 1991 (i.e., a $100 decrease in U.S. net equity) and a $90 deficit in ECEP for 1991. A's dividend equivalent amount is $10 for 1991, i.e., A's deficit of $90 in ECEP for 1991 increased by $100, the decrease in A's U.S. net equity during 1991. A portion of the reduction in U.S. net equity in 1991 ($90) is attributable to A's deficit in ECEP for that year. The reduction in U.S. net equity in 1991 ($100) triggers a dividend equivalent amount only to the extent it exceeds the $90 current year deficit in ECEP for 1991. As of the beginning of 1992, A has $50 of accumulated ECEP (i.e., $110 aggregate ECEP less $60 aggregate dividend equivalent amounts for years preceding 1992).

Example (6). Nimble dividend equivalent amount. Foreign corporation A, a calendar year taxpayer, had a deficit in ECEP of $100 for 1987 and $100 for 1988, and has $90 of ECEP for 1989. A had $2,000 U.S. net equity as of the close of 1988 and has $2,000 U.S. net equity as of the close of 1989. A has a dividend equivalent amount of $90 for 1989, its ECEP for the year, even though it has a net deficit of $110 in ECEP for the period 1987-1989.

(c) U.S. net equity. *(1) Definition.* The term "U.S. net equity" means the aggregate amount of the U.S. assets (as defined in paragraphs (c)(2) and (d)(1) of this section) of a foreign corporation as of the determination date (as defined in paragraph (c)(3) of this section), reduced (including below zero) by the U.S. liabilities (as defined in paragraph (e) of this section) of the foreign corporation as of the determination date.

(2) Definition of the amount of a U.S. asset. (i) In general. For purposes of this section, the term "amount of a U.S. asset" means the U.S. asset's adjusted basis for purposes of computing earnings and profits ("E&P basis") multiplied by the proportion of the asset that is treated as a U.S. asset under paragraphs (d)(1) through (4) of this section. The amount of a U.S. asset that is money shall be its face value. See paragraph (d)(6) of this section for rules concerning the computation of the E&P basis of a U.S. asset.

(ii) Bad debt reserves. A bank described in section 585(a)(2)(B) (without regard to the second sentence thereof) that uses the reserve method of accounting for bad debts for U.S. federal income tax purposes shall decrease the amount of loans that qualify as U.S. assets by any reserve that is permitted under section 585.

(3) Definition of determination date. For purposes of this section, the term "determination date" means the close of the day on which the amount of U.S. net equity is required to be determined. Unless otherwise provided, the U.S. net equity of a foreign corporation is required to be determined as of the close of the foreign corporation's taxable year.

(d) U.S. assets. *(1) Definition of a U.S. asset.* (i) General rule. Except as provided in paragraph (d)(5) of this section, the term "U.S. asset" means an asset of a foreign corporation (other than an interest in a partnership, trust, or estate) that is held by the corporation as of the determination date if—

(A) All income produced by the asset on the determination date is ECI (as defined in paragraph (d)(1)(iii) of this section) (or would be ECI if the asset produced income on that date); and

(B) All gain from the disposition of the asset would be ECI if the asset were disposed of on that date and the disposition produced gain.

For purposes of determining whether income or gain from an asset would be ECI under this paragraph (d)(1)(i), it is immaterial whether the asset is of a type that is unlikely to, or cannot, produce income or gain. For example, money may be a U.S. asset although it does not produce income or gain. In the case of an asset that does not produce income, however, the determination of whether income from the asset would be ECI shall be made under the principles of section 864 and the regulations thereunder, but without regard to § 1.864-4(c)(2)(iii)(b). For purposes of determining whether an asset is a U.S. asset under this paragraph (d)(1), a foreign corporation may presume, unless it has reason to know otherwise, that gain from the sale of personal property (including inventory property) would be U.S. source if gain from the sale of that type of property would ordinarily be attributable to an office or other fixed place of business of the foreign corporation within the United States (within the meaning of section 865(e)(2)).

(ii) Special rules for assets not described in paragraph (d)(1)(i) of this section. An asset of a foreign corporation that is held by the corporation as of the determination date and is not described in paragraph (d)(1)(i) of this section shall be treated as a U.S. asset to the extent provided in paragraph (d)(2) of this section (relating to special rules for certain assets, including assets that produce income or gain at least a portion of which is ECI), and in paragraphs (d)(3) and (4) of this section (relating to special rules for interests in a partnership, trust, and estate).

(iii) Definition of ECI. For purposes of the regulations under section 884, the term "ECI" means income that is effectively connected with the conduct of a trade or business in the United States and income that is treated as effectively connected with the conduct of a trade or business in the United States under any provision of the Code. The term "ECI" also includes all income that is or is treated as effectively connected with the conduct of a U.S. trade or business whether or not the income is included in gross income (for example, interest income earned with respect to tax-exempt bonds).

(2) Special rules for certain assets. (i) Depreciable and amortizable property. An item of depreciable personal property or an item of amortizable intangible property shall be treated as a U.S. asset of a foreign corporation in the same proportion that the amount of the depreciation or amortization with respect to the item of property that is allowable as a deduction, or is includible in cost of goods sold, for the taxable year in computing the effectively connected taxable income of the foreign corporation bears to the total amount of depreciation or amortization computed for the taxable year with respect to the item of property.

(ii) Inventory. An item or pool of inventory property (as defined in section 865(i)(1)) shall be treated as a U.S. asset in the same proportion as the amount of gross receipts from the sale or exchange of such property for the three preceding taxable years (or for such part of the three-year period as the corporation has been in existence) that is effectively connected with the conduct of a U.S. trade or business bears to the total amount of gross receipts from the sale or exchange of such property during such period (or part thereof). If a foreign corporation has not sold or exchanged such property during such three-year period (or part thereof), then the property shall be treated as a U.S. asset in the same proportion that the anticipated amount of gross receipts from the sale or exchange of the property that is reasonably anticipated to be ECI bears to the anticipated total amount of gross receipts from the sale or exchange of the property.

(iii) Installment obligations. An installment obligation received in connection with an installment sale (as defined in section 453(b)) for which an election under section 453(d) has not been made shall be treated as a U.S. asset to the extent that it is received in connection with the sale of a U.S. asset. If an obligation is received in connection with the sale of an asset that is wholly a U.S. asset, it shall be treated as a U.S. asset in its entirety. If a single obligation is received in connection with the sale of an asset that is in part a U.S. asset under the rules of paragraphs (d)(2) through (4) of this section, or in connection with the sale of several assets including one or more non-U.S. assets, the obligation shall be treated as U.S. asset in the same proportion as—

(A) The sum of the amount of gain from the installment sale that would be ECI if the obligation were satisfied in full on the determination date and the adjusted basis of the obligation on such date (as determined under section 453B) attributable to the amount of gain that would be ECI bears to

(B) The sum of the total amount of gain from the sale if the obligation were satisfied in full and the adjusted basis of the obligation on such date (as determined under section 453B).

However, the obligation will only be treated as a U.S. asset if the interest income or original issue discount with respect to the obligation is ECI or the foreign corporation elects to treat the interest or original issue discount as ECI in the same proportion that the obligation is treated as a U.S. asset. A foreign corporation may elect to treat interest income or original issue discount as ECI by reporting such interest income or original issue discount as ECI on its income tax return or an amended return for the taxable year. See paragraph (d)(6)(ii) of this section to determine the E&P basis of an installment obligation for purposes of this paragraph (d)(2)(iii).

(iv) Receivables. (A) Receivables arising from the sale or exchange of inventory property. An account or note receivable (whether or not bearing stated interest) with a maturity not exceeding six months that arises from the sale or exchange of inventory property (as defined in section 865(i)(1)) shall be treated as a U.S. asset in the proportion determined under paragraph (d)(2)(iii) of this section as if the receivable were an installment obligation.

(B) Receivables arising from the performance of services or leasing of property. An account or note receivable (whether or not bearing stated interest) with a maturity not exceeding six months that arises from the performance of services or the leasing of property in the ordinary course of a foreign corporation's trade or business shall be treated as a U.S. asset in the same proportion that the amount of gross income represented by the receivable that is ECI bears to the total amount of gross income represented by the receivable. For purposes of this paragraph (d)(2)(iv)(B), the amount of income represented by a receivable shall not include interest income or original issue discount.

(v) Bank and other deposits. A deposit or credit balance with a person described in section 871(i)(3) or a Federal Reserve Bank that is interest-bearing shall be treated as a U.S. asset if all income derived by the foreign corporation with respect to the deposit or credit balance during the taxable year is ECI. Any other deposit or credit balance shall only be treated as a U.S. asset if the deposit or credit balance is needed in a U.S. trade or business within the meaning of § 1.864-4(c)(2)(iii)(a).

(vi) Debt instruments. A debt instrument, as defined in section 1275(a)(1) (other than an asset treated as a U.S. asset under any other subdivision of this paragraph (d)) shall be treated as a U.S. asset, notwithstanding the fact that gain from the sale or exchange of the obligation on the determination date would not be ECI, if—

(A) All income derived by the foreign corporation from such obligation during the taxable year is ECI; and

(B) The yield for the period that the instrument was held during the taxable year equals or exceeds the Applicable Federal Rate for instruments of similar type and maturity.

Shares in a regulated investment company that purchases solely instruments that, under this paragraph (d)(2)(vi), would be U.S. assets if held directly by the foreign corporation shall also be treated as a U.S. asset.

(vii) Securities held by a foreign corporation engaged in a banking, financing or similar business.

Securities described in § 1.864-4(c)(5)(ii)(b)(3) held by a foreign corporation engaged in the active conduct of a banking, financing, or similar business in the United States during the taxable year shall be treated as U.S. assets in the same proportion that income, gain, or loss from such securities is ECI for the taxable year under § 1.864-4(c)(5)(ii).

(viii) Federal income taxes. An overpayment of Federal income taxes shall be treated as a U.S. asset to the extent that the tax would reduce a foreign corporation's ECEP for the taxable year but for the fact that the tax does not accrue during the taxable year.

(ix) Losses involving U.S. assets. A foreign corporation that sustains, with respect to a U.S. asset, a loss for which a deduction is not allowed under section 165 (in whole or in part) because there exists a reasonable prospect of recovering compensation for the loss shall be treated as having a U.S. asset ("loss property") from the date of the loss in the same proportion that the asset was treated as a U.S. asset immediately before the loss. See paragraph (d)(6)(iv) of this section to determine the E&P basis of the loss property.

(x) Ruling for involuntary conversion. If property that is a U.S. asset of a foreign corporation is compulsorily or involuntarily converted into property not similar or related in service or use (within the meaning of section 1033), the foreign corporation may apply to the Commissioner for a ruling to determine its U.S. assets for the taxable year of the involuntary conversion.

(xi) Examples. The principles of paragraphs (c) and (d)(1) and (2) of this section are illustrated by the following examples.

Example (1). Depreciable property. Foreign corporation A, a calendar year taxpayer, is engaged in a trade or business in the United States. A owns equipment that is used in its manufacturing business in country X and in the United States. Under § 1.861-8, A's depreciation deduction with respect to the equipment is allocated to sales income and is apportioned 70 percent to ECI and 30 percent to income that is not ECI. Under paragraph (d)(2)(ii) of this section, the equipment is 70 percent a U.S. asset. The equipment has an E&P basis of $100 at the beginning of 1993. A's depreciation deduction (for purposes of computing earnings and profits) with respect to the equipment is $10 for 1993. To determine the amount of A's U.S. asset at the close of 1993, the equipment's $90 E&P basis at the close of 1993 is multiplied by 70 percent (the proportion of the asset that is a U.S. asset). The amount of the U.S. asset as of the close of 1993 is $63.

Example (2). U.S. real property interest connected to a U.S. business. FC is a foreign corporation that is a bank, within the meaning of section 585(a)(2)(B) (without regard to the second sentence thereof), and is engaged in the business of taking deposits and making loans through its branch in the United States. In 1996, FC makes a loan in the ordinary course of its lending business in the United States, securing the loan with a mortgage on the U.S. real property being financed by the borrower. In 1997, after the borrower has defaulted on the loan, FC takes title to the real property that secures the loan. On December 31, 1997, FC continues to hold the property, classifying it on its financial statement as Other Real Estate Owned. Because all income and gain from the property would be ECI to FC under the principles of section 864(c)(2), the U.S. real property constitutes a U.S. asset within the meaning of paragraph (d) of this section.

Example (3). U.S. real property interest not connected to a U.S. business. Foreign corporation A owns a condominium apartment in the United States. Assume that holding the apartment does not constitute a U.S. trade or business and the foreign corporation has not made an election under section 882(d) to treat income with respect to the property as ECI. The condominium apartment is not a U.S. asset of A because the income, if any, from the asset would not be ECI. However, the disposition by A of the condominium apartment at a gain will give rise to ECEP.

Example (4). Stock in a domestically-controlled REIT. As an investment, foreign corporation A owns stock in a domestically-controlled REIT, within the meaning of section 897(h)(4)(B). Under section 897(h)(2), gain on disposition of stock in the REIT is not treated as ECI. For this reason the stock does not qualify as a U.S. asset under paragraph (d)(1) of this section even if dividend distributions from the REIT are treated as ECI. Thus, A will have a dividend equivalent amount based on the ECEP attributable to a distribution of ECI from the REIT, even if A invests the proceeds from the dividend in additional stock of the REIT. (Stock in a REIT that is not a domestically-controlled REIT is also not a U.S. asset. See § 1.884-1(d)(5)).

Example (5). Section 864(c)(7) property. Foreign corporation A is engaged in the equipment leasing business in the United States and Canada. A transfers the equipment leased by its U.S. trade or business to its Canadian business after the equipment is fully depreciated in the United States. The Canadian business sells the equipment two years later. Section 864(c)(7) would treat the gain on the disposition of the equipment by A as taxable under section 882 as if the sale occurred immediately before the equipment was transferred to the Canadian business. The equipment would not be treated as a U.S. asset even if the gain was ECI because the income from the equipment in the year of the sale in Canada would not be ECI.

(3) Interest in a partnership. (i) In general. A foreign corporation that is a partner in a partnership must take into account its interest in the partnership (and not the partnership assets) in determining its U.S. assets. For purposes of determining the proportion of the partnership interest that is a U.S. asset, a foreign corporation may elect to use either the asset method described in paragraph (d)(3)(ii) of this section or the income method described in paragraph (d)(3)(iii) of this section.

(ii) Asset method. (A) In general. A partner's interest in a partnership shall be treated as a U.S. asset in the same proportion that the sum of the partner's proportionate share of the adjusted bases of all partnership assets as of the determination date, to the extent that the assets would be treated as U.S. assets if the partnership were a foreign corporation, bears to the sum of the partner's proportionate share of the adjusted bases of all partnership assets as of the determination date. Generally a partner's proportionate share of a partnership asset is the same as its proportionate share of all items of income, gain, loss, and deduction that may be generated by the asset.

(B) Non-uniform proportionate shares. If a partner's proportionate share of all items of income, gain, loss, and deduction that may be generated by a single asset of the partnership throughout the period that includes the taxable year of the partner is not uniform, then, for purposes of determining the partner's proportionate share of the adjusted basis of that asset, a partner must take into account the portion of the adjusted basis of the asset that reflects the partner's economic interest in that asset. A partner's economic interest in an asset of the partnership must be determined by applying the following presumptions. These presumptions may, however, be rebutted if the partner or the Internal Revenue Service shows that the presumption is inconsistent with the partner's true economic interest in the asset during the corporation's taxable year.

(1) If a partnership asset ordinarily generates directly identifiable income, a partner's economic interest in the asset is determined by reference to its proportionate share of income that may be generated by the asset for the partnership's taxable year ending with or within the partner's taxable year.

(2) If a partnership asset ordinarily generates current deductions and ordinarily generates no directly identifiable income, for example because the asset contributes equally to the generation of all the income of the partnership (such as an asset used in general and administrative functions), a partner's economic interest in the asset is determined by reference to its proportionate share of the total deductions that may be generated by the asset for the partnership's taxable year ending with or within the partner's taxable year.

(3) For other partnership assets not described in paragraph (d)(3)(ii)(B)(1) or (2) of this section, a partner's economic interest in the asset is determined by reference to its proportionate share of the total gain or loss to which it would be entitled if the asset were sold at a gain or loss in the partnership's taxable year ending with or within the partner's taxable year.

(C) Partnership election under section 754. If a partnership files an election in accordance with section 754, then for purposes of this paragraph (d)(3)(ii), the basis of partnership property shall reflect adjustments made pursuant to sections 734 (relating to distributions of property to a partner) and 743 (relating to the transfer of an interest in a partnership). However, adjustments made pursuant to section 743 may be made with respect to a transferee partner only.

(iii) Income method. Under the income method, a partner's interest in a partnership shall be treated as a U.S. asset in the same proportion that its distributive share of partnership ECI for the partnership's taxable year that ends with or within the partner's taxable year bears to its distributive share of all partnership income for that taxable year.

(iv) Manner of election. (A) In general. In determining the proportion of a foreign corporation's interest in a partnership that is a U.S. asset, a foreign corporation must elect one of the methods described in paragraph (d)(3) of this section on a timely filed return for the first taxable year beginning on or after the effective date of this section. An amended return does not qualify for this purpose, nor shall the provisions of § 301.9100-1 of this chapter and any guidance promulgated thereunder apply. An election shall be made by the foreign corporation calculating its U.S. assets in accordance with the method elected. An elected method must be used for a minimum period of five years before the foreign corporation may elect a different method. To change an election before the end of the requisite five-year period, a foreign corporation must obtain the consent of the Commissioner or her delegate. The Commissioner or her delegate will generally consent to a foreign corporation's request to change its election only in rare and unusual circumstances. A foreign corporation that is a partner in more than one partnership is not required to elect to use the same method for each partnership interest.

(B) Elections with tiered partnerships. If a foreign corporation elects to use the asset method with respect to an interest in a partnership, and that partnership is a partner in a lower-tier partnership, the foreign corporation may apply either the asset method or the income method to determine the proportion of the upper-tier partnership's interest in the lower-tier partnership that is a U.S. asset.

(v) Failure to make proper election. If a foreign corporation, for any reason, fails to make an election to use one of the methods required by paragraph (d)(3) of this section in a timely fashion, the district director or the Assistant Commissioner (International) may make the election on behalf of the foreign corporation and such election shall be binding as if made by that corporation.

(vi) Special rule for determining a partner's adjusted basis in a partnership interest. For purposes of paragraphs (d)(3) and (6) of this section, a partner's adjusted basis in a partnership interest shall be the partner's basis in such interest (determined under section 705) reduced by the partner's share of the liabilities of the partnership determined under section 752 and increased by a proportionate share of each liability of the partnership equal to the partner's proportionate share of the expense, for income tax purposes, attributable to such liability for the taxable year. A partner's adjusted basis in a partnership interest cannot be less than zero.

(vii) E&P basis of a partnership interest. See paragraph (d)(6)(iii) of this section for special rules governing the calculation of a foreign corporation's E&P basis in a partnership interest.

(viii) The application of this paragraph (d)(3) is illustrated by the following examples:

Example (1). General rule.

(i) Facts. Foreign corporation, FC, is a partner in partnership ABC, which is engaged in a trade or business within the United States. FC and ABC are both calendar year taxpayers. ABC owns and manages two office buildings located in the United States, each with an adjusted basis of $50. ABC also owns a non-U.S. asset with an adjusted basis of $100. ABC has no liabilities. Under the partnership agreement, FC has a 50 percent interest in the capital of ABC and a 50 percent interest in all items of income, gain, loss, and deduction that may be generated by the partnership's assets. FC's adjusted basis in ABC is $100. In determining the proportion of its interest in ABC that is a U.S. asset, FC elects to use the asset method described in paragraph (d)(3)(ii) of this section.

(ii) Analysis. FC's interest in ABC is treated as a U.S. asset in the same proportion that the sum of FC's proportionate share of the adjusted bases of all ABC's U.S. assets (50% of $100), bears to the sum of FC's proportionate share of the adjusted bases of all of ABC's assets (50% of $200). Under the asset method, the amount of FC's interest in ABC that is a U.S. asset is $50 ($100 × $50/$100).

Example (2). Special allocation of gain with respect to real property.

(i) Facts. The facts are the same as in Example 1, except that under the partnership agreement, FC is allocated 20 percent of the income from the partnership property but 80 percent of the gain on disposition of the partnership property.

(ii) Analysis. Assuming that the buildings ordinarily generate directly identifiable income, there is a rebuttable presumption under paragraph (d)(3)(ii)(B)(1) of this section that FC's proportionate share of the adjusted basis of the buildings is FC's proportionate share of the income generated by the buildings (20%) rather than the total gain that it would be entitled to under the partnership agreement (80%) if the buildings were sold at a gain on the determination date. Thus, the sum of FC's proportionate share of the adjusted bases in ABC's U.S. assets (the buildings) is presumed to be $20 [(20% of $50) + (20% of $50)]. Assuming that the non-U.S. asset is not income producing and does not generate current deductions, there is a rebuttable presumption under paragraph (d)(3)(ii)(B)(3) of this section that FC's proportionate share of the adjusted basis of that asset is FC's interest in the gain on the disposition of the asset (80%) rather than its proportionate share of the income that may be generated by the asset (20%). Thus, FC's proportionate share of the adjusted basis of ABC's non-U.S. asset is presumed to be $80 (80% of $100). FC's proportionate share of the adjusted bases of all of the assets of ABC is $100 ($20 + $80). The amount of FC's interest in ABC that is a U.S. asset is $20 ($100 × $20/$100).

Example (3). Tiered partnerships (asset method).

(i) Facts. The facts are the same as in Example 1, except that FC's adjusted basis in ABC is $175 and ABC also has a 50 percent interest in the capital of partnership DEF. DEF owns and operates a commercial shopping center in the United States with an adjusted basis of $200 and also owns non-U.S. assets with an adjusted basis of $100. DEF has no liabilities. ABC's adjusted basis in its interest in DEF is $150 and ABC has a 50 percent interest in all the items of income, gain, loss and deduction that may be generated by the assets of DEF.

(ii) Analysis. Because FC has elected to use the asset method described in paragraph (d)(3)(ii) of this section, it must determine what proportion of ABC's partnership interest in DEF is a U.S. asset. As permitted by paragraph (d)(3)(iv)(B) of this section, FC also elects to use the asset method with respect to ABC's interest in DEF. ABC's interest in DEF is treated as a U.S. asset in the same proportion that the sum of ABC's proportionate share of the adjusted bases of all DEF's U.S. assets (50% of $200), bears to the sum of ABC's proportionate share of the adjusted bases of all of DEF's assets (50% of $300). Thus, the amount of ABC's interest in DEF that is a U.S. asset is $100 ($150 × $100/$150). FC must then apply the rules of paragraph (d)(3)(ii) of this section to all the assets of ABC, including ABC's interest in DEF that is treated in part as a U.S. asset ($100) and in part as a non-U.S. asset ($50). FC's interest in ABC is treated as a U.S. asset in the same proportion that the sum of FC's proportionate share of the adjusted bases of the U.S. assets of ABC (including ABC's interest in DEF), bears to the sum of FC's proportionate share of the adjusted bases of all ABC's assets (including ABC's interest in DEF). Thus, the amount of FC's interest in ABC that is a U.S. asset is $100 (FC's adjusted basis in ABC ($175) multiplied by FC's proportionate share of the sum of the adjusted bases of ABC's U.S. assets ($100)) over FC's proportionate share of the sum of the adjusted bases of ABC's assets ($175)).

Example (4). Tiered partnerships (income method).

(i) Facts. The facts are the same as in Example 3, except that FC has elected to use the income method described in paragraph (d)(3)(iii) of this section to determine the proportion of its interest in ABC that is a U.S. asset. The two office buildings located in the United States generate $60 of income that is ECI for the taxable year. The non-U.S. asset is not-income producing. In addition ABC's distributive share of income from DEF consists of $40 of income that is ECI and $140 of income that is not ECI.

(ii) Analysis. Because FC has elected to use the income method it does need to determine what proportion of ABC's partnership interest in DEF is a U.S. asset. FC's interest in ABC is treated as a U.S. asset in the same proportion that its distributive share of ABC's income for the taxable year that is ECI ($50) ($30 earned directly by ABC + $20 distributive share from DEF) bears to its distributive share of all ABC's income for the taxable year ($55) ($30 earned directly by ABC + $25 distributive share from DEF). Thus, FC's interest in ABC that is a U.S. asset is $159 ($175 × $50/$55).

(4) Interest in a trust or estate. (i) Estates and non-grantor trusts. A foreign corporation that is a beneficiary of a trust or estate shall not be treated as having a U.S. asset by virtue of its interest in the trust or estate.

(ii) Grantor trusts. If, under sections 671 through 678, a foreign corporation is treated as owning a portion of a trust that includes all the income and gain that may be generated by a trust asset (or pro rata portion of a trust asset), the foreign corporation will be treated as owning the trust asset (or pro rata portion thereof) for purposes of determining its U.S. assets under this section.

(5) Property that is not a U.S. asset. (i) Property that does not give rise to ECEP. Property described in paragraphs (d)(1) through (4) of this section shall not be treated as a U.S. asset of a foreign corporation if, on the determination date, income from the use of the property, or gain or loss from the disposition of the property, would be described in paragraph (f)(2) of this section (relating to certain income that does not produce ECEP).

(ii) Assets acquired to increase U.S. net equity artificially. U.S. assets shall not include assets acquired or used by a foreign corporation if one of the principal purposes of such acquisition or use is to increase artificially the U.S. assets of a foreign corporation on the determination date. Whether assets are acquired or used for such purpose will depend upon all the facts and circumstances of each case. Factors to be considered in determining whether one of the principal purposes in acquiring or using an asset is to increase artificially the U.S. assets of a foreign corporation include the length of time during which the asset was used in a U.S. trade or business, whether the asset was acquired from, or disposed of to, a related person, and whether the aggregate value of the U.S. assets of the foreign corporation increased temporarily on the determination date. For purposes of this paragraph (d)(5)(ii), to be one of the principal purposes, a purpose must be important, but it is not necessary that it be the primary purpose.

(iii) Interbranch transactions. A transaction of any type between separate offices or branches of the same taxpayer does not create a U.S. asset.

(6) E&P basis of a U.S. asset. (i) General rule. The E&P basis of a U.S. asset for purposes of this section is its adjusted basis for purposes of computing the foreign corporation's earnings and profits. In determining the E&P basis of a U.S. asset, the adjusted basis of the asset (for purposes of computing taxable income) must be increased or decreased to take into account inclusions of income or gain, and deductions or similar charges, that affect the basis of the asset where such items are taken into account in a different manner for purposes of computing earnings and profits than for purposes of computing taxable income. For example, if section 312(k) requires that depreciation with respect to a U.S. asset be determined using the straight line method for purposes of computing earnings and profits, but depreciation with respect to the asset is determined using a different method for purposes of computing taxable income, the E&P basis of the property for purposes of this section must be computed using the straight line method of depreciation.

(ii) Installment obligations. (A) Sales in taxable year beginning on or after January 1, 1987. For purposes of this section, the E&P basis of an installment obligation described in paragraph (d)(2)(iii) of this section that arises in connection with an installment sale occurring in a taxable year beginning on or after January 1, 1987, shall equal the sum of the total amount of gain from the sale if the obligation were satisfied in full and the adjusted basis of the property sold as of the date of sale, reduced by payments received with respect to the obligation that are not interest or original issue discount. See paragraph (j)(2)(ii) of this section, however, for a special E&P basis rule for an installment obligation arising in connection with a sale of a U.S. asset by a foreign corporation described in section 312(k)(4), where such sale occurs in a taxable year beginning in 1987.

(B) Sales in taxable year prior to January 1, 1987. For purposes of this section, the E&P basis of an installment obligation described in paragraph (d)(2)(iii) of this section that arises in connection with an installment sale occurring in a taxable year beginning before January 1, 1987, shall equal zero.

(iii) Computation of E&P basis in a partnership. For purposes of this section, a foreign corporation's E&P basis in a partnership interest shall be the foreign corporation's adjusted basis in such interest (as determined under paragraph (d)(3)(vi) of this section), further adjusted to take into account any differences between the foreign corporation's distributive share of items of partnership income, gain, loss, and deduction for purposes of computing the taxable income of the foreign corporation and the foreign corporation's distributive share of items of partnership income, gain, loss, and deduction for purposes of computing the earnings and profits of the foreign corporation.

(iv) Computation of E&P basis of a loss property. The E&P basis of a loss property (as defined in paragraph (d)(2)(ix) of this section) shall equal the E&P basis, immediately before the loss, of the U.S. asset with respect to which the loss was sustained, reduced (but not below zero) by—

(A) The amount of any deduction claimed under section 165 by the foreign corporation with respect to the loss for earnings and profits purposes; and

(B) Any compensation received with respect to the loss.

(v) Computation of E&P basis of financial instruments. [Reserved]

(vi) Example. The application of paragraph (d)(6)(ii) of this section is illustrated by the following example.

Example. Sale in taxable year beginning on or after January 1, 1987. Foreign corporation A, a calendar year taxpayer, sells a U.S. asset on the installment method in 1993. Under the terms of the sale, A is to receive $100, payable in ten annual installments of $10 beginning in 1994, plus an arm's-length rate of interest on the unpaid balance of the sales price. A's adjusted basis in the property sold is $70. The obligation received in connection with the installment sale is treated as a U.S. asset with an E&P basis of $100 ($30 (the amount of gain from the sale if the obligation were satisfied in full) + $70 (the adjusted basis of the property sold)). If A receives a payment of $10 (not including interest) in 1994 with respect to the obligation, the obligation is treated as a U.S. asset with an E&P basis of $90 ($100 – $10) as of the close of 1994.

(e) U.S. liabilities. The term "U.S. liabilities" means the amount of liabilities determined under paragraph (e)(1) of this section decreased by the amount of liabilities determined under paragraph (e)(3) of this section, and increased by the amount of liabilities determined under paragraph (e)(2) of this section.

(1) Liabilities based on § 1.882-5. The amount of liabilities determined under this paragraph (e)(1) is the amount of U.S.-connected liabilities of a foreign corporation under § 1.882-5 if the U.S.-connected liabilities were computed using the assets and liabilities of the foreign corporation as of the determination date (rather than the average of such assets and liabilities for the taxable year) and without regard to paragraph (e)(3) of this section.

(2) Additional liabilities. (i) Insurance reserves.The amount of liabilities determined under this paragraph (e)(2)(i) is the amount (as of the determination date) of the total insurance liabilities on United States business (within the meaning of section 842(b)(2)(B)) of a foreign corporation described in section 842(a) (relating to foreign corporations carrying on an insurance business in the United States) to the extent that such liabilities are not otherwise treated as U.S. liabilities by reason of paragraph (e)(1) of this section.

(ii) Liabilities described in § 1.882-5(a)(1)(ii). The amount of liabilities determined under this paragraph (e)(2)(ii) is the amount (as of the determination date) of liabilities described in § 1.882-5(a)(1)(ii) (relating to liabilities giving rise to interest expense that is directly allocated to income from a U.S. asset).

(3) Election to reduce liabilities. (i) General rule. The amount of liabilities determined under this paragraph (e)(3) is the amount by which a foreign corporation elects to reduce its liabilities under paragraph (e)(1) of this section.

(ii) [Reserved]. For further guidance, see entry in § 1.884-1T(e)(3)(ii).

(iii) Effect of election on interest deduction and branch-level interest tax. A foreign corporation that elects to reduce its liabilities under this paragraph (e)(3) must, for purposes of computing the amount of its interest apportioned to ECI under § 1.882-5, reduce its U.S.-connected liabilities for the taxable year of the election by the amount of the reduction in liabilities under this paragraph (e)(3). The reduction of its U.S.-connected liabilities will also require a corresponding decrease in the amount of its interest apportioned to ECI under § 1.882-5 for purposes of § 1.884-4(a) and for all other Code sections for which the amount of interest apportioned under § 1.882-5 is relevant.

(iv) [Reserved]. For further guidance, see entry in § 1.884-1T(e)(3)(iv).

(v) Effect of election on complete termination. If a foreign corporation completely terminates its U.S. trade or business (within the meaning of § 1.884-2T(a)(2)), notwithstanding § 1.884-2T(a), the foreign corporation will be subject to tax on a dividend equivalent amount that equals the lesser of—

(A) The foreign corporation's accumulated ECEP that is attributable to an election to reduce liabilities; or

(B) The amount by which the corporation elected to reduce liabilities at the end of the taxable year preceding the year of complete termination.

For purposes of the preceding sentence, accumulated ECEP is attributable to an election to reduce liabilities to the extent that the ECEP was accumulated because of such an election rather than because of an increase in U.S. assets. For example, if a foreign corporation did not have positive ECEP in any year for which an election was made, it would not be required to include an amount as a dividend equivalent amount under this paragraph (e)(3)(v) because any accumulated ECEP that it may have is not attributable to an election to reduce liabilities.

(4) Artificial decrease in U.S. liabilities. If a foreign corporation repays or otherwise decreases its U.S. liabilities and one of the principal purposes of such decrease is to decrease artificially its U.S. liabilities on the determination date, then such decrease shall not be taken into account for purposes of computing the foreign corporation's U.S. net equity. Whether the U.S. liabilities of a foreign corporation are artificially decreased will depend on all the facts and circumstances of each case. Factors to be considered in determining whether one of the principal purposes for the repayment or decrease of the liabilities is to decrease artificially the U.S. liabilities of a foreign corporation shall include whether the aggregate liabilities are temporarily decreased on or before the determination date by, for example, the repayment of liabilities, or U.S. liabilities are temporarily decreased on or before the determination date by the acquisition with contributed funds of passive-type assets that are not U.S. assets. For purposes of this paragraph (e)(4), to be one of the principal purposes, a purpose must be important, but it is not necessary that it be the primary purpose.

(5) Examples. The application of this paragraph (e) is illustrated by the following examples.

Example (1). General rule for computation of U.S. liabilities. For purposes of computing its U.S.-connected liabilities under § 1.882-5(c), A must determine the average total value of its assets that are U.S. assets. Assume that the average value of such assets is $100, while the amount of such assets as of the close of 1997 is $125. For purposes of § 1.882-5(c)(2), A must determine the ratio of the average of its worldwide liabilities for the year to the average total value of worldwide assets for the taxable year. Assume that A's average liabilities-to-assets ratio under § 1.882-5(c)(2) is 55 percent, while its liabilities-to-assets ratio at the close of 1997 is only 50 percent. Thus, assuming no further adjustments under paragraph (e)(3) of this section, A's U.S.-connected liabilities for purposes of § 1.882-5 are $55 ($100 × 55%). However, A's U.S. liabilities are $62.50 for purposes of this section, the value of its assets determined under § 1.882-5(b)(2) as of the close of December ($125) multiplied by the liabilities-to-assets ratio (50%) as of such date.

Example (2). [Reserved]. For further guidance, see entry in § 1.884-1T(e)(5) Example 2.

(f) Effectively connected earnings and profits. *(1) In general.* Except as provided in paragraph (f)(2) of this section and as modified by § 1.884-2T (relating to the incorporation or complete termination of a U.S. trade or business or the reorganization or liquidation of a foreign corporation or its domestic subsidiary), the term "effectively connected earnings and profits" ("ECEP") means the earnings and profits (or deficits therein) determined under section 312 and this paragraph (f) that are attributable to ECI (within the meaning of paragraph (d)(1)(iii) of this section). Because the term "ECI" includes income treated as effectively connected, income that is ECI under section 842(b) (relating to minimum net investment income of an insurance business) or 864(c)(7) (relating to gain from property formerly held for use in a U.S. trade or business) gives rise to ECEP. ECEP also includes earnings and profits attributable to ECI of a foreign corporation earned through a partnership, and through a trust or estate. For purposes of section 884, gain on the sale of a U.S. real property interest by a foreign corporation that has made an election to be treated as a domestic corporation under section 897(i) will also give rise to ECEP. ECEP is not reduced by distributions made by the foreign corporation during any taxable year or by the amount of branch profits tax or tax on excess interest (as defined in § 1.884-4(a)(2)) paid by the foreign corporation. Earnings and profits are treated as attributable to ECI even if the earnings and profits are taken into account under section 312 in an earlier or later taxable year than the taxable year in which the ECI is taken into account.

(2) Income that does not produce ECEP. The term "ECEP" does not include any earnings and profits attributable to—

(i) Income excluded from gross income under section 883(a)(1) or 883(a)(2) (relating to certain income derived from the operation of ships or aircraft);

(ii) Income that is ECI by reason of section 921(d) or 926(b) (relating to certain income of a FSC and certain dividends paid by a FSC to a foreign corporation or nonresident alien) that is not otherwise ECI;

(iii) Gain on the disposition of a U.S. real property interest described in section 897(c)(1)(A)(ii) (relating to certain interests in a domestic corporation);

(iv) Income that is ECI by reason of section 953(c)(3)(C) (relating to certain income of a captive insurance company that a corporation elects to treat as ECI) that is not otherwise ECI;

(v) Income that is exempt from tax under section 892 (relating to certain income of foreign governments); and

(vi) Income that is ECI by reason of section 882(e) (relating to certain interest income of banks organized under the laws of a possession of the United States) that is not otherwise ECI.

(3) Allocation of deductions attributable to income that does not produce ECEP. In determining the amount of a foreign corporation's ECEP for the taxable year, deductions and other adjustments shall be allocated and apportioned under the principles of § 1.861-8 between ECI that gives rise to ECEP and income described in paragraph (f)(2) of this section (relating to income that is ECI but does not give rise to ECEP).

(4) Examples. The principles of paragraph (f) of this section are illustrated by the following examples.

Example (1). Tax-exempt income. Foreign corporation A owns a tax-exempt municipal bond that is a U.S. asset as of the close of its 1989 taxable year. The municipal bond gives rise in 1989 to ECI (even though the income is excluded from gross income under section 103(a) and is not gross income of a foreign corporation by reason of section 882(b)), and therefore gives rise to ECEP in 1989.

Example (2). Income exempt under a treaty. Foreign corporation A derives ECI that constitutes business profits that are not attributable to a permanent establishment maintained by A in the United States. The ECI is exempt from taxation under section 882(a) by reason of an income tax treaty and section 894(a). The income nevertheless gives rise to ECEP under this paragraph (f). However, a dividend equivalent amount attributable to such ECEP may be exempt from the branch profits tax by reason of paragraph (g) of this section (relating to the application of the branch profits tax to corporations that are residents of countries with which the United States has an income tax treaty).

(g) Corporations resident in countries with which the United States has an income tax treaty. *(1) General rule.* Except as provided in paragraph (g)(2) of this section, a foreign corporation that is a resident of a country with which the United States has an income tax treaty in effect for a taxable year in which it has a dividend equivalent amount and that meets the requirements, if any, of the limitation on benefits provisions of such treaty with respect to the dividend equivalent amount shall not be subject to the branch profits tax on such amount (or will qualify for a reduction in the amount of tax with respect to such amount) only if—

(i) The foreign corporation is a qualified resident of such country for the taxable year, within the meaning of § 1.884-5(a); or

(ii) The limitation on benefits provision, or an amendment to that provision, entered into force after December 31, 1986.

If, after application of § 1.884-5(e)(4)(iv), a foreign corporation is a qualified resident under § 1.884-5(e) (relating to the active trade or business test) only with respect to one of its trades or businesses in the United States, i.e., the trade or business that is an integral part of its business conducted in its country of residence, and not with respect to another, the rules of this paragraph shall apply only to that portion of its dividend equivalent amount attributable to the trade or business for which the foreign corporation is a qualified resident.

(2) Special rules for foreign corporations that are qualified residents on the basis of their ownership. (i) General rule. A foreign corporation that, in any taxable year, is a qualified resident of a country with which the United States has an income tax treaty in effect solely by reason of meeting the requirements of § 1.884-5(b) and (c) (relating, respectively, to stock ownership and base erosion) shall be exempt from the branch profits tax or subject to a reduced rate of branch profits tax under paragraph (g)(1) of this section with respect to the portion of its dividend equivalent amount for the taxable year attributable to accumulated ECEP only if the foreign corporation is a qualified resident of such country within the meaning of § 1.884-5(a) for the taxable years includible, in whole or in part, in a consecutive 36-month period that includes the taxable year of the dividend equivalent amount. A foreign corporation that fails the 36-month test described in the preceding sentence shall be exempt from the branch profits tax or subject to the branch profits tax at a reduced rate under paragraph (g)(1) of this section with respect to accumulated ECEP (determined on a last-in-first-out basis) accumulated only during prior years in which the foreign corporation was a qualified resident of such country within the meaning of § 1.884-5(a).

(ii) Rules of application. A foreign corporation that has not satisfied the 36-month test as of the close of the taxable year of the dividend equivalent amount but satisfies the test with respect to such dividend equivalent amount by meeting the 36-month test by the close of the second taxable year succeeding the taxable year of the dividend equivalent amount shall be subject to the branch profits tax for the year of the dividend equivalent amount without regard to paragraph (g)(1) of this section on the portion of the dividend equivalent amount attributable to accumulated ECEP derived in a taxable year in which the foreign corporation was not a qualified resident within the meaning of § 1.884-5(a). Upon meeting the 36-month test, the foreign corporation shall be entitled to claim by amended return a refund of the tax paid with respect to the dividend equivalent amount in excess of the branch profits tax calculated by taking into account paragraph (g)(2)(i) of this section, provided the foreign corporation establishes in the amended return for the taxable year that it has met the requirements of such paragraph. For purposes of section 6611 (dealing with interest on overpayments), any overpayment of branch profits tax by reason of this paragraph (g)(2)(ii) shall be deemed not to have been made before the filing date for the taxable year in which the foreign corporation establishes that it has met the 36-month test.

(iii) Example. The application of this paragraph (g)(2) is illustrated by the following example.

Example. (i) Foreign corporation A, a calendar year taxpayer, is a resident of the United Kingdom. A has a dividend equivalent amount for its taxable year 1991 of $300, of which $100 is attributable to 1991 ECEP and $200 to accumulated ECEP. A is a qualified resident for its taxable year 1991 because for that year it meets the requirements of § 1.884-5(b) and (c), relating, respectively, to stock ownership and base erosion. For 1991 A does not meet the requirements of § 1.884-5(d), (e), or (f) for qualified residence. A is not a qualified resident of the United Kingdom for any taxable year prior to 1990 but is a qualified resident for its taxable years 1990 and 1992.

(ii) Because A is a qualified resident for the 3-year period (1990, 1991, and 1992) that includes the taxable year of the dividend equivalent amount (1991), A satisfies the 36-month test of this paragraph (g)(2) and no branch profits tax is imposed on the total $300 dividend equivalent amount. However, since A was not a qualified resident for any taxable year prior to 1990 and therefore cannot establish that it has satisfied the 36-month test until the taxable year following the year of the dividend equivalent amount, A must pay the branch profits tax for its taxable year 1991 with respect to the portion of the dividend equivalent amount attributable to accumulated ECEP relating to years prior to 1990 without regard to paragraph (g)(1) of this section. A may file for a refund of the branch profits tax paid with respect to its 1991 taxable year at any time after it establishes that it is a qualified resident for its 1992 taxable year.

(3) Exemptions for foreign corporations resident in certain countries with income tax treaties in effect on January 1, 1987. The branch profits tax shall not be imposed on the portion of the dividend equivalent amount with respect to which a foreign corporation satisfies the requirements of paragraphs (g)(1) and (2) of this section for a country listed below, so long as the income tax treaty between the United States and that country, as in effect on January 1, 1987, remains in effect, except to the extent the treaty is modified on or after January 1, 1987, to expressly provide for the imposition of the branch profits tax:

Aruba	Germany	Malta
Austria	Greece	Morocco
Belgium	Hungary	Netherlands
People's Republic of China	Iceland	Netherlands Antilles
	Ireland	Norway
	Italy	
Cyprus	Jamaica	Pakistan
Denmark	Japan	Philippines
Egypt	Korea	Sweden
Finland	Luxembourg	Switzerland

United Kingdom

(4) Modifications with respect to other income tax treaties. (i) Limitation on rate of tax. (A) General rule. If, under paragraphs (g)(1) and (2) of this section, a corporation qualifies for a reduction in the amount of the branch profits tax and paragraph (g)(3) of this section does not apply, the rate of tax shall be the rate of tax on branch profits specified in the treaty between the United States and the corporation's country of residence or, if no rate of tax on branch profits is specified, the rate of tax that would apply under such treaty to dividends paid to the foreign corporation by a wholly-owned domestic corporation.

(B) Certain treaties in effect on January 1, 1987. The branch profits tax shall generally be imposed at the following rates on the portion of the dividend equivalent amount with respect to which a foreign corporation satisfies the requirements of paragraphs (g)(1) and (2) of this section for a country listed below, for as long as the relevant provisions of those income tax treaties remain in effect and are not modified or superseded by subsequent agreement:

Australia (15%)	New Zealand (5%)	Trinidad & Tabago (10%)
Barbados (5%)	Poland (5%)	U.S.S.R. (30%)
Canada (10%)	Romania (10%)	
France (5%)	South Africa (30%)	

However, for special rates imposed on corporations resident in France and Trinidad & Tobago that have certain amounts of dividend and interest income, see the dividend articles of the income tax treaties with those countries.

(ii) Limitations other than rate of tax. If, under paragraphs (g)(1) and (2) of this section, a foreign corporation qualifies for a reduction in the amount of branch profits tax and paragraph (g)(3) of this section does not apply, then—

(A) The foreign corporation shall be entitled to the benefit of any limitations on imposition of a tax on branch profits (in addition to any limitations on the rate of tax) contained in the treaty; and

(B) No branch profits tax shall be imposed with respect to a dividend equivalent amount out of ECEP or accumulated ECEP of the foreign corporation unless the ECEP or accumulated ECEP is attributable to a permanent establishment in the United States or, if not otherwise prohibited under the treaty, to gain from the disposition of a U.S. real property interest described in section 897(c)(1)(A)(i), except to the extent the treaty specifically permits the imposition of the branch profits tax on such earnings and profits.

No article in such treaty shall be construed to provide any limitations on imposition of the branch profits tax other than as provided in this paragraph (g)(4).

(iii) Computation of the dividend equivalent amount if a foreign corporation has both ECEP attributable to a permanent establishment and not attributable to a permanent establishment. To determine the dividend equivalent amount of a foreign corporation out of ECEP that is attributable to a permanent establishment, the foreign corporation may only take into account its U.S. assets, U.S. liabilities, U.S. net equity and ECEP attributable to its permanent establishment. Thus, a foreign corporation may not reduce the amount of its ECEP attributable to its permanent establishment by reinvesting all or a portion of that amount in U.S. assets not attributable to the permanent establishment.

(iv) Limitations under the Canadian treaty. The limitations on the imposition of the branch profits tax under the Canadian treaty include, but are not limited to, those described in paragraphs (g)(4)(iv)(A) and (B).

(A) Effect of deficits in earnings and profits. In the case of a foreign corporation that is a qualified resident of Canada, the dividend equivalent amount for any taxable year shall not exceed the foreign corporation's accumulated ECEP as of the beginning of the taxable year plus the corporation's ECEP for the taxable year. Thus, for example, if a foreign corporation that is a qualified resident of Canada has a deficit in accumulated ECEP of $200 as of the beginning of the taxable year and ECEP of $100 for the taxable year, it will have no dividend equivalent amount for the taxable year because it would have a cumulative deficit in ECEP of $100 as of the close of the taxable year. For purposes of this paragraph (g)(4)(iii)(A), any net deficit in accumulated earnings and profits attributable to taxable years beginning before January 1, 1987, shall be includible in determining accumulated ECEP.

(B) One-time exemption of Canadian $500,000. (1) General rule. In the case of a foreign corporation that is a qualified resident of Canada, the branch profits tax shall be imposed only with respect to that portion of the dividend equivalent amount for the taxable year that, when translated into Canadian dollars and added to the dividend equivalent amounts for preceding taxable years translated into Canadian dollars, exceeds Canadian $500,000. The value of the dividend equivalent amount in Canadian currency shall be determined by translating the ECEP for each taxable year that is includible in the dividend equivalent amount (as determined in U.S. dollars under the currency translation method used in determining the foreign corporation's taxable income for U.S. tax purposes) by the weighted average exchange rate for the taxable year (determined under the rules of section 989(b)(3)) during which the earnings and profits were derived.

(2) Reduction in amount of exemption in the case of related corporations. The amount of a foreign corporation's exemption under this paragraph (g)(4)(iii)(B) shall be reduced by the amount of any exemption that reduced the dividend equivalent amount of an associated foreign corporation with respect to the same or a similar business. For purposes of this paragraph (g)(4)(iii)(B), a foreign corporation is an associated foreign corporation if it is related to the foreign corporation for purposes of section 267(b) or it and the foreign corporation are stapled entities (within the meaning of section 269B(c)(2)) or are effectively stapled entities. A business is the same as or similar to another business if it involves the sale, lease, or manufacture of the same or a similar type of property or the provision of the same or a similar type of services. A U.S. real property interest described in section 897(c)(1)(A)(i) shall be treated as a business and all such U.S. real property interests shall be treated as businesses that are the same or similar.

(3) Coordination with second-tier withholding tax. The value of the dividend equivalent amount that is exempt from the branch profits tax by reason of paragraph (g)(4)(iii)(B)(1) of this section shall not be subject to tax under section 871(a) or 881, or to withholding under section 1441 or 1442, when distributed by the foreign corporation.

(5) Benefits under treaties other than income tax treaties. A treaty that is not an income tax treaty does not exempt a foreign corporation from the branch profits tax or reduce the amount of the tax.

(h) Stapled entities. Any foreign corporation that is treated as a domestic corporation by reason of section 269B (relating to stapled entities) shall continue to be treated as a foreign corporation for purposes of section 884 and the regulations thereunder, notwithstanding section 269B or the regulations thereunder. Dividends paid by such foreign corporation shall be treated as paid by a domestic corporation and shall be subject to the tax imposed by section 871(a) or 881(a), and to withholding under section 1441 or 1442, as applicable, to the extent paid out of earnings and profits that are not subject to tax under section 884(a). Dividends paid by such foreign corporation out of earnings and profits subject to tax under section 884(a) shall be exempt from the tax imposed by sections 871(a) and 881(a) and shall not be subject to withholding under section 1441 or 1442. Whether dividends are paid out of earnings and profits that are subject to tax under section 884(a) shall be determined under section 884(e)(3)(A) and the regulations thereunder. The limitation on the application of treaty benefits in section 884(e)(3)(B) (relating to qualified residents) shall apply to a foreign corporation described in this paragraph (h).

(i) Effective date. *(1) General rule.* This section is effective for taxable years beginning on or after October 13, 1992. With respect to a taxable year beginning before October 13, 1992 and after December 31, 1986, a foreign corporation may elect to apply this section in lieu of § 1.884-1T of the temporary regulations (as contained in the CFR edition revised as of April 1, 1992), but only if the foreign corporation also makes an election under § 1.884-4(e) to apply § 1.884-4 in lieu of § 1.884-4T (as contained in the CFR edition revised as of April 1, 1992) for that taxable year, and the statute of limitations for assessment of a deficiency has not expired for that taxable year. Once an election has been made, an election under this section shall apply to all subsequent taxable years. However, paragraph (f)(2)(vi) of this section (relating to certain interest income of Possessions banks) shall not apply for taxable years beginning before January 1, 1990.

(2) Election to reduce liabilities. A foreign corporation may make an election to reduce its liabilities under paragraph (e)(3) of this section with respect to a taxable year for which an election under paragraph (i)(1) of this section is in effect by filing an amended return for the taxable year and recomputing its interest deduction and any other item affected by the election on an amended Form 1120F to take into account the reduction in liabilities for such year.

(3) Separate election for installment obligations. A foreign corporation may make a separate election to apply paragraphs (d)(2)(iii) and (d)(6)(ii) of this section (relating to installment obligations treated as U.S. assets) to any prior taxable year without making an election under paragraph (i)(1) of this section, provided the statute of limitations for assessment of a deficiency has not expired for that taxable year and each succeeding taxable year. Once an election under this paragraph (i)(3) has been made, it shall apply to all subsequent taxable years.

(4) Special rules for certain U.S. assets and liabilities. Paragraphs (c)(2)(i) and (ii), (d)(3), (d)(4), (d)(5)(iii), (d)(6)(iii), (d)(6)(vi), (e)(2), and (e)(3)(ii), of this section are effective for taxable years beginning on or after June 6, 1996.

(j) Transition rules. *(1) General rule.* Except as provided in paragraph (j)(2) of this section, in order to compute its dividend equivalent amount in the first taxable year to which this section applies (whether or not such year begins before October 13, 1992), a foreign corporation must recompute its U.S. net equity as of close of the preceding taxable year using the rules of this section and use such recomputed amount, rather than the amount computed under § 1.884-1T (as contained in the CFR edition revised as of April 1,

1992), to determine the amount of any increase or decrease in the U.S. net equity as of the close of that taxable year.

(2) Installment obligations. (i) Interest election. In recomputing its U.S. net equity as of the close of the preceding taxable year, a foreign corporation that holds an installment obligation treated as a U.S. asset under § 1.884-1T(d)(7) (as contained in the CFR edition revised as of April 1, 1992) as of such date may apply the rules of paragraph (d)(2)(iii) of this section without regard to the rule in that paragraph that requires interest or original issue discount on the obligation to be treated as ECI in order for such obligation to be treated as a U.S. asset.

(ii) 1987 sales by certain foreign corporations. The E&P basis of an installment obligation arising in connection with a sale of property by a foreign corporation described in section 312(k)(4), where such sale occurs in a taxable year beginning in 1987, shall equal the E&P basis of the property sold as of the determination date reduced by payments received with respect to the obligation that do not represent gain for earnings and profits purposes, interest or original issue discount.

T.D. 8432, 9/10/92, amend T.D. 8657, 3/5/96, T.D. 9281, 8/16/2006.

PAR. 3. Section 1.884-1 is amended by revising the entries for paragraphs § 1.884-1(e)(3)(ii), (e)(3)(iv) and (e)(5) Example 2 to read as follows:

Proposed § 1.884-1 Determination of interest deduction [*For Preamble, see ¶ 152,789*]

* * * * *

(e) *(3)* (ii) [The text of this proposed amendment is the same as the text of § 1.884-1T(e)(3)(ii) published elsewhere in this issue of the Federal Register]. [See T.D. 9281, 08/17/2006, 71 Fed. Reg. 159.]

***** (ii) [The text of this proposed amendment is the same as the text of § 1.884-1T(e)(3)(iv) published elsewhere in this issue of the Federal Register]. [See T.D. 9281, 08/17/2006, 71 Fed. Reg. 159.]

* * * * *

(5)

Example (2). [The text of this proposed amendment is the same as the text of § 1.884-1T(e)(5) Example 2 published elsewhere in this issue of the Federal Register]. [See T.D. 9281, 08/17/2006, 71 Fed. Reg. 159.]

* * * * *

PAR. 3. Section 1.884-1 is amended as follows:

1. Paragraph (c)(2)(iii) is added.

2. Paragraph (d)(2) is amended as follows:

a. Paragraph (d)(2)(vii) is revised.

b. In paragraph (d)(2)(xi), Example 6 through Example 8 are added.

3. The text of paragraph (d)(6)(v) is added.

4. In paragraph (i)(4), a sentence is added at the end of the existing text.

The revised and added provisions read as follows:

Proposed § 1.884-1 Branch profits tax. [*For Preamble, see ¶ 151,713*]

* * * * *

(c) * * *

(2) * * *

(iii) Hedging transactions. A transaction that hedges a U.S. asset, or a pool of U.S. assets, will be taken into account in determining the amount of that asset (or pool of assets) to the extent that income or loss from the hedging transaction produces ECI or reduces ECI. A transaction that hedges a U.S. asset, or pool of U.S. assets, is also taken into account in determining the currency denomination of the U.S. asset (or pool of U.S. assets). A transaction will be considered to hedge a U.S. asset only if the transaction meets the requirements of § 1.1221-2(a), (b), and (c), and is identified in accordance with the requirements of § 1.1221-2(e).

(d) * * *

(2) * * *

(vii) Financial instruments. A financial instrument, including a security as defined in section 475 and a section 1256 contract, shall be treated as a U.S. asset of a foreign corporation in the same proportion that the income, gain, or loss from such security is ECI for the taxable year.

* * * * *

(xi) * * *

Example (6). Hedging transactions. (i) Facts. FC is a foreign corporation engaged in a trade or business in the United States through a U.S. branch. The functional currency of FC's U.S. branch is the U.S. dollar. On January 1, 1997, in the ordinary course of its business, the U.S. branch of FC enters into a forward contract with an unrelated party to purchase 100 German marks (DM) on March 31, 1997, for $50. To hedge the risk of currency fluctuation on this transaction, the U.S. branch also enters into a forward contract with another unrelated party to sell 100 DM on March 31, 1997, for $52, identifying this contract as a hedging transaction in accordance with the requirements of § 1.1221-2(e). FC marks its foreign currency transactions to market for U.S. tax purposes.

(ii) Net assets. At the end of FC's taxable year, the value of the forward contract to purchase 100 DM is marked to market, resulting in gain of $10 being realized and recognized as U.S. source effectively connected income by FC. Similarly, FC marks to market the contract to sell 100 DM, resulting in $8 of realized and recognized loss by FC. Pursuant to paragraph (c)(2)(iii) of this section, FC must increase or decrease the amount of its U.S. assets to take into account any transaction that hedges the contract to purchase 100 DM. Consequently, FC has a U.S. asset of $2 ($10 (the adjusted basis of the contract to purchase 100 DM) − $8 (the loss on the contract to sell 100 DM)).

Example (7). Split hedge. The facts are the same as in Example 5, except that the contract to sell 100 DM is entered into with an unrelated third party by the home office of FC. FC includes the contract to sell 100 DM in a pool of assets treated as producing income effectively connected with the U.S. trade or business of FC. Therefore, under paragraph (c)(2)(iii) of this section, at its next determination date FC will report a U.S. asset of $2, computed as in Example 5.

Example (8). Securities. FC is a foreign corporation engaged in a U.S. trade or business through a branch in the United States. During the taxable year 1997, FC derives $100 of income from securities, of which $60 is treated as U.S. source effectively connected income under the terms of an Advance Pricing Agreement that uses a profit split methodology. Accordingly, pursuant to paragraph (d)(2)(vii) of this section, FC has a U.S. asset equal to 60% ($60 of ECI divided by $100 of gross income from securities) of the value of the securities.

*   *   *   *   *

(6) * * *

(v) Computation of E&P basis of financial instruments. For purposes of this section, the E&P basis of a security that is marked to market under section 475 and a section 1256 contract shall be adjusted to take into account gains and losses recognized by reason of section 475 or section 1256. The E&P basis must be further adjusted to take into account a transaction that hedges a U.S. asset, as provided in paragraph (c)(2)(ii) of this section.

*   *   *   *   *

(i) * * *

(4) * * * Paragraphs (c)(2)(iii), (d)(2)(vii), and (d)(6)(v) of this section will be effective for taxable years beginning on or after the date these regulations are published as final regulations in the Federal Register.

*   *   *   *   *

§ 1.884-1T Branch profits tax (temporary).

(a) through (e)(3)(i) [Reserved]. For further guidance, see § 1.884-1(a) through (e)(3)(i).

(e) *(3)* (ii) Limitation. For any taxable year, a foreign corporation may elect to reduce the amount of its liabilities determined under paragraph § 1.884-1(e)(1) of this section by an amount that does not exceed the lesser of the amount of U.S. liabilities as of the determination date, or the amount of U.S. liability reduction needed to reduce a dividend equivalent amount as of the determination date to zero.

(iii) [Reserved]. For further guidance, see § 1.884-1(e)(3)(iii).

(iv) Method of election. A foreign corporation that elects the benefits of this paragraph (e)(3) for a taxable year shall state on its return for the taxable year (or on a statement attached to the return) that it has elected to reduce its liabilities for the taxable year under this paragraph (e)(3) and that it has reduced the amount of its U.S.-connected liabilities as provided in § 1.884-1(e)(3)(iii), and shall indicate the amount of such reductions on the return or attachment. An election under this paragraph (e)(3) must be made before the due date (including extensions) for the foreign corporation's income tax return for the taxable year, except that for the first tax year for which the original tax return due date (including extensions) is after August 17, 2006 and not later than December 31, 2006, an election under this paragraph (e)(3) may be made on an amended return within 180 days after the original due date (including extensions).

(v) through (e)(5) Example 1 [Reserved]. For further guidance, see § 1.884-1(e)(3)(v) through (e)(5) Example 1.

(5) (v)

Example (2). Election made to reduce liabilities. (i) As of the close of 2007, foreign corporation A, a real estate company, owns U.S. assets with an E&P basis of $1000. A has $800 of liabilities under paragraph (e)(1) of this section. A has accumulated ECEP of $500 and in 2008, A has $60 of ECEP that it intends to retain for future expansion of its U.S. trade or business. A elects under paragraph (e)(3) of this section to reduce its liabilities by $60 from $800 to $740. As a result of the election, assuming A's U.S. assets and U.S. liabilities would otherwise have remained constant, A's U.S. net equity as of the close of 1994 will increase by the amount of the decrease in liabilities ($60) from $200 to $260 and its ECEP will be reduced to zero. Under § 1.884-1(e)(3)(iii), A's interest expense for the taxable year is reduced by the amount of interest attributable to $60 of liabilities and A's excess interest is reduced by the same amount. A's taxable income and ECEP are increased by the amount of the reduction in interest expense attributable to the liabilities, and A may make an election under paragraph (e)(3) of this section to further reduce its liabilities, thus increasing its U.S. net equity and reducing the amount of additional ECEP created for the election.

(ii) In 2009, assuming A again has $60 of ECEP, A may again make the election under paragraph (e)(3) to reduce its liabilities. However, assuming A's U.S. assets and liabilities under paragraph (e)(1) of this section remain constant, A will need to make an election to reduce its liabilities by $120 to reduce to zero its ECEP in 2009 and to continue to retain for expansion (without the payment of the branch profits tax) the $60 of ECEP earned in 2008. Without an election to reduce liabilities, A's dividend equivalent amount for 2009 would be $120 ($60 of ECEP plus the $60 reduction in U.S. net equity from $260 to $200). If A makes the election to reduce liabilities by $120 (from $800 to $680), A's U.S. net equity will increase by $60 (from $260 at the end of the previous year to $320), the amount necessary to reduce its ECEP to $0. However, the reduction of liabilities will itself create additional ECEP subject to section 884 because of the reduction in interest expense attributable to the $120 of liabilities. A can make the election to reduce liabilities by $120 without exceeding the limitation on the election provided in paragraph (e)(3)(ii) of this section because the $120 reduction does not exceed the amount needed to treat the 2009 and 2008 ECEP as reinvested in the net equity of the trade or business within the United States.

(iii) If A terminates its U.S. trade or business in 2009 in accordance with the rules in § 1.884-2T(a), A would not be subject to the branch profits tax on the $60 of ECEP earned in that year. Under paragraph § 1.884-1(e)(3)(v) of this section, however, it would be subject to the branch profits tax on the portion of the $60 of ECEP that it earned in 2008 that became accumulated ECEP because of an election to reduce liabilities.

(f) through (j)(2)(ii) [Reserved]. For further guidance, see § 1.884-1(f) through (j)(2)(ii).

T.D. 9281, 8/16/2006.

§ 1.884-2 Special rules for termination or incorporation of a U.S. trade or business or liquidation or reorganization of a foreign corporation or its domestic subsidiary.

(a) through (a)(2)(i) [Reserved] For further information, see § 1.884-2T(a) through (a)(2)(ii).

(2) (ii) Waiver of period of limitations. The waiver referred to in § 1.884-2T(a)(2)(i)(D) shall be executed on Form 8848, or substitute form, and shall extend the period for assessment of the branch profits tax for the year of complete termination to a date not earlier than the close of the sixth taxable year following that taxable year. This form shall include such information as is required by the form and accompanying instructions. The waiver must be signed by the person authorized to sign the income tax returns for the foreign corporation (including an agent authorized to do so under a general or specific power of attorney). The waiver must be filed on or before the date (including extensions) prescribed for filing the foreign corporation's income tax return for the year of complete termination. With respect to a complete termination occurring in a taxable year ending

prior to June 6, 1996, a foreign corporation may also satisfy the requirements of this paragraph (a)(2)(ii) by applying § 1.884-2T(a)(2)(ii) of the temporary regulations (as contained in the CFR edition revised as of April 1, 1995). A properly executed Form 8848, substitute form, or other form of waiver authorized by this paragraph (a)(2)(ii) shall be deemed to be consented to and signed by a Service Center Director or the Assistant Commissioner (International) for purposes of § 301.6501(c)-1(d) of this chapter.

(3) through (a)(4) [Reserved] For further information, see § 1.884-2T(a)(3) through (a)(4).

(5) Special rule if a foreign corporation terminates an interest in a trust. A foreign corporation whose beneficial interest in a trust terminates (by disposition or otherwise) in any taxable year shall be subject to the branch profits tax on ECEP attributable to amounts (including distributions of accumulated income or gain) treated as ECI to such beneficiary in such taxable year notwithstanding any other provision of § 1.884-2T(a).

(b) through (c)(2)(ii) [Reserved] For further information, see § 1.884-2T(b) through (c)(2)(ii).

(c) *(2)* (iii) Waiver of period of limitations and transferee agreement. In the case of a transferee that is a domestic corporation, the provisions of § 1.884-2T(c)(2)(i) shall not apply unless, as part of the section 381(a) transaction, the transferee executes a Form 2045 (Transferee Agreement) and a waiver of period of limitations as described in this paragraph (c)(2)(iii), and files both documents with its timely filed (including extensions) income tax return for the taxable year in which the section 381(a) transaction occurs. The waiver shall be executed on Form 8848, or substitute form, and shall extend the period for assessment of any additional branch profits tax for the taxable year in which the section 381(a) transaction occurs to a date not earlier than the close of the sixth taxable year following the taxable year in which such transaction occurs. This form shall include such information as is required by the form and accompanying instructions. The waiver must be signed by the person authorized to sign Form 2045. With respect to a complete termination occurring in a taxable year ending prior to June 6, 1996, a foreign corporation may also satisfy the requirements of this paragraph (c)(2)(iii) by applying § 1.884-2T(c)(2)(iii) of the temporary regulations (as contained in the CFR edition revised as of April 1, 1995). A properly executed Form 8848, substitute form, or other form of waiver authorized by this paragraph (c)(2)(iii) shall be deemed to be consented to and signed by a Service Center Director or the Assistant Commissioner (International) for purposes of § 301.6501(c)-1(d) of this chapter.

(3) through (c)(6)(i)(A) [Reserved]. For further guidance, see § 1.884-2T(c)(3) through (c)(6)(i)(A).

(6) (i) (B) Shareholders of the transferee (or of the transferee's parent in the case of a triangular reorganization described in section 368(a)(1)(C) or a reorganization described in sections 368(a)(1)(A) and 368(a)(2)(D) or (E)) who in the aggregate owned more than 25 percent of the value of the stock of the transferor at any time within the 12-month period preceding the close of the year in which the section 381(a) transaction occurs sell, exchange or otherwise dispose of their stock or securities in the transferee at any time during a period of three years from the close of the taxable year in which the section 381(a) transaction occurs.

(C) In the case of a triangular reorganization described in section 368(a)(1)(C) or a reorganization described in sections 368(a)(1)(A) and 368(a)(2)(D) or (E), the transferee's parent sells, exchanges, or otherwise disposes of its stock or securities in the transferee at any time during a period of three years from the close of the taxable year in which the section 381(a) transaction occurs.

(D) A corporation related to any such shareholder or the shareholder itself if it is a corporation (subsequent to an event described in paragraph (c)(6)(i)(A) or (B) of this section) or the transferee's parent (subsequent to an event described in paragraph (c)(6)(i)(C) of this section), uses, directly or indirectly, the proceeds or property received in such sale, exchange or disposition, or property attributable thereto, in the conduct of a trade or business in the United States at any time during a period of three years from the date of sale in the case of a disposition of stock in the transferor, or from the close of the taxable year in which the section 381(a) transaction occurs in the case of a disposition of the stock or securities in the transferee (or the transferee's parent in the case of a triangular reorganization described in section 368(a)(1)(C) or a reorganization described in sections 368(a)(1)(A) and (a)(2)(D) or (E)). Where this paragraph (c)(6)(i) applies, the transferor's branch profits tax liability for the taxable year in which the section 381(a) transaction occurs shall be determined under § 1.884-1, taking into account all the adjustments in U.S. net equity that result from the transfer of U.S. assets and liabilities to the transferee pursuant to the section 381(a) transaction, without regard to any provisions in this paragraph (c). If an event described in paragraph (c)(6)(i)(A), (B), or (C) of this section occurs after the close of the taxable year in which the section 381(a) transaction occurs, and if additional branch profits tax is required to be paid by reason of the application of this paragraph (c)(6)(i), then interest must be paid on that amount at the underpayment rates determined under section 6621(a)(2), with respect to the period between the date that was prescribed for filing the transferor's income tax return for the year in which the section 381(a) transaction occurs and the date on which the additional tax for that year is paid. Any such additional tax liability together with interest thereon shall be the liability of the transferee within the meaning of section 6901 pursuant to section 6901 and the regulations thereunder.

(ii) through (f) [Reserved]. For further guidance, see § 1.884-2T(c)(6)(ii) through (f).

(g) Effective dates. Paragraphs (a)(2)(ii) and (c)(2)(iii) of this section are effective for taxable years beginning after December 31, 1986. Paragraph (a)(5) of this section is effective for taxable years beginning on or after June 6, 1996. Paragraphs (c)(6)(i)(B), (C), and (D), are applicable for tax years beginning after December 31, 1986, except that such paragraphs are applicable to transactions occurring on or after January 23, 2006, in the case of reorganizations described in sections 368(a)(1)(A) and 368(a)(2)(D) or (E).

T.D. 8657, 3/5/96, amend T.D. 9243, 1/23/2006.

§ 1.884-2T Special rules for termination or incorporation of a U.S. trade or business or liquidation or reorganization of a foreign corporation or its domestic subsidiary (temporary).

(a) Complete termination of a U.S. trade or business. *(1) General rule.* A foreign corporation shall not be subject to the branch profits tax for the taxable year in which it completely terminates all of its U.S. trade or business within the meaning of paragraph (a)(2) of this section. A foreign corporation's non-previously taxed accumulated effectively connected earnings and profits as of the close of the taxable year of complete termination shall be extinguished for purposes of section 884 and the regulations thereunder, but not for other purposes (for example, sections 312, 316 and 381).

(2) Operating rules. (i) Definition of complete termination. A foreign corporation shall have completely terminated all of its U.S. trade or business for any taxable year ("the year of complete termination") only if—

(A) As of the close of that taxable year, the foreign corporation either has no U.S. assets, or its shareholders have adopted an irrevocable resolution in that taxable year to completely liquidate and dissolve the corporation and, before the close of the immediately succeeding taxable year (also a "year of complete termination" for purposes of applying this paragraph (a)(2)), all of its U.S. assets are either distributed, used to pay off liabilities, or cease to be U.S. assets;

(B) Neither the foreign corporation nor a related corporation uses, directly or indirectly, any of the U.S. assets of the terminated U.S. trade or business, or property attributable thereto or to effectively connected earnings and profits earned by the foreign corporation in the year of complete termination, in the conduct of a trade or business in the United States at any time during a period of three years from the close of the year of complete termination;

(C) The foreign corporation has no income that is, or is treated as, effectively connected with the conduct of a trade or business in the United States (other than solely by reason of section 864(c)(6) or (c)(7)) during the period of three years from the close of the year of complete termination; and

(D) The foreign corporation attaches to its income tax return for each year of complete termination a waiver of the period of limitations, as described in paragraph (a)(2)(ii) of this section.

If a foreign corporation fails to completely terminate all of its U.S. trade or business because of the failure to meet any of the requirements of this paragraph (a)(2), then its branch profits tax liability for the taxable year and all subsequent taxable years shall be determined under the provisions of § 1.884-1, without regard to any provisions in this paragraph (a), taking into account any reduction in U.S. net equity that results from a U.S. trade or business of the foreign corporation ceasing to have U.S. assets. Any additional branch profits tax liability that may result, together with interest thereon (charged at the underpayment rates determined under section 6621(a)(2) with respect to the period between the date that was prescribed for filing the foreign corporation's income tax return for the taxable year with respect to which the branch profits tax liability arises and the date on which the additional tax for that year is paid), and applicable penalties, if any, shall be the liability of the foreign corporation (or of any person who is a transferee of the foreign corporation within the meaning of section 6901).

(ii) Waiver of period of limitations. [Reserved] See § 1.884-2(a)(2)(ii) for rules relating to this paragraph.

(iii) Property subject to reinvestment prohibition rule. For purposes of paragraph (a)(2)(i)(B) of this section—

(A) The term "U.S. assets of the terminated U.S. trade or business" shall mean all the money and other property that qualified as U.S. assets of the foreign corporation as of the close of the taxable year immediately preceding the year of complete termination; and

(B) Property attributable to U.S. assets or to effectively connected earnings and profits earned by the foreign corporation in the year of complete termination shall mean money or other property into which any part or all of such assets or effectively connected earnings and profits are converted at any time before the expiration of the three-year period specified in paragraph (a)(2)(i)(B) of this section by way of sale, exchange, or other disposition, as well as any money or other property attributable to the sale by a shareholder of the foreign corporation of its interest in the foreign corporation (or a successor corporation) at any time after a date which is 12 months before the close of the year of complete termination (24 months in the case of a foreign corporation that makes an election under paragraph (b) of this section).

(iv) Related corporation. For purposes of paragraph (a)(2)(i)(B) of this section, a corporation shall be related to a foreign corporation if either corporation is a 10-percent shareholder of the other corporation or, where the foreign corporation completely liquidates, if either corporation would have been a 10-percent shareholder of the other corporation had the foreign corporation remained in existence. For this purpose, the term "10-percent shareholder" means any person described in section 871(h)(3)(B) as well as any person who owns 10 percent or more of the total value of the stock of the corporation, and stock ownership shall be determined on the basis of the attribution rules described in section 871(h)(3)(C).

(v) Direct or indirect use of U.S. assets. The use of any part or all of the property referred to in paragraph (a)(2)(i)(B) of this section shall include the loan thereof to a related corporation or the use thereof as security (as a pledge, mortgage, or otherwise) for any indebtedness of a related corporation.

(3) Complete termination in the case of a section 338 election. A foreign corporation whose stock is acquired by another corporation that makes (or is deemed to make) an election under section 338 with respect to the stock of the foreign corporation shall be treated as having completely liquidated as of the close of the acquisition date (as defined in section 338(h)(2)) and to have completely terminated all of its U.S. trade or business with respect to the taxable year ending on such acquisition date provided the foreign corporation that exists prior to the section 338 transaction complies with the requirements of paragraph (a)(2)(i)(B) and (D) of this section. For purposes of the preceding sentence, any of the money or other property paid as consideration for the acquisition of the stock in the foreign corporation (and for any debt claim against the foreign corporation) shall be treated as property attributable to the U.S. assets of the terminated U.S. trade or business and to the effectively connected earnings and profits of the foreign corporation earned in the year of complete termination.

(4) Complete termination in the case of a foreign corporation with income under section 864(c)(6) or 864(c)(7). No branch profits tax shall be imposed on effectively connected earnings and profits attributable to income that is treated as effectively connected with the conduct of a trade or business in the United States solely by reason of section 864(c)(6) or 864(c)(7) if—

(i) No income of the foreign corporation for the taxable year is, or is treated as, effectively connected with the conduct of a trade or business in the United States, without regard to section 864(c)(6) or 864(c)(7),

(ii) The foreign corporation has no U.S. assets as of the close of the taxable year, and

(iii) Such effectively connected earnings and profits would not have been subject to branch profits tax pursuant to the complete termination provisions of paragraph (a)(1) of this section if income or gain subject to section 864(c)(6) had not been deferred or if property subject to section 864(c)(7) had been sold immediately prior to the date the property ceased to have been used in the conduct of a trade or business in the United States.

(5) Special rule if a foreign corporation terminates an interest in a trust. [Reserved] See § 1.884-2(a)(5) for rules relating to this paragraph.

(6) Coordination with second-level withholding tax. Effectively connected earnings and profits and non-previously taxed accumulated effectively connected earnings and profits of a foreign corporation that are exempt from branch profits tax by reason of the provisions of paragraph (a)(1) of this section shall not be subject to tax under section 871(a), 881(a), 1441 or 1442 when paid as a dividend by such foreign corporation (or a successor-in-interest).

(b) Election to remain engaged in a U.S. trade or business. *(1) General rule.* A foreign corporation that would be considered to have completely terminated all of its U.S. trade or business for the taxable year under the provisions of paragraph (a)(2)(i) of this section, but for the provisions of paragraph (a)(2)(i)(B) of this section that prohibit reinvestment within a three-year period, may make an election under this paragraph (b) for the taxable year in which it completely terminates all its U.S. trade or business (as determined without regard to paragraph (a)(2)(i)(B) of this section) and, if it so chooses, for the following taxable year (but not for any succeeding taxable year). The election under this paragraph (b) is an election by the foreign corporation to designate an amount of marketable securities as U.S. assets for purposes of § 1.884-1. The marketable securities identified pursuant to the election under paragraph (b)(3) of this section shall be treated as being U.S. assets in an amount equal, in the aggregate, to the lesser of the adjusted basis of the U.S. assets that ceased to be U.S. assets during the taxable year in which the election is made (determined on the date or dates the U.S. assets ceased to be U.S. assets) or the adjusted basis of the marketable securities as of the end of the taxable year. The securities must be held from the date that they are identified until the end of the taxable year for which the election is made, or if disposed of during the taxable year, must be replaced on the date of disposition with other marketable securities that are acquired on or before that date and that have a fair market value as of the date of substitution not less than their adjusted basis.

(2) Marketable security. For purposes of this paragraph (b), the term "marketable security" means a security (including stock) that is part of an issue any portion of which is regularly traded on an established securities market (within the meaning of § 1.884-5(d)(2) and (4)) and a deposit described in section 871(i)(3)(A) or (B).

(3) Identification requirements. In order to qualify for this election—

(i) The marketable securities must be identified on the books and records of the U.S. trade or business within 30 days of the date an equivalent amount of U.S. assets ceases to be U.S. assets; and

(ii) On the date a marketable security is identified, its adjusted basis must not exceed its fair market value.

(4) Treatment of income from deemed U.S. assets. The income or gain from the marketable securities (or replacement securities) subject to an election under this paragraph (b) that arises in a taxable year for which an election is made shall be treated as ECI (other than for purposes of section 864(c)(7)), and losses from the disposition of such marketable securities shall be allocated entirely to income that is ECI. In addition, all such securities shall be treated as if they had been sold for their fair market value on the earlier of the last business day of a taxable year for which an election is in effect or the day immediately prior to the date of substitution by the foreign corporation of a U.S. asset for the marketable security, and any gain (but not loss) and accrued interest on the securities shall also be treated as ECI. The adjusted basis of such property shall be increased by the amount of any gain recognized by reason of this paragraph (b).

(5) Method of election. A foreign corporation may make an election under this paragraph (b) by attaching to its income tax return for the taxable year a statement—

(i) Identifying the marketable securities treated as U.S. assets under this paragraph (b);

(ii) Setting forth the E&P bases of such securities; and

(iii) Agreeing to treat any income, gain or loss as provided in paragraph (b)(4) of this section. Such statement must be filed on or before the due date (including extensions) of the foreign corporation's income tax return for the taxable year. A foreign corporation shall not be permitted to make an election under this paragraph (b) more than once.

(6) Effective date. This paragraph (b) is effective for taxable years beginning on or after October 13, 1992. However, if a foreign corporation has made a valid election under § 1.884-1(i) to apply that section with respect to a taxable year beginning before October 13, 1992 and after December 31, 1986, this paragraph (b) shall be effective beginning with such taxable year.

(c) Liquidation, reorganization, etc. of a foreign corporation. The following rules apply to the transfer by a foreign corporation engaged (or deemed engaged) in the conduct of a U.S. trade or business (the "transferor") of its U.S. assets to another corporation (the "transferee") in a complete liquidation or reorganization described in section 381(a) (a "section 381(a) transaction") if the transferor is engaged (or deemed engaged) in the conduct of a U.S. trade or business immediately prior to the section 381(a) transaction. For purposes of this paragraph (c), a section 381(a) transaction is considered to occur in the taxable year that ends on the date of distribution or transfer (as defined in § 1.381(b)-1(b)) pursuant to the section 381(a) transaction.

(1) Inapplicability of paragraph (a)(1) of this section to section 381(a) transactions. Paragraph (a)(1) of this section (relating to the complete termination of a U.S. trade or business of a foreign corporation) does not apply to exempt the transferor from branch profits tax liability for the taxable year in which the section 381(a) transaction occurs or in any succeeding taxable year.

(2) Transferor's dividend equivalent amount for the taxable year in which a section 381(a) transaction occurs. The dividend equivalent amount for the taxable year, including a short taxable year, in which a section 381(a) transaction occurs shall be determined under the provisions of § 1.884-1, as modified under the provisions of this paragraph (c)(2).

(i) U.S. net equity. The transferor's U.S. net equity as of the close of the taxable year shall be determined without regard to any transfer in that taxable year of U.S. assets to or from the transferee pursuant to a section 381(a) transaction, and without regard to any U.S. liabilities assumed or acquired by the transferee from the transferor in that taxable year pursuant to a section 381(a) transaction. The transferor's adjusted basis (for earnings and profits purposes) in U.S. assets transferred to the transferee pursuant to a section 381(a) transaction shall be the adjusted basis of those assets (for earnings and profits purposes) immediately prior to the section 381(a) transaction, adjusted as provided under section 362(b), treating the transferor, for that purpose, as though it were the transferee and treating the gain taken into account for earnings and profits purposes as gain recognized.

(ii) Effectively connected earnings and profits. The transferor's effectively connected earnings and profits for the taxable year in which the section 381(a) transaction occurs and its non-previously taxed accumulated effectively connected earnings and profits shall be determined without regard to the carryover to the transferee of the transferor's earnings and profits under section 381(a) and (c)(2) and paragraph (c)(4) of this section. Effectively connected earnings and profits for the taxable year in which a section 381(a) transaction occurs shall be adjusted by the amount of any gain recognized to the transferor in that year pursuant to the section 381(a) transaction (to the extent taken into account for earnings and profits purposes).

(iii) Waiver of period of limitations and transferee agreement. [Reserved] See § 1.884-2(c)(2)(iii) for rules relating to this paragraph.

(3) Transferor's dividend equivalent amount for any taxable year succeeding the taxable year in which the section 381(a) transaction occurs. Any decrease in U.S. net equity in any taxable year succeeding the taxable year in which the section 381(a) transaction occurs shall increase the transferor's dividend equivalent amount for those years without regard to the limitation in § 1.884-1(b)(3)(ii), to the extent such decrease in U.S. net equity does not exceed the balance of effectively connected earnings and profits and non-previously taxed accumulated effectively connected earnings and profits carried over to the transferee pursuant to section 381(a) and (c)(2), as determined under paragraph (c)(4) of this section.

(4) Earnings and profits of the transferor carried over to the transferee pursuant to the section 381(a) transaction. (i) Amount. The amount of effectively connected earnings and profits and non-previously taxed accumulated effectively connected earnings and profits of the transferor that carry over to the transferee under section 381(a) and (c)(2) shall be the effectively connected earnings and profits and the non-previously taxed accumulated effectively connected earnings and profits of the transferor immediately before the close of the taxable year in which the section 381(a) transaction occurs. For this purpose, the provisions in § 1.381(c)(2)-1 shall generally apply with proper adjustments to reflect the fact that effectively connected earnings and profits and non-previously taxed accumulated effectively connected earnings and profits are not affected by distributions to shareholders but, rather, by dividend equivalent amounts. Therefore, the amounts of effectively connected earnings and profits and non-previously taxed accumulated effectively connected earnings and profits that carry over to the transferee pursuant to those provisions are reduced by the transferor's dividend equivalent amount for the taxable year in which the section 381(a) transaction occurs. Such amounts are also reduced to the extent of any dividend equivalent amount determined for any succeeding taxable year solely as a result of the provisions of paragraph (c)(3) of this section. For purposes of this paragraph (c)(4)(i), if the transferor accumulates non-previously taxed effectively connected earnings and profits, or incurs a deficit in effectively connected earnings and profits, attributable to a period that is after the close of the taxable year in which the section 381(a) transaction occurs and before the liquidation of the transferor, then such effectively connected earnings and profits, or deficits therein, shall be deemed to have been accumulated or incurred on or before the close of the taxable year in which the section 381(a) transaction occurs.

(ii) Retention of character. All of the transferor's effectively connected earnings and profits and non-previously taxed accumulated effectively connected earnings and profits that carry over to the transferee shall constitute non-previously taxed accumulated effectively connected earnings and profits of the transferee. In the case of a domestic transferee, such non-previously taxed accumulated effectively connected earnings and profits shall also constitute accumulated earnings and profits of the transferee for purposes of section 316(a)(2).

(iii) Treatment of distributions by a domestic transferee out of non-previously taxed accumulated effectively connected earnings and profits. In the event the transferee is a domestic corporation, distributions out of the transferee's non-previously taxed accumulated effectively connected earnings and profits that are received by a foreign distributee shall qualify for benefits under an applicable income tax treaty only (A) if the distributee qualifies for the benefits under such treaty and (B) to the extent that the transferor foreign corporation would have qualified under the principles of § 1.884-1(g)(1) and (2)(i) for an exemption or reduction in rate with respect to the branch profits tax if the non-previously taxed accumulated effectively connected earnings and profits had been reflected in a dividend equivalent amount for the taxable year in which the section 381(a) transaction occurs. (The tax rate on dividends specified in the treaty between the distributee's country of residence and the United States shall apply to any dividends received by a distributee who qualifies for a treaty benefit under the preceding sentence.) In addition, distributions out of such non-previously taxed accumulated effectively connected earnings and profits shall retain their character in the hands of any domestic distributee up a chain of corporate shareholders for purposes of applying this paragraph (c)(4)(iii) to distributions made by any such person to a foreign distributee. If a domestic transferee has non-previously taxed accumulated effectively connected earnings and profits carried over from the transferor as well as accumulated earnings and profits, then each category of earnings and profits shall be accounted for in two separate pools, and any distribution of earnings and profits shall be treated as a distribution out of each pool in proportion to the respective amount of undistributed earnings and profits in each pool. Section 871(i) (relating, in part, to dividends paid by a domestic corporation meeting the 80-percent foreign business requirements of section 861(c)(1)) shall not apply to any dividends paid by a domestic transferee out of its non-previously taxed accumulated effectively connected earnings and profits.

(5) Determination of U.S. net equity of a transferee that is a foreign corporation. In the event the transferee is a foreign corporation, then for purposes of determining the transferee's increase or decrease in U.S. net equity under § 1.884-1 for its taxable year during which the section 381(a) transaction occurs, its U.S. net equity as of the close of its immediately preceding taxable year shall be increased by the amount of U.S. net equity acquired by the transferee from the transferor pursuant to the section 381(a) transaction, taking into account the adjustments to the basis (for earnings and profits purposes) of U.S. assets under the principles of section 362(b).

(6) Special rules in the case of the disposition of stock or securities in a domestic transferee or in the transferor. (i) General rule. This paragraph (c)(6)(i) shall apply where the

transferee is a domestic corporation, subdivision (A), (B), or (C) of this paragraph applies and subdivision (D) of this paragraph applies.

(A) Shareholders of the transferor sell, exchange or otherwise dispose of stock in the transferor at any time during a 12-month period before the date of distribution or transfer (as defined in § 1.381(b)-1(b)) and the aggregate amount of such stock sold, exchanged or otherwise disposed of exceeds 25 percent of the value of the stock of the transferor, determined on a date that is 12 months before the date of distribution or transfer.

(B) , (C), and (D) [Reserved]. For further guidance, see § 1.884-2(c)(6)(i)(B), (C), and (D).

(ii) Operating rule. For purposes of paragraph (c)(6)(i) of this section paragraphs (a)(2)(iii)(B), (iv) and (v) of this section shall apply for purposes of making the determinations under paragraph (c)(6)(i)(D) of this section.

(d) Incorporation under section 351. *(1) In general.* The following rules apply to the transfer by a foreign corporation engaged (or deemed engaged) in the conduct of a U.S. trade or business (the "transferor") of part or all of its U.S. assets to a U.S. corporation (the "transferee") in exchange for stock or securities in the transferee in a transaction that qualifies under section 351(a) (a "section 351 transaction"), provided that immediately after the transaction, the transferor is in control (as defined in section 368(c)) of the transferee, without regard to other transferors.

(2) Inapplicability of paragraph (a)(1) of this section to section 351 transactions. Paragraph (a)(1) of this section does not apply to exempt the transferor from branch profits tax liability for the taxable year in which a section 351 transaction described in paragraph (d)(1) of this section occurs and shall not apply for any subsequent taxable year of the transferor in which it, or a successor-in-interest, owns stock or securities of a transferee as of the close of the transferor's taxable year.

(3) Transferor's dividend equivalent amount for the taxable year in which a section 351 transaction occurs. The dividend equivalent amount of the transferor for the taxable year in which a section 351 transaction described in paragraph (d)(1) of this section occurs shall be determined under the provisions of § 1.884-1, as modified by the provisions of this paragraph (d)(3) provided that the transferee elects under paragraph (d)(4) of this section to be allocated a proportionate amount of the transferor's effectively connected earnings and profits and non-previously taxed accumulated effectively connected earnings and profits and the foreign corporation files a statement as provided in paragraph (d)(5)(i) of this section and complies with the agreement included in such statement with respect to a subsequent disposition of the transferee's stock.

(i) U.S. net equity. The transferor's U.S. net equity as of the close of the taxable year shall be determined without regard to any transfer in that taxable year of U.S. assets to or from the transferee pursuant to a section 351 transaction, and without regard to any U.S. liabilities assumed or acquired by the transferee from the transferor in that taxable year pursuant to a section 351 transaction. The transferor's adjusted basis for earnings and profits purposes in U.S. assets transferred to the transferee pursuant to a section 351 transaction shall be the adjusted basis of those assets for earnings and profits purposes immediately prior to the section 351 transaction, increased by the amount of any gain recognized by the transferor on the transfer of such assets in the section 351 transaction to the extent taken into account for earnings and profits purposes.

(ii) Effectively connected earnings and profits. Subject to the limitation in paragraph (d)(3)(iii) of this section, the calculation of the transferor's dividend equivalent amount shall take into account the transferor's effectively connected earnings and profits for the taxable year in which a section 351 transaction occurs (including any amount of gain recognized to the transferor pursuant to the section 351 transaction to the extent the gain is taken into account for earnings and profits purposes) and, for purposes of applying the limitation of § 1.884-1(b)(3)(ii), its non-previously taxed accumulated effectively connected earnings and profits, determined without regard to the allocation to the transferee of the transferor's effectively connected earnings and profits and non-previously taxed accumulated effectively connected earnings and profits pursuant to the election under paragraph (d)(4)(i) of this section.

(iii) Limitation on dividend equivalent amount. The dividend equivalent amount determined under this paragraph (d)(3) shall not exceed the sum of the transferor's effectively connected earnings and profits and non-previously taxed accumulated effectively connected earnings and profits determined after taking into account the allocation to the transferee of the transferor's earnings pursuant to an election under paragraph (d)(4)(i) of this section.

(4) Election to increase earnings and profits. (i) General rule. The election referred to in paragraph (d)(3) of this section is an election by the transferee to increase its earnings and profits by the amount determined under paragraph (d)(4)(ii) of this section. An election under this paragraph (d)(4)(i) shall be effective only if the transferee attaches a statement to its timely filed (including extensions) income tax return for the taxable year in which the section 351 transaction occurs, in which—

(A) It agrees to be subject to the rules of paragraph (c)(4)(ii) and (iii) of this section with respect to the transferor's effectively connected earnings and profits and non-previously taxed accumulated effectively connected earnings and profits allocated to the transferee pursuant to the election under this paragraph (d)(4)(i) in the same manner as if such earnings and profits had been carried over to the transferee pursuant to section 381(a) and (c)(2), and

(B) It identifies the amount of effectively connected earnings and profits and non-previously taxed accumulated effectively connected earnings and profits that are allocated from the transferor.

An election with respect to a taxable year ending on or before December 1, 1988, may be made by filing an amended Form 1120F on or before January 3, 1988, to which the statement described in this paragraph (d)(4)(i) shall be attached.

(ii) Amount of the transferor's effectively connected earnings and profits and non-previously taxed accumulated effectively connected earnings and profits allocated to the transferee. The amount referred to in paragraph (d)(4)(i) of this section is equal to the same proportion of the transferor's effectively connected earnings and profits and non-previously taxed accumulated effectively connected earnings and profits (determined immediately prior to the section 351 transaction and without regard to this paragraph (d)(4) or any dividend equivalent amount for the taxable year) that the adjusted bases for purposes of computing earnings and profits in all the U.S. assets transferred to the transferee by the transferor pursuant to the section 351 transaction bear to the adjusted bases for purposes of computing earnings and profits in all the U.S. assets of the transferor, determined immediately prior to the section 351 transaction.

(iii) Effect of election on transferor. For purposes of computing the transferor's dividend equivalent amount for the taxable year succeeding the taxable year in which a section 351 transaction occurs, the transferor's effectively connected earnings and profits and non-previously taxed accumulated effectively connected earnings and profits as of the close of the taxable year in which the section 351 transaction occurs shall be reduced by the amount of its effectively connected earnings and profits and non-previously taxed accumulated effectively connected earnings and profits allocated to the transferee pursuant to the election under paragraph (d)(4)(i) of this section (and by its dividend equivalent amount for the taxable year in which the section 351 transaction occurs).

(5) Dispositions of stock or securities of the transferee by the transferor. (i) General rule. The statement referred to in paragraph (d)(3) of this section is a statement executed by the transferor stating the transferor's agreement that, upon the disposition of part or all of the stock or securities it owns in the transferee (or a successor-in-interest), it shall treat as a dividend equivalent amount for the taxable year in which the disposition occurs an amount equal to the lesser of (A) the amount realized upon such disposition or (B) the total amount of effectively connected earnings and profits and non-previously taxed accumulated effectively connected earnings and profits that was allocated from the transferor to that transferee pursuant to an election under paragraph (d)(4)(i) of this section, which amount shall be reduced to the extent previously taken into account by the transferor as dividends or dividend equivalent amounts for tax or branch profits, tax purposes. The extent and manner in which such dividend equivalent amount may be subject to the branch profits tax in the taxable year of disposition shall be determined under the provisions of section 884 and the regulations thereunder, including the provisions of paragraph (a) of this section (relating to complete terminations), as limited under paragraph (d)(2) of this section. Except as otherwise provided in paragraph (d)(5)(ii) of this section, the term "disposition" means any transfer that would constitute a disposition by the transferor for any purpose of the Internal Revenue Code and the regulations thereunder. This paragraph (d)(5)(i) shall apply regardless of whether the stock or securities of the transferee are U.S. assets in the hands of the transferor at the time of sale, exchange or disposition.

(ii) Exception for certain tax-free dispositions. For purposes of paragraph (d)(5)(i) of this section, a disposition does not include a transfer of stock or securities of the transferee by the transferor in a transaction that qualifies as a transfer pursuant to a complete liquidation described in section 332(b) or a transfer pursuant to a reorganization described in section 368(a)(1)(F). Any other transfer that qualifies for non-recognition of gain or loss shall be treated as a disposition for purposes of paragraph (d)(5)(i) of this section, unless the Commissioner has, by published guidance or by prior ruling issued to the taxpayer upon its request, determined such transfer not to be a disposition for purposes of paragraph (d)(5)(i) of this section.

(iii) Distributions governed by section 355. In the case of a distribution or exchange of stock or securities of a transferee to which section 355 applies (or so much of section 356 as relates to section 355) and that is not in pursuance of a plan meeting the requirements of a reorganization as defined in section 368(a)(1)(D), § 1.312-10(b) (relating to the allocation of earnings and profits in certain corporate separations) shall not apply to reduce the transferor's effectively connected earnings and profits or non-previously taxed accumulated effectively connected earnings and profits.

(iv) Filing of statement. The statement referred to in paragraph (d)(5)(i) of this section shall be attached to a timely filed (including extensions) income tax return of the transferor for the taxable year in which the section 351 transaction occurs. An election with respect to a taxable year ending on or before December 1, 1988, may be made by filing an amended Form 1120F on or before January 3, 1988, to which the statement described in this paragraph (d)(5)(iv) shall be attached.

(6) Example. The provisions of this paragraph (d) are illustrated by the following example.

Example. Foreign corporation X has a calendar taxable year. X's only assets are U.S. assets and X computes its interest deduction using the actual ratio of liabilities to assets under § 1.882-5(b)(2)(ii). X's U.S. net equity as of the close of its 1988 taxable year is $2,000, resulting from the following amounts of U.S. assets and liabilities:

U.S. assets		U.S. liabilities	
U.S. building A.	$1,000	Mortgage A	800
U.S. building B.	2,500	Mortgage B	1,500
Other U.S. assets	800		
Total	4,300		2,300

Assume that X's adjusted basis in its assets is equal to X's adjusted basis in its assets for earnings and profits purposes. On September 30, 1989, X transfers building A, which has a fair market value of $1,800, to a newly created U.S. corporation Y under section 351 in exchange for 100% of the stock of Y with a fair market value of $800, other property with a fair market value of $200, and the assumption of Mortgage A. Assume that under sections 11 and 351(b), tax of $30 is imposed with respect to the $200 of other property received by X. X's non-previously taxed accumulated effectively connected earnings and profits as of the close of its 1988 taxable year are $200 and its effectively connected earnings and profits for its 1989 taxable year are $330, including $170 of gain recognized to X on the transfer as adjusted for earnings and profits purposes (i.e., $200 of gain recognized minus $30 of tax paid with respect to the gain). Y takes a $1,200 basis in the building transferred from X, equal to the basis in the hands of X ($1,000) increased by the amount of gain recognized to X in the section 351 transaction ($200). Y makes an election in the manner described in paragraph (d)(4)(i) of this section to increase its earnings and profits by the amount described in paragraph (d)(4)(ii) of this section and X files a statement as provided in paragraph (d)(5)(i) of this section. The branch profits tax consequences to X and Y in the taxable year in which the section 351 transaction occurs and in subsequent taxable years are as follows:

(i) X's dividend equivalent amount for 1989. The determination of X's dividend equivalent amount for 1989 is a three-step process: determining X's U.S. net equity as of the close of its 1989 taxable year under paragraph (d)(3)(i) of this section; determining the amount of X's effectively connected earnings and profits and non-previously taxed accumulated effectively connected earnings and profits for its 1989 taxable year under paragraph (d)(3)(ii) of this section; and applying the limitation in paragraph (d)(3)(iii) of this section.

Step one: Pursuant to paragraph (d)(3)(i) of this section, X's U.S. net equity as of the close of its 1989 taxable year is calculated without regard to the section 351 transaction except that X's basis in its U.S. assets is increased by the $170 amount of gain it has recognized for earnings and profits purposes in connection with the section 351 transaction. Thus, X's U.S. net equity as of the close of its 1989 taxable year is $1,870, consisting of the following U.S. assets and liabilities, taking into account the fact that X's other U.S. assets have decreased to $500:

U.S. assets		U.S. liabilities	
Building A	$1,170	Mortgage A	800
Building B	2,500	Mortgage B	1,500
Other U.S. assets	500		
Total	4,170		2,300

Thus, X's U.S. net equity as of the close of its 1989 taxable year has decreased by $130 relative to its U.S. net equity as of the close of its 1988 taxable year.

Step two: Pursuant to paragraph (d)(3)(ii) of this section, X's effectively connected earnings and profits and non-previously taxed accumulated effectively connected earnings and profits for the taxable year are determined without taking into account the allocation to Y of X's effectively connected earnings and profits and non-previously taxed accumulated effectively connected earnings and profits pursuant to the election under paragraph (d)(4)(i) of this section. Thus, X's effectively connected earnings and profits for its 1989 taxable year are $330 and X's non-previously taxed accumulated effectively connected earnings and profits are $200. Thus, but for the limitation in paragraph (d)(3)(iii) of this section, X's dividend equivalent amount for the taxable year would be $460, equal to X's effectively connected earnings and profits for the taxable year ($330), increased by the decrease in X's U.S. net equity ($130).

Step three: Pursuant to paragraph (d)(3)(iii) of this section, X's dividend equivalent amount for its 1989 taxable year may not exceed the sum of the transferor's effectively connected earnings and profits and non-previously taxed accumulated effectively connected earnings and profits, determined as of the close of its 1989 taxable year, after taking into account the allocation of the transferor's earnings and profits pursuant to the election under paragraph (d)(4)(i) of this section. Based upon subdivision (ii) of this example, X's dividend equivalent amount for 1989 cannot exceed $423, which is equal to the total amount of X's effectively connected earnings and profits and non-previously taxed accumulated effectively connected earnings and profits, determined as of the close of its 1989 taxable year without regard to the allocation of earnings and profits to Y pursuant to Y's election under paragraph (d)(4)(i) of this section ($530), reduced by the amount of X's effectively connected earnings and profits and non-previously taxed accumulated effectively connected earnings and profits allocated to Y pursuant to Y's election under paragraph (d)(4)(i) of this section ($107). Thus, X's dividend equivalent amount for its 1989 taxable year is limited to $423.

(ii) Amount of X's effectively connected earnings and profits and non-previously taxed accumulated effectively connected earnings and profits transferred to Y. Pursuant to Y's election under paragraph (d)(4)(i) of this section, Y increases its earnings and profits by the amount prescribed in paragraph (d)(4)(ii) of this section. This amount is equal to the sum of X's effectively connected earnings and profits and non previously taxed accumulated effectively connected earnings and profits determined immediately before the section 351 transaction, without regard to X's dividend equivalent amount for the year, allocated in the same proportion that X's basis in the U.S. assets transferred to Y bears to the bases of all of X's U.S. assets, which bases are determined immediately prior to the section 351(a) transaction. The amount of X's effectively connected earnings and profits immediately before the section 351 transaction is assumed to be $260. The total amount of effectively connected earnings and profits ($260) and non-previously taxed accumulated effectively connected earnings and profits ($200) determined immediately before the section 351 transaction is, therefore, $460. The portion of $460 that is allocated to Y pursuant to Y's election under paragraph (d)(4)(i) of this section is $107, calculated as $46? multiplied by a fraction, the numerator of which is the basis of the U.S. assets transferred to Y pursuant to the section 351 transaction ($1,000), and the denominator of which is the basis of X's U.S. assets determined immediately before the section 351 transaction ($4,300). Pursuant to paragraph (d)(4)(i) of this section, the amount of $107 of X's effectively connected earnings and profits and non-previously taxed accumulated effectively connected earnings and profits allocated to Y pursuant to paragraph (d)(4)(i) of this section constitutes non-previously taxed accumulated effectively connected earnings and profits of Y.

(iii) X's non-previously taxed accumulated effectively connected earnings and profits for 1990. Pursuant to paragraph (d)(4)(iii) of this section, X's non-previously taxed accumulated effectively connected earnings and profits as of the close of its 1989 taxable year for purposes of computing its dividend equivalent amount for its taxable year 1990 are zero, i.e., $530 of effectively connected earnings and profits and non-previously taxed accumulated effectively connected earnings and profits reduced by $107 of effectively connected earnings and profits and non-previously taxed accumulated effectively connected earnings and profits allocated to Y, and further reduced by X's $423 dividend equivalent amount for its 1989 taxable year.

(iv) X's U.S. net equity for purposes of determining the dividend equivalent amount for succeeding taxable years. For 1990, X must determine its U.S. net equity as of December 31, 1989, in order to determine whether there has been an increase or decrease in its U.S. net equity as of December 31, 1990. For this purpose, X's U.S. net equity as of December 31, 1989 is determined under the provisions of § 1.884-1 without regard to the special rules in paragraph (d)(3)(i) of this section. Thus, X's U.S. net equity as of December 31, 1989 is $1,500, consisting of the following. U.S. assets and liabilities:

U.S. assets		U.S. liabilities	
Building B	$2,500	Mortgage B	1,500
Other U.S. assets	500		
Total	$3,000		1,500

(e) Certain transactions with respect to a domestic subsidiary. In the case of a section 381(a) transaction in which a domestic subsidiary of a foreign corporation transfers assets to that foreign corporation or to another foreign corporation with respect to which the first foreign corporation owns stock (directly or indirectly) meeting the requirements of section 1504(a)(2), the transferee's non-previously taxed accumulated effectively connected earnings and profits for the taxable year in which the section 381(a) transaction occurs shall be increased by all of the domestic subsidiary's current earnings and profits and earnings and profits accumulated after December 31, 1986, that carry over to the transferee under sections 381(a) and (c)(1) (including non-previously taxed accumulated effectively connected earnings and profits, if any, transferred to the domestic subsidiary under paragraphs (c)(4) and (d)(4) of this section and treated as earnings and profits under paragraphs (c)(4)(ii) and (d)(4)(ii) of this section). For purposes of determining the transferee's dividend equivalent amount for the taxable year in which the section 381(a) transaction occurs, the transferee's U.S. net equity as of the close of its taxable year immediately preceding the taxable year during which the section 381(a) transaction occurs shall be increased by the greater of

(1) The amount by which the transferee's U.S. net equity computed immediately prior to the transfer would have increased due to the transfer of the subsidiary's assets and liabilities if U.S. net equity were computed immediately prior to the transfer and immediately after the transfer (taking into account in the earnings and profits basis of the assets transferred any gain recognized on the transfer to the extent reflected in earnings and profits), or

(2) The total amount of U.S. net equity transferred (directly or indirectly) by the foreign parent to the domestic subsidiary in one or more prior section 351 or 381(a) transactions.

(f) Effective date. This section is effective for taxable years beginning after December 31, 1986.

T.D. 8223, 8/29/88, amend T.D. 8432, 9/10/92, T.D. 8657, 3/5/96, T.D. 9243, 1/23/2006.

§ 1.884-3T Coordination of branch profits tax with second-tier withholding (temporary).[Reserved]

§ 1.884-4 Branch-level interest tax.

(a) General rule. *(1) Tax on branch interest.* In the case of a foreign corporation that, during the taxable year, is engaged in trade or business in the United States or has gross income that is ECI (as defined in § 1.884-1(d)(1)(iii)), any interest paid by such trade or business (hereinafter "branch interest," as defined in paragraph (b) of this section) shall, for purposes of subtitle A (Income Taxes), be treated as if it were paid by a domestic corporation (other than a corporation described in section 861(c)(1), relating to a domestic corporation that meets the 80 percent foreign business requirement). Thus, for example, whether such interest is treated as income from sources within the United States by the person who receives the interest shall be determined in the same manner as if such interest were paid by a domestic corporation (other than a corporation described in section 861(c)(1)). Such interest shall be subject to tax under section 871(a) or 881, and to withholding under section 1441 or 1442, in the same manner as interest paid by a domestic corporation (other than a corporation described in section 861(c)(1)) if received by a foreign person and not effectively connected with the conduct by the foreign person of a trade or business in the United States, unless the interest, if paid by a domestic corporation, would be exempt under section 871(h) or 881(c) (relating to exemption for certain portfolio interest received by a foreign person), section 871(i) or 881(d) (relating, in part, to exemption for certain bank deposit interest received by a foreign person), or another provision of the Code. Such interest shall also be treated as interest paid by a domestic corporation (other than a corporation described in section 861(c)(1)) for purposes of sections 864(c), 871(b) and 882(a) (relating to income that is effectively connected with the conduct of a trade or business within the United States) and section 904 (relating to the limitation on the foreign tax credit). For purposes of this section, a foreign corporation also shall be treated as engaged in trade or business in the United States if, at any time during the taxable year, it owns an asset taken into account under § 1.882-5(a)(1)(ii) or (b)(1) for purposes of determining the amount of the foreign corporation's interest expense allocated or apportioned to ECI. See paragraph (b)(8) of this section for the effect of income tax treaties on branch interest.

(2) Tax on excess interest. (i) Definition of excess interest. For purposes of this section, the term "excess interest" means—

(A) The amount of interest allocated or apportioned to ECI of the foreign corporation under § 1.882-5 for the taxable year, after application of § 1.884-1(e)(3); minus

(B) The foreign corporation's branch interest (as defined in paragraph (b) of this section) for the taxable year, but not including interest accruing in a taxable year beginning before January 1, 1987; minus

(C) The amount of interest determined under paragraph (c)(2) of this section (relating to interest paid by a partnership).

(ii) Imposition of tax. A foreign corporation shall be liable for tax on excess interest under section 881(a) in the same manner as if such excess interest were interest paid to the foreign corporation by a wholly-owned domestic corporation (other than a corporation described in section 861(c)(1)) on the last day of the foreign corporation's taxable year. Excess interest shall be exempt from tax under section 881(a) only as provided in paragraph (a)(2)(iii) of this section (relating to treatment of certain excess interest of banks as interest on deposits) or paragraph (c)(3) of this section (relating to income tax treaties).

(iii) Treatment of a portion of the excess interest of banks as interest on deposits. A portion of the excess interest of a foreign corporation that is a bank (as defined in section 585(a)(2)(B) without regard to the second sentence thereof) provided that a substantial part of its business in the United States, as well as all other countries in which it operates, consists of receiving deposits and making loans and discounts, shall be treated as interest on deposits (as described in section 871(i)(3)), and shall be exempt from the tax imposed by section 881(a) as provided in such section. The portion of the excess interest of the foreign corporation that is treated as interest on deposits shall equal the product of the foreign corporation's excess interest and the greater of—

(A) The ratio of the amount of interest-bearing deposits, within the meaning of section 871(i)(3)(A), of the foreign corporation as of the close of the taxable year to the amount of all interest-bearing liabilities of the foreign corporation on such date; or

(B) 85 percent.

(iv) Reporting and payment of tax on excess interest. The amount of tax due under section 884(f) and this section with respect to excess interest of a foreign corporation shall be reported on the foreign corporation's income tax return for the taxable year in which the excess interest is treated as paid to the foreign corporation under section 884(f)(1)(B) and paragraph (a)(2) of this section, and shall not be subject to withholding under section 1441 or 1442. The tax shall be due and payable as provided in section 6151 and such other sections of Subtitle F of the Internal Revenue Code as apply, and estimated tax payments shall be due with respect to a foreign corporation's liability for the tax on excess interest as provided in section 6655.

(3) Original issue discount. For purposes of this section, the term "interest" includes original issue discount, as defined in section 1273(a)(1).

(4) Examples. The application of this paragraph (a) is illustrated by the following examples.

Example (1). Taxation of branch interest and excess interest. Foreign corporation A, a calendar year taxpayer that is not a corporation described in paragraph (a)(2)(iii) of this section (relating to banks), has $120 of interest allocated or apportioned to ECI under § 1.882-5 for 1997. A's branch interest (as defined in paragraph (b) of this section) for 1997 is as follows: $55 of portfolio interest (as defined in section 871(h)(2)) to B, a nonresident alien; $25 of interest to foreign corporation C, which owns 15 percent of the combined voting power of A's stock, with respect to bonds issued by A; and $20 to D, a domestic corporation. B and C are not engaged in the conduct of a trade or business in the United States. A, B and C are residents of countries with which the United States does not have an income tax treaty. The interest payments made to B and D are not subject to tax under section 871(a) or 881 and are not subject to withholding under section 1441 or 1442. The payment to C, which does not qualify as portfolio interest because C owns at least 10 percent of the combined voting power of A's stock, is subject to withholding of $7.50 ($25 × 30%). In addition, because A's interest allocated or apportioned to ECI under § 1.882-5 ($120) exceeds its branch interest ($100), A has excess interest of $20, which is subject to a tax of $6 ($20 × 30%) under section 881. The tax on A's excess interest must be reported on A's income tax return for 1997.

Example (2). Taxation of excess interest of a bank. Foreign corporation A, a calendar year taxpayer, is a corporation described in paragraph (a)(2)(iii) of this section (relating to banks) and is a resident of a country with which the United States does not have an income tax treaty. A has excess interest of $100 for 1997. At the close of 1997, A has $10,000 of interest-bearing liabilities (including liabilities that give rise to branch interest), of which $8,700 are interest-bearing deposits. For purposes of computing the tax on A's excess interest, $87 of the excess interest ($100 excess interest × ($8,700 interest-bearing deposits/$10,000 interest-bearing liabilities)) is treated as interest on deposits. Thus, $87 of A's excess interest is exempt from tax under section 881(a) and the remaining $13 of excess interest is subject to a tax of $3.90 ($13 × 30%) under section 881(a).

(b) Branch interest. *(1) Definition of a branch interest.* For purposes of this section, the term "branch interest" means interest that is—

(i) Paid by a foreign corporation with respect to a liability that is—

(A) A U.S. booked liability within the meaning of § 1.882-5(d)(2) (other than a U.S. booked liability of a partner within the meaning of § 1.882-5(d)(2)(vii)); or

(B) Described in § 1.884-1(e)(2) (relating to insurance liabilities on U.S. business and liabilities giving rise to interest expense that is directly allocated to income from a U.S. asset); or

(ii) In the case of a foreign corporation other than a corporation described in paragraph (a)(2)(iii) of this section, a liability specifically identified (as provided in paragraph (b)(3)(i) of this section) as a liability of a U.S. trade or business of the foreign corporation on or before the earlier of the date on which the first payment of interest is made with respect to the liability or the due date (including extensions) of the foreign corporation's income tax return for the taxable year, provided that—

(A) The amount of such interest does not exceed 85 percent of the amount of interest of the foreign corporation that would be excess interest before taking into account interest treated as branch interest by reason of this paragraph (b)(1)(ii);

(B) The requirements of paragraph (b)(3)(ii) of this section (relating to notification of recipient of interest) are satisfied; and

(C) The liability is not described in paragraph (b)(3)(iii) of this section (relating to liabilities incurred in the ordinary course of a foreign business or secured by foreign assets) or paragraph (b)(1)(i) of this section.

(2) [Reserved]

(3) Requirements relating to specifically identified liabilities. (i) Method of identification. A liability described in paragraph (b)(1)(ii) of this section is identified as a liability of a U.S. trade or business only if the liability is shown on the records of the U.S. trade or business, or is identified as a liability of the U.S. trade or business on other records of the foreign corporation or on a schedule established for the purpose of identifying the liabilities of the U.S. trade or business. Each such liability must be identified with sufficient specificity so that the amount of branch interest attributable to the liability, and the name and address of the recipient, can be readily identified from such records or schedule. However, with respect to liabilities that give rise to portfolio interest (as defined in sections 871(h) and 881(c)) or that are payable 183 days or less from the date of original issue, and form part of a larger debt issue, such liabilities may be identified by reference to the issue and maturity date, principal amount and interest payable with respect to the entire debt issue. Records or schedules described in this paragraph that identify liabilities that give rise to branch interest must be maintained in the United States by the foreign corporation or an agent of the foreign corporation for the entire period commencing with the due date (including extensions) of the income tax return for the taxable year to which the records or schedules relate and ending with the expiration of the period of limitations for assessment of tax for such taxable year. A foreign corporation that is subject to this section may identify a liability under paragraph (b)(1)(ii) of this section whether or not it is actually engaged in the conduct of a trade or business in the United States.

(ii) Notification to recipient. Interest with respect to a liability described in paragraph (b)(1)(ii) of this section shall not be treated as branch interest unless the foreign corporation paying the interest either—

(A) Makes a return, pursuant to section 6049, with respect to the interest payment; or

(B) Sends a notice to the person who receives such interest in a confirmation of the transaction, a statement of account, or a separate notice, within two months of the end of the calendar year in which the interest was paid, stating that the interest paid with respect to the liability is from sources within the United States.

(iii) Liabilities that do not give rise to branch interest under paragraph (b)(1)(ii) of this section. A liability is described in this paragraph (b)(3)(iii) (and interest with respect to the liability may not be treated as branch interest of a foreign corporation by reason of paragraph (b)(1)(ii) of this section) if—

(A) The liability is directly incurred in the ordinary course of the profit-making activities of a trade or business of the foreign corporation conducted outside the United States, as, for example, an account or note payable arising from the purchase of inventory or receipt of services by such trade or business; or

(B) The liability is secured (during more than half the days during the portion of the taxable year in which the interest accrues) predominantly by property that is not a U.S. asset (as defined in § 1.884-1(d)) unless such liability is secured by substantially all the property of the foreign corporation.

(4) [Reserved]

(5) Increase in branch interest where U.S. assets constitute 80 percent or more of a foreign corporation's assets. (i) General rule. If a foreign corporation would have excess interest before application of this paragraph (b)(5) and the amount of the foreign corporation's U.S. assets as of the close of the taxable year equals or exceeds 80 percent of all money and the aggregate E&P basis of all property of the foreign corporation on such date, then all interest paid and accrued by the foreign corporation during the taxable year that was not treated as branch interest before application of this paragraph (b)(5) and that is not paid with respect to a liability described in paragraph (b)(3)(iii) of this section (relating to liabilities incurred in the ordinary course of a foreign business or secured by non-U.S. assets) shall be treated as branch interest. However, if application of the preceding sentence would cause the amount of the foreign corporation's branch interest to exceed the amount permitted by paragraph (b)(6)(i) of this section (relating to branch interest in excess of a foreign corporation's interest allocated or apportioned to ECI under § 1.882-5) the amount of branch interest arising by reason of this paragraph shall be reduced as provided in paragraphs (b)(6)(ii) and (iii) of this section, as applicable.

(ii) Example. The application of this paragraph (b)(5) is illustrated by the following example.

Example. Application of 80 percent test. Foreign corporation A, a calendar year taxpayer, has $90 of interest allocated or apportioned to ECI under § 1.882-5 for 1993. Before application of this paragraph (b)(5), A has $40 of branch interest in 1993. A pays $60 of other interest during 1993, none of which is attributable to a liability described in paragraph (b)(3)(iii) of this section (relating to liabilities incurred in the ordinary course of a foreign business and liabilities predominantly secured by foreign assets). As of the close of 1993, A has an amount of U.S. assets that exceeds 80 percent of the money and E&P bases of all A's property. Before application of this paragraph (b)(5), A would have $50 of excess interest (i.e., the $90 interest allocated or apportioned to its ECI under § 1.882-5 less $40 of branch interest). Under this paragraph (b)(5), the $60 of additional interest paid by A is also treated as branch interest. However, to the extent that treating the $60 of additional interest as branch interest would create an amount of branch interest that would exceed the amount of branch interest permitted under paragraph (b)(6) of this section (relating to branch interest that exceeds a foreign corporation's interest allocated or apportioned to ECI under § 1.882-5) the amount of the additional branch interest is reduced under paragraph (b)(6)(iii) of this section, which generally allows a foreign corporation to specify certain liabilities that do not give rise to branch interest or paragraph (b)(6)(ii) of this section, which generally specifies liabilities that do not give rise to branch interest beginning with the most-recently incurred liability.

(6) Special rule where branch interest exceeds interest allocated or apportioned to ECI of a foreign corporation. (i) General rule. If the amount of branch interest that is both paid and accrued by a foreign corporation during the taxable year (including interest that the foreign corporation elects under paragraph (c)(1) of this section to treat as paid during the taxable year) exceeds the amount of interest allocated or apportioned to ECI of a foreign corporation under § 1.882-5 for the taxable year, then the amount of the foreign corporation's branch interest shall be reduced by the amount of such excess as provided in paragraphs (b)(6)(ii) and (iii) of this section, as applicable. The rules of paragraphs (b)(6)(ii) and (iii) of this section shall also apply where the amount of branch interest with respect to liabilities identified under paragraph (b)(1)(ii) of this section exceeds the maximum amount that may be treated as branch interest under that paragraph. This paragraph (b)(6) shall apply whether or not a reduction in the amount of branch interest occurs as a result of adjustments made during the examination of the foreign corporation's income tax return, such as a reduction in the amount of interest allocated or apportioned to ECI of the foreign corporation under § 1.882-5.

(ii) Reduction of branch interest beginning with most-recently incurred liability. Except as provided in paragraph (b)(6)(iii) of this section (relating to an election to specify liabilities that do not give rise to branch interest), the amount of the excess in paragraph (b)(6)(i) of this section shall first reduce branch interest attributable to liabilities described in paragraph (b)(1)(ii) of this section (relating to liabilities identified as giving rise to branch interest) and then, if such excess has not been reduced to zero, branch interest attributable to the group of liabilities described in paragraph (b)(1)(i) of this section. The reduction of branch interest attributable to each group of liabilities (i.e., liabilities described in paragraph (b)(1)(ii) of this section and liabilities described in paragraph (b)(1)(i) of this section) shall be made beginning with interest attributable to the latest-incurred liability and continuing, in reverse chronological order, with branch interest attributable to the next-latest incurred liability. The branch interest attributable to a liability must be reduced to zero before a reduction is made with respect to branch interest attributable to the next-latest incurred liability. Where only a portion of the branch interest attributable to a liability is reduced by reason of this paragraph (b)(6)(ii), the reduction shall be made beginning with the last interest payment made with respect to the liability during the taxable year and continuing, in reverse chronological order, with the next-latest payment until the amount of branch interest has been reduced by the amount specified in paragraph (b)(6)(i) of this section. The amount of interest that is not treated as branch interest by reason of this paragraph (b)(6)(ii) shall not be treated as paid by a domestic corporation and thus shall not be subject to tax under section 871(a) or 881(a).

(iii) Election to specify liabilities that do not give rise to branch interest. For purposes of reducing the amount of branch interest under paragraph (b)(6)(i) of this section, a foreign corporation may, instead of using the method described in paragraph (b)(6)(ii) of this section, elect for any taxable year to specify which liabilities will not be treated as giving rise to branch interest or will be treated as giving rise only in part to branch interest. Branch interest paid during the taxable year with respect to a liability specified under this paragraph (b)(6)(iii) must be reduced to zero before a reduction is made with respect to branch interest attributable to the next-specified liability. If all interest payments with respect to a specified liability, when added to all interest payments with respect to other liabilities specified under this paragraph (b)(6)(iii), would exceed the amount of the reduction under paragraph (b)(6)(i) of this section, then only a portion of the branch interest attributable to that specified liability shall be reduced under this paragraph (b)(6)(iii), and the reduction shall be made beginning with the last interest payment made with respect to the liability during the taxable year and continuing, in reverse chronological order, with the next-latest payment until the amount of branch interest has been reduced by the amount of the reduction under paragraph (b)(6)(i) of this section. A foreign corporation that elects to have this paragraph (b)(6)(iii) apply shall note on its books and records maintained in the United States that the liability is not to be treated as giving rise to branch interest, or is to be treated as giving rise to branch interest only in part. Such notation must be made after the close of the taxable year in which the foreign corporation pays the interest and prior to the due date (with extensions) of the foreign corporation's income tax return for the taxable year. However, if the excess interest in paragraph (b)(6)(i) of this section occurs as a result of adjustments made during the examination of the foreign corporation's income tax return, the election and notation may be made at the time of examination. The amount of interest that is not treated as branch interest by reason of this paragraph (b)(6)(iii) shall not be treated as paid by a domestic corporation and thus shall not be subject to tax under section 871(a) or 881(a).

(iv) Examples. The application of this paragraph (b)(6) is illustrated by the following examples.

Example (1). Branch interest exceeds interest apportioned to ECI with no election in effect. Foreign corporation A, a calendar year, accrual method taxpayer, has interest expense apportioned to ECI under § 1.882-5 of $230 for 1997. A's branch interest for 1993 is as follows:

(i) $130 paid to B, a domestic corporation, with respect to a note issued on March 10, 1997, and secured by real property located in the United States;

(ii) $60 paid to C, an individual resident of country X who is entitled to a 10 percent rate of withholding on interest payments under the income tax treaty between the United States and X, with respect to a note issued on October 15, 1996, which gives rise to interest subject to tax under section 871(a);

(iii) $80 paid to D, an individual resident of country Y who is entitled to a 15 percent rate of withholding on interest payments under the income tax treaty between the United States and Y, with respect to a note issued on February 15, 1997, which gives rise to interest subject to tax under section 871(a); and

(iv) $70 of portfolio interest (as defined in section 871(h)(2)) paid to E, a nonresident alien, with respect to a bond issued on March 1, 1997.

A's branch interest accrues during 1997 for purposes of calculating the amount of A's interest apportioned to ECI under § 1.882-5. A has identified under paragraph (b)(1)(ii) of this section the liabilities described in paragraphs (ii), (iii) and (iv) of this example. A has not made an election under paragraph (b)(6)(iii) of this section to specify liabilities that do not give rise to branch interest. The amount of A's branch interest in 1997 is limited under paragraph (b)(6)(i) of this section to $230, the amount of the interest apportioned to A's ECI for 1997. The amount of A's branch interest must thus be reduced by $110 ($340 – $230) under paragraph (b)(6)(ii) of this section. The reduction is first made with respect to interest attributable to liabilities described in paragraph (b)(1)(v) of this section (i.e., liabilities identified as giving rise to branch interest) and, within the group of liabilities described in paragraph (b)(1)(v) of this section, is first made with respect to the latest-incurred liability. Thus, the $70 of interest paid to E with respect to the bond issued on March 1, 1997, and $40 of the $80 of interest paid to D with respect to the note issued on February 15, 1997, are not treated as branch interest. The interest paid to D is no longer subject to tax under section 871(a), and D may claim a refund of amounts withheld with respect to the interest payments. There is no change in the tax consequences to E because the interest received by E was portfolio interest and was not subject to tax when it was treated as branch interest.

Example (2). Effect of election to specify liabilities. Assume the same facts as in Example 1 except that A makes an election under paragraph (b)(6)(iii) of this section to specify which liabilities are not to be treated as giving rise to branch interest. A specifies the liability to D, who would be taxable at a rate of 15 percent on interest paid with respect to the liability, as a liability that does not give rise to branch interest, and D is therefore not subject to tax under section 871(a) and is entitled to a refund of amounts withheld with respect to the interest payments. A also specifies the liability to C as a liability that gives rise to branch interest only in part. As a result, $30 of the $60 of interest paid to C is not treated as branch interest, and C is entitled to a refund with respect to the $30 of interest that is not treated as branch interest.

(7) Effect of election under paragraph (c)(1) of this section to treat interest as if paid in year of accrual. If a foreign corporation accrues an interest expense in a taxable year earlier than the taxable year of payment and elects under paragraph (c)(1) of this section to compute its excess interest as if the interest expense were branch interest paid in the year of accrual, the interest expense shall be treated as branch interest that is paid at the close of such year (and not in the actual year of payment) for all purposes of this section. Such interest shall thus be subject to tax under section 871(a) or 881(a) and withholding under section 1441 or section 1442, as if paid on the last day of the taxable year of accrual. Interest that is treated under paragraph (c)(1) of this section as paid in a later year for purposes of computing excess interest shall be treated as paid only in the actual year of payment for all purposes of this section other than paragraphs (a)(2) and (c)(1) of this section (relating to excess interest).

(8) Effect of treaties. (i) Payor's treaty. In the case of a foreign corporation's branch interest, relief shall be available under an article of an income tax treaty between the United States and the foreign corporation's country of residence relating to interest paid by the foreign corporation only if, for the taxable year in which the branch interest is paid (or if the branch interest is treated as paid in an earlier taxable year under paragraph (b)(7) of this section, for the earlier taxable year)—

(A) The foreign corporation meets the requirements of the limitation on benefits provision, if any, in the treaty, and either—

(1) The corporation is a qualified resident (as defined in § 1.884-5(a)) of that foreign country in such year; or

(2) The corporation meets the requirements of paragraph (b)(8)(iii) of this section in such year; or

(B) The limitation on benefits provision, or an amendment to that provision, entered into force after December 31, 1986.

(ii) Recipient's treaty. A foreign person (other than a foreign corporation) that derives branch interest is entitled to claim benefits under provisions of an income tax treaty between the United States and its country of residence relating to interest derived by the foreign person. A foreign corporation may claim such benefits if it meets, with respect to the branch interest, the requirements of the limitation on benefits provision, if any, in the treaty and—

(A) The foreign corporation meets the requirements of paragraphs (b)(8)(i)(A) or (B) of this section; and

(B) In the case of interest paid in a taxable year beginning after December 31, 1988, with respect to an obligation with a maturity not exceeding one year, each foreign corporation that beneficially owned the obligation prior to maturity was a qualified resident (for the period specified in paragraph (b)(8)(i) of this section) of a foreign country with which the United States has an income tax treaty or met the requirements of the limitation on benefits provision in a treaty with respect to the interest payment and such provision entered into force after December 31, 1986.

(iii) Presumption that a foreign corporation continues to be a qualified resident. For purposes of this paragraph (b)(8), a foreign corporation that was a qualified resident for the prior taxable year because it fulfills the requirements of § 1.884-5 shall be considered a qualified resident with respect to branch interest that is paid or received during the current taxable year if—

(A) In the case of a foreign corporation that met the stock ownership and base erosion tests in § 1.884-5(b) and (c) for the preceding taxable year, the foreign corporation does not know, or have reason to know, that either 50 percent of its stock (by value) is not beneficially owned (or treated as beneficially owned by reason of § 1.884-5(b)(2)) by qualifying shareholders at any time during the portion of the taxable year that ends with the date on which the interest is paid, or that the base erosion test is not met during the portion of the taxable year that ends with the date on which the interest is paid;

(B) In the case of a foreign corporation that met the requirements of § 1.884-5(d) (relating to publicly-traded corporations) for the preceding taxable year, the foreign corporation is listed on an established securities exchange in the United States or its country of residence at all times during the portion of the taxable year that ends with the date on which the interest is paid and does not fail the requirements of § 1.884-5(d)(4)(iii) (relating to certain closely-held corporations) at any time during such period; or

(C) In the case of a foreign corporation that met the requirements of § 1.884-5(e) (relating to the active trade or business test) for the preceding taxable year, the foreign corporation continues to operate (other than in a nominal degree), at all times during the portion of the taxable year that ends with the date on which the interest is paid, the same business in the U.S. and its country of residence that caused it to meet such requirements for the preceding taxable year.

(iv) Treaties other than income tax treaties. A treaty that is not an income tax treaty does not provide any benefits with respect to branch interest.

(v) Effect of income tax treaties on interest paid by a partnership. If a foreign corporation is a partner (directly or indirectly) in a partnership that is engaged in a trade or business in the United States and owns an interest of 10 percent or more (as determined under the attribution rules of section 318) in the capital, profits, or losses of the partnership at any time during the partner's taxable year, the relief that may be claimed under an income tax treaty with respect to the foreign corporation's distributive share of interest paid or treated as paid by the partnership shall not exceed the relief that would be available under paragraphs (b)(8)(i) and (ii) of this section if such interest were branch interest of the foreign corporation. See paragraph (c)(2) of this section for the effect on a foreign corporation's excess interest of interest paid by a partnership of which the foreign corporation is a partner.

(vi) Examples. The following examples illustrate the application of this paragraph (b)(8).

Example (1). Payor's treaty. The income tax treaty between the United States and country X provides that the United States may not impose a tax on interest paid by a corporation that is a resident of that country (and that is not a domestic corporation) if the recipient of the interest is a nonresident alien or a foreign corporation. Corp A is a qualified resident of country X and meets the limitation on benefits provision in the treaty. A's branch interest is not subject to tax under section 871(a) or 881(a) regardless of whether the recipient is entitled to benefits under an income tax treaty.

Example (2). Recipient's treaty and interest received from a partnership. A, a foreign corporation, and B, a nonresident alien, are partners in a partnership that owns and operates U.S. real estate and each has a distributive share of partnership interest deductions equal to 50 percent of the interest deductions of the partnership. There is no income tax treaty between the United States and the countries of residence of A and B. The partnership pays $1,000 of interest to a bank that is a resident of a foreign country, Y, and that qualifies under an income tax treaty in effect with the United States for a 5 percent rate of tax on U.S. source interest paid to a resident of country Y. However, the bank is not a qualified resident of country Y and the limitation on benefits provision of the treaty has not been amended since December 31, 1986. The partnership is required to withhold at a rate of 30 percent on $500 of the interest paid to the bank (i.e., A's 50 percent distributive share of interest paid by the partnership) because the bank cannot, under paragraph (b)(8)(iv) of this section, claim greater treaty benefits by lending money to the partnership than it could claim if it lent money to A directly and the $500 were branch interest of A.

(c) Rules relating to excess interest. *(1) Election to compute excess interest by treating branch interest that is paid and accrued in different years as if paid in year of accrual.* (i) General rule. If branch interest is paid in one or more taxable years before or after the year in which the interest accrues, a foreign corporation may elect to compute its excess interest as if such branch interest were paid on the last day of the taxable year in which it accrues, and not in the taxable year in which it is actually paid. The interest expense will thus reduce the amount of the foreign corporation's excess interest in the year of accrual rather than in the year of actual payment. Except as provided in paragraph (c)(1)(ii) of this section, if an election is made for a taxable year, this paragraph (c)(1)(i) shall apply to all branch interest that is paid or accrued during that year. See paragraph (b)(7) of this section for the effect of an election under this paragraph (c)(1) on branch interest that accrues in a taxable year after the year of payment.

(ii) Election not to apply in certain cases. An election under this paragraph (c)(1) shall not apply to an interest expense that accrued in a taxable year beginning before January 1, 1987, and shall not apply to an interest expense that was paid in a taxable year beginning before such date unless the interest was income from sources within the United States. An election under this paragraph (c)(1) shall not apply to branch interest that accrues during the taxable year and is paid in an earlier taxable year if the branch interest reduced excess interest in such earlier year. However, a foreign corporation may amend its income tax return for such earlier taxable year so that the branch interest does not reduce excess interest in such year.

(iii) Requirements for election. A foreign corporation that elects to apply this paragraph (c)(1) shall attach to its income tax return (or to an amended income tax return) a statement that it elects to have the provisions of this paragraph (c)(1) apply, or shall provide written notice to the Commissioner during an examination that it elects to apply this paragraph (c)(1). The election shall be effective for the taxable year to which the return relates and for all subsequent taxable years unless the Commissioner consents to revocation of the election.

(iv) Examples. The following examples illustrate the application of this paragraph (c)(1).

Example (1). Interest accrued before paid. Foreign corporation A, a calendar year, accrual method taxpayer, has $100 of interest allocated or apportioned to ECI under § 1.882-5 for 1997. A has $60 of branch interest in 1997 before application of this paragraph (c)(1). A has an interest expense of $20 that properly accrues for tax purposes in 1997 but is not paid until 1998. When the interest is paid in 1998 it will meet the requirements for branch interest under paragraph (b)(1) of this section. A makes a timely election under this paragraph (c)(1) to treat the accrued interest as if it were paid in 1997. A will be treated as having branch interest of $80 for 1997 and excess interest of $20 in 1997. The $20 of interest treated as branch interest of A in 1997 will not again be treated as branch interest in 1998.

Example (2). Interest paid before accrued. Foreign corporation A, a calendar year, accrual method taxpayer, has $60 of branch interest in 1997. The interest expense does not accrue until 1998 and the amount of interest allocated or apportioned to A's ECI under § 1.882-5 is zero for 1997 and $60 for 1998. A makes an election under this paragraph (c)(1) with respect to 1997. As a result of the election, A's $60 of branch interest in 1997 reduces the amount of A's excess interest for 1998 rather than in 1997.

(2) Interest paid by a partnership. (i) General rule. Except as otherwise provided in paragraphs (c)(2)(i) and (ii) of this section, if a foreign corporation is a partner in a partnership that is engaged in trade or business in the United States, the amount of the foreign corporation's distributive share of interest paid or accrued by the partnership shall reduce (but not below zero) the amount of the foreign corporation's excess interest for the year to the extent such interest is taken into account by the foreign corporation in that year for purposes of calculating the interest allocated or apportioned to the ECI of the foreign corporation under § 1.882-5. A foreign corporation's excess interest shall not be reduced by its distributive share of partnership interest that is attributable to a liability described in paragraph (b)(3)(iii) of this section (relating to interest on liabilities incurred in the ordinary course of a foreign business or secured predominantly by assets that are not U.S. assets) or would be described in paragraph (b)(3)(iii) of this section if entered on the partner's books. See paragraph (b)(8)(v) of this section for the effect of income tax treaties on interest paid by a partnership.

(ii) Special rule for interest that is paid and accrued in different years. Paragraph (c)(2)(i) of this section shall not apply to any portion of a foreign corporation's distributive share of partnership interest that is paid and accrued in different taxable years unless the foreign corporation has an election in effect under paragraph (c)(1) of this section that is effective with respect to such interest and any tax due under section 871(a) or 881(a) with respect to such interest has been deducted and withheld at source in the earlier of the taxable year of payment or accrual.

(3) Effect of treaties. (i) General rule. The rate of tax imposed on the excess interest of a foreign corporation that is a resident of a country with which the United States has an income tax treaty shall not exceed the rate provided under such treaty that would apply with respect to interest paid by a domestic corporation to that foreign corporation if the foreign corporation meets, with respect to the excess interest, the requirements of the limitation on benefits provision, if any, in the treaty and either—

(A) The corporation is a qualified resident (as defined in § 1.884-5 (a)) of that foreign country for the taxable year in which the excess interest is subject to tax; or

(B) The limitation on benefits provision, or an amendment to that provision, entered into force after December 31, 1986.

(ii) Provisions relating to interest paid by a foreign corporation. Any provision in an income tax treaty that exempts or reduces the rate of tax on interest paid by a foreign corporation does not prevent imposition of the tax on excess interest or reduce the rate of such tax.

(4) Example. The application of paragraphs (c)(2) and (3) of this section is illustrated by the following example.

Example. Interest paid by a partnership. Foreign corporation A, a calendar year taxpayer, is not a resident of a foreign country with which the United States has an income tax treaty. A is engaged in the conduct of a trade or business both in the United States and in foreign countries, and owns a 50 percent interest in X, a calendar year partnership engaged in the conduct of a trade or business in the United States. For 1997, all of X's liabilities are of a type described in paragraph (b)(1) of this section (relating to liabilities on U.S. books) and none are described in paragraph (b)(3)(iii) of this section (relating to liabilities that may not give rise to branch interest). A's distributive share of interest paid by X in 1997 is $20. For 1997, A has $150 of interest allocated or apportioned to its ECI under § 1.882-5, $120 of which is attributable to branch interest. Thus, the amount of A's excess interest for 1997, before application of paragraph (c)(2)(i) of this section, is $30. Under paragraph (c)(2)(i) of this section, A's $30 of excess interest is reduced by $20, representing A's share of interest paid by X. Thus, the amount of A's excess interest for 1998 is reduced to $10. A is subject to a tax of 30 percent on its $10 of excess interest.

(d) Stapled entities. A foreign corporation that is treated as a domestic corporation by reason of section 269B (relating to stapled entities) shall continue to be treated as a foreign corporation for purposes of section 884(f) and this section, notwithstanding section 269B and the regulations thereunder. Interest paid by such foreign corporation shall be treated as paid by a domestic corporation and shall be subject to the tax imposed by section 871(a) or 881(a), and to withholding under section 1441 and 1442, as applicable, to the extent such interest is not subject to tax by reason of section 884(f) and this section.

(e) Effective dates. *(1) General rule.* Except as provided in paragraph (e)(2) of this section, this section is effective for taxable years beginning October 13, 1992 and for payments of interest described in section 884(f)(1)(A) made (or treated as made under paragraph (b)(7) of this section) during taxable years of the payor beginning after such date. With respect to taxable years beginning before October 13,

1992 and after December 31, 1986, a foreign corporation may elect to apply this section in lieu of § 1.884-4T of the temporary regulations (as contained in the CFR edition revised as of April 1, 1992) as they applied to the foreign corporation after issuance of Notice 89-80, 1989-2 C.B. 394, but only if the foreign corporation has made an election under § 1.884-1(i) to apply § 1.884-1 in lieu of § 1.884-1T (as contained in the CFR edition revised as of April 1, 1992) for that year, and the statute of limitations for assessment of a deficiency has not expired for that taxable year. Once an election has been made, an election under this section shall apply to all subsequent taxable years.

(2) Special rule. Paragraphs (a)(1), (a)(2)(iii), (b)(1), (b)(3), (b)(5)(i), (b)(6)(i), (b)(6)(ii), and (c)(2)(i) of this section are effective for taxable years beginning on or after June 6, 1996.

(f) Transition rules. *(1) Election under paragraph (c)(1) of this section.* If a foreign corporation has made an election described in § 1.884-4T(b)(7) (as contained in the CFR edition revised as of April 1, 1992) with respect to interest that has accrued and been paid in different taxable years, such election shall be effective for purposes of paragraph (c)(1) of this section as if the corporation had made the election under paragraph (c)(1) of this section of these regulations.

(2) Waiver of notification requirement for non-banks under Notice 89-80. If a foreign corporation that is not a bank has made an election under Notice 89-80 to apply the rules in Part 2 of Section I of the Notice in lieu of the rules in § 1.884-4T(b) (as contained in the CFR edition revised as of April 1, 1992) to determine the amount of its interest paid and excess interest in taxable years beginning prior to 1990, the requirement that the foreign corporation satisfy the notification requirements described in paragraph (b)(3)(ii) of this section is waived with respect to interest paid in taxable years ending on or before the date the Notice was issued.

(3) Waiver of legending requirement for certain debt issued prior to January 3, 1989. For purposes of sections 871(h), 881(c), and this section, branch interest of a foreign corporation that would be treated as portfolio interest under section 871(h) or 881(c) but for the fact that it fails to meet the requirements of section 163(f)(2)(B)(ii)(II) (relating to the legend requirement), shall nevertheless be treated as portfolio interest provided the interest arises with respect to a liability incurred by the foreign corporation before January 3, 1989, and interest with respect to the liability was treated as branch interest in a taxable year beginning before January 1, 1990.

T.D. 8432, 9/10/92, amend T.D. 8657, 3/5/96.

§ 1.884-5 Qualified resident.

(a) Definition of qualified resident. A foreign corporation is a qualified resident of a foreign country with which the United States has an income tax treaty in effect if, for the taxable year, the foreign corporation is a resident of that country (within the meaning of such treaty) and either—

(1) Meets the requirements of paragraphs (b) and (c) of this section (relating to stock ownership and base erosion);

(2) Meets the requirements of paragraph (d) of this section (relating to publicly-traded corporations);

(3) Meets the requirements of paragraph (e) of this section (relating to the conduct of an active trade or business); or

(4) Obtains a ruling as provided in paragraph (f) of this section that it shall be treated as a qualified resident of its country of residence.

(b) Stock ownership requirement. *(1) General rule.* (i) Ownership by qualifying shareholders. A foreign corporation satisfies the stock ownership requirement of this paragraph (b) for the taxable year if more than 50 percent of its stock (by value) is beneficially owned (or is treated as beneficially owned by reason of paragraph (b)(2) of this section) during at least half of the number of days in the foreign corporation's taxable year by one or more qualifying shareholders. A person shall be treated as a qualifying shareholder only if such person meets the requirements of paragraph (b)(3) of this section and is either—

(A) An individual who is either a resident of the foreign country of which the foreign corporation is a resident or a citizen or resident of the United States;

(B) The government of the country of which the foreign corporation is a resident (or a political subdivision or local authority of such country), or the United States, a State, the District of Columbia, or a political subdivision or local authority of a State;

(C) A corporation that is a resident of the foreign country of which the foreign corporation is a resident and whose stock is primarily and regularly traded on an established securities market (within the meaning of paragraph (d) of this section) in that country or the United States or a domestic corporation whose stock is primarily and regularly traded on an established securities market (within the meaning of paragraph (d) of this section) in the United States;

(D) A not-for-profit organization described in paragraph (b)(1)(iv) of this section that is not a pension fund as defined in paragraph (b)(8)(i)(A) of this section and that is organized under the laws of the foreign country of which the foreign corporation is a resident or the United States; or

(E) A beneficiary of certain pension funds (as defined in paragraph (b)(8)(i)(A) of this section) administered in or by the country in which the foreign corporation is a resident to the extent provided in paragraph (b)(8) of this section.

Beneficial owners of an association taxable as a corporation shall be treated as shareholders of such association for purposes of this paragraph (b)(1). If stock of a foreign corporation is owned by a corporation that is treated as a qualifying shareholder under paragraph (b)(1)(i)(C) of this section, such stock shall not also be treated as owned, directly or indirectly, by any qualifying shareholders of such corporation for purposes of this paragraph (b). Notwithstanding the above, a foreign corporation will not be treated as a qualified resident unless it obtains the documentation described in paragraph (b)(3) of this section to show that the requirements of this paragraph (b)(1)(i) have been met and maintains the documentation as provided in paragraph (b)(9) of this section. See also paragraph (b)(1)(iii) of this section, which treats certain publicly-traded classes of stock as owned by qualifying shareholders.

(ii) Special rules relating to qualifying shareholders. For purposes of applying paragraph (b)(1)(i) of this section—

(A) Stock owned on any day shall be taken into account only if the beneficial owner is a qualifying shareholder on that day or, in the case of a corporation or not-for-profit organization that is a qualifying shareholder under paragraph (b)(1)(i)(C) or (D) of this section, for a one-year period that includes such day; and

(B) An individual, corporation or not-for-profit organization is a resident of a foreign country if it is a resident of that country for purposes of the income tax treaty between the United States and that country.

(iii) Publicly-traded class of stock treated as owned by qualifying shareholders. A class of stock of a foreign corporation shall be treated as owned by qualifying shareholders if—

(A) The class of stock is listed on an established securities market in the United States or in the country of residence of the foreign corporation seeking qualified resident status; and

(B) The class of stock is primarily and regularly traded on such market (within the meaning of paragraphs (d)(3) and (4) of this section, applied as if the class of stock were the sole class of stock relied on to meet the requirements of paragraph (d)(4)(i)(A)).

For purposes of this paragraph (b), stock in such class shall not also be treated as owned by any qualifying shareholders who own such stock, either directly or indirectly.

(iv) Special rule for not-for-profit organizations. A not-for-profit organization is described in paragraph (b)(1)(iv) of this section if it meets the following requirements—

(A) It is a corporation, association taxable as a corporation, trust, fund, foundation, league or other entity operated exclusively for religious, charitable, educational, or recreational purposes, and it is not organized for profit;

(B) It is generally exempt from tax in its country of organization by virtue of its not-for-profit status; and

(C) Either—

(1) More than 50 percent of its annual support is expended on behalf of persons described in paragraphs (b)(1)(i)(A) through (E) of this section or on qualified residents of the country in which the organization is organized; or

(2) More than 50 percent of its annual support is derived from persons described in paragraphs (b)(1)(i)(A) through (E) of this section or from persons who are qualified residents of the country in which the organization is organized.

For purposes of meeting the requirements of paragraph (b)(1)(iv)(C) of this section, a not-for-profit organization may rely on the addresses of record of its individual beneficiaries and supporters to determine if such persons are resident in the country in which the not-for-profit organization is organized, provided that the addresses of record are not nonresidential addresses such as a post office box or in care of a financial intermediary, and the officers, directors or administrators of the organization do not know or have reason to know that the individual beneficiaries or supporters do not reside at that address.

(2) Rules for determining constructive ownership. (i) General rules for attribution. For purposes of this section, stock owned by a corporation, partnership, trust, estate, or mutual insurance company or similar entity shall be treated as owned proportionately by its shareholders, partners, beneficiaries, grantors or other interest holders as provided in paragraph (b)(2)(ii) through (v) of this section. The proportionate interest rules of this paragraph (b)(2) shall apply successively upward through a chain of ownership, and a person's proportionate interest shall be computed for the relevant days or period that is taken into account in determining whether a foreign corporation is a qualified resident. Except as otherwise provided, stock treated as owned by a person by reason of this paragraph (b)(2) shall, for purposes of applying this paragraph (b)(2), be treated as actually owned by such person.

(ii) Partnerships. A partner shall be treated as having an interest in stock of a foreign corporation owned by a partnership in proportion to the least of—

(A) The partner's percentage distributive share of the partnership's dividend income from the stock;

(B) The partner's percentage distributive share of gain from disposition of the stock by the partnership;

(C) The partner's percentage distributive share of the stock (or proceeds from the disposition of the stock) upon liquidation of the partnership.

For purposes of this paragraph (b)(2)(ii), however, all qualifying shareholders that are partners of a partnership shall be treated as one partner. Thus, the percentage distributive shares of dividend income, gain and liquidation rights of all qualifying shareholders that are partners in a partnership are aggregated prior to determining the least of the three percentages.

(iii) Trusts and estates. (A) Beneficiaries. In general, a person shall be treated as having an interest in stock of a foreign corporation owned by a trust or estate in proportion to the person's actuarial interest in the trust or estate, as provided in section 318(a)(2)(B)(i), except that an income beneficiary's actuarial interest in the trust will be determined as if the trust's only asset were the stock. The interest of a remainder beneficiary in stock will be equal to 100 percent minus the sum of the percentages of any interest in the stock held by income beneficiaries. The ownership of an interest in stock owned by a trust shall not be attributed to any beneficiary whose interest cannot be determined under the preceding sentence, and any such interest, to the extent not attributed by reason of this paragraph (b)(2)(iii)(A), shall not be considered owned by a beneficiary unless all potential beneficiaries with respect to the stock are qualifying shareholders. In addition, a beneficiary's actuarial interest will be treated as zero to the extent that a grantor is treated as owning the stock under paragraph (b)(2)(iii)(B) of this section. A substantially separate and independent share of a trust, within the meaning of section 663(c), shall be treated as a separate trust for purposes of this paragraph (b)(2)(iii)(A), provided that payment of income, accumulated income or corpus of a share of one beneficiary (or group of beneficiaries) cannot affect the proportionate share of income, accumulated income or corpus of another beneficiary (or group of beneficiaries).

(B) Grantor trusts. A person is treated as the owner of stock of a foreign corporation owned by a trust to the extent that the stock is included in the portion of the trust that is treated as owned by the person under sections 671 to 679 (relating to grantors and others treated as substantial owners).

(iv) Corporations that issue stock. A shareholder of a corporation that issues stock shall be treated as owning stock of a foreign corporation that is owned by such corporation on any day in a proportion that equals the value of the stock owned by such shareholder to the value of all stock of such corporation. If there is an agreement, express or implied, that a shareholder of a corporation will not receive distributions from the earnings of stock owned by the corporation, the shareholder will not be treated as owning that stock owned by the corporation.

(v) Mutual insurance companies and similar entities. Stock held by a mutual insurance company, mutual savings bank, or similar entity (including an association taxable as a corporation that does not issue stock interests) shall be considered owned proportionately by the policy holders, depositors, or other owners in the same proportion that such persons share in the surplus of such entity upon liquidation or dissolution.

(vi) Pension funds. See paragraphs (b)(8)(ii) and (iii) of this section for the attribution of stock owned by a pension fund (as defined in paragraph (b)(8)(i)(A)) to beneficiaries of the fund.

(vii) Examples. The rules of paragraph (b)(2)(ii) of this section are illustrated by the following examples.

Example (1). Stock held solely by qualifying shareholders through a partnership. A and B, residents of country X, are qualifying shareholders, within the meaning of paragraphs (b)(1)(i)(A) through (E) of this section, and the sole partners of partnership P. P's only asset is the stock of foreign corporation Z, a country X corporation seeking qualified resident status under this section. A's distributive share of P's income and gain on the disposition of P's assets is 80 percent, but A's distributive share of P's assets (or the proceeds therefrom) on P's liquidation is 20 percent. B's distributive share of P's income and gain is 20 percent and B is entitled to 80 percent of the assets (or proceeds therefrom) on P's liquidation. Under the attribution rules of paragraph (b)(2)(ii) of this section, A and B will be treated as a single partner owning in the aggregate 100 percent of the stock of Z owned by P.

Example (2). Stock held by both qualifying and non-qualifying shareholders through a partnership. Assume the same facts as in Example 1 except that C, an individual who is not a qualifying shareholder, is also a partner in P and that C's distributive share of P's income is 60 percent. The distributive shares of A and B are the same as in Example 1 except that A's distributive share of income is 20 percent. Under the attribution rules of paragraph (b)(2)(ii) of this section, A and B will be treated as a single partner owning in the aggregate 40 percent of the stock of Z owned by P (i.e., the least of A and B's aggregate distributive shares of dividend income (40 percent), gain (100 percent), and liquidation rights (100 percent) with respect to the Z stock).

Example (3). Stock held through tiered partnerships. Assume the same facts as in Example 1, except that P does not own the stock of Z directly, but rather is a partner in partnership P1, which owns the stock of Z. Assume that P's distributive share of the dividend income, gain and liquidation rights with respect to the Z stock held by P1 is 40 percent. Assume that of the remaining partners of P1 only D is a qualifying shareholder. D's distributive share of P1's dividend income and gain is 15 percent; D's distributive share of P1's assets on liquidation is 25 percent. Under the attribution rules of paragraph (b)(2)(ii) of this section, A and B, treated as a single partner, will own 40 percent of the Z stock owned by P1 (100 percent × 40 percent) and D will be treated as owning 15 percent of the Z stock owned by P1 (the least of D's dividend income (15 percent), gain (15 percent), and liquidation rights (25 percent) with respect to the Z stock). Thus, 55 percent of the Z stock owned by P1 is treated as owned by qualifying shareholders under paragraph (b)(2)(ii) of this section.

(3) Required documentation. (i) Ownership statements, certificates of residency and intermediary ownership statements. Except as provided in paragraphs (b)(3)(ii), (iii) and (iv) and paragraph (b)(8) of this section, a person shall only be treated as a qualifying shareholder of a foreign corporation if—

(A) For the relevant period, the person completes an ownership statement described in paragraph (b)(4) of this section and, in the case of an individual who is not a U.S. citizen or resident, also obtains a certificate of residency described in paragraph (b)(5) of this section;

(B) In the case of a person owning stock in the foreign corporation indirectly through one or more intermediaries (including mere legal owners or recordholders acting as nominees), each intermediary completes an intermediary ownership statement described in paragraph (b)(6) of this section; and

(C) Such ownership statements and certificates of residency are received by the foreign corporation on or before the earlier of the date it files its income tax return for the taxable year to which the statements relate or the due date (including extensions) for filing such return or, in the case of a foreign corporation claiming treaty benefits under § 1.884-4(b)(8)(i) or (ii) (relating to branch interest) on or before the date on which such interest is paid.

(ii) Substitution of intermediary verification statement for ownership statements and certificates of residency. If a qualifying shareholder owns stock through an intermediary that is either a domestic corporation, a resident of the United States, or a resident (for treaty purposes) of a country with which the United States has an income tax treaty in effect, the intermediary may provide an intermediary verification statement (as described in paragraph (b)(7) of this section) in place of any relevant ownership statements and certificates of residency from qualifying shareholders, and in place of intermediary ownership statements (or, where applicable, intermediary verification statements) from all intermediaries standing in the chain of ownership between the qualifying shareholders and the intermediary issuing the intermediary verification statement. An intermediary verification statement generally certifies that the verifying intermediary holds the documentation described in the preceding sentence and agrees to make it available to the District Director on request. Such intermediary verification statements, along with an intermediary ownership statement from the verifying intermediary, must be received by the foreign corporation on or before the earlier of the date it files its income tax return for the taxable year to which the statements relate or the due date (including extensions) for filing such return. An indirect owner of a foreign corporation is thus treated as a qualifying shareholder of a foreign corporation if the foreign corporation receives, on or before the time specified above, an intermediary verification statement and an intermediary ownership statement from the verifying intermediary and an intermediary ownership statement from all intermediaries standing in the chain of the verifying intermediary's ownership of its interest in the foreign corporation.

(iii) Special rule for registered shareholders of widely-held corporations. An ownership statement and a certificate of residency shall not be required in the case of an individual who is a shareholder of record of a corporation that has at least 250 shareholders if—

(A) The individual owns less than one percent of the stock (by value) (applying the attribution rules of section 318) of the corporation at all times during the taxable year;

(B) The individual's address of record is in the corporation's country of residence and is not a nonresidential address such as a post office box or in care of a financial intermediary or stock transfer agent; and

(C) The officers and directors of the corporation do not know or have reason to know that the individual does not reside at that address.

The rule in this paragraph (b)(3)(iii) may also be applied with respect to individual owners of mutual insurance companies, mutual savings banks or similar entities, provided that the same conditions set forth in this paragraph (b)(3)(iii) are met with respect to such individuals.

(iv) Special rule for pension funds. See paragraphs (b)(8)(ii) through (v) of this section for special documentation rules applicable to pension funds (as defined in paragraph (b)(8)(i)(A) of this section).

(v) Reasonable cause exception. If a foreign corporation does not obtain the documentation described in this paragraph (b)(3) or (b)(8) of this section in a timely manner but is able to show prior to notification of an examination of the return for the taxable year that the failure was due to reasonable cause and not willful neglect, the foreign corporation may perfect the documentation after the deadlines specified in paragraph this (b)(3) or (b)(8) of this section. It may make such a showing by providing a written statement to the District Director having jurisdiction over the taxpayer's return or the Office of the Assistant Commissioner (International), as applicable, setting forth the reasons for the failure to obtain the documentation in a timely manner and describing the documentation that was received after the deadline had passed. Whether a failure to obtain the documentation in a timely manner was due to reasonable cause shall be determined by the District Director or the Office of the Assistant Commissioner (International), as applicable, under all the facts and circumstances.

(4) Ownership statements from qualifying shareholders. (i) Ownership statements from individuals. An ownership statement from an individual is a written statement signed by the individual under penalties of perjury stating—

(A) The name, permanent address, and country of residence of the individual and, if the individual was not a resident of the country for the entire taxable year of the foreign corporation seeking qualified resident status, the period during which it was a resident of the foreign corporation's country of residence;

(B) If the individual is a direct beneficial owner of stock in the foreign corporation, the name of the corporation, the number of shares in each class of stock of the corporation that are so owned, and the period of time during the taxable year of the foreign corporation during which the individual owned the stock (or, in the case of an association taxable as a corporation, the amount and nature of the owner's interest in such association);

(C) If the individual directly owns an interest in a corporation, partnership, trust, estate or other intermediary that owns (directly or indirectly) stock in the foreign corporation, the name of the intermediary, the number and class of shares or amount and nature of the interest of the individual in such intermediary (that is relevant for purposes of attributing ownership in paragraph (b)(2) of this section), and the period of time during the taxable year of the foreign corporation during which the individual held such interest; and

(D) To the extent known by the individual, a description of the chain of ownership through which the individual owns stock in the foreign corporation, including the name and address of each intermediary standing between the intermediary described in paragraph (b)(4)(i)(C) of this section and the foreign corporation.

(ii) Ownership statements from governments. An ownership statement from a government that is a qualifying shareholder is a written statement signed by either—

(A) An official of the governmental authority, agency or office that has supervisory authority with respect to the government's ownership interest who is authorized to sign such a statement on behalf of the authority, agency or office; or

(B) The competent authority of the foreign country (as defined in the income tax treaty between the United States and the foreign country).

Such statement shall provide the title of the official signing the statement and the name and address of the government agency, and shall provide the information described in paragraphs (b)(4)(i)(B) through (D) of this section (substituting "government" for "individual") with respect to the government's direct or indirect ownership of stock in the foreign corporation seeking qualified resident status.

(iii) Ownership statements from publicly-traded corporations. An ownership statement from a corporation that is a qualifying shareholder under paragraph (b)(1)(i)(C) of this section is a written statement signed by a person authorized to sign a tax return on behalf of the corporation under penalties of perjury stating—

(A) The name, permanent address, and principal place of business of the corporation (if different from its permanent address);

(B) The information described in paragraphs (b)(4)(i)(B) through (D) of this section (substituting "corporation" for "individual"); and

(C) That the corporation's stock is primarily and regularly traded on an established securities exchange (within the meaning of paragraph (d) of this section) in the United States or its country of residence.

(iv) Ownership statements from not-for-profit organizations. An ownership statement from a not-for-profit organization (other than a pension fund as defined in paragraph (b)(8)(i)(A) of this section) is a written statement signed by a person authorized to sign a tax return on behalf of the organization under penalties of perjury stating—

(A) The name, permanent address, and principal location of the activities of the organization (if different from its permanent address);

(B) The information described in paragraphs (b)(4)(i)(B) through (D) of this section (substituting "not-for-profit organization" for "individual") with respect to the not-for-profit organization's direct or indirect ownership of stock in the foreign corporation seeking qualified resident status; and

(C) That the not-for-profit organization satisfies the requirements of paragraph (b)(1)(iv) of this section.

(v) Ownership through a nominee. For purposes of this paragraph (b)(4) and paragraph (b)(6) of this section, a person who owns either stock in a foreign corporation seeking qualified resident status or an interest in an intermediary described in paragraph (b)(4)(i)(C) of this section through a nominee shall be treated as owning such stock or interest directly and must, therefore, provide the information described in paragraphs (b)(4)(i) through (iv) of this section, as applicable. Such person must also provide the name and address of the nominee.

(5) Certificate of residency. A certificate of residency must be signed by the relevant authorities (as described below) of the country of residence of the individual shareholder and must state that the individual is a resident of that country for purposes of its income tax laws or, if the authorities do not customarily make such a determination, that the individual has filed a tax return claiming resident status and subjecting the individual's income to tax on a resident basis for the taxable year or period that ends with or within the taxable year for which the corporation is seeking qualified resident status. In the case of an individual who is not legally required to file a tax return in his or her country of

residence or in any other country, a certificate of residency of a parent or guardian residing at such individual's address shall be considered sufficient to meet that individual's obligation under this paragraph (b)(5). The relevant authorities shall be the competent authority of the foreign country of which the foreign corporation is a resident, as defined in the income tax treaty between the foreign country and the United States, or such other governmental office of the foreign country (or political subdivision thereof) that customarily provides statements of residence. Notwithstanding the foregoing, the Commissioner may consult with the competent authority of a country regarding the procedures set forth in this paragraph (b)(5) and if necessary agree on additional or alternative procedures under which these certificates may be issued.

(6) Intermediary ownership statement. An intermediary ownership statement is a written statement signed under penalties of perjury by the intermediary (if the intermediary is an individual) or a person that would be authorized to sign a tax return on behalf of the intermediary (if the intermediary is not an individual) containing the following information:

(i) The name, address, country of residence, and principal place of business (in the case of a corporation or partnership) of the intermediary and, if the intermediary is a trust or estate, the name and permanent address of all trustees or executors (or equivalent under foreign law);

(ii) The information described in paragraphs (b)(4)(i)(B) through (D) (substituting "intermediary making the ownership statement" for "individual") with respect to the intermediary's direct or indirect ownership in the stock in the foreign corporation seeking qualified resident status;

(iii) If the intermediary is a nominee for a qualifying shareholder or another intermediary, the name and permanent address of the qualifying shareholder, or the name and principal place of business of such other intermediary;

(iv) If the intermediary is not a nominee for a qualifying shareholder or another intermediary, the proportionate interest in the intermediary of each direct shareholder, partner, beneficiary, grantor, or other interest holder (or if the direct holder is a nominee, of its beneficial shareholder, partner, beneficiary, grantor, or other interest holder) from which the intermediary received an ownership statement and the period of time during the taxable year for which the interest in the intermediary was owned by such shareholder, partner, beneficiary, grantor or other interest holder. For purposes of this paragraph (b)(6)(iv), the proportionate interest of a person in an intermediary is the percentage interest (by value) held by such person, determined using the principles for attributing ownership in paragraph (b)(2) of this section. If an intermediary is not required to receive an ownership statement from its individual registered shareholders or other interest holders by reason of paragraph (b)(3)(iii) of this section, then it must provide a list of the names and addresses of such registered shareholders or other interest holders and the aggregate proportionate interest in the intermediary of such registered shareholders or other interest holders.

(7) Intermediary verification statement. An intermediary verification statement that may be substituted for certain documentation under paragraph (b)(3)(ii) of this section is a written statement signed under penalties of perjury by the intermediary (if the intermediary is an individual) or by a person that would be authorized to sign a tax return on behalf of the intermediary (if the verifying intermediary is not an individual) containing the following information—

(i) The name, principal place of business, and country of residence of the verifying intermediary;

(ii) A statement that the verifying intermediary has obtained either—

(A) An ownership statement and, if applicable, a certificate of residency from a qualifying shareholder with respect to the foreign corporation seeking qualified resident status, and an intermediary ownership statement from each intermediary standing in the chain of ownership between the verifying intermediary and the qualifying shareholder; or

(B) An intermediary verification statement substituting for the documentation described in paragraph (b)(7)(ii)(A) and an intermediary ownership statement from such intermediary and each intermediary standing in the chain of ownership between such intermediary and the verifying intermediary;

(iii) The proportionate interest (as computed using the documentation described in paragraph (b)(7)(ii) of this section) in the intermediary owned directly or indirectly by qualifying shareholders;

(iv) An agreement to make available to the Commissioner at such time and place as the Commissioner may request the underlying documentation described in paragraph (b)(7)(ii) of this section; and

(v) A specific and valid waiver of any right to bank secrecy or other secrecy under the laws of the country in which the verifying intermediary is located, with respect to any qualifying shareholder ownership statements, certificates of residency, intermediary ownership statements or intermediary verification statements that the verifying intermediary has obtained pursuant to paragraph (b)(7)(ii) of this section.

A foreign corporation may combine, in a single statement, the information in an intermediary ownership statement and the information in an intermediary verification statement.

(8) Special rules for pension funds. (i) Definitions. (A) Pension fund. For purposes of this section, the term "pension fund" shall mean a trust, fund, foundation, or other entity that is established exclusively for the benefit of employees or former employees of one or more employers, the principal purpose of which is to provide retirement, disability, and death benefits to beneficiaries of such entity and persons designated by such beneficiaries in consideration for prior services rendered.

(B) Beneficiary. For purposes of this section, the term "beneficiary" of a pension fund shall mean any person who has made contributions to the pension fund, or on whose behalf contributions have been made, and who is currently receiving retirement, disability, or death benefits from the pension fund or can reasonably be expected to receive such benefits in the future, whether or not the person's right to receive benefits from the fund has vested.

(ii) Government pension funds. An individual who is a beneficiary of a pension fund that would be a controlled entity of a foreign sovereign within the principles of § 1.892-2T(c)(1) of the regulations (relating to pension funds established for the benefit of employees or former employees of a foreign government) shall be treated as a qualifying shareholder of a foreign corporation in which the pension fund owns a direct or indirect interest without having to meet the documentation requirements under paragraph (b)(3)(i)(A) of this section, if the foreign corporation is resident in the country of the foreign sovereign and the trustees, directors, or other administrators of the pension fund provide, with the pension fund's intermediary ownership statement described in paragraph (b)(6) of this section, a written statement that the fund is a controlled entity described in this paragraph (b)(8)(ii). See paragraph (b)(4)(ii) of this section regarding an ownership statement from a pension fund that is an integral part of a foreign government.

(iii) Non-government pension funds. For purposes of this section, an individual who is a beneficiary of a pension fund not described in paragraph (b)(8)(ii) of this section shall be treated as a qualifying shareholder of a foreign corporation owned directly or indirectly by such pension fund without having to meet the documentation requirements under paragraph (b)(3)(i)(A) of this section, if—

(A) The pension fund is administered in the foreign corporation's country of residence and is subject to supervision or regulation by a governmental authority (or other authority delegated to perform such supervision or regulation by a governmental authority) in such country;

(B) The pension fund is generally exempt from income taxation in its country of administration;

(C) The pension fund has 100 or more beneficiaries;

(D) The beneficiary's address, as it appears on the records of the fund, is in the foreign corporation's country of residence or the United States and is not a nonresidential address, such as a post office box or in care of a financial intermediary, and none of the trustees, directors or other administrators of the pension fund know, or have reason to know, that the beneficiary is not an individual resident of such foreign country or the United States;

(E) In the case of a pension fund that has fewer than 500 beneficiaries, the beneficiary's employer provides (if the beneficiary is currently contributing to the fund) to the trustees, directors or other administrators a written statement that the beneficiary is currently employed in the country in which the fund is administered or is usually employed in such country but is temporarily employed by the company outside of the country; and

(F) The trustees, directors or other administrators of the pension fund provide, with the pension fund's intermediary ownership statement described in paragraph (b)(6) of this section, a written statement signed under penalties of perjury declaring that the pension fund meets the requirements in paragraphs (b)(8)(iii)(A), (B) and (C) of this section and giving the number of beneficiaries who meet the requirements of paragraph (b)(8)(iii)(D) of this section, and, if applicable, paragraph (b)(8)(iii)(E) of this section.

(iv) Computation of beneficial interests in non-government pension funds. The number of shares in a foreign corporation that are held indirectly by beneficiaries of a pension fund who are qualifying shareholders may be computed based on the ratio of the number of such beneficiaries to all beneficiaries of the pension fund (rather than on the basis of the rules in paragraph (b)(2) of this section) if—

(A) The pension fund meets the requirements of paragraphs (b)(8)(iii)(A), (B) and (C) of this section;

(B) The trustees, directors or other administrators of the pension fund have no knowledge, and no reason to know, that the ratio of the pension fund's beneficiaries who are residents of either the country in which the pension fund is administered or of the United States to all beneficiaries of the pension fund would differ significantly from the ratio of the sum of the actuarial interests of such residents in the pension fund to the actuarial interests of all beneficiaries in the pension fund (or, if the beneficiaries' actuarial interest in the stock held directly or indirectly by the pension fund differs from the beneficiaries's actuarial interest in the pension fund, the ratio of actuarial interests computed by reference to the beneficiaries' actuarial interest in the stock);

(C) Either—

(1) Any overfunding of the pension fund would be payable, pursuant to the governing instrument or the laws of the foreign country in which the pension fund is administered, only to, or for the benefit of, one or more corporations that are qualified residents of the country in which the pension fund is administered, individual beneficiaries of the pension fund or their designated beneficiaries, or social or charitable causes (the reduction of the obligation of the sponsoring company or companies to make future contributions to the pension fund by reason of overfunding shall not itself result in such overfunding being deemed to be payable to or for the benefit of such company or companies); or

(2) The foreign country in which the pension fund is administered has laws that are designed to prevent overfunding of a pension fund and the funding of the pension fund is within the guidelines of such laws; or

(3) The pension fund is maintained to provide benefits to employees in a particular industry, profession, or group of industries or professions and employees of at least 10 companies (other than companies that are owned or controlled, directly or indirectly, by the same interests) contribute to the pension fund or receive benefits from the pension fund; and

(D) The trustees, directors or other administrators provide, with the pension fund's intermediary ownership statement described in paragraph (b)(6) of this section, a written statement signed under penalties of perjury certifying that the requirements in paragraphs (b)(8)(iv)(A), (B), and either (C)(1), (C)(2) or (C)(3) of this section have been met.

The statement described in paragraph (b)(8)(iv)(D) of this section may be combined, in a single statement, with the information required in paragraph (b)(8)(iii)(F) of this section.

(v) Time for making determinations. The determinations required to be made under this paragraph (b)(8) shall be made using information shown on the records of the pension fund for a date on or after the beginning of the foreign corporation's taxable year to which the determination is relevant.

(9) Availability of documents for inspection. (i) Retention of documents by the foreign corporation. The documentation described in paragraphs (b)(3) and (b)(8) of this section must be retained by the foreign corporation until expiration of the period of limitations for the taxable year to which the documentation relates and must be made available for inspection by the District Director at such time and place as the District Director may request.

(ii) Retention of documents by an intermediary issuing an intermediary verification statement. The documentation upon which an intermediary relies to issue an intermediary verification statement under paragraph (b)(7) of this section must be retained by the intermediary for a period of six years from the date of issuance of the intermediary verification statement and must be made available for inspection by the District Director at such time and place as the District Director may request.

(10) Examples. The application of this paragraph (b) is illustrated by the following examples.

Example (1). Foreign corporation A is a resident of country L, which has an income tax treaty in effect with the United States. Foreign corporation A has one class of stock issued and outstanding consisting of 1,000 shares, which are beneficially owned by the following alien individuals, directly or by application of paragraph (b)(2) of this section:

Individual	Shares owned, directly or indirectly by application of paragraph (b)(2) of this section	Percentage
T - resident of the U.S.	200	20%
U - resident of country L................	400	40%
V - resident of country M	100	10%
W - resident of country L	210	21%
X - resident of country N	90	9%
Total....................................	1,000	100%

(i) T owns his 200 shares directly and is a beneficial owner.

(ii) U and V own, respectively, an 80 percent and a 20 percent actuarial interest in foreign trust FT, (which interest does not differ from their respective interests in the stock owned by FT), which beneficially owns 100 percent of the stock of a foreign corporation B with bearer shares, which beneficially owns 500 shares of foreign corporation A. Foreign corporation B is incorporated in a country that does not have an income tax treaty with the United States. The foreign trust has deposited the bearer shares it owns in B with a bank in a foreign country that has an income tax treaty with the United States.

(iii) W beneficially owns all the shares of foreign corporation C, which are registered in the name of individual Z, a nominee, who resides in country L; foreign corporation C beneficially owns a 70 percent interest in foreign corporation D, which beneficially owns 300 shares of A. D's shares are bearer shares that C (not a resident of a country with which the United States has an income tax treaty) has deposited with a bank in a foreign country that has an income tax treaty with the United States.

(iv) X beneficially owns a 30 percent interest in foreign corporation D.

(v) A is a qualified resident of country L if it obtains the applicable documentation described in paragraph (b)(3) of this section either with respect to ownership by individuals U and W or with respect to ownership by individuals T and U, since either combination of qualifying shareholders of foreign corporation A will exceed 50 percent.

Example (2). Assume the same facts as in Example 1 and assume that foreign corporation A chooses to obtain documentation with respect to individuals T and U.

(i) A must obtain, pursuant to paragraph (b)(3)(i) of this section, an ownership statement (as described in paragraph (b)(4)(i) of this section) signed by T. T is not required to furnish a certificate of residency because T is a U.S. resident.

(ii) U must provide foreign trust FT with an ownership statement and certificate of residency, as described in paragraphs (b)(4) and (b)(5) of this section. The trustees of FT must provide the depository bank holding foreign corporation B's bearer shares with an intermediary ownership statement concerning its beneficial ownership of B's shares and must attach to it the documentation provided by U. The depository bank must provide B with an intermediary ownership statement regarding its holding of B shares on behalf of FT and has the choice of attaching—

(A) The documentation from U and the intermediary ownership statement from FT; or

(B) An intermediary verification statement described in paragraph (b)(7) of this section, in which case foreign corporation B would not be provided with U's individual documentation or FT's intermediary ownership statement, both of which are retained by the depository bank.

(iii) In either case, B must then provide foreign corporation A with an intermediary ownership statement regarding its direct beneficial ownership of shares in A and, as the case may be, either—

(A) U's documentation and the intermediary ownership statements by FT and the depository bank; or

(B) The depository bank's intermediary ownership and verification statements.

(iv) Thus, with respect to U, A must obtain under paragraph (b)(3)(i) of this section the individual documentation regarding U and an intermediary ownership statement from each intermediary standing in the chain of U's indirect beneficial ownership of shares in A, i.e., from FT, the depository bank and B. In the alternative, A must obtain under paragraph (b)(3)(ii) of this section an intermediary verification statement issued by the depository bank and an intermediary ownership statement from the bank and from B, which, in this example, are the only intermediaries standing in the chain of ownership of the verifying intermediary (i.e., the depository bank).

Example (3). Assume the same facts as in Example 1. In addition, assume that foreign corporation A chooses to obtain documentation with respect to individuals U and W. With respect to U, A must obtain the same documentation that is described in Example 2. With respect to W, A must obtain, under paragraph (b)(3)(i) of this section, individual documentation regarding W and an intermediary ownership statement from each intermediary standing in the chain of W's indirect beneficial ownership of shares in A, i.e., from individual Z, foreign corporation C, the depository bank in the foreign treaty country, and foreign corporation D. In the alternative, A must obtain, under paragraph (b)(3)(ii) of this section, either—

(i) An intermediary verification statement by the depository bank in the foreign treaty country and an intermediary ownership statement from the bank and from D; or

(ii) An intermediary verification statement from Z and an intermediary ownership statement from Z and from each intermediary standing in the chain of ownership of shares in foreign corporation A, i.e., from C, the depository bank in the foreign treaty country and D. C may not issue an intermediary verification statement because it is not a resident of a country with which the United States has an income tax treaty.

(c) Base erosion. A foreign corporation satisfies the requirement relating to base erosion for a taxable year if it establishes that less than 50 percent of its income for the taxable year is used (directly or indirectly) to make deductible payments in the current taxable year to persons who are not residents (or, in the case of foreign corporations, qualified residents) of the foreign country of which the foreign corporation is a resident and who are not citizens or residents (or, in the case of domestic corporations, qualified residents) of the United States. Whether a domestic corporation is a qualified resident of the United States shall be determined under the principles of this section. For purposes of this paragraph (c), the term "deductible payments" includes payments that would be ordinarily deductible under U.S. income tax principles without regard to other provisions of the Code that may require the capitalization of the expense, or disallow or defer the deduction. Such payments include, for example, interest, rents, royalties and reinsurance premiums. For purposes of this paragraph (c), the income of a foreign corporation means the corporation's gross income for the taxable year (or, if the foreign corporation has no gross income for the taxable year, the average of its gross income for the three previous taxable years) under U.S. tax principles, but not excluding items of income otherwise excluded from gross income under U.S. tax principles.

(d) Publicly-traded corporations. *(1) General rule.* A foreign corporation that is a resident of a foreign country shall be treated as a qualified resident of that country for any taxable year in which—

(i) Its stock is primarily and regularly traded (as defined in paragraphs (d)(3) and (4) of this section) on one or more established securities markets (as defined in paragraph (d)(2) of this section) in that country, or in the United States, or both; or

(ii) At least 90 percent of the total combined voting power of all classes of stock of such foreign corporation entitled to vote and at least 90 percent of the total value of the stock of such foreign corporation is owned, directly or by application of paragraph (b)(2) of this section, by a foreign corporation that is a resident of the same foreign country or a domestic corporation and the stock of such parent corporation is primarily and regularly traded on an established securities market in that foreign country or in the United States, or both.

(2) Established securities market. (i) General rule. For purposes of section 884, the term "established securities market" means, for any taxable year—

(A) A foreign securities exchange that is officially recognized, sanctioned, or supervised by a governmental authority of the country in which the market is located, is the principal exchange in that country, and has an annual value of shares traded on the exchange exceeding $1 billion during each of the three calendar years immediately preceding the beginning of the taxable year;

(B) A national securities exchange that is registered under section 6 of the Securities Act of 1934 (15 U.S.C. 78f); and

(C) A domestic over-the-counter market (as defined in paragraph (d)(2)(iv) of this section).

(ii) Exchanges with multiple tiers. If a principal exchange in a foreign country has more than one tier or market level on which stock may be separately listed or traded, each such tier shall be treated as a separate exchange.

(iii) Computation of dollar value of stock traded. For purposes of paragraph (d)(2)(i)(A) of this section, the value in U.S. dollars of shares traded during a calendar year shall be determined on the basis of the dollar value of such shares traded as reported by the International Federation of Stock Exchanges, located in Paris, or, if not so reported, then by converting into U.S. dollars the aggregate value in local currency of the shares traded using an exchange rate equal to the average of the spot rates on the last day of each month of the calendar year.

(iv) Definition of over-the-counter market. An over-the-counter market is any market reflected by the existence of an interdealer quotation system. An interdealer quotation system is any system of general circulation to brokers and dealers that regularly disseminates quotations of stocks and securities by identified brokers or dealers, other than by quotation sheets that are prepared and distributed by a broker or dealer in the regular course of business and that contain only quotations of such broker or dealer.

(v) Discretion to determine that an exchange qualifies as an established securities market. The Commissioner may, in his sole discretion, determine in a published document that a securities exchange that does not meet the requirements of paragraph (d)(2)(i)(A) of this section qualifies as an established securities market. Such a determination will be made only if it is established that—

(A) The exchange, in substance, has the attributes of an established securities market (including adequate trading volume, and comparable listing and financial disclosure requirements);

(B) The rules of the exchange ensure active trading of listed stocks; and

(C) The exchange is a member of the International Federation of Stock Exchanges.

(vi) Discretion to determine that an exchange does not qualify as an established securities market. The Commissioner may, in his sole discretion, determine in a published document that a securities exchange that meets the requirements of paragraph (d)(2)(i) of this section does not qualify as an established securities market. Such determination shall be made if, in the view of the Commissioner—

(A) The exchange does not have adequate listing, financial disclosure, or trading requirements (or does not adequately enforce such requirements); or

(B) There is no clear and convincing evidence that the exchange ensures the active trading of listed stocks.

(3) Primarily traded. For purposes of this section, stock of a corporation is "primarily traded" on one or more established securities markets in the corporation's country of residence or in the United States in any taxable year if, with respect to each class described in paragraph (d)(4)(i)(A) of this section (relating to classes of stock relied on to meet the regularly traded test)—

(i) The number of shares in each such class that are traded during the taxable year on all established securities markets in the corporation's country of residence or in the United States during the taxable year exceeds

(ii) The number of shares in each such class that are traded during that year on established securities markets in any other single foreign country.

(4) Regularly traded. (i) General rule. For purposes of this section, stock of a corporation is "regularly traded" on one or more established securities markets in the foreign corporation's country of residence or in the United States for the taxable year if—

(A) One or more classes of stock of the corporation that, in the aggregate, represent 80 percent or more of the total combined voting power of all classes of stock of such corporation entitled to vote and of the total value of the stock of such corporation are listed on such market or markets during the taxable year;

(B) With respect to each class relied on to meet the 80 percent requirement of paragraph (d)(4)(i)(A) of this section—

(1) Trades in each such class are effected, other than in de minimis quantities, on such market or markets on at least 60 days during the taxable year (or ⅙ of the number of days in a short taxable year); and

(2) The aggregate number of shares in each such class that is traded on such market or markets during the taxable year is at least 10 percent of the average number of shares outstanding in that class during the taxable year (or, in the case of a short taxable year, a percentage that equals at least 10 percent of the number of days in the short taxable year divided by 365).

If stock of a foreign corporation fails the 80 percent requirement of paragraph (d)(4)(i)(A) of this section, but a class of such stock meets the trading requirements of paragraph (d)(4)(i)(B) of this section, such class of stock may be taken into account under paragraph (b)(1)(iii) of this section as owned by qualifying shareholders for purposes of meeting the ownership test of paragraph (b)(1) of this section.

(ii) Classes of stock traded on a domestic established securities market treated as meeting trading requirements. A class of stock that is traded during the taxable year on an established securities market located in the United States shall be treated as meeting the trading requirements of paragraph (d)(4)(i)(B) of this section if the stock is regularly quoted by brokers or dealers making a market in the stock. A broker or dealer makes a market in a stock only if the broker or dealer holds himself out to buy or sell the stock at the quoted price.

(iii) Closely-held classes of stock not treated as meeting trading requirement (A) General rule. A class of stock shall not be treated as meeting the trading requirements of paragraph (d)(4)(i)(B) of this section (or the requirements of paragraph (d)(4)(ii) of this section) for a taxable year if, at any time during the taxable year, one or more persons who are not qualifying shareholders (as defined in paragraph (b)(1) of this section) and who each beneficially own 5 percent or more of the value of the outstanding shares of the class of stock own, in the aggregate, 50 percent or more of the outstanding shares of the class of stock for more than 30 days during the taxable year. For purposes of the preceding sentence, shares shall not be treated as owned by a qualifying shareholder unless such shareholder provides to the foreign corporation, by the time prescribed in paragraph (b)(3) of this section, the documentation described in paragraph (b)(3) of this section necessary to establish that it is a qualifying shareholder. For purposes of this paragraph (d)(4)(iii)(A), shares of stock owned by a pension fund, as defined in paragraph (b)(8)(i)(A) of this section, shall be treated as beneficially owned by the beneficiaries of such fund, as defined in paragraph (b)(8)(i)(B) of this section.

(B) Treatment of related persons. Persons related within the meaning of section 267(b) shall be treated as one person for purposes of this paragraph (d)(4)(iii). In determining whether two or more corporations are members of the same controlled group under section 267(b)(3), a person is considered to own stock owned directly by such person, stock owned with the application of section 1563(e)(1), and stock owned with the application of section 267(c). Further, in determining whether a corporation is related to a partnership under section 267(b)(10), a person is considered to own the partnership interest owned directly by such person and the partnership interest owned with the application of section 267(e)(3).

(iv) Anti-abuse rule. Trades between persons described in section 267(b) (as modified in paragraph (d)(4)(iii)(B) of this section) and trades conducted in order to meet the requirements of paragraph (d)(4)(i)(B) of this section shall be disregarded. A class of stock shall not be treated as meeting the trading requirements of paragraph (d)(4)(i)(B) of this section if there is a pattern of trades conducted to meet the requirements of that paragraph. For example, trades between two persons that occur several times during the taxable year may be treated as an arrangement or a pattern of trades conducted to meet the trading requirements of paragraph (d)(4)(i)(B) of this section.

(5) Burden of proof for publicly-traded corporations. A foreign corporation that relies on this paragraph (d) to establish that it is a qualified resident of a country with which the United States has an income tax treaty shall have the burden of proving all the facts necessary for the corporation to be treated as a qualified resident, except that with respect to paragraphs (d)(4)(iii) and (iv) of this section, a foreign corporation, with either registered or bearer shares, will meet the burden of proof if it has no reason to know and no actual knowledge of facts that would cause the corporation's stock not to be treated as regularly traded under such paragraphs. A foreign corporation that has shareholders of record must also maintain a list of such shareholders and, on request, make available to the District Director such list and any other relevant information known to the foreign corporation.

(e) Active trade or business. *(1) General rule.* A foreign corporation that is a resident of a foreign country shall be treated as a qualified resident of that country with respect to any U.S. trade or business if, during the taxable year—

(i) It is engaged in the active conduct of a trade or business (as defined in paragraph (e)(2) of this section) in its country of residence;

(ii) It has a substantial presence (within the meaning of paragraph (e)(3) of this section) in its country of residence; and

(iii) Either—

(A) Such U.S. trade or business is an integral part (as defined in paragraph (e)(4) of this section) of an active trade or business conducted by the foreign corporation in its country of residence; or

(B) In the case of interest received by the foreign corporation for which a treaty exemption or rate reduction is claimed pursuant to § 1.884-4(b)(8)(ii), the interest is derived in connection with, or is incidental to, a trade or business described in paragraph (e)(1)(i) of this section.

A foreign corporation may determine whether it is a qualified resident under this paragraph (e) by applying the rules of this paragraph (e) to the entire affiliated group (as defined in section 1504(a) without regard to section 1504(b)(2) or (3)) of which the foreign corporation is a member rather than to the foreign corporation separately. If a foreign corporation chooses to apply the rules of this paragraph (e) to its entire affiliated group as provided in the preceding sentence, then it must apply such rules consistently to all of its U.S. trades or businesses conducted during the taxable year.

(2) Active conduct of a trade or business. A foreign corporation is engaged in the active conduct of a trade or business only if either—

(i) It is engaged in the active conduct of a trade or business within the meaning of section 367(a)(3) and the regulations thereunder; or

(ii) It qualifies as a banking or financing institution under the laws of the foreign country of which it is a resident, it is licensed to do business with residents of its country of residence, and it is engaged in the active conduct of a banking, financing, or similar business within the meaning of § 1.864-4(c)(5)(i) in its country of residence.

A foreign corporation that is an insurance company within the meaning of § 1.801-3(a) or (b) is engaged in the active conduct of a trade or business only if it is predominantly engaged in the active conduct of an insurance business within the meaning of section 952(c)(1)(B)(v) and the regulations thereunder.

(3) Substantial presence test. (i) General rule. Except as provided in paragraph (e)(3)(ii) of this section, a foreign corporation that is engaged in the active conduct of a trade or business in its country of residence has a substantial presence in that country if, for the taxable year, the average of the following three ratios exceeds 25 percent and each ratio is at least equal to 20 percent—

(A) The ratio of the value of the assets of the foreign corporation used or held for use in the active conduct of a trade or business in its country of residence at the close of the taxable year to the value of all assets of the foreign corporation at the close of the taxable year;

(B) The ratio of gross income from the active conduct of the foreign corporation's trade or business in its country of residence that is derived from sources within such country for the taxable year to the worldwide gross income of the foreign corporation for the taxable year; and

(C) The ratio of the payroll expenses in the foreign corporation's country of residence for the taxable year to the foreign corporation's worldwide payroll expenses for the taxable year.

(ii) Special rules. (A) Asset ratio. For purposes of paragraph (e)(3)(i)(A) of this section, the value of an asset shall be determined using the method used by the taxpayer in keeping its books for purposes of financial reporting in its country of residence. An asset shall be treated as used or held for use in a foreign corporation's trade or business if it meets the requirements of § 1.367(a)-2T(b)(5). Stock held by a foreign corporation shall not be treated as an asset of the foreign corporation for purposes of paragraph (e)(3)(i)(A) of this section if the foreign corporation owns 10 percent or more of the total combined voting power of all classes of stock of such corporation entitled to vote. The rules of § 1.954-2T(b)(3) (other than § 1.954-2T(b)(3)(x)) shall apply to determine the location of assets used or held for use in a trade or business. Loans originated or acquired in the course of the normal customer loan activities of a banking, financing or similar institution, and securities and derivative financial instruments held by dealers, traders and insurance companies for use in a trade or business shall be treated as located in the country in which an office or other fixed place of business is primarily responsible for the acquisition of the asset and the realization of income, gain or loss with respect to the asset.

(B) Gross income ratio. (1) General rule. For purposes of paragraph (e)(3)(i)(B) of this section, the term "gross income" means the gross income of a foreign corporation for purposes of financial reporting in its country of residence. Gross income shall not include, however, dividends, interest, rents, or royalties unless such corporation derives such dividends, interest, rents, or royalties in the active conduct of its trade or business. Gross income shall also not include gain from the disposition of stock if the foreign corporation owns 10 percent or more of the total combined voting power of all classes of stock of such corporation entitled to vote. Except as provided in this paragraph (e)(3)(ii)(B), the principles of sections 861 through 865 shall apply to determine the amount of gross income of a foreign corporation derived within its country of residence.

(2) Banks, dealers and traders. Dividend income and gain from the sale of securities, or from entering into or disposing of derivative financial instruments by dealers and traders in such securities or derivative financial instruments shall be treated as derived within the country where the assets are located under paragraph (e)(3)(ii)(A) of this section. Other income, including interest and fees, earned in the active conduct of a banking, financing or similar business shall be treated as derived within the country where the payor of such interest or other income resides. For purposes of the preceding sentence, if a branch or similar establishment outside the country in which the payor resides makes a payment of interest or other income, such amounts shall be treated as derived within the country in which the branch or similar establishment is located.

(3) Insurance companies. The gross income of a foreign insurance company shall include only gross premiums received by the company.

(4) Other corporations. Gross income from the performance of services, including transportation services, shall be treated as derived within the country of residence of the person for whom the services are performed. Gross income from the sale of property by a foreign corporation shall be treated as derived within the country in which the purchaser resides.

(5) Anti-abuse rule. The Commissioner may disregard the source of income from a transaction determined under this paragraph (e)(3)(ii)(B) if it is determined that one of the principal purposes of the transaction was to increase the source of income derived within the country of residence of the foreign corporation for purposes of this section.

(C) Payroll ratio. For purposes of paragraph (e)(3)(i)(C) of this section, the payroll expenses of a foreign corporation shall include expenses for "leased employees" (within the meaning of section 414(n)(2) but without regard to subdivision (B) of that section) and commission expenses paid to employees and agents for services performed for or on behalf of the corporation. Payroll expense for an employee, agent or a "leased employee" shall be treated as incurred where the employee, agent or "leased employee" performs services on behalf of the corporation.

(iii) Exception to gross income test for foreign corporations engaged in certain trades or businesses. In determining whether a foreign corporation engaged primarily in selling tangible property or in manufacturing, producing, growing, or extracting tangible property has a substantial presence in its country of residence for purposes of paragraph (e)(3)(i) of this section, the foreign corporation may apply the ratio provided in this paragraph (e)(3)(iii) instead of the ratio described in paragraph (e)(3)(i)(B) of this section (relating to the ratio of gross income derived from its country of residence). This ratio shall be the ratio of the direct material costs of the foreign corporation with respect to tangible property manufactured, produced, grown, or extracted in the foreign corporation's country of residence to the total direct material costs of the foreign corporation.

(4) Integral part of an active trade or business in a foreign corporation's country of residence. (i) In general. A U.S. trade or business of a foreign corporation is an integral part of an active trade or business conducted by a foreign corporation in its country of residence if the active trade or business conducted by the foreign corporation in both its country of residence and in the United States comprise, in principal part, complementary and mutually interdependent steps in the United States and its country of residence in the production and sale or lease of goods or in the provision of services. Subject to the presumption and de minimis rule in paragraphs (e)(4)(iii) and (iv) of this section, if a U.S. trade or business of a foreign corporation sells goods that are not, in principal part, manufactured, produced, grown, or extracted by the foreign corporation in its country of residence, such business shall not be treated as an integral part of an active trade or business conducted in the foreign corporation's country of residence unless the foreign corporation takes physical possession of the goods in a warehouse or other storage facility that is located in its country of residence and in which goods of such type are normally stored prior to sale to customers in such country.

(ii) Presumption for banks. A U.S. trade or business of a foreign corporation that is described in § 1.884-4(a)(2)(iii) shall be presumed to be an integral part of an active banking business conducted by the foreign corporation in its country of residence provided that a substantial part of the business of the foreign corporation in both its country of residence and the United States consists of receiving deposits and making loans and discounts. This paragraph shall be effective for taxable years beginning on or after June 6, 1996.

(iii) Presumption if business principally conducted in country of residence. A U.S. trade or business of a foreign corporation shall be treated as an integral part of an active trade or business of a foreign corporation in its country of residence with respect to the sale or lease of property (or the performance of services) if at least 50 percent of the foreign corporation's worldwide gross income from the sale or lease of property of the type sold in the United States (or from the performance of services of the type performed in the United States) is derived from the sale or lease of such property for consumption, use, or disposition in the foreign corporation's country of residence (or from the performance of such services in the foreign corporation's country of residence). In determining whether property or services are of the same type, a foreign corporation shall follow recognized industry or trade usage or the three-digit major groups (or any narrower classification) of the Standard Industrial Classification as prepared by the Statistical Policy Division of the Office of Management and Budget, Executive Office of the President. The determination of whether income is of the same kind must be made in a consistent manner from year to year.

(iv) De minimis rule. If a foreign corporation is engaged in more than one U.S. trade or business and if at least 80 percent of the sum of the ECEP from the current year and the preceding two years is attributable to one or more trades or businesses that meet the integral part test of this paragraph (e)(4), all of the U.S. trades or businesses of the foreign corporation shall be treated as an integral part of an active trade or business conducted by the foreign corporation. If a foreign corporation has more than one U.S. trade or business and does not meet the requirements of the preceding sentence but otherwise meets the requirements of this paragraph (e)(4) with regard to one or more trade or business, see § 1.884-1(g)(1) to determine the extent to which treaty benefits apply to such corporation.

(f) Qualified resident ruling. *(1) Basis for ruling.* In his or her sole discretion, the Commissioner may rule that a foreign corporation is a qualified resident of its country of residence if the Commissioner determines that individuals who are not residents of the foreign country of which the foreign corporation is a resident do not use the treaty between that country and the United States in a manner inconsistent with the purposes of section 884. The purposes of section 884 include, but are not limited to, the prevention of treaty shopping by an individual with respect to any article of an income tax treaty between the country of residence of the foreign corporation and the United States.

(2) Factors. In order to make this determination, the Commissioner may take into account the following factors, including, but not limited to:

(i) The business reasons for establishing and maintaining the foreign corporation in its country of residence;

(ii) The date of incorporation of the foreign corporation in relation to the date that an income tax treaty between the United States and the foreign corporation's country of residence entered into force;

(iii) The continuity of the historical business and ownership of the foreign corporation;

(iv) The extent to which the foreign corporation meets the requirements of one or more of the tests described in paragraphs (b) through (e) of this section;

(v) The extent to which the U.S. trade or business is dependent on capital, assets, or personnel of the foreign trade or business;

(vi) The extent to which the foreign corporation receives special tax benefits in its country of residence;

(vii) Whether the foreign corporation is a member of an affiliated group (as defined in section 1504(a) without regard to section 1504(b)(2) or (3)), that has no members resident outside the country of residence of the foreign corporation; and

(viii) The extent to which the foreign corporation would be entitled to comparable treaty benefits with respect to all articles of an income tax treaty that would apply to that corporation if it had been incorporated in the country or countries of residence of the majority of its shareholders. For purposes of the preceding sentence, shareholders taken into account shall generally be limited to persons described in paragraph (b)(1)(i) of this section but for the fact that they are not residents of the foreign corporation's country of residence.

(3) Procedural requirements. A request for a ruling under this paragraph (f) must be submitted on or before the due date (including extensions) of the foreign corporation's income tax return for the taxable year for which the ruling is requested. A foreign corporation receiving a ruling will be treated as a qualified resident of its country of residence for the taxable year for which the ruling is requested and for the succeeding two taxable years. If there is a material change in any fact that formed the basis of the ruling, such as the ownership or the nature of the trade or business of the foreign corporation, the foreign corporation must notify the Secretary within 90 days of such change and submit a new private letter ruling request. The Commissioner will then rule whether the change affects the foreign corporation's status as a qualified resident, and such ruling will be valid for the taxable year in which the material change occurred and the two succeeding taxable years, subject to the requirement in the preceding sentence to notify the Commissioner of a material change.

(g) Effective dates. Except as provided in paragraph (e)(4)(ii) of this section, this section is effective for taxable years beginning on or after October 13, 1992. With respect to a taxable year beginning before October 13, 1992 and af ter December 31, 1986, a foreign corporation may elect to apply this section in lieu of the temporary regulations under 1.884-5T (as contained in the CFR edition revised as of April 1, 1992), but only if the statute of limitations for as sessment of a deficiency has not expired for that taxable year. Once an election has been made, an election shall ap ply to all subsequent taxable years.

(h) Transition rule. If a foreign corporation elects to apply this section in lieu of § 1.884-5T (as contained in the CFR edition revised as of April 1, 1992) as provided in paragraph (g) of this section, and the application of paragraph (b) of this section results in additional documentation requirements in order for the foreign corporation to be treated as a qualified resident, the foreign corporation must obtain the documentation required under that paragraph on or before March 11, 1993.

T.D. 8432, 9/10/92, amend T.D. 8657, 3/5/96.

---

§ 1.892-1T Purpose and scope of regulations (temporary).

(a) In general. These regulations provide guidance with respect to the taxation of income derived by foreign governments and international organizations from sources within the United States. Under section 892, certain specific types of income received by foreign governments are excluded from gross income and are exempt, unless derived from the conduct of a commercial activity or received from or by a controlled commercial entity. This section sets forth the effective date of the regulations. Section 1.892-2T defines a foreign government. In particular it describes the extent to which either an integral part of a foreign sovereign or an entity which is not an integral part of a foreign sovereign will be treated as a foreign government for purposes of section 892. Section 1.892-3T describes the types of income that generally qualify for exemption and certain limitations on the exemption. Section 1.892-4T provides rules concerning the characterization of activities as commercial activities. Section 1.892-5T defines a controlled commercial entity. Section 1.892-6T sets forth the extent to which income of international organizations from sources within the United States is excluded from gross income and is exempt from taxation. Section 1.892-7T sets forth the relationship of section 892 to other Internal Revenue Code sections.

(b) Effective date. The regulations set forth in §§ 1.892-1T through 1.892-7T apply to income received by a foreign government on or after July 1, 1986. No amount of income shall be required to be deducted and withheld, by reason of the amendment of section 892 by section 1247 of the Tax Reform Act of 1986 (Pub. L. 99-514, 100 Stat. 2085, 2583) from any payment made before October 22, 1986.

T.D. 8211, 6/24/88.

---

§ 1.892-2T Foreign government defined (temporary).

> ***Caution:*** The Treasury has not yet amended Reg § 1.892-2T to reflect changes made by P.L. 100-647.

(a) Foreign government. *(1) Definition.* The term "foreign government" means only the integral parts or controlled entities of a foreign sovereign.

(2) Integral part. An "integral part" of a foreign sovereign is any person, body of persons, organization, agency, bureau, fund, instrumentality, or other body, however designated, that constitutes a governing authority of a foreign country. The net earnings of the governing authority must be credited to its own account or to other accounts of the foreign sovereign, with no portion inuring to the benefit of any private person. An integral part does not include any individual who is a sovereign, official, or administrator acting in a private or personal capacity. Consideration of all the facts and circumstances will determine whether an individual is acting in a private or personal capacity.

(3) Controlled entity. The term "controlled entity" means an entity that is separated in form from a foreign sovereign or otherwise constitute a separate juridical entity if it satisfies the following requirements:

(i) It is wholly owned and controlled by a foreign sovereign directly or indirectly through one or more controlled entities;

(ii) It is organized under the laws of the foreign sovereign by which owned;

(iii) Its net earnings are credited to its own account or to other accounts of the foreign sovereign, with no portion of its income inuring to the benefit of any private person; and

(iv) Its assets vest in the foreign sovereign upon dissolution.

A controlled entity does not include partnerships or any other entity owned and controlled by more than one foreign sovereign. Thus, a foreign financial organization organized and wholly owned and controlled by several foreign sovereigns to foster economic, financial, and technical cooperation between various foreign nations is not a controlled entity for purposes of this section

(b) Inurement to the benefit of private persons. For purposes of this section, income will be presumed not to inure to the benefit of private persons if such persons (within the meaning of section 7701(a)(1)) are the intended beneficiaries of a governmental program which is carried on by the foreign sovereign and the activities of which constitute governmental functions (within the meaning of § 1.892-4T(c)(4)). Income will be considered to inure to the benefit of private persons if such income benefits:

(1) Private persons through the use of a governmental entity as a conduit for personal investment; or

(2) Private persons who divert such income from its intended use by the exertion of influence or control through means explicitly or implicitly approved of by the foreign sovereign.

(c) Pension trusts. *(1) In general.* A controlled entity includes a separately organized pension trust if it meets the following requirements:

(i) The trust is established exclusively for the benefit of (A) employees or former employees of a foreign government or (B) employees or former employees of a foreign government and non-governmental employees or former employees that perform or performed governmental or social services;

(ii) The funds that comprise the trust are managed by trustees who are employees of, or persons appointed by, the foreign government;

(iii) The trust forming a part of the pension plan provides for retirement, disability, or death benefits in consideration for prior services rendered; and

(iv) Income of the trust satisfies the obligations of the foreign government to participants under the plan, rather than inuring to the benefit of a private person.

Income of a pension trust is subject to the rules of § 1.892-5T(b)(3) regarding the application of the rules for controlled commercial entities to pension trusts. Income of a superannuation or similar pension fund of an integral part or controlled entity (which is not a separate pension trust as defined in this paragraph (c)(1)) is subject to the rules that generally apply to a foreign sovereign. Such a pension fund may also benefit non-governmental employees or former employees that perform or performed governmental or social services.

(2) Illustrations. The following examples illustrate the application of paragraph (c)(1).

Example (1). The Ministry of Welfare (MW), an integral part of foreign sovereign FC, instituted a retirement plan for FC's employees and former employees. Retirement benefits under the plan are based on a percentage of the final year's salary paid to an individual, times the number of years of government service. Pursuant to the plan, contributions are made by MW to a pension trust managed by persons appointed by MW to the extent actuarially necessary to fund accrued pension liabilities. The pension trust in turn invests such contributions partially in United States Treasury obligations. The income of the trust is credited to the trust's account and subsequently used to satisfy the pension plan's obligations to retired employees. Under these circumstances, the income of the trust is not deemed to inure to the benefit of private persons. Accordingly, the trust is considered a controlled entity of FC.

Example (2). The facts are the same as in Example (1), except that the retirement plan also benefits employees performing governmental or social services for the following non-government institutions: (i) A university in a local jurisdiction; (ii) a harbor commission; and (iii) a library system. The retirement benefits under the plan are based on the total amounts credited to an individual's account over the term of his or her employment. MW makes annual contributions to each covered employee's account equal to a percentage of annual compensation. In addition, the income derived from investment of the annual contributions is credited annually to individual accounts. The annual contributions do not exceed an amount that is determined to be actuarially necessary to provide the employee with reasonable retirement benefits. Notwithstanding that retirement benefits vary depending upon the investment experience of the trust, no portion of the income of the trust is deemed to inure to the benefit of private persons. Accordingly, the trust is considered a controlled entity of FC.

Example (3). The facts are the same as in Example (1), except that employees are allowed to make unlimited contributions to the trust, and such contributions are credited to the employee's account as well as interest accrued on such contributions. Retirement benefits will reflect the amounts credited to the individual accounts in addition to the usual annuity computation based on the final year's salary and years of service. A pension plan established under these rules is in part acting as an investment conduit. As a result, the income of the trust is deemed to inure to the benefit of private persons. Accordingly, the trust is not considered a controlled entity of FC.

Example (4). (a) The facts are the same as in Example (2), except that MW establishes a pension fund rather than a separate pension trust. A pension fund is merely assets of an integral part or controlled entity allocated to a separate account and held and invested for purposes of providing retirement benefits. Under these circumstances, the income of the pension fund is not deemed to inure to the benefit of private persons. Accordingly, income earned from the United States Treasury obligations by the pension fund is considered to be received by a foreign government and is exempt from taxation under section 892.

(b) The facts are the same as in Example (4)(a), except that MW is a controlled entity of foreign sovereign FC. The result is the same as in Example (4)(a). However, should MW engage in commercial activities (whether within or outside the United States), the income from the Treasury obligations earned by the pension fund will not be exempt from taxation under section 892 since MW will be considered a controlled commercial entity within the meaning of § 1.892-5T(a).

(d) Political subdivision and transnational entity. The rules that apply to a foreign sovereign apply to political subdivisions of a foreign country and to transnational entities. A transnational entity is an organization created by more than one foreign sovereign that has broad powers over external and domestic affairs of all participating foreign countries stretching beyond economic subjects to those concerning legal relations and transcending state or political boundaries.

T.D. 8211, 6/24/88.

§ 1.892-3T Income of foreign governments (temporary).

(a) Types of income exempt. *(1) In general.* Subject to the exceptions contained in §§ 1.892-4T and 1.892-5T for income derived from the conduct of a commercial activity or received from or by a controlled commercial entity, the following types of income derived by a foreign government (as defined in § 1.892-2T) are not included in gross income and are exempt:

(i) Income from investments in the United States in stocks, bonds, or other securities;

(ii) Income from investments in the United States in financial instruments held in the execution of governmental financial or monetary policy; and

(iii) Interest on deposits in banks in the United States of moneys belonging to such foreign government.

Income derived from sources other than described in this paragraph (such as income earned from a U.S. real property interest described in section 897(c)(1)(A)(i)) is not exempt from taxation under section 892. Furthermore, any gain derived from the disposition a U.S. real property interest defined in section 897(c)(1)(A)(i) shall in no event qualify for exemption under section 892.

(2) Income from investments. For purposes of paragraph (a) of this section, income from investments in stocks, bonds or other securities includes gain from their disposition and income earned from engaging in section 1058 securities lending transactions. Gain on the disposition of an interest in a partnership or a trust is not exempt from taxation under section 892.

(3) Securities. For purposes of paragraph (a) of this section, the term "other securities" includes any note or other evidence of indebtedness. Thus, an annuity contract, a mortgage, a banker's acceptance or a loan are securities for purposes of this section.

However, the term "other securities" does not include partnership interests (with the exception of publicly traded partnerships within the meaning of section 7704) or trust interests. The term also does not include commodity forward or futures contracts and commodity options unless they constitute securities for purposes of section 864(b)(2)(A).

(4) Financial instrument. For purposes of paragraph (a) of this section, the term "financial instrument" includes any forward, futures, options contract, swap agreement or similar instrument in a functional or nonfunctional currency (see section 985(b) for the definition of funotional currency) or in precious metals when held by a foreign government or central bank of issue (as defined in § 1.895-1(b)). Nonfunctional currency or gold shall be considered a "financial instrument" also when physically held by a central bank of issue.

(5) Execution of financial or monetary policy. (i) Rule. A financial instrument shall be deemed held in the execution of governmental financial or monetary policy if the primary purpose for holding the instrument is to implement or effectuate such policy.

(ii) Illustration. The following example illustrates the application of this paragraph (a)(5).

Example. In order to ensure sufficient currency reserves, the monetary authority of foreign country FC issues short-term government obligations. The amount received from the obligations is invested in U.S. financial instruments. Since the primary purpose for obtaining the U.S. financial instruments is to implement FC's monetary policy, the income received from the financial instruments is exempt from taxation under section 892.

(b) Illustrations. The principles of paragraph (a) of this section may be illustrated by the following examples.

Example (1). X, a foreign corporation not engaged in commercial activity anywhere in the world, is a controlled entity of a foreign sovereign within the meaning of § 1.892-2T(a)(3). X is not a Central bank of issue as defined in § 1.895-1(b). In 1987, X received the following items of income from investments in the United States: (i) Dividends from a portfolio of publicly traded stocks in U.S. corporations in which X owns less than 50 percent of the stock; (ii) dividends from BTB Corporation, an automobile manufacturer, in which X owns 50 percent of the stock; (iii) interest from bonds issued by noncontrolled entities and from interest-bearing bank deposits in noncontrolled entities; (iv) rents from a net lease on real property; (v) gains from silver futures contracts; (vi) gains from wheat futures contracts; (vii) gains from spot sales of nonfunctional foreign currency in X's possession; (viii) gains from the disposition of a publicly traded partnership interest, and (ix) gains from the disposition of the stock of Z Corporation, a United States real property holding company as defined in section 897, of which X owns 12 percent of the stock. Only income derived from sources described in paragraph (a)(1) of this section is treated as income of a foreign government eligible for exemption from taxation. Accordingly, only income received by X from items (i), (iii), (v) provided that the silver futures contracts are held in the execution of governmental financial or monetary policy, and (ix) is exempt from taxation under section 892.

Example (2). The facts are the same as in Example (1), except that X is also a central bank of issue within the meaning of section 895. Since physical possession of nonfunctional foreign currency when held by a central bank of issue is considered a financial instrument, the item (vii) gains from spot sales of nonfunctional foreign currency are exempt from taxation under paragraph (a)(1) of this section, if physical possession of the currency was an essential part of X's reserve policy in the execution of its governmental financial or monetary policy.

Example (3). State Concert Bureau, an integral part of a foreign sovereign within the meaning of § 1.892-2T(a)(2), entered into an agreement with a U.S. corporation engaged in the business of promoting international cultural programs. Under the agreement the State Concert Bureau agreed to send a ballet troupe on tour for 5 weeks in the United States. The Bureau received approximately $60,000 from the performances. Regardless of whether the performances themselves constitute commercial activities under § 1.892-4T, the income received by the Bureau is not exempt from taxation under section 892 since the income is from sources other than described in paragraph (a)(1) of this section.

T.D. 8211, 6/24/88.

§ 1.892-4T Commercial activities (temporary).

(a) Purpose. The exemption generally applicable to a foreign government (as defined in § 1.892-2T) for income described in § 1.892-3T does not apply to income derived from the conduct of a commercial activity or income received by a controlled commercial entity or received (directly or indirectly) from a controlled commercial entity. This section provides rules for determining whether income is derived from the conduct of a commercial activity. These rules also apply in determining under § 1.892-5T whether an entity is a controlled commercial entity.

(b) In general. Except as provided in paragraph (c) of this section, all activities (whether conducted within or outside the United States) which are ordinarily conducted by the taxpayer or by other persons with a view towards the current or future production of income or gain are commercial activities. An activity may be considered a commercial activity even if such activity does not constitute the conduct of a trade or business in the United States under section 864(b).

(c) Activities that are not commercial. *(1) Investments.* (i) In general. Subject to the provisions of paragraphs (ii) and (iii) of this paragraph (c)(1), the following are not commercial activities: Investments in stocks, bonds, and other securities; loans; investments in financial instruments held in the execution of governmental financial or monetary policy; the holding of net leases on real property or land which is not producing income (other than on its sale or from an investment in net leases on real property); and the holding of bank deposits in banks. Transferring securities under a loan agreement which meets the requirements of section 1058 is an investment for purposes of this paragraph (c)(1)(i). An activity will not cease to be an investment solely because of the volume of transactions of that activity or because of other unrelated activities.

(ii) Trading. Effecting transactions in stocks, securities, or commodities for a foreign government's own account does not constitute a commercial activity regardless of whether such activities constitute a trade or business for purposes of section 162 or a U.S. trade or business for purposes of section 864. Such transactions are not commercial activities regardless of whether they are effected by the foreign government through its employees or through a broker, commission agent, custodian, or other independent agent and regardless of whether or not any such employee or agent has discretionary authority to make decisions in effecting the transactions. An activity undertaken as a dealer, however, as defined in § 1.864-2(c)(2)(iv)(a) will not be an investment for purposes of this paragraph (c)(1)(i). For purposes of this paragraph (c)(1)(ii), the term "commodities" means commodities of a kind customarily dealt in on an organized commodity exchange but only if the transaction is of a kind customarily consummated at such place.

(iii) Banking, financing, etc. Investments (including loans) made by a banking, financing, or similar business constitute commercial activities, even if the income derived from such investments is not considered to be income effectively connected to the active conduct of a banking, financing, or similar business in the U.S. by reason of the application of § 1.864-4(c)(5).

(2) Cultural events. Performances and exhibitions within or outside the United States of amateur athletic events and events devoted to the promotion of the arts by cultural organizations are not commercial activities.

(3) Non-profit activities. Activities that are not customarily attributable to or carried on by private enterprise for profit are not commercial activities. The fact that in some instances Federal, State, or local governments of the United States also are engaged in the same or similar activity does not mean necessarily that it is a non-profit activity. For example, even though the United States Government may be engaged in the activity of operating a railroad, operating a railroad is not a non-profit activity.

(4) Governmental functions. Governmental functions are not commercial activities. The term "governmental functions" shall be determined under U.S. standards. In general, activities performed for the general public with respect to the common welfare or which relate to the administration of some phase of government will be considered governmental functions. For example, the operation of libraries, toll bridges, or local transportation services and activities substantially equivalent to the Federal Aviation Authority, Interstate Commerce Commission, or United States Postal Service will all be considered governmental functions for purposes of this section.

(5) Purchasing. The mere purchasing of goods for the use of a foreign government is not a commercial activity.

T.D. 8211, 6/24/88.

§ 1.892-5 Controlled commercial entity.

(a) through (a)(2) [Reserved]. For further information, see § 1.892-5T(a) through (a)(2).

(3) For purposes of section 892(a)(2)(B), the term entity means and includes a corporation, a partnership, a trust (including a pension trust described in § 1.892-2T(c)) and an estate.

(4) Effective date. This section applies on or after January 14, 2002. See § 1.892-5T(a) for the rules that apply before January 14, 2002.

(b) through (d) [Reserved]. For further information, see §§ 1.892-5T(b) through (d).

T.D. 9012, 7/31/2002.

§ 1.892-5T Controlled commercial entity (temporary).

(a) In general. The exemption generally applicable to a foreign government (as defined in § 1.892-2T) for income described in § 1.892-3T does not apply to income received by a controlled commercial entity or received (directly or indirectly) from a controlled commercial entity. The term "controlled commercial entity" means any entity engaged in commercial activities as defined in § 1.892-4T (whether conducted within or outside the United States) if the government—

(1) Holds (directly or indirectly) any interest in such entity which (by value or voting power) is 50 percent or more of the total of such interests in such entity, or

(2) Holds (directly or indirectly) a sufficient interest (by value or voting power) or any other interest in such entity which provides the foreign government with effective practical control of such entity.

(3) [Reserved]. For further information, see § 1.892-5(a)(3).

(b) Entities treated as engaged in commercial activity. *(1) U.S. real property holding corporations.* A United States real property holding corporation, as defined in section 897(c)(2) or a foreign corporation that would be a United States real property holding corporation if it was a United States corporation, shall be treated as engaged in commercial activity and, therefore, is a controlled commercial entity if the requirements of paragraph (a)(1) or (a)(2) of this section are satisfied.

(2) Central banks. Notwithstanding paragraph (a) of this section, a central bank of issue (as defined in § 1.895-1(b)) shall be treated as a controlled commercial entity only if it engages in commercial activities within the United States.

(3) Pension trusts. A pension trust, described in § 1.892-2T(c), which engages in commercial activities within or outside the United States, shall be treated as a controlled commercial entity. Income derived by such a pension trust is not income of a foreign government for purposes of the exemption from taxation provided in section 892. A pension trust described in § 1.892-2T(c) shall not be treated as a controlled commercial entity if such trust solely earns income which would not be unrelated business taxable income (as defined in section 512(a)(1)) if the trust were a qualified trust described in section 401(a). However, only income derived by a pension trust that is described in § 1.892-3T and which is not from commercial activities as defined in § 1.892-4T is exempt from taxation under section 892.

(c) Control. *(1) Attribution.* (i) Rule. In determining for purposes of paragraph (a) of this section the interest held by a foreign government, any interest in an entity (whether or not engaged in commercial activity) owned directly or indirectly by an integral part or controlled entity of a foreign sovereign shall be treated as actually owned by such foreign sovereign.

(ii) Illustration. The following example illustrates the application of paragraph (c)(1)(i) of this section.

Example. FX, a controlled entity of foreign sovereign FC, owns 20 percent of the stock of Corp 1. Neither FX nor Corp 1 is engaged in commercial activity anywhere in the world. Corp 1 owns 60 percent of the stock of Corp 2, which is engaged in commercial activity. The remaining 40 percent of Corp 2's stock is owned by Bureau, an integral part of foreign sovereign FC. For purposes of determining whether Corp 2 is a controlled commercial entity of FC, Bureau will be treated as actually owning the 12 percent of Corp 2's stock indirectly owned by FX. Therefore, since Bureau directly and indirectly owns 52 percent of the stock of Corp 2, Corp 2 is a controlled commercial entity of FC within the meaning of paragraph (a) of this section. Accordingly, dividends or other income received, directly or indirectly, from Corp 2 by either Bureau or FX will not be exempt from taxation under section 892. Furthermore, dividends from Corp 1 to the extent attributable to dividends from Corp 2 will not be exempt from taxation. Thus, a distribution from Corp 1 to FX shall be exempt only to the extent such distribution exceeds Corp 1's earnings and profits attributable to the Corp 2 dividend amount received by Corp 1.

(2) Effective practical control. An entity engaged in commercial activity may be treated as a controlled commercial entity if a foreign government holds sufficient interests in such entity to give it "effective practical control" over the entity. Effective practical control may be achieved through a minority interest which is sufficiently large to achieve effective control, or through creditor, contractual, or regulatory relationships which, together with ownership interests held by the foreign government, achieve effective control. For example, an entity engaged in commercial activity may be treated as a controlled commercial entity if a foreign government, in addition to holding a small minority interest (by value or voting power), is also a substantial creditor of the entity or controls a strategic natural resource which such entity uses in the conduct of its trade or business, giving the foreign government effective practical control over the entity.

(d) Related controlled entities. *(1) Brother/sister entities.* Commercial activities of a controlled entity are not attributed to such entity's other brother/sister related entities. Thus, investment income described in § 1.892-2T that is derived by a controlled entity that is not itself engaged in commercial activity within or outside the United States is exempt from taxation notwithstanding the fact that such entity's brother/sister related entity is a controlled commercial entity.

(2) Parent/subsidiary entities. (i) Subsidiary to parent attribution. Commercial activities of a subsidiary controlled entity are not attributed to its parent. Thus, investment income described in § 1.892-3T that is derived by a parent controlled entity that is not itself engaged in commercial activity within or outside the United States is exempt from taxation notwithstanding the fact that its subsidiary is a controlled commercial entity. Dividends or other payments of income received by the parent controlled entity from the subsidiary are not exempt under section 892, because it constitutes income received from a controlled commercial entity. Furthermore, dividends paid by the parent are not exempt to the extent attributable to the dividends received by the parent from the subsidiary. Thus, a distribution by the parent shall be exempt only to the extent such distribution exceeds earnings and profits attributable to the dividend received from its subsidiary.

(ii) Parent to subsidiary attribution. Commercial activities of a parent controlled entity are attributed to its subsidiary. Thus, investment income described in § 1.892-3T that is derived by a subsidiary controlled entity (not engaged in commercial activity within or outside the United States) is not exempt from taxation under section 892 if its parent is a controlled commercial entity.

(3) Partnerships. Except for partners of publicly traded partnerships, commercial activities of a partnership are attributable to its general and limited partners for purposes of section 892. For example, where a controlled entity is a general partner in a partnership engaged in commercial activities, the controlled entity's distributive share of partnership income (including income described in § 1.892-3T) will not be exempt from taxation under section 892.

(4) Illustrations. The principles of this section may be illustrated by the following examples.

Example (1). (a) The Ministry of Industry and Development is an integral part of a foreign sovereign under § 1.892-2T(a)(2). The Ministry is engaged in commercial activity within the United States. In addition, the Ministry receives income from various publicly traded stocks and bonds, soybean futures contracts and net leases on U.S. real property. Since the Ministry is an integral part, and not a controlled entity, of a foreign sovereign, it is not a controlled commercial entity within the meaning of paragraph (a) of this section. Therefore, income described in § 1.892-3T is ineligible for exemption under section 892 only to the extent derived from the conduct of commercial activities. Accordingly, the Ministry's income from the stocks and bonds is exempt from U.S. tax.

(b) The facts are the same as in Example (1)(a), except that the Ministry also owns 75 percent of the stock of R, a U.S. holding company that owns all the stock of S, a U.S. operating company engaged in commercial activity. Ministry's dividend income from R is income received indirectly from a controlled commercial entity. The Ministry's income from the stocks and bonds, with the exception of dividend income from R, is exempt from U.S. tax.

(c) The facts are the same as in Example (1)(a), except that the Ministry is a controlled entity of a foreign sovereign. Since the Ministry is a controlled entity and is engaged in commercial activity, it is a controlled commercial entity within the meaning of paragraph (a) of this section, and none of its income is eligible for exemption.

Example (2). (a) Z, a controlled entity of a foreign sovereign, has established a pension trust as part of a pension plan for the benefit of its employees and former employees. The pension trust (T), which meets the requirements of § 1.892-2T(c), has investments in the U.S. in various stocks, bonds, annuity contracts, and a shopping center which is leased and managed by an independent real estate management firm. T also makes securities loans in transactions that qualify under section 1058. T's investment in the shopping center is not considered an unrelated trade or business within the meaning of section 513(b). Accordingly, T will not be treated as engaged in commercial activity. Since T is not a controlled commercial entity, its investment income described in § 1.892-3T, with the exception of income received from the operations of the shopping center, is exempt from taxation under section 892.

(b) The facts are the same as Example (2)(a), except that T has an interest in a limited partnership which owns the shopping center. The shopping center is leased and managed by the partnership rather than by an independent management firm. Managing a shopping center, directly or indirectly through a partnership of which a trust is a member, would be considered an unrelated trade or business within the meaning of section 513(b) giving rise to unrelated business taxable income. Since the commercial activities of a partnership are attributable to its partners, T will be treated as engaged in commercial activity and thus will be considered a controlled commercial entity. Accordingly, none of T's income will be exempt from taxation under section 892.

(c) The facts are the same as Example (2)(a), except that Z is a controlled commercial entity. The result is the same as in Example (2)(a).

Example (3). (a) The Department of Interior, an integral part of foreign sovereign FC, wholly owns corporations G and H. G, in turn, wholly owns S. G, H and S are each controlled entities. G, which is not engaged in commercial activity anywhere in the world, receives interest income from deposits in banks in the United States. Both H and S do not have any investments in the U.S. but are both engaged in commercial activities. However, only S is engaged in commercial activities within the United States. Because neither the commercial activities of H nor the commercial activities of S are attributable to the Department of Interior or G, G's interest income is exempt from taxation under section 892.

(b) The facts are the same as Example (3)(a), except that G rather than S is engaged in commercial activities and S rather than G receives the interest income from the United States. Since the commercial activities of G are attributable to S, S's interest income is not exempt from taxation.

Example (4). (a) K, a controlled entity of a foreign sovereign, is a general partner in the Daj partnership. The Daj partnership has investments in the U.S. in various stocks and bonds and also owns and manages an office building in New York. K will be deemed to be engaged in commercial activity by being a general partner in Daj even if K does not actually make management decisions with regard to the partnership's commercial activity, the operation of the office building. Accordingly K's distributive share of partnership income (including income derived from stocks and bonds) will not be exempt from taxation under section 892.

(b) The facts are the same as in Example (4)(a), except that the Daj partnership has hired a real estate management firm to lease offices and manage the building. Notwithstanding the fact that an independent contractor is performing the activities, the partnership shall still be deemed to be engaged in commercial activity. Accordingly, K's distributive share of partnership income (including income derived from stocks and bonds) will not be exempt from taxation under section 892.

(c) The facts are the same as in Example (4)(a), except that K is a partner whose partnership interest is considered a publicly traded partnership interest within the meaning of section 7704. Under paragraph (d)(3) of this section, the partnership's commercial activity will not be attributed to K. Since K will not be deemed to be engaged in commercial activity, K's distributive share of partnership income derived from stocks and bonds will be exempt from taxation under section 892.

T.D. 8211, 6/24/88, amend T.D. 9012, 7/31/2002.

§ 1.892-6T Income of international organizations (temporary).

(a) Exempt from tax. Subject to the provisions of section 1 of the International Organizations Immunities Act (22 U.S.C. 288) (the provisions of which are set forth in paragraph (b)(3) of § 1.893-1), the income of an international organization (as defined in section 7701(a)(18)) received from investments in the United States in stocks, bonds, or other domestic securities, owned by such international organization, or from interest on deposits in banks in the United States of moneys belonging to such international organization, or from any other source within the United States, is exempt from Federal income tax.

(b) Income received prior to Presidential designation. An organization designated by the President through appropriate Executive order as entitled to enjoy the privileges, exemptions, and immunities provided in the International Organizations Immunities Act may enjoy the benefits of the exemption with respect to income of the prescribed character received by such organization prior to the date of the issuance of such Executive order, if (i) the Executive order does not provide otherwise and (ii) the organization is a public international organization in which the United States participates, pursuant to a treaty or under the authority of an act of Congress authorizing such participation or making an appropriation for such participation, at the time such income is received.

T.D. 8211, 6/24/88.

§ 1.892-7T Relationship to other Internal Revenue Code sections (temporary).

(a) Section 893. The term "foreign government" referred to in section 893 (relating to the exemption for compensation of employees of foreign governments) has the same meaning as given such term in § 1.892-2T.

(b) Section 895. A foreign central bank of issue (as defined in § 1.895-1(b)) that fails to qualify for the exemption from tax provided by this section (for example, it is not wholly owned by a foreign sovereign) may nevertheless be exempt from tax on the items of income described in section 895.

(c) Section 883(b). Nothing in section 892 or these regulations shall limit the exemption provided under section 883(b) relating generally to the exemption of earnings derived by foreign participants from the ownership or operation of communications satellite systems.

(d) Section 884. Earnings and profits attributable to income of a controlled entity of a foreign sovereign which is exempt from taxation under section 892 shall not be subject to the tax imposed by section 884(a).

(e) Sections 1441 and 1442. No withholding is required under sections 1441 and 1442 in the case of income exempt from taxation under section 892.

T.D. 8211, 6/24/88.

§ 1.893-1 Compensation of employees of foreign governments or international organizations.

Caution: The Treasury has not yet amended Reg § 1.893-1 to reflect changes made by P.L. 100-647.

(a) Employees of foreign governments. *(1) Exempt from tax.* Except to the extent that the exemption is limited by the execution and filing of the waiver provided for in section 247(b) of the Immigration and Nationality Act (8 U.S.C. 1257(b)), all employees of a foreign government (including consular or other officers, or nondiplomatic representatives) who are not citizens of the United States, or are citizens of the Republic of the Philippines (whether or not citizens of the United States), are exempt from Federal income tax with respect to wages, fees, or salaries received by them as compensation for official services rendered to such foreign government, provided (i) the services are of a character similar to those performed by employees of the Government of the United States in that foreign country and (ii) the foreign government whose employees are claiming exemption grants an equivalent exemption to employees of the Government of the United States performing similar services in that foreign country.

(2) Certificate by Secretary of State. Section 893(b) provides that the Secretary of State shall certify to the Secretary of the Treasury the names of the foreign countries which grant an equivalent exemption to the employees of the Government of the United States performing services in such foreign countries, and the character of the services performed by employees of the Government of the United States in foreign countries.

(3) Items not exempt. The income received by employees of foreign governments from sources other than their salaries, fees, or wages, referred to in subparagraph (1) of this paragraph, is subject to Federal income tax.

(4) Immigration and Nationality Act. Section 247(b) of the Immigration and Nationality Act provides as follows:

Sec. 247. Adjustment of status of certain resident aliens. . . .

(b) The adjustment of status required by subsection (a) [of section 247 of the Immigration and Nationality Act] shall not be applicable in the case of any alien who requests that he be permitted to retain his status as an immigrant and who, in such form as the Attorney General may require, executes and files with the Attorney General a written waiver of all rights, privileges, exemptions, and immunities under any law or any executive order which would otherwise accrue to him because of the acquisition of an occupational status entitling him to a nonimmigrant status under paragraph (15)(A), (15)(E), (15)(G) of section 101(a).

(5) Effect of waiver. An employee of a foreign government who executes and files with the Attorney General the waiver provided for in section 247(b) of the Immigration and Nationality Act thereby waives the exemption conferred by section 893 of the Code. As a consequence, that exemption does not apply to income received by that alien after the date of filing of the waiver.

(6) Citizens of the United States. The compensation of citizens of the United States (other than those who are also citizens of the Republic of the Philippines) who are officers or employees of a foreign government is not exempt from income tax pursuant to this paragraph. But see section 911 and the regulations thereunder.

(b) Employees of international organizations. *(1) Exempt from tax.* Except to the extent that the exemption is limited by the execution and filing of the waiver provided for in section 247(b) of the Immigration and Nationality Act and subject to the provisions of sections 1, 8, and 9 of the International Organizations Immunities Act (22 U.S.C. 288, 288e, 288f), wages, fees, or salary of any officer or employee of an international organization (as defined in section 7701(a)(18)) received as compensation for official services to that international organization is exempt from Federal income tax, if that officer or employee (i) is not a citizen of the United States or (ii) is a citizen of the Republic of the Philippines (whether or not a citizen of the United States).

(2) Income earned prior to executive action. An individual of the prescribed class who receives wages, fees, or salary as compensation for official services to an organization designated by the President through appropriate Executive order as entitled to enjoy the privileges, exemptions, and immunities provided in the International Organizations Immunities Act and who has been duly notified to, and accepted by, the Secretary of State as an officer or employee of that organization, or who has been designated by the Secretary of State prior to formal notification and acceptance, as a prospective officer or employee of that organization, may enjoy the benefits of the exemption with respect to compensation of the prescribed character earned by that individual, either prior to the date of the issuance of the Executive order, or prior to the date of the acceptance or designation by the Secretary of State, for official services to that organization, if (i) the Executive order does not provide otherwise, (ii) the organization is a public international organization in which the United States participates, pursuant to a treaty or under the authority of an act of Congress authorizing such participation or making an appropriation for such participation, at the time the compensation is earned, and (iii) the individual is an officer or employee of that organization at that time.

(3) International Organizations Immunities Act. Sections 1, 8, and 9 of the International Organizations Immunities Act (22 U.S.C. 288, 288e, 288f) provide in part as follows:

Section 1. For the purposes of this title [International Organizations Immunities Act], the term "international organization" means a public international organization in which the United States participates pursuant to any treaty or under the authority of any Act of Congress authorizing such participation or making an appropriation for such participation, and which shall have been designated by the President through appropriate Executive order as being entitled to enjoy the privileges, exemptions, and immunities herein provided. The President shall be authorized, in the light of the functions performed by any such international organization, by appropriate Executive order to withhold or withdraw from any such organization or its officers or employees any of the privileges, exemptions, and immunities provided for in this title (including the amendments made by this title) or to condition or limit the enjoyment by any such organization or its officers or employees of any such privilege, exemption, or immunity. The President shall be authorized, if in his judgment such action should be justified by reason of the abuse by an international organization or its officers and employees of the privileges, exemptions, and immunities herein provided or for any other reason, at any time to revoke the designation of any international organization under this section, whereupon the international organization in question shall cease to be classed as an international organization for the purposes of this title. Sec. 8. (a) No person shall be entitled to the benefits of this title [International Organizations Immunities Act] unless he (1) shall have been duly notified to and accepted by the Secretary of State as a . . . officer, or employee; or (2) shall have been designated by the Secretary of State, prior to formal notification and acceptance, as a prospective . . . officer, or employee; . . . .

(b) Should the Secretary of State determine that the continued presence in the United States of any person entitled to the benefits of this title is not desirable, he shall so inform the . . . international organization concerned . . . , and after such person shall have had a reasonable length of time, to be determined by the Secretary of State, to depart from the United States, he shall cease to be entitled to such benefits.

(c) No person shall, by reason of the provisions of this title, be considered as receiving diplomatic status or as receiving any of the privileges incident thereto other than such as are specifically set forth herein.

Sec. 9. The privileges, exemptions, and immunities of international organizations and of their officers and employees . . . provided for in this title [International Organizations Immunities Act], shall be granted notwithstanding the fact that the similar privileges, exemptions, and immunities granted to a foreign government, its officers, or employees, may be conditioned upon the existence of reciprocity by that foreign government: Provided. That nothing contained in this title shall be construed as precluding the Secretary of State from withdrawing the privileges, exemptions and immunities herein provided from persons who are nationals of any foreign country on the ground that such country is failing to accord corresponding privileges, exemptions, and immunities to citizens of the United States.

(4) Effect of waiver. An officer or employee of an international organization who executes and files with the Attorney General the waiver provided for in section 247(b) of the Immigration and Nationality Act (8 U.S.C. 1257(b)) thereby waives the exemption conferred by section 893 of the Code. As a consequence, that exemption does not apply to income

received by that individual after the date of filing of the waiver.

(5) Citizens of the United States. The compensation of citizens of the United States (other than those who are citizens of the Republic of the Philippines) who are officers or employees of an international organization is not exempt from income tax pursuant to this paragraph. But see section 911 and the regulations thereunder.

(c) Tax conventions, consular conventions, and international agreements. *(1) Exemption dependent upon internal revenue laws.* A tax convention or consular convention between the United States and a foreign country, which provides that the United States may include in the tax base of its residents all income taxable under the internal revenue laws, and which makes no specific exception for the income of the employees of that foreign government, does not provide any exemption (with respect to residents of the United States) beyond that which is provided by the internal revenue laws. Accordingly, the effect of the execution and filing of a waiver under section 247(b) of the Immigration and Nationality Act by an employee of a foreign government which is a party to such a convention is to subject the employee to tax to the same extent as provided in paragraph (a)(5) of this section with respect to the waiver of exemption under section 893.

(2) Exemption not dependent upon internal revenue laws. If a tax convention, consular convention, or international agreement provides that compensation paid by the foreign government or international organization to its employees is exempt from Federal income tax, and the application of this exemption is not dependent upon the provisions of the internal revenue laws, the exemption so conferred is not affected by the execution and filing of a waiver under section 247(b) of the Immigration and Nationality Act. For examples of exemptions which are not affected by the Immigration and Nationality Act, see article X of the income tax convention between the United States and the United Kingdom (60 Stat. 1383); article IX, section 9(b), of the Articles of Agreement of the International Monetary Fund (60 Stat. 1414); and article VII, section 9(b), of the Articles of Agreement of the International Bank for Reconstruction and Development (60 Stat. 1458).

T.D. 6258, 10/23/57.

§ 1.894-1 Income affected by treaty.

Caution: The Treasury has not yet amended Reg § 1.894-1 to reflect changes made by P.L. 100-647.

(a) Income exempt under treaty. Income of any kind is not included in gross income and is exempt from tax under subtitle A (relating to income taxes), to the extent required by any income tax convention to which the United States is a party. However, unless otherwise provided by an income tax convention, the exclusion from gross income under section 894(a) and this paragraph does not apply in determining the accumulated taxable income of a foreign corporation under section 535 and the regulations thereunder or the undistributed personal holding company income of a foreign corporation under section 545 and the regulations thereunder. Moreover, the distributable net income of a foreign trust is determined without regard to section 894 and this paragraph, to the extent provided by section 643(a)(6)(B). Further, the compensating tax adjustment required by section 819(a)(3) in the case of a foreign life insurance company is to be determined without regard to section 894 and this paragraph, to the extent required by section 819(a)(3)(A). See § 1.871-12 for the manner of determining the tax liability of a nonresident alien individual or foreign corporation whose gross income includes income on which the tax is reduced under a tax convention.

(b) Taxpayer treated as having no permanent establishment in the United States. *(1) In general.* A nonresident alien individual or a foreign corporation, that is engaged in trade or business in the United States through a permanent establishment located therein at any time during a taxable year beginning after December 31, 1966, shall be deemed not to have a permanent establishment in the United States at any time during that year for purposes of applying any exemptions from, or reduction in the rate of any tax under subtitle A of the Code which is provided by any income tax convention with respect to income which is not effectively connected for that year with the conduct of a trade or business in the United States by the taxpayer. This paragraph applies to all treaties or conventions entered into by the United States, whether entered into before, on, or after November 13, 1966, the date of enactment of the Foreign Investors Tax Act of 1966 (80 Stat. 1539). This paragraph is not considered to be contrary to any obligation of the United States under an income tax convention to which it is a party. The benefit granted under section 894(b) and this paragraph applies only to those items of income derived from sources within the United States which are subject to the tax imposed by section 871(a) or 881(a), and section 1441, 1442, or 1451, on the noneffectively connected income received from sources within the United States by a nonresident alien individual or a foreign corporation. The benefit does not apply to any income from real property in respect of which an election is in effect for the taxable year under § 1.871-10 or in determining under section 877(b) the tax of a nonresident alien individual who has lost United States citizenship at any time after March 8, 1965. The benefit granted by section 894(b) and this paragraph is not elective.

(2) Illustrations. The application of this paragraph may be illustrated by the following examples:

Example (1). M, a corporation organized in foreign country X, uses the calendar year as the taxable year. The United States and country X are parties to an income tax convention which provides in part that dividends received from sources within the United States by a corporation of country X not having a permanent establishment in the United States are subject to tax under chapter 1 of the Code at a rate not to exceed 15 percent. During 1967, M is engaged in business in the United States through a permanent establishment located therein and receives $100,000 in dividends from domestic corporation B, which under section 861(a)(2)(A) constitutes income from sources within the United States. Under section 864(c)(2) and § 1.864-4(c), the dividends received from B are not effectively connected for 1967 with the conduct of a trade or business in the United States by M. Although M has a permanent establishment in the United States during 1967, it is deemed, under section 894(b) and this paragraph, not to have a permanent establishment in the United States during that year with respect to the dividends. Accordingly, in accordance with paragraph (c)(3) of § 1.871-12 the tax on the dividends is $15,000, that is, 15 percent of $100,000, determined without the allowance of any deductions.

Example (2). T, a corporation organized in foreign country X, uses the calendar year as the taxable year. The United States and country X are parties to an income tax convention which provides in part that an enterprise of country X is not subject to tax under chapter 1 of the Code in respect of its industrial or commercial profits unless it is engaged in trade or business in the United States during the taxable year through a permanent establishment located therein and that, if it is so engaged, the tax may be imposed upon the entire income of that enterprise from sources within the United States. The convention also provides that the tax imposed by chapter 1 of the Code on dividends received from sources within the United States by a corporation of X which is not engaged in trade or business in the United States through a permanent establishment located therein shall not exceed 15 percent of the dividend. During 1967, T is engaged in a business (business A) in the United States which is carried on through a permanent establishment in the United States; in addition, T is engaged in a business (business B) in the United States which is not carried on through a permanent establishment. During 1967, T receives from sources within the United States $60,000 in service fees through the operation of business A and $10,000 in dividends through the operation of business B, both of which amounts are, under section 864(c)(2)(B) and § 1.864-4(c)(3), effectively connected for that year with the conduct of a trade or business in the United States by that corporation. The service fees are considered to be industrial or commercial profits under the tax convention with country X. Since T has no income for 1967 which is not effectively connected for that year with the conduct of a trade or business in the United States by that corporation section 894(b), this paragraph, and § 1.871-12 do not apply. Accordingly, for 1967 T's entire income of $70,000 from sources within the United States is subject to tax, after allowance of deductions, in accordance with section 882(a)(1) and paragraph (b)(2) of § 1.882-1.

Example (3). S, a corporation organized in foreign country W, uses the calendar year as the taxable year. The United States and country W are parties to an income tax convention which provides in part that a corporation of a country W is not subject to tax under Chapter 1 of the Code in respect of its industrial or commercial profits unless it is engaged in trade or business in the United States during the taxable year through a permanent establishment located therein and that, if it is so engaged, the tax may be imposed upon the entire income of that corporation from sources within the United States. The convention also provides that the tax imposed by chapter 1 of the Code on dividends received from sources within the United States by a corporation of country W which is not engaged in trade or business in the United States through a permanent establishment located therein shall not exceed 15 percent of the dividend. During 1967, S is engaged in business in the United States through a permanent establishment located therein and derives from sources within the United States $100,000 in service fees which, under section 864(c)(2)(B) and § 1.864-4(c)(3), are effectively connected for that year with the conduct of a trade or business in the United States by S and which are considered to be industrial or commercial profits under the tax convention with country W. During 1967, S also derives from sources within the United States, through another business it carries on in foreign country X, $10,000 in sales income which, under section 864(c)(3) and § 1.864-4(b), is effectively connected for that year with the conduct of a trade or business in the United States by S and $5,000 in dividends which, under section 864(c)(2)(A) and § 1.864-4(c)(2), are not effectively connected for that year with the conduct of a trade or business in the United States by S. The sales income is considered to be industrial or commercial profits under the tax convention with country W. Although S is engaged in a trade or business in the United States during 1967 through a permanent establishment located therein, it is deemed, under section 894(b) and this paragraph, not to have a permanent establishment therein with respect to the $5,000 in dividends. Accordingly, in accordance with paragraph (c) of § 1.871-12, for 1967 S is subject to a tax of $750 on the dividends ($5,000 × .15) and a tax, determined under section 882(a) and § 1.882-1, on its $110,000 industrial or commercial profits.

Example (4). (a) N, a corporation organized in foreign country Z, uses the calendar year as the taxable year. The United States and country Z are parties to an income tax convention which provides in part that the tax imposed by chapter 1 of the Code on dividends received from sources within the United States by a corporation of country Z shall not exceed 15 percent of the amount distributed if the recipient does not have a permanent establishment in the United States or, where the recipient does have a permanent establishment in the United States, if the shares giving rise to the dividends are not effectively connected with the permanent establishment. The tax convention also provides that if a corporation of country Z is engaged in industrial or commercial activity in the United States through a permanent establishment in the United States, income tax may be imposed by the United States on so much of the industrial or commercial profits of such corporation as are attributable to the permanent establishment in the United States.

(b) During 1967, N is engaged in a business (business A) in the United States which is not carried on through a permanent establishment in the United States. In addition, N has a permanent establishment in the United States through which it carries on another business (business B) in the United States. During 1967, N holds shares of stock in domestic corporation D which are not effectively connected with N's permanent establishment in the United States. During 1967, N receives $100,000 in dividends from D which, pursuant to section 864(c)(2)(A) and § 1.864-4(c)(2), are effectively connected for that year with the conduct of business A. Under section 861(a)(2)(A) these dividends are treated as income from sources within the United States. In addition, during 1967, N receives from sources within the United States $150,000 in sales income which, pursuant to section 864(c)(3) and § 1.864-4(b), is effectively connected with the conduct of a trade or business in the United States and which is considered to be industrial or commercial profits under the tax convention with country Z. Of these total profits, $70,000 is from business A and $80,000 is from business B. Only the $80,000 of industrial or commercial profits is attributable to N's permanent establishment in the United States.

(c) Since N has no income for 1967 which is not effectively connected for that year with the conduct of a trade or business in the United States by that corporation, section 894(b) and this paragraph do not apply. However, N is entitled to the reduced rate of tax under the tax convention with country Z with respect to the dividends because the shares of stock are not effectively connected with N's permanent establishment in the United States. Accordingly, assuming that there are no deductions connected with N's industrial or commercial profits, the tax for 1967, determined as provided in paragraph (c) of § 1.871-12, is $46,900 as follows:

Tax on nontreaty income:	
$80,000 × .48	$38,400
Less $25,000 × .26	6,500
	31,900
Tax on treaty income:	
$100,000 (gross dividends) × .15	15,000
Total tax	46,900

Example (5). M, a corporation organized in foreign country Z, uses the calendar year as the taxable year. The United States and country Z are parties to an income tax convention which provides in part that a corporation of country Z is not subject to tax under chapter 1 of the Code in respect of its commercial and industrial profits except such profits as are allocable to its permanent establishment in the United States. The regulations in this chapter under the tax convention with country Z provides that a corporation of country Z having a permanent establishment in the United States is subject to U.S. tax upon its industrial and commercial profits from sources within the United States and that its industrial and commercial profits from such sources are deemed to be allocable to the permanent establishment in the United States. During 1967, M is engaged in a business (business A) in the United States which is carried on through a permanent establishment in the United States; in addition, M is engaged in a business (business B) in foreign country X and none of such business is carried on in the United States. During 1967, M receives from sources within the United States $40,000 in sales income through the operation of business A and $10,000 in sales income through the operation of business B, both of which amounts are, under section 864(c)(3) and § 1.864-4(b), effectively connected for that year with the conduct of a trade or business in the United States by that corporation. The sales income is considered to be industrial and commercial profits under the tax convention with country Z. Since M has no income for 1967 which is not effectively connected for that year with the conduct of a trade or business in the United States by that corporation, section 894(b) and this paragraph do not apply. Accordingly, for 1967 M's entire income of $50,000 from sources within the United States is subject to tax, after allowance of deductions, in accordance with section 882(a)(1) and paragraph (b)(2) of § 1.882-1.

(c) Substitute interest and dividend payments. The provisions of an income tax convention dealing with interest or dividends paid to or derived by a foreign person include substitute interest or dividend payments that have the same character as interest or dividends under § 1.864-5(b)(2)(ii), 1.871-7(b)(2) or 1.881-2(b)(2). The provisions of this paragraph (c) shall apply for purposes of securities lending transactions or sale-repurchase transactions as defined in § 1.861-2(a)(7) and § 1.861-3(a)(6).

(d) Special rule for items of income received by entities.

(1) In general. The tax imposed by sections 871(a), 881(a), 1443, 1461, and 4948(a) on an item of income received by an entity, wherever organized, that is fiscally transparent under the laws of the United States and/or any other jurisdiction with respect to an item of income shall be eligible for reduction under the terms of an income tax treaty to which the United States is a party only if the item of income is derived by a resident of the applicable treaty jurisdiction. For this purpose, an item of income may be derived by either the entity receiving the item of income or by the interest holders in the entity or, in certain circumstances, both. An item of income paid to an entity shall be considered to be derived by the entity only if the entity is not fiscally transparent under the laws of the entity's jurisdiction, as defined in paragraph (d)(3)(ii) of this section, with respect to the item of income. An item of income paid to an entity shall be considered to be derived by the interest holder in the entity only if the interest holder is not fiscally transparent in its jurisdiction with respect to the item of income and if the entity is considered to be fiscally transparent under the laws of the interest holder's jurisdiction with respect to the item of income, as defined in paragraph (d)(3)(iii) of this section. Notwithstanding the preceding two sentences, an item of income paid directly to a type of entity specifically identified in a treaty as a resident of a treaty jurisdiction shall be treated as derived by a resident of that treaty jurisdiction.

(2) Application to domestic reverse hybrid entities. (i) In general. An income tax treaty may not apply to reduce the amount of federal income tax on U.S. source payments received by a domestic reverse hybrid entity. Further, notwithstanding paragraph (d)(1) of this section, the foreign interest holders of a domestic reverse hybrid entity are not entitled to the benefits of a reduction of U.S. income tax under an income tax treaty on items of income received from U.S. sources by such entity. A domestic reverse hybrid entity is a domestic entity that is treated as not fiscally transparent for U.S. tax purposes and as fiscally transparent under the laws of the interest holder's jurisdiction, with respect to the item of income received by the domestic entity.

(ii) Payments by domestic reverse hybrid entities. (A) General rule. Except as otherwise provided in paragraph (d)(2)(ii)(B) of this section, an item of income paid by a domestic reverse hybrid entity to an interest holder in such entity shall have the character of such item of income under U.S. law and shall be considered to be derived by the interest holder, provided the interest holder is not fiscally transparent in its jurisdiction, as defined in paragraph (d)(3)(iii) of this section, with respect to the item of income. In determining whether the interest holder is fiscally transparent with respect to the item of income under this paragraph (d)(2)(ii)(A), the determination under paragraph (d)(3)(ii) of this section shall be made based on the treatment that would have resulted had the item of income been paid by an entity that is not fiscally transparent under the laws of the interest holder's jurisdiction with respect to any item of income.

(B) Payment made to related foreign interest holder. (1) General rule. If—

(i) A domestic entity makes a payment to a related domestic reverse hybrid entity that is treated as a dividend under either the laws of the United States or the laws of the jurisdiction of a related foreign interest holder in the domestic reverse hybrid entity, and under the laws of the jurisdiction of the related foreign interest holder in the domestic reverse hybrid entity, the related foreign interest holder is treated as deriving its proportionate share of the payment under the principles of paragraph (d)(1) of this section; and

(ii) The domestic reverse hybrid entity makes a payment of a type that is deductible for U.S. tax purposes to the related foreign interest holder or to a person, wherever organized, the income and losses of which are available, under the laws of the jurisdiction of the related foreign interest holder, to offset the income and losses of the related foreign interest holder, and for which a reduction in U.S. withholding tax would be allowed under an applicable income tax treaty; then

(iii) To the extent the amount of the payment described in paragraph (d)(2)(ii)(B)(1)(ii) of this section does not exceed the sum of the portion of the payment described in paragraph (d)(2)(ii)(B)(1)(i) of this section treated as derived by the related foreign interest holder and the portion of any other prior payments described in paragraph (d)(2)(ii)(B)(1)(i) of this section treated as derived by the related foreign interest holder, the amount of the payment described in (d)(2)(ii)(B)(1)(ii) of this section will be treated for all purposes of the Internal Revenue Code and any applicable income tax treaty as a distribution within the meaning of section 301(a) of the Internal Revenue Code, and the tax to be withheld from the payment described in paragraph (d)(2)(ii)(B)(1)(ii) of this section (assuming the payment is a dividend under section 301(c)(1) of the Internal Revenue Code) shall be determined based on the appropriate rate of withholding that would be applicable to dividends paid from the domestic reverse hybrid entity to the related foreign interest holder in accordance with the principles of paragraph (d)(2)(ii)(A) of this section.

(2) Determining amount to be recharacterized under paragraph (d)(2)(ii)(B)(1)(iii). For purposes of determining the amount to be recharacterized under paragraph (d)(2)(ii)(B)(1)(iii) of this section, the portion of the payment described in paragraph (d)(2)(ii)(B)(1)(i) of this section treated as derived by the related foreign interest holder shall be increased by the portion of the payment derived by any other person described in paragraph (d)(2)(ii)(B)(1)(ii), and shall be reduced by the amount of any prior section 301(c) distributions made by the domestic reverse hybrid entity to the related foreign interest holder or any other person described in paragraph (d)(2)(ii)(B)(1)(ii) and by the amount of any payments from the domestic reverse hybrid entity previously recharacterized under paragraph (d)(2)(ii)(B)(1)(iii) of this section.

(3) Tiered entities. The principles of this paragraph (d)(2)(ii)(B) also shall apply to payments referred to in this paragraph (d)(2)(ii)(B) made among related entities when there is more than one domestic reverse hybrid entity or other fiscally transparent entity involved.

(4) Definition of related. For purposes of this section, a person shall be treated as related to a domestic reverse hybrid entity if it is related by reason of the ownership requirements of section 267(b) or 707(b)(1), except that the language "at least 80 percent" applies instead of "more than 50 percent," where applicable. For purposes of determining whether a person is related by reason of the ownership requirements of section 267(b) or 707(b)(1), the constructive ownership rules of section 318 shall apply, and the attribution rules of section 267(c) also shall apply to the extent they attribute ownership to persons to whom section 318 does not attribute ownership.

(C) Payments to persons not described in paragraph (d)(2)(ii)(B)(1)(ii). (1) Related persons. The Commissioner may treat a payment by a domestic reverse hybrid entity to a related person (who is neither the related foreign interest holder nor otherwise described in paragraph (d)(2)(ii)(B)(1)(ii) of this section), in whole or in part, as being made to a related foreign interest holder for purposes of applying paragraph (d)(2)(ii)(B) of this section, if—

(i) The payment to the related person is of a type that is deductible by the domestic reverse hybrid entity; and

(ii) The payment is made in connection with one or more transactions the effect of which is to avoid the application of paragraph (d)(2)(ii)(B) of this section.

(2) Unrelated persons. The Commissioner may treat a payment by a domestic reverse hybrid entity to an unrelated person, in whole or in part, as being made to a related foreign interest holder for purposes of applying paragraph (d)(2)(ii)(B) of this section, if—

(i) The payment to the unrelated person is of a type that is deductible by the domestic reverse hybrid entity;

(ii) The unrelated person (or other person (whether related or not) which receives a payment in a series of transactions that includes a transaction involving such unrelated person) makes a payment to the related foreign interest holder (or other person described in paragraph (d)(2)(ii)(B)(1)(ii));

(iii) The foregoing payments are made in connection with a series of transactions which constitute a financing arrangement, as defined in § 1.881-3(a)(2)(i); and

(iv) The transactions have the effect of avoiding the application of paragraph (d)(2)(ii)(B) of this section.

(iii) Examples. The rules of this paragraph (d)(2) are illustrated by the following examples:

Example (1). Dividend paid by unrelated entity to domestic reverse hybrid entity.

(i) Facts. Entity A is a domestic reverse hybrid entity, as defined in paragraph (d)(2)(i) of this section, with respect to the U.S. source dividends it receives from B, a domestic corporation to which A is not related within the meaning of paragraph (d)(2)(ii)(B)(4) of this section. A's 85-percent shareholder, FC, is a corporation organized under the laws of Country X, which has an income tax treaty in effect with the United States. A's remaining 15-percent shareholder is an unrelated domestic corporation. Under Country X law, FC is not fiscally transparent with respect to the dividend, as defined in paragraph (d)(3)(ii) of this section. In year 1, A receives $100 of dividend income from B. Under Country X law, FC is treated as deriving $85 of the $100 dividend payment received by A. The applicable rate of tax on dividends under the U.S.-Country X income tax treaty is 5 percent with respect to a 10-percent or more corporate shareholder.

(ii) Analysis. Under paragraph (d)(2)(i) of this section, the U.S.-Country X income tax treaty does not apply to the dividend income received by A because the payment is made by B, a domestic corporation, to A, another domestic corporation. A remains fully taxable under the U.S. tax laws as a domestic corporation with regard to that item of income. Further, pursuant to paragraph (d)(2)(i) of this section, notwithstanding the fact that A is treated as fiscally transparent with respect to the dividend income under the laws of Country X, FC may not claim a reduced rate of taxation on its share of the U.S. source dividend income received by A.

Example (2). Interest paid by domestic reverse hybrid entity to related foreign interest holder where dividend is paid by unrelated entity.

(i) Facts. The facts are the same as in Example 1. Both the United States and Country X characterize the payment by B in year 1 as a dividend. In addition, in year 2, A makes a payment of $25 to FC that is characterized under the Internal Revenue Code as interest on a loan from FC to A. Under the U.S.-Country X income tax treaty, the rate of tax on interest is zero. Under Country X laws, had the interest been paid by an entity that is not fiscally transparent under Country X's laws with respect to any item of income, FC would not be fiscally transparent as defined in paragraph (d)(2)(ii) of this section with respect to the interest.

(ii) Analysis. The analysis is the same as in Example 1 with respect to the $100 payment from B to A. With respect to the $25 payment from A to FC, paragraph (d)(2)(ii)(B) of this section will not apply because, although

FC is a related foreign interest holder in A, A is not related to B, the payor of the dividend income it received. Under paragraph (d)(2)(ii)(A) of this section, the $25 of interest paid by A to FC in year 2 is characterized under U.S. law as interest. Accordingly, in year 2, A is entitled to an interest deduction with respect to the $25 interest payment from A to FC, and FC is entitled to the reduced rate of withholding applicable to interest under the U.S.-Country X income tax treaty, assuming all other requirements for claiming treaty benefits are met.

Example (3). Interest paid by domestic reverse hybrid entity to related foreign interest holder where dividend is paid by a related entity.

(i) Facts. The facts are the same as in Example 2, except the $100 dividend income received by A in year 1 is from A's wholly-owned subsidiary, S.

(ii) Analysis. The analysis is the same as in Example 1 with respect to the $100 dividend payment from S to A. However, the $25 interest payment in year 2 by A to FC will be treated as a dividend for all purposes of the Internal Revenue Code and the U.S.-Country X income tax treaty because $25 does not exceed FC's share of the $100 dividend payment made by S to A ($85). Since FC is not fiscally transparent with respect to the payment as determined under paragraph (d)(2)(ii)(A) of this section, FC is entitled to the reduced rate applicable to dividends under the U.S.-Country X income tax treaty with respect to the $25 payment. Because the $25 payment in year 2 is recharacterized as a dividend for all purposes of the Internal Revenue Code and the U.S.-Country X income tax treaty, A is not entitled to an interest deduction with respect to that payment and FC is not entitled to claim the reduced rate of withholding applicable to interest.

Example (4). Definition of related foreign interest holder.

(i) Facts. The facts are the same as in Example 3, except that A has two 50-percent shareholders, FC1 and FC2. In year 2, A makes an interest payment of $25 to both FC1 and FC2. FC1 is a corporation organized under the laws of Country X, which has an income tax treaty in effect with the United States. FC2 is a corporation organized under the laws of Country Y, which also has an income tax treaty in effect with the United States. FP owns 100-percent of both FC1 and FC2, and is organized under the laws of Country X. Under Country X law, FC1 is not fiscally transparent with respect to the dividend, as defined in paragraph (d)(3)(ii) of this section. Under Country X law, FC1 is treated as deriving $50 of the $100 dividend payment received by A because A is fiscally transparent under the laws of Country X, as determined under paragraph (d)(3)(iii) of this section. The applicable rate of tax on dividends under the U.S.-Country X income tax treaty is 5-percent with respect to a 10-percent or more corporate shareholder. Under Country Y law, FC2 is not treated as deriving any of the $100 dividend payment received by A because, under the laws of Country Y, A is not a fiscally transparent entity.

(ii) Analysis. The analysis is the same as in Example 1 with respect to the $100 dividend payment from S to A. With respect to the $25 payment in year 2 by A to FC1, the payment will be treated as a dividend for all purposes of the Internal Revenue Code and the U.S.-Country X income tax treaty because FC1 is a related foreign interest holder as determined under paragraph (d)(2)(ii)(B)(4) of this section, and because $25 does not exceed FC1's share of the dividend payment made by S to A ($50). FC1 is a related foreign interest holder because FC1 is treated as owning the stock of A owned by FC2 under section 267(b)(3). Since FC1 is not fiscally transparent with respect to the payment as determined under paragraph (d)(2)(ii)(A) of this section, FC1 is entitled to the 5-percent reduced rate applicable to dividends under the U.S.-Country X income tax treaty with respect to the $25 payment. Because the $25 payment in year 2 is recharacterized as a dividend for all purposes of the Internal Revenue Code and the U.S.-Country X income tax treaty, A is not entitled to an interest deduction with respect to that payment. Even though FC2 is also a related foreign interest holder, the $25 interest payment by A to FC2 in year 2 is not recharacterized because A is not fiscally transparent under the laws of Country Y, and FC2 is not treated as deriving any of the $100 dividend payment received by A. Thus, the U.S.-Country Y income tax treaty is not implicated.

Example (5). Higher treaty withholding rate on dividends.

(i) Facts. The facts are the same as in Example 3, except that under the U.S.-Country X income tax treaty, the rate of tax on interest is 10-percent and the rate of tax on dividends is 5-percent.

(ii) Analysis. The analysis is the same as in Example 1 with respect to the $100 dividend payment from S to A. The analysis is the same as in Example 3 with respect to the $25 interest payment in year 2 from A to FC.

Example (6). Foreign sister corporation the income and losses of which may offset the income and losses of related foreign interest holder.

(i) Facts. The facts are the same as Example 3, except that in year 2, A makes the interest payment of $25 to FS, a subsidiary of FC also organized in Country X. Under the laws of Country X, FS is not fiscally transparent with respect to the interest payment, and the income and losses of FS may be used to offset the income and losses of FC.

(ii) Analysis. The analysis is the same as in Example 1 with respect to the $100 dividend payment from S to A. With respect to the $25 interest payment from A to FS in year 2, FS is a person described in paragraph (d)(2)(ii)(B)(1)(ii) of this section because the income and losses of FS may be used under the laws of Country X to offset the income and losses of FC, the related foreign interest holder that derived its proportionate share of the payment from S to A. Therefore, paragraph (d)(2)(ii)(B) of this section applies, and the $25 interest payment in year 2 by A to FS is treated as a dividend for all purposes of the Internal Revenue Code and the U.S.-Country X income tax treaty because the $25 payment does not exceed FC's share of the $100 dividend payment made by S to A ($85). Since FS is not fiscally transparent with respect to the payment as determined under paragraph (d)(2)(ii)(A) of this section, FS is entitled to obtain the rate applicable to dividends under the U.S.-Country X income tax treaty with respect to the $25 payment. Because the $25 payment in year 2 is recharacterized as a dividend for all purposes of the Internal Revenue Code and the U.S.-Country X income tax treaty, A is not entitled to an interest deduction with respect to the payment and FS is not entitled to claim the reduced rate of withholding applicable to interest under the U.S.-Country X income tax treaty.

Example (7). Interest paid by domestic reverse hybrid entity to unrelated foreign bank.

(i) Facts. The facts are the same as in Example 3, except that in year 2, A makes the interest payment of $25 to FB, a Country Y unrelated foreign bank, on a loan from FB to A.

(ii) Analysis. The analysis is the same as in Example 1 with respect to the $100 dividend payment from S to A.

With respect to the payment from A to FB, paragraph (d)(2)(ii)(B) of this section will not apply because, although A is related to S, the payor of the dividend income it received, A is not related to FB under paragraph (d)(2)(ii)(B)(4) of this section. Under paragraph (d)(2)(ii)(A) of this section, the $25 interest payment made from A to FB in year 2 is characterized as interest under the Internal Revenue Code.

Example (8). Interest paid by domestic reverse hybrid to an unrelated entity pursuant to a financing arrangement.

(i) Facts. The facts are the same as in Example 7, except that in year 3, FB makes an interest payment of $25 to FC on a deposit made by FC with FB.

(ii) Analysis. The analysis is the same as in Example 1 with respect to the $100 dividend payment from S to A. With respect to the $25 payment from A to FB in year 2, because the payment is made in connection with a transaction that consititutes a financing arrangement within the meaning of paragraph (d)(2)(ii)(C)(2) of this section, the payment may be treated by the Commissioner as being made directly to FC. If the Commissioner disregards FB, then the analysis is the same as in Example 3 with respect to the $25 interest payment in year 2 from A to FC.

Example (9). Royalty paid by related entity to domestic reverse hybrid entity.

(i) Facts. The facts are the same as in Example 3, except the $100 income received by A from S in year 1 is a royalty payment under both the laws of the United States and the laws of Country X. The royalty rate under the treaty is 10 percent and the interest rate is 0 percent.

(ii) Analysis. The analysis as to the royalty payment from S to A is the same as in Example 1 with respect to the $100 dividend payment from S to A. With respect to the $25 payment from A to FC, paragraph (d)(2)(ii)(B) of this section will not apply because the payment from S to A is not treated as a dividend under the Internal Revenue Code or the laws of Country X. Under paragraph (d)(2)(ii)(A) of this section, the $25 of interest paid by A to FC in year 2 is characterized as interest under the Internal Revenue Code. Accordingly, in year 2, FC may obtain the reduced rate of withholding applicable to interest under the U.S.-Country X income tax treaty, assuming all other requirements for claiming treaty benefits are met.

(3) Definitions. (i) Entity. For purposes of this paragraph (d), the term entity shall mean any person that is treated by the United States or the applicable treaty jurisdiction as other than an individual. The term entity includes disregarded entities, including single member disregarded entities with individual owners.

(ii) Fiscally transparent under the law of the entity's jurisdiction. (A) General rule. For purposes of this paragraph (d), an entity is fiscally transparent under the laws of the entity's jurisdiction with respect to an item of income to the extent that the laws of that jurisdiction require the interest holder in the entity, wherever resident, to separately take into account on a current basis the interest holder's respective share of the item of income paid to the entity, whether or not distributed to the interest holder, and the character and source of the item in the hands of the interest holder are determined as if such item were realized directly from the source from which realized by the entity. However, the entity will be fiscally transparent with respect to the item of income even if the item of income is not separately taken into account by the interest holder, provided the item of income, if separately taken into account by the interest holder, would not result in an income tax liability for that interest holder different from that which would result if the interest holder did not take the item into account separately, and provided the interest holder is required to take into account on a current basis the interest holder's share of all such non-separately stated items of income paid to the entity, whether or not distributed to the interest holder. In determining whether an entity is fiscally transparent with respect to an item of income in the entity's jurisdiction, it is irrelevant that, under the laws of the entity's jurisdiction, the entity is permitted to exclude such item from gross income or that the entity is required to include such item in gross income but is entitled to a deduction for distributions to its interest holders.

(B) Special definitions. For purposes of this paragraph (d)(3)(ii), an entity's jurisdiction is the jurisdiction where the entity is organized or incorporated or may otherwise be considered a resident under the laws of that jurisdiction. An interest holder will be treated as taking into account that person's share of income paid to an entity on a current basis even if such amount is taken into account by the interest holder in a taxable year other than the taxable year of the entity if the difference is due solely to differing taxable years.

(iii) Fiscally transparent under the law of an interest holder's jurisdiction. (A) General rule. For purposes of this paragraph (d), an entity is treated as fiscally transparent under the law of an interest holder's jurisdiction with respect to an item of income to the extent that the laws of the interest holder's jurisdiction require the interest holder resident in that jurisdiction to separately take into account on a current basis the interest holder's respective share of the item of income paid to the entity, whether or not distributed to the interest holder, and the character and source of the item in the hands of the interest holder are determined as if such item were realized directly from the source from which realized by the entity. However, an entity will be fiscally transparent with respect to the item of income even if the item of income is not separately taken into account by the interest holder, provided the item of income, if separately taken into account by the interest holder, would not result in an income tax liability for that interest holder different from that which would result if the interest holder did not take the item into account separately, and provided the interest holder is required to take into account on a current basis the interest holder's share of all such nonseparately stated items of income paid to the entity, whether or not distributed to the interest holder. An entity will not be treated as fiscally transparent with respect to an item of income under the laws of the interest holder's jurisdiction, however, if, under the laws of the interest holder's jurisdiction, the interest holder in the entity is required to include in gross income a share of all or a part of the entity's income on a current basis year under any type of anti-deferral or comparable mechanism. In determining whether an entity is fiscally transparent with respect to an item of income under the laws of an interest holder's jurisdiction, it is irrelevant how the entity is treated under the laws of the entity's jurisdiction.

(B) Special definitions. For purposes of this paragraph (d)(3)(iii), an interest holder's jurisdiction is the jurisdiction where the interest holder is organized or incorporated or may otherwise be considered a resident under the laws of that jurisdiction. An interest holder will be treated as taking into account that person's share of income paid to an entity on a current basis even if such amount is taken into account by such person in a taxable year other than the taxable year of the entity if the difference is due solely to differing taxable years.

(iv) Applicable treaty jurisdiction. The term applicable treaty jurisdiction means the jurisdiction whose income tax treaty with the United States is invoked for purposes of reducing the rate of tax imposed under sections 871(a), 881(a), 1461, and 4948(a).

(v) Resident. The term resident shall have the meaning assigned to such term in the applicable income tax treaty.

(4) Application to all income tax treaties. Unless otherwise explicitly agreed upon in the text of an income tax treaty, the rules contained in this paragraph (d) shall apply in respect of all income tax treaties to which the United States is a party. Notwithstanding the foregoing sentence, the competent authorities may agree on a mutual basis to depart from the rules contained in this paragraph (d) in appropriate circumstances. However, a reduced rate under a tax treaty for an item of U.S. source income paid will not be available irrespective of the provisions in this paragraph (d) to the extent that the applicable treaty jurisdiction would not grant a reduced rate under the tax treaty to a U.S. resident in similar circumstances, as evidenced by a mutual agreement between the relevant competent authorities or by a public notice of the treaty jurisdiction. The Internal Revenue Service shall announce the terms of any such mutual agreement or public notice of the treaty jurisdiction. Any denial of tax treaty benefits as a consequence of such a mutual agreement or notice shall affect only payment of U.S. source items of income made after announcement of the terms of the agreement or of the notice.

(5) Examples. This paragraph (d) is illustrated by the following examples:

Example (1). Treatment of entity treated as partnership by U.S. and country of organization.

(i) Facts. Entity A is a business organization formed under the laws of Country X that has an income tax treaty in effect with the United States. A is treated as a partnership for U.S. federal income tax purposes. A is also treated as a partnership under the laws of Country X, and therefore Country X requires the interest holders in A to separately take into account on a current basis their respective shares of the items of income paid to A, whether or not distributed to the interest holders, and the character and source of the items in the hands of the interest holders are determined as if such items were realized directly from the source from which realized by A. A receives royalty income from U.S. sources that is not effectively connected with the conduct of a trade or business in the United States.

(ii) Analysis. A is fiscally transparent in its jurisdiction within the meaning of paragraph (d)(3)(ii) of this section with respect to the U.S. source royalty income in Country X and, thus, A does not derive such income for purposes of the U.S.-X income tax treaty.

Example (2). Treatment of interest holders in entity treated as partnership by U.S. and country of organization.

(i) Facts. The facts are the same as under Example 1. A's partners are M, a corporation organized under the laws of Country Y that has an income tax treaty in effect with the United States, and T, a corporation organized under the laws of Country Z that has an income tax treaty in effect with the United States. M and T are not fiscally transparent under the laws of their respective countries of incorporation. Country Y requires M to separately take into account on a current basis M's respective share of the items of income paid to A, whether or not distributed to M, and the character and source of the items of income in M's hands are determined as if such items were realized directly from the source from which realized by A. Country Z treats A as a corporation and does not require T to take its share of A's income into account on a current basis whether or not distributed.

(ii) Analysis. M is treated as deriving its share of the U.S. source royalty income for purposes of the U.S.-Y income tax treaty because A is fiscally transparent under paragraph (d)(3)(iii) with respect to that income under the laws of Country Y. Under Country Z law, however, because T is not required to take into account its share of the U.S. source royalty income received by A on a current basis whether or not distributed, A is not treated as fiscally transparent. Accordingly, T is not treated as deriving its share of the U.S. source royalty income for purposes of the U.S.-Z income tax treaty.

Example (3). Dual benefits to entity and interest holder.

(i) Facts. The facts are the same as under Example 2, except that A is taxable as a corporation under the laws of Country X. Article 12 of the U.S.-X income tax treaty provides for a source country reduced rate of taxation on royalties of 5-percent. Article 12 of the U.S.-Y income tax treaty provides that royalty income may only be taxed by the beneficial owner's country of residence.

(ii) Analysis. A is treated as deriving the U.S. source royalty income for purposes of the U.S.-X income tax treaty because it is not fiscally transparent with respect to the item of income within the meaning of paragraph (d)(3)(ii) of this section in Country X, its country of organization. M is also treated as deriving its share of the U.S. source royalty income for purposes of the U.S.-Y income tax treaty because A is fiscally transparent under paragraph (d)(3)(iii) of this section with respect to that income under the laws of Country Y. T is not treated as deriving the U.S. source royalty income for purposes of the U.S.-Z income tax treaty because under Country Z law A is not fiscally transparent. Assuming all other requirements for eligibility for treaty benefits have been satisfied, A is entitled to the 5-percent treaty reduced rate on royalties under the U.S.-X income tax treaty with respect to the entire royalty payment. Assuming all other requirements for treaty benefits have been satisfied, M is also entitled to a zero rate under the U.S.-Y income tax treaty with respect to its share of the royalty income.

Example (4). Treatment of grantor trust.

(i) Facts. Entity A is a trust organized under the laws of Country X, which does not have an income tax treaty in effect with the United States. M, the grantor and owner of A for U.S. income tax purposes, is a resident of Country Y, which has an income tax treaty ineffect with the United States. M is also treated as the grantor and owner of the trust under the laws of Country Y. Thus, Country Y requires M to take into account all items of A's income in the taxable year, whether or not distributed to M, and determines the character of each item in M's hands as if such item was realized directly from the source from which realized by A. Country X does not treat M as the owner of A and does not require M to account for A's income on a current basis whether or not distributed to M. A receives interest income from U.S. sources that is neither portfolio interest nor effectively connected with the conduct of a trade or business in the United States.

(ii) Analysis. A is not fiscally transparent under the laws of Country X within the meaning of paragraph (d)(3)(ii) of this section with respect to the U.S. source interest income, but A may not claim treaty benefits because there is no

U.S.-X income tax treaty. M, however, does derive the income for purposes of the U.S.-Y income tax treaty because under the laws of Country Y, A is fiscally transparent.

Example (5). Treatment of complex trust.

(i) Facts. The facts are the same as in Example 4 except that M is treated as the owner of the trust only under U.S. tax law, after application of section 672(f), but not under the law of Country Y. Although the trust document governing A does not require that A distribute any of its income on a current basis, some distributions are made currently to M. There is no requirement under Country Y law that M take into account A's income on a current basis whether or not distributed to him in that year. Under the laws of Country Y, with respect to current distributions, the character of the item of income in the hands of the interest holder is determined as if such item were realized directly from the source from which realized by A. Accordingly, upon a current distribution of interest income to M, the interest income retains its source as U.S. source income.

(ii) Analysis. M does not derive the U.S. source interest income because A is not fiscally transparent under paragraph (d)(3)(ii) of this section with respect to the U.S. source interest income under the laws of Country Y. Although the character of the interest in the hands of M is determined as if realized directly from the source from which realized by A, under the laws of Country Y, M is not required to take into account his share of A's interest income on a current basis whether or not distributed. Accordingly, neither A nor M is entitled to claim treaty benefits, since A is a resident of a non-treaty jurisdiction and M does not derive the U.S. source interest income for purposes of the U.S.-Y income tax treaty.

Example (6). Treatment of interest holders required to include passive income under anti-deferral regime.

(i) Facts. The facts are the same as under Example 2. However, Country Z does require T, who is treated as owning 60-percent of the stock of A, to take into account its respective share of the royalty income of A under an anti-deferral regime applicable to certain passive income of controlled foreign corporations.

(ii) Analysis. T is still not eligible to claim treaty benefits with respect to the royalty income. T is not treated as deriving the U.S. source royalty income for purposes of the U.S.-Z income tax treaty under paragraph (d)(3)(iii) of this section because T is only required to take into account its pro rata share of the U.S. source royalty income by reason of Country Z's anti-deferral regime.

Example (7). Treatment of contractual arrangements operating as collective investment vehicles.

(i) Facts. A is a contractual arrangement without legal personality for all purposes under the laws of Country X providing for joint ownership of securities. Country X has an income tax treaty in effect with the United States. A is a collective investment fund which is of a type known as a Common Fund under Country X law. Because of the absence of legal personality in Country X of the arrangement, A is not liable to tax as a person at the entity level in Country X and is thus not a resident within the meaning of the Residence Article of the U.S.-X income tax treaty. A is treated as a partnership for U.S. income tax purposes and receives U.S. source dividend income. Under the laws of Country X, however, investors in A only take into account their respective share of A's income upon distribution from the Common Fund. Some of A's interest holders are residents of Country X and some of Country Y. Country Y has no income tax treaty in effect with the United States.

(ii) Analysis. A is not fiscally transparent under paragraph (d)(3)(ii) of this section with respect to the U.S. source dividend income because the interest holders in A are not required to take into account their respective shares of such income in the taxable year whether or not distributed. Because A is an arrangement without a legal personality that is not considered a person in in Country X and thus not a resident of Country X under the Residence Article of the U.S.-X income tax treaty, however, A does not derive the income as a resident of Country X for purposes of the U.S.-X income tax treaty. Further, because A is not fiscally transparent under paragraph (d)(3)(iii) of this section with respect to the U.S. source dividend income, A's interest holders that are residents of Country X do not derive the income as residents of Country X for purposes of the U.S.-X income tax treaty.

Example (8). Treatment of person specifically listed as resident in applicable treaty.

(i) Facts. The facts are the same as in Example 7 except that A (the Common Fund) is organized in Country Z and the Residence Article of the U.S.-Z income tax treaty provides that "the term 'resident of a Contracting State' includes, in the case of Country Z, Common Funds. * * *"

(ii) Analysis. A is treated, for purposes of the U.S.-Z income tax treaty as deriving the dividend income as a resident of Country Z under paragraph (d)(1) of this section because the item of income is paid directly to A, A is a Common Fund under the laws of Country Z, and Common Funds are specifically identified as residents of Country Z in the U.S.-Z treaty. There is no need to determine whether A meets the definition of fiscally transparent under paragraph (d)(3)(ii) of this section.

Example (9). Treatment of investment company when entity receives distribution deductions, and all distributions sourced by residence of entity.

(i) Facts. Entity A is a business organization formed under the laws of Country X, which has an income tax treaty in effect with the United States. A is treated as a partnership for U.S. income tax purposes. Under the laws of Country X, A is an investment company taxable at the entity level and a resident of Country X. It is also entitled to a distribution deduction for amounts distributed to its interest holders on a current basis. A distributes all its net income on a current basis to its interest holders and, thus, in fact, has no income tax liability to Country X. A receives U.S. source dividend income. Under Country X law, all amounts distributed to interest holders of this type of business entity are treated as dividends from sources within Country X and Country X imposes a withholding tax on all payments by A to foreign persons. Under Country X laws, the interest holders in A do not have to separately take into account their respective shares of A's income on a current basis if such income is not, in fact, distributed.

(ii) Analysis. A is not fiscally transparent under paragraph (d)(3)(ii) of this section with respect to the U.S. source dividends because the interest holders in A do not have to take into account their respective share of the U.S. source dividends on a current basis whether or not distributed. A is also not fiscally transparent under paragraph (d)(3)(ii) of this section because there is a change in source of the income received by A when A distributes the income to its interest holders and, thus, the character and source of the income in the hands of A's interest holder are not determined as if such income were realized directly from the source from which realized by A. Accordingly, A is treated as deriving the U.S. source dividends for purposes of the U.S.-Country X treaty.

Example (10). Item by item determination of fiscal transparency.

(i) Facts. Entity A is a business organization formed under the laws of Country X, which has an income tax treaty in effect with the United States. A is treated as a partnership for U.S. income tax purposes. Under the laws of Country X, A is an investment company taxable at the entity level and a resident of Country X. It is also entitled to a distribution deduction for amounts distributed to its interest holders on a current basis. A receives both U.S. source dividend income and interest income from U.S. sources that is neither portfolio interest nor effectively connected with the conduct of a trade or business in the United States. Country X law sources all distributions attributable to dividend income based on the residence of the investment company. In contrast, Country X law sources all distributions attributable to interest income based on the residence of the payor of the interest. No withholding applies with respect to distributions attributable to U.S. source interest and the character of the distributions attributable to the interest income remains the same in the hands of A's interest holders as if such items were realized directly from the source from which realized by A. However, under Country X law the interest holders in A do not have to take into account their respective share of the interest income received by A on a current basis whether or not distributed.

(ii) Analysis. An item by item analysis is required under paragraph (d) of this section. The analysis is the same as Example 9 with respect to the dividend income. A is also not fiscally transparent under paragraph (d)(3)(ii) of this section with respect to the interest income because, although the character of the distributions attributable to the interest income in the hands of A's interest holders is determined as if realized directly from the source from which realized by A, under Country X law the interest holders in A do not have to take into account their respective share of the interest income received by A on a current basis whether or not distributed. Accordingly, A derives the U.S. source interest income for purpose of the U.S.-X treaty.

Example (11). Treatment of charitable organizations.

(i) Facts. Entity A is a corporation organized under the laws of Country X that has an income tax treaty in effect with the United States. Entity A is established and operated exclusively for religious, charitable, scientific, artistic, cultural, or educational purposes. Entity A receives U.S. source dividend income from U.S. sources. A provision of Country X law generally exempts Entity A's income from Country X tax due to the fact that Entity A is established and operated exclusively for religious, charitable, scientific, artistic, cultural, or educational purposes. But for such provision, Entity A's income would be taxed by Country X.

(ii) Analysis. Entity A is not fiscally transparent under paragraph (d)(3)(ii) of this section with respect to the U.S. source dividend income because, under Country X law, the dividend income is treated as an item of income of A and no other persons are required to take into account their respective share of the item of income on a current basis, whether or not distributed. Accordingly, Entity A is treated as deriving the U.S. source dividend income.

Example (12). Treatment of pension trusts.

(i) Facts. Entity A is a trust established and operated in Country X exclusively to provide pension or other similar benefits to employees pursuant to a plan. Entity A receives U.S. source dividend income. A provision of Country X law generally exempts Entity A's income from Country X tax due to the fact that Entity A is established and operated exclusively to provide pension or other similar benefits to employees pursuant to a plan. Under the laws of Country X, the beneficiaries of the trust are not required to take into account their respective share of A's income on a current basis, whether or not distributed and the character and source of the income in the hands of A's interest holders are not determined as if realized directly from the source from which realized by A.

(ii) Analysis. A is not fiscally transparent under paragraph (d)(3)(ii) of this section with respect to the U.S. source dividend income because under the laws of Country X, the beneficiaries of A are not required to take into account their respective share of A's income on a current basis, whether or not distributed. A is also not fiscally transparent under paragraph (d)(3)(ii) of this section with respect to the U.S. source dividend income because under the laws of Country X, the character and source of the income in the hands of A's interest holders are not determined as if realized directly from the source from which realized by A. Accordingly, A derives the U.S. source dividend income for purposes of the U.S.-X income tax treaty.

(6) Effective date. This paragraph (d) applies to items of income paid on or after June 30, 2000, except paragraphs (d)(2)(ii) and (d)(2)(iii) of this section apply to items of income paid by a domestic reverse hybrid entity on or after June 12, 2002, with respect to amounts received by the domestic reverse hybrid entity on or after June 12, 2002.

(e) Effective dates. Paragraphs (a) and (b) of this section apply for taxable years beginning after December 31, 1966. For corresponding rules applicable to taxable years beginning before January 1, 1967, (see 26 CFR part 1 revised April 1, 1971). Paragraph (c) of this section is applicable to payments made after November 13, 1997. See paragraph (d)(6) of this section for applicability dates for paragraph (d) of this section.

T.D. 6258, 10/23/57, amend T.D. 7293, 11/27/73, T.D. 8735, 10/6/97, T.D. 8889, 6/30/2000, T.D. 8999, 6/11/2002.

PAR. 11. Section 1.894-1 is amended as follows:

1. Paragraph (d) is redesignated as paragraph (e).

2. New paragraph (d) is added.

The addition reads as follows:

Proposed § 1.894-1 Income affected by treaty. [*For Preamble, see ¶ 151,855*]

* * * * *

(d) Income from a global dealing operation. If a taxpayer that is engaged in a global dealing operation, as defined in § 1.482-8(a)(2)(i), has a permanent establishment in the United States under the principles of an applicable U.S. income tax treaty, the principles of § 1.863-3(h), § 1.864-4(c)(2)(iv), § 1.864-4(c)(3)(ii), § 1.864-4(c)(5)(vi)(a) or § 1.864-6(b)(2)(ii)(d)(3) shall apply for purposes of determining the income attributable to that U.S. permanent establishment.

* * * * *

§ 1.895-1 Income derived by a foreign central bank of issue, or by bank for international settlements, from obligations of the United States.

(a) In general. Income derived by a foreign central bank of issue from obligations of the United States or of any agency or instrumentality thereof, or from interest on deposits with persons carrying on the banking business, is excluded from the gross income of such bank and is exempt from income tax if the bank is the owner of the obligations or deposits and does not hold the obligations or deposits for, or use them in connection with, the conduct of a commercial banking function or other commercial activity by such bank. For purposes of this section and paragraph (i) of § 1.1441-4, obligations of the United States or of any agency or instrumentality thereof include beneficial interests, participations, and other instruments issued under section 302(c) of the Federal National Mortgage Association Charter Act (12 U.S.C. 1717). See 24 CFR Part 1600 *et seq.*

(b) Foreign central bank of issue. *(1)* A foreign central bank of issue is a bank which is by law or government sanction the principal authority, other than the government itself, issuing instruments intended to circulate as currency. Such a bank is generally the custodian of the banking reserves of the country under whose law it is organized. See also paragraph (b)(5) of § 1.861-2.

(2) The exclusion granted by section 895 applies to an instrumentality that is separate from a foreign government, whether or not owned in whole or in part by a foreign government. For example, foreign banks organized along the lines of, and performing functions similar to, the Federal Reserve System qualify as foreign central banks of issue for purposes of this section.

(3) The Bank for International Settlements shall be treated as though it were a foreign central bank of issue for purposes of obtaining the exclusion granted by section 895.

(c) Ownership of United States obligations or bank deposits. The exclusion does not apply if the obligations or bank deposits from which the income is derived are not owned by the foreign central bank of issue. Obligations held, or deposits made, by a foreign central bank of issue as agent, custodian, trustee, or in any other fiduciary capacity, shall be considered as not owned by such bank for purposes of this section.

(d) Commercial banking function or other commercial activity. The exclusion applies only to obligations of the United States or of any agency or instrumentality thereof, or to bank deposits, held for, or used in connection with, the conduct of a central banking function and not to obligations or deposits held for, or used in connection with, the conduct of commercial banking functions or other commercial activities by the foreign central bank.

(e) Other exclusions. See section 861(a)(1)(A) and (E) and § 1.861-2(b)(1) and (4), for special rules relating to interest paid or credited before January 1, 1977, on deposits and on similar amounts and for rules on interest derived from bankers' acceptances. For exemption from withholding under § 1.1441-1 on income derived by a foreign central bank of issue, or by the Bank for International Settlements, from obligations of the United States or of any agency or instrumentality thereof, or from bank deposits, see § 1.1441-4(i).

(f) Effective date. This section shall apply with respect to taxable years beginning after December 31, 1966. For corresponding rules applicable to taxable years beginning before January 1, 1967, see 26 CFR 1.85-1 (Rev. as of Jan. 1, 1972).

T.D. 6636, 2/25/63, amend T.D. 7378, 9/29/75.

---

§ 1.897-1 Taxation of foreign investment in United States real property interests, definition of terms.

(a) In general. *(1) Purpose and scope of regulations.* These regulations provide guidance with respect to the taxation of foreign investments in U.S. real property interests and related matters. This section defines various terms for purposes of sections 897, 1445, and 6039C and the regulations thereunder. Section 1.897-2 provides rules regarding the definition of, and consequences of, U.S. real property holding corporation status. Section 1.897-3 sets forth rules pursuant to which certain foreign corporations may elect under section 897(i) to be treated as domestic corporations for purposes of sections 897 and 6039C. Finally, § 1.987-4 provides rules concerning the similar election under section 897(k) for certain foreign corporations in the process of liquidation.

(2) Effective date. The regulations set forth in §§ 1.897-1 through 1.897-4 are effective for transactions occurring after June 18, 1980. However, with respect to all transactions occurring after June 18, 1980 and before January 30, 1985, taxpayers may at their option choose to apply the Temporary Regulations under section 897 (in their entirety). The Temporary Regulations are located at 26 CFR §§ 6a. 897-1 through 6a.897-4 (Revised as of April 1, 1983), and were originally published in the Federal Register for September 21, 1982 (47 FR 41532) and amended by T.D. 7890, published in the Federal Register on April 28, 1983 (48 FR 19163).

(b) Real property. *(1) In general.* The term "real property" includes the following three categories of property: Land and unsevered natural products of the land, improvements, and personal property associated with the use of real property. The three categories of real property are defined in subparagraphs (2), (3), and (4) of this paragraph (b). Local law definitions will not be controlling for purposes of determining the meaning of the term "real property" as it is used in sections 897, 1445, and 6039C and the regulations thereunder.

(2) Land and unsevered natural products of the land. The term "real property" includes land, growing crops and timber, and mines, wells, and other natural deposits. Crops and timber cease to be real property at the time that they are severed from the land. Ores, minerals, and other natural deposits cease to be real property when they are extracted from the ground. The storage of severed or extracted crops, timber, or minerals in or upon real property will not cause such property to be recharacterized as real property.

(3) Improvements. (i) In general. The term "real property" includes improvements on land. An improvement is a building, any other inherently permanent structure, or the structural components of either, as defined in subdivisions (ii) through (iv) of this paragraph (b)(3).

(ii) Building. The term "building" generally means any structure or edifice enclosing a space within its walls, and usually covered by a roof, the purpose of which is, for example, to provide shelter or housing or to provide working, office, parking, display, or sales space. The term includes, for example, structures such as apartment houses, factory and office buildings, warehouses, barns, garages, railway or bus stations, and stores. Any structure that is classified as a building for purposes of section 48(a)(1)(B) and § 1.48-1 shall be treated as such for purposes of this section.

(iii) Inherently permanent structure. (A) In general. The term "inherently permanent structure" means any property not otherwise described in this paragraph (b)(3) that is affixed to real property and that will ordinarily remain affixed for an indefinite period of time. Property that is not classified as a building for purposes of section 48(a)(1)(B) and § 1.48-1 may nevertheless constitute an inherently permanent structure. For purposes of this section, affixation to real property may be accomplished by weight alone.

(B) Use of precedents under section 48. Any property not otherwise described in this paragraph (b)(3) that constitutes "other tangible property" under the principles of section 48(a)(1)(B) and § 1.48-1(c) and (d) shall be treated for purposes of this section as an inherently permanent structure. Thus, for example, the term includes swimming pools, paved parking areas and other pavements, special foundations for heavy equipment, wharves and docks, bridges, fences, inherently permanent advertising displays, inherently permanent outdoor lighting facilities, railroad tracks and signals, telephone poles, permanently installed telephone and television cables, broadcasting towers, oil derricks, oil and gas pipelines, oil and gas storage tanks, grain storage bins, and silos. However, property that is determined to be either property in the nature of machinery under § 1.48-1(c) or property which is essentially an item of machinery or equipment under § 1.48-1(e)(1)(i) shall not be treated as an inherently permanent structure.

(C) Absence of precedents under section 48. Where precedents developed under the principles of section 48 fail to provide adequate guidance with respect to the classification of particular property, the determination of whether such property constitutes an inherently permanent structure shall be made in view of all the facts and circumstances. In particular, the following factors must be taken into account:

(1) The manner in which the property is affixed to real property;

(2) Whether the property was designed to be easily removable or to remain in place indefinitely;

(3) Whether the property has been moved since its initial installation;

(4) Any circumstances that suggest the expected period of affixation (e.g., a lease that requires removal of the property upon its expiration);

(5) The amount of damage that removal of the property would cause to the property itself or to the real property to which it is affixed; and

(6) The extent of the effort that would be required to remove the property, in terms of time and expense.

(iv) Structural components of buildings and other inherently permanent structures. Structural components of buildings and other inherently permanent structures, as defined in § 1.48-1(e)(2), themselves constitute improvements. Structural components include walls, partitions, floors, ceilings, windows, doors, wiring, plumbing, central heating and central air conditioning systems, lighting fixtures, pipes, ducts, elevators, escalators, sprinkler systems, fire escapes and other components relating to the operation or maintenance of a building. However, the term "structural components" does not include machinery the sole justification for the installation of which is the fact that such machinery is required to meet temperature or humidity requirements which are essential for the operation of other machinery or the processing of materials or foodstuffs. Machinery may meet the "sole justification" test provided by the preceding sentence even though it incidentally provides for the comfort of employees or serves to an insubstantial degree areas where such temperature or humidity requirements are not essential.

(4) Personal property associated with the use of the real property. (i) In general. The term "real property" includes movable walls, furnishings, and other personal property associated with the use of the real property. Personal property is associated with the use of real property only if it is described in one of the categories set forth in subdivisions (A) through (D) of this paragraph (b)(4)(i). "Personal property" for purposes of this section means any property that constitutes "tangible personal property" under the principles of § 1.48-1(c), without regard to whether such property qualifies as section 38 property. Such property will be associated with the use of the real property only where both the personal property and the United States real property interest with which it is associated are held by the same person or by related persons within the meaning of § 1.897-1(i). For purposes of this paragraph (b)(4)(i), property is used "predominantly" in a named activity if it is devoted to that activity during at least half of the time in which it is in use during a calendar year.

(A) Property used in mining, farming, and forestry. Personal property is associated with the use of real property if it is predominantly used to exploit unsevered natural products in or upon the land. Such property includes mining equipment used to extract ores, minerals, and other natural deposits from the ground. It also includes any property used to cultivate the soil and harvest its products, such as farm machinery, draft animals, and equipment used in the growing and cutting of timber. However, personal property used to process or transport minerals, crops, or timber after they are severed from the land is not associated personal property.

(B) Property used in the improvement of real property. Personal property is associated with the use of real property if it is predominantly used to construct or otherwise carry out improvements to real property. Such property includes equipment used to alter the natural contours of the land, equipment used to clear and prepare raw land for construction, and equipment used to carry out the construction of improvements.

(C) Property used in the operation of a lodging facility. Personal property is associated with the use of real property if it is predominantly used in connection with the operation of a lodging facility. Property that is used in connection with the operation of a lodging facility includes property used in the living quarters of such facility, such as beds and other furniture, refrigerators, ranges and other equipment, as well as property used in the common areas of such facility, such as lobby furniture and laundry equipment. Such property constitutes personal property associated with the use of real property in the hands of the owner or operator of the facility, not of the tenant or guest. A lodging facility is an apartment house or apartment, hotel, motel, dormitory, residence, or any other facility (or part of a facility) predominantly used to provide, at a charge, living and/or sleeping accommodations, whether on daily, weekly, monthly, annual, or other basis. The term "lodging facility" does not include a personal residence occupied solely by its owner, or a facility used primarily as a means of transportation (such as an aircraft, vessel, or a railroad car) or used primarily to provide medical or convalescent services, even though sleeping accommodations are provided. Nor does the term include temporary living quarters provided by an employer due to the unavailability of lodgings within a reasonable distance of a worksite (such as a mine or construction project). The term "lodging facility" does not include any portion of a facility that constitutes a nonlodging commercial facility and that is available to persons not using the lodging facility on the same basis that it is available to tenants of the lodging facility. Examples of nonlodging commercial facilities include restaurants, drug stores, and grocery stores located in a lodging facility.

(D) Property used in the rental of furnished office and other work space. Personal property is associated with the use of real property if it is predominantly used by a lessor to provide furnished office or other work space to lessees. Property that is so used includes office furniture and equipment included in the rental of furnished space. Such property constitutes personal property associated with the use of real property in the hands of the lessor, not of the lessee.

(ii) Dispositions of associated personal property. (A) In general. Personal property that has become associated with the use of a real property interest shall itself be treated as a real property interest upon its disposition, unless either:

(1) The personal property is disposed of more than one year before the disposition of any present right to use or occupy the real property with which it was associated (and subject to the provisions of subdivision (B) of this paragraph (b)(4)(ii);

(2) The personal property is disposed of more than one year after the disposition of all present rights to use or occupy the real property with which it was associated (and subject to the provisions of subdivision (C) of this paragraph (b)(4)(ii)); or

(3) The personal property and the real property with which it was associated are separately sold to persons that are related neither to the transferor not to one another (and subject to the provisions of subdivision (D) of this paragraph (b)(4)(ii)).

(B) Personal property disposed of one year before realty. A transferor of personal property associated with the use of real property need not treat such property as a real property interest upon disposition if on the date of disposition the transferor does not expect or intend to dispose of the real property until more than one year later.

However, if the real property is in fact disposed of within the following year, the transferor must treat the personal property as having been a real property interest as of the date on which the personalty was disposed of. If the transferor had not previously filed an income tax return, a return must be filed and tax paid, together with any interest due thereon, by the later of the date on which a tax return or payment is actually due (with extensions), or the 60th day following the date of disposition. If the transferor had previously filed an income tax return, an amended return must be filed and tax paid, together with any interest due thereon, by the later of the dates specified above. Such a transferor may be liable to penalties for failure to file, for late payment of tax, or for understatement of liability, but only if the transferor knew or had reason to anticipate that the real property would be disposed of within one year of the disposition of the associated personal property.

(C) Personalty disposed of one year after realty. A disposition of real property shall be disregarded for purposes of subdivision (A)(2) of this paragraph (b)(4)(ii) if any right to use or occupy the real property is reacquired within the one-year period referred to in that subdivision. However, the disposition shall not be disregarded if such reacquisition is made in foreclosure of a mortgage or other security interest, in the exercise of a contractual remedy, or in the enforcement of a judgment. If, however, the reacquisition of the property is made pursuant to a plan the principal purpose of which is the avoidance of the provisions of section 897, 1445, or 6039C and the regulations thereunder, then the initial disposition shall be disregarded for purposes of subdivision (A)(2) of this paragraph (b)(4)(ii).

(D) Separate dispositions of personalty and realty. A transferor of personal property associated with the use of real property need not treat such property as a real property interest upon disposition if within 90 days before or after such disposition the transferor separately disposes of the real property interest to persons that are related neither to the transferor nor to the purchaser of the personal property. A transferor may rely upon this rule unless the transferor knows or has reason to know that the purchasers of the real property and the personal property—

(1) Are related persons of; or

(2) Intend to reassociate the personal property with the use of the real property within one year of the date of disposition of the personal property.

(E) Status of property in hands of transferee. Personal property that has been associated with the use of real property and that is sold to an unrelated party will be treated as real property in the hands of the transferee only if the personal property becomes associated with the use of real property held or acquired by the transferee, in the manner described in paragraph (b)(4)(i) of this section.

(iii) Determination dates. The determination of whether personal property is personal property associated with the use of real property as defined in this paragraph (b)(4) is to be made on the date the personal property is disposed of and on each applicable determination date. See § 1.897-2(c).

(c) United States real property interest. *(1) In general.* The term "United States real property interest" means any interest, other than an interest solely as a creditor, in either:

(i) Real property located in the United States or the Virgin Islands, or

(ii) A domestic corporation unless it is established that the corporation was not a U.S. real property holding corporation within the period described in section 897(c)(1)(A)(ii). In addition, for the limited purpose of determining whether any corporation is a U.S. real property holding corporation, the term "United States real property interest" means an interest, other than an interest solely as a creditor, in a foreign corporation unless it is established that the foreign corporation is not a U.S. real property holding corporation within the period prescribed in section 897(c)(1)(A)(ii). See § 1.897-2 for rules regarding the manner of establishing that a corporation is not a United States real property holding corporation.

(2) Exceptions and special rules. (i) Domestically-controlled REIT. An interest in a domestically-controlled real estate investment trust (REIT) is not a U.S. real property interest. A domestically-controlled REIT is one in which less than 50 percent of the fair market value of the outstanding stock was directly or indirectly held by foreign persons during the five-year period ending on the applicable determination date (or the period since June 18, 1980, if shorter). For purposes of this determination the actual owners of stock, as determined under § 1.857-8, must be taken into account.

(ii) Corporation that has disposed of all U.S. real property interests. The term "United States real property interest" does not include an interest in a corporation which has disposed of all its U.S. real property interests in transactions in which the full amount of gain, if any, was recognized, as provided as section 897(c)(1)(B). See § 1.897-2(f) for rules regarding the requirements of section 897(c)(1)(B).

(iii) Publicly-traded corporations. If, at any time during the calendar year, any class of stock of a domestic corporation is regularly traded on an established securities market, an interest in such corporation shall be treated as a U.S. real property interest only in the case of:

(A) A regularly traded interest owned by a person who beneficially owned more than 5 percent of the total fair market value of that class of interests at any time during the five-year period ending either on the date of disposition of such interest or other applicable determination date (or the period since June 18, 1980, in shorter), or

(B) [Reserved]

(iv) Publicly traded partnerships and trusts. If any class of interests in a partnership or trust is, within the meaning of § 1.897-1(m) and (n), regularly on an established securities market, then for purposes of sections 897(g) and 1445 and § 1.897-2(d) and (e) an interest in the entity shall not be treated as an interest in a partnership or trust. Instead, such an interest shall be subject to the rules applicable to interests in publicly traded corporations pursuant to paragraph (c)(2)(iii) of this section. Such interests can be real property interests in the hands of a person that holds a greater than 5 percent interest. Therefore, solely for purposes of determining whether greater than 5 percent interests in such an entity constitute U.S. real property interests the disposition of which is subject to tax, the entity is required to determine pursuant to the provisions of § 1.897-2 whether the assets it holds would cause it to be classified as a U.S. real property holding corporation if it were a corporation. The treatment of dispositions of U.S. real property interests by publicly traded partnerships and trusts is not affected by the rules of this paragraph (c)(2)(iv); by reason of the operation of section 897(a), foreign partners or beneficiaries are subject to tax upon their distributive share of any gain recognized upon such dispositions by the partnership or trust. The rules of this paragraph (c)(2)(iv) are illustrated by the following example.

Example. PTP is a partnership one class of interests in which is regularly traded on an established securities market. A is a nonresident alien individual who owns 1 percent of a class of limited partnership interests in PTP. B is a nonresident alien individual who owns 10 percent of the same class of limited partnership interests in PTP. On July 1, 1986, A and B sell their interests in PTP. Pursuant to the rules of this paragraph (c)(2)(iv), neither disposition is treated as the disposition of a partnership interest subject to the provisions of section 897(g). Instead, A and B are treated as having disposed of interests in a publicly traded corporation. Therefore, pursuant to the rule of paragraph (c)(2)(iii) of this section, A's disposition of a 1 percent interest has no consequences under section 897. However, B's disposition of a 10 percent interest will constitute the disposition of a U.S. real property interest subject to tax by reason of the operation of section 897 unless it is established pursuant to the rules of § 1.897-2 that the interest is not a U.S. real property interest.

(d) Interest other than an interest solely as a creditor. *(1) In general.* This paragraph defines an interest other than an interest solely as a creditor, with respect to real property, and with respect to corporations, partnerships, trusts, and estates. An interest solely as a creditor either in real property or in a domestic corporation does not constitute a United States real property interest. Similarly, where one corporation holds an interest solely as a creditor in a second corporation or in a partnership, trust, or estate, that interest will be disregarded for purposes of determining whether the first corporation is a U.S. real property holding corporation (except to the extent that such interest constitutes an asset used or held for use in a trade or business, in accordance with rules of § 1.897-1(f)). In addition, the disposition of an interest solely as a creditor in a partnership, trust, or estate is not subject to sections 897, 1445, and 6039C. Whether an interest is considered debt under any provisions of the Code is not determinative of whether it constitutes an interest solely as a creditor for purpose of sections 897, 1445, and 6039C and the regulations thereunder.

(2) Interests in real property other than solely as creditor. (i) In general. An interest in real property other than an interest solely as a creditor includes a fee ownership, co-ownership, or leasehold interest in real property, a time sharing interest in real property, and a life estate, remainder, or reversionary interest in such property. The term also includes any direct or indirect right to share in the appreciation in the value, or in the gross or net proceeds or profits generated by, the real property.

A loan to an individual or entity under the terms of which a holder of the indebtedness has any direct or indirect right to share in the appreciation in value of, or the gross or net proceeds or profits generated by, an interest in real property of the debtor or of a related person is, in its entirety, an interest in real property other than solely as a creditor. An interest in production payments described in section 636 does not generally constitute an interest in real property other than solely as a creditor. However, a right to production payments shall constitute an interest in real property other than solely as a creditor if it conveys a right to share in the appreciation in value of the mineral property. A production payment that is limited to a quantum of mineral (including a percentage of recoverable reserves produced) or a period of time will be considered to convey a right to share in the appreciation in value of the mineral property. The rules of this paragraph (d)(2)(i) are illustrated by the following example.

Example. A, a U.S. citizen, purchases a condominium unit located in the United States for $500,000. A makes a $100,000 down payment and borrows $400,000 from B, a foreign person, to pay the balance of the purchase price. Under the terms of the loan. A is to pay B 13 percent annual interest each year for 10 years and 35 percent of the appreciation in the fair market value of the condominium at the end of the 10-year period. Because B has a right to share in the appreciation in value of the condominium, B has an interest other than solely as a creditor in the condominium. B's entire interest in the obligation from A, therefore, is a United States real property interest.

(ii) Special rule. (A) Installment obligations. A right to installment or other deferred payments from the disposition of an interest in real property will constitute an interest solely as a creditor if the transferor elects not to have the installment method of section 453(a) apply, any gain or loss is recognized in the year of disposition, and all tax due is timely paid. See section 1445 and regulations thereunder for further guidance concerning the availability of installment sale treatment under section 453. If an agreement for the payment of tax with respect to an installment sale is entered into with the Internal Revenue Service pursuant to section 1445, that agreement may specify whether or not the installment obligation will constitute an interest solely as a creditor. If an installment obligation constitutes an interest other than solely as a creditor then the receipt of each payment shall be treated as the disposition of an interest in real property that is subject to section 897(a) to the extent of any gain required to be taken into account pursuant to section 453. If the original holder of an installment obligation that constitutes an interest other than solely as a creditor subsequently disposes of the obligation to an unrelated party and recognizes gain or loss pursuant to section 453B, the obligation will constitute an interest in real property solely as a creditor in the hands of the subsequent holder. However, if the obligation is disposed of to a related person and the full amount of gain realized upon the disposition of the real property has not been recognized upon such disposition of the installment obligation, then the obligation shall continue to be an interest in real property other than solely as a creditor in the hands of the subsequent holder subject to the rules of this paragraph (d)(2)(ii)(A). In addition, if the obligation is disposed of to any person for a principal purpose of avoiding the provisions of sections 897, 1445, or 6039C, then the obligation shall continue to be an interest in real property other than solely as a creditor in the hands of the subsequent holder subject to the rules of this paragraph (d)(2)(ii)(A). However, rights to payments arising from dispositions that took place before June 19, 1980, shall in no event constitute interests in real property other than solely as a creditor, even if such payments are received after June 18, 1980. In addition, rights to payments arising from dispositions to unrelated parties that took place before January 1, 1985, and that were not subject to U.S. tax pursuant to the provisions of a U.S. income tax treaty, shall not constitute interests in real property other than solely as a creditor, even if such payments are received after December 31, 1984.

(B) Options. An option, a contract or a right of first refusal to acquire any interest in real property (other than an interest solely as a creditor) will itself constitute an interest in real property other than solely as a creditor.

(C) Security interests. A right to repossess or foreclose on real property under a mortgage, security agreement, financing statement, or other collateral instrument securing a debt will not be considered a reversionary interest in, or a right to share in the appreciation in value of or gross or net proceeds or profits generated by, an interest in real property. Thus, no such right of repossession or foreclosure will of itself cause an interest in real property which is otherwise an interest solely as a creditor to become an interest other than solely as a creditor. In addition, a person acting as mortgagee in possession shall not be considered to hold an interest in real property other than solely as a creditor, if the mortgagee's interest in the property otherwise constitutes an interest solely as a creditor.

(D) Indexed interest rates. An interest will not constitute a right to share in the appreciation in the value of, or gross or net proceeds or profits generated by, real property solely because it bears a rate of interest that is tied to an index of any kind that is intended to reflect general inflation or deflation of prices and interest rates (e.g., the Consumer Price Index). However, where an interest in real property bears a rate of interest that is tied to an index the principal purpose of which is to reflect changes in real property values, the real property interest will be considered an indirect right to share in the appreciation in value of, or gross or net proceeds or profits generated by, real property. Such an indirect right constitutes an interest in real property other than solely as a creditor.

(E) Commissions. A right to payment of a commission, brokerage fee, or similar charge for professional services rendered in connection with the arrangement or financing of a purchase, sale, or lease of real property does not constitute a right to share in the appreciation in value of, or gross or net proceeds or profits of, real property solely because it is based upon a percentage of the purchase price or rent. Thus, a right to a commission earned by a real estate agent based on a percentage of the sales price does not constitute an interest in real property other than solely as a creditor. However, a right to a commission, brokerage fee, or similar charge will constitute an interest other than solely as a creditor if the total amount of the payment is contingent upon appreciation, proceeds, or profits of the real property occurring or arising after the date of the transaction with respect to which the professional services were rendered. For example, a commission earned in connection with the purchase of a real property interest that is contingent upon the amount of gain ultimately realized by the purchaser will constitute an interest in real property other than solely as a creditor.

(F) Trustees' fees, etc. A right to payment of reasonable compensation for services rendered as a trustee, as an administrator of an estate, or in a similar capacity does not constitute a right to share in the appreciation in the value of, or gross or net proceeds or profits of, real property solely because the assets of the trust or estate include U.S. real property interests.

(3) Interest in an entity other than solely as a creditor. (i) In general. For purposes of sections 897, 1445, and 6039C, an interest in an entity other than an interest solely as a creditor is—

(A) Stock of a corporation;

(B) An interest in a partnership as a partner within the meaning of section 761(b) and the regulations thereunder;

(C) An interest in a trust or estate as a beneficiary within the meaning of section 643(c) and the regulations thereunder or an ownership interest in any portion of a trust as provided in section 671 through 679 and the regulations thereunder;

(D) An interest which is, in whole or in part, a direct or indirect right to share in the appreciation in value of an interest in an entity described in subdivision (A), (B), or (C) of this paragraph (d)(3)(i) or a direct or indirect right to share in the appreciation in value of assets of, or gross or net proceeds or profits derived by, the entity; or

(E) A right (whether or not presently exercisable) directly or indirectly to acquire, by purchase, conversion, exchange, or in any other manner, an interest described in subdivision (A), (B), (C), or (D) of this paragraph (d)(3)(i).

(ii) Special rules. (A) Installment obligations. A right to installment or other deferred payments from the disposition of an interest in an entity will constitute an interest solely as a creditor if the transferor elects not to have the installment method of section 453(a) apply, any gain or loss is recognized in the year of disposition, and tax due is timely paid. See section 1445 and regulations thereunder for further guidance concerning the availability of installment sale treatment under section 453. If an agreement for the payment of tax with respect to an installment sale is entered into with the Internal Revenue Service pursuant to section 1445, that agreement may specify whether or not the installment obligation will constitute an interest solely as a creditor. If an installment obligation constitutes an interest other than solely as a creditor then the receipt of each payment shall be treated as the disposition of such an interest and shall be subject to section 897(a) to the extent that: (1) It constitutes the disposition of a U.S. real property interest and (2) Gain or loss is required to be taken into account pursuant to section 453. Such treatment shall apply to payments arising from dispositions of interests in a corporation any class of the stock of which is regularly traded on an established securities market, but only in the case of a disposition of any portion of an interest described in paragraph (c)(2)(iii)(A) or (B) of this section. If the original holder of an installment obligation that constitutes an interest other than solely as a creditor subsequently disposes of the obligation to an unrelated party and recognizes gain or loss pursuant to section 453B, the obligation will constitute an interest in the entity solely as a creditor in the hands of the subsequent holder. However, if the obligation is disposed of to a related person and the full amount of grain realized upon the disposition of the interest in the entity has not been recognized upon such disposition of the installment obligation, then the obligation shall continue to be an interest in the entity other than solely as a creditor in the hands of the subsequent holder subject to the rules of this paragraph (d)(3)(ii)(A). In addition, if the obligation is disposed of to any person for a principal purpose of avoiding the provisions of section 897, 1445, or 6039C, then the obligation shall continue to be an interest in the entity other than solely as a creditor in the hands of the subsequent holder subject to the rules of this paragraph (d)(3)(ii)(A). However, rights to payments arising from dispositions that took place before June 19, 1980, shall in no event constitute interests in an entity other than solely as a creditor, even if such payments are received after June 18, 1980. In addition, such treatment shall not apply to payments arising from dispositions to unrelated parties that took place before January 1, 1985, and that were not subject to U.S. tax pursuant to the provisions of a U.S. income tax treaty, regardless of when such payments are received.

(B) Contingent interests. The interests described in subdivision (D) of paragraph (d)(3)(i) of this section include any right to a payment from an entity the amount of which is contingent on the appreciation in value of an interest described in subdivision (A), (B), or (C) of paragraph (d)(3)(i) of this section or which is contingent on the appreciation in value of assets of, or the general gross or net proceeds or profits derived by, such entity. The right to such a payment is itself an interest in the entity other than solely as a creditor, regardless of whether the holder of such right actually holds an interest in the entity described in subdivision (A), (B), or (C) of paragraph (d)(3)(i) of this section. For example, a stock appreciation right constitutes an interest in a corporation other than solely as a creditor even if the holder of such right actually holds no stock in the corporation. However, the interests described in subdivision (D) of paragraph (d)(3)(i) of this section do not include any right to a payment that is (1) exclusively contingent upon and exclusively paid out of revenues from sales of personal property (whether tangible or intangible) or from services, or (2) exclusively contingent upon the resolution of a claim asserted against the entity by a person related neither to the entity nor to the holder of the interest.

(C) Security interests. A right to repossess or foreclose on an interest in an entity under a mortgage, security agreement, financing statement, or other collateral instrument securing a debt will not of itself cause an interest in an entity which is otherwise an interest solely as a creditor to become an interest other than solely as a creditor.

(D) Royalties. The interests described in subdivision (D) of paragraph (d)(3)(i) of this section do not include rights to payments representing royalties, license fees, or similar charges for the use of patents, inventions, formulas, copyrights, literary, musical or artistic compositions, trademarks, trade names, franchises, licenses, or similar intangible property.

(E) Commissions. The interests described in subdivision (D) of paragraph (d)(3)(i) of this section do not include a right to a commission, brokerage fee or similar charge for professional services rendered in connection with the purchase or sale of an interest in an entity. However, a right to such a payment will constitute an interest other than solely as a creditor if the total amount of the payment is contingent upon appreciation in value of assets of, or proceeds or profits derived by, the entity after the date of the transaction with respect to which the payment was earned.

(F) Trustee's fees. The interests described in subdivision (D) of paragraph (d)(3)(i) of this section do not include a right to payment representing reasonable compensation for services rendered as a trustee, as an administrator of an estate, or in a similar capacity.

(4) Aggregation of interests. If a person holds both interests solely as a creditor and interests other than solely as a creditor in real property or in an entity, those interests will generally be treated as separate and distinct interests. However, such interests shall be aggregated and treated as interests other than solely as a creditor in their entirety if the interest solely as a creditor has been separated from, or acquired separately from, the interest other than solely as a creditor, for a principal purpose of avoiding the provisions of section 897, 1445, or 6039C by causing one or more of such interests to be an interest solely as a creditor. The existence of such a purpose will be determined with reference to all the facts and circumstances. Where an interest solely as a creditor has arm's-length interest and repayment terms it shall in no event be aggregated with and treated as an interest other than solely as a creditor. For purposes of this paragraph (d)(4), an interest rate that does not exceed 120 percent of the applicable Federal rate (as defined in section 1274(d)) shall be presumed to be an arm's-length interest rate. For purposes of applying the rules of this paragraph (d)(4), a person shall be treated as holding any interests held by a related person within the meaning of § 1.897-1(i).

(5) "Interest" means "interest other than solely as a creditor." Unless otherwise stated, the term "interest" as used with regard to real property or with regard to an entity hereafter in the regulations under sections 897, 1445, and 6039C, means an interest in such real property or entity other than an interest solely as a creditor.

(e) Proportionate share of assets held by an entity. *(1) In general.* A person that holds an interest in an entity is for certain purposes treated as holding a proportionate or pro rata share of the assets held by the entity. Such proportionate share must be calculated, in accordance with the rules of this paragraph, for the following purposes.

(i) In determining whether a corporation is a U.S. real property holding corporation—

(A) A person holding an interest in a partnership, trust, or estate is treated as holding a proportionate share of the assets held by the partnership, trust, or estate (see section 897-2(e)(2)), and

(B) A corporation that holds a controlling interest in a second corporation is treated as holding a proportionate share of the assets held by the second corporation (see § 1.897-2(e)(3)).

(ii) In determining reporting obligations that may be imposed under section 6039C, the holder of an interest in a partnership, trust, or estate is treated as owning a proportionate share of the U.S. real property interests held by the partnership, trust, or estate.

(2) Proportionate share of assets held by a corporation or partnership. (i) In general. A person's proportionate or pro

rata share of assets held by a corporation or partnership is determined by multiplying—

(A) The person's percentage ownership interest in the entity, by

(B) The fair market value of the assets held by the entity (or the book value of such assets, in the case of a determination pursuant to § 1.897-2(b)(2)).

(ii) Percentage ownership interest. A person's percentage ownership interest in a corporation or partnership is the percentage equal to the ratio of (A) the sum of the liquidation values of all interests in the entity held by the person to (B) the sum of the liquidation values of all outstanding interest in the entity. The liquidation value of an interest in an entity is the amount of cash and the fair market value of any property that would be distributed with respect to such interest upon the liquidation of the entity after satisfaction of liabilities to persons having interests in the entity solely as creditors. With respect to an entity that has interests outstanding that grant a presently-exercisable option to acquire or right to convert into or otherwise acquire an interest in the entity other than solely as a creditor, the liquidation value of all interests in such entity shall be calculated as though such option or right had been exercised, giving effect both to the payment of any consideration required to exercise the option or right and to the issuance of the additional interest.

The fair market value of the assets of the entity, the amount of cash held by the entity, and the amount of liabilities to persons having interests solely as creditors if determined for this purpose on the date with respect to which the percentage ownership interest is determined.

(iii) Examples. The rules of this paragraph (e)(2) are illustrated by the following examples.

Example (1). Corporation K's only assets are stock and securities with a fair market value as of the applicable determination date of $20,000,000 K's assets are subject to liabilities of $10,000,000. Among K's liabilities are a $1,000,000 loan from L, under the terms of which L is entitled, upon payment of the loan principal, to a profit share equal to 10 percent of the excess of the fair market value of K's assets over $18,000,000, but only if all other corporate liabilities have been paid. K has two classes of stock, common and preferred. PS1 and PS2 each own 100 of the 200 outstanding shares of preferred stock. CS1 and CS2 each own 500 of the 1,000 outstanding shares of common stock. Each preferred shareholder is entitled to $10,000 per share of preferred stock upon liquidation, subject to payment of all corporate liabilities and to any amount owed to L, but before any common shareholder is paid. The liquidation value of L's interest in K, which constitutes an interest other than an interest solely as a creditor, is $1,200 ($1,000,000 principal of the loan to K plus $200,000 (10 percent of the excess of $20,000,000 over $18,000,000). The liquidation value of each of PS1's and PS2's blocks of preferred stock is $1,000,000 ($10,000 times 100 shares each). The liquidation value of each of CS1's and CS2's blocks of common stock is $3,900,000 [$20,000,000 (the total fair market value of K's assets) – $9,000,000 (liabilities to creditors other than L) – $1,200,000 (L's liquidation value) – $2,000,000 (PS1's and PS2's liquidation value)) times 50 percent (the percentage of common stock owned by each)]. The sum of the liquidation values of all of the outstanding interests in K (i.e., interests other than solely as a creditor) is $11,000,000 [$1,200,000 (L's liquidation value) + $2,000,000 (PS1's and PS2's liquidation values) + $7,800,000 (CS1's and CS2's liquidation values)]. Each of CS1's and CS2's percentage ownership interests in K is 35.5 percent ($3,900,000 divided by $11,000,000). Each of PS1's and PS2's percentage ownership interests in K is 9 percent ($1,000,000 divided by $11,000,000). L's percentage ownership interest in K is 11 percent ($1,200,000 divided by $11,000,000).

Example (2). A, a U.S. person, and B, a foreign person are partners in a partnership the only asset of which is a parcel of undeveloped land purchased by the partnership in 1980 for $300,000. The partnership has no liabilities, and its capital is $300,000. A's and B's interests in the capital of the partnership are 25 percent and 75 percent, respectively, and A and B each has a 50 percent profit interest in the partnership. The partnership agreement provides that upon liquidation any unrealized gain will be distributed in accordance with the partners' profit interest. In 1984 the partnership has no items of income or deduction, and the fair market value of its parcel of undeveloped land is $500,000. In 1984 the percentage ownership interest of A in the partnership is 35 percent [the ratio of $100,000 (the liquidation value of A's profit interest in 1984) plus $75,000 (the liquidation value of A's 25 percent interest in the partnership's $300,000 capital) to $500,000 (the sum of the liquidation values of all outstanding interests in the partnership)]. The percentage ownership interest of B in the partnership in 1984 is 65 percent [the ratio of $325,000 (B's $100,000 profit interest plus his $225,00 capital interest) to $500,000]

(3) Proportionate share of assets held by trusts and estates. (i) In general. A person's proportionate or pro rata share of assets held by a trust or estate is determined by multiplying—

(A) The person's percentage ownership interest in the trust or estate, by

(B) The fair market value of the assets held by the trust or estate (or the book value of such assets, in the case of a determination pursuant to § 1.897-2(b)(2)).

(ii) percentage ownership interest. (A) General rule. A person's percentage ownership interest in a trust or an estate—is the percentage equal to the ratio of:

(*1*) The sum of the actuarial values of such person's interests in the cash and other assets held by the trust or estate after satisfaction of the liabilities of the trust or estate to persons holding interests in the trust or estate solely as creditors, to

(*2*) the entire amount of such cash and other assets after satisfaction of liabilities to persons holding interests in the trust or estate solely as creditors. For purposes of calculating this ratio, the fair market value of the trust's or estate's assets, the amount of cash held by the trust or estate, and the amount of the liabilities to persons having interests solely as creditors is determined on the date with respect to which the percentage ownership interest is determined. With respect to a trust or estate that has interests outstanding that grant a presently-exercisable option to acquire or right to convert into or otherwise acquire an interest in the trust or estate other than solely as a creditor, the liquidation value of all interests in such entity shall be calculated as though such option or right had been exercised, giving effect both to the payment of any consideration required to exercise the option or right and to the issuance of the additional interest. With respect to a trust or estate that has interests outstanding that entitle any person to a distribution of U.S. real property interests upon liquidation that is disproportionate to such person's interest in the total assets of the trust or estate, such disproportionate right shall be disregarded in the calculation of the interest-holders' proportionate share of the U.S. real property interests held by the entity. For purposes of determining his own percentage ownership interest in a trust, a grantor or other person will be treated as owning any portion of the trust's cash and other assets which such person is treated as owning under sections 671 through 679.

(B) Discretionary trusts and estates. In determining percentage ownership interest in a trust or an estate, the sum of the definitely ascertainable actuarial values of interests in the cash and the other assets of the trust or estate held by persons in existence on the date with respect to which such determination is made must equal the amount in paragraph (e)(3)(ii)(A)(2) of this section. If the amount in paragraph (e)(3)(ii)(A)(2) of this section exceeds the sum of the definitely ascertainable actuarial values of the interests held by persons in existence on the determination date, the excess will be considered to be owned in total by each beneficiary who is in existence on such date, whose interest in the excess is not definitely ascertainable and who is potentially entitled to such excess. However, such excess shall not be considered to be owned in total by each beneficiary if the discretionary terms of the trust or estate were included for a principal purpose of avoiding the provisions of section 897, 1445, or 6039C by causing assets other than U.S. real property interests to be attributed in total to each beneficiary. The rules of this paragraph (e)(3) are illustrated by the following example.

Example. A, a U.S. person, established a trust on December 31, 1984, and contributed real property with a fair market value of $10,000 to the trust. The terms of that trust provided that the trustee, a bank that is unrelated to A, at its discretion may retain trust income or may distribute it to X, a foreign person, or to the head of state of any country other than the United States. The remainder upon the death of X is to go in equal shares to such of Y and Z, both foreign persons, as survive X. On December 31, 1984, the total value of the trust's assets is $10,000. On the same date, the actuarial values of the remainder interests of Y and Z in the corpus of the trust are definitely ascertainable. They are $1,000 and $500, respectively. Neither the income interest of X nor of the head of state of any country other than the United States has a definitely ascertainable actuarial value on December 31, 1984. The interests of Y and Z in the income portion of the trust similarly have no definitely ascertainable actuarial values on such date since the income may be distributed rather than retained by the trust. Since the sum of the actuarial values of definitely ascertainable interests of persons in existence ($1,500) is less than $10,000, the difference ($8,500) is treated as owned by each beneficiary who is in existence on December 31, 1984, and who is potentially entitled to such excess. Therefore, X, Y, Z, and the head of state of any country other than the United States are each considered as owning the entire $8,500 income interest in the trust. On December 31, 1984, the total actuarial value of X's interest is $8,500, and his percentage ownership interest is 85 percent. The total actuarial value of Y's interest in the trust is $9,500 ($1,000 plus $8,500), and his percentage ownership interest is 95 percent. The total actuarial value of Z's interest is $9,000 ($500 plus $8,500), and his percentage ownership interest is 90 percent. The actuarial value of the interest of the head of state of each country other than the United States is $8,500, and his percentage ownership interest is 85 percent.

(4) Dates with respect to which percentage ownership interests are determined. The dates with respect to which percentage ownership interests are determined are the applicable determination dates outlined in §§ 1.897-2 or in regulations under section 6039C.

(f) Asset used or held for use in a trade or business. *(1) In general.* The term "asset used or held for use in a trade or business" means—

(i) Property, other than a U.S. real property interest, that is—

(A) Stock in trade of an entity or other property of a kind which would properly be included in the inventory of the entity if on hand at the close of the taxable year, or property held by the entity primarily for sale to customers in the ordinary course of its trade or business, or

(B) Depreciable property used or held for use in the trade or business, as described in section 1231(b)(1) but without regard to the holding period limitations of section 1231(b), or

(C) Livestock, including poultry, used or held for use in a trade or business for draft, breeding, dairy, or sporting purposes, and

(ii) Goodwill and going concern value, patents, inventions, formulas copyrights, literary, musical, or artistic compositions, trademarks, trade names, franchises, licenses, customer lists, and similar intangible property, but only to the extent that such property is used or held for use in the entity's trade or business and subject to the valuation rules of § 1.897-1(o)(4), and

(iii) Cash, securities, receivables of all kinds, options or contracts to acquire any of the foregoing, and options or contracts to acquire commodities, but only to the extent that such assets are used or held for use in the corporation's trade or business and do not constitute U.S. real property interests.

(2) Used or held for use in a trade or business. An asset is used or held for use in an entity's trade or business if it is, under the principles of § 1.864-4(c)(2)—

(i) Held for the principal purpose of promoting the present conduct of the trade or business,

(ii) Acquired and held in the ordinary course of the trade or business, as, for example, in the case of an account or note receivable arising from that trade or business (including the performance of services), or

(iii) Otherwise held in a direct relationship to the trade or business. In determining whether an asset is held in a direct relationship to the trade or business, consideration shall be given to whether the asset is needed in that trade or business. An asset shall be considered to be needed in a trade or business only if the asset is held to meet the present needs of that trade or business and not its anticipated future needs. An asset shall be considered as needed in the trade or business if, for example, the asset is held to meet the operating expenses of that trade or business. Conversely, an asset shall be considered as not needed in the trade or business if, for example, the asset is held for the purpose of providing for future diversification into a new trade or business, future expansion of trade or business activities, future plant replacement, or future business contingencies. An asset that is held to meet reserve or capitalization requirements imposed by applicable law shall be presumed to be held in a direct relationship to the trade or business.

(3) Special rules concerning liquid assets. (i) Safe harbor amount. Assets described in paragraph (f)(1)(iii) of this section shall be presumed to be used or held for use in a trade or business, in an amount up to 5 percent of the fair market value of other assets used or held for use in the trade or business. However, the rule of this paragraph (f)(3)(i) shall not apply with respect to any assets described in paragraph

(f)(1)(iii) of this section that are held or acquired for the principal purpose of avoiding the provisions of section 897 or 1445.

(ii) Investment companies. Assets described in paragraph (f)(1)(iii) of this section shall be presumed to be used or held for use in an entity's trade or business if the principal business of the entity is trading or investing in such assets for its own account. An entity's principal business shall be presumed to be trading or investing in assets described in paragraph (f)(1)(iii) of this section if the fair market value of such assets held by the entity equals or exceeds 90 percent of the sum of the fair market values of the entity's U.S. real property interests, interests in real property located outside the United States, assets otherwise used or held for use in trade or business, and assets described in paragraph (f)(1)(iii) of this section.

(4) Examples. The application of this paragraph (f) may be illustrated by the following examples:

Example (1). M, a domestic corporation engaged in industrial manufacturing, is required to hold a large current cash balance for the purposes of purchasing materials and meeting its payroll. The amount of the cash balance so required varies because of the fluctuating seasonal nature of the corporation's business. In months when large cash balances are not required, the corporation invests the surplus amount in U.S. Treasury bills. Since both the cash and the Treasury bills are held to meet the present needs of the business, they are held in a direct relationship to that business, and, therefore, constitute assets used or held for use in the trade or business.

Example (2). R, a domestic corporation engaged in the manufacture of goods, engages a stock brokerage firm to manage securities which were purchased with funds from R's general surplus reserves. The funds invested in these securities are intended to provide for the future expansion of R into a new trade or business. Thus, the funds are not necessary for the present needs of the business; they are accordingly not held in a direct relationship to the business and do not constitute assets used or held for use in the trade or business.

Example (3). B, a federally chartered and regulated bank, is required by law to hold substantial reserves of cash, stock, and securities. Pursuant to the rule of paragraph (f)(2) of this section, such assets are presumed to be held in a direct relationship to B's business, and thus constitute assets used or held for use in the trade or business. In addition, B holds substantial loan receivables which are acquired and held in the ordinary course of its banking business. Pursuant to the rule of paragraph (f)(1)(iii) of this section, such receivables constitute assets used or held for use in the trade or business.

(g) Disposition: For purposes of sections 897, 1445, and 6039C, the term "disposition" means any transfer that would constitute a disposition by the transferor for any purpose of the Internal Revenue Code and regulations thereunder. The severance of crops or timber and the extraction of minerals do not alone constitute the disposition of a U.S. real property interest.

(h) Gain or loss. The amount of gain or loss arising from the disposition of the U.S. real property interest shall be determined as provided in section 1001(a) and (b). Such gain or loss shall be subject to the provisions of section 897(a) and (b), unless a nonrecognition provision is applicable pursuant to section 897(d) or (e) and regulations thereunder. Amounts otherwise treated for Federal income tax purposes as principal and interest payments on debt obligations of all kinds (including obligations that are interests other than solely as a creditor) do not give rise to gain or loss that is subject to section 987(a). However, principal payments on installment obligations described in §§ 1.897-1(d)(2)(ii)(A) and 1.897-1(d)(3)(ii)(A) do give rise to gain or loss that is subject to section 897(a), to the extent such gain or loss is required to be recognized pursuant to section 453. The rules of paragraphs (g) and (h) are illustrated by the following examples.

Example (1). Foreign individual C has an undivided fee interest in a parcel of real property located in the United States. The fair market value of C's interest is $70,000, and C's basis in such interest is $50,000. The only liability to which the real property is subject is the liability of $65,000 secured by a mortgage in the same amount. C transfers his fee interest in the property subject to the mortgage by gift to D. C realizes $15,000 of gain upon such transfer. As a transfer by gift constitutes a disposition for purposes of the Code, and as gain is realized upon that transfer, the gift is a disposition for purposes of sections 897, 1445, and 6039C and is subject to section 897(a) to the extent of the gain realized. However, section 897(a) would not be applicable to the transfer if the mortgage on the U.S. real property were equal to or less than C's $50,000 basis, since the transfer then would not give rise to the realization of gain or loss under the Internal Revenue Code.

Example (2). Foreign corporation Y makes a loan of $1 million to domestic individual Z, secured by a mortgage on residential real property purchased with the loan proceeds. The loan agreement provides that Y is entitled to receive fixed monthly payments from Z, constituting repayment of principal plus interest at a fixed rate. In addition, the agreement provides that Y is entitled to receive a percentage of the appreciation value of the real property as of the time that the loan is retired. The obligation in its entirety is considered debt for Federal income tax purposes. However, because of Y's right to share in the appreciation in value of the real property, the debt obligation gives Y an interest in the real property other than solely as a creditor. Nevertheless, as principal and interest payments do not constitute gain under section 1001 and paragraph (h) of this section, and both the monthly and final payments received by Y are considered to consist solely of principal and interest for Federal income tax purposes, section 897(a) shall not apply to Y's receipt of such payments. However, Y's sale of the debt obligation to foreign corporation A would give rise to gain that is subject to section 897(a).

(i) Related person. For purposes of sections 897, 1445, and 6039C, persons are considered to be related if they are partners or partnerships described in section 707(b)(1) of the Code or if they are related within the meaning of section 267(b) and (c) of the Code (except that section 267(f) shall apply without regard to section 1563(b)(2)).

(j) Domestic corporation. The term "domestic corporation" has the same meaning as set forth in section 7701(a)(3) and (4) and § 301.7701-5. For purposes of sections 897 and 6039C, it also includes a foreign corporation with respect to which an election under section 897(i) and § 1.897-3 or section 897(k) and § 1.897-4 to be treated as domestic corporation is in effect.

(k) [Reserved]

(l) Foreign corporation. The term "foreign corporation" has the meaning ascribed to such term in section 7701(a) (3) and (5) and § 301.7701-5. For purposes of sections 897 and 6039C, however, the term does not include a foreign corporation with respect to which there is in effect an election under section 897(i) and § 1.897-3 or section 897(k) and § 1.897-4 to be treated as a domestic corporation.

(m) Established securities market. For purposes of sections 897, 1445, and 6039C, the term "established securities market" means—

(1) A national securities exchange which is registered under section 6 of the Securities Exchange Act of 1934 (15 U.S.C. 78f),

(2) A foreign national securities exchange which is officially recognized, sanctioned, or supervised by governmental authority, and

(3) Any over-the-counter market. An over-the-counter market is any market reflected by the existence of an interdealer quotation system. An interdealer quotation system is any system of general circulation to brokers and dealers which regularly disseminates quotations of stocks and securities by identified brokers or dealers, other than by quotation sheets which are prepared and distributed by a broker or dealer in the regular course of business and which contain only quotations of such broker or dealer.

(n) [Reserved]

(o) Fair market value. *(1) In general.* For purposes of sections 897, 1445, and 6039C only, the term "fair market value" means the value of the property determined in accordance with the rules, contained in this paragraph (o). The definition of fair market value provided herein is not to be used in the calculation of gain or loss from the disposition of a U.S. real property interest pursuant to section 1001. An independent professional appraisal of the value of property must be submitted only if such an appraisal is specifically requested in connection with the negotiation of a security agreement pursuant to section 1445.

(2) Method of calculating fair market value. (i) In general. The fair market value of property is its gross value (as defined in paragraph (o)(2)(ii) of this section) reduced by the outstanding balance of any debts secured by the property which are described in paragraph (o)(2)(iii) of this section. See § 1.897-2(b) for the alternative use of book values in certain limited circumstances.

(ii) Gross value. Gross value is the price at which the property would change hands between an unrelated willing buyer and willing seller, neither being under any compulsion to buy or to sell and both having reasonable knowledge of all relevant facts. Generally, with respect to trade or business assets, going concern value should be used as it will provide the most accurate reflection of such a price. However, taxpayers may use other methods of valuation if they can establish that such method will provide a more accurate determination of gross value and if they consistently apply such method to all assets to be valued. See subdivisions (3) and (4) of this paragraph (o) for special rules with respect to the valuation of leases and of intangible assets.

(iii) Debts secured by the property. The gross value of property shall be reduced by the outstanding balance of debts that are:

(A) Secured by a mortgage or other security interest in the property that is valid and enforceable under the law of the jurisdiction in which the property is located, and

(B) Either (1) Incurred to acquire the property (including long-term financing obtained in replacement of construction loans or other short-term debt within one year of the acquisition or completion of the property), or (2) otherwise incurred in direct connection with the property, such as property tax liens upon real property or debts incurred to maintain or improve property.

In addition, if any debt described in this paragraph (o)(2)(iii) is refinanced for a valid business purpose (such as obtaining a more favorable rate of interest), the principal amount of the replacement debt does not exceed the outstanding balance of the original debt, and the replacement debt is secured by the property, then the gross value of the property shall be reduced by the replacement debt. Obligations to related persons shall not be taken into account for purposes of this paragraph (o)(2)(iii) unless such obligations constitute interests solely as a creditor pursuant to the provisions of paragraph (d)(4) of this section and unless the related person has made similar loans to unrelated persons on similar terms and conditions.

(iv) Anti-abuse rule. The gross value of real property located outside the United States and of assets used or held for use in a trade or business shall be reduced by the outstanding balance of any debt that was entered into for the principal purpose of avoiding the provisions of section 897, 1445, or 6039C by enabling the corporation to acquire such assets. The existence of such a purpose shall be determined with reference to all the facts and circumstances. Debts that a particular corporation routinely enters into in the ordinary course of its acquisition of assets used or held for use in its trade or business will not be considered to be entered into for the principal purpose of avoiding the provisions of section 897, 1445, or 6039C.

(3) Fair market value of leases and options. For purposes of sections 897, 1445, and 6039C, the fair market value of a leasehold interest in real property is the price at which the lease could be assigned or the property sublet, neither party to such transaction being under any compulsion to enter into the transaction and both having reasonable knowledge of all relevant facts. Thus, the value of a leasehold interest will generally consist of the present value, over the period of the lease remaining, of the difference between the rental provided for in the lease and the current rental value of the real property. A leasehold interest bearing restrictions on its assignment or sublease has a fair market value of zero, but only if those restrictions in practical effect preclude (rather than merely condition) the lessee's ability to transfer, at a gain, the benefits of a favorable lease. The normal commercial practice of lessors may be used to determine whether restrictions in a lease have the practical effect of precluding transfer at a gain. The fair market value of an option to purchase any property is, similarly, the price at which the option could be sold, consisting generally of the difference between the option price and the fair market value of the property, taking proper account of any restrictions upon the transfer of the option.

(4) Fair market value of intangible assets. For purposes of determining whether a corporation is a U.S. real property holding corporation, the fair market value of intangible assets described in § 1.897-1(f)(1)(ii) may be determined in accordance with the following rules.

(i) Purchase price. Intangible assets described in § 1.897-1(f)(1)(ii) that were acquired by purchase from a person not related to the purchaser within the meaning of § 1.897-1(i) may be valued at their purchase price. However, such purchase price must be adjusted to reflect any amortization required by generally accepted accounting principles applied in the United States. Intangible assets acquired by purchase shall include any amounts allocated to goodwill or going concern valued pursuant to section 338(b)(3) and regulations thereunder. Intangible assets acquired by purchase shall not include assets that were acquired indirectly through an acquisition of stock to which section 338 does not apply. Such assets must be value pursuant to a method described in subdivision (ii) or (iii) of this paragraph (o)(4).

(ii) Book value. Intangible assets described in § 1.897-1(f)(1)(ii) (other than good will and going concern value) may be valued at the amount at which such assets are carried on the financial accounting records of the holder of such assets, provided that such amount is determined in accordance with generally accepted accounting principles applied in the United States. However, this method may not be used with respect to assets acquired by purchase from a related person within the meaning of § 1.897-1(i).

(iii) Other methods. Intangible assets described in § 1.897-1(f)(1)(ii) may be valued pursuant to any other reasonable method at an amount reflecting the price at which the asset would change hands between an unrelated willing buyer and willing seller, neither being under any compulsion to buy or to sell and both having reasonable knowledge of all relevant facts. However, a corporation that uses a method of valuation other than the purchase price or book value methods may be required to comply with the special notification requirements of § 1.897-2(h)(1)(iii)(A).

(p) Identifying number. The "identifying number" of an individual is the individual's United States social security number or the identification number assigned by the Internal Revenue Service (see § 301.6109-1 of this chapter). The "identifying number" of any other person is its United States employer identification number.

T.D. 7999, 12/26/84, amend T.D. 8113, 12/18/86, T.D. 8198, 5/4/88, T.D. 8657, 3/5/96, T.D. 9082, 8/4/2003.

§ 1.897-2 United States real property holding corporations.

(a) Purpose and scope. This section provides rules regarding the definition and consequences of U.S. real property holding corporation status. U.S. real property holding corporation status is important for determining whether gain from the disposition by a foreign person of an interest in a domestic corporation is taxable. Such status is also important for purposes of the withholding and reporting requirements of sections 1445 and 6039C. For example, a person that buys stock of a U.S. real property holding corporation from a foreign person is required to withhold under section 1445. In addition, for purposes of determining whether another corporation is a U.S. real property holding corporation, an interest in a foreign corporation is a U.S. real property interest unless it is established that the foreign corporation is not a U.S. real property holding corporation. The general definition of a U.S. real property holding corporation is provided in paragraph (b) of this section. Paragraph (c) provides rules regarding the dates on which U.S. real property holding corporation status must be determined. The assets that must be included in making the determination of a corporation's status are set forth in paragraph (d), while paragraph (e) provides special rules regarding the treatment of interests held by a corporation in partnerships, trusts, estates, and other corporations. Rules regarding the termination of U.S. real property holding corporation status are set forth in paragraph (f). Paragraph (g) explains the manner in which an interest-holder can establish that a corporation is not a U.S. real property holding corporation, and paragraph (h) provides rules regarding certain notification requirements applicable to corporations.

(b) U.S. real property holding corporation. *(1) In general.* A corporation is a U.S. real property holding corporation if the fair market value of the U.S. real property interests held by the corporation on any applicable determination date equals or exceeds 50 percent of the sum of the fair market values of its—

(i) U.S. real property interests;

(ii) Interests in real property located outside the United States; and

(iii) Assets other than those described in subdivision (i) or (ii) of this paragraph (b)(1) that are used or held for use in its trade or business.

See paragraphs (d) and (e) of this section for rules regarding the directly and indirectly held assets that must be included in the determination of whether a corporation is a U.S. real property holding corporation. The term "interest in real property located outside the United States" means an interest other than solely as a creditor (as defined in § 1.897-1(d)) in real property (as defined in § 1.897-(b)) that is located outside the United States or the Virgin Islands. If a corporation qualifies as a U.S. real property holding corporation on any applicable determination date after June 18, 1980, any interest in it shall be treated as a U.S. real property interest for a period of five years from that date, unless the provisions of paragraph (f)(2) of this section are applicable.

(2) Alternative test. (i) In general. The fair market value of a corporation's U.S. real property interests shall be presumed to be less than 50 percent of the fair market value of the aggregate of its assets described in paragraphs (d) and (e) of this section if on an applicable determination date the total book value of the U.S. real property interests held by the corporation is 25 percent or less of the book value of the aggregate of the corporation's assets described in paragraphs (d) and (e) of this section.

(ii) Definition of book value. For purposes of this section and § 1.897-1(e) the term "book value" shall be defined as follows. In the case of assets that are held directly by the corporation, the term means the value at which an item is carried on the financial accounting records of the corporation, if such value is determined in accordance with generally accepted accounting principles applied in the United States. In the case of assets of which a corporation is treated as holding a pro rata share pursuant to paragraphs (e)(2) and (3) of this section and § 1.897-1(e), the term "book value" means the corporation's share of the value at which the asset is carried on the financial accounting records of the entity that directly holds the asset, if such value is determined in accordance with generally accepted accounting principles applied in the United States. For purposes of this paragraph (b)(2)(ii), an entity need not keep all of its books in accordance with U.S. accounting principles, so long as the value of the relevant assets is determined in accordance therewith.

(iii) Denial of presumption. If the Internal Revenue Service determines, on the basis of information as to the fair market values of a corporation's assets, that the presumption allowed by this paragraph (b)(2) may not accurately reflect the status of the corporation, the Service will notify the corporation that it may not rely upon the presumption. The Service will provide a written notice to the corporation that sets forth the general grounds for the Service's conclusion that the presumption may be inaccurate. By the 90th day following the date on which the corporation receives the Service's notification, the corporation must determine whether on its most recent determination date it was a U.S. real property holding corporation pursuant to the general rule set forth in paragraph (b)(1) of this section and must notify the Service of its determination. If the corporation determines that it was not a U.S. real property holding corporation pursuant to the general rule, then the corporation may upon future determination dates rely upon the presumption allowed by this paragraph (b)(2), unless on the basis of additional information the Service again requests that the determination be made pursuant to the general rule. If the corporation determines that it was a U.S. real property holding corporation on its most recent determination date, then by the 180th day following the date on which the corporation received the Service's notification the corporation (if a domestic corporation) must notify each holder of an interest in it that contrary to any prior representations it was a U.S. real property holding corporation as of its most recent determination date.

(iv) Applicability of penalties. A corporation that had previously relied upon the presumption allowed by this paragraph (b)(2) but that is determined to be a U.S. real property holding corporation shall not be subject to penalties for any incorrect notice previously given pursuant to the requirements of paragraph (h) of this section, if:

(A) The corporation in fact carried out the necessary calculations enabling it to rely upon the presumption allowed by this paragraph (b)(2); and

(B) The corporation complies with the provisions of paragraph (b)(2)(iii) of this section. However, a corporation shall remain subject to any applicable penalties if at the time of its reliance on the presumption allowed by this paragraph (b)(2) the corporation knew that the book value of relevant assets was substantially higher or lower than the fair market value of those assets and therefore had reason to believe that under the general test of paragraph (b)(1) of this section the corporation would probably be a U.S. real property holding corporation. Information with respect to the fair market value of its assets is known by a corporation if such information is included on any books and records of the corporation or its agent, is known by its directors or officers, or is known by employees who in the course of their employment have reason to know such information. A corporation relying upon the presumption allowed by this paragraph (b)(2) has no affirmative duty to determine the fair market values of assets if such values are not otherwise known to it in accordance with the preceding sentence. The rules of this paragraph (b)(2)(iv) may be illustrated by the following examples.

Example (1). DC is a domestic corporation engaged in light manufacturing that knows that it has foreign shareholders. On its December 31, 1985 determination date DC held assets used in its trade or business, consisting largely of recently-purchased equipment, with a book value of $500,000. DC's only real property interest was a factory that it had occupied for over 50 years, which had a book value of $200,000. The factory was located in a deteriorated downtown area, and DC had no knowledge of any facts indicating that the fair market value of the property was substantially higher than its book value. Therefore, DC was entitled to rely upon the presumption allowed by § 1.897-2(b)(2) and any incorrect statement pursuant to § 1.897-2(h) that arose out of such reliance would not give rise to penalties.

Example (2). The facts are the same as in Example 1, except as follows. By the time of DC's December 31, 1989 determination date, the downtown area in which DC's factory was located had become the subject of an extensive urban renewal program. On December 1, 1989, the president of DC was offered $750,000 for the factory by a developer who planned to convert the property into condominiums. Because DC thus had knowledge of the fair market value of its assets which made it clear that the corporation would probably be a U.S. real property holding corporation under the general rule of § 1.897-2(b)(1), DC was not entitled to rely upon the presumption allowed by § 1.897-2(b)(2) after December 1, 1989, and any false statements arising out of such reliance thereafter would give rise to penalties.

(v) Effect on interest-holders and related persons. For the effect on interest holders and related persons of reliance on a statement issued by a corporation that made a determination as to whether it was a U.S. real property holding corporation under the provisions of § 1.897-2(b), see §§ 1.897-2(g)(1)(ii)(A) and 1.897-2(g)(2)(ii).

(c) Determination dates for applying U.S. real property holding corporation test. *(1) In general.* Whether a corporation is a U.S. real property holding corporation is to be determined as of the following dates:

(i) The last day of the corporation's taxable year;

(ii) The date on which the corporation acquires any U.S. real property interest;

(iii) The date on which the corporation disposes of an interest in real property located outside the United States or disposes of other assets used or held for use in a trade or business during the calendar year, subject to the provisions of paragraph (c)(2)(i) of this section; and

(iv) In the case of a corporation that is treated pursuant to paragraph (d)(4) or (5) of this section as owning a portion of the assets held by an entity in which the corporation directly or indirectly holds an interest, the date on which that entity either (A) acquires a U.S. real property interest, (B) disposes of an interest in real property located outside the United States or (C) disposes of other assets used or held for use in a trade or business during the calendar year, subject to the provisions of paragraph (c)(2)(ii) of this section. A determination that is triggered by a transaction described in subdivision (ii), (iii), or (iv) of this paragraph (c)(1) must take such transaction into account. However, the first determination of a corporation's status need not be made until the 120th day after the later of the date of incorporation or of the date on which the corporation first acquires a shareholder. In addition, no determination of a corporation's status need be made during the 12-month period beginning on the date on which a corporation adopts a plan of complete liquidation, provided that all the assets of the corporation (other than assets retained to meet claims) are distributed within such period.

(2) Transactions not requiring a determination. (i) Transactions by corporation. Notwithstanding the provisions of paragraph (c)(1) of this section, a determination of U.S. real property holding corporation status need not be made on the date of:

(A) A corporation's disposition of inventory or livestock (as described in § 1.897-1(f)(1)(i)(A) and (C));

(B) The satisfaction of accounts receivable arising from the disposition of inventory or livestock or from the performance of services;

(C) The disbursement of cash to meet the regular operating needs of the business (e.g., to acquire inventory or to pay wages and salaries);

(D) A corporation's disposition of assets used or held for use in a trade or business (other than inventory or livestock) not in excess of a limitation amount determined in accordance with the rules of subdivision (iii) of this paragraph (c)(2); or

(E) A corporation's acquisition of U.S. real property interests not in excess of a limitation amount determined in accordance with the rules of subdivision (iii) of this paragraph (c)(2).

(ii) Transactions by entity other than corporation. Notwithstanding the provisions of paragraph (c)(1)(iv) or (c)(2)(v) of this section, in the case of a corporation that is treated as owning a portion of the assets held by an entity in which the corporation directly or indirectly holds an interest, a determination of U.S. property holding corporation status need not be made on the date of:

(A) The entity's disposition of inventory or livestock (as described in § 1.897-1(f)(1)(i)(A) and (C));

(B) The satisfaction of accounts receivable arising from the entity's disposition of inventory or livestock or from the performance of personal services;

(C) The entity's disbursement of cash to meet the regular operating needs of its business (e.g. to acquire inventory or to pay wages and salaries);

(D) The entity's disposition of assets used or held for use in a trade or business (other than inventory or livestock) not in excess of a limitation amount determined in accordance with the rules of subdivision (iii) of this paragraph (c)(2); or

(E) The entity's acquisition of U.S. real property interests not in excess of a limitation amount determined in accordance with the rules of subdivision (iii) of this paragraph (c)(2).

(iii) Calculation of limitation amount. The amount of assets used or held for use in a trade or business that may be disposed of, and the amount of U.S. real property interests that may be acquired, by a corporation or other entity without triggering a determination date shall be calculated in accordance with the following rules:

(A) If, in accordance with the provisions of paragraphs (d) and (e) of this section, a corporation on its most recent determination date was considered to hold U.S. real property interests having a fair market value that was less than 25 percent of the aggregate fair market value of all the assets it was considered to hold, then the applicable limitation amount shall be 10 percent of the fair market value of all trade or business assets or all U.S. real property interests (as applicable) held directly by the corporation or by another entity described in paragraph (c)(1)(iv) of this section on that determination date.

(B) If, in accordance with the provisions of paragraphs (d) and (e) of this section, a corporation on its most recent determination date was considered to hold U.S. real property interests having a fair market value that was equal to or greater than 25 and less than 35 percent of the aggregate fair market value of all the assets it was considered to hold, then the applicable limitation amount shall be 5 percent of the fair market value of all trade or business assets or all U.S. real property interests (as applicable) held directly by the corporation or by another entity described in paragraph (c)(1)(iv) of this section on that determination date.

(C) If, in accordance with the provisions of paragraphs (d) and (e) of this section, a corporation on its most recent determination date was considered to hold U.S. real property interests having a fair market value that was equal to or greater than 35 percent of the aggregate fair market value of all the assets it was considered to hold, then the applicable limitation amount shall be 2 percent of the fair market value of all trade or business assets or all U.S. real property interests (as applicable) held directly by the corporation or by another entity described in paragraph (c)(1)(iv) of this section on that determination date.

(D) If a corporation is not a U.S. real property holding corporation under the alternative test of paragraph (b)(2) of this section (relating to the book value of the corporation's assets), then the applicable limitation shall be 10 percent of the book value of all trade or business assets or all U.S. real property interests (as applicable) held directly by the corporation or by another entity described in paragraph (c)(1)(iv) of this section on the most recent determination date.

Dispositions or acquisitions by the corporation or other entity of assets having a value less than the applicable limitation amount must be cumulated by the corporation or entity making such dispositions or acquisitions, and a determination must be made on the date of a transaction that causes the total of either type to exceed the applicable limitation. Once a determination is triggered by a transaction that causes the applicable limitation to be exceeded, the computation of the amount of trade or business assets disposed of or real property interests required after that date shall begin again at zero.

The rules of this paragraph (c)(2) may be illustrated by the following examples.

Example (1). DC is a domestic corporation, no class of stock of which is regularly traded on an established securities market, that knows that it has several foreign shareholders. As of December 31, 1984, DC holds U.S. real property interests with a fair market value of $500,000, no real property interests located outside the U.S. and other assets used in its trade or business with a fair market value of $1,600,000. Thus, the fair market value of DC's U.S. real property interests ($500,000) is less than 25% ($525,000) of the total ($2,100,000) of DC's U.S. real property interests ($500,000), interests in real property located outside the United States (zero), and assets used or held for use in a trade or business ($1,600,000). DC is not a U.S. real property holding corporation, and under the rule of paragraph (c)(2)(i) of this section it may dispose of trade or business assets with a fair market value equal to 10 percent ($160,000) of the total fair market value ($1,600,000) of such assets held by it on its most recent determination date (December 31, 1984), without triggering a determination of its U.S. real property holding corporation status. Therefore, when DC disposes of $60,000 worth of trade or business assets (other than inventory or livestock) on March 1, 1985, and again on April 1, 1985, no determination of its status is required on either date. However, when DC disposes of a further $60,000 worth of such trade or business assets on May 1, its total dispositions of such assets ($180,000) exceeds its applicable limitation amount, and DC is therefore required to determine its U.S. real property holding corporation status. On May 1, 1985, the fair market value of DC's U.S. real property interests ($500,000) is greater than 25 percent ($480,000) and less than 35 percent ($672,000) of the total ($1,920,000) of DC's U.S. real property interests ($500,000), interests in real property located outside the United States (zero), and assets used or held for use in a trade or business ($1,420,000). DC is still not a U.S. real property holding corporation, but must now compute its applicable limitation amount as of the May 1 determination date. Under the rule of paragraph (c)(2)(iii)(B) of this section. DC could now dispose of trade or business assets other than inventory or livestock with a total fair market value equal to 5 percent of the fair market value of all trade or business assets held by DC on the May 1 determination date. Therefore, disposition of such trade or business assets with a fair market value of more than $71,000 (5 percent of $1,420,000) will trigger a further determination date for DC.

Example (2). DC is a domestic corporation, no class of stock of which is regularly traded on an established securities market, that knows that it has several foreign shareholders. As of December 31, 1986, DC's only assets are a U.S. real property interest with a fair market value of $300,000 other assets used or held for use in its trade or business with a fair market value of $600,000, and a 50 percent partnership interest in domestic partnership DP. DC's interest in DP constitutes a percentage ownership interest in the partnership of 50 percent, and pursuant to the rules of paragraph (e)(2) of this section DC is treated as owning a portion of the assets of DP determined by multiplying that percentage by the fair market value of DP's assets. As of December 31, 1986, DP's only assets are U.S. real property interests with a fair market value of $120,000 and other assets used in its trade or business with a fair market value of $380,000. As of its December 31, 1986, determination date, the fair market value ($360,000) of the U.S. real property interests DC holds ($300,000) and is treated as holding ($80,000 [The fair market value of DP's U.S. real property interest ($120,000) multiplied by DC's percentage ownership interest in DP (50 percent)]), is equal to 31 percent of the sum of the fair market values ($1,150,000) of the U.S. real property interests DC holds and is treated as holding ($360,000) DC's interest in real property located outside the United States (zero), and assets used or held for use in a trade or business that DC holds or is treated as holding ($790,000 [$600,000 (held directly) plus $190,000 (DC's 50 percent share of assets used or held for use in a trade or business by DP)]). Thus, under the rules of paragraph (c)(2)(i) and (iii)(B) of this section DC may dispose of assets used or held for use in its trade or business with a fair market value equal to 5 percent ($30,000) of the total fair market value ($600,000) of such assets held directly by it on its most recent determination date (December 31, 1986), without triggering a determination of its U.S. real property holding corporation status. In addition, under the rules of paragraph (c)(2)(ii) and (iii)(A) of this section, a determination date for DC would not be triggered by DP's disposition of trade or business assets (other than inventory or livestock) with a fair market value equal to 5 percent ($19,000) of the total fair market value ($380,000) of such assets held by it as of DC's most recent determination date (December 31, 1986). However, any disposition of such assets by DP exceeding that limitation would trigger a determination of DC's U.S. real property holding corporation status. In addition under the rule of paragraph (c)(1)(iv) of this section, any disposition of a U.S. real property interest by DP would trigger a determination date for DC, while under the rule of paragraph (c)(2)(ii) of this section no disposition of inventory or livestock by DP would trigger a determination for DC.

(3) Alternative monthly determination dates. (i) In general. Notwithstanding the provisions of paragraph (c)(1) and (2) of this section, a corporation may choose to determine its U.S. real property holding corporation status in accordance with the rules of this paragraph (c)(3). In the case of a corporation that has determined that it is not a U.S. real property holding corporation pursuant to the alternative test of paragraph (b)(2) of this section (relating to the book value of the corporation's assets), the rules of this paragraph (c)(3) may be applied by using book values rather than fair market values in all relevant calculations.

(ii) Monthly determinations. A corporation that determines its U.S. real property holding corporation status in accordance with the rules of this paragraph (c)(3) must make a determination at the end of each calendar month.

(iii) Transactional determinations. A corporation that determines its U.S. real property holding corporation status in accordance with the rules of this paragraph (c)(3) must make a determination as of the date on which, pursuant to a single transaction (consisting of one or more transfers):

(A) U.S. real property interests are acquired, and/or

(B) Interests in real property located outside the U.S. and/or assets used or held for use in a trade or business are disposed of, if the total fair market value of the assets acquired and/or disposed of exceeds 5 percent of the sum of the fair market values of the U.S. real property interests, interests in real property located outside the U.S., and assets used or held for use in a trade or business held by the corporation.

(iv) Exceptions. Notwithstanding any other provision of this paragraph (c)(3), the first determination of a corporation's status need not be made until the 120th day after the later of the date of incorporation or the date on which the corporation first acquires a shareholder. In addition, no determination of a corporation's status need be made during the 12-month period beginning on the date on which a corporation adopts a plan of complete liquidation, if all the assets of the corporation (other than assets retained to meet claims) are distributed within such period.

(4) Valuation date methods. (i) In general. For purposes of determining whether a corporation is a U.S. real property holding corporation on any applicable determination date, the fair market value of the assets held by the corporation (in accordance with § 1.897-2(d)) as of that determination date must be used.

(ii) Alternative valuation date method for determination dates other than the last day of the taxable year. For purposes of paragraph (c)(4)(i) of this section, if an applicable determination date under paragraph (c)(1), (2), or (3) of this section is other than the last day of the taxable year, property may be valued as of the later of the last day of the previous taxable year or the date such property was acquired. For purposes of the determination date that falls on the last day of the taxable year, fair market value as of that date must always be used.

(iii) Consistent methods. The valuation date method selected under this paragraph (c)(4) for the first determination date in a taxable year must be used for all subsequent determination dates for such year. In addition, the valuation date method selected must be used for all property with respect to which the determination is made. The use of one method for one taxable year does not preclude the use of the other method for any other taxable year.

(5) Illustrations. The rules of this paragraph (c) are illustrated by the following examples:

Example (1). Nonresident alien individual C purchased 100 shares of stock of domestic corporation K on July 26, 1965. Although K has additional shares of common stock outstanding, its stock has never been traded on an established securities market. At all times during calendar year 1985, K's only assets were a parcel of U.S. real estate (parcel A) and a parcel of country Z real estate (parcel B). On December 31, 1985, the fair market value of parcel A was $1,000,000 and the fair market value of parcel B was $2,000,000. For purposes of determining whether K was a U.S. real property holding corporation during 1985, the only applicable determination date was December 31, 1985, because K did not make any acquisitions or dispositions described in paragraph (c)(1) of this section during the year. The test of paragraph (b) of this section is applied using the fair market value of the property held on that date. K was not a U.S. real property holding corporation during 1985 because as of December 31, 1985, the fair market value ($1,000,000) of the U.S. real property interests held by K did not equal or exceed 50 percent ($1,500,000) of the sum ($3,000,000) of the fair market value of K's U.S. real property interest ($1,000,000), the interests in real property located outside the United States ($2,000,000), plus other assets used or held for use by K in a trade or business (zero).

Example (2). The facts are the same as in example (1), except that on April 7, 1986, K purchased another parcel of U.S. real estate for $2,000,000. K's purchase of real property on April 7 triggered a determination on that date. As provided in paragraph (c)(3)(ii) of this section, K chooses to use the value of parcels A and B as of the previous December 31, while newly acquired parcel C must be valued as of its acquisition on April 7, 1986. On that date, K qualifies as a U.S. real property holding corporation, since the fair market value of its U.S. real property interests ($3,000,000) exceeds 50 percent ($2,500,000) of the sum ($5,000,000) of the fair market value of K's U.S. real property interests ($3,000,000), its interests in real property located outside the U.S. ($2,000,000), and its other assets used or held for use in a trade or business (zero).

(d) Assets held by a corporation. The assets that must be included in the determination of whether a corporation is a U.S. real property holding corporation are the following:

(1) U.S. real property interests that are held directly by the corporation (including directly-held interests in foreign corporations that are treated as U.S. real property interests pursuant to the rules of paragraph (e)(1) of this section);

(2) Interests in real property located outside the United States that are held directly by the corporation;

(3) Assets used or held for use in a trade or business that are held directly by the corporation;

(4) A proportionate share of assets held through a partnership, trust, or estate pursuant to the rules of paragraph (e)(2) of this section; and

(5) A proportionate share of assets held through a domestic or foreign corporation in which a corporation holds a controlling interest, pursuant to the rules of paragraph (e)(3) of this section.

(e) Special rules regarding assets held by a corporation. *(1) Interests in foreign corporations.* For purposes only of determining whether any corporation is a U.S. real property holding corporation, an interest in a foreign corporation shall be treated as a U.S. real property interest unless it is established that the interest was not a U.S. real property interest under the rules of this section on the applicable determination date. The rules of paragraph (g)(2) of this section must be complied with to establish that the interest is not a U.S. real property interest. However, regardless of whether an interest in a foreign corporation is treated as a U.S. real property interest for this purpose, gain or loss from the disposition of an interest in such corporation will not be treated as effectively connected with the conduct of a U.S. trade or business by reason of section 897(a). The rules of this paragraph (e)(1) are illustrated by the following examples. In each example, fair market value is determined as of the applicable determination dates under paragraph (c)(4)(i) of this section.

Example (1). Nonresident alien individual F holds all of the stock of domestic corporation DC. DC's only assets are 40 percent of the stock of foreign corporation FC, with a fair market value of $500,000, and a parcel of country W real estate, with a fair market value of $400,000. Foreign corporation FP, unrelated to DC, holds the other 60 percent of the stock of FC. FC's only asset is a parcel of U.S. real estate with a fair market value of $1,250,000. FC is a U.S. real property holding corporation because the fair market value of its U.S. real property interests ($1,250,000) exceeds 50 percent ($625,000) of the sum of the fair market values of its U.S. real property interests ($1,250,000), its interests in real property located outside the United States (zero), plus its other assets used or held for use in a trade or business (zero). Consequently DC's interest in FC is treated as a U.S. real property interest under the rules of this paragraph (e)(1). DC is a U.S. real property holding corporation because the fair market value ($500,000) of its U.S. real property interest (the stock of FC) exceeds 50 percent ($450,000) of the sum ($900,000) of the fair market value of its U.S. real property interests ($500,000), its interests in real property located outside the United States ($400,000), plus its other assets used or held for use in a trade or business (zero). If F disposes of her stock within 5 years of the current determination date, her gain or loss on the disposition of her stock in DC will be treated as effectively connected with a U.S. trade or business under section 897(a). However, FP's gain on the disposition of its FC stock would not be subject to the provisions of section 897(a) because the stock of FC is a U.S. real property interest only for purposes of determining whether DC is a U.S. real property holding corporation.

Example (2). Nonresident alien individual B holds all of the stock of domestic corporation US. US's only assets are 40 percent of the stock of foreign corporation FC1. Nonresident alien individual N, unrelated to US, holds the other 60 percent of FC1's stock. FC1's only assets are 40 percent of the stock of foreign corporation FC2. The remaining 60 percent of the stock of FC2 is owned by nonresident alien individual X, who is unrelated to FC1. FC2's only asset is a parcel of U.S. real estate with fair market value of $1,000,000. FC2, therefore, is a U.S. real property holding corporation, and the stock of FC2 held by FC1 is a U.S. real property interest for purposes of determining whether FC1 is a U.S. real property interest for purposes of determining whether US is a U.S. real property holding corporation (but not for purposes of treating FC1's gain from the disposition of FC2 stock as effectively connected with a U.S. trade or business under section 897(a)). As all of FC1's assets are U.S. real property interests, the stock of FC1 held by US is a U.S. real property holding corporation (but not for purposes of subjecting N's gain on the disposition of FC1 stock to the provisions of section 897(a)). As US is a domestic corporation and as all of its assets are U.S. real property interests, US is a U.S. real property holding corporation, and the stock of US held by B is a U.S. real property interest for purposes of section 897(a)). Therefore, B's gain or loss upon the disposition of the stock of US within 5 years of the most recent determination date is subject to the provisions of section 897(a).

(2) Proportionate ownership of assets held by partnerships, trusts, and estates. For purposes of determining whether a corporation is a U.S. real property holding corporation, a holder of an interest in a partnership, a trust, or an estate (whether domestic or foreign) shall be treated pursuant to section 897(c)(4)(B) as holding a proportionate share of the assets held by the entity.

However, a holder of an interest shall not be treated as holding a proportionate share of assets that in the hands of the entity are subject to the rule of § 1.897-1(f)(3)(ii) (concerning the trade or business assets of investment companies). Such proportionate share is to be determined in accordance with the rules of § 1.897-1(e) on each applicable determination date. The interest in the entity shall itself be disregarded when a proportionate share of the entity's assets is attributed to the interest-holder pursuant to the rule of this paragraph (e)(2). Any asset treated as held by a holder of an interest by reason of this paragraph (e)(2) which is used or held for use in an trade or business by the partnership, trust, or estate shall be treated as so used or held for use by the holder of the interest. The proportionate ownership rule of this paragraph (e)(2) applies successively upward through a chain of ownership. The proportionate ownership rule of this paragraph (e)(2) is illustrated by the following examples. In each example fair market value is determined as of the applicable determination date under paragraph (c)(4)(i) of this section.

Example (1). Nonresident alien individual F holds all of the stock of domestic corporation DC. DC is a partner in foreign partnership FP, and DC's percentage ownership interest in FP is 50 percent. DC's other assets are a parcel of country F real estate with a fair market value of $500,000 and other assets which it uses in its business with a fair market value of $100,000, FP's assets are a parcel of country Z real estate with a fair market value of $300,000 and a parcel of U.S. real estate with a fair market value of $2,000,000. For purposes of determining whether DC is a U.S. real property holding corporation, DC is treated as holding its pro rata share of the assets held by FP. DC's pro rata share of the U.S. real estate held by FP is $1,000,000, determined by multiplying the fair market value ($2,000,000) of the U.S. real property interests held by FP by DC's percentage ownership interest in FP (50 percent). DC's pro rata share of the country Z real estate held by FP is $150,000, determined in the same manner. DC is a U.S. real property holding corporation because the fair market value ($1,000,000) of its U.S. real property interests (the U.S. real estate it is treated as holding proportionately) exceeds 50 percent ($875,000) of the sum ($1,750,000) of the fair market value of its U.S. real property interests ($1,000,000), its interests in real property located outside the United States [($650,000) (its country F real estate and its pro rata share of the country Z real estate)], plus its other assets which are used or held for use in a trade or business ($100,000). Because DC is a domestic U.S. real property holding corporation, the stock of DC is a U.S. real property interest and F's gain or loss on the disposition of this DC stock within 5 years of the current determination date will be treated as effectively connected with a U.S. trade or business under section 897(a).

Example (2). Nonresident alien individual B holds all of the stock of domestic corporation US. US is a beneficiary of foreign trust FT. US's percentage ownership interest in FT is 90 percent. US has no other assets. FT is a partner in domestic partnership DP. FT's percentage ownership interest in DP is 30 percent. FT has no other assets. DP's only asset is a parcel of U.S. real estate with a fair market value of $1,000,000. FT is treated as holding U.S. real estate with a fair market value of $300,000 (30 percent of the U.S. real estate held by DP with a fair market value of $1,000,000). For purposes of determining whether US is a U.S. real property holding corporation, the proportionate ownership rule is applied successively upward through the chain of ownership. Thus, US is treated as holding 90 percent of FT's $300,000 pro rata share of the U.S. real estate held by DP. US is a U.S. real property holding corporation because the fair market value ($270,000) of its U.S. real property interests (its pro rata share of the U.S. real estate held by DP) exceeds 50 percent ($135,000) of the sum of the fair market values of its U.S. real property interests ($270,000), its interests in real property located outside the United States (zero), plus its other assets used or held for use in a trade or business (zero). Because US is a domestic U.S. real property holding corporation, the stock of US is a U.S. real property interest, and B's gain or loss from the disposition of US stock within 5 years of the current determination date will be treated as effectively connected with a U.S. trade or business under section 807(a).

(3) Controlling interests in corporations. For purposes only of determining whether a corporation is a U.S. real property holding corporation, if the corporation (the "first corporation") holds a controlling interest in a second corporation—

(i) The first corporation is treated as holding a proportionate share of each asset (i.e., U.S. real property interests, interests in real property located outside the United States, and assets used or held for use in a trade or business) held by the second corporation, determined in accordance with the rules of § 1.897-1(e);

(ii) Any asset so treated as held proportionately by the first corporation which is used or held for use by the second corporation in a trade or business shall be treated as so used or held for use by the first corporation; and

(iii) Interests in the second corporation held by the first corporation are not themselves taken into account as U.S. real property interests (regardless of whether the second corporation is a U.S. real property holding corporation) or as trade or business assets. However, the first corporation shall not be treated as holding a proportionate share of assets that in the hands of the second corporation are subject to the rules of § 1.897-1(f)(3)(ii) (concerning the trade or business assets of investment companies). A determination of what portion of the assets of the second corporation are considered to be held by the first corporation shall be made as of the applicable dates for determining whether the first corporation is a U.S. real property holding corporation. A "controlling interest" means 50 percent or more of the fair market value of all classes of stock of the corporation, determined as of the applicable determination date. In determining whether a corporation holds a controlling interest in another corporation, section 318(a) shall apply (except that sections 318(a)(2)(C) and (3)(C) are applied by substituting the phrase "5 percent" for "50 percent"). However, a corporation that does not directly hold any interest in a second corporation shall not be treated as holding a controlling interest in the second corporation by reason of the application of section 318(a)(3)(C). The rules of this paragraph (e)(3) apply successively upward through a chain of ownership. For example, if the second corporation owns a controlling interest in a third corporation, the rules of this paragraph shall be applied first to determine the portion of the assets of the third corporation that is considered to be held by the second corporation and then to determine the portion of the assets held and considered to be held by the second corporation that is considered to be held by the first corporation. The controlling interest rules of this paragraph (e)(3) apply, regardless of whether a corporation is domestic or foreign, whenever it is necessary to determine whether a corporation is a U.S. real property holding corporation. The rules of this paragraph (e)(3) are illustrated by the following examples. In each example fair market value is determined as of the applicable determination date under paragraph (c)(4)(i) of this section and no corporation holds constructively any interest not specified in the example.

Example (1). Nonresident alien individual N owns all of the stock of domestic corporation DC. DC's only assets are 60 percent of the fair market value of all classes of stock of foreign corporation FS and 60 percent of the fair market value of all classes of stock of domestic corporation DS. The percentage ownership interest of DC in each of FS and DS is 60 percent. The balance of the stock in FS and DS is held by nonresident alien individual B, who is unrelated to DC. FS's only asset is a parcel of country F real estate with a fair market value of $1,000,000. DS's only asset is a parcel of U.S. real estate with a fair market value of $2,000,000. The value of DC stock in FS and DS is not taken into account for purposes of determining whether DC is a U.S. real property holding corporation. Rather, because DC holds a controlling interest (60 percent) in each of FS and DS, DC is treated as holding a portion of each asset held by FS and DS. DC's portion of the country F real estate held by FS is $600,000, determined by multiplying the fair market value ($1,000,000) of the country F real estate by DC's percentage ownership interest (60 percent). Similarly, DC's portion of the U.S. real estate held by DS is $1,200,000 (60 percent of $2,000,000). DC is a U.S. real property holding corporation, because the fair market value ($1,200,000) of its U.S. real property interests (its portion of the U.S. real estate) exceeds 50 percent ($900,000) of the sum ($1,800,000) of the fair market values of its U.S. real property interests ($1,200,000), its interests in real property located outside the United States (the $600,000 portion of country F real estate), plus its other assets used or held for use in a trade or business (zero). Because DC is a domestic U.S. real property holding corporation, the stock of DC is a U.S. real property interest, and N's gain or loss on the disposition of DC stock within 5 years of the current determination date would be treated as effectively connected with a U.S. trade or business under section 897(a).

Example (2). (i) Nonresident alien individual F owns all of the stock of domestic corporation US1. US1's only asset is 85 percent of the fair market value of all classes of stock of domestic corporation US2. US2's only assets are 60 percent of the fair market value of all classes of stock of domestic corporation US3, with a fair market value of $600,000, and a parcel of country D real estate with a fair market value of $800,000. US3's only asset is a parcel of U.S. real estate with a fair market value of $2,000,000. The percentage ownership interest of F in US1 is 100 percent.

Although US1 owns 85 percent of the stock of US2, US1's percentage ownership interest in US2 is 75 percent, because US2 has other interests other than solely as a creditor outstanding. US2's percentage ownership interest in US3 is 60 percent.

(ii) US2 holds a controlling interest in US3, since it holds more than 50 percent of the fair market value of all classes of stock of US3. Consequently, the value of US2's stock in US3 is not taken into account in determining whether US2 is a U.S. real property holding corporation, even though US3 is a U.S. real property holding corporation. Instead, US2 is treated as holding a portion of the U.S. real estate held by US3. US2's portion of the U.S. real estate is $1,200,000, determined by multiplying US2's percentage ownership interest (60 percent) by the fair market value ($2,000,000) of the U.S. real estate. US1 holds a controlling interest in US2 (75 percent.). By reapplying the rules of paragraph (e)(3) of this section successively upward through the chain of ownership, US1's stock in US2 is not taken into account, and US1 is treated as holding a portion of the country D real estate held by US2 and the U.S. real estate which US2 is treated as holding proportionately. US1's portion of the country D real estate is $600,000, determined by multiplying US1's percentage ownership interest (75 percent) by the fair market value ($800,000) of the country D real estate. US1's portion of the U.S. real estate which US2 is treated as owning is $900,000, determined by multiplying US1's percentage ownership interest (75 percent) by the fair market value ($1,200,000) of US2's portion of U.S. real estate held by US3. US1 is a U.S. real property holding corporation, because the fair market value ($900,000) of its U.S. real property interests (its portion of US2's portion of U.S. real estate) is more than 50 percent ($750,000) of the sum ($1,500,000) of fair market values of its U.S. real property interests ($900,000), its interests in real property located outside the United States ($800,000), plus its other assets need or held for use in a trade or business (zero). Because US1 is a U.S. real property holding corporation and is a domestic corporation, the stock of US1 is a U.S. real property interest, and F's gain or loss on the disposition of US1 stock within 5 years of the current determination date will be treated as effectively connected with a U.S. trade or business under section 897(a).

Example (3). Nonresident alien individual B holds all of the stock of domestic corporation DC. DC's only assets are 40 percent of the fair market value of all classes of stock of foreign corporation FC and a parcel of country R real estate with a fair market value of $100,000. FC's only asset is one parcel of U.S. real estate with a fair market value of $1,000,000. The fair market value of the FC stock held by DC is $200,000. FC is a U.S. real property holding corporation. Since DC does not hold a controlling interest in FC, the controlling interest rules of paragraph (e)(3) of this section do not apply to treat DC as holding a portion of the U.S. real estate held by FC. However, because FC is a U.S. real property holding corporation, the stock of FC is a U.S. real property interest for purposes of determining whether DC is a U.S. real property holding corporation because the fair market value ($200,000) of its U.S. real property interest (the stock of FC) exceeds 50 percent ($150,000) of the sum ($300,000) of the fair market values of its U.S. real property interest ($200,000), its interests in real property located outside the United States ($100,000), plus its other assets used or held for use in a trade or business (zero). Because DC is a U.S. real property holding corporation and is a domestic corporation, its stock is a U.S. real property interest, and B's gain or loss on the disposition of DC stock within 5 years of the current determination date would be subject to the provisions of section 897(a).

Example (4). Nonresident alien individual C owns all of the stock of domestic corporation DC1. DC1's only assets are 25 percent of the fair market value of all classes of stock of domestic corporation DC2, and a parcel of U.S. real estate with a fair market value of $100,000. The stock of DC2 is not an asset used or held for use in DC1's trade or business. DC2's only assets are a building located in the U.S. with a fair market value of $100,000 and manufacturing equipment and inventory with a fair market value of $200,000, DC2 is not a U.S. real property holding corporation. Since DC1 does not hold a controlling interest in DC2, the rules of this paragraph (e)(3) do not apply to treat DC1 as holding a portion of the assets held by DC2. In addition, since DC2 is not a U.S. real property corporation, its stock does not constitute a U.S. real property interest. Therefore, for purposes of determining whether DC1 is a real property holding corporation, its interest in DC2 is not taken into account. Since DC1's only other asset is a parcel of U.S. real estate, DC1 is a U.S. real property holding corporation, and

C's gain or loss on the disposition of DC1 stock within 5 years of the current determination date would be subject to the provisions of section 897(a).

(4) Co-application of rules of this paragraph (e). The rules of this paragraph (e) apply in conjunction with one another for purposes of determining whether a corporation is a U.S. real property holding corporation. The rule of this paragraph (e)(4) is illustrated by the following example. In the example fair market value is determined as of the applicable determination date in accordance with paragraph (c)(4)(i) of this section.

Example. Nonresident alien individual B holds 100 percent of the stock of domestic corporation US. US's only asset is 10 percent of the stock of foreign corporation FC1. FC1's only asset is 100 percent of the stock of foreign corporation FC2. FC2's only asset is a 50 percent interest in domestic partnership DP. FC2's percentage ownership interest in DP is 50 percent. DP's only asset is a parcel of U.S. real estate with a fair market value of $10,000,000. In determining whether US is a U.S. real property holding corporation, the rules of this paragraph (e) apply in conjunction with one another. Consequently, under paragraph (e)(2) of the section FC2 is treated as holding U.S. real estate with a fair market value of $5,000,000 (50 percent of $10,000,000, its pro rata share of real estate held by DP). Under paragraph (e)(3) of this section, FC1 is treated as holding 100 percent of the assets of FC2 (U.S. real estate with a fair market value of $5,000,000). FC1, therefore, is a U.S. real property holding corporation. Under paragraph (e)(1) of this section, the stock of FC1 is treated as U.S. real property interest. US is a U.S. real property holding corporation because 100 percent of its assets (the stock of FC1) are U.S. real property interests. As US is a U.S. real property holding corporation and is a domestic corporation, the stock of US is a U.S. real property interest, and B's gain or loss from the disposition of stock of US within 5 years of the current determination date will be subject to the provisions of section 897(a).

(f) Termination of U.S. real property holding corporation status. *(1) In general.* A U.S. real property holding corporation may voluntarily determine its status as of the date of any acquisition or disposition of assets. If the fair market value of its U.S. real property interests on such date no longer equals or exceeds 50 percent of the fair market value of all assets described in paragraphs (d) and (e) of this section, such corporation shall cease to be U.S. real property holding corporation as of such date, and on the day that is five years after such date interests in such corporation shall cease to be treated as U.S. real property interests (unless subsequent transactions within the five-year period have caused the fair market value of the corporation's U.S. real property interests to equal or exceed 50 percent of the fair market value of assets described in paragraphs (d) and (e) of this section). A corporation that determines that interests in it have ceased to be U.S. real property interests pursuant to the rules of this paragraph (f) may so inform the Internal Revenue Service, as provided in paragraph (h) of this section.

(2) Early termination. Interests in a U.S. real property holding corporation shall immediately cease to be U.S. real property interests as of the first date on which the following conditions are met—

(i) The corporation does not hold any U.S. real property interests, and

(ii) All of the U.S. real property interests directly or indirectly held by such corporation at any time during the previous five years (but disregarding any disposed of before June 19, 1980) either (A) were directly of indirectly disposed of in transactions in which the full amount of the gain (if any) was recognized or (B) ceased to be U.S. real property interests by reason of the application of this paragraph (f) to one or more other corporations. For purposes of this paragraph (f)(2), a corporation that disposes of all U.S. real property interests other than a lease that has a fair market value of zero will be considered to have disposed of all of its U.S. real property interests, provided that the leased property is used in the conduct by the corporation of a trade or business in the United States. Such a lease may include an option to renew, but only if such option is for a renewal at fair market rental rates prevailing at the time of renewal.

(g) Establishing that a corporation is not a U.S. real property holding corporation. *(1) Foreign persons disposing of interests.* (i) In general. A foreign person disposing of an interest in a domestic corporation (other than an interest solely as a creditor) must establish that the interest was not a U.S. real property interest as of the date of disposition, either by:

(A) Obtaining a statement from the corporation pursuant to the provisions of subdivision (ii) of this paragraph (g)(1), or

(B) Obtaining a determination by the Commissioner, Small Business/Self Employed Division (SB/SE) pursuant to the provisions of subdivision (iii) of this paragraph (g)(1). If the foreign person does not establish by either method that the interest disposed of was not a U.S. real property interest then the interest shall be presumed to have been a U.S. real property interest the disposition of which is subject to section 897(a). See paragraph (g)(3) of this section for certain exceptions to this rule. It should be noted that the rules of this section relate solely to interests in a corporation that are interests other than solely as a creditor. Therefore, a statement by a corporation or a determination by the Commissioner (under paragraphs (g) or (h) of this section) that an interest is not a U.S. real property interest depends solely upon whether or not the corporation was a U.S. real property holding corporation during the period described in section 897(c)(1)(A)(ii) (subject to certain special rules). The determination of whether an interest is one solely as a creditor is made under the rules of § 1.897-1(d).

(ii) Statement from corporation. (A) In general. A foreign person disposing of an interest in a domestic corporation may establish that the interest was not a U.S. real property interest as of the date of the disposition by requesting and obtaining from the corporation a statement that the interest was not a U.S. real property interest as of that date. However, a corporation's statement shall not be valid for purposes of this rule, and thus may not be relied upon for purposes of establishing that an interest was not a U.S. real property interest, unless the corporation complies with the notice requirements of paragraph (h)(2) or (h)(4) of this section. A foreign person that requests and obtains such a statement is not required to forward the statement to the Internal Revenue Service and is not required to take any further action to establish that the interest disposed of was not a U.S. real property interest. To qualify under this rule, the foreign person must obtain the corporation's statement no later than the date, including any extensions, on which a tax return would be due with respect to a disposition. A foreign person that relies in good faith upon a statement from the corporation is not thereby excused from filing a return and paying any taxes and interest due thereon if the corporation's statement is later found to have been incorrect. However, such reliance shall be taken into account in determining whether the foreign person shall be subject to any penalty for the previous failure to file. However, a foreign person that knew or had reason to know that a corporation's statement was incorrect is not entitled to rely upon such statement and shall remain liable for all applicable penalties.

(B) Coordination with section 1445. Pursuant to section 1445 and regulations thereunder, withholding of tax is not required with respect to a foreign person's disposition of an interest in a domestic corporation, if the transferee is furnished with a statement by the corporation under paragraph (h) of this section that the interest is not a U.S. real property interest. A foreign person that obtains a corporation's statement for that purpose prior to the date of disposition may also rely upon the statement for purposes of this paragraph (g)(h)(ii), unless the corporation informs the foreign person (pursuant to paragraph (h)(1)(iv)(C) of this section) that it became a U.S. real property holding corporation after the date of the notice but prior to the actual date of disposition.

(iii) Determination by Commissioner. (A) In general. A foreign person disposing of an interest in a domestic corporation may establish that the interest was not a U.S. real property interest as of the date of disposition by requesting and obtaining a determination to that effect from the Commissioner. Such a determination may be requested pursuant to the provisions of subdivision (B) or (C) of this paragraph (g)(1)(iii). A request for a determination should be addressed to: Commissioner, Small Business/Self Employed Division (SB/SE); S C3-413 NCFB, 500 Ellin Road, Lanham, MD 20706. A foreign transferor who has requested a determination by the Commissioner pursuant to the rules of this paragraph (g)(1)(iii) is not thereby excused from filing a return and paying any tax due by the date, including any extensions, on which such return and payment would otherwise be due with respect to a disposition. If the Commissioner subsequently determines and notifies the foreign transferor that the interest was not a U.S. real property interest, the foreign transferor shall be entitled to a refund of any taxes, penalties, and interest paid by reason of the application of section 897(a) pursuant to the rules of paragraph (g)(1)(i) of this section, together with any interest otherwise due on such refund, if a claim for refund is made within the applicable time limits.

(B) Determination based on Commissioner's information. A foreign person may request that the Commissioner make a determination based on information contained in the Director's records, if:

(1) The foreign person made a request to the corporation for information as to the status of its interest no later than the 90th day before the date, including any extensions, on which a tax return would otherwise be due with respect to a disposition, and

(2) The corporation failed to respond to such request by the 30th day following the date the request was delivered to the corporation. If the Commissioner is unable to make a determination based on information available to him, he shall inform the foreign person that the interest must be treated as a U.S. real property interest unless the person subsequently obtains either the necessary statement from the corporation or a determination pursuant to subdivision (C) of this paragraph (g)(1)(iii).

(C) Determination based on information supplied by foreign person. A foreign person may request that the Commissioner make a determination based on information supplied by the foreign person. Such information may be drawn, for example, from annual reports, financial statements, or records of the corporation, and must establish to the satisfaction of the Commissioner that the foreign person's interest was not a U.S. real property interest as of the date of disposition.

(D) Determination by Commissioner on his own motion. Notwithstanding any other provision of this section, a foreign person shall not treat the disposition of an interest in a domestic corporation as a disposition of a U.S real property interest if such person is notified that the Commissioner has upon his own motion determined that the interest was not a U.S. real property interest as of the date of disposition.

(2) Corporations determining U.S. real property holding corporation status. (i) In general. A corporation that must determine whether it is a U.S. real property holding corporation, and that holds an interest in another corporation (other than a controlling interest as defined in paragraph (e)(3) of this section), must determine whether or not that interest was a U.S. real property interest as of its own determination date, by either:

(A) Obtaining a statement from the second corporation pursuant to the provisions of subdivision (ii) of this paragraph (g)(2);

(B) Obtaining a determination by the Commissioner pursuant to the provisions of subdivision (iii) of this paragraph (g)(2); or

(C) Making an independent determination pursuant to the provisions of subdivision (iv) of this paragraph (g)(2).

A corporation that is unable to determine by any of the above methods whether its interest in a second corporation is a U.S. real property interest must presume that such interest is a U.S. real property interest.

(ii) Statement from corporation. A corporation may determine whether or not an interest in a second corporation was a U.S. real property interest as of its own determination date by obtaining from the second corporation's a statement that the interest was not a U.S. real property interest as of that date. However, the second corporation statement shall not be valid for purposes of this rule, and thus may not be relied upon for purposes of establishing that an interest was not a U.S. real property interest, unless such corporation complies with the notice requirements of paragraph (h)(2) or (h)(4) of this section.

(iii) Determination by Commissioner. (A) In general. A corporation may determine whether or not an interest in a second corporation was a U.S. real property interest as of its own determination date by requesting and obtaining a determination to that effect from the Commissioner. Such a determination may be requested pursuant to the provisions of subdivision (B) or (C) of this paragraph (g)(2)(iii). A request for a determination must be addressed to: Commissioner, Small Business/Self Employed Division SB/SE); S C3-413 NCFB, 500 Ellin Road, Lanham, MD 20706. A corporation that has requested a determination by the Commissioner pursuant to the provisions of this paragraph is not thereby excused from taking any action required by section 897 or 1445 by the date on which such action would otherwise be due. However, the Commissioner may grant a reasonable extension of time for the satisfaction of any requirement if the Commissioner is satisfied that the corporation has not sought a determination pursuant to this paragraph (g)(2)(iii) for a principal purpose of delay.

(B) Determination based on Commissioner's information. A corporation may request that the Commissioner make a determination based on information contained in the Director's records, if:

(1) The corporation made a request to the second corporation for information as to the status of its interest no later than the fifth day following the first corporation's determination date, and

(2) The second corporation failed to respond to such request by the 30th day following the date the request was delivered to the second corporation. Pending his resolution of such a request, the Commissioner will generally grant an extension with respect to the change-of-status notification that may otherwise be required pursuant to paragraph (h)(1)(ii) of this section. If the Director is unable to make a determination based on information available to him, he shall inform the corporation that the interest must be treated as a U.S. real property interest unless the corporation subsequently obtains either the necessary statement from the second corporation or a determination pursuant to paragraph (g)(2)(iii)(C) or (g)(2)(iv) of this section.

(C) Determination based on information supplied by corporation. A corporation may request that the Commissioner make a determination based on information supplied by the corporation. Such information may be drawn, for example, from annual reports, financial statements, or records of the second corporation, and must establish to the satisfaction of the Commissioner that the interest in the second corporation was not a U.S. real property interest as of the first corporation's determination date.

(D) Determination by Commissioner on his own motion. Notwithstanding any other provision of this section, a corporation shall not treat an interest in a second corporation as a U.S. real property interest if the corporation is notified that the Commissioner has upon his own motion determined that the interest in the second corporation is not a U.S. real property interest.

(iv) Independent determination by corporation. A corporation may independently determine whether or not an interest in a second corporation was a U.S. real property interest as of the first corporation's own determination date. Such determination must be based upon the best evidence available, drawn from annual reports, financial statements, records of the second corporation, or from any other source, that demonstrates to a reasonable certainty that the interest in the second corporation was not a U.S. real property interest. A corporation that makes an independent determination pursuant to this paragraph (g)(2)(iv) shall be subject to the special notification rule of paragraph (h)(1)(iii)(D) of the section. If the Commissioner subsequently determines that the corporation's independent determination was incorrect, the corporation shall be subject to penalties for any past failure to comply with the requirements of section 897 or 1445 only if the corporation's determination was unreasonable in view of facts that the corporation knew or had reason to know.

(3) Requirements not applicable. If at any time during the calendar year any class of stock of a corporation is regularly traded on an established securities market, the requirements of this paragraph (g) shall not apply with respect to any holder of an interest in such corporation other than a person who holds an interest described in § 1.897-1(c)(2)(iii)(A) or (B). For example, a corporation determining whether it is a U.S. real property holding corporation need not ascertain from a regularly traded corporation in which it neither holds, nor has held during the period described in section 897(c)(1)(A)(ii), more than a 5 percent interest whether that regularly traded corporation is itself a U.S. real property holding corporation. In addition, the requirements of this paragraph (g) do not apply to any holder of an interest in a domestically-controlled RETT (REIT), as defined in section 897(h)(4)(B).

(h) Notice requirements applicable to corporations. *(1) Statement to foreign interest-holder.* (i) In general. A domestic corporation must, within a reasonable period after receipt of a request from a foreign person holding an interest in it, inform that person whether the interest constitutes a U.S. real property interest. No particular form is required for this statement, which need only indicate the corporation's determination. The statement must be dated and signed by a responsible corporate officer who must verify under penalties of perjury that the statement is correct to his knowledge and belief.

(ii) Required determination. For purposes of the statement required by paragraph (h)(1)(i) of this section, an interest in a corporation is a U.S. real property interest if the corporation was a U.S. real property holding corporation on any determination date during the 5-year period ending on the date specified in the interest-holder's request, or on the date such request was received if no date is specified (or during such shorter period ending on the date that is applicable pursuant to section 897(c)(1)(A)(ii). However, an interest in a corporation is not a U.S. real property interest if such interest is excluded under section 897(c)(1)(B).

(2) Notice to the Internal Revenue Service. If a foreign interest holder requests that a domestic corporation provide a statement described in paragraph (h)(1) of this section, then such corporation must provide a notice to the Internal Revenue Service in accordance with this paragraph (h)(2). No particular form is required for such notice, but the following must be provided:

(i) A statement that the notice is provided pursuant to the requirements of § 1.897-2(h)(2);

(ii) The name, address, and identifying number of the corporation providing the notice;

(iii) The name, address, and identifying number (if any) of the foreign interest holder that requested the statement (this information may be omitted from the notice if fully set forth in the statement to the foreign interest holder attached to the notice).

(iv) Whether the interest in question is a U.S. real property interest;

(v) A statement signed by a responsible corporate officer verifying under penalties of perjury that the notice (including any attachments thereto) is correct to his knowledge and belief. A copy of any statement provided to the foreign interest holder must be attached to the notice. The notice must be mailed to the Director, Philadelphia Service Center, P.O. Box 21086, Drop Point 8731, FIRPTA Unit, Philadelphia, PA 19114-0586 on or before the 30th day after the statement referred to in § 1.897-2(h)(1) is mailed to the interest holder that requested it. Failure to mail such notice within the time period set forth in the preceding sentence will cause the statement provided pursuant to § 1.897-2(h)(1) to become an invalid statement.

(3) Requirements not applicable. The requirements of this paragraph (h) do not apply to domestically-controlled REITs, as defined in section 897(h)(4)(B). These requirements also do not apply to a corporation any class of stock in which is regularly traded on an established securities market at any time during the calendar year. However, such a corporation may voluntarily choose to comply with the requirements of paragraph (h)(4) of this section.

(4) Voluntary notice to Internal Revenue Service. (i) In general. A domestic corporation which determines that it is not a U.S. real property holding corporation—

(A) on each of the applicable determination dates in a taxable year, or

(B) pursuant to section 897(c)(1)(B), may attach to its income tax return for that year a statement informing the Internal Revenue Service of its determination. A corporation that has provided a voluntary notice described in this § 1.897-2(h)(4)(i) for the immediately preceding taxable year and that does not have an event described in § 1.897-2(c)(1)(ii), (iii) or (iv) prior to receiving a request from a foreign person under § 1.897-2(h)(1), is exempt from the notice requirement of § 1.897-2(h)(2).

(ii) Early termination of real property holding corporation status. A corporation that determines during the course of its taxable year that interests in it have ceased to be U.S. real property interests pursuant to the rules of section 897(c)(1)(B) may, on the day of its determination or thereafter, provide a statement to the Director, Philadelphia Service Center, P.O. Box 21086, Drop Point 8731, FIRPTA Unit, Philadelphia, PA 19114-0586, informing the Service of its determination. No particular form is required but the statement must set forth the corporation's name, address, identification number, a brief statement regarding its determination and the date such determination was made. Such statement will enable foreign interest-holders to dispose of their interests without being subject to section 897(a), as provided in paragraph (g) of this section.

(5) Supplemental statements. (i) By corporations with substantial intangible assets. A corporation that is subject to the requirements of paragraph (h)(2) of this section (or that voluntarily complies with the requirements of paragraph (h)(4) of this section) must submit a supplemental statement to the Internal Revenue Service if—

(A) Such corporation values any of the intangible assets described in § 1.897-1(f)(1)(ii) (other than goodwill or going concern value) by a method other than the purchase price or book value methods described in § 1.897-1(o)(4); and

(B) The fair market value of such intangible assets equals or exceeds 25 percent of the total of the fair market values of the assets the corporation is considered to hold in accordance with the provisions of paragraphs (d) and (e) of this section.

The supplemental statement must inform the Internal Revenue Service that the corporation meets the criteria of subdivisions (A) and (B) of this paragraph (h)(5)(i), and must summarize the methods and calculations upon which the corporation's determination of the fair market value of its intangible assets is based. In addition, the supplemental statement must list any intangible assets that were purchased from any person that have been valued by the corporation at an amount other than their purchase price, and must provide a justification for such a departure from the purchase price. The supplemental statement must be attached to or incorporated in the statement provided under paragraph (h)(2) or (h)(4) of this section.

(ii) Corporation not valuing goodwill or going concern value at purchase price. A corporation that is subject to the requirements of paragraph (h)(2) of this section (or that voluntarily complies with the requirements of paragraph (h)(4) of this section) must submit a supplemental statement to the Internal Revenue Service if such corporation values goodwill or going concern value pursuant to § 1.897-1(o)(4)(iii). The supplemental statement must set forth that it is made pursuant to this paragraph (h)(5)(ii), and must summarize the methods and calculations upon which the corporation's determination of the fair market value of such intangible assets is based. In addition, the supplemental statement must list any such assets that were purchased from any person that have been valued by the corporation at an amount other than their purchase price, and must provide a justification for such a departure from the purchase price. The supplemental statement must be attached to or incorporated in the statement provided under paragraph (h)(2) or (h)(4) of this section.

(iii) Corporation using alternative U.S. real property holding corporation test. A corporation that is subject to the requirements of paragraph (h)(2) of this section (or that voluntarily complies with the requirements of paragraph (h)(4) of this section) must submit a supplemental statement to the Internal Revenue Service if—

(A) Such corporation utilizes the rule of paragraph (b)(2) of this section (regarding the book values of assets held by the corporation) to presume that it is not a U.S. real property holding corporation; and

(B) Such corporation is engaged in or is planning to engage in a trade or business of mining, farming, or forestry, or of buying and selling or developing real property, or of leasing real property to tenants.

The supplemental statement must inform the Internal Revenue Service that the corporation meets the criteria of subdivisions (A) and (B) of this paragraph (h)(5)(iii), and must be attached to or incorporated in the statement provided under paragraph (h)(2) or (h)(4) of this section.

(iv) Corporation determining real property holding corporation status of second corporation. A corporation that is subject to the requirements of paragraph (h)(2) of this section (or that voluntarily complies with the requirements of paragraph (h)(4) of this section) must submit a supplemental statement to the Internal Revenue Service if such corporation independently determines whether or not an interest in a second corporation is a U.S. real property interest, pursuant to paragraph (g)(2)(iv) of this section. The supplemental statement must set forth that it is made pursuant to this paragraph (h)(5)(iv) and must briefly summarize the facts upon which the corporation's determination is based and the sources of the information relied upon by the corporation. The supplemental statement must be attached to or incorporated in the statement provided under paragraph (h)(2) or (h)(4) of this section.

(i) Transition Rules. *(1) General waiver of penalties for failure to file.* If a foreign person disposed of an interest in a domestic corporation between June 18, 1980 and January 23, 1987, and such person establishes under the rules of paragraph (g) of this section at any time that the interest disposed of was not a U.S. real property interest, then such person shall not be subject to tax under section 897 and shall not be subject to penalties (or interest) for failure to file an income tax return with respect to such disposition.

(2) Foreign persons that met the requirements of prior regulations. A foreign person that disposed of an interest in a domestic corporation between June 18, 1980 and January 23, 1987, shall be deemed to have satisfied the requirements of paragraph (g) of this section with respect to such disposition if such person established under prior temporary or prior final regulations issued under section 897 that the interest disposed of was not a U.S. real property interest.

T.D. 7999, 12/26/84, amend T.D. 8113, 12/18/86, T.D. 9082, 8/4/2003.

§ 1.897-3 Election by foreign corporation to be treated as a domestic corporation under section 897(i).

(a) Purpose and scope. This section provides rules pursuant to which a foreign corporation may elect under section 897(i) to be treated as a domestic corporation for purposes of sections 897, 1445, and 6039C and the regulations thereunder. A foreign corporation with respect to which an election under section 897(i) is in effect is subject to all rules under section 897 and 1445 that apply to domestic corporations. Thus, for example, if a foreign corporation that has made an election under section 897(i) is a U.S. real property holding corporation, interests in it are U.S. real property interests that are subject to withholding under section 1445, and any gain or loss from the disposition of such interests by a foreign person will be treated as effectively connected with a U.S. trade or business under section 897(a). Similarly, if a foreign corporation makes an election under section 897(i), its distribution of a U.S. real property interest pursuant to section 301 will be subject to the carryover basis rule of section 897(f). However, an interest in an electing corporation is not a U.S. real property interest if following the election the interest is described in section 897(c)(1)(B) or § 1.897-1(c)(2) (subject to the exceptions of subdivisions (i) and (ii) of that section). In addition, section 897(d) will not apply to any distribution of a U.S. real property interest by such corporation or to any sale or exchange of such interest pursuant to a plan of complete liquidation under section 337. A foreign corporation that makes an election under section 897(i) shall not be treated as a domestic corporation for purposes of any other provision of the Code or regulations, except to the extent that it is required to consent to such treatment as a condition to making the election. For further information concerning the effect of an election under section 897(i) upon the withholding requirements of section 1445, see § 1.1445-7. An election under section 897(i) is the exclusive remedy of any foreign person claiming discriminatory treatment under any treaty with respect to the application of sections 897, 1445, and 6039C to a foreign corporation. Therefore, if a corporation does not make an effective election, relief under a nondiscrimination article of any treaty shall not be otherwise available with respect to the application of sections 897, 1145, and 6039C to such corporation.

(b) General conditions. A foreign corporation may make an election under section 897(i) only if it meets all three of the following conditions.

(1) Holding a U.S. real property interest. The foreign corporation must hold a U.S. real property interest at the time of the election. This condition is satisfied when a U.S. real property interest is acquired simultaneously with the effective date of an election. For example, this condition is satisfied when real property is acquired in an exchange described in section 351 that is carried out simultaneously with the effective date of the election. This condition is also satisfied by a corporation that indirectly holds a U.S. real property interest through a partnership, trust, or estate.

(2) Entitlement to nondiscriminatory treatment. The foreign corporation must be entitled to nondiscriminatory treatment with respect to its U.S. real property interest under any treaty to which the United States is a party. Where the corporation indirectly holds a U.S. real property interest through a partnership, trust, or estate, the corporation itself must be entitled to nondiscriminatory treatment with respect to such property interest.

(3) Submission of election in proper form. The foreign corporation must comply with the requirements of paragraph (c) of this section respecting the manner and form in which an election must be submitted.

(c) Manner and form of election. An election under section 897(i) is made by filing the materials described in subparagraphs (1) through (5) of this paragraph (c) with the Director, Philadelphia Service Center, P.O. Box 21086, Drop Point 8731, FIRPTA Unit, Philadelphia, PA 19114-0586. The required items may be incorporated in a single document.

(1) General statement. The foreign corporation must supply a general statement indicating that an election under section 897(i) is being made. The general statement must be signed by a responsible corporate officer, who must verify under penalty of perjury that the statement and all other documents submitted pursuant to the requirements of this paragraph (c) are true and correct to his knowledge and belief. No particular form is required for the statement, which must contain all the following information—

(i) The name, address, identifying number, and place and date of incorporation of the foreign corporation;

(ii) The treaty and article under which the foreign corporation is seeking nondiscriminatory treatment;

(iii) A description of the U.S. real property interests held by the corporation, either directly or through a partnership, trust, or estate, including the dates such interests were acquired, the corporation's adjusted bases in such interests, and their fair market values as of the date of the election (or book values if the corporation is not a U.S. real property holding corporation under the alternative test of § 1.897-2(b)(2)); and

(iv) A list of all dispositions of any interests in the foreign corporation after December 31, 1979, and before June 19, 1980, between related persons (as defined in section 453(f)(1)), giving the type and the amount of any interest transferred, the name and address of the related person to whom the interest was transferred, the transferor's basis in the interest transferred, and the amount of any nontaxed gain as defined in section 1125(d) of Pub. L. 96-499.

(2) Waiver of treaty benefits. The foreign corporation must submit a binding waiver of the benefits of any U.S. treaty with respect to any gain or loss from the disposition of a U.S. real property interest during the period in which the election is in effect.

(3) Consent to be taxed. The foreign corporation must submit a binding agreement to treat as though it were a domestic corporation any gain or loss that is recognized upon—

(i) The disposition of any U.S. real property interest during the period in which the election is in effect, and

(ii) The disposition of any property that it acquired in exchange for a U.S. real property interest in a nonrecognition transaction (as defined under section 897(e)) during the period in which the election is in effect.

(4) Interest-holders' consent to election. (i) In general. The foreign corporation must submit both a signed consent to the making of the election and a waiver of U.S. treaty benefits with respect to any gain or loss from the disposition of an interest in the corporation from each person who holds an interest in the corporation on the date the election is made. In the case of a corporation any class of stock of which is regularly traded on an established securities market at any time during the calendar year, the signed consent and

waiver need only be provided by a person who holds an interest described in § 1.897-1(c)(2)(iii)(A) or (B) (determined after application of the constructive ownership rules of section 897(c)(6)(C). The foreign corporation must also include with the signed consents and waivers a list that identifies and describes the interest in the corporation held by each interest holder, including the type and amount of such interest and its fair market value as of the date of the election.

(ii) Corporation's retention of interest-holders' consents. A corporation need not file the consents and waivers of its interest-holders as required by paragraph (c)(4)(i) of this section, if it instead complies with the requirements of subdivisions (A) through (D) of this paragraph (c)(4)(ii).

(A) The corporation must place a legend on each outstanding certificate for shares of its stock that reads substantially as follows: "(Name of corporation) has made an election under section 897(i) of the United States Internal Revenue Code to be treated as a U.S. corporation for certain tax purposes, and any purchaser of this interest may therefore be required to withhold tax at the time of the purchase." The corporation must certify that the foregoing requirement has been met and that it will place an equivalent legend on every stock certificate that is issued while the election under section 897(i) is in effect and the corporation retains the consents and waivers of its interest-holders under the rules of this paragraph (c)(4)(ii). However, with respect to any registered certificate issued prior to January 30, 1985, in lieu of placing a legend on the certificate the corporation may certify that it will provide the purchaser of the interest with a copy of the legend at the time the certificate is surrendered for issuance of a new certificate.

(B) The corporation must include with its election a statement that the corporation has received both a signed consent to the making of the election and a waiver of U.S. treaty benefits with respect to any gain or loss from the disposition of an interest in the corporation from each person who holds an interest in the corporation on the date the election is made. In the case of a corporation any class of stock of which is regularly traded on an established securities market at any time during the calendar year, the signed consent and waiver need only be provided by a person who holds or has held an interest described in § 1.897-1(c)(2)(iii)(A) or (B) (determined after application of the constructive ownership rules of section 897(c)(6)(C).

(C) The corporation must include with its election a list that describes the interests in the corporation held by each interest-holder. The list need not identify the interest-holders by name, but must set forth the type, amount, and fair market value of the interests held by each.

(D) The corporation must include with its election an agreement that the corporation will retain all signed consents and waivers for a period of three years from the date of the election and supply such documents to the Director within 30 days of his request for production thereof. The Director's review of the signed consents and waivers pursuant to this provision shall not constitute an examination for purposes of section 7605(b).

(5) Statement regarding prior dispositions. The foreign corporation must state that no interest in the corporation was disposed of during the shortest of (A) the period from June 19, 1980, through the date of the election, (B) the period from the date on which the corporation first holds a U.S. real property interest through the date of the election or (C) the five-year period ending on the date of the election. If the corporation cannot state that no such dispositions have been made, it may make the section 897(i) election only if it states that it has complied with the requirements of paragraph (d)(2) of this section.

(d) Time and duration of election. *(1) In general.* A foreign corporation that meets the conditions of paragraph (b) of this section may make an election under section 897(i) at any time before the first disposition of an interest in the corporation which would be subject to section 897(a) if the election had been made before that disposition, except as otherwise provided in paragraph (d)(2) of this section. The period to which the election applies begins on the date on which the election is made, or such earlier date as is specified in the election, but not earlier than June 19, 1980. Unless revoked, an election applies for the duration of the time for which the corporation remains in existence. An election is made on the date that the statements described in paragraph (c) of this section are delivered to the Philadelphia Service Center. If the election is delivered by United States mail, the provisions of section 7502 and the regulations thereunder shall apply in determining the date of delivery.

(2) Election after disposition of stock. An election under section 897(i) may be made after any disposition of an interest in the corporation which would have been subject to section 897(a) if the election had been made before that disposition, but only if the requirements of either subdivision (i) or (ii) of this paragraph (d)(2) are met with respect to all dispositions of interests during the period described in paragraph (c)(5) of this section.

(i) There is a payment of an amount equal to any taxes which would have been imposed by reason of the application of section 897 upon all persons who had disposed of interests in the corporation during the period described in paragraph (c)(5) of this section had the corporation made the election prior to such dispositions. Such payment must be made by the later of the date the election is made, or the date on which payment of such taxes would otherwise have been due, and must include any interest that would have accrued had tax actually been due with respect to the disposition. As an election made prior to any disposition of interests in the corporation would have been conditioned on a waiver of treaty benefits by the interest-holders, payment of an amount equal to tax and any interest with respect to such prior disposition is required as a condition to making a subsequent election under this subdivision (i) irrespective of the application of any treaty provision. For this purpose, it is not necessary that the payment be made by the person who would have owned the tax if the election under this section had been made prior to the disposition, and that person is under no obligation to supply any information to the present holders of interests in the electing corporation. The payment shall be made to the U.S. Treasury. Where the payment is made by a present holder of an interest, the basis of the person's interest in the corporation shall be increased to the extent of the amount paid.

(ii) Each person that acquired an interest in the electing corporation took a basis in the interest that was equal to the basis of the interest in the hands of the person from which the interest was acquired, increased by the sum of any gain recognized by the transferor of the interest and any tax paid under chapter 1 by the person that acquired the interest, if such interest was acquired after June 18, 1980.

(3) Adequate proof of basis. For purposes of meeting the conditions of paragraph (d)(2)(i) or (ii) of this section, a corporation must establish the bases of and amount of gain realized by all persons who disposed of interests in the corporation during the period described in paragraph (c)(5) of this

section. See paragraph (g)(3) of this section for an exception to this rule.

(4) Acknowledgment of receipt. Within 60 days after its receipt of an election under section 897(i), the Internal Revenue Service will acknowledge receipt of the election. Such acknowledgment either will indicate that the information submitted with the election is complete or will specify any documents that remain to be submitted pursuant to the requirements of paragraph (c) of this section respecting the manner and form in which an election must be made.

(e) Anti-abuse rule. *(1) In general.* A corporation that is otherwise eligible to make an election under section 897(i) may do so only by complying with the requirements of subdivision (2) of this paragraph, if during the period described in paragraph (c)(5) of this section—

(i) Prior to receipt of a U.S. real property interest by the corporation seeking to make the election, stock in such corporation (or in any corporation controlled by such corporation) was acquired in a transaction in which the person acquiring such stock obtained an increase in basis in the stock over the adjusted basis of the stock in the hands of the person from whom it was acquired;

(ii) The full amount of gain realized by the person from whom the stock was acquired was not subject to U.S. tax; and

(iii) The corporation seeking to make the election received the U.S. real property interest in a transaction or series of transactions to which section 897(d)(1)(B) or (e)(1) applies to allow for nonrecognition of gain.

(2) Recognition of gain. A corporation described in subparagraph (1) of this paragraph (e) may make an election under section 897(i) only if it pays an amount equal to the tax on the full amount of gain realized by the transferors of the stock of such corporation (or of any corporation controlled by it) in the transaction described in paragraph (e)(1)(i) of this section. However, such amount must be paid only if the stock of the corporation seeking to make the election (or the stock of a corporation controlled by it) would have constituted a U.S. real property interest had it (or a corporation controlled by it) made the election before that acquisition. Such amount must be paid by the later of the date of the election or the date on which such tax would otherwise be due, and must include any interest that would have accrued had tax actually been due with respect to the disposition.

(3) Definition of control. For purposes of this paragraph, a corporation controls a second corporation if it holds 80 percent or more of the total combined voting power of all classes of stock entitled to vote, and 80 percent or more of the total number of shares of all other classes of stock of the second corporation. In a chain of corporations where each succeeding corporation is controlled within the meaning of this subparagraph (3) by the corporation immediately above it in the chain, each corporation in the chain shall be considered to be controlled by all corporations that preceded it in the chain.

(4) Examples. The rules of this paragraph (e) are illustrated by the following examples.

Example (1). Nonresident alien individual X owns 100 percent of the stock of foreign corporation L which was organized in 1981. L's only asset is a parcel of U.S. real property which it has held since 1981. The fair market value of the U.S. real property held by L on January 1, 1984, is $1,000,000. L's basis in the property is $200,000. X's basis in the L stock is $500,000. On June 1, 1984, M corporation, a foreign corporation owned by foreign persons who are unrelated to X, purchases the stock of L from X for $1,000,000 with title passing outside of the United States. Since the stock of L is not a U.S. real property interest, X's gain from the disposition of the L stock ($500,000) is not treated as effectively connected with a U.S. trade or business under section 897(a). In addition, since X was neither engaged in a U.S. trade or business nor present in the U.S. at any time during 1984, such gain is not subject to U.S. tax under section 871. On January 1, 1987, M liquidates L under a plan of liquidation adopted on that same date. Under section 332 of the Code M recognizes no gain on receipt of the parcel of U.S. real property distributed by L in liquidation. Under section 334(b)(1) M takes $200,000 as its basis in the U.S. real property received from L. Under section 897(d)(1)(B) no gain would be recognized to L under section 897(d)(1)(A) on the liquidating distribution. As a consequence, no gain is recognized to L under section 336 of the Code. After its receipt of the U.S. real property from L, M seeks to make an election to be treated as a domestic corporation. Thus, M acquired the L stock in a transaction in which it obtained a basis in such stock in excess of the adjusted basis of X in the stock, U.S. tax was not paid on the full amount of the gain realized by X, and M has received the property in a distribution to which section 897(d)(1)(B) applied to provide for nonrecognition of gain to L. Therefore, M may make the election only if it pays an amount equal to the tax on the full amount of X's gain, pursuant to the rule of subparagraph (e)(2) of this section.

Example (2). Nonresident alien individual X owns 100 percent of the stock of foreign corporation A which owns 100 percent of the stock of foreign corporation B. X's basis in the A stock is $500,000. A's basis in the B stock is $500,000. B owns U.S. real property with a fair market value of $1,000,000. B's basis in the U.S. real property is $500,000. On January 1, 1985, X sells the stock of A to Y, an unrelated individual, for $1,000,000 with title passing outside of the United States. In addition, X was neither engaged in a U.S. trade or business nor present in the U.S. at any time during 1985. Since the A stock is not a U.S. real property interest, X's gain on such disposition is not treated as effectively connected with a U.S. trade or business under section 897(a) and is therefore not subject to U.S. tax under section 871. On July 1, 1987, a plan of liquidation is adopted, and B is liquidated into A. Under sections 332, 334(b)(1), 336, and 897(d)(1)(B), there is no tax to A on receipt of U.S. real property from B and no tax to B on the distribution of the U.S. real property interest to A. After receipt of the property A seeks to make an election under section 897(i). Under the rules of paragraph (e) of this section, A may make the election only if it pays an amount equal to the tax on the full amount of X's gain. (Assuming that A is a U.S. real property holding corporation, the same result would be required by the rule of paragraph (d)(2) of this section.)

(f) Revocation of election. *(1) In general.* An election under section 897(i) may be revoked only with the consent of the Commissioner. A request for revocation shall be in writing and shall be addressed to the Director, Philadelphia Service Center, P.O. Box 21086, Drop Point 8731, FIRPTA Unit, Philadelphia, PA 19114-0586. The request shall include the name, address, and identifying number of the corporation seeking to revoke the election, and a description of all U.S. real property interests held by the corporation on the date of the request for revocation, including the dates such interests were acquired, the corporation's adjusted bases in such interests, and their fair market values as of the date of the request (or book value if the corporation is not a U.S. real property holding corporation under the alternative test of § 1.897-2(b)(2)). The request shall be signed by a responsible officer of the corporation under penalty of perjury and shall contain a statement either that the corporation has made no distributions described in subparagraph (2) of this paragraph (f) or that the conditions of that subparagraph have been satisfied. A revocation will be effective as of the date the request is delivered to the Philadelphia Service Center, unless the Commissioner provides otherwise in his consent to the revocation. If the request is delivered by United States mail, the provisions of section 7502 and the regulations thereunder shall apply in determining the date of delivery. The Commissioner will generally consent to a revocation, provided either that there have been no distributions described in subparagraph (2) of this paragraph (f), or that the conditions of that subparagraph have been satisfied. Within 90 days after its receipt of a request to revoke an election under section 897(i), the Internal Revenue Service will acknowledge receipt of the request. Such acknowledgment either will indicate that the information submitted with the request is complete or will specify any information that remains to be submitted pursuant to the requirements of this paragraph (f).

(2) Revocation after distribution. If there have been any distributions of U.S. real property interests by the corporation during the period to which an election made under section 897(i) applies, the Commissioner shall consent to the revocation of such election only if one of the following conditions is met.

(i) The full amount of gain realized by the corporation upon the distribution was subject to U.S. income tax.

(ii) There is a payment of an amount equal to the taxes that would have been imposed upon the corporation by reason of the application of section 897 if the election had not been in effect on the date of the distribution. Such payment must be made by the later of the date of the request for revocation or the date on which payment of such tax would otherwise have been due, and must include any interest that would have accrued had tax actually been due with respect to the distribution. If under the terms of any treaty to which the United States is a party such distribution would not have been subject to U.S. income tax notwithstanding the provisions of section 897, then this condition may be satisfied by providing a statement with the request for revocation setting forth the treaty and article which would have exempted the distribution from U.S. tax had the election under section 897(i) not been in effect on the date thereof.

(iii) At the time of the receipt of the distributed property, the distributee would be subject to taxation under chapter 1 of the Code on a subsequent disposition of the distributed property, and the basis of the distributed property in the hands of the distributee is no greater than the adjusted basis of such property before the distribution, increased by the amount of gain (if any) recognized by the distributing corporation. For purposes of this paragraph (f)(2)(i)(C), a distributee shall be considered to be subject to taxation upon a subsequent disposition of distributed property only if such distributee waives the benefits of any U.S. treaty that would otherwise render such disposition not taxable by the United States. Such waiver must be attached to the corporation's request for revocation.

(g) Transitional rules. *(1) In general.* An election under section 897(i) that was made at any time after June 18, 1980, must be amended to comply with the requirements of paragraphs (b), (c), and (d) of this section. Such amendment must be delivered in writing to the Director, Philadelphia Service Center by [the date which is 3 months after the date of publication of this document in the FEDERAL REGISTER]. If the amendment is delivered by United States mail, the provisions of section 7502 and the regulations thereunder shall apply in determining the date of delivery. An election that is properly amended pursuant to the requirements of this section shall be effective as of the date of the original election.

(2) Corporations previously entitled to make election. A foreign corporation that would have been entitled under the rules of this section to make a section 897(i) election at any time between June 19, 1980, and January 30, 1985, may retroactively make such an election pursuant to the requirements of this section. Such election must be delivered to the Director, Foreign Operations District, by March 1, 1985.

(3) Interests in corporation disposed of prior to publication. Where interests in a corporation were disposed of before January 3, 1984, the requirement of paragraph (d)(2) of this section may be met, notwithstanding the requirement of paragraph (d)(3), by paying a tax that is based upon a reasonable estimate of the gain upon the prior dispositions. Such estimate must be based on all facts and circumstances known to, and ascertainable through the exercise of reasonable diligence by, the corporation seeking to make the election.

(h) Effective date. The requirement in paragraph (c)(1)(i) of this section that the statement making the section 897(i) election contain the identifying number of the foreign corporation (in all cases) is applicable November 3, 2003.

T.D. 7999, 12/26/84, amend T.D. 8113, 12/18/86, T.D. 9082, 8/4/2003.

§ 1.897-4AT Table of contents (temporary).

T.D. 8198, 5/4/88.

§ 1.897-5 Corporate distributions.

(a) through (d)(1)(iii)(E) [Reserved]. For further guidance, see § 1.897-5T(a) through (d)(1)(iii)(E).

(d)

(1)

(iii)

(F) Identification by name and address of the distributee or transferee, including the distributee's or transferee's taxpayer identification number;

(G) through (d)(4) [Reserved]. For further guidance, see § 1.897-5T(d)(1)(iii)(G) through (d)(4).

(e) Effective date. This section is applicable to transfers and distributions after November 3, 2003.

T.D. 9082, 8/4/2003.

§ 1.897-5T Corporate distributions (temporary).

Caution: The Treasury has not yet amended Reg § 1.897-5T to reflect changes made by P.L. 108-357, P.L. 104-191.

(a) Purpose and scope. This section provides rules concerning the recognition of gain or loss and adjustments to basis required with respect to certain corporate distributions that are subject to section 897. Paragraph (b) of this section provides rules concerning such distributions by domestic corporations, including distributions under section 301, distributions in redemption of stock, and distributions in liquidation. Paragraph (c) sets forth rules concerning distributions by foreign corporations, including distributions under sections 301 and 355, distributions in redemption of stock, and distributions in liquidation. Finally, various rules generally applicable to distributions subject to this section, as well as to transfers subject to § 1.897-6T, are set forth in paragraph (d). The rules contained in this section are also subject to the tax avoidance rules of § 1.897-6T(c).

(b) Distributions by domestic corporations. *(1) Limitation of basis upon dividend distribution of U.S. real property interest.* Under section 897(f), if any domestic corporation (distributing corporation) distributes a U.S. real property interest to a shareholder that is a foreign person (distributee) in a distribution to which section 301 applies, then the basis of the distributed U.S. real property interest in the hands of the foreign distributee shall be determined in accordance with the provisions of section 301(d), and shall not exceed—

(i) The adjusted basis of the property before the distribution in the hands of the distributing corporation, increased by

(ii) The sum of—

(A) Any gain recognized by the distributing corporation on the distribution, and

(B) Any U.S. tax paid by or on behalf of the distributee with respect to the distribution.

(2) Distributions by U.S. real property holding corporations which are taxable exchanges of stock under generally applicable rules. If a domestic corporation, stock in which is treated as a U.S. real property interest, distributes property with respect to such stock to a foreign shareholder, the distributee shall be treated as having disposed of a U.S. real property interest, and shall recognize gain or loss on the stock of such domestic corporation to the extent that, with respect to the distributees—

(i) Part of all of the distribution is treated pursuant to section 301(c)(3)(A) as a sale or exchange of stock;

(ii) Part or all of the distribution is treated pursuant to section 302(a) as made in part or full payment in exchange for stock; or

(iii) Part or all of the distribution is treated pursuant to section 331(a) as made in full payment in exchange for stock.

Stock in a domestic corporation shall not be considered a U.S. real property interest pursuant to the provisions of § 1.897-2(f)(2) if the corporation does not hold any U.S. real property interests and has disposed of all of its U.S. real property interests owned within the previous five years in transactions in which the full amount of gain was recognized under the rules of § 1.897-2(f)(2). If gain is recognized at the corporate level on either a distribution of a U.S. real property interest or a sale of a U.S. real property interest in a liquidation, such distribution or sale shall be considered a disposition for purposes of § 1.897-2(f)(2). With regard to the consequences of a distribution from a U.S. real property holding corporation under section 355(a), see § 1.897-6T(a)(1) and (4).

(3) Section 332 liquidations of U.S. real property holding corporations. (i) General rules. Exchanges that are subject to section 897(e) are normally covered by § 1.897-6T(a)(1), (2) and (3). This paragraph (b)(3) provides rules concerning the application of section 897(e) and the general principles of § 1.897-6T(a)(1), (2) and (3) to section 332 liquidations of U.S. real property holding corporations.

(ii) Distribution to a foreign corporation under section 332 after June 18, 1980, and before the repeal of the General Utilities doctrine. Except for distributions under paragraph (b)(3)(iii) of this section (relating to section 332 and former section 334(b)(2)), the rules of this paragraph (b)(3)(ii) shall apply to section 332 distributions after June 18, 1980, and before January 1, 1990, pursuant to section 336(a) as in effect prior to the effective dates of the amendments made by section 631 of the Tax Reform Act of 1986. A foreign corporation that meets the stock ownership requirements of section 332(b) with respect to stock in a domestic corporation that is a U.S. real property interest shall not, after December 31, 1984, be subject to taxation by reason of section 367(a). The foreign corporation shall recognize gain pursuant to section 897(e)(1) on such stock upon the receipt of property in a section 332(a) liquidation from such domestic corporation, but only to the extent that the property received constitutes property other than a U.S. real property interest. The gain on the stock in the domestic corporation to be recognized by the foreign corporation pursuant to section 897(e)(1) shall be determined by multiplying the gain realized on the distribution by a fraction. The numerator of the fraction shall be the fair market value of the property other than U.S. real property interests received by the foreign corporation on the distribution, and the denominator shall be the fair market value of all property received by the foreign corporation on the distribution. The bases of the distributed U.S. real property interests in the hands of the foreign corporation shall be the same as the bases in the hands of the domestic corporation. The bases of the property other than U.S. real property interests in the hands of the foreign corporation shall be the same as the bases in the hands of the domestic corporation, plus any gain recognized by the foreign corporation on the distribution allocated among such assets in proportion to the potential gain inherent in each such asset at the time of distribution. However, the basis of each asset is limited to its fair market value. Property, other than a U.S. real property interest that is distributed by the domestic corporation, shall not be considered to be distributed by the domestic corporation pursuant to a section 332 liquidation (that is, the foreign corporation shall not be considered to be a corporation for purposes of section 332) if the requirements of section 367(a) are not satisfied. See, for example, sections 1245(b)(3) and 1250(d)(3) regarding the consequences to the distributing domestic corporation if the requirements of section 367(a) are not satisfied.

(iii) Distribution to a foreign corporation under section 332 and former section 334(b)(2) after June 18, 1980. The rules of this paragraph (b)(2)(iii) shall apply to section 332 distributions after June 18, 1980 where the basis of the distributed property in the hands of the foreign corporation is determined under section 334(b)(2) as in effect prior to the Tax Equity and Fiscal Responsibility Act of 1982. A foreign corporation that meets the stock ownership requirements of section 332(b) with respect to stock in a domestic corporation that is a U.S. real property interest recognize gain on the receipt of property in a section 332(a) liquidation where section 334(b)(2) applies to the extent that the fair market value of the distributed assets that are not U.S. real property interests exceeds the basis of such assets determined under section 334(b)(2) (for example, if the liquidation does not occur immediately upon the purchase of stock in the domestic corporation). The gain recognized shall not exceed the excess of the fair market value of the stock of the domestic corporation in the hands of foreign at the time of the distribution over the shareholder's adjusted basis in such stock. The basis of the distributed U.S. real property interests in the hands of the foreign corporation shall be determined under section 334(b)(2), by reference to the adjusted basis of the stock with respect to which the distribution was made. The basis of such property other than U.S. real property interests shall be tentatively determined under section 334(b)(2), and then increased by any gain recognized by the foreign corporation on the distribution allocated among such assets in proportion to the potential gain inherent in each such asset at the time of distribution (computed using the tentative basis as determined under section 334(b)(2)). The basis of each asset is limited, however, to its fair market value.

(iv) Distribution to a foreign corporation under section 332 after July 31, 1986 and after the repeal of the General Utilities doctrine. The rules of this subdivision (iv) shall apply to section 332 distributions after July 31, 1986, pursuant to section 337(a) as in effect after the effective dates of the amendments of section 631 of the Tax Reform Act of 1986.

(A) Liquidation of domestic corporation. A foreign corporation that meets the stock ownership requirements of section 332(b) with respect to stock in a domestic corporation that is a U.S. real property interest (except a foreign corporation that has made an effective election under section 897(i) and the stock of which is treated as a U.S. real property interest) shall not recognize any gain under sections 367(a) or 897(e)(1) on the receipt of property in a section 332(a) liquidation. The domestic corporation shall not recognize gain under section 367(e)(2) on the distribution of U.S. real property interests (other than stock in a former U.S. real property holding corporation which is treated as a U.S. real property interest) to the foreign corporation. The domestic corporation shall recognize gain under section 367(e)(2) on the distribution of stock in a former U.S. real property holding corporation which is treated as a U.S. real property interest. With respect to recognition of gain or loss by the domestic corporation under section 367(e)(2) on the distribution of property other than U.S. real property interests, see the regulations under section 367(e)(2). The basis of the distributed U.S. real property interests (other than stock in a former U.S. real property holding corporation) in the hands of the foreign corporation shall be the same as it was in the hands of the domestic corporation. The basis of any property (other than U.S. real property interests) and stock in a former U.S. real property holding corporation that is a U.S. real property interest in the hands of the foreign corporation shall be the same as it was in the hands of the domestic corporation increased by any gain recognized by the distributing corporation on the distribution that was subject to U.S. taxation.

(B) Liquidation of certain foreign corporations making a section 897(i) election. A foreign corporation that meets the stock ownership requirements of section 332(b) with respect to stock in another foreign corporation, that has made an effective election under section 897(i) and the stock of which is treated as a U.S. real property interest, shall recognize gain pursuant to section 897(e)(1) on such stock upon the receipt from the distributing foreign corporation of property that is not a U.S. real property interest, and that is not used by the distributee foreign corporation in the conduct of a trade or business within the United States (if the distributee foreign corporation is not a resident of a country with which the United States maintains an income tax treaty) or in a permanent establishment within the United States (if the distributee foreign corporation is a resident of a country with which the United States maintains an income tax treaty). The gain on the stock in the foreign corporation (making an effective election under section 897(i)) to be recognized by the distributee foreign corporation pursuant to section 897(e)(1) shall be determined by multiplying the gain realized on the distribution by a fraction. The numerator of the fraction shall be the fair market value of the property received by the distributee foreign corporation upon which it must recognize gain, and the denominator of the fraction shall be the fair market value of all property received by the distributee foreign corporation on the distribution. The distributing foreign corporation shall not recognize gain under section 367(e)(2) on the distribution of U.S. real property interests to the distributee foreign corporation. With respect to the recognition of gain or loss under section 367(e)(2) on the distribution of property other than U.S. real property interests, see the regulations under section 367(e)(2). The basis of the distributed U.S. real property interests in the hands of the distributee foreign corporation shall be the same as it was in the hands of the distributing foreign corporation. The basis of the property upon which the distributee foreign corporation recognized gain in the hands of the distributee foreign corporation shall be the same as the basis in the hands of the distributing foreign corporation, plus any gain recognized by the distributee foreign corporation on the receipt of such property allocated among such property in proportion to the potential gain inherent in each such property at the time of the distribution. In regard to the basis of any other property received by the distributee foreign corporation in the liquidation, see the regulations under section 367(e)(2). However, the basis of each asset is limited to its fair market value.

(v) Transfer of foreign corporation stock followed by a section 332 liquidation treated as a reorganization. If a nonresident alien or foreign corporation transfers the stock of a foreign-corporation that owns a U.S. real property interest to a domestic corporation in exchange for stock of the domestic corporation (or its domestic or foreign parent corporation) in a reorganization under section 368(a)(1)(B) or in an exchange under section 351(a), and if the foreign corporation then distributes the U.S. real property interest to the domestic corporation in a liquidation described in section 332(a) within five years of the transfer of the stock of the foreign corporation to the domestic corporation, then the transfer of the foreign corporation stock and the liquidation shall be treated as a reorganization described in section 368(a)(1)(C) or (D). The rules of § 1.897-6T(a)(1) shall apply to the transfer of the U.S. real property interest to the domestic corporation in exchange for domestic corporation stock, and the rules of § 1.897-5T(c)(4) shall apply to the distribution of domestic corporation stock by the foreign corporation. However, the rules of this paragraph (b)(3)(v) shall not apply if the transfer of the foreign corporation stock and the liquidation under section 332(a) are separate and independent transactions justified by substantial and verifiable business purposes.

(4) Section 897(i) companies. Except as otherwise provided herein for purposes of this section and § 1.897-6T, a foreign corporation that has made a valid election under section 897(i) shall be treated as a domestic corporation and not

as a foreign corporation in determining the application of section 897. For rules concerning the making of a section 897(i) election, see §§ 1.897-3 and 1.897-8T. In regard to section 367(e)(2) and foreign corporations that have made an effective election under section 897(i), see paragraph (b)(3)(iv) of this section.

(5) Examples. The following examples illustrate the rules of this paragraph (b). In each example there is no applicable income tax treaty to which the United States is a party.

Example (1). (i) A is a nonresident alien who owns 100 percent of the stock of DC, a U.S. real property holding corporation. DC's only asset is Parcel P, a U.S. real property interest, with a fair market value of $500,000 and an adjusted basis of $300,000. DC completely liquidates in 1987 and distributes Parcel P to A in exchange for the DC stock held by A.

(ii) Under section 336(a), DC must recognize gain to the extent of the excess of the fair market value ($500,000) over the adjusted basis ($300,000), or $200,000.

(iii) A does not recognize any gain under section 897(a) because the DC stock in the hands of A is no longer a U.S. real property interest under paragraph (b)(2) of this section and paragraph 2(f) of § 1.897-2. A does recognize gain (if any) under section 331(a); however, the gain is not subject to taxation under section 871(a). A's adjusted basis in Parcel P is $500,000.

(iv) If DC did not recognize all of the gain on the disposition under a transitional rule to section 631 of the Tax Reform Act of 1986, then paragraph (b)(2) of this section and paragraph 2(f) of § 1.897-2 would not apply to A. A would recognize gain (if any) under paragraph (b)(2) because the distribution is treated as in full payment in exchange for the DC stock under section 897(a).

Example (2). (i) FC, a Country F corporation, owns 100 percent of the stock of DC, a U.S. real property holding corporation. FC's basis in the stock of DC is $400,000, and the fair market value of the DC stock is $800,000. DC owns a U.S. real property interest with an adjusted basis of $350,000 and a fair market value of $600,000. DC also owns other assets that are not U.S. real property interests that have an adjusted basis of $125,000 and a fair market value of $200,000. DC completely liquidates in 1985 and distributes all of its property to FC in exchange for the DC stock held by FC.

(ii) Under paragraph (b)(3)(ii) of this section, FC recognizes $100,000 of gain under section 897(a) on the disposition of the DC stock. This is determined by multiplying FC's gain realized ($400,000) by a fraction. The numerator of the fraction is the fair market value of the property other than U.S. real property interests ($200,000), and the denominator of the fraction is the fair market value of all property received ($800,000). FC takes a carryover adjusted basis in the U.S. real property interest ($350,000). FC's adjusted basis in the assets that are not U.S. real property interests ($200,000) is the basis of those assets in the hands of DC ($125,000) plus the gain recognized by FC on the distribution ($100,000) not to exceed the fair market value ($200,000).

Example (3). (i) FC, a Country F corporation, owns 100 percent of the stock of DC, a U.S. real property holding corporation. FC's basis in the stock of DC is $300,000, and the fair market value of the DC stock is $500,000. DC owns Parcel P, a U.S. real property interest, with an adjusted basis of $250,000 and a fair market value of $400,000. DC also owns all of the stock of DX, a former U.S. real property holding corporation whose stock is a U.S. real property interest, with an adjusted basis of $50,000 and a fair market value of $100,000. DC completely liquidates in 1987 and distributes all of its property to FC in exchange for the DC stock held by FC.

(ii) Under paragraph (b)(3)(iv)(A) of this section, DC recognizes $50,000 of gain on the distribution to FC of the DX stock. DC does not recognize any gain for purposes of section 367(e)(2) on the distribution to FC of Parcel P.

(iii) Under paragraph (b)(3)(iv)(A) of this section, FC's disposition of its DC stock is not treated as a disposition of a U.S. real property interest. Under section 334(b)(1), FC takes a carryover adjusted basis of $250,000 in Parcel P. FC takes an increased basis of $100,000 in the DX stock which is equal to DC's basis ($50,000) increased by the gain recognized by DC ($50,000).

(iv) The result would be the same if FC had made an effective election under section 897(i).

(6) Section 333 elections. (i) General rule. A foreign shareholder that elects section 333 as in effect prior to its repeal by the Tax Reform Act of 1986 upon the distribution of property in a liquidation by a domestic corporation whose stock is treated as a U.S. real property interest shall recognize gain on such stock to the extent that—

(A) The property received by the foreign shareholder constitutes property other than U.S. real property interests subject to U.S. taxation upon its disposition as specified by paragraph (a)(1) of this section, or

(B) The basis of a U.S. real property interest subject to U.S. taxation upon its disposition in the hands of the recipient foreign shareholder exceeds the basis of the U.S. real property interest in the hands of the liquidating domestic corporation.

In determining the amount of gain recognized by the foreign shareholder, the foreign shareholder shall be considered to have exchanged the domestic corporation stock for all the property distributed on a proportionate fair market value basis. The gain recognized on a respective portion of domestic corporation stock shall not exceed the gain realized on that portion. Property other than U.S. real property interests subject to U.S. taxation upon disposition shall have a fair market value basis in the hands of the foreign shareholder. The basis of U.S. real property interests subject to U.S. taxation upon disposition shall be the basis of the proportionate part of the domestic corporation stock cancelled or redeemed in the liquidation, increased in the amount of gain recognized (other than gain recognized under this section) by the shareholder in respect to that proportionate part of the domestic corporation stock.

(ii) Example. The rules of paragraph (b)(6)(i) of this section may be illustrated by the following example.

Example. (i) A is a citizen and resident of Country F with which the U.S. does not have an income tax treaty. A owns all of the stock of DC, a U.S. real property holding corporation. The DC stock has a fair market value of $1,000,000. A acquired the DC stock in two purchases. The basis of one lot of the DC stock is $150,000, and the basis of the other lot is $650,000.

(ii) DC owns Parcel P, a U.S. real property interest, with a fair market value of $750,000 and an adjusted basis of $400,000. DC's only other property is equipment with a fair market value of $250,000 and an adjusted basis of $100,000. DC does not have any earnings and profits.

(iii) DC completely liquidates in 1985 in accordance with section 333 by distributing Parcel P and the equipment to A. A elects section 333 treatment.

(iv) A is considered as having exchanged 75 percent (fair market value of Parcel P/fair market value of all property distributed) of the DC stock for Parcel P. A realized gain of $150,000 on that portion of the DC stock ($750,000-$600,000). All of the gain of $150,000 is recognized under section 897 (a) because A's basis in Parcel P under section 334 (c) ($600,000) would exceed DC's basis in Parcel P ($400,000) by at least the amount of realized gain. A takes a basis of $750,000 in Parcel P.

(v) A is considered as having exchanged 25 percent (fair market value of equipment/fair market value of all property distributed) of the DC stock for the equipment. A realized gain of $50,000 on that portion of the DC stock ($250,000-$200,000). All of the gain of $50,000 is recognized under section 897 (a). A takes a basis of $250,000 in the equipment.

(c) Distributions of U.S. real property interests by foreign corporations. *(1) Recognition of gain required.* If a foreign corporation makes a distribution (including a distribution in liquidation or redemption) of a U.S. real property interest to a shareholder (whether foreign or domestic), then, except as provided in paragraph (c)(2), (3), or (4) of this section, the distributing corporation shall recognize gain (but not loss) on the distribution under section 987 (d)(1). The gain recognized shall be equal to the excess of the fair market value of the U.S. real property interest (as of the time of the distribution) over its adjusted basis. Except as otherwise provided, the distributee's basis in the distributed U.S. real property interest shall be determined under the otherwise applicable sections of the Code. The distributee (whether domestic or foreign) of a foreign corporation in a liquidation under section 332 shall take the foreign corporation's basis in the distributed U.S. real property interest increased by any gain recognized (and subject to U.S. income taxation) by the foreign corporation on the distribution of such U.S. real property interest.

(2) Recognition of gain not required. (i) Statutory exception rule. Under section 897(d)(2)(A), gain shall not be recognized by a distributing foreign corporation if—

(A) At the time of the receipt of the distributed U.S. real property interest, the distributee would be subject to U.S. income taxation on a subsequent disposition of the U.S. real property interest, determined in accordance with the rules of paragraph (d)(1) of this section;

(B) The basis of the distributed U.S. real property interest in the hands of the distributee is no greater than the adjusted basis of such property before the distribution, increased by the amount of gain (if any) recognized by the distributing corporation upon the distribution and added to the adjusted basis under the otherwise applicable provisions; and

(C) The distributing corporation complies with the filing requirements of paragraph (d)(1)(iii) of this section.

(ii) Section 332 liquidations. (A) In general. A distributing foreign corporation that meets the requirements of paragraph (c)(2)(i) in a section 332(a) liquidation shall not recognize gain on the distribution of U.S. real property interests to a foreign corporation meeting the stock ownership requirements of section 332(b) if the distributing corporation complies with the procedural requirements of paragraph (d)(1)(iii). Whether a foreign corporation recognizes gain on the distribution of U.S. real property interests to a U.S. corporation meeting the stock ownership requirements of section 332(b) depends upon whether the U.S. corporation satisfies the subject to tax requirement provided in paragraph (d)(1)(i) (in addition to the procedural requirements of paragraph (d)(1)(iii)). With respect to section 332 distributions by a foreign corporation occurring after July 31, 1986, section 367(e)(2) shall not affect the application of section 337(a) (as in effect after the Tax Reform Act of 1986) and paragraph (c)(2)(i) of this section to the distribution of a U.S. real property interest.

(B) Recognition of gain required in certain section 332 liquidations. Notwithstanding the other rules of this paragraph (c), a foreign corporation shall, pursuant to the authority conferred by section 897(e)(2), recognize gain on its distribution after May 5, 1988 of a U.S. real property interest to a domestic corporation meeting the stock ownership requirements of section 332(b) if—

(1) The foreign corporation has not made an election under section 897(i), and any gain on the stock in the foreign corporation would be subject to U.S. taxation if an election were made on the date of the liquidation; and

(2) The distribution of the U.S. real property interest by the foreign corporation to the domestic corporation pursuant to section 332(a) occurs less than five years after the date of the last gain from the disposition of stock of the foreign corporation that would be subject to payment of tax under § 1.897-3(d)(2)(i) if an election under section 897(i) were made by the foreign corporation on the date of its liquidation.

With regard to the treatment of certain foreign corporations as domestic corporations under section 897(i), however, see §§ 1.897-3 and 1.897-8T.

(iii) Examples. The rules of this paragraph (c)(2) may be illustrated by the following examples.

Example (1). (i) DC, a domestic corporation, owns 100 percent of the stock of FC, a Country F corporation, FC's only asset is Parcel P, a U.S. real property interest, with a fair market value of $500x and an adjusted basis of $100x. In September 1987, FC liquidates under section 332(a) and transfers Parcel P to DC. The transitional rules contained in section 633 of the Tax Reform Act of 1986 concerning the repeal of the General Utilities doctrine would not be applicable to a subsequent distribution or disposition of assets by DC.

(ii) Assume that FC complies with the filing requirements of paragraph (d)(1)(iii). DC will be subject to U.S. income taxation on a subsequent disposition of Parcel P under the rules of paragraph (d)(1). The basis of Parcel P in the hands of DC will be $100x under section 334(b)(1), and thus no greater than the basis of Parcel P in the hands of FC. FC does not recognize any gain under the rules of paragraph (c)(1) of this section on the distribution because the exception of paragraph (d)(2)(1) applies.

Example (2). If in Example (1) the distribution by FC to DC occurred in September 1985, and DC sold or exchanged Parcel P under sections 336(a) or 337(a) as in effect prior to the Tax Reform Act of 1986, then FC must recognize gain of $400x on the distribution of Parcel P. The gain must be recognized because Parcel P in the hands of DC is not considered subject to U.S. income taxation on a subsequent disposition under the rules of paragraph (d)(1) of this section.

(3) Limitation of gain recognized under paragraph (c)(1) of this section for certain section 355 distributions. (i) In general. Under paragraph (c)(1) of this section, a foreign corporation that distributes stock in a domestic corporation that constitutes a U.S. real property interest in a distribution

to which section 355 applies shall recognize gain on the distribution to the extent that the fair market value of the distributed stock exceeds its adjusted basis in the hands of the distributing foreign corporation. The gain recognized shall be limited under this paragraph (c)(3), however, to the amount by which the aggregate basis of the distributed stock in the hands of the distributees exceeds the aggregate adjusted basis of the distributed stock in the hands of the distributing corporation. The distributees' basis in the distributed U.S. real property interest shall be determined under the otherwise applicable provisions of section 358. (Thus, the distributees' basis in the distributed U.S. real property interest shall be determined without any increase for any gain recognized by the foreign corporation).

(ii) Example. The rules of paragraph (c)(3)(i) of this section may be illustrated by the following example.

Example. (i) C is a citizen and resident of Country F. C owns all of the stock of FC, a Country F corporation. The fair market value of the FC stock is 1000x, and C has a basis of 600x in the FC stock. Country F does not have an income tax treaty with the United States.

(ii) In a transaction qualifying as a distribution of stock of a controlled corporation under section 355(a), FC distributes to C all of the stock of DC, a U.S. real property holding corporation. C does not surrender any of the FC stock. The DC stock has a fair market value of 600x, and FC has an adjusted basis of 200x in the DC stock. After the distribution, the FC stock has a fair market value of 400x.

(iii) Under paragraph (c)(3)(i) of this section, FC must recognize gain on the distribution of the DC stock to C equal to the difference between the fair market value of the DC stock (600x) and FC's adjusted basis in the DC stock (200x). This results in a potential gain of 400x. Under section 358, C takes a 360x adjusted basis in the DC stock. Provided that FC complies with the filing requirements of paragraph (d)(1)(iii) of this section, the gain recognized by FC is limited under paragraph (c)(3)(i) to 160x because (A) this is the amount by which the basis of the DC stock in the hands of C (360x) exceeds the adjusted basis of the DC stock in the hands of FC (200x), and (B) at the time of receipt of the DC stock, C would be subject to U.S. taxation on a subsequent disposition of the stock.

(iv) C's adjusted basis in the DC stock is not increased by the 160x recognized by FC.

(4) Distribution by a foreign corporation in certain reorganizations. (i) In general. Under paragraph (c)(1) of this section, a foreign corporation that transfers property to another corporation in an exchange under section 361(a) for stock of a domestic corporation which is a United States real property holding corporation immediately after the transfer in a reorganization under section 368(a)(1)(C), (D), or (F) shall recognize gain under section 897(d)(1) on the distribution (whether actual or deemed) of the stock of the domestic corporation received by the foreign corporation to its shareholders (whether domestic or foreign). See § 1.897-6T(a) of the regulations for the consequences to the foreign corporation of the exchange of its property for the domestic corporation stock.

(ii) Statutory exception. Pursuant to the exception provided in section 897(d)(2)(A), no gain shall be recognized by the foreign corporation on its distribution of the domestic corporation stock if—

(A) At the time of the distribution, the distributee (i.e., the exchanging shareholder in the section 354 exchange) would be subject to U.S. taxation on a subsequent disposition of the stock of the domestic corporation, determined in accordance with the rules of paragraph (d)(1) of this section;

(B) The distributee's adjusted basis in the stock of the foreign corporation immediately before the distribution was no greater than the foreign corporation's basis in the stock of the domestic corporation determined under section 358; and

(C) The distributing corporation complies with the filing requirements of paragraph (d)(1)(iii) of this section.

(iii) Regulatory limitation on gain recognized. If the requirements of subdivisions (A) and (C) of paragraph (c)(4)(ii) are met, the amount of any gain recognized by the foreign corporation shall not exceed the excess of the distributee's adjusted basis in the stock of the foreign corporation immediately before the distribution over the foreign corporation's basis in the stock of the domestic corporation immediately before the distribution as determined under section 358.

(iv) Examples. The rules of paragraph (c)(4) of this section may be illustrated by the following examples.

Example (1). (i) A, a nonresident alien, organized FC, a Country W corporation, in September 1980 to invest in U.S. real estate. In 1986, FC's only asset is Parcel P, a U.S. real property interest with a fair market value of $600,000 and an adjusted basis to FC of $200,000. Parcel P is subject to a mortgage with an outstanding balance of $100,000. The fair market value of the FC stock is $500,000, and A's adjusted basis in the stock is $100,000. FC does not have liabilities in excess of the adjusted basis in Parcel P. The United States does not have a treaty with Country W that entitles FC to nondiscriminatory treatment as described in section 1.897-3(b)(2) of the regulations.

(ii) Pursuant to a plan of reorganization under section 368(a)(1)(D), FC transfers Parcel P to DC, a newly formed domestic corporation, in exchange for DC stock. FC distributes the DC stock to A in exchange for A's FC stock.

(iii) FC's exchange of Parcel P for the DC stock is a disposition of a U.S. real property interest. Under § 1.897-6T(a)(1), there is an exchange of a U.S. real property interest (Parcel P) for another U.S. real property interest (DC stock) so that no gain is recognized on the exchange under section 897(e). DC takes FC's basis of $200,000 in Parcel P under section 362(b). Under section 358(a)(1), FC takes a $100,000 basis in the DC stock because FC's substituted basis of $200,000 in the DC stock is reduced by the $100,000 of liabilities to which Parcel P is subject.

(iv) Under section 897(d)(1) and paragraph (c)(4)(i) of this section, FC generally must recognize gain on the distribution of the DC stock received in exchange for FC's assets equal to the difference between the fair market value of the DC stock ($500,000) and FC's adjusted basis in the DC stock prior to the distribution ($100,000). This results in a potential gain of $400,000. Under section 358(a)(1), A takes a basis in the DC stock equal to its basis in the FC stock of $100,000. Provided that FC complies with the filing requirements of paragraph (d)(1)(iii) of this section, no gain is recognized by FC on the distribution of the DC stock under the statutory exception to the general rule of section 897(d)(1) provided in section 897(d)(2)(A) and paragraph (c)(4)(ii) of this section because (1) A's basis in the DC stock ($100,000) does not exceed FC's adjusted basis in the DC stock ($100,000) immediately prior to the distribution and (2) A, at the time of receipt of the DC stock, would be subject to U.S. taxation on a subsequent disposition of the stock.

(v) The FC stock in the hands of A is not a U.S. real property interest because FC is a foreign corporation that has not elected to be treated as a domestic corporation under section 897(i). Accordingly, the exchange of the FC stock by A for DC stock is not a disposition of a U.S. real property interest under section 897(a).

Example (2). The facts are the same as in Example (1), except that A purchased the FC stock in September 1983 for $100,000 from S, a nonresident alien, and that S had a basis of $40,000 in the FC stock at the time of the sale to A. The results are the same as in Example 1.

Example (3). (i) The facts are the same as in Example 1, except that A's adjusted basis in the FC stock prior to the reorganization is $300,000. Following the distribution, A takes its basis of $300,000 in the FC stock as its basis in the DC stock pursuant to section 358(a)(1).

(ii) FC does not qualify under the statutory exception of paragraph (c)(4)(ii) to the general recognition rule of section 897(d)(1) and paragraph (c)(4)(i) of this section because A's basis in the DC stock ($300,000) exceeds FC's adjusted basis in the DC stock ($100,000) immediately prior to the distribution. However, provided that FC complies with the filing requirements of paragraph (d)(1)(iii) of this section, the gain recognized by FC is limited to $200,000 under the regulatory limitation of gain provided by paragraph (c)(4)(iii). This is the excess of A's basis in the FC stock immediately before the distribution ($300,000) over A's adjusted basis in the DC stock immediately before the distribution ($100,000).

(iii) A takes a basis of $300,000 in the DC stock under section 358(a)(1). A's basis in the DC stock is not increased by the gain recognized by FC. DC takes a basis of $200,000 in Parcel P under section 362(b).

Example (4). (i) The facts are the same as in Example (3), except that the United States has an income tax treaty with Country W entitling FC to nondiscriminatory treatment under section 1.897-3(b)(2) of the regulations. A valid election under section 897(i) is made to treat FC as a U.S. corporation.

(ii) FC is treated as a domestic corporation for purposes of section 897 and is not required to recognize gain under section 897(d)(1) and paragraph (c)(4)(i) of this section on the distribution of the DC stock as described in Example 3. (If a valid section 897(i) election were not made, the result would be same as in Example (3).)

(iii) The FC stock in the hands of A is a U.S. real property interest because an election was made under section 897(i) to treat FC as a U.S. corporation. The exchange of the FC stock for DC stock by A is a disposition of a U.S. real property interest. Under section 897(e)(1) and paragraph (a) of § 1.897-6T, A does not recognize gain on the exchange because there is an exchange of a U.S. real property interest (the FC stock) for another U.S. real property interest (the DC stock). Under section 358(a)(1), A takes as its basis in the DC stock A's basis in the FC stock ($300,000).

(5) Sales of U.S. real property interests by foreign corporations under section 337. Section 337 as in effect prior to the Tax Reform Act of 1986 shall not apply to any sale or exchange (including a deemed section 337 sale pursuant to an election under section 338(a) to treat a stock purchase as an asset acquisition) of a U.S. real property interest by a foreign corporation.

(6) Section 897(l) credit. If a foreign corporation adopts a plan of complete liquidation and if, solely by reason of section 897(d) and this section, section 337(a) (as in effect before the Tax Reform Act of 1986) does not apply to sales or exchanges of, or section 336 (as in effect before the Tax Reform Act of 1986) does not apply to distributions of, United States real property interests by the liquidating corporation, then—

(i) The amount realized by the shareholder on the distribution shall be increased by its proportionate share of the amount by which the tax imposed by chapter 1 of the Code, as modified by the provisions of any applicable U.S. income tax treaty, on the liquidating corporation would have been reduced if section 897(d) and this section had not been applicable, and

(ii) For purposes of the Code, the shareholder shall be deemed to have paid, on the last day prescribed by law for the payment of the tax imposed by subtitle A of the Code on the shareholder for the taxable year, an amount of tax equal to the amount of increase in the amount realized described in subdivision (i) of this paragraph (c).

The special rule provided by this paragraph (c)(5) applies only to shareholders who are United States citizens or residents, and who have held stock in the liquidating corporation continuously since June 18, 1980. This special rule also only applies for the first taxable year of any such shareholder in which the shareholder receives a distribution in complete liquidation from the foreign corporation.

(7) Other applicable rules. For rules concerning exemption of gain pursuant to a U.S. income tax treaty, withholding of tax from distributions, and other applicable rules, see paragraph (d) of this section. For the treatment of liquidations described in section 334(b)(2)(A) of certain foreign corporations acquired before November 6, 1980, see § 1.897-4.

(d) Rules of general application. *(1) Interests subject to taxation upon later disposition.* (i) In general. Pursuant to the otherwise applicable rules of this section and § 1.897-6T, nonrecognition of gain or loss may apply with respect to certain distribution or exchanges of U.S. real property interests if any gain from a subsequent disposition of the interests that are distributed or received by the transferor in the exchange would be included in the gross income of the distributee or transferor and be subject to U.S. taxation. Gain is considered subject to U.S. taxation if the gain is included on the income tax return of a U.S. tax paying entity even if there is no U.S. tax liability (for example, because of net operating losses or an investment tax credit). Gain is not considered subject to U.S. taxation if the gain is derived by a tax exempt entity. A real estate investment trust is considered to be a passthrough entity for purposes of the rule of taxability of this paragraph (d)(1)(i). Thus, for example, a tax exempt entity holding an interest in a real estate investment trust is not subject to tax. A domestic corporation (including a foreign corporation that makes an effective section 897(i) election after receipt of the U.S. real property interest) shall not be considered subject to U.S. taxation on a subsequent disposition of a U.S. real property interest if it received the U.S. real property interest prior to the effective date of the repeal of section 336(a) or 337(a) as in effect prior to the Tax Reform Act of 1986, unless the U.S. real property interest has not been sold or exchanged by the domestic corporation prior to such effective date in a transaction to which either section 336(a) or section 337(a) (as in effect prior to such effective date) applied. In addition, an interest shall be considered to be subject to U.S. taxation upon its subsequent disposition only if the requirements set forth in subdivision (iii) of this paragraph (d)(1) are met.

(ii) Effects of income tax treaties. (A) Effect of treaty exemption from tax. Except as otherwise provided in subdivision (C) of this paragraph (d)(1)(ii), a U.S. real property interest shall not be considered to be subject to U.S. taxation upon a subsequent disposition if, at the time of its distribution or exchange, the recipient is entitled pursuant to the provisions of a U.S. income tax treaty to an exemption from U.S. taxation upon a disposition of the interest.

(B) Effect of treaty reduction of tax. If, at the time of a distribution or exchange, a distributee of a U.S. real property interest in a distribution or a transferor who receives a U.S. real property interest in an exchange would be entitled pursuant to the provisions of a U.S. income tax treaty to reduced U.S. taxation upon the disposition of the interest, then a portion of the interest received shall be treated as an interest subject to U.S. taxation upon its disposition, and, therefore, that portion shall be entitled to nonrecognition treatment under the rules of this section or § 1.897-6T. The portion of the interest that is treated as subject to U.S. taxation is determined by multiplying the fair market value of the interest by a fraction. The numerator of the fraction is the amount of tax that would be due pursuant to the provisions of the applicable U.S. income tax treaty upon the recipient's disposition of the interest, determined as of the date of the distribution or transfer. The denominator of the fraction is the amount of tax that would be due upon such disposition but for the provisions of the treaty. However, nonrecognition treatment may be preserved in accordance with the provisions of subdivision (C) of this paragraph (d)(1)(ii). With regard to the provisions of this paragraph, see Article XIII (9) of the United States-Canada Income Tax Convention.

(C) Waiver of treaty benefits to preserve nonrecognition. Notwithstanding the provisions of subdivisions (A) and (B) of this paragraph (d)(1)(ii), an interest shall be considered to be subject to U.S. taxation upon its subsequent disposition if, in accordance with paragraph (d)(1)(iii)(F) of this section, the recipient waives the benefits of a U.S. income tax treaty that would otherwise entitle the recipient to an exemption from (or reduction of) U.S. tax upon a disposition of the interest.

(iii) Procedural requirements. If a U.S. real property interest is distributed or transferred after December 31, 1987, the transferor or distributor (that is a nonresident alien individual or a foreign corporation) shall file an income tax return for the taxable year of the distribution or transfer. Also, if a U.S. real property interest is distributed or transferred in a transaction before January 1, 1988, with respect to which nonrecognition treatment would not have been available under the express provisions of section 897 (d) or (e) of the Code but is available under the provisions of this section or § 1.897-6T, then the person that would otherwise be subject to tax by reason of the operation of section 897 must file an income tax return for the taxable year of the distribution or transfer. This requirement is satisfied by filing a tax return or an amended tax return for the year of the distribution or transfer by May 5, 1989, or by the date that the filing of the return is otherwise required. The person filing the return must attach thereto a document setting forth the following:

(A) A statement that the distribution or transfer is one to which section 897 applies;

(B) A description of the U.S. real property interest distributed or transferred, including its location, its adjusted basis in the hands of the distributor or transferor immediately before the distribution or transfer, and the date of the distribution or transfer;

(C) A description of the U.S. real property interest received in an exchange;

(D) A declaration signed by an officer of the corporation that the distributing foreign corporation has substantiated the adjusted basis of the shareholder in its stock if the distributing corporation has nonrecognition or recognition limitation under paragraph (c)(3) or (4) of this section;

(E) The amount of any gain recognized and tax withheld by any person with respect to the distribution or transfer;

(F) [Reserved]. For further guidance, see § 1.897-5(d)(1)(iii)(F).

(G) The treaty and article (if any) under which the distributee or transferor would be exempt from U.S. taxation on a sale of the distributed U.S. real property interest or the U.S. real property interest received in the transfer; and

(H) A declaration, signed by the distributee or transferor or its authorized legal representative, that the distributee or transferor shall treat any subsequent sale, exchange, or other disposition of the U.S. real property interest as a disposition that is subject to U.S. taxation, notwithstanding the provisions of any U.S. income tax treaty or intervening change in circumstances. A person who has provided or filed a notice described in § 1.1445-2(d)(2)(iii) or § 1.1445-5(b)(2)(ii) in connection with a transaction may satisfy the requirement of this paragraph (d)(1)(iii) by attaching to his return a copy of that notice together with any information or declaration required by this subdivision not contained in that notice.

(2) Treaty exception to imposition of tax. If gain that would be currently recognized pursuant to the provisions of this section or § 1.897-6T is subject to an exemption from (or reduction of) U.S. tax pursuant to a U.S. income tax treaty, then gain shall be recognized only as provided by that treaty, for dispositions occurring before January 1, 1985. For dispositions occurring after December 31, 1984, all gain shall be recognized as provided in section 897 and the regulations thereunder, except as provided by Articles XIII(9) and XXX(5) of the United States-Canada Income Tax Convention or other income tax treaty entered into force after June 6, 1988.

With regard to Article XXX(5) of the Income Tax Treaty with Canada, see, Rev. Rul. 85-76, 1985-1 C.B. 409. With regard to basis adjustments for certain related person transactions, see, § 1.897-6T(c)(3).

(3) Withholding. Under sections 1441 and 1442, as modified by the provisions of any applicable U.S. income tax treaty, a corporation must withhold tax from a dividend distribution to which section 301 applies to a shareholder that is a foreign person, if the dividend is considered to be from sources inside the United States. For a description of dividends that are considered to be from sources inside the United States, see section 861(a)(2). Under section 1445, withholding is required with respect to certain dispositions and distributions of U.S. real property interests.

(4) Effect on earnings and profits. With respect to adjustments to earnings and profits for gain recognized to a distributing corporation on a distribution, see section 312 and the regulations thereunder.

(e) Effective date. Except as otherwise specifically provided in the text of these regulations, this section shall be effective for transfers, exchanges, distributions and other dispositions occurring after June 18, 1980.

T.D. 8198, 5/4/88, amend T.D. 9082, 8/4/2003.

§ 1.897-6T Nonrecognition exchanges applicable to corporations, their shareholders, and other taxpayers, and certain transfers of property in corporate reorganizations (Temporary).

(a) Nonrecognition exchanges. *(1) In general.* Except as otherwise provided in this section and in § 1.897-5T, for purposes of section 897(e) any nonrecognition provision shall apply to a transfer by a foreign person of a U.S. real property interest on which gain is realized only to the extent that the transferred U.S. real property interest is exchanged for a U.S. real property interest which, immediately following the exchange, would be subject to U.S. taxation upon its disposition, and the transferor complies with the filing requirements of paragraph (d)(1)(iii) of § 1.897-5T. No loss shall be recognized pursuant to section 897(e) or the rules of this section unless such loss is otherwise permitted to be recognized. In the case of an exchange of a U.S. real property interest for stock in a domestic corporation (that is otherwise treated as a U.S. real property interest), such stock shall not be considered a U.S. real property interest unless the domestic corporation is a U.S. real property holding corporation immediately after the exchange. Whether an interest would be subject to U.S. taxation in the hands of the transferor upon its disposition shall be determined in accordance with the rules of § 1.897-5T(d)(1).

(2) Definition of "nonrecognition" provision. A "nonrecognition provision" is any provision of the Code which provides that gain or loss shall not be recognized if the requirements of that provision are met. Nonrecognition provisions relevant to this section include, but are not limited to, sections 332, 351, 354, 355, 361, 721, 731, 1031, 1033 and 1036. For purposes of section 897(e), sections 121 and 453 are not nonrecognition provisions.

(3) Consequence of nonapplication of nonrecognition provisions. If a nonrecognition provision does not apply to a transaction, then the U.S. real property interest transferred shall be considered exchanged pursuant to a transaction that is subject to U.S. taxation by reason of the operation of section 897. See, however, § 1.897-5T(d)(2) with respect to the treaty exceptions to the imposition of tax. If a U.S. real property interest is exchanged for an interest the disposition of which is only partially subject to taxation under chapter 1 of the Code (as modified by the provisions of any applicable U.S. income tax treaty), then any nonrecognition provision shall apply only to the extent that the interest received in the exchange would be subject to taxation under chapter 1 of the Code, as modified. For example, the exchange of a U.S. real property interest for an interest in a partnership will receive nonrecognition treatment pursuant to section 721 only to the extent that a disposition of the partnership interest will be subject to U.S. taxation by reason of the operation of section 897(g).

(4) Section 355 distributions treated as exchanges. If a domestic corporation, stock in which is treated as a U.S. real property interest, distributes stock in a foreign corporation or stock in a domestic corporation that is not a U.S. real property holding corporation to a foreign person under section 355(a), then the foreign person shall be considered as having exchanged a proportionate part of the stock in the domestic corporation that is treated as a U.S. real property interest for stock that is not treated as a U.S. real property interest.

(5) [Reserved.]

(6) Determination of basis. If a nonrecognition provision applies to the transfer of a U.S. real property interest pursuant to the provisions of this section, then the basis of the property received in the exchange shall be determined in accordance with the rules generally applicable with respect to such nonrecognition provision. Similarly, the basis of the exchanged property in the hands of the transferee shall be determined in accordance with the rules that generally apply to such transfer.

(7) Examples. The rules of paragraphs (a)(1) through (6) of this section may be illustrated by the following examples. In each instance, the filing requirements of paragraph (d)(1)(iii) of § 1.897-5T have been satisfied.

Example (1). (i) A is a citizen and resident of Country F with which the U.S. does not have an income tax treaty. A owns Parcel P, a U.S. real property interest, with a fair market value of $500,000 and an adjusted basis of $300,000. A transfers Parcel P to DC, a newly formed U.S. real property holding corporation wholly owned by A, in exchange for DC stock.

(ii) Under paragraph (a)(1) of this section, A has exchanged a U.S. real property interest (Parcel P) for another U.S. real property interest (DC stock) which is subject to U.S. taxation upon its disposition. The nonrecognition provisions of section 351(a) apply to A's transfer of Parcel P.

(iii) Under paragraph (a)(6) of this section, the basis of the DC stock received by A is determined in accordance with the rules generally applicable to the transfer. A takes a $300,000 adjusted basis in the DC stock under the rules of section 358(a)(1).

Example (2). [Reserved.]

Example (3). [Reserved.]

Example (4). (i) B is a citizen and resident of Country F with which the U.S. does not have an income tax treaty. B owns stock in DC1, a U.S. real property holding corporation. In a reorganization qualifying for nonrecognition under section 368(a)(1)(B), B exchanges the DC1 stock under section 354(a) for stock in DC2, a U.S. real property holding corporation.

(ii) A does not recognize any gain under paragraph (a)(1) of this section on the exchange of the DC1 stock for DC2 stock because there is an exchange of a U.S. real property interest (the DC1 stock) for another U.S. real property interest (the DC2 stock) which is subject to U.S. taxation upon its disposition.

Example (5). (i) C is a citizen and resident of Country F with which the U.S. does not have an income tax treaty. C owns all of the stock of DC, a U.S. real property holding corporation. The fair market value of the DC stock is 500x, and C has a basis of 100x in the DC stock.

(ii) In a transaction qualifying as a distribution of stock of a controlled corporation under section 355(a), DC distributes to C all of the stock of FC, a foreign corporation that has not made a section 897(i) election. C does not surrender any of the DC stock. The FC stock has a fair market value of 200x. After the distribution, the DC stock has a fair market value of 300x.

(iii) Under the rules of paragraph (a)(4) of this section, C is considered to have exchanged DC stock with a fair market value of 200x and an adjusted basis of 40x for FC stock with a fair market value of 200x. Because the FC stock is not a U.S. real property interest, C must recognize gain of 160x under section 897(a) on the distribution. C takes a basis of 200x in the FC stock. C's basis in the DC stock is reduced to 60x pursuant to section 358(c).

Example (6). (i) A is an individual citizen and resident of Country F. F has an income tax treaty with the United States that exempts gain from the sale of stock, but not real property, by a resident of F from U.S. taxation. In 1981, A transferred Parcel P, an appreciated U.S. real property interest, to

DC, a U.S. real property holding corporation, in exchange for DC stock. A owned all of the stock of DC.

(ii) Under the rules of paragraph (a)(1) of this section, A must recognize gain on the transfer of Parcel P. Even though there is an exchange of a U.S. real property interest for another U.S. real property interest, there is gain recognition because the U.S. real property interest received (the DC stock) would not have been subject to U.S. taxation upon a disposition immediately following the exchange. A may not convert a U.S. real property interest that was subject to taxation under section 897 into a U.S. real property interest that could be sold without taxation under section 897 due to a treaty exemption.

Example (7). (i) A, a nonresident alien, organized FC1, a Country W corporation in September 1980 to invest in U.S. real property. FC1's only asset is Parcel P, a U.S. real property interest with a fair market value of $500,000 and an adjusted basis of $200,000. The FCI stock has a fair market value of $500,000 and A's basis in the FC1 stock is $100,000. The United States does not have a treaty with Country W.

(ii) A, organized FC2, a Country W corporation in July 1987. FC2 organized DC in August 1987. Pursuant to a plan of reorganization under section 368(a)(1)(C), FC1 transfers Parcel P to DC in exchange for FC2 voting stock. As a result of the transfer, DC is a U.S. real property holding corporation wholly owned by FC2. The FC2 stock used by DC in the acquisition had been transferred by FC2 to DC as part of the plan of reorganization. FC1 distributes the FC2 stock to A in exchange for A's FC1 stock.

(iii) FC1's exchange of Parcel P for the FC2 stock under section 361(a) is a disposition of a U.S. real property interest. FC1 must recognize gain of $300,000 under section 897(e) and paragraph (a)(1) of this section on the exchange because the FC2 stock received in exchange for Parcel P is not a U.S. real property interest.

(iv) Under section 362(b), DC takes a basis of $500,000 in Parcel P. FC2 takes a basis of $500,000 in the DC stock. A takes a basis of $100,000 in the FC2 stock under section 358(a)(1). Section 897(d) and paragraph (c)(1) of § 1.897-5T do not apply to FC1's distribution of the FC2 stock because the FC2 stock is not a U.S. real property interest.

Example (8). (i) The facts are the same as in Example 7, except that the United States has a treaty with Country W that entitles FC1 and FC2 to nondiscriminatory treatment as described in § 1.897-3(b)(2). FC1, but not FC2, makes a valid section 897(i) election prior to the transaction.

(ii) FC1's transfer of Parcel P to DC in exchange for FC2 stock is not subject to section 897(e) and paragraph (a)(1) of this section because FC1 made an election under section 897(i). DC takes a basis of $200,000 in Parcel P under section 362(b).

(iii) FC1's distribution of the FC2 stock to A in exchange for the FC1 stock is not subject to the section 897(d) and paragraph (c)(1) of § 1.897-5T because FC1 made an election under section 897(i).

(iv) A must recognize gain on the exchange under section 354(a) of the FC1 stock for the FC2 stock. A exchanged a U.S. real property interest (the FC1 stock) for an interest which is not a U.S. real property interest (the FC2 stock). A recognizes gain of $400,000. Under section 1012, A takes a $500,000 basis in the FC2 stock.

Example (9). (i) The facts are the same as in Example 7 except that the United States has a treaty with Country W that entitles FC1 and FC2 to nondiscriminatory treatment as described in § 1.897-3(b)(2). FC2, but not FC1, makes a valid section 897(i) election prior to the transaction.

(ii) FC1's exchange of Parcel P for the FC2 stock under section 361(a) is a disposition of a U.S. real property interest. FC1 does not recognize any gain under section 897(e) and paragraph (a)(1) of this section because there is an exchange of a U.S. real property interest (Parcel P) for another U.S. real property interest (the FC2 stock). DC takes a basis of $200,000 in Parcel P under section 362(b). FC2 takes a basis of $200,000 in the DC stock.

(iii) FC1's distribution of the FC2 stock to A in exchange for the FC1 stock is subject to section 897(d) and paragraph (c)(1) of § 1.897-5T. Because A takes a basis of $100,000 in the FC2 stock under section 358(a) (which is less than the $200,000 basis of the FC2 stock in the hands of FC1), and A would be subject to U.S. taxation under section 897(a) on a subsequent disposition of the FC2 stock, FC1 does not recognize any gain under paragraph (c)(1) of § 1.897-5T due to the statutory exception of paragraph (c)(2)(i) of that section, provided that FC1 complies with the filing requirements of paragraph (d)(i)(C) of § 1.897-5T.

(iv) Since, the FC1 stock was not a U.S. real property interest, its disposition by A in the section 354(a) exchange for FC2 stock is not subject to section 897(e) and paragraph (a)(1) of this section.

Example (10). (i) The facts are the same as in Example 7, except that the United States has a treaty with Country W that entitles FC1 and FC2 to nondiscriminatory treatment as described in § 1.897-3(b)(2). FC1 and FC2 made valid section 897(i) elections prior to the transactions.

(ii) FC1's transfer of Parcel P to DC in exchange for FC2 stock is not subject to section 897(e) and paragraph (a)(1) of this section because FC1 made an election under section 897(i). DC takes a basis of $200,000 in Parcel P under section 362(a). FC2 takes a basis of $200,000 in the DC stock.

(iii) FC1's distribution of the FC2 stock to A in exchange for the FC1 stock is not subject to section 897(d) and paragraph (c)(1) of § 1.897-5T because FC1 made an election under section 897(i).

(iv) A does not recognize any gain on the exchange of the FC1 stock for the FC2 stock under section 354(a). Under paragraph (a)(1) of this section, there is an exchange of a U.S. real property interest (FCl stock) for another U.S. real property interest (FC2 stock). A takes a basis of $100,000 in the FC2 stock under section 358(a).

(8) Treatment of nonqualifying property. (i) In general. If, under paragraph (a)(1) of this section, a nonrecognition provision would apply to an exchange but for the fact that nonqualifying property (cash or property other than U.S. real property interests) is received in addition to property (U.S. real property interests) that is permitted to be received under paragraph (a)(1) of this section, then the transferor shall recognize gain under this section equal to the lesser of—

(A) The sum of the cash received plus the fair market value of the nonqualifying property received, or

(B) The gain realized with respect to the U.S. real property interest transferred. However, no loss shall be recognized pursuant to this paragraph (a)(8) unless such loss is otherwise permitted to be recognized.

(ii) Treatment of mixed exchanges. In a mixed exchange where both a U.S. real property interest and other property (including cash) is transferred in exchange both for property the receipt of which would qualify for nonrecognition treatment pursuant to paragraph (a)(1) of this section and for other property (including cash) which would not so qualify, the transferor will recognize gain in accordance with the rules set forth in subdivisions (A) through (C) of this paragraph (a)(8)(ii).

(A) Allocation of nonqualifying property. The amount of nonqualifying property (including cash) considered to be received in exchange for U.S. real property interests shall be determined by multiplying the fair market value of the nonqualifying property received by a fraction ("real property fraction"). The numerator of the fraction is the fair market value of the U.S. real property interest transferred in the exchange. The denominator of the fraction is the fair market value of all property transferred in the exchange.

(B) Recognition of gain. The amount of gain that must be recognized, and that shall be subject to U.S. taxation by reason of the operation of section 897, shall be equal to the lesser of:

(1) The amount determined under subdivision (A) of this paragraph (a)(8)(ii), or

(2) The gain or loss realized with respect to the U.S. real property interest exchanged.

(C) Treatment of other amounts. The treatment of other amounts received in a mixed exchange shall be determined as follows:

(1) The amount of nonqualifying property (including cash) considered to be received in exchange for property (including cash) other than U.S. real property interests shall be treated in the manner provided in the relevant nonrecognition provision. Such amounts shall be determined by subtracting the amount determined under subdivision (A) of this paragraph (a)(8)(ii) from the total amount of nonqualifying property received in the exchange.

(2) The amount of qualifying property considered to be received in exchange for U.S. real property interests shall be treated in the manner provided in paragraph (a)(1) of this section. Such amount shall be determined by multiplying the total fair market value of qualifying property received in the exchange by the real property fraction described in subdivision (A) of this paragraph (a)(8)(ii).

(3) The amount of qualifying property considered to be received in exchange for property other than U.S. real property interests shall be treated in the manner provided in the relevant nonrecognition provision. Such amount shall be determined by subtracting the amount determined under subdivision (2) of this paragraph (a)(8)(ii)(C) from the total fair market value of qualifying property received in the exchange.

(iii) Example. The rules of paragraph (a)(8)(ii) of this section may be illustrated by the following example.

Example. (i) A is an individual citizen and resident of country F. Country F does not have an income tax treaty with the United States. A is the sole proprietor of a business located in the United States, the assets of which consist of a U.S. real property interest with a fair market value of $1,000,000 and an adjusted basis of $700,000, and equipment used in the business with a fair market value of $500,000 and an adjusted basis of $250,000. A decides to incorporate the business, and on January 1, 1987, A transfers his assets to domestic corporation DC in exchange for 100 percent of the stock of DC, with a fair market value of $900,000. In addition, A receives a long term note (constituting a security) from DC for $600,000, bearing arm's length interest and repayment terms. DC has no assets other than those received in the exchange with A. Pursuant to section 897(c)(2) and § 1.897-2, DC is a U.S. real property holding corporation. Therefore, the stock of DC is a U.S. real property interest. Assume that the note from DC constitutes an interest in the corporation solely as a creditor as provided by § 1.897-1(d)(4) of the regulation. A complies with the filing requirements of paragraph (d)(1)(iii) of § 1.897-5T.

(ii) Because the note from DC would not be subject to U.S. taxation upon its disposition, it is nonqualifying property for purposes of determining whether A is entitled to receive nonrecognition treatment pursuant to section 351 with respect to his exchange of the U.S. real property interest. Thus, A must recognize gain in the manner provided in paragraph (a)(8)(ii) of this section. Pursuant to paragraph (a)(8)(ii)(A), the amount of nonqualifying property received in exchange for the real property interests is determined by multiplying the fair market value of such property ($600,000) by the real property fraction. The numerator of the fraction is $1,000,000, the fair market value of the real property transferred by A. The denominator is $1,500,000, the fair market value of all property transferred by A. Thus, A is considered to have received $400,000 of the note in exchange for the real property ($600,000 × $1,000,000/$1,500,000). Pursuant to paragraph (a)(8)(ii)(B), A must recognize the lesser of the amount initially determined or the gain realized with respect to the U.S. real property interest. Therefore, A must recognize the $300,000 gain realized with respect to the real property.

(iii) Pursuant to paragraph (a)(8)(ii)(C) of this section, A is considered to have received $200,000 of the note in exchange for equipment ($600,000 [total value of note received] minus $400,000 [portion of note received in exchange for real property]), $600,000 of the stock in exchange for real property ($900,000 [total value of stock received] times $1,000,000/1,500,000) [proportion of property exchanged consisting of real property]), and $300,000 of the stock in exchange for equipment ($900,000 [total value of stock received] minus $600,000 [portion of stock received in exchange for real property]). All three amounts are entitled to nonrecognition treatment pursuant to section 351.

(iv) Pursuant to paragraph (a)(2) of this section, A's basis in the stock and note received and DC's basis in the U.S. real property interest and equipment will be determined in accordance with the generally applicable rules. The $400,000 portion of the note received in exchange for the real property interest is other property. Pursuant to section 358(a)(2), A takes a fair market value ($400,000) basis for that portion of the note. Pursuant to section 358(a)(1), A's basis in the property received without the recognition of gain (the DC stock and the other portion of the note) will be equal to the basis of the property transferred ($950,000 [$700,000 basis of U.S. real property interest plus $250,000 basis of equipment]), decreased by the fair market value of the other property received ($400,000 portion of the note), and increased by the amount of gain recognized to A on the transaction ($300,000). Thus, A's basis in the stock and the nonrecognition portion of the note is $850,000 ($950,000 − $400,000 $850,000 is allocated between the stock and the nonrecognition portion of the note in proportion to their fair market values. A takes a basis of $697,000 in the DC stock ($850,000 × 900,000/1,100,000). A takes a basis of $153,000 in the nonrecognition portion of the note $850,000 × 200,000/1,100,000). A's basis in the note is $553,000 ($400,000 + $153,000). DC's basis in the property received from A will be determined under section 362(a). DC takes a basis of $1,000,000 in the real property interest (A's basis of

$700,000 increased by the $300,000 of gain recognized by A on it). DC takes a basis of $250,000 in the equipment (A's basis of $250,000).

(9) Treaty exception to imposition of tax. If gain that would be currently recognized pursuant to the provisions of this section is subject to an exemption from, or reduction of, U.S. tax pursuant to a U.S. income tax treaty, then gain shall be recognized only as provided by that treaty for dispositions occurring before January 1, 1985. For dispositions occurring after December 31, 1984, all gain shall be recognized as provided in section 897 and the regulations thereunder, except as provided by Articles XII (9) and XXX (5) of the United States-Canada Income Tax Convention or other income tax treaty entered into after June 6, 1988. In regard to Article XXX (5) the Income Tax Treaty with Canada, see, Rev. Rul. 85-76, 1985-1 C.B. 409.

(b) Certain foreign to foreign exchanges. *(1) Exceptions to the general rule.* Notwithstanding the provisions of paragraph (a)(1) of this section and pursuant to authority conferred by section 897(e)(2), a foreign person shall not recognize gain, in the instances described in paragraph (b)(2) of this section, on the transfer of a U.S. real property interest to a foreign corporation in exchange for stock in a foreign corporation, but only if the transferee's subsequent disposition of the transferred U.S. real property interest would be subject to U.S. taxation, as determined in accordance with the provisions of § 1.897-5T(d)(1), if the filing requirements of paragraph (d)(1)(iii) of § 1.897-5T have been satisfied, if one of the five conditions set forth in paragraph (b)(2) exists, and if one of the following three forms of exchange takes place.

(i) The exchange is made by a foreign corporation pursuant to section 361(a) in a reorganization described in section 368(a)(1)(D) or (F) and there is an exchange of the transferor corporation stock for the transferee corporation stock under section 354(a); or

(ii) The exchange is made by a foreign corporation pursuant to section 361(a) in a reorganization described in section 368(a)(1)(C); there is an exchange of the transferor corporation stock for the transferee corporation stock (or stock of the transferee corporation's parent in the case of a parenthetical C reorganization) under section 354(a); and the transferor corporation's shareholders own more than fifty percent of the voting stock of the transferee corporation (or stock of the transferee corporation's parent in the case of a parenthetical C reorganization) immediately after the reorganization; or

(iii) The U.S. real property interest exchanged is stock in a U.S. real property holding corporation; the exchange qualifies under section 351(a) of section 354(a) in a reorganization described in section 368(a)(1)(B); and immediately after the exchange, all of the outstanding stock of the transferee corporation (or stock of the transferee corporation's parent in the case of a parenthetical B reorganization) is owned in the same proportions by the same nonresident alien individuals and foreign corporations that, immediately before the exchange, owned the stock of the U.S. real property holding corporation.

If, however, a nonresident alien individual or foreign corporation which received stock in an exchange described in subdivision (iii) of this paragraph (b)(1) (or the transferee corporation's parent) disposes of any of such foreign stock within three years from the date of its receipt, then that individual or corporation shall recognize that portion of the gain realized with respect to the stock in the U.S. real property holding corporation for which foreign stock disposed of was received.

(2) Applicability of exception. The exception to the provisions of paragraph (a)(1) provided by paragraph (b)(1) shall apply only if one of the following five conditions exists.

(i) Each of the interests exchanged or received in a transferor corporation or transferee corporation would not be a U.S. real property interest as defined in § 1.897-1(c)(1) if such corporations were domestic corporations; or

(ii) The transferee corporation (and the transferee corporation's parent in the case of a parenthetical B or C reorganization) is incorporated in a foreign country that maintains an income tax treaty with the United States that contains an information exchange provision; the transfer occurs after May 5, 1988; and the transferee corporation (and the transferee corporation's parent in the case of a parenthetical B or C reorganization) submit a binding waiver of all benefits of the respective income tax treaty (including the opportunity to make an election under section 897(i)), which must be attached to each of the transferor and transferee corporation's income tax returns for the year of the transfer; or

(iii) The transferee foreign corporation (and the transferee corporation's parent in the case of a parenthetical B or C reorganization) is a qualified resident as defined in section 884(e) and any regulations thereunder of the foreign country in which it is incorporated; or

(iv) The transferee foreign corporation (and the transferee corporation's parent in the case of a parenthetical B or C reorganization) is incorporated in the same foreign country as the transferor foreign corporation; and there is an income tax treaty in force between that foreign country and the United States at the time of the transfer that contains an exchange of information provision; or

(v) The transferee foreign corporation is incorporated in the same foreign country as the transferor foreign corporation; and the transfer is incident to a mere change in identity, form, or place of organization of one corporation under section 368(a)(1)(F).

For purposes of any election by a transferee foreign corporation (or the transferee corporation's parent in the case of a parenthetical C reorganization) to be treated as a domestic corporation under section 897(i) and § 1.897-3 where the exchange was described in subdivisions (i) or (ii) of paragraph (b)(1) of this section, any prior dispositions of the transferor foreign corporation stock will be subject to the requirements of § 1.897-3(d)(2) upon an election under section 897(i) by the transferee foreign corporation (or the transferee corporation's parent in the case of a parenthetical C reorganization).

(3) No exceptions. No exception to recognition of gain under paragraph (a)(1) of this section is provided for the transfer of a U.S. real property interest by a foreign person to a foreign corporation in exchange for stock in a foreign corporation other than as provided in this paragraph (b). Thus, no exception is provided where—

(i) Such exchange is made pursuant to section 351 and the U.S. real property interest transferred is not stock in a U.S. real property holding corporation; or

(ii) Such exchange is made pursuant to section 361(a) in a reorganization described in section 368(a)(1) that does not qualify for nonrecognition of gain under this paragraph (b). With regard to the treatment of certain foreign corporations as domestic corporations under section 897(i), see §§ 1.897-3 and 1.897-8T.

(4) Examples. The rules of paragraph (b)(1) and (2) of this section may be illustrated by the following examples. In each instance, the filing requirements of paragraph (d)(1)(iii) of § 1.897-5T have been satisfied.

Example (1). (i) FC is a Country F corporation that has not made a section 897(i) election. FC owns Parcel P, a U.S. real property interest, with a fair market value of $450x and an adjusted basis of 100x.

(ii) FC transfers Parcel P to FS, its wholly owned Country F subsidiary, in exchange for FS stock under section 351(a). FS has not made a section 897(i) election. Under the rules of paragraph (a)(1) of this section, FC must recognize gain of 350x under section 897(a) because the FS stock received in the exchange is not a U.S. real property interest. No exception to the recognition rule of paragraph (a)(1) is provided under this paragraph (b) for a transfer under section 351(a) of a U.S. real property interest (that is not stock in a U.S. real property holding corporation) by a foreign corporation to another foreign corporation in exchange for stock to the transferee corporation.

Example (2). (i) FC is a Country F corporation that has not made a section 897(i) election. FC owns several U.S. real property interests that have appreciated in value since FC purchased the interests. FP, a Country F corporation, owns all of the outstanding stock of FC. Country F maintains an income tax treaty with the United States.

(ii) For valid business purposes, FC transferred substantially all of its assets including all of its U.S. real property interests to FS in 1989 under section 361(a) in a reorganization in exchange for FS stock. FS is a newly formed Country F corporation that is owned by FC. The transfer qualifies as a reorganization under section 368(a)(1)(D). FC immediately distributes the FS stock to FP in exchange for the FC stock and FC dissolves. FP has no gain or loss on the exchange of the FC stock for the FS stock under section 354(a).

(iii) Under the rules of paragraph (b)(1)(i) of this section, FC does not recognize any gain on the transfer of the U.S. real property interests to FS under section 361(a) in the reorganization under section 368(a)(1)(D) because FS would be subject to U.S. taxation on a subsequent disposition of the interests, as required by paragraph (b)(1) of this section; there is an exchange of stock under section 354(a), as required by paragraph (b)(1)(i); and FC and FS are incorporated in Country F which maintains an income tax treaty with the United States, as required by paragraph (b)(2)(iv).

(5) Contributions of property. A foreign person that contributes a U.S. real property interest to a foreign corporation as paid in surplus or as a contribution to capital (including a contribution provided in section 304(a)) shall be treated, for purposes of section 897(j) and this section, as exchanging the U.S. real property interest for stock in the foreign corporation.

(c) Denial of nonrecognition with respect to certain tax avoidance transfers. *(1) In general.* The provisions of § 1.897-5T and paragraphs (a) and (b) of this section are subject to the rules of this paragraph (c).

(2) Certain transfers to domestic corporations. (i) General rule. If a foreign person transfers property, that is not a U.S. real property interest, to a domestic corporation in a nonrecognition exchange, where—

(A) The adjusted basis of such property transferred exceeded its fair market value on the date of the transfer to the domestic corporation;

(B) The property transferred will not immediately be used in, or held by the domestic corporation for use in, the conduct of a trade or business as defined in § 1.897-1(f); and

(C) Within two years of the transfer to the domestic corporation, the property transferred is sold at a loss; then, it will be presumed, absent clear and convincing evidence to the contrary, that the purpose for transferring the loss property was the avoidance of taxation on the disposition of U.S. real property interests by the domestic corporation. Any loss recognized by the domestic corporation on the sale or exchange of such property shall not be used by the domestic corporation, either by direct offset or as part of a net operating loss or capital loss carryback or carryover to offset any gain recognized from the sale or exchange of a U.S. real property interest by the domestic corporation.

(ii) Example. The rules of paragraph (c)(2)(i) of this section may be illustrated by the following example.

Example. A is an individual citizen and resident of country F, which does not have an income tax treaty with the U.S. On January 1, 1987, A transfers a U.S. real property interest with a basis of $100,000 and a fair market value of $600,000 to domestic corporation DC in exchange for all of the stock of DC. On October 20, 1987, A transfers stock of a publicly traded domestic corporation with a basis in his hands of $900,000 and a fair market value of $500,000, in exchange for additional stock of DC. The stock of the publicly traded domestic corporation does not constitute an asset used or held for use in DC's trade or business. If DC sells the stock of the publicly traded domestic corporation before October 20, 1989 and recognizes a loss, the loss may not be used to offset any gain recognized on the sale of the U.S. real property interests by DC.

(3) Basis adjustment for certain related person transactions. In the case of any disposition after December 31, 1979, of a U.S. real property interest to a related person (within the meaning of section 453(f)(1)), the basis of the interest in the hands of the person acquiring such interest shall be reduced by the amount of any gain which is not subject to taxation under section 871(b)(1) or 882(a)(1) because the disposition occurred before June 19, 1980 or because of any treaty obligation of the United States. If a foreign corporation makes an election under section 897(i), and the stock of such corporation was transferred between related persons after December 31, 1979 and before June 19, 1980, then such stock shall be treated as a U.S. real property interest solely for purposes of this paragraph (c)(3).

(4) Rearrangement of ownership to gain treaty benefit. A foreign person who directly or indirectly owns a U.S. real property interest may not directly or indirectly rearrange the incidents of ownership of the U.S. real property interest through the use of nonrecognition provisions in order to gain the benefit of a treaty exemption from taxation. Such nonrecognition will not apply to the foreign transferor. The transferor will recognize gain but not loss on the transfer under section 897(a).

(d) Effective date. Except as specifically provided otherwise in the text of the regulations, paragraphs (a) through (c) shall be effective for transfers, exchanges and other dispositions occurring after June 18, 1980. Paragraph (a)(5)(ii) of this section shall be effective for exchanges and elections occurring after June 6, 1988.

T.D. 8198, 5/4/88, amend T.D. 9082, 8/4/2003.

---

§ 1.897-7T Treatment of certain partnership interests as entirely U.S. real property interests under sections 897(g) and 1445(e) (temporary).

(a) Rule. Pursuant to section 897(g), an interest in a partnership in which, directly or indirectly, fifty percent or more of the value of the gross assets consist of U.S. real property interests, and ninety percent or more of the value of the gross assets consist of U.S. real property interests plus any cash or cash equivalents shall, for purposes of section 1445, be treated as entirely a U.S. real property interest. For purposes of section 897(g), such interest shall be treated as a U.S. real property interest only to the extent that the gain on the disposition is attributable to U.S. real property interests (and not cash, cash equivalents or other property). Consequently, a disposition of any portion of such partnership interest shall be subject to partial taxation under section 897(a) and full withholding under section 1445(a). For purposes of this paragraph, cash equivalent means any asset readily convertible into cash (whether or not denominated in U.S. dollars) including, but not limited to, bank accounts, certificates of deposit, money market accounts, commercial paper, U.S. and foreign treasury obligations and bonds, corporate obligations and bonds, precious metals or commodities, and publicly traded instruments.

(b) Effective date. Section 1.897-7T shall be effective for transfers, exchanges, distributions and other dispositions occurring after June 6, 1988.

T.D. 8198, 5/4/88.

§ 1.897-8T Status as a U.S. real property holding corporation as a condition for electing section 897(i) pursuant to § 1.897-3 (Temporary).

(a) Purpose and scope. This section provides a temporary regulation that if and when adopted as a final regulation, will be added to paragraph (b) of § 1.897-3. Paragraph (b) of this section would then appear as paragraph (b)(4) of § 1.897-3.

(b) General conditions. The foreign corporation upon making an election under section 897(i) (including any retroactive election) must qualify as a U.S. real property holding corporation as defined in paragraph (b)(1) of § 1.897-2.

(c) Effective Date. Section 1.897-8T shall be effective as of June 6, 1988, with respect to foreign corporations making an election under section 897(i) after May 5, 1988.

T.D. 8198, 5/4/88.

§ 1.897-9T Treatment of certain interest in publicly traded corporations, definition of foreign person, and foreign governments and international organizations. (Temporary).

(a) Purpose and scope. This section provides a temporary regulation that, if and when adopted as a final regulation will be added as new paragraphs (c)(2)(iii)(B), (k), (n) and (q) of § 1.897-1. Paragraph (b) of this section would then appear as paragraph (c)(2)(iii)(B) of § 1.897-1. Paragraph (c) of this section would then appear as paragraph (k) of § 1.897-1. Paragraph (d) of this section would then appear as paragraph (n) of § 1.897-1. Paragraph (e) of this section would then appear as paragraph (q) of § 1.897-1.

(b) Any other interest in the corporation (other than an interest solely as a creditor) if on the date such interest was acquired by its present holder it had a fair market value greater than the fair market value on that date of 5 percent of the regularly traded class of the corporation's stock with the lowest fair market value. However, if a non-regularly traded class of interests in the corporation is convertible into a regularly traded class of interests in the corporation, an interest in such non-regularly traded class shall be treated as a U.S. real property interest if on the date it was acquired by its present holder it had a fair market value greater than the fair market value on that date of 5 percent of the regularly traded class of the corporation's stock into which it is convertible. If a person holds interests in a corporation of a class that is not regularly traded, and subsequently acquires additional interests of the same class, then all such interests must be aggregated and valued as of the date of the subsequent acquisition. If the subsequent acquisition causes that person's interests to exceed the applicable limitation, then all such interests shall be treated as U.S. real property interests, regardless of when acquired. In addition, if a person holds interests in a corporation of separate classes that are not regularly traded, and if such interests were separately acquired for a principal purpose of avoiding the applicable 5 percent limitation of this paragraph, then such interests shall be aggregated for purposes of applying that limitation. This rule shall not apply to interests of separate classes acquired in transactions more than three years apart. For purposes of paragraph (c)(2)(iii) of § 1.897-1, section 318(a) shall apply (except that section 318(a)(2)(C) and (3)(C) shall each be applied by substituting "5 percent" for "50 percent").

(c) Foreign person. The term "foreign person" means a nonresident alien individual (including an individual subject to the provisions of section 877), a foreign corporation as defined in paragraph (1) of this section, a foreign partnership, a foreign trust or a foreign estate, as such persons are defined respectively by § 1.871-2 and by 7701 and the regulations thereunder. A resident alien individual, including a nonresident alien with respect to whom there is in effect an election under section 6013(g) or (h) to be treated as United States resident, is not a foreign person. With respect to the status of foreign governments and international organizations, see paragraph (e) of this section.

(d) Regularly traded. *(1) General rule.* (i) Trading requirements. A class of interests that is traded on one or more established securities markets is considered to be regularly traded on such market or markets for any calendar quarter during which—

(A) Trades in such class are effected, other than in de minimis quantities, on at least 15 days during the calendar quarter;

(B) The aggregate number of the interests in such class traded is at least 7.5 percent or more of the average number of interests in such class outstanding during the calendar quarter; and

(C) The requirements of paragraph (d)(3) of this section are met.

(ii) Exceptions. (A) in the case of the class of interests which is held by 2,500 or more record shareholders, the requirements of paragraph (d)(1)(i)(B) of this section shall be applied by substituting "2.5 percent" for "7.5 percent" .

(B) If at any time during the calendar quarter 100 or fewer persons own 50 percent or more of the outstanding shares of a class of interests, such class shall not be considered to be regularly traded for purposes of sections 897, 1445 and 6039C. Related persons shall be treated as one person for purposes of this paragraph (d)(1)(ii)(B).

(iii) Anti-abuse rule. Trades between related persons shall be disregarded. In addition, a class of interests shall not be treated as regularly traded if there is an arrangement or a pattern of trades designed to meet the requirements of this paragraph (d)(1). For example, trades between two persons that occur several times during the calendar quarter may be treated as an arrangement or a pattern of trades designed to meet the requirements of this paragraph (d)(1).

(2) Interests traded on domestic established securities markets. For purposes of sections 897, 1445 and 6039C, a class of interests that is traded on an established securities market located in the United States is considered to be regularly traded for any calendar quarter during which it is regularly quoted by brokers or dealers making a market in such interests. A broker or dealer makes a market in a class of interests only if the broker or dealer holds himself out to buy or sell interests in such class at the quoted price. Stock of a corporation that is described in section 851(a)(1) and units of a unit investment trust registered under the Investment Company Act of 1940 (15 U.S.C. sections 80a-1 to 80a-2) shall be treated as regularly traded within the meaning of this paragraph.

(3) Reporting requirement for interests traded on foreign securities markets. A class of interests in a domestic corporation that is traded on one or more established securities markets located outside the United States shall not be considered to be regularly traded on such market or markets unless such class is traded in registered form, and—

(i) The corporation registers such class of interests pursuant to section 12 of the Securities Exchange Act of 1934, 15 U.S.C. section 78, or

(ii) The corporation attaches to its Federal income tax return a statement providing the following:

(A) A caption which states "The following information concerning certain shareholders of this corporation is provided in accordance with the requirements of § 1.897-9T."

(B) The name under which the corporation is incorporated, the state in which such corporation is incorporated, the principal place of business of the corporation, and its employer identification number, if any;

(C) The identity of each person who, at any time during the corporation's taxable year, was the beneficial owner of more than 5 percent of any class of interests of the corporation to which this paragraph (d)(3) applies;

(D) The title, and the total number of shares issued, of any class of interests so owned; and

(E) With respect to each beneficial owner of more than 5 percent of any class of interests of the corporation, the number of shares owned, the percentage of the class represented thereby, and the nature of the beneficial ownership of each class of shares so owned.

Interests in a domestic corporation which has filed a report pursuant to this paragraph (d)(3)(ii) shall be considered to be regularly traded on an established securities market only for the taxable year of the corporation with respect to which such a report is filed.

(4) Coordination with section 1445. For purposes of section 1445, a class of interests in a corporation shall be presumed to be regularly traded during a calendar quarter if such interests were regularly traded within the meaning of this paragraph during the previous calendar quarter.

(e) Foreign governments and international organizations. A foreign government shall be treated as a foreign person with respect to U.S. real property interests, and shall be subject to sections 897, 1445, and 6039C on the disposition of a U.S. real property interest except to the extent specifically otherwise provided in the regulations issued under section 892. An international organization (as defined in section 7701(a)(18)) is not a foreign person with respect to U.S. real property interests, and is not subject to sections 897, 1445, and 6039C on the disposition of a U.S. real property interest. Buildings or parts of buildings and the land ancillary thereto (including the residence of the head of the diplomatic mission) used by the foreign government for a diplomatic mission shall not be a U.S. real property interest in the hands of the respective foreign government.

(f) Effective date. Section 1.897-9T with the exception of paragraph (e) shall be effective for transfers, exchanges, distributions and other dispositions occurring on or after June 6, 1988. Paragraph (e) of this section shall be effective for transfers, exchanges, distributions and other dispositions occurring on or after July 1, 1986.

T.D. 8198, 5/4/88.

Proposed § 1.898-0 Outline of regulations for section 898. [*For Preamble, see ¶ 151,485*]

This section lists the major paragraphs contained in §§ 1.898-1 through 1.898-4.

§ 1.898-1 Taxable year of certain foreign corporations.

(a) In general.

(b) Effective dates.

(c) Exceptions to section 898.

(1) Specified foreign corporations with no section 951(a) or foreign personal holding company income.

(2) Elections to be treated as domestic corporations.

§ 1.898-2 Definition of specified foreign corporation.

(a) In general.

(b) Ownership requirements.

(1) In general.

(2) Ownership by attribution.

(3) Definition of United States shareholder.

(i) In general.

(ii) Certain captive insurance companies.

(iii) Foreign personal holding companies.

(4) Illustrations.

(c) Special rule for foreign personal holding companies that are not controlled foreign corporations.

(1) In general.

(2) Illustrations.

§ 1.898-3 Determining the required year.

(a) Controlled foreign corporations.

(1) In general.

(2) One-month deferral election.

(3) Majority U.S. shareholder year.

(i) In general.

(ii) Passthrough entities.

(4) Inconsistent majority U.S. shareholder years.

(i) In general.

(ii) Formula for determining least aggregate deferral.

(iii) Illustrations.

(iv) Procedural requirements and effective date.

(5) Testing days.

(i) In general.

(ii) Illustration.

(iii) Additional testing days.

(iv) Illustration.

(v) Anti-abuse rule.

(b) Foreign personal holding companies.

(1) In general.

(2) One-month deferral election not available.

(3) Testing days.

§ 1.898-4 Special rules.

(a) Changes in the required year of a specified foreign corporation for its first taxable year beginning after July 10, 1989.

(1) In general.

(2) Procedure for a specified foreign corporation to conform to the required year for the first taxable year beginning after July 10, 1989.

(i) No section 898(c)(1)(B) election.

(ii) With section 898(c)(1)(B) election.

(iii) Filing requirement.

(b) Changes in the required year of a specified foreign corporation during a taxable year of a specified foreign corporation subsequent to its first taxable year beginning after July 10, 1989.

(1) In general.

(2) Procedure for the change to a new required year of a specified foreign corporation for taxable years subsequent to its first taxable year beginning after July 10, 1989.

(i) Different majority U.S. shareholder year.

(ii) Election under section 898(c)(1)(B).

(iii) Procedure for prior years.

(iv) Making a second election under section 898(c)(1)(B).

(v) Procedure for obtaining the consent of the Commissioner to change the required year of specified foreign corporations.

(3) Short period.

(i) In general.

(ii) Illustrations.

(4) Conforming changes in the majority U.S. shareholder year.

(c) Nonconforming foreign and United States taxable years of a specified foreign corporation.

(1) In general.

(2) Computation of income and earnings and profits of a specified foreign corporation.

(i) Separate books of account.

(ii) Income and earnings and profits computation in lieu of separate books.

(iii) Illustration.

(3) 52-53-week taxable year.

(i) In general.

(ii) Majority United States shareholder with a 52-53-week taxable year.

(iii) Specified foreign corporation with a 52-53-week taxable year.

(iv) Illustrations.

(4) Certain captive insurance companies that elect to treat their related person insurance income as income effectively connected with the conduct of a United States trade or business.

(d) Four-year income spread.

Proposed § 1.898-1 Taxable year of certain foreign corporations. [*For Preamble, see ¶ 151,485*]

(a) In general. Pursuant to section 898(a), the taxable year of a specified foreign corporation is the required year. The required year is generally the majority U.S. shareholder year. These regulations define specified foreign corporation and United States shareholder, for purposes of these rules, at § 1.898-2(a) and (b)(3), respectively. The ownership requirements of a specified foreign corporation, which are a part of the definition of specified foreign corporation, are set forth at § 1.898-2(b)(1) and (2). A special rule for determining whether a foreign corporation that meets the ownership requirements of a foreign personal holding company is a specified foreign corporation is located at § 1.898-2(c). Section 1.898-3 sets forth the rules for the determination of the required year, including rules by which a specified foreign corporation that is a controlled foreign corporation may elect a taxable year beginning one month earlier than the majority U.S. shareholder year. Section 1.898-4 sets forth special rules including rules at paragraphs (a) and (b) of that section on changes in the required year, rules at paragraph (c) of that section covering situations where the required year under section 898 is different from the specified foreign corporation's foreign taxable year (the taxable year for purposes of computing income tax liabilities due a foreign country), and rules at paragraph (d) of that section regarding the four-year spread of certain income.

(b) Effective dates. Sections 1.898-1 through 1.898-4 are effective for taxable years of specified foreign corporations beginning after July 10, 1989. However, §§ 1.898-3(a)(4) (regarding situations in which inconsistent majority U.S. shareholder years exist) and 1.898-3(a)(5)(iii) (regarding situations in which additional testing days are required) are effective for taxable years beginning after [INSERT DATE 120 DAYS AFTER DATE OF PUBLICATION OF FINAL REGULATIONS IN THE FEDERAL REGISTER], and section 1.898-4(b) is effective for changes in the required year of a specified foreign corporation subsequent to its first taxable year beginning after July 10, 1989.

(c) Exceptions to section 898. *(1) Specified foreign corporations with no section 951(a) or foreign personal holding company income.* A specified foreign corporation is not required to conform its taxable year to the required year so long as its United States shareholders do not have any amount includible in gross income pursuant to section 951(a) and do not receive any actual or deemed distributions attributable to amounts described in section 553 with respect to that corporation. Once any United States shareholder of that specified foreign corporation has any amount includible in gross income pursuant to section 951(a) or receives any actual or deemed distributions attributable to amounts described in section 553 with respect to that corporation, then the specified foreign corporation must comply with section 898 and §§ 1.898-3 and 1.898-4 beginning with its first taxable year subsequent to the taxable year to which that shareholder's income is attributable. Once the specified foreign corporation is required to conform its taxable year to the required year, the fact that the shareholders of the corporation cease to have any such amount includible in gross income pursuant to section 951(a) or section 553 is not relevant. Section 898 continues to apply.

(2) Elections to be treated as domestic corporations. A foreign corporation that is a foreign insurance company and that elects to be treated as a domestic corporation pursuant

to section 953(d) is treated as a domestic corporation for all purposes of the Code and, thus, is not subject to section 898. Likewise, a foreign corporation organized under the laws of a contiguous foreign country and described in section 1504(d) is not subject to section 898 if the foreign corporation is treated as a domestic corporation in accordance with section 1504(d).

Proposed § 1.898-2 Definition of specified foreign corporation. [*For Preamble, see ¶ 151,485*]

(a) In general. For purposes of section 898 and §§ 1.898-1 through 1.898-4, a specified foreign corporation means any foreign corporation with respect to which the ownership requirements of section 898(b)(2) and paragraph (b) of this section are met and which either is treated as a controlled foreign corporation for any purpose under sections 951 through 964 of the Code (including sections 957(a), 957(b) and 953(c)), or is a foreign personal holding company, as defined in section 552.

(b) Ownership requirements. *(1) In general.* The ownership requirements of section 898(b)(2) and this paragraph (b)(1) are met with respect to any foreign corporation if a United States shareholder owns, or is considered to own by applying the attribution rules set forth in paragraph (b)(2) of this section, on each testing day, more than 50 percent of the total voting power of all classes of stock of the foreign corporation entitled to vote, or more than 50 percent of the total value of all classes of stock of the foreign corporation.

(2) Ownership by attribution. For purposes of section 898(b)(2)(A) and paragraph (b)(1) of this section, the rules contained in the following sections of the Internal Revenue Code apply in determining ownership—

(i) Section 958(a) and (b) for determining direct, indirect, and constructive stock ownership of a controlled foreign corporation;

(ii) Section 551(f) pertaining to the stock of a foreign personal holding company held through a foreign entity; and,

(iii) Section 554 for determining stock ownership of a foreign personal holding company.

(3) Definition of United States shareholder. (i) In general. For purposes of §§ 1.898-1 through 1.898-4, United States shareholder has the meaning given to it by section 951(b), except that, in the case of a foreign corporation having related person insurance income, as defined in section 953(c)(2), a person will be treated as a United States shareholder for purposes of section 898 if that person is treated as a United States shareholder under section 953(c)(1). See section 898(b)(3)(A).

(ii) Certain captive insurance companies. The determination of whether certain shareholders are United States shareholders under section 953(c)(1) and, consequently, whether the foreign corporation is a controlled foreign corporation for a particular taxable year, depends on the proportion of related person insurance income to total insurance income earned by the foreign corporation during the taxable year. If the related person insurance income of the foreign corporation is less than 20 percent of its total insurance income for the year, then the special rules of section 953(c) for captive insurance companies will not apply. The determination of whether the related person insurance income of a foreign corporation is less than 20 percent of its total insurance income for a particular taxable year cannot be made until the end of that year. Consequently, a foreign corporation that derives related person insurance income generally will not be required to consider non-10 percent United States shareholders (i.e., persons who are United States shareholders only because of the special captive insurance rules) in determining whether it is a controlled foreign corporation on the first day of the foreign corporation's taxable year to determine further whether it is a specified foreign corporation and, therefore, subject to section 898, unless the foreign corporation was treated as a controlled foreign corporation because of the special captive insurance rules for the immediately preceding taxable year. When a foreign corporation is both a captive insurance company and a specified foreign corporation, it must consider all persons who are United States shareholders under both sections 951(b) and 953(c) in determining its required year.

(iii) Foreign personal holding companies. In the case of any foreign personal holding company as defined in section 552, which is not also a specified foreign corporation by reason of being a controlled foreign corporation under section 898(b)(1)(A)(i), United States shareholder means any person who is treated as a United States shareholder under section 551(a).

(4) Illustrations. The application of this paragraph (b) may be illustrated by the following examples:

Example (1). Z is a publicly traded United States corporation that owns all of the outstanding stock of FY, a foreign corporation. FY is not a foreign personal holding company. FY owns 51 percent (of both voting power and value) of all of the outstanding stock of FX, which is also a foreign corporation. The remainder of the stock is owned by an unrelated foreign corporation. FY is a controlled foreign corporation and a specified foreign corporation. In addition, pursuant to section 958(a)(2), Z is considered to own its proportionate share (i.e., 51 percent) of the stock of FX which is owned by FY. Thus, FX is also both a controlled foreign corporation and specified foreign corporation, as defined in section 898(b) and this section.

Example (2). Z is a United States citizen who owns 51 percent of the value, but none of the voting stock, of FY, a foreign corporation. The remaining 49 percent of the value of FY, as well as all of FY's voting stock, is owned by a nonresident alien individual who is not related to Z. FY owns 51 percent (of both voting power and value) of all of the outstanding stock of FX, which is also a foreign corporation. FY is not a controlled foreign corporation because it does not have a United States shareholder within the meaning of section 951(b) (although if FY had related person insurance income it may be a controlled foreign corporation under the rules of section 953(c)). FY was a foreign personal holding company for its prior year. FY is a foreign personal holding company and a specified foreign corporation for the current year for purposes of section 898 because Z is a United States shareholder within the meaning of section 551(a) who owns 51 percent of the total value of the stock of FY. See section 552(a)(2)(B). Under section 551(f), however, the stock of FX owned by FY is not treated as being owned proportionately by Z. Accordingly, FX is not subject to section 898.

Example (3). FX has 20 equal shareholders, all of whom are related United States persons. Thus, FX does not qualify as a controlled foreign corporation under the general subpart F rules applicable to insurance companies because none of the United States persons are United States shareholders. However, if FX earns related person insurance income in a particular taxable year, then it will be considered a controlled foreign corporation for that year, unless the amount of the related person insurance income was less than 20 percent of its total insurance income for that year. If, in its taxable year ending December 31, 1990, FX earns related person insurance income in an amount that is less than 20 percent of its total insurance income and, thus, is not considered a controlled foreign corporation, then FX would not be required to determine its required year on January 1, 1991. Alternatively, if FX earns related person insurance income in its taxable year ending December 31, 1990, in excess of the 20 percent de minimis amount and, thus, is considered a controlled foreign corporation, FX would be required to determine whether it is a specified foreign corporation on January 1, 1991, and in making that determination, would be required to treat all United States persons owning its stock as United States shareholders.

(c) Special rule for foreign personal holding companies that are not controlled foreign corporations. *(1) In general.* A foreign corporation that is not a controlled foreign corporation for 30 days or more during the current taxable year will be required to determine whether it is a specified foreign corporation on any testing day during the current year only if the foreign corporation—

(i) meets the ownership requirements of section 552(a)(2) (ownership requirements for a foreign personal holding company) for the current taxable year, and

(ii) was a foreign personal holding company for its taxable year immediately preceding the current taxable year.

(2) Illustrations. The application of this paragraph (c) may be illustrated by the following examples:

Example (1). (i) FX is a foreign corporation that uses the calendar year as its taxable year. For calendar year 1989, its last taxable year beginning before the effective date of section 898, FX met the stock ownership requirements of section 552(a)(2) for a foreign personal holding company. More than 50 percent of the total value of all classes of stock of FX is owned by Y, a United States shareholder with a taxable year ending June 30. The remaining value of FX stock, and all of FX's voting stock, is owned by Z, a nonresident alien individual who is unrelated to Y. FX is not a controlled foreign corporation.

(ii) On January 1, 1990 (FX's first testing day after the effective date of section 898), FX examined its gross income for the taxable year ending December 31, 1989. FX met the gross income requirement of section 552(a)(1) for a foreign personal holding company for that year. Therefore, under the rules of this paragraph (c), FX was deemed to be a foreign personal holding company, for purposes of section 898, for the current taxable year beginning January 1, 1990. Accordingly, FX was required to determine whether it was a specified foreign corporation on January 1, 1990. FX was a specified foreign corporation on that date and, therefore, was required to change its taxable year to the required year ending on June 30.

Example (2). The facts are the same as in Example 1, with the additional fact that FX did not meet the gross income requirement for a foreign personal holding company for the short taxable year beginning January 1, 1990, and ending June 30, 1990. Nevertheless, FX will be required to maintain a taxable year beginning July 1, 1990, as its required year under section 898(c).

Proposed § 1.898-3 Determining the required year. [*For Preamble, see ¶ 151,485*]

(a) Controlled foreign corporations. *(1) In general.* The required year is the majority U.S. shareholder year prescribed in section 898(c)(1)(C) and paragraph (a)(3) of this section. If, however, there are inconsistent majority U.S. shareholder years, then the required year is the taxable year prescribed in section 898(c)(1)(A)(ii) and paragraph (a)(4) of this section.

(2) One-month deferral election. A specified foreign corporation that is a controlled foreign corporation may elect under section 898(c)(1)(B) and § 1.898-4(a)(2)(ii) and (b)(2)(ii) of this section a taxable year beginning one month earlier than the majority U.S. shareholder year. The specified foreign corporation may revoke this election; see § 1.898-4(b). If the specified foreign corporation revokes the election, it may re-elect the one-month deferral only if it follows the procedures set forth in § 1.898-4(b)(2)(iv) and (v). A specified foreign corporation that is a foreign personal holding company, but is not a controlled foreign corporation, may not make this election. Also, this election may not be made by a specified foreign corporation that is a controlled foreign corporation, but whose required year is the taxable year prescribed by section 898(c)(1)(A)(ii) and paragraph (a)(4) of this section because there are inconsistent majority U.S. shareholder years.

(3) Majority U.S. shareholder year. (i) In general. For the purpose of determining the required year of a specified foreign corporation, the majority U.S. shareholder year under section 898(c)(1)(C)(i) means the taxable year (if any) which, on each testing day as defined in paragraph (a)(5) of this section, constitutes the taxable year of a United States shareholder described in either paragraph (a)(3)(i)(A) or (B) of this section.

(A) Each United States shareholder, as defined in section 898(b)(3)(A) and § 1.898-2(b)(3), that owns more than 50 percent of the voting power of all classes of stock of the specified foreign corporation entitled to vote, or more than 50 percent of the total value of all classes of stock of the specified foreign corporation, after application of the attribution rules of section 898(b)(2)(B). This shareholder is described in section 898(b)(2)(A) and is referred to in this section as a "more than 50 percent United States shareholder."

(B) Each United States shareholder, as defined in section 898(b)(3)(A) and § 1.898-2(b)(3), that is not a more than 50 percent United States shareholder and whose stock was treated as owned under section 898(b)(2)(B) (the attribution rules) by a more than 50 percent United States shareholder.

(ii) Passthrough entities. For the purpose of determining the required year of a specified foreign corporation, if each United States shareholder described in paragraph (a)(3)(i)(A) or (B) of this section is a passthrough entity, such as an S corporation, partnership, trust, or estate, then the majority U.S. shareholder year is the taxable year which, on a testing day, constitutes the taxable year of the passthrough entity and not the taxable year or years of the passthrough entity's shareholders, partners, or beneficiaries.

(4) Inconsistent majority U.S. shareholder years. (i) In general. There may exist more than one majority U.S. shareholder year under section 898(c)(1)(C)(i) and paragraph (a)(3) of this section because the taxable years of shareholders described in paragraph (a)(3)(i)(A) or (B) of this section may be different taxable years. If the majority U.S. shareholder years are inconsistent, then the specified foreign corporation must adopt the taxable year that results in the least aggregate deferral of income to all United States shareholders of the specified foreign corporation, even if that taxable year is not a majority U.S. shareholder year. See paragraph (a)(4)(iii), Example 2, of this section. If the required year is the taxable year prescribed by this paragraph (a)(4) because there are inconsistent majority U.S. shareholder years, then

the one-month deferral election under section 898(c)(1)(B) and paragraph (a)(2) of this section is not available.

(ii) Formula for determining least aggregate deferral. The aggregate deferral of income for a particular year is equal to the sum of the products determined by multiplying, on each testing day as defined in paragraph (a)(5) of this section, the number of month(s) of deferral for each United States shareholder, that are shareholders on the testing day, that would be generated by that year end by that United States shareholder's percentage interest in deemed distributions from the specified foreign corporation. The United States shareholder's taxable year that produces the lowest sum when compared to the other United States shareholders' taxable years is the taxable year that results in the least aggregate deferral of income to the United States shareholders. For purposes of this section, the number of months of deferral for a United States shareholder of a specified foreign corporation is measured by the number of months from the end of the taxable year of the specified foreign corporation to the end of the taxable year of the United States shareholder. Part of a month is treated as a month. If the calculation results in more than one taxable year qualifying as the taxable year with the least aggregate deferral, the specified foreign corporation may select any one of such taxable years as its required year. However, if one of such qualifying taxable years is also the specified foreign corporation's existing taxable year, the specified foreign corporation must maintain its existing taxable year.

(iii) Illustrations. The application of this paragraph (a)(4) may be illustrated by the following examples:

Example (1). (i) FX is a foreign corporation with two classes of stock, only one of which is voting stock. Each class of stock shares equally in distributions. FX has a June 30 taxable year. FX's shareholders, A, B and C are U.S. citizens. A owns 45 percent of each class of stock, B owns 35 percent of each class of stock, and C owns the remaining 20 percent of each class of stock. A is B's grandfather and C is unrelated to A and B. A and C are calendar year taxpayers. B's taxable year ends on June 30. Under sections 958(b)(1) and 318(a)(1)(A), A is considered to own the stock owned by B. Under section 898(c)(1)(C)(i)(I), A is a more than 50 percent United States shareholder and under section 898(c)(1)(C)(i)(II), B is a United States shareholder whose stock is considered to be owned by a more than 50 percent United States shareholder. Accordingly, FX has two majority U.S. shareholder years, the calendar year and the fiscal year ending June 30. These majority U.S. shareholder years are inconsistent.

(ii) Beginning July 1, 1990, the first day of FX's first taxable year beginning after July 10, 1989, FX must conform its taxable year to the required year by adopting the taxable year that results in the least aggregate deferral of income, taking into consideration the taxable year of each United States shareholder, including C. The taxable year ending December 31 produces .35 × 6 (B's percentage share of distributions from FX multiplied by the number of months of deferral if December 31 is the required year), or a product of 2.1. The taxable year ending June 30 produces [.45 × 6] plus [.20 × 6] (A and C's percentage shares of distributions from FX multiplied by the number of months of deferral if June 30 is the required year), or a product of 3.9. Accordingly, the taxable year ending December 31 is the required year. However, if C's year end were also June 30, or if only the nonvoting stock shared in distributions and B owned all of the nonvoting stock, then the taxable year ending June 30 would produce the least aggregate deferral of income, and would be the required year.

Example (2). (i) LX is a calendar year foreign corporation with one class of stock. LX's shareholders, A, B and C are U.S. citizens. A is B's grandfather and C is unrelated to A and B. A owns 10 percent of LX's stock and has a taxable year ending June 30. B owns 45 percent of LX's stock and has a taxable year ending March 31. C owns the remaining 45 percent of LX and has a September 30 taxable year. Under sections 958(b)(1) and 318(a)(1)(A), A is considered to own the stock owned by B. Under section 898(c)(1)(C)(i)(I), A is a more than 50 percent United States shareholder and under section 898(c)(1)(C)(i)(II), B is a United States shareholder whose stock is considered to be owned by a more than 50 percent United States shareholder. Accordingly, LX has two inconsistent majority U.S. shareholder years, the fiscal year ending June 30 and the fiscal year ending March 31.

(ii) Beginning January 1, 1990, the first day of LX's first taxable year beginning after July 10, 1989, LX must conform its taxable year to the required year by adopting the taxable year that results in the least aggregate deferral of income, taking into consideration the taxable year of each United States shareholder. The taxable year ending June 30 produces [.45 × 3] plus [.45 × 9] (B and C's, respective percentage shares of distributions multiplied by the number of months of deferral), or a product of 5.4. The taxable year ending March 31 produces [.1 × 9] plus [.45 × 6] (A and C's percentage shares of distributions multiplied by the number of months of deferral), or a product of 3.6. The taxable year ending September 30 produces [.1 × 3] plus [.45 × 6] (A and B's percentage shares of distributions multiplied by the number of months of deferral), or a product of 3.0. Accordingly, September 30 is the required year.

(iv) Procedural requirements and effective date. This paragraph (a)(4) is effective for taxable years beginning after [INSERT DATE 120 DAYS AFTER DATE OF PUBLICATION OF FINAL REGULATIONS IN THE FEDERAL REGISTER]. In order to show that the requirements of this paragraph (a)(4) are satisfied, a statement setting forth the computations required to establish the taxable year that results in the least aggregate deferral of income to the United States shareholders of the specified foreign corporation must be attached to Form 5471 and, if applicable, to Form 1120F, and must indicate the following at the top of page one of the statement: "FILED UNDER § 1.898-3(a)(4)."

(5) Testing days. (i) In general. A specified foreign corporation must identify its majority U.S. shareholder year(s), if any, for the purpose of determining its required year. The specified foreign corporation must determine its majority U.S. shareholder year on each testing day. In general, the testing day is the first day of the specified foreign corporation's taxable year for U.S. tax purposes, determined without regard to section 898. See section 898(c)(1)(C)(ii).

(ii) Illustration. The application of paragraph (a)(5)(i) of this section may be illustrated by the following example:

Example. FX is a foreign corporation that, prior to the effective date of section 898, used the calendar year as its taxable year. Thus, on January 1, 1990, the first day of FX's first taxable year beginning after July 10, 1989, FX determined whether it was a specified foreign corporation and, thus, required to change its taxable year to the required year under section 898(c). Based on this test, FX changed to a taxable year ending on June 30 (because FX was a specified foreign corporation and its majority U.S. shareholder year ends on June 30). Accordingly, FX had a short period taxable year for the period beginning January 1, 1990, and ending June 30, 1990. On July 1, 1990, the first day of its new taxable year, FX again tested to determine whether it was using the required year.

(iii) Additional testing days. For taxable years of specified foreign corporations beginning after [INSERT DATE THAT IS 120 DAYS AFTER FINAL REGULATIONS ARE PUBLISHED IN THE FEDERAL REGISTER], a specified foreign corporation must determine its majority U.S. shareholder year on each day, since the most recent testing day described in paragraph (a)(5)(i) of this section, on which a substantial change occurs in the United States ownership of the stock of the specified foreign corporation. A substantial change in the United States ownership of the stock of a specified foreign corporation is a change that results in a new more than 50 percent United States shareholder of the foreign corporation.

(iv) Illustration. The application of paragraph (a)(5)(iii) of this section may be illustrated by the following example:

Example. FX is a controlled foreign corporation with one class of stock and a taxable year ending on June 30. Y, the majority United States shareholder of FX, owns 51 percent of the stock of FX. Y also has a taxable year ending June 30. Thus, FX is a specified foreign corporation subject to section 898. On May 1, 1994, Y sold 10 percent of the stock in FX to Z, an unrelated United States corporation that owned 41 percent of the stock of FX before the sale. Z obtained, therefore, a sufficient amount of FX stock to qualify as a "more than 50 percent United States shareholder" of FX. Z has a taxable year ending on April 30. Consequently, on May 1, 1994, FX determined that its new required year was a taxable year ending April 30. FX has a taxable year ending June 30, 1994, and a short taxable year beginning July 1, 1994, and ending April 30, 1995. See § 1.898-4(b)(3).

(v) Anti-abuse rule. The district director may require the use of a testing day other than that identified in paragraph (a)(5)(i) or (iii) of this section that will reflect more accurately the ownership of the specified foreign corporation and thereby the aggregate deferral of income to the United States shareholders of the specified foreign corporation where the United States shareholders engage in a transaction (or transactions) that has as its principal purpose the avoidance of the principles of this section. Thus, the anti-abuse rule of the preceding sentence would apply, for example, when there is a transfer of an interest in a specified foreign corporation that results in a temporary transfer of that interest principally for the purpose of qualifying for a specific taxable year under the principles of this section.

(b) Foreign personal holding companies. *(1) In general.* The required year is the majority U.S. shareholder year prescribed by section 898(c)(1)(A) and paragraph (a)(3) of this section. If, however, there are inconsistent majority U.S. shareholder years, then the required year is the taxable year determined under the provisions of paragraph (a)(4) of this section.

(2) One-month deferral election not available. A specified foreign corporation that is a foreign personal holding company, but is not a controlled foreign corporation, may not make the one-month deferral election of paragraph (a)(2) of this section.

(3) Testing days. See paragraph (a)(5) of this section.

PAR. 9. Section 1.898-4, as proposed to be added at 58 FR 297, January 5, 1993, is amended by adding paragraph (c)(3)(iv) to read as follows:

Proposed § 1.898-4 Special rules. [*For Preamble, see ¶ 152,177*]

* * * * *

(c) * * *

(3) * * *

(iv) Recognition of income and deductions. See § 1.441-2(e) for rules regarding the recognition of income and deductions (e.g., amounts includible in gross income pursuant to sections 951(a) or 553) if either the majority United States shareholder, or the specified foreign corporation, or both, elect to use a 52-53-week taxable year under this paragraph (c)(3).

* * * * *

Proposed § 1.898-4 Special rules. [*For Preamble, see ¶ 151,485*]

(a) Changes in the required year of a specified foreign corporation for its first taxable year beginning after July 10, 1989. *(1) In general.* A specified foreign corporation must conform its taxable year to the required year as defined in section 898(c) for taxable years beginning after July 10, 1989. In addition, section 898(c)(1)(B) permits a specified foreign corporation that is a controlled foreign corporation to elect a taxable year beginning one month earlier than the majority U.S. shareholder year.

(2) Procedure for a specified foreign corporation to conform to the required year for the first taxable year beginning after July 10, 1989. (i) No section 898(c)(1)(B) election. If no election under section 898(c)(1)(B) can be made because the specified foreign corporation is a foreign personal holding company, or no election is being made for a specified foreign corporation that is a controlled foreign corporation, but the specified foreign corporation is changing its first taxable year beginning after July 10, 1989, to conform to the required year, then unless the instructions to the forms provide otherwise, the words "Change in Taxable Year" must be placed in the upper left hand corner of the first page of Form 5471 and, if applicable, on Form 1120F, with respect to the specified foreign corporation for the taxable year for which the change is made. If a specified foreign corporation is not required to change its taxable year, then no notation concerning this fact need appear on Form 5471 and, if applicable, on Form 1120F.

(ii) With section 898(c)(1)(B) election. The election under section 898(c)(1)(B) may be made for a specified foreign corporation that is a controlled foreign corporation for its first taxable year beginning after July 10, 1989, by indicating on Form 5471 and, if applicable, on Form 1120F, that the taxable year shown on the form with respect to the controlled foreign corporation was determined in accordance with section 898(c)(1)(B). The following words must be used unless the instructions to the forms provide otherwise:

(A) If the election involves a change in the taxable year of the controlled foreign corporation, the words "Section 898(c)(1)(B) Election - Change in Taxable Year" must be placed in the upper left hand corner of the first page of Form 5471 and, if applicable, on Form 1120F; and

(B) If the election does not involve a change in the taxable year of the controlled foreign corporation, the words, "Section 898(c)(1)(B) Election" must be placed in the upper left hand corner of the first page of Form 5471 and, if applicable, on Form 1120.

(iii) Filing requirement. If a specified foreign corporation changed its required year for its first taxable year beginning after July 10, 1989, to conform to the requirements of section 898 and § 1.898-3 but did not follow the procedures set forth in Rev. Proc. 90-26 and this paragraph (a)(2), a statement must be attached to the first Form 5471 and, if applicable,, Form 1120F, to be filed after [INSERT DATE THAT IS 120 DAYS AFTER DATE OF PUBLICATION OF FINAL REGULATIONS IN THE FEDERAL REGISTER] indicating that the corporation's taxable year was changed to conform to the requirements of section 898. If a specified foreign corporation has not conformed its first taxable year beginning after July 10, 1989, to the taxable year required by section 898 and § 1.898-3, an amended return with an amended Form 5471 (or Form 1120F) must be filed to satisfy the requirements of section 898, § 1.898-3 and this paragraph (a)(2).

(b) Changes in the required year of a specified foreign corporation during a taxable year of a specified foreign corporation subsequent to its first taxable year beginning after July 10, 1989. *(1) In general.* A specified foreign corporation must conform its taxable year to a different required year should circumstances arise in which the required year changes under the rules of § 1.898-3, such as when a substantial change in ownership of a specified foreign corporation results in a new more than 50 percent United States shareholder with a different majority U.S. shareholder year. The change in taxable year of a specified foreign corporation made to conform to a different required year shall be treated as initiated by the taxpayer and as having been made with the consent of the Commissioner. The requirements set forth in this paragraph (b) are effective for taxable years subsequent to a specified foreign corporation's first taxable year beginning after July 10, 1989.

(2) Procedure for the change to a new required year of a specified foreign corporation for taxable years subsequent to its first taxable year beginning after July 10, 1989. (i) Different majority U.S. shareholder year. If the specified foreign corporation is changing its taxable year to conform to a different required year under paragraph (b)(1) of this section, unless the instructions to the forms provide otherwise, the words "Change in Taxable Year" must be placed in the upper left hand corner of the first page of Form 5471 and, if applicable, on Form 1120F, with respect to the specified foreign corporation for the taxable year for which the change is made. This paragraph covers terminations of prior elections under section 898(c)(1)(B) made in conjunction with that change.

(ii) Election under section 898(c)(1)(B). If the specified foreign corporation that is a controlled foreign corporation is changing its taxable year to conform to a different required year under paragraph (b) of this section and an election under section 898(c)(1)(B) is made, the change in taxable year and the election under section 898(c)(1)(B) are to be noted on Form 5471 and, if applicable, on Form 1120F, with respect to that corporation for the taxable year for which the change and election are made. Unless the instructions to the forms provide otherwise, the words "Section 898(c)(1)(B) Election - Change in Taxable Year" must be placed in the upper left hand corner of the first page of each form. This paragraph covers terminations of prior elections under section 898(c)(1)(B) made in conjunction with that election.

(iii) Procedure for prior years. If a specified foreign corporation conformed its taxable year to that required by section 898 and § 1.898-3 prior to [INSERT DATE THAT IS 120 DAYS AFTER DATE OF PUBLICATION OF FINAL REGULATIONS IN THE FEDERAL REGISTER] but did not follow the procedures set forth in this paragraph (b)(2), a statement must be attached to the first Form 5471 and, if applicable, Form 1120F, to be filed after [INSERT DATE THAT IS 120 DAYS AFTER DATE OF PUBLICATION OF FINAL REGULATIONS IN THE FEDERAL REGISTER] indicating that the corporation's taxable year was changed to conform to the requirements of section 898 and § 1.898-3. If a specified foreign corporation has not conformed a taxable year subsequent to its first taxable year beginning after July 10, 1989, to the taxable year required by section 898 and § 1.898-3, an amended return, with an amended Form 5471 (or Form 1120F) must be filed to satisfy the requirements of section 898, § 1.898-3 and this paragraph (b)(2).

(iv) Making a second election under section 898(c)(1)(B). Except for an election under section 898(c)(1)(B) that is made in conjunction with a change in its taxable year to conform to a different required year under paragraph (b)(2)(ii) of this section, a specified foreign corporation that has elected the one-month deferral under section 898(c)(1)(B) and subsequently revoked that election shall not be eligible to make an election under section 898(c)(1)(B) for any taxable year before its fifth taxable year which begins after the first taxable year for which the revocation is effective, unless the consent of the Commissioner pursuant to the procedures set forth in paragraph (b)(2)(v) of this section is obtained.

(v) Procedure for obtaining the consent of the Commissioner to change the required year of specified foreign corporations. In the circumstance described in paragraph (b)(2)(iv) of this section, a specified foreign corporation must request the approval of the Commissioner for a change in taxable year by completing and filing Form 1128 (Application for Change in Accounting Period) with the Commissioner of Internal Revenue. The application may be filed either by the majority United States shareholder on behalf of the specified foreign corporation or by the specified foreign corporation. The application must be filed on or before the 15th day of the second calendar month following the close of the short period for which a return is required to effect the change in taxable year. Reference to this regulation must be made part of the application by placing the following statement at the top of page one of the application: "FILED UNDER § 1.898-4." Approval of a change in taxable year described in paragraph (b)(2)(iv) of this section will not be granted unless the taxpayer agrees to the terms, conditions, and adjustments, as set forth by the Commissioner, under which the change will be effected. Unless the instructions to the forms indicate otherwise, re-election of section 898(c)(1)(B) must be noted on Form 5471 and, if applicable, on Form 1120F, for the taxable year for which the re-election is made. Unless the instructions to the forms indicate otherwise, the words "Re-elected Section 898(c)(1)(B) Election - Change in Taxable Year" must be placed in the upper left hand corner of the first page of each form.

(3) Short period. (i) In general. Any short period required for a specified foreign corporation to effect the change in taxable year described in paragraph (b)(1) of this section will begin on the first day of the specified foreign corporation's current taxable year and will end on the last day of the new required year within which the change in ownership of the specified foreign corporation (or other event that necessitates a change in taxable year) occurs. If, however, the last day of the specified foreign corporation's current taxable year occurs prior to the last day of the new required year within which the change in ownership of the specified foreign corporation (or other event resulting in a new required year) oc-

curs, then the short period will begin the day following the last day of the specified foreign corporation's current taxable year and end on the last day of the new required year subsequent to the required year within which the change in ownership of the specified foreign corporation (or other event resulting in a new required year) occurred. In no case shall the taxable year of the specified foreign corporation be in excess of one year.

(ii) Illustrations. The application of this paragraph (b)(3) may be illustrated by the following examples:

Example (1). FX is a foreign corporation that is a specified foreign corporation within the meaning of section 898(b). FX had been a calendar year taxpayer. On July 1, 1991, FX was purchased by a United States shareholder with a September 30 fiscal year. Accordingly, the short period required to change the taxable year of FX to the required year began on January 1, 1991, the first day of FX's current taxable year, and ended on September 30, 1991, the last day of the new required year within which the change in ownership of FX occurred.

Example (2). The facts are the same as in Example 1 except that on July 1, 1991, FX was purchased by a United States shareholder with a June 30 fiscal year. Accordingly, the short period required to change the taxable year of FX to the required year did not begin until January 1, 1992, the day following the last day of FX's current taxable year because the last day of FX's current taxable year occurs prior to the last day of the new required year within which the change in ownership occurred. The short period will begin January 1, 1992, and will end June 30, 1992.

(4) Conforming changes in the majority U.S. shareholder year. The requirements of section 898 and §§ 1.898-3 and 1.898-4 may be satisfied by a majority United States shareholder of a specified foreign corporation changing its taxable year to conform to the taxable year of the specified foreign corporation. However, any change to the United States shareholder's taxable year requires the approval of the Commissioner, and must be made in accordance with section 442 and the regulations under that section, relating to changes of annual accounting period.

(c) Nonconforming foreign and United States taxable years of a specified foreign corporation. *(1) In general.* If a specified foreign corporation's foreign taxable year (for purposes of computing income tax liabilities due a foreign country) does not conform to the required year pursuant to section 898(c) and § 1.898-3, then the United States shareholders must compute any income inclusion relating to the specified foreign corporation including, but not limited to, subpart F income, increase in earnings invested in United States property, foreign personal holding company income, and section 864(d) income in accordance with the rules set forth in paragraphs (c)(2) and (3) of this section. However, see section 338 and the regulations under that section for rules applicable to certain domestic and foreign corporations, and the shareholders of those corporations where an election under that section is made.

(2) Computation of income and earnings and profits of a specified foreign corporation. (i) Separate books of account. A specified foreign corporation that has a foreign taxable year different from its required year, as determined under section 898(c) and § 1.898-3, will have portions of two foreign annual accounting periods in each required year. In this case, either separate books of account for the specified foreign corporation based upon the required year may be maintained, or income (and earnings and profits) shall be computed as set forth in paragraph (c)(2)(ii) of this section. Books of account must be maintained on a consistent basis for each foreign annual accounting period.

(ii) Income and earnings and profits computation in lieu of separate books. In lieu of maintaining separate books of account, income and earnings and profits shall be computed in two steps. First, for the foreign annual accounting period of the specified foreign corporation which ends within its required year, the income (and earnings and profits) of the specified foreign corporation is the entire income (or earnings and profits) of the foreign annual accounting period, less the income (or earnings and profits), if any, of that foreign annual accounting period properly allocable to the preceding taxable year, determined under a consistent application of the principles of section 964 and the regulations under that section. Second, for the foreign annual accounting period of the specified foreign corporation which ends after its required year, the income (and earnings and profits) of the specified foreign corporation is the income (and earnings and profits) of each month (or quarter) which has ended within the required year determined on the basis of interim actual book closings and computed by a consistent application of the principles of section 964 and the regulations under that section. If the amount of income properly includable in the gross income of United States shareholders in the preceding taxable year is different from the amount of income actually included by United States shareholders in the preceding taxable year, then an adjustment must be made by each United States person affected by means of an amended return for that preceding taxable year.

(iii) Illustration. The application of this paragraph (c)(2) may be illustrated by the following example:

Example. (i) FX is a specified foreign corporation organized in foreign country, FC. FX's annual accounting period and taxable year, for FC purposes, end March 31. FX's required year is the calendar year. FX did not conform its FC taxable year to the required year. Separate books for United States tax purposes are not maintained. Accordingly, FX's required year, Calendar Year 1, will include portions of two FC annual accounting periods and FC taxable years.

(ii) For the FC period ending March 31, during Calendar Year 1, FX's income (in U.S. dollars) was $1,000, all of which was foreign personal holding company income. This amount was determined on the basis of FX's annual March 31, FC financial reports, adjusted in accordance with section 964 and the regulations under that section. Of the $1,000, it was determined from the annual financial reports that $350 was earned during the months ending in Calendar Year 1. For the period April 1, during Calendar Year 1, to the end of Calendar Year 1, FX's income was $1,200, determined on the basis of FX's monthly interim FC books of account. Accordingly, the income of FX subject to inclusion in the gross income of United States shareholders for Calendar Year 1, is $1,550. However, based on FX's annual March 31, Year 2, financial reports (adjusted in accordance with section 964 and the regulations under that section), FX's income for the period April 1, during Calendar Year 1, to the end of Calendar Year 1 was $1,300, not $1,200. Accordingly, each United States shareholder of FX must file an amended return for Calendar Year 1 showing its portion of the additional $100 of income.

(3) 52-53-week taxable year. (i) Majority United States shareholder with a 52-53-week taxable year. If a majority United States shareholder elects to follow a 52-53-week taxable year (determined under section 441(f) and the regulations under that section), and the specified foreign corporation does not intend to follow a 52-53-week taxable year,

then the required year of the specified foreign corporation, as determined under section 898(c) and § 1.898-3, shall be a 12-month taxable year, which must end on the last day of the same month used in determining the 52-53-week taxable year of its majority United States shareholder. If the election of the one-month deferral under section 898(c)(1)(B) and § 1.898-3(a)(2) is made, the election will be valid, and the specified foreign corporation may retain a 12-month taxable year, subject to the condition that the 12-month taxable year must end on the last day of the month which immediately precedes the month used in determining the 52-53-week taxable year of its majority United States shareholder.

(ii) Specified foreign corporation with a 52-53-week taxable year. If a specified foreign corporation elects to follow a 52-53-week taxable year, and the majority United States shareholder does not intend to follow a 52-53-week taxable year, then the required year, as determined under section 898(c) and § 1.898-3, of the specified foreign corporation shall be a 52-53-week taxable year, which must end within a seven-day period from the last day of the 12-month taxable year of its majority United States shareholder. If the election of the one-month deferral under section 898(c)(1)(B) and § 1.898-3(a)(2) is made, the election will be valid and the specified foreign corporation may retain a 52-53-week taxable year, subject to the condition that the 52-53-week taxable year must end within a seven-day period from the last day of the month which immediately precedes the 12-month taxable year of its majority United States shareholder.

(iii) Illustrations. The application of this paragraph (c)(3) may be illustrated by the following examples:

Example (1). X is a United States corporation created on January 1, 1990, that elected to follow a 52-53-week taxable year which ends on the Friday nearest the end of December. Thus, X's first United States taxable year began on Monday, January 1, 1990, and ended on Friday, December 28, 1990; its next taxable year began on Saturday, December 29, 1990, and ended on Friday, January 3, 1992. X owns 100 percent of FY, a specified foreign corporation that is a controlled foreign corporation which follows a 12-month taxable year ending on November 30. In these circumstances, X's taxable year may end either earlier or later than one month after the end of FY's taxable year. Nonetheless, an election under section 898(c)(1)(B), which would permit FY to retain its current taxable year, will be effective because FY's taxable year ends on the last day of the month which immediately precedes the same month used in determining the 52-53-week taxable year of X, its majority United States shareholder.

Example (2). Y is a United States person with a taxable year ending September 30. Y also is the majority United States shareholder of FX, a specified foreign corporation which is a controlled foreign corporation that wishes to make the one-month deferral election under section 898(c)(1)(B). FX follows a 52-53-week taxable year that ends on the Monday closest to the last day of August. In 1990, the last day of August fell on a Friday. Thus, FX's taxable year ended on Monday, September 3, 1990, a date within a seven-day period from the last day of the month which immediately precedes the 12-month taxable year of its majority United States shareholder, Y. In 1994, FX's taxable year will end on Monday, August 29, and its next taxable year will begin on August 30, 1994. Thus, in 1994, FX's taxable year will begin more than one month before the beginning of Y's United States taxable year. Nevertheless, the election made under section 898(c)(1)(B) will be effective because FX's taxable year will end within a seven-day period from the last day of the month which immediately precedes the 12-month taxable year of its majority United States shareholder.

(4) Certain captive insurance companies that elect to treat their related person insurance income as income effectively connected with the conduct of a United States trade or business. Section 953(c)(3)(C) permits a foreign corporation to elect to treat its related person insurance income as income effectively connected with the conduct of a trade or business in the United States. Under § 1.953-7(c)(3) of proposed regulations, such a foreign corporation must utilize the calendar year as its annual accounting period for United States tax purposes, as required by section 843. Further, if an election is made for the first taxable year beginning after December 31, 1987, or any subsequent taxable year, the election is effective from the first day of the taxable year for which the election is made (and all subsequent taxable years). Therefore, a foreign corporation that has a fiscal taxable year prior to making the election must file a short-year return for the period from the first day the election becomes effective to the last day of the calendar year in which the election is made. The rules under section 953(c)(3)(C) and § 1.953-7 will prevail over the rules under section 898 and this section. Thus, if a captive insurance company that is a specified foreign corporation makes an election pursuant to section 953(c)(3)(C) and § 1.953-7(c), it must use the calendar year as its annual accounting period for United States tax purposes, regardless of the taxable year of its majority United States shareholder. However, if a captive insurance company that is a specified foreign corporation does not make the election pursuant to section 953(c)(3)(C) and the regulations thereunder, it must conform its United States taxable year to that of its majority United States shareholder.

(d) Four-year income spread. For its first taxable year beginning after July 10, 1989, if, because of the change necessitated by section 898 in the taxable year of the specified foreign corporation, any United States person was required to include in gross income for one taxable year amounts attributable to two taxable years of the specified foreign corporation, the amount that the United States person would otherwise have included in gross income for the one taxable year by reason of the short taxable year of the specified foreign corporation resulting from the change shall be included in that person's gross income ratably over a four-taxable-year period beginning with that one taxable year. A United States person who is required by reason of section 898 to include in gross income amounts attributable to two taxable years of a specified foreign corporation may not waive the four-year ratable inclusion of such gross income.

§ 1.901-1 Allowance of credit for taxes.

Caution: The Treasury has not yet amended Reg § 1.901-1 to reflect changes made by P.L. 100-647, P.L. 100-203, P.L. 99-509, P.L. 98-369, P.L. 97-248.

(a) In general. Citizens of the United States, domestic corporations, and certain aliens resident in the United States or Puerto Rico may choose to claim a credit, as provided in section 901, against the tax imposed by chapter 1 of the Code for taxes paid or accrued to foreign countries and possessions of the United States, subject to the conditions prescribed in the following subparagraphs:

(1) Citizen of the United States. A citizen of the United States, whether resident or nonresident, may claim a credit for (i) the amount of any income, war profits, and excess profits taxes paid or accrued (or deemed paid or accrued under section 905(b)) during the taxable year to any foreign

country or to any possession of the United States; and (ii) his share of any such taxes of a partnership of which he is a member, or of an estate or trust of which he is a beneficiary.

(2) Domestic corporation. A domestic corporation may claim a credit for (i) the amount of any income, war profits, and excess profits taxes paid or accrued during the taxable year to any foreign country or to any possession of the United States; and (ii) the taxes deemed to have been paid or accrued under section 902, 905(b), or 960.

(3) Alien resident of the United States or Puerto Rico. An alien resident of the United States, or an alien individual who is a bona fide resident of Puerto Rico during the entire taxable year, may claim a credit for—

(i) The amount of any income, war profits, and excess profits taxes paid or accrued during the taxable year to any possession of the United States;

(ii) The amount of any such taxes paid or accrued (or deemed paid or accrued under section 905(b)) during the taxable year to any foreign country, if the foreign country of which such alien resident is a citizen or subject, in imposing such taxes, allows a similar credit to citizens of the United States residing in such country; and

(iii) His share of any such taxes of a partnership of which he is a member, or of an estate or trust of which he is a beneficiary, paid or accrued (or deemed paid or accrued under section 905(b)) during the taxable year,

(a) To any foreign country, if the foreign country of which such alien resident is a citizen or subject, in imposing such taxes, allows a similar credit to citizens of the United States residing in such country, or

(b) To any possession of the United States, as the case may be.

(4) Limitation. Section 907(a) limits the credit against the tax imposed by chapter 1 of the Code for certain foreign taxes paid or accrued with respect to foreign oil or gas extraction income. See § 1.907(a)-1.

(b) Foreign countries which satisfy the similar credit requirement. *(1) Taxes of foreign country of which alien resident is citizen or subject.* A foreign country of which an alien resident is a citizen or subject allows a similar credit, within the meaning of section 901(b)(3), to a United States citizen residing in such country either—

(i) If such country allows him a credit against its income taxes for the amount of income taxes paid or accrued to the United States; or

(ii) If, in imposing such taxes, such country exempts from taxation the income received by him from sources within the United States (as determined under Part I (section 861 and following), subchapter N, chapter 1 of the Code).

(2) Taxes of foreign country other than one of which alien resident is citizen or subject. An alien resident of the United States may claim a credit for income taxes paid or accrued by him to a foreign country other than the one of which he is a citizen or subject if the country of which he is a citizen or subject either—

(i) Allows a credit to a United States citizen residing therein for income taxes paid or accrued by him to such other foreign country; or

(ii) In imposing its income taxes, exempts from taxation the income of a United States citizen residing therein from sources within such other foreign country.

(c) Deduction denied if credit claimed. If a taxpayer chooses with respect to any taxable year to claim a credit for taxes to any extent, such choice will be considered to apply to income, war profits, and excess profits taxes paid or accrued in such taxable year to all foreign countries and possessions of the United States, and no portion of any such taxes shall be allowed as a deduction from gross income in such taxable year or any succeeding taxable year. See section 275(a)(4).

(d) Period during which election can be made or changed. The taxpayer may, for a particular taxable year, claim the benefits of section 901 (or claim a deduction in lieu of a foreign tax credit) at any time before the expiration of the period prescribed by section 6511(d)(3)(A) (or section 6511(c) if the period is extended by agreement).

(e) Joint return. In the case of a husband and wife making a joint return, credit for taxes paid or accrued to any foreign country or to any possession of the United States shall be computed upon the basis of the total taxes so paid by or accrued against the spouses.

(f) Taxes against which credit not allowed. The credit for taxes shall be allowed only against the tax imposed by chapter 1 of the Code, but it shall not be allowed against the following taxes imposed under that chapter:

(1) The minimum tax for tax preferences imposed by section 56;

(2) The 10 percent tax on premature distributions to owner-employees imposed by section 72(m)(5)(B);

(3) The tax on lump sum distributions imposed by section 402(e);

(4) The additional tax on income from certain retirement accounts imposed by section 408(f);

(5) The tax on accumulated earnings imposed by section 531;

(6) The personal holding company tax imposed by section 541;

(7) The additional tax relating to war loss recoveries imposed by section 1333; and

(8) The additional tax relating to recoveries of foreign expropriation losses imposed by section 1351.

(g) [Reserved]. For further guidance, see § 1.901-1T(g).

(h) Taxpayers denied credit in a particular taxable year. Taxpayers who are denied the credit for taxes for particular taxable years are the following:

(1) An individual who elects to pay the optional tax imposed by section 3, or one who elects under section 144 to take the standard deduction (see section 36);

(2) A taxpayer who elects to deduct taxes paid or accrued to any foreign country or possession of the United States (see sections 164 and 275);

(3) A regulated investment company which has exercised the election under section 853.

(i) Dividends from a DISC treated as foreign. For purposes of sections 901 through 906 and the regulations thereunder, any amount treated as a dividend from a corporation which is a DISC or former DISC (as defined in section 992(a)(1) or (3) as the case may be) will be treated as a dividend from a foreign corporation to the extent such dividend is treated under section 861(a)(2)(D) as income from sources without the United States.

T.D. 6275, 12/2/57, amend T.D. 6466, 5/12/60, T.D. 6780, 12/21/64, T.D. 6789, 12/30/64, T.D. 6795, 1/28/65, T.D. 7283, 8/2/73, T.D. 7564, 9/11/78, T.D. 7636, 8/9/79, T.D. 7961, 6/20/84, T.D. 8160, 9/8/87, T.D. 9194, 4/6/2005.

PAR. 10. In § 1.901-1, paragraph (g) is revised to read as follows:

Proposed § 1.901-1 Allowance of credit for taxes. [*For Preamble, see ¶ 152,645*]

• ***Caution:*** This Notice of Proposed Rulemaking was partially finalized by TD 9248, 01/30/2006. Regs. §§ 1.1-1, 1.170A-1, 1.861-3, 1.861-8, 1.871-1, 1.876-1, 1.881-5, 1.884-0, 1.901-1, 1.931-1, 1.932-1, 1.933-1, 1.934-1, 1.935-1, 1.937-2, 1.937-3, 1.957-3, 1.1402(a)-12, 1.6038-2, 1.6046-1, 301.6688-1, 301.7701-3, and 301.7701(b)-1 remain proposed.

(g) [The text of the proposed amendment to § 1.901-1(g) is the same as the text of § 1.901-1T(g) published elsewhere in this issue of the Federal Register]. [*See T.D. 9194, 4/11/2005, 70 Fed. Reg. 68.*]

§ 1.901-1T Allowance of credit for taxes (temporary).

• ***Caution:*** Under Code Sec. 7805, temporary regulations expire within three years of the date of issuance. This temporary regulation was issued on 4/6/2005.

(a) through (f) [Reserved]. For further guidance, see § 1.901-1(a) through (f).

(g) Taxpayers to whom credit not allowed. Among those to whom the credit for taxes is not allowed are the following7mdash;

(1) Except as provided in section 906, a foreign corporation;

(2) Except as provided in section 906, a nonresident alien individual who is not described in section 876 (see sections 874(c) and 901(b)(4));

(3) A nonresident alien individual described in section 876 other than a bona fide resident (as defined in section 937(a) and the regulations thereunder) of Puerto Rico during the entire taxable year (see sections 901(b)(3) and (4)); and

(4) A U.S. citizen or resident alien individual who is a bona fide resident of a section 931 possession (as defined in § 1.931-1T(c)(1)), the U.S. Virgin Islands, or Puerto Rico, and who excludes certain income from U.S. gross income to the extent of taxes allocable to the income so excluded (see sections 931(b)(2), 933(1), and 932(c)(4)).

(h) [Reserved]. For further guidance, see § 1.901-1(h).

(i) [Reserved]. For further guidance, see § 1.901-1(i).

(j) Effective date. This section shall apply for taxable years ending after October 22, 2004.

T.D. 9194, 4/6/2005.

§ 1.901-2 Income, war profits, or excess profits tax paid or accrued.

Caution: The Treasury has not yet amended Reg § 1.901-2 to reflect changes made by P.L. 105-34, P.L. 100-203, P.L. 99-514, P.L. 99-509.

(a) Definition of income, war profits, or excess profits tax. *(1) In general.* Section 901 allows a credit for the amount of income, war profits or excess profits tax (referred to as "income tax" for purposes of this section and §§ 1.901-2A and 1.903-1) paid to any foreign country. Whether a foreign levy is an income tax is determined independently for each separate foreign levy. A foreign levy is an income tax if and only if—

(i) It is a tax; and

(ii) The predominant character of that tax is that of an income tax in the U.S. sense.

Except to the extent otherwise provided in paragraphs (a)(3)(ii) and (c) of this section, a tax either is or is not an income tax, in its entirety, for all persons subject to the tax. Paragraphs (a), (b) and (c) of this section define an income tax for purposes of section 901. Paragraph (d) of this section contains rules describing what constitutes a separate foreign levy. Paragraph (e) of this section contains rules for determining the amount of tax paid by a person. Paragraph (f) of this section contains rules for determining by whom foreign tax is paid. Paragraph (g) of this section contains definitions of the terms "paid by," "foreign country," and "foreign levy." Paragraph (h) of this section states the effective date of this section.

(2) Tax. (i) In general. A foreign levy is a tax if it requires a compulsory payment pursuant to the authority of a foreign country to levy taxes. A penalty, fine, interest, or similar obligation is not a tax, nor is a customs duty a tax. Whether a foreign levy requires a compulsory payment pursuant to a foreign country's authority to levy taxes is determined by principles of U.S. law and not by principles of law of the foreign country. Therefore, the assertion by a foreign country that a levy is pursuant to the foreign country's authority to levy taxes is not determinative that, under U.S. principles, it is pursuant thereto. Notwithstanding any assertion of a foreign country to the contrary, a foreign levy is not pursuant to a foreign country's authority to levy taxes, and thus is not a tax, to the extent a person subject to the levy receives (or will receive), directly or indirectly, a specific economic benefit (as defined in paragraph (a)(2)(ii)(B) of this section) from the foreign country in exchange for payment pursuant to the levy. Rather, to that extent, such levy requires a compulsory payment in exchange for such specific economic benefit. If, applying U.S. principles, a foreign levy requires a compulsory payment pursuant to the authority of a foreign country to levy taxes and also requires a compulsory payment in exchange for a specific economic benefit, the levy is considered to have two distinct elements: a tax and a requirement of compulsory payment in exchange for such specific economic benefit. In such a situation, these two distinct elements of the foreign levy (and the amount paid pursuant to each such element) must be separated. No credit is allowable for a payment pursuant to a foreign levy by a dual capacity taxpayer (as defined in paragraph (a)(2)(ii)(A) of this section) unless the person claiming such credit establishes the amount that is paid pursuant to the distinct element of the foreign levy that is a tax. See paragraph (a)(2)(ii) of this section and § 1.901-2A.

(ii) Dual capacity taxpayers. (A) In general. For purposes of this section and §§ 1.901-2A and 1.903-1, a person who is subject to a levy of a foreign state or of a possession of the United States or of a political subdivision of such a state or possession and who also, directly or indirectly (within the meaning of paragraph (a)(2)(ii)(E) of this section) receives (or will receive) a specific economic benefit from the state or possession or from a political subdivision of such state or possession or from an agency or instrumentality of any of the foregoing is referred to as a "dual capacity taxpayer."

Dual capacity taxpayers are subject to the special rules of § 1.901-2A.

(B) Specific economic benefit. For purposes of this section and §§ 1.901-2A and 1.903-1, the term "specific economic benefit" means an economic benefit that is not made available on substantially the same terms to substantially all persons who are subject to the income tax that is generally imposed by the foreign country, or, if there is no such generally imposed income tax, an economic benefit that is not made available on substantially the same terms to the population of the country in general. Thus, a concession to extract government-owned petroleum is a specific economic benefit, but the right to travel or to ship freight on a government-owned airline is not, because the latter, but not the former, is made generally available on substantially the same terms. An economic benefit includes property; a service; a fee or other payment; a right to use, acquire or extract resources, patents or other property that a foreign country owns or controls (within the meaning of paragraph (a)(2)(ii)(D) of this section); or a reduction or discharge of a contractual obligation. It does not include the right or privilege merely to engage in business generally or to engage in business in a particular form.

(C) Pension, unemployment, and disability fund payments. A foreign levy imposed on individuals to finance retirement, old-age, death, survivor, unemployment, illness, or disability benefits, or for some substantially similar purpose, is not a requirement of compulsory payment in exchange for a specific economic benefit, as long as the amounts required to be paid by the individuals subject to the levy are not computed on a basis reflecting the respective ages, life expectancies or similar characteristics of such individuals.

(D) Control of property. A foreign country controls property that it does not own if the country exhibits substantial indicia of ownership with respect to the property, for example, by both regulating the quantity of property that may be extracted and establishing the minimum price at which it may be disposed of.

(E) Indirect receipt of a benefit. A person is considered to receive a specific economic benefit indirectly if another person receives a specific economic benefit and that other person—

(1) Owns or controls, directly or indirectly, the first person or is owned or controlled, directly or indirectly, by the first person or by the same persons that own or control, directly or indirectly, the first person; or

(2) Engages in a transaction with the first person under terms and conditions such that the first person receives, directly or indirectly, all or part of the value of the specific economic benefit.

(3) Predominant character. The predominant character of a foreign tax is that of an income tax in the U.S. sense—

(i) If, within the meaning of paragraph (b)(1) of this section, the foreign tax is likely to reach net gain in the normal circumstances in which it applies,

(ii) But only to the extent that liability for the tax is not dependent, within the meaning of paragraph (c) of this section, by its terms or otherwise, on the availability of a credit for the tax against income tax liability to another country.

(b) Net gain. *(1) In general.* A foreign tax is likely to reach net gain in the normal circumstances in which it applies if and only if the tax, judged on the basis of its predominant character, satisfies each of the realization, gross receipts, and net income requirements set forth in paragraphs (b)(2), (b)(3) and (b)(4), respectively, of this section.

(2) Realization. (i) In general. A foreign tax satisfies the realization requirement if, judged on the basis of its predominant character, it is imposed—

(A) Upon or subsequent to the occurrence of events ("realization events") that would result in the realization of income under the income tax provisions of the Internal Revenue Code;

(B) Upon the occurrence of an event prior to a realization event (a "prerealization event") provided the consequence of such event is the recapture (in whole or part) of a tax deduction, tax credit or other tax allowance previously accorded to the taxpayer; or

(C) Upon the occurrence of a prerealization event, other than one described in paragraph (b)(2)(i)(B) of this section, but only if the foreign country does not, upon the occurrence of a later event (other than a distribution or a deemed distribution of the income), impose tax ("second tax") with respect to the income on which tax is imposed by reason of such prerealization event (or, if it does impose a second tax, a credit or other comparable relief is available against the liability for such a second tax for tax paid on the occurrence of the prerealization event) and—

(1) The imposition of the tax upon such prerealization event is based on the difference in the values of property at the beginning and end of a period; or

(2) The prerealization event is the physical transfer, processing, or export of readily marketable property (as defined in paragraph (b)(2)(iii) of this section).

A foreign tax that, judged on the basis of its predominant character, is imposed upon the occurrence of events described in this paragraph (b)(2)(i) satisfies the realization requirement even if it is also imposed in some situations upon the occurrence of events not described in this paragraph (b)(2)(i). For example, a foreign tax that, judged on the basis of its predominant character, is imposed upon the occurrence of events described in this paragraph (b)(2)(i) satisfies the realization requirement even though the base of that tax also includes imputed rental income from a personal residence used by the owner and receipt of stock dividends of a type described in section 305(a) of the Internal Revenue Code. As provided in paragraph (a)(1) of this section, a tax either is or is not an income tax, in its entirety, for all persons subject to the tax; therefore, a foreign tax described in the immediately preceding sentence satisfies the realization requirement even though some persons subject to the tax will on some occasions not be subject to the tax except with respect to such imputed rental income and such stock dividends. However, a foreign tax based only or predominantly on such imputed rental income or only or predominantly on receipt of such stock dividends does not satisfy the realization requirement.

(ii) Certain deemed distributions. A foreign tax that does not satisfy the realization requirement under paragraph (b)(2)(i) of this section is nevertheless considered to meet the realization requirement if it is imposed with respect to a deemed distribution (e.g., by a corporation to a shareholder) of amounts that meet the realization requirement in the hands of the person that, under foreign law, is deemed to distribute such amount, but only if the foreign country does not, upon the occurrence of a later event (e.g., an actual distribution), impose tax ("second tax") with respect to the income on which tax was imposed by reason of such deemed distribution (or, if it does impose a second tax, a credit or other comparable relief is available against the liability for such a second tax for tax paid with respect to the deemed distribution)..

(iii) Readily marketable property. Property is readily marketable if—

(A) It is stock in trade or other property of a kind that property would be included in inventory if on hand at the close of the taxable year or if it is held primarily for sale to customers in the ordinary course of business, and

(B) It can be sold on the open market without further processing or it is exported from the foreign country.

(iv) Examples. The provisions of paragraph (b)(2) of this section may be illustrated by the following examples:

Example (1). Residents of country X are subject to a tax of 10 percent on the aggregate net appreciation in fair market value during the calendar year of all shares of stock held by them at the end of the year. In addition, all such residents are subject to a country X tax that qualifies as an income tax within the meaning of paragraph (a)(1) of this section. Included in the base of the income tax are gains and losses realized on the sale of stock, and the basis of stock for purposes of determining such gain or loss is its cost. The operation of the stock appreciation tax and the income tax as applied to sales of stock is exemplified as follows: a resident of country X, purchases stock in June, 1983 for 100u (units of country X currency) and sells it in May, 1985 for 160u. On December 31, 1983, the stock is worth 120u and on December 31, 1984, it is worth 155u. Pursuant to the stock appreciation tax, A pays 2u for 1983 (10 percent of (120u – 100u)), 3.5u for 1984 (10 percent of (155u – 120u)), and nothing in 1985 because no stock was held at the end of that year. For purposes of the income tax, A must include 60u (160u – 100u) in his income for 1985, the year of sale. Pursuant to paragraph (b)(2)(i)(C) of this section, the stock appreciation tax does not satisfy the realization requirement because country X imposes a second tax upon the occurrence of a later event (i.e., the sale of stock) with respect to the income that was taxed by the stock appreciation tax and no credit or comparable relief is available against such second tax for the stock appreciation tax paid.

Example (2). The facts are the same as in example 1 except that if stock was held on the December 31 last preceding the date of its sale, the basis of such stock for purposes of computing gain or loss under the income tax is the value of the stock on such December 31. Thus, in 1985, A includes only 5u (160u – 155u) as income from the sale for purposes of the income tax. Because the income tax imposed upon the occurrence of a later event (the sale) does not impose a tax with respect to the income that was taxed by the stock appreciation tax, the stock appreciation tax satisfies the realization requirement. The result would be the same if, instead of a basis adjustment to reflect taxation pursuant to the stock appreciation tax, the country X income tax allowed a credit (or other comparable relief) to take account of the stock appreciation tax. If a credit mechanism is used, see also paragraph (e)(4)(i) of this section.

Example (3). Country X imposes a tax on the realized net income of corporations that do business in country X. Country X also imposes a branch profits tax on corporations organized under the law of a country other than country X that do business in country X. The branch profits tax is imposed when realized net income is remitted or deemed to be remitted by branches in country X to home offices outside of country X. The branch profits tax is imposed subsequent to the occurrence of events that would result in realization of income (i.e., by corporations subject to such tax) under the income tax provisions of the Internal Revenue Code; thus, in accordance with paragraph (b)(2)(i)(A) of this section, the branch profits tax satisfies the realization requirement.

Example (4). Country X imposes a tax on the realized net income of corporations that do business in country X (the "country X corporate tax"). Country X also imposes a separate tax on shareholders of such corporations (the "country X shareholder tax"). The country X shareholder tax is imposed on the sum of the actual distributions received during the taxable year by such a shareholder from the corporation's realized net income for that year (i.e., income from past years is not taxed in a later year when it is actually distributed) plus the distributions deemed to be received by such a shareholder. Deemed distributions are defined as (A) a shareholder's pro rata share of the corporation's realized net income for the taxable year, less (B) such shareholder's pro rata share of the corporation's country X corporate tax for that year, less (C) actual distributions made by such corporation to such shareholder from such net income. A shareholder's receipt of actual distributions is a realization event within the meaning of paragraph (b)(2)(i)(A) of this section. The deemed distributions are not realization events, but they are described in paragraph (b)(2)(ii) of this section. Accordingly, the country X shareholder tax satisfies the realization requirement.

(3) Gross receipts. (i) In general. A foreign tax satisfies the gross receipts requirement if, judged on the basis of its predominant character, it is imposed on the basis of—

(A) Gross receipts; or

(B) Gross receipts computed under a method that is likely to produce an amount that is not greater than fair market value.

A foreign tax that, judged on the basis of its predominant character, is imposed on the basis of amounts described in this paragraph (b)(3)(i) satisfies the gross receipts requirement even if it is also imposed on the basis of some amounts not described in this paragraph (b)(3)(i).

(ii) Examples. The provisions of paragraph (b)(3)(i) of this section may be illustrated by the following examples:

Example (1). Country X imposes a "headquarters company tax" on country X corporations that serve as regional headquarters for affiliated nonresident corporations, and this tax is a separate tax within the meaning of paragraph (d) of this section. A headquarters company for purposes of this tax is a corporation that performs administrative, management or coordination functions solely for nonresident affiliated entities. Due to the difficulty of determining on a case-by-case basis the arm's length gross receipts that headquarters companies would charge affiliates for such services, gross receipts of a headquarters company are deemed, for purposes of this tax, to equal 110 percent of the business expenses incurred by the headquarters company. It is established that this formula is likely to produce an amount that is not greater than the fair market value of arm's length gross receipts from such transactions with affiliates. Pursuant to paragraph (b)(3)(i)(B) of this section, the headquarters company tax satisfies the gross receipts requirement.

Example (2). The facts are the same as in Example 1, with the added fact that in the case of a particular taxpayer, A, the formula actually produces an amount that is substantially greater than the fair market value of arm's length gross receipts from transactions with affiliates. As provided in paragraph (a)(1) of this section, the headquarters company tax either is or is not an income tax, in its entirety, for all persons subject to the tax. Accordingly, the result is the same as in example 1 for all persons subject to the headquarters company tax, including A.

Example (3). Country X imposes a separate tax (within the meaning of paragraph (d) of this section) on income from the extraction of petroleum. Under that tax, gross receipts from extraction income are deemed to equal 105 percent of the fair market value of petroleum extracted. This computation is designed to produce an amount that is greater than the fair market value of actual gross receipts; therefore, the tax on extraction income is not likely to produce an amount that is not greater than fair market value. Accordingly, the tax on extraction income does not satisfy the gross receipts requirement. However, if the tax satisfies the criteria of § 1.903-1(a), it is a tax in lieu of an income tax.

(4) Net income. (i) In general. A foreign tax satisfies the net income requirement if, judged on the basis of its predominant character, the base of the tax is computed by reducing gross receipts (including gross receipts as computed under paragraph (b)(3)(i)(B) of this section) to permit—

(A) Recovery of the significant costs and expenses (including significant capital expenditures) attributable, under reasonable principles, to such gross receipts; or

(B) Recovery of such significant costs and expenses computed under a method that is likely to produce an amount that approximates, or is greater than, recovery of such significant costs and expenses.

A foreign tax law permits recovery of significant costs and expenses even if such costs and expenses are recovered at a different time than they would be if the Internal Revenue Code applied, unless the time of recovery is such that under the circumstances there is effectively a denial of such recovery. For example, unless the time of recovery is such that under the circumstances there is effectively a denial of such recovery, the net income requirement is satisfied where items deductible under the Internal Revenue Code are capitalized under the foreign tax system and recovered either on a recurring basis over time or upon the occurrence of some future event or where the recovery of items capitalized under the Internal Revenue Code occurs less rapidly under the foreign tax system. A foreign tax law that does not permit recovery of one or more significant costs or expenses, but that provides allowances that effectively compensate for nonrecovery of such significant costs or expenses, is considered to permit recovery of such costs or expenses. Principles used in the foreign tax law to attribute costs and expenses to gross receipts may be reasonable even if they differ from principles that apply under the Internal Revenue Code (e.g., principles that apply under section 265, 465 or 861(b) of the Internal Revenue Code). A foreign tax whose base, judged on the basis of its predominant character, is computed by reducing gross receipts by items described in paragraph (b)(4)(i)(A) or (B) of this section satisfied the net income requirement even if gross receipts are not reduced by some such items. A foreign tax whose base is gross receipts or gross income does not satisfy the net income requirement except in the rare situation where that tax is almost certain to reach some net gain in the normal circumstances in which it applies because costs and expenses will almost never be so high as to offset gross receipts or gross income, respectively, and the rate of the tax is such that after the tax is paid persons subject to the tax are almost certain to have net gain. Thus, a tax on the gross receipts or gross income of businesses can satisfy the net income requirement only if businesses subject to the tax are almost certain never to incur a loss (after payment of the tax). In determining whether a foreign tax satisfied the net income requirement, it is immaterial whether gross receipts are reduced, in the base of the tax, by another tax, provided that other tax satisfies the realization, gross receipts and net income requirements.

(ii) Consolidation of profits and losses. In determining whether a foreign tax satisfies the net income requirement, one of the factors to be taken into account is whether, in computing the base of the tax, a loss incurred in one activity (e.g., a contract area in the case of oil and gas exploration) in a trade or business is allowed to offset profit earned by the same person in another activity (e.g., a separate contract area) in the same trade or business. If such an offset is allowed, it is immaterial whether the offset may be made in the taxable period in which the loss is incurred or only in a different taxable period, unless the period is such that under the circumstances there is effectively a denial of the ability to offset the loss against profit. In determining whether a foreign tax satisfies the net income requirement, it is immaterial that no such offset is allowed if a loss incurred in one such activity may be applied to offset profit earned in that activity in a different taxable period, unless the period is such that under the circumstances there is effectively a denial of the ability to offset such loss against profit. In determining whether a foreign tax satisfies the net income requirement, it is immaterial whether a person's profits and losses from one trade or business (e.g., oil and gas extraction) are allowed to offset its profits and losses from another trade or business, (e.g., oil and gas refining and processing) or whether a person's business profits and losses and its passive investment profits and losses are allowed to offset each other in computing the base of the foreign tax. Moreover, it is immaterial whether foreign law permits or prohibits consolidation of profits and losses of related persons, unless foreign law requires separate entities to be used to carry on separate activities in the same trade or business. If foreign law requires that separate entities carry on such separate activities, the determination whether the net income requirement is satisfied is made by applying the same considerations as if such separate activities were carried on by a single entity.

(iii) Carryovers. In determining whether a foreign tax satisfies the net income requirement, it is immaterial, except as otherwise provided in paragraph (b)(4)(ii) of this section, whether losses incurred during one taxable period may be carried over to offset profits incurred in different taxable periods.

(iv) Examples. The provisions of this paragraph (b)(4) may be illustrated by the following examples:

Example (1). Country X imposes an income tax on corporations engaged in business in country X; however, that income tax is not applicable to banks. Country X also imposes a tax (the "bank tax") of 1 percent on the gross amount of interest income derived by banks from branches in country X; no deductions are allowed. Banks doing business in country X incur very substantial costs and expenses (e.g. interest expense) attributable to their interest income. The bank tax neither provides for recovery of significant costs and expenses nor provides any allowance that significantly compensates for the lack of such recovery. Since such banks are not almost certain never to incur a loss on their interest income from branches in country X, the bank tax does not satisfy the net income requirement. However, if the tax on corporations is generally imposed, the bank tax satisfies the criteria of § 1.903-1(a) and therefore is a tax in lieu of an income tax.

Example (2). Country X law imposes an income tax on persons engaged in business in country X. The base of that tax is realized net income attributable under reasonable principles to such business. Under the tax law of country X, a bank is not considered to be engaged in business in country X unless it has a branch in country X and interest income earned by a bank from a loan to a resident of country X is not considered attributable to business conducted by the bank in country X unless a branch of the bank in country X performs certain significant enumerated activities, such as negotiating the loan. Country X also imposes a tax (the "bank tax") of 1 percent on the gross amount of interest income earned by banks from loans to residents of country X if such banks do not engage in business in country X or if such interest income is not considered attributable to business conducted in country X. For the same reasons as are set forth in example 1, the bank tax does not satisfy the net income requirement. However, if the tax on persons engaged in business in country X is generally imposed, the bank tax satisfies the criteria of § 1.903-1(a) and therefore is a tax in lieu of an income tax.

Example (3). A foreign tax is imposed at the rate of 40 percent on the amount of gross wages realized by an employee; no deductions are allowed. Thus, the tax law neither provides for recovery of costs and expenses nor provides any allowance that effectively compensates for the lack of such recovery. Because costs and expenses of employees attributable to wage income are almost always insignificant compared to the gross wages realized, such costs and expenses will almost always not be so high as to offset the gross wages and the rate of the tax is such that, under the circumstances, after the tax is paid, employees subject to the tax are almost certain to have net gain. Accordingly, the tax satisfies the net income requirement.

Example (4). Country X imposes a tax at the rate of 48 percent of the "taxable income" of nonresidents of country X who furnish specified types of services to customers who are residents of country X. "Taxable income" for purposes of the tax is defined as gross receipts received from residents of country X (regardless of whether the services to which the receipts relate are performed within or outside country X) less deductions that permit recovery of the significant costs and expenses (including significant capital expenditures) attributable under reasonable principles to such gross receipts. The country X tax satisfies the net income requirement.

Example (5). Each of country X and province Y (a political subdivision of country X) imposes a tax on corporations, called the "country X income tax" and the "province Y income tax," respectively. Each tax has an identical base, which is computed by reducing a corporation's gross receipts by deductions that, based on the predominant character of the tax, permit recovery of the significant costs and expenses (including significant capital expenditures) attributable under reasonable principles to such gross receipts. The country X income tax does not allow a deduction for the province Y income tax for which a taxpayer is liable, nor does the province Y income tax allow a deduction for the country X income tax for which a taxpayer is liable. As provided in paragraph (d)(1) of this section, each of the country X income tax and the province Y income tax is a separate levy. Both of these levies satisfy the net income requirement; the fact that neither levy's base allows a deduction for the other levy is immaterial in reaching that determination.

(c) Soak-up taxes. *(1) In general.* Pursuant to paragraph (a)(3)(ii) of this section, the predominant character of a foreign tax that satisfies the requirement of paragraph (a)(3)(i) of this section is that of an income tax in the U.S. sense only to the extent that liability for the foreign tax is not dependent (by its terms or otherwise) on the availability of a credit for the tax against income tax liability to another country. Liability for foreign tax is dependent on the availability of a credit for the foreign tax against income tax liability to another country only if and to the extent that the foreign tax would not be imposed on the taxpayer but for the availability of such a credit. See also § 1.903-1(b)(2).

(2) Examples. The provisions of paragraph (c)(1) of this section may be illustrated by following examples:

Example (1). Country X imposes a tax on the receipt of royalties from sources in country X by nonresidents of country X. The tax is 15 percent of the gross amount of such royalties unless the recipient is a resident of the United States or of country A, B, C, or D, in which case the tax is 20 percent of the gross amount of such royalties. Like the United States, each of countries A, B, C, and D allows its residents a credit against the income tax otherwise payable to it for income taxes paid to other countries. Because the 20 percent rate applies only to residents of countries which allow a credit for taxes paid to other countries and the 15 percent rate applies to residents of countries which do not allow such a credit, one-fourth of the country X tax would not be imposed on residents of the United States but for the availability of such a credit. Accordingly, one-fourth of the country X tax imposed on residents of the United States who receive royalties from sources in country X is dependent on the availability of a credit for the country X tax against income tax liability to another country.

Example (2). Country X imposes a tax on the realized net income derived by all nonresidents from carrying on a trade or business in country X. Although country X law does not prohibit other nonresidents from carrying on business in country X, United States persons are the only nonresidents of country X that carry on business in country X in 1984. The country X tax would be imposed in its entirety on a nonresident of country X irrespective of the availability of a credit for country X tax against income tax liability to another country. Accordingly, no portion of that tax is dependent on the availability of such a credit.

Example (3). Country X imposes tax on the realized net income of all corporations incorporated in country X. Country X allows a tax holiday to qualifying corporations incorporated in country X that are owned by nonresidents of country X, pursuant to which no country X tax is imposed on the net income of a qualifying corporation for the first ten years of its operations in country X. A corporation qualifies for the tax holiday if it meets certain minimum investment criteria and if the development office of country X certifies that in its opinion the operations of the corporation will be consistent with specified development goals of country X. The development office will not so certify to any corporation owned by persons resident in countries that allow a credit (such as that available under section 902 of the Internal Revenue Code) for country X tax paid by a corporation incorporated in country X. In practice, tax holidays are granted to a large number of corporations, but country X tax is imposed on a significant number of other corporations incorporated in country X (e.g., those owned by country X persons and those which have had operations for more than 10 years) in addition to corporations denied a tax holiday because their shareholders qualify for a credit for the country X tax against income tax liability to another country. In the case of corporations denied a tax holiday because they have U.S. shareholders, no portion of the country X tax during the period of the denied 10-year tax holiday is dependent on the availability of a credit for the country X tax against income tax liability to another country.

Example (4). The facts are the same as in example 3, except that corporations owned by persons resident in countries that will allow a credit for country X tax at the time when dividends are distributed by the corporations are granted a provisional tax holiday. Under the provisional tax holiday, instead of relieving such a corporation from country X tax for 10 years, liability for such tax is deferred until the corporation distributes dividends. The result is the same as in example 3.

(d) Separate levies. *(1) In general.* For purposes of sections 901 and 903, whether a single levy or separate levies are imposed by a foreign country depends on U.S. principles and not on whether foreign law imposes the levy or levies in a single or separate statutes. A levy imposed by one taxing authority (e.g., the national government of a foreign country) is always separate for purposes of sections 901 and 903 from a levy imposed by another taxing authority (e.g., a political subdivision of that foreign country). Levies are not separate merely because different rates apply to different taxpayers. For example, a foreign levy identical to the tax imposed on U.S. citizens and resident alien individuals by section 1 of the Internal Revenue Code is a single levy notwithstanding the levy has graduated rates and applies different rate schedules to unmarried individuals, married individuals who file separate returns and married individuals who file joint returns. In general, levies are not separate merely because some provisions determining the base of the levy apply, by their terms or in practice, to some, but not all, persons subject to the levy. For example, a foreign levy identical to the tax imposed by section 11 of the Internal Revenue Code is a single levy even though some provisions apply by their terms to some but not all corporations subject to the section 11 tax (e.g., section 465 is by its terms applicable to corporations described in sections 465(a)(1)(B) and 465(a)(1)(C), but not to other corporations), and even though some provisions apply in practice to some but not all corporations subject to the section 11 tax (e.g., section 611 does not, in practice, apply to any corporation that does not have a qualifying interest in the type of property described in section 611(a)). However, where the base of a levy is different in kind, and not merely in degree, for different classes of persons subject to the levy, the levy is considered for purposes of sections 901 and 903 to impose separate levies for such classes of persons. For example, regardless of whether they are contained in a single or separate foreign statutes, a foreign levy identical to the tax imposed by section 871(b) of the Internal Revenue Code is a separate levy from a foreign levy identical to the tax imposed by section 1 of the Internal Revenue Code as it applies to persons other than those described in section 871(b), and foreign levies identical to the taxes imposed by sections 11, 541, 881, 882, 1491 and 3111 of the Internal Revenue Code are each separate levies, because the base of each of those levies differs in kind, and not merely in degree, from the base of each of the others. Accordingly, each such levy must be analyzed separately to determine whether it is an income tax within the meaning of paragraph (a)(1) of this section and whether it is a tax in lieu of an income tax within the meaning of paragraph (a) of § 1.903-1. Where foreign law imposes a levy that is the sum of two or more separately computed amounts, and each such amount is computed by reference to a separate base, separate levies are considered, for purposes of sections 901 and 903, to be imposed. A separate base may consist, for example, of a particular type of income or of an amount unrelated to income, e.g., wages paid. Amounts are not separately computed if they are computed separately merely for purposes of a preliminary computation and are then combined as a single base. In the case of levies that apply to dual capacity taxpayers, see also § 1.901-2A(a).

(2) Contractual modifications. Notwithstanding paragraph (d)(1) of this section, if foreign law imposing a levy is modified for one or more persons subject to the levy by a contract entered into by such person or persons and the foreign country, then foreign law is considered for purposes of sections 901 and 903 to impose a separate levy for all persons to whom such contractual modification of the levy applies, as contrasted to the levy as applied to all persons to whom such contractual modification does not apply. In applying the provisions of paragraph (c) of this section to a tax as modified by such a contract, the provisions of § 1.903-1(b)(2) shall apply.

(3) Examples. The provisions of paragraph (d)(1) of this section may be illustrated by the following examples:

Example (1). A foreign statute imposes a levy on corporations equal to the sum of 15% of the corporation's realized net income plus 3% of its net worth. As the levy is the sum of two separately computed amounts, each of which is computed by reference to a separate base, each of the portion of the levy based on income and the portion of the levy based on net worth is considered, for purposes of sections 901 and 903, to be a separate levy.

Example (2). A foreign statute imposes a levy on nonresident alien individuals analogous to the taxes imposed by section 871 of the Internal Revenue Code. For the same reasons as set forth in example 1, each of the portion of the foreign levy analogous to the tax imposed by section 871(a) and the portion of the foreign levy analogous to the tax imposed by sections 871(b) and 1, is considered, for purposes of sections 901 and 903, to be a separate levy.

Example (3). A single foreign statute or separate foreign statutes impose a foreign levy that is the sum of the products of specified rates applied to specified bases, as follows:

Bases	Rate (percent)
Net income from mining	45
Net income from manufacturing	50
Net income from technical services	50
Net income from other services	45
Net income from investment	15
All other net income	50

In computing each such base, deductible expenditures are allocated to the type of income they generate. If allocated deductible expenditures exceed the gross amount of a specified type of income, the excess may not be applied against income of a different specified type. Accordingly, the levy is the sum of several separately computed amounts, each of which is computed by reference to a separate base. Each of the levies on mining net income, manufacturing net income, technical services net income, other services net income, investment net income and other net income is, therefore, considered, for purposes of sections 901 and 903, to be a separate levy.

Example (4). The facts are the same as in example 3, except that excess deductible expenditures allocated to one type of income are applied against other types of income to which the same rate applies. The levies on mining net income and other services net income together are considered, for purposes of sections 901 and 903, to be a single levy since, despite a separate preliminary computation of the bases, by reason of the permitted application of excess allocated deductible expenditures, the bases are not separately computed. For the same reason, the levies on manufacturing net income, technical services net income and other net income together are considered, for purposes of sections 901 and 903, to be a single levy. The levy on investment net income is considered, for purposes of sections 901 and 903, to be a separate levy. These results are not dependent on whether the application of excess allocated deductible expenditures to a different type of income, as described above, is permitted in the same taxable period in which the expenditures are taken into account for purposes of the preliminary computation, or only in a different (e.g., later) taxable period.

Example (5). The facts are the same as in example 3, except that excess deductible expenditures allocated to any type of income other than investment income are applied against the other types of income (including investment income) according to a specified set of priorities of application. Excess deductible expenditures allocated to investment income are not applied against any other type of income. For the reason expressed in example 4, all of the levies are together considered, for purposes of sections 901 and 903, to be a single levy.

(e) Amount of Income tax that is creditable. *(1) In general.* Credit is allowed under section 901 for the amount of income tax (within the meaning of paragraph (a)(1) of this section) that is paid to a foreign country by the taxpayer. The amount of income tax paid by the taxpayer is determined separately for each taxpayer.

(2) Refunds and credits. (i) In general. An amount is not tax paid to a foreign country to the extent that it is reasonably certain that the amount will be refunded, credited, rebated, abated, or forgiven. It is not reasonably certain that an amount will be refunded, credited, rebated, abated, or forgiven if the amount is not greater than a reasonable approximation of final tax liability to the foreign country.

(ii) Examples, the provisions of paragraph (e)(2)(i) of this section may be illustrated by the following examples:

Example (1). The internal law of country X imposes a 25 percent tax on the gross amount of interest from sources in country X that is received by a nonresident of country X. Country X law imposes the tax on the nonresident recipient and requires any resident of country X that pays such interest to a nonresident to withhold and pay over to country X 25 percent of such interest, which is applied to offset the recipient's liability for the 25 percent tax. A tax treaty between the United States and country X overrides internal law of country X and provides that country X may not tax interest received by a resident of the United States from a resident of country X at a rate in excess of 10 percent of the gross amount of such interest. A resident of the United States may claim the benefit of the treaty only by applying for refund of the excess withheld amount (15 percent of the gross amount of interest income) after the end of the taxable year. A, a resident of the United States, receives a gross amount of 100u (units of country X currency) of interest income from a resident of country X from sources in country X in the taxable year 1984, from which 25u of country X tax is withheld. A files a timely claim for refund of the 15u excess withheld amount. 15u of the amount withheld (25u – 10u) is reasonably certain to be refunded; therefore 15u is not considered an amount of tax paid to country X.

Example (2). A's initial income tax liability under country X law is 100u (units of country X currency). However, under country X law A's initial income tax liability is reduced in order to compute its final tax liability by an investment credit of 15u and a credit for charitable contributions of 5u. The amount of income tax paid by A is 80u.

Example (3). A computes his income tax liability in country X for the taxable year 1984 as 100u (units of country X currency), files a tax return on that basis, and pays 100u of tax. The day after A files that return, A files a claim for refund of 90u. The difference between the 100u of liability reflected in A's original return and the 10u of liability reflected in A's refund claim depends on whether a particular expenditure made by A is nondeductible or deductible, respectively. Based on an analysis of the country X tax law, A's country X tax advisors have advised A that it is not clear whether or not that expenditure is deductible. In view of the uncertainty as to the proper treatment of the item in question under country X tax law, no portion of the 100u paid by A is reasonably certain to be refunded. If A receives a refund, A must treat the refund as required by section 905(c) of the Internal Revenue Code.

Example (4). A levy of country X, which qualifies as an income tax within the meaning of paragraph (a)(1) of this section, provides that each person who makes payment to country X pursuant to the levy will receive a bond to be issued by country X with an amount payable at maturity equal to 10 percent of the amount paid pursuant to the levy. A pays 38,000u (units of country X currency) to country X and is entitled to receive a bond with an amount payable at maturity of 3800u. It is reasonably certain that a refund in the form of property (the bond) will be made. The amount of that refund is equal to the fair market value of the bond. Therefore, only the portion of the 38,000u payment in excess of the fair market value of the bond is an amount of tax paid.

(3) Subsidies. (i) General rule. An amount of foreign income tax is not an amount of income tax paid or accrued by a taxpayer to a foreign country to the extent that—

(A) The amount is used, directly or indirectly, by the foreign country imposing the tax to provide a subsidy by any means (including, but not limited to, a rebate, a refund, a credit, a deduction, a payment, a discharge of an obligation, or any other method) to the taxpayer, to a related person (within the meaning of section 482), to any party to the transaction, or to any party to a related transaction; and

(B) The subsidy is determined, directly or indirectly, by reference to the amount of the tax or by reference to the base used to compute the amount of the tax.

(ii) Subsidy. The term "subsidy" includes any benefit conferred, directly or indirectly, by a foreign country to one of the parties enumerated in paragraph (e)(3)(i)(A) of this section. Substance and not form shall govern in determining whether a subsidy exists. The fact that the U.S. taxpayer may derive no demonstrable benefit from the subsidy is irrelevant in determining whether a subsidy exists.

(iii) Official exchange rate. A subsidy described in paragraph (e)(3)(i)(B) of this section does not include the actual use of an official foreign government exchange rate converting foreign currency into dollars where a free exchange rate also exists if—

(A) The economic benefit represented by the use of the official exchange rate is not targeted to or tied to transactions that give rise to a claim for a foreign tax credit;

(B) The economic benefit of the official exchange rate applies to a broad range of international transactions, in all cases based on the total payment to be made without regard to whether the payment is a return of principal, gross income, or net income, and without regard to whether it is subject to tax; and

(C) Any reduction in the overall cost of the transaction is merely coincidental to the broad structure and operation of the official exchange rate.

In regard to foreign taxes paid or accrued in taxable years beginning before January 1, 1987, to which the Mexican Exchange Control Decree, effective as of December 20, 1982, applies, see Rev. Rul. 84-143, 1984-2 C.B. 127.

(iv) Examples. The provisions of this paragraph (e)(3) may be illustrated by the following examples:

Example (1). (i) Country X imposes a 30 percent tax on nonresident lenders with respect to interest which the nonresident lenders receive from borrowers who are residents of Country X, and it is established that this tax is a tax in lieu of an income tax within meaning of § 1.903-1(a). Country X provides the nonresident lenders with receipts upon their payment of the 30 percent tax. Country X remits to resident borrowers an incentive payment for engaging in foreign loans, which payment is an amount equal to 20 percent of the interest paid to nonresident lenders.

(ii) Because the incentive payment is based on the interest paid, it is determined by reference to the base used to compute the tax that is imposed on the nonresident lender. The incentive payment is considered a subsidy under this paragraph (e)(3) since it is provided to a party (the borrower) to the transaction and is based on the amount of tax that is imposed on the lender with respect to the transaction. Therefore, two-thirds (20 percent/30 percent) of the amount withheld by the resident borrower from interest payments to the nonresidential lender is not an amount of income tax paid or accrued for purposes of section 901(b).

Example (2). (i) A U.S. bank lends money to a development bank in Country X. The development bank relends the money to companies resident in Country X. A withholding tax is imposed by Country X on the U.S. bank with respect to the interest that the development bank pays to the U.S. bank, and appropriate receipts are provided. On the date that the tax is withheld, fifty percent of the tax is credited by Country X to an account of the development bank. Country X requires the development bank to transfer the amount credited to the borrowing companies.

(ii) The amount successively credited to the account of the development bank and then to the account of the borrowing companies is determined by reference to the amount of the tax and the tax base. Since the amount credited to the borrowing companies is a subsidy provided to a party (the borrowing companies) to a related transaction and is based on the amount of tax and the tax base, it is not an amount paid or accrued as an income tax for purposes of section 901(b).

Example (3). (i) A U.S. bank lends dollars to a Country X borrower. Country X imposes a withholding tax on the lender with respect to the interest. The tax is to be paid in Country X currency, although the interest is payable in dollars. Country X has a dual exchange rate system, comprised of a controlled official exchange rate and a free exchange rate. Priority transactions such as exports of merchandise, imports of merchandise, and payments of principal and interest on foreign currency loans payable abroad to foreign lenders are governed by the official exchange rate which yields more dollars per unit of Country X currency than the free exchange rate. The Country X borrower remits the net amount of dollar interest due to the U.S. bank (interest due less withholding tax), pays the tax withheld in Country X currency to the Country X government, and provides to the U.S. bank a receipt for payment of the Country X taxes.

(ii) The use of the official exchange rate by the U.S. bank to determine foreign taxes with respect to interest is not a subsidy described in paragraph (e)(3)(i)(B) of this section. The official exchange rate is not targeted to or tied to transactions that give rise to a claim for a foreign tax credit. The use of the official exchange rate applies to the interest paid and to the principal paid. Any benefit derived by the U.S. bank through the use of the official exchange rate is merely coincidental to the broad structure and operation of the official exchange rate.

Example (4). (i) B, a U.S. corporation, is engaged in the production of oil and gas in Country X pursuant to a production sharing agreement between B, Country X, and the state petroleum authority of Country X. The agreement is approved and enacted into law by the Legislature of Country X. Both B and the petroleum authority are subject to the Country X income tax. Each entity files an annual income tax return and pays, to the tax authority of Country X, the amount of income-tax due on its annual income. B is a dual capacity taxpayer as defined in § 1.901-2(a)(2)(ii)(A). Country X has agreed to return to the petroleum authority one-half of the income taxes paid by B by allowing it a credit in calculating its own its own tax liability to Country X.

(ii) The petroleum authority is a party to a transaction with B and the amount returned by Country X to the petroleum authority is determined by reference to the amount of the tax imposed on B. Therefore, the amount returned is a subsidy as described in this paragraph (e)(3) and one-half the tax imposed on B is not an amount of income tax paid or accrued.

Example (5). Assume the same facts as in *Example 4,* except that the state petroleum authority of Country X does not receive amounts from Country X related to tax paid by B. Instead, the authority of Country X receives a general appropriation from Country X, which is not calculated with reference to the amount of tax paid by B. The general appropriation is therefore not a subsidy described in this paragraph (e)(3).

(v) Effective Date. This paragraph (e)(3) shall apply to foreign taxes paid or accrued in taxable years beginning after December 31, 1986.

(4) Multiple levies. (i) In general. If, under foreign law, a taxpayer's tentative liability for one levy (the "first levy") is or can be reduced by the amount of the taxpayer's liability for a different levy (the "second levy"), then the amount considered paid by the taxpayer to the foreign country pursuant to the second levy is an amount equal to its entire liability for that levy, and the remainder of the amount paid is considered paid pursuant to the first levy. This rule applies regardless of whether it is or is not likely that liability for one such levy will always exceed liability for the other such levy. For an example of the application of this rule, see example (5) of § 1.903-1(b)(3). If, under foreign law, the amount of a taxpayer's liability is the greater or lesser of amounts computed pursuant to two levies, then the entire amount paid to the foreign country by the taxpayer is considered paid pursuant to the levy that imposes such greater or lesser amount, respectively, and no amount is considered paid pursuant to such other levy.

(ii) Integrated tax systems. [Reserved]

(5) Noncompulsory amounts. (i) In general. An amount paid is not a compulsory payment, and thus is not an amount of tax paid, to the extent that the amount paid exceeds the

amount of liability under foreign law for tax. An amount paid does not exceed the amount of such liability if the amount paid is determined by the taxpayer in a manner that is consistent with a reasonable interpretation and application of the substantive and procedural provisions of foreign law (including applicable tax treaties) in such a way as to reduce, over time, the taxpayer's reasonably expected liability under foreign law for tax, and if the taxpayer exhausts all effective and practical remedies, including invocation of competent authority procedures available under applicable tax treaties, to reduce, over time, the taxpayer's liability for foreign tax (including liability pursuant to a foreign tax audit adjustment). Where foreign tax law includes options or elections whereby a taxpayer's tax liability may be shifted, in whole or part, to a different year or years, the taxpayer's use or failure to use such options or elections does not result in a payment in excess of the taxpayer's liability for foreign tax. An interpretation or application of foreign law is not reasonable if there is actual notice or constructive notice (e.g., a published court decision) to the taxpayer that the interpretation or application is likely to be erroneous. In interpreting foreign tax law, a taxpayer may generally rely on advice obtained in good faith from competent foreign tax advisors to whom the taxpayer has disclosed the relevant facts. A remedy is effective and practical only if the cost thereof (including the risk of offsetting or additional tax liability) is reasonable in light of the amount at issue and the likelihood of success. A settlement by a taxpayer of two or more issues will be evaluated on an overall basis, not on an issue-by-issue basis, in determining whether an amount is a compulsory amount. A taxpayer is not required to alter its form of doing business, its business conduct, or the form of any business transaction in order to reduce its liability under foreign law for tax.

(ii) Examples. The provisions of paragraph (e)(5)(i) of this section may be illustrated by the following examples:

Example (1). A, a corporation organized and doing business solely in the United States, owns all of the stock of B, a corporation organized in country X. In 1984 A buys merchandise from unrelated persons for $1,000,000, shortly thereafter resells that merchandise to B for $600,000, and B later in 1984 resells the merchandise to unrelated persons for $1,200,000. Under the country X income tax, which is an income tax within the meaning of paragraph (a)(1) of this section, all corporations organized in country X are subject to a tax equal to 3 percent of their net income. In computing its 1984 country X income tax liability B reports $600,000 ($1,200,000 – $600,000) of profit from the purchase and resale of the merchandise referred to above. The country X income tax law requires that transactions between related persons be reported at arm's length prices, and a reasonable interpretation of this requirement, as it has been applied in country X, would consider B's arm's length purchase price of the merchandise purchased from A to be $1,050,000. When it computes its country X tax liability B is aware that $600,000 in not an arm's length price (by country X standards). B's knowing use of a non-arm's length price (by country X standards) of $600,000, instead of a price of $1,050,000 (an arm's length price under country X's law), is not consistent with a reasonable interpretation and application of the law of country X, determined in such a way as to reduce over time B's reasonably expected liability for country X income tax. Accordingly, $13,500 (3 percent of $450,000 ($1,050,000 – $600,000)), the amount of country X income tax paid by B to country X that is attributable to the purchase of the merchandise from B's parent at less than an arm's length price, is in excess of the amount of B's liability for country X tax, and thus is not an amount of tax.

Example (2). A, a corporation organized and doing business solely in the United States, owns all of the stock of B, a corporation organized in country X. Country X has in force an income tax treaty with the United States. The treaty provides that the profits of related persons shall be determined as if the persons were not related. A and B deal extensively with each other. A and B, with respect to a series of transactions involving both of them, treat A as having $300,000 of income and B as having $700,000 of income for purposes of A's United States income tax and B's country X income tax, respectively. B has no actual or constructive notice that its treatment of these transactions under country X law is likely to be erroneous. Subsequently, the Internal Revenue Service reallocates $200,000 of this income from B to A under the authority of section 482 and the treaty. This reallocation constitutes actual notice to A and constructive notice to B that B's interpretation and application of country X's law and the tax treaty is likely to be erroneous. B does not exhaust all effective and practical remedies to obtain a refund of the amount of country X income tax paid by B to country X that is attributable to the reallocated $200,000 of income. This amount is in excess of the amount of B's liability for country X tax and thus is not an amount of tax.

Example (3). The facts are the same as in example 2, except that B files a claim for refund (an administrative proceeding) of country X tax and A or B invokes the competent authority procedures of the treaty, the cost of which is reasonable in view of the amount at issue and the likelihood of success. Nevertheless, B does not obtain any refund of country X tax. The cost of pursuing any judicial remedy in country X would be unreasonable in light of the amount at issue and the likelihood of B's success, and B does not pursue any such remedy. The entire amount paid by B to country X is a compulsory payment and thus is an amount of tax paid by B.

Example (4). The facts are the same as in example 2, except that, when the Internal Revenue Service makes the reallocation, the country X statute of limitations on refunds has expired; and neither the internal law of the country X nor the treaty authorizes the the country X tax authorities to pay a refund that is barred by the statute of limitations. B does not file a claim for refund, and neither A nor B invokes the competent authority procedures of the treaty. Because the country X tax authorities would be barred by the statute of limitations from paying a refund, B has no effective and practicable remedies. The entire amount paid by B to country X is a compulsory payment and thus is an amount of tax paid by B.

Example (5). A is a U.S. person doing business in country X. In computing its income tax liability to the country X. A is permitted, at its election to recover the cost of machinery used in its business either by deducting that cost in the year of acquisition or by depreciating that cost on the straight line method over a period of 2, 4, 6 or 10 years. A elects to depreciate machinery over 10 years. This election merely shifts A's tax liability to different years (compared to the timing of A's tax liability under a different depreciation period); it does not result in a payment in excess of the amount of A's liability for the country X income tax in any year since the amount of the country X tax paid by A is consistent with a reasonable interpretation of the country X law in such a way as to reduce over time A's reasonably expected liability for the country X tax. Because the standard of paragraph (e)(5(i) of this section refers to A's reasonably expected liability, not its actual liability, events actually occurring in subsequent years (e.g., whether A has sufficient profit in such years so that such depreciation deductions actually reduce A's country X tax liability or whether the country X tax rates change) are immaterial.

Example (6). The internal law of country X imposes a 25 percent tax on the gross amount of interest from sources in country X that is received by a nonresident of country X. Country X law imposes the tax on the nonresident recipient and requires any resident of country X that pays such interest to a nonresident to withhold and pay over to country X 25 percent of such interest, which is applied to offset the recipient's liability for the 25 percent tax. A tax treaty between the United States and country X overrides internal law of country X and provides that country X may not tax interest received by a resident of the United States from a resident of country X at a rate in excess of 10 percent of the gross amount of such interest. A resident of the United States may claim the benefit of the treaty only by applying for a refund of the excess withheld amount (15 percent of the gross amount of interest income) after the end of the taxable year, A, a resident of the United States, receives a gross amount of 100u (units of country X currency) of interest income from a resident of country X from sources in country X in the taxable year 1984, from which 25u of country X tax is withheld. A does not file a timely claim for refund. 15u of the amount withheld (25u − 10u) is not a compulsory payment and hence is not an amount of tax.

(f) Taxpayer. *(1) In general.* The person by whom tax is considered paid for purposes of sections 901 and 903 is the person on whom foreign law imposes legal liability for such tax, even if another person (e.g., a withholding agent) remits such tax. For purposes of this section, § 1.901-2A and § 1.903-1, the person on whom foreign law imposes such liability is referred to as the "taxpayer." A foreign tax of a type described in paragraph (a)(2)(ii)(c) of this section is considered to be imposed on the recipients of wages if such tax is deducted from such wages under provisions that are comparable to section 3102(a) and (b) of the Internal Revenue Code.

(2) Party undertaking tax obligation as part of transaction. (i) In general. Tax is considered paid by the taxpayer even if another party to a direct or indirect transaction with the taxpayer agrees, as a part of the transaction, to assume the taxpayer's foreign tax liability. The rules of the foregoing sentence apply notwithstanding anything to the contrary in paragraph (e)(3) of this section. See § 1.901-2A for additional rules regarding dual capacity taxpayers.

(ii) Examples. The provisions of paragraphs (f)(1) and (f)(2)(i) of this section may be illustrated by the following examples:

Example (1). Under a loan agreement between A, a resident of county X, and B, a United States person, A agrees to pay B a certain amount of interest net of any tax that country X may impose on B with respect to its interest income. Country X imposes a 10 percent tax on the gross amount of interest income received by nonresidents of country X from sources in country X, and it is established that this tax is a tax in lieu of an income tax within the meaning of § 1.903-1(a). Under the law of country X this tax is imposed on the nonresident recipient, and any resident of country X that pays such interest to a nonresident is required to withhold and pay over to country X 10 percent of the amount of such interest, which is applied to offset the recipient's liability for the tax. Because legal liability for the tax is imposed on the recipient of such interest income, B is the taxpayer with respect to country X tax imposed on B's interest income from B's loan to A. Accordingly, B's interest income for federal income tax purposes includes the amount of country X tax that is imposed on B with respect to such interest income and that is paid on B's behalf by A pursuant to the loan agreement, and, under paragraph (f)(2)(i) of this section, such tax is considered for purposes of section 903 to be paid by B.

Example (2). The facts are the same as in example (1), except that in collecting and receiving the interest B is acting as a nominee for, or agent of, C, who is a United States person. Because C (not B) is the beneficial owner of the interest, legal liability for the tax is imposed on C, not B (C's nominee or agent). Thus, C is the taxpayer with respect to country X tax imposed on C's interest income from C's loan to A. Accordingly, C's interest income for federal income tax purposes includes the amount of country X tax that is imposed on C with respect to such interest income and that is paid on C's behalf by A pursuant to the loan agreement. Under paragraph (f)(2)(i) of this section, such tax is considered for purposes of section 903 to be paid by C. No such tax is considered paid by B.

Example (3). Country X imposes a tax called the "country X income tax." A, a United States person engaged in construction activities in country X, is subject to that tax. Country X has contracted with A for A to construct a naval base. A is a dual capacity taxpayer (as defined in paragraph (a)(2)(ii)(A) of this section) and, in accordance with paragraphs (a)(1) and (c)(1) of § 1.901-2A, A has established that country X income tax as applied to dual capacity persons and country X income tax as applied to persons other than dual capacity persons together constitute a single levy. A has also established that that levy is an income tax within the meaning of paragraph (a)(1) of this section. Pursuant to the terms of the contract, country X has agreed to assume any country X tax liability that A may incur with respect to A's income from the contract. For federal income tax purposes, A's income from the contract includes the amount of tax liability that is imposed by country X on A with respect to its income from the contract and that is assumed by country X; and for purposes of section 901 the amount of such tax liability assumed by country X is considered to be paid by A. By reason of paragraph (f)(2)(i) of this section, country X is not considered to provide a subsidy, within the meaning of paragraph (e)(3) of this section, to A.

(3) Taxes paid on combined income. If foreign income tax is imposed on the combined income of two or more related persons (for example, a husband and wife or a corporation and one or more of its subsidiaries) and they are jointly and severally liable for the income tax under foreign law, foreign law is considered to impose legal liability on each such person for the amount of the foreign income tax that is attributable to its portion of the base of the tax, regardless of which person actually pays the tax.

(g) Definitions. For purposes of this section and §§ 1.901-2A and 1.903-1, the following definitions apply:

(1) The term "paid" means "paid or accrued"; the term "payment" means "payment or accrual"; and the term "paid by" means "paid or accrued by or on behalf of."

(2) The term "foreign country" means any foreign state, any possession of the United States, and any political subdivision of any foreign state or of any possession of the United States. The term "possession of the United States" includes Puerto Rico, the Virgin Islands, Guam, the Northern Mariana Islands and American Samoa.

(3) The term "foreign levy" means a levy imposed by a foreign country.

(h) Effective date. *(1) In general.* This section, § 1.901-2A, and § 1.903-1 apply to taxable years beginning after November 14, 1983. In addition, a person may elect to apply the provisions of this section, § 1.901-2A, and § 1.903-1 to earlier years. See paragraph (h)(2) of this section.

(2) Election to apply regulations to earlier years. (i) Scope of election. An election to apply the provisions of this section, § 1.901-2A, and § 1.903-1 to taxable years beginning on or before November 14, 1983, is made with respect to one or more foreign states and possessions of the United States with respect to a taxable year of the person making the election beginning on or before November 14, 1983. Such election requires all of the provisions of this section, § 1.901-2A, and § 1.903-1 to be applied to such taxable year and to all subsequent taxable years of the person making the election ("elected years"). If an election applies to a foreign state or to a possession of the United States ("election country"), it applies to all taxes of the election country and to all taxes of all political subdivisions of the election country. An election does not apply to foreign taxes carried forward to any elected year from any taxable year to which the election does not apply. Such election does apply to foreign taxes carried back or forward from any elected year to any taxable year.

(ii) Effect of election. An election to apply the regulations to earlier years has no effect on the limitations on assessment and collection or on the limitations on credit or refund (see Chapter 66 of the Internal Revenue Code).

(iii) Manner of making election. An election to apply the regulations to one or more earlier taxable years is made by attaching a statement to a return, amended return, or claim for refund for the earliest taxable year to which the election relates. Such statement shall state that the election is made and, unless the election is to apply to all foreign countries, the statement shall designate the election countries. In the absence of such a designation of the election countries, all foreign countries shall be election countries.

(iv) Time for making election. An election to apply the regulations to earlier taxable years must be made by October 12, 1984, except that if a person who has deducted (instead of credited) foreign taxes in its United States income tax return for such an earlier taxable year validly makes an election to credit (instead of deduct) such taxes in a timely filed amended return for such earlier taxable year and such amended return is filed after such date, an election to apply the regulations to such earlier taxable year must be made in such amended return.

(v) Revocation of election. An election to apply the regulations to earlier taxable years may not be revoked.

(vi) Affiliated groups. A member of an affiliated group that files a consolidated United States income tax return may apply the regulations to earlier years only if an election to so apply them has been made by the common parent of such affiliated group on behalf of all members of the group.

T.D. 7918, 10/6/83, amend T.D. 8372, 10/30/91.

PAR. 3. In § 1.901-2, paragraphs (f) and (h) are revised to read as follows:

Proposed § 1.901-2 Income, war profits, or excess profits tax paid or accrued. [*For Preamble, see ¶ 152,781*]

* * * * *

(f) Taxpayer. *(1) In general.* (i) Income taxes. Income tax (within the meaning of paragraphs (a) through (c) of this section) is considered paid for U.S. income tax purposes by the person on whom foreign law imposes legal liability for such tax. In general, foreign law is considered to impose legal liability for tax on income on the person who is required to take the income into account for foreign income tax purposes (paragraph (f)(4) of this section reserves with respect to certain related party hybrid payments). This rule applies even if under foreign law another person is obligated to remit the tax, another person (e.g., a withholding agent) actually remits the tax, or foreign law permits the foreign country to proceed against another person to collect the tax in the event the tax is not paid. However, see section 905(b) and the regulations thereunder for rules relating to proof of payment. Except as provided in paragraph (f)(2)(i) of this section, for purposes of this section the term person has the meaning set forth in section 7701(a)(1), and so includes an entity treated as a corporation, trust, estate or partnership for U.S. tax purposes, but not a disregarded entity described in § 301.7701-2(c)(2)(i) of this chapter. The person on whom foreign law imposes legal liability is referred to as the "taxpayer" for purposes of this section, § 1.901-2A, and § 1.903-1.

(ii) Taxes in lieu of income taxes. The principles of paragraph (f)(1)(i) and paragraphs (f)(2) through (f)(5) of this section shall apply to determine the person who is considered to have legal liability for, and thus to have paid, a tax in lieu of an income tax (within the meaning of § 1.903-1(a)). Accordingly, foreign law is considered to impose legal liability for any such tax on the person who is the owner of the base on which the tax is imposed for foreign tax purposes.

(2) Taxes on combined income of two or more persons. (i) In general. If foreign tax is imposed on the combined income of two or more persons (for example, a husband and wife or a corporation and one or more of its subsidiaries), foreign law is considered to impose legal liability on each such person for the amount of the tax that is attributable to such person's portion of the base of the tax. Therefore, if foreign tax is imposed on the combined income of two or more persons, such tax shall be allocated among, and considered paid by, such persons on a pro rata basis. For this purpose, the term pro rata means in proportion to each person's portion of the combined income, as determined under paragraph (f)(2)(iv) of this section and, generally, under foreign law. The rules of this paragraph (f)(2) apply regardless of which person is obligated to remit the tax, which person actually remits the tax, or which person the foreign country could proceed against to collect the tax in the event all or a portion of the tax is not paid. For purposes of this paragraph (f)(2), the term person shall include a disregarded entity described in § 301.7701-2(c)(2)(i) of this chapter. In determining the amount of tax paid by an owner of a hybrid partnership or disregarded entity (as defined in paragraph (f)(3) of this section), this paragraph (f)(2) shall first apply to determine the amount of tax paid by the hybrid partnership or disregarded entity, and then paragraph (f)(3) of this section shall apply to allocate the amount of such tax to the owner.

(ii) Combined income. For purposes of this paragraph (f)(2), foreign tax is imposed on the combined income of two or more persons if such persons compute their taxable income on a combined basis under foreign law. Foreign tax is considered to be imposed on the combined income of two or more persons even if the combined income is computed under foreign law by attributing to one such person (e.g., the foreign parent of a foreign consolidated group) the income of other such persons. However, foreign tax is not considered to be imposed on the combined income of two or more persons solely because foreign law:

(A) Permits one person to surrender a net loss to another person pursuant to a group relief or similar regime;

(B) Requires a shareholder of a corporation to include in income amounts attributable to taxes imposed on the corporation with respect to distributed earnings, pursuant to an integrated tax system that allows the shareholder a credit for such taxes; or

(C) Requires a shareholder to include, pursuant to an anti-deferral regime (similar to subpart F of the Internal Revenue Code (sections 951 through 965)), income attributable to the shareholder's interest in the corporation.

(iii) Reverse hybrid entities. For purposes of this paragraph (f)(2), if an entity is a corporation for U.S. income tax purposes and a person is required to take all or a part of the income of one or more such entities into account under foreign law because the entity is treated as a branch or a pass-through entity under foreign law (a reverse hybrid), tax imposed on the person's share of income from each reverse hybrid and tax imposed by the foreign country on other income of the person, if any, is considered to be imposed on the combined income of the person and each reverse hybrid. Therefore, under paragraph (f)(2)(i) of this section, foreign tax imposed on the combined income of the person and each reverse hybrid shall be allocated between the person and the reverse hybrid on a pro rata basis. For this purpose, the term pro rata means in proportion to the portion of the combined income included in the foreign tax base that is attributable to the person's share of income from each reverse hybrid and the portion of the combined income that is attributable to the other income of the person (including income received from a reverse hybrid other than in the owner's capacity as an owner). If the person has a share of income from the reverse hybrid but no other income on which tax is imposed by the foreign country, the entire amount of foreign tax is allocated to and considered paid by the reverse hybrid.

(iv) Portion of combined income. (A) In general. Except with respect to income attributable to related party hybrid payments or accrued amounts described in paragraph (f)(4) of this section, each person's portion of the combined income shall be determined by reference to any return, schedule or other document that must be filed or maintained with respect to a person showing such person's income for foreign tax purposes, as properly amended or adjusted for foreign tax purposes. If no such return, schedule or document must be filed or maintained with respect to a person for foreign tax purposes, then, for purposes of this paragraph (f)(2), such person's income shall be determined from the books of account regularly maintained by or on behalf of the person for purposes of computing its taxable income under foreign law.

(B) Effect of certain payments. Each person's portion of the combined income shall be determined by giving effect to payments and accrued amounts of interest, rents, royalties, and other amounts to the extent such payments or accrued amounts are taken into account in computing the separate taxable income of such person both under foreign law and under U.S. tax principles. With respect to certain related party hybrid payments, see the reservation in paragraph (f)(4) of this section. Thus, for example, interest paid by a reverse hybrid to one of its owners with respect to an instrument that is treated as debt for both U.S. and foreign tax purposes would be considered income of the owner and would reduce the taxable income of the reverse hybrid. However, each person's portion of the combined income shall be determined without taking into account any payments from other persons whose income is included in the combined base that are treated as dividends under foreign law, and without taking into account deemed dividends or any similar attribution of income made for purposes of computing the combined income under foreign law. This rule applies regardless of whether any such dividend, deemed dividend or attribution of income results in a deduction or inclusion under foreign law.

(C) Net losses. If tax is considered to be imposed on the combined income of three or more persons and one or more of such persons has a net loss for the taxable year for foreign tax purposes, the following rules apply. If foreign law provides mandatory rules for allocating the net loss among the other persons, then the rules that apply for foreign tax purposes shall apply for purposes of paragraph (f)(2)(iv) of this section. If foreign law does not provide mandatory rules for allocating the net loss, the net loss shall be allocated among all other such persons pro rata based on the amount of each person's income, as determined under paragraphs (f)(2)(iv)(A) and (B) of this section. For purposes of this paragraph (f)(2)(iv)(C), foreign law shall not be considered to provide mandatory rules for allocating a loss solely because such loss is attributed from one person to a second person for purposes of computing combined income, as described in paragraph (f)(2)(ii) of this section.

(v) Collateral consequences. U.S. tax principles shall apply to determine the tax consequences if one person remits a tax that is the legal liability of, and thus is considered paid by, another person. For example, a payment of tax for which a corporation has legal liability by a shareholder of that corporation (including an owner of a reverse hybrid) will ordinarily result in a deemed capital contribution and deemed payment of tax by the corporation. If the corporation reimburses the shareholder for the tax payment, such reimbursement would ordinarily be treated as a distribution for U.S. tax purposes.

(3) Taxes on income of hybrid partnerships and disregarded entities. (i) Hybrid partnerships. If foreign law imposes tax at the entity level on the income of an entity that is treated as a partnership for U.S. income tax purposes (a hybrid partnership), the hybrid partnership is considered to be legally liable for such tax under foreign law. Therefore, the hybrid partnership is considered to pay the tax for U.S. income tax purposes. See § 1.704-1(b)(4)(viii) for rules relating to the allocation of such tax among the partners of the partnership. If the hybrid partnership's U.S. taxable year closes for all partners due to a termination of the partnership under section 708 and the regulations thereunder (other than in the case of a termination under section 708(b)(1)(A)) and the foreign taxable year of the partnership does not close, then foreign tax paid or accrued by the partnership with respect to the foreign taxable year that ends with or within the new partnership's first U.S. taxable year shall be allocated between the terminating partnership and the new partnership. The allocation shall be made under the principles of § 1.1502-76(b) based on the respective portions of the taxable income of the partnership (as determined under foreign law) for the foreign taxable year that are attributable to the period ending on and the period ending after the last day of the terminating partnership's U.S. taxable year. The principles of the preceding sentence shall also apply if the hybrid partnership's U.S. taxable year closes with respect to one or more, but less than all, partners or, except as otherwise pro-

vided in section 706(d)(2) or (d)(3) (relating to certain cash basis items of the partnership), there is a change in any partner's interest in the partnership during the partnership's U.S. taxable year. If, as a result of a change in ownership during a hybrid partnership's foreign taxable year, the hybrid partnership becomes a disregarded entity and the entity's foreign taxable year does not close, foreign tax paid or accrued by the disregarded entity with respect to the foreign taxable year shall be allocated between the hybrid partnership and the owner of the disregarded entity under the principles of this paragraph (f)(3)(i).

(ii) Disregarded entities. If foreign tax is imposed at the entity level on the income of an entity described in § 301.7701-2(c)(2)(i) of this chapter (a disregarded entity), foreign law is considered to impose legal liability for the tax on the person who is treated as owning the assets of the disregarded entity for U.S. income tax purposes. Such person shall be considered to pay the tax for U.S. income tax purposes. If there is a change in the ownership of such disregarded entity during the entity's foreign taxable year and such change does not result in a closing of the disregarded entity's foreign taxable year, foreign tax paid or accrued with respect to such foreign taxable year shall be allocated between the old owner and the new owner. The allocation shall be made under the principles of § 1.1502-76(b) based on the respective portions of the taxable income of the disregarded entity (as determined under foreign law) for the foreign taxable year that are attributable to the period ending on the date of the ownership change and the period ending after such date. If, as a result of a change in ownership, the disregarded entity becomes a hybrid partnership and the entity's foreign taxable year does not close, foreign tax paid or accrued by the hybrid partnership with respect to the foreign taxable year shall be allocated between the old owner and the hybrid partnership under the principles of this paragraph (f)(3)(ii). If the person who owns a disregarded entity is a partnership for U.S. income tax purposes, see § 1.704-1(b)(4)(viii) for rules relating to the allocation of such tax among the partners of the partnership.

(4) Tax on income attributable to related party payments or accrued amounts that are deductible for foreign (or U.S.) tax law purposes and that are nondeductible for U.S. (or foreign) tax law purposes or that are disregarded for U.S. tax law purposes. [Reserved].

(5) Party undertaking tax obligation as part of transaction. Tax is considered paid by the taxpayer even if another party to a direct or indirect transaction with the taxpayer agrees, as a part of the transaction, to assume the taxpayer's foreign tax liability. The rules of the foregoing sentence apply notwithstanding anything to the contrary in paragraph (e)(3) of this section. See § 1.901-2A for additional rules regarding dual capacity taxpayers.

(6) Examples. The following examples illustrate the rules of paragraphs (f)(1) through (f)(5) of this section.

Example (1). (i) Facts. Under a loan agreement between A, a resident of country X, and B, a United States person, A agrees to pay B a certain amount of interest net of any tax that country X may impose on B with respect to its interest income. Country X imposes a 10 percent tax on the gross amount of interest income received by nonresidents of country X from sources in country X, and it is established that this tax is a tax in lieu of an income tax within the meaning of § 1.903-1(a). Under the law of country X this tax is imposed on the interest income of the nonresident recipient, and any resident of country X that pays such interest to a nonresident is required to withhold and pay over to country X 10 percent of the amount of such interest. Under the law of country X, the country X taxing authority may proceed against A, but not B, if A fails to withhold and pay over the tax to country X.

(ii) Result. Under paragraph (f)(1)(ii) of this section, B is considered legally liable for the country X tax because such tax is imposed on B's interest income. Therefore, for U.S. income tax purposes, B is considered to pay the country X tax, and B's interest income includes the amount of country X tax that is imposed with respect to such interest income and paid on B's behalf by A. No portion of such tax is considered paid by A.

Example (2). (i) Facts. The facts are the same as in Example 1, except that in collecting and receiving the interest B is acting as a nominee for, or agent of, C, who is a United States person. Accordingly, C, not B, is the beneficial owner of the interest for U.S. income tax purposes. Country X law also recognizes the nominee or agency arrangement and, thus, considers C to be the beneficial owner of the interest income.

(ii) Result. Under paragraph (f)(1)(ii) of this section, legal liability for the tax is considered to be imposed on C, not B (C's nominee or agent). Thus, C is the taxpayer with respect to the country X tax imposed on C's interest income from C's loan to A. Accordingly, C's interest income for U.S. income tax purposes includes the amount of country X tax that is imposed on C with respect to such interest income and that is paid on C's behalf by A pursuant to the loan agreement. Under paragraph (f)(1)(ii) of this section, such tax is considered for U.S. income tax purposes to be paid by C. No such tax is considered paid by B.

Example (3). (i) Facts. A, a U.S. person, owns a bond issued by C, a resident of country X. On January 1, 2008, A and B enter into a transaction in which A, in form, sells the bond to B, also a U.S. person. As part of the transaction, A and B agree that A will repurchase the bond from B on December 31, 2013 for the same amount. In addition, B agrees to make payments to A equal to the amount of interest B receives from C. As a result of the arrangement, legal title to the bond is transferred to B. The transfer of legal title has the effect of transferring ownership of the bond to B for country X tax purposes. A remains the owner of the bond for U.S. income tax purposes. Country X imposes a 10 percent tax on the gross amount of interest income received by nonresidents of country X from sources in country X, and it is established that this tax is a tax in lieu of an income tax within the meaning of § 1.903-1(a). Under the law of country X this tax is imposed on the interest income of the nonresident recipient, and any resident of country X that pays such interest to a nonresident is required to withhold and pay over to country X 10 percent of the amount of such interest. On December 31, 2008, C pays B interest on the bond and withholds 10 percent of country X tax.

(ii) Result. Under paragraph (f)(1)(ii) of this section, B is considered legally liable for the country X tax because B is the owner of the interest income for country X tax purposes, even though A and not B recognizes the interest income for U.S. tax purposes. The result would be the same if the transaction had the effect of transferring ownership of the bond to B for U.S. income tax purposes.

Example (4). (i) Facts. On January 1, 2007, A, a United States person, purchases a bond issued by X, a foreign person resident in country Y. A accrues interest income on the bond for U.S. tax purposes from January 1, 2007, until A sells the bond to B, another United States person, on July 1, 2007. On December 31, 2007, X pays interest on the bond that accrued for the entire year to B. Country Y imposes a 10 percent tax on the gross amount of interest income received by nonresidents of country Y from sources in country Y, and it is established that this tax is a tax in lieu of an income tax within the meaning of § 1.903-1(a). Under the law of country Y this tax is imposed on the interest income of the nonresident recipient, and any resident of country Y that pays such interest to a nonresident is required to withhold and pay over to country Y 10 percent of the amount of such interest. Pursuant to the law of country Y, X withholds tax from the interest paid to B.

(ii) Result. Under paragraph (f)(1)(ii) of this section, legal liability for the tax is considered to be imposed on B. Thus, B is the taxpayer with respect to the entire amount of the country Y tax even though, for U.S. income tax purposes, B only recognizes interest that accrues on the bond on and after July 1, 2007. No portion of the country Y tax is considered to be paid by A even though, for U.S. income tax purposes, A recognizes interest on the bond that accrues prior to July 1, 2007.

Example (5). (i) Facts. A, a United States person and resident of country X, is an employee of B, a corporation organized in country X. Under the laws of country X, B is required to withhold from A's wages and pay over to country X foreign social security tax of a type described in paragraph (a)(2)(ii)(C) of this section, and it is established that this tax is an income tax described in paragraph (a)(1) of this section.

(ii) Result. Under paragraph (f)(1)(i) of this section, A is considered legally liable for the country X tax because such tax is imposed on A's wages. Therefore, for U.S. income tax purposes, A is considered to pay the country X tax.

Example (6). (i) Facts. A, a United States person, owns 100 percent of B, an entity organized in country X. B is a corporation for country X tax purposes, and a disregarded entity for U.S. income tax purposes. B owns 100 percent of corporation C and corporation D, both of which are also organized in country X. B, C and D use the "u" as their functional currency and file on a combined basis for country X income tax purposes. Country X imposes an income tax described in paragraph (a)(1) of this section at the rate of 30 percent on the taxable income of corporations organized in country X. Under the country X combined reporting regime, income (or loss) of C and D is attributed to, and treated as income (or loss) of, B. B has the sole obligation to pay country X income tax imposed with respect to income of B and income of C and D that is attributed to, and treated as income of, B. Under the law of country X, country X may proceed against B, but not C or D, if B fails to pay over to country X all or any portion of the country X income tax imposed with respect to such income. In year 1, B has taxable income of 100u, C has taxable income of 200u, and D has a net loss of (60u). Under the law of country X, B is considered to have 240u of taxable income with respect to which 72u of country X income tax is imposed. Country X does not provide mandatory rules for allocating D's loss.

(ii) Result. Under paragraph (f)(2)(ii) of this section, the 72u of country X tax is considered to be imposed on the combined income of B, C, and D. Because country X law does not provide mandatory rules for allocating D's loss between B and C, under paragraph (f)(2)(iv)(C) of this section D's (60u) loss is allocated pro rata: 20u to B ((100u/300u) x 60u) and 40u to C ((200u/300u) x 60u). Under paragraph (f)(2)(i) of this section, the 72u of country X tax must be allocated pro rata among B, C, and D. Because D has no income for country X tax purposes, no country X tax is allocated to D. Accordingly, 24u (72u x (80u/240u)) of the country X tax is allocated to B, and 48u (72u x (160u/240u)) of such tax is allocated to C. Under paragraph (f)(3)(ii) of this section, A is considered to have legal liability for the 24u of country X tax allocated to B under paragraph (f)(2) of this section.

Example (7). (i) Facts. A, a domestic corporation, owns 95 percent of the voting power and value of C, an entity organized in country Z that uses the "u" as its functional currency. B, a domestic corporation, owns the remaining 5 percent of the voting power and value of C. Pursuant to an election made under § 301.7701-3(a), C is treated as a corporation for U.S. income tax purposes, but as a partnership for country Z income tax purposes. Accordingly, under country Z law, A and B are required to take into account their respective shares of the taxable income of C. Country Z imposes an income tax described in paragraph (a)(1) of this section at the rate of 30 percent on such taxable income. For 2007, C has 500u of taxable income for country Z tax purposes. A's and B's shares of such income are 475u and 25u, respectively. In addition, A has 125u of taxable income attributable to a permanent establishment in country Z. Income of nonresidents that is attributable to a permanent establishment in country Z is also subject to the country Z income tax at a rate of 30 percent. Accordingly, country Z imposes 180u of tax on A's total taxable income of 600u (475u of income from C and 125u of income from the permanent establishment). Country Z imposes 7.5u of tax on B's 25u of taxable income from C.

(ii) Result. Under paragraph (f)(2)(iii) of this section, the 180u of tax imposed on the taxable income of A is considered to be imposed on the combined income of A and C. Under paragraph (f)(2)(i) of this section, such tax must be allocated between A and C on a pro rata basis. Accordingly, C is considered to be legally liable for the 142.5u (180u x (475u/600u)) of country Z tax imposed on A's 475u share of C's income, and A is considered to be legally liable for the 37.5u (180u x (125u/600u)) of the country Z tax imposed on A's 125u of income from its permanent establishment. Under paragraph (f)(2)(iii) of this section, the 7.5u of tax imposed on the taxable income of B is considered to be imposed on the combined income of B and C. Since B has no other income on which income tax is imposed by country Z, under paragraph (f)(2)(iii) of this section the entire amount of such tax is allocated to and considered paid by C. C's post-1986 foreign income taxes include the U.S. dollar equivalent of 150u of country Z income tax C is considered to pay for U.S. income tax purposes. A, but not B, is eligible to compute deemed-paid taxes under section 902(a) in connection with dividends received from C. Under paragraph (f)(2)(v) of this section, the payment by A or B of tax for which C is considered legally liable is treated as a capital contribution by A or B to C.

Example (8). (i) Facts. A, B, and C are U.S. persons that each use the calendar year as their taxable year. A and B each own 50 percent of the capital and profits of D, an entity organized in country M. D is a partnership for U.S. income tax purposes, but is a corporation for country M tax purposes. D uses the "u" as its functional currency and the calendar year as its taxable year for both U.S. tax purposes and country M tax purposes. Country M imposes an income tax described in paragraph (a)(1) of this section at a rate of 30 percent at the entity level on the taxable income of D. On September 30, 2008, A sells its 50 percent interest in D to C. A's sale of its partnership interest results in a termination of the partnership under section 708(b) for U.S. tax purposes. As a result of the termination, "old" D's taxable year closes on September 30, 2008 for U.S. tax purposes. "New"' D also has a short U.S. taxable year, beginning on October 1, 2008, and ending on December 31, 2008. The sale of A's interest does not close D's taxable year for country M tax purposes. D has 400u of taxable income for its 2008 foreign taxable year with respect to which country M imposes 120u equal to $120 of income tax.

(ii) Result. Under paragraph (f)(3)(i) of this section, hybrid partnership D is legally liable for the $120 of country M income tax imposed on its net income. Because D's taxable year closes on September 30, 2008, for U.S. tax purposes, but does not close for country M tax purposes, under paragraph (f)(3)(i) of this section the $120 of country M tax must be allocated under the principles of § 1.1502-76(b) between the short U.S. taxable years of old D and new D. See § 1.704-1(b)(4)(viii) for rules relating to the allocation of old D's country M taxes between A and B and the allocation of new D's country M taxes between B and C.

Example (9). (i) Facts. A, a United States person engaged in construction activities in country X, is subject to the country X income tax. Country X has contracted with A for A to construct a naval base. A is a dual capacity taxpayer (as defined in paragraph (a)(2)(ii)(A) of this section) and, in accordance with paragraphs (a)(1) and (c)(1) of § 1.901-2A, A has established that the country X income tax as applied to dual capacity persons and the country X income tax as applied to persons other than dual capacity persons together constitute a single levy. A has also established that that levy is an income tax within the meaning of paragraph (a)(1) of this section. Pursuant to the terms of the contract, country X has agreed to assume any country X income tax liability that A may incur with respect to A's income from the contract.

(ii) Result. For U.S. income tax purposes, A's income from the contract includes the amount of tax that is imposed by country X on A with respect to its income from the contract and that is assumed by country X; and the amount of the tax liability assumed by country X is considered to be paid by A. By reason of paragraph (f)(5) of this section, country X is not considered to provide a subsidy, within the meaning of section 901(i) and paragraph (e)(3) of this section, to A.

* * * * *

(h) Effective date. Paragraphs (a) through (e) and paragraph (g) of this section, § 1.901-2A and § 1.903-1 apply to taxable years beginning after November 14, 1983. Paragraph (f) of this section is effective for foreign taxes paid or accrued during taxable years of the taxpayer beginning on or after January 1, 2007.

PAR. 2. Section 1.901-2 is amended by adding paragraphs (e)(5)(iii) and (iv), and revising paragraph (h) to read as follows:

Proposed § 1.901-2 Income, war profits, or excess profits tax paid or accrued. [*For Preamble, see ¶ 152,845*]

* * * * *

(e) *(5)* * * *

(iii) U.S.-owned foreign entities. (A) In general. If a U.S. person described in section 901(b) directly or indirectly owns stock possessing 80 percent or more of the total voting power and total value of one or more foreign corporations (or, in the case of a non-corporate foreign entity, directly or indirectly owns an interest in 80 percent or more of the income of one or more such foreign entities), the group comprising such foreign corporations and entities (the "U.S.-owned group") shall be treated as a single taxpayer for purposes of paragraph (e)(5) of this section. Therefore, if one member of such a U.S.-owned group transfers or surrenders a net loss for the taxable year to a second member of the U.S.-owned group and the loss reduces the foreign tax due from the second member pursuant to a foreign law group relief or similar regime, foreign tax paid by the first member in a different year does not fail to be a compulsory payment solely because such tax would not have been due had the member that transferred or surrendered the net loss instead carried over the loss to reduce its own income and foreign tax liability in that year. Similarly, if one or more members of the U.S.-owned group enter into a combined settlement under foreign law of two or more issues involving different members of the group, such settlement will be evaluated on an overall basis, not on an issue-by-issue or entity-by-entity basis, in determining whether an amount is a compulsory amount. The provisions of this paragraph (e)(5)(iii) apply solely for purposes of determining whether amounts paid are compulsory payments of foreign tax and do not, for example, modify the provisions of section 902 requiring separate pools of post-1986 undistributed earnings and post-1986 foreign income taxes for each member of a qualified group.

(B) Special rules. All domestic corporations that are members of a consolidated group (as that term is defined in § 1.1502-1(h)) shall be treated as one domestic corporation for purposes of this paragraph (e)(5)(iii). For purposes of this paragraph (e)(5)(iii), indirect ownership of stock or another equity interest (such as an interest in a partnership) shall be determined in accordance with the principles of section 958(a)(2), whether the interest is owned by a U.S. or foreign person.

(C) Examples. The following examples illustrate the rules of this paragraph (e)(5)(iii):

Example (1). (i) Facts. A, a domestic corporation, wholly owns B, a country X corporation. B, in turn, wholly owns several country X corporations, including C and D. B, C, and D participate in group relief in country X. Under the country X group relief rules, a member with a net loss may choose to surrender the loss to another member of the group. In year 1, C has a net loss of (1,000x) and D has net income of 5,000x for country X tax purposes. Pursuant to the group relief rules in country X, C agrees to surrender its year 1 net loss to D and D agrees to claim the net loss. D uses the net loss to reduce its year 1 net income to 4,000x for country X tax purposes, which reduces the amount of country X tax D owes in year 1 by 300x. In year 2, C earns 3,000x with respect to which it pays 900x of country X tax. Country X permits a taxpayer to carry forward net losses for up to ten years.

(ii) Result. Paragraph (e)(5)(i) of this section provides, in part, that an amount paid to a foreign country does not exceed the amount of liability under foreign law for tax if the taxpayer determines such amount in a manner that is consistent with a reasonable interpretation and application of the substantive and procedural provisions of foreign law (including applicable tax treaties) in such a way as to reduce, over time, the taxpayer's reasonably expected liability under foreign law for tax. Under paragraph (e)(5)(iii)(A) of this section, B, C, and D are treated as a single taxpayer for purposes of testing whether the reasonably expected foreign tax liability has been minimized over time, because A directly and indirectly owns 100 percent of each of B, C, and D. Accordingly, none of the 900x paid by C in year 2 fails to be a compulsory payment solely because C could have reduced its year 2 country X tax liability by 300x by choosing to carry forward its year 1 net loss to year 2 instead of surrendering it to D to reduce D's country X liability in year 1.

Example (2). (i) Facts. L, M, and N are country Y corporations. L owns 100 percent of the common stock of M, which owns 100 percent of the stock of N. O, a domestic corporation, owns a security issued by M that is treated as debt for country Y tax purposes and as stock for U.S. tax purposes. As a result, L owns 100 percent of the stock of M for country Y purposes while O owns 99 percent of the stock of M for U.S. tax purposes. L, M, and N participate in group relief in country Y. Pursuant to the group relief rules in country Y, M may surrender its loss to any member of the group. In year 1, M has a net loss of $10 million, N has net income of $25 million, and L has net income of $15 million. M chooses to surrender its year 1 net loss to L. Country Y imposes tax of 30 percent on the net income of country Y corporations. Accordingly, in year 1, the loss surrender has the effect of reducing L's country Y tax by $3 million. In year 1, N makes a payment of $7.5 million to country Y with respect to its net income of $25 million. If M had surrendered its net loss to N instead of L, N would have had net income of $15 million, with respect to which it would have owed only $4.5 million of country Y tax.

(ii) Result. M and N, but not L, are treated as a single taxpayer for purposes of paragraph (e)(5) of this section because O directly and indirectly owns 99 percent of each of M and N, but owns no direct or indirect interest in L. Accordingly, in testing whether M and N's reasonably expected foreign tax liability has been minimized over time, L is not considered the same taxpayer as M and N, collectively, and the $3 million reduction in L's year 1 country Y tax liability through the surrender to L of M's $10 million country Y net loss in year 1 is not considered to reduce M and N's collective country Y tax liability.

(iv) Certain structured passive investment arrangements. (A) In general. Notwithstanding paragraph (e)(5)(i) of this section, an amount paid to a foreign country (a "foreign payment") is not a compulsory payment, and thus is not an amount of tax paid, if the foreign payment is attributable to an arrangement described in paragraph (e)(5)(iv)(B) of this section. For purposes of this paragraph (e)(5)(iv), a foreign payment is attributable to an arrangement described in paragraph (e)(5)(iv)(B) of this section if the foreign payment is described in paragraph (e)(5)(iv)(B)(1)(ii) of this section.

(B) Conditions. An arrangement is described in this paragraph (e)(5)(iv)(B) if all of the following conditions are satisfied:

(1) Special purpose vehicle (SPV). An entity that is part of the arrangement meets the following requirements:

(i) Substantially all of the gross income (for United States tax purposes) of the entity is passive investment income as defined in paragraph (e)(5)(iv)(C)(4) of this section, and substantially all of the assets of the entity are assets held to produce such passive investment income. As provided in paragraph (e)(5)(iv)(C)(4)(ii) of this section, passive investment income generally does not include income of a holding company from qualified equity interests in lower-tier entities that are predominantly engaged in the active conduct of a trade or business. Thus, except as provided in paragraph (e)(5)(iv)(C)(4)(ii) of this section, qualified equity interests of a holding company in such lower-tier entities are not held to produce passive investment income and the ownership of such interests will not cause the holding company to satisfy this paragraph (e)(5)(iv)(B)(1)(i).

(ii) There is a foreign payment attributable to income of the entity (as determined under the laws of the foreign country to which such foreign payment is made), including the entity's share of income of a lower-tier entity that is a branch or pass-through entity under the laws of such foreign country. A foreign payment attributable to income of an entity includes a foreign payment attributable to income that is required to be taken into account by an owner of the entity, if the entity is a branch or pass-through entity under the laws of such foreign country. A foreign payment attributable to income of an entity also includes a foreign payment attributable to income of a lower-tier entity that is a branch or pass-through entity for U.S. tax purposes. A foreign payment attributable to income of the entity does not include a withholding tax (within the meaning of section 901(k)(1)(B)) imposed on a distribution or payment from the entity to a U.S. party (as defined in paragraph (e)(5)(iv)(B)(2) of this section).

(2) U.S. party. A person (a "U.S. party") would be eligible to claim a credit under section 901(a) (including a credit for foreign taxes deemed paid under section 902 or 960) for all or a portion of the foreign payment described in paragraph (e)(5)(iv)(B)(1)(ii) of this section if the foreign payment were an amount of tax paid.

(3) Direct investment. The foreign payment or payments described in paragraph (e)(5)(iv)(B)(1)(ii) of this section are (or are expected to be) substantially greater than the amount of credits, if any, the U.S. party would reasonably expect to be eligible to claim under section 901(a) for foreign taxes attributable to income generated by the U.S. party's proportionate share of the assets owned by the SPV if the U.S. party directly owned such assets. For this purpose, direct ownership shall not include ownership through a branch, a permanent establishment or any other arrangement (such as an agency arrangement) that would result in the income generated by the U.S. party's proportionate share of the assets being subject to tax on a net basis in the foreign country to which the payment is made. A U.S. party's proportionate share of the assets of the SPV shall be determined by reference to such U.S. party's proportionate share of the total value of all of the outstanding interests in the SPV that are held by its equity owners and creditors.

(4) Foreign tax benefit. The arrangement is structured in such a manner that it results in a foreign tax benefit (such as a credit, deduction, loss, exemption or a disregarded payment) for a counterparty described in paragraph (e)(5)(iv)(B)(5) of this section or for a person that is related to the counterparty (determined under the principles of paragraph (e)(5)(iv)(C)(6) of this section by applying the tax laws of a foreign country in which the counterparty is subject to tax on a net basis) but is not related to the U.S. party (within the meaning of paragraph (e)(5)(iv)(C)(6) of this section).

(5) Unrelated counterparty. The arrangement involves a counterparty. A counterparty is a person (other than the SPV) that is not related to the U.S. party (within the meaning of paragraph (e)(5)(iv)(C)(6) of this section) and that meets one of the following conditions:

(i) The person is considered to own directly or indirectly 10 percent or more of the equity of the SPV under the tax laws of a foreign country in which the person is subject to tax on the basis of place of management, place of incorporation or similar criterion or otherwise subject to a net basis tax.

(ii) In a single transaction or series of transactions, the person directly or indirectly acquires 20 percent or more of the value of the assets of the SPV under the tax laws of a foreign country in which the person is subject to tax on the basis of place of management, place of incorporation or similar criterion or otherwise subject to a net basis tax. For purposes of determining the percentage of assets of the SPV acquired by the person, an asset of the SPV shall be disregarded if a principal purpose for transferring such asset to the SPV was to avoid this paragraph (e)(5)(iv)(B)(5)(ii).

(6) Inconsistent treatment. The U.S. and an applicable foreign country (as defined in paragraph (e)(5)(iv)(C)(1) of this section) treat one or more of the following aspects of the arrangement differently under their respective tax systems, and the U.S. treatment of the inconsistent aspect would materially affect the amount of income recognized by the U.S. party or the amount of credits claimed by the U.S. party if the foreign payment described in paragraph (e)(5)(iv)(B)(1)(ii) of this section were an amount of tax paid:

(i) The classification of the SPV (or an entity that has a direct or indirect ownership interest in the SPV) as a corporation or other entity subject to an entity-level tax, a partnership or other flow-through entity or an entity that is disregarded for tax purposes.

(ii) The characterization as debt, equity or an instrument that is disregarded for tax purposes of an instrument issued by the SPV (or an entity that has a direct or indirect ownership interest in the SPV) to the U.S. party, the counterparty or a person related to the U.S. party or the counterparty.

(iii) The proportion of the equity of the SPV (or an entity that directly or indirectly owns the SPV) that is considered to be owned directly or indirectly by the U.S. party and the counterparty.

(iv) The amount of taxable income of the SPV for one or more tax years during which the arrangement is in effect.

(C) Definitions. (1) Applicable foreign country. An applicable foreign country means each foreign country to which a foreign payment described in paragraph (e)(5)(iv)(B)(1)(ii) of this section is made or which confers a foreign tax benefit described in paragraph (e)(5)(iv)(B)(4) of this section.

(2) Entity. For purposes of paragraph (e)(5)(iv)(B)(1) and (e)(5)(iv)(C)(4) of this section, the term entity includes a corporation, trust, partnership or disregarded entity described in § 301.7701-2(c)(2)(i) of this chapter.

(3) Indirect ownership. For purposes of paragraph (e)(5)(iv) of this section, indirect ownership of stock or another equity interest (such as an interest in a partnership) shall be determined in accordance with the principles of section 958(a)(2), whether the interest is owned by a U.S. or foreign entity.

(4) Passive investment income. (i) In general. For purposes of paragraph (e)(5)(iv) of this section, the term passive investment income means income described in section 954(c), as modified by this paragraph (e)(5)(iv)(C)(4)(i) and paragraph (e)(5)(iv)(C)(4)(ii) of this section. In determining whether income is described in section 954(c), sections 954(c)(3) and 954(c)(6) shall be disregarded, and sections 954(h) and (i) shall be taken into account by applying those provisions at the entity level as if the entity were a controlled foreign corporation (as defined in section 957(a)). In addition, for purposes of the preceding sentence, any income of an entity attributable to transactions with a person that would be a counterparty (as defined in paragraph (e)(5)(iv)(B)(5) of this section) if the entity were an SPV, or with other persons that are described in paragraph (e)(5)(iv)(B)(4) of this section and that are eligible for a foreign tax benefit described in such paragraph (e)(5)(iv)(B)(4), shall not be treated as qualified banking or financing income or as qualified insurance income, and shall not be taken into account in applying sections 954(h) and (i) for purposes of determining whether other income of the entity is excluded from section 954(c)(1) under section 954(h) or (i).

(ii) Income attributable to lower-tier entities. Except as provided in this paragraph (e)(5)(iv)(C)(4)(ii), income of an entity that is attributable to an equity interest in a lower-tier entity is passive investment income. If the entity is a holding company and directly owns a qualified equity interest in another entity (a "lower-tier entity") that is engaged in the active conduct of a trade or business and that derives more than 50 percent of its gross income from such trade or business, then none of the entity's income attributable to such interest is passive investment income, provided that there are no arrangements whereby substantially all of the entity's opportunity for gain and risk of loss with respect to such interest is borne by the U.S. party (or a related person) or the counterparty (or a related person), but not both parties. For purposes of the preceding sentence, an entity is a holding company, and is considered to be engaged in the active conduct of a trade or business and to derive more than 50 percent of its gross income from such trade or business, if substantially all of its assets consist of qualified equity interests in one or more entities, each of which is engaged in the active conduct of a trade or business and derives more than 50 percent of its gross income from such trade or business and with respect to which there are no arrangements whereby substantially all of the entity's opportunity for gain and risk of loss with respect to such interest is borne by the U.S. party (or a related person) or the counterparty (or a related person), but not both parties. For purposes of this paragraph (e)(5)(iv)(C)(4)(ii), a lower-tier entity that is engaged in a banking, financing, or similar business shall not be considered to be engaged in the active conduct of a trade or business unless the income derived by such entity would be excluded from section 954(c)(1) under section 954(h) or (i), determined by applying those provisions at the lower-tier entity level as if the entity were a controlled foreign corporation (as defined in section 957(a)). In addition, for purposes of the preceding sentence, any income of an entity attributable to transactions with a person that would be a counterparty (as defined in paragraph (e)(5)(iv)(B)(5) of this section) if the entity were an SPV, or with other persons that are described in paragraph (e)(5)(iv)(B)(4) of this section and that are eligible for a foreign tax benefit described in such paragraph (e)(5)(iv)(B)(4), shall not be treated as qualified banking or financing income or as qualified insurance income, and shall not be taken into account in applying sections 954(h) and (i) for purposes of determining whether other income of the entity is excluded from section 954(c)(1) under section 954(h) or (i).

(5) Qualified equity interest. With respect to an interest in a corporation, the term qualified equity interest means stock representing 10 percent or more of the total combined voting power of all classes of stock entitled to vote and 10 percent or more of the total value of the stock of the corporation or disregarded entity, but does not include any preferred stock (as defined in section 351(g)(3)). Similar rules shall apply to determine whether an interest in an entity other than a corporation is a qualified equity interest.

(6) Related person. Two persons are related for purposes of paragraph (e)(5)(iv) of this section if—

(i) One person directly or indirectly owns stock (or an equity interest) possessing more than 50 percent of the total value of the other person; or

(ii) The same person directly or indirectly owns stock (or an equity interest) possessing more than 50 percent of the total value of both persons.

(7) Special purpose vehicle (SPV). For purposes of this paragraph (e)(5)(iv), the term SPV means the entity described in paragraph (e)(5)(iv)(B)(1) of this section.

(D) Examples. The following examples illustrate the rules of paragraph (e)(5)(iv) of this section. No inference is intended as to whether a taxpayer would be eligible to claim a credit under section 901(a) if a foreign payment were an amount of tax paid.

Example (1). U.S. borrower transaction. (i) Facts. A domestic corporation (USP) forms a country M corporation (Newco), contributing $1.5 billion in exchange for 100 percent of the stock of Newco. Newco, in turn, loans the $1.5 billion to a second country M corporation (FSub) wholly owned by USP. FSub is engaged in the active conduct of manufacturing and selling widgets and derives more than 50 percent of its gross income from such business. USP then sells its entire interest in Newco to a country M corporation (FP) for the original purchase price of $1.5 billion, subject to an obligation to repurchase the interest in five years for $1.5 billion. The sale has the effect of transferring ownership of the Newco stock to FP for country M tax purposes. The sale-repurchase transaction is structured in a way that qualifies as a collateralized loan for U.S. tax purposes. Therefore, USP remains the owner of the Newco stock for U.S. tax purposes. In year 1, FSub pays Newco $120 million of interest. Newco pays $36 million to country M with respect to such interest income and distributes the remaining $84 million to FP. Under country M law, the $84 million distribution is excluded from FP's income. FP is not related to USP within the meaning of paragraph (e)(5)(iv)(C)(6) of this section. Under an income tax treaty between country M and the U.S., country M does not impose country M tax on interest received by U.S. residents from sources in country M.

(ii) Result. The payment by Newco to country M is not a compulsory payment, and thus is not an amount of tax paid. First, Newco is an SPV because all of Newco's income is passive investment income described in paragraph (e)(5)(iv)(C)(4) of this section, Newco's only asset, a note, is held to produce such income, and the payment to country M is attributable to such income. Second, if the foreign payment were treated as an amount of tax paid, USP would be deemed to pay the foreign payment under section 902(a) and, therefore, would be eligible to claim a credit for such payment under section 901(a). Third, USP would not pay any country M tax if it directly owned Newco's loan receivable. Fourth, distributions from Newco to FP are exempt from tax under country M law. Fifth, FP is a counterparty because FP and USP are unrelated and FP owns more than 10 percent of the stock of Newco under country M law. Sixth, FP is the owner of 100 percent of Newco's stock for country M tax purposes, while USP is the owner of 100 percent of Newco's stock for U.S. tax purposes, and USP's ownership of the stock would materially affect the amount of credits claimed by USP if the payment to country M were an amount of tax paid. If the foreign payment were treated as an amount of tax paid, USP's ownership of the stock for U.S. tax purposes would make USP eligible to claim a credit for such amount under sections 901(a) and 902(a). Because the payment to country M is not an amount of tax paid, USP has dividend income of $84 million and is not deemed to pay any country M tax under section 902(a). USP also has interest expense of $84 million. FSub's post-1986 undistributed earnings are reduced by $120 million of interest expense.

Example (2). U.S. borrower transaction. (i) Facts. The facts are the same as in Example 1, except that FSub is a wholly-owned subsidiary of Newco. In addition, FSub agrees not to pay, and Newco and FP agree not to cause FSub to pay, dividends during the five-year period in which FP holds the Newco stock subject to the obligation of USP to repurchase the stock.

(ii) Result. The results are the same as in Example 1. Although Newco wholly owns FSub, which is engaged in the active conduct of manufacturing and selling widgets and derives more than 50 percent of its income from such business, income attributable to Newco's stock in FSub is passive investment income because there are arrangements whereby substantially all of Newco's opportunity for gain and risk of loss with respect to its stock in FSub is borne by USP.

See paragraph (e)(iv)(C)(4)(ii) of this section. Accordingly, Newco's stock in FSub is held to produce passive investment income. Thus, Newco is an SPV because all of Newco's income is passive investment income described in paragraph (e)(5)(iv)(C)(4) of this section, Newco's assets are held to produce such income, and the payment to country M is attributable to such income.

Example (3). Active business; no SPV. (i) Facts. A, a domestic corporation, wholly owns B, a country X corporation engaged in the manufacture and sale of widgets. On January 1, 2008, C, also a country X corporation, loans $400 million to B in exchange for an instrument that is debt for U.S. tax purposes and equity for country X tax purposes. As a result, C is considered to own 20 percent of the stock of B for country X tax purposes. B loans $55 million to D, a country Y corporation wholly owned by A. For its 2008 tax year, B has $166 million of net income attributable to its sales of widgets and $3.3 million of interest income attributable to the loan to D. Country Y does not impose tax on interest paid to nonresidents. B makes a payment of $50.8 million to country X with respect to B's net income. Country X does not impose tax on dividend payments between country X corporations. A and C are not related within the meaning of paragraph (e)(5)(iv)(C)(6) of this section.

(ii) Result. B is not an SPV within the meaning of paragraph (e)(5)(iv)(B)(1) of this section because the amount of interest income received from D does not constitute substantially all of B's income and the $55 million loan to D does not constitute substantially all of B's assets. Accordingly, the $50.8 million payment to country X is not attributable to an arrangement described in paragraph (e)(5)(iv) of this section.

Example (4). U.S. lender transaction. (i) Facts. (A) A country X corporation (foreign bank) contributes $2 billion to a newly-formed country X corporation (Newco) in exchange for 100 percent of Newco's common stock. A U.S. bank (USB) contributes $1 billion to Newco in exchange for securities that are treated as stock of Newco for U.S. tax purposes and debt of Newco for country X tax purposes. The securities represent 10 percent of the total voting power of Newco. Newco contributes the entire $3 billion to a newly-formed country X entity (RH) in exchange for 99 percent of RH's equity. Foreign bank owns the remaining 1 percent of RH. RH is treated as a corporation for U.S. tax purposes and a partnership for country X tax purposes. RH loans the entire $3 billion it receives from Newco to foreign bank in exchange for a note that pays interest currently and a zero-coupon note. Under an income tax treaty between country X and the U.S., country X does not impose country X tax on interest received by U.S. residents from sources in country X. Country X does not impose tax on dividend payments between country X corporations. USB and the foreign bank are not related within the meaning of paragraph (e)(5)(iv)(C)(6) of this section.

(B) In year 1, foreign bank pays RH $92 million of interest and accrues $113 million of interest on the zero-coupon note. RH distributes the $92 million of cash it receives to Newco. Newco distributes $44 million to USB. Because RH is a partnership for country X purposes, Newco is required to report for country X purposes 99 percent ($203 million) of the income recognized by RH. Newco is entitled to interest deductions of $44 million for distributions to USB on the securities for country X tax purposes and, thus, has $159 million of net income for country X tax purposes. Newco makes a payment to country X of $48 million with respect to its net income. For U.S. tax purposes, Newco's post-1986 undistributed earnings pool for year 1 is $44 million ($92 million-$48 million). For country X tax purposes, foreign bank is entitled to interest expense deductions of $205 million.

(ii) Result. (A) The payment to country X is not a compulsory payment, and thus is not an amount of tax paid. First, Newco is an SPV because all of Newco's income is passive investment income described in paragraph (e)(5)(iv)(C)(4) of this section, Newco's sole asset, stock of RH, is held to produce such income, and the payment to country X is attributable to such income. Second, if the foreign payment were treated as an amount of tax paid, USB would be deemed to pay the $48 million under section 902(a) and, therefore, would be eligible to claim a credit under section 901(a). Third, USB would not pay any country X tax if it directly owned its proportionate share of Newco's asset, the 99 percent interest in RH, because under the U.S.-country X tax treaty country X would not impose tax on USB's distributive share of RH's interest income. Fourth, foreign bank is entitled to interest deductions under country X law for interest it pays and accrues to RH, and will receive tax-free dividends from Newco upon payment of the accrued interest. Fifth, foreign bank and USB are unrelated and foreign bank is considered to own more than 10 percent of Newco under country X law. Sixth, the U.S. and country X view several aspects of the transaction differently, and the U.S. treatment would materially affect the amount of credits claimed by USB if the country X payment were an amount of tax paid. If the country X payment were treated as an amount of tax paid, the equity treatment of the securities for U.S. tax purposes would make USB eligible to claim a credit for the payment under sections 901(a) and 902(a). Moreover, the fact that Newco recognizes a smaller amount of income for U.S. tax purposes than it does for country X tax purposes would increase the amount of credits USB would be eligible to claim upon receipt of the $44 million distribution. Because the $48 million payment to country X is not an amount of tax paid, USB has dividend income of $44 million. It is not deemed to pay tax under section 902(a).

(B) In addition, RH is an SPV because all of RH's income is passive investment income described in paragraph (e)(5)(iv)(C)(4) of this section, RH's sole assets, notes of foreign bank, are held to produce such income, and Newco's payment to country X is attributable to such income. Second, if the foreign payment were treated as an amount of tax paid, USB would be deemed to pay the $48 million under section 902(a) and, therefore, would be eligible to claim a credit under section 901(a). Third, USB would not pay any country X tax if it directly owned its proportionate share of RH's assets, notes of foreign bank, because under the U.S.-country X tax treaty country X would not impose tax on interest paid by foreign bank to USB. Fourth, foreign bank is entitled to interest deductions under country X law for interest it pays and accrues to RH, and will receive tax-free dividends from Newco upon payment of the accrued interest. Fifth, foreign bank and USB are unrelated and foreign bank is considered to own directly or indirectly more than 10 percent of RH under country X law. Sixth, the U.S. and country X view several aspects of the transaction differently, and the U.S. treatment would materially affect the amount of credits claimed by USB if the country X payment were an amount of tax paid. If the country X payment were treated as an amount of tax paid, the equity treatment of the Newco securities for U.S. tax purposes would make USB eligible to claim a credit for the payment under sections 901(a) and 902(a). Moreover, the entity classification of RH for U.S. tax purposes results in Newco recognizing a smaller amount of income for U.S. tax purposes than it does for country X tax purposes, which would increase the amount of credits USB would be eligible to claim upon receipt of the $44 million distribution. Because the $48 million payment to country X is not an amount of tax paid, USB has dividend income of $44 million. It is not deemed to pay tax under section 902(a).

Example (5). Active business; no SPV. (i) Facts. A, a country X corporation, and B, a domestic corporation, each contribute $1 billion to a newly-formed country X entity (C) in exchange for stock of C. C is treated as a corporation for country X purposes and a partnership for U.S. tax purposes. C contributes $1.95 billion to a newly-formed country X corporation (D) in exchange for 100 percent of D's stock. It loans its remaining $50 million to D. Accordingly, C's sole assets are stock and debt of D. D uses the entire $2 billion to engage in the business of manufacturing and selling widgets. For the 2015 tax year, D derives $300 million of income from its widget business and derives $2 million of interest income. For the 2015 tax year, C has dividend income of $200 million and interest income of $3.2 million with respect to its investment in D. Country X does not impose tax on dividends received by one country X corporation from a second country X corporation. C makes a payment of $960,000 to country X with respect to C's net income.

(ii) Result. C's dividend income is not passive investment income, and C's stock in D is not held to produce such income, because C owns at least 10 percent of D and D derives more than 50 percent of its income from the active conduct of its widget business. See paragraph (e)(5)(iv)(C)(4)(ii) of this section. As a result, less than substantially all of C's income is passive investment income and less than substantially all of C's assets are held to produce passive investment income. Accordingly, C is not an SPV within the meaning of paragraph (e)(5)(iv)(B)(1) of this section, and the $960,000 payment to country X is not attributable to an arrangement described in paragraph (e)(5)(iv) of this section.

Example (6). Active business; no SPV. (i) Facts. The facts are the same as in Example 5, except that instead of loaning $50 million to D, C contributes the $50 million to E in exchange for 10 percent of the stock of E. E is a country Y entity that in not engaged in the active conduct of a trade or business. Also, for the 2015 tax year, D pays no dividends to C, E pays $3.2 million in dividends to C, and C makes a payment of $960,000 to country X with respect to C's net income.

(ii) Result. C's dividend income attributable to its stock in E is passive investment income, and C's stock in E is held to produce such income. C's stock in D is not held to produce passive investment income because C owns at least 10 percent of D and D derives more than 50 percent of its income from the active conduct of its widget business. See paragraph (e)(5)(iv)(C)(4)(ii) of this section. As a result, less than substantially all of C's assets are held to produce passive investment income. Accordingly, C does not meet the requirements of paragraph (e)(5)(iv)(B)(1) of this section, and the $960,000 payment to country X is not attributable to an arrangement described in paragraph (e)(5)(iv) of this section.

Example (7). Asset holding transaction. (i) Facts. (A) A domestic corporation (USP) contributes $6 billion of country Z debt obligations to a country Z entity (DE) in exchange for all of the class A and class B stock of DE. A corporation unrelated to USP and organized in country Z (Fcorp) contributes $1.5 billion to DE in exchange for all of the class C stock of DE. DE uses the $1.5 billion contributed by Fcorp to redeem USP's class B stock. The class C stock is entitled to "all" income from DE. However, Fcorp is obligated immediately to contribute back to DE all distributions on the class C stock. USP and Fcorp enter into—

(1) A forward contract under which USP agrees to buy after five years the class C stock for $1.5 billion; and

(2) An agreement under which USP agrees to pay Fcorp interest at a below-market rate on $1.5 billion.

(B) For U.S. tax purposes, these steps create a secured loan of $1.5 billion from Fcorp to USP. Therefore, for U.S. tax purposes, USP is the owner of both the class A and class C stock. DE is a disregarded entity for U.S. tax purposes and a corporation for country Z tax purposes. In year 1, DE earns $400 million of interest income on the country Z debt obligations. DE makes a payment to country Z of $100 million with respect to such income and distributes the remaining $300 million to Fcorp. Fcorp contributes the $300 million back to DE. USP and Fcorp are not related within the meaning of paragraph (e)(5)(iv)(C)(6) of this section. Country Z does not impose tax on interest income derived by U.S. residents.

(C) Country Z treats Fcorp as the owner of the class C stock. Pursuant to country Z tax law, Fcorp is required to report the $400 million of income with respect to the $300 million distribution from DE, but is allowed to claim credits for DE's $100 million payment to country Z. For country Z tax purposes, Fcorp's contribution increases its basis in the class C stock. When the class C stock is later "sold" to USP for $1.5 billion, the increase in tax basis will result in a country Z tax loss for Fcorp. Each year, the amount of the basis increase (and, thus, the amount of the loss generated) will be approximately $300 million.

(ii) Result. The payment to country Z is not a compulsory payment, and thus is not an amount of tax paid. First, DE is an SPV because all of DE's income is passive investment income described in paragraph (e)(5)(iv)(C)(4) of this section, all of DE's assets are held to produce such income, and the payment to country Z is attributable to such income. Second, if the payment were treated as an amount of tax paid, USP would be eligible to claim a credit for such amount under section 901(a). Third, USP would not pay any country Z tax if it directly owned DE's assets. Fourth, Fcorp is entitled to claim a credit under country Z tax law for the payment and will recognize a loss under country Z law upon the "sale" of the class C stock. Fifth, Fcorp and USP are not related within the meaning of paragraph (e)(5)(iv)(C)(6) of this section and Fcorp is considered to own more than 10 percent of DE under country Z law. Sixth, the United States and country X view certain aspects of the transaction differently and the U.S. treatment would materially affect the amount of credits claimed by USP if the country Z payment were an amount of tax paid. USP's ownership of the class C stock for U.S. tax purposes would make USP eligible to claim a credit for the country Z payment if the payment were treated as an amount of tax paid.

* * * * *

(h) Effective date. Paragraphs (a) through (e)(5)(ii) and paragraph (g) of this section, § 1.901-2A, and § 1.903-1 apply to taxable years beginning after November 14, 1983. Paragraphs (e)(5)(iii) and (iv) of this section are effective for foreign taxes paid or accrued during taxable years of the taxpayer ending on or after the date on which these regulations are published as final regulations in the Federal Register.

§ 1.901-2A Dual capacity taxpayers.

(a) Application of separate levy rules as applied to dual capacity taxpayers. *(1) In general.* If the application of a foreign levy (as defined in § 1.901-2(g)(3)) is different, either by the terms of the levy or in practice, for dual capacity taxpayers (as defined in § 1.901-2(a)(2)(ii)(A)) from its application to other persons, then unless the only such difference is that a lower rate (but the same base) applies to dual capacity taxpayers, such difference is considered to be related to the fact that dual capacity taxpayers receive, directly or indirectly, a specific economic benefit (as defined in § 1.901-2(a)(2)(ii)(B)) from the foreign country and thus to be a difference in kind, and not merely of degree. In such a case, notwithstanding any contrary provision of § 1901-2(d), the levy as applicable to such dual capacity tax payers is a separate levy (within the meaning of § 1.901-2(d)) from the levy as applicable to such other persons, regardless of whether such difference is in the base of the levy, in the rate of the levy, or both. In such a case, each of the levy as applied to dual capacity taxpayers and the levy as applied to other persons must be analyzed separately to determine whether it is an income tax within the meaning of § 1.901-2(a)(1) and whether it is a tax in lieu of an income tax within the meaning of § 1.903-1(a). However, if the application of the levy is neither different by its terms nor different in practice for dual capacity taxpayers from its application to other persons, or if the only difference is that a lower rate (but the same base) applies to dual capacity taxpayers, then, in accordance with § 1.901-2(d), such foreign levy as applicable to dual capacity taxpayers and such levy as applicable to other persons together constitute a single levy. In such a case, no amount paid (as defined in § 1.901-2(g)(1)) pursuant to such levy by any such dual capacity taxpayer is considered to be paid in exchange for a specific economic benefit, and such levy, as applicable in the aggregate to such dual capacity taxpayers and to such other persons, is analyzed to determine whether it is an income tax within the meaning of § 1.901-2(a)(1) or a tax in lieu of an income tax within the meaning of § 1.903-1(a). Application of a foreign levy to dual capacity taxpayers will be considered to be different in practice from application of that levy to other persons, even if no such difference is apparent from the terms of the levy, unless it is established that application of that levy to dual capacity taxpayers does not differ in practice from its application to other persons.

(2) Examples. The provisions of paragraph (a)(1) of this section may be illustrated by the following examples:

Example (1). Under a levy of country X called the country X income tax, every corporation that does business in country X is required to pay to country X 40 percent of its income from its business in country X. Income for purposes of the country X income tax is computed by subtracting specified deductions from the corporation's gross income derived from its business in country X. The specified deductions include the corporation's expenses attributable to such gross income and allowances for recovery of the cost of capital expenditures attributable to such gross income, except that under the terms of the country X income tax a corporation engaged in the exploitation of minerals K, L or M in country X is not permitted to recover, currently or in the future, expenditures it incurs in exploring for those minerals. In practice, the only corporations that engage in exploitation of the specified minerals in country X are dual capacity taxpayers. Thus, the application of the country X income tax to dual capacity taxpayers is different from its application to other corporations. The country X income tax as applied to corporations that engage in the exploitation of minerals K, L or M (dual capacity taxpayers) is, therefore, a separate levy from the country X income tax as applied to other corporations. Accordingly, each of (i) the country X income tax as applied to such dual capacity taxpayers and (ii) the country X income tax as applied to such other persons, must be analyzed separately to determine whether it is an income tax within the meaning of § 1.901-2(a)(1) and whether it is a tax in lieu of an income tax within the meaning of § 1.903-1(a).

Example (2). The facts are the same as in example (1), except that it is demonstrated that corporations that engage in exploitation of the specified minerals in country X and that are subject to the levy include both dual capacity taxpayers and other persons. The country X income tax as applied to all corporations is, therefore, a single levy. Accordingly, no amount paid pursuant to the country X income tax by a dual capacity taxpayer is considered to be paid in exchange for a specific economic benefit; and, if the country X income tax is an income tax within the meaning of § 1.901-2(a)(1) or a tax in lieu of an income tax within the meaning of § 1.903-1(a), it will be so considered in its entirely for all corporations subject to it.

Example (3). Under a levy of country Y called the country Y income tax, each corporation incorporated in country Y is required to pay to country Y a percentage of its worldwide income. The applicable percentage is greater for such corporations that earn more than a specified amount of income than for some corporations that earn less than that amount. Income for purposes of the levy is computed by deducting from gross income specified types of expenses and specified allowances for capital expenditures. The expenses for which deductions are permitted differ depending on the type of business in which the corporation subject to the levy is engaged, e.g., a deduction for interest paid to a related party is not allowed for corporations engaged in enumerated types of activities. In addition, carryover of losses from one taxable period to another is permitted for corporations engaged in specified types of activities, but not for corporations engaged in other activities. By its terms, the foreign levy makes no distinction between dual capacity taxpayers and other persons. It is established that in practice the higher rate of the country Y income tax applies to both dual capacity taxpayers and other persons and that in practice the differences in the base of the country Y income tax (e.g., the lack of a deduction for interest paid to related parties for some corporations subject to the levy and the lack of a carryover provision for some corporations subject to the levy) apply to both dual capacity taxpayers and other persons. The country Y income tax as applied to all corporations incorporated in country Y is therefore a single levy. Accordingly, no amount paid pursuant to the country Y income tax by a dual capacity taxpayer is considered to be paid in exchange for a specific economic benefit; and if the country Y income tax is an income tax within the meaning of § 1.901-2(a)(1) or a tax in lieu of an income tax within the meaning of § 1.903-1(a), it will be so considered in its entirety for all persons subject to it.

Example (4). The facts are the same as in example (3), except that it is not established that in practice the higher rate does not apply only to dual capacity taxpayers. By reason of such higher rate, application of the country Y income tax to dual capacity taxpayers is different in practice from application of the country Y income tax to other persons subject to it. The country Y income tax as supplied to dual capacity taxpayers is therefore a separate levy from the country Y income tax as applied to other corporations incorporated in country Y. Accordingly, each of (i) the country Y income tax as applied to dual capacity taxpayers and (ii) the country Y income tax as applied to other corporations incorporated in country Y, must be analyzed separately to determine whether it is an income tax within the meaning of § 1.901-2(a)(1) and whether it is a tax in lieu of an income tax within the meaning of § 1.903-1(a).

Example (5). Under a levy of country X called the country X tax, all persons who do not engage in business in country X and who receive interest income from residents of country X are required to pay to country X 25 percent of the gross amount of such interest income. It is established that the country X tax applies by its terms and in practice to certain banks that are dual capacity taxpayers and to persons who are not dual capacity taxpayers and that application to such dual capacity taxpayers does not differ by its terms or in practice from application to such other persons. The country X tax as applied to all such persons (both the dual capacity taxpayers and the other persons) is, therefore, a single levy. Accordingly, no amount paid pursuant to the country X tax by such a dual capacity taxpayer is considered to be paid in exchange for a specific economic benefit; and, if the country X tax is a tax in lieu of an income tax within the meaning of § 1.903-1(a), it will be so considered in its entirety for all persons subject to it.

Example (6). Under a levy of country X called the country X tax, every corporation incorporated outside of country X ("foreign corporation") that maintains a branch in country X is required annually to pay to country X 52 percent of its net income attributable to that branch. It is established that the application of the country X tax is neither different by its terms nor different in practice for certain banks that are dual capacity taxpayers from its application to persons (which may, but do not necessarily, include other banks) that are not dual capacity taxpayers. The country X tax as applied to all foreign corporations with branches in country X (i.e., both those banks that are dual capacity taxpayers and the foreign corporations that are not dual capacity taxpayers) is, therefore, a single levy. Accordingly, no amount paid pursuant to the country X tax by a bank that is a dual capacity taxpayer is considered to be paid in exchange for a specific economic benefit; and, if the country X tax is an income tax within the meaning of § 1.901-2(a)(1) or a tax in lieu of an income tax within the meaning of § 1.903-1(a), it will be so considered in its entirety for all persons subject to it.

Example (7). Under a levy of country H called the country H tax, all corporations that are organized outside country H and that do not engage in business in country H are required to pay to country H a percentage of the gross amount of interest income derived from residents of country H. The percentage is 30 percent, except that it is 15 percent for a specified category of corporations. All corporations in that category are dual capacity taxpayers. It is established that the country H tax applies by its terms and in practice to dual capacity taxpayers and to persons that are not dual capacity taxpayers and that the only difference in application between such dual capacity taxpayers and such other persons is that a lower rate (but the same base) applies to such dual capacity taxpayers. The country H tax as applied to all such persons (both the dual capacity taxpayers and the other persons) is, therefore, a single levy. Accordingly, no amount paid pursuant to the country H tax by such a dual capacity taxpayer is considered to be paid in exchange for a specific economic benefit, and if the country H tax is a tax in lieu of an income tax within the meaning of § 1.903-1(a), it will be so considered in its entirety for all persons subject to it.

(b) Burden of proof for dual capacity taxpayers. *(1) In general.* For credit to be allowable under section 901 or 903, the person claiming credit must establish that the foreign levy with respect to which credit is claimed is an income tax within the meaning of § 1.901-2(a)(1) or a tax in lieu of an income tax within the meaning of § 1.903-1(a), respectively. Thus, such person must establish, among other things, that such levy is a tax. See § 1.901-2(a)(2)(i) and § 1.903-1(a). Where a person claims credit under section 901 or 903 for an amount paid by a dual capacity taxpayer pursuant to a foreign levy, § 1.901-2(a)(2)(i) and § 1.903-1(a), respectively, require such person to establish the amount, if any, that is paid pursuant to the distinct element of the levy that is a tax. If, pursuant to paragraph (a)(1) of this section and § 1.901-2(d), such levy as applicable to dual capacity taxpayers and such levy as applicable to other persons together constitute a single levy, then no amount paid pursuant to that levy by any such dual capacity taxpayer is considered to be paid in exchange for a specific economic benefit. Accordingly, such levy has only one distinct element, and the levy either is or is not, in its entirety, a tax. If, however, such levy as applicable to dual capacity taxpayers is a separate levy from such levy as applicable to other persons, then a person claiming credit under section 901 or 903 for an amount paid by a dual capacity taxpayer pursuant to such separate levy may establish the amount, if any, that is paid pursuant to the distinct element of the levy that is a tax only by the facts and circumstances method or the safe harbor method described in paragraph (c) of this section. If such person fails to so establish such amount, no portion of the amount that is paid pursuant to the separate levy by the dual capacity taxpayer to such foreign country shall be treated as an amount of tax. Any amount that, either by reason of application of the methods of paragraph (c) of this section or by reason of the immediately preceding sentence, is not treated as an amount of tax shall (i) be considered to have been paid in exchange for a specific economic benefit; (ii) be characterized (e.g., as royalty, purchase price, cost of sales, reduction of the proceeds of a sale, or reduction of interest income) according to the nature of the transaction and of the specific economic benefit received; and (iii) be treated according to such characterization for all purposes of Chapter 1 of the Internal Revenue Code, except that any determination that an amount is not tax for purposes of section 901 or 903 by reason of application of the safe harbor method shall not be taken into account in determining whether or not such an amount is to be characterized and treated as tax for purposes of computing an allowance for percentage depletion under sections 611 and 613.

(2) Effect of certain treaties. If, irrespective of whether such credit would be allowable under section 901 or 903 in the absence of a treaty, the United States has in force a treaty with a foreign country that treats a foreign levy as an income tax for purposes of allowing credit for United States tax and if the person claiming credit is entitled to the benefit of such treaty, then, unless such person claims credit not under the treaty but under section 901 or 903, and except to the extent the treaty provides otherwise and subject to all terms, conditions and limitations provided in the treaty, no portion of an amount paid with respect to such levy by a dual capacity taxpayer shall be considered to be paid in exchange for a specific economic benefit. If, however, such person claims credit not under such treaty but rather under section 901 or 903 (e.g., so as not to be subject to a limitation contained in such treaty), the provisions of this section apply to such levy.

(c) Satisfaction of burden of proof. *(1) In general.* This paragraph (c) sets out the methods by which a person who claims credit under section 901 or 903 for an amount paid by a dual capacity taxpayer pursuant to a foreign levy that satisfies all of the criteria of section 901 or 903 other than the determination of the distinct element of the levy that is a tax and of the amount that is paid pursuant to that distinct element (a "qualifying levy") may establish such distinct element and amount. Such person must establish the amount paid pursuant to a qualifying levy that is paid pursuant to the distinct element of the levy that is a tax (which amount therefore is an amount of income tax within the meaning of § 1.901-2(a)(1) or an amount of tax in lieu of income tax within the meaning of § 1.903-1(a) (a "qualifying amount")) only by the facts and circumstances method set forth in paragraph (c)(2) of this section or the safe harbor method set forth in paragraph (c)(3) of this section. A levy is not a qualifying levy, and neither the facts and circumstances method nor the safe harbor method applies to an amount paid by a dual capacity taxpayer pursuant to a foreign levy, if it has been established pursuant to § 1.901-2(d) and paragraph (a)(1) of this section that that levy as applied to that dual capacity taxpayer and that levy as applied to persons other than dual capacity taxpayers together constitute a single levy, or if it has been established in accordance with the first sentence of paragraph (b)(2) of this section that credit is allowable by reason of a treaty for an amount paid with respect to such levy.

(2) Facts and circumstances method. (i) In general. If the person claiming credit establishes, based on all of the relevant facts and circumstances, the amount, if any, paid by the dual capacity taxpayer pursuant to the qualifying levy that is not paid in exchange for a specific economic benefit, such amount is the qualifying amount with respect to such qualifying levy. In determining the qualifying amount with respect to a qualifying levy under the facts and circumstances method, neither the methodology nor the results that would have obtained if a person had elected to apply the safe harbor method to such qualifying levy is a relevant fact or circumstance. Accordingly, neither such methodology nor such results shall be taken into account in applying the facts and circumstances method.

(ii) Examples. The application of the facts and circumstances method is illustrated by the following examples:

Example (1). Country A which does not have a generally imposed income tax, imposes a levy called the country A income tax, on corporations that carry on the banking business through a branch in country A. All such corporations lend money to the government of country A, and the consideration (interest) paid by the government of country A for the loans is not made available by the government on substantially the same terms to the population of country A in general. Thus, the country A income tax is imposed only on dual capacity taxpayers. L, a corporation that carries on the banking business through a branch in country A and that is a dual capacity taxpayer, establishes that all of the criteria of section 901 are satisfied by the country A income tax, except for the determination of the distinct element of the levy that is a tax and of L's qualifying amount with respect thereto. The country A income tax is, therefore a qualifying levy. L establishes that, although all persons subject to the country A income tax are dual capacity taxpayers, the country A income tax applies in the same manner to income from such persons' transactions with the government of country A as it does to income from their transactions with private persons; that there are significant transactions (either in volume or in amount) with private persons; and that the portion of such persons' income that is derived from transactions with the government of country A on the one hand or private persons on the other varies greatly among persons subject to the country A income tax. By making this showing, L has demonstrated that no portion of the amount paid by it to country A pursuant to the levy is paid in exchange for a specific economic benefit (the interest income). Accordingly, L has demonstrated under the facts and circumstances method that the entire amount it has paid pursuant to the country A income tax is a qualifying amount.

Example (2). A, a domestic corporation that is a dual capacity taxpayer subject to a qualifying levy of country X, pays 1000u (units of country X currency) to country X in 1986 pursuant to the qualifying levy. A does not elect to apply the safe harbor method to country X, but if had so elected, 800u would have been A's qualifying amount with respect to the levy. Based on all of the relevant facts and circumstances (which do not include either the methodology of the safe harbor method or the qualifying amount that would have obtained under that method), A establishes that 628u of such 1000u is not paid in exchange for a specific economic benefit. A has demonstrated under the facts and circumstances method that 628u is a qualifying amount. Pursuant to paragraph (b)(1) of this section, 372u (1000u-628u) is considered to have been paid by A in exchange for a specific economic benefit. That amount is characterized and treated as provided in paragraph (b)(1) of this section.

Example (3). The facts are the same as in example (2) except that under the safe harbor method 580u would have been A's qualifying amount with respect to the levy. That amount is not a relevant fact or circumstance and the result is the same as in example (2).

(3) Safe harbor method. Under the safe harbor method, the person claiming credit makes an election as provided in paragraph (d) of this section and, pursuant to such election, applies the safe harbor formula described in paragraph (e) of this section to the qualifying levy or levies to which the election applies.

(d) Election to use the safe harbor method. *(1) Scope of election.* An election to use the safe harbor method is made with respect to one or more foreign states and possessions of the United States with respect to a taxable year of the person making the election (the "electing person"). Such election applies to such taxable year and to all subsequent taxable years of the electing person (" election years"), unless the election is revoked in accordance with paragraph (d)(4) of this section. If an election applies to a foreign state or possession of the United States ("elected country"), it applies to all qualifying levies of the elected country and to all qualifying levies of all political subdivisions of the elected country with respect to which the electing person claims credit for amounts paid (or deemed to be paid) by any dual capacity taxpayer. A member of an affiliated group that files a consolidated United States income tax return may use the safe harbor method for a foreign state or U.S. possession only if an election to use the safe harbor method for that state or possession has been made by the common parent of such affiliated group on behalf of all members of the group. Similarly, a member of an affiliated group that does not file a consolidated United States income tax return may elect to use the safe harbor method for a foreign state or U.S. possession only if an election to use the safe harbor method for that state or possession is made by each member of the affiliated group which claims credit for taxes paid to such state or possession or to any political subdivision thereof. An election to use the safe harbor method for an elected country does not apply to foreign taxes carried back or forward to any election year from any taxable year to which the election does not apply. Such election does apply to foreign taxes carried back or forward from any election year to any taxable year. A person who elects to use the safe harbor method for one or more foreign countries may, in a later taxable year, also elect to use that method for other foreign countries.

(2) Effect of election. An election to use the safe harbor method described in paragraph (c)(3) of this section requires the electing persons to apply the safe harbor formula of paragraph (e) of this section to all qualifying levies of all elected countries and their political subdivisions, and constitutes a specific waiver by such person of the right to use the facts and circumstances method described in paragraph (c)(2) of this section with respect to any levy of any elected country or any political subdivision thereof.

(3) Time and manner of making election. (i) In general. To elect to use the safe harbor method, an electing person must attach a statement to its United States income tax return for the taxable year for which the election is made and must file such return by the due date (including extensions) for the filing thereof. Such statement shall state—

(A) That the electing person elects to use the safe harbor method for the foreign states and the possessions of the United States designated in the statement and their political subdivisions, and

(B) That the electing person waives the right, for any election year, to use the facts and circumstances method for any levy of the designated states, possessions and political subdivisions. Notwithstanding the foregoing, a person may, with the consent of the Commissioner, elect to use the safe harbor method for a taxable year for one or more foreign states or possessions of the United States, at a date later than that specified in the first sentence of this paragraph (d)(3)(i) e.g., upon audit of such person's United States income tax return for such taxable year. The Commissioner will normally consent to such a later election if such person demonstrates that it failed to make a timely election for such a foreign state or possession for such taxable year because such person reasonably believed either that it was not a dual capacity taxpayer with respect to such state or possession or any political subdivision thereof was possession or any political subdivision thereof was a qualifying levy (for example, because it reasonably, but incorrectly, believed that the levy it paid was not a separate levy from that applicable to persons other than dual capacity taxpayers). The Commissioner will not, however, consent to such a later election with respect to any state or possession for a taxable year if such person (or any other member of an affiliated group of which such person is a member) applied the facts and circumstances method to any levy of such state or possession or any political subdivision thereof for such taxable year.

(ii) Certain retroactive elections. Not withstanding the requirements of paragraph (d)(3)(i) of this section relating to the time and manner of making an election, an election may be made for a taxable year beginning on or before November 14, 1983, provided the electing person elects in accordance with § 1.901-2(h) to apply all of the provisions of this section, § 1.901-2 and § 1.903-1 to such taxable year and provided all of the requirements set forth in this paragraph (d)(3)(ii) are satisfied. Such an election shall be made by timely (including extensions) filing a federal income tax return or an amended federal income tax return for such taxable year; by attaching to such return a statement containing the statements and information set forth in paragraph (d)(3)(i) of this section; and by filing amended income tax returns for all subsequent election years for which income tax returns have previously been filed in which credit is claimed under section 901 or 903 and applying the safe harbor method in such amended returns. All amended returns referred to in the immediately preceding sentence must be filed on or before October 12, 1984, (unless the Commissioner consents to a later filing in circumstances similar to those provided in paragraph (d)(3)(i)) and at a time when neither assessment of a deficiency for any of such election years nor the filing of a claim for any refund claimed in any such amended return is barred.

(iii) Election to credit taxes made in amended return. If a person has filed a United States income tax return for a taxable year to which this § 1.901-2A applies (including application by reason of the election provided in § 1.901-2(h)(2)) in which such person has deducted (instead of credited) qualifying foreign taxes and such person validly makes an election to credit (instead of deduct) such taxes in a timely filed amended return for such taxable year, an election to use the safe harbor method may be made in such amended return provided all of the requirements of paragraph (d)(3)(ii) of this section are satisfied other than the requirement that such amended return and the other amended returns referred to in that paragraph be filed on or before October 12, 1984.

(4) Revocation of election. An election to use the safe harbor method described in paragraph (c)(3) of this section may not be revoked without the consent of the Commissioner. An application for consent to revoke such election with respect to one or more elected countries shall be made to the Commissioner of Internal Revenue, Washington, D.C. 20224. Such application shall be made not later than the 30th day before the due date (including extensions) for the filing of the income tax return for the first taxable year for which the revocation is sought to be effective, except in the case of an event described in (i), (ii), (iii), or (iv) below, in which case an application for revocation with retroactive effect may be made within a reasonable time after such event. The Commissioner may make his consent to any revocation conditioned upon adjustments being made in one or more taxable years so as to prevent the revocation from resulting in a distortion of the amount of any item relating to tax liability in any taxable year. The Commissioner will normally consent to a revocation (including, in the case of (i), (ii), (iii) or (iv) below, one with retroactive effect), if—

(i) An amendment to the Internal Revenue Code or the regulations thereunder is made which applies to the taxable year for which the revocation is to be effective and the amendment substantially affects the taxation of income from sources outside the United States under subchapter N of Chapter 1 of the Internal Revenue Code; or

(ii) After a safe harbor election is made with respect to a foreign state, a tax treaty between the United States and that state enters into force; that treaty covers a foreign tax to which the safe harbor election applies; and that treaty applies to the taxable year for which the revocation is to be effective; or

(iii) After a safe harbor election is made with respect to a foreign state or possession of the United States, a material change is made in the tax law of that state or possession or of a political subdivision of that state or possession; and the changed law applies to the taxable year for which the revocation is to be effective and has a material effect on the taxpayer; or

(iv) With respect to a foreign country to which a safe harbor election applies, the Internal Revenue Service issues a letter ruling to the electing person and that letter ruling (A) relates to the availability or application of the safe harbor method to one or more levies of such foreign country; (B) does not relate to the facts and circumstances method described in paragraph (c)(2) of this section; and (C) fails to include a ruling requested by the electing person or includes a ruling contrary to one requested by such person (in either case, other than one relating to the facts and circumstances method) and such failure or inclusion has a material adverse effect on the amount of such electing person's credit for taxes paid to such foreign country for the taxable year for which the revocation is to be effective; or

(v) A corporation ("new member") becomes a member of an affiliated group; the new member and one or more pre-existing members of such group are dual capacity taxpayers with respect to the same foreign country; and, with respect to such country, either the new member or the pre-existing members (but not both) have made a safe harbor election; and the Commissioner in his discretion determines that obtaining the benefit of the right to revoke the safe harbor election with respect to such foreign country was not the principal purpose of the affiliation between such new member and such group; or

(vi) The election has been in effect with respect to at least three taxable years prior to the taxable year for which the revocation is to be effective. The Commissioner may, in his discretion, consent to a revocation even if none of the foregoing subdivisions (i) through (vi) is applicable, if an election has been revoked with respect to an elected country, a subsequent election to apply the safe harbor method with respect to such elected country may be made only with the consent of the Commissioner and upon such terms and conditions as the Commissioner in his discretion may require.

(e) Safe harbor formula. *(1) In general.* The safe harbor formula applies to determine the distinct element of a qualifying levy that is a tax and the amount paid by a dual capacity taxpayer pursuant to such qualifying levy that is the qualifying amount with respect to such levy. Under the safe harbor formula the amount paid in a taxable year pursuant to a qualifying levy that is the qualifying amount with respect to such levy is an amount equal to:

$(A - B - C) \times D/(1 - D)$ where: (except as otherwise provided in paragraph (e)(5) of this section)

A = the amount of gross receipts as determined under paragraph (e)(2) of this section
B = the amount of costs and expenses as determined under paragraph (e)(2) of this section

C = the total amount paid in the taxable year by the dual capacity taxpayer pursuant to the qualifying levy (the "actual payment amount")

D = the tax rate as determined under paragraph (e)(3) of this section

In no case, however, shall the qualifying amount exceed the actual payment amount; and the qualifying amount is zero if the safe harbor formula yields a qualifying amount less than zero. The safe harbor formula is intended to yield a qualifying amount equal to the amount of generally imposed income tax within the meaning of paragraphs (a) and (b)(1) of § 1.903-1 ("general tax") of the foreign country that would have been required to be paid in the taxable year by the dual capacity taxpayer if it has not been a dual capacity taxpayer and if the base of the general tax had allowed a deduction in such year for the amount (" specific economic benefit amount") by which the actual payment amount exceeds the qualifying amount. See, however, paragraph (e)(5) of this section if an elected country has no general tax. The specific economic benefit amount is considered to be the portion of the actual payment amount that is paid pursuant to the distinct portion of the qualifying levy that imposes an obligation in exchange for a specific economic benefit. The specific economic benefit amount is therefore considered to be an amount paid by the dual capacity taxpayer in exchange for such specific economic benefit, which amount must be treated for purposes of chapter 1 of the Internal Revenue Code as provided in paragraph (b)(1) of this section.

(2) Determination of gross receipts and costs and expenses. For purposes of the safe harbor formula, gross receipts and costs and expenses are, except as otherwise provided in this paragraph (e), the gross receipts and the deductions for costs and expenses, respectively, as determined under the foreign law applicable in computing the actual payment amount of the qualifying levy to which the safe harbor formula applies. However, except as otherwise provided in this paragraph (e), if provisions of the qualifying levy increase or decrease the liability imposed on dual capacity taxpayers compared to the general tax liability of persons other than dual capacity taxpayers by reason of the determination or treatment of gross receipts or of costs or expenses, the provisions generally applicable in computing such other persons' tax base under the general tax shall apply to determine gross receipts and costs and expenses for purposes of computing the qualifying amount. If provisions of the qualifying levy relating to gross receipts meet the requirements of § 1.901-2(b)(3)(i), such provisions shall apply to determine gross receipts for purposes of computing the qualifying amount. If neither the general tax nor the qualifying levy permits recovery of one or more costs or expenses, and by reason of the failure to permit such recovery the qualifying levy does not satisfy the net income requirement of § 1.901-2(b)(4) (even though the general tax does satisfy that requirement), then such cost or expense shall be considered a cost or expense for purposes of computing the qualifying amount. If the qualifying levy does not permit recovery of one or more significant costs or expenses, but provides allowances that effectively compensate for nonrecovery of such significant costs or expenses, then, for purposes of computing the qualifying amount, costs and expenses shall not include the costs and expenses under the general tax whose nonrecovery under the qualifying levy is compensated for by such allowances but shall instead include such allowances. In determining costs and expenses for purposes of computing the qualifying amount with respect to a qualifying levy, the actual payment amount with respect to such levy shall not be considered a cost or expense. For purposes of this paragraph, the following differences in gross receipts and costs and expenses between the qualifying levy and the general tax shall not be considered to increase the liability imposed on dual capacity taxpayers compared to the general tax liability of persons other than dual capacity taxpayers, but only if the general tax would be an income tax within the meaning of § 1.901-2(a)(1) if such different treatment under the qualifying levy had also applied under the general tax:

(i) Differences in the time of realization or recognition of one or more items of income or in the time when recovery of one or more costs and expenses is allowed (unless the period of recovery of such costs and expenses pursuant to the qualifying levy is such that it effectively is a denial of recovery of such costs and expenses, as described in § 1.901-2(b)(4)(i)); and

(ii) Differences in consolidation or carryover provisions of the types described in paragraphs (b)(4)(ii) and (b)(4)(iii) of § 1.901-2.

(3) Determination of tax rate. The tax rate for purposes of the safe harbor formula is the tax rate (expressed as a decimal) that is applicable in computing tax liability under the general tax. If the rate of the general tax varies according to the amount of the base of that tax, the rate to be applied in computing the qualifying amount is the rate that applies under the general tax to a person whose base is, using the terminology of paragraph (e)(1) of this section, "A" minus "B" minus the specific economic benefit amount paid by the dual capacity taxpayer pursuant to the qualifying levy, provided such rate applies in practice to persons other than dual capacity taxpayers, or, if such rate does not so apply in practice, the next lowest rate of the general tax that does so apply in practice.

(4) Determination of applicable provisions of general tax. (i) In general. If the general tax is a series of income taxes (e.g., on different types of income), or if the application of the general tax differs by its terms for different classes of persons subject to the general tax (e.g., for persons in different industries), then, except as otherwise provided in this paragraph (e), the qualifying amount shall be computed by reference to the income tax contained in such series of income taxes, or in the case of such different applications the application of the general tax, that by its terms and in practice imposes the highest tax burden on persons other than dual capacity taxpayers. Notwithstanding the preceding sentence, the general tax amount shall be computed by reference to the application of the general tax to entities of the same type (as determined under the general tax) as the dual capacity taxpayer and to persons of the same resident or nonresident status (as determined under the general tax) as the dual capacity taxpayer; and, if the general tax treats business income differently from non-business (e.g., investment) income (as determined under the general tax), the dual capacity taxpayer's business and non-business income shall be treated as the general tax treats such income. If, for example the dual capacity taxpayer would, under the general tax, be treated as a resident (e.g., because the general tax treats an entity that is organized in the foreign country or managed or controlled there as a resident) and as a corporation (i.e., because the rules of the general tax treat an entity like the dual capacity taxpayer as a corporation), and if some of the dual capacity taxpayer's income would, under the general tax, be treated as business income and some as non-business income, the dual capacity taxpayer and its income shall be so treated in computing the qualifying amount.

(ii) Establishing that provisions apply in practice. For purposes of the safe harbor formula a provision (including tax rate) shall be considered a provision of the general tax only if it is reasonably likely that that provision applies by its terms and in practice to persons other than dual capacity taxpayers. In general, it will be assumed that a provision (including tax rate) that by its terms applies to persons other than dual capacity taxpayers is reasonably likely to apply in practice to such other persons, unless the person claiming credit knows or has reason to know otherwise. However, in cases of doubt, the person claiming credit may be required to demonstrate that such provision is reasonably likely so to apply in practice.

(5) No general tax. If a foreign country does not impose a general tax (and thus a levy, in order to be a qualifying levy must satisfy all of the criteria of section 901 (because section 903 cannot apply), other than the determination of the distinct element of the levy that is a tax and of the amount that is paid pursuant to that distinct element), paragraphs (e)(2), (3) and (4) of this section do not apply to a qualifying levy of such country, and the terms of the safe harbor formula set forth in paragraph (e)(1) of this section are defined with respect to such levy as follows:

A = the amount of gross receipts as determined under the qualifying levy;
B = the amount of deductions for costs and expenses as determined under the qualifying levy;
C = the actual payment amount; and
D = the lower of the rate of the qualifying levy, or the rate of tax specified in section 1(b)(5) (or predecessor or successor section, as the case may be) of the Internal Revenue Code as applicable to the taxable year in which the actual payment amount is paid.

(6) Certain taxes in lieu of an income tax. To the extent a tax in lieu of an income tax (within the meaning of § 1.903-1(a)) that applies in practice to persons other than dual capacity taxpayers would actually have been required to be paid in the taxable year by a dual capacity taxpayer if it had not been a dual capacity taxpayer (e.g., in substitution for the general tax with respect to a type of income, such as interest income, dividend income, royalty income, insurance income), such tax in lieu of an income tax shall be treated as if it were an application of the general tax for purposes of applying the safe harbor formula of this paragraph (e) to such dual capacity taxpayer, and such formula shall be applied to yield a qualifying amount that is approximately equal to the general tax (so defined) that would have been required to be paid in the taxable year by such dual capacity taxpayer if the base of such general tax had allowed a deduction in such year for the specific economic benefit amount.

(7) Multiple levies. If, in any election year of an electing person, with respect to any elected country and all of its political subdivisions,

(i) Amounts are paid by a dual capacity taxpayer pursuant to more than one qualifying levy or pursuant to one or more levies that are qualifying levies and one or more levies that are not qualifying levies by reason of the last sentence of paragraph (c)(1) of this section but with respect to which credit is allowable, or

(ii) More than one general tax (including a tax treated as if it were an application of the general tax under paragraph (e)(6)) would have been required to be paid by a dual capacity taxpayer (or taxpayers) if it (or they) had not been a dual capacity taxpayer (or taxpayers), or

(iii) Credit is claimed with respect to amounts paid by more than one dual capacity taxpayer, the provisions of this paragraph (e) shall be applied such that the aggregate qualifying amount with respect to such qualifying levy or levies plus the aggregate amount paid with respect to levies referred to in (e)(7)(i) that are not qualifying levies shall be the aggregate amount that would have been required to be paid in the taxable year by such dual capacity taxpayer (or taxpayers) pursuant to such general tax or taxes if it (or they) had not been a dual capacity taxpayer (or taxpayers) and if the base of such general tax or taxes had allowed a deduction in such year for the aggregate specific economic benefit amount (except that, if paragraph (e)(5) applies to any levy of such elected country or any political subdivision thereof, the aggregate qualifying amount for qualifying levies of such elected country and all of its political subdivisions plus the aggregate amount paid with respect to levies referred to the paragraph (e)(7)(i) that are not qualifying levies shall not exceed the greater of the aggregate amount paid with respect to levies referred to in paragraph (e)(7)(i) that are not qualifying levies and the amount determined in accordance with paragraph (e)(5) where "D" is the rate of tax specified in section 11(b)(5) (or predecessor or successor section, as the case may be) of the Internal Revenue Code as applicable to the taxable year in which the actual payment amount is paid). However, in no event shall such aggregate amount exceed the aggregate actual payment amount plus the aggregate amount paid with respect to levies referred to in (e)(7)(i) that are not qualifying levies, nor be less than the aggregate amount paid with respect to levies referred to in (e)(7)(i) that are not qualifying levies. In applying (e)(7)(ii) a person who is not subject to a levy but who is considered to receive a specific economic benefit by reason of § 1.901-2(a)(2)(ii)(E) shall be treated as a dual capacity taxpayer. See example (12) in paragraph (e)(8) of this section.

(8) Examples. The provisions of this paragraph (e) may be illustrated by the following examples:

Example (1). Under a levy of country X called the country X income tax, every corporation that does business in country X is required to pay to country X 40% of its income from its business in country X. Income for purposes of the country X income tax is computed by subtracting specified deductions from the corporation's gross income derived from its business in country X. The specified deductions include the corporation's expenses attributable to such gross income and allowances for recovery of the cost of capital expenditures attributable to such gross income, except that under the terms of the country X income tax a corporation engaged in the exploitation of minerals K, L or M in country X is not permitted to recover, currently or in the future, expenditures it incurs in exploring for those minerals. Under the terms of the country X income tax interest is not deductible to the extent it exceeds an arm's length amount (e.g., if the loan to which the interest relates is not in accordance with normal commercial practice or to the extent the interest rate exceeds an arm's length rate). In practice, the only corporations that engage in exploitation of the specified minerals in country X are dual capacity taxpayers. Because no other persons subject to the levy engage in exploitation of minerals K, L or M, in country X, the application of the country X income tax to dual capacity taxpayers is different from its application to other corporations. The country X income tax as applied to corporations that engage in the exploitation of minerals K, L, or M (dual capacity taxpayers) is, therefore, a separate levy from the country X income tax as applied to other corporations.

A is a U.S. corporation that is engaged in country X in exploitation of mineral K. Natural deposits of mineral K in country X are owned by country X, and A has been allowed to extract mineral K in consideration of payment of a bonus and of royalties to an instrumentality of country X. Therefore, A is a dual capacity taxpayer. In 1984, A does business in country X within the meaning of the levy. A has validly elected the safe harbor method for country X for 1984. In 1984, as determined in accordance with the country X income tax as applied to A, A has gross receipts of 120u (units of country X currency), deducts 20u of costs and expenses, and pays 40u (40% of (120u – 20u)) to country X pursuant to the levy. A also incurs in 1984, 10u of nondeductible expenditures for exploration for mineral K and 2u of nondeductible interest costs attributable to an advance of funds from a related party to finance an undertaking relating to the exploration for mineral K for which normal commercial financing was unavailable because of the substantial risk inherent in the undertaking. A establishes that the country X income tax as applied to persons other than dual capacity taxpayers is an income tax within the meaning of § 1.901-2(a)(1), that it is the generally imposed income tax of country X and hence the general tax, and that all of the criteria of section 903 are satisfied with respect to the country X income tax as applied to dual capacity taxpayers, except for the determination of the distinct element of the levy that is a tax and of A's qualifying amount with respect thereto. (No conclusion is reached whether the country X income tax as applied to dual capacity taxpayers is an income tax within the meaning of § 1.901-2(a)(1). Such a determination would require, among other things, that the country X income tax as so applied, judged on the basis of its predominant character, meets the net income requirement of § 1.901-2(b)(4) notwithstanding its failure to permit recovery of exploration expenses.) A has therefore demonstrated that the country X income tax as applied to dual capacity taxpayers is a qualifying levy.

In applying the safe harbor formula, in accordance with paragraph (e)(2), the amount of A's costs and expenses includes the 10u of nondeductible exploration expenses. The failure to permit recovery of interest in excess of arm's length amounts, a provision of both the general tax and the qualifying levy, does not cause the qualifying levy to fail to satisfy the net income requirement of § 1.901-2(b)(4); therefore, the amount of A's cost and expenses does not include the 2u of nondeductible interest costs. Thus, under the safe harbor method, A's qualifying amount with respect to the levy is 33.33u ((120u – 30u – 40u) amount is 6.67u (A's actual payment amount (40u) less A's qualifying amount (33.33u)). Under paragraph (a) of this section, this 6.67u is considered to be consideration paid by A for the right to extract mineral K. Pursuant to paragraph (b) of this section, this amount is characterized according to the nature of A's transactions with country X and its instrumentality and of the specific economic benefit received (the right to extract mineral K), as an additional royalty or other business expense paid or accrued by A and is so treated for all purposes of Chapter 1 of the Internal Revenue Code, except that if an allowance for percentage depletion is allowable to A under sections 611 and 613 with respect to A's interest in mineral K, the determination whether this 6.67u is tax or royalty for purposes of computing the amount of such allowance shall be made under sections 611 and 613 without regard to the determination that under the safe harbor formula such 6.67u is not tax for purposes of section 901 or 903.

Example (2). Under a levy of country Y called the country Y income tax, each corporation incorporated in country Y is required to pay to country Y a percentage of its worldwide income. The applicable percentage is 40 percent of the first 1,000u (units of country Y currency) of income and 50 percent of income in excess of 1,000u. Income for purposes of the levy is computed by deducting from gross income specified types of expenses and specified allowances for capital expenditures. The expenses for which deductions are permitted differ depending on the type of business in which the corporation subject to the levy is engaged, e.g., a deduction for interest paid to a related party is not allowed for corporations engaged in enumerated types of activities. In addition, carryover of losses from one taxable period to another is permitted for corporations engaged in specified types of activities, but not for corporations engaged in other activities. By its terms, the foreign levy makes no distinction between dual capacity taxpayers and other persons. In practice the differences in the base of the country Y income tax (e.g., the lack of a deduction for interest paid to related parties for some corporations subject to the levy and the lack of a carryover provision for some corporations subject to the levy) apply to both dual capacity taxpayers and other persons, but the 50 percent rate applies only to dual capacity taxpayers. By reason of such higher rate, application of the country Y income tax to dual capacity taxpayers is different in practice from application of the country Y income tax to other persons subject to it. The country Y income tax as applied to dual capacity taxpayers is therefore a separate levy from the country Y income tax as applied to other corporations incorporated in country Y.

B is a corporation incorporated in country Y that is engaged in construction activities in country Y. B has a contract with the government of country Y to build a hospital in country Y for a fee that is not made available on substantially the same terms to substantially all persons who are subject to the general tax of country X. Accordingly, B is a dual capacity taxpayer. B has validly elected the safe harbor method for country Y for 1985. In 1985, as determined in accordance with the country Y income tax as applied to B, B has gross receipts of 10,000u, deducts 6,000u of costs and expenses, and pays 1900u ((1,000u × 40%)

It is assumed that B has established that the country Y income tax as applied to persons other than dual capacity taxpayers is an income tax within the meaning of § 1.901-2(a)(1) and is the general tax. It is further assumed that B has demonstrated that all of the criteria of section 901 are satisfied with respect to the country Y income tax as applied to dual capacity taxpayers, except for the determination of the distinct element of such levy that is a tax and of B's qualifying amount with respect to that levy, and therefore that the country Y income tax as applied to dual capacity taxpayers is a qualifying levy.

In applying the safe harbor formula, in accordance with paragraph (e)(3), the 50 percent rate is not used because it does not apply in practice to persons other than dual capacity taxpayers. The next lowest rate of the general tax that does apply in practice to such persons, 40 percent, is used. Accordingly, under the safe harbor formula, B's qualifying amount with respect to the levy is 1400u ((10,000u – 6000u – 1900u) × .40/(1 actual payment amount (1900u) less B's qualifying amount (1400u)). Pursuant to paragraph (b) of this section, B's specific economic benefit amount is characterized according to the nature of B's transactions with country Y and of the specific economic benefit received, as a reduction of B's proceeds of its contract with country Y; and this amount is so treated for all purposes of Chapter 1 of the

Code, including the computation of B's accumulated profits for purposes of section 902.

Example (3). The facts are the same as in example (2), with the following additional facts: The contract between B and country Y is a cost plus contract. One of the costs of the contract which country Y is required to pay or for which it is required to reimburse B is any tax of country Y on B's income or receipts from the contract. Instead of reimbursing B therefor, country Y agrees with B to assume any such tax liability. Under country Y tax law, B is not considered to have additional income or receipts by reason of country Y's assumption of B's country Y tax liability. In 1985, B's gross receipts of 10,000u include 3000u from the contract, and its costs and expenses of 6000u include 2000u attributable to the contact. B's other gross receipts and expenses do not relate to any transaction in which B receives a specific economic benefit. In accordance with the contract, country Y, and not B, is required to bear the amount of B's country Y income tax liability on B's 1000u (3000u − 2000u) income from the contract. In accordance with the contract B computes its country Y income tax without taking this 1000u into account and therefore pays 1400u ((1000u × 40%) ÷ (2000u × 50%)) to country Y pursuant to the levy.

In accordance with § 1.901-2(f)(2)(i), the country Y income tax which country Y is, under the contract, required to bear is considered to be paid by country Y on behalf of B. B's proceeds of its contract, for all purposes of Chapter 1 of the Code (including the computation of B's accumulated profits for purposes of section 902), therefore, are increased by the additional 500u (1900u computed as in example (2) less 1400u as computed above) of B's liability under the country Y income tax that is assumed by country Y and such 500u is considered to be paid pursuant to the levy by country Y on behalf of B. In applying the safe harbor formula, therefore, the computation is exactly as in example (2) and the results are the same as in example (2).

Example (4). Country L issues a decree (the "April 11 decree."), in which it states it is exercising its tax authority to impose a tax on all corporations on their "net income" from country L. "Net income" is defined as actual gross receipts less all expenses attributable thereto, except that in the case of income from extraction of petroleum, gross receipts are defined as 105 percent of actual gross receipts, and no deduction is allowed for interest incurred on loans whose proceeds are used for exploration for petroleum. Under the April 11 decree, wages paid by corporations subject to the decree are deductible in the year of payment, except that corporations engaged in the extraction of petroleum may deduct such wages only by amortization over a 5-year period and, to the extent such wages are paid to officers, they may be deducted only by amortization over a period of 50 years. The April 11 decree permits related corporations subject to the decree to file consolidated returns in which net income and net losses of related corporations offset each other in computing net income for purposes of the April 11 decree, except that corporations engaged in petroleum exploration or extraction activities are not eligible for inclusion in such a consolidated return. The law of country L does not require separate entities to carry on separate activities in connection with exploring for or extracting petroleum. Net losses of a taxable year may be carried over for 10 years to offset income, except that no more than 25% of net income (before deducting the loss carryover) in any such future year may be offset by a carryover of net loss, and, in the case of any corporation engaged in exploration or extraction of petroleum, losses incurred prior to such a corporation's having net income from production may be carried forward for only 8 years and no more than 15% of net income in any such future year may be offset by such a net loss. The rate to be paid under the April 11 decree is 50% of net income (as defined in the levy), except that if net income exceeds 10,000u (units of country L currency), the rate is 75% of the corporation's net income (including the first 10,000u thereof). In practice, no corporations other than corporations engaged in extraction of petroleum have net income in excess of 10,000u. All petroleum resources of country L are owned by the government of country L, whose petroleum ministry licenses corporations to explore for and extract petroleum in consideration for payment of royalties as petroleum is produced.

J is a U.S. corporation that is engaged in country L in the exploration and extraction of petroleum and therefore is a dual capacity taxpayer. J has validly elected the safe harbor method for country L for the year 1986, the year that J commenced activities in country L, and has not revoked such election. For the years 1983 through 1988, J's gross receipts, deductions and net income before application of the carryover provisions, determined in accordance with the April 11 decree, are as follows:

Year	Gross receipts (105 percent of actual gross receipts)	Deductions other than wages	Wages paid other than to officers (amortizable at 20 percent)	Wages paid to officers (amortizable at 2 percent)	Nondeductible exploration interest expense	Net Income (loss) (B-C—amortization of cumulative D-amortization of cumulative E)
A.	B.	C.	D.	E.	F.	G.
1983..........	0	13,000u	100u	50u	1,000u	(13,021u)
1984..........	0	17,000u	100u	50u	2,800u	(17,042u)
1985..........	42,000u	15,000u	100u	50u	2,800u	28,937u
1986..........	105,000u	20,000u	100u	50u	2,800u	84,916u

After application of the carryover provisions, J's net income and actual payment amounts pursuant to the April 11 levy are as follows:

Year	Net income (loss)	Actual payment amount (tax 75 percent)
H	L	J

1983	(13,021u)	0
1984	(17,042u)	0
1985	22,896u	17,172u
1986	72,179u	54,134u

Pursuant to paragraph (a)(1) of this section, the April 11 decree as applied to corporations engaged in the exploration or extraction of petroleum in country L is a separate levy from the April 11 decree as applied to all other corporations. J establishes that the April 11 decree, as applied to such other corporations, is an income tax within the meaning of § 1.901-2(a)(1) and that the decree as so applied is the general tax.

The April 11 decree as applied to corporations engaged in the exploration or extraction of petroleum in country L does not meet the gross receipts requirement of § 1.901-2(b)(3); therefore, irrespective of whether it meets the other requirements of § 1.901-2(b)(1), it is not an income tax within the meaning of § 1.901-2(a)(1). However, the April 11 decree as applied to such corporations is a qualifying levy because J has demonstrated that all of the criteria of section 903 are satisfied with respect to the April 11 decree as applied to such corporations, except for the determination of the distinct element of such levy that imposes a tax and of J's qualifying amount with respect thereto.

In applying the safe harbor formula, in accordance with paragraph (e)(2), gross receipts are computed by reference to the general levy, and thus are 100%, not 105%, of actual gross receipts. Similarly, costs and expenses include exploration interest expense. In accordance with paragraph (e)(2)(i) of this section the difference between the general tax and the qualifying levy in the timing of the deduction for wages, other than wages of officers, is not considered to increase the liability of dual capacity taxpayers because the general tax would not have failed to be an income tax within the meaning of § 1.901-2(a)(1) if it had provided for 5-year amortization of such wages instead of for current deduction. See § 1.901-2(b)(4)(i). However, amortization of wages paid to officers over a 50-year period is such A deferred recovery of such wages that it effectively is a denial of the deduction of the excess of such wages paid in any year over the amortization of such cumulative wages permitted in such year. See § 1.901-2(b)(4)(i). The different treatment of wages paid to officers under the general tax and the qualifying levy is thus not merely a difference in timing within the meaning of paragraph (e)(2)(i) of this section. Accordingly, the difference between the amount of wages paid by J to officers in any year and J's deduction (in computing the actual payment amount) for amortization of such cumulative wages allowed in such year is, pursuant to paragraph (e)(2) of this section, treated as a cost and expense in computing J's qualifying amount for such year with respect to the April 11 decree. The differences in the consolidation and carryover provisions between the general tax and the qualifying levy are of the types described in paragraph (e)(2)(ii) of this section and pursuant to paragraphs (b)(4)(ii) and (b)(4)(iii) of § 1.901-2, the general tax would not fail to be an income tax within the meaning of § 1.901-2(a)(i) even if it contained the consolidation and carryover provisions of the qualifying levy. Thus such differences are not considered to increase the liability of dual capacity taxpayers pursuant to the qualifying levy as compared to the general tax liability of persons other than dual capacity taxpayers.

Accordingly, in applying the safe harbor formula to the qualifying levy for 1985 and 1986, gross receipts and costs and expenses are computed as follows:

Gross receipts

1985: 42,000u × (100/105) = 40,000u

1986: 105,000u × (100/105) = 100,000u

COSTS AND EXPENSES

Item	1985	1986
1. Deductions other than wages (column C in the preceding chart)	15,000u	20,000u
2. Amortization of cumulative wages paid in 1983 and thereafter other than to officers	60u	80u
3. Deduction of wages to officers paid in current year, instead of amortization allowed in current year of such cumulative wages paid in 1983 and thereafter	50u	50u
4. Deduction of exploration interest expense	2,800u	2,800u
5. Costs and expenses before carryover of net loss (sum of lines 1 through 4)	17,910u	22,930u
6. Recalculation of loss carryover by recalculating 1983 and 1984 net income (loss) to reflect current deduction of wages to officers and exploration interest expense: 1983 adjusted net loss carryover (13,021u) + (49u) + (1000u) = (14,070u); 1984 adjusted net loss carryover (17,042u) + (48u) + (2800u) = (19,890u)		
7. Recalculation of limitation on use of net loss carryover deduction:		
Gross receipts	40,000u	100,000u
Less costs and expenses	(17,910u)	(22,930)
Total	22,090u	77,070u
Times 15 percent limitation	3,314u	11,561u
8. Costs and expenses including net loss carryover deduction (line 5 plus line 7)	21,224u	34,491u

In years after 1986, costs and expenses for purposes of determining the qualifying amount would reflect net loss carryforward deductions based on the recomputed losses carried forward from 1983 and 1984 (14,070u and 19,890u, respectively) less the amounts thereof that were utilized in determining costs and expenses for 1985 and 1986 (3,314u and 11,561u, respectively). The 1983 and 1984 loss carryforwards would be considered utilized in accordance with the order of priority in which such losses are utilized under the terms of the qualifying levy.

In applying the safe harbor formula, the tax rate to be used, in accordance with paragraph (e)(3) of this section, is 50.

Accordingly, under the safe harbor method J's qualifying amounts with respect to the April 11 decree for 1985 and 1986 are computed as follows:

1985: (40,000u − 21,224u − 17,172u) × .50/(1 − .50 = 1604u)
1986: (100,000u − 34,491u − 54,134u) × .50/(1 − .50 = 11,375u)

Under the safe harbor method J's qualifying amounts with respect to the April 11 decree for 1985 and 1986 are thus 1604u and 11,375u, respectively; and its specific economic benefit amounts are 15,568u (17,172u − 1604u) and 42,759uc, 54.134u − 11,375u), respectively. Pursuant to paragraph (b) of this section J's specific economic benefit amounts are characterized according to the nature of J's transactions with country L and of the specific economic benefit received by L as additional royalties paid to country L with respect to the petroleum extracted by J in country L in 1985 and 1986, and these amounts are so treated for all purposes of Chapter 1 of the Code.

Example (5). Country E, which has no generally imposed income tax, imposes a levy called the country E income tax only on corporations carrying on the banking a business through a branch in country E and on corporations engaged in the extraction of petroleum in country E. All of the petroleum resources of country E are owned by the government of country E, whose petroleum ministry licenses corporations to explore for petroleum and extract petroleum in consideration of payment of royalties as petroleum is extracted. The base of the country E income tax is a corporation's actual gross receipts from sources in country E less all expenses attributable, on reasonable principles, to such gross receipts; the rate of tax is 29 percent.

A is a U.S. corporation that carries on the banking business through a branch in country E, B is a U.S. corporation (unrelated to A) that is engaged in the extraction of petroleum in country E. In 1984 A receives interest on loans it has made to 160 borrowers in country E, seven of which are agencies and instrumentalities of the government of country E. The economic benefits received by A and B (i.e., the interest received by A from the government and B's license to extract petroleum owned by the government) are not made available on substantially the same terms to the population of country E in general.

A and B are dual capacity taxpayers. Each of them has validly elected the safe harbor method for country E for 1984. A demonstrates that the country E income tax, as applied to it (a dual capacity taxpayer) is not different by its terms or in practice from the country E income tax as applied to persons (in this case other banks) that are not dual capacity taxpayers. A has therefore established pursuant to paragraph (a)(1) of this section and § 1.901-2(d) that the country E income tax as applied to it and the country E income tax as applied to persons other than dual capacity taxpayers are together a single levy. A establishes that such levy is an income tax within the meaning of § 1.901-2(a)(1). In accordance with paragraph (a)(1) of this section, no portion of the amount paid by A pursuant to such levy is considered to be paid in exchange for a specific economic benefit. Thus, the entire amount paid by A pursuant to this levy is an amount of income tax paid.

B does not demonstrate that the country E income tax as applied to corporations engaged in the extraction of petroleum in country E (dual capacity taxpayers) is not different by its terms or in practice from the country E income tax as applied to persons other than dual capacity taxpayers (i.e., banks that are not dual capacity taxpayers). Accordingly, pursuant to paragraph (a)(1) of this section and § 1.901-2(d), the country E income tax as applied to corporations engaged in the extraction of petroleum in country E is a separate levy from the country E income tax as applied to other persons.

B demonstrates that all of the criteria of section 901 are satisfied with respect to the country E income tax as applied to corporations engaged in the exploration of petroleum in country E, except for the determination of the distinct element of such levy that imposes a tax and of B's qualifying amount with respect to the levy. Pursuant to paragraph (e)(5) of this section, in applying the safe harbor formula to B, "A" is the amount of B's gross receipts as determined under the country E income tax as applied to B; "B" is the amount of B's costs and expenses as determined thereunder; "C" is B's actual payment amount; and "D" is .29, the lower of the rate (29 percent) of the qualifying levy (the country E income tax as applied to corporations engaged in the extraction of petroleum in country E) or the rate (46 percent) of tax specified for 1984 in section 11(b)(5) of the Internal Revenue Code. Thus, B's qualifying amount is equal to its actual payment amount.

Example (6). The facts are the same as in example (5), except that the rate of the country E income tax is 55 percent. For the reasons stated in example (5), the results with respect to A are the same as in example (5). In applying the safe harbor formula to B, "A," "B," and "C" are the same as in example (5), but "D" is .46, as that rate is less than .55. Thus, B's qualifying amount is less than B's actual payment amount, and the difference is B's specific economic benefit amount.

Example (7). Country E imposes a tax (called the country E income tax) on the realized net income derived by corporations from sources in country E, except that, with respect to interest income received from sources in country E and certain insurance income, nonresident corporations are instead subject to other levies. With respect to such interest income a levy (called the country E interest tax) requires nonresident corporations to pay to country E 20 percent of such gross interest income unless the nonresident corporation falls within a specified category of corporations ("special corporations"), all of which are dual capacity taxpayers, in which case the rate is instead 25 percent. With respect to such insurance income nonresident corporations are subject to a levy (called the country E insurance tax), which is not an income tax within the meaning of § 1.901-2(a)(1).

The country E interest tax applies at the 20 percent rate by its terms and in practice to persons other than dual capacity taxpayers. The country E interest tax as applied at the 25 percent rate to special corporations applies only to dual capacity taxpayers; therefore, the country E interest tax as applied to special corporations is a separate levy from the country E interest tax as applied at the 20 percent rate.

A is a U.S. corporation which is a special corporation subject to the 25 percent rate of the country E interest tax. A does not have any insurance income that is subject to the country E insurance tax. A, a dual capacity taxpayer, has validly elected the safe harbor formula for 1984. In 1984 A receives 100u (units of country E currency) of gross interest income subject to the country E interest tax and pays 25u to country E.

A establishes that the country E income tax is the general imposed income tax of country E; that all of the criteria of section 903 are satisfied with respect to the country E interest tax as applied to special corporations except for the determination of the distinct element of the levy that is a tax and of A's qualifying amount with respect thereto. A has therefore demonstrated that the country E interest tax as applied to special corporations is a qualifying levy. A establishes that the country E interest tax at the 20 percent rate is a tax in lieu of an income tax within the meaning of § 1.903-1(a). Pursuant to paragraph (e)(6) of this section the country E interest tax at the 20 percent rate is treated as if it were an application of the general tax for purposes of the safe harbor formula of this paragraph (e), since that tax would actually have been required to have been paid by A with respect to its interest income had A not been a dual capacity taxpayer (special corporation) instead subject to the qualifying levy (the country E interest tax at the 25 percent rate).

Even if the country E insurance tax is a tax in lieu of an income tax within the meaning of § 1.903-1(a), that tax is not treated as if it were an application of the general tax for purposes of applying the safe harbor formula to A since A had no insurance income in 1984 and hence such tax would not actually have been required to be paid by A had A not been a dual capacity taxpayer.

Example (8). Under a levy of country S called the country S income tax, each corporation operating in country S is required to pay country S 50 percent of its income from operations in country S. Income for purposes of the country S income tax is computed by subtracting all attributable costs and expenses from a corporation's gross receipts derived from its business in country S. Among corporations on which the country S income tax is imposed are corporations engaged in the owned by country S, and all corporations engaged in the exploitation of mineral K in country S. Natural deposits of mineral K in country S are exploitation thereof do so under concession agreements with an instrumentality of country S. Such corporations, in addition to the 50 percent country S income tax, are also subject to a levy called a surtax, which is equal to 60 percent of posted price net income less the amount of the country S income tax. The surtax is not deductible in computing the country S income tax of corporations engaged in the exploitation of mineral K in country S.

A is a U.S. corporation engaged in country S in the exploitation of mineral K, and A has been allowed to extract mineral K under a concession agreement with an instrumentality of country S. Therefore, A is a dual capacity taxpayer. In accordance with a term of the concession agreement, certain of A's income (net of expenses attributable thereto) is exempted from the income tax and surtax.

The results for A in 1984 are as follows:

	Income tax	Surtax
Gross Receipts:		
Realized—Taxable	120u	—
Realized—Exempt	15u	—
Posted Price Taxable	—	145u
Costs:		
Attributable to Taxable Receipts	20u	20u
Attributable to Exempt Receipts	5u	—
Taxable Income	100u	125u
Tentative Surtax (60 percent)	—	75u
Petroleum Levy at 50 percent	50u	50u
Surtax	—	25u

Because of the difference (nondeductibility of the surtax) in the country S income tax as applied to dual capacity taxpayers from its application to other persons, the country S income tax as applied to dual capacity taxpayers and the country S income tax as applied to persons other than dual capacity taxpayers are separate levies. Moreover, because A's concession agreement provides for a modification (exemption of certain income) of the country S income tax and surtax as they otherwise apply to other persons engaged in the exploitation of mineral K in country S, those levies (contractual levies) as applied to A are separate levies from those levies as applied to other persons engaged in the exploitation of mineral K in country S.

A establishes that the country S income tax as applied to persons other than dual capacity taxpayers is an income tax within the meaning of § 1.901-2(a)(1) and is the general tax. A demonstrates that all the criteria of section 903 are satisfied with respect to the country S income tax as applied to A and with respect to the surtax as applied to A, except for the determination of the distinct elements of such levies that are taxes and of A's qualifying amounts with respect to such levies. Therefore, both the country S income tax as applied to A and the surtax as applied to A are qualifying levies.

In applying the safe harbor formula, in accordance with paragraph (e)(2), the amount of A's gross receipts includes the exempt realized income, and the amount of A's costs and expenses includes the costs attributable to such exempt income. In accordance with paragraph (e)(7)(i), the amount of the qualifying levy for purposes of the formula is the sum of A's liability for the country S income tax and A's liability for the surtax. Accordingly, under the safe harbor formula, A's qualifying amount with respect to the country S income tax and the surtax is 35u ((135u − 25u − 75u) × .50/(1 − .50)). A's specific economic benefit amount is 40u (A's actual payment amount (75u) less A's qualifying amount (35u)).

Example (9). Country T imposes a levy on corporations, called the country T income tax. The country T income tax is imposed at a rate of 50 percent on gross receipts less all costs and expenses, and affiliated corporations are allowed to consolidate their results in applying the country T income tax. Corporations engaged in the exploitation of mineral L in country T are subject to a levy that is identical to the country T income tax except that no consolidation among affiliated corporations is allowed. The levy allows unlimited loss carryforwards.

C and D are affiliated U.S. corporations engaged in country T in the exploitation of mineral L. Natural deposits of mineral L in country T are owned by country T, and C and D have been allowed to extract mineral L in consideration of certain payments to an instrumentality of country T. Therefore, C and D are dual capacity taxpayers.

The results for C and D in 1984 and 1985 are as follows:

	1984		1985	
	C	D	CD	
Gross Receipts	120u	0	120u	120u
Costs	20u	50u	20u	20u
Loss Carryforward				50u
Net Income (Loss)	100u	(50u)	100u	50u
Income Tax	50u		50u	25u

C and D establish that the country T income tax as applied to persons other than dual capacity taxpayers is an income tax within the meaning of § 1.901-2(a)(1) and is the general tax. C and D demonstrate that all, of the criteria of section 901 are satisfied with respect to the country T income tax as applied to dual capacity taxpayers, except for the determination of the distinct element of such levy that is a tax and of C and D's qualifying amounts with respect to that levy. Therefore, the country T income tax as applied to dual capacity taxpayers is a qualifying levy.

In applying the safe harbor formula, in accordance with paragraphs (e)(2)(ii) and (e)(7)(iii), the gross receipts, costs and expenses, and actual payment amounts of C and D are aggregated, except that in D's loss year (1984) its gross receipts and costs and expenses are disregarded. The results of any loss year are disregarded since the country T income tax as applied to dual capacity taxpayers does not allow consolidation, and, pursuant to paragraph (e)(2)(ii), differences in consolidation provisions between such levy and the country T income tax as applied to persons that are not dual capacity taxpayers are not considered. Accordingly, in 1984 the qualifying amount with respect to the country T income tax is 50u ((120u − 20u considered paid by C. In 1985 the qualifying amount is 75u ((120u carry forward) − 50u − 25u) × .50/(1 D.

Example (10). Country W imposes a levy called the country W income tax on corporations doing business in country W. The country W income tax is imposed at a 50 percent rate on gross receipts less all costs and expenses. Corporations engaged in the exploitation of mineral M in country W are subject to a levy that is identical in all respects to the country W income tax except that it is imposed at a rate of 80 percent (the "80 percent levy").

A is a U.S. corporation engaged in country W in exploitation of mineral M and is subject to the 80 percent levy. Natural deposits of mineral M in country W are owned by country W, and A has been allowed to extract mineral M in consideration of certain payments to an instrumentality of country W. Therefore, A is a dual capacity taxpayer. B, a U.S. corporation affiliated with A, also is engaged in business in country W, but has no transactions with country W. B is subject to the country W income tax. B is a dual capacity taxpayer within the meaning of § 1.901-2(a)(2)(ii)(A) by virtue of its affiliation with A.

The results for A and B in 1984 are as follows:

	A	B
Gross Receipts ...	120u	100u
Costs	20u	40u
Net Income	100u	80u
Tax Rate	80	.50
Tax............	80u	30u

A and B establish that the country W income tax as applied to persons other than dual capacity taxpayers is an income tax within the meaning of § 1.901-2(a)(1) and is the general tax. It is assumed that B has demonstrated that the country W income tax as applied to B does not differ by its terms or in practice from the country W income tax as applied to persons other than dual capacity taxpayers and hence that the country W income tax as applied to B, a dual capacity taxpayer, and the country W income tax as applied to such other persons is a single levy. Thus, with respect to B, the country W income tax is not a qualifying levy by reason of the last sentence of paragraph (c)(1) of this section. A demonstrates that all the criteria of section 901 are satisfied with respect to the 80 percent levy, except for the determination of the distinct element of such levy that is a tax and of A's qualifying amount with respect thereto. Accordingly, the 80 percent levy as applied to A is a qualifying levy.

In applying the safe harbor formula in accordance with paragraphs (e)(7)(i) and (e)(7)(iii) in the instant case, it is not necessary to incorporate B's results in the safe harbor formula because B's taxation in country W is identical to the taxation of persons other than dual capacity taxpayers and because neither A's and B's results nor their taxation in country W interact in any way to change A's taxation. All of the amount paid by B, 30u, is an amount of income tax paid by B within the meaning of § 1.901-2(a)(1). Accordingly, under the safe harbor formula, the qualifying amount for A with respect to the 80 percent levy is 20u ((120u .50)). The remaining 60u paid by A (80u − 20u) is A's specific economic benefit amount.

Example (11). The facts are the same as in example (10), except that it is assumed that B has not demonstrated that the country W income tax as applied to B does not differ by its terms or in practice from the country W income tax as applied to persons other than dual capacity taxpayers. In addition, A and B demonstrate that all the criteria of section 901 are satisfied with respect to each of the country W income tax and the 80 percent levy as applied to dual capacity taxpayers, except for the determination of the distinct elements of such levies that are taxes of A and B's qualifying amounts with respect to such levies. Therefore, the country W income tax and 80 percent levy as applied to dual capacity taxpayers are qualifying levies.

In applying the safe harbor formula in accordance with paragraphs (e)(7)(i) and (e)(7)(iii), the results of A and B are aggregated. Accordingly, under the safe harbor formula, the aggregate qualifying amount for A and B with respect to the country W income tax and 80 percent levy is 50u ([(120u ÷ 100u) − (20u ÷ 40u) − (80u ÷ 30u)] × .50/(1 − .50)).

Example (12). Country Y imposes a levy on corporations operating in country Y, called the country Y income tax. Income for purposes of the country Y income tax is computed by subtracting all costs and expenses from a corporation's gross receipts derived from its business in country Y. The rate of the country Y income tax is 50 percent. Country Y also imposes a 20 percent tax (the "withholding tax") on the gross amount of certain income, including dividends, received by persons who are not residents of country Y from persons who are residents of country Y and from corporations that operate there. Corporations engaged in the exploitation of mineral K in country Y are subject to a levy (the "75 percent levy") that is identical in all respects to the country Y income tax except that it is imposed at a rate of 75 percent. Dividends received from such corporations are not subject to the withholding tax.

C, a wholly-owned country Y subsidiary of D, a U.S. corporation, is engaged in country Y in the exploitation of mineral K. Natural deposits of mineral K in country Y are owned by country Y, and C has been allowed to extract mineral K in consideration of certain payments to an instrumentality of country Y. Therefore, C is a dual capacity taxpayer. D has elected the safe harbor method for country Y for 1984. In 1984, C's gross receipts are 120u (units of country Y currency), its costs and expenses are 20u, and its liability under the 75 percent levy is 75u. C distributes the amount that remains, 25u, as a dividend to D.

D establishes that the country Y income tax as applied to persons other than dual capacity taxpayers is an income tax within the meaning of § 1.901-2(a)(1) and the general tax, and that all the criteria of section 901 are satisfied with respect to the 75 percent levy, except for the determination of the distinct element of such levy that is tax and of C's qualifying amount with respect thereto. Accordingly, the 75 percent levy is a qualifying levy.

Pursuant to paragraph (e)(7), D (which is not subject to a levy of country Y but is considered to receive a specific economic benefit by reason of § 1.901-2(a)(2)(ii)(E)) is treated as a dual capacity taxpayer in applying paragraph (e)(7)(ii). D demonstrates that the withholding tax is a tax in lieu of an income tax within the meaning of § 1.903-1, which tax applies in practice to persons other than dual capacity taxpayers, and that such tax actually would have applied to D had D not been a dual capacity taxpayer (i.e., had C not been a dual capacity taxpayer, in which case D also would not have been one). Accordingly, the withholding tax is treated for purposes of the safe harbor formula as if it were an application of the general tax.

In applying the safe harbor formula to this situation in accordance with paragraph (e)(7)(ii), the rates of the country Y income tax and the withholding tax are aggregated into a single effective general tax rate. In this case, the rate is .60 (.50 ÷ [(1 − .50) × .20]). Accordingly, under the safe harbor formula, C's qualifying amount with respect to the 75 percent levy is 37.5u [(120u − 20u amount that C and D would have paid if C had been subject to the country Y income tax and had distributed to D as a dividend subject to the withholding tax the entire amount that remained for the year after payment of the country Y income tax. Because C is in fact the only taxpayer, the entire qualifying amount is paid by C.

Example (13). The facts are the same as in example (12), except that dividends received from corporations engaged in the exploitation of mineral K in country Y are subject to the withholding tax. Thus, C's liability under the 75 percent tax on the 75u, and D's liability under the withholding tax on the 25u distribution is 5u.

D, which is a dual capacity taxpayer, demonstrates that the withholding tax as applied to D does not differ by its terms or in practice from the withholding tax as applied to persons other than dual capacity taxpayers and hence that the withholding tax as applied to D and that levy as applied to such other persons is a single levy. D demonstrates that all of the criteria of section 903 are satisfied with respect to the withholding tax. The withholding tax is not a qualifying levy by reason of the last sentence of paragraph (c)(1) of this section.

Paragraphs (e)(7)(i), (e)(7)(ii) and (e)(7)(iii) all apply in this situation. As in example (10), it is not necessary to incorporate the withholding tax into the safe harbor formula. All of the amount paid by D, 5u, is an amount of tax paid by D in lieu of an income tax. In applying the safe harbor formula to C, therefore, with respect to the 75 percent levy, "A" is 120, "B" is "20", "C" is 75 and "D" is .50. Accordingly, C's qualifying amount with respect to the 75 percent levy is 25u; the remaining 50u that it paid is its specific economic benefit amount.

Example (14). The facts are the same as in example (12), except that dividends received from corporations engaged in the exploitation of mineral K in country Y are subject to a 10 percent withholding tax (the "10 percent withholding tax"). Thus, C's liability under the 75 percent levy is 75u, and D's liability under the 10 percent withholding tax on the 25u distribution is 2.5u.

The only difference between the withholding tax and the 10 percent withholding tax applicable only to dual capacity taxpayers (including D) is that a lower rate (but the same base) applies to dual capacity taxpayers. Although the withholding tax and the 10 percent withholding tax are together a single levy, this difference makes it necessary, when dealing with multiple levies, to incorporate the withholding tax and D's payment pursuant to the 10 percent withholding tax in the safe harbor formula. Accordingly, as in example (12), the safe harbor formula is applied by aggregation.

The aggregate effective rate of the general taxes for purposes of the safe harbor formula is .60 (.50 ÷ [(1 − .50) payment amount of the qualifying levies for purposes of the formula is the sum of C and D's liability for the 75 percent levy and the 10 percent withholding tax. Accordingly, under the safe harbor formula, the aggregate qualifying amount with respect to the 75 percent levy on C and the 10 percent withholding tax on D is 33.75u ((120u − 20u − [75u ÷ 2.5u]) × .60/(1 − .60)), which is the aggregate amount of tax that C and D would have paid if C had been subject to the country Y income tax and had paid out its entire amount remaining after payment of the tax to D as a dividend subject to the withholding tax.

Example (15). The facts are the same as in example (5), except that the rate of the country E income tax is 45 percent and a political subdivision of country E also imposes a levy, called the "local tax," on all corporations subject to the country E income tax. The base of the local tax is the same as the base of the country E income tax; the rate is 10 percent.

The reasoning of example (5) with regard to the country E income tax as applied to A and B, respectively, applies equally with regard to the local tax as applied to A and B, respectively. Accordingly, the entire amount paid by A pursuant to each of the country E income tax and the local tax is an amount of income tax paid, and both the country E income tax as applied to B and the local tax as applied to B are qualifying levies.

Pursuant to paragraph (e)(7), in applying the safe harbor formula to B, "A" is the amount of B's gross receipts as determined under the (identical) country E income tax and local tax as applied to B; "B" is the amount of B's costs and expenses thereunder; and "C" is the sum of B's actual payment amounts with respect to the two levies. Pursuant to paragraph (e)(7), in applying the safe harbor formula to B, B's aggregate qualifying amount with respect to the two levies is limited to the amount determined in accordance with paragraph (e)(5) where "D" is the rate of tax specified in section 11(b)(5) of the Internal Revenue Code. Accordingly, "D" is .46, which is the lower of the aggregate rate (55 percent) of the qualifying levies or the section 11(b)(5) rate (46 percent). B's aggregate qualifying amount is, therefore, identical to B's qualifying amount in example (6), which is less than its aggregate actual payment amount, and the difference is B's specific economic benefit amount.

(f) Effective date. The effective date of this section is as provided in § 1.901-2(h).

T.D. 7918, 10/6/83.

§ 1.901-3 Reduction in amount of foreign taxes on foreign mineral income allowed as a credit.

(a) Determination of amount of reduction. *(1) In general.* For purposes of determining the amount of taxes which are allowed as a credit under section 901(a) for taxable years beginning after December 31, 1969, the amount of any income, war profits, and excess profits taxes paid or accrued, or deemed to be paid under section 902, during the taxable year to any foreign country or possession of the United States with respect to foreign mineral income (as defined in paragraph (b) of this section) from sources within such country or possession shall be reduced by the amount, if any, by which—

(i) The smaller of—

(a) The amount of such foreign income, war profits, and excess profits taxes, or

(b) The amount of the tax which would be computed under chapter 1 of the Code for such year with respect to such foreign mineral income if the deduction for depletion were determined under section 611 without regard to the deduction for percentage depletion under section 613, exceeds

(ii) The amount of the tax computed under chapter 1 of the Code for such year with respect to such foreign mineral income.

The reduction required by this subparagraph must be made on a country-by-country basis whether the taxpayer uses for the taxable year the per-country limitation under section 904(a)(1), or the overall limitation under section 904(a)(2), on the amount of taxes allowed as credit under section 901(a).

(2) Determination of amount of tax on foreign mineral income. (i) Foreign tax. For purposes of subparagraph (1)(i)(a) of this paragraph, the amount of the income, war profits, and excess profits taxes paid or accrued during the taxable year to a foreign country or possession of the United States with respect to foreign mineral income from sources within such country or possession is an amount which is the greater of—

(a) The amount by which the total amount of the income, war profits, and excess profits taxes paid or accrued during the taxable year to such country or possession exceeds the amount of such taxes that would be paid or accrued for such year to such country or possession without taking into account such foreign mineral income, or

(b) The amount of the income, war profits, and excess profits taxes that would be paid or accrued to such country or possession if such foreign mineral income were the taxpayer's only income for the taxable year,

except that in no case shall the amount so determined exceed the total of all income, war profits, and excess profits taxes paid or accrued during the taxable year to such country or possession. For such purposes taxes which are paid or accrued also include taxes which are deemed paid under section 902. In the case of a dividend described in paragraph (b)(2)(i)(a) of this section which is from sources within a foreign country or possession of the United States and is attributable in whole or in part to foreign mineral income, the amount of the income, war profits, and excess profits taxes deemed paid under section 902 during the taxable year to such country or possession with respect to foreign mineral income from sources within such country or possession is an amount which bears the same ratio to the amount of the income, war profits, and excess profits taxes deemed paid under section 902 during such year to such country or possession with respect to such dividend as the portion of the dividend which is attributable to foreign mineral income bears to the total dividend. For purposes of (a) and (b) of this subdivision, foreign mineral income is to be reduced by any credits, expenses, losses, and other deductions which are properly allocable to such income under the law of the foreign country or possession of the United States from which such income is derived.

(ii) U.S. tax. For purposes of subparagraph. *(l)* (ii) of this paragraph, the amount of the tax computed under chapter 1 of the Code for the taxable year with respect to foreign mineral income from sources within a foreign country or possession of the United States is the greater of—

(a) The amount by which the tax under chapter 1 of the Code on the taxpayer's taxable income for the taxable year exceeds a tax determined under such chapter on the taxable income for such year determined without regard to such foreign mineral income, or

(b) The amount of tax that would be determined under chapter 1 of the Code if such foreign mineral income were the taxpayer's only income for the taxable year.

For purposes of this subdivision the tax is to be determined without regard to any credits against the tax and without taking into account any tax against which a credit is not allowed under section 901(a). For purposes of (b) of this subdivision, the foreign mineral income is to be reduced only by expenses, losses, and other deductions properly allocable under chapter 1 of the Code to such income and is to be computed without any deduction for personal exemptions under section 151 or 642(b).

(iii) U.S. income tax computed without deduction allowed by section 613. For purposes of subparagraph (1)(i)(b) of this paragraph, the amount of the tax which would be computed under chapter 1 of the Code (without regard to section 613) for the taxable year with respect to foreign mineral income from sources within a foreign country or possession of the United States is the amount of the tax on such income that would be computed under such chapter by using as the allowance for depletion cost depletion computed upon the adjusted depletion basis of the property. For purposes of this subdivision the tax is to be determined without regard to any credits against the tax and without taking into account any tax against which credit is not allowed under section 901(a). If the greater tax with respect to the foreign mineral income under subdivision (ii) of this subparagraph is the tax determined under (a) of such subdivision, the tax determined for purposes of subparagraph (1)(i)(b) of this paragraph is to be determined by applying the principles of (a) (rather than of (b)) of subdivision (ii) of this subparagraph. On the other hand, if the greater tax with respect to the foreign mineral income under subdivision (ii) of this subparagraph is the tax determined under (b) of such subdivision, the tax determined for purposes of subparagraph (1)(i)(b) of this paragraph is to be determined by applying the principles of (b) rather than of (a)) of subdivision (ii) of this subparagraph.

(3) Special rules. (i) The reduction required by this paragraph in the amount of taxes paid, accrued, or deemed to be paid to a foreign country or possession of the United States applies only where the taxpayer is allowed a deduction for percentage depletion under section 613 with respect to any part of his foreign mineral income for the taxable year from sources within such country or possession, whether or not such deduction is allowed with respect to the entire foreign mineral income from sources within such country or possession for such year.

(ii) For purposes of this section, the term "foreign country" or "possession of the United States" includes the adjacent continental shelf areas to the extent, and in the manner, provided by section 638(2) and the regulations thereunder.

(iii) The provisions of this section are to be applied before making any reduction required by section 1503(b) in the amount of income, war profits, and excess profits taxes paid or accrued to foreign countries or possessions of the United States by a Western Hemisphere trade corporation.

(iv) If a taxpayer chooses with respect to any taxable year to claim a credit under section 901 and has any foreign mineral income from sources within a foreign country or possession of the United States with respect to which the deduction under section 613 is allowed, he must attach to his return a schedule showing the computations required by subdivisions (i), (ii), and (iii) of subparagraph (2) of this paragraph.

(v) A taxpayer who has elected to use the overall limitation under section 904(a)(2) on the amount of the foreign tax credit for any taxable year beginning before January 1, 1970, may, for his first taxable year beginning after December 31, 1969, revoke his election without first securing the consent of the Commissioner. See paragraph (d) of § 1.904-1.

(b) Foreign mineral income defined. *(1) In general.* The term "foreign mineral income" means income (determined under chapter 1 of the Code) from sources within a foreign country or possession of the United States derived from—

(i) The extraction of minerals from mines, wells, or other natural deposits,

(ii) The processing of minerals into their primary products, or

(iii) The transportation, distribution, or sale of minerals or of the primary products derived from minerals.

Any income of the taxpayer derived from an activity described in either subdivision (i), (ii), or (iii) of this subparagraph is foreign mineral income, since it is not necessary that the taxpayer extract, process, and transport, distribute, or sell minerals or their primary products for the income derived from any such activity to be foreign mineral income. Thus, for example, an integrated oil company must treat as foreign mineral income from sources within a foreign country or possession of the United States all income from such sources derived from the production of oil, the refining of crude oil into gasoline, the distribution of gasoline to marketing outlets, and the retail sale of gasoline. Similarly, income from such sources from the refining, distribution, or marketing of fuel oil by the taxpayer is foreign mineral income, whether or not the crude oil was extracted by the taxpayer. In further illustration, income from sources within a foreign country or possession of the United States derived from the processing of minerals into their primary products by the taxpayer is foreign mineral income, whether or not the minerals were extracted, or the primary products were sold, by the taxpayer. Section 901(e) and this section apply whether or not the extraction, processing, transportation, distribution, or selling of the minerals or primary products is done by the taxpayer. Thus, for example, an individual who derives royalty income from the extraction of oil from an oil well in a foreign country has foreign mineral income for purposes of this paragraph. Income from the manufacture, distribution, and marketing of petrochemicals is not foreign mineral income. Foreign mineral income is not limited to gross income from the property within the meaning of section 613(c) and § 1.613-3.

(2) Income included in foreign mineral income. (i) In general. Foreign mineral income from sources within a foreign country or possession of the United States includes, but is not limited to—

(a) Dividends from such sources, as determined under § 1.902-1(h)(1), received from a foreign corporation in respect of which taxes are deemed paid by the taxpayer under section 902, to the extent such dividends are attributable to foreign mineral income described in subparagraph (1) of this paragraph. The portion of such a dividend which is attributable to such income is that amount which bears the same ratio to the total dividend received as the earnings and profits out of which such dividend is paid that are attributable to foreign mineral income bear to the total earnings and profits out of which such dividend is paid. For such purposes, the foreign mineral income of a foreign corporation is its foreign mineral income described in this paragraph (including any dividends described in this (a) which are received from another foreign corporation), whether or not such income is derived from sources within the foreign country or possession of the United States in which, or under the laws of which, the former corporation is created or organized. A foreign corporation is considered to have no foreign mineral income for any taxable year beginning before January 1, 1970.

(b) Any section 78 dividend to which a dividend described in (a) of this subdivision gives rise, but only to the extent such section 78 dividend is deemed paid under paragraph (a)(2)(i) of this section with respect to foreign mineral income from sources within such country or possession and to the extent it is treated under § 1.902-1(h)(1) as income from sources within such country or possession.

(c) Any amounts includible in income of the taxpayer under section 702(a) as his distributive share of the income of a partnership consisting of income described in subparagraph (1) of this paragraph.

(d) Any amounts includible in income of the taxpayer by virtue of section 652(a), 662(a), 671, 682(a), or 691(a), to the extent such amounts consist of income described in subparagraph (1) of this paragraph.

(ii) Illustration. The provisions of this subparagraph may be illustrated by the following example:

Example. (a) Throughout 1974, M, a domestic corporation, owns all the one class of stock of N, a foreign corporation which is not a less developed country corporation within the meaning of section 902(d). Both corporations use the calendar year as the taxable year. N is incorporated in foreign country Y. During 1974, N has income from sources within foreign country X, all of which is foreign mineral income. During 1974, N also has income from sources within country Y, none of which is foreign mineral income. N is taxed in each foreign country only on income derived from sources within that country. Neither country X nor country Y allows a credit against its tax for foreign income taxes. N pays a dividend of $40,000 to M for 1974.

For purposes of section 902, the dividend is paid from earnings and profits for 1974.

(b) N's earnings and profits and taxes for 1974 are determined as follows:

Foreign mineral income from country X		$100,000
Less:		
Intangible drilling and development costs	$21,000	
Cost depletion	3,000	24,000
Taxable income from country X		76,000
Income tax rate of country X		× 50%
Tax paid to country X		38,000
Income from country Y		100,000
Less deductions		25,000
Taxable income from country Y		75,000
Income tax rate of country Y		× 60%
Tax paid to country Y		45,000
Total taxable income		151,000
Less total foreign income taxes		83,000
Total earnings and profits		68,000
Taxable income from foreign mineral income		76,000
Less: Tax paid on foreign mineral income		38,000
Earnings and profits from foreign mineral income		38,000

(c) For 1974, M has foreign mineral income from country Y of $49,636.68, determined in the following manner and by applying this section, § 1.78-1, and § 1.902-1(h)(1):

Portion of dividend from country Y attributable to foreign mineral income (subdivision (i)(a) of this subparagraph) ($40,000 × $38,000/$68,000)	$ 22,352.94
Foreign income tax deemed paid by M to country Y under section 902(a)(1) ($83,000 × $40,000/$68,000)	48,823.53
Foreign income tax deemed paid by M to country Y with respect to foreign mineral income from country Y (paragraph (a)(2)(i) of this section) ($48,823.53 × $22,352.94/$40,000)	$ 27,283.74
Foreign mineral income from country Y:	
Dividend attributable to foreign mineral income from country Y	22,352.94
Sec. 78 dividend deemed paid with respect to foreign mineral income (subdivision (i)(b) of this subparagraph)	27,283.74
Total foreign mineral income	49,636.68

(c) Limitations on foreign tax credit. *(1) In general.* The reduction under section 901(e) and paragraph (a)(1) of this section in the amount of foreign taxes allowed as a credit under section 901(a) is to be made whether the per-country limitation under section 904(a)(1) or the overall limitation under section 904(a)(2) is used for the taxable year, but the reduction in the amount of foreign taxes allowed as a credit under section 901(a) must be made on a country-by-country basis before applying the limitation under section 904(a) to the reduced amount of taxes. If for the taxable year the separate limitation under section 904(f) applies to any foreign mineral income, that limitation must also be applied after making the reduction under section 901(e) and paragraph (a)(1) of this section.

(2) Carrybacks and carryovers of excess tax paid. (i) In general. Any amount by which (a) any income, war profits, and excess profits taxes paid or accrued, or deemed to be paid under section 902, during the taxable year to any foreign country or possession of the United States with respect to foreign mineral income from sources within such country or possession exceed (b) the reduced amount of such taxes as determined under paragraph (a)(1) of this section may not be deemed paid or accrued under section 904(d) in any other taxable year. See § 1.904-2(b)(2)(iii). However, to the extent such reduced amount of taxes exceeds the applicable limitation under section 904(a) for the taxable year it shall be deemed paid or accrued under section 904(d) in another taxable year as a carryback or carryover of an unused foreign tax. The amount so deemed paid or accrued in another taxable year is not, however, deemed paid or accrued with respect to foreign mineral income in such other taxable year. See § 1.904-2(c)(3).

(ii) Carryovers to taxable years beginning after December 31, 1969. Where, under the provisions of section 904(d), taxes paid or accrued, or deemed to be paid under section 902, to any foreign country or possession of the United States in any taxable year beginning before January 1, 1970, are deemed paid or accrued in one or more taxable years beginning after December 31, 1969, the amount of such taxes so deemed paid or accrued with respect to foreign mineral income and shall not be reduced under section 901(e) and paragraph (a)(1) of this section.

(iii) Carrybacks to taxable years beginning before January 1, 1970. Where income, war profits, and excess profits taxes are paid or accrued, or deemed to be paid under section 902, to any foreign country or possession of the United States in any taxable year beginning after December 31, 1969, with respect to foreign mineral income from sources within such country or possession, they must first be reduced under section 901(e) and paragraph (a)(1) of this section before they may be deemed paid or accrued under section 904(d) in one or more taxable years beginning before January 1, 1970.

(d) Illustrations. The application of this section may be illustrated by the following examples, in which the surtax exemption provided by section 11(d) and the tax surcharge provided by section 51(a) are disregarded for purposes of simplification:

Example (1). (a) M, a domestic corporation using the calendar year as the taxable year, is an operator drilling for oil in foreign country W. For 1971, M's gross income under chapter 1 of the Code is $100,000, all of which is foreign mineral income from a property in country W and is subject to the allowance for depletion. During 1971, M incurs intangible drilling and development costs of $15,000, which are currently deductible for purposes of the tax of both countries. Cost depletion amounts to $2,000 for purposes of the tax of both countries, and only cost depletion is allowed as a deduction under the law of country W. It is assumed that no other deductions are allowable under the law of either country. Based upon the facts assumed, the income tax paid to country W on such foreign mineral income is $41,500, and the U.S. tax on such income before allowance of the foreign tax credit is $30,240, determined as follows:

	U.S. tax	W tax
Foreign mineral income	$100,000	$100,000
Less:		
Intangible drilling and development costs	15,000	15,000
Cost depletion	—	2,000
Percentage depletion (22% of $100,000, but not to exceed 50% of $85,000)	22,000	—
Taxable income	63,000	83,000
Income tax rate	48%	50%
Tax	30,240	41,500

(b) Without taking this section into account, M would be allowed a foreign tax credit for 1971 of $30,240 ($30,240 × $63,000/$63,000), and foreign income tax in the amount of $11,260 ($41,500 less $30,240) would first be carried back to 1969 under section 904(d).

(c) Pursuant to paragraph (a)(1) of this section, however, the foreign income tax allowable as a credit against the U.S. tax is reduced to $31,900, determined as follows:

Foreign income tax paid on foreign mineral income		$41,500
Less reduction under sec. 901(e):		
Smaller of $41,500 (tax paid to country W on foreign mineral income) or $39,840 (U.S. tax on foreign mineral income of $83,000 ($83,000 X 48%), determined by deducting cost depletion of $2,000 in lieu of percentage depletion of $22,000)	$39,840	

Less: U.S. tax on foreign mineral income (before credit)	$30,240	$ 9,600
Foreign income tax allowable as a credit		31,900

(d) After taking this section into account, M is allowed a foreign tax credit for 1971 of $30,240 ($30,240 × $63,000/63,000). The amount of foreign income tax which may be first carried back to 1969 under section 904(d) is reduced from $11,260 to $1,660 ($31,900 less $30,240).

Example (2). (a) M, a domestic corporation using the calendar year as the taxable year, is an operator drilling for oil in foreign country X. For 1972, M has gross income under chapter 1 of the Code of $100,000, all of which is foreign mineral income from a property in country X and is subject to the allowance for depletion. During 1972, M incurs intangible drilling and development costs of $50,000 which are currently deductible for purposes of the U.S. tax but which must be amortized for purposes of the tax of country X. Percentage depletion of $22,000 is allowed as a deduction by both countries. For purposes of the U.S. tax, cost depletion for 1972 amounts to $15,000. It is assumed that no other deductions are allowable under the law of either country. Based upon these facts, the income tax paid to country X on such foreign mineral income is $27,200, and the U.S. tax on such income before allowance of the foreign tax credit is $13,440, determined as follows:

	U.S. tax	X tax
Foreign mineral income	$100,000	$100,000
Less:		
Intangible drilling & development costs	50,000	10,000
Percentage depletion	22,000	22,000
Taxable income	28,000	68,000
Income tax rate	48%	40%
Tax	13,440	27,200

(b) Without taking this section into account, M would be allowed a foreign tax credit for 1972 of $13,440 ($13,440 × $28,000/$28,000), and foreign income tax in the amount of $13,760 ($27,200 less $13,440) would first be carried back to 1970 under section 904(d).

(c) Pursuant to paragraph (a)(1) of this section, however, the foreign income tax allowable as a credit against the U.S. tax is reduced to $23,840, determined as follows:

Foreign income tax paid on foreign mineral income		$27,200
Less reduction under sec. 901(e):		
Smaller of $27,200 (tax paid to country × on foreign mineral income) or $16,800 (U.S. tax on foreign mineral income of $35,000 ($35,000 × 48%), determined by deducting cost depletion of $15,000 in lieu of percentage depletion of $22,000)	$16,800	
Less: U.S. tax on foreign mineral income (before credit)	13,440	3,360
Foreign income tax allowable as a credit		23,840

(d) After taking this section into account, M is allowed a foreign tax credit of $13,440 ($13,440 × $28,000/$28,000). The amount of foreign income tax which may be first carried back to 1970 under section 904(d) is reduced from $13,760 to $10,400 ($23,840 less $13,440).

Example (3). (a) N, a domestic corporation using the calendar year as the taxable year, is an operator drilling for oil in foreign country Y. For 1972, N's gross income under chapter 1 of the Code is $100,000, all of which is foreign mineral income from a property in country Y and is subject to the allowance for depletion. During 1972, N incurs intangible drilling and development costs of $15,000, which are currently deductible for purposes of the U.S. tax but are not deductible under the law of country Y. Depreciation of $40,000 is allowed as a deduction for purposes of the U.S. tax; and of $20,000, for purposes of the Y tax. Cost depletion amounts to $10,000 for purposes of the tax of both countries, and only cost depletion is allowed as a deduction under the law of country Y. It is assumed that no other deductions are allowable under the law of either country. Based upon the facts assumed, the income tax paid to country Y on such foreign mineral income is $14,000, and the U.S. tax on such income before allowance of the foreign tax credit is $11,040, determined as follows:

	U.S. tax	Y tax
Foreign mineral income	$100,000	$100,000
Less:		
Intangible drilling and development costs	15,000	—
Depreciation	40,000	20,000
Cost depletion	—	10,000
Percentage depletion (22% of $100,000, but not to exceed 50% of $45,000)	22,000	—
Taxable income	23,000	70,000
Income tax rate	48%	20%
Tax	11,040	14,000

(b) Without taking this section into account, N would be allowed a foreign tax credit for 1972 of $11,040 ($11,040 × $23,000/$23,000), and foreign income tax in the amount of $2,960 ($14,000 less $11,040) would first be carried back to 1970 under section 904(d).

(c) Pursuant to paragraph (a)(1) of this section, however, the foreign income tax allowable as a credit against the U.S. tax is reduced to $11,040, determined as follows:

Foreign income tax paid on foreign mineral income		$14,000
Less reduction under sec. 901(e):		
Smaller of $14,000 (tax paid to country Y on foreign mineral income) or $16,800 (U.S. tax on foreign mineral income of $35,000 ($35,000 × 48%), determined by deducting cost depletion of $10,000 in lieu of percentage depletion of $22,000)	$14,000	
Less: U.S. tax on foreign mineral income (before credit)	11,040	2,960
Foreign income tax allowable as a credit		11,040

(d) After taking this section into account, N is allowed a foreign tax credit for 1972 of $11,040 ($11,040 × $23,000/$23,000), but no foreign income tax is carried back to 1970 under section 904(d) since the allowable credit of $11,040 does not exceed the limitation of $11,040.

Example (4). (a) D, a domestic corporation using the calendar year as the taxable year, is an operator drilling for oil in foreign country Z. For 1971, D's gross income under chapter 1 of the Code is $100,000, all of which is foreign mineral income from a property in country Z and is subject to the allowance for depletion. During 1971, D incurs intangible drilling and development costs of $85,000, which are currently deductible for purposes of the U.S. Tax but are not deductible under the law of country Z. Cost depletion in the amount of $10,000 is allowed as a deduction for purposes of both the U.S. tax and the tax of country Z. Percentage depletion is not allowed as a deduction under the law of country Z and is not taken as a deduction for purposes of the U.S. tax. It is assumed that no other deductions are allowable under the law of either country. Based upon the facts assumed, the income tax paid to country Z on such foreign mineral income is $27,000, and the U.S. tax on such income before allowance of the foreign tax credit is $2,400, determined as follows:

	U.S. tax	Z tax
Foreign mineral income	$100,000	$100,000
Less:		
Intangible drilling & development costs	85,000	—
Cost depletion	10,000	10,000
Taxable income	5,000	90,000
Income tax rate	48%	30%
Tax	2,400	27,000

(b) Section 901(e) and this section do not apply to reduce the amount of the foreign income tax paid to country Z with respect to the foreign mineral income since for 1971 D is not allowed the deduction for percentage depletion with respect to any foreign mineral income from sources within country Z. Accordingly, D is allowed a foreign tax credit of $2,400 ($2,400 × $5,000/$5,000), and foreign income tax in the amount of $24,600 ($27,000 less $2,400) is first carried back to 1969 under section 904(d).

Example (5). (a) R, a domestic corporation using the calendar year as the taxable year, is an operator drilling for oil in the United States and in foreign country Z. For 1971, R's gross income under chapter 1 of the Code is $250,000, of which $100,000 is foreign mineral income from a property in foreign country Z and $150,000 is from a property in the United States, all being subject to the allowance for depletion. During 1971, R incurs intangible drilling and development costs of $125,000 in the United States and of $25,000 in country Z, all of which are currently deductible for purposes of the U.S. tax. Of these costs of $25,000 incurred in country Z, only $2,500 is currently deductible under the law of country Z. Cost depletion in the case of the U.S. property amounts to $60,000; and in the case of the property in country Z, to $5,000, which is allowed as a deduction under the laws of such country. Percentage depletion is not allowed as a deduction under the law of country Z. In computing the U.S. tax for 1971, R is required to use cost depletion with respect to the mineral income from the U.S. property and percentage depletion with respect to the foreign mineral income from the property in country Z. It is assumed that no other deductions are allowed under the law of either country. Based upon the facts assumed, the income tax paid to country Z on the foreign mineral income from sources therein is $37,000, and the U.S. tax on the entire mineral income before allowance of the foreign tax credit is $8,640, determined as follows:

	U.S. tax	Z tax
Gross income (including foreign mineral income)	$250,000	$100,000
Less:		
Intangible drilling and development costs	150,000	2,500
Cost depletion	60,000	5,000
Percentage depletion on foreign mineral income (22% of $100,000, but not to exceed 50% of [$100,000 – $25,000])	22,000	—
Taxable income	18,000	92,500
Income tax rate	48%	40%
Tax	8,640	37,000

(b) Without taking this section into account, R would be allowed a foreign tax credit for 1971 of $8,640 ($8,640 × $18,000/$18,000), and foreign income tax in the amount of $28,360 ($37,000 less $8,640) would first be carried back to 1969 under section 904(d).

(c) Under paragraph (a)(2)(ii) of this section, the amount of the U.S. tax for 1971 with respect to foreign mineral income from country Z is $25,440, which is the greater of the amounts of tax determined under subparagraphs (1) and (2):

(1) U.S. tax on total taxable income in excess of U.S. tax on taxable income excluding foreign mineral income from country Z (determined under paragraph (a)(2)(ii)(a) of this section):

U.S. tax on total income		$8,640
Less U.S. tax on taxable income other than foreign mineral income from Country Z:		
Income from U.S. property	$150,000	
Intangible drilling and development costs	125,000	
Cost depletion	60,000	
Taxable income	0	
Income tax rate	48%	
U.S. tax	0	0
Excess tax		8,640

(2) U. S. tax on foreign mineral income from country Z (determined under paragraph (a)(2)(ii)(b) of this section):

Foreign mineral income	$100,000
Intangible drilling and development costs	25,000
Percentage depletion (22% of $100,000, but not to exceed 50% of $75,000)	22,000
Taxable income	53,000
Income tax rate	48%
U.S. tax	25,440

(d) Under paragraph (a)(2)(iii) of this section, the amount of the U.S. tax which would be computed for 1971 (without regard to section 613) with respect to foreign mineral income from sources within country Z is $33,600, computed by applying the principles of paragraph (a)(2)(ii)(b) of this section:

Foreign mineral income	$100,000
Intangible drilling and development costs	25,000
Cost depletion	5,000
Taxable income	70,000
Income tax rate	48%
U.S. tax	33,600

(e) Pursuant to paragraph (a)(1) of this section, the foreign income tax allowable as a credit against the U.S. tax for 1971 is reduced to $28,840, determined as follows:

Foreign income tax paid on foreign mineral income		$37,000
Less reduction under sec. 901(e):		
Smaller of $37,000 (tax paid to country Z on foreign mineral income) or $33,600 (U.S. tax on foreign mineral income of $70,000, as determined under paragraph (d) of this example,	$33,600	
Less: U.S. tax on foreign mineral income of $53,000, as determined under paragraph (c) of this example	25,440	8,160
Foreign income tax allowable as a credit		$28,840

(f) After taking this section into account, R is allowed a foreign tax credit for 1971 of $8,640 ($8,640 × $18,000/$18,000). The amount of foreign income tax which may be first carried back to 1969 under section 904(d) is reduced from $28,360 to $20,200 ($28,840 less $8,640).

Example (6). (a) B, a single individual using the calendar year as the taxable year, is an operator drilling for oil in foreign countries X and Y. For 1972, B's gross income under chapter 1 of the Code is $250,000, of which $150,000 is foreign mineral income from a property in country X and $100,000 is foreign mineral income from a property in country Y, all being subject to the allowance for depletion. The assumption is made that B's earned taxable income for 1972 is insufficient to cause section 1348 to apply. During 1972, B incurs intangible drilling and development costs of $16,000 in country X and of $9,000 in country Y, which are currently deductible for purposes of both the U.S. tax and the tax of countries X and Y, respectively. For purposes of both the U.S. tax and the tax of countries X and Y, respectively, cost depletion in the case of the X property amounts to $8,000, and in the case of Y property, to $7,000; and only cost depletion is allowed as a deduction under the law of countries X and Y. For 1972, B uses the overall limitation under section 904(a)(2) on the foreign tax credit. Percentage depletion is not allowed as a deduction under the law of countries X and Y. It is assumed that the only other allowable deductions amount to $2,250. None of these deductions is attributable to the income from the properties in countries X and Y, and none is deductible under the laws of country X or country Y. Based upon the facts assumed, the income tax paid to countries X and Y on the foreign mineral income from each such country is $71,820 and $25,200, respectively, and the U.S. tax on B's total taxable income before allowance of the foreign tax credit is $99,990, determined as follows:

	U.S. tax	X tax	Y tax
Total income (including foreign mineral income from countries X and Y)	$250,000	$150,000	$100,000
Intangible drilling and development costs	25,000	16,000	9,000
Cost depletion		8,000	7,000
Percentage depletion (22% of $150,000, but not to exceed 50% of $134,000; plus 22% of $100,000, but not to exceed 50% of $91,000)	55,000		
Adjusted gross income	170,000		
Other deductions	2,250		
Personal exemption	750		
Taxable income	167,000	126,000	84,000
Income tax rate		57%	30%
Foreign tax		71,820	25,200
U.S. tax ($53,090 plus 70% of $67,000)	99,990		

(b) Without taking this section into account, B would be allowed a foreign tax credit for 1972 of $97,020 ($71,820 + $25,200), but not to exceed the overall limitation under section 904(a)(2) of $99,990 ($99,990 × $167,750/$167,750). There would be no foreign income tax carried back to 1970 under section 904(d) since the allowable credit of $97,020 does not exceed the limitation of $99,990.

(c) Under paragraph (a)(2)(ii) of this section, the amount of the U.S. tax for 1972 with respect to foreign mineral income from sources within country X is $69,760, which is the greater of the amounts of tax determined under subparagraphs (1) and (2):

(1) U.S. tax on total taxable income in excess of U.S. tax on taxable income excluding foreign mineral income from country X (determined under paragraph (a)(2)(ii)*(a)* of this section):

U.S. tax on total taxable income		$99,990
Less U.S. tax on taxable income other than foreign mineral income from country X:		
Foreign mineral income from country Y	$100,000	
Intangible drilling and development costs	9,000	
Percentage depletion (22% of $100,000, but not to exceed 50% of $91,000)	22,000	
Adjusted gross income	69,000	
Other deductions	2,250	
Personal exemption	750	
Taxable income	66,000	
U.S. tax ($26,390 plus 64% of $6,000)		30,230
Excess tax		69,760

(2) U.S. tax on foreign mineral income from country X (determined under paragraph (a)(2)(ii)*(b)* of this section):

Foreign mineral income from country X	$150,000.00
Intangible drilling and development costs	16,000.00
Percentage depletion (22% of $150,000, but not to exceed 50% of $134,000)	33,000.00
Adjusted gross income	101,000.00
Other deductions	
Taxable income	101,000.00
U.S. tax ($53,090 plus 70% of excess over $100,000)	53,790.00

(d) Under paragraph (a)(2)(iii) of this section, and by applying the principles of paragraph (a)(2)(ii)*(a)* of this section, the amount of the U.S. tax which would be computed for 1972 (without regard to section 613) with respect to foreign mineral income from sources within country X is $87,920, which is the excess of the U.S. tax ($127,990) determined under subparagraph (1) over the U.S. tax ($40,070) determined under subparagraph (2):

(1) U.S. tax on total taxable income determined without regard to section 613:

Total income	$250,000
Intangible drilling and development costs	25,000
Cost depletion	15,000
Adjusted gross income	210,000
Other deductions	2,250
Personal exemption	750
Taxable income	207,000
U.S. tax ($53,090 plus 70% of $107,000).	127,990

(2) U.S. tax on total taxable income other than foreign mineral income from country X, determined without regard to section 613:

Foreign mineral income from country Y	$100,000
Intangible drilling and development costs	9,000
Cost depletion	7,000
Adjusted gross income	84,000
Other deductions	2,250
Personal exemption	750
Taxable income	81,000
U.S. tax ($39,390 plus 68% of $1,000)	40,070

(e) Under paragraph (a)(2)(i) of this section, the amount of income tax paid to country X for 1972 with respect to foreign mineral income from sources within such country is $71,820. This is the amount determined under both (a) and (b) of paragraph (a)(2)(i) of this section, since, in this case, there is no income from sources within country X other than foreign mineral income, and there are no deductions allowed under the law of country X which are not allocable to such foreign mineral income.

(f) Pursuant to paragraph (a)(1) of this section, the foreign income tax with respect to foreign mineral income from sources within country X which is allowable as a credit against the U.S. tax for 1972 is reduced to $69,760, determined as follows:

Foreign income tax paid to country X on foreign mineral income		$71,820
Less reduction under sec. 901(e): to country X on		
Smaller of $71,620 (tax paid to country X on foreign mineral income) or $87,920 (U.S. tax on foreign mineral income from sources within country X, as determined under paragraph (d) of this example)	$71,820	
Less: U.S. tax on foreign mineral income from source within country X determined under paragraph (c) of this example	69,760	2,060
Foreign income tax of country X allowable as a credit		69,760

(g) Under paragraph (a)(2)(ii) of this section, the amount of the U.S. tax for 1972 with respect to foreign mineral income from sources within country Y is $48,280, which is the greater of the amounts of tax determined under subparagraphs (1) and (2):

(1) U.S. tax on total taxable income in excess of U.S. tax on taxable income excluding foreign mineral income from country Y (determined under paragraph (a)(2)(ii)(a) of this section):

U.S. tax on total taxable income		$99,990
Less U.S. tax on taxable income other than foreign mineral income from country Y:		
Foreign mineral income from country X	$150,000	
Intangible drilling and development costs	16,000	
Percentage depletion (22% of $150,000, but not to exceed 50% of $134,000)	33,000	
Adjusted gross income	101,000	
Other deductions	2,250	
Personal exemption	750	
Taxable income	98,000	
U.S. tax ($46,190 plus 69% of $8,000)		51,710
Excess tax		48,280

(2) U.S. tax on foreign mineral income from country Y (determined under paragraph (a)(2)(ii)*(b)* of this section):

Foreign mineral income from country Y	$100,000
Intangible drilling and development costs	9,000
Percentage depletion (22% of $100,000, but not to exceed 50% of $91,000)	22,000
Adjusted gross income	69,000
Other deductions	
Taxable income	69,000
U.S. tax ($26,390 plus 64% of $9,000)	32,150

(h) Under paragraph (a)(2)(iii) of this section, and by applying the principles of paragraph (a)(2)(ii)(a) of this section, the amount of the U.S. tax which would be computed for 1972 (without regard to section 613) with respect to foreign mineral income from sources within country Y is $58,800, which is the excess of the U.S. tax ($127,990) determined under paragraph (d)(1) of this example over the U.S. tax ($69,190) on total taxable income other than foreign mineral income from country Y, determined without regard to section 613, as follows:

Foreign mineral income from country X	$ 150,000
Intangible drilling and development costs	16,000
Cost depletion	8,000
Adjusted gross income	126,000
Personal exemption	2,250
Other deductions	(750)
Taxable income	123,000
U.S. tax ($53,090 plus 70% of $23,000)	69,190

(i) Under paragraph (a)(2)(i) of this section, the amount of income tax paid to country Y for 1972 with respect to foreign mineral income from sources within such country is $25,200. This is the amount determined under both (a) and (b) of paragraph (a)(2)(i) of this section, since, in this case, there is no income from sources within country Y other than foreign mineral income, and there are no deductions allowed under the law of country Y which are not allocable to such foreign mineral income.

(j) Pursuant to paragraph (a)(1) of this section, the foreign income tax with respect to foreign mineral income from sources within country Y which is allowable as a credit against the U.S. tax for 1972 is not reduced from $25,200, as follows:

Foreign income tax paid to country Y on foreign mineral income	$25,200
Less reduction under sec. 901(e):	

Smaller of $25,200 (tax paid to country Y on foreign mineral income) or $58,800 (U.S. tax on foreign mineral income from sources within country Y, as determined under paragraph (h) of this example)	$25,200	
Less: U.S. tax on foreign mineral income from sources within country Y, as determined under paragraph (g) of this example	48,280	
Foreign income tax of country Y allowable as a credit		25,200

(k) After taking this section into account, B is allowed a foreign tax credit for 1972 of $94,960 ($69,760 + $25,200), but not to exceed the overall limitation under section 904(a)(3) of $99,990 ($99,990 × $167,750/$167,750). There would be no foreign income tax carried back to 1970 under section 904(d) since the allowable credit of $94,960 does not exceed the limitation of $99,990.

Example (7). (a) P, a domestic corporation using the calendar year as the taxable year, is an operator mining for iron ore in foreign country X. For 1971, P's gross income under chapter 1 of the Code is $100,000, all of which is foreign mineral income from a property in country X and is subject to the allowance for depletion. For 1971, cost depletion amounts to $5,000 for purposes of the tax of both countries, and only cost depletion is allowed as a deduction under the law of country X. It is assumed that deductions (other than for depletion) attributable to the mineral property in country X amount to $8,000, and these deductions are allowable under the law of both countries. Based upon the facts assumed, the income tax paid to country X on such foreign mineral income is $39,150, and the U.S. tax on such income before allowance of the foreign tax credit is $37,440 determined as follows:

	U.S. tax	X tax
Foreign mineral income	$100,000	$100,000
Less:		
Percentage depletion (14% of $100,000, but not to exceed 50% of $92,000)	14,000	
Cost depletion		5,000
Other deductions	8,000	8,000
Taxable income	78,000	87,000
Income tax rate	48%	45%
Tax	37,440	30,150

(b) Without taking this section into account, P would be allowed a foreign tax credit for 1971 of $37,440 ($37,440 × $78,000/$78,000), and foreign income tax in the amount of $1,710 ($39,150 less $37,440) would first be carried back to 1969 under section 904(d).

(c) Pursuant to paragraph (a)(1) of this section, however, the foreign income tax allowable as a credit against the U.S. tax is reduced to $37,440, determined as follows:

Foreign income tax paid on foreign mineral income		$ 39,150
Less reduction under sec. 901(e):		
Smaller of $39,150 (tax paid to country X on foreign mineral income) or $41,760 (U.S. tax on foreign mineral income of $87,000 ($87,000 × 48%), determined by deducting cost depletion of $5,000 in lieu of percentage depletion of $14,000)	$39,150	
Less: U.S. tax on foreign mineral income (before credit)	37,440	1,710
Foreign income tax allowable as a credit		37,440

(d) After taking this section into account, P is allowed a foreign tax credit for 1971 of $37,440 ($37,440 × $78,000/$78,000), but no foreign income tax is carried back to 1969 under section 904(d) since the allowable credit of $37,440 does not exceed the limitation of $37,440.

Example (8). (a) The facts are the same as in example (7), except that P is assumed to have received dividends for 1971 of $25,000 from R, a foreign corporation incorporated in country X which is not a less developed country corporation within the meaning of section 902(d). Income tax of $2,500 ($25,000 × 10%) on such dividends is withheld at the source in country X. It is assumed that P is deemed under section 902(a)(1) and § 1.902-1(h) to have paid income tax of $22,500 to country X in respect of such dividends and that under paragraphs (a)(2)(i) and (b)(2)(i) of this section such dividends are deemed to be attributable to foreign mineral income from sources in country X and that such tax is deemed to be paid with respect to such foreign mineral income. Based upon the facts assumed, the U.S. tax on the foreign mineral income from sources in country X is $60,240 before allowance of the foreign tax credit, determined as follows:

Foreign mineral income from country X:		
Income from mining property	$100,000	
Dividends from R	25,000	
Sec. 78 dividend	22,500	$147,500
Less:		
Percentage depletion (14% of $100,000, but not to exceed 50% of $92,000)		$ 14,000
Other deductions		8,000
Taxable income		125,500
Income tax rate		48%
U.S. tax		60,240

(b) Without taking this section into account, P would be allowed a foreign tax credit for 1971 of $60,240 ($60,240 × $125,500/$125,500), and foreign income tax in the amount of $3,910 ([$39,150 + $22,500 + $2,500] less $60,240) would first be carried back to 1969 under section 904(d).

(c) Pursuant to paragraph (a)(1) of this section, however, the foreign income tax allowable as a credit against the U.S. tax is reduced from $64,150 to $60,240, determined as follows:

Foreign income tax paid, and deemed to be paid, to country X on foreign mineral income ($39,150 + $22,500 + $2,500)	$64,150
Less reduction under sec. 901(e):	

Smaller of $64,150 (tax paid and deemed paid to country X on foreign mineral income) or $64,560 (U.S. tax on foreign mineral income of $134,500 ($134,500 × 48%), determined by deducting cost depletion of $5,000 in lieu of percentage depletion of $14,000) . . .	$64,150	
Less: U.S. tax on foreign mineral income (before credit)	60,240	3,910
Foreign income tax allowable as a credit		60,240

(c) After taking this section into account, P is allowed a foreign tax credit for 1971 of $60,240 ($60,240 × $125,500/$125,500), but no foreign income tax is carried back to 1969 under section 904(d) since the allowable credit of $60,240 does not exceed the limitation of $60,240.

T.D. 7294, 11/29/73, amend T.D. 7481, 4/15/77.

§ 1.902-0 Outline of regulations provisions for section 902.

Caution: The Treasury has not yet amended Reg § 1.902-0 to reflect changes made by P.L. 105-34.

This section lists the provisions under section 902.

§ 1.902-1 Credit for domestic corporate shareholder of a foreign corporation for foreign income taxes paid by the foreign corporation.

(a) Definitions and special effective date.

(1) Domestic shareholder.

(2) First-tier corporation.

(3) Second-tier corporation.

(4) Third- or lower-tier corporation.

(i) Third-tier corporation.

(ii) Fourth-, fifth-, or sixth-tier corporation.

(5) Example.

(6) Upper- and lower-tier corporations.

(7) Foreign income taxes.

(8) Post-1986 foreign income taxes.

(i) In general.

(ii) Distributions out of earnings and profits accumulated by a lower-tier corporation in its taxable years beginning before January 1, 1987, and included in the gross income of an upper-tier corporation in its taxable year beginning after December 31, 1986.

(iii) Foreign income taxes paid or accrued with respect to high withholding tax interest.

(9) Post-1986 undistributed earnings.

(i) In general.

(ii) Distributions out of earnings and profits accumulated by a lower-tier corporation in its taxable years beginning before January 1, 1987, and included in the gross income of an upper-tier corporation in its taxable year beginning after December 31, 1986.

(iii) Reduction for foreign income taxes paid or accrued.

(iv) Special allocations.

(10) Pre-1987 accumulated profits.

(i) Definition.

(ii) Computation of pre-1987 accumulated profits.

(iii) Foreign income taxes attributable to pre-1987 accumulated profits.

(11) Dividend.

(12) Dividend received.

(13) Special effective date.

(i) Rule.

(ii) Example.

(b) Computation of foreign income taxes deemed paid by a domestic shareholder, first-tier corporation, or lower-tier corporation.

(1) General rule.

(2) Allocation rule for dividends attributable to post-1986 undistributed earnings and pre-1987 accumulated profits.

(i) Portion of dividend out of post-1986 undistributed earnings.

(ii) Portion of dividend out of pre-1987 accumulated profits.

(3) Dividends paid out of pre-1987 accumulated profits.

(4) Deficits in accumulated earnings and profits.

(5) Examples.

(c) Special rules.

(1) Separate computations required for dividends from each first-tier and lower-tier corporation.

(i) Rule.

(ii) Example.

(2) Section 78 gross-up.

(i) Foreign income taxes deemed paid by a domestic shareholder.

(ii) Foreign income taxes deemed paid by an upper-tier corporation.

(iii) Example.

(3) Creditable foreign income taxes.

(4) Foreign mineral income.

(5) Foreign taxes paid or accrued in connection with the purchase or sale of certain oil and gas.

(6) Foreign oil and gas extraction income.

(7) United States shareholders of controlled foreign corporations.

(8) Effect of certain liquidations, reorganizations, or similar transactions on certain foreign taxes paid or accrued in taxable years beginning on or before August 5, 1997.

(i) General rule.

(ii) Example.

(d) Dividends from controlled foreign corporations and noncontrolled section 902 corporations.

(1) General rule.

(2) Look-through.

(i) Dividends.

(ii) Coordination with section 960.

(e) Information to be furnished.

(f) Examples.

(g) Effective date.

§ 1.902-2 Treatment of deficits in post-1986 undistributed earnings and pre-1987 accumulated profits of a first- or lower-tier corporation for purposes of computing an amount of foreign taxes deemed paid under § 1.902-1.

(a) Carryback of deficits in post-1986 undistributed earnings of a first- or lower-tier corporation to pre-effective date taxable years.

(1) Rule.

T.D. 8708, 1/6/97, amend T.D. 9260, 4/24/2006.

§ 1.902-1 Credit for domestic corporate shareholder of a foreign corporation for foreign income taxes paid by the foreign corporation.

Caution: The Treasury has not yet amended Reg § 1.902-1 to reflect changes made by P.L. 108-357, P.L. 105-34.

(a) Definitions and special effective date. For purposes of section 902, this section, and § 1.902-2, the definitions provided in paragraphs (a)(1) through (12) of this section and the special effective date of paragraph (a)(13) of this section apply.

(1) Domestic shareholder. In the case of dividends received by a domestic corporation from a foreign corporation after December 31, 1986, the term domestic shareholder means a domestic corporation, other than an S corporation as defined in section 1361(a), that owns at least 10 percent of the voting stock of the foreign corporation at the time the domestic corporation receives a dividend from that foreign corporation.

(2) First-tier corporation. In the case of dividends received by a domestic shareholder from a foreign corporation in a taxable year beginning after December 31, 1986, the term first-tier corporation means a foreign corporation, at least 10 percent of the voting stock of which is owned by a domestic shareholder at the time the domestic shareholder receives a dividend from that foreign corporation. The term first-tier corporation also includes a DISC or former DISC, but only with respect to dividends from the DISC or former DISC that are treated under sections 861(a)(2)(D) and 862(a)(2) as income from sources without the United States.

(3) Second-tier corporation. In the case of dividends paid to a first-tier corporation by a foreign corporation in a taxable year beginning after December 31, 1986, the foreign corporation is a second-tier corporation if, at the time a first-tier corporation receives a dividend from that foreign corporation, the first-tier corporation owns at least 10 percent of the foreign corporation's voting stock and the product of the following equals at least 5 percent—

(i) The percentage of voting stock owned by the domestic shareholder in the first-tier corporation; multiplied by

(ii) The percentage of voting stock owned by the first-tier corporation in the second-tier corporation.

(4) Third- or lower-tier corporation. (i) Third-tier corporation. In the case of dividends paid to a second-tier corporation by a foreign corporation in a taxable year beginning after December 31, 1986, a foreign corporation is a third-tier corporation if, at the time a second-tier corporation receives a dividend from that foreign corporation, the second-tier corporation owns at least 10 percent of the foreign corporation's voting stock and the product of the following equals at least 5 percent—

(A) The percentage of voting stock owned by the domestic shareholder in the first-tier corporation; multiplied by

(B) The percentage of voting stock owned by the first-tier corporation in the second-tier corporation; multiplied by

(C) The percentage of voting stock owned by the second-tier corporation in the third-tier corporation.

(ii) Fourth-, fifth-, or sixth-tier corporation. [Reserved]. For further guidance, see § 1.902-1T(a)(4)(ii).

(5) Example. The following example illustrates the ownership requirements of paragraphs (a)(1) through (4) of this section:

Example. (i) Domestic corporation M owns 30 percent of the voting stock of foreign corporation A on January 1, 1991, and for all periods thereafter. Corporation A owns 40 percent of the voting stock of foreign corporation B on January 1, 1991, and continues to own that stock until June 1, 1991, when Corporation A sells its stock in Corporation B. Both Corporation A and Corporation B use the calendar year as the taxable year. Corporation B pays a dividend out of its post-1986 undistributed earnings to Corporation A, which Corporation A receives on February 16, 1991. Corporation A pays a dividend out of its post-1986 undistributed earnings to Corporation M, which Corporation M receives on January 20, 1992. Corporation M uses a fiscal year ending on June 30 as the taxable year.

(ii) On February 16, 1991, when Corporation B pays a dividend to Corporation A, Corporation M satisfies the 10-percent stock ownership requirement of paragraphs (a)(1) and (2) of this section with respect to Corporation A. Therefore, Corporation A is a first-tier corporation within the meaning of paragraph (a)(2) of this section and Corporation M is a domestic shareholder of Corporation A within the meaning of paragraph (a)(1) of this section. Also on February 16, 1991, Corporation B is a second-tier corporation within the meaning of paragraph (a)(3) of this section because Corporation A owns at least 10 percent of its voting stock, and the percentage of voting stock owned by Corporation M in Corporation A on February 16, 1991 (30 percent) multiplied by the percentage of voting stock owned by Corporation A in Corporation B on February 16, 1991 (40 percent) equals 12 percent. Corporation A shall be deemed to have paid foreign income taxes of Corporation B with respect to the dividend received from Corporation B on February 16, 1991.

(iii) On January 20, 1992, Corporation M satisfies the 10-percent stock ownership requirement of paragraphs (a)(1) and (2) of this section with respect to Corporation A. Therefore, Corporation A is a first-tier corporation within the meaning of paragraph (a)(2) of this section and Corporation M is a domestic shareholder within the meaning of paragraph (a)(1) of this section. Accordingly, for its taxable year ending on June 30, 1992, Corporation M is deemed to have paid a portion of the post-1986 foreign income taxes paid, accrued, or deemed to be paid, by Corporation A. Those taxes will include taxes paid by Corporation B that were deemed paid by Corporation A with respect to the dividend paid by Corporation B to Corporation A on February 16, 1991, even though Corporation B is no longer a second-tier corporation with respect to Corporations A and M on January 20, 1992, and has not been a second-tier corporation with respect to Corporations A and M at any time during the taxable years of Corporations A and M that include January 20, 1992.

(6) Upper- and lower-tier corporations. [Reserved]. For further guidance, see § 1.902-1T(a)(6).

(7) Foreign income taxes. [Reserved]. For further guidance, see § 1.902-1T(a)(7).

(8) Post-1986 foreign income taxes. (i) In general. [Reserved]. For further guidance, see § 1.902-1T(a)(8)(i).

(ii) Distributions out of earnings and profits accumulated by a lower-tier corporation in its taxable years beginning before January 1, 1987, and included in the gross income of an upper-tier corporation in its taxable year beginning after December 31, 1986. Post-1986 foreign income taxes shall include foreign income taxes that are deemed paid by an upper-tier corporation with respect to distributions from a lower-tier corporation out of non-previously taxed pre-1987 accumulated profits, as defined in paragraph (a)(10) of this section, that are received by an upper-tier corporation in any taxable year of the upper-tier corporation beginning after December 31, 1986, provided the upper-tier corporation's earnings and profits in that year are included in its post-1986 undistributed earnings under paragraph (a)(9) of this section. Foreign income taxes deemed paid with respect to a distribution of pre-1987 accumulated profits shall be translated from the functional currency of the lower-tier corporation into dollars at the spot exchange rate in effect on the date of the distribution. To determine the character of the earnings and profits and associated taxes for foreign tax credit limitation purposes, see section 904 and § 1.904-7(a).

(iii) Foreign income taxes paid or accrued with respect to high withholding tax interest. Post-1986 foreign income taxes shall not include foreign income taxes paid or accrued by a noncontrolled section 902 corporation (as defined in section 904(d)(2)(E)(i)) in a taxable year beginning on or before December 31, 2002 with respect to high withholding tax interest (as defined in section 904(d)(2)(B)) to the extent the foreign tax rate imposed on such interest exceeds 5 percent. See section 904(d)(2)(E)(ii) and § 1.904-4(g)(2)(iii) (26 CFR revised as of April 1, 2006). The reduction in foreign income taxes paid or accrued by the amount of tax in excess of 5 percent imposed on high withholding tax interest income must be computed in functional currency before foreign income taxes are translated into U.S. dollars and included in post-1986 foreign income taxes.

(9) Post-1986 undistributed earnings. (i) In general. Except as provided in paragraphs (a)(10) and (13) of this section, the term post-1986 undistributed earnings means the amount of the earnings and profits of a foreign corporation (computed in accordance with sections 964(a) and 986) accumulated in taxable years of the foreign corporation beginning after December 31, 1986, determined as of the close of the taxable year of the foreign corporation in which it distributes a dividend. Post-1986 undistributed earnings shall not be reduced by reason of any earnings distributed or otherwise included in income, for example under section 304, 367(b), 551, 951(a), 1248 or 1293, during the taxable year. Post-1986 undistributed earnings shall be reduced to account for distributions or deemed distributions that reduced earnings and profits and inclusions that resulted in previously-taxed amounts described in section 959(c)(1) and (2) or section 1293(c) in prior taxable years beginning after December 31, 1986. Thus, post-1986 undistributed earnings shall not be reduced to the extent of the ratable share of a controlled foreign corporation's subpart F income, as defined in section 952, attributable to a shareholder that is not a United States shareholder within the meaning of section 951(b) or section 953(c)(1)(A), because that amount has not been included in a shareholder's gross income. Post-1986 undistributed earnings shall be reduced as provided herein regardless of whether any shareholder is deemed to have paid any foreign taxes, and regardless of whether any domestic shareholder chose to claim a foreign tax credit under section 901(a) for the year of the distribution. For rules on carrybacks and carryforwards of deficits and their effect on post-1986 undistributed earnings, see section 1.902-2. In the case of a foreign corporation the foreign income taxes of which are computed based on an accounting period of less than one

year, the term year means that accounting period. See sections 441(b)(3) and 443.

(ii) Distributions out of earnings and profits accumulated by a lower-tier corporation in its taxable years beginning before January 1, 1987, and included in the gross income of an upper-tier corporation in its taxable year beginning after December 31, 1986. Distributions by a lower-tier corporation out of non-previously taxed pre-1987 accumulated profits, as defined in paragraph (a)(10) of this section, that are received by an upper-tier corporation in any taxable year of the upper-tier corporation beginning after December 31, 1986, shall be treated as post-1986 undistributed earnings of the upper-tier corporation, provided the upper-tier corporation's earnings and profits for that year are included in its post-1986 undistributed earnings under paragraph (a)(9)(i) of this section. To determine the character of the earnings and profits and associated taxes for foreign tax credit limitation purposes, see section 904 and § 1.904-7(a).

(iii) Reduction for foreign income taxes paid or accrued. In computing post-1986 undistributed earnings, earnings and profits shall be reduced by foreign income taxes paid or accrued regardless of whether the taxes are creditable. Thus, earnings and profits shall be reduced by foreign income taxes paid with respect to high withholding tax interest even though a portion of the taxes is not creditable pursuant to section 904(d)(2)(E)(ii) and is not included in post-1986 foreign income taxes under paragraph (a)(8)(iii) of this section. Earnings and profits of an upper-tier corporation, however, shall not be reduced by foreign income taxes paid by a lower-tier corporation and deemed to have been paid by the upper-tier corporation.

(iv) Special allocations. The term post-1986 undistributed earnings means the total amount of the earnings of the corporation determined at the corporate level. Special allocations of earnings and taxes to particular shareholders, whether required or permitted by foreign law or a shareholder agreement, shall be disregarded. If, however, the Commissioner establishes that there is an agreement to pay dividends only out of earnings in the separate categories for passive or high withholding tax interest income, then only taxes imposed on passive or high withholding tax interest earnings shall be treated as related to the dividend. See § 1.904-6(a)(2).

(10) Pre-1987 accumulated profits. (i) Definition. The term pre-1987 accumulated profits means the amount of the earnings and profits of a foreign corporation computed in accordance with section 902 and attributable to its taxable years beginning before January 1, 1987. If the special effective date of paragraph (a)(13) of this section applies, pre-1987 accumulated profits also includes any earnings and profits (computed in accordance with sections 964(a) and 986) attributable to the foreign corporation's taxable years beginning after December 31, 1986, but before the first day of the first taxable year of the foreign corporation in which the ownership requirements of section 902(c)(3)(B) and paragraphs (a)(1) through (4) of this section are met with respect to that corporation.

(ii) Computation of pre-1987 accumulated profits. Pre-1987 accumulated profits must be computed under United States principles governing the computation of earnings and profits. Pre-1987 accumulated profits are determined at the corporate level. Special allocations of accumulated profits and taxes to particular shareholders with respect to distributions of pre-1987 accumulated profits in taxable years beginning after December 31, 1986, whether required or permitted by foreign law or a shareholder agreement, shall be disregarded. Pre-1987 accumulated profits of a particular year shall be reduced by amounts distributed from those accumulated profits or otherwise included in income from those accumulated profits, for example under sections 304, 367(b), 551, 951(a), 1248 or 1293. If a deficit in post-1986 undistributed earnings is carried back to offset pre-1987 accumulated profits, pre-1987 accumulated profits of a particular taxable year shall be reduced by the amount of the deficit carried back to that year. See section 1.902-2. The amount of a distribution out of pre-1987 accumulated profits, and the amount of foreign income taxes deemed paid under section 902, shall be determined and translated into United States dollars by applying the law as in effect prior to the effective date of the Tax Reform Act of 1986. See §§ 1.902-3, 1.902-4 and 1.964-1.

(iii) Foreign income taxes attributable to pre-1987 accumulated profits. The term pre-1987 foreign income taxes means any foreign income taxes paid, accrued, or deemed paid by a foreign corporation on or with respect to its pre-1987 accumulated profits. Pre-1987 foreign income taxes of a particular year shall be reduced by the amount of taxes paid or deemed paid by the foreign corporation on or with respect to amounts distributed or otherwise included in income from pre-1987 accumulated profits of that year. Thus, pre-1987 foreign income taxes shall be reduced by the amount of taxes deemed paid by a domestic shareholder (regardless of whether the shareholder chose to credit foreign income taxes under section 901 for the year of the distribution or inclusion) or a first-tier or second-tier corporation, and by the amount of taxes that would have been deemed paid had any other shareholder been eligible to compute an amount of foreign taxes deemed paid under section 902. Foreign income taxes deemed paid with respect to a distribution of pre-1987 accumulated profits shall be translated from the functional currency of the distributing corporation into United States dollars at the spot exchange rate in effect on the date of the distribution.

(11) Dividend. For purposes of section 902, the definition of the term dividend in section 316 and the regulations under that section applies. Thus, for example, distributions and deemed distributions under sections 302, 304, 305(b) and 367(b) that are treated as dividends within the meaning of section 301(c)(1) also are dividends for purposes of section 902. In addition, the term dividend includes deemed dividends under sections 551 and 1248, but not deemed inclusions under sections 951(a) and 1293. For rules concerning excess distributions from section 1291 funds that are treated as dividends solely for foreign tax credit purposes, (see Regulation Project INTL-656-87 published in 1992-1 C.B. 1124; see § 601.601(d)(2)(ii)(b) of this chapter).

(12) Dividend received. A dividend shall be considered received for purposes of section 902 when the cash or other property is unqualifiedly made subject to the demands of the distributee. See § 1.301-1(b). A dividend also is considered received for purposes of section 902 when it is deemed received under section 304, 367(b), 551, or 1248.

(13) Special effective date. (i) Rule. If the first day on which the ownership requirements of section 902(c)(3)(B) and paragraphs (a)(1) through (4) of this section are met with respect to a foreign corporation, without regard to whether a dividend is distributed, is in a taxable year of the foreign corporation beginning after December 31, 1986, then—

(A) The post-1986 undistributed earnings and post-1986 foreign income taxes of the foreign corporation shall be determined by taking into account only taxable years beginning on and after the first day of the first taxable year of the foreign corporation in which the ownership requirements are met, including subsequent table years in which the ownership requirements of section 902(c)(3)(B) and paragraphs (a)(1) through (4) of this section are not met; and

(B) Earnings and profits accumulated prior to the first day of the first taxable year of the foreign corporation in which the ownership requirements of section 902(c)(3)(B) and paragraphs (a)(1) through (4) of this section are met shall be considered pre-1987 accumulated profits.

(ii) Example. The following example illustrates the special effective date rules of this paragraph (a)(13):

Example. As of December 31, 1991, and since its incorporation, foreign corporation A has owned 100 percent of the stock of foreign corporation B. Corporation B is not a controlled foreign corporation. Corporation B uses the calendar year as its taxable year, and its functional currency is the u. Assume 1u equals $1 at all relevant times. On April 1, 1992, Corporation B pays a 200u dividend to Corporation A and the ownership requirements of section 902(c)(3)(B) and paragraphs (a)(1) through (4) of this section are not met at that time. On July 1, 1992, domestic corporation M purchases 10 percent of the Corporation B stock from Corporation A and, for the first time, Corporation B meets the ownership requirements of section 902(c)(3)(B) and paragraph (a)(2) of this section. Corporation M uses the calendar year as its taxable year. Corporation B does not distribute any dividends to Corporation M during 1992. For its taxable year ending December 31, 1992, Corporation B has 500u of earnings and profits (after foreign taxes but before taking into account the 200u distribution to Corporation A) and pays 100u of foreign income taxes that is equal to $100. Pursuant to paragraph (a)(13)(i) of this section, Corporation B's post-1986 undistributed earnings and post-1986 foreign income taxes will include earnings and profits and foreign income taxes attributable to Corporation B's entire 1992 taxable year and all taxable years thereafter. Thus, the April 1, 1992, dividend to Corporation A will reduce post-1986 undistributed earnings to 300u (500u − 200u) under paragraph (a)(9)(i) of this section. The foreign income taxes attributable to the amount distributed as a dividend to Corporation A will not be creditable because Corporation A is not a domestic shareholder. Post-1986 foreign income taxes, however, will be reduced by the amount of foreign taxes attributable to the dividend. Thus, as of the beginning of 1993, Corporation B has $60 ($100 − [$100 × 40% (200u/500u)]) of post-1986 foreign income taxes. See paragraphs (a)(8)(i) and (b)(1) of this section.

(b) Computation of foreign income taxes deemed paid by a domestic shareholder, first-tier corporation, or lower-tier corporation. *(1) General rule.* If a foreign corporation pays a dividend in any taxable year out of post-1986 undistributed earnings to a shareholder that is a domestic shareholder or an upper-tier corporation at the time it receives the dividend, the recipient shall be deemed to have paid the same proportion of any post-1986 foreign income taxes paid, accrued or deemed paid by the distributing corporation on or with respect to post-1986 undistributed earnings which the amount of the dividend out of post-1986 undistributed earnings (determined without regard to the gross-up under section 78) bears to the amount of the distributing corporation's post-1986 undistributed earnings. An upper-tier corporation shall not be entitled to compute an amount of foreign taxes deemed paid on a dividend from a lower-tier corporation, however, unless the ownership requirements of paragraphs (a)(1) through (4) of this section are met at each tier at the time the upper-tier corporation receives the dividend. Foreign income taxes deemed paid by a domestic shareholder or an upper-tier corporation must be computed under the following formula:

$$\text{Foreign income taxes deemed paid by domestic shareholder (or upper-tier corporation)} = \text{Post-1986 foreign income taxes of first-tier corporation (or lower-tier corporation)} \times \frac{\text{Dividend paid to domestic shareholder (or upper-tier corporation) by first-tier corporation (or lower-tier corporation)}}{\text{Post-1986 undistributed earnings of first-tier corporation (or lower-tier corporation)}}$$

(2) Allocation rule for dividends attributable to post-1986 undistributed earnings and pre-1987 accumulated profits. (i) Portion of dividend out of post-1986 undistributed earnings. Dividends will be deemed to be paid first out of post-1986 undistributed earnings to the extent thereof. If dividends exceed post-1986 undistributed earnings and dividends are paid to more than one shareholder, then the dividend to each shareholder shall be deemed to be paid pro rata out of post-1986 undistributed earnings, computed as follows:

$$\text{Portion of Dividend to a Shareholder Attributable to Post-1986 Undistributed Earnings} = \text{Post-1986 Undistributed Earnings} \times \frac{\text{Dividend to Shareholder}}{\text{Total Dividends Paid to all Shareholders}}$$

(ii) Portion of dividend out of pre-1987 accumulated profits. After the portion of the dividend attributable to post-1986 undistributed earnings is determined under paragraph (b)(2)(i) of this section, the remainder of the dividend received by a shareholder is attributable to pre-1987 accumulated profits to the extent thereof. That part of the dividend attributable to pre-1987 accumulated profits will be treated as paid first from the most recently accumulated earnings and profits. See § 1.902-3. If dividends paid out of pre-1987 accumulated profits are attributable to more than one pre-1987 taxable year and are paid to more than one shareholder, then the dividend to each shareholder attributable to earnings and profits accumulated in a particular pre-1987 taxable year shall be deemed to be paid pro rata out of accumulated profits of that taxable year, computed as follows:

$$\text{Portion of Dividend to a Shareholder Attributable to Accumulated Profits of a Particular Pre-1987 Taxable Year} = \text{Dividend Paid Out of Pre-1987 Accumulated Profits With Respect to the Particular Pre-1987 Taxable Year} \times \frac{\text{Dividend to Shareholder}}{\text{Total Dividends Paid to all Shareholders}}$$

(3) Dividends paid out of pre-1987 accumulated profits. If dividends are paid by a first-tier corporation or a lower-tier corporation out of pre-1987 accumulated profits, the domestic shareholder or upper-tier corporation that receives the dividends shall be deemed to have paid foreign income taxes to the extent provided under section 902 and the regulations thereunder as in effect prior to the effective date of the Tax Reform Act of 1986. See paragraphs (a)(10) and (13) of this section and §§ 1.902-3 and 1.902-4.

(4) Deficits in accumulated earnings and profits. No foreign income taxes shall be deemed paid with respect to a distribution from a foreign corporation out of current earnings and profits that is treated as a dividend under section 316(a)(2), and post-1986 foreign income taxes shall not be reduced, if as of the end of the taxable year in which the dividend is paid or accrued, the corporation has zero or a deficit in post-1986 undistributed earnings and the sum of current plus accumulated earnings and profits is zero or less than zero. The dividend shall reduce post-1986 undistributed earnings and accumulated earnings and profits.

(5) Examples. The following examples illustrate the rules of this paragraph (b):

Example (1). Domestic corporation M owns 100 percent of foreign corporation A. Both Corporation M and Corporation A use the calendar year as the taxable year, and Corporation A uses the u as its functional currency. Assume that 1u equals $1 at all relevant times. All of Corporation A's pre-1987 accumulated profits and post-1986 undistributed earnings are non-subpart F general limitation earnings and profits under section 904(d)(1)(I). As of December 31, 1992, Corporation A has 100u of post-1986 undistributed earnings and $40 of post-1986 foreign income taxes. For its 1986 taxable year, Corporation A has accumulated profits of 200u (net of foreign taxes) and paid 60u of foreign income taxes on those earnings. In 1992, Corporation A distributes 150u to Corporation M. Corporation A has 100u of post-1986 undistributed earnings and the dividend, therefore, is treated as paid out of post-1986 undistributed earnings to the extent of 100u. The first 100u distribution is from post-1986 undistributed earnings, and, because the distribution exhausts those earnings, Corporation M is deemed to have paid the entire amount of post-1986 foreign income taxes of Corporation A ($40). The remaining 50u dividend is treated as a dividend out of 1986 accumulated profits under paragraph (b)(2) of this section. Corporation M is deemed to have paid $15 (60u × 50u/200u, translated at the appropriate exchange rates) of Corporation A's foreign income taxes for 1986. As of January 1, 1993, Corporation A's post-1986 undistributed earnings and post-1986 foreign income taxes are 0. Corporation A has 150u of accumulated profits and 45u of foreign income taxes remaining in 1986.

Example (2). Domestic corporation M (incorporated on January 1, 1987) owns 100 percent of foreign corporation A (incorporated on January 1, 1987). Both Corporation M and Corporation A use the calendar year as the taxable year, and Corporation A uses the u as its functional currency. Assume that 1u equals $1 at all relevant times. Corporation A has no pre-1987 accumulated profits. All of Corporation A's post-1986 undistributed earnings are non-subpart F general limitation earnings and profits under section 904(d)(1)(I). On January 1, 1992, Corporation A has a deficit in accumulated earnings and profits and a deficit in post-1986 undistributed earnings of (200u). No foreign taxes have been paid with respect to post-1986 undistributed earnings. During 1992, Corporation A earns 100u (net of foreign taxes), pays $40 of foreign taxes on those earnings and distributes 50u to Corporation M. As of the end of 1992, Corporation A has a deficit of (100u)((200u) post-1986 undistributed earnings + 100u current earnings and profits) in post-1986 undistributed earnings. Corporation A, however, has current earnings and profits of 100u. Therefore, the 50u distribution is treated as a dividend in its entirety under section 316(a)(2). Under paragraph (b)(4) of this section, Corporation M is not deemed to have paid any of the foreign taxes paid by Corporation A because post-1986 undistributed earnings and the sum of current plus accumulated earnings and profits are (100u). The dividend reduces both post-1986 undistributed earnings and accumulated earnings and profits. Therefore, as of January 1, 1993, Corporation A's post-1986 undistributed earnings are (150u) and its accumulated earnings and profits are (150u). Corporation A's post-1986 foreign income taxes at the start of 1993 are $40.

(c) Special rules. *(1) Separate computations required for dividends from each first-tier and lower-tier corporation.* (i) Rule. If in a taxable year dividends are received by a domestic shareholder or an upper-tier corporation from two or more first-tier corporations or two or more lower-tier corporations, the foreign income taxes deemed paid by the domestic shareholder or the upper-tier corporation under sections 902(a) and (b) and paragraph (b) of this section shall be computed separately with respect to the dividends received from each first-tier corporation or lower-tier corporation. If a domestic shareholder receives dividend distributions from one or more first-tier corporations and in the same taxable year the first-tier corporation receives dividends from one or more lower-tier corporations, then the amount of foreign income taxes deemed paid shall be computed by starting with the lowest-tier corporation and working upward.

(ii) Example. The following example illustrates the application of this paragraph (c)(1):

Example. P, a domestic corporation, owns 40 percent of the voting stock of foreign corporation S. S owns 30 percent of the voting stock of foreign corporation T, and 30 percent of the voting stock of foreign corporation U. Neither S, T, nor U is a controlled foreign corporation. P, S, T and U all use the calendar year as their taxable year. In 1993, T and U both pay dividends to S and S pays a dividend to P. To compute foreign taxes deemed paid, paragraph (c)(1) of this section requires P to start with the lowest tier corporations and to compute foreign taxes deemed paid separately for dividends from each first-tier and lower-tier corporation. Thus, S first will compute foreign taxes deemed paid separately on its dividends from T and U. The deemed paid taxes will be added to S's post-1986 foreign income taxes, and the dividends will be added to S's post-1986 undistributed earnings. Next, P will compute foreign taxes deemed paid with respect to the dividend from S. This computation will take into account the taxes paid by T and U and deemed paid by S.

(2) Section 78 gross-up. (i) Foreign income taxes deemed paid by a domestic shareholder. Except as provided in section 960(b) and the regulations under that section (relating to amounts excluded from gross income under section 959(b)), any foreign income taxes deemed paid by a domestic shareholder in any taxable year under section 902(a) and paragraph (b) of this section shall be included in the gross income of the domestic shareholder for the year as a dividend under section 78. Amounts included in gross income under section 78 shall, for purposes of section 904, be deemed to be derived from sources within the United States to the extent the earnings and profits on which the taxes were paid are treated under section 904(g) as United States source earnings and profits. Section 1.904-5(m)(6). Amounts included in gross income under section 78 shall be treated for purposes of section 904 as income in a separate category to the extent that the foreign income taxes were allocated and apportioned to income in that separate category. See section 904(d)(3)(G) and § 1.904-6(b)(3).

(ii) Fourteen income taxes deemed paid by an upper-tier corporation. Foreign income taxes deemed paid by an upper-tier corporation on a distribution from a lower-tier corporation are not included in the earnings and profits of the upper-tier corporation. For purposes of section 904, foreign income taxes shall be allocated and apportioned to income in a separate category to the extent those taxes were allocated to the earnings and profits of the lower-tier corporation in that separate category. See section 904(d)(3)(G) and § 1.904-6(b)(3). To the extent that section 904(g) treats the earnings of the lower-tier corporation on which those foreign income taxes were paid as United States source earnings and profits, the foreign income taxes deemed paid by the upper-tier corporation on the distribution from the lower-tier corporation shall be treated as attributable to United States source earnings and profits. See section 904(g) and § 1.904-5(m)(6).

(iii) Example. The following example illustrates the rules of this paragraph (c)(2):

Example. P, a domestic corporation, owns 100 percent of the voting stock of controlled foreign corporation S. Corporations P and S use the calendar year as their taxable year, and S uses the u as its functional currency. Assume that 1u equals $1 at all relevant times. As of January 1, 1992, S has -0- post-1986 undistributed earnings and -0-post-1986 foreign income taxes. In 1992, S earns 150u of non-subpart F general limitation income net of foreign taxes and pays 60u of foreign income taxes. As of the end of 1992, but before dividend payments, S has 150u of post-1986 undistributed earnings and $60 of post-1986 foreign income taxes. Assume that 50u of S's earnings for 1992 are from United States sources. S pays P a dividend of 75u which P receives in 1992. Under § 1.904-5(m)(4), one-third of the dividend, or 25u (75u × 50u/150u), is United States source income to P. P computes foreign taxes deemed paid on the dividend under paragraph (b)(1) of this section of $30 ($60 × 50% [75u/150u]) and includes that amount in gross income under section 78 as a dividend. Because 25u of the 75u dividend is United States source income to P, $10 ($30 × 33.33% [25u/75u]) of the section 78 dividend will be treated as United States source income to P under this paragraph (c)(2).

(3) Creditable foreign income taxes. The amount of creditable foreign income taxes under section 901 shall include, subject to the limitations and conditions of sections 902 and 904, foreign income taxes actually paid and deemed paid by a domestic shareholder that receives a dividend from a first-tier corporation. Foreign income taxes deemed paid by a domestic shareholder under paragraph (b) of this section shall be deemed paid by the domestic shareholder only for purposes of computing the foreign tax credit allowed under section 901.

(4) Foreign mineral income. Certain foreign income, war profits and excess profits taxes paid or accrued with respect to foreign mineral income will not be considered foreign income taxes for purposes of section 902. See section 901(e) and § 1.901-3.

(5) Foreign taxes paid or accrued in connection with the purchase or sale of certain oil and gas. Certain income, war profits, or excess profits taxes paid or accrued to a foreign country in connection with the purchase and sale of oil or gas extracted in that country will not be considered foreign income taxes for purposes of section 902. See section 901(f).

(6) Foreign oil and gas extraction income. For rules relating to reduction of the amount of foreign income taxes deemed paid with respect to foreign oil and gas extraction income, see section 907(a) and the regulations under that section.

(7) United States shareholders of controlled foreign corporations. See paragraph (d) of this section and sections 960 and 962 and the regulations under those sections for special rules relating to the application of section 902 in computing foreign income taxes deemed paid by United States shareholders of controlled foreign corporations.

(8) Effect of certain liquidations, reorganizations, or similar transactions on certain foreign taxes paid or accrued in taxable years beginning on or before August 5, 1997. [Reserved]. For further guidance, see § 1.902-1T(c)(8).

(d) Dividends from controlled foreign corporations and noncontrolled section 902 corporations. *(1) General rule.* [Reserved]. For further guidance, see § 1.902-1T(d)(1).

(2) Look-through. (i) Dividends. [Reserved]. For further guidance, see § 1.902-1T(d)(2)(i).

(ii) Coordination with section 960. For rules coordinating the computation of foreign taxes deemed paid with respect to amounts included in gross income under section 951(a) and dividends distributed by a controlled foreign corporation, see section 960 and the regulations under that section.

(e) Information to be furnished. If the credit for foreign income taxes claimed under section 901 includes foreign income taxes deemed paid under section 902 and paragraph (b) of this section, the domestic shareholder must furnish the same information with respect to the foreign income taxes deemed paid as it is required to furnish with respect to the foreign income taxes it directly paid or accrued and for which the credit is claimed. See § 1.905-2. For other information required to be furnished by the domestic shareholder for the annual accounting period of certain foreign corporations ending with or within the shareholder's taxable year, and for reduction in the amount of foreign income taxes paid, accrued, or deemed paid for failure to furnish the required information, see section 6038 and the regulations under that section.

(f) Examples. The following examples illustrate the application of this section:

Example (1). Since 1987, domestic corporation M has owned 10 percent of the one class of stock of foreign corporation A. The remaining 90 percent of Corporation A's stock is owned by Z, a foreign corporation. Corporation A is not a controlled foreign corporation. Corporation A uses the u as its functional currency, and 1u equals $1 at all relevant times. Both Corporation A and Corporation M use the calendar year as the taxable year. In 1992, Corporation A pays a 30u dividend out of post-1986 undistributed earnings, 3u to Corporation M and 27u to Corporation Z. Corporation M is deemed, under paragraph (b) of this section, to have paid a portion of the post-1986 foreign income taxes paid by Corporation A and includes the amount of foreign taxes deemed paid in gross income under section 78 as a dividend. Both the foreign taxes deemed paid and the dividend would be subject to a separate limitation for dividends from Corporation A, a noncontrolled section 902 corporation. Under paragraph (a)(9)(i) of this section, Corporation A must reduce its post-1986 undistributed earnings as of January 1, 1993, by the total amount of dividends paid to Corporation M and Corporation Z in 1992. Under paragraph (a)(8)(i) of this section, Corporation A must reduce its post-1986 foreign income taxes as of January 1, 1993, by the amount of foreign income taxes that were deemed paid by Corporation M and by the amount of foreign income taxes that would have been deemed paid by Corporation Z had Corporation Z been eligible to compute an amount of foreign income taxes deemed paid with respect to the dividend received from Corporation A. Foreign income taxes deemed paid by Corporation M and Corporation A's opening balances in post-1986 undistributed earnings and post-1986 foreign income taxes for 1993 are computed as follows:

1. Assumed post-1986 undistributed earnings of Corporation A at start of 1992	25u
2. Assumed post-1986 foreign income taxes of Corporation A at start of 1992	$25
3. Assumed pre-tax earnings and profits of Corporation A for 1992	50u
4. Assumed foreign income taxes paid or accrued by Corporation A in 1992	15u
5. Post-1986 undistributed earnings in Corporation A for 1992 (pre-dividend) (Line 1 plus Line 3 minus Line 4)	60u
6. Post-1986 foreign income taxes in Corporation A for 1992 (pre-dividend) (Line 2 plus Line 4 translated at the appropriate exchange rates)	$40
7. Dividends paid out of post-1986 undistributed earnings of Corporation A to Corporation M in 1992	3u
8. Percentage of Corporation A's post-1986 undistributed earnings paid to Corporation M (Line 7 divided by Line 5)	5%
9. Foreign income taxes of Corporation A deemed paid by Corporation M under section 902(a) (Line 6 multiplied by Line 8)	$2
10. Total dividends paid out of post-1986 undistributed earnings of Corporation A to all shareholders in 1992	30u
11. Percentage of Corporation A's post-1986 undistributed earnings paid to all shareholders in 1992 (Line 10 divided by Line 5)	50%
12. Post-1986 foreign income taxes paid with respect to post-1986 undistributed earnings distributed to all shareholders in 1992 (Line 6 multiplied by Line 11)	$20
13. Corporation A's post-1986 undistributed earnings at the start of 1993 (Line 5 minus Line 10)	30u
14. Corporation A's post-1986 foreign income taxes at the start of 1993 (Line 6 minus Line 12)	$20

Example (2). (i) The facts are the same as in Example 1, except that Corporation M has also owned 10 percent of the one class of stock of foreign corporation B since 1987. Corporation B uses the calendar year as the taxable year. The remaining 90 percent of Corporation B's stock is owned by Corporation Z. Corporation B is not a controlled foreign corporation. Corporation B uses the u as its functional currency, and 1u equals $1 at all relevant times. In 1992, Corporation B has earnings and profits and pays foreign income taxes, a portion of which are attributable to high withholding tax interest, as defined in section 904(d)(2)(B)(i). Corporation B must reduce its pool of post-1986 foreign income taxes by the amount of tax imposed on high withholding tax interest in excess of 5 percent because that amount is not treated as a tax for purposes of section 902. See section 904(d)(2)(E)(ii) and paragraph (a)(8)(iii) of this section. Corporation B pays 50u in dividends in 1992, 5u to Corporation M and 45u to Corporation Z. Corporation M must compute its section 902(a) deemed paid taxes separately for the dividends it receives in 1992 from Corporation A (as computed in Example 1) and from Corporation B. Foreign income taxes of Corporation B deemed paid by Corporation M, and Corporation B's opening balances in post-1986 undistributed earnings and post-1986 foreign income taxes for 1993 are computed as follows:

1. Assumed post-1986 undistributed earnings of Corporation B at start of 1992	(100u)
2. Assumed post-1986 foreign income taxes of Corporation B at start of 1992	$0
3. Assumed pre-tax earnings and profits of Corporation B for 1992 (including 50u of high withholding tax interest on which 5u of tax is withheld)	302.50u
4. Assumed foreign income taxes paid or accrued by Corporation B in 1992	102.50u
5. Post-1986 undistributed earnings in Corporation B for 1992 (pre-dividend) (Line 1 plus Line 3 minus Line 4)	100u
6. Amount of foreign income tax of Corporation B imposed on high withholding tax interest in excess of 5% (5u withholding tax – [5% × 50u high withholding tax interest])	2.50u
7. Post-1986 foreign income taxes in Corporation B for 1992 (pre-dividend) (Line 2 plus [Line 4 minus Line 6 translated at the appropriate exchange rate])	$100
8. Dividends paid out of post-1986 undistributed earnings to Corporation M in 1992	5u
9. Percentage of Corporation B's post-1986 undistributed earnings paid to Corporation M (Line 8 divided by Line 5)	5%
10. Foreign income taxes of Corporation B deemed paid by Corporation M under section 902(a) (Line 7 multiplied by Line 9)	$5
11. Total dividends paid out of post-1986 undistributed earnings of Corporation B to all shareholders in 1992	50u
12. Percentage of Corporation B's post-1986 undistributed earnings paid to all shareholders in 1992 (Line 11 divided by Line 5)	50%

13. Post-1986 foreign income taxes of Corporation B paid on or with respect to post-1986 undistributed earnings distributed to all shareholders in 1992 (Line 7 multiplied by Line 12) $50
14. Corporation B's post-1986 undistributed earnings at start of 1993 (Line 5 minus Line 11) 50u
15. Corporation B's post-1986 foreign income taxes at start of 1993 (Line 7 minus Line 13) $50

(ii) For 1992, as computed in Example 1, Corporation M is deemed to have paid $2 of the post-1986 foreign income taxes paid by Corporation A and includes $2 in gross income as a dividend under section 78. Both the income inclusion and the credit are subject to a separate limitation for dividends from Corporation A, a noncontrolled section 902 corporation. Corporation M also is deemed to have paid $5 of the post-1986 foreign income taxes paid by Corporation B and includes $5 in gross income as a deemed dividend under section 78. Both the income inclusion and the foreign taxes deemed paid are subject to a separate limitation for dividends from Corporation B, a noncontrolled section 902 corporation.

Example (3). (i) Since 1987, domestic corporation M has owned 50 percent of the one class of stock of foreign corporation A. The remaining 50 percent of Corporation A is owned by foreign corporation Z. For the same time period, Corporation A has owned 40 percent of the one class of stock of foreign corporation B, and Corporation B has owned 30 percent of the one class of stock of foreign corporation C. The remaining 60 percent of Corporation B is owned by foreign corporation Y, and the remaining 70 percent of Corporation C is owned by foreign corporation X. Corporations A, B, and C are not controlled foreign corporations. Corporations A, B, and C use the u as their functional currency, and 1u equals $1 at all relevant times. Corporation B uses a fiscal year ending June 30 as its taxable year; all other corporations use the calendar year as the taxable year. On February 1, 1992, Corporation C pays a 500u dividend out of post-1986 undistributed earnings, 150u to Corporation B and 350u to Corporation X. On February 15, 1992, Corporation B pays a 300u dividend out of post-1986 undistributed earnings computed as of the close of Corporation B's fiscal year ended June 30, 1992, 120u to Corporation A and 180u to Corporation Y. On August 15, 1992, Corporation A pays a 200u dividend out of post-1986 undistributed earnings, 100u to Corporation M and 100u to Corporation Z. In computing foreign taxes deemed paid by Corporations B and A, section 78 does not apply and Corporations B and A thus do not have to include the foreign taxes deemed paid in earnings and profits. See paragraph (c)(2)(ii) of this section. Foreign income taxes deemed paid by Corporations B, A and M, and the foreign corporations' opening balances in post-1986 undistributed earnings and post-1986 foreign income taxes for Corporation B's fiscal year beginning July 1, 1992, and Corporation C's and Corporation A's 1993 calendar years are computed as follows:

A. CORPORATION C (THIRD-TIER CORPORATION):

1. Assumed post-1986 undistributed earnings in Corporation C at start of 1992 .... 1300u
2. Assumed post-1986 foreign income taxes in Corporation C at start of 1992 .... $500
3. Assumed pre-tax earnings and profits of Corporation C for 1992 .... 500u
4. Assumed foreign income taxes paid or accrued in 1992 .... 300u
5. Post-1986 undistributed earnings in Corporation C for 1992 (pre-dividend) (Line 1 plus Line 3 minus Line 4) 1500u
6. Post-1986 foreign income taxes in Corporation C for 1992 (pre-dividend) (Line 2 plus Line 4 translated at the appropriate exchange rates) $800
7. Dividends paid out of post-1986 undistributed earnings of Corporation C to Corporation B in 1992 .... 150u
8. Percentage of Corporation C's post-1986 undistributed earnings paid to Corporation B (Line 7 divided by Line 5) 10%
9. Foreign income taxes of Corporation C deemed paid by Corporation B under section 902(b)(2) (Line 6 multiplied by Line 8) $80
10. Total dividends paid out of post-1986 undistributed earnings of Corporation C to all shareholders in 1992 .... 500u
11. Percentage of Corporation C's post-1986 undistributed earnings paid to all shareholders in 1992 (Line 10 divided by Line 5) 33.33%
12. Post-1986 foreign income taxes paid with respect to post-1986 undistributed earnings distributed to all shareholders in 1992 (Line 6 multiplied by Line 11) $266.66
13. Post-1986 undistributed earnings in Corporation C at start of 1993 (Line 5 minus Line 10) 1000u
14. Post-1986 foreign income taxes in Corporation C at start of 1993 (Line 6 minus Line 12) $533.34

B. CORPORATION B (SECOND-TIER CORPORATION):

1. Assumed post-1986 undistributed earnings in Corporation B as of July 1, 1991 0
2. Assumed post-1986 foreign income taxes in Corporation B as of July 1, 1991 0
3. Assumed pre-tax earnings and profits of Corporation B for fiscal year ended June 30, 1992, (including 150u dividend from Corporation B) 1000u
4. Assumed foreign income taxes paid or accrued by Corporation B in fiscal year ended June 30, 1992 .... 200u
5. Foreign income taxes of Corporation C deemed paid by Corporation B in its fiscal year ended June 30, 1992 (Part A, Line 9 of paragraph (i) of this Example 3) $80
6. Post-1986 undistributed earnings in Corporation B for fiscal year ended June 30, 1992 (pre-dividend) (Line 1 plus Line 3 minus Line 4) 800u
7. Post-1986 foreign income taxes in Corporation B for fiscal year ended June 30, 1992 (pre-dividend) (Line 2 plus Line 4 translated at the appropriate exchange rates plus Line 5) $280
8. Dividends paid out of post-1986 undistributed earnings of Corporation B to Corporation A on February 15, 1992 .... 120u
9. Percentage of Corporation B's post-1986 undistributed earnings for fiscal year ended June 30, 1992, paid to Corporation A (Line 8 divided by Line 6) 15%

10. Foreign income taxes paid and deemed paid by Corporation B as of June 30, 1992, deemed paid by Corporation A under section 902(b)(1) (Line 7 multiplied by Line 9)	$42
11. Total dividends paid out of post-1986 undistributed earnings of Corporation B for fiscal year ended June 30, 1992	300u
12. Percentage of Corporation B's post-1986 undistributed earnings for fiscal year ended June 30, 1992, paid to all shareholders (Line 11 divided by Line 6)	37.5%
13. Post-1986 foreign income taxes paid and deemed paid with respect to post-1986 undistributed earnings distributed to all shareholders during Corporation B's fiscal year ended June 30, 1992 (Line 7 multiplied by Line 12)	$105
14. Post-1986 undistributed earnings in Corporation B as of July 1, 1992 (Line 6 minus Line 11)	500u
15. Post-1986 foreign income taxes in Corporation B as of July 1, 1992 (Line 7 minus Line 13)	$175
C. CORPORATION A (FIRST-TIER CORPORATION):	
1. Assumed post-1986 undistributed earnings in Corporation A at start of 1992	250u
2. Assumed post-1986 foreign income taxes in Corporation A at start of 1992	$100
3. Assumed pre-tax earnings and profits of Corporation A for 1992 (including 120u dividend from Corporation B)	250u
4. Assumed foreign income taxes paid or accrued by Corporation A in 1992	100u
5. Foreign income taxes paid or deemed paid by Corporation B as of June 30, 1992, that are deemed paid by Corporation A in 1992 (Part B, Line 10 of paragraph (i) of this Example 3)	$42
6. Post-1986 undistributed earnings in Corporation A for 1992 (pre-dividend) (Line 1 plus Line 3 minus Line 4)	400u
7. Post-1986 foreign income taxes in Corporation A for 1992 (pre-dividend) (Line 2 plus Line 4 translated at the appropriate exchange rates plus Line 5)	$242
8. Dividends paid out of post-1986 undistributed earnings of Corporation A to Corporation M on August 15, 1992	100u
9. Percentage of Corporation A's post-1986 undistributed earnings paid to Corporation M in 1992 (Line 8 divided by Line 6)	25%
10. Foreign income taxes paid and deemed paid by Corporation A in 1992 that are deemed paid by Corporation M under section 902(a) (Line 7 multiplied by Line 9)	$60.50
11. Total dividends paid out of post-1986 undistributed earnings of Corporation A to all shareholders in 1992	200u
12. Percentage of Corporation A's post-1986 undistributed earnings paid to all shareholders in 1992 (Line 11 divided by Line 6)	50%
13. Post-1986 foreign income taxes paid and deemed paid by Corporation A with respect to post-1986 undistributed earnings distributed to all shareholders in 1992 (Line 7 multiplied by Line 12)	$121
14. Post-1986 undistributed earnings in Corporation A at start of 1993 (Line 6 minus Line 11)	200u
15. Post-1986 foreign income taxes in Corporation A at start of 1993 (Line 7 minus Line 13)	$121

(ii) Corporation M is deemed, under section 902(a) and paragraph (b) of this section, to have paid $60.50 of post-1986 foreign income taxes paid, or deemed paid, by Corporation A on or with respect to its post-1986 undistributed earnings (Part C, Line 10) and Corporation M includes that amount in gross income as a dividend under section 78. Both the income inclusion and the credit are subject to a separate limitation for dividends from Corporation A, a noncontrolled section 902 corporation.

Example (4). (i) Since 1987, domestic corporation M has owned 100 percent of the voting stock of controlled foreign corporation A, and Corporation A has owned 100 percent of the voting stock of controlled foreign corporation B. Corporations M, A and B use the calendar year as the taxable year. Corporations A and B are organized in the same foreign country and use the u as their functional currency. 1u equals $1 at all relevant times. Assume that all of the earnings of Corporations A and B are general limitation earnings and profits within the meaning of section 904(d)(2)(I), and that neither Corporation A nor Corporation B has any previously taxed income accounts. In 1992, Corporation B pays a dividend of 150u to Corporation A out of post-1986 undistributed earnings, and Corporation A computes an amount of foreign taxes deemed paid under section 902(b)(1). The dividend is not subpart F income to Corporation A because section 954(c)(3)(B)(i) (the same country dividend exception) applies. Pursuant to paragraph (c)(2)(ii) of this section, Corporation A is not required to include the deemed paid taxes in earnings and profits. Corporation A has no pre-1987 accumulated profits and a deficit in post-1986 undistributed earnings for 1992. In 1992, Corporation A pays a dividend of 100u to Corporation M out of its earnings and profits for 1992 (current earnings and profits). Under paragraph (b)(4) of this section, Corporation M is not deemed to have paid any of the foreign income taxes paid or deemed paid by Corporation A because Corporation A has a deficit in post-1986 undistributed earnings as of December 31, 1992, and the sum of its current plus accumulated profits is less than zero. Note that if instead of paying a dividend to Corporation A in 1992, Corporation B had made an additional investment of $150 in United States property under section 956, that amount would have been included in gross income by Corporation M under section 951(a)(1)(B) and Corporation M would have been deemed to have paid $50 of foreign income taxes paid by Corporation B. See sections 951(a)(1)(B) and 960. Foreign income taxes of Corporation B deemed paid by Corporation A and the opening balances in post-1986 undistributed earnings and post-1986 foreign income taxes for Corporation A and Corporation B for 1993 are computed as follows:

A. CORPORATION B (SECOND-TIER CORPORATION):
1. Assumed post-1986 undistributed earnings in Corporation B at start of 1992 .... 200u
2. Assumed post-1986 foreign income taxes in Corporation B at start of 1992 .... $50
3. Assumed pre-tax earnings and profits of Corporation B for 1992 .... 150u
4. Assumed foreign income taxes paid or accrued in 1992 .... 50u
5. Post-1986 undistributed earnings in Corporation B for 1992 (pre-dividend) (Line 1 plus Line 3 minus Line 4) 300u
6. Post-1986 foreign income taxes in Corporation B for 1992 (pre-dividend) (Line 2 plus Line 4 translated at the appropriate exchange rates) $100
7. Dividends paid out of post-1986 undistributed earnings of Corporation B to Corporation A in 1992 .... 150u
8. Percentage of Corporation B's post-1986 undistributed earnings paid to Corporation A (Line 7 divided by Line 5) 50%
9. Foreign income taxes of Corporation B deemed paid by Corporation A under section 902(b)(1) (Line 6 multiplied by Line 8) $50
10. Post-1986 undistributed earnings in Corporation B at start of 1993 (Line 5 minus Line 7) 150u
11. Post-1986 foreign income taxes in Corporation B at start of 1993 (Line 6 minus Line 9) $50

B. CORPORATION A (FIRST-TIER CORPORATION):
1. Assumed post-1986 undistributed earnings in Corporation A at start of 1992 .... (200u)
2. Assumed post-1986 foreign income taxes in Corporation A at start of 1992 0
3. Assumed pre-tax earnings and profits of Corporation A for 1992 (including 150u dividend from Corporation B) 200u
4. Assumed foreign income taxes paid or accrued by Corporation A in 1992 .... 40u
5. Foreign income taxes paid by Corporation B in 1992 that are deemed paid by Corporation A (Part A, Line 9 of paragraph (i) of this Example 4) $50
6. Post-1986 undistributed earnings in Corporation A for 1992 (pre-dividend) (Line 1 plus Line 3 minus Line 4) . (40u)
7. Post-1986 foreign income taxes in Corporation A for 1992 (pre-dividend) (Line 2 plus Line 4 translated at the appropriate exchange rates plus Line 5) $90
8. Dividends paid out of current earnings and profits of Corporation A for 1992 .... 100u
9. Percentage of post-1986 undistributed earnings of Corporation A paid to Corporation M in 1992 (Line 8 divided by the greater of Line 6 or zero) 0
10. Foreign income taxes paid and deemed paid by Corporation A in 1992 that are deemed paid by Corporation M under section 902 (a) (Line 7 multiplied by Line 9) 0
11. Post-1986 undistributed earnings in Corporation A at start of 1993 (line 6 minus line 8) .... (140u)
12. Post-1986 foreign income taxes in Corporation A at start of 1993 (Line 7 minus Line 10) $90

(ii) For 1993, Corporation A has 500u of earnings and profits on which it pays 160u of foreign income taxes. Corporation A receives no dividends from Corporation B, and pays a 100u dividend to Corporation M. The 100u dividend to Corporation M carries with it some of the foreign income taxes paid and deemed paid by Corporation A in 1992, which were not deemed paid by Corporation M in 1992 because Corporation A had no post-1986 undistributed earnings. Thus, for 1993, Corporation M is deemed to have paid $125 of post-1986 foreign income taxes paid and deemed paid by Corporation A and includes that amount in gross income as a dividend under section 78, determined as follows:

1. Post-1986 undistributed earnings in Corporation A at start of 1993 .... (140u)
2. Post-1986 foreign income taxes in Corporation A at start of 1993 .... $90
3. Pre-tax earnings and profits of Corporation A for 1993 .... 500u
4. Foreign income taxes paid or accrued by Corporation A in 1993 .... 160u
5. Post-1986 undistributed earnings in Corporation A for 1993 (pre-dividend) (Line 1 plus Line 3 minus Line 4) 200u
6. Post-1986 foreign income taxes in Corporation A for 1993 (pre-dividend) (Line 2 plus Line 4 translated at the appropriate exchange rates) $250
7. Dividends paid out of post-1986 undistributed earnings of Corporation A to Corporation M in 1993 .... 100u
8. Percentage of post-1986 undistributed earnings of Corporation A paid to Corporation M in 1993 (Line 7 divided by Line 5) 50%
9. Foreign income taxes paid and deemed paid by Corporation A that are deemed paid by Corporation M in 1993 (Line 6 multiplied by Line 8) $125
10. Post-1986 undistributed earnings in Corporation A at start of 1994 (Line 5 minus Line 7) 100u
11. Post-1986 foreign income taxes in Corporation A at start of 1994 (Line 6 minus Line 9) $125

Example (5). (i) Since 1987, domestic corporation M has owned 100 percent of the voting stock of controlled foreign corporation A. Corporation M also conducts operations through a foreign branch. Both Corporation A and Corporation M use the calendar year as the taxable year. Corporation A uses the u as its functional currency and 1u equals $1 at all relevant times. Corporation A has no subpart F income, as defined in section 952, and no increase in earnings invested in United States property under section 956 for 1992. Corporation A also has no previously taxed income accounts. Corporation A has general limitation income and high withholding tax interest income that, by operation of section 954(b)(4), does not constitute foreign base company income under section 954(a). Because Corporation A is a controlled foreign corporation, it is not required to reduce post-1986 foreign income taxes by foreign taxes paid or accrued with respect to high withholding tax interest in excess of 5 percent. See § 1.902-1(a)(8)(iii). Corporation A pays a 60u dividend to Corporation M in 1992. For 1992, Corporation M is deemed, under paragraph (b) of this section, to have paid $24 of the post-1986 foreign income taxes paid by Corporation A and includes that amount in gross income under section 78 as a dividend, determined as follows:

1. Assumed post-1986 undistributed earnings in Corporation A at start of 1992 attributable to:	
(a) Section 904(d)(1)(B) high withholding tax interest	20u
(b) Section 904(d)(1)(I) general limitation income	55u
2. Assumed post-1986 foreign income taxes in Corporation A at start of 1992 attributable to:	
(a) Section 904(d)(1)(B) high withholding tax interest	$5
(b) Section 904(d)(1)(I) general limitation income	$20
3. Assumed pre-tax earnings and profits of Corporation A for 1992 attributable to:	
(a) Section 904(d)(1)(B) high withholding tax interest	20u
(b) Section 904(d)(1)(I) general limitation income	20u
4. Assumed foreign income taxes paid or accrued in 1992 on or with respect to:	
(a) Section 904(d)(1)(B) high withholding tax interest	10u
(b) Section 904(d)(1)(I) general limitation income	5u
5. Post-1986 undistributed earnings in Corporation A for 1992 (pre-dividend) attributable to:	
(a) Section 904(d)(1)(B) high withholding tax interest (Line 1(a) + Line 3(a) minus Line 4(a))	30u
(b) Section 904(d)(1)(I) general limitation income (Line 1(b) + Line 3(b) minus Line 4(b))	70u
(c) Total	100u
6. Post-1986 foreign income taxes in Corporation A for 1992 (pre-dividend) attributable to:	
(a) Section 904(d)(1)(B) high withholding tax interest (Line 2(a) + Line 4(a) translated at the appropriate exchange rates)	$15
(b) Section 904(d)(1)(I) general limitation income (Line 2(b) + Line 4(b) translated at the appropriate exchange rates)	$25
7. Dividends paid to Corporation M in 1992	60u
8. Dividends paid to Corporation M in 1992 attributable to section 904(d) separate categories pursuant to § 1.904-5(d):	
(a) Dividends paid to Corporation M in 1992 attributable to section 904(d)(1)(B) high withholding tax interest (Line 7 multiplied by Line 5(a) divided by Line 5(c)	18u
(b) Dividends paid to Corporation M in 1992 attributable to section 904(d)(1)(I) general limitation income (Line 7 multiplied by Line 5(b) divided by Line 5(c)	42u
9. Percentage of Corporation A's post-1986 undistributed earnings for 1992 paid to Corporation M attributable to:	
(a) Section 904(d)(1)(B) high withholding tax interest (Line 8(a) divided by Line 5(a))	60%
(b) Section 904(d)(1)(I) general limitation income (Line 8(b) divided by Line 5(b)	60%
10. Foreign income taxes of Corporation A deemed paid by Corporation M under section 902(a) attributable to:	
(a) Foreign income taxes of Corporation A deemed paid by Corporation M under section 902(a) with respect to section 904(d)(1)(B) high withholding tax interest (Line 6(a) multiplied by Line 9(a))	$9
(b) Foreign income taxes of Corporation A deemed paid by Corporation M under section 902(a) with respect to section 904(d)(1)(I) general limitation income (Line 6(b) multiplied by Line 9(b)	$15
11. Post-1986 undistributed earnings in Corporation A at start of 1993 attributable to:	
(a) Section 904(d)(1)(B) high withholding tax interest (Line 5(a) minus Line 8(a))	12u
(b) Section 904(d)(1)(I) general limitation income (Line 5(b) minus Line 8(b))	28u
12. Post-1986 foreign income taxes in Corporation A at start of 1989 allocable to:	
(a) Section 904(d)(1)(B) high withholding tax interest (Line 6(a) – Line 10(a))	$6
(b) Section 904(d)(1)(I) general limitation income (Line 6(b) – Line 10(b))	$10

(ii) For purposes of computing Corporation M's foreign tax credit limitation, the post-1986 foreign income taxes of Corporation A deemed paid by Corporation M with respect to income in separate categories will be added to the foreign income taxes paid or accrued by Corporation M associated with income derived from Corporation M's branch operation in the same separate categories. The dividend (and the section 78 inclusion with respect to the dividend) will be treated as income in separate categories and added to Corporation M's other income, if any, attributable to the same separate categories. See section 904(d) and § 1.904-6.

(g) Effective date. [Reserved]. For further guidance, see § 1.902-1T(g).

T.D. 8708, 1/6/97, amend T.D. 8916, 12/27/2000, T.D. 9260, 4/24/2006.

PAR. 4. In § 1.902-1, paragraphs (a), (c), (d) and (g) are revised to read as follows:

Proposed § 1.902-1 Credit for domestic corporate shareholder of a foreign corporation for foreign income taxes paid by the foreign corporation. [*For Preamble, see ¶ 152,753*]

[The text of the proposed amendments to § 1.902-1(a), (c), (d), and (g) are the same as the text of § 1.902-1T(a), (c), (d), and (g) published elsewhere in this issue of the Federal Register.] [*See T.D. 9260, 04/24/2006, 71 Fed. Reg. 79.*]

* * * * *

§ 1.902-1T Credit for domestic corporate shareholder of a foreign corporation for foreign income taxes paid by the foreign corporation (temporary).

• ***Caution:*** Under Code Sec. 7805, temporary regulations expire within three years of the date of issuance. This temporary regulation was issued on 4/24/2006.

(a) *(1)* through (a)(3) [Reserved]. For further guidance, see § 1.902-1(a)(1) through (a)(3).

(4) (i) [Reserved]. For further guidance, see § 1.902-1(a)(4)(i).

(ii) Fourth-, fifth-, or sixth-tier corporation. In the case of dividends paid to a third-, fourth-, or fifth-tier corporation by a foreign corporation in a taxable year beginning after August 5, 1997, the foreign corporation is a fourth-, fifth-, or sixth-tier corporation, respectively, if at the time the dividend is paid, the corporation receiving the dividend owns at least 10 percent of the foreign corporation's voting stock, the chain of foreign corporations that includes the foreign corporation is connected through stock ownership of at least 10 percent of their voting stock, the domestic shareholder in the first-tier corporation in such chain indirectly owns at least 5 percent of the voting stock of the foreign corporation through such chain, such corporation is a controlled foreign corporation (as defined in section 957) and the domestic shareholder is a United States shareholder (as defined in section 951(b)) in the foreign corporation. Taxes paid by a fourth-, fifth-, or sixth-tier corporation shall be taken into account in determining post-1986 foreign income taxes only if such taxes are paid with respect to taxable years beginning after August 5, 1997, in which the corporation was a controlled foreign corporation.

(5) [Reserved]. For further guidance, see § 1.902-1(a)(5).

(6) Upper- and lower-tier corporations. In the case of a sixth-tier corporation, the term upper-tier corporation means a first-, second-, third-, fourth-, or fifth-tier corporation. In the case of a fifth-tier corporation, the term upper-tier corporation means a first-, second-, third-, or fourth-tier corporation. In the case of a fourth-tier corporation, the term upper-tier corporation means a first-, second-, or third-tier corporation. In the case of a third-tier corporation, the term upper-tier corporation means a first- or second-tier corporation. In the case of a second-tier corporation, the term upper-tier corporation means a first-tier corporation. In the case of a first-tier corporation, the term lower-tier corporation means a second-, third-, fourth-, fifth-, or sixth-tier corporation. In the case of a second-tier corporation, the term lower-tier corporation means a third-, fourth-, fifth-, or sixth-tier corporation. In the case of a third-tier corporation, the term lower-tier corporation means a fourth-, fifth-, or sixth-tier corporation. In the case of a fourth-tier corporation, the term lower-tier corporation means a fifth- or sixth-tier corporation. In the case of a fifth-tier corporation, the term lower-tier corporation means a sixth-tier corporation.

(7) Foreign income taxes. The term foreign income taxes means income, war profits, and excess profits taxes as defined in § 1.902-1(a), and taxes included in the term income, war profits, and excess profits taxes by reason of section 903, that are imposed by a foreign country or a possession of the United States, including any such taxes deemed paid by a foreign corporation under this section. Foreign income, war profits, and excess profits taxes shall not include amounts excluded from the definition of those taxes pursuant to section 901 and the regulations under that section. See sections 901(f) and (i) and paragraph (c)(5) of this section. Foreign income, war profits, and excess profits taxes also shall not include taxes for which a credit is disallowed under section 901 and the regulations thereunder. See sections 901(e), (h), (j), (k), and (l), and paragraphs (c)(4) and (c)(8) of this section.

(8) Post-1986 foreign income taxes. (i) In general. Except as provided in paragraphs (a)(10) and (a)(13) of this section, the term post-1986 foreign income taxes of a foreign corporation means the sum of the foreign income taxes paid, accrued, or deemed paid in the taxable year of the foreign corporation in which it distributes a dividend plus the foreign income taxes paid, accrued, or deemed paid in the foreign corporation's prior taxable years beginning after December 31, 1986, to the extent the foreign taxes were not attributable to dividends distributed to, or earnings otherwise included (e.g., under section 304, 367(b), 551, 951(a), 1248, or 1293) in the income of, a foreign or domestic shareholder in prior taxable years. Except as provided in paragraph (b)(4) of this section, foreign taxes paid or deemed paid by the foreign corporation on or with respect to earnings that were distributed or otherwise removed from post-1986 undistributed earnings in prior post-1986 taxable years shall be removed from post-1986 foreign income taxes regardless of whether the shareholder is eligible to compute an amount of foreign taxes deemed paid under section 902, and regardless of whether the shareholder in fact chose to credit foreign income taxes under section 901 for the year of the distribution or inclusion. Thus, if an amount is distributed or deemed distributed by a foreign corporation to a United States person that is not a domestic shareholder within the meaning of paragraph (a)(1) of this section (e.g., an individual or a corporation that owns less than 10% of the foreign corporation's voting stock), or to a foreign person that does not meet the definition of an upper-tier corporation under paragraph (a)(6) of this section, then although no foreign income taxes shall be deemed paid under section 902, foreign income taxes attributable to the distribution or deemed distribution that would have been deemed paid had the shareholder met the ownership requirements of paragraphs (a)(1) through (4) of this section shall be removed from post-1986 foreign income taxes. Further, if a domestic shareholder chooses to deduct foreign taxes paid or accrued for the taxable year of the distribution or inclusion, it shall nonetheless be deemed to have paid a proportionate share of the foreign corporation's post-1986 foreign income taxes under section 902(a), and the foreign income taxes deemed paid must be removed from post-1986 foreign income taxes. In the case of a foreign corporation the foreign income taxes of which are determined based on an accounting period of less than one year, the term year means that accounting period. See sections 441(b)(3) and 443.

(ii) through (c)(7) [Reserved]. For guidance, see § 1.902-1(a)(8)(ii) through (c)(7).

(c) *(8) Effect of certain liquidations, reorganizations, or similar transactions on certain foreign taxes paid or accrued in taxable years beginning on or before August 5, 1997.* (i) General rule. Notwithstanding the effect of any liquidation, reorganization, or similar transaction, foreign taxes paid or accrued by a member of a qualified group (as defined in section 902(b)(2)) shall not be eligible to be deemed paid if they were paid or accrued in a taxable year beginning on or before August 5, 1997, by a corporation that was a fourth-, fifth- or sixth-tier corporation with respect to the taxpayer on the first day of the corporation's first taxable year beginning after August 5, 1997.

(ii) Example. P, a domestic corporation, has owned 100 percent of the voting stock of foreign corporation S at all times since January 1, 1987. Until June 30, 2002, S owned 100 percent of the voting stock of foreign corporation T, T owned 100 percent of the voting stock of foreign corporation U, and U owned 100 percent of the voting stock of foreign corporation V. P, S, T, U, and V each use the calendar year as their U.S. taxable year. Thus, beginning in 1998 V was a fourth-tier controlled foreign corporation, and its foreign taxes paid or accrued in 1998 and later taxable years were eligible to be deemed paid. On June 30, 2002, T was liquidated, causing S to acquire 100 percent of the stock of U. As a result, V became a third-tier controlled foreign corporation. In 2003, V paid a dividend to U. Under paragraph (c)(8) of this section, foreign taxes paid by V in taxable years beginning before 1998 are not taken into account in computing the foreign taxes deemed paid with respect to the dividend paid by V to U.

(d) Dividends from controlled foreign corporations and noncontrolled section 902 corporations. *(1) General rule.* If a dividend is described in paragraphs (d)(1) (A) through (D) of this section, the following rules apply. If a dividend is paid out of post-1986 undistributed earnings or pre-1987 accumulated profits of a foreign corporation attributable to more than one separate category, the amount of foreign income taxes deemed paid by the domestic shareholder or the upper-tier corporation under section 902 and paragraph (b) of this section shall be computed separately with respect to the post-1986 undistributed earnings or pre-1987 accumulated profits in each separate category out of which the dividend is paid. See §§ 1.904-5T(c)(4), 1.904-5(i), and paragraph (d)(2) of this section. The separately computed deemed-paid taxes shall be added to other taxes paid by the domestic shareholder or upper-tier corporation with respect to income in the appropriate separate category. The rules of this paragraph (d)(1) apply to dividends received by—

(A) A domestic shareholder that is a United States shareholder (as defined in section 951(b) or section 953(c)) from a first-tier corporation that is a controlled foreign corporation;

(B) A domestic shareholder from a first-tier corporation that is a noncontrolled section 902 corporation;

(C) An upper-tier controlled foreign corporation from a lower-tier controlled foreign corporation if the corporations are related look-through entities within the meaning of § 1.904-5(i) (see § 1.904-5T(i)(3)); or

(D) A foreign corporation that is eligible to compute an amount of foreign taxes deemed paid under section 902(b)(1), from a controlled foreign corporation or a noncontrolled section 902 corporation (i.e., both the payor and payee corporations are members of the same qualified group as defined in section 902(b)(2) (see § 1.904-5T(i)(4)).

(2) Look-through. (i) Dividends. Any dividend distribution by a controlled foreign corporation or noncontrolled section 902 corporation to a domestic shareholder or a foreign corporation that is eligible to compute an amount of foreign taxes deemed paid under section 902(b)(1) shall be deemed paid pro rata out of each separate category of income. Any dividend distribution by a controlled foreign corporation to a controlled foreign corporation that is a related look-through entity within the meaning of § 1.904-5T(i)(3) shall also be deemed to be paid pro rata out of each separate category of income. See §§ 1.904-5T(c)(4), 1.904-5(i), and 1.904-7. The portion of the foreign income taxes attributable to a particular separate category that shall be deemed paid by the domestic shareholder or upper-tier corporation must be computed under the following formula:

$$\text{Foreign taxes deemed paid by domestic shareholder or upper-tier corporation with respect to a separate category} = \text{Post-1986 foreign income taxes of first-tier or lower-tier corporation allocated and apportioned to the separate category under § 1.904-6} \times \frac{\text{Dividend amount attributable to the separate category}}{\text{Post-1986 undistributed earnings of first-tier or lower-tier corporation in the separate category.}}$$

(e) through (f). [Reserved] For further guidance, see § 1.902-1(e) through (f).

(g) Effective dates. This section and § 1.902-1 apply to any distribution made in and after a foreign corporation's first taxable year beginning on or after January 1, 1987, except that the provisions of paragraphs (a)(4)(ii), (a)(6), (a)(7), (a)(8)(i), and (c)(8) of this section apply to distributions made in taxable years of foreign corporations beginning after April 25, 2006, and, except as provided in § 1.904-7T(f)(9), the provisions of paragraph (d) of this section apply to distributions in taxable years of foreign corporations beginning after December 31, 2002.

T.D. 9260, 4/24/2006.

§ 1.902-2 Treatment of deficits in post-1986 undistributed earnings and pre-1987 accumulated profits of a first- or lower-tier corporation for purposes of computing an amount of foreign taxes deemed paid under Sec. 1.902-1.

Caution: The Treasury has not yet amended Reg § 1.902-2 to reflect changes made by P.L. 105-34.

(a) Carryback of deficits in post-1986 undistributed earnings of a first- or lower-tier corporation to pre-effective date taxable years. *(1) Rule.* For purposes of computing foreign income taxes deemed paid under § 1.902-1(b) with respect to dividends paid by a first- or lower-tier corporation, when there is a deficit in the post-1986 undistributed earnings of that corporation and the corporation makes a distribution to shareholders that is a dividend or would be a dividend if there were current or accumulated earnings and profits, then the post-1986 deficit shall be carried back to the most recent pre-effective date taxable year of the first- or lower-tier corporation with positive accumulated profits computed under section 902. See § 1.902-3(e). For purposes of this § 1.902-2, a pre-effective date taxable year is a taxable year beginning before January 1, 1987, or a taxable year beginning after December 31, 1986, if the special effective date of § 1.902-1(a)(13) applies. The deficit shall reduce the section 902 accumulated profits in the most recent pre-effective date year to the extent thereof, and any remaining deficit shall be carried back to the next preceding year or years until the deficit is completely allocated. The amount carried back shall reduce the deficit in post-1986 undistributed earnings. Any foreign income taxes paid in a post-effective date year will not be carried back to pre-effective date taxable years or removed from post-1986 foreign income taxes. See section 960 and the regulations under that section for rules governing the carryback of deficits and the computation of foreign income taxes deemed paid with respect to deemed income inclusions from controlled foreign corporations.

(2) Examples. The following examples illustrate the rules of this paragraph (a):

Example (1). (i) From 1985 through 1990, domestic corporation M owns 10 percent of the one class of stock of foreign corporation A. The remaining 90 percent of Corporation A's stock is owned by Z, a foreign corporation. Corporation A is not a controlled foreign corporation and uses the u as its functional currency. 1u equals $1 at all relevant times. Both Corporation A and Corporation M use the calendar year as the taxable year. Corporation A has pre-1987 accumulated profits and post-1986 undistributed earnings or deficits in post-1986 undistributed earnings, pays pre-1987 and post-1986 foreign income taxes, and pays dividends as summarized below:

Taxable year	1985	1986	1987	1988	1989	1990
Current E & P (Deficits) of Corp. A	150u	150u	(100u)	100u	0	0
Current Plus Accumulated E & P of Corp. A	150u	300u	200u	250u	250u	200u
Post-'86 Undistributed Earnings of Corp. A			(100u)	100u	100u	50u
Post-'86 Undistributed Earnings of Corp. A Reduced By Current Year Dividend Distributions (increased by deficit carryback)			0	100u	50u	50u
Foreign Income Taxes of Corp. A (Annual)	120u	120u	$10	$50	0	0
Post-'86 Foreign Income Taxes of Corp. A			$10	$60	$60	$30
12/31 Distributions to Corp. M	0	0	5u	0	5u	0
12/31 Distributions to Corp. Z	0	0	45u	0	45u	0

(ii) On December 31, 1987, Corporation A distributes a 5u dividend to Corporation M and a 45u dividend to Corporation Z. At that time Corporation A has a deficit of (100u) in post-1986 undistributed earnings and $10 of post-1986 foreign income taxes. The (100u) deficit (but not the post-1986 foreign income taxes) is carried back to offset the accumulated profits of 1986 and removed from post-1986 undistributed earnings. The accumulated profits for 1986 are reduced to 50u (150u − 100u). The dividend is paid out of the reduced 1986 accumulated profits. Foreign taxes deemed paid by Corporation M with respect to the 5u dividend are 12u (120u × (5u/50u)). See § 1.902-1(b)(3). Corporation M must include 12u in gross income (translated under the rule applicable to foreign income taxes paid on earnings accumulated in pre-effective date years) under section 78 as a dividend. Both the income inclusion and the foreign taxes deemed paid are subject to a separate limitation for dividends from Corporation A, a noncontrolled section 902 corporation. No accumulated profits remain in Corporation A with respect to 1986 after the carryback of the 1987 deficit and the December 31, 1987, dividend distributions to Corporations M and Z.

(iii) On December 31, 1989, Corporation A distributes a 5u dividend to Corporation M and a 45u dividend to Corporation Z. At that time Corporation A has 100u of post-1986 undistributed earnings and $60 of post-1986 foreign income taxes. Therefore, the dividend is considered paid out of Corporation A's post-1986 undistributed earnings. Foreign taxes deemed paid by Corporation M with respect to the 5u dividend are $3 ($60 × 5%[5u/100u]). Corporation M must include $3 in gross income under section 78 as a dividend. Both the income inclusion and the foreign taxes deemed paid are subject to a separate limitation for dividends from noncontrolled section 902 corporation A. Corporation A's post-1986 undistributed earnings as of January 1, 1990, are 50u (100u − 50u). Corporation A's post-1986 foreign income taxes must be reduced by the amount of foreign taxes that would have been deemed paid if both Corporations M and Z were eligible to compute an amount of deemed paid taxes. Section 1.902-1(a)(8)(i). The amount of foreign income taxes that would have been deemed paid if both Corporations M and Z were eligible to compute an amount of deemed paid taxes on the 50u dividend distributed by Corporation A is $30 ($60 × 50%[50u/100u]). Thus, post-1986 foreign income taxes as of January 1, 1990, are $30 ($60 − $30).

Example (2). The facts are the same as in Example 1, except that Corporation A has a deficit in its post-1986 undistributed earnings of (150u) on December 31, 1987. The deficit is carried back to 1986 and reduces accumulated profits for that year to -0-. Thus, the foreign income taxes paid with respect to the 1986 accumulated profits will never be deemed paid. The 1987 dividend is deemed to be out of Corporation A's 1985 accumulated profits. Foreign taxes deemed paid by Corporation M under section 902 with respect to the 5u dividend paid on December 31, 1987, are 4u (120u × 5u/150u). See § 1.902-1(b)(3). As a result of the December 31, 1987, dividend distributions, 100u (150u − 50u) of accumulated profits and 80u (120u reduced by 40u[120u × 50u/150u] of foreign taxes that would have been deemed paid had all of Corporation A's shareholders been eligible to compute an amount of foreign taxes deemed paid with respect to the dividend paid out of 1985 accumulated profits) remain in Corporation A, with respect to 1985.

Example (3). (i) From 1986 through 1991, domestic corporation M owns 10 percent of the one class of stock of foreign corporation A. The remaining 90 percent of Corporation A's stock is owned by Corporation Z, a foreign corporation. Corporation A is not a controlled foreign corporation and uses the u as its functional currency. 1u equals $1 at all relevant times. Both Corporation A and Corporation M use the calendar year as the taxable year. Corporation A has pre-1987 accumulated profits and post-1986 undistributed earnings or deficits in post-1986 undistributed earnings, pays pre-1987 and post-1986 foreign income taxes, and pays dividends as summarized below:

Taxable year	1986	1987	1988	1989	1990	1991
Current E & P (Deficits) of Corp. A	100u	(50u)	150u	75u	25u	0
Current Plus Accumulated E & P of Corp. A	100u	50u	200u	175u	200u	80u
Post-'86 Undistributed Earnings of Corp. A		(50u)	100u	75u	100u	0
Post-'86 Undistributed Earnings of Corp. A Reduced By Current Year Dividend Distributions (increased by deficit carryback)		(50u)	0	75u	0	0
Foreign Income Taxes (Annual) of Corp. A	80u	0	$120	$20	$20	0
Post-'86 Foreign Income Taxes of Corp. A		0	$120	$20	$40	0
12/31 Distributions to Corp. M	0	0	10u	0	12u	0
12/31 Distributions to Corp. Z	0	0	90u	0	108u	0

(ii) On December 31, 1988, Corporation A distributes a 10u dividend to Corporation M and a 90u dividend to Corporation Z. At that time Corporation A has 100u in its post-1986 undistributed earnings and $120 in its post-1986 foreign income taxes. Corporation M is deemed, under section 1.902-1(b)(1), to have paid $12 ($120 × 10% [10u/100u]) of the post-1986 foreign income taxes paid by Corporation A and includes that amount in gross income under section 78 as a dividend. Both the income inclusion and the foreign taxes deemed paid are subject to a separate limitation for dividends from noncontrolled section 902 corporation A. Corporation A's post-1986 undistributed earnings as of January 1, 1989, are -0- (100u − 100u). Its post-1986 foreign taxes as of January 1, 1989, also are -0-, $120 reduced by $120 of foreign income taxes paid that would have been deemed paid if both Corporations M and Z were eligible to compute an amount of foreign taxes deemed paid on the dividend from Corporation A ($120 × 100% [100u/100u]).

(iii) On December 31, 1990, Corporation A distributes a 12u dividend to Corporation M and a 108u dividend to Corporation Z. At that time Corporation A has 100u in its post-1986 undistributed earnings and $40 in its post-1986 foreign income taxes. The dividend is paid out of post-1986 undistributed earnings to the extent thereof (100u), and the remainder of 20u is paid out of 1986 accumulated profits. Under § 1.902-1(b)(2), the 12u dividend to Corporation M is deemed to be paid out of post-1986 undistributed earnings to the extent of 10u (100u × 12u/120u) and the remaining 2u is deemed to be paid out of Corporation A's 1986 accumulated profits. Similarly, the 108u dividend to Corporation Z is deemed to be paid out of post-1986 undistributed earnings to the extent of 90u (100u x 108u/120u) and the remaining 18u is deemed to be paid out of Corporation A's 1986 accumulated profits. Foreign income taxes deemed paid by Corporation M under section 902 with respect to the portion of the dividend paid out of post-1986 undistributed earnings are $4 ($40 × 10% [10u/100u]), and foreign taxes deemed paid by Corporation M with respect to the portion of the dividend deemed paid out of 1986 accumulated profits are 1.6u (80u × 2u/100u). Corporation M must include $4 plus 1.6u translated under the rule applicable to foreign income taxes paid on earnings accumulated in taxable years prior to the effective date of the Tax Reform Act of 1986 in gross income as a dividend under section 78. The income inclusion and the foreign income taxes deemed paid are subject to a separate limitation for dividends from noncontrolled section 902 Corporation A. As of January 1, 1991, Corporation A's post-1986 undistributed earnings are -0-(100u − 100u). 80u (100u − 20u) of accumulated profits remain with respect to 1986. Post-1986 foreign income taxes as of January 1, 1991, are -0-, $40 reduced by $40 of foreign income taxes paid that would have been deemed paid if both Corporations M and Z were eligible to compute an amount of deemed paid taxes on the 100u dividend distributed by Corporation A out of post-1986 undistributed earnings ($40 × 100% [100u/100u]). Corporation A has 64u of foreign income taxes remaining with respect to 1986, 80u reduced by 16u [80u × 20u/100u] of foreign income taxes that would have been deemed paid if Corporations M and Z both were eligible to compute an amount of deemed paid taxes on the 20u dividend distributed by Corporation A out of 1986 accumulated profits.

(b) Carryforward of deficit in pre-1987 accumulated profits of a first- or lower-tier corporation to post-1986 undistributed earnings for purposes of section 902. *(1) General rule.* For purposes of computing foreign income taxes deemed paid under § 1.902-1(b) with respect to dividends paid by a first- or lower-tier corporation out of post-1986 undistributed earnings, the amount of a deficit in accumulated profits of the foreign corporation determined under section 902 as of the end of its last pre-effective date taxable year is carried forward and reduces post-1986 undistributed earnings on the first day of the foreign corporation's first taxable year beginning after December 31, 1986, or on the first day of the first taxable year in which the ownership requirements of section 902(c)(3)(B) and § 1.902-1(a)(1) through (4) are met if the special effective date of § 1.902-1(a)(13) applies. Any foreign income taxes paid with respect to a pre-effective date year shall not be carried forward and included in post-1986 foreign income taxes. Post-1986 undistributed earnings may not be reduced by the amount of a pre-1987 deficit in earnings and profits computed under section 964(a). See section 960 and the regulations under that section for rules governing the carryforward of deficits and the computation of foreign income taxes deemed paid with respect to deemed income inclusions from controlled foreign corporations. For translation rules governing carryforwards of deficits in pre-1987 accumulated profits to post-1986 taxable years of a foreign corporation with a dollar functional currency, see § 1.985-6(d)(2).

(2) Effect of pre-effective date deficit. If a foreign corporation has a deficit in accumulated profits as of the end of its last pre-effective date taxable year, then the foreign corporation cannot pay a dividend out of pre-effective date years unless there is an adjustment made (for example, a refund of foreign taxes paid) that restores section 902 accumulated profits to a pre-effective date taxable year or years. Moreover, if a foreign corporation has a deficit in section 902 accumulated profits as of the end of its last pre-effective date taxable year, then no deficit in post-1986 undistributed earnings will be carried back under paragraph (a) of this section. For rules concerning carrybacks of eligible deficits from post-1986 undistributed earnings to reduce pre-1987 earnings and profits computed under section 964(a), see section 960 and the regulations under that section.

(3) Examples. The following examples illustrate the rules of this paragraph (b):

Example (1). (i) From 1984 through 1988, domestic corporation M owns 10 percent of the one class of stock of foreign corporation A. The remaining 90 percent of Corporation A's stock is owned by Corporation Z, a foreign corporation. Corporation A is not a controlled foreign corporation and uses the u as its functional currency. 1u equals $1 at all relevant times. Both Corporation A and Corporation M use the calendar year as the taxable year. Corporation A has pre-1987 accumulated profits or deficits in accumulated profits and post-1986 undistributed earnings, pays pre-1987 and post-1986 foreign income taxes, and pays dividends as summarized below:

Taxable year	1984	1985	1986	1987	1988
Current E & P (Deficits) of Corp. A	25u	(100u)	(25u)	200u	100u
Current Plus Accumulated E & P (Deficits) of Corp. A	25u	(75u)	(100u)	100u	50u
Post-'86 Undistributed Earnings of Corp. A				100u	50u
Post-'86 Undistributed Earnings of Corp. A Reduced By Current Year Dividend Distributions (reduced by deficit carryforward)				(50u)	50u
Foreign Income Taxes (Annual) of Corp. A	20u	5u	0	$100	$50
Post-'86 Foreign Income Taxes of Corp. A				$100	$50
12/31 Distributions to Corp. M	0	0	0	15u	0
12/31 Distributions to Corp. Z	0	0	0	135u	0

(ii) On December 31, 1987, Corporation A distributes a 150u dividend, 15u to Corporation M and 135u to Corporation Z. Corporation A has 200u of current earnings and profits for 1987, but its post-1986 undistributed earnings are only 100u as a result of the reduction for pre-1987 accumulated deficits required under paragraph (b)(1) of this section. Corporation A has $100 of post-1986 foreign income taxes. Only 100u of the 150u distribution is a dividend out of post-1986 undistributed earnings. Foreign income taxes deemed paid by Corporation M in 1987 with respect to the 10u dividend attributable to post-1986 undistributed earnings, computed under section 1.902-1(b), are $10 ($100 × 10% [10u/100u]). Corporation M includes this amount in gross income under section 78 as a dividend. Both the income inclusion and the foreign taxes deemed paid are subject to a separate limitation for dividends from noncontrolled section 902 corporation A. After the distribution, Corporation A has (50u) of post-1986 undistributed earnings (100u - 150u) and -0- post-1986 foreign income taxes, $100 reduced by $100 of foreign income taxes paid that would have been deemed paid if both Corporations M and Z were eligible to compute an amount of deemed paid taxes on the 100u dividend distributed by Corporation A out of post-1986 undistributed earnings ($100 × 100% [100u/100u]).

(iii) The remaining 50u of the 150u distribution cannot be deemed paid out of accumulated profits of a pre-1987 year because Corporation A has an accumulated deficit as of the end of 1986 that eliminated all pre-1987 accumulated profits. See paragraph (b)(2) of this section. The 50u is a dividend out of current earnings and profits under section 316(a)(2), but Corporation M is not deemed to have paid any additional foreign income taxes paid by Corporation A with respect to that 50u dividend out of current earnings and profits. See § 1.902-1(b)(4).

Example (2). (i) From 1986 through 1991, domestic corporation M owns 10 percent of the one class of stock of foreign corporation A. The remaining 90 percent of Corporation A's stock is owned by Corporation Z, a foreign corporation. Corporation A is not a controlled foreign corporation and uses the u as its functional currency. 1u equals $1 at all relevant times. Both Corporation A and Corporation M use the calendar year as the taxable year. Corporation A has pre-1987 accumulated profits or deficits in accumulated profits and post-1986 undistributed earnings, pays post-1986 foreign income taxes, and pays dividends as summarized below:

Taxable year	1986	1987	1988	1989	1990
Current E & P (Deficits) of Corp. A	(100u)	150u	(150u)	100u	250u
Current Plus Accumulated E & P (Deficits) of Corp. A	(100u)	50u	(200u)	(100u)	50u
Post-'86 Undistributed Earnings of Corp. A		50u	(200u)	(100u)	50u
Post-'86 Undistributed Earnings of Corp. A Reduced By Current Year Dividend Distributions (reduced by deficit carryforward)		(50u)	(200u)	(200u)	0
Foreign Income Taxes (Annual) of Corp. A	0	$120	0	$50	$100
Post-'86 Foreign Income Taxes of Corp. A		$120	0	$50	$150
12/31 Distributions to Corp. M	0	10u	0	10u	5u
12/31 Distributions to Corp. Z	0	90u	0	90u	45u

(ii) On December 31, 1987, Corporation A distributes a 10u dividend to Corporation M and a 90u dividend to Corporation Z. At the time of the distribution, Corporation A has 50u of post-1986 undistributed earnings and 150u of current earnings and profits. Thus, 50u of the dividend distribution (5u to Corporation M and 45u to Corporation Z) is a dividend out of post-1986 undistributed earnings. The remaining 50u is a dividend out of current earnings and profits under section 316(a)(2), but Corporation M is not deemed to have paid any additional foreign income taxes paid by Corporation A with respect to that 50u dividend out of current earnings and profits. See § 1.902-1(b)(4). Note that even if there were no current earnings and profits in Corporation A, the remaining 50u of the 100u distribution cannot be deemed paid out of accumulated profits of a pre-1987 year because Corporation A has an accumulated deficit as of the end of 1986 that eliminated all pre-1987 accumulated profits. See paragraph (b)(2) of this section. Corporation A has $120 of post-1986 foreign income taxes. Foreign taxes deemed paid by Corporation M under section 902 with respect to the 5u dividend out of post-1986 undistributed earnings are $12 ($120 × 10% [5u/50u]). Corporation M includes this amount in gross income as a dividend under section 78. Both the foreign taxes deemed paid and the deemed dividend are subject to a separate limitation for dividends from noncontrolled section 902 corporation A. As of January 1, 1988, Corporation A has (50u) in its post-1986 undistributed earnings (50u – 100u) and -0- in its post-1986 foreign income taxes, $120 reduced by $120 of foreign taxes that would have been deemed paid if both Corporations M and Z were eligible to compute an amount of deemed paid taxes on the dividend distributed by Corporation A out of post-1986 undistributed earnings ($120 × 100% [50u/50u]).

(iii) On December 31, 1989, Corporation A distributes a 10u dividend to Corporation M and a 90u dividend to Corporation Z. Although the distribution is considered a dividend in its entirety out of 1989 earnings and profits pursuant to section 316(a)(2), post-1986 undistributed earnings are (100u). Accordingly, for purposes of section 902, Corporation M is deemed to have paid no post-1986 foreign income taxes. See § 1.902-1(b)(4). Corporation A's post-1986 undistributed earnings as of January 1, 1990, are (200u) ((100u) – 100u). Corporation A's post-1986 foreign income taxes are not reduced because no taxes were deemed paid.

(iv) On December 31, 1990, Corporation A distributes a 5u dividend to Corporation M and a 45u dividend to Corporation Z. At that time Corporation A has 50u of post-1986 undistributed earnings, and $150 of post-1986 foreign income taxes. Foreign taxes deemed paid by Corporation M under section 902 with respect to the 5u dividend are $15 ($150 × 10% [5u/50u]). Post-1986 undistributed earnings as of January 1, 1991, are -0-(50u – 50u). Post-1986 foreign income taxes as of January 1, 1991, also are -0-, $150 reduced by $150 ($150 × 100% [50u/50u]) of foreign income taxes that would have been deemed paid if both Corporations M and Z were eligible to compute an amount of deemed paid taxes on the 50u dividend.

T.D. 8708, 1/6/97, amend T.D. 9260, 4/24/2006.

§ 1.902-3 Credit for domestic corporate shareholder of a foreign corporation for foreign income taxes paid with respect to accumulated profits of taxable years of the foreign corporation beginning before January 1, 1987.

Caution: The Treasury has not yet amended Reg § 1.902-3 to reflect changes made by P.L. 105-34.

(a) Definitions. For purposes of section 902 and §§ 1.902-3 and 1.902-4:

(1) Domestic shareholder. In the case of dividends received by a domestic corporation after December 31, 1964, from a foreign corporation, the term "domestic shareholder" means a domestic corporation which owns at least 10 percent of the voting stock of the foreign corporation at the time it receives a dividend from such foreign corporation.

(2) First-tier corporation. In the case of dividends received by a domestic shareholder after December 31, 1964, from a foreign corporation, the term "first-tier corporation" means a foreign corporation at least 10 percent of the voting stock of which is owned by a domestic shareholder at the time it receives a dividend from such foreign corporation. The term "first-tier corporation" also means a DISC or former DISC, but only with respect to dividends from the DISC or former DISC to the extent they are treated under sections 861(a)(2)(D) and 862(a)(2) as income from sources without the United States.

(3) Second-tier corporation. (i) In the case of dividends paid to a first-tier corporation by a foreign corporation after January 12, 1971 (i.e., the date of enactment of Pub. L. 91-684, 84 Stat. 2068), but only for purposes of applying this section for a taxable year of a domestic shareholder ending after that date, the foreign corporation is a "second-tier corporation" if at least 10 percent of its voting stock is owned by the first-tier corporation at the time the first-tier corporation receives the dividend.

(ii) In the case of dividends paid to a first-tier corporation by a foreign corporation after January 12, 1971, but only for purposes of applying this section for a taxable year of a domestic shareholder ending before January 13, 1971, or in the case of any dividend paid to a first-tier corporation by a foreign corporation before January 13, 1971, the foreign corporation is a "second-tier corporation" if at least 50 percent of its voting stock is owned by the first-tier corporation at the time the first-tier corporation receives the dividend.

(4) Third-tier corporation. In the case of dividends paid to a second-tier corporation (as defined in paragraph (a)(3)(i) or (ii) of this section) by a foreign corporation after January 12, 1971, but only for purposes of applying this section for a taxable year of a domestic shareholder ending after that date, the foreign corporation is a "third-tier corporation" if at least 10 percent of its voting stock is owned by the second-tier corporation at the time the second-tier corporation receives the dividend.

(5) Foreign income taxes. The term "foreign income taxes" means income, war profits, and excess profits taxes, and taxes included in the term "income, war profits, and excess profits taxes" by reason of section 903, imposed by a foreign country or a possession of the United States.

(6) Dividend. For the definition of the term "dividend" for purposes of applying section 902 and this section, see section 316 and the regulations thereunder.

(7) Dividend received. A dividend shall be considered received for purposes of section 902 and this section when the cash or other property is unqualifiedly made subject to the demands of the distributee. See § 1.301-1(b).

(b) Domestic shareholder owning stock in a first-tier corporation. *(1) In general.* (i) If a domestic shareholder receives dividends in any taxable year from its first-tier corporation, the credit for foreign income taxes allowed by section 901 includes, subject to the conditions and limitations of this section, the foreign income taxes deemed, in accordance with paragraph (b)(2) of this section, to be paid by such domestic shareholder for such year.

(ii) If dividends are received by a domestic shareholder from more than one first-tier corporation, the taxes deemed to be paid by such shareholder under section 902(a) and this paragraph (b) shall be computed separately with respect to the dividends received from each of such first-tier corporations.

(iii) Any taxes deemed paid by a domestic shareholder for the taxable year pursuant to section 902(a) and paragraph (b)(2) of this section shall, except as provided in § 1.960-3(b), be included in the gross income of such shareholder for such year as a dividend pursuant to section 78 and § 1.78-1. For the source of such a section 78 dividend, see paragraph (h)(1) of this section.

(iv) Any taxes deemed, under paragraph (b)(2) of this section, to be paid by the domestic shareholder shall be deemed to be paid by such shareholder only for purposes of the foreign tax credit allowed under section 901. See section 904 for other limitations on the amount of the credit.

(v) For rules relating to reduction of the amount of foreign income taxes deemed paid or accrued with respect to foreign mineral income, see section 901(e) and § 1.901-3.

(vi) For the nonrecognition as a foreign income tax for purposes of this section of certain income, profits, or excess profits taxes paid or accrued to a foreign country in connection with the purchase and sale of oil or gas extracted in such country, see section 901(f) and the regulations thereunder.

(vii) For rules relating to reduction of the amount of foreign income taxes deemed paid with respect to foreign oil and gas extraction income, see section 907(a) and the regulations thereunder.

(viii) See the regulations under sections 960, 962, and 963 for special rules relating to the application of section 902 in computing the foreign tax credit of United States shareholders of controlled foreign corporations.

(2) Amount of foreign taxes deemed paid by a domestic shareholder. To the extent dividends are paid by a first-tier corporation to its domestic shareholder out of accumulated profits, as defined in paragraph (e) of this section, for any taxable year, the domestic shareholder shall be deemed to have paid the same proportion of any foreign income taxes paid, accrued or deemed, in accordance with paragraph (c)(2) of this section, to be paid by such first-tier corporation on or with respect to such accumulated profits for such year which the amount of such dividends (determined without regard to the gross-up under section 78) bears to the amount by which such accumulated profits exceed the amount of such taxes (other than those deemed, under paragraph (c)(2) of this section, to be paid). For determining the amount of foreign income taxes paid or accrued by such first-tier corporation on or with respect to the accumulated profits for the taxable year of such first-tier corporation, see paragraph (f) of this section.

(c) First-tier corporation owning stock in a second-tier corporation. *(1) In general.* For purposes of applying section 902(a) and paragraph (b)(2) of this section, if a first-tier corporation receives dividends in any taxable year from its second-tier corporation, the foreign income taxes deemed to be paid by the first-tier corporation on or with respect to its own accumulated profits for such year shall be the amount determined in accordance with paragraph (c)(2) of this section. This paragraph (c) shall not apply unless the product of—

(i) The percentage of voting stock owned by the domestic shareholder in the first-tier corporation at the time that the domestic shareholder receives dividends from the first-tier corporation in respect of which foreign income taxes are deemed to be paid by the domestic shareholder under paragraph (b)(1) of this section, and

(ii) The percentage of voting stock owned by the first-tier corporation in the second-tier corporation equals at least 5 percent. The percentage under paragraph (c)(1)(ii) of this section of voting stock owned by the first-tier corporation in the second-tier corporation is determined as of the time that the dividend distributed by the second-tier corporation is received by the first-tier corporation and thus included in accumulated profits of the first-tier corporation out of which dividends referred to in paragraph (c)(1)(i) of this section are distributed by the first-tier corporation to the domestic shareholder.

Example. On February 10, 1976, foreign corporation B pays a dividend out of its accumulated profits for 1975 to foreign corporation A. On February 16, 1976, the date on which it receives the dividend, A Corporation owns 40 percent of the voting stock of B Corporation. Both corporations use the calendar year as the taxable year. On June 1, 1976, A Corporation sells its stock in B Corporation. On January 17, 1977, A Corporation pays a dividend out of its accumulated profits for 1976 to domestic corporation M. M Corporation owns 30 percent of the voting stock of A Corporation on January 20, 1977, the date on which it receives the dividend. M Corporation uses a fiscal year ending on April 30 as the taxable year. On February 16, 1976, A Corporation satisfies the 10-percent stock ownership requirement referred to in paragraph (a)(3) of this section with respect to B Corporation, and on January 20, 1977, M Corporation satisfies the 10-percent stock-ownership requirement referred to in paragraph (a)(2) of this section with respect to A Corporation. The 5-percent requirement of this paragraph (c)(1) is also satisfied since 30 percent (the percentage of voting stock owned by M Corporation in A Corporation on January 20, 1977), when multiplied by 40 percent (the percentage of voting stock owned by A Corporation in B Corporation on February 16, 1976), equals 12 percent. Accordingly, for its taxable year ending on April 30, 1977, M Corporation is entitled to a credit for a portion of the foreign income taxes paid, accrued, or deemed to be paid, by A Corporation for 1976; and for 1976 A Corporation is deemed to have paid a portion of the foreign income taxes paid or accrued by B Corporation for 1975.

(2) Amount of foreign taxes deemed paid by a first-tier corporation. A first-tier corporation which receives dividends in any taxable year from its second-tier corporation shall be deemed to have paid for such year the same proportion of any foreign income taxes paid, accrued, or deemed, in accordance with paragraph (d)(2) of this section, to be paid by its second-tier corporation on or with respect to the accumulated profits, as defined in paragraph (e) of this section, for the taxable year of the second-tier corporation from which such dividends are paid which the amount of such dividends bears to the amount by which such accumulated profits of the second-tier corporation exceed the taxes so paid or accrued. For determining the amount of the foreign income taxes paid or accrued by such second-tier corporation on or with respect to the accumulated profits for the taxable year of such second-tier corporation, see paragraph (f) of this section.

(d) Second-tier corporation owning stock in a third-tier corporation. *(1) In general.* For purposes of applying section 902(b)(1) and paragraph (c)(2) of this section, if a second-tier corporation receives dividends in any taxable year from its third-tier corporation, the foreign income taxes deemed to be paid by the second-tier corporation on or with respect to its own accumulated profits for such year shall be the amount determined in accordance with paragraph (d)(2) of this section. This paragraph (d) shall not apply unless the product of—

(i) The percentage of voting stock arrived at in applying the 5-percent requirement of paragraph (c)(1) of this section with respect to dividends received by the first-tier corporation from the second-tier corporation, and

(ii) the percentage of voting stock owned by the second-tier corporation in the third-tier corporation equals at least 5 percent. The percentage under paragraph (d)(1)(ii) of this section of voting stock owned by the second-tier corporation in the third-tier corporation is determined as of the time that the dividend distributed by the third-tier corporation is received by the second-tier corporation and thus included in accumulated profits of the second-tier corporation out of which dividends referred to in paragraph (d)(1)(i) of this section are distributed by the second-tier corporation to the first-tier corporation.

Example. On February 27, 1975, foreign corporation C pays a dividend out of its accumulated profits for 1974 to foreign corporation B. On March 3, 1975, the date on which it receives the dividend, B Corporation owns 50 percent of the voting stock of C Corporation. On February 10, 1976, B Corporation pays a dividend out of its accumulated profits for 1975 to foreign corporation A. On February 16, 1976, the date on which it receives the dividend, A Corporation owns 40 percent of the voting stock of B Corporation. All three corporations use the calendar year as the taxable year. On January 17, 1977, A Corporation pays a dividend out of its accumulated profits for 1976 to domestic corporation M. M Corporation owns 30 percent of the voting stock of A Corporation on January 20, 1977, the date on which it receives the dividend. M Corporation uses a fiscal year ending on April 30 as the taxable year. On February 16, 1976, A Corporation satisfies the 10-percent stock ownership requirement referred to in paragraph (a)(3) of this section with respect to B Corporation, and on January 20, 1977, M Corporation satisfies the 10-percent stock-ownership requirement referred to in paragraph (a)(2) of this section with respect to A Corporation. The 5-percent requirement of paragraph (c)(1) of this section is also satisfied since 30 percent (the percentage of voting stock owned by M Corporation in A Corporation on January 20, 1977), when multiplied by 40 percent (the percentage of voting stock owned by A Corporation in B Corporation on February 16, 1976), equals 12 percent. On March 3, 1975, B Corporation satisfies the 10 percent stock ownership requirement referred to in paragraph (a)(4) of this section with respect to C Corporation. The 5-percent requirement of this paragraph (d)(1) is also satisfied since 12 percent (the percentage of voting stock arrived at in applying the 5-percent requirement of paragraph (c)(1) of this section with respect to the dividends received by A Corporation from B Corporation on February 16, 1976), when multiplied by 50 percent (the percentage of voting stock owned by B Corporation in C Corporation on March 3, 1975), equals 6 percent. Accordingly, for its taxable year ending on April 30, 1977, M Corporation is entitled to a credit for a portion of the foreign income taxes paid, accrued, or deemed to be paid, by A Corporation for 1976; for 1976 A Corporation is deemed to have paid a portion of the foreign income taxes paid, accrued, or deemed to be paid, by B Corporation for 1975; and for 1975 B Corporation is deemed to have paid a portion of the foreign income taxes paid or accrued by C Corporation for 1974.

(2) Amount of foreign taxes deemed paid by a second-tier corporation. For purposes of applying paragraph (c)(2) of this section to a first-tier corporation, a second-tier corporation which receives dividends in its taxable year from its third-tier corporation shall be deemed to have paid for such year the same proportion of any foreign income taxes paid or accrued by its third-tier corporation on or with respect to the accumulated profits, as defined in paragraph (e) of this section, for the taxable year of the third-tier corporation from which such dividends are paid which the amount of such dividends bears to the amount by which such accumulated profits of the third-tier corporation exceed the taxes so paid or accrued. For determining the amount of the foreign income taxes paid or accrued by such third-tier corporation on or with respect to the accumulated profits for the taxable year of such third-tier corporation, see paragraph (f) of this section.

(e) Determination of accumulated profits of a foreign corporation. The accumulated profits for any taxable year of a first-tier corporation and the accumulated profits for any taxable year of a second-tier or third-tier corporation, which are taken into account in applying paragraph (c)(2) or (d)(2) of this section with respect to such first-tier corporation, shall be the sum of—

(1) The earnings and profits of such corporation for such year, and

(2) The foreign income taxes imposed on or with respect to the gains, profits, and income to which such earnings and profits are attributable.

(f) Taxes paid on or with respect to accumulated profits of a foreign corporation. For purposes of this section, the amount of foreign income taxes paid or accrued on or with respect to the accumulated profits of a foreign corporation for any taxable year shall be the entire amount of the foreign income taxes paid or accrued for such year on or with respect to such gains, profits, and income. For purposes of this paragraph (f), the gains, profits, and income of a foreign corporation for any taxable year shall be determined after reduction by any income, war profits, or excess profits taxes imposed on or with respect to such gains, profits, and income by the United States.

(g) Determination of earnings and profits of a foreign corporation. *(1) Taxable year to which section 963 does not apply.* For purposes of this section, the earnings and profits of a foreign corporation for any taxable year beginning after December 31, 1962, other than a taxable year to which paragraph (g)(2) of this section applies, may, if the domestic shareholder chooses, be determined under the rules provided by § 1.964-1 exclusive of paragraphs (d) and (e) of such section. The translation of amounts so determined into United States dollars or other foreign currency shall be made at the proper exchange rate for the date of distribution with respect to which the determination is made.

(2) Taxable year to which section 963 applies. For any taxable year of a foreign corporation with respect to which there applies under § 1.963-1(c)(1) an election by a corporate United States shareholder to exclude from its gross income for the taxable year the subpart F income of a controlled foreign corporation, the earnings and profits of such foreign corporation for such year with respect to such shareholder must be determined, for purposes of this section, under the rules provided by § 1.964-1, even though the amount of the minimum distribution required under § 1.963-2(a) to be received by such shareholder from such earnings and profits of such foreign corporation, or from the consolidated earnings and profits of the chain or group which includes such foreign corporation, is zero. Effective for taxable years of foreign corporations beginning after December 31, 1975, section 963 is repealed by section 602(a)(1) of the Tax Reduction Act of 1975 (89 Stat. 58); accordingly, this paragraph (g)(2) is inapplicable with respect to computing earnings and profits for such taxable years.

(3) Time and manner of making choice. The controlling United States shareholders (as defined in § 1.964-1(c)(5)) of a foreign corporation shall make the choice referred to in paragraph (g)(1) of this section (including the elections permitted by § 1.964-1(b) and (c)) by filing a written statement to such effect with the Director of the Internal Revenue Service Center, 11601 Roosevelt Boulevard, Philadelphia, Pennsylvania 19155, within 180 days after the close of the first taxable year of the foreign corporation during which such shareholders receive a distribution of earnings and profits with respect to which the benefits of this section are claimed

or on or before November 15, 1965, whichever is later. For purposes of this paragraph (g)(3), the 180-day period shall commence on the date of receipt of any distribution which is considered paid from the accumulated profits of a preceding year or years under paragraph (g)(4) of this section. See § 1.964-1(c)(3)(ii) and (iii) for procedures requiring notification of the Director of the Internal Revenue Service Center and noncontrolling shareholders of action taken.

(4) Determination by district director. The district director in whose district is filed the income tax return of the domestic shareholder claiming a credit under section 901 for foreign income taxes deemed, under section 902 and this section, to be paid by such shareholder shall have the power to determine, with respect to a foreign corporation, from the accumulated profits of what taxable year or years the dividends were paid. In making such determination the district director shall, unless it is otherwise established to his satisfaction, treat any dividends which are paid in the first 60 days of any taxable year of such a corporation as having been paid from the accumulated profits of the preceding taxable year or years of such corporation and shall, in other respects, treat any dividends as having been paid from the most recently accumulated profits. For purposes of this paragraph (g)(4), in the case of a foreign corporation the foreign income taxes of which are determined on the basis of an accounting period of less than 1 year, the term "year" shall mean such accounting period. See sections 441(b)(3) and 443.

(h) Source of income from first-tier corporation and country to which tax is deemed paid. *(1) Source of income.* For purposes of section 904(a)(1) (relating to the per-country limitation), in the case of a dividend received by a domestic shareholder from a first-tier corporation there shall be deemed to be derived from sources within the foreign country or possession of the United States under the laws of which the first-tier corporation is created or organized the sum of the amounts which under paragraph (a)(3)(ii) of § 1.861-3 are treated, with respect to such dividend, as income from sources without the United States.

(2) Country to which taxes deemed paid. For purposes of section 904, all foreign income taxes paid, or deemed under paragraph (c) of this section to be paid, by a first-tier corporation shall be deemed to be paid to the foreign country or possession of the United States under the laws of which such first-tier corporation is created or organized.

(i) United Kingdom income taxes paid with respect to royalties. A taxpayer shall not be deemed under section 902 and this section to have paid any taxes with respect to which a credit is allowable to such taxpayer or any other taxpayer by virtue of section 905(b).

(j) Information to be furnished. If the credit for foreign income taxes claimed under section 901 includes taxes deemed, under paragraph (b)(2) of this section, to be paid, the domestic shareholder must furnish the same information with respect to such taxes as it is required to furnish with respect to the taxes actually paid or accrued by it and for which credit is claimed. See § 1.905-2. For other information required to be furnished by the domestic shareholder for the annual accounting period of certain foreign corporations ending with or within such shareholder's taxable year, and for reduction in the amount of foreign income taxes paid or deemed to be paid for failure to furnish such information, see section 6038 and the regulations thereunder.

(k) Illustrations. The application of this section may be illustrated by the following examples:

Example (1). Throughout 1978, domestic corporation M owns all the one class of stock of foreign corporation A. Both corporations use the calendar year as the taxable year. Corporation A has accumulated profits, pays foreign income taxes, and pays dividends for 1978 as summarized below. For 1978, M Corporation is deemed, under paragraph (b)(2) of this section, to have paid $20 of the foreign income taxes paid by A Corporation for 1978 and includes such amount in gross income under section 78 as a dividend, determined as follows:

Gains, profits, and income of A Corp	$100
Foreign income taxes imposed on or with respect to gains, profits, and income	40
Accumulated profits	100
Foreign income taxes paid on or with respect to accumulated profits (total foreign income taxes)	40
Accumulated profits in excess of foreign income taxes	60
Dividends paid to M Corp	30
Foreign income taxes of A Corp. deemed paid by M Corp. under sec. 902(a) ($40 × $30 ÷ $60)	20

Example (2). The facts are the same as in example (1), except that M Corporation also owns all the one class of stock of foreign corporation B which also uses the calendar year as the taxable year. Corporation B has accumulated profits, pays foreign income taxes, and pays dividends for 1978 as summarized below. For 1978, M Corporation is deemed under paragraph (b)(2) of this section, to have paid $20 of the foreign income taxes paid by A Corporation for 1978 and to have paid $50 of the foreign income taxes paid by B Corporation for 1978, and includes $70 in gross income as a dividend under section 78, determined as follows:

B Corporation

Gains, profits and income	$200
Foreign income taxes imposed on or with respect to gains, profits, and income	100
Accumulated profits	200
Foreign income taxes paid by B Corp. on or with respect to accumulated profits	100
Accumulated profits in excess of foreign income taxes	100
Dividends paid to M Corp	50
Foreign income taxes of B Corporation deemed paid by M Corporation under section 902(a) ($100 × $50/$100)	50

M Corporation

Foreign income taxes deemed paid under sec. 902(a):	
Taxes of A Corp (from example (1))	$ 20
Taxes of B Corp (as determined above)	50
Total	70
Foreign income taxes included in gross income under sec. 78 as a dividend:	
Taxes of A Corp (from example(1))	20
Taxes of B Corp	50
Total	70

Example (3). For 1978, domestic corporation M owns all the one class of stock of foreign corporation A, which in turn owns all the one class of stock of foreign corporation B. All corporations use the calendar year as the taxable year. For 1978, M Corporation is deemed under paragraph (b)(2) of this section to have paid $50 of the foreign income taxes paid, or deemed under paragraph (c)(2) of this section to be paid, by A Corporation for such year and includes such amount in gross income as a dividend under section 78, determined as follows upon the basis of the facts assumed:

B Corp. (second-tier corporation):

Gains, profits, and income	$300
Foreign income taxes imposed on or with respect to gains, profits, and income	120
Accumulated profits	300
Foreign income taxes paid by B Corp. on or with respect to its accumulated profits (total foreign income taxes)	120
Accumulated profits in excess of foreign income taxes	180
Dividends paid on Dec. 31, 1978 to A Corp	90
Foreign income taxes of B Corp. deemed paid by A Corp. for 1978 under sec. 902(b)(1) ($120 × $90 ÷ $180)	60

A Corp. (first-tier corporation):

Gains, profits, and income:	
Business operations	200
Dividends from B Corp	90
Total	290
Foreign income taxes imposed on or with respect to gains, profits, and income	40
Accumulated profits	290
Foreign income taxes paid by A Corp. on or with respect to its accumulated profits (total foreign income taxes)	40
Accumulated profits in excess of foreign income taxes	250
Foreign income taxes paid, and deemed to be paid, by A Corp. for 1978 on or with respect to its accumulated profits for such year ($60 + $40)	100
Dividends paid on Dec. 31, 1978, to M Corp	125

M Corp. (domestic shareholder):

Foreign income taxes of A Corp. deemed paid by M Corp. for 1978 under sec. 902(a) ($100 × $125 ÷ $250)	50
Foreign income taxes included in gross income of M Corp. under sec. 78 as a dividend received from A Corp.	50

Example (4). Throughout 1978, domestic corporation M owns 50 percent of the voting stock of foreign corporation A. A Corporation has owned 40 percent of the voting stock of foreign corporation B, since 1970; B Corporation has owned 30 percent of the voting stock of foreign corporation C, since 1972. B Corporation uses a fiscal year ending on June 30 as its taxable year; all other corporations use the calendar year as the taxable year. On February 1, 1977, B Corporation receives a dividend from C Corporation out of C Corporation's accumulated profits for 1976. On February 15, 1977, A Corporation receives a dividend from B Corporation out of B Corporation's accumulated profits for its fiscal year ending in 1977. On February 15, 1978, M Corporation receives a dividend from A Corporation out of A Corporation's accumulated profits for 1977. For 1978, M Corporation is deemed under paragraph (b)(2) of this section to have paid $81.67 of the foreign income taxes paid, or deemed under paragraph (c)(2) of this section to be paid, by A Corporation on or with respect to its accumulated profits for 1977, and M Corporation includes that amount in gross income as a dividend under section 78, determined as follows upon the basis of the facts assumed:

C Corp. (third-tier corporation):

Gains, profits, and income for 1976	$2,000.00
Foreign income taxes imposed on or with respect to such gains, profits, and income	800.00
Accumulated profits	2,000.00
Foreign income taxes paid by C Corp. on or with respect to its accumulated profits (total foreign income taxes	800.00
Accumulated profits in excess of foreign income taxes	1,200.00
Dividends paid on Feb. 1, 1977 to B Corp	150.00
Foreign income taxes of C Corp. for 1976 deemed paid by B Corp. for its fiscal year ending in 1977 ($800 × $150 ÷ $1,200)	100.00

B Corp. (second-tier corporation):

Gains, profits, and income for fiscal year ending in 1977:	
Business operations	850.00
Dividends from C Corp	150.00
Total	1,000.00
Foreign income taxes imposed on or with respect to gains, profits, and income	200.00
Accumulated profits	1,000.00
Foreign income taxes paid by B Corp. on or with respect to its accumulated profits (total foreign income taxes)	200.00
Accumulated profits in excess of foreign income taxes	800.00
Foreign income taxes paid, and deemed to be paid, by B Corp. for its fiscal year on or with respect to its accumulated profits for such year ($100 + $200)	300.00
Dividends paid on Feb. 15, 1977 to A Corp	120.00
Foreign income taxes of B Corp. for its fiscal year deemed paid by A Corp. for 1977 ($300 × $120 ÷ $800)	45.00

A Corp. (first-tier corporation):

Gains, profits, and income for 1977:	
Business operations	380.00
Dividends from B Corp	120.00
Total	500.00
Foreign income taxes imposed on or with respect to gains, profits, and income	200.00
Accumulated profits	500.00
Foreign income taxes paid by A Corp. on or with respect to its accumulated profits (total foreign income taxes)	200.00
Accumulated profits in excess of foreign taxes	300.00
Foreign income taxes paid, and deemed to be paid, by A Corp. for 1977 on or with respect to its accumulated profits for such year ($45 + $200)	245.00
Dividends paid on Feb. 15, 1978 to M Corp	100.00

M Corp. (domestic shareholder):

Foreign income taxes of A Corp. for 1977 deemed paid by M Corp. for 1978 under sec. 902(a) ($245 × $100 ÷ $300)	81.67
Foreign income taxes included in gross income of M Corp. under sec. 78 as a dividend received from A Corp	81.67

(l) Effective date. Except as provided in § 1.902-4, this section applies to any distribution received from a first-tier corporation by its domestic shareholder after December 31, 1964, and before the beginning of the foreign corporation's first taxable year beginning after December 31, 1986. If, however, the first day on which the ownership requirements of section 902(c)(3)(B) and § 1.902-1(a)(1) through (4) are met with respect to the foreign corporation is in a taxable year of the foreign corporation beginning after December 31, 1986, then this section shall apply to all taxable years beginning after December 31, 1964, and before the year in which the ownership requirements are first met. See § 1.902-1(a)(13)(i). For corresponding rules applicable to distributions received by the domestic shareholder prior to January 1, 1965, see § 1.902-5 as contained in the 26 CFR part 1 edition revised April 1, 1976.

T.D. 6275, 12/2/57, amend T.D. 6310, 9/10/58, T.D. 6462, 5/5/60, T.D. 6466, 5/12/60, T.D. 6789, 12/30/64, T.D. 6805, 3/8/65, T.D. 7378, 9/29/75, T.D. 7481, 4/15/77, T.D. 7490, 6/10/77, T.D. 7649, 10/17/79, T.D. 8708, 1/6/97.

§ 1.902-4 Rules for distributions attributable to accumulated profits for taxable years in which a first-tier corporation was a less developed country corporation.

Caution: The Treasury has not yet amended Reg § 1.902-4 to reflect changes made by P.L. 94-455.

(a) In general. If a domestic shareholder receives a distribution from a first-tier corporation before January 1, 1978, in a taxable year of the domestic shareholder beginning after December 31, 1964, which is attributable to accumulated profits of the first-tier corporation for a taxable year beginning before January 1, 1976, in which the first-tier corporation was a less developed country corporation (as defined in 26 CFR § 1.902-2 rev. as of April 1, 1978), then the amount of the credit deemed paid by the domestic shareholder with respect to such distribution shall be calculated under the rules relating to less developed country corporations contained in (26 CFR § 1.902-1 rev. as of April 1, 1978).

(b) Combined distributions. If a domestic shareholder receives a distribution before January 1, 1978, from a first-tier corporation, a portion of which is described in paragraph (a) of this section, and a portion of which is attributable to accumulated profits of the first-tier corporation for a year in which the first-tier corporation was not a less developed country corporation, then the amount of taxes deemed paid by the domestic shareholder shall be computed separately on each portion of the dividend. The taxes deemed paid on that portion of the dividend described in paragraph (a) shall be computed as specified in paragraph (a). The taxes deemed paid on that portion of the dividend described in this paragraph (b), shall be computed as specified in § 1.902-3.

(c) Distributions of a first-tier corporation attributable to certain distributions from second- or third-tier corporations. Paragraph (a) shall apply to a distribution received by a domestic shareholder before January 1, 1978, from a first-tier corporation out of accumulated profits for a taxable year beginning after December 31, 1975, if:

(1) The distribution is attributable to a distribution received by the first-tier corporation from a second- or third-tier corporation in a taxable year beginning after December 31, 1975.

(2) The distribution from the second- or third-tier corporation is made out of accumulated profits of the second- or third-tier corporation for a taxable year beginning before January 1, 1976, and

(3) The first-tier corporation would have qualified as a less developed country corporation under section 902(d) (as in effect on December 31, 1975), in the taxable year in which it received the distribution.

(d) Illustrations. The application of this section may be illustrated by the following examples:

Example (1). M, a domestic corporation owns all of the one class of stock of foreign corporation A. Both corporations use the calendar year as the taxable year. A Corporation pays a dividend to M Corporation on January 1, 1977, partly out of its accumulated profits for calendar year 1976 and partly out of its accumulated profits for calendar year 1975. For 1975 A Corporation qualified as a less developed country corporation under the former section 902(d) (as in effect on December 31, 1975). M Corporation is deemed under paragraphs (a) and (b) of this section to have paid $63 of foreign income taxes paid by A Corporation on or with respect to its accumulated profits for 1976 and 1975 and M Corporation includes $36 of that amount in gross income as a dividend under section 78, determined as follows upon the basis of the facts assumed:

1976	
Gains, profits, and income of A Corp. for 1976	$120.00
Foreign income taxes imposed on or with respect to such gains, profits, and income	36.00
Accumulated profits	120.00
Foreign income taxes paid by A Corp. on or with respect to its accumulated profits (total foreign income taxes)	36.00
Accumulated profits in excess of foreign income taxes	84.00
Dividend to M Corp. out of 1976 accumulated profits	84.00
Foreign income taxes of A for 1976 deemed paid by M Corp. ($84/$84 × $36)	36.00
Foreign income taxes included in gross income of M Corp. under sec. 78 as a dividend from A Corp	36.00

1975	
Gains, profits, and income of A Corp for 1975	$257.14
Foreign income taxes imposed on or with respect to such gains, profits, and income	77.14
Accumulated profits (under sec. 902(c)(1)(B) as in effect prior to amendment by the Tax Reform Act of 1976)	180.00
Foreign income taxes paid by A Corp. on or with respect to its accumulated profits ($77.14 × $180/$257.14)	54.00
Dividends paid to M Corp. out of accumulated profits of A Corp. for 1975	90.00
Foreign income taxes of A Corp. for 1975 deemed paid by M Corp. (under sec 902(a)(2) as in effect prior to amendment by the Tax Reform Act of 1976) ($54 × $90/$180)	27.00
Foreign income taxes included in gross income of M Corp. under sec. 78 as a dividend from A Corp	0

Example (2). The facts are the same as in example (1), except that the distribution from A Corporation to M Corporation on January 1, 1977, was from accumulated profits of A Corporation for 1976. A Corporation's accumulated profits for 1976 were made up of income from its trade or business, and a dividend paid by B, a second-tier corporation in 1976. The dividend from B Corporation to A Corporation was from accumulated profits of B Corporation for 1975. A Corporation would have qualified as a less developed country corporation for 1976 under the former section 902(d) (as in effect on December 31, 1975). M Corporation is deemed under paragraphs (b) and (c) of this section to have paid

$543 of the foreign taxes paid or deemed paid by A Corporation on or with respect to its accumulated profits for 1976, and M Corporation includes $360 of that amount in gross income as a dividend under section 78, determined as follows upon the basis of the facts assumed:

Total gains, profits and income of A Corp. for 1976	$1,500
Gains and profits from business operations	1,200
Gains and profits from dividend A Corp. received in 1976 from B Corp out of accumulated profits of B Corp. for 1975	300
Foreign taxes imposed on or with respect to such profits and income	450
Foreign taxes paid by A Corp. attributable to gains and profits from A Corp.'s business operations	360
Foreign taxes paid by A Corp. attributable to dividend from B Corp. in 1976	90
Dividends from A Corp. to M Corp. on Jan. 1, 1977	1,050
Portion of dividend attributable to gains and profits of A Corp. from business operations. ($1,200/$1,500 × $1,050)	840
Portion of dividends attributable to gains on profits of A Corp. from dividend from B Corp. ($300/$1,500 × $1,050	210

(a) Amount of foreign taxes of A Corp. deemed paid by M Corp. on A Corp.'s gains and profits for 1976 from business operations.

Gains, profits, and income of A Corp. from business operations	$1,200
Foreign income taxes imposed on or with respect to gains, profits, and income	360
Accumulated profits	1,200
Foreign income taxes paid by A Corp. on or with respect to its accumulated profits (total foreign income taxes)	360
Accumulated profits in excess of foreign income taxes	840
Dividend to M Corp	840
Foreign taxes of A Corp. deemed paid by M Corp. ($360 × $840/$840)	360
Foreign taxes included in gross income of M Corp. under sec. 78 as a dividend	360

(b) Amount of foreign taxes of A Corp. deemed paid by M Corp. on portion of the dividend attributable to B Corp.'s accumulated profits for 1975.

B Corp. (second-tier corporation):	
Gains, profits, and income for calendar year 1975	$1,000
Foreign income taxes imposed on or with respect to gains, profits, and income	400
Accumulated profits (under sec. 902(c)(1)(B) as in effect prior to amendment by the Tax Reform Act of 1976)	600
Foreign income taxes paid by B Corp. on or with respect to its accumulated profits ($400 × $600/$1,000)	240
Dividend to A Corp. in 1976	300
Foreign taxes of B Corp. for 1975 deemed paid by A Corp. (under sec. 902(b)(1)(B) as in effect prior to amendment by the Tax Reform Act of 1976) ($240 × $300/$600)	120
A Corp. (first-tier corporation):	
Gains, profits, and income for 1976 attributable to dividend from B Corp.'s accumulated profits for 1975	300
Foreign income taxes imposed on or with respect to such gains, profits, and income	90
Accumulated profits (under sec. 902(c)(1)(B) as in effect prior to amendment by the Tax Reform Act of 1976)	210
Foreign taxes paid by A Corp. on or with respect to such accumulated profits ($90 × $210/$300)	63
Foreign income taxes paid and deemed to be paid by A Corp. for 1976 on or with respect to such accumulated profits ($120 + $63)	183
Dividend paid to M Corp. attributable to dividend from B Corp. out of accumulated profits for 1975)	210
Foreign taxes of A Corp. deemed paid by M Corp. (under sec. 902(a)(2) as in effect prior to amendment by the Tax Reform Act of (1976) ($183 × $210/$210)	183
Amount included in gross income of M Corp. under sec. 78	0

T.D. 6805, 3/8/65, amend T.D. 7283, 8/2/73, T.D. 7481, 4/15/77, T.D. 7646, 10/17/79, T.D. 8708, 1/6/97.

§ 1.903-1 Taxes in lieu of income taxes.

(a) In general. Section 903 provides that the term "income, war profits, and excess profits taxes", shall include a tax paid in lieu of a tax on income, war profits, or excess profits (" income tax") otherwise generally imposed by any foreign country. For purposes of this section and §§ 1.901-2 and 1.901-2A, such a tax is referred to as a "tax in lieu of an income tax"; and the terms "paid" and "foreign country" are defined in § 1.901-2(g). A foreign levy (within the meaning of § 1.901-2(g)(3)) is a tax in lieu of an income tax if and only if—

(1) It is a tax within the meaning of § 1.901-2(a)(2): and

(2) It meets the substitution requirement as set forth in paragraph (b) of this section.

The foreign country's purpose in imposing the foreign tax (e.g., whether it imposes the foreign tax because of administrative difficulty in determining the base of the income tax otherwise generally imposed) is immaterial. It is also immaterial whether the base of the foreign tax bears any relation to realized net income. The base of the tax may, for example, be gross income, gross receipts or sales, or the number of units produced or exported. Determinations of the amount of a tax in lieu of an income tax that is paid by a person and determinations of the person by whom such tax is paid are made under § 1.901-2(e) and (f), respectively, substituting the phrase "tax in lieu of an income tax" for the phrase "income tax" wherever the latter appears in those sections. Section 1.901-2A contains additional rules applicable to dual capacity taxpayers (as defined in § 1.901-2(a)(2)(ii)(A)). The rules of this section are applied independently to each separate levy (within the meaning of §§ 1.901-2(d) and 1.901-2A(a)) imposed by the foreign country. Except as otherwise provided in paragraph (b)(2) of this section, a foreign tax either is or is not a tax in lieu of an income tax in its entirety for all persons subject to the tax.

(b) Substitution. *(1) In general.* A foreign tax satisfies the substitution requirement if the tax in fact operates as a tax imposed in substitution for, and not in addition to, an income tax or a series of income taxes otherwise generally imposed. However, not all income derived by persons subject to the foreign tax need be exempt from the income tax. If, for example, a taxpayer is subject to a generally imposed income tax except that, pursuant to an agreement with the foreign country, the taxpayer's income from insurance is subject to a gross receipts tax and not to the income tax, then the gross receipts tax meets the substitution requirement notwithstanding the fact that the taxpayer's income from other activities, such as the operation of a hotel, is subject to the generally imposed income tax. A comparison between the tax burden of this insurance gross receipts tax and the tax burden that would have obtained under the generally imposed income tax is irrelevant to this determination.

(2) Soak-up taxes. A foreign tax satisfies the substitution requirement only to the extent that liability for the foreign tax is not dependent (by its terms or otherwise) on the availability of a credit for the foreign tax against income tax liability to another country. If, without regard to this paragraph (b)(2), a foreign tax satisfies the requirement of paragraph (b)(1) of this section (including for this purpose any foreign tax that both satisfies such requirement an also is and income tax within the meaning of § 1.901-2(a)(1)), liability for the foreign tax is dependent on the availability of a credit for the foreign tax against income tax liability to another country only to the extent of the lesser of—

(i) The amount of foreign tax that would not be imposed on the taxpayer but for the availability of such a credit to the taxpayer (within the meaning of § 1.901-2(c)), or

(ii) The amount, if any, by which the foreign tax paid by the taxpayer exceeds the amount of foreign income tax that would have been paid by the taxpayer if it had instead been subject to the generally imposed income tax of the foreign country.

(3) Examples. The provisions of this paragraph (b) may be illustrated by the following examples:

Example (1). Country X has a tax on realized net income that is generally imposed except that nonresidents are not subject to that tax. Nonresidents are subject to a gross income tax on income from country X that is not attributable to a trade or business carried on in country X. The gross income tax Imposed on nonresidents satisfies the substitution requirement set forth in this paragraph (b). See also examples (1) and (2) of § 1.901-2(b)(4)(iv).

Example (2). The facts are the same as in example (1), with the additional fact that payors located in country X are required by country X law to withhold the gross income tax from payments they make to nonresidents, and to remit such withheld tax to the government of country X. The result is the same as in example (1).

Example (3). The facts are the same as in example (2), with the additional fact that the gross income tax on nonresidents applies to payments for technical services performed by them outside of country X. The result is the same as in example (2).

Example (4). Country X has a tax that is generally imposed on the realized net income of nonresident corporations that is attributable to trade or business carried on in country X. The tax applies to all nonresident corporations that engage in business in country X except for such corporations that engage in contracting activities, each of which is instead subject to two different taxes. The taxes applicable to nonresident corporations that engage in contracting activities satisfy the substitution requirement set forth in this paragraph (b).

Example (5). Country X imposes both an excise tax and an income tax. The excise tax, which is payable independently of the income tax, is allowed as a credit against the income tax. For 1984 A has a tentative income tax liability of 100u (units of country X currency) but is allowed a credit for 30u of excise tax that it has paid. Pursuant to paragraph (e)(4)(i) of § 1.901-2, the amount of excise tax A has paid to country X is 30u and the amount of income tax A has paid to country X is 70u. The excise tax paid by A does not satisfy the substitution requirement set forth in this paragraph (b) because the excise tax is imposed on A in addition to, and not insubstitution for, the generally imposed income tax.

Example (6). Pursuant to a contract with country X, A, a domestic corporation engaged in manufacturing activities in country X, must pay tax to country X equal to the greater of (i) 5u (units of country X currency) per item produced, or (ii) the maximum amount creditable by A against its U.S. income tax liability for that year with respect to income from its country X operation. Also pursuant to the contract, A is exempted from otherwise generally imposed income tax. A produces 16 items in 1984 and the maximum amount creditable by A against its U.S. income tax liability for 1984 is 125u. If A had been subject to country X's otherwise generally imposed income tax it would have paid a tax of 150u. Pursuant to paragraph (b)(2) of this section, the amount of tax paid by A that is dependent on the availability of a credit against income tax of another country is 0 (lesser of (i) 45u, the amount that would not be imposed but for the availability of a credit (125u– 80u) or (ii) 0, the amount by which the contractual tax (125u) exceeds the generally imposed income tax (150u)).

Example (7). The facts are the same as in example (6) except that, of the 150u A would have paid if it had been subject to the otherwise generally imposed income tax, 6 is dependent on the availability of a credit against income tax of another country. The amount of tax actually paid by A (i.e., 125u) that is dependent on the availability of a credit against income tax of another country is 35u (lesser of (i) 45u, computed as in example (6), or (ii) 35u, the amount by which the contractual tax (125u) exceeds the amount A would have paid as income tax if had been subject to the otherwise generally imposed income tax (90u, i.e., 150u–60u).

(c) Effective date. The effective date of this section is as provided in § 1.901-2(h).

T.D. 7918, 10/6/83.

§ 1.904-0 Outline of regulation provisions.

Caution: The Treasury has not yet amended Reg § 1.904-0 to reflect changes made by P.L. 100-647.

This section lists the headings for §§ 1.904-1 through 1.904-7.

§ 1.904-1 Limitation on credit for foreign taxes.

(a) Per-county limitation.

(1) General.

(2) Illustration of principles.

(b) Overall limitation.

(1) General.

(2) Illustration of principles.

(c) Special computation of taxable income.

(d) Election of overall limitation.

(1) In general.

(i) Manner of making election.

(ii) Revocation for first taxable year beginning after December 31, 1969.

(2) Method of making the initial election.

(3) Method of revoking an election and making a new election.

(e) Joint return.

(1) General.

(2) Electing the overall limitation.

§ 1.904-2 Carryback and carryover of unused foreign tax.

(a) Credit for foreign tax carryback or carryover.

(b) Years to which carried.

(1) General.

(2) Definitions.

(3) Taxable years beginning before January 1, 1958.

(c) Tax deemed paid or accrued.

(1) Unused foreign tax for per-country limitation year.

(2) Unused foreign tax for overall limitation year.

(3) Unused foreign tax with respect to foreign mineral income.

(d) Determination of excess limitation for certain years.

(e) Periods of less than 12 months.

(f) Statement with tax return.

(g) Illustration of carrybacks and carryovers.

(h) Transition rules for carryovers and carrybacks of pre-2003 and post-2002 unused foreign tax paid or accrued with respect to dividends from noncontrolled section 902 corporations.

(1) Carryover of unused foreign tax.

(2) Carryback of unused foreign tax.

(i) [Reserved].

§ 1.904-3 Carryback and carryover of unused foreign tax by husband and wife.

(a) In general.

(b) Joint unused foreign tax and joint excess limitation.

(c) Continuous use of joint return.

(d) From separate to joint return.

(e) Amounts carried from or through a joint return year to or through a separate return year.

(f) Allocation of unused foreign tax and excess limitation.

(1) Limitation.

(i) Per-country limitation.

(ii) Overall limitation.

(2) Unused foreign tax.

(i) Per-country limitation.

(ii) Overall limitation.

(3) Excess limitation.

(i) Per-country limitation taxpayer.

(ii) Overall limitation.

(4) Excess limitation to be applied.

(5) Reduction of excess limitation.

(6) Spouses using different limitations.

(g) Illustrations.

§ 1.904-4 Separate application of section 904 with respect to certain categories of income.

(a) [Reserved].

(b) [Reserved].

(c) High-taxed income.

(1) In general.

(2) Grouping of items of income in order to determine whether passive income is high-taxed income.

(i) Effective dates.

(A) In general.

(B) Application to prior periods.

(ii) Grouping rules.

(A) Initial allocation and apportionment of deductions and taxes.

(B) Reallocation of loss groups.

(3) Amounts received or accrued by United States persons.

(4) Dividends and inclusions from controlled foreign corporations, dividends from noncontrolled section 902 corporations, and income of foreign QBUs.

(5) Special rules.

(i) Certain rents and royalties.

(ii) Treatment of partnership income.

(iii) Currency gain or loss.

(iv) Coordination with section 954(b)(4).

(6) Application of this paragraph to additional taxes paid or deemed paid in the year of receipt of previously taxed income.

(i) Determination made in year of inclusion.

(ii) Exception.

(iii) Allocation of foreign taxes imposed on distributions of previously taxed income.

(iv) Increase in taxes paid by successors.

(A) General rule.

(B) Exception for U.S. shareholders not entitled to look-through.

(7) Application of this paragraph to certain reductions of tax on distributions of income.

(i) In general.

(ii) Allocation of reductions of foreign tax.

(iii) Interaction with section 954(b)(4).

(8) Examples.

(d) [Reserved].

(e) Financial services income.

(1) In general.

(2) Active financing income.

(i) Income included.

(3) Financial services entities.

(i) In general.

(ii) Special rule for affiliated groups.

(iii) Treatment of partnerships and other pass-through entities.

(A) Rule.

(B) Examples.

(iv) Examples.

(4) Definition of incidental income.

(i) In general.

(A) Rule.

(B) Examples.

(2) Rules for noncontrolled section 902 corporations.

(3) [Reserved].

§ 1.904-6 Allocation and apportionment of taxes.

(a) Allocation and apportionment of taxes to a separate category or categories of income.

(1) Allocation of taxes to a separate category or categories of income.

(i) Taxes related to a separate category of income.

(ii) Apportionment of taxes related to more than one separate category.

(iii) Apportionment of taxes for purposes of applying the high tax income test.

(iv) Special rule for base and timing differences.

(2) Reserved.

(b) Application of paragraph (a) to sections 902 and 960.

(1) Determination of foreign taxes deemed paid.

(2) Distributions received from foreign corporations that are excluded from gross income under section 959(b).

(3) Application of section 78.

(4) Increase in limitation.

(c) Examples.

§ 1.904-7 Transition rules.

(a) Characterization of distributions and section 951(a)(1)(A)(ii) and (iii) and (B) inclusions of earnings of a controlled foreign corporation accumulated in taxable years beginning before January 1, 1987, during taxable years of both the payor controlled foreign corporation and the recipient which begin after December 31, 1986.

(1) Distributions and section 951(a)(1)(A)(ii) and (iii) and (B) inclusions.

(2) Limitation on establishing the character of earnings and profits.

(b) Application of look-through rules to distributions (including deemed distributions) and payments by an entity to a recipient when one's taxable year begins before January 1, 1987 and the other's taxable year begins after December 31, 1986.

(1) In general.

(2) Payor of interest, rents, or royalties is subject to the Act and recipient is not subject to the Act.

(3) Recipient of interest, rents, or royalties is subject to the Act and payor is not subject to the Act.

(4) Recipient of dividends and subpart F inclusions is subject to the Act and payor is not subject to the Act.

(5) Examples.

(c) Installment sales.

(d) Special effective date for high withholding tax interest earned by persons with respect to qualified loans described in section 1201(e)(2) of the Act.

(e) Treatment of certain recapture income.

(f) Treatment of non-look-through pools of a noncontrolled section 902 corporation or a controlled foreign corporation in post-2002 taxable years.

(g) [Reserved].

T.D. 8214, 7/15/88, amend T.D. 8412, 5/13/92, T.D. 8627, 11/6/95, T.D. 8805, 1/8/99, T.D. 8916, 12/27/2000, T.D. 9141, 7/19/2004, T.D. 9260, 4/24/2006, T.D. 9368, 12/20/2007, T.D. 9371, 12/20/2007.

PAR. 2. Section 1.904-0 is amended by revising the entries for § 1.904(f)-1(a), (d)(2), (d)(3), and (d)(4), and for § 1.904(f)-2(c) and (c)(1), and adding entries for Sec. § 1.904(f)-7 and 1.904(f)-8 to read as follows:

Proposed § 1.904-0 (12/21/2007) Outline of regulation provisions for section 904. [*For Preamble, see ¶ 152,941*]

* * * * *

§ 1.904(f)-1 Overall foreign loss and the overall foreign loss account.

* * * * *

(a)(1) and (a)(2) [The text of these entries is the same as the text of the entries for § 1.904(f)-1T(a)(1) and (a)(2) in § 1.904(f)-0T published elsewhere in this issue of the Federal Register.] [*See T.D. 9371, 12/21/2007, 72 Fed. Reg. 245.*]

* * * * *

(d)(2) (d)(3), and (d)(4) [The text of these entries is the same as the text of the entries for § 1.904(f)-1T(d)(2), (d)(3), and (d)(4) in § 1.904(f)-0T published elsewhere in this issue of the Federal Register.] [*See T.D. 9371, 12/21/2007, 72 Fed. Reg. 245.*]

* * * * *

§ 1.904(f)-2 Recapture of overall foreign losses.

* * * * *

(c) and (c)(1) [The text of these entries is the same as the text of the entries for § 1.904(f)-2T(c) and (c)(1) in § 1.904(f)-0T published elsewhere in this issue of the Federal Register.] [*See T.D. 9371, 12/21/2007, 72 Fed. Reg. 245.*]

* * * * *

§ 1.904(f)-7 Separate limitation loss and the separate limitation loss account. [The text of the entries for this section is the same as the text of the entries for § 1.904(f)-7T(a) through (f) in § 1.904(f)-0T published elsewhere in this issue of the Federal Register.] [*See T.D. 9371, 12/21/2007, 72 Fed. Reg. 245.*]

§ 1.904(f)-8 Recapture of separate limitation loss accounts. [The text of the entries for this section is the same as the text of the entries for § 1.904(f)-8T(a) through (c) in § 1.904(f)-0T published elsewhere in this issue of the Federal Register.] [*See T.D. 9371, 12/21/2007, 72 Fed. Reg. 245.*]

§ 1.904-1 Limitation on credit for foreign taxes.

Caution: The Treasury has not yet amended Reg § 1.904-1 to reflect changes made by P.L. 108-311, P.L. 107-147, P.L. 101-239, P.L. 100-647, P.L. 99-514, P.L. 98-369, P.L. 98-21, P.L. 97-448, P.L. 97-248, P.L. 96-222, P.L. 95-600, P.L. 94-455.

(a) Per-country limitation. *(1) General.* In the case of any taxpayer who does not elect the overall limitation under section 904(a)(2), the amount allowable as a credit for income or profits taxes paid or accrued to a foreign country or a possession of the United States is subject to the per-country limitation prescribed in section 904(a)(1). Such limitation provides that the credit for such taxes paid or accrued (including those deemed to have been paid or accrued other than by reason of section 904(d) to each foreign country or possession of the United States shall not exceed that proportion of the tax against which credit is taken which the taxpayer's taxable income from sources within such country or possession (but not in excess of the taxpayer's entire taxable income) bears to his entire taxable income for the same taxable year. For special rules regarding the application of the per-country limitation when the taxpayer has derived section 904(f) interest or section 904(f) dividends, see § 1.904-4 or § 1.904-5.

(2) Illustration of principles. The operation of the per-country limitation under section 904(a)(1) on the credit for foreign taxes paid or accrued may be illustrated by the following examples:

Example (1). The credit for foreign taxes allowable for 1954 in the case of X, an unmarried citizen of the United States who in 1954 received the income shown below and had three exemptions under section 151, is $14,904, computed as follows:

Taxable income (computed without deductions for personal exemptions) from sources within the United States	$50,000
Taxable income (computed without deductions for personal exemptions) from sources within Great Britain	25,000
Total taxable income	75,000
United States income tax (based on taxable income computed with the deductions for personal exemptions)	44,712
British income and profits taxes	18,000
Per-country limitation $\left(\frac{25,000}{75,000} \text{ of } \$44,712\right)$	14,904
Credit for British income and profits taxes (total British income and profits taxes, reduced in accordance with the per-country limitation)	14,904

Example (2). Assume the same facts as in example (1), except that the sources of X's income and taxes paid are as shown below. The credit for foreign taxes allowable to X is $13,442.40, computed as follows:

Taxable income (computed without deductions for personal exemptions) from sources within the United States	$ 50,000
Taxable income (computed without deductions for personal exemptions) from sources within Great Britain	$ 15,000
Taxable income (computed without deductions for personal exemptions) from sources within Canada	10,000
Total taxable income	75,000
United States income tax (based on taxable income computed with the deductions for personal exemptions)	44,712
British income and profits taxes	10,800
Per-country limitation on British income and profits taxes $\left(\frac{15,000}{75,000} \text{ of } \$44,712\right)$	8,942.40
Credit for British income and profits taxes as limited by per-country limitation	8,942.40
Canadian income and profits taxes	4,500.00
Per-country limitation on Canadian income and profits taxes $\left(\frac{10,000}{75,000} \text{ of } \$44,712\right)$	5,961.60
Credit for Canadian income and profits taxes (total Canadian income and profits taxes, since such amount does not exceed the per-country limitation)	4,500.00
Total amount of credit allowable (sum of credits—$8,942.40 plus $4,500)	13,442.40

Example (3). A domestic corporation realized taxable income in 1954 in the amount of $100,000, consisting of $50,000 from United States sources and dividends of $50,000 from a Brazilian corporation, more than 10 percent of whose voting stock it owned. The Brazilian corporation paid income and profits taxes to Brazil on its income and in addition paid a dividend tax for the account of its shareholders on income distributed to them, the latter tax being withheld and paid at the source. The domestic corporation's credit for foreign taxes is $23,250, computed as follows:

Taxable income from sources within the United States		$ 50,000
Taxable income from sources within Brazil		50,000
Total taxable income		100,000
United States income tax		46,500
Dividend tax paid at source to Brazil		19,000
Income and profits taxes deemed under section 902 to have been paid to Brazil, computed as follows:		
Dividends received from Brazilian corporation during 1954	$ 50,000	
Income of Brazilian corporation during 1954	200,000	
Income and profits taxes paid to Brazil on $200,000	30,000	
Accumulated profits ($200,000 minus $30,000)	170,000	
Brazilian taxes applicable to accumulated profits distributed: $\frac{50,000}{170,000} \text{ of } \frac{170,000}{200,000} \text{ of } \$30,000$		7,500
Total income and profits taxes paid and deemed to have been paid to Brazil		26,500
Per-country limitation $\left(\frac{50,000}{100,000} \text{ of } \$46,500\right)$		23,250
Credit for Brazilian income and profits taxes as limited by per-country limitation		23,250

(b) Overall limitation. *(1) General.* In the case of any taxpayer who elects the overall limitation provided by section 904(a)(2), the total credit for taxes paid or accrued (including those deemed to have been paid or accrued other than by reason of section 904(d)) shall not exceed that proportion of the tax against which such credit is taken which the taxpayer's taxable income from sources without the United States (but not in excess of the taxpayer's entire taxable income) bears to his entire taxable income for the same taxable year. For special rules regarding the application of the overall limitation when the taxpayer has derived section 904(f) interest or section 904(f) dividends, see § 1.904-4 or § 1.904-5.

(2) Illustration of principles. The operation of the overall limitation under section 904(a)(2) may be illustrated by the following example.

Example. Corporation X, a domestic corporation, for its taxable year beginning January 1, 1961, elects the overall limitation provided by section 904(a)(2). For taxable year

	Per country	Overall	Overall	Overall	Overall	Per country
Taxable years	1961	1962	1963	1964	1965	1966
Limitations:						
Country X	$175					$290
Country Y	125					95
Overall		$250	$800	$300	$400	
Taxes actually accrued:						
Country X	325					200
Country Y	85					100
Aggregate		350	380	425	450	
Unused foreign tax to be carried back or over from year of origin:						
Country X	150					
Country Y						5
Aggregate		100		125	50	
Excess limitations:						
Country X						90
Country Y	40					
Overall			420			
Unused foreign tax absorbed as taxes deemed accrued under section 904(d) and carried from—						
1961 (Country X)						(90)
1962 (Overall)			(100)			
1964 (Overall)			(125)			
1965 (Overall)			(50)			

(ii) Since the per-country limitation is applicable for 1961 and 1966 only, any unused foreign tax with respect to such years may not be deemed accrued in 1962, 1963, 1964, or 1965, years for which the overall limitation applies. However, the excess limitation for 1966 with respect to country X ($90) is available to absorb a part of the unused foreign tax for 1961 with respect to country X. The difference with respect to country X between the unused foreign tax for 1961 ($150) and the amount absorbed as taxes deemed accrued ($90) in 1966, or $60, may not be carried beyond 1966 since the unused foreign tax may be carried forward only 5 taxable years. There is no excess limitation with respect to country Y for 1961 in respect of the unused foreign tax of country Y for 1966, since the unused foreign tax may be carried back only 2 taxable years.

(iii) Since the overall limitation is applicable for 1962, 1963, 1964, and 1965, any unused foreign tax with respect to such years may not be absorbed as taxes deemed accrued in 1961 or 1966, years for which the per-country limitation applies. However, the excess limitation for 1963 ($420) computed on the basis of the overall limitation is available to absorb the unused foreign tax for 1962 ($100), the unused foreign tax for 1964 ($125), and the unused foreign tax for 1965 ($50), leaving an excess limitation above such absorption of $145 ($420−$275).

(h) Transition rules for carryovers and carrybacks of pre-2003 and post-2002 unused foreign tax paid or accrued with respect to dividends from noncontrolled section 902 corporations. [Reserved]. For further guidance, see § 1.904-2T(h).

(i) [Reserved.] For further guidance, see § 1.904-2T(i).

T.D. 6789, 12/30/64, amend T.D. 7292, 11/30/73, T.D. 7490, 6/10/77, T.D. 7961, 6/20/84, T.D. 9260, 4/24/2006, T.D. 9368, 12/20/2007.

PAR. 2. Section 1.904-2(i) is added to read as follows:

Proposed § 1.904-2 Carryback and carryover of unused foreign tax. [*For Preamble, see ¶ 152,939*]

* * * * *

(i) [The text of proposed § 1.904-2(i) is the same as the text of § 1.904-2T(i)(1) through (3) published elsewhere in this issue of the Federal Register.] [*See T.D. 9368, 12/21/2007, 72 Fed. Reg. 245.*]

PAR. 5. In § 1.904-2, paragraph (a) is revised and paragraph (h) is added to read as follows:

Proposed § 1.904-2 Carryback and carryover of unused foreign tax. [*For Preamble, see ¶ 152,753*]

[The text of the proposed amendment to § 1.904-2(a) and the text of proposed § 1.904-2(h) are the same as the text of § 1.904-2T(a) and (h) published elsewhere in this issue of the Federal Register.] [*See T.D. 9260, 04/24/2006, 71 Fed. Reg. 79.*]

§ 1.904-2T Carryback and carryover of unused foreign tax (temporary).

• ***Caution:*** Under Code Sec. 7805, temporary regulations expire within three years of the date of issuance. This temporary regulation was issued on 4/24/2006.

(a) Credit for foreign tax carryback or carryover (temporary). A taxpayer who chooses to claim a credit under section 901 for a taxable year is allowed a credit under that section not only for taxes otherwise allowable as a credit but also for taxes deemed paid or accrued in that year as a result of a carryback or carryover of an unused foreign tax under section 904(c). However, the taxes so deemed paid or accrued shall not be allowed as a deduction under section 164(a). Paragraphs (b) through (g) of § 1.904-2 and § 1.904-

3, providing rules for the computation of carryovers and carrybacks, do not reflect a number of intervening statutory amendments, including the redesignation of section 904(d) as section 904(c) for taxable years beginning after 1975, amendments to sections 904(d) and (f) regarding the application of separate limitations in taxable years beginning after 1986, the limitation of the carryback period to one year for unused foreign taxes arising in taxable years beginning after October 22, 2004, and the extension of the carryover period to ten years for unused foreign taxes that may be carried to any taxable year ending after October 22, 2004. However, the principles of paragraphs (b) through (g) of § 1.904-2 and § 1.904-3 shall apply in determining carrybacks and carryovers of unused foreign taxes, modified so as to take into account the effect of statutory amendments. For transition rules relating to the carryover and carryback of unused foreign tax paid with respect to dividends from noncontrolled section 902 corporations, see paragraph (h) of this section. For special rules regarding these computations in case of taxes paid, accrued, or deemed paid with respect to foreign oil and gas extraction income or foreign oil related income, see section 907(f) and the regulations under that section.

(b) through (g) [Reserved]. For further guidance, see § 1.904-2(b) through (g).

(h) Transition rules for carryovers and carrybacks of pre-2003 and post-2002 unused foreign tax paid or accrued with respect to dividends from noncontrolled section 902 corporations (temporary). *(1) Carryover of unused foreign tax.* Except as provided in §§ 1.904-7T(f)(9)(iv) and 1.904(f)-12T(g)(3), the rules of this paragraph (h)(1) apply to reallocate to the taxpayer's other separate categories any unused foreign taxes (as defined in § 1.904-2(b)(2)) that were paid or accrued or deemed paid under section 902 with respect to a dividend from a noncontrolled section 902 corporation paid in a taxable year of the noncontrolled section 902 corporation beginning before January 1, 2003, which taxes were subject to a separate limitation for dividends from that noncontrolled section 902 corporation. To the extent any such unused foreign taxes are carried forward to a taxable year of a domestic shareholder beginning on or after the first day of the noncontrolled section 902 corporation's first taxable year beginning after December 31, 2002, such taxes shall be allocated among the taxpayer's separate categories in the same proportions as the related dividend would have been assigned had such dividend been eligible for look-through treatment when paid. Accordingly, the taxes shall be allocated in the same percentages as the reconstructed earnings in the noncontrolled section 902 corporation's non-look-through pool and pre-1987 accumulated profits that were accumulated in taxable years beginning before January 1, 2003, out of which the dividend was paid, in accordance with the rules of § 1.904-7T(f), or, if the taxpayer elects the safe harbor of § 1.904-7T(f)(4)(ii), in the same percentages as the taxpayer properly characterizes the stock of the noncontrolled section 902 corporation for purposes of apportioning its interest expense in its first taxable year ending after the first day of the noncontrolled section 902 corporation's first taxable year beginning after December 31, 2002. See § 1.904-7T(f)(2) and (f)(4). In the case of unused foreign taxes allocable to dividends from a noncontrolled section 902 corporation with respect to which the taxpayer was no longer a domestic shareholder (as defined in § 1.902-1(a)) as of the first day of such taxable year, such taxes shall be allocated among the taxpayer's separate categories in the same percentages as the earnings in the noncontrolled section 902 corporation's non-look-through pool or pre-1987 accumulated profits would have been assigned had they been distributed in the last taxable year in which the taxpayer was a domestic shareholder in such corporation. The unused foreign taxes that are carried forward shall be treated as allocable to general limitation income to the extent that such taxes would otherwise have been allocable to passive income, either on a look-through basis or as a result of inadequate substantiation under the rules of § 1.904-7T(f)(4).

(2) Carryback of unused foreign tax. The rules of this paragraph (h)(2) apply to any unused foreign taxes that were paid or accrued or deemed paid under section 902 with respect to a dividend from a noncontrolled section 902 corporation paid in a taxable year of a noncontrolled section 902 corporation beginning after December 31, 2002, which dividends were eligible for look-through treatment. To the extent any such unused foreign taxes are carried back to a prior taxable year of a domestic shareholder, a credit for such taxes shall be allowed only to the extent of the excess limitation in the same separate category or categories to which the related look-through dividend was assigned and not in any separate category for dividends from noncontrolled section 902 corporations.

(i) Transition rules for carryovers and carrybacks of pre-2007 and post-2006 unused foreign tax. *(1) Carryover of unused foreign tax.* (i) General rule. For purposes of this paragraph (i), the terms post-2006 separate category and pre-2007 separate category have the meanings set forth in § 1.904-7T(g)(1)(ii) and (iii). The rules of this paragraph (i)(1) apply to reallocate to the taxpayer's post-2006 separate categories for general category income and passive category income any unused foreign taxes (as defined in § 1.904-2(b)(2)) that were paid or accrued or deemed paid under section 902 with respect to income in a pre-2007 separate category (other than a category described in § 1.904-4(m)). To the extent any such unused foreign taxes are carried forward to a taxable year beginning after December 31, 2006, such taxes shall be allocated to the taxpayer's post-2006 separate categories to which those taxes would have been allocated if the taxes were paid or accrued in a taxable year beginning after December 31, 2006. For example, any foreign taxes paid or accrued or deemed paid with respect to financial services income in a taxable year beginning before January 1, 2007, that are carried forward to a taxable year beginning after December 31, 2006, will be allocated to the general category because the financial services income to which those taxes relate would have been allocated to the general category if it had been earned in a taxable year beginning after December 31, 2006.

(ii) Safe harbor. In lieu of applying the rules of paragraph (i)(1)(i) of this section, a taxpayer may allocate all unused foreign taxes in the pre-2007 separate category for passive income to the post-2006 separate category for passive category income, and allocate all other unused foreign taxes described in paragraph (i)(1)(i) of this section to the post-2006 separate category for general category income.

(2) Carryback of unused foreign tax. (i) General rule. The rules of this paragraph (i)(2) apply to any unused foreign taxes that were paid or accrued or deemed paid under section 902 with respect to income in a post-2006 separate category (other than a category described in § 1.904-4(m)). To the extent any such unused foreign taxes are carried back to a taxable year beginning before January 1, 2007, a credit for such taxes shall be allowed only to the extent of the excess limitation in the pre-2007 separate category, or categories, to which the taxes would have been allocated if the taxes were paid or accrued in a taxable year beginning before January 1, 2007. For example, any foreign taxes paid or accrued or

deemed paid with respect to income in the general category in a taxable year beginning after December 31, 2006, that are carried back to a taxable year beginning before January 1, 2007, will be allocated to the same separate categories to which the income would have been allocated if it had been earned in a taxable year beginning before January 1, 2007.

(ii) Safe harbor. In lieu of applying the rules of paragraph (i)(2)(i) of this section, a taxpayer may allocate all unused foreign taxes in the post-2006 separate category for passive category income to the pre-2007 separate category for passive income, and may allocate all other unused foreign taxes described in paragraph (i)(2)(i) of this section to the pre-2007 separate category for general limitation income.

(3) Effective/applicability date. This paragraph (i) applies to taxable years of United States taxpayers beginning after December 31, 2006 and ending on or after December 21, 2007.

(4) Expiration date. The applicability of this paragraph (i) expires on December 20, 2010.

T.D. 9260, 4/24/2006, amend T.D. 9368, 12/20/2007.

---

§ 1.904-3 Carryback and carryover of unused foreign tax by husband and wife.

Caution: The Treasury has not yet amended Reg § 1.904-3 to reflect changes made by P.L. 101-239, P.L. 100-647, P.L. 99-514, P.L. 98-369.

(a) In General. This section provides rules, in addition to those prescribed in § 1.904-2, for the carryback and carryover of the unused foreign tax paid or accrued to a foreign country or possession by a husband and wife making a joint return for one or more of the taxable years involved in the computation of the carryback or carryover.

(b) Joint unused foreign tax and joint excess limitation. In the case of a husband and wife the joint unused foreign tax or the joint excess limitation for a taxable year for which a joint return is made shall be computed on the basis of the combined income, deductions, taxes, and credit of both spouses as if the combined income, deductions, taxes, and credit were those of one individual.

(c) Continuous use of joint return. If a husband and wife make a joint return for the current taxable year, and also make joint returns for each of the other taxable years involved in the computation of the carryback or carryover of the unused foreign tax to the current taxable year, the joint carryback or the joint carryover to the current taxable year shall be computed on the basis of the joint unused foreign tax and the joint excess limitations.

(d) From separate to joint return. If a husband and wife make a joint return for the current taxable year, but make separate returns for all of the other taxable years involved in the computation of the carryback or carryover of the unused foreign tax to the current taxable year, the separate carrybacks or separate carryovers shall be a joint carryback or a joint carryover to the current taxable year. If for such current year the per-country limitation applies, then only the unused foreign tax for a taxable year of a spouse for which the per-country limitation applied to such spouse may constitute a carryover or carryback to the current taxable year. If for such current taxable year the overall limitation applies, then only the unused foreign tax for a taxable year of a spouse for which the overall limitation applied to such spouse may constitute a carryover or carryback to the current taxable year.

(e) Amounts carried from or through a joint return year to or through a separate return year. It is necessary to allocate to each spouse his share of an unused foreign tax or excess limitation for any taxable year for which the spouses filed a joint return if—

(1) The husband and wife file separate returns for the current taxable year and an unused foreign tax is carried thereto from a taxable year for which they filed a joint return;

(2) The husband and wife file separate returns for the current taxable year and an unused foreign tax is carried to such taxable year from a year for which they filed separate returns but is first carried through a year for which they filed a joint return; or

(3) The husband and wife file a joint return for the current taxable year and an unused foreign tax is carried from a taxable year for which they filed joint returns but is first carried through a year for which they filed separate returns.

In such cases, the separate carryback or carryover of each spouse to the current taxable year shall be computed in the manner described in § 1.904-2 but with the modifications set forth in paragraph (f) of this section. Where applicable, appropriate adjustments shall be made to take into account the fact that, for any taxable year involved in the computation of the carryback or the carryover, either spouse has interest income described in section 904(f)(2) with respect to which the provisions of section 904(f) and § 1.904-4 apply, or dividends described in section 904(f)(1)(B) with respect to which the provisions of section 904(f) and § 1.904-5 apply, or foreign oil related income described in section 907(c) with respect to which the separate limitation in section 907(b) applies.

(f) Allocation of unused foreign tax and excess limitation. *(1) Limitation.* (i) Per-country limitation. The per-country limitation of a particular spouse with respect to a foreign country or United States possession for a taxable year for which a joint return is made shall be the portion of the limitation on the joint return which bears the same ratio to such limitation as such spouse's taxable income (with gross income and deductions taken into account to the same extent as taken into account on the joint return) from sources within such country or possession (but not in excess of the joint taxable income from sources within such country or possession) bears to the joint taxable income from such sources.

(ii) Overall limitation. The overall limitation of a particular spouse for a taxable year for which a joint return is made shall be the portion of the limitation on the joint return which bears the same ratio to such limitation as such spouse's taxable income (with gross income and deductions taken into account to the same extent as taken into account on the joint return) from sources without the United States (but not in excess of the joint taxable income from such sources) bears to the joint taxable income from such sources.

(2) Unused foreign tax. (i) Per-country limitation. The unused foreign tax of a particular spouse with respect to a foreign country or United States possession for a taxable year for which a joint return is made shall be the excess of his tax paid or accrued to such country or possession over his limitation determined under subparagraph (1)(i) of this paragraph.

(ii) Overall limitation. The unused foreign tax of a particular spouse for a taxable year to which the overall limitation applies and for which a joint return is made shall be the excess of his tax paid or accrued to foreign countries and

United States possessions over his limitation determined under subparagraph (1)(ii) of this paragraph.

(3) Excess limitation. (i) Per-country limitation taxpayer. A spouse's excess limitation with respect to a foreign country or possession for a taxable year for which a joint return is made shall be the excess of his limitation determined under subparagraph (1)(i) of this paragraph over his taxes paid or accrued to such country or possession for such taxable year.

(ii) Overall limitation. A spouse's excess limitation for a taxable year to which the overall limitation applies and for which a joint return is made shall be the excess of his limitation determined under subparagraph (1)(ii) of this paragraph over his taxes paid or accrued to foreign countries and United States possessions for such taxable year.

(4) Excess limitation to be applied. The excess limitation of the particular spouse for any taxable year which is applied against the unused foreign tax of that spouse for another taxable year in order to determine the amount of the unused foreign tax which shall be carried back or over to a third taxable year shall be, in a case in which the excess limitation is determined on a joint return, the sum of the following amounts:

(i) Such spouse's excess limitation determined under subparagraph (3) of this paragraph reduced as provided in subparagraph (5)(i) of this paragraph, and

(ii) The excess limitation of the other spouse determined under subparagraph (3) of this paragraph for that taxable year reduced as provided in subparagraph (5)(i) and (ii) of this paragraph.

(5) Reduction of excess limitation. (i) The part of the excess limitation which is attributable to each spouse for the taxable year, as determined under subparagraph (3) of this paragraph, shall be reduced by absorbing as taxes deemed paid or accrued under section 904(d) in that year the unabsorbed separate unused foreign tax of such spouse, and the unabsorbed unused foreign tax determined under subparagraph (2) of this paragraph of such spouse, for taxable years which begin before the beginning of the year of origin of the unused foreign tax of the particular spouse against which the excess limitation so determined is being applied.

(ii) In addition, the part of the excess limitation which is attributable to the other spouse for the taxable year, as determined under subparagraph (3) of this paragraph, shall be reduced by absorbing as taxes deemed paid or accrued under section 904(d) in that year the unabsorbed unused foreign tax, if any, of such other spouse for the taxable year which begins on the same date as the beginning of the year of origin of the unused foreign tax of the particular spouse against which the excess limitation so determined is being applied.

(6) Spouses using different limitations. If an unused foreign tax is carried through a taxable year for which spouses made a joint return and the credit under section 901 for such taxable year is not claimed, and in the prior taxable year separate returns are made in which the per-country limitation applies to one spouse and the overall limitation applies to the other spouse, the amount treated as absorbed in the taxable year for which a joint return is made—

(i) With respect to the spouse for which the per-country limitation applies shall be determined on the basis of the excess limitation which would be allocated to such spouse under subparagraph (3)(i) of this paragraph had the per-country limitation applied for such year to both spouses;

(ii) With respect to the other spouse for which the overall limitation applies shall be determined on the basis of the excess limitation which would be allocated to such spouse under subparagraph (3)(ii) of this paragraph had the overall limitation applied for such year to both spouses.

This subparagraph shall be applied without regard to subparagraph (4)(ii) of this paragraph.

(g) Illustrations. This section may be illustrated by the following examples:

Example (1). (a) H and W, calendar year taxpayers, file joint returns for 1961 and 1963, and separate returns for 1962, 1964, and 1965; and for each of those taxable years they choose to claim a credit under section 901. For the taxable years involved, they had unused foreign tax, excess limitations, and carrybacks and carryovers of unused foreign tax as set forth below. The overall limitation applies to both spouses for all taxable years involved in this example. Neither H nor W had an unused foreign tax or excess limitation for any year before 1961 or after 1965. For purposes of this example, any reference to an excess limitation means such a limitation as determined under paragraph (c)(2)(ii) of § 1.904-2 but without regard to any taxes deemed paid or accrued under section 904(d):

Taxable year	1961	1962	1963	1964	1965
Return	Joint	Separate	Joint	Separate	Separate
H's unused foreign tax to be carried over or back, or excess limitation (enclosed in parentheses)	$500	$250	($650)	$400	($500)
W's unused foreign tax to be carried over or back, or excess limitation (enclosed in parentheses)	300	(200)	(300)	150	(100)
Total	800		(950)		
Carryovers absorbed:					
W's, from 1961		200W[1]	100W		
H's, from 1961			500H[2]		
H's, from 1962			150H		
			100W		
W's, from 1964					50W
H's, from 1964					400H
Carrybacks absorbed:					
W's, from 1964		0	100W		
H's, from 1964			0		

[1] W—absorbed by W's excess limitation.
[2] H—absorbed by H's excess limitation

(b) Two hundred dollars of the $300 constituting W's part of the joint unused foreign tax for 1961 is absorbed by her separate excess limitation of $200 for 1962, and the remaining $100 of such part is absorbed by her part ($300) of the joint excess limitation for 1963. The excess limitation of $300 for 1963 is not required first to be reduced by any amount, since neither H nor W has any unused foreign tax for taxable years beginning before 1961.

(c) H's part ($500) of the joint unused foreign tax for 1961 is absorbed by his part ($650) of the joint excess limitation for 1963. The excess limitation of $650 for 1963 is not required first to be reduced by any amount, since neither H nor W has any unused foreign tax for taxable years beginning before 1961.

(d) H's unused foreign tax of $250 for 1962 is first absorbed (to the extent of $150) by H's part of the joint excess limitation for 1963, which must first be reduced from $650 to $150 by the absorption as taxes deemed paid or accrued in 1963 of H's unused foreign tax of $500 for 1961, which is a taxable year beginning before 1962. The remaining part ($100) of H's unused foreign tax for 1962 is then absorbed by W's part of the joint excess limitation for 1963, which must first be reduced from $300 to $200 by the absorption as taxes deemed paid or accrued in 1963 of the unabsorbed part ($100) of W's unused foreign tax for 1961, which is a taxable year beginning before 1962.

(e) W's unused foreign tax of $150 for 1964 is first absorbed (to the extent of $100) by W's part of the joint excess limitation for 1963, which must first be reduced from $300 to $100 by the absorption as taxes deemed paid or accrued in 1963 of the unabsorbed part ($100) of W's unused foreign tax for 1961 and the unabsorbed part ($100) of H's unused foreign tax for 1962, which are taxable years beginning before 1964. No part of W's unused foreign tax for 1964 is absorbed by H's part of the joint excess limitation for 1963, since H's part of that excess must first be reduced from $650 to $0 by the absorption as taxes deemed paid or accrued in 1963 of H's unused foreign tax of $500 for 1961 and of the unabsorbed part ($150) of H's unused foreign tax for 1962, which are taxable years beginning before 1964. The unabsorbed part ($50) of W's unused foreign tax for 1964 is then absorbed by W's excess limitation of $100 for 1965. No part of W's unused foreign tax for 1964 is absorbed by W's excess limitation for 1962, since that excess limitation must first be reduced from $200 to $0 by W's unused foreign tax for 1961, which is a taxable year beginning before 1964.

(f) No part of H's unused foreign tax of $400 for 1964 is absorbed by H's part of the joint excess limitation for 1963, since H's part of that excess must first be reduced from $650 to $0 by the absorption as taxes deemed paid or accrued in 1963 of H's unused foreign tax of $500 for 1961 and of a part ($150) of H's unused foreign tax for 1962, which are taxable years beginning before 1964. Moreover, no part of H's unused foreign tax of $400 for 1964 is absorbed by W's part of the joint excess limitation for 1963, since W's part of that excess must first be reduced from $300 to $0 by the absorption as taxes deemed paid or accrued in 1963 of the unabsorbed part ($100) of W's unused foreign tax for 1961 and of the unabsorbed part ($100) of H's unused foreign tax for 1962, which are taxable years beginning before 1964, and also by the absorption of a part ($100) of W's unused foreign tax of $150 for 1964, which is a taxable year beginning on the same date as the beginning of H's taxable year 1964. The unabsorbed part ($400) of H's unused foreign tax for 1964 is then absorbed by H's excess limitation of $500 for 1965.

Example (2). (a) Assume the same facts as those in example (1) except that for 1964 W's unused foreign tax is $20, instead of $150. The carrybacks and carryovers absorbed are the same as in example (1) except as indicated in paragraphs (b) and (c) of this example.

(b) No part of W's unused foreign tax of $20 for 1964 is absorbed by W's excess limitation for 1962, since that excess must first be reduced from $200 to $0 by W's unused foreign tax for 1961, which is a taxable year beginning before 1964. W's unused foreign tax of $20 for 1964 is absorbed by W's part of the joint excess limitation for 1963, which must first be reduced from $300 to $100 by the absorption as taxes deemed paid or accrued in 1963 of the unabsorbed part ($100) of W's unused foreign tax for 1961 and the unabsorbed part ($100) of H's unused foreign tax for 1962, which are taxable years beginning before 1964.

(c) For the reason given in paragraph (f) of example (1), no part of H's unused foreign tax of $400 for 1964 is absorbed by H's part of the joint excess limitation for 1963. H's unused foreign tax of $400 for 1964 is first absorbed (to the extent of $80) by W's part of the joint excess limitation for 1963, which must first be reduced from $300 to $80 by the absorption as taxes deemed paid or accrued in 1963 of the unabsorbed part ($100) of W's unused foreign tax for 1961 and of the unabsorbed part ($100) of H's unused foreign tax for 1962, which are taxable years beginning before 1964, and also by the absorption of W's unused foreign tax of $20 for 1964, which is a taxable year beginning on the same date as the beginning of H's taxable year 1964. The unabsorbed part ($320) of H's unused foreign tax for 1964 is then absorbed by H's excess limitation of $500 for 1965.

Example (3). The facts are the same as in example (1) except that the per-country limitation applies to both spouses for all taxable years involved in the example and that excess limitations and the unused foreign taxes relate to a single foreign country. The carryovers and carrybacks are the same as in example (1).

T.D. 6789, 12/30/64, amend T.D. 7292, 11/30/73, T.D. 7490, 6/10/77, T.D. 7961, 6/20/84.

§ 1.904-4 Separate application of section 904 with respect to certain categories of income.

Caution: The Treasury has not yet amended Reg § 1.904-4 to reflect changes made by P.L. 109-135, P.L. 108-357, P.L. 105-34, P.L. 103-66, P.L. 100-647.

(a) [Reserved]. For further guidance, see § 1.904-4T(a).

(b) [Reserved]. For further guidance, see § 1.904-4T(b).

(c) High-taxed income. *(1) In general.* Income received or accrued by a United States person that would otherwise be passive income shall not be treated as passive income if the income is determined to be high-taxed income. Income shall be considered to be high-taxed income if, after allocating expenses, losses and other deductions of the United States person to that income under paragraph (c)(2)(ii) of this section, the sum of the foreign income taxes paid or accrued by the United States person with respect to such income and the foreign taxes deemed paid or accrued by the United States person with respect to such income under section 902 or section 960 exceeds the highest rate of tax specified in section 1 or 11, whichever applies (and with reference to section 15 if applicable), multiplied by the amount of such income (including the amount treated as a dividend under section 78). If, after application of this paragraph (c), income that would otherwise be passive income is determined to be high-taxed income, such income shall be treated as general category income, and any taxes imposed on that income shall be considered related to general category income under § 1.904-6. If, after application of this paragraph (c), passive income is zero or less than zero, any taxes imposed on the passive income shall be considered related to general category income. For additional rules regarding losses related to passive income, see paragraph (c)(2) of this section. Income and taxes shall be translated at the appropriate rates, as determined under sections 986, 987 and 989 and the regulations under those sections, before application of this paragraph (c). For purposes of allocating taxes to groups of income, United States source passive income is treated as any other passive income. In making the determination whether income is high-taxed, however, only foreign source income, as determined under United States tax principles, is relevant. See paragraph (c)(8) Examples 10 through 13 of this section for examples illustrating the application of this paragraph (c)(1) and paragraph (c)(2) of this section. This paragraph (c)(1) is applicable for taxable years beginning after March 12, 1999.

(2) Grouping of items of income in order to determine whether passive income is high-taxed income. (i) Effective dates. [Reserved]. For further guidance, see § 1.904-4T(c)(2)(i).

(ii) Grouping rules. (A) Initial allocation and apportionment of deductions and taxes. For purposes of determining whether passive income is high-taxed, expenses, losses and other deductions shall be allocated and apportioned initially to each of the groups of passive income (described in paragraphs (c)(3), (4), and (5) of this section) under the rules of §§ 1.861-8 through 1.861-14T and 1.865-1 and 1.865-2. Taxpayers that allocate and apportion interest expense on an asset basis may nevertheless apportion passive interest expense among the groups of passive income on a gross income basis. Foreign taxes are allocated to groups under the rules of § 1.904-6(a)(iii). If a loss on a disposition of property gives rise to foreign tax (i.e., the transaction giving rise to the loss is treated under foreign law as having given rise to a gain), the foreign tax shall be allocated to the group of passive income to which gain on the sale would have been assigned under paragraph (c)(3) or (4) of this section. A determination of whether passive income is high-taxed shall be made only after application of paragraph (c)(2)(ii)(B) of this section (if applicable).

(B) Reallocation of loss groups. If, after allocation and apportionment of expenses, losses and other deductions under paragraph (c)(2)(ii)(A) of this section, the sum of the allocable deductions exceeds the gross income in one or more groups, the excess deductions shall proportionately reduce income in the other groups (but not below zero).

(3) and (4) [Reserved]. For further guidance, see § 1.904-4T(c)(3) and (4) introductory text.

(4) (i) Income from sources within the QBU's country of operation. Passive income from sources within the QBU's country of operation shall be treated as one item of income.

(ii) Income from sources without the QBU's country of operation. Passive income from sources without the QBU's country of operation shall be grouped on the basis of the tax imposed on that income as provided in § 1.904-4T(c)(3)(i) through (iv).

(iii) Determination of the source of income. For purposes of this paragraph (c)(4), income will be determined to be from sources within or without the QBU's country of operation under the laws of the foreign country of the payor of the income.

(5) Special rules. (i) Certain rents and royalties. All items of rent or royalty income to which an item of rent or royalty expense is directly allocable shall be treated as a single item of income and shall not be grouped with other amounts.

(ii) Treatment of partnership income. A partner's distributive share of income from a foreign or United States partnership that is not subject to the look-through rules and that is treated as passive income under § 1.904-5(h)(2)(i) (generally providing that a less than 10 percent partner's distributive share of partnership income is passive income) shall be treated as a single item of income and shall not be grouped with other amounts. A distributive share of income from a foreign partnership that is treated as passive income under the look-through rules shall be grouped according to the rules in paragraph (c)(4) of this section. A distributive share of income from a United States partnership that is treated as passive income under the look-through rules shall be grouped according to the rules in paragraph (c)(3) of this section, except that the portion, if any, of the distributive share of income attributable to income earned by a United States partnership through a foreign QBU shall be grouped under the rules of paragraph (c)(4) of this section.

(iii) Currency gain or loss. (A) Section 986(c). Any currency gain or loss with respect to a distribution received by a United States shareholder (other than a foreign QBU of that shareholder) of previously taxed earnings and profits that is recognized under section 986(c) and that is treated as an item of passive income shall be subject to the rules provided in paragraph (c)(3)(iii) of this section. If that item, however, is received or accrued by a foreign QBU of the United States shareholder, it shall be treated as an item of passive income from sources within the QBU's country of operation for purposes of paragraph (c)(4)(i) of this section. This paragraph (c)(5)(iii)(A) shall be applied separately for each foreign QBU of a United States shareholder.

(B) Section 987(3). Any currency gain or loss with respect to remittances or transfers of property between QBUs of a United States shareholder that is recognized under section 987(3)(B) and that is treated as an item of passive income shall be subject to the rules provided in paragraph (c)(3)(iii) of this section. If that item, however, is received or accrued by a foreign QBU of the United States shareholder, it shall be treated as an item of passive income from sources within the QBU's country of operation for purposes of paragraph (c)(4)(i) of this section. This paragraph (c)(5)(iii)(B) shall be applied separately for each foreign QBU of a United States shareholder.

(C) Example. The following example illustrates the provisions of this paragraph (c)(5)(iii).

Example. P, a domestic corporation, owns all of the stock of S, a controlled foreign corporation that uses x as its functional currency. In 1993, S earns 100x of passive foreign personal holding company income. When included in P's income under subpart F, the exchange rate is 1x equals $1. Therefore, P's subpart F inclusion is $100. At the end of 1993, S has previously taxed earnings and profits of 100x and P's basis in those earnings is $100. In 1994, S has no earnings and distributes 100x to P. The value of the earnings when distributed is $150. Assume that under section 986(c), P must recognize $50 of passive income attributable to the appreciation of the previously taxed income. Country X does not recognize any gain or loss on the distribution. Therefore, the section 986(c) gain is not subject to any foreign withholding tax or other foreign tax. Thus, under paragraph (c)(3)(iii) of this section, the section 986(c) gain shall be grouped with other items of P's income that are subject to no withholding tax or other foreign tax.

(iv) Coordination with section 954(b)(4). For rules relating to passive income of a controlled foreign corporation that is exempt from subpart F treatment because the income is subject to high foreign tax, see section 904(d)(3)(E), § 1.904-4(c)(7)(iii), and § 1.904-5(d)(2).

(6) Application of this paragraph to additional taxes paid or deemed paid in the year of receipt of previously taxed income. (i) Determination made in year of inclusion. The determination of whether an amount included in gross income under section 951(a) is high-taxed income shall be made in the taxable year the income is included in the gross income of the United States shareholder under section 951(a) (hereinafter the "taxable year of inclusion"). Any increase in foreign taxes paid or accrued, or deemed paid or accrued, when the taxpayer receives an amount that is excluded from gross income under section 959(a) and that is attributable to a controlled foreign corporation's earnings and profits relating to the amount previously included in gross income will not be considered in determining whether the amount included in income in the taxable year of inclusion is high-taxed income.

(ii) Exception. Paragraph (c)(6)(i) of this section shall not apply to an increase in tax in a case in which the taxpayer is required to adjust its foreign taxes in the year of inclusion under section 905(c).

(iii) Allocation of foreign taxes imposed on distributions of previously taxed income. If an item of income is considered high-taxed income in the year of inclusion and paragraph (c)(6)(i) of this section applies, then any increase in foreign income taxes imposed with respect to that item shall be considered to be related to general category income. If an item of income is not considered to be high-taxed income in the taxable year of inclusion and paragraph (c)(6)(i) of this section applies, the following rules shall apply. The taxpayer shall treat an increase in taxes paid or accrued, or deemed paid or accrued, on any distribution of the earnings and profits attributable to the amount included in gross income in the taxable year of inclusion as taxes related to passive income to the extent of the excess of the product of (A) the highest rate of tax in section 11 (determined with regard to section 15 and determined as of the year of inclusion) and (B) the amount of the inclusion (after allocation of parent expenses) over (C) the taxes paid or accrued, or deemed paid or accrued, in the year of inclusion. The taxpayer shall treat any taxes paid or accrued, or deemed paid or accrued, on the distribution in excess of this amount as taxes related to general category income. If these additional taxes are not creditable in the year of distribution the carryover rules of section 904(c) apply. For purposes of this paragraph, the foreign tax on a subpart F inclusion shall be considered increased on distribution of the earnings and profits associated with that inclusion if the total of taxes paid and deemed paid on the inclusion and the distribution (taking into account any reductions in tax and any withholding taxes) is greater than the total taxes deemed paid in the year of inclusion. Any foreign currency loss associated with the earnings and profits that are distributed with respect to the inclusion is not to be considered as giving rise to an increase in tax.

(iv) Increase in taxes paid by successors. (A) General rule. Except as provided in paragraph (c)(6)(iv)(B) of this section, if passive earnings and profits previously included in income of a United States shareholder are distributed to a person that was not a United States shareholder of the distributing corporation in the year the earnings were included, any increase in foreign taxes paid or accrued, or deemed paid or accrued, on that distribution shall be treated as taxes related to general category income, regardless of whether the previously-taxed income was considered high-taxed income under section 904(d)(2)(F) in the year of inclusion.

(B) Exception. For a special rule applicable to distributions prior to August 6, 1997, to U.S. shareholders not entitled to look-through treatment, see 26 CFR 1.904-4(c)(6)(iv)(B) (revised as of April 1, 2006).

(C) Effective date. This paragraph (c)(6)(iv) applies to taxable years beginning after December 31, 1986. However, for taxable years beginning before January 1, 2001, taxpayers may rely on § 1.904-4(c)(6)(iv) of regulations project INTL-1-92, published at 1992-1 C.B. 1209. See § 601.601(d)(2) of this chapter.

(7) Application of this paragraph to certain reductions of tax on distributions of income. (i) In general. If the effective rate of tax imposed by a foreign country on income of a foreign corporation that is included in a taxpayer's gross income is reduced under foreign law on distribution of such income, the rules of this paragraph (c) apply at the time that the income is included in the taxpayer's gross income without regard to the possibility of subsequent reduction of foreign tax on the distribution. If the inclusion is considered to be high-taxed income, then the taxpayer shall treat the inclusion as general category income. When the foreign corporation distributes the earnings and profits to which the inclusion was attributable and the foreign tax on the inclusion is reduced, then the taxpayer shall redetermine whether the inclusion should be considered to be high-taxed income provided that a redetermination of United States tax liability is required under section 905(c). If, taking into account the reduction in foreign tax, the inclusion would not have been considered high-taxed income, then the taxpayer, in redetermining its United States tax liability for the year or years affected, shall treat the inclusion and the associated taxes (as reduced on the distribution) as passive income and taxes. See section 905(c) and the regulations thereunder regarding the method of adjustment. For this purpose, the foreign tax on a subpart F inclusion shall be considered reduced on distribution of the earnings and profits associated with the inclusion if the total of taxes paid and deemed paid on the inclusion and the distribution (taking into account any reductions in tax and any withholding taxes) is less that the total taxes deemed paid in the year of inclusion. Any foreign currency gain associated with the earnings and profits that are distributed with respect to the inclusion is not to be considered a reduction of tax.

(ii) Allocation of reductions of foreign tax. For purposes of paragraph (c)(7)(i) of this section, reductions in foreign tax shall be allocated among the separate categories under the same principles as those of § 1.904-6 for allocating taxes among the separate categories. Thus, for purposes of determining to which year's taxes the reduction in taxes relates, foreign law shall apply. If, however, foreign law does not attribute a reduction in taxes to a particular year or years, then the reduction in taxes shall be attributable, on an annual last in-first out (LIFO) basis, to foreign taxes potentially subject to reduction that are associated with previously taxed income, then on a LIFO basis to foreign taxes associated with income that under paragraph (c)(7)(iii) of this section remains as passive income but that was excluded from subpart F income under section 954(b)(4), and finally on a LIFO basis to foreign taxes associated with other earnings and profits. Furthermore, in applying the ordering rules of section

959(c), distributions shall be considered made on a LIFO basis first out of earnings described in section 959(c)(1) and (2), then on a LIFO basis out of earnings and profits associated with income that remains passive income under paragraph (c)(7)(iii) of this section but that was excluded from subpart F under section 954(b)(4), and finally on a LIFO basis out of other earnings and profits. For purposes of this paragraph (c)(7)(ii), foreign law is not considered to attribute a reduction in tax to a particular year or years if foreign law attributes the tax reduction to a pool or group containing income from more than one taxable year and such pool or group is defined based on a characteristic of the income (for example, the rate of tax paid with respect to the income) rather than on the taxable year in which the income is derived.

(iii) Interaction with section 954(b)(4). If a taxpayer excludes passive income from a controlled foreign corporation's foreign personal holding company income under these circumstances, then, notwithstanding the general rule of § 1.904-5(d)(2), the income shall be considered to be passive income until distribution of that income. If a taxpayer excludes passive income from a controlled foreign corporation's foreign personal holding company income under these circumstances, then the income shall be considered to be passive income until distribution of that income. At that time, the rules of this paragraph shall apply to determine whether the income is high-taxed income and, therefore, general category income. For purposes of determining whether a reduction in tax is attributable to taxes on income excluded under section 954(b)(4), the rules of paragraph (c)(7)(ii) of this section apply. The rules of paragraph (c)(7)(ii) of this section shall apply for purposes of ordering distributions to determine whether such distributions are out of earnings and profits associated with such excluded income. For an example illustrating the operation of this paragraph (c)(7)(iii), see paragraph (c)(8) Example (7) of this section.

(8) Examples. The following examples illustrate the application of this paragraph (c).

Example (1). Controlled foreign corporation S is a wholly-owned subsidiary of domestic corporation P. S is a single qualified business unit (QBU) operating in foreign country X. In 1988, S earns $130 of gross passive royalty income from country X sources, and incurs $30 of expenses that do not include any payments to P. S's $100 of net passive royalty income is subject to $30 of foreign tax, and is included under section 951 in P's gross income for the taxable year. The royalty income is not subject to a withholding tax, and is not taxed by Country X, and the interest and the rental income are subject to a 4 percent and 10 percent withholding tax, respectively. After application of the high-tax kick-out rules of paragraph (c)(1) of this section, the $50 inclusion is treated as general category income, and the $30 of taxes deemed paid are treated as taxes imposed on general category income, because the foreign taxes paid and deemed paid on the income exceed the highest United States tax rate multiplied by the $50 inclusion ($30 > $17 (.34 × $50)).

Example (2). The facts are the same as in Example (1) except that instead of earning $130 of gross passive royalty income, S earns $65 of gross passive royalty income from country X sources and $65 of gross passive interest income from country Y sources. S incurs $15 of expenses and $5 of foreign tax with regard to the royalty income and incurs $15 of expenses and $10 of foreign tax with regard to the interest income. P allocates $50 of expenses pro rata to the $50 inclusion ($45 section 951 inclusion and $5 section 78 amount) attributable to the royalty income earned by S and the $50 inclusion ($40 section 951 inclusion and $10 section 78 amount) attributable to the interest income earned by S. Under paragraph (c)(4) of this section, the high-tax test is applied separately to the section 951 inclusion attributable to the income from X sources and the section 951 inclusion attributable to the income from Y sources. Therefore, after allocation of P's $50 of expenses, the resulting $25 inclusion attributable to the royalty income from X sources is still treated as passive income because the foreign taxes paid and deemed paid on the income do not exceed the highest United States tax rate multiplied by the $25 inclusion ($5 > $8.50 (.34 × $25)). The $25 inclusion attributable to the interest income from Y sources is treated as general category income because the foreign taxes paid and deemed paid exceed the highest United States tax rate multiplied by the $25 inclusion ($10 > $8.50 (.34 × $25)).

Example (3). Controlled foreign corporation S is a wholly-owned subsidiary of domestic corporation P. S is incorporated and operating in country Y and has a branch in country Z. S has two QBUs (QBU Y and QBU Z). In 1988, S earns $65 of gross passive royalty income in country Y through QBU Y and $65 of gross passive royalty income in country Z through QBU Z. S allocates $15 of expenses to the gross passive royalty income earned by each QBU, resulting in net income of $50 in each QBU. Country Y imposes $5 of foreign tax on the royalty income earned in Y, and country Z imposes $10 of tax on royalty income earned in Z. All of S's income constitutes subpart F foreign personal holding company income that is passive income and is included in P's gross income for the taxable year. P allocates $50 of expenses pro rata to the $100 subpart F inclusion attributable to the QBUs (consisting of the $45 section 951 inclusion derived through QBU Y, the $5 section 78 amount attributable to QBU Y, the $40 section 951 inclusion derived through QBU Z, and the $10 section 78 amount attributable to QBU Z), resulting in a net inclusion of $50. Pursuant to paragraph (c)(4) of this section, the high-tax kickout rules must be applied separately to the subpart F inclusion attributable to the income earned by QBU Y and the income earned by QBU Z. After application of the high-tax kickout rules, the $25 inclusion attributable to Y will still be treated as passive income because the foreign taxes paid and deemed paid on the income do not exceed the highest United States tax rate multiplied by the $25 inclusion ($5 > $8.50 (.34 × $25)). The $25 inclusion attributable to Z will be treated as general category income because the foreign taxes paid and deemed paid on the income exceed the highest United States tax rate multiplied by the $25 inclusion ($10 > $8.50 (.34 × $25)).

Example (4). Domestic corporation M operates in branch form in foreign countries X and Y. The branches are qualified business units (QBUs), within the meaning of section 989(a). In 1988, QBU X earns passive royalty income, interest income and rental income. All of the QBU X passive income is from Country Z sources. The royalty income is not subject to a withholding tax, and is not taxed by Country X, and the interest and the rental income are subject to a 4 percent and 10 percent withholding tax, respectively. QBU Y earns interest income in Country Y that is not subject to foreign tax. For purposes of determining whether M's foreign source passive income is high-taxed income, the rental income and the interest income earned in QBU X are treated as one item of income pursuant to paragraphs (c)(4)(ii) and (3)(ii) of this section. The interest income earned in QBU Y and the royalty income earned in QBU X are each treated as a separate item of income under paragraphs (c)(4)(i) (with respect to QBU Y's interest income) and (c)(4)(ii) and

(3)(iii) (with respect to QBU X's royalty income) of this section.

Example (5). S, a controlled foreign corporation incorporated in foreign country R, is a wholly-owned subsidiary of P, a domestic corporation. For 1988, P is required under section 951(a) to include in gross income $80 (not including the section 78 amount) attributable to the earnings and profits of S for such year, all of which is foreign personal holding company income that is passive rent or royalty income. S does not make any distributions in 1988 or 1989. Foreign income taxes paid by S for 1988 that are deemed paid by P for such year under section 960(a) with respect to the section 951(a) inclusion equal $20. Twenty dollars ($20) of P's expenses are properly allocated to the section 951(a) inclusion. The foreign income tax paid with respect to the section 951(a) inclusion does not exceed the highest United States tax rate multiplied by the amount of income after allocation of parent expenses ($20 > $27.20 (.34 × $80)). Thus, P's section 951(a) inclusion for 1988 is included in P's passive income and the $20 of taxes attributable to that inclusion are treated as taxes related to passive income. In 1990, S distributes $80 to P, and under section 959 that distribution is treated as attributable to the earnings and profits with respect to the amount included in income by P in 1988 and is excluded from P's gross income. Foreign country R imposes a withholding tax of $15 on the distribution in 1990. Under paragraph (c)(6)(i) of this section, the withholding tax in 1990 does not affect the characterization of the 1988 inclusion as passive income nor does it affect the characterization of the $20 of taxes paid in 1988 as taxes paid with respect to passive income. No further parent expenses are allocable to the receipt of that distribution. In 1990, the foreign taxes paid ($15) exceed the product of the highest United States tax rate and the amount of the inclusion reduced by taxes deemed paid in the year of inclusion ($15 > ((.34 × $80) – $20)). Thus, under paragraph (c)(6)(iii) of this section, $7.20 ((.34 × $80) – $20)) of the $15 withholding tax paid in 1990 is treated as taxes related to passive income and the remaining $7.80 ($15 – $7.20) of the withholding tax is treated as related to general category income.

Example (6). S, a controlled foreign corporation, is a wholly-owned subsidiary of P, a domestic corporation. P and S are calendar year taxpayers. In 1987, S's only earnings consist of $200 of passive income that is foreign personal holding company income that is earned in a foreign country X. Under country X's tax system, the corporate tax on particular earnings is reduced on distribution of those earnings and no withholding tax is imposed. In 1987, S pays $100 of foreign tax. P does not elect to exclude this income from subpart F under section 954(b)(4) and includes $200 in gross income ($100 of net foreign personal holding company income and $100 of the section 78 amount). At the time of the inclusion, the income is considered to be high-taxed income under paragraphs (c)(1) and (c)(6)(i) of this section and is general category income to P. S does not distribute any of its earnings in 1987. In 1988, S has no earnings. On December 31, 1988, S distributes the $100 of earnings from 1987. At that time, S receives a $50 refund from X attributable to the reduction of the country X corporate tax imposed on those earnings. Under paragraph (c)(7)(i) of this section, P must redetermine whether the 1987 inclusion should be considered to be high-taxed income. By taking into account the reduction in foreign tax, the inclusion would not have been considered high-taxed income. Therefore, P must redetermine its foreign tax credit for 1987 and treat the inclusion and the taxes associated with the inclusion as passive income and taxes. P must follow the appropriate section 905(c) procedures.

Example (7). The facts are the same as in Example (6) except that P elects to apply section 954(b)(4) to S's passive income that is subpart F income. Although the income is not considered to be subpart F income, it remains passive income until distribution. In 1988, S distributes $150 to P. The distribution is a dividend to P because S has $150 of accumulated earnings and profits (the $100 of earnings in 1987 and the $50 refund in 1988). P has no expenses allocable to the dividend from S. In 1988, the income is subject to the high-tax kick-out rules under paragraph (c)(7)(iii) of this section. The income is passive income to P because the foreign taxes paid and deemed paid by P with respect to the income do not exceed the highest United States tax rate on that income.

Example (8). The facts are the same as in Example (6) except that the distribution in 1988 is subject to a withholding tax of $25. Under paragraph (c)(7)(i) of this section, P must redetermine whether the 1987 inclusion should be considered to be high-taxed income because there is a net $25 reduction of foreign tax. By taking into account both the reduction in foreign corporate tax and the withholding tax, the inclusion would continue to be considered high-taxed income. P must follow the appropriate section 905(c) procedures. P must redetermine its foreign tax credit for 1987, but the inclusion and the $75 taxes ($50 of deemed paid tax and $25 withholding tax) will continue to be treated as general category income and taxes.

Example (9). (i) S, a controlled foreign corporation operating in country G, is a wholly-owned subsidiary of P, a domestic corporation. P and S are calendar year taxpayers. Country G imposes a tax of 50 percent on S's earnings. Under country G's system, the foreign corporate tax on particular earnings is reduced on distribution of those earnings to 30 percent and no withholding tax is imposed. Under country G's law, distributions are treated as made out of a pool of undistributed earnings subject to the 50% tax rate. For 1987, S's only earnings consist of passive income that is foreign personal holding company income that is earned in foreign country G. S has taxable income of $110 for United States purposes and $100 for country G purposes. Country G, therefore, imposes a tax of $50 on the 1987 earnings of S. P does not elect to exclude this income from subpart F under section 954(b)(4) and includes $110 in gross income ($60 of net foreign personal holding company income and $50 of the section 78 amount). At the time of the inclusion, the income is considered to be high-taxed income under paragraph (c) of this section and is general limitation income to P. S does not distribute any of its taxable income in 1987.

(ii) In 1988, S earns general category income that is not subpart F income. S again has $110 in taxable income for United States purposes and $100 in taxable income for country G purposes, and S pays $50 of tax to foreign country G. In 1989, S has no taxable income or earnings. On December 31, 1989, S distributes $60 of earnings and receives a refund of foreign tax of $24. Country G treats the distribution of earnings as out of the 50% tax rate pool of earnings accumulated in 1987 and 1988. However, under paragraph (c)(7)(ii) of this section, the distribution, and, therefore, the reduction of tax is treated as first attributable to the $60 of passive earnings attributable to income previously taxed in 1987. However, because, under foreign law, only 40 percent (the reduction in tax rates from 50 percent to 30 percent is a 40 percent reduction in tax) of the $50 of foreign taxes on the passive earnings can be refunded, $20 of the $24 foreign tax refund reduces foreign taxes on passive earnings. The other $4 of the tax refund reduces the general category taxes from $50 to $46 (even though for United States purposes the $60 distribution is entirely out of passive earnings).

(iii) Under paragraph (c)(7) of this section, P must redetermine whether the 1987 inclusion should be considered to be high-taxed income. By taking into account the reduction in foreign tax, the inclusion would not have been considered high-taxed income ($30 > .34 × $110). Therefore, P must redetermine its foreign tax credit for 1987 and treat the inclusion and the taxes associated with the inclusion as passive income and taxes. P must follow the appropriate section 905(c) procedures.

Example (10). P, a domestic corporation, earns $100 of passive royalty income from sources within the United States. Under the laws of Country X, however, that royalty is considered to be from sources within Country X and Country X imposes a 10 percent withholding tax on the payment of the royalty. P also earns $100 of passive foreign source dividend income subject to a 10 percent withholding tax to which $15 of expenses are allocated. In determining whether P's passive income is high-taxed, the $10 withholding tax on P's royalty income is allocated to passive income, and within the passive category to the group of income described in paragraph (c)(3)(ii) of this section (passive income subject to a withholding tax of less than 15 percent (but greater than zero)). For purposes of determining whether the income is high-taxed, however, only the foreign source dividend income is taken into account. The foreign source dividend income will still be treated as passive income because the foreign taxes paid on the passive income in the group ($20) do not exceed the highest United States tax rate multiplied by the $85 of net foreign source income in the group ($20 is less than $28.90 ($100 − $15) × .34).

Example (11). In 2001, P, a U.S. citizen with a tax home in Country X, earns the following items of gross income: $400 of foreign source, passive limitation interest income not subject to foreign withholding tax but subject to Country X income tax of $100, $200 of foreign source, passive limitation royalty income subject to a 5 percent foreign withholding tax (foreign tax paid is $10), $1,300 of foreign source, passive limitation rental income subject to a 25 percent foreign withholding tax (foreign tax paid is $325), $500 of foreign source, general category income that gives rise to a $250 foreign tax, and $2,000 of U.S. source capital gain that is not subject to any foreign tax. P has a $900 deduction allocable to its passive rental income. P's only other deduction is a $700 capital loss on the sale of stock that is allocated to foreign source passive limitation income under § 1.865-2(a)(3)(i). The $700 capital loss is initially allocated to the group of passive income subject to no withholding tax but subject to foreign tax other than withholding tax. The $300 amount by which the capital loss exceeds the income in the group must be reapportioned to the other groups under paragraph (c)(2)(ii)(B) of this section. The royalty income is thus reduced by $100 to $100 ($200 − ($300 × (200/600))) and the rental income is thus reduced by $200 to $200 ($400 − ($300 × (400/600))). The $100 royalty income is not high-taxed and remains passive income because the foreign taxes do not exceed the highest United States rate of tax on that income. Under the high-tax kick-out, the $200 of rental income and the $325 of associated foreign tax are assigned to the general category category.

Example (12). The facts are the same as in Example 11 except the amount of the capital loss that is allocated under § 1.865-2(a)(3)(i) and paragraph (c)(2) of this section to the group of foreign source passive income subject to no withholding tax but subject to foreign tax other than withholding tax is $1,200. Under paragraph (c)(2)(ii)(B) of this section, the excess deductions of $800 must be reapportioned to the $200 of net royalty income subject to a 5 percent withholding tax and the $400 of net rental income subject to a 15 percent or greater withholding tax. The income in each of these groups is reduced to zero, and the foreign taxes imposed on the rental and royalty income are considered related to general category income. The remaining loss of $200 constitutes a separate limitation loss with respect to passive income.

Example (13). In 2001, P, a domestic corporation, earns a $100 dividend that is foreign source passive limitation income subject to a 30-percent withholding tax. A foreign tax credit for the withholding tax on the dividend is disallowed under section 901(k). A deduction for the tax is allowed, however, under sections 164 and 901(k)(7). In determining whether P's passive income is high-taxed, the $100 dividend and the $30 deduction are allocated to the first group of income described in paragraph (c)(3)(iv) of this section (passive income subject to no withholding tax or other foreign tax).

(d) [Reserved].

(e) Financial services income. *(1) In general.* The term "financial services income" means income derived by a financial services entity, as defined in paragraph (e)(3) of this section, that is:

(i) Income derived in the active conduct of a banking, insurance, financing, or similar business (active financing income as defined in paragraph (e)(2) of this section), except income described in paragraph (e)(2)(i)(W) of this section (high withholding tax interest);

(ii) Passive income as defined in section 904(d)(2)(A) and paragraph (b) of this section as determined before the application of the exception for high-taxed income;

(iii) Export financing interest as defined in section 904(d)(2)(G) and paragraph (h) of this section that, but for section 904(d)(2)(B)(ii), would also meet the definition of high withholding tax interest; or

(iv) Incidental income as defined in paragraph (e)(4) of this section.

(2) Active financing income. (i) Income included. For purposes of paragraph (e)(1) and (e)(3) of this section, income is active financing income only if it is described in any of the following subdivisions.

(A) Income that is of a kind that would be insurance income as defined in section 953(a) (including related party insurance income as defined in section 953(c)(2)) and determined without regard to those provisions of section 953(a)(1)(A) that limit insurance income to income from countries other than the country in which the corporation was created or organized.

(B) Income from the investment by an insurance company of its unearned premiums or reserves ordinary and necessary to the proper conduct of the insurance business, income from providing services as an insurance underwriter, income from insurance brokerage or agency services, and income from loss adjuster and surveyor services.

(C) Income from investing funds in circumstances in which the taxpayer holds itself out as providing a financial service by the acceptance or the investment of such funds, including income from investing deposits of money and income earned investing funds received for the purchase of traveler's checks or face amount certificates.

(D) Income from making personal, mortgage, industrial, or other loans.

(E) Income from purchasing, selling, discounting, or negotiating on a regular basis, notes, drafts, checks, bills of exchange, acceptances, or other evidences of indebtedness.

(F) Income from issuing letters of credit and negotiating drafts drawn thereunder.

(G) Income from providing trust services.

(H) Income from arranging foreign exchange transactions, or engaging in foreign exchange transactions.

(I) Income from purchasing stock, debt obligations, or other securities from an issuer or holder with a view to the public distribution thereof or offering or selling stock, debt obligations, or other securities for an issuer or holder in connection with the public distribution thereof, or participating in any such undertaking.

(J) Income earned by broker-dealers in the ordinary course of business (such as commissions) from the purchase or sale of stock, debt obligations, commodities futures, or other securities or financial instruments and dividend and interest income earned by broker dealers on stock, debt obligations, or other financial instruments that are held for sale.

(K) Service fee income from investment and correspondent banking.

(L) Income from interest rate and currency swaps.

(M) Income from providing fiduciary services.

(N) Income from services with respect to the management of funds.

(O) Bank-to-bank participation income.

(P) Income from providing charge and credit card services or for factoring receivables obtained in the course of providing such services.

(Q) Income from financing purchases from third parties.

(R) Income from gains on the disposition of tangible or intangible personal property or real property that was used in the active financing business (as defined in paragraph (e)(3)(i) of this section) but only to the extent that the property was held to generate or generated active financing income prior to its disposition.

(S) Income from hedging gain with respect to other active financing income.

(T) Income from providing traveller's check services.

(U) Income from servicing mortgages.

(V) Income from a finance lease. For this purpose, a finance lease is any lease that is a direct financing lease or a leveraged lease for accounting purposes and is also a lease for tax purposes.

(W) High withholding tax interest that would otherwise be described as active financing income.

(X) Income from providing investment advisory services, custodial services, agency paying services, collection agency services, and stock transfer agency services.

(Y) Any similar item of income that is disclosed in the manner provided in the instructions to the Form 1118 or 1116 or that is designated as a similar item of income in guidance published by the Internal Revenue Service.

(3) Financial services entities. (i) In general. The term "financial services entity" means an individual or entity that is predominantly engaged in the active conduct of a banking, insurance, financing, or similar business (active financing business) for any taxable Year. Except as provided in paragraph (e)(3)(ii) of this section, a determination of whether an entity is a financial services entity shall be done on an entity-by-entity basis. An individual or entity is predominantly engaged in the active financing business for any year if for that year at least 80 percent of its gross income is income described in paragraph (e)(2)(i) of this section. For this purpose, gross income includes all income realized by an individual or entity, whether includible or excludible from gross income under other operative provisions of the Code, but excludes gain from the disposition of stock of a corporation that prior to the disposition of its stock is related to the transferor within the meaning of section 267(b). For this purpose, income received from a related person that is a financial services entity shall be excluded if such income is characterized under the look-through rules of section 904(d)(3) and § 1.904-5. In addition, income received from a related person that is not a financial services entity but that is characterized as financial services income under the look-through rules shall be excluded. See paragraph (e)(3)(iv) Example (5) of this section. Any income received from a related person that is characterized under the look-through rules and that is not otherwise excluded by this paragraph will retain its character either as active financing income or other income in the hands of the recipient for purposes of determining if the recipient is a financial services entity and if the income is financial services income to the recipient. For purposes of this paragraph, related person is defined in § 1.904-5(i)(1).

(ii) Special rule for affiliated groups. In the case of any corporation that is not a financial services entity under paragraph (e)(3)(i) of this section, but is a member of an affiliated group, such corporation will be deemed to be a financial services entity if the affiliated group as a whole meets the requirements of paragraph (e)(3)(i) of this section. For purposes of this paragraph (e)(3)(ii), affiliated group means an affiliated group as defined in section 1504(a), determined without regard to section 1504(b)(3). In counting the income of the group for purposes of determining whether the group meets the requirements of paragraph (e)(3)(i) of this section, the following rules apply. Only the income of group members that are United States corporations or foreign corporations that are controlled foreign corporations in which United States members of the affiliated group own, directly or indirectly, at least 80 percent of the total voting power and value of the stock shall be included. For purposes of this paragraph (e)(3)(ii), indirect ownership shall be determined under section 318 and the regulations under that section. The income of the group will not include any income from transactions with other members of the group. Passive income will not be considered to be active financing income merely because that income is earned by a member of the group that is a financial services entity without regard to the rule of this paragraph (e)(3)(ii). This paragraph (e)(3)(ii) applies to taxable years beginning after December 31, 2000.

(iii) Treatment of partnerships and other pass-through entities. For purposes of determining whether a partner (including a partnership that is a partner in a second partnership) is a financial services entity, all of the partner's income shall be taken into account, except that income that is excluded under paragraph (e)(3)(i) of this section shall not be taken into account. Thus, if a partnership is determined to be a financial services entity none of the income of the partner received from the partnership that is characterized under the look-through rules shall be included for purpose of determining if the partner is a financial services entity. If a partnership is determined not to be a financial services entity, then income of the partner from the partnership that is characterized under the look-through rules will be taken into account (unless such income is financial services income) and such income will retain its character either as active financing income or as other income in the hands of the partner for purposes of determining if the partner is a financial service entity and if the income is financial services income to the partner. If a partnership is a financial services entity and the partner's income from the partnership is characterized as financial services income under the look-through rules, then, for purposes of determining a partner's foreign tax credit limitation, the income from the partnership shall be considered to be financial services income to the partner regardless of whether the partner is itself a financial services entity. The rules of this paragraph (e)(3)(iii) will apply for purposes of determining whether an owner of an interest in any other pass-through entity the character of the income of which is preserved when such income is included in the income of the owner of the interest is a financial services entity.

(iv) Examples. The principles of paragraph (e)(3) of this section are illustrated by the following examples.

Example (1). P is a domestic corporation that owns 100 percent of the stock of S, a controlled foreign corporation incorporated in Country X. For the 1990 taxable year, 60 percent of S's income is active financing income that consists of income that will be considered general limitation or passive income if S is not a financial services entity. The other 40 percent of S's income is passive non-active financing income. S is not a financial services entity and its active financing income thus retains its character as general limitation and passive income. S makes an interest payment to P in 1990 that is characterized under the look-through rules. Although the interest is not financial services income to S under the look-through rules, it retains it character as active financing income when paid to P and P must take that income into account in determining whether it is a financial services entity under paragraph (e)(3)(i) of this section. If P is determined to be a financial services entity, both the portion of the interest payment characterized as active financing income (whether general limitation or passive income in S's hands) and the portion characterized as passive non-active financing income received from S will be recharacterized as financial services income.

Example (2). Foreign corporation A, which is not a controlled foreign corporation, owns 100 percent of the stock of domestic corporation B, which owns 100 percent of the stock of domestic corporation C. A also owns 100 percent of the stock of foreign corporation D. D owns 100 percent of the stock of domestic corporation E, which owns 100 percent of the stock of controlled foreign corporation F. All of the corporations are members of an affiliated group within the meaning of section 1504(a) (determined without regard to section 1504(b)(3)). Pursuant to paragraph (e)(3)(ii) of this section, however, only the income of B, C, E, and F is counted in determining whether the group meets the requirements of paragraph (e)(3)(i) of this section. For the 2001 taxable year, B's income consists of $95 of active financing income and $5 of passive non-active financing income. C has $40 of active financing income and $20 of passive non-active financing income. E has $70 of active financing income and $15 of passive non-active financing income. F has $10 of passive income. B and E qualify as financial services entities under the entity test of paragraph (e)(3)(i) of this section. Therefore, B and E are financial services entities without regard to whether the group as a whole is a financial services entity and all of the income of B and E shall be treated as financial services income. C and F do not qualify as financial services entities under the entity test of paragraph (e)(3)(i) of this section. However, under the affiliated group test of paragraph (e)(3)(ii) of this section, C and F are financial services entities because at least 80 percent of the group's total income consists of active financing income ($205 of active financing income is 80.4 percent of $255 total income). B's and E's passive income is not treated as active financing income for purposes of the affiliated group test of paragraph (e)(3)(ii) of this section even though it is treated as financial services income without regard to whether the group satisfies the affiliated group test. Once C and F are determined to be financial services entities under the affiliated group test, however, all of the passive income of the group is treated as financial services income. Thus, 100 percent of the income of B, C, E, and F for 2001 is financial services income.

Example (3). PS is a domestic partnership operating in branch form in foreign country X. PS has two equal general partners, A and B. A and B are domestic corporations that each operate in branch form in foreign countries Y and Z. All of A's income, except that derived through PS, is manufacturing income. All of B's income, except that derived through PS, is active financing income. A and B's only income from PS are distributive shares of PS's income. PS is a financial services entity and all of its income is financial services income. The income from PS is excluded in determining if A or B are financial services entities. Thus, A is not a financial services entity because none of A's income is active financing income and B is a financial services entity because all of B's income is active financing income. However, both A and B's distributive shares of PS's taxable income consist of financial services income even though A is not a financial services entity.

Example (4). PS is a domestic partnership operating in foreign country X. A and B are domestic corporations that are equal general partners in PS and, therefore, the look-through rules apply for purposes of characterizing A's and B's distributive shares of PS's income. Fifty (50) percent of PS's gross income is active financing income that is not high withholding tax interest. The active financing income includes income that also meets the definition of passive income and income that meets the definition of general limitation income. The other 50 percent of PS's income is from manufacturing. PS is, therefore, not a financial services entity. A's and B's distributive shares of partnership taxable income consist of general limitation manufacturing income and active financing income. Under paragraph (c)(3)(i) of this section, the active financing income shall be financial services income to A or B if either A or B is determined to be a financial services entity. If A or B is not a financial services entity, the distributive shares of income from PS will not be financial services income to A or B and will consist of passive and general limitation income. All of the income from PS is included in determining if A or B are financial services entities.

Example (5). P is a United States corporation that is not a financial services entity. P owns 100 percent of the stock of S, a controlled foreign corporation that is not a financial services entity. S owns 100 percent of the stock of T, a controlled foreign corporation that is a financial services entity. In 1991, T pays a dividend to S. The dividend from T is characterized under the look-through rules of section 904(d)(3). Pursuant to paragraph (e)(3)(i) of this section, the dividend from T is excluded in determining whether S is a financial services entity. S is determined not to be a financial services entity but the dividend retains its character as financial services income in S's hands. Any subpart F inclusion or dividend to P out of earnings and profits attributable to the dividend from T will be excluded in determining whether P is a financial services entity but the inclusion or dividend will retain its character as financial services income.

(4) Definition of incidental income. (i) In general. (A) Rule. Incidental income is income that is integrally related to active financing income of a financial services entity. Such income includes, for example, income from precious metals trading and commodity trading that is integrally related to futures income. If securities, shares of stock, or other types of property are acquired by a financial services entity as an ordinary and necessary incident to the conduct of a active financing business, the income from such property will be considered to be financial services income but only so long as the retention of such property remains an ordinary or necessary incident to the conduct of such business. Thus property, including stock, acquired as the result of, or in order to prevent, a loss in an active financing business upon a loan held by the taxpayer in the ordinary course of such business will be considered ordinary and necessary to the conduct of such business, but income from such property will be considered financial services income only so long as the holding of such property remains an ordinary and necessary incident to the conduct of such business. If an entity holds such property for five years or less then the property is considered held incident to the financial services business. If an entity holds such property for more than five years, a presumption will be established that the entity is not holding such property incident to its financial services business. An entity will be able to rebut the presumption by demonstrating that under the facts and circumstances it is not holding the property as an investment. However, the fact that an entity holds the property for more than five years and is not able to rebut the presumption that it is not holding the property incident to its financial services business will not affect the characterization of any income received from the property during the first five years as financial services income.

(B) Examples. The following examples illustrate the application of paragraph (e)(4)(i) of this section.

Example (1). X is a financial services entity within the meaning of paragraph (e)(3)(i) of this section. In 1987, X made a loan in the ordinary course of its business to an unrelated foreign corporation, Y. As security for that loan, Y pledged certain operating assets. Those assets generate income of a type that would be subject to the general limitation. In January 1989, Y defaulted on the loan and forfeited the collateral. During the period X held the assets, X earned operating income generated by those assets. This income was applied in partial satisfaction of Y's obligation. In 1993, X sold the forfeited assets. The sales proceeds were in excess of the remainder of Y's obligation. The operating income received in the period from 1989 to 1993 and the income on the sale of the assets in 1993 are financial services income of X.

Example (2). The facts are the same as in *Example* (1), except that instead of pledging its operating assets as collateral for the loan, Y pledged the stock of its operating subsidiary Z. In 1993 X sold the stock of Z in complete satisfaction of Y's obligation. X's income from the sale of Z stock in satisfaction of Y's obligation is financial services income.

Example (3). P, a domestic corporation, is a financial services entity within the meaning of paragraph (e)(3)(i) of this section. P holds a United States dollar denominated debt (the "obligation") of the Central Bank of foreign country X. The obligation evidences a loan of $100 made by P to the Central Bank. In 1988, pursuant to a program of country X, P delivers the obligation to the Central Bank which credits 70 units of country X currency to M, a country X corporation. M issues all of its only class of capital stock to P. M invests the 70 units of country X currency in the construction and operation of a new hotel in X. In 1994, M distributes 10 units of country X currency to P as a dividend. P is not able to rebut the presumption that it is not holding the stock of M incident to its financial services business. The dividend to P is, therefore, not financial services income.

(ii) Income that is not incidental income. Income that is attributable to non-financial activity is not incidental income within the meaning of paragraph (e)(4)(i) and (ii) of this section solely because such income represents a relatively small proportion of the taxpayer's total income or that the taxpayer engages in non-financial activity on a sporadic basis. Thus, for example, income from data processing services provided to related or unrelated parties or income from the sale of goods or non-financial services (for example travel services) is not financial services income, even if the recipient is a financial services entity.

(5) Exceptions. Financial services income does not include income that is:

(i) Export financing interest as defined in section 904(d)(2)(G) and paragraph (h) of this section unless that income would be high withholding tax interest as defined in section 904(d)(2)(B) but for paragraph (d)(2)(B)(ii) of that section;

(ii) High withholding tax interest as defined in section 904(d)(2)(B) unless that income also meets the definition of export financing interest; and

(iii) Dividends from noncontrolled section 902 corporations as defined in section 904(d)(2)(E) paid in taxable years beginning before January 1, 2003

(f) [Reserved]. For further guidance, see § 1.904-4T(f).

(g) [Reserved]. For further guidance, see § 1.904-4T(g).

(h) Export financing interest. *(1) Definitions.* (i) Export financing interest. The term "export financing interest" means any interest derived from financing the sale (or other disposition) for use or consumption outside the United States of any property that is manufactured, produced, grown, or extracted in the United States by the taxpayer or a related person, and not more than 50 percent of the fair market value of which is attributable to products imported into the United States. For purposes of this paragraph, the term "United States" includes the fifty States, the District of Columbia, and the Commonwealth of Puerto Rico.

(ii) Fair market value. For purposes of this paragraph, the fair market value of any property imported into the United States shall be its appraised value, as determined by the Secretary under section 402 of the Tariff Act of 1930 (19 U.S.C. 1401a) in connection with its importation. For purposes of determining the foreign content of an item of property imported into the United States, see section 927 and the regulations thereunder.

(iii) Related person. For purposes of this paragraph, the term "related person" has the meaning given it by section 954(d)(3) except that such section shall be applied by substituting "the person with respect to whom the determination is being made" for "controlled foreign corporation" each place it applies.

(2) Treatment of export financing interest. Except as provided in paragraph (h)(3) of this section, if a taxpayer (including a financial services entity) receives or accrues export financing interest from an unrelated person, then that interest shall be treated as general category income.

(3) [Reserved]. For further guidance, see § 1.904-4T(h)(3).

(4) Examples. The following examples illustrate the operation of paragraph (h)(3) of this section:

Example (1). Controlled foreign corporation S is a wholly-owned subsidiary of domestic corporation P. S is not a financial services entity and has accumulated cash reserves. P has uncollected trade and service receivables of foreign obligors. P sells the receivables at a discount (" factors") to S. The income derived by S on the receivables is related person factoring income. The income is also export financing interest. Because the income is related person factoring income, the income is passive income to S.

Example (2). The facts are the same as in Example (1) except that S is a financial services entity and derives the income in an active financing business. The income derived by S on the receivables is related person factoring income and is also export financing interest. Therefore, pursuant to paragraph (h)(3)(iii) of this section, the income is financial services income to S.

Example (3). Domestic corporation S is a wholly-owned subsidiary of domestic corporation P. S is not a financial services entity and has accumulated cash reserves. P has uncollected trade and service receivables of foreign obligors. P factors the receivables to S. The income derived by S on the receivables is related person factoring income. The income is also export financing interest. The income will be passive income to S.

Example (4). The facts are the same as in *Example (3)* except that instead of factoring P's receivables, S finances the sales of P's goods by making loans to the purchasers of P's goods. The interest derived by S on these loans is export financing interest and is not related person factoring income. The income will be general limitation income to S.

(5) Income eligible for section 864(d)(7) exception (same country exception) from related person factoring treatment. (i) Income other than interest. If any foreign person receives or accrues income that is described in section 864(d)(7) (income on a trade or service receivable acquired from a related person in the same foreign country as the recipient) and such income would also meet the definition of export financing interest if section 864(d)(1) applied to such income (income on a trade or service receivable acquired from a related person treated as interest), then the income shall be considered to be export financing interest and shall be treated as general category income.

(ii) Interest income. If export financing interest is received or accrued by any foreign person and that income would otherwise be treated as related person factoring income under section 864(d)(6) if section 864(d)(7) did not apply, section 904(d)(2)(B)(iii)(I) shall apply, and the interest shall be treated as general category income. If that interest is received or accrued by a financial services entity, section 904(d)(2)(C)(iii)(III) shall apply and the interest shall be treated as general limitation income.

(iii) Examples. The following examples illustrate the operation of this paragraph (h)(5):

Example (1). Controlled foreign corporation S is a wholly-owned subsidiary of domestic corporation P. Controlled foreign corporation T is a wholly-owned subsidiary of controlled foreign corporation S. S and T are incorporated in Country M. In 1987, P sells tractors to T, which T sells to X, an unrelated foreign corporation organized in country M. The tractors are to be used in country M. T uses a substantial part of its assets in its trade or business located in Country M. T has uncollected trade receivables from X that it factors to S. S derived more than 20 percent of its gross income for 1987 other than from an active financing business and the income derived by S from the receivables is not derived in an active financing business. Thus, pursuant to paragraph (e)(3)(i) of this section, S is not a financial services entity. The income is not related person factoring income because it is described in section 864(d)(7) (income eligible for the same country exception). If section 864(d)(1) applied, the income S derived from the receivables would meet the definition of export financing interest. The income, therefore, is considered to be export financing interest and is general category income to S.

Example (2). The facts are the same as in Example (1) except that S is a financial services entity and derives the income on the receivables from the conduct of an active financing business. The income S derives from the receivables is not related person factoring income because it is described in section 864(d)(7). If the income would be high withholding tax interest but for section 904(d)(2)(B)(ii), then the income will not be considered to be export financing interest and will be financial services income to S. Otherwise, the income will be considered to be export financing interest and will be general limitation income to S.

Example (3). Controlled foreign corporation S is a wholly-owned subsidiary of domestic corporation, P. Controlled foreign corporation T is a wholly-owned subsidiary of controlled foreign corporation S. S and T are incorporated in country M. S is not a financial services entity. In 1987, P sells tractors to T, which T sells to X, a foreign partnership that is organized in country M and is related to S and T. S makes a loan to X to finance the tractor sales. The interest earned by S from financing the sales is described in section 864(d)(7) and is export financing interest. Therefore, the income shall be general limitation income to S.

Example (4). The facts are the same as in Example (3) except that S is a financial services entity and derives the interest on the loan to X in an active financing business. The interest S earns is export financing interest that is not described in section 864(d)(1) because it is described in section 864(d)(7). Because the interest is described in section 864(d)(7) and is export financing interest, section 904(d)(2)(C)(iii)(III) shall apply and the income shall be general limitation income to S, unless it would also be high withholding tax interest but for section 904(d)(2)(B)(ii), in which case it will be financial services income to S.

(i) Interaction of section 907(c) and income described in this section. If a person receives or accrues income that is income described in section 907(c) (relating to oil and gas income), the rules of section 907(c) and the regulations thereunder, as well as the rules of this section, shall apply to the income. The reduction in amount allowed as foreign tax provided by section 907(a) shall therefore be calculated separately for dividends received or accrued by the taxpayer from each separate noncontrolled section 902 corporation.

(j) Special rule for DASTM gain or loss. Any DASTM gain or loss computed under § 1.985-3(d) must be allocated among the categories of income under the rules of § 1.985-3(e)(2)(iv) or (e)(3). The rules of § 1.985-3(e) apply before the rules of section 904(d)(2)(B)(iii)(II) (the exception from passive income for high-taxed income).

(k) Special rule for alternative minimum tax foreign tax credit. For purposes of computing the alternative minimum tax foreign tax credit under section 59(a), items included in alternative minimum taxable income by reason of section 56(g) (adjustments based on adjusted current earnings) shall be characterized as income described in a separate category under section 904(d) and this section based on the character of the underlying items of income.

(l) [Reserved]. For further guidance, see § 1.904-4T(l).

(m) Income treated as allocable to an additional separate category. If section 904(a), (b), and (c) are applied separately to any category of income under the Internal Revenue Code (for example, under section 56(g)(4)(C)(iii)(IV), 245(a)(10), 865(h), 901(j), or 904(h)(10)), that category of income will be treated for all purposes of the Internal Revenue Code and regulations as if it were a separate category listed in section 904(d)(1).

T.D. 8214, 7/15/88, amend T.D. 8412, 5/13/92, T.D. 8556, 7/22/94, T.D. 8805, 1/8/99, T.D. 8916, 12/27/2000, T.D. 8973, 12/27/2001, T.D. 9141, 7/19/2004, T.D. 9260, 4/24/2006, T.D. 9368, 12/20/2007.

PAR. 3. In § 1.904-4, paragraphs (a), (b), (h)(3), and (l) are revised and paragraph (n) is added to read as follows:

Proposed § 1.904-4 Separate application of section 904 with respect to certain categories of income. [*For Preamble, see ¶ 152,939*]

(a) [The text of the proposed amendment to § 1.904-4(a) is the same as the text of § 1.904-4T(a) published elsewhere in this issue of the Federal Register.] [*See T.D. 9368, 12/21/2007, 72 Fed. Reg. 245.*]

(b) [The text of the proposed amendment to § 1.904-4(b) is the same as the text of § 1.904-4T(b) published elsewhere in this issue of the Federal Register.] [*See T.D. 9368, 12/21/2007, 72 Fed. Reg. 245.*]

* * * * *

(h) * * *

(3) [The text of the proposed amendment to § 1.904-4(h)(3) is the same as the text of § 1.904-4T(h)(3) published elsewhere in this issue of the Federal Register.] [*See T.D. 9368, 12/21/2007, 72 Fed. Reg. 245.*]

* * * * *

(l) [The text of the proposed amendment to § 1.904-4(l) is the same as the text of § 1.904-4T(l) published elsewhere in this issue of the Federal Register.] [*See T.D. 9368, 12/21/2007, 72 Fed. Reg. 245.*]

* * * * *

(n) [The text of proposed § 1.904-4(n) is the same as the text of § 1.904-4T(n) published elsewhere in this issue of the Federal Register.] [*See T.D. 9368, 12/21/2007, 72 Fed. Reg. 245.*]

PAR. 6. In § 1.904-4, paragraph (c) is revised to read as follows:

Proposed § 1.904-4 Separate application of section 904 with respect to certain categories of income. [*For Preamble, see ¶ 152,753*]

* * * * *

(c) [The text of the proposed amendments to § 1.904-4(c) is the same as the text of § 1.904-4T(c) published elsewhere in this issue of the Federal Register.] [*See T.D. 9260, 04/24/2006, 71 Fed. Reg. 79.*]

§ 1.904-4T Separate application of section 904 with respect to certain categories of income (temporary).

• ***Caution:*** Under Code Sec. 7805, temporary regulations expire within three years of the date of issuance. This temporary regulation was issued on 4/24/2006.

(a) In general. A taxpayer is required to compute a separate foreign tax credit limitation for income received or accrued in a taxable year that is described in section 904(d)(1)(A) (passive category income), 904(d)(1)(B) (general category income), or § 1.904-4(m) (additional separate categories).

(b) Passive category income. *(1) In general.* The term passive category income means passive income and specified passive category income.

(2) Passive income. (i) In general. The term passive income means any--

(A) Income received or accrued by any person that is of a kind that would be foreign personal holding company income (as defined in section 954(c)) if the taxpayer were a controlled foreign corporation, including any amount of gain on the sale or exchange of stock in excess of the amount treated as a dividend under section 1248; or

(B) Amount includible in gross income under section 1293.

(ii) Exceptions. Passive income does not include any export financing interest (as defined in section 904(d)(2)(G) and paragraph (h) of this section), any high-taxed income (as defined in section 904(d)(2)(F) and paragraph (c) of this section), or any active rents and royalties (as defined in paragraph (b)(2)(iii) of this section). In addition, passive income does not include any income that would otherwise be passive but is characterized as income in another separate category under the look-through rules of section 904(d)(3), (d)(4), and (d)(6)(C) and the regulations under those provisions. In determining whether any income is of a kind that would be foreign personal holding company income, the rules of section 864(d)(5)(A)(i) and (6) (treating related person factoring income of a controlled foreign corporation as foreign personal holding company income that is not eligible for the export financing income exception to the separate limitation for passive income) shall apply only in the case of income of a controlled foreign corporation (as defined in section 957). Thus, income earned directly by a United States person that is related person factoring income may be eligible for the exception for export financing interest.

(iii) Active rents or royalties. (A) In general. For rents and royalties paid or accrued after September 20, 2004, passive income does not include any rents or royalties that are derived in the active conduct of a trade or business, regardless of whether such rents or royalties are received from a related or an unrelated person. Except as provided in paragraph (b)(2)(iii)(B) of this section, the principles of section 954(c)(2)(A) and the regulations under that section shall apply in determining whether rents or royalties are derived in the active conduct of a trade or business. For this purpose, the term taxpayer shall be substituted for the term controlled foreign corporation if the recipient of the rents or royalties is not a controlled foreign corporation.

(B) Active conduct of trade or business. Rents and royalties are considered derived in the active conduct of a trade or business by a United States person or by a controlled foreign corporation (or other entity to which the look-through rules apply) for purposes of section 904 (but not for purposes of section 954) if the requirements of section 954(c)(2)(A) are satisfied by one or more corporations that are members of an affiliated group of corporations (within the meaning of section 1504(a), determined without regard to section 1504(b)(3)) of which the recipient is a member. For purposes of this paragraph (b)(2)(iii)(B), an affiliated group includes only domestic corporations and foreign corporations that are controlled foreign corporations in which domestic members of the affiliated group own, directly or indirectly, at least 80 percent of the total voting power and value of the stock. For purposes of this paragraph (b)(2)(iii)(B), indirect ownership shall be determined under section 318 and the regulations under that section.

(iv) Examples. The following examples illustrate the application of paragraph (b)(2) of this section.

Example (1). P is a domestic corporation with a branch in foreign country X. P does not have any financial services income. For 2008, P has a net foreign currency gain that would not constitute foreign personal holding company income if P were a controlled foreign corporation because the gain is directly related to the business needs of P. The currency gain is, therefore, general category income to P because it is not income of a kind that would be foreign personal holding company income.

Example (2). Controlled foreign corporation S is a wholly-owned subsidiary of P, a domestic corporation. S is regularly engaged in the restaurant franchise business. P licenses trademarks, tradenames, certain know-how, related services, and certain restaurant designs for which S pays P an arm's length royalty. P is regularly engaged in the development and licensing of such property. The royalties received by P for the use of its property are allocable under the look-through rules of § 1.904-5 to the royalties S receives from the franchisees. Some of the franchisees are unrelated to S and P. Other franchisees are related to S or P and use the licensed property outside of S's country of incorporation. S does not satisfy, but P does satisfy, the active trade or business requirements of section 954(c)(2)(A) and the regulations under that section. The royalty income earned by S with regard to both its related and unrelated franchisees is foreign personal holding company income because S does not satisfy the active trade or business requirements of section 954(c)(2)(A) and, in addition, the royalty income from the related franchisees does not qualify for the same country exception of section 954(c)(3). However, all of the royalty income earned by S is general category income to S under § 1.904-4(b)(2)(iii) because P, a member of S's affiliated group (as defined therein), satisfies the active trade or business test (which is applied without regard to whether the royalties are paid by a related person). S's royalty income that is taxable to P under subpart F and the royalties paid to P are general category income to P under the look-through rules of § 1.904-5(c)(1)(i) and (c)(3), respectively.

(3) Specified passive category income means

(i) Dividends from a DISC or former DISC (as defined in section 992(a)) to the extent such dividends are treated as income from sources without the United States;

(ii) Taxable income attributable to foreign trade income (within the meaning of section 923(b)); or

(iii) Distributions from a FSC (or a former FSC) out of earnings and profits attributable to foreign trade income (within the meaning of section 923(b)) or interest or carrying charges (as defined in section 927(d)(1)) derived from a transaction which results in foreign trade income (as defined in section 923(b)).

(c) *(1)* [Reserved]. For further guidance, see § 1.904-4(c)(1).

(2) Grouping of items of income in order to determine whether passive income is high-taxed income. (i) Effective dates. For purposes of determining whether passive income is high-taxed income, the grouping rules of paragraphs (c)(3) and (c)(4) of this section apply to taxable years beginning after December 31, 2002. For corresponding rules applicable to taxable years beginning before January 1, 2003, see 26 CFR § 1.904-4(c)(2)(i) (revised as of April 1, 2006).

(ii) [Reserved]. For further guidance, see § 1.904-4(c)(2)(ii).

(3) Amounts received or accrued by United States persons. Except as otherwise provided in § 1.904-4(c)(5), all passive income received by a United States person shall be subject to the rules of this paragraph (c)(3). However, subpart F inclusions that are passive income, dividends from a controlled foreign corporation or noncontrolled section 902 corporation that are passive income, and income that is earned by a United States person through a foreign qualified business unit (foreign QBU) that is passive income shall be subject to the rules of this paragraph only to the extent provided in paragraph (c)(4) of this section. For purposes of this section, a foreign QBU is a QBU (as defined in section 989(a)), other than a controlled foreign corporation or noncontrolled section 902 corporation, that has its principal place of business outside the United States. These rules shall apply whether the income is received from a controlled foreign corporation of which the United States person is a United States shareholder, from a noncontrolled section 902 corporation of which the United States person is a domestic corporation meeting the stock ownership requirements of section 902(a), or from any other person. For purposes of determining whether passive income is high-taxed income, the following rules apply:

(i) All passive income received during the taxable year that is subject to a withholding tax of fifteen percent or greater shall be treated as one item of income.

(ii) All passive income received during the taxable year that is subject to a withholding tax of less than fifteen percent (but greater than zero) shall be treated as one item of income.

(iii) All passive income received during the taxable year that is subject to no withholding tax or other foreign tax shall be treated as one item of income.

(iv) All passive income received during the taxable year that is subject to no withholding tax but is subject to a foreign tax other than a withholding tax shall be treated as one item of income.

(4) Dividends and inclusions from controlled foreign corporations, dividends from noncontrolled section 902 corporations, and income of foreign QBUs. Except as provided in paragraph (c)(5) of this section, all dividends and all amounts included in gross income of a United States shareholder under section 951(a)(1) with respect to the foreign corporation that (after application of the look-through rules of section 904(d)(3) and § 1.904-5) are attributable to passive income received or accrued by a controlled foreign corporation, all dividends from a noncontrolled section 902 corporation that are received or accrued by a domestic corporate shareholder meeting the stock ownership requirements of section 902(a) that (after application of the look-through

rules of section 904(d)(4) and § 1.904-5) are treated as passive income, and all amounts of passive income received or accrued by a United States person through a foreign QBU shall be subject to the rules of this paragraph (c)(4). This paragraph (c)(4) shall be applied separately to dividends and inclusions with respect to each controlled foreign corporation of which the taxpayer is a United States shareholder and to dividends with respect to each noncontrolled section 902 corporation of which the taxpayer is a domestic corporate shareholder meeting the stock ownership requirements of section 902(a). This paragraph (c)(4) also shall be applied separately to income attributable to each QBU of a controlled foreign corporation, noncontrolled section 902 corporation, or any other look-through entity as defined in § 1.904-5(i), except that if the entity subject to the look-through rules is a United States person, then this paragraph (c)(4) shall be applied separately only to each foreign QBU of that United States person.

(i) through (h)(2) [Reserved]. For further guidance, see § 1.904-4(c)(i) through (h)(2).

(h) *(3) Exception.* Unless it is received or accrued by a financial services entity, export financing interest shall be treated as passive category income if that income is also related person factoring income. For this purpose, related person factoring income is--

(i) Income received or accrued by a controlled foreign corporation that is income described in section 864(d)(6) (income of a controlled foreign corporation from a loan for the purpose of financing the purchase of inventory property of a related person); or

(ii) Income received or accrued by any person that is income described in section 864(d)(1) (income from a trade receivable acquired from a related person).

(4) through (k) [Reserved]. For further guidance, see § 1.904-4(h)(3)(iii) through (k).

(l) Priority rule. Income that meets the definitions of a separate category described in paragraph (m) of this section and another category of income described in section 904(d)(2)(A)(i) and (ii) will be subject to the separate limitation described in paragraph (m) of this section and will not be treated as general category income described in section 904(d)(2)(A)(ii).

(m) [Reserved]. For further guidance, see § 1.904-4(m).

(n) Effective/applicability date. Paragraphs (a), (b), (h)(3), and (l) of this section shall apply to taxable years of United States taxpayers beginning after December 31, 2006 and ending on or after December 21, 2007, and to taxable years of a foreign corporation which end with or within taxable years of its domestic corporate shareholder beginning after December 31, 2006 and ending on or after December 21, 2007.

(o) Expiration date. The applicability of paragraphs (a), (b), (h)(3)(ii) and (l) of this section expires on December 20, 2010.

T.D. 9260, 4/24/2006, amend T.D. 9368, 12/20/2007.

§ 1.904-5 Look-through rules as applied to controlled foreign corporations and other entities.

Caution: The Treasury has not yet amended Reg § 1.904-5 to reflect changes made by P.L. 100-647.

(a) and (a)(1) [Reserved]. For further guidance, see § 1.904-5T(a) introductory text and (a)(1).

(2) The term "controlled foreign corporation" has the meaning given such term by section 957 (taking into account the special rule for certain captive insurance companies contained in section 953(c)).

(3) The term "United States shareholder" has the meaning given such term by section 951(b) (taking into account the special rule for certain captive insurance companies contained in section 953(c)), except that for purposes of this section, a United States shareholder shall include any member of the controlled group of the United States shareholder. For this purpose the controlled group is any member of the affiliated group within the meaning of section 1504(a)(1) except that "more than 50 percent" shall be substituted for "at least 80 percent" wherever it appears in section 1504(a)(2). For taxable years beginning before January 1, 2001, the preceding sentence shall be applied by substituting "50 percent" for "more than 50 percent".

(4) [Reserved]. For further guidance, see § 1.904-5T(a)(4).

(b) [Reserved]. For further guidance, see § 1.904-5T(b).

(c) Rules for specific types of inclusions and payments. *(1) Subpart F inclusions.* (i) Rule. Any amount included in gross income under section 951(a)(1)(A) shall be treated as income in a separate category to the extent the amount so included is attributable to income received or accrued by the controlled foreign corporation that is described as income in such category. For purposes of this § 1.904-5, income shall be characterized under the rules of § 1.904-4 prior to the application of the rules of paragraph (c) of this section. For rules concerning inclusions under section 951(a)(1)(B), see paragraph (c)(4)(i) of this section.

(ii) Examples. The following examples illustrate the application of this paragraph (c)(1):

Example (1). Controlled foreign corporation S is a wholly-owned subsidiary of P, a domestic corporation. S earns $200 of net income, $85 of which is foreign base company shipping income, $15 of which is foreign personal holding company income, and $100 of which is non-subpart F general limitation income. No foreign tax is imposed on the income. One hundred dollars ($100) of S's income is subpart F income taxed currently to P under section 951(a)(1)(A). Because $85 of the subpart F inclusion is attributable to shipping income of S, $85 of the subpart F inclusion is shipping income to P. Because $15 of the subpart F inclusion is attributable to passive income of S, $15 of the subpart F inclusion is passive income to P.

Example (2). Controlled foreign corporation S is a wholly-owned subsidiary of domestic corporation P. S is a financial services entity. P manufactures cars and is not a financial services entity. In 1987, S earns $200 of interest income unrelated to its banking business and $900 of interest income related to its banking business. Assume that S pays no foreign taxes and has no expenses. All of S's income is included in P's gross income as foreign personal holding company income. Because S is a financial services entity, income that would otherwise be passive income is considered to be financial services income. P, therefore, treats the entire subpart F inclusion as financial services income.

Example (3). Controlled foreign corporation S is a wholly-owned subsidiary of domestic corporation P. P is a financial services entity. S manufactures cars and is not a financial services entity. In 1987, S earns $200 of passive income that is subpart F income and $900 of general limitation non-subpart F income. Assume that S pays no foreign taxes on its passive earnings and has no expenses. P includes the $200 of subpart F income in gross income. Because P is a financial services entity, the inclusion will be financial services income to P.

Example (4). Controlled foreign corporation S is a wholly-owned subsidiary of domestic corporation P. Neither P nor S is a financial services entity. Controlled foreign corporation T is a wholly-owned subsidiary of controlled foreign corporation S. T is a financial services entity. In 1991, T pays a dividend to S. For purposes of determining whether S is a financial services entity under § 1.904-4(e)(3)(i), the dividend from T is ignored. For purposes of characterizing the dividend in S's hands under the look-through rules of paragraph (c)(4) of this section, however, the dividend retains its character as financial services income. Similarly, any subpart F inclusion or dividend to P out of the earnings and profits attributable to the dividend from S is excluded in determining whether P is a financial services entity under § 1.904-4(e)(3)(i), but retains its character in P's hands as financial services income under paragraph (c)(4) of this section.

Example (5). Controlled foreign corporation S is a wholly-owned subsidiary of domestic corporation P. S owns 40 percent of foreign corporation A, 45 percent of foreign corporation B, 30 percent of foreign corporation C and 20 percent of foreign corporation D. A, B, C, and D are noncontrolled section 902 corporations. In 1987, S's only income is a $100 dividend from each foreign corporation. Assume that S pays no foreign taxes and has no expenses. All $400 of the income is foreign personal holding company income and is included in P's gross income. P must include $100 in its separate limitation for dividends from A, $100 in its separate limitation for dividends from B, $100 in its separate limitation for dividends from C, and $100 in its separate limitation for dividends from D.

(2) Interest. (i) In general. For purposes of this paragraph, related person interest is any interest paid or accrued by a controlled foreign corporation to any United States shareholder in that corporation (or to any other related person) to which the look-through rules of section 904(d)(3) and this section apply. Unrelated person interest is all interest other than related person interest. Related person interest shall be treated as income in a separate category to the extent it is allocable to income of the controlled foreign corporation in that category. If related person interest is received or accrued from a controlled foreign corporation by two or more persons, the amount of interest received or accrued by each person that is allocable to any separate category of income shall be determined by multiplying the amount of related person interest allocable to that separate category of income by a fraction. The numerator of the fraction is the amount of related person interest received or accrued by that person and the denominator is the total amount of related person interest paid or accrued by the controlled foreign corporation.

(ii) Allocating and apportioning expenses of a controlled foreign corporation including interest paid to a related person. Related person interest and other expenses of a controlled foreign corporation shall be allocated and apportioned in the following manner:

(A) Gross income in each separate category shall be determined;

(B) Any expenses that are definitely related to less than all of gross income as a class, including unrelated person interest that is directly allocated to income from a specific property, shall be allocated and apportioned under the principles of §§ 1.861-8 or 1.861-10T, as applicable, to income in each separate category;

(C) Related person interest shall be allocated to and shall reduce (but not below zero) the amount of passive foreign personal holding company income as determined after the application of paragraph (c)(2)(ii)(B) of this section;

(D) To the extent that related person interest exceeds passive foreign personal holding company income as determined after the application of paragraphs (c)(2)(ii)(B) and (C) of this section, the related person interest shall be apportioned under the rules of this paragraph to separate categories other than passive income.

(1) If under § 1.861-9T, the modified gross income method of apportioning interest expense is elected, related person interest shall be apportioned as follows:

$$\text{Related person interest—Related person interest allocated under paragraph (c)(2)(ii)(C) of this section} \times \frac{\text{Gross income in a separate category (other than passive)}}{\text{Total gross income (other than passive)}}$$

(2) If under § 1.861-9T, the asset method of apportioning interest expense is elected, related person interest shall be apportioned according to the following formula:

$$\text{Related person interest minus Related person interest minus allocated under paragraph (c)(2)(ii)(C) of this section} \times \frac{\text{Value of assets in a separate category (other than passive)}}{\text{Value of total assets (other than passive)}}$$

(E) Any other expenses (including unrelated person interest that is not directly allocated to income from a specific property) that are not definitely related expenses or that are definitely related to all of gross income as a class shall be apportioned under the rules of this paragraph to reduce income in each separate category.

(1) If under § 1.861-9T, the modified gross income method of apportioning interest expense is elected, the interest expense shall be apportioned as follows:

Expense apportionable to a separate category =

$$\text{Expense} \times \frac{\text{Gross income in a separate category (minus related person interest allocated under paragraph (c)(2)(ii)(C) of this section if the category is passive)}}{\text{Total gross income minus related person interest allocated to passive income under paragraph (c)(2)(ii)(C) of this section}}$$

(2) If under § 1.861-9T, the asset method of apportioning interest expense is elected, then the expense shall be apportioned as follows:

Expense apportionable to a separate category =

$$\text{Expense} \times \frac{\text{Value of assets in a separate category (minus related person debt allocated to passive assets if the category is passive)}}{\text{Value of total assets minus related person debt allocated to passive assets}}$$

(3) Expenses other than interest shall be apportioned in a similar manner depending on the apportionment method used. See § 1.861-8T(c)(1)(i)-(vi).

(iii) [Reserved]. For further guidance, see § 1.904-5T(c)(2)(iii).

(iv) Definitions. (A) Value of assets and reduction in value of assets and gross income. For purposes of paragraph (c)(2)(ii)(D) and (E) of this section, the value of total assets is the value of assets in all categories (determined under the principles of § 1.861-9T(g). See § 1.861-10T(d)(2) to determine the reduction in value of assets and gross income for purposes of apportioning additional third person interest expense that is not directly allocated when some interest expense has been directly allocated. For purposes of this paragraph and paragraph (c)(2)(ii)(E) of this section, any reduction in the value of assets for indebtedness that relates to interest allocated under paragraph (c)(2)(ii)(C) of this section is made before determining the average of asset values. For rules relating to the averaging of reduced asset values see § 1.861-9T(g)(2).

(B) Related person debt allocated to passive assets. For purposes of paragraph (c)(2)(ii)(E) of this section, related person debt allocated to passive assets is determined as follows:

$$\text{Related person debt allocated to the passive category} = \text{Total related person debt} \times \frac{\text{Related person interest allocable to passive income under paragraph (c)(2)(ii)(C)}}{\text{All related person interest}}$$

For this purpose, the term "total related person debt" means the sum of the principal amounts of obligations of a controlled foreign corporation owed to any United States shareholder of such corporation or to any related entity (within the meaning of paragraph (g) of this section) determined at the end of the taxable year.

(v) Examples. The following examples illustrate the operation of this paragraph (c)(2).

Example (1). (i) Controlled foreign corporation S is a wholly-owned subsidiary of P, a domestic corporation. In 1987, S earns $200 of foreign personal holding company income that is passive income. S also earns $100 of foreign base company sales income that is general limitation income. S has $2000 of passive assets and $2000 of general limitation assets. In 1987, S makes a $150 interest payment to P with respect to a $1500 loan from P. S also pays $100 of interest to an unrelated person on a $1000 loan from that person. S has no other expenses. S uses the asset method to apportion interest expense.

(ii) Under paragraph (c)(2)(ii)(C) of this section, the $150 related person interest payment is allocable to S's passive foreign personal holding company income. Therefore, the $150 interest payment is passive income to P. Because the entire related person interest payment is allocated to passive income under paragraph (c)(2)(ii)(C) of this section, none of the related person interest payment is apportioned to general limitation income under paragraph (c)(2)(ii)(D) of this section. Under paragraph (c)(2)(iii)(B) of this section, the entire amount of the related person debt is allocable to passive assets ($1500 = $1500 × $150/$150). Under paragraph (c)(2)(ii)(E) of this section, $20 of interest expense paid to an unrelated person is apportioned to passive income ($20 = $100 × ($2000 − $1500)/($4000 − $1500)). Eighty dollars ($80) of the interest expense paid to an unrelated person is apportioned to general limitation income ($80 = $100 × $2000/($4000 − $1500)).

Example (2). The facts are the same as in Example (1), except that S uses the gross income method to apportion interest expense. Under paragraph (c)(2)(ii)(E) of this section, the unrelated person interest expense would be apportioned on a gross income method. Therefore, $33 of interest expense paid to unrelated persons would be apportioned to passive income ($33 = $100 × ($200 − $150)/($300 − $150) and $67 of interest expense paid to unrelated persons would be allocated to general limitation income ($67 = $100 × $100/($300 − $150).

Example (3). (i) The facts are the same as in *Example* (1), except that S has an additional $50 of third person interest expense that is directly allocated to income from a specific property that produces only passive income. The principal amount of indebtedness to which the interest relates is $500. S also has $50 of additional non-interest expenses that are not definitely related expenses and that are apportioned on an asset basis.

(ii) Under paragraph (c)(2)(ii)(B) of this section, the $50 of directly allocated third person interest is first allocated to reduce the passive income of S. Under paragraph (c)(2)(ii)(C) of this section, the $150 of related person interest is allocated to the remaining $150 of passive income. Under paragraph (c)(2)(iii)(B) of this section, all of the related person debt is allocated to passive assets. ($1500 = $1500 × $150/$150).

(iii) Under paragraph (c)(2)(ii)(E) of this section, the noninterest expenses that are not definitely related are apportioned on the basis of the asset values reduced by the allocated related person debt. Therefore, $10 of these expenses are apportioned to the passive category ($50 × ($2000 − $1500)/($4000 − $1500)) and $40 are apportioned to the general limitation category ($50 × $2000/($4000 − $1500)).

(iv) In order to apportion third person interest between the categories of assets, the value of assets in a separate category must also be reduced under the principles of § 1.861-8 by the indebtedness relating to the specifically allocated interest. Therefore, under paragraph (c)(2)(iii)(B) of this section, the value of assets in the passive category for purposes of apportioning the additional third person interest = 0 ($2000 minus $500 (the principal amount of the debt, the interest payment on which is directly allocated to specific interest producing properties) minus $1500 (the related person debt allocated to passive assets)). Under paragraph (c)(2)(ii)(E) of this section, all $100 of the non-definitely related third person interest is apportioned to the general limitation category ($100 = $100 × $2000/($4000 − $500 − $1500)).

Example (4). (i) Controlled foreign corporation S is a wholly-owned subsidiary of P, a domestic corporation. In 1987, S earns $100 of foreign personal holding company income that is passive income. S also earns $100 of foreign base company sales income that is general limitation income. S has $1000 of general limitation assets and $1000 of passive assets. In 1987, S makes a $150 interest payment to P on a $1500 loan from P and has $20 of general and administrative expenses (G & A) that under the principles of §§ 1.861-8 through 1.861-14T is treated as directly allocable to all of P's gross income. S also makes a $25 interest payment to an unrelated person on a $250 loan from the unrelated person. S has no other expenses. S uses the asset method to apportion interest expense. S uses the gross income method to apportion G & A.

(ii) Under paragraph (c)(2)(ii)(C) of this section, $100 of the interest payment to P is allocable to S's passive foreign personal holding company income. Under paragraph (c)(2)(ii)(D) of this section, the additional $50 of related person interest expense is apportioned to general limitation income ($50 = $50 × $1000/$1000). Under paragraph (c)(2)(iii)(B) of this section, related person debt allocated to passive assets equals $1000 ($1000 = $1500 × $100/$150).

(iii) Under paragraph (c)(2)(ii)(E) of this section, none of the $25 of interest expense paid to an unrelated person is apportioned to passive income ($0 = $25 × ($1000 − $1000)/($2000 − $1000). Twenty-five dollars ($25) of the interest expense paid to an unrelated person is apportioned to general limitation income ($25 = $25 × $1000/$2000 − $1000). Under paragraph (c)(2)(ii)(E) of this section, none of the G & A is allocable to S's passive foreign personal holding company income ($0 = $20 × ($100 − $100)/($200 − $100). All $20 of the G & A is apportioned to S's general limitation income ($20 = $20 × $100/($200 − $100).

Example (5). The facts are the same as in *Example* (4), except that S uses the gross income method to apportion interest expense. As in *Example* (4), $100 of the interest payment to P is allocated to passive income under paragraph (c)(2)(ii)(C) of this section. Under paragraph (c)(2)(ii)(D) of this section, the additional $50 of related person interest expense is apportioned to general limitation income ($150 − 100 × $100/$100). Under paragraph (c)(2)(ii)(E) of this section, none of the unrelated person interest expense and none of the G & A is apportioned to passive income, because after the application of paragraph (c)(2)(ii)(C) of this section, no passive income remains in the passive income category.

Example (6). Controlled foreign corporation T is a wholly-owned subsidiary of S, a controlled foreign corporation. S is a wholly-owned subsidiary of P, a domestic corporation. S is not a financial services entity. S and T are incorporated in the same country. In 1987, P sells tractors to T, which T sells to X, a foreign corporation that is related to both S and T and is organized in the same country as S and T. S makes a loan to X to finance the tractor sales. Assume that the interest earned by S from financing the sales is export financing interest that is neither related person factoring income nor foreign personal holding company income. The export financing interest earned by S is, therefore, general limitation income. S earns no other income. S makes a $100 interest payment to P. The $100 of interest paid is allocable under the look-through rules of paragraph (c)(2)(ii) of this section to the general limitation income earned by S and is therefore general limitation income to P.

(3) Rents and royalties. Any rents or royalties received or accrued from a controlled foreign corporation in which the taxpayer is a United States shareholder shall be treated as income in a separate category to the extent they are allocable to income of the controlled foreign corporation in that category under the principles of §§ 1.861-8 through 1.861-14T.

(4) Dividends. (i) Look-through rule for controlled foreign corporations. Any dividend paid or accrued out of the earnings and profits of any controlled foreign corporation, shall be treated as income in a separate category in proportion to the ratio of the portion of earnings and profits attributable to income in such category to the total amount of earnings and profits of the controlled foreign corporation. For purposes of this paragraph, the term "dividend" includes any amount included in gross income under section 951(a)(1)(B) as a pro rata share of a controlled foreign corporation's increase in earnings invested in United States property.

(ii) Special rule for dividends attributable to certain loans. If a dividend is distributed to a taxpayer by a controlled foreign corporation, that controlled foreign corporation is the recipient of loan proceeds from a related look-through entity (within the meaning of § 1.904-5(i)), and the purpose of such loan is to alter the characterization of the dividend for purposes of this section, then, to the extent of the principal amount of the loan, the dividend shall be characterized with respect to the earnings and profits of the related person lender rather than with respect to the earnings and profits of the dividend payor. A loan will not be considered made for the purpose of altering the characterization of a dividend if the loan would have been made or maintained on substantially the same terms irrespective of the dividend. The determination of whether a loan would have been made or maintained on substantially the same terms irrespective of the dividend will be made taking into account all the facts and circumstances of the relationship between the lender and the borrower. Thus, for example, a loan by a related party lender to a controlled foreign corporation that arises from the sale of inventory in the ordinary course of business will not be considered a loan made for the purpose of altering the character of any dividend paid by the borrower.

(iii) [Reserved]. For further guidance, see § 1.904-5T(c)(4)(iii).

(iv) Examples. The following examples illustrate the application of this paragraph (c)(4).

Example (1). Controlled foreign corporation S is a wholly-owned subsidiary of P, a domestic corporation. In 1987, S has earnings and profits of $1,000, $600 of which is attributable to general limitation income and $400 of which is attributable to dividends received by S from its wholly-owned subsidiary, T. T is a controlled foreign corporation and is incorporated and operates in the same country as S. All of T's income is financial services income. Neither S's general limitation income nor the dividend from T is subpart F income. In December 1987, S pays a dividend to P of $200, all of which is attributable to earnings and profits earned in 1987. Six-tenths of the dividend ($120) is treated as general limitation income because six-tenths of S's earnings and profits are attributable to general limitation income. Four-tenths of the dividend ($80) is treated as financial services income because four-tenths of S's earnings and profits are attributable to dividends from T, and all of T's earnings are financial services income.

Example (2). A, a United States person, has been the sole shareholder in controlled foreign corporation X since its organization on January 1, 1963. Both X and A are calendar year taxpayers. X's earnings and profits for 1963 through the end of 1987 totaled $3,000. A sells his stock in X at the end of 1987 and realizes a gain of $4,000. Of the total $4,000 gain, $3,000 (A's share of the post-1962 earnings and profits) is includible in A's gross income as a dividend and is subject to the look-through rules including the transition rule of § 1.904-7(a) with respect to the portion of the distribution out of pre-87 earnings and profits. The remaining $1,000 of the gain is includible as gain from the sale or exchange of the X stock and is passive income to A.

(d) Effect of exclusions from subpart F income. *(1) De minimis amount of subpart F income.* If the sum of a controlled foreign corporation's gross foreign base company income (determined under section 954(a) without regard to section 954(b)(5)) and gross insurance income (determined under section 953(a)) for the taxable year is less than the lesser of 5 percent of gross income or $1,000,000, then all of that income (other than income that would be financial services income without regard to this paragraph (d)(1)) shall be treated as general limitation income. In addition, if the test in the preceding sentence is satisfied, for purposes of paragraphs (c)(2)(ii)(D) and (E) of this section (apportionment of interest expense to passive income using the asset method), any passive limitation assets shall be treated as general limitation assets. The determination in the first sentence shall be made prior to the application of the exception for certain income subject to a high rate of foreign tax described in paragraph (d)(2) of this section.

(2) Exception for certain income subject to high foreign tax. Except as provided in § 1.904-4(c)(7)(iii) (relating to reductions in tax upon distribution), for purposes of the dividend look-through rule of paragraph (c)(4)(i) of this section, an item of net income that would otherwise be passive income (after application of the priority rules of § 1.904-4(l) and that is received or accrued by a controlled foreign corporation shall be treated as general limitation income, and the earnings and profits attributable to such income shall be treated as general limitation earnings and profits, if the taxpayer establishes to the satisfaction of the Secretary that such income was subject to an effective rate of income tax imposed by a foreign country greater than 90 percent of the maximum rate of tax specified in section 11 (with reference to section 15, if applicable). The preceding sentence has no effect on amounts (other than dividends) paid or accrued by a controlled foreign corporation to a United States shareholder of such controlled foreign corporation to the extent those amounts are allocable to passive income of the controlled foreign corporation.

(3) Examples. The following examples illustrate the application of this paragraph.

Example (1). Controlled foreign corporation S is a wholly-owned subsidiary of P, a domestic corporation. In 1987, S earns $100 of gross income, $4 of which is interest that is subpart F foreign personal holding company income and $96 of which is gross manufacturing income that is not subpart F income. S has no other earnings for 1987. S has no expenses and pays no foreign taxes. S pays P a $100 dividend. Under the de minimis rule of section 954(b)(3), none of S's income is treated as foreign base company income. All of S's income, therefore, is treated as general limitation income. The entire $100 dividend is general limitation income to P.

Example (2). (i) Controlled foreign corporation S is a wholly-owned subsidiary of P, a domestic corporation. In 1987, S earns $50 of shipping income of a type that is foreign base company shipping income. S also earns $50 of dividends from T, a foreign corporation in which S owns 45 percent of the voting stock, and receives a $50 of dividends from U, a foreign corporation in which S owns 5% of the voting stock. Foreign persons hold the remaining voting stock of both T and U. S, T, and U are all incorporated in different foreign countries. The dividends S receives from T and U are of a type that normally would be subpart F foreign personal holding company income that is passive income. Under § 1.904-4(l)(1)(iv), however, the dividends from T are dividends from a noncontrolled section 902 corporation rather than passive income. S has no expenses. The earnings and profits of S are equal to the net income after taxes of S. The dividends and the shipping income are taxed abroad by S's country of incorporation at an effective rate of 40 percent. P establishes to the satisfaction of the Secretary that the effective rate of tax on both the dividends and the shipping income exceeds 90 percent of the maximum United States tax rate. Thus, under section 954(b)(4), neither the shipping income nor the dividends are taxed currently to P under subpart F. S's earnings attributable to shipping income and dividends from a noncontrolled section 902 corporation retain their character as such. Under paragraph (d)(2) of this section, S's earnings attributable to the dividends from U are treated as earnings attributable to general limitation income. See §§ 1.905-3T and 1.905-4T, however, for rules concerning adjustments to the pools of earnings and profits and foreign taxes and redeterminations of United States tax liability when foreign taxes are refunded in a later year.

(ii) In 1988, S has no earnings and pays a $150 dividend (including gross-up) to P. The dividend is paid out of S's post-1986 pool of earnings and profits. One-third of the dividend ($50) is attributable to S's shipping earnings, one-third ($50) is attributable to the dividend from T, and one-third ($50) is attributable to the dividend from U. Pursuant to section 904(d)(3)(E) and paragraph (c)(4) of this section, one-third of the dividend is shipping income, one-third is a dividend from a noncontrolled section 902 corporation, T, and one-third is general limitation income to P.

(e) Treatment of subpart F income in excess of 70 percent of gross income. *(1) Rule.* If the sum of a controlled foreign corporation's gross foreign base company income (determined without regard to section 954(b)(5)) and gross insurance income for the taxable year exceeds 70 percent of the gross income, then all of the controlled foreign corporation's gross income shall be treated as foreign base company income or gross insurance income (whichever is appropriate) and, thus, included in a United States shareholder's gross income. However, the inclusion in gross income of an amount that would not otherwise be subpart F income does not affect its character for purposes of determining whether the income is within a separate category. The determination of whether the controlled foreign corporation's gross foreign base company income and gross insurance income exceeds 70 percent of gross income is made before the exception for certain income subject to a high rate of foreign tax.

(2) Example. The following example illustrates the application of this paragraph.

Example. Controlled foreign corporation S is a wholly-owned subsidiary of P, a domestic corporation. S earns $100, $75 of which is foreign personal holding company income and $25 of which is non-subpart F services income. S is not a financial services entity. S's gross and net income are equal. Under the 70 percent full inclusion rule of section 954(b)(3)(B), the entire $100 is foreign base company income currently taxable to P under section 951. Because $75 of the $100 section 951 inclusion is attributable to S's passive income, $75 of the inclusion is passive income to P. The remaining $25 of the inclusion is treated as general limitation income to P because $25 is attributable to S's general limitation income.

(f) Modification of look-through rules for certain income. *(1) High withholding tax interest.* If a taxpayer receives or accrues interest from a controlled foreign corporation that is a financial services entity, and the interest would be described as high withholding tax interest if section 904(d)(3) and paragraph (c)(2) of this section (the look-through rules for interest) did not apply, then the interest shall be treated as high withholding tax interest to the extent that the interest is allocable under section 904(d)(3) and paragraph (c)(2)(i) of this section to financial services income of the controlled foreign corporation. See section 904(d)(3)(H). The amount treated as high-withholding tax interest under this paragraph (f)(1) shall not exceed the interest, or equivalent income, of the payor that would be taken into account in determining the financial services income of the payor if the look-through rules applied.

(2) Distributions from a FSC. Income received or accrued by a taxpayer that, under the rules of paragraph (c)(4) of this section (look-through rules for dividends), would be treated as foreign trade income or as passive income that is interest and carrying charges (as defined in section 927(d)(1)), and

that is also a distribution from a FSC (or a former FSC), shall be treated as a distribution from a FSC (or a former FSC).

(3) Example. The following example illustrates the operation of paragraph (f)(1) of this section.

Example. Controlled foreign corporation S is a wholly-owned subsidiary of P, a domestic corporation. S is a financial services entity. In 1988, S earns $80 of interest that meets the definition of financial services income and $20 of high withholding tax interest. S makes a $100 interest payment to P. The interest payment to P is subject to a withholding tax of 15 percent. Twenty dollars ($20) of the interest payment to P is considered to be high withholding tax interest because, under section 904(d)(3), it is allocable to the high withholding tax interest earned by S. The remaining eighty dollars ($80) of the interest payment is also treated as high withholding tax interest to P because, under paragraph (f)(1) of this section, interest that is subject to a high withholding tax but would not be considered to be high withholding tax interest under the look-through rules of paragraph (c)(2) of this section, shall be treated as high withholding tax interest to the extent that the interest would have been treated as financial services interest income under the look-through rules of paragraph (c)(2)(i) of this section.

(g) Application of look-through rules to certain domestic corporations. The principles of section 904(d)(3) and this section shall apply to any foreign source interest, rents and royalties paid by a United States corporation to a related corporation. For this purpose, a United States corporation and another corporation are considered to be related if one owns, directly or indirectly, stock possessing more than 50 percent of the total voting power of all classes of stock of the other corporation or more than 50 percent of the total value of the other corporation. In addition, a United States corporation and another corporation shall be considered to be related if the same United States shareholders own, directly or indirectly, stock possessing more than 50 percent of the total voting power of all classes of stock or more than 50 percent of the total value of each corporation. For purposes of this paragraph, the constructive stock ownership rules of section 318 and the regulations under that section apply. For taxable years beginning before January 1, 2001, this paragraph (g) shall be applied by substituting "50 percent or more" for "more than 50 percent" each place it appears.

(h) Application of look-through rules to partnerships and other pass-through entities. *(1) General rule.* Except as provided in paragraph (h)(2) of this section, a partner's distributive share of partnership income shall be characterized as income in a separate category to the extent that the distributive share is a share of income earned or accrued by the partnership in such category. Payments to a partner described in section 707 (e.g., payments to a partner not acting in capacity as a partner) shall be characterized as income in a separate category to the extent that the payment is attributable under the principles of § 1.861-8 and this section to income earned or accrued by the partnership in such category, if the payments are interest, rents, or royalties that would be characterized under the look-through rules of this section if the partnership were a foreign corporation, and the partner who receives the payment owns 10 percent or more of the value of the partnership. A payment by a partnership to a member of the controlled group (as defined in paragraph (a)(3) of this section) of the partner shall be characterized under the look-through rules of this section if the payment would be a section 707 payment entitled to look-through treatment if it were made to the partner.

(2) Exception for certain partnership interests. (i) Rule. Except as otherwise provided, if any limited partner or corporate general partner owns less than 10 percent of the value in a partnership, the partner's distributive share of partnership income from the partnership shall be passive income to the partner, and the partner's distributive share of partnership deductions from the partnership shall be allocated and apportioned under the principles of § 1.861-8 only to the partner's passive income from that partnership.

(ii) Exceptions. To the extent a partner's distributive share of income from a partnership is a share of high withholding tax interest received or accrued by the partnership, that partner's distributive share of partnership income will be high withholding tax interest regardless of the partner's level of ownership in the partnership. If a partnership interest described in paragraph (h)(2)(i) of this section is held in the ordinary course of a partner's active trade or business, the rules of paragraph (h)(1) of this section shall apply for purposes of characterizing the partner's distributive share of the partnership income. A partnership interest will be considered to be held in the ordinary course of a partner's active trade or business if the partner (or a member of the partner's affiliated group of corporations (within the meaning of section 1504(a) and without regard to section 1504(b)(3))) engages (other than through a less than 10 percent interest in a partnership) in the same or related trade or business as the partnership.

(3) [Reserved]. For further guidance, see § 1.904-5T(h)(3).

(4) Value of a partnership interest. For purposes of paragraphs (i), (h)(1), and (h)(2) of this section, a partner will be considered as owning 10 percent of the value of a partnership for a particular year if the partner has 10 percent of the capital and profits interest of the partnership. Similarly, a partnership (first partnership) is considered as owning 50 percent of the value of another partnership (second partnership) if the first partnership owns 50 percent of the capital and profits interests of another partnership. For this purpose, value will be determined at the end of the partnership's taxable year. Similarly, a partnership (first partnership) is considered as owning more than 50 percent of the value of another partnership (second partnership) if the first partnership owns more than 50 percent of the capital and profits interests of the second partnership. For this purpose, value will be determined at the end of the partnership's taxable year. For taxable years beginning before January 1, 2001, the second preceding sentence shall be applied by substituting "50 percent" for "more than 50 percent".

(i) Application of look-through rules to related entities. *(1)* [Reserved]. For further guidance, see § 1.904-5T(i)(1).

(2) Exception for distributive shares of partnership income. In the case of tiered partnership arrangements, a distributive share of partnership income will be characterized under the look-through rules of section 904(d)(3) and this section if the partner meets the requirements of paragraph (h)(1) of this section with respect to the partnership (first partnership), whether or not the income is received through another partnership or partnerships (second partnership) and whether or not the first partnership and the second partnership are considered to be related under the rules of paragraph (i)(1) of this section.

(3) and (4) [Reserved]. For further guidance, see § 1.904-5T(i)(3) and (4).

(5) Examples. The following examples illustrate the provisions of this paragraph (i):

Example (1). P, a domestic corporation, owns all of the stock of S, a controlled foreign corporation. S owns 40 percent of the stock of T, a Country X corporation that is a controlled foreign corporation. The remaining 60 percent of the stock of T is owned by V, a domestic corporation. The percentages of value and voting power of T owned by S and V correspond to their percentages of stock ownership. T owns 40 percent (by vote and value) of the stock of U, a Country Z corporation that is a controlled foreign corporation. The remaining 60 percent of U is owned by unrelated U.S. persons. U earns exclusively general limitation non-subpart F income. In 2001, U makes an interest payment of $100 to T. Look-through principles do not apply because T and U are not related look-through entities under paragraph (i)(1) of this section (because T does not own more than 50 percent of the voting power or value of U). The interest is passive income to T, and is subpart F income to P and V. Under paragraph (c)(1) of this section, look-through principles determine P and V's characterization of the subpart F inclusion from T. P and therefore must characterize the inclusion as passive income.

Example (2). The facts are the same as in Example 1 except that instead of a $100 interest payment, U pays a $50 dividend to T in 2001. P and V each own, directly or indirectly, more than 10 percent of the voting power of all classes of stock of both T and U. Pursuant to paragraph (i)(3) of this section, for purposes of applying this section to the dividend from U to T, U and T are treated as related look-through entities. Therefore, look-through principles apply to characterize the dividend income as general limitation income to T. The dividend is subpart F income of T that is taxable to P and V. The subpart F inclusions of P and V are also subject to look-through principles, under paragraph (c)(1) of this section, and are characterized as general limitation income to P and V because the income is general limitation income of T.

Example (3). The facts are the same as in Example 1, except that U pays both a $100 interest payment and a $50 dividend to T, and T owns 80 percent (by vote and value) of U. Under paragraph (i)(1) of this section, T and U are related look-through entities, because T owns more than 50 percent (by vote and value) of U. Therefore, look-through principles apply to both the interest and dividend income paid or accrued by U to T, and T treats both types of income as general limitation income. Under paragraph (c)(1) of this section, P and V apply look-through principles to the resulting subpart F inclusions, which therefore are also general limitation income to P and V.

Example (4). and 5 [Reserved]. For further guidance, see § 1.904-5T(i)(5) Examples 4 and 5.

(j) Look-through rules applied to passive foreign investment company inclusions. If a passive foreign investment company is a controlled foreign corporation and the taxpayer is a United States shareholder in that passive foreign investment company, any amount included in gross income under section 1293 shall be treated as income in a separate category to the extent the amount so included is attributable to income received or accrued by that controlled foreign corporation that is described as income in the separate category. For purposes of this paragraph (j), the priority rules of § 1.904-4(l) shall apply prior to the application of the rules of this paragraph.

(k) Ordering rules. *(1) In general.* Income received or accrued by a related person to which the look-through rules apply is characterized before amounts included from, or paid or distributed by that person and received or accrued by a related person. For purposes of determining the character of income received or accrued by a person from a related person if the payor or another related person also receives or accrues income from the recipient and the look-through rules apply to the income in all cases, the rules of paragraph (k)(2) of this section apply.

(2) Specific rules. For purposes of characterizing income under this paragraph, the following types of income are characterized in the order stated:

(i) Rents and royalties;

(ii) Interest;

(iii) Subpart F inclusions and distributive shares of partnership income;

(iv) Dividend distributions.

If an entity is both a recipient and a payor of income described in any one of the categories described in (k)(2)(i) through (iv) of this section, the income received will be characterized before the income that is paid. In addition, the amount of interest paid or accrued, directly or indirectly, by a person to a related person shall be offset against and eliminate any interest received or accrued, directly or indirectly, by a person from that related person before application of the ordering rules of this paragraph. In a case in which a person pays or accrues interest to a related person, and also receives or accrues interest indirectly from the related person, the smallest interest payment is eliminated and the amount of all other interest payments are reduced by the amount of the smallest interest payment.

(l) Examples. The following examples illustrate the application of paragraphs (g), (h), (i), and (k) of this section.

Example (1). S and T, controlled foreign corporations, are wholly-owned subsidiaries of P, a domestic corporation. S and T are incorporated in two different foreign countries and T is a financial services entity. In 1987, S earns $100 of income that is general limitation foreign base company sales income. After expenses, including a $50 interest payment to T, S's income is subject to foreign tax at an effective rate of 40 percent. P elects to exclude S's $50 of net income from subpart F under section 954(b)(4). T earns $350 of income that consists of $300 of subpart F financial services income and $50 of interest received from S. The $50 of interest is foreign personal holding company income in T's hands because section 954(c)(3)(A)(i) (same country exception for interest payments) does not apply. The $50 of interest is also general limitation income to T because S and T are related look-through entities within the meaning of paragraph (i)(1) of this section and, therefore the look-through rules of paragraph (c)(2)(i) of this section apply to characterize the interest payment. Thus, with respect to T, P includes in its gross income $50 of general limitation foreign personal holding company income and $300 of financial services income.

Example (2). The facts are the same as in Example (1) except that instead of earning $100 of general limitation foreign base company sales income, S earns $100 of foreign personal holding company income that is passive income. Although the interest payment to T would otherwise be passive income, T is a financial services entity and, under § 1.904-4(e)(1), the income is treated as financial services income in T's hands. Thus, P's entire $350 section 951 inclusion consists of financial services income.

Example (3). P, a domestic corporation, wholly-owns S, a domestic corporation that is a 80/20 corporation. In 1987, S's earnings consist of $100 of foreign source shipping income and $100 of foreign source high withholding tax interest. S makes a $100 foreign source interest payment to P.

The interest payment to P is subject to the look-through rules of paragraph (c)(2)(i) of this section, and is characterized as shipping income and high withholding tax interest to the extent that it is allocable to such income in S's hands.

Example (4). PS is a domestic partnership that is the sole shareholder of controlled foreign corporation S. PS has two general partners, A and B. A and B each have a greater than 10 percent interest in PS. PS also has two limited partners, C and D. C has a 50 percent interest in the partnership and D has a 9 percent interest. A, B, C and D are all United States persons. In 1987, S has $100 of general limitation non-subpart F income on which it pays no foreign tax. S pays a $100 dividend to PS. The dividend is the only income of PS. Under the look-through rule of paragraph (c)(4) of this section, the dividend to PS is general limitation income. Under paragraph (h)(1) of this section, A's, B's, and C's distributive shares of PS's income are general limitation income. Under paragraph (h)(2) of this section, because D is a limited partner with a less than 10 percent interest in PS, D's distributive share of PS's income is passive income.

Example (5). P has a 25 percent interest in partnership PS that he sells to X for $110. P's basis in his partnership interest is $35. P recognizes $75 of gain on the sale of its partnership interest and is subject to no foreign tax. Under paragraph (h)(3) of this section, the gain is treated as passive income.

Example (6). P, a domestic corporation, owns 100 percent of the stock of S, a controlled foreign corporation, and S owns 100 percent of the stock of T, a controlled foreign corporation. S has $100 of passive foreign personal holding company income from unrelated persons and $100 of general limitation income. S also has $50 of interest income from T. S pays T $100 of interest. Under paragraph (k)(2) of this section, the $100 interest payment from S to T is reduced for limitation purposes to the extent of the $50 interest payment from T to S before application of the rules in paragraph (c)(2)(ii) of this section. Therefore, the interest payment from T to S is disregarded. S is treated as if it paid $50 of interest to T, all of which is allocable to S's passive foreign personal holding company income. Therefore the $50 interest payment from S to T is passive income.

Example (7). P, a domestic corporation, owns 100 percent of the stock of S, a controlled foreign corporation. S owns 100 percent of the stock of T, a controlled foreign corporation and 100 percent of the stock of U, a controlled foreign corporation. In 1988, T pays S $5 of interest. S pays U $10 of interest and U pays T $20 of interest. Under paragraph (k)(2) of this section, the interest payments from S to U must be offset by the amount of interest that S is considered as receiving indirectly from U and the interest payment from U to T is offset by the amount of the interest payment that U is considered as receiving indirectly from T. The $10 payment by S to U is reduced by $5, the amount of the interest payment from T to S that is treated as being paid indirectly by U to S. Similarly, the $20 interest payment from U to T is reduced by $5, the amount of the interest payment from S to U that is treated as being paid indirectly by T to U. Therefore, under paragraph (k)(2) of this section, T is treated as having made no interest payment to S, S is treated as having paid $5 of interest to U, and U is treated as having paid $15 to T.

Example (8). (i) P, a domestic corporation, owns 100 percent of the stock of S, a controlled foreign corporation, and S owns 100 percent of the stock of T, a controlled foreign corporation. In 1987, S earns $100 of passive foreign personal holding company income and $100 of general limitation non-subpart F sales income from unrelated persons and $100 of general limitation non-subpart F interest income from a related person, W. S pays $150 of interest to T. T earns $200 of general limitation sales income from unrelated persons and the $150 interest payment from S. T pays S $100 of interest.

(ii) Under paragraph (k)(2) of this section, the $100 interest payment from T to S reduces the $150 interest payment from S to T. S is treated as though it paid $50 of interest to T. T is treated as though it made no interest payment to S.

(iii) Under paragraph (k)(2)(ii) of this section, the remaining $50 interest payment from S to T is then characterized. The interest payment is first allocable under the rules of paragraph (c)(2)(ii)(C) of this section to S's passive income. Therefore, the $50 interest payment to T is passive income. The interest income is foreign personal holding company income in T's hands. T, therefore, has $50 of subpart F passive income and $200 of non-subpart F general limitation income.

(iv) Under paragraph (k)(2)(iii) of this section, subpart F inclusions are characterized next. P has a subpart F inclusion with respect to S of $50 that is attributable to passive income of S and is treated as passive income to P. P has a subpart F inclusion with respect to T of $50 that is attributable to passive income of T and is treated as passive income to P.

Example (9). (i) P, a domestic corporation, owns 100 percent of the stock of S, a controlled foreign corporation, and S owns 100 percent of the stock of T, a controlled foreign corporation. P also owns 100 percent of the stock of U, a controlled foreign corporation. In 1987, S earns $100 of passive foreign personal holding company income and $200 of non-subpart F general limitation income from unrelated persons. S also receives $150 of dividend income from T. S pays $100 of interest to T and $100 of interest to U. U earns $300 of non-subpart F general limitation income and the $100 of interest received from S. U pays a $100 royalty to T. T earns the $100 interest payment received from S and the $100 royalty received from U.

(ii) Under paragraph (k)(2)(i) of this section, the royalty paid by U to T is characterized first. Assume that the royalty is directly allocable to U's general limitation income. Also assume that the royalty is not subpart F income to T. With respect to T, the royalty is general limitation income.

(iii) Under paragraph (k)(2)(ii) of this section, the interest payments from S to T and U are characterized next. This characterization is done without regard to any dividend income received by S because, under paragraph (k)(2) of this section, dividends are characterized after interest payments from a related person. The interest payments are first allocable to S's passive income under paragraph (c)(2)(ii)(C) of this section. Therefore, $50 of the interest payment to T is passive and $50 of the interest payment to U is passive. The remaining $50 paid to T is general limitation income and the remaining $50 paid to U is general limitation income. All of the interest payments to T and U are subpart F foreign personal holding company income to both recipients.

(iv) Under paragraph (k)(2)(iii) of this section, P has a $100 subpart F inclusion with respect to T that is characterized next. Fifty dollars ($50) of the subpart F inclusion is passive income to P because it is attributable to the passive income portion of the interest income received by T from S, and $50 of the inclusion is treated as general limitation income to P because it is attributable to the general limitation portion of the interest income received by T from S. Under paragraph (k)(2)(iii) of this section, P also has a $100 subpart F inclusion with respect to U. Fifty dollars ($50) of the subpart F inclusion is passive income to P because it is attributable to the passive portion of the interest income received by U from S, and $50 of the inclusion is general limitation income to P because it is attributable to the general limitation portion of the interest income received by U from S.

(v) Under paragraph (k)(2)(iv) of this section, the $150 distribution from T to S is characterized next. One-hundred dollars ($100) of the distribution is out of earnings and profits attributable to previously taxed income. Therefore, only $50 is a dividend that is subject to the look-through rules of paragraph (d) of this section. The $50 dividend is attributable to T's general limitation income and is general limitation income to S in its entirety.

Example (10). (i) P, a domestic corporation, owns 100 percent of the stock of S, a controlled foreign corporation, and S owns 100 percent of the stock of T, a controlled foreign corporation. P also owns 100 percent of the stock of U, a controlled foreign corporation. S, T and U are all incorporated in the same foreign country. In 1987, S earns $100 of passive foreign personal holding income and $200 of general limitation non-subpart F income from unrelated persons. S pays $100 of interest to T and $100 of interest to U. U earns $300 of general limitation non-subpart F income and the $100 of interest received from S. T's only income is the $100 interest payment received from S.

(ii) Under paragraph (k)(2)(ii) of this section, the interest payments from S to T and U are characterized first. The interest payments are first allocated under the rule of paragraph (c)(2)(ii)(C) of this section to S's passive income. Therefore, under that provision and paragraph (c)(2)(i) of this section, $50 of the interest payment to T is passive income to T and $50 of the interest payment to U is passive income to U. The remaining $50 paid to T is general limitation income and the remaining $50 paid to U is general limitation income.

(iii) Under paragraph (k)(2)(iii) of this section, any subpart F inclusion of P is determined and characterized next. Under paragraph (c)(1)(i) of this section, paragraphs (c)(2)(i) and (c)(2)(ii) apply not only for purposes of determining the separate category of income of S to which the interest payments from S to T and U are allocable but also for purposes of determining the subpart F income of T and U. Although the interest payments from S to T and U are "same country" interest payments that would otherwise be excludible from T's and U's subpart F income under section 954(c)(3)(A)(i), section 954(c)(3)(B) provides that the exception for same country payments between related persons shall not apply to the extent such payments have reduced the subpart F income of the payor. In this case, $50 of the $100 interest payment from S to T reduced S's subpart F income and $50 of the $100 interest payment from S to U reduced the remaining $50 of S's subpart F income. Therefore, T has $50 of subpart F income that is passive income and U has $50 of subpart F income that is passive income. P includes $100 of subpart F income in gross income that is passive income to P.

(iv) The remaining $50 of interest paid by S to T and the remaining $50 of interest paid by S to U is not subpart F income to T or U because it did not reduce S's subpart F income and is therefore eligible for the same country exception.

Example (11). P, a domestic corporation, owns 100 percent of the stock of S, a controlled foreign corporation, and S owns 100 percent of the stock of T, a controlled foreign corporation. P also owns 100 percent of the stock of U, a controlled foreign corporation. In 1991, T earns $100 of general limitation income that is not subpart F income and distributes the entire amount to S as a dividend. S earns $100 of passive foreign personal holding company income and the $100 dividend from T. S pays $100 of interest to U. U earns $200 of general limitation income that is foreign base company income and $100 of interest income from S. This transaction does not involve circular payments and, therefore, the ordering rules of paragraph (k)(2) of this section do not apply. Instead, pursuant to paragraph (k)(1) of this section, income received is characterized first. T's earnings and, thus, the dividend from T to S are characterized first. S includes the $100 dividend from T in gross income as general limitation income because all of T's earnings are general limitation income. S thus has $100 of passive foreign personal holding company income and $100 of general limitation income. The interest payment to U is then characterized as $100 passive income under paragraph (c)(2)(ii)(C) of this section (allocation of related person interest to passive foreign personal holding company income). For 1991, U thus has $200 of general limitation income that is subpart F income, and $100 of passive foreign personal holding company income. For 1991, P includes in its gross income $200 of general limitation subpart F income from U, $100 of passive subpart F income from U (relating to the interest payment from S to U), and $100 of general limitation subpart F income from S (relating to the dividend from T to S).

(m) Application of section 904(g). *(1)* [Reserved]. For further guidance, see § 1.904-5T(m)(1).

(2) Treatment of interest payments.

(i) Interest payments from controlled foreign corporations. If interest is received or accrued by a United States shareholder or a person related to a United States shareholder (within the meaning of paragraph (c)(2)(ii) of this section) from a controlled foreign corporation, the interest shall be considered to be allocable to income of the controlled foreign corporation from sources within the United States for purposes of section 904(d) to the extent that the interest is allocable under paragraph (c)(2)(ii)(C) of this section to passive income that is from sources within the United States. If related person interest is less than or equal to passive income, the related person interest will be allocable to United States source passive income based on the ratio of United States source passive income to total passive income. To the extent that related person interest exceeds passive income, and, therefore, is allocated under paragraph (c)(2)(ii)(D) of this section to income in a separate category other than passive, the following formulas apply in determining the portion of the interest payment that is from sources within the United States. If the taxpayer uses the gross income method to allocate interest, the portion of the interest payment from sources within the United States is determined as follows:

$$\text{The amount of the interest payment allocated to the separate category under paragraph (c)(2)(ii)(D) of this section} \times \frac{\text{Gross income from United States sources in that category}}{\text{Gross income from all sources in that category}}$$

If the taxpayer uses the asset method to allocate interest, then the portion of the interest payment from sources within the United States is determined as follows:

$$\text{The amount of the interest payment allocated to the separate category under paragraph (c)(2)(ii)(D) of this section} \times \frac{\text{Value of domestic assets in that category}}{\text{Value of total assets in that category}}$$

For purposes of this paragraph, the value of assets in a separate category is the value of assets as determined under the principles of § 1.861-9T(g). See § 1.861-10T(d)(2) for purposes of determining the value of assets and gross income in a separate category as reduced for indebtedness the interest on which is directly allocated.

(ii) [Reserved]. For further guidance, see § 1.904-5T(m)(2)(ii).

(3) Examples. The following examples illustrate the application of this paragraph.

Example (1). Controlled foreign corporation S is a wholly-owned subsidiary of P, a domestic corporation. In 1988, S pays P $300 of interest. S has no other expenses. In 1988, S has $3000 of assets that generate $650 of foreign source general limitation sales income and a $1000 loan to an unrelated foreign person that generates $20 of foreign source passive interest income. S also has a $4000 loan to an unrelated United States person that generates $70 of United States source passive income and $4000 of inventory that generates $100 of United States source general limitation income. S uses the asset method to allocate interest expense. The following chart summarizes S's assets and income:

	Foreign	U.S.	Totals
Assets:			
Passive	1000	4000	5000
General	3000	4000	7000
Total	4000	8000	2000
Income:			
Passive	20	70	90
General	650	100	750
Total	670	170	840

Under paragraph (c)(2)(ii)(C) of this section, $90 of the related person interest payment is allocable to S's passive income. Under paragraph (m)(2) of this section, $70 is from sources within the United States and $20 is from foreign sources. Under paragraph (c)(2)(ii)(D) of this section, the remaining $210 of the related person interest payment is allocated to general limitation income. Under paragraph (m)(2) of this section, $120 of the remaining $210 is treated as income from sources within the United States ($120 = $210 × $4000/$7000) and $90 is treated as income from foreign sources. ($90 = $210 × $3000/$7000).

Example (2). The facts are the same as in *Example* (1) except that S uses the gross income method to allocate interest expense. The first $90 of related person interest expense is allocated to passive income in the same manner as in Example (1). Under paragraph (c)(2)(ii)(D) of this section, the remaining $210 of the related person interest expense is allocated to general limitation income. Under paragraph (m)(2) of this section, $28 of the remaining $210 is treated as income from United States sources ($28 = $210 × $100/$750) and $182 is treated as income from foreign sources ($182 = $210 × $650/$750).

Example (3). Controlled foreign corporation S is a wholly-owned subsidiary of P, a domestic corporation. In 1988, S pays $300 of interest to P. S has no other expenses. S uses the asset method to allocate interest expense. In 1988, S has $4000 of assets that generate $650 of foreign source general limitation manufacturing income and a $1000 loan to an unrelated foreign person that generates $100 of foreign source passive interest income. S has $500 of shipping assets that generate $200 of foreign source shipping income and $500 of shipping assets that generate $200 of United States source shipping income. S also has a $1000 loan to an unrelated United States person that generates $100 of United States source passive income. S's passive income is not also described as shipping income. The following chart summarizes S's assets and income:

	Foreign	U.S.	Totals
Assets:			
Passive	1000	1000	2000
Shipping	500	500	1000
General	4000	0	4000
Total	5500	1500	7000
Income:			
Passive	100	100	200
Shipping	200	200	400
General	650	0	650
Total	950	300	1250

Under paragraph (c)(2)(ii)(C) of this section, $200 of the related person interest payment is allocable to S's passive income. Under paragraph (m)(2) of this section, $100 of this amount is from foreign sources and $100 is from sources within the United States.

Under paragraph (c)(2)(ii)(D) of this section, $80 of the remaining $100 of the related person interest payment is allocated to general limitation income ($80 = $100 × $4000/$5000) and $20 is allocated to shipping income ($20 = $100 × $1000/$5000).

Under paragraph (m)(2) of this section, none of $80 of the interest payment allocated to general limitation income is treated as income from United States sources ($0 = $80 × $0/$4000). Therefore, the entire $80 is treated as income from foreign sources.

Under paragraph (m)(2) of this section, $10 of the $20 of the interest payment allocated to the shipping income is treated as income from United States sources ($10 = $20 × $500/$1000) and $10 of the $20 is treated as income from foreign sources ($10 = $20 × $500/$1000).

Example (4). The facts are the same as in Example (3) except that S uses the gross income method to allocate interest expense. The interest allocated to passive income under paragraph (c)(2)(ii)(C) of this section is the same, $200, $100 from United States sources and $100 from foreign sources.

Under paragraph (c)(2)(ii)(D) of this section, the remaining $100 of related person interest is allocated between the shipping and general limitation categories based on the gross income in those categories. Therefore, $38 of the remaining $100 interest payment is allocated to shipping income ($38 = $100 × $400/($1250 − $200)) and $62 is treated as allocated to general limitation income ($62 = $100 × $650/($1250 − $200)).

Under paragraph (m)(2) of this section, $19 of the $38 allocable to shipping income is treated as income from United States sources ($19 = $38 × $200/$400) and $19 is treated as income from foreign sources ($19 = $38 × $200/$400).

Under paragraph (m)(2) of this section, all of the $62, allocated to general limitation income is treated as income from foreign sources ($62 = $62 × $650/$650).

(4) Treatment of dividend payments. (i) [Reserved]. For further guidance, see § 1.904-5T(m)(4)(i).

(ii) Determination of earnings and profits from United States sources. In order to determine the portions of earnings and profits from United States sources and from foreign sources within each separate category, related person interest shall be allocated to the United States source portion of income in a separate category by applying the rules of paragraph (m)(2) of this section. Other expenses shall be allocated by applying the rules of paragraph (c)(2)(ii) of this section separately to the United States source income and the foreign source income in each category. For example, unrelated person interest expense that is allocated among categories of income based upon the relative amounts of assets in a category must be allocated between United States and foreign source income within each category by applying the rules of paragraph (c)(2)(ii)(E) of this section separately to United States source and foreign source assets in the separate category.

(iii) Example. The following example illustrates the application of this paragraph.

Example. Controlled foreign corporation, S, is a wholly owned subsidiary of P, a domestic corporation. S is a financial services entity. In 1987, S has $100 of non-subpart F general limitation earnings and profits and $100 of non-subpart F financial services income. None of the general limitation earnings and profits are from sources within the United States, and $50 of the financial services earnings and profits are from United States sources. In 1988, S earns $300 of non-subpart F general limitation earnings and profits and $500 of non-subpart F financial services earnings and profits. One hundred dollars ($100) of the general limitation earnings and profits are from sources within the United States. None of the financial services earnings and profits are from United States sources. In 1988, S pays P a $500 dividend. Under paragraph (c)(4) of this section, $200 of the dividend is attributable to general limitation earnings and profits ($200 = $500 × $400/$1000). Under this paragraph (m)(3), the portion of the dividend that is attributable to general limitation earnings and profits from sources within the United States is $50 ($200 × $100/$400). Under paragraph (c)(4) of this section, $300 of the dividend is attributable to financial services earnings and profits ($300 = $500 × $600/$1000). Under this paragraph (m)(3), the portion of the dividend that is attributable to financial services earnings and profits from sources within the United States is $25 ($300 × $50/$600).

(5) Treatment of subpart F inclusions. (i) Rule. Any amount included in the gross income of a United States shareholder of a controlled foreign corporation under section 951(a) shall be treated as income subject to a separate limitation that is derived from sources within the United States to the extent such amount is attributable to income of the controlled foreign corporation in the corresponding category of income from sources within the United States. In order to determine a controlled foreign corporation's taxable income and earnings and profits from sources within the United States in each separate category, the principles of paragraph (m)(4)(ii) of this section shall apply.

(ii) Example. The following example illustrates the application of this paragraph (m)(5).

Example. Controlled foreign corporation S is a wholly-owned subsidiary of domestic corporation, P. In 1987, S earns $100 of subpart F foreign personal holding company income that is passive income. Of this amount, $40 is derived from sources within the United States. S also earns $50 of subpart F general limitation income. None of this income is from sources within the United States. Assume that S pays no foreign taxes and has no expenses. P is required to include $150 in gross income under section 951(a). Of this amount, $60 will be foreign source passive income to P and $40 will be United States source passive income to P. Fifty dollars ($50) will be foreign source general limitation income to P.

(6) Treatment of section 78 amount. For purposes of treating taxes deemed paid by a taxpayer under section 902(a) and section 960(a)(1) as a dividend under section 78, taxes that are paid or accrued with respect to United States source income in a separate category shall be treated as United States source income in that separate category.

(7) Coordination with treaties. (i) Rule. If any amount of income derived from a United States-owned foreign corporation, as defined in section 904(g)(6), would be treated as derived from sources within the United States under section 904(g) and this paragraph (m) and, pursuant to an income tax convention with the United States, the taxpayer chooses to avail itself of benefits of the convention that treat that amount as arising from sources outside the United States under a rule explicitly treating the income as foreign source, then that amount will be treated as foreign source income. However, sections 904(a), (b), (c), (d) and (f), 902, 907, and 960 shall be applied separately to amounts described in the preceding sentence with respect to each treaty under which the taxpayer has claimed benefits and, within each treaty, to each separate category of income.

(ii) Example. The following example illustrates the application of this paragraph (m)(7).

Example. Controlled foreign corporation S is incorporated in Country A and is a wholly-owned subsidiary of P, a domestic corporation. In 1990, S earns $80 of foreign base company sales income in Country A which is general limitation income and $40 of U.S. source interest income. S incurs $20 of expenses attributable to its sales business. S pays P $40 of interest that is allocated to U.S. source passive income under paragraphs (c)(2)(ii)(C) and (m)(2) of this section. Assume that earnings and profits equal net income. All of S's net income of $60 is includible in P's gross income under subpart F (section 951(a)(1)). For 1990, P also has $100 of passive income derived from investments in Country B. Pursuant to section 904(g)(3) and paragraph (m)(2) of this section, the $40 interest payment from S is United States source income to P because it is attributable to United States source interest income of S. The United States-Country A income tax treaty, however, treats all interest payments by residents of Country A as Country A sourced and P elects to apply the treaty. Pursuant to section 904(g)(10) and this paragraph (m)(7), the entire interest payment will be treated as foreign source income to P. P thus has $60 of foreign source general limitation income, $40 of foreign source passive income from S, and $100 of other foreign source passive income. In determining P's foreign tax credit limitation on passive income, the passive income from Country A shall be treated separately from any other passive income.

(n) [Reserved]. For further guidance, see § 1.904-5T(n).

(o) Effective dates.

(1) Rules for controlled foreign corporations and other look-through entities. Section 904(d)(3) and this section apply to distributions and section 951 inclusions of earnings and profits of a controlled foreign corporation (or other entity to which this section applies) derived during the first taxable year of the controlled foreign corporation (or other entity) beginning after December 31, 1986, and thereafter, and to payments made by a controlled foreign corporation (or other entity) during such taxable years, without regard to whether the corresponding taxable year of the recipient of the distribution or payment or of one or more of the United States shareholders of the controlled foreign corporation begins after December 31, 1986.

(2) [Reserved]. For further guidance, see § 1.904-5T(o)(2).

(3) [Reserved]. For further guidance, see § 1.904-5T(o)(3).

T.D. 8214, 7/15/88, amend T.D. 8412, 5/13/92, T.D. 8767, 3/23/98, T.D. 8827, 7/12/99, T.D. 8916, 12/27/2000, T.D. 9141, 7/19/2004, T.D. 9260, 4/24/2006, T.D. 9368, 12/20/2007.

PAR. 4. In § 1.904-5, paragraph (h)(3) is revised and paragraph (o)(3) is added to read as follows:

Proposed § 1.904-5 Look-through rules as applied to controlled foreign corporations and other entities. [*For Preamble, see ¶ 152,939*]

* * * * *

(h) * * *

(3) [The text of the proposed amendment to § 1.904-5(h)(3) is the same as the text of § 1.904-5T(h)(3) published elsewhere in this issue of the Federal Register.] [*See T.D. 9368, 12/21/2007, 72 Fed. Reg. 245.*]

* * * * *

(o) * * *

(3) [The text of proposed § 1.904-5(o)(3) is the same as the text of § 1.904-5T(o)(3) published elsewhere in this issue of the Federal Register.] [*See T.D. 9368, 12/21/2007, 72 Fed. Reg. 245.*]

PAR. 7. In § 1.904-5, paragraphs (a), (b), (c), (i), (m), (n), and (o) are revised to read as follows:

Proposed § 1.904-5 Look-through rules as applied to controlled foreign corporations and other entities. [*For Preamble, see ¶ 152,753*]

* * * * * [The text of the proposed amendments to § 1.904-5(a), (b), (c), (i), (m), (n), and (o) are the same as the text of § 1.904-5T(a), (b), (c), (i), (m), (n), and (o) published elsewhere in this issue of the Federal Register.] [*See T.D. 9260, 04/24/2006, 71 Fed. Reg. 79.*]

PAR. 2. In § 1.904-5, paragraph (k)(1) is revised to read as follows:

Proposed § 1.904-5 Look-through rules as applied to controlled foreign corporations and other entities. [*For Preamble, see ¶ 151,985*]

* * * * *

(k) Ordering rules. *(1) In general.* Income received or accrued by a related person to which the look-through rules apply is characterized before amounts included from, or paid or distributed by, that person and received or accrued by a related person. For purposes of determining the character of income received or accrued by a person from a related person if the payor or another related person also receives or accrues income from the recipient and the look-through rules apply to the income in all cases, the rules of paragraph (k)(2) of this section apply. Notwithstanding any other provision of this section, the principles of § 1.954-1(c)(1)(i) will apply to any expense subject to § 1.954-1(c)(1)(i).

* * * * *

§ 1.904-5T Look-through rules as applied to controlled foreign corporations and other entities (temporary).

• ***Caution:*** Under Code Sec. 7805, temporary regulations expire within three years of the date of issuance. This temporary regulation was issued on 4/24/2006.

(a) Definitions. For purposes of sections 904(d)(3) and 904(d)(4) and the regulations under section 904, the following definitions apply:

(1) The term separate category means, as the context requires, any category of income described in section 904(d)(1)(A), (B), (C), (D), (F), (G), (H), or (I) and in § 1.904-4(b), (d), (e), and (f), any category of income described in § 1.904-4(m), or any category of earnings and profits to which income described in such provisions is attributable.

(2) and (3) [Reserved]. For further guidance, see § 1.904-5(a)(2) and (3).

(4) The term noncontrolled section 902 corporation means any foreign corporation with respect to which the taxpayer meets the stock ownership requirements of section 902(a), or, with respect to a lower-tier foreign corporation, the taxpayer meets the requirements of section 902(b). Except as provided in section 902 and the regulations under that section and paragraphs (i)(3) and (i)(4) of this section, a controlled foreign corporation shall not be treated as a noncontrolled section 902 corporation with respect to any distributions out of its earnings and profits for periods during which it was a controlled foreign corporation. In the case of a partnership owning a foreign corporation, the determination of whether a taxpayer meets the ownership requirements of section 902(a) or (b) will be made with respect to the taxpayer's indirect ownership, and not the partnership's direct ownership, in the foreign corporation. See section 902(b)(7).

(b) In general. Except as otherwise provided in section 904(d)(3) and (4) and this section, dividends, interest, rents, and royalties received or accrued by a taxpayer from a controlled foreign corporation in which the taxpayer is a United States shareholder shall be treated as general limitation income. See § 1.904-5T(c)(4)(iii) for the treatment of dividends received by a domestic corporation from a noncontrolled section 902 corporation in which the domestic corporation meets the stock ownership requirements of section 902(a).

(c) *(1)* through (c)(2)(ii) [Reserved]. For further guidance, see § 1.904-5(c)(1) through (c)(2)(ii).

(2) (iii) Allocating and apportioning expenses of a noncontrolled section 902 corporation. Expenses of a noncontrolled section 902 corporation shall be allocated and apportioned in the same manner as expenses of a controlled foreign corporation under § 1.904-5(c)(2)(ii), except that the related person interest rule of § 1.904-5(c)(2)(ii)(C) and (D) shall not apply.

(iv) through (c)(4)(ii) [Reserved]. For further guidance, see § 1.904-5(c)(2)(iv) through (c)(4)(ii).

(3) (iii) Look-through rule for dividends from noncontrolled section 902 corporations. Except as otherwise provided in this subparagraph (iii), any dividend that is distributed by a noncontrolled section 902 corporation and received or accrued by a domestic corporation that meets the stock ownership requirements of section 902(a) shall be treated as income in a separate category in proportion to the ratio of the portion of earnings and profits attributable to income in such category to the total amount of earnings and profits of the noncontrolled section 902 corporation. A dividend distributed by a noncontrolled section 902 corporation shall be treated as passive income if the look-through characterization of such dividend is not substantiated to the satisfaction of the Commissioner, or if such dividend is received or accrued by a shareholder that is neither a domestic corporation meeting the stock ownership requirements of section 902(a) nor a foreign corporation meeting the requirements of section 902(b). See § 1.904-5T(i)(4). See § 1.904-7T for transition rules concerning the treatment of undistributed earnings (or a deficit) of a noncontrolled section 902 corporation that were accumulated in taxable years beginning before January 1, 2003.

(4) (iv) through (h)(2) [Reserved]. For further guidance, see § 1.904-5(c)(4)(iv) through (h)(2).

(h) *(3) Income from the sale of a partnership interest.* (i) In general. To the extent a partner recognizes gain on the sale of a partnership interest, that income shall be treated as passive category income to the partner, unless the income is considered to be high-taxed under section 904(d)(2)(B)(iii)(II) and § 1.904-4(c).

(ii) Exception for 25-percent owned partnership. In the case of a sale of an interest in a partnership by a partner that is a 25-percent owner of the partnership under the principles of section 954(c)(4)(B), income recognized on the sale of the partnership interest shall be treated as general category income to the extent that such gain would not be classified as foreign personal holding company income under the look-through rule of section 954(c)(4).

(i) Application of look-through rules to related entities. *(1) In general.* Except as provided in paragraphs (i)(2), (3), and (4) of this section, the principles of this section shall apply to distributions and payments that are subject to the look-through rules of section 904(d)(3) and this section from a controlled foreign corporation or other entity otherwise entitled to look-through treatment (a ''look-through entity'') under this section to a related look-through entity. A noncontrolled section 902 corporation shall be considered a look-through entity only to the extent provided in paragraph (i)(4) of this section. Two look-through entities shall be considered to be related to each other if one owns, directly or indirectly, stock possessing more than 50 percent of the total voting power of all classes of voting stock of the other entity or more than 50 percent of the total value of such entity. In addition, two look-through entities are related if the same United States shareholders own, directly or indirectly, stock possessing more than 50 percent of the total voting power of all voting classes of stock (in the case of a corporation) or more than 50 percent of the total value of each look-through entity. In the case of a corporation, value shall be determined by taking into account all classes of stock. In the case of a partnership, value shall be determined under the rules in paragraph (h)(4) of this section. For purposes of this section, indirect ownership shall be determined under section 318 and the regulations thereunder.

(2) [Reserved]. For further guidance, see § 1.904-5(i)(2).

(3) Special rule for dividends between controlled foreign corporations. Solely for purposes of dividend payments between controlled foreign corporations, two controlled foreign corporations shall be considered related look-through entities if the same United States shareholder owns, directly or indirectly, at least 10 percent of the total voting power of all classes of stock of each foreign corporation. If two controlled foreign corporations are not considered related look-through entities for purposes of this section because a United States shareholder does not satisfy the ownership requirement set forth in this paragraph (i)(3), the dividend payment will be characterized under the look-through rules of section 904(d)(4) and this section if the requirements set forth in paragraph (i)(4) of this section are satisfied.

(4) Payor and recipient of dividend are members of same qualified group. Solely for purposes of dividend payments in taxable years beginning after December 31, 2002, between controlled foreign corporations, noncontrolled section 902 corporations, or a controlled foreign corporation and a noncontrolled section 902 corporation, the payor and recipient corporations shall be considered related look-through entities if the corporations are members of the same qualified group as defined in section 902(b)(2) and the recipient corporation is eligible to compute foreign taxes deemed paid with respect to the dividend under section 902(b)(1).

(5) Examples. The following examples illustrate the provisions of this paragraph (i):

Example (1). through 3 [Reserved]. For further guidance, see § 1.904-5(i)(5) Examples 1 through 3.

Example (4). P, a domestic corporation, owns all of the voting stock of S, a controlled foreign corporation. S owns 5 percent of the voting stock of T, a controlled foreign corporation. The remaining 95 percent of the stock of T is owned by P. In 2006, T pays a $50 dividend to S and a $950 dividend to P. The dividend to S is not eligible for look-through treatment under paragraph (i)(4) of this section, and S is not eligible to compute an amount of foreign taxes deemed paid with respect to the dividend from T, because S and T are not members of the same qualified group (S owns less than 10 percent of the voting stock of T). See section 902(b) and § 1.902-1(a)(3). However, the dividend is eligible for look-through treatment under paragraph (i)(3) of this section because P owns at least 10 percent of the voting power of all classes of stock of both S and T. The dividend is subpart F income of S that is taxable to P.

Example (5). P, a domestic corporation, owns 50 percent of the voting stock of S, a controlled foreign corporation. S owns 10 percent of the voting stock of T, a controlled foreign corporation. The remaining 50 percent of the stock of S and the remaining 90 percent of the stock of T are owned, respectively, by X and Y. X and Y are each United States shareholders of T but are not related to P, S, or each other. In 2006, T pays a $100 dividend to S. The dividend is not eligible for look-through treatment under paragraph (i)(3) of this section because no United States shareholder owns at least 10 percent of the voting power of all classes of stock of both S and T (P and X each own only 5 percent of T). However, the dividend is eligible for look-through treatment under paragraph (i)(4) of this section, and S is eligible to compute an amount of foreign taxes deemed paid with respect to the dividend from T, because S and T are members of the same qualified group. See section 902(b) and § 1.902-1(a)(3). The dividend is subpart F income of S that is taxable to P and X.

(j) through (l) [Reserved]. For further guidance, see § 1.904-5(j) through (l).

(m) Application of section 904(g). *(1) In general.* This paragraph (m) applies to certain amounts derived from controlled foreign corporations and noncontrolled section 902 corporations that are treated as United States-owned foreign corporations as defined in section 904(g)(6). For purposes of determining the portion of an interest payment that is allocable to income earned or accrued by a controlled foreign corporation or noncontrolled section 902 corporation from sources within the United States under section 904(g)(3), the rules in paragraph (m)(2) of this section apply. For purposes of determining the portion of a dividend (or amount treated as a dividend, including amounts described in section 951(a)(1)(B)) paid or accrued by a controlled foreign corporation or noncontrolled section 902 corporation that is treated as from sources within the United States under section 904(g)(4), the rules in paragraph (m)(4) of this section apply. For purposes of determining the portion of an amount included in gross income under section 951(a)(1)(A) that is attributable to income of the controlled foreign corporation from sources within the United States under section 904(g)(2), the rules in paragraph (m)(5) of this section apply. In order to determine whether section 904(g) applies, section 904(g)(5) (exception if a United States-owned foreign corporation has a de minimis amount of United States source income) shall be applied to the total amount of earnings and profits of a controlled foreign corporation or noncontrolled section 902 corporation for a taxable year without regard to the characterization of those earnings under section 904(d).

(2) (1) [Reserved]. For further guidance, see § 1.904-5(m)(2)(i).

(ii) Interest payments from noncontrolled section 902 corporations. If interest is received or accrued by a shareholder from a noncontrolled section 902 corporation (where the shareholder is a domestic corporation that meets the stock ownership requirements of section 902(a)), the rules of subparagraph (m)(2)(i) apply in determining the portion of the interest payment that is from sources within the United States, except that the related party interest rules of subparagraph (c)(2)(ii)(C) shall not apply.

(3) [Reserved]. For further guidance, see § 1.904-5(m)(3).

(4) Treatment of dividend payments. (i) Rule. Any dividend or distribution treated as a dividend under this section (including an amount included in gross income under section 951(a)(1)(B)) that is received or accrued by a United States shareholder from a controlled foreign corporation, or any dividend that is received or accrued by a domestic corporate shareholder meeting the stock ownership requirements of section 902(a) from a noncontrolled section 902 corporation, shall be treated as income in a separate category derived from sources within the United States in proportion to the ratio of the portion of the earnings and profits of the controlled foreign corporation or noncontrolled section 902 corporation in the corresponding separate category from United States sources to the total amount of earnings and profits of the controlled foreign corporation or noncontrolled section 902 corporation in that separate category.

(ii) through (7). [Reserved] For further guidance, see § 1.904-5(m)(4)(ii) through (7).

(n) Order of application of sections 904(d) and (g). In order to apply the rules of this section, section 904(d)(1) shall first be applied to the controlled foreign corporation or noncontrolled section 902 corporation to determine the amount of income and earnings and profits derived by the controlled foreign corporation or noncontrolled section 902 corporation in each separate category. The income and earnings and profits in each separate category that are from United States sources shall then be determined. Sections 904(d)(3), 904(d)(4), and 904(g), and this section shall then be applied for purposes of characterizing and sourcing income received, accrued, or included by a United States shareholder in the controlled foreign corporation or a domestic corporate shareholder that meets the stock ownership requirements of section 902(a) with respect to a noncontrolled section 902 corporation that is attributable or allocable to income or earnings and profits of the foreign corporation.

(o) *(1)* [Reserved]. For further guidance, see § 1.904-5(o)(1).

(2) Rules for noncontrolled section 902 corporations. Except as provided in § 1.904-7T(f)(9), section 904(d)(4) and this section apply to distributions from a noncontrolled section 902 corporation that are paid during the first taxable year of the noncontrolled section 902 corporation beginning after December 31, 2002, and thereafter, without regard to whether the corresponding taxable year of the recipient of the distribution begins after December 31, 2002, except that the provisions of paragraphs (m)(1), (m)(2)(ii), (m)(4)(i), and (n) apply to distributions from a noncontrolled section 902 corporation paid in taxable years of such corporation beginning after April 25, 2006. For corresponding rules applicable to taxable years beginning before January 1, 2003, see 26 CFR § 1.904-5 (revised as of April 1, 2006).

(3) Rules for income from the sale of a partnership interest. (i) Effective/applicability date. Paragraph (h)(3) of this section shall apply to taxable years of United States taxpayers beginning after December 31, 2006 and ending on or after December 21, 2007, and to taxable years of a foreign corporation which end with or within taxable years of its domestic corporate shareholder beginning after December 31, 2006 and ending on or after December 21, 2007.

(ii) Expiration date. The applicability of paragraph (h)(3) of this section expires on December 20, 2010.

T.D. 9260, 4/24/2006, amend T.D. 9368, 12/20/2007.

§ 1.904-6 Allocation and apportionment of taxes.

Caution: The Treasury has not yet amended Reg § 1.904-6 to reflect changes made by P.L. 105-34, P.L. 100-647.

(a) Allocation and apportionment of taxes to a separate category or categories of income. *(1) In general.* (i) Taxes related to a separate category of income. The amount of foreign taxes paid or accrued with respect to a separate category of income (including United States source income) shall include only those taxes that are related to income in that separate category. Taxes are related to income if the income is included in the base upon which the tax is imposed. If, for example, foreign law exempts certain types of income from foreign taxes, or certain types of income are exempt from foreign tax under an income tax convention, then no taxes are considered to be related to such income for purposes of this paragraph. As another example, if foreign law provides for a specific rate of tax with respect to certain types of income (e.g., capital gains), or certain expenses, deductions, or credits are allowed under foreign law only with respect to a particular type of income, then such provisions shall be taken into account in determining the amount of foreign tax imposed on such income. A withholding tax (unless it is a withholding tax that is not the final tax payable on the income as described in § 1.904-4(d)) is related to the income from which it is withheld. A tax that is imposed on a base that includes more than one separate category of income is considered to be imposed on income in all such categories, and, thus, the taxes are related to all such categories included within the foreign country or possession's taxable income base.

(ii) Apportionment of taxes related to more than one separate category. If a tax is related to more than one separate category, then, in order to determine the amount of the tax paid or accrued with respect to each separate category, the tax shall be apportioned on an annual basis among the separate categories on the basis of the following formula:

$$\text{Foreign tax related to more than one separate category} \times \frac{\text{Net income subject to that foreign tax included in a separate category}}{\text{Net income subject to that foreign tax}}$$

For purposes of apportioning foreign taxes among the separate categories, gross income is determined under the law of the foreign country or a possession of the United States to which the foreign income taxes have been paid or accrued. Gross income, as determined under foreign law, in the passive category shall first be reduced by any related person interest expense that is allocated to the income under the principles of section 954(b)(5) and § 1.904-5(c)(2)(ii)(C) (adjusted gross passive income). Gross income in all separate categories (including adjusted gross passive income) is next reduced by deducting any expenses, losses, or other amounts that are deductible under foreign law that are specifically allocable to the gross amount of such income under the laws of that foreign country or possession. If expenses are not specifically allocated under foreign law then the expenses will be apportioned under the principles of foreign law but only after taking into account the reduction of passive income by the application of section 954(b)(5). Thus, for example, if foreign law provides that expenses will be apportioned on a gross income basis, the gross income amounts will be those amounts determined under foreign law except that, in the case of passive income, the amount will be adjusted gross passive income. If foreign law does not provide for the direct allocation or apportionment of expenses, losses, or other deductions to a particular category of income, then the principles of §§ 1.861-8 through 1.861-14T and section 954(b)(5) shall apply in allocating §§ 1.861-8 through 1.861-14T such expenses, losses, or other deductions to gross income as determined under foreign law after reduction of passive income by the amount of related person interest allocated to passive income under section 954(b)(5) and § 1.904-5(c)(2)(ii)(C). For example, the principles of §§ 1.861-8 through 1.861-14T apply to require definitely related expenses to be directly allocated to particular categories of gross income and provide the methods of apportioning expenses that are definitely related to more than one category of gross income or that are not definitely related to any particular category of gross income. For this purpose, the apportionment of expenses required to be made under §§ 1.861-8 through 1.861-14T need not be made on other than a separate company basis. The rules in this paragraph apply only for purposes of the apportionment of taxes among separate categories of income and do not affect the computation of a taxpayer's foreign tax credit limitation with respect to a specific category of income. If the taxpayer applies the principles of §§ 1.861-8 through 1.861-14T for purposes of allocating expenses at the level of the taxpayer (or at the level of the qualified business unit, foreign subsidiary, or other entity that paid or accrued the foreign taxes) under this paragraph (a)(1)(ii), such principles shall be applied (for such purposes) in the same manner as the taxpayer applies such principles in determining the income or earnings and profits for United States tax purposes of the taxpayer (or of the qualified business unit, foreign subsidiary, or other entity that paid or accrued the foreign taxes, as the case may be). For example, a taxpayer must use the modified gross income method under § 1.861-9T when applying the principles of that section for purposes of this paragraph (a)(1)(ii) to determine the amount of a controlled foreign corporation's income, in each separate category, that is taxed by a foreign country, if the taxpayer applies the modified gross income method under § 1.861-9T(f)(3) when applying § 1.861-9T to determine the income and earnings and profits of the controlled foreign corporation for United States tax purposes.

(iii) Apportionment of taxes for purposes of applying the high-tax income test. If taxes have been allocated and apportioned to passive income under the rules of paragraph (a)(1)(i) or (ii) of this section, the taxes must further be apportioned to the groups of income described in § 1.904-4(c)(3), (4) and (5) for purposes of determining if the group is high-taxed income. Taxes will be related to income in a particular group under the same rules as those in paragraph (a)(1)(i) and (ii) of this section except that those rules shall be applied by substituting the term "group" for the term "category."

(iv) Special rule for base and timing differences. If, under the law of a foreign country or possession of the United States, a tax is imposed on an item of income that does not constitute income under United States tax principles, that tax shall be treated as imposed with respect to general limitation income. If, under the law of a foreign country or possession of the United States, a tax is imposed on an item that would be income under United States tax principles in another year, that tax will be allocated to the appropriate separate category or categories as if the income were recognized under United States tax principles in the year in which the tax was imposed.

(2) [Reserved].

(b) Application of paragraph (a) to sections 902 and 960. *(1) Determination of foreign taxes deemed paid.* If, for the taxable year, there is included in the gross income of a domestic corporation under section 951 an amount attributable to the earnings and profits of a controlled foreign corporation for any taxable year and the amount included consists of income in more than one separate category of the controlled foreign corporation, then the domestic corporation shall be deemed to have paid only a portion of the taxes paid or accrued, or deemed paid or accrued, by the controlled foreign corporation that are allocated to each separate category to which the inclusion is attributable. The portion of the taxes allocated to a particular separate category that shall be deemed paid by the United States shareholder shall be equal to the taxes allocated to that separate category multiplied by the amount of the inclusion with respect to that category (as determined under § 1.904-5(c)(1)) and divided by the earnings and profits of the controlled foreign corporation with respect to that separate category (in accordance with § 1.904-5(c)(2)(ii)). The rules of this paragraph (b)(1) also apply for purposes of computing the foreign taxes deemed paid by United States shareholders of controlled foreign corporations under section 902.

(2) Distributions received from foreign corporations that are excluded from gross income under section 959(b). The principles of this paragraph shall be applied to—

(i) Any portion of a distribution received from a first-tier corporation by a domestic corporation or individual that is excluded from the domestic corporation's or individual's income under section 959(a) and § 1.959-1; and

(ii) Any portion of a distribution received from an immediately lower-tier corporation by a second- or first-tier corporation that is excluded from such foreign corporation's gross income under section 959(b) and § 1.959-2, if such distribution is treated as a dividend pursuant to § 1.960-2(a).

(3) Application of section 78. For purposes of treating taxes deemed paid by a taxpayer under section 902(a) and section 960(a)(1) as a dividend under section 78, taxes that were allocated to income in a separate category shall be treated as income in that same separate category.

(4) Increase in limitation. The amount of the increase in the foreign tax credit limitation allowed by section 960(b) and § 1.960-4 shall be determined with regard to the applicable category of income under section 904(d).

(c) Examples. The following examples illustrate the application of this section.

Example (1). M, a domestic corporation, conducts business in foreign country X. M earns $400 of shipping income, $200 of general limitation income and $200 of passive income as determined under foreign law. Under foreign law, none of M's expenses are directly allocated or apportioned to a particular category of income. Under the principles of §§ 1.861-8 through 1.861-14T, M allocates $75 of directly allocable expenses to shipping income, $10 of directly allocable expenses to general limitation income, and no such expenses to passive income. M also apportions expenses that are not directly allocable to a specific class of gross income—$40 to shipping income, $20 to general limitation income, and $20 to passive income. Therefore, for purposes of paragraph (a) of this section, M has $285 of net shipping income, $170 of net general limitation income, and $180 of net passive income. Country X imposes tax of $100 on a base that includes M's shipping income and general limitation income. Country X exempts passive income from tax. The tax paid by M is related to M's shipping and general limitation income. The $100 tax is apportioned between those limitations. Thus, M is considered to have paid $63 of X tax on its shipping income ($100 × $285/$455) and $37 of tax on its general limitation income ($100 × $170/$455). None of the X tax is allocated to M's passive income.

Example (2). The facts are the same as in example (1) except that X does not exempt all passive income from tax but only exempts interest income. M's passive income consists of $100 of gross dividend income, to which $10 of expenses that are not directly allocable are apportioned, and $100 of interest income, to which $10 of expenses that are not directly allocable are apportioned. The $90 of net dividend income is subject to X tax, and $90 of net interest income is exempt from X tax. M pays $130 of tax to X. The $130 of tax is related to M's general, shipping, and passive income. The tax is apportioned among those limitations as follows: $68 to shipping income ($130 × $285/$545) $41 to general limitation income ($130 × $170/$545), and $21 to passive income ($130 × $90/$545).

Example (3). P, a domestic corporation, owns 100 percent of s, a controlled foreign corporation organized in country X. S owns 100 percent of T, a controlled foreign corporation that is also organized in country X. Country X grants group relief to S and T. In 1987, S earns $100 of income and T incurs an $80 loss. Under country X's group relief provisions, only $20 of S's income is subject to country X tax. Country X imposes a 30 percent tax on this income ($6). P includes $100 of S's income in gross income under section 951. Six dollars($6) of foreign tax is related to that income for purposes of section 960.

Example (4). P, a domestic corporation, owns 100 percent of S, a controlled foreign corporation organized in country X and 100 percent of T, a controlled foreign corporation organized in country Y. T has $200 of gross manufacturing general limitation income and $50 of passive income. T also pays S $100 for shipping T's goods, a price that may be justified under section 482. T has no other expenses and S has no other income or expense. T's income and earnings and profits are the same. Foreign country X does not tax S on its shipping income. Foreign country Y taxes all of T's income at a rate of 20 percent. Under the law of foreign country Y, T is only allowed a $50 deduction for the payment to S. Therefore, for foreign law purposes, T has $150 of manufacturing income and earnings and profits and $50 of passive income and earnings and profits upon which it pays $40 of tax. Under the principles of foreign law, $30 of that tax is imposed on the general limitation manufacturing income and $10 of the tax is imposed on passive income. Therefore, the foreign effective rate on the general limitation income is 30 percent and the foreign effective rate on the passive income is 20 percent. T has $100 of general limitation income and $50 of passive income and pays $30 of general limitation taxes and $10 of passive taxes. S has $100 of shipping income and pays no foreign tax.

Example (5). R, a domestic corporation, owns 50 percent of T, a foreign corporation that is not a controlled foreign corporation and that is organized in foreign country X. R licenses certain property to T. T then relicenses this property to a third person. In 1987, T paid R a royalty of $100 all of which is treated as passive income to R because it was not an active royalty as defined in § 1.904-4(b)(2). R has $10 of expenses associated with the royalty income and no foreign tax was imposed on the royalty so the high-tax kickout does not apply. In 1988, the Commissioner determined that the correct arm's length royalty was $150 and under the authority of section 482 reallocated an additional $50 of income to R for 1987. Under a closing agreement with the Commissioner, R elected the benefits of Rev. Proc. 65-17 in relation to the income reallocated from R and established an account receivable from T. In 1988, T paid R an additional $50 to reflect the section 482 adjustment and the account receivable that was established because of the adjustment. Foreign country X treats the $50 payment in 1988 as a dividend by T and imposes a $10 withholding tax on the payment. Under paragraph (a)(1) of this section, the $10 of withholding tax is treated as fully allocable to the $50 payment because under foreign law the tax is imposed only on that income. For U.S. purposes, the income is not characterized as a dividend but as a repayment of a bona fide debt and, therefore, the $50 of income is not required to be recognized by R in 1988. The $10 of tax is treated as a tax paid in 1988 on the $50 of passive income included by R in 1987 pursuant to the section 482 adjustment rather than as a tax associated with a dividend from a noncontrolled section 902 corporation. The $10 tax is a tax imposed on passive income under paragraph (a)(1)(iv) of this section.

Example (6). P, a domestic corporation, owns all of the stock of S, a controlled foreign corporation that is incorporated in country X. In 2004, S has $100 of passive income, $200 of shipping income and $200 of general limitation income. S also has $100 of related person interest expense and $100 of other expenses that under foreign law are directly allocable to the general limitation income of S. S has no other expenses. Country X imposes a tax of 25 percent on all of the net income of S and S, therefore, pays $75 in foreign tax. Under paragraph (a)(1)(ii) of this section, the passive income of S is first reduced by the amount of related person interest for purposes of determining the net amount for purposes of allocating the $75 of tax. Under paragraph (a)(1)(ii) of this section, the general limitation income of S is reduced by the $100 of other expenses. Therefore, $50 of the foreign tax is allocated to the shipping income of S ($50 = $75 x $200/$300), $25 is allocated to the general limitation income of S ($25 = $75 x $100/$300), and no taxes are allocated to S's passive income.

Example (7). Domestic corporation P owns all of the stock of a controlled foreign corporation S, which owns all of the stock of controlled foreign corporation T. All such corporations use the calendar year as the taxable year. Assume that earnings and profits are equal to net income and that the income amounts are identical under United States and foreign law principles. In 1987, T earns (before foreign taxes) $187.50 of net passive income and $62.50 of net general limitation income and pays $50 of foreign taxes. S earns no income in 1987 and pays no foreign taxes. For 1987, P is required under section 951 to include in gross income $175 attributable to the earnings and profits of T for that year. One hundred and fifty dollars ($150) of the subpart F inclusion is attributable to passive income earned by T, and $25 of the subpart F inclusion is attributable to general limitation income earned by T. In 1988, T earns no income and pays no foreign taxes. T pays a $200 dividend to S, consisting of $175 from its earnings and profits attributable to amounts required to be included in P's gross income with respect to T and $25 from its other earnings and profits. Assume that no withholding tax is imposed with respect to the distribution from T to S. In 1988, S earns $100 of net general limitation income and receives a $200 dividend from T. S pays $30 in foreign taxes. For 1988, P is required under section 951 to include in gross income $22.50 attributable to the earnings and profits of S for such year. The entire subpart F inclusion is attributable to general limitation income earned by S. In 1988, S pays P a dividend of $247.50, consisting of $157.50 from its earnings and profits attributable to the amount required under section 951 to be included in P's gross income with respect to T, $22.50 from its earnings and profits attributable to the amount required under section 951 to be included in P's gross income with respect to S, and $67.50 from its other earnings and profits. Assume the de minimis rule of section 954(b)(3)(A) and the full inclusion rule of section 954(b)(3)(B) do not apply to the gross amounts of income earned by S and T. The foreign income taxes deemed paid by P for 1987 and 1988 under section 960(a)(1) and section 902(a) are determined as follows on the basis of the following facts and computations.

T corporation (second-tier corporation):

1. Pre-tax earnings and profits:
   - (a) Passive income (p.i.) 187.50
   - Plus:
   - (b) General limitation income (g.l.i.) 62.50
   - (c) Total 250.00
   - Less:
   - (d) Foreign income taxes paid on or with respect to T's earnings and profits (20%) 50.00
   - (e) Earnings and profits 200.00
2. Allocation of taxes:
   - (a) Foreign income taxes paid by T that are allocable to p.i. earned by T:
     - Line 1(d) taxes 50.00
     - Multiplied by: foreign law net p.i. 187.50
     - Divided by: foreign law total net income 250.00
     - Result.............................. 37.50
   - (b) Foreign income taxes paid by T that are allocable to q.l.i. earned by T:
     - Line 1(d) taxes 50.00
     - Multiplied by: foreign law net g.l.i. 62.50
     - Divided by: foreign law total net income 250.00
     - Result.............................. 12.50
3. T's earnings and profits:
   - (a) Earnings and profits attributable to T's p.i.:
     - Line (1)(a) e & p 187.50
     - Less: line 2(a) taxes 37.50
     - Result.............................. 150.00
   - (b) Earnings and profits attributable to T's g.l.i.:
     - Line (1)(b) e & p 62.50
     - Less: line 2(b) taxes 12.50
     - Result.............................. 50.00
4. Subpart F inclusion attributable to T:
   - (a) Amount required to be included in P's gross income for 1987 under section 951 with respect to T that is attributable to T's p.i. 150.00
   - (b) Amount required to be included in P's gross income for 1987 under section 951 with respect to T that is attributable to T's g.l.i. 25.00
5. Foreign income taxes deemed paid by P under section 960(a)(1) with respect to T:
   - (a) Taxes deemed paid that are attributable to T's subpart F inclusion that are attributable to T's p.i.:

Line 2(a) taxes 37.50
Multiplied by:
line 4(a) sec. 951 incl. 150.00
Divided by:
line 3(a) e & p 150.00
Result: 37.50

(b) Taxes deemed paid that are attributable to T's subpart F inclusion that are attributable to T's g.l.i.:
Line 2(b) taxes 12.50
Multiplied by:
line 4(b) sec. 951 incl. 25.00
Divided by:
line 3(b) e & p 50.00
Result.............................. 6.25

6. Dividends paid to S:
(a) Dividends attributable to T's previously taxed p.i. 150.00
Plus:
(b) Dividends attributable to T's previously taxed g.l.i. 25.00
Plus:
(c) Dividends from T's non-previously taxed earnings and profits attributable to p.i. 0
Plus:
(d) Dividends from T's non-previously taxed earnings and profits attributable to g.l.i. 25.00
(e) Total dividends paid to S................ 200.00

7. Taxes deemed paid by S:
(a) Taxes of T deemed paid by S for 1987 under section 902(b)(1) with regard to T's p.i.:
Line 2(a) taxes 37.50
Multiplied by:
line 6(c) dividend 0
Dividend by:
line 3(a) e & p 150.00
Result.............................. 0

(b) Taxes of T deemed paid by S for 1987 under section 902(b)(1) with regard to T's g.l.i.:
Line 2(b) taxes 12.50
Multiplied by:
line 6(d) dividend 25.00
Dividend by:
line 3(b) e & p 50.00
Result.............................. 6.25

S corporation (first-tier corporation):

8. Pre-tax earnings and profits:
(a) Dividends from T attributable to T's non-previously taxed p.i. 0
Plus:
(b) Dividends from T attributable to T's non-previously taxed g.l.i. 25
Plus:
(c) Dividends from T attributable to T's previously taxed p.i. 150
Plus:
(d) Dividends from T attributable to T's previously taxed g.l.i. 25
Plus:
(e) Passive income other than dividend from T 0
Plus:
(f) General limitation income other than dividend from T .. 100.00
(g) Total pre-tax earnings and profits ... 300.00
(h) Foreign income taxes paid on or with respect to S's earnings and profits (10%) 30.00
(i) Earnings and profits 270.00

9. Allocation of taxes:
(a) Foreign income taxes paid by S that are allocable to non-previously taxed p.i. earned by S:
Line 8(h) taxes 30.00
Multiplied by:
foreign law line 8(a) & 8(e) p.i. amounts 0
Dividend by:
foreign law total net income 300.00
Result................................. 0

(b) Foreign income taxes paid by S that are allocable to S's previously taxed p.i. received from T:
Line 8(h) taxes 30.00
Multiplied by:
foreign law line 8(c) p.i. amount 150.00
Divided by:
foreign law total net income 300.00
Result................................. 15.00

(c) Foreign income taxes paid by S that are allocable to non-previously taxed g.l.i. earned by S:
Line 8(h) taxes 30.00
Multiplied by:
foreign law line 8(b) & line 8(f) g.l.i. amounts 125.00
Divided by:
foreign law total net income 300.00
Result................................. 12.50

(d) Foreign income taxes paid by S that are allocable to S's previously taxed g.l.i. received from T:
Line 8(h) taxes 30.00
Multiplied by:
foreign law line 8(d) amount 25.00
Divided by:
foreign law total net income 300.00
Result................................. 2.50

10. (a) Non-previously taxed earnings and profits of S:
Lines 8(a), 8(b), 8(e), & 8(f) e & p 125.00
Less: lines 9(a) & 9(c) taxes 12.50

Result 112.50
(b) Portion of result in 10(a) attributable to S's p.i. 0
(c) Portion of result in 10(a) attributable to S's g.l.i. 112.50

11. (a) Previously taxed earnings and profits of S:
Lines 8(c) and 8(d) e & p 175.00
Less: lines 9(b) & 9(d) taxes 17.50
Result 157.50
(b) Portion of result in 11(a) attributable to T's p.i.:
Line 8(c) 150.00
Less: line 9(b) taxes 15.00
Result 135.00
(c) Portion of result in 11(a) attributable to T's g.l.i.:
Line 8(d) 25.00
Less: line 9(d) taxes 2.50
Result 22.50

12. Subpart F inclusion attributable to S:
(a) Amount required to be included in P's gross income for 1988 under section 951 with respect to S that is attributable to S's p.i. 0
(b) Amount required to be included in P's gross income for 1988 under section 951 with respect to S that is attributable to S's g.l.i. 22.50

13. Foreign income taxes deemed paid by P under section 960(a)(1) with respect to S:
(a) Taxes deemed paid that are attributable to S's subpart F inclusion that are attributable to S's p.i.:
Line 9(a) taxes 0
Multiplied by:
line 12(a) sec. 951 incl. 0
Divided by:
line 10(b) e & p 0
Result 0
(b) Taxes deemed paid that are attributable to S's subpart F inclusion that are attributable to S's g.l.i.:
Line 9(c) taxes 12.50
Multiplied by:
line 12(b) sec. 951 incl. 22.50
Divided by:
line 10(c) e & p 112.50
Result 2.50
(c) Foreign income taxes deemed paid by S deemed paid by P that are allocable to S's p.i.:
Line 7(a) taxes deemed paid by S ... 0
Multiplied by:
line 12(a) sec. 951 incl. 0
Divided by:
line 10(b) e & p 0
Result 0
(d) Foreign income taxes deemed paid by S deemed paid by P that are allocable to S's g.l.i.:
Line 7(b) taxes deemed paid by S .. 6.25
Multiplied by:
line 12(b) sec. 951 incl. 22.50
Divided by: line 10(c) e & p 112.50
Result 1.25

14. Dividends paid to P:
(a) Dividends from S attributable to S's previously taxed p.i. 0
Plus:
(b) Dividends from S attributable to S's previously taxed g.l.i. 22.50
Plus:
(c) Dividends to which section 902(a) applies:
(i) Consisting of S's earnings and profits attributable to T's previously taxed p.i. 135.00
Plus:
(ii) Consisting of S's earnings and profits attributable to T's previously taxed g.l.i. 22.50
Plus:
(iii) Consisting of S's other p.i. earnings and profits .. 0
Plus:
(iv) Consisting of S's other g.l.i. earnings and profits 67.50
(v) Total section 902 dividend 225.00
(d) Total dividends paid to P 247.50

15. Foreign income taxes deemed paid by P under section 902 and section 960(a)(3) with respect to S:
(a) Taxes paid by S deemed paid by P under section 902(a) with regard to S's p.i.:
Line 9(a) taxes 0
Multiplied by:
line 14(c)(iii) div. 0
Divided by:
line 10(b) e & p 0
Result 0
(b) Taxes paid by S deemed paid by P under section 902(a) with regard to S's g.l.i.:
Line 9(c) taxes 12.50
Multiplied by:
line 14(c)(iv) div. 67.50
Divided by:
line 10(c) e & p 112.50
Result 7.50
(c) Taxes deemed paid by S deemed paid by P under section 902(a) with regard to S's p.i.:
Line 7(a) deemed paid taxes 0
Multiplied by:

line 14(c)(iii) div. 0
Divided by:
line 10(b) e & p 0
Result.................................. 0
(d) Taxes deemed paid by S deemed paid by P under section 902(a) with regard to S's g.l.i.:
Line 7(b) deemed paid taxes 6.25
Multiplied by:
line 14(c)(iv) div. 67.50
Divided by:
line 10(c) e & p 112.50
Result.................................. 3.75
(e) Foreign income taxes paid by S under section 960(a)(3) deemed paid by P with regard to S's previously taxed p.i.:
Line 9(b) taxes 15.00
Multiplied by:
line 14(c)(i) div. 135.00
Divided by:
line 11(b) e & p 135.00
Result.................................. 15.00
(f) Foreign income taxes paid by S under section 960(a)(3) deemed paid by P with regard to S's previously taxed g.l.i.:
Line 9(d) taxes 2.50
Multiplied by:
line 14(c)(ii) div.............. 22.50
Divided by:
line 11(c) e & p 22.50
Result.................................. 2.50
Summary:
Total taxes deemed paid by P under section 960(a)(1) with respect to—
Passive income of S and T included under section 951 in income of P:
Line 5(a) 37.50
Plus:
Line 13(a) 0
Plus:
Line 13(c) 0
Result.......................... 37.50
General limitation income of S and T included under section 951 in income of P:
Line 5(b) 6.25
Plus:
Line 13(b) 2.50
Plus:
Line 13(d) 1.25
Result.......................... 10.00
Total deemed paid taxes under section 960(a)(1) 47.50
Total taxes deemed paid by P under section 902 and section 960(a)(3) attributable to passive income of S and T (line 15(e)) 15.00
Total taxes deemed paid by P under section 902 and section 960(a)(3) attributable to general limitation income of S and T:
Line 15(b) 7.50
Plus:
Line 15(d) 3.75
Plus:
Line 15(f) 2.50
Result.......................... 13.75

T.D. 8214, 7/15/88, amend T.D. 8412, 5/13/92, T.D. 9141, 7/19/2004, T.D. 9260, 4/24/2006.

§ 1.904-7 Transition rules.

Caution: The Treasury has not yet amended Reg § 1.904-7 to reflect changes made by P.L. 105-34, P.L. 100-647.

(a) Characterization of distributions and section 951(a)(1) (A) (ii) and (iii) and (B) inclusions of earnings of a controlled foreign corporation accumulated in taxable years beginning before January 1, 1987, during taxable years of both the payor controlled foreign corporation and the recipient which begin after December 31, 1986. *(1) Distributions and section 951(a)(1) (A) (ii) and (iii) and (B) inclusions.* Earnings accumulated in taxable years beginning before January 1, 1987, by a foreign corporation that was a controlled foreign corporation when such earnings were accumulated are characterized in that foreign corporation's hands under section 904(d)(1)(A) (separate limitation interest income) or section 904(d)(1)(E) (general limitation income) (prior to their amendment by the Tax Reform Act of 1986 (the Act)) after application of the de minimis rule of former section 904(d)(3)(C) (prior to its amendment by the Act). When, in a taxable year after the effective date of the Act, earnings and profits attributable to such income are distributed to, or included in the gross income of, a United States shareholder under section 951(a)(1) (A) (ii) or (iii) or (B) (hereinafter in this section "inclusions"), the ordering rules of section 904(d)(3)(D) and § 1.904-5(c)(4) shall be applied in determining initially the character of the income of the distributee or United States shareholder. Thus, a proportionate amount of a distribution described in this paragraph initially will be characterized as separate limitation interest income in the hands of the distributee based on the ratio of the separate limitation interest earnings and profits out of which the dividend was paid to the total earnings and profits out of which the dividend was paid. The distribution or inclusions must then be recharacterized in the hands of the distributee or United States shareholder on the basis of the following principles:

(i) Distributions and inclusions that initially are characterized as separate limitation interest income shall be treated as passive income;

(ii) Distributions and inclusions that initially are characterized as old general limitation income shall be treated as general limitation income, unless the taxpayer establishes to the satisfaction of the Commissioner that the distribution or inclusion is attributable to:

(A) Earnings and profits accumulated with respect to shipping income, as defined in section 904(d)(2)(D) and § 1.904-4(f); or

(B) In the case of a financial services entity, earnings and profits accumulated with respect to financial services income, as defined in section 904(d)(2)(C)(ii) and § 1.904-4(e)(1); or

(C) Earnings and profits accumulated with respect to high withholding tax interest, as defined in section 904(d)(2)(B) and § 1.904-4(d).

(2) Limitation on establishing the character of earnings and profits. In order for a taxpayer to establish that distributions or inclusions that are attributable to general limitation earnings and profits of a particular taxable year beginning before January 1, 1987, are attributable to shipping, financial services or high withholding tax interest earnings and profits, the taxpayer must establish the amounts of foreign taxes paid or accrued with respect to income attributable to those earnings and profits that are to be treated as taxes paid or accrued with respect to shipping, financial services or high withholding tax interest income, as the case may be, under section 904(d)(2)(I). Conversely, in order for a taxpayer to establish the amounts of general limitation taxes paid or accrued in a taxable year beginning before January 1, 1987, that are to be treated as taxes paid or accrued with respect to shipping, financial services or high withholding tax interest income, as the case may be, the taxpayer must establish the amount of any distributions or inclusions that are attributable to shipping, financial services or high withholding tax interest earnings and profits. For purposes of establishing the amounts of general limitation taxes that are to be treated as taxes paid or accrued with respect to shipping, financial services or high withholding tax interest income, the principles of § 1.904-6 shall be applied.

(b) Application of look-through rules to distributions (including deemed distributions) and payments by an entity to a recipient when one's taxable year begins before January 1, 1987 and the other's taxable year begins after December 31, 1986. *(1) In general.* This paragraph provides rules relating to the application of section 904(d)(3) to payments made by a controlled foreign corporation or other entity to which the look-through rules apply during its taxable year beginning after December 31, 1986, but received in a taxable year of the recipient beginning before January 1, 1987. The paragraph also provides rules relating to distributions (including deemed distributions) or payments made by a controlled foreign corporation to which section 904(d)(3) (as in effect before the Act) applies during its taxable year beginning before January 1, 1987, and received in a taxable year of the recipient beginning after December 31, 1986.

(2) Payor of interest, rents, or royalties is subject to the Act and recipient is not subject to the Act. If interest, rents, or royalties are paid or accrued on or after the start of the payor's first taxable year beginning on or after January 1, 1987, but prior to the start of the recipient's first taxable year beginning on or after January 1, 1987, such interest, rents, or royalties shall initially be characterized in accordance with section 904(d)(3) and § 1.904-5. To the extent that interest payments in the hands of the recipient are initially characterized as passive income under these rules, they will be treated as separate limitation interest in the hands of the recipient. To the extent that rents or royalties in the hands of the recipient are initially characterized as passive income under these rules, they will be recharacterized as general limitation income in the hands of the recipient.

(3) Recipient of interest, rents, or royalties is subject to the Act and payor is not subject to the Act. If interest, rents, or royalties are paid or accrued before the start of the payor's first taxable year beginning on or after January 1, 1987, but on or after the start of the recipient's first taxable year beginning after January 1, 1987, the income in the recipient's hands shall be initially characterized in accordance with former section 904(d)(3) (prior to its amendment by the Act). To the extent interest income is characterized as separate limitation interest income under these rules, that income shall be recharacterized as passive income in the hands of the recipient. Rents or royalties will be characterized as general limitation income.

(4) Recipient of dividends and subpart F inclusions is subject to the Act and payor is not subject to the Act. If dividends are paid or accrued or section 951(a)(1) inclusions occur before the start of the first taxable year of a controlled foreign corporation beginning on or after January 1, 1987, but on or after the start of the first taxable year of the distributee or United States shareholder beginning on or after January 1, 1987, the dividends or section 951(a)(1) inclusions in the hands of the distributee or United States shareholder shall be initially characterized in accordance with former section 904(d)(3) (including the ordering rules of section 904(d)(3)(A). Therefore, under former section 904(d)(3)(A), dividends are considered to be paid or derived first from earnings attributable to separate limitation interest income. To the extent the dividend or section 951(a)(1) inclusion is initially characterized under these rules as separate limitation interest income in the hands of the distributee or United States shareholder, the dividend or section 951(a)(1) inclusion shall be recharacterized as passive income in the hands of the distributee or United States shareholder. The portion, if any, of the dividend or section 951(a)(1) inclusion that is not characterized as passive income shall be characterized according to the rules in paragraph (a) of this section. Therefore, a taxpayer may establish that income that would otherwise be characterized as general limitation income is shipping or financial services income. Rules comparable to the rules contained in section 904(d)(2)(I) shall be applied for purposes of characterizing foreign taxes deemed paid with respect to distributions and section 951(a)(1) inclusions covered by this paragraph (b)(4).

(5) Examples. The following examples illustrate the application of this paragraph (b).

Example (1). P is a domestic corporation that is a fiscal year taxpayer (July 1-June 30). S, a controlled foreign corporation, is a wholly-owned subsidiary of P and has a calendar taxable year. On June 1, 1987, S makes a $100 interest payment to P. Because the payment is made after January 1, 1987 (the first day of S's first taxable year beginning after December 31, 1986), the look-through rules of section 904(d)(3) apply to characterize the payment made by S. To the extent, however, that the interest payment to P is allocable to passive income earned by S, the payment will be included in P's separate limitation for interest as provided in former section 904(d)(1)(A).

Example (2). P is a domestic corporation that is a calendar year taxpayer. S, a controlled foreign corporation, is a wholly-owned subsidiary of P and has a July 1-June 30 taxable year. On June 1, 1987, S makes a $100 interest payment to P. Because the payment is made prior to July 1, 1987 (the first day of S's first taxable year beginning after December 31, 1986), the look-through rules of section 904(d)(3) do not apply. Assume that, under former section 904(d)(3), the interest payment would be characterized as separate limitation interest income. For purposes of determining P's foreign tax credit limitation, the interest payment will be passive income as provided in section 904(d)(1)(A).

Example (3). The facts are the same as in Example (2) except that on June 1, 1987, S makes a $100 dividend distribution to P. Because the dividend is paid prior to July 1, 1987 (the first day of S's first taxable year beginning after December 31, 1986), the look-through rules of section 904(d)(3) do not apply. Assume that, under former section 904(d)(3), S's earnings and profits for the taxable year ending June 30, 1987, consist of $200 of earnings attributable to general limitation income and $75 of earnings attributable to separate limitation interest income. The portion of the dividend that is attributable to S's separate limitation interest and is treated as separate limitation interest income under former section 904(d)(3) is $75. The remaining $25 of the dividend is treated as general limitation income under former section 904(d)(3). For purposes of determining P's foreign tax credit limitation, $75 of the dividend will be recharacterized as passive income. The remaining $25 of the dividend will be characterized as general limitation income, unless P can establish that the general limitation portion is attributable to shipping or financial services income.

(c) Installment sales. If income is received or accrued by any person on or after the effective date of the Act (as applied to such person) that is attributable to a disposition of property by such person with regard to which section 453 or section 453A applies (installment sale treatment), and the disposition occurred prior to the effective date of the Act, that income shall be characterized according to the rules of §§ 1.904-4 through 1.904-7.

(d) Special effective date for high withholding tax interest earned by persons with respect to qualified loans described in section 1201(e)(2) of the Act. For purposes of characterizing interest received or accrued by any person, the definition of high withholding tax interest in § 1.904-4(d) shall apply to taxable years beginning after December 31, 1986, except as provided in section 1201(e)(2) of the Act.

(e) Treatment of certain recapture income. Except as otherwise provided, if income is subject to recapture under section 585(c), the income shall be general limitation income. If the income is recaptured by a taxpayer that is a financial services entity, the entity may treat the income as financial services income if the taxpayer establishes to the satisfaction of the Secretary that the deduction to which the recapture amount is attributable is allocable to financial services income. If the taxpayer establishes to the satisfaction of the Secretary that the deduction to which the recapture amount is attributable is allocable to high-withholding tax interest income, the taxpayer may treat the income as high-withholding tax interest.

(f) [Reserved]. For further guidance, see § 1.904-7T(f).

(g) [Reserved.] For further guidance, see § 1.904-7T(g).

T.D. 8214, 7/15/88, amend T.D. 8412, 5/13/92, T.D. 9260, 4/24/2006, T.D. 9368, 12/20/2007.

PAR. 5. Section 1.904-7(g) is added to read as follows:

Proposed § 1.904-7 Transition rules. [*For Preamble, see ¶ 152,939*]

* * * * *

(g) [The text of proposed § 1.904-7(g) is the same as the text of § 1.904-7T(g)(1) through (6) published elsewhere in this issue of the Federal Register.] [*See T.D. 9368, 12/21/2007, 72 Fed. Reg. 245.*]

PAR. 8. In Sec. 1.904-7, paragraph (f) is added as follows:

Proposed § 1.904-7 Transition rules. [*For Preamble, see ¶ 152,753*]

* * * * *

(f) [The text of proposed § 1.904-7(f) is the same as the text of § 1.904-7T(f) published elsewhere in this issue of the Federal Register.] [*See T.D. 9260, 04/24/2006, 71 Fed. Reg. 79.*]

§ 1.904-7T Transition rules (temporary).

• ***Caution:*** Under Code Sec. 7805, temporary regulations expire within three years of the date of issuance. This temporary regulation was issued on 4/24/2006.

(a) through (e) [Reserved]. For further guidance, see § 1.904-7(a) through (e).

(f) Treatment of non-look-through pools of a noncontrolled section 902 corporation or a controlled foreign corporation in post-2002 taxable years. *(1) Definition of non-look-through pools.* The term non-look-through pools means the pools of post-1986 undistributed earnings (as defined in § 1.902-1(a)(9)) that were accumulated, and post-1986 foreign income taxes (as defined in § 1.902-1(a)(8)) paid, accrued, or deemed paid, in and after the first taxable year in which the foreign corporation had a domestic shareholder (as defined in § 1.902-1(a)(1)) but before any such shareholder was eligible for look-through treatment with respect to dividends from the foreign corporation.

(2) Treatment of non-look-through pools of a noncontrolled section 902 corporation. Any undistributed earnings in the non-look-through pool that were accumulated in taxable years beginning before January 1, 2003, by a noncontrolled section 902 corporation as of the last day of the corporation's last taxable year beginning before January 1, 2003, shall be treated in taxable years beginning after December 31, 2002, as if they were accumulated during a period when a dividend paid by the noncontrolled section 902 corporation to a domestic shareholder would have been eligible for look-through treatment under section 904(d)(4) and § 1.904-5. Post-1986 foreign income taxes paid, accrued or deemed paid with respect to such earnings shall be treated as if they were paid, accrued or deemed paid during a period when the related earnings were eligible for look-through treatment. Any such earnings and taxes in the non-look-through pools shall constitute the opening balance of the noncontrolled section 902 corporation's pools of post-1986 undistributed earnings and post-1986 foreign income taxes on the first day of the foreign corporation's first taxable year beginning after December 31, 2002, in accordance with the rules of paragraph (f)(4) of this section.

(3) Treatment of non-look-through pools of a controlled foreign corporation. A controlled foreign corporation may have non-look-through pools of post-1986 undistributed earnings and post-1986 foreign income taxes that were accumulated and paid in a taxable year beginning before January 1, 2003, in which it was a noncontrolled section 902 corporation. Any such undistributed earnings in the non-look-through pool as of the last day of the controlled foreign corporation's last taxable year beginning before January 1, 2003, shall be treated in taxable years beginning on or after January 1, 2003, as if they were accumulated during a period when a dividend paid by the controlled foreign corporation out of such earnings, or an amount included in the gross income of a United States shareholder under section 951 that is attributable to such earnings, would have been eligible for look-through treatment. Any post-1986 foreign income taxes paid, accrued, or deemed paid with respect to such earnings

shall be treated in taxable years beginning on or after January 1, 2003, as if they were paid, accrued, or deemed paid during a period when a dividend or inclusion out of such earnings would have been eligible for look-through treatment. Any such undistributed earnings and taxes in the non-look-through pools shall be added to the pools of post-1986 undistributed earnings and post-1986 foreign income taxes of the controlled foreign corporation in the appropriate separate categories on the first day of the controlled foreign corporation's first taxable year beginning after December 31, 2002, in accordance with the rules of paragraph (f)(4) of this section. Similar rules shall apply to characterize any previously-taxed earnings and profits described in section 959(c)(1)(A) that are attributable to earnings in the non-look-through pool.

(4) Substantiation of look-through character of undistributed earnings and taxes in a non-look-through pool. (i) Reconstruction of earnings and taxes pools. In order to substantiate the look-through characterization of undistributed earnings and taxes in a non-look-through pool under section 904(d)(4) and § 1.904-5, the taxpayer shall make a reasonable, good-faith effort to reconstruct the non-look-through pools of post-1986 undistributed earnings and post-1986 foreign income taxes (and previously-taxed earnings and profits, if any) on a look-through basis for each year in the non-look-through period, beginning with the first taxable year in which post-1986 undistributed earnings were accumulated in the non-look-through pool. Reconstruction shall be based on reasonably available books and records and other relevant information, and it must account for earnings distributed and taxes deemed paid in these years as if they were distributed and deemed paid pro rata from the amounts that were added to the non-look-through pools during the non-look-through period.

(ii) Safe harbor method. A taxpayer may allocate the undistributed earnings and taxes in the non-look-through pools to the foreign corporation's look-through pools of post-1986 undistributed earnings and post-1986 foreign income taxes in other separate categories on the first day of the foreign corporation's first taxable year beginning after December 31, 2002, in the same percentages as the taxpayer properly characterizes the stock of the foreign corporation in the separate categories for purposes of apportioning the taxpayer's interest expense in its first taxable year ending after the first day of the foreign corporation's first taxable year beginning after December 31, 2002, under § 1.861-12T(c)(3) or (c)(4), as the case may be. If the modified gross income method described in § 1.861-9T(j) is used to apportion interest expense of the foreign corporation in its first taxable year beginning after December 31, 2002, the taxpayer must allocate the undistributed earnings and taxes in the non-look-through pools to the foreign corporation's look-through pools of post-1986 undistributed earnings and post-1986 foreign income taxes based on an average of the foreign corporation's modified gross income ratios for the foreign corporation's taxable years beginning in 2003 and 2004. A taxpayer may also use the safe harbor method described in this paragraph (f)(4)(ii) to allocate to separate categories any previously-taxed earnings and profits described in section 959(c)(1)(A) that are attributable to the non-look-through pool.

(iii) Inadequate substantiation. If a taxpayer does not elect the safe harbor method described in paragraph (f)(4)(ii) of this section and the Commissioner determines that the look-through characterization of earnings and taxes in the non-look-through pools cannot reasonably be determined based on the available information, the Commissioner shall allocate the undistributed earnings and taxes in the non-look-through pools to the foreign corporation's passive category.

(iv) Examples. The following examples illustrate the application of this paragraph (f)(4):

Example (1). P, a domestic corporation, has owned 50 percent of the voting stock of S, a foreign corporation, at all times since January 1, 1987, and S has been a noncontrolled section 902 corporation with respect to P since that date. P and S each use the calendar year as their U.S. taxable year. 1987 was the first year in which post-1986 undistributed earnings were accumulated in the non-look-through pool of S. As of December 31, 2002, S had 200u of post-1986 undistributed earnings and $100 of post-1986 foreign income taxes in its non-look-through pools. P does not elect the safe harbor method under paragraph(f)(4)(ii) of this section to allocate the earnings and taxes in the non-look-through pools to S's other separate categories and does not attempt to substantiate the look-through characterization of S's non-look-through pools. The Commissioner, however, reasonably determines, based on information used to characterize S's stock for purposes of apportioning P's interest expense in P's 2003 and 2004 taxable years, that 100u of the earnings and all $100 of the taxes in the non-look-through pools are properly assigned on a look-through basis to the general limitation category, and 100u of earnings and no taxes are properly assigned on a look-through basis to the passive category. Therefore, in accordance with the Commissioner's look-through characterization of the earnings and taxes in S's non-look-through pools, on January 1, 2003, S has 100u of post-1986 undistributed earnings and $100 of post-1986 foreign income taxes in the general limitation category and 100u of post-1986 undistributed earnings and no post-1986 foreign income taxes in the passive category.

Example (2). The facts are the same as in Example 1, except that the Commissioner cannot reasonably determine, based on the available information, the proper look-through characterization of the 200u of undistributed earnings and $100 of taxes in S's non-look-through pools. Accordingly, the Commissioner will assign such earnings and taxes to the passive category, so that as of January 1, 2003, S has 200u of post-1986 undistributed earnings and $100 of post-1986 foreign income taxes in the passive category, and the Commissioner will treat S as a passive category asset for purposes of apportioning P's interest expense.

(5) Treatment of a deficit accumulated in a non-look-through pool. Any deficit in the non-look-through pool of a noncontrolled section 902 corporation or a controlled foreign corporation as of the end of its last taxable year beginning before January 1, 2003, shall be treated in taxable years beginning after December 31, 2002, as if the deficit had been accumulated during a period in which a dividend paid by the foreign corporation would have been eligible for look-through treatment. In the case of a noncontrolled section 902 corporation, the deficit and taxes, if any, in the non-look-through pools shall constitute the opening balance of the look-through pools of post-1986 undistributed earnings and post-1986 foreign income taxes of the noncontrolled section 902 corporation in the appropriate separate categories on the first day of its first taxable year beginning after December 31, 2002. In the case of a controlled foreign corporation, the deficit and taxes, if any, in the non-look-through pools shall be added to the balance of the look-through pools of post-1986 undistributed earnings and post-1986 foreign income taxes of the controlled foreign corporation in the appropriate separate categories on the first day of its first taxable year beginning after December 31, 2002. The taxpayer must sub-

stantiate the look-through characterization of the deficit and taxes in accordance with the rules of paragraph (f)(4) of this section. If a taxpayer does not elect the safe harbor described in paragraph (f)(4)(ii) of this section and the Commissioner determines that the look-through characterization of the deficit and taxes cannot reasonably be determined based on the available information, the Commissioner shall allocate the deficit and taxes, if any, in the non-look-through pools to the foreign corporation's passive category. If, as of the end of a taxable year beginning after December 31, 2002, in which it pays a dividend, the foreign corporation has zero or a deficit in post-1986 undistributed earnings (taking into account any earnings or a deficit accumulated in taxable years beginning before January 1, 2003), the deficit in post-1986 undistributed earnings shall be carried back to reduce pre-1987 accumulated profits, if any, on a last-in first-out basis. See § 1.902-2(a)(1). If, as of the end of a taxable year beginning after December 31, 2002, in which the foreign corporation pays a dividend out of current earnings and profits, it has zero or a deficit in post-1986 undistributed earnings (taking into account any earnings or a deficit accumulated in taxable years beginning before January 1, 2003), and the sum of current plus accumulated earnings and profits is zero or less than zero, no foreign taxes shall be deemed paid with respect to the dividend. See § 1.902-1(b)(4).

(6) Treatment of pre-1987 accumulated profits. Any pre-1987 accumulated profits (as defined in § 1.902-1(a)(10)) of a controlled foreign corporation or noncontrolled section 902 corporation shall be treated in taxable years beginning after December 31, 2002, as if they were accumulated during a period in which a dividend paid by the foreign corporation would have been eligible for look-through treatment. Any pre-1987 foreign income taxes (as defined in § 1.902-1(a)(10)(iii)) shall be treated as if they were paid, accrued or deemed paid during a year when a dividend out of the related pre-1987 accumulated profits would have been eligible for look-through treatment. The taxpayer must substantiate the look-through characterization of the pre-1987 accumulated profits and pre-1987 foreign income taxes in accordance with the rules of paragraph (f)(4) of this section. If a taxpayer does not elect the safe harbor described in paragraph (f)(4)(ii) of this section and the Commissioner determines that the look-through characterization of the pre-1987 accumulated profits and pre-1987 foreign income taxes cannot reasonably be determined based on the available information, the pre-1987 accumulated profits and pre-1987 foreign income taxes shall be allocated to the foreign corporation's passive category.

(7) Treatment of post-1986 undistributed earnings or a deficit of a controlled foreign corporation attributable to dividends from a noncontrolled section 902 corporation paid in taxable years beginning before January 1, 2003. (i) Look-through treatment of post-1986 undistributed earnings at controlled foreign corporation level. Dividends paid by a noncontrolled section 902 corporation to a controlled foreign corporation in post-1986 taxable years of the noncontrolled section 902 corporation beginning before January 1, 2003, were assigned to a separate category for dividends from that noncontrolled section 902 corporation. Beginning on the first day of the controlled foreign corporation's first taxable year beginning on or after the first day of the lower-tier corporation's first taxable year beginning after December 31, 2002, any post-1986 undistributed earnings, or previously-taxed earnings and profits described in section 959(c)(1) or (2), of the controlled foreign corporation in such a separate category shall be treated as if they were accumulated during a period when a dividend paid by the noncontrolled section 902 corporation would have been eligible for look-through treatment. Any post-1986 foreign income taxes in such a separate category shall also be treated as if they were paid, accrued or deemed paid during a period when such a dividend would have been eligible for look-through treatment. Any such post-1986 undistributed earnings and post-1986 foreign income taxes in a separate category for dividends from a noncontrolled section 902 corporation shall be added to the opening balance of the controlled foreign corporation's look-through pools of post-1986 undistributed earnings and post-1986 foreign income taxes in the appropriate separate categories on the first day of the controlled foreign corporation's first taxable year beginning on or after the first day of the lower-tier corporation's first taxable year beginning after December 31, 2002. The taxpayer must substantiate the look-through characterization of such earnings and taxes in accordance with the rules of paragraph (f)(7)(iii) of this section.

(ii) Look-through treatment of deficit in post-1986 undistributed earnings at controlled foreign corporation level. If a controlled foreign corporation has a deficit in a separate category for dividends from a lower-tier noncontrolled section 902 corporation that is a member of the controlled foreign corporation's qualified group as defined in section 902(b)(2), such deficit shall be treated in taxable years of the upper-tier corporation beginning on or after the first day of the lower-tier corporation's first taxable year beginning after December 31, 2002, as if the deficit had been accumulated during a period in which a dividend from the lower-tier corporation would have been eligible for look-through treatment. Any post-1986 foreign income taxes in the separate category for dividends from the noncontrolled section 902 corporation shall also be treated as if they were paid, accrued or deemed paid during a period when the dividends were eligible for look-through treatment. The deficit and related post-1986 foreign income taxes, if any, shall be added to the opening balance of the controlled foreign corporation's look-through pools of post-1986 undistributed earnings and post-1986 foreign income taxes in the appropriate separate categories on the first day of the controlled foreign corporation's first taxable year beginning on or after the first day of the lower-tier corporation's first taxable year beginning after December 31, 2002. The taxpayer must substantiate the look-through characterization of the deficit and taxes in accordance with the rules of paragraph (f)(7)(iii) of this section.

(iii) Substantiation required for look-through treatment. The taxpayer must substantiate the look-through characterization of post-1986 undistributed earnings, previously-taxed earnings and profits, or a deficit in post-1986 undistributed earnings in a separate category for dividends paid by a noncontrolled section 902 corporation in taxable years beginning before January 1, 2003, by making a reasonable, good-faith effort to reconstruct the earnings (or deficit) and taxes in the separate category at the level of the controlled foreign corporation on a look-through basis, in accordance with the principles of paragraph (f)(4)(i) of this section. Alternatively, the taxpayer may allocate the earnings (or deficit) and taxes to the controlled foreign corporation's look-through pools by electing to apply the safe harbor described in paragraph (f)(4)(ii) at the level of the controlled foreign corporation. If the taxpayer so elects, the earnings (or deficit) and taxes shall be allocated to the controlled foreign corporation's look-through pools in the appropriate separate categories on the first day of the controlled foreign corporation's first taxable year beginning on or after the first day of the lower-tier corporation's first taxable year beginning after December 31, 2002. The allocation shall be made in the same percentages as the controlled foreign corporation would properly characterize the stock of the lower-tier noncontrolled section 902 corporation in the separate categories for purposes of apportioning the controlled foreign corporation's interest expense in its first taxable year ending after the first day of the noncontrolled section 902 corporation's first taxable year beginning after December 31, 2002. Under § 1.861-12T(c)(3), the apportionment ratios properly used by the controlled foreign corporation are in turn based on the apportionment ratios properly used by the noncontrolled section 902 corporation to apportion its interest expense in its first taxable year beginning after December 31, 2002. In the case of a taxpayer that elects to use the safe harbor rule where the lower-tier noncontrolled section 902 corporation uses the modified gross income method described in § 1.861-9T(j) to apportion interest expense for its first taxable year beginning after December 31, 2002, earnings (or a deficit) and taxes in the separate category for dividends from the noncontrolled section 902 corporation shall be allocated to the look-through pools based on the average of the noncontrolled section 902 corporation's modified gross income ratios for its taxable years beginning in 2003 and 2004. In the case of a controlled foreign corporation that has in its qualified group a chain of lower-tier noncontrolled section 902 corporations, the safe harbor applies first to characterize the stock of the third-tier corporation and then to characterize the stock of the second-tier corporation. Where a taxpayer elects the safe harbor with respect to a lower-tier noncontrolled section 902 corporation with respect to which the taxpayer did not meet the requirements of section 902(a) as of the end of the upper-tier controlled foreign corporation's last taxable year beginning before January 1, 2003, the earnings (or deficit) and taxes in the separate category for dividends from the lower-tier corporation shall be allocated to the upper-tier corporation's look-through pools in the separate categories in the same percentages as the stock of the lower-tier corporation would have been characterized for purposes of apportioning the upper-tier corporation's interest expense in the last year the taxpayer met the ownership requirements of section 902(a) with respect to the lower-tier corporation if the look-through rules had applied in that year. If a taxpayer does not elect the safe harbor method described in this subparagraph (f)(7)(iii), and the Commissioner determines that the look-through characterization of the earnings (or deficit) and taxes cannot reasonably be determined based on the available information, the Commissioner shall allocate the earnings (or deficit) and associated foreign income taxes to the controlled foreign corporation's passive category.

(8) Treatment of distributions received by an upper-tier corporation from a lower-tier noncontrolled section 902 corporation when the corporations do not have the same taxable years. (i) Rule. In the case of dividends paid by a lower-tier noncontrolled section 902 corporation to an upper-tier corporation where both are members of the same qualified group as defined in section 902(b)(2), the following rules apply. Dividends paid by the lower-tier corporation in taxable years beginning before January 1, 2003, are assigned to a separate category for dividends from that corporation, regardless of whether the corresponding taxable year of the recipient corporation began after December 31, 2002. Post-1986 undistributed earnings, previously-taxed earnings and profits, and post-1986 foreign income taxes in such a separate category shall be treated, beginning on the first day of the upper-tier corporation's first taxable year beginning on or after the first day of the lower-tier corporation's first taxable year beginning after December 31, 2002, as if they were accumulated during a period when a dividend paid by the lower-tier corporation would have been eligible for look-through treatment under section 904(d)(4) and § 1.904-5. Dividends paid by a lower-tier corporation in taxable years beginning after December 31, 2002, are eligible for look-through treatment when paid, without regard to whether the corresponding taxable year of the recipient upper-tier corporation began after December 31, 2002.

(ii) Example. The following example illustrates the application of paragraph (f) of this section:

Example. M, a domestic corporation, has directly owned 50 percent of the stock of X, and X has directly owned 50 percent of the stock of Y, at all times since X and Y were organized on January 1, 1990. Accordingly, X and Y are noncontrolled section 902 corporations with respect to M, and X and Y are members of the same qualified group. M and Y use the calendar year as their U.S. taxable year, and X uses a taxable year beginning on July 1. Under § 1.904-4(g) and paragraph (f)(10) of this section, a dividend paid to M by X on January 15, 2003 (during X's last pre-2003 taxable year) is not eligible for look-through treatment in 2003. However, under § 1.861-12T(c)(4), M will characterize the stock of X on a look-through basis for purposes of interest expense apportionment in its 2003 taxable year. Under § 1.904-4T(h)(1), any unused foreign taxes in M's separate category for dividends from X will be carried over to M's other separate categories on a look-through basis for M's taxable years beginning on and after January 1, 2004. Under paragraph (f)(2) of this section, any undistributed earnings and taxes in X's non-look-through pools will be allocated to X's other separate categories on July 1, 2003. Under § 1.904-5(i)(4) and paragraphs (f)(8)(i) and (f)(10) of this section, a dividend paid to X by Y on January 15, 2003 (during Y's first post-2002 taxable year) is eligible for look-through treatment when paid, notwithstanding that it is received in a pre-2003 taxable year of X.

(9) Election to apply pre-AJCA rules to 2003 and 2004 taxable years. (i) Definition. The term single category for dividends from all noncontrolled section 902 corporations means the separate category described in section 904(d)(1)(E) as in effect for taxable years beginning after December 31, 2002, and prior to its repeal by the American Jobs Creation Act (AJCA), Public Law 108-357, 118 Stat. 1418 (October 22, 2004).

(ii) Time, manner, and form of election. A taxpayer may elect not to apply the provisions of section 403 of the AJCA and to apply the rules of this paragraph (f)(9) to taxable years of noncontrolled section 902 corporations beginning after December 31, 2002, and before January 1, 2005, without regard to whether the corresponding taxable years of the taxpayer or any upper-tier corporation begin before or after such dates. A taxpayer shall be eligible to make such an election provided that--

(A) The taxpayer's tax liability as shown on an original or amended tax return for each of its affected taxable years is consistent with the rules of this paragraph (f)(9), the guidance set forth in Notice 2003-5 (2003-1 C.B. 294) (see § 601.601(d)(2) of this chapter), and the principles of § 1.861-12T(c)(4) for each such year for which the statute of limitations does not preclude the filing of an amended return;

(B) The taxpayer makes appropriate adjustments to eliminate any double benefit arising from the application of this paragraph (f)(9) to years that are not open for assessment; and

(C) The taxpayer attaches a statement to its next tax return for which the due date (with extensions) is more than 90 days after April 25, 2006, indicating that the taxpayer elects not to apply the provisions of section 403 of the AJCA to taxable years of its noncontrolled section 902 corporations beginning in 2003 and 2004, and that the taxpayer has filed original returns or will file amended returns reflecting tax liabilities for each affected year that satisfy the requirements described in this paragraph (f)(9)(ii).

(iii) Treatment of non-look-through pools in taxable years beginning after December 31, 2004. Undistributed earnings (or a deficit) and taxes in the non-look-through pools of a controlled foreign corporation or a noncontrolled section 902 corporation as of the end of its last taxable year beginning before January 1, 2005, shall be treated in taxable years beginning after December 31, 2004, as if they were accumulated and paid during a period in which a distribution out of earnings in the non-look-through pool would have been eligible for look-through treatment. Such earnings (or deficit) and taxes shall be added to the foreign corporation's pools of post-1986 undistributed earnings and post-1986 foreign income taxes in the appropriate separate categories on the first day of the foreign corporation's first taxable year beginning after December 31, 2004. In accordance with the principles of paragraph (f)(4) of this section, the taxpayer must reconstruct the non-look-through pools or, if the taxpayer elects the safe harbor, allocate the earnings and taxes in the non-look-through pools to the foreign corporation's look-through pools in the appropriate separate categories on the first day of the foreign corporation's first taxable year beginning after December 31, 2004. Under the safe harbor, this allocation is made in the same percentages as the taxpayer properly characterized the stock of the foreign corporation for purposes of apportioning the taxpayer's interest expense in the taxpayer's first taxable year ending after the first day of the foreign corporation's first taxable year beginning after December 31, 2002. See § 1.861-12T(c)(3) and (4). If a taxpayer does not elect the safe harbor described in paragraph (f)(4)(ii) and the Commissioner determines that the look-through characterization of the earnings (or deficit) and taxes cannot reasonably be determined based on the available information, the earnings (or deficit) and taxes shall be allocated to the foreign corporation's passive category.

(iv) Carryover of unused foreign tax. To the extent that a taxpayer has unused foreign taxes in the single category for dividends from all noncontrolled section 902 corporations, such taxes shall be carried forward to the appropriate separate categories in the taxpayer's taxable years beginning on or after the first day of the relevant noncontrolled section 902 corporation's first taxable year beginning after December 31, 2004. Such unused taxes shall be carried forward in the same manner as § 1.904-2T(h)(1) provides that unused foreign taxes in the separate categories for dividends from each noncontrolled section 902 corporation are carried over to taxable years beginning on or after the first day of the noncontrolled section 902 corporation's first taxable year beginning after December 31, 2002, in the case of a taxpayer that does not make the election under paragraph (f)(9) of this section. The electing taxpayer shall determine which noncontrolled section 902 corporations paid the dividends to which the unused foreign taxes are attributable and assign the taxes to the appropriate separate categories as if such dividends had been eligible for look-through treatment when paid. Accordingly, the taxpayer must substantiate the look-through characterization of the unused foreign taxes in accordance with paragraph (f)(4) of this section by reconstructing the non-look-through pools or, if the taxpayer elects the safe harbor, by allocating the unused foreign taxes to other separate categories in the same percentages as the taxpayer properly characterized the stock of the noncontrolled section 902 corporation for purposes of apportioning the taxpayer's interest expense for its first taxable year ending after the first day of the noncontrolled section 902 corporation's first taxable year beginning after December 31, 2002. The rule described in this paragraph (f)(9)(iv) shall apply only to unused foreign taxes attributable to dividends out of earnings that were accumulated by noncontrolled section 902 corporations in taxable years of such corporations beginning before January 1, 2003, because only unused foreign taxes attributable to distributions out of pre-2003 earnings are included in the single category for dividends from all noncontrolled section 902 corporations. To the extent that unused foreign taxes carried forward to the single category for dividends from all noncontrolled section 902 corporations under the rules of Notice 2003-5 (see § 601.601(d)(2) of this chapter) were either absorbed by low-taxed dividends paid by noncontrolled section 902 corporations out of the non-look-through pool in taxable years of such corporations beginning in 2003 or 2004, or expired unused, the amount of taxes carried forward to the separate categories on a look-through basis will be smaller than the aggregate amount of taxes initially carried forward to the single category for dividends from all noncontrolled section 902 corporations. In this case, the unused foreign taxes arising in each taxable year shall be deemed attributable to each noncontrolled section 902 corporation in the same ratio as the dividends included in the separate category that were paid by such corporation in such year bears to all such dividends paid by all noncontrolled section 902 corporations in such year. Unused foreign taxes carried forward from the separate categories for dividends from each noncontrolled section 902 corporation to the single category for dividends from all noncontrolled section 902 corporations will similarly be deemed to have been utilized on a pro rata basis. The remaining unused foreign taxes are then assigned to the appropriate separate categories under the rules of paragraph (f)(4) of this section. Unused foreign taxes shall be treated as allocable to general limitation income to the extent that such taxes would otherwise have been allocable to passive income (based on reconstructed pools or the safe harbor method), or to the extent that, under paragraph (f)(4)(iii) of this section, the Commissioner determines that the look-through characterization cannot reasonably be determined based on the available information.

(v) Carryback of unused foreign tax. To the extent that a taxpayer has unused foreign taxes attributable to a dividend paid by a noncontrolled section 902 corporation that was eligible for look-through treatment under section 904(d)(4) and § 1.904-5, any such unused foreign taxes shall be carried back to prior taxable years within the same separate category and not to the single category for dividends from all noncontrolled section 902 corporations or any separate category for dividends from a noncontrolled section 902 corporation. See Notice 2003-5 (see § 601.601(d)(2) of this chapter) for rules relating to the carryback of unused foreign taxes in the single category for dividends from all noncontrolled section 902 corporations.

(vi) Recapture of overall foreign loss or separate limitation loss in the single category for dividends from all noncontrolled section 902 corporations. To the extent that a taxpayer has a balance in a separate limitation loss or overall foreign loss account in the single category for dividends from all noncontrolled section 902 corporations under section 904(d)(1)(E) (prior to its repeal by the AJCA), at the end of the taxpayer's last taxable year beginning before January 1, 2005 (or a later taxable year in which the taxpayer received a dividend subject to the separate limitation for dividends from all noncontrolled section 902 corporations), the amount of such balance shall be allocated on the first day of the taxpayer's next taxable year to the taxpayer's other separate categories. The amount of such balance that is attributable to each noncontrolled section 902 corporation shall be allocated in the same percentages as the taxpayer properly characterized the stock of such corporation for purposes of apportioning the taxpayer's interest expense for its first taxable year ending after the first day of such corporation's first taxable year beginning after December 31, 2002, under § 1.861-12T(c)(3) or (c)(4), as the case may be. To the extent that a taxpayer has a balance in a separate limitation loss account for the single category for dividends from all noncontrolled section 902 corporations with respect to another separate category, and the separate limitation loss account would otherwise be assigned to that other category under this paragraph (f)(9)(vi), such balance shall be eliminated.

(vii) Recapture of separate limitation losses in other separate categories. To the extent that a taxpayer has a balance in any separate limitation loss account in a separate category with respect to the single category for dividends from all noncontrolled section 902 corporations at the end of the taxpayer's last taxable year with or within which ends the last taxable year of the relevant noncontrolled section 902 corporation beginning before January 1, 2005, such loss shall be recaptured in subsequent taxable years as income in the appropriate separate category. The separate limitation loss account shall be deemed attributable on a pro rata basis to those noncontrolled section 902 corporations that paid dividends out of earnings accumulated in taxable years beginning before January 1, 2003, in the years in which the separate limitation loss in the other separate category arose. The ratable portions of the separate limitation loss account shall be recaptured as income in the taxpayer's separate categories in the same percentages as the taxpayer properly characterized the stock of the relevant noncontrolled section 902 corporation for purposes of apportioning the taxpayer's interest expense in its first taxable year ending after the first day of such corporation's first taxable year beginning after December 31, 2002, under § 1.861-12T(c)(3) or (c)(4), as the case may be. To the extent that a taxpayer has a balance in any separate limitation loss account in any separate category that would have been recaptured as income in that same category under this paragraph (f)(9)(vii), such balance shall be eliminated.

(viii) Treatment of undistributed earnings in an upper-tier corporation-level single category for dividends from lower-tier noncontrolled section 902 corporations. Where a controlled foreign corporation or noncontrolled section 902 corporation has a single category for dividends from all noncontrolled section 902 corporations containing earnings attributable to dividends paid by one or more lower-tier corporations, the following rules apply. The post-1986 undistributed earnings, previously-taxed earnings and profits described in section 959(c)(1) or (2), if any, and associated post-1986 foreign income taxes shall be allocated to the upper-tier corporation's other separate categories in the same manner as earnings and taxes in a separate category for dividends from each noncontrolled section 902 corporation maintained by the upper-tier corporation are allocated under paragraph (f)(7) of this section. Accordingly, post-1986 undistributed earnings, previously-taxed earnings and profits, if any, and post-1986 foreign income taxes in the single category for dividends from all noncontrolled section 902 corporations shall be treated as if they were accumulated and paid, accrued or deemed paid during a period when a dividend paid by each lower-tier corporation that paid dividends included in the single category would have been eligible for look-through treatment. If the taxpayer elects the safe harbor rule described in paragraph (f)(7)(iii) of this section, the earnings and taxes shall be allocated based on the apportionment ratios properly used by the lower-tier corporation to apportion its interest expense for its first taxable year beginning after December 31, 2002. The taxpayer must substantiate the look-through characterization of the earnings and taxes in accordance with the rules of paragraph (f)(7)(iii) of this section. If the taxpayer does not elect the safe harbor and the Commissioner determines that the look-through characterization of the earnings cannot reasonably be determined based on the available information, the earnings and taxes shall be assigned to the upper-tier corporation's passive category.

(ix) Treatment of a deficit in the single category for dividends from lower-tier noncontrolled section 902 corporations. Where a controlled foreign corporation or noncontrolled section 902 corporation had an aggregate deficit in the single category for dividends from all noncontrolled section 902 corporations as of the end of the upper-tier corporation's last taxable year beginning before January 1, 2005, such deficit and the associated post-1986 foreign income taxes, if any, shall be allocated to the upper-tier corporation's other separate categories in the same percentages in which the non-look-through pools of each lower-tier corporation to which the deficit is attributable were assigned to such corporation's other separate categories in its first taxable year beginning after December 31, 2002. If the taxpayer elects the safe harbor rule described in paragraph (f)(7)(iii) of this section, the deficit and taxes shall be allocated based on how the taxpayer properly characterized the stock of the lower-tier noncontrolled section 902 corporation for purposes of apportioning the upper-tier corporation's interest expense for the upper-tier corporation's first taxable year ending after the first day of the lower-tier corporation's first taxable year beginning after December 31, 2002. The taxpayer must substantiate the look-through characterization of the deficit and taxes in accordance with the rules of paragraph (f)(7)(iii) of this section. If the taxpayer does not elect the safe harbor and the Commissioner determines that the look-through characterization of the deficit cannot reasonably be determined based on the available information, the deficit and taxes shall be assigned to the upper-tier corporation's passive category.

(10) Effective date. Except in the case of a taxpayer that makes the election under paragraph (f)(9) of this section, section 904(d)(4) and this paragraph (f) shall apply to dividends from a noncontrolled section 902 corporation that are paid during the first taxable year of the noncontrolled section 902 corporation beginning after December 31, 2002, and thereafter, without regard to whether the corresponding taxable year of the recipient of the dividend begins after December 31, 2002. In the case of a taxpayer that makes the election under paragraph (f)(9) of this section, the provisions of section 403 of the AJCA, including section 904(d)(4), and this paragraph (f) shall apply to dividends from a noncontrolled section 902 corporation that are paid in taxable years of the noncontrolled section 902 corporation beginning after December 31, 2004, without regard to whether the corresponding taxable year of the recipient of the dividend begins after December 31, 2004.

(g) Treatment of earnings and foreign taxes of a controlled foreign corporation or a noncontrolled section 902 corporation accumulated in taxable years beginning before January 1, 2007. *(1) Definitions.* (i) Pre-2007 pools means the pools in each separate category of post-1986 undistributed earnings (as defined in § 1.902-1(a)(9)) that were accumulated, and post-1986 foreign income taxes (as defined in § 1.902-1(a)(8)) paid, accrued, or deemed paid, in taxable years beginning before January 1, 2007.

(ii) Pre-2007 separate categories means the separate categories of income described in section 904(d) as applicable to taxable years beginning before January 1, 2007, and any other separate category of income described in § 1.904-4(m).

(iii) Post-2006 separate categories means the separate categories of income described in section 904(d) as applicable to taxable years beginning after December 31, 2006, and any other separate category of income described in § 1.904-4(m).

(2) Treatment of pre-2007 pools of a controlled foreign corporation or a noncontrolled section 902 corporation. Any post-1986 undistributed earnings in a pre-2007 pool of a controlled foreign corporation or a noncontrolled section 902 corporation shall be treated in taxable years beginning after December 31, 2006, as if they were accumulated during a period in which the rules governing the determination of post-2006 separate categories applied. Post-1986 foreign income taxes paid, accrued, or deemed paid with respect to such earnings shall be treated as if they were paid, accrued, or deemed paid during a period in which the rules governing the determination of post-2006 separate categories (including the rules of section 904(d)(3)(E)) applied as well. Any such earnings and taxes in pre-2007 pools shall constitute the opening balance of the foreign corporation's post-1986 undistributed earnings and post-1986 foreign income taxes on the first day of the foreign corporation's first taxable year beginning after December 31, 2006, in accordance with the rules of paragraph (g)(3) of this section. Similar rules shall apply to characterize any deficits in the pre-2007 pools and previously-taxed earnings and profits described in section 959(c)(1)(A) that are attributable to earnings in the pre-2007 pools.

(3) Substantiation of post-2006 character of earnings and taxes in a pre-2007 pool. (i) Reconstruction of earnings and taxes pools. In order to substantiate the post-2006 characterization of post-1986 undistributed earnings (as well as deficits and previously-taxed earnings, if any) and post-1986 foreign income taxes in pre-2007 pools of a controlled foreign corporation or a noncontrolled section 902 corporation, the taxpayer shall make a reasonable, good-faith effort to reconstruct the pre-2007 pools of post-1986 undistributed earnings (as well as deficits and previously-taxed earnings, if any) and post-1986 foreign income taxes following the rules governing the determination of post-2006 separate categories for each taxable year beginning before January 1, 2007, beginning with the first year in which post-1986 undistributed earnings were accumulated in the pre-2007 pool. Reconstruction shall be based on reasonably available books and records and other relevant information. To the extent any pre-2007 separate category includes earnings that would be allocated to more than one post-2006 separate category, the taxpayer must account for earnings distributed and taxes deemed paid in these years for such category as if they were distributed and deemed paid pro rata from the amounts that were added to that category during each taxable year beginning before January 1, 2007.

(ii) Safe harbor method. (A) In general. Subject to the rules of paragraph (g)(3)(iii) of this section, a taxpayer may allocate the post-1986 undistributed earnings and post-1986 foreign income taxes in pre-2007 pools of a controlled foreign corporation or a noncontrolled section 902 corporation (as well as deficits and previously-taxed earnings, if any) under one of the safe harbor methods described in paragraphs (g)(3)(ii)(B) and (g)(3)(ii)(C) of this section.

(B) General safe harbor method. (1) Any post-1986 undistributed earnings (as well as deficits and previously-taxed earnings, if any) and post-1986 foreign income taxes of a noncontrolled section 902 corporation or a controlled foreign corporation in a pre-2007 separate category for passive income, certain dividends from a DISC or former DISC, taxable income attributable to certain foreign trade income, or certain distributions from a FSC or former FSC shall be allocated to the post-2006 separate category for passive category income.

(2) Any post-1986 undistributed earnings (as well as deficits and previously-taxed earnings, if any) and post-1986 foreign income taxes of a noncontrolled section 902 corporation or a controlled foreign corporation in a pre-2007 separate category for financial services income, shipping income or general limitation income shall be allocated to the post-2006 separate category for general category income.

(3) Except as provided in paragraph (g)(3)(ii)(B)(4) of this section, any post-1986 undistributed earnings (as well as deficits and previously-taxed earnings, if any) and post-1986 foreign income taxes of a noncontrolled section 902 corporation or a controlled foreign corporation in a pre-2007 separate category for high withholding tax interest shall be allocated to the post-2006 separate category for passive category income.

(4) If a controlled foreign corporation has positive post-1986 undistributed earnings and post-1986 foreign income taxes in a pre-2007 separate category for high withholding tax interest, such earnings and taxes shall be allocated to the post-2006 separate category for general category income if the earnings would qualify as income subject to high foreign taxes under section 954(b)(4) if the entire amount of post-1986 undistributed earnings were treated as a net item of income subject to the rules of § 1.954-1(d). If the high withholding tax interest earnings would not qualify as income subject to high foreign taxes under section 954(b)(4), then the earnings and taxes shall be allocated to the post-2006 separate category for passive category income.

(C) Interest apportionment safe harbor. A taxpayer may allocate the post-1986 undistributed earnings (as well as deficits and previously-taxed earnings, if any) and post-1986 foreign income taxes in pre-2007 pools of a controlled foreign corporation or a noncontrolled section 902 corporation following the principles of paragraph (f)(4)(ii) of this section.

(iii) Consistency rule. The election to apply a safe harbor method under paragraph (g)(3)(ii) of this section in lieu of the rules described in paragraph (g)(3)(i) of this section may be made on a separate category by separate category basis. However, if a taxpayer elects to apply a safe harbor to allocate pre-2007 pools of more than one pre-2007 separate category of a controlled foreign corporation or a noncontrolled section 902 corporation, such safe harbor (the general safe harbor described in paragraph (g)(3)(ii)(B) of this section or the interest apportionment safe harbor described in paragraph (g)(3)(ii)(C) of this section) shall apply to allocate post-1986 undistributed earnings (as well as deficits and previously-taxed earnings, if any) and post-1986 foreign income taxes for the pre-2007 pools in each pre-2007 separate category of the foreign corporation for which the taxpayer elected to apply a safe harbor method in lieu of reconstructing the pre-2007 pools.

(4) Treatment of pre-1987 accumulated profits. Any pre-1987 accumulated profits (as defined in § 1.902-1(a)(10)) of a noncontrolled section 902 corporation or a controlled foreign corporation shall be treated in taxable years beginning after December 31, 2006, as if they had been accumulated during a period in which the rules governing the determination of post-2006 separate categories applied. Foreign income taxes paid, accrued, or deemed paid with respect to such earnings shall be treated as if they were paid, accrued, or deemed paid during a period in which the rules governing the determination of post-2006 separate categories applied as well. The taxpayer must substantiate the post-2006 characterization of the pre-1987 accumulated profits and pre-1987 foreign income taxes in accordance with the rules of paragraph (g)(3) of this section, including the safe harbor provisions. Similar rules shall apply to characterize any deficits or previously-taxed earnings and profits described in section 959(c)(1)(A) that are attributable to pre-1987 accumulated profits.

(5) Treatment of earnings and foreign taxes in pre-2007 pools of a lower-tier controlled foreign corporation or noncontrolled section 902 corporation. The rules of paragraphs (g)(1) through (4) of this section apply to post-1986 undistributed earnings (as well as deficits and previously-taxed earnings, if any) and post-1986 foreign income taxes in pre-2007 pools, and pre-1987 accumulated profits and pre-1987 foreign income taxes, of a lower-tier controlled foreign corporation or noncontrolled section 902 corporation.

(6) Effective/applicability date. This paragraph (g) shall apply to taxable years of United States taxpayers beginning after December 31, 2006 and ending on or after December 21, 2007, and to taxable years of a foreign corporation which end with or within taxable years of its domestic corporate shareholder beginning after December 31, 2006 and ending on or after December 21, 2007.

(7) Expiration date. The applicability of this paragraph (g) expires on December 20, 2010.

T.D. 9260, 4/24/2006, amend T.D. 9368, 12/20/2007.

§ 1.904(b)-0 Outline of regulation provisions.

This section lists the headings for §§ 1.904(b)-1 and 1.904(b)-2.

§ 1.904(b)-1 Special rules for capital gains and losses.

(a) Capital gains and losses included in taxable income from sources outside the United States.

(1) Limitation on capital gain from sources outside the United States when the taxpayer has net capital losses from sources within the United States.

(i) In general.

(ii) Allocation of reduction to separate categories or rate groups.

(A) In general.

(B) Taxpayer with capital gain rate differential.

(2) Exclusivity of rules; no reduction by reason of net capital loss from sources outside the United States in a different separate category.

(3) Capital losses from sources outside the United States in the same separate category.

(4) Examples.

(b) Capital gain rate differential.

(1) Application of adjustments only if capital gain rate differential exists.

(2) Determination of whether capital gain rate differential exists.

(3) Special rule for certain noncorporate taxpayers.

(c) Rate differential adjustment of capital gains.

(1) Rate differential adjustment of capital gains in foreign source taxable income.

(i) In general.

(ii) Special rule for taxpayers with a net long-term capital loss from sources within the United States.

(iii) Examples.

(2) Rate differential adjustment of capital gains in entire taxable income.

(d) Rate differential adjustment of capital losses from sources outside the United States.

(1) In general.

(2) Determination of which capital gains are offset by net capital losses from sources outside the United States.

(e) Qualified dividend income.

(1) In general.

(2) Exception.

(f) Definitions.

(1) Alternative tax rate.

(2) Net capital gain.

(3) Rate differential portion.

(4) Rate group.

(i) Short-term capital gains or losses.

(ii) Long-term capital gains.

(iii) Long-term capital losses.

(5) Terms used in sections 1(h), 904(b) or 1222.

(g) Examples.

(h) Coordination with section 904(f).

(1) In general.

(2) Examples.

(i) Effective date.

§ 1.904(b)-2 Special rules for application of section 904(b) to alternative minimum tax foreign tax credit.

(a) Application of section 904(b)(2)(B) adjustments.

(b) Use of alternative minimum tax rates.

(1) Taxpayers other than corporations.

(2) Corporate taxpayers.

(c) Effective date.

T.D. 9371, 12/20/2007.

§ 1.904(b)-1 Special rules for capital gains and losses.

Caution: The Treasury has not yet amended Reg § 1.904(b)-1 to reflect changes made by P.L. 100-647.

(a) Capital gains and losses included in taxable income from sources outside the United States. *(1) Limitation on capital gain from sources outside the United States when the taxpayer has net capital losses from sources within the United States.* (i) In general. Except as otherwise provided in this section, for purposes of section 904 and this section, taxable income from sources outside the United States (in all of the taxpayer's separate categories in the aggregate) shall include capital gain net income from sources outside the United States (determined by considering all of the capital gain and loss items in all of the taxpayer's separate categories in the aggregate) only to the extent of capital gain net income from all sources. Thus, capital gain net income from sources outside the United States (determined by considering all of the capital gain and loss items in all of the taxpayer's separate categories in the aggregate) shall be reduced to the extent such amount exceeds capital gain net income from all sources.

(ii) Allocation of reduction to separate categories or rate groups. (A) In general. If capital gain net income from sources outside the United States exceeds capital gain net income from all sources, and the taxpayer has capital gain net income from sources outside the United States in only one separate category, such excess is allocated as a reduction to that separate category. If a taxpayer has capital gain net income from foreign sources in two or more separate categories, such excess must be apportioned on a pro rata basis as a reduction to each such separate category. For purposes of the preceding sentence, pro rata means based on the relative amounts of the capital gain net income from sources outside the United States in each separate category.

(B) Taxpayer with capital gain rate differential. If a taxpayer with a capital gain rate differential for the year (within the meaning of paragraph (b) of this section) has capital gain net income from foreign sources in only one rate group within a separate category, any reduction to such separate category pursuant to paragraph (a)(1)(ii)(A) of this section must be allocated to such rate group. If a taxpayer with a capital gain rate differential for the year (within the meaning of paragraph (b) of this section) has capital gain net income from foreign sources in two or more rate groups within a separate category, any reduction to such separate category pursuant to paragraph (a)(1)(ii)(A) of this section must be apportioned on a pro rata basis among such rate groups. For purposes of the preceding sentence, pro rata means based on the relative amounts of the capital gain net income from sources outside the United States in each rate group within the applicable separate category.

(2) Exclusivity of rules; no reduction by reason of net capital losses from sources outside the United States in a different separate category. Capital gains from sources outside the United States in any separate category shall be limited by reason of section 904(b)(2)(A) and the comparable limitation of section 904(b)(2)(B)(i) only to the extent provided in paragraph (a)(1) of this section (relating to limitation on capital gain from sources outside the United States when taxpayer has net capital losses from sources within the United States).

(3) Capital losses from sources outside the United States in the same separate category. Except as otherwise provided in paragraph (d) of this section, taxable income from sources outside the United States in each separate category shall be reduced by any capital loss that is allocable or apportionable to income from sources outside the United States in such separate category to the extent such loss is allowable in determining taxable income for the taxable year.

(4) Examples. The following examples illustrate the application of this paragraph (a) to taxpayers that do not have a capital gain rate differential for the taxable year. See paragraph (g) of this section for examples that illustrate the application of this paragraph (a) to taxpayers that have a capital gain rate differential for the year. The examples are as follows:

Example (1). Taxpayer A, a corporation, has a $3,000 capital loss from sources outside the United States in the general limitation category, a $6,000 capital gain from sources outside the United States in the passive category, and a $2,000 capital loss from sources within the United States. A's capital gain net income from sources outside the United States in the aggregate, from all separate categories, is $3,000 ($6,000 - $3,000). A's capital gain net income from all sources is $1,000 ($6,000 - $3,000 - $2,000). Thus, for purposes of section 904, A's taxable income from sources outside the United States in all of A's separate categories in the aggregate includes only $1,000 of capital gain net income from sources outside the United States. See paragraph (a)(1)(i) of this section. Pursuant to paragraphs (a)(1)(i) and (a)(1)(ii)(A) of this section, A must reduce the $6,000 of capital gain net income from sources outside the United States in the passive category by $2,000 ($3,000 of capital gain net income from sources outside the United States - $1,000 of capital gain net income from all sources). After the adjustment, A has $4,000 of capital gain from sources outside the United States in the passive category and $3,000 of capital loss from sources outside the United States in the general limitation category.

Example (2). Taxpayer B, a corporation, has a $300 capital gain from sources outside the United States in the general limitation category and a $200 capital gain from sources outside the United States in the passive category. B's capital gain net income from sources outside the United States is $500 ($300 + $200). B also has a $150 capital loss from sources within the United States and a $50 capital gain from sources within the United States. Thus, B's capital gain net income from all sources is $400 ($300 + $200 - $150 + $50). Pursuant to paragraph (a)(1)(ii)(A) of this section, the $100 excess of capital gain net income from sources outside the United States over capital gain net income from all sources ($500 - $400) must be apportioned, as a reduction, three-fifths ($300/$500 of $100, or $60) to the general limitation category and two-fifths ($200/$500 of $100, or $40) to the passive category. Therefore, for purposes of section 904, the general limitation category includes $240 ($300 - $60) of capital gain net income from sources outside the United States and the passive category includes $160 ($200 - $40) of capital gain net income from sources outside the United States.

Example (3). Taxpayer C, a corporation, has a $10,000 capital loss from sources outside the United States in the general limitation category, a $4,000 capital gain from sources outside the United States in the passive category, and a $2,000 capital gain from sources within the United States. C's capital gain net income from sources outside the United States is zero, since losses exceed gains. C's capital gain net income from all sources is also zero. C's capital gain net income from sources outside the United States does not exceed its capital gain net income from all sources, and therefore paragraph (a)(1) of this section does not require any reduction of C's passive category capital gain. For purposes of section 904, C's passive category includes $4,000 of capital gain net income. C's general limitation category includes a capital loss of $6,000 because only $6,000 of capital loss is allowable as a deduction in the current year. The entire $4,000 of capital loss in excess of the $6,000 of capital loss that offsets capital gain in the taxable year is carried back or forward under section 1212(a), and none of such $4,000 is taken into account under section 904(a) or (b) for the current taxable year.

(b) Capital gain rate differential. *(1) Application of adjustments only if capital gain rate differential exists.* Section 904(b)(2)(B) and paragraphs (c) and (d) of this section apply only for taxable years in which the taxpayer has a capital gain rate differential.

(2) Determination of whether capital gain rate differential exists. For purposes of section 904(b) and this section, a capital gain rate differential is considered to exist for the taxable year only if the taxpayer has taxable income (excluding net capital gain and qualified dividend income) for the taxable year, a net capital gain for the taxable year and—

(i) In the case of a taxpayer other than a corporation, tax is imposed on the net capital gain at a reduced rate under section 1(h) for the taxable year; or

(ii) In the case of a corporation, tax is imposed under section 1201(a) on the taxpayer at a rate less than any rate of tax imposed on the taxpayer by section 11, 511, or 831(a) or (b), whichever applies (determined without regard to the last sentence of section 11(b)(1)), for the taxable year.

(3) Special rule for certain noncorporate taxpayers. A taxpayer that has a capital gain rate differential for the taxable year under paragraph (b)(2)(i) of this section and is not subject to alternative minimum tax under section 55 for the taxable year may elect not to apply the rate differential adjustments contained in section 904(b)(2)(B) and paragraphs (c) and (d) of this section if the highest rate of tax imposed on such taxpayer's taxable income (excluding net capital gain and any qualified dividend income) for the taxable year under section 1 does not exceed the highest rate of tax in effect under section 1(h) for the taxable year and the amount of the taxpayer's net capital gain from sources outside the United States, plus the amount of the taxpayer's qualified dividend income from sources outside the United States, is less than $20,000. A taxpayer that has a capital gain rate differential for the taxable year under paragraph (b)(2)(i) of this section and is subject to alternative minimum tax under section 55 for the taxable year may make such election if the rate of tax imposed on such taxpayer's alternative minimum taxable income (excluding net capital gain and any qualified dividend income) under section 55 does not exceed 26 percent, the highest rate of tax imposed on such taxpayer's taxable income (excluding net capital gain and any qualified dividend income) for the taxable year under section 1 does not exceed the highest rate of tax in effect under section 1(h) for the taxable year and the amount of the taxpayer's net capital gain from sources outside the United States, plus the amount of the taxpayer's qualified dividend income from sources outside the United States, is less than $20,000. A taxpayer who makes this election shall apply paragraph (a) of this section as if such taxpayer does not have a capital gain rate differential for the taxable year. An eligible taxpayer shall be presumed to have elected not to apply the rate differential adjustments, unless such taxpayer applies the rate differential adjustments contained in section 904(b)(2)(B) and paragraphs (c) and (d) of this section in determining its foreign tax credit limitation for the taxable year.

(c) Rate differential adjustment of capital gains. *(1) Rate differential adjustment of capital gains in foreign source taxable income.* (i) In general. Subject to paragraph (c)(1)(ii) of this section, in determining taxable income from sources outside the United States for purposes of section 904 and this section, capital gain net income from sources outside the United States in each long-term rate group in each separate category (separate category long-term rate group), shall be reduced by the rate differential portion of such capital gain net income. For purposes of paragraph (c)(1) of this section, references to capital gain net income are references to capital gain net income remaining after any reduction to such income pursuant to paragraph (a)(1) of this section (i.e., paragraph (a)(1) of this section applies before paragraphs (c) and (d) of this section).

(ii) Special rule for taxpayers with a net long-term capital loss from sources within the United States. If a taxpayer has a net long-term capital loss from sources within the United States (i.e., the taxpayer's long-term capital losses from sources within the United States exceed the taxpayer's long-term capital gains from sources within the United States) and also has any short-term capital gains from sources within or without the United States, then capital gain net income from sources outside the United States in each separate category long-term rate group shall be reduced by the rate differential portion of the applicable rate differential amount. The applicable rate differential amount is determined as follows:

(A) Step 1: Determine the U.S. long-term capital loss adjustment amount. The U.S. long-term capital loss adjustment amount is the excess, if any, of the net long-term capital loss from sources within the United States over the amount, if any, by which the taxpayer reduced long-term capital gains from sources without the United States pursuant to paragraph (a)(1) of this section.

(B) Step 2: Determine the applicable rate differential amount. If a taxpayer has capital gain net income from sources outside the United States in only one separate category long-term rate group, the applicable rate differential amount is the excess of such capital gain net income over the U.S. long-term capital loss adjustment amount. If a taxpayer has capital gain net income from sources outside the United States in more than one separate category long-term rate group, the U.S. long-term capital loss adjustment amount shall be apportioned on a pro rata basis to each separate category long-term rate group with capital gain net income. For purposes of the preceding sentence, pro rata means based on the relative amounts of capital gain net income from sources outside the United States in each separate category long-term rate group. The applicable rate differential amount for each separate category long-term rate group with capital gain net income is the excess of such capital gain net income over the portion of the U.S. long-term capital loss adjustment amount apportioned to the separate category long-term rate group pursuant to this Step 2.

(iii) Examples. The following examples illustrate the provisions of paragraph (c)(1)(ii) of this section. The taxpayers in the examples are assumed to have taxable income (excluding net capital gain and qualified dividend income) subject to a rate of tax under section 1 greater than the highest rate of tax in effect under section 1(h) for the applicable taxable year. The examples are as follows:

Example (1). (i) M, an individual, has $300 of long-term capital gain from foreign sources in the passive category, $200 of which is subject to tax at a rate of 15 percent under section 1(h) and $100 of which is subject to tax at a rate of 28% under section 1(h). M has $150 of short-term capital gain from sources within the United States. M has a $100 long-term capital loss from sources within the United States.

(ii) M's capital gain net income from sources outside the United States ($300) does not exceed M's capital gain net income from all sources ($350). Therefore, paragraph (a)(1) of this section does not require any reduction of M's capital gain net income in the passive category.

(iii) Because M has a net long-term capital loss from sources within the United States ($100) and also has a short-term capital gain from U.S. sources ($150), M must apply the provisions of paragraph (c)(1)(ii) of this section to determine the amount of the $300 of capital gain net income in the passive category that is subject to a rate differential adjustment. Under Step 1, the U.S. long-term capital loss adjustment amount is $100 ($100 - $0). Under Step 2, M must apportion this amount to each rate group in the passive category pro rata based on the amount of capital gain net income in each rate group. Thus, $66.67 ($200/$300 of $100) is apportioned to the 15 percent rate group and $33.33 ($100/$300 of $100) is apportioned to the 28 percent rate group. The applicable rate differential amount for the 15 percent rate group is $133.33 ($200 - $66.67). Thus, $133.33 of the $200 of capital gain net income in the 15 percent rate group is subject to a rate differential adjustment pursuant to paragraph (c)(1) of this section. The remaining $66.67 is not subject to a rate differential adjustment. The applicable rate differential amount for the 28 percent rate group is $66.67 ($100 - $33.33). Thus, $66.67 of the $100 of capital gain net income in the 28 percent rate group is subject to a rate differential adjustment pursuant to paragraph (c)(1) of this section. The remaining $33.33 is not subject to a rate differential adjustment.

Example (2). (i) N, an individual, has $300 of long-term capital gain from foreign sources in the passive category, all of which is subject to tax at a rate of 15 percent under section 1(h). N has $50 of short-term capital gain from sources within the United States. N has a $100 long-term capital loss from sources within the United States.

(ii) N's capital gain net income from sources outside the United States ($300) exceeds N's capital gain net income from all sources ($250). Pursuant to paragraph (a)(1) of this section, N must reduce the $300 capital gain in the passive category by $50. N has $250 of capital gain remaining in the passive category.

(iii) Because N has a net long-term capital loss from sources within the United States ($100) and also has a short-term capital gain from U.S. sources ($50), N must apply the provisions of paragraph (c)(1)(ii) of this section to determine the amount of the $250 of capital gain in the passive category that is subject to a rate differential adjustment. Under Step 1, the U.S. long-term capital loss adjustment amount is $50 ($100 - $50). Under Step 2, the applicable rate differential amount is $200 ($250 - $50). Thus, $200 of the capital gain in the passive category is subject to a rate differential adjustment under paragraph (c)(1) of this section. The remaining $50 is not subject to a rate differential adjustment.

Example (3).

(i) O, an individual, has a $100 short-term capital gain from foreign sources in the passive category. O has $300 of long-term capital gain from foreign sources in the passive category, all of which is subject to tax at a rate of 15 percent under section 1(h). O has a $100 long-term capital loss from sources within the United States.

(ii) O's capital gain net income from sources outside the United States ($400) exceeds O's capital gain net income from all sources ($300). Pursuant to paragraph (a)(1) of this section, O must reduce the $400 capital gain net income in the passive category by $100. Because C has capital gain net income in two or more rate groups in the passive category, O must apportion such amount, as a reduction, to each rate group on a pro rata basis pursuant to paragraph (a)(1)(ii)(B) of this section. Thus, $25 ($100/$400 of $100) is apportioned to the short-term capital gain and $75 ($300/$400 of $100) is apportioned to the long-term capital gain in the 15 percent rate group. After application of paragraph (a)(1) of this section, O has $75 of short-term capital gain in the passive category and $225 of long-term capital gain in the 15 percent rate group in the passive category.

(iii) Because O has a net long-term capital loss from sources within the United States ($100) and also has a short-term capital gain from foreign sources ($100), O must apply the provisions of paragraph (c)(1)(ii) of this section to determine the amount of the $225 of long-term capital gain in the 15 percent rate group that is subject to a rate differential adjustment. Under Step 1, the U.S. long-term capital loss adjustment amount is $25 ($100 - $75). Under Step 2, the applicable rate differential amount is $200 ($225 - $25). Thus, $200 of the long-term capital gain is subject to a rate differential adjustment under paragraph (c)(1) of this section. The remaining $25 of long-term capital gain is not subject to a rate differential adjustment.

(2) Rate differential adjustment of capital gains in entire taxable income. For purposes of section 904 and this section, entire taxable income shall include gains from the sale or exchange of capital assets only to the extent of capital gain net income reduced by the sum of the rate differential portions of each rate group of net capital gain.

(d) Rate differential adjustment of capital losses from sources outside the United States. *(1) In general.* In determining taxable income from sources outside the United States for purposes of section 904 and this section, a taxpayer with a net capital loss in a separate category rate group shall reduce such net capital loss by the sum of the rate differential portions of the capital gain net income in each long-term rate group offset by such net capital loss. A net capital loss in a separate category rate group is the amount, if any, by which capital losses in a rate group from sources outside the United States included in a separate category exceed capital gains from sources outside the United States in the same rate group and the same separate category.

(2) Determination of which capital gains are offset by net capital losses from sources outside the United States. For purposes of paragraph (d)(1) of this section, in order to determine the capital gain net income offset by net capital losses from sources outside the United States, the following rules shall apply in the following order:

(i) Net capital losses from sources outside the United States in each separate category rate group shall be netted against capital gain net income from sources outside the United States from the same rate group in other separate categories.

(ii) Capital losses from sources within the United States shall be netted against capital gains from sources within the United States in the same rate group.

(iii) Net capital losses from sources outside the United States in excess of the amounts netted against capital gains under paragraph (d)(2)(i) of this section shall be netted against the taxpayer's remaining capital gains from sources within and outside the United States in the following order, and without regard to any net capital losses, from any rate group, from sources within the United States—

(A) First against capital gain net income from sources within the United States in the same rate group;

(B) Next, against capital gain net income in other rate groups, in the order in which capital losses offset capital gains for purposes of determining the taxpayer's taxable income and without regard to whether such capital gain net income derives from sources within or outside the United States, as follows:

(1) A net capital loss in the short-term rate group is used first to offset any capital gain net income in the 28 percent rate group, then to offset capital gain net income in the 25 percent rate group, then to offset capital gain net income in the 15 percent rate group, and finally to offset capital gain net income in the 5 percent rate group.

(2) A net capital loss in the 28 percent rate group is used first to offset capital gain net income in the 25 percent rate group, then to offset capital gain net income in the 15 percent rate group, and finally to offset capital gain net income in the 5 percent rate group.

(3) A net capital loss in the 15 percent rate group is used first to offset capital gain net income in the 5 percent rate group, and then to offset capital gain net income in the 28 percent rate group, and finally to offset capital gain net income in the 25 percent rate group.

(iv) Net capital losses from sources outside the United States in any rate group, to the extent netted against capital gains in any other separate category under paragraph (d)(2)(i) of this section or against capital gains in the same or any other rate group under paragraph (d)(2)(iii) of this section, shall be treated as coming pro rata from each separate category that contains a net capital loss from sources outside the United States in that rate group. For example, assume that the taxpayer has $20 of net capital losses in the 15 percent rate group in the passive category and $40 of net capital losses in the 15 percent rate group in the general limitation category, both from sources outside the United States. Further assume that $50 of the total $60 net capital losses from sources outside the United States are netted against capital gain net income in the 28 percent rate group (from other separate categories or from sources within the United States). One-third of the $50 of such capital losses would be treated as coming from the passive category, and two-thirds of such $50 would be treated as coming from the general limitation category.

(v) In determining the capital gain net income offset by a net capital loss from sources outside the United States pursuant to this paragraph (d)(2), a taxpayer shall take into account any reduction to capital gain net income from sources outside the United States pursuant to paragraph (a) of this section and shall disregard any adjustments to such capital gain net income pursuant to paragraph (c)(1) of this section.

(vi) If at any time during a taxable year, tax is imposed under section 1(h) at a rate other than a rate of tax specified in this paragraph (d)(2), the principles of this paragraph (d)(2) shall apply to determine the capital gain net income offset by any net capital loss in a separate category rate group.

(vii) The determination of which capital gains are offset by capital losses from sources outside the United States under this paragraph (d)(2) is made solely in order to determine the appropriate rate-differential-based adjustments to such capital losses under this section and section 904(b), and does not change the source, allocation, or separate category of any such capital gain or loss for purposes of computing taxable income from sources within or outside the United States or for any other purpose.

(e) Qualified dividend income. *(1) In general.* A taxpayer that has taxable income (excluding net capital gain and qualified dividend income) for the taxable year and that qualifies for a reduced rate of tax under section 1(h) on its qualified dividend income (as defined in section 1(h)(11)) for the taxable year shall adjust the amount of such qualified dividend income in a manner consistent with the rules of paragraphs (c)(1)(i) (first sentence) and (c)(2) of this section irrespective of whether such taxpayer has a net capital gain for the taxable year. For purposes of making adjustments pursuant to this paragraph (e), the special rule in paragraph (c)(1)(ii) of this section for taxpayers with a net long-term capital loss from sources within the United States shall be disregarded.

(2) Exception. A taxpayer that makes the election provided for in paragraph (b)(3) of this section shall not make adjustments pursuant to paragraph (e)(1) of this section. Additionally, a taxpayer other than a corporation that does not have a capital gain rate differential for the taxable year within the meaning of paragraph (b)(2) of this section may elect not to apply paragraph (e)(1) of this section if such taxpayer would have qualified for the election provided for in paragraph (b)(3) of this section had such taxpayer had a capital gain rate differential for the taxable year. Such a taxpayer shall be presumed to make the election provided for in the preceding sentence unless such taxpayer applies the rate differential adjustments provided for in paragraph (e)(1) of this section to the qualified dividend income in determining its foreign tax credit limitation for the taxable year.

(f) Definitions. For purposes of section 904(b) and this section, the following definitions apply:

(1) Alternative tax rate. The term alternative tax rate means, with respect to any rate group, the rate applicable to that rate group under section 1(h) (for taxpayers other than corporations) or section 1201(a) (for corporations). For example, the alternative tax rate for unrecaptured section 1250 gain is 25 percent.

(2) Net capital gain. For purposes of this section, net capital gain shall not include any qualified dividend income (as defined in section 1(h)(11)). See paragraph (e) of this section for rules relating to qualified dividend income.

(3) Rate differential portion. The term rate differential portion with respect to capital gain net income from sources outside the United States in a separate category long-term rate group (or the applicable portion of such amount), net capital gain in a rate group, or capital gain net income in a long-term rate group, as the case may be, means the same proportion of such amount as—

(i) The excess of the highest applicable tax rate (as defined in section 904(b)(3)(E)(ii)) over the alternative tax rate; bears to

(ii) The highest applicable tax rate (as defined in section 904(b)(3)(E)(ii)).

(4) Rate group. For purposes of this section, the term rate group means:

(i) Short-term capital gains or losses. With respect to a short-term capital gain or loss, the rate group is the short-term rate group.

(ii) Long-term capital gains. With respect to a long-term capital gain, the rate group is the particular rate of tax to which such gain is subject under section 1(h). Such a rate group is a long-term rate group. For example, the 28 percent rate group of capital gain net income from sources outside the United States consists of the capital gain net income from sources outside the United States that is subject to tax at a rate of 28 percent under section 1(h). Such 28 percent rate group is a long-term rate group. If a taxpayer has long-term capital gains that may be subject to tax at more than one rate under section 1(h) and the taxpayer's net capital gain attributable to such long-term capital gains and any qualified dividend income are taxed at one rate of tax under section 1(h), then all of such long-term capital gains shall be treated as long-term capital gains in that one rate group. If a taxpayer has long-term capital gains that may be subject to tax at more than one rate of tax under section 1(h) and the taxpayer's net capital gain attributable to such long-term capital gains and any qualified dividend income are taxed at more than one rate pursuant to section 1(h), the taxpayer shall determine the rate group for such long-term capital gains from sources within or outside the United States (and, to the extent from sources outside the United States, from each separate category) ratably based on the proportions of net capital gain and any qualified dividend income taxed at each applicable rate. For example, under the section 1(h) rates in effect for tax years beginning in 2004, a long-term capital gain (other than a long-term capital gain described in section 1(h)(4)(A) or (h)(6)) may be subject to tax at 5 percent or 15 percent.

(iii) Long-term capital losses. With respect to a long-term capital loss, a loss described in section 1(h)(4)(B)(i) (collectibles loss) or (iii) (long-term capital loss carryover) is a loss in the 28 percent rate group. All other long-term capital losses shall be treated as losses in the highest rate group in effect under section 1(h) for the tax year with respect to long-term capital gains other than long-term capital gains described in section 1(h)(4)(A) or (h)(6). For example, under the section 1(h) rates in effect for tax years beginning in 2004, a long-term capital loss not described in section 1(h)(4)(B)(i) or (iii) shall be treated as a loss in the 15 percent rate group.

(5) Terms used in sections 1(h), 904(b) or 1222. For purposes of this section, any term used in this section and also used in section 1(h), section 904(b) or section 1222 shall have the same meaning given such term by section 1(h), 904(b) or 1222, respectively, except as otherwise provided in this section.

(g) Examples. The following examples illustrate the provisions of this section. In these examples, the rate differential adjustment is shown as a fraction, the numerator of which is the alternative tax rate percentage and the denominator of which is 35 percent (assumed to be the highest applicable tax rate for individuals under section 1). Finally, all dollar amounts in the examples are abbreviated from amounts in the thousands (for example, $50 represents $50,000). The examples are as follows:

Example (1). (i) AA, an individual, has items from sources outside the United States only in the passive category for the taxable year. AA has $1000 of long-term capital gains from sources outside the United States that are subject to tax at a rate of 15 percent under section 1(h). AA has $700 of long-term capital losses from sources outside the United States, which are not described in section 1(h)(4)(B)(i) or (iii). For the same taxable year, AA has $800 of long-term capital gains from sources within the United States that are taxed at a rate of 28 percent under section 1(h). AA also has $100 of long-term capital losses from sources within the United States, which are not described in section 1(h)(4)(B)(i) or (iii). AA also has $500 of ordinary income from sources within the United States. The highest tax rate in effect under section 1(h) for the taxable year with respect to long-term capital gains other than long-term capital gains described in section 1(h)(4)(A) or (h)(6) is 15 percent. Accordingly, AA's long-term capital losses are in the 15 percent rate group.

(ii) AA's items of ordinary income, capital gain and capital loss for the taxable year are summarized in the following table:

	U.S. source	Foreign source: passive
15% rate group	($100)	$1,000 (700)
28% rate group	800	
Ordinary income	500	

(iii) AA's capital gain net income from sources outside the United States ($300) does not exceed AA's capital gain net income from all sources ($1,000). Therefore, paragraph (a)(1) of this section does not require any reduction of AA's capital gain net income in the passive category.

(iv) In computing AA's taxable income from sources outside the United States in the numerator of the section 904(a) foreign tax credit limitation fraction for the passive category, AA's $300 of capital gain net income in the 15 rate group in the passive category must be adjusted as required under paragraph (c)(1) of this section. AA adjusts the $300 of capital gain net income using 15 percent as the alternative tax rate, as follows: $300 (15%/35%).

(v) In computing AA's entire taxable income in the denominator of the section 904(a) foreign tax credit limitation fraction, AA combines the $300 of capital gain net income from sources outside the United States and the $100 net capital loss from sources within the United States in the same rate group (15 percent). AA must adjust the resulting $200 ($300 - $100) of net capital gain in the 15 percent rate group as required under paragraph (c)(2) of this section, using 15 percent as the alternative tax rate, as follows: $200 (15%/35%). AA must also adjust the $800 of net capital gain in the 28 percent rate group, using 28 percent as the alternative tax rate, as follows: $800 (28%/35%). AA must also include ordinary income from sources outside the United States in the numerator, and ordinary income from all sources in the denominator, of the foreign tax credit limitation fraction.

(vi) AA's passive category foreign tax credit limitation fraction is $128.58/$1225.72, computed as follows:

$$\frac{\$300(15\%/35\%)}{\$500 + \$200(15\%/35\%) + \$800(28\%/35\%)}$$

Example (2). (i) BB, an individual, has the following items of ordinary income, capital gain, and capital loss for the taxable year:

	U.S. source	Foreign source	
		General	Passive
15% rate group	$300	($500)	$100
25% rate group	200	....	....
28% rate group	500	(300)	....
Ordinary income	1,000	500	500

(ii) BB's capital gain net income from sources outside the United States in the aggregate (zero, since losses exceed gains) does not exceed BB's capital gain net income from all sources ($300). Therefore, paragraph (a)(1) of this section does not require any reduction of BB's capital gain net income in the passive category.

(iii) In computing BB's taxable income from sources outside the United States in the numerators of the section 904(a) foreign tax credit limitation fractions for the passive and general limitation categories, BB must adjust capital gain net income from sources outside the United States in each separate category long-tem rate group and net capital losses from sources outside the United States in each separate category rate group as provided in paragraphs (c)(1) and (d) of this section.

(A) The $100 of capital gain net income in the 15 percent rate group in the passive category is adjusted under paragraph (c)(1) of this section as follows: $100 (15%/35%).

(B) BB must adjust the net capital losses in the 15 percent and 28 percent rate groups in the general limitation category in accordance with the ordering rules contained in paragraph (d)(2) of this section. Under paragraph (d)(2)(i) of this section, BB's net capital loss in the 15 percent rate group is netted against capital gain net income from sources outside the United States in other separate categories in the same rate group. Thus, $100 of the $500 net capital loss in the 15 percent rate group in the general limitation category offsets $100 of capital gain net income in the 15 percent rate group in the passive category. Accordingly, $100 of the $500 net capital loss is adjusted under paragraph (d)(1) of this section as follows: $100 (15%/35%).

(C) Next, under paragraph (d)(2)(iii)(A) of this section, BB's net capital losses from sources outside the United States in any separate category rate group are netted against capital gain net income in the same rate group from sources within the United States. Thus, $300 of the $500 net capital loss in the 15 percent rate group in the general limitation category offsets $300 of capital gain net income in the 15 percent rate group from sources within the United States. Accordingly, $300 of the $500 net capital loss is adjusted under paragraph (d)(1) of this section as follows: $300 (15%/35%). Similarly, the $300 of net capital loss in the 28 percent rate group in the general limitation category offsets $300 of capital gain net income in the 28 percent rate group from sources within the United States. The $300 net capital loss is adjusted under paragraph (d)(1) of this section as follows: $300 (28%/35%).

(D) Finally, under paragraph (d)(2)(iii)(B) of this section, the remaining net capital losses in a separate category rate group are netted against capital gain net income from other rate groups from sources within and outside the United States. Thus, the remaining $100 of the $500 net capital loss in the 15 percent rate group in the general limitation category offsets $100 of the remaining capital gain net income in the 28 percent rate group from sources within the United States. Accordingly, the remaining $100 of net capital loss is adjusted under paragraph (d)(1) of this section as follows: $100 (28%/35%).

(iv) In computing BB's entire taxable income in the denominator of the section 904(a) foreign tax credit limitation fractions, BB must adjust net capital gain by netting all of BB's capital gains and losses, from sources within and outside the United States, and adjusting any remaining net capital gains, based on rate group, under paragraph (c)(2) of this section. BB must also include foreign source ordinary income in the numerators, and ordinary income from all sources in the denominator, of the foreign tax credit limitation fractions. The denominator of BB's foreign tax credit limitation fractions reflects $2,000 of ordinary income from all sources, $100 of net capital gain taxed at the 28% rate and adjusted as follows: $100 (28%/35%), and $200 of net capital gain taxed at the 25% rate and adjusted as follows: $200 (25%/35%).

(v) BB's foreign tax credit limitation fraction for the general limitation category is $8.56/$2222.86, computed as follows:

$$\frac{\$500 - \$100(15\%/35\%) - \$300(15\%/35\%) - \$300(28\%/35\%) - \$100(28\%/35\%)}{\$1{,}000 + \$500 + \$500 + \$100(28\%/35\%) + \$200(25\%/35\%)}$$

(vi) BB's foreign tax credit limitation fraction for the passive category is $542.86/$2222.86, computed as follows:

$$\frac{\$500 + \$100(15\%/35\%)}{\$1{,}000 + \$500 + \$500 + \$100(28\%/35\%) + \$200(25\%/35\%)}$$

Example (3). (i) CC, an individual, has the following items of ordinary income, capital gain, and capital loss for the taxable year:

	U.S. source	Foreign source General	Foreign source Passive
15% rate group	$300	($720)	($80)
25% rate group	200	....	....
28% rate group	500	(150)	50
Ordinary income	1,000	1,000	500

(ii) CC's capital gain net income from sources outside the United States (zero, since losses exceed gains) does not exceed CC's capital gain net income from all sources ($100). Therefore, paragraph (a)(1) of this section does not require any adjustment.

(iii) In computing CC's taxable income from sources outside the United States in the numerators of the section 904(a) foreign tax credit limitation fractions for the passive and general limitation categories, CC must adjust capital gain net income from sources outside the United States in each separate category long-tem rate group and net capital losses from sources outside the United States in each separate category rate group as provided in paragraphs (c)(1) and (d) of this section.

(A) CC must adjust the $50 of capital gain net income in the 28 percent rate group in the passive category pursuant to paragraph (c)(1) of this section as follows: $50 (28%/35%).

(B) Under paragraph (d)(2)(i) of this section, $50 of CC's $150 net capital loss in the 28 percent rate group in the general limitation category offsets $50 of capital gain net income in the 28 percent rate group in the passive category. Thus, $50 of the $150 net capital loss is adjusted as follows: $50 (28%/35%). Next, under paragraph (d)(2)(iii)(A) of this section, the remaining $100 of net capital loss in the 28 percent rate group in the general limitation category offsets $100 of capital gain net income in the 28 percent rate group from sources within the United States. Thus, the remaining $100 of net capital loss is adjusted as follows: $100 (28%/35%).

(C) Under paragraphs (d)(2)(iii)(A) and (d)(2)(iv) of this section, the net capital losses in the 15 percent rate group in the passive and general limitation categories offset on a pro rata basis the $300 of capital gain net income in the 15 percent rate group from sources within the United States. The proportionate amount of the $720 net capital loss ($720/$800 of $300, or $270) is adjusted as follows: $270 (15%/35%). The proportionate amount of the $80 net capital loss ($80/$800 of $300, or $30) is adjusted as follows $30 (15%/35%).

(D) Of the remaining $500 of net capital loss in the 15 percent rate group in the general limitation and passive categories, $400 offsets the remaining $400 of capital gain net income in the 28 percent rate group from sources within the United States under paragraph (d)(2)(iii)(B)(3) of this section. The proportionate amount of the $720 net capital loss ($720/$800 of $400, or $360) is adjusted as follows: $360 (28%/35%). The proportionate amount of the $80 net capital loss ($80/$800 of $400, or $40) is adjusted as follows: $40 (28%/35%).

(E) Under paragraph (d)(2)(iii)(B)(3) of this section, the remaining $100 of net capital loss in the 15 percent rate group in the general limitation and passive limitation categories offsets $100 of capital gain net income in the 25 percent rate group from sources within the United States. The proportionate amount of the $720 net capital loss ($720/$800 of $100, or $90) is adjusted as follows: $90 (25%/35%). The proportionate amount of the $80 net capital loss ($80/$800 of $100 of $10) is adjusted as follows: $10 (25%/35%).

(iv) In computing CC's entire taxable income in the denominator of the section 904(a) foreign tax credit limitation fractions, CC must adjust capital gain net income by netting all of CC's capital gains and losses, from sources within and outside the United States, and adjusting any remaining net capital gains, based on rate group, under paragraph (c)(2) of this section. The denominator of CC's foreign tax credit limitation fractions reflects $2,500 of ordinary income from all sources and $100 of net capital gain taxed at the 25% rate and adjusted as follows: $100 (25%/35%).

(v) CC's foreign tax credit limitation fraction for the general limitation category is $412/$2571.42, computed as follows:

$$\frac{\$1{,}000 - \$50\ (28\%/35\%) - \$100(28\%/35\%) - \$270(15\%/35\%) - \$360(28\%/35\%) - \$90(25\%/35\%)}{\$1{,}000 + \$1{,}000 + \$500 + \$100(25\%/35\%)}$$

(vi) CC's foreign tax credit limitation fraction for the passive category is $488.00/$2571.42, computed as follows:

$$\frac{\$500 + \$50(28\%/35\%) - \$30(15\%/35\%) - \$40(28\%/35\%) - \$10(25\%/35\%)}{\$1{,}000 + \$1{,}000 + \$500 + \$100(25\%/35\%)}$$

Example (4). (i) DD, an individual, has the following items of ordinary income, capital gain and capital loss for the taxable year:

	U.S. source	Foreign source: General	Foreign source: Passive
15% rate group	($80)	($100)	$300
Short-term	....	500	100
Ordinary income	500	....	....

(ii) DD's capital gain net income from outside the United States ($800) exceeds DD's capital gain net income from all sources ($720). Pursuant to paragraph (a)(1)(ii)(A) of this section, DD must apportion the $80 of excess of capital gain net income from sources outside the United States between the general limitation and passive categories based on the amount of capital gain net income in each separate category. Thus, one-half ($400/$800 of $100, or $40) is apportioned to the general limitation category and one-half ($400/ $800 of $80, or $40) is apportioned to the passive category. The $40 apportioned to the general limitation category reduces DD's $500 short-term capital gain in the general limitation category to $460. Pursuant to paragraph (a)(1)(ii)(B) of this section, the $40 apportioned to the passive category must be apportioned further between the capital gain net income in the short-term rate group and the 15 percent rate group based on the relative amounts of capital gain net income in each rate group. Thus, one-fourth ($100/$400 of $40 or $10) is apportioned to the short-term rate group and three-fourths ($300/$400 of $40 or $30) is apportioned to the 15 percent rate group. DD's passive category includes $90 of short-term capital gain and $270 of capital gain net income in the 15% rate group.

(iii) Because DD has a net long-term capital loss from sources within the United States ($80) and also has short-term capital gains, DD must apply the provisions of paragraph (c)(1)(ii) of this section to determine the amount of DD's $270 of capital gain net income in the 15% rate group that is subject to a rate differential adjustment under paragraph (c)(1) of this section. Under Step 1, the U.S. long-term capital loss adjustment amount is $50 ($80-$30). Under Step 2, the applicable rate differential amount is the excess of the remaining capital gain net income over the U.S. long-term adjustment amount. Thus, the applicable rate differential amount is $220 ($270 - $50). In computing DD's taxable income from sources outside the United States in the numerator of the section 904(a) foreign tax credit limitation fraction for the passive category, DD must adjust this amount as follows: $220 (15%/35%). DD does not adjust the remaining $50 of capital gain net income in the 15% rate group.

(iv) The amount of capital gain net income in the 15% rate group in the passive category, taking into account the adjustment pursuant to paragraph (a)(1) of this section and disregarding the adjustment pursuant to paragraph (c)(1) of this section, is $270. Under paragraphs (d)(2)(i) and (d)(2)(v) of this section, DD's $100 net capital loss in the 15% rate group in the general limitation category offsets capital gain net income in the 15% rate group in the passive category. Accordingly, the $100 of net capital loss is adjusted as follows: $100 (15%/35%).

(v) In computing DD's entire taxable income in the denominator of the section 904(a) foreign tax credit limitation fractions, DD must adjust capital gain net income by netting all of DD's capital gains and losses from sources within and outside the United States, and adjusting the remaining net capital gain in each rate group pursuant to paragraph (c)(2) of this section. The denominator of DD's foreign tax credit limitation fraction reflects $500 of ordinary income from all sources, $600 of short-term capital gain and $120 of net capital gain in the 15 percent rate group adjusted as follows: $120 (15%/35%).

(vi) DD's foreign tax credit limitation fraction for the general limitation category is $417.14/$1151.43, computed as follows:

$$\frac{\$460 - \$100(15\%/35\%)}{\$500 + \$600 + \$120(15\%/35\%)}$$

(vii) DD's foreign tax credit limitation fraction for the passive category is $234.29/$1151.43, computed as follows:

$$\frac{\$90 + \$220(15\%/35\%) + \$50}{\$500 + \$600 + \$120(15\%/35\%)}$$

Example (5). (i) EE, an individual, has the following items of ordinary income, capital gain and capital loss for the taxable year:

	U.S. source	Foreign source: passive
15% rate group	($150)	$300
28% rate group	....	200
Short-term	30	100
Ordinary income	500	....

(ii) EE's capital gain net income from sources outside the United States ($600) exceeds EE's capital gain net income from all sources ($480). Pursuant to paragraph (a)(1)(ii) of this section, the $120 of excess capital gain net income from sources outside the United States is allocated as a reduction to the passive category and must be apportioned pro rata to each rate group within the passive category with capital gain net income. Thus, $20 ($100/$600 of $120) is apportioned to the short-term rate group, $60 ($300/$600 of $120) is apportioned to the 15 percent rate group and $40 ($200/ $600 of $120) is apportioned to the 28 percent rate group. After application of paragraph (a)(1) of this section, EE has $80 of capital gain net income in the short-term rate group, $240 of capital gain net income in the 15 percent rate group and $160 of capital gain net income in the 28 percent rate group.

(iii) Because EE has a net long-term capital loss from sources within the United States ($150) and also has short-term capital gains, EE must apply the provisions of paragraph (c)(1)(ii) of this section to determine the amount of EE's remaining $400 ($240 + $160) of capital gain net income in long-term rate groups in the passive category that is subject to a rate differential adjustment. to a rate differential adjustment. Under Step 1, the U.S. long-term capital loss adjustment amount is $50 ($150-$100). Under Step 2, EE must apportion this amount pro rata to each long-term rate group within the passive category with capital gain net income. Thus, $30 ($240/$400 of $50) is apportioned to the 15 percent rate group and $20 ($160/$400 of $50) is apportioned to the 28 percent rate group. The applicable rate differential amount for the 15 percent rate group is $210 ($240 - $30). The applicable rate differential amount for the 28 percent rate group is $140 ($160 - $20).

(iv) Pursuant to paragraph (c)(1)(ii) of this section, EE must adjust $210 of the $240 capital gain in the 15 percent rate group as follows: $210 (15%/35%). EE does not adjust the remaining $30. Pursuant to paragraph (c)(1)(ii) of this section, EE must adjust $140 of the $160 capital gain in the 28 percent rate group as follows: $140 (28%/35%). EE does not adjust the remaining $20.

(v) In computing EE's entire taxable income in the denominator of the section 904(a) foreign tax credit limitation fractions, EE must adjust capital gain net income by netting all of EE's capital gains and losses from sources within and outside the United States, and adjusting the remaining net capital gain in each rate group pursuant to paragraph (c)(2) of this section. The denominator of EE's foreign tax credit limitation fraction reflects $500 of ordinary income from all sources, $130 of short-term capital gain, $150 of net capital gain in the 15 percent rate group adjusted as follows: $150 (15%/35%), and $200 of net capital gain in the 28 percent rate group adjusted as follows: $200 (28%/35%).

(vi) EE's foreign tax credit limitation fraction for the passive category is $332/$854.29, computed as follows:

$$\frac{\$80 + \$210\ (15\%/35\%) + \$30 + \$140\ (28\%/35\%) + \$20}{\$500 + \$130 + \$150\ (15\%/35\%) + \$200\ (28\%/35\%)}$$

(h) Coordination with section 904(f). *(1) In general.* Section 904(b) and this section shall apply before the provisions of section 904(f) as follows:

(i) The amount of a taxpayer's separate limitation income or loss in each separate category, the amount of overall foreign loss, and the amount of any additions to or recapture of separate limitation loss or overall foreign loss accounts pursuant to section 904(f) shall be determined after applying paragraphs (a), (c)(1), (d) and (e) of this section to adjust capital gains and losses and qualified dividend income from sources outside the United States in each separate category.

(ii) To the extent a capital loss from sources within the United States reduces a taxpayer's foreign source taxable income under paragraph (a)(1) of this section, such capital loss shall be disregarded in determining the amount of a taxpayer's taxable income from sources within the United States for purposes of computing the amount of any additions to the taxpayer's overall foreign loss accounts.

(iii) In determining the amount of a taxpayer's loss from sources in the United States under section 904(f)(5)(D) (section 904(f)(5)(D) amount), the taxpayer shall make appropriate adjustments to capital gains and losses from sources within the United States to reflect adjustments pursuant to section 904(b)(2) and this section. Therefore, for purposes of section 904, a taxpayer's section 904(f)(5)(D) amount shall be equal to the excess of the taxpayer's foreign source taxable income in all separate categories in the aggregate for the taxable year (taking into account any adjustments pursuant to paragraphs (a)(1), (c)(1), (d) and (e) of this section) over the taxpayer's entire taxable income for the taxable year (taking into account any adjustments pursuant to paragraphs (c)(2) and (e) of this section).

(2) Examples. The following examples illustrate the application of paragraph (h) of this section:

Example (1). (i) W, an individual, has the following items of ordinary income, capital gain, and capital loss for the taxable year:

	U.S. source	Foreign source	
		General	Passive
15% rate group	$500	$100	($400)
Ordinary income	900	100	....

(ii) In computing W's taxable income from sources outside the United States for purposes of section 904 and this section, W must adjust the capital gain net income and net capital loss in each separate category as provided in paragraphs (c)(1) and (d) of this section. Thus, W must adjust the $100 of capital gain net income in the general limitation category and the $400 of net capital loss in the passive category as follows: $100 (15%/35%) and $400 (15%/35%).

(iii) After the adjustment to W's net capital loss in the passive category, W has a $171.43 separate limitation loss in the passive category. After the adjustment to W's capital gain in the general limitation category, W has $142.86 of foreign source taxable income in the general limitation category. Thus, $142.86 of the separate limitation loss reduces foreign source taxable income in the general limitation category. See section 904(f)(5)(B). W adds $142.86 to the separate limitation loss account for the passive category. The remaining $28.57 of the separate limitation loss reduces income from sources within the United States. See section 904(f)(5)(A). Thus, W adds $28.57 to the overall foreign loss account for the passive category.

Example (2). (i) X, a corporation, has the following items of ordinary income, ordinary loss, capital gain and capital loss for the taxable year: foreign source:

	U.S. source	Foreign source: general
Capital gain	($500)	$700
Ordinary income	1100	(1000)

(ii) X's capital gain net income from sources outside the United States ($700) exceeds X's capital gain net income from all sources ($200). Pursuant to paragraph (a)(1) of this section, X must reduce the $700 capital gain in the general limitation category by $500. After the adjustment, X has $200 of capital gain net income remaining in the general limitation category. Thus, X has an overall foreign loss attributable to the general limitation category of $800.

(iii) For purposes of computing the amount of the addition to X's overall foreign loss account for the general limitation category, the $500 capital loss from sources within the United States is disregarded and X's taxable income from sources within the United States is $1100. Accordingly, X must increase its overall foreign loss account for the general limitation category by $800.

Example (3). (i) Y, a corporation, has the following items of ordinary income, ordinary loss, capital gain and capital loss for the taxable year:

	U.S. source	Foreign source: passive
Capital gain	($100)	$200
Ordinary income	(200)	500

(ii) Y's capital gain net income from sources outside the United States ($200) exceeds Y's capital gain net income from all sources ($100). Pursuant to paragraph (a)(1) of this section, Y must reduce the $200 capital gain in the passive category by $100. Y has $100 of capital gain net income remaining in the passive category.

(iii) Y is not required to make adjustments pursuant to paragraph (c), (d) or (e) of this section. See paragraphs (b) and (e) of this section. Y's foreign source taxable income in the passive category after the adjustment pursuant to paragraph (a)(1) of this section is $600. Y's entire taxable income for the taxable year is $400.

(iv) Y's section 904(f)(5)(D) amount is the excess of Y's foreign source taxable income in all separate categories in the aggregate for the taxable year after taking into account the adjustment pursuant to paragraph (a)(1) of this section ($600) over Y's entire taxable income for the taxable year ($400). Therefore, Y's section 904(f)(5)(D) amount is $200 and Y's foreign source taxable income in the passive category is reduced to $400. See section 904(f)(5)(D).

Example (4). (i) Z, an individual, has the following items of ordinary income, ordinary loss and capital gain for the taxable year:

	U.S. source	Foreign source	
		General	Passive
15% rate group	$100	....	....
Ordinary income	(200)	$300	$300

(ii) Z's foreign source taxable income in all of Z's separate categories in the aggregate for the taxable year is $600. (There are no adjustments to Z's foreign source taxable income pursuant to paragraph (a)(1), (c)(1), (d) or (e) of this section.)

(iii) In computing Z's entire taxable income in the denominator of the section 904(d) foreign tax credit limitation fractions, Z must adjust the $100 of net capital gain in the 15 percent rate group pursuant to paragraph (c)(2) of this section as follows: $100 (15%/35%). Thus, Z's entire taxable income for the taxable year, taking into account the adjustment pursuant to paragraph (c)(2) of this section, is $442.86.

(iv) Z's section 904(f)(5)(D) amount is the excess of Z's foreign source taxable income in all separate categories in the aggregate for the taxable year ($600) over Z's entire taxable income for the taxable year after the adjustment pursuant to paragraph (c)(2) of this section ($442.86). Therefore, Z's section 904(f)(5)(D) amount is $157.32. This amount must be allocated pro rata to the passive and general limitation categories in accordance with section 904(f)(5)(D).

Example (5). (i) O, an individual, has the following items of ordinary income, ordinary loss and capital gain for the taxable year:

	U.S. source	Foreign source General	Foreign source Passive
15% rate group	$1100	($500)	....
Ordinary income	(1000)	1000	$500

(ii) In determining O's taxable income from sources outside the United States, O must reduce the $500 capital loss in the general limitation category to $214.29 ($500 x 15%/35%) pursuant to paragraph (d) of this section. Taking this adjustment into account, O's foreign source taxable income in all of O's separate categories in the aggregate is $1285.71 ($1000 - $214.29 + $500).

(iii) In computing O's entire taxable income in the denominator of the section 904(a) foreign tax credit limitation fraction, O must reduce the $600 of net capital gain for the year to $257.14 ($600 x 15%/35%) pursuant to paragraph (c)(2) of this section. Taking this adjustment into account, O's entire taxable income for the year is $757.14 ($500 + $257.14).

(iv) Therefore, O's section 904(f)(5)(D) amount is $528.57 ($1285.71 - $757.14). This amount must be allocated pro rata to O's $500 of income in the passive category and O's $785.71 of adjusted income in the general limitation category in accordance with section 904(f)(5)(D).

(i) Effective date. This section shall apply to taxable years beginning after July 20, 2004. Taxpayers may choose to apply this section and § 1.904(b)-2 to taxable years ending after July 20, 2004.

T.D. 7914, 9/28/83, amend T.D. 9141, 7/19/2004.

§ 1.904(b)-2 Special rules for application of section 904(b) to alternative minimum tax foreign tax credit.

Caution: The Treasury has not yet amended Reg § 1.904(b)-2 to reflect changes made by P.L. 100-647, P.L. 99-514.

(a) Application of section 904(b)(2)(B) adjustments. Section 904(b)(2)(B) shall apply for purposes of determining the alternative minimum tax foreign tax credit under section 59 (regardless of whether or not the taxpayer has made an election under section 59(a)(4)).

(b) Use of alternative minimum tax rates. *(1) Taxpayers other than corporations.* In the case of a taxpayer other than a corporation, for purposes of determining the alternative minimum tax foreign tax credit under section 59—

(i) Section 904(b)(3)(D)(i) shall be applied by using the language "section 55(b)(3)" instead of "subsection (h) of section 1";

(ii) Section 904(b)(3)(E)(ii)(I) shall be applied by using the language "section 55(b)(1)(A)(i)" instead of "subsection (a), (b), (c), (d), or (e) of section 1 (whichever applies)"; and

(iii) Section 904(b)(3)(E)(iii)(I) shall be applied by using the language "the alternative rate of tax determined under section 55(b)(3)" instead of "the alternative rate of tax determined under section 1(h)".

(2) Corporate taxpayers. In the case of a corporation, for purposes of determining the alternative minimum tax foreign tax credit under section 59, section 904(b)(3)(E)(ii)(II) shall be applied by using the language "section 55(b)(1)(B)" instead of "section 11(b)".

(c) Effective date. This section shall apply to taxable years beginning after July 20, 2004. See § 1.904(b)-1(i) for a rule permitting taxpayers to choose to apply § 1.904(b)-1 and this § 1.904(b)-2 to taxable years ending after July 20, 2004.

T.D. 7914, 9/28/83, amend T.D. 9141, 7/19/2004.

§ 1.904(f)-0 Outline of regulation provisions.

This section lists the headings for §§ 1.904(f)-1 through 1.904(f)-8 and 1.904(f)-12.

§ 1.904(f)-1 Overall foreign loss and the overall foreign loss account.

(a)(1) Overview of regulations.

(2) [Reserved]. For further guidance, see the entry for § 1.904(f)-1T(a)(2) in § 1.904(f)-0T.

(b) Overall foreign loss accounts.

(c) Determination of a taxpayer's overall foreign loss.

(1) Overall foreign loss defined.

(2) Separate limitation defined.

(3) Method of allocation and apportionment of deductions.

(d) Additions to the overall foreign loss account.

(1) General rule.

(2) Overall foreign losses of another taxpayer.

(3) Additions to overall foreign loss account created by loss carryovers.

(4) [Reserved]. For further guidance, see the entry for § 1.904(f)-1T(d)(4) in § 1.904(f)-0T.

(e) Reductions of overall foreign loss accounts.

(1) Pre-capture reduction for amounts allocated to other taxpayers.

(2) Reduction for amounts recaptured.

(f) Illustrations.

§ 1.904(f)-2 Recapture of overall foreign losses.

(a) In general.

(b) Determination of taxable income from sources without the United States for purposes of recapture.

(1) In general.

(c) and (c)(1) [Reserved]. For further guidance, see the entries for § 1.904(f)-2T(c) and (c)(1) in § 1.904(f)-0T.

(2) Election to recapture more of the overall foreign loss than is required under paragraph (c)(1).

(3) Special rule for recapture of losses incurred prior to section 936 election.

(4) Recapture of pre-1983 overall foreign losses determined on a combined basis.

(5) Illustrations.

(d) Recapture of overall foreign losses from dispositions under section 904(f)(3).

(1) In general.

(2) Treatment of net capital gain.

(3) Dispositions where gain is recognized irrespective of section 904(f)(3).

(4) Dispositions in which gain would not otherwise be recognized.

(i) Recognition of gain to the extent of the overall foreign loss account.

(ii) Basis adjustment.

(iii) Recapture of overall foreign loss to the extent of amount recognized.

(iv) Priorities among dispositions in which gain is deemed to be recognized.

(5) Definitions.

(i) Disposition.

(ii) Property used in a trade or business.

(iii) Property used predominantly outside the United States.

(iv) Property which is a material factor in the realization of income.

(6) Carryover of overall foreign loss accounts in a corporate acquisition to which section 381(a) applies.

(7) Illustrations.

§ 1.904(f)-4 Recapture of foreign losses out of accumulation distributions from a foreign trust.

(a) In general.

(b) Effect of recapture on foreign tax credit limitation under section 667(d).

(c) Recapture if taxpayer deducts foreign taxes deemed distributed.

(d) Illustrations.

§ 1.904(f)-5 Special rules for recapture of overall foreign losses of a domestic trust.

(a) In general.

(b) Recapture of trust's overall foreign loss.

(1) Trust accumulates income.

(2) Trust distributes income.

(3) Trust accumulates and distributes income.

(c) Amounts allocated to beneficiaries.

(d) Section 904(f)(3) dispositions to which § 1.904(f)-2(d)(4)(i) is applicable.

(e) Illustrations.

§ 1.904(f)-6 Transitional rule for recapture of FORI and general limitation overall foreign losses incurred in taxable year beginning before January 1, 1983, from foreign source taxable income subject to the general limitation in taxable years beginning after December 31, 1982.

(a) General rule.

(b) Recapture of pre-1983 FORI and general limitation overall foreign losses from post-1982 income.

(1) Recapture from income subject to the same limitation.

(2) Recapture from income subject to the other limitation.

(c) Coordination of recapture of pre-1983 and post-1982 overall foreign losses.

(d) Illustrations.

§ 1.904(f)-7 Separate limitation loss and the separate limitation loss account. [Reserved]. For further guidance, see the entries for § 1.904(f)-7T in § 1.904(f)-0T.

§ 1.904(f)-8 Recapture of separate limitation loss accounts. [Reserved]. For further guidance, see the entries for § 1.904(f)-8T in § 1.904(f)-0T.

§ 1.904(f)-12 Transition rules.

(a) Recapture in years beginning after December 31, 1986, of overall foreign losses incurred in taxable years beginning before January 1, 1987.

(1) In general.

(2) Rule for general limitation losses.

(i) In general.

(ii) Exception.

(3) Priority of recapture of overall foreign losses incurred in pre-effective date taxable years.

(4) Examples.

(b) Treatment of overall foreign losses that are part of net operating losses incurred in pre-effective date taxable years which are carried forward to post-effective date taxable years.

(1) Rule.

(2) Example.

(c) Treatment of overall foreign losses that are part of net operating losses incurred in post-effective date taxable years which are carried back to pre-effective date taxable years.

(1) Allocation to analogous income category.

(2) Allocation to U.S. source income.

(3) Allocation to other separate limitation categories.

(4) Examples.

(d) Recapture of FORI and general limitation overall foreign losses incurred in taxable years beginning before January 1, 1983.

(e) Recapture of pre-1983 overall foreign losses determined on a combined basis.

(f) Transition rules for taxable years beginning before December 31, 1990.

(g) Recapture in years beginning after December 31, 2002, of separate limitation losses and overall foreign losses incurred in years beginning before January 1, 2003, with respect to the separate category for dividends from a noncontrolled section 902 corporation.

(h) [Reserved].

T.D. 9371, 12/20/2007.

§ 1.904(f)-0T Outline of regulation provisions (temporary).

This section lists the headings for Sec. § 1.904(f)-1T, 1.904(f)-2T, 1.904(f)-7T and 1.904(f)-8T.

§ 1.904(f)-1T Overall foreign loss and the overall foreign loss account (temporary).

(a)(1) [Reserved]. For further guidance, see the entry for § 1.904(f)-1(a)(1) in § 1.904(f)-0.

(2) Application to post-1986 taxable years.

(b) through (d)(3) [Reserved]. For further guidance, see the entries for § 1.904(f)-1(b) through (d)(3) in § 1.904(f)-0.

(d)(4) Adjustments for capital gains and losses.

(e) through (f) [Reserved]. For further guidance, see the entries for § 1.904(f)-1(e) through (f) in § 1.904(f)-0.

(g) Effective/applicability date.

(h) Expiration date.

§ 1.904(f)-2T Recapture of overall foreign loss (temporary).

(a) and (b) [Reserved]. For further guidance, see the entries for § 1.904(f)-2(a) and (b) in § 1.904(f)-0.

(c) Section 904(f)(1) recapture.

(1) In general.

(2) through (d) [Reserved]. For further guidance, see the entries for § 1.904(f)-2(c)(2) through (d) in § 1.904(f)-0.

(e) Effective/applicability date.

(f) Expiration date.

§ 1.904(f)-7T Separate limitation loss and the separate limitation loss account (temporary).

(a) Overview of regulations.

(b) Definitions.

(1) Separate category.

(2) Separate limitation income.

(3) Separate limitation loss.

(c) Separate limitation loss account.

(d) Additions to separate limitation loss accounts.

(1) General rule.

(2) Separate limitation losses of another taxpayer.

(3) Additions to separate limitation loss account created by loss carryovers.

(e) Reductions of separate limitation loss accounts.

(1) Pre-recapture reduction for amounts allocated to other taxpayers.

(2) Reduction for offsetting loss accounts.

(3) Reduction for amounts recaptured.

(f) Effective/applicability date.

(g) Expiration date.

§ 1.904(f)-8T Recapture of separate limitation loss accounts (temporary).

(a) In general.

(b) Effect of recharacterization of separate limitation income on associated taxes.

(c) Effective/applicability date.

(d) Expiration date.

T.D. 9371, 12/20/2007.

---

§ 1.904(f)-1 Overall foreign loss and the overall foreign loss account.

Caution: The Treasury has not yet amended Reg § 1.904(f)-1 to reflect changes made by P.L. 104-188, P.L. 100-647, P.L. 99-514.

(a) *(1) Overview of regulations.* In general, section 904(f) and these regulations apply to any taxpayer that sustains an overall foreign loss (as defined in paragraph (c)(1) of this section) in a taxable year beginning after December 31, 1975. For taxable years ending after December 31, 1984, and beginning before January 1, 1987, there can be five types of overall foreign losses; a loss under each of the five separate limitations contained in former section 904(d)(1)(A) (passive interest limitation), (d)(1)(B) (DISC dividend limitation), (d)(1)(C) (foreign trade income limitation), (d)(1)(D) (foreign sales corporation (FSC) distributions limitation), and (d)(1)(E) (general limitation). For taxable years beginning after December 31, 1982, and ending before January 1, 1985, there can be three types of overall foreign losses under former section 904(d)(1)(A) (passive interest limitation), former section 904(d)(1)(B) (DISC dividend limitation) and former section 904(d)(1)(C) (general limitation). For taxpayers subject to section 907, the post-1982 general limitation overall foreign loss account may be further subdivided, as provided in § 1.904(f)-6. For taxable years beginning after December 31, 1975, and before January 1, 1983, taxpayers should have computed overall foreign losses separately under the passive interest limitation, the DISC dividend limitation, the general limitation, and the section 907(b) (FORI) limitation. However, for taxable years beginning after December 31, 1975, and before January 1, 1983, taxpayers may have computed only two types of overall foreign losses: A foreign oil related loss under the FORI limitation and an overall foreign loss computed on a combined basis for the passive interest limitation, the DISC dividend limitation, and the general limitation. A taxpayer that computed overall foreign losses for these years on a combined basis will not be required to amend its return to recompute such losses on a separate basis. If a taxpayer computed its overall foreign losses for these years separately under the passive interest limitation, the DISC dividend limitation, and the general limitation, on returns previously filed, a taxpayer may not amend those returns to compute such overall foreign losses on a combined basis. Section 1.904(f)-1 provides rules for determining a taxpayer's overall foreign losses, for establishing overall foreign loss accounts, and for making additions to and reductions of such accounts for purposes of section 904(f). Section 1.904(f)-2 provides rules for recapturing the balance in any overall foreign loss account under the general recapture rule of section 904(f)(1) and under the special recapture rule of section 904(f)(3) when the taxpayer disposes of property used predominantly outside the United States in a trade or business. Section 1.904(f)-3 provides rules for allocating overall foreign losses that are part of net operating losses or net capital losses to foreign source income in years to which such losses are carried. In addition, § 1.904(f)-3 provides transition rules for the treatment of net operating losses incurred in taxable years beginning after December 31, 1982, and carried back to taxable years beginning before January 1, 1983, and of net operating losses incurred in taxable years beginning before January 1, 1983, and carried forward to taxable years beginning after December 31, 1982. Section 1.904(f)-4 provides rules for recapture out of an accumulation distribution of a foreign trust. Section 1.904(f)-5 provides rules for recapture of overall foreign losses of domestic trusts. Section 1.904(f)-6 provides a transition rule for recapturing a taxpayer's pre-1983 overall foreign losses under the general limitation and the FORI limitation out of taxable income subject to the general limitation in taxable years beginning after December 31, 1982. Section § 1.1502-9 provides rules concerning the application of these regulations to corporations filing consolidated returns.

(2) [Reserved]. For further guidance, see § 1.904(f)-1T(a)(2).

(b) Overall foreign loss accounts. Any taxpayer that sustains an overall foreign loss under paragraph (c) of this section must establish an account for such loss. Separate types of overall foreign losses must be kept in separate accounts. For taxable years beginning prior to January 1, 1983, taxpayers that computed losses on a combined basis in accordance with § 1.904(f)-1(c)(1) will keep one overall foreign loss account for such overall foreign loss. The balance in each overall foreign loss account represents the amount of such overall foreign loss subject to recapture by the taxpayer in a given year. From year to year, amounts may be added to or subtracted from the balances in such accounts as provided in paragraphs (d) and (e) of this section. The taxpayer must report the balances (if any) in its overall foreign loss accounts annually on a Form 1116 or 1118. Such forms must be filed for each taxable year ending after September 24, 1987. The balance in each account does not have to be attributed to the year or years in which the loss was incurred.

(c) Determination of a taxpayer's overall foreign loss. *(1) Overall foreign loss defined.* For taxable years beginning after December 31, 1982, and before January 1, 1987, a taxpayer sustains an overall foreign loss in any taxable year in which its gross income from sources without the United States subject to a separate limitation (as defined in paragraph (c)(2) of this section) is exceeded by the sum of the deductions properly allocated and apportioned thereto. Such losses are to be determined separately in accordance with the principles of the separate limitations. Accordingly, income and deductions subject to a separate limitation are not to be netted with income and deductions subject to another separate limitation for purposes of determining the amount of an overall foreign loss. A taxpayer may, for example, have an overall foreign loss under the general limitation in the same taxable year in which it has taxable income under the DISC dividend limitation. The same principles of calculating overall foreign losses on a separate limitation basis apply for taxable years beginning before January 1, 1983, except that a taxpayer shall determine its overall foreign losses on a combined basis, except for income subject to the FORI limitation, if the taxpayer filed its pre-1983 returns on such basis. Thus, for taxable years beginning prior to January 1, 1983, a taxpayer can net income and losses among the passive interest limitation, the DISC dividend limitation, and the general limitation if the taxpayer calculated its overall foreign losses that way at the time. Taxpayers that computed overall foreign losses separately under each of the separate limitations on their returns filed for taxable years beginning prior to January 1, 1983, may not amend such returns to compute their overall foreign losses for pre-1983 years on a combined basis.

(2) Separate limitation defined. For purposes of paragraph (c)(1) of this section and these regulations, the term separate limitation means any of the separate limitations under former section 904(d)(1)(A) (passive interest limitation), (B) (DISC dividend limitation), (C) (foreign trade income limitation), (D) (FSC distributions limitation), and (E) (general limitation) and the separate limitation under section 907(b) (FORI limitation) (for taxable years ending after December 31, 1975, and beginning before January 1, 1983).

(3) Method of allocation and apportionment of deductions. In determining its overall foreign loss, a taxpayer shall allocate and apportion expenses, losses, and other deductions to the appropriate category of gross income in accordance with section 862(b) and § 1.861-8 of the regulations. However, the following deductions shall not be taken into account:

(i) The amount of any net operating loss deduction for such year under section 172(a); and

(ii) To the extent such losses are not compensated for by insurance or otherwise, the amount of any—

(A) Expropriation losses for such year (as defined in section 172(h)), or

(B) Losses for such year which arise from fire, storm, shipwreck, or other casualty, or from theft.

(d) Additions to the overall foreign loss account. *(1) General rule.* A taxpayer's overall foreign loss as determined under paragraph (c) of this section shall be added to the applicable overall foreign loss account at the end of its taxable year to the extent that the overall foreign loss has reduced United States source income during the taxable year or during a year to which the loss has been carried back. For rules with respect to carryovers see paragraph (d)(3) of this section and § 1.904(f)-3.

(2) Overall foreign losses of another taxpayer. If any portion of any overall foreign loss of another taxpayer is allocated to the taxpayer in accordance with § 1.904(f)-5 (relating to overall foreign losses of domestic trusts) or § 1.1502-9 (relating to consolidated overall foreign losses), the taxpayer shall add such amount to its applicable overall foreign loss account.

(3) Additions to overall foreign loss account created by loss carryovers. Subject to the adjustments under § 1.904(f)-1(d)(4), the taxpayer shall add to each overall foreign loss account—

(i) All net operating loss carryovers to the current taxable year attributable to the same limitation to the extent that overall foreign losses included in the net operating loss carryovers reduced United States source income for the taxable year, and

(ii) All capital loss carryovers to the current taxable year attributable to the same limitation to the extent that foreign source capital loss carryovers reduced United States source capital gain net income for the taxable year.

(4) [Reserved]. For further guidance, see § 1.904(f)-1T(d)(4).

(e) Reductions of overall foreign loss accounts. The taxpayer shall subtract the following amounts from its overall foreign loss accounts at the end of its taxable year in the following order, if applicable:

(1) Pre-recapture reduction for amounts allocated to other taxpayers. An overall foreign loss account is reduced by the amount of any overall foreign loss which is allocated to another taxpayer in accordance with § 1.904(f)-5 (relating to overall foreign losses of domestic trusts) or § 1.1502-9 (relating to consolidated overall foreign losses).

(2) Reduction for amounts recaptured. An overall foreign loss account is reduced by the amount of any foreign source income that is subject to the same limitation as the loss that resulted in the account and that is recaptured in accordance with § 1.904(f)-2(c) (relating to recapture under section 904(f)(1)); 1.904(f)-2(d) (relating to recapture when the taxpayer disposes of certain properties under section 904(f)(3)); and 1.904(f)-4 (relating to recapture when the taxpayer receives an accumulation distribution from a foreign trust under section 904(f)(4)).

(f) Illustrations. The rules of this section are illustrated by the following examples.

Example (1). X Corporation is a domestic corporation with foreign branch operations in country C. X's taxable income and losses for its taxable year 1983 are as follows:

U.S. Source taxable income	$1,000
Foreign source taxable income (loss) subject to the general limitation	($ 500)
Foreign source taxable income subject to the passive interest limitation	$ 200

X has a general limitation overall foreign loss of $500 for 1983 in accordance with paragraph (c)(1) of this section. Since the general limitation overall foreign loss is not considered to offset income under the separate limitation for passive interest income, it therefore offsets $500 of United States source taxable income. This amount is added to X's general limitation overall foreign loss account at the end of 1983 in accordance with paragraphs (c)(1) and (d)(1) of this section.

Example (2). Y Corporation is a domestic corporation with foreign branch operations in Country C. Y's taxable income and losses for its taxable year 1982 are as follows:

U.S. source taxable income	$1,000
Foreign source taxable income subject to the general limitation	($ 500)
Foreign source taxable income subject to the passive interest limitation	$ 250

For its pre-1983 taxable years, Y filed its returns determining its overall foreign losses on a combined basis. In accordance with paragraphs (a) and (c)(1) of this section, Y may net the foreign source income and loss before offsetting the United States source income. Y therefore has a section 904(d)(1)(A-C) overall foreign loss account of $250 at the end of 1982.

Example (3). X Corporation is a domestic corporation with foreign branch operations in country C. For its taxable year 1985, X has taxable income (loss) determined as follows:

U.S. source taxable income	$200
Foreign source taxable income (loss) subject to the general limitation	($1,000)
Foreign source taxable income (loss) subject to the passive limitation	$1,800

X has a general limitation overall foreign loss of $1,000 in accordance with paragraph (c)(1) of this section. The overall foreign loss offsets $200 of United States source taxable income in 1985 and, therefore, X has a $200 general limitation overall foreign loss account at the end of 1985. The remaining $800 general limitation loss is offset by the passive interest limitation income 1985 so that X has no net operating loss carryover that is attributable to the general limitation loss and no additional amount attributable to that loss will be added to the overall foreign loss account in 1985 or in any other year.

(g) [Reserved]. For further guidance, see § 1.904(f)-1T(g).

T.D. 8153, 8/21/87, amend T.D. 9371, 12/20/2007.

PAR. 3. In § 1.904(f)-1, paragraph (a)(2) is added, and paragraph (d)(4) is revised, to read as follows:

Proposed § 1.904(f)-1 (12/21/2007) Overall foreign loss and the overall foreign loss account. [*For Preamble, see ¶ 152,941*]

(a) *(1)* * * *

(2) [The text of the proposed amendments to § 1.904(f)-1(a)(2) is the same as the text of § 1.904(f)-1T(a)(2) published elsewhere in this issue of the Federal Register.] [*See T.D. 9371, 12/21/2007, 72 Fed. Reg. 245.*]

* * * * *

(d) * * *

(4) [The text of the proposed amendments to § 1.904(f)-1(d)(4) is the same as the text of § 1.904(f)-1T(d)(4) published elsewhere in this issue of the Federal Register.] [*See T.D. 9371, 12/21/2007, 72 Fed. Reg. 245.*]

* * * * *

§ 1.904(f)-1T Overall foreign loss and the overall foreign loss account (temporary).

(a) *(1)* [Reserved]. For further guidance, see § 1.904(f)-1(a)(1).

(2) Application to post-1986 taxable years. The principles of §§ 1.904(f)-1 through 1.904(f)-5 shall apply to overall foreign loss sustained in taxable years beginning after December 31, 1986, modified so as to take into account the effect of statutory amendments.

(b) through (d)(3) [Reserved]. For further guidance, see § 1.904(f)-1(b) through (d)(3).

(d) *(4) Adjustments for capital gains and losses.* If a taxpayer has capital gains or losses, the taxpayer shall make adjustments to such capital gains and losses to the extent required under section 904(b)(2) and § 1.904(b)-1 before applying the provisions of § 1.904(f)-1T. See § 1.904(b)-1(h).

(e) and (f) [Reserved]. For further guidance, see § 1.904(f)-1(e) and (f).

(g) Effective/applicability date. This section applies to taxable years beginning after December 21, 2007.

(h) Expiration date. The applicability of this section expires on December 20, 2010.

T.D. 9371, 12/20/2007.

§ 1.904(f)-2 Recapture of overall foreign losses.

Caution: The Treasury has not yet amended Reg § 1.904(f)-2 to reflect changes made by P.L. 100-647, P.L. 99-514.

(a) In general. A taxpayer shall be required to recapture an overall foreign loss as provided in this section. Recapture is accomplished by treating as United States source income a portion of the taxpayer's foreign source taxable income of the same limitation as the foreign source loss that resulted in an overall foreign loss account. As a result, if the taxpayer elects the benefits of section 901 or section 936, the taxpayer's foreign tax credit limitation with respect to such income is decreased. As provided in § 1.904(f)-1(e)(2), the balance in a taxpayer's overall foreign loss account is reduced by the amount of loss recaptured. Recapture continues until such time as the amount of foreign source taxable income recharacterized as United States source income equals the amount in the overall foreign loss account. As provided in § 1.904(f)-1(e)(2), the balance in a overall foreign loss account is reduced at the end of each taxable year by the amount of the loss recaptured during that taxable year. Regardless of whether recapture occurs in a year in which a taxpayer elects the benefits of section 901 or in a year in which a taxpayer deducts its foreign taxes under section 164, the overall foreign loss account is recaptured only to the extent of foreign source taxable income remaining after applying the appropriate section 904(b) adjustments, if any, as provided in paragraph (b) of this section.

(b) Determination of taxable income from sources without the United States for purposes of recapture. *(1) In general.* For purposes of determining the amount of an overall foreign loss subject to recapture, the taxpayer's taxable income from sources without the United States shall be computed with respect to each of the separate limitations described in § 1.904(f)-1(c)(2) in accordance with the rules set forth in § 1.904(f)-1(c)(1) and (3). This computation is made without taking into account foreign source taxable income (and deductions properly allocated and apportioned thereto) subject to other separate limitations. Before applying the recapture rules to foreign source taxable income, the following provisions shall be applied to such income in the following order:

(i) Former section 904(b)(3)(C) (prior to its removal by the Tax Reform Act of 1986) and the regulations thereunder shall be applied to treat certain foreign source gain as United States source gain; and

(ii) Section 904(b)(2) and the regulations thereunder shall be applied to make adjustments in the foreign tax credit limitation fraction for certain capital gains and losses.

(c) Section 904(f)(1) recapture. *(1)* [Reserved]. For further guidance, see § 1.904(f)-2T(c)(1).

(2) Election to recapture more of the overall foreign loss than is required under paragraph (c)(1). In a year in which a taxpayer elects the benefits of sections 901 or 936, a taxpayer may make an annual revocable election to recapture a greater portion of the balance in an overall foreign loss account than is required to be recaptured under paragraph (c)(1) of this section. A taxpayer may make such an election or amend a prior election by attaching a statement to its annual Form 1116 or 1118. If an amendment is made to a prior year's election, an amended tax return should be filed. The statement attached to the Form 1116 or 1118 must indicate the percentage and dollar amount of the taxpayer's foreign source taxable income that is being recharacterized as United States source income and the percentage and dollar amount of the balance (both before and after recapture) in the overall foreign loss account that is being recaptured. Except for the special recapture rules for section 936 corporations and for recapture of pre-1983 overall foreign losses determined on a combined basis, the taxpayer that elects to credit its foreign taxes may not elect to recapture an amount in excess of the taxpayer's foreign source taxable income subject to the same limitation as the loss that resulted in the overall foreign loss account.

(3) Special rule for recapture of losses incurred prior to section 936 election. If a corporation elects the application of section 936 and at the time of the election has a balance in any overall foreign loss account, such losses will be recaptured from the possessions source income of the electing section 936 corporation that qualifies for the section 936 credit, including qualified possession source investment income as defined in section 936(d)(2), even though the overall foreign loss to be recaptured may not be attributable to a loss in an income category of a type that would meet the definition of qualified possession source investment income. For purposes of recapturing an overall foreign loss incurred by a consolidated group including a corporation that subsequently elects to use section 936, the electing section 936 corporation's possession source income that qualifies for the section 936 credit, including qualified possession source investment income, shall be used to recapture the section 936 corporation's share of previously incurred overall foreign loss accounts. Rules for determining the section 936 corporation's share of the consolidated groups overall foreign loss accounts are provided in § 1.1502-9(c).

(4) Recapture of pre-1983 overall foreign losses determined on a combined basis. If a taxpayer computed its overall foreign losses on a combined basis in accordance with § 1.904(f)-1(c)(1) for taxable years beginning before January 1, 1983, any losses recaptured in taxable years beginning after December 31, 1982, shall be recaptured from income subject to the general limitation, subject to the rules in § 1.904(f)-6(a) and (b). Ordering rules for recapture of these losses are provided in § 1.904(f)-6(c).

(5) Illustrations. The rules of this paragraph (c) are illustrated by the following examples, all of which assume a United States corporate tax rate of 50 percent unless otherwise stated.

Example (1). X Corporation is a domestic corporation that does business in the United States and abroad. On December 31, 1983, the balance in X's general limitation overall foreign loss account is $600, all of which is attributable to a loss incurred in 1983. For 1984, X has United States source taxable income of $500 and foreign source taxable income subject to the general limitation of $500. For 1984, X pays $200 in foreign taxes and elects section 901. Under paragraph (c)(1) of this section, X is required to recapture $250 (the lesser of $600 or 50 percent of $500) of its overall foreign loss. As a consequence, X's foreign tax credit limitation under the general limitation is $250/$1,000 × $500, or $125, instead of $500/$1,000 × $500, or $250. The balance in X's general limitation overall foreign loss account is reduced by $250 in accordance with § 1.904(f)-1(e)(2).

Example (2). The facts are the same as in example (1) except that X makes an election to recapture its overall foreign loss to the extent of 80 percent of its foreign source taxable income subject to the general limitation (or $400) in accordance with paragraph (c)(2) of this section. As a result of recapture, X's 1984 foreign tax credit limitation for income subject to the general limitation is $100/$1,000 × $500, or $50, instead of $500/$1,000 × $500, or $250. X's general limitation overall foreign loss account is reduced by $400 in accordance with § 1.904(f)-1(e)(2).

Example (3). The facts are the same as in example (1) except that X does not elect the benefits of section 901 in 1984 and instead deducts its foreign taxes paid. In 1984, X recaptures $300 of its overall foreign loss, the difference between X's foreign source taxable income of $500 and $200 of foreign taxes paid. The balance in X's general limitation overall foreign loss account is reduced by $300 in accordance with § 1.904(f)-1(e)(2).

Example (4). [Reserved]. For further guidance see § 1.904(f)-2T(c)(5) Example 4.

Example (5). On December 31, 1980, V, a domestic corporation that does business in the United States and abroad, has a balance in its section 904(d)(1)(A-C) overall foreign loss account of $600. V also has a balance in its FORI limitation overall foreign loss account of $900. For 1981, V has foreign source taxable income subject to the general limitation of $500 and $500 of United States source income. V also has foreign source taxable income subject to the FORI limitation of $800. V is required to recapture $250 of its section 904(d)(1)(A-C) overall foreign loss account (the lesser of $600 or 50% of $500) and its general limitation foreign tax credit limitation is $250/$1,800 × $900, or $125 instead of $500/$1,800 × $900, or $250. V is also required to recapture $400 of its FORI limitation overall foreign loss account (the lesser of $900 or 50% of $800). V's foreign tax credit limitation for FORI is $400/$1,800 × $900, or $200, instead of $800/$1,800 × $900, or $400. The balance in V's FORI limitation overall foreign loss account is reduced to $500 and the balance in V's section 904(d)(1)(A-C) account is reduced to $350, in accordance with § 1.904(f)-1(e)(2).

Example (6). This example assumes a United States corporate tax rate of 46 percent (under section 11(b)) and an alternative rate of tax under section 1201(a) of 28 percent. W is a domestic corporation that does business in the United States and abroad. On December 31, 1984, W has $350 in its general limitation overall foreign loss account. For 1985, W has $500 of United States source taxable income, and has foreign source income subject to the general limitation as follows:

Foreign source taxable income other than net capital gain	$720
Foreign source net capital gain	$460

Under paragraph (b)(2) of this section, foreign source taxable income for purposes of recapture includes foreign source capital gain net income, reduced, under section 904(b)(2), by the rate differential portion of foreign source net capital gain, which adjusts for the reduced tax rate for net capital gain under section 1201(a):

Foreign source capital gain net income	$460
Rate differential portion of foreign source net capital gain (18/46 of $460)	−180
Foreign source capital gain included in foreign source taxable income	$280

The total foreign source taxable income of W for purposes of recapture in 1985 in $1,000 ($720 + $280). Under paragraph (c)(1) of this section, W is required to recapture $350 (the lesser of $350 or 50 percent of $1,000), and W's general limitation overall foreign loss account is reduced to zero. W's foreign tax credit limitation for income subject to the general limitation is $650/$1,500 × $690 ((.46) (500 + 720) + (.28) (460)), or $299, instead of $1,000/$1,500 × $690, or $460.

(d) Recapture of overall foreign losses from dispositions under section 904(f)(3). *(1) In general.* If a taxpayer disposes of property used or held for use predominantly without the United States in a trade or business during a taxable year and that property generates foreign source taxable income subject to a separate limitation to which paragraph (a) of this section is applicable, (i) gain will be recognized on the disposition of such property, (ii) such gain will be treated as foreign source income subject to the same limitation as the income the property generated, and (iii) the applicable overall foreign loss account shall be recaptured as provided in paragraphs (d)(2), (d)(3), and (d)(4) of this section. See paragraph (d)(5) of this section for definitions.

(2) Treatment of net capital gain. If the gain from a disposition of property to which this paragraph (d) applies is treated as net capital gain, all references to such gain in paragraphs (d)(3) and (d)(4) of this section shall mean such gain as adjusted under paragraph (b) of this section. The amount by which the overall foreign loss account shall be reduced shall be determined from such adjusted gain.

(3) Dispositions where gain is recognized irrespective of section 904(f)(3). If a taxpayer recognizes foreign source gain subject to a separate limitation on the disposition of property described in paragraph (d)(1) of this section, and there is a balance in a taxpayer's overall foreign loss account that is attributable to a loss under such limitation after applying paragraph (c) of this section, an additional portion of such balance shall be recaptured in accordance with paragraphs (a) and (b) of this section. The amount recaptured shall be the lesser of such balance or 100 percent of the foreign source gain recognized on the disposition that was not previously recharacterized.

(4) Dispositions in which gain would not otherwise be recognized. (i) Recognition of gain to the extent of the overall foreign loss account. If a taxpayer makes a disposition of property described in paragraph (d)(1) of this section in which any amount of gain otherwise would not be recognized in the year of the disposition, and such property was used or held for use to generate foreign source taxable income subject to a separate limitation under which the taxpayer had a balance in its overall foreign loss account (including a balance that arose in the year of the disposition), the taxpayer shall recognize foreign source taxable income in an amount equal to the lesser of:

(A) The sum of the balance in the applicable overall foreign loss account (but only after such balance has been increased by amounts added to the account for the year of the disposition or has been reduced by amounts recaptured for the year of the disposition under paragraph (c) and paragraph (d)(3) of this section) plus the amount of any overall foreign loss that would be part of a net operating loss for the year of the disposition if gain from the disposition were not recognized under section 904(f)(3), plus the amount of any overall foreign loss that is part of a net operating loss carryover from a prior year, or

(B) The excess of the fair market value of such property over the taxpayer's adjusted basis in such property.

The excess of the fair market value of such property over its adjusted basis shall be determined on an asset by asset basis. Losses from the disposition of an asset shall not be recognized. Any foreign source taxable income deemed received and recognized under this paragraph (d)(4)(i) will have the same character as if the property had been sold or exchanged in a taxable transaction and will constitute gain for all purposes.

(ii) Basis adjustment. The basis of the property received in an exchange to which this paragraph (d)(4) applies shall be increased by the amount of gain deemed recognized, in accordance with applicable sections of subchapters C (relating to corporate distributions and adjustments), K (relating to partners and partnerships), O (relating to gain or loss on the disposition of property), and P (relating to capital gains and losses). If the property to which this paragraph (d)(4) applies was transferred by gift, the basis of such property in the hands of the donor immediately preceding such gift shall be increased by the amount of the gain deemed recognized.

(iii) Recapture of overall foreign loss to the extent of amount recognized. The provisions of paragraphs (a) and (b) of this section shall be applied to the extent of 100 percent of the foreign source taxable income which is recognized under paragraph (d)(4)(i) of this section. However, amounts of foreign source gain that would not be recognized except by application of section 904(f)(3) and paragraph (d)(4)(i) of this section, and which are treated as United States source gain by application of section 904(b)(3)(C) (prior to its removal by the Tax Reform Act of 1986) and paragraph (b)(1) of this section, shall reduce the overall foreign loss account (subject to the adjustments described in paragraph (d)(2) of this section) if such gain is net capital gain, notwithstanding the fact that such amounts would otherwise not be recaptured under the ordering rules in paragraph (b) of this section.

(iv) Priorities among dispositions in which gain is deemed to be recognized. If, in a single taxable year, a taxpayer makes more than one disposition to which this paragraph (d)(4) is applicable, the rules of this paragraph (d)(4) shall be applied to each disposition in succession starting with the disposition which occurred earliest, until the balance in the applicable overall foreign loss account is reduced to zero. If the taxpayer simultaneously makes more than one disposition to which this paragraph (d)(4) is applicable, the rules of paragraph (d)(4) shall be applied so that the balance in the applicable overall foreign loss account to be recaptured will be allocated pro rata among the assets in proportion to the excess of the fair market value of each asset over the adjusted basis of each asset.

(5) Definitions. (i) Disposition. A disposition to which this paragraph (d) applies includes a sale; exchange; distribution; gift; transfer upon the foreclosure of a security interest (but not a mere transfer of title to a creditor upon creation of a security interest or to a debtor upon termination of a security interest); involuntary conversion; contribution to a partnership, trust, or corporation; transfer at death; or any other transfer of property whether or not gain or loss is recognized under other provisions of the Code. However, a disposition to which this paragraph (d) applies does not include:

(A) A distribution or transfer of property to a domestic corporation described in section 381(a) (provided that paragraph (d)(6) of this section (d)(5)(iv) of this section);

(B) A disposition of property which is not a material factor in the realization of income by the taxpayer (as defined in paragraph (d)(5)(iv) of this section);

(C) A transaction in which gross income is not realized; or

(D) The entering into a unitization or pooling agreement (as defined in § 1.614-8(b)(6) of the regulations) containing a valid election under section 761(a)(2), and in which the source of the entire gain from any disposition of the interest created by the agreement would be determined to be foreign source under section 862(a)(5) if the disposition occurred presently.

(ii) Property used in a trade or business. Property is used in a trade or business if it is held for the principal purpose of promoting the present or future conduct of the trade or business. This generally includes property acquired and held in the ordinary course of a trade or business or otherwise held in a direct relationship to a trade or business. In determining whether an asset is held in a direct relationship to a trade or business, principal consideration shall be given to whether the asset is used in the trade or business. Property will be treated as held in a direct relationship to a trade or business if the property was acquired with funds generated by that trade or business or if income generated from the asset is available for use in that trade or business. Property used in a trade or business may be tangible or intangible, real or personal property. It includes property, such as equipment, which is subject to an allowance for depreciation under section 167 or cost recovery under section 168. Property may be considered used in a trade or business even if it is a capital asset in the hands of the taxpayer. However, stock of another corporation shall not be considered property used in a trade or business if a substantial investment motive exists for acquiring and holding the stock. On the other hand, stock acquired or held to assure a source of supply for a trade or business shall be considered property used in that trade or business. Inventory is generally not considered property used in a trade or business. However, when disposed of in a manner not in the ordinary course of a trade or business, inventory will be considered property used in the trade or business. A partnership interest will be treated as property used in a trade or business if the underlying assets of the partnership would be property used in a trade or business. For purposes of section 904(f)(3) and § 1.904(f)-2(d)(1) and (5), a disposition of a partnership interest to which this section applies will be treated as a disposition of a proportionate share of each of the assets of the partnership. For purposes of allocating the purchase price of the interest and the seller's basis in the interest to those assets, the principles of § 1.751-1(a) will apply.

(iii) Property used predominantly outside the United States. Property will be considered used predominantly outside the United States if for a 3-year period ending on the date of the disposition (or, if shorter, the period during which the property has been used in the trade or business) such property was located outside the United States more than 50 percent of the time. An aircraft, railroad rolling stock, vessel, motor vehicle, container, or other property used for transportation purposes is deemed to be used predominantly outside the United States if, during the 3-year (or shorter) period, either such property is located outside the United States more than 50 percent of the time or more than 50 percent of the miles traversed in the use of such property are traversed outside the United States.

(iv) Property which is a material factor in the realization of income. For purposes of this section, property used in a trade or business will be considered a material factor in the realization of income unless the taxpayer establishes that it is not (or, if the taxpayer did not realize income from the trade or business in the taxable year, would not be expected to be) necessary to the realization of income by the taxpayer.

(6) Carryover of overall foreign loss accounts in a corporate acquisition to which section 381(a) applies. In the case of a distribution or transfer described in section 381(a), an overall foreign loss account of the distributing or transferor corporation shall be treated as an overall foreign loss account of the acquiring or transferee corporation as of the close of the date of the distribution or transfer. If the transferee corporation had an overall foreign loss account under the same separate limitation prior to the distribution or transfer, the balance in the transferor's account must be added to the transferee's account. If not, the transferee must adopt the transferor's overall foreign loss account. An overall foreign loss of the transferor will be treated as incurred by the transferee in the year prior to the year of the transfer.

(7) Illustrations. The rules of this paragraph (d) are illustrated by the following examples which assume that the United States corporate tax rate is 50 percent (unless otherwise stated). For purposes of these examples, none of the foreign source gains are treated as net capital gains (unless so stated).

Example (1). X Corporation has a balance in its general limitation overall foreign loss account of $600 at the close of its taxable year ending December 31, 1984. In 1985, X sells assets used predominantly outside the United States in a trade or business and recognizes $1,000 of gain on the sale under section 1001. This gain is subject to the general limitation. This sale is a disposition within the meaning of paragraph (d)(5)(i) of this section, and to which this paragraph (d) applies. X has no other foreign source taxable income in 1985 and has $1,000 of United States source taxable income. Under paragraph (c), X is required to recapture $500 (the lesser of the balance in X's general limitation overall foreign loss account ($600) or 50 percent of $1,000) of its overall foreign loss account. The balance in X's general limitation overall foreign loss account is reduced to $100 in accordance with § 1.904(f)-1(e)(2). In addition, under paragraph (d)(3) of this section, X is required to recapture $100 (the lesser of the remaining balance in its general limitation overall foreign loss account ($100) or 100 percent of its foreign source taxable income recognized on such disposition that has not been previously recharacterized ($500)). The total amount recaptured is $600. X's foreign tax credit limitation for income subject to the general limitation in 1985 is $200 ($400/$2,000 × $1,000) instead of $500 ($1,000/$2,000 foreign loss account is reduced to zero in accordance with § 1.904(f)-1(e)(2).

Example (2). On December 31, 1984, Y Corporation has a balance in its general limitation overall foreign loss account of $1,500. In 1985, Y has $500 of United States source taxable income and $200 of foreign source taxable income subject to the general limitation. Y's foreign source taxable income is from the sale of property used predominantly outside of the United States in a trade or business. This sale is a disposition to which this paragraph (d) is applicable. In 1985, Y also transferred property used predominantly outside of the United States in a trade or business to another corporation. Under section 351, no gain was recognized on this transfer. Such property had been used to generate foreign source taxable income subject to the general limitation. The excess of the fair market value of the property transferred over Y's adjusted basis in such property was $2,000. In accordance with paragraph (c) of this section, Y is required to recapture $100 (the lesser of $1,500, the amount in Y's general limitation overall foreign loss account, or 50 percent of $200, the amount of general limitation foreign source taxable income for the current year) of its general limitation overall foreign loss. Y is then required to recapture an additional $100 of its general limitation overall foreign loss account under paragraph (d)(3) of this section out of the remaining gain recognized on the sale of assets, because 100 percent of such gain is subject to recapture. The balance in Y's general limitation overall foreign loss account is reduced to $1,300 in accordance with § 1.904(f)-1(e)(2). Y corporation is then required to recognize $1,300 of foreign source taxable income on its section 351 transfer under paragraph (d)(4) of this section. The remaining $700 of potential gain associated with the section 351 transfer is not recognized. Under paragraph (d)(4), 100 percent of the $1,300 is recharacterized as United States source taxable income, and Y's general limitation overall foreign loss account is reduced to zero. Y's entire taxable income for 1985 is:

U.S. source taxable income	$ 500
Foreign source taxable income subject to the general limitation that is recharacterized as U.S. source income by paragraphs (c) and (d)(3) of this section	200
Gain recognized under section 904(f)(3) and paragraph (d)(4) of this section, and recharacterized as U.S. source income	1,300
Total	$2,000

Y's foreign tax credit limitation for 1985 for income subject to the general limitation to $0 ($0/$2,000 × $1,000) instead of $100 ($200/$700 × $350).

Example (3). W Corporation is a calendar year domestic corporation with foreign branch operations in country C. As of December 31, 1984, W has no overall foreign loss accounts and has no net operating loss carryovers. W's entire taxable income in 1985 is:

U.S. source taxable income	$800
Foreign source taxable income (loss) subject to the general limitation	($1,000)

W cannot carry back its 1985 NOL to any earlier year. As of December 31, 1985, W therefore has $800 in its general limitation overall foreign loss account. In 1986, W earns $400 United States source taxable income and has an additional $1,000 loss from the operations of the foreign branch. Income in the loss category would be subject to the general limitation. Also in 1986, W disposes of property used predominately outside the United States in a trade or business. Such property generated income subject to the general limitation. The excess of the property's fair market value over its adjusted basis is $3,000. The disposition is of a type described in § 1.904(f)-2(d)(4)(i). W has no other income in 1986. Under § 1.904(f)-2(d)(4)(i), W is required to recognize foreign source taxable income on the disposition in an amount equal to the lesser of $2,000 ($800 (the balance in the general limitation overall foreign loss account as of 1985) × $400 (the increase in the general limitation overall foreign loss account attributable to the disposition year) × $600 (the general limitation overall foreign loss that is part of the NOL from 1986) part of the NOL from 1985)) or $3,000. The $2,000 foreign source income required to be recognized under section 904(f)(3) is reduced to $1,200 by the remaining $600 loss in 1986 and the $200 net operating loss carried forward from 1985. This $1,200 of income is subject to the general limitation. In computing foreign tax credit limitation for general limitation income, the $1,200 of foreign source income is treated as United States source income and, therefore, W's foreign tax credit limitation for income subject to the general limitation is zero. W's overall foreign loss account is reduced to zero.

Example (4). Z Corporation has a balance in its FORI overall foreign loss account of $1,500 at the end of its taxable year 1980. In 1981, Z has $1,600 of foreign oil related income subject to the separate limitation for FORI income and no United States source income. In addition, in 1981, Z makes two dispositions of property used predominantly outside the United States in a trade or business on which no gain was recognized. Such property generated foreign oil related income. The excess of the fair market value of the property transferred in the first disposition over Z's adjusted basis in such property is $575. The excess of the fair market value of the property transferred in the second disposition over Z's adjusted basis in such property is $1,000. Under paragraph (c) of this section, Z is required to recapture $800 (the lesser of 50 percent of its foreign oil related income of $1,600 or the balance ($1,500) in its FORI overall foreign loss account) of its foreign oil related loss. In accordance with paragraphs (d)(4)(i) and (iv) of this section, Z is required to recognize foreign oil related income in the amount of $575 on the first disposition and, since the foreign oil related loss account is now reduced by $1,375 (the $800 and $575 amounts previously recaptured), Z is required to recognize foreign oil related income in the amount of $125 on the second disposition. In accordance with paragraph (d)(4)(iii) of this section, the entire amount recognized is treated as United States source income and the balance in the FORI overall foreign loss account is reduced to zero under § 1.904(f)-1(e)(2). Z's foreign tax credit limitation for FORI is $400 ($800/$2,300 × $1,150) instead of $800 ($1,600/$1,600

Example (5). The facts are the same as in example (4), except that the gain from the two dispositions of property is treated as net capital gain and the United States corporate tax rate is assumed to be 46 percent. As in example (4), Z is required to recapture $800 of its foreign oil related loss from its 1981 ordinary foreign oil related income. In accordance with paragraph (d)(4)(i) and (iv) of this section, Z is first required to recognize foreign oil related income (which is net capital gain) on the first disposition in the amount of $575. Under paragraphs (b) and (d)(2) of this section, this net capital gain is adjusted by subtracting the rate differential portion of such gain from the total amount of such gain to determine the amount by which the foreign oil related loss account is reduced, which is $350 ($575 − ($575 × 18/46)). The balance remaining in Z's foreign oil related loss account after this step is $350. Therefore, this process will be repeated, in accordance with paragraph (d)(4)(iv) of this section, to recapture that remaining balance out of the gain deemed recognized on the second disposition, resulting in reduction of the foreign oil related loss account to zero and net capital gain required to be recognized from the second disposition in the amount of $575, which must also be adjusted by subtracting the rate differential portion to determine the amount by which the foreign oil related loss account is reduced (which is $350). The $575 of net capital gain from each disposition is recharacterized as United States source net capital gain. Z's section 907 (b) foreign tax credit limitation is the same as in example (4), and Z has $1,150 ($575 + $575) of United States source net capital gain.

(e) [Reserved]. For further guidance, see § 1.904(f)-2T(e).

T.D. 8153, 8/21/87, amend T.D. 9371, 12/20/2007.

PAR. 4. Section 1.904(f)-2(c)(1) and (c)(5) Example 4. are revised to read as follows:

Proposed § 1.904(f)-2 (12/21/2007) Recapture of overall foreign losses. [*For Preamble, see ¶ 152,941*]

* * * * *

(c) * * * *(1)* [The text of the proposed amendments to § 1.904(f)-2(c)(1) is the same as the text of § 1.904(f)-2T(c)(1) published elsewhere in this issue of the Federal Register.] [*See T.D. 9371, 12/21/2007, 72 Fed. Reg. 245.*]

* * * * *

(5) * * *

Example (4). [The text of the proposed amendments to § 1.904(f)-2(c)(5) Example 4. is the same as the text of § 1.904(f)-2T(c)(5) Example 4. published elsewhere in this issue of the Federal Register.] [*See T.D. 9371, 12/21/2007, 72 Fed. Reg. 245.*]

* * * * *

§ 1.904(f)-2T Recapture of overall foreign losses (temporary).

(a) and (b) [Reserved]. For further guidance, see § 1.904(f)-2(a) and (b).

(c) Section 904(f)(1) recapture. *(1) In general.* In a year in which a taxpayer elects the benefits of section 901 or 30A, the amount of foreign source taxable income subject to recharacterization in a taxable year in which paragraph (a) of this section is applicable is the lesser of the aggregate amount of maximum potential recapture in all overall foreign loss accounts or fifty percent of the taxpayer's total foreign source taxable income. If the aggregate amount of maximum potential recapture in all overall foreign loss accounts exceeds fifty percent of the taxpayer's total foreign source taxable income, foreign source taxable income in each separate category with an overall foreign loss account is recharacterized in an amount equal to the section 904(f)(1) recapture amount, multiplied by the maximum potential recapture in the overall foreign loss account, divided by the aggregate amount of maximum potential recapture in all overall foreign loss accounts. The maximum potential recapture in any account is the lesser of the balance in that overall foreign loss account (after reduction of such accounts in accordance with § 1.904(f)-1(e)) or the foreign source taxable income for the year in the same separate category as the loss account. If, in any year, in accordance with section 164(a) and section 275(a)(4)(A), a taxpayer deducts rather than credits its foreign taxes, recapture is applied to the extent of the lesser of--

(i) The balance in the overall foreign loss account in each separate category; or

(ii) Foreign source taxable income minus foreign taxes in each separate category.

(2) through (5) Example 3 [Reserved]. For further guidance, see § 1.904(f)-2(c)(2) through (5) Example 3.

(5)

Example (4). Y Corporation is a domestic corporation that does business in the United States and abroad. On December 31, 2007, the balance in Y's general category overall foreign loss account is $500, all of which is attributable to a loss incurred in 2007. Y has no other loss accounts subject to recapture. For 2008, Y has U.S. source taxable income of $400 and foreign source taxable income of $300 in the general category and $900 in the passive category. Under paragraph (c)(1) of this section, the amount of Y's general category income subject to recharacterization is the lesser of the aggregate maximum potential recapture or 50 percent of the total foreign source taxable income. In this case Y's aggregate maximum potential recapture is $300 (the lesser of the $500 balance in the general category overall foreign loss account or $300 foreign source income in the general category for the year), which is less than $600, or 50 percent of total foreign source taxable income ($1200 x 50%). Therefore, pursuant to paragraph (c) of this section, $300 of foreign source income in the general category is recharacterized as U.S. source income. The balance in Y's general category overall foreign loss account is reduced by $300 to $200 in accordance with § 1.904(f)-1(e)(2).

Example (5). through (d) [Reserved]. For further guidance, see § 1.904(f)-2(c)(5) Example 5 through § 1.904(f)-2(d).

(e) Effective/applicability date. This section applies to taxable years beginning after December 21, 2007.

(f) Expiration date. The applicability of this section expires on December 20, 2010.

T.D. 9371, 12/20/2007.

§ 1.904(f)-3 Allocation of net operating losses and net capital losses.

Caution: The Treasury has not yet amended Reg § 1.904(f)-3 to reflect changes made by P.L. 100-647, P.L. 99-514.

For rules relating to the allocation of net operating losses and net capital losses, see § 1.904(g)-3T.

T.D. 8153, 8/21/87, amend T.D. 8677, 6/26/96, T.D. 8823, 6/25/99, T.D. 9371, 12/20/2007.

§ 1.904(f)-4 Recapture of foreign losses out of accumulation distributions from a foreign trust.

Caution: The Treasury has not yet amended Reg § 1.904(f)-4 to reflect changes made by P.L. 100-647, P.L. 99-514.

(a) In general. If a taxpayer receives a distribution of foreign source taxable income subject to a separate limitation in which the taxpayer had a balance in an overall foreign loss account and that income is treated under section 666 as having been distributed by a foreign trust in a preceding taxable year, a portion of the balance in the taxpayer's applicable overall foreign loss account shall be subject to recapture under this section. The amount subject to recapture shall be the lesser of the balance in the taxpayer's overall foreign loss account (after applying §§ 1.904(f)-1, 1.904(f)-2, 1.904(f)-3, and 1.904(f)-6 to the taxpayer's other income or loss in the current taxable year) or the entire amount of foreign source taxable income deemed distributed in a preceding year or years under section 666.

(b) Effect of recapture on foreign tax credit limitation under section 667(d). If paragraph (a) of this section is applicable, then in applying the separate limitation (in accordance with section 667(d)(1)(A) and (C)) to determine the amount of foreign taxes deemed distributed under section 666(b) and (c) that can be credited against the increase in tax in a computation year, a portion of the foreign source taxable income deemed distributed in such computation year shall be treated as United States source income. Such portion shall be determined by multiplying the amount of foreign source taxable income deemed distributed in the computation year by a fraction. The numerator of this fraction is the balance in the taxpayer's overall foreign loss account (after application of §§ 1.904(f)-1, 1.904(f)-2, 1.904(f)-3, and 1.904(f)-6), and the denominator of the fraction is the entire amount of foreign source taxable income deemed distributed under section 666. However, the numerator of this fraction shall not exceed the denominator of the fraction.

(c) Recapture if taxpayer deducts foreign taxes deemed distributed. If paragraph (a) of this section is applicable and if, in accordance with section 667(d)(1)(B), the beneficiary deducted rather than credited its taxes in the computation year, the beneficiary shall reduce its overall foreign loss account (but not below zero) by an amount equal to the lesser of the balance in the applicable overall foreign loss account or the amount of the actual distribution deemed distributed in the computation year (without regard to the foreign taxes deemed distributed).

(d) Illustrations. The provisions of this section are illustrated by the following examples:

Example (1). X Corporation is a domestic corporation that has a balance of $10,000 in its general limitation overall foreign loss account on December 31, 1980. For its taxable year beginning January 1, 1981, X's only income is an accumulation distribution from a foreign trust of $20,000 of general limitation foreign source taxable income. Under section 666, the amount distributed and the foreign taxes paid on such amount ($4,000) are deemed distributed in two prior taxable years. In determining the partial tax on such distribution under section 667(b), the amount added to each computation year is $12,000 (the sum of the actual distribution plus the taxes deemed distributed ($24,000) divided by the number of accumulation years (2)). Of that amount, $5,000 ($10,000/$24,000 × $12,000) is treated as United States source taxable income in accordance with paragraph (b) of this section. Assuming the United States tax rate is 50 percent, X's separate foreign tax credit limitation against the increase in tax in each computation year is $3,500 ($7,000/$12,000 × $6,000) instead of $6,000 ($12,000/$12,000 × $6,000). X's overall foreign loss account is reduced to zero in accordance with paragraph (a) of this section.

Example (2). Assume the same facts as in Example (1), except that X deducted rather than credited its foreign taxes in the computation years. In 1979, the amount added to X's income is $12,000 under section 667(b), $2,000 of which is deductible under section 667(d)(1)(B). X must reduce its overall foreign loss account by $10,000, the amount of the actual distribution that is deemed distributed in 1979 (without regard to the $2,000 foreign taxes also deemed distributed). The entire overall foreign loss account is therefore reduced to $0 in 1979.

T.D. 8153, 8/21/87.

§ 1.904(f)-5 Special rules for recapture of overall foreign losses of a domestic trust.

Caution: The Treasury has not yet amended Reg § 1.904(f)-5 to reflect changes made by P.L. 100-647, P.L. 99-514.

(a) In general. Except as provided in this section, the rules contained in §§ 1.904(f)-1, 1.904(f)-2, 1.904(f)-3, 1.904(f)-4, and 1.904(f)-s6 apply to domestic trusts.

(b) Recapture of trust's overall foreign loss. In taxable years in which a trust has foreign source taxable income subject to a separate limitation in which the trust has a balance in its overall foreign loss account, the balance in the trust's overall foreign loss account shall be recaptured as follows:

(1) Trust accumulates income. If the trust accumulates all of its foreign source taxable income subject to the same limitation as the loss that created the balance in the overall foreign loss account, its overall foreign loss shall be recaptured out of such income in accordance with §§ 1.904(f)-1, 1.904(f)-2, 1.904(f)-3, 1.904(f)-4, and 1.904(f)-6.

(2) Trust distributes income. If the trust distributes all of its foreign source taxable income subject to the same limitation as the loss that created the overall foreign loss account, the amount of the overall foreign loss that would be subject to recapture by the trust under paragraph (b)(1) of this section shall be allocated to the beneficiaries in proportion to the amount of such income which is distributed to each beneficiary in that year.

(3) Trust accumulates and distributes income. If the trust accumulates part of its foreign source taxable income subject to the same limitation as the loss that created the overall foreign loss account and distributes part of such income, the portion of the overall foreign loss that would be subject to recapture by the trust under paragraph (b)(1) of this section if the distributed income were accumulated shall be allocated to the beneficiaries receiving income distributions. The amount of overall foreign loss to be allocated to such beneficiaries shall be the same portion of the total amount of such overall foreign loss that would be recaptured as the amount of such income which is distributed to each beneficiary bears to the total amount of such income of the trust for such year. That portion of the overall foreign loss subject to recapture in such year that is not allocated to the beneficiaries in accordance with this paragraph (b)(3) shall be recaptured by the trust in accordance with paragraph (b)(1).

(c) Amounts allocated to beneficiaries. Amounts of a trust's overall foreign loss allocated to any beneficiary in accordance with paragraph (b)(2) or (3) of this section shall be added to the beneficiary's applicable overall foreign loss account and treated as an overall foreign loss of the beneficiary incurred in the taxable year preceding the year of such allocation. Such amounts shall be recaptured in accordance with §§ 1.904(f)-1, 1.904(f)-2, 1.904(f)-3, 1.904(f)-4, and 1.904(f)-6 out of foreign source taxable income distributed by the trust which is subject to the same separate limitation.

(d) Section 904(f)(3) dispositions to which § 1.904(f)-2(d)(4)(i) is applicable. Foreign source taxable income recognized by a trust under § 1.904(f)-2(d)(4) on a disposition of property used in a trade or business outside the United States shall be deemed to be accumulated by the trust. All such income shall be used to recapture the trust's overall foreign loss in accordance with § 1.904(f)-2(d)(4).

(e) Illustrations. The provisions of this section are illustrated by the following examples:

Example (1). T, a domestic trust, has a balance of $2,000 in a general limitation overall foreign loss account on December 31, 1983. For its taxable year ending on December 31, 1984, T has foreign source taxable income subject to the general limitation of $1,600, all of which it accumulates. Under paragraph (b)(1) of this section, T is required to recapture $800 in 1984 (the lesser of the overall foreign loss or 50 percent of the foreign source taxable income). This amount is treated as United States source income for purposes of taxing T in 1984 and upon subsequent distribution to T's beneficiaries. At the end of its 1984 taxable year, T has a balance of $1,200 in its overall foreign loss account.

Example (2). The facts are the same as in example (1). In 1985, T has general limitation foreign source taxable income of $1,000, which it distributes to its beneficiaries as follows: $500 to A, $250 to B, and $250 to C. Under paragraph (b)(1) of this section, T would have been required to recapture $500 of its overall foreign loss if it had accumulated all of such income. Therefore, under paragraph (b)(2) of this section, T must allocate $500 of its overall foreign loss to A, B, and C as follows: $250 to A ($500 $250/$1,000), and $125 to C ($500 × $250/$1,000). Under paragraph (c) of this section and § 1.904(f)-1(d)(4), A, B, and C must add the amounts of general limitation overall foreign loss allocated to them from T to their overall foreign loss accounts and treat such amounts as overall foreign losses incurred in 1984. A, B, and C must then apply the rules of §§ 1.904(f)-1, 1.904(f)-2, 1.904(f)-3, 1.904(f)-4, and 1.904(f)-6 to recapture their overall foreign losses. T's overall foreign loss account is reduced in accordance with § 1.904(f)-1(e)(1) by the $500 that is allocated to A, B, and C. At the end of 1985, T's general limitation overall foreign loss account has a balance of $700.

Example (3). The facts are the same as in example (2), including an overall foreign loss account at the end of 1984 of $1,200, except that in 1985 T's general limitation foreign source taxable income is $1,500 instead of $1,000, and T accumulates the additional $500. Under paragraph (b)(1) of this section, T would be required to recapture $750 of its overall foreign loss if it accumulated all of the $1,500. Under paragraph (b)(3) of this section, T must allocate $500 of its overall foreign loss to A, B, and C as follows: $250 to A ($750 × $500/$1,500) and $125 each to B and C (750 – $250/$1,500). T must also recapture $250 of its overall foreign loss, which is the amount subject to recapture in 1985 that is not allocated to the beneficiaries ($750 – $500 = $250). Under § 1.904(f)-1(e)(1), T reduces its general limitation overall foreign loss account by $500. Under § 1.904(f)-1(e)(2), T reduces its general limitation overall foreign loss account by $250. At the end of 1985 there is a balance in the general limitation overall foreign loss account of $450 (($1,200 – $500) – $250).

T.D. 8153, 8/21/87.

§ 1.904(f)-6 Transitional rule for recapture of FORI and general limitation overall foreign losses incurred in taxable years beginning before January 1, 1983, from foreign source taxable income subject to the general limitation in taxable years beginning after December 31, 1982.

Caution: The Treasury has not yet amended Reg § 1.904(f)-6 to reflect changes made by P.L. 100-647, P.L. 99-514.

(a) General rule. For taxable years beginning after December 31, 1982, foreign source taxable income subject to the general limitation includes foreign oil related income (as defined in section 907(c)(2) prior to its amendment by section 211 of the Tax Equity and Fiscal Responsibility Act of 1982). However, for purposes of recapturing general limitation overall foreign losses incurred in taxable years beginning before January 1, 1983 (pre-1983) out of foreign source taxable income subject to the general limitation in taxable years beginning after December 31, 1982 (post-1982), the taxpayer shall make separate determinations of foreign oil related income and other general limitation income (as if the FORI limitation under "old section 907(b)" (prior to its amendment by section 211 of the Tax Equity and Fiscal Responsibility Act of 1982) were still in effect), and shall apply the rules set forth in this section. The taxpayer shall maintain separate accounts for its pre-1983 FORI limitation overall foreign losses, its pre-1983 general limitation overall foreign losses (or its pre-1983 section 904(d)(1)(A-C) overall foreign losses if such losses were computed on a combined basis), and its post-1982 general limitation overall foreign losses. The taxpayer shall continue to maintain such separate accounts, make such separate determinations, and apply the rules of this section separately to each account until the earlier of—

(1) Such time as the taxpayer's entire pre-1983 FORI limitation overall foreign loss account and pre-1983 general limitation overall foreign loss account (or, if the taxpayer determined pre-1983 overall foreign losses on a combined basis, the section 904(d)(1)(A-C) account) have been recaptured, or

(2) The end of the taxpayer's 8th post-1982 taxable year, at which time the taxpayer shall add any remaining balance in its pre-1983 FORI limitation account and pre-1983 general limitation overall foreign loss account (or the section 904(d)(1)(A-C) account) to its post-1982 general limitation overall foreign loss account.

(b) Recapture of pre-1983 FORI and general limitation overall foreign losses from post-1982 income. A taxpayer having a balance in its pre-1983 FORI limitation overall foreign loss account or its pre-1983 general limitation overall foreign loss account (or its pre-1983 section 904(d)(1)(A-C) account) in a post-1982 taxable year shall recapture such overall foreign loss as follows:

(1) Recapture from income subject to the same limitation. The taxpayer shall first apply the rules of §§ 1.904(f)-1 through 1.904(f)-5 to the taxpayer's separately determined foreign oil related income to recapture the pre-1983 FORI limitation overall foreign loss account, and shall apply such rules to the taxpayer's separately determined general limitation income (exclusive of foreign oil related income) to recapture the pre-1983 general limitation overall foreign loss account (or the section 904(d)(1)(A-C) overall foreign loss account. Rules for determining the recapture of the pre-1983 section 904(d)(1)(A-C) losses are contained in § 1.904(f)-2(c)(4).

(2) Recapture from income subject to the other limitation. The taxpayer shall next apply the rules of § 1.904(f)-1 through -5 to the taxpayer's separately determined foreign oil related income to recapture the pre-1983 general limitation overall foreign loss account (or the section 904(d)(1)(A-C) overall foreign loss account) and shall apply such rules to the taxpayer's separately determined general limitation income to recapture foreign oil related losses to the extent that—

(i) The amount recaptured from such separately determined income under paragraph (b)(1) of this section is less than 50 percent (or such larger percentage as the taxpayer elects) of such separately determined income, and

(ii) The amount recaptured from such separately determined income under this paragraph (b)(2) does not exceed an amount equal to 12½ percent of the balance in the taxpayer's pre-1983 FORI limitation overall foreign loss account or the pre-1983 general limitation overall foreign loss account (or the section 904(d)(1)(A-C) overall foreign loss account) at the beginning of the taxpayer's first post-1982 taxable year, multiplied by the number of post-1982 taxable years (including the year to which this rule is being applied) which have elapsed, less the amount (if any) recaptured in prior post-1982 taxable years under this paragraph (b)(2) from such separately determined income.

The taxpayer may elect to recapture a pre-1983 overall foreign loss from post-1982 income subject to the general limitation at a faster rate than is required by this paragraph (b)(2). This election shall be made in the same manner as an election to recapture more than 50 percent of the income subject to recapture under section 904(f)(1), as provided in § 1.904(f)-2(c)(2).

(c) Coordination of recapture of pre-1983 and post-1982 overall foreign losses. A taxpayer incurring a general limitation overall foreign loss in any post-1982 taxable year in which the taxpayer has a balance in a pre-1983 FORI limitation or its pre-1983 general limitation overall foreign loss account (or the section 904(d)(1)(A-C) overall foreign loss account) shall establish a separate overall foreign loss account for such loss. The taxpayer shall recapture its overall foreign losses in succeeding taxable years by first applying the rules of this section to recapture its pre-1983 overall foreign losses, and then applying the rules of §§ 1.904(f)-1 through 1.904(f)-5 to recapture its post-1982 general limitation overall foreign loss. A post-1982 general limitation overall foreign loss is required to be recaptured only to the extent that the amount of foreign source taxable income recharacterized under paragraph (b) of this section is less than 50 percent of the taxpayer's total general limitation foreign source taxable income (including foreign oil related income)) for such taxable year (except as required by section 904(f)(3)). However, a taxpayer may elect to recapture at a faster rate.

(d) Illustrations. The provisions of this section are illustrated by the following examples:

Example (1). X Corporation is a domestic corporation which has the calendar year as its taxable year. On December 31, 1982, X has a balance of $1,000 in its section 904(d)(1)(A-C) overall foreign loss account. X does not have a balance in a FORI limitation overall foreign loss account. For 1983, X has income of $1,200, which was subject to the general limitation and includes foreign oil related income of $1,000 and other general limitation income of $200. In 1983, X is required to recapture $225 of its pre-1983 section 904(d)(1)(A-C) overall foreign loss account computed as follows:

Amount recaptured under paragraph (b)(1) of this section $100

The amount recaptured from general limitation income exclusive of foreign oil related income is the lesser of $1,000 (the pre-1983 loss reflected in the section 904(d)(1)(A-C) overall foreign loss account) or 50 percent of $200 (the separately determined general limitation income (exclusive of foreign oil related income).

Amount recaptured under paragraph (b)(2) of this section $125

The amount recaptured from foreign oil related income is the lesser of $900 (the remaining pre-1983 section 904(d)(1)(A-C) overall foreign loss account after recapture under paragraph (b)(1) of this section) or 50 percent of $1,000 (the separately determined foreign oil related income), but as limited by paragraph (b)(2)(ii) of this section to (12½ percent of $1,000×1)–$0, which is $125.

Total amount recaptured in 1983 .... $225

Example (2). The facts are the same as in example (1), except that X has general limitation income of $50 for 1984 and $600 for 1985, all of which is foreign oil related income. X is required to recapture $25 in 1984 and $225 in 1985 of its pre-1983 section 904(d)(1)(A-C) overall foreign loss account computed as follows:

Amount recaptured under paragraph (b)(2) of this section in 1984 .... $25

The amount recaptured from foreign oil related income is the lesser of $775 (the remaining pre-1983 section 904(d)(1)(A-C) overall foreign loss account or 50 percent of $50 (the separately determined foreign oil related income). This amount is within the limitation of paragraph (b)(2)(ii) of this section, (12½ percent of $1,000 × 2)

Amount recaptured under paragraph (b)(2) of this section in 1985 .... $225

The amount recaptured from foreign oil related income is the lesser of $750 (the remaining pre-1983 section 904(d)(1)(A-C) overall foreign loss account) or 50 percent of $600 (the separately determined foreign oil related income), but as limited by paragraph (b)(2)(ii) of this section to (12½ percent of $1,000 × 3) – ($125 1983 under paragraph (b)(2) of this section, and $25 is the amount recaptured in 1984 under paragraph (b)(2) of this section.)

Example (3). Y Corporation is a domestic corporation which has the calendar year as its taxable year. On December 31, 1982, Y has a balance of $400 in its section 904(d)(1)(A-C) overall foreign loss account. Y does not have a balance in a FORI overall foreign loss account. For 1983, Y has a general limitation overall foreign loss of $200. For 1984, Y has general limitation income of $1,200, all of which is foreign oil related income. In 1984, Y is required to recapture a total of $300 computed as follows:

Amount of pre-1983 overall foreign loss recaptured under paragraph (b)(2) of this section $100

The amount of pre-1983 section 904(d)(1)(A-C) overall foreign loss account attributable to a general limitation loss recaptured from foreign oil related income is the lesser of $400 (the loss) or 50 percent of $1,200 (the separately determined foreign oil related income), but as limited by paragraph (b)(2)(ii) of this section to (12½ percent of $400 × 2) – $0, which is $100.

Amount of post-1982 overall foreign loss recaptured under paragraph (c) of this section $200

The amount of post-1982 general limitation overall foreign loss recaptured is the amount computed under § 1.904(f)-2(c)(1), which is the lesser of $200 (the post-1982 loss) or 50 percent of $1,200 (the income), but only to the extent that the amount of pre-1983 loss recaptured under paragraph (b) of this section is less than 50 percent of such income ((50 percent of $1,200) – $100 recaptured under paragraph (b) = $500).

Total amount recaptured in 1984	$300

At the end of 1984, Y has a balance in its pre-1983 section 904(d)(1)(A-C) overall foreign loss account of $300, and has reduced its post-1982 general limitation overall foreign loss account to zero.

Example (4). Z is a domestic corporation which has the calendar year as its taxable year. On December 31, 1982, Z has a balance of $400 in its section 904(d)(1)(A-C) overall foreign loss account, and a balance of $1,000 in its FORI limitation overall foreign loss account. For 1983, Z has general limitation income of $2,000, which includes foreign oil related income of $1,000 and other general limitation income of $1,000. Keeping these amounts separate for purposes of this section, Z is required to recapture a total of $1,000 in 1983, computed as follows:

Amount recaptured under paragraph (b)(1) of this section	$900

The amount of pre-1983 section 904(d)(1)(A-C) overall foreign loss account recaptured from general limitation income exclusive of foreign oil related income, in accordance with § 1.904(f)-2(c)(1), is the lesser of $400 (the section 904(d)(1)(A-C) overall foreign loss) or 50 percent of $1,000, the general limitation income exclusive of foreign oil related income), which is $400.

The amount of pre-1983 FORI overall foreign loss recaptured from foreign oil related income, in accordance with § 1.904(f)-2(c)(1), is the lesser of $1,000 (the FORI overall foreign loss) or 50 percent of $1,000 (the foreign oil related income), which is $500.

Amount recaptured under paragraph (b)(2) of this section	$100

The amount of pre-1983 FORI 907(b) overall foreign loss recaptured from section general limitation income exclusive of foreign oil related income is the lesser of $500 (the remaining balance in that loss account) or 50 percent of $1,000 (the general limitation income exclusive of foreign oil related income), but only to the extent that the amount recaptured from such income under paragraph (b)(1) of this section is less than 50 percent of such income, or $100 (50 percent of $1,000) foreign loss account, and only up to the amount permitted by paragraph (b)(2)(ii) of this section, which is (12½ percent of $1,000

Total amount recaptured in 1983	$1,000

At the end of 1983, Z has reduced its pre-1983 section 904(d)(1)(A-C) overall foreign loss account to zero, and has a balance in its pre-1983 FORI overall foreign loss account of $400.

T.D. 8153, 8/21/87.

§ 1.904(f)-7 Separate limitation loss and the separate limitation loss account. [Reserved].

For further guidance, see § 1.904(f)-7T.

T.D. 9371, 12/20/2007.

PAR. 5.

Sections 1.904(f)-7 and 1.904(f)-8 are added to read as follows:

Proposed § 1.904(f)-7 Separate limitation loss and the separate limitation loss account. [*For Preamble, see ¶ 152,941*]

[The text of proposed § 1.904(f)-7 is the same as the text of § 1.904(f)-7T(a) through (f) published elsewhere in this issue of the Federal Register.] [*See T.D. 9371, 12/21/2007, 72 Fed. Reg. 245.*]

§ 1.904(f)-7T Separate limitation loss and the separate limitation loss account (temporary).

(a) Overview of regulations. This section provides rules for determining a taxpayer's separate limitation losses, for establishing separate limitation loss accounts, and for making additions to and reductions from such accounts for purposes of section 904(f). Section 1.904(f)-8T provides rules for recharacterizing the balance in any separate limitation loss account under the general recharacterization rule of section 904(f)(5)(C).

(b) Definitions. The definitions in paragraphs (b)(1) through (4) of this section apply for purposes of this section and §§ 1.904(f)-8T and 1.904(g)-3T.

(1) Separate category means each separate category of income described in section 904(d) and any other category of income described in § 1.904-4(m). For example, income subject to section 901(j) or 904(h)(10) is income in a separate category.

(2) Separate limitation income means, with respect to any separate category, the taxable income from sources outside the United States, separately computed for that category for the taxable year. Separate limitation income shall be determined by taking into account any adjustments for capital gains and losses under section 904(b)(2) and § 1.904(b)-1. See § 1.904(b)-1(h)(1)(i).

(3) Separate limitation loss means, with respect to any separate category, the amount by which the foreign source gross income in that category is exceeded by the sum of expenses, losses and other deductions (not including any net operating loss deduction under section 172(a) or any expropriation loss or casualty loss described in section 907(c)(4)(B)(iii)) properly allocated and apportioned thereto for the taxable year. Separate limitation losses are determined separately for each separate category. Accordingly, income and deductions attributable to a separate category are not netted with income and deductions attributable to another separate category for purposes of determining the amount of a separate limitation loss. Separate limitation losses shall be determined by taking into account any adjustments for capital gains and losses under section 904(b)(2) and § 1.904(b)-1. See § 1.904(b)-1(h)(1)(i).

(c) Separate limitation loss account. Any taxpayer that sustains a separate limitation loss that is allocated to reduce separate limitation income of the taxpayer under the rules of § 1.904(g)-3T must establish a separate limitation loss account for the loss. The taxpayer must establish separate loss accounts for each separate category in which a separate limitation loss is incurred that is allocated to reduce other separate limitation income. A separate account must then be established for each separate category to which a portion of the loss is allocated. The balance in any separate limitation loss account represents the amount of separate limitation income that is subject to recharacterization (as income in another separate category) in a subsequent year pursuant to § 1.904(f)-8T and section 904(f)(5)(F). From year to year, amounts may be added to or subtracted from the balance in such loss accounts, as provided in paragraphs (d) and (e) of this section.

(d) Additions to separate limitation loss accounts. *(1) General rule.* A taxpayer's separate limitation loss as defined in paragraph (b)(3) of this section shall be added to the applicable separate limitation loss accounts at the end of the taxable year to the extent that the separate limitation loss has reduced separate limitation income in one or more other separate categories of the taxpayer during the taxable year. For rules with respect to net operating loss carryovers, see paragraph (d)(3) of this section and § 1.904(g)-3T.

(2) Separate limitation losses of another taxpayer. If any portion of any separate limitation loss account of another taxpayer is allocated to the taxpayer in accordance with § 1.1502-9T (relating to consolidated separate limitation losses) the taxpayer shall add such amount to its applicable separate limitation loss account.

(3) Additions to separate limitation loss account created by loss carryovers. The taxpayer shall add to each separate limitation loss account all net operating loss carryovers to the current taxable year to the extent that separate limitation losses included in the net operating loss carryovers reduced foreign source income in other separate categories for the taxable year.

(e) Reductions of separate limitation loss accounts. The taxpayer shall subtract the following amounts from its separate limitation loss accounts at the end of its taxable year in the following order as applicable:

(1) Pre-recapture reduction for amounts allocated to other taxpayers. A separate limitation loss account is reduced by the amount of any separate limitation loss account which is allocated to another taxpayer in accordance with § 1.1502-9T (relating to consolidated separate limitation losses).

(2) Reduction for offsetting loss accounts. A separate limitation account is reduced to take into account any netting of separate limitation loss accounts under § 1.904(g)-3T(c).

(3) Reduction for amounts recaptured. A separate limitation loss account is reduced by the amount of any separate limitation income that is earned in the same separate category as the separate limitation loss that resulted in the account and that is recharacterized in accordance with § 1.904(f)-8T (relating to recapture of separate limitation losses) or section 904(f)(5)(F) (relating to recapture of separate limitation loss accounts out of gain realized from dispositions).

(f) Effective/applicability date. This section applies to taxpayers that sustain separate limitation losses in taxable years beginning after December 21, 2007. For taxable years beginning after December 31, 1986, and on or before December 21, 2007, see section 904(f)(5).

(g) Expiration date. The applicability of this section expires on December 20, 2010.

T.D. 9371, 12/20/2007.

§ 1.904(f)-8 Recapture of separate limitation loss accounts.

[Reserved]. For further guidance, see § 1.904(f)-8T. For further guidance, see § 1.904(f)-7T.

T.D. 9371, 12/20/2007.

PAR. 5.

Sections 1.904(f)-7 and 1.904(f)-8 are added to read as follows:

Proposed § 1.904(f)-8 Recapture of separate limitation loss accounts. [*For Preamble, see ¶ 152,941*]

[The text of proposed § 1.904(f)-8 is the same as the text of § 1.904(f)-8T(a) through (c) published elsewhere in this issue of the Federal Register.] [*See T.D. 9371, 12/21/2007, 72 Fed. Reg. 245.*]

§ 1.904(f)-8T Recapture of separate limitation loss accounts (temporary).

(a) In general. A taxpayer shall recapture a separate limitation loss account as provided in this section. If the taxpayer has a separate limitation loss account or accounts in any separate category (the ''loss category'') and the loss category has income in a subsequent taxable year, the income shall be recharacterized as income in that other category or categories. The amount of income recharacterized shall not exceed the separate limitation loss accounts for the loss category as determined under § 1.904(f)-7T, including the aggregate separate limitation loss accounts from the loss category not previously recaptured under this paragraph (a). If the taxpayer has more than one separate limitation loss account in a loss category, and there is not enough income in the loss category to recapture the entire amount in all the loss accounts, then separate limitation income in the loss category shall be recharacterized as separate limitation income in the separate limitation loss categories on a proportionate basis. This is determined by multiplying the total separate limitation income subject to recapture by a fraction, the numerator of which is the amount in a particular loss account and the denominator of which is the total amount in all loss accounts for the separate category.

(b) Effect of recapture of separate limitation income on associated taxes. Recharacterization of income under paragraph (a) of this section shall not result in the recharacterization of any tax. The rules of § 1.904-6, including the rules that the taxes are allocated on an annual basis and that foreign taxes paid on U.S. source income shall be allocated to the separate category that includes that U.S. source income (see § 1.904-6(a)), shall apply for purposes of allocating taxes to separate categories. Allocation of taxes pursuant to § 1.904-6 shall be made before the recapture of any separate limitation loss accounts of the taxpayer pursuant to the rules of this section.

(c) Effective/applicability date. This section applies to taxpayers that sustain separate limitation losses in taxable years beginning after December 21, 2007. For taxable years beginning after December 31, 1986, and on or before December 21, 2007, see section 904(f)(5).

(d) Expiration date. The applicability of this section expires on December 20, 2010.

T.D. 9371, 12/20/2007.

§ 1.904(f)-9 [Reserved]
§ 1.904(f)-10 [Reserved]
§ 1.904(f)-11 [Reserved]
§ 1.904(f)-12 Transition rules.

(a) Recapture in years beginning after December 31, 1986, of overall foreign losses incurred in taxable years beginning before January 1, 1987. *(1) In general.* If a taxpayer has a balance in an overall foreign loss account at the end of its last taxable year beginning before January 1, 1987 (pre-effective date years), the amount of that balance shall be recaptured in subsequent years by recharacterizing income received in the income category described in section 904(d) as in effect for taxable years beginning after December 31, 1986 (post-effective date years), that is analogous to the income category for which the overall foreign loss account was established, as follows:

(i) Interest income as defined in section 904(d)(1)(A) as in effect for pre-effective date taxable years is analogous to passive income as defined in section 904(d)(1)(A) as in effect for post-effective date years;

(ii) Dividends from a DISC or former DISC as defined in section 904(d)(1)(B) as in effect for pre-effective date taxable years is analogous to dividends from a DISC or former DISC as defined in section 904(d)(1)(F) as in effect for post-effective date taxable years;

(iii) Taxable income attributable to foreign trade income as defined in section 904(d)(1)(C) as in effect for pre-effective date taxable years is analogous to taxable income attributable to foreign trade income as defined in section 904(d)(1)(G) as in effect for post-effective date years;

(iv) Distributions from a FSC (or former FSC) as defined in section 904(d)(1)(D) as in effect for pre-effective date taxable years is analogous to distributions from a FSC (or former FSC) as defined in section 904(d)(1)(H) as in effect for post-effective date taxable years;

(v) For general limitation income as described in section 904(d)(1)(E) as in effect for pre-effective date taxable years, see the special rule in paragraph (a)(2) of this section.

(2) Rule for general limitation losses. (1) In general. Overall foreign losses incurred in the general limitation category of section 904(d)(1)(E), as in effect for pre-effective date taxable years, that are recaptured in post-effective date taxable years shall be recaptured from the taxpayer's general limitation income, financial services income, shipping income, and dividends from each noncontrolled section 902 corporation. If the sum of the taxpayer's general limitation income, financial services income, shipping income and dividends from each noncontrolled section 902 corporation for a taxable year subject to recapture exceeds the overall foreign loss to be recaptured, then the amount of each type of separate limitation income that will be treated as U.S. source income shall be determined as follows:

$$\text{Overall foreign loss subject to recapture} \times \frac{\text{Amount of income in each separate category from which the loss may be recaptured}}{\text{Sum of income in all separate categories from which the loss may be recaptured}}$$

This recapture shall be made after the allocation of separate limitation losses pursuant to section 904(f)(5)(B) and before the recharacterization of post-effective date separate limitation income pursuant to section 904(f)(5)(C).

(ii) Exception. If a taxpayer can demonstrate to the satisfaction of the district director that an overall foreign loss in the general limitation category of section 904(d)(1)(E), as in effect for pre-effective date taxable years, is attributable, in sums certain, to losses in one or more separate categories of section 904(d)(1) (including for this purpose the passive income category and the high withholding tax interest category), as in effect for post-effective date taxable years, then the taxpayer may recapture the loss (in the amounts demonstrated) from those separate categories only.

(3) Priority of recapture of overall foreign losses incurred in pre-effective date taxable years. An overall foreign loss incurred by a taxpayer in pre-effective date taxable years shall be recaptured to the extent thereof before the taxpayer recaptures an overall foreign loss incurred in a post-effective date taxable year.

(4) Examples. The following examples illustrate the application of this paragraph (a).

Example (1). X corporation is a domestic corporation which operates a branch in Country Y. For its taxable year ending December 31, 1988, X has $800 of financial services income, $100 of general limitation income and $100 of shipping income. X has a balance of $100 in its general limitation overall foreign loss account which resulted from an overall foreign loss incurred during its 1986 taxable year. X is unable to demonstrate to which of the income categories set forth in section 904(d)(1) as in effect for post-effective date taxable years the loss is attributable. In addition, X has a balance of $100 in its shipping overall foreign loss account attributable to a shipping loss incurred during its 1987 taxable year. X has no other overall foreign loss accounts. Pursuant to section 904(f)(1), the full amount in each of X corporation's overall foreign loss accounts is subject to recapture since $200 (the sum of those amounts) is less than 50% of X's foreign source taxable income for its 1988 taxable year, or $500. X's overall foreign loss incurred during its 1986 taxable year is recaptured before the overall foreign loss incurred during its 1987 taxable year, as follows: $80 ($100 × 800/1000) of X's financial services income, $10 ($100 × 100/1000) of X's general limitation income, and $10 (100 × 100/1000) of X's shipping income will be treated as U.S. source income. The remaining $90 of X corporation's 1988 shipping income will be treated as U.S. source income for the purpose of recapturing X's 100 overall foreign loss attributable to the shipping loss incurred in 1987. $10 remains in X's shipping overall foreign loss account for recapture in subsequent taxable years.

Example (2). The facts are the same as in Example (1) except that X has $800 of financial services income, $100 of general limitation income, a $100 dividend from a noncontrolled section 902 corporation and a ($100) shipping loss for its taxable year ending December 31, 1988. Separate limitation losses are allocated pursuant to the rules of section 904(f)(5) before the recapture of overall foreign losses. Therefore, the ($100) shipping loss incurred by X will be allocated to its separate limitation income as follows: $80 ($100 × 800/1000) will be allocated to X's financial services income, $10 ($100 × 100/1000) will be allocated to its general limitation income and $10 ($100 × 100/1000) will be allocated to X's dividend from the noncontrolled section 902 corporation. Accordingly, after allocation of the 1988 shipping loss, X has $720 of financial services income, $90 of general limitation income, and a $90 dividend from the noncontrolled section 902 corporation. Pursuant to section 904(f)(1), the full amount in each of X corporation's overall foreign loss accounts is subject to recapture since $200 (the sum of those amounts) is less than 50% of X's net foreign source taxable income for its 1988 taxable year, or $450. X's overall foreign loss incurred during its 1986 taxable year is recaptured as follows: $80 ($100 × 720/900) of X's financial services income, $10 ($100 × 90/900) of its general limitation income and $10 ($100 × 90/900) of its dividend from the noncontrolled section 902 corporation will be treated as U.S. source income. Accordingly, after application of section 904(f), X has $100 of U.S. source income, $640 of financial services income, $80 of general limitation income and a $80 dividend from the noncontrolled section 902 corporation for its 1988 taxable year. X must establish a separate limitation loss account for each portion of the 1988 shipping loss that was allocated to its financial services income, general limitation income and dividends from the noncontrolled section 902 corporation. X's overall foreign loss account for the 1986 general limitation loss is reduced to zero. X still has a

$100 balance in its overall foreign loss account that resulted from the 1987 shipping loss.

Example (3). Y is a domestic corporation which has a branch operation in Country Z. For its 1988 taxable year, Y has $5 of shipping income, $15 of general limitation income and $100 of financial services income. Y has a balance of $100 in its general limitation overall foreign loss account attributable to its 1986 taxable year. Y has no other overall foreign loss accounts. Pursuant to section 904(f)(1), $60 of the overall foreign loss is subject to recapture since 50% of Y's foreign source income for 1988 is less than the balance in its overall foreign loss account. Y can demonstrate that the entire $100 overall foreign loss was attributable to a shipping limitation loss incurred in 1986. Accordingly, only Y's $5 of shipping limitation income received in 1988 will be treated as U.S. source income. Because Y can demonstrate that the 1986 loss was entirely attributable to a shipping loss, none of Y's general limitation income or financial services income received in 1988 will be treated as U.S. source income.

Example (4). The facts are the same as in Example (3) except that Y can only demonstrate that $50 of the 1986 overall foreign loss account was attributable to a shipping loss incurred in 1986. Accordingly, Y's $5 of shipping limitation income received in 1988 will be treated as U.S. source income. The remaining $50 of the 1986 overall foreign loss that Y cannot trace to a particular separate limitation will be recaptured and treated as U.S. source income as follows: $43 ($50 × 100/115) of Y's financial services income will be treated as U.S. source income and $7 ($50 × 15/115) of Y's general limitation income will be treated as U.S. source income. Y has $45 remaining in its overall foreign loss account to be recaptured from shipping income in a future year.

(b) Treatment of overall foreign losses that are part of net operating losses incurred in pre-effective date taxable years which are carried forward to post-effective date taxable years. *(1) Rule.* An overall foreign loss that is part of a net operating loss incurred in a pre-effective date taxable year which is carried forward, pursuant to section 172, to a post-effective date taxable year will be carried forward under the rules of section 904(f)(5) and the regulations under that section. See also Notice 89-3, 1989-1 C.B. 623. For this purpose the loss must be allocated to income in the category analogous to the income category set forth in section 904(d) as in effect for pre-effective date taxable years in which the loss occurred. The analogous category shall be determined under the rules of paragraph (a) of this section.

(2) Example. The following example illustrates the rule of paragraph (b)(1) of this section.

Example. Z is a domestic corporation which has a branch operation in Country D. For its taxable year ending December 31, 1988, Z has $100 of passive income and $200 of general limitation income. Z also has a $60 net operating loss which was carried forward pursuant to section 172 from its 1986 taxable year. The net operating loss resulted from an overall foreign loss attributable to the general limitation income category. Z can demonstrate that the loss is a shipping loss. Therefore, the net operating loss will be treated as a shipping loss for Z's 1988 taxable year. Pursuant to section 904(f)(5), the shipping loss will be allocated as follows: $20 ($60 × 100/300) will be allocated to Z's passive income and $40 ($60 × 200/300) will be allocated to Z's general limitation income. Accordingly, after application of section 904(f), Z has $80 of passive income and $160 of general limitation income for its 1988 taxable year. Although no addition to Z's overall foreign loss account for shipping income will result from the NOL carry forward, shipping income earned by Z in subsequent taxable years, will be subject to recharacterization as a passive income and general limitation income pursuant to the rules set forth in section 904(f)(5).

(c) Treatment of overall foreign losses that are part of net operating losses incurred in post-effective date taxable years which are carried back to pre-effective date taxable years. *(1) Allocation to analogous income category.* An overall foreign loss that is part of a net operating loss incurred by the taxpayer in a post-effective date taxable year which is carried back, pursuant to section 172, to a pre-effective date taxable year shall be allocated first to income in the pre-effective date income category analogous to the income category set forth in section 904(d) as in effect for post-effective date taxable years in which the loss occurred. Except for the general limitation income category, the pre-effective date income category that is analogous to a post-effective date income category shall be determined under paragraphs (a)(1)(i) through (iv) of this section. The general limitation income category for pre-effective date years shall be treated as the income category that is analogous to the post-effective date categories for general limitation income, financial services income, shipping income, dividends from each noncontrolled section 902 corporation and high withholding tax interest income. If the net operating loss resulted from separate limitation losses in more than one post-effective date income category and more than one loss is carried back to pre-effective date general limitation income, then the losses shall be allocated to the pre-effective date general limitation income based on the following formula:

$$\text{Pre-effective date general limitation income} \times \frac{\text{Loss in each post-effective date separate limitation category that is analogous to pre-effective date general limitation income}}{\text{Losses in all post-effective categories that are analogous to pre-effective date general limitation income}}$$

(2) Allocation to U.S. source income. If an overall foreign loss is carried back to a pre-effective date taxable year and the loss exceeds the foreign source income in the analogous category for the carry back year, the remaining loss shall be allocated against U.S. source income as set forth in § 1.904(f)-3. The amount of the loss that offsets U.S. source income must be added to the taxpayer's overall foreign loss account. An addition to an overall foreign loss account resulting from the carry back of a net operating loss incurred by a taxpayer in a post-effective date taxable year shall be treated as having been incurred by the taxpayer in the year in which the loss arose and shall be subject to recapture pursuant to section 904(f) as in effect for post-effective date taxable years.

(3) Allocation to other separate limitation categories. To the extent that an overall foreign loss that is carried back as part of a net operating loss exceeds the separate limitation income to which it is allocated and the U.S. source income of the taxpayer for the taxable year to which the loss is car-

ried, the loss shall be allocated pro rata to other separate limitation income of the taxpayer for the taxable year. However, there shall be no recharacterization of separate limitation income pursuant to section 904(f)(5) as a result of the allocation of such a net operating loss to other separate limitation income of the taxpayer.

(4) Examples. The following examples illustrate the rules of paragraph (c) of this section.

Example (1). X is a domestic corporation which has a branch operation in Country A. For its taxable year ending December 31, 1987, X has a $60 net operating loss which is carried back pursuant to section 172 to its taxable year ending December 31, 1985. The net operating loss resulted from a shipping loss; X had no U.S. source income in 1987. X had $20 of general limitation income, $40 of DISC limitation income and $10 of U.S. source income for its 1985 taxable year. The $60 NOL is allocated first to X's 1985 general limitation income to the extent thereof ($20) since the general limitation income category of section 904(d) as in effect for pre-effective date taxable years is the income category that is analogous to shipping income for post-effective date taxable years. Therefore, X has no general limitation income for its 1985 taxable year. Next, pursuant to section 904(f) as in effect for pre-effective date taxable years, the remaining $40 of the NOL is allocated first to X's $10 of U.S. source income and then to $30 of X's DISC limitation income for its 1985 taxable year. Accordingly, X has no U.S. source income and $10 of DISC limitation income for its 1985 taxable year after allocation of the NOL. X has a $10 balance in its shipping overall foreign loss account which is subject to recapture pursuant to section 904(f) as in effect for post-effective date taxable years. X will not be required to recharacterize, pursuant to section 904(f)(5), subsequent shipping income as DISC limitation income.

Example (2). Y is a domestic corporation which has a branch operation in Country B. For its taxable year ending December 31, 1987, X has a $200 net operating loss which is carried back pursuant to section 172 to its taxable year ending December 31, 1986. The net operating loss resulted from a ($100) general limitation loss and a ($100) shipping loss. Y had $100 of general limitation income and $200 of U.S. source income for its taxable year ending December 31, 1986. The separate limitation losses for 1987 are allocated pro rata to Y's 1986 general limitation income as follows: $50 of the ($100) general limitation loss ($100 × 100/200) and $50 of the ($100) shipping loss ($100 × 100/200) is allocated to Y's $100 of 1986 general limitation income. The remaining $50 of Y's general limitation loss and the remaining $50 of Y's shipping loss are allocated to Y's 1986 U.S. source income. Accordingly, Y has no foreign source income and $100 of U.S. source income for its 1986 taxable year. Y has a $50 balance in its general limitation overall foreign loss account and a $50 balance in its shipping overall foreign loss account, both of which will be subject to recapture pursuant to section 904(f) as in effect for post-effective date taxable years.

(d) Recapture of FORI and general limitation overall foreign losses incurred in taxable years beginning before January 1, 1983. For taxable years beginning after December 31, 1986, and before January 1, 1991, the rules set forth in § 1.904(f)-6 shall apply for purposes of recapturing general limitation and foreign oil related income (FORI) overall foreign losses incurred in taxable years beginning before January 1, 1983 (pre-1983). For taxable years beginning after December 31, 1990, the rules set forth in this section shall apply for purposes of recapturing pre-1983 general limitation and FORI overall foreign losses.

(e) Recapture of pre-1983 overall foreign losses determined on a combined basis. The rules set forth in paragraph (a)(2) of this section shall apply for purposes of recapturing overall foreign losses incurred in taxable years beginning before January 1, 1983, that were computed on a combined basis in accordance with § 1.904(f)-1(c)(1).

(f) Transition rules for taxable years beginning before December 31, 1990. For transition rules for taxable years beginning before January 1, 1990, see 26 CFR § 1.904(f)-13T as it appeared in the Code of Federal Regulations revised as of April 1, 1990.

(g) Recapture in years beginning after December 31, 2002, of separate limitation losses and overall foreign losses incurred in years beginning before January 1, 2003, with respect to the separate category for dividends from a noncontrolled section 902 corporation. [Reserved] For further guidance, see § 1.904(f)-12T(g).

(h) [Reserved.] For further guidance, see § 1.904(f)-12T(h).

T.D. 8306, 8/1/90, amend T.D. 9260, 4/24/2006, T.D. 9368, 12/20/2007.

PAR. 6. § 1.904(f)-12(h) is added to read as follows:

Proposed § 1.904(f)-12 Transition rules. [*For Preamble, see ¶ 152,939*]

* * * * *

(h) [The text of proposed § 1.904-12(h) is the same as the text of § 1.904-12T(h)(1) through (h)(6) published elsewhere in this issue of the Federal Register.] [*See T.D. 9368, 12/21/2007, 72 Fed. Reg. 245.*]

PAR. 9. In § 1.904(f)-12, paragraph (g) is added as follows:

Proposed § 1.904(f)-12 Transition rules. [*For Preamble, see ¶ 152,753*]

* * * * *

(g) [The text of proposed § 1.904(f)-12(g) is the same as the text of § 1.904(f)-12T(g) published elsewhere in this issue of the Federal Register.] [*See T.D. 9260, 04/24/2006, 71 Fed. Reg. 79.*]

§ 1.904(f)-12T Transition rules (temporary).

• ***Caution:*** Under Code Sec. 7805, temporary regulations expire within three years of the date of issuance. This temporary regulation was issued on 4/24/2006.

(a) through (f) [Reserved]. For further guidance, see § 1.904(f)-12(a) through (f).

(g) Recapture in years beginning after December 31, 2002, of separate limitation losses and overall foreign losses incurred in years beginning before January 1, 2003, with respect to the separate category for dividends from a noncontrolled section 902 corporation. *(1) Recapture of separate limitation loss or overall foreign loss in a separate category for dividends from a noncontrolled section 902 corporation.* To the extent that a taxpayer has a balance in any separate limitation loss or overall foreign loss account in a separate category for dividends from a noncontrolled section 902 corporation under section 904(d)(1)(E) (prior to its repeal by Public Law 108-357, 118 Stat. 1418 (October 22, 2004)) at the end of the taxpayer's last taxable year beginning before January 1, 2003 (or a later taxable year in which the taxpayer received a dividend subject to a separate limitation for dividends from that noncontrolled section 902 corporation), the amount of such balance shall be allocated on the first day of the taxpayer's next taxable year to the taxpayer's other separate categories. The amount of such balance shall be allocated in the same percentages as the taxpayer properly characterized the stock of the noncontrolled section 902 corporation for purposes of apportioning the taxpayer's interest expense for its first taxable year ending after the first day of such corporation's first taxable year beginning after December 31, 2002, under § 1.861-12T(c)(3) or (c)(4), as the case may be. To the extent a taxpayer has a balance in any separate limitation loss account in a separate category for dividends from a noncontrolled section 902 corporation with respect to another separate category, and the separate limitation loss would otherwise be assigned to that other category under this paragraph (g)(1), such balance shall be eliminated.

(2) Recapture of separate limitation loss in another separate category. To the extent that a taxpayer has a balance in any separate limitation loss account in a separate category with respect to a separate category for dividends from a noncontrolled section 902 corporation under section 904(d)(1)(E) (prior to its repeal by Public Law 108-357, 118 Stat. 1418 (October 22, 2004)) at the end of the taxpayer's last taxable year with or within which ends the last taxable year of the noncontrolled section 902 corporation beginning before January 1, 2003, such loss shall be recaptured in subsequent taxable years as income in the appropriate separate categories. The separate limitation loss shall be recaptured as income in other separate categories in the same percentages as the taxpayer properly characterizes the stock of the noncontrolled section 902 corporation for purposes of apportioning the taxpayer's interest expense in its first taxable year ending after the first day of the foreign corporation's first taxable year beginning after December 31, 2002, under § 1.861-12T(c)(3) or (c)(4), as the case may be. To the extent a taxpayer has a balance in a separate limitation loss account in a separate category that would have been recaptured as income in that same category under this paragraph (g)(2), such balance shall be eliminated.

(3) Exception. Where a taxpayer formerly met the stock ownership requirements of section 902(a) with respect to a foreign corporation, but did not meet the requirements of section 902(a) on December 20, 2002 (or on the first day of the taxpayer's first taxable year beginning after December 31, 2002, in the case of a transaction that was the subject of a binding contract in effect on December 20, 2002), if the taxpayer has a balance in any separate limitation loss or overall foreign loss account for a separate category for dividends from that foreign corporation under section 904(d)(1)(E) (prior to its repeal by Public Law 108-357, 118 Stat. 1418 (October 22, 2004)) at the end of the taxpayer's last taxable year beginning before January 1, 2003, then the amount of such balance shall not be subject to recapture under section 904(f) and this section. If a separate limitation loss or overall foreign loss account for such category is not subject to recapture under this paragraph (g)(3), the taxpayer cannot carry over any unused foreign taxes in such separate category to any other limitation category. However, a taxpayer may elect to recapture the balances of all separate limitation loss and overall foreign loss accounts for all separate categories for dividends from such formerly-owned noncontrolled section 902 corporations under the rules of paragraphs (g)(1) and (2) of this section. If a taxpayer so elects, it may carry over any unused foreign taxes in these separate categories to the appropriate separate categories as provided in § 1.904-2T(h).

(4) Examples. The following examples illustrate the application of this paragraph (g):

Example (1). X is a domestic corporation that meets the ownership requirements of section 902(a) with respect to Y, a foreign corporation the stock of which X owns 50 percent. Therefore, Y is a noncontrolled section 902 corporation with respect to X. Both X and Y use the calendar year as their taxable year. As of December 31, 2002, X had a $100 balance in its separate limitation loss account for the separate category for dividends from Y, of which $60 offset general limitation income and $40 offset passive income. For purposes of apportioning X's interest expense for its 2003 taxable year, X properly characterized the stock of Y as a multiple category asset (80% general and 20% passive). Under paragraph (g)(1) of this section, on January 1, 2003, $80 ($100 x 80/100) of the $100 balance in the separate limitation loss account is assigned to the general limitation category. Of this $80 balance, $32 ($80 x 40/100) is with respect to the passive category, and $48 ($80 x 60/100) is with respect to the general limitation category and therefore is eliminated. The remaining $20 balance ($100 x 20/100) of the $100 balance is assigned to the passive category. Of this $20 balance, $12 ($20 x 60/100) is with respect to the general limitation category, and $8 ($20 x 40/100) is with respect to the passive category and therefore is eliminated.

Example (2). The facts are the same as in Example 1, except that as of December 31, 2002, X had a $30 balance in its separate limitation loss account in the general limitation category, and a $20 balance in its separate limitation loss account in the passive category, both of which offset income in the separate category for dividends from Y. Under paragraph (g)(2) of this section, the separate limitation loss accounts in the general limitation and passive categories with respect to the separate category for dividends from Y will be recaptured on and after January 1, 2003, from income in other separate categories, as follows. Of the $30 balance in X's separate limitation loss account in the general category with respect to the separate category for dividends from Y, $6 ($30 x 20/100) is with respect to the passive category, and $24 ($30 x 80/100) is with respect to the general limitation category and therefore is eliminated. Of the $20 balance in X's separate limitation loss account in the passive category with respect to the separate category for dividends from Y, $16 ($20 x 80/100) will be recaptured out of general limitation income, and $4 ($20 x 20/100) would otherwise be recaptured out of passive income and therefore is eliminated.

(5) Effective date. This paragraph (g) shall apply for taxable years beginning after December 31, 2002.

(h) Recapture in years beginning after December 31, 2006, of separate limitation losses and overall foreign losses incurred in years beginning before January 1, 2007. *(1) Losses related to pre-2007 separate categories for passive income, certain dividends from a DISC or former DISC, taxable income attributable to certain foreign trade income or certain distributions from a FSC or former FSC.* (i) Recapture of separate limitation loss or overall foreign loss incurred in a pre-2007 separate category for passive income, certain dividends from a DISC or former DISC, taxable income attributable to certain foreign trade income or certain distributions from a FSC or former FSC. To the extent that a taxpayer has a balance in any separate limitation loss or overall foreign loss account in a pre-2007 separate category (as defined in § 1.904-7T(g)(1)(ii)) for passive income, certain dividends from a DISC or former DISC, taxable income attributable to certain foreign trade income or certain distributions from a FSC or former FSC, at the end of the taxpayer's last taxable year beginning before January 1, 2007, the amount of such balance, or balances, shall be allocated on the first day of the taxpayer's next taxable year to the taxpayer's post-2006 separate category (as defined in § 1.904-7T(g)(1)(iii)) for passive category income.

(ii) Recapture of separate limitation loss with respect to a pre-2007 separate category for passive income, certain dividends from a DISC or former DISC, taxable income attributable to certain foreign trade income or certain distributions from a FSC or former FSC. To the extent that a taxpayer has a balance in any separate limitation loss account in any pre-2007 separate category with respect to a pre-2007 separate category for passive income, certain dividends from a DISC or former DISC, taxable income attributable to certain foreign trade income or certain distributions from a FSC or former FSC at the end of the taxpayer's last taxable year beginning before January 1, 2007, such loss shall be recaptured in subsequent taxable years as income in the post-2006 separate category for passive category income.

(2) Losses related to pre-2007 separate categories for shipping, financial services income or general limitation income. (i) Recapture of separate limitation loss or overall foreign loss incurred in a pre-2007 separate category for shipping income, financial services income or general limitation income. To the extent that a taxpayer has a balance in any separate limitation loss or overall foreign loss account in a pre-2007 separate category for shipping income, financial services income or general limitation income at the end of the taxpayer's last taxable year beginning before January 1, 2007, the amount of such balance, or balances, shall be allocated on the first day of the taxpayer's next taxable year to the taxpayer's post-2006 separate category for general category income.

(ii) Recapture of separate limitation loss with respect to a pre-2007 separate category for shipping income, financial services income or general limitation income. To the extent that a taxpayer has a balance in any separate limitation loss account in any pre-2007 separate category with respect to a pre-2007 separate category for shipping income, financial services income or general limitation income at the end of the taxpayer's last taxable year beginning before January 1, 2007, such loss shall be recaptured in subsequent taxable years as income in the post-2006 separate category for general category income.

(3) Losses related to a pre-2007 separate category for high withholding tax interest. (i) Recapture of separate limitation loss or overall foreign loss incurred in a pre-2007 separate category for high withholding tax interest. To the extent that a taxpayer has a balance in any separate limitation loss or overall foreign loss account in a pre-2007 separate category for high withholding tax interest at the end of the taxpayer's last taxable year beginning before January 1, 2007, the amount of such balance shall be allocated on the first day of the taxpayer's next taxable year on a pro rata basis to the taxpayer's post-2006 separate categories for general category and passive category income, based on the proportion in which any unused foreign taxes in the same pre-2007 separate category for high withholding tax interest are allocated under § 1.904-2T(i)(1). If the taxpayer has no unused foreign taxes in the pre-2007 separate category for high withholding tax interest, then any loss account balance in that category shall be allocated to the post-2006 separate category for passive category income.

(ii) Recapture of separate limitation loss with respect to a pre-2007 separate category for high withholding tax interest. To the extent that a taxpayer has a balance in a separate limitation loss account in any pre-2007 separate category with respect to a pre-2007 separate category for high withholding tax interest at the end of the taxpayer's last taxable year beginning before January 1, 2007, such loss shall be recaptured in subsequent taxable years on a pro rata basis as income in the post-2006 separate categories for general category and passive category income, based on the proportion in which any unused foreign taxes in the pre-2007 separate category for high withholding tax interest are allocated under § 1.904-2T(i)(1). If the taxpayer has no unused foreign taxes in the pre-2007 separate category for high withholding tax interest, then the loss account balance shall be recaptured in subsequent taxable years solely as income in the post-2006 separate category for passive category income.

(4) Elimination of certain separate limitation loss accounts. After application of paragraphs (h)(1) through (h)(3) of this section, any separate limitation loss account allocated to the post-2006 separate category for passive category income for which income is to be recaptured as passive category income, as determined under those same provisions, shall be eliminated. Similarly, after application of paragraphs (h)(1) through (h)(3) of this section, any separate limitation loss account allocated to the post-2006 separate category for general category income for which income is to be recaptured as general category income, as determined under those same provisions, shall be eliminated.

(5) Alternative method. In lieu of applying the rules of paragraphs (h)(1) through (h)(3) of this section, a taxpayer may apply the principles of paragraphs (g)(1) and (g)(2) of this section to determine recapture in taxable years beginning after December 31, 2006, of separate limitation losses and overall foreign losses incurred in taxable years beginning before January 1, 2007.

(6) Effective/applicability date. This paragraph (h) shall apply to taxable years of United States taxpayers beginning after December 31, 2006 and ending on or after December 21, 2007.

(7) Expiration date. The applicability of this paragraph (h) expires on December 20, 2010.

T.D. 9260, 4/24/2006, amend T.D. 9368, 12/20/2007.

§ 1.904(g)-0 Outline of regulation provisions.

This section lists the headings for §§ 1.904(g)-1 through 1.904(g)-3.

§ 1.904(g)-1 Overall domestic loss and the overall domestic loss account.

[Reserved]. For further guidance, see the entries for § 1.904(g)-1T in § 1.904(g)-0T.

§ 1.904(g)-2 Recapture of overall domestic losses.

[Reserved]. For further guidance, see the entries for § 1.904(g)-2T in § 1.904(g)-0T.

§ 1.904(g)-3 Ordering rules for the allocation of net operating losses, net capital losses, U.S. source losses, and separate limitation losses, and for recapture of separate limitation losses, overall foreign losses, and overall domestic losses.

[Reserved]. For further guidance, see the entries for § 1.904(g)-3T in § 1.904(g)-0T.

T.D. 9371, 12/20/2007.

Proposed § 1.904(g)-0 Outline of regulation provisions. [*For Preamble, see ¶ 152,941*]

* * * * *

§ 1.904(g)-1 Overall domestic loss and the overall domestic loss account. [The text of the entries for this section is the same as the text for § 1.904(g)-1T(a) through (f) in § 1.904(g)-0T published elsewhere in this issue of the Federal Register.] [*See T.D. 9371, 12/21/2007, 72 Fed. Reg. 245.*]

§ 1.904(g)-2 Recapture of overall domestic losses. [The text of the entries for this section is the same as the text for § 1.904(g)-2T(a) through (d) in § 1.904(g)-0T published elsewhere in this issue of the Federal Register.] [*See T.D. 9371, 12/21/2007, 72 Fed. Reg. 245.*]

§ 1.904(g)-3 Ordering rules for the allocation of net operating losses, net capital losses, U.S. source losses, and separate limitation losses, and for recapture of separate limitation losses, overall foreign losses, and overall domestic losses. [The text of the entries for this section is the same as the text for § 1.904(g)-3T(a) through (i) in § 1.904(g)-0T published elsewhere in this issue of the Federal Register.] [*See T.D. 9371, 12/21/2007, 72 Fed. Reg. 245.*]

§ 1.904(g)-0T Outline of regulation provisions (temporary).

This section lists the headings for §§ 1.904(g)-1T through 1.904(g)-3T.

§ 1.904(g)-1T Overall domestic loss and the overall domestic loss account (temporary).

(a) Overview of regulations.

(b) Overall domestic loss accounts.

(1) In general.

(2) Taxable year in which overall domestic loss is sustained.

(c) Determination of a taxpayer's overall domestic loss.

(1) Overall domestic loss defined.

(2) Domestic loss defined.

(3) Qualified taxable year defined.

(4) Method of allocation and apportionment of deductions.

(d) Additions to overall domestic loss accounts.

(1) General rule.

(2) Overall domestic loss of another taxpayer.

(3) Adjustments for capital gains and losses.

(e) Reductions of overall domestic loss accounts.

(1) Pre-recapture reduction for amounts allocated to other taxpayers.

(2) Reduction for amounts recaptured.

(f) Effective/applicability date.

(g) Expiration date.

§ 1.904(g)-2T Recapture of overall domestic losses (temporary).

(a) In general.

(b) Determination of U.S. source taxable income for purposes of recapture.

(c) Section 904(g)(1) recapture.

(d) Effective/applicability date.

(e) Expiration date.

§ 1.904(g)-3T Ordering rules for the allocation of net operating losses, net capital losses, U.S. source losses, and separate limitation losses, and for recapture of separate limitation losses, overall foreign losses, and overall domestic losses (temporary).

(a) In general.

(b) Step One: Allocation of net operating loss and net capital loss carryovers.

(1) In general.

(2) Full net operating loss carryover.

(3) Partial net operating loss carryover.

(4) Net capital loss carryovers.

(c) Step Two: Allocation of separate limitation losses.

(d) Step Three: Allocation of U.S. source losses.

(e) Step Four: Recapture of overall foreign loss accounts.

(f) Step Five: Recapture of separate limitation loss accounts.

(g) Step Six: Recapture of overall domestic loss accounts.

(h) Examples.

(i) Effective/applicability date.

(j) Expiration date.

T.D. 9371, 12/20/2007.

§ 1.904(g)-1 Overall domestic loss and the overall domestic loss account.

[Reserved]. For further guidance, see § 1.904(g)-1T.

T.D. 9371, 12/20/2007.

Proposed § 1.904(g)-1 Overall domestic loss and the overall domestic loss account. [*For Preamble, see ¶ 152,941*]

[The text of proposed § 1.904(g)-1 is the same text of § 1.904(g)-1T(a) through (f) published elsewhere in this issue of the Federal Register.] [*See T.D. 9371, 12/21/2007, 72 Fed. Reg. 245.*]

§ 1.904(g)-1T Overall domestic loss and the overall domestic loss account (temporary).

(a) Overview of regulations. This section provides rules for determining a taxpayer's overall domestic losses, for establishing overall domestic loss accounts, and for making additions to and reductions from such accounts for purposes of section 904(g). Section 1.904(g)-2T provides rules for recapturing the balance in any overall domestic loss account under the general recharacterization rule of section 904(g)(1). Section 1.904(g)-3T provides ordering rules for the allocation of net operating losses, net capital losses, U.S. source losses, and separate limitation losses, and the recapture of separate limitation losses, overall foreign losses and overall domestic losses.

(b) Overall domestic loss accounts. *(1) In general.* Any taxpayer that sustains an overall domestic loss under paragraph (c) of this section must establish an account for such loss. Separate overall domestic loss accounts must be maintained with respect to each separate category in which foreign source income is offset by the domestic loss. The balance in each overall domestic loss account represents the amount of such overall domestic loss subject to recapture in a given year. From year to year, amounts may be added to or subtracted from the balances in such accounts as provided in paragraphs (d) and (e) of this section.

(2) Taxable year in which overall domestic loss is sustained. When a taxpayer incurs a domestic loss that is carried back as part of a net operating loss to offset foreign source income in a qualified taxable year, as defined in paragraph (c)(3) of this section, the resulting overall domestic loss is treated as sustained in the later year in which the domestic loss was incurred and not in the earlier year in which the loss offset foreign source income. Similarly, when a taxpayer incurs a domestic loss that is carried forward as part of a net operating loss and applied to offset foreign source income in a later taxable year, the resulting overall domestic loss is treated as sustained in the later year in which the domestic loss offsets foreign source income and not in the earlier year in which the loss was incurred. For example, if a taxpayer incurs a domestic loss in the 2007 taxable year that is carried back to the 2006 qualified taxable year and offsets foreign source income in 2006, the resulting overall domestic loss is treated as sustained in the 2007 taxable year. If a taxpayer incurs a domestic loss in a pre-2007 taxable year that is carried forward to a post-2006 qualified taxable year and offsets foreign source income in the post-2006 year, the resulting overall domestic loss is treated as sustained in the post-2006 year. The overall domestic loss account is established at the end of the later of the taxable year in which the domestic loss arose or the qualified taxable year to which the loss is carried and applied to offset foreign source income, and will be recaptured from U.S. source income arising in subsequent taxable years.

(c) Determination of a taxpayer's overall domestic loss. *(1) Overall domestic loss defined.* For taxable years beginning after December 31, 2006, a taxpayer sustains an overall domestic loss--

(i) In any qualified taxable year in which its domestic loss for such taxable year offsets foreign source taxable income for the taxable year or for any preceding qualified taxable year by reason of a carryback; and

(ii) In any other taxable year in which the domestic loss for such taxable year offsets foreign source taxable income for any preceding qualified taxable year by reason of a carryback.

(2) Domestic loss defined. For purposes of this section and §§ 1.904(g)-2T and 1.904(g)-3T, the term domestic loss means the amount by which the U.S. source gross income for the taxable year is exceeded by the sum of the expenses, losses and other deductions properly apportioned or allocated to such income, taking into account any net operating loss carried forward from a prior taxable year, but not any loss carried back. If a taxpayer has any capital gains or losses, the amount of the taxpayer's domestic loss shall be determined by taking into account adjustments under section 904(b)(2) and § 1.904(b)-1. See § 1.904(b)-1(h)(1)(iii).

(3) Qualified taxable year defined. For purposes of this section and §§ 1.904(g)-2T and 1.904(g)-3T, the term qualified taxable year means any taxable year for which the taxpayer chooses the benefits of section 901.

(4) Method of allocation and apportionment of deductions. In determining its overall domestic loss, a taxpayer shall allocate and apportion expenses, losses, and other deductions to U.S. gross income in accordance with sections 861(b) and 865 and the regulations thereunder, including §§ 1.861-8T through 1.861-14T.

(d) Additions to overall domestic loss accounts. *(1) General rule.* A taxpayer's overall domestic loss as determined under paragraph (c) of this section shall be added to the applicable overall domestic loss account at the end of its taxable year to the extent that the overall domestic loss either reduces foreign source income for the year (but only if such year is a qualified taxable year) or reduces foreign source income for a qualified taxable year to which the loss has been carried back.

(2) Overall domestic loss of another taxpayer. If any portion of any overall domestic loss of another taxpayer is allocated to the taxpayer in accordance with § 1.1502-9T (relating to consolidated overall domestic losses) the taxpayer shall add such amount to its applicable overall domestic loss account.

(3) Adjustments for capital gains and losses. If the taxpayer has capital gains or losses, the amount by which an overall domestic loss reduces foreign source income in a taxable year shall be determined in accordance with § 1.904(b)-1(h)(1)(i) and (iii).

(e) Reductions of overall domestic loss accounts. The taxpayer shall subtract the following amounts from its overall domestic loss accounts at the end of its taxable year in the following order, if applicable:

(1) Pre-recapture reduction for amounts allocated to other taxpayers. An overall domestic loss account is reduced by the amount of any overall domestic loss which is allocated to another taxpayer in accordance with § 1.1502-9T (relating to consolidated overall domestic losses).

(2) Reduction for amounts recaptured. An overall domestic loss account is reduced by the amount of any U.S. source income that is recharacterized in accordance with § 1.904(g)-2T(c) (relating to recapture under section 904(g)(1)).

(f) Effective/applicability date. This section applies to any taxpayer that sustains an overall domestic loss for a taxable year beginning after December 21, 2007. Taxpayers may choose to apply this section to overall domestic losses sustained in other taxable years beginning after December 31, 2006, as well.

(g) Expiration date. The applicability of this section expires on December 20, 2010.

T.D. 9371, 12/20/2007.

---

§ 1.904(g)-2 Recapture of overall domestic losses.

[Reserved]. For further guidance, see § 1.904(g)-2T.

T.D. 9371, 12/20/2007.

Proposed § 1.904(g)-2 Recapture of overall domestic losses. [*For Preamble, see ¶ 152,941*]

[The text of proposed § 1.904(g)-2 is the same text of § 1.904(g)-2T(a) through (d) published elsewhere in this issue of the Federal Register.] [*See T.D. 9371, 12/21/2007, 72 Fed. Reg. 245.*]

§ 1.904(g)-2T Recapture of overall domestic losses (temporary).

(a) In general. A taxpayer shall recapture an overall domestic loss as provided in this section. Recapture is accomplished by treating a portion of the taxpayer's U.S. source taxable income as foreign source income. The recharacterized income is allocated among and increases foreign source income in separate categories in proportion to the balances of the overall domestic loss accounts with respect to those separate categories. As a result, if the taxpayer elects the benefits of section 901, the taxpayer's foreign tax credit limitation is increased. As provided in § 1.904(g)-1T(f)(2), the balance in a taxpayer's overall domestic loss account with respect to a separate category is reduced at the end of each taxable year by the amount of loss recaptured during that taxable year. Recapture continues until such time as the amount of U.S. source income recharacterized as foreign source income equals the amount in the overall domestic loss account.

(b) Determination of U.S. source taxable income for purposes of recapture. For purposes of determining the amount of an overall domestic loss subject to recapture, the taxpayer's taxable income from U.S. sources shall be computed in accordance with the rules set forth in § 1.904(g)-1T(c)(4).

(c) Section 904(g)(1) recapture. The amount of any U.S. source taxable income subject to recharacterization in a taxable year in which paragraph (a) of this section is applicable is the lesser of the aggregate balance in taxpayer's overall domestic loss accounts in each separate category (after reduction of such account in accordance with § 1.904(g)-1T(e)) or fifty percent of the taxpayer's U.S. source taxable income (as determined under paragraph (b) of this section).

(d) Effective/applicability date. This section applies to any taxpayer that sustains an overall domestic loss for a taxable year beginning after December 21, 2007. Taxpayers may choose to apply this section to overall domestic losses sustained in other taxable years beginning after December 31, 2006, as well.

(e) Expiration date. The applicability of this section expires on December 20, 2010.

T.D. 9371, 12/20/2007.

§ 1.904(g)-3 Ordering rules for the allocation of net operating losses, net capital losses, U.S. source losses, and separate limitation losses, and for recapture of separate limitation losses, overall foreign losses, and overall domestic losses.

[Reserved]. For further guidance, see § 1.904(g)-3T.

T.D. 9371, 12/20/2007.

Proposed § 1.904(g)-3 Ordering rules for the allocation of net operating losses, net capital losses, U.S. source losses, and separate limitation losses, and for recapture of separate limitation losses, overall foreign losses, and overall domestic losses. [*For Preamble, see ¶ 152,941*]

[The text of proposed § 1.904(g)-3 is the same text of § 1.904(g)-3T(a) through (i) published elsewhere in this issue of the Federal Register.] [*See T.D. 9371, 12/21/2007, 72 Fed. Reg. 245.*]

§ 1.904(g)-3T Ordering rules for the allocation of net operating losses, net capital losses, U.S. source losses, and separate limitation losses, and for recapture of separate limitation losses, overall foreign losses, and overall domestic losses (temporary).

(a) In general. This section provides ordering rules for the allocation of net operating losses, net capital losses, U.S. source losses, and separate limitation losses, and for recapture of separate limitation losses, overall foreign losses, and overall domestic losses. The rules must be applied in the order set forth in paragraphs (b) through (g) of this section.

(b) Step One: Allocation of net operating loss and net capital loss carryovers. *(1) In general.* Net operating losses from a current taxable year are carried forward or back to a taxable year in the following manner. Net operating losses that are carried forward pursuant to section 172 are combined with income or loss in the carryover year in the manner described in this paragraph (b). The combined amounts are then subject to the ordering rules provided in paragraphs (c) through (g) of this section. Net operating losses that are carried back to a prior taxable year pursuant to section 172 are allocated to income in the carryback year in the manner set forth in paragraphs (b)(2) and (3), (c), and (d) of this section. The income in the carryback year to which the net operating loss is allocated is the foreign source income in each separate category and the U.S. source income after the application of sections 904(f) and 904(g) to income and loss in that previous year, including as a result of net operating loss carryovers or carrybacks from taxable years prior to the current taxable year.

(2) Full net operating loss carryover. If the full net operating loss (that remains after carryovers to other taxable years) is less than or equal to the taxable income in a particular taxable year (carryover year), and so can be carried forward in its entirety to such carryover year, U.S. source losses and foreign source losses in separate categories that are part of a net operating loss from a particular taxable year that is carried forward in its entirety shall be combined with the U.S. income or loss and the foreign source income or loss in the same separate categories in the carryover year.

(3) Partial net operating loss carryover. If the full net operating loss (that remains after carryovers to other taxable years) exceeds the taxable income in a carryover year, and so cannot be carried forward in its entirety to such carryover year, the following rules apply:

(i) First, any U.S. source loss (not to exceed the net operating loss carryover) shall be carried over to the extent of any U.S. source income in the carryover year.

(ii) If the net operating loss carryover exceeds the U.S. source loss carryover determined under paragraph (b)(3)(i) of this section, then separate limitation losses that are part of the net operating loss shall be tentatively carried over to the extent of separate limitation income in the same separate category in the carryover year. If the sum of the potential separate limitation loss carryovers determined under the preceding sentence exceeds the amount of the net operating loss carryover reduced by any U.S. source loss carried over under paragraph (b)(3)(i) of this section, then the potential separate limitation loss carryovers shall be reduced pro rata so that their sum equals such amount.

(iii) If the net operating loss carryover exceeds the sum of the U.S. and separate limitation loss carryovers determined under paragraphs (b)(3)(i) and (ii) of this section, then a proportionate part of the remaining loss from each separate category shall be carried over to the extent of such excess and combined with the foreign source loss, if any, in the same separate categories in the carryover year.

(iv) If the net operating loss carryover exceeds the sum of all the loss carryovers determined under paragraphs (b)(3)(i), (ii), and (iii) of this section, then any U.S. source loss not carried over under paragraph (b)(3)(i) of this section shall be carried over to the extent of such excess and combined with the U.S. source loss, if any, in the carryover year.

(4) Net capital loss carryovers. Rules similar to the rules of paragraphs (b)(1) through (3) of this section apply for

purposes of determining the components of a net capital loss carryover to a taxable year.

(c) Step Two: Allocation of separate limitation losses. The taxpayer shall allocate separate limitation losses sustained during the taxable year (increased, if appropriate, by any losses carried over under paragraph (b) of this section), in the following manner:

(1) the taxpayer shall allocate its separate limitation losses for the year to reduce its separate limitation income in other separate categories on a proportionate basis, and increase its separate limitation loss accounts appropriately. To the extent a separate limitation loss in one separate category is allocated to reduce separate limitation income in a second separate category, and the second category has a separate limitation loss account from a prior taxable year with respect to the first category, the two separate limitation loss accounts shall be netted one against the other.

(2) If the taxpayer's separate limitation losses for the taxable year exceed the taxpayer's separate limitation income for the year, so that the taxpayer has separate limitation losses remaining after the application of paragraph (c)(1) of this section, the taxpayer shall allocate those losses to its U.S. source income for the taxable year, to the extent thereof, and shall increase its overall foreign loss accounts appropriately.

(d) Step Three: Allocation of U.S. source losses. The taxpayer shall allocate U.S. source losses sustained during the taxable year (increased, if appropriate, by any losses carried over under paragraph (b) of this section) to separate limitation income on a proportionate basis, and shall increase its overall domestic loss accounts appropriately.

(e) Step Four: Recapture of overall foreign loss accounts. If the taxpayer's separate limitation income for the taxable year (reduced by any losses carried over under paragraph (b) of this section) exceeds the sum of the taxpayer's U.S. source loss and separate limitation losses for the year, so that the taxpayer has separate limitation income remaining after the application of paragraphs (c)(1) and (d) of this section, then the taxpayer shall recapture prior year overall foreign losses, if any, in accordance with §§ 1.904(f)-2 and 1.904(f)-2T.

(f) Step Five: Recapture of separate limitation loss accounts. To the extent the taxpayer has remaining separate limitation income for the year after the application of paragraph (e) of this section, then the taxpayer shall recapture prior year separate limitation loss accounts, if any, in accordance with § 1.904(f)-8T.

(g) Step Six: Recapture of overall domestic loss accounts. If the taxpayer's U.S. source income for the year (reduced by any losses carried over under paragraph (b) of this section or allocated under paragraph (c) of this section, but not increased by any recapture of overall foreign loss accounts under paragraph (e) of this section) exceeds the taxpayer's separate limitation losses for the year, so that the taxpayer has U.S. source income remaining after the application of paragraph (c)(2) of this section, then the taxpayer shall recapture its prior year overall domestic losses, if any, in accordance with § 1.904(g)-2T.

(h) Examples. The following examples illustrate the rules of this section. Unless otherwise noted, all corporations use the calendar year as the U.S. taxable year.

Example (1). (i) Facts. (A) Z Corporation is a domestic corporation with foreign branch operations in Country B. For 2009, Z has a net operating loss of ($500), determined as follows:

General	Passive	US
($300)	$0	($200)

(B) For 2008, Z had the following taxable income and losses after application of section 904(f) and (g) to income and loss in 2008:

General	Passive	US
$400	$200	$110

(ii) Net operating loss allocation. Because Z's taxable income for 2008 exceeds its total net operating loss for 2009, the full net operating loss is carried back. Under Step 1, each component of the net operating loss is carried back and combined with its same category in 2008. See paragraph (b)(2) of this section. After allocation of the net operating loss, Z has the following taxable income and losses for 2008:

General	Passive	US
$100	$200	($90)

(iii) Loss allocation. Under Step 3, the ($90) of U.S. loss is allocated proportionately to reduce the general category and passive category income. Accordingly, $30 ($90 x $100/$300) of the U.S. loss is allocated to general category income and $60 ($90 x $200/$300) of the U.S. loss is allocated to passive category income, with a corresponding creation or increase to Z's overall domestic loss accounts.

Example (2). (i) Facts. (A) X Corporation is a domestic corporation with foreign branch operations in Country C. As of January 1, 2007, X has no loss accounts subject to recapture. For 2007, X has a net operating loss of ($1400), determined as follows:

General	Passive	US
($400)	($200)	($800)

(B) X has no taxable income in 2005 or 2006 available for offset by a net operating loss carryback. For 2008, X has the following taxable income and losses:

General	Passive	US
$500	($100)	$1200

(ii) Net operating loss allocation. Under Step 1, because X's total taxable income for 2008 of $1600 ($1200 + $500 - $100) exceeds the total 2007 net operating loss, the full $1400 net operating loss is carried forward. Under paragraph (b)(2) of this section, each component of the net operating loss is carried forward and combined with its same category in 2008. After allocation of the net operating loss, X has the following taxable income and losses:

General	Passive	US
$100	($300)	$400

(iii) Loss allocation. Under Step 2, $100 of the passive category loss offsets the $100 of general category income, resulting in a passive category separate limitation loss account with respect to general category income, and the other $200 of passive category loss offsets $200 of the U.S. source taxable income, resulting in the creation of an overall foreign loss account in the passive category.

Example (3). (i) Facts. Assume the same facts as in Example 2, except that in 2008, X had the following taxable income and losses:

General	Passive	US
$200	($100)	$1200

(ii) Net operating loss allocation. Under Step 1, because the total net operating loss for 2007 of ($1400) exceeds total taxable income for 2008 of $1300 ($1200 + $200 - $100), X has a partial net operating loss carryover to 2008 of $1300. Under paragraph (b)(3)(i) of this section, first, the $800 U.S. source component of the net operating loss is allocated to U.S. income for 2008. The tentative general category carryover under paragraph (b)(3)(ii) of this section ($200) does not exceed the remaining net operating loss carryover amount ($500). Therefore, $200 of the general category component of the net operating loss is next allocated to the general category income for 2008. Under paragraph (b)(3)(iii) of this section, the remaining $300 of net operating loss carryover ($1300 - $800 - $200) is carried over proportionally from the remaining net operating loss components in the general category ($200, or $400 total general category loss--$200 general category loss already allocated) and passive category ($200). Therefore, $150 ($300x$200x$400) of the remaining net operating loss carryover is carried over from the general category for 2007 and combined with the general category for 2008, and $150 ($300x$200x$400) of the remaining net operating loss carryover is carried over from the passive category for 2007 and combined with the passive category for 2008. After allocation of the net operating loss carryover from 2007 to the appropriate categories for 2008, X has the following taxable income and losses:

General	Passive	US
($150)	($250)	$400

(iii) Loss allocation. Under Step 2, the losses in the general and passive categories fully offset the U.S. source income, resulting in the creation of general category and passive category overall foreign loss accounts.

Example (4). (i) Facts. Assume the same facts as in Example 2, except that in 2008, X has the following taxable income and losses:

General	Passive	US
$200	$200	($200)

(ii) Net operating loss allocation. Under Step 1, because the total net operating loss of ($1400) exceeds total taxable income for 2008 of $200 ($200 + $200 - $200), X has a partial net operating loss carryover to 2008 of $200. Because X has no U.S. source income in 2008, under paragraph (b)(3)(i) of this section no portion of the U.S. source component of the net operating loss is initially carried into 2008. Because the total tentative carryover under paragraph (b)(3)(ii) of this section of $400 ($200 in each of the general and passive categories) exceeds the net operating loss carryover amount, the tentative carryover from each separate category is reduced proportionately by $100 ($200 x $200/$400). Accordingly, $100 ($200 - $100) of the general category component of the net operating loss is carried forward and $100 ($200 - $100) of the passive category component of the net operating loss is carried forward and combined with income in the same respective categories for 2008. After allocation of the net operating loss carryover from 2007, X has the following taxable income and losses:

General	Passive	US
$100	$100	($200)

(iii) Loss allocation. Under Step 3, the $200 U.S. source loss offsets the remaining $100 of general category income and $100 of passive category income, resulting in the creation of overall domestic loss accounts with respect to the general and passive categories.

Example (5). (i) Facts. Assume the same facts as in Example 2, except that in 2008, X has the following taxable income and losses:

General	Passive	US
$800	($100)	$100

(ii) Net operating loss allocation. Under Step 1, because X's total net operating loss in 2007 of ($1400) exceeds its total taxable income for 2008 of $800 ($100 + $800 - $100), X has a partial net operating loss carryover to 2008 of $800. Under paragraph (b)(3)(i) of this section, $100 of the U.S. source component of the net operating loss is allocated to U.S. income for 2008. The tentative general category carryover under paragraph (b)(3)(ii) of this section does not exceed the remaining net operating loss carryover amount. Therefore, $400 of the general category component of the net operating loss is allocated to reduce general category income in 2008. Under paragraph (b)(3)(iii) of this section, of the remaining $300 of net operating loss carryover ($800 - $100 - $400), $200 is carried forward from the passive category component of the net operating loss and combined with the passive category for 2008. Under paragraph (b)(3)(iv) of this section, the remaining $100 ($300 - $200) of net operating loss carryover is carried forward from the U.S. source component of the net operating loss and combined with the U.S. source income (loss) for 2008. After allocation of the net operating loss carryover from 2007, X has the following taxable income and losses:

General	Passive	US
$400	($300)	($100)

(iii) Loss allocation. (A) Under Step 2, the $300 passive category loss offsets the $300 of income in the general category, resulting in the creation of a passive category separate limitation loss account with respect to the general category.

(B) Under Step 3, the $100 U.S. source loss offsets the remaining $100 of the general category income, resulting in the creation of an overall domestic loss account with respect to the general category.

Example (6). (i) Facts. (A) Y Corporation is a domestic corporation with foreign branch operations in Country D. Y has no net operating losses and does not make an election to recapture more than the required amount of overall foreign losses. As of January 1, 2007, Y has a ($200) general category overall foreign loss (OFL) account and a ($200) general category separate limitation loss (SLL) account with respect to the passive category. For 2007, Y has $400 of passive category income that is fully offset by a ($400) domestic loss in that taxable year, giving rise to the creation of an overall domestic loss (ODL) account with respect to the passive category. As of January 1, 2008, Y has the following balances in its OFL, SLL, and ODL accounts:

General		US
OFL	Passive SLL	US Passive ODL
$200	$200	$400

(B) In 2008, Y has the following taxable income and losses:

General	Passive	US
$400	($100)	$600

(ii) Loss allocation. Under Step 2, the $100 of passive category loss offsets $100 of the general category income, creating a passive category SLL account of $100 with respect to the general category. Because there is an offsetting general category SLL account of $200 with respect to the passive category from a prior taxable year, the two accounts are netted against each other so that all that remains is a $100 general category SLL account with respect to the passive category.

(iii) OFL account recapture. Under Step 4, 50 percent of the remaining $300, or $150, of income in the general category is subject to recharacterization as U.S. source income as a recapture of part of the OFL account in the general category.

(iv) SLL account recapture. Under Step 5, $100 of the remaining $150 of income in the general category is recharacterized as passive category income as a recapture of the general category SLL account with respect to the passive category.

(v) ODL account recapture. Under Step 6, 50 percent of the $600, or $300, of U.S. source income is subject to recharacterization as foreign source passive category income as a recapture of a part of the ODL account with respect to the passive category. None of the $150 of general category income that was recharacterized as U.S. source income under Step 5 is included here as income subject to recharacterization in connection with recapture of the overall domestic loss account.

(v) Results. (A) After the allocation of loss and recapture of loss accounts, X has the following taxable income and losses for 2008:

General	Passive	US
$50	$400	$450

(B) As of January 1, 2009, Y has the following balances in its OFL, SLL and ODL accounts:

General		Passive	US
OFL	Passive SLL	General SLL	Passive ODL
$50	$0	$0	$100

(i) Effective/applicability date. This section applies to taxable years beginning after December 21, 2007. Taxpayers may choose to apply this section to other taxable years beginning after December 31, 2006, as well.

(j) Expiration date. The applicability of this section expires on December 20, 2010.

T.D. 9371, 12/20/2007.

§ 1.904(i)-0 Outline of regulation provisions.

This section lists the headings for Sec. 1.904(i)-1.

§ 1.904(i)-1 Limitation on use of deconsolidation to avoid foreign tax credit limitations.

(a) General rule.

(1) Determination of taxable income.

(2) Allocation.

(b) Definitions and special rules.

(1) Affiliate.

(i) Generally.

(ii) Rules for consolidated groups.

(iii) Exception for newly acquired affiliates.

(2) Includible corporation.

(c) Taxable years.

(d) Consistent treatment of foreign taxes paid.

(e) Effective date.

T.D. 9371, 12/20/2007.

§ 1.904(i)-1 Limitation on use of deconsolidation to avoid foreign tax credit limitations.

(a) General rule. If two or more includible corporations are affiliates, within the meaning of paragraph (b)(1) of this section, at any time during their taxable years, then, solely for purposes of applying the foreign tax credit provisions of section 59(a), sections 901 through 908, and section 960, the rules of this section will apply.

(1) Determination of taxable income. (i) Each affiliate must compute its net taxable income or loss in each separate category (as defined in § 1.904-5(a)(1), and treating U.S. source income or loss as a separate category) without regard to sections 904(f) and 907(c)(4). Only affiliates that are members of the same consolidated group use the consolidated return regulations (other than those under sections 904(f) and 907(c)(4)) in computing such net taxable income

or loss. To the extent otherwise applicable, other provisions of the Internal Revenue Code and regulations must be used in the determination of an affiliate's net taxable income or loss in a separate category.

(ii) The net taxable income amounts in each separate category determined under paragraph (a)(1)(i) of this section are combined for all affiliates to determine one amount for the group of affiliates in each separate category. However, a net loss of an affiliate (first affiliate) in a separate category determined under paragraph (a)(1)(i) of this section will be combined under this paragraph (a) with net income or loss amounts of other affiliates in the same category only if, and to the extent that, the net loss offsets taxable income, whether U.S. or foreign source, of the first affiliate. The consolidated return regulations that apply the principles of sections 904(f) and 907(c)(4) to consolidated groups will then be applied to the combined amounts in each separate category as if all affiliates were members of a single consolidated group.

(2) Allocation. Any net taxable income in a separate category calculated under paragraph (a)(1)(ii) of this section for purposes of the foreign tax credit provisions must then be allocated among the affiliates under any consistently applied reasonable method, taking into account all of the facts and circumstances. A method is consistently applied if used by all affiliates from year to year. Once chosen, an allocation method may be changed only with the consent of the Commissioner. This allocation will only affect the source and foreign tax credit separate limitation character of the income for purposes of the foreign tax credit separate limitation of each affiliate, and will not otherwise affect an affiliate's total net income or loss. This section applies whether the federal income tax consequences of its application favor, or are adverse to, the taxpayer.

(b) Definitions and special rules. For purposes of this section only, the following terms will have the meanings specified.

(1) Affiliate. (i) Generally. Affiliates are includible corporations—

(A) That are members of the same affiliated group, as defined in section 1504(a); or

(B) That would be members of the same affiliated group, as defined in section 1504(a) if—

(1) Any non-includible corporation meeting the ownership test of section 1504(a)(2) with respect to any such includible corporation was itself an includible corporation; or

(2) The constructive ownership rules of section 1563(e) were applied for purposes of section 1504(a).

(ii) Rules for consolidated groups. Affiliates that are members of the same consolidated group are treated as a single affiliate for purposes of this section. The provisions of paragraph (a) of this section shall not apply if the only affiliates under this definition are already members of the same consolidated group without operation of this section.

(iii) Exception for newly acquired affiliates. (A) With respect to acquisitions after December 7, 1995, an includible corporation acquired from unrelated third parties (First Corporation) will not be considered an affiliate of another includible corporation (Second Corporation) during the taxable year of the First Corporation beginning before the date on which the First Corporation originally becomes an affiliate with respect to the Second Corporation.

(B) With respect to acquisitions on or before December 7, 1995, an includible corporation acquired from unrelated third parties will not be considered an affiliate of another includible corporation during its taxable year beginning before the date on which the first includible corporation first becomes an affiliate with respect to that other includible corporation.

(C) This exception does not apply where the acquisition of an includible corporation is used to avoid the application of this section.

(2) Includible corporation. The term includible corporation has the same meaning it has in section 1504(b).

(c) Taxable years. If all of the affiliates use the same U.S. taxable year, then that taxable year must be used for purposes of applying this section. If, however, the affiliates use more than one U.S. taxable year, then an appropriate taxable year must be used for applying this section. The determination whether a taxable year is appropriate must take into account all of the relevant facts and circumstances, including the U.S. taxable years used by the affiliates for general U.S. income tax purposes. The taxable year chosen by the affiliates for purposes of applying this section must be used consistently from year to year. The taxable year may be changed only with the prior consent of the Commissioner. Those affiliates that do not use the year determined under this paragraph (c) as their U.S. taxable year for general U.S. income tax purposes must, for purposes of this section, use their U.S. taxable year or years ending within the taxable year determined under this paragraph (c). If, however, the stock of an affiliate is disposed of so that it ceases to be an affiliate, then the taxable year of that affiliate will be considered to end on the disposition date for purposes of this section.

(d) Consistent treatment of foreign taxes paid. All affiliates must consistently either elect under section 901(a) to claim a credit for foreign income taxes paid or accrued, or deemed paid or accrued, or deduct foreign taxes paid or accrued under section 164. See also § 1.1502-4(a); § 1.905-1(a).

(e) Effective date. Except as provided in paragraph (b)(1)(iii) of this section (relating to newly acquired affiliates), this section is effective for taxable years of affiliates beginning after December 31, 1993.

T.D. 8627, 11/6/95.

---

§ 1.904(j)-0 Outline of regulation provisions.

This section lists the headings for Sec. 1.904(j)-1.

T.D. 9371, 12/20/2007.

---

§ 1.904(j)-1 Certain individuals exempt from foreign tax credit limitation.

(a) Election available only if all foreign taxes are creditable foreign taxes. A taxpayer may elect to apply section 904(j) for a taxable year only if all of the taxes for which a credit is allowable to the taxpayer under section 901 for the taxable year (without regard to carryovers) are creditable foreign taxes (as defined in section 904(j)(3)(B)).

(b) Coordination with carryover rules. *(1) No carryovers to or from election year.* If the taxpayer elects to apply section 904(j) for any taxable year, then no taxes paid or accrued by the taxpayer during such taxable year may be deemed paid or accrued under section 904(c) in any other taxable year, and no taxes paid or accrued in any other taxable year may be deemed paid or accrued under section 904(c) in such taxable year.

(2) Carryovers to and from other years determined without regard to election years. The amount of the foreign taxes paid or accrued, and the amount of the foreign source taxable income, in any year for which the taxpayer elects to apply section 904(j) shall not be taken into account in determining the amount of any carryover to or from any other taxable year. However, an election to apply section 904(j) to any year does not extend the number of taxable years to which unused foreign taxes may be carried under section 904(c) and § 1.904-2(b). Therefore, in determining the number of such carryover years, the taxpayer must take into account years to which a section 904(j) election applies.

(3) Determination of amount of creditable foreign taxes. Otherwise allowable carryovers of foreign tax credits from other taxable years shall not be taken into account in determining whether the amount of creditable foreign taxes paid or accrued by an individual during a taxable year exceeds $300 ($600 in the case of a joint return) for purposes of section 904(j)(2)(B).

(c) Examples. The following examples illustrate the provisions of this section:

Example (1). In 2006, X, a single individual using the cash basis method of accounting for income and foreign tax credits, pays $100 of foreign taxes with respect to general limitation income that was earned and included in income for United States tax purposes in 2005. The foreign taxes would be creditable under section 901 but are not shown on a payee statement furnished to X. X's only income for 2006 from sources outside the United States is qualified passive income, with respect to which X pays $200 of creditable foreign taxes shown on a payee statement. X may not elect to apply section 904(j) for 2006 because some of X's foreign taxes are not creditable foreign taxes within the meaning of section 904(j)(3)(B).

Example (2). (i) In 2009, A, a single individual using the cash basis method of accounting for income and foreign tax credits, pays creditable foreign taxes of $250 attributable to passive income. Under section 904(c), A may also carry forward to 2009 $100 of unused foreign taxes paid in 2005 with respect to passive income, $300 of unused foreign taxes paid in 2005 with respect to general limitation income, $400 of unused foreign taxes paid in 2006 with respect to passive income, and $200 of unused foreign taxes paid in 2006 with respect to general limitation income. In 2009, A's only foreign source income is passive income described in section 904(j)(3)(A)(i), and this income is reported to A on a payee statement (within the meaning of section 6724(d)(2)). If A elects to apply section 904(j) for the 2009 taxable year, the unused foreign taxes paid in 2005 and 2006 are not deemed paid in 2009, and A therefore cannot claim a foreign tax credit for those taxes in 2009.

(ii) In 2010, A again is eligible for and elects the application of section 904(j). The carryforwards from 2005 expire in 2010. The carryforward period established under section 904(c) is not extended by A's election under section 904(j). In 2011, A does not elect the application of section 904(j). The $600 of unused foreign taxes paid in 2006 on passive and general limitation income are deemed paid in 2011, under section 904(c), without any adjustment for any portion of those taxes that might have been used as a foreign tax credit in 2009 or 2010 if A had not elected to apply section 904(j) to those years.

(d) Effective date. Section 1.904(j)-1 applies to taxable years beginning after July 20, 2004.

T.D. 9141, 7/19/2004.

§ 1.905-1 When credit for taxes may be taken.

(a) In general. The credit for taxes provided in subpart A (section 901 and following), part III, subchapter N, chapter 1 of the Code, may ordinarily be taken either in the return for the year in which the taxes accrued or in which the taxes were paid, dependent upon whether the accounts of the taxpayer are kept and his returns filed using an accrual method or using the cash receipts and disbursements method. Section 905(a) allows the taxpayer, at his option and irrespective of the method of accounting employed in keeping his books, to take such credit for taxes as may be allowable in the return for the year in which the taxes accrued. An election thus made under section 905(a) (or under the corresponding provisions of prior internal revenue laws) must be followed in returns for all subsequent years, and no portion of any such taxes accrued in a year in which a credit is claimed will be allowed as a deduction from gross income in any year. See also § 1.905-4.

(b) Foreign income subject to exchange controls. If, however, under the provisions of the regulations under section 461, an amount otherwise constituting gross income for the taxable year from sources without the United States is, owing to monetary, exchange, or other restrictions imposed by a foreign country, not includible in gross income of the taxpayer for such year, the credit for income taxes imposed by such foreign country with respect to such amount shall be taken proportionately in any subsequent taxable year in which such amount or portion thereof is includible in gross income.

T.D. 6275, 12/2/57.

§ 1.905-2 Conditions of allowance of credit.

(a) Forms and information. *(1)* Whenever the taxpayer chooses, in accordance with paragraph (d) of § 1.901-1, to claim the benefits of the foreign tax credit, the claim for credit shall be accompanied by Form 1116 in the case of an individual or by Form 1118 in the case of a corporation.

(2) The form must be carefully filled in with all the information called for and with the calculations of credits indicated. Except where it is established to the satisfaction of the district director that it is impossible for the taxpayer to furnish such evidence, the taxpayer must provide upon request the receipt for each such tax payment if credit is sought for taxes already paid or the return on which each such accrued tax was based if credit is sought for taxes accrued. The receipt or return must be either the original, a duplicate original, or a duly certified or authenticated copy. The preceding two sentences are applicable for returns whose original due date falls on or after January 1, 1988. If the receipt or the return is in a foreign language, a certified translation thereof must be furnished by the taxpayer. Any additional information necessary for the determination under part I (section 861

and following), subchapter N, chapter 1 of the Code, of the amount of income derived from sources without the United States and from each foreign country shall, upon the request of the district director, be furnished by the taxpayer. If the taxpayer upon request fails without justification to furnish any such additional information which is significant, including any significant information which he is requested to furnish pursuant to § 1.861-8(f)(5) as proposed in the FEDERAL REGISTER for November 8, 1976, the District Director may disallow the claim of the taxpayer to the benefits of the foreign tax credit.

(b) Secondary evidence. Where it has been established to the satisfaction of the district director that it is impossible to furnish a receipt for such foreign tax payment, the foreign tax return, or direct evidence of the amount of tax withheld at the source, the district director, may, in his discretion, accept secondary evidence thereof as follows:

(1) Receipt for payment. In the absence of a receipt for payment of foreign taxes there shall be submitted a photostatic copy of the check, draft, or other medium of payment showing the amount and date thereof, with certification identifying it with the tax claimed to have been paid, together with evidence establishing that the tax was paid for taxpayer's account as his own tax on his own income. If credit is claimed on an accrual method, it must be shown that the tax accrued in the taxable year.

(2) Foreign tax return. If the foreign tax return is not available, the foreign tax has not been paid, and credit is claimed on an accrual method, there shall be submitted—

(i) A certified statement of the amount claimed to have accrued,

(ii) Excerpts from the taxpayer's accounts showing amounts of foreign income and tax thereon accrued on its books,

(iii) A computation of the foreign tax based on income from the foreign country carried on the books and at current rates of tax to be established by data such as excerpts from the foreign law, assessment notices, or other documentary evidence thereof,

(iv) A bond, if deemed necessary by the district director, filed in the manner provided in cases where the foreign return is available, and

(v) In case a bond is not required, a specific agreement wherein the taxpayer shall recognize its liability to report the correct amount of tax when ascertained, as required by the provisions of section 905(c).

If at any time the foreign tax receipts or foreign tax returns become available to the taxpayer, they shall be promptly submitted to the district director.

(3) Tax withheld at source. In the case of taxes withheld at the source from dividends, interest, royalties, compensation, or other form of income, where evidence of withholding and of the amount withheld cannot be secured from those who have made the payments, the district director may, in his discretion, accept secondary evidence of such withholding and of the amount of the tax so withheld, having due regard to the taxpayer's books of account and to the rates of taxation prevailing in the particular foreign country during the period involved.

(c) Credit for taxes accrued but not paid. In the case of a credit sought for a tax accrued but not paid, the district director may, as a condition precedent to the allowance of a credit, require a bond from the taxpayer, in addition to Form 1116 or 1118. If such a bond is required, Form 1117 shall be used by an individual or by a corporation. It shall be in such sum as the Commissioner may prescribe, and shall be conditioned for the payment by the taxpayer of any amount of tax found due upon any redetermination of the tax made necessary by such credit proving incorrect, with such further conditions as the district director may require. This bond shall be executed by the taxpayer, or the agent or representative of the taxpayer, as principal, and by sureties satisfactory to and approved by the Commissioner. See also 6 U.S.C. 15.

T.D. 6275, 12/2/57, amend T.D. 6789, 12/30/64, T.D. 7292, 11/30/73, T.D. 7456, 1/3/77, T.D. 8210, 6/22/88, T.D. 8412, 5/13/92, T.D. 8759, 1/26/98.

Proposed § 1.905-3 Adjustments to United States tax liability and to the pools of post-1986 undistributed earnings and post-1986 foreign income taxes as a result of a foreign tax redetermination. [*For Preamble, see ¶ 152,925*]

[The text of this section is the same as the text of § 1.905-3T(a) through (e) published elsewhere in this issue of the Federal Register.] [*See T.D. 9362, 11/07/2007, 72 Fed. Reg. 215.*]

§ 1.905-3T Adjustments to the pools of foreign taxes and earnings and profits when the allowable foreign tax credit changes (temporary).

Caution: The Treasury has not yet amended Reg § 1.905-3T to reflect changes made by P.L. 105-34.

(a) Effective/applicability dates. *(1) Currency translation.* Except as provided in § 1.905-5T, paragraph (b) of this section applies to taxes paid or accrued in taxable years of United States taxpayers beginning on or after November 7, 2007 and to taxes paid or accrued by a foreign corporation in its taxable years which end with or within a taxable year of the domestic corporate shareholder beginning on or after November 7, 2007. For taxable years beginning after December 31, 1997, and before November 7, 2007, section 986(a), as amended by the Taxpayer Relief Act of 1997 and the American Jobs Creation Act of 2004, shall apply. For taxable years beginning after December 31, 1986, and before January 1, 1998, § 1.905-3T (as contained in 26 CFR part 1, revised as of April 1, 2007) shall apply.

(2) Foreign tax redeterminations. Paragraphs (c) and (d) of this section apply to foreign tax redeterminations occurring in taxable years of United States taxpayers beginning on or after November 7, 2007 where the foreign tax redetermination affects the amount of foreign taxes paid or accrued by a United States taxpayer. Where the redetermination of foreign tax paid or accrued by a foreign corporation affects the computation of foreign taxes deemed paid under section 902 or 960 with respect to post-1986 undistributed earnings of the foreign corporation, paragraphs (c) and (d) of this section apply to foreign tax redeterminations occurring in taxable years of a foreign corporation which end with or within a taxable year of the domestic corporate shareholder beginning on or after November 7, 2007. For corresponding rules applicable to foreign tax redeterminations occurring in taxable years beginning before November 7, 2007, see Sec. § 1.905-3T and 1.905-5T (as contained in 26 CFR part 1, revised as of April 1, 2007).

(b) Currency translation rules. *(1) Translation of foreign taxes taken into account when accrued.* (i) In general. Except as provided in paragraph (b)(1)(ii) of this section, in the case of a taxpayer or a member of a qualified group (as defined in section 902(b)(2)) that takes foreign income taxes into account when accrued, the amount of any foreign taxes denominated in foreign currency that have been paid or accrued, additional tax liability denominated in foreign currency, taxes withheld in foreign currency, or estimated taxes paid in foreign currency shall be translated into dollars using the average exchange rate (as defined in § 1.989(b)-1) for the United States taxable year to which such taxes relate.

(ii) Exceptions. (A) Taxes not paid within two years. Any foreign income taxes denominated in foreign currency that are paid more than two years after the close of the United States taxable year to which they relate shall be translated into dollars using the exchange rate as of the date of payment of the foreign taxes. To the extent any accrued foreign income taxes denominated in foreign currency remain unpaid two years after the close of the taxable year to which they relate, see paragraph (b)(3) of this section for translation rules for the required adjustments.

(B) Taxes paid before taxable year begins. Any foreign income taxes paid before the beginning of the United States taxable year to which such taxes relate shall be translated into dollars using the exchange rate as of the date of payment of the foreign taxes.

(C) Inflationary currency. Any foreign income taxes the liability for which is denominated in any inflationary currency shall be translated into dollars using the exchange rate as of the date of payment of the foreign taxes. For this purpose, the term inflationary currency means the currency of a country in which there is cumulative inflation during the base period of at least 30 percent, as determined by reference to the consumer price index of the country listed in the monthly issues of International Financial Statistics, or a successor publication, of the International Monetary Fund. For purposes of this paragraph (b)(1)(ii)(C), base period means, with respect to any taxable year, the thirty-six calendar months immediately preceding the last day of such taxable year (see § 1.985-1(b)(2)(ii)(D)). Accrued but unpaid taxes denominated in an inflationary currency shall be translated into dollars at the exchange rate on the last day of the United States taxable year to which such taxes relate.

(D) Election to translate taxes using exchange rate for date of payment. A taxpayer that is otherwise required to translate foreign income taxes that are denominated in foreign currency using the average exchange rate may elect to translate foreign income taxes described in this paragraph (b)(1)(ii)(D) into dollars using the exchange rate as of the date of payment of the foreign taxes, provided that the liability for such taxes is denominated in nonfunctional currency. A taxpayer may make an election under this paragraph (b)(1)(ii)(D) for all foreign income taxes, or for only those foreign income taxes that are denominated in nonfunctional currency and are attributable to qualified business units with United States dollar functional currencies. The election must be made by attaching a statement to the taxpayer's timely filed return (including extensions) for the first taxable year to which the election applies. The statement must identify whether the election is made for all foreign taxes or only for foreign taxes attributable to qualified business units with United States dollar functional currencies. Once made, the election shall apply for the taxable year for which made and all subsequent taxable years unless revoked with the consent of the Commissioner. Accrued but unpaid taxes subject to an election under this paragraph (b)(1)(ii)(D) shall be translated into dollars at the exchange rate on the last day of the United States taxable year to which such taxes relate. For taxable years beginning after December 31, 2004, and before November 7, 2007, the rules of Notice 2006-47, 2006-20 IRB 892 (see § 601.601(d)(2)(ii)(b)), shall apply.

(E) Regulated investment companies. In the case of a regulated investment company (as defined in section 851 and the regulations under that section) which takes into account income on an accrual basis, foreign income taxes paid or accrued with respect to such income shall be translated into dollars using the exchange rate as of the date the income accrues.

(2) Translation of foreign taxes taken into account when paid. In the case of a taxpayer that takes foreign income taxes into account when paid, the amount of any foreign tax liability denominated in foreign currency, additional tax liability denominated in foreign currency, or estimated taxes paid in foreign currency shall be translated into dollars using the exchange rate as of the date of payment of such foreign taxes. Foreign taxes withheld in foreign currency shall be translated into dollars using the exchange rate as of the date on which such taxes were withheld.

(3) Refunds or other reductions of foreign tax liability. In the case of a taxpayer that takes foreign income taxes into account when accrued, a reduction in the amount of previously-accrued foreign taxes that is attributable to a refund of foreign taxes denominated in foreign currency, a credit allowed in lieu of a refund, the correction of an overaccrual, or an adjustment on account of accrued taxes denominated in foreign currency that were not paid by the date two years after the close of the taxable year to which such taxes relate, shall be translated into dollars using the exchange rate that was used to translate such amount when originally claimed as a credit or added to post-1986 foreign income taxes. In the case of foreign income taxes taken into account when accrued but translated into dollars on the date of payment, see paragraph (d) of this section for required adjustments to reflect a reduction in the amount of previously-accrued foreign taxes that is attributable to a difference in exchange rates between the date of accrual and date of payment. In the case of a taxpayer that takes foreign income taxes into account when paid, a refund or other reduction in the amount of foreign taxes denominated in foreign currency shall be translated into dollars using the exchange rate that was used to translate such amount when originally claimed as a credit. If a refund or other reduction of foreign taxes relates to foreign taxes paid or accrued on more than one date, then the refund or other reduction shall be deemed to be derived from, and shall reduce, the last payment of foreign taxes first, to the extent of that payment. See paragraphs (d)(1) (redetermination of United States tax liability for foreign taxes paid directly by a United States person) and (d)(2)(ii) (method of adjustment of a foreign corporation's pools of post-1986 undistributed earnings and post-1986 foreign income taxes) of this section.

(4) Allocation of refunds of foreign tax. Refunds of foreign tax shall be allocated to the same separate category as foreign taxes to which the refunded taxes relate. Refunds are related to foreign taxes of a separate category if the foreign tax that was refunded was imposed with respect to that separate category. See section 904(d) and § 1.904-6 concerning the allocation of taxes to separate categories of income. Earnings and profits of a foreign corporation in the separate category to which the refund relates shall be increased to reflect the foreign tax refund.

(5) Basis of foreign currency refunded. (i) In general. A recipient of a refund of foreign tax shall determine its basis in the currency refunded under the following rules.

(ii) United States dollar functional currency. If the functional currency of the qualified business unit (QBU) (as defined in section 989 and the regulations under that section) that paid the tax and received the refund is the United States dollar or the person receiving the refund is not a QBU, then the recipient's basis in the foreign currency refunded shall be the dollar value of the refund determined under paragraph (b)(3) of this section by using, as appropriate, either the average exchange rate for the taxable year to which such taxes relate or the other exchange rate that was used to translate such amount when originally claimed as a credit or added to post-1986 foreign income taxes.

(iii) Nondollar functional currency. If the functional currency of the QBU receiving the refund is not the United States dollar and is different from the currency in which the foreign tax was paid, then the recipient's basis in the foreign currency refunded shall be equal to the functional currency value of the non-functional currency refund translated into functional currency at the exchange rate between the functional currency and the non-functional currency. Such exchange rate is determined under paragraph (b)(3) of this section by substituting the words "functional currency" for the word "dollar" and by using, as appropriate, either the average exchange rate for the taxable year to which such taxes relate or the other exchange rate that was used to translate such amount when originally claimed as a credit or added to post-1986 foreign income taxes.

(iv) Functional currency tax liabilities. If the functional currency of the QBU receiving the refund is the currency in which the refund was made, then the recipient's basis in the currency received shall be the amount of the functional currency received.

(v) Foreign currency gain or loss. For purposes of determining foreign currency gain or loss on the initial payment of accrued foreign tax in a non-functional currency, see section 988. For purposes of determining subsequent foreign currency gain or loss on the disposition of non-functional currency the basis of which is determined under this paragraph (b)(5), see section 988(c)(1)(C).

(c) Foreign tax redetermination. For purposes of this section and § 1.905-4T, the term foreign tax redetermination means a change in the foreign tax liability that may affect a taxpayer's foreign tax credit. A foreign tax redetermination includes: accrued taxes that when paid differ from the amounts added to post-1986 foreign income taxes or claimed as credits by the taxpayer (such as corrections to overaccruals and additional payments); accrued taxes that are not paid before the date two years after the close of the taxable year to which such taxes relate; any tax paid that is refunded in whole or in part; and, for taxes taken into account when accrued but translated into dollars on the date of payment, a difference between the dollar value of the accrued tax and the dollar value of the tax paid attributable to fluctuations in the value of the foreign currency relative to the dollar between the date of accrual and the date of payment.

(d) Redetermination of United States tax liability. *(1) Foreign taxes paid directly by a United States person.* If a foreign tax redetermination occurs with respect to foreign tax paid or accrued by or on behalf of a United States taxpayer, then a redetermination of the United States tax liability is required for the taxable year for which the foreign tax was claimed as a credit. See § 1.905-4T(b) which requires notification to the IRS of a foreign tax redetermination with respect to which a redetermination of United States liability is required, and see section 905(b) and the regulations under that section which require that a taxpayer substantiate that a foreign tax was paid and provide all necessary information establishing its entitlement to the foreign tax credit. However, a redetermination of United States tax liability is not required (and a taxpayer need not notify the IRS) if the foreign taxes are taken into account when accrued but translated into dollars as of the date of payment, the difference between the dollar value of the accrued tax and the dollar value of the tax paid is attributable to fluctuations in the value of the foreign currency relative to the dollar between the date of accrual and the date of payment, and the amount of the foreign tax redetermination with respect to each foreign country is less than the lesser of ten thousand dollars or two percent of the total dollar amount of the foreign tax initially accrued with respect to that foreign country for the United States taxable year. In such case, an appropriate adjustment shall be made to the taxpayer's United States tax liability in the taxable year during which the foreign tax redetermination occurs.

(2) Foreign taxes deemed paid under sections 902 or 960. (i) Redetermination of the United States tax liability not required. Subject to the special rule of paragraph (d)(4), a redetermination of United States tax liability is not required to account for the effect of a redetermination of foreign tax paid or accrued by a foreign corporation on the foreign taxes deemed paid by a United States corporation under sections 902 or 960. Instead, adjustments shall be made, and notification of such adjustments shall be filed, as required by paragraphs (d)(2) and (3) of this section.

(ii) Adjustments to the pools of post-1986 undistributed earnings and post-1986 foreign income taxes.

(A) Reduction in foreign tax paid or accrued. A foreign corporation's pool of post-1986 foreign income taxes in the appropriate separate category shall be reduced by the United States dollar amount of a foreign tax refund or other reduction in the amount of foreign tax paid or accrued, translated into United States dollars as provided in paragraph (b)(3) of this section. A foreign corporation's pool of post-1986 undistributed earnings in the appropriate separate category shall be increased by the functional currency amount of the foreign tax refund or other reduction in the amount of foreign tax paid or accrued. The allocation of the refund or other adjustment to the appropriate separate categories shall be made in accordance with paragraph (b)(4) of this section and § 1.904-6. If a foreign corporation receives a refund of foreign tax in a currency other than its functional currency, that refund shall be translated into its functional currency, for purposes of computing the increase to its pool of post-1986 undistributed earnings, at the exchange rate between the functional currency and the non-functional currency, as determined under paragraph (b)(3) of this section, by substituting the words "functional currency" for the word "dollar" and by using the same average or spot rate exchange rate convention that applies for purposes of translating such foreign taxes into United States dollars.

(B) Additional foreign tax paid or accrued. A foreign corporation's pool of post-1986 foreign income taxes in the appropriate separate category shall be increased by the United States dollar amount of the additional foreign tax paid or accrued, translated in accordance with the rules of paragraphs (b)(1) and (b)(2) of this section. A foreign corporation's pool of post-1986 undistributed earnings in the appropriate separate category shall be decreased by the functional currency amount of the additional foreign tax paid or accrued. The allocation of the additional amount of foreign tax among the separate categories shall be made in accordance with § 1.904-6. If a foreign corporation pays or accrues foreign tax in a currency other than its functional currency, that tax shall be translated into its functional currency, for purposes of computing the decrease to its pool of post-1986 undistributed earnings, at the exchange rate between the functional currency and the non-functional currency, as determined under paragraph (b)(3) of this section, by substituting the words "functional currency" for the word "dollar" and by using the same average or spot rate exchange rate convention that applies for purposes of translating such foreign taxes into United States dollars.

(C) Refunds of foreign taxes of lower tier foreign corporations that cause deficits in foreign tax pools. If a lower tier foreign corporation receives a refund of foreign tax after making a distribution to an upper tier foreign corporation and the refund would have the effect of reducing below zero the lower tier corporation's pool of foreign taxes in any separate category, then both the lower tier and upper tier corporations shall adjust the appropriate pool of foreign taxes to reflect that refund. The upper tier foreign corporation shall adjust its pool of foreign taxes by the difference between the United States dollar amount of foreign tax deemed paid by the upper tier foreign corporation prior to the refund and the United States dollar amount of foreign tax recomputed as if the refund occurred prior to the distribution. The upper tier foreign corporation shall not make any adjustment to its earnings and profits because foreign taxes deemed paid by the upper tier corporation are not included in the upper tier corporation's earnings and profits. The lower tier foreign corporation shall adjust its pool of foreign taxes by the difference between the United States dollar amount of the refund and the United States dollar amount of the adjustment to the upper tier foreign corporation's pool of foreign taxes. The earnings and profits of the lower tier foreign corporation shall be adjusted to reflect the full amount of the refund. The provisions of this paragraph (d)(2)(ii)(C) do not apply to distributions or inclusions to a United States person. See paragraph (d)(3)(iv) of this section for rules relating to actual or deemed distributions made to a United States person.

(D) Examples. The following examples illustrate the application of this paragraph (d)(2):

Example (1). Controlled foreign corporation (CFC) is a wholly-owned subsidiary of its domestic parent, P. Both CFC and P are calendar year taxpayers. CFC has a functional currency, the u, other than the dollar and its pool of post-1986 undistributed earnings is maintained in that currency. CFC and P use the average exchange rate to translate foreign taxes. In 2008, CFC accrued and paid 100u of foreign income taxes with respect to non-subpart F income. The average exchange rate for 2008 was $1:1u. In 2009, CFC received a refund of 50u of foreign taxes with respect to its non-subpart F income in 2008. CFC made no distributions to P in 2008. In accordance with paragraph (d)(2)(ii)(A) of this section and subject to paragraph (d)(3) of this section, in 2009 CFC's pool of post-1986 foreign income taxes must be reduced by $50 (because the refund must be translated into dollars using the exchange rate that was used to translate such amount when added to CFC's post-1986 foreign income taxes, that is, $1:1u, the average exchange rate for 2008) and the CFC's pool of post-1986 undistributed earnings must be increased by 50u (because the post-1986 undistributed earnings must be increased by the functional currency amount of the refund received). An income adjustment reflecting foreign currency gain or loss under section 988 with respect to the refund of foreign taxes received by CFC is not required because the foreign taxes are denominated and paid in CFC's functional currency.

Example (2). The facts are the same as in Example 1, except that in 2008, CFC had general category post-1986 undistributed earnings attributable to non-subpart F income of 200u (net of foreign taxes), and CFC accrued and paid 160u in foreign income taxes with respect to those earnings. The average exchange rate for 2008 was $1:1u. Also in 2008, CFC made a distribution to P of 50u, and P was deemed to have paid $40 of foreign taxes with respect to that distribution (50u/200u x $160). In 2009, CFC received a refund of foreign taxes of 5u with respect to its nonsubpart F income in 2008. Also in 2009, CFC made a distribution to P of 50u. CFC had no income and paid no foreign taxes in 2009. In accordance with paragraph (d)(2)(ii) of this section, CFC's pool of general category post-1986 foreign income taxes is reduced in 2009 by $5 to $115 (because the refund must be translated into dollars using the exchange rate that was used to translate such amount when added to CFC's post-1986 foreign income taxes, that is, $1:1u, the average exchange rate for 2008), and CFC's pool of general category post-1986 undistributed earnings must be increased in 2009 by 5u to 155u (because the post-1986 undistributed earnings must be increased by the functional currency amount of the refund received). (An income adjustment reflecting foreign currency gain or loss under section 988 with respect to the refund of foreign taxes received by CFC is not required because the foreign taxes are denominated and paid in CFC's functional currency.) A redetermination of P's deemed paid credit and U.S. tax for 2008 is not required, because the 5u refund, if taken into account in 2008, would have reduced P's deemed paid taxes by less than 10% (50u/205u x $155 = $37.80). See paragraph (d)(3)(ii) of this section. P is deemed to pay $37.10 of foreign taxes with respect to the distribution in 2009 of 50u (50u/155u x $115).

Example (3). (i) CFC1 is a foreign corporation that is wholly-owned by P, a domestic corporation. CFC2 is a foreign corporation that is wholly-owned by CFC1. The functional currency of CFC1 and CFC2 is the u, and the pools of post-1986 undistributed earnings of CFC1 and CFC2 are maintained in that currency. CFC1, CFC2, and P use the average exchange rate to translate foreign income taxes. In 2008, CFC2 had post-1986 undistributed earnings attributable to non-subpart F income of 100u (net of foreign taxes) and paid 100u in foreign income taxes with respect to those earnings. The average exchange rate for 2008 was $1:1u. CFC1 had no income and no earnings and profits other than those resulting from distributions from CFC2, as provided in either Situation 1 or Situation 2. CFC1 paid no foreign taxes.

(ii) Situation 1. In 2009, CFC2 received a refund of foreign taxes of 25u with respect to its 2008 taxable year. As of the close of 2009, CFC2 had 125u of post-1986 undistributed earnings (100u + 25u) and $75 of post-1986 foreign income taxes ($100-$25). In 2010, CFC2 made a distribution to CFC1 of 50u. CFC1 was deemed to have paid $30 of foreign taxes with respect to that distribution (50u/ 125u x $75). (An income adjustment reflecting foreign currency gain or loss under section 988 with respect to the refund of foreign taxes received by CFC1 is not required because the foreign taxes are denominated and paid in CFC1's functional currency.) At the end of 2010, CFC2 had 75u of post-1986 undistributed earnings (125u-50u) and $45 of post-1986 foreign income taxes ($75-$30).

(iii) Situation 2. The facts are the same as in Example 3(ii), Situation 1, except that CFC2 made a distribution of 50u in 2009 and received a refund of 75u of foreign tax in 2010. In 2009, the amount of foreign taxes deemed paid by

CFC1 is $50 (50u/100u x $100). In accordance with paragraph (d)(2)(ii)(C) of this section, the pools of post-1986 foreign income taxes of CFC1, as well as CFC2, must be adjusted in 2010, because the 2010 refund would otherwise have the effect of reducing below zero CFC2's pool of post-1986 foreign income taxes. Under paragraph (d)(3)(iv) of this section, the pools would have to be adjusted in 2009, and a redetermination of P's United States tax liability would be required, if P had received or accrued a distribution or inclusion from CFC1 or CFC2 in 2009 and computed an amount of foreign taxes deemed paid. CFC1's pool of post-1986 foreign income taxes must be reduced in 2010 by $42.86, determined as follows: $50 (foreign taxes deemed paid on the distribution from CFC2) minus $7.14 (the foreign taxes that would have been deemed paid had the refund occurred prior to the distribution (50u/175u x $25)). CFC2's pool of foreign taxes must be reduced in 2010 by $32.14, determined as follows: $75 (75u refund translated into dollars using the exchange rate that was used to translate such amount when originally added to post-1986 foreign income taxes, that is, $1:1u, the average exchange rate for 2008) minus $42.86 (the adjustment to CFC1's pool of post-1986 foreign income taxes). (An income adjustment reflecting foreign currency gain or loss under section 988 with respect to the refund of foreign taxes received by CFC1 is not required because the foreign taxes are denominated and paid in CFC1's functional currency.) The following reflects the pools of post-1986 undistributed earnings and post-1986 foreign income taxes of CFC1 and CFC2.

	Post-1986 earnings (u)	Foreign taxes ($)
CFC2:		
2008 . . .	100	100
2009 . . .	100 − 50 = 50	100 − 50 = 50
2010 . . .	50 + 75 > = 125	50 − 32.14 = 17.86
CFC1:		
2009 . . .	50	50
2010 . . .	50	50 − 42.86 = 7.14

(3) Exceptions. The provisions of paragraph (d)(2) of this section shall not apply and a redetermination of United States tax liability is required to account for the effect of a redetermination of foreign tax on foreign taxes deemed paid by a United States corporation under section 902 or section 960 to the extent provided in this paragraph (d)(3).

(i) Hyperinflationary currencies. A redetermination of United States tax liability is required if the foreign tax liability is in a hyperinflationary currency. The term "hyperinflationary currency" means the currency of a country in which there is cumulative inflation during the base period of at least 100% as determined by reference to the consumer price index of the country listed in the monthly issues of International Financial Statistics, or a successor publication, of the International Monetary Fund. "Base period" means, with respect to any taxable year, the thirty-six calendar months immediately preceding the last day of such taxable year (see § 1.985-2T(b)(2)).

(ii) Deemed paid foreign tax adjustment of ten percent or more. A redetermination of United States tax liability is required if a foreign tax redetermination occurs with respect to foreign taxes paid by a foreign corporation and such foreign tax redetermination, if taken into account in the taxable year of the foreign corporation to which the foreign tax redetermination relates, has the effect of reducing by ten percent or more the domestic corporate shareholder's foreign taxes deemed paid under section 902 or 960 with respect to a distribution or inclusion from the foreign corporation in any taxable year of the domestic corporate shareholder. If a redetermination of United States tax is required under the preceding sentence for any taxable year, a redetermination of United States tax is also required for all subsequent taxable years in which the domestic corporate shareholder received or accrued a distribution or inclusion from the foreign corporation.

(iii) Example. The following example illustrates the application of paragraph (d)(3)(ii) of this section:

Example. (i) Facts. Controlled foreign corporation (CFC) is a wholly-owned subsidiary of its domestic parent, P. Both CFC and P use the calendar year as their taxable year. CFC has a functional currency, the u, other than the dollar, and its pool of post-1986 undistributed earnings is maintained in that currency. CFC and P use the average exchange rate to translate foreign income taxes. As of January 1, 2008, CFC had 500u of general category post-1986 undistributed earnings and $200 of general category post-1986 foreign income taxes. In 2008, when the average exchange rate for the year was $1:1u, CFC earned general category income of 600u, accrued 100u of foreign income tax with respect to that income, and made a distribution to P of 100u, 10% of CFC's post-1986 undistributed earnings of 1,000u. P was deemed to have paid $30 of foreign income taxes in 2008 with respect to that distribution (100u/1,000u x $300). In 2009, CFC paid its actual foreign tax liability for 2008 of 80u. Also in 2009, for which the average exchange rate was $1:1.5u, CFC earned 500u of general category income, accrued 150u of tax with respect to that income, and distributed 100u to P. In 2010, CFC incurred a general category loss of (500u) and accrued no foreign tax. The loss was carried back to 2008 for foreign tax purposes, and CFC received a refund in 2011 of all 80u of foreign taxes paid for its 2008 taxable year.

(ii) Result in 2009. If the 20u overaccrual of tax for 2008 were taken into account in 2008, CFC's general category post-1986 undistributed earnings would be 1,020u, CFC's general category post-1986 foreign income taxes would be $280, and P would be deemed to pay $27.45 of tax with respect to the 2008 distribution of 100u (100u/1020u x $280 = $27.45). Because $2.55 is less than 10% of the $30 of foreign taxes deemed paid as originally calculated in 2008, P is not required to redetermine its deemed paid credit and U.S. tax liability for 2008 in 2009. Instead, CFC's general category post-1986 foreign income taxes are reduced by $20 in 2009 (because the overaccrual for 2008 is translated into dollars using the exchange rate that was used to translate such amount when originally added to post-1986 foreign income taxes, that is, $1:1u, the average exchange rate for 2008), and the corresponding pool of general category post-1986 undistributed earnings is increased by 20u in 2009 (because the post-1986 undistributed earnings pool is increased by the functional currency amount of the overaccrual). CFC's general category post-1986 undistributed earnings are also increased in 2009 to 1270u by the 350u earned in 2009 (900u + 20u + 350u = 1270u), and CFC's general category post-1986 foreign income taxes are increased by $100 to $350 ($270 - $20 + $100). P is deemed to pay $27.56 of foreign income taxes in 2009 with respect to the 100u distribution from CFC in that year (100u/1270u x $350).

(iii) Result in 2011. If the 80u refund of tax for 2008 were taken into account in 2008, CFC's general category post-1986 undistributed earnings would be 1,100u, CFC's general category post-1986 foreign income taxes would be $200, and P would be deemed to pay $18.18 of tax with respect to the 2008 distribution of 100u (100u/1,100u x $200

= $18.18). Because $11.82 is more than 10% of the $30 of foreign taxes deemed paid as originally calculated in 2008, under paragraph (d)(3)(ii) of this section, P is required to redetermine its deemed paid credit and U.S. tax liability for 2008 and 2009 in 2011. As determined in 2011, CFC's post-1986 undistributed earnings for 2009 are 1350u (1,100u as revised for 2008, less 100u distributed in 2008, plus 350u earned in 2009), and its post-1986 foreign income taxes for 2009 are $281.82 ($200 as revised for 2008, less $18.18 deemed paid in 2008, plus $100 accrued for 2009). As redetermined in 2011, P's deemed paid credit with respect to the 100u distribution from CFC in 2009 is $20.88 (100u/1350u x $281.82).

(iv) Deficit in foreign tax pool. A redetermination of United States tax liability is required if a foreign tax redetermination occurs with respect to foreign taxes deemed paid with respect to a Subpart F inclusion or an actual distribution which has the effect of reducing below zero the distributing foreign corporation's pool of foreign taxes in any separate category. Whether a foreign corporation's pool of foreign taxes is reduced below zero shall be determined at the close of the taxable year of the foreign corporation in which the foreign tax redetermination occurred. In no case shall taxes paid or accrued with respect to one separate category be applied to offset a negative balance in any other separate category.

(v) Example. The following example illustrates the application of paragraph (d)(3)(iv) of this section:

Example. Controlled foreign corporation (CFC) is a wholly-owned subsidiary of its domestic parent, P. Both CFC and P are calendar year taxpayers. CFC has a functional currency, the u, other than the dollar, and its pool of post-1986 undistributed earnings is maintained in that currency. CFC and P use the average exchange rate to translate foreign taxes. The average exchange rate for both 2008 and 2009 was $1:1u. In 2008, CFC earned 200u of general category income, accrued and paid 100u of foreign taxes with respect to that income, and made a distribution to P of 50u, half of CFC's post-1986 undistributed earnings of 100u. P is deemed to have paid $50 of foreign taxes with respect to that distribution (50u/100u x $100). In 2009, CFC received a refund of all 100u of foreign taxes related to the general category income for 2008. In 2009, CFC earned an additional 290u of income, 200u of which was passive category income and 90u of which was general category income, and accrued and paid 95u of foreign tax, 40u of which was with respect to the passive category income and 45u of which was with respect to the general category income. In accordance with paragraph (d)(3)(iv) of this section, P is required to redetermine its United States tax liability for 2008 to account for the foreign tax redetermination occurring in 2009 because, if an adjustment to CFC's pool of post-1986 foreign income taxes in the general category were made, the pool would be ($5). A deficit is not permitted to be carried in CFC's pool of post-1986 foreign income taxes in any separate category.

(vi) Reduction of corporate level tax on distribution of earnings and profits. If a United States shareholder of a controlled foreign corporation receives a distribution out of previously taxed earnings and profits and a foreign country has imposed tax on the income of the controlled foreign corporation, which tax is reduced on distribution of the earnings and profits of the corporation, then the United States shareholder shall redetermine its United States tax liability for the year or years affected.

(e) Foreign tax imposed on foreign refund. If the redetermination of foreign tax for a taxable year or years is occasioned by the refund to the taxpayer of taxes paid to a foreign country or possession of the United States and the foreign country or possession imposed tax on the refund, then the amount of the refund shall be considered to be reduced by the amount of any tax described in section 901 imposed by the foreign country or possession of the United States with respect to such refund. In such case, no other credit under section 901, and no deduction under section 164, shall be allowed for any taxable year with respect to such tax imposed on such refund.

(f) Expiration date. The applicability of this section expires on or before November 5, 2010.

T.D. 8210, 6/22/88, amend T.D. 9362, 11/6/2007.

Proposed § 1.905-4 Notification of foreign tax redetermination. [*For Preamble, see ¶ 152,925*]

[The text of this section is the same as the text of § 1.905-4T(a) through (f)(2) published elsewhere in this issue of the Federal Register.] [*See T.D. 9362, 11/07/2007, 72 Fed. Reg. 215.*]

§ 1.905-4T Notification of foreign tax redetermination (temporary).

Caution: The Treasury has not yet amended Reg § 1.905-4T to reflect changes made by P.L. 105-34.

(a) Application of this section. The rules of this section apply if, as a result of a foreign tax redetermination (as defined in § 1.905-3T(c)), a redetermination of United States tax liability is required under section 905(c) and § 1.905-3T(d).

(b) Time and manner of notification. *(1) Redetermination of United States tax liability.* (i) In general. Except as provided in paragraphs (b)(1)(iv), (v), and (b)(3) of this section, any taxpayer for which a redetermination of United States tax liability is required must notify the Internal Revenue Service (IRS) of the foreign tax redetermination by filing an amended return, Form 1118 (Foreign Tax Credit—Corporations) or Form 1116 (Foreign Tax Credit), and the statement required under paragraph (c) of this section for the taxable year with respect to which a redetermination of United States tax liability is required. Such notification must be filed within the time prescribed by this paragraph (b) and contain the information described in paragraph (c) of this section. Where a foreign tax redetermination requires an individual to redetermine the individual's United States tax liability, and as a result of such foreign tax redetermination the amount of creditable taxes paid or accrued by such individual during the taxable year does not exceed the applicable dollar limitation in section 904(k), the individual shall not be required to file Form 1116 with the amended return for such taxable year if the individual satisfies the requirements of section 904(k).

(ii) Reduction in amount of foreign tax liability. Except as provided in paragraphs (b)(1)(iv), (v), and (b)(3) of this section, for each taxable year of the taxpayer with respect to which a redetermination of United States tax liability is required by reason of a foreign tax redetermination that reduces the amount of foreign taxes paid or accrued, or included in the computation of foreign taxes deemed paid, the taxpayer must file a separate notification for each such taxable year by the due date (with extensions) of the original return for the taxpayer's taxable year in which the foreign tax redetermination occurred.

(iii) Increase in amount of foreign tax liability. Except as provided in paragraphs (b)(1)(iv), (v), and (b)(3) of this section, for each taxable year of the taxpayer with respect to which a redetermination of United States tax liability is required by reason of a foreign tax redetermination that increases the amount of foreign taxes paid or accrued, or included in the computation of foreign taxes deemed paid, the taxpayer must notify the Internal Revenue Service within the period provided by section 6511(d)(3)(A). Filing of such notification within the prescribed period shall constitute a claim for refund of United States tax.

(iv) Multiple redeterminations of United States tax liability for same taxable year. Where more than one foreign tax redetermination requires a redetermination of United States tax liability for the same taxable year of the taxpayer and those redeterminations occur within two consecutive taxable years of the taxpayer, the taxpayer may file for such taxable year one amended return, Form 1118 or 1116, and the statement required under paragraph (c) of this section that reflect all such foreign tax redeterminations. If the taxpayer chooses to file one notification for such redeterminations, the taxpayer must file such notification by the due date (with extensions) of the original return for the taxpayer's taxable year in which the first foreign tax redetermination that reduces foreign tax liability occurred. Where a foreign tax redetermination with respect to the taxable year for which a redetermination of United States tax liability is required occurs after the date for providing such notification, more than one amended return may be required with respect to that taxable year.

(v) Carryback and carryover of unused foreign tax. Where a foreign tax redetermination requires a redetermination of United States tax liability that would otherwise result in an additional amount of United States tax due, but such amount is eliminated as a result of a carryback or carryover of an unused foreign tax under section 904(c), the taxpayer may, in lieu of applying the rules of paragraphs (b)(1)(i) and (ii) of this section, notify the IRS of such redetermination by attaching a statement to the original return for the taxpayer's taxable year in which the foreign tax redetermination occurs. Such statement must be filed by the due date (with extensions) of the original return for the taxpayer's taxable year in which the foreign tax redetermination occurred and contain the information described in § 1.904-2(f).

(vi) Example. The following example illustrates the application of this paragraph (b)(1):

Example. (i) X, a domestic corporation, is an accrual basis taxpayer and uses the calendar year as its United States taxable year. X conducts business through a branch in Country M, the currency of which is the m, and also conducts business through a branch in Country N, the currency of which is the n. X uses the average exchange rate to translate foreign income taxes. Assume that X is able to claim a credit under section 901 for all foreign taxes paid or accrued.

(ii) In 2008, X accrued and paid 100m of Country M taxes with respect to 400m of foreign source general category income. The average exchange rate for 2008 was $1:1m. Also in 2008, X accrued and paid 50n of Country N taxes with respect to 150n of foreign source general category income. The average exchange rate for 2008 was $1:1n. X claimed a foreign tax credit of $150 ($100 (100m at $1:1m) + $50 (50n at $1:1n)) with respect to its foreign source general category income on its United States tax return for 2008.

(iii) In 2009, X accrued and paid 100n of Country N taxes with respect to 300n of foreign source general category income. The average exchange rate for 2009 was $1.50:1n. X claimed a foreign tax credit of $150 (100n at $1.5:1n) with respect to its foreign source general category income on its United States tax return for 2009.

(iv) On June 15, 2012, when the spot exchange rate was $1.40:1n, X received a refund of 10n from Country N, and, on March 15, 2013, when the spot exchange rate was $1.20:1m, X was assessed by and paid Country M an additional 20m of tax. Both payments were with respect to X's foreign source general category income in 2008. On May 15, 2013, when the spot exchange rate was $1.45:1n, X received a refund of 5n from Country N with respect to its foreign source general category income in 2009.

(v) X must redetermine its United States tax liability for both 2008 and 2009. With respect to 2008, X must notify the IRS of the June 15, 2012, refund of 10n from Country N that reduced X's foreign tax liability by filing an amended return, Form 1118, and the statement required in paragraph (c) of this section for 2008 by the due date of the original return (with extensions) for 2012. The amended return and Form 1118 must reduce the amount of foreign taxes claimed as a credit under section 901 by $10 (10n refund translated at the average exchange rate for 2008, or $1:1n (see § 1.905-3T(b)(3)). X will recognize foreign currency gain or loss under section 988 in or after 2012 on the conversion of the 10n refund into dollars. With respect to the March 15, 2013, additional assessment of 20m by Country M, X must notify the IRS within the time period provided by section 6511(d)(3)(A), increasing the foreign taxes available as a credit by $24 (20m translated at the exchange rate on the date of payment, or $1.20:1m). See sections 986(a)(1)(B)(i) and 986(a)(2)(A) and § 1.905-3T(b)(1)(ii)(A). X may so notify the IRS by filing a second amended return, Form 1118, and the statement required in paragraph (c) of this section for 2008, within the time period provided by section 6511(d)(3)(A). Alternatively, when X redetermines its United States tax liability for 2008 to take into account the 10n refund from Country N which occurred in 2012, X may also take into account the 20m additional assessment by Country M which occurred on March 15, 2013. See § 1.905-4T(b)(1)(iv). Where X reflects both foreign tax redeterminations on the same amended return, Form 1118, and in the statement required in paragraph (c) of this section for 2008, the amount of X's foreign taxes available as a credit would be:

(A) Reduced by $10 (10n refund translated at $1:1n) and

(B) Increased by $24 (20m additional assessment translated at the exchange rate on the date of payment, March 15, 2013, or $1.20:1m). The foreign taxes available as a credit therefore would be increased by $14 ($24 (additional assessment) - $10 (refund)). The due date of the 2008 amended return, Form 1118, and the statement required in paragraph (c) of this section reflecting foreign tax redeterminations in both years would be the due date (with extensions) of X's original return for 2012.

(vi) With respect to 2009, X must notify the IRS by filing an amended return, Form 1118, and the statement required in paragraph (c) of this section for 2009 that is separate from that filed for 2008. The amended return, Form 1118, and the statement required in paragraph (c) of this section for 2009 must be filed by the due date (with extensions) of X's original return for 2013. The amended return and Form 1118 must reduce the amount of foreign taxes claimed as a credit under section 901 by $7.50 (5n refund translated at the average exchange rate for 2009, or $1.50:1n). X will recognize foreign currency gain or loss under section 988 in or after 2013 on the conversion of the 5n refund into dollars.

(2) Pooling adjustment in lieu of redetermination of United States tax liability. Where a redetermination of foreign tax paid or accrued by a foreign corporation affects the computation of foreign taxes deemed paid under section 902 or 960, and the taxpayer is required to adjust the foreign corporation's pools of post-1986 undistributed earnings and post-1986 foreign income taxes under § 1.905-3T(d)(2), the taxpayer is required to notify the IRS of such redetermination by reflecting the adjustments to the foreign corporation's pools of post-1986 undistributed earnings and post-1986 foreign income taxes on a Form 1118 for the taxpayer's first taxable year with respect to which the redetermination affects the computation of foreign taxes deemed paid. Such Form 1118 must be filed by the due date (with extensions) of the original return for such taxable year. In the case of multiple redeterminations that affect the computation of foreign taxes deemed paid for the same taxable year and that are required to be reported under this paragraph (b)(2), a taxpayer may file one notification for all such redeterminations in lieu of filing a separate notification for each such redetermination. See section 905(b) and the regulations under that section which require that a taxpayer substantiate that a foreign tax was paid and provide all necessary information establishing its entitlement to the foreign tax credit.

(3) Taxpayers under the jurisdiction of the Large and Mid-Size Business Division. The rules of this paragraph (b)(3) apply where a redetermination of United States tax liability is required by reason of a foreign tax redetermination that results in a reduction in the amount of foreign taxes paid or accrued, or included in the computation of foreign taxes deemed paid, and such foreign tax redetermination occurs while a taxpayer is under the jurisdiction of the Large and Mid-Size Business Division (or similar program). The taxpayer must, in lieu of applying the rules of paragraphs (b)(1)(i) and (ii) of this section (requiring the filing of an amended return, Form 1118, and a statement described in paragraph (c) of this section by the due date (with extensions) of the original return for the taxpayer's taxable year in which the foreign tax redetermination occurred), notify the IRS of such redetermination by providing to the examiner the statement described in paragraph (c) of this section during an examination of the return for the taxable year for which a redetermination of United States tax liability is required by reason of such foreign tax redetermination. The taxpayer must provide the statement to the examiner no later than 120 days after the latest of the date the foreign tax redetermination occurs, the opening conference of the examination, or the hand-delivery or postmark date of the opening letter concerning the examination. If, however, the foreign tax redetermination occurs more than 180 days after the latest of the opening conference or the hand-delivery or postmark date of the opening letter, the taxpayer may, in lieu of applying the rules of paragraphs (b)(1)(i) and (ii) of this section, provide the statement to the examiner within 120 days after the date the foreign tax redetermination occurs, and the IRS, in its discretion, may accept such statement or require the taxpayer to comply with the rules of paragraphs (b)(1)(i) and (ii) of this section. A taxpayer subject to the rules of this paragraph (b)(3) must satisfy the rules of this paragraph (b)(3) (in lieu of the rules of paragraphs (b)(1)(i) and (ii) of this section) in order not to be subject to the penalty relating to the failure to file notice of a foreign tax redetermination under section 6689 and the regulations under that section. This paragraph (b)(3) shall not apply where the due date specified in paragraph (b)(1)(ii) of this section for providing notice of the foreign tax redetermination precedes the latest of the opening conference or the hand-delivery or postmark date of the opening letter concerning an examination of the return for the taxable year for which a redetermination of United States tax liability is required by reason of such foreign tax redetermination. In addition, any statement that would otherwise be required to be provided under this paragraph (b)(3) on or before May 5, 2008 will be considered timely if provided on or before May 5, 2008.

(4) Example. The following example illustrates the application of paragraph (b)(3) of this section:

Example. X, a taxpayer under the jurisdiction of the Large and Mid-Size Business Division, uses the calendar year as its United States taxable year. On October 15, 2009, X receives a refund of foreign tax that constitutes a foreign tax redetermination that necessitates a redetermination of United States tax liability for X's 2008 taxable year. Under paragraph (b)(1)(ii) of this section, X is required to notify the IRS of the foreign tax redetermination by filing an amended return, Form 1118, and the statement required in paragraph (c) of this section for its 2008 taxable year by September 15, 2010 (the due date (with extensions) of the original return for X's 2009 taxable year). On December 15, 2010, the IRS hand delivers an opening letter concerning the examination of the return for X's 2008 taxable year, and the opening conference for such examination is scheduled for January 15, 2011. Because the date for notifying the IRS of the foreign tax redetermination under paragraph (b)(1)(ii) of this section precedes the date of the opening conference concerning the examination of the return for X's 2008 taxable year, paragraph (b)(3) of this section does not apply, and X must notify the IRS of the foreign tax redetermination by filing a amended return, Form 1118, and the statement required in paragraph (c) of this section for the 2008 taxable year by September 15, 2010.

(c) Notification contents. *(1) In general.* In addition to satisfying the requirements of paragraph (b) of this section, the taxpayer must furnish a statement that contains information sufficient for the IRS to redetermine the taxpayer's United States tax liability where such a redetermination is required under section 905(c), and to verify adjustments to the pools of post-1986 undistributed earnings and post-1986 foreign income taxes where such adjustments are required under § 1.905-3T(d)(2). The information must be in a form that enables the IRS to verify and compare the original computations with respect to a claimed foreign tax credit, the revised computations resulting from the foreign tax redetermination, and the net changes resulting therefrom. The statement must include the taxpayer's name, address, identifying number, and the taxable year or years of the taxpayer that are affected by the foreign tax redetermination. In addition, the taxpayer must provide the information described in paragraph (c)(2) or (c)(3) of this section, as appropriate. If the statement is submitted to the IRS under paragraph (b)(3) of this section, which provides requirements with respect to reporting by taxpayers under the jurisdiction of the Large and Mid-Size Business Division, the statement must also include the following declaration signed by a person authorized to sign the return of the taxpayer: "Under penalties of perjury, I declare that I have examined this written statement, and to the best of my knowledge and belief, this written statement is true, correct, and complete."

(2) Foreign taxes paid or accrued. Where a redetermination of United States tax liability is required by reason of a foreign tax redetermination as defined in § 1.905-3T(c), in

addition to the information described in paragraph (c)(1) of this section, the taxpayer must provide the following: the date or dates the foreign taxes were accrued, if applicable; the date or dates the foreign taxes were paid; the amount of foreign taxes paid or accrued on each date (in foreign currency) and the exchange rate used to translate each such amount, as provided in § 1.905-3T(b)(1) or (b)(2); and information sufficient to determine any interest due from or owing to the taxpayer, including the amount of any interest paid by the foreign government to the taxpayer and the dates received. In addition, in the case of any foreign tax that is refunded in whole or in part, the taxpayer must provide the date of each such refund; the amount of such refund (in foreign currency); and the exchange rate that was used to translate such amount when originally claimed as a credit (as provided in § 1.905-3T(b)(3)) and the exchange rate for the date the refund was received (for purposes of computing foreign currency gain or loss under section 988). In addition, in the case of any foreign taxes that were not paid before the date two years after the close of the taxable year to which such taxes relate, the taxpayer must provide the amount of such taxes in foreign currency, and the exchange rate that was used to translate such amount when originally added to post-1986 foreign income taxes or claimed as a credit. Where a redetermination of United States tax liability results in an amount of additional tax due, but the carryback or carryover of an unused foreign tax under section 904(c) only partially eliminates such amount, the taxpayer must also provide the information required in § 1.904-2(f).

(3) Foreign taxes deemed paid. Where a redetermination of United States tax liability is required under § 1.905-3T(d)(3) to account for the effect of a redetermination of foreign tax paid or accrued by a foreign corporation on foreign taxes deemed paid under section 902 or 960, in addition to the information described in paragraphs (c)(1) and (c)(2) of this section, the taxpayer must provide the balances of the pools of post-1986 undistributed earnings and post-1986 foreign income taxes before and after adjusting the pools in accordance with the rules of § 1.905-3T(d)(2), the dates and amounts of any dividend distributions or other inclusions made out of earnings and profits for the affected year or years, and the amount of earnings and profits from which such dividends were paid for the affected year or years.

(d) Payment or refund of United States tax. The amount of tax, if any, due upon a redetermination of United States tax liability shall be paid by the taxpayer after notice and demand has been made by the IRS. Subchapter B of chapter 63 of the Internal Revenue Code (relating to deficiency procedures) shall not apply with respect to the assessment of the amount due upon such redetermination. In accordance with sections 905(c) and 6501(c)(5), the amount of additional tax due shall be assessed and collected without regard to the provisions of section 6501(a) (relating to limitations on assessment and collection). The amount of tax, if any, shown by a redetermination of United States tax liability to have been overpaid shall be credited or refunded to the taxpayer in accordance with the provisions of section 6511(d)(3)(A) and § 301.6511(d)-3 of this chapter.

(e) Interest and penalties. *(1) In general.* If a redetermination of United States tax liability is required by reason of a foreign tax redetermination, interest shall be computed on the underpayment or overpayment in accordance with sections 6601 and 6611 and the regulations under these sections. No interest shall be assessed or collected on any underpayment resulting from a refund of foreign tax for any period before the receipt of the refund, except to the extent interest was paid by the foreign country or possession of the United States on the refund for the period. In no case, however, shall interest assessed and collected pursuant to the preceding sentence for any period before receipt of the foreign tax refund exceed the amount that otherwise would have been assessed and collected under section 6601 and the regulations under this section for that period. Interest shall be assessed from the time the taxpayer (or the foreign corporation of which the taxpayer is a shareholder) receives a refund until the taxpayer pays the additional tax due the United States.

(2) Adjustments to pools of foreign taxes. No underpayment or overpayment of United States tax liability results from a redetermination of foreign tax unless a redetermination of United States tax liability is required. Consequently, no interest shall be paid by or to a taxpayer as a result of adjustments to a foreign corporation's pools of post-1986 undistributed earnings and post-1986 foreign income taxes made in accordance with § 1.905-3T(d)(2).

(3) Imposition of penalty. Failure to comply with the provisions of this section shall subject the taxpayer to the penalty provisions of section 6689 and the regulations under that section.

(f) Effective/applicability date. *(1) In general.* This section applies to foreign tax redeterminations (defined in § 1.905-3T(c)) occurring in taxable years of United States taxpayers beginning on or after November 7, 2007, where the foreign tax redetermination affects the amount of foreign taxes paid or accrued by a United States taxpayer. Where the redetermination of foreign tax paid or accrued by a foreign corporation affects the computation of foreign taxes deemed paid under section 902 or 960 with respect to pre-1987 accumulated profits or post-1986 undistributed earnings of the foreign corporation, this section applies to foreign tax redeterminations occurring in a taxable year of the foreign corporation which ends with or within a taxable year of its domestic corporate shareholder beginning on or after November 7, 2007. In no case, however, shall this paragraph (f)(1) operate to extend the statute of limitations provided by section 6511(d)(3)(A).

(2) Foreign tax redeterminations occurring in taxable years beginning before November 7, 2007. (i) Scope. This paragraph (f)(2) applies to any foreign tax redetermination (as defined in § 1.905-3T(c)) which occurred in any of the three taxable years of a United States taxpayer immediately preceding the taxpayer's first taxable year beginning on or after November 7, 2007; reduced the amount of foreign taxes paid or accrued by the taxpayer; and requires a redetermination of United States tax liability for any taxable year. This paragraph (f)(2) also applies to any redetermination of foreign tax paid or accrued by a foreign corporation which occurred in a taxable year of the foreign corporation which ends with or within any of the three taxable years of a domestic corporate shareholder immediately preceding such shareholder's first taxable year beginning on or after November 7, 2007; reduced foreign taxes included in the computation of foreign taxes deemed paid by such shareholder under section 902 or 960; and requires a redetermination of United States tax liability under § 1.905-3T(d)(3) for any taxable year. For corresponding rules applicable to foreign tax redeterminations occurring in taxable years beginning before the third taxable year immediately preceding the taxable year beginning on or after November 7, 2007, see 26 CFR 1.905-4T and 1.905-5T (as contained in 26 CFR part 1, revised as of April 1, 2007).

(ii) Notification required. If, as of November 7, 2007, the taxpayer has not satisfied the notification requirements described in § 1.905-3T and this section (as contained in 26 CFR part 1, revised as of April 1, 2007, as modified by Notice 90-26, 1990-1 CB 336, see § 601.601(d)(2)(ii)(b) of this chapter), with respect to a foreign tax redetermination described in paragraph (f)(2)(i) of this section, the taxpayer must notify the IRS of the foreign tax redetermination by filing an amended return, Form 1118 or 1116, and the statement required in paragraph (c) of this section for the taxable year with respect to which a redetermination of United States tax liability is required. Such notification must be filed no later than the due date (with extensions) of the original return for the taxpayer's first taxable year following the taxable year in which these regulations are first applicable. Where the foreign tax redetermination requires an individual to redetermine the individual's United States tax liability, and as a result of such foreign tax redetermination the amount of creditable taxes paid or accrued by such individual during the taxable year does not exceed the applicable dollar limitation in section 904(k), the individual shall not be required to file Form 1116 with the amended return for such taxable year if the individual satisfies the requirements of section 904(k). The rules of paragraphs (b)(1)(iv) and (v) of this section (concerning multiple redeterminations of United States tax liability for the same taxable year, and the carryback and carryover of unused foreign tax) shall apply.

(iii) Taxpayers under the jurisdiction of the Large and Mid-Size Business Division. If a taxpayer under the jurisdiction of the Large and Mid-Size Business Division is otherwise required under paragraph (f)(2)(ii) of this section to notify the IRS of a foreign tax redetermination described in paragraph (f)(2)(ii) of this section by filing an amended return, Form 1118, and the statement required in paragraph (c) of this section, such taxpayer may, in lieu of applying the rules of paragraph (f)(2)(ii) of this section, provide to the examiner the information described in paragraph (c) of this section during an examination of the return for the taxable year for which a redetermination of United States tax liability is required by reason of such foreign tax redetermination. The taxpayer must provide the information to the examiner on or before the date that is the later of May 5, 2008 or 120 days after the latest of the opening conference or the hand-delivery or postmark date of the opening letter concerning an examination of the return for the taxable year for which a redetermination of United States tax liability is required. However, if November 7, 2007 is more than 180 days after the latest of the opening conference or the hand-delivery or postmark date of the opening letter, the IRS, in its discretion, may accept such statement or require the taxpayer to comply with the rules of paragraph (f)(2)(ii) of this section. This paragraph (f)(2)(iii) shall not apply where the due date specified in paragraph (f)(2)(ii) of this section for providing notice of the foreign tax redetermination precedes the latest of the opening conference or the hand-delivery or postmark date of the opening letter concerning an examination of the return for the taxable year for which a redetermination of United States tax liability is required.

(iv) Interest and penalties. Interest shall be computed in accordance with paragraph (e) of this section. Failure to comply with the provisions of this paragraph (f)(2) shall subject the taxpayer to the penalty provisions of section 6689 and the regulations under that section.

(3) Expiration date. The applicability of this section expires on or before November 5, 2010.

T.D. 8210, 6/22/88, amend T.D. 9362, 11/6/2007.

Proposed § 1.905-5 Foreign tax redeterminations and currency translation rules for foreign tax redeterminations occurring in taxable years beginning prior to January 1, 1987. [*For Preamble, see ¶ 152,925*]

[The text of this section is the same as the text of § 1.905-5T(a) through (f) published elsewhere in this issue of the Federal Register.] [*See T.D. 9362, 11/07/2007, 72 Fed. Reg. 215.*]

§ 1.905-5T Foreign tax redeterminations and currency translation rules for foreign tax redeterminations occurring in taxable years beginning prior to January 1, 1987 (Temporary).

(a) In general. This section sets forth rules governing the application of section 905(c) to foreign tax redeterminations occurring prior to January 1, 1987. However, the rules of this section also apply to foreign tax redeterminations occurring after December 31, 1986 with respect to foreign tax deemed paid under section 902 or section 960 with respect to pre-1987 accumulated profits (as defined in § 1.902-1(a)(10)(i).

(b) Currency translation rules. *(1) Foreign taxes paid by the taxpayer and certain foreign taxes deemed paid.* Foreign taxes paid in foreign currency that are paid by or on behalf of a taxpayer or deemed paid under section 960 (or under section 902 in a deemed distribution under section 1248) shall be translated into dollars at the rate of exchange for the date of the payment of the foreign tax. Refunds of such taxes shall be translated into dollars at the rate of exchange for the date of the refund.

(2) Foreign taxes deemed paid on an actual distribution. Foreign taxes deemed paid by a taxpayer under section 902 with respect to an actual distribution and refunds of such taxes shall be translated into dollars at the rate of exchange for the date of the distribution of the earnings to which the taxes relate.

(c) Foreign tax redetermination. The term "foreign tax redetermination" means a foreign tax redetermination as defined in § 1.905-3T(c).

(d) Redetermination of United States tax liability. *(1) In general.* A redetermination of United States tax liability is required with respect to any foreign tax redetermination subject to this section and shall be subject to the requirements of § 1.905-4T(b). The content of the notification required by this paragraph (d) shall be the same as provided in § 1.905-4T(c), except as modified by paragraphs (d)(2), (3), and (4) of this section.

(2) Refunds. In the case of any refund of foreign tax, the rate of exchange on the date of the refund shall be included in the information required by § 1.905-4T(c)(2).

(3) Foreign taxes deemed paid under section 902. In the case of foreign taxes paid or accrued by a foreign corporation that are deemed paid or accrued under section 902 with respect to an actual distribution and with respect to which there was a redetermination of foreign tax, the United States taxpayer's information shall include, in lieu of the information required by § 1.905-4T(c)(3), the following: the foreign corporation's name and identifying number (if any); the date on which the foreign taxes were accrued and the dates on which the foreign taxes were paid; the amounts of the foreign taxes accrued or paid in foreign currency on each such date; the dates on which any foreign taxes were refunded and the amounts thereof; the dates and amounts of any dividend distributions made out of earnings and profits for the affected year or years; the rate of exchange on the date of any such distribution; and the amount of earnings and profits

from which such dividends were paid for the affected year or years.

(4) Foreign taxes deemed paid under section 960. In the case of foreign taxes paid under section 960 (or under section 902 in the case of an amount treated as a dividend under section 1248), the rate of exchange determined under § 1.964-1 for translating accrued foreign taxes shall be included in the information required by § 1.905-4T(c)(4).

(e) Exception for de minimis currency fluctuations. A United States taxpayer need not notify the Service of a foreign tax redetermination that results solely from a currency fluctuation if the amount of such redetermination with respect to the foreign country is less than the lesser of ten thousand dollars or two percent of the total dollar amount of the foreign tax, prior to the adjustment, initially accrued with respect to that foreign country for the taxable year.

(f) Special effective/applicability date. See § 1.905-4T(f) for the applicability date of notification requirements relating to foreign tax redeterminations that affect foreign taxes deemed paid under section 902 or section 960 with respect to pre-1987 accumulated profits accumulated in taxable years of a foreign corporation beginning on or after January 1, 1987. Failure to comply with the provisions of this section shall subject the taxpayer to the penalty provisions of section 6689 and the regulations thereunder. In no case, however, shall this paragraph operate to extend the statute of limitations provided by section 6511(d)(3)(A).

(g) Expiration date. The applicability of this section expires on or before November 5, 2010.

T.D. 8210, 6/22/88, amend T.D. 9362, 11/6/2007.

§ 1.907-0 Outline of regulation provisions for section 907.

This section lists the paragraphs contained in §§ 1.907(a)-0 through 1.907(f)-1.

§ 1.907(a)-0 Introduction (for taxable years beginning after December 31, 1982).

(a) Effective dates.

(b) Key terms.

(c) FOGEI tax limitation.

(d) Reduction of creditable FORI taxes.

(e) FOGEI and FORI.

(f) Posted prices.

(g) Transitional rules.

(h) Section 907(f) carrybacks and carryovers.

(i) Statutes covered.

§ 1.907(a)-1 Reduction in taxes paid on FOGEI (for taxable years beginning after December 31, 1982).

(a) Amount of reduction.

(b) Foreign taxes paid or accrued.

(1) Foreign taxes.

(2) Foreign taxes paid or accrued.

(c) Limitation level.

(1) In general.

(2) Limitation percentage of corporations.

(3) Limitation percentage of individuals.

(4) Losses.

(5) Priority.

(d) Illustrations.

(e) Effect on other provisions.

(1) Deduction denied.

(2) Reduction inapplicable.

(3) Section 78 dividend.

(f) Section 904 limitation.

§ 1.907(b)-1 Reduction of creditable FORI taxes (for taxable years beginning after December 31, 1982).

§ 1.907(c)-1 Definitions relating to FOGEI and FORI (for taxable years beginning after December 31, 1982).

(a) Scope.

(b) FOGEI.

(1) General rule.

(2) Amount.

(3) Other circumstances.

(4) Income directly related to extraction.

(5) Income not included.

(6) Fair market value.

(7) Economic interest.

(c) Carryover of foreign oil extraction losses.

(1) In general.

(2) Reduction.

(3) Foreign oil extraction loss defined.

(4) Affiliated groups.

(5) FOGEI taxes.

(6) Examples.

(d) FORI.

(1) In general.

(2) Transportation.

(3) Distribution or sale.

(4) Processing.

(5) Primary product from oil.

(6) Primary product from gas.

(7) Directly related income.

(e) Assets used in a trade or business.

(1) In general.

(2) Section 907(c) activities.

(3) Stock.

(4) Losses on sale of stock.

(5) Character of gain or loss.

(6) Allocation of amount realized.

(7) Interest.

(f) Terms and items common to FORI and FOGEI.

(1) Minerals

(2) Taxable income.

(3) Interest on working capital.

(4) Exchange gain or loss.

(5) Allocation.

(6) Facts and circumstances.

(g) Directly related income.

(1) In general.

(2) Directly related services.

(3) Leases and licenses.

(4) Related person.

(5) Gross income.

T.D. 8240, 1/19/89, amend T.D. 8338, 3/14/91, T.D. 8655, 1/5/96.

§ 1.907(a)-0 Introduction (for taxable years beginning after December 31, 1982).

Caution: The Treasury has not yet amended Reg § 1.907(a)-0 to reflect changes made by 103-66.

(a) Effective dates. The provisions of §§ 1.907(a)-0 through § 1.907(f)-1 apply to taxable years beginning after December 31, 1982. For provisions that apply to taxable years beginning before January 1, 1983, see §§ 1.907(a)-0A through 1.907(f)-1A.

(b) Key terms. For purposes of the regulations under section 907—

(1) FOGEI means foreign oil and gas extraction income.

(2) FORI means foreign oil related income.

(3) FOGEI taxes mean foreign oil and gas extraction taxes as defined in section 907(c)(5).

(4) FORI taxes means foreign taxes on foreign oil related income. See § 1.907(c)-3.

(c) FOGEI tax limitation. Section 907(a) limits the foreign tax credit for taxes paid or accrued on FOGEI. See § 1.907(a)-1.

(d) Reduction of creditable FORI taxes. Section 907(b) recharacterizes FORI taxes as non-creditable deductible expenses to the extent that the foreign law imposing the FORI taxes is structured, or in fact operates, so that the amount of tax imposed with respect to FORI will be materially greater, over a reasonable period of time, than the amount generally imposed on income that is neither FOGEI nor FORI. See § 1.907(b)-1.

(e) FOGEI and FORI. FOGEI includes the taxable income from the extraction of minerals from oil or gas wells by a taxpayer (or another person) and from the sale or exchange of assets used in the extraction business. FORI includes taxable income from the activities of processing oil and gas into their primary products, transporting or distributing oil and gas and their primary products, and from the disposition of assets used in these activities. For this purpose, a disposition includes only a sale or exchange. FOGEI and FORI may also include taxable income from the performance of related services or from the lease of related property and certain dividends, interest, or amounts described in section 951(a). See §§ 1.907(c)-1 through 1.907(c)-3.

(f) Posted prices. Certain sales prices are disregarded when computing FOGEI for purposes of chapter 1 of the Code. See § 1.907(d)-1.

(g) Transitional rules. Section 907(e) provides rules for the carryover of unused FOGEI taxes from taxable years beginning before January 1, 1983, and carryback of FOGEI taxes arising in taxable years beginning after December 31, 1982. See § 1.907(e)-1.

(h) Section 907(f) carrybacks and carryovers. FOGEI taxes disallowed under section 907(a) may be carried back or forward to other taxable years. These FOGEI taxes may be absorbed in another taxable year to the extent of the lesser of the separate excess extraction limitation or the excess limitation in the general limitation category (section 904(d)(1)(I)) for the carryback or carryover year. See § 1.907(f)-1.

(i) Statutes covered. The regulations under section 907 are issued as a result of the enactment of section 601 of the Tax Reduction Act of 1975, of section 1035 of the Tax Reform Act of 1976, of section 301(b)(14) of the Revenue Act of 1978, of section 211 of the Tax Equity and Fiscal Responsibility Act of 1982 and of section 1012(g)(6)(A)-(B) of the Technical and Miscellaneous Revenue Act of 1988.

T.D. 8338, 3/14/91.

---

§ 1.907(a)-1 Reduction in taxes paid on FOGEI (for taxable years beginning after December 31, 1982).

(a) Amount of reduction. FOGEI taxes are reduced by the amount by which they exceed a limitation level (as defined in paragraph (c) of this section).

(b) Foreign taxes paid or accrued. For purposes of the regulations under section 907—

(1) Foreign taxes. The term "foreign taxes" means income, war profits, or excess profits taxes of foreign countries or possessions of the United States otherwise creditable under section 901 (including those creditable by reason of section 903).

(2) Foreign taxes paid or accrued. The terms "foreign taxes paid or accrued," "FOGEI taxes paid or accrued," and "FORI taxes paid or accrued" include foreign taxes deemed paid under sections 902 and 960. Unless otherwise expressly provided, these terms do not include foreign taxes deemed paid by reason of sections 904(c) and 907(f).

(c) Limitation level. *(1) In general.* The limitation level is FOGEI for the taxable year multiplied by the limitation percentage for that year.

(2) Limitation percentage for corporations. A corporation's limitation percentage is the highest rate of tax specified in section 11(b) for the particular year.

(3) Limitation percentage for individuals. Section 907(a)(2)(B) provides that the limitation percentage for individual taxpayers is the effective rate of tax for those taxpayers. The effective rate of tax is computed by dividing the entire tax, before the credit under section 901(a) is taken, by the taxpayer's entire taxable income.

(4) Losses. (i) For purposes of determining whether income is FOGEI, a taxpayer's FOGEI will be recharacterized as foreign source non-FOGEI to the extent that FOGEI losses for preceding taxable years beginning after December 31, 1982, exceed the amount of FOGEI already recharacterized. See § 1.907(c)-1(c). However, taxes that were paid or accrued on the recharacterized FOGEI will remain FOGEI taxes.

(ii) Taxes paid or accrued by a person to a foreign country may be FOGEI taxes even though that person has under U.S. law a net operating loss from sources within that country.

(iii) For purposes of determining whether income is FOGEI, a taxpayer's income will be treated as income from sources outside the United States even though all or a portion of that income may be resourced as income from sources within the United States under section 904(f)(1) and (4).

(5) Priority. (i) Section 907(a) applies before section 908, relating to reduction of credit for participation in or cooperation with an international boycott.

(ii) Section 901(f) (relating to certain payments with respect to oil and gas not considered as taxes) applies before section 907.

(d) Illustrations. Paragraphs (a) through (c) of this section are illustrated by the following examples.

Example (1). M, a U.S. corporation, uses the accrual method of accounting and the calendar year as its taxable year. For 1984, M has $20,000 of FOGEI, derived from operations in foreign countries X and Y, and has accrued $11,500 of foreign taxes with respect to FOGEI. The highest tax rate specified in section 11(b) for M's 1984 taxable year is 46 percent. Pursuant to section 907(a), M's FOGEI taxes limitation level for 1984 is $9,200 (46% × $20,000). The foreign taxes in excess of this limitation level ($2,300) may be carried back or forward. See section 907(f) and § 1.907(f)-1 and section 907(e) and § 1.907(e)-1.

Example (2). The facts are the same as in Example 1 except that M is a partnership owned equally by U.S. citizens A and B who each file as unmarried individuals and do not itemize deductions. Pursuant to section 905(a), A and B have elected to credit foreign taxes in the year accrued. The total amount of foreign taxes accrued by A and B with respect to their distributive shares of M's FOGEI is $11,500 ($5,750 accrued by A and $5,750 accrued by B). A and B have no other FOGEI. A's only taxable income for 1984 is his 50% distributive share ($10,000) of M's FOGEI and A has a preliminary U.S. tax liability of $1,079. B has $112,130 of taxable income for 1984 (including his 50% distributive share ($10,000) of M's FOGEI) and has a preliminary U.S. tax liability of $44,000. Pursuant to section 907(a), A's FOGEI taxes limitation level for 1984 is $1,079 (($1,079/$10,000) × $10,000) and B's FOGEI taxes limitation level for 1984 is $3,924 (($44,000/$112,130) × $10,000).

(e) Effect on other provisions. *(1) Deduction denied.* If a credit is claimed under section 901, no deduction under section 164(a)(3) is allowed for the amount of the FOGEI taxes that exceed a taxpayer's limitation level for the taxable year. See section 275(a)(4)(A). Thus, FOGEI taxes disallowed under section 907(a) are not added to the cost or inventory amount of oil or gas.

(2) Reduction inapplicable. The reduction under section 907(a) does not apply to a taxpayer that deducts foreign taxes and does not claim the benefits of section 901 for a taxable year.

(3) Section 78 dividend. The reduction under section 907(a) has no effect on the amount of foreign taxes that are treated as dividends under section 78.

(f) Section 904 limitation. FOGEI taxes as reduced under section 907(a) are creditable only to the extent permitted by the general limitation of section 904(d)(1)(I).

T.D. 8338, 3/14/91.

---

§ 1.907(b)-1 Reduction of creditable FORI taxes (for taxable years beginning after December 31, 1982).

If the foreign law imposing a FORI tax (as defined in § 1.907(c)-3) is either structured in a manner, or operates in a manner, so that the amount of tax imposed on FORI is generally materially greater than the tax imposed by the foreign law on income that is neither FORI nor FOGEI ("described manner"), section 907(b) provides a special rule which limits the amount of FORI taxes paid or accrued by a person to a foreign country which will be considered income, war profits, or excess profits taxes. Section 907(b) will apply to a person regardless of whether that person is a dual capacity taxpayer as defined in § 1.901-2(a)(2)(ii)(A). (In general, a dual capacity taxpayer is a person who pays an amount to a foreign country part of which is attributable to an income tax and the remainder of which is a payment for a specific economic benefit derived from that country.) Foreign law imposing a tax on FORI will be considered either to be structured in or to operate in the described manner only if, under the facts and circumstances, there has been a shifting of tax by the foreign country from a tax on FOGEI to a tax on FORI.

T.D. 8338, 3/14/91.

---

§ 1.907(c)-1 Definitions relating to FOGEI and FORI (for taxable years beginning after December 31, 1982).

Caution: The Treasury has not yet amended Reg § 1.907(c)-1 to reflect changes made by P.L. 104-188, P.L. 103-66.

(a) Scope. This section explains the meaning to be given certain terms and items in section 907(c)(1), (2), and (4). See also §§ 1.907(a)-0(b) and 1.907(c)-2 for further definitions.

(b) FOGEI. *(1) General rule.* Under section 907(c)(1), FOGEI means taxable income (or loss) derived from sources outside the United States and its possessions from the extraction (by the taxpayer or any other person) of minerals from oil or gas wells located outside the United States and its possessions or from the sale or exchange of assets used by the taxpayer in the trade or business of extracting those minerals. Extraction of minerals from oil or gas wells will result in gross income from extraction in every case in which that person has an economic interest in the minerals in place. For other circumstances in which gross income from extraction may arise, see paragraph (b)(3) of this section. For determination of the amount of gross income from extraction, see paragraph (b)(2) of this section. For definition of the phrase "assets used by the taxpayer in the trade or business" and for rules relating to that type of FOGEI, see paragraph (e)(1) of this section. The term "minerals" is defined in paragraph (f)(1) of this section, For determination of taxable income, see paragraph (f)(2) of this section. FOGEI includes, in addition, items listed in section 907(c)(3) (relating to dividends, interest, partnership distributions, etc.) and explained in § 1.907(c)-2. For the reduction of what would otherwise be FOGEI by losses incurred in a prior year, see section 907(c)(4) and paragraph (c) of this section.

(2) Amount. The gross income from extraction is determined by reference to the fair market value of the minerals in the immediate vicinity of the well. Fair market value is determined under paragraph (b)(6) of this section.

(3) Other circumstances. Gross income from extraction or the sale or exchange of assets described in section 907(c)(1)(B) includes income from any arrangement, or a combination of arrangements or transactions, to the extent the income is in substance attributable to the extraction of minerals or such a sale or exchange. For instance, a person may have gross income from such a sale or exchange if the person purchased minerals from a foreign government at a discount and the discount reflects an arm's-length amount in consideration for the government's nationalization of assets that person owned and used in the extraction of minerals.

(4) Income directly related to extraction. Gross income from extraction includes directly related income under paragraph (g) of this section.

(5) Income not included. FOGEI as otherwise determined under this paragraph (b), nevertheless, does not include income to the extent attributable to marketing, distributing, processing or transporting minerals or primary products. Income from the purchase and sale of minerals is not ordinarily FOGEI. If the foreign taxes paid or accrued in connection with income from a purchase and sale are not creditable by reason of section 901(f), that income is not FOGEI. A taxpayer to whom section 901(f) applies is not a producer.

(6) Fair market value. For purposes of this paragraph (b), the fair market value of oil or gas in the immediate vicinity of the well depends on all of the facts and circumstances as they exist relative to a party in any particular case. The facts and circumstances that may be taken into account include, but are not limited to, the following—

(i) The facts and circumstances pertaining to an independent market value (if any) in the immediate vicinity of the well,

(ii) The facts and circumstances pertaining to the relationships between the taxpayer and the foreign government. If an independent fair market value in the immediate vicinity of the well cannot be determined but fair market value at the port, or a similar point, in the foreign country can be determined (port price), an analysis of the arrangement between the taxpayer and the foreign government that retains a share of production could be evidence of the appropriate, arm's-length difference between the port price and the field price, and

(iii) The other facts and circumstances pertaining to any difference in the producing country between the field and port prices.

(7) Economic interest. For purposes of this paragraph (b), the term "economic interest" means an economic interest as defined in § 1.611-1(b)(1), whether or not a deduction for depletion is allowable under section 611.

(c) Carryover of foreign oil extraction losses. *(1) In general.* Pursuant to section 907(c)(4), the determination of FOGEI for a particular taxable year takes into account a foreign oil extraction loss incurred in prior taxable years beginning after December 31, 1982. There is no time limitation on this carryover of foreign oil extraction losses. Section 907(c)(4) does not provide for any carryback of these losses. Section 907(c)(4) operates solely for purposes of determining FOGEI and thus operates independently of section 904(f).

(2) Reduction. That portion of the income of the taxpayer for the taxable year which but for this paragraph (c) would be treated as FOGEI is reduced (but not below zero) by the excess of—

(i) The aggregate amount of foreign oil extraction losses for preceding taxable years beginning after December 31, 1982, over

(ii) The aggregate amount of reductions under this paragraph (c) for preceding taxable years beginning after December 31, 1982.

(3) Foreign oil extraction loss defined. (i) In general. For purposes of this paragraph (c), the term "foreign oil extraction loss" means the amount by which the gross income for the taxable year that is taken into account in determining FOGEI for that year is exceeded by the sum of the deductions properly allocated and apportioned to that gross income as determined under paragraph (f)(2) of this section). A person can have a foreign oil extraction loss for a taxable year even if the person has not chosen the benefits of section 901 for that year.

(ii) Items not taken into account. For purposes of paragraph (c)(3)(i) of this section, the following items are not taken into account—

(A) The net operating loss deduction allowable for the taxable year under section 172(a),

(B) Any foreign expropriation loss (as defined in section 172(h)) for the taxable year, and

(C) Any loss for the taxable year which arises from fire, storm, shipwreck, or other casualty, or from theft.

A loss mentioned in paragraph (c)(3)(ii)(B) or (C) of this section is taken into account, however, to the extent compensation (for instance by insurance) for the loss is included in gross income.

(4) Affiliated groups. The foreign oil extraction loss of an affiliated group of corporations (within the meaning of section 1504(a)) that files a consolidated return is determined on a group basis. If the group does not have a foreign oil extraction loss, the foreign oil extraction loss of a member of that group will not reduce on a separate basis that member's FOGEI for a later taxable year. For special rules affecting the foreign oil extraction loss in the case of certain related domestic corporations that are not members of the same affiliated group, see section 904(i).

(5) FOGEI taxes. If FOGEI is reduced pursuant to this paragraph (c) (and thereby recharacterized as non-FOGEI income), any foreign taxes imposed on the FOGEI that is recharacterized as other income retain their character as FOGEI taxes. See section 907(c)(5).

(6) Examples. The provisions of this paragraph (c) may be illustrated by the following examples.

Example (1). (i) Facts. X, a U.S. corporation using the accrual method of accounting and the calendar year as its taxable year, is engaged in extraction activities in three foreign countries. X has only the following combined foreign tax items for the three countries (prior to the application of this paragraph (c)) for 1983, 1984, and 1985:

	1983	1984	1985
FOGEI	$(700)	$100	$450
FOGEI taxes	10	60	200
Net operating loss deduction	(200)	0	0
Foreign oil extraction loss allowable after adjustment for paragraph (c)(3)(ii) amounts	(500)	0	0
General limitation taxes other than FOGEI taxes	30	90	230

(ii) 1983. Because X's FOGEI for 1983 is a loss of $(700), X's section 907(a) limitation for 1983 is $0 (.46 × $0). Thus, none of the FOGEI taxes paid or accrued in 1983 ($10) can be credited in 1983. They can, however, be carried back to 1981 or 1982 pursuant to the provisions of section 907(e)(2) and § 1.907(e)-1 and carried forward pursuant to the provisions of section 907(f) and § 1.907(f)-1.

(iii) 1984. X's FOGEI for 1984, prior to the application of this paragraph (c), is $100. X has a foreign oil extraction loss for 1983 of $(500). This loss must be applied against X's preliminary FOGEI of $100 for 1984. Thus, X's FOGEI for 1984 is $0 and X has $(400) ($500 − $100) of foreign oil extraction loss from 1983 to be carried to 1985. Since X's FOGEI for 1984 is $0, its section 907(a) limitation is $0 (.46 × $0). Therefore, none of the FOGEI taxes paid or accrued in 1984 ($60) can be credited in 1984. They can, however, be carried back pursuant to the provisions of section 907(e)(2) and § 1.907(e)-1 and carried forward pursuant to the provisions of section 907(f) and § 1.907(f)-1.

(iv) 1985. X's FOGEI for 1985, prior to the application of this paragraph (c), is $450. X's remaining foreign oil extraction loss carryover from 1983 is $(400) ad this must be applied against X's preliminary FOGEI of $450 for 1985. Thus, X's FOGEI for 1984 is $50 ($450 − $400). X's section 907(a) limitation is $23 (.46 × $50). Therefore, $23 of the FOGEI taxes paid or accrued in 1985, together with the other $230 of general limitation taxes, can be credited in 1985, subject to the general limitation of section 904(d)(1)(E) (as in effect prior to 1987). The excess of FOGEI taxes, $177 ($200 − $23), can be carried back pursuant to the provisions of section 907(e)(2) and § 1.907(e)-1 and carried forward pursuant to the provisions of section 907(f) and § 1.907(f)-1.

Example (2). (i) Facts. The facts are the same as in Example 1 except that X's paragraph (c)(3)(ii) items for 1983 allocable to FOGEI are $(800) instead of $(200). FOGEI remains a loss of $(700). Thus, X does not have a foreign oil extraction loss for 1983 because it has $100 of FOGEI when its paragraph (c)(3)(ii) items are not taken into account ($(700) + $800).

(ii) 1983. The results are the same as in Example 1.

(iii) 1984. Although X had FOGEI loss of $(700) in 1983, there is not a loss that can be carried forward after adjustment for paragraph (c)(3)(ii) items. Thus, X's FOGEI for 1984 is not reduced by the 1983 loss. X's section 907(a) limitation for 1984 is $46 (.46 × $100). Therefore, $46 of the FOGEI taxes paid or accrued in 1984, together with the other $90 of general limitation taxes, can be credited in 1984, subject to the general limitation of section 904(d)(1)(E) (as in effect prior to 1987). The excess of $14 ($60 − $46) can be carried back to 1982 pursuant to the provisions of section 907(e)(2) and § 1.907(e)-1 and carried forward pursuant to the provisions of section 907(f) and § 1.907(f)-1.

(iv) 1985. Since there is no foreign oil extraction loss for either 1983 or 1984 to be applied in 1985, X's FOGEI for 1985 is $450. Thus, its section 907(a) limitation for 1985 is $207 (.46 × $450) and all of its FOGEI taxes paid or accrued in 1985 ($200), together with the other $230 of general limitation taxes, can be credited in 1985, subject to the general limitation of section 904(d)(1)(E) (as in effect prior to 1987). FOGEI taxes in the amount of $10 from 1983 and $14 from 1984 may be carried forward to 1985 if they have not been used in carryback years. However, because the excess section 907(a) limitation for 1985 is only $7, that is the maximum potential FOGEI taxes from 1983 or 1984 that may be used in 1985.

Example (3). (i) Facts. Y, a U.S. corporation using the accrual method of accounting and the calendar year as its taxable year, is engaged in extraction activities in three foreign countries. Y's only foreign taxable income is income subject to the general limitation of section 904(d)(1)(E) (as in effect prior to 1987). Y has no paragraph (c)(3)(ii) items. Y has the following foreign tax items for 1983 and 1984:

	1983	1984
FOGEI	$ (400)	$300
Other foreign taxable income	250	200
U.S. taxable income	1,000	1,100
Worldwide taxable income	850	1,600
FOGEI taxes	10	180
Other general limitation taxes	50	40
Foreign oil extraction loss	(400)	0

(ii) 1983.

(A) Section 907(a) limitation. Because Y's FOGEI for 1983 is a loss of $(400), Y's section 907(a) limitation for 1983 is $0. Thus, none of the FOGEI taxes paid or accrued in 1983 ($10) can be credited in 1983. They can, however, be carried back to 1981 or 1982 pursuant to the provisions of section 907(e)(2) and § 1.907(e)-1 and carried forward pursuant to the provisions of section 907(f) and § 1.907(f)-1.

(B) Section 904(d) fraction. Y has a foreign loss of $(150) ($(400 + $250) for 1983. Thus, its fraction for purposes of determining its general limitation of section 904(d)(1)(E) is $0/$850.

(C) Section 907(a) limitation. Y's foreign oil extraction loss for 1983 is $(400). Applying this loss to its preliminary FOGEI for 1984 ($300) eliminates all of Y's FOGEI for 1984. Because Y's FOGEI for 1984 is $0, its section 907(a) limitation is also $0. Thus, none of the FOGEI taxes paid or accrued in 1984 ($180) can be credited in 1984. They can, however, be carried back to 1982 pursuant to the provisions of section 907(e)(2) and § 1.907(e)-1 and carried forward pursuant to the provisions of section 907(f) and § 1.907(f)-1. Y has a remaining foreign oil extraction loss of $(100) from 1983 to be carried to 1985.

(D) Section 904(d) fraction. Y's preliminary foreign taxable income for purposes of determining its general limitation of section 904(d)(1)(E) is $500 ($300 + $200). However, Y has an overall foreign loss from 1983 of $(150) ($(400) + $250) and thus, pursuant to section 904(f), Y must recharacterize $150 (lesser of $150 or 50% of $500) of its 1984 foreign taxable income as U.S. taxable income. Thus, Y's fraction for purposes of determining its general limitation of section 904(d)(1)(E) for 1984 is $350/$1,600.

Example (4). (i) Facts. Assume the same facts as in Example 3 except that Y has the following foreign tax items:

(ii) 1983. For 1983, Y has a section 904(d)(1)(E) overall foreign loss account of $50; see section 904(f) and § 1.904(f)-1(b).

(iii) 1984. Because Y's FOGEI for 1984 is a loss of $(100), Y's section 907(a) limitation for 1984 is $0. Thus, none of the FOGEI taxes paid or accrued in 1984 ($10) can be credited in 1984. They can, however, be carried back under the provisions of section 907(e)(2) and § 1.907(e)-1 and carried forward under the provisions of section 907(f) and § 1.907(f)-1.

(iv) 1985. Y's FOGEI loss of $(100) for 1984 is carried forward to 1985 and offsets FOGEI income in that amount in 1985. The entire section 904(d)(1)(E) overall foreign loss account of $50 is recaptured in 1985; therefore, Y has $75 of foreign source income and $50 of U.S. source income. However, Y has $125 of FOGEI since, for purposes of section 907(a), the $50 resourced by section 904(f) will be treated as income from sources outside the United States; see § 1.907(a)-1(c)(4)(iii). Accordingly, Y's section 907(a) limitation is $57.50 (.46 × $125). Y's section 904(d)(1)(E) limitation is, however, only $34.50 (.46 × $75). Thus, Y may claim a foreign tax credit of $34.50 in 1985. Y may carry back or carry forward $23 ($57.50 − $34.50) and that amount is not subject to the section 907(a) limitation in the carry to year. In addition, $67.50 ($125 − $57.50) may be carried back pursuant to the provisions of section 907(e)(2) and § 1.907(e)-1 and carried forward pursuant to the provisions of section 907(f) and § 1.907(f)-1. This amount is subject to the section 907(a) limitation in the carry to year.

(d) FORI. *(1) In general.* Section 907(c)(2) defines FORI to include taxable income from the processing of oil and gas into their primary products, from the transportation or distribution and sale of oil and gas and their primary products, from the disposition of assets used in these activities and from the performance of any other related service. FORI may also include, under section 907(c)(3), certain dividends, interest, or amounts described in section 951(a). This paragraph (d) defines certain terms and items applicable to FORI.

(2) Transportation. Gross income from transportation of minerals or primary products ("gross transportation income") is gross income arising from carrying minerals or primary products between two places (including time or voyage charter hires) by any means of transportation, such as a vessel, pipeline, truck, railroad, or aircraft. Except for directly related income under paragraphs (d)(7) and (g) of this section, gross transportation income does not include gross income received by a lessor from a bareboat charter hire of a means of transportation, certain other rental income, or income from the performance of certain services.

(3) Distribution or sale. The term "distribution or sale" means the sale or exchange of minerals or primary products to processors, users who purchase, store, or use in bulk quantities, other persons for further distribution, retailers, or consumers. Gross income from distribution or sale includes interest income attributable to the distribution of minerals or primary products on credit.

(4) Processing. The term "processing" means the destructive distillation, or a process similar in effect to destructive distillation, of crude oil and the processing of natural gas into their primary products including processes used to remove pollutants from crude oil or natural gas.

(5) Primary product from oil. The term "primary product" (in the case of oil) means all products derived from the processing of crude oil, including volatile products, light oils (such as motor fuel and kerosene), distillates (such as naphtha), lubricating oils, greases and waxes, and residues (such as fuel oil).

(6) Primary product from gas. The term "primary product" (in the case of gas) means all gas and associated hydrocarbon components from gas wells or oil wells, whether recovered at the lease or upon further processing, including natural gas, condensates, liquefiable petroleum gases (such as ethane, propane, and butane), and liquid products (such as natural gasoline).

(7) Directly related income. FORI also includes directly related income under paragraph (g) of this section.

(e) Assets used in a trade or business. *(1) In general.* The term "assets used by the taxpayer in the trade or business" in section 907(c)(1)(B) and (2)(D) means property primarily used in one or more of the trades or businesses that are section 907(c) activities. For purposes of this paragraph (e), assets used in a trade or business are assets described in section 1231(b) (applied without regard to any holding period or the character of the asset as being subject to the allowance for depreciation under section 167).

(2) Section 907(c) activities. Section 907(c) activities are those described in section 907(c)(1)(A) (for FOGEI) or (c)(2)(A) through (C) (for FORI). If an asset is used primarily in one or more section 907(c) activities, then the entire gain (or loss) will be considered attributable to those activities. For example, if a person uses a service station primarily to distribute primary products from oil, then all of the gain (or loss) on the sale of the station is FORI even though the person uses the station to distribute products that are not primary products (such as tires or batteries). If an asset is not primarily used in one or more section 907(c) activities, then the entire gain or loss will not be FOGEI or FORI.

(3) Stock. Stock of any corporation (whether foreign or domestic) will not be treated as an asset used by a person in section 907(c) activities.

(4) Losses on sale of stock. If, under § 1.861-8(e)(7), a loss on the sale, exchange, or disposition of stock is considered a deduction which is definitely related and allocable to FOGEI or FORI, then notwithstanding § 1.861-8(e)(7) and paragraph (f)(2) of this section, this loss shall be allocated and apportioned to the same class of income that would have been produced if there were capital gain from the sale, exchange or disposition.

(5) Character of gain or loss. Except in the case of stock, gain or loss from the sale, exchange or disposition of assets used in the trade or business may be FORI or FOGEI to the extent taken into account in computing taxable income for the taxable year, whether or not the gain or loss is ordinary income or ordinary loss.

(6) Allocation of amount realized. The amount realized from the sale, exchange or disposition of several assets in one transaction is allocated among them in proportion to their respective fair market values. This allocation is made under the principles set forth in § 1.1245-1(a)(5) (relating to allocation between section 1245 property and non-section 1245 property).

(7) Interest. Gross income from the sale, exchange or disposition of on asset used in a section 907(c) activity includes interest income from such a sale, exchange or disposition.

(f) Terms and items common to FORI and FOGEI. *(1) Minerals.* The term "minerals" means hydrocarbon minerals extracted from oil and gas wells, including crude oil or natural gas (as defined in section 613A(e)). The term includes incidental impurities from these wells, such as sulphur, nitrogen, or helium. The term does not include hydrocarbon minerals derived from shale oil or tar sands.

(2) Taxable income. Deductions to be taken into account in computing taxable income or net operating loss attributable to FOGEI or FORI are determined under the principles of § 1.861-8. For an exception with regard to losses, see paragraph (e)(4) of this section.

(3) Interest on working capital. FORI and FOGEI may include interest on bank deposits or on any other temporary investment which is not in excess of funds reasonably necessary to meet the working capital requirements and the specifically anticipated business needs of the person that is engaged in the conduct of the activities described in section 907(c)(1) or (2).

(4) Exchange gain or loss. Exchange gain (and loss) may be FORI and FOGEI. For taxable years beginning after 1986, exchange gain or loss from a section 988 transaction may be FORI or FOGEI only if directly related to the business needs (under the principles of section 954(c)(1)(D)) attributable to the conduct of the section 907(c) activity.

(5) Allocation. Interest income and exchange gain (or loss) described, respectively, in paragraph (f)(3) and (4) of this section are allocated among FORI, FOGEI, and any other class of income relevant for purposes of the foreign tax credit limitations under any reasonable method which is consistently applied from year-to-year.

(6) Facts and circumstances. Income not described elsewhere in this section may be FOGEI or FORI if, under the facts and circumstances in the particular case, the income is in substance directly attributable to the activities described in section 907(c)(1) or (2). For example, assume that a producer in the North Sea suffers a casualty caused by an explosion, fire, and resulting destruction of a drilling platform. Insurance proceeds received for the platform's destruction in excess of the producer's basis is extraction income if the excess constitutes income from sources outside the United States. In addition, income from an insurance policy for business interruption may be extraction income to the extent the payments under the policy are geared directly to the loss of income from production and are treated as income from sources outside the United States. Also, if an oil company's oil concession or assets used in extraction activities described in section 907(c)(1)(A) and located outside the United States are nationalized or expropriated by a foreign government, or instrumentality thereof, income derived from that nationalization or expropriation (including interest on the income paid pursuant to the nationalization or expropriation) is FOGEI. Likewise, if a company's assets used in the activities described in section 907(c)(2)(A) through (C) and located outside the United States are nationalized or expropriated by a foreign government, or instrumentality thereof, income (including interest on the income paid pursuant to the nationalization or expropriation) derived from the nationalization or expropriation will be FORI. Nationalization or expropriation is deemed to be a sale or exchange for purposes of section 907(c)(1)(B) and a disposition for purposes of section 907(c)(2)(D). In further example, assume that an oil company has an exclusive right to buy all the oil in country X from Y, an instrumentality of the foreign sovereign which owns all of the oil in X. The oil company does not have an economic interest in any oil in country X. Y has a temporary cash-flow problem and demands that the oil company make advance deposits for the purchase of oil not yet delivered. In return, Y grants the oil company a discount on the price of the oil when delivered. Income represented by the discount on the later disposition of the oil is FORI described in section 907(c)(2)(C). The result would be the same if Y credited the oil company with interest on the advance deposits, which had to be used to purchase oil (the interest income would be FORI).

(g) Directly related income. *(1) In general.* Section 907(c)(2)(E) and this paragraph (g) include in FORI, and this paragraph (g) includes in FOGEI, income from the performance of directly related services (as defined in paragraph (g)(2) of this section). This paragraph (g) also includes in FORI and FOGEI income from the lease or license of related property (as defined in paragraph (g)(3) of this section). Section 907(c)(2)(E) with regard to FORI and this paragraph (g) with regard to both FORI and FOGEI do not apply to a person if—

(i) Neither that person nor a related person (as defined in paragraph (g)(4) of this section) has FOGEI described in paragraph (b) of this section (other than paragraph (b)(4) of this section relating to directly related income) or FORI described in paragraph (d) of this section (other than paragraph (d)(7) of this section relating to directly related income), or

(ii) Less than 50 percent of that person's gross income from sources outside the United States which is related exclusively to the performance of services and from the lease or license of property described in paragraph (g)(2) and (3) of this section, respectively, is attributable to services performed for (or on behalf of), leases to, or licenses with, related persons, but

(iii) Paragraph (g)(1)(ii) of this section will not apply to a person if 50 percent or more of that person's total gross income from sources outside the United States is FOGEI and FORI (as both are described in paragraph (g)(1)(i) of this section).

A person described in paragraph (g)(1)(i) or (ii) of this section will, however, have directly related services income which is FOGEI if the income is so classified by reason of the income based on output test set forth in paragraph (g)(2)(i)(B) of this section.

(2) Directly related services. (i) FOGEI. (A) Income from directly related services will be FOGEI, as that term is defined in paragraph (b)(1) and (3) of this section, if those services are directly related to the active conduct of extraction (including exploration) of minerals from oil and gas wells. Paragraph (b)(1) of this section provides that, in order to have extraction income, a person must have an economic interest in the minerals in place. However, paragraph (b)(3) of this section recognizes that income arising from "other circumstances" is extraction income if that income is in substance attributable to the extraction of minerals.

(B) An example of "other circumstances" under paragraph (b)(3) of this section is the "income based on output test." This income based on output test provides that, if the amount of compensation paid or credited to a person for services is dependent on the amount of minerals discovered or extracted, the income of the person from the performance of the services will be directly related services income which is FOGEI. This test will apply whether or not the person performing the services has, or had, an economic interest in the minerals discovered or extracted.

(ii) FORI. With regard to the determination of directly related services income which is FORI, directly related services are those services directly related to the active conduct of the operations described in section 907(c)(2)(A) through (C). Those services include, for example, services performed in relation to the distribution of minerals or primary products or in connection with the operation of a refinery, or the types of services described in § 1.954-6(d) (other than § 1.954-6(d)(4) which relate to foreign base company shipping income.

(iii) Recipient of the services. Directly related services described in paragraph (g)(2)(i) and (ii) of this section may be performed for any person without regard to whether that person is a related person.

(iv) Excluded services. (A) FOGEI. Directly related services which produce FOGEI do not include insurance, accounting or managerial services.

(B) FORI. Directly related services which produce FORI do not, generally, include insurance, accounting or managerial services. These services will, however, produce FORI if they are performed by the person performing the operations described in section 907(c)(2)(A) through (C). For these purposes, insurance income which is FORI means taxable income as defined in section 832(a).

(3) Leases and licenses. A lease or license of related property is the lease or license of assets used (or held for use) by the lessor, licensor, or another person (including the lessee or a sublessee) in the active conduct of the activities described in section 907(c)(1)(A) or (c)(2)(A) through (C). The leases or licenses described in this paragraph (g)(3) include, for example, a lease of a means of transportation under a bareboat charger hire, of drilling equipment used in extraction operations, or the license of a patent, know-how, or similar intangible property used in extracting, transporting, distributing or processing minerals or primary products. This paragraph (g)(3) applies without regard to whether the parties are related persons.

(4) Related person. A person will be treated as a related person for purposes of this paragraph (g) if that person would be so treated within the meaning of section 954(d)(3) (as applied by substituting the word "corporation" for the word "controlled foreign corporation") or that person is a partnership or partner described in section 707(b)(1).

(5) Gross income. A foreign corporation shall be treated as a domestic corporation for the purpose of applying the gross-income rules in paragraph (g)(1)(ii) and (iii) of this section.

(h) Coordination with other provisions. *(1) Certain adjustments.* The character of income as FOGEI or FORI is determined before making any adjustment under section 482 or section 907(d). For example, assume that X and Y are related parties, Y's only income is from the sale of oil that Y purchased from X, and FOGEI from X is diverted to Y through an arrangement described in paragraph (b)(3) of this section. Accordingly, Y has FOGEI. If under section 482 the Commissioner reallocates the FOGEI from Y to X, then Y's remaining income represents only a profit from distributing the oil, and thus is FORI. If the foreign taxes paid by Y on this income are otherwise creditable under section 901, the foreign taxes that are not refunded to Y retain their characterization as FOGEI taxes.

(2) Section 901(f). Section 901(f) (relating to certain payments with respect to oil and gas not considered as taxes) applies before section 907. Taxes disallowed by section 901(f) are added to the cost or inventory amount of oil or gas.

T.D. 8338, 3/14/91.

§ 1.907(c)-2 Section 907(c)(3) items (for taxable years beginning after December 31, 1982).

Caution: The Treasury has not yet amended Reg § 1.907(c)-2 to reflect changes made by P.L. 105-34.

(a) Scope. This section provides rules relating to certain items listed in section 907(c)(3). The rules of this section are expressed in terms of FORI but apply for determining FOGEI by substituting "FOGEI" for "FORI" whenever appropriate. FOGEI does not include interest described in section 907(c)(3)(A). Dividends paid prior to January 1, 1987, and described in section 907(c)(3)(B), as in effect prior to amendment by the Technical and Miscellaneous Revenue Act of 1988, are included in FORI and not FOGEI.

(b) Dividend. *(1) Section 1248 dividend.* A section 1248 dividend is a dividend described in section 907(c)(3)(A). Except as otherwise provided in this paragraph (b)(1), gain (or loss) from the disposition of stock in any corporation is not FOGEI or FORI. See § 1.907(c)-1(e)(3) and (4).

(2) Section 78 dividend. A section 78 dividend is FORI to the extent it arises from a dividend described in section 907(c)(3)(A), or an amount described in section 907(c)(3)(C).

(c) Taxes deemed paid. *(1) Voting stock test.* Items described in section 907(c)(3)(A) or (C) are FORI only if a deemed- paid-tax test is met under the criteria of section 902 or 960. The purpose of this test is to require minimum direct or indirect ownership by a domestic corporation in the voting stock of a foreign corporation as a prerequisite for the item to qualify as FORI in the hands of the domestic corporation. The test is whether a domestic corporation would be deemed to pay any taxes of a foreign corporation when a dividend or an amount described in section 907(c)(3)(A) or (C), respectively, is included in the domestic corporation's gross income. In the case of interest described in section 907(c)(3)(A), the test is whether any taxes would be deemed paid if there were a hypothetical dividend.

(2) Dividends and interest. For purposes of section 907(c)(3)(A), a domestic corporation is deemed under section 902 to pay taxes in respect of dividends and interest received from a foreign corporation whether or not the foreign corporation:

(i) Actually pays or is deemed to pay taxes, or

(ii) In the case of interest, actually pays dividends.

This paragraph (c)(2) also applies to dividends received by a foreign corporation from a second-tier or third-tier foreign corporation (as defined in § 1.902-1(a)(3)(i) and (4), respectively).

In the case of interest received by a foreign corporation from another foreign corporation, this paragraph (c)(2) applies if the taxes of both foreign corporations would be deemed paid under section 902(a) or (b) for purposes of applying section 902(a) to the same taxpayer which is a domestic corporation. In the case of interest received by any corporation (whether foreign or domestic), all members of an affiliated group filing a consolidated return will be treated as the same taxpayer under section 907(c)(3)(A) if the foreign taxes of the payor and (if the recipient is a foreign corporation) the foreign taxes of the recipient would be deemed paid under section 902 by at least one member. The term "member" is defined in § 1.1502-1(b). Thus, for example, assume that P owns all of the stock of D1 and D2 and P, D1, and D2 are members of an affiliated group filing o consolidated return. Assume further that D1 owns all of the stock of F1 and D2 owns all of the stock of F2, where F1 and F2 are foreign corporations. Interest paid by F1 to P, D2, or F2 may be FORI.

(3) Amounts included under section 951(a). For purposes of section 907(c)(3)(C), a domestic corporation is deemed under section 960 to pay taxes in respect of a foreign corporation, whether or not the foreign corporation actually pays taxes on the amounts included in gross income under section 951(a).

(d) Amount attributable to certain items. *(1) Certain dividends.* (i) General rule. The portion of a dividend described in section 907(c)(3)(A) that is FORI equals—

Amount of dividend x a/b

a = FORI accumulated profits in excess of FORI taxes paid or accrued, and

b = Total accumulated profits in excess of total foreign taxes paid or accrued.

This paragraph (d)(1)(i) applies even though the FORI accumulated profits arose in a taxable year of a foreign corporation beginning before January 1, 1983. Determination of the FORI amount of dividends under this paragraph (d)(1)(i) must be made separately for FORI accumulated profits and total accumulated profits that arose in taxable years beginning before January 1, 1987, and for FORI accumulated profits and total accumulated profits that arose in taxable years beginning after December 31, 1986. Dividends are deemed to be paid first out of FORI and total accumulated profits that arose in table years beginning after December 31, 1986. With regard to FORI accumulated profits and total accumulated profits that arose in taxable years beginning after December 31, 1986, the portion of a dividend that is FORI equals—

Amount of dividend x a/b

a = Post-1986 undistributed FORI earning determined under the principles of section 902(c)(1), and

b = Post-1986 undistributed earnings determined under the principles of section 902(c)(1).

(ii) Cross-references. See § 1.902-1(g) for the determination of a foreign corporation's earnings and profits and of those out of which a dividend is paid. See § 1.1248-2 or 1.1248-3 for the determination of the earnings and profits attributable to the sale or exchange of stock in certain foreign corporations.

(2) Interest received from certain foreign corporations. Interest described in section 907(c)(3)(A) is FORI to the extent the corresponding interest expense of the paying corporation is properly allocable and apportionable to the gross income of the paying corporation that would be FORI were that corporation a domestic corporation. This allocation and apportionment is made in a manner consistent with the rules of section 954(b)(5) and § 1.861-8(e)(2).

(3) Dividends from domestic corporation. The amount of a dividend from a corporation described in section 907(c)(3)(B), as in effect prior to amendment by the Technical and Miscellaneous Revenue Act of 1988, paid in a taxable year of that corporation beginning before December 31, 1986, that is FORI is determined under the principles of paragraph (d)(1)(i) of this section with respect to its current earnings and profits under section 316(a)(2) or its accumulated earnings and profits under section 316(a)(1), as the case may be.

(4) Amounts with respect to which taxes are deemed paid under section 906(a). (i) Portion attributable to FORI. The portion of an amount described in section 907(c)(3)(C) that is FORI equals:

A × B/C

A = Amount described in section 907(c)(3)(C)

B = FORI earnings and profits

C = Total earnings and profits

For taxable years ending after January 23, 1989, the facts and circumstances will be used to determined what part of the amount of the section 907(c)(3)(C) amount is directly attributable to FOGEI, FORI and other income.

(ii) Earnings and profits. Total earnings and profits are those of the foreign corporation for a taxable year under section 964 and the regulations under that section.

(5) Section 78 dividend. The portion of a section 78 dividend that will be considered FORI will equal the amount of taxes deemed paid under either section 902(a) or section 960(a)(1) with respect to the dividend to the extent the taxes deemed paid are FORI taxes under § 1.907(c)-3 (b) or (c). See § 1.907(c)-3(a)(1).

(6) Special rule. (i) No item in the formula described in paragraph (d)(1)(i) of this section includes amounts excluded from the gross income of a United States shareholder under section 959(a)(1).

(ii) With respect to a foreign corporation, earnings and profits in the formula described in paragraph (d)(4)(i) of this section do not include amounts excluded under section 959(b) from its gross income.

(7) Deficits. (i) Allocation of deficits within a separate category. In a taxable year in which a foreign corporation described in section 907(c)(3)(A) pays a dividend or has income that is subject to inclusion under section 951, if the foreign corporation has positive post-1986 undistributed earnings in a separate category but within that separate category there is a deficit in post-1986 undistributed earnings attributable to earnings other than FOGEI and FORI, that deficit shall be allocated ratably between the FOGEI and FORI post-1986 undistributed earnings within that separate category. Any deficit in post-1986 undistributed earnings attributable to either FOGEI or FORI shall be allocated first to FOGEI or FORI post-1986 undistributed earnings (as the case may be) to the extent thereof. Post-1986 undistributed FORI earnings are the post-1986 undistributed earnings (as defined in section 902 and the regulations under that section) attributable to FORI as defined in section 907(c)(2) and (3). Post-1986 undistributed FOGEI earnings are the post-1986 undistributed earnings (as defined in section 902 and the regulations under that section) attributable to FOGEI as defined in section 907(c)(1) and (3).

Example. Foreign corporation X for years 1987 and 1988 had the following undistributed earnings (none of which is income that is subject to inclusion under section 951) and foreign taxes:

	Earnings	Taxes
FOGEI	$800	$400
FORI	(750)	—
Other	700	250
Total	$750	$650

On December 31, 1988, X paid a dividend of all of its post-1986 undistributed earnings to its sole shareholder Y. Under paragraph (d)(5) and (7)(i) of this section and § 1.907(c)-2(d)(5), $450 of Y's dividend is attributable to FOGEI ($50 from undistributed earnings plus a $400 section 78 dividend) and $950 is attributable to other earnings ($700 from undistributed earnings plus a $250 section 78 dividend).

(ii) Deficits allocated among separate categories. If a deficit in a separate category ("first separate category") is allocated to another separate category ("second separate category") under sections 902 and 960 pursuant to notice 88-71, 1988-2 CB 374 and the regulations under those sections, the following rules shall apply. Any deficit in post-1986 undistributed earnings attributable to either FOGEI (or FORI) from the first separate category shall be allocated to post-1986 undistributed earnings in the second separate category to the extent thereof in the following order:

(A) FOGEI (or FORI),

(B) FORI (or FOGEI), and

(C) Other income.

Any deficit in post-1986 undistributed earnings attributable to other income from the first separate category shall be allocated first to other post-1986 undistributed earnings and then ratably to FOGEI and FORI post-1986 undistributed earnings in the second separate category.

(iii) Pre-1987 deficits. The amount of a dividend paid by a foreign corporation described in section 907(c)(3)(A) out of positive pre-1987 earnings that is attributable to FOGEI and FORI shall be determined in a manner similar to that used in paragraph (d)(7)(i) and (ii) of this section except that the determinations shall be made on an annual basis.

(8) Illustrations. The application of this paragraph (d) is illustrated by the following examples.

Example (1). X, a domestic corporation, owns all of the stock of Y, a foreign corporation organized in country S. Y owns all of the stock of Z, a foreign corporation also organized in country S. Each corporation uses the calendar year as its taxable year. In 1983, Z has $150 of FOGEI earnings and profits and $250 of earnings and profits other than FOGEI or FORI. Assume that Z paid no taxes to S and X must include $100 in its gross income under section 951(a) with respect to Z. Under paragraph (d)(4)(i) of this section, $37.50 of the amount described in section 951(a) is FOGEI ($100 × $150/$400). The remaining $62.50 of the section 951(a) amount represents other income.

Example (2). Assume the same facts as in Example 1 except that the taxable year in question is 1988. In addition, under the facts and circumstances, it is determined that of the $100 section 951(a) amount included in X's gross income, $30 is directly attributable to Z's FOGEI activity, $60 is directly attributable to Z's FORI activity and $10 is directly attributable to Z's other activity. Accordingly. under paragraph (d)(4)(i), $30 will be FOGEI and $60 will be FORI to X.

Example (3). (i) Assume the same facts as in Example 1. Assume further that, in 1983, Z distributes its entire earnings and profits ($400) to Y which consists of a dividend of $300 and a section 959(a)(1) distribution of $100. Y has no other earnings and profits during 1983. Assume that the dividend and distribution are not foreign personal holding company income under section 954(c). Y pays no taxes to S. In 1983, Y distributes its entire earnings and profits to X.

(ii) Under paragraphs (c)(2) and (d)(1)(i) of this section, Y has FOGEI of $112.50, i.e., the amount of the dividend received by Y ($300) multiplied by the fraction described in paragraph (d)(1)(i). The numerator of the fraction is Z's FOGEI accumulated profits in excess of the FOGEI taxes paid ($112.50) and the denominator is Z's total accumulated profits in excess of total foreign taxes paid ($400) minus the amount excluded from Y's gross income under section 959(a)(1) ($100). The rule of paragraph (d)(6)(ii) of this section does not apply since X does not include any amount in its gross income under section 951(a) with respect to Y. If Y paid taxes to S, this paragraph (d) would apply to characterize those taxes as FOGEI taxes or other taxes. See § 1.907(c)-3(a)(8) and Example 2 (iii) under § 1.907(c)-3(e).

(iii) The distribution from Y to X is a dividend to the extent of $300, i.e., the amount of the distribution ($400) minus the amount excluded from X's gross income under section 959(a)(1) ($100). Under paragraphs (d)(1)(i) and (6)(i) of this section, $112.50 of the dividend is FOGEI, i.e., the amount of the dividend ($300) multiplied by a fraction. The numerator of the fraction is $112.50, i.e., the FOGEI accumulated profits of Y in excess of FOGEI taxes paid ($150) minus the FOGEI accumulated profits of Y in excess of FOGEI taxes paid excluded from X's gross income under section 959(a)(1) ($37.50). The denominator of the fraction is $300, i.e., the total accumulated profits of Y in excess of taxes paid ($400) minus the amount excluded from X's gross income under section 959(a)(1) ($100).

Example (4). Assume the same facts as in Example 1 with the following modifications: in 1983, Z's only earnings and profits are FORI earnings and profits which are included in X's gross income under section 951(a). Z distributes its entire earnings and profits to Y. In 1983, Y has total earnings and profits of $100 without regard to the dividend from Z, $60 of which are FORI earnings and profits. Y also has $40 which is included in X's gross income under section 951(a). Under paragraph (d)(6)(ii) of this section, the dividend from Z is disregarded for purposes of applying paragraph (d)(4)(i) of this section to the $40 included in X's gross income under section 951(a) with respect to Y. Accordingly, $24 of the amount described in section 951(a) is FORI ($40 × $60/$100). Had these circumstances existed in 1988, and if the $40 included in X's gross income under section 951(a) was directly attributable to FORI activity, all of that income would be FORI to X.

(e) Dividends, interest, and other amounts from sources within a possession. FORI includes the items listed in sections 907(c)(3)(A) and (C) to the extent attributable to FORI of a corporation that is created or organized in or under the laws of a possession of the United States.

(f) Income from partnerships, trusts, etc. FORI and FOGEI include a person's distributive share (determined under the principles of section 704) of the income of any partnership and amounts included in income under subchapter J of chapter 1 of the Code (relating to the taxation of trusts, estates, and beneficiaries) to the extent the income and amounts are attributable to FORI and FOGEI. For taxable years beginning after 1986, the principles of §§ 1.904-5(h) and (i) shall be applied to determine whether (and to what extent) a person's distributive share is FORI and FOGEI. Thus, for example, a less-than-10 percent corporate partner's share of income of the partnership would generally be treated as passive income to the partner, and not as FORI or FOGEI, unless an exception under §§ 1.904-5(h) and (i) applies.

T.D. 8338, 3/14/91.

---

§ 1.907(c)-3 FOGEI and FORI taxes (for taxable years beginning after December 31, 1982).

(a) Tax characterization, allocation and apportionment. *(1) Scope.* Paragraphs (a)(2) through (6) of this section provides rules for the characterization, allocation, and apportionment of the income taxes (other than withholding taxes) paid or accrued to a foreign country among FOGEI, FORI, and other income relevant for purposes of sections 907 and 904. Some of the rules in this section are expressed in terms of FOGEI taxes but they apply to FORI taxes by substituting "FORI taxes" for "FOGEI taxes" whenever appropriate. For the treatment of withholding taxes, see paragraph (a)(8) of this section. FOGEI taxes are determined without any reduction under section 907(a). In addition, determination of FOGEI taxes will not be affected by recharacterization of FOGEI by section 907(c)(4). See § 1.907(c)-1(c)(5). Foreign taxes will not be characterized as creditable FORI taxes if section 907(b) and § 1.907(b)-1 apply.

(2) Three classes of income. There are three classes of income: FOGEI, FORI, and other income.

(3) More than one class in a foreign tax base. If more than one class of income is taxed under one tax base under the law of a foreign country, the amount of pre-credit foreign tax for each base must be determined. This amount is the foreign taxes paid or accrued to that country for the base as increased by the tax credits (if any) which reduced those taxes and were allowed in the country for that tax. More than one class of income is taxed under the same base, if, under a foreign country's law, deductions from one class of income may reduce the income of any other class and the classes are subject to foreign tax at the same rates.

(4) Allocation of tax within a base. If more than one class of income is taxed under the same base under a foreign country's law, the pre-credit foreign tax for the base is apportioned to each class of income in proportion to the income of each class. Tax credits are than allocated (under paragraph (a)(6) of this section) to the apportioned pre-credit tax. Income of a class over the deductions allowed under foreign law for, and which are attributable to, that class.

(5) Modified gross income. Modified gross income is not necessarily the same as gross income as defined for purposes of chapter 1 of the Internal Revenue Code. Modified gross income is determined with reference to the foreign tax base for gross income (or its equivalent). However, the characterization of the base as a particular class of income is governed by general principles of U.S. tax law. Thus, for example—

(i) Gross income from extraction is the fair market value of oil or gas in the immediate vicinity of the well (as determined under § 1.907(c)-1(b)(6) (without any deductions)).

(ii) Whether cost of goods sold (or any other deduction) is a deduction from modified gross income and the amount of such a deduction is determined under foreign law.

(iii) Modified gross income includes items that are part of the foreign tax base even though they are not gross income under U.S. law so long as the foreign taxes paid on the base constitute creditable taxes under section 901 (including taxes described in section 903). For example, if a foreign country imposes a tax (creditable under section 901) on a tax base that includes in small part a percentage of the value of a company's oil reserves in place, modified gross income from extraction includes such a percentage of value solely for purposes of making the tax allocation in paragraph (a)(4) of this section.

(iv) Modified gross income from extraction is increased for purposes of this paragraph (a)(5) by the entire excess of the posted price over fair market value if the foreign country uses a posted price system or other pricing arrangement described in section 907(d) in imposing its income tax.

(v) Modified gross income from FORI is that income attributable to the activities in sections 907(c)(2)(A) through (C) and (E).

(vi) Modified gross income for any class may not include gross income that is not subject to taxation by the foreign country.

(6) Allocation of tax credits. The foreign taxes paid or accrued on a particular class of income equals the precredit tax on the class reduced (but not below zero) by the credits allowed under foreign law against the foreign tax on the particular class. Any tax credit attributable to a class that is not allocated to that class is allocated to the other class in the base or, if there are three classes in the base, is apportioned ratably among the taxes paid or accrued on the other two

classes (as reduced in accordance with the preceding sentence).

(7) Withholding taxes. Paragraph (a)(2) through (6) of this section does not apply to withholding taxes imposed by a foreign country. FOGEI taxes may include withholding taxes imposed with respect to a distribution from a corporation. The portion of the total withholding taxes on a distribution that constitutes FOGEI taxes is determined by the portion of the distribution that is FOGEI. In addition, FOGEI taxes may include taxes imposed one distribution described in section 959(a)(1) or on amounts described in section 959(b). The portion of the total withholding taxes imposed on a distribution described in section 959(a)(1) or on amounts described In section 959(b) is determined by reference to the portion of the amount included in gross income under section 951(a) that was FOGEI.

(b) Dividends. *(1) In general.*

(i) FOGEI taxes deemed paid with respect to a dividend equal the total taxes deemed paid with respect to the dividend multiplied by the fraction:

FOGEI taxes paid or accrued by payor
———
Total foreign taxes paid or accrued by the payor

(ii) With regard to dividends received in taxable years beginning after December 31, 1986, FOGEI taxes deemed paid with respect to a dividend equal the total taxes deemed paid with respect to the portion of the dividend within a separate category multiplied by the fraction:

Post-1986 FOGEI taxes as determined under the principles of section 902(c)(2) that are allocable to that separate category
———
Post-1986 foreign income taxes as determined under the principles of section 902(c)(2) that are allocable to that separate category.

(iii) This paragraph (b) applies to a dividend described in section 907(c)(3)(A) (including a section 1248 dividend) with reference to the particular taxable year or years of those accumulated profits out of which a dividend is paid. Determination of FOGEI taxes under this paragraph (b) must be made separately.

(A) For FOGEI taxes paid on FOGEI accumulated profits and total taxes paid on accumulated profits that arose in taxable years beginning before January 1, 1987, to which paragraph (b)(1)(i) of this section applies, and

(B) For FOGEI taxes paid on FOGEI accumulated profits and total taxes paid on accumulated profits that arose in taxable years beginning after December 31, 1986, to which paragraph (b)(1)(ii) of this section applies.

For purposes of these determinations, dividends are deemed to be paid first out of FOGEI and total accumulated profits that arose in taxable years beginning after December 31, 1986. See § 1.907(c)-2(d)(1)(i). See section 960(a)(3) and § 1.960-2 relating to distributions that are treated as dividends for purposes of section 902.

(2) Section 78 dividend. There are no FOGEI taxes with respect to section 78 dividends.

(c) Includable amounts under section 951(a). (1) FOGEI taxes deemed paid with respect to an amount includable in gross income under section 951(a) equal the total taxes deemed paid with respect to that amount multiplied by the fraction:

FOGEI taxes paid or accrued by the foreign corporation
———
Total foreign taxes paid or accrued by the foreign corporation

(2) With regard to an amount includable in gross income under section 951(a) in taxable years beginning after December 31, 1986, FOGEI taxes deemed paid with respect to that amount equal the total taxes deemed paid with respect to that amount within a separate category multiplied by the fraction:

Post-1986 FOGEI foreign income taxes as determined under the principles of section 902(c)(2) that are allocable to that separate category
———
Post-1986 foreign income taxes as determined under the principles of section 902(c)(2) that are allocable to that separate category

Taxes in the fraction in this paragraph (c)(2) include only those foreign taxes that may be deemed paid under section 960(a) by reason of such inclusion. See §§ 1.960-1(c)(3) and 1.960-2(c).

(d) Partnerships. A partner's distributive share of the partnership's FOGEI taxes is determined under the principles of section 704.

(e) Illustrations. The application of this section maybe illustrated by the following examples.

Example (1). X, a domestic corporation, owns all of the stock of Y, a foreign corporation organized in country S. Y owns all of the stock of Z, a foreign corporation organized in country T. Each corporation used the calendar year as its taxable year. In 1983, X includes in its gross income an amount described in section 951(a) with respect to Z. Assume that the taxes deemed paid under section 902(a) by X by reason of such an inclusion is $70. Assume further that Z paid total taxes of $120, $80 of which is FOGEI tax. Under paragraph (c) of this section, the FOGEI tax deemed paid is $46.67 (i.e., $70 × $80/$120). This $46.67 is also FOGEI under § 1.907(c)-2(d)(5) because it must be included in X's gross income under section 78.

Example (2). (i) Assume the same facts as in Example 1. Assume further that in 1983, Z distributes its entire earnings and profits to Y. Y has no earnings and profits during 1983 other than this dividend. Y paid a tax of $50 to S. Assume that Y is deemed under section 902(b)(1) to pay $50 of the tax paid by Z, which was not deemed paid by X under section 960(a)(1) in 1983. In 1983, Y distributes its entire earnings and profits to X. Assume that X is deemed under section 902(a) to pay $100 of the taxes actually paid, and deemed paid, by Y.

(ii) Paragraph (b)(1) of this section applies to characterize the $50 tax of Z that Y is deemed to pay under section 902(b)(1). Y is deemed to pay $33.33 of FOGEI tax, i.e., the amount of the tax deemed paid by Y ($50) multiplied by a fraction. The numerator of the fraction is the amount of Z's FOGEI tax ($80) and the denominator is the total taxes paid by Z ($120).

(iii) Under paragraph (a)(8) of this section, a portion of the $50 tax actually paid by Y on the earnings and profits received from Z is FOGEI tax. The amount of tax actually paid by Y that is FOGEI tax depends on the amount of the distribution from Z that is FOGEI (see § 1.907(c)-2(d)(1)(i) and Example 2(ii) under § 1.907(c)-2(d)(8)). This result does not depend upon whether a portion of the distribution from Z is described in section 959(b) and it follows even though a portion of Y's earnings and profits will be excluded from X's gross income under section 959(a)(1) when distributed by Y. Assume that $12.50 of the $50 tax actually paid by Y is FOGEI tax.

(iv) Under paragraph (b)(1) of this section, X is deemed to pay $45.83 of FOGEI tax by reason of the distribution from Y. This amount is determined by multiplying the total taxes deemed paid by X by reason of such distribution ($100) by a fraction. The numerator of the fraction is the FOGEI tax paid, and deemed paid, by Y ($45.83, i.e., $33.33 under paragraph (ii) of this example plus $12.50 under paragraph (iii) of this example). The denominator of the fraction is the total taxes paid, and deemed paid, by Y ($100). This $45.83 is FOGEI under § 1.907(c)-2(d)(5) because it is included in X's gross income as a section 78 dividend.

Example (3). (i) X, a domestic corporation, has a concession with foreign country Y that gives it the exclusive right to extract and export the crude oil and natural gas owned by Y. The concession agreement and location of the oil and gas wells mandate that X construct a system of pipelines to transport the minerals that are extracted to a port where they are loaded onto tankers for export. X owns the transportation facilities. Y has an income tax system under which income from mineral operations is subject to a 50 percent tax rate. The taxation by Y of the mineral operations is a separate tax base under paragraph (a)(3) of this section. Under this system, Y imposes the tax at the port prior to export and it establishes a posted price of $12 per barrel. Y also collects royalties of $1.44 per barrel (i.e., 12 percent of this posted price) which is deductible in computing the petroleum tax. Y also allows X deductible lifting costs of $.20 per barrel and deductible transporting costs of $.80 per barrel. Y does not allow any credits against the mineral tax. Assume that X does not have any income in Y other than the mineral income. (In 1983, X extracts, transports, and exports 10,000,000 barrels of crude oil, but for convenience, all computations are in terms of one barrel). X pays foreign taxes of $4.78 per barrel, computed as follows:

Sales		$12.00
Royalties	$1.44	.....
Lifting	.20	.....
Transporting	.80	.....
	2.44	(2.44)
Income base		9.56
Tax rate (percent)		.50
Tax		4.78

Assume that these taxes are creditable taxes under section 901, that the fair market value of the oil at the port is $10 per barrel, and that under § 1.907(c)-1(b)(6) fair market value in the immediate vicinity of the oil wells is $9 per barrel. Thus, at the port, the excess of posted price ($12) over fair market value ($10) is $2.

(ii) The $4.78 foreign tax paid to Y is allocated to FOGEI and FORI in accordance with the rules in paragraph (a)(2) through (5) of this section.

(iii) Under paragraph (a)(3) of this section, FOGEI and FORI are subject to foreign taxation under one tax base. This foreign tax is allocated between FOGEI tax and FORI tax in accordance with paragraph (a)(4) and (5) of this section.

(iv) The modified gross income for FOGEI is $11, i.e., fair market value in the immediate vicinity of the well ($9) plus the excess at the port of posted price over fair market value ($2). The modified gross income for FORI is $1, i.e., value added to the oil beyond the well-head which is part of Y's tax base ($10-$9).

(v) The royalty deductions are all directly attributable to FOGEI.

(vi) Under paragraph (a)(4) of this section, the income of each class is determined as follows:

	FOGEI	FORI
Modified gross income	$11.00	$1.00
Deductions:		
Royalties	1.44	0
Lifting	.20	0
Transporting	0	.80
Total	1.64	.80
Net income	9.36	.20

(vii) Under paragraph (a)(4) of this section, the total tax paid to Y is allocated to FOGEI and FORI in proportion to the income in each class. The calculation is as follows: FOGEI tax = $4.78 × $9.36/$9.56 = $4.68

FORI tax = $4.78 × $0.20/$9.56 = $0.10

Thus, for the 10,000,000 barrels, the FOGEI tax is $46,800,000 and the FORI tax is $1,000,000.

(viii) The allocation under paragraph (a)(4) of this section, rather than the direct application of stated foreign tax rates to foreign-law taxable income in each class of income (which would produce the same results in the facts of this example), is necessary when a foreign country taxes more than one class of income under a progressive rate structure. See Example 4 in this paragraph (e).

Example (4). Assume the same facts as in Example 3 except that Y's tax is imposed at 40 percent for the first $20,000,000 of income and at 60 percent for all other income. The foreign taxes are allocated under paragraph (a)(4) of this section between FOGEI and FORI in the same manner as in paragraphs (vi) and (vii) of Example 3, as follows:

(1) Taxable income	$95,600,000
(2) Tax:	
(a) 40% of $20,000,000	8,000,000
(b) 60% of $75,600,000	45,360,000
(c) Total tax	53,360,000
(3) FOGEI tax (line 2(c) × $9.36/$9.56)	52,243,680
(4) FORI tax (line 2(c) × $0.20/$9.56)	1,116,320

Example (5). Assume the same facts as in Example 3. Assume further that X refines the crude oil into primary products prior to export and Y imposes its tax on the basis of crude oil equivalences of $12 per barrel, rather than the value of the primary products, to establish port prices. Assume that this arrangement is a pricing arrangement described in section 907(d). Thus, Y does not tax the refinery income. The results are the same as in Example 3 even if $12 per barrel is equal to, more than, or less than, the value of the primary products at the port. See paragraph (a)(5)(vi) of this section.

T.D. 8338, 3/14/91.

§ 1.907(d)-1 Disregard of posted prices for purposes of chapter 1 of the Code (for taxable years beginning after December 31, 1982).

(a) In general. *(1) Scope.* Section 907(d) applies if a person has FOGEI from the—

(i) Acquisition (other than from a foreign government) or

(ii) Disposition of minerals at a posted price that differs from the fair market value at the time of the transaction. Also, if a seller (other than a foreign government) derives FOGEI upon a disposition described in the preceding sentence, section 907(d) applies to the acquisition by the purchaser whether or not the purchaser has FOGEI. Thus, section 907(d) may apply in determining a person's FORI.

(2) Initial computation requirement. If section 907(d) applies to any person, income on the transaction as initially reflected on the person's return shall be computed as if the transaction were effected at fair market value. This requirement applies the first time a person has taxable income derived from either the transaction or an item (such as a dividend described in section 907(c)(3)(A)) determined with reference to that income.

(3) Burden of proof. The taxpayer must be able to demonstrate the transaction as it actually occurred and the basis for reporting the transaction under the principles of paragraph (a)(2) of this section.

(4) Related parties. Section 907(d) (as a rule of characterization) applies whether or not the parties to the transaction are related. Thus, the excess of the posted price over the fair market value may never be taken into account in determining a person's FOGEI under section 907(a) but may be taken into account in determining a person's FORI.

(b) Adjustments. If a taxpayer does not comply with the initial requirement of paragraph (a)(2) of this section, adjustments under section 907(d) may be made only by the Commissioner in the same manner that section 482 is administered. Correlative and similar adjustments consistent with the substantive and procedural principles of section 482 and § 1.482-1(d) apply. However, section 907(d) is not a limitation on section 482. If a taxpayer disposing of minerals at a posted price does comply with the initial computation requirement of this section, adjustments and correlative and similar adjustments consistent with the substantive and procedural aspects of section 482 and § 1.482-1(d) shall apply, whether made on the return by the taxpayer or on a later audit. This paragraph (b) does not apply to an actual sale or exchange of minerals made between persons with respect to whom adjustments under section 482 would never apply (but see paragraph (a)(4) of this section).

(c) Definitions. For purposes of this section—

(1) Foreign government. The term foreign government means only the integral parts or controlled entities of a foreign sovereign and political subdivisions of a foreign country.

(2) Minerals. The term minerals has the same meaning as in § 1.907(c)-1(f)(1).

(3) Posted price. The term posted price means the price set by, or at the direction of, a foreign government to calculate income for purposes of its tax or at which minerals must be sold.

(4) Other pricing arrangement. The term other pricing arrangement in section 907(d) means a pricing arrangement having the effect of a posted price.

(5) Fair market value. The term fair market value, whether or not at the port prior to export, is determined in the same way that the wellhead price is determined under § 1.907(c)-1(b)(6).

T.D. 8338, 3/14/91.

§ 1.907(f)-1 Carryback and carryover of credits disallowed by section 907(a) (for amounts carried between taxable years that each begin after December 31, 1982).

(a) In general. If a taxpayer chooses the benefits of section 901, any unused FOGEI tax paid or accrued in a taxable year beginning after December 31, 1982, may be carried to the taxable years specified in section 907(f) under the carryback and carryover principles of this section § 1.904-2(b). See section 907(e) and § 1.907(e)-1 for transitional rules that apply to unused FOGEI taxes carried back or forward between a taxable year beginning before January 1, 1983, and a taxable year beginning after December 31, 1982.

(b) Unused FOGEI tax. *(1) In general.* The "unused FOGEI tax" for purposes of this section is the excess of the FOGEI taxes for a taxable year (year of origin) over that year's limitation level (as defined in § 1.907(a)-1(b)).

(2) Year of origin. The term "year of origin" in the regulations under section 904 corresponds to the term "unused credit year" under section 907(f).

(c) Tax deemed paid or accrued. The unused FOGEI tax from a year of origin that may be deemed paid or accrued under section 907(f) in any preceding or succeeding taxable year (" excess limitation year") may not exceed the lesser of—

(1) The excess extraction limitation for the excess limitation year, or

(2) The excess general section 904 limitation for the excess limitation year.

(d) Excess extraction limitation. Under section 907(f)(2)(A), the "excess extraction limitation" for an excess limitation year is the amount by which that year's section 907(a) extraction limitation exceeds the sum of—

(1) The FOGEI taxes paid or accrued, and

(2) The FOGEI taxes deemed paid or accrued in that year by reason of a section 907(f) carryback or carryover from preceding years of origin.

(e) Excess general section 904 limitation. Under section 907(f)(2)(B), the "excess general section 904 limitation" for an excess limitation year is the amount by which that year's section 904 general limitation exceeds the sum of—

(1) The general limitation taxes paid or accrued (or deemed to have been paid under section 902 or 960) to all foreign countries and possessions of the United States during the taxable year,

(2) The general limitation taxes deemed paid or accrued in such taxable year under section 904(c) and which are attributable to taxable years preceding the unused credit year, plus

(3) The FOGEI taxes deemed paid or accrued in that year by reason of a section 907(f) carryover (or carryback) from preceding years of origin.

(f) Section 907(f) priority. If a taxable year is a year of origin under both section 907(f) and section 904(c), section 907(f) applies first. See section 907(f)(3)(A).

(g) Cross-reference. In computing the carryback and carryover of disallowed credits under section 907(f), the principles of § 1.904-2(d), (e), and (f) apply.

(h) Example. The following example illustrates the application of section 907(f).

Example. X, a U.S. corporation organized on January 1, 1983, uses the accrual method of accounting and the calendar year as its taxable year. X's only income is income which is not subject to a separate tax limitation under section 904(d). X's preliminary U.S. tax liability indicates an effective rate of 46% for taxable years 1983-1985. X has the following foreign tax items for 1983-1985:

	1983	1984	1985
1. FOGEI	$15,000	$20,000	$10,000
2. FOGEI taxes	7,500	9,200	4,200
3. Other foreign taxable income	8,000	5,000	10,000
4. Other foreign taxes	3,200	2,000	3,000
5. (a) Section 907(a) limitation (.46 × (line 1))	6,900	9,200	4,600
(b) General section 904 limitation (.46 × (line 1 + line 3))	10,580	11,500	9,200
6. (a) Unused FOGEI taxes (excess of line 2 over line 5(a))	600	0	0
(b) Unused general limitation taxes (excess of line 4 + lesser of line 2 or line 5(a) over line 5(b))	0	0	0
7. (a) FOGEI taxes from years preceding 1983 deemed accrued under section 907(f)	0	0	0
(b) Section 904 general limitation taxes from years preceding 1983 deemed accrued under section 904(c)	0	0	0
8. (a) Excess section 907(a) limitation (excess of line 5(a) over sum of line 2 and line 7(a))	0	0	400
(b) Excess section 904 general limitation (excess of line 5(b) over sum of line 4, lesser of line 2 and line 5(a) and line 7(b))	480	300	2,000
9. Limit on FOGEI taxes that will be deemed accrued under section 907(f) (lesser of line 8(a) and line 8(b))	0	0	400

X has unused 1983 FOGEI taxes of $600. Since the excess section 907(a) limitation for 1984 is zero, the unused FOGEI taxes are carried to 1985. Of the $600 carryover, $400 is deemed accrued in 1985 and the balance of $200 is carried to following years (but not to a year after 1988). After the carryover from 1983 to 1985, the excess section 904 general limitation for 1985 (line 8(b)) is reduced by $400 to $1,600 to reflect the amount of 1983 FOGEI taxes deemed accrued in 1985 under section 907(f).

T.D. 8338, 3/14/91.

§ 1.911-1 Partial exclusion for earned income from sources within a foreign country and foreign housing costs.

Caution: The Treasury has not yet amended Reg § 1.911-1 to reflect changes made by P.L. 109-222.

(a) In general. Section 911 provides that a qualified individual may elect to exclude the individual's foreign earned income and the housing cost amount from the individual's gross income for the taxable year. Foreign earned income is excludable to the extent of the applicable limitation for the taxable year. The housing cost amount for the taxable year is excludable to the extent attributable to employer provided amounts. If a portion of the housing cost amount for the taxable year is attributable to non-employer provided amounts, such amount may be deductible by the qualified individual subject to a limitation. The amounts excluded under section 911(a) and the amount deducted under section 911(c)(3)(A) for the taxable year shall not exceed the individual's foreign earned income for such taxable year. Foreign earned income must be earned during a period for which the individual qualifies to make an election under section 911(d)(1). A housing cost amount that would be deductible except for the application of this limitation may be carried over to the next taxable year and is deductible to the extent of the limitation for that year. Except as otherwise provided, §§ 1.911-1 through 1.911-7 apply to taxable years beginning after December 31, 1981. These sections do not apply to any item of income, expense, deduction, or credit arising before January 1, 1982, even if such item is attributable to services performed after December 31, 1981.

(b) Scope. Section 1.911-2 provides rules for determining whether an individual qualifies to make an election under section 911. Section 1.911-3 provides rules for determining the amount of foreign earned income that is excludable under section 911(a)(1). Section 1.911-4 provides rules for determining the housing cost amount and the portions excludable under section 911(a)(2) or deductible under section 911(c)(3). Section 1.911-5 provides special rules applicable to married couples. Section 1.911-6 provides for the disallowance of deductions, exclusions, and credits attributable to amounts excluded under section 911. Section 1.911-7 provides procedural rules for making or revoking an election under section 911.

Section 1.911-8 provides a reference to rules applicable to taxable years beginning before January 1, 1982.

T.D. 8006, 1/17/85.

§ 1.911-2 Qualified individuals.

(a) In general. An individual is a qualified individual if:

(1) The individual's tax home is in a foreign country or countries throughout—

(i) The period of bona fide residence described in paragraph (a)(2)(i) of this section, or

(ii) The 330 full days of presence described in paragraph (a)(2)(ii) of this section, and

(2) The individual is either—

(i) A citizen of the United States who establishes to the satisfaction of the Commissioner or his delegate that the individual has been a bona fide resident of a foreign country or countries for an uninterrupted period which includes an entire taxable year, or

(ii) A citizen or resident of the United States who has been physically present in a foreign country or countries for at least 330 full days during any period of twelve consecutive months.

(b) Tax home. For purposes of paragraph (a)(i) of this section, the term "tax home" has the same meaning which it has for purposes of section 162(a)(2) (relating to travel expenses away from home). Thus, under section 911, an individual's tax home is considered to be located at his regular or principal (if more than one regular) place of business or, if the individual has no regular or principal place of business because of the nature of the business, then at his regular place of abode in a real and substantial sense. An individual shall not, however, be considered to have a tax home in a foreign country for any period for which the individual's abode is in the United States. Temporary presence of the individual in the United States does not necessarily mean that the individual's abode is in the United States during that time. Maintenance of a dwelling in the United States by an individual, whether or not that dwelling is used by the individual's spouse and dependents, does not necessarily mean that the individual's abode is in the United States.

(c) Determination of bona fide residence. For purposes of paragraph (a)(2)(i) of this section, whether an individual is a bona fide resident of a foreign country shall be determined by applying, to the extent practical, the principles of section 871 and the regulations thereunder, relating to the determination of the residence of aliens. Bona fide residence in a foreign country or countries for an uninterrupted period may be established, even if temporary visits are made during the period to the United States or elsewhere on vacation or business. An individual with earned income from sources within a foreign country is not a bona fide resident of that country if:

(1) The individual claims to be a nonresident of that foreign country in a statement submitted to the authorities of that country, and

(2) The earned income of the individual is not subject, by reason of nonresidency in the foreign country, to the income tax of that country.

If an individual has submitted a statement of nonresidence to the authorities of a foreign country the accuracy of which has not been resolved as of any date when a determination of the individual's bona fide residence is being made, then the individual will not be considered a bona fide resident of the foreign country as of that date.

(d) Determination of physical presence. For purposes of paragraph (a)(2)(ii) of this section, the following rules apply.

(1) Twelve-month test. A period of twelve consecutive months may begin with any day but must end on the day before the corresponding day in the twelfth succeeding month. The twelve-month period may begin before or after arrival in a foreign country and may end before or after departure.

(2) 330-day test. The 330 full days need not be consecutive but may be interrupted by periods during which the individual is not present in a foreign country. In computing the minimum 330 full days of presence in a foreign country or countries, all separate periods of such presence during the period of twelve consecutive months are aggregated. A full day is a continuous period of twenty-four hours beginning with midnight and ending with the following midnight. An individual who has been present in a foreign country and then travels over areas not within any foreign country for less than twenty-four hours shall not be deemed outside a foreign country during the period of travel. If an individual who is in transit between two points outside the United States is physically present in the United States for less than twenty-four hours, such individual shall not be treated as present in the United States during such transit but shall be treated as travelling over areas not within any foreign country. For purposes of this paragraph (d)(2), the term "transit between two points outside the United States" has the same meaning that it has when used in section 7701(b)(6)(C).

(3) Illustrations of the physical presence requirement. The physical presence requirement of paragraph (a)(2)(ii) of this section is illustrated by the following examples:

Example (1). B, a U.S. citizen, arrives in Venezuela from New York at 12 noon on April 24, 1982. B remains in Venezuela until 2 p.m. on March 21, 1983, at which time B departs for the United States. Among other possible twelve month periods, B is present in a foreign country an aggregate of 330 full days during each of the following twelve month periods: March 21, 1982 through March 20, 1983; and April 25, 1982 through April 24, 1983.

Example (2). C, a U.S. citizen, travels extensively from the time C leaves the United States on March 5, 1982, until the time C departs the United Kingdom on January 1, 1984, to return to the United States permanently. The schedule of C's travel and the number of full days at each location are listed below:

Country	Time and date of arrival	Time and date of departure	Full days in foreign country
United States		10 p.m. (by air) Mar. 5, 1982	
United Kingdom	9 a.m. Mar. 6, 1982	10 p.m. (by ship) June 25, 1982	110
United States	11 a.m. June 30, 1982	1 p.m. (by ship) July 19, 1982	0
France	3 p.m. July 24, 1982	11 a.m. (by air) Aug. 22, 1983	393
United States	4 p.m. Aug. 22, 1983	9 a.m. (by air) Sept. 4, 1983	0
United Kingdom	9 a.m. Sept. 5, 1983	9 a.m. (by air) Jan. 1, 1984	117
United States	1 p.m. Jan. 1, 1984		

Among other possible twelve month periods, C is present in a foreign country or countries an aggregate of 330 full days during the following twelve month periods: March 2, 1982 through March 1, 1983; and January 21, 1983 through January 20, 1984. The computation of days with respect to each twelve month period may be illustrated as follows:

First twelve month period (March 2, 1982 through March 1, 1983):

	Full days in foreign country
Mar. 2, 1982 through Mar. 6, 1982	0
Mar. 7, 1982 through June 24, 1982	110
June 25, 1982 through July 24, 1982	0
July 25, 1982 through Mar. 1, 1983	220
Total full days	330

Second twelve month period (January 21, 1983 through January 20, 1984):

	Full days in foreign country
Jan. 21, 1983 through Aug. 21, 1983	213
Aug. 22, 1983 through Sept. 5, 1983	0
Sept. 6, 1983 through Dec. 31, 1983	117
Jan. 1, 1984 through Jan. 20, 1984	0
Total full days	330

(e) Special rules. For purposes only of establishing that an individual is a qualified individual under paragraph (a) of this section, residence or presence in a foreign country while there employed by the U.S. government or any agency or instrumentality of the U.S. government counts towards satisfaction of the requirements of § 1.911-2(a). (But see section 911(b)(1)(B)(ii) and § 1.911-3(c)(3) for the rule excluding amounts paid by the U.S. government to an employee from the definition of foreign earned income.) Time spent in a foreign country prior to January 1, 1982, counts toward satisfaction of the bona fide residence and physical presence requirements, even though no exclusion or deduction may be allowed under section 911 for income attributable to services performed during that time. For purposes or paragraph (a)(2)(ii) of this section, the term "resident of the United States" includes an individual for whom a valid election is in effect under section 6013(g) or (h) for the taxable year or years during which the physical presence requirement is satisfied.

(f) Waiver of period of stay in foreign country due to war or civil unrest. Notwithstanding the requirements of paragraph (a) of this section, an individual whose tax home is in, a foreign country, and who is a bona fide resident of, or present in a foreign country for any period, who leaves the foreign country after August 31, 1978, before meeting the requirements of paragraph (a) of this section, may as provided in this paragraph, qualify to make an election under section 911(a) and § 1.911-7(a). If the Secretary determines, after consultation with the Secretary of State or his delegate, that war, civil unrest, or similar adverse conditions existed in a foreign country, then the Secretary shall publish the name of the foreign country and the dates between which such conditions were deemed to exist. In order to qualify to make an election under this paragraph, the individual must establish to the satisfaction of the Secretary that the individual left a foreign country, the name of which has been published by the Secretary, during the period when adverse conditions existed and that the individual could reasonably have expected to meet the requirements of paragraph (a) of this section but for the adverse conditions. The individual shall attach to his return for the taxable year a statement that the individual expected to meet the requirements of paragraph (a) of this section but for the conditions in the foreign country which precluded the normal conduct of business by the individual. Such individual shall be treated as a qualified individual, but only for the actual period of residence or presence. Thus, in determining the number of the individual's qualifying days, only days within the period of actual residence or presence shall be counted.

(g) United States. The term "United States" when used in a geographical sense includes any territory under the sovereignty of the United States. It includes the states, the District of Columbia, the possessions and territories of the United States, the territorial waters of the United States, the air space over the United States, and the seabed and subsoil of those submarine areas which are adjacent to the territorial waters of the United States and over which the United States has exclusive rights, in accordance with international law, with respect to the exploration and exploitation of natural resources.

(h) Foreign country. The term "foreign country when used in a geographical sense includes any territory under the sovereignty of a government other than that of the United States. It includes the territorial waters of the foreign country (determined in accordance with the laws of the United States), the air space over the foreign country, and the seabed and subsoil of those submarine areas which are adjacent to the territorial waters of the foreign country and over which the foreign country has exclusive rights, in accordance with international law, with respect to the exploration and exploitation of natural resources.

T.D. 8006, 1/17/85.

§ 1.911-3 Determination of amount of foreign earned income to be excluded.

Caution: The Treasury has not yet amended Reg § 1.911-3 to reflect changes made by P.L. 105-34.

(a) Definition of foreign earned income. For purposes of section 911 and the regulations thereunder, the term "foreign earned income" means earned income (as defined in paragraph (b) of this section) from sources within a foreign country (as defined in § 1.911-2(h)) that is earned during a period for which the individual qualifies under § 1.911-2(a) to make an election. Earned income is from sources within a foreign country if it is attributable to services performed by an individual in a foreign country or countries. The place of receipt of earned income is immaterial in determining whether earned income is attributable to services performed in a foreign country or countries.

(b) Definition of earned income. *(1) In general.* The term "earned income" means wages, salaries, professional fees, and other amounts received as compensation for personal services actually rendered including the fair market value of all remuneration paid in any medium other than cash. Earned income does not include any portion of an amount paid by a corporation which represents a distribution of earnings and profits rather than a reasonable allowance as compensation for personal services actually rendered to the corporation.

(2) Earned income from business in which capital is material. In the case of an individual engaged in a trade or business (other than in corporate form) in which both personal services and capital are material income producing factors, a reasonable allowance as compensation for the personal services actually rendered by the individual shall be considered earned income, but the total amount which shall be treated as the earned income of the individual from such trade or business shall in no case exceed thirty percent of the individual's share of the net profits of such trade or business.

(3) Professional fees. Earned income includes all fees received by an individual engaged in a professional occupation (such as doctor or lawyer) in the performance of professional activities. Professional fees constitute earned income even though the individual employs assistants to perform part or all of the services, provided the patients or clients are those of the individual and look to the individual as the person responsible for the services rendered.

(c) Amounts not included in foreign earned income. Foreign earned income does not include an amount:

(1) Excluded from gross income under section 119;

(2) Received as a pension or annuity (including social security benefits);

(3) Paid to an employee by an employer which is the U.S. government of any U.S. government agency or instrumentality;

(4) Included in the individual's gross income by reason of section 402(b) (relating to the taxability of a beneficiary of a nonexempt trust) or section 403(c) (relating to the taxability of a beneficiary under a nonqualified annuity or under annuities purchased by exempt organizations);

(5) Included in gross income by reason of § 1.911-6(b)(4)(ii); or

(6) Received after the close of the first taxable year following the taxable year in which the services giving rise to the amounts were performed. For treatment of amounts received after December 31, 1962, which are attributable to services performed on or before December 31, 1962, and with respect to which there existed on March 12, 1962, a right (whether forfeitable or nonforfeitable) to receive such amounts, see § 1.72-8.

(d) Determination of the amount of foreign earned income that may be excluded under section 911(a)(1). *(1) In general.* Foreign earned income described in this section may be excluded under section 911(a)(1) and this paragraph only to the extent of the limitation specified in paragraph (d)(2) of this section. Income is considered to be earned in the taxable year in which the services giving rise to the income are performed. The determination of the amount of excluded earned income in this manner does not affect the time for reporting any amounts included in gross income.

(2) Limitation. (i) In general. The term "section 911(a)(1) limitation" means the amount of foreign earned income for a taxable year which may be excluded under section 911(a)(1). The section 911(a)(1) limitation shall be equal to the lesser of the qualified individual's foreign earned income for the taxable year in excess of amounts that the individual elected to exclude from gross income under section 911(a)(2) or the product of the annual rate for the taxable year (as specified in paragraph (d)(2)(ii) of this section) multiplied by the following fraction:

$$\frac{\text{The number of qualifying days in the taxable year}}{\text{The number of days in the taxable year}}$$

(ii) Annual rate for the taxable year. The annual rate for the taxable year is the rate set forth in section 911(b)(2)(A).

(3) Number of qualifying days. For purposes of section 911 and the regulations thereunder, the number of qualifying days is the number of days in the taxable year within the period during which the individual met the tax home requirement and either the bona fide residence requirement or the physical presence requirement of § 1.911-2(a). Although the period of bona fide residence must include an entire taxable year, the entire uninterrupted period of residence may include fractional parts of a taxable year. For instance, if an individual who was a calendar year taxpayer established a tax home and a residence in a foreign country as of November 1, 1982, and maintained the tax home and the residence through March 31, 1984, then the uninterrupted period of bona fide residence includes fractional parts of the years 1982 and 1984, and all of 1983. The number of qualifying days in 1982 is sixty-one. The number of qualifying days in 1983 is 365. The number of qualifying days in 1984 is ninety-one. The period during which the physical presence requirement of § 1.911-2(a)(2)(ii) is met is any twelve consecutive month period during which the individual is physically present in one or more foreign countries for 330 days and the individual's tax home is in a foreign country during each day of such physical presence. Such period may include days when the individual is not physically present in a foreign country, and days when the individual does not maintain a tax home in a foreign country. Such period may include fractional parts of a taxable year. Thus, if an individual's period of physical presence is the twelve-month period beginning June 1, 1982, and ending May 31, 1983, the number of qualifying days in 1982 is 214 and the number of qualifying days in 1983 is 151.

(e) Attribution rules. *(1) In general.* Foreign earned income is considered to be earned in the taxable year in which the individual performed the services giving rise to the income. If income is earned in one taxable year and received in another taxable year, then, for purposes of determining the amount of foreign earned income that the individual may exclude under section 911(a), the individual must attribute the income to the taxable year in which the services giving rise to the income were performed. Thus, any reimbursement would be attributable to the taxable year in which the services giving rise to the obligation to pay the reimbursement were performed, not the taxable year in which the reimbursement was received. For example, tax equalization payments are normally received in the year after the year in which the services giving rise to the obligation to pay the tax equalization payment were performed. Therefore, such payments will almost always have to be attributed to the prior year. Foreign earned income attributable to services performed in a preceding taxable year shall be excludable from gross income in the year of receipt only to the extent such amount could have been excluded under paragraph (d)(1) in the preceding taxable year, had such amount been received in the preceding taxable year. The taxable year to which income is attributable will be determined on the basis of all the facts and circumstances.

(2) Priority of use of the section 911(a)(1) limitation. Foreign earned income received in the year in which it is earned shall be applied to the section 911(a)(1) limitation for that year before applying income earned in that year that is received in any other year. Foreign earned income that is earned in one year and received in another year shall be applied to the section 911(a)(1) limitation for the year in which it was earned, on a year by year basis, in any order that the individual chooses. (But see section 911(b)(1)(B)(iv)). An individual may not amend his return to change the treatment of income with respect to the section 911(a)(1) exclusion after the period provided by section 6511(a). The special period of limitation provided by section 6511(d)(3) does not apply for this purpose. For example, C, a qualified individual, receives an advance bonus of $10,000 in 1982, salary of $70,000 in 1983, and a performance bonus of $10,000 in 1984, all of which are foreign earned income for 1983. C has a section 911(a)(1) limitation for 1983 of $80,000, and has no housing cost amount exclusion. On his income tax return for 1983, C elects to exclude foreign earned income of $70,000 received in 1983. C may also exclude his $10,000 advance bonus received in 1982 (by filing an amended return for 1982), or he may exclude the $10,000 performance bonus received in 1984 on his 1984 income tax return. However, C may not exclude part of the 1982 bonus and part of the 1984 bonus.

(3) Exception for year-end payroll period. Notwithstanding paragraph (e)(1) of this section, salary or wage payments of a cash basis taxpayer shall be attributed entirely to the year of receipt under the following circumstances:

(i) The period for which the payment is made is a normal payroll period of the employer which regularly applies to the employee;

(ii) The payroll period includes the last day of the employee's taxable year;

(iii) The payroll period does not exceed 16 days; and

(iv) The payment is part of a normal payroll of the employer that is distributed at the same time, in relation to the payroll period, that such payroll would normally be distributed, and is distributed before the end of the next succeeding payroll period.

(4) Attribution of bonuses and substantially nonvested property to periods in which services were performed. (i) In general. Bonuses and substantially nonvested property are attributable to all of the services giving rise to the income on the basis of all the facts and circumstances. If an individual receives a bonus or substantially nonvested property (as defined in § 1.83-3(b)) and it is determined to be attributable to services performed in more than one taxable year, then, for purposes of determining the amount eligible for exclusion from gross income in the year the bonus is received or the property vests, a portion of such amount shall be treated as attributable to services performed in each taxable year (or portion thereof) during the period when services giving rise to the bonus or the substantially nonvested property were performed. Such portion shall be determined by dividing the amount of the bonus or the excess of the fair market value of the vested property over the amount paid, if any, for the vested property, by the number of months in the period when services giving rise to such amount were performed, and multiplying the quotient by the number of months in such period in the taxable year. For purposes of this section, the term "month" means a calendar month. A fraction of a calendar month shall be deemed a month if it includes fifteen or more days.

(ii) Examples. The following examples illustrate the application of this paragraph (e)(4).

Example (1). A, an employee of M Corporation during all of 1983 and 1984, worked in the United States from January 1 through April 30, 1983, and received $12,000 of salary for that period. A worked in country F from May 1, 1983 through the end of 1984, and is a qualified individual under § 1.911-2(a) for that period. For the period from May 1 through December 31, 1983, A received $32,000 of salary. M pays a bonus on December 20, 1983 to each of M's employees in an amount equal to 10 percent of the employee's regular wages or salary for the 1983 calendar year. The amount of A's bonus is $4,400 for 1983. The portion of A's bonus that is attributable to services performed in country F and is foreign earned income for 1983 is $3,200, or $32,000 attributable to services performed in the United States, and is not foreign earned income.

Example (2). The facts are the same as in example (1), except that M determines bonuses separately for each country based on the productivity of the employees in that country. M pays a bonus to employees in country F, in the amount of 15 percent of each employee's wages or salary earned in country F. A's country F bonus is $4,800 for 1983 ($32,000 × 15 percent), and is foreign earned income for 1983. If A also receives a bonus (or if A's bonus is increased) for working in the United States during 1983, that amount is not foreign earned income.

Example (3). X corporation offers its employees a bonus of $40,000 if the employee accepts employment in a foreign country and remains in a foreign country for a period of at least four years. A, an employee of X, is a calendar year and cash basis taxpayer. A accepts employment with X in foreign country F. A begins work in F on July 1, 1983 and continues to work in F for X until June 30, 1987. In 1987 X pays A a $40,000 bonus. The bonus is attributable to services A performed from July 1, 1983 through June 30, 1987. The amount of the bonus attributable to 1987 is $5,000 (($40,000 ÷ 48) × 6). The amount of the bonus attributable to 1986 is $10,000 (($40,000 attributable to 1986 only to the extent that amount could have been excluded under section 911(a)(1) had A received it in 1986. The remaining $25,000 is attributable to services performed in taxable years before 1986. Such amounts may not be excluded under section 911 because they are received after the close of the taxable year following the taxable year in which the services giving rise to the income were performed.

(iii) Special rule for elections under section 83(b). If an individual receives substantially nonvested property and makes an election under section 83(b) and § 1.83-2(a) to include in his gross income the amount determined under section 83(b)(1)(A) and (B) and § 1.83-2(a) for the taxable year in which the property is transferred (as defined in § 1.83-3(a)), then, for the purpose of determining the amount eligible for exclusion in the year of receipt, the individual may elect either of the following options:

(A) Substantially nonvested property may be treated as attributable entirely to services performed in the taxable year in which an election to include it in income is made. If so treated, then the amount otherwise included in gross income as determined under § 1.83-2(a) will be excludable under section 911(a) for such year subject to the limitation provided in § 1.911-3(d)(2) for such year.

(B) A portion of the substantially nonvested property may be treated as attributable to services performed or to be performed in each taxable year during which the substantial risk of forfeiture (as defined in section 83(c) and § 1.83-3(c)) exists. The portion treated as attributable to services performed or to be performed in each taxable year is determined by dividing the amount of the substantially nonvested property included in gross income as determined under § 1.83-2(a) by the number of months during the period when a substantial risk of forfeiture exists. The quotient is multiplied by the total number of months in the taxable year during which a substantial risk of forfeiture exists. The amount determined to be attributable to services performed in the year the election is made shall be excluded from gross income for such year as provided in paragraph (d)(2) of this section. Amounts treated as attributable to services performed in subsequent taxable years shall be excludable in the year of receipt only to the extent such amounts could be excluded under paragraph (d)(2) of this section in such subsequent years. An individual may obtain such additional exclusion by filing an amended return for the taxable year in which the property was transferred. The individual may only amend his or her return within the period provided by section 6511(a) and the regulations thereunder.

(5) Moving expense reimbursements. (i) Source of reimbursements. For the purpose of determining whether a moving expense reimbursement is attributable to services performed within a foreign country or within the United States, in the absence of evidence to the contrary, the reimbursement shall be attributable to future services to be performed at the new principal place of work. Thus, a reimbursement received by an employee from his employer for the expenses of a move to a foreign country will generally be attributable to services performed in the foreign country. A reimbursement received by an employee from his employer for the expenses of a move from a foreign country to the United States will generally be attributable to services performed in

the United States. For purposes of this paragraph (e)(5), evidence to the contrary includes, but is not limited to, an agreement, between the employer and the employee, or a statement of company policy, which is reduced to writing before the move to the foreign country and which is entered into or established to induce the employee or employees to move to a foreign country. The writing must state that the employer will reimburse the employee for moving expenses incurred in returning to the United States regardless of whether the employee continues to work for the employer after the employee returns to the United States. The writing may contain conditions upon which the right to reimbursement is determined as long as the conditions set forth standards that are definitely ascertainable and the conditions can only be fulfilled prior to, or through completion of the employee's return move to the United States that is the subject of the writing. In no case will an oral agreement or statement of company policy concerning moving expenses be considered evidence to the contrary. For the purpose of determining whether a storage expense reimbursement is attributable to services performed within a foreign country, in the case of storage expenses incurred after December 31, 1983, the reimbursement shall be attributable to services performed during the period of time for which the storage expenses are incurred.

(ii) Attribution of foreign source reimbursements to taxable years in which services are performed. (A) In general. If a reimbursement for moving expenses is determined to be from foreign sources under paragraph (e)(5)(i) of this section, then for the purpose of determining the amount eligible for exclusion in accordance with paragraphs (d)(2) and (e)(2) of this section, the reimbursement shall be considered attributable to services performed in the year of the move as long as the individual is a qualified individual for a period that includes 120 days in the year of the move. The period that is used in determining the number of qualifying days for purposes of the individual's section 911(a)(1) limitation (under paragraph (d)(2) of this section) must also be used in determining whether the individual is a qualified individual for a period that includes 120 days in the year of the move. If the individual is not a qualified individual for such period, then the individual shall treat a portion of the reimbursement as attributable to services performed in the year of the move, and a portion as attributable to services performed in the succeeding taxable year, if the move is from the United States to a foreign country, or to the prior taxable year, if the move is from a foreign country to the United States. The portion of the reimbursement treated as attributable to services performed in the year of the move shall be determined by multiplying the total reimbursement by the following fraction:

$$\frac{\text{The number of qualifying days (as defined in paragraph (d)(3) of this section) in the year of the move}}{\text{The number of days in the taxable year of the move}}$$

The remaining portion of the reimbursement shall be treated as attributable to services performed in the year succeeding or preceding the year of the move. Amounts treated as attributable to services performed in a year succeeding or preceding the year of the move shall be excludable in the year of receipt only to the extent such amounts could be excluded under paragraph (d)(2) of this section in such succeeding or preceding year.

(B) Moves beginning before January 1, 1984. Notwithstanding paragraph (e)(5)(ii)(A) of this section, this paragraph (e)(5)(ii)(B) shall apply for moves begun before January 1, 1984. If a reimbursement for moving expenses is determined to be from foreign sources under paragraph (e)(5)(i) of this section, then for the purpose of determining the amount eligible for exclusion in accordance with paragraphs (d)(2) and (e)(2) of this section, the reimbursement shall be considered attributable to services performed in the year of the move. However, if the individual does not qualify under section 911(d)(1) and § 1.911-2(a) for the entire taxable year of the move, then the individual shall treat a portion of the reimbursement as attributable to services performed in the succeeding taxable year, if the move is from the United States to a foreign country, or to the prior taxable year, if the move is from a foreign country to the United States. The portion of the reimbursement treated as attributable to services performed in the year succeeding or preceding the move shall be determined by multiplying the total reimbursement by the following fraction:

$$\frac{\text{The number of qualifying days (as defined in paragraph (d)(3) of this section) in the year of the move}}{\text{The number of days in the taxable year of the move}}$$

and subtracting the product from the total reimbursement.

Amounts treated as attributable to services performed in a year succeeding or preceding the year of the move shall be excludable in the year of receipt only to the extent such amounts could be excluded under paragraph (d)(2) of this section in such succeeding or preceding year.

(f) Examples. The following examples illustrate the application of this section.

Example (1). A is a U.S. citizen and calendar year taxpayer. A's tax home was in foreign country F and A was physically present in F for 330 days during the period from July 4, 1982 through July 3, 1983. The number of A's qualifying days in 1982 as determined under paragraph (d)(2) of this section is 181. In 1982 A receives $40,000 attributable to services performed in foreign country F in 1982. Under paragraph (d)(2) of this section A's section 911(a)(1) limitation is $37,192, that is the lesser of $40,000 (foreign earned income) or

$$\$75{,}000 \text{ (annual rate)} \times \frac{181 \text{ (qualifying days)}}{365 \text{ (days in taxable year)}}$$

Example (2). The facts are the same as in example (1) except that in 1982 A receives $30,000 attributable to services performed in foreign country F. A excludes this amount from gross income under paragraph (d) of this section. In addition, in 1983 A receives $10,000 attributable to services performed in F in 1982 and $35,000 attributable to services performed in F in 1983. On his return for 1983, A must report $45,000 of income. A's section 911(a)(1) limitation for 1983 is the lesser of $35,000 (foreign earned income) or $49,329, the annual rate for the taxable year multiplied by a fraction the numerator of which is A's qualifying days in the taxable year and the denominator of which is the number of days in the taxable year ($80,000 × 184/365). On his tax return for 1983 A may exclude $35,000 attributable to services performed in 1983. A may only exclude $7,192 of the $10,000 received in 1983 attributable to services performed in 1982 because such amount is only excludable in 1983 to the extent such amount could have been excluded in 1982 subject to the section 911(a)(1) limitation for 1982 which is $37,192 ($75,000 × 181/365). No portion of amounts attributable to services performed in 1982 may be used in calculating A's section 911(a)(1) limitation for 1983. Thus, even though A could have excluded an additional $5,329 in 1983 if A had had more foreign earned income attributable to

1983, A may not exclude the $2,808 of remaining foreign earned income attributable to 1982.

Example (3). C is a U.S. citizen and calendar year taxpayer. C establishes a bona fide residence and a tax home in foreign country J on March 1, 1982, and maintains a tax home and a residence in J until December 31, 1986. In March of 1982 C's employer, Y corporation, transfers stock in Y to C. The stock is subject to forfeiture if C returns to the U.S. before January 1, 1985. C elects under section 83(b) to include $15,000, the amount determined with respect to such stock under section 83(b)(1), in gross income in 1982. C's other foreign earned income in 1982 is $58,000. C elects under paragraph (e)(4)(iii)(B) of this section to treat the stock as if earned over the period of the substantial risk of forfeiture. The number of months in the period of the substantial risk of forfeiture is thirty-four. The number of months in the taxable year 1982 within the period of foreign employment is ten. For purposes of determining C's section 911(a)(1) limitation, $4,412 (($15,000/34) × 10) of the amount included in gross income under section 83(b) is treated as attributable to services performed in 1982, $5,294 is treated as attributable to services to be performed in 1983, and $5,294 is treated as attributable to services to be performed in 1984. In 1982, C excludes $62,412 under section 911(a)(1). That is the lesser of foreign earned income for 1982 ($58,000 + $4,412) or the annual rate for the taxable year multiplied by a fraction the numerator of which is C's qualifying days in the taxable year and the denominator of which is the number of days in the taxable year ($75,000 × 306/365). C continues to perform services in foreign country J throughout 1983 and 1984. C would be able to exclude the remaining $5,294 attributable to services performed in 1983 and $5,294 attributable to services performed in 1984 if those amounts would be excludable if they had been received in 1983 or 1984 respectively. If C is entitled to exclude the additional amounts, C must claim the exclusion by filing an amended return for 1982.

Example (4). D is a U.S. citizen and a calendar year taxpayer. In September, 1984 D moves to a foreign country K. D is physically present in K, and D's tax home is in K, from September 15, 1984 through December 31, 1985. D receives $6,000 in April, 1985 from his employer, as a reimbursement for expenses of moving to K, pursuant to a written agreement that such moving expenses would be reimbursed to D upon successful completion of 6 months employment in K. Under paragraph (e)(15)(i) of this section, the reimbursement is attributable to services performed in K. Under the physical presence test of § 1.911-2(a)(2)(ii), among other periods D is a qualified individual for the period of August 10, 1984 through August 9, 1985, which includes 144 days in 1984. Under paragraph (e)(5)(ii)(A) of this section, for the purpose of determining the amount eligible for exclusion, the reimbursement is considered attributable to services performed in 1984 (the year of the move) because D is a qualified individual under § 1.911-2(a) for a period that includes 120 days in 1984. The reimbursement may be excluded under paragraphs (d)(2) and (e)(2) of this section, to the extent that D's foreign earned income for 1984 that was earned and received in 1984 was less than the annual rate for the taxable year multiplied by the number of D's qualifying days in the taxable year over the number of days in D's taxable year ($80,000 × 144/366), or $31,475.

Example (5). The facts are the same as in example (4) except that D is not a qualified individual under the physical presence test, but is a qualified individual under the bona fide residence test for the period of September 15, 1984 through December 31, 1985. Under paragraph (e)(5)(ii)(A) of this section, for the purpose of determining the amount eligible for exclusion, the reimbursement is considered attributable to services performed in 1984 and 1985 because D is not a qualified individual for a period that includes 120 days in 1984 (the year of the move). The portion of the reimbursement treated as attributable to services performed in 1984 is $6,000 × 108/366, or $1,770, and may be excluded, subject to D's 1984 section 911(a)(1) limitation. The balance of the reimbursement, $4,230, is treated as attributable to services performed in 1985, and may be excluded to the extent provided in paragraphs (d)(2) and (e)(2) of this section.

Example (6). The facts are the same as in example (4), with the following additions. Before D moved to K, D and his employer signed a written agreement that D would perform services for the employer for at least one year, primarily in country K, and, if D did not voluntarily cease to work for the employer primarily in country K before one year had elapsed, the employer would reimburse D for one half of D's expenses, up to a maximum of $4,000, of moving back to the United States. The agreement also stated that, if D did not voluntarily leave the employment in K before two years had elapsed, the employer would reimburse D for all of D's reasonable expenses of moving back to the United States. The agreement further stated that D's right to reimbursement would not be conditioned upon the performance of services after D ceased to work in K. D worked in country K for all of 1985. On January 1, 1986, D left K and moved to the United States. In February, 1986 the employer paid D $3,500 as reimbursement for one-half of D's expenses of moving to the United States. Although D did not fulfill the condition in the agreement to receive full reimbursement, all of the conditions in the agreement set forth definitely ascertainable standards and no condition could be fulfilled after D moved back to the United States. The agreement fulfills the requirements of paragraph (e)(5)(i) of this section, and therefore is evidence that the reimbursement should not be attributable to future services to be performed at D's new principal place of work. Under the facts and circumstances, the reimbursement is attributable to services performed in K. Under paragraph (e)(5)(ii)(A) of this section, the entire reimbursement is attributable to services performed in 1985. The amount attributable to 1985 may be excluded to the extent provided in paragraphs (d)(2) and (e)(2) of this section.

T.D. 8006, 1/17/85.

§ 1.911-4 Determination of housing cost amount eligible for exclusion or deduction.

Caution: The Treasury has not yet amended Reg § 1.911-4 to reflect changes made by P.L. 109-222.

(a) Definition of housing cost amount. The term "housing cost amount" means an amount equal to the reasonable expenses paid or incurred (as defined in section 7701(a)(25)) during the taxable year by or on behalf of the individual attributable to housing in a foreign country for the individual and any spouse or dependents who reside with the individual (or live in a second foreign household described in paragraph (b)(5) of this section) less the base housing amount as defined in paragraph (c) of this section. The housing cost amount must be reduced by the amount of any military or section 912 allowance or similar allowance excludable from gross income that is intended to compensate the individual or the individual's spouse in whole or in part for the expenses of housing during the same period for which the individual claims a housing cost amount exclusion or deduction.

(b) Housing expenses. *(1) Included expenses.* For purposes of paragraph (a) of this section, housing expenses include rent, the fair rental value of housing provided in kind by the employer, utilities (other than telephone charges), real and personal property insurance, occupancy taxes not described in paragraph (b)(2)(v) of this section, nonrefundable fees paid for securing a leasehold, rental of furniture and accessories, household repairs, and residential parking.

(2) Excluded expenses. Housing expenses do not include:

(i) The cost of house purchase, improvements, and other costs that are capital expenditures;

(ii) The cost of purchased furniture or accessories or domestic labor (maids, gardeners, etc.);

(iii) Amortized payments of principal with respect to an evidence of indebtedness secured by a mortgage on the taxpayer's housing;

(iv) Depreciation of housing owned by the taxpayer, or amortization or depreciation of capital improvements made to housing leased by the taxpayer;

(v) Interest and taxes deductible under section 163 or 164 or other amounts deductible under section 216(a) (relating to deduction of interest and taxes by cooperative housing corporation tenant);

(vi) The expenses of more than one foreign household except as provided in paragraph (b)(5) of this section;

(vii) Expenses excluded from gross income under section 119;

(viii) Expenses claimed as deductible moving expenses under section 217; or

(ix) The cost of a pay television subscription.

(3) Limitation. Housing expenses are taken into account for purposes of this section only to the extent attributable to housing for portions of the taxable year within the period during which the individual satisfies the requirements of § 1.911-2(a). Housing expenses are not taken into account for the period during which the value of the individual's housing is excluded from gross income under section 119, unless the individual maintains a second foreign household described in paragraph (b)(5) of this section. If an individual maintains two foreign households, only expenses incurred with respect to the abode which bears the closest relationship, not necessarily geographic, with respect to the individual's tax home shall be taken into account, unless one of the households is a second foreign household.

(4) Reasonableness. An amount paid for housing shall not be treated as reasonable, for purposes of paragraph (a) of this section, to the extent that the expense is lavish or extravagant under the circumstances.

(5) Expenses of a second foreign household. (i) In general. The term "second foreign household" means a separate abode maintained by an individual outside of the U.S. for his or her spouse or dependents (who, if minors, are in the individual's legal custody or the joint custody of the individual and the individual's spouse) at a place other than the tax home of the individual because of adverse living conditions at the individual's tax home. If an individual maintains a second foreign household the expenses of the second foreign household may be included in the individual's housing expenses under paragraph (b)(1) of this section. Under no circumstances shall an individual be considered to maintain more than one second foreign household at the same time.

(ii) Adverse living conditions. Solely for purposes of paragraph (b)(5)(i) of this section, adverse living conditions are living conditions which are dangerous, unhealthful, or otherwise adverse. Adverse living conditions include a state of warfare or civil insurrection in the general area of the individual's tax home. Adverse living conditions exist if the individual resides on the business premises of the employer for the convenience of the employer and, because of the nature of the business (for example, a construction site or drilling rig), it is not feasible for the employer to provide housing for the individual's spouse or dependents. The criteria used by the Department of State in granting a separate maintenance allowance are relevant, but not determinative, for purposes of determining whether a separate household is provided because of adverse living conditions.

(c) Base housing amount. *(1) In general.* The base housing amount is equal to the product of 16 percent of the annual salary of an employee of the United States who is compensated at a rate equal to the annual salary rate paid for step 1 of grade GS-14, multiplied by the following fraction:

$$\frac{\text{The number of qualifying days}}{\text{The number of days in the taxable year}}$$

For purposes of the above fraction, the number of qualifying days is determined in accordance with § 1.911-3(d)(3).

(2) Annual salary of step 1 of grade GS-14. The annual salary rate for a step 1 of grade GS-14 is determined on January first of the calendar year in which the individual's taxable year begins.

(d) Housing cost amount exclusion. *(1) Limitation.* A qualified individual who has elected to exclude his or her housing cost amount may only exclude the lesser of the full amount of either the individual's housing cost amount attributable to employer provided amounts or the individual's foreign earned income for the taxable year. A qualified individual who elects to exclude his or her housing cost amount may not claim less than the full amount of the housing cost exclusion determined under this paragraph.

(2) Employer provided amounts. For purposes of this section, the term "employer provided amounts" means any amounts paid or incurred on behalf of the individual by the individual's employer which are foreign earned income included in the individual's gross income for the taxable year (without regard to section 911). Employer provided amounts include, but are not limited to, the following amounts: any salary paid by the employer to the employee; any reimbursement paid by the employer to the employee for housing expenses, educational expenses for the individual's dependents, or as part of a tax equalization plan; the fair market value of compensation provided in kind (including lodging, unless excluded under section 119, relating to meals and lodging furnished for the convenience of the employer); and any amount paid by the employer to any third party on behalf of the employee. An individual will only have earnings that are not employer provided amounts if the individual has earnings from self-employment.

(3) Housing cost amount attributable to employer provided amounts. For the purpose of determining what portion of the housing cost amount is excludable and what portion is deductible the following rules apply. If the individual has no income from self-employment, then the entire housing cost amount is attributable to employer provided amounts and is, therefore, excludable to the extent of the limitation provided in paragraph (d)(1) of this section. If the individual only has income from self-employment, then the entire housing cost amount is attributable to non-employer provided amounts and is, therefore, deductible to the extent of the limitation provided in paragraph (e) of this section. In all other instances, the housing cost amount attributable to employer provided amounts shall be determined by multiplying the

housing cost amount by the following fraction: Employer provided amounts over foreign earned income for the taxable year. The housing cost amount attributable to non-employer provided amounts shall be determined by subtracting the portion of the housing cost amount attributable to employer provided amounts from the total housing cost amount.

(e) Housing cost amount deduction. *(1) In general.* If a portion of the individual's housing cost amount is determined under paragraph (d)(3) of this section to be attributable to non-employer provided amounts, the individual may deduct that amount from gross income for the taxable year but only to the extent of the individual's foreign earned income (as defined in § 1.911-3) for the taxable year in excess of foreign earned income excluded and the housing cost amount excluded from gross income for the taxable year under § 1.911-3 and this section.

(2) Carryover. If any portion of the individual's housing cost amount deduction is disallowed for the taxable year under paragraph (e)(1) of this section, such portion shall be carried over and treated as a deduction from gross income for the succeeding taxable year (but only for the succeeding taxable year) to the extent of the excess, if any, of:

(i) The amount of foreign earned income for the succeeding taxable year less the foreign earned income and the housing cost amount excluded from gross income under § 1.911-3 and this section for the succeeding taxable year over,

(ii) The portion, if any, of the housing cost amount that is deductible under paragraph (e)(1) of this section for the succeeding taxable year.

(f) Examples. The following examples illustrate the application of this section. In all examples the annual rate for a step 1 of GS-14 as of January first of the calendar year in which the individual's taxable year begins is $39,689.

Example (1). B, a U.S. citizen is a calendar year taxpayer who was a bona fide resident of and whose tax home was located in foreign country G for the entire taxable year 1982. B receives an $80,000 salary from B's employer for services performed in G. B incurs no business expenses. B receives housing provided by B's employer with a fair rental value of $15,000. The value of the housing furnished by B's employer is not excluded from gross income under section 119. B pays $10,000 for housing expenses. B's gross income and foreign earned income for 1982 is $95,000. B elects the foreign earned income exclusion of section 911(a)(1) and the housing cost amount exclusion of section 911(a)(2). B must first compute his housing cost amount exclusion. B's housing cost amount is $18,650 determined by reducing B's housing expenses, $25,000 ($15,000 fair rental value of housing and $10,000 of other expenses), by the base housing amount of $6,350 (($39,689 × .16) × 365/365). Because B has no income from self-employment, the entire amount is attributable to employer provided amounts and therefore, is excludable. B's section 911(a)(1) limitation is $75,000. That is the lesser of $75,000 × 365/365 or $95,000 – 18,650. B's total exclusion for 1982 under section 911(a)(1) and (2) is $93,650.

Example (2). The facts are the same as in example (1) except that B's salary for 1982 is $70,000. B's foreign earned income for 1982 is $85,000. B's housing cost amount is $18,650, all of which is attributable to employer provided amounts. B's housing cost amount is excludable to the extent of the lesser of B's housing cost amount attributable to employer provided amounts, $18,650, or the foreign earned income for the taxable year, $85,000. Thus, B excludes $18,650 under section 911(a)(2). B's section 911(a)(1) limitation for 1982 is $66,350 (the lesser of $75,000 × 365/365 or $85,000 – 18,650). B's total exclusion for 1982 under section 911(a)(1) and (2) is $85,000.

Example (3). The facts are the same as in example (2) except that in 1983, B receives $5,000 attributable to services performed in 1982. B may exclude the entire $5,000 in 1983 because such amount would have been excludable under § 1.911-3(d)(1) had it been received in 1982.

Example (4). C is a U.S. citizen self-employed and a calendar year and cash basis taxpayer. C arrived in foreign country H on October 3, 1982, and departed from H on March 8, 1984. C's tax home was located in H throughout that period. C was physically present for 330 full days during the twelve consecutive month period August 30, 1982, through August 29, 1983. The number of C's qualifying days in 1982 is 124. During 1982 C had $35,000 of foreign earned income, none of which was attributable to employer provided amounts and $8,000 of reasonable housing expenses. C's housing cost amount is $5,843 ($8,000 – ((39,689 × .16) × 124/365)). C elects to exclude her foreign earned income under § 1.911-3(d)(1). C's section 911(a)(1) limitation for 1982 is $25,479 (the lesser of C's foreign earned income for the taxable year ($35,000) or the annual rate for the taxable year multiplied by the number of C's qualifying days over the number of days in the taxable year ($75,000 × 124/365 = $25,479). C may not claim the housing cost amount exclusion under section 911(a)(2) because no portion of the housing cost amount is attributable to employer provided amounts. C may deduct the lesser of her housing cost amount ($5,843) or her foreign earned income in excess of amounts excluded under section 911(a) ($35,000 – 25,479 = $9,521). Thus, C's housing cost amount deduction is $5,843.

Example (5). The facts are the same as in example (4) except that C had $30,000 of foreign earned income for 1982, none of which was attributable to employer provided amounts. C elects to exclude $25,479 under § 1.911-3(d)(1). C may only deduct $4,521 of her housing cost amount under paragraph (e)(1) of this section because her foreign earned income in excess of amounts excluded under section 911(a) is $4,521 ($30,000 – 25,479). The $1,322 of unused housing cost amount deduction may be carried over to the subsequent taxable year.

Example (6). The facts are the same as in example (4) except that C had $15,000 of foreign earned income of 1982, none of which was attributable to employer provided amounts. C elects to exclude the entire $15,000 under § 1.911-3(d)(1). C is not entitled to a housing cost amount deduction for 1982 since she has no foreign earned income in excess of amounts excluded under section 911(a). C may carry over her entire housing cost amount deduction to 1983.

Example (7). The facts are the same as in example (6). In addition, during taxable year 1983 C had $115,000 of foreign earned income, none of which was attributable to employer provided amounts, and $40,000 of reasonable housing expenses C elects to exclude her foreign earned income under § 1.911-3(d)(1). C's section 911(a)(1) limitation is the lesser of $115,000 or $80,000 ($80,000 × 365/365). C's housing cost amount for 1983 is $33,650 (40,000 – (39,689 × .16) × 365/365). Since no portion of that amount is attributable to employer provided amounts, C may not claim a housing cost amount exclusion. C may deduct the lesser of her housing cost amount ($33,650) or her foreign earned income in excess of amounts excluded under section 911(a) ($115,000 – 80,000 = 35,000). Thus, C may deduct her

$33,650 housing cost amount in 1983. In addition, C may deduct $1,350 of the housing cost amount deduction carried over from taxable year 1982. (($115,000 – 80,000 – 33,650 = $1,350). The remaining $4,493 ($5,843 – 1,350) of the housing cost amount deduction carried over from taxable year 1982 may not be deducted in 1983 or carried over to 1984.

Example (8). D is a U.S. citizen and a calendar year and cash basis taxpayer. D is a bona fide resident of and maintains his tax home in foreign country J for all of taxable year 1984. In 1984, D earns $80,000 of foreign earned income, $60,000 of which is an employer provided amount and $20,000 of which is a non-employer provided amount. D's total housing cost amount for 1984 is $25,000. D elects to exclude, under section 911(a)(2), the portion of his housing cost amount that is attributable to employer provided amounts. D's excludable housing cost amount is $18,750; that is the total housing cost amount ($25,000) multiplied by employer provided amounts for the taxable year ($60,000) over foreign earned income for the taxable year ($80,000). D also elects to exclude his foreign earned income under § 1.911-3(d)(1). D's section 911(a)(1) limitation for 1984 is $61,250 (the lesser of $80,000 – $18,750 or $80,000 × 366/366). D's total exclusion for 1984 under section 911(a)(1) and (2) is $80,000. D cannot claim a housing cost amount deduction in 1984 because D has no foreign earned income in excess of his foreign earned income and housing cost amount excluded from gross income for the taxable year under § 1.911-3 and this section. D may carry over his housing cost amount deduction of $6,250, the total housing cost amount less the portion attributable to employer provided amounts ($25,000 – 18,750), to taxable year 1985.

T.D. 8006, 1/17/85.

§ 1.911-5 Special rules for married couples.

(a) Married couples with two qualified individuals. *(1) In general.* In the case in which a husband and wife both are qualified individuals under § 1.911-2(a), each individual may make one or more elections under § 1.911-7 and exclude from gross income foreign earned income and exclude or deduct housing cost amounts subject to the rules of paragraph (a)(2) and (3) of this section.

(2) Computation of excluded foreign earned income. The amount of excludable foreign earned income is determined separately for each spouse under the rule of § 1.911-3 on the basis of the income attributable to the services of that spouse. If the spouses file separate returns each may exclude the amount of his or her foreign earned income attributable to his or her services subject to the limitations of § 1.911-3(d)(2). If the spouses file a joint return, the sum of these foreign earned income amounts so determined for each spouse may be excluded. For example, H and W both qualify under § 1.911-2(a)(2)(i) for the entire 1983 taxable year. During 1983 W earns $100,000 of foreign earned income and H earns $45,000 of foreign earned income. H and W file a joint return for 1983. On their joint return H and W may exclude from gross income a total of $125,000. That amount is determined by adding W's section 911(a)(1) limitation, $80,000 (the lesser of $80,000 × 365/365 or $100,000), and H's section 911(a)(1) limitation, $45,000 (the lesser of $80,000 × 365/365 or $45,000).

(3) Computation of housing cost amount. (i) Spouses residing together. If the spouses reside together, and file a joint return, they may compute their housing cost amount either jointly or separately. If the spouses reside together and file separate returns, they must compute their housing cost amounts separately. If the spouses compute their housing cost amounts separately, they may allocate the housing expenses to either of them or between them for the purpose of calculating separate housing cost amounts, but each spouse claiming a housing cost amount exclusion or deduction must use his or her full base housing amount in such computation. If the spouses compute their housing, cost amount jointly, then only one of the spouses may claim the housing cost amount exclusion or deduction. Either spouse may claim the housing cost amount exclusion or deduction; however, if the spouses have different periods of residence or presence and the spouse with the shorter period of residence or presence claims the exclusion or deduction, then only the expenses incurred in that shorter period may be claimed as housing expenses. The spouse claiming the exclusion or deduction may aggregate the couple's housing expenses, and subtract his or her base housing amount. For example, H and W reside together and file a joint return. H was a bona fide resident of and maintained his tax home in foreign country M from August 17, 1982 through December 31, 1983. W was a bona fide resident of and maintained her tax home in foreign country M from September 15, 1982 through December 31, 1983. During 1982, H and W earn and receive, respectively, $25,000 and $10,000 of foreign earned income. H paid $10,000 for qualified housing expenses in 1982, $7,500 of that was for qualified housing expenses incurred from September 15, 1982 through December 31, 1982. W paid $3,000 for qualified housing expenses in 1982 all of which were incurred during her period of residence. H and W may choose to compute their housing cost amount jointly. If they do so and H claims the housing cost amount exclusion his exclusion would be $10,617. H's housing expenses would be $13,000 ($10,000 + $3,000) and his base housing amount would be $2,383 ((39,689 × .16) × 137/365 = $2,383). If instead W claims the housing cost amount exclusion her exclusion would be $8,621. W's housing expenses would be $10,500 ($7,500 + 3,000) and her base housing amount would be $1,879 (($39,689 × .16) × 108/365 = $1,879). If H and W file jointly and both claim a housing cost amount exclusion, then H's and W's housing cost amounts would be, respectively, $7,617 ($10,000 – 2,383) and $1,121 ($3000 – 1,879).

(ii) Spouses residing apart. If the spouses reside apart, both spouses may exclude or deduct their housing cost amount if the spouses have different tax homes that are not within reasonable commuting distance (as defined in § 1.119-1(d)(4)) of each other and neither spouse's residence is within a reasonable commuting distance of the other spouse's tax home. If the spouse's tax homes, or one spouse's residence and the other spouse's tax home, are within a reasonable commuting distance of each other, only one spouse may exclude or deduct his or her housing cost amount. Regardless of whether the spouses file joint or separate returns, the amount of the housing cost amount exclusion or deduction must be determined separately for each spouse under the rules of § 1.911-4. If both spouses claim a housing cost amount exclusion or deduction directly as qualified individuals, neither may claim any such exclusion or deduction under section 911(c)(2)(B)(ii), relating to a second foreign household maintained for the other spouse. If one spouse fails to claim a housing cost amount exclusion or deduction which that spouse could claim directly, the other spouse may claim such exclusion or deduction under section 911(c)(2)(B)(ii), relating to a second foreign household maintained for the first spouse, provided that all the requirements of that section are met. Spouses may not claim more than one second foreign household and the expenses of such household may only be claimed by one spouse. For example, if both H and W are qualified individuals and H's tax home is in London and W's tax home is in Paris, then both H and W may exclude or deduct their housing cost amounts; however, H and W must compute these amounts separately regardless of whether they file joint or separate returns. If instead of living in Paris, W lives in an area where there are adverse living conditions and W maintains H's home in London, then W may add those housing expenses to her housing expenses and compute one base housing amount. In that case H may not claim a housing cost amount exclusion or deduction.

(iii) Housing cost amount attributable to employer provided amounts. Each spouse claiming a housing cost amount exclusion or deduction shall compute the portion of the housing cost amount that is attributable to employer provided amounts separately, based on his or her separate foreign earned income, in accordance with § 1.911-4(d)(3).

(b) Married couples with community income. The amount of excludable foreign earned income of a husband and wife with community income is determined separately for each spouse in accordance with paragraph (a) of this section on the basis of income attributable to that spouse's services without regard to community property laws. See sections 879 and 6013(g) and (h) for special rules regarding treatment of community income of a nonresident alien individual married to a U.S. citizen or resident.

T.D. 8006, 1/17/85.

§ 1.911-6 Disallowance of deductions, exclusions, and credits.

Caution: The Treasury has not yet amended Reg § 1.911-6 to reflect changes made by P.L. 109-222.

(a) In general. No deduction or exclusion from gross income under Subtitle A of the Code or credit against the tax imposed by chapter 1 of the Code shall be allowed to the extent the deduction, exclusion, or credit is properly allocable to or chargeable against amounts excluded from gross income under section 911(a). For purposes of the preceding sentence, deductions, exclusions, and credits which are definitely related (as provided in § 1.861-8), in whole or in part, to earned income shall be allocated and apportioned to foreign earned income and U.S. source earned income in accordance with the rules contained in § 1.861-8. Deductions, exclusions, and credits which are definitely related to all gross income under § 1.861-8, including deductions for interest described in § 1.861-8(e)(2)(ii), are definitely related, in whole or in part, to earned income. In the case of interest expense allocable, in whole or in part, to foreign earned income under § 1.861-8(e)(2)(ii), the expense shall normally be apportioned under option one of the optional gross income methods of apportionment (§ 1.861-8(e)(2)(vi)(A)), but without regard to conditions (1) and (2) of subdivision (vi)(A) (the fifty percent conditions). Such interest expense shall not normally be apportioned under the asset method of § 1.861-8(e)(2)(v). This is because, where section 911 is the operative section, the expense normally relates more closely to gross income generated from activities than to the amount of capital utilized or invested in activities or property. Deductions that are allocated and apportioned to foreign earned income must then be allocated and apportioned to foreign earned income that is excluded under section 911(a). If an individual has foreign earned income from both self-employment and other employment, the amount excluded under section 911(a)(1) shall be deemed to include a pro rata amount of the self-employment income and the income from other employment; thus, a pro rata portion of deductible expenses attributable to self-employment income must be disallowed. For purposes of section 911(d)(6) and this section only, deductions, exclusions, or credits which are not definitely related to any class of gross income shall not be allocable or chargeable to excluded amounts and are, therefore, deductible to the extent allowed by chapter 1 of the Code. Examples of deductions that are not definitely related to a class of gross income are personal and family medical expenses, qualified retirement contributions (but see section 219(b)(1)), real estate taxes and mortgage interest on a personal residence, charitable contributions, alimony payments, and deductions for personal exemptions. In addition, for purposes of this section, amounts excludable or deductible under section 911 or 119 shall not be allocable or chargeable to other amounts excluded under section 911(a). Thus, an individual's housing cost amount which is excludable or deductible under § 1.911-4(d) for a taxable year is not apportioned in part to the individual's foreign earned income which is excluded for such year under § 1.911-3(d). Therefore, the entire amount of such exclusion or deduction is allowed to the extent provided in § 1.911-4. This section does not affect the time for claiming any deduction, exclusion, or credit that is not allocated or apportioned to excluded amounts.

(b) Moving expenses. *(1) In general.* No deduction shall be allowed for moving expenses under section 217 to the extent the deduction is properly allocable to or chargeable against amounts of foreign earned income excluded from gross income under section 911(a). If an individual's new principal place of work is in a foreign country, deductible moving expenses will be allocable to foreign earned income. If an individual treats a reimbursement from his employer for the expenses of a move from a foreign country to the United States as attributable to services performed in a foreign country under § 1.911-3(e)(5)(i), then deductible moving expenses attributable to that move will be allocable to foreign earned income. If the individual is a qualified individual who elects to exclude foreign earned income under section 911(a), then some or all of such moving expenses must be disallowed as a deduction.

(2) Attribution of moving expense deduction to taxable years in which services are performed. If a moving expense deduction is properly allocable to foreign earned income, the deduction shall be considered attributable to services performed in the year of the move as long as the individual is a qualified individual under § 1.911-2(a) for a period that includes 120 days in the year of the move. If the individual is not a qualified individual for such period, then the individual shall treat the deduction as attributable to services performed in both the year of the move and the succeeding taxable year, if the move is from the United States to the foreign country, or the prior taxable year, if the move is from a foreign country to the United States. Notwithstanding the preceding two sentences, storage expenses incurred after December 31, 1983 shall be treated as attributable to services performed in the year in which the expenses are incurred.

(3) Formula for disallowance of moving expense deduction. The portion of the moving expense deduction that is disallowed shall be determined by multiplying the moving expense deduction by a fraction the numerator of which is all amounts excluded under section 911(a) for the year or years to which the deduction is attributable (under paragraph (b)(2) of this section) and the denominator of which is for-

eign earned income (as defined in § 1.911-3(a)) for that year or years.

(4) Effect of disallowance based on attribution of deduction to subsequent year's income. An individual may claim a moving expense deduction in the taxable year in which the amount of the expense is paid or incurred even if attributable, in part, to the succeeding year. However, at such time as the individual excludes income under section 911(a) for the year or years to which the deduction is attributable, the individual shall either—

(i) File an amended return for the year in which the deduction was claimed that does not claim the portion of the deduction that is disallowed because it is chargeable against excluded income, or

(ii) Include in income for the year following the year in which the deduction was claimed an amount equal to the amount of the deduction that is disallowed.

Any amount included in income under paragraph (b)(4)(ii) of this section is not foreign earned income.

(5) Moves beginning before January 1, 1984. Notwithstanding paragraph (b)(1) through (3) of this section, the rules of this paragraph (b)(5) shall apply for moves beginning before January 1, 1984.

(i) Individual qualifies for the entire taxable year of the move. If the individual is a qualified individual for the entire taxable year of the move, then the amount of moving expense disallowed shall be determined by multiplying the moving expense deduction otherwise allowable by a fraction the numerator of which is the foreign earned income excluded under section 911(a) for the taxable year of the move and the denominator of which is the foreign earned income for the same taxable year.

(ii) Individual qualifies for less than the entire taxable year of the move. If the individual is a qualified individual for less than the entire taxable year of the move, then, for the purpose of determining the portion of the otherwise allowable moving expense deduction that is disallowed, the individual must attribute a portion of the otherwise allowable moving expense deduction either to the succeeding taxable year, if the move is from the United States to a foreign country, or to the prior taxable year, if the move is from a foreign country to the United States. The portion of the moving expense deduction treated as attributable to services performed in the year of the move shall be determined by multiplying the otherwise allowable moving expense deduction by the following fraction:

$$\frac{\text{The number of qualifying days (as defined in § 1.911-3(d)(3)) in the year of the move}}{\text{The number of days in the taxable year of the move}}$$

The portion of the moving expense deduction treated as attributable to the year succeeding or preceding the move shall be determined by subtracting the portion of the moving expense deduction that is attributable to the year of the move from the total moving expense deduction. The allocation of a portion of the moving expense deduction to a succeeding or preceding taxable year does not affect the time for claiming the allowable moving expense deduction. The portion of the moving expense deduction that is disallowed shall be determined by multiplying the moving expense deduction attributable to the year of the move or the succeeding or preceding year, as the case may be, by a fraction the numerator of which is amounts excluded under section 911(a) for that year and the denominator of which is foreign earned income for that year.

(c) Foreign taxes. *(1) Amount disallowed.* No deduction or credit is allowed for foreign income, war profits, or excess profits taxes paid or accrued with respect to amounts excluded from gross income under section 911. To determine the amount of disallowed foreign taxes, multiply the foreign tax imposed on foreign earned income (as defined in § 1.911-3(a)) received or accrued during the taxable year by a fraction, the numerator of which is amounts excluded under section 911(a) in such taxable year less deductible expenses properly allocated to such amounts (see paragraphs (a) and (b) of this section), and the denominator of which is foreign earned income (as defined in § 1.911-3(a)) received or accrued during the taxable year less deductible expenses properly allocated or apportioned thereto. For the purpose of determining the extent to which foreign taxes are disallowed, the housing cost amount deduction is treated as definitely related to foreign earned income that is not excluded. If the foreign tax is imposed on foreign earned income and some other income (for example earned income from sources within the United States or an amount not subject to tax in the United States), and the taxes on the other amount cannot be segregated, then the denominator equals the total of the amounts subject to tax less deductible expenses allocable to all such amounts.

(2) Definitions and special rules. (i) Taxable year. For purposes of paragraph (c)(1) of this section, the term "taxable year" means the individual's taxable year for U.S. tax purposes. Such term includes the portion of any foreign taxable year within the individual's U.S. taxable year and excludes the portion of any foreign taxable year not within the individual's U.S. taxable year.

(ii) Apportionment of foreign taxes. For purposes of this paragraph (c), foreign taxes imposed on foreign earned income shall be deemed to accrue, on a pro rata basis, to income as the income is received or accrued. The taxes so accrued shall be apportioned to the taxable year during which the income is received or accrued. This rule applies for all individuals, regardless of their method of accounting.

(iii) Effect of disallowance. The disallowance of foreign taxes under this paragraph (c) shall not affect the time for claiming any deduction or credit for foreign taxes paid. Rather, the disallowance shall only affect the amount of taxes considered paid or accrued to any foreign country.

(iv) Interest on foreign taxes. Any interest expense incurred on a liability for foreign taxes is allocated and apportioned not under this paragraph (c) but under paragraph (a) of this section to foreign earned income and then to excluded foreign earned income and to that extent disallowed as a deduction under paragraph (a). In that regard, see also § 1.861-8(e)(2) for the specific rules for allocation and apportionment of interest expense.

(d) Examples. The following examples illustrate the application of this section.

Example (1). In 1982 A, an architect, operates his business as a sole proprietorship in which capital is not a material income producing factor. A receives $1,000,000 in gross receipts, all of which is foreign source earned income, and incurs $500,000 of otherwise deductible business expenses definitely related to the foreign earned income. A elects to exclude $75,000 under section 911(a)(1). The expenses must be apportioned to excluded earned income as follows: $500,000 × $75,000/1,000,000. Thus, $37,500 of the business expenses are not deductible.

Example (2). The facts are the same as in example (1), except that $100,000 of A's gross receipts is U.S. source earned income and $68,000 of A's business expenses are attributable to the U.S. source earned income. Thus, A has $900,000 of foreign earned income and $432,000 of deductions allocated to foreign earned income. The expenses apportioned to excluded earned income are $432,000 × $75,000/$900,000, or $36,000, which are not deductible.

Example (3). B is a U.S. citizen, calendar year and cash basis taxpayer. B moves to foreign country N and maintains a tax home and is physically present there from July 1, 1984 through May 26, 1985. Among other possible periods, B is a qualified individual for 219 days in the year of the move. B pays $6,000 of otherwise deductible moving expenses in 1984. For 1984, B's foreign earned income is $60,000 and B excludes $47,869 ($80,000 × 219/366) under section 911(a). Under paragraph (b)(2) of this section, B's moving expenses are attributable to services performed in 1984. Under paragraph (b)(3) of this section, $6,000 × $47,869/$60,000, or $4,789, of B's moving expense deduction is disallowed. B may deduct $1,211 of moving expenses on his 1984 return.

Example (4). The facts are the same as in example (3) except that B maintains a tax home and is physically present in foreign country N from October 9, 1984 through September 3, 1985. Among other possible periods, B is a qualified individual for no more than 119 days in 1984 and 281 days in 1985. B's foreign earned income for 1984 is $60,000. B's foreign earned income for 1985 is $150,000. Because B is a qualified individual for less than 120 days in the year of the move, under paragraph (b)(2) of this section, B's moving expenses are attributable to services performed in 1984 and 1985. At the close of 1984, B may either seek an extension of time to file under § 1.911-7(c) or may file an income tax return without claiming the exclusions or deduction under section 911. B does not seek an extension and files without excluding foreign earned income; thus B may deduct his moving expenses in full. B later amends his 1984 return and excludes foreign earned income for that year. B excludes foreign earned income for 1985. B must determine the portion of the moving expense deduction that is disallowed. The portion of the moving expense deduction that is disallowed is determined by multiplying the otherwise allowable moving expense deduction by a fraction. The numerator of the fraction is the sum of amounts excluded under section 911(a) for 1984 and 1985, that is $26,082 or $80,000 × 119/365, plus $61,589, or $80,000 × 281/365, which totals $87,671. The denominator of the fraction is the sum of foreign earned income for 1984 and 1985, that is $60,000 plus $150,000, or $210,000. B's allowable moving expense deduction is $3,495, or $6,000 – ($6,000 × $87,671/$210,000). If B does not file an amended 1984 return (and does not exclude foreign earned income for 1984), but excludes foreign earned income under section 911(a) for 1985, a portion of his moving expense deduction is disallowed, based on the same formula. The amount disallowed is $6,000 × $61,589/$210,000, or $1,760. This amount may be recaptured either by filing an amended return for 1984 or by including it in income for 1985 (in which case it is not foreign earned income).

Example (5). C is a U.S. citizen, a self-employed individual, and a cash basis and calendar year taxpayer. For the entire 1982 taxable year C maintained his tax home and his bona fide residence in foreign country P. During 1982 C earned and received $120,000 of foreign earned income, none of which was attributable to employer provided amounts. C paid $40,000 of business expenses. C elected to exclude foreign earned income under section 911(a)(1) and claimed a housing cost amount deduction of $15,000. C received $10,000 of foreign source interest income which was included with C's earned income in a single tax base and taxed at graduated rates. For 1982, C paid $30,000 in income tax to foreign country P. The amount of C's business expenses that is properly apportioned to excluded amounts (and therefore, not deductible) equals $25,000, which is determined by multiplying the otherwise allowable deductions by C's excluded amounts over C's foreign earned income ($40,000 × 75,000/120,000). The amount of country P tax that is properly apportioned to excluded amounts (and therefore, not deductible or creditable) equals $20,000, which is determined by multiplying the tax of $30,000 by the following fraction:

$$\frac{\text{\$50,000 (\$75,000 excluded amounts less \$25,000 of deductible expenses allocable thereto)}}{\text{\$75,000 (((\$120,000 foreign earned income less \$40,000 of deductible expenses allocable thereto) less \$15,000 housing cost amount deduction allocable thereto) plus \$10,000 other taxable income)}}$$

Example (6). D is a U.S. citizen and an accrual basis and calendar year taxpayer for U.S. tax purposes. For the entire period from January 1, 1982 through December 31, 1983, D maintains his tax home and his bona fide residence in foreign country R. For purposes of R's income tax, D is a cash basis taxpayer and uses a fiscal year that begins on April 1 and ends on the following March 31. During his entire period of residence in R, D receives foreign earned income of $10,000 each month, all of which is attributable to employer provided amounts. For his foreign taxable year ending March 31, 1982, D pays $10,000 of income tax to R. For his foreign taxable year ending March 31, 1983, D pays $54,000 of income tax to R. Under paragraph (c)(2)(ii) of this section, all of the $10,000 of tax paid for this foreign taxable year ending March 31, 1982 is imposed on foreign earned income received in 1982, as is $40,500, or 9/12 × $54,000, of tax paid for his foreign taxable year ending March 31, 1983. (D received $10,000 per month for the last 3 months of his foreign taxable year ending March 31, 1982, all of which are within his U.S. taxable year ending December 31, 1982 under paragraph (c)(2)(i) of this section, and $10,000 per month for each month of his foreign taxable year ending March 31, 1983, of which the first 9 months are within his U.S. taxable year ending December 31, 1982. Under paragraph (c)(2)(ii) of this section, foreign taxes are deemed to accrue on a pro rata basis to income as it is received or accrued. Thus, all of the $10,000 of foreign taxes imposed on the income received during D's foreign taxable year ending March 31, 1982 accrue to D's 1982 foreign earned income, as do 9/12 (or $90,000/120,000) of foreign taxes imposed on income received during D's foreign taxable year ending March 31, 1983, for purposes of determining the amount of D's foreign taxes that is disallowed.) For 1982, D has no deductible expenses, and elects to exclude his housing cost amount of $21,000 under section 911(a)(2) and foreign earned income of $75,000 under section 911(a)(1). The amount of D's foreign taxes disallowed for deduction or credit purposes for 1982 is $8,000 (that is, $10,000 × $96,000/$120,000) of the taxes for his foreign taxable year ending March 31, 1982, plus $32,400 (that is, $40,500 × $96,000/$120,000) of the taxes for his foreign taxable year ending March 31, 1983, or $40,400. From 1982, D has $2,000 ($10,000 – $8,000) of deductible or creditable taxes accrued on March 31, 1982, and $8,100 ($40,500 – $32,400) of deductible or creditable taxes accrued on March 31, 1983, after the disallowance based on his 1982 excluded income.

Example (7). E is a United States citizen, calendar year and cash basis taxpayer. E is physically present in and establishes his tax home in foreign country S on May 1, 1981. For purposes of country S, E's taxable year begins on April 1 and ends the following March 31. E receives foreign earned income of $15,000 each month beginning on May 1, 1981. At the end of his foreign taxable year ending on March 31, 1982, E pays $70,000 of income tax to S on $165,000 of foreign earned income. Under section 911, as in effect for taxable years beginning before January 1, 1982, E may not exclude any income that is earned or received during 1981. None of E's taxes paid in 1982 that are attributable to income earned or received in 1981 are subject to disallowance because, under paragraph (c)(2)(ii) of this section, the only taxes disallowed are those deemed to accrue on income earned and received after December 31, 1981, and excluded from gross income. The amount of E's taxes paid in 1982 that are attributable to 1981 is $50,909, or $70,000 × $120,000/$165,000. E elects to exclude foreign earned income for 1982. The amount of E's taxes paid to S in 1982 that accrue to 1982 foreign earned income, and are therefore subject to disallowance based on excluded income, is $19,091, or $70,000 × $45,000/$165,000.

T.D. 8006, 1/17/85.

§ 1.911-7 Procedural rules.

(a) Elections of a qualified individual. *(1) In general.* In order to receive either exclusion provided by section 911(a), a qualified individual must elect, separately with respect to each exclusion, to exclude foreign earned income under section 911(a)(1) and the housing cost amount under section 911(a)(2). Any such elections may be made on Form 2555 or on a comparable form. Each election must be filed either with the income tax return, or with an amended return, for the first taxable year of the individual for which the election is to be effective. An election once made remains in effect for that year and all subsequent years unless revoked under paragraph (b) of this section. Each election shall contain information sufficient to determine whether the individual is a qualified individual as provided in § 1.911-2. The statement shall include the following information:

(i) The individual's name, address, and social security number;

(ii) The name of the individual's employer;

(iii) Whether the individual claimed exclusions under section 911 for earlier years after 1981 and within the five preceding taxable years;

(iv) Whether the individual has revoked a previously made election and the taxable year for which such revocation was effective;

(v) The exclusion or exclusions the individual is electing;

(vi) The foreign country or countries in which the individual's tax home is located and the date when such tax home was established;

(vii) The status (either bona fide residence or physical presence) under which the individual claims the exclusion;

(viii) The individual's qualifying period of residence or presence;

(ix) The individual's foreign earned income for the taxable year including the fair market value of all noncash remuneration; and,

(x) If the individual elects to exclude the housing cost amount, the individual's housing expenses.

(2) Requirement of a return. (i) In general. In order to make a valid election under this paragraph (a), the election must be made:

(A) With an income tax return that is timely filed (including any extensions of time to file),

(B) With a later return filed within the period prescribed in section 6511(a) amending the foregoing timely filed income tax return,

(C) With an original income tax return that is filed within one year after the due date of the return (determined without regard to any extension of time to file); this one year period does not constitute an extension of time for any purpose—it is merely a period during which a valid election may be made on a late return, or

(D) With an income tax return filed after the period described in paragraphs (a)(2)(i)(A), (B), or (C) of this section provided—

(1) The taxpayer owes no federal income tax after taking into account the exclusion and files Form 1040 with Form 2555 or a comparable form attached either before or after the Internal Revenue Service discovers that the taxpayer failed to elect the exclusion; or

(2) The taxpayer owes federal income tax after taking into account the exclusion and files Form 1040 with Form 2555 or a comparable form attached before the Internal Revenue Service discovers that the taxpayer failed to elect the exclusion.

(3) A taxpayer filing an income tax return pursuant to paragraph (a)(2)(i)(D)(1) or (2) of this section must type or legibly print the following statement at the top of the first page of the Form 1040: "Filed Pursuant to Section 1.911-7(a)(2)(i)(D)."

(ii) Election for 1982 and 1983 taxable years. Solely for purposes of paragraph (a)(2)(i)(A) of this section, an income tax return for any taxable year beginning before January 1, 1984 shall be considered timely filed if it is filed on or before July 23, 1985.

(3) Housing cost amount deduction. An individual does not have to make an election in order to claim the housing cost amount deduction. However, such individual must provide the Commissioner with information sufficient to determine the individual's correct amount of tax. Such information shall include the following: The individual's name, address, and social security number; the name of the individual's employer; the foreign country in which the individual's tax home was established; the status under which the individual claims the deduction; the individual's qualifying period of residence or presence; the individual's foreign earned income for the taxable year; and the individual's housing expenses.

(4) Effect of immaterial error or omission. An inadvertent error or omission of information required to be provided to make an election under this paragraph (a) shall not render the election invalid if the error or omission is not material in determining whether the individual is a qualified individual or whether the individual intends to make the election.

(b) Revocation of election. *(1) In general.* An individual may revoke any election made under paragraph (a) of this section for any taxable year. A revocation must be made separately with respect to each election. The individual may revoke an election for any taxable year, including the first taxable year for which an election was effective, by filing a statement that the individual is revoking one or more of the previously made elections. The statement must be filed with the income tax return, or with an amended return, for the first taxable year of the individual for which the revocation is to be effective. A revocation once made is effective for that year and all subsequent years. If an election is revoked for any taxable year, including the first taxable year for which the election was effective, the individual may not, without the consent of the Commissioner, again make the same election until the sixth taxable year following the taxable year for which the revocation was first effective. For example, a qualified individual makes an election to exclude foreign earned income under section 911(a)(1) and files it with his 1982 income tax return. The individual files 1983 and 1984 income tax returns on which he excludes his foreign earned income. Then, within 3 years after filing his 1982 income tax return, the individual files an amended 1982 income tax return with a statement revoking his election to exclude foreign earned income under section 911(a)(1). The revocation of the election is effective for taxable years 1982, 1983, and 1984. The individual may not elect to exclude income under section 911(a)(1) for any taxable year before 1988, unless he obtains consent to reelect under paragraph (b)(2) of this section.

(2) Reelection before sixth taxable year after revocation. If an individual revoked an election under paragraph (b)(1) of this section and within five taxable years the individual wishes to reelect the same exclusion, then the individual may apply for consent to the reelection. The application for consent shall be made by requesting a ruling from the Associate Chief Counsel (Technical), National Office, Internal Revenue Service, 1111 Constitution Avenue NW., Washington, D.C. 20224. In determining whether to consent to reelection the Associate Chief Counsel or his delegate shall consider any facts and circumstances that may be relevant to the determination. Relevant facts and circumstances may include the following: a period of United States residence, a move from one foreign country to another foreign country with differing tax rates, a substantial change in the tax laws of the foreign country of residence or physical presence, and a change of employer.

(c) Returns and extensions. *(1) In general.* Any return filed before completion of the period necessary to qualify an individual for any exclusion of deduction provided by section 911 shall be filed without regard to any exclusion or deduction provided by that section. A claim for a credit or refund of any overpayment of tax may be filed, however, if the taxpayer subsequently qualifies for any exclusion or deduction under section 911. See section 6012(c) and § 1.6012-1(a)(3), relating to returns to be filed and information to be furnished by individuals who qualify for any exclusion or deduction under section 911.

(2) Extensions. An individual desiring an extension of time (in addition to the automatic extension of time granted by § 1.6081-2) for filing a return until after the completion of the qualifying period described in paragraph (c)(1) of this section for claiming any exclusion or deduction under section 911 may apply for an extension. An individual whose moving expense deduction is attributable to services performed in two years may apply for an extension of time for filing a return until after the end of the second year. The individual may make such application on Form 2350 or a comparable form. The application must be filed with the Director, Internal Revenue Service Center, Philadelphia, Pennsylvania 19255. The application must set forth the facts relied on to justify the extension of time requested and must include a statement as to the earliest date the individual expects to become entitled to any exclusion or deduction by reason of completion of the qualifying period.

(d) Declaration of estimated tax. In estimating gross income for the purpose of determining whether a declaration of estimated tax must be made for any taxable year, an individual is not required to take into account income which the individual reasonably believes will be excluded from gross income under the provisions of section 911. In computing estimated tax, however, the individual must take into account, among other things, the denial of the foreign tax credit for foreign taxes allocable to the excluded income (see § 1.911-6(c)).

T.D. 8006, 1/17/85, amend T.D. 8480, 6/29/93.

§ 1.911-8 Former deduction for certain expenses of living abroad.

For rules relating to the deduction for certain expenses of living abroad applicable to taxable years beginning before January 1, 1982, see 26 CFR 1.913-1 through 1.913-13 as they appeared in the Code of Federal Regulations revised as of April 1, 1982.

T.D. 8006, 1/17/85.

§ 1.912-1 Exclusion of certain cost-of-living allowances.

Caution: The Treasury has not yet amended Reg § 1.912-1 to reflect changes made by P.L. 100-647, P.L. 87-293, P.L. 86-707.

(a) Amounts received by Government civilian personnel stationed outside the continental United States as cost-of-living allowances in accordance with regulations approved by the President are, by the provisions of section 912(1), excluded from gross income. Such allowances shall be considered as retaining their characteristics under section 912(1) notwithstanding any combination thereof with any other allowance. For example, the cost-of-living portion of a "living and quarters allowance" would be excluded from gross income whether or not any other portion of such allowance is excluded from gross income.

(b) For purposes of section 912(1), the term "continental United States" includes only the 48 States existing on February 25, 1944 (the date of the enactment of the Revenue Act of 1943 (58 Stat. 21)) and the District of Columbia.

T.D. 6249, 8/21/57, amend T.D. 6365, 2/13/59.

§ 1.912-2 Exclusion of certain allowances of Foreign Service personnel.

Amounts received by personnel of the Foreign Service of the United States as allowances or otherwise under the terms of title IX of the Foreign Service Act of 1946 (22 U.S.C. 1131–1158) are, by the provisions of section 912(2), excluded from gross income.

T.D. 6249, 8/21/57.

§ 1.921-1T Temporary regulations providing transition rules for DISCs and FSCs (temporary).

Caution: The Treasury has not yet amended Reg § 1.921-1T to reflect changes made by P.L. 106-519.

(a) Termination of a DISC. *(1) At end of 1984.*

Q-1. What is the effect of the termination on December 31, 1984 of a DISC's taxable year?

A-1. Without regard to the annual accounting period of the DISC, the last taxable year of each DISC beginning during 1984 shall be deemed to close on December 31, 1984. The corporation's DISC election also shall be deemed revoked at the close of business on December 31, 1984. (A DISC that does not elect to be an interest charge DISC as of January 1, 1985, in addition to a corporation described in section 992(a)(3), shall be referred to as a "former DISC".) A corporation which wishes to be treated as a FSC, a small FSC, or an interest charge DISC must make an election as provided under paragraph (b) (Q & A #1) of this section.

(2) Deemed distributions for short taxable years.

Q-2. If the termination of the DISC's taxable year on December 31, 1984, results in a short taxable year, how are the deemed distributions under section 995(b)(1)(E) determined?

A-2. The deemed distributions are determined on the basis of the DISC's taxable income for its short taxable year ending on December 31, 1984. In computing the incremental distribution under section 995(b)(1)(E), the export gross receipts for the short taxable year must be annualized.

(3) Qualification as a DISC for 1984.

Q-3. Must the DISC satisfy all the tests set forth in section 992(a)(1) for the DISC's taxable year ending December 31, 1984?

A-3. All of the tests under section 992(a)(1), except the qualified assets test under section 992(a)(1)(B), must be satisfied.

(4) Commissions for 1984.

Q-4. Must commissions be paid by a related supplier to a DISC with respect to the DISC's taxable year ending December 31, 1984?

A-4. No.

(5) Producer's loans of 1984.

Q-4A. Must commissions which were earned prior to January 1, 1985, be paid by a related supplier if the last date payment is required (as set forth in § 1.994-1(e)(3)) is after December 31, 1984?

A-4A. No.

Q-5. Must the producer's loan rules under section 993(d) be satisfied with respect to the DISC's taxable year ending December 31, 1984?

A-5. Yes.

(6) Accumulated DISC income.

Q-6. Under what circumstances is any remaining accumulated DISC income treated as previously taxed income (and not taxed)?

A-6. The accumulated DISC income of a DISC (but not a DISC described in section 992(a)(3)) as of December 31, 1984, is treated as previously taxed income when actually distributed after December 31, 1984. Any amounts distributed by the former DISC (including a DISC which has elected to be an interest charge DISC) after December 31, 1984, shall be treated as made first out of current earnings and profits and then out of previously taxed income to the extent thereof. For purposes of the preceding sentence, amounts distributed before July 1, 1985 shall be treated as made first out of previously taxed income to the extent thereof. If property other than money is distributed and if such property was a qualified export asset within the meaning of section 993(b) on December 31, 1984, then for purposes of section 311, no gain or loss will be recognized on the distribution and the distributee will have the same basis in the property as the distributor.

Q-7. May a DISC that was previously disqualified, but has requalified as of December 31, 1984, treat any accumulated DISC income as previously taxed income?

A-7. If a DISC was previously disqualified, but has requalified as of December 31, 1984, any accumulated DISC income previously required to be taken into income upon prior disqualification shall not be treated as previously taxed income. All accumulated DISC income derived since requalification, however, will be treated as previously taxed income.

(7) Distribution of previously taxed income.

Q-8. What effect will the distribution of previously taxed income have on the earnings and profits of corporate shareholders of the former DISC?

A-8. The earnings and profits of the corporate shareholders of the former DISC will be increased by the amount of money and the adjusted basis of any property which is distributed out of previously taxed income.

Q-9. Will the distribution of the former DISC's accumulated DISC income as previously taxed income after December 31, 1984, result in a reduction in the shareholder's basis of the stock of the former DISC and consequent taxation of the excess of the distribution over such basis as capital gain under section 996(d)?

A-9. No. This distribution will be treated both as amounts representing deemed distributions under section 995(b)(1) and as previously taxed income. Thus, no capital gain will arise.

(8) Qualifying distributions.

Q-10. How is a qualifying distribution to satisfy the qualified export receipts tests under section 992(c)(1)(A) which is made with respect to the DISC's taxable year ending on December 31, 1984, treated?

A-10. The distribution will not be treated as previously taxed income but will be taxed to the shareholder of the former DISC, as provided under section 992(c) and 996(a)(2) and the regulations thereunder, in the shareholder's taxable year in which the distribution is made.

(9) Deficiency distributions.

Q-11. With respect to an audit adjustment made after December 31, 1984, may a deficiency distribution be made, and if so, in what manner may it be made?

A-11. A deficiency distribution may be made notwithstanding the fact that after December 31, 1984 the former DISC is a taxable corporation under Subchapter C, has elected to be treated as an interest charge DISC, or has been liquidated, reorganized or is otherwise no longer in existence. However, such deficiency distribution shall be treated as made out of accumulated DISC income which is not previously taxed income because it will be treated as distributed prior to December 31, 1984 to the DISC's shareholders.

Q-11A. Must a former DISC remain in existence in order for a former DISC shareholder to take advantage of the spread provided in section 995(b)(2) with respect to DISC disqualification?

A-11A. No. With respect to distributions deemed to be received by a former DISC shareholder under section 995(b)(2) for taxable years beginning after December 31, 1984, if the former DISC shareholder elects, the rules of section 995(b)(2)(B) shall apply even though the former DISC does not continue in existence. If the former DISC is no longer in existence, the former DISC's shareholders will be deemed to have received the distribution on the last day of their taxable years over the applicable period of time determined under section 995(b)(2) as if the former DISC had remained in existence.

(10) Deemed distribution for 1984.

Q-12. How is the deemed distribution to a shareholder for the DISC's taxable year ending December 31, 1984, taken into account?

A-12. (i) If the taxable year of the DISC ending on December 31, 1984, (A) is the first taxable year of the DISC which begins in 1984, (B) begins after the date in 1984 on which the taxable year of the DISC's shareholder begins, and (C) if the DISC's shareholder makes an election under section 805(b)(3) of the Tax Reform Act of 1984, the deemed distribution under section 995(b) with respect to income derived by the DISC for such taxable year of the DISC shall be treated as received by the shareholder in 10 equal installments (unless the shareholder elects to be treated as receiving the deemed distribution in income over a smaller number of equal installments). The first installment shall be treated as received by the shareholder on the last day of the shareholder's second taxable year beginning in 1984 (if any), or if the shareholder had only one taxable year which began in 1984, on the last day of the shareholder's first taxable year beginning in 1985. One installment shall be treated as received by the shareholder on the last day of each succeeding taxable year of the shareholder until the entire amount of the DISC's 1984 deemed distribution has been included in the shareholder's taxable income. To make the election under section 805(b)(3) of the Tax Reform Act of 1984, the DISC shareholder must attach a statement to its timely filed tax return (including extensions) for its taxable year which includes December 31, 1984, indicating the total amount of the shareholder's pro rata share of the DISC's deemed distribution for 1984 (determined under section 995(b) of the Code without regard to the election under section 805(b)(3) of the Tax Reform Act of 1984), and the number of equal installments, if less than 10, over which the shareholder wishes to spread its pro rata share of the deemed distribution for 1984. If the election under section 805(b)(3) of the Tax Reform Act of 1984 is made, it may not be changed or revoked. In determining estimated tax payments, the portion of the deemed distribution includible in the shareholder's taxable income for any taxable year under this subdivision (i) shall be treated as received by the shareholder on the last day of such taxable year.

(ii) Except as provided in subdivision (i), the deemed distribution under section 995(b) with respect to income derived by the DISC for its taxable year ending on December 31, 1984, shall be included in the shareholder's taxable income for its taxable year which includes December 31, 1984. Thus, if the taxable year of the DISC and the DISC's shareholder both begin on January 1, 1984, and end on December 31, 1984 (or, if the taxable year of the DISC beginning in 1984 begins before the taxable year of the DISC's shareholder), the deemed distribution with respect to the DISC's taxable year ending on December 31, 1984, will be included in the DISC shareholder's taxable year ending on (or including) December 31, 1984, and the election described in subdivision (i) may not be made.

(iii) The provisions of this Question and Answer-12 apply without regard to any existence of the DISC after December 31, 1984, as an interest charge DISC.

Q-12A. If under section 805(b)(3) of the Tax Reform Act of 1984 the shareholders of the DISC are permitted to make an election to treat the DISC's 1984 deemed distribution as received over a 10-year period, must the DISC distribute that amount to its shareholders ratably over the 10-year period?

A-12A. No. Under section 805(b)(3) of the Tax Reform Act of 1984, if the DISC's deemed distribution for its taxable year which ended on December 31, 1984, is a qualified distribution, the shareholders of the DISC are permitted to make an election to treat the distribution as received over a 10-year period. The 10-year treatment applies even though the amount of the deemed distribution is distributed to the DISC's shareholders prior to the period in which the distribution is taken into income by the shareholders. In addition, under section 996(e) of the Code, the shareholder's basis in the stock of the DISC will be considered as increased, as of the date of liquidation, by the shareholder's pro rata share of the amount of the undistributed qualified distribution even though that amount is treated as received by the shareholder in later years. Further, the actual distribution in liquidation of the former DISC after 1984 will increase the earnings and profits of a corporate distributee, and the amount actually distributed shall be treated under the rules of section 996.

(11) Conformity of accounting period.

Q-13. May a DISC be established or change its annual accounting period for taxable years beginning after March 21, 1984, and before January 1, 1985?

A-13. A DISC that is established or that changes its annual accounting period after March 21, 1984, must conform its annual accounting period to that of its principal shareholder (the shareholder with the highest percentage of voting power as defined in section 441(h)).

(12) DISC gains and distributions from U.S. sources.

Q-14. What is the effective date of the amendment to section 996(g), made by section 801(d)(10) of the Tax Reform Act of 1984, which treats certain DISC gains and distributions as derived from sources within the United States?

A-14. Under section 805(a)(3) of the Act, the amendment to section 996(g) shall apply to all gains referred to in section 995(c) and all distributions out of accumulated DISC income including deemed distributions made on or after June 22, 1984.

(b) Establishing and electing status as a FSC, small FSC or interest charge DISC. *(1) Ninety-day period.*

Q-1. How does a corporation elect to be treated as a FSC, a small FSC, or an interest charge DISC?

A-1. A corporation electing FSC or small FSC status must file Form 8279. A corporation electing interest charge DISC status must file Form 4876A. A corporation electing to be treated as an FSC, small FSC, or interest charge DISC for its first taxable year shall make its election within 90 days after the beginning of that year. A corporation electing to be treated as an FSC, small FSC, or interest charge DISC for any taxable year other than its first taxable year shall make its election during the 90-day period immediately preceding the first day of that taxable year. The election to be an FSC, small FSC, or interest charge DISC may be made by the corporation, however, during the first 90 days of a taxable year, even if that taxable year is not the corporation's first taxable year, if that taxable year begins before July 1, 1985. Likewise, the election to be an FSC (or a small FSC) may be made during the first 90 days of any taxable year of a corporation if the corporation had in a prior taxable year elected small FSC (or FSC) status and the corporation revokes the small FSC (or FSC) election within the 90 day period. A corporation which was a DISC for its taxable year ending December 31, 1984, which wishes to be treated as an interest charge DISC beginning with its first taxable year beginning after December 31, 1984, may make the election to be treated as an interest charge DISC by filing Form 4876A on or before July 1, 1987. Also, if a corporation which has elected FSC, small FSC or interest charge DISC status, or a shareholder of that corporation, is acquired in a qualified stock purchase under section 338(d)(3), and if an election under section 338(a) is effective with regard to that corporation, the corporation may re-elect FSC, small FSC or interest charge DISC status, (whichever is applicable,) not later than the date of the election under section 338(a), see section 338(g)(i) and § 1.338-2(d). This re-election is necessary because the original elections are deemed terminated if an election is made under section 338(a). The rules contained in § 1.992-2(a)(1), (b)(1) and (b)(3) shall apply to the manner of making the election and the manner and form of shareholder consent.

(2) FSC incorporated in a possession.

Q-2. Where does a FSC which is incorporated in a U.S. possession file its election?

A-2. The election is filed with the Internal Revenue Service Center, Philadelphia, Pennsylvania 19255.

(3) Information returns.

Q-3. Must Form 5471 be filed with respect to the organization of a FSC pursuant to section 6046 or to provide information with respect to a FSC pursuant to section 6038?

A-3. A Form 5471 required under section 6046 need not be filed with respect to the organization of a FSC. The requirements of section 6046 shall be satisfied by the filing of a Form 8279 dealing with the election to be treated as a FSC or small FSC. However, a Form 5471 will be required with respect to a reorganization of a FSC (or small FSC) or an acquisition of stock of a FSC (or small FSC), as required under section 6046 and the regulations thereunder. Provided that a Form 1120 FSC is filed, a Form 5471 need not be filed to satisfy the requirements of section 6038.

(4) Conformity of accounting period.

Q-4. Since a FSC, small FSC, and interest charge DISC must use the same annual accounting period as the principal shareholder, must such corporation delay the beginning of its first taxable year beyond January 1, 1985 if the principal shareholder (the shareholder with the highest percentage of voting power as defined in section 441(h)) is not a calendar year taxpayer?

A-4. No. Where the principal shareholder is not a calendar year taxpayer, a corporation may elect to be treated as a FFSC, small FSC, or interest charge DISC for a taxable year beginning January 1, 1985. However, such corporation must close its first taxable year and adopt the annual accounting period of its principal shareholder as of the first day of the principal shareholder's first taxable year beginning in 1985. A FSC, small FSC, or interest charge DISC need not obtain the consent of the Commissioner under section 442 to conform its annual accounting period to the annual accounting period of its principal shareholder.

(5) Dollar limitations for short taxable years.

Q-5. If a small FSC or an interest charge DISC has a short taxable year, how are the dollar limitations on foreign trading export gross receipts and qualified export gross receipts, respectively, determined for small FSCs and interest charge DISCs?

A-5. The dollar limitations are to be prorated on a daily basis. Thus, for example, if for its 1985 taxable year a small FSC has a short taxable year of 73 days, then in determining exempt foreign trade income, any foreign trading gross receipts that exceed $1 million (73/365 × $5 million) will not be taken into account.

(6) Change of accounting period.

Q-6. The principal shareholder of a FSC, a small FSC, or an interest charge DISC (hereinafter referred to as a "FSC") changes its annual accounting period or is replaced by a new principal shareholder during a taxable year, is it necessary for the FSC to change its annual accounting period?

A-6. If the principal shareholder changes its annual accounting period, the FSC must also change its annual accounting period to conform to that of its principal shareholder. If the voting power of the principal shareholder is reduced by an amount equal to at least 10 percent of the total shares entitled to vote and such shareholder is no longer the principal shareholder, the FSC must conform its accounting period to that of its new principal shareholder. However, in determining whether a shareholder is a principal shareholder, the voting power of the shareholders is determined as of the beginning of the FSC's taxable year. Thus, for example, assume that for 1985 a FSC adopts a calendar year period as its annual accounting period to conform to that of its principal shareholder. Assume further than in March 1985 there is a 10 percent change in voting power and a different shareholder whose annual accounting period begins on July 1 becomes the new principal shareholder. The FSC will not be required to adopt the annual accounting period of its new principal shareholder until July 1, 1986. The FSC will have a short taxable year for the period January 1 to June 30, 1986.

(7) Transition transfers.

Q-7. Under what circumstances may a DISC or former DISC transfer its assets to a FSC or small FSC without incurring any tax liability on the transfer?

A-7. A DISC or former DISC will recognize no income, gain, or loss on a transfer of its qualified assets (as defined in section 993(b)) to a FSC or small FSC if all of the following conditions are met:

(1) The assets transferred were held by the DISC on August 4, 1983, and were transferred by the DISC or former DISC to the FSC or small FSC in a transfer completed before January 1, 1986; and

(2) The assets are transferred in a transaction which would qualify for nonrecognition under subchapter C of Chapter 1 of the Code, or would so qualify but for section 367 of the Code.

In such case, section 367 shall not apply to the transfer.

In addition, other provisions of subchapter C will apply to the transfer, such as section 358 (basis to shareholders), section 362 (basis to corporations), and section 381 (carryovers in corporate acquisitions). In determining whether a transfer by a DISC to a FSC or small FSC qualifies for nonrecognition under subchapter C, a liquidation of the assets of the DISC into a parent corporation followed by a transfer by the parent of those assets to the FSC or small FSC will be treated as a transaction described in section 368(a)(1)(D).

Notwithstanding the foregoing answer, a taxpayer which transfers a right to use its corporate name to a FSC in a transaction described in sections 332, 351, 354, 356 and 361 shall not be treated as having sold that right under section 367(d) or as having transferred that right to an entity that is not a corporation under section 367(a) provided that the corporate name is used only by the FSC and is not licensed or otherwise made available to others by the FSC.

(8) Completed contract method.

Q-8. Under what conditions is a taxpayer using the completed contract method of accounting as defined in § 1.451-

3(d) exempted from satisfying the foreign management and foreign economic process requirements of subsections (c) and (d) of section 924?

A-8. If the taxpayer has entered into a binding contract before March 16, 1984, or has on March 15, 1984, and at all times thereafter a firm plan, evidenced in writing, to enter the contract and enters into a binding contract by December 31, 1984, then the taxpayer will be treated as having satisfied the foreign management tests of section 924(c) for periods before December 31, 1984, and the foreign economic process tests of section 924(d) with respect to costs incurred before December 31, 1984, with respect to the transaction. The FSC rules will apply to the income from the long-term contract if an election is made and the general FSC requirements under section 922 are satisfied. However, such taxpayer need not satisfy the activities test under section 925(c) for activities which occur before January 1, 1985 in order to use the transfer pricing rules under section 925.

(9) Long-term contract—before March 15, 1984.

Q-9. Under what conditions is a taxpayer who enters into a binding long-term contract (i.e., a contract which is not completed in the taxable year in which it is entered into) before March 15, 1984, but does not use the completed contract method of accounting exempted from satisfying the foreign management and economic process requirements of subsections (c) and (d) of section 924?

A-9. If a taxpayer enters into a binding contract before March 15, 1984, the taxpayer will be treated as having satisfied the foreign management tests of section 924(c) for periods before December 31, 1984, and the foreign economic process tests of section 924(d) with respect to costs incurred before December 31, 1984, but only with respect to income attributable to such contracts that is recognized before December 31, 1986. The FSC rules will apply to the income from the long-term contract if an election is made and the general FSC requirements under section 922 are satisfied. However, such taxpayer need not satisfy the activities test under section 925(c) for activities which occur before January 1, 1985, in order to use the transfer pricing rules under section 925.

(10) Long-term contract—after March 15, 1984.

Q-10. Under what conditions is a taxpayer who has a long-term contract (i.e., a contract which is not completed in the taxable year in which it is entered into) but does not use the completed contract method of accounting exempted from satisfying the foreign management and economic process requirements of subsections (c) and (d) of section 924 if such taxpayer enters into a binding contract after March 15, 1984 and before January 1, 1985?

A-10. If a taxpayer enters into a contract after March 15, 1984, and before January 1, 1985, the taxpayer will be treated as having satisfied the foreign management tests of section 924(c) for periods before December 31, 1984, and the foreign economic process tests of section 924(d) with respect to costs incurred before December 31, 1984, but only with respect to income attributable to such contract that is recognized before December 31, 1985.

The FSC rules will apply to the income from the long-term contract if an election is made and the general requirements under section 922 are satisfied. However, such taxpayer need not satisfy the activities test under section 925(c) for activities which occur before January 1, 1985 in order to use the transfer pricing rules under section 925.

(11) Incomplete transactions.

Q-11. In computing its foreign trade income, how should a FSC treat transfers of export property from a related supplier to a DISC which is subsequently resold by a FSC after the DISC's termination?

A-11. In applying the gross receipts and combined taxable income methods under section 925(a)(1) and (a)(2), the transaction is treated as if the transfer of export property were made by the related supplier to the FSC except that the foreign management and economic processes tests under section 924 and the activities test under section 925(c) shall be deemed to be satisfied for purposes of the transaction.

(12) Pre-effective date costs and activities.

Q-12. Are costs incurred and activities performed prior to January 1, 1985 taken into account for purposes of satisfying the foreign management and foreign economic processes requirements of subsections (c) and (d) of section 924 and the activities test under section 925(c)?

A-12. For purposes of determining the costs incurred and the activities performed to be taken into account with respect to contracts entered into after December 31, 1984, only those costs incurred and activities performed after December 31, 1984 are taken into consideration. Costs incurred and activities performed by a related supplier prior to January 1, 1985 (or prior to the effective date of a corporation's election to be treated as a FSC if other than January 1, 1985) with respect to transactions occurring after January 1, 1985 (or after the effective date of a corporation's election to be treated as a FSC) need not be taken into account for purposes of computing the FSC's profit under section 925 but are treated for section 925(c) purposes as if they were performed on behalf of the FSC.

(13) FSC and interest charge DISC.

Q-13. Can a FSC and an interest charge DISC be members of the same controlled group?

A-13. A FSC and an interest charge DISC cannot be members of the same controlled group. If any controlled group of corporations of which an interest charge DISC is a member establishes a FSC, then any interest charge DISC which is a member of such group shall be treated as having terminated its status as an interest charge DISC.

(c) Export Trade Corporations. *(1) Previously taxed income.*

Q-1. Under what circumstances are earnings of an export trade corporation that have not been included in income under section 951 treated as previously taxed income previously included in the income of a U.S. shareholder for purposes of section 959 (and not taxed)?

A-1. A corporation which qualifies as an export trade corporation (ETC) with respect to its last taxable year beginning before January 1, 1985, and elects to discontinue operations as an ETC for all taxable years beginning after December 31, 1984, shall not be required to take into income earnings attributable to previously excluded export trade income, as defined in § 1.970-1(b), derived with respect to taxable years beginning before January 1, 1985. However, any amounts distributed by the former ETC (i.e. a corporation which was an ETC for its last taxable year beginning before January 1, 1985) shall be treated as being made out of current earnings and profits and then out of previously taxed income. For purposes of determining the shareholder's basis in the ETC stock, distributions of previously excluded export trade income shall be treated as if made out of previously taxed income which has already been included in gross income under section 951(a)(1)(B). Thus, no basis adjustment under section 961 is necessary. In addition, upon the sale or exchange of the stock of such corporation in a transaction described in section 1248(a), the earnings and profits of the corporation attributable to such previously untaxed income shall not be subject to section 1248(a).

(2) Qualification as an ETC for last year.

Q-2. Must an ETC satisfy all of the tests set forth in section 971(a)(1) for the ETC's last taxable year beginning before January 1, 1985?

A-2. All of the tests in section 971(a)(1) must be satisfied, except that for purposes of the working capital requirements set forth in section 971(c)(1), the working capital of the ETC at the close of its last taxable year beginning before January 1, 1985 shall be deemed reasonable.

(3) Continuation of ETC status.

Q-3. May a corporation which chooses to remain an ETC after December 31, 1984 continue to do so?

A-3. Yes. However, previously untaxed income of such ETC shall not be treated as previously taxed income in accordance with Q&A #1 of this section.

(4) Discontinuation of ETC status.

Q-4. How does an ETC make an election to discontinue its operation as an ETC?

A-4. The United States shareholders (as defined in section 951(b)) must file a statement of election on behalf of the ETC indicating the intent of the ETC to discontinue operations as an ETC for taxable years beginning after December 31, 1984. In addition, the statement of election must include the name, address, taxpayer identification number and stock interest of each United States shareholder. The statement must also indicate that the corporation on behalf of which the shareholders are making the election qualified as an ETC for its last taxable year beginning before January 1, 1985, and also the amount of earnings attributable to previously excluded export trade income. The statement must be jointly signed by each United States shareholder with each shareholder stating under penalties of perjury that he or she holds the stock interest specified for such shareholder in the statement of election. A copy of the statement of election must be attached to Form 5471 (information return with respect to a foreign corporation) filed with respect to the ETC's last taxable year beginning before January 1, 1985.

(5) Transition transfers.

Q-5. Under what circumstances may an electing ETC transfer its assets to a FSC without incurring any tax liability on the transfer?

A-5. An electing ETC will recognize no income, gain, or loss on a transfer of its assets to a FSC but only if all of the following conditions are met:

(1) The assets transferred were held by the ETC on August 4, 1983, and were transferred by the ETC to the FSC in a transfer completed before January 1, 1986; and

(2) The assets are transferred in a transaction which would qualify for nonrecognition under subchapter C of Chapter 1 of the Code, or would so qualify but for section 367 of the Code.

In such case, section 367 shall not apply to the transfer. In addition, other provisions of Subchapter C will apply to the transfer such as section 358 (basis to shareholders), section 362 (basis to corporation) and section 381 (carryovers in corporate acquisitions). In determining whether a transfer by an ETC to a FSC qualifies for nonrecognition under Subchapter C, a liquidation of the assets of the ETC into a parent corporation followed by a transfer by the parent of those assets to the FSC will be treated as a transaction described in section 368(a)(1)(D).

T.D. 7983, 10/5/84, amend T.D. 7992, 12/6/84, T.D. 7993 12/7/84, T.D. 8126, 3/2/87, T.D. 8515, 1/12/94, T.D. 8858, 1/5/2000, T.D. 8940, 2/12/2001.

PAR. 3. Paragraph (b)(6) of § 1.921-1T is removed.

Proposed § 1.921-1T [Amended] [*For Preamble, see ¶ 151,083*]

§ 1.921-2 Foreign Sales Corporation—general rules.

Caution: The Treasury has not yet amended Reg § 1.921-2 to reflect changes made by P.L. 106-519.

(a) Definition of a FSC and the Effect of a FSC Election.

Q-1. What is the definition of a Foreign Sales Corporation (hereinafter referred to as a "FSC" (All references to FSCs include small FSCs unless indicated otherwise)?

A-1. As defined in section 922(a), an FSC must satisfy the following eight requirements.

(i) The FSC must be a corporation organized or created under the laws of a foreign country that meets the requirements of section 927(e)(3) (a "qualifying foreign country") or a U.S. possession other than Puerto Rico (an "eligible possession"). See Q&As 3, 4, and 5 of § 1.922-1.

(ii) A FSC may not have more than 25 shareholders at any time during the taxable year. See Q&A 6 of § 1.922-1.

(iii) A FSC may not have any preferred stock outstanding during the taxable year. See Q&As 7 and 8 of § 1.922-1.

(iv) A FSC must maintain an office outside of the United States in a qualifying foreign country or an eligible possession and maintain a set of permanent books of account (including invoices or summaries of invoices) at such office. See Q&As 9, 10, 11, 12, 13, 14, and 15 of § 1.922-1.

(v) A FSC must maintain within the United States the records required under section 6001. See Q&A 16 of § 1.922-1.

(vi) The FSC must have a board of directors which includes at least one individual who is not a resident of the United States at all times during the taxable year. See Q&As 17, 18, 19, 20, and 21 of § 1.922-1.

(vii) A FSC may not be a member, at any time during the taxable year, of any controlled group of corporations of which an interest charge DISC is a member. See Q&A 2 of this section and Q&A 13, of § 1.921-1T(b)(13).

(viii) A FSC must have made an election under section 927(f)(1) which is in effect for the taxable year. See Q& A 1 of § 1.921-1T(b)(1) and § 1.927(f)-1.

In addition, under section 441(h), the taxable year of a FSC must conform to the taxable year of its principal shareholder. See Q&A 4 of § 1.921-1T(b)(4).

Q-2. Does the reference to a DISC under section 922(a)(1)(F) which provides that a FSC cannot be a member, at any time during the taxable year, of any controlled group of corporations of which a DISC is a member refer solely to an interest charge DISC?

A-2. Yes.

(b) Small FSC.

Q-3. What is a small FSC?

A-3. A small FSC is a Foreign Sales Corporation which meets the requirements of section 922(a)(1) enumerated in Q&A 1 of this section as well as the requirements of section

922(b). Section 922(b) requires that a small FSC make a separate election to be treated as a small FSC. See Q&A 1 of § 1.921-1T(b) and § 1.927(f)-1. In addition, section 922(b) requires that the small FSC not be a member, at any time during the taxable year, of a controlled group of corporations which includes a FSC unless such FSC is a small FSC.

Q-4. What is the effect of an election as a small FSC?

A-4. Under section 924(b)(2), a small FSC need not meet the foreign management and economic processes tests of section 924(b)(1) in order to have foreign trading gross receipts. However, in determining the exempt foreign trade income of a small FSC, any foreign trading gross receipts for the taxable year in excess of $5 million are not taken into account. If the foreign trading gross receipts of a small FSC for the taxable year exceed the $5 million limitation, the FSC may select the gross receipts to which the limitation is allocated. In order to use the administrative pricing rules under section 925(a), a small FSC must satisfy the activities test under section 925(c). In addition, under section 441(h), the taxable year of a small FSC must conform to the taxable year of its principal shareholder (defined in Q&A 4 of § 1.921-1T(b)(4) as the shareholder with the highest percentage of its voting power).

Q-5. What is the effect on a small FSC (or FSC) ("target") if it is acquired, directly or indirectly, by a corporation if that acquiring corporation (" acquiring"), or a member of the acquiring corporation's controlled group, is a FSC (or small FSC)?

A-5. Unless the corporations in the controlled group elect to terminate the FSC (or small (FSC) election of the acquiring corporation, the target's small FSC's (or FSC's) taxable year and election will terminate as of the day preceding the date the target small FSC and acquiring FSC became members of the same controlled group. The target small FSC will receive FSC benefits for the period prior to termination, but the $5 million small FSC limitation will be reduced to the amount which bears the same ratio to the $5 million as the number of days in the short year created by the termination bears to 365. The due date of the income tax return for the short taxable year created by this provision will be the date prescribed by section 6072(b), including extensions, starting with the last day of the short taxable year. If the short taxable year created by this provision ends prior to March 3, 1987, the filing date of the tax return for the short taxable year will be automatically extended until the earlier of May 18, 1987 or the date under section 6072(b) assuming a short taxable year had not been created by these regulations.

(c) Comparison of FSC to DISC.

Q-6. How does a FSC differ from a DISC?

A-6. A DISC is a domestic corporation which is not itself taxable while a FSC must be created or organized under the laws of a jurisdiction which is outside of the United States (including certain U.S. possessions) and may be taxable on its income except for its exempt foreign trade income. The DISC provisions enable a shareholder to obtain a partial deferral of tax on income from export sales and certain services, if 95 percent of its receipts and assets are export related. The FSC provisions contain no assets test, but a portion of income for export sales and certain services is exempt from U.S. taxes if the FSC satisfies certain foreign presence, foreign management, and foreign economic processes tests.

(d) Organization of a FSC.

Q-7. Under the laws of what countries may a FSC be organized?

A-7. A FSC may not be created or organized under the laws of the United States, a state, or other political subdivision. However, a FSC may be created or organized under the laws of a possession of the United States, including Guam. American Samoa, the Commonwealth of the Northern Mariana Islands and the Virgin Islands of the United States, but not Puerto Rico. These eligible possessions are located outside the U.S. customs territory. In addition, a FSC may incorporate under the laws of a foreign country that is a party to—

(i) an exchange of information agreement that meets the standards of the Caribbean Basin Economic Recovery Act of 1983 (Code section 274(h)(6)(C)), or

(ii) a bilateral income tax treaty with the United States if the Secretary certifies that the exchange of information program under the treaty carries out the purpose of the exchange of information requirements of the FSC legislation as set forth in section 927(e)(3), if the company is covered under the exchange of information program under subdivision (i) or (ii). The Secretary may terminate the certification. Any termination by the Secretary will be effective six months after the date of the publication of the notice of such termination in the **Federal Register**.

(e) Foreign trade income.

Q-8. How is foreign trade income defined?

A-8. Foreign trade income, defined in section 923(b), is gross income of an FSC attributable to foreign trading gross receipts. It includes both the profits earned by the FSC itself from exports and commissions earned by the FSC from products and services exported by others.

(f) Investment Income and Carrying Charges.

Q-9. What do the terms "investment income" and "carrying charges" mean?

A-9.

(i) Investment income means:

(A) Dividends,

(B) Interest,

(C) Royalties,

(D) Annuities,

(E) Rents (other than rents from the lease or rental of export property for use by the lessee outside of the United States);

(F) Gains from the sale of stock or securities,

(G) Gains from future transactions in any commodity on, or subject to the rules of, a board of trade or commodity exchange (other than gains which arise out of a bona fide hedging transaction reasonably necessary to conduct the business of the FSC in the manner in which such business is customarily conducted by others),

(H) Amounts includable in computing the taxable income of the corporation under part I of subchapter J, and

(I) Gains from the sale or other disposition of any interest in an estate or trust.

(ii) Carrying charges means:

(A) Charges that are imposed by a FSC or a related supplier and that are identified as carrying charges, (" stated carrying charges") and

(B)(1) Charges that are considered to be included in the price of the property or services sold by an FSC or a related supplier, as provided under Q&As 1 and 2 of § 1.927(d)-1, and (2) any other unstated interest.

Q-10. How are investment income and carrying charges treated?

A-10. Investment income and carrying charges are not foreign trading gross receipts. Investment income and carrying charges are includable in the taxable income of an FSC, except in the case of a commission FSC where carrying charges are treated as income of the related supplier, and are treated as income effectively connected with a trade or business conducted through a permanent establishment within the United States. The source of investment income and carrying charges is determined under sections 861, 862, and 863 of the Code.

(g) Small Businesses.

Q-11. What options are available to small businesses engaged in exporting?

A-11. A small business may elect to be treated as either a small FSC or an interest charge DISC. See Q&As 3 & 4 of § 1.921-2 relating to a small FSC. Rules with respect to interest charge DISCs are the subject of another regulations project.

T.D. 8127, 3/2/87.

§ 1.921-3T Foreign sales corporation general rules (temporary).

Caution: The Treasury has not yet amended Reg § 1.921-3T to reflect changes made by P.L. 106-519.

(a) Exclusion. *(1) Classifications of income.* The extent to which income of a FSC (any further reference to a FSC in this section shall include a small FSC unless indicated otherwise) is subject to the corporate income tax of section 11, or, in the alternative, section 1201(a), is dependent upon the allocation of the FSC's income to the following five categories:

(i) Exempt foreign trade income determined under section 923 and § 1.923-1T;

(ii) Non-exempt foreign trade income determined with regard to the administrative pricing rules of section 925(a)(1) or (2);

(iii) Non-exempt foreign trade income determined without regard to the administrative pricing rules of section 925(a)(1) or (2) (section 923(a)(2) non-exempt income as defined in section 927(d)(6));

(iv) Investment income and carrying charges; and

(v) Other non-foreign trade income.

(2) Source and characterization of FSC income. (i) Exempt foreign trade income. The exempt foreign trade income of a FSC determined under section 923 and § 1.923-1T is treated as foreign source income which is not effectively connected with a United States trade or business. See § 1.923-1T(a) for the definition of foreign trade income and § 1.923-1T(b) for the definition of exempt foreign trade income.

(ii) Non-exempt foreign trade income determined with regard to the administrative pricing rules. The FSC's non-exempt foreign trade income with respect to a transaction or group of transactions will be treated as United States source income which is effectively connected with the FSC's trade or business which is conducted through its permanent establishment within the United States if either of the administrative pricing rules of section 925(a)(1) or (2) is used to determine the FSC's foreign trade income from a transaction or group of transactions. See § 1.923-1T(b) for the definition of non-exempt foreign trade income.

(iii) Non-exempt foreign trade income determined without regard to the administrative pricing rules. The source and taxation of the FSC's non-exempt foreign trade income not classified in paragraph (a)(2)(ii) of this section will be determined under the appropriate sections of the Internal Revenue Code and the regulations under those sections. This type of income (section 923(a)(2) non-exempt income) includes both income that is not effectively connected with the conduct of a trade or business in the United States and income that is effectively connected.

(iv) Investment income and carrying charges. All of the FSC's investment income and carrying charges will be treated as income which is effectively connected with the FSC's trade or business which is conducted through its permanent establishment within the United States. The source of that income will be determined under the appropriate sections of the Internal Revenue Code and the regulations under those sections. See § 1.921-2(f) (Q & A9) for definition of investment income and carrying charges.

(v) Non-foreign trade income (other than investment income and carrying charges). The source and taxation of the FSC's non-foreign trade income (other than investment income and carrying charges) will be determined under the appropriate sections of the Internal Revenue Code and the regulations under those sections.

(b) Allocation and apportionment of deductions. Expenses, losses and deductions incurred by the FSC shall be allocated and apportioned under the rules set forth in § 1.861-8 to the FSC's foreign trade income and to the FSC's non-foreign trade income. Any deductions incurred by the FSC on a transaction, or group of transactions, which are allocated and apportioned to the FSC's foreign trade income from that transaction, or group of transactions, shall be allocated on a proportionate basis between exempt foreign trade income and non-exempt foreign trade income.

(c) Net operating losses and capital losses. *(1) General rule.* (i) If an FSC for any taxable year incurs a deficit in earnings and profits attributable to foreign trade income determined without regard to the administrative pricing rules of section 925(a)(1) or (2), that deficit shall be applied to reduce current earnings and profits, if any, attributable to—

(A) First, exempt foreign trade income determined with regard to the administrative pricing rules,

(B) Second, non-exempt foreign trade income determined with regard to the administrative pricing rules,

(C) Third, investment income and carrying charges, and

(D) Fourth, other non-foreign trade income.

(ii) If an FSC for any taxable year incurs a deficit in earnings and profits attributable to non-foreign trade income (other than investment income, carrying charges and net capital losses), that deficit shall be applied to reduce current earnings and profits, if any, attributable to—

(A) First, investment income and carrying charges,

(B) Second, exempt foreign trade income determined with regard to the administrative pricing rules,

(C) Third, exempt foreign trade income determined without regard to the administrative pricing rules,

(D) Fourth, non-exempt foreign trade income determined with regard to the administrative pricing rules, and

(E) Fifth, section 923(a)(2) non-exempt income.

(iii) If an FSC for any taxable year incurs a deficit in earnings and profits attributable to investment income and carrying charges, that deficit shall be applied to reduce current earnings and profits, if any, attributable to—

(A) First, non-foreign trade income other than capital gains,

(B) Second, exempt foreign trade income determined with regard to the administrative pricing rules,

(C) Third, exempt foreign trade income determined without regard to the administrative pricing rules,

(D) Fourth, non-exempt foreign trade income determined with regard to the administrative pricing rules, and

(E) Fifth, section 923(a)(2) non-exempt income.

(iv) Net capital losses will be available for carryback or carryover pursuant to paragraph (c)(2) of this section.

(v) Because the no-loss rules provide that a related supplier may always compensate the FSC for its expenses either as part of the commission payment or as part of the transfer price if the administrative pricing rules are used (see § 1.925(a)-1T(e)(1)(i)), an FSC will not have a deficit in its earnings and profits relating to foreign trade income determined with regard to the administrative pricing rules. To determine the amount of any division of earnings and profits for the purpose of determining under § 1.926(a)-1T(a) and (b) the treatment and order of distributions, the portion of a deficit in earnings and profits chargeable under this paragraph to such division prior to such distribution shall be determined in a manner consistent with the rules in § 1.316-2(b) for determining the amount of earnings and profits available on the date of any distribution.

(2) Carryback or carryover of net operating losses and capital losses to other taxable years of an FSC (or former FSC). (i) The amount of the deduction for the taxable year under section 172 for a net operating loss carryback or carryover, or under section 1212 for a capital loss carryback or carryover, shall be determined in the same manner as if the FSC were a foreign corporation which had not elected to be treated as an FSC. Thus, the amount of the deduction will be the same whether or not the corporation was an FSC in the year of the loss or in the year to which the loss is carried.

(ii) Any carryback or carryover of an FSC's (or former FSC's) net operating loss which is attributable to transactions which give rise to foreign trade income shall be charged—

(A) First, to earnings and profits attributable to exempt foreign trade income which is determined without regard to the administrative pricing rules,

(B) Second, to earnings and profits attributable to section 923(a)(2) non-exempt income,

(C) Third, to earnings and profits attributable to exempt foreign trade income determined with regard to the administrative pricing rules,

(D) Fourth, to earnings and profits attributable to non-exempt foreign trade income determined with regard to the administrative pricing rules,

(E) Fifth, to earnings and profits attributable to investment income and carrying charges (other than capital gain income), and

(F) Sixth, to earnings and profits attributable to non-foreign trade income (other than investment income, carrying charges and capital gain income).

(iii) Any carryback or carryover of an FSC's (or former FSC's) net operating loss which is attributable to non-foreign trade income (other than capital gain income) shall be charged—

(A) First, to earnings and profits attributable to non-foreign trade income (other than investment income, carrying charges and capital gain income),

(B) Second, to earnings and profits attributable to investment income and carrying charges,

(C) Third, to earnings and profits attributable to exempt foreign trade income determined with regard to the administrative pricing rules,

(D) Fourth, to earnings and profits attributable to non-exempt foreign trade income determined with regard to the administrative pricing rules,

(E) Fifth, to earnings and profits attributable to exempt foreign trade income which is determined without regard to the administrative pricing rules, and

(F) Sixth, to earnings and profits attributable to section 923(a)(2) non-exempt income.

(iv) Any carryback or carryover of a net operating loss to a year in which the corporation was (or is) an FSC from a taxable year in which the corporation was not an FSC shall be applied in a manner consistent with subdivision (iii) of this paragraph.

(d) Credits against tax. *(1) General rule.* Notwithstanding any other provision of chapter 1, subtitle A, an FSC is allowed under section 921(c) as credits against tax only the following credits:

(i) The foreign tax credit, section 27(a);

(ii) The credit for tax withheld at source on foreign corporations, section 33; and

(iii) The certain uses of gasoline and special fuels credit, section 34.

(2) Foreign tax credit. (i) The direct foreign tax credit of section 901(b)(4) as determined under section 906 for income, war profits, and excess profits taxes (or taxes in lieu thereof) paid or accrued to any foreign country or possession of the United States is allowed an FSC only to the extent that those taxes are attributable to the FSC's foreign source non-foreign trade income which is effectively connected with its conduct of a trade or business within the United States. See section 906(b)(5).

(ii) The foreign tax credit for domestic corporate shareholders in foreign corporations (the deemed paid credit) provided under section 901(a) as determined under section 902 is allowed for income, war profits, and excess profits taxes deemed paid or accrued by an FSC (or former FSC) only to the extent those taxes are deemed paid or accrued with respect to the FSC's (or former FSC's) section 923(a)(2) non-exempt income and its non-foreign trade income.

(iii) The foreign tax credit allowed by sections 901 and 903 for tax withheld at source is allowed only to the extent the dividends paid to the FSC's (or former FSC's) shareholder are attributable to the FSC's (or former FSC's) section 923(a)(2) non-exempt income and its non-foreign trade income.

(3) Foreign tax credit limitation. (i) For purposes of computation of the direct foreign tax credit of section 901(b)(4) as determined under section 906, the separate limitation of section 904(d)(1)(C) for the FSC's taxable income attributable to its foreign trade income will apply. The direct foreign tax credit is not allowed to an FSC with regard to taxes it paid which are attributable to its foreign trade income. Since the foreign tax credit is not allowed for that type of income,

the effect of the separate limitation is to remove the FSC's foreign trade income from the numerator of the fraction used to compute the FSC's overall foreign tax credit limitation.

(ii) A separate limitation under section 904(d)(1)(D) is provided for distributions from an FSC (or former FSC) that arise through operation of the deemed paid credit of section 902 and are attributable to foreign trade income earned during the period when the distributing corporation was an FSC. This limitation is computed by multiplying the FSC's shareholder's tentative United States tax by a fraction the numerator of which is the foreign source dividend (determined with regard to section 78) attributable to the foreign trade income less dividends received deductions and other expenses allocated and apportioned under § 1.861-8 allowed to the shareholder and the denominator of which is the shareholder's worldwide income. The effect of this separate limitation is to remove dividends attributable to the FSC's foreign trade income from the numerator of the fraction used to compute the overall foreign tax credit limitation of the FSC's shareholder.

(iii) The separate limitation under section 904(d)(1)(D) also applies to the foreign tax credit allowed to an FSC shareholder by sections 901 and 903 for tax withheld at source on dividends paid by the FSC. The numerator of this fraction is the part of the dividend attributable to the FSC's foreign trade income and the denominator is the shareholder's worldwide income. The effect of this separate limitation is to remove dividends attributable to foreign trade income of an FSC (or former FSC) from the numerator of the fraction used to compute the overall foreign tax credit limitation of the FSC's shareholder.

(e) Deduction for foreign income, war profits and excess profits taxes. Under section 275(a)(4)(B), income, war profits and excess profits taxes imposed by a foreign country or possession of the United States may not be deducted by an FSC to the extent those taxes are paid or accrued with respect to its foreign trade income.

(f) Payment of estimated tax. Every FSC which is subject to tax under section 11 or 1201(a) and section 882 must make payment of its estimated tax in accordance with section 6154 and the regulations under that section. In determining the amount of the estimated tax, the FSC must treat the tax imposed by section 881 as though it were a tax imposed by section 11. See section 6154(g).

(g) Accumulated earnings, personal holding company and foreign personal holding company. The provisions covering the accumulated earnings tax (sections 531 through 537), personal holding companies (sections 541 through 547) and foreign personal holding companies (sections 551 through 558) apply to FSCs to the extent they would apply to foreign corporations that are not FSCs.

(h) Subpart F income and increase of earnings invested in U.S. property. For the mandatory inclusion in the gross income of the U.S. shareholders of the Subpart F income and of the increase in earnings invested in U.S. property of an FSC, see sections 951 through 964 and the regulations under those sections. However, the foreign trade income (other than section 923(a)(2) non-exempt income) and, generally, the investment income and carrying charges of an FSC and any deductions which are allocated and apportioned to those classes of income, are not taken into account under sections 951 through 964. See sections 951(e) and 952(b).

(i) Certain accumulations of earnings and profits. For the inclusion in the gross income of U.S. persons as a dividend on the gain recognized on certain sales or exchanges of stock in an FSC, to the extent of certain earnings and profits attributable to the stock which were accumulated while the FSC was a controlled foreign corporation, see section 1248 and the regulations under that section. However, section 1248 and the regulations under that section do not apply to an FSC's earnings and profits attributable to foreign trade income, see section 1248(d)(6).

(j) Limitations on certain multiple tax benefits. The provisions of section 1561, Limitations on Certain Multiple Tax Benefits in the Case of Certain Controlled Corporations, and section 1563, Definitions and Special Rules, and the regulations under those sections apply to an FSC and its controlled group.

T.D. 8126, 3/2/87.

§ 1.922-1 Requirements that a corporation must satisfy to be a FSC or a small FSC.

Caution: The Treasury has not yet amended Reg § 1.922-1 to reflect changes made by P.L. 106-519.

(a) FSC requirements.

Q-1. What are the requirements that a corporation must satisfy to be an FSC?

A-1. A corporation must satisfy all of the requirements of section 922(a).

(b) Small FSC requirements.

Q-2. What are the requirements that a corporation must satisfy to be a small FSC?

A-2. A corporation must satisfy all of the requirements of sections 922(a)(1) and (b).

(c) Definition of corporation.

Q-3. What type of entity is considered a corporation for purposes of qualifying as an FSC or a small FSC under section 922?

A-3. A foreign entity that is classified as a corporation under section 7701(a)(3) (other than an insurance company) is considered a corporation for purposes of this requirement.

(d) Eligible possession.

Q-4. For purposes of meeting the place of incorporation requirement of section 922(a)(1)(A), what is a possession of the United States?

A-4. For purposes of section 922(a)(1)(A), the possessions of the United States are Guam, American Samoa, the Commonwealth of the Northern Mariana Islands, and the Virgin Islands of the United States ("eligible possessions"). Puerto Rico, although a possession for certain tax purposes, does not qualify as a jurisdiction in which a FSC or small FSC may be incorporated.

(e) Qualifying countries.

Q-5. For purposes of meeting the place of incorporation requirement of section 922(a)(1)(A), what is a foreign country and which foreign countries meet the requirements of section 927(e)(3)?

A-5. (i) A foreign country is a jurisdiction outside the 50 states, the District of Columbia, the Commonwealth of Puerto Rico, and the possessions of the United States.

(ii) A list of the foreign countries that meet the requirements of section 927(e)(3) ("qualifying countries") will be published from time to time in the **Federal Register** and the Internal Revenue Bulletin. A corporation is considered to be created or organized under the laws of a foreign country that meets the requirements of section 927(e)(3) only if the foreign country is a party to (A) an exchange of information agreement under the Caribbean Basin Economic Recovery Act (Code section 274(h)((6)(C)), or (B) a bilateral income tax treaty with the United States if the Secretary certifies that the exchange of information program under the treaty carries out the purposes of the exchange of information requirements of the FSC legislation as set forth in Code section 927(e)(3) and if the corporation is covered under exchange of information program under subdivision (A) or (B).

(f) Number of shareholders.

Q-6. Who is counted as a shareholder of a corporation for purposes of determining whether a corporation meets the limitation on the number of shareholders to no more than 25 under section 922(a)(1)(B)?

A-6. Solely for purposes of the limitation on the number of shareholders, the following rules apply:

(i) In general, an individual who owns an interest in stock of the corporation is counted as a shareholder. In the case of joint owners, each joint owner is counted as a shareholder. A member of a corporation's board of directors who holds qualifying shares that are required to be owned by a resident of the country of incorporation is not counted as a shareholder.

(ii) A corporation that owns an interest in stock of the corporation is counted as a single shareholder.

(iii) An estate that owns an interest in stock of the corporation is counted as a single shareholder. If the limitation on number of shareholders is not satisfied by reason of the closing of an estate, the FSC will continue to qualify for the taxable year of the FSC in which the estate is closed.

(iv) A trust is not counted as a shareholder. In the case of a trust all of which is treated as owned by one or more persons under sections 671 through 679, those persons are counted as shareholders. In the case of all other trusts, a beneficiary is counted as a shareholder.

(v) A partnership is not counted as a shareholder. A general or limited partner is counted as a shareholder if it is a corporation, an individual, or an estate, under the rules contained in subdivisions (i) through (iii). A general or limited partner is not counted as a shareholder if it is a partnership or a trust; the rules contained in subdivision (iv) and this subdivision (v) apply to the determination of who is counted as a shareholder.

(g) Class of stock.

Q-7. What is preferred stock for purposes of determining whether a corporation satisfies the requirement under section 922(a)(1)(C) that no preferred stock be outstanding?

A-7. Preferred stock is stock that is limited and preferred as to dividends or distributions in liquidation.

Q-8. Can a corporation have outstanding more than one class of common stock?

A-8. Yes. However, the rights of a class of stock will be disregarded if the right has the effect of avoidance of Federal income tax. For instance, dividend rights may not be used to direct dividends from exempt foreign trade income to shareholders that have taxable income and to direct other dividends to shareholders that have met operating loss carryovers.

(h) Office.

Q-9. What is an office for purposes of determining whether a corporation satisfies the requirement of section 922(a)(1)(D)(i)?

A-9. An office is a place for the transaction of the business of the corporation. To be an office a place must meet all of the following requirements;

(i) It must have a fixed location. A transient location is not a fixed location.

(ii) It must be a building or a portion of a building consisting of at least one room. A room is a partitioned part of the inside of a building. The building or portion thereof used as the corporation's office must be large enough to accommodate the equipment required in subdivision (iii) of this answer 9 and the activity required in subdivision (iv) of this answer 9. However, an office is not limited to a room with communication equipment or an adjacent room. Noncontiguous space within the same building will also constitute an office if it is equipped for the retention of the documentation required to be stored by the FSC and if access to the necessary communication equipment is available for use by the FSC.

(iii) It must be equipped for the performance of the corporation's business. An office must be equipped for the communication and retention of information and must be supplied with communication services.

(iv) It must be regularly used for some business activity of the corporation. A corporation's business activities must include the maintenance of the documentation described in Q&A 12 of this section. These documents need not be prepared at the office. Any person, whether or not related to the corporation, may perform the business activities of the corporation at the office if the activity is performed pursuant to a contract, oral or written, for the performance of the activity on behalf of the corporation.

(v) It must be operated, and owned or leased, by the corporation or by a person, whether or not related to the corporation, under contract to the corporation.

(vi) It must be maintained by the corporation or by a person, whether or not related, to the corporation, under contract to the corporation at all times during the taxable year. In the case of a corporation newly organized as a FSC, thirty days may elapse between the time the corporation is organized as a FSC *(i.e.,* the first day for which the FSC election is effective) and the time an office is maintained by the corporation or a person under contract with the corporation. A place that meets the requirements in subdivision (i) through (vi) of this answer 9 can also be used for activities that are unrelated to the business activity of the corporation.

Q-10. Can a corporation locate an office in any foreign country if it has at least one office in a U.S. possession or in a foreign country that meets the requirements of section 927(e)(3) as provided Q&A 5 of this section?

A-10. Yes.

Q-11. Must a corporation locate the office that is required under section 922(a)(1)(D)(i) in the country or possession of its incorporation?

A-11. No.

(i) Documentation.

Q-12. What documentation must be maintained at the corporation's office for purposes of section 922(a)(1)(D)(ii)?

A-12. At least the following documentation must be maintained at the corporation's office under section 922(a)(1)(D)(ii):

(i) The quarterly income statements, a final year-end income statement and a year-end balance sheet of the FSC; and

(ii) All final invoices (or a summary of them) or statements of account with respect to (A) sales by the FSC, and (B) sales by a related person if the FSC realizes income with respect to such sales. A final invoice is an invoice upon which payment is made by the customer. A invoice must contain, at a minimum, the customer's name or identifying number and, with respect to the transaction or transactions, the date, product or product code or service of service code, quantity, price, and amount due. In the alternative, a document will be acceptable as a final invoice even though it does not include all of the above listed information if the FSC establishes that the document is considered to be a final invoice under normal commercial practices. An invoice forwarded to the customer after payment has been tendered or received pursuant to a letter of credit, as a receipt for payment, satisfies this definition. A single final invoice may cover more than one transaction with a customer.

(iii) A summary of final invoices may be in any reasonable form provided that the summary contains all substantive information from the invoices. All substantive information includes the customer's name or identifying number, the invoice number, date, product or product code, and amount owed. In the alternative, all substantive information includes a summary of the information that is included on documents considered to be final invoices under normal commercial practice. A statement of account is any summary statement forwarded to a customer to inform of, or confirm, the status of transactions occurring within an accounting period during a taxable year that is not less than one month. A statement of account must contain, at a minimum, the customer's name or identifying number, date of the statement of account and the balance due (even if the balance due is zero) as of the last day of the accounting period covered by the statement of account. In the alternative, a document will be accepted as a statement of account even though it does not include all of the above listed information if the FSC establishes that the document is considered a statement of account under normal commercial practice. For these purposes, a document will be considered to be a statement of account under normal commercial practice if it is sent to domestic as well as to export customers in order to inform the customers of the status of transactions during an accounting period. With regard to quarterly income statements, a reasonable estimate of the FSC's income and expense items will be acceptable. If the FSC is a commission FSC, 1.83% of the related supplier's gross receipts will be considered a reasonable estimate of the FSC's income. The documents required by this Q&A 12 need not be prepared by the FSC. In addition they need not be prepared at the FSC's office.

(iv) The FSC will satisfy the requirement that the documents be maintained at its office even if not all final invoices (or summaries) or statements of account or items to be included on statements of account are maintained at its office as long as it makes a good faith effort to do so and provided that any failure to maintain the required documents is cured within a reasonable time of discovery of the failure.

Q-13. If the required documents are not prepared at the FSC's office, by what date must the documents be maintained at its office?

A-13. With regard to the applicable quarters of years prior to March 3, 1987, the quarterly income statements, final invoices (or summaries), or statements of account and the year-end balance sheet must be maintained at the FSC's office no later than the due date, including extensions, of the FSC tax return for the applicable taxable year in which the period ends. With regard to the applicable quarters or years ending after March 3, 1987, the quarterly income statements for the first three quarters of the FSC year must be maintained at the FSC's office no later than 90 days after the end of the quarter. The quarterly income statement for the fourth quarter of the FSC year, the final year-end income statement, the year-end balance sheet, and the final invoices (or summaries) or statements of account must be maintained at the FSC's office no later than the due date, including extensions, of the FSC tax return for the applicable taxable year.

Q-14. In what form must the documentation required under section 922(a)(1)(D)(ii) be maintained?

A-14. The documentation required to be maintained by the office may be originals or duplicates and may be in any form that qualifies as a record under Rev. Rul. 71-20, 1971-1 C.B. 392. Therefore, documentation may be maintained in the form of punch cards, magnetic tapes, disks, and other machine-sensible media used for recording, consolidating, and summarizing accounting transactions and records within a taxpayer's automatic data processing system. The corporation need not maintain at its office equipment capable of reading the machine-sensible media. That equipment, however, must be situated in a location that is readily accessible to the corporation. The equipment need not be owned by the corporation.

Q-15. How long must the documentation required under section 922(a)(1)(D)(ii) be maintained?

A-15. The documentation required under section 922(a)(1)(D)(ii) for a taxable year must be maintained at the FSC's office described in section 922(a)(1)(D)(i) until the period of limitations for assessment of tax for the taxable year has expired under section 6501.

Q-16. Under what circumstances will a corporation be considered to satisfy the requirement of section 922(a)(1)(D)(iii) that it maintain the records it is required to keep under section 6001 at a location within the United States?

A-16. A corporation will be considered to satisfy this requirement if the records required under section 6001 are kept by any person at any location in the United States provided that the records are retained in accordance with section 6001 and the regulations thereunder.

(j) Board of directors.

Q-17. What is a corporation's "board of directors" for purposes of the requirement under section 922(a)(1)(E) that, at all times during the taxable year, the corporation must have a board of directors which includes at least one individual who is not a resident of the United States?

A-17. The "board of directors" is the body that manages and directs the corporation according to the law of the qualifying country or eligible possession under the laws of which the corporation was created or organized.

Q-18. Can the member of the board of directors who is a nonresident of the United States be a citizen of the United States?

A-18. Yes. For purposes of meeting the requirement under section 922(a)(1)(E), the member of the board who cannot be a United States resident can be a United States citizen. The principles of section 7701(b) shall be used to determine whether a United States citizen is a United States resident.

Q-19. If the only member of the board of directors who is not a resident of the United States dies, or resigns, is removed from the board or becomes a resident of the United States will the corporation be considered to fail the requirement under section 922(a)(1)(E)?

A-19. If the corporation appoints a new member who is a nonresident of the United States to the board within 30 days after the death, resignation or removal of the former nonresident member, the corporation will be considered to satisfy the requirement under section 922(a)(1)(E). Also, the corporation will be considered to satisfy the requirement under section 922(a)(1)(E) if the corporation appoints a new member who is a nonresident of the United States to the board within 30 days after the corporation has knowledge, or reason to know, that the board's former nonresident member was in fact a resident of the United States.

Q-20. Is a nonresident alien individual who elects to be treated as a resident of the United States for a taxable year under section 6013(g) considered a nonresident of the United States for purposes of the requirement under section 922(a)(1)(E)?

A-20. Yes.

Q-21. Will the requirement that a FSC's board of directors have a nonresident member at all times during the taxable year be satisfied if the nonresident member is elected or appointed to the board of directors no later than 30 days after the first day for which the FSC election is effective?

A-21. Yes.

T.D. 8127, 3/2/87.

§ 1.923-1T Exempt foreign trade income (temporary).

Caution: The Treasury has not yet amended Reg § 1.923-1T to reflect changes made by P.L. 106-519, P.L. 99-514.

(a) Foreign trade income. Foreign trade income of a FSC is the FSC's gross income attributable to its foreign trading gross receipts. (Any further reference to a FSC in this section shall include a small FSC unless indicated otherwise.) If the FSC is the principal on the sale of export property which it purchased from a related supplier, the FSC's gross income is determined by subtracting from its foreign trading gross receipts the transfer price determined under the transfer pricing methods of section 925(a). If the FSC is the commission agent on the sale of export property by its related supplier, the FSC's gross income is the commission paid or payable by the related supplier to the FSC with respect to the transactions that would have generated foreign trading gross receipts had the FSC been the principal on the transaction. See § 1.925(a)-1T(f) Examples (1) and (6) for illustrations of the computation of a FSC's foreign trade income, exempt foreign trade income and taxable income.

(b) Exempt foreign trade income. *(1) Determination.* (i) If a FSC uses either of the two administrative pricing rules, provided for by sections 925(a)(1) and (2), to determine its income from a transaction, or group of transactions, to which section 925 applies (see § 1.925(a)-1T(b)(2)(ii) and (iii)), $^{15}/_{23}$ of the foreign trade income that it earns from the transaction, or group of transactions, will be exempt foreign trade income. If a FSC has a noncorporate shareholder (shareholders), $^{16}/_{23}$ of its foreign trade income attributable to the noncorporate shareholder's (shareholders') proportionate interest in the FSC will be exempt foreign trade income. See section 291(a)(4).

(ii) If a FSC does not use the administrative pricing rules to determine its income from a transaction, or group of transactions, which gives rise to foreign trade income, 30 percent of its foreign trade income will be exempt foreign trade income. If a FSC has a noncorporate shareholder (shareholders), 32 percent of its foreign trade income attributable to the non-corporate shareholder's (shareholders') proportionate interest in the FSC will be exempt foreign trade income. See section 291(a)(4).

(iii) Exempt foreign trade income so determined under subdivisions (1)(i) and (ii) of this paragraph is treated as foreign source income which is not effectively connected with the conduct of a trade or business within the United States. See section 921(a).

(2) Special rule for foreign trade income allocable to a qualified cooperative. (i) Pursuant to section 923(a)(4), if a qualified cooperative is a shareholder of a FSC, the FSC's nonexempt foreign trade income determined by use of either of the administrative pricing methods of section 925(a)(1) or (2) which is allocable to the marketing of agricultural or horticultural products, or the providing of related services, for any taxable year will be treated as exempt foreign trade income to the extent that it is distributed to the qualified cooperative shareholder. A qualified cooperative is defined as any organization to which chapter 1, subchapter T, part 1 of the Code applies. See section 1381(a).

(ii) This special rule of section 923(a)(4) shall apply only if the distribution is made before the due date under section 6072(b), including extensions, for filing the FSC's income tax return for that year. Any distribution which satisfies this requirement will be treated as made on the last day of the FSC's taxable year. In addition, this special rule shall apply only if the income of the cooperative is based on arm's length transactions between the cooperative and its members or patrons.

(iii) Income attributable to the marketing of agricultural or horticultural products, or the providing of related services, shall be allocated to the FSC shareholders on a per share basis. See § 1.926(a)-1T(b) for ordering rules for distributions from a FSC.

(3) Special rule for military property. (i) Under section 923(a)(5), the exempt foreign trade income of an FSC relating to the disposition of, or services relating to, military property shall be equal to 50 percent of the amount which, but for section 923(a)(5), would be treated as exempt foreign trade income under section 923(a)(2) or (3). The foreign trade income no longer treated as exempt because of this special rule of section 923(a)(5) will remain income of the FSC and will be treated as nonexempt foreign trade income.

(ii) The term "military property" is defined in section 995(b)(3)(B) and includes any property which is an arm, ammunition, or implement of war designated in the munitions list published pursuant to section 38 of the International Security Assistance and Arms Export Control Act of 1976 (22 U.S.C. 2778) (which repealed and replaced the Military Security Act of 1954).

T.D. 8126, 3/2/87.

§ 1.924(a)-1T Temporary regulations; definition of foreign trading gross receipts.

Caution: The Treasury has not yet amended Reg § 1.924(a)-1T to reflect changes made by P.L. 106-519, P.L. 99-514.

(a) In general. The term "foreign trading gross receipts" means any of the five amounts described in paragraphs (b) through (f) of this section, except to the extent that any of the five amounts is an excluded receipt within the meaning of paragraph (g) of this section. These amounts will not be foreign trading gross receipts if the FSC is not managed outside the United States, pursuant to section 924(c), or if the economic processes with regard to a transaction, or group of transactions, that are required of an FSC by section 924(d) do not take place outside the United States. The requirement that these activities take place outside the United States does not apply to a small FSC. The activities required by sections 924(c) and (d) may be performed either by the FSC or by any person (whether or not related to the FSC) acting under contract with the FSC for the performance of the required activities. Sections 1.924(c)-1 and 1.924(d)-1 provide rules to determine whether these requirements have been met. For purposes of this section—

(1) FSC. All references to a FSC in this section mean a FSC, except when the context indicates that such term means a corporation in the process of meeting the conditions necessary for that corporation to become an FSC. All references to a FSC in this section shall include a small FSC unless indicated otherwise.

(2) Sale and lease. The term "sale" includes an exchange or other disposition and the term "lease" includes a rental or a sublease. The term "license" includes a sublicense. All rules under this section applicable to leases of export property apply in the same manner to licenses of export property. See § 1.927(a)-1T(f)(3) for a description of intangible property which cannot be export property.

(3) Gross receipts. The term "gross receipts" is defined by section 927(b) and § 1.927(b)-1T.

(4) Export property. The term "export property" is defined by section 927(a) and § 1.927(a)-1T.

(5) Controlled group. The term "controlled group" is defined by paragraph (h) of this section.

(6) Related supplier and related party. The terms related supplier and related party are defined by § 1.927(d)-2T.

(b) Sales of export property. Foreign trading gross receipts of a FSC include gross receipts from the sale of export property by the FSC, or by any principal for whom the FSC acts as a commission agent (whether or not the principal is a related supplier), pursuant to the terms of a contract entered into with a purchaser by the FSC or by the principal at any time or by any other person and assigned to the FSC or the principal at any time prior to the shipment of the property to the purchaser. Any agreement, oral or written, which constitutes a contract at law, satisfies the contractual requirements of this paragraph. Gross receipts from the sale of export property, whenever received, do not constitute foreign trading gross receipts unless the seller (or the corporation acting as commission agent for the seller) is an FSC at the time of the shipment of the property to the purchaser. For example, if a corporation which sells export property under the installment method is not an FSC for the taxable year in which the property is shipped to the purchaser, gross receipts from the sale do not constitute foreign trading gross receipts for any taxable year of the corporation.

(c) Leases of export property. *(1) In general.* Foreign trading gross receipts of an FSC include gross receipts from the lease of export property provided that—

(i) The property is held by the FSC (or by a principal for whom the FSC acts as commission agent with respect to the lease) either as an owner or lessee at the beginning of the term of the lease, and

(ii) The FSC qualified (or was treated) as a FSC for its taxable year in which the term of the lease began.

(2) Prepayment of lease receipts. If the gross receipts from a lease of export property are prepaid, then—

(i) All the prepaid gross receipts are foreign trading gross receipts of an FSC if it is reasonably expected at the time of the prepayment that, throughout the term of the lease, the lease will meet the requirements of this paragraph and the property will be export property; or

(ii) If it is reasonably expected at the time of the prepayment that the prepaid receipts would not be foreign trading gross receipts throughout the term of the lease if those receipts were not received as a prepayment, then only those prepaid receipts, for the taxable years of the FSC for which they would be foreign trading gross receipts, are foreign trading gross receipts. Thus, for example, if a lessee makes a prepayment of the first and last years' rent, and it is reasonably expected that the leased property will be export property for the first half of the lease period but not the second half of such period, the amount of the prepayment which represents the first year's rent will be considered foreign trading gross receipts if it would otherwise qualify, whereas the amount of the prepayment which represents the last year's rent will not be considered foreign trading gross receipts.

(d) Related and subsidiary services. *(1) In general.* Foreign trading gross receipts of an FSC include gross receipts from services furnished by the FSC which are related and subsidiary to any sale or lease (as described in paragraph (b) or (c) of this section) of export property by the FSC or with respect to which the FSC acts as a commission agent, provided that the FSC derives foreign trading gross receipts from the sale or lease. The services may be performed within or without the United States.

(2) Services furnished by the FSC. Services are considered to be furnished by an FSC for purposes of this paragraph if the services are provided by—

(i) The person who sold or leased the export property to which the services are related and subsidiary, provided that the FSC acts as a commission agent with respect to the sale or lease of the property and with respect to the services,

(ii) The FSC as principal, or any other person pursuant to a contract with the FSC, provided the FSC acted as principal or commission agent with respect to the sale or lease of the property, or

(iii) A member of the same controlled group as the FSC if the sale or lease of the export property is made by another member of the controlled group provided, however, that the FSC acts as principal or commission agent with respect to the sale or lease and as commission agent with respect to the services.

(3) Related services. Services which may be related to a sale or lease of export property include but are not limited to warranty service, maintenance service, repair service, and installation service. Transportation (including insurance related to such transportation) will be related to a sale or lease of export property, if the cost of the transportation is included in the sale price or rental of the property or, if the cost is separately stated, is paid by the FSC (or its principal) which sold or leased the property to the person furnishing the transportation service. Financing or the obtaining of financing for a sale or lease is not a related service for purposes of this paragraph. A service is related to a sale or lease of export property if—

(i) The service is of the type customarily and usually furnished with the type of transaction in the trade or business in which the sale or lease arose, and

(ii) The contract to furnish the service—

(A) Is expressly provided for in or is provided for by implied warranty under the contract of sale or lease,

(B) Is entered into on or before the date which is 2 years after the date on which the contract under which the sale or lease was entered into, provided that the person described in paragraph (d)(2) of this section which is to furnish the service delivers to the purchaser or lessor a written offer or option to furnish the services on or before the date on which the first shipment of goods with respect to which the service is to be performed is delivered, or

(C) Is a renewal of the services contract described in subdivisions (ii)(A) and (B) of this paragraph.

(4) Subsidiary services. (i) In general. Services related to a sale or lease of export property are subsidiary to the sale or lease only if it is reasonably expected at the time of the sale or lease that the gross receipts from all related services furnished by the FSC (as defined in this paragraph (d)(2)) will not exceed 50 percent of the sum of the gross receipts from the sale or lease and the gross receipts from related services furnished by the FSC (as described in this paragraph (d)(2)). In the case of a sale, reasonable expectations at the time of the sale are based on the gross receipts from all related services which may reasonably be performed at any time before the end of the 10-year period following the date of the sale. In the case of a lease, reasonable expectations at the time of the lease are based on the gross receipts from all related services which may reasonably be performed at any time before the end of the term of the lease (determined without regard to renewal options).

(ii) Allocation of gross receipts from services. In determining whether the services related to a sale or lease of export property are subsidiary to the sale or lease, the gross receipts to be treated as derived from the furnishing of services may not be less than the amount of gross receipts reasonably allocated to the services as determined under the facts and circumstances of each case without regard to whether—

(A) The services are furnished under a separate contract or under the same contract pursuant to which the sale or lease occurs, or

(B) The cost of the services is specified in the contract of sale or lease.

(iii) Transactions involving more than one item of export property. If more than one item of export property is sold or leased in a single transaction pursuant to one contract, the total gross receipts from the transaction and the total gross receipts from all services related to the transaction are each taken into account in determining whether the services are subsidiary to the transaction. However, the provisions of this subdivision apply only if the items could be included in the same product line, as determined under § 1.925(a)-1T(c)(8).

(iv) Renewed service contracts. If under the terms of a contract for related services, the contract is renewable within 10 years after a sale of export property, or during the term of a lease of export property, related services to be performed under the renewed contract are subsidiary to the sale or lease if it is reasonably expected at the time of the renewal that the gross receipts from all related services which have been and which are to be furnished by the FSC (as described in paragraph (d)(2) of this section) will not exceed 50 percent of the sum of the gross receipts from the sale or lease and the gross receipts from related services furnished by the FSC (as so described). Reasonable expectations are determined as provided in subdivision (i) of this paragraph.

(v) Parts used in services. If a services contract described in paragraph (d)(3) of this section provides for the furnishing of parts in connection with the furnishing of related services, gross receipts from the furnishing of the parts are not taken into account in determining whether under this paragraph (d)(4) the services are subsidiary. See paragraph (b) or (c) of this section to determine whether the gross receipts from the furnishing of parts constitute foreign trading gross receipts. See § 1.927(a)-1T(c)(2) and (e)(3) for rules regarding the treatment of the parts with respect to the manufacture of export property and the foreign content of the property, respectively.

(5) Relation to leases. If the gross receipts for services which are related and subsidiary to a lease of property have been prepaid at any time for all the services which are to be performed before the end of the term of the lease, then the rules in paragraph (c)(2) of this section (relating to prepayment of lease receipts) will determine whether prepaid services under this paragraph (d)(5) are foreign trading gross receipts Thus, for example, if it is reasonably expected that leased property will be export property for the first year of the term of the lease but will not be export property for the second year of the term, prepaid gross receipts for related and subsidiary services to be furnished in the first year may be foreign trading gross receipts. However, any prepaid gross receipts for the services to be furnished in the second year cannot be foreign trading gross receipts.

(6) Relation with export property determination. The determination as to whether gross receipts from the sale or lease of export property constitute foreign trading gross receipts does not depend upon whether services connected with the sale or lease are related and subsidiary to the sale or lease. Thus, for example, assume that an FSC receives gross receipts of $1,000 from the sale of export property and gross receipts of $1,100 from installation and maintenance services which are to be furnished by the FSC within 10 years after the sale and which are related to the sale. The $1,100 which the FSC receives for the services would not be foreign trading gross receipts since the gross receipts from the services exceed 50 percent of the sum of the gross receipts from the sale and the gross receipts from the related services furnished by the FSC. The $1,000 which the FSC receives from the sale of export property would, however, be foreign trading gross receipts if the sale met the requirements of paragraph (b) of this section.

(e) Engineering and architectural services. *(1) In general.* Foreign trading gross receipts of an FSC include gross receipts from engineering services (as described in paragraph (e)(5) of this section) or architectural services (as described in paragraph (e)(6) of this section) furnished by such FSC (as described in paragraph (e)(7) of this section) for a construction project (as defined in paragraph (e)(8) of this section) located, or proposed for location, outside the United States. Such services may be performed within or without the United States.

(2) Services included. Engineering and architectural services include feasibility studies for a proposed construction project whether or not such project is ultimately initiated.

(3) Excluded services. Engineering and architectural services do not include—

(i) Services connected with the exploration for oil or gas, or

(ii) Technical assistance or knowhow. For purposes of this paragraph, the term "technical assistance or knowhow" includes activities or programs designed to enable business, commerce, industrial establishments, and governmental organizations to acquire or use scientific, architectural, or engineering information.

(4) Other services. Receipts from the performance of construction activities other than engineering and architectural services constitute foreign trading gross receipts to the extent that the activities are related and subsidiary services (within the meaning of paragraph (d) of this section) with respect to a sale or lease of export property.

(5) Engineering services. For purposes of this paragraph, engineering services in connection with any construction project (within the meaning of paragraph (e)(8) of this section) include any professional services requiring engineering education, training, and experience and the application of special knowledge of the mathematical, physical, or engineering sciences to those professional services as consultation, investigation, evaluation, planning, design, or responsible supervision of construction for the purpose of assuring compliance with plans, specifications, and design.

(6) Architectural services. For purposes of this paragraph, architectural services include the offering or furnishing of any professional services such as consultation, planning, aesthetic and structural design, drawings and specifications, or responsible supervision of construction (for the purpose of assuring compliance with plans, specifications, and design) or erection, in connection with any construction project (within the meaning of paragraph (e)(8) of this section).

(7) Definition of "furnished by the FSC". For purposes of this paragraph, the term "furnished by the FSC" means architectural and engineering services furnished:

(i) By the FSC,

(ii) By another person (whether or not that person is a United States person) pursuant to a contract entered into with the FSC at any time prior to the furnishing of the services, provided that the FSC acts as principal, or

(iii) By another person (whether or not that person is a United States person) pursuant to a contract for the furnishing of the services entered into by, or assigned to, the person at any time, provided that the FSC acts as a commission agent for the furnishing of the services.

(8) Definition of "construction project". For purposes of this paragraph, the term "construction project" includes the erection, expansion, or repair (but not including minor remodeling or minor repairs) of new or existing buildings or other physical facilities including, for example, roads, dams, canals, bridges, tunnels, railroad tracks, and pipelines. The term also includes site grading and improvement and installation of equipment necessary for the construction. Gross receipts from the sale or lease of construction equipment are not foreign trading gross receipts unless the equipment is export property.

(f) Managerial services. *(1) In general.* Foreign trading gross receipts of a first FSC for its taxable year include gross receipts from the furnishing of managerial services provided for an unrelated FSC or unrelated interest charge DISC to aid the unrelated FSC or unrelated interest charge DISC in deriving foreign trading gross receipts or qualified export receipts, as the case may be, provided that at least 50 percent of the first FSC's gross receipts for such year consists of foreign trading gross receipts derived from the sale or lease of export property and the furnishing of related and subsidiary services. For purposes of this paragraph, managerial services are considered furnished by an FSC if the services are provided—

(i) By the first FSC,

(ii) By another person (whether or not a United States person) pursuant to a contract entered into by that person with the first FSC at any time prior to the furnishing of the services, provided that the first FSC acts as principal with respect to the furnishing of the services, or

(iii) By another person (whether or not a United States person) pursuant to a contract for the furnishing of services entered into at any time prior to the furnishing of the services provided that the first FSC acts as commission agent with respect to those services.

(2) Definition of "managerial services". The term "managerial services" as used in this paragraph means activities relating to the operation of an unrelated FSC or an unrelated interest charge DISC which derives foreign trading gross receipts or qualified export receipts as the case may be from the sale or lease of export property and from the furnishing of services related and subsidiary to those sales or leases. The term includes staffing and operational services necessary to operate the unrelated FSC or unrelated interest charge DISC, but does not include legal, accounting, scientific, or technical services. Examples of managerial services are: conducting export market studies, making shipping arrangements, and contacting potential foreign purchasers.

(3) Status of recipient of managerial services. Foreign trading gross receipts of a first FSC include receipts from the furnishing of managerial services during any taxable year of a recipient of such services if the recipient qualifies as an FSC or interest charge DISC for the taxable year. For purposes of this paragraph, a recipient is deemed to qualify as an FSC or interest charge DISC for its taxable year if the first FSC obtains from the recipient a copy of the recipient's election to be treated as an FSC or interest charge DISC together with the recipient's sworn statement that an election has been timely filed with the Internal Revenue Service Center. The recipient may mark out the names of its shareholders on a copy of its election to be treated as an FSC or interest charge DISC before submitting it to the first FSC. The copy of the election and the sworn statement of the recipient must be received by the first FSC within six months after the first FSC furnishes managerial services for the recipient. The copy of the election and the sworn statement of the recipient need not be obtained by the first FSC for subsequent taxable years of the recipient. A recipient of managerial services is not treated as an FSC or interest charge DISC with respect to the services performed during a taxable year for which the recipient does not qualify as an FSC or interest charge DISC if the first FSC performing such services does not believe or if a reasonable person would not believe (taking into account the furnishing FSC's managerial relationship with such recipient FSC or interest charge DISC) at the beginning of such taxable year that the recipient will qualify as an FSC or an interest charge DISC for such taxable year.

(g) Excluded receipts. *(1) In general.* Notwithstanding the provisions of paragraphs (b) through (f) of this section, foreign trading gross receipts of an FSC do not include any of the six amounts described in paragraphs (g)(2) through (7) of this section.

(2) Sales and leases of property for ultimate use in the United States. Property which is sold or leased for ultimate use in the United States does not constitute export property. See § 1.927(a)-1T(d)(4) relating to determination of where the ultimate use of the property occurs. Thus, foreign trading gross receipts of an FSC described in paragraph (b) or (c) of this section do not include gross receipts of the FSC from the sale or lease of this property.

(3) Sales or leases of export property and furnishing of services accomplished by subsidy. Foreign trading gross receipts of an FSC do not include gross receipts described in

paragraphs (b) through (f) of this section if the sale or lease of export property or the furnishing of services is accomplished by a subsidy granted by the United States or any instrumentality thereof, see section 924(f)(1)(B). Subsidies covered by section 924(f)(1)(B) are listed in subdivisions (i) through (vi) of this paragraph.

(i) The development loan program, or grants under the technical cooperation and development grants program of the Agency for International Development, or grants under the military assistance program administered by the Department of Defense, pursuant to the Foreign Assistance Act of 1961, as amended (22 U.S.C. 2151) unless the FSC shows to the satisfaction of the Commissioner that, under the conditions existing at the time of the sale (or at the time of lease or at the time the services were rendered), the purchaser (or lessor or recipient of the services) had a reasonable opportunity to purchase (or lease or contract for services) on competitive terms and from a seller (or lessor or performer of services) who was not a U.S. person, goods (or services) which were substantially identical to such property (or services) and which were not manufactured, produced, grown, or extracted in the United States (or performed by a U.S. person);

(ii) The Pub. L. 480 program authorized under Title I of the Agricultural Trade Development and Assistance Act of 1954, as amended (7 U.S.C. 1691, 1701-1714);

(iii) The Export Payment program of the Commodity Credit Corporation authorized by sections 5(d) and (f) of the Commodity Credit Corporation Charter Act, as amended (15 U.S.C. 714c(d) and (f);

(iv) The section 32 export payment programs authorized by section 32 of the Act of August 24, 1935, as amended (7 U.S.C. 612c);

(v) The Export Sales program of Commodity Credit Corporation authorized by sections 5(d) and (f) of the Commodity Credit Corporation Charter Act, as amended (15 U.S.C. 714c(d) and (f)), other than the GSM-4 program provided under 7 CFR Part 1488, and section 407 of the Agricultural Act of 1949, as amended (7 U.S.C. 1427), for the purpose of disposing of surplus agricultural commodities and exporting or causing to be exported agricultural commodities; and

(vi) The Foreign Military Sales direct credit program (22 U.S.C. 2763) or the Foreign Military Sales loan guaranty program (22 U.S.C. 2764) if—

(A) The borrowing country is released from its contractual liability to repay the United States government with respect to those credits or guaranteed loans;

(B) The repayment period exceeds twelve years; or

(C) The interest rate charged is less than the market rate of interest as defined in 22 U.S.C. 2763(c)(2)(B); unless the FSC shows to the satisfaction of the Commissioner that, under the conditions existing at the time of the sale, the purchaser had a reasonable opportunity to purchase, on competitive terms from a seller who was not a U.S. person, goods which were substantially identical to this property and which were not manufactured, produced, grown, or extracted in the United States. Information regarding whether an export is financed, in whole or in part, with funds derived from the programs identified in this subdivision may be obtained from the Comptroller, Defense Security Assistance Agency, Department of Defense, Washington, DC 20301.

(4) Sales or leases of export property and furnishing of architectural or engineering services for use by the United States. (i) In general. Foreign trading gross receipts of a FSC do not include gross receipts described in paragraph (b), (c), or (e) of this section if a sale or lease of export property, or the furnishing of architectural or engineering services, is for use by the United States or an instrumentality thereof in any case in which any law or regulation requires in any manner the purchase or lease of property manufactured, produced, grown, or extracted in the United States or requires the use of architectural or engineering services performed by a United States person. See section 924(f)(1)(A)(ii). For example, a sale by a FSC of export property to the Department of Defense for use outside the United States would not produce foreign trading gross receipts for the FSC if the Department of Defense purchased the property from appropriated funds subject to either any provision of the Department of Defense Federal Acquisition Regulations Supplement (48 CFR Chapter 2) or any appropriations act for the Department of Defense for the applicable year if the regulations or appropriations act requires that the items purchased must have been grown, reprocessed, reused, or produced in the United States. The Department of Defense's regulations do not require that items purchased by the Department for resale in post or base exchanges and commissary stores located on United States military installations in foreign countries be items grown, reprocessed, reused or produced in the United States. Therefore, receipts arising from the sale by an FSC to those post or base exchanges and commissary stores will not be excluded from the definition of foreign trading gross receipts by this paragraph (g)(4).

(ii) Direct or indirect sales or leases. Any sale or lease of export property is for use by the United States or an instrumentality thereof if such property is sold or leased by a FSC (or by a principal for whom the FSC acts as commission agent) to—

(A) A person who is a related person with respect to the FSC or such principal and who sells or leases the property for use by the United States or an instrumentality thereof, or

(B) A person who is not a related person with respect to the FSC or such principal if, at the time of the sale or lease, there is an agreement or understanding that the property will be sold or leased for use by the United States or an instrumentality thereof (or if a reasonable person would have known at the time of the sale or lease that the property would be sold or leased for use by the United States or an instrumentality thereof) within 3 years after the sale or lease.

(iii) Excluded programs. The provisions of subdivisions (4)(i) and (ii) of this paragraph do not apply in the case of a purchase by the United States or an instrumentality thereof if the purchase is pursuant to—

(A) The Foreign Military Sales Act, as amended (22 U.S.C. 2751 *et seq.*), or a program under which the United States government purchases property for resale, on commercial terms, to a foreign government or agency or instrumentality thereof, or

(B) A program (whether bilateral or multilateral) under which sales to the United States government are open to international competitive bidding.

(5) Services. Foreign trading gross receipts of a FSC do not include gross receipts described in paragraph (d) of this section (concerning related and subsidiary services) if the services from which such gross receipts are derived are related and subsidiary to the sale or lease of property which results in excluded receipts under this paragraph.

(6) Receipts within controlled group. (i) For purposes of the transfer pricing methods of section 925(a), gross receipts of a corporation do not constitute foreign trading gross receipts for any taxable year of the corporation if at the time of the sale, lease, or other transaction resulting in the gross

receipts, the corporation and the person from whom the gross receipts are directly or indirectly derived (whether or not such corporation and such person are the same person) are members of the same controlled group, and either

(A) The corporation and the person each qualifies as a FSC (or if related FSCs are commission agents of each party to the transaction) for its taxable year in which its receipts arise, or

(B) With regard to sale transactions, a sale of export property to a FSC (or to a related person if the FSC is the commission agent of the related person) by a non-FSC within the same controlled group follows any sale of the export property to a FSC (or to a related person if the FSC is the commission agent of the related person) within the same controlled group if foreign trading gross receipts resulted from the sale. Thus for example, assume that R, S, X, and Y are members of the same controlled group and that X and Y are FSCs. If R sells property to S and pays X a commission relating to that sale and if S sells the same property to an unrelated foreign party and pays Y a commission relating to that sale, the receipts received by X from the sale of such property by R to S will be considered to be derived from Y, a FSC which is a member of the same controlled group as X, and thus will not result in foreign trading gross receipts to X. The receipts received by Y from the sale to an unrelated foreign party may, however, result in foreign trading gross receipts to Y. For another example, if R and S both assign the commissions to X, receipts derived from the sale from R to S will be considered to be derived from X acting as commission agent for S and will not result in foreign trading gross receipts to X. Receipts derived by X from the sale of property by S to an unrelated foreign party may, however, constitute foreign trading gross receipts.

(ii) Section 1.927(a)-1T(f)(2) provides rules regarding property not constituting export property in certain cases where such property is leased to any corporation which is a member of the same controlled group as the lessor.

(7) Factoring of receivables by a related supplier. If an account receivable arising with respect to export property is transferred to any person for an amount reflecting a discount from the selling price of the export property, then the gross receipts from the sale which are treated as foreign trading gross receipts for purposes of computing a FSC's profit under the administrative pricing methods of section 925(a)(1) and (2) shall be reduced by the amount of the discount. See § 1.925(a)-1T(f) Example (11) for illustration of how this special rule affects computation of combined taxable income of a FSC and its related supplier.

(h) Definition of "controlled group". For purposes of sections 921 through 927 and the regulations under those sections, the term "controlled group" has the same meaning as is assigned to the term "controlled group of corporations" by section 1563(a), except that (1) the phrase "more than 50 percent" is substituted for the phrase "at least 80 percent" each place the latter phrase appears in section 1563(a), and (2) section 1563(b) shall not apply. Thus, for example, a foreign corporation subject to tax under section 882 may be a member of a controlled group. Furthermore, two or more corporations (including a foreign corporation) are members of a controlled group at any time such corporations meet the requirements of section 1563(a) (as modified by this paragraph).

(i) FSC's entitlement to income. *(1) Application of administrative pricing rules of section 925(a).* A corporation which meets the requirements of section 922(a) (or section 922(b) if the corporation elects small FSC status) and § 1.921-2(a) (Q&A1) to be treated as an FSC (or small FSC) for a taxable year is entitled to income, and the administrative pricing rules of section 925(a)(1) or (2) apply, in the case of any transaction described in § 1.925(a)-1T(b)(iii) between the FSC and its related supplier (as defined in § 1.927(d)-2T(a)) as long as the FSC, or someone under contract to it, satisfies the requirements of section 925(c). The requirements of section 925(c) must be met by a commission FSC as well as by a buy-sell FSC. See § 1.925(a)-1T(a)(3)(i) and (b)(2)(ii).

(2) Other transactions. In the case of a transaction to which the provisions of paragraph (i)(1) of this section do not apply but from which an FSC derives gross receipts, the income to which the FSC is entitled as a result of the transaction is determined pursuant to the terms of the contract for the transaction and, if applicable, section 482 and the regulations under that section. For applicability of the section 482 transfer pricing method, see § 1.925(a)-1T(a)(3)(ii) and (b)(2)(i).

(j) Small FSC limitation. *(1) In general.* Under section 924(b)(2)(B), in determining exempt foreign trade income of a small FSC, the foreign trading gross receipts of the small FSC for the taxable year which exceed $5 million are not taken into account. The foreign trading gross receipts of the small FSC not taken into account for purposes of computing the small FSC's exempt foreign trade income shall be taken into account in computing the small FSC's non-exempt foreign trade income. If the foreign trading gross receipts of the small FSC exceed the $5 million limitation, the small FSC may select the gross receipts to which the limitation is allocated. See section 922(b) and § 1.921-2(b) (Q&A3) for a definition of a small FSC.

(2) Members of a controlled group limited to one $5 million amount. (i) General rule. All small FSCs which are members of a controlled group on a December 31, shall, for their taxable years which include that December 31, be limited to one $5 million amount. The $5 million amount shall be allocated equally among the member small FSCs of the controlled group for their taxable years including that December 31, unless all of the member small FSCs consent to an apportionment plan providing for an unequal allocation of the $5 million amount. The apportionment plan shall provide for the apportionment of a fixed dollar amount to one or more of the corporations, and the sum of the amounts so apportioned shall not exceed the $5 million amount. If the taxable year including the December 31 of any member small FSC is a short period (as defined in section 443), the portion of the $5 million amount allocated to that member small FSC for that short period under the preceding sentence shall be reduced to the amount which bears the same ratio to the amount so allocated as the number of days in such short period bears to 365. The consent of each member small FSC to the apportionment plan for the taxable year shall be signified by completing the form (i.e., Schedule O or any successor to that form) which satisfies the requirements of and is filed in the manner specified in § 1.1561-3T. An apportionment plan may be amended in the manner prescribed in § 1.1561-3T(a), except that an original or an amended plan may not be adopted with respect to a particular December 31 if at the time the original or amended plan is sought to be adopted, less than 12 full months remain in the statutory period (including extensions) for the assessment of a deficiency against any shareholder of a member small FSC the tax liability of which would change by the adoption of the original or amended plan. If less than 12 full months of the period remain with respect to any such shareholder, the director of

the service center with which the shareholder files its income tax return will, upon request, enter into an agreement extending the statutory period for the limited purpose of assessing any deficiency against that shareholder attributable to the adoption of the original or amended apportionment plan.

(ii) Membership determined under section 1563(b). For purposes of this paragraph (j)(2), the determination of whether a small FSC is a member of a controlled group of corporations with respect to any taxable year shall be made in the manner prescribed in section 1563(b) and the regulations under that section.

(iii) Certain short taxable years. (A) General rule. If a small FSC has a short period (as defined in section 443) which does not include a December 31, and that small FSC is a member of a controlled group of corporations which includes one or more other small FSC's with respect to the short period, then the amount described in section 924(b)(2)(B) with respect to the short period of that small FSC shall be determined by—

(1) Dividing $5 million by the number of small FSCs which are members of that group on the last day of the short period, and

(2) Multiplying the result by a fraction, the numerator of which is the number of days in the short period and the denominator of which is 365. For purposes of the preceding sentence, section 1563(b) shall be applied as if the last day of the short period were substituted for December 31. Except as provided in subdivision (2)(iii)(B) of this paragraph, the small FSC having a short period not including a December 31 may not enter into an apportionment plan with respect to the short period.

(B) Exception. If the short period not including a December 31 of two or more small FSCs begins on the same date and ends on the same date and those small FSCs are members of the same controlled group, those small FSCs may enter into an apportionment plan for such short period in the manner provided in subdivision (2)(i) of this paragraph with respect to the combined amount allowed to each of those small FSCs under subdivision (2)(iii)(A) of this paragraph.

T.D. 8126, 3/2/87, amend T.D. 9304, 12/21/2006.

---

§ 1.924(c)-1 Requirement that a FSC be managed outside the United States.

Caution: The Treasury has not yet amended Reg § 1.924(c)-1 to reflect changes made by P.L. 106-519.

(a) In general. Section 924(b)(1)(A) provides that a FSC shall be treated as having foreign trading gross receipts for the taxable year only if the management of the FSC during the year takes place outside the United States, as provided in section 924(c). Section 924(c) and this section set forth the management activities that must take place outside the United States in order to satisfy the requirement of section 924(b)(1)(A). Paragraph (b) of this section provides rules for determining whether the requirements of section 924(c)(1) have been met. Section 924(c)(1) requires that all meetings of the board of directors of the FSC during the taxable year and all meetings of the shareholders of the FSC during the taxable year take place outside the United States. Paragraph (c) of this section provides rules for maintaining the FSC's principal bank account outside the United States as provided in section 924(c)(2). Paragraph (d) of this section provides rules for disbursements required by section 924(c)(3) to be made from bank accounts of the FSC maintained outside the United States.

(b) Meetings of board of directors and meetings of shareholders must be outside the United States. All meetings of the board of directors of the FSC and all meetings of the shareholders of the FSC that take place during a taxable year must take place outside the United States to meet the requirements of section 924(c)(1). Only meetings that are formally convened as meetings of the board of directors or as shareholder meetings will be taken into account in determining whether those requirements have been met. In addition, all such meetings must comply with the local laws of the foreign country or possession of the United States in which the FSC was created or organized. The local laws determine whether a meeting must be held, when and where it must be held (if it is held at all), who must be present, quorum requirements, use of proxies, and so on. Where the local law permits action by the board of directors or shareholders to be taken by written consent without a meeting, use of such procedure will not constitute a meeting for purposes of section 924(c)(1). Section 924(c)(1) and this section impose no other requirements except the requirement that meetings that are actually held take place outside the United States. If the participants in a meeting are not all physically present in the same location, the location of the meeting is determined by the location of the persons exercising a majority of the voting power (including proxies) participating in the meeting. For example, a FSC has five directors, and is organized in country A. Country A's law requires that a majority of the directors of a corporation must participate in a meeting to constitute a quorum (and, thus, a meeting), but there is no requirement that the meeting be held in country A or that the directors must be physically present to participate. One director is in country A, another director is in country B, and a third director is in the United States.

These three directors convene a meeting by telephone that constitutes a meeting under the law of country A. The meeting occurs outside the United States because the persons exercising a majority of the voting power participating in the meeting are located outside the United States.

(c) Maintenance of the principal bank account outside the United States. *(1) In general.* For purposes of section 924(c), the bank account that shall be regarded as the principal bank account of a FSC is the bank account from which the disbursements described in paragraph (d) of this section are made. A FSC may have more than one principal bank account. The bank account that is regarded as the principal bank account must be maintained in a foreign country which meets the requirements of section 927(e)(3), or in any possession of the United States (as defined in section 927(d)(5)), and it must be so maintained at all times during the taxable year. For taxable years beginning on or after February 19, 1987, a principal bank account or accounts must be designated on the annual return of the FSC by providing the bank name(s) and account number(s).

(2) Maintenance of the account in a bank. The bank account that is regarded as the principal bank account must be maintained in an institution that is engaged in the conduct of a banking, financing, or similar business, as defined in § 1.954-2(d)(2)(ii) (without regard to whether it is a controlled foreign corporation). The institution may be a U.S. bank, provided that the account is maintained in a branch outside the United States.

(3) Maintenance of an account outside the United States. Maintenance of the principal bank account outside the United States means that the account regarded as the principal bank account must be an account maintained on the books of the banking institution at an office outside the

United States, but does not require that access to the account may be made only outside the United States. Instructions providing for deposits into or disbursements from the account may originate in the United States without affecting the status of maintenance of the account outside the United States.

(4) Maintenance of the account at all times during the taxable year. The term "at all times during the taxable year" generally means for each day of the taxable year. In the case of a newly created or organized corporation, thirty days may elapse between the effective date of the corporation's election to be treated as a FSC and the date a bank account is opened without causing the FSC to fail the requirement that it maintain its principal bank account outside the United States at all times during the taxable year. For example, if a corporation is created or organized prior to January 1, 1985 and makes an election to be treated as a FSC within the first 90 days of 1985, the election is effective as of January 1, 1985. Thus, the FSC must open a bank account within 30 days of January 1, or as of January 31, 1985, to satisfy this requirement. Also, a FSC shall be treated as satisfying this requirement if the account that is regarded as its principal bank account is terminated during the taxable year, provided that (i) such termination is the result of circumstances beyond the FSC's control, and (ii) the FSC establishes a new principal bank account within thirty days after such termination. A FSC may close its principal bank account and replace it with another account that qualifies under this paragraph (c) as a principal bank account at any time provided that no lapse of time occurs between the closing of the principal bank account and the opening of the replacement account.

(5) Other accounts. The FSC may maintain other bank accounts in addition to its principal bank account. Such other accounts may be located anywhere, without limitation. The mere existence of such other accounts will not cause the FSC to fail to satisfy the requirements of section 924(c).

(d) Disbursement of dividends, legal and accounting fees, and salaries of officers and directors out of the principal bank account of the FSC. *(1) In general.* All dividends, legal fees, accounting fees, salaries of officers of the FSC, and salaries or fees paid to members of the board of directors of the FSC that are disbursed during the taxable year must be disbursed out of bank account(s) of the FSC maintained outside the United States. Such an account is treated as the principal bank account of the FSC for purposes of section 924(c). Dividends, however, may be netted against amounts owed to the FSC (e.g., commissions) by a related supplier through book entries. If the FSC regularly disburses its legal or accounting fees, salaries of officers, and salaries or fees of directors out of its principal bank account, the occasional, inadvertent payment by mistake of fact or law of such amounts out of another bank account will not be considered a disbursement by the FSC if, upon determination that such payment was made from another account, reimbursement to such other account is made from the principal bank account of the FSC within a reasonable period from the date of the determination. Disbursement out of the principal bank account of the FSC may be made by transferring funds from the principal bank account to a U.S. account of the FSC provided that (i) the payment of the dividends, salaries or fees to the recipients is made within 12 months of the transfer, (ii) the purpose of the expenditures is designated and, (iii) the payment of the dividends, salaries or fees is actually made out of the same U.S. account that received the disbursement from the principal bank account.

(2) Reimbursement. Legal or accounting fees, salaries of officers, and salaries or fees of directors that are paid by a related person wholly or partially on behalf of a FSC must be reimbursed by the FSC. The amounts paid by the related person are not considered disbursed by the FSC until the related person is reimbursed by the FSC. The related person must be reimbursed no later than the last date prescribed for filing the FSC's tax return (including extensions) for the taxable year to which the reimbursement relates. Any reimbursement for amounts paid on behalf of the FSC must be disbursed out of the FSC's principal bank account (and not netted against any obligation owed by the related person to the FSC), as set forth in paragraph (c) of this section. To determine the amounts paid on behalf of the FSC, the FSC may rely upon a written statement or invoice furnished to it by the related person which shows the following:

(i) The actual fees charged for performing the legal or accounting services for the FSC or, if such fees cannot be ascertained by the related person, a good faith estimate thereof, and the actual salaries or fees paid for services as officers and directors of the FSC, and

(ii) The person who performed or provided the services.

(3) Good Faith Exception. If, after the FSC has filed its tax return, a determination is made by the Commissioner that all or a part of the legal or accounting fees, salaries of officers, and salaries or fees of directors of the FSC were paid by a related person without receiving reimbursement, the FSC may, nonetheless, satisfy the requirements of section 924(c)(3) if the fees and salaries were paid by the related person in good faith, and the FSC reimburses the related person for the fees and salaries paid within 90 days after the determination. The reimbursement shall be treated as made as of the end of the taxable year of the FSC for which the reimbursement is made.

(4) Dividends. (i) Definition. For purposes of section 924(c) and this section only, the term "dividends" refers solely to cash dividends (including a dividend paid in a foreign functional currency) actually paid pursuant to a declaration or authorization by the FSC. Accordingly, a "dividend" will not include a constructive dividend that is deemed to be paid (regardless of the source of such constructive dividend) or a distribution of property that is a dividend under section 316 other than a distribution of U.S. dollars or a foreign functional currency.

(ii) Offset accounting entries. Payment of dividends by the FSC to its related supplier may be in the form of an accounting entry offsetting an amount payable to the related supplier for the dividend against an existing debt owed to the FSC. The offset accounting entries must be clearly identified in the books of account of both the related supplier and the FSC.

(5) Legal and accounting fees. For purposes of this section, legal and accounting fees do not include salaries paid to legal and accounting employees of the FSC (or a related person). Legal and accounting fees are limited to fees paid to independent persons performing legal or accounting services for or with respect to the FSC.

(6) Salaries of officers and directors. For purposes of this section, salaries of officers and salaries or fees of directors are only those salaries or fees paid for services as officers or directors of the FSC. Salaries do not include reimbursed travel and entertainment expenses. If an individual officer, director, or employee of a related person is also an officer or director of a FSC and receives additional compensation for services performed for the FSC, the portion of the compen-

sation paid to the individual which is for services performed for the FSC is required to be disbursed out of the FSC's principal bank account. For purposes of this section, the term "compensation" is defined as set forth in 1.415(c)-2(b) and (c).

T.D. 8125, 2/13/87, amend T.D. 9319, 4/4/2007.

§ 1.924(d)-1 Requirement that economic processes take place outside the United States.

Caution: The Treasury has not yet amended Reg § 1.924(d)-1 to reflect changes made by P.L. 106-519.

(a) In general. Section 924(b)(1)(B) provides that a FSC has foreign trading gross receipts from any transaction only if economic processes with respect to such transaction take place outside the United States as provided in section 924(d). Section 924(d) and this section set forth the rules for determining whether a sufficient amount of the economic processes of a transaction take place outside the United States. Generally, a transaction will qualify if the FSC satisfies two different requirements: Participation outside the United States in the sales portion of the transaction, and satisfaction of either the 50-percent or the 85-percent foreign direct cost test. The activities comprising these economic processes may be performed by the FSC or by any other person acting under contract with the FSC. (All references to "FSC" in §§ 1.924(d)-1 and 1.924(e)-1 shall mean the FSC or, if applicable, the person performing the relevant activity under contract on behalf of the FSC). The FSC may act upon standing instructions from another person in the performance of any activity, whether a sales activity under paragraph (c) of this section or an activity relating to the disposition of export property under paragraph (d) of this section and § 1.924(e)-1. The identity of the FSC as a separate entity is not required to be disclosed in the performance of any of the activities comprising the economic processes. Except as otherwise provided, the location of any activity is determined by the place where the activity is initiated by the FSC, and not by the location of any person transmitting instructions to the FSC.

(b) Activities performed by another person. *(1) In general.* Any person, whether domestic or foreign, and whether related or unrelated to the FSC, may perform any activity required to satisfy this section, provided that the activity is performed pursuant to a contract for the performance of that activity on behalf of the FSC. Such a contract may be any oral or written agreement which constitutes a contract at law. The person performing the activity is not required to enter into a contract directly with the FSC and, thus, may be a direct or indirect subcontractor of a person under contract with the FSC. For example, assume that a buy-sell FSC enters into an agreement with its related supplier in which the related supplier agrees to perform on behalf of the FSC all sales activities with respect to the FSC's transactions with its foreign customers. Through its existing agreements with a domestic unrelated person, the related supplier subcontracts the performance of these activities to the domestic unrelated person, who, in turn, subcontracts the performance of the sales activities to foreign sales agents. The sales activities performed by the foreign sales agents are considered to be performed on behalf of the FSC for purposes of meeting the requirements of section 924(d)(1)(A).

(2) Proof of Compliance. If the FSC does not perform the activity itself, it must maintain records adequate to establish, with respect to each transaction or group of transactions, that the activity was performed and that the performance of such activity took place outside the United States. If the person who performed the activity on behalf of the FSC is an independent contractor, the FSC may rely upon a written declaration from that person stating that the activities were performed by that person on behalf of the FSC, and were performed outside the United States. An invoice or a receipt for payment will be considered to be such a written declaration if it specifies that the activities were performed outside the United States or specifies a particular place outside the United States where the activities were performed. If the person performing the activities on behalf of the FSC is a related person, the FSC must maintain records adequate to establish that the activities were actually performed and where the activities were performed. Such records may be stored with the related person provided that the FSC makes such records available to the Commissioner upon request.

(c) Participation outside the United States in the sales portion of the transaction. *(1) In general.* The requirement of section 924(d)(1)(A) is met with respect to the gross receipts of a FSC derived from any transaction if the FSC has participated outside the United States in the solicitation, the negotiation, or the making of the contract relating to such transaction (hereinafter described as "sales activities"), as provided in this paragraph (c). A sale need not occur in order that the solicitation or negotiation tests be satisfied. Once the FSC has participated outside the United States in an activity that constitutes the solicitation, negotiation, or the making of the contract with respect to a transaction, any prior or subsequent activity by the FSC with respect to such transaction that would otherwise constitute the sales activity will be disregarded for purposes of determining whether the FSC has met the requirements of section 924(d)(1)(A). For example, if a FSC sells a product to a foreign customer by first meeting with the customer in New York to discuss the product and then by mailing to it from outside the United States a brochure describing the product, the prior meeting is disregarded and only the mailing is considered in determining whether there was solicitation outside the United States by the FSC with respect to the transaction which has occurred.

(2) Solicitation (other than advertising). For purposes of this paragraph (c), "solicitation" refers to any communication (by any method, including, but not limited to, telephone, telegraph, mail, or in person) by the FSC, at any time during the 12 month period (measured from the date the communication is mailed or transmitted) immediately preceding the execution of a contract relating to the transaction to a specific, targeted customer or potential customer, that specifically addresses the customer's attention to the product or service which is the subject of the transaction. For purposes of paragraph (c)(2) of this section, communication by mail means depositing the communication in a mailbox. Except as provided in § 1.924(e)-1(a)(1) with respect to second mailings, activities that would otherwise constitute advertising (such as sending sales literature to a customer or potential customer) will be considered solicitation if the activities are directed at a specific, targeted customer or potential customer, and the costs of the activity are not taken into account as advertising under the foreign direct cost tests. Activities that would otherwise constitute sales promotion (such as a promotional meeting in person with a customer) will be considered to be solicitation if the activities are directed at a specific, targeted customer or potential customer, and the costs of the activity are not taken into account as sales promotion under the foreign direct cost tests. Except as provided in § 1.924(e)-1(a)(1) with respect to second mailings,

the same or similar activities cannot be considered both solicitation and advertising, or both solicitation and sales promotion, with respect to the same customer. Solicitation, however, may take place at the same time as, and in conjunction with, another sales activity. Additionally, it may take place with respect to any person, whether domestic or foreign, and whether or not related to the FSC.

(3) Negotiation. For purposes of this paragraph (c), "negotiation" refers to any communication by the FSC to a customer or potential customer aimed at an agreement on one or more of the terms of a transaction, including, but not limited to, price, credit terms, quantity, or time or manner of delivery. For purposes of this paragraph (c)(3), communication by mail has the same meaning as provided in paragraph (c)(2) of this section. Negotiation does not include the mere receipt of a communication from a customer (such as an order) that includes terms of a sale. Negotiation may take place at the same time as, and in conjunction with, another sales activity. Additionally, it may take place with respect to any person, whether domestic or foreign, and whether or not related to the FSC.

(4) Making of a contract. For purposes of this paragraph (c), "making of a contract" refers to performance by the FSC of any of the elements necessary to complete a sale, such as making an offer or accepting an offer. A requirements contract is considered an open offer to be accepted from time to time when the customer submits an order for a specified quantity. Thus, the acceptance of such an order will be considered the making of a contract. The written confirmation by the FSC to the customer of the acceptance of the open order will also be considered the making of a contract. Acceptance of an unsolicited bid or order is considered the "making of a contract" even if no solicitation or negotiation occurred with respect to the transaction. The written confirmation by the FSC to the customer of an oral or written agreement which confirms variable contract terms, such as price, credit terms, quantity, or time or manner of delivery, or specifies (directly or by cross-reference) additional contract terms will be considered the making of a contract. A written confirmation is any confirmation expressed in writing, including a telegram, telex, or other similar written communciation. The making of a contract may take place at the same time as, and in conjunction with, another sales activity. Additionally, it may take place with respect to any person, whether domestic or foreign, and whether or not related to the FSC.

(5) Grouping transactions. Generally, the sales activities under this paragraph (c) are to be applied on a transaction-by-transaction basis. By annual election of the FSC, however, any of the sales activities may be applied on the basis of a group as set forth in this paragraph (c)(5). Any groupings used must be supported by adequate documentation of performance of activities relating to the groupings used. An election by the FSC to group transactions must be made on its annual income tax return. The FSC, however, may amend its tax return to group in a manner different from that elected on its original return before the expiration of the statute of limitations.

(i) Standards of groups. A determination by a FSC as to a grouping will be accepted by a district director if such determination conforms to any of the following standards:

(A) Product or product line groupings. A product or product line grouping may be based upon either a recognized trade or industry usage, or upon a two digit major group (or on any inferior classification or combination of inferior classifications within a major group) of the Standard Industrial Classification as prepared by the Statistical Policy Division of the Office of Management and Budget, Executive Office of the President. For taxable years beginning on or before February 19, 1987, any sales activity that is performed outside the United States with respect to any transaction covered by the product or product line grouping during the FSC's taxable year shall apply to all transactions covered by the product or product line. However, for taxable years beginning after February 19, 1987, the requirement of section 924(d)(1)(A) is met with respect to all transactions covered by the product or product line grouping only if the sales activities are performed outside the United States with respect to customers with sales representing either: (i) 20 percent or more of the foreign trading gross receipts of the product or product line grouping during the current year or (ii) 50 percent or more of the foreign trading gross receipts of the product or product line grouping for the prior year irrespective of whether any sales occurred within the current year to the prior year customers. If during the prior taxable year, the controlled group of which the FSC is a member had a DISC or interest charge DISC, the FSC may use the 50 percent rule with respect to the preceding DISC or interest charge DISC year, substituting qualified export receipts for foreign trading gross receipts. A corporation which has not been treated in the prior year as a FSC, interest charge DISC, or DISC does not have to meet either the 20 percent test or the 50 percent test for the first year in which it is treated as a FSC.

(B) Customer groupings. A customer grouping includes all transactions of the FSC with a particular customer during the FSC's taxable year. Thus, any sales activity that is performed outside the United States with respect to any transaction with the customer during the taxable year shall apply to all transactions within the customer grouping.

(C) Contract groupings. A contract grouping includes all transactions of the FSC under a particular contract for a taxable year. Thus, any sales activity that is performed outside the United States with respect to any transaction under the contract will apply to all transactions under the contract for such taxable year. For long-term contracts between unrelated parties, the sales activities tests need be satisfied only once for the life of the contract. With respect to requirements contracts and long-term contracts between related parties, the sales activities test must be satisfied annually.

(D) Product or product line groupings within customer or contract groupings. Groupings may be based upon product or product line groupings within customer or contract groupings. If, however, the primary groupings is a customer or contract grouping, the 20 percent test set forth in subdivision (A) of this paragraph relating to product or product line grouping will not be applicable.

(ii) Transactions included in a grouping. A choice by a FSC to group transactions shall generally apply to all transactions within the scope of that grouping. The choice of a grouping, however, applies only to transactions covered by the grouping and, for transactions not encompassed by the grouping, the determinations may be made on a transaction-by-transaction basis or other grouping basis. For example, a FSC may choose a product grouping with respect to one product and use the transaction-by-transaction method for another product within the same taxable year. In addition, if a FSC applies sales activity rules on the basis of other types of groupings, such as all sales to a particular customer, transactions included in those other groupings shall be excluded from product groupings.

(iii) Different groupings allowed for different purposes. A choice by the FSC to group transactions may be made separately for each of the sales activities under section 924(d)(1)(A). Groupings used for purposes of section 924(d)(1)(A) will have no relationship to groupings used for other purposes, such as satisfying the foreign direct cost tests. This paragraph (c)(5) does not apply for purposes of section 925.

(6) Examples. The provisions of this paragraph (c) may be illustrated by the following examples:

Example (1). In November, a calendar year FSC mailed from its foreign office its catalog to a potential foreign customer. The catalog displayed numerous products along with a brief description and the price of each. In February of the following year, the FSC sold to the customer a product displayed in the catalog. Since the FSC communicated with the customer during the 12-month period prior to the sale, although during the previous taxable year, the FSC participated outside the United States in the solicitation relating to the transaction.

Example (2). A FSC with a taxable year ending April 30, 1986, solicits customer X during that taxable year with respect to Product A. In the previous taxable year, the FSC sold product A to customers V, W, X, Y, Z, none of whom were customers in the taxable year ending April 30, 1986. The sales proceeds from sales to customer X represented 50 percent of the foreign trading gross receipts for the previous FSC year. The FSC meets the 50 percent test for product or product line grouping for the taxable year ending April 30, 1986. If the facts were changed so that there was not a FSC, DISC or interest charge DISC in the same controlled group in the previous taxable year, the single solicitation directed to any customer would qualify all transactions within the product group as meeting the solicitation requirement for that taxable year. For subsequent taxable years, the 50 percent test or the 20 percent test would be applicable.

Example (3). A FSC earns commissions on the sale of export property by its domestic related supplier to United States wholesalers for final sale to foreign customers. The related supplier receives an order from one of its United States wholesalers. The related supplier telephones the United States wholesaler to inform it of the new price and the probability of another price increase soon. The United States wholesaler orally agrees to the new price and the related supplier instructs the FSC to telex the wholesaler from its foreign office a confirmation that the product will be sold at the current new price. The written confirmation by the FSC of an oral agreement on a variable contract term constitutes the making of a contract. Thus, the requirements of section 924(d)(1)(A) are met with respect to the transaction relating to the product.

(d) Satisfaction of either the 50-percent or the 85-percent foreign direct cost test. *(1) In general.* Section 924(d)(1)(B) requires, in order for the gross receipts of a transaction to qualify as foreign trading gross receipts, that the foreign direct costs incurred by the FSC attributable to the transaction equal or exceed 50 percent of the total direct costs incurred by the FSC attributable to the transaction. The direct costs are those costs attributable to activities described in the five categories of section 924(e). Section 924(d)(2) provides that, instead of satisfying the 50-percent foreign direct cost test of section 924(d)(1)(B), the FSC may incur foreign direct costs attributable to activities described in each of two of those categories that equal or exceed 85 percent of the total direct costs incurred by the FSC attributable to the activity described in each of the two categories. If no direct costs are incurred by the FSC in a particular category, that category shall not be taken into account for purposes of determining satisfaction of either the 50-percent or the 85-percent foreign direct cost test. If any amount of direct costs is incurred in a particular category, that category shall be taken into account for purposes of the foreign direct costs tests.

(2) Direct costs. (i) Definition of direct costs. For purposes of section 924(d), direct costs are those costs which are incident to and necessary for the performance of any activity described in section 924(e). Direct costs include the cost of materials which are consumed in the performance of the activity, and the cost of labor which can be identified or associated directly with the performance of the activity, (but only to the extent of wages, salaries, fees for professional services, and other amounts paid for personal services actually rendered, such as bonuses or compensation paid for services on the basis of a percentage of profits). Direct costs also include the allowable depreciation deduction for equipment or facilities (or the rental cost for use thereof) that can be specifically identified or associated with the activity, as well as the contract price of an activity performed on behalf of the FSC by a contractor. If costs of services or the use of facilities are only incidentally related to the performance of an activity described in section 924(e), only the incremental cost is considered to be identified directly with the activity. For example, supervisory, administrative, and general overhead expenses, such as telephone service, normally are not identified directly with particular activities described in section 924(e). The cost of a long distance telephone call made to arrange for delivery of export property, however, is identified directly with the activities described in section 924(e)(2). Direct costs for purposes of section 924(d) do not necessarily include all of the expenses taken into account for purposes of determining the taxable income of the FSC or the combined taxable income of the FSC and its related supplier.

(ii) Allocation of direct costs. For purposes of this section only, if costs are identified with more than one activity (whether or not all of the activities are described in section 924(e)), the portion of the costs attributable to each activity shall be determined by allocating the costs among the activities in any manner that is consistently applied and, if applicable, that reasonably reflects relative costs that would be incurred by performing each activity independently. If costs of an activity are attributable to more than one transaction or grouping of transactions, the portion of the costs attributable to each transaction or grouping shall be determined by allocating the costs among the transactions or groupings in any manner that is consistently applied and, if applicable, that reasonably reflects relative costs that would be incurred by performing the activity independently with respect to each transaction or grouping.

(3) Total direct costs. The term "total direct costs" means all of the direct costs of any transaction attributable to activities described in any paragraph of section 924(e). For purposes of the 50-percent foreign direct cost test of section 924(d)(1)(B), total direct costs are determined based on the direct costs of all activities described in all of the paragraphs of section 924(e). For purposes of the 85-percent foreign direct cost test of section 924(d)(2), however, the total direct costs are determined separately for each paragraph of section 924(e). If more than one activity is included within a paragraph of section 924(e), direct costs must be incurred with respect to at least one activity listed in the paragraph. If costs are incurred with respect to more than one activity, all

direct costs must be considered for purposes of satisfying the direct costs test.

(4) Foreign direct costs. The term "foreign direct costs" means the portion of the total direct costs of any transaction which is attributable to activities performed outside the United States. For purposes of the 50-percent foreign direct cost test, foreign direct costs are determined based on the direct costs of all activities described in all of the paragraphs of section 924(e). For purposes of the 85-percent foreign direct cost test, however, foreign direct costs are determined separately for each paragraph of section 924(e).

(5) Fifty percent foreign direct cost test. To satisfy the requirement of section 924(d)(1)(B), the foreign direct costs incurred by the FSC attributable to the transaction must equal or exceed 50 percent of the total direct costs attributable to the transaction. This test looks to the cost of the activities described in section 924(e) on an aggregate basis; therefore, it is not necessary that the foreign direct costs of each activity, or of each paragraph of section 924(e), equal or exceed 50 percent of the total direct costs of that activity or paragraph.

(6) Eighty-five percent foreign direct cost test. (i) General rule. To satisfy the requirement of section 924(d)(2), the foreign direct costs of a transaction incurred by the FSC attributable to activities described in each of at least two paragraphs of section 924(e) must equal or exceed 85 percent of the total direct costs attributable to activities described in that paragraph. This test looks to costs of the activities on a paragraph-by-paragraph basis (but not on an activity-by-activity basis). As an example, the foreign direct costs of advertising and sales promotion are aggregated with each other for this purpose, but they are not aggregated with the foreign direct costs of transportation.

(ii) Satisfaction of the 85-percent test. If, after the FSC files its tax return indicating that it has satisfied the 85-percent foreign direct cost test with respect to each of at least two paragraphs of subsection 924(e) and a determination is made by the Commissioner that the foreign direct costs attributable to one or both of the two paragraphs of section 924(e) specified on the return did not equal or exceed 85 percent of the total direct costs attributable to such activities, the FSC may, nonetheless, satisfy the 85-percent foreign direct cost test if the foreign direct costs attributable to any two paragraphs of section 924(e) equal or exceed 85 percent of the total direct costs attributable to those other paragraphs.

(e) Grouping transactions. Generally, the foreign direct cost tests under paragraph (d) of this section are to be applied on a transaction-by-transaction basis. By annual election of the FSC, however, the foreign direct cost tests may be applied on a customer, contract or product or product line grouping basis. Any groupings used must be supported by adequate documentation of performance of activities and costs of activities relating to the groupings used. An election by the FSC to group transactions must be made on its annual income tax return. The FSC may, however, amend its tax return before the expiration of the statute of limitations under section 6501 of the Code to group in a manner different from that elected on its original return.

(1) Standards for groupings. A determination by a FSC as to a grouping will be accepted by the district director if such determination conforms to any of the following standards:

(i) Product or product line groupings. A product or product line grouping may be based either on a recognized trade or industry usage, or on a two digit major grouping (or on any inferior classification or combination of inferior classifications within a major grouping) of the Standard Industrial Classification as prepared by the Statistical Policy Division of the Office of Management and Budget, Executive Office of the President.

(ii) Customer groupings. A customer grouping includes all transactions of the FSC with a particular customer during the FSC's taxable year.

(iii) Contract groupings. A contract grouping includes all transactions of the FSC under a particular contract, including a requirements contract. The tests will be applied to all transactions within a contract grouping during each taxable year of the FSC; however, by election of the FSC, all transactions under a contract that occur in the first or the last year of the contract may be included with, respectively, the next succeeding or the immediately preceding taxable year in applying these tests. For example, if with respect to transactions during the first calendar year of a 5-year contract, a calendar year FSC incurs direct costs attributable to the transactions of $100X for advertising, all of which are foreign direct costs, and $10X for processing of customers orders and for arranging for delivery, $9X (or 90 percent of the total direct costs) of which are foreign direct costs, the FSC has satisfied the 85-percent foreign direct cost test with respect to those transactions for the taxable year. If with respect to transactions during the second year of the contract, the FSC only incurs $18X of direct costs for processing of customer orders and arranging for delivery, $15X (83.3 percent of the total direct costs) of which are foreign direct costs, the FSC may include the transactions from the first year of the contract to meet the 85-percent foreign direct cost test in the second taxable year. Thus, with respect to the transactions in the second year, the FSC satisfies the foreign direct costs test for advertising (because the entire $100X of direct costs are foreign direct costs) and for processing of customer orders and arranging for delivery (because of the $28X of direct costs, $24X or 85.7 percent of the total direct costs are foreign direct costs). If, however, with respect to transactions in the third year, the FSC satisfies the foreign direct costs test, those transactions cannot be included with the transactions in the fourth year. The FSC may aggregate the direct costs in the fourth and fifth years in the same manner as for the first and second years as described above in order to satisfy the 85 percent foreign direct costs test.

(iv) Product or product line groupings within customer or contract groupings. Groupings may be based on product or product line groupings within customer or contract groupings.

(2) Transactions included in a grouping. An election by the FSC to group transactions shall generally apply to all transactions within the scope of that grouping. The election of a grouping, however, applies only to transactions covered by the grouping and, as to transactions not encompassed by the grouping, the determinations may be made on a transaction-by-transaction basis or other grouping basis. For example, the FSC may elect a product grouping with respect to one product and elect the transaction-by-transaction method for another product within the same taxable year. In addition, if a FSC is permitted to apply either the 50-percent or the 85-percent foreign direct cost test on the basis of other types of groupings, such as all transactions with respect to a particular customer, transactions included in those other groupings shall be excluded from product groupings.

(3) Different groupings allowed for different purposes. An election by the FSC to group transactions may be made separately for each of the activities relating to disposition of ex-

port property under section 924(d)(1)(B) or section 924(d)(2). Groupings used for purposes of section 924 will have no bearing on groupings for other purposes. This paragraph (e) does not apply for purposes of section 925.

(f) Exception for foreign military property. *(1) General rule.* The requirements of this section do not apply to any activities performed in connection with foreign military sales except those activities described in section 924(e). The FSC is deemed to have satisfied the requirements of section 924(d)(1)(A).

(2) Example. The principles of paragraph (f)(1) of this section may be illustrated by the following example:

Example. A FSC earns commissions on foreign military sales by its related supplier. All solicitation, negotiation, and contract making activities occur in the United States solely between the related supplier and the United States government. The property is delivered, title passes, and payment is made in the United States in accordance with standard United States government practices. The FSC incurs direct costs in the amount of $155X to process the government's orders and arrange for delivery of the goods, all of which are foreign direct costs. In addition, it incurs foreign direct costs in the amount of $250X for assembling and transmitting its final invoice to the government from outside the U.S. and foreign direct costs of $200X associated with receiving payment from the related supplier in accordance with the rules of § 1.924(e)-1(d)(2)(iii). No other activities occur with respect to the foreign military sales. The FSC has satisfied the 85-percent foreign direct cost test and thus has foreign trading gross receipts with respect to the foreign military sales. The fact that the FSC did not participate outside the United States in any of the sales activities has no bearing on the qualification of the receipts since the FSC is deemed to have met the requirements of § 924(d)(1)(A).

T.D. 8125, 2/13/87.

---

§ 1.924(e)-1 Activities relating to the disposition of export property.

Caution: The Treasury has not yet amended Reg § 1.924(e)-1 to reflect changes made by P.L. 106-519.

(a) Advertising and sales promotion. For purposes of section 924(e), advertising and sales promotion are defined as follows.

(1) Advertising. (i) Advertising defined. (A) General rule. Advertising means the announcement or description of property or services described in section 924(a), in some medium of mass communication (such as radio, television, newspaper, trade journals, mass mailings, or billboards), in order to induce multiple customers or potential customers to buy or rent the property or services from the FSC or related supplier. Advertising is not required to be directed to the general public, but may be focused toward any group of export customers or potential export customers. Advertising except for the advertising described in § 1.924(e)-1(a)(1)(B) must describe one or more specific products or product lines (or services) and identify the product as a product offered by the FSC or related supplier. Advertising intended solely to build a favorable image of a company or group of companies is not included in this definition of advertising. Additionally, advertising primarily directed at customers or potential customers in the United States is not included in this definition of advertising, nor is advertising related to property or services not described in section 924(a).

(B) Special rules for sales to distributors. If the customer is a distributor (whether domestic or foreign, related or unrelated to the FSC), an expense that is incurred by the distributor and charged to the FSC or related supplier as a reduction in the purchase price or as a separate charge for an announcement or description described in paragraph (a)(1)(A) of this section to induce the distributor's customers, potential customers, or the ultimate users to buy or rent the property or services is advertising for these purposes (i) if the FSC incurs 20 percent or more of the total advertising costs of the distributor or (ii) if the FSC pays the total charge of an advertisement either directly or indirectly. For these purposes, a distributor is anyone other than an end user or a final consumer. A FSC may incur direct advertising costs to a foreign end consumer even though the FSC sells to a U.S. distributor.

(ii) Direct costs of advertising. Direct costs of advertising include costs of transmitting, displaying, or distributing the advertising to customers or potential customers and the costs of printing in the case of sales literature, but do not include fees paid to an independent advertising agency to develop the announcement or description, translation costs, or costs of preparing the announcement or description for potential use as advertising. Direct costs of sending sales literature to customers or potential customers may be taken into account as advertising costs as long as the activity is not taken into account for purposes of the sales activity requirements of § 1.924(d)-1(c).

(iii) Location of advertising. (A) General Rule. The location of advertising activity is the place to which the advertising is transmitted, displayed, distributed, mailed, or otherwise conveyed to the customers or potential customers (or in the case of advertising described in paragraph (a)(i)(B) of this section, the distributor's customers, or the ultimate users). For example, a television advertisement that is broadcast to a foreign country constitutes advertising activity outside the United States even though the broadcast signal originates in the United States. Therefore, the cost of that advertising activity is a foreign cost. The FSC may rely upon the distribution statistics of the publisher of print media or the broadcaster of broadcast media through which the advertising is distributed. If the distribution statistics show that 85 percent or more of the readership, radio listeners, or viewership are outside the United States, all direct costs of advertising are considered foreign direct costs of advertising.

(B) Foreign editions of journals, magazines, etc. Costs related to advertising in foreign English editions of U.S. publications as well as advertising in any publication in a foreign language are foreign direct costs.

(C) United States editions. Costs related to advertising in United States publications are not treated as direct costs even if the publication also has a foreign edition in English.

(iv) Second mailings. In general, direct costs of sending sales literature to customers may be treated as solicitation or advertising, but not both. A distinction may be made, however, between a first and second mailing so that one may be treated as advertising and the other may be treated as solicitation. To qualify under this second mailing rule, the two mailings must be generically different items such as a price list and a description of the product itself. An amended price list would not be distinguishable from an original price list and would, therefore, not constitute a second mailing.

(v) Examples. The principles of paragraph (a)(1) of this section may be illustrated by the following examples:

Example (1). The related supplier, under contract with a buy-sell FSC to advertise export product D on the "FSC's" behalf to its foreign unrelated customers, engaged a French advertising agency to develop an advertising campaign to induce French customers to buy the product. As a part of the advertising campaign, the agency places a one-page advertisement in a relevant French trade journal. The advertisement constitutes advertising within the meaning of paragraph (a)(1) of this section.

Example (2). A United States weekly magazine publishes, in addition to its United States edition, a Canadian edition in English and a Mexican edition in Spanish. A FSC incurs costs of $200 X for a one-page display in each of the three editions for a total advertising cost of $600 X. The $200 X cost relating to the advertising in the United States edition is not a direct cost because it relates to United States sales. The total costs of $400 X relating to advertising in the English language Canadian edition and the Spanish language Mexican edition are foreign direct costs.

Example (3). A FSC earns commissions on the sale of export product E by its domestic related supplier to United States distributors for resale to Canadian retail customers. The related supplier, under contract with the FSC to advertise product E, pays an amount equal to 1 percent of its annual gross receipts with respect to product E under a cooperative advertising arrangement with the distributor. The amount, which represents 20 percent of the total advertising costs for product E, is reimbursed by the FSC. The 20-percent amount represents a significant portion of the total advertising costs and thus constitutes advertising within the meaning of paragraph (a)(1)(i) of this section.

Example (4). A FSC mails two items to each customer on its customer list within one taxable year. The first mailing consists of a price list which merely lists the various products by name and provides a price next to each product name. The second mailing consists of a brochure which fully describes and illustrates each product. The two mailings are generically different. Therefore, one mailing may be counted as advertising while the other mailing may be counted as solicitation.

(2) Sales promotion. (i) Sales promotion defined. Sales promotion means an appeal made in person to an export customer or potential export customer for the sale or rental of property or services described in section 924(a), made in the context of a trade show or customer meeting. A customer meeting means a periodic meeting (*e.g.*, quarterly, semi-annual, or annual) in which 10 or more customers or potential customers are reasonably expected to attend. However, for taxable years beginning before February 19, 1987, a customer meeting may, at the option of the taxpayer, mean any meeting with a customer or potential customer regardless of the frequency of the meetings or the number of customers or potential customers in attendance. A meeting, show or event in the United States that is primarily aimed at the export of goods or services described in section 924(a) constitutes sales promotion. Sales promotion does not include an appeal made in the context of any meeting, show or event primarily aimed at U.S. customers or an appeal for the sale or rental of property or services not described in section 924(a). Whether any meeting, show or event is primarily aimed at U.S. customers or at the export of goods or services described in section 924(a) shall be determined by all of the facts and circumstances including the announced objective of the meeting, show or event; the attendees; the location of the meeting, show or event; and the product or special feature of the product.

(ii) Direct costs of sales promotion. Direct costs of sales promotion include costs such as rental of space at trade shows, payments to organizers or other persons hired for the event, rental of display equipment and decorations for the event, and costs of maintaining a showroom. Direct costs of sales promotion also include costs for travel, meals, and lodging for direct sales people attending the event if these costs are paid by the FSC or related supplier. In the case of a customer meeting, direct costs of sales promotion include the costs of materials printed specifically for the meeting and the costs of travel, lodging, and food for both the direct sales people and customers or potential customers attending the meeting. Direct costs of sales promotion do not include the cost of salaries and commissions of direct sales people or the cost of discount coupons, samples of the product, or printed advertising materials that are used for general advertising as well as sales promotion.

(iii) Location of sales promotion. The location of sales promotion activity is the place where the trade show or customer meeting is held.

(iv) Examples. The principles of paragraph (a)(2)(i) of this section may be illustrated by the following examples:

Example (1). The related supplier sells various export products described in section 924(a) to its foreign customers. As a commission agent for the related supplier with respect to such sales, the FSC performs sales promotion. It contracts with the related supplier to serve as its agent for such purposes. To stimulate the sale of its export products, the related supplier conducts semi-annual meetings with the purchasing agents of its customers at its Kansas City headquarters. Ten or more purchasing agents are reasonably expected to attend each meeting. At such meetings, the purchasing agents see the related supplier's manufacturing facilities, visit with its executives, attend technical updates, and see new export products. These semi-annual customer meetings constitute sales promotion within the meaning of paragraph (a)(2)(i) of this section. Direct costs incurred with respect to the customer meetings are U.S. direct costs because the sales promotion activities occur within the United States.

Example (2). Assume the same facts as in *Example (1)*, except that the related supplier exhibits products that only operate on 220 volts at a trade show in the United States. According to the trade show sponsors, the purpose of the show is to increase sales abroad of United States-manufactured products. Since the products exhibited are designed for operation in foreign countries and the purpose of the trade show is to boost sales in those countries, the trade show held in the United States is primarily aimed at the export products described in section 924(a) and not at United States customers. Thus, the trade show constitutes sales promotion within the meaning of paragraph (a)(2)(i) of this section and the direct costs incurred in connection with the trade show are treated as United States direct costs.

(b) Processing of customer orders and arranging for delivery of the export property. For purposes of section 924(e), the processing of customer orders and the arranging for delivery of the export property are defined in paragraph (b)(1) and paragraph (b)(2), respectively, of this section. For taxable years beginning after February 19, 1987, if the FSC performs the activities of processing of customer orders and arranging for delivery of the export property and elects to group its transactions, it is considered to have performed the activities with respect to all transactions in the grouping elected by the FSC under § 1.924(d)-1(e) during the taxable year if it performs the activities of processing of customer orders and arranging for delivery of the export property with respect to customers generating 20 percent or more of foreign trading gross receipts within the elected grouping.

(1) Processing of customer orders. (i) Processing of customer orders defined. The processing of customer orders means notification by the FSC to the related supplier of the order and of the requirements for delivery. The related supplier may have independent knowledge of the order and requirements for delivery. If the FSC does not have a related supplier, the processing of customer orders means communication with the customer by any method such as telephone, telegram, or mail to acknowledge receipt of the order and requirements for delivery. Once the related supplier has been notified by the FSC, or the customer has received an acknowledgement from the FSC, of the order and requirements for delivery, subsequent or prior communications with respect to an order (such as changes in quantity or prospective delivery date) are not included in the definition of processing of customer orders.

(ii) Direct costs of processing customer orders. Direct costs of processing of customer orders include salaries of clerical personnel and costs of telephone, telegram, mail, or other communication media (including the costs of operating transmission equipment).

(iii) Location of processing of customer orders. The location of this activity is the place where the communication is initiated by the FSC.

(iv) Examples. The principles of paragraph (b)(1) of this section may be illustrated by the following examples:

Example (1). A domestic related supplier, using a FSC as its commission agent on the sale of export property to foreign customers, receives an order from one of its foreign customers. Information concerning the receipt of such order and its requirements for delivery are transmitted to the FSC. The FSC from its office outside the United States notifies the related supplier of the order and the requirements for delivery by telex. This notification by the FSC to the related supplier constitutes the processing of the customer's order within the meaning of paragraph (b)(1)(i) of this section. In addition, its direct costs of processing the customer's order are foreign direct costs because the communication is initiated by the FSC from outside the United States.

Example (2). A domestic unrelated supplier manufactures a product which it sells to a buy-sell FSC located in Germany for resale to the FSC's German customers. Upon receiving an order from one of its customers, the FSC telephones the customer from its German office to acknowledge receipt of the order and the requirements for delivery. The acknowledgement constitutes the processing of the customer's order within the meaning of paragraph (b)(1)(i) of this section and the direct costs attributable thereto are foreign direct costs.

(2) Arranging for delivery. (i) Arranging for delivery defined. The arranging for delivery of export property means the taking of necessary steps to have the export property delivered to the customer in accordance with the requirements of the order. Arranging for delivery does not include preparation of shipping documents (*e.g.,* bill of lading) or the property for shipment (*i.e.,* packaging or crating), or shipment of property (*i.e.,* transportation). Arranging for delivery does include communications with a carrier or freight forwarder to provide transportation (as defined in § 1.924(e)-1(c)(1), but without regard to when the commission relationship for purposes of transportation begins) for the export property from the FSC or related supplier to the place where the customer takes possession of the property. Arranging for delivery also includes communications with the customer to notify the customer of the time and place of delivery. The carrier or freight forwarder and the customer may already have knowledge of the information communicated. If the FSC has communicated with the carrier or freight forwarder, where applicable, and the customer to notify it of the time and place of delivery, prior or subsequent communications to either about delivery are not included in the definition of arranging for delivery.

(ii) Direct costs of arranging for delivery. The direct costs of arranging for delivery include salaries of clerical personnel and costs of telephone, telegraph, mail, and other communications media, but do not include any actual shipping costs.

(iii) Location of arranging for delivery. The location of arranging for delivery activity is the place where the activity is initiated by the FSC.

(iv) Examples. The principles of paragraph (b)(2)(i) of this section may be illustrated by the following examples:

Example (1). A FSC earns commissions on the sale of export property by its domestic related supplier to foreign customers. The shipment term of all of the related supplier's sales is F.O.B. (Free on Board) its manufacturing plant in Gary, Indiana. Thus, there is no transportation as defined in § 1.924(e)-1(c)(1) with respect to its sales. From its shipping department at the plant, the related supplier telephones carriers to arrange for delivery. It also notifies the FSC by mail of the time and place of delivery of the customer's orders. The FSC from its office outside the United States transmits the received information to the customers. Because there is no transportation to be arranged, this communication alone by the FSC to the customers to notify them of the time and place of delivery constitutes arranging for delivery within the meaning of paragraph (b)(2)(i) of this section.

Example (2). Assume the same facts as in *Example (1),* except that the shipment term of all of the related supplier's sales is C.I.F. (Cost, Insurance, Freight) and that the commission relationship for transportation begins after the export property leaves the United States customs territory. The related supplier telephones a trucking firm and an overseas carrier from its plant in Gary, Indiana to ascertain information on transporting its property by truck to the docks, and by overseas carrier from the docks to the place where the customer takes possession. Upon receiving the necessary information, the related supplier electronically transmits to the FSC the shipping information and the time and place of delivery to the customer. In addition, it instructs the FSC to communicate the necessary shipping information to the carriers to ensure shipment and to notify the customer of the time and place of delivery. The FSC does both from its office located outside of the United States. The communications by the FSC to the carriers and the customer constitute arranging for delivery within the meaning of paragraph (b)(2)(i) of this section.

(c) Transportation. *(1) Transportation defined.* For purposes of section 924(e), transportation means moving or shipping the export property during the period when the FSC owns or is responsible for the property, or, if the FSC is acting as a commission agent, during the period when the related supplier owns or is responsible for the property but after the commission relationship for purposes of transportation begins (even if the relationship begins after the property leaves the U.S. customs territory). The FSC or related supplier is treated as responsible for the property when it either has title, bears the risk of loss, or insures the property during shipment. Since a commission FSC will not generally have title or bear the risk of loss, it will, nevertheless, satisfy the transportation test if the related supplier has either title, bears the risk of loss, or insures the property during shipment. Examples of methods of shipping which would qualify as transportation include F.O.B. (Free on Board) destination, C.I.F. (Cost, Insurance, Freight), Ex Ship, and Ex Quay, but do not include C. & F. (Cost and Freight) or F.O.B. shipping point.

(2) Direct costs of transportation. The direct costs of transportation include the expenses of shipping, such as fees paid to carriers and freight forwarders, costs of freight insurance, and documentation fees. With respect to fungible commodities, direct costs include only those costs incurred after the goods have been identified to a contract. Transportation costs do not include any of the costs of arranging for delivery. The FSC is considered to engage in transportation activity whenever it pays the costs of shipping the export property and the property is shipped during the period when the FSC owns or is responsible for the property as provided in paragraph (c)(1) of this section. If the customer pays the shipping costs directly, the FSC is not considered to engage in transportation activity. If, however, the FSC pays the shipping costs, the ultimate transfer of those costs to the customer will not disqualify the FSC from engaging in transportation for purposes of section 924(e) regardless of whether the costs are included in the sale price of the export property or separately stated.

(3) Location of transportation. The location of transportation activity is the area over which the property is transported. Thus, the portion of total direct costs of transportation treated as foreign direct costs is the portion attributable to transportation outside the United States, determined on the basis of the ratio of mileage outside the U.S. customs territory to total mileage. For purposes of determining mileage outside U.S. customs territory, goods are treated as leaving U.S. customs territory when they have been tendered to an international carrier for shipment to a foreign location, as long as they are not removed from the custody of the carrier before they reach a point outside U.S. customs territory. The same rule for determining mileage outside the U.S. customs territory will apply to freight forwarders if (i) the forwarder has the risk of loss or is an insurer of the goods, and (ii) the property is shipped on a single bill of lading issued to the FSC or its agent as the shipper.

(4) Examples. The principles of paragraph (c) of this section may be illustrated by the following examples:

Example (1). A buy-sell FSC sells export property to a customer located in Canada. The contract between the FSC and the customer requires that the property be shipped F.O.B. its Canadian destination. Under this shipment term, the FSC holds title and bears the risk of loss until the property is tendered at its Canadian destination. Thus, it is responsible for the property during shipment. The FSC instructs its related supplier to ship the property from its manufacturing facilities in St. Louis. The related supplier negotiates two contracts, one for domestic transportation and the second for foreign transportation. A domestic trucking firm transports the property to the Canadian border where a Canadian trucking company is used to transport the property to its Canadian destination. The documentation fees and the fees for the two trucking firms are paid by the FSC. Because the FSC paid the costs of shipping and the property was shipped during the period when the FSC was responsible for the property, the FSC has engaged in transportation activity, the direct costs of which are the fees paid by the FSC. If 70 percent of the mileage from St. Louis to the Canadian destination is associated with the transportation from the Canadian border to the Canadian destination, 70 percent of the FSC's direct transportation costs are foreign direct costs. If, instead of using two trucking firms, the FSC had tendered the goods to a freight forwarder for shipment to a foreign location and the freight forwarder assumed the risk of loss for the goods and issued a single bill of lading, all of the fees paid by the FSC to the freight forwarder would be foreign direct costs.

Example (2). A related supplier sells export property to its foreign customer in Liverpool, England. The contract between the related supplier and the customer requires that the property be shipped C.I.F. Liverpool. The related supplier engages the FSC as its commission agent with respect to its sales to the customer, requiring the FSC to provide transportation to the customer. The FSC contracts with the related supplier to provide the transportation on behalf of the FSC. The commission agreement between the related supplier and the FSC provides that the FSC's responsibilities with respect to transportation of the export property begins after the property leaves the U.S. customs territory. The related supplier hires a domestic trucking firm to transport the shipment to a New York City port where it is loaded on a cargo ship destined for Liverpool at a total cost of $3,000X, $2,750X of which is allocable to mileage from the U.S. customs territory to Liverpool, England. Because the related supplier insures the property during shipment under C.I.F., the property is shipped during the period when the related supplier is treated as responsible for the property. Thus, the FSC, as the related supplier's commission agent, has satisfied the transportation test. In addition, because the FSC's responsibilities with respect to transportation begins when the property leaves U.S. customs territory, the FSC's payment of $2,750X is a foreign direct cost of transportation. The remaining $250X is not a direct cost of transportation to the FSC because the amount was expended before the commission relationship between the FSC and related supplier began.

Example (3). A FSC earns commissions on sales by the related supplier of export property, all of which falls within a single two-digit SIC group. The related supplier is under contract to the FSC to perform on the FSC's behalf all of the section 924(e) activities attributable to the sales. Of all of the sales made during the year, the FSC has no transportation costs with respect to the sales to customer R because the shipment term is F.O.B. the related supplier's Chicago plant. With respect to the sales to customer S, the FSC ships the property F.O.B. its destination and pays 100 percent of the transportation costs, all of which are foreign direct costs because the commission relationship for transportation begins outside the U.S. customs territory. For purposes of determining whether the FSC has satisfied the 85-percent foreign direct cost test for transportation, the FSC groups the sales by product. Because the transportation costs for sales to customer S are 100-percent foreign direct costs and because there are no transportation costs on sales to customer R, the FSC is considered to have met the 85-percent foreign direct cost test for transportation for all the sales in the single two-digit SIC group.

(d) Determination and transmittal of a final invoice or statement of account and receipt of payment. For purposes of section 924(e), the determination and transmittal of a final invoice or statement of account and the receipt of payment are defined as follows.

(1) Determination and transmittal of a final invoice or statement of account. (i) Definitions. (A) In general. The

determination and transmittal of a final invoice or statement of account means the assembly of either a final invoice or statement of account and the forwarding of that document to the customer. A FSC may elect to send either final invoices or statements of account and disregard any costs of the alternative not elected. For taxable years beginning after February 19, 1987, a special grouping rule is provided. If the FSC assembles and forwards either a statement of account or a final invoice from outside the United States to customers with sales representing 50 percent of the current year foreign trading gross receipts within a product or product line grouping or to customers with sales representing 50 percent of the prior year foreign trading gross receipts within a product or product line grouping utilized for the current year, all other U.S. costs will be disregarded and the FSC will be deemed to have no U.S. costs with respect to the determination and transmittal of a final invoice or statement of account. If, during the prior taxable year, the controlled group of which the FSC is a member had a DISC or interest charge DISC, the FSC may apply the 50 percent rule by taking into account the customers and sales of the DISC or interest charge DISC for the preceding taxable year. If no foreign trading gross receipts (or qualified export receipts for DISC purposes) were received in the prior year either by the FSC or by a DISC or interest charge DISC within the controlled group of which the FSC is a member, the FSC must apply the 50 percent rule taking into account customers and foreign trading gross receipts for the current year. In the event that the 50 percent rule is not satisfied, all costs associated with assembly and forwarding of the selected documents (invoices or statements of account) must be included in the costs attributable to activities described in section 924(e)(4).

(B) Final invoice defined. A final invoice is an invoice upon which payment is made by the customer. A final invoice must contain the customer's name or identifying number and, with respect to the transaction or transactions, the date, product or service, quantity, price, and amount due. In the alternative, a document will be acceptable as a final invoice even though it does not include all of the above listed information if the FSC establishes that the document is considered to be a final invoice under normal commercial practices. An invoice forwarded to the customer after payment has been tendered or received pursuant to a letter of credit as a receipt for payment satisfies this definition.

(C) Statement of account defined. A statement of account is any summary statement forwarded to a customer to inform of, or confirm, the status of transactions occurring within an accounting period during a taxable year that is not less than one month. A statement of account must contain, at a minimum, the customer's name or identifying number, date of the statement of account as of the last day of the accounting period covered by the statement of account and the balance due (even if the balance due is zero). A single final invoice or statement of account can cover more than one transaction with one customer. In the alternative, a document will be accepted as a statement of account even though it does not include all of the above listed information if the FSC establishes that the document is considered a statement of account under normal commercial practice. For these purposes, a document will be considered to be a statement of account under normal commercial practices if it is sent to domestic as well as to export customers in order to inform the customers of the status of transactions during an accounting period. Additional information may be sent separately, such as summary statements forwarded to a related party for purposes of reconciling intercompany accounts for financial reporting requirements. If the information is sent separately, the direct costs associated with the assembly and forwarding of that information are not considered for purposes of section 924(d).

(D) Assembly and forwarding defined. Assembly means folding the documents (where applicable), filing envelopes, and addressing envelopes (if window envelopes are not used). Forwarding means mailing or delivery.

(ii) Direct costs of determination and transmittal of final invoice or statement of account. Direct costs of this activity include costs of office supplies, office equipment, clerical salaries and costs of mailing or other delivery services, if the costs can be identified or associated directly with the assembly and transmittal of a final invoice or statement of account. Costs of establishing a price, or of communicating prices or other billing information between the FSC and a related supplier are not direct costs of this activity. In addition, the costs of preparing and mailing the final invoices or statements of account to the FSC and the costs of accumulating and formatting data for invoicing or statements of account on computer discs, tapes, or some other storage media along with the costs of transmitting or transporting this data to the FSC are not direct costs of this activity.

(iii) Location of determination and transmittal of a final invoice or statement of account. For taxable years beginning before February 19, 1987, the location of this activity is the place where the final invoice or statement of account is assembled for forwarding to the customer or the place from which it is forwarded to the customer. Thus, the forwarding of the final invoice or statement of account from outside the United States is sufficient to source this activity outside the United States. For all other taxable years, the location of this activity is the place where the final invoice or statement of account is both assembled and forwarded to the customer.

(iv) Examples. The principles of paragraph (d)(1) of this section may be illustrated by the following examples, all of which apply to taxable years beginning on or after February 19, 1987.

Example (1). A related supplier sells export property to its foreign customers. The related supplier engages the FSC as its commission agent with respect to the sales, requiring the FSC to determine and transmit final invoices or statements of account to the customers with respect to the sales. Annually, the FSC assembles and forwards statements of account to customers representing 40 percent of current year export sales and 35 percent of prior year sales. The statements are sent from its office outside of the United States. The remaining statements of account are sent from the Albany, New York office of the related supplier. The statements are recognized in its industry as a statement of account. Although the statement does not contain all of the information described in § 1.924(e)-1(d)(1)(i), it is sent to both domestic and foreign customers of the related supplier to inform the customer of the status of its transactions with the related supplier. The document qualifies as a statement of account under § 1.924(e)-1(d)(1)(i); however, the 50 percent test set forth in § 1.924(e)-1(d)-1(d)(1)(i)(A) is not satisfied. Therefore, the FSC must take into account all domestic direct costs attributable to assembly and forwarding of statements of account from its domestic office in determining whether the FSC has satisfied the direct costs test with respect to section 924(e)(4) and § 924(e)-1(d).

Example (2). Employees of a FSC, in the FSC's foreign office, fold and place in envelopes the sheet or sheets that constitute the final invoices provided by the related supplier. In addition, the employees address, affix postage to, and mail the envelopes. These activities constitute the determination and transmittal of the final invoices within the meaning of paragraph (d)(1)(i) of this section and, because the final invoices are assembled and forwarded to the customers from outside the United States, all the direct costs of the activities are foreign direct costs.

Example (3). The related supplier sends to the FSC's foreign office a computer tape to be used to prepare a statement of account. A management company, working under contract with the FSC, transcribes the data to a piece of paper which is a statement of account for purposes of § 1.924(d)(1)(i), folds the document, and fills, affixes postage to, and mails the envelopes. Only the costs performed by the management company under contract with the FSC that constitute the assembly and forwarding of a statement of account under § 1.924(e)-1(d)(1)(i)(D) are direct costs. Therefore, the costs attributable to transcribing the data to a piece of paper are not direct costs for purposes of section 924(e)(4).

(2) Receipt of payment. (i) Receipt of payment defined. Receipt of payment means the crediting of the FSC's bank account by an amount which is not less than 1.83 percent of the gross receipts ("gross receipts amount") associated with the transaction. The FSC's bank account is not credited unless the FSC has the authority to withdraw the amount deposited. Where sales proceeds are factored or where payments from related foreign subsidiaries are netted against amounts owed to these foreign subsidiaries in an intercompany account, crediting of the FSC's bank account with no less than the gross receipts amount of the factoring proceeds or the proceeds, net of offsets, respectively, qualifies as receipt of payment. In addition, where a FSC is precluded from receiving a portion of the proceeds of the export transaction, the FSC may satisfy receipt of payment by receiving no less than the gross receipts amount of the remaining portion of the proceeds in its bank account. In the case of advance or progress payments, each payment constitutes a payment for receipt of payment purposes.

(ii) Direct costs of receipt of payment. Direct costs of receiving payment include the expenses of maintaining a bank account of the FSC in which payment is deposited, any fees or service charges incurred for converting the payment into U.S. currency, and any transfer fees incurred with respect to the transfer of funds into and out of the FSC's bank account in accordance with the 35 calendar day rule in paragraph (d)(2)(iii) of this section. The transfer fees and the fees or service charges incurred for currency conversion are considered to be foreign direct costs of receiving payment; however, exchange losses are not costs of receiving payment.

(iii) Location of receipt of payment. The location of this activity is the office of the banking institution at which the account is maintained. If payment is made by the purchaser directly to the FSC or the related supplier in the United States, and the FSC or related supplier transfers the gross receipts amount associated with the transaction to a bank account of the FSC outside the United States after receipt of payment (*i.e.,* cash, check, wire transfer, etc.), but no later than 35 calendar days after receipt of good funds (*i.e.,* the clearance of the check) the FSC is considered to have received payment outside the United States. Therefore, all transfer fees and the costs of the foreign bank account are treated as foreign direct costs. The United States bank costs are disregarded. If, however, the related supplier does not transfer the gross receipts amount within 35 calendar days, United States bank costs are not disregarded and are domestic direct costs. In either case, the transfer costs, currency conversion charges, and foreign bank costs remain foreign direct costs. The preceding rules apply both to commission FSCs and buy-sell FSCs.

(iv) Examples. The principles of paragraph (d)(2) of this section may be illustrated by the following examples:

Example (1). A FSC earns commissions on sales of export property by its related supplier. The related supplier manufactures and sells its export property to its foreign subsidiaries for resale in their respective countries. From time to time, the foreign subsidiaries will return products to the related supplier for credit and, from time to time, the foreign subsidiaries purchase products in their respective countries and sell such products to the related supplier. These transactions result in various amounts being owed to the foreign subsidiaries. Each month the various inter-company obligations are reviewed. The result of such review of inter-company indebtedness is a netting out of the various intercompany liabilities on the books, to the extent possible, and a flow of funds for the net obligation. Due to the nature of these transactions, the amounts owed by the foreign subsidiaries exceed the amounts which the related supplier owes to the foreign subsidiaries. The gross receipts amount (*i.e.,* 1.83 percent of this net amount) is credited to the FSC's bank account. This constitutes receipt of payment for purposes of paragraph (d)(2)(i) of this section.

Example (2). In a leveraged lease transaction, a FSC-lessor obtains purchase financing from a lending institution. The lending institution retains a security interest in the proceeds and requires that a portion of each rental payment be paid by the lessee directly to the lending institution. Since the FSC is precluded from receiving a portion of the proceeds of the export transaction, the FSC may satisfy the receipt of payment requirement by receiving the gross receipts amount with respect to the remaining proceeds.

Example (3). A buy-sell FSC sells its export property to a foreign customer and is paid by means of a "draw-down" letter of credit. Over a substantial period of time prior to delivery of the export property, amounts are advanced to the FSC under the letter of credit. At delivery, the remaining amount available is paid. Each payment made to the FSC constitutes a payment for receipt of payment purposes and thus the gross receipts amount related to each payment must be credited to the FSC's bank account.

Example (4). An FSC earns commissions on sales of export property by its related supplier. The related supplier regularly collects payments from its foreign customers in a San Francisco bank account and, after the San Francisco bank has collected on the checks, transfers, within 35 calendar days, the gross receipts amounts from its New York bank account to the FSC's bank account located outside the United States. The FSC incurred transfer fees of $160X in addition to a fee of $35X for the maintenance of the FSC's bank account outside the United States during the 35 calendar day period. The maintenance fee relating to the United States bank account for the 35 calendar day period is $45X. The receipt of payment test is met because the gross receipts amounts are transferred after payment but within 35 calendar days to the FSC's bank account located outside the United States. The transfer fees of $160X and the maintenance fee of $35X relating to the FSC's foreign bank account are foreign direct costs. The $45X maintenance fee related to the United States bank account is not a direct cost. If the gross receipts amounts had not been transferred to the FSC's foreign bank account within 35 calendar days, the $45X maintenance fee related to the United States bank account would be considered a United States direct cost. The transfer fee of $160X and the maintenance fee of $35X relating to the

FSC's foreign bank account, however, would, nonetheless, be considered as foreign direct costs. The same funds received in San Francisco need not be transferred to the FSC's foreign bank account because money is fungible. For the same reason, the gross receipts amounts need not be transferred from the same bank account in which the payments are received.

(e) Assumption of credit risk. *(1) Assumption of credit risk defined.* For purposes of section 924(e), the assumption of credit risk means bearing the economic risk of nonpayment with respect to a transaction. If the FSC is acting as a commission agent for the related supplier, this risk is borne by the FSC if the commission contract transfers the costs of the economic risk of nonpayment with respect to the transaction from the related supplier to the FSC. The FSC may elect on its annual return to bear the economic risk of nonpayment with respect to its transactions during a taxable year by either—

(i) Assuming the risk of a bad debt in accordance with the rules of paragraph (e)(4)(i) of this section,

(ii) Obtaining insurance to cover nonpayment,

(iii) Investigating credit of a customer or a potential customer,

(iv) Factoring trade receivables, or

(v) Selling by means of letters of credit or banker's acceptances.

Only the alternative elected to be performed by the FSC during a taxable year is relevant for purposes of section 924(d). For example, if a buy-sell FSC elects to bear the economic risk of nonpayment with respect to its transaction during a taxable year by assuming the risk of a bad debt in accordance with the rules of paragraph (e)(4)(i) of this section, and also factors the transaction's trade receivables, only the direct costs of assuming the risk of a bad debt are relevant for purposes of section 924(d). For purposes of this paragraph, a potential customer is an unrelated person who is engaged in the purchase or sale of export property on whom an investigation is performed, but with whom no export sales contract is executed.

(2) Direct costs of assumption of credit risk. (i) With respect to assuming the risk of a bad debt, the direct costs of the assumption of credit risk in the case of a buy-sell FSC include debts that become uncollectible and charges taken into account in determining additions to bad debt reserves of the FSC. In the case of a commission FSC, the direct costs of the assumption of credit risk include the assumption of the debts and charges of the related supplier attributable to export sales that are allowed as deductions under section 166.

(ii) With respect to insurance, the direct costs of the assumption of credit risk are the costs of obtaining insurance against the risk of nonpayment. Qualifying insurance must be obtained from an unrelated insurer and must cover the risk of nonpayment due to default and bankruptcy by the purchaser. Insurance obtained from a related insurer, or insurance that covers default and bankruptcy due to risks of war or political unrest without covering ordinary default or bankruptcy is not sufficient.

(iii) With respect to investigating credit, the direct costs of assumption of credit risk are the external costs of investigating credit for customers or potential customers, including costs of membership in a credit agency or association for that purpose (but not the costs of approving credit by an internal credit agency).

(iv) With respect to factoring trade receivables, the direct costs of assumption of credit risk are the costs of factoring trade receivables of related and unrelated customers (e.g. the amount of the discount and the fees relating to factoring).

(v) With respect to letters of credit or banker's acceptances, the direct costs of assumption of credit risk are the costs of letters of credit or banker's acceptances and the documentary collection costs.

(3) Location of assumption of credit risk. The location of the activity of assumption of credit risk is the location of the customer or obligor whose payment is at risk, except that the location of investigating credit is the location of the credit agency or association performing the investigation. A foreign branch of a United States corporation and a foreign office of the United States government are not foreign obligors for purposes of this test. A foreign branch of a United States credit investigation agency or association, however, is treated as located outside the United States.

(4) Special rules. (i) Assuming the risk of a bad debt.

(A) In general. If a FSC chooses to bear the economic risk of nonpayment by assuming the risk of a bad debt with respect to a transaction or grouping of transactions and an actual bad debt loss on a foreign trading gross receipt is not incurred in any three consecutive years, the FSC will be deemed to have performed this activity during the first two years of the three year period. For the third year, the FSC will not be deemed to have performed this activity and must satisfy the 85 percent foreign direct costs test by satisfying any two paragraphs included within section 924(e) other than assumption of credit risk activity under section 924(e)(5). An actual bad debt loss will only satisfy the activity test with respect to a single three consecutive year period.

(B) Example. The principles of this paragraph may be illustrated by the following example:

Example. In year 1, a related supplier of a commission FSC incurs a bad debt with respect to foreign trading gross receipts owed by a foreign obligor. This expense is the only bad debt incurred with respect to foreign trading gross receipts in year 1. Therefore, the direct costs for the bearing of the economic risk of nonpayment for year 1 are all foreign direct costs and the 85-percent test is satisfied. In year 2, the FSC incurs a bad debt with respect to a U.S. broker/consolidator. The direct costs for year 2 are U.S. direct costs and, therefore, the 85-percent test is not satisfied. No bad debt is incurred in year 3. Because a bad debt with respect to a foreign obligor is incurred in year 1, the FSC is deemed to have satisfied the economic risk of nonpayment for each of years 1, 2 and 3.

(ii) Grouping with respect to other risk activities. For taxable years beginning after February 19, 1987, if a FSC elects to bear the economic risk of nonpayment by performing one of the activities described in paragraph (e) of this section and elects to group transactions, it is considered to have performed the elected activity with respect to all transactions within the group during the taxable year if it performs the activity in accordance with the following rules. If a FSC elects to factor trade receivables, at least 20 percent of the face amount of a group's receivables must be factored. If a FSC elects to sell by means of letters of credit or banker's acceptances, a fee must be incurred with respect to 20 percent of the foreign trading gross receipts attributable to sales within the group. If the FSC elects to obtain insurance to cover nonpayment, 20 percent of the face amount of receivables attributable to sales included in the § 1.924(d)-1(e) grouping elected by the FSC must be insured. If a FSC elects to investigate credit of customers or potential customers, 20 percent of new or potential customers for which a credit investigation is performed must be investigated.

T.D. 8125, 2/13/87.

§ 1.925(a)-1 Transfer pricing rules for FSCs.

(a) through (c)(7) [Reserved]. For further guidance, see § 1.925(a)-1T(a) through (c)(7).

(c) *(8) Grouping transactions.* (i) The determinations under this section are to be made on a transaction-by-transaction basis. However, at the annual choice made by the related supplier if the administrative pricing methods are used, some or all of these determinations may be made on the basis of groups consisting of products or product lines. The election to group transactions shall be evidenced on Schedule P of the FSC's U.S. income tax return for the taxable year. No untimely or amended returns filed later than one year after the due date of the FSC's timely filed (including extensions) U.S. income tax return will be allowed to elect to group, to change a grouping basis, or to change from a grouping basis to a transaction-by-transaction basis (collectively "grouping redeterminations"). The rule of the previous sentence is applicable to taxable years beginning after December 31, 1999. For any taxable year beginning before January 1, 2000, a grouping redetermination may be made no later than the due date of the FSC's timely filed (including extensions) U.S. income tax return for the FSC's first taxable year beginning on or after January 1, 2000. Notwithstanding the time limits for filing grouping redeterminations otherwise specified in the previous three sentences, a grouping redetermination may be made at any time during the one-year period commencing upon notification of the related supplier by the Internal Revenue Service of an examination, provided that both the FSC and the related supplier agree to extend their respective statutes of limitations for assessment by one year. In addition, any grouping redeterminations made under this paragraph must meet the requirements under § 1.925(a)-1T(e)(4) with respect to redeterminations other than grouping. The language "or grouping of transactions" is removed from the fourth sentence of § 1.925(a)-1T(e)(4), applicable to taxable years beginning after December 31, 1997. See also § 1.925(b)-1T(b)(3)(i).

(ii) through (f) [Reserved] For further guidance, see § 1.925(a)-1T(c)(8)(ii) through (f).

(g) Effective date. The provisions of this section apply on or after March 2, 2001.

T.D. 8944, 3/2/2001.

§ 1.925(a)-1T Transfer pricing rules for FSCs (temporary).

Caution: The Treasury has not yet amended Reg § 1.925(a)-1T to reflect changes made by P.L. 106-519.

(a) Scope. *(1) Transfer pricing rules.* In the case of a transaction described in paragraph (b) of this section, section 925 permits a related party to a FSC to determine the allowable transfer price charged the FSC (or commission paid to the FSC) by its choice of the three transfer pricing methods described in paragraphs (c)(2), (3), and (4) of this section: The "1.83 percent" gross receipts method and the "23 percent" combined taxable income method (the administrative pricing rules) of section 925(a)(1) and (2), respectively, and the section 482 method of section 925(a)(3). (Any further reference to a FSC in this section shall include a small FSC unless indicated otherwise.) Subject to the special no-loss rule of § 1.925(a)-1T(e)(1)(iii), any, or all, of the transfer pricing methods may be used in the same taxable year of the FSC for separate transactions (or separate groups of transactions). If either of the administrative pricing methods (the gross receipts method or combined taxable income method) is applied to a transaction, the Commissioner may not make distributions, apportionments, or allocations as provided by section 482 and the regulations under that section. The transfer price charged the FSC (or the commission paid to the FSC) on a transaction with a person that is not a related party to the FSC may be determined in any manner agreed to by the FSC and that person. However, the Commissioner will use special scrutiny to determine whether a person selling export property to an FSC (or paying a commission to an FSC) is a related party to the FSC with respect to a transaction if the FSC earns a profit on the transaction in excess of the profit it would have earned had the administrative pricing rules applied to the transaction.

(2) Special rules. For rules as to certain "incomplete transactions" and for computing full costing combined taxable income, see paragraphs (c)(5) and (6) of this section. For a special rule as to cooperatives and computation of their combined taxable incomes, see paragraph (c)(7) of this section. Grouping of transactions for purposes of applying the administrative pricing method chosen is provided for by paragraph (c)(8) of this section. The rules in paragraph (c) of this section are directly applicable only in the case of sales or exchanges of export property to an FSC for resale, and are applicable by analogy to leases, commissions, and services as provided in paragraph (d) of this section. For a rule providing for the recovery of the FSC's costs in an overall loss situation, see paragraph (e)(1)(i) of this section. Paragraph (e)(2) of this section provides for the applicability of section 482 to resales by the FSC to related persons or to sales between related persons prior to the sale to the FSC. Paragraph (e)(3) of this section provides for the creation of receivables if the transfer price, rental payment, commission or payment for services rendered is not paid by the due date of the FSC's income tax return for the taxable year under section 6072(b), including extensions provided for by section 6081. Provisions for the subsequent determination and further adjustment to the relevant amounts are set forth in paragraphs (e)(4) and (5) of this section. Paragraph (f) of this section has several examples illustrating the provisions of this section. Section 1.925(b)-1T prescribes the marginal costing rules authorized by section 925(b)(2). Section 1.927(d)-2T provides definitions of related supplier and related party.

(3) Performance of substantial economic functions. (i) Administrative pricing methods. The application of the administrative pricing methods of section 925(a)(1) and (2) does not depend on the extent to which the FSC performs substantial economic functions beyond those required by section 925(c). See paragraph (b)(2)(ii) of this section and § 1.924(a)-1T(i)(1).

(ii) Section 482 method. In order to apply the section 482 method of section 925(a)(3), the arm's length standards of section 482 and the regulations under that section must be satisfied. In applying the standards of section 482, all of the rules of section 482 will apply. Thus, if the FSC would not be recognized as a separate entity, it would also not be recognized on application of the section 482 method. Similarly, if a FSC performs no substantial economic function with respect to a transaction, no income will be allocable to the

FSC under the section 482 method. See § 1.924(a)-1T(i)(2). If a related supplier performs services under contract with a FSC, the FSC will not be deemed to have performed substantial economic functions for purposes of the section 482 method unless it compensates the related supplier under the provisions of § 1.482-2(b)(1) through (7). See § 1.925(a)-1T(c)(6)(ii) for the applicability of the regulations under section 482 in determination of the FSC's profit under the administrative pricing methods.

(b) Transactions to which section 925 applies. *(1) In general.* The transfer pricing methods of section 925 (the administrative pricing methods and the section 482 method) will apply, generally, only if a transaction, or group of transactions, gives rise to foreign trading gross receipts (within the meaning of section 924(a) and § 1.924(a)-1T) to the FSC (or small FSC, as defined in section 922(b) and § 1.921-2(b) (Q&A3)). However, the transfer pricing methods will apply as well if the FSC is acting as commission agent for a related supplier with regard to a transaction, or group of transactions, on which the related supplier is the principal if the transaction, or group of transactions, would have resulted in foreign trading gross receipts had the FSC been the principal

(2) Application of the transfer pricing rules. (i) Section 482 method. The section 482 transfer pricing method may be applied to any transaction between a related supplier and a FSC if the requirements of paragraph (a)(3)(ii) of this section have been met.

(ii) Administrative pricing methods. The administrative pricing methods may be applied in situations in which the FSC is either the principal or commission agent on the transaction, or group of transactions, only if the requirements of section 925(c) are met. Section 925(c) requires that the FSC performs all the activities described in subsections (d)(1)(A) and (e) of section 924 that are attributable to a particular transaction, or group of transactions. The FSC need not perform any activities with respect to a particular transaction merely to comply with section 925(c) if that activity would not have been performed but for the requirements of that subsection. The FSC need not perform all of the activities outside the United States. None of the activities need be performed outside the United States by a small FSC. Rather than the FSC itself performing the activities required by section 925(c), another person under contract, written or oral, directly or indirectly, with the FSC may perform the activities (see § 1.924(d)-1(b)). If a related supplier is performing the required activities on behalf of the FSC with regard to a transaction, or group of transactions, the requirements of section 925(c) will be met if the FSC pays the related supplier an amount equal to the direct and indirect expenses related to the required activities. See paragraph (c)(6)(ii) of this section for the amount of compensation due the related supplier. The payment made to the related supplier must be reflected on the FSC's books and must be taken into account in computing the FSC's and related supplier's combined taxable income. If it is determined that the related supplier was not compensated for all the expenses related to the required activities or if the entire payment is not reflected on the FSC's books or in computing combined taxable income, the administrative pricing methods may be used but proper adjustments will be made to the FSC's and related supplier's books or income. At the election of the FSC and related supplier, the requirements of section 925(c) will be deemed to have been met if the related supplier is paid by the FSC an amount equal to all of the costs under paragraph (c)(6)(iii)(D) of this section (limited by paragraph (c)(6)(ii) of this section) related to the export sale, other than expenses relating to activities performed directly by the FSC or by a person other than the related supplier, and if that payment is reflected on the FSC's books and in computing the FSC's and related supplier's combined taxable income on the transaction, or group of transactions. If it is determined that the related supplier was not compensated for all its expenses or if the entire payment is not reflected on the FSC's books or in computing combined taxable income, the administrative pricing methods may be used but proper adjustments will be made to the FSC's and related supplier's books or income. All activities that are performed in connection with foreign military sales are considered to be performed by the FSC, or under contract with the FSC, if they are performed by the United States government even though the United States government has not contracted for the performance of those activities. All actual costs incurred by the FSC and related supplier in connection with the performance of those activities must be taken into account, however, in determining the combined taxable income of the FSC and related supplier.

(iii) Allowable transactions for purposes of the administrative pricing methods. If the required performance of activities has been met, the administrative pricing methods may be applied to a transaction between a related supplier and an FSC only in the following circumstances.

(A) The related supplier sells export property (as defined in section 927(a) and § 1.927(a)-1T) to the FSC for resale or the FSC acts as a commission agent for the related supplier on sales by the related supplier of export property to third parties, whether or not related parties. For purposes of this section, references to sales include references to exchanges or other dispositions.

(B) The related supplier leases export property to the FSC for sublease for a comparable period with comparable terms of payment, or the FSC acts as commission agent for the related supplier on leases of export property by the related supplier, to third parties whether or not related parties.

(C) Services are furnished by an FSC as principal or by a related supplier if an FSC is a commission agent for the related supplier which are related and subsidiary to any sale or lease by the FSC, acting as principal or commission agent, of export property under subdivision (iii)(A) and (B) of this paragraph.

(D) Engineering or architectural services for construction projects located (or proposed for location) outside of the United States are furnished by the FSC if the FSC is acting as principal, or by the related supplier if the FSC is a commission agent for the related supplier, with respect to the furnishing of the services to a third party whether or not a related party.

(E) The FSC acting as principal, or the related supplier where the FSC is a commission agent, furnishes managerial services in furtherance of the production of foreign trading gross receipts of an unrelated FSC or the production of qualified export receipts of an unrelated interest charge DISC.

This subdivision (iii)(E) shall not apply for any taxable year unless at least 50 percent of the gross receipts for such taxable year of the FSC or of the related supplier, whichever party furnishes the managerial services, is derived from activities described in subdivisions (iii)(A), (B), or (C) of this paragraph.

(c) Transfer price for sales of export property. *(1) In general.* Under this paragraph, rules are prescribed for computing the allowable price for a transfer from a related supplier to an FSC in the case of a sale, described in paragraph (b)(2)(iii)(A) of this section, of export property.

(2) The "1.83 percent" gross receipts method. Under the gross receipts method of pricing, described in section 925(a)(1), the transfer price for a sale by the related supplier to the FSC is the price as a result of which the profit derived by the FSC from the sale will not exceed 1.83 percent of the foreign trading gross receipts of the FSC derived from the sale of the export property. Pursuant to section 925(d), the amount of profit derived by the FSC under this method may not exceed twice the amount of profit determined under, at the related supplier's election, either the combined taxable income method of § 1.925(a)-1T(c)(3) or the marginal costing rules of § 1.925(b)-1T. For FSC taxable years beginning after December 31, 1986, if the related supplier elects to determine twice the profit determined under the combined taxable income method using the marginal costing rules, because of the no-loss rule of § 1.925(a)-1T(e)(1)(i), the profit that may be earned by the FSC is limited to 100% of the full costing combined taxable income as determined under § 1.925(a)-1T(c)(3) and (6). Interest or carrying charges with respect to the sale are not foreign trading gross receipts.

(3) The "23 percent" combined taxable income method. Under the combined taxable income method of pricing, described in section 925(a)(2), the transfer price for a sale by the related supplier to the FSC is the price as a result of which the profit derived by the FSC from the sale will not exceed 23 percent of the full costing combined taxable income (as defined in paragraph (c)(6) of this section) of the FSC and the related supplier attributable to the foreign trading gross receipts from such sale.

(4) Section 482 method. If the methods of paragraph (c)(2) and (3) of this section are inapplicable to a sale or if the related supplier does not choose to use them, the transfer price for a sale by the related supplier to the FSC is to be determined on the basis of the sales price actually charged but subject to the rules provided by section 482 and the regulations for that section and by § 1.925(a)-1T(a)(3)(ii).

(5) Incomplete transactions. (i) For purposes of the gross receipts and combined taxable income methods, if export property which the FSC purchased from the related supplier is not resold by the FSC before the close of either the FSC's taxable year or the taxable year of the related supplier during which the export property was purchased by the FSC from the related supplier, then—

(A) The transfer price of the export property sold by the FSC during that year shall be computed separately from the transfer price of the export property not sold by the FSC during that year.

(B) With respect to the export property not sold by the FSC during that year, the transfer price paid by the FSC for that year shall be the related supplier's cost of goods sold (see paragraph (c)(6)(iii)(C) of this section) with respect to the property.

(C) For the subsequent taxable year during which the export property is resold by the FSC, an additional amount shall be paid by the FSC (to be treated as income for the later year in which it is received or accrued by the related supplier) equal to the excess of the amount which would have been the transfer price under this section had the transfer to the FSC by the related supplier and the resale by the FSC taken place during the taxable year of the FSC during which it resold the property over the amount already paid under subdivision (B) of this paragraph.

(D) The time and manner of payment of transfer prices required by subdivisions (i)(B) and (C) of this paragraph shall be determined under paragraphs (e)(3), (4) and (5) of this section.

(ii) For purposes of this paragraph, a FSC may determine the year in which it received property from a related supplier and the year in which it resells property in accordance with the method of identifying goods in its inventory properly used under section 471 or section 472 (relating respectively to the general rule for inventories and to the rule for LIFO inventories). Transportation expense of the related supplier in connection with a transaction to which this paragraph applies shall be treated as an item of cost of goods sold with respect to the property if the related supplier includes the cost of intracompany transportation between its branches, divisions, plants, or other units in its cost of goods sold (see paragraph (c)(6)(iii)(C) of this section).

(6) Full costing combined taxable income. (i) In general. For purposes of section 925 and this section, if a FSC is the principal on the sale of export property, the full costing combined taxable income of the FSC and its related supplier from the sale is the excess of the foreign trading gross receipts of the FSC from the sale over the total costs of the FSC and related supplier including the related supplier's cost of goods sold and its and the FSC's noninventoriable costs (see § 1.471-11(c)(2)(ii)) which relate to the foreign trading gross receipts. Interest or carrying charges with respect to the sale are not foreign trading gross receipts.

(ii) Section 482 applicability. Combined taxable income under this paragraph shall be determined after taking into account under paragraph (e)(2) of this section all adjustments required by section 482 with respect to transactions to which the section is applicable. If a related supplier performs services under contract with a FSC, the FSC shall compensate the related supplier an arm's length amount under the provisions of § 1.482-2(b)(1) through (6). Section 1.482-2(b)(7), which provides that an arm's length charge shall not be deemed equal to costs or deductions with respect to services which are an integral part of the business activity of either the member rendering the services (i.e., the related supplier) or the member receiving the benefit of the services (i.e., the FSC), shall not apply if the administrative pricing methods of section 925(a)(1) and (2) are used to compute the FSC's profit and if the related supplier is the person rendering the services. Section 1.482-2(b)(7) shall apply, however, if a related person other than the related supplier is the person rendering the services or if the section 482 method of section 925(a)(3) is used to compute the FSC's profit. See § 1.925(a)-1T(a)(3)(ii). For a special rule for computation of combined taxable income where the related supplier is a qualified cooperative shareholder of the FSC, see paragraph (c)(7) of this section.

(iii) Rules for determination of gross receipts and total costs. In determining the gross receipts of the FSC and the total costs of the FSC and related supplier which relate to such gross receipts, the rules set forth in subdivisions (iii)(A) through (E) of this paragraph shall apply.

(A) Subject to the provisions of subdivisions (iii)(B) through (E) of this paragraph, the methods of accounting used by the FSC and related supplier to compute their taxable incomes will be accepted for purposes of determining the amounts of items of income and expense (including depreciation) and the taxable year for which those items are taken into account.

(B) A FSC may, generally, choose any method of accounting permissible under section 446(c) and the regulations under that section. However, if a FSC is a member of a controlled group (as defined in section 927(d)(4) and § 1.924(a)-1T(h)), the FSC may not choose a method of accounting which, when applied to transactions between the FSC and other members of the controlled group, will result in a material distortion of the income of the FSC or of any other member of the controlled group. Changes in the method of accounting of a FSC are subject to the requirements of section 446(e) and the regulations under that section.

(C) Cost of goods sold shall be determined in accordance with the provisions of § 1.61-3. See sections 471 and 472 and the regulations thereunder with respect to inventories. With respect to property to which an election under section 631 applies (relating to cutting of timber considered as a sale or exchange), cost of goods sold shall be determined by applying § 1.631-1(d)(3) and (e) (relating to fair market value as of the beginning of the taxable year of the standing timber cut during the year considered as its cost).

(D) Costs (other than cost of goods sold) which shall be treated as relating to gross receipts from sales of export property are the expenses, losses, and deductions definitely related, and therefore allocated and apportioned thereto, and a ratable part of any other expenses, losses, or deductions which are not definitely related to any class of gross income, determined in a manner consistent with the rules set forth in § 1.861-8. The deduction for depletion allowed by section 611 relates to gross receipts from sales of export property and shall be taken into account in computing the combined taxable income of the FSC and its related supplier.

(7) Cooperatives and combined taxable income method. If a qualified cooperative, as defined in section 1381(a), sells export property to a FSC of which it is a shareholder, the combined taxable income of the FSC and the cooperative shall be computed without taking into account deductions allowed under section 1382(b) and (c) for patronage dividends, per-unit retain allocations and nonpatronage distributions. The FSC and cooperative must take into account, however, when computing combined taxable income, the cooperative's cost of goods sold, or cost of purchases.

(8) Grouping transactions. (i) [Reserved] For further guidance, see § 1.925(a)-1(c)(8)(i).

(ii) A determination by the related supplier as to a product or a product line will be accepted by a district director if such determination conforms to either of the following standards: Recognized trade or industry usage, or the two-digit major groups (or any inferior classifications or combinations thereof, within a major group) of the Standard Industrial Classification as prepared by the Statistical Policy Division of the Office of Management and Budget, Executive Office of the President. A product shall be included in only one product line for purposes of this section if a product otherwise falls within more than one product line classification.

(iii) A choice by the related supplier to group transactions for a taxable year on a product or product line basis shall apply to all transactions with respect to that product or product line consummated during the taxable year. However, the choice of a product or product line grouping applies only to transactions covered by the grouping and, as to transactions not encompassed by the grouping, the determinations are to be made on a transaction-by-transaction basis. For example, the related supplier may choose a product grouping with respect to one product and use the transaction-by-transaction method for another product within the same taxable year. Sale transactions may not be grouped, however, with lease transactions.

(iv) For purposes of this section, transactions involving military property, as defined in section 923(a)(5) and § 1.923-1T(b)(3)(ii), may be grouped only with other military property included within the same product or product line grouping determined under the standards of subdivision (8)(ii) of this paragraph. Non-military property included within a product or product line grouping which includes military property may be grouped, at the election of the related supplier, under the general grouping rules of subdivisions (i) through (iii) of this paragraph.

(v) A special grouping rule applies to agricultural and horticultural products sold to the FSC by a qualified cooperative if the FSC satisfies the requirements of section 923(a)(4). Section 923(a)(4) increases the amount of the FSC's exempt foreign trade income with regard to sales of these products, see § 1.923-1T(b)(2). This special grouping rule provides that if the related supplier elects to group those products that no other export property may be included within that group. Export property which would have been grouped under the general grouping rules of subdivisions (i) through (iii) of this paragraph with the export property covered by this special grouping rule may be grouped, however, at the election of the related supplier, under the general grouping rules.

(vi) For rules as to grouping certain related and subsidiary services, see paragraph (d)(3)(ii) of this section.

(vii) If there is more than one FSC (or more than one small FSC) within a controlled group of corporations, the same grouping of transactions, if any, must be used by all FSCs (or small FSCs) within the controlled group. If the same grouping of transactions is required by this subdivision, and if grouping is elected, the same transfer pricing method must be used to determine each FSC's (or small FSC's) taxable income with respect to that grouping.

(viii) The product or product line groups that are established for purposes of determining combined taxable income may be different from the groups that are established with regard to economic processes (see § 1.924(d)-1(e)).

(d) Rules under section 925(a)(1) and (2) for transactions other than sales by an FSC. The following rules are prescribed for purposes of applying the gross receipts method or combined taxable income method to transactions other than sales by an FSC.

(1) Leases. In the case of a lease of export property by a related supplier to a FSC for sublease by the FSC, the amount of rent the FSC must pay to the related supplier shall be computed in a manner consistent with the rules in paragraph (c) of this section for computing the transfer price in the case of sales and resales of export property under the gross receipts method or combined taxable income method. Transactions may not be so grouped on a product or product line basis under the rules of paragraph (c)(8) of this section as to combine in any one group of transactions both lease transactions and sale transactions.

(2) Commissions. If any transaction to which section 925 applies is handled on a commission basis for a related supplier by a FSC and if commissions paid to the FSC give rise to gross receipts to the related supplier which would have been foreign trading gross receipts under section 924(a) had the FSC made the sale directly then—

(i) The administrative pricing methods of section 925(a)(1) and (2) may be used to determine the FSC's commission income only if the requirements of section 925(c) (relating to activities that must be performed in order to use the administrative pricing methods) are met, see § 1.925(a)-1T(b)(2)(ii).

(ii) The amount of the income that may be earned by the FSC in any year is the amount, computed in a manner consistent with paragraph (c) of this section, which the FSC would have been permitted to earn under the gross receipts method, the combined taxable income method, or the section 482 method if the related supplier had sold (or leased) the property or service to the FSC and the FSC had in turn sold (or subleased) to a third party, whether or not a related party.

(iii) The combined taxable income of a FSC and the related supplier from the transaction is the excess of the related supplier's gross receipts from the transaction which would have been foreign trading gross receipts had the sale been made by the FSC directly over the related supplier's and the FSC's total costs, excluding the commission paid or payable to the FSC, but including the related supplier's cost of goods sold and its and the FSC's noninventoriable costs (see § 1.471-11(c)(2)(ii)) which relate to the gross receipts from the transaction. The related supplier's gross receipts for purposes of the administrative pricing methods shall be reduced by carrying charges, if any, as computed under § 1.927(d)-1(a)(Q&A2). These carrying charges shall remain income of the related supplier.

(iv) The maximum commission the FSC may charge the related supplier is the amount of income determined under subdivisions (ii) and (iii) of this paragraph plus the FSC's total costs for the transaction as determined under paragraph (c)(6) of this section.

(3) Receipts from services. (i) Related and subsidiary services attributable to the year of the export transaction. The gross receipts for related and subsidiary services described in paragraph (b)(2)(iii)(C) of this section shall be treated as part of the receipts from the export transaction to which such services are related and subsidiary, but only if, under the arrangement between the FSC and its related supplier and the accounting method otherwise employed by the FSC, the income from such services is includible for the same taxable year as income from such export transaction.

(ii) Other services. Income from the performance of related and subsidiary services will be treated as a separate type of income if subdivision (i) of this paragraph does not apply. Income from the performance of engineering and architectural services and certain managerial services, as defined in paragraphs (b)(2)(iii)(D) and (E), respectively, of this section, will in all situations be treated as separate types of income. If this subdivision (ii) applies, the amount of taxable income which the FSC may derive for any taxable year shall be determined under the arrangement between the FSC and its related supplier and shall be computed in a manner consistent with the rules in paragraph (c) of this section for computing the transfer price in the case of sales for resale of export property under the transfer pricing rules of section 925. Related and subsidiary services to which the above subdivision (i) of this paragraph does not apply may be grouped, under the rules for grouping of transactions in paragraph (c)(8) of this section, with the products or product lines to which they are related and subsidiary, so long as the grouping of services chosen is consistent with the grouping of products or product lines chosen for the taxable year in which either the products or product lines were sold or in which payment for the services is received or accrued. Grouping of transactions shall not be allowed with respect to the determination of taxable income which the FSC may derive from services described in paragraph (b)(2)(iii)(D) or (E) of this section whether performed by the FSC or by the related supplier. Those determinations shall be made only on a transaction-by-transaction basis.

(e) Special rules for applying paragraphs (c) and (d) of this section. *(1) Limitation on FSC income ("no loss" rules).* (i) If there is a combined loss on a transaction or group of transactions, a FSC may not earn a profit under either the combined taxable income method or the gross receipts method. Also, for FSC taxable years beginning after December 31, 1986, in applying the gross receipts method, the FSC's profit may not exceed 100% of full costing combined taxable income determined under the full costing method of § 1.925(a)-1T(c) (3) and (6). This rule prevents pricing at a loss to the related supplier. The related supplier may in all situations set a transfer price or rental payment or pay a commission in an amount that will allow the FSC to recover an amount not in excess of its costs, if any, even if to do so would create, or increase, a loss in the related supplier.

(ii) For purposes of determining whether a combined loss exists, the basis for grouping transactions chosen by the related supplier under paragraph (c)(8) of this section for the taxable year shall apply.

(iii) If a FSC recognizes income while the related supplier recognizes a loss on a sale transaction under the section 482 method, neither the combined taxable income method nor the gross receipts method may be used by the FSC and related supplier (or by a FSC in the same controlled group and the related supplier) for any other sale transaction, or group of sale transactions, during a year which fall within the same three digit Standard Industrial Classification as the subject sale transaction. The reason for this rule is to prevent the segregation of transactions for the purposes of allowing the related supplier to recognize a loss on the subject transactions, while allowing the FSC to earn a profit under the administrative pricing methods on other transactions within the same three digit Standard Industrial Classification.

(2) Relationship to section 482. In applying the administrative pricing methods, it may be necessary to first take into account the price of a transfer (or other transaction) between the related supplier (or FSC) and a related party which is subject to the arm's length standard of section 482. Thus, for example, if a related supplier sells to a FSC export property which the related supplier purchased from related parties, the costs taken into account in computing the combined taxable income of the FSC and the related supplier are determined after any necessary adjustment under section 482 of the price paid by the related supplier to the related parties. In applying section 482 to a transfer by a FSC to a related party, the parties are treated as if they were a single entity carrying on all the functions performed by the FSC and the related supplier with respect to the transaction. The FSC shall be allowed to receive under the section 482 standard the amount the related supplier would have received had there been no FSC.

(3) Creation of receivables. (i) If the amount of the transfer price or rental payment actually charged by a related supplier to a FSC or the sales commission actually charged by a FSC to a related supplier has not been paid, an account receivable and payable will be deemed created as of the due date under section 6072(b), including extensions provided for under section 6081, of the FSC's tax return for the taxable year of the FSC during which a transaction to which section 925 is applicable occurs. The receivable and payable will be in an amount equal to the difference between the amount of the transfer price or rental payment or commission determined under section 925 and this section and the

amount (if any) actually paid or received. For example, a calendar year FSC's related supplier paid the FSC on July 1, 1985, a commission of $50 on the sale of export property. On September 15, 1986, the extended due date of the FSC's income tax return for taxable year 1985, the related supplier determined that the commission should have been $60. The additional $10 of commission had not been paid. Accordingly, an interest-bearing payable to the FSC from the related supplier in the amount of $10 was created as of September 15, 1986. A $10 interest bearing receivable was also created on the FSC's books.

(ii) An indebtedness arising under the above subdivision (i) shall bear interest at an arm's length rate, computed in the manner provided by § 1.482-2(a)(2), from the due date under section 6072(b), including extensions provided for under section 6081, of the FSC's tax return for the taxable year of the FSC in which the transaction occurred which gave rise to the indebtedness to the date of payment of the indebtedness. The interest so computed shall be accrued and included in the taxable income of the person to whom the indebtedness is owed for each taxable year during which the indebtedness is unpaid if that person is an accrual basis taxpayer or when the interest is paid if a cash basis taxpayer. Because the transactions covered by this subdivision are between the related supplier and FSC, the carrying charges provisions of § 1.927(d)-1(a) do not apply.

(iii) Payment of dividends, transfer prices, rents, commissions, service fees, receivables, or payables may be in the form of money, property, sales discount, or an accounting entry offsetting the amount due the related supplier, or FSC, whichever applies, against an existing debt of the other party to the transaction. This provision does not eliminate the requirement that actual cash payments be made by the related supplier to a commission FSC if the receipt of payment test of section 924(e)(4) is used to meet the foreign economic process requirements of section 924(d). The offset accounting entries must be clearly identified in both the related supplier's and FSC's books of account.

(4) Subsequent determination of transfer price, rental income or commission. The FSC and its related supplier would ordinarily determine under section 925 and this section the transfer price or rental payment payable by the FSC or the commission payable to the FSC for a transaction before the FSC files its return for the taxable year of the transaction. After the FSC has filed its return, a redetermination of those amounts by the Commissioner may only be made if specifically permitted by a Code provision or regulations under the Code. Such a redetermination would include a redetermination by reason of an adjustment under section 482 and the regulations under that section or section 861 and § 1.861-8 which affects the amounts which entered into the determination. In addition, a redetermination may be made by the FSC and related supplier if their taxable years are still open under the statute of limitations for making claims for refund under section 6511 if they determine that a different transfer pricing method may be more beneficial. Also, the FSC and related supplier may redetermine the amount of foreign trading gross receipts and the amount of the costs and expenses that are used to determine the FSC's and related supplier's profits under the transfer pricing methods. Any redetermination shall affect both the FSC and the related supplier. The FSC and the related supplier may not redetermine that the FSC was operating as a commission FSC rather than a buy-sell FSC, and vice versa.

(5) Procedure for adjustments to redeterminations. (i) If a redetermination under paragraph (e)(4) of this section is made of the transfer price, rental payment or commission for a transaction, or group of transactions, the person who was underpaid under this redetermination shall establish (or be deemed to have established), at the date of the redetermination, an account receivable from the person with whom it engaged in the transaction equal to the difference between the amounts as redetermined and the amounts (if any) previously paid and received, plus the amount (if any) of the account receivable determined under paragraph (e)(3) of this section that remains unpaid. A corresponding account payable will be established by the person who underpaid the amount due.

(ii) An account receivable established in accordance with the above subdivision (5)(i) of this paragraph shall bear interest at an arm's length rate, computed in the manner provided by § 1.482-2(a)(2), from the day after the date the account receivable is deemed established to the date of payment. The interest so computed shall be accrued and included in the taxable income for each taxable year during which the account receivable is outstanding of an accrual basis taxpayer or when paid if a cash basis taxpayer.

(iii) In lieu of establishing an account receivable in accordance with the above subdivision (5)(i) of this paragraph for all or part of an amount due a related supplier, the related supplier and FSC are permitted to treat all or part of any current or prior distribution which was made by the FSC as an additional payment of transfer price or rental payment or repayment of commission (and not as a distribution) made as of the date the distribution was made. Any additional amount arising on the redetermination due the related supplier after this treatment shall be represented by an account receivable established under the above subdivision (5)(i) of this paragraph. To the extent that a distribution is so treated under this subdivision (5)(iii), it shall cease to qualify as a distribution for any Federal income tax purpose. If all or part of any distribution made to a shareholder other than the related supplier is recharacterized under this subdivision (5)(iii), the related supplier shall establish an account receivable from that shareholder for the amount so recharacterized. The Commissioner may prescribe by Revenue Procedure conditions and procedures that must be met in order to obtain the relief provided by this subdivision (5)(iii).

(iv) The procedure for adjustments to transfer price provided by this paragraph does not apply to incomplete transactions described in paragraph (c)(5) of this section. Such procedure will, however, be applied to any such transaction with respect to the taxable year in which the transaction is completed.

(f) Examples. The provisions of this section may be illustrated by the following examples:

Example (1). In 1985, F, a FSC, purchases export property from R, a domestic manufacturer of export property A. R is F's related supplier. The sale from R to F is made under a written agreement which provides that the transfer price between R and F shall be that price which allocates to F the maximum amount permitted to be received under the transfer pricing rules of section 925. F resells property A in 1985 to an unrelated purchaser for $1,000. The terms of the sales contract between F and the unrelated purchaser provide that payment of the $1,000 sales price will be made within 90 days after sale. The purchaser pays the entire sales price within 60 days. F incurs indirect and direct expenses in the amount of $260 attributable to the sale which relate to the activities and functions referred to in section 924(c), (d) and (e). In addition, F incurs additional expenses attributable to the sale in the amount of $35. R's cost of goods sold attributable to the export property is $550. R incurred direct selling expenses in connection with the sale of $50. R's deductible general and administrative expenses allocable to all gross income are $200. Apportionment of those supportive expenses on the basis of gross income does not result in a material distortion of income and is a reasonable method of apportionment. R's direct selling expenses and its general and administrative expenses were not required to be incurred by F. R's gross income from sources other than the transaction is $17,550 resulting in total gross income of R and F (excluding the transfer price paid by F) of $18,000 ($450 plus $17,550). For purposes of this example, it is assumed that if R sold the export property to F for $690, the price could be justified as satisfying the standards of section 482. Under these facts, F may earn, under the combined taxable income method, the more favorable of the three transfer pricing rules, a profit of $23 on the sale. (Unless otherwise indicated, all examples in this section assume that the marginal costing method of § 1.925(b)-1T does not result in a higher profit than the profit under the full costing combined taxable income method of paragraphs (c)(3) and (6) of this section.) F's profit and the transfer price to F from the transaction, using the administrative pricing methods, and F's profit if the transfer price is determined under section 482, would be as follows:

Combined taxable income:	
F's foreign trading gross receipts	$1,000.00
R's cost of goods sold	(550.00)
Combined gross income	450.00
Less:	
R's direct selling expenses	50.00
F's expenses	295.00
Apportionment of R's general and administrative expenses:	
R's total G/A expenses	200.00
Combined gross income	450.00
R's and F's total gross income (foreign and domestic)	18,000.00
Apportionment of G/A expenses:	
$200 × $450/$18,000	5.00
Total	(350.00)
Combined taxable income	100.00
The section 482 method—Transfer price to F and F's profit:	
Transfer price to F	$ 690.00
F's profit:	
F's foreign trading gross receipts	1,000.00
Less:	
F's cost of goods sold	690.00
F's expenses	295.00
Total	(985.00)
F's profit	15.00
The gross receipts method—	
F's profit and transfer price to F:	
F's profit— lesser of 1.83% of F's foreign trading gross receipts ($18.30) or two times F's profit under the combined taxable income method ($46.00) (See below) (Unless otherwise indicated, all examples in this section assume that the marginal costing method of § 1.925(b)-1T does not result in a higher profit than the profit under the full costing combined taxable income method)	18.30
Transfer price to F:	
F's foreign trading gross receipts	1,000.00
Less:	
F's expenses	295.00
F's profit	18.30
Total	(313.30)
Transfer price	686.70
The combined taxable income method—F's profit and transfer price to F:	
F's profit—23% of combined taxable income ($100)	$ 23.00
Transfer price to F:	
F's foreign trading gross receipts	1,000.00
Less:	
F's expenses	295.00
F's profit	23.00
Total	(318.00)
Transfer price	682.00

With a profit of $23 under the most favorable of the transfer pricing methods, F's exempt foreign trade income under section 923 would be $207.39, computed as follows:

F's foreign trading gross receipts	$1,000.00
F's costs of purchases (transfer price)	(682.00)
F's foreign trade income	318.00
F's exempt foreign trade income $318 × 15/23	207.39

F's taxable income would be $8.00, computed as follows:

F's foreign trade income	$ 318.00
F's exempt foreign trade income	(207.39)
F's non-exempt foreign trade income	110.61
Less:	
F's expenses allocable to non-exempt foreign trade income $295 × $110.61/$318	(102.61)
F's taxable income	8.00

Of F's total expenses, $192.39 ($295 × $207.39/$318) are allocated to F's exempt foreign trade income and are disallowed for purposes of computing F's taxable income.

Example (2). Assume the same facts as in Example (1) except that the purchaser pays the entire sales price 96 days after delivery, well beyond the 60 day period in which payment must be made to avoid recharacterization of part of the contract price as carrying charges. Therefore, the contract price of $1,000 includes $10 of carrying charges, assuming a discount rate of 10%. See § 1.927(d)-1(a) (Q & A2) for computation method for determining amount of carrying charges. Under these facts, F may earn, under the combined taxable income method, the most favorable of the three transfer pricing rules, a profit of $20.73 on the sale. F's profit and the transfer price to F under the transfer pricing rules, assuming that a carrying charge is incurred, would be as follows:

Combined taxable income:	
F's foreign trading gross receipts	$990.00
R's cost of goods sold	(550.00)
Combined gross income	440.00
Less:	
R's direct selling expenses	50.00
R's apportioned G/A expenses:	
$200 × $440/$18,000	4.89
F's expenses	295.00
Total	(349.89)
Combined taxable income	90.11
The combined taxable income method—F's profit and transfer price to F:	
F's profit—23% of combined taxable income ($90.11)	$ 20.73
Transfer price to F:	
F's foreign trading gross receipts	990.00
Less:	
F's expenses	295.00
F's profit	20.73
Total	(315.73)
Transfer price	674.27
The gross receipts method—F's profit and transfer price to F:	
F's profit—lesser of 1.83% of F's foreign trading gross receipts ($18.12) or two times F's profit under the combined taxable income method ($41.46)	$ 18.12
Transfer price to F:	
F's foreign trading gross receipts	990.00
Less:	
F's expenses	295.00
F's profit	18.12
Total	(313.12)
Transfer price	676.88
The section 482 method—Transfer price to F and F's profit:	
Transfer price to F	690.00
F's profit:	
F's foreign trading gross receipts	990.00
Less:	
F's cost of goods sold	690.00
F's expenses	295.00
Total	(985.00)
F's profit	5.00

Example (3). R and F are calendar year taxpayers. R, a domestic manufacturing company, owns all the stock of F, a FSC for the taxable year. During 1985, R produces and sells a product line of export property to F for $157, a price which can be justified as satisfying the arm's length price standard of section 482. The sale from R to F is made under a written agreement which provides that the transfer price between R and F shall be that price which allocates to F the maximum amount permitted to be received under the transfer pricing rules of section 925. F resells the export property for $200. R's cost of goods sold attributable to the export property is $115 so that the combined gross income from the sale of the export property is $85 (i.e., $200 minus $115). R incurs $18 in direct selling expenses in connection with the sale of the property. R's deductible general and administrative expenses allocable to all gross income are $120. R's direct selling and its general and administrative expenses were not required to be incurred by F. R's gross income from sources other than the transaction is $5,015 resulting in total gross income of R and F (excluding the transfer price paid by F) of $5,100 (i.e., $85 plus $5,015). F incurs $50 in direct and indirect expenses attributable to resale of the export property. Of those expenses, $45 relate to activities and functions referred to in section 924(c), (d) and (e). The maximum profit which F may earn with respect to the product line is $3.66, computed as follows:

Combined taxable income:	
F's foreign trading gross receipts	$200.00
R's cost of goods sold	(115.00)
Combined gross income	85.00
Less:	
R's direct selling expenses	18.00
R's apportioned G/A expenses: $120 × $85/$5,100	2.00
F's expenses	50.00
Total	(70.00)
Combined taxable income	15.00
The combined taxable income method—F's profit:	
F's profit—23% of combined taxable income ($15)	$ 3.45
The gross receipts method—F's profit:	
F's profit— lesser of 1.83% of F's foreign trading gross receipts ($3.66) or two times F's profit under the combined taxable income method ($6.90)	$ 3.66
The section 482 method—F's profit:	
F's foreign trading gross receipts	200.00
Less:	
F's cost of goods sold	157.00
F's expenses	50.00
Total	(207.00)
F's profit (loss)	(7.00)

Since the gross receipts method results in a greater to F ($3.66) than does either the combined taxable income method ($3.45) or the section 482 method (a loss of $7), and does not exceed twice the profit under the combined taxable income method, F may earn a maximum profit of $3.66. Accordingly, the transfer price from R to F may be readjusted as long as the transfer price is not readjusted below $146.34, computed as follows:

Transfer price to F:	
F's foreign trading gross receipts	$200.00
Less:	
F's expenses	50.00
F's profit	3.66
Total	(53.66)

Transfer price	146.34

Example (4). R and F are fiscal year May 31 year-end taxpayers. R, a domestic manufacturing company, owns all the stock of F, a FSC for the taxable year. During August of 1987, R produces and sells 100 units of export property A to F under a written agreement which provides that the transfer price between R and F shall be that price which allocates to F the maximum profit permitted to be received under the transfer pricing rules of section 925. Thereafter, the 100 units are resold for export by F for $950. R's cost of goods sold attributable to the 100 units is $650. R incurs costs, both direct and indirect, in the amount of $270 with regard to activities and functions referred to in section 924(c), (d) and (e) which it was under contract with F to perform for F. R's direct selling expenses are $40. Those expenses were not required to be incurred by F. For purposes of this example, assume that R has no general and administrative expenses other than those relating to the section 924(c), (d) and (e) activities and functions. F incurs expenses in the amount of $290 attributable to the resale which relate to the activities and functions referred to in section 924(c), (d) and (e). Of that amount, $270 was paid to R under contract to perform the activities in section 924. The remaining $20 was paid to independent contractors. R chooses not to apply the section 482 transfer pricing method to determine F's profit on the transaction. F may not earn any income under either the gross receipts (see the special no-loss rule of paragraph (e)(1)(i) of this section) or the combined taxable income administrative pricing methods with respect to resale of the 100 units because there is a combined loss of $(30) on the transaction, computed as follows:

Combined taxable income:	
F's foreign trading gross receipts	$950.00
R's cost of goods sold	(650.00)
Combined gross income	300.00
Less:	
R's direct selling expenses	40.00
F's expenses	290.00
Total	(330.00)
Combined taxable income (loss)	(30.00)

Under paragraph (e)(1)(i) of this section, F is permitted to recover its expenses attributable to the sale ($290) even though such recovery results in a loss or increased loss to the related supplier. Accordingly, the transfer price from R to F may be readjusted as long as the transfer price is not readjusted below $660, computed as follows:

Transfer price to F:	
F's foreign trading gross receipts	$950.00
Less:	
F's expenses	(290.00)
Transfer price	660.00

Example (5). Assume the same facts as in Example (4) except that F performs the section 924(c), (d) and (e) activities and functions and that R chooses to apply the section 482 transfer pricing method. Under the standards of section 482, a transfer price from R to F of $650 is an arm's length price. Accordingly, the transfer price to F and F's profit on the subsequent resale of product A ($10) are as follows:

The section 482 method—Transfer price to F and F's profit:

Transfer price to F	$650.00
F's profit:	
F's foreign trading gross receipts	950.00
F's cost of purchases	(650.00)
F's gross income	300.00
Less:	
F's expenses	(290.00)
F's profit	10.00

This sale of product A results in a loss to R of $40 (transfer price of $650 less R's cost of goods sold of $650 and direct selling expenses of $40). Since R chose to use the section 482 transfer pricing method on this loss transaction, under the special no loss rule of paragraph (e)(1)(iii) of this section, the administrative pricing methods of section 925(a)(1) and (2) may not be used for any other sale transactions, or group of sale transactions, during the same year of other products which fall within the same three digit Standard Industrial Classification as product A. F's profit, if any, on these sales must be computed under the section 482 transfer pricing method.

Example (6). R and F are calendar year taxpayers. R, a domestic manufacturing company, owns all the stock of F, a FSC for the taxable year. During 1985, R manufactures 100 units of export property A. R enters into a written agreement with F whereby F is granted a sales franchise with respect to export property A and F will receive commissions with respect to these exports equal to the maximum amount permitted to be received under the administrative pricing rules of section 925(a)(1) and (2). Thereafter, the 100 units are sold for export by R for $1,000. The total sales price of $1,000 was paid by the purchaser to R within 60 days of the sales transaction. The entire $1,000 would have been foreign trading gross receipts had F been the principal on the sale. R's cost of goods sold attributable to the 100 units is $650. R's direct selling expenses so attributable are $50. R's deductible general and administrative expenses, other than those attributable to the section 924 (c), (d) and (e) activities and functions, allocable to all gross income are $200. Apportionment of those supportive expenses on the basis of gross income does not result in a material distortion of income and is a reasonable method of apportionment. R's direct selling expenses and the portion of the general and administrative expenses not relating to the activities and functions referred to in section 924(c), (d) and (e) were not required to be incurred by F. R's gross income from sources other than the transaction is $17,650 resulting in total gross income of $18,000 ($350 plus $17,650). R and a related person perform on F's behalf the activities and functions referred to in section 924(c), (d) and (e). In performing these activities, R and the related person incurred expenses, both direct and indirect, of $200 and $45, respectively. F pays $200 to R under contract and $50 to the related person. The maximum profit which F may earn under the franchise pursuant to the administrative pricing rules is $18.30, computed as follows:

Combined taxable income:	
R's gross receipts from the sale	$ 1,000.00
R's costs of goods sold	(650.00)
Combined gross income	350.00
Less:	
R's direct selling expenses	50.00
F's expenses	250.00

Apportionment of R's general and administrative expenses:	
R's total G/A expenses	200.00
Combined gross income	350.00
R's and F's total gross income (foreign and domestic)	18,000.00
Apportionment of G/A expenses: $200 × 350/$18,000	3.89
Total	(303.89)
Combined taxable income	46.11

As reflected in the above computation, F included on its books $200 of expenses related to the section 924 activities and performed by R on behalf of F. R incurred $253.89 of expenses. These expenses were reflected on its books. Under paragraph (b)(2)(ii) of this section, R and F may elect to include all of the expenses related to the export sales on F's books. This will satisfy the requirements of section 925(c) without requiring an allocation of the expenses between R and F. Under this election, as reflected in the following computation, combined taxable income will still be $46.11 but, as reflected in a later part of this example, the commission due F will be increased by $253.89:

Combined taxable income:	
R's gross receipts from the sale	$1,000.00
R's cost of goods sold	(650.00)
Combined gross income	350.00
Less:	
F's expenses	(303.89)
Combined taxable income	46.11
The combined taxable income method—F's profit:	
F's profit—23% of combined taxable income ($46.11)	$ 10.61
The gross receipts method—F's profit:	
F's profit—lesser of 1.83% of R's gross receipts ($18.30) or two times F's profit under the combined taxable income method ($21.22)	$ 18.30

If the election provided for in paragraph (b)(2)(ii) of this section is not made, F may receive a commission from R in the amount of $268.30, computed as follows:

F's expenses	$ 250.00
F's profit	18.30
F's commission	268.30

This $268.30 is F's foreign trade income. F's exempt foreign trade income is $174.98 ($268.30 × 15/23). F's taxable income is $6.37, computed as follows:

F's foreign trade income	$ 268.30
F's exempt foreign trade income	(174.98)
F's non-exempt foreign trade income	93.32
Less:	
F's expenses allocable to non-exempt foreign trade income $250 × $93.32/$268.30	(86.95)
F's taxable income	6.37

Of F's total expenses, $163.05 ($250 × $174.98/$268.30) are allocated to F's exempt foreign trade income and are disallowed for purposes of computing F's taxable income.

If R and F make the election provided for in paragraph (b)(2)(ii) of this section, F may receive a commission from R in the amount of $322.19, computed as follows:

F's expenses	$303.89
F's profit	18.30
F's commission	322.19

With this election, this $322.19 is F's foreign trade income. F's exempt foreign trade income is $210.12 ($322.19 × 15/23). F's taxable income is still $6.37, computed as follows:

F's foreign trade income	$322.19
F's exempt foreign trade income	(210.12)
F's non-exempt foreign trade income	112.07
Less:	
F's expenses allocable to non-exempt foreign trade income $303.89 × $112.07/$322.19	(105.70)
F's taxable income	6.37

Of F's total expenses, $198.19 ($303.89 × $210.12/$322.19) are allocated to F's exempt foreign trade income and are disallowed for purposes of computing F's taxable income.

Example (7). Assume the same facts as in Example (6) except that R's direct selling expenses are $60. The profit which F may earn under the franchise pursuant to the administrative pricing rules is $16.62, computed as follows:

Combined taxable income:		
R's gross receipts from the sale		$1,000.00
R's cost of goods sold		(650.00)
Combined gross income		350.00
Less:		
R's direct selling expenses	60.00	
R's apportioned G/A expenses	3.89	
F's expenses	250.00	
		(313.89)
Combined taxable income		36.11
The combined taxable income method—F's profit:		
F's profit—23% of combined taxable income ($36.11)		8.31
The gross receipts method—F's profit:		
F's profit—lesser of 1.83% of R's gross receipts ($18.30) or two times F's profit under the combined taxable income method ($16.62)		16.62

F may receive a commission from R in the amount of $266.62, computed as follows:

F's expenses	$ 250.00
F's profit	16.62
F's commission	266.62

If the election provided for in paragraph (b)(2)(ii) of this section is made by R and F, the profit which F may earn under the franchise pursuant to the administrative pricing rules will remain at $16.62 but will be computed as follows:

Combined taxable income:	
R's gross receipts from the sale	$1,000.00
R's cost of goods sold	(650.00)
Combined gross income	350.00
Less:	
F's expenses	(313.89)
Combined taxable income	36.11

The combined taxable income method—F's profit:	
F's profit—23% of combined taxable income ($36.11)	8.31

The gross receipts method—F's profit:	
F's profit—lesser of 1.83% of R's gross receipts ($18.30) or two times F's profit under the combined taxable income method ($16.62)	16.62

F may receive a commission from R in the amount of $330.51, computed as follows:	
F's expenses	313.89
F's profit	16.62
F's commission	330.51

As illustrated by Example (6), F's exempt taxable income and taxable income will be the same regardless of which method is used to compute F's commission.

Example (8). Assume the same facts as in Example (6) except that F's expenses are $300. With this assumption, there is a combined loss of $(3.89) on the transaction under the full costing combined taxable income method, computed as follows:

Combined taxable income:		
R's gross receipts from the sale		$1,000.00
R's cost of goods sold		(650.00)
Combined gross income		350.00
Less:		
R's direct selling expenses	50.00	
R's appointed G/A expenses	3.89	
F's expenses	300.00	
		(353.89)
Combined taxable income (loss)		(3.89)

Since there is a combined loss, F will not have a profit under the full costing combined taxable income method. However, for purposes of this example, it is assumed that under the marginal costing rules of § 1.925(b)-1T the maximum combined taxable income is $75 and the overall profit percentage limitation is $30. Accordingly, F's profit would be $6.90 (23% of $30) under the marginal costing rules. F's profit under the gross receipts method will be $13.80 (1.83% of $1,000 limited by section 925(d) to two times the profit determined under marginal costing). The commission F may receive from R is $313.80. Had all of the expenses been reflected on F's books pursuant to the election of paragraph (b)(2)(ii) of this section, F's commission would have been $367.69.

Example (9). Assume the same facts as in Example (6) except that F's expenses are $300 and that the transaction occurred in 1987. F will not earn a profit under the sales franchise pursuant to the administrative pricing rules. This is shown by the following computation:

Combined taxable income:		
R's gross receipts from the sale		$1,000.00
R's cost of goods sold		(650.00)
Combined gross income		350.00
Less:		
R's direct selling expenses	50.00	
R's appointed G/A expenses	3.89	
F's expenses	300.00	
		(353.89)
Combined taxable income (loss)		(3.89)

F will not have a profit under the full costing combined taxable income method since there is a combined loss of $(3.89). Also, F will not have a profit under the gross receipts method due to section 925(d) and the special no loss rule of paragraph (e)(1)(i) of this section. In addition, F will not have a profit under the marginal costing rules because the profit may not exceed full costing combined taxable income, see § 1.925(b)-1T(b)(4). Although F may not earn a profit, it is entitled to recoup its expenses. Therefore, the commission F may receive from R is $300.00. R will bear the entire loss. Had all of the expenses been reflected on F's books pursuant to the election of paragraph (b)(2)(ii) of this section, F's commission would have been $353.89.

Example (10). Assume the same facts as in Example (6) except that R receives total payment of the sale price of $1,000 on the 96th day after delivery, well beyond the 60 day period in which payment must be made to avoid recharacterization of part of the contract price as carrying charges. Therefore, the contract price of $1,000 includes $10 of carrying charges, assuming a discount rate of 10%. See § 1.927(d)-1(a) (Q & A2) for computation method for determining amount of carrying charges. This $10 of carrying charges is R's income. The profit which F may earn under the franchise pursuant to the administrative pricing rules is $16.66, computed as follows (the election of paragraph (b)(2)(ii) of this section is not made by R and F):

Combined taxable income:	
R's gross receipts from the sale	$990.00
R's cost of goods sold	(650.00)
Combined gross income	340.00
Less:	
R's direct selling expenses	50.00
R's apportioned G/A expenses: $200 × $340/$18,000	3.78
F's expenses	250.00
Total	(303.78)
Combined taxable income	36.22

The combined taxable income method—F's profit:	
F's profit—23% of combined taxable income ($36.22)	$ 8.33

The gross receipts method—F's profit:	
F's profit—lesser of 1.83% of R's gross receipts ($18.12) or two times F's profit under the combined taxable income method ($16.66)	$ 16.66

F may receive a commission from R in the amount of $266.66, computed as follows:	
F's expenses	$250.00
F's profits	16.66

F's commission	266.66

Example (11). Assume the same facts as in Example (6). In addition, assume that R also manufactures products K, L, M, N, and P all of which are export property as defined in section 927(a). Product K is military property as defined in section 923(a)(5) and § 1.923-1T(b)(3)(ii). Assume further that products A, L, and P are included within product line X and that products K, L, M, and N are included within product line W. R has entered into a written agreement with F under which F is granted a sales franchise with respect to exporting the products. Under this agreement, F will receive commissions with respect to those exports equal to the maximum amount permitted to be received under the administrative pricing rules. The table set forth below details F's foreign trading gross receipts, R's cost of goods sold and R's and F's expenses allocable and apportioned under § 1.861-8 to the sale of products A, L, M, N, and P. For purposes of this example, it is assumed that R does not incur any general and administrative expenses. Because of the special grouping rule of paragraph (c)(8)(ii) of this section, product L may be included for purposes of the administrative pricing rules in only one product line, at the option of R. Also for these purposes, product K, which is military property, may not be grouped with products L, M, and N. See paragraph (c)(8)(iv) of this section. Under these facts, F will have profits under the franchise agreement from the sale of products A, L, M, N, and P and may receive commissions from R relating to the sale of those products, assuming the election of paragraph (b)(2)(ii) of this section is not made, in the following amounts:

	Profit	F's Expenses	Commissions
Product Line X (products A and P)	$36.34	$490.00	$526.34
Product Line W (products L, M, and N)	$40.48	$421.00	$461.48

On the sale of product K, R received gross receipts of $150. R's cost of goods sold was $130. R's and F's expenses allocable to product K totaled $10 ($7 of R's expenses and $3 of F's). Under the gross receipts method, F earned a profit of $2.75 (1.83% of $150) and $2.30 under the combined taxable income method. F may receive a commission, assuming the election of paragraph (b)(2)(ii) of this section is made by R and F, from R in the amount of $12.75, computed as follows:

F's expenses	$10.00
F's profit	2.75
F's commission	$12.75

	Product A	Product L	Product M	Product N	Product P	Total
Product Line X						
Combined Taxable Income						
R's GR From sale	$1,000				$1,000	$2,000
R's cost of goods sold	(650)				(650)	(1,300)
Combined gross income	350				350	700
Less:						
R's expenses	50				81	131
F's expenses	250				240	490
Total	(300)				(321)	(621)
Combined taxable income (loss)	$50				$29	$79
23% of CTI	$11.50				$6.67	$18.17
1.83% of GR from sale	$18.30				$13.34	$36.34
Product Line W						
Combined Taxable Income						
R's GR from sale		$1,000	$625	$1,800		$3,425
R's cost of goods sold		(650)	(445)	(1,600)		(2,695)
Combined gross income		350	180	200		730
Less:						
R's expenses		81	70	70		221
F's expenses		230	60	131		421
Total		(311)	(130)	(201)		(642)
Combined taxable income (loss)		$39	$50	$(1)		$88
23% of CTI		$8.97	$11.50	$0		$20.24
1.83% of GR from sale		$17.94	$11.44	$0		$40.48

Example (12). R and F are calendar year taxpayers. R owns all the stock of F, an FSC for the taxable year. During 1985, R purchases 100 units of export property A from B, an unrelated domestic manufacturing company for $850. R's direct selling expenses so attributable are $20. R enters into a written agreement with F whereby F is granted a sales franchise with respect to export product A and F will receive commissions with respect to these exports equal to the maximum amount permitted to be received under the administrative pricing rules of section 925. Thereafter, the 100 units are sold for export by R for $1,050. R factors the trade receivable to unrelated person X for $1,000. Under § 1.924(a)-1T(g)(7), total gross receipts for purposes of computing R's and F's combined taxable income is $1,000 (total receipts ($1,050) less the discount ($50)). This $1,000 would have been foreign trading gross receipts had F been the principal on the sale. For purposes of this example, it is assumed that R did not incur any general and administrative expenses. F incurs expenses in the amount of $110, all of which were performed by R under contract to F. The profit which F may earn under the franchise pursuant to the administrative pricing rules is $9.20 computed as follows:

Combined taxable income:	
R's gross receipts from the sale	$1,000.00
R's cost of goods sold	(850.00)
	(150.00)
Less:	
R's direct selling expenses	20.00
F's expenses	110.00
Total	130.00
Combined taxable income	$ 20.00

The combined taxable income method—F's profit:	
F's profit—23% of combined taxable income ($20)	$ 4.60
The gross receipts method—F's profit:	
F's profit—lesser of 1.83% of R's gross receipts ($18.30) or two times F's profit under the combined taxable income method ($9.20)	$ 9.20

F may receive a commission from R in the amount of $119.20, computed as follows (the election of § 1.925(a)-1T(b)(2)(ii) has not been made):	
F's expenses	$ 110.00
F's profit	9.20
F's commission	$ 119.20

Example (13). R and F are calendar year taxpayers. R, a domestic manufacturing company, owns all the stock of F, an FSC for the taxable year. During March 1985, R manufactures office equipment, export property within the definition of section 927(a)(1), which it leases on April 1, 1985, to F for a term of 1 year at a monthly rental of $1,000, a rent which satisfies the standard of arm's length rental under section 482. F subleases the product on April 1, 1985, for a term of 1 year at a monthly rental of $1,200. R's cost for the product leased is $40,000. R's other deductible expenses attributable to the product are $200, all of which are incurred in 1985. Those expenses were not incurred under contract to F. F's expenses attributable to sublease of the export property are $1,150, all of which are incurred in 1985 directly by F. R depreciates the property on a straight line basis, using a half-year convention, assuming a 10 year recovery period (see section 168(f)(2)(C), § 1.48-1(g)). The profit which F may earn with respect to the transaction is $1,483.50 for 1985 and $600 for 1986, computed as follows:

Computation for 1985

Combined taxable income:	
F's sublease rental receipts for year ($1,200 × 9 months)	$10,800.00
Less:	
R's depreciation (($40,000 × 1/10) × 9/12)	3,000.00
R's expenses	200.00
F's expense	1,150.00
Total	(4,350.00)
Combined taxable income	6,450.00

The combined taxable income method—F's profit:	
F's profit—23% of combined taxable income ($6,450)	$ 1,483.50
The gross receipts method—F's profit:	
F's profit—lesser of 1.83% of F's foreign trading gross receipts ($197.64) or two times F's profit under the combined taxable income method ($2,967)	$ 197.64

The section 482 method—F's profit:	
F's sublease rental receipts for year	$10,800.00
Less:	
F's lease rental payments for year	9,000.00
F's expenses	1,150.00
Total	(10,150.00)
F's profit	650.00

Since the combined taxable income method results in greater profit to F ($1,483.50) than does either the gross receipts method ($197.64) or the section 482 method ($650), F may earn a profit of $1,483.50 for 1985. Accordingly, the monthly rental payable by F to R for 1985 may be readjusted as long as the monthly rental payable is not readjusted below $907.39, computed as follows:

Monthly rental payable by F to R for 1985:	
F's sublease rental receipts for year	$10,800.00
Less:	
F's expenses	1,150.00
F's profit	1,483.50
Total	(2,633.50)
Rental payable for 1985	8,166.50
Rental payable each month ($8,166.50 ÷ 9 months)	$ 907.39

Computation for 1986

Combined taxable income:	
F's sublease rental receipts for year ($1,200 × 3 months)	$3,600.00
Less:	
R's depreciation (($40,000 × 1/10) × 3/12)	(1,000.00)
Combined taxable income	2,600.00

The combined taxable income method—F's profit:	
F's profit—23% of combined taxable income ($2,600)	598.00
The gross receipts method—F's profit:	
F's profit—lesser of 1.83% of F's foreign trading gross receipts ($3,600) or two times F's profit under the combined taxable income method ($1,196)	65.88

The section 482 method—F's profit:	
F's sublease rental receipts for year	$3,600.00
Less:	
F's lease rental payments for year	(3,000.00)
F's profit	600.00

Since the section 482 method results in a greater profit to F ($600) than does either the combined taxable income method ($598) or the gross receipts method ($65.88), F may earn a profit of $600 for 1986. Accordingly, the monthly rental payable by F to R for 1986 may be readjusted as long as the monthly rental payable is not readjusted below $1,000, computed as follows:

Monthly rental payable by F to R for 1986:	
F's sublease rental receipts for year	$3,600.00
Less:	
F's profit	(600.00)
Rental payable for 1986	3,000.00
Rental payable for each month ($3,000 ÷ 3 months)	1,000.00

(g) Effective date. The provisions of this section and § 1.925(b)-1T apply with respect to taxable year ending after 2/2/2001..

T.D. 8126, 3/2/87, amend T.D. 8764, 3/2/98, T.D. 8944, 3/2/2001, T.D. 8956, 7/2/2001.

§ 1.925(b)-1T Temporary regulations; marginal costing rules.

Caution: The Treasury has not yet amended Reg § 1.925(b)-1T to reflect changes made by P.L. 106-519.

(a) In general. This section prescribes the marginal costing rules authorized by section 925(b)(2). If under paragraph (c)(1) of this section a FSC is treated for its taxable year as seeking to establish or maintain a foreign market for sales of an item, product, or product line of export property (as defined in § 1.927(a)-1T) from which foreign trading gross receipts (as defined in § 1.924(a)-1T) are derived, the marginal costing rules prescribed in paragraph (b) of this section may be applied at the related supplier's election to compute combined taxable income of the FSC and related supplier derived from those sales. (Any further reference to a FSC in this section shall include a small FSC unless indicated otherwise.) The combined taxable income determined under these marginal costing rules may be used to determine whether the "twice the amount determined under the combined taxable income method" limitation for the 1.83% of gross receipts test of section 925(d) has been met.

For FSC taxable years beginning after December 31, 1986, if the marginal costing rules are used to determine the section 925(d) limitation, the FSC may not earn more than 100% of full costing combined taxable income determined under the full costing combined taxable income method of § 1.925(a)-1T(c)(3) and (6). The marginal costing rules may be applied even if the related supplier does not manufacture, produce, grow, or extract the export property sold. The marginal costing rules do not apply to sales of export property which in the hands of a purchaser related under section 954(d)(3) to the seller give rise to foreign base company sales income as described in section 954(d) unless, for the purchaser's year in which it resells the export property, section 954(b)(3)(A) is applicable or that income is under the exceptions in section 954(b)(4). In addition, the marginal costing rules do not apply to leases of property or to the performances of any services even if they are related and subsidiary services (as defined in § 1.924(a)-1T(d) and § 1.925(a)-1T(b)(2)(iii)(C)).

(b) Marginal costing rules. *(1) In general.* Marginal costing is a method under which only direct production costs of producing a particular item, product, or product line are taken into account for purposes of computing the combined taxable income of the FSC and its related supplier under section 925(a)(2). The costs to be taken into account are the related supplier's direct material and labor costs (as defined in § 1.471-11(b)(2)(i)). Costs which are incurred by the FSC and which are not taken into account in computing combined taxable income are deductible by the FSC only to the extent of the FSC's non-foreign trade income. If the related supplier is not the manufacturer or producer of the export property that is sold, the related supplier's purchase price shall be taken into account.

(2) Overall profit percentage limitation. Under marginal costing, the combined taxable income of the FSC and its related supplier may not exceed the overall profit percentage (determined under paragraph (c)(2) of this section) multiplied by the FSC's foreign trading gross receipts if the FSC is the principal on the sale (or the related supplier's gross receipts if the FSC is a commission agent) from the sale of export property.

(3) Grouping of transactions. (i) In general, for purposes of this section, an item, product, or product line is the item or group consisting of the product or product line pursuant to § 1.925(a)-1T(c)(8) used by the taxpayer for purposes of applying the full costing combined taxable income method of § 1.925(a)-1T(c)(3) and (6).

(ii) However, for purposes of determining the overall profit percentage under paragraph (c)(2) of this section, any product or product line grouping permissible under § 1.925(a)-1T(c)(8) may be used at the annual choice of the FSC even though it may not be the same item or grouping referred to in subdivision (i) of this paragraph as long as the grouping chosen for determining the overall profit percentage is at least as broad as the grouping referred to in the above subdivision (i) of this paragraph. A product may be included for this purpose, however, in only one product group even though under the grouping rules it would otherwise fall in more than one group. Thus, the marginal costing rules will not apply with respect to any regrouping if the regrouping does not include any product (or products) that was included in the group for purposes of the full costing method.

(4) Application of limitation on FSC income ("no loss" rules). The marginal costing rules of this section will not apply if there is a combined loss of the related supplier and the FSC determined in accordance with paragraph (b)(1) of this section. In addition, for FSC taxable years beginning after December 31, 1986, the profit determined under the marginal costing method may be allowed to the FSC only to the extent it does not exceed the FSC's and the related supplier's full costing combined taxable income determined under the full costing combined taxable income method of § 1.925(a)-1T(c)(3) and (6). This rule prevents pricing at a loss to the related supplier. If either of these "no loss" rules apply, the related supplier may nonetheless charge a transfer price or pay a commission in an amount that will allow the FSC to recover an amount not in excess of its full costs, if any, even if to do so would create or increase a loss in the related supplier. The effect of these no-loss rules and of the overall profit percentage limitation of paragraph (c)(2) of this section is that the FSC's profit under these marginal costing rules is limited to the lesser of the following:

(i) 23% of maximum combined taxable income determined under the marginal costing rules,

(ii) 23% of the overall profit percentage limitation, or

(iii) For FSC taxable years beginning after December 31, 1986, 100% of the full costing combined taxable income determined under the full costing combined taxable income method of § 1.925(a)-1T(c)(3) and (6).

(c) Definitions. *(1) Establishing or maintaining a foreign market.* An FSC shall be treated for its taxable year as seeking to establish or maintain a foreign market with respect to sales of an item, product, or product line of export property from which foreign trading gross receipts are derived if the combined taxable income computed under paragraph (b) of this section is greater than the full costing combined taxable income computed under the full costing combined taxable income method of § 1.925(a)-1T(c)(3) and (6).

(2) Overall profit percentage. (i) For purposes of this section, the overall profit percentage for a taxable year of the FSC for a product or product line is the percentage which—

(A) The combined taxable income of the FSC and its related supplier from the sale of export property plus all other taxable income of its related supplier from all sales (domestic and foreign) of such product or product line during the FSC's taxable year, computed under the full costing method, is of

(B) The total gross receipts (determined under § 1.927(b)-1T) of the FSC and related supplier from all sales of the product or product line.

(ii) At the annual option of the related supplier, the overall profit percentage for the FSC's taxable year for all products and product lines may be determined by aggregating the amounts described in subdivisions (i)(A) and (B) of this paragraph of the FSC, and all domestic members of the controlled group (as defined in section 927(d)(4) and § 1.924(a)-1T(h)) of which the FSC is a member, for the FSC's taxable year and for taxable years of the members ending with or within the FSC's taxable year.

(iii) For purposes of determining the amounts in subdivisions (i) and (ii) of this paragraph, a sale of property between an FSC and its related supplier or between domestic members of the controlled group shall be taken into account only during the FSC's taxable year (or taxable year of the member ending within the FSC's taxable year) during which the property is ultimately sold to a person which is not related to the FSC or if related, is a foreign person that is not an FSC.

(3) Full costing method. For purposes of section 925 and this section, the term "full costing combined taxable income method" is the method for determining full costing combined taxable income set forth in § 1.925(a)-1T(c)(3) and (6).

(d) Examples. The provisions of this section may be illustrated by the following examples:

Example (1). R and F are calendar year taxpayers. R, a domestic manufacturing company, owns all the stock of F, an FSC for the taxable year. During 1985, R produces and sells 100 units of export property A to F under a written agreement which provides that the transfer price between R and F shall be that price which allocates to F the maximum profit permitted to be received under the administrative pricing rules of section 925(a)(1) and (2). Thereafter, the 100 units are resold for export by F for $950. R's cost of goods sold attributable to the 100 units is $650 consisting in part of $400 of direct materials and $200 of direct labor. R incurs selling expenses directly attributable to the sale in the amount of $100. Those expenses were not required to be incurred by F. For purposes of this example, it is assumed that R does not have general and administrative expenses that are not definitely allocable to any item of gross income. F's expenses attributable to the resale of the 100 units are $120. For purposes of this example, R and F have gross receipts of $4,000 from all domestic and foreign sales. R's total cost of goods sold and total expenses relating to its foreign and domestic sales are $2,730 and $450, respectively. Under full costing, the combined taxable income will be $80, computed as follows:

Combined taxable income—full costing:	
F's foreign trading gross receipts	$950.00
R's cost of goods sold	(650.00)
Combined gross income	300.00
Less:	
R's direct selling expenses	100.00
F's expenses	120.00
Total	(220.00)
Combined taxable income (loss)	80.00

F's profit under the full costing combined taxable income method is $18.40, i.e., 23% of full costing combined taxable income ($80). F's profit under the gross receipts method will be $17.39, i.e., 1.83% of F's foreign trading gross receipts ($950). However, under the marginal costing rules, F would have a profit attributable to the export sale in the amount of $38.24, i.e., 23% of combined taxable income as determined under the marginal costing rules (23% of $166.25). As shown by the computation below, the combined taxable income under marginal costing is limited to the overall profit percentage limitation ($166.25) since that amount is less than the maximum combined taxable income amount ($350):

Maximum combined taxable income (determined under paragraph (b)(1) of this section):	
F's foreign trading gross receipts	$ 950.00
Less:	
R's direct materials	400.00
R's direct labor	200.00
Total	(600.00)
Maximum combined total income	350.00
Overall profit percentage limitation calculation (determined under paragraph (c)(2) of this section):	
Gross receipts of R and F from all domestic and foreign sales	$4,000.00
R's cost of goods sold	(2,730.00)
Combined gross income	1,270.00
Less:	
R's expenses	450.00
F's expenses	120.00
Total	(570.00)
Total taxable income from all sales computed on a full costing method	700.00
Overall profit percentage (total taxable income ($700) divided by total gross receipts ($4,000))	17.5%
Overall profit percentage limitation: Overall profit percentage times F's foreign trading gross receipts (17.5% × $950.00)	$ 166.25

The transfer price from R to F may be set at $791.76, computed as follows:

Transfer price to F:	
F's foreign trading gross receipts	$950.00
Less:	
F's expenses	120.00
F's profit	38.24
Total	(158.24)
Transfer price	791.76

Example (2). Assume the same facts as in *Example (1)* except that F's expenses are $170. Under full costing, the combined taxable income will be $30, computed as follows:

Combined taxable income—full costing:	
F's foreign trading gross receipts	$950.00
R's cost of goods sold	(650.00)
Combined gross income	300.00
Less:	
R's expenses	100.00
F's expenses	170.00
Total	(270.00)
Combined taxable income (loss)	30.00

F's profit under the full costing combined taxable income method is $6.90, i.e., 23% of combined taxable income, $30. Under the marginal costing rules, F may earn a profit attributable to the export sale in the amount of $35.51, i.e., 23% of combined taxable income as determined under the marginal costing rules (23% of $154.38). Had the transaction occurred in 1987, F would have had a profit attributable to the export sale under these marginal costing rules of only $30, i.e., 23% of combined taxable income as determined under the marginal costing rules (23% of $154.38) limited, for FSC taxable years beginning after December 31, 1986, to combined taxable income determined under full costing ($30), see paragraph (b)(4) of this section. F's profit under the gross receipts method will be $17.39 i.e., 1.83% of F's foreign trading gross receipts ($950). The computations are as follows:

Maximum combined taxable income (determined under paragraph (b)(1) of this section):	
F's foreign trading gross receipts	$ 950.00
Less:	
R's direct materials	400.00
R's direct labor	200.00
Total	(600.00)
Maximum combined taxable income	350.00
Overall profit percentage limitation calculation (determined under paragraph (c)(2) of this section):	
Gross receipts of R and F from all domestic and foreign sales	4,000.00
R's cost of goods sold	(2,730.00)
Combined gross income	1,270.00
Less:	
R's expenses	450.00
F's expenses	170.00
Total	(620.00)
Total taxable income from all sales computed on a full costing method	650.00
Overall profit percentage (total taxable income ($650) divided by total gross receipts ($4,000))	16.25%
Overall profit percentage limitation. Overall profit percentage times F's foreign trading gross receipts (16.25% × $950.00)	154.38

The transfer price from R to F may be set at $744.49, computed as follows:

Transfer price to F:	
F's foreign trading gross receipts	950.00
Less:	
F's expenses	170.00
F's profit	35.51
Total	(205.51)
Transfer price	744.49

Example (3). Assume the same facts as in Example (1) except that the transaction occurs in 1987 and that F incurs expenses in the amount of $250. Since a $50 combined loss, as computed below, is incurred, F will not have any profit under either the full costing combined taxable income method, the gross receipts method or the marginal costing rules:

Combined taxable income—full costing:	
F's foreign trading gross receipts	$950.00
R's cost of goods sold	(650.00)
Combined gross income	300.00
Less:	
R's expenses	100.00
F's expenses	250.00
Total	(350.00)
Combined taxable income (loss)	(50.00)

The transfer price to R may be set at $700 so that F may recover its expenses.

Example (4). R and F are calendar year taxpayers. R, a domestic manufacturing company, owns all the stock of F, a FSC for the taxable year. During 1985, R manufactures export property A. R enters into a written agreement with F whereby F will receive a commission with respect to sales of export property A by R which result in gross receipts to R which would have been foreign trading gross receipts had F and not R been the principal on the sale. F will receive commissions with respect to such export sales equal to the maximum amount permitted to be received under the transfer pricing rules of section 925. The maximum commission may be earned by F under these marginal costing rules. In this example, R received $950 from the sale of export property A. R's cost of goods sold for that property was $620. R incurred direct selling expenses of $20. Also, it is assumed that R incurred total general and administrative expenses, in addition to those incurred relating to its contract to perform on behalf of F the functions and activities of section 924(c), (d) and (e), of $50. R incurred direct and indirect expenses of $130 in performing those functions and activities on behalf of F. During 1985, R had gross receipts from all domestic and foreign sales of $3,500, total cost of goods sold and total expenses relating to the domestic and foreign sales of $1,600 and $259, respectively. The election provided for in § 1.925(a)-1T(b)(2)(ii) was not made by R and F.

Combined taxable income—full costing:

F's gross receipts from the sale of the export property		$ 950.00
R's cost of goods sold		(620.00)
Combined gross income		330.00
Less:		
R's direct selling expenses		20.00
F's expenses		130.00
Apportionment of R's general and administrative expenses:		
R's total G/A expenses	$ 50	—
Combined gross income	330	—
R's total gross income	1,900	—
Apportionment of G/A expenses $50 × $330/$1,900		8.68
Total		(158.68)
Combined taxable income (loss)		171.32

Maximum combined taxable income (determined under paragraph (b)(1) of this section):

R's gross receipts from the sale of the export property	$ 950.00
Less:	
R's direct materials	450.00
R's direct labor	100.00
Total	(550.00)
Maximum combined taxable income	400.00

Overall profit percentage limitation calculation (determined under paragraph (c)(2) of this section):

Gross receipts of R from all domestic and foreign sales	3,500.00
R's cost of goods sold	(1,600.00)
Combined gross income	1,900.00
Less:	
R's total expenses	259.00
F's total expenses	130.00
Total	(450.00)
Total taxable income from all sales computed on a full costing method	1,511.00
Overall profit percentage (total taxable income ($1,511) divided by total gross receipts ($3,500))	43.17%
Overall profit percentage limitation. Overall profit percentage times R's gross receipts from the sale of export property (i.e., 43.17% × $950.00)	410.12

Since the overall profit percentage limitation ($410.12) is greater than the maximum combined taxable income ($400), combined taxable income under marginal costing and for purposes of computing F's commission is limited to $400. Under these marginal costing rules, F will have a profit attributable to the sale of $92, i.e., 23% of combined taxable income as determined under the marginal costing rules (23% of $400). Accordingly, the commission F receives from R is $222, i.e., F's expenses ($130) plus F's profit ($92).

Example (5). Assume the same facts as in Example (4), except that R's gross receipts from the sale of export property which would have been foreign trading gross receipts had F been the principal on the sale are $1,050 and gross receipts from all sales, domestic and foreign, remain at $3,500. For purposes of applying the combined taxable income method, R and F may compute their combined taxable income attributable to the product line of export property under the marginal costing rules as follows:

Combined taxable income—full costing:

R's gross receipts from the sale of the export property	$1,050.00
R's cost of goods sold	(620.00)
Combined gross income	430.00
Less:	
R's direct selling expenses	20.00
F's expenses	130.00
Apportionment of R's G/A expenses $50 × $430/$1,900	11.32
Total	(161.32)
Combined taxable income (loss)	268.68

Maximum combined taxable income (determined under paragraph (b)(1) of this section):

R's gross receipts from the sale of export property	$1,050.00
Less:	
R's direct materials	450.00
R's direct labor	100.00
Total	(550.00)
Maximum combined taxable income	500.00
Overall profit percentage (see example (4))	43.17%
Overall profit percentage limitation (determined under paragraph (c)(2) of this section) (R's gross receipts from sale ($1,050.00) times the overall profit percentage (43.17%))	453.29

Since maximum combined taxable income ($500) is greater than the overall profit percentage limitation ($453.29), combined taxable income under marginal costing and for purposes of computing F's commission is limited to $453.29. Under these marginal costing rules, F will have a profit attributable to the sales of $104.26, i.e., 23% of combined taxable income (23% of $453.29). Accordingly, the commission F receives from R is $234.26, i.e., F's expenses ($130) plus F's profit ($104.26).

Example (6). Assume the same facts as in Example (5), except that F has expenses of $140 and R's cost of goods sold for the export sale was $900. R does not incur any direct selling expenses. Since cost of goods sold has increased by $280, R's total gross income has been reduced from $1,900 to $1,620. For purposes of applying the combined taxable income method, R and F may compute their combined taxable income under the marginal costing rules as follows:

Combined taxable income—full costing:

R's gross receipts from the sale of export property	$1,050.00
R's cost of goods sold	(900.00)
Combined gross income	150.00
Less:	

F's expenses	140.00
Apportionment of R's G/A expenses $50 × $150/$1,620	4.63
Total	(144.63)
Combined taxable income (loss)	5.37
Maximum combined taxable income (determined under paragraph (b)(1) of this section):	
R's gross receipts from the sale of export property	$1,050.00
Less:	
R's direct materials	630.00
R's direct labor	200.00
Total	(830.00)
Maximum combined taxable income	220.00
Overall profit percentage limitation calculation (determined under paragraph (c)(2) of this section):	
Gross receipts of R and F from all domestic and foreign sales	$3,500.00
R's cost of goods sold	(1,880.00)
Combined gross income	1,620.00
Less:	
R's total expenses	259.00
F's total expenses	140.00
Total	(399.00)
Total taxable income from all sales computed on a full costing method	$1,221.00
Overall profit percentage (total taxable income ($1,221) divided by total gross receipts ($3,500))	34.89%
Overall profit percentage limitation—overall profit percentage times R's gross receipts from the sale of export property (i.e., 34.89% × $1,050)	$ 366.35

Since the overall profit percentage limitation ($366.35) is greater than the maximum combined taxable income ($220), combined taxable income under marginal costing and for purposes of computing F's commission is limited to $220. Under these marginal costing rules, F will have a profit attributable to the sale of $50.60, i.e., 23% of combined taxable income as determined under the marginal costing rules (23% of $220). If the transaction occurred in 1987, F's profit would be limited, however, by paragraph (b)(4) of this section to full costing combined taxable income of $5.37.

T.D. 8126, 3/2/87, amend T.D. 8764, 3/2/98, T.D. 8944, 3/2/2001.

§ 1.926(a)-1 Distributions to shareholders.

Caution: The Treasury has not yet amended Reg § 1.926(a)-1 to reflect changes made by P.L. 106-519.

(a) Treatment of distributions.[Reserved] For guidance, see § 1.926(a)-1T(a).

(b) Order of distribution. *(1) In general.* (i) Distributions by a FSC received by a shareholder in a taxable year of the shareholder beginning before January 1, 1990. Any actual distribution to a shareholder by a FSC (all references to a FSC in this section shall include a small FSC and a former FSC) that is received by the shareholder in a taxable year of the shareholder beginning before January 1, 1990, and made out of earnings and profits shall be treated as made in the following order, to the extent thereof—

(A) Out of earnings and profits attributable to exempt foreign trade income determined solely because of operation of section 923(a)(4),

(B) Out of earnings and profits attributable to other exempt foreign trade income,

(C) Out of earnings and profits attributable to non-exempt foreign trade income determined under either of the administrative pricing methods of section 925(a)(1) or (2),

(D) Out of earnings and profits attributable to section 923(a)(2) non-exempt income, and

(E) Out of other earnings and profits.

(ii) Distributions by a FSC received by a shareholder in a taxable year of the shareholder beginning after December 31, 1989. Any actual distribution to a shareholder by a FSC that is received by the shareholder in a taxable year beginning after December 31, 1989, and that is made out of earnings and profits shall be treated as made in the following order, to the extent thereof—

(A) Out of earnings and profits attributable to exempt foreign trade income determined solely because of the operation of section 923(a)(4),

(B) Out of earnings and profits attributable to foreign trade income (other than exempt foreign trade income determined solely because of the operation of section 923(a)(4)) allocable to the marketing of agricultural or horticultural products (or the providing of related services) by a qualified cooperative which is a shareholder of the FSC,

(C) Out of earnings and profits attributable to non-exempt foreign trade income and other exempt foreign trade income determined under either of the administrative pricing methods of section 925(a)(1) and (2). Distributions out of this classification will be made on a pro rata basis so that 15/23 (16/23 with regard to distribution to a non-corporate shareholder of each distribution will be out of earnings and profits attributable to exempt foreign trade income and the remainder will be out of earnings and profits attributable to non-exempt foreign trade income. To the extent the distributions are out of earnings and profits attributable to the disposition of, or services related to, military property, 7.5/23 (8/23 with regard to distributions to a non-corporate shareholder) of each distribution will be out of earnings and profits attributable to exempt foreign trade income and the remainder will be out of earnings and profits attributable to non-exempt foreign trade income,

(D) Out of earnings and profits attributable to other exempt foreign trade income determined under the transfer pricing method of section 925(a)(3),

(E) Out of earnings and profits attributable to section 923(a)(2) non-exempt income,

(F) Out of earnings and profits attributable to effectively connected income, as defined in section 245(c)(4)(B), and

(G) Out of other earnings and profits.

(2) Determination of earnings and profits.[Reserved] For guidance, see § 1.926(a)-1T(b)(1).

(c) Definition of "former FSC".[Reserved] For guidance, see § 1.926(a)-1T(c).

(d) Personal holding company income.[Reserved] For guidance, see § 1.926(a)-1T(d).

(e) Sale of stock if section 1248 applies.[Reserved] For guidance, see § 1.926(a)-1T(e).

T.D. 8340, 3/14/91.

§ 1.926(a)-1T Distributions to shareholders (temporary).

Caution: The Treasury has not yet amended Reg § 1.926(a)-1T to reflect changes made by P.L. 106-519.

(a) Treatment of distributions. Any distribution by an FSC (or former FSC) to its shareholder with respect to its stock will be includible in the shareholder's gross income in accordance with the provisions of section 301. (Any further reference to an FSC in this section shall include a small FSC unless indicated otherwise.) See section 245(c) for treatment of distributions to domestic corporate shareholders of the FSC. If earnings and profits of an FSC (or former FSC) attributable to foreign trade income are distributed to a shareholder which is a foreign person (or a nonresident alien individual), that distribution shall be treated as United States source income which is effectively connected with the conduct of a trade or business conducted through a permanent establishment of such shareholder within the United States. For this purpose, distributions to a foreign partnership, foreign trust, foreign estate or other foreign entities that would be treated as pass-through entities under U.S. law shall be treated as made directly to the partners of beneficiaries in proportion to their respective interest in the entity.

(b) Order of distributions. *(1) In general.* For guidance, see § 1.926(a)-1(b)(1).

(2) Determination of earnings and profits. For purposes of this section, the earnings and profits of a FSC (or former FSC) shall be the earnings and profits computed in accordance with the rules, where applicable, prescribed in § 1.964-1 (relating to determination of the earnings and profits of a foreign corporation) other than subsections (d) and (e) of that section.

(c) Definition of "former FSC". Under section 926(c), the term "former FSC" refers to a corporation which is not a FSC for a taxable year but which was a FSC for a prior taxable year. However, a corporation is not a former FSC for a taxable year unless such corporation has, at the beginning of such taxable year, earnings and profits attributable to foreign trade income. A corporation which is a former FSC for a taxable year is a former FSC for all purposes of the Code.

(d) Personal holding company income. *(1) Treatment of dividends.* Any amount includible in a shareholder's gross income as a dividend with respect to the stock of a FSC (or former FSC) under paragraph (a) of this section shall be treated as a dividend for all purposes of the Code, except that that part of the dividend attributable to foreign trade income, other than an amount attributable to section 923(a)(2) non-exempt income, shall not be considered in applying the personal holding company and foreign personal holding company provisions (sections 541 through 547 and 551 through 558, respectively).

(2) Look through option. With regard to distributions from a FSC (or former FSC) which are not treated as personal holding company income under paragraph (d)(1) of this section, the shareholder may, however, treat any amount of that distribution as an item of income described under section 543 (or section 553) (for example, rents) if it establishes to the satisfaction of the Commissioner that such amount is attributable to earnings and profits of the FSC derived from such item of income. For example, distributions from a FSC relating to section 923(a)(2) non-exempt income will be treated as dividends for purposes of the personal holding company provisions of sections 541 through 547 unless the look through option is elected. Under this option, if earnings and profits out of which those distributions are made are attributable to the lease of export property, the FSC shareholder may treat the distribution for purposes of the personal holding company provisions as rents rather than as dividends. This may be beneficial to the shareholder because rents are not considered under section 543(a)(2) as personal holding company income, if in general, rents constitute 50% or more of the shareholder's adjusted ordinary gross income.

(e) Sale of stock if section 1248 applies. For purposes of section 1248, the earnings and profits of a FSC (or former FSC) shall not include earnings and profits attributable to foreign trade income.

T.D. 8126, 3/2/87, amend T.D. 8340, 3/14/91.

§ 1.927(a)-1T Temporary Regulations; Definition of export property.

Caution: The Treasury has not yet amended Reg § 1.927(a)-1T to reflect changes made by P.L. 106-519, P.L. 105-34, P.L. 103-66.

(a) General rule. Under section 927 (a), except as otherwise provided with respect to excluded property in paragraphs (f), (g) and (h) of this section and with respect to certain short supply property in paragraph (i) of this section, export property is property in the hands of any person (whether or not an FSC) (any further reference to an FSC in this section shall include a small FSC unless indicated otherwise)—

(1) U.S. manufactured, produced, grown or extracted. Manufactured, produced, grown, or extracted in the United States by any person or persons other than an FSC (see paragraph (c) of this section),

(2) Foreign use, consumption or disposition. Held primarily for sale, lease or rental in the ordinary course of a trade or business by an FSC to an FSC or to any other person for direct use, consumption, or disposition outside the United States (see paragraph (d) of this section),

(3) Foreign content. Not more than 50 percent of the fair market value of which is attributable to articles imported into the United States (see paragraph (e) of this section), and

(4) Non-related FSC purchaser or user. Which is not sold, leased or rented by an FSC, or with an FSC as commission agent, to another FSC which is a member of the same controlled group (as defined in section 927(d)(4) and § 1.924(a)-1T(h)) as the FSC.

(b) Services. For purposes of this section, services (including the written communication of services in any form) are not export property. Whether an item is property or services shall be determined on the basis of the facts and circumstances attending the development and disposition of the item. Thus, for example, the preparation of a map of a particular construction site would constitute services and not export property, but standard maps prepared for sale to customers generally would not constitute services and would be export property if the requirements of this section were otherwise met.

(c) Manufacture, production, growth, or extraction of property. *(1) By a person other than a FSC.* Export property may be manufactured, produced, grown, or extracted in the United States by any person, provided that that person does not qualify as a FSC. Property held by a FSC which was manufactured, produced, grown or extracted by it at a time when it did not qualify as a FSC is not export property of the FSC. Property which sustains further manufacture, production or processing outside the United States prior to sale or lease by a person but after manufacture, production, processing or extraction in the United States will be considered as manufactured, produced, grown or extracted in the United States by that person only if the property is reimported into the United States for further manufacturing, production or processing prior to final export sale. In order to be considered export property, the property manufactured, produced, grown or extracted in the United States must satisfy all of the provisions of section 927(a) and this section.

(2) Manufactured, produced or processed. For purposes of this section, property which is sold or leased by a person is considered to be manufactured, produced or processed by that person or by another person pursuant to a contract with that person if the property is manufactured or produced, as defined in § 1.954-3(a)(4). For purposes of this section, however, in determining if the 20% conversion test of § 1.954-3(a)(4)(iii) has been met, conversion costs include assembly and packaging costs but do not include the value of parts provided pursuant to a services contract as described in § 1.924(a)-1T(d)(3). In addition, for purposes of this section, the 20% conversion test is extended and applied to the export property's adjusted basis rather than to its cost of goods sold if it is leased or held for lease.

(d) Foreign use, consumption or disposition. *(1) In general.* (i) Under paragraph (a)(2) of this section, export property must be held primarily for the purpose of sale, lease or rental in the ordinary course of a trade or business, by a FSC to a FSC or to any other person, and the sale or lease must be for direct use, consumption, or disposition outside the United States. Thus, property cannot qualify as export property unless it is sold or leased for direct use, consumption, or disposition outside the United States. Property is sold or leased for direct use, consumption, or disposition outside the United States if the sale or lease satisfies the destination test described in subdivision (2) of this paragraph, the proof of compliance requirements described in subdivision (3) of this paragraph, and the use outside the United States test described in subdivision (4) of this paragraph.

(ii) Factors not taken into account. In determining whether property which is sold or leased to a FSC is sold or leased for direct use, consumption, or disposition outside the United States, the fact that the acquiring FSC holds the property in inventory or for lease prior to the time it sells or leases it for direct use, consumption, or disposition outside the United States will not affect the characterization of the property as export property. Fungible export property must be physically segregated from non-export property at all times after purchase by or rental by a FSC or after the start of the commission relationship between the FSC and related supplier with regard to the export property. Non-fungible export property need not be physically segregated from non-export property.

(2) Destination test. (i) For purposes of paragraph (d)(1) of this section, the destination test of this paragraph is satisfied with respect to property sold or leased by a seller or lessor only if it is delivered by the seller or lessor (or an agent of the seller or lessor) regardless of the F.O.B. point or the place at which title passes or risk of loss shifts from the seller or lessor—

(A) Within the United States to a carrier or freight forwarder for ultimate delivery outside the United States to a purchaser or lessee (or to a subsequent purchaser or sublessee),

(B) Within the United States to a purchaser or lessee, if the property is ultimately delivered outside the United States (including delivery to a carrier or freight forwarder for delivery outside the United States) by the purchaser or lessee (or a subsequent purchaser or sublessee) within 1 year after the sale or lease,

(C) Within or outside the United States to a purchaser or lessee which, at the time of the sale or lease, is a FSC or an interest charge DISC and is not a member of the same controlled group as the seller or lessor,

(D) From the United States to the purchaser or lessee (or a subsequent purchaser or sublessee) at a point outside the United States by means of the seller's or lessor's own ship, aircraft, or other delivery vehicle, owned, leased, or chartered by the seller or lessor,

(E) Outside the United States to a purchaser or lessee from a warehouse, storage facility, or assembly site located outside the United States, if the property was previously shipped by the seller or lessor from the United States, or

(F) Outside the United States to a purchaser or lessee if the property was previously shipped by the seller or lessor from the United States and if the property is located outside the United States pursuant to a prior lease by the seller or lessor, and either (1) the prior lease terminated at the expiration of its term (or by the action of the prior lessee acting alone), (2) the sale occurred or the term of the subsequent lease began after the time at which the term of the prior lease would have expired, or (3) the lessee under the subsequent lease is not a related person with respect to the lessor and the prior lease was terminated by the action of the lessor (acting alone or together with the lessee).

(ii) For purposes of this paragraph (d)(2) (other than paragraphs (d)(2)(i)(C) and (F)(3)), any relationship between the seller or lessor and any purchaser, subsequent purchaser, lessee, or sublessee is immaterial.

(iii) In no event is the destination test of this paragraph (d)(2) satisfied with respect to property which is subject to any use (other than a resale or sublease), manufacture, assembly, or other processing (other than packaging) by any person between the time of the sale or lease by such seller or lessor and the delivery or ultimate delivery outside the United States described in this paragraph (d)(2).

(iv) If property is located outside the United States at the time it is purchased by a person or leased by a person as lessee, such property may be export property in the hands of such purchaser or lessee only if it is imported into the United States prior to its further sale or lease (including a sublease) outside the United States. Paragraphs (a)(3) and (e) of this section (relating to the 50 percent foreign content test) are applicable in determining whether such property is export property. Thus, for example, if such property is not subjected to manufacturing or production (as defined in paragraph (c) of this section) within the United States after such importation, it does not qualify as export property.

(3) Proof of compliance with destination test. (i) Delivery outside the United States. For purposes of paragraph (d)(2) of this section (other than subdivision (i)(C) thereof), a seller or lessor shall establish ultimate delivery, use, or consumption of property outside the United States by providing—

(A) A facsimile or carbon copy of the export bill of lading issued by the carrier who delivers the property,

(B) A certificate of an agent or representative of the carrier disclosing delivery of the property outside the United States,

(C) A facsimile or carbon copy of the certificate of lading for the property executed by a customs officer of the country to which the property is delivered,

(D) If that country has no customs administration, a written statement by the person to whom delivery outside the United States was made,

(E) A facsimile or carbon copy of the Shipper's Export Declaration, a monthly shipper's summary declaration filed with the Bureau of Customs, or a magnetic tape filed in lieu of the Shipper's Export Declaration, covering the property, or

(F) Any other proof (including evidence as to the nature of the property or the nature of the property or the nature of the transaction) which establishes to the satisfaction of the Commissioner that the property was ultimately delivered, or directly sold, or directly consumed outside the United States within 1 year after the sale or lease.

(ii) The requirements of subdivision (i) (A), (B), (C), or (E) of this paragraph will be considered satisfied even though the name of the ultimate consignee and the price paid for the goods is marked out provided that, in the case of a Shipper's Export Declaration or other document listed in subdivision (i)(E) of this paragraph or a document such as an export bill of lading, such document still indicates the country in which delivery to the ultimate consignee is to be made and, in the case of a certificate of an agent or representative of the carrier, that the document indicates that the property was delivered outside the United States.

(iii) A seller or lessor shall also establish the meeting of the requirement of paragraph (d)(2)(i) of this section (other than subdivision (i)(C) thereof), that the property was delivered outside the United States without further use, manufacture, assembly, or other processing within the United States.

(iv) For purposes of paragraph (d)(2)(i)(C) of this section, a purchaser or lessee of property is deemed to qualify as an FSC or an interest charge DISC for its taxable year if the seller or lessor obtains from the purchaser or lessee a copy of the purchaser's or lessee's election to be treated as an FSC or interest charge DISC together with the purchaser's or lessee's sworn statement that the election has been timely filed with the Internal Revenue Service Center. The copy of the election and the sworn statement of the purchaser or lessee must be received by the seller or lessor within 6 months after the sale or lease. A purchaser or lessee is not treated as an FSC or interest charge DISC with respect to a sale or lease during a taxable year for which the purchaser or lessee does not qualify as a FSC or interest charge DISC if the seller or lessor does not believe or if a reasonable person would not believe at the time the sale or lease is made that the purchaser or lessee will qualify as an FSC or interest charge DISC for the taxable year.

(v) If a seller or lessor fails to provide proof of compliance with the destination test as required by this paragraph (d)(3), the property sold or leased is not export property.

(4) Sales and leases of property for ultimate use in the United States. (i) In general. For purposes of paragraph (d)(1) of this section, the use test in this paragraph (d)(4) is satisfied with respect to property which—

(A) Under subdivision (4)(ii) through (iv) of this paragraph is not sold for ultimate use in the United States, or

(B) Under subdivision (4)(v) of this paragraph is leased for ultimate use outside the United States.

(ii) Sales of property for ultimate use in the United States. For purposes of subdivision (4)(i) of this paragraph, a purchaser of property (including components, as defined in subdivision (4)(vii) of this paragraph) is deemed to use the property ultimately in the United States if any of the following conditions exist:

(A) The purchaser is a related party with respect to the seller and the purchaser ultimately uses the property, or a second product into which the property is incorporated as a component, in the United States.

(B) At the time of the sale, there is an agreement or understanding that the property, or a second product into which the property is incorporated as a component, will be ultimately used by the purchaser in the United States.

(C) At the time of the sale, a reasonable person would have believed that the property or the second product would be ultimately used by the purchaser in the United States unless, in the case of a sale of components, the fair market value of the components at the time of delivery to the purchaser constitutes less than 20 percent of the fair market value of the second product into which the components are incorporated (determined at the time of completion of the production, manufacture, or assembly of the second product).

For purposes of subdivision (4)(ii)(B) of this paragraph, there is an agreement or understanding that property will ultimately be used in the United States if, for example, a component is sold abroad under an express agreement with the foreign purchaser that the component is to be incorporated into a product to be sold back to the United States. As a further example, there would also be such an agreement or understanding if the foreign purchaser indicated at the time of the sale or previously that the component is to be incorporated into a product which is designed principally for the United States market. However, such an agreement or understanding does not result from the mere fact that a second product, into which components exported from the United States have been incorporated and which is sold on the world market, is sold in substantial quantities in the United States.

(iii) Use in the United States. For purposes of subdivision (4)(ii) of this paragraph, property (including components incorporated into a second product) is or would be ultimately used in the United States by the purchaser if, at any time within 3 years after the purchase of such property or components, either the property is or the components (or the second product into which the components are incorporated) are resold by the purchaser for use by a subsequent purchaser within the United States or the purchaser or subsequent purchaser fails, for any period of 365 consecutive days, to use the property or second product predominantly outside the United States (as defined in subdivision (4)(vi) of this paragraph).

(iv) Sales to retailers. For purposes of subdivision (4)(ii)(C) of this paragraph, property sold to any person whose principal business consists of selling from inventory to retail customers at retail outlets outside the United States will be considered to be used predominantly outside the United States.

(v) Leases of property for ultimate use outside the United States. For purposes of subdivision (4)(i) of this paragraph, a lessee of property is deemed to use property ultimately outside the United States during a taxable year of the lessor if the property is used predominantly outside the United States (as defined in subdivision (4)(vi) of this paragraph) by the lessee during the portion of the lessor's taxable year which is included within the term of the lease. A determination as to whether the ultimate use of leased property satisfies the requirements of this subdivision is made for each taxable year of the lessor. Thus, leased property may be used predominantly outside the United States for a taxable year of the lessor (and thus, constitute export property if the remaining requirements of this section are met) even if the property is not used predominantly outside the United States in earlier taxable years or later taxable years of the lessor.

(vi) Predominant use outside the United States. For purposes of this paragraph (d)(4), property is used predominantly outside the United States for any period if, during that period, the property is located outside the United States more than 50 percent of the time. An aircraft, railroad rolling stock, vessel, motor vehicle, container, or other property used for transportation purposes is deemed to be used predominantly outside the United States for any period if, during that period, either the property is located outside the United States more than 50 percent of the time or more than 50 percent of the miles traversed in the use of the property are traversed outside the United States. However, property is deemed to be within the United States at all times during which it is engaged in transport between any two points within the United States, except where the transport constitutes uninterrupted international air transportation within the meaning of section 4262(c)(3) and the regulations under that section (relating to tax on air transportation of persons). An orbiting satellite is deemed to be located outside the United States. For purposes of applying section 4262(c)(3) to this subdivision, the term "United States" includes the Commonwealth of Puerto Rico.

(vii) Component. For purposes of this paragraph (d)(4), a component is property which is (or is reasonably expected to be) incorporated into a second product by the purchaser of such component by means of production, manufacture, or assembly.

(e) Foreign content of property. *(1) The 50 percent test.* Under paragraph (a)(3) of this section, no more than 50 percent of the fair market value of export property may be attributable to the fair market value of articles which were imported into the United States. For purposes of this paragraph (e), articles imported into the United States are referred to as "foreign content." The fair market value of the foreign content of export property is computed in accordance with paragraph (e)(4) of this section. The fair market value of export property which is sold to a person who is not a related person with respect to the seller is the sale price for such property (not including interest, finance or carrying charges, or similar charges.)

(2) Application of 50 percent test. The 50 percent test is applied on an item-by-item basis. If, however, a person sells or leases a large volume of substantially identical export property in a taxable year and if all of that property contains substantially identical foreign content in substantially the same proportion, the person may determine the portion of foreign content contained in that property on an aggregate basis.

(3) Parts and services. If, at the time property is sold or leased the seller or lessor agrees to furnish parts pursuant to a services contract (as provided in § 1.924(a)-1T(d)(3)) and the price for the parts is not separately stated, the 50 percent test is applied on an aggregate basis to the property and parts. If the price for the parts is separately stated, the 50 percent test is applied separately to the property and to the parts.

(4) Computation of foreign content. (i) Valuation. For purposes of applying the 50 percent test, it is necessary to determine the fair market value of all articles which constitutes foreign content of the property being tested to determine if it is export property. The fair market value of the imported articles is determined as of the time the articles are imported into the United States.

(A) General rule. Except as provided in paragraph (e)(4)(i)(B), the fair market value of the imported articles which constitutes foreign content is their appraised value, as determined under section 403 of the Tariff Act of 1930 (19 U.S.C. 1401a) in connection with their importation. The appraised value of the articles is the full dutiable value of the articles, determined, however, without regard to any special provision in the United States tariff laws which would result in a lower dutiable value.

(B) Special election. If all or a portion of the imported article was originally manufactured, produced, grown, or extracted in the United States, the taxpayer may elect to determine the fair market value of the imported articles which constitutes foreign content under the provisions of this paragraph (e)(4)(i)(B) if the property is subjected to manufacturing or production (as defined in paragraph (c) of this section) within the United States after importation. A taxpayer making the election under this paragraph may determine the fair market value of the imported articles which constitutes foreign content to be the fair market value of the imported articles reduced by the fair market value at the time of the initial export of the portion of the property that was manufactured, produced, grown, or extracted in the United States. The taxpayer must establish the fair market value of the imported articles and of the portion of the property manufactured, produced, grown, or extracted in the United States at the time of the initial export in accordance with subdivision (4)(ii)(B) of this paragraph.

(ii) Evidence of fair market value. (A) General rule. For purposes of subdivision (4)(i)(A) of this paragraph, the fair market value of the imported articles is their appraised value, which may be evidenced by the customs invoice issued on the importation of such articles into the United States. If the holder of the articles is not the importer (or a related person with respect to the importer), the appraised value of the articles may be evidenced by a certificate based upon information contained in the customs invoice and furnished to the holder by the person from whom the articles (or property incorporating the articles) were purchased. If a customs invoice or certificate described in the preceding sentences is not available to a person purchasing property, the person shall establish that no more than 50 percent of the fair market value of such property is attributable to the fair market value of articles which were imported into the United States.

(B) Special election. For purposes of the special election set forth in subdivision (4)(i)(B) of this paragraph, if the initial export is made to a controlled person within the meaning of section 482, the fair market value of the imported articles and of the portion of the articles that are manufactured, produced, grown, or extracted within the United States shall be established by the taxpayer in accordance with the rules under section 482 and the regulations under that section. If the initial export is not made to a controlled person, the fair market value must be established by the taxpayer under the facts and circumstances.

(iii) Interchangeable component articles. (A) If identical or similar component articles can be incorporated interchangeably into property and a person acquires component articles that are imported into the United States and other component articles that are not imported into the United States, the determination whether imported component articles were incorporated in the property that is exported from the United States shall be made on a substitution basis as in the case of the rules relating to drawback accounts under the customs laws. See section 313(b) of the Tariff Act of 1930, as amended (19 U.S.C. 1313(b)).

(B) The provisions of subdivision (4)(iii)(A) of this paragraph may be illustrated by the following example:

Example. Assume that a manufacturer produces a total of 20,000 electronic devices. The manufacturer exports 5,000 of the devices and subsequently sells 11,000 of the devices to a FSC which exports the 11,000 devices. The major single component article in each device is a tube which represents 60 percent of the fair market value of the device at the time the device is sold by the manufacturer. The manufacturer imports 8,000 of the tubes and produces the remaining 12,000 tubes. For purposes of this subdivision, in accordance with the substitution principle used in the customs drawback laws, the 5,000 devices exported by the manufacturer are each treated as containing an imported tube because the devices were exported prior to the sale to the FSC. The remaining 3,000 imported tubes are treated as being contained in the first 3,000 devices purchased and exported by the FSC. Thus, since the 50 percent test is not met with respect to the first 3,000 devices purchased and exported by the FSC, those devices are not export property. The remaining 8,000 devices purchased and exported by the FSC are treated as containing tubes produced in the United States, and those devices are export property (if they otherwise meet the requirements of this section).

(f) Excluded property. *(1) In general.* Notwithstanding any other provision of this section, the following property is not export property—

(i) Property described in subdivision (2) of this paragraph (relating to property leased to a member of controlled group),

(ii) Property described in subdivision (3) of this paragraph (relating to certain types of intangible property),

(iii) Products described in paragraph (g) of this section (relating to oil and gas products), and

(iv) Products described in paragraph (h) of this section (relating to certain export controlled products).

(2) Property leased to member of controlled group. (i) In general. Property leased to a person (whether or not a FSC) which is a member of the same controlled group as the lessor constitutes export property for any period of time only if during the period—

(A) The property is held for sublease, or is subleased, by the person to a third person for the ultimate use of the third person;

(B) The third person is not a member of the same controlled group; and

(C) The property is used predominantly outside the United States by the third person.

(ii) Predominant use. The provisions of paragraph (d)(4)(vi) of this section apply in determining under subdivision (2)(i)(C) of this paragraph whether the property is used predominantly outside the United States by the third person.

(iii) Leasing rule. For purposes of this paragraph (f)(2), leased property is deemed to be ultimately used by a member of the same controlled group as the lessor if such property is leased to a person which is not a member of the controlled group but which subleases the property to a person which is a member of the controlled group. Thus, for example, if X, a FSC for the taxable year, leases a movie film to Y, a foreign corporation which is not a member of the same controlled group as X, and Y then subleases the film to persons which are members of the controlled group for showing to the general public, the film is not export property. On the other hand, if X, a FSC for the taxable year, leases a movie film to Z, a foreign corporation which is a member of the same controlled group as X, and Z then subleases the film to Y, another foreign corporation, which is not a member of the same controlled group for showing to the general public, the film is not disqualified from being export property.

(iv) Certain copyrights. With respect to a copyright which is not excluded by subdivision (3) of this paragraph from being export property, the ultimate use of the property is the sale or exhibition of the property to the general public. Thus, if A, a FSC for the taxable year, leases recording tapes to B, a foreign corporation which is a member of the same controlled group as A, and if B makes records from the recording tape and sells the records to C, another foreign corporation, which is not a member of the same controlled group, for sale by C to the general public, the recording tape is not disqualified under this paragraph from being export property, notwithstanding the leasing of the recording tape by A to a member of the same controlled group, since the ultimate use of the tape is the sale of the records (i.e., property produced from the recording tape).

(3) Intangible property. Export property does not include any patent, invention, model, design, formula, or process, whether or not patented, or any copyright (other than films, tapes, records, or similar reproductions, for commercial or home use), goodwill, trademark, tradebrand, franchise, or other like property. Although a copyright such as a copyright on a book or computer software does not constitute export property, a copyrighted article (such as a book or standardized, mass marketed computer software) if not accompanied by a right to reproduce for external use is export property if the requirements of this section are otherwise satisfied. Computer software referred to in the preceding sentence may be on any medium, including, but not limited to, magnetic tape, punched cards, disks, semi-conductor chips and circuit boards. A license of a master recording tape for reproduction outside the United States is not disqualified under this paragraph from being export property.

(g) Oil and Gas. *(1) In general.* Under section 927(a)(2)(C), export property does not include oil or gas (or any primary product thereof).

(2) Primary product from oil or gas. A primary product from oil or gas is not export property. For purposes of this paragraph—

(i) Primary product from oil. The term "primary product from oil" means crude oil and all products derived from the destructive distillation of crude oil, including—

(A) Volatile products,

(B) Light oils such as motor fuel and kerosene,

(C) Distillates such as naphtha,

(D) Lubricating oils,

(E) Greases and waxes, and

(F) Residues such as fuel oil.

For purposes of this paragraph, a product or commodity derived from shale oil which would be a primary product from oil if derived from crude oil is considered a primary product from oil.

(ii) Primary product from gas. The term "primary product from gas" means all gas and associated hydrocarbon components from gas wells or oil wells, whether recovered at the lease or upon further processing, including—

(A) Natural gas,

(B) Condensates,

(C) Liquefied petroleum gases such as ethane, propane, and butane, and

(D) Liquid products such as natural gasoline.

(iii) Primary products and changing technology. The primary products from oil or gas described in subdivisions (2) (i) and (ii) of this paragraph and the processes described in those subdivisions are not intended to represent either the only primary products from oil or gas, or the only processes from which primary products may be derived under existing and future technologies. For example, petroleum coke, although not derived from the destructive distillation of crude oil, is a primary product from oil derived from an existing technology.

(iv) Non-primary products. For purposes of this paragraph, petrochemicals, medicinal products, insecticides and alcohols are not considered primary products from oil or gas.

(h) Export controlled products. *(1) In general.* Section 927(a)(2)(D) provides that an export controlled product is not export property. A product or commodity may be an export controlled product at one time but not an export controlled product at another time. For purposes of this paragraph, a product or commodity is an "export controlled product" at a particular time if at that time the export of such product or commodity is prohibited or curtailed under section 7(a) of the Export Administration Act of 1979, to effectuate the policy relating to the protection of the domestic economy set forth in paragraph (2)(C) of section 3 of the Export Administration Act of 1979. That policy is to use export controls to the extent necessary to protect the domestic economy from the excessive drain of scarce materials and to reduce the serious inflationary impact of foreign demand.

(2) Products considered export controlled products. (i) In general. For purposes of this paragraph, an export controlled product is a product or commodity, which is subject to short supply export controls under 15 CFR Part 377. A product or commodity is considered an export controlled product for the duration of each control period which applies to such product or commodity. A control period of a product or commodity begins on and includes the initial control date (as defined in subdivision (2)(ii) of this paragraph) and ends on and includes the final control date (as defined in subdivision (2)(iii) of this paragraph).

(ii) Initial control date. The initial control date of a product or commodity which is subject to short supply export controls is the effective date stated in the regulations to 15 CFR Part 377 which subjects the product or commodity to short supply export controls. If there is no effective date stated in these regulations, the initial control date of the product or commodity will be thirty days after the effective date of the regulations which subject the product or commodity to short supply export controls.

(iii) Final control date. The final control date of a product or commodity is the effective date stated in the regulations to 15 CFR Part 377 which removes the product or commodity from short supply export controls. If there is no effective date stated in those regulations, the final control date of the product or commodity is the date which is thirty days after the effective date of the regulations which remove the product or commodity from short supply export control.

(iv) Expiration of Export Administration Act. An initial control date and final control date cannot occur after the expiration date of the Export Administration Act under the authority of which the short supply export controls were issued.

(3) Effective dates. (i) Products controlled on January 1, 1985. If a product or commodity was subject to short supply export controls on January 1, 1985, this paragraph shall apply to all sales, exchanges, other dispositions, or leases of the product or commodity made after January 1, 1985, by the FSC or by the FSC's related supplier if the FSC is the commission agent on the transaction.

(ii) Products first controlled after January 1, 1985. If a product or commodity becomes subject to short supply export controls after January 1, 1985, this paragraph applies to sales, exchanges, other dispositions, or leases of such product or commodity made on or after the initial control date of such product or commodity, and to owning such product or commodity on or after such date.

(iii) Date of sales, exchange, lease, or other disposition. For purposes of this paragraph (h)(3), the date of sale, exchange, or other disposition of a product or commodity is the date as of which title to such product or commodity passes. The date of a lease is the date as of which the lessee takes possession of a product or commodity. The accounting method of a person is not determinative of the date of sale, exchange, other disposition, or lease.

(i) Property in short supply. If the President determines that the supply of any property which is otherwise export property as defined in this section is insufficient to meet the requirements of the domestic economy, he may by Executive Order designate such property as in short supply. Any property so designated will be treated under section 927(a)(3) as property which is not export property during the period beginning with the date specified in such Executive Order and ending with the date specified in an Executive Order setting forth the President's determination that such property is no longer in short supply.

T.D. 8126, 3/2/87.

§ 1.927(b)-1T Temporary Regulations; Definition of gross receipts.

Caution: The Treasury has not yet amended Reg § 1.927(b)-1T to reflect changes made by P.L. 106-519.

(a) General rule. Under section 927(b), for purposes of sections 921 through 927, the gross receipts of a person for a taxable year are—

(1) Business income. The total amounts received or accrued by the person from the sale or lease of property held primarily for sale or lease in the ordinary course of a trade or business, and

(2) Other income. Gross income recognized from whatever source derived, such as, for example, from—

(i) The furnishing of services (whether or not related to the sale or lease of property described in subdivision (1) of this paragraph),

(ii) Dividends and interest (including tax exempt interest),

(iii) The sale at a gain of any property not described in subdivision (1) of this paragraph, and

(iv) Commission transactions to the extent described in paragraph (e) of this section.

(b) Non-gross receipts items. For purposes of paragraph (a) of this section, gross receipts do not include amounts received or accrued by a person from—

(1) Loan transactions. The proceeds of a loan or the repayment of a loan, or

(2) Non-taxable transactions. A receipt of property in a transaction to which section 118 (relating to contribution to capital) or section 1032 (relating to exchange of stock for property) applies.

(c) Non-reduction of total amounts. For purposes of paragraph (a) of this section, the total amounts received or accrued by a person are not reduced by costs of goods sold, expenses, losses, a deduction for dividends received, or any other deductible amounts. The total amounts received or accrued by a person are reduced by returns and allowances.

(d) Method of accounting. For purposes of paragraph (a) of this section, the total amounts received or accrued by a person shall be determined under the method of accounting used in computing its taxable income. If, for example, a FSC receives advance or installment payments for the sale or lease of property described in paragraph (a)(1) of this section, for the furnishing of services, or which represent recognized gain from the sale of property not described in paragraph (a)(1) of this section, any amount of such advance payments is considered to be gross receipts of the FSC for the taxable year for which such amount is included in the gross income of the FSC.

(e) Commission transactions. *(1) In general.* (i) With a related supplier. In the case of transactions which give rise to a commission from the FSC's related supplier on the sale or lease of property or the furnishing of services by a principal, the FSC's gross income from all such transactions is the commission paid or payable to the FSC by the related supplier. The FSC's gross receipts for purposes of computing its profit under the administrative pricing methods of section 925(a)(1) and (2) shall be the gross receipts (other than gross receipts which would not be foreign trading gross receipts had they been received by the FSC) derived by the related supplier from the sale or lease of the property or from the furnishing of services, with respect to which the commissions are derived. Also, in determining whether the 50% test in section 924(a) has been met, the relevant gross receipts are the gross receipts of the related supplier.

(ii) With an unrelated principal. In the case of transactions which give rise to a commission from an unrelated principal to a FSC on the sale or lease of property or the furnishing of services by a principal, the amount recognized by the FSC as gross income from all such transactions shall be the commission received from the principal.

(2) Selective commission arrangements. (i) In general. A commission arrangement between the FSC and its related supplier may provide that the FSC will not be the related supplier's commission agent with respect to sales or leases of export property, or the furnishing of services, which do not result in foreign trading gross receipts. In addition, the commission agreement may provide that the FSC will not be the related supplier's commission agent on transactions which would result in a loss to the related supplier under the transfer pricing rules of section 925(a). In a buy-sell FSC situation, selective commission arrangements are not applicable. Determination of which transactions fall within the selective commission arrangement may be made up to the due date under section 6072(b), including extensions provided for under section 6081, of the FSC's income tax return for the taxable year of the FSC during which a transaction occurs.

(ii) Example. The treatment of a selective commission arrangement may be illustrated by the following example:

Example. A calendar year commission FSC ("F") entered into a selective commission arrangement with related supplier RS which provided that F will not be RS's commission agent on transactions which would result in a loss to RS under the transfer pricing rules of section 925(a). During 1987, RS sold three different articles of export property A, B and C, all of which fall within the same three digit Standard Industrial Classification. In July of 1988, while preparing the FSC's 1987 income tax return, RS determined that the sale of export property A resulted in a loss to RS under the section 482 method of section 925(a)(3) and that applying that method to the sales of export property B and C resulted in only a small amount of income to both RS and F. In addition, RS determined that grouping export property B and C, while excluding export property A from the grouping, resulted in the highest profit to F under the combined taxable income administrative pricing method of section 925(a)(2). Using the same grouping, the gross receipts method of section 925(a)(1) would result in a lower profit to F. Under the special no-loss rule of § 1.925(a)-1T(e)(1)(iii), RS would be prohibited from using the combined taxable income administrative pricing method to determine F's profit for the grouping of export property B and C if it used the section 482 method on the sale of export property A. This results because there was a loss to RS on the sale of export property A. Under the selective commission arrangement, RS could exercise its option and exclude the sale of export property A. Since F is no longer deemed to have been operating as RS's commission agent on that sale, the combined taxable income method may be used to compute F's profit on the grouping of the sales of export property B and C.

(f) Example. The definition of gross receipts under this section may be illustrated by the following example:

Example. During 1985, M, a related supplier of N, is engaged in the manufacture of machines in the United States. N, a calendar year FSC, is engaged in the sale and lease of such machines in foreign countries. N furnishes services which are related and subsidiary to its sale and lease of those machines. N also acts as a commission agent in foreign countries for Z, an unrelated supplier, with respect to Z's sale of products. N receives dividends on stock owned by it, interest on loans, and proceeds from sales of business assets located outside the United States resulting in recognized gains and losses. N's gross receipts for 1985 are $3,550, computed on the basis of the additional facts assumed in the table below:

N's sales receipts for machines manufactured by M (without reduction for cost of goods sold and selling expenses)	$1,500
N's lease receipts for machines manufactured by M (without reduction for depreciation and leasing expenses)	500
N's gross income from related and subsidiary services for machines manufactured by M (without reduction for service expenses)	400
N's sales receipts for products manufactured by Z (without reduction for Z's cost of goods sold, commissions on sales and commission sales expenses)	550
Dividends received by N	150
Interest received by N	200

Proceeds received by N representing recognized gain (but not losses) for sales of business assets located outside the United States	250
N's gross receipts	3,550

T.D. 8126, 3/2/87.

§ 1.927(d)-1 Other definitions.

Caution: The Treasury has not yet amended Reg § 1.927(d)-1 to reflect changes made by P.L. 106-519.

(a) Carrying Charges.

Q-1. Under what circumstances is the sales price of property or services sold by a FSC or a related supplier considered to include carrying charges as defined in subdivision (ii)(B)(1) of Q&A-9 of § 1.921-2?

A-1. (i) The proceeds received from a sale of export property by a FSC or a related supplier (or the amount paid for services rendered or from rental of export property) may include carrying charges if any part of the sale proceeds (or service or rental payment) is paid after the end of the normal payment period. If the export property is sold or leased by, or if the services are rendered by, the FSC, the entire carrying charges amount as determined in Q&A-2 of this section will be the income of the FSC. If, however, the FSC is the commission agent of a related supplier on these transactions, the carrying charges amount so determined is income of the related supplier. The commission payable to the FSC will be computed by reducing the related supplier's gross receipts from the transaction by the amount of the carrying charges. No carrying charges will be assessed on the commissions paid by the related supplier to the FSC. The carrying charges provisions, likewise, do not apply to any other transaction that does not give rise to foreign trading gross receipts.

(ii) The normal payment period for a sale transaction is 60 days from the earlier of date of sale or date of exchange of property under the contract. For this purpose, the date of sale will be the date the sale is recorded on the seller's books of account under its normal accounting method. The date the transaction was recorded on the seller's books of account shall be disregarded if recording is delayed in order to delay the start of the normal payment period. In these circumstances, the earlier of the date of the contract or date of exchange of property will be deemed the date of sale. For related and subsidiary services that are not separately stated from the sale or lease transaction, the earlier of the date of the sale or date the export property is delivered to the purchaser is the applicable date. For related and subsidiary services which are separately stated from the sale or lease transaction and for other services, such as engineering and architectural services, the normal payment period is 60 days from the earlier of the date payment is due for the services or the date services under the contract are completed. The date of completion of a services contract is the date of final approval of the services by the recipient. With regard to transactions involving the lease or rental of export property, the normal payment period will begin on the date the rental payment is due under the lease. The date the normal payment period begins under this subdivision (ii) will be the same whether or not the transaction is with a related person.

(iii) The carrying charges are computed for the period beginning with the first day after the end of the normal payment period and ending with the date of payment. A FSC may elect at any time prior to the close of the statute of limitations of section 6501(a) for the FSC taxable year to treat the final date of payment stated in the contract as the date of payment if—

(A) the contracts for all transactions completed during the taxable year require that payment be received within the normal payment period,

(B) no more than 20% of transactions for which final payment is received in the taxable year involve payment after the end of the normal payment period. For FSC taxable years beginning after March 3, 1987, the 20% test will apply only to the dollar value of the transactions and not to the number of transactions. For prior taxable years, the 20% test will apply to either the dollar value of the transactions or to the number of transactions. The special grouping rules applicable to determination of the FSC's profit under the administrative pricing rules of section 925 may be applied to this elective provision. Accordingly, transactions may be grouped into product or product-line groupings to determine whether 20% or less of the dollar value (or number of transactions, if applicable) of the grouped transactions involve payment after the end of the normal payment period.

Q-2. How are carrying charges as defined in subdivision (ii)(B)(1) of Q&A 9 of § 1.921-9 computed?

A-2. If carrying charges as defined in subdivision (ii)(B)(1) of Q&A of § 1.921-9 are considered to be included in the sale price of property income or rental payment services, the amount of the carrying charges is equal to the amount in subdivision (i) of this answer if the contract provides for stated interest or the amount in subdivisions (ii) or (iii) of this answer, whichever is applicable, if the contract does not so provide.

(i) If a contract provides for stated interest beginning on the day after the end of the normal payment period, carrying charges will accrue only if the stated interest rate is less than the short-term, monthly Federal rate as of the day after the end of normal payment period and then only to the extent the stated interest is less than the short-term, monthly Federal rate. The short-term, monthly Federal rate is that rate as determined for purposes of section 1274(d) and which is published in the Internal Revenue Bulletin. Carrying charges will not accrue, however, unless payments are made after the end of the normal payment period.

(ii) If a contract for a transaction does not provide for stated interest, and if the taxpayer does not elect the method described in subdivision (iii) of this answer, the amount of carrying charges is equal to the excess of—

(A) The amount of the sales price of property, services income or rental payment that is unpaid on the day after the end of the normal payment period, over

(B) The present value, as of the day after the end of the normal payment period, of all payments that are required to be made under the contract and that are unpaid on the day after the end of the normal payment period. The amount of the sales price of property, service income or rental payment is the amount under the contract whether it be the sales price, amount paid for services or the rental amount determined as of the actual payment date unless a FSC makes the election provided under subdivision (iii) of Q&A 1. If a FSC makes the election provided under subdivision (III) of Q&A 1, the amount of the sales price is the sales price, services income or rental payment under the contract determined as of the final payment date stated in the contract. All payments that are required to be made under the contract include the stated sales price, services income or rental payment as well as stated amounts of interest and carrying charges. The discount rate for the present value computation is simple interest at the short-term monthly Federal rate published in the Internal Revenue Bulletin, determined as of the day after the end of the normal payment period. The present value of a payment is calculated as follows:

$$P = S \frac{1}{(1 + (i \times t))}$$

P = present value of a payment that is required and unpaid after the end of the normal payment period
S = amount of a payment that is required and unpaid after the end of the normal payment period
i = the short-term monthly Federal rate
t = the number of days after the end of the normal payment period and before date of payment divided by 365

If a sale is made, or if services are completed, or if rent is due under a lease in a taxable year and the required date of payment is in a later taxable year, carrying charges for the first taxable year are computed for the number of days after the end of the normal payment period and before the end of the taxable year. For the following taxable year, carrying charges are computed for the number of days after the beginning of the taxable year and before the date of payment.

(iii) At the election of the taxpayer, the amount of carrying charges may be determined under the method described in this subdivision (iii). If the taxpayer elects this method, it must be used for all applicable transactions within the taxable year of the FSC. If this optional method is used, the computation of carrying charges must be made separately for transactions involving related persons and for those transactions involving unrelated persons. In addition, the computation of carrying charges must be made separately for each of the five types of income of the FSC (or of the related supplier if the related supplier is the principal on the transaction) listed in subparagraph (1) through (5) of section 924(a). These groupings are separate and distinct from the groupings that are established for purposes of determining the FSC's profit on the export transactions. The optional method allowed in this subdivision provides that the amount of carrying charges for a taxable year of a FSC (or related supplier if the related supplier is the principal on the export transaction) is computed using the average of receivables of unrelated persons (or of related persons) and the average time those receivables are outstanding. Receivables are included in this computation only if they are from transactions on which foreign trading gross receipts, as defined in section 924(a), are received by the FSC (or which are received by a related supplier of a FSC and which would have been foreign trading gross receipts had they been received by the FSC). Carrying charges are calculated under this method as follows:

CC = (AR) (I/365) (X) (Y)
CC = Carrying charges
AR = Average monthly receivables balance for the taxable year
I = The average short-term, monthly Federal rate for the year
X = The number of times receivables turn over in the year
Y = The number of days the average receivables are outstanding over 60 days

This optional method is illustrated in Example (5) in subdivision (v) of this answer.

(iv) The computation of carrying charges under this answer 2 applies only to the determination of carrying charges under subdivision (ii)(B)(1) of Q&A 9 of § 1.921-2 and does not apply to the determination of any other unstated interest or for any other purpose.

(v) The following examples illustrate the computation of carrying charges under this section:

Example (1). On January 1, 1985, a FSC sells export property for $10,000. The export property is delivered to the purchaser on January 10, 1985. The terms of the contract require payment within 90 days after sale. The normal payment period is 60 days. The FSC does not make an election under subdivision (iii) of Q&A. The contract does not require the payment of any interest or carrying charges. The purchaser pays the entire sales price on March 1, 1985. The sales price is not considered to include any carrying charges because the purchase paid the entire sales price within the normal payment period.

Example (2). The facts are the same as in example (1) except that the purchaser pays the entire sales price on April 6, 1985, 96 days after the earlier of the date of sale or date of delivery (i.e., January 1, 1985). Therefore, the sales price is considered to include carrying charges computed as follows:

Step 1: Determines the short-term monthly Federal rate as of the earlier of date of sale or date of delivery. For purposes of this example, the rate is 10%.

Step 2: Determine the fraction of the year represented by the number of days after 60 days and before date of payment. In this example, the number of days beyond 60 is 96 − 60 = 36, which is divided by 365

$$\frac{36 \text{ days}}{365 \text{ days}} = .099 \text{ fraction of the year}$$

Step 3: Using the short-term monthly Federal rate and the fraction of the year, compute the present value of the payment.

$$P = S \frac{1}{(1 + (i \times t))}$$

$$P = \$10{,}000 \frac{1}{(1 + (.10 \times .099))}$$

P = $10,000 (.99)
P = $9,900

Step 4: Using the present value of all payments, compute the carrying charges.

Carrying Charges = Sales Price Value

$10,000	Sales Price
− 9,900	Present Value
$ 100	Carrying charges

Example (3). On October 15, 1985, F, a FSC, leases export property to X for one month with a total rental due of $20,000. Under the terms of the lease, A agreed to pay F $10,000 on October 15, 1985, and the remaining $10,000 on January 15, 1986. The contract does not require the payment of any interest or carrying charges. The second $10,000 payment is made on January 3, 1986. This payment does not include any carrying charges because X paid the $10,000 before the start of the normal payment period.

Example (4). On October 15, 1985, F, a FSC, leases export property to X, for one month with a total amount due under the lease of $10,000, payable on October 15, 1985. X delays payment until January 19, 1986, which was 96 days after the start of the normal payment period. The 60 day normal payment period terminated on December 14, 1985. Therefore, the lease payment is considered to include carrying charges of $100 computed in the same manner as in Example (2). Of this $100, 17/36, or $47.22, is carrying charges for 1985 (i.e., 17 days in December), and 19/36, or $52.78, is carrying charges for 1986.

Example (5). During 1986, F, a FSC, sold on account export properties A and B to related and unrelated persons.

(A) Unrelated persons. During 1986, the sales on account to unrelated persons totaled $6,000. On the last day of each of the months of 1986, F had total receivables from unrelated persons from sales of export properties A and B, as follows:

January 31	$1,400
February 28	1,400
March 31	1,000
April 30	1,000
May 31	1,200
June 30	1,300
July 31	1,000
August 31	1,300
September 30	1,500
October 31	1,100
November 30	1,200
December 31	1,000
	14,400

Carrying charges for 1986 with unrelated persons under the optional method of subdivision (iii) of this answer will be $19.23, computed as follows:

Step 1: Determine the average short-term, monthly Federal rate for the year. For purposes of this example, the rate is assumed to be 9%.

Step 2: Determine the average receivables for the year. This average is calculated by totaling the end of the month receivables balance of each month of the year and dividing by twelve. In this example, the average monthly receivables balance is $1,200, calculated as follows:

$$\$1,200 = \$14,400/12$$

Step 3: Determine the number of times the receivables turn over during the year. This is calculated by dividing the sales on account for the year by the average monthly receivables balance for the year. For purposes of this example, receivables turned over 5 times for 1986, computed as follows:

$$5 = \frac{\$6,000}{\$1,200}$$

Step 4: Determine the number of days the average receivables are outstanding in excess of 60 days. In this example, there are 13 receivable days in excess of 60 days, computed as follows:

$$13 \text{ days} = (365/5) - 60 \text{ days}$$

Step 5: The amount of carrying charges, $19.23, is calculated by using the following equation:

CC = (AR) (I/365) (X) (Y)

CC = Carrying charges

AR = Average monthly receivables balance for the taxable year (step 2)

I = The average short-term monthly Federal rate for the year (step 1)

X = The number of times receivables turn over in the year (step 3)

Y = The number of days the average receivables are outstanding over 60 days (step 4)

CC = $19.23 = ($1,200) (.09/365) (5)(13)

(B) Related persons. Carrying charges, if any, on the sales on account to related persons must be computed separately using this optional method.

Q-3. Is a discount from the sales price of property or services for prompt payment considered to be stated carrying charges as defined in subdivision (ii)(A) of Q&A 9 of § 1.921-2?

A-3. No.

Q-4. Is the receipt of an arm's length factoring payment from an unrelated person considered a payment of the sales proceeds for purposes of determining whether payment is made within the normal payment period and the possible imposition of carrying charges?

A-4. Yes.

T.D. 8127, 3/2/87.

§ 1.927(d)-2T Definitions and special rules relating to Foreign Sales Corporation (temporary).

Caution: The Treasury has not yet amended Reg § 1.927(d)-2T to reflect changes made by P.L. 106-519.

(a) Definition of related supplier. For purposes of sections 921 through 927 and the regulations under those sections, the term "related supplier" means a related party which directly supplies to a FSC any property or services which the FSC disposes of in a transaction producing foreign trading gross receipts, or a related party which uses the FSC as a commission agent in the disposition of any property or services producing foreign trading gross receipts. A FSC may have different related suppliers with respect to different transactions. If, for example, X owns all the stock of Y, a corporation, and of F, a FSC, and X sells a product to Y which is resold to F, only Y is the related supplier of F. If, however, X sells directly to F and Y also sells directly to F, then, as to the transactions involving direct sales to F, each of X and Y is a related supplier of F.

(b) Definition of related party. The term "related party" means a person which is owned or controlled directly or indirectly by the same interests as the FSC within the meaning of section 482 and § 1.482-1(a).

T.D. 8126, 3/2/87.

§ 1.927(e)-1 Special sourcing rule.

Caution: The Treasury has not yet amended Reg § 1.927(e)-1 to reflect changes made by P.L. 106-519.

(a) Source rules for related persons. *(1) In general.* The income of a person described in section 482 from a sale of export property giving rise to foreign trading gross receipts of a FSC that is treated as from sources outside the United States shall not exceed the amount that would be treated as foreign source income earned by such person if the pricing rule under section 994 that corresponds to the rule used under section 925 with respect to such transaction applied to such transaction. This special sourcing rule also applies if the FSC is acting as a commission agent for the related supplier with respect to the transaction described in the first sentence of this paragraph (a)(1) that gives rise to foreign trading gross receipts and the transfer pricing rules of section 925 are used to determine the commission payable to the FSC. No limitation results under this section with respect to a transaction to which the section 482 pricing rule under section 925(a)(3) applies.

(2) Grouping of transactions. If, for purposes of determining the FSC's profits under the administrative pricing rules of sections 925(a) (1) and (2), grouping of transactions under

§ 1.925(a)-1T(c)(8) was elected, the same grouping shall be used for making the determinations under the special sourcing rule in this section.

(3) Corresponding DISC pricing rules. (i) In general. For purposes of this section—

(A) The DISC gross receipts pricing rule of section 994(a)(1) corresponds to the gross receipts pricing rule of section 925(a)(1);

(B) The DISC combined taxable income pricing rule of section 994(a)(2) corresponds to the combined taxable income pricing rule of section 925(a)(2); and

(C) The DISC section 482 pricing rule of section 994(a)(3) corresponds to the section 482 pricing rule of section 925(a)(3).

(ii) Special rules. For purposes of this section—

(A) The DISC pricing rules of section 994(a)(1) and (2) shall be determined without regard to export promotion expenses;

(B) Qualified export receipts under section 994(a)(1) and (2) shall be deemed to be an amount equal to the foreign trading gross receipts arising from the transaction; and

(C) Combined taxable income for purposes of section 994(a)(2) shall be deemed to be an amount equal to the combined taxable income for purposes of section 925(a)(2) arising from the transaction.

(b) Examples. The provisions of this section may be illustrated by the following examples:

Example (1). (i) R and F are calendar year taxpayers. R, a domestic manufacturing company, owns all the stock of F, which is a FSC acting as a commission agent for R. For the taxable year, R and F used the combined taxable income pricing rule of section 925(a)(2). For the taxable year, the combined taxable income of R and F is $100 from the sale of export property, as defined in section 927(a), manufactured by R using production assets located in the United States. Title to the export property passed outside of the United States.

(ii) Under section 925(a)(2), 23 percent of the $100 combined taxable income of R and F ($23) is allocated to F and the remaining $77 is allocated to R. Absent the special sourcing rule, under section 863(b) the $77 income allocated to R would be sourced $38.50 U.S. source and $38.50 foreign source. Under the special sourcing rule, the amount of foreign source income earned by a related supplier of a FSC shall not exceed the amount that would result if the corresponding DISC pricing rule applied. The DISC combined taxable income pricing rule of section 994(a)(2) corresponds to the combined taxable income pricing rule of section 925(a)(2). Under section 994(a)(2), $50 of the combined taxable income ($100 × .50) would be allocated to the DISC and the remaining $50 would be allocated to the related supplier. Under section 863(b), the $50 income allocated to the DISC's related supplier would be sourced $25 U.S. source and $25 foreign source. Accordingly, under the special sourcing rule, the foreign source income of R shall not exceed $25.

Example (2). (i) Assume the same facts as in Example 1 except that R and F used the gross receipts pricing rule of section 925(a)(1). In addition, for the taxable year foreign trading gross receipts derived from the sale of the export property are $2,000.

(ii) Under section 925(a)(1), 1.83 percent of the $2,000 foreign trading gross receipts ($36.60) is allocated to F and the $63.40 remaining combined taxable income ($100–$36.60) is allocated to R. Absent the special sourcing rule, under section 863(b) the $63.40 income allocated to R would be sourced $31.70 U.S. source and $31.70 foreign source. Under the special sourcing rule, the amount of foreign source income earned by a related supplier of a FSC shall not exceed the amount that would result if the corresponding DISC pricing rule applied. The DISC gross receipts pricing rule of section 994(a)(1) corresponds to the gross receipts pricing rule of section 925(a)(1). Under section 994(a)(1), $80 ($2,000 × .04) would be allocated to the DISC and the $20 remaining combined taxable income would be allocated to the related supplier. Under section 863(b), the $20 income allocated to the DISC's related supplier would be sourced $10 U.S. source and $10 foreign source. Accordingly, under the special sourcing rule, the foreign source income of R shall not exceed $10.

(c) Effective date. The rules of this section are applicable to taxable years beginning after December 31, 1997.

T.D. 8782, 9/17/98.

§ 1.927(e)-2T Effect of boycott participation on FSC and small FSC benefits (temporary).

Caution: The Treasury has not yet amended Reg § 1.927(e)-2T to reflect changes made by P.L. 106-519.

(a) International boycott factor. If the FSC (or small FSC) or any member of the FSC's (or small FSC's) controlled group participates in or cooperates with an international boycott within the meaning of section 999, the FSC's (or small FSC's) exempt foreign trade income as determined under section 923(a) shall be reduced by an amount equal to the product of the FSC's (or small FSC's) exempt foreign trade income multiplied by the international boycott factor determined under section 999. The amount of the reduction will be considered as non-exempt foreign trade income.

(b) Specifically attributable taxes and income method. If the taxpayer clearly demonstrates that the income earned for the taxable year is attributable to specific operations, then in lieu of applying the international boycott factor for such taxable year, the amount of the exempt foreign trade income as determined under section 923(a) that will be reduced by this section shall be the amount specifically attributable to the operations in which there was participation in or cooperation with an international boycott under section 999(b)(1). The amount of the reduction will be considered as non-exempt foreign trade income.

T.D. 8126, 3/2/87.

§ 1.927(f)-1 Election and termination of status as a Foreign Sales Corporation.

Caution: The Treasury has not yet amended Reg § 1.927(f)-1 to reflect changes made by P.L. 106-519.

(a) Election of status as a FSC or a small FSC.

Q-1. What is the effect of an election by a corporation to be treated as a FSC or small FSC?

A-1. A valid election to be treated as a FSC or a small FSC applies to the taxable year of the corporation for which made and remains in effect for all succeeding taxable years in which the corporation qualifies to be a FSC unless revoked by the corporation or unless the corporation fails for five consecutive years to qualify as a FSC (in case of a FSC election) or a small FSC (in case of a small FSC election).

Q-2. Can a corporation established prior to January 1, 1985 be treated as a FSC or a small FSC prior to making a FSC or a small FSC election?

A-2. A corporation cannot be treated as a FSC or a small FSC until it has made a FSC or a small FSC election. An election made within the first 90 days of 1985 relates back to January 1, 1985 unless the taxpayer indicates otherwise.

Q-3. If a shareholder who has not consented to a FSC or small FSC election transfers some or all of its shares before or during the first taxable year for which the election is made, may the holder of the transferred shares consent to the election?

A-3. A holder of the transferred shares may consent to a FSC or small FSC election under the circumstances described in § 1.922-2(c)(1). The rules contained in § 1.992-(c) shall apply to the consent by a holder of transferred shares.

Q-4. If a shareholder who has consented to a FSC or a small FSC election transfers some or all of its shares before the first taxable year for which the election is made, must the holder of the transferred shares consent to the election?

A-4. Yes. Consent must be made by any recipient of such shares on or before the 90th day after the first day of such first taxable year. If such recipient fails to file his consent on or before such 90th day, and extension of time for filing such consent may be granted in the manner, and subject to the conditions, described in paragraph (b)(3) of § 1.992-2.

Q-5. May an election of a corporation to be a FSC or a small FSC be effective as of a time other than the start of the corporation's taxable year?

A-5. No.

Q-6. If a fiscal year foreign corporation was in existence on December 31, 1984, must it wait until the first day of its taxable year beginning after January 1, 1985, to elect FSC status?

A-6. No. If a fiscal year foreign corporation was in existence on December 31, 1984, its taxable year will be deemed to have terminated on that date if the foreign corporation elects FSC status to be effective January 1, 1985. An income tax return will be required for any short years created by the deemed closing of the taxable year unless the corporation is relieved from the necessity of making a return by section 6012 and the regulations under that section. If the corporation's taxable year is deemed closed by operation of this regulation, the filing date of tax returns for the short taxable year ended on December 31, 1984, will be automatically extended until May 18, 1987.

Q-7. What is the effect of an election to be treated as a FSC or as a small FSC if the corporation or any other member of the controlled group has in effect an election to be treated as an interest charge DISC?

A-7. The interest charge DISC election shall be treated as revoked for all purposes under the Code as of the date the FSC election is effective. An affirmative revocation of the DISC election is unnecessary. The FSC election shall take effect. As long as the FSC election remains in effect, neither the corporation nor any other member of the controlled group is permitted to elect to be treated as an interest charge DISC for any taxable year including any part of a taxable year during which the corporation's FSC election continues to be effective.

Q-8. What is the effect of an election to be treated as a small FSC if the corporation or any other member of the controlled group has in effect an election to be treated as a FSC?

A-8. As long as a FSC election remains in effect, neither the corporation nor any other member of the controlled group is permitted to elect to be treated as a small FSC for any taxable year including any part of a taxable year during which a FSC election continues to be effective. Any FSC within the controlled group must affirmatively revoke its FSC election for a taxable year including any part of a taxable year for which small FSC status is elected.

Q-9. What is the effect of an election to be treated as a FSC if the corporation or any other member of the controlled group has in effect an election to be treated as a small FSC?

A-9. As long as a small FSC election remains in effect, neither the corporation nor any other member of the controlled group is permitted to elect to be treated as a FSC for any taxable year including any part of the taxable year during which a small FSC election continues to be effective. Any small FSC within the controlled group must affirmatively revoke its small FSC election for a taxable year including any part of a taxable year for which FSC status is elected. An election to be treated as a small FSC is permitted if the corporation or any other member of the controlled group has in effect an election to be treated as a small FSC. For a special rule providing for conversion of a small FSC to a FSC within one taxable year, see § 1.921-1T(b)(1) (Q&A-1).

(b) Termination of election of status as a FSC or a small FSC.

Q-10. How is the status of a corporation as a FSC or as a small FSC terminated?

A-10. The status of a corporation as a FSC or as a small FSC is terminated through revocation or by its continued failure to be a FSC.

Q-11. For what taxable year may a corporation revoke its election to be treated as a FSC or as a small FSC?

A-11. A corporation may revoke its election to be treated as a FSC or as a small FSC for any taxable year of the corporation after the first taxable year for which the election is effective.

Q-12. When must a corporation revoke a FSC or a small FSC election if revocation is to be effective for the taxable year in which revocation takes place?

A-12. If a corporation files a statement revoking its election to be treated as a FSC or as a small FSC during the first 90 days of a taxable year (other than the first taxable year for which such election is effective), such revocation will be effective for such taxable year and all taxable years thereafter. If the corporation files a statement revoking its election to be treated as a FSC or a small FSC after the firs 90 days of a taxable year, the revocation will be effective for all taxable years following such taxable year.

Q-13. Can a FSC change its status to a small FSC, or can a small FSC change its status to a FSC as of a date other than the first day of a taxable year?

A-13. No. Since a revocation of an election to be a FSC or a small FSC is effective only for entire taxable year, a corporation's change between FSC and small FSC status is effective as of the first day of a taxable year.

Q-14. How may a corporation revoke an election by a corporation to be treated as a FSC or a small FSC?

A-14. A corporation may revoke its election by filing a statement that the corporation revokes its election under section 922(a) to be treated as a FSC or under section 922(b) to be treated as a small FSC. Such statement shall indicate the corporation's name, address, employer identification number, and the first taxable year of the corporation for which the revocation is to be effective. The statement shall be signed by any person authorized to sign a corporate return under section 6062. Such revocation shall be filed with the Service Center with which the corporation filed its return.

Q-15. What if the effect is a corporation that has elected to be treated as a FSC or a small FSC fails to qualify as a FSC because it does not meet the requirements of section 922 for a taxable year?

A-15. If a corporation that has elected to be treated as a FSC or a small FSC does not qualify as a FSC or a small FSC for a taxable year, the corporation will not be treated as a FSC or a small FSC for the taxable year. However, the failure of a corporation to qualify to be treated as a FSC or a small FSC for a taxable year does not terminate the election of the corporation to be treated as FSC or a small FSC unless the corporation does not qualify under section 922 for each of 5 consecutive taxable years, as provided in Q&A 16 of this section.

Q-16. Under what circumstances is the FSC or small FSC election terminated for continued failure to be a FSC?

A-16. If a corporation that has elected to be treated as a FSC or a small FSC does not qualify under section 922 to be treated as a FSC or small FSC for each of 5 consecutive taxable years, such election terminates and will not be effective for any taxable year after such fifth taxable year. Such termination will be effective automatically without notice to such corporation or to the Internal Revenue Service.

T.D. 8127, 3/2/87.

§ 1.931-1 Exclusion of certain income from sources within Guam, American Samoa, or the Northern Mariana Islands.

[Reserved]. For further guidance, see § 1.931-1T.

T.D. 6249, 8/21/57, amend T.D. 7283, 8/2/73, T.D. 7385, 10/28/75, T.D. 9194, 4/6/2005.

PAR. 11.

Section 1.931-1 is revised to read as follows:

Proposed § 1.931-1 Exclusion of certain income from sources within Guam, American Samoa, or the Northern Mariana Islands. [*For Preamble, see ¶ 152,645*]

• ***Caution:*** This Notice of Proposed Rulemaking was partially finalized by TD 9248, 01/30/2006. Regs. §§ 1.1-1, 1.170A-1, 1.861-3, 1.861-8, 1.871-1, 1.876-1, 1.881-5, 1.884-0, 1.901-1, 1.931-1, 1.932-1, 1.933-1, 1.934-1, 1.935-1, 1.937-2, 1.937-3, 1.957-3, 1.1402(a)-12, 1.6038-2, 1.6046-1, 301.6688-1, 301.7701-3, and 301.7701(b)-1 remain proposed.

[The text of the proposed amendment to § 1.931-1 is the same as the text of § 1.931-1T published elsewhere in this issue of the Federal Register]. [*See T.D. 9194, 4/11/2005, 70 Fed. Reg. 68.*]

§ 1.931-1T Exclusion of certain income from sources within Guam, American Samoa, or the Northern Mariana Islands (temporary).

• ***Caution:*** Under Code Sec. 7805, temporary regulations expire within three years of the date of issuance. This temporary regulation was issued on 4/6/2005.

(a) General rule.

(1) An individual (whether a United States citizen or an alien), who is a bona fide resident of a section 931 possession during the entire taxable year, shall exclude from gross income the income derived from sources within any section 931 possession and the income effectively connected with the conduct of a trade or business by such individual within any section 931 possession, except amounts received for services performed as an employee of the United States or any agency thereof.

(2) The following example illustrates the application of the general rule in paragraph (a)(1) of this section:

Example. [Reserved]

(b) Deductions and credits. In any case in which any amount otherwise constituting gross income is excluded from gross income under the provisions of section 931, there shall not be allowed as a deduction from gross income any items of expenses or losses or other deductions (except the deduction under section 151, relating to personal exemptions), or any credit, properly allocable to, or chargeable against, the amounts so excluded from gross income. For purposes of the preceding sentence, the rules of § 1.861-8 shall apply (with creditable expenditures treated in the same manner as deductible expenditures).

(c) Definitions. For purposes of this section:

(1) The term section 931 possession means a possession that is a specified possession and that has entered into an implementing agreement, as described in section 1271(b) of the Tax Reform Act of 1986 (Public Law 99-514 (100 Stat. 2085)), with the United States that is in effect for the entire taxable year.

(2) The term specified possession means Guam, American Samoa, or the Northern Mariana Islands.

(3) The rules of § 1.937-1T shall apply for determining whether an individual is a bona fide resident of a section 931 possession.

(4) The rules of § 1.937-2T shall apply for determining whether income is from sources within a section 931 possession.

(5) The rules of § 1.937-3T shall apply for determining whether income is effectively connected with the conduct of a trade or business within a section 931 possession.

(d) Effective date. This section shall apply for taxable years ending after October 22, 2004.

T.D. 9194, 4/6/2005, amend T.D. 9248, 1/30/2006.

§ 1.932-1 Coordination of United States and Virgin Islands income taxes.

Caution: The Treasury has not yet amended Reg § 1.932-1 to reflect changes made by P.L. 99-272.

[Reserved]. For further guidance, see § 1.932-1T.

T.D. 6249, 8/21/57, amend T.D. 6462, 5/5/60, T.D. 7332, 12/20/74, T.D. 7385, 10/28/75, T.D. 9194, 4/6/2005.

PAR. 12. Section 1.932-1 is revised to read as follows:

Proposed § 1.932-1 Coordination of United States and Virgin Islands income taxes. [*For Preamble, see ¶ 152,645*]

• ***Caution:*** This Notice of Proposed Rulemaking was partially finalized by TD 9248, 01/30/2006. Regs. §§ 1.1-1, 1.170A-1, 1.861-3, 1.861-8, 1.871-1, 1.876-1, 1.881-5, 1.884-0, 1.901-1, 1.931-1, 1.932-1, 1.933-1, 1.934-1, 1.935-1, 1.937-2, 1.937-3, 1.957-3, 1.1402(a)-12, 1.6038-2, 1.6046-1, 301.6688-1, 301.7701-3, and 301.7701(b)-1 remain proposed.

[The text of the proposed amendment to § 1.932-1 is the same as the text of § 1.932-1T published elsewhere in this issue of the Federal Register]. [*See T.D. 9194, 4/11/2005, 70 Fed. Reg. 68.*]

§ 1.932-1T Coordination of United States and Virgin Islands income taxes (temporary).

• ***Caution:*** Under Code Sec. 7805, temporary regulations expire within three years of the date of issuance. This temporary regulation was issued on 4/6/2005.

(a) Scope. *(1) In general.* Section 932 and this section set forth the special rules relating to the filing of income tax returns and income tax liabilities of individuals described in paragraph (a)(2) of this section. Paragraph (h) of this section also provides special rules requiring consistent treatment of business entities in the United States and in the United States Virgin Islands (Virgin Islands).

(2) Individuals covered. This section shall apply to any individual who:

(i) Is a bona fide resident of the Virgin Islands during the entire taxable year;

(ii) (A) Is a citizen or resident of the United States (other than a bona fide resident of the Virgin Islands) during the entire taxable year; and

(B) Has income derived from sources within the Virgin Islands, or effectively connected with the conduct of a trade or business within the Virgin Islands, for the taxable year; or

(iii) Files a joint return for the taxable year with any individual described in paragraph (a)(2)(i) or (ii) of this section.

(3) Definitions. For purposes of this section:

(i) The rules of § 1.937-1T shall apply for determining whether an individual is a bona fide resident of the Virgin Islands.

(ii) The rules of § 1.937-2T shall apply for determining whether income is from sources within the Virgin Islands.

(iii) The rules of § 1.937-3T shall apply for determining whether income is effectively connected with the conduct of a trade or business within the Virgin Islands.

(b) U.S. individuals with V.I. income. *(1) Dual filing requirement.* Subject to paragraph (d) of this section, an individual described in paragraph (a)(2)(ii) of this section shall make an income tax return for the taxable year to the United States and file a copy of such return with the Virgin Islands. Such individuals must also attach Form 8689, "Allocation of Individual Income Tax to the Virgin Islands," to the U.S. income tax return and to the income tax return filed with the Virgin Islands.

(2) Tax payments. (i) Each individual to whom this paragraph (b) applies for the taxable year shall pay the applicable percentage of the taxes imposed by this chapter for such taxable year (determined without regard to paragraph (b)(2)(ii) of this section) to the Virgin Islands.

(ii) There shall be allowed as a credit against the tax imposed by this chapter for the taxable year an amount equal to the taxes required to be paid to the Virgin Islands under paragraph (b)(2)(i) of this section which are so paid. Such taxes shall be considered creditable in the same manner as taxes paid to the United States (e.g., under section 31) and not as taxes paid to a foreign government (e.g., under sections 27 and 901).

(iii) For purposes of this paragraph (b)(2):

(A) The term applicable percentage means the percentage which Virgin Islands adjusted gross income bears to adjusted gross income.

(B) The term Virgin Islands adjusted gross income means adjusted gross income determined by taking into account only income derived from sources within the Virgin Islands and deductions properly apportioned or allocable thereto. For purposes of the preceding sentence, the rules of § 1.861-8 shall apply.

(C) Pursuant to § 1.937-2T(a), the rules of § 1.937-2T(c)(1)(ii) and (c)(2) do not apply.

(c) Bona fide residents of the Virgin Islands. Subject to paragraph (d) of this section, an individual described in paragraph (a)(2)(i) of this section shall be subject to the following income tax return filing requirements:

(1) V.I. filing requirements. An individual to whom this paragraph (c) applies shall file an income tax return for the taxable year with the Virgin Islands. On this return, the individual shall report income from all sources and identify the source of each item of income shown on the return.

(2) U.S. filing requirements. For purposes of calculating the income tax liability to the United States of an individual to whom this paragraph (c) applies, gross income shall not include any amount included in gross income on the return filed with the Virgin Islands pursuant to paragraph (c)(1) of this section, and deductions and credits allocable to such income shall not be taken into account, provided that--

(i) The individual fully satisfied the reporting requirements of paragraph (c)(1) of this section; and

(ii) The individual fully paid the tax liability referred to in section 934(a) to the Virgin Islands with respect to such income.

(d) Joint returns. In the case of married persons, if one or both spouses is an individual described in paragraph (a)(2) of this section and they file a joint return of income tax, the spouses shall file their joint return with, and pay the tax due on such return to, the jurisdiction (or jurisdictions) where the spouse who has the greater adjusted gross income for the taxable year would be required under paragraph (b) or (c) of this section to file a return if separate returns were filed and all of their income were the income of such spouse. For this purpose, adjusted gross income of each spouse is determined under section 62 and the regulations thereunder but without regard to community property laws; and, if one of the spouses dies, the taxable year of the surviving spouse shall be treated as ending on the date of such death.

(e) Place for filing returns. *(1) U.S. returns.* A return required under the rules of paragraphs (b) and (c) of this section to be filed with the United States shall be filed as directed in the applicable forms and instructions.

(2) V.I. returns. A return required under the rules of paragraphs (b) and (c) of this section to be filed with the Virgin Islands shall be filed as directed in the applicable forms and instructions.

(f) Tax accounting standards. *(1) In general.* A dual filing taxpayer must use the same tax accounting standards on the returns filed with the United States and the Virgin Islands. A taxpayer who has filed a return only with the United States or only with the Virgin Islands as a single filing taxpayer for a prior taxable year and is required to file a return only with the other jurisdiction as a single filing taxpayer for a later taxable year may not, for such later taxable year, use different tax accounting standards unless the second jurisdiction consents to such change. However, such change will not be effective for returns filed thereafter with the first jurisdiction unless before such later date of filing the taxpayer also obtains the consent of the first jurisdiction to make such change. Any request for consent to make a change pursuant to this paragraph (f) must be made to the office where the return is required to be filed under paragraph (e) of this section and in sufficient time to permit a copy of the consent to be attached to the return for the taxable year.

(2) Definitions. For purposes of this paragraph (f):

(i) The term dual filing taxpayer means a taxpayer who is required to file returns with the United States and the Virgin Islands for the same taxable year under the rules of paragraph (b) or (c) of this section.

(ii) The term single filing taxpayer means a taxpayer who is required to file a return only with the United States (because the individual is not described in paragraph (a)(2) of this section) or only with the Virgin Islands (because the individual is described in paragraph (a)(2)(i) of this section and satisfies the conditions of paragraphs (c)(2)(i) and (ii) of this section) for the taxable year.

(iii) The term tax accounting standards includes the taxpayer's accounting period, methods of accounting, and any election to which the taxpayer is bound with respect to the reporting of taxable income.

(g) Extension of territory. *(1) Section 932(a) taxpayers.* (i) General rule. With respect to an individual to whom section 932(a) applies for a taxable year, for purposes of taxes imposed by Chapter 1 of the Internal Revenue Code, the United States generally shall be treated, in a geographical and governmental sense, as including the Virgin Islands. The purpose of this rule is to facilitate the coordination of the tax systems of the United States and the Virgin Islands. Accordingly, the rule will have no effect where it is manifestly inapplicable or its application would be incompatible with the intent of any provision of the Internal Revenue Code.

(ii) Application of general rule. Contexts in which the general rule of paragraph (g)(1)(i) of this section apply include:

(A) The characterization of taxes paid to the Virgin Islands. An individual to whom section 932(a) applies may take income tax required to be paid to the Virgin Islands under section 932(b) into account under sections 31, 6315, and 6402(b) as payments to the United States. Taxes paid to the Virgin Islands and otherwise satisfying the requirements of section 164(a) will be allowed as a deduction under that section, but income taxes required to be paid to the Virgin Islands under section 932(b) will be disallowed as a deduction under section 275(a).

(B) The determination of the source of income for purposes of the foreign tax credit (e.g., sections 901 through 904). Thus, for example, after an individual to whom section 932(a) applies determines which items of income constitute income from sources within the Virgin Islands under the rules of section 937(b), such income shall be treated as income from sources within the United States for purposes of section 904.

(C) The eligibility of a corporation to make a subchapter S election (sections 1361 through 1379). Thus, for example, for purposes of determining whether a corporation created or organized in the Virgin Islands may make an election under section 1362(a) to be a subchapter S corporation, it shall be treated as a domestic corporation and a shareholder to whom section 932(a) applies shall not be treated as a nonresident alien individual with respect to such corporation. While such an election is in effect, the corporation shall be treated as a domestic corporation for all purposes of the Internal Revenue Code. For the consistency requirement with respect to entity status elections, see paragraph (h) of this section.

(D) The treatment of items carried over from other tax years. Thus, for example, if an individual to whom section 932(a) applies has for a taxable year a net operating loss carryback or carryover under section 172, a foreign tax credit carryback or carryover under section 904, a business credit carryback or carryover under section 39, a capital loss carryover under section 1212, or a charitable contributions carryover under section 170, the carryback or carryover will be reported on the return filed in accordance with paragraph (b)(1) of this section, even though the return of the taxpayer for the taxable year giving rise to the carryback or carryover was required to be filed with the Virgin Islands under section 932(c).

(E) The treatment of property exchanged for property of a like kind (section 1031). Thus, for example, if an individual to whom section 932(a) applies exchanges real property located in the United States for real property located in the Virgin Islands, notwithstanding the provisions of section 1031(h), such exchange may qualify as a like-kind exchange under section 1031 (provided that all the other requirements of section 1031 are satisfied).

(iii) Nonapplication of the general rule. Contexts in which the general rule of paragraph (g)(1)(i) of this section does not apply include:

(A) The application of any rules or regulations that explicitly treat the United States and any (or all) of its possessions as separate jurisdictions (e.g., sections 931 through 937, 7651, and 7654).

(B) The determination of any aspect of an individual's residency (e.g., sections 937(a) and 7701(b)). Thus, for example, an individual whose principal place of abode is in the Virgin Islands is not considered to have a principal place of abode in the United States for purposes of section 32(c).

(C) The characterization of a corporation for purposes other than subchapter S (e.g., sections 367, 951 through 964, 1291 through 1298, 6038, and 6038B). Thus, for example, if an individual to whom section 932(a) applies transfers appreciated tangible property to a corporation created or organized in the Virgin Islands in a transaction described in section 351, he or she must recognize gain unless an exception under section 367(a) applies. Also, if a corporation created or organized in the Virgin Islands qualifies as a passive foreign investment company under sections 1297 and 1298 with respect to an individual to whom section 932(a) applies, a dividend paid to such shareholder does not constitute qualified dividend income under section 1(h)(11)(B).

(2) Section 932(c) taxpayers. (i) General rule. With respect to an individual to whom section 932(c) applies for a taxable year, for purposes of the territorial income tax of the Virgin Islands (i.e., mirrored sections of the Internal Revenue Code), the Virgin Islands generally shall be treated, in a geographical and governmental sense, as including the United States. The purpose of this rule is to facilitate the coordination of the tax systems of the United States and the Virgin Islands. Accordingly, the rule will have no effect where it is manifestly inapplicable or its application would be incompatible with the intent of any provision of the Internal Revenue Code.

(ii) Application of general rule. Contexts in which the general rule of paragraph (g)(2)(i) of this section apply include:

(A) The characterization of taxes paid to the United States. A taxpayer described in section 932(c)(1) may take income tax paid to the United States into account under mirrored sections 31, 6315, and 6402(b) as payments to the Virgin Islands.

(B) The determination of the source of income for purposes of the foreign tax credit (e.g., mirrored sections 901 through 904). Thus, for example, any item of income that constitutes income from sources within the United States under the rules of sections 861 through 865 shall be treated as income from sources within the Virgin Islands for purposes of mirrored section 904.

(C) The eligibility of a corporation to make a subchapter S election (mirrored sections 1361 through 1379). Thus, for example, for purposes of determining whether a corporation created or organized in the United States may make an election under mirrored section 1362(a) to be a subchapter S corporation, it shall be treated as a domestic corporation and a shareholder to whom section 932(c) applies shall not be treated as a nonresident alien individual with respect to such corporation. While such an election is in effect, the corporation shall be treated as a domestic corporation for all purposes of the territorial income tax. For the consistency requirement with respect to entity status elections, see paragraph (h) of this section.

(D) The treatment of items carried over from other tax years. Thus, for example, if an individual to whom section 932(c) applies has for a taxable year a net operating loss carryback or carryover under mirrored section 172, a foreign tax credit carryback or carryover under mirrored section 904, a business credit carryback or carryover under mirrored section 39, a capital loss carryover under mirrored section 1212, or a charitable contributions carryover under mirrored section 170, the carryback or carryover will be reported on the return filed in accordance with paragraph (c)(1) of this section, even though the return of the taxpayer for the taxable year giving rise to the carryback or carryover was required to be filed with the United States.

(E) The treatment of property exchanged for property of a like kind (mirrored section 1031). Thus, for example, if an individual to whom section 932(c) applies exchanges real property located in the United States for real property located in the Virgin Islands, notwithstanding the provisions of mirrored section 1031(h), such exchange may qualify as a like-kind exchange under mirrored section 1031 (provided that all the other requirements of mirrored section 1031 are satisfied).

(iii) Nonapplication of general rule. Contexts in which the general rule of paragraph (g)(2)(i) of this section does not apply include:

(A) The determination of any aspect of an individual's residency (e.g., mirrored section 7701(b)). Thus, for example, an individual whose principal place of abode is in the United States is not considered to have a principal place of abode in the Virgin Islands for purposes of mirrored section 32(c).

(B) The determination of the source of income for purposes other than the foreign tax credit (e.g., sections 932(a) and (b), 934(b), and 937). Thus, for example, compensation for services performed in the United States and rentals or royalties from property located in the United States do not constitute income from sources within the Virgin Islands for purposes of section 934(b).

(C) The definition of wages (mirrored section 3401). Thus, for example, services performed by an employee for an employer in the United States do not constitute services performed in the Virgin Islands under mirrored section 3401(a)(8).

(h) Entity status consistency requirement. *(1) In general.* Taxpayers should make consistent entity status elections (as defined in paragraph (h)(3) of this section), where applicable, in both the United States and the Virgin Islands. In the case of a business entity to which this paragraph (h) applies:

(i) If an entity status election is filed with the Internal Revenue Service but not with the Virgin Islands Bureau of Internal Revenue (BIR), the Director of the BIR or his delegate, at his discretion, may deem the election also to have been made for Virgin Islands tax purposes.

(ii) If an entity status election is filed with the BIR but not with the Internal Revenue Service, the Commissioner, at his discretion, may deem the election also to have been made for U.S. Federal tax purposes.

(iii) If inconsistent entity status elections are filed with the BIR and the Internal Revenue Service, both the Commissioner and the Director of the BIR or his delegate may, at their individual discretion, treat the elections they each received as invalid and may deem the election filed in the other jurisdiction to have been made also for tax purposes in their own jurisdiction. (See Rev. Proc. 89-8 (1989-1 C.B. 778) for procedures for requesting the assistance of the Internal Revenue Service when a taxpayer is or may be subject to inconsistent tax treatment by the Internal Revenue Service and a U.S. possession tax agency.)

(2) Scope. This paragraph (h) applies to the following business entities:

(i) A business entity (as defined in § 301.7701-2(a) of this chapter) that is domestic (as defined in § 301.7701-5 of this chapter), or otherwise treated as domestic for purposes of the Internal Revenue Code, and that is owned in whole or in part by any person who is either a bona fide resident of the Virgin Islands or a business entity created or organized in the Virgin Islands.

(ii) A business entity that is created or organized in the Virgin Islands and that is owned in whole or in part by any

U.S. person (other than a bona fide resident of the Virgin Islands).

(3) Definition. For purposes of this section, the term entity status election includes an election under § 301.7701-3(c) of this chapter, an election under section 1362(a), and any other similar elections.

(4) Default status. Solely for the purpose of determining classification of an eligible entity under § 301.7701-3(b), and § 301.7701-3(b) as mirrored in the Virgin Islands, an eligible entity subject to this paragraph (h) shall be classified for both U.S. Federal and Virgin Islands tax purposes using the rule that applies to domestic eligible entities.

(5) Transition rules. (i) In the case of an election filed prior to April 11, 2005, except as provided in paragraph (h)(5)(ii) of this section, the rules of paragraph (h)(1) of this section shall apply as of the first day of the first taxable year of the entity beginning after April 11, 2005.

(ii) In the unlikely circumstance that inconsistent elections described in paragraph (h)(1)(iii) are filed prior to April 11, 2005, and the entity cannot change its classification to achieve consistency because of the sixty-month limitation described in § 301.7701-3(c)(1)(iv) of this chapter, then the entity may nevertheless request permission from the Commissioner or the Director of the BIR or his delegate to change such election to avoid inconsistent treatment by the Commissioner and the Director of the BIR or his delegate.

(iii) Except as provided in paragraphs (h)(5)(i) and (h)(5)(ii) of this section, in the case of an election filed with respect to an entity before it became an entity described in paragraph (h)(2) of this section, the rules of paragraph (h)(1) of this section shall apply as of the first day that such entity is described in paragraph (h)(2) of this section.

(iv) In the case of an entity created or organized prior to April 11, 2005, paragraph (h)(4) of this section shall take effect for U.S. Federal income tax purposes (or Virgin Islands income tax purposes, as the case may be) as of the first day of the first taxable year of the entity beginning after April 11, 2005.

(i) Examples. The rules of this section are illustrated by the following examples:

Example (1). (i) A is a U.S. citizen who resides in State R. The Federal Individual Income Tax Return, Form 1040, that A prepares for 2004 reports adjusted gross income of $90x, including $30x from sources in the U.S. Virgin Islands (USVI). The income tax liability reported on A's Form 1040 is $18x. A files a copy of his Federal Form 1040 with the USVI Bureau of Internal Revenue as required by section 932(a)(2) and paragraph (b)(1) of this section, and pays the applicable percentage of his Federal income tax liability to the USVI as required by section 932(b) and paragraph (b)(2) of this section, computed as follows:

30/90 x 18x = $6x income tax liability to the USVI

(ii) A claims a credit against his Federal income tax liability reported on his Form 1040 in the amount of $6x. A attaches a Form 8689, "Allocation of Individual Income Tax to the Virgin Islands," to the Form 1040 filed with the Internal Revenue Service and to the copy of the Form 1040 filed with the USVI.

Example (2). [Reserved].

Example (3). H and W are U.S. citizens. H resides in State T and W is a bona fide resident of the U.S. Virgin Islands (USVI). For 2004, H and W prepare a joint Individual Income Tax Return, Form 1040, which reports total adjusted gross income of $75x of which $40x is attributable to compensation that W received for services performed in the USVI and $35x to compensation that H received for services performed in State T. Pursuant to section 932(d) and paragraph (d) of this section, the joint income tax return of H and W is filed with the USVI as required by section 932(c) and paragraph (c) of this section. H and W may claim a tax credit on such return for income tax withheld during 2004 and paid to the Internal Revenue Service.

Example (4). (i) The facts are the same as in example 3, except that H also earns $25x for services performed in the USVI, so that H and W's total adjusted gross income is $100x, and their total income tax liability is $20x.

(ii) Pursuant to section 932(d) and paragraph (d) of this section, H and W must file a copy of their joint Federal Form 1040 with the Bureau of Internal Revenue of the USVI as required by section 932(a)(2) and paragraph (b)(1) of this section, and pay the applicable percentage of their Federal income tax liability to the USVI as required by section 932(b) and paragraph (b)(2) of this section, computed as follows:

65/100 x 20x = $13x income tax liability to the USVI

(iii) H and W claim a credit against their Federal income tax liability reported on the Form 1040 in the amount of $13x, the portion of their Federal income tax liability required to be paid to the USVI. H and W attach a Form 8689, "Allocation of Individual Income Tax to the Virgin Islands," to the Form 1040 filed with the Internal Revenue Service and to the copy of the Form 1040 filed with the USVI.

Example (5). J is a U.S. citizen and a bona fide resident of the U.S. Virgin Islands (USVI). In 2005, J receives compensation for services performed in the USVI in the amount of $40x. J prepares and files an Individual Income Tax Return, Form 1040, with the USVI and reports gross income of only $30x. J has not satisfied the conditions of section 932(c)(4) and paragraph (c) of this section for an exclusion from gross income for U.S. Federal income tax purposes and, therefore, must file a Federal income tax return in accordance with the Internal Revenue Code and the regulations.

Example (6). (i) N is a U.S. citizen and a bona fide resident of the U.S. Virgin Islands. In 2004, N receives compensation for services performed in Country M. N prepares and files an Individual Income Tax Return, Form 1040, with the USVI and reports the compensation as income effectively connected with the conduct of a trade or business in the USVI. N claims a special credit against the tax on this compensation purportedly pursuant to a USVI law enacted within the limits of its authority under section 934.

(ii) Under the principles of section 864(c)(4) as applied pursuant to section 937(b)(1) and § 1.937-3T(b), compensation for services performed outside the USVI may not be treated as income effectively connected with the conduct of a trade or business in the USVI for purposes of section 934(b). Consequently, N is not entitled to claim the special credit under USVI law with respect to N's income from services performed in Country M. Given that N has not fully paid his tax liability referred to in section 934(a), he has not satisfied the conditions of section 932(c)(4) and paragraph (c) of this section for an exclusion from gross income for U.S. Federal income tax purposes. Accordingly, N must file a Federal income tax return in accordance with the Internal Revenue Code and the regulations.

(j) Effective date. This section shall apply for taxable years ending after October 22, 2004.

T.D. 9194, 4/6/2005, amend T.D. 9248, 1/30/2006.

§ 1.933-1 Exclusion of certain income from sources within Puerto Rico.

(a) [Reserved]. For further guidance, see § 1.933-1T(a).

(b) Taxable year of change of residence from Puerto Rico. A citizen of the United States who changes his residence from Puerto Rico after having been a bona fide resident thereof for a period of at least two years immediately preceding the date of such change in residence shall exclude from his gross income the income derived from sources within Puerto Rico which is attributable to that part of such period of Puerto Rico residence which preceded the date of such change in residence, except amounts received for services performed as an employee of the United States or any agency thereof.

(c) [Reserved]. For further guidance, see § 1.933-1T(c).

(d) [Reserved]. For further guidance, see § 1.933-1T(d).

(e) [Reserved]. For further guidance, see § 1.933-1T(e).

T.D. 6249, 8/21/57, amend T.D. 9194, 4/6/2005.

PAR. 13. Section 1.933-1 is amended by revising paragraphs (a) and (c) and adding paragraphs (d) and (e) to read as follows:

Proposed § 1.933-1 Exclusion of certain income from sources within Puerto Rico. [*For Preamble, see ¶ 152,645*]

• ***Caution:*** This Notice of Proposed Rulemaking was partially finalized by TD 9248, 01/30/2006. Regs. §§ 1.1-1, 1.170A-1, 1.861-3, 1.861-8, 1.871-1, 1.876-1, 1.881-5, 1.884-0, 1.901-1, 1.931-1, 1.932-1, 1.933-1, 1.934-1, 1.935-1, 1.937-2, 1.937-3, 1.957-3, 1.1402(a)-12, 1.6038-2, 1.6046-1, 301.6688-1, 301.7701-3, and 301.7701(b)-1 remain proposed.

(a) [The text of the proposed amendment to § 1.933-1(a) is the same as the text of § 1.933-1T(a) published elsewhere in this issue of the Federal Register]. [*See T.D. 9194, 4/11/2005, 70 Fed. Reg. 68.*]

* * * * *

(c) [The text of the proposed amendment to § 1.933-1(c) is the same as the text of § 1.933-1T(c) published elsewhere in this issue of the Federal Register]. [*See T.D. 9194, 4/11/2005, 70 Fed. Reg. 68.*]

(d) [The text of the proposed amendment to § 1.933-1(d) is the same as the text of § 1.933-1T(d) published elsewhere in this issue of the Federal Register]. [*See T.D. 9194, 4/11/2005, 70 Fed. Reg. 68.*]

(e) [The text of the proposed amendment to § 1.933-1(e) is the same as the text of § 1.933-1T(e) published elsewhere in this issue of the Federal Register]. [*See T.D. 9194, 4/11/2005, 70 Fed. Reg. 68.*]

§ 1.933-1T Exclusion of certain income from sources within Puerto Rico (temporary).

• ***Caution:*** Under Code Sec. 7805, temporary regulations expire within three years of the date of issuance. This temporary regulation was issued on 4/6/2005.

(a) General rule. *(1)* An individual (whether a United States citizen or an alien), who is a bona fide resident of Puerto Rico during the entire taxable year, shall exclude from gross income the income derived from sources within Puerto Rico, except amounts received for services performed as an employee of the United States or any agency thereof.

(2) The following example illustrates the application of the general rule in paragraph (a)(1) of this section:

Example. [Reserved].

(b) [Reserved]. For further guidance, see § 1.933-1(b).

(c) Deductions and credits. In any case in which any amount otherwise constituting gross income is excluded from gross income under the provisions of section 933, there shall not be allowed as a deduction from gross income any items of expenses or losses or other deductions (except the deduction under section 151, relating to personal exemptions), or any credit, properly allocable to, or chargeable against, the amounts so excluded from gross income. For purposes of the preceding sentence, the rules of § 1.861-8 shall apply (with creditable expenditures treated in the same manner as deductible expenditures).

(d) Definitions. For purposes of this section:

(1) The rules of § 1.937-1T shall apply for determining whether an individual is a bona fide resident of Puerto Rico.

(2) The rules of § 1.937-2T shall apply for determining whether income is from sources within Puerto Rico.

(e) Effective date. This section shall apply for taxable years ending after October 22, 2004.

T.D. 9194, 4/6/2005, amend T.D. 9248, 1/30/2006.

§ 1.934-1 Limitation on reduction in income tax liability incurred to the Virgin Islands.

[Reserved]. For further guidance, see § 1.934-1T.

T.D. 6629, 12/27/62, amend T.D. 9194, 4/6/2005.

PAR. 14.

Section 1.934-1 is revised to read as follows:

Proposed § 1.934-1 Limitation on reduction in income tax liability incurred to the Virgin Islands. [*For Preamble, see ¶ 152,645*]

• ***Caution:*** This Notice of Proposed Rulemaking was partially finalized by TD 9248, 01/30/2006. Regs. §§ 1.1-1, 1.170A-1, 1.861-3, 1.861-8, 1.871-1, 1.876-1, 1.881-5, 1.884-0, 1.901-1, 1.931-1, 1.932-1, 1.933-1, 1.934-1, 1.935-1, 1.937-2, 1.937-3, 1.957-3, 1.1402(a)-12, 1.6038-2, 1.6046-1, 301.6688-1, 301.7701-3, and 301.7701(b)-1 remain proposed.

[The text of the proposed amendment to § 1.934-1 is the same as the text of § 1.934-1T published elsewhere in this issue of the Federal Register]. [*See T.D. 9194, 4/11/2005, 70 Fed. Reg. 68.*]

§ 1.934-1T Limitation on reduction in income tax liability incurred to the Virgin Islands (temporary).

• ***Caution:*** Under Code Sec. 7805, temporary regulations expire within three years of the date of issuance. This temporary regulation was issued on 4/6/2005.

(a) General rule. Section 934(a) provides that tax liability incurred to the United States Virgin Islands (Virgin Islands) shall not be reduced or remitted in any way, directly or indirectly, whether by grant, subsidy, or other similar payment, by any law enacted in the Virgin Islands, except to the extent provided in section 934(b). For purposes of the preceding sentence, the term "tax liability" means the liability incurred to the Virgin Islands pursuant to subtitle A of the Internal Revenue Code, as made applicable in the Virgin Islands by the Act of July 12, 1921 (48 U.S.C. 1397), or pursuant to section 28(a) of the Revised Organic Act of the Virgin Islands (48 U.S.C. 1642), as modified by section 7651(5)(B).

(b) Exception for V.I. income. *(1) In general.* Section 934(b)(1) provides an exception to the application of section 934(a). Under this exception, section 934(a) does not apply with respect to tax liability incurred to the Virgin Islands to the extent that such tax liability is attributable to income derived from sources within the Virgin Islands or income effectively connected with the conduct of a trade or business within the Virgin Islands.

(2) Limitation. Section 934(b)(2) limits the scope of the exception provided by section 934(b)(1). Pursuant to this limitation, the exception does not apply with respect to an individual who is a citizen or resident of the United States (other than a bona fide resident of the Virgin Islands). For the rules for determining tax liability incurred to the Virgin Islands by such an individual, see section 932(a) and the regulations thereunder.

(3) Computation rule. (i) Operative rule. For purposes of section 934(b)(1) and this paragraph (b), tax liability incurred to the Virgin Islands for the taxable year attributable to income derived from sources within the Virgin Islands or income effectively connected with the conduct of a trade or business within the Virgin Islands shall be computed as follows:

(A) Add to the income tax liability incurred to the Virgin Islands any credit against the tax allowed under mirrored section 901(a);

(B) Multiply by taxable income from sources within the Virgin Islands and income effectively connected with the conduct of a trade or business within the Virgin Islands (applying the rules of § 1.861-8 to determine deductions allocable to such income);

(C) Divide by total taxable income; and

(D) Subtract the portion of any credit allowed under mirrored section 901 (other than credits for taxes paid to the United States) determined by multiplying the amount of taxable income from sources outside the Virgin Islands or the United States that is effectively connected to the conduct of a trade or business in the Virgin Islands divided by the total amount of taxable income from such sources.

(ii) Limitation. Tax liability incurred to the Virgin Islands attributable to income derived from sources within the Virgin Islands or income effectively connected with the conduct of a trade or business within the Virgin Islands, as computed in this paragraph (b)(3), however, shall not exceed the total amount of income tax liability actually incurred.

(4) Definitions. For purposes of this section:

(i) Bona fide resident. The rules of § 1.937-1T shall apply for determining whether an individual is a bona fide resident of the Virgin Islands.

(ii) Source. The rules of § 1.937-2T shall apply for determining whether income is from sources within the Virgin Islands.

(iii) Effectively connected income. The rules of § 1.937-3T shall apply for determining whether income is effectively connected with the conduct of a trade or business in the Virgin Islands.

(c) Exception for qualified foreign corporations. *(1) In general.* Section 934(b)(3) provides an exception to the application of section 934(a). Under this exception, section 934(a) does not apply with respect to tax liability incurred to the Virgin Islands by a qualified foreign corporation to the extent that such tax liability is attributable to income which is derived from sources outside the United States and which is not effectively connected with the conduct of a trade or business within the United States.

(2) Qualified foreign corporation. For purposes of paragraph (c)(1) of this section, the term qualified foreign corporation means any foreign corporation if 1 or more United States persons own or are treated as owning (within the meaning of section 958) less than 10 percent of—

(i) The total voting power of the stock of such corporation; and

(ii) The total value of the stock of such corporation,

(3) Computation rule. (i) Operative rule. For purposes of section 934(b)(3) and this paragraph (c), tax liability incurred to the Virgin Islands for the taxable year attributable to income which is derived from sources outside the United States and which is not effectively connected with the conduct of a trade or business within the United States shall be computed as follows—

(A) Add to the income tax liability incurred to the Virgin Islands any credit against the tax allowed under mirrored section 901(a);

(B) Multiply by taxable income which is derived from sources outside the United States and which is not effectively connected with the conduct of a trade or business within the United States (applying the rules of § 1.861-8 to determine deductions allocable to such income);

(C) Divide by total taxable income; and

(D) Subtract any credit allowed under mirrored section 901 (other than credits for taxes paid to the United States or taxes for which a credit is allowable for U.S. Federal income tax purposes under section 906 of the Internal Revenue Code).

(ii) Limitation Tax liability incurred to the Virgin Islands attributable to income which is derived from sources outside the United States and which is not effectively connected with the conduct of a trade or business within the United States, as computed in this paragraph (c)(3), however, shall not exceed the total amount of income tax liability actually incurred.

(4) U.S. income. (i) In general. For purposes of this section, except as provided in paragraph (c)(4)(ii) of this section, the rules of sections 861 through 865 and the regulations thereunder shall apply for determining whether income is from sources outside the United States or effectively connected with the conduct of a trade or business within the United States.

(ii) Conduit arrangements. Income shall be considered to be from sources within the United States for purposes of paragraph (c)(1) of this section if, pursuant to a plan or arrangement—

(A) The income is received in exchange for consideration provided to another person; and

(B) Such person (or another person) provides the same consideration (or consideration of a like kind) to a third person in exchange for one or more payments constituting income from sources within the United States.

(d) Examples. The rules of this section are illustrated by the following examples:

Example (1). (i) S is a U.S. citizen and a bona fide resident of the U.S. Virgin Islands (USVI). For 2005, S files a Form 1040INFO, "Non-Virgin Islands Source Income of Virgin Islands Residents," with the USVI on which S reports total gross income as follows:

Compensation for services performed in the USVI	$50,000
Compensation for services performed in the United States	40,000
Compensation for services performed in Mexico	30,000
Income from inventory sales in Latin America attributable to USVI Office	20,000
Interest on a U.S. bank account	6,000
Interest on a V.I. bank account	5,000
Dividends from a U.S. corporation	4,000

(ii) Accordingly, S has total gross income of $155,000, comprising income from sources within the USVI or effectively connected to the conduct of a trade or business in the USVI (USVI ECI) of $75,000, income from sources within the United States of $50,000, and income from other sources (not USVI ECI) of $30,000. After taking into account allowable deductions, S's total taxable income is $120,000, of which $45,000 is taxable income from sources within the USVI, $15,000 is taxable income from other sources that is USVI ECI under the rules of section 937(b) and Sec. § 1.937-2T and 1.937-3T, and $22,500 is taxable income from sources outside the USVI (and outside the United States) that is not USVI ECI. S's tax liability incurred to the USVI pursuant to the Internal Revenue Code as applicable in the USVI (mirror code) is $30,000. S is entitled to claim a credit under section 901 of the mirror code in the amount of $10,000 for income tax paid to Mexico and other Latin American countries, for a net income tax liability of $20,000.

(iii) Pursuant to a USVI law that was duly enacted within the limits of its authority under section 934, S may claim a special deduction relating to his business activities in the USVI. However, under section 934(b), S's ability to claim this special deduction is limited. Specifically, the maximum amount of the reduction in S's mirror code tax liability that may result from claiming this deduction, computed in accordance with paragraph (b)(3) of this section, is as follows:

(20,000 + 10,000) x ((45,000 + 15,000) / (120,000)) - 10,000 x ((15,000) / (15,000 + 22,500)) = 30,000 x (.5) - 10,000 x (.4) = 15,000 - 4,000 = $11,000

(iv) Accordingly, S's net tax liability incurred to the USVI must be at least $19,000 (30,000 - 11,000), prior to taking into account any foreign tax credit.

Example (2). The facts are the same as Example 1, except that S is a U.S. citizen who resides in the United States. As required by section 932(a) and (b), S files with the U.S. Virgin Islands (USVI) a copy of his Federal income tax return and pays to the USVI the portion of his Federal income tax liability that his Virgin Islands adjusted gross income bears to his adjusted gross income. Under section 934(b)(2), S may not claim the special deduction offered under USVI law relating to business activities like his in the USVI to reduce any of his tax liability payable to the USVI under section 932(b).

Example (3). (i) Z is a nonresident alien who resides in Country FC. In 2005, Z receives dividends from a corporation organized under the law of the U.S. Virgin Islands (USVI) in the amount of $90x. Z's tax liability incurred to the USVI pursuant to section 871(a) of the Internal Revenue Code as applicable in the USVI (mirror code) is $27x.

(ii) Pursuant to a USVI law that was duly enacted within the limits of its authority under section 934, Z may claim a special exemption for income relating to his investment in the USVI. The maximum amount of the reduction in Z's mirror code tax liability that may result from claiming this exemption, computed in accordance with paragraph (b)(3) of this section, is as follows:

27x (90x /90x) = $27x

(iii) Accordingly, depending on the terms of the exemption as provided under USVI law, Z's net tax liability incurred to the USVI may be reduced or eliminated entirely.

Example (4). (i) A Corp is organized under the laws of the U.S. Virgin Islands (USVI) and is engaged in a trade or business in the United States through an office in State N. All of A Corp's outstanding stock is owned by U.S. citizens who are bona fide residents of the USVI. During 2005, A Corp had $50x in gross income from sources within the USVI (as determined under section 937(b) and § 1.937-2T) that is not effectively connected with the conduct of a trade or business in the United States; $20x in gross income from sources in Country H that is effectively connected with the conduct of A Corp's trade or business in the United States; and $10x in gross income from sources in Country R that is not effectively connected with the conduct of A Corp's trade or business in the United States.

(ii) Section 934(b)(3) permits the USVI to reduce or remit the income tax liability of a qualified foreign corporation arising under the Internal Revenue Code as applicable in the USVI (mirror code) with respect to income that is derived from sources outside the United States and that is not effectively connected with the conduct of a trade or business in the United States. A foreign corporation constitutes a "qualified foreign corporation" under section 934(b)(3)(B) if less than 10 percent of the total voting power and value of the stock of the corporation is owned or treated as owned (within the meaning of section 958) by one or more United States persons. A U.S. citizen is a United States person as defined in section 7701(a)(30)(A). Given that 10 percent or more of the voting power and value of its stock is owned by U.S. citizens, A Corp does not constitute a "qualified foreign corporation" under section 934(b)(3)(B). Accordingly, the USVI may only reduce or remit A Corp's mirror code income tax liability with respect to its $50x in gross income from sources within the USVI.

Example (5). (i) The facts are the same as in Example 4, except that the outstanding stock of A Corp is owned by the following individuals:

U.S. citizens who are bona fide residents of the USVI . .	5%
U.S. citizens who are not bona fide residents of the USVI	3%
Nonresident aliens who are bona fide residents of the USVI	42%
Nonresident aliens who are not bona fide residents of the USVI	50%

(ii) Given that less than 10 percent of the voting power and value of its stock is owned by United States persons, A Corp constitutes a qualified foreign corporation under section 934(b)(3)(B). Accordingly, the USVI may reduce or remit A Corp's mirror code income tax liability with respect to its $50x in gross income from sources within the USVI and its $10x in gross income from sources in Country R that is not effectively connected with the conduct of A Corp's trade or business in the United States. In no event, however, may the USVI reduce or remit A Corp's mirror code income tax liability with respect to its $20x in gross income from sources in Country H that is effectively connected with the conduct of A Corp's trade or business in the United States.

(e) Effective date. Except as otherwise provided in this paragraph (e), this section applies for taxable years ending after October 22, 2004. Paragraph (c)(4)(ii) of this section applies to amounts paid or accrued after April 11, 2005.

T.D. 9194, 4/6/2005.

§ 1.935-1 Coordination of individual income taxes with Guam and the Northern Mariana Islands.

(a) Application of section.

(1) through (a)(3) [Reserved]. For further guidance, see § 1.935-1T(a)(1) through (a)(3).

(b) Filing requirement. *(1)* [Reserved]. For further guidance, see § 1.935-1T(b)(1).

(2) Joint returns. In the case of married persons, if one or both spouses is an individual described in paragraph (a)(2) of this section and they file a joint return of income tax, the spouses shall file their joint return with, and pay the tax due on such return to, the jurisdiction where the spouse who has the greater adjusted gross income for the taxable year would be required under subparagraph (1) of this paragraph to file his return if separate returns were filed. For this purpose, adjusted gross income of each spouse is determined under section 62 and the regulations thereunder but without regard to community property laws; and, if one of the spouses dies, the taxable year of the surviving spouse shall be treated as ending on the date of such death.

(3) [Reserved]. For further guidance, see § 1.935-1T(b)(3).

(4) Tax accounting standards. A taxpayer who has filed his return with one of the jurisdictions named in subparagraph (1) of this paragraph for a prior taxable year and is required to file his return for a later taxable year with the other such jurisdiction may not, for such later taxable year, change his accounting period, method of accounting, or any election to which he is bound with respect to his reporting of taxable income to the first jurisdiction unless he obtains the consent of the second jurisdiction to make such change. However, such change will not be effective for returns filed thereafter with the first jurisdiction unless before such later date of filing he also obtains the consent of the first jurisdiction to make such change. Any request for consent to make a change pursuant ot this subparagraph must be made to the office where the return is required to be filed under subparagraph (3) of this paragraph and in sufficient time to permit a copy of the consent to be attached to the return for the taxable year.

(5) through (b)(7) [Reserved]. For further guidance, see § 1.935-1T(b)(5) through (b)(7).

(c) through (f) [Reserved]. For further guidance, see § 1.935-1T(c) through (f).

(g) [Reserved]. For further guidance, see § 1.935-1T(g).

T.D. 7385, 10/28/75, amend T.D. 9194, 4/6/2005.

PAR. 15. Section 1.935-1 is amended is amended as follows:

1. Revise paragraphs (a)(1) through (a)(3).

2. Revise paragraphs (b)(1) and (b)(3), and add paragraphs (b)(5) through (b)(7).

3. Revise paragraphs (c) through (f).

4. Add paragraph (g).

The revisions and additions are as follows:

Proposed § 1.935-1 Coordination of individual income taxes with Guam and the Northern Mariana Islands.

[*For Preamble, see ¶ 152,645*]

• ***Caution:*** This Notice of Proposed Rulemaking was partially finalized by TD 9248, 01/30/2006. Regs. §§ 1.1-1, 1.170A-1, 1.861-3, 1.861-8, 1.871-1, 1.876-1, 1.881-5, 1.884-0, 1.901-1, 1.931-1, 1.932-1, 1.933-1, 1.934-1, 1.935-1, 1.937-2, 1.937-3, 1.957-3, 1.1402(a)-12, 1.6038-2, 1.6046-1, 301.6688-1, 301.7701-3, and 301.7701(b)-1 remain proposed.

(a) *(1)* through (a)(3) [The text of the proposed amendment to § 1.935-1(a)(1) through (a)(3) is the same as the text of § 1.935-1T(a)(1) through (a)(3) published elsewhere in this issue of the Federal Register]. [*See T.D. 9194, 4/11/2005, 70 Fed. Reg. 68.*]

(b) *(1)* [The text of the proposed amendment to § 1.935-1(b)(1) is the same as the text of § 1.935-1T(b)(1) published elsewhere in this issue of the Federal Register]. [*See T.D. 9194, 4/11/2005, 70 Fed. Reg. 68.*]

* * * * *

(3) [The text of the proposed amendment to § 1.935-1(b)(3) is the same as the text of § 1.935-1T(b)(3) published elsewhere in this issue of the Federal Register]. [*See T.D. 9194, 4/11/2005, 70 Fed. Reg. 68.*]

* * * * *

(5) through (b)(7) [The text of the proposed § 1.935-1(b)(5) through (b)(7) is the same as the text of § 1.935-1T(b)(5) through (b)(7) published elsewhere in this issue of the Federal Register]. [*See T.D. 9194, 4/11/2005, 70 Fed. Reg. 68.*]

(c) [The text of the proposed amendment to § 1.935-1(c) is the same as the text of § 1.935-1T(c) published elsewhere in this issue of the Federal Register]. [*See T.D. 9194, 4/11/2005, 70 Fed. Reg. 68.*]

(d) [The text of the proposed amendment to § 1.935-1(d) is the same as the text of § 1.935-1T(d) published elsewhere in this issue of the Federal Register]. [*See T.D. 9194, 4/11/2005, 70 Fed. Reg. 68.*]

(e) [The text of the proposed amendment to § 1.935-1(e) is the same as the text of § 1.935-1T(e) published elsewhere in this issue of the Federal Register]. [*See T.D. 9194, 4/11/2005, 70 Fed. Reg. 68.*]

(f) [The text of the proposed amendment to § 1.935-1(f) is the same as the text of § 1.935-1T(f) published elsewhere in this issue of the Federal Register]. [*See T.D. 9194, 4/11/2005, 70 Fed. Reg. 68.*]

(g) [The text of the proposed § 1.935-1(g) is the same as the text of § 1.935-1T(g) published elsewhere in this issue of the Federal Register]. [*See T.D. 9194, 4/11/2005, 70 Fed. Reg. 68.*]

§ 1.935-1T Coordination of individual income taxes with Guam and the Northern Mariana Islands (temporary).

• ***Caution:*** Under Code Sec. 7805, temporary regulations expire within three years of the date of issuance. This temporary regulation was issued on 4/6/2005.

(a) Application of section. *(1) Scope.* Section 935 and this section set forth the special rules relating to the filing of income tax returns, income tax liabilities, and estimated income tax of individuals described in paragraph (a)(2) of this section. Paragraph (e) of this section also provides special rules requiring consistent treatment of business entities in the United States and in section 935 possessions.

(2) Individuals covered. This section shall apply to any individual who—

(i) Is a bona fide resident of a section 935 possession during the entire taxable year, whether or not such individual is a citizen of the United States or a resident alien (as defined in section 7701(b)(1)(A));

(ii) Is a citizen of a section 935 possession but not otherwise a citizen of the United States;

(iii) Has income from sources within a section 935 possession for the taxable year, is a citizen of the United States or a resident alien (as defined in section 7701(b)(1)(A)) and is not a bona fide resident of a section 935 possession during the entire taxable year; or

(iv) Files a joint return for the taxable year with any individual described in paragraph (a)(2)(i), (ii), or (iii) of this section.

(3) Definitions. For purposes of this section:

(i) The term section 935 possession means Guam or the Northern Mariana Islands, unless such possession has entered into an implementing agreement, as described in section 1271(b) of the Tax Reform Act of 1986 (Pub. L. 99-514 (100 Stat. 2085)), with the United States that is in effect for the entire taxable year.

(ii) The term relevant possession means:

(A) With respect to an individual described in paragraph (a)(2)(i) of this section, the section 935 possession of which such individual is a bona fide resident.

(B) With respect to an individual described in paragraph (a)(2)(ii) of this section, the section 935 possession of which such individual is a citizen.

(C) With respect to an individual described in paragraph (a)(2)(iii) of this section, the section 935 possession from which such individual derives income.

(iii) The rules of § 1.937-1T shall apply for determining whether an individual is a bona fide resident of a section 935 possession.

(iv) The rules of § 1.937-2T generally shall apply for determining whether income is from sources within a section 935 possession. Pursuant to § 1.937-2T(a), however, the rules of § 1.937-2T(c)(1)(ii) and (c)(2) do not apply for purposes of section 935(a)(3) (as in effect before the effective date of its repeal) and paragraph (a)(2)(iii) of this section.

(v) The term citizen of the United States means any individual who is a citizen within the meaning of § 1.1-1(c), except that the term does not include an individual who is a citizen of a section 935 possession but not otherwise a citizen of the United States. The term citizen of a section 935 possession but not otherwise a citizen of the United States means any individual who has become a citizen of the United States by birth or naturalization in the section 935 possession.

(vi) With respect to the United States, the term resident means an individual who is a citizen (as defined in § 1.1-1(c)) or resident alien (as defined in section 7701(b)) and who does not have a tax home (as defined in section 911(d)(3)) in a foreign country during the entire taxable year. The term does not include an individual who is a bona fide resident of a section 935 possession.

(vii) The term U.S. taxpayer means an individual described in paragraph (b)(1)(i) or (iii)(B) of this section.

(b) Filing requirement. *(1) Tax jurisdiction.* An individual described in paragraph (a)(2) of this section shall file an income tax return for the taxable year—

(i) With the United States if such individual is a resident of the United States;

(ii) With the relevant possession if such individual is described in paragraph (a)(2)(i) of this section; or

(iii) If neither paragraph (b)(1)(i) nor paragraph (b)(1)(ii) of this section applies—

(A) With the relevant possession if such individual is described in paragraph (a)(2)(ii) of this section; or

(B) With the United States if such individual is a citizen of the United States, as defined in paragraph (a)(3) of this section.

(2) [Reserved]. For further guidance, see § 1.935-1(b)(2).

(3) Place for filing returns. (i) U.S. returns. A return required under this paragraph (b) to be filed with the United States shall be filed as directed in the applicable forms and instructions.

(ii) Guam returns. A return required under this paragraph (b) to be filed with Guam shall be filed as directed in the applicable forms and instructions.

(iii) NMI returns. A return required under this paragraph (b) to be filed with the Northern Mariana Islands shall be filed as directed in the applicable forms and instructions.

(4) [Reserved]. For further guidance, see § 1.935-1(b)(4).

(5) Tax payments. The tax shown on the return shall be paid to the jurisdiction with which such return is required to be filed and shall be determined by taking into account any credit under section 31 for tax withheld by the relevant pos-

session or the United States on wages, any credit under section 6402(b) for an overpayment of income tax to the relevant possession or the United States, and any payments under section 6315 of estimated income tax paid to the relevant possession or the United States.

(6) Liability to other jurisdiction. (i) Filing with the relevant possession. In the case of an individual who is required under paragraph (b)(1) of this section to file a return with the relevant possession for a taxable year, if such individual properly files such return and fully pays his or her income tax liability to the relevant possession, such individual is relieved of liability to file an income tax return with, and to pay an income tax to, the United States for the taxable year.

(ii) Filing with the United States. In the case of an individual who is required under paragraph (b)(1) of this section to file a return with the United States for a taxable year, such individual is relieved of liability to file an income tax return with, and to pay an income tax to, the relevant possession for the taxable year.

(7) Information reporting. [Reserved].

(c) Extension of territory. *(1) U.S. taxpayers.* (i) General rule. With respect to a U.S. taxpayer, for purposes of taxes imposed by Chapter 1 of the Internal Revenue Code, the United States generally shall be treated, in a geographical and governmental sense, as including the relevant possession. The purpose of this rule is to facilitate the coordination of the tax systems of the United States and the relevant possession. Accordingly, the rule will have no effect where it is manifestly inapplicable or its application would be incompatible with the intent of any provision of the Internal Revenue Code.

(ii) Application of general rule. Contexts in which the general rule of paragraph (c)(1)(i) of this section apply include:

(A) The characterization of taxes paid to the relevant possession. Income tax paid to the relevant possession may be taken into account under sections 31, 6315, and 6402(b) as payments to the United States. Taxes paid to the relevant possession and otherwise satisfying the requirements of section 164(a) will be allowed as a deduction under that section, but income taxes paid to the relevant possession will be disallowed as a deduction under section 275(a).

(B) The determination of the source of income for purposes of the foreign tax credit (e.g.,, sections 901 through 904). Thus, for example, after a U.S. taxpayer determines which items of income constitute income from sources within the relevant possession under the rules of section 937(b), such income shall be treated as income from sources within the United States for purposes of section 904.

(C) The eligibility of a corporation to make a subchapter S election (sections 1361 through 1379). Thus, for example, for purposes of determining whether a corporation created or organized in the relevant possession may make an election under section 1362(a) to be a subchapter S corporation, it shall be treated as a domestic corporation and a U.S. taxpayer shareholder shall not be treated as a nonresident alien individual with respect to such corporation. While such an election is in effect, the corporation shall be treated as a domestic corporation for all purposes of the Internal Revenue Code. For the consistency requirement with respect to entity status elections, see paragraph (e) of this section.

(D) The treatment of items carried over from other tax years. Thus, for example, if a U.S. taxpayer has for a taxable year a net operating loss carryback or carryover under section 172, a foreign tax credit carryback or carryover under section 904, a business credit carryback or carryover under section 39, a capital loss carryover under section 1212, or a charitable contributions carryover under section 170, the carryback or carryover will be reported on the return filed with the United States in accordance with paragraph (b)(1)(i) or (b)(1)(iii)(B) of this section, even though the return of the taxpayer for the taxable year giving rise to the carryback or carryover was required to be filed with a section 935 possession.

(E) The treatment of property exchanged for property of a like kind (section 1031). Thus for example, if a U.S. taxpayer exchanges real property located in the United States for real property located in the relevant possession, notwithstanding the provisions of section 1031(h), such exchange may qualify as a like-kind exchange under section 1031 (provided that all the other requirements of section 1031 are satisfied).

(iii) Nonapplication of general rule. Contexts in which the general rule of paragraph (c)(1)(i) of this section does not apply include:

(A) The application of any rules or regulations that explicitly treat the United States and any (or all) of its possessions as separate jurisdictions (e.g.,, sections 931 through 937, 7651, and 7654).

(B) The determination of any aspect of an individual's residency (e.g., sections 937(a) and 7701(b)). Thus, for example, an individual whose principal place of abode is in the relevant possession is not considered to have a principal place of abode in the United States for purposes of section 32(c).

(C) The determination of the source of income for purposes other than the foreign tax credit (e.g., sections 935, 937, and 7654). Thus, for example, income determined to be derived from sources within the relevant possession under section 937(b) shall not be considered income from sources within the United States for purposes of Form 5074, "Allocation of Individual Income Tax to Guam or the Commonwealth of the Northern Mariana Islands".

(D) The definition of wages (section 3401). Thus, for example, services performed by an employee for an employer in the relevant possession do not constitute services performed in the United States under section 3401(a)(8).

(E) The characterization of a corporation for purposes other than subchapter S (e.g., sections 367, 951 through 964, 1291 through 1298, 6038, and 6038B). Thus, for example, if a U.S. taxpayer transfers appreciated tangible property to a corporation created or organized in the relevant possession in a transaction described in section 351, he or she must recognize gain unless an exception under section 367(a) applies. Also, if a corporation created or organized in the relevant possession qualifies as a passive foreign investment company under sections 1297 and 1298 with respect to a U.S. taxpayer, a dividend paid to such shareholder does not constitute qualified dividend income under section 1(h)(11)(B).

(2) Application in relevant possession. In applying the territorial income tax of the relevant possession, such possession generally shall be treated, in a geographical and governmental sense, as including the United States. Thus, for example, income tax paid to the United States may be taken into account under sections 31, 6315, and 6402(b) as payments to the relevant possession. Moreover, a citizen of the United States (as defined in paragraph (a)(3) of this section) not a resident of the relevant possession will not be treated as a nonresident alien individual for purposes of the territorial income tax of the relevant possession. Thus, for exam-

ple, a citizen of the United States (as so defined), or a resident of the United States, will not be treated as a nonresident alien individual for purposes of section 1361(b)(1)(C) of the Guamanian Territorial income tax.

(d) Special rules for estimated income tax. *(1) In general.* An individual must make each payment of estimated income tax (and any amendment to the estimated tax payment) to the jurisdiction with which the individual reasonably believes, as of the date of that payment (or amendment), that he or she will be required to file a return for the taxable year under paragraph (b)(1) of this section. In determining the amount of such estimated income tax, income tax paid to the relevant possession may be taken into account under sections 31 and 6402(b) as payments to the United States, and vice versa. For other rules relating to estimated income tax, see section 6654.

(2) Joint estimated income tax. In the case of married persons making a joint payment of estimated income tax, the taxpayers must make each payment of estimated income tax (and any amendment to the estimated tax payment) to the jurisdiction where the spouse who has the greater estimated adjusted gross income for the taxable year would be required under paragraph (d)(1) of this section to pay estimated income tax if separate payments were made. For this purpose, estimated adjusted gross income of each spouse for the taxable year is determined without regard to community property laws.

(3) Erroneous payment. If the individual or spouses erroneously pay estimated income tax to the United States instead of the relevant possession or vice versa, only subsequent payments or amendments of the payments are required to be made pursuant to paragraph (d)(1) or (d)(2) of this section with the other jurisdiction.

(4) Place for payment. Estimated income tax required under this paragraph (d) to be paid to Guam or the Northern Mariana Islands shall be paid as directed in the applicable forms and instructions issued by the relevant possession. Estimated income tax required under paragraph (d)(1) of this section to be paid to the United States shall be paid as directed in the applicable forms and instructions.

(5) Liability to other jurisdiction. (i) Filing with Guam or the Northern Mariana Islands. Subject to paragraph (d)(6) of this section, an individual required under this paragraph (d) to pay estimated income tax (and amendments thereof) to Guam or the Northern Mariana Islands is relieved of liability to pay estimated income tax (and amendments thereof) to the United States.

(ii) Filing with the United States. Subject to paragraph (d)(6) of this section, an individual required under this paragraph (d) to pay estimated income tax (and amendments thereof) to the United States is relieved of liability to pay estimated income tax (and amendments thereof) to the relevant possession.

(6) Underpayments. The liability of an individual described in paragraph (a)(2) of this section for underpayments of estimated income tax for a taxable year, as determined under section 6654, shall be to the jurisdiction with which the individual is required under paragraph (b) of this section to file his or her return for the taxable year.

(e) Entity status consistency requirement. *(1) In general.* Taxpayers should make consistent entity status elections (as defined in paragraph (e)(3)(ii) of this section), when applicable, in both the United States and section 935 possessions. In the case of a business entity to which this paragraph (e) applies:

(i) If an entity status election is filed with the Internal Revenue Service but not with the relevant possession, the appropriate tax authority of the relevant possession, at his discretion, may deem the election also to have been made for the relevant possession tax purposes.

(ii) If an entity status election is filed with the relevant possession but not with the Internal Revenue Service, the Commissioner, at his discretion, may deem the election also to have been made for U.S. Federal tax purposes.

(iii) If inconsistent entity status elections are filed with the relevant possession and the Internal Revenue Service, both the Commissioner and the appropriate tax authority of the relevant possession may, at their individual discretion, treat the elections they each received as invalid and may deem the election filed in the other jurisdiction to have been made also for tax purposes in their own jurisdiction. (See Rev. Proc. 89-8 (1989-1 C.B. 778) for procedures for requesting the assistance of the Internal Revenue Service when a taxpayer is or may be subject to inconsistent tax treatment by the Internal Revenue Service and a U.S. possession tax agency.)

(2) Scope. This paragraph (e) applies to the following business entities:

(i) A business entity (as defined in § 301.7701-2(a) of this chapter) that is domestic (as defined in § 301.7701-5 of this chapter), or otherwise treated as domestic for purposes of the Internal Revenue Code, and that is owned in whole or in part by any person who is either a bona fide resident of a section 935 possession or a business entity created or organized in a section 935 possession.

(ii) A business entity that is created or organized in a section 935 possession and that is owned in whole or in part by any U.S. person (other than a bona fide resident of such possession).

(3) Definitions. For purposes of this section—

(i) The term appropriate tax authority of the relevant possession means the individual responsible for tax administration in such possession or his delegate.

(ii) The term entity status election includes an election under § 301.7701-3(c) of this chapter, an election under section 1362(a), and any other similar elections.

(4) Default status. Solely for the purpose of determining classification of an eligible entity under § 301.7701-3(b), and § 301.7701-3(b) as mirrored in the relevant possession, an eligible entity subject to this paragraph (e) shall be classified for both U.S. Federal and the relevant possession tax purposes using the rule that applies to domestic eligible entities.

(5) Transition rules. (i) In the case of an election filed prior to April 11, 2005, except as provided in paragraph (e)(5)(ii) of this section, the rules of paragraph (e)(1) of this section shall apply as of the first day of the first taxable year of the entity beginning after April 11, 2005.

(ii) In the unlikely circumstance that inconsistent elections described in paragraph (e)(1)(iii) are filed prior to April 11, 2005, and the entity cannot change its classification to achieve consistency because of the sixty-month limitation described in § 301.7701-3(c)(1)(iv) of this chapter, then the entity may nevertheless request permission from the Commissioner or appropriate tax authority of the relevant possession to change such election to avoid inconsistent treatment by the Commissioner and the appropriate tax authority of the relevant possession.

(iii) Except as provided in paragraphs (e)(5)(i) and (e)(5)(ii) of this section, in the case of an election filed with respect to an entity before it became an entity described in paragraph (e)(2) of this section, the rules of paragraph (e)(1) of this section shall apply as of the first day that such entity is described in paragraph (e)(2) of this section.

(iv) In the case of an entity created or organized prior to April 11, 2005, paragraph (e)(4) of this section shall take effect for U.S. Federal income tax purposes (or the relevant possession income tax purposes, as the case may be) as of the first day of the first taxable year of the entity beginning after April 11, 2005.

(f) Examples. The application of this section is illustrated by the following examples:

Example (1). [Reserved].

Example (2). [Reserved].

(g) Effective date. This section shall apply for taxable years ending after October 22, 2004.

T.D. 9194, 4/6/2005, amend T.D. 9248, 1/30/2006.

§ 1.936-1 Elections.

Caution: The Treasury has not yet amended Reg § 1.936-1 to reflect changes made by P.L. 104-188.

(a) Making an election. A domestic corporation shall make an election under section 936(e), for any taxable year beginning after December 31, 1975, by filing Form 5712 on or before the later of—

(1) The date on which such corporation is required, pursuant to sections 6072(b) and 6081, to file its Federal income tax return for the first taxable year for which the election is made; or

(2) April 8, 1980.

Form 5712 shall be filed with the Internal Revenue Service Center, 11601 Roosevelt Boulevard, Philadelphia, Pennsylvania 19155 (Philadelphia Center).

(b) Revoking an election. Any corporation to which an election under section 936(e) applies on April 8, 1980 is hereby granted the consent of the Secretary to revoke that election for the first taxable year to which the election applied. (The corporation may make a new election under § 1.936-1(a) for any subsequent taxable year.) The corporation shall make this revocation by sending to the Philadelphia Center a written statement of revocation on or before February 8, 1980.

T.D. 7673, 2/7/80.

§ 7.936-1 Qualified possession source investment income.

Caution: The Treasury has not yet amended Reg § 7.936-1 to reflect changes made by P.L. 104-188.

For purposes of this section, interest earned after September 30, 1976 (less applicable deductions), by a domestic corporation, engaged in the active conduct of a trade or business in Puerto Rico, which elects the application of section 936 with respect to deposits with certain Puerto Rican financial institutions will be treated as qualified possession source investment income within the meaning of section 936(d)(2) if (1) the interest qualifies for exemption from Puerto Rican income tax under regulations issued by the Secretary of the Treasury of Puerto Rico, as in effect on September 28, 1976, under the authority of section 2(j) of the Puerto Rico Industrial Incentive Act of 1963, as amended, (2) the interest is from sources within Puerto Rico (within the meaning of section 936(d)(2)(A)), and (3) the funds with respect to which the interest is earned are derived from the active conduct of a trade or business in Puerto Rico or from investment of funds so derived.

Because of the need for immediate guidance with respect to the provision contained in this Treasury Decision, it is found impracticable to issue it with notice and public procedure thereon under subsection (b) of section 553 of Title 5 of the United States Code or subject to the effective date limitation of subsection (d) of that section.

T.D. 7452, 12/29/76.

PAR. 4. Section 7.936-1 is removed.

Proposed § 7.936-1 [Removed] [*For Preamble, see ¶ 151,049*]

Proposed § 1.936-2 Source of income. [*For Preamble, see ¶ 151,049*]

Caution: The Treasury has not yet amended Reg § 1.936-2 to reflect changes made by P.L. 104-188, P.L. 100-647, P.L. 99-514, P.L. 95-600.

(a) In general. Except as provided in § 1.936-2(b) (relating to certain interest), for purposes of section 936(d)(2), the determination as to whether gross income is from sources within a particular possession shall be made in accordance with § 1.863-6.

(b) Certain interest. *(1)* Interest paid by a possessions corporation that meets the condition of section 936(a)(2)(A) with respect to a particular possession is from sources within that possession.

(2) Interest paid or credited on deposit accounts with a possession branch of a corporation or partnership is from sources within the possession if, at the time of payment or crediting, the branch is engaged within the possession in the commercial banking business or the business of a savings and loan or similar association.

Proposed § 1.936-3 Investment in a possession (for use therein). [*For Preamble, see ¶ 151,049*]

Caution: The Treasury has not yet amended Reg § 1.936-3 to reflect changes made by P.L. 104-188, P.L. 100-647, P.L. 99-514, P.L. 95-600.

For purposes of section 936(d)(2), interest and certain dividends derived after April 17, 1984 (less deductions allocable and apportionable thereto) by a domestic corporation engaged in the active conduct of a trade or business in Puerto Rico shall be treated as attributable to investment in Puerto Rico (for use therein) if the interest or certain dividends qualify for exemption from Puerto Rican Income Tax under regulations issued by the Secretary of the Treasury of Puerto Rico, as in effect on April 17, 1984 under the authority of the Acts No. 6 of December 15, 1953, 57 of June 13, 1963, and 25 of June 2, 1978, as amended, to determine the institutions which are eligible to receive funds from exempted businesses under those Acts. In the case of any investment of funds made by the possessions corporation after [Date that is 30 days after the date of publication in the Federal Register of this regulation as a Treasury decision], the preceding sentence shall not apply unless the possessions corporation receives, at the time the funds are delivered for investment, the written agreement of the institution receiving the funds that the funds will be invested by the institution so as to qualify for exemption under the foregoing regulations of Puerto Rico. Interest derived after September 30, 1976 and before April 18, 1984 shall be treated as attributable to investment in Puerto Rico (for use therein) if the interest qualifies for exemption from Puerto Rican Income Tax under regulations issued by the Secretary of the Treasury of Puerto Rico as in effect on September 28, 1976 under the authority of section 2(j) of the Puerto Rico Industrial Incentive Act of 1963, as amended.

Proposed § 1.936-3A Funds derived from a possession. [*For Preamble, see ¶ 151,049*]

Caution: The Treasury has not yet amended Reg § 1.936-3A to reflect changes made by P.L. 104-188, P.L. 100-647, P.L. 99-514, P.L. 95-600.

(a) In general. Funds treated as derived from the active conduct of a trade or business in a possession or from investment of such funds in a possession ("qualified funds") include—

(1) Taxable income from sources without the United States derived from the active conduct of a trade or business in the possession, and

(2) Qualified possession source investment income, reduced by any distributions paid with respect to such income and by any losses (not otherwise taken into account under subparagraph (1) or (2) from such activity or investment. The amount of any capital contributions to a possessions corporation is not treated as qualified funds.

(b) Limitation on investment. Notwithstanding paragraph (a), the amount of qualified funds which may be invested in a possession and give rise to income which is treated as qualified possession source investment income is limited to the total qualified funds for the taxable year and for all prior taxable years which are not already invested in a possession. For this purpose, qualified possession source investment income is not included in total qualified funds for the current taxable year, but is included with respect to prior taxable years.

(c) Illustration: The principles of paragraphs (a) and (b) of this section are illustrated by the following example:

Example. X has operated in Puerto Rico as a section 936 corporation since January 1, 1980. In 1980 X earned $30,000 from the active conduct of a business in Puerto Rico and paid a dividend of $20,000. On January 1, 1981 X invested $20,000 in a Puerto Rican financial institution. For the year 1981 X had a loss of $10,000 from the conduct of its business and received $1500 in interest. For the years 1982 and 1983 X earned $40,000 and $60,000 respectively from its business and $2000 each year from its investments which qualify under § 1.936-3 and paid dividends of $20,000 and $30,000 respectively. On January 1, 1984 X deposited $80,000 in the same Puerto Rican financial institution for a total deposit of $100,000. For 1984 X had a $5000 loss from its business, but received $15,000 of interest from its investments.

For 1981, the interest received from the investment in the Puerto Rican financial institution was not qualified possession source investment income since there were no qualified funds for 1981. The $30,000 of income received by X from the active conduct of its business in 1980 was reduced to zero by a $20,000 dividend in 1980 and a $10,000 loss in 1981.

For 1982 and 1983 the $20,000 originally deposited in 1981 and not withdrawn are treated as qualified funds and all of the income derived therefrom as qualified possession source investment income assuming the requirements of §§ 1.936-2 and 1.936-3 are met. The zero qualified funds at the end of 1981 were increased to $20,000 in 1982, representing $40,000 of active business income less $20,000 of dividends; in 1983, the qualified funds available for investment were further increased to $52,000, representing $60,000 of active business income in 1983 less dividend payment of $30,000 (or $30,000) plus $2000 of qualified possession source investment income accrued in 1982). The $1500 of interest earned in 1981 was not derived from qualified funds and, therefore, was not qualified possession source investment income. In addition, this amount and any amount of interest derived therefrom can never be qualified funds since the $1500 was neither derived initially from the active conduct of a trade or business in Puerto Rico nor was it qualified possession source investment income.

For 1984, $7350 of the $15,000 of interest received on the $100,000 investment constitutes qualified possession source investment income since only $49,000 of the $100,000 deposited was from qualified funds ($52,000 of qualified funds at the end of 1983 reduced by the $5000 of loss incurred in 1984 and increased by the $2000 of qualified possession source investment income accrued in 1983).

§ 1.936-4 Intangible property income in the absence of an election out.

Caution: The Treasury has not yet amended Reg § 1.936-4 to reflect changes made by P.L. 104-188, P.L. 100-647, P.L. 99-514.

The rules in this section apply for purposes of section 936(h) and also for purposes of section 934(e), where applicable.

Question 1: If a possessions corporation and its affiliates do not make an election under either the cost sharing or 50/50 profit split option, what rules will govern the treatment of income attributable to intangible property owned or leased by the possessions corporation?

Answer 1: Intangible property income will be allocated to the possessions corporation's U.S. shareholders with the proration of income based on shareholdings. If a shareholder of the possessions corporation is a foreign person or a tax-exempt person, the possessions corporation will be taxable on that shareholder's pro rata amount of the intangible property income. If any class of the stock of a possessions corporation is regularly traded on an established securities market, then the intangible property income will be taxable to the possessions corporation rather than the corporation's U.S. shareholders. For these purposes, a United States shareholder includes any shareholder who is a United States person as described under section 7701(a)(30). The term "intangible property income" means the gross income of a possessions corporation attributable to any intangible property other than intangible property which has been licensed to such corporation since prior to 1948 and which was in use by such corporation on September 3, 1982.

Question 2: What is the source of the intangible property income described in question 1?

Answer 2: The intangible property income is U.S. source, whether taxed to U.S. shareholders or taxed to the possessions corporation. Such intangible property income, if treated as income of the possessions corporation, does not enter into the calculation of the 80-percent possessions source test or the 65-percent active trade or business test of section 936(a)(2)(A) and (B).

Question 3: How will the amount of income attributable to intangible property be measured?

Answer 3: Income attributable to intangible property includes the amount received by a possessions corporation from the sale, exchange, or other disposition of any product or from the rendering of a service which is in excess of the reasonable costs it incurs in manufacturing the product or rendering the service (other than costs incurred in connection with intangibles) plus a reasonable profit margin. A reasonable profit margin shall be computed with respect to direct and indirect costs other than (i) costs incurred in connection with intangibles, (ii) interest expense, and (iii) the cost of materials which are subject to processing or which are components in a product manufactured by the possessions corporation. Notwithstanding the above, certain taxpayers who have been permitted by the Internal Revenue Service in taxable years beginning before January 1, 1983, to use the cost-plus method of pricing without reflecting a return from intangibles, but including the cost of materials in the cost base, will not be precluded from doing so. (Sec. 3.02(3), Rev. Proc. 63-10, 1963-1 C.B. 490.) Thus, the Internal Revenue Service may continue in appropriate cases to permit such taxpayers to continue to report their income as they have been under existing procedures described in the previous sentence if it is appropriate under all the facts and circumstances and does not distort the income of the taxpayer.

Question 4: If there is no intangible property related to a product produced in whole or in part by a possessions corporation, what method may the possessions corporation use to compute its income?

Answer 4: The taxpayer may compute its income using the appropriate method as provided under section 482 and the regulations thereunder. The taxpayer may also elect the cost sharing or profit split method.

T.D. 8090, 6/9/86.

§ 1.936-5 Intangible property income when an election out is made: product, business presence, and contract manufacturing.

Caution: The Treasury has not yet amended Reg § 1.936-5 to reflect changes made by P.L. 104-188, P.L. 100-647, P.L. 99-514.

The rules in this section apply for purposes of section 936(h) and also for purposes of section 934(e), where applicable.

(a) Definition of product.

Q-1. What does the term "product" mean?

A-1. The term "product" means an item of property which is the result of a production process. The term "product" includes component products, integrated products, and end-product forms. A component product is a product which is subject to further processing before sale to an unrelated party. A component product may be produced from other items of property, and if it is so produced, may be treated as including or not including (at the choice of the possessions corporation) one or more of such other items of property for all purposes of section 936(h)(5). An integrated product is a product which is not subject to any further processing before sale to an unrelated party and which includes all component products from which it is produced. An end-product form is a product which—

(1) Is not subject to any further processing before sale to an unrelated party;

(2) Is produced from a component product or products; and

(3) Is treated as not including certain component products for all purposes of section 936(h)(5).

A possessions corporation may treat a component product, integrated product, or end-product form as its possession product even though the final stage or stages of production occur outside the possession. Further processing includes transformation; incorporation, assembly, or packaging.

Q-2. If a possessions corporation produces both a component product and an integrated product (which by definition includes the end-product form), may the possessions corporation use the options under section 936(h)(5) to compute its income with respect to either the component product, the integrated product or the end-product form?

A-2. Yes. The possessions corporation may choose to treat the component product, the integrated product, or the end-product form as the product for purposes of determining whether the possessions corporation satisfies the significant business presence test. The possessions corporation must treat the same item of property as its product (the possession product) for all purposes of section 936(h)(5) for that taxable year, including the significant business presence test under section 936(h)(5)(B)(ii), the possessions sales calculation under section 936(h)(5)(C)(i)(I), the determination of income under section 936(h)(5)(C)(i)(II), and the combined taxable income computations under section 936(h)(5)(C)(ii). Although the possessions corporation must treat the same item of property as its product for all purposes of section 936(h)(5) in a particular taxable year, its choice of the component product, integrated product or end-product form may be different from year to year. The possessions corporation must specify the possession product on a statement attached to its return (Schedule P of Form 5735). The possessions corporation may specify its choice by either listing the components that are included in the possession product or the components that are excluded from the possession product. The possessions corporation must file a separate Schedule P with respect to each possession product. The possessions corporation must attach to each Schedule P detailed computations indicating how the significant business presence test is satisfied with respect to the possession product identified in that Schedule P.

Q-3. A possessions corporation produces a product that is sometimes sold to unrelated parties without further processing and is sometimes sold to unrelated parties after further processing. May the possessions corporation choose to treat the same item of property as the possession product even though in some cases it is an integrated product and in some cases it is a component product?

A-3. Yes. Except as provided in questions and answers 4 and 5, the possessions corporation must designate a single possession product even though it is sometimes a component product and sometimes an integrated product.

Q-4. A possessions corporation produces a product that is sometimes sold without further processing by any member of the affiliated group to unrelated parties or to related parties for their own consumption and is sometimes sold after further processing by any member of the affiliated group to unrelated parties or to related parties for their own consumption. May the possessions corporation designate two products as possession products?

A-4. The possessions corporation may designate two or more possession products. The possessions corporation must use a consistent definition of the possession product for all items of property that are sold to unrelated parties or consumed by related parties at the same stage in the production process. The significant business presence test shall apply separately to each product designated by the possessions corporation. The possessions corporation shall compute its income separately with respect to each product.

Q-5. A possessions corporation produces a product in one taxable year and does not sell all of the units that it produced. In the next taxable year the possessions corporation produces a product which includes the product produced in the prior year. The possessions corporation could not have satisfied the significant business presence test with respect to the units produced the first taxable year if the larger possession product had been designated. May the possessions corporation designate two possession products in the second year?

A-5. Yes. The possessions corporation may designate two possession products. However, once a product has been designated for a particular year all sales of units produced in that year must be defined in the same manner. In addition, the taxpayer must maintain a significant business presence in a possession with respect to that product. Sales shall be deemed made first out of the current year's production. If all of the current year's production is sold and some inventory is liquidated, then the taxpayer's method of inventory accounting shall be applied to determine what year's layer of inventory is liquidated.

Example (1). A possessions corporation S, manufactures a bulk pharmaceutical in a possession. S transfers the bulk pharmaceutical to its U.S. parent, P, for encapsulation and sale by P to customers. S satisfies the significant business presence test with respect to the bulk pharmaceutical (the component product) and the combination of the bulk pharmaceutical and the capsule (the integrated product). S may use the cost sharing or profit split method to compute its income with respect to either the component product or the integrated product.

Example (2). The facts are the same as in example (1) except that S does not satisfy the significant business presence test with respect to the integrated product. S may use the cost sharing or profit split method to compute its income only with respect to the component product. However, if in a later taxable year S satisfies the significant business presence test with respect to the integrated product, then S may use the cost sharing or profit split method to compute its income with respect to that integrated product for that later taxable year.

Example (3). P, a domestic corporation, produces in bulk form in the United States the active ingredient for a pharmaceutical product, P transfers the bulk form to S, a wholly owned possessions corporation. S uses the bulk form to produce in Puerto Rico the finished dosage form drug. S transfers the drug in finished dosage form to P, which sells the drug to unrelated customers in the U.S. The direct labor costs incurred in Puerto Rico by S during its taxable year in formulating, filling and finishing the dosage form are at least 65 percent of the total direct labor costs incurred by the affiliated group in producing the bulk and finished forms during that period. S manufactures (within the meaning of section 954(d)(1)(A)) the finished dosage form. S has elected out under section 936(h)(5) under the profit split option for the drug product area (SIC 283). P and S may treat the bulk and finished dosage forms as parts of an integrated product. Since S satisfies the significant business presence requirement with respect to the integrated product, it is entitled to 50 percent of the combined taxable income on the integrated product.

Example (4). A possessions corporation, S. produces the keyboard of an electric typewriter and incorporates the keyboard with components acquired from a related corporation into finished typewriters. S does not satisfy the significant business presence test with respect to the typewriters (the integrated product). Therefore, S may use the cost sharing or profit split method to compute its income only with respect to a component product or end-product form. For taxable year 1983, S specifies on a statement attached to its return (Schedule P of Form 5735) that the possession product is the end-product form. The statement identifys the components—for example, the keyboard structure and frame—which are included in the possession product. S's definition of the possession product will apply to all units of the electric typewriters which S produces in whole or in part in the possession and which are sold in 1983. Thus, all units of a given component incorporated into such typewriters will be treated in the same way. For example, all keyboards and all frames will be included in the possession product, and all electric drive mechanisms and rollers will be excluded from the possession product.

Example (5). Possessions corporation A produces printed circuit boards in a possession. The printed circuit boards are sold to unrelated parties. A also uses the boards to produce personal computers in the possession. A may designate two possession products: printed circuit boards and personal computers. The significant business presence test applies separately with respect to each of these products. Thus, for those printed circuit boards that are sold to unrelated parties, only the costs of the possessions corporation and the other members of the affiliated group that are incurred with respect to units of the printed circuit boards which are produced in whole or in part in the possessions and sold to third parties shall be taken into account. Conversely, with respect to personal computers, only the costs incurred with respect to the personal computers shall be taken into account. This would include the costs with respect to printed circuit boards that are incorporated into personal computers but not the costs incurred with respect to printed circuit boards that are sold without further processing to unrelated parties.

Example (6). Possessions corporation S produces integrated circuits in a possession. P, an affiliate of S, produces circuit boards in the United States. P transfers the circuit boards to S. S assembles the integrated circuits and the circuit boards. S sells some of the loaded circuit boards to third parties. S retains some of the loaded circuit boards and incorporates them into central processing units. The central processing units are then sold to third parties. S may designate two possession products. S must use a consistent definition of the possession product for all units that are sold at the same stage in the production process. Thus, with respect to those units sold after assembly of the integrated circuits and the printed circuits boards, if S cannot satisfy the significant business presence test with respect to all the loaded circuit boards (the integrated product), then S must designate a lesser product, either the integrated circuit (the component product) or the loaded circuit board less the printed circuit board (the end-product form) as its possession product. With respect to the central processing units sold the same rule would apply. Thus, if S cannot satisfy the significant business presence test with respect to the entire central processing unit for all of the central processing units sold, S must designate some lesser product as its possession product.

Example (7). S is a possession corporation. In 1985, S produced 100 units of product X. Those units were finished into product Y in 1985 by affiliates of S. Product X is a component of product Y. In 1985, S satisfies the direct labor test with respect to product X but not with respect to product Y. S designates the component product X as its possession product. In 1986 S produces 100 units of product X and finishes those units into product Y. S would have satisfied the significant business presence test with respect to product X if S had designated product X as its possession product in 1986. In addition, in 1986 S satisfies the significant business presence test with respect to the integrated product Y. In 1986, S sells 150 units of Y. One hundred of those units would be deemed to be produced in 1986. With respect to those units S may designate the integrated product Y as its possession product. Under S's method of inventory accounting the remaining 50 units were determined to have been produced in 1985. With respect to those units S must define its possession product as it did for the taxable year in which those units were produced. Thus, S's possession product would be the component product X.

Q-6. May an affiliated group establish groupings of possession products and treat the groupings as single products?

A-6. An affiliated group may establish reasonable groupings of possession products based on similarities in the production processes of the possession products. Possession products that are grouped shall be treated as a single product. The determination of whether the production processes involved in producing the products that are to be grouped are similar is based on the production processes of the components that are included in the possession product. The affiliated group may establish new groupings each year. Any grouping which materially distorts a taxpayer's income or the application of the significant business presence test may be disallowed by the Commissioner. The mere fact that a grouping results in an increased allocation of income to the possessions corporation does not, of itself, create a material distortion of income. If the Commissioner determines that the taxpayer's grouping is improper with respect to one or more products in a group, then those products shall be excluded from the group. The effect of excluding a product or products from the group is that the taxpayer must demonstrate that the group without the excluded products (and each excluded product itself) satisfies the significant business presence test. If the group without the excluded products, or any of the excluded products themselves, fails to satisfy the significant business presence test, then the possessions corporation's income from those products shall be determined under section 936(h)(1) through (4) and the regulations thereunder.

Example (1). The following are examples of possession products the processes of production of which are sufficiently similar that they may be grouped and treated as a single product:

(A) Beverage bases or concentrates for different soft drinks or soft drink syrups, regardless of whether some include sweeteners and some do not;

(B) Different styles of clothing;

(C) Different styles of shoes;

(D) Equipment which relies on gravity to deliver solutions to patients intravenously;

(E) Equipment which relies on machines to deliver solutions to patients intravenously;

(F) Video game cartridges, even though the concept and design of each game title is, in part, protected against infringement by separate copyrights;

(G) All integrated circuits;

(H) All printed circuit boards; and

(I) Hardware and software if the software is one of several alternative types of software offered by the manufacturer and sold only with the hardware, and a purchaser of the hardware would ordinarily purchase one or more of the manufacturer-provided alternative types of software. In all other cases, hardware and software may not be grouped and treated as a single product.

Groupings (D) and (E) do not include any solutions which are delivered through the equipment described therein.

Example (2). A possessions corporation produces in Puerto Rico non-programmable, interactive cathode ray tube computer terminals that vary in price. These terminals all interact with a computer or controller to perform their functions of data entry, graphics word processing, and program development. The terminals can be purchased with options that include a built-in printer, different language keyboards, specialized cathode ray tubes, and different power supply features. All terminals are produced in one integrated process requiring the same skills and operations. The differences in the production of the terminals include differences in the number of printed circuit boards incorporated in each terminal, the use of unique keyboards, and the installation and testing of the built-in printer. Some difference in direct labor time to manufacture the terminals occurs, primarily due to the differing number and complexity of printed circuit boards incorporated into each terminal. Different model numbers are assigned to various computer terminals. A grouping by the taxpayer of all of the terminals as one product will be respected by the Service, unless the Service establishes that substantial distortion results. This grouping is proper because the processes of producing each of the terminals are similar.

Example (3). A possessions corporation, S produces several models of serial matrix impact printers and teleprinters. These products have differing performance standards based on such factors as speed (in characters per second), numbers of columns, and cost. The production process for all types of printers involves production of three basic elements: electronic circuitry, the printing head, and the mechanical parts. The process of producing all the printers is similar. Thus, all printers could be grouped and treated as a single product. S purchases electronic circuitry and mechanical parts from a U.S. affiliate. S performs manufacturing functions relative to the printing head and assembles and tests the finished printers. S does not satisfy the significant business presence test with respect to the integrated products. S therefore specifies on a statement attached to its return (Schedule P of Form 5735) that the possession product for both the serial matrix printers and the teleprinters is the end-product form. The statement identifies the components which are included in each possession product. S may group and treat as a single product the serial matrix printers and the teleprinters if both end-product forms include and exclude similar components. Thus, if the end-product form for both the serial matrix printers and the teleprinters includes the mechanical parts and excludes the electronic circuitry, then S may group and treat as a single product the two end-product forms. If, however, the end-product forms for the two items of property contain components that are not similar and as a result of this definition of the end-product forms the production processes involved in producing the two end-product forms are not similar, then S may not group the end-product forms.

Q-7. Is the affiliated group permitted to include in a group an item of property that is not produced in whole or in part in a possession?

A-7. No.

Example (1). Possessions corporation S produces 70 units of product A in a possession. P, an affiliate of S, produces

30 units of product A entirely in the United States. All of the units are sold to unrelated parties. The affiliated group is not permitted to group the 30 units of product A produced in the United States with the 70 units produced in the possession because those units are not produced in whole or in part in a possession.

Example (2). The facts are the same as in example (1) except that the 30 units of product A are transferred to possessions corporation S. S incorporates the 100 units of product A into product B. This incorporation takes place in the possession. S may group and treat as a single product all of the units of product B even though some of those units contain units of product A that were produced in the possession and some that were produced in the United States.

Q-8. What factors should be disregarded in determining whether a particular grouping of similar items of property is reasonable?

A-8. In general, differences in the following factors will be disregarded in determining whether a particular grouping of items of property is reasonable:

(1) Differences in testing requirements (e.g., some products sold for military use may require more extensive or different testing than products sold for commercial use);

(2) Differences in the product specifications that are designed to accommodate the product to its area of use or for conditions under which used (e.g., electrical products designed for ultimate use in the United States differ from electrical products designed for ultimate use in Europe);

(3) Differences in packaging or labeling (e.g., differences in the number of units of the items shipped in one package); and

(4) Minor differences in the operations of the items of property.

Q-9. What rules apply for purposes of determining whether pharmaceutical products are properly grouped and treated as a single product?

A-9. The rules contained in questions and answers 6 through 8 of this section shall apply. Thus, an affiliated group may establish reasonable groupings based on similarities in the production processes of two or more possession products. In establishing a group the affiliated group may only compare the production processes involved in producing the possession products. The fact that two pharmaceutical products contain different active or inert ingredients is not relevant to the determination of whether the pharmaceutical products may be grouped. For example, if the possession products are bulk chemicals and the production processes involved in producing the bulk chemicals are similar, those bulk chemicals may be grouped and treated as a single product even though they contain different active or inert ingredients. The affiliated group may also group and treat as a single product the finished dosage form drug as long as the production processes involved in producing the finished dosage forms are similar. For these purposes, the production processes involved in producing the following classes of items shall be considered to be sufficiently similar that possession products delivered in a form described in one of the categories may be grouped with other possession products delivered in a form described in the same category.

The categories are:

(1) Capsules, tablets, and pills;

(2) Liquids, ointments, and creams; or

(3) Injectable and intravenous preparations.

No distinctions should be based on packaging, list numbers, or size of dosage. The affiliated group may group and treat as a single product the integrated product (combination of the bulk and the delivery form) only if all the production processes involved in producing the integrated products are similar. The rules of this question and answer are illustrated by the following examples.

Example (1). Possessions corporation S produces two chemical active ingredients X and Y. Both chemical ingredients are produced through the process of fermentation. The affiliated group is permitted to group and treat as a single product the two chemical ingredients.

Example (2). The facts are the same as in example (1) and possessions corporation S finishes chemical ingredient X into tablets and chemical ingredient Y into capsules. The affiliated group is permitted to group and treat as a single product the combination of the bulk pharmaceutical and the finishing because the production processes involved in producing the integrated products are similar.

Example (3). Possessions corporation S produces in a possession a bulk chemical X by fermentation. A United States affiliate, P, produces in the United States a bulk chemical, Y, by fermentation. Both bulk chemicals are finished by S in the possession. The finished dosage form of X is in pill form. The finished dosage form of Y is in injectable form. If S's possession product is the integrated product or the end-product form then S may not group X and Y because the production processes involved in producing the finished dosage form of X and Y are not similar. If S's possession product is the component then S may not group X and Y because the bulk chemical Y is not produced in whole or in part in a possession.

Q-10. Will the fact that a manufacturer of a drug must submit a New Drug Application ("NDA") or a supplemental NDA to the Food and Drug Administration have any effect on the definition or grouping of a product?

A-10. No.

Q-11. A possessions corporation which produced a product or rendered a type of service in a possession on or before September 3, 1982, is not required to meet the significant business presence test in a possession with respect to such product or type of service for its taxable years beginning before January 1, 1986 (the interim period). During such interim period, how will the term "product" be defined for purposes of allocating income under the cost sharing or profit split methods?

A-11. During the interim period the product will be determined based on the activities performed by the possessions corporation within a possession on September 3, 1982. During the interim period the possessions corporation may compute its income under the cost sharing or profit split method only with respect to the product that is produced or manufactured within the meaning of section 954(d)(1)(A) within the possession. If the product is manufactured from a component or components produced by an affiliated corporation or a contract manufacturer, then the product will not be treated as including such component or components for purposes of the computation of income under the cost sharing or profit split methods. Thus, the possessions corporation is not entitled to any return on the intangibles associated with the component or components. Notwithstanding the preceding sentences, for taxable years beginning before January 1, 1986, a possessions corporation may compute its income under the cost sharing or profit split method with respect to a product which includes a component or components produced by an affiliated corporation or contract manufacturer if the possessions corporation satisfies with respect to such product the significant business presence test described in section 936(h)(5)(B)(ii) and the regulations thereunder.

Example (1). A possessions corporation, S, was manufacturing (within the meaning of section 954(d)(1)(A)) integrated circuits in a possession on September 3, 1982. S transferred those integrated circuits to related corporation P. P incorporated the integrated circuits into central processing units (CPUs in the United States) and sold the CPUs to unrelated parties. S continued to manufacture integrated circuits in the possession through January 1, 1986. For taxable years beginning before January 1, 1986, S may compute its income under the cost sharing or profit split method with respect to the integrated circuits regardless of whether S satisfies the significant business presence test. However, unless S satisfies the significant business presence test with respect to the central processing units, S may not compute its income under the cost sharing or profit split methods with respect to the CPUs, and thus, S is not entitled to any return on manufacturing intangibles associated with CPUs to the extent that they are not related to the integrated circuits produced by S, nor (except as provided in the profit split methods) to any return on marketing intangibles.

Example (2). A possessions corporation S, was engaged on September 3, 1982, in the manufacture (within the meaning of section 954(d)(1)(A)) of a bulk pharmaceutical in Puerto Rico from raw materials. S sold the bulk pharmaceutical to its U.S. parent, P, for encapsulation and sale by P to customers as the product X. Because S was not engaged in the encapsulation of X, S is not considered to have manufactured the integrated product, X, in Puerto Rico. During the interim period, S may compute its income under the cost sharing or profit split methods with respect to the integrated product, X, only if S satisfies the significant business presence test with respect to X. S may compute its income under the cost sharing or profit split methods with respect to the component product (the bulk pharmaceutical).

Example (3). P is a domestic corporation that is not a possessions corporation. P manufactures a bulk pharmaceutical in the United States. P transfers the bulk pharmaceutical to its wholly owned subsidiary, S, a possessions corporation. On September 3, 1982, S was engaged in the encapsulation of the bulk pharmaceutical in Puerto Rico in a manner which satisfies the test of section 954(d)(1)(A). For taxable years beginning before January 1, 1986, S may compute its income under the cost sharing or profit split methods with respect to the end-product form the (the encapsulated drug) regardless of whether S meets the significant business presence test. However, unless S satisfies the significant business presence test with respect to the integrated product, S may not compute its income under the cost sharing or profit split methods with respect to the integrated product, and thus, S is not entitled to any return on the intangibles associated with the bulk pharmaceutical.

Q-12. On September 3, 1982, a possessions corporation, S was engaged in the manufacture (within the meaning of section 954(d)(1)(A)) of X in a possession. During the interim period, after September 3, 1982, but before January 1, 1986, S produced Y, which differs from X in terms of minor design features. S did not produce Y in a possession on September 3, 1982. Will S be considered to have commenced production of a new product after September 3, 1982, for purposes of the application of the significant business presence test for the interim period?

A-12. No. X and Y will be considered to be a single product, and therefore S will not be required to satisfy the business presence test separately with respect to Y during the interim period. In all cases in which the items of property produced on or before September 3, 1982 and the items of property produced after that date could have been grouped together under the guidelines provided in § 1.936-5(a) questions and answers 6 through 10, the possessions corporation will not be considered to manufacture a new product after September 3, 1982.

Q-13. May the term "product" be defined differently for export sales than for domestic sales?

A-13. Yes. For rules concerning the application of the separate election for export sales see § 1.936-7(b).

(b) Requirement of significant business presence. *(1) General rules.*

Q-1. In general, a possessions corporation may compute its income under the cost sharing or profit split methods with respect to a product only if the possessions corporation has a significant business presence in a possession with respect to that product. When will a possession corporation be considered to have a significant business presence in a possession?

A-1. For purposes of the cost sharing method, the significant business presence test is met if the possessions corporation satisfies either a value added test or a direct labor test. For purposes of the profit split method, the significant business presence test is met if the possessions corporation satisfies either a value added test or a direct labor test and also manufactures the product in the possession within the meaning of section 954(d)(1)(A).

Q-2. How may a possessions corporation satisfy the direct labor test with respect to a product?

A-2. The possessions corporation will satisfy the direct labor test with respect to a product if the direct labor costs incurred by the possessions corporation as compensation for services performed in a possession are greater than or equal to 65 percent of the direct labor costs of the affiliated group for units of the possession product produced during the taxable year in whole or in part by the possessions corporation.

Q-3. How may a possessions corporation satisfy the value added test?

A-3. In order to satisfy the value added test, the production costs of the possessions corporation incurred in the possession with respect to units of the possession product produced in whole or in part by the possessions corporation in the possession and sold or otherwise disposed of during the taxable year by the affiliated group to unrelated parties must be greater than or equal to twenty-five percent of the difference between gross receipts from such sales or other dispositions and the direct material costs of the affiliated group for materials purchased for such units from unrelated parties.

Q-4. Must the significant business presence test be met with respect to all units of the product produced during the taxable year by the affiliated group?

A-4. No. The significant business presence test must be met with respect to only those units of the product produced during the taxable year in whole or in part by the possessions corporation in a possession.

Q-5. For purposes of determining whether a possessions corporation satisfies the significant business presence test, how shall the possessions corporation treat the cost of components transferred to the possessions corporation by a member of the affiliated group?

A-5. The treatment of the cost of components transferred from an affiliate depends on whether the possession product is treated as including the components for purposes of section 936(h). If it is, then for purposes of the value added test, the production costs associated with the component shall be treated as production costs of the affiliated group that are not incurred by the possessions corporation. Those production costs, other than the cost of materials, shall not be treated as a cost of materials. For purposes of the direct labor test and the alternative significant business presence test, the direct labor costs associated with such components shall be treated as direct labor costs of the affiliated group that are not incurred by the possessions corporation. If the possession product is treated as not including such component for purposes of section 936(h), then, solely for purposes of determining whether the possessions corporation satisfies the value added test, the cost of the component shall not be treated as either a cost of materials or as a production cost. For purposes of the direct labor test and the alternative significant business presence test, the direct labor costs associated with such component shall not be treated as direct labor costs of the affiliated group. If the possession product is treated as not including such component, then the possessions corporation shall not be entitled to any return on the intangibles associated with the manufacturing or marketing of the component.

Q-6. May two or more related possessions corporations aggregate their production or direct labor costs for purposes of determining whether they satisfy the significant business presence test with respect to a single product?

A-6. No.

Q-7. A possessions corporation, S, purchases raw materials and components from an unrelated corporation which conducts business outside of a possession. The unrelated corporation is not a contract manufacturer. What is the treatment of such raw materials and components for purposes of the significant business presence test?

A-7. Where Company S purchases raw materials or components from an unrelated corporation which is not a contract manufacturer, the raw materials and components are treated as materials, and the costs related thereto are treated as a cost of materials.

(2) Direct labor costs.

Q-1. How is the term "direct labor costs" to be defined?

A-1. The term "direct labor costs" has the same meaning which it has for purposes of § 1.471-11(b)(2)(i). Thus, direct labor costs include the cost of labor which can be identified or associated with particular units or groups of units of a specific product. The elements of direct labor include such items as basic compensation, overtime pay, vacation and holiday pay, sick leave pay (other than payments pursuant to a wage continuation plan under section 105(d)), shift differential, payroll taxes, and payments to a supplemental unemployment benefit plan paid or incurred on behalf of employees engaged in direct labor.

Q-2. May a taxpayer treat a cost as a direct labor cost if it is not included in inventoriable costs under section 471 and the regulations thereunder?

A-2. No. A cost may be treated as a direct labor cost only if it is included in inventoriable costs. However, a cost may be considered a direct labor cost even though the activity to which it relates would not constitute manufacturing under section 954(d)(1)(A) as long as the cost is included in inventoriable costs.

Q-3. May the members of the affiliated group include as direct labor costs the labor element in indirect production costs?

A-3. No. The labor element of indirect production costs may not be considered as part of direct labor costs.

Q-4. Do direct labor costs include the costs which can be identified or associated with particular units or groups of units of a specific product if those costs could also be described as quality control and inspection?

A-4. Yes. Direct labor costs include costs which can be identified or associated with particular units or groups of units of a specific product. Thus, if quality control and inspection is an integral part of the production process, then the labor associated with that quality control and inspection shall be considered direct labor. For example, integrated circuits are soldered to printed circuit boards by passing the boards over liquid solder. Employees inspect each of the boards and repair any imperfectly soldered joints discovered on that inspection. The labor associated with this process is direct labor. However, if a person performs random inspections on limited numbers of products, then that labor associated with those inspections shall be considered quality control and therefore indirect labor.

Q-5. Do direct labor costs of the possessions corporation include only the costs which were actually incurred or do they take into account, in addition, any labor savings which result because the activities were performed in a possession rather than in the United States?

A-5. Direct labor costs include only the costs which were actually incurred.

Q-6. For purposes of determining whether a possessions corporation satisfies the significant business presence test for a taxable year with respect to a product, how shall the possessions corporation compute its direct labor costs of units of the product?

A-6. The direct labor test shall be applied separately to products produced in whole or in part by the possessions corporation in the possession during each taxable year. Sales shall be deemed to be made first out of the current year's production. If sales are made only out of the current year's production, then the direct labor costs of producing those units that are sold shall be the pro rata portion of the total direct labor costs of producing all the units that are produced in whole or in part in the possession by the possessions corporation during the current year. If all of the current year's production is sold and some inventory is liquidated, then the direct labor test shall be applied separately to the current year's production and the liquidated inventory. The direct labor costs of producing the liquidated inventory shall be the pro rata portion of the total direct labor costs that were incurred in producing all the units that were produced in whole or in part by the possessions corporation in the possessions in the layer of liquidated inventory determined under the member's method of inventory accounting.

Example. S is a cash basis calendar year taxpayer that has made an election under section 936(a). In 1985 S produced 100 units of product X. Fifty percent of the direct labor costs of the affiliated group were incurred by S and were compensation for services performed in the possession. Thus, S did not satisfy the significant business presence test with respect to product X in taxable year 1985. During 1986 S produced 100 units of product X. One hundred percent of the direct labor costs of the affiliated group were incurred by S and were compensation for services performed in the possession. In 1986 S sells 150 units of product X. One hundred of those units are deemed to be from the units produced in 1986. With respect to those units S satisfies the significant business presence test. Under S's method of inventory accounting the remaining 50 units were determined to be produced in 1985. With respect to those units S does not satisfy the significant business presence test because only 50% of the direct labor costs incurred in producing those units were incurred by S and were compensation for services performed in the possession.

Q-7. What is the result if in a particular taxable year the possessions corporation satisfies the significant business presence test with respect to units of the product produced in one year and fails the significant business with respect to units produced in another year?

A-7. For those units of the product with respect to which the possession corporation satisfies the significant business presence test, the possessions corporation may compute its income under the provisions of section 936(h)(5). For those units of the product with respect to which the possessions corporations fails the significant business presence test, the possessions corporation must compute its income under section 936(h)(1) through (4).

Q-8. Do direct labor costs include costs incurred in a prior taxable year with respect to units of the possession product that are finished in a later taxable year?

A-8. Yes.

(3) Direct material costs.

Q-1. How is the term "direct material costs" to be defined?

A-1. Direct material costs include the cost of those materials which become an integral part of the specific product and those materials which are consumed in the ordinary course of manufacturing and can be identified or associated with particular units or groups of units of that product. See § 1.471-3 for the elements of direct material costs.

Q-2. May a taxpayer treat a cost as a direct material cost if it is not included in inventoriable costs under section 471 and the regulations thereunder?

A-2. A taxpayer may not treat such costs as direct material costs.

(4) Production costs.

Q-1. How is the term "production costs" defined?

A-1. The term "production costs" has the same meaning which it has for purposes of § 1.471-11(b) except that the term does not include direct material costs and interest. Thus, production costs include direct labor costs and fixed and variable indirect production costs (other than interest).

Q-2. With respect to indirect production costs described in § 1.471-11(c)(2)(ii) and (iii), may a possessions corporation include these costs in production costs for purposes of section 936, if they are not included in inventoriable costs under section 471 and the regulations thereunder?

A-2. No. A possessions corporation may include these costs only if they are included for purposes of section 471 and the regulations thereunder. If a possessions corporation and the other members of the affiliated group include and exclude different indirect production costs in their inventoriable costs, then, for purposes of the significant business presence test, the possessions corporation shall compute its production costs and the production costs of the other members of the affiliated group by subtracting from the production costs of each member all indirect costs included by that member that are not included in production costs by all other members of the affiliated group.

Q-3. Does a change in a taxpayer's method of accounting for purposes of section 471 affect the taxpayer's computation of production costs for purposes of section 936?

A-3. Yes. If a taxpayer changes its method of accounting for purposes of section 471, then the same change shall apply for purposes of section 936.

Q-4. For purposes of determining whether a possessions corporation satisfies the significant business presence test for a taxable year with respect to a product, how shall the possessions corporation compute its costs of producing units of the product sold or otherwise disposed to unrelated parties during the taxable year?

A-4. All members of the affiliated group may elect to use their current year production costs regardless of whether the members use the FIFO or LIFO method of inventory accounting. If some or all of the current year's production of a product is sold, then the production costs of producing those units sold shall be the pro rata portion of the total production costs of producing all the units produced in the current year. If all of the current year's production of a product is sold and some inventory is liquidated, then the production costs of producing the liquidated inventory shall be the pro rata portion of the production costs incurred in producing the layer of liquidated inventory as determined under the member's method of inventory accounting.

Q-5. How should the members of the affiliated group determine the portion of their production costs that is allocable to units of the product sold or otherwise disposed of during the taxable year?

A-5. The members of the affiliated group may use either standard production costs (so long as variances are not material), average production costs, or FIFO production costs to determine the production costs that will be considered to be attributable to units of the product sold or otherwise disposed of during the taxable year. However, all members of the affiliated group must use the same method.

Q-6. When is the quality control and inspection of a product considered to be part of the production activity for that product?

A-6. Quality control and inspection of a manufactured product before its sale or other disposition by the manufacturer, or before its incorporation into other products, is considered to be part of the indirect production activity for that initial product. Subsequent testing of a product to ensure that the product is compatible with other products is not a part of the production activity for the initial product.

When a component is incorporated into an end-product form and the end-product form is then tested, the latter testing will be considered to be a part of the indirect production activity for the end-product form and will not be considered to be a part of the production activity for the component.

Q-7. For purposes of the significant business presence test and the allocation of income to a possessions corporation, what is the treatment of the cost of installation of a product?

A-7. For purposes of the significant business presence test and the allocation of income to a possessions corporation, product installation costs need not be taken into account as costs incurred in the manufacture of that product, if the taxpayer keeps such permanent books of account or records as are sufficient to establish the fair market price of the uninstalled product. In such a case, the cost of installation materials, the cost of the labor for installation, and a reasonable profit for installation will not be included in the costs and income associated with the possession product. If the taxpayer does not keep such permanent books of account or records, then the cost of installation materials and the cost of labor for installation shall be treated as costs associated with the possession product and income will be allocated to the possessions corporation and its affiliates under the rules provided in these regulations.

Q-8. For purposes of the significant business presence test and the allocation of income to a product or service, what is the treatment of the cost of servicing and maintaining a possession product that is sold to an unrelated party?

A-8. The cost of servicing and maintaining a possession product after it is sold is not associated with the production of that product.

Q-9. For purposes of the significant business presence test and the allocation of income to a possessions corporation, what is the treatment of the cost of samples?

A-9. The cost of producing samples will be treated as a marketing expense and not as inventoriable costs for these purposes. However, for taxable years beginning prior to January 1, 1986, the cost of producing samples may be treated as either a marketing expense or as inventoriable costs.

(5) Gross receipts.

Q-1. How shall the affiliated group determine gross receipts from sales or other dispositions by the affiliated group to unrelated parties of the possession product?

A-1. Gross receipts shall be determined in the same manner as possession sales under the rules contained in § 1.936-6(a)(2).

(6) Manufacturing within the meaning of section 954(d)(1)(A).

Q-1. What is the test for determining, within the meaning of section 954(d)(1)(A), whether a product is manufactured or produced by a possessions corporation in a possession?

A-1. A product is considered to have been manufactured or produced by a possessions corporation in a possession within the meaning of section 954(d)(1)(A) and § 1.954-3(a)(4) if—

(i) The property has been substantially transformed by the possessions corporation in the possession;

(ii) The operations conducted by the possessions corporation in the possession in connection with the property are substantial in nature and are generally considered to constitute the manufacture or production of property; or

(iii) The conversion costs sustained by the possessions corporation in the possession, including direct labor, factory burden, testing of components before incorporation into an end product and testing of the manufactured product before sales account for 20 percent or more of the total cost of goods sold of the possessions corporation.

In no event, however, will packaging, repackaging, labeling, or minor assembly operations constitute manufacture or production of property. See particularly examples (2) and (3) of § 1.954-3(a)(4)(iii).

Q-2. Does the requirement that a possession product be produced or manufactured in a possession within the meaning of section 954(d)(1)(A) apply to taxable years beginning before January 1, 1986?

A-2. A possessions corporation must satisfy this requirement for taxable years beginning before January 1, 1986, in the following cases:

(7) Start-up operations.

Q-1. With respect to products not produced (and types of services not rendered) in the possession on or before September 3, 1982, when must a possessions corporation first satisfy the 25 percent value added test or the 65 percent direct labor test?

A-1. A transitional period is established such that a possessions corporation engaged in start-up operations with respect to a product or service need not satisfy the 25 percent value added test or the 65 percent labor test until the third taxable year following the taxable year in which such product is first sold by the possessions corporation or such service is first rendered by the possessions corporation. During the transitional period, the applicable percentages for these tests will be as follows:

	Any year after 1982		
	1	2	3
Value added test	10	15	20
Labor test	35	45	55

Q-2. Does the requirement that a possession product be produced or manufactured in a possessions within the meaning of section 954(d)(1)(A) apply to a product if the possessions corporation is engaged in start-up operations with respect to that product?

A-2. The possessions corporation must produce or manufacture the possessions product within the meaning of section 954(d)(1)(A) if the possessions corporation computes its income with respect to that product under the profit split method.

Q-3. When will a possessions corporation be considered to be engaged in start-up operations?

A-3. A possessions corporation is engaged in start-up operations if it begins operations in a possession with respect to a product or type of service after September 3, 1982. Subject to the further provisions of this answer, a possessions corporation will be considered to begin operations with respect to a product if, under the rules of § 1.936-5(a) questions and answers (6) through (10), such product could not be grouped with any other item of property manufactured in whole or in part in the possessions by any member of the affiliated group in any preceding taxable year. Any improvement or other change in a possession product which does not substantially change the production process would not be deemed to create a new product. A change in the division of manufacturing activity between the possessions corporation and its affiliates with respect to an item of property will not give rise to a new product. If a possessions corporation was producing a possession product that was either a component product or an end-product form and the possessions corporation expands its operations in the same possession so that it is now producing a product that includes the earlier possession product, the possessions corporation will not be entitled to use the start-up significant business presence test unless the production costs incurred by the possessions corporation in the possession in producing a unit of its new possession product are at least double the production costs incurred by the possessions corporation in the possession in producing a unit of the earlier possession product. If any member of an affiliated group actually groups two or more items of property then, solely for the purposes of determining whether any item of property in that group is a new product, that grouping shall be respected. However, the fact that an affiliated group does not actually group two or more items of property shall be disregarded in determining whether any item of property is a new product. Notwithstanding the above, if a possessions corporation is producing a possession product in one possession and such corporation or a member of its affiliated group begins operations in a different possession, regardless of whether the items of property could be grouped, the affiliated group may treat the units of the item of property produced at the new site of operations in the different possession as a new product.

(8) Alternative significant business presence test.

Q-1. Will the Secretary adopt a significant business presence test other than those set forth in section 936(h)(5)(B)(ii)?

A-1. Yes. The following significant business presence test is adopted both for the transitional period and thereafter. A possessions corporation will have a significant business presence in a possession for a taxable year with respect to a product or type of service if—

(i) No less than 50 percent of the direct labor costs of the affiliated group for units of the product produced, in whole or in part, during the taxable year by the possessions corporation or for the type of service rendered by the possessions corporation during the taxable year are incurred by the possessions corporation as compensation for services performed in the possession; and

(ii) The direct labor costs of the possessions corporation for units of the product produced or the type of service rendered plus the base period construction costs are no less than 70 percent of the sum of such base period construction costs and the direct labor costs of the affiliated group for such units of the product produced or the type of service rendered.

Notwithstanding satisfaction of the above test, for purposes of determining whether a possessions corporation may compute its income under the profit split method, a possessions corporation will not be treated as having a significant business presence in a possession with respect to a product unless the possessions corporation manufactures the product in the possession within the meaning of section 954(d)(1)(A).

Q-2. How is the term "base period construction costs" defined?

A-2. The term "base period construction costs" means the average construction costs incurred by or on behalf of the possessions corporation for services in the possession during the taxable year and the preceding four taxable years for section 1250 property (as defined in section 1250(c) and the regulations thereunder) that is used for the production of the product or the rendering of the service in the possession, and which represents the original use of the section 1250 property. For purposes of the preceding sentence, if the possessions corporation was not in existence during one or more of the four preceding taxable years, its construction costs for that year or years shall be deemed to be zero. Construction costs include architects' and engineers' fees, labor costs, and overhead and profit (if the construction is performed by a person that is not a member of the affiliated group).

(c) Definition and treatment of contract manufacturing.

Q-1. For purposes of determining whether a possessions corporation satisfies the significant business presence test with respect to a product, the costs incurred by the possessions corporation or by any of its affiliates in connection with contract manufacturing which is related to that product and is performed outside the possession shall be treated as direct labor costs of the affiliated group and shall not be treated as production costs of the possessions corporation or as material costs. How is the term "contract manufacturing" to be defined?

A-1. The term "contract manufacturing" includes any arrangement between a possessions corporation (or another member of the affiliated group) and an unrelated person if the unrelated person:

(1) Performs work on inventory owned by a member of the affiliated group for a fee without the passage of title;

(2) Performs production activities (including manufacturing, assembling, finishing, or packaging) under the direct supervision and control of a member of the affiliated group; or

(3) Does not undertake any significant risk in manufacturing its product (e.g., it is paid by the hour).

Q-2. Does an arrangement between a member of the affiliated group and an unrelated party constitute contract manufacturing if the unrelated party uses an intangible owned or licensed by a member of the affiliated group?

A-2. Such an arrangement will be treated as contract manufacturing if the unrelated party makes use of a patent owned or licensed by a member of the affiliated group in producing the product which becomes part of the possession product of the possessions corporation. In addition, such use of manufacturing intangibles other than patents may be treated as contract manufacturing if it is established that the arrangement has the effect of materially distorting the application of the significant business presence test. However, the preceding sentence shall not apply if the possessions corporation establishes that the arrangement was entered into for a substantial business purpose (e.g., to obtain the benefit of special expertise of the manufacturer or economies of scale). These rules shall not apply to such contract manufacturing performed in taxable years beginning before January 1, 1986, nor shall the rules apply to binding contracts for the performance of such contract manufacturing entered into before June 13, 1986.

Q-3. For purposes of the significant business presence test, how shall a possessions corporation treat the cost of contract manufacturing performed within a possession?

A-3. If the possessions corporation uses the value added test, it will be permitted to treat the cost of the contract manufacturing performed in a possession, not including material costs, as a production cost of the possessions corporation. If it uses the direct labor test or the alternative significant business presence test set forth in § 1.936-5(b)(8), it is permitted to treat the direct labor costs of the contract manufacturer associated with such contract manufacturing as a cost of direct labor of the possessions corporation. The allowable amount of the direct labor cost shall be determined in accordance with question and answer 4 below.

Q-4. How are the amounts paid by a possessions corporation to a contract manufacturer for services rendered in a possession to be treated by the possessions corporation in computing the direct labor cost of the product to which such contract manufacturing relates?

A-4. If the possessions corporation can establish the contract manufacturer's direct labor cost which was incurred in the possession, such cost will be treated as incurred by the possessions corporation as compensation for services performed in the possession. If the possessions corporation cannot establish such cost, then 50 percent of the amount paid to such contract manufacturer may be treated as incurred by the possessions corporation as compensation for services performed in the possession: provided, that not more than 50 percent of the fair market value of the product manufactured by the contract manufacturer is attributable to articles shipped into the possession, and the possessions corporation receives a statement from the contract manufacturer that this test has been satisfied. If this fair market value test is not satisfied, then the cost of contract manufacturing performed within a possession shall not be treated as a production cost or a direct labor cost of either the possessions corporation or the affiliated group.

Q-5. For purposes of the significant business presence test, what is the treatment of costs which are incurred by a member of the affiliated group (including the possessions corporation) for contract manufacturing performed outside of the possession with respect to an item of property which is a component of the possession product?

A-5. If the possession product is treated as including such component, the cost of the contract manufacturing shall be treated as a direct labor cost of members of the affiliated group other than the possessions corporation for purposes of the direct labor test and the alternative significant business presence test, and shall not be treated as a production cost of the possessions corporation or as a cost of materials for purposes of the value added test. If the possession product is treated as not including such component, the cost of the contract manufacturing shall not be treated as a direct labor cost of any member of the affiliated group for purposes of the direct labor test and the alternative significant business presence test, and shall not be treated as a production cost of the possessions corporation or as a cost of materials for purposes of the value added test.

T.D. 8090, 6/9/86.

§ 1.936-6 Intangible property income when an election out is made: cost sharing and profit split options; covered intangibles.

Caution: The Treasury has not yet amended Reg § 1.936-6 to reflect changes made by P.L. 104-188, P.L. 100-647, P.L. 99-514.

The rules in this section apply for purposes of section 936(h) and also for purposes of section 934(e) where applicable.

(a) Cost sharing option. *(1) Product area research.* Question 1: Cost sharing payments are based on research undertaken by the affiliated group in the "product area" which includes the possession product. The term "product area" is defined by reference to the three-digit classification under the Standard Industrial Classification (SIC) code. Which governmental agency has jurisdiction to decide the proper SIC category for any specific product?

Answer 1: Solely for the purpose of determining the tax consequences of operating in a possession, the Secretary or his delegate has exclusive jurisdiction to decide the proper SIC category under which a product is classified. For this purpose, the product area under which a product is classified will be determined according to the 1972 edition of the SIC code. From time to time and in appropriate cases, the Secretary may prescribe regulations or issue rulings determining the proper SIC category under which a particular product is to be classified, and may prescribe regulations for aggregating two or more three-digit classifications of the SIC code and for classifying product areas according to a system other than under the SIC code.

Question 2: How is the term "affiliated group" defined for purposes of the cost sharing option?

Answer 2: For purposes of the cost sharing option, the term "affiliated group" means the possessions corporation and all other organizations, trades or businesses (whether or not incorporated, whether or not organized in the United States, and whether or not affiliated) owned or controlled directly or indirectly by the same interests, within the meaning of section 482.

Question 3: Are research and development expenditures that are included in product area research limited to research and development expenditures that are deductible under section 174 or that are incurred by U.S. affiliates?

Answer 3: No, product area research is not limited to product area research expenditures deductible under section 174 or to expenses incurred by U.S. affiliates. Product area research also includes deductions permitted under section 168 with respect to research property which are not deductible under section 174; qualified research expenses within the meaning of section 30(b); payments (such as royalties) for the use of, or right to use, a patent, invention, formula, process, design, pattern or know-how; and a proper allowance for amounts incurred in the acquisition of manufacturing intangible property. In the case of an acquisition of depreciable or amortizable manufacturing intangible property, the annual amount of product area research shall be equal to the allowable depreciation or amortization on the intangible property for the taxable year. In the case of an acquisition of nondepreciable or nonamortizable manufacturing intangible property, the amount expended for the acquisition shall be deemed to be amortized over a five year period and included in product area research in the year of the deemed amortization. Any contingent payment made with respect to the acquisition of nonamortizable manufacturing intangible property shall be treated as amounts incurred in the acquisition of nonamortizable manufacturing intangible property when paid or accrued.

Question 4: Does royalty income from a person outside the affiliated group with respect to the manufacturing intangibles within a product area reduce the product area research pool within the same product area?

Answer 4: Yes.

Question 5: Does income received from a person outside the affiliated group from the sale of a manufacturing intangible reduce the product area research pool within the same product area?

Answer 5: In determining product area research, the income from the sale attributable to noncontingent payments will reduce product area research ratably over the remaining useful life of the property in the case of an amortizable intangible and ratably over a 5-year period in the case of a nonamortizable intangible. Any income attributable to contingent amounts received with respect to the sale of manufacturing intangible property shall be treated as amounts received from the sale of the manufacturing intangible property in the year in which such contingent amounts are received or accrued.

Question 6: If a member of an affiliated group incurs research and development expenses pursuant to a contract with an unrelated person who is entitled to exclusive ownership of all the technology resulting from the expenditures, is the amount of product area research reduced by the amount of such expenditures?

Answer 6: To the extent that the product area research expenditures can be allocated solely to the technology produced for the unrelated person, such expenditures will not be included in product area research expenditures provided, however, that the unrelated person has exclusive ownership of all the technology resulting from these expenditures, and further that no member of the affiliated group has a right to use any of the technology.

Question 7: What is the treatment of product area research expenditures attributable to a component where the component and the integrated product fall within different product areas?

Answer 7: For purposes of the computation of product area research expenditures in the product area by the affiliated group, the product area in which the component falls is aggregated with the product area in which the integrated product falls. However, if the component product and integrated product are in separate SIC codes and if the component product is not included in the definition of the possession product, then the product area research expenditures are not aggregated. The same rule applies where the taxpayer elects a component product which encompasses another component product and the two component products fall into separate SIC codes. In such case, the product area in which the first component falls is aggregated with the product area in which the second component falls.

(2) Possession sales and total sales. Question 1: The cost sharing payment is the same proportion of the total cost of product area research which the amount of "possession sales" of the affiliated group bears to the "total sales" of the affiliated group within the product area. How are "possession sales" defined for purposes of the cost sharing fraction?

Answer 1: The term "possession sales" means the aggregate sales or other dispositions of the possession product, to persons who are not members of the affiliated group, less returns and allowances and less indirect taxes imposed on the production of the product, for the taxable year. Except as otherwise indicated in § 1.936-6(a)(2), the sales price to be used is the sales price received by the affiliated group from persons who are not members of the affiliated group.

Question 2: For purposes of the numerator of the cost sharing fraction, how are possession sales computed where the possession product is a component product or an end-product form?

Answer 2: (i) The sales price of the component product or end-product form is determined as follows. With respect to a component product, an independent sales price from comparable uncontrolled transactions must be used if such price can be determined in accordance with § 1.482-2(e)(2). If an independent sales price of the component product from comparable uncontrolled transactions cannot be determined, then the sales price of the component product shall be deemed to be equal to the transfer price, determined under the appropriate section 482 method, which the possessions corporation uses under the cost sharing method in computing the income it derives from the active conduct of a trade or business in the possession with respect to the component product. The possessions corporation in lieu of using the transfer price determined under the preceding sentence may treat the sales price for the component product as equal to the same proportion of the third party sales price of the integrated product which the production costs attributable to the component product bear to the total production cost for the integrated product. Production cost will be the sum of direct and indirect production costs as defined in § 1.936-5(b)(4). If the possessions corporation determines the sales price of the component product using the production cost ratio, the transfer price used by the possessions corporation in computing its income from the component product under the cost sharing method may not be greater than such sales price. (ii) With respect to an end-product form, the sales price of the end-product form is equal to the difference between the third party sales price of the integrated product and the independent sales price of the excluded component(s) from comparable uncontrolled transactions, if such price can be determined under § 1.482-2(e)(2). If an independent sales price of the excluded component(s) from uncontrolled transactions cannot be determined, then the sales price of the end-product form shall be deemed to be equal to the transfer price, determined under the appropriate section 482 method, which the possessions corporation uses under the cost sharing method in computing the income it derives from the active conduct of a trade or business in the possession with respect to such end-product form. The possessions corporation in lieu of using the transfer price determined under the preceding sentence may use the production cost ratio method described above to determine the sales price of the end-product form (i.e., the same proportion of the third party sales price of the integrated product which the production costs attributable to the end-product form bear to the total production costs for the integrated product). If the possessions corporation determines the sales price of the end-product form using the production cost ratio, the transfer price used by the possessions corporation in computing its income from the end-product form under the cost sharing method may not be greater than such sales price. For similar rules applicable to the profit split option see § 1.936-6(b)(1), question and answer 12.

Question 3: For purposes of determining possessions sales in the numerator of the cost sharing fraction, will the replacement part price of the product be treated as a price from comparable uncontrolled transactions?

Answer 3: Prices for replacement parts are generally higher than prices for equipment sold as part of an original system. Thus, prices for replacement parts cannot generally be used directly as prices for comparable uncontrolled transactions. However, replacement part prices may be used for estimating comparable uncontrolled prices where the price differential can be reasonably determined and taken into account under § 1.482-2(e)(2).

Question 4: For purposes of determining possession sales in the cost sharing fraction, what is the treatment of components that are purchased by one possessions corporation from an affiliated possessions corporation and which are incorporated into a possession product where the transferor possessions corporation treats the transferred component as a possession product?

Answer 4: When one possessions corporation purchases components from a second possessions corporation which is an affiliated corporation, the purchase price of the components paid to the second possessions corporation shall be subtracted from the sales proceeds of the product produced in the possession by the first possessions corporation, and only the remainder is included in the numerator of the cost sharing formula for the first corporation. For example, assume that N corporation manufactures a component for sale to O corporation for $100 (a price which reflects prices in comparable uncontrolled transactions). Both N and O are affiliated possessions corporations. N has designated that component product as its possession product. O then incorporates that product into a second product which is sold to customers for $300 N and O must make separate cost sharing payments. The cost sharing payment of N corporation is determined by including $100 as possession sales, and the payment of O is determined by subtracting that $100 purchase price from the $300 received from customers. Thus, the possessions sales amount of O is $200. This rule is intended to prevent the double counting of the sales of a component produced by one possessions corporation and incorporated into another product by an affiliated possessions corporation.

Question 5: Are pre-TEFRA sales included in the cost sharing fraction?

Answer 5: No. Pre-TEFRA sales are sales of products produced by the possessions corporation and transferred to an affiliate prior to a possessions corporation's first taxable year beginning after December 31, 1982. Pre-TEFRA sales are not included in either the numerator or denominator of the cost sharing fraction. If the U.S. affiliate uses the FIFO method of costing inventory, the pre-TEFRA inventory will be treated as the first inventory sold by the U.S. affiliate during the first year in which section 936(h) applies. If the U.S. affiliate uses the LIFO method of costing inventory (either dollar-value or specific goods LIFO), pre-TEFRA inventor will be treated as inventory sold by the U.S. affiliate in the year in which the U.S. affiliate's LIFO layer containing pre-TEFRA LIFO inventory is liquidated.

Question 6: How are "possession sales" determined under the cost sharing formula if members of the affiliated group (other than the possessions corporation) include purchases of the possession product, X, in a dollar-value LIFO inventory pool (as provided under § 1.472-8)?

Answer 6: Possession sales may be determined by applying the revenue identification method provided under paragraph (b)(1) Question and Answer 18 of this section.

Question 7: Do possession sales include excise taxes paid by the possessions corporation when the product is sold for ultimate use or consumption in the possession?

Answer 7: No. The amount of excise taxes is excluded from both the numerator and denominator of the cost sharing fraction.

Question 8: How are "total sales" defined for purposes of the cost sharing fraction?

Answer 8: The term "total sales" means aggregate sales or other dispositions of products in the same product area as the possession product, less returns and allowances and less indirect taxes imposed on the production of the product, for the taxable year to persons who are not members of the affiliated group. The sales price to be used is the sales price received by the affiliated group from persons who are not members of the affiliated group.

Question 9: In computing that cost sharing payment, how are "total sales" computed if the dollar-value LIFO inventory pool includes some products which are not included in the product area (determined under the 3-digit SIC code) on which the denominator of the cost sharing fraction is based?

Answer 9: In such case, the amount of the total sales within the product area to persons who are not members of the affiliated group by persons who are members of the affiliated group is determined by multiplying the total sales of the products within the dollar-value LIFO inventory pool by a fraction. The numerator of the fraction includes the dollar-value of purchases by members of the affiliated group (including the possessions corporation) of products within the product area made during the year, plus any added production costs (as defined in § 1.471-11(b), (c), and (d) but not including the costs of materials) incurred by the affiliates during the same period. The denominator of the fraction includes the dollar-value of purchases by members of the affiliated group (including the possessions corporation) of products within the dollar-value LIFO inventory pool made during the same period (including any production costs, as described above, incurred by the affiliate during the same period). For these purposes, purchases of a possession product are determined on the basis of the possessions corporation's cost for its inventory purposes.

Question 10: May a possessions corporation compute its income under the cost sharing method with respect to a possession product which the possessions corporation sells to a member of its affiliated group and which that member then leases to an unrelated person or uses in its own trade or business?

Answer 10: Yes, provided that an independent sales price for the possession product from comparable uncontrolled transactions can be determined in accordance with § 1.482-2(e)(2), and, provided further, that such member complies with the requirements of § 1.936-6(a)(2), question and answer 14. If, however, there is a comparable uncontrolled price for an integrated product and the possession product is a component product or end-product form thereof, the possessions corporation may, if such member complies with the requirements of § 1.936-6(a)(2), question and answer 14, compute its income under the cost sharing method with respect to such possession product. In that case, the cost sharing payment shall be computed under the following question and answer.

Question 11: How are possession sales and total sales to be determined for purposes of computing the cost sharing payment with respect to a possession product which the possessions corporation sells to a member of its affiliated group where that member then leases the possession product to unrelated persons or uses it in its own trade or business?

Answer 11: If the possessions corporation is entitled to compute its income from such sales of the possession product under the cost sharing method, both possession sales and total sales shall be determined as if the possession product had been sold by the affiliate to an unrelated person at the time the possession product was first leased or otherwise placed in service by the affiliate. The sales price on such deemed sale shall be equal to the independent sales price from comparable uncontrolled transactions determined in accordance with § 1.482-2(e)(2), if any. If the possession product is a component product or an end-product form for which there is no such independent sales price but there is a comparable uncontrolled price for the integrated product which includes the possession product, the deemed sales price of the possession product shall be computed under the rules of § 1.936-6(a)(2) question and answer 2. The full amount of income received under the lease shall be treated as income of (and taxed to) the affiliate and not the possessions corporation.

Question 12: When may a possessions corporation take into account in computing total sales under the cost sharing method products in the same product area as the possession product (other than the possession product itself) where such products are leased by members of the affiliated group to unrelated persons or used by any such member in its own trade or business?

Answer 12: For purposes of computing total sales under the cost sharing method, the possessions corporation may take into account products in the same product area as the possession product itself where such products are leased by members of the affiliated group to unrelated persons or used in the trade or business of any such member, but only if an independent sales price of such products from comparable uncontrolled transactions may be determined under § 1.482-2(e)(2). In such cases, the units of such products which are leased or otherwise used internally by members of the affiliated group may be treated as sold to unrelated persons for such independent sales price for purposes of computing total sales.

Question 13: Assuming that a possessions corporation is entitled to compute its income under the cost sharing method with respect to sales of a possession product to affiliates in cases where those affiliates lease units of the possession product to unrelated persons or use them internally, is the possessions corporation's income from the possession product any different than if the affiliates had sold the product to unrelated parties?

Answer 13: No.

Question 14: If a possessions corporation sells units of a possession product to a member of its affiliated group and that affiliate then leases those units to an unrelated person or uses the units in its own trade or business, what requirements must the affiliate meet in order for the possessions corporation to be entitled to the benefits of the cost sharing method with respect to such units?

Answer 14: (i) For taxable years of the possessions corporation beginning on or before June 13, 1986, the affiliate need not meet any special requirements in order for the possessions corporation to be entitled to the benefits of the cost sharing method with respect to such units. Thus, the affiliate's basis in such units shall be equal to the transfer price used for computing the possessions corporation's gross income with respect to such units under section 936(h)(5)(C)(i)(II), and the income derived by the affiliate from such lease or internal use shall be reported by the affiliate when and to the extent actually derived. The affiliate shall not be deemed to have sold such units to an unrelated party at the time they were first leased or otherwise placed in service for any purpose other than the computation of possession sales and total sales. A similar rule applies to other products in the same product area as the possession product which are sold by any member in its own trade or business and which the possessions corporation takes into account in computing total sales under the cost sharing method.

(ii) For taxable years of the possessions corporations beginning after June 13, 1986, a possessions corporations will not be entitled to the benefits of the cost sharing method with respect to units of the possession product which the possessions corporation sells to an affiliate where the affiliate then leases such units to an unrelated person or uses them in its own trade or business, unless the affiliate agrees to be treated for all tax purposes as having sold such units to an unrelated party at the time they were first leased or otherwise placed in service by such affiliate. The affiliate must demonstrate such agreement by reporting its income from such units as if: (A) it had sold such units to an unrelated person at such time at a price equal to the price used to compute possessions sales under § 1.936-6(a)(2), question and answer 11; (B) it had immediately repurchased such units for the same price; and (C) its basis in such units for all subsequent purposes was equal to its cost basis from such deemed repurchase. For treatment of other products in the same product area as the possession product see § 1.936-6(a)(2), question and answer 12.

(iii) The principles contained in questions and answers 11, 12, 13, and 14 are illustrated by the following example:

Example. Possessions corporation S and its affiliate A are calendar year taxpayers. In 1985, S manufactures 100 units of possession product X. S sells 50 units of X to unrelated persons in arm's length transactions for $10 per unit. In applying the cost sharing method to determine the portion of its gross income from such sales which qualifies for the possessions tax credit, S determines that $8 of the $10 sales price may be taken into account. S sells the remaining 50 units of X to A, and A then leases such units to unrelated persons. In 1985, A also manufacturers 100 units of product Y, the only other product in the same product area as X manufactured or sold by any member of the affiliated group. A manufactured the 100 units of Y at a cost of $15 per unit, sold 50 units of Y to unrelated persons in arm's length transactions for $20 per unit, and leased the remaining 50 units of Y to unrelated persons.

S may compute its income under the cost sharing method with respect to the 50 units of X it sold to A because S can determine an independent sales price of X from comparable uncontrolled transactions under § 1.482-2(e)(2). For purposes of computing both possessions sales and total sales, the 50 units of X sold to A will be deemed to have been sold by A to an unrelated person for $10 per unit. The income of S qualifying for the possessions tax credit from the sale of those 50 units of X to A, and A's basis in those units, will both be determined using the $8 transfer price determined under section 936(h)(5)(C)(i)(II). For purposes of computing total sales in the denominator of the cost sharing fraction, S may also take into account the 50 units of Y leased by A to unrelated persons, as if A had sold those units for $20 per unit. A's basis in those units of Y will continue to be its actual cost basis of $15 per unit.

If all of the above transactions had occurred in 1987, S would be entitled to compute its income under the cost sharing method with respect to the 50 units of X it sold to A only if A agreed to be treated for all tax purposes as if it had sold such units for $10 per unit, realized income on such deemed sale of $2 per unit, repurchased such units immediately for $10 per unit, and then leased such units, which would then have a $10 per unit basis in A's hands. For purposes of computing total sales, S would be entitled to take into account the 50 units of X leased by A to unrelated persons as if A had sold such units for $20 per unit.

(3) Credits against cost sharing payments. Question 1: Is the cost of product area research paid or accrued by the possessions corporation in a taxable year creditable against the cost sharing payment?

Answer 1: Yes, if the cost of the product area research is paid or accrued solely by the possessions corporation. Thus, payments by the possessions corporation under cost sharing arrangements with, or royalties paid to, unrelated persons are so creditable. Amounts (such as royalties) paid directly or indirectly to, or on behalf of, related persons and amounts paid under any cost sharing agreements with related persons are not creditable against the cost sharing payment.

Question 2: Do royalties or other payments made by an affiliate of the possessions corporation to another member of the affiliated group reduce the cost sharing payment if such royalties or other payments are based, in part, on activity of the possessions corporation?

Answer 2: No. Payments made between affiliated corporations do not reduce the cost sharing payment. Thus, for example, if a possessions corporation sells a component to a foreign affiliate for incorporation by the foreign affiliate into an integrated product sold to unrelated persons, and the foreign affiliate pays a royalty to the U.S. parent of the possessions corporation based on the total value of the integrated product, the cost sharing payment of the possessions corporation is not reduced.

(4) Computation of cost sharing payment. Question 1: S is a possessions corporation engaged in the manufacture and sale of four products (A, B, C, and D) all of which are classified under the same three-digit SIC code. S sells its pro-

duction to a U.S. affiliate, P, which resells it to unrelated parties in the United States. P's third party sales of each of these products produced in whole or in part by S (computed as provided under paragraph (a)(2) of § 1.936-6) are $1 million or a total of $4 million for A, B, C, and D. P's other sales of products in the same SIC code are $3,000,000; and the defined worldwide product area research of the affiliated group is $350,000. How should S compute the cost sharing amount for products A, B, C, and D?

Answer 1: The cost sharing amount is computed separately for each product on Schedule P of Form 5735. S should use the following formula for each of the products A, B, C, and D:

$$\frac{\text{Sales to unrelated persons of possession product}}{\text{Total sales of products in SIC code}} \times \text{Worldwide product area research}$$

$$\frac{\$1{,}000{,}000}{\$7{,}000{,}000} \times \$350{,}000 = \$50{,}000$$

Question 2: The facts are the same as in question 1 except that S manufactures product D under a license from an unrelated person. S pays the unrelated party an annual license fee of $20,000. Thus, the worldwide product area research expense of the affiliated group is $370,000. How should the cost sharing payment be adjusted?

Answer 2: The cost sharing fee should be reduced by the $20,000 license fee made as a direct annual payment to a third party on account of product D. The cost sharing payment with respect to product D in this example will be adjusted as follows:

$$\frac{\text{Sales to unrelated persons of possession product}}{\text{Total sales of products in SIC code}} \times \text{Worldwide product area research} - \text{Amount paid by the possessions corporation to an unrelated party}$$

$$\left(\frac{1{,}000{,}000}{\$7{,}000{,}000} \times \$370{,}000\right) - \$20{,}000 = \$32{,}857$$

Question 3: The facts are the same as in question 1 except that S also manufactures and exports product E to a foreign affiliate, which resells it to unrelated persons for $1 million. S makes a separate election for its export sales. How should S compute the cost sharing amount for product E?

Answer 3: The numerator of the cost sharing fraction is the aggregate sales or other dispositions by members of the affiliated group of the units of product E produced in whole or in part in the possession to persons who are not members of the affiliated group. The cost sharing amount for product E would be computed as follows:

$$\frac{\text{Export sales of E}}{\text{Total sales of products in SIC code (In this example, U.S. Sales of A, B, C, and D + export sales of E)}} \times \text{Worldwide product area research}$$

or

$$\frac{\$1{,}000{,}000}{(\$7{,}000{,}000 + \$1{,}000{,}000)} \times \$350{,}000 = \$43{,}750$$

Question 4: The facts are the same as in question 1, except that S also receives $10,000 in royalty income from unrelated persons for the licensing of certain manufacturing intangible property rights. What is the amount of the product area research that must be allocated in determining the cost sharing amount?

Answer 4: If the affiliated group receives royalty income from unrelated persons with respect to manufacturing intangibles in the same product area, then the product area research to be considered shall be first reduced by such royalty income. In this case, the amount of product area research to be used in determining S's cost sharing payment should be reduced by the $10,000 royalty payment received to $340,000.

Question 5: May a possessions corporation redetermine the amount of its required cost sharing payment after filing its tax return?

Answer 5: If after filing its tax return, a possessions corporation files an amended return, or if an adjustment is made on audit, either of which affects the amount of the cost sharing payment required, then a redetermination of the cost sharing payment must be made. See, however, section 936(h)(5)(C)(i)(III)(a) with respect to the increase in the cost sharing payment due to interest imposed under section 6601(a).

(5) Effect of election under the cost sharing method. Question 1: What is the effect of the cost sharing method?

Answer 1: The cost sharing payment reduces the amount of deductions (and the amount of reductions in earnings and profits) otherwise allowable to the U.S. affiliates (other than tax-exempt affiliates) within the affiliated group as determined under section 936(h)(5)(C)(i)(I)(b) which have incurred research expenditures (as defined in § 1.936-6(a)(1), question and answer (3) in the same product area for which the cost sharing option is elected, during the taxable year in which the cost sharing payment accrues. If there are no such U.S. affiliates, the reductions with respect to deductions and earnings and profits, as the case may be, are made with respect to foreign affiliates within the same affiliated group which have incurred product area research expenditures in such product area attributable to a U.S. trade or business. If there are no affiliates which have incurred research expenditures in such product area, the reductions are then made with respect to any other U.S. affiliate and, if there is no such U.S. affiliate, then to any other foreign affiliate. The allocations of these reductions in each case shall be made in proportion to the gross income of the affiliates. In the case of foreign affiliates, the allocation shall be made in proportion to gross income attributable to the U.S. trade or business or worldwide gross income, as the case may be. With respect to each group above, the reduction of deductions shall be applied first to deductions under section 174, then to deductions under section 162, and finally to any other deductions on a pro rata basis.

Question 2: For purposes of estimated tax payments, when is the cost sharing amount deemed to accrue?

Answer 2: The cost sharing amount is deemed to accrue to the appropriate affiliate on the last day of the taxable year of each such affiliate in which or with which the taxable year of the possessions corporation ends.

Question 3: If the cost sharing method is elected and the year of accrual of the cost sharing payment to the appropriate affiliate (described in question and answer 1 of this paragraph (a)(5)) differs from the year of actual payment by the possessions corporation, in what year are the deductions of the recipients reduced?

Answer 3: In the year the cost sharing payment has accrued.

Question 4: What is the treatment of income from intangibles under the cost sharing method?

Answer 4: Under the cost sharing method, a possessions corporation is treated as the owner, for purposes of obtaining a return thereon, of manufacturing intangibles related to a possession product. The term "manufacturing intangible" means any patent, invention, formula, process, design, pattern, or know-how. The possessions corporation will not be treated as the owner, for purposes of obtaining a return thereon, of any manufacturing intangibles related to a component product produced by an affiliated corporation and transferred to the possessions corporation for incorporation into the possession product, except in the case that the possession product is treated as including such component product for all purposes of section 936(h)(5). Further, the possessions corporation will not be treated as the owner, for purposes of obtaining a return thereon, of any marketing intangibles except "covered intangibles." (See § 1.936-6(c).)

Question 5: If the cost sharing option is elected, is it necessary for the possessions corporation to be the legal owner of the manufacturing intangibles related to the possession product in order for the possessions corporation to receive a full return with respect to such intangibles?

Answer 5: No. There is no requirement that manufacturing intangibles be owned by the possessions corporation.

Question 6: How is income attributable to marketing intangibles treated under the cost sharing method?

Answer 6: Except in the case of "covered intangibles" (see § 1.936-6(c)), the possessions corporation is not treated as the owner of any marketing intangibles, and income attributable to marketing intangible of the possessions corporation will be allocated to the possessions corporation's U.S. shareholders with the proration of income based on shareholdings. If a shareholder of the possessions corporation is a foreign, person or is otherwise tax exempt, the possessions corporation is taxable on that shareholder's pro rata amount of the intangible property income. If the possessions corporation is a corporation any class of the stock of which is regularly traded on an established securities market, then the income attributable to marketing intangibles will be taxable to the possessions corporation rather than the corporation's U.S. shareholders.

Question 7: What is the source of the intangible property income described in question and answer 6?

Answer 7: The intangible property income is U.S. source whether taxed to the U.S. shareholder or taxed to the possessions corporation and section 863(b) does not apply for this purpose. However, such intangible property income, if treated as income of the possessions corporation, does not enter into the calculation of the 80-percent possession source test or the 65-percent active trade or business test.

Question 7a: What is the source of the taxpayer's gross income derived from a sale in the United States of a possession product purchased by the taxpayer (or an affiliate) from a corporation that has an election in effect under section 936, if the income from such sale is taken into account to determine benefits under cost sharing for the section 936 corporation? Is the result different if the taxpayer (or an affiliate) derives gross income from a sale in the United States of an integrated product incorporating a possession product purchased by the taxpayer (or an affiliate) from the section 936 corporation, if the taxpayer (or an affiliate) processes the possession product or an excluded component in the United States?

Answer 7a: Under either scenario, the income is U.S. source, without regard to whether the possession product is a component, end-product, or integrated product. Section 863 does not apply in determining the source of the taxpayer's income. This Q&A 7a is applicable for taxable years beginning on or after November 13, 1998.

Question 8: May marketing intangible income, if any, be allocated to the possessions corporation with respect to custom-made products?

Answer 8: No. If the cost sharing option is elected, then income attributable to marketing intangibles (other than "covered intangibles" described in § 1.936-6(c)) will be taxed as discussed in questions and answers 6 and 7 of paragraph (a)(5) of this section. It is immaterial whether the product is custom-made.

Question 9: In order to sell a pharmaceutical product in the United States, a New Drug Application ("NDA") for the product must be approved by the U.S. Food and Drug Administration. Is an NDA considered a manufacturing or marketing intangible for purposes of the allocation of income under the cost sharing method?

Answer 9: A manufacturing intangible.

Question 10: Can a copyright be, in whole or in part, a manufacturing intangible for purposes of the allocation of income under the cost sharing method?

Answer 10: In general, a copyright is a marketing intangible. See section 936(h)(3)(B)(ii). However, copyrights may be treated either as manufacturing intangibles or nonmanufacturing intangibles (or as partly each) depending upon the function or the use of the copyright. If the copyright is used in manufacturing, it will be treated as a manufacturing intangible; but if it is used in marketing, even if it is also classified as know-how, it will be treated as a marketing intangible.

Question 11: If the cost sharing option is elected and a patent is related to the product produced by the possessions corporation, does the return to the possessions corporation with respect to the manufacturing intangible include the make, use, and sell elements of the patent?

Answer 11: Yes. A patent confers an exclusive right for 17 years to sell a product covered by the patent. During this period, the return to the possessions corporation includes the make, use and sell elements of the patent.

Question 12: For purposes of the cost sharing option, may a safe haven rule be applied to determine the amount of marketing intangible income?

Answer 12: No. The amount of marketing intangible income is determined on the basis of all relevant facts and circumstances. The section 482 regulations will continue to apply except to the extent modified by the election. Rev. Proc. 63-10 and Rev. Proc. 68-22 do not apply for this purpose.

Question 13: If a product covered by the cost sharing election is sold by a possessions corporation to an affiliated corporation for resale to an unrelated party, may the resale price method under section 482 be used to determine the intercompany price of the possessions corporation?

Answer 13: In general, the resale price method may be used if (a) no comparable uncontrolled price for the product exists, and (b) the affiliated corporation does not add a substantial amount of value to the product by manufacturing or by the provision of services which are reflected in the sales price of the product to the customer. The possessions corporation will not be denied use of the resale price method for purposes of such inter-company pricing merely because the reseller adds more than an insubstantial amount to the value of the product by the use of intangible property.

Question 14: If a possessions corporation makes the cost sharing election and uses the cost-plus method under section 482 to determine the arm's-length price of a possession product, will the cost base include the cost of materials which are subject to processing or which are components in the possession product?

Answer 14: A taxpayer may include the cost of materials in the cost base if it is appropriate under the regulations under § 1.482-2(e)(4).

Question 15: If the possessions corporation computes its income with respect to a product under the cost sharing method, and the price of the product is determined under the cost-plus method under section 482, does the cost base used in computing cost-plus under section 482 include the amount of the cost sharing payment?

Answer 15: The amount of the cost sharing payment is included in the cost base. However, no profit with respect to the cost sharing payment will be allowed.

Question 16: If a member of the affiliated group transfers to a possessions corporation a component which is incorporated into a possession product, how will the transfer price for the component be determined?

Answer 16: The transfer price for the component will be determined under section 482, and as follows. If the possession product is treated as not including such component for purposes of section 936(h)(5), the transfer price paid for the component will include a return on all intangibles related to the component product. It the possession product is treated as including such component for purposes of section 936(h)(5), then the transfer price paid for the component by the possessions corporation will not include a return on any manufacturing intangible related to the component product, and the possessions corporation will obtain the return on the manufacturing intangibles associated with the component.

Question 17: If the possessions corporation computes its income with respect to a product under the cost sharing method, with respect to which units of the product shall the possessions corporation be treated as owning intangible property as a result of having made the cost sharing election?

Answer 17: The possessions corporation shall not be treated as owning intangible property, as a result of having made the cost sharing election, with respect to any units of a possession product which were not taken into account by the possessions corporation in applying the significant business presence test for the current taxable year or for any prior taxable year in which the possessions corporation also had a significant business presence in the possession with respect to such product.

(b) Profit split option. *(1) Computation of combined taxable income.* Question 1: In determining combined taxable income from sales of a possession product, how are the allocations and apportionments of expenses, losses, and other deductions to be determined?

Answer 1: (i) Expenses, losses, and other deductions are to be allocated and apportioned on a "fully-loaded" basis under § 1.861-8 to the combined gross income of the possessions corporation and other members of the affiliated group (other than foreign affiliates). For purposes of the profit split option, the term "affiliated group" is defined the same as under § 1.936-6(a)(1) question and answer 2. The amount of research, development, and experimental expenses allocated and apportioned to combined gross income is to be determined under § 1.861-8(e)(3). The amount of research, development and experimental expenses and related deductions (such as royalties paid or accrued with respect to manufacturing intangibles by the possessions corporation or other domestic members of the affiliated group to unrelated persons or to foreign affiliates) allocated and apportioned to combined gross income shall in no event be less than the amount of the cost sharing payment that would have been required under the rules set forth in section 936(h)(5)(C)(i)(II) and paragraph (a) of this section if the cost sharing option had been elected. Other expenses which are subject to § 1.861-8(e) are to be allocated and apportioned in accordance with that section. For example, interest expense (including payments made with respect to bonds issued by the Puerto Rican Industrial, Medical and Environmental Control Facilities Authority (AFICA)) is to be allocated and apportioned under § 1.861-8(e)(2). With the exception of marketing and distribution expenses discussed below, the other remaining expenses which are definitely related to a class of gross income shall be allocated to that class of gross income and shall be apportioned on the basis of any reasonable method, as described in § 1.861-8(b)(3) and (c)(1). Examples of such methods may include, but are not limited to, those specified in § 1.861-8(c)(1)(i) through (vi).

(ii) The class of gross income to which marketing and distribution expenses relate and shall be allocated is generally to be defined by the same "product area" as is determined for the relevant research, development, and experimental expenses (i.e., the appropriate 3-digit SIC code), but shall include only gross income generated or reasonably expected to be generated from the geographic area or areas to which the expenses relate. It shall be presumed that marketing and distribution expenses relate to all product sales within the same product area. If, however, it can be established that any of these expenses are separately identifiable expenses, such as advertising, and relate, directly or indirectly, solely to a specific product or a specific group of products, such expenses shall be allocated to the class of gross income defined by the specific product or group of products. Thus, advertising and other separately identifiable marketing expenses which relate specifically and exclusively to a particular product must be allocated entirely to the gross income from that product, even though the taxpayer or other members of an affiliated group which includes the taxpayer produce and market other products in the same 3-digit SIC code classification. The mere display of a company logo or mention of a company name solely in the context of identifying the manufacturer shall not prevent an advertisement from relating specifically and exclusively to a particular product or group of products.

(iii) If marketing and distribution expenses are allocated to a class of gross income which consists both of income from sales of possession products (the statutory grouping) and other income such as from sale by U.S. affiliates of products not produced in the possession (the residual grouping), then these marketing and distribution expenses shall be apportioned on a "fully loaded" basis which reflects, to a reasonably close extent, the factual relationship between these deductions and the statutory and residual groupings of gross income. Apportionment methods based upon comparisons of amounts incurred before ultimate sale of a product (including apportionment on a comparison of costs of goods sold, other expenses incurred, or other comparisons set forth in § 1.861-8(c)(1)(v), such as time spent) are not on a "fully-loaded" basis and do not reflect this required factual relationship. These deductions shall be apportioned on a basis of comparison of the amount of gross sales or receipts or another method if it is established that such method similarly reflects the required factual relationship. Thus, for example, a comparison of units sold may be used only where the units are of the same or similar value and are, thus, in fact comparable.

(iv) The rules for allocation and apportionment of marketing and distribution expenses may be illustrated by the following examples:

Example (1). Assume that possessions corporation A manufacturers prescription pharmaceutical product #1 for resale by P, its U.S. parent corporation, in the United States. Additionally, assume that P manufactures prescription pharmaceutical products #2 and #3 in the United States for sale there. Further, assume that all three products are within the same product area, and that marketing and distribution expenses are internally divided by P among the three products on the basis of time spent by sales persons of P on marketing of the three products, as follows:

Product #1	50X
Product #2	80X
Product #3	110X
Total	240X

These expenses of 240X are allocated to gross income generated by all three products and shall be apportioned on the basis of gross sales or receipts of product #1 as compared to products #2 and #3 or another method which similarly reflects the factual relationship between these expenses and gross income derived from product #1 and products #2 and #3. Thus, if a sales method were used and sales of product #1 accounted for one-third of sales receipts from the three products, 80X (240 ÷ 3) of marketing and distribution expenses would be apportioned to the combined gross income from product #1.

Example (2). Corporation B produces and sells Brand W whiskey, in the United States. B's subsidiary, S, which is a possessions corporation, produces soft drink extract in Puerto Rico which it sells to independent bottlers to produce Brand S soft drinks for sale in the United States. Corporation B's advertisements and other promotional materials for Brand W whiskey make no reference to Brand S soft drinks (or any other Corporation B products), and Brand S soft drink advertisements and other promotional materials make no reference to Brand W whiskey (or any other corporation B products). For purposes of section 936(h), the advertising and other promotional expenses for Brand W whiskey must be allocated entirely to the gross income from sales of Brand W whiskey and the advertising and other promotional expenses for Brand S soft drink must be allocated entirely to the gross income from the sales of soft drink extract, notwithstanding the fact that whiskey and soft drink extract are both included in SIC code 208. A similar result would apply, for example, to separately identifiable advertising and other marketing expenses which relate specifically and exclusively to one or the other of the following pairs of products: chewing gum and granulated sugar (SIC code 206); canned tuna fish and freeze-dried coffee (SIC code 209); children's underwear and ladies' brassieres (SIC code 234); aspirin tablets and prescription antibiotic tablets (SIC code 283); floor wax and perfume (SIC code 284); adhesives and inks (SIC code 289); semi-conductors and cathode-ray tubes (SIC code 367); batteries and extension cords (SIC code 369); bandages and dental supplies (SIC code 384); stainless steel flatware and jewelry parts (SIC code 391); children's toys and sporting goods (SIC code 394); hair curlers and zippers (SIC code 396); and paint brushes and linoleum tiles (SIC code 399).

Example (3). Assume the same facts as in Example (1) and that possessions corporation A also manufactures aspirin, a non-prescription product, for resale by its U.S. parent corporation, P. Further, assume that the advertising and separately identifiable marketing expenses which relate specifically and exclusively to aspirin sales total $100 and that these expenses are allocable solely to gross income derived from aspirin sales. The sales method continues to be used to apportion the marketing and distribution expenses related, directly or indirectly, to products #1, #2, and #3, and the apportionment of such expenses to product #1 for purposes of determining combined taxable income from product #1 will remain as stated in Example (1). None of the advertising and other separately identifiable marketing expenses which relate specifically and exclusively to aspirin will be taken into account in allocating and apportioning the marketing and distribution expenses relating to the gross income attributable to products #1, #2, and #3. Gross income attributable to aspirin will be considered as a separate class of gross income, and all the advertising and separately identifiable marketing expenses which relate specifically and exclusively to aspirin sales of $100 will be allocated to the class of gross income derived from aspirin sales. Similarly, none of the marketing and distribution expenses, directly or indirectly, related solely to the group of products #1, #2, and #3 will be taken into account in determining the combined taxable income from aspirin sales, the remaining marketing and distribution expenses which do not, directly or indirectly, relate solely to any specific product or group of products (e.g., the salaries of a Vice-President of Marketing who has responsibility for marketing all products and his staff) shall be allocated and apportioned on the basis of the gross receipts from the sales of all of the products (or a similar method) in determining combined taxable income of any product.

Question 2: How may the allocation and apportionment of expenses to combined gross income be verified?

Answer 2: Substantiation of the allocation and apportionment of expenses will be required upon audit of the possessions corporation and affiliates. Detailed substantiation may be necessary, particularly where the entities are engaged in multiple lines of business involving distinct product areas. Sources of substantiation may include certified financial reports. Form 10-K's, annual reports, internal production reports, product line assembly work papers, and other relevant materials. In this regard, see § 1.861-8(f)(5).

Question 3: Does section 936(h) override the moratorium provided by section 223 of the Economic Recovery Tax Act of 1981 and any subsequent similar moratorium?

Answer 3: Yes. Thus, the allocation and apportionment of product area research described in question and answer 1 must be made without regard to the moratorium.

Question 4: Is the cost of samples treated as a marketing expense?

Answer 4: Yes. The cost of producing samples will be treated as a marketing expense and not as inventoriable costs for purposes of determining combined taxable income (and compliance with the significant business presence test). However, for taxable years beginning prior to January 1, 1986, the cost of producing samples may be treated as either a marketing expense or as inventoriable costs.

Question 5: If a possessions corporation uses the profit split method to determine its taxable income from sales of a product, how does it determine its gross income for purposes of the 80-percent possession source test and the 65-percent active trade or business test of section 936(a)(2)?

Answer 5: One-half of the deductions of the affiliated group (other than foreign affiliates) which are used in determining the combined taxable income from sales of the product are added to the portion of the combined taxable income allocated to the possessions corporation in order to determine the possessions corporation's gross income from sales of such product.

Question 6: How will income from intangibles related to a possession product be treated under the profit split method?

Answer 6: Combined taxable income of the possessions corporation and affiliates from the sale of the possession product will include income attributable to all intangibles, including both manufacturing and marketing intangibles, associated with the product.

Question 7: Can a possessions corporation apply the profit split option to a possession product if no U.S. affiliates derive income from the sale of the possession product?

Answer 7: Yes.

Question 8: With respect to the factual situation discussed in question and answer 7 how is combined taxable income computed?

Answer 8: The profit split option is applied to the taxable income of the possessions corporation from sales of the possession product to foreign affiliates and unrelated persons. Fifty percent of that income is allocated to the possessions corporation, and the remainder is allocated to the appropriate affiliates as described in question and answer 13 of this paragraph (b)(1).

Question 9: May a possessions corporation compute its income under the profit split method with respect to units of a possession product which it sells to a U.S. affiliate if the U.S. affiliate leases such units to unrelated persons or to foreign affiliates or uses such units in its own trade or business?

Answer 9: Yes, provided that an independent sales price for the possession product from comparable uncontrolled transactions can be determined in accordance with § 1.482-2(e)(2). If, however, there is a comparable uncontrolled price for an integrated product and the possession product is a component product or end-product form thereof, the possessions corporation may compute its income under the profit split method with respect to such units. In either case, the possessions corporation shall compute combined taxable income with respect to such units under the following question and answer.

Question 10: If the possessions corporation is entitled to use the profit split method in the situation described in Q. 9 (leasing units of the possession product or use of such units in the taxpayer's own trade or business), how should it compute combined taxable income with respect to such units?

Answer 10:

(i) Combined taxable income shall be computed as if the U.S. affiliate had sold the units to an unrelated person (or to a foreign affiliate) at the time the units were first leased or otherwise placed in service by the U.S. affiliate. The sales price on such deemed sale shall be equal to the independent sales price from comparable uncontrolled transactions determined in accordance with § 1.482-2(e)(2), if any.

(ii) If the possession product is a component product or an end-product form, the combined taxable income with respect to the possession product shall be determined under Q&A. 12 of this paragraph (b)(1).

(iii) For purposes of determining the basis of a component product or an end-product form, the deemed sales price of such product must be determined. The deemed sales price of the component product shall be determined by multiplying the deemed sales price of the integrated product that includes the component product by a ratio, the numerator of which is the production costs of the component product and the denominator of which is the production costs of the integrated product that includes the component product. The deemed sales price of an end-product form shall be determined by multiplying the deemed sales price of the integrated product that includes the end-product form by a ratio, the numerator of which is the production costs of the end-product form and the denominator of which is the production costs of the integrated product that includes the end-product form. For the definition of production costs, see Q&A. 12 of this paragraph (b)(1).

(iv)

(A) If combined taxable income is determined under paragraph (v) of A. 12 of this paragraph (b)(1), in the case of a component product, the deemed sales price shall be determined by using the actual sales price of that product when sold as an integrated product (as adjusted under the rules of the fourth sentence of § 1.482-3(b)(2)(ii)(A)).

(B) If combined taxable income is determined under paragraph (v) of A. 12 of this paragraph (b)(1), in the case of an end-product form, the deemed sales price shall be determined by subtracting from the deemed sales price of the integrated product that includes the end-product form (e.g., the leased property) the actual sales price of the excluded component when sold as an integrated product to an unrelated person (as adjusted under the rules of the fourth sentence of § 1.482-3(b)(2)(ii)(A)).

(v) The full amount of income received under the lease shall be treated as income of (and be taxed to) the U.S. affiliate and not the possessions corporation.

Question 11: In the situation described in question 9, how does the U.S. affiliate determine its basis in such units for purposes of computing depreciation and similar items?

Answer 11: The U.S. affiliate shall be treated, for purposes of computing its basis in such units, as if it had repurchased such units immediately following the deemed sale and at the deemed sales price as provided in Q&A. 10 of this paragraph (b)(1).

The principles of questions and answers 10 and 11 are illustrated by the following example:

Example. Possessions corporation S manufactures 100 units of possession product X. S sells 50 units of X to an unrelated person in an arm's length transaction for $10 per unit. S sells the remaining 50 units to its U.S. affiliate, A, which leases such units to unrelated persons. The combined taxable income for the 100 units of X is computed below on the basis of the given production, sales, and cost data:

Sales:	
1. Total sales by S to unrelated persons (50 × $10)	$500
2. Total deemed sales by A to unrelated persons (50 × $10)	500
3. Total gross receipts (line 1 plus line 2)	1,000
Total costs:	
4. Material costs	200
5. Production costs	300
6. Research expenses	0
7. Other expenses	100
8. Total (add lines 4 through 7)	600
Combined taxable income attributable to the 100 units of X:	

9. Combined taxable income (line 3 minus line 8) 400
10. Share of combined taxable income apportioned to S (50% of line 9) 200
11. Share of combined taxable income apportioned to A (line 9 minus line 10). 200

A's basis in 50 units of X leased by it to unrelated persons:

12. 50 units times $10 deemed repurchase price . . . 500

Subsequent leasing income is entirely taxed to A.

Question 12: If the possession product is a component product or an end-product form, how is the combined taxable income for such product to be determined?

Answer 12:

(i) Except as provided in paragraph (v) of this A. 12, combined taxable income for a component product or an end-product form is computed under the production cost ratio (PCR) method.

(ii) Under the PCR method, the combined taxable income for a component product will be the same proportion of the combined taxable income for the integrated product that includes the component product that the production costs attributable to the component product bear to the total production costs (including costs incurred by the U.S. affiliates) for the integrated product that includes the component product. Production costs will be the sum of the direct and indirect production costs as defined under § 1.936-5(b)(4) except that the costs will not include any costs of materials. If the possession product is a component product that is transformed into an integrated product in whole or in part by a contract manufacturer outside of the possession, within the meaning of § 1.936-5(c), the denominator of the PCR shall be computed by including the same amount paid to the contract manufacturer, less the costs of materials of the contract manufacturer, as is taken into account for purposes of the significant business presence test under § 1.936-5(c) Q&A. 5.

(iii) Under the PCR method the combined taxable income for an end-product form will be the same proportion of the combined taxable income for the integrated product that includes the end-product form that the production costs attributable to the end-product form bear to the total production costs (including costs incurred by the U.S. affiliates) for the integrated product that includes the end-product form. Production costs will be the sum of the direct and indirect production costs as defined under § 1.936-5(b)(4) except that the costs will not include any costs of materials. If the possession product is an end-product form and an excluded component is contract manufactured outside of the possession, within the meaning of § 1.936-5(c), the denominator shall be computed by including the same amount paid to the contract manufacturer, less cost of materials of the contract manufacturer, as is also taken into account for purposes of the significant business presence test under § 1.936-5(c) Q&A. 5.

(iv) This paragraph (iv) of A. 12 illustrates the computation of combined taxable income for a component product or end-product form under the PCR method. S, a possessions corporation, is engaged in the manufacture of microprocessors. S obtains a component from a U.S. affiliate, O. S sells its production to another U.S. affiliate, P, which incorporates the microprocessors into central processing units (CPUs). P transfers the CPUs to a U.S. affiliate, Q, which incorporates the CPUs into computers for sale to unrelated persons. S chooses to define the possession product as the CPUs. The combined taxable income for the sale of the possession product on the basis of the given production, sales, and cost data is computed as follows:

Production costs (excluding costs of materials):

1. O's costs for the component 100
2. S's costs for the microprocessors 500
3. P's costs for the CPU's (the possession product) 200
4. Q's costs for the computers 400
5. Total production costs for the computer (Add lines 1 through 4) 1,200
6. Combined production costs for the CPU (the possession product) (Add lines 1 through 3) 800
7. Ratio of production costs for the CPUs (the possession product) to the production costs for the computer 0.667

Determination of combined taxable income for computers:

Sales:

8. Total possession sales of computers to unrelated customers and foreign affiliates 7,500

Total costs of O, S, P, and Q incurred in production of a computer:

9. Production costs (enter from line 5) 1,200
10. Material costs 100
11. Total costs (line 9 plus line 10) 1,300
12. Combined gross income from sale of computers (line 8 minus line 11) 6,200

Expenses of the affiliated group (other than foreign affiliates) allocable and apportionable to the computers or any component thereof under the rules of §§ 1.861-8 through 1.861-14T and 1.936-6(b)(1), Q&A. 1:

13. Expenses (other than research expenses) 980

Research expenses of the affiliated group allocable and apportionable to the computers:

14. Total sales in the 3-digit SIC Code 12,500
15. Possession sales of the computers (enter from line 8) 7,500
16. Cost sharing fraction (divide line 15 by line 14) 0.6
17. Research expenses incurred by the affiliated group in 3-digit SIC Code multiplied by 120 percent 700
18. Cost sharing amount (multiply line 16 by line 17) 420
19. Research of the affiliated group (other than foreign affiliates) allocable and apportionable under §§ 1.861-17(e)(3) and 1.861-14T(e)(2) to the computers . . . 300
20. Enter the greater of line 18 or line 19 420

Computation of combined taxable income of the computer and the CPU:

21. Combined taxable income attributable to the computer (line 12 minus line 13 and line 20) 4,800
22. Combined taxable income attributable to CPUs (multiply line 21 by line 7) (production cost ratio) 3,200
23. Share of combined taxable income apportioned to S (50 percent of line 22) 1,600

Share of combined taxable income apportioned to U.S. affiliate(s) of S:

24. Adjustments for research expenses (line 18 minus line 19 multiplied by line 7) ..	80
25. Adjusted combined taxable income (line 22 plus line 24)	3,280
26. Share of combined taxable income apportioned to affiliates of S (line 25 minus line 23)	1,680

(v)

(A) If a possession product is sold by a taxpayer or its affiliate to unrelated persons in covered sales both as an integrated product and as a component product and the conditions of paragraph (v)(C) of this A. 12 are satisfied, the taxpayer may elect to determine the combined taxable income derived from covered sales of the component product under this paragraph (v). In that case, the combined taxable income derived from covered sales of the component product shall be determined by using the same per unit combined taxable income as is derived from covered sales of the product as an integrated product, but subject to the limitation of paragraph (v)(D) of this A. 12.

(B) In the case of a possession product that is an end-product form, if all of the excluded components are also separately sold by the taxpayer or its affiliate to unrelated persons in uncontrolled transactions and the conditions of paragraph (v)(C) of this A. 12 are satisfied, the taxpayer may elect to determine the combined taxable income of such end-product form under this paragraph (v). In that case, the combined taxable income derived from covered sales of the end-product form shall be determined by reducing the per unit combined taxable income from the integrated product that includes the end-product form by the per unit combined taxable income for excluded components determined under the rules of this paragraph (v), but subject to the limitation of paragraph (v)(D) of this A. 12. For this purpose, combined taxable income of the excluded components must be determined under section 936 as if the excluded components were possession products.

(C) In the case of component products, this paragraph (v) applies only if the sales price of the possession product sold in covered sales as an integrated product (i.e., in uncontrolled transactions) would be the most direct and reliable measure of an arm's length price within the meaning of the fourth sentence of § 1.482-3(b)(2)(ii)(A) for the component product. For purposes of applying the fourth sentence of § 1.482-3(b)(2)(ii)(A), the sale of the integrated product that includes the component product is treated as being immediately preceded by a sale of the component (i.e. without further processing) in a controlled transaction. In the case of end-product forms, this paragraph (v) applies only if the sales price of excluded components separately sold in uncontrolled transactions would be the most direct and reliable measure of an arm's length price within the meaning of the fourth sentence of § 1.482-3(b)(2)(ii)(A) for all excluded components of an integrated product that includes an end-product form. For purposes of applying the fourth sentence of § 1.482-3(b)(2)(ii)(A), the sale of the integrated product that includes excluded components is treated as being immediately preceded by a sale of the excluded components (i.e. without further processing) in a controlled transaction. Under the fourth sentence of § 1.482-3(b)(2)(ii)(A), the uncontrolled transactions referred to in this paragraph (v)(C) must have no differences with the controlled transactions that would affect price, or have only minor differences that have a definite and reasonably ascertainable effect on price and for which appropriate adjustments are made (resulting in appropriate adjustments to the computation of combined taxable income). If such adjustments cannot be made, or if there are more than minor differences between the controlled and uncontrolled transactions, the method provided by this paragraph (v)(C) cannot be used. Thus, for example, these uncontrolled transactions must involve substantially identical property in the same or a substantially identical geographic market, and must be substantially identical to the controlled transaction in terms of their volumes, contractual terms, and market level. See § 1.482-3(b)(2)(ii)(B).

(D) In no case can the per unit combined taxable income as determined under paragraph (v)(A) or (B) of this A. 12 be greater than the per unit combined taxable income of the integrated product that includes the component product or end-product form.

(E) The provisions of this paragraph (v) are illustrated by the following example. Taxpayer manufactures product A in a U.S. possession. Some portion of product A is sold to unrelated persons as an integrated product and the remainder is sold to related persons for transformation into product AB. The combined taxable income of integrated product A is $400 per unit and the combined taxable income of product AB is $300 per unit. The production cost ratio with respect to product A when sold as a component of product AB, is 2/3. Unless the taxpayer elects and satisfies the conditions of this paragraph (v), the combined taxable income with respect to A will be $200 per unit (combined taxable income for AB of $300 × the production cost ratio of 2/3). If, however, the comparability standards of paragraph (v)(C) of this A. 12 are met, the taxpayer may elect to determine combined taxable income of product A when sold as a component of product AB using the same per unit combined taxable income as product A when sold as an integrated product. However, the per unit combined taxable income from sales of product A as a component product may not exceed the per unit combined taxable income on the sale of product AB. Therefore, the combined taxable income of component product A may not exceed $300 per unit.

(vi) Taxpayers that have not elected the percentage limitation under section 936(a)(1) for the first taxable year beginning after December 31, 1993, may do so if the taxpayer has elected the profit split method and computation of combined taxable income is affected by Q&A. 12 of this paragraph (b)(1).

(vii) The rules of Q&A. 12 of this paragraph (b)(1) apply for taxable years ending 30 days after May 10, 1996. If, however, the election under paragraph (v) of A. 12 of § 1.936-6(b)(1) is made, this election must be made for the taxpayer's first taxable year beginning after December 31, 1993, and if not made effective for that year, the election cannot be made for any later taxable year. A successor corporation that makes the same or substantially similar products as its predecessor corporation cannot make an election under paragraph (v) of A. 12 of § 1.936-6(b)(1) unless the election was made by its predecessor corporation for its first taxable year beginning after December 31, 1993. Question 13: If the profit split option is elected, how is the portion of combined taxable income not allocated to the possessions corporation to be treated?

Answer 13: (i) The income shall be allocated to affiliates in the following order, but no allocations will be made to affiliates described in a later category if there are any affiliates in a prior category—

(A) First, to U.S. affiliates (other than tax exempt affiliates) within the group (as determined under section 482) that derive income with respect to the product produced in whole or in part in the possession;

(B) Second, to U.S. affiliates (other than tax exempt affiliates) that derive income from the active conduct of a trade or business in the same product area as the possession product;

(C) Third, to other U.S. affiliates (other than tax-exempt affiliates);

(D) Fourth, to foreign affiliates that derive income from the active conduct of a U.S. trade or business in the same product area as the possession product (or, if the foreign members are resident in a country with which the U.S. has an income tax convention, then to those foreign members that have a permanent establishment in the United States that derives income in the same product area as the possession product); and

(E) Fifth, to all other affiliates.

(ii) The allocations made under paragraph (i)(A) of this A. 13 shall be made on the basis of the relative gross income derived by each such affiliate with respect to the product produced in whole or in part in the possession. For this purpose, gross income must be determined consistently for each affiliate and consistently from year to year.

(iii) The allocations made under paragraphs (i)(B) and (i)(D) of this A. 13 shall be made on the basis of the relative gross income derived by each such affiliate from the active conduct of the trade or business in the same product area.

(iv) The allocations made under paragraphs (i)(C) and (i)(E) of this A. 13 shall be made on the basis of the relative total gross income of each such affiliate before allocating income under this section.

(v) Income allocated to affiliates shall be treated as U.S. source and section 863(b) does not apply for this purpose.

(vi) For purposes of determining an affiliate's estimated tax liability for income thus allocated for taxable years beginning prior to January 1, 1995, the income shall be deemed to be received on the last day of the taxable year of each such affiliate in which or with which the taxable year of the possessions corporation ends. For taxable years beginning after December 31, 1994, quarterly estimated tax payments will be required as provided under section 711 of the Uruguay Round Agreements, Public Law 103-465 (1994), page 230, and any administrative guidance issued by the Internal Revenue Service thereunder.

Question 14: What is the source of the portion of combined taxable income allocated to the possessions corporation?

Answer 14: Income allocated to the possessions corporation shall be treated as possession source income and as derived from the active conduct of a trade or business within the possession.

Question 15: How is the profit split option to be applied to properly account for costs incurred in a year with respect to products which are sold by the possessions corporation to a U.S. affiliate during such year, but are not resold by the U.S. affiliate to persons who are not members of the affiliated group or to foreign affiliates until a later year?

Answer 15: The rules under § 1.994-1(c)(5) are to be applied. Incomplete transactions will not be taken into consideration in computing combined taxable income. Thus, for example, if in 1983, A, a possessions corporation, sells units of a product with a cost to A of $5000 to B corporation, its U.S. affiliate, which use the dollar-value LIFO method of costing inventory, and B sells units with a cost of $4000 (representing A's cost) to C corporation, a foreign affiliate, only $4000 of such costs shall be taken into consideration in computing the combined taxable income of the possessions corporation and U.S. affiliates for 1983. If a specific goods LIFO inventory method is used by B, the determination of whether A's goods remain in B's inventory shall be based on whether B's specific goods LIFO grouping has experienced an increment or decrement for the year on the specific LIFO cost of such units, rather than on an average unit cost of such units. If the FIFO method of costing inventory is used by B, transfers may be based on the cost of the specific units transferred or on the average unit production cost of the units transferred, but in each case a FIFO flow assumption shall be used to identify the units transferred. For a determination of which goods are sold by taxpayers using the LIFO method, see question and answer 19.

Question 16: If a possessions corporation purchases materials from an affiliate and computes combined taxable income for a possession product which includes such materials, how are those materials to be treated in the possessions corporation's inventory?

Answer 16: The cost of those materials is considered to be equal to the affiliate's cost using the affiliate's method of costing inventory.

Question 17: If the possessions corporation uses the FIFO method of costing inventory and the U.S. affiliate uses the LIFO method of costing inventory, or vice versa, what method of costing inventory should be used in computing combined taxable income?

Answer 17: The transferor corporation's method of costing inventory determines the cost of inventory for purposes of combined taxable income while the transferee corporation's method of costing inventory determines the flow. Assume, for example, that X corporation, a possessions corporation, using the FIFO method of costing inventory purchases materials from Y corporation, U.S. affiliate, also using the FIFO method. X corporation produces a product which it transfers to Z corporation, another U.S. affiliate using the LIFO method. Assume also that the final product satisfies the significant business presence test. Under the facts, the cost of the materials purchased by X from Y is Y's FIFO cost. The costs of the inventory transferred by X to Z are determined under X's FIFO method of accounting as is the flow of the inventory from X to Z. The costs added by Z are determined under Z's LIFO method of inventory, as is the flow of the inventory from Z to unrelated persons or foreign affiliates.

Question 18: How are the costs of a possession product and the revenues derived from the sale of a possession product determined if the U.S. affiliate includes purchases of the possessions product in a dollar-value LIFO inventory pool (as provided under § 1.472-8)?

Answer 18: The following method will be accepted in determining the revenues derived from the sale of a possession product and the costs of a possession product if the U.S. affiliate includes purchases of the possession product in a dollar-value LIFO inventory pool. The rules apply solely for the cost sharing and profit split options under section 936(h).

(i) Revenue Identification: The identification of revenues derived from sales of a possession product must generally be made on a specific identification basis. The particular method employed by a taxpayer for valuing its inventory will have no impact on the determination of what units are sold or how much revenue is derived from such sales. Thus, if a U.S. affiliate sells both item A (a possession product) and item B (a non-possession product), the actual sales revenues received by the U.S. affiliate from item A sales would constitute possession product revenue for purposes of the profit split option and possession sales for purposes of the cost sharing option regardless of whether the U.S. affiliate values its inventories on the FIFO or the LIFO method. In instances where sales of item A (i.e., the possession product) cannot be determined by use of specific identification (for example, in cases where items A and B are identical except that one is produced in the possession (item A) and the other (item B) is produced outside of the possession and it is not possible to segregate these items in the hands of the U.S. affiliate), it will be necessary to identify the portion of the combined sales of items A and B (which together can be identified on a specific identification basis) which is attributed to item A sales and the portion which is attributed to item B sales. The determination of the portion of aggregated sales attributable to item A and item B is independent of the LIFO method used to determine the cost of such sales and may be made under the following approach. A taxpayer may, for purposes of this section of the regulations, use the relative purchases (in units) of items A and B by the U.S. affiliate during the taxable year (or other appropriate measuring period such as the period during the taxable year used to determine current-year costs, i.e., earliest acquisitions period, latest acquisitions period, etc.) in determining the ratio to apply against the combined items A and B sales revenue. If the sales exceed current purchases, the taxpayer can use a FIFO unit approach which identifies actual unit sales on a first-in, first-out basis. Revenue determination where specific identification is not possible is illustrated by the following example:

Example. At the end of year 1, there are 600 units of combined items A and B which are to be allocated between A and B on the basis of annual purchases of A and B units during year 1. During year 1, 1,000 units of item A, a possession product, and 2,000 units of item B, a non-possession product, were purchased. Thus, the 600 units in year 1 ending inventory are allocated 200 (i.e. ⅓) to item A units and 400 (i.e. ⅔) to item B units based on the relative purchases of A (1,000) and B (2,000) in year 1. These units appear as beginning inventory in year 2.

In year 2, 1,500 units of item A are purchased and 1,500 units of item B are purchased. However, 3,300 units of items A and B in the aggregate are sold for $600,000. The relative proportion of the $600,000 attributable to item A and to item B sales would be determined as follows:

Year Two sales	Item A	Item B
Unit sales from opening inventory	200	400
Unit sale from current-year purchases	1,350	1,350
Total unit sales (3,300)	1,550	1,750
Percentage	47	53

Revenues from item A sales	281,818	$\left\{ \$600{,}000 \times \frac{1550}{3300} \right\}$
Revenues from item B sales	318,182	$\left\{ \$600{,}000 \times \frac{1750}{3300} \right\}$

Year 2 Closing Inventory	Units
A	150
B	150

Thus, revenues from Item A sales for purposes of computing possession sales for the cost sharing option and revenues for the profit split option are $281,818.

(ii) Cost Identification: The determination of the cost of possession product sales by the U.S. affiliate must be based on the LIFO inventory method of the U.S. affiliate. The LIFO cost of possession product sales will, for purposes of this section of the regulations, be determined by maintaining a separate LIFO cost for possession products in a taxpayer's opening and closing LIFO inventory and using this cost to calculate an independent cost of possession product sales. This separate LIFO cost for possession products in the LIFO pool of a taxpayer is to be determined as follows:

(A) Determine the base-year cost of possession products in ending inventory in a LIFO pool.

(B) Determine the percentage of the base-year cost of possession products in the pool as compared to the total base-year cost of all items in the pool.

(C) Multiply the percentage determined in step (B) above by the ending LIFO inventory value of the pool to determine the deemed LIFO cost attributable to possession products in the pool.

(D) Subtract the LIFO cost of possession products in ending inventory in the pool (as calculated in step (c) above) from the sum of: (1) possession product purchases for the year, plus (2) the portion of the opening LIFO inventory value of the pool attributed to possession products (i.e., the result obtained in step (c) above for the prior year). The number determined by this calculation is the LIFO cost of possession product sales from the taxpayer's LIFO pool.

Example. Assume that item A is a possession product and item B is a non-possession product and also assume the inventory and purchases with respect to the LIFO pool as provided below:

Year 1—Ending Inventory

	No. of Units	Base-year cost/unit	Base-year cost	Percent
Item A	100	$2.00	$200	20
Item B	200	4.00	800	80

Year 1—LIFO Value

	Base year cost	Index	LIFO cost
Increment layer 2	$ 300	3.0	$ 900
Increment layer 1	400	2.0	800
Base layer	300	1.0	300
Pool total	$1,000		$2,000

Year 1—LIFO Value Per Item

	Base year cost	LIFO value
Total pool	$1,000	$2,000
Item A	200	400
Item B	800	1,600

Year 2—Purchases

	Total purchases
Item A	$6,000
Item B	4,000

Year 2—Ending Inventory

	No. of units	Base year cost/unit	Base year cost	Percent
Item A	200	$2.00	$400	50
Item B	100	4.00	400	50

Year 2—LIFO Value

	Base year cost	Index	LIFO cost
Increment layer 2	$100	3.0	$ 300
Increment layer 1	400	2.0	800
Base layer	$300	1.0	300
Pool total	800		1,400

The year 2 LIFO cost of possession product A sales will be calculated as follows:

(1) Base-year cost of item in year 2 ending inventory = $400

(2) Percentage of Item A base-year cost to total base-year cost ($400 ÷ $800) = 50%

(3) LIFO value of Item A ($1,400 × 50%) = $700

(4) LIFO cost of Item A sales is determined by adding to the beginning inventory in year 2 the purchases of item A in year 2 and subtracting from this amount the ending inventory in year 2 ($400 + $6000 − $700 = $5700). The beginning inventory in year 2 is determined by multiplying the LIFO cost of the year 1 ending inventory by a percentage of item A base-year cost to the total base-year cost in year 1. The ending inventory in year 2 is determined under (3) above.

Question 19: If a possession product is purchased from a possessions corporation by a U.S. affiliate using the dollar-value LIFO method of costing its inventory and is included in a LIFO pool of the U.S. affiliate which includes products purchased from the possessions corporation in pre-TEFRA years, how should the LIFO index computation of the U.S. affiliate be made in the first year in which section 936(h) applies and in subsequent taxable years?

Answer 19: The U.S. affiliate should treat the first taxable year for which section 936(h) applies as a new base year in accordance with procedures provided by regulations under section 472. Thus, the opening inventory for the first year for which section 936(h) applies (valuing possession products purchased from the possessions corporation on the basis of the cost of such possession products), would equal the new base year cost of the inventory of such pool of the U.S. affiliate. Increments and decrements at new base year cost would be valued for LIFO purposes pursuant to the procedures provided by regulations under section 472.

Question 20: If the possessions corporation computes its income with respect to a product under the profit split method, with respect to which units of the product shall the profit split method apply?

Answer 20: The profit split method shall apply to units of the possession product produced in whole or in part by the possessions corporation in the possession and sold during the taxable year by members of the affiliated group (other than foreign affiliates) to unrelated parties or to foreign affiliates. In no event shall the profit split method apply to units of the product which were not taken into account by the possessions corporation in applying the significant business presence test for the current taxable year or for any prior taxable year in which the possessions corporation also had a significant business presence in the possession with respect to such product.

(2) Pre-TEFRA inventory. Question 1: How is pre-TEFRA inventory to be determined if the profit split option is elected and the FIFO method of costing inventory is used by the U.S. affiliate?

Answer 1: Pre-TEFRA inventory is inventory which was produced by the possessions corporation and transferred to a U.S. affiliate prior to the possessions corporation's first taxable year beginning after December 31, 1982. Pre-TEFRA inventory will not be included for purposes of the profit split option. If the U.S. affiliate uses the FIFO method of costing inventory, the pre-TEFRA inventory will be treated as the first inventory sold by the U.S. affiliate during the first year in which section 936(h) applies and will not be included in the computation of combined taxable income for purposes of the profit split option. The treatment of pre-TEFRA inventory when FIFO costing is used by both the U.S. affiliate and the possessions corporation is illustrated by the following example in which FIFO unit costing is used:

Example. Assume the following:

	X		Y	
	Possessions corporation		U.S. Affiliate	
	Number of Units	Cost per Unit	Number of Units	Cost per Unit
Beginning inventory	500	$150	200	$225
Units produced during 1983	1,000	200	—	—
Ending inventory	400	200	300	—

In 1983, the beginning inventory of X, a possessions corporation, is 500 units with a unit cost of $150 and the beginning inventory of Y, the U.S. affiliate, is 200 units with a unit cost of $225, which represents the section 482 price paid by Y. Y's beginning inventory in 1983 represents purchases made in 1982 of products produced by X in that year. Y sells all the units it purchases from X to Z, a foreign affiliate. In 1983, X produces 1000 units at a unit cost of $200 and sells 1100 units to Y (the difference between 1500 units, representing X's 1983 beginning inventory (500) and the units produced by X in 1983 (1000), and X's ending inventory of 400 units). Of the 1100 units sold by X to Y in 1983 only 800 units (and not 1000 units) which were sold by Y to Z are taken into consideration in computing combined taxable income for 1983. Since FIFO costing by the possessions corporation is used, the cost is $150 per unit for the first 500 units and $200 per unit for the remaining 300 units. The 200 units sold by X to Y in 1982 are pre-TEFRA inventory and are not included in the computation of combined taxable income for 1983. They are also treated as the first units sold by Y to Z in 1983. This inventory has a unit cost of $225, which reflects the section 482 transfer price from X to Y in 1982. Y's 1983 ending inventory of 300 units will not be taken into consideration in computing the combined taxable income of X and Y for 1983 because the units have not been sold to a foreign affiliate or to persons who are not members of the affiliated group. In a subsequent year when the units are sold to Z, the cost to X and selling price to Z of these units will enter into the computation of combined taxable income for that year.

(c) Covered intangibles. Question 1: What are "covered intangibles" under section 936(h)(5)(C)(i)(II)?

Answer 1: The term "covered intangibles" means (1) intangible property developed in a possession solely by the possessions corporation and owned by it, (2) manufacturing intangible property (described in section 936(h)(3)(B)(i)) which is acquired by the possessions corporation from unrelated persons, and (3) any other intangible property (described in section 936(h)(3)(B)(ii) through (v), to the extent not described in section 936(h)(3)(B)(i)) which relates to sales of products or services to unrelated persons for ultimate consumption or use in the possession in which the possessions corporation conducts its business. The possessions corporation is treated as the owner of covered intangibles for purposes of obtaining a return thereon.

Question 2: Do covered intangibles include manufacturing intangible property which is acquired by an affiliate and subsequently transferred to the possessions corporation?

Answer 2: No. In order for a manufacturing intangible to be treated as a covered intangible, the intangible property must be acquired directly by the possessions corporation from an unrelated person unless the manufacturing intangible was acquired by an affiliate from an unrelated person and was transferred to the possessions corporation by the affiliate prior to September 3, 1982.

Question 3: If a possessions corporation licenses a manufacturing intangible from an unrelated party, will the licensed intangible be treated as a covered intangible?

Answer 3: No.

Question 4: How is ultimate consumption or use determined for purposes of the definition of covered intangibles?

Answer 4: A product will be treated as having its ultimate use or consumption in a possession if it is sold by the possessions corporation to a related or unrelated person in a possession and is not resold or used or consumed outside of the possession within one year after the date of the sale.

Question 5: Are sales of products that relate to covered intangibles excluded from the cost sharing fraction?

Answer 5: If no manufacturing intangibles other than covered intangibles are associated with the possession product, then sales of such product will be excluded from the cost sharing fraction. If both covered and non-covered manufacturing intangibles are associated with the possession product, then sales of such product will be included in the cost sharing fraction.

Question 6: If the cost sharing option is elected, is it necessary for the possessions corporation to be the legal owner of covered intangibles described in section 936(h)(5)(C)(i)(II)(c) related to the product in order for the possessions corporation to receive a full return with respect to such intangibles?

Answer 6: No. For purposes of section 936(h), it is immaterial whether such covered intangibles are owned by the possessions corporation or by another member of the affiliated group. Moreover, if the legal owner of such covered intangibles which are subject to section 936(h)(5) is an affiliate of the possessions corporation, such person will not be required to charge an arm's-length royalty under section 482 to the possessions corporation.

T.D. 8090, 6/9/86, amend T.D. 8669, 5/9/96, T.D. 8786, 10/13/98.

§ 1.936-7 Manner of making election under section 936(h)(5); special election for export sales; revocation of election under section 936(a).

Caution: The Treasury has not yet amended Reg § 1.936-7 to reflect changes made by P.L. 104-188, P.L. 100-647, P.L. 99-514.

(a) The rules in this section apply for purposes of section 936(h) and also for purposes of section 934(e), where applicable.

(b) Manner of making election. Question 1: How does a possessions corporation make an election to use the cost sharing method or profit split method?

Answer 1: A possessions corporation makes an election to use the cost sharing or profit split method by filing Form 5712-A ("Election and Verification of the Cost Sharing or Profit Split Method Under Section 936(h)(5)") and attaching it to its tax return. Form 5712-A must be filed on or before the due date (including extensions) of the tax return of the possessions corporation for its first taxable year beginning after December 31, 1982. The electing corporation must set forth on the form the name and the taxpayer identification number or address of all members of the affiliated group (including foreign affiliates not required to file a U.S. tax return). All members of the affiliated group must consent to the election. For elections filed with respect to taxable years beginning before January 1, 2003, an authorized officer of the electing corporation must sign the statement of election and must declare that he has received a signed statement of consent from an authorized officer, director, or other appropriate official of each member of the affiliated group. Elections filed for taxable years beginning after December 31, 2002, must incorporate a declaration by the electing corporation that it has received a signed consent from an authorized officer, director, or other appropriate official of each member of the affiliated group and will be verified by signing the return. The election is not valid for a taxable year unless all affiliates consent. A failure to obtain an affiliate's written consent will not invalidate the election out if the possessions corporation made a good faith effort to obtain all the necessary consents or the failure to obtain the missing consent was inadvertent. Subsequently created or acquired affiliates are bound by the election. If an election out is revoked under section 936(h)(5)(F)(iii), a new election out with respect to that product area cannot be made without the consent of the Commissioner. The possessions corporation shall file an amended Form 5712-A with its timely filed (including extensions) income tax return to reflect any changes in the names or number of the members of the affiliated group for any taxable year after the first taxable year to which the election out applies. By consenting to the election out, all affiliates agree to provide information necessary to compute the cost sharing payment under the cost sharing method or combined taxable income under the profit split method, and failure to provide such information shall be treated as a request to revoke the election out under section 936(h)(5)(F)(iii).

Question 2: May the "election out" under section 936(h)(5) be made on a product-by-product basis, or must it be made on a wide basis?

Answer 2: An electing corporation is required to treat products in the same product area in the same manner. Similarly, all possessions corporations in the same affiliated group that produce any products or render any services in the same product area must make the same election for all products that fall within the same product area. However, § 1.936-7(b) provides that the electing corporation may make a different election for export sales than for domestic sales. The electing corporation or corporations may also make different elections for products that fall within different product areas.

Question 3: May the possessions corporation elect to define product area more narrowly than the 3-digit SIC code?

Answer 3: No. Certain alternatives, such as the 4-digit SIC code, would not be permitted under the statute. However, other methods for defining product area may be considered by the Commissioner in the future.

Question 4: May a possessions corporation make an election out under the cost sharing method with respect to a product area if the affiliated group incurs no research, development or experimental costs in the product area?

Answer 4: Yes. In that case the cost sharing payment will be zero.

Question 5: If the significant business presence test is not satisfied for a product or type of service within the product area covered by the election out under section 936(h)(5) what rules will apply with respect to that product?

Answer 5: With respect to the product which does not satisfy the significant business presence test, the provisions of section 936(h)(1) through (h)(4) will apply to the allocation of income. However, if a cost sharing or a profit split election has been made with respect to the product area, the cost sharing payment or the research and development floor under section 936(h)(5)(C)(ii)(II) will not be reduced.

Question 6: Is a taxpayer permitted to make a change of election with respect to the cost sharing and profit split methods?

Answer 6: In general, once the election is properly made, it is binding for the first year in which it applies and all subsequent years (including upon any later created or acquired affiliates), and revocation is only permitted with the consent of the Commissioner of Internal Revenue. However, a taxpayer will be permitted to change its election once from the cost sharing method to the profit split method or vice versa, or from the method permitted under section 936(h)(1) through (h)(4) to cost sharing or profit split or vice versa, without the consent of the Commissioner if the change is made on the taxpayer's return for its first taxable year ending after June 13, 1986. Such change will apply to such taxable year and all subsequent taxable years, and, at the taxpayer's option, may also apply to all prior taxable years for which section 936(h) was in effect. A change of election will be treated as an election subject to the procedures set forth above and to section 481 of the Internal Revenue Code.

Question 7: If the Commissioner determines that a possessions corporation does not meet the 80-percent possession source test or the 65-percent active trade or business test (the "qualification tests") for any taxable year beginning after 1982, under what circumstances is the possessions corporation permitted to make a distribution of property after the close of its taxable year to meet the qualification tests?

Answer 7: A possessions corporation may make a pro rata distribution of property to its shareholders after the close of the taxable year if the Commissioner determines that the possessions corporation does not satisfy the qualification tests (a) by reason of the exclusion from gross income of intangible income under section 936(h)(1)(B) or Section 936(h)(5)(C)(i)(II) or (b) by reason of the allocation to the shareholders of the possessions corporation of income under section 936(h)(5)(C)(ii)(III); provided, however, that the determination of the Commissioner does not contain a finding that the failure of such corporation to satisfy the qualification tests was due, in whole or in part, to fraud with intent to evade tax or willful neglect on the part of the possessions corporation. The possessions corporation must designate the distribution at the time the distribution is made as a distribution to meet qualification requirements, and it will be subject to the provisions of section 936(h)(4). Such distributions will not qualify for the dividends received deduction.

Question 8: If a possessions corporation owns stock in a subsidiary possessions corporation, any intangible property income allocated to the parent possessions corporation under section 936(h) will be treated as U.S. source income and taxable to the parent possessions corporation. Is the intangible property income taken into consideration in determining whether the parent possessions corporation meets the income tests of section 936(a)(2)?

Answer 8: While taxable to the parent possessions corporation, the intangible property income does not enter into the calculation of the 80-percent possession source test or the 65-percent active trade or business test of section 936(a)(2)(A) and (B). This would also be the case if the subsidiary possessions corporation made a qualifying distribution under section 936(h)(4).

(c) Separate election for export sales. Question 1: What methods of computing income can a possessions corporation use under the separate election for export sales?

Answer 1: The only two methods which are available under the separate election for export sales are the cost sharing method and the profit split method.

Question 2: What is the definition of export sales for purposes of the separate election for export sales?

Answer 2: The determination of export sales is based upon the destination of the product, i.e., where it is to be used or consumed. If the product is sold to a U.S. affiliate, it will be treated as an export sale only if resold or otherwise transferred abroad to a foreign person (including a foreign affiliate or foreign branch of a U.S. affiliate) within one year from the date of sale to the U.S. affiliate for ultimate use or consumption outside the United States as provided under § 1.954-3(a)(3)(ii).

Question 3: Assume that a possessions corporation sells a product to both foreign affiliates and foreign branches of U.S. affiliates. In addition, it sells the product to its U.S. parent for resale in the U.S. The possessions corporation makes a profit split election for domestic sales and a cost sharing election of export sales. Will the sales to foreign branches of U.S. affiliates be treated as exports subject to the cost sharing method or as domestic sales subject to the profit split method?

Answer 3: The sales to a foreign branch of a U.S. corporation are exports if for ultimate use or consumption outside of the United States as provided under § 1.954-3(a)(3)(ii).

Question 4: Under what circumstances may a possessions corporation make the separate election under section 936(h)(5)(F)(iv)(II) for computing its income from products exported to a foreign person when the income derived by such foreign person on the resale of such products is included in foreign base company income under section 954(a)?

Answer 4: If the income derived by a foreign person on the resale of products manufactured, in whole or in part, by a possessions corporation is included in foreign base company income under section 954(a), then the possessions corporation may make the separate export election under section 936(h)(5)(F)(iv)(II) for computing its income from such products only if such foreign person has been formed or is availed of for substantial business reasons that are unrelated to an affiliated corporation's U.S. tax liability. For purposes of the preceding sentence, a foreign person will be considered to be formed or availed of for such substantial business reasons if the foreign person in the normal course of business purchases substantial quantities of products from both the possessions corporation and its affiliates for resale, and, in addition provides support services for affiliated companies such as centralized testing, marketing of products, management of local currency exposures, or other similar services. However, a foreign person that purchases and resells products only from a possessions corporation is presumed to be formed or availed of for other than such substantial business reasons, even if the foreign person provides additional services.

Question 5: When will the "manufacturing" test set forth in subsection (d)(1)(A) of section 954 be applicable to the export sales of a product of a possessions corporation which makes a separate election for export sales?

Answer 5: An electing corporation will be required to meet the "manufacturing" test set forth in subsection (d)(1)(A) of section 954 with respect to export sales of its product in each taxable year in which the separate election for export sales is in effect.

(d) Revocation of election under section 936(a). Question 1: When may an election under section 936(a) be revoked?

Answer 1: An election under section 936(a) may be revoked during the first ten years of section 936 status only with the consent of the Commissioner, and without the Commissioner's consent after that time. The Commissioner hereby consents to all requests for revocation that are made with respect to the taxpayer's first taxable year beginning after December 31, 1982 provided that the section 936(a) election was in effect for the corporation's last taxable year beginning before January 1, 1983, if the taxpayer agrees not to re-elect section 936(a) prior to its first taxable year beginning after December 31, 1988. A taxpayer that wishes to revoke a section 936(a) election under the terms of the blanket revocation must attach a "Statement of Revocation—Section 936" to the taxpayer's timely filed return (including extensions) and must state that in revoking the election the taxpayer agrees not to re-elect section 936(a) prior to its first taxable year beginning after December 31, 1988. Other requests to revoke not covered by the Commissioner's blanket consent should be addressed to the District Director having jurisdiction over the taxpayer's tax return.

T.D. 8090, 6/9/86, amend T.D. 9100, 12/18/2003, T.D. 9300, 12/7/2006.

---

§ 1.936-8T Qualified possession source investment income (Temporary). [Reserved]

§ 1.936-9T Source of qualified possession source investment income (Temporary regulations). [Reserved]

§ 1.936-10 Qualified investments.

Caution: The Treasury has not yet amended Reg § 1.936-10 to reflect changes made by P.L. 104-188, P.L. 101-382.

(a) In general. [Reserved]

(b) Qualified investments in Puerto Rico. [Reserved]

(c) Qualified investment in certain Caribbean Basin countries. *(1) General rule.* An investment of qualified funds described in this section shall be treated as a qualified investment of funds for use in Puerto Rico if the funds are used for a qualified investment in a qualified Caribbean Basin country. A qualified investment in a qualified Caribbean Basin country is a loan of qualified funds by a qualified financial institution (described in paragraph (c)(3) of this section) directly to a qualified recipient (described in paragraph (c)(9) of this section) or indirectly through a single financial intermediary for investment in active business assets (as defined in paragraph (c)(4) of this section) in a qualified Caribbean Basin country (described in paragraph (c)(10)(ii) of this section) or for investment in development projects (as defined in paragraph (c)(5) of this section) in a qualified Caribbean Basin country, provided—

(i) The investment is authorized, prior to disbursement of the funds, by the Commissioner of Financial Institutions of Puerto Rico (or his delegate) pursuant to regulations issued by such Commissioner; and

(ii) The agreement, certification, and due diligency requirements under paragraphs (c)(11), (12), and (13) of this section are met.

A loan by a qualified financial institution shall not be disqualified merely because the loan transaction is processed by the central bank of issue of the country into which the loan is made pursuant to, and solely for purposes of complying with, the exchange control laws or regulations of such country. Further, a loan by a qualified financial institution shall not be disqualified merely because the loan is acquired by another person, provided such other person is also a qualified financial institution.

(2) Termination of qualification. (i) In general. An investment that, at any time after having met the requirements for a qualified investment ins qualified Caribbean Basin country under the terms of this paragraph (c), fails to meet any of the conditions enumerated in this paragraph (c) shall no longer be considered a qualified investment in a qualified Caribbean Basin country from the time of such failure, unless the investment satisfies the requirements for a timely cure described in paragraph (c)(2)(ii) of this section. Such a failure includes, but is not limited to, the occurrence of any of the following events:

(A) Active business assets cease to qualify as such;

(B) Proceeds from the investment are diverted for the financing of assets, projects, or operations that are not active business assets or development projects or are not the assets or the project of the qualified recipient;

(C) The holder of the qualified recipient's obligation is not a qualified financial institution;

(D) The qualified recipient's qualified business activity ceases to qualify as such; or

(E) The qualified Caribbean Basin country ceases to be a country described in paragraph (c)(10)(ii) of this section.

(ii) Timely cure. (A) In general. A timely cure shall be considered to have been made if the event or events that cause disqualification of the investment are corrected within a reasonable period of time. For purposes of this section, a reasonable period of time shall not exceed 60 days after such event or events come to the attention of the qualified recipient or the qualified financial institution or should have come to their attention by the exercise of reasonable diligence.

(B) Due diligence requirements. A time cure of a failure to comply with the due diligence requirements of paragraphs (c)(11), (12), and (13) of this section shall be considered to be made if the failure to comply is due to reasonable cause and, upon request of the Commissioner of Financial Institutions of Puerto Rico (or his delegate) or of the Assistant Commissioner (International) (or his authorized representative), the qualified financial institution (and its trustee or agent), if any), the financial intermediary, or the qualified recipient establishes to the satisfaction of the Commissioner of Financial Institutions of Puerto Rico (or his delegate) or of the Assistant Commissioner (International) (or his authorized representative) that it has exercised due diligence in ensuring that the funds were property disbursed to a qualified recipient and applied by or on behalf of such qualified recipient to uses that qualify the investment as an investment in qualified business assets or a development project under the provisions of this paragraph (c).

(iii) Assumption of qualified recipient's obligation. An investment shall not cease to qualify merely because the qualified recipient's obligation to the qualified financial institution (or to a financial intermediary, if any) is assumed by another person, provided such other person assumes the qualified recipient's agreement and certification requirements under paragraph (c)(11)(i) of this section and is either—

(A) A qualified recipient on the date of assumption, in which case such person shall be treated for purposes of this section as the original qualified recipient and shall be subject to all the requirements of this section for continued qualification of the loan as a qualified investment in a qualified Caribbean Basin country; or

(B) An international organization, the principal purpose of which is to foster economic development in developing countries and which is described in section 1 of the International Organizations Immunities Act (22 U.S.C. 288), if the assumption of the obligation is pursuant to a bona fide guarantee agreement.

(3) Qualified financial institution. (i) General rule. For purposes of section 936(d)(4)(A) and this section, a qualified financial institution includes only—

(A) A banking, financing, or similar business defined in § 1.864-4(c)(5)(i) that is an eligible institution described in paragraph (c)(3)(ii) of this section, but not including branches of such institution outside of Puerto Rico;

(B) A single-purpose entity described in paragraph (c)(3)(iii) of this section;

(C) The Government Development Bank for Puerto Rico;

(D) The Puerto Rico Economic Development Bank; and

(E) Such other entity as may be determined by the Commissioner by Revenue Procedure or other guidance published in the Internal Revenue Bulletin.

(ii) Eligible institution. An eligible institution means an institution—

(A) That is an entity organized under the laws of the Commonwealth of Puerto Rico or is the Puerto Rican branch of an entity organized under the laws of another jurisdiction, if such entity is engaged in a banking, financing, or similar business defined in § 1.864-4(c)(5)(i), and

(B) That is licensed as an eligible institution under Regulation No. 3582 (or any successor regulation) issued by the Commissioner of Financial Institutions of Puerto Rico (hereinafter "Puerto Rico Regulation No. 3582").

(iii) Single-purpose entity. A single purpose entity is an entity that is an entity that meets all of the following conditions:

(A) The entity is organized under the laws of the Commonwealth of Puerto Rico and is a corporation, a partnership or a trust, which conducts substantially all of its activities in Puerto Rico.

(B) The sole purpose of the entity is to use qualified funds from possessions corporations to make one or more qualified investments in a qualified Caribbean Basin country and the entity actually uses such funds only for such purpose.

(C) In the case of an entity that is a trust, one of the trustees is a qualified financial institution described in paragraph (c)(3)(i) of this section.

(D) The entity is licensed as an eligible institution under Puerto Rican Regulation No. 3582 (or any successor regulation).

(E) Any temporary investment by the entity for its own account of funds received from a possessions corporation, and the income from the investment thereof, and any temporary investment by the entity for its own account of principal and interest paid by a borrower to the entity, and the income from the investment thereof, are limited to investments in eligible activities, as described in section 6.2.4 of Puerto Rican Regulation No. 3582, as in effect on September 22, 1989.

(4) Investments in active business assets. (i) In general. For purposes of section 936(d)(4)(A)(i)(I) and this section and subject to the provisions of paragraph (c)(8) of this section, a loan qualifies as an investment in active business assets if—

(A) The amounts disbursed to a qualified recipient under the loan or bond issue are promptly applied (as defined in paragraphs (c)(6) and (7) of this section) by (or on behalf of) the qualified recipient solely for capital expenditures for the construction, rehabilitation (including demolition associated therewith), improvement, or upgrading of qualified assets described in paragraphs (c)(4)(ii)(A), (B), (E), and (F) of this section, for the acquisition of qualified assets described in paragraphs (c)(4)(ii)(B), (C), (E), and (F) of this section, for the expenditures described in paragraphs (c)(4)(ii) (D), (E), and (F) of this section, and, if applicable, for the financing of incidental expenditures described in paragraph (c)(4)(iii) of this section;

(B) The qualified recipient owns the assets for United States income tax purposes and uses them in a qualified business activity (as defined in paragraph (c)(4)(iv)); and

(C) The requirements of paragraph (c)(6) of this section (regarding temporary investments and time periods within which the funds must be invested) and of paragraph (c)(7) of this section (regarding the refinancing of existing funding and the time periods within which funding for investments must be secured) are satisfied.

(ii) Definition of qualified assets. For purposes of this paragraph (c), qualified assets mean—

(A) Real property;

(B) Tangible personal property (such as furniture, machinery, or equipment) that is not property described in section 1221(1) and that is either new property or property which at no time during the period specified in paragraph (c)(4)(v) of this section was used in a business activity in the qualified Caribbean Basin country in which the property is to be used;

(C) Rights to intangible property that is a patent, invention, formula, process, design, pattern, know-how, or similar item, or rights under a franchise agreement, provided that such rights—

(1) Were not at any time during the period specified in paragraph (c)(4)(v) of this section used in a business activity

in the qualified Caribbean Basin country in which the rights are to be used,

(2) Are not rights the use of which gives rise, or would give rise if used, to United States source income, and

(3) Are not rights acquired by the qualified recipient from a person related (within the meaning of section 267(b), using "10 percent" instead of "50 percent" in the places where it appears) to the qualified recipient;

(D) Exploration and development expenditures incurred by a qualified recipient for the purpose of ascertaining the existence, location, extent or quality of any deposit of ore, oil, gas, or other mineral in a qualified Caribbean Basin country, as well as for purposes of developing such deposit (within the meaning of section 616 of the Code and the regulations thereunder);

(E) Living plants and animals (other than crops, plants, and animals that are acquired primarily to hold as inventory by the qualified recipient for resale in the ordinary course of trade or business) acquired in connection with a farming business (as defined in § 1.263-1T(c)(4)(i)), expenditures of a preparatory nature to prepare the land or area for farming (such as planting trees, drilling wells, clearing brush, leveling land, laying pipes, building roads, constructing tanks and reservoirs), expenditures for soil and water conservation of a type described in section 175(c)(1), and expenditures of a development nature incurred in connection with, and during, the preproductive period of property produced in a farming business (as defined in § 1.263-1T(c)(4)(ii));

(F) Other assets or expenditures that are not described in paragraphs (c)(4)(ii)(A) through (E) of this section and that the Commissioner may, by Revenue Procedure or other guidance published in the Internal Revenue Bulletin or by ruling issued to a qualified financial institution or qualified recipient upon its request, determine to be qualified assets.

(iii) Incidental expenditures. An amount in addition to the loan proceeds borrowed to make an investment in active business assets shall be considered an investment in active business assets if such amount is applied to finance expenditures that are incidental to making the investment in active business assets, provided such amount is disbursed at or about the same time the proceeds for making the investment in active business assets are disbursed. For purposes of this section, expenditures incidental to an investment in active business assets include only the following items:

(A) A reasonable amount of costs (other than the cost of credit enhancement or bond insurance premiums) associated with arranging the financing of an investment in active business assets, not to exceed 3.5 percent of the proceeds of the loan or bond issue.

(B) A reasonable amount of installation costs and other reasonable costs associated with placing an active business asset in service in the qualified business activity.

(C) An amount not in excess of 10 percent of the total amount of investment in qualified assets to finance the acquisition of inventory, and other working capital requirements, but if an investment is in connection with a manufacturing or farming business, the percentage limitation shall be 50 percent rather than 10 percent provided the excess over the 10 percent limitation is used to finance inventory property. For purposes of this paragraph (c), whether a business is a manufacturing business shall be determined under principles similar to those described in section 954(d)(1)(A) and the regulations thereunder; whether a business is a farming business shall be determined under § 1.263-1T(c)(4)(i).

(D) An amount not in excess of 5 percent of the sum of the investment in active business assets and the costs described in paragraphs (c)(4)(iii)(A), (B), and (C) of this section for the refinancing of an existing debt of the qualified recipient if such refinancing is incidental to an investment in active business assets. For this purpose, the replacement of an existing loan arrangement shall not be considered the refinancing of an existing indebtedness to the extent that the funds under such loan arrangement have not yet been disbursed to the qualified recipient.

(iv) Qualified business activity. A qualified business activity is a lawful industrial or commercial activity that is conducted as an active trade or business (under principles similar to those described in § 1.367(a)-2T(b)(2) and (3)) in a qualified Caribbean Basin country. A trade or business for purposes of this paragraph (c)(4)(iv) is any business activity meeting the principles of section 367 of the Code and described in Divisions A through I (excluding group 43 in Division E (relating to the United States Postal Service) and groups 84 (relating to museums, art galleries, and botanical and zoological gardens), 86 (relating to membership organizations), and 88 (relating to private households) in Division I) of the 1987 Standard Industrial Classification Manual issued by the Executive Office of the President, Office of Management and Budget, or in the comparable provisions of any successor Standard Industrial Classification Manual that is adopted by the Commissioner of Internal Revenue in a notice, regulation, or other document published in the Internal Revenue Cumulative Bulletin.

(v) Period of use. The period referred to in paragraphs (c)(4)(ii)(B) and (C) of this section shall be a five year period preceding the date of acquisition with the loan proceeds, if the date of acquisition is on or before May 13, 1991. If the date of acquisition is after May 13, 1991, then the period specified in this paragraph (c)(4)(v) shall be three years preceding the date of acquisition with the loan proceeds.

(5) Investments in development projects. (i) In general. Subject to the provisions of paragraph (c)(8) of this section, this paragraph (c)(5)(i) describes the requirements in order for a loan by a qualified financial institution to qualify as an investment in a development project for purposes of section 936(d)(4)(A)(i)(II) and for this section.

(A) The amounts disbursed under the loan or bond issue must be promptly applied (as defined in paragraphs (c)(6) and (7) of this section) by (or on behalf of) the qualified recipient solely for one or more investments described in paragraph (c)(4)(i)(A) of this section and in any land, buildings, or other property functionally related and subordinate to a facility described in paragraph (c)(5)(ii) of this section (determined under principles similar to those described in § 1.103-8(a)(3)), for use (under principles similar to those described in § 1.367(a)-2T(b)(5)) in connection with one or more activities described in paragraph (c)(5)(i)(B) of this section.

(B) The activities referred to in paragraph (c)(5)(i)(A) of this section are—

(1) A development project described in paragraph (c)(5)(ii) of this section in a qualified Caribbean Basin country; or

(2) The performance in a qualified Caribbean Basin country of a non-commercial governmental function described in paragraph (c)(5)(iv) of this section;

(C) The qualified recipient must own the assets for United States income tax purposes;

(D) The requirements of paragraph (c)(6) of this section (regarding temporary investments and time periods within which the funds must be invested) and of paragraph (c)(7) of this section (regarding the refinancing of existing funding and time periods within which funding for investments must be secured) must be satisfied.

(ii) Development project. For purposes of this paragraph (c), a development project is one or more facilities in a qualified Caribbean Basin country that support economic development in that country and that satisfy the public use requirement of paragraph (c)(5)(iii) of this section. Examples of facilities that may meet the public use requirement include, but are not limited to—

(A) Transportation systems and equipment, including sea, surface, and air, such as roads, railways, air terminals, runways, harbor facilities, and ships and aircraft;

(B) Communications facilities;

(C) Training and education facilities related to qualified business activities;

(D) Industrial parks, including necessary support facilities such as roads, transmission lines for water, gas, electricity, and sewage; docks; plant sites preparations; power generation; sewage disposal; and water treatment;

(E) Sports facilities;

(F) Convention or trade show facilities;

(G) Sewage, solid waste, water, and electric facilities;

(H) Housing projects pursuant to a government program designed to provide affordable housing to low or moderate income families, based upon local standards; and

(I) Hydroelectric generating facilities.

(iii) Public use requirement. To satisfy the public use requirement in paragraph (c)(5)(ii) of this section, a facility must serve or be available on a regular basis for general public use, as contrasted with similar types of facilities which are constructed for the exclusive use of a limited number of persons as determined under principles similar to those described in § 1.103-8(a)(2).

(iv) Non-commercial governmental functions. For purposes of paragraph (c)(5)(i)(B) of this section, the term "non-commercial governmental functions" refers to activities that, under U.S. standards, are not customarily attributable to or carried on by private enterprises for profit and are performed for the general public with respect to the common welfare or which relate to the administration of some phase of government. For example, the operation of libraries, toll bridges, or local transportation services, and activities substantially equivalent to those carried out by the Federal Aviation Authority, Interstate Commerce Commission, or United States Postal Service, are considered non-commercial governmental functions. For purposes of this section, non-commercial government functions shall not include military activities.

(v) [Reserved]

(6) Prompt application of borrowed proceeds. This paragraph (c)(6) provides rules for determining whether amounts disbursed to a qualified recipient by a qualified financial institution (or a financial intermediary) shall be considered to have been promptly applied for the purpose of paragraphs (c)(4)(i)(A) and (c)(5)(i)(A) of this section.

(i) In general. Except as otherwise provided in paragraphs (c)(6)(ii) and (c)(7)(iii)(B) of this section, amounts disbursed to a qualified recipient by a qualified financial institution (or a financial intermediary) shall be considered to have been promptly applied for the purpose of paragraphs (c)(4)(i)(A) and (c)(5)(i)(A) of this section if the amounts are fully expended for any of the purposes described in paragraphs (c)(4)(i)(A) or (c)(5)(i)(A) of this section no later than six months from the date of such disbursement and any temporary investment of such funds by the qualified recipient during such period complies with the rules of paragraph (c)(6)(iii)(A) of this section. Where the amounts disbursed are bond proceeds described in paragraph (c)(6)(iv)(A) of this section, the six-month period shall begin on the date of issuance of the bonds. In the event the qualified financial institution (or financial intermediary) invests any part of the bond proceeds before disbursement of those proceeds to the qualified recipient, all earnings from any such investment shall be paid to the qualified recipient or applied for its benefit.

(ii) Special rules for long term projects financed out of bond proceeds. In the case of a long term project described in paragraph (c)(6)(iv)(B) of this section that is financed out of bond proceeds, the six-month period described in paragraph (c)(6)(i) of this section shall be extended with respect to the amount of bond proceeds used to fund the project for such reasonable period of time as shall be necessary until completion of the project or until beginning of production (in the case of a farming business), but, in any event, not to exceed three years from the date of issuance of the bonds, and only if—

(A) The project that is financed out of bond proceeds was identified as of the date of issue;

(B) A construction and expenditure plan certified by an independent expert (such as an engineer, an architect, or a farming expert) is filed with, and approved by, the Commissioner of Financial Institutions of Puerto Rico (or his delegate) prior to the date of issue, which makes a reasonable estimate, as of the date of filing of the plan, of the amounts and uses of the bond proceeds and the time of completion or production, and includes a schedule of progress payments until such time;

(C) The terms of the construction and expenditure plan are disclosed in the public offering memorandum, private placement memorandum, or similar document prepared for information or disclosure purposes in relation to the issuance of bonds; and

(D) Any temporary investment of the bond proceeds complies with the rules of paragraph (c)(6)(iii)(A) and (B) of this section.

(iii) Temporary investments. (A) During six-month period. During the six-month period described in paragraph (c)(6)(i) of this section, during the first six months of the period described in paragraph (c)(6)(ii) of this section, and during the 30-day period described in paragraph (c)(7)(iii)(A) of this section, loan proceeds disbursed to a qualified recipient, bond proceeds, and income from the investment thereof, may be held in unrestricted yield investments, provided such yield reflects normal market yield for such type of investments and provided the income from such investments, if any, is or would be sourced either in Puerto Rico or in a country in which the investment in active business assets or development project is to be made.

(B) During other periods. During any other period, any temporary investment of bond proceeds, and of income from such investments, shall be limited to investments in eligible activities. For purposes of this paragraph (c)(6)(iii)(B), the term "eligible activities" shall mean those investments described in section 6.2.4 of Puerto Rican Regulation No. 3582, as in effect on September 22, 1989.

(iv) Definitions. (A) Bond proceeds. For purposes of this paragraph (c), bond proceeds shall mean the proceeds from the issuance of obligations by way of a public offering or a private placement by a qualified financial institution for investment in active business assets or a development project that has been identified at the time of issue and is described in a public offering memorandum, private placement memorandum, or similar document prepared for information or disclosure purposes in relation to the issuance of the bonds.

(B) Long term project. For purposes of this section, the term long term project means—

(1) A project, whether or not under a contract, for the construction, rehabilitation, improvement, upgrading, or production of qualified assets, or for expenditures, described in paragraph (c)(4)(ii) of this section (other than paragraph (c)(4)(ii)(C) of this section), which is reasonably expected to require more than 12 months to complete; or

(2) The production of property in a farming business referred to in paragraph (c)(4)(ii)(E) of this section, which is reasonably expected to require a preproductive period in excess of 12 months.

(7) Financing of previously incurred costs. Loan or bond proceeds which are disbursed after a qualified recipient has paid or incurred part or all of the costs of acquiring active business assets or investing in a development project shall be considered to have been applied for such purposes only as provided in this paragraph (c)(7).

(i) Replacement of temporary non-section 936 financing of a qualified investment. This paragraph (c)(7)(i) prescribes the maximum time limits within which temporary non-section 936 financing of qualified investments may be replaced with section 936 funds without being considered a prohibited refinancing transaction. This paragraph (c)(7)(i) applies to the refinancing of costs incurred with respect to investments that, at the time the costs were first incurred, were either qualified investments in a qualified Caribbean Basin country or were investments by a qualified recipient in active business assets or a development project in a qualified Caribbean Basin country. This paragraph (c)(7)(i) applies also to the refinancing of costs incurred with respect to any other investment. However, in the latter case, the amount of costs that may be refinanced with section 936 funds is limited to the amount of costs that are incurred with respect to the investment after the investment becomes a qualified investment in a qualified Caribbean Basin country. For purposes of this paragraph (c)(7)(i), the time when costs are incurred shall be determined under principles similar to those applicable under section 461(h) dealing with the economic performance test for the accrual of deductible liabilities. This paragraph (c)(7)(i) applies only to the situations described in this paragraph (c)(7)(i).

(A) In the case of an investment in active business assets or a development project, a loan shall be a qualified investment for purposes of this paragraph (c) if the loan proceeds are disbursed, or the obligations are issued, no later than six months after the date on which the qualified recipient takes possession of the asset or the facility or, if earlier, places the asset or the facility in service. However, in the case of a small project described In paragraph (c)(8)(v) of this section, the six-month period shall be one year.

(B) In the case of an investment in active business assets or a development project that is part of a long term project described in paragraph (c)(6)(iv)(B) of this section, a loan shall also be a qualified investment for purposes of this paragraph (c) if the loan proceeds are disbursed, or the obligations are issued, no later than six months after completion of the project or, in the case of a farming business, after the beginning of production, and in any event, no later than three years after the date on which the first payment is made toward the eligible costs of the project. The amount of the qualified investment may not exceed the sum of—

(1) The eligible costs relating to investments described in paragraph (c)(4)(i)(A) in the case of an investment in active business assets, or the eligible costs relating to investments described in paragraph (c)(5)(i) of this section in the case of a development project, but only to the extent of the costs that are incurred after the date described in paragraph (c)(7)(i)(D) of this section, and

(2) the portion of unpaid interest that would be required to be capitalized under U.S. tax rules and that accrued on prior temporary non-section 936 financing from the date described in paragraph (c)(7)(i)(D) of this section through the date the section 936 loan proceeds are disbursed or the section 936 obligations are issued.

(C) In order to qualify for the special rules of this paragraph (c)(7)(i), a plan must be filed with the Commissioner of Financial Institutions of Puerto Rico (or his delegate) stating the qualified recipient's intention to refinance the costs of the long term project with section funds.

(D) The date referred to in paragraph (c)(7)(i)(B)(1) and (2) of this section is a date that is the later of—

(1) the date the plan described in paragraph (c)(7)(i)(C) is filed, or

(2) the date the investment becomes a qualified investment by a qualified recipient in active business assets or a development project in a qualified Caribbean Basin country.

(ii) Refinancing of section 936 financing. A section 936 loan or bond issue used to finance a qualified investment described in paragraph (c)(1) of this section may be refinanced with section 936 funds through a new loan or bond issue to the extent of the remaining principal balance on such existing qualified financing, increased by the amount of unpaid interest accrued through the date the new loan proceeds are disbursed or the new obligations are issued and that would be required to be capitalized under U.S. tax rules.

(iii) Prompt application of borrowed proceeds. (A) In general. In the case of a loan or bond issue described in paragraphs (c)(7)(i) or (ii) of this section, the rules of paragraph (c)(6) of this section shall apply but the six-month period described in paragraph (c)(6)(i) of this section shall be limited to 30 days from the date of disbursement of loan proceeds to the qualified recipient or from the date of issuance in the case of a bond issue.

(B) Special rules for long term projects financed out of bond proceeds. In the case of a long term project described in paragraph (c)(6)(iv)(B) of this section that is financed out of bond proceeds, the 30-day period described in paragraph (c)(7)(iii)(A) of this section shall be extended with respect to the amount of bond proceeds used for the permanent financing of the long term project for such reasonable period of time as shall be necessary until completion of the project or beginning of production (in the case of a farming business), but, in any event, not to exceed three years from the date of issuance of the bonds. For purposes of this paragraph (c)(7)(iii)(B), the period of time shall be considered reasonable only if—

(1) A construction and expenditure plan certified by an independent expert (such as an engineer, an architect, or a

farming expert) is filed with, and approved by, the Commissioner of Financial Institutions of Puerto Rico (or his delegate) prior to the date of issue, which makes a reasonable estimate, as of the date of issue, of the amounts and uses of the bond proceeds and the time of completion or production, and includes a schedule of progress payments until such time; and

(2) The terms of the construction and expenditure plan are disclosed in the public offering memorandum, private placement memorandum, or similar document prepared for information or disclosure purposes in relation to the bond issue.

(8) Miscellaneous operating rules. (i) Sale and leaseback. An asset that is acquired and leased back to the person from whom acquired does not constitute an investment in an active business asset or an investment in a development project.

(ii) Use of asset in qualified business activity. For purposes of paragraph (c)(4)(i)(B), an asset shall be considered used or held for use in a qualified business activity if it is used or held for use in such activity under principles similar to those described in § 1.367(a)-2T(b)(5), or a successor provision.

(iii) Definition of capital expenditures. For purposes of this paragraph (c), capital expenditures mean those expenditures described in section 263(a) of the Code (without regard to paragraphs (A) through (G) of section 263(a)(1)), and those costs required to be capitalized under section 263A with respect to property described in section 263A(b)(1), relating to self-constructed assets.

(iv) Loans through certain financial intermediaries. A loan by a qualified financial institution shall not be disqualified from being an investment in active business assets or in a development project merely because the proceeds are first lent to a financial intermediary (as defined in paragraph (c)(8)(iv)(H) of this section) which, in turn, on-lends the proceeds directly to a qualified recipient, provided the requirements of this paragraph (c)(8)(iv) are satisfied.

(A) The loan to the qualified recipient must satisfy the requirements of paragraph (c)(4)(i) of this section in the case of an investment in active business assets, or of paragraph (c)(5)(i) of this section in the case of an investment in a development project.

(B) The qualified recipient and the active business assets or development project in which the proceeds are to be invested must be identified prior to disbursement of any part of the proceeds by the qualified financial institution to the financial intermediary.

(C) The effective interest rate charged by the qualified financial institution to the financial intermediary must not exceed the average interest rate paid by the qualified financial institution with respect to its eligible funds, increased by such number of basis points as is required to provide reasonable compensation to the qualified financial institution for services performed and risks assumed with respect to the loan to the financial intermediary that are not ordinarily required to be performed or assumed with respect to a deposit, loan, repurchase agreement or other transfer of eligible funds with another qualified financial institution. The average interest rate shall be the average rate, determined on a daily basis, paid by the qualified financial institution on its eligible funds over the most recent quarter preceding the date on which the rate on the loan to the financial intermediary is committed.

(D) The effective interest rate charged by the financial intermediary to the qualified recipient must not exceed the effective interest rate charged to the financial intermediary by the qualified financial institution, increased by such number of basis points as is required to provide reasonable compensation to the financial intermediary for services performed and risks assumed with respect to the loan to the qualified recipient.

(E) The financial intermediary must borrow from the qualified financial institution under substantially the same terms as it lends to the qualified recipient. In particular, both loans must have disbursement terms, repayment schedules and maturity dates for interest and principal amounts such that the financial intermediary does not retain for more than 48 hours any of the funds disbursed by the qualified financial institution nor any of the funds paid by the qualified recipient in repayment of principal or interest on the loan.

(F) The financial institution and the financial intermediary must agree to comply with the due diligence requirements described in paragraphs (c)(11), (12), and (13) of this section;

(G) The time periods and temporary investments rules in paragraphs (c)(6) and (7) of this section must be complied with; and

(H) For purposes of this paragraph (c), the financial intermediary must be—

(1) An active trade or business which a person maintains in a qualified Caribbean Basin country and which consists of a banking, financing or similar business as defined in § 1.864-4(c)(5)(i) (other than a central bank of issue); or

(2) A public international organization, the principal purpose of which is to foster economic development in developing countries and which is described in section 1 of the International Organizations Immunities Act (22 U.S.C. § 288).

For purposes of paragraphs (c)(8)(iv)(C) and (D) of this section, the determination of whether compensation is reasonable shall be made in relation to normal commercial practices for comparable transactions carrying a similar degree of commercial, currency and political risk. Reasonable credit enhancement fees and other reasonable fees and amounts charged to the financial intermediary or the qualified recipient with respect to the loan transaction in addition to interest shall be added to the interest cost in determining the effective interest rate.

(v) Small project. For purposes of this paragraph (c), a small project shall be a project (including the acquisition of an asset) for which the total amount of section 936 funds used for its financing does not exceed $1,000,000 in the aggregate, or such other amount as the Commissioner may publish, from time to time, in the Internal Revenue Bulletin.

(9) Qualified recipient. For purposes of this section, a qualified recipient is any person described in paragraphs (c)(9)(i) or (ii) of this section. The term "person" means a person described in section 7701(a)(1) or a government (within the meaning of § 1.892-2T(a)(1)) of a qualified Caribbean Basin country.

(i) In the case of an investment described in paragraph (c)(4) of this section (relating to investments in active business assets), a qualified recipient is a person that carries on a qualified business activity in a qualified Caribbean Basin country, and complies with the agreement and certification requirements described in paragraph (c)(11)(i) of this section at all times during the period in which the investment remains outstanding.

(ii) In the case of an investment described in paragraph (c)(5) of this section (relating to investments in development projects), a qualified recipient is the borrower (including a person empowered by the borrower to authorize expenditures for the investment in the development project) that has authority to comply, and complies, with the agreement and certification requirements described in paragraph (c)(11)(i) of this section at all times during the period in which the investment remains outstanding.

(10) Investments in a qualified Caribbean Basin country. (i) Rules for determining the place of an investment. The rules of this paragraph (c)(10)(i) shall apply to determine the extent to which an investment in an active business asset or a development project will be considered made in qualified Caribbean Basin Country.

(A) An investment in real property is considered made in the qualified Caribbean Basin country in which the real property is located.

(B) Except as otherwise provided in this paragraph (c)(10)(i)(B), an investment in tangible personal property is considered made in a qualified Caribbean Basin Country so long as the tangible personal property is predominantly used in that country. Whether property is used predominantly in a qualified Caribbean Basin country shall be determined under principles similar to those described in § 1.48-1(g)(1), (g)(2)(ii), (g)(2)(iv), (g)(2)(vi), (g)(2)(viii), and (g)(2)(x) (relating to investment tax credits for property used outside the United States) as in effect on December 31, 1985. A vessel, container, or aircraft shall be considered for use predominantly in a qualified Caribbean Basin country in any year if it is used for transport to and from such country with some degree of frequency during that year and at least 30 percent of the income from the use of such vessel, container or aircraft for that year is sourced in such country under principles similar to those described in section 863(c)(1) and (2) (relating to source rules for certain transportation income). Cables and pipelines which are permanently installed as part of a communication or transportation system between a qualified Caribbean Basin country and another country or among several countries which include a qualified Caribbean Basin country shall be considered used in a qualified Caribbean Basin country to the extent of 50 percent of the portion of the facility that directly links the qualified country to another country or to a hub, unless it is established by notice or other guidance published in the Internal Revenue Bulletin or by ruling issued to a qualified institution or qualified recipient upon request that it is appropriate to attribute a greater portion of the cost of the facility to the qualified Caribbean Basin country.

(C) An investment in rights to intangible property is considered made in a qualified Caribbean Basin country to the extent such rights are used in that country. Where rights to intangible property are used shall be determined under principles similar to those described in § 1.954-2T(b)(3)(vii) or a successor provision.

(ii) Qualified Caribbean Basin Country. For purposes of this section, the term "qualified Caribbean Basin country" means any beneficiary country (within the meaning of section 212(a)(1)(A) of the Caribbean Basin Economic Recovery Act, Public Law 98-67 (Aug. 5, 1983), 97 Stat. 384, 19 U.S.C. 2702(a)(1)(A)), which meets the requirements of section 274(h)(6)(A)(i) and (ii) and the U.S. Virgin Islands, and includes the territorial waters and continental shelf thereof.

(11) Agreements and certifications by qualified recipients and financial intermediaries. (i) In general. In order for an investment to be considered a qualified investment under section 936(d)(4) and paragraph (c)(1) of this section, a qualified recipient must certify to the qualified financial institution (or to the financial intermediary, if the loan is made through a financial intermediary) on the date of closing of the loan agreement and on each anniversary date thereof, that it is a qualified recipient described in paragraph (c)(9) of this section. In addition, the qualified recipient must agree in the loan agreement with the qualified financial institution (or with the financial intermediary, if the loan is made through a financial intermediary)—

(A) To use the funds at all times during the period the loan is outstanding solely for the purposes and in the manner described in paragraph (c)(4) of this section (regarding investment in active business assets) or in paragraph (c)(5) of this section (regarding investment in development projects);

(B) To comply with the requirements of paragraph (c)(6) of this section (regarding temporary investments and time periods within which the funds must be invested) and paragraph (c)(7) of this section (regarding the refinancing of existing funding and the time periods within which funding for investments must be secured);

(C) To notify the Assistant Commissioner (International), the qualified financial institution (or the financial intermediary, if the loan is made through a financial intermediary), and the Commissioner of Financial Institutions of Puerto Rico (or his delegate) pursuant to paragraph (c)(14) of this section if it no longer is a qualified recipient or if, for any other reason, the investment has ceased to qualify as a qualified investment described in paragraph (c)(1) of this section, promptly upon the occurrence of such disqualifying event; and

(D) To permit examination by the office of the Assistant Commissioner (International) (or by the office of any District Director authorized by the Assistant Commissioner (International)) and the Commissioner of Financial Institutions of Puerto Rico (or his delegate) of all necessary books and records that are sufficient to verify that the funds were used for investments in active business assets or development projects in conformity with the terms of the loan agreement.

(ii) Certification by a financial intermediary. In the case of a loan by a qualified financial institution to a financial intermediary, the financial intermediary must certify to the qualified financial institution (using the procedures described in paragraph (c)(11)(i) of this section) that it is a financial intermediary described in paragraph (c)(8)(iv)(H) of this section, and must furnish to the qualified financial institution a copy of the qualified recipient's certification described in paragraph (c)(11)(i) of this section and of its loan agreement with the qualified recipient. In addition, the financial intermediary must agree in the loan agreement with the qualified financial institution:

(A) To comply with the requirements of paragraph (c)(8)(iv) of this section; and

(B) To permit examination by the office of the Assistant Commissioner (International) (or by the office of any District Director authorized by the Assistant Commissioner (International)) and the Commissioner of Financial Institutions of Puerto Rico (or his delegate) of all its necessary books and records that are sufficient to verify that the funds were used in conformity with the terms of the loan agreements.

(12) Certification requirements. In order for an investment to be considered a qualified investment under section 936(d)(4), section 936(d)(4)(C)(i) requires that both the person in whose trade or business such investment is made and the financial institution certify to the Secretary of the Treasury and the Commissioner of Financial Institutions of Puerto Rico that the proceeds of the loan will be promptly used

to acquire active business assets or to make other authorized expenditures. This certification requirement is satisfied as to the qualified financial institution, the financial intermediary (if any), and the qualified recipient if the qualified financial institution submits a certificate to both the Assistant Commissioner (International) and to the Commissioner of Financial Institutions of Puerto Rico (or his delegate) pursuant to paragraph (c)(14) of this section upon authorization of the investment by the Commissioner of Financial Institutions and, in any event, prior to the first disbursement of the loan proceeds to the qualified recipient or to the financial intermediary (if any), in which the qualified financial institution—

(i) Represents that, as of the date of the certification, the qualified recipient and the financial intermediary (if any) have complied with the requirements described in paragraph (c)(11) of this section;

(ii) Describes the important terms of the loan to the financial intermediary (if any) and to the qualified recipient, including the amount of the loan, the nature of the investment, the basis for its qualification as an investment in active business assets or a development project under this section, the identity of the financial intermediary (if any) and of the qualified recipient, the qualified Caribbean Basin country involved, and the nature of the collateral or other security used, including any guarantee;

(iii) Agrees to permit examination by the Assistant Commissioner (International) (or by the office of any District Director authorized by the Assistant Commissioner (International)) and the Commissioner of Financial Institutions of Puerto Rico (or his delegate) of all its necessary books and records that are sufficient to verify that the funds were used for investments in active business assets or development projects in conformity with the terms of the loan agreement or agreements with the financial intermediary (if any) and with the qualified recipient; and

(iv) In the case of a single-purpose entity that is a qualified financial institution, discloses the name and address of the entity's trustee or agent, if any, that assists the qualified financial institution in the performance of its due diligence requirement under paragraph (c) of this section, and represents that the trustee or agent has agreed with the qualified financial institution to permit examination by the Assistant Commissioner (International) (or by the office of any District Director authorized by the Assistant Commissioner (International)) and the Commissioner of Financial Institutions of Puerto Rico (or his delegate) of all necessary books and records of such trustee or agent that are sufficient to verify that the funds were used for investments in active business assets or development projects in conformity with the terms of the loan agreement or agreements with the financial intermediary (if any) and with the qualified recipient.

(13) Continuing due diligence requirements. In order to maintain the qualification for an investment under paragraph (c)(1) of this section, the continuing due diligence requirements described in this paragraph (c)(13) must be satisfied.

(i) Requirements of qualified recipient. A qualified recipient must—

(A) Submit annually to the qualified financial institution or to the financial intermediary from which its qualified funds were obtained a copy of its most recent annual financial statement accompanied by an opinion of an independent accountant familiar with the financials of the qualified recipient disclosing the amount of the loan, the current outstanding balance of the loan, describing the assets financed with such loan and the qualified business activity in which such assets are used or the development project for which the loan is used, and stating that there are no reasons to doubt that the loan proceeds have been properly used and continue to be properly used, and

(B) Act in a manner consistent with its representations and agreements described in paragraph (c)(11) of this section.

(ii) Requirements of qualified financial institutions. Except as otherwise provided in paragraph (c)(13)(iii) of this section, a qualified financial institution described in paragraph (c)(3) of this section must maintain in its records and have available for inspection the documentation described in paragraph (c)(13)(ii)(A) or (B) of this section. In addition, the qualified financial institution is required to notify the Assistant Commissioner (International) and the Commissioner of Financial Institutions of Puerto Rico (or his delegate) pursuant to paragraph (c)(14) of this section upon becoming aware that a loan has ceased to be an investment in active business assets or a development project under this section. For purposes of this paragraph (c)(13)(ii), multiple loans for investment in a single qualified business activity or development project will be aggregated in determining what due diligence requirements apply.

(A) In the case of a small project described in paragraph (c)(8)(v) of this section, the following documents must be maintained and available for inspection:

(1) The loan application or other similar document;

(2) The financial statements of the qualified recipient filed as part of the loan application;

(3) The statement required by section 6.4.3(a)(iii) of Puerto Rican Regulation No. 3582; or any successor thereof, signed by the qualified recipient (or its duly authorized representative), acknowledging the receipt of the loan proceeds, describing the assets financed with such loan and the business activity in which such assets are to be used or the development project for which the funds will be utilized, the collateral to be provided for the transaction including any guarantee, and the basis for its qualification as a qualified recipient;

(4) The loan documents; and

(5) In the case of a qualified financial institution that is a single-purpose entity, a copy of the agreement with the entity's trustee or agent, if any, described in paragraph (c)(12)(iv) of this section.

(B) In the case of a disbursement concerning a project that is not a small project described in paragraph (c)(8)(v) of this section, the following documents must be maintained and available for inspection, in addition to the documents required by paragraph (c)(13)(ii)(A) of this section:

(1) A memorandum of credit prepared by an officer of the qualified financial institution (or, in the case of a single purpose entity, an agent of the entity or a trustee for the entity, if any) and signed by the officer of the qualified financial institution, containing the details of the investigation and review that the qualified financial institution, or its trustee or agent, if any, conducted in order to evaluate whether the investment is qualified under paragraph (c)(1) of this section and the opinion of the officer of the qualified financial institution, or the opinion of an officer of the agent of, or of the trustee for, the qualified financial institution, if any, that there is no reasonable ground for belief that the qualified funds will be diverted to a use that is not permitted under the provisions of this section; in making this investigation and review, factors that must be utilized are ones similar to

those listed in Puerto Rico Regulation No. 3582, section 6.4.2;

(2) The annual financial statement of the qualified recipient; and

(3) The written report of an officer of the qualified financial institution, or of an officer of an agent of, or of the trustee for, the qualified financial institution, if any, documenting discussions, both before and after the disbursement of the loan proceeds, with each recipient's accounting, financial and executive personnel with respect to the proposed and actual use of the loan proceeds and his analysis of the annual financial statements of the qualified recipient including an analysis of the statement of sources and uses of funds. After the loan disbursement, such discussions and review shall occur annually during the term of the loan. Such report shall include the conclusion that in such officer's opinion there is no reasonable ground for belief that the qualified recipient is improperly utilizing the funds.

(iii) Requirements in the case of a financial intermediary. Where a qualified financial institution lends funds to a financial intermediary which are on-lent to a qualified recipient—

(A) The obligation to maintain the documentation described in paragraph (c)(13)(ii)(A) or (B) of this section shall apply only to the financial intermediary and not to the qualified financial institution and the provisions of paragraph (c)(13)(ii)(A) or (B) of this section shall be read so as to impose on the financial intermediary any obligation imposed on the qualified financial institution.

(B) The financial intermediary shall forward annually to the qualified financial institution a copy of the documentation it is required to maintain in its records pursuant to the provisions of this paragraph (c)(13)(iii) and shall notify the Assistant Commissioner (International), the Commissioner of Financial Institutions of Puerto Rico (or his delegate) and the qualified financial institution pursuant to paragraph (c)(14) of this section upon becoming aware that a loan has ceased to be an investment in active business assets or a development project under this section. The qualified financial institution must maintain in its records and have available for inspection the documentation furnished by the financial intermediary pursuant to this paragraph (c)(13)(iii)(B).

(C) The qualified financial institution shall cause one of its officers (or one of the officers of its agent or trustee, if any) to prepare a written report documenting his analysis of the documentation furnished by the financial intermediary pursuant to paragraph (c)(13)(iii)(B) of this section, his discussions, both before and after the disbursement of the loan proceeds, with the financial intermediary's accounting, financial and executive personnel with respect to the proposed and actual use of the loan proceeds, and his analysis of the annual financial statements of the qualified recipient including an analysis of the statement of sources and uses of funds. After the loan disbursement, such discussions and review shall occur annually during the term of the loan. Such report shall include the conclusion that in such officer's opinion there is no reasonable ground for belief that the qualified recipient is improperly utilizing the funds.

(14) Procedures for notices and certifications. Notices and certifications to the Assistant Commissioner (International) required under paragraphs (c)(11), (12) and (13) of this section shall be addressed to the attention of the Assistant Commissioner (International), Office of Taxpayer Service and Compliance, IN:C, 950 L'Enfant Plaza South, SW., Washington, DC 20024. Notices and certifications to the Commissioner of Financial Institutions of Puerto Rico required under paragraphs (c)(11), (12), and (13) of this section shall be addressed as follows: Commissioner of Financial Institutions, GPO Box 70324, San Juan, Puerto Rico 00936.

(15) Effective date. This paragraph (c) is effective May 13, 1991. It is applicable to investments by a possessions corporation in a financial institution that are used by a financial institution for investments in accordance with a specific authorization granted by the Commissioner of Financial Institutions of Puerto Rico (or his delegate) after September 22, 1989. However, the taxpayer may choose to apply § 1.936-10T(c) for periods before June 12, 1991.

T.D. 8350, 5/10/91.

PAR. 2. Section 1.936-10 is amended as follows:

1. Paragraph (c)(5)(i)(A) is amended by adding a new sentence at the end of the paragraph to read as set forth below;

2. Paragraph (c)(5)(i)(B)(1) is amended by removing the word "or" at the end of the paragraph.

3. Paragraph (c)(5)(i)(B)(2) is amended by adding the word "or" at the end of the paragraph and paragraph (c)(5)(i)(B)(3) is added to read as set forth below.

4. Paragraph (c)(5)(v) is added to read as set forth below.

5. Paragraphs (c)(9)(i) and (ii) are revised to read as set forth below.

Proposed § 1.936-10 Qualified investments. [*For Preamble, see ¶ 151,269*]

* * * * *

(c) * * *

(5) * * *

(i) * * *

(A) * * * Solely for purposes of a qualified privatization described in paragraph (c)(5)(v) of this section, the amounts disbursed under the loan or bond issue may also be applied to an investment in a corporation, partnership, or trust.

(B) * * *

(3) A qualified privatization described in paragraph (c)(5)(v) of this section;

* * * * *

(v) Qualified privatization. This paragraph (c)(5)(v) is effective for investments made by a possessions corporation in a financial institution for investments in accordance with a specific authorization granted by the Commissioner of Financial Institutions of Puerto Rico (or his delegate) on or after [insert date that is 30 days after publication of the final regulations in the FEDERAL REGISTER] . For purposes of this section, a qualified privatization is a financing transaction that satisfies all of the requirements of this paragraph (c)(5)(v).

(A) The loan must be made to finance the acquisition, directly or through an investment in a corporation, partnership or trust, of any assets that are currently used in a trade or business or were used in a trade or business but are no longer so used at the time of acquisition and a plan exists to continue or resume using those assets in the conduct of an active trade or business. The loan can also be used to finance other costs associated with acquiring the trade or business or placing assets back in service, within the limits set forth in paragraph (c)(4)(iii) of the section.

(B) After the acquisition, the assets must be used in a trade or business conducted as a qualified business activity.

(C) The United States Agency for International Development (USAID) or the Overseas Private Investment Corporation (OPIC) must certify, prior to the acquisition, that, as a result of the transfer of the activity from the public to the private sector, the acquisition is expected to have a significant positive developmental impact in the qualified Caribbean Basin country where the trade or business is conducted. The determination of whether an acquisition has significant positive developmental impact depends upon an analysis measuring the extent to which incremental developmental benefits exceed incremental negative effects. Generally, developmental effects will be measured in relation to the impact of the acquisition on those economic factors generally used to measure the effect of an activity on the economy of a qualified Caribbean Basin country. Those factors include (but are not limited to) increased economic efficiency and innovation conducive to self-sustaining growth, decreased government expenditures or increased direct revenues to the government, an improved balance of payments of the qualified Caribbean Basin country (through expanded exports of goods or services), increased employment over time, reduced cost of capital, increased expenditures for maintenance and operations, increased capital expenditures, increased net output and improved market competitiveness. Negative factors include (but are not limited to) increased capital outflows (e.g., expenditures abroad and repatriation to any foreign shareholders).

(D) During the 3-year period preceding the acquisition, the government of the qualified Caribbean Basin country must have owned an interest, directly or indirectly, in the acquired assets that, by value or voting interest, represented 50 percent or more of the total of such interests in the acquired assets, and such government must have exercised effective control over such assets.

(E) After the acquisition and during all the time that the loan is outstanding, no government or government-controlled entity may own, directly or indirectly, any interest in the acquired assets.

(F) No government or government-controlled entity may exercise any effective control, or managerial or operational responsibility or authority, over the acquired assets at any time during the time that the loan is outstanding. This restriction is not intended to restrict the normal exercise of regulatory authority by a government, provided such power is not exercised in a way that would defeat the intent of the provisions in this paragraph (c)(5)(v)(F).

* * * * *

(9) * * *

(i) In the case of an investment described in paragraph (c)(4) of this section (relating to investments in active business assets) or in paragraph (c)(5)(v) of this section (relating to qualified privatization), a qualified recipient is a person that carries on a qualified business activity in a qualified Caribbean Basin country, and complies with the agreement and certification requirements described in paragraph (c)(11)(i) of this section at all times during the period in which the investment remains outstanding.

(ii) In the case of an investment described in paragraph (c)(5) of this section (relating to investments in development projects), other than an investment described in paragraph (c)(5)(v) of this section, a qualified recipient is the borrower (including a person empowered by the borrower to authorize expenditures for the investment in the development project) that has authority to comply, and complies, with the agreement and certification requirements described in paragraph (c)(11)(i) of this section at all times during the period in which the investment remains outstanding.

§ 1.936-11 New lines of business prohibited.

(a) In general. A possessions corporation that is an existing credit claimant, as defined in section 936(j)(9)(A) and this section, that adds a substantial new line of business during a taxable year, or that has a new line of business that becomes substantial during the taxable year, loses its status as an existing credit claimant for that year and all years subsequent.

(b) New line of business. *(1) In general.* A new line of business is any business activity of the possessions corporation that is not closely related to a pre-existing business of the possessions corporation. The term closely related is defined in paragraph (b)(2) of this section. The term pre-existing business is defined in paragraph (b)(3) of this section.

(2) Closely related. To determine whether a new activity is closely related to a pre-existing business of the possessions corporation all the facts and circumstances must be onsidered, including those set forth in paragraphs (b)(2)(i)(A) through (G) of this section.

(i) Factors. The following factors will help to establish that a new activity is closely related to a pre-existing business activity of the possessions corporation—

(A) The new activity provides products or services very similar to the products or services provided by the pre-existing business;

(B) The new activity markets products and services to the same class of customers;

(C) The new activity is of a type that is normally conducted in the same business location;

(D) The new activity requires the use of similar operating assets;

(E) The new activity's economic success depends on the success of the pre-existing business;

(F) The new activity is of a type that would normally be treated as a unit with the pre-existing business' in the business accounting records; and

(G) The new activity and the pre-existing business are regulated or licensed by the same or similar governmental authority.

(ii) Safe harbors. An activity is not a new line of business if—

(A) If the activity is within the same six-digit North American Industry Classification System (NAICS) code (or four-digit Standard Industrial Classification (SIC) code). The similarity of the NAICS or SIC codes may not be relied upon to determine whether the activity is closely related to a pre-existing business where the code indicates a miscellaneous category;

(B) If the new activity is within the same five-digit NAICS code (or three-digit SIC code) and the facts relating to the new activity also satisfy at least three of the factors listed in paragraphs (b)(2)(i)(A) through (G) of this section; or

(C) If the pre-existing business is making a component product or end-product form, as defined in § 1.936-5(a)(1),Q&A1, and the new business activity is making an integrated product, or an end-product form with fewer excluded components, that is not within the same six-digit NAICS code (or four-digit SIC code) as the pre-existing business solely because the component product and the integrated product (or two end-product forms) have different end-uses.

(3) Pre-existing business. (i) In general. Except as provided in paragraph (b)(3)(ii) of this section, a business activity is a pre-existing business of the existing credit claimant if—

(A) The existing credit claimant was actively engaged in the activity within the possession on or before October 13, 1995; and

(B) The existing credit claimant had elected the benefits of the Puerto Rico and possession tax credit pursuant to an election which was in effect for the taxable year that included October 13, 1995.

(ii) Acquisition of an existing credit claimant. (A) If all the assets of one or more trades or businesses of a corporation of an existing credit claimant are acquired by an affiliated or non-affiliated existing credit claimant which carries on the business activity of the predecessor existing credit claimant, the acquired business activity will be treated as a pre-existing business of the acquiring corporation. A non-affiliated acquiring corporation will not be bound by any section 936(h) election made by the predecessor existing credit claimant with respect to that business activity.

(B) Where all of the assets of one or more trades or businesses of a corporation of an existing credit claimant are acquired by a corporation that is not an existing credit claimant, the acquiring corporation may make a section 936(e) election for the taxable year in which the assets are acquired with the following effects—

(1) The acquiring corporation will be treated as an existing credit claimant for the year of acquisition;

(2) The activity will be considered a pre-existing business of the acquiring corporation;

(3) The acquiring corporation will be deemed to satisfy the rules of section 936(a)(2) for the year of acquisition; and

(4) After making an election under section 936(e), a non-affiliated acquiring corporation will not be bound by elections under sections 936(a)(4) and (h) made by the predecessor existing credit claimant.

(C) For purposes of this section the assets of a trade or business are determined at the time of acquisition provided that the transferee actively conducts the trade or business acquired.

(D) A mere change in the stock ownership of a possessions corporation will not affect its status as an existing credit claimant for purposes of this section.

(4) Leasing of assets. (i) The leasing of assets (and employees to operate leased assets) will not, for purposes of this section, be considered a new line of business of the existing credit claimant if—

(A) the existing credit claimant used the leased assets in an active trade or business for at least five years;

(B) the existing credit claimant does not through its own officers or staff of employees perform management or operational functions (but not including operational functions performed through leased employees) with respect to the leased assets; and

(C) the existing credit claimant does not perform marketing functions with respect to the leasing of the assets.

(ii) Any income from the leasing of assets not considered a new line of business pursuant to paragraph (b)(4)(i) of this section will not be income from the active conduct of a trade or business (and, therefore, the existing credit claimant may not receive a possession tax credit with respect to such income).

(5) Timing rule. The tests for a new line of business in this paragraph (whether the new activity is closely related to a pre-existing business) are applied only at the end of the taxable year during which the new activity is added.

(c) Substantial. *(1) In general.* A new line of business is considered to be substantial as of the earlier of—

(i) The taxable year in which the possessions corporation derives more than 15 percent of its gross income from that new line of business (gross income test); or

(ii) The taxable year in which the possessions corporation directly uses in that new line of business more than 15 percent of its assets (assets test).

(2) Gross income test. The denominator in the gross income test is the amount that is the gross income of the possessions corporation for the current taxable year, while the numerator is the amount that is the gross income of the new line of business for the current taxable year. The gross income test is applied at the end of each taxable year. For purposes of this test, if a new line of business is added late in the taxable year, the income is not to be annualized in that year. In the case of a new line of business acquired through the purchase of assets, the gross income of such new line of business for the taxable year of the acquiring corporation that includes the date of acquisition is determined from the date of acquisition through the end of the taxable year. In the case of a consolidated group election made pursuant to section 936(i)(5), the test applies on a company by company basis and not on a consolidated basis.

(3) Assets test. (i) Computation. The denominator is the adjusted tax basis of the total assets of the possessions corporation for the current taxable year. The numerator is the adjusted tax basis of the total assets utilized in the new line of business for the current taxable year. The assets test is computed annually using all assets including cash and receivables.

(ii) Exception. A new line of business of a possessions corporation will not be treated as substantial as a result of meeting the assets test if an event that is not reasonably anticipated causes assets used in the new line of business of the possessions corporation to exceed 15 percent of the adjusted tax basis of the possessions corporation's total assets. For example, an event that is not reasonably anticipated would include the destruction of plant and equipment of the pre-existing business due to a hurricane or other natural disaster, or other similar circumstances beyond the control of the possessions corporation. The expiration of a patent is not such an event and will not permit use of this exception.

(d) Examples. The following examples illustrate the rules described in paragraphs (a), (b), and (c) of this section. In the following examples, X Corp. is an existing credit claimant unless otherwise indicated:

Example (1). X Corp. is a pharmaceutical corporation which manufactured bulk chemicals (a component product). In March 1997, X Corp. began to also manufacture pills (e.g., finished dosages or an integrated product). The new activity provides products very similar to the products provided by the pre-existing business. The new activity is of a type that is normally conducted in the same business location as the pre-existing business. The activity's economic success depends on the success of the pre-existing business. The manufacture of bulk chemicals is in NAICS code 325411, Medicinal and Botanical Manufacturing, while the manufacture of the pills is in NAICS code 325412, Pharmaceutical Preparation Manufacturing. Although the products have a different end-use, may be marketed to a different class of customers, and may not use similar operating assets, they are within the same five-digit NAICS code and the activity also satisfies paragraphs (b)(2)(i)(A), (C), and (E) of this section. The manufacture of the pills by X Corp. will be considered closely related to the manufacture of the bulk chemicals. Therefore, X Corp. will not be considered to have added a new line of business for purposes of paragraph (b) of this section because it falls within the safe harbor rule of (b)(2)(ii)(B).

Example (2). X Corp. currently manufactures printed circuit boards in a possession. As a result of a technological breakthrough, X Corp. could produce the printed circuit boards more efficiently if it modified its existing production methods. Because demand for its products was high, X Corp. expanded when it modified its production methods. After these modifications to the facilities and production methods, the products produced through the new technology were in the same six-digit NAICS code as products produced previously by X Corp. See paragraph (b)(2)(ii)(A) of this section. Therefore, X Corp. will not be considered to have added a new line of business for purposes of paragraph (b) of this section because it falls within the safe harbor rule of (b)(2)(ii)(A).

Example (3). X Corp. has manufactured Device A in Puerto Rico for a number of years and began to manufacture Device B in Puerto Rico in 1997. Device A and Device B are both used to conduct electrical current to the heart and are both sold to cardiologists. There is no significant change in the type of activity conducted in Puerto Rico after the transfer of the manufacturing of Device B to Puerto Rico. Similar manufacturing equipment, manufacturing processes and skills are used in the manufacture of both devices. Both are regulated and licensed by the Food and Drug Administration. The economic success of Device B is dependent upon the success of Device A only to the extent that the liability and manufacturing prowess with respect to one reflects favorably on the other. Depending upon the heart abnormality, the cardiologist may choose to use Device A, Device B or both on a patient. The manufacture of Device B is treated as a unit with the manufacture of Device A in X Corp.'s accounting records. The manufacture of Device A is in the six-digit NAICS code 339112, Surgical and Medical Instrument Manufacturing. The manufacture of Device B is in the six-digit NAICS code 334510, Electromedical and Electrotherapeutic Apparatus Manufacturing. (The manufacture of Device A is in the four-digit SIC code 3845, Electromedical and Electrotherapeutic Apparatus. The manufacture of Device B is in the four-digit SIC code 3841, Surgical and Medical Instruments and Apparatus.) The safe harbor of paragraph (b)(2)(ii)(B) of this section applies because the two activities are within the same three-digit SIC code and Corp. X satisfies paragraphs (b)(2)(i)(A), (B), (C), (D), (F), and (G) of this section.

Example (4). X Corp. has been manufacturing house slippers in Puerto Rico since 1990. Y Corp. is a U.S. corporation that is not affiliated with X Corp. and is not an existing credit claimant. Y Corp. has been manufacturing snack food in the United States. In 1997, X Corp. purchased the assets of Y Corp. and began to manufacture snack food in Puerto Rico. House slipper manufacturing is in the six-digit NAICS code 316212 (Four-digit SIC code 3142, House Slippers). The manufacture of snack foods falls under the six-digit NAICS code 311919, Other Snack Food Manufacturing (four-digit SIC code 2052, Cookies and Crackers (pretzels)). Because these activities are not within the same five or six digit NAICS code (or the same three or four-digit SIC code), and because snack food is not an integrated product that contains house slippers, the safe harbor of paragraph (b)(2)(ii) of this section cannot apply. Considering all the facts and circumstances, including the seven factors of paragraph (b)(2)(i) of this section, the snack food manufacturing activity is not closely related to the manufacture of house slippers, and is a new line of business, within the meaning of paragraph (b) of this section.

Example (5). X Corp., a calendar year taxpayer, is an existing credit claimant that has elected the profit-split method for computing taxable income. P Corp. was not an existing credit claimant and manufactured a product in a different five-digit NAICS code than the product manufactured by X Corp. In 1997, X Corp. acquired the stock of P Corp. and liquidated P Corp. in a tax-free liquidation under section 332, but continued the business activity of P Corp. as a new business segment. Assume that this new business segment is a new line of business within the meaning of paragraph (c) of this section. In 1997, X Corp. has gross income from the active conduct of a trade or business in a possession computed under section 936(a)(2) of $500 million and the adjusted tax basis of its assets is $200 million. The new business segment had gross income of $60 million, or 12 percent of the X Corp. gross income, and the adjusted basis of the new segment's assets was $20 million, or 10 percent of the X Corp. total assets. In 1997, X Corp. does not derive more than 15 percent of its gross income, or directly use more that 15 percent of its total assets, from the new business segment. Thus, the new line of business acquired from P Corp. is not a substantial new line of business within the meaning of paragraph (c) of this section, and the new activity will not cause X Corp. to lose its status as an existing credit claimant during 1997. In 1998, however, the gross income of X Corp. grew to $750 million while the gross income of the new line of business grew to $150 million, or 20% of the X Corp. 1998 gross income. Thus, in 1998, the new line of business is substantial within the meaning of paragraph (c) of this section, and X Corp. loses its status as an existing credit claimant for 1998 and all years subsequent.

(e) Loss of status as existing credit claimant. An existing credit claimant that adds a substantial new line of business in a taxable year, or that has a new line of business that becomes substantial in a taxable year, loses its status as an existing credit claimant for that year and all years subsequent.

(f) Effective date. *(1) General rule.* This section applies to taxable years of a possessions corporation beginning on or after January 25, 2000.

(2) Election for retroactive application. Taxpayers may elect to apply retroactively all the provisions of this section for any open taxable year beginning after December 31, 1995. Such election will be effective for the year of the election and all subsequent taxable years. This section will not apply to activities of pre-existing businesses for taxable years beginning before January 1, 1996.

T.D. 8868, 1/21/2000.

§ 1.937-1 Bona fide residency in a possession.

(a) Scope. *(1) In general.* Section 937(a) and this section set forth the rules for determining whether an individual qualifies as a bona fide resident of a particular possession (the relevant possession) for purposes of subpart D, part III, Subchapter N, Chapter 1 of the Internal Revenue Code as well as section 865(g)(3), section 876, section 881(b), paragraphs (2) and (3) of section 901(b), section 957(c), section 3401(a)(8)(C), and section 7654(a).

(2) Definitions. For purposes of this section and §§ 1.937-2 and 1.937-3—

(i) Possession means one of the following United States possessions: American Samoa, Guam, the Northern Mariana Islands, Puerto Rico, or the Virgin Islands. When used in a geographical sense, the term comprises only the territory of each such possession (without application of sections 932(c)(3) and 935(c)(2) (as in effect before the effective date of its repeal)).

(ii) United States, when used in a geographical sense, is defined in section 7701(a)(9), and without application of sections 932(a)(3) and 935(c)(1) (as in effect before the effective date of its repeal).

(b) Bona fide resident. *(1) General rule.* An individual qualifies as a bona fide resident of the relevant possession if such individual satisfies the requirements of paragraphs (c) through (e) of this section with respect to such possession.

(2) Special rule for members of the Armed Forces. A member of the Armed Forces of the United States who qualified as a bona fide resident of the relevant possession in a prior taxable year is deemed to have satisfied the requirements of paragraphs (c) through (e) of this section for a subsequent taxable year if such individual otherwise is unable to satisfy such requirements by reason of being absent from such possession or present in the United States during such year solely in compliance with military orders. Conversely, a member of the Armed Forces of the United States who did not qualify as a bona fide resident of the relevant possession in a prior taxable year is not considered to have satisfied the requirements of paragraphs (c) through (e) of this section for a subsequent taxable year by reason of being present in such possession solely in compliance with military orders. Armed Forces of the United States is defined (and members of the Armed Forces are described) in section 7701(a)(15).

(3) Juridical persons. Except as provided in § 1.881-5(f):

(i) Only natural persons may qualify as bona fide residents of a possession; and

(ii) The rules governing the tax treatment of bona fide residents of a possession do not apply to juridical persons (including corporations, partnerships, trusts, and estates).

(4) Transition rule. For taxable years beginning before October 23, 2004, and ending after October 22, 2004, an individual is considered to qualify as a bona fide resident of the relevant possession if that individual would be a bona fide resident of the relevant possession by applying the principles of §§ 1.871-2 through 1.871-5.

(5) Special rule for cessation of bona fide residence in Puerto Rico. See paragraph (f)(2)(ii) of this section for a special rule applicable to a citizen of the United States who ceases to be a bona fide resident of Puerto Rico during a taxable year.

(c) Presence test. *(1) In general.* A United States citizen or resident alien individual (as defined in section 7701(b)(1)(A)) satisfies the requirements of this paragraph (c) for a taxable year if that individual—

(i) Was present in the relevant possession for at least 183 days during the taxable year;

(ii) Was present in the relevant possession for at least 549 days during the three-year period consisting of the taxable year and the two immediately preceding taxable years, provided that the individual was also present in the relevant possession for at least 60 days during each taxable year of the period;

(iii) Was present in the United States for no more than 90 days during the taxable year;

(iv) During the taxable year had earned income (as defined in § 1.911-3(b)) in the United States, if any, not exceeding in the aggregate the amount specified in section 861(a)(3)(B) and was present for more days in the relevant possession than in the United States; or

(v) Had no significant connection to the United States during the taxable year. See paragraph (c)(5) of this section.

(2) Special rule for alien individuals. A nonresident alien individual (as defined in section 7701(b)(1)(B)) satisfies the requirements of this paragraph (c) for a taxable year if during that taxable year that individual satisfies the substantial presence test of § 301.7701(b)-1(c) of this chapter (except for the substitution of the name of the relevant possession for the term United States where appropriate).

(3) Days of presence. For purposes of paragraph (c)(1) of this section—

(i) An individual is considered to be present in the relevant possession on:

(A) Any day that the individual is physically present in that possession at any time during the day;

(B) Any day that an individual is outside of the relevant possession to receive, or to accompany on a full-time basis a parent, spouse, or child (as defined in section 152(f)(1)) who is receiving, qualifying medical treatment as defined in paragraph (c)(4) of this section; and

(C) Any day that an individual is outside the relevant possession because the individual leaves or is unable to return to the relevant possession during any—

(*1*) 14-day period within which a major disaster occurs in the relevant possession for which a Federal Emergency Management Agency Notice of a Presidential declaration of a major disaster is issued in the Federal Register; or

(*2*) Period for which a mandatory evacuation order is in effect for the geographic area in the relevant possession in which the individual's place of abode is located.

(ii) An individual is considered to be present in the United States on any day that the individual is physically present in the United States at any time during the day. Notwithstanding the preceding sentence, the following days will not count as days of presence in the United States:

(A) Any day that an individual is temporarily present in the United States under circumstances described in paragraph (c)(3)(i)(B) or (C) of this section;

(B) Any day that an individual is in transit between two points outside the United States (as described in § 301.7701(b)-3(d) of this chapter), and is physically present in the United States for fewer than 24 hours;

(C) Any day that an individual is temporarily present in the United States as a professional athlete to compete in a charitable sports event (as described in § 301.7701(b)-3(b)(5) of this chapter);

(D) Any day that an individual is temporarily present in the United States as a student (as defined in section 152(f)(2)); and

(E) In the case of an individual who is an elected representative of the relevant possession, or who serves full time as an elected or appointed official or employee of the government of the relevant possession (or any political subdivision thereof), any day spent serving the relevant possession in that role.

(iii) If, during a single day, an individual is physically present—

(A) In the United States and in the relevant possession, that day is considered a day of presence in the relevant possession;

(B) In two possessions, that day is considered a day of presence in the possession where the individual's tax home is located (applying the rules of paragraph (d) of this section).

(4) Qualifying medical treatment. (i) In general. The term qualifying medical treatment means medical treatment provided by (or under the supervision of) a physician (as defined in section 213(d)(4)) for an illness, injury, impairment, or physical or mental condition that satisfies the documentation and production requirements of paragraph (c)(4)(iii) of this section and that involves—

(A) Any period of inpatient care in a hospital or hospice and any period immediately before or after that inpatient care to the extent it is medically necessary; or

(B) Any temporary period of inpatient care in a residential medical care facility for medically necessary rehabilitation services;

(ii) Inpatient care. The term inpatient care means care requiring an overnight stay in a hospital, hospice, or residential medical care facility, as the case may be.

(iii) Documentation and production requirements. In order to satisfy the documentation and production requirements of this paragraph, an individual must, with respect to each qualifying medical treatment, prepare (or obtain), maintain, and, upon a request by the Commissioner (or the person responsible for tax administration in the relevant possession), make available within 30 days of such request:

(A) Records that provide—

(1) The patient's name and relationship to the individual (if the medical treatment is provided to a person other than the individual);

(2) The name and address of the hospital, hospice, or residential medical care facility where the medical treatment was provided;

(3) The name, address, and telephone number of the physician who provided the medical treatment;

(4) The date(s) on which the medical treatment was provided; and

(5) Receipt(s) of payment for the medical treatment;

(B) Signed certification by the providing or supervising physician that the medical treatment was qualified medical treatment within the meaning of paragraph (c)(4)(i) of this section, and setting forth—

(1) The patient's name;

(2) A reasonably detailed description of the medical treatment provided by (or under the supervision of) the physician;

(3) The dates on which the medical treatment was provided; and

(4) The medical facts that support the physician's certification and determination that the treatment was medically necessary; and

(C) Such other information as the Commissioner may prescribe by notice, form, instructions, or other publication (see § 601.601(d)(2) of this chapter).

(5) Significant connection. For purposes of paragraph (c)(1)(v) of this section—

(i) The term significant connection to the United States means—

(A) A permanent home in the United States;

(B) Current registration to vote in any political subdivision of the United States; or

(C) A spouse or child (as defined in section 152(f)(1)) who has not attained the age of 18 whose principal place of abode is in the United States other than—

(1) A child who is in the United States because the child is living with a custodial parent under a custodial decree or multiple support agreement; or

(2) A child who is in the United States as a student (as defined in section 152(f)(2)).

(ii) Permanent home. (A) General rule. For purposes of paragraph (c)(5)(i)(A) of this section, except as provided in paragraph (c)(5)(ii)(B) of this section, the term permanent home has the same meaning as in § 301.7701(b)-2(d)(2) of this chapter.

(B) Exception for rental property. If an individual or the individual's spouse owns property and rents it to another person at any time during the taxable year, then notwithstanding that the rental property may constitute a permanent home under § 301.7701(b)-2(d)(2) of this chapter, it is not a permanent home under this paragraph (c)(5)(ii) unless the taxpayer uses any portion of it as a residence during the taxable year under the principles of section 280A(d). In applying the principles of section 280A(d) for this purpose, an individual is treated as using the rental property for personal purposes on any day determined under the principles of section 280A(d)(2) or on any day that the rental property (or any portion of it) is not rented to another person at fair rental for the entire day. The rental property is not used for personal purposes on any day on which the principal purpose of the use of the rental property is to perform repair or maintenance work on the property. Whether the principal purpose of the use of the rental property is to perform repair or maintenance work is determined in light of all the facts and circumstances including, but not limited to, the following: The amount of time devoted to repair and maintenance work, the frequency of the use for repair and maintenance purposes during a taxable year, and the presence and activities of companions.

(iii) For purposes of this paragraph (c)(5), the term spouse does not include a spouse from whom the individual is legally separated under a decree of divorce or separate maintenance.

(d) Tax home test. *(1) General rule.* Except as provided in paragraph (d)(2) of this section, an individual satisfies the requirements of this paragraph (d) for a taxable year if that individual did not have a tax home outside the relevant possession during any part of the taxable year. For purposes of section 937 and this section, an individual's tax home is determined under the principles of section 911(d)(3) without regard to the second sentence thereof. Thus, under section 937, an individual's tax home is considered to be located at the individual's regular or principal (if more than one regular) place of business. If the individual has no regular or principal place of business because of the nature of the business, or because the individual is not engaged in carrying on any trade or business within the meaning of section 162(a), then the individual's tax home is the individual's regular place of abode in a real and substantial sense.

(2) Exceptions. (i) Year of move. See paragraph (f) of this section for a special rule applicable to an individual who becomes or ceases to be a bona fide resident of the relevant possession during a taxable year.

(ii) Special rule for seafarers. For purposes of section 937 and this section, an individual is not considered to have a tax home outside the relevant possession solely by reason of employment on a ship or other seafaring vessel that is predominantly used in local and international waters. For this purpose, a vessel is considered to be predominantly used in local and international waters if, during the taxable year, the aggregate amount of time it is used in international waters and in the waters within three miles of the relevant possession exceeds the aggregate amount of time it is used in the territorial waters of the United States, another possession, and a foreign country.

(iii) Special rule for students and government officials. Any days described in paragraphs (c)(3)(ii)(D) and (E) of this section are disregarded for purposes of determining whether an individual has a tax home outside the relevant possession under paragraph (d)(1) of this section during any part of the taxable year.

(e) Closer connection test. *(1) General rule.* Except as provided in paragraph (e)(2) of this section, an individual satisfies the requirements of this paragraph (e) for a taxable year if that individual did not have a closer connection to the United States or a foreign country than to the relevant possession during any part of the taxable year. For purposes of this paragraph (e)—

(i) The principles of section 7701(b)(3)(B)(ii) and § 301.7701(b)-2(d) of this chapter apply (without regard to the final sentence of § 301.7701(b)-2(b) of this chapter); and

(ii) An individual's connections to the relevant possession are compared to the aggregate of the individual's connections with the United States and foreign countries.

(2) Exception for year of move. See paragraph (f) of this section for a special rule applicable to an individual who becomes or ceases to be a bona fide resident of the relevant possession during a taxable year.

(f) Year of move. *(1) Move to a possession.* For the taxable year in which an individual's residence changes to the relevant possession, the individual satisfies the requirements of paragraphs (d)(1) and (e)(1) of this section if—

(i) For each of the 3 taxable years immediately preceding the taxable year of the change of residence, the individual is not a bona fide resident of the relevant possession;

(ii) For each of the last 183 days of the taxable year of the change of residence, the individual does not have a tax home outside the relevant possession or a closer connection to the United States or a foreign country than to the relevant possession; and

(iii) For each of the 3 taxable years immediately following the taxable year of the change of residence, the individual is a bona fide resident of the relevant possession.

(2) Move from a possession. (i) General rule. Except for a bona fide resident of Puerto Rico to whom § 1.933-1(b) and paragraph (f)(2)(ii) of this section apply, for the taxable year in which an individual ceases to be a bona fide resident of the relevant possession, the individual satisfies the requirements of paragraphs (d)(1) and (e)(1) of this section if—

(A) For each of the 3 taxable years immediately preceding the taxable year of the change of residence, the individual is a bona fide resident of the relevant possession;

(B) For each of the first 183 days of the taxable year of the change of residence, the individual does not have a tax home outside the relevant possession or a closer connection to the United States or a foreign country than to the relevant possession; and

(C) For each of the 3 taxable years immediately following the taxable year of the change of residence, the individual is not a bona fide resident of the relevant possession.

(ii) Year of move from Puerto Rico. Notwithstanding an individual's failure to satisfy the presence, tax home, or closer connection test prescribed under paragraph (b)(1) of this section for the taxable year, the individual is a bona fide resident of Puerto Rico for that part of the taxable year described in paragraph (f)(2)(ii)(E) of this section if the individual—

(A) Is a citizen of the United States;

(B) Is a bona fide resident of Puerto Rico for a period of at least 2 taxable years immediately preceding the taxable year;

(C) Ceases to be a bona fide resident of Puerto Rico during the taxable year;

(D) Ceases to have a tax home in Puerto Rico during the taxable year; and

(E) Has a closer connection to Puerto Rico than to the United States or a foreign country throughout the part of the taxable year preceding the date on which the individual ceases to have a tax home in Puerto Rico.

(g) Examples. The principles of this section are illustrated by the following examples:

Example (1). Presence test. H, a U.S. citizen, is engaged in a profession that requires frequent travel. H spends 195 days of each of the years 2005 and 2006 in Possession N. In 2007, H spends 160 days in Possession N. Under paragraph (c)(1)(ii), H satisfies the presence test of paragraph (c) of this section with respect to Possession N for taxable year 2007. Assuming that in 2007 H does not have a tax home outside of Possession N and does not have a closer connection to the United States or a foreign country under paragraphs (d) and (e) of this section respectively, then regardless of whether H was a bona fide resident of Possession N in 2005 and 2006, H is a bona fide resident of Possession N for taxable year 2007.

Example (2). Presence test. W, a U.S. citizen, lives for part of the taxable year in a condominium, which she owns, located in Possession P. W also owns a house in State N where she lives for 120 days every year to be near her grown children and grandchildren. W is retired and her income consists solely of pension payments, dividends, interest, and Social Security benefits. For 2006, W is only present in Possession P for a total of 175 days because of a 70-day vacation to Europe and Asia. Thus, for taxable year 2006, W is not present in Possession P for at least 183 days, is present in the United States for more than 90 days, and has a significant connection to the United States by reason of her permanent home. However, under paragraph (c)(1)(iv) of this section, W still satisfies the presence test of paragraph (c) of this section with respect to Possession P because she has no earned income in the United States and is present for more days in Possession P than in the United States.

Example (3). Presence test. T, a U.S. citizen, was born and raised in State A, where his mother still lives in the house in which T grew up. T is a sales representative for a company based in Possession V. T lives with his wife and minor children in their house in Possession V. T is registered to vote in Possession V and not in the United States. In 2006, T spends 120 days in State A and another 120 days in foreign countries. When traveling on business to State A, T often stays at his mother's house in the bedroom he used when he was a child. T's stays are always of short duration, and T asks for his mother's permission before visiting to make sure that no other guests are using the room and that she agrees to have him as a guest in her house at that time. Therefore, under paragraph (c)(5)(ii) of this section, T's mother's house is not a permanent home of T. Assuming that no other accommodations in the United States constitute a permanent home with respect to T, then under paragraphs (c)(1)(v) and (c)(5) of this section, T has no significant connection to the United States. Accordingly, T satisfies the presence test of paragraph (c) of this section for taxable year 2006.

Example (4). Alien resident of possession— presence test. F is a citizen of Country G. F's tax home is in Possession C and F has no closer connection to the United States or a foreign country than to Possession C. F is present in Possession C for 123 days and in the United States for 110 days every year. Accordingly, F is a nonresident alien with respect to the United States under section 7701(b), and a bona fide resident of Possession C under paragraphs (b), (c)(2), (d), and (e) of this section.

Example (5). Seafarers— tax home. S, a U.S. citizen, is employed by a fishery and spends 250 days at sea on a fishing vessel in 2006. When not at sea, S resides with his wife at a house they own in Possession G. The fishing vessel upon which S works departs and arrives at various ports in Possession G, other possessions, and foreign countries, but is in international and local waters (within the meaning of paragraph (d)(2) of this section) for 225 days in 2006. Under paragraph (d)(2) of this section, for taxable year 2006, S will not be considered to have a tax home outside Possession G for purposes of section 937 and this section solely by reason of S's employment on board the fishing vessel.

Example (6). Seasonal workers—tax home and closer connection. P, a U.S. citizen, is a permanent employee of a hotel in Possession I, but works only during the tourist season. For the remainder of each year, P lives with her husband and children in Possession Q, where she has no outside employment. Most of P's personal belongings, including her automobile, are located in Possession Q. P is registered to vote in, and has a driver's license issued by, Possession Q. P does her personal banking in Possession Q and P routinely lists her address in Possession Q as her permanent address on forms and documents. P satisfies the presence test of paragraph (c) of this section with respect to both Possession Q and Possession I, because, among other reasons, under paragraph (c)(1)(iii) of this section she does not spend more than 90 days in the United States during the taxable year. P satisfies the tax home test of paragraph (d) of this section only with respect to Possession I, because her regular place of business is in Possession I. P satisfies the closer connection test of paragraph (e) of this section with respect to both Possession Q and Possession I, because she does not have a closer connection to the United States or to any foreign country (and possessions generally are not treated as foreign countries). Therefore, P is a bona fide resident of Possession I for purposes of the Internal Revenue Code.

Example (7). Closer connection to United States than to possession. Z, a U.S. citizen, relocates to Possession V in a prior taxable year to start an investment consulting and venture capital business. Z's wife and two teenage children remain in State C to allow the children to complete high school. Z travels back to the United States regularly to see his wife and children, to engage in business activities, and to take vacations. He has an apartment available for his full-time use in Possession V, but he remains a joint owner of the residence in State C where his wife and children reside. Z and his family have automobiles and personal belongings such as furniture, clothing, and jewelry located at both residences. Although Z is a member of the Possession V Chamber of Commerce, Z also belongs to and has current relationships with social, political, cultural, and religious organizations in State C. Z receives mail in State C, including brokerage statements, credit card bills, and bank advices. Z conducts his personal banking activities in State C. Z holds a State C driver's license and is registered to vote in State C. Based on the totality of the particular facts and circumstances pertaining to Z, Z is not a bona fide resident of Possession V because he has a closer connection to the United States than to Possession V and therefore fails to satisfy the requirements of paragraphs (b)(1) and (e) of this section.

Example (8). Year of move to possession. D, a U.S. citizen, files returns on a calendar year basis. From January 2003 through May 2006, D resides in State R. In June 2006, D moves to Possession N, purchases a house, and accepts a permanent position with a local employer. D's principal place of business from July 1 through December 31, 2006 is in Possession N, and during that period (which totals at least 183 days) D does not have a closer connection to the United States or a foreign country than to Possession N. For the remainder of 2006, and throughout years 2007 through 2009, D continues to live and work in Possession N and maintains a closer connection to Possession N than to the United States or any foreign country. D satisfies the tax home and closer connection tests for 2006 under paragraphs (d)(2), (e)(2), and (f)(1) of this section. Accordingly, assuming that D also satisfies the presence test in paragraph (c) of this section, D is a bona fide resident of Possession N for all of taxable year 2006.

Example (9). Year of move from possession (other than Puerto Rico). J, a U.S. citizen, files returns on a calendar year basis. From January 2007 through December 2009, J is a bona fide resident of Possession C because she satisfies the requirements of paragraph (b)(1) of this section for each year. J continues to reside in Possession C until September 6, 2010, when she accepts new employment and moves to State H. J's principal place of business from January 1 through September 5, 2010 is in Possession C, and during that period (which totals at least 183 days) J does not have a closer connection to the United States or a foreign country than to Possession C. For the remainder of 2010 and throughout years 2011 through 2013, D continues to live and work in State H and is not a bona fide resident of Possession C. J satisfies the tax home and closer connection tests for 2010 with respect to Possession C under paragraphs (d)(2)(i), (e)(2), and (f)(2)(i) of this section. Accordingly, assuming that J also satisfies the presence test of paragraph (c) of this section, J is a bona fide resident of Possession C for all of taxable year 2010.

Example (10). Year of move from Puerto Rico. R, a U.S. citizen who files returns on a calendar year basis satisfies the requirements of paragraphs (b) through (e) of this section for years 2006 and 2007. From January through April 2008, R continues to reside and maintain his principal place of business in and closer connection to Puerto Rico. On May 5, 2008, R moves and changes his principal place of business (tax home) to State N and later that year establishes a closer connection to the United States than to Puerto Rico. R does not satisfy the presence test of paragraph (c) for 2008 with respect to Puerto Rico. Moreover, because R had a tax home outside of Puerto Rico and establishes a closer connection to the United States in 2008, R does not satisfy the requirements of paragraph (d)(1) or (e)(1) of this section for 2008. However, because R was a bona fide resident of Puerto Rico for at least two taxable years before his change of residence to State N in 2008, he is a bona fide resident of Puerto Rico from January 1 through May 4, 2008 under paragraphs (b)(5) and (f)(2)(ii) of this section. See section 933(2) and § 1.933-1(b) for rules on attribution of income.

(h) Information reporting requirement. The following individuals are required to file notice of their new tax status in such time and manner as the Commissioner may prescribe by notice, form, instructions, or other publication (see § 601.601(d)(2) of this chapter):

(1) Individuals who take the position for U.S. tax reporting purposes that they qualify as bona fide residents of a possession for a tax year subsequent to a tax year for which they were required to file Federal income tax returns as citizens or residents of the United States who did not so qualify.

(2) Citizens and residents of the United States who take the position for U.S. tax reporting purposes that they do not qualify as bona fide residents of a possession for a tax year subsequent to a tax year for which they were required to file income tax returns (with the Internal Revenue Service, the tax authorities of a possession, or both) as individuals who did so qualify.

(3) Bona fide residents of Puerto Rico or a section 931 possession (as defined in § 1.931-1T(c)(1)) who take a position for U.S. tax reporting purposes that they qualify as bona fide residents of that possession for a tax year subsequent to a tax year for which they were required to file income tax returns as bona fide residents of the United States Virgin Islands or a section 935 possession (as defined in § 1.935-1T(a)(3)(i)).

(i) Effective date. Except as provided in this paragraph (i), this section applies to taxable years ending after January 31, 2006. Paragraph (h) of this section also applies to a taxpayer's 3 taxable years immediately preceding the taxpayer's first taxable year ending after October 22, 2004. Taxpayers also may choose to apply this section in its entirety to all taxable years ending after October 22, 2004 for which the statute of limitations under section 6511 is open.

T.D. 9248, 1/30/2006, amend T.D. 9297, 11/13/2006.

Proposed § 1.937-1 Bona fide residency in a possession. [*For Preamble, see ¶ 152,645*]

• ***Caution:*** This Notice of Proposed Rulemaking was partially finalized by TD 9248, 01/30/2006. Regs. §§ 1.1-1, 1.170A-1, 1.861-3, 1.861-8, 1.871-1, 1.876-1, 1.881-5, 1.884-0, 1.901-1, 1.931-1, 1.932-1, 1.933-1, 1.934-1, 1.935-1, 1.937-2, 1.937-3, 1.957-3, 1.1402(a)-12, 1.6038-2, 1.6046-1, 301.6688-1, 301.7701-3, and 301.7701(b)-1 remain proposed.

[The text of the proposed § 1.937-1 is the same as the text of § 1.937-1T published elsewhere in this issue of the Federal Register]. [*See T.D. 9194, 4/11/2005, 70 Fed. Reg. 68.*]

Proposed § 1.937-2 Income from sources within a possession. [*For Preamble, see ¶ 152,645*]

• ***Caution:*** This Notice of Proposed Rulemaking was partially finalized by TD 9248, 01/30/2006. Regs. §§ 1.1-1, 1.170A-1, 1.861-3, 1.861-8, 1.871-1, 1.876-1, 1.881-5, 1.884-0, 1.901-1, 1.931-1, 1.932-1, 1.933-1, 1.934-1, 1.935-1, 1.937-2, 1.937-3, 1.957-3, 1.1402(a)-12, 1.6038-2, 1.6046-1, 301.6688-1, 301.7701-3, and 301.7701(b)-1 remain proposed.

[The text of the proposed § 1.937-2 is the same as the text of § 1.937-2T published elsewhere in this issue of the Federal Register]. [*See T.D. 9194, 4/11/2005, 70 Fed. Reg. 68.*]

§ 1.937-2T Income from sources within a possession (temporary).

• ***Caution:*** Under Code Sec. 7805, temporary regulations expire within three years of the date of issuance. This temporary regulation was issued on 4/6/2005.

(a) Scope. Section 937(b) and this section set forth the rules for determining whether income is considered to be from sources within a particular possession (the relevant possession) for purposes of the Internal Revenue Code, including section 957(c) and Subpart D, Part III, Subchapter N, Chapter 1 of the Internal Revenue Code, as well as section 7654(a) of the 1954 Internal Revenue Code (until the effective date of its repeal). Paragraphs (c)(1)(ii) and (c)(2) of this section do not apply, however, for purposes of sections 932(a) and (b) and 935(a)(3) (as in effect before the effective date of its repeal). In the case of a possession or territory that administers income tax laws that are identical (except for the substitution of the name of the possession or territory for the term United States where appropriate) to those in force in the United States, these rules do not apply for purposes of the application of such laws. These rules also do not affect the determination of whether income is considered to be from sources without the United States for purposes of the Internal Revenue Code.

(b) In general. Except as provided in paragraphs (c) through (i) of this section, the principles of sections 861 through 865 and the regulations thereunder (relating to the determination of the gross and the taxable income from sources within and without the United States) generally shall be applied in determining the gross and the taxable income from sources within and without the relevant possession. In the application of such principles, the name of the relevant possession shall be used instead of the term United States, the term bona fide resident of followed by the name of the relevant possession shall be used instead of the term United States resident, and the term domestic shall be construed to mean created or organized in such possession.

(c) U.S. income. *(1) In general.* Except as provided in paragraph (d) of this section, income from sources within the relevant possession shall not include any item of income determined under the rules of sections 861 through 865 and the regulations thereunder to be—

(i) From sources within the United States; or

(ii) Effectively connected with the conduct of a trade or business within the United States.

(2) Conduit arrangements. Income shall be considered to be from sources within the United States for purposes of paragraph (c)(1) of this section if, pursuant to a plan or arrangement—

(i) The income is received in exchange for consideration provided to another person; and

(ii) Such person (or another person) provides the same consideration (or consideration of a like kind) to a third person in exchange for one or more payments constituting income from sources within the United States.

(d) Income from certain sales of inventory property. For special rules that apply to determine the source of income from certain sales of inventory property, see § 1.863-3(f).

(e) Income from services. *(1) No de minimis rule.* In applying the principles of section 861 and the regulations thereunder pursuant to paragraph (b) of this section, the exception in section 861(a)(3) shall not apply.

(2) Service in the Armed Forces. In the case of a member of the Armed Forces of the United States, the following rules shall apply for determining the source of compensation for services performed in compliance with military orders:

(i) If the individual is a bona fide resident of a possession and such services are performed in the United States or in another possession, the compensation constitutes income from sources within the possession of which the individual is a bona fide resident (and not from sources within the United States or such other possession).

(ii) If the individual is not a bona fide resident of a possession and such services are performed in a possession, the compensation constitutes income from sources within the United States (and not from sources within such possession).

(f) Gains from certain dispositions of property. *(1) Property of former U.S. residents.*

(i) Income from sources within the relevant possession shall not include gains from the disposition of property described in paragraph (f)(1)(ii) of this section by an individual described in paragraph (f)(1)(iii) of this section. See also section 1277(e) of Public Law 99-514 (100 Stat. 2985) (providing that gains from the disposition of certain property by individuals who acquired residency in certain possessions shall be considered to be from sources within the United States).

(ii) Property is described in this paragraph (f)(1)(ii) when the following conditions are satisfied—

(A) The property is of a kind described in section 731(c)(3)(C)(i) or 954(c)(1)(B); and

(B) The property was owned by the individual before such individual became a bona fide resident of the relevant possession.

(iii) An individual is described in this paragraph (f)(1)(iii) when the following conditions are satisfied—

(A) For the taxable year for which the source of the gain must be determined, the individual is a bona fide resident of the relevant possession; and

(B) For any of the 10 years preceding such year, the individual was a citizen or resident of the United States (other than a bona fide resident of the relevant possession).

(iv) If an individual described in paragraph (f)(1)(iii) of this section exchanges property described in paragraph (f)(1)(ii) of this section for other property in a transaction in which gain or loss is not required to be recognized (in whole or in part) under U.S. income tax principles, such other property shall also be considered property described in paragraph (f)(1)(ii) of this section.

(v) If an individual described in paragraph (f)(1)(iii) of this section owns, directly or indirectly, at least 10 percent (by value) of any entity to which property described in paragraph (f)(1)(ii) of this section is transferred in a transaction in which gain or loss is not required to be recognized (in whole or in part) under U.S. income tax principles, any gain recognized upon a disposition of the property by such entity shall be treated as income from sources outside the relevant possession if any gain recognized upon a direct or indirect disposition of the individual's interest in such entity would have been so treated under paragraph (f)(1)(iv) of this section.

(2) Special rules under section 865 for possessions. (i) Except as provided in paragraph (f)(1) of this section—

(A) Gain that is considered to be derived from sources outside of the United States under section 865(g)(3) shall be considered income from sources within Puerto Rico; and

(B) Gain that is considered to be derived from sources outside of the United States under section 865(h)(2)(B) shall be considered income from sources within the possession in which the liquidating corporation is created or organized.

(ii) In applying the principles of section 865 and the regulations thereunder pursuant to paragraph (b) of this section, the rules of section 865(g) shall not apply, but the special rule of section 865(h)(2)(B) shall apply with respect to gain recognized upon the liquidation of corporations created or organized in the United States.

(g) Dividends. *(1) Dividends from certain possessions corporations.* (i) In general. Except as provided in paragraph (g)(1)(ii) of this section, with respect to any possessions shareholder, only the possessions source ratio of any dividend paid or accrued by a corporation created or organized in a possession (possessions corporation) shall be treated as income from sources within such possession. For purposes of this paragraph (g)—

(A) The possessions source ratio shall be a fraction, the numerator of which equals the gross income of the possessions corporation from sources within the possession in which it is created or organized (applying the rules of this section) for the testing period, and the denominator of which equals the total gross income of the corporation for the testing period; and

(B) The term possessions shareholder means any individual who is a bona fide resident of the possession in which the corporation is created or organized and who owns, directly or indirectly, at least 10 percent of the total voting stock of the corporation.

(ii) Dividends from corporations engaged in the active conduct of a trade or business in the relevant possession. The entire amount of any dividend paid or accrued by a possessions corporation shall be treated as income from sources within the possession in which it is created or organized when the following conditions are met—

(A) 80 percent or more of the gross income of the corporation for the testing period was derived from sources within such possession (applying the rules of this section) or was effectively connected with the conduct of a trade or business in such possession (applying the rules of § 1.937-3T); and

(B) 50 percent or more of the gross income of the corporation for the testing period was derived from the active conduct of a trade or business within such possession.

(iii) Testing period. For purposes of this paragraph (g)(1), the term testing period means the 3-year period ending with the close of the taxable year of the payment of the dividend (or for such part of such period as the corporation has been in existence).

(iv) Subsidiary look-through rule. For purposes of this paragraph (g)(1), if a possessions corporation owns (directly or indirectly) at least 25 percent (by value) of the stock of another corporation, such possessions corporation shall be treated as if it—

(A) Directly received its proportionate share of the income of such other corporation; and

(B) Actively conducted any trade or business actively conducted by such other corporation.

(2) Dividends from other corporations. In applying the principles of section 861 and the regulations thereunder pursuant to paragraph (b) of this section, the special rules relating to dividends for which deductions are allowable under section 243 or 245 shall not apply.

(h) Income inclusions. For purposes of determining whether an amount described in section 904(h)(1)(A) constitutes income from sources within the relevant possession—

(1) If the individual owns (directly or indirectly) at least 10 percent of the total voting stock of the corporation from which such amount is derived, the principles of section 904(h)(2) shall apply. In the case of an individual who is not a possessions shareholder (as defined in paragraph (g)(1)(i)(B) of this section), the preceding sentence shall apply only if the corporation qualifies as a United States-owned foreign corporation for purposes of section 904(h); and

(2) In all other cases, the amount shall be considered income from sources in the jurisdiction in which the corporation is created or organized.

(i) Interest. *(1) Interest from certain possessions corporations.* (i) In general. Except as provided in paragraph (i)(1)(ii) of this section, with respect to any possessions shareholder (as defined in paragraph (g)(1)(i)(B) of this section), interest paid or accrued by a possessions corporation shall be treated as income from sources within the possession in which it is created or organized to the extent that such interest is allocable to assets that generate, have generated, or could reasonably have been expected to generate income from sources within such possession (under the rules of this section) or income effectively connected with the conduct of a trade or business within such possession (under the rules of § 1.937-3T). For purposes of the preceding sentence, the principles of §§ 1.861-9 through 1.861-12 shall apply.

(ii) Interest from corporations engaged in the active conduct of a trade or business in the relevant possession. The entire amount of any interest paid or accrued by a possessions corporation shall be treated as income from sources within the possession in which it is created or organized when the conditions of paragraphs (g)(1)(ii) (A) and (B) of this section are met (applying the rules of paragraphs (g)(1)(iii) and (iv) of this section).

(2) Interest from partnerships. Interest paid or accrued by a partnership shall be treated as income from sources within a possession only to the extent that such interest is allocable to income effectively connected with the conduct of a trade or business in such possession. For purposes of the preceding sentence, the principles of § 1.882-5 shall apply (as if the partnership were a foreign corporation and as if the trade or business in the possession were a trade or business in the United States).

(j) Indirect ownership. For purposes of this section, the rules of section 318(a)(2) shall apply except that the language "5 percent" shall be used instead of "50 percent" in section 318(a)(2)(C).

(k) Examples. The provisions of this section may be illustrated by the following examples:

Example (1). X, a U.S. citizen, resides in State N and acquires the stock of Corporation C, a domestic corporation, in 2000. X moves to the Northern Mariana Islands (NMI) in 2003. In 2004, while a bona fide resident of the NMI, X recognizes gain on the sale of the Corporation C stock. Pursuant to section 1277(e) of the Tax Reform Act of 1986, Public Law 99-514 (100 Stat. 2085) (October 22, 1986), this gain is treated as income from sources within the United States for all purposes of the Internal Revenue Code (including section 7654, as in effect with respect to the NMI), and not as income from sources in the NMI.

Example (2). X, a U.S. citizen, resides in State F and acquires a 5 percent interest in Partnership P in 2003. X moves to the U.S. Virgin Islands (USVI) in 2004. In 2006, while a bona fide resident of the USVI, X recognizes gain on the sale of the interest in Partnership P. Pursuant to paragraph (f)(1) of this section, the gain shall not be treated as income from sources within the USVI for purposes of the Internal Revenue Code (for example, for purposes of section 934(b)).

Example (3). X, a bona fide resident of Possession I, a section 931 possession (as defined in § 1.931-1T(c)(1)), is engaged in a trade or business in the United States through an office in State H. In 2005, this office materially participates in the sale of inventory property in Possession I, such that the income from these inventory sales is considered effectively connected to this trade or business in the United States under section 864(c)(4)(B)(iii). This income shall not be treated as income from sources within Possession I for purposes of section 931(a)(1) pursuant to paragraph (c)(1)(ii) of this section, but nonetheless shall continue to be treated as income from sources without the United States under section 862 (for example, for purposes of section 904).

Example (4). (i) X, a bona fide resident of Possession I, owns 25 percent of the outstanding shares of A Corp, a corporation organized under the laws of Possession I. In 2006, X receives a dividend of $70x from A Corp. During 2004 through 2006, A Corp has gross income from the following sources:

Year	Possession I sources	Sources outside possession I
2004	$10x	$20x
2005	20x	10x
2006	25x	15x

(ii) A Corp owns 50 percent of the outstanding shares of B Corp, a corporation organized under the laws of Country

FC. During 2004 through 2006, B Corp has gross income from the following sources:

Year	Possession I sources	Sources outside possession I
2004	$10x	$6x
2005	14x	8x
2006	10x	4x

(iii) A Corp is treated as having received 50 percent of the gross income of B Corp. Therefore, for 2004 through 2006, the gross income of A Corp is from the following sources:

Year	Possession I sources	Sources outside possession I
2004	$15x	$23x
2005	27x	14x
2006	30x	17x
Totals	72x	54x

(iv) Pursuant to paragraph (g) of this section, the portion of the dividend of $70x that X receives from Corp A in 2006 that is treated as income from sources within Possession I is 72/126 of $70x, or $40x.

Example (5). X is a U.S. citizen and a bona fide resident of the Northern Mariana Islands (NMI). In 2005, X receives compensation for services performed as a member of the crew of a fishing boat. Ten percent of the services for which X receives compensation are performed in the NMI, and 90 percent of X's services are performed in international waters. X is a "United States person" as defined in section 7701(a)(30)(A). Accordingly, pursuant to section 863(d)(1)(A), the compensation that X receives for services performed in international waters is treated as income from sources within the United States for purposes of the Internal Revenue Code (including section 7654, as in effect with respect to the NMI). Under the principles of section 861(a)(3) as applied pursuant to paragraph (b) of this section, the compensation that X receives for services performed in the NMI is treated as income from sources within the NMI.

(l) Effective date. Except as otherwise provided in this paragraph (l), this section applies to income earned in tax years ending after October 22, 2004. Paragraph (c)(1) of this section applies to income earned after December 31, 2004. Paragraph (f) of this section applies to dispositions after April 11, 2005. Paragraphs (c)(2), (g)(1), (h), and (i) of this section apply to amounts paid or accrued after April 11, 2005.

T.D. 9194, 4/6/2005.

Proposed § 1.937-3 Income effectively connected with the conduct of a trade or business in a possession. [*For Preamble, see ¶ 152,645*]

• ***Caution:*** This Notice of Proposed Rulemaking was partially finalized by TD 9248, 01/30/2006. Regs. §§ 1.1-1, 1.170A-1, 1.861-3, 1.861-8, 1.871-1, 1.876-1, 1.881-5, 1.884-0, 1.901-1, 1.931-1, 1.932-1, 1.933-1, 1.934-1, 1.935-1, 1.937-2, 1.937-3, 1.957-3, 1.1402(a)-12, 1.6038-2, 1.6046-1, 301.6688-1, 301.7701-3, and 301.7701(b)-1 remain proposed.

[The text of the proposed § 1.937-3 is the same as the text of § 1.937-3T published elsewhere in this issue of the Federal Register]. [*See T.D. 9194, 4/11/2005, 70 Fed. Reg. 68.*]

§ 1.937-3T Income effectively connected with the conduct of a trade or business in a possession (temporary).

• ***Caution:*** Under Code Sec. 7805, temporary regulations expire within three years of the date of issuance. This temporary regulation was issued on 4/6/2005.

(a) Scope. Section 937(b) and this section set forth the rules for determining whether income is effectively connected with the conduct of a trade or business within a particular possession (the relevant possession) for purposes of the Internal Revenue Code, including sections 881(b) and 957(c) and Subpart D, Part III, Subchapter N, Chapter 1 of the Internal Revenue Code. Paragraph (c) of this section does not apply, however, for purposes of section 881(b). In the case of a possession or territory that administers income tax laws that are identical (except for the substitution of the name of the possession or territory for the term United States where appropriate) to those in force in the United States, these rules do not apply for purposes of the application of such laws.

(b) In general. Except as provided in paragraphs (c) and (d) of this section, the principles of section 864(c) and the regulations thereunder (relating to the determination of income, gain or loss which is effectively connected with the conduct of a trade or business within the United States) shall generally be applied in determining whether income is effectively connected with the conduct of a trade or business within the relevant possession (except for the substitution of the name of the relevant possession for the term United States where appropriate), without regard to whether the taxpayer qualifies as a nonresident alien individual or a foreign corporation with respect to such possession. For purposes of the preceding sentence, all income other than income from sources within the relevant possession (as determined under the rules of § 1.937-2T) shall be considered income from sources without the relevant possession, and subject to the rules of this section, the principles of section 864(c)(4) shall apply for purposes of determining whether such income constitutes income effectively connected with the conduct of a trade or business in the relevant possession.

(c) U.S. income. *(1) In general.* Except as provided in paragraph (d) of this section, income considered to be effectively connected with the conduct of a trade or business within the relevant possession shall not include any item of income determined under the rules of sections 861 through 865 and the regulations thereunder to be—

(i) From sources within the United States; or

(ii) Effectively connected with the conduct of a trade or business within the United States.

(2) Conduit arrangements. Income shall be considered to be from sources within the United States for purposes of paragraph (c)(1) of this section if, pursuant to a plan or arrangement—

(i) The income is received in exchange for consideration provided to another person; and

(ii) Such person (or another person) provides the same consideration (or consideration of a like kind) to a third person in exchange for one or more payments constituting income from sources within the United States.

(d) Income from certain sales of inventory property. Paragraph (c) of this section shall not apply to income from sales of inventory property described in § 1.863-3(f).

(e) Examples. The provisions of this section may be illustrated by the following examples:

Example (1). X is a bona fide resident of Possession I, a section 931 possession (as defined in § 1.931-1T(c)(1)). X has an office in Possession I from which X conducts a business consisting of the development and sale of specialized computer software. A purchaser of software will frequently pay X an additional amount to install the software on the purchaser's operating system and to ensure that the software is functioning properly. X performs the installation services at the purchaser's place of business which may be in Possession I, in the United States, or in another country. The provision of such services is not de minimis and constitutes a separate transaction under the rules of § 1.861-18. Under the principles of section 864(c)(4) as applied pursuant to paragraph (b) of this section, the compensation that X receives for personal services performed outside of Possession I is not considered to be effectively connected with the conduct of a trade or business in Possession I for purposes of section 931(a)(2).

Example (2). (i) F Bank is organized under the laws of Country FC and operates an active banking business from offices in the U.S. Virgin Islands (USVI). In connection with this banking business, F Bank makes loans to and receives interest payments from borrowers who reside in the USVI, in the United States, and in Country FC.

(ii) Under the principles of section 861(a)(1) as applied pursuant to § 1.937-2T(b), interest payments received by F Bank from borrowers who reside in the United States or in Country FC constitute income from sources outside of the USVI. Under the principles of section 864(c)(4) as applied pursuant to paragraph (b) of this section, interest income from sources outside of the USVI generally may constitute income that is effectively connected with the conduct of a trade or business within the USVI for purposes of the Internal Revenue Code. However, interest payments received by F Bank from borrowers who reside in the United States constitute income from sources within the United States under section 861(a)(1). Accordingly, under paragraph (c)(1) of this section, such interest income shall not be treated as effectively connected with the conduct of a trade or business in the USVI for purposes of the Internal Revenue Code (for example, for purposes of section 934(b)). Interest payments received by F Bank from borrowers who reside in Country FC, however, may be treated as effectively connected with the conduct of a trade or business in the USVI for purposes of the Internal Revenue Code (including section 934(b)).

(iii) To the extent that, as described in section 934(a), the USVI administers income tax laws that are identical (except for the substitution of the name of the USVI for the term United States where appropriate) to those in force in the United States, interest payments received by F Bank from borrowers who reside in the United States or in Country FC may be treated as income that is effectively connected with the conduct of a trade or business in the USVI for purposes of F Bank's income tax liability to the USVI under mirrored section 882.

Example (3). (i) G is a partnership that is organized under the laws of, and that operates an active financing business from offices in, Possession I. Interests in G are owned by D, a bona fide resident of Possession I, and N, an alien individual who resides in Country FC. Pursuant to a pre-arrangement, G loans $x to T, a business entity organized under the laws of Country FC, and T in turn loans $y to E, a U.S. resident. In accordance with the arrangement, E pays interest to T, which in turn pays interest to G.

(ii) The arrangement constitutes a conduit arrangement under paragraph (c)(2) of this section, and the interest payments received by G are treated as income from sources within the United States for purposes of paragraph (c)(1) of this section. Accordingly, the interest received by G shall not be treated as effectively connected with the conduct of a trade or business in Possession I for purposes of the Internal Revenue Code (including sections 931(a)(2) and 934(b), if applicable with respect to D). Whether such interest constitutes income from sources within the United States for other purposes of the Internal Revenue Code under generally applicable conduit principles will depend on the facts and circumstances. See, for example, Aiken Indus., Inc. v. Commissioner, 56 T.C. 925 (1971).

(iii) If Possession I administers income tax laws that are identical (except for the substitution of the name of the possession for the term ''United States'' where appropriate) to those in force in the United States, the interest received by G may be treated as income effectively connected with the conduct of a trade or business in Possession I under mirrored section 864(c)(4) for purposes of determining the Possession I territorial income tax liability of N under mirrored section 871.

(f) Effective date. Except as otherwise provided in this paragraph (f), this section applies to income earned in taxable years ending after October 22, 2004. Paragraph (c)(1) of this section applies to income earned after December 31, 2004. Paragraph (c)(2) of this section applies to amounts paid or accrued after April 11, 2005.

T.D. 9194, 4/6/2005.

---

§ 1.951-1 Amounts included in gross income of United States shareholders.

Caution: The Treasury has not yet amended Reg § 1.951-1 to reflect changes made by P.L. 105-34, P.L. 103-66, P.L. 100-647, P.L. 99-514, P.L. 98-369.

(a) In general. If a foreign corporation is a controlled foreign corporation (within the meaning of section 957) for an uninterrupted period of 30 days or more (determined under paragraph (f) of this section) during any taxable year of such corporation beginning after December 31, 1962, every person—

(1) Who is a United States shareholder (as defined in section 951(b) and paragraph (g) of this section) of such corporation at any time during such taxable year, and

(2) Who owns (within the meaning of section 958(a)) stock in such corporation on the last day, in such year, on which such corporation is a controlled foreign corporation shall include in his gross income for his taxable year in which or with which such taxable year of the corporation ends, the sum of—

(i) Such shareholder's pro rata share (determined under paragraph (b) of this section) of the corporation's subpart F income (as defined in section 952) for such taxable year of the corporation,

(ii) Such shareholder's pro rata share (determined under paragraph (b) of this section) of the corporation's subpart F income (as defined in section 952) for such taxable year of the corporation,

(iii) Such shareholder's pro rata share (determined under paragraph (c)(2) of this section) of the corporation's previously excluded subpart F income withdrawn from investment in foreign base company shipping operations for such taxable year of the corporation, and

(iv) The amount determined under section 956 with respect to such shareholder for such taxable year of the corporation (but only to the extent not excluded from gross income under section 959(a)(2)).

(3) For purposes of determining whether a United States shareholder which is a domestic corporation is a personal holding company under section 542 and § 1.542-1, the character of the amount includible in gross income of such domestic corporation under this paragraph shall be determined as if such amount were realized directly by such corporation from the source from which it is realized by the controlled foreign corporation. See paragraph (a) of § 1.957-2 for special limitation on the amount of subpart F income in the case of a controlled foreign corporation described in section 957(b). See section 970(a) and § 1.970-1 which provides for the reduction of subpart F income of export trade corporations.

(b) Limitation on a United States shareholder's pro rata share of subpart F income. *(1) In general.* For purposes of paragraph (a)(2)(i) of this section, a United States shareholder's pro rata share (determined in accordance with the rules of paragraph (e) of this section) of the foreign corporation's subpart F income for the taxable year of such corporation is—

(i) The amount which would have been distributed with respect to the stock which such shareholder owns (within the meaning of section 958(a)) in such corporation if on the last day, in such corporation's taxable year, on which such corporation is a controlled foreign corporation it had distributed pro rata to its shareholders an amount which bears the same ratio to its subpart F income for such taxable year as the part of such year during which such corporation is a controlled foreign corporation bears to the entire taxable year, reduced by—

(ii) The amount of distributions received by any other person during such taxable year as a dividend with respect to such stock, but only to the extent that such distributions do not exceed the dividend which would have been received by such other person if the distributions by such corporation to all its shareholders had been the amount which bears the same ratio to the subpart F income of such corporation for the taxable year as the part of such year during which such shareholder did not own (within the meaning of section 958(a)) such stock bears to the entire taxable year.

(2) Illustrations. The application of this paragraph may be illustrated by the following examples:

Example (1). A, a United States shareholder, owns 100 percent of the only class of stock of M, a controlled foreign corporation throughout 1963. Both A and M Corporation use the calendar year as a taxable year. For 1963, M Corporation derives $100 of subpart F income, has $100 of earnings and profits, and makes no distributions. A must include $100 in his gross income for 1963 under section 951(a)(1)(A)(i).

Example (2). The facts are the same as in example (1), except that instead of holding 100 percent of the stock of M Corporation for the entire year, A sells 60 percent of such stock to B, a nonresident alien, on May 26, 1963. Thus, M Corporation is a controlled foreign corporation for the period January 1, 1963, through May 26, 1963. A must include $40 ($100 × 146/365) in his gross income for 1963 under section 951(a)(1)(A)(i).

Example (3). The facts are the same as in example (1), except that instead of holding 100 percent of the stock of M Corporation for the entire year, A holds 60 percent of such stock on December 31, 1963, having acquired such interest on May 26, 1963, from B, a nonresident alien, who owned such interest from January 1, 1963. Before A's acquisition of such stock, M Corporation had distributed a dividend of $15 to B in 1963 with respect to such stock. A must include $21 in his gross income for 1963 under section 951(a)(1)(A)(i), such amount being determined as follows:

Corporation M's subpart F income for 1963		$100
Less: Reduction under sec. 951(a)(2)(A) for period (1-1-63 through 5-26-63) during which M Corporation is not a controlled foreign corporation ($100 × 146/365)		40
Subpart F income for 1963 as limited by sec. 951(a)(2)(A)		60
A's pro rata share of subpart F income as determined under sec. 951(a)(2)(A) (60 percent of $60)		36
Less: Reduction under sec. 951(a)(2)(B) for dividends received by B during 1963 with respect to the stock acquired by A in M Corporation:		
(i) Dividend received by B	$15	
(ii) B's pro rata share of the amount which bears the same ratio to M Corporation's subpart F income for 1963 ($100) as the period during which A did not own (within the meaning of sec. 958(a)) his stock (146 days) bears to the entire taxable year (365 days) (60 percent of $100 × 146/365))	24	
(iii) Amount of reduction (lesser of (i) or (ii)) . .		15

A's pro rata share of subpart F income as determined under sec. 951(a)(2) 21

Example (4). A, a United States shareholder, owns 100 percent of the only class of stock of P, a controlled foreign corporation throughout 1963, and P owns 100 percent of the only class of stock of R, a controlled foreign corporation throughout 1963. A and Corporations P and R each use the calendar year as a taxable year. For 1963, R Corporation derives $100 of subpart F income, has $100 of earnings and profits, and distributes a dividend of $20 to P Corporation. Corporation P has no income for 1963 other than the dividend received from R Corporation. A must include $100 in his gross income for 1963 under section 951(a)(1)(A)(i) as subpart F income of R Corporation for such year. Such subpart F income is not reduced under sec. 951(a)(2)(B) for the dividend of $20 paid to P Corporation because there was no part of the year 1963 during which A did not own (within the meaning of section 958(a)) the stock of R Corporation. By reason of the application of section 959(b), the $20 distribution from R Corporation to P Corporation is not again includible in the gross income of A under section 951(a).

Example (5). The facts are the same as in example (4), except that instead of holding the stock of R Corporation for the entire year, P Corporation acquires 60 percent of the only class of stock of R Corporation on March 14, 1963, from C, a nonresident alien, after R Corporation distributes in 1963 a dividend of $35 to C with respect to the stock so acquired by P Corporation. The stock interest so acquired by P Corporation was owned by C from January 1, 1963, until acquired by P Corporation. A must include $36 in his gross income for 1963 under section 951(a)(1)(A)(i), such amount being determined as follows:

Corporation R's subpart F income for 1963		$100
Less: Reduction under sec. 951(a)(2)(A) for period (1-1-63 through 3-14-63) during which R Corporation is not a controlled foreign corporation ($100 × 73/365)		20
Subpart F income for 1963 as limited by sec. 951(a)(2)(A)		80
A's pro rata share of subpart F income as determined under sec. 951(a)(2)(A) (60 percent of $80)		48
Less: Reduction under sec. 951(a)(2)(B) for dividends received by C during 1963 with respect to the stock indirectly acquired by A in R Corporation.		
(i) Dividend received by C	$35	
(ii) C's pro rata share of the amount which bears the same ratio to R Corporation's subpart F income for 1963 ($100) as the period during which A did not indirectly own (within the meaning of section 958(a)(2)) his stock (73 days) bears to the entire taxable year (365 days) (60 percent of ($100 × 73/365))	12	
(iii) Amount of reduction (lesser of (i) or (ii)) . . .		12
A's pro rata share of subpart F income as determined under sec. 951(a)(2)		36

(c) Limitation on a United States shareholder's pro rata share of previously excluded subpart F income withdrawn from investments. *(1) Investments in less developed countries.* For purposes of paragraph (a)(2)(ii) of this section, a United States shareholder's pro rata share (determined in accordance with the rules of paragraph (e) of this section) of the foreign corporation's previously excluded subpart F income withdrawn from investment in less developed countries for the taxable year of such corporation shall not exceed an amount which bears the same ratio to such shareholder's pro rata share of such income withdrawn (as determined under section 955(a)(3), as in effect before the enactment of the Tax Reduction Act of 1975, and paragraph (c) of § 1.955-1) for such taxable year as the part of such year during which such corporation is a controlled foreign corporation bears to the entire taxable year. See paragraph (c)(2) of § 1.955-1 for a special rule applicable to exclusions and withdrawals occurring before the date on which the United States shareholder acquires his stock.

(2) Investments in foreign base company shipping operations. For purposes of paragraph (a)(2)(iii) of this section, a United States shareholder's pro rata share (determined in accordance with the rules of paragraph (e) of this section) of the foreign corporation's previously excluded subpart F income withdrawn from investment in foreign base company shipping operations for the taxable year of such corporation shall not exceed an amount which bears the same ratio to such shareholder's pro rata share of such income withdrawn (as determined under section 955(a)(3) and paragraph (c) of § 1.955A-1) for such taxable year as the part of such year during which such corporation is a controlled foreign corporation bears to the entire taxable year. See paragraph (c)(2) of § 1.955A-1 for a special rule applicable to exclusions and withdrawals occurring before the date on which the United States shareholder acquires his stock.

(d) [Reserved].

(e) "Pro rata share" defined. *(1) In general.* For purposes of paragraphs (b) and (c) of this section, a United States shareholder's pro rata share of the controlled foreign corporation's subpart F income, previously excluded subpart F income withdrawn from investment in less developed countries, or previously excluded subpart F income withdrawn from investment in foreign base company shipping operations, respectively, for any taxable year is his pro rata share determined under § 1.952-1(a), § 1.955-1(c), or § 1.955A-1(c), respectively.

(2) One class of stock. If a controlled foreign corporation for a taxable year has only one class of stock outstanding, each United States shareholder's pro rata share of such corporation's subpart F income or withdrawal for the taxable year under paragraph (e)(1) of this section shall be determined by allocating the controlled foreign corporation's earnings and profits on a per share basis.

(3) More than one class of stock. (i) In general. Subject to paragraphs (e)(3)(ii) through (e)(3)(v) of this section, if a controlled foreign corporation for a taxable year has more than one class of stock outstanding, the amount of such corporation's subpart F income or withdrawal for the taxable year taken into account with respect to any one class of stock for purposes of paragraph (e)(1) of this section shall be that amount which bears the same ratio to the total of such subpart F income or withdrawal for such year as the earnings and profits which would be distributed with respect to such class of stock if all earnings and profits of such corporation for such year (not reduced by actual distributions during the year) were distributed on the last day of such corporation's taxable year on which such corporation is a controlled foreign corporation (the hypothetical distribution date), bear to the total earnings and profits of such corporation for such taxable year.

(ii) Discretionary power to allocate earnings to different classes of stock. (A) In general. Subject to paragraph (e)(3)(iii) of this section, the rules of this paragraph apply for purposes of paragraph (e)(1) of this section if the allocation of a controlled foreign corporation's earnings and profits for the taxable year between two or more classes of stock depends upon the exercise of discretion by that body of persons which exercises with respect to such corporation the powers ordinarily exercised by the board of directors of a domestic corporation (discretionary distribution rights). First, the earnings and profits of the corporation are allocated under paragraph (e)(3)(i) of this section to any class or classes of stock with non-discretionary distribution rights (e.g., preferred stock entitled to a fixed return). Second, the amount of earnings and profits allocated to a class of stock with discretionary distribution rights shall be that amount which bears the same ratio to the remaining earnings and profits of such corporation for such taxable year as the value of all shares of such class of stock, determined on the hypothetical distribution date, bears to the total value of all shares of all classes of stock with discretionary distribution rights of such corporation, determined on the hypothetical distribution date. For purposes of the preceding sentence, in the case where the value of each share of two or more classes of stock with discretionary distribution rights is substantially the same on the hypothetical distribution date, the allocation of earnings and profits to such classes shall be made as if such classes constituted one class of stock in which each share has the same rights to dividends as any other share.

(B) Special rule for redemption rights. For purposes of paragraph (e)(3)(ii)(A) of this section, discretionary distribution rights do not include rights to redeem shares of a class of stock (even if such redemption would be treated as a distribution of property to which section 301 applies pursuant to section 302(d)).

(iii) Special allocation rule for stock with mixed distribution rights. For purposes of paragraphs (e)(3)(i) and (e)(3)(ii) of this section, in the case of a class of stock with both discretionary and non-discretionary distribution rights, earnings and profits shall be allocated to the non-discretionary distribution rights under paragraph (e)(3)(i) of this section and to the discretionary distribution rights under paragraph (e)(3)(ii) of this section. In such a case, paragraph (e)(3)(ii) of this section will be applied such that the value used in the ratio will be the value of such class of stock solely attributable to the discretionary distribution rights of such class of stock.

(iv) Dividend arrearages. For purposes of paragraph (e)(3)(i) of this section, if an arrearage in dividends for prior taxable years exists with respect to a class of preferred stock of such corporation, the earnings and profits for the taxable year shall be attributed to such arrearage only to the extent such arrearage exceeds the earnings and profits of such corporation remaining from prior taxable years beginning after December 31, 1962, or the date on which such stock was issued, whichever is later.

(v) Earnings and profits attributable to certain section 304 transactions. For taxable years of a controlled foreign corporation beginning on or after January 1, 2006, if a controlled foreign corporation has more than one class of stock outstanding and the corporation has earnings and profits and subpart F income for a taxable year attributable to a transaction described in section 304, and such transaction is part of a plan a principal purpose of which is the avoidance of Federal income taxation, the amount of such earnings and profits allocated to any one class of stock shall be that amount which bears the same ratio to the remainder of such earnings and profits as the value of all shares of such class of stock, determined on the hypothetical distribution date, bears to the total value of all shares of all classes of stock of the corporation, determined on the hypothetical distribution date.

(4) Scope of hypothetical distribution. (i) Redemption rights. Notwithstanding the terms of any class of stock of the controlled foreign corporation or any agreement or arrangement with respect thereto, no amount shall be considered to be distributed as part of the hypothetical distribution with respect to a particular class of stock for purposes of paragraph (e)(3) of this section to the extent that a distribution of such amount would constitute a distribution in redemption of stock (even if such redemption would be treated as a distribution of property to which section 301 applies pursuant to section 302(d)), a distribution in liquidation, or a return of capital.

(ii) Certain cumulative preferred stock. For taxable years of a controlled foreign corporation beginning on or after January 1, 2006, if a controlled foreign corporation has one or more classes of preferred stock with cumulative dividend rights, such stock shall be considered for the purposes of this section as stock with discretionary distribution rights. As a result, the provisions of paragraph (e)(3)(ii) of this section shall apply for purposes of allocating earnings and profits to such stock, except that earnings and profits shall first be allocated to the stock under paragraph (e)(3)(i) of this section to the extent of any dividends paid with respect to the stock during the taxable year. Additional earnings and profits will be allocated to the stock only in an amount equal to the excess (if any) of the amount of earnings and profits allocated to the stock under paragraph (e)(3)(ii) of this section over the amount of such dividends. Notwithstanding the foregoing, if a class of redeemable preferred stock with cumulative dividend rights has a mandatory redemption date, and all dividend arrearages with respect to such stock compound at least annually at a rate that is not lower than the applicable Federal rate (as defined in section 1274(d)(1)) (AFR) that applies on the date the stock is issued for the term from such issue date to the mandatory redemption date, based on a comparable compounding assumption, such stock shall not be considered for purposes of this section as stock with discretionary distribution rights.

(5) Restrictions or other limitations on distributions. (i) In general. A restriction or other limitation on distributions of earnings and profits by a controlled foreign corporation will not be taken into account, for purposes of this section, in determining the amount of earnings and profits that shall be allocated to a class of stock of the controlled foreign corporation or the amount of the United States shareholder's pro rata share of the controlled foreign corporation's subpart F income or withdrawal for the taxable year.

(ii) Definition. For purposes of this section, a restriction or other limitation on distributions includes any limitation that has the effect of limiting the allocation or distribution of earnings and profits by a controlled foreign corporation to a United States shareholder, other than currency or other restrictions or limitations imposed under the laws of any foreign country as provided in section 964(b).

(iii) Exception for certain preferred distributions. The right to receive periodically a fixed amount (whether determined by a percentage of par value, a reference to a floating coupon rate, a stated return expressed in terms of a certain amount of dollars or foreign currency, or otherwise) with respect to a class of stock the distribution of which is a condition precedent to a further distribution of earnings or profits that year with respect to any class of stock (not including a distribution in partial or complete liquidation) is not a restriction or other limitation on the distribution of earnings and profits by a controlled foreign corporation under paragraph (e)(5) of this section.

(iv) Illustrative list of restrictions and limitations. Except as provided in paragraph (e)(5)(iii) of this section, restrictions or other limitations on distributions include, but are not limited to—

(A) An arrangement that restricts the ability of the controlled foreign corporation to pay dividends on a class of shares of the corporation owned by United States shareholders until a condition or conditions are satisfied (e.g., until another class of stock is redeemed);

(B) A loan agreement entered into by a controlled foreign corporation that restricts or otherwise affects the ability to make distributions on its stock until certain requirements are satisfied; or

(C) An arrangement that conditions the ability of the controlled foreign corporation to pay dividends to its shareholders on the financial condition of the controlled foreign corporation.

(6) Examples. The application of this section may be illustrated by the following examples:

Example (1). (i) Facts. FC1, a controlled foreign corporation within the meaning of section 957(a), has outstanding 100 shares of one class of stock. Corp E, a domestic corporation and a United States shareholder of FC1, within the meaning of section 951(b), owns 60 shares. Corp H, a domestic corporation and a United States shareholder of FC1, within the meaning of section 951(b), owns 40 shares. FC1, Corp E, and Corp H each use the calendar year as a taxable year. Corp E and Corp H are shareholders of FC1 for its entire 2005 taxable year. For 2005, FC1 has $100x of earnings and profits, and income of $100x with respect to which amounts are required to be included in gross income of United States shareholders under section 951(a). FC1 makes no distributions during that year.

(ii) Analysis. FC1 has one class of stock. Therefore, under paragraph (e)(2) of this section, FC1's earnings and profits are allocated on a per share basis. Accordingly, for the taxable year 2005, Corp E's pro rata share of FC1's subpart F income is $60x (60/ 100 x $100x) and Corp H's pro rata share of FC1's subpart F income is $40x (40/100 x $100x).

Example (2). (i) Facts. FC2, a controlled foreign corporation within the meaning of section 957(a), has outstanding 70 shares of common stock and 30 shares of 4-percent, nonparticipating, voting, preferred stock with a par value of $10x per share. The common shareholders are entitled to dividends when declared by the board of directors of FC2. Corp A, a domestic corporation and a United States shareholder of FC2, within the meaning of section 951(b), owns all of the common shares. Individual B, a foreign individual, owns all of the preferred shares. FC2 and Corp A each use the calendar year as a taxable year. Corp A and Individual B are shareholders of FC2 for its entire 2005 taxable year. For 2005, FC2 has $50x of earnings and profits, and income of $50x with respect to which amounts are required to be included in gross income of United States shareholders under section 951(a). In 2005, FC2 distributes as a dividend $12x to Individual B with respect to Individual B's preferred shares. FC2 makes no other distributions during that year.

(ii) Analysis. FC2 has two classes of stock, and there are no restrictions or other limitations on distributions within the meaning of paragraph (e)(5) of this section. If the total $50x of earnings were distributed on December 31, 2005, $12x would be distributed with respect to Individual B's preferred shares and the remainder, $38x, would be distributed with respect to Corp A's common shares. Accordingly, under paragraph (e)(3)(i) of this section, Corp A's pro rata share of FC1's subpart F income is $38x for taxable year 2005.

Example (3). (i) Facts. The facts are the same as in Example 2, except that the shares owned by Individual B are Class B common shares and the shares owned by Corp A are Class A common shares and the board of directors of FC2 may declare dividends with respect to one class of stock without declaring dividends with respect to the other class of stock. The value of the Class A common shares on the last day of FC2's 2005 taxable year is $680x and the value of the Class B common shares on that date is $300x. The board of directors of FC2 determines that FC2 will not make any distributions in 2005 with respect to the Class A and B common shares of FC2.

(ii) Analysis. The allocation of FC2's earnings and profits between its Class A and Class B common shares depends solely on the exercise of discretion by the board of directors of FC2. Therefore, under paragraph (e)(3)(ii)(A) of this section, the allocation of earnings and profits between the Class A and Class B common shares will depend on the value of each class of stock on the last day of the controlled foreign corporation's taxable year. On the last day of FC2's taxable year 2005, the Class A common shares had a value of $9.30x/share and the Class B common shares had a value of $10x/ share. Because each share of the Class A and Class B common stock of FC2 has substantially the same value on the last day of FC2's taxable year, under paragraph (e)(3)(ii)(A) of this section, for purposes of allocating the earnings and profits of FC2, the Class A and Class B common shares will be treated as one class of stock. Accordingly, for FC2's taxable year 2005, the earnings and profits of FC2 are allocated $35x (70/100 x $50x) to the Class A common shares and $15x (30/100 x $50x) to the Class B common shares. For its taxable year 2005, Corp A's pro rata share of FC2's subpart F income will be $35x.

Example (4). (i) Facts. FC3, a controlled foreign corporation within the meaning of section 957(a), has outstanding 100 shares of Class A common stock, 100 shares of Class B common stock and 10 shares of 5-percent nonparticipating, voting preferred stock with a par value of $50x per share. The value of the Class A shares on the last day of FC3's 2005 taxable year is $800x. The value of the Class B shares on that date is $200x. The Class A and Class B shareholders each are entitled to dividends when declared by the board of directors of FC3, and the board of directors of FC3 may declare dividends with respect to one class of stock without declaring dividends with respect to the other class of stock. Corp D, a domestic corporation and a United States shareholder of FC3, within the meaning of section 951(b), owns all of the Class A shares. Corp N, a domestic corporation and a United States shareholder of FC3, within the meaning of section 951(b), owns all of the Class B shares. Corp S, a domestic corporation and a United States shareholder of FC3, within the meaning of section 951(b), owns all of the preferred shares. FC3, Corp D, Corp N, and Corp S each use the calendar year as a taxable year. Corp D, Corp N, and Corp S are shareholders of FC3 for all of 2005. For 2005, FC3 has $100x of earnings and profits, and income of $100x with respect to which amounts are required to be included in gross income of United States shareholders under section 951(a). In 2005, FC3 distributes as a dividend $25x to Corp S with respect to the preferred shares. The board of directors of FC3 determines that FC3 will make no other distributions during that year.

(ii) Analysis. The distribution rights of the preferred shares are not a restriction or other limitation within the meaning of paragraph (e)(5) of this section. Pursuant to paragraph (e)(3)(i) of this section, if the total $100x of earnings were distributed on December 31, 2005, $25x would be distributed with respect to Corp S's preferred shares and the remainder, $75x would be distributed with respect to Corp D's Class A shares and Corp N's Class B shares. The allocation of that $75x between its Class A and Class B shares depends solely on the exercise of discretion by the board of directors of FC3. The value of the Class A shares ($8x/share) and the value of the Class B shares ($2x/share) are not substantially the same on the last day of FC3's taxable year 2005. Therefore for FC3's taxable year 2005, under paragraph (e)(3)(ii)(A) of this section, the earnings and profits of FC3 are allocated $60x ($800/ $1,000 x $75x) to the Class A shares and $15x ($200/$1,000 x $75x) to the Class B shares. For the 2005 taxable year, Corp D's pro rata share of FC3's subpart F income will be $60x, Corp N's pro rata share of FC3's subpart F income will be $15x and Corp S's pro rata share of FC3's subpart F income will be $25x.

Example (5). (i) Facts. FC4, a controlled foreign corporation within the meaning of section 957(a), has outstanding 40 shares of participating, voting, preferred stock and 200 shares of common stock. The owner of a share of preferred stock is entitled to an annual dividend equal to 0.5-percent of FC4's retained earnings for the taxable year and also is entitled to additional dividends when declared by the board of directors of FC4. The common shareholders are entitled to dividends when declared by the board of directors of FC4. The board of directors of FC4 has discretion to pay dividends to the participating portion of the preferred shares (after the payment of the preference) and the common shares. The value of the preferred shares on the last day of FC4's 2005 taxable year is $600x ($100x of this value is attributable to the discretionary distribution rights of these shares) and the value of the common shares on that date is $400x. Corp E, a domestic corporation and United States shareholder of FC4, within the meaning of section 951(b), owns all of the preferred shares. FC5, a foreign corporation that is not a controlled foreign corporation within the meaning of section 957(a), owns all of the common shares. FC 4 and Corp E each use the calendar year as a taxable year. Corp E and FC5 are shareholders of FC4 for all of 2005. For 2005, FC4 has $100x of earnings and profits, and income of $100x with respect to which amounts are required to be included in gross income of United States shareholders under section 951(a). In 2005, FC4's retained earnings are equal to its earnings and profits. FC4 distributes as a dividend $20x to Corp E that year with respect to Corp E's preferred shares. The board of directors of FC4 determines that FC4 will not make any other distributions during that year.

(ii) Analysis. The non-discretionary distribution rights of the preferred shares are not a restriction or other limitation within the meaning of paragraph (e)(5) of this section. The allocation of FC4's earnings and profits between its preferred shares and common shares depends, in part, on the exercise of discretion by the board of directors of FC4 because the preferred shares are shares with both discretionary distribution rights and non-discretionary distribution rights. Paragraph (e)(3)(i) of this section is applied first to determine the allocation of earnings and profits of FC4 to the non-discretionary distribution rights of the preferred shares. If the total $100x of earnings were distributed on December 31, 2005, $20x would be distributed with respect to the non-discretionary distribution rights of Corp E's preferred shares. Accordingly, $20x would be allocated to such shares under paragraphs (e)(3)(i) and (iii) of this section. The remainder, $80x, would be allocated under paragraph (e)(3)(ii)(A) and (e)(3)(iii) of this section between the preferred and common shares by reference to the value of the discretionary distribution rights of the preferred shares and the value of the common shares. Therefore, the remaining $80x of earnings and profits of FC4 are allocated $16x ($100x/$500x x $80x) to the preferred shares and $64x ($400x/$500x x $80) to the common shares. For its taxable year 2005, Corp E's pro rata share of FC4's subpart F income will be $36x ($20x + $16x).

Example (6). (i) Facts. FC6, a controlled foreign corporation within the meaning of section 957(a), has outstanding 10 shares of common stock and 400 shares of 2-percent nonparticipating, voting, preferred stock with a par value of $1x per share. The common shareholders are entitled to dividends when declared by the board of directors of FC6. Corp M, a domestic corporation and a United States shareholder of FC6, within the meaning of section 951(b), owns all of the common shares. FC7, a foreign corporation that is not a controlled foreign corporation within the meaning of section 957(a), owns all of the preferred shares. Corp M and FC7 cause the governing documents of FC6 to provide that no dividends may be paid to the common shareholders until FC6 cumulatively earns $100,000x of income. FC6 and Corp M each use the calendar year as a taxable year. Corp M and FC7 are shareholders of FC6 for all of 2005. For 2005, FC6 has $50x of earnings and profits, and income of $50x with respect to which amounts are required to be included in gross income of United States shareholders under section 951(a). In 2005, FC6 distributes as a dividend $8x to FC7 with respect to FC7's preferred shares. FC6 makes no other distributions during that year.

(ii) Analysis. The agreement restricting FC6's ability to pay dividends to common shareholders until FC6 cumulatively earns $100,000x of income is a restriction or other limitation, within the meaning of paragraph (e)(5) of this section, and will be disregarded for purposes of calculating Corp M's pro rata share of subpart F income. The non-discretionary distribution rights of the preferred shares are not a restriction or other limitation within the meaning of paragraph (e)(5) of this section. If the total $50x of earnings were distributed on December 31, 2005, $8x would be distributed with respect to FC7's preferred shares and the remainder, $42x, would be distributed with respect to Corp M's common shares. Accordingly, under paragraph (e)(3)(i) of this section, Corp M's pro rata share of FC6's subpart F income is $42x for taxable year 2005.

Example (7). (i) Facts. FC8, a controlled foreign corporation within the meaning of section 957(a), has outstanding 40 shares of common stock and 10 shares of 4-percent voting preferred stock with a par value of $50x per share. Pursuant to the terms of the preferred stock, FC8 has the right to redeem at any time, in whole or in part, the preferred stock. FP, a foreign corporation, owns all of the preferred shares. Corp G, a domestic corporation wholly owned by FP and a United States shareholder of FC8, within the meaning of section 951(b), owns all of the common shares. FC8 and Corp G each use the calendar year as a taxable year. FP and Corp G are shareholders of FC8 for all of 2005. For 2005, FC8 has $100x of earnings and profits, and income of $100x with respect to which amounts are required to be included in gross income of a United States shareholder under section 951(a). In 2005, FC8 distributes as a dividend $20x to FP with respect to FP's preferred shares. FC8 makes no other distributions during that year.

(ii) Analysis. Pursuant to paragraph (e)(3)(ii)(B) of this section, the redemption rights of the preferred shares will not be treated as a discretionary distribution right under paragraph (e)(3)(ii)(A) of this section. Further, if FC8 were treated as having redeemed any preferred shares under paragraph (e)(3)(i) of this section, the redemption would be treated as a distribution to which section 301 applies under section 302(d) due to FP's constructive ownership of the common shares. However, pursuant to paragraph (e)(4) of this section, no amount of earnings and profits would be allocated to the preferred shareholders on the hypothetical distribution date, under paragraph (e)(3)(i) of this section, as a result of FC8's right to redeem, in whole or in part, the preferred shares. FC8's redemption rights with respect to the preferred shares cannot affect the allocation of earnings and profits between FC8's shareholders. Therefore, the redemption rights are not restrictions or other limitations within the meaning of paragraph (e)(5) of this section. Additionally, the non-discretionary distribution rights of the preferred shares are not restrictions or other limitations within the meaning of paragraph (e)(5) of this section. Therefore, if the total $100x of earnings were distributed on December 31, 2005, $20x would be distributed with respect to FP's preferred shares and the remainder, $80x, would be distributed with respect to Corp G's common shares. Accordingly, under paragraph (e)(3)(i) of this section, Corp G's pro rata share of FC8's subpart F income is $80 for taxable year 2005.

Example (8). (i) Facts. FC9, a controlled foreign corporation within the meaning of section 957(a), has outstanding 40 shares of common stock and 60 shares of 6-percent, nonparticipating, nonvoting, preferred stock with a par value of $100x per share. Individual J, a United States shareholder of FC9, within the meaning of section 951(b), who uses the calendar year as a taxable year, owns 30 shares of the common stock, and 15 shares of the preferred stock during tax year 2005. The remaining 10 common shares and 45 preferred shares of FC9 are owned by Individual N, a foreign individual. Individual J and Individual N are shareholders of FC9 for all of 2005. For taxable year 2005, FC9 has $1,000x of earnings and profits, and income of $500x with respect to which amounts are required to be included in gross income of United States shareholders under section 951(a).

(ii) Analysis. The non-discretionary distribution rights of the preferred shares are not a restriction or other limitation within the meaning of paragraph (e)(5) of this section. If the total $1,000x of earnings and profits were distributed on December 31, 2005, $360x (0.06 x $100x x 60) would be distributed with respect to FC9's preferred stock and $640x ($1,000x minus $360x) would be distributed with respect to its common stock. Accordingly, of the $500x with respect to which amounts are required to be included in gross income of United States shareholders under section 951(a), $180x ($360x/$1,000x x $500x) is allocated to the outstanding preferred stock and $320x ($640x/$1,000x x $500x) is allocated to the outstanding common stock. Therefore, under paragraph (e)(3)(i) of this section, Individual J's pro rata share of such amounts for 2005 is $285x [($180x x 15/60)+($320x x 30/40)].

Example (9). (i) Facts. In 2006, FC10, a controlled foreign corporation within the meaning of section 957(a), has outstanding 100 shares of common stock and 100 shares of 6-percent, voting, preferred stock with a par value of $10x per share. All of the common stock is held by Corp H, a foreign corporation, which invested $1000x in FC10 in exchange for the common stock. All of the preferred stock is held by Corp J, a domestic corporation, which invested $5000x in FC10 in exchange for the preferred stock. Corp H is unrelated to Corp J. In 2006, FC10 borrows $3000x from a bank and invests $5000x in preferred stock issued by FC11, a foreign corporation the common stock of which is owned by Corp J. Corp J's adjusted basis in its FC 11 common stock is $5000x. FC11, which has no current or accumulated earnings and profits, distributes the $5000x to Corp J. Subsequently, in 2007, FC10 sells the FC11 preferred stock to FC12, a wholly-owned foreign subsidiary of FC11 that has $5000x of accumulated earnings and profits, for $5000x in a transaction described in section 304. FC10 repays the bank loan in full. For 2007, FC10 has $5000x of earnings and profits, all of which is subpart F income attributable to a section 304 dividend arising from FC10's sale of the FC11 preferred stock to FC12. At all relevant times, the value of the common stock of FC10 is $1000x and the value of the preferred stock of FC10 is $5000x.

(ii) Analysis. The acquisition and sale of the FC11 preferred stock by FC10 was part of a plan a principal purpose of which was the avoidance of Federal income tax by depleting the earnings and profits of FC12 and allowing FC11 to make a distribution to Corp J that it characterizes entirely as a return of basis. FC10 has $5000x of earnings and profits for 2007 attributable to a dividend from a section 304 transaction which was part of such plan. Under paragraph (e)(3)(v) of this section, these earnings and profits are allocated to the common and preferred stock of FC10 in accordance with the relative value of each class of stock ($1000x and $5000x, respectively). Thus, for taxable year 2007, $833x (⅙ x $5000x = $833x) of these earnings and profits is allocated to FC10's common stock and $4167x (⅚ x $5000x = $4167x) is allocated to its preferred stock.

(7) Effective dates. Except as provided in paragraphs (e)(3)(v) and (e)(4)(ii) of this section, this paragraph (e) applies for taxable years of a controlled foreign corporation beginning on or after January 1, 2005. However, if the application of this paragraph (e) for purposes of a related Internal Revenue Code provision, such as section 1248, results in an allocation to the stock of such corporation of earnings and profits that have already been allocated to the stock for an earlier year under the prior rules of § 1.951-1(e), as contained in 26 CFR part 1 revised April 1, 2005, then the prior rules will continue to apply to the extent necessary to avoid such duplicative allocation.

(f) Determination of holding period. For purposes of sections 951 through 964, the holding period of an asset (including stock of a controlled foreign corporation) shall be determined by excluding the day on which such asset is acquired and including the day on which such asset is disposed of. The application of this paragraph may be illustrated by the following example:

Example. On June 30, 1963, United States person E acquires 70 of the 100 shares of the only class of stock of foreign corporation A from nonresident alien B, who until such time owns all such 100 shares. E sells 10 shares of stock of such corporation on November 30, 1963, and 60 shares on December 31, 1963, to nonresident alien F. Corporation A is a controlled foreign corporation for the period beginning with July 1, 1963, and extending through December 31, 1963. As to the 10 shares of stock sold on November 30, 1963, E is treated as not owning such shares at any time after November 30, 1963, nor before July 1, 1963. As to the remaining 60 shares of stock, E is treated as not owning them before July 1, 1963, or after December 31, 1963.

(g) United States shareholder defined. *(1) In general.* For purposes of sections 951 through 964, the term "United States shareholder" means, with respect to a foreign corporation, a United States person (as defined in section 957(d)) who owns within the meaning of section 958(a), or is considered as owning by applying the rules of ownership of section 958(b), 10 percent or more of the total combined voting power of all classes of stock entitled to vote of such foreign corporation.

(2) Percentage of total combined voting power owned by United States person. (i) Meaning of combined voting power. In determining for purposes of subparagraph (1) of this paragraph whether a United States person owns the requisite percentage of voting power of all classes of stock entitled to vote, consideration will be given to all the facts and circumstances in each case. In any case where—

(a) A foreign corporation has more than one class of stock outstanding, and

(b) One or more United States persons own (within the meaning of section 958) shares of any one class of stock which possesses the power to elect, appoint, or replace a person, or persons, who with respect to such corporation, exercise the powers ordinarily exercised by a member of the board of directors of a domestic corporation,

the percentage of the total combined voting power with respect to such corporation owned by any such United States person shall be his proportionate share of the percentage of the persons exercising the powers ordinarily exercised by members of the board of directors of a domestic corporation (described in (b) of this subdivision) which such class of stock (as a class) possesses the power to elect, appoint, or replace. In all cases, however, a United States person will be deemed to own 10 percent or more of the total combined voting power with respect to a foreign corporation if such person owns (within the meaning of section 958) 20 percent or more of the total number of shares of a class of stock of such corporation possessing one or more powers enumerated in paragraph (b)(1) of § 1.957-1. Whether a foreign corporation is a controlled foreign corporation for purposes of sections 951 through 964 shall be determined by applying the rules of section 957 and §§ 1.957-1 through 1.957-4.

(ii) Illustration. The application of this paragraph may be illustrated by the following examples:

Example (1). Foreign corporation S has two classes of capital stock outstanding, consisting of 60 shares of class A stock and 40 shares of class B stock. Each class of the outstanding stock is entitled to participate on a share for share basis in any dividend distributions by S Corporation. The owners of a majority of the class A stock are entitled to elect 7 of the 10 corporate directors, and the owners of a majority of the class B stock are entitled to elect the other 3 of the 10 directors. Thus, the class A stock (as a class) possesses 70 percent of the total combined voting power of all classes of stock entitled to vote of S Corporation, and the class B stock (as a class) possesses 30 percent of such voting power. D, a United States person, owns 31 shares of the class A stock and thus owns 36.167 percent (31/60 × 70 percent) of the total combined voting power of all classes of stock entitled to vote of S Corporation. By reason of the ownership of such voting power, D is a United States shareholder of S Corporation under section 951(b). For purposes of section 957, S Corporation is a controlled foreign corporation by reason of D's ownership of a majority of the class A stock, as illustrated in example (2) of paragraph (c) of § 1.957-1. E, a United States person, owns eight shares of the class A stock and thus owns 9.333 percent (8/60 × 70 percent) of the total combined voting power of all classes of stock entitled to vote of S Corporation. Since E owns only 9.333 percent of such voting power and less than 20 percent of the number of shares of the class A stock, he is not a United States shareholder of S Corporation under section 951(b). F, a United States person, owns 14 shares of the class B stock and thus owns 10.5 percent (14/40 × 30 percent) of the total combined voting power of all classes of stock entitled to vote of S Corporation. By reason of the ownership of such voting power, F is a United States shareholder of S Corporation under section 951(b).

Example (2). Foreign corporation R has three classes of stock outstanding, consisting of 10 shares of class A stock, 20 shares of class B stock, and 300 shares of class C stock. Each class of the outstanding stock is entitled to participate on a share for share basis in any distribution by R Corporation. The owners of a majority of the class A stock are entitled to elect 6 of the 10 corporate directors, and the owners of a majority of the class B stock are entitled to elect the other 4 of the 10 directors. The class C stock is not entitled to vote. D, E, and F, United States persons, each own 2 shares of the class A stock and 100 shares of the class C stock. As owners of a majority of the class A stock, D, E, and F elect 6 members of the board of directors. D, E, and F are United States shareholders of R Corporation under section 951(b) since each owns 20 percent of the total number of shares of the class A stock which possesses the power to elect a majority of the board of directors of R Corporation. For purposes of section 957, R Corporation is a controlled foreign corporation by reason of the ownership by D, E, and F of a majority of the class A stock, as illustrated in example (2) of paragraph (c) of § 1.957-1.

T.D. 6795, 1/28/65, amend T.D. 7893, 5/11/83, T.D. 9222, 8/24/2005, T.D. 9251, 2/21/2006.

§ 1.951-2 Coordination of subpart F with election of a foreign investment company to distribute income.

A United States shareholder who for his taxable year is a qualified shareholder (within the meaning of section 1247(c)) of a foreign investment company with respect to which an election under section 1247(a) and the regulations thereunder is in effect for the taxable year of such company which ends with or within such taxable year of such shareholder shall not be required to include any amount in his gross income for his taxable year under paragraph (a) of § 1.951-1 with respect to such company for that taxable year of such company.

T.D. 6795, 1/28/65.

§ 1.951-3 Coordination of subpart F with foreign personal holding company provisions.

Caution: The Treasury has not yet amended Reg § 1.951-3 to reflect changes made by P.L. 98-369.

A United States shareholder (as defined in section 951(b)) who is required under section 551(b) to include in his gross income for his taxable year his share of the undistributed foreign personal holding company income for the taxable year of a foreign personal holding company (as defined in section 552) which for that taxable year is a controlled foreign corporation (as defined in section 957) shall not be required to include in his gross income for his taxable year under section 951(a) and paragraph (a) of § 1.951-1 any amount attributable to the earnings and profits of such corporation for that taxable year of such corporation. If a foreign corporation is both a foreign personal holding company and a controlled foreign corporation for the same period which is only a part of its taxable year, then, for purposes of applying the immediately preceding sentence, such corporation shall be deemed to be, for such part of such year, a foreign personal holding company and not a controlled foreign corporation and the earning and profits of such corporation for the taxable year shall be deemed to be that amount which bears the same ratio to its earnings and profits for the taxable year as such part of the taxable year bears to the entire taxable year. The application of this section may be illustrated by the following examples:

Example (1). A, a United States shareholder owns 100 percent of the only class of stock of controlled foreign corporation M which, in turn, owns 100 percent of the only class of stock of controlled foreign corporation N. A and Corporations M and N use the calendar year as a taxable year. During 1963, N Corporation derives $40,000 of gross income all of which is foreign personal holding company income within the meaning of section 553; thus, N Corporation is a foreign personal holding company for such year within the meaning of section 552(a). For 1963, N Corporation has undistributed foreign personal holding company income (as defined in section 556(a)) of $30,000, derives $25,000 of subpart F income, and has earnings and profits of $32,000. During 1963, M Corporation derives $100,000 of gross income (including as a dividend under section 555(c)(2) the $30,000 of N Corporation's undistributed foreign personal holding company income), 65 percent of which is foreign personal holding company income within the meaning of section 553. Therefore, M Corporation is a foreign personal holding company for such year. For 1963, M Corporation has undistributed foreign personal holding company income (as defined in section 556(a)) of $90,000, determined by taking into account under section 552(c)(1) N Corporation's $30,000 of undistributed foreign personal holding company income for such year; in addition, M Corporation derives $50,000 of subpart F income and has earnings and profits of $92,000. Neither M Corporation nor N Corporation makes any actual distributions during 1963. A is required under section 551(b) to include in his gross income for 1963 as a dividend the $90,000 of M Corporation's undistributed foreign personal holding company income for such year. For 1963, A is not required to include in his gross income under section 951(a) any of the $50,000 subpart F income of M Corporation or of the $25,000 subpart F income of N Corporation.

Example (2). The facts are the same as in example (1), except that only 45 percent of M Corporation's gross income (determined by including under section 555(c)(2) the $30,000 of N Corporation's undistributed foreign personal holding company income) is foreign personal holding company income within the meaning of section 553; accordingly, M Corporation is not a foreign personal holding company for 1963. Since for such year M Corporation is not a foreign personal holding company, the undistributed foreign personal holding company income ($30,000) of N Corporation is not required under section 555(b) to be included in the gross income of M Corporation for 1963; as a result, such income is not required under section 551(b) to be included in the gross income of A for such year even though N Corporation is a foreign personal holding company for that year. For 1963, A is required to include $75,000 in his gross income under section 951(a)(1)(A)(i) and paragraph (a) of § 1.951-1, consisting of the $50,000 subpart F income of M Corporation and the $25,000 subpart F income of N Corporation.

Example (3). The facts are the same as in example (1), except that in 1963 N Corporation actually distributes $30,000 to M Corporation and M Corporation, in turn actually distributes $90,000 to A. Under section 556 the undistributed foreign personal holding company income of both M Corporation and N Corporation is thus reduced to zero; accordingly, no amount is included in the gross income of A under section 551(b) by reason of his interest in corporations M and N. A must include $75,000 in his gross income for 1963 under section 951(a)(1)(A)(i) and paragraph (a) of § 1.951-1, consisting of the $50,000 subpart F income of M Corporation and the $25,000 subpart F income of N Corporation. Of the $90,000 distribution received by A from M Corporation, $75,000 is excludable from his gross income under section 959(a)(1) as previously taxed earnings and profits; the remaining $15,000 is includible in his gross income for 1963 as a dividend.

Example (4). (a) A, a United States shareholder, owns 100 percent of the only class of stock of controlled foreign corporation P, organized on January 1, 1963. Both A and P Corporation use the calendar year as a taxable year. During 1963, 1964, and 1965, P Corporation is not a foreign personal holding company as defined in section 552(a); in each of such years, P Corporation derives dividend income of $10,000 which constitutes foreign personal holding company income (within the meaning of § 1.954-2) but under 26 CFR § 1.954-1(b)(1) (Rev. as of Apr. 1, 1975) excludes such amounts from foreign base company income as dividends received from, and reinvested in, qualified investments in less developed countries. Corporation P's earnings and profits accumulated for 1963, 1964, and 1965 and determined under paragraph (b)(2) of § 1.955-1 are $40,000. For 1966, P Corporation is a foreign personal holding company, has predistribution earnings and profits of $10,000, derives $10,000 of income which is both foreign personal holding company income within the meaning of section 553 and subpart F income within the meaning of section 952, distributes $8,000 to A, and has undistributed foreign personal holding company income of $2,000 within the meaning of section 556. In addition, for 1966 P Corporation has a withdrawal (determined under section 955(a), as in effect before the enactment of the Tax Reduction Act of 1975, but without regard to its earnings and profits for such year) of $25,000 of previously excluded subpart F income from investment in less developed countries. A is required under section 551(b) to include in his gross income for 1966 as a dividend the $2,000 undistributed foreign personal holding company income. The $8,000 distribution is includible in A's gross income for 1966 under sections 61(a)(7) and 301 as a distribution to which section 316(a)(2) applies. Corporation P's $25,000 withdrawal of previously excluded subpart F income from investment in less developed countries is includible in A's gross income for 1966 under section 951(a)(1)(A)(ii) and paragraph (a)(2) of § 1.951-1.

(b) If P Corporation's earnings and profits accumulated for 1963, 1964, and 1965 were $15,000 instead of $40,000, the result would be the same as in paragraph (a) of this example, except that a withdrawal of only $15,000 of previously excluded subpart F income from investment in less developed countries would be includible in A's gross income for 1966 under section 915(a)(1)(A)(ii) and paragraph (a)(2) of § 1.951-1.

(c) The principles of this example also apply to withdrawals (determined under section 955(a), as in effect before the enactment of the Tax Reduction Act of 1975) of previously excluded subpart F income from investment in less developed countries effected after the effective date of such Act, and to withdrawals (determined under section 955(a), as amended by such Act) of previously excluded subpart F income from investment in foreign base company shipping operations.

Example (5). (a) The facts are the same as in paragraph (a) of example (4), except that, instead of having $25,000 decrease in qualified investments in less developed countries for 1966, P Corporation invests $20,000 in tangible property (not described in section 956(b)(2)) located in the United States and such investment constitutes an increase (determined under section 956(a) but without regard to the earnings and profits of P Corporation for 1966) in earnings invested in United States property. Corporation P's earnings and profits accumulated for 1963, 1964 and 1965 and determined under paragraph (b)(1) of § 1.956-1 are $22,000. The result is the same as in paragraph (a) of example (4), except that instead of including the $25,000 withdrawal, A must include $20,000 in his gross income for 1966 under section 951(a)(1)(B) and paragraph (a)(2)(iv) of § 1.951-1 as an investment of earnings in United States property.

(b) If P Corporation's earnings and profits accumulated for 1963, 1964, and 1965 were $9,000 instead of $22,000, the result would be the same as in paragraph (a) of this example, except that only $9,000 would be includible in A's gross income for 1966 under section 951(a)(1)(B) and paragraph (a)(2)(iv) of § 1.951-1 as an investment of earnings in United States property.

T.D. 6795, 1/28/65, amend T.D. 7893, 5/11/83.

---

§ 1.952-1 Subpart F income defined.

Caution: The Treasury has not yet amended Reg § 1.952-1 to reflect changes made by P.L. 105-34, P.L. 100-647, P.L. 99-514, P.L. 99-509.

(a) In general. For purposes of sections 951 through 964, a controlled foreign corporation's subpart F income for any taxable year shall, except as provided in paragraph (b) of this section and subject to the limitations of paragraphs (c) and (d) of this section, consist of the sum of—

(1) The income derived by such corporation for such year from the insurance of United States risks (determined in accordance with the provisions of section 953 and §§ 1.953-1 through 1.953-6),

(2) The income derived by such corporation for such year which constitutes foreign base company income (determined in accordance with the provisions of section 954 and §§ 1.954-1 through 1.954-8),

(3) (i) An amount equal to the product of—

(A) The income of such corporation other than income which—

(1) Is attributable to earnings and profits of the foreign corporation included in the gross income of a United States person under section 951 (other than by reason of this paragraph) (determined in accordance with the provisions of section 951 and § 1.951-1), or

(2) Is described in section 952(b), multiplied by

(B) The international boycott factor determined in accordance with the provisions of section 999(c)(1), or

(ii) In lieu of the amount determined under paragraph (a)(3)(i) of this section, the amount described under section 999(c)(2) of such international boycott income, and

(4) The sum of the amount of any illegal bribes, kickbacks, or other payments paid after November 3, 1976, by or on behalf of the corporation during the taxable year of the corporation directly or indirectly to an official, employee, or agent in fact of a government. An amount is paid by a controlled foreign corporation where it is paid by an officer, director, employee, shareholder or agent of such corporation for the benefit of such corporation. For purposes of this section, the principles of section 162(c) and the regulations thereunder shall apply. In the case of payments made after September 3, 1982, a payment is illegal if the payment would be unlawful under the Foreign Corrupt Practices Act of 1977 if the payor were a United States person. The fair market value of an illegal payment made in the form of property or services shall be considered the amount of such illegal payment.

Pursuant to section 951(a)(1)(A)(i) and § 1.951-1, a United States shareholder of such controlled foreign corporation must include his pro rata share of such subpart F income in his gross income for his taxable year in which or with which such taxable year of the foreign corporation ends. See section 952(a). However, see paragraph (a) of § 1.957-2 for special rule limiting the subpart F income to the income derived from the insurance of United States risks in the case of certain controlled foreign corporations described in section 957(b).

(b) Exclusion of U.S. income. *(1) Taxable years beginning before January 1, 1967.* For rules applicable to taxable years beginning before January 1, 1967, see 26 CFR § 1.952-1(b)(1) (Rev. as of Apr. 1, 1975).

(2) Taxable years beginning after December 31, 1966. Notwithstanding paragraph (a) of this section, a controlled foreign corporation's subpart F income for any taxable year beginning after December 31, 1966, shall not include any item of income from sources within the United States which is effectively connected for that year with the conduct by such corporation of a trade or business in the United States unless, pursuant to a treaty to which the United States is a party, such item of income either is exempt from the income tax imposed by chapter 1 (relating to normal taxes and surtaxes) of the Code or is subject to such tax at a reduced rate. Thus, for example, dividends received from sources within the United States during the taxable year, which are not effectively connected for that year with the conduct of a trade or business in the United States by that corporation, shall not be excluded from subpart F income under section 952(b) and this subparagraph even though such dividends are subject to the tax of 30 percent imposed by section 881(a). Also, for example, if, by reason of an income tax convention to which the United States is a party, an amount of interest from sources within the United States by a foreign corporation is subject to tax under chapter 1 at a flat rate of 15 percent, as provided in § 1.871-12, such interest is not excluded from subpart F income under section 952(b) and this subparagraph. The deductions attributable to items of income which are excluded from subpart F income under this subparagraph shall not be taken into account for purposes of section 952.

(3) Rule applicable under section 956(b)(2). For purposes only of paragraph (b)(1)(viii) of § 1.956-2, an item of income derived by a controlled foreign corporation from sources with the United States with respect to which for the taxable year a tax is imposed in accordance with section 882(a) shall be considered described in section 952(b) whether or not such item of income would have constituted subpart F income for such year.

(c) Limitation on a controlled foreign corporation's subpart F income. *(1) In general.* A United States shareholder's pro rata share (determined in accordance with the rules of paragraph (e) of § 1.951-1) of a controlled foreign corporation's subpart F income for any taxable year shall not exceed his pro rata share of the earnings and profits (as defined in section 964(a) and § 1.964-1) of such corporation for such taxable year, computed as of the close of such taxable year without diminution by reason of any distributions made during such taxable year, minus the sum of—

(i) The amount, if any, by which such shareholder's pro rata share of—

(a) The sum of such corporation's deficits in earnings and profits for prior taxable years beginning after December 31, 1962, plus

(b) The sum of such corporation's deficits in earnings and profits for taxable years beginning after December 31, 1959, and before January 1, 1963 (reduced by the sum of the earnings and profits (as so defined) of such corporation for any of such taxable years) exceeds

(c) The sum of such corporation's earnings and profits for prior taxable years beginning after December 31, 1962, which, with respect to such shareholder, are allocated to other earnings and profits under section 959(c)(3) and § 1.959-3; and

(ii) Such shareholder's pro rata share of any deficits in earnings and profits of other foreign corporations for a taxable year beginning after December 31, 1962, which are attributable to stock of such other foreign corporations owned by such shareholder within the meaning of section 958(a) and which, in accordance with section 952(d) and paragraph (d) of this section, are taken into account as a reduction in the controlled foreign corporation's earnings and profits for such taxable year.

For purposes of applying this subparagraph, the reduction (if any) provided by subdivision (i) of this subparagraph in a United States shareholder's pro rata share of the earnings and profits of a controlled foreign corporation shall be taken into account before the reduction provided by subdivision (ii) of this subparagraph. See section 952(c).

(2) Special rules. For purposes only of determining the limitation under subparagraph (1) of this paragraph on a United States shareholder's pro rata share of a controlled foreign corporation's subpart F income for any taxable year—

(i) Status of foreign corporation. The earnings and profits, or deficit in earnings and profits, of a foreign corporation for any taxable year shall be taken into account whether or not such foreign corporation is a controlled foreign corporation at the time such earnings and profits are derived or such deficit in earnings and profits is incurred.

(ii) Deficits in earnings and profits taken into account only once. A controlled foreign corporation's deficit in earnings and profits for any taxable year preceding the taxable year shall be taken into account for the taxable year only to the extent such deficit has not been taken into account under this paragraph, paragraph (d) of this section, or paragraph (d)(2)(ii) of § 1.963-2 (applied as if section 963 had not been repealed by the Tax Reduction Act of 1975) in computing a minimum distribution, for any taxable year preceding the taxable year, to reduce earnings and profits of such preceding year of such controlled foreign corporation or of any other controlled foreign corporation. To the extent a controlled foreign corporation's (the "first corporation") excess foreign base company shipping deductions for any taxable year (determined under § 1.955A-3(c)(2)(i)) reduce the foreign base company shipping income of another member of a related group (as defined in § 1.955A-2(b)), such deductions shall not be taken into account in determining the earnings and profits or deficits in earnings and profits of such first corporation for such taxable year for purposes of this paragraph (c) and paragraph (d) of this section. The rule of the preceding sentence shall not apply to the extent the excess foreign base company shipping deductions of the first corporation reduce the foreign base company shipping income of another member of a related group below zero.

(iii) Determination of pro rata share. A United States shareholder's pro rata share of a controlled foreign corporation's earnings and profits, or deficit in earnings and profits, for any taxable year shall be determined in accordance with the principles of paragraph (e) of § 1.951-1 and paragraph (d)(2)(ii) of § 1.963-2.

(3) Illustrations. The application of this paragraph may be illustrated by the following examples:

Example (1). (a) A is a United States shareholder who owns 100 percent of the only class of stock of M Corporation, a controlled foreign corporation organized on January 1, 1963. Both A and M Corporation use the calendar year as a taxable year.

(b) During 1963, M Corporation derives $20,000 of subpart F income and has earnings and profits of $30,000. Corporation M makes no distributions to A during such year. The limitation under section 952(c) on M Corporation's subpart F income for 1963 is $30,000; and $20,000 is includible in A's gross income for such year under section 951(a)(1)(A)(i).

(c) On January 1, 1964, M Corporation acquires 100 percent of the only class of stock of N Corporation, a controlled foreign corporation which uses the calendar year as a taxable year. During 1964, N Corporation derives $6,000 of subpart F income, has $7,000 of earnings and profits, and distributes $5,000 to M Corporation. The limitation under section 952(c) on N Corporation's subpart F income for 1964 is $7,000; and $6,000 of subpart F income is includible in A's gross income for such year under section 951(a)(1)(A)(i).

(d) During 1964, M Corporation derives $8,000 of rents which constitute subpart F income, makes a $10,000 distribution to A, and has earnings and profits of $12,000 (including the $5,000 dividend received from N Corporation). The limitation under section 952(c) on M Corporation's subpart F income for 1964 is $7,000, determined as follows:

Corporation M's earnings and profits for 1964 (determined under section 964(a) and Sec. 1.964-1 as of the close of such year without diminution for any distributions made during such year)	$12,000
Less: Corporation M's earnings and profits for 1964 described in section 959(b)	5,000
Limitation on M Corporation's subpart F income for 1964	7,000

Thus, for 1964 with respect to A's interest in M Corporation, $7,000 of subpart F income is includible in his gross income under section 951(a)(1)(A)(i). The $10,000 dividend received from M Corporation is excludible from A's gross income for 1964 under section 959(a)(1) and paragraph (b) of § 1.959-1.

Example (2). A is a United States shareholder who owns 100 percent of the only class of stock of R Corporation which was organized on January 1, 1961. R Corporation is a controlled foreign corporation for the entire period after December 31, 1962, here involved. Both A and R Corporation use the calendar year as a taxable year. During 1963, R Corporation derives $25,000 of subpart F income and has $50,000 of earnings and profits. Corporation R has $15,000 of earnings and profits for 1961, and a deficit in earnings and profits of $45,000 for 1962. Thus, R Corporation has as of December 31, 1963, a net deficit in earnings and profits of $30,000 for the years 1961 and 1962. Corporation R makes no distributions to A during 1963. The limitation under section 952(c) on R Corporation's subpart F income for 1963 is $20,000 ($50,000 minus $30,000), and $20,000 of subpart F income is includible in A's gross income for 1963 under section 951(a)(1)(A)(i). During 1964, R Corporation derives $18,000 of subpart F income and has $30,000 of earnings and profits. Corporation R makes no distributions to A during 1964. The entire $18,000 of subpart F income is includible in A's gross income for 1964 under section 951(a)(1)(A)(i).

(d) Treatment of deficits in earnings and profits attributable to stock of other foreign corporation indirectly owned by a United States shareholder. *(1) In general.* For purposes of paragraph (c)(1)(ii) of this section, if—

(i) A United States shareholder owns (within the meaning of section 958(a)) stock in two or more foreign corporations in a chain of foreign corporations (as defined in subparagraph (2)(ii) of this paragraph), and

(ii) Any of the corporations in such chain has a deficit in earnings and profits for a taxable year beginning after December 31, 1962,

then, with respect to such shareholder and only for purposes of determining the limitation on subpart F income under paragraph (c) of this section, the earnings and profits for the taxable year of each such foreign corporation which is a controlled foreign corporation shall, in accordance with the rules of subparagraph (2) of this paragraph, be reduced to take into account any deficit in earnings and profits referred to in subdivision (ii) of this subparagraph. See section 952(d).

(2) Special rules. For purposes of this paragraph—

(i) Applicable rules. The special rules set forth in paragraph (c)(2) of this section shall apply.

(ii) "Chain" defined. A chain of foreign corporations shall, with respect to a United States shareholder, include—

(a) Any foreign corporation in which such shareholder owns (within the meaning of section 958(1)(A)) stock, but only to the extent of the stock so owned, and

(b) All foreign corporations in which such shareholder owns (within the meaning of section 958(a)(2)) stock, but only to the extent of the stock so owned by reason of his ownership of the stock referred to in (a) of this subdivision.

(iii) Allocation of deficit. If one or more foreign corporations (whether or not a controlled foreign corporation) includible in a chain of foreign corporations has a deficit in earnings and profits (determined under section 964(a) and § 1.964-1) for the taxable year, the amount of deficit taken into account under section 952(d) with respect to a United States shareholder in such chain as a reduction in earnings and profits for the taxable year of a controlled foreign corporation includible in such chain shall be an amount which bears the same ratio to such shareholder's pro rata share of the total deficit in earnings and profits for the taxable year of all includible foreign corporations as his pro rata share of the earnings and profits (determined under paragraph (c) of this section but without regard to the provisions of subparagraph (1)(ii) of such paragraph) for the taxable year of such includible controlled foreign corporation bears to his pro rata share of the total earnings and profits (as so determined under paragraph (c) of this section) for the taxable year of all includible controlled foreign corporations. The amount of deficit taken into account under this subdivision with respect to any controlled foreign corporation includible in a chain of foreign corporations shall not exceed the United States shareholder's pro rata share of the controlled foreign corporation's earnings and profits for the taxable year.

(iv) Taxable year. The taxable year from which a deficit is allocated under this paragraph, and the taxable year to which such deficit is allocated to reduce earnings and profits, shall be the taxable year of the foreign corporation ending with or within the taxable year of the United States shareholder described in subparagraph (1)(i) of this paragraph.

(3) Illustration. The application of this paragraph may be illustrated by the following examples:

Example (1). (a) Domestic corporation M owns 100 percent, 20 percent, and 100 percent, respectively, of the only class of stock of foreign corporations A, B, and F, respectively. Corporation A owns 80 percent of the only class of stock of each of foreign corporations B and C, respectively. Corporation F owns 20 percent of such stock of C Corporation. Corporation B owns 75 percent of the only class of stock of foreign corporation D, and 50 percent of the only class of stock of each of foreign corporations G and H, respectively. C Corporation owns 75 percent of the only class of stock of foreign corporation E. All the corporations use the calendar year as a taxable year, and all of the foreign corporations, except corporations G and H, are controlled foreign corporations throughout the period here involved.

(b) The subpart F income, and the earnings and profits (determined under paragraph (c) of this section but without regard to subparagraph (1)(ii) of such paragraph) or deficit in earnings and profits (determined under section 964(a) and § 1.964-1), of each of the foreign corporations for 1963 are as follows, the deficits being set forth in parenthesis:

	Subpart F income	Earnings and profits (deficits)
A Corporation	$ 6,000	$18,000
B Corporation		(7,500)
C Corporation		(2,500)
D Corporation	4,000	5,000
E Corporation	12,000	15,000
F Corporation	8,000	20,250
G Corporation		(10,000)
H Corporation		7,000

(c) The chains of foreign corporations (within the meaning of subparagraph (2)(ii) of this paragraph) for 1963 are the "A" chain, consisting of corporations A, B, C, D, E, G, and H, but only to the extent of M Corporation's stock interest in such corporations under section 958(a) by reason of its ownership of stock in A Corporation; the "B" chain, consisting of corporations B, D, G, and H, but only to the extent of M Corporation's stock interest in such corporations under section 958(a) by reason of its ownership of stock in B Corporation; and the "F" chain, consisting of corporations F, C, and E, but only to the extent of M Corporation's stock interest in such corporations under section 958(a) by reason of its ownership of stock in F Corporation.

(d) Corporation M's stock interest under section 958(a) in each of the chains of foreign corporations is as follows for 1963:

	A	B	C	D	E	F	G	H
				Percent				
A chain:								
Direct interest	100							
(100% × 80%)		80						
(100% × 80%)			80					
(80% × 75%)				60				
(80% × 75%)					60			
(80% × 50%)							40	
(80% × 50%)								40
B chain:								
Direct interest	20							
(20% × 75%)				15				
(20% × 50%)							10	
(20% × 50%)								10
F chain:								
Direct interest						100		
(100% × 20%)			20					
(20% × 75%)					15			
Total interests	100	100	100	75	75	100	50	50

(e) Corporation M's pro rata share of the earnings and profits (determined under paragraph (c) of this section but without regard to subparagraph (1)(ii) of such paragraph), or of the deficit, of each controlled foreign corporation or each foreign corporation, respectively, includible in the respective chains for 1963 is as follows:

	Earnings and profits	Deficit
A chain:		
A Corporation (100%)	$18,000	
B Corporation (80%)		($6,000)
C Corporation (80%)		(2,000)
D Corporation (60%)	3,000	
E Corporation (60%)	9,000	
G Corporation (40%)		(4,000)
H Corporation (40%)	([1])	
Total	30,000	(12,000)
B chain:		
B Corporation (20%)		(1,500)
D Corporation (15%)	750	
G Corporation (10%)		(1,000)
H Corporation (10%)	([1])	
Total	$ 750	(2,500)
F chain:		
F Corporation (100%)	20,250	
C Corporation (20%)		(500)
E Corporation (15%)	2,250	
Total	$22,500	(500)

[1] The earnings and profits of H Corporation are not included in the total earnings and profits for the chain because H Corporation is not a controlled foreign corporation.

(f) The amount by which M Corporation's pro rata share of the earnings and profits for 1963 of the controlled foreign corporations in each respective chain shall be reduced under section 952(d) by M Corporation's pro rata share of the deficits of corporations B, C, and G for 1963 is determined as follows:

	Amount of reduction	
A chain:		
A Corporation ($12,000 × $18,000/$30,000)	$ 7,200	
D Corporation ($12,000 × $3,000/$30,000)	1,200	
E Corporation ($12,000 × $9,000/$30,000)	3,600	
Total	12,000	
B chain:		
D Corporation ($2,500 × $750/$750)	$2,500	
Limitation: M Corporation's pro rata share of D Corporation's earnings and profits	750	
Allocation of used deficit ($750) to M Corporation's pro rata share of the deficits of corporations B and G:		
B Corporation ($750 × ($1,500/$2,500))	450	
G Corporation ($750 × ($1,000/$2,500))	300	
Total	750	750
F chain:		
F Corporation ($500 × $20,250/$22,500)		450
E Corporation ($500 × $2,250/$22,500)		50
Total		500

(g) Corporation M's pro rata share of the earnings and profits (determined after reduction for deficits under section 952(d)) for 1963 of each controlled foreign corporation in the respective chains, determined on a chain-by-chain basis, is determined as follows:

	Earnings and profits before reduction	Reduction (sec. 952(d)	Reduced earnings and profits
A chain:			
A Corporation	$18,000	$7,200	$10,800
D Corporation	3,000	1,200	1,800
E Corporation	9,000	3,600	5,400
B chain:			
D Corporation	750	750	
F chain:			
F Corporation	20,250	450	19,800
E Corporation	2,250	50	2,200

(h) Corporation M's pro rata share of each controlled foreign corporation's subpart F income, limited as provided by section 952(c) and paragraph (c) of this section, for 1963 which is includible in its gross income for such year under section 951(a)(1)(A)(i) and § 1.951-1 is determined as follows:

	Subpart F income (before limitation)	Earnings and profits (sec. 952 (c))	Amount includible in income
A Corporation (100%)	$6,000	$10,800	$ 6,000
D Corporation (75%)	3,000	1,800	1,800
E Corporation (75%)	9,000	7,600	7,600
F Corporation (100%)	8,000	19,800	8,000

Total includible under sec. 951(a)(1)(A)(i) ...	23,400

Example (2). The facts are the same as in example (1) except that, in addition, for 1964, foreign corporations C, D, and E have no subpart F income and no earnings and profits and foreign corporations G and H have no earnings and profits. For 1964, B Corporation has subpart F income of $1,000 and earnings and profits (determined in accordance with section 964(a) and § 1.964-1) of $1,500; A Corporation has subpart F income of $800 and earnings and profits of $1,000; and F Corporation has subpart F income of $500 and earnings and profits of $1,000. Such earnings and profits are determined without regard to distributions for 1964. Corporation B has an unused deficit in earnings and profits of $1,050 for 1963 ($1,500 minus $450) applicable to M Corporation's interest in such corporation (paragraph (f) of example (1)), and, under paragraph (c)(1)(i)(a) of this section, with respect to M Corporation, such deficit reduces B Corporation's earnings and profits for 1964 to $450. Inasmuch as G Corporation is not a controlled foreign corporation for 1964, such corporation's unused deficit in earnings and profits of $700 for 1963 ($1,000 minus $300) applicable to M Corporation's interest in such corporation (paragraph (f) of example (1)) may be used under paragraph (c)(1)(i)(a) of this section to reduce M Corporation's interest in G Corporation's earnings and profits in a later year or years for which G Corporation is a controlled foreign corporation. Corporation M's pro rata share of each controlled foreign corporation's subpart F income, limited as provided by section 952(c) and para- graph (c) of this section, for 1964 which is includible in its gross income for such year under section 951(a)(1)(A)(i) and § 1.951-1 is determined as follows:

	Subpart F income (before limitation)	Earnings and profits (sec. 952 (c))	Amount includible in income
A Corporation	$ 800	$1,000	$800
B Corporation	1,000	450	450
F Corporation	500	1,000	500

Example (3). The facts are the same as in example (2), except that for 1964 B Corporation has subpart F income of $550 and earnings and profits (determined in accordance with section 964(a) and § 1.964-1) of $550; such earnings and profits are determined without regard to distributions for 1964. Under paragraph (c)(1)(i)(a) of this section, B Corporation's unused deficit of $1,050 for 1963 reduces its earnings and profits for 1964 with respect to M Corporation to zero. The remaining $500 of the unused deficit for 1963 applicable to M Corporation's interest in B Corporation may be used under paragraph (c)(1)(i)(a) of this section in later years to reduce M Corporation's interest in B Corporation's earnings and profits.

(e) Application of current earnings and profits limitation. *(1) In general.* If the subpart F income (as defined in section 952(a)) of a controlled foreign corporation exceeds the foreign corporation's earnings and profits for the taxable year, the subpart F income includible in the income of the corporation's United States shareholders is reduced under section 952(c)(1)(A) in accordance with the following rules. The excess of subpart F income over current year earnings and profits shall—

(i) First, proportionately reduce subpart F income in each separate category of the controlled foreign corporation, as defined in § 1.904-5(a)(1), in which current earnings and profits are zero or less than zero;

(ii) Second, proportionately reduce subpart F income in each separate category in which subpart F income exceeds current earnings and profits; and

(iii) Third, proportionately reduce subpart F income in other separate categories.

(2) Allocation to a category of subpart F income. An excess amount that is allocated under paragraph (e)(1) of this section to a separate category must be further allocated to a category of subpart F income if the separate category contains more than one category of subpart F income described in section 952(a) or, in the case of foreign base company income, described in § 1.954-1(c)(1)(iii)(A)(1) or (2). In such case, the excess amount that is allocated to the separate category must be allocated to the various categories of subpart F income within that separate category on a proportionate basis.

(3) Recapture of subpart F income reduced by operation of earnings and profits limitation. Any amount in a category of subpart F income described in section 952(a) or, in the case of foreign base company income, described in § 1.954-1(c)(1)(iii)(A)(1) or (2) that is reduced by operation of the current year earnings and profits limitation of section 952(c)(1)(A) and this paragraph (e) shall be subject to recapture in a subsequent year under the rules of section 952(c)(2) and paragraph (f) of this section.

(4) Coordination with sections 953 and 954. The rules of this paragraph (e) shall be applied after the application of sections 953 and 954 and the regulations under those sections, except as provided in § 1.954-1(d)(4)(ii).

(5) Earnings and deficits retain separate limitation character. The income reduction rules of paragraph (e)(1) of this section shall apply only for purposes of determining the amount of an inclusion under section 951(a)(1)(A) from each separate category as defined in § 1.904-5(a)(1) and the separate categories in which recapture accounts are established under section 952(c)(2) and paragraph (f) of this section. For rules applicable in computing post-1986 undistributed earnings, see generally section 902 and the regulations under that section. For rules relating to the allocation of deficits for purposes of computing foreign taxes deemed paid under section 960 with respect to an inclusion under section 951(a)(1)(A), see § 1.960-1(i).

(f) Recapture of subpart F income in subsequent taxable year. *(1) In general.* If a controlled foreign corporation's subpart F income for a taxable year is reduced under the current year earnings and profits limitation of section 952(c)(1)(A) and paragraph (e) of this section, recapture accounts will be established and subject to recharacterization in any subsequent taxable year to the extent the recapture accounts were not previously recharacterized or distributed, as provided in paragraphs (f)(2) and (3) of this section.

(2) Rules of recapture. (i) Recapture account. If a category of subpart F income described in section 952(a) or, in the case of foreign base company income, described in § 1.954-1(c)(1)(iii)(A)(1) or (2) is reduced under the current year earnings and profits limitation of section 952(c)(1)(A) and paragraph (e) of this section for a taxable year, the amount of such reduction shall constitute a recapture account.

(ii) Recapture. Each recapture account of the controlled foreign corporation will be recharacterized, on a proportionate basis, as subpart F income in the same separate category (as defined in § 1.904-5(a)(1)) as the recapture account to the extent that current year earnings and profits exceed subpart F income in a taxable year. The United States shareholder must include his pro rata share (determined under the rules of § 1.951-1(e)) of each recharacterized amount in income as subpart F income in such separate category for the taxable year.

(iii) Reduction of recapture account and corresponding earnings. Each recapture account, and post-1986 undistributed earnings in the separate category containing the recapture account, will be reduced in any taxable year by the amount which is recharacterized under paragraph (f)(2)(ii) of this section. In addition, each recapture account, and post-1986 undistributed earnings in the separate category containing the recapture account, will be reduced in the amount of any distribution out of that account (as determined under the ordering rules of section 959(c) and paragraph (f)(3)(ii) of this section).

(3) Distribution ordering rules. (i) Coordination of recapture and distribution rules. If a controlled foreign corporation distributes an amount out of earnings and profits described in section 959(c)(3) in a year in which current year earnings and profits exceed subpart F income and there is an amount in a recapture account for such year, the recapture rules will apply first.

(ii) Distributions reduce recapture accounts first. Any distribution made by a controlled foreign corporation out of earnings and profits described in section 959(c)(3) shall be treated as made first on a proportionate basis out of the recapture accounts in each separate category to the extent thereof (even if the amount in the recapture account exceeds post-1986 undistributed earnings in the separate category containing the recapture account). Any remaining distribution shall be treated as made on a proportionate basis out of the remaining earnings and profits of the controlled foreign corporation in each separate category. See section 904(d)(3)(D).

(4) Examples. The application of paragraphs (e) and (f) of this section may be illustrated by the following examples:

Example (1). (i) A, a U.S. person, is the sole shareholder of CFC, a controlled foreign corporation formed on January 1, 1998, whose functional currency is the u. In 1998, CFC earns 100u of foreign base company sales income that is general limitation income described in section 904(d)(1)(I) and incurs a (200u) loss attributable to activities that would have produced general limitation income that is not subpart F income. In 1998 CFC also earns 100u of foreign personal holding company income that is passive income described in section 904(d)(1)(A), and 100u of foreign personal holding company income that is dividend income subject to a separate limitation described in section 904(d)(1)(E) for dividends from a noncontrolled section 902 corporation. CFC's subpart F income for 1998, 300u, exceeds CFC's current earnings and profits, 100u, by 200u. Under section 952(c)(1)(A) and paragraph (e) of this section, subpart F income is limited to CFC's current earnings and profits of 100u, all of which is included in A's gross income under section 951(a)(1)(A). The 200u of CFC's 1998 subpart F income that is not included in A's income in 1998 by reason of section 952(c)(1)(A) is subject to recapture under section 952(c)(2) and paragraph (f) of this section.

(ii) For purposes of determining the amount and type of income included in A's gross income and the amount and type of income in CFC's recapture account, the rules of paragraphs (e)(1) and (2) of this section apply. Under paragraph (e)(1)(i) of this section, the amount by which CFC's subpart F income exceeds its earnings and profits for 1998, 200u, first reduces from 100u to 0 CFC's subpart F income in the general limitation category, which has a current year deficit of (100u) in earnings and profits. Next, under paragraph (e)(1)(iii) of this section, the remaining 100u by which CFC's 1998 subpart F income exceeds earnings and profits is applied proportionately to reduce CFC's subpart F income in the separate categories for passive income (100u) and dividends from the noncontrolled section 902 corporation (100u). Thus, A includes 50u of passive limitation/foreign personal holding company income and 50u of dividends from the noncontrolled section 902 corporation/foreign personal holding company income in gross income in 1998. CFC has 100u in its general limitation/foreign base company sales income recapture account attributable to the 100u of foreign base company sales income that is not included in A's income by reason of the earnings and profits limitation of section 952(c)(1)(A). CFC also has 50u in its passive limitation recapture account, all of which is attributable to foreign personal holding company income, and 50u in its recapture account for dividends from the noncontrolled section 902 corporation, all of which is attributable to foreign personal holding company income.

(iii) For purposes of computing post-1986 undistributed earnings, the rules of sections 902 and 960, including the rules of § 1.960-1(i), apply. Under § 1.960-1(i), the general limitation deficit of (100u) is allocated proportionately to reduce passive limitation earnings of 100u and noncontrolled section 902 dividend earnings of 100u. Thus, passive limitation earnings are reduced by 50u to 50u (100u passive limitation earnings/200u total earnings in positive separate categories × (100u) general limitation deficit = 50u reduction), and the noncontrolled section 902 corporation earnings are reduced by 50u to 50u (100u noncontrolled section 902 corporation earnings/200u total earnings in positive separate categories + (100u) general limitation deficit = 50u reduction). All of CFC's post-1986 foreign income taxes with respect to passive limitation income and dividends from the noncontrolled section 902 corporation are deemed paid by A under section 960 with respect to the subpart F inclusions (50u inclusion/50u earnings in each separate category). After the inclusion and deemed-paid taxes are computed, at the close of 1998 CFC has a (100u) deficit in general limitation earnings (100u subpart F earnings + (200u) nonsubpart F loss), 50u of passive limitation earnings (100u of earnings attributable to foreign personal holding company income – 50u inclusion) with a corresponding passive limitation/foreign personal holding company income recapture account of 50u, and 50u of earnings subject to a separate limitation for dividends from the noncontrolled section 902 corporation (100u earnings – 50u inclusion) with a corresponding noncontrolled section 902 corporation/foreign personal holding company income recapture account of 50u.

Example (2). (i) The facts are the same as in Example 1 with the addition of the following facts. In 1999, CFC earns 100u of foreign base company sales income that is general limitation income and 100u of foreign personal holding company income that is passive limitation income. In addition, CFC incurs (10u) of expenses that are allocable to its separate limitation for dividends from the noncontrolled section 902 corporation. Thus, CFC's subpart F income for 1999, 200u, exceeds CFC's current earnings and profits, 190u, by 10u. Under section 952(c)(1)(A) and paragraph (e) of this section, subpart F income is limited to CFC's current earnings and profits of 190u, all of which is included in A's gross income under section 951(a)(1)(A).

(ii) For purposes of determining the amount and type of income included in A's gross income and the amount and type of income in CFC's recapture accounts, the rules of paragraphs (e)(1) and (2) of this section apply. While CFC's general limitation post-1986 undistributed earnings for 1999 are 0 ((100u) opening balance + 100u subpart F income), CFC's general limitation subpart F income (100u) does not exceed its general limitation current earnings and profits (100u) for 1999. Accordingly, under paragraph (e)(1)(iii) of this section, the amount by which CFC's subpart F income exceeds its earnings and profits for 1999, 10u, is applied proportionately to reduce CFC's subpart F income in the separate categories for general limitation income, 100u, and passive income, 100u. Thus, A includes 95u of general limitation foreign base company sales income and 95u of passive limitation foreign personal holding company income in gross income in 1999. At the close of 1999 CFC has 105u in its general limitation/foreign base company sales income recapture account (100u from 1998 + 5u from 1999), 55u in its passive limitation/foreign personal holding company income recapture account (50u from 1998 + 5u from 1999), and 50u in its dividends from the noncontrolled section 902 corporation/foreign personal holding company income recapture account (all from 1998).

(iii) For purposes of computing post-1986 undistributed earnings in each separate category, the rules of sections 902 and 960, including the rules of § 1.960-1(i), apply. Thus, post-1986 undistributed earnings (or an accumulated deficit) in each separate category are increased (or reduced) by current earnings and profits or current deficits in each separate category. The accumulated deficit in CFC's general limitation earnings and profits (100u) is reduced to 0 by the addition of 100u of 1999 earnings and profits. CFC's passive limitation earnings of 50u are increased by 100u to 150u, and CFC's noncontrolled section 902 corporation earnings of 50u are decreased by (10u) to 40u. After the addition of current year earnings and profits and deficits to the separate categories there are no deficits remaining in any separate category. Thus, the allocation rules of § 1.960-1(i)(4) do not apply in 1999. Accordingly, in determining the post-1986 foreign income taxes deemed paid by A, post-1986 undistributed earnings in each separate category are unaffected by earnings in the other categories. Foreign taxes deemed paid under section 960 for 1999 would be determined as follows for each separate category: with respect to the inclusion of 95u of foreign base company sales income out of general limitation earnings, the section 960 fraction is 95u inclusion/0 total earnings; with respect to the inclusion of 95u of passive limitation income the section 960 fraction is 95u inclusion/150u passive earnings. Thus, no general limitation taxes would be associated with the inclusion of the general limitation earnings because there are no accumulated earnings in the general limitation category. After the deemed-paid taxes are computed, at the close of 1999 CFC has a (95u) deficit in general limitation earnings and profits ((100u) opening balance + 100u current earnings − 95u inclusion), 55u of passive limitation earnings and profits (50u opening balance + 100u current foreign personal holding company income − 95u inclusion), and 40u of earnings and profits subject to the separate limitation for dividends from the noncontrolled section 902 corporation (50u opening balance + (10u) expense).

Example (3). (i) A, a U.S. person, is the sole shareholder of CFC, a controlled foreign corporation whose functional currency is the u. At the beginning of 1998, CFC has post-1986 undistributed earnings of 275u, all of which are general limitation earnings described in section 904(d)(1)(I). CFC has no previously-taxed earnings and profits described in section 959(c)(1) or (c)(2). In 1998, CFC has a (200u) loss in the shipping category described in section 904(d)(1)(D), 100u of foreign personal holding company income that is passive income described in section 904(d)(1)(A), and 125u of general limitation manufacturing earnings that are not subpart F income. CFC's subpart F income for 1998, 100u, exceeds CFC's current earnings and profits, 25u, by 75u. Under section 952(c)(1)(A) and paragraph (e) of this section, subpart F income is limited to CFC's current earnings and profits of 25u, all of which is included in A's gross income under section 951(a)(1)(A). The 75u of CFC's 1998 subpart F income that is not included in A's income in 1998 by reason of section 952(c)(1)(A) is subject to recapture under section 952(c)(2) and paragraph (f) of this section.

(ii) For purposes of determining the amount and type of income included in A's gross income and the amount and type of income in CFC's recapture account, the rules of paragraphs (e)(1) and (2) of this section apply. Under paragraph (e)(1) of this section, the amount of CFC's subpart F income in excess of earnings and profits for 1998, 75u, reduces the 100u of passive limitation foreign personal holding company income. Thus, A includes 25u of passive limitation foreign personal holding company income in gross income, and CFC has 75u in its passive limitation/foreign personal holding company income recapture account.

(iii) For purposes of computing post-1986 undistributed earnings in each separate category the rules of sections 902 and 960, including the rules of § 1.960-1(i), apply. Under § 1.960-1(i), the shipping limitation deficit of (200u) is allocated proportionately to reduce general limitation earnings of 400u and passive limitation earnings of 100u. Thus, general limitation earnings are reduced by 160u to 240u (400u general limitation earnings/500u total earnings in positive separate categories × (200u) shipping deficit = 160u reduction), and passive limitation earnings are reduced by 40u to 60u (100u passive earnings/500u total earnings in positive separate categories × (200u) shipping deficit = 40u reduction). Five-twelfths of CFC's post-1986 foreign income taxes with respect to passive limitation earnings are deemed paid by A under section 960 with respect to the subpart F inclusion (25u inclusion/60u passive earnings). After the inclusion and deemed-paid taxes are computed, at the close of 1998 CFC has 400u of general limitation earnings (275u opening balance + 125u current earnings), 75u of passive limitation earnings (100u of foreign personal holding company income − 25u inclusion), and a (200u) deficit in shipping limitation earnings.

Example (4). (i) The facts are the same as in Example 3 with the addition of the following facts. In 1999, CFC earns 50u of general limitation earnings that are not subpart F income and 75u of passive limitation income that is foreign personal holding company income. Thus, CFC has 125u of current earnings and profits. CFC distributes 200u to A. Under paragraph (f)(3)(i) of this section, the recapture rules are applied first. Thus, the amount by which 1999 current earnings and profits exceed subpart F income, 50u, is recharacterized as passive limitation foreign personal holding company income. CFC's total subpart F income for 1999 is 125u of passive limitation foreign personal holding company income (75u current earnings plus 50u recapture account), and the passive limitation/foreign personal holding company income recapture account is reduced from 75u to 25u.

(ii) CFC has 150u of previously-taxed earnings and profits described in section 959(c)(2) (25u attributable to 1998 and 125u attributable to 1999), all of which is passive limitation earnings and profits. Under section 959(c), 150u of the 200u distribution is deemed to be made from earnings and profits described in section 959(c)(2). The remaining 50u is deemed to be made from earnings and profits described in section 959(c)(3). Under paragraph (f)(3)(ii) of this section, the dividend distribution is deemed to be made first out of the passive limitation recapture account to the extent thereof (25u). Under paragraph (f)(2)(iii) of this section, the passive limitation recapture account is reduced from 25u to 0. The remaining distribution of 25u is treated as made out of CFC's general limitation earnings and profits.

(iii) For purposes of computing post-1986 undistributed earnings, the rules of section 902 and 960, including the rules of § 1.960-1(i), apply. Thus, the shipping limitation accumulated deficit of (200u) reduces general limitation earnings and profits of 450u and passive limitation earnings and profits of 150u on a proportionate basis. Thus, 100% of CFC's post-1986 foreign income taxes with respect to passive limitation earnings are deemed paid by A under section 960 with respect to the 1999 subpart F inclusion of 125u (100u inclusion (numerator limited to denominator)/100u passive earnings). No post-1986 foreign income taxes remain to be deemed paid under section 902 in connection with the 25u distribution from the passive limitation/foreign personal holding company income recapture account. One-twelfth of CFC's post-1986 foreign income taxes with respect to general limitation earnings are deemed paid by A under section 902 with respect to the distribution of 25u general limitation earnings and profits described in section 959(c)(3) (25u inclusion/300u general limitation earnings). After the deemed-paid taxes are computed, at the close of 1999 CFC has 425u of general limitation earnings and profits (400u opening balance + 50u current earnings – 25u distribution), 0 of passive limitation earnings (75u recapture account + 75u current foreign personal holding company income – 125u inclusion – 25u distribution), and a (200u) deficit in shipping limitation earnings.

(5) Effective date. Paragraph (e) of this section and this paragraph (f) apply to taxable years of a controlled foreign corporation beginning after March 3, 1997.

(g) Treatment of distributive share of partnership income. *(1) In general.* A controlled foreign corporation's distributive share of any item of income of a partnership is income that falls within a category of subpart F income described in section 952(a) to the extent the item of income would have been income in such category if received by the controlled foreign corporation directly. For specific rules regarding the treatment of a distributive share of partnership income under certain provisions of subpart F, see §§ 1.954-1(g), 1.954-2(a)(5), 1.954-3(a)(6), and 1.954-4(b)(2)(iii).

(2) Example. The application of this paragraph (g) may be illustrated by the following example:

Example. CFC, a controlled foreign corporation, is an 80-percent partner in PRS, a foreign partnership. PRS earns $100 of interest income that is not export financing interest as defined in section 954(c)(2)(B), or qualified banking or financing income as defined in section 954(h)(3)(A), from a person unrelated to CFC. This interest income would have been foreign personal holding company income to CFC, under section 954(c), if it had received this income directly. Accordingly, CFC's distributive share of this interest income, $80, is foreign personal holding company income.

(3) Effective date. This paragraph (g) applies to taxable years of a controlled foreign corporation beginning on or after July 23, 2002.

T.D. 6795, 1/28/65, amend T.D. 6892, 8/22/66, T.D. 7293, 11/27/73, T.D. 7545, 5/5/78, T.D. 7862, 12/16/82, T.D. 7893, 5/11/83, T.D. 7894, 5/11/83, T.D. 8331, 1/24/91, T.D. 8704, 12/31/96, T.D. 9008, 7/22/2002.

---

§ 1.952-2 Determination of gross income and taxable income of a foreign corporation.

Caution: The Treasury has not yet amended Reg § 1.952-2 to reflect changes made by P.L. 105-34.

(a) Determination of gross income. *(1) In general.* Except as provided in subparagraph (2) of this paragraph, the gross income of a foreign corporation for any taxable year shall, subject to the special rules of paragraph (c) of this section, be determined by treating such foreign corporation as a domestic corporation taxable under section 11 and by applying the principles of section 61 and the regulations thereunder.

(2) Insurance gross income. (i) Life insurance gross income. The gross income for any taxable year of a controlled foreign corporation which is engaged in the business of reinsuring or issuing insurance or annuity contracts and which, if it were a domestic corporation engaged only in such business, would be taxable as a life insurance company to which part I (sections 801 through 820) of subchapter L of chapter 1 of the Code applies, shall, subject to the special rules of paragraph (c) of this section, be the sum of—

(a) The gross investment income, as defined under section 804(b), except that interest which is excluded from gross income under section 103 shall not be taken into account;

(b) The sum of the items taken into account under section 809(c), except that advance premiums shall not be taken into account; and

(c) The amount by which the net long-term capital gain exceeds the net short-term capital loss.

(ii) Mutual and other insurance gross income. The gross income for any taxable year of a controlled foreign corporation which is engaged in the business of reinsuring or issuing insurance or annuity contracts and which, if it were a domestic corporation engaged only in such business, would be taxable as a mutual insurance company to which part II (sections 821 through 826) of subchapter L of chapter 1 of the Code applies or as a mutual marine insurance or other insurance company to which part III (sections 831 and 832) of subchapter L of chapter 1 of the Code applies, shall, subject to the special rules of paragraph (c) of this section, be—

(a) The sum of—

(1) The gross income, as defined in section 832(b)(1);

(2) The amount of losses incurred, as defined in section 832(b)(5); and

(3) The amount of expenses incurred, as defined in section 832(b)(6); reduced by

(b) The amount of interest which under section 103 is excluded from gross income.

(b) Determination of taxable income. *(1) In general.* Except as provided in subparagraph (2) of this paragraph, the taxable income of a foreign corporation for any taxable year shall, subject to the special rules of paragraph (c) of this section, be determined by treating such foreign corporation as a domestic corporation taxable under section 11 and by applying the principles of section 63.

(2) Insurance taxable income. The taxable income for any taxable year of a controlled foreign corporation which is engaged in the business of reinsuring or issuing insurance or annuity contracts and which, if it were a domestic corpora-

tion engaged only in such business, would be taxable as an insurance company to which subchapter L of chapter 1 of the Code applies shall, subject to the special rules of paragraph (c) of this section, be determined by treating such corporation as a domestic corporation taxable under subchapter L of chapter 1 of the Code and by applying the principles of §§ 1.953-4 and 1.953-5 for determining taxable income.

(c) Special rules for purposes of this section. *(1) Nonapplication of certain provisions.* Except where otherwise distinctly expressed, the provisions of subchapters F, G, H, L, M, N, S, and T of chapter 1 of the Internal Revenue Code shall not apply and, for taxable years of a controlled foreign corporation beginning after March 3, 1997, the provisions of section 103 of the Internal Revenue Code shall not apply.

(2) Application of principles of § 1.964-1. The determinations with respect to a foreign corporation shall be made as follows:

(i) Books of account. The books of account to be used shall be those regularly maintained by the corporation for the purpose of accounting to its shareholders.

(ii) Accounting principles. Except as provided in subparagraphs (3) and (4) of this paragraph, the accounting principles to be employed are those described in paragraph (b) of § 1.964-1. Thus, in applying accounting principles generally accepted in the United States for purposes of reflecting in the financial statements of a domestic corporation the operations of foreign affiliates, no adjustment need be made unless such adjustment will have a material effect, within the meaning of paragraph (a) of § 1.964-1.

(iii) Translation into United States dollars. (a) In general. Except as provided in (b) of this subdivision, the amounts determined in accordance with subdivision (ii) of this subparagraph shall be translated into United States dollars in accordance with the principles of paragraph (d) of § 1.964-1.

(b) Special rule. In any case in which the value of the foreign currency in relation to the United States dollar fluctuates more than 10 percent during any translation period (within the meaning of paragraph (d)(6) of § 1.964-1), the subpart F income and non-subpart F income shall be separately translated as if each constituted all the income of the controlled foreign corporation for the translation period.

(iv) Tax accounting methods. The tax accounting methods to be employed are those established or adopted by or on behalf of the foreign corporation under paragraph (c) of § 1.964-1. Thus, such accounting methods must be consistent with the manner of treating inventories, depreciation, and elections referred to in subdivisions (ii), (iii), and (iv) of paragraph (c)(1) of § 1.964-1 and used for purposes of such paragraph; however, if, in accordance with paragraph (c)(6) of § 1.964-1, a foreign corporation receives foreign base company income before any elections are made or before an accounting method is adopted by or on behalf of such corporation under paragraph (c)(3) of § 1.964-1, the determinations of whether an exclusion set forth in section 954(b) applies shall be made as if no elections had been made and no accounting method had been adopted.

(v) Exchange gain or loss. (a) Exchange gain or loss, determined in accordance with the principles of § 1.964-1(e), shall be taken into account for purposes of determining gross income and taxable income.

(b) Exchange gain or loss shall be treated as foreign base company shipping income (or as a deduction allocable thereto) to the extent that it is attributable to foreign base company shipping operations. The extent to which exchange gain or loss is attributable to foreign base company shipping operations may be determined under any reasonable method which is consistently applied from year to year. For example, the extent to which the exchange gain or loss is attributable to foreign base company shipping operations may be determined on the basis of the ratio which the foreign based company shipping income of the corporation for the taxable year bears to its total gross income for the taxable year, such ratio to be determined without regard to the subdivision (v).

(c) The remainder of the exchange gain or loss shall be allocated between subpart F income and non-subpart F income under any reasonable method which is consistently applied from year to year. For example, such remainder may be allocated to subpart F income in the same ratio that the gross subpart F income (exclusive of foreign base company shipping income) of the corporation for the taxable year bears to its total gross income (exclusive of foreign base company shipping income) for the taxable year, such ratio to be determined without regard to this subdivision (v).

(3) Necessity for recognition of gain or loss. Gross income of a foreign corporation (including an insurance company) includes gain or loss only if such gain or loss would be recognized under the provisions of the Internal Revenue Code if the foreign corporation were a domestic corporation taxable under section 11 (subject to the modifications of subparagraph (1) of this paragraph). See section 1002. However, a foreign corporation shall not be treated as a domestic corporation for purposes of determining whether section 367 applies.

(4) Gross income and gross receipts. The term "gross income" may not have the same meaning as the term "gross receipts". For example, in a manufacturing, merchandising, or mining business, gross income means the total sales less the cost of goods sold, plus any income from investments and from incidental or outside operations or sources.

(5) Treatment of capital loss and net operating loss. In determining taxable income of a foreign corporation for any taxable year—

(i) Capital loss carryback and carryover. The capital loss carryback and carryover provided by section 1212(a) shall not be allowed.

(ii) Net operating loss deduction. The net operating loss deduction under section 172(a) or the operations loss deduction under section 812 shall not be allowed.

(6) Corporations which have insurance income. For purposes of paragraphs (a)(2) and (b)(2) of this section, in determining whether a controlled foreign corporation which is engaged in the business of reinsuring or issuing insurance or annuity contracts and which, if it were a domestic corporation engaged only in such business, would be taxable as an insurance company to which subchapter L of chapter 1 of the Code applies, it is immaterial that—

(i) The corporation would be exempt from taxation as an organization described in section 501(a),

(ii) The corporation would not be taxable as an insurance company to which subchapter L of the Code applies, or

(iii) The corporation would be subject to the alternative tax for small mutual insurance companies provided by section 821(c).

T.D. 6795, 1/28/65, amend T.D. 7893, 5/11/83, T.D. 7894, 5/11/83, T.D. 8704, 12/31/96.

PAR. 2. Section 1.952-2(c)(2)(iv) is revised to read as follows:

Proposed § 1.952-2 Determination of gross income and taxable income of a foreign corporation. [*For Preamble, see ¶ 151,393*]

* * * * *

(c) * * *

(2) * * *

(iv) Tax accounting methods. The tax accounting methods to be employed are those established or adopted by or on behalf of the foreign corporation under § 1.964-1(c), except that the provisions of § 1.964-1(c)(1)(ii)(B) and (c)(1)(iii)(D) shall not apply in determining the gross income or the taxable income of the foreign corporation. Thus, such accounting methods must be consistent with the manner of treating inventories, depreciation, and elections referred to in § 1.964-1(c)(1)(ii)(A), (iii)(A) through (C) and (iv) and used for purposes of such paragraphs; however, if, in accordance with § 1.964-1(c)(6), a foreign corporation receives foreign base company income before any elections are made or before an accounting method is adopted by or on behalf of such corporation under § 1.964-1(C)(3), the determinations of whether an exclusion set forth in section 954(b) applies shall be made as if no elections had been made and no accounting method had been adopted.

PAR. 2. Sections 1.953-1 through 1.953-6 are redesignated as §§ 1.953-1A through 1.953-6A and a new center heading is added preceding newly designated § 1.953-1A to read as follows:

REGULATIONS APPLICABLE TO TAXABLE YEARS BEGINNING BEFORE JANUARY 1,1987

PAR. 3. A new center heading and new §§ 1.953-0 through 1.953-7 are added to read as follows:

REGULATIONS APPLICABLE TO TAXABLE YEARS BEGINNING AFTER DECEMBER 31, 1986

Proposed § 1.953-0 Introduction. [*For Preamble, see ¶ 151,253*]

(a) This paragraph lists the topics covered in §§ 1.953-0 through 1.953-7.

§ 1.953-0 Introduction.

(a) Outline.

(b) Effective dates.

§ 1.953-1 Taxation of foreign insurance operations.

(a) In general.

(b) Determining subpart F inclusions of income from insurance operations.

(1) Procedure.

(2) Cross reference to additional provisions.

(c) Effective date.

§ 1.953-2 Premiums attributable to the section 953 insurance income category and the SCI income category.

(a) In general.

(1) Section 953 insurance income premiums.

(2) SCI income premiums.

(b) Method of attributing premiums to the section 953 insurance income or SCI income categories.

(1) In general.

(2) Examples.

(c) Definition of premiums.

(d) Allocation and apportionment of premiums.

(1) Risks both in and outside the home country.

(2) Examples.

(3) 80 percent rule.

(i) In general.

(ii) Example.

(e) Location of risks in connection with property.

(1) In general.

(2) Specific rules for locating certain types of property.

(i) Commercial transportation property.

(ii) Examples.

(iii) Noncommercial transportation property.

(iv) Property exported by ship or aircraft.

(v) Property imported by ship or aircraft.

(vi) Shipments originating and terminating in the home country.

(vii) Shipments originating and terminating in a country other than the home country.

(3) Related assets and certain moveable property.

(i) Related assets.

(ii) Example.

(iii) Moveable property.

(iv) Example.

(f) Location of risks in connection with liability arising out of activity.

(1) Definition of risks in connection with liability.

(2) Location of risk.

(i) In general.

(ii) Examples.

(3) Specific rules locating certain activities.

(i) Liability with respect to property manufactured, produced, constructed, or assembled.

(ii) Examples.

(iii) Location of activities in connection with transportation property.

(iv) Example.

(v) Selling activity.

(vi) Example.

(g) Location of risks in connection with life or health.

(1) In general.

(2) Example.

(h) Risks deemed to be located in a country other than the home country.

(1) Artificial arrangements.

(2) Evidence of arrangements.

(3) Examples.

§ 1.953-3 Allocation of premiums to the RPII or nonRPII categories of section 953 insurance income.

(a) In general.

(b) Related person insurance income.

(1) In general.

(2) Definitions.

(i) United States shareholder, related person, and controlled foreign corporation.

(ii) Examples.

(iii) United States shareholder: exception for indirect ownership; publicly traded stock.

(iv) Example.

(v) Controlled foreign corporation: shipowner's protection and indemnity association.

(3) Reinsurance.

(i) In general.

(ii) Examples.

(4) Indirectly insuring a related insured: fronting.

(i) In general.

(ii) Example.

(5) Cross-insurance arrangements.

(i) In general.

(ii) Example.

(6) Specific premium rules.

(i) Premiums received prior to January 1, 1987.

(ii) Apportionment of premiums if stock owned for less than entire taxable year.

(iii) Examples.

(iv) Anti-abuse rule.

(v) Example.

§ *1.953-4 Allocation and apportionment of items of investment income.*

(a) In general.

(1) Investment income.

(2) Decreases in reserves.

(i) In general.

(ii) Examples.

(b) Allocation of investment income.

(1) In general.

(2) Examples.

(c) Apportionment of investment income.

(1) Life insurance companies.

(i) In general.

(ii) Section 807(c) items attributable to RPII, nonRPII, and SCI contracts.

(2) Property and casualty companies.

(i) In general.

(ii) Unpaid losses attributable to a particular category.

(3) Examples.

§ *1.953-5 Allocation and apportionment of expenses.*

(a) Allocation of deductions to RPII, nonRPII, and SCI categories.

(b) Apportionment of expenses to RPII, nonRPII, and SCI categories.

(1) In general.

(2) Life insurance companies.

(i) Investment deductions.

(ii) Other deductions.

(3) Property and casualty companies.

(i) Investment deductions.

(ii) Other deductions.

(c) Allocation and apportionment of deductions between premium and investment income after the deductions have been allocated or apportioned to the SCI or RPII categories.

(1) In general.

(2) Examples.

(3) Apportionment of reserves, losses, policyholder dividends, and policy acquisition expenses and certain other deductions between investment and premium income.

(i) In general.

(ii) Deduction for reserves and losses defined.

(iii) Investment income required to be added to reserves and required to fund losses.

(iv) Investment income's proportionate share of policyholder dividends.

(v) Apportionment of policy acquisition expenses and certain other deductions.

(vi) Example.

(4) Alternative method for life insurance companies.

(i) In general.

(ii) Example.

(5) Losses in excess of premium or investment income.

(6) Losses within the RPII, nonRPII, and SCI categories.

§ *1.953-6 Application of subchapter L and certain sections of subchapter N of the Code.*

(a) Applicability of subchapter L.

(1) In general.

(2) Applicability of section 7702. [Reserved]

(3) Applicability of section 817. [Reserved]

(b) Special rules regarding use of subchapter L to compute RPII, nonRPII, and SCI income.

(1) Certain provisions not to apply.

(2) Allocation and apportionment of certain items.

(c) Alternative tax for certain small companies.

(d) Computation of reserves to determine applicability of part I of subchapter L.

(1) Reserves required by law.

(i) Reserves with respect to United States business.

(ii) Reserves deemed to be required.

(iii) Reserves with respect to foreign business.

(2) SCI reserves to be taken into account.

(e) Computation of reserves for purposes of computing taxable income.

(1) Actual reserves required.

(2) Life insurance reserves.

(3) Discounted unpaid losses of a property and casualty company.

(4) Interest rates used for determining reserves.

(i) Qualified foreign contracts and property and liability contracts.

(ii) Nonqualified foreign contracts.

(f) Corporations not qualifying as insurance companies.

(1) In general.

(2) Items of gross income attributable to insurance operations of a non-insurance company.

(i) Corporations computing taxable income under part I of subchapter L.

(ii) Example.

(iii) Corporations computing taxable income under part II of subchapter L.

(g) Relationship between sections 953 and 954.

(1) Priority of application.

(i) In general.

(ii) Examples.

(2) Decrease or increase in income not material.

(i) In general.

(ii) Examples.

(h) Inclusion of pro rata share of subpart F income derived from insurance operations.

(1) Inclusion of pro rata share of related person insurance income.

(2) Inclusion of subpart F income other than related person insurance income.

(3) Earnings and profits limitation.

(4) Examples.

(5) Controlled foreign corporation for less than entire year.

(i) In general.

(ii) Example.

(6) Distributions.

(i) In general.

(ii) Example.

(7) Mutual insurance companies.

(i) Application of sections 959, 961, and 1248.

(j) Application of section 367(b). [Reserved]

(k) Interaction with section 954(b)(3).

§ 1.953-7 Exceptions to inclusion of related person insurance income for certain shareholders.

(a) Corporation not held by insureds.

(1) In general.

(2) Examples.

(b) De minimis insurance exception.

(1) In general.

(2) Examples.

(3) Anti-abuse rule.

(i) In general.

(ii) Examples.

(c) Election to treat income as effectively connected.

(1) In general.

(2) Corporations which may make the election.

(i) In general.

(ii) Successor corporation.

(iii) Examples.

(3) Taxable year of corporation making election.

(4) Period during which election is in effect.

(i) Elections that become effective in taxable years beginning after December 31, 1987.

(ii) Examples.

(iii) Elections that become effective in first taxable year beginning after December 31, 1986.

(iv) Examples.

(5) Effect of election: taxation under section 882; alternative minimum tax; dividends received deduction; pre-1987 deficits in earnings and profits, and net operating losses.

(6) Exemption from tax imposed by section 4371.

(7) Procedure for making election under section 953(c)(3)(C).

(i) In general.

(ii) When election must be made.

(iii) Election.

(8) Closing agreement.

(9) Letter of credit.

(i) In general.

(ii) Changes in the amount of the letter of credit.

(10) Underpayment of tax due.

(11) Termination or revocation of election.

(i) Termination.

(ii) Revocation with consent.

(iii) Unilateral revocation by Commissioner.

(b) Effective dates. *(1)* The provisions of §§ 1.953-1 through 1.953-7 apply to taxable years of a controlled foreign corporation beginning after December 31, 1986. However, the amendments to section 953(c)(2) and (c)(3) by section 1012(i)(3)(A) and (B)(i) and (ii) of the Technical and Miscellaneous Revenue Act of 1988 shall apply to taxable years beginning after December 31, 1987 to the extent such amendments add the phrase "(directly or indirectly)." Further, the risk location rules of § 1.953-2 shall apply only to periods of coverage that begin on or after June 17, 1991. Prior to the effective date of § 1.953-2, taxpayers may determine the location of risks by using the principles of § 1.953-2A of the regulations, but those principles shall be applied to determine whether risks are located in or outside the controlled foreign corporation's country of incorporation rather than in or outside the United States. Finally, the apportionment of reserves, losses, policyholder dividends, and policy acquisition expenses between premium and investment income within the SCI, and, in certain circumstances, within the RPII category as provided in § 1.953-5(c)(3) shall apply to taxable years beginning on or after April 17, 1991. For taxable years beginning prior to April 17, 1991, taxpayers may use a reasonable apportionment formula.

(2) The provisions of §§ 1.953-1A through 1.953-6A apply to taxable years of a controlled foreign corporation beginning before January 1, 1987. All references therein to sections of the Code are to the Internal Revenue Code of 1954 prior to the amendments made by the Tax Reform Act of 1986.

§ 1.953-1 Income from insurance of United States risks.

> ***Caution:*** The Treasury has not yet amended Reg § 1.953-1 to reflect changes made by P.L. 100-647, P.L. 99-514, P.L. 98-369.

(a) In general. The subpart F income of a controlled foreign corporation for any taxable year includes its income derived from the insurance of United States risks for such taxable year. See section 952(a)(1). A controlled foreign corporation shall have income derived from the insurance of United States risks for such purpose if it has taxable income, as determined under § 1.953-4 or § 1.953-5, which is attributable to the reinsuring or the issuing of any insurance or annuity contract in connection with United States risks, as defined in § 1.953-2 or § 1.953-3, and if it satisfies the 5-percent minimum premium requirement prescribed in paragraph (b) of this section. It is immaterial for purposes of this section whether the person insured or the beneficiary of any insurance, annuity, or reinsurance contract is, as to such corporation, a related person or a United States shareholder. For definition of the term "controlled foreign corporation" for purposes of taking into account income derived from the insurance of United States risks under section 953, see section 957(a) and (b) and §§ 1.957-1 and 1.957-2.

(b) 5-percent minimum premium requirement. A controlled foreign corporation shall not have income derived from the insurance of United States risks for purposes of this section unless the premiums received by such corporation during the taxable year which are attributable to the reinsuring and the issuing of insurance and annuity contracts in connection with the United States risks exceed 5 percent of the total premiums which are received by such corporation during such taxable year and which are attributable to the reinsuring and the issuing of insurance and annuity contracts in connection with all risks.

(c) General definitions. For purposes of §§ 1.953-1 to 1.953-6, inclusive—

(1) Reinsurance, etc. The terms "reinsurance", "insurance", and "annuity contract" have the same meaning which they have for purposes of applying section 809(c)(1) or section 832(b)(4), as the case may be.

(2) Premiums. The term "premiums" means the items taken into account for the taxable year under section 809(c)(1), or the amount computed for the taxable year under section 832(b)(4) without the application of subparagraph (B) thereof, as the case may be; except that, for purposes of determining the amount of premiums received in applying paragraph (b) of this section or paragraph (a) of § 1.953-3, advance premiums and deposits shall not be taken into account.

(3) Insurance company. The term "insurance company" has the same meaning which it has for purposes of applying section 801(a), determined by applying the principles of paragraph (a) of § 1.801-3.

(4) Related person. The term "related person", when used with respect to a controlled foreign corporation, shall have the meaning assigned to it by paragraph (e) of § 1.954-1.

(5) Policy period. With respect to any insurance or annuity contract under which a corporation is potentially liable at any time during its taxable year, the term "policy period" means with respect to such year each period of coverage under the contract if such period begins or ends with or within the taxable year, except that, if such period of coverage is more than one year, such term means such of the following periods as are applicable, each one of which is a policy period with respect to the taxable year:

(i) The one-year period which begins with the effective date of the contract and begins or ends with or within the taxable year,

(ii) The one-year period which begins with an anniversary of the contract and begins or ends with or within the taxable year, and

(iii) The period of less than one year if such period begins with an anniversary of the contract, ends with the date on which coverage under the contract terminates, and begins or ends with or within the taxable year.

For such purposes, the effective date of the contract is the date on which coverage under the contract beings, and the anniversary of the contract is the annual return of the effective date. The period of coverage under a contract is the period beginning with the effective date of the contract and ending with the date on which the coverage under the contract expires; except that, if the risk under the contract has been transferred by assumption reinsurance, the period of coverage shall end with the effective date of such transfer or, if the contract is cancelled, with the effective date of cancellation. For this purpose, the term "assumption reinsurance" shall have the meaning provided by paragraph (a)(7)(ii) of § 1.809-5. The application of this subparagraph may be illustrated by the following examples:

Example (1). Controlled foreign corporation A issues to domestic corporation M an insurance contract which provides coverage for the 2½ year period beginning on July 1, 1963. Corporation A uses the calendar year as the taxable year. For 1963, the policy period under such contract as to A Corporation is July 1, 1963, to June 30, 1964. For 1964, the policy periods under such contract as to A Corporation are July 1, 1963, to June 30, 1964, and July 1, 1964, to June 30, 1965. For 1965, the policy periods under such contract as to A Corporation are July 1, 1964, to June 30, 1965, and July 1, 1965, to December 31, 1965.

Example (2). The facts are the same as in example (1) except that M Corporation cancels the contract on August 31, 1963. For 1963, the policy period under such contract as to A Corporation is July 1, 1963, to August 31, 1963.

Example (3). The facts are the same as in example (1) except that on January 15, 1965, A Corporation cedes insurance under the contract to controlled foreign corporation B, which also uses the calendar year as the taxable year. For 1964, the policy periods under such contract as to A Corporation are July 1, 1963, to June 30, 1964, and July 1, 1964, to June 30, 1965. For 1965, the policy periods under such contract as to both A Corporation and B Corporation are July 1, 1964, to June 30, 1965, and July 1, 1965, to December 31, 1965.

Example (4). Controlled foreign corporation C, which uses the calendar year as the taxable year, issues to domestic corporation N an insurance contract which covers the marine risks in connection with shipping a machine to Europe. The contract does not specify the dates during which the machine is covered, but provides coverage from the time the machine is delivered alongside a named vessel in Hoboken, New Jersey, until the machine is delivered alongside such vessel in Liverpool, England. Such deliveries in New Jersey and England take place on February 1, and February 28, 1963, respectively. For 1963, the policy period under such contract as to C Corporation is February 1, to February 28, 1963.

(6) Foreign country. The term "foreign country" includes, where not otherwise expressly provided, a possession of the United States.

T.D. 6781, 12/22/64.

Proposed § 1.953-1 Taxation of foreign insurance operations. [*For Preamble, see ¶ 151,253*]

(a) In general. The income from the insurance operations of a controlled foreign corporation may be subject to inclusion in the gross income of a United States shareholder under subpart F of the Code either as insurance income under section 953 or as foreign personal holding company income under section 954(a)(1) and (c). Section 953 insurance income is income (including premium and investment income) attributable to the issuing or reinsuring of any insurance or annuity contract in connection with risks located in a country other than the country (the "home country") under the laws of which the controlled foreign corporation is created or organized and which would be taxed under subchapter L of the Code if the income were the income of a domestic insurance company. The term "home country" includes any area within the jurisdiction (as recognized by the United States) of the country of incorporation of a controlled foreign corporation or within the jurisdiction of a possession of such country. A risk is located in a country other than the home country if it is located on the high seas outside the home country. Insurance income exists only with respect to bona fide contracts of insurance (or reinsurance) or annuity contracts. There are two categories of section 953 insurance income: income that constitutes related person insurance income under § 1.953-3(b)(1) (the "RPII category") and income that is subject to section 953 but is not related person insurance income (the "nonRPII category"). Income, whether premium or investment income, derived from issuing or reinsuring insurance or annuity contracts in connection with risks located in the country in which the controlled foreign corporation is created or organized is referred to as same country insurance ("SCI") income. Investment income attributable to premiums that constitute SCI income may be includable in the gross income of the United States shareholders of a controlled foreign corporation as foreign personal holding company income under sections 954(a)(1) and (c). However, the premiums attributable to issuing or reinsuring insurançe or annuity contracts in connection with risks located in the controlled foreign corporation's home country are not generally treated as subpart F income.

(b) Determining subpart F inclusions of income from insurance operations. *(1) Procedure.* The following procedures are used to determine the amount of a controlled foreign corporation's section 953 insurance income and its foreign personal holding company income derived from insurance operations:

(i) Determine whether premiums from insurance, reinsurance, and annuity contracts issued by the controlled foreign corporation constitute section 953 insurance income or SCI income by determining the location of the risks under the contracts (see § 1.953-2);

(ii) Determine whether the premiums that constitute section 953 insurance income are attributable to the RPII or nonRPII categories (see § 1.953-3);

(iii) Allocate and apportion investment income to the RPII, nonRPII, and SCI categories (see § 1.953-4); and

(iv) Allocate and apportion deductions to the RPII, nonRPII, and SCI categories; within the SCI category and, under certain circumstances, within the RPII category, further allocate and apportion deductions between SCI premium income and SCI investment income (see § 1.953-5).

(2) Cross reference to additional provisions. Section 1.953-6 contains rules relating to the application of subchapter L of the Code (insurance companies), subpart F of part III of subchapter N (controlled foreign corporations), and certain additional Code provisions to income derived from the conduct of insurance operations. Section 1.953-7 contains rules regarding certain exceptions to the inclusion of related person insurance income in the gross income of certain United States shareholders.

(c) Effective date. For regulations under section 953 that apply to the taxable years of a controlled foreign corporation beginning before January 1, 1987, see §§ 1.953-1A through 1.953-6A. The provisions of § 1.953-1 and §§ 1.953-3 through 1.953-7 apply to the taxable years of a controlled foreign corporation beginning after December 31, 1986. However, the amendments to section 953(c)(2) and (c)(3) by section 1012(i)(3)(A) and (B)(i) and (ii) of the Technical and Miscellaneous Revenue Act of 1988 shall apply to taxable years beginning after December 31, 1987 to the extent such amendments add the phrase "(directly or indirectly)." Also, the regulations under § 1.953-2 regarding the location of risks will apply only to periods of coverage, regardless of when the contract was issued, that begin on or after June 17, 1991. Prior to the effective date of § 1.953-2, taxpayers may determine the location of risks by using the principles of § 1.953-2A of the regulations, but those principles shall be applied to determine whether risks are located in or outside the controlled foreign corporation's country of incorporation rather than in or outside the United States. Finally, the apportionment of reserves, losses, policyholder dividends, and policy acquisition expenses between premium and investment income within the SCI, and, in certain circumstances, within the RPII category as provided in § 1.953-5(c)(3) shall apply to taxable years beginning on or after April 17, 1991. For taxable years beginning prior to April 17, 1991, taxpayers may use a reasonable apportionment formula.

§ 1.953-2 Actual United States risks.

Caution: The Treasury has not yet amended Reg § 1.953-2 to reflect changes made by P.L. 100-647, P.L. 99-514, P.L. 98-369.

(a) In general. For purposes of paragraph (a) of § 1.953-1, the term "United States risks" means risks described in section 953(a)(1)(A)—

(1) In connection with property in the United States (as defined in paragraph (b) of this section),

(2) In connection with liability arising out of activity in the United States (as defined in paragraph (c) of this section), or

(3) In connection with the lives or health of residents of the United States (as defined in paragraph (d) of this section)..

For purposes of section 953(a), the term "United States" is used in a geographical sense and includes only the States and the District of Columbia. Therefore, the reinsuring or the issuing of insurance or annuity contracts by a controlled foreign corporation in connection with property located in a foreign country or a possession of the United States, in connection with activity in a foreign country or a possession, or in connection with the lives or health of citizens of the United States who are not residents of the United States will not give rise to income to which paragraph (a) of § 1.953-1 applies, unless the income derived by the controlled foreign corporation from such contracts constitutes income derived in connection with risks which are deemed to be United States risks, as defined in § 1.953-3.

(b) Property in the United States. The term "property in the United States" means property, as defined in subparagraph (1) of this paragraph, which is in the United States, within the meaning of subparagraph (2) of this paragraph.

(1) Property defined. The term "property" means any interest of an insured in tangible (including real and personal) or intangible property. Such interests include, but are not limited to, those of an owner, landlord, tenant, mortgagor, mortgagee, trustee, beneficiary, or partner. Thus, for example, if insurance is issued against loss from fire and theft with respect to an insured's home and its contents, such risks are risks in connection with property, whether the insured is the owner or lessee and whether the contents include furniture or cash and securities. Furthermore, if insurance is issued against all risks of damage or loss with respect to the automobile of an insured, such risks are risks in connection with property, whether the risks insured against may be caused by the insured, another person, or natural forces.

(2) United States location. (i) In general. Property will be considered property in the United States when it is exclusively located in the United States. Conversely, property will be considered property not in the United States when it is exclusively located outside the United States. In addition, property which is ordinarily located in, but temporarily lo-

cated outside, the United States will be considered property in the United States both when it is ordinarily located in, and when it is temporarily located outside, the United States if the premium which is attributable to the reinsuring or issuing of any insurance contract in connection with such property cannot be allocated to, or apportioned between, risks incurred when such property is actually located in the United States and risks incurred when it is actually located outside the United States. If such premium can be so allocated or apportioned on a reasonable basis, however, such property will be considered property not in the United States when it is actually located outside the United States. However, property will not be considered property in the United States if it is neither property which is exclusively located in the United States nor property which is ordinarily located in, but temporarily located outside, the United States. The rules prescribed in subdivision (ii) of this subparagraph shall apply in determining whether a premium can be allocated or apportioned on a reasonable basis to or between risks incurred when property is actually located in the United States and risks incurred when such property is actually located outside the United States. The rules prescribed in subdivisions (iii) through (x) of this subparagraph shall apply in determining whether property is, or will be considered, exclusively located in or outside the United States and whether property is, or will be considered, ordinarily located in the United States; such rules also limit the rule of premium allocation and apportionment prescribed in this subdivision and subdivision (ii) of this subparagraph. The determinations required by this subparagraph shall be made with respect to the location of property during the policy period applicable to the taxable year of the insuring or reinsuring corporation, or, if more than one policy period exists with respect to such taxable year, such determinations shall be made separately with respect to the location of property during each such policy period.

(ii) Premium allocation or apportionment. Whether a premium can be allocated or apportioned on a reasonable basis to or between risks incurred when property is actually located in the United States and risks incurred when such property is actually located outside the United States shall depend on the intention of the parties to the insurance contract, as determined from its provisions and the facts and circumstances preceding its execution. Contract provisions on the basis of which the premium reasonably may be so allocated or apportioned include, but are not limited to, provisions which separately describe each risk covered, the period of coverage of each risk, the special warranties for each risk, the premium for each risk (or the basis for determining such premium), and the conditions of paying the premium for each risk. For purposes of this subdivision, it shall be unnecessary formally to make a separate policy with respect to each risks covered or with respect to each clause attached to the policy, provided that the intention of the parties to the contract is reasonably clear. For example, if in the ordinary course of carrying on an insurance business an insurance policy is issued which covers fire, theft, and water damage risks incurred when property is actually located in the United States and marine risks incurred when such property is actually located outside the United States and which, pursuant to accepted insurance principles, properly describes the premium rates as percentages of the amount of coverage as ".825% plus .3% fire, etc. risks plus .12% water risks = 1.245%", a reasonable basis exists to allocate a $124.50 premium paid for $10,000 of such coverage to $82.50 for foreign risks and $42.00 ($30.00 + $12.00) to United States risks.

(iii) Property in general. (a) Ordinary and temporary location. Except as otherwise provided in subdivisions (iv) through (x) of this subparagraph, the determination of whether property is ordinarily located in the United States will depend on all the facts and circumstances in each case. Property is ordinarily located in the United States if its location in the United States is regular, usual, or often occurring. However, in all cases property will be considered ordinarily located in the United States if it is actually located in the United States for an aggregate of more than 50 percent of the days in the applicable policy period whereas property will, under no circumstances, be considered ordinarily located in the United States if it is actually located in the United States for an aggregate of not more than 30 percent of the days in the applicable policy period. Property which is ordinarily located in the United States is temporarily located outside the United States when it is actually located outside the United States. For purposes of determining the number and percent of the days in an applicable policy period, the term "day" means, not any 24-consecutive-hour period, but a continuous period of twenty-four hours commencing from midnight and ending with the following midnight; in determining the location of property for such purposes, an amount of time which is at least one-half of such a day, but less than the entire day, shall be considered a day, and an amount of time which is less than one-half of such a day shall not be considered a day.

(b) Illustrations. The application of this subdivision may be illustrated by the following examples:

Example (1). Controlled foreign corporation A issues to domestic corporation M a comprehensive blanket or floater insurance policy which, for one year, covers inventory samples which M Corporation regularly ships from the United States in order to encourage sales. Such shipments are made on the condition that they be returned to the United States within 5 days after they are received. During the one-year policy period, such samples are sent from, and returned to, the United States 50 times, and during such one-year period are actually located in the United States for an aggregate of 120 days. Since the location of the samples in the United States during such one-year period is often recurring, they are property ordinarily located in, but temporarily located outside, the United States. Therefore, they will be considered property in the United States even though for such one-year period their location in the United States is not regular or usual and is not for an aggregate of more than 50 percent of the days in the policy period. However, if, by considering such factors as the terms and premium schedule of the insurance contract as well as the number, value, and duration of the location in and outside the United States, of such samples, the premium which is attributable to the issuing of such contract can be allocated to, or apportioned between, risks occurring when such samples are actually located in the United States and risks occurring when they are actually located outside the United States, such samples will be considered property not in the United States when they are actually located outside the United States.

Example (2). A machine, located for several years in a foreign branch of a United States manufacturer, is permanently transferred to the home office of such manufacturer, where it arrives on January 1, 1963, and remains for the remainder of 1963. Under a separate insurance contract issued by a controlled foreign corporation, which uses the calendar year as the taxable year, such machine is insured against damage for the three-year period commencing on May 1, 1962. Because of the change in location of the machine, the premiums are increased as of January 1, 1963. Since the machine is in the United States from January 1, 1963, to April 30, 1963, its location in the United States is regular and usual during the policy period of May 1, 1962, to April 30, 1963. Accordingly, the machine is ordinarily located in the United States for such policy period. However, since the premium which is attributable to the issuing of such contract is allocable to risks occurring when the machine is actually located in, and when it is actually located outside, the United States, such machine will be considered property not in the United States from May 1, 1962, through December 31, 1962.

(iv) Commercial motor vehicle, ships, aircraft, railroad rolling stock, and containers. Any motor vehicle, ship, aircraft, railroad rolling stock, or any container transported thereby, which is used exclusively in the commercial transportation of persons or property to or from the United States (including such transportation from one place to another in the United States and is ordinarily located in the United States will be considered property in the United States both when such property is ordinarily located in, and when such property is temporarily located outside, the United States. Whether such property is used in the transportation of persons or property to or from the United States and is ordinarily located in the United States are issues to be determined from all the facts and circumstances in each case. However, in all cases such transportation property will be considered ordinarily located in the United States if either more than 50 percent of the miles traversed during the applicable policy period in the use of such property are traversed within the United States or such property is located in the United States more than 50 percent of the time during such period. Further, such transportation property will not at any time be considered property in the United States if either not more than 30 percent of the miles traversed during the applicable policy period in the use of such property are traversed within the United States or such property is located in the United States for not more than 30 percent of the time during such period. Nevertheless, if not more than 30 percent of the miles traversed during the applicable policy period in the use of such transportation property are traversed within the United States such property will be considered ordinarily located in the United States if it is located in the United States more than 50 percent of the time during such period. Moreover, if such transportation property is located in the United States for not more than 30 percent of the time during the applicable policy period, such property will be considered ordinarily located in the United States if more than 50 percent of the miles traversed during such period in the use of such property are traversed within the United States. If such transportation property is considered property in the United States because more than 50 percent of the miles traversed during the applicable policy period in the use of such property are traversed within the United States, the apportionment of premium provided in subdivision (i) of this subparagraph shall be made on a mileage basis. If, however, such property is considered property in the United States because such property is located in the United States more than 50 percent of the time during the applicable policy period, the apportionment of premium provided in subdivision (i) of this subparagraph shall be made on a time basis.

(v) Noncommercial motor vehicles, ships, aircraft, and railroad rolling stock. Except as provided in subdivision (iv) of this subparagraph, any motor vehicle, ship or boat, aircraft, or railroad rolling stock which at any time is actually located in the United States and which either (a) is registered with the United States, a State (including any political subdivision thereof), or any agency thereof or (b), if not so registered, is owned by a citizen, resident, or corporation of the United States will be considered property which is ordinarily located in the United States. Unless the premium which is attributable to the reinsuring or issuing of any insurance contract in connection with such property considered ordinarily located in the United States is specifically allocated under the contract to risks incurred when such property is actually located in the United States and to risks incurred when it is actually located outside the United States, such property will be considered property in the United States both when it is ordinarily located in, and when it is temporarily located outside, the United States; under no circumstances will such property be considered outside the United States on the basis of any apportionment of such premium.

(vi) Property exported or imported by railroad or motor vehicle. Any property which is exported from, or imported to, the United States by railroad or motor vehicle will be considered property ordinarily located in the United States which, when such property is not actually located in the United States, is temporarily located outside the United States. For example, if an insurance contract reinsured or issued in connection with property exported from the United States by motor vehicle covers risks commencing when such property is loaded on the motor vehicle at the United States warehouse and terminating when such property is unloaded at the foreign warehouse, and if the premium payable with respect to risks incurred when the property is in the United States and risks incurred when the property is in the foreign country is not separately stated, such property will be considered property in the United States only until such property is actually located outside the United States, provided that the premium can be properly apportioned (for example) on the basis of time or mileage, between risks incurred when the property is actually located in the United States and risks incurred when it is actually located outside the United States. If in such case the premium is not so apportionable, such property will be considered property in the United States both when such property is ordinarily located in, and when it is temporarily located outside, the United States.

(vii) Property exported by ship or aircraft. If an insurance contract which is reinsured or issued in connection with property which is exported from the United States by ship or aircraft covers risks all of which terminate when such property is placed aboard a ship or aircraft at the United States port of exit for shipment from the United States, such property will be considered property in the United States. If such insurance contract covers risks all of which commence when such property is placed aboard a ship or aircraft at the United States port of exit for shipment from the United States, such property will be considered property not in the United States. If such insurance contract covers risks commencing before, and terminating after, such property is placed aboard a ship or aircraft at the United States port of exit for shipment from the United States, such property will be considered property ordinarily located in the United States which, after such property is placed aboard such ship or aircraft at the United States port of exit, is temporarily located outside the United States. The application of this subdivision may be illustrated by the following example:

Example. A controlled foreign corporation issues an insurance contract in connection with property exported from the United States by ship. The contract covers risks commencing after such property is removed from the United States warehouse and terminating when such property is unloaded at the foreign port of entry. Assuming that the premium payable with respect to the risks incurred before and the risks incurred after the property is placed aboard the ship at the United States port of exit for shipment from the United States or with respect to the steps in handling such property during such coverage, such as transporting the property to the United States port of exit, unloading the property there, placing the property aboard the ship, holding the property aboard the ship in port, the actual voyage, and unloading the property at the foreign port of entry, is separately stated in, or is determinable from, such contract, the property will be considered property in the United States only until such property is placed aboard the ship at the United States port of exit for shipment from the United States. Assuming, however, that the premiums payable with respect to such steps, or with respect to the risks incurred before and the risks incurred after the property is placed aboard the ship at the United States port of exit, are not allocable or apportionable under the contract, such property will be considered property in the United States both before and after such property is placed aboard the ship at the United States port of exit.

(viii) Property imported by ship or aircraft. If an insurance contract which is reinsured or issued in connection with property which is imported to the United States by ship or aircraft covers risks all of which terminate when such property is unloaded at the United States port of entry, such property will be considered property not in the United States. If such insurance contract covers risks all of which commence after such property is unloaded at the United States port of entry, such property will be considered property in the United States. If such insurance contract covers risks commencing before, and terminating after, such property is unloaded at the United States port of entry, such property will be considered property ordinarily located in the United States which, before such property is unloaded at the United States port of entry, is temporarily located outside the United States. For an illustration pertaining to the allocation or apportionment of the premium, see the example in subdivision (vii) of this subparagraph.

(ix) Shipments originating and terminating in the United States. Any property which is shipped from one place in the United States to another place in the United States, on or over a foreign country, the high seas, or the coastal waters of the United States will be considered property actually located at all times in the United States. For example, property which is shipped from New York City to Los Angeles via the Panama Canal or from San Francisco to Hawaii or Alaska will be considered property actually located at all times in the United States.

(x) Shipments originating and terminating in a foreign country. Any property which is shipped by any means, or a combination of means, of transportation from one foreign country to another foreign country, or from a contiguous foreign country to the same contiguous foreign country, on or over the United States will be considered property exclusively located outside the United States. Notwithstanding the foregoing, any property which is shipped by any means, or a combination of means, of transportation from one contiguous foreign country to another contiguous foreign country on or over the United States will be considered property ordinarily located in the United States which, when such property is not actually located in the United States, is temporarily located outside the United States.

(c) Liability from United States activity. The term "liability arising out of activity in the United States" means a loss, as described in subparagraph (1) of this paragraph, or a liability, as described in subparagraph (2) of this paragraph, which could arise from activity performed in the United States, as defined in subparagraph (3) of this paragraph.

(1) Loss described. The term "loss" includes all loss of an insured which could arise from the occurrence of the event insured against except that such term does not include any loss in connection with property described in paragraph (b) of this section. For example, such term includes, in the case of a promoter of outdoor sporting events, the loss which could arise from the cancellation of such an event because of inclement weather.

(2) Liability described. The term "liability" includes all liability of an insured in tort, contract, property, or otherwise. It includes, for example, the liability of a principal for the acts of his agent, of a husband for the acts of his spouse, and of a parent for the acts of his child. The term not only includes the direct liability which may be incurred, for example, by a tortfeasor to the person harmed, but also the indirect liability which may be incurred, for example, by a manufacturer to the purchaser at retail for a breach of warranty.

(3) Activity in the United States. (i) In general. A loss or liability will be considered a loss or liability which could arise from activity performed in the United States if the loss or liability would result, if at all, from an activity exclusively carried on in the United States. Conversely, a loss or liability will be considered a loss or liability which could not arise from activity performed in the United States if the loss or liability would result, if at all, from an activity exclusively carried on outside the United States. In addition, a loss or liability will be considered a loss or liability which could arise from activity performed in the United States if the loss or liability would result, if at all, from an activity ordinarily carried on in, but partly carried on outside, the United States. If the premium which is attributable to the reinsuring or issuing of any insurance contract in connection with an activity ordinarily carried on in, but partly carried on outside, the United States can, on a reasonable basis, be allocated to, or apportioned between, the risks incurred with respect to the activity carried on in, and the risks incurred with respect to the activity carried on outside, the United States, such loss or liability will be considered a loss or liability which could not arise from activity performed in the United States to the extent the loss or liability would result, if at all, from that activity carried on outside the United States. However, a loss or liability will not be considered a loss or liability which could arise from an activity performed in the United States if such loss or liability would result, if at all, from an activity which is neither exclusively carried on in the United States nor ordinarily carried on in, but partly carried on outside, the United States. The principles of paragraph (b)(2)(ii) of this section for allocating or apportioning a premium on a reasonable basis to or between risks incurred when property is actually located in the United States and risks incurred when such property is actually located outside the United States shall apply for allocating or apportioning a premium on a reasonable basis to or between the risks incurred with respect to the activity carried on in, and the risks incurred with respect to the activity carried on outside, the United States. The rules prescribed in subdivisions (ii) through (vi) of this subparagraph shall apply in determining whether an activity is, or will be considered, exclusively carried on in or outside the United States and whether an activity is, or will be considered, ordinarily carried on in the United States and in determining what is the activity which is performed by the insured from which a loss or liability results or could result; such rules also limit the

rule of premium allocation and apportionment prescribed in this subdivision. The determinations required by this subparagraph shall be made with respect to the location of an activity of the insured performed during the policy period applicable to the taxable year of the insuring or reinsuring corporation, or, if more than one policy period exists with respect to such taxable year, such determinations shall be made separately with respect to the location of the activity during each such policy period.

(ii) Substantial activity carried on in the United States. The term "activity" is used in its broadest sense and includes the performance of an act unlawfully undertaken, the wrongful performance of an act lawfully undertaken, and the wrongful failure to perform an act lawfully required to be undertaken. With respect to a loss described in subparagraph (1) of this paragraph, the term "activity" includes the occurrence of the event insured against. The determination of whether an activity ordinarily is carried on in, but is partly carried on outside, the United States will depend on all the facts and circumstances in each case. An activity ordinarily is carried on in the United States if a substantial amount of such activity is carried on in the United States. Factors which will be taken into account in determining whether a substantial amount of activity is carried on in the United States are those which are connected with the activity and include, but are not limited to, the location of the insured's assets, the place where personal services are performed, and the place where sales occur, but only if such assets, services, and sales are connected with the activity. In all cases an activity will be considered substantially carried on in the United States if more than 50 percent of the insured's total assets, personal services, and sales, if any, connected with such activity are located, performed, or occur in the United States. On the other hand, an activity will, under no circumstances, be considered substantially carried on in the United States if not more than 30 percent of the insured's total assets, personal services, and sales, if any, connected with such activity are located, performed, or occur in the United States. For this purpose, the mean of the value of the total assets at the beginning and end of the policy period shall be used, determined by taking assets into account at their actual value (not reduced by liabilities), which, in the absence of affirmative evidence to the contrary, shall be deemed to be (a) face value in the case of bills receivable, accounts receivable, notes receivable, and open accounts held by an insured using the cash receipts and disbursements method of accounting and (b) adjusted basis in the case of all other assets. Personal services shall be measured by the amount of compensation paid or accrued for such services, and sales shall be measured by the volume of gross sales. An activity is carried on partly outside the United States if it is carried on, whether substantially or insubstantially, outside the United States.

(iii) Manufacturing, producing, constructing, or assembling activity. If a person who manufactures, produces, constructs, or assembles property is liable with regard to the consumption or use of such property, such liability will be considered to result from the activity performed of manufacturing, producing, constructing, or assembling such property. If such person manufactures, produces, constructs, or assembles more than one type of product, the liability with regard to the consumption on use of one of such products will be considered to result from the activity performed of manufacturing, producing, constructing, or assembling that particular product. For example, the liability of a building contractor, which constructs apartment buildings only in the United States, for the improper construction of, or the failure to construct, an apartment building, will be considered to result from an activity exclusively carried on in the United States and will be considered a liability which could arise from activity performed in the United States. In further illustration, the liability (which is covered by a single policy of insurance) of a domestic corporation, which assembles refrigerators exclusively in the United States and manufactures automobiles both in a foreign country and in the United States through substantial activity carried on in each of such countries, for the negligent manufacturing of a part of one of the automobiles by the foreign branch, will be considered to result from an activity ordinarily carried on in, but partly carried on outside, the United States and will be considered a liability which could arise from activity performed in the United States.

(iv) Selling activity. If a person is liable with regard to selling activity performed, such liability will be considered, except as provided in subdivisions (iii), (v), and (vi) of this subparagraph, to result from such selling activity. A person will be considered to be engaged in selling activity if such person engages in an activity resulting in the sale of property. Thus, it is immaterial that, under the Code, such activity would not constitute engaging in or carrying on a trade or business in the country in which such activity is carried on, the property in the goods does not pass in such country, or delivery of the property is not made in such country. For example, if a foreign wholesale distributor, which manages its entire business operations in a foreign country and sells its inventory exclusively in the United States—its only contact in the United States being the promotion of such sales to United States retail outlets by advertising in trade publications and distributing sales catalogues—is liable for a breach of warranty with regard to the sale of property to a United States retail outlet, such liability will be considered to result from an activity exclusively carried on in the United States and will be considered a liability which could arise from activity performed in the United States.

(v) Liability from service or driving activity. (a) In general. If a person is liable with regard to any service activity performed, or is liable with regard to driving activity performed in connection with a motor vehicle, ship or boat, aircraft, or railroad rolling stock, whether or not exclusively used in the commercial transportation of persons or property, such liability will be considered to result from such service or driving activity. For example, if an oil company which drills for oil exclusively in a foreign country is liable with regard to the negligent handling by its employees of explosives in the course of such drilling there, such liability will be considered to result from an activity exclusively carried on outside the United States and will be considered a liability which could not arise from activity performed in the United States. In further illustration, if a corporation which services machinery exclusively in a foreign country under servicing contracts is liable with regard to the negligent repairing of a machine under such a contract, such liability will be considered to result from an activity exclusively carried on outside the United States and will be considered a liability which could not arise from activity performed in the United States.

(b) Location of activities in connection with transportation property. For purposes of subdivision (a) of this subdivision, service or driving activity performed in connection with a motor vehicle, ship or boat, aircraft, or railroad rolling stock, whether or not exclusively used in the commercial transportation of persons or property, will be considered activity performed in the United States if the activity is carried on at a time when such property is or will be considered, in accordance with subdivision (iv) or (v) of paragraph (b)(2) of this section, actually in the United States or ordinarily located in the United States. However, if the premium which is attributable to the reinsuring or issuing of any insurance contract in connection with such service or driving activity which is carried on at a time when such property is, or will be considered, ordinarily located in the United States can be allocated to, or apportioned between, the risks incurred when such property is actually located in the United States and risks incurred when it is actually located in the United States and risks incurred when it is actually located outside the United States, such liability will be considered a liability which could arise from activity performed in the United States only when such property is actually located in the United States. Any allocation or apportionment of premium under the preceding sentence shall be made in accordance with the rules of allocation and apportionment provided in subdivision (iv) or (v) of paragraph (b)(2) of this section. For example, if a person is liable with regard to the performance of services outside the United States in the operation of a motor vehicle which is used exclusively in the commercial transportation of persons to and from the United States and which, because more than 50 percent of the miles traversed during the applicable policy period in the use of such property are traversed within the United States, is considered ordinarily located in the United States, such liability will be considered to be a liability which could not arise from activity performed in the United States only to the extent that the premium which is attributable to the reinsuring or issuing of any insurance contract in connection with such service activity is apportioned on a mileage basis between the risks insured when such motor vehicle is actually located in the United States and when such vehicle is actually located outside the United States. See paragraph (b)(2)(iv) of this section. In further illustration, if a person is liable with regard to his negligent driving of a motor vehicle which is not used exclusively in the commercial transportation of persons or property, which is registered with any State, and which is driven both in the United States and a foreign country, such liability will be considered a liability which could arise from activity performed in the United States, unless the premium which is attributable to the reinsuring or issuing of an insurance contract in connection with such driving performed in such motor vehicle ordinarily located in the United States is specifically allocated under the contract to risks incurred with respect to driving performed in, and to risks incurred with respect to driving performed outside, the United States. See paragraph (b)(2)(v) of this section.

(c) Illustration. The application of this subdivision may be further illustrated by the following example:

Example. Controlled foreign corporation A is a wholly owned subsidiary of domestic corporation M. Both corporations are insurance companies and use the calendar year as the taxable year. Corporation M is exclusively engaged in issuing to owners of commercial rental property which is located in the United States insurance contracts which cover any harm which may be caused in 1963 by the tortious conduct of the owners' employees in managing and maintaining such property. The owners insured under such contracts include both residents and nonresidents of the United States. In 1963, M Corporation cedes to A Corporation one-half of the insurance contracts issued by M Corporation in that year, including the contracts issued to nonresidents. Income of A Corporation derived in 1963 from reinsuring the risks of M Corporation is income from the insurance of United States risks since all the insurance contracts reinsured by it are in connection with a liability which could arise from service activity performed in the United States.

(vi) Liability from delivery of property. If the person who is obligated to delivery property is liable with regard to such delivery, such liability will be considered to result from the activity performed of delivering such property. For example, if a corporation which exports all of its inventory from the United States to foreign countries or possessions of the United States is liable with regard to its failure to make delivery outside the United States of inventory it has sold, such liability will be considered to result from an activity exclusively carried on outside the United States and will be considered a liability which could not arise from activity performed in the United States. In further illustration, if a corporation which exports all of its inventory from a foreign country to the United States is liable with regard to its improper delivery in the United States of inventory it has sold, such liability will be considered to result from an activity exclusively carried on in the United States and will be considered a liability which could arise from activity performed in the United States.

(d) Lives or health of United States residents. Risks in connection with the lives or health of residents of the United States include those risks which are the subject of insurance contracts referred to in section 801(a), relating to the definition of a life insurance company. If the insured is a resident of the United States at the time the insurance contract is approved, the risk is in connection with the life or health of a resident of the United States for the period of coverage under the contract. However, if during such period of coverage the insured notifies the insurer, or circumstances known to the insurer indicate, that the insured is no longer a resident of the United States, the risk shall cease to be a risk in connection with the life or health of a resident of the United States for the policy period in which the insured gives such notice or such circumstances are known to the insurer, and for each subsequent policy period. Conversely, if the insured is a resident of a particular foreign country at the time the insurance contract is approved, the risk is in connection with the life or health of a resident of such foreign country for the period of coverage under the contract. However, if during such period of coverage the insured notifies the insurer, or circumstances known to the insurer indicate, that the insured is no longer a resident of such foreign country, the insured notifies the insurer, or circumstances known to the insurer indicate, that the insured is no longer a resident of such foreign country, the risk shall cease to be a risk in connection with the life or health of a resident of such particular foreign country for the policy period in which the insured gives such notice or such circumstances are known to the insurer, and for each subsequent policy period. In determining the country of residence of an insured, the principles of §§ 301.7701(b)-1 through 301.7701(b)-9 of this chapter, relating to the determination of residence and nonresidence in the United States and of foreign residence, shall apply. Citizens of the United States are not residents of the United States merely because of their citizenship. The application of this paragraph may be illustrated by the following example:

Example. Controlled foreign corporation A is a wholly owned subsidiary of domestic corporation M. Corporation A uses the calendar year as the taxable year and is engaged in the life insurance business in foreign country X. In 1963, A Corporation issues ordinary life insurance contracts on the lives of residents of the United States, including one issued on February 1, 1963, to R, a citizen of foreign country Y and a resident of the United States on such date. All activity in connection with the issuing of such contracts is transacted by mail. On May 1, 1963, R abandons his United States residence and establishes residence in foreign country Z. There are no circumstances known to A Corporation that R has changed his residence until R, on March 1, 1964, actually notifies A Corporation of that change. Income of A Corporation for the policy period of February 1, 1963, to January 31, 1964, from issuing such insurance contracts is income derived from the insurance of United States risks. However, income of A Corporation derived for the policy period of February 1, 1964, to January 31, 1965, from R's insurance contract is not income derived from the insurance of United States risks.

T.D. 6781, 12/22/64, amend T.D. 7736, 11/14/80, T.D. 8411, 4/24/92.

Proposed § 1.953-2 Premiums attributable to the section 953 insurance income category and the SCI income category. [*For Preamble, see ¶ 151,253*]

(a) In general. Premiums on any insurance, reinsurance, or any annuity contract (including an annuity certain, which is an annuity that guarantees payments for a fixed period without reference to life contingencies) must be classified as either section 953 insurance income or SCI income. To determine whether premiums paid for an annuity certain are section 953 insurance income or SCI income, the annuity certain shall be treated as a contract covering risks in connection with life or health. Premiums written (less return premiums and premiums paid for reinsurance) before the first taxable year of the controlled foreign corporation beginning after December 31, 1986 that become earned under section 832(b)(4) in such taxable year or succeeding taxable years must be classified as either section 953 insurance income or SCI income. (See § 1.953-3, below, for rules allocating premiums that constitute section 953 insurance income to the RPII or nonRPII categories.) .

(1) Section 953 insurance income premiums. Premiums constitute section 953 insurance income if they relate to risks that are—

(i) In connection with property located in a country other than the home country, as described in paragraph (e) of this section;

(ii) In connection with a liability arising out of an activity conducted in a country other than the home country, as described in paragraph (f) of this section;

(iii) In connection with the life or health of a resident of a country other than the home country, as described in paragraph (g) of this section; or

(iv) In connection with risks not described in paragraph (a)(1)(i) through (iii) of this section as a result of any arrangement whereby another person receives a substantially equal amount of premiums or other consideration in respect of issuing (or reinsuring) a contract described in paragraph (a)(1)(i) through (iii) of this section. (See paragraph (h) of this section).

(2) SCI income premiums. Premiums constitute SCI income if they relate to risks that are—

(i) In connection with property located in the home country, as described in paragraph (e) of this section;

(ii) In connection with a liability arising out of an activity conducted in the home country, as described in paragraph (f) of this section; or

(iii) In connection with the life or health of a resident of the home country, as described in paragraph (g) of this section.

(b) Method of attributing premiums to the section 953 insurance income or SCI income categories. *(1) In general.* Whether the premiums from an insurance, reinsurance, or annuity contract constitute section 953 insurance income or SCI income is determined by the location of the risks during the period or periods of coverage under the contract to which the premiums relate. A period of coverage is a period no longer than one year during which insurance coverage is provided or an annuity contract is in force and which begins or ends with or within the taxable year of the controlled foreign corporation. A period of coverage begins when coverage under the contract commences or on the anniversary of that date. A period of coverage ends on the last day preceding a new period of coverage, on the day the contract terminates or is canceled, or on the day the risk under the contract has been transferred in a reinsurance transaction in which the reinsurer assumes all rights and obligations under the reinsured policies. The determination of where a risk is located must be made separately for each period of coverage applicable to the taxable year.

(2) Examples. The following examples illustrate the principles of paragraph (b)(1) of this section.

Example (1). Controlled foreign corporation X, incorporated in country M, issues to corporation Z an insurance contract which provides coverage for a 2½ year period beginning on July 1, 1987. Under the insurance contract, premiums are paid monthly. Corporation X uses the calendar year as the taxable year. For premiums included in gross income for the 1987 taxable year, the period of coverage under the contract is July 1, 1987 to June 30, 1988. For premiums included in gross income for the 1988 taxable year, there are two applicable periods of coverage: July 1, 1987 to June 30, 1988 and July 1, 1988 to June 30, 1989. Whether the premiums attributable to each such period of coverage constitute section 953 insurance income or SCI insurance income must be made by considering only the facts pertinent to each period of coverage separately. For the 1989 taxable year, the periods of coverage are July 1, 1988 to June 30, 1989 and July 1, 1989 to December 31, 1989. Again, whether the premiums attributable to each such period of coverage constitute section 953 insurance income or SCI insurance income must be made by considering only the facts pertinent to each period of coverage separately.

Example (2). The facts are the same as in Example 1 except that Z cancels the contract on August 31, 1987. For the 1987 taxable year, the period of coverage is July 1, 1987 to August 31, 1987.

Example (3). The facts are the same as in Example 1 except that on January 15, 1989, X cedes risks under the insurance contract in a reinsurance transaction (other than a reinsurance transaction in which the reinsurer assumes all rights and obligations under the reinsured contracts) to controlled foreign corporation W, which also uses the calendar year as the taxable year. For the 1988 taxable year, the periods of coverage for X are July 1, 1987 to June 30, 1988 and July 1, 1988 to June 30, 1989. For 1989, the periods of coverage for both X and W are July 1, 1988 to June 30, 1989 and July 1, 1989 to December 31, 1989.

Example (4). The facts are the same as in Example 1 except that corporation X issues to corporation Z an insurance contract which covers the marine risks of shipping a machine to and from countries other than country M. The contract does not specify the dates during which the machine is covered, but provides coverage from the time the machine is delivered alongside a named vessel at the port of embarkation until the time the machine is delivered alongside the vessel at the port of debarkation. The deliveries are commenced and completed during the period beginning February 1, 1987 and ending February 28, 1987. For the 1987 taxable year, the period of coverage is February 1 to February 28, 1987.

(c) Definition of premiums. For a controlled foreign corporation that would be taxed as a life insurance company under part I of subchapter L (relating to life insurance companies) of the Code if it were a domestic insurance company, the term "premiums," for purposes of this section and § 1.953-3, means the items taken into account for the taxable year under section 803(a)(1). For a controlled foreign corporation that would be taxed under part II of subchapter L (relating to insurance companies other than life insurance companies), the term "premiums," for purposes of this section and § 1.953-3, means premiums written, as defined in section 832(b)(4)(A). If a policy of insurance, such as a reporting form policy or other policy, does not require premiums to be paid until the policy term expires, then the deposits required during the term of the policy must be included in premiums. In the case of a mutual fire or flood insurance company described in section 832(b)(1)(D), the term "premiums," for purposes of this section and § 1.953-3, means the entire amount of premiums deposited. In addition, for taxable years beginning after December 31, 1986 and before January 1, 1993, if the foreign corporation was a controlled foreign corporation (as defined in section 957 of the Code prior to its amendment by the Tax Reform Act of 1986) in the most recent taxable year beginning before January 1, 1987, the term "premiums" also includes an amount equal to 3⅓ percent of the unearned premiums at the end of the most recent taxable year beginning before January 1, 1987 that are sourced within the United States under section 861(a)(7). See section 832(b)(4)(C). Premiums included in gross income by virtue of the preceding sentence are attributable to risks located outside the controlled foreign corporation's home country.

(d) Allocation and apportionment of premiums. *(1) Risks both in and outside the home country.* If the risks covered by a contract of insurance or reinsurance or annuity contract are located both in and outside the home country during any period of coverage, the premium for insuring the risks must be allocated to or apportioned between risks incurred in the home country and risks incurred outside the home country. Allocation of a premium means that there is a direct correlation between the premium charged and the location of the insured risks in or outside the home country. Apportionment means that there is a reasonable basis for dividing the premium between risks incurred in the home country and risks incurred outside the home country, but there is no direct correlation between the premium charged and the location of the risks. If a premium is apportioned between home country risks and risks incurred outside the home country, each premium payment shall be considered to be partly related to home country risks and partly related to risks incurred outside the home country. The allocation or apportionment of premiums to or between risks located in the home country and risks located outside the home country must be reasonable in relation to the location of the insured risks during the period of coverage. In considering whether a method of allocation or apportionment is reasonable, consideration shall be given to the types of risks covered and the terms of the insurance, reinsurance, or annuity contract including, but not limited to, provisions which separately describe each risk covered, the period of coverage of each risk, the special warranties for each risk, the premium for each risk, and the conditions for paying the premium for each risk. The allocation and apportionment of premiums must be consistent with the rules prescribed in paragraphs (e), (f), and (g) of this section. In addition, once a particular method has been adopted for allocating and apportioning premiums under a contract, that method must be used as long as the contract is in force.

(2) Examples. The following examples illustrate the rules of paragraph (d)(1) of this section.

Example (1). X is a country F controlled foreign corporation with a calendar taxable year. X insures from July 1, 1987 through June 30, 1988 a particular piece of machinery that is located in country F. The machine is moved outside country F on January 1, 1988. The contract provides for $500 in premiums to be paid on June 30, 1987 and $1,000 on January 1, 1988. The larger premium payment on January 1, 1988 reflects the increased risks associated with locating the machine outside country F. For the 1987 and 1988 taxable years, the period of coverage is July 1, 1987 to June 30, 1988. Because there is a direct correlation between the premium payments and the location of the risks, the premiums must be allocated. The $500 premium payment included in X's gross income for the 1987 taxable year relates to risks incurred while the property is located in country F; therefore, all $500 in premiums constitute SCI income. The $1,000 included in X's gross income in the 1988 taxable year relates to coverage while the property is outside country F; therefore, all $1,000 constitutes section 953 insurance income.

Example (2). Z is a country F controlled foreign corporation with a calendar taxable year. Z issues a policy of insurance covering risks of damage to railroad rolling stock that only travels a particular route between country F and country M. The railroad rolling stock travels an equal number of miles in both countries. A $1,000 premium is required by Z to insure the railroad rolling stock from July 1, 1987 through June 30, 1988. The premium is paid in two installments: $500 on June 30, 1987 and $500 on January 1, 1988. Based on the types of risks covered by the contract of insurance and the terms of the contract, Z, in conformance with paragraph (e)(2)(i) of this section, chooses an apportionment method based on mileage. Because the premium is apportioned, $250 of the $500 premium included in the gross income of Z in the 1987 taxable year is attributable to home country risks and $250 is attributable to risks outside the home country. The result for the 1988 taxable year is the same.

(3) 80 percent rule. (i) In general. If 80 percent or more of the premiums for a period of coverage of a particular contract are apportioned to risks located in the home country or to risks located outside the home country, then all of the premiums for the period of coverage are apportioned to risks incurred in or outside the home country, as the case may be.

(ii) Example. The following example illustrates the operation of the 80 percent rule of paragraph (d)(3)(i) of this section.

Example. Controlled foreign corporation X, which is incorporated in country F and uses the calendar year as its taxable year, issues an insurance contract insuring a machine owned by Y against damage for a one year period commencing on May 1, 1987. When the contract was issued, the machine was located in country F; however, on April 1, 1988, Y moved the machine to a branch located outside country F. Y is required to pay premiums of $100 per month under the terms of the insurance contract. For the taxable years ending December 31, 1987 and December 31, 1988, the period of coverage is May 1, 1987 to April 30, 1988. For that period of coverage 1/12 ($100/$1200) of the premiums are related to risks located outside country F. Because approximately 92% of the premiums are related to home country risks, all the premiums under the contract are attributable to home country risks. Therefore, the $800 of premiums received by X from Y in the taxable year ending December 31, 1987 and the $400 of premiums received in the taxable year ending December 31, 1988 are attributable entirely to home country risks and constitute SCI income.

(e) Location of risks in connection with property. *(1) In general.* Risks in connection with property covered by a contract of insurance or reinsurance are located where the property is located during the period or periods of coverage applicable to the taxable year. A risk is in connection with property if it is related to an interest of an insured in tangible (whether real or personal) or intangible property. An interest in real property includes, but is not limited to, the interest of an owner, landlord, tenant, licensee, licensor, mortgagor, mortgagee, trustee, beneficiary, or partner. Where property is located depends on all the facts and circumstances. (See paragraph (e)(2) of this section for specific rules locating certain types of property.) The determination of where property is located must be made separately under each contract of insurance or reinsurance and for each item of property covered by the contract for each period of coverage applicable to the taxable year. (However, see paragraph (e)(3)(i) of this section which permits property to be aggregated in certain circumstances for purposes of determining location of risks.)

(2) Specific rules for locating certain types of property. (i) Commercial transportation property. Premiums related to insuring or reinsuring risks in connection with any motor vehicle, ship or boat, aircraft, railroad rolling stock, or any container transported thereby ("commercial transportation property") that is used predominantly in the commercial transportation of persons or property are attributable to risks located in the home country if the property is located in the home country for the entire period of coverage, or outside the home country if the property is located outside the home country for the entire period of coverage. If the commercial transportation property is located both in and outside the home country, then the premiums shall be allocated or apportioned between risks located in the home country and risks located outside the home country on any reasonable basis (such as time or mileage) that gives due regard to the risk being insured and that complies with the requirements of paragraphs (d)(1) and (d)(3) of this section. See paragraph (e)(3)(iii) of this section for rules relating to the location of moveable property, which includes commercial transportation property, if the location of such property cannot be determined by the end of the taxable year.

(ii) Examples. The following examples illustrate the operation of paragraph (e)(2)(i) of this section.

Example (1). Controlled foreign corporation Y, which is incorporated in country F, issues a property and liability insurance contract covering a helicopter that is used in rescue operations in country F as well as other countries. More than 60 percent of the miles traversed by the helicopter are outside country F. However, the helicopter is located in a hanger in country F for more than 90 percent of the period of coverage. Y apportions the premiums based on the time the helicopter is located in and outside the country of incorporation. An apportionment based on the amount of time that the helicopter is located in and outside country F is not reasonable in light of the types of risks insured and the activities in which the helicopter is engaged. Therefore, Y's apportionment of the premium will not be respected.

Example (2). Corporation Y, a country F controlled foreign corporation, insures an airplane that is used exclusively for the commercial transportation of persons or property. Of the total miles travelled by the airplane, 60 percent are traversed outside country F, and 40 percent are traversed in country F. The airplane is grounded only for repairs, and the repairs are made at the location of the airplane at the time the repairs are needed. The premiums must be apportioned on a reasonable basis between risks incurred while the plane is in country F and risks incurred while it is outside country F. On the facts presented in this example, an apportionment based on total miles traversed in and outside country F would be reasonable. Thus, 60 percent of the premiums would constitute section 953 insurance income and 40 percent of the premiums would constitute SCI income.

Example (3). The facts are the same as in Example 2 except that of the total miles travelled by the airplane, 85 percent are traversed outside the home country and 15 percent are traversed in the home country. Under the 80 percent rule of paragraph (d)(3) of this section, all of the premiums are apportioned to risks located outside country F.

(iii) Noncommercial transportation property. Premiums related to risks incurred in connection with any motor vehicle, ship or boat, aircraft, or railroad rolling stock not used predominantly in the commercial transportation of persons or property are attributable to risks located outside the home country if the noncommercial transportation property is registered during the period of coverage with a country other than the home country (including any political subdivision or agency of such country) or if the owner of the property is a citizen of, resident of, or entity organized under the laws of a country other than the home country. In all other cases, noncommercial transportation property shall be deemed to be located in the home country.

(iv) Property exported by ship or aircraft. Premiums related to risks in connection with property exported from the home country by ship or aircraft are attributable to risks incurred while the exported property is located in the home country if the insured risks terminate when the exported property is placed aboard the ship or aircraft for export. Premiums are attributable to risks incurred while the exported property is located outside the home country if the insured risks commence when the exported property is placed aboard the ship or aircraft for export. If the insured risks commence before the exported property is placed aboard the ship or aircraft for export and terminate after the departure of the ship or aircraft from the home country, the premiums must be allocated or apportioned between risks incurred while the exported property is located in the home country and risks incurred while the property is located outside the home country on any reasonable basis (such as time or mileage) that gives due regard to the risk being insured and that complies with the requirements of paragraphs (d)(1) and (d)(3) of this section.

(v) Property imported by ship or aircraft. Premiums related to risks in connection with property imported into the home country by ship or aircraft are attributable to risks incurred outside the home country if the insured risks terminate when the imported property is unloaded at the home country port of entry. If the insured risks commence after the imported property is unloaded from the ship or aircraft at the home country port of entry, the premiums are attributable to risks incurred while the imported property is in the home country. If the insured risks commence before and terminate after the imported property is unloaded from the ship or aircraft at the home country port of entry, the premiums must be allocated or apportioned to or between risks incurred while the imported property is located in the home country and risks incurred while the imported property is located outside the home country on any reasonable basis (such as time or mileage) that gives due regard to the risk being insured and that complies with the requirements of paragraphs (d)(1) and (d)(3) of this section.

(vi) Shipments originating and terminating in the home country. Premiums related to risks incurred in connection with property transported from one place in the home country to another place in the home country on or over another country, or on or over the high seas outside the territorial waters of the home country are attributable to risks in the home country unless the premiums are allocated, in a reasonable manner, under the terms of the insurance contract to risks incurred while the property is located in the home country and risks incurred while the property is located outside the home country.

(vii) Shipments originating and terminating in a country other than the home country. Premiums related to risks in connection with property transported on or over the home country to and from points outside the home country are attributable to risks located outside the home country unless the premiums are allocated, in a reasonable manner, under the terms of the insurance contract to risks incurred while the property is located in the home country and risks incurred while the property is located outside the home country.

(3) Related assets and certain moveable property. (i) Related assets. If a contract of insurance or reinsurance covers a group of related assets, such as inventory, which are located in and outside the home country, premiums under the contract may be allocated or apportioned, on any reasonable basis, between risks located in the home country and risks located outside the home country by reference to such property taken in the aggregate.

(ii) Example. The following example illustrates the related assets rule of paragraph (e)(3)(i) of this section.

Example. X is a controlled foreign corporation incorporated in country F. X issues a contract of insurance to M covering M's inventory. M maintains its inventory in warehouses in country F and other countries. The risks to which the inventory is exposed are similar in each country in which the inventory is stored. For the applicable period of coverage, 40 percent of M's inventory is located in country F and 60 percent is located outside country F. The location of the property is determined on the basis of the average value of inventory warehoused in and outside of country F during the period of coverage. X may apportion 40 percent of the premiums under the contract with M to the SCI income category and 60 percent to the section 953 insurance income category.

(iii) Moveable property. In any case in which a contract of insurance or reinsurance covers moveable property (other than noncommercial transportation property) and the determination of the location of the property in or outside the home country during a period of coverage cannot practicably be made by the close of the controlled foreign corporation's taxable year, the controlled foreign corporation may apportion the premiums in conformance with a reasonable expectation of where the property will be located during the period of coverage, provided that the apportionments made on all contracts to which this paragraph (e)(3)(iii) applies do not result in a material distortion. A material distortion results if the amount of premiums apportioned to the SCI or section 953 insurance income category determined by reference to the actual facts pertinent to the period of coverage, as ascertained within 90 days after the end of the period of coverage, would result in at least a 10 percentage point difference when compared to the amount of premiums apportioned to those categories under a reasonable expectation of where the property will be located during the period of coverage. In order to avail itself of this method, the controlled foreign corporation must maintain records that demonstrate the reasonableness of its apportionment, disclose the actual location of the property as ascertained within 90 days after the end of the period of coverage, and demonstrate that the apportionment did not result in a material distortion. If such records are not maintained, the apportionment method of this paragraph may not be used and the property shall be located under the rule of this paragraph (e) that would apply in absence of the method prescribed by this paragraph (e)(2)(iii). In the event of a material distortion, the United States shareholders or, if an election is made under § 1.953-7(c), the controlled foreign corporation must file amended income tax returns and apportion premiums based on the actual location of the property and the rules of paragraphs (d) and (e) of this section.

(iv) Example. The following example illustrates the moveable property rule of paragraph (e)(3)(iii) of this section.

Example. X is a controlled foreign corporation incorporated in country F. It uses the calendar year as its taxable year. X issues a contract of insurance covering a ship from July 1, 1988 to June 30, 1989. The contract is the only one issued by X that covers moveable property. The owner of the ship leases the ship to third persons on a per voyage basis. Based on information provided by the shipowner, 30 percent of the total miles traversed during the 12 month period immediately preceding the issuance of the contract were in home country waters and 70 percent outside the home country. X may apportion 30 percent of the premiums received to the SCI income category and 70 percent to the section 953 insurance income category. Within 90 days after the end of the policy period, X obtains information demonstrating that the ship was used in the territorial waters of the home country 25 percent of the time and outside the territorial waters 75 percent of the time. The apportionment method used by X is reasonable and does not result in a material distortion because an apportionment based on the facts pertinent to the period of coverage would not have resulted in at least a 10 percentage point difference in the amount of premiums apportioned to the SCI or section 953 insurance income categories. Thus, X may use the apportionment method described in paragraph (e)(3)(iii) of this section provided it maintains the records required by that paragraph.

(f) Location of risks in connection with liability arising out of activity. *(1) Definition of risks in connection with liability.* A risk covered by a contract of insurance or reinsurance is in connection with liability arising out of an activity if the insured is covered against a liability resulting from the actions of a person or a juridical entity, including actions that result in a tort, violation of contract, violation of property rights, or any other cause of action pursuant to the operation of law. The term not only includes a direct liability, which, for example, may be incurred by a tortfeasor to the person harmed, but also an indirect liability, such as the liability of one person to another resulting from the actions of an independent contractor. Moreover, a risk in connection with liability includes any loss of an insured (except a loss in connection with property described in paragraph (e) of this section) which could arise from the occurrence of an event insured against. For example, in the case of a promoter of outdoor sporting events, a risk in connection with liability arising out of an activity includes the loss that could arise from the cancellation of a sporting event because of inclement weather.

(2) Location of risk. (i) In general. A risk in connection with an activity is located where the activity that could give rise to a liability or loss is performed. For purposes of allocating and apportioning premiums between risks located in and outside the home country, where an activity is performed depends on the facts and circumstances of each case. Among the factors to be considered in making the determination are the location of the assets associated with the activity, the place where services comprising the activity are performed, the place where activities intended to result in a sale occur, and the place where sales actually occur.

(ii) Examples. The following examples illustrate the location of risk rules of paragraph (f)(2)(i) of this section.

Example (1). X is a controlled foreign corporation that issues liability insurance and is incorporated in country M. It uses a calendar year as its taxable year. X issues a contract of insurance to Z, which owns and operates department stores in country M and other countries. The contract covers all of Z's stores. It provides coverage against "liability for bodily injury or property damage arising out of the ownership, maintenance, or use of the insured premises and all operations necessary or incidental thereto." Assuming X cannot allocate the premiums between home country and other country risks, it must apportion the premiums between those risks on a reasonable basis taking into account where the stores are located and the level of covered activities in each of those stores.

Example (2). Y is a controlled foreign corporation incorporated in country F. Y writes worker's compensation coverage. Y issues a contract to Z, which has employees in country F and other countries, covering all of Z's employees. The premiums paid by Z are not allocable to risks located in the home country and risks located outside the home country. Z must apportion the premiums on a reasonable basis taking into account where Z's employees perform services.

(3) Specific rules locating certain activities. (i) Liability with respect to property manufactured, produced, constructed, or assembled. Premiums under a policy of insurance or reinsurance that insures a person that manufactures, produces, constructs, or assembles property against claims arising from the consumption or use of such property are attributable to risks from an activity performed where the consumption or use of the property takes place, or if the place of consumption or use cannot be known, where the property is manufactured, produced, constructed, or assembled. If the consumption or use of the property could arise in or outside the home country, the premiums must be allocated to or apportioned between risks located in the home country and risks located outside the home country on any reasonable basis that gives due regard to the risk being insured and that complies with the requirements of paragraphs (d)(1) and (d)(3) of this section.

(ii) Examples. The following examples illustrate the rule of paragraph (f)(3)(i) of this section.

Example (1). X is a contractor that constructs apartment buildings. X uses a system of pre—fabricated construction that entails constructing parts of the apartment buildings in country F and assembling them outside of country F. The only completed apartment buildings constructed by X are outside of country F. X is insured by Z, a country F controlled foreign corporation, against liability for the improper construction of, or the failure to construct, an apartment building. Z is insuring risks in connection with an activity that arises outside of country F because that is where the use of the property takes place.

Example (2). M manufactures automobiles in facilities located in country W. M is covered by a single policy of insurance issued by F, a controlled foreign corporation organized in country W. M sells its automobiles through independent dealers all over the world including country W. F charges a single premium to insure M against any liability for harm to persons or damage to property arising from a manufacturing defect. F must apportion the premium between risks located in W and risks located outside W on a reasonable basis because the use of the automobiles occurs in and outside of country W. However, if it cannot be known where the automobiles are used, then F is deemed to be insuring risks in connection with an activity that arises in country W because that is where the automobiles are manufactured.

(iii) Location of activities in connection with transportation property. Premiums under a contract of insurance or reinsurance covering risks in connection with the operation of a motor vehicle, ship or boat, aircraft, or railroad rolling stock are attributable to risks in connection with an activity performed where the transportation property is located under the principles of paragraph (e)(2)(i) and (iii) of this section relating to the location of transportation property.

(iv) Example. The following example illustrates the rule of paragraph (f)(3)(iii) of this section.

Example. X is a controlled foreign corporation created under the laws of country F and uses the calendar year as its taxable year. X insures B, a pilot for a commercial airline, against any damage to persons or property arising from B's professional activities. X charges a $10,000 premium, payable $5,000 at the inception of the policy and $5,000 on January 1, 1988, for a one year policy providing coverage from July 1, 1987 to June 30, 1988. B always pilots the same round trip flight from country F to country R and back. For both the 1987 and 1988 taxable years, the period of coverage is July 1, 1987 to June 30, 1988. On each trip from F to R the aircraft traverses half of the total mileage in country F and half in country R. Because the aircraft B flies is located in the home country one-half of the time, a reasonable basis exists for apportioning one-half of the premiums paid by B to risks arising from his activities outside the home country and one-half to activities arising in the home country. Thus, for the 1987 taxable year, the $5,000 of premiums are apportioned so that $2,500 of the premiums are attributable to home country risks and $2,500 of the premiums are attributable to risks located outside the home country. For the 1988 taxable year, the results are the same.

(v) Selling activity. The liability of a person arises from selling activity only if, and to the extent that, the liability does not relate to liability in connection with property manufactured, produced, constructed, or assembled, as described in paragraph (f)(3)(i) of this section, or liability for activities in connection with transportation property, as described in paragraph (f)(3)(iii) of this section. A person is engaged in selling activity if the person engages in any activity which is intended to result in the sale of property. Premiums received on a contract of insurance or reinsurance covering risks in connection with selling activity are attributable to risks incurred where the selling activity takes place regardless of whether the property passes through, or is delivered in, the country in which the selling activity is carried on. Selling activity takes place where the activities preparatory to the sale, such as advertising, negotiating, and distributing, take place.

(vi) Example. The following example illustrates the rule of paragraph (f)(3)(v) of this section.

Example. Corporation M, a country W corporation, insures a wholesale distributor against liability arising out of a breach of warranty. The wholesale distributor negotiates and processes orders in country W, but sells its inventory exclusively in countries other than country W by advertising in trade publications and distributing sales catalogues in those countries. The premiums on the policy issued to M are attributable to risks arising from activities performed both in and outside country W and M must allocate and apportion, on a reasonable basis, the premiums received for insuring the wholesale distributor between risks located in country W and risks located outside country W.

(g) Location of risks in connection with life or health. *(1) In general.* Risks in connection with life or health include risks under contracts of insurance, reinsurance, annuity contracts, or noncancelable health and accident contracts defined in section 816(a) (relating to the definition of a life insurance company). Risks under cancelable health and accident contracts are also risks in connection with life or health. An annuity certain, under which annuity payments are not determined by reference to life contingencies, is treated, for purposes of section 953 as a contract covering risks in connection with life or health. The risk under any insurance, reinsurance, or annuity contract covered by this paragraph (g)(1) is located in the country where the person with respect to whom the risk is located (the "determining life") is resident. The determining life with respect to any life, accident, or health insurance or reinsurance contract is the person whose life or health is covered by the contract. The determining life with respect to a life annuity contract is the person by whose life the annuity payments are measured. The determining life with respect to an annuity certain is the life of the person who purchases the annuity contract and the life of the person for whose benefit the annuity was purchased. Thus, risks in connection with an annuity certain are deemed to be located in their entirety outside a controlled foreign corporation's home country if either the purchaser of the contract or the recipient of the annuity payments resides outside the home country, as determined in accordance with the rules of this paragraph. The person with the determining life is presumed to be resident at the last address given to the controlled foreign corporation as such person's residence, unless the controlled foreign corporation knows or has reason to know that such person is resident at a different address. Premiums received under a contract of group life or health insurance must be apportioned between risks located in the home country and risks outside the home country on the basis of the last known addresses of the residences of the persons insured under the contract or, in the case where the contract is issued to an employer, where the persons covered by the contract are employed.

(2) Example. The following example illustrates the rules of paragraph (g)(1) of this section.

Example. Controlled foreign corporation X, a country F corporation and a calendar year taxpayer, is engaged in the life insurance business. On July 1, 1987, X issues a three year term life insurance contract on the life of B. Premiums under the contract are payable on July 1 and December 31 of each year the contract is in force. B gives to X an address in country F as the address of his primary residence. On November 1, 1987, B changes his primary residence from country F to country Z. B notifies X of the change of address on February 1, 1988. For X's 1987 taxable year the premiums received on July 1, 1987 and December 31, 1987 are allocable to the SCI income category. Because X did not have knowledge, and had no reason to know, of B's change of address until February 1, 1988, it may rely, for all premium payments received before February 1, 1988, on the address B initially provided at the time the contract was approved. However, all premiums received after February 1, 1988 constitute section 953 insurance income because X had knowledge at the time those premiums were received that B had his or her primary residence outside of country F.

(h) Risks deemed to be located in a country other than the home country. *(1) Artificial arrangements.* The section 953 insurance income of a controlled foreign corporation includes any insurance income from issuing or reinsuring insurance policies or annuity contracts covering risks located in the home country if the insurance, reinsurance, or annuity contracts are attributable to any direct or indirect cross-insurance arrangement whereby the controlled foreign corporation provides insurance, reinsurance, or annuity contracts relating to home country risks and, in exchange, another person provides insurance, reinsurance, or annuity contracts relating to risks located outside the home country. Arrangements to which this rule applies include those entered into by the controlled foreign corporation, persons related (within the meaning of section 954(d)(3)) to the controlled foreign corporation, the United States shareholders of the controlled foreign corporation, and persons related to such shareholders.

(2) Evidence of arrangements. The determination of whether an arrangement referred to in paragraph (h)(1) of this section exists depends on all the facts and circumstances. Facts to be considered in determining the existence of such an arrangement include the premiums charged in relation to the risks insured, the profit margin expected from the contracts, and the loss experience of the risks which the other person insures or reinsures compared with the loss experience of the risks which the controlled foreign corporation insures or reinsures. Further, consideration will be given to the existence of common directors or owners between the parties executing the reciprocal insurance arrangement. The period in which the controlled foreign corporation receives premiums and the period of coverage for which the premiums are received need not be the same as, or identical in length with, that of the other person or limited to a single taxable year of the controlled foreign corporation.

(3) Examples. The following examples illustrate the principles of paragraph (h) of this section.

Example (1). Controlled foreign corporation X is incorporated in country F and is a wholly-owned subsidiary of corporation M, a United States corporation. Foreign corporation Y is a wholly owned subsidiary of foreign corporation R. R is not a controlled foreign corporation. Corporations M and R, which are not related, agree that from July 1, 1987 through December 31, 1987, Y corporation will reinsure certain policies issued by M covering risks that are located outside country F, and that from January 1, 1988 through June 30, 1988, X will reinsure certain policies issued by R covering risks that are located in country F. The premiums received by X corporation from reinsuring the risks of R are attributable to risks located outside country F and constitute section 953 insurance income.

Example (2). The facts are the same as in Example 1 except that one-third of the risks of M to be reinsured are reinsured with Y and two-thirds of the risks are reinsured with Z, another wholly owned foreign subsidiary of R. The premiums received by X from reinsuring the policies of R are attributable to risks located outside country F and constitute section 953 insurance income.

Example (3). The facts are the same as in Example 1 except that X and V, another wholly-owned foreign subsidiary of M, reinsure the risks of R. The premiums received by X and V from reinsuring the policies of R are attributable to risks located outside country F and constitute section 953 insurance income.

§ 1.953-3 Risks deemed to be United States risks.

Caution: The Treasury has not yet amended Reg § 1.953-3 to reflect changes made by P.L. 100-647, P.L. 99-514, P.L. 98-369.

(a) Artificial arrangements. For purposes of paragraph (a) of § 1.953-1, the term "United States risks" also includes under section 953(a)(1)(B) risks which are deemed to be United States risks. They are risks (other than United States risks described in section 953(a)(1)(A) and § 1.953-2) which a controlled foreign corporation reinsures under an insurance or annuity contract, or with respect to which a controlled foreign corporation issues any insurance or annuity contract, in accordance with any arrangement whereby another corporation which is not a controlled foreign corporation receives an amount of premiums (for reinsuring or issuing any insurance or annuity contract in connection with the United States risks described in section 953(a)(1)(A) and § 1.953-2) which is substantially equal to the amount of premiums which the controlled foreign corporation receives under its contracts. Arrangements to which this rule applies include those entered into by the controlled foreign corporation, by its United States shareholders, or by a related person.

(b) Evidence of arrangements. The determination of the existence of an arrangement referred to in paragraph (a) of this section shall depend on all the facts and circumstances in each case. In making this determination, it will be recognized that arrangements of this type generally are orally entered into outside the United States and that direct evidence of such an arrangement is not ordinarily available. Therefore, in determining the existence of such an arrangement, consideration will be given to whether or not there is substantial similarity between the type, location, profit margin expected, and loss experience of the risks which the corporation which is not a controlled foreign corporation insures or reinsures and the risks which the controlled foreign corporation insures or reinsures. Further, consideration will be given to the existence of prior similar arrangements between, and the identity of the directors or shareholders of, the corporation which is not a controlled foreign corporation, its shareholders, or related persons and the controlled foreign corporation, its shareholders, or related persons. However, the absence of such prior arrangements or identity of directors or shareholders will not of itself establish the nonexistence of an arrangement referred to in paragraph (a) of this section. In determining whether the amounts received by the controlled foreign corporation and the corporation which is not a controlled foreign corporation are substantially equal, the period in which the controlled foreign corporation receives premiums need not be the same as, or identical in length with, that of the corporation which is not a controlled foreign corporation nor limited to a taxable year of the controlled foreign corporation.

(c) Illustrations. The application of this section may be illustrated by the following examples:

Example (1). Controlled foreign corporation A is a wholly owned subsidiary of domestic corporation M. Foreign corporation B is a wholly owned subsidiary of foreign corporation R. All corporations use the calendar year as the taxable year. Corporations M and R, which are not related persons, agree that from July 1, 1963, through December 31, 1963, B Corporation will reinsure all risks of M Corporation which are United States risks described in section 953(a)(1)(A), and that from January 1, 1964, through June 30, 1964, A Corporation will reinsure all risks of R Corporation which are not United States risks described in section 953(a)(1)(A). The amount of premiums received by A Corporation and B Corporation, respectively, as a result of the agreement are substantially equal. The income of A Corporation derived in 1964 from reinsuring the risks of R Corporation is income derived from the insurance of United States risks described in section 953(a)(1)(B).

Example (2). Assume the same facts as in example (1), except that M and R Corporations also agree, as part of their arrangement, that from July 1, 1964, through December 31, 1964, B Corporation will reinsure all risks of M Corporation which are United States risks described in section 953(a)(1)(A), and that from January 1, 1965, through June 30, 1965, A Corporation will reinsure all risks of R Corporation which are not United States risks described in section 953(a)(1)(A). The amount of premiums derived by B Corporation from July 1, 1963, through December 31, 1963, under the agreement is not substantially equal to the amount of premiums derived by B Corporation from July 1, 1964, through December 31, 1964, is not substantially equal to the amount of premiums derived by A Corporation from January 1, 1965, through June 30, 1965. However, the aggregate amount of premiums received by B Corporation under the arrangement is substantially equal to the aggregate amount of premiums received by A Corporation. The income of A Corporation derived in 1964 and 1965 from reinsuring the risks of R Corporation is income derived from the insurance of United States risks described in section 953(a)(1)(B).

Example (3). Assume the same facts as in example (1), except that foreign corporation C is also a wholly owned subsidiary of R Corporation. Assume that C Corporation uses the calendar year as its taxable year. Assume further that M Corporation and R Corporation agree that from July 1, 1963, through December 31, 1963, B Corporation and C Corporation together will reinsure the United States risks described in section 953(a)(1)(A) of M Corporation. The amount of premiums received by B Corporation in respect of such United States risks is equal to one-third of the amount received by A Corporation in respect of the risks which are not United States risks described in section 953(a)(1)(A), and the amount of premiums received by C Corporation in respect of such United States risks is equal to two-thirds of the amount so received by A Corporation. The income of A Corporation derived in 1964 from reinsuring the risks of R Corporation is income derived from the insurance of United States risks described in section 953(a)(1)(B).

Example (4). Assume the same facts as in example (3), except that controlled foreign corporation D is also a wholly owned subsidiary of M Corporation and uses the calendar year as its taxable year. Assume further that M Corporation and R Corporation agree that in 1964 R Corporation will pay premiums of $300,000 to A Corporation and $700,000 to D Corporation to reinsure all risks of R Corporation which are not United States risks described in section 953(a)(1)(A), and that in 1963 M Corporation will pay premiums of $400,000 to B Corporation and $600,000 to C Corporation to reinsure all risks of M Corporation which are United States risks described in section 953(a)(1)(A). The income of A Corporation and D Corporation derived in 1964 from reinsuring the risks of R Corporation is income derived from the insurance of United States risks described in section 953(a)(1)(B).

Example (5). Controlled foreign corporation A is a wholly owned subsidiary of domestic insurance corporation M. Controlled foreign corporation B is a wholly owned subsidiary of domestic insurance corporation N. All corporations use the calendar year as the taxable year. As a result of an arrangement between M Corporation and N Corporation, in 1963 A Corporation reinsures all the United States risks described in section 953(a)(1)(A) of N Corporation, and B Corporation reinsures all the United States risks described in section 953(a)(1)(A) of M Corporation. The premiums and other consideration received by A Corporation and B Corporation in respect of such reinsurance are not substantially equal. The income of A Corporation and B Corporation in 1963 from reinsuring the risks of N Corporation and M Corporation, respectively, is income derived from the insurance of United States risks described in section 953(a)(1)(A) and is not income derived from the insurance of United States risks described in section 953(a)(1)(B).

Example (6). Assume the same facts as in example (5), except that B Corporation is not a controlled foreign corporation. The income of A Corporation in 1963 from reinsuring the risks of N Corporation is income derived from the insurance of United States risks described in section 953(a)(1)(A) and is not income derived from the insurance of United States risks described in section 953(a)(1)(B).

T.D. 6781, 12/22/64.

Proposed § 1.953-3 Allocation of premiums to the RPII or nonRPII categories of section 953 insurance income. [*For Preamble, see ¶ 151,253*]

(a) In general. All premiums that constitute section 953 insurance income are included within one of two categories: premiums that constitute related person insurance income ("RPII premiums") under paragraph (b) of this section and premiums that do not constitute RPII premiums ("nonRPII premiums"). RPII premiums are not recharacterized as nonRPII premiums even though the exceptions of § 1.953-7 are applicable. However, if the exceptions of § 1.953-7(a) or (b) apply, persons that are United States shareholders solely by virtue of section 953(c)(1)(A) and paragraph (b)(2) of this section of a controlled foreign corporation, as defined in section 953(c)(1)(B) and paragraph (b)(2) of this section, do not include RPII income in their gross income. Persons that are United States shareholders within the meaning of section 951(b) of a controlled foreign corporation as defined in section 957 must always include RPII income in their gross income, regardless of whether the exceptions of § 1.953-7(a) or (b) apply. However, the special pro rata share rules of section 953(c)(5) and § 1.953-6(h)(1) shall not apply if the conditions of section 953(c)(3)(A) and (B) and § 1.953-7(a) and (b) are met.

(b) Related person insurance income. *(1) In general.* Related person insurance income is included within the meaning of the term "insurance income" as that term is used in section 953. Related person insurance income is premium and investment income attributable to a policy of insurance or reinsurance that provides insurance coverage to a related insured on risks located outside the controlled foreign corporation's country of incorporation, or premium and investment income attributable to an annuity contract that is purchased by or for the benefit of a related insured if the determining life is located outside the controlled foreign corporation's country of incorporation. For this purpose, a related insured is any insured, purchaser of an annuity contract, or recipient of annuity payments that is a United States shareholder of the controlled foreign corporation or a related person (within the meaning of section 954(d)(3)) to a United States shareholder.

(2) Definitions. (i) United States shareholder, related person, and controlled foreign corporation. For purposes of determining whether insurance income is related person insurance income, the terms "United States shareholder," "related person to a United States shareholder," and "controlled foreign corporation" are specifically defined. The term "controlled foreign corporation" means any foreign corporation if 25 percent or more of the total combined voting power of all classes of stock of the foreign corporation entitled to vote or 25 percent or more of the total value of the stock of the foreign corporation is owned (within the meaning of section 958(a)), or is considered as owned by applying the rules of ownership of section 958(b), by United States shareholders on any day during the taxable year of the foreign corporation. For purposes of applying this section to a foreign mutual insurance company, the term stock includes any certificate entitling the holder to voting power in the mutual company. See section 958(a)(3). A "United States shareholder" for these purposes is any United States person (as defined in section 957(c)) who owns (within the meaning of section 958(a)) any stock of the foreign corporation at any time during the foreign corporation's taxable year. A person is a related person to a United States shareholder if the person is related within the meaning of section 954(d)(3) of the Code to the United States shareholder. Thus, a person is related to a United States shareholder if the person controls (within in the meaning of section 954(d)(3)), or is controlled by, the United States shareholder, or the person is controlled by the same person (or persons) that controls the United States shareholder. In addition, in the case of any policy of insurance covering liability arising from services performed as a director, officer, or employee of a corporation, or as a partner or employee of a partnership, the person performing such services and the entity for which such services are performed shall be treated as related persons.

(ii) Examples. The following examples illustrate the definitions of paragraph (b)(2)(i) of this section.

Example (1). X is a country F corporation that provides insurance coverage to its 100 shareholders. X has voting common stock and nonvoting preferred stock issued and outstanding. All of the voting common stock is owned by 75 foreign persons. None of the foreign shareholders are related persons within the meaning of section 954(d)(3). All of the nonvoting preferred stock is owned by 25 United States persons. The nonvoting preferred stock accounts for 25 percent of the total value of both classes of stock outstanding. Therefore, each United States person is a United States shareholder and X is a controlled foreign corporation under section 953(c)(2)(B). The premiums from policies of insurance issued to the twenty-five United States shareholders constitute RPII premiums to the extent those premiums relate to risks located outside country F. The premiums from the 75 foreign shareholders constitute nonRPII premiums to the extent those premiums relate to risks located outside country F.

Example (2). The facts are the same as in Example 1 except that all of the nonvoting preferred stock is owned by a foreign corporation, all of the stock of which is owned by the 25 United States persons. Under section 958(a)(2), the United States persons are considered as owning the stock owned by the foreign corporation. Therefore, X is a controlled foreign corporation and the 25 United States persons are United States shareholders.

Example (3). The facts are the same as in Example 1 except that 5 of the nonvoting preferred stock shareholders are insured by X and 20 are not. X is a controlled foreign corporation and all 25 United States persons are United States shareholders. A United States person need not be insured by the controlled foreign corporation to be a United States shareholder of that corporation.

Example (4). Y is a foreign corporation that issues policies of insurance and reinsurance. The one class of Y stock outstanding is owned equally by 25 shareholders who are United States persons. None of the shareholders of Y are insured by Y; however, five of the policies issued by Y are issued to wholly-owned foreign subsidiaries of five of Y's shareholders. The premiums attributable to the policies of insurance issued with respect to the foreign subsidiaries constitute RPII premiums. The insured foreign subsidiaries are related persons to United States shareholders because those subsidiaries are controlled, within the meaning of section 954(d)(3), by United States shareholders.

(iii) United States shareholder: exception for indirect ownership; publicly traded stock. A United States person who is not insured or reinsured (directly or indirectly) by a foreign corporation (the "insuring foreign corporation") and is not related to a person insured (directly or indirectly) by the insuring foreign corporation shall not be treated as a United States shareholder of the insuring foreign corporation by virtue of section 958(a)(2) because of such person's ownership of stock in another foreign corporation which owns stock (directly or indirectly) in the insuring foreign corporation if:

(A) The stock of the other foreign corporation is publicly traded;

(B) The United States person owns less than five percent of the combined voting power of all classes of stock entitled to vote and less than five percent of the total value of the stock of the other foreign corporation; and

(C) The stock of the insuring foreign corporation constitutes less than five percent of the gross value of all the assets of the other foreign corporation.

(iv) Example. The following example illustrates the indirect ownership exception of paragraph (b)(2)(iii) of this section.

Example. X is a foreign corporation which writes policies of insurance for its shareholders and unrelated persons. X has one class of stock outstanding. Five shareholders of X, who are United States persons, each own 4 percent of X's stock. These shareholders are also insured by X. The remaining 80 percent of the X stock is owned by corporation Y, a foreign corporation the stock of which is publicly traded. X insures certain risks of Y. All of the stock of Y is owned by United States persons, but no shareholder of Y owns more than 5 percent of the stock of Y by vote or value or is insured by X. None of the United States persons are related to Y or to each other. The X stock owned by Y constitutes less than five percent of the total value of all of Y's assets. The United States persons who own the stock of Y are not considered United States shareholders of X under section 958(a)(2) because the requirements of paragraph (b)(2)(iii) of this section are met. Therefore, only 20 percent of the X stock is owned by United States persons and X is not a controlled foreign corporation.

(v) Controlled foreign corporation: shipowner's protection and indemnity association. A controlled foreign corporation meeting the definition of paragraph (b)(2)(i) of this section and also qualifying as a shipowner's protection and indemnity association under section 526 of the Code is a controlled foreign corporation subject to the provisions of §§ 1.953-1 through 1.953-7. Thus, a United States shareholder of such an association must include its pro rata share of the receipts of such an association that constitute section 953 insurance income, including premiums, dues, and assessments, less appropriately allocated and apportioned expenses, losses and other deductions, in such shareholder's gross income as required by § 1.953-6(h) notwithstanding section 526. See § 1.952-2(c)(1) which states that subchapter F does not apply in determining the gross income of a controlled foreign corporation.

(3) Reinsurance. (i) In general. Related person insurance income includes income attributable to contracts of reinsurance, including reinsurance arrangements in which the reinsurer accepts all the rights and obligations under the reinsured contracts, pursuant to which the controlled foreign corporation reinsures contracts issued by its United States shareholders, or related persons to such shareholders.

(ii) Examples. The following examples illustrate the rule of paragraph (b)(3)(i) of this section.

Example (1). Twenty-five domestic corporations, which are engaged in the business of issuing property insurance policies to unrelated commercial entities, formed Z under the laws of country W to reinsure a portion of the risks insured by the domestic corporations. Each of the twenty-five domestic corporations owns an equal amount of the one class of stock of Z outstanding. Z has no business other than reinsuring the policies issued by its shareholders. The premiums received by Z constitute RPII premiums.

Example (2). The facts are the same as in Example 1. However, X, one of the shareholders of Z, enters a portfolio (assumption) reinsurance agreement with Z under which Z assumes all of the rights and obligations under certain policies issued by X. Z notifies the policyholders that it is assuming all the rights and obligations under the policies issued by X. The premiums from the reinsured policies constitute related person insurance income even though X no longer has any rights or obligations under the policies.

(4) Indirectly insuring a related insured: Fronting. (i) In general. For taxable years beginning after December 31, 1987, premiums received on insurance contracts, or contracts reinsuring insurance contracts, that indirectly insure United States shareholders of a controlled foreign corporation or persons related to such shareholders are included within the definition of related person insurance income. A contract indirectly insures a United States shareholder or person related to such shareholder if the contract is issued by an unrelated person and the contract is ultimately reinsured with the controlled foreign corporation in which the United States shareholder owns stock. For taxable years beginning after December 31, 1987, premiums received on annuity contracts, or contracts reinsuring annuity contracts, that are indirectly purchased by, or indirectly provide annuity benefits to, a United States shareholder or persons related to such shareholders are included within the definition of related person insurance income.

(ii) Example. The following example illustrates the rule of paragraph (b)(4)(i) of this section.

Example. Z is a domestic corporation that has issued a policy of insurance to Y. Y is a domestic corporation which owns stock in X, a controlled foreign corporation within the meaning of section § 1.953-3(b)(2)(i). Z does not own any of the stock of X. Z reinsures with X part of the risk it insures under the policy issued to Y. The premiums received by X for reinsuring the policy issued to Y are RPII premiums because one of its United States shareholders, Y, is indirectly an insured of X.

(5) Cross-insurance arrangements. (i) In general. Related person insurance income includes insurance income attributable to a direct or indirect cross-insurance arrangement whereby the controlled foreign corporation issues an insurance, reinsurance, or annuity contract to a person other than a related insured (as defined in paragraph (b)(1) of this section) in return for another person issuing an insurance, reinsurance, or annuity contract to a person that would be a related insured if the controlled foreign corporation were to issue an insurance, reinsurance, or annuity contract to such person. See § 1.953-2(h).

(ii) Example. The following example illustrates the rule of paragraph (b)(5)(i) of this section.

Example. Controlled foreign corporation X is owned by 30 United States shareholders engaged in a similar line of business. Controlled foreign corporation Y is owned by 32 United States shareholders engaged in the same line of business as the 30 shareholders of X. Both X and Y provide insurance to businesses engaged in the line of business in which their shareholders are engaged as well as other types of business. X agrees to provide insurance protection to Y's shareholders and Y agrees to provide insurance to X's shareholders. The premiums of both X and Y that relate to insuring the shareholders of the other corporation constitute related person insurance income.

(6) Specific premium rules. (i) Premiums received prior to January 1, 1987. Related person insurance income includes premiums written (less return premiums and premiums paid for reinsurance) before the first taxable year of the controlled foreign corporation beginning after December 31, 1986 that become earned under section 832(b)(4) in a taxable year beginning after December 31, 1986, or succeeding taxable years, provided that the premiums otherwise qualify as related person insurance income.

(ii) Apportionment of premiums if stock owned for less than entire taxable year. If, during a taxable year of a controlled foreign corporation, an insurance, reinsurance, or annuity contract that relates to a United States shareholder remains in force beyond the period during which the United States shareholder owns stock in the controlled foreign corporation, the amount of the premiums, as defined in § 1.953-2(c), attributable to the contract must be apportioned between the RPII category and the nonRPII category. The amount apportioned to the RPII category is equal to the amount of premiums on the contract included in the gross income of the controlled foreign corporation in the taxable year multiplied by a fraction, the numerator of which is the number of days in the period of coverage which fall within the taxable year during which the United States shareholder owned stock in the controlled foreign corporation, and the denominator of which is the total number of days in the period of coverage that fall within the taxable year. The remainder of the premiums on the contract are apportioned to the nonRPII category.

(iii) Examples. The following examples illustrate the rule of paragraph (b)(6)(ii) of this section.

Example (1). Y is a country F controlled foreign corporation with a calendar taxable year. Y issues a policy of insurance to M, one of its United States shareholders, covering risks of property damage to a plant owned by M. The plant is located outside country F. The policy covers risks incurred from July 1, 1987 to June 30, 1988. M pays premiums of $1,000 on July 1, 1987 and $1,000 on January 1, 1988. On September 30, 1987, M sells all of its stock in Y. In Y's 1987 taxable year, there are 183 days during which M is insured. M is a stockholder in Y for 92 days during the 1987 taxable year. Therefore, of the $1,000 of premiums from M included in Y's gross income in its 1987 taxable year, $503 ($1,000 × 92/183) is allocated to the RPII premium category and $497 is allocated to the nonRPII premium category. For the 1988 taxable year, all $1,000 of premiums from M are allocated to the nonRPII premium category because M owns no stock in Y on any day of the period of coverage falling within the 1988 taxable year.

Example (2). The facts are the same as in Example 1 except that M sells only a part of its Y stock on September 30, 1987. Because M remains a shareholder in Y, all the premiums received from M in the 1987 and 1988 taxable years are allocated to the RPII premium category.

(iv) Anti-abuse rule. If the facts and circumstances indicate that the premiums charged on an insurance, reinsurance, or annuity contract that gives rise to related person insurance income are below the premium rate charged on comparable contracts issued to unrelated persons, then the district director can recast capital contributions or other amounts paid or deposited by the United States shareholder as premiums on an insurance, reinsurance, or annuity contract. See also section 482 (allocation of income and deductions among taxpayers) and section 845 (certain reinsurance agreements).

(v) Example. The following example illustrates the anti-abuse rule of paragraph (b)(6)(iv) of this section.

Example. X is a controlled foreign corporation incorporated in country F that insures the risks of its shareholders, all of whom are United States persons, as well as the risks of unrelated persons. In 1987, X issued fire insurance policies to some of its shareholders and to unrelated persons covering property located outside country F. The premium rates charged to the shareholders under the policies were less than those charged to similarly situated unrelated persons. The shareholders who are insured under the fire insurance policies also purchased preferred stock on which X has call rights which become effective on the same dates that the policies expire. The facts indicate that the amounts paid for the preferred stock are actually part of the cost of the insurance provided to the shareholders. All or part of the amounts paid for the preferred stock may be recharacterized as premiums paid on insurance policies.

§ 1.953-4 Taxable income to which section 953 applies.

Caution: The Treasury has not yet amended Reg § 1.953-4 to reflect changes made by P.L. 100-647, P.L. 99-514, P.L. 98-369.

(a) Taxable income defined. *(1) Life insurance taxable income.* For a controlled foreign corporation which is engaged in the business of reinsuring or issuing insurance or annuity contracts and which, if it were a domestic corporation engaged only in such business, would be taxable as a life insurance company to which part I (sections 801 through 820) of subchapter L of the Code applies, the term "taxable income" means for purposes of paragraph (a) of § 1.953-1 the gain from operations, as defined in section 809(b) and as modified by this section, derived from, and attributable to, the insurance of United States risks. For purposes of determining such taxable income, the provisions of section 802(b) (relating to the definition of life insurance company taxable income) shall not apply. Determinations for purposes of this subparagraph shall be made without regard to section 501(a).

(2) Mutual and other insurance taxable income. For a controlled foreign corporation which is engaged in the business of reinsuring or issuing insurance or annuity contracts and which, if it were a domestic corporation engaged only in such business, would be taxable as a mutual insurance company to which part II (sections 821 through 826) of subchapter L of the Code applies or a mutual marine insurance or other insurance company to which part III (sections 831 and 832) of subchapter L of the Code applies, the term "taxable income" means for purposes of paragraph (a) of § 1.953-1 taxable income, as defined in section 832(a) and as modified by this section, derived from, and attributable to, the insurance of United States risks. Determinations for purposes of this subparagraph shall be made without regard to section 501(a).

(3) Corporations not qualifying as insurance companies. For special rules applicable under this section in the case of a controlled foreign corporation which, if it were a domestic corporation, would not qualify as an insurance company, see § 1.953-5.

(b) Certain provisions inapplicable. In determining taxable income under this section, the following provisions of subchapter L of the Code shall not apply:

(1) Section 809(d)(4), relating to the operations loss deduction;

(2) Section 809(d)(5), relating to certain nonparticipating contracts;

(3) Section 809(d)(6), relating to certain accident and health insurance and group life insurance;

(4) Section 809(d)(10), relating to small business deduction;

(5) Section 817(b), relating to gain on property held on December 31, 1958, and certain substituted property acquired after 1958; and

(6) Section 832(c)(5), relating to capital losses.

(c) Computation of reserves required by law. *(1) Law applicable in determining reserves.* The reserves which will be taken into account as reserves required by law under section 801(b)(2), both in determining for any taxable year whether a controlled foreign corporation is a controlled foreign corporation described in paragraph (a)(1) or (2) of this section and in determining taxable income of such corporation for the taxable year under paragraph (a) of this section, shall be the following reserves:

(i) Reserves required by the law of a State. The reserves which are required by the law of the State or States to which the insurance business of the controlled foreign corporation is subject, but only with respect to its United States business, if any, which is taxable under section 819(a).

(ii) Reserves deemed to be required. To the extent of such controlled foreign corporation's insurance business not taxable under section 819(a)—

(a) Except as provided in subdivision (b) of this subdivision (ii), the reserves which would result if such reserves were determined by applying the minimum standards of the law of New York as if such controlled foreign corporation were an insurance company transacting all of its insurance business (other than its United States business which is taxable under section 819(a) for such taxable year in such State, and

(b) With respect to all risks covered by insurance ceded to such controlled foreign corporation by an insurance company to which apply the provisions of subchapter L of the Code (determined without regard to section 501(a)) and in respect of which an election is made by or on behalf of such controlled foreign corporation to determine its reserves in accordance with this subdivision (b), the amount of reserves against such risks which would result if all of such reserves were determined by applying the law of the State, to which the risks in the hands of such insurance company are subject, as if such controlled foreign corporation were an insurance company engaged in reinsuring such risks in such State.

(2) Rules of application. For purposes of subparagraph (1) of this paragraph, the following rules shall apply:

(i) Life insurance reserves computed on preliminary term basis. For purposes of determining under paragraph (a) of this section the taxable income of a controlled foreign corporation, an election may be made by or on behalf of such corporation that the amount of reserves which are taken into account as life insurance reserves with respect to contracts for which reserves are computed on a preliminary term basis shall be determined as provided in section 818(c). This election shall apply, subject to section 818(c), to all life insurance reserves of the controlled foreign corporation, whether or not reserves applicable to the United States business taxable under section 819(a). However, reserves determined as provided in section 818(c) shall not be taken into account in determining whether a controlled foreign corporation is a controlled foreign corporation described in paragraph (a)(1) or (2) of this section.

(ii) Actual reserves required. (a) A controlled foreign corporation will be considered to have a reserve only to the extent the reserve has been actually held during the taxable year for which such reserve is claimed.

(b) For determining when reserves are required by the law of a State, see paragraph (b) of § 1.801-5 of this chapter.

(iii) Total reserves to be taken into account. The total reserves of a controlled foreign corporation shall be taken into account in determining whether such corporation is a controlled foreign corporation described in paragraph (a)(1) or (2) of this section. Therefore, in making such determination, the reserves which, under subparagraph (1)(i) of this paragraph, are required by the law of any State shall be taken into account together with the reserves which, under subparagraph (1)(ii) of this paragraph, are deemed to be required. Moreover, reserves applicable to the reinsuring or the issuing of insurance or annuity contracts of both United States risks and foreign risks shall be taken into account. Finally, except as provided in subdivision (i) of this subparagraph, the reserves which are taken into account in determining whether a controlled foreign corporation is a controlled foreign corporation described in paragraph (a)(1) or (2) of this section shall be the same reserves which are taken into account in determining under paragraph (a) of this section the taxable income of such corporation.

(iv) Method of comparing reserves when subject ot more than one State. If the insurance business of a controlled foreign corporation is subject to the law of more than one State, the amount of reserves taken into account under subparagraph (1)(i) of this paragraph shall be the amount of the highest aggregate reserve required by any State, determined as provided in paragraph (a) of § 1.801-5 of this chapter.

(d) Domestic corporation tax attributes. In determining taxable income of a controlled foreign corporation under this section there shall be allowed, except as provided in section 953(b), this section, and § 1.953-5, the exclusions and deductions from gross income which would be allowed if such corporation were a domestic insurance company engaged in the business of only reinsuring or issuing the insurance or annuity contracts which have been reinsured or issued by such corporation. For this purpose, the provisions of sections 819, 821(e), 822(e), 831(b), and 832(d), relating to foreign insurance companies, shall not apply; however, for the exclusion from the taxable income determined under section 953 of amounts derived from sources within the United States, see section 952(b) and paragraph (b) of § 1.952-1. Furthermore, taxable income shall be determined under this section without regard to section 882(b) and (c), relating to gross income and deductions of a foreign corporation, and without regard to whether the controlled foreign corporation is carrying on an insurance business in the United States. For other rules relating to the determination of gross income and taxable income of a foreign corporation for purposes of subpart F, see § 1.952-2.

(e) Limitation on certain amounts in respect of United States risks. In determining taxable income under this section the following amounts shall not, in accordance with section 953(b)(4), be taken into account except to the extent they are attributable to the reinsuring or issuing of any insurance or annuity contract in connection with United States risks described in § 1.953-2 or § 1.953-3:

(1) The amount of premiums determined under section 809(c)(1);

(2) The net decrease in reserves determined under section 809(c)(2);

(3) The net increase in reserves determined under section 809(d)(2); and

(4) The premiums earned on insurance contracts during the taxable year, as determined under section 832(b)(4).

For the allocation and apportionment of such amounts to income from the insurance of United States risks, see paragraphs (f) and (g) of this section.

(f) Items allocated or apportioned. *(1) Rules of allocation or apportionment.* In determining taxable income under this section, first determine all items of income, expenses, losses, and other deductions which directly relate to the premiums received for the reinsuring or the issuing of any insurance or annuity contract in connection with United States risks, as defined in §§ 1.953-2 and 1.953-3, and allocate such items to the insurance of United States risks. For example, the deductions allowed by section 809(d)(1), relating to death benefits, section 809(d)(3), relating to dividends to policyholders, and section 809(d)(7), relating to the assumption by another person of liabilities under insurance contracts, shall be allocated to the insurance of United States risks to the extent they relate directly to the premiums received for reinsuring or issuing insurance or annuity contracts in connection with United States risks. Next, determine all items of income, expenses, losses, and other deductions which directly relate to the premiums received for the reinsuring or the issuing of any insurance or annuity contract in connection with foreign risks and allocate such items to the reinsuring of foreign risks. Finally, determine all items of income, expenses, losses, and other deductions which relate to the premiums received for the reinsuring or the issuing of any insurance or annuity contract in connection with both United States risks and foreign risks, and, except as provided in paragraph (g) of this section, apportion such items between the insurance of United States risks and the insurance of foreign risks in the manner prescribed in subparagraph (2) or (3) of this paragraph, as the case may be. As used in this section, the term "foreign risks" means risks which are not United States risks as defined in § 1.953-2 or § 1.953-3.

(2) Method of apportionment in determination of life insurance taxable income. (i) Investment yield and net long-term capital gain. Unless they can be allocated to the insurance of United States risks, as provided in subparagraph (1) of this paragraph, in determining a controlled foreign corporation's taxable income for any taxable year under paragraph (a)(1) of this section—

(a) The investment yield under section 804(c),

(b) The amount (if any) under section 809(b)(1)(B) by which the net long-term capital gain exceeds the net short-term capital loss, and

(c) Those deductions allowed under section 809(d)(8), (9), and (12) which relate to gross investment income

shall be apportioned to the reinsuring and issuing of insurance and annuity contracts in connection with United States risks in an amount which bears the same ratio to each of such amounts of investment yield, excess gain, and deductions as the sum of the mean of each of the items described in section 810(c) at the beginning and end of the taxable year attributable to reinsuring and issuing any insurance and annuity contracts in connection with United States risks bears to the sum of the mean of each of the items described in section 810(c) at the beginning and end of the taxable year attributable to reinsuring and issuing all insurance and annuity contracts. Thus, for example, if the ratio which the sum of the mean of each of the items described in section 810(c) at the beginning and end of the taxable year attributable to reinsuring and issuing insurance and annuity contracts in connection with United States risks bears to the sum of the mean of each of the items described in section 810(c) at the beginning and end of the taxable year attributable to reinsuring and issuing all insurance and annuity contracts in one to three, then, unless an allocation to the insurance of United States risks can be made as provided in subparagraph (1) of this paragraph, one-third of each of such amounts of investment yield, excess gain, and deductions shall be apportioned to the reinsuring and issuing of insurance and annuity contracts in connection with United States risks, and two-thirds of each of such amounts shall be apportioned to the reinsuring and issuing of insurance and annuity contracts in connection with foreign risks.

(ii) Other income and deductions. (a) Amount taken into account. In determining a controlled foreign corporation's taxable income for any taxable year under paragraph (a)(1) of this section, all items of income taken into account under section 809(c)(3), relating to other amounts of gross income, and the other deductions allowed under section 809(d)(12) to the extent that such other deductions do not relate to gross investment income shall be apportioned to the reinsuring and issuing of insurance and annuity contracts in connection with United States risks in an amount which bears the same ratio to each of such items of income or of such other deductions as the numberator determined under (b) of this subdivision bears to the denominator determined under (c) of this subdivision.

(b) Numerator. The numerator used for purposes of the apportionment under (a) of this subdivision shall be an amount which equals the amount determined under (c) of this subdivision, but only to the extent that the amount so determined is taken into account under paragraph (e) of this section in determining taxable income for the taxable year.

(c) Denominator. The denominator used for purposes of the apportionment under (a) of this subdivision shall be an amount which equals—

(1) The amount of premiums determined under section 809(c)(1) for the taxable year, plus

(2) The net decrease in reserves determined under section 809(c)(2) for such year, minus

(3) The net increase in reserves determined under section 809(d)(2) for such year.

(iii) Reserves used in apportionment formula. The rules for determining which reserves are taken into account in determining the taxable income of a controlled foreign corporation under paragraph (a) of this section shall also apply under subdivision (ii)(b) and (c) of this subparagraph in determining the net decrease in reserves under section 809(c)(2) or the net increase in reserves under section 809(d)(2). See paragraph (c) of this section.

(3) Method of apportionment in determination of mutual and other insurance income. (i) In general. In determining a controlled foreign corporation's taxable income for any taxable year under paragraph (a)(2) of this section, any item which is required to be apportioned under subparagraph (1) of this paragraph shall be apportioned to the reinsuring and issuing of insurance and annuity contracts in connection with United States risks in an amount which bears the same ratio to the total amount of such item as the amount of premiums earned on insurance contracts during the taxable year which is required to be taken into account by such corporation under paragraph (e)(4) of this section in determining such taxable income bears to the total amount of all its premiums earned (as determined under section 832(b)(4)) on insurance contracts during the taxable year.

(ii) Reserves used in apportionment formula. The principles of subparagraph (2)(iii) of this paragraph shall apply in determining the reserves included in premiums earned on insurance contracts during the taxable year for purposes of subdivision (i) of this subparagraph.

(g) Separate accounting. The methods of apportionment prescribed in subparagraphs (2) and (3) of paragraph (f) of this section for determining taxable income under this section shall not apply if the district director determines that the controlled foreign corporation, in good faith and unaffected by considerations of tax liability, regularly employs in its books of account a detailed segregation of receipts, expenditures, assets, liabilities, and net worth which clearly reflects the income derived from the reinsuring or issuing of insurance or annuity contracts in connection with United States risks. The district director, in making such determination, shall give effect to any foreign law, satisfactory evidence of which is presented by the United States shareholder to the district director, which requires a reasonable segregation of those items of income, expense, losses, and other deductions which relate to determining such taxable income.

(h) Illustration. The application of paragraphs (e) and (f) of this section may be illustrated by the following example:

Example. Controlled foreign corporation A, incorporated under, and engaged in an insurance business subject to, the laws of foreign country X, is a wholly owned subsidiary of domestic corporation M. Both corporations use the calendar year as the taxable year. Corporation M is a life insurance company as defined in section 801(a); A Corporation would, if it were a domestic corporation, be taxable under part I of subchapter L of the Code. In 1963, A Corporation derives income from the insurance of United States risks as a result of reinsuring the life insurance policies issued by M Corporation on lives of residents of the United States. In 1963, A Corporation also issues policies of life insurance on individuals who are not residents of the United States, but its premiums from the reinsuring of United States risks exceed the 5-percent minimum premium requirement prescribed in paragraph (b) of § 1.953-1. Based upon the facts set forth in paragraph (a) of this example, A Corporation for 1963 has taxable income under this section of $40,200, which is attributable to the reinsuring of life insurance contracts in connection with United States risks, determined in the manner provided in paragraphs (b), (c), and (d) of this example.

(a) A summary of the entire operations of A Corporation for 1963, determined under this section as though such corporation were a domestic life insurance company but without applying paragraph (f) of this section, is as follows:

Item	Attributable to all insurance	Attributable to reinsuring U.S. risks	Attributable to insuring foreign risks
Investment Income:			
(1) Investment yield under sec. 804(c)	$ 90,000	Unallocable	Unallocable
(2) Sum of the mean of each of the items described in sec. 810(c) at beginning and end of 1963	2,500,000	$1,000,000	$1,500,000
(3) Required interest under sec. 809(a)(2)	60,000	25,000	35,000
(4) Deductions allowed under sec. 809(d)(8), (9), and (12) which relate to gross investment income	10,000	Unallocable	Unallocable
Underwriting Income:			
(5) Premiums under sec. 809(c)(1)	600,000	200,000	400,000
(6) Net decrease in reserves under sec. 809(c)(2)	10,000	None	10,000
(7) Net increase in reserves under sec. 809(d)(2)	40,000	40,000	None
(8) Deductions allowed under sec. 809(d) (other than deduction allowed under sec. 809(d)(2) and other than those deductions allowed under sec. 809(d)(8), (9), and (12) which relate to gross investment income):			
(i) allocable	330,000	110,000	220,000
(ii) unallocable	60,000	Unallocable	Unallocable

(b) The unallocable investment yield ($90,000) under paragraph (a)(1) of this example and the unallocable deductions ($10,000) under paragraph (a)(4) relating to gross investment income are apportioned to the reinsuring of United States risks under paragraph (f)(1)(i) of this section in the amounts of $36,000, and $4,000, respectively, determined as follows:

(1) Sum of the mean of each of the items described in sec. 810(c) at beginning and end of 1963, attributable to reinsuring U.S. risks (paragraph (a)(2))	$1,000,000
(2) Sum of the mean of each of the items described in sec. 810(c) at beginning and end of 1963, attributable to all insurance (paragraph (a)(2))	$2,500,000
(3) Ratio of amount under subparagraph (1) to amount under subparagraph (2) ($1,000,000/$2,500,000)	40%
(4) Amount of investment yield attributable to reinsuring of U.S. risks (40% of $90,000)	$ 36,000
(5) Amount of such deductions attributable to reinsuring of U.S. risks (40% of $10,000)	$ 4,000

(c) The unallocable deductions ($60,000) under paragraph (a)(8)(ii) of this example which do not relate to gross investment income are apportioned to the reinsuring of United States risks under paragraph (f)(2)(ii) of this section in the amount of $16,800, determined as follows:

(1) The numerator determined under paragraph (f)(2)(ii)(b) of this section is $160,000, determined as follows:

(i) Premiums under sec. 809(c)(1) attributable to reinsuring U.S. risks (paragraph (a)(5))	$200,000
(ii) Plus: Net decrease in reserves under sec. 809(c)(2) attributable to reinsuring U.S. risks (paragraph (a)(6))	none
	$200,000
(iii) Less: Net increase in reserves under sec. 809(d)(2) attributable to reinsuring U.S. risks (paragraph (a)(7))	$ 40,000
	$160,000

(2) The denominator determined under paragraph (f)(2)(ii)(c) of this section is $570,000, determined as follows:

(i) Premiums under sec. 809(c)(1) attributable to all insurance (paragraph (a)(5))	$600,000
(ii) Plus: Net decrease in reserves under sec. 809(c)(2) attributable to all insurance (paragraph (a)(6))	10,000
	$610,000
(iii) Less: Net increase in reserves under sec. 809(d)(2) attributable to all insurance (paragraph (a)(7))	$ 40,000
	$570,000

(3) Ratio which the numerator determined under subparagraph (1) bears to the denominator determined under subparagraph (2) ($160,000/$570,000)—28%.

(4) Amount of deductions attributable to reinsuring of U.S. risks (28% of $60,000)—$16,800.

(d) The taxable income of A Corporation for 1963 which constitutes its income derived from the insurance of United States risks for purposes of paragraph (a) of § 1.953-1 is $40,200, determined as follows:

Item	Attributable to all insurance		Attributable to reinsuring U.S. risks		Attributable to insuring foreign risks	
Item:						
(1) Investment yield under sec. 804(c) (paragraph (a)(1), unallocable but as apportioned under paragraph (b)(4))	$ 90,000		$ 36,000		$ 54,000	
(2) Less: Required interest under sec. 809(a)(2) (paragraph (a)(3))	60,000		25,000		35,000	
(3) Life insurance company's share of investment yield under sec. 809(b)(1)(A)		$ 30,000		$ 11,000		$ 19,000
Plus sum of:						
(4) Premiums under sec. 809(c)(1) (paragraph (a)(5))	600,000		200,000		400,000	
(5) Net decrease in reserves under sec. 809(c)(2) (paragraph (a)(6))	10,000	610,000	None	200,000	10,000	410,000
Sum determined under sec. 809(b)(1)		640,000		211,000		429,000
Less sum of:						
(6) Net increase in reserves under sec. 809(b)(2) (paragraph (a)(7))	40,000		40,000		None	
(7) Deductions allowed under sec. 809(d)(8), (9), and (12) which relate to gross investment income (paragraph (a)(4)), unallocable but as apportioned under paragraph (b)(5)	10,000		4,000		6,000	
(8) Deductions allowed under sec. 809(d) (other than deduction allowed under sec. 809(d)(2) and other than those deductions allowed under sec. 809(d)(8), (9), and (12) which relate to gross investment income) (paragraph (a)(8)):						

(i) allocable	330,000		110,000		220,000	
(ii) unallocable, but as apportioned under paragraph (c)(4)	60,000	440,000	16,800	170,800	43,200	269,200
Gain from operations		200,000		40,200		159,800

T.D. 6781, 12/22/64.

Proposed § 1.953-4 Allocation and apportionment of items of investment income. [*For Preamble, see ¶ 151,253*]

(a) In general. *(1) Investment income.* This section prescribes the rules for determining the amount of investment income within the RPII, nonRPII, and SCI categories. Except as provided in paragraph (a)(2) of this section, investment income for this purpose is any type of income of a controlled foreign corporation for the taxable year other than premiums as defined in § 1.953-2(c). Thus, investment income includes, but is not limited to, gain from the sale or disposition of property under section 832(b)(1)(B), interest, dividends, and rents. Investment income also includes, to the extent prescribed in paragraph (a)(2) of this section, income resulting from the decrease in section 807(c) items under section 807(a), income resulting from the decrease in section 807(c)(1) items included in unearned premiums of a property and casualty insurance company under section 832(b)(4), and income resulting from a reduction of discounted unpaid losses under section 832(b)(5). An item of investment income is allocated to a particular category, whether the RPII, nonRPII, or SCI category, only if the income results from a decrease in reserves attributable under the principles of § 1.953-5(a) to a particular category or if the requirements of paragraph (b) of this section are met. If an item of investment income cannot be allocated to the RPII, nonRPII, or SCI categories, it is apportioned to the different categories in accordance with paragraph (c) of this section. If the investment income within each of the RPII, nonRPII, and SCI categories is determined under the apportionment method of paragraph (c) of this section, then the investment income within each category shall be deemed to consist of each type of investment income (e.g., dividends, interest, tax-exempt interest, and capital gains) in the same proportion that the aggregate amount of a particular type of investment income earned during the taxable year bears to the total amount of all types of investment income earned during the taxable year.

(2) Decreases in reserves. (i) In general. In the case of each of the RPII, nonRPII, and SCI categories of income, if a decrease in section 807(c) items or a decrease in section 846 discounted unpaid losses occurs as the result of the payment of claims and benefits accrued and losses incurred, as described in section 805(a)(1), or as the result of losses paid, as described in section 832(b)(5)(A)(i), then the income resulting from the decrease in reserves shall be deemed to consist of premium and investment income in the same proportion that the claims, benefits, or losses that result in the decrease in the reserve are apportioned between premium and investment income under § 1.953-5(c)(3)(iii)(A). Section 807(c) items include section 807(c)(1) reserves included in the unearned premiums of a property and casualty insurance company under section 832(b)(4). If a decrease in section 807(c) items and section 846 unpaid losses attributable under the principles of § 1.953-5(a) to the SCI category and to the RPII category (if the elections under section 953(c)(3)(C) and section 831(b) are made) occurs as the result of any actuarial redetermination, the amount of income included in gross income in accordance with section 807(f), in the case of a foreign life insurance company, or in accordance with section 481, in the case of a foreign property and casualty insurance company, shall be considered investment income equal to the amount obtained by multiplying the decrease in section 807(c) items or section 846 discounted unpaid losses by a fraction. The numerator of the fraction shall be the amount of the increase in section 807(c) items or section 846 discounted unpaid losses that have been apportioned against investment income under § 1.953-5(c)(3)(iii)(B) and (C) during the five taxable years (or the period during which the controlled foreign corporation has been in existence, if less than five taxable years) preceding the current taxable year. The denominator of the fraction shall be the total amount of deductions attributable to the increases in section 807(c) items and section 846 discounted unpaid losses during the five taxable years (or shorter period, if applicable) preceding the current taxable year. The remainder of the decrease in section 807(c) items and section 846 discounted unpaid losses attributable to the SCI category and, if appropriate, the RPII category shall be treated as giving rise to premium income. In the case of section 807(c) items and section 846 discounted unpaid losses attributable to the nonRPII category and the RPII category, if the section 953(c)(3)(C) and section 831(b) elections have not been made, the entire decrease in section 807(c) items and section 846 discounted unpaid losses shall be treated as investment income.

(ii) Examples. The following examples illustrate the principles of paragraph (a)(2)(i) of this section.

Example (1). Y is a life insurance company and is a controlled foreign corporation. In 1988 Y's section 807(c)(1) life insurance reserves decrease from $10,000 to $8,000, resulting in $2,000 of income under sections 803(a)(2) and 807(a). The decrease resulted from the payment of a death benefit that, under § 1.953-5(c)(3)(iii)(A), is apportioned against investment income and premium income in the amount of $1,500 and $500, respectively. The $2,000 decrease results in $1,500 of investment income ($2,000 × $1,500/$2,000) and $500 of premium income ($2,000 × $500/$2,000).

Example (2). X is a property and casualty insurance company and is a controlled foreign corporation. Under section 832(b)(5), X had, for its 1987 taxable year, discounted unpaid losses of $100,000 attributable to contracts the premiums from which were allocable to the SCI category of income. For 1988, X had losses paid of $50,000 and discounted unpaid losses of $25,000 allocable to contracts giving rise to SCI premiums. Section 832(b)(5) requires X to reduce its 1988 losses paid by the excess of discounted unpaid losses for 1987 over the current year discounted unpaid losses. Thus, X has $25,000 of income resulting from the decrease in discounted unpaid losses computed as follows: 1988 losses paid of $50,000 minus the difference between 1987 discounted unpaid losses of $100,000 and 1988 discounted unpaid losses of $25,000 ($50,000 − [$100,000 − $25,000]) = $25,000. Assuming that section 481 applies, X will take the premium and investment income into account in accordance with that section. If over the past five years, the increase in discounted unpaid losses is $50,000, of which

$10,000 was allocated to investment income and $40,000 to premium income under § 1.953-5(c)(3)(iii)(B) and (C), then ⅕th ($10,000/$50,000) of the amounts taken into income in each taxable year in accordance with section 481 will be treated as investment income and ⅘ths ($40,000/$50,000) will be treated as premium income.

(b) Allocation of investment income. *(1) In general.* An item of investment income is allocated to a particular category of income if the item directly relates to a contract (or that part of a contract) which gives rise to premiums allocable to the same category of income. An item of investment income is considered to be directly related to a contract (or that part of a contract) which gives rise to premiums allocable to a particular category if the income is derived from an asset which is identified on the controlled foreign corporation's books and records as an asset relating to RPII, nonRPII, or SCI contracts and the controlled foreign corporation separately accounts for the various income, exclusion, deduction, reserve, and other liability items properly attributable to such contracts.

(2) Examples. The following examples illustrate the rules of paragraph (b)(1) of this section.

Example (1). The facts are the same as in Example 2 of paragraph (a)(2)(ii) of this section. The amount of investment income included in gross income in each taxable year in accordance with section 481 is allocable to the SCI category.

Example (2). Z is a country F controlled foreign corporation which issues life insurance contracts. Among the contracts issued by Z are variable life insurance contracts issued to residents of country F. The life insurance contracts qualify as variable contracts under section 817(d) of the Code. The amounts received under the contracts are allocated pursuant to country F law to an account which is segregated from the general asset accounts of Z, and the amount of the death benefits under the contracts are adjusted on the basis of the investment return and the market value of the segregated asset account. Z's books of account identify the assets relating to the variable life insurance contracts issued to residents of country F, and Z separately accounts for the various income, exclusion, deduction, reserve, and other liability items properly attributable to such contracts. Therefore, all of the investment income attributable to the variable contracts is allocable to the SCI income category.

(c) Apportionment of investment income. *(1) Life insurance companies.* (i) In general. A foreign corporation that would determine its insurance income under part I of subchapter L (relating to life insurance companies) if it were a domestic company shall apportion its investment income to each of the RPII, nonRPII, and SCI categories, in the same proportion that—

(A) The sum of the means of each of the items described in section 807(c) attributable to contracts which give rise to premiums within the particular income category bears to

(B) The sum of the means of the items described in section 807(c) for the taxable year attributable to all contracts.

(ii) Section 807(c) items attributable to RPII, nonRPII, and SCI contracts. The amount of an item described in section 807(c) that is attributable to a particular income category is that amount which would result if the section 807(c) item were computed, using the assumptions required under section 807, as modified by § 1.953-6(e), only with respect to the contracts the premiums from which are apportioned to that particular income category.

(2) Property and casualty companies. (i) In general. A foreign corporation that would determine its insurance income under part II of subchapter L (relating to insurance companies other than life insurance companies) if it were a domestic company shall apportion its investment income to each of the RPII, nonRPII, and SCI categories, in the same proportion that—

(A) The sum of the premiums written, as defined in section 832(b)(4)(A), for the current taxable year, plus the amount of unearned premiums as of the close of the previous taxable year, plus the amount of the section 846 discounted unpaid losses as of the close of the previous taxable year attributable to the particular income category, bears to

(B) The sum of the premiums written as defined in section 832(b)(4)(A), for the current taxable year, plus the amount of unearned premiums as of the close of the previous taxable year, plus the amount of the section 846 discounted unpaid losses as of the close of the previous taxable year attributable to all categories of income.

(ii) Unpaid losses attributable to a particular category. The amount of the section 846 discounted unpaid losses that are attributable to a particular income category is that amount which would result if the unpaid losses were computed, using the assumptions required by section 846, as modified by § 1.953-6(e), only with respect to the contracts the premiums from which are apportioned to that particular income category.

(3) Examples. The following examples illustrate the principles of paragraph (c) of this section.

Example (1). X is a property and casualty insurance company and a controlled foreign corporation that is not engaged in a trade or business in the United States. X is a calendar year taxpayer. In 1987, X had $600 of premiums written from contracts issued to related insureds and $300 of premiums written from contracts issued to unrelated persons. At the end of 1986, X had $400 in unearned premiums from contracts issued to related insureds and $200 of unearned premiums from contracts issued to unrelated persons. X also had unpaid losses at the end of 1986 of $500 with respect to its related insured contracts and $250 with respect to its contracts issued to unrelated persons. In 1987, X had $1,000 of taxable interest income and $2,000 of tax exempt income. The total of X's premiums written for the current year, plus previous year unearned premiums, plus previous year unpaid loss reserves on RPII business is $1,500 ($600 + $400 + $500) and on nonRPII business is $750 ($300 + $200 + $250). Therefore, $2,000 of investment income ($1,500/$2,250 × $3,000) is apportioned to the RPII category and $1,000 ($750/$2,250 × $3,000) is apportioned to the nonRPII category. Pursuant to paragraph (a)(1) of this section, of the $2,000 apportioned to the RPII category, $666.67 ($2,000 × $1,000/$3,000) is taxable interest income and $1,333.33 ($2,000 × $2,000/$3,000) is tax- exempt interest. Of the $1,000 apportioned to the nonRPII category, $333.33 ($1,000 × $1,000/$3,000) is taxable interest income and $666.67 ($1,000 × $2,000/$3,000) is tax-exempt interest income.

Example (2). (i) Y is a controlled foreign corporation that issues life insurance policies and would, if it were a domestic corporation, be taxable under part I of subchapter L of the Code. Y is not engaged in a trade or business within the United States. In 1987, its first year in business, Y only issues insurance policies to its United States shareholders or persons related to its United States shareholders. Y received $3,000 in premiums for the year and at the end of the year had a reserve under section 807(c)(1) of $2,000. In 1988, Y only issues life insurance policies to persons other than its United States shareholders or persons related to those shareholders. Y receives $5,000 in premiums in 1988. In 1988, Y's year-end section 807(c)(1) reserves with respect to contracts issued to related persons is $1,000 and with respect to unrelated persons is $4,000. Investment income in 1988 is $1,000, all of which is taxable interest income. The mean of the 807(c) items for 1988 are computed in Table 1 below.

Table 1

Mean section 807(c) attributable to RPII contracts in force in 1988:	
Mean of life insurance reserves attributable to nonRPII policies:	
1987 closing reserve	$2,000
1988 closing reserve	$1,000
Mean = ($2,000 + $1,000) ÷2	$1,500
Mean of life insurance reserves attributable to nonRPII policies:	
1987 closing reserve	$ 0
1988 closing reserve	$4,000
Mean = $4,000 ÷ 2	$2,000

(ii) Based on the computations in Table 1, the investment income apportioned to the RPII category equals $1,000 × ($1,500/3,500) or $428.57, and investment income apportioned to the nonRPII category equals $1,000 × ($2,000/$3,500) or $571.42.

§ 1.953-5 Corporations not qualifying as insurance companies.

Caution: The Treasury has not yet amended Reg § 1.953-5 to reflect changes made by P.L. 100-647, P.L. 99-514, P.L. 98-369.

(a) In general. A controlled foreign corporation is not excluded from the application of paragraph (a) of § 1.953-1 because such corporation, if it were a domestic corporation, would not be taxable as an insurance company to which subchapter L of the Code applies. Thus, if a controlled foreign corporation reinsures or issues insurance or annuity contracts in connection with United States risks, as defined in § 1.953-2 or § 1.953-3, and satisfies the 5-percent minimum premium requirement prescribed in paragraph (b) of § 1.953-1, such corporation may derive income from the insurance of United States risks even though the primary and predominant business activity of such corporation during the taxable year is not the issuing of insurance or annuity contracts or the reinsuring of risks underwritten by insurance companies.

(b) Income from insurance of United States risks by noninsurance company. For purposes of paragraph (a) of § 1.953-1, the taxable income derived from the reinsuring or the issuing of any insurance or annuity contract in connection with United States risks by a controlled foreign corporation which, if it were a domestic corporation, would not be taxable as an insurance company to which subchapter L of the Code applies shall be determined under § 1.953-4, subject to, and to the extent not inconsistent with, the special rules prescribed in paragraph (c) or (d) of this section, whichever applies.

(c) Special rules in determining taxable income. *(1) In general.* The rules prescribed in this paragraph apply in order to exclude from the determination under § 1.953-4 of the taxable income described in paragraph (b) of this section those items of the controlled foreign corporation's gross income and deductions which are not attributable to the reinsuring and issuing of insurance and annuity contracts.

(2) Life insurance taxable income. (i) Amount of investment yield take into account. For purposes of determining the taxable income of a controlled foreign corporation which would not be taxable as an insurance company to which subchapter L of the Code applies if it were a domestic corporation but would be taxable as an insurance company to which part I of such subchapter applies if it were a domestic insurance company engaged in the business of only reinsuring or issuing the insurance or annuity contracts which have been reinsured or issued by such corporation, the investment yield under section 804(c), the amount (if any) by which the net long-term capital gain exceeds the net short-term capital loss, and all items of income taken into account under section 809(c)(3) shall be taken into account, subject to the provisions of paragraphs (e) and (f) of § 1.953-4, in an amount which bears the same ratio to each of such amounts of investment yield, excess gain, and income items, as the case may be, as the numerator determined under subdivision (ii) of this subparagraph bears to the denominator determined under subdivision (iii) of this subparagraph.

(ii) Numerator. The numerator used for purposes of the apportionment under subdivision (i) of this subparagraph shall be the sum of—

(a) The mean of each of the items described in section 810(c) at the beginning and end of the taxable year, determined in accordance with the rules prescribed in paragraph (c) of § 1.953-4 for purposes of determining taxable income of a controlled foreign corporation under paragraph (a) of § 1.953-4,

(b) The mean of other liabilities at the beginning and end of the taxable year which are attributable to the reinsuring and issuing of insurance and annuity contracts, and

(c) The mean of the earnings and profits accumulated by the controlled foreign corporation at the beginning and end of the taxable year (determined without diminution by reason of any distributions made during the taxable year) which are attributable to the reinsuring and issuing of insurance and annuity contracts.

(iii) Denominator. The denominator used for purposes of the apportionment under subdivision (i) of this subparagraph shall be the mean of the value of the total assets held by the controlled foreign corporation at the beginning and end of the taxable year, determined by taking assets into account at their actual value (not reduced by liabilities), which, in the absence of affirmative evidence to the contrary, shall be deemed to be (a) face value in the case of bills receivable, accounts receivable, notes receivable, and open accounts held by a controlled foreign corporation using the cash receipts and disbursements method of accounting and (b) adjusted basis in the case of all other assets.

(3) Mutual and other insurance taxable income. (i) Amount of insurance income taken into account. For purposes of determining the taxable income of a controlled foreign corporation which, if it were a domestic corporation, would not be taxable as an insurance company to which subchapter L of the Code applies but which if it were a domestic insurance company engaged in the business of only reinsuring or issuing the insurance or annuity contracts which have been reinsured or issued by such corporation, would be taxable as a mutual insurance company to which part II of subchapter L of the Code applies, or would be taxable as a mutual marine insurance or other insurance company to which part III of subchapter L of the Code applies, the sum of the items of gross income referred to in section 832(b)(1) (except the gross amount earned during the taxable year from underwriting income described in section 832(b)(1)(A))

reduced by the deductions allowable under section 832(c) which are related to such items of gross income shall be taken into account, subject to the provisions of paragraphs (e) and (f) of § 1.953-4, in an amount which bears the same proportion to the sum of such items of gross income reduced by such deductions as the numerator determined under subdivisions (ii) of this subparagraph bears to the denominator determined under subdivision (iii) of this subparagraph.

(ii) Numerator. The numerator used for purposes of the apportionment under subdivision (i) of this subparagraph shall be the sum of—

(a) The mean of the controlled foreign corporation's unearned premiums at the beginning and end of the taxable year, determined under section 832(b)(4)(B) and in accordance with the rules prescribed in paragraph (c) of § 1.953-4 for purposes of determining taxable income of a controlled foreign corporation under paragraph (a) of § 1.953-4,

(b) The mean of such corporation's unpaid losses at the beginning and end of the taxable year, determined under section 832(b)(5)(B),

(c) The mean of the items described in section 810(c)(4) at the beginning and end of the taxable year, to the extent allowable to such corporation under section 832(c)(11),

(d) The mean of other liabilities at the beginning and end of the taxable year which are attributable to the reinsuring and issuing of insurance and annuity contracts, and

(e) The mean of the earnings and profits accumulated by such corporation at the beginning and end of the taxable year (determined without diminution by reason of any distributions made during the taxable year) which are attributable to the reinsuring and issuing of insurance and annuity contracts.

(iii) Denominator. The denominator used for purposes of the apportionment under subdivision (i) of this subparagraph shall be the mean of the value of the total assets held by the controlled foreign corporation at the beginning and end of the taxable year, determined in the manner prescribed in subparagraph (2)(iii) of this paragraph.

(d) Separate accounting. The special rules described in paragraph (c) of this section shall not apply if the district director determines that the controlled foreign corporation, in good faith and unaffected by considerations of tax liability, regularly employs in its books of account a detailed segregation of receipts, expenditures, assets, liabilities, and net worth which clearly reflects the income derived from the reinsuring or issuing of insurance or annuity contracts. The district director, in making such determination, shall give effect to any foreign law, satisfactory evidence of which is presented by the United States shareholder to the district director, which requires a reasonable segregation of the insurance assets of the controlled foreign corporation.

T.D. 6781, 12/22/64.

Proposed § 1.953-5 Allocation and apportionment of expenses. [*For Preamble, see ¶ 151,253*]

(a) Allocation of deductions to RPII, nonRPII, and SCI categories. To compute the amount of section 953 insurance income or foreign personal holding company income that a controlled foreign corporation has derived from insurance operations, items of expenses, losses, and other deductions (collectively referred to as "deductions") must be allocated to and apportioned among the RPII, nonRPII, and SCI categories of income. Allocation of expenses shall be made in accordance with §§ 1.861-8, 1.861-8T, 1.861-9T, 1.861-10T, and 1.861-12T, and this section. The deduction under section 832(b)(4)(B) for unearned premiums is allocable to the categories to which the unearned premiums relate as determined by §§ 1.953-2 and 1.953-3. The deductions for death benefits, increases in reserves, policyholder dividends, consideration in respect of the assumption by another person of liabilities, and reimbursable dividends under section 805(a)(1), (2), (3), (6), and (7) are allocable to the particular category of income to which those deductions relate. The deductions for losses paid and discounted unpaid losses, under section 832(b)(5), and dividends and similar distributions paid or declared to policyholders in their capacity as such, under section 832(c)(11), are also allocable to the particular category of income to which those deductions relate. The amount of the deductions specified in the preceding two sentences of this paragraph shall be considered to relate to the RPII, nonRPII, and SCI categories to the extent the deduction is attributable to contracts that give rise to premiums allocated to a particular category. Deductions not specifically addressed in this paragraph (a) may be allocated to the RPII, nonRPII, or SCI category of income if the controlled foreign corporation identifies on its books and records the assets which relate to RPII, nonRPII, or SCI contracts, and the controlled foreign corporation separately accounts for the various income, exclusion, deduction, reserve, and other liability items properly attributable to such contracts.

(b) Apportionment of expenses to RPII, nonRPII, and SCI categories. *(1) In general.* Those expenses which cannot be allocated must be apportioned among the RPII, nonRPII, and SCI categories.

(2) Life insurance companies. (i) Investment deductions. A controlled foreign corporation that would be taxable under part I of subchapter L (relating to life insurance companies) if it were a domestic insurance company shall apportion to the RPII, nonRPII, and SCI categories its deductions that are allocable or apportionable to investment income under §§ 1.861-8, 1.861-8T, 1.861-9T, 1.861-10T, and 1.861-12T in the same proportion that investment income for the current taxable year is apportioned to those categories under § 1.953-4(c).

(ii) Other deductions. A controlled foreign corporation that would be taxable under part I of subchapter L (relating to life insurance companies) if it were a domestic insurance company shall apportion to the RPII, nonRPII, and SCI categories a deduction that is not allocable or apportionable to investment income under §§ 1.861-8, 1.861-8T, 1.861-9T, 1.861-10T, and 1.861-12T in the same proportion as the numerator in paragraph (b)(2)(ii)(A) of this section bears to the denominator in paragraph (b)(2)(ii)(B) of this section.

(A) Numerator. For purposes of this paragraph (b)(2)(ii) the numerator equals:

(1) The amount of premiums determined under section 803(a)(1) allocable to the income category, plus

(2) The decrease in section 807(c) items allocable to the income category as determined under section 807(a), minus

(3) The increase in section 807(c) items allocable to the income category as determined under section 807(b).

(B) Denominator. For purposes of this paragraph (b)(2)(ii) the denominator equals:

(1) The amount of premiums determined under section 803(a)(1) for all categories of income, plus

(2) The decrease in section 807(c) items for all categories of income as determined under section 807(a), minus

(3) The increase in section 807(c) items for all categories of income as determined under section 807(b).

(3) Property and casualty companies. (i) Investment deductions. A controlled foreign corporation that would be taxable under part II of subchapter L (relating to insurance companies other than life companies) if it were a domestic insurance company shall apportion to the RPII, nonRPII, and SCI categories its deductions that are allocable or apportionable to investment income under §§ 1.861-8, 1.861-8T, 1.861-9T, 1.861-10T, and 1.861-12T in the same proportion that investment income for the current taxable year is apportioned to those categories under § 1.953-4(c).

(ii) Other deductions. A controlled foreign corporation that would be taxable under part II of subchapter L (relating to insurance companies other than life insurance companies) if it were a domestic insurance company shall apportion to the RPII, nonRPII, and SCI categories a deduction that is not allocable or apportionable to investment income under §§ 1.861-8, 1.861-8T, 1.861-9T, 1.861-10T, and 1.861-12T in the same proportion that the premiums earned, as defined in section 832(b)(4), allocated to a particular income category bears to the total of the premiums earned in all of the income categories.

(c) Allocation and apportionment of deductions between premium and investment income after the deductions have been allocated or apportioned to the SCI or RPII categories. *(1) In general.* Deductions within the SCI category must be allocated to or apportioned between premium income and investment income. Deductions within the RPII category must be allocated to or apportioned between premium and investment income if an election is made under section 953(c)(3)(C) (relating to the treatment of RPII income as effectively connected with the conduct of a United States trade or business) and under section 831(b) (alternative tax for certain small companies). Allocation and apportionment of deductions to or between premium and investment income within the SCI category and, if applicable, the RPII category is made in accordance with §§ 1.861-8, 1.861-8T, 1.861-9T, 1.861-10T, 1.861-12T and paragraph (c)(3) of this section.

(2) Examples. The following examples illustrate the rule of paragraph (c)(1) of this section.

Example (1). X is a life insurance company that issues policies insuring the lives of persons residing in X's country of incorporation. X requires its insureds to undergo medical examinations by physicians approved and paid by X. Under the principles of §§ 1.861-8, 1.861-8T, 1.861-9T, 1.861-10T, and 1.861-12T and this section, the medical expenses paid by X are allocable to the class of gross income consisting of X's SCI premiums.

Example (2). Z is a life insurance company that issues policies only in its country of incorporation. Z has an investment department that is in charge of investing Z's funds. The amount expended by Z in compensating the employees of its investment department is allocable under the principles of § 1.861-8 and this section to the class of gross income consisting of Z's SCI investment income.

(3) Apportionment of reserves, losses, policyholder dividends, and policy acquisition expenses and certain other deductions between investment and premium income. (i) In general. For taxable years beginning on or after April 17, 1991, the amount of the deduction for reserves, the deduction for losses, the deduction for policyholder dividends, the deduction for policy acquisition expenses, and certain other deductions apportioned against investment income within the SCI category and, if applicable, within the RPII category, shall be—

(A) The amount of investment income required to be added to reserves and required to fund losses without the SCI and, if applicable, the RPII category as computed in paragraph (c)(3)(iii) of this section;

(B) Investment income's proportionate share of policyholder dividends within the SCI and, if applicable, the RPII category as determined under paragraph (c)(3)(iv) of this section; and

(C) The amount of policy acquisition expenses and certain other deductions determined under paragraph (c)(3)(v) of this section.

The remainder of the deductions for reserves, losses, policyholder dividends, policy acquisition expenses, and certain other deductions within the SCI and, if applicable, the RPII category shall be apportioned against and reduce premium income. For taxable years beginning prior to April 17, 1991, taxpayers may use a reasonable apportionment formula.

(ii) Deduction for reserves and losses defined. For purposes of paragraph (c)(3)(i) of this section, the phrase "deduction for losses" means current year deductions for claims, benefits, and losses under section 805(a)(1) (other than discounted unpaid losses under section 846), losses paid under section 832(b)(5)(A)(i), and unpaid losses on life insurance contracts. The phrase "deduction for reserves" means, for purposes of paragraph (c)(3)(i) of this section: the increase in section 807(c) reserves, as adjusted by section 807(b), of a foreign life insurance company; the increase in section 807(c)(1) reserves, as adjusted under section 807(b), included in unearned premiums of a foreign property and casualty company; and the increase in section 846 discounted unpaid losses as computed under section 832(b)(5)(ii).

(iii) Investment income required to be added to reserves and required to fund losses. The total amount of investment income required to be added to reserves and to fund current year losses within the SCI and, if applicable, the RPII category is computed as the sum of the following:

(A) The investment income portion of current year losses within the SCI and, if applicable, the RPII category: This amount is the excess of—

(1) The amount of current year losses within the appropriate category, less

(2) The amount of current year losses within the appropriate category divided by one plus one-half of the annual interest rate specified in § 1.953-6(e)(4) for computing reserves.

(B) The investment income portion attributable to current-year premiums that have been added to reserves within the SCI and, if applicable, the RPII category: This amount shall be computed as—

(1) The amount of current-year premiums added to reserves within the appropriate category multiplied by one-half of the annual interest rate specified in § 1.953-6(e)(4) for computing reserves, or

(2) If the amount of current-year premiums added to the reserves is not known, the excess of—

(i) The year-end reserves within the appropriate category attributable to current-year premiums within the appropriate category, less

(ii) The year-end reserves within the appropriate category divided by one plus one-half of the annual interest rate specified in § 1.953-6(e)(4) for computing reserves.

(C) The investment income portion attributable to reserves within the SCI and, if applicable, the RPII category existing as of the end of the preceding taxable year and still in existence as of the end of the current taxable year: This amount shall be computed as the excess of—

(1) The amount of the reserves within the appropriate category at the end of the taxable year, less the sum of the amount of reserves within the appropriate category attributable to current-year premiums plus the investment income portion attributable to current-year premiums as computed under paragraph (c)(3)(iii)(B) of this section, over

(2) The amount obtained by dividing the amount computed under paragraph (c)(3)(iii)(C)(1) of this section by one plus the annual interest rate specified in § 1.953-6(e)(4) for computing reserves.

(D) If the amount of a reserve within the SCI and, if applicable, the RPII category is increased because of any actuarial redetermination, the investment income portion of the increase shall be treated as the amount of the adjustment multiplied by a fraction, the numerator of which is the amount of reserves within the appropriate category that have been deducted against gross investment income under paragraph (c)(3)(iii)(B) and (D) of this section during the five taxable years preceding the current taxable year (or for the life of the corporation preceding the current taxable year if the foreign corporation has been in existence for less than five taxable years), and the denominator of which is the total amount of deductions attributable to reserves within the appropriate category during the five taxable years preceding the current taxable year (or for the life of the corporation preceding the current taxable year, as may be applicable).

(iv) Investment income's proportionate share of policyholder dividends. For purposes of this paragraph (c)(3), investment income's proportionate share of policyholder dividends, as defined in section 808(a) and (b) and section 832(c)(11), is an amount equal to the deduction for policyholder's dividends determined under sections 808, 809, and 832(c)(11) for the taxable year multiplied by a fraction, the numerator of which is gross investment income within the SCI and, if applicable, the RPII category, for the taxable year, reduced by the amounts determined under paragraph (c)(3)(i)(A) of this section, and the denominator of which is total gross income within the appropriate category reduced by the excess, if any, of the closing balance of items described in section 807(c) or discounted unpaid losses under section 846 within the appropriate category, over the opening balance of such items and losses within the appropriate category. For purposes of paragraph (c)(3)(iv) of this section, the denominator of the fraction shall be determined by including tax-exempt interest and by applying section 807(a)(2)(B) as if it did not contain section 807(a)(2)(B)(i) thereof.

(v) Apportionment of policy acquisition expenses and certain other deductions. For purposes of this paragraph (c)(3), specified policy acquisition expenses, as defined in section 848(c)(1), and general deductions, as defined in section 848(c)(2), shall be apportioned to investment income within the SCI category and, if applicable, the RPII category, in the same proportion as the numerator in paragraph (c)(3)(v)(A) of this section bears to the denominator in paragraph (c)(3)(v)(B) of this section.

(A) Numerator. For purposes of this paragraph (c)(3)(v), the numerator equals the amount of investment income allocated or apportioned to the SCI category and, if applicable, the RPII category, minus the amount of the deduction for reserves apportioned to investment income under this paragraph (c)(3), to the extent that such reserves qualify as life insurance reserves within the meaning of section 816(b).

(B) Denominator. For purposes of this paragraph (c)(3)(v), the denominator equals the amount of premium income allocated or apportioned to the SCI category and, if applicable, the RPII category, plus the amount determined under paragraph (c)(3)(v)(A) of this section. For purposes of paragraph (c)(3)(v)(B) of this section, premium income is the amount of premiums without the meaning of section 803(a)(1) and (b), in the case of a controlled foreign corporation that would be taxable under part I of subchapter L (relating to life insurance companies) if it were a domestic insurance company. In the case of a controlled foreign corporation that would be taxable under part II of subchapter L (relating to insurance companies other than life companies) if it were a domestic insurance company, premium income is the amount of premiums within the meaning of section 832(b)(4). All computations entering into the determination of premium income for purposes of paragraph (c)(3)(v)(B) of this section shall be made in the manner required under section 811(a) for life insurance companies.

The fraction set forth in this paragraph (c)(3)(v), determined for each taxable year, applies to the amount of specified policy acquisition expenses computed under section 848(c)(1) for that taxable year, which are capitalized and allowed as a deduction in such taxable year and in subsequent taxable years in accordance with section 848(a). The fraction set forth in this paragraph (c)(3)(v), determined for each taxable year, also applies to the amount, if any, by which general deductions (as defined in section 848(c)(2)) deductible in such taxable year exceed specified policy acquisition expenses for such year (as computed and capitalized under section 848). Such general deductions are subject to the apportionment formula set forth in this paragraph (c)(3)(v), even if the capitalization requirements of section 848 do not apply to the company or to certain contracts issued by it. For purposes of this paragraph (c)(3)(v), the terms "net premiums" and "general deductions," as defined in sections 848(d) and 848(c)(2), respectively, shall be computed by taking into account only amounts that have been allocated or apportioned to the SCI category and, if applicable, the RPII category.

(vi) Example. The following example demonstrates the calculation of the amount of investment income required to be added to reserves and fund losses under paragraph (c)(3)(i) of this section.

Example. X is a country F controlled foreign corporation that has income from issuing life insurance contracts to persons who reside in country F. At the end of its 1988 taxable year, X has a reserve under section 807(c)(1) of $12,292 of which $7,000 is from the addition of current-year premiums plus $350 of investment income attributable to those premiums. At the end of the 1987 taxable year X's reserves were $7,350. Thus, X's reserves have increased a total of $4,942. X paid $3,000 in death benefits in 1988. The appropriate interest rate for computing X's life insurance reserves on all of X's policies is 10% per annum. The amount of reserves and losses apportioned to premium and investment income is computed as follows:

(i) The investment income portion of X's current year losses paid:

Losses − [Losses/(1 + .5(10%)] $3,000 − (3,000/1.05) = $142.86

(ii) The investment income portion of X's current year premiums that have been added to reserves:

There are two methods for computing this amount:

(a) Current year premiums added to reserves × .5 (annual interest rate for determining reserves). $7,000 × .05 = $350

(b) Year-end reserves attributable to current-year premiums less [such year-end reserves divided by 1 + .5 (annual interest rate)].

$7,350 – [$7,350/(1 + .5(10%)] = $7,350 – $7,000 = $350.

(iii) The investment income portion attributable to section 807(c) reserves existing at the end of the preceding taxable year that were in existence at the end of the current taxable year.

[Year-end reserves less the sum of reserves attributable to current-year premiums plus the investment income portion attributable to current-year premiums minus the amount obtained in the previous term divided by (1 + 10%)]

[$12,292 – ($7,000 + $350)] – [($12,292 – ($7,000 + $350))/1.10] = $4,942 – $4,492.72 = $449.28

Thus, of $3,000 in losses, $142.86 is apportioned to gross investment income and $2,857.14 is allocated to premium income. Of the $4,942 increase in reserves, $350 is the amount of investment income required to be added to current-year premiums and $449.28 is the amount of investment income required to be added to reserves that were in existence throughout the year.

Thus, $799.28 of the $4,942.28 increase in reserves is apportioned to investment income and $4,142.72 ($4,942 – $799.28) of the increase in reserves is apportioned to premium income.

(4) Alternative method for life insurance companies. (i) In general. As an alternative to the computations required by paragraph (c)(3)(i) of this section, a controlled foreign corporation that would be subject to part I of subchapter L if it were a domestic insurance company may apportion against investment income within the SCI and, if applicable, the RPII category, the deductions for reserves, losses, and policyholder dividends in an amount equal to the policy interest plus gross investment income's proportionate share of policyholder dividends as computed under section 812(b). The remaining amount, if any, of the deductions for reserves, losses, and policyholder dividends shall be apportioned to gross premium income.

(ii) Example. The following example demonstrates the principles of paragraph (c)(4)(i) of this section.

Example. X is a controlled foreign corporation that would be taxable as a life insurance company under part I of subchapter L if it were a domestic insurance company. In 1988, X has a reserve of $1,000. In 1989, X has a reserve of $1,500. Under section 812(b)(2)(A), and using the interest rate prescribed in § 1.953-6(e)(4) for computing reserves, X has policy interest equal to $200. Rather than using the method set forth in paragraph (c)(3)(i) of this section, the increase in reserves may be apportioned between premium and investment income by apportioning the policy interest to investment income and by apportioning the increase in the reserves less the policy interest against premium income. Thus, $200 is apportioned to investment income and $300 ($500 – $200) is apportioned to premium income.

(5) Losses in excess of premium or investment income. If the total amount of deductions allocated and apportioned to premium income within the RPII and nonRPII categories exceeds the amount of premium income within those categories, then the excess shall be allocated to investment income within the same category. If the total amount of deductions allocated and apportioned to premium income within the SCI category exceeds the amount of premium income within that category, then the excess shall not be allocated to investment income within the SCI category and shall not be allocated to any other category of subpart F income. However, if an election is made under section 952(c)(1)(B)(vii), the deductions allocated and apportioned to premium income within the SCI category shall be allocated to investment income within the SCI category. If the total amount of deductions allocated or apportioned to investment income within each of the RPII and nonRPII categories exceeds the amount of investment income within those categories, then the excess deductions shall be allocated to premium income within the same category. If the total amount of deductions allocated or apportioned to investment income within the SCI category exceeds the amount of investment income within that category, then the excess deductions shall be allocated to the RPII or nonRPII categories in accordance with paragraph (c)(6) of this section. However, if an election is made under section 952(c)(1)(B)(vii), deductions allocated or apportioned to investment income with the SCI category that exceed the income within that category shall first reduce premium income within the same category.

(6) Losses within the RPII, nonRPII, and SCI categories. If, after allocating and apportioning deductions, there is a loss within the RPII or nonRPII categories, within the investment income portion of the SCI category, or, if an election is made under section 952(c)(1)(B)(vii), within the entire SCI category, then a loss in one category will be treated as reducing income in another category only for purposes of calculating the pro rata share of RPII, nonRPII, or SCI income to be included by United States shareholders as defined in section 951(b). Thus, persons that are United States shareholders solely by virtue of section 953(c)(1)(A) may not use a loss within the nonRPII or SCI categories to reduce income within the RPII category.

§ 1.953-6 Relationship of sections 953 and 954.

> ***Caution:*** The Treasury has not yet amended Reg § 1.953-6 to reflect changes made by P.L. 100-647, P.L. 99-514, P.L. 98-369.

(a) Priority of application. For purposes of determining the subpart F income of a controlled foreign corporation under section 952 for any taxable year, the provisions of section 954, relating to foreign base company income, shall be applied, after first applying section 953, only with respect to income which is not income derived from the insurance of United States risks under section 953. For example, the provisions of section 954 may be applied with respect to the income of a controlled foreign corporation which is not income derived from the insurance of United States risks under section 953 because such corporation does not satisfy the 5-percent minimum premium requirement prescribed in paragraph (b) of § 1.953-1, even though such corporation has taxable income, as determined under § 1.953-4, which is attributable to the reinsuring or the issuing of any insurance or annuity contracts in connection with United States risks. In addition, the provisions of section 954 may apply with respect to the income of a controlled foreign corporation to the extent such income is not allocated or apportioned under § 1.953-4 to the insurance of United States risks.

(b) Decrease in income not material. It is not material that the income of a controlled foreign corporation is decreased as a result of the application of paragraph (a) of this section. Thus, in applying § 1.953-4 to the income of a controlled foreign corporation described in paragraph (c)(2) of § 1.953-5 which would, but for paragraph (a) of this section, be subject to the provisions of section 954, there shall be allowed, in determining the taxable income derived from the insurance of United States risks under § 1.953-4, a deduction under section 809(a)(1) for the share of each and every item of investment yield set aside for policyholders; it is not material that in determining foreign base company income such deduction would not be allowed under section 954(b)(5). Further, income of a controlled foreign corporation which is required to be taken into account under section 953 in determining income derived from the insurance of United States risks and would, but for the provisions of paragraph (a) of this section, constitute foreign base company income under section 954 shall not be taken into account under section 954(b)(3)(B) in determining whether foreign base company income exceeds 70 percent of gross income for the taxable year.

(c) Increase in income not material. It is not material that the income of a controlled foreign corporation is increased as a result of the application of paragraph (a) of this section. Thus, in applying § 1.953-4 to income of a controlled foreign corporation which would, but for paragraph (a) of this section, be subject to the provisions of section 954, it is not material that the dividends, interest, and gains from the sale or exchange of stock or securities derived from certain investments which would not be included in foreign personal holding company income under section 954(c)(3)(B) are included under section 953 in income derived from the insurance of United States risks. Further, income of a controlled foreign corporation which is required to be taken into account under section 953 in determining income derived from the insurance of United States risks and would, but for paragraph (a) of this section, constitute foreign base company income shall not be excluded under section 954(b)(3)(A) for the taxable year.

T.D. 6781, 12/22/64.

Proposed § 1.953-6 Application of subchapter L and certain sections of subchapter N of the Code. [*For Preamble, see ¶ 151,253*]

(a) Applicability of subchapter L. *(1) In general.* A controlled foreign corporation which has insurance income under section 953 or foreign personal holding company income that is SCI investment income shall compute its insurance income or SCI investment income either under part I of subchapter L of the Code (relating to life insurance companies) or under part II of subchapter L of the Code (relating to other insurance companies) as modified by this section and § 1.952-2. If a controlled foreign corporation does not file an annual statement with an insurance regulatory authority of any State, such corporation must complete those portions of the annual statement prescribed by the National Association of Insurance Commissioners which are necessary to make the determinations and computations required under subchapter L of the Code. If a controlled foreign corporation uses the reserves described in paragraph (d)(1)(ii) of this section (relating to reserves on United States business for which no NAIC statement is required) to qualify as a life insurance company subject to part I under subchapter L, then the foreign corporation shall compute its reserves, for purposes of the NAIC annual statement, by following the laws and regulations of New York or the laws of the State of the United States where the insured risks are located, whichever is applicable under paragraph (d)(1)(ii) of this section. In all other circumstances, the controlled foreign corporation shall complete the necessary portion of the NAIC annual statement by following the rules prescribed in §§ 1.953-1 through 1.953-7 and, to the extent not inconsistent with those sections, the rules prescribed by the National Association of Insurance Commissioners.

(2) Applicability of section 7702. [Reserved]

(3) Applicability of section 817. [Reserved]

(b) Special rules regarding use of subchapter L to compute RPII, nonRPII, and SCI income. *(1) Certain provisions not to apply.* The following provisions of subchapter L do not apply in computing section 953 insurance income or foreign personal holding company income that is SCI investment income:

(i) Section 806, relating to the small life insurance company deduction;

(ii) Section 805(a)(5), relating to the operations loss deduction; and

(iii) Section 832(c)(5), relating to certain capital losses.

(2) Allocation and apportionment of certain items. The items referred to in section 803(a)(1) (relating to gross amount of premiums and other considerations), section 803(a)(2) (relating to net decrease in reserves), section 805(a)(2) (relating to net increase in reserves), and section 832(b)(4) (relating to premiums earned on insurance contracts) shall be taken into account in computing income within a particular category, whether the RPII, nonRPII, and SCI categories, only to the extent they relate to a contract issued or reinsured by the controlled foreign corporation that gives rise to premiums within that particular category. For rules relating to the allocation of premiums, see §§ 1.953-2 and 1.953-3. For rules relating to increases or decreases in reserves, see §§ 1.953-4 and 1.953-5.

(c) Alternative tax for certain small companies. Any controlled foreign corporation that computes its taxable income under part II of subchapter L (relating to insurance companies other than life insurance companies) and makes the election under § 1.953-7(c) to have its related person insurance income treated as effectively connected with the conduct of a trade or business in the United States may elect to have its related person insurance income, as well as its income effectively connected with the conduct of a United States trade or business that is excluded from subpart F income under section 952(b), taxed under section 831(b) (alternative tax for certain small companies) if the requirements of that section are met. To determine whether a corporation meets the net written premium requirement of section 831(b), the premiums on all policies (including SCI policies) of insurance or reinsurance or annuity contracts issued by the corporation must be taken into account.

(d) Computation of reserves to determine applicability of part I of subchapter L. *(1) Reserves required by law.* The reserves set forth in this paragraph (d)(1) are the only reserves to be taken into account as reserves required by law under section 816(b)(2) to determine for any taxable year whether a controlled foreign corporation is subject to part I of subchapter L (relating to life insurance companies):

(i) Reserves with respect to United States business. The reserves which are required by the law of the state or states of the United States, including the District of Columbia, to which the business of the controlled foreign corporation is subject, but only with respect to its United States business, if any, which is taxable under section 842(a).

(ii) Reserves deemed to be required. To the extent the controlled foreign corporation is not subject to section 842(a) but issues a policy of insurance or an annuity contract to a resident of the United States—

(A) Except as provided in paragraph (d)(1)(ii)(B) of this section, the reserves that would be required by applying the minimum standards of the law of New York as if the controlled foreign corporation were an insurance company transacting all of its insurance business (other than its insurance business carried on within the United States that is subject to section 842(a)) for the taxable year in New York, and

(B) With respect to all United States risks covered by insurance ceded to the controlled foreign corporation by an insurance company subject to subchapter L of the Code, determined without regard to section 501, and in respect of which an election is made by or on behalf of the controlled foreign corporation to determine its reserves in accordance with paragraph (d)(1)(ii)(B) of this section, the amount of reserves against such risks which would result if the reserves were determined by applying the law of the state of the United States where the risks are located as if the controlled foreign corporation were an insurance company in that state engaged in reinsuring the risks.

(iii) Reserves with respect to foreign business. In the case of a reserve on a contract that is not described in paragraph (d)(1)(i) and (ii) of this section, the reserve determined under the laws, regulations, or administrative guidance of the insurance regulatory authority of the home country, or the reserve determined under the laws of the country of residence of the insured, if the controlled foreign corporation is subject to the insurance regulatory authority of the insured's country of residence. If the reserves of a controlled foreign corporation are subject to the laws of more than one foreign jurisdiction, the amount of reserves taken into account shall be the largest reserve required by any such foreign jurisdiction. If neither the home country nor the country of residence of the insured require reserves to be established, then the reserve shall be computed using the mortality tables prescribed by section 807(d) but using the interest rate prescribed in paragraph (e)(4) of this section applicable to qualified contracts.

(2) SCI reserves to be taken into account. The total reserves of a controlled foreign corporation are taken into account to determine whether the corporation is to compute its taxable income under part I of subchapter L. Thus, reserves which relate to the lives or health of residents of the home country are taken into account.

(e) Computation of reserves for purposes of computing taxable income. *(1) Actual reserves required.* For all purposes of §§ 1.953-1 through 1.953-7, a controlled foreign corporation will be considered to have a reserve only to the extent the reserve has been actually held during the taxable year for which the reserve is claimed.

(2) Life insurance reserves. For purposes of computing the taxable income from insurance operations, the section 807(c)(1) items of a controlled foreign corporation that would be taxable under part I or part II of subchapter L of the Code if it were a domestic insurance company that are related to a nonqualified contract, as defined in this paragraph, shall be determined under the rules of section 807(d). The amount of life insurance reserves under section 807(c)(1) relating to qualified foreign contracts shall be determined under the rules of section 807(e)(4) and paragraph (e)(4) of this section. For purposes of this paragraph, a qualified foreign contract means a contract insuring life or health issued by a controlled foreign corporation if the person with the determining life, as defined in § 1.953-2(g)(1), is a resident of the country in which the controlled foreign corporation is incorporated and such country is not contiguous to the United States. A nonqualified foreign contract is any contract that is not a qualified foreign contract.

(3) Discounted unpaid losses of a property and casualty company. If a controlled foreign corporation would be taxable under part II of subchapter L of the Code if it were a domestic insurance company or if it would be subject to part I but has discounted unpaid losses as defined in section 846, the amount of its discounted unpaid losses shall be determined under the rules of section 846 except to the extent modified by paragraph (e)(4) of this section.

(4) Interest rates used for determining reserves. (i) Qualified foreign contracts and property and liability contracts. For purposes of applying section 807(d)(2)(B) and section 812(b)(2)(A) to qualified foreign contracts as defined in paragraph (e)(2) of this section, the term "prevailing State assumed interest rate" shall mean the highest assumed interest rate permitted to be used in computing life insurance reserves for insurance contracts or annuity contracts under the laws of each country in which the controlled foreign corporation conducts an insurance business. For purposes of applying sections 807 and 812 to qualified foreign contracts, as defined in paragraph (e)(2) of this section, and for purposes of applying section 846 to contracts covering risks located outside the United States, the applicable federal interest rate shall be a foreign currency rate of interest analogous to the applicable federal mid- term rates as defined in section 1274(d), but based on annual compounding. An analogous foreign currency rate of interest is a rate of interest based on yields (with an appropriate compounding period) of the highest grade of outstanding marketable obligations denominated in the currency of the country pursuant to the laws of which the controlled foreign corporation computes its reserves (excluding any obligations that benefit from special tax exemptions or preferential tax rates not available to debt instruments generally) with due consideration given to the maturities of the obligations. If a controlled foreign corporation that would be subject to part II of subchapter L if it were a domestic insurance company uses the loss payment patterns prescribed by the Secretary under section 846(d) for discounting unpaid losses (rather than the company's historical payment pattern as permitted under section 846(e)), the company must compute the year-end discounted fraction of unpaid losses and the reserve discount factors by using the applicable federal interest rate required by this paragraph and may not use the year-end discounted fraction of unpaid losses and the reserve discount factors prescribed by the Secretary for any accident year.

(ii) Nonqualified foreign contracts. For purposes of applying sections 807 and 812 to nonqualified foreign contracts, as defined in paragraph (e)(2) of this section, the prevailing state assumed interest rate shall be the rate defined in section 807(d)(4)(B) and the applicable federal interest rate shall be the rate defined in section 807(d)(4)(A).

(f) Corporations not qualifying as insurance companies. *(1) In general.* The United States shareholders of a controlled foreign corporation must include their pro rata share of that corporation's section 953 insurance income even if the foreign corporation would not be taxed under subchapter L of the Code if it were a domestic corporation. Such a corporation shall compute its section 953 insurance income and its foreign personal holding company income that is SCI investment income under the rules of part I or part II of subchapter L as modified by section 953(b) and §§ 1.953-1 through 1.953-7, to the extent not inconsistent with the rules of this paragraph, as if it were a domestic insurance company. A controlled foreign corporation will compute its insurance income as if it were a domestic insurance company subject to part I of subchapter L (relating to life insurance companies) only if it can meet the requirements of section 816(a) of the Code taking into account only that portion of its business which involves the issuing or reinsuring of insurance or annuity contracts. If the requirements of section 816(a) cannot be met, then the controlled foreign corporation must compute its insurance income under part II of subchapter L.

(2) Items of gross income attributable to insurance operations of a non-insurance company. (i) Corporations computing taxable income under part I of subchapter L. The taxable income of a controlled foreign corporation described under paragraph (f)(1) of this section that computes its insurance income under part I of subchapter L, shall include in its insurance income, together with the items of gross income that directly relate to its life insurance business, the items of income described in section 803(a)(3) which are not directly related to its insurance business, and which are not directly related to any other trade or business, in the proportion that the numerator determined under paragraph (f)(2)(i)(A) of this section bears to the denominator determined under paragraph (f)(2)(i)(B) of this section.

(A) Numerator. The numerator used for the apportionment under paragraph (f)(2)(i) of this section is the sum of the means of the items described in section 807(c) at the beginning and end of the taxable year.

(B) Denominator. The denominator used for the apportionment under paragraph (f)(2)(ii) of this section is the mean of the value of the total assets held by the controlled foreign corporation at the beginning and the end of the taxable year, determined by taking bills, accounts, notes receivable, and open accounts at face value and all other assets at their adjusted basis under section 1011 of the Code, unless there is affirmative evidence that more accurately reflects the value of the assets.

(ii) Example. The following example illustrates the principles of paragraph (f)(2)(i) of this section.

Example. X is a controlled foreign corporation incorporated in country M engaged in the business of selling product V. It uses the calendar year as its taxable year. All of X's sales are to persons who reside outside of country M. A division of X issues contracts of credit life insurance to ensure payment of the purchase price of X's products. X does not, however, do enough business as an insurer to qualify as an insurance company under subchapter L of the Code. In 1988, X receives $500 in premiums and $3,000 in sales from product V. X also has interest, dividends, and gains from the sale of investment properties in the amount of $10,000. The investment income is not specifically allocable to the insurance or non-insurance businesses. The mean of X's reserves under section 807(c) determined as of the beginning and end of 1988 is $1,000. The mean of the value of X's total assets held at the beginning and the end of the taxable year is $5,000. The $3,000 received as part of the sales price of product in are directly related to V's non-insurance business and do not constitute insurance income. The $500 in premiums are directly related to V's insurance business and do constitute insurance income under section 953. Of X's $10,000 in investment income $2,000 ($10,000 × $1,000/$5,000) is insurance income under section 953.

(iii) Corporations computing taxable income under part II of subchapter L. The taxable income of a controlled foreign corporation described in paragraph (f)(1) of this section that computes its insurance income as if it were a domestic insurance company subject to part II of subchapter L shall include in its insurance income, together with the items of gross income that directly relate to its insurance business, the items of income described in section 832(b)(1) which are not directly related to its insurance business, and which are not directly related to any other trade or business, in the proportion that the numerator determined under paragraph (f)(2)(iii)(A) of this section bears to the denominator determined under paragraph (f)(2)(iii)(B) of this section.

(A) Numerator. The numerator used for the apportionment under paragraph (f)(2)(iii) of this section is the sum of—

(1) The mean of the controlled foreign corporation's unearned premiums at the beginning and end of the taxable year, determined under section 832(b)(4)(B);

(2) The mean of the controlled foreign corporation's discounted unpaid losses at the beginning and end of the taxable year, determined under section 846; plus

(3) The mean of the items described in section 807(c)(4) at the beginning and end of the taxable year, to the extent allowable under section 832(c)(11).

(B) Denominator. The denominator used for the apportionment under paragraph (f)(2)(iii) of this section is the mean of the value of the total assets held by the controlled foreign corporation at the beginning and the end of the taxable year, determined by taking bills, accounts, notes receivable, and open accounts at face value and all other assets at their adjusted basis under section 1011 of the Code, unless there is affirmative evidence that more accurately reflects the value of the assets.

(g) Relationship between sections 953 and 954. *(1) Priority of application.* (i) In general. For purposes of determining the subpart F income of a controlled foreign corporation, the provisions of section 953 and §§ 1.953-1 through 1.953-7 must be applied before the provisions of section 954 (relating to foreign base company income). Further, the provisions of section 954 apply only to income that is not insurance income under section 953. For example, the provisions of section 954 are applied to the investment income attributable to premiums received with respect to insured risks located in the controlled foreign corporation's country of incorporation only after §§ 1.953-1 through 1.953-7 have been applied to determine the amount of section 953 insurance income and SCI income and the deductions allocated and apportioned to those categories of income. Notwithstanding the foregoing, foreign base company oil related income as defined in section 954(a)(5) and (g) shall not be treated as insurance income subject to section 953 and shall not be subject to §§ 1.953-1 through 1.953-7.

(ii) Examples. The following examples illustrate the principles of paragraph (g)(1)(i) of this section.

Example (1). X is a controlled foreign corporation incorporated in country F. X's only trade or business is the insurance business. All of X's premiums are received under contracts insuring risks located outside country F. X earns interest, dividends, and rents from the investment of the premiums it receives. The interest, dividends, and rents are insurance income under section 953 and not foreign personal holding company income under section 954.

Example (2). Y is a controlled foreign corporation incorporated in country W. Y owns all of the outstanding stock of Z, also a country W corporation. Y writes contracts that give rise to premiums allocable to the nonRPII and SCI categories. In its taxable year ending in 1988, Y receives a dividend from Z. Y must allocate or apportion that dividend income to the nonRPII and SCI categories under § 1.953-4 before applying the exception of section 954(c)(3) (relating to dividends from same-country related corporations) to the SCI investment income.

(2) Decrease or increase in income not material. (i) In general. For purposes of computing the subpart F income of a controlled foreign corporation deriving income from insurance, reinsurance, or annuity contracts, deductions are allowed if they are allowed under subchapter L of the Code as modified by section 953 regardless of whether they are allocated or apportioned to section 953 insurance income or SCI investment income which constitutes section 954(c) foreign personal holding company income. Further, the amount of section 953 insurance income and the amount of foreign personal holding company income attributable to SCI investment income shall be determined in accordance with subchapter L of the Code, as modified by section 953, even though those rules result in a greater amount of subpart F income compared to the amount determined under section 954. Thus, in applying section 953 to income of a controlled foreign corporation that would, but for section 953, be subject to the provisions of section 954, the exceptions under section 954(c) which would not require a United States shareholder to include in gross income dividends, interest, rents, royalties, gains from the sale or exchange of property described in section 954(c)(1)(B), net gains from commodities transactions described in section 954(c)(1)(C), and net gains from foreign currency transactions described in section 954(c)(1)(D), are irrelevant.

(ii) Examples. The principles of this paragraph (g)(2) are illustrated in the following examples.

Example (1). Z is a controlled foreign corporation that only issues and reinsures property and casualty insurance policies covering home country risks. Z may allocate a part of its discounted unpaid losses under section 846 to its SCI investment income which is foreign personal holding company income under section 954(c).

Example (2). Y, a controlled foreign corporation, receives dividends and interest from a subsidiary which is incorporated in the same country as X and has a substantial part of its trade or business assets located in that country. All of X's income is attributable to the RPII or nonRPII categories. The dividends, after the appropriate allocation and apportionment, are included in the gross income of X's United States shareholders without regard to section 954(c)(3) (relating to dividends and interest from same-country related corporations).

(h) Inclusion of pro rata share of subpart F income derived from insurance operations. *(1) Inclusion of pro rata share of related person insurance income.* Each section 953(c) shareholder, as defined in this paragraph (h)(1), must include in its gross income (subject to the section 952(c) earnings and profits limitation) the lesser of—

(i) The "pro rata amount," which is the amount that would be determined under section 951(a)(2) if only related person insurance income were taken into account; if the number of shares of stock owned (within the meaning of section 958(a)) by section 953(c) shareholders in the aggregate on the last day of the taxable year were the total number of shares in the foreign corporation; and if only distributions received by section 953(c) shareholders were taken into account under section 951(a)(2)(B); or

(ii) The "limitation amount," which is the amount that would be determined under section 951(a)(2) if all of the taxable income of the foreign corporation for the taxable year were subpart F income. A section 953(c) shareholder is a United States shareholder as defined in section 953(c)(1)(A) and § 1.953-3(b)(2) and includes a United States shareholder as defined in section 951(b).

(2) Inclusion of subpart F income other than related person insurance income. Each United States shareholder as defined in section 951(b) (a "section 951(b) shareholder") must include, in addition to its pro rata share of income within the RPII category computed under paragraph (h)(1) of this section, its pro rata share of subpart F income other than related person insurance income, as computed under section 951(a)(2) and paragraph (h)(3) of this section. A section 951(b) shareholder must include its pro rata share of income within the RPII category as computed under this paragraph (h)(2) regardless of whether the exceptions of section 953(c)(3)(A) and (B) and § 1.953-7(a) and (b) apply.

(3) Earnings and profits limitation. Pursuant to section 952(c)(1)(A), the subpart F income of any controlled foreign corporation for any taxable year shall not exceed the earnings and profits of such corporation for such taxable year. Thus, a United States shareholder's inclusion of subpart F income shall not exceed such shareholder's pro rata share, computed under the principles of section 951(a)(2), of the earnings and profits of the controlled foreign corporation. If the sum of a United States shareholder's pro rata share of related person insurance income and subpart F income other than related person insurance income exceeds such shareholder's pro rata share of the controlled foreign corporation's earnings and profits, then the section 952(c)(1)(A) earnings and profits limitation shall be applied by first including the United States shareholder's pro rata share of related person insurance income.

(4) Examples. The following examples illustrate the principles of paragraph (h) of this section.

Example (1). X is a country M corporation and is a controlled foreign corporation under section 957, section 953(c)(1)(B), and § 1.953-3(b)(2). It has 100 shares of one class of stock outstanding. A owns 5 shares, B owns 5 shares, C owns 70 shares, and F owns 20 shares. A, B, and C are unrelated United States persons; F is a foreign person. A, B and C are considered section 953(c) shareholders. Only C, however, is a section 951(b) shareholder. During the current taxable year, X has $1,000 of related person insurance income and $1,000 of earnings and profits. A and B will each include $50 and C will include $700 of related person insurance income in gross income, computed as set forth below.

Computation of pro rata share of related person insurance income.

Lesser of:

Pro rata amount:					
A:	5/80	×	$1,000	=	$ 62.50
B:	5/80	×	$1,000	=	$ 62.50
C:	70/80	×	$1,000	=	$875.00
or					
Limitation amount:					
A:	5/100	×	$1,000	=	$ 50
B:	5/100	×	$1,000	=	$ 50
C:	70/100	×	$1,000	=	$ 700

Example (2). The facts are the same as in Example 1 except that there is $2,000 of related person insurance income and $1,500 of earnings and profits. The amount of related person insurance income included in gross income of A, B, and C is $75, $75, and $1,050, respectively, as computed below.

(i) Computation of pro rata share of related person insurance income.

Lesser of:

Pro rata amount:

A:	5/80	×	$2,000	=	$ 125
B:	5/80	×	$2,000	=	$ 125
C:	70/80	×	$2,000	=	$1,750

or

Limitation amount:

A:	5/100	×	$2,000	=	$ 100
B:	5/100	×	$2,000	=	$ 100
C:	70/100	×	$2,000	=	$1,400

(ii) Computation of section 952(c)(1)(A) earnings and profits limitation.

A:	5/100	×	$1,500	=	$ 75
B:	5/100	×	$1,500	=	$ 75
C:	70/100	×	$1,500	=	$1,050

The amount of related person insurance income included in the gross income of each shareholder is limited by their pro rata share of earnings and profits as computed under section 952(c) because that amount is less than both the pro rata amount and the limitation amount.

Example (3). The facts are the same as in Example 1 except that X has $1,000 in related person insurance income, $1,000 in subpart F income other than related person insurance income, and $1,500 in earnings and profits.

(i) Computation of pro rata share of related person insurance income.

Lesser of:

Pro rata amount:

A:	5/80	×	$1,000	=	$ 62.50
B:	5/80	×	$1,000	=	$ 62.50
C:	70/80	×	$1,000	=	$875.00

or

Limitation amount:

A:	5/100	×	$2,000	=	$ 100
B:	5/100	×	$2,000	=	$ 100
C:	70/100	×	$2,000	=	$1,400

(ii) Computation of the pro rata share of subpart F income other than related person insurance income.

C is the only section 951(b) shareholder.

C: 70/100 × $1,000 = $700

(iii) Computation of pro rata share of earnings and profits.

A:	5/100	×	$1,500	=	$ 75
B:	5/100	×	$1,500	=	$ 75
C:	70/100	×	$1,500	=	$1,050

With respect to A and B, the pro rata amount of related person insurance income is less than their pro rata share of X's earnings and profits. Thus, A and B will each include $62.50 in gross income as related person insurance income. The sum of C's pro rata share of related person insurance income (the pro rata amount of $875) and subpart F income other than related person insurance income ($700) equals $1,575. That sum exceeds C's pro rata share of X's earnings and profits ($1,050). Thus, C must include $875 of related person insurance income and $175 ($1,050 – $875) of subpart F income other than related person insurance income.

(5) Controlled foreign corporation for less than entire year. (i) In general. If a foreign corporation with related person insurance income is a controlled foreign corporation for less than the entire taxable year, for purposes of computing the limitation amount, only the taxable income of the foreign corporation for that portion of the taxable year during which the foreign corporation was a controlled foreign corporation, computed as if such income were earned ratably throughout the taxable year, shall be treated as subpart F income.

(ii) Example. The rule of this paragraph (h)(5) is illustrated in the following example.

Example. X, a foreign corporation, was incorporated on January 1, 1987 by A, B and F. As of that date, A and B, who are United States persons, each own 5 shares and F, who is not a United States person, owns 90 shares of the 100 shares of the single class of stock issued and outstanding. On July 1, 1987, F sells 70 of his shares to C, a United States person. At the end of the calendar year, which is also X's taxable year, X has $1,000 of income from providing insurance to its United States shareholders and persons related to those shareholders. X also has $1,000 of earnings and profits for the year. A and B must each include $25.00 in gross income and C must include $349.00. The computations necessary to determine related person insurance income are set forth below.

Computation of the pro rata share of related person insurance income.

Lesser of:

Pro rata amount:

A:	5/80 × (182/365 × $1,000)	=	$ 31.00
B:	5/80 × (182/365 × $1,000)	=	$ 31.00
C:	70/80 × (182/365 × $1,000)	=	$436.00

or

Limitation amount:

A:	5/100 × (182/365 × $1,000)	=	$ 25.00
B:	5/100 × (182/365 × $1,000)	=	$ 25.00
C:	70/100 × (182/365 × $1,000)	=	$349.00

Thus, the amount of related person insurance income to be included by A, B, and C is the limitation amount.

(6) Distributions. (i) In general. Only distributions to United States shareholders, as defined in section 951(b) or section 953(c)(1)(A), are to be taken into account for purposes of computing the pro rata amount, as defined in paragraph (h)(1)(i) of this section. However, for purposes of computing the limitation amount under paragraphs (h)(1)(ii) of this section, distributions to shareholders other than United States shareholders shall be taken into account.

(ii) Example. The following example illustrates the rule of paragraph (h)(6)(i) of this section.

Example. X is a controlled foreign corporation within the meaning of section 953(c)(1) and § 1.953-3(b)(2) and has 100 shares of one class of stock outstanding. F, who is not a United States person, owned all 100 shares of X's outstanding stock until July 1, 1987, when A, a United States person, acquired 60 shares of the stock from F. On June 30, 1987, before A had acquired X's stock from F, X made a distribution of $2 per share for a total of $200 to F. At the end of the calendar year, which is also X's taxable year, X had $2,000 of taxable income, of which $1,000 is related person insurance income. X also had earnings and profits for the taxable year of $2,000. The computation for determining A's pro rata share of related person insurance income is set forth below.

Computation of the pro rata share of related person insurance income.

(i) Pro rata amount:
A: $^{60}/_{60} \times {}^{182}/_{365} \times \$1{,}000 = \$499.00$
(ii) Limitation amount:
A: $^{60}/_{100} \times {}^{182}/_{365} \times \$2{,}000 = \$598.00$
minus lesser of:
$120 dividend on
shares purchased
$60\% \times {}^{182}/_{365} \times \$2{,}000$ ($598.00) = ($120.00)/$478.00

Thus, A must include $478 of related person insurance income in gross income.

(7) Mutual insurance companies. For purposes of sections 951(a)(2) and 953(c)(5) and paragraph (h) of this section, a United States shareholder that is a policyholder in a mutual insurance company shall compute its pro rata share by reference to the amount that would be distributed with respect to the United States shareholder's policy or policies owned on the last day of the controlled foreign corporation's taxable year if all the related person insurance income and all the subpart F income other than related person insurance income were distributed to the policyholders. In making the determination of a mutual policyholder's pro rata share of subpart F income the rules set forth in paragraph (h)(7)(i) through (iii) of this section are applied in the order given and the first rule to result in the determination of a specific amount to be included in the policyholder's gross income is the rule that shall be applied. The mutual policyholder's pro rata share of subpart F income shall be determined as:

(i) The amount that would be distributed annually under the terms of the policy or the by-laws of the corporation;

(ii) The amount that would be distributed if the mutual company were liquidated; or

(iii) The amount that would be distributed to a policyholder if earnings and profits were distributed in the same proportion that premiums paid by the policyholder over a five-year period ending on the last day of the controlled foreign corporation's taxable year bears to the total amount of premiums paid by all policyholders who hold ownership interests on the last day of the taxable year and have held their interest over the five-year period.

(i) Application of sections 959, 961, and 1248. If a foreign corporation that is a controlled foreign corporation under section 953(c) makes a distribution with respect to its stock, section 959(a)(1) shall apply to any United States shareholder as defined in section 953(c)(1)(A) and § 1.953-3(b)(2). Earnings and profits attributable to related person insurance income included in the gross income of a United States shareholder with less than 10 percent of the combined voting power of the stock of the controlled foreign corporation shall be treated as earnings and profits which have been included in the gross income of a United States shareholder for purposes of sections 956 and 959(a)(2). In addition, the adjustments made to the basis of stock in a controlled foreign corporation required by section 961 shall apply to any United States shareholder as defined in section 953(c)(1)(A) and § 1.953-3(b)(2). Any United States person who is a United States shareholder, as defined in section 953(c)(1)(A) and § 1.953-3(b)(2), of a controlled foreign corporation, as defined in section 953(c)(1)(B) and § 1.953-3(b)(2), shall be treated as meeting the stock ownership requirements of section 1248(a)(2). In addition, any controlled foreign corporation, within the meaning of section 953(c)(1)(B) and § 1.953-3(b)(2), shall be treated as a controlled foreign corporation for purposes of section 1248.

(j) Application of section 367(b). [Reserved]

(k) Interaction with section 954(b)(3). Income that would not be considered subpart F income but for the operation of section 954(b)(3)(B) shall not be considered related person insurance income. Thus, if foreign base company income and insurance income exceed 70 percent of gross income, United States persons who are United States shareholders solely by operation of section 953(c)(1)(A) and § 1.953-3(b)(2) must include in their gross income only their pro rata share of related person insurance income. Any person who is a United States shareholder as defined in section 951(b) shall, however, include his pro rata share, as determined under this section, of the entire amount of subpart F income of the controlled foreign corporation.

Proposed § 1.953-7 Exceptions to inclusion of related person insurance income for certain shareholders.
[*For Preamble, see ¶ 151,253*]

(a) Corporation not held by insureds. *(1) In general.* A person that is a United States shareholder solely by virtue of section 953(c)(1) shall not include in gross income such person's pro rata share of income that qualifies as related person insurance income if, at all times during the taxable year of the foreign corporation, less than 20 percent of the total combined voting power of all classes of stock of the corporation entitled to vote and less than 20 percent of the total value (both stock and policies) of the corporation is owned (directly or indirectly under the principles of section 883(c)(4)) by persons who are the insured under any insurance or reinsurance contract, who are the purchasers or beneficiaries of any annuity contract issued or reinsured by the foreign corporation, or who are related persons (within the meaning of section 954(d)(3)) to any such insured. For purposes of this paragraph, the term "insured" means only United States persons, as defined in section 957(c), or persons related to United States persons (within the meaning of section 954(d)(3)) who are insured or reinsured by the foreign corporation, persons who have purchased or are beneficiaries under any annuity contract issued or reinsured by the foreign corporation, or persons insured by the foreign corporation in a cross-insurance arrangement described in § 1.953-3(b)(5).

(2) Examples. The principles of this paragraph (a) are illustrated in the following examples.

Example (1). X is a country Y corporation which issues property and liability insurance policies for risks located outside country Y. X has one class of voting stock outstanding. Z, a domestic corporation, owns 60 percent of X's stock. Z has 100 shareholders each of which owns one percent of Z. Of the remaining shareholders of X, four are foreign corporations, each of which owns five percent of the X stock, and four are domestic corporations which also own five percent each. X has issued policies of insurance to 25 of Z's shareholders, the four foreign corporations which own stock in X, and to W, one of the domestic corporate shareholders of X. None of the other shareholders of X are insured by X. The 25 insureds who own stock in Z own, indirectly under the principles of section 883(c)(4), 15 percent of the stock of X (25% × 60%). The insurance income attributable to the policy of insurance issued to W is related person insurance income that is includable in the gross income of the four domestic corporate shareholders of X because 20 percent of the stock of X is owned directly or indirectly by insureds who are United States persons: 15 percent by 25 of the shareholders of Z plus 5 percent owned by W. In addition, because Z is a United States shareholder as defined in section 951(b), as well as in section 953(c)(1), it must include its pro rata share of the related person insurance of income of X, plus the section 953(a) insurance income that is not related person insurance income, regardless of whether 20 percent or more of the corporation is owned, directly or indirectly, by insureds who are United States persons.

Example (2). Y is a controlled foreign corporation. Its one class of stock outstanding is owned equally by 20 domestic corporations, none of which are insured by Y. Nine of the shareholder corporations are the parent corporations of nine unrelated, wholly-owned foreign subsidiaries which are insured by Y. Because the insureds are related persons, within the meaning of section 954(d)(3), to United States shareholders (the domestic corporate shareholders), the income from insuring the foreign subsidiaries is related person insurance income. Moreover, because nine domestic corporate shareholders of Y control the subsidiaries, within the meaning of section 954(d)(3), they are related persons. Therefore, 45 percent (9 × 5%) of the stock of Y is owned by United States shareholders that are related to the insureds and the exception to inclusion in gross income of paragraph (a)(1) of this section is inapplicable. The 20 domestic shareholders must include Y's related person insurance income in their gross income.

(b) De minimis insurance exception. *(1) In general.* A person that is a United States shareholder solely by virtue of section 953(c)(1) shall not include in gross income such person's pro rata share of income that qualifies as related person insurance income if the related person insurance income, determined on a gross basis, of the foreign corporation is less than 20 percent of the foreign corporation's total insurance income for the taxable year, determined on a gross basis, without regard to those provisions of section 953(a)(1) and § 1.953-2(a)(1) which limit section 953 insurance income to income from countries other than the country in which the corporation was created or organized. Related person insurance income determined on a gross basis means life insurance gross income within the meaning of section 803 or gross income within the meaning of section 832(b)(1), whichever is applicable, except that the phrase "premiums earned (within the meaning of section 832(b)(4)" shall be substituted for the term "underwriting income," where that term appears in section 832(b)(1)(A).

(2) Examples. The following examples illustrate the principles of paragraph (b)(1) of this section.

Example (1). X is a country Y corporation engaged in the business of issuing liability insurance. All of the stock of X is owned by United States shareholders. Each of the United States shareholders owns less than 10 percent of X's one class of stock outstanding. For its 1987 taxable year, X has $100,000 of gross income of which $10,000 constitutes section 953 insurance income within the RPII category and $50,000 constitutes section 953 insurance income within the nonRPII category. Of the remaining $40,000 of income, $10,000 would have been premium and investment income within the RPII category of section 953 insurance income and $30,000 would have been premium and investment income within the nonRPII category of insurance income except that those amounts relate to contracts insuring risks located in the home country. Thus, without regard to the same country exception, $20,000 of income ($10,000 from the RPII category and $10,000 from the SCI category) would have been within the RPII category of section 953 insurance income. X does not meet the de minimis insurance exception of paragraph (b)(1) of this section because 20 percent ($20,000/$100,000) of its insurance income, determined without regard to those provisions of section 953(a)(1) and § 1.953-2(a)(3) which limit insurance income to income from insuring risks located outside the home country, is related person insurance income.

Example (2). The facts are the same as in Example 1 except that $3,000 of premiums that constitute income within the RPII category is paid to another insurer pursuant to a reinsurance contract. X does meet the de minimis insurance exception because under section 832(b)(4)(A) premiums paid for reinsurance are deducted from premiums written in arriving at premiums earned. Thus, approximately 17.5 percent ($17,000/$97,000) of X's insurance income is related person insurance income.

(3) Anti-abuse rule. (i) In general. In determining insurance income on a gross basis, the District Director may exclude income attributable to an insurance or reinsurance contract covering the life, health, property, or liability of a person other than a United States shareholder, or person related to such shareholder, or attributable to an annuity contract, or a contract reinsuring annuity contracts, that are purchased by, or provide annuity payments to, a person other than a United States shareholder or person related to such shareholder, if the primary purpose for entering into the contract is to qualify for the de minimis insurance exception. See also section 845. In making this determination, the District Director will consider all the facts and circumstances. Among the factors to be considered are whether there is a true transfer of risk, whether the predominant purpose for the transaction is a bona fide business purpose, and whether the terms of the insurance or reinsurance contract reflect the terms that unrelated parties would agree to in a similar transaction. (ii) (ii) Examples. The following examples illustrate the principles of paragraph (b)(3) of this section.

Example (1). The facts are the same as in Example 1 in paragraph (b)(2) of this section, except that near the end of its taxable year, X cedes to another insurance company, Z, under a contract of reinsurance some of the insurance policies that were issued by X to persons other than related insureds. X receives a ceding commission from Z of $30,000 and thereby increases its gross income other than RPII income by $30,000. Thus, approximately 15 percent ($20,000/$130,000) of X's income is RPII income without regard to the same country exception. At the beginning of the following taxable year, Z reinsures with S, a subsidiary controlled by X, a block of insurance which is similar to the policies X reinsured with Z. W pays Z a ceding commission of $30,000. Based on the facts and circumstances, X will be regarded as having engaged in the reinsurance transaction with Z in order to qualify for the de minimis exception. Therefore, the $30,000 of income from the reinsurance transaction will be ignored in determining whether X qualifies for the de minimis exception.

Example (2). The facts are the same as in Example 1 in paragraph (b)(2) of this section except, that near the end of the taxable year, X enters a reinsurance agreement with M under which X receives $30,000 in nonRPII premiums. At the beginning of the following taxable year, X cedes to F all of the risks of M that X reinsured at the end of 1988, transferring the $30,000 in premiums to F. The $30,000 in nonRPII premiums received by X under the reinsurance agreement will be ignored for purposes of determining whether X qualifies for the de minimis related person insurance income exception.

(c) Election to treat income as effectively connected. *(1) In general.* A controlled foreign corporation, other than a disqualified corporation, may elect in accordance with the procedures set forth in this paragraph to treat its related person insurance income that is not actually effectively connected income under section 864(c) as if it were income effectively connected with the conduct of a trade or business in the United States. To make the election, the foreign corporation must waive all benefits (other than with respect to section 884) with respect to related person insurance income granted by the United States under any treaty, including any friendship, commerce and navigation treaty, between the United States and any foreign country.

(2) Corporations which may make the election. (i) In general. The election may be made by any corporation that is not a disqualified corporation. A corporation is a disqualified corporation if, for any taxable year beginning after December 31, 1986, it is a controlled foreign corporation as defined in section 957(a) or (b) (without regard to section 953(c)(1)(B) and § 1.953-3(b)(2)) for an uninterrupted period of 30 days or more during the taxable year and a United States shareholder, as defined in section 951(b), owns, directly or indirectly, within the meaning of section 958(a) (without regard to the constructive ownership rules of section 958(b)), stock in the corporation at some time during the taxable year.

(ii) Successor corporation. A corporation that is a successor to another corporation that, during any taxable year beginning after December 31, 1986, was a disqualified corporation may not make the election. The term "successor corporation" means any foreign corporation that acquires assets of another foreign corporation having a fair market value of 50 percent or more of the fair market value of all the assets held by the acquired foreign corporation immediately before the acquisition, if 50 percent or more of the combined voting power of all classes of stock entitled to vote or 50 percent or more of the value of all classes of stock in the acquiring corporation is owned, directly or indirectly, at the time of the acquisition by one or more persons who at any time during which the acquired foreign corporation was a disqualified corporation owned, directly or indirectly, 50 percent or more of the combined voting power of all classes of stock entitled to vote or 50 percent or more of the value of all classes of stock in the acquired foreign corporation.

(iii) Examples. The following examples illustrate the principles of paragraph (c)(2) of this section.

Example (1). Subsequent to December 31, 1986, 50 domestic corporations, all engaged in business within the same industry, form M, a foreign corporation to insure the risks of the 50 corporations and their subsidiaries. Each of the corporations owns two percent of the one class of voting stock of M outstanding. M may make the election under section 953(c)(3)(C) to have its related person insurance income treated as if it were effectively connected with the conduct of a trade or business within the United States because it has never been a controlled foreign corporation within the meaning of section 957(a) or (b).

Example (2). The facts are the same as in Example 1, except that four of the 50 domestic corporate shareholders, W, X, Y, and Z, each own 7 percent of the stock of M and are wholly-owned subsidiaries of V, a domestic corporation. None of the other shareholders of M are 10 percent or greater shareholders. M is a controlled foreign corporation under section 957(b) because more than 25 percent of its stock is owned by United States shareholders as defined in section 951(b). Under the attribution rules of section 958(b), W, X, Y, and Z are each considered as owning 28 percent of the stock of M and therefore are United States shareholders under section 951(b) because each is considered as owning the stock of the others by attribution through V. Because each of W, X, Y, and Z own stock in M directly under section 958(a), M is a disqualified corporation.

Example (3). On January 1, 1987, X, a domestic corporation, formed Z under the laws of country F as a reinsurance company constituting a mutual insurance company under the laws of country F. X capitalized Z by contributing interest bearing reserve fund certificates which entitle X to 30 percent of the voting power in Z. Z reinsures policies issued by X, none of which relate to risks located in country F. Under the laws of country F, the policyholders under the policies issued by X and reinsured by Z are members of Z and have voting rights. None of these policyholders hold 10 percent or more of the voting power of Z. However, only those policyholders may receive policyholder dividends from Z. X is not entitled to any non-liquidating distributions from Z. Z is a controlled foreign corporation within the meaning of section 957(b). Even though neither X nor the United States policyholders have had inclusions of insurance income in their gross income by virtue of subpart F of the Code, because Z is a controlled foreign corporation under section 957(b) it cannot make the election under section 953(c)(3)(C) to have its related person insurance income treated as if it were effectively connected with the conduct of a trade or business within the United States.

(3) Taxable year of corporation making election. A corporation making the election to treat related person insurance income as income effectively connected with the conduct of a trade or business in the United States must utilize the calendar year as its annual accounting period for United States tax purposes, as required by section 843.

(4) Period during which election is in effect. (i) Elections that become effective in taxable years beginning after December 31, 1987. If an election under paragraph (c)(3) of this section is made for the first taxable year beginning after December 31, 1987 or any subsequent taxable year, the election is effective from the first day of the taxable year for which the election is made (and all subsequent taxable years). Therefore, a foreign corporation that has a fiscal taxable year prior to making the election must file a short-year return for the period from the first day the election becomes effective to the last day of the calendar year in which the election is made.

(ii) Examples. The following examples illustrate the rule of paragraph (c)(4)(i) of this section.

Example (1). X is a controlled foreign corporation that keeps its books and records on a calendar year basis. X makes an election under paragraph (c)(3) of this section for the 1988 taxable year. X's election is effective as of January 1, 1988.

Example (2). Y is a controlled foreign corporation that keeps its books and records on a July 1 to June 30 fiscal year basis. Y makes an election under paragraph (c)(3) of this section for the 1988 taxable year. Y's election is effective as of July 1, 1988. Y must file a short-year return covering the period from July 1, 1988 to December 31, 1988.

(iii) Elections that become effective in first taxable year beginning after December 31, 1986. For any foreign corporation that makes an election under paragraph (c) of this section for the first taxable year beginning after December 31, 1986, the election is effective as of the date indicated by the corporation on its election statement and for all subsequent taxable years. A foreign corporation that had a fiscal taxable year prior to making the election must file a short-year return covering the period from the beginning of its 1987 fiscal year to the last day of its 1987 fiscal year. The foreign corporation must include in its gross income for the taxable year in which the election becomes effective the amount of related person insurance income that is attributable to the period from the date the election becomes effective through the last day of the calendar year. The amount of the related person insurance income attributable to such period is that amount determined by allocating to each day in the taxable year its ratable portion of related person insurance income. However, if the corporation keeps adequate books and records that, in the district director's discretion, accurately reflect the actual amount of the income earned in such period, the corporation may include such amount in gross income rather than the daily pro rata amount.

(iv) Examples. The following examples illustrate the principles of paragraph (c)(4)(iii) of this section.

Example (1). X is a controlled foreign corporation that keeps its books and records on a calendar year basis. X makes an election under paragraph (c) of this section for the 1987 taxable year. In its election statement, X chose September 15, 1987 as the effective date of its election. X must include in gross income the related person insurance income attributable to the period from September 15, 1987 to December 31, 1987 in its calendar year 1987 tax return.

Example (2). Y is a controlled foreign corporation that keeps its books and records on a July 1 to June 30 fiscal year basis. Y makes an election under this paragraph (c) of this section for the 1987 taxable year and chooses to make the election effective as of September 1, 1987. Y must file a short-year return covering the period from July 1, 1987 to August 31, 1987. The related person insurance income of Y that, under Y's method of accounting, is attributable to the period from July 1, 1987 to August 31, 1987 must be included in the gross income of Y's United States shareholders. In addition, X must also file another short-year return covering the period from September 1, 1987 to December 31, 1987 and must include in its gross income for that period the related person insurance income attributable to that period.

(5) Effect of election: taxation under section 882; alternative minimum tax; dividends received deduction; pre-1987 deficits in earnings and profits; and net operating losses. If a foreign corporation makes an election under paragraph (c) of this section, all income that is actually effectively connected with the conduct of a trade or business in the United States (as determined under sections 864(c) and 842) and all related person insurance income that is not effectively connected with the conduct of a trade or business within the United States but is treated as if it were effectively connected by virtue of the election under this paragraph (c) of this section will be taxable under section 882. The branch profits tax imposed by section 884 and the tax imposed on interest described in section 884(f) will apply to an electing corporation to the same extent and in the same manner that those taxes would have applied if the corporation had not made the election. Thus, the exclusion from the branch profits tax contained in section 884(d)(2)(D) (relating to income treated as effectively connected under section 953(c)(3)(C)) does not apply to income which is actually effectively connected with the conduct of a trade or business within the United States under sections 864(c) and 842. Further, a controlled foreign corporation that makes the election under section 953(c)(3)(C) shall continue to be treated as a controlled foreign corporation for purposes of section 864(c)(4)(D)(ii). Thus, related person insurance income that is treated as income effectively connected with the conduct of a United States trade or business shall not be subject to the branch profits tax under section 884 solely by virtue of making the election under section 953(c)(3)(C). But see section 842(b) with respect to the minimum effectively connected net investment income of a foreign corporation conducting an insurance business within the United States. Related person insurance income that is treated as if it were effectively connected with the conduct of a United States trade or business is subject to the alternative minimum tax provisions of sections 55 and 56 of the Code. For purposes of section 245 (dividends from certain foreign corporations), related person insurance income that is treated as if it were effectively connected by virtue of an election under paragraph (c)(3) of this section shall be treated as effectively connected for purposes of determining post- 1986 undistributed U.S. earnings under section 245(a)(5). Net operating loss deductions and deficits in earnings and profits of a corporation making the election under paragraph (c)(3) of this section that would be carried over from, or incurred in, taxable years beginning before January 1, 1986 cannot be carried over to, or used in, taxable years beginning after December 31, 1986.

(6) Exemption from tax imposed by section 4371. The tax imposed by section 4371 (relating to policies issued or reinsured by foreign insurers) shall not apply to premiums that are subject to the election under paragraph (c) of this section to treat related person insurance income which is not otherwise effectively connected income under section 864(c) as if it were effectively connected with the conduct of a trade or business within the United States. The exemption from the tax imposed by section 4371 begins after the later of the date of acceptance of the election or the first day of the first taxable year for which the election is made. An election is accepted on the date when the closing agreement has been executed by the taxpayer and the Commissioner. A copy of the election statement that has been stamped as accepted by the Commissioner will serve to place others on notice of the exemption. If an election has an effective date prior to the date on which the election is accepted, any excise taxes that have been paid on any related person insurance income received prior to the acceptance of the election may be refunded to the person who remitted the taxes. See also section 4373, which exempts from the excise tax under section 4371 income which is effectively connected with the conduct of a trade or business within the United States.

(7) Procedure for making election under section 953(c)(3)(C). (i) In general. In order to make a valid election to treat related person insurance income as income effectively connected with the conduct of a trade or business in the United States, a foreign corporation must provide the Internal Revenue Service with a signed election statement, a signed closing agreement, and a letter of credit.

(ii) When election must be made. In order for the election to be effective for a taxable year, an election statement must be filed on or before the due date of the electing corporation's tax return reporting the related person insurance income earned during the taxable year.

(iii) Election. An election is made by mailing an original and one copy of an election statement to the Internal Revenue Service, Assistant Commissioner (International), IN:C:C:51, 950 L'Enfant Plaza South, SW Washington, DC 20024. The statement must be signed under penalty of perjury by a responsible corporate officer, within the meaning of section 6062, stating that the statement and accompanying documents are true and complete to the best of the officer's knowledge and belief. A copy of the accepted election statement must be attached to the first tax return of the electing corporation that includes related person insurance income to which the election under paragraph (c) of this section applies. The election statement must be made in the following (or substantially similar) form:

FOREIGN CAPTIVE INSURANCE

Company Election Under Section 953(c)(3)(C)

(1) __________ (Name, address, tax identification number [a number will automatically be assigned to those corporations not already having a number], and place of incorporation of the corporation) hereby elects under section 953(c)(3)(C) to treat its related person insurance income, as defined in section 953(c)(2), that is not actually effectively connected with the conduct of a trade or business in the United States under sections 864 or 842, as income effectively connected with the conduct of a trade or business within the United States.

(2) (Name of corporation) waives all benefits (other than with respect to section 884) with respect to related person insurance income under any treaty, including any friendship, commerce and navigation treaty, between the United States and any foreign country.

(3) (Name of corporation) agrees to timely file a United States income tax return and timely remit the income tax due on its related person insurance income, determined as if all such income were effectively connected with the conduct of a United States trade or business.

(4) Attached to this election statement is a complete list of all United States shareholders, as defined in section 953(c)(1)(A) and § 1.953-3(b)(2), which own stock in (Name of corporation) as of a date no more than 90 days prior to the date this election statement is mailed. The list includes the name, address, tax identification number, and ownership percentage for each such United States shareholder. (Name of corporation) agrees to file an updated list containing the information prescribed in this paragraph determined as of the last day of each taxable year. This updated list will be filed with the United States tax return reporting the related person insurance income earned by the corporation for each taxable year the election is in effect. [Attach listing].

(5) (Name of corporation) agrees to file a complete list of all United States persons (whether or not listed as United States persons who own stock in (Name of corporation)) whose risks are insured or reinsured by (Name of corporation), or who have purchased annuities or will receive annuity payments from (Name of corporation) as of the last day of each taxable year. The list will include the name, address, and tax identification number of each United States person so insured or reinsured. The list will be filed with the United States tax return reporting related person insurance income earned by (Name of corporation) for each taxable year the election is in effect.

(6) (Name of corporation) agrees to provide security for the payment of tax due on its related person insurance income. The security will be in an amount and upon the terms as stated in a closing agreement to be executed between the Internal Revenue Service and (Name of corporation).

(7) Attached is the power of attorney, Form 2848, of the person authorized to negotiate a closing agreement on behalf of (Name of corporation).

The undersigned declares under penalty of perjury that the statements contained in this election and accompanying documents are true and complete to the best of his/her knowledge and belief.

__________ ____________________

Date (Title)
(Name of Corporation)

(8) Closing agreement. After the receipt of the election statement, the controlled foreign corporation's designated representative will be provided with a model closing agreement and further instructions on completing the election process.

(9) Letter of credit. (i) In general. A foreign corporation that makes the election under paragraph (c)(3) of this section must provide a letter of credit issued in favor of the Internal Revenue Service. The letter of credit must generally be in an amount equal to 10 percent of the gross premium income from insuring or reinsuring the risks of United States shareholders and persons related to such shareholders in the 12 month period preceding the filing of the election. In the case of a corporation that did not receive gross premiums from United States shareholders or related persons in the previous 12 month period, the amount of the letter of credit required will be based on an estimate of the projected gross premiums of the corporation for the first year of the election. For purposes of paragraph (c)(9)(i) and (ii) of this section, the term "gross premiums" means the amount of gross premiums written on insurance contracts during the taxable year without adjustment for return premiums, premiums for reinsurance, premiums and other consideration arising out of indemnity reinsurance, or increases in unearned premiums. In all cases, a minimum amount of $75,000 will be required and the maximum amount required will not exceed $10,000,000. The foreign corporation must provide, under penalty of perjury, evidence to support the computation of the amount of the letter of credit it proposes as security under paragraph (c) of this section.

(ii) Changes in the amount of the letter of credit. Once the amount of the letter of credit has been determined for a taxable year, no change in the amount of the letter of credit is required unless in a subsequent taxable year there is an increase in gross premiums to more than 120 percent of the amount of the gross premiums used to compute the letter of credit (the "base year gross premiums"). If for any taxable year, the foreign corporation has gross premium income constituting more than 120 percent of the base year gross premiums, the amount of the letter of credit must be increased within 30 days of the filing of the tax return for that year. If a letter of credit in a greater amount must be provided, it must be in the amount of 10 percent of the gross premiums for the taxable year. No change in the letter of credit is required if gross premiums for a taxable year decline from the base year premium level; however, the taxpayer may submit a new letter of credit equal to 10 percent of the gross premiums for the taxable year in replacement of the outstanding letter of credit.

(10) Underpayment of tax due. If it is determined that there is a deficiency or underpayment of any tax due pursuant to the election, the Commissioner will issue a notice of deficiency or notice and demand in the amount of the deficiency or underpayment determined, plus any applicable interest and penalties. Assessment and collection of any deficiency or underpayment of tax will be as provided by the Internal Revenue Code and payment of all additional amounts due will be in accordance with the terms specified in any statement of notice and demand sent to the foreign corporation. If the tax is not paid in accordance with the terms of the statement of notice and demand, collection of the deficiency will be made by resorting to the letter of credit before any levy or proceeding in court for collection is instituted against the controlled foreign corporation or its

shareholders. However, nothing in paragraph (c)(3)(10) of this section shall be construed to preclude the Secretary's ability to use the jeopardy assessment procedures of sections 6861 through 6864 of the Code. If the letter of credit is drawn upon, it must be reinstated to the level as provided for under the closing agreement within 60 days after the date drawn upon.

(11) Termination or revocation of election. (i) Termination. If a controlled foreign corporation that made the election to treat its related person insurance income as effectively connected income for any taxable year becomes a disqualified corporation, as defined in paragraph (c)(2) of this section, in any subsequent taxable year, the election will not apply to any taxable year beginning after the taxable year in which the corporation becomes a disqualified corporation. If a foreign corporation's election is terminated by virtue of the corporation's becoming a disqualified corporation, the corporation will be barred from making another election under section 953(c)(3)(C).

(ii) Revocation with consent. The election to treat related person insurance income as effectively connected with the conduct of a trade or business within the United States can be revoked only with the consent of the Commissioner. In order to obtain a revocation, the taxpayer must request a ruling from the Associate Chief Counsel (International). To determine whether a request for revocation should be granted, consideration will be given to all the facts and circumstances. Among the circumstances that will be considered as favorable to a determination to allow revocation of an election will be whether the foreign corporation would qualify for the de minimis ownership exception of paragraph (a)(1) of this section or the de minimis related person insurance exception of paragraph (b)(2) of this section. If after having made an election under paragraph (c) of this section the foreign corporation makes an election under section 953(d) (relating to the election of a foreign insurance company to be treated as a domestic corporation), the election under this paragraph shall be treated as revoked with the Commissioner's consent beginning with the period that the election under section 953(d) is in effect. The revocation of an election is effective for the taxable year indicated by the Commissioner in the consent. Any foreign corporation that receives the consent of the Commissioner to revoke an election may not make a subsequent election for a period of four years from the end of the first taxable year in which the election is not in effect.

(iii) Unilateral revocation by Commissioner. If an electing corporation fails to timely file a return, fails to pay the tax due with respect to related person insurance income that it elects to have taxed as effectively connected income, fails to make the estimated tax payments required by section 6655, or fails to maintain or provide a letter of credit in the appropriate amount, the election may be revoked by the Commissioner for the taxable year in which the electing corporation fails to file a return, pay the tax due, pay the estimated tax, or fails to maintain or provide the appropriate letter of credit or in any subsequent taxable year. If the revocation is made in a taxable year subsequent to the taxable year in which the failure occurs, the Commissioner can make the revocation effective retroactively to the taxable year in which the failure occurred or any subsequent taxable year. Revocation of the election may cause the United States shareholders of the foreign corporation to be liable for subpart F inclusions and make the foreign corporation liable for the unpaid excise tax on premiums under section 4371 for insurance or reinsurance issued by the foreign corporation. Funds obtained under the letter of credit will be applied to the taxes due from the foreign corporation, its shareholders, or both, with respect to related person insurance income. Any foreign corporation (or successor corporation, as defined in paragraph (c)(2)(ii) of this section) the election of which is unilaterally revoked by the Commissioner shall be barred from making another election under section 953(c)(3)(C).

§ 1.954-0 Introduction.

(a) Effective dates. *(1) Final regulations.* (i) In general. Except as otherwise specifically provided, the provisions of §§ 1.954-1 and 1.954-2 apply to taxable years of a controlled foreign corporation beginning after November 6, 1995. If any of the rules described in §§ 1.954-1 and 1.954-2 are inconsistent with provisions of other regulations under subpart F, these final regulations are intended to apply instead of such other regulations.

(ii) Election to apply final regulations retroactively. (A) Scope of election. An election may be made to apply the final regulations retroactively with respect to any taxable year of the controlled foreign corporation beginning on or after January 1, 1987. If such an election is made, these final regulations must be applied in their entirety for such taxable year and all subsequent taxable years. All references to section 11 in the final regulations shall be deemed to include section 15, where applicable.

(B) Manner of making election. An election under this paragraph (a)(1)(ii) is binding on all United States shareholders of the controlled foreign corporation and must be made—

(1) By the controlling United States shareholders, as defined in § 1.964-1(c)(5), by attaching a statement to such effect with their original or amended income tax returns for the taxable year of such United States shareholders in which or with which the taxable year of the CFC ends, and including any additional information required by applicable administrative pronouncements, or

(2) In such other manner as may be prescribed in applicable administrative pronouncements.

(C) Time for making election. An election may be made under this paragraph (a)(1)(ii) with respect to a taxable year of the controlled foreign corporation beginning on or after January 1, 1987 only if the time for filing a return or claim for refund has not expired for the taxable year of any United States shareholder of the controlled foreign corporation in which or with which such taxable year of the controlled foreign corporation ends.

(D) Revocation of election. An election made under this paragraph (a)(1)(ii) may not be revoked.

(2) Temporary regulations. The provisions of §§ 4.954-1 and 4.954-2 of this chapter apply to taxable years of a controlled foreign corporation beginning after December 31, 1986 and on or before November 6, 1995. However, the provisions of § 4.954-2(b)(6) of this chapter continue to apply. For transactions entered into on or before October 9, 1995, taxpayers may rely on Notice 89-90, 1989-2 C.B. 407, in applying the temporary regulations.

(3) §§ 1.954A-1 and 1.954A-2. The provisions of §§ 1.954A-1 and 1.954A-2 (as contained in 26 CFR part 1 edition revised April 1, 1995) apply to taxable years of a controlled foreign corporation beginning before January 1, 1987. All references therein to sections of the Code are to the Internal Revenue Code of 1954 prior to the amendments made by the Tax Reform Act of 1986.

(b) Outline of §§ 1.954-0, 1.954-1 and 1.954-2.

(4) Inadvertent error.

(5) Anti-abuse rule.

(iii) Inventory and similar property.

(A) Definition.

(B) Hedging transactions.

(iv) Regular dealer.

(v) Dealer property.

(A) Definition.

(B) Securities dealers.

(C) Hedging transactions.

(vi) Examples.

(vii) Debt instrument.

(b) Dividends, interest, rents, royalties and annuities.

(1) In general.

(2) Exclusion of certain export financing interest.

(i) In general.

(ii) Exceptions.

(iii) Conduct of a banking business.

(iv) Examples.

(3) Treatment of tax-exempt interest. [Reserved]

(4) Exclusion of dividends or interest from related persons.

(i) In general.

(A) Corporate payor.

(B) Payment by a partnership.

(ii) Exceptions.

(A) Dividends.

(B) Interest paid out of adjusted foreign base company income or insurance income.

(1) In general.

(2) Rule for corporations that are both recipients and payors of interest.

(C) Coordination with sections 864(d) and 881(c).

(iii) Trade or business requirement.

(iv) Substantial assets test.

(v) Valuation of assets.

(vi) Location of tangible property.

(A) In general.

(B) Exception.

(vii) Location of intangible property.

(A) In general.

(B) Exception for property located in part in the payor's country of incorporation.

(viii) Location of inventory and dealer property.

(A) In general.

(B) Inventory and dealer property located in part in the payor's country of incorporation.

(ix) Location of debt instruments.

(x) Treatment of certain stock interests.

(xi) Treatment of banks and insurance companies. [Reserved]

(5) Exclusion of rents and royalties derived from related persons.

(i) In general.

(A) Corporate payor.

(B) Payment by a partnership.

(ii) Exceptions.

(A) Rents or royalties paid out of adjusted foreign base company income or insurance income.

(B) Property used in part in the controlled foreign corporation's country of incorporation.

(6) Exclusion of rents and royalties derived in the active conduct of a trade or business.

(c) Excluded rents.

(1) Active conduct of a trade or business.

(2) Special rules.

(i) Adding substantial value.

(ii) Substantiality of foreign organization.

(iii) Active leasing expenses.

(iv) Adjusted leasing profit.

(3) Examples.

(d) Excluded royalties.

(1) Active conduct of a trade or business.

(2) Special rules.

(i) Adding substantial value.

(ii) Substantiality of foreign organization.

(iii) Active licensing expenses.

(iv) Adjusted licensing profit.

(3) Examples.

(e) Certain property transactions.

(1) In general.

(i) Inclusions.

(ii) Exceptions.

(iii) Treatment of losses.

(iv) Dual character property.

(2) Property that gives rise to certain income.

(i) In general.

(ii) Gain or loss from the disposition of a debt instrument.

(3) Property that does not give rise to income.

(f) Commodities transactions.

(1) In general.

(i) Inclusion in foreign personal holding company income.

(ii) Exception.

(iii) Treatment of losses.

(2) Definitions.

(i) Commodity.

(ii) Commodities transaction.

(iii) Qualified active sale.

(A) In general.

(B) Active conduct of a commodities business.

(C) Substantially all.

(D) Activities of employees of a related entity.

(iv) Qualified hedging transaction entered into prior to January 31, 2003.

(A) In general.

(B) Exception.

(C) Effective date.

(v) Qualified hedging transaction entered into on or after January 31, 2003.

(A) In general.

(B) Exception.
(C) Examples.
(D) Effective date.
(vi) Financial institutions not a producer, etc.
(g) Foreign currency gain or loss.
(1) Scope and purpose.
(2) In general.
(i) Inclusion.
(ii) Exclusion for business needs.
(A) General rule.
(B) Business needs.
(C) Regular dealers.
(1) General rule.
(2) Certain interest-bearing liabilities treated as dealer property.
(i) In general.
(ii) Failure to identify certain liabilities.
(iii) Effective date.
(D) Example.
(iii) Special rule for foreign currency gain or loss from an interest-bearing liability.
(3) Election to characterize foreign currency gain or loss that arises from a specific category of subpart F income as gain or loss in that category.
(i) In general.
(ii) Time and manner of election.
(iii) Revocation of election.
(iv) Example.
(4) Election to treat all foreign currency gains or losses as foreign personal holding company income.
(i) In general.
(ii) Time and manner of election.
(iii) Revocation of election.
(5) Gains and losses not subject to this paragraph.
(i) Capital gains and losses.
(ii) Income not subject to section 988.
(iii) Qualified business units using the dollar approximate separate transactions method.
(iv) Gain or loss allocated under § 1.861-9. [Reserved]
(h) Income equivalent to interest.
(1) In general.
(i) Inclusion in foreign personal holding company income.
(ii) Exceptions.
(A) Liability hedging transactions.
(B) Interest.
(2) Definition of income equivalent to interest.
(i) In general.
(ii) Income from the sale of property.
(3) Notional principal contracts.
(i) In general.
(ii) Regular dealers.
(4) Income equivalent to interest from factoring.
(i) General rule.
(ii) Exceptions.
(iii) Factored receivable.
(iv) Examples.
(5) Receivables arising from performance of services.
(6) Examples.

T.D. 8618, 9/6/95, amend T.D. 8767, 3/23/98, T.D. 9039, 1/30/2003.

PAR. 3. Section 1.954-0 (b) is amended as follows:

1. The entry for § 1.954-1(c)(1)(i) is revised.

2. Entries for § 1.954-1(c)(1)(i)(A) through (c)(1)(i)(E) are added.

3. An entry for § 1.954-2(a)(5) is added.

4. An entry for § 1.954-2(a)(6) is added.

The revision and additions read as follows:

Proposed § 1.954-0 Introduction. [*For Preamble, see ¶ 151,985*]

* * * * *

(b) * * *

§ 1.954-1 Foreign Base Company Income

* * * * *

(c) * * *
(1) * * *
(i) Deductions.
(A) Deductions against gross foreign base company income.
(B) Special rule for deductible payments to certain non-fiscally transparent entities.
(C) Limitations.
(D) Example.
(E) Effective date.

* * * * *

§ 1.954-2 Foreign Personal Holding Company Income

(a) * * *
(5) Special rules applicable to distributive share of partnership income.
(i) Application of related person exceptions where payment reduces foreign tax of payor.
(ii) Certain other exceptions applicable to foreign personal holding company income. [Reserved]
(iii) Effective date.
(6) Special rules applicable to exceptions from foreign personal holding company income treatment in circumstances involving hybrid branches.
(i) In general.
(ii) Exception where no tax reduction or tax disparity.
(iii) Effective date.

* * * * *

§ 4.954-0 Introduction.

(a) Effective date. *(1)* The provisions of §§ 4.954-1 and 4.954-2 apply to taxable years of a controlled foreign corporation beginning after December 31, 1986. Consequently, any gain or loss (including foreign currency gain or loss as defined in section 988(b)) recognized during such taxable years of a controlled foreign corporation is subject to these provisions. For further guidance, see § 1.954-0(a) of this chapter.

(2) The provisions of §§ 1.954A-1 and 1.954A-2 apply to taxable years of a controlled foreign corporation beginning before January 1, 1987. All references therein to sections of the Code are to the Internal Revenue Code of 1954 prior to the amendments made by the Tax Reform Act of 1986.

(b) Outline of regulation provisions for sections 954(b)(3), 954(b)(4), 954(b)(5) and 954(c) for taxable years of a controlled foreign corporation beginning after December 31, 1986.

§ 4.954-0 Introduction.

(a) Effective dates.

(b) Outline.

§ 4.954-1 Foreign base company income.

(a) In general.

(1) Purpose and scope.

(2) Definition of gross foreign base company income.

(3) Definition of adjusted gross foreign base company income.

(4) Definition of net foreign base company income.

(5) Definition of adjusted net foreign base company income.

(6) Insurance income definitions.

(7) Additional items of adjusted net foreign base company income or adjusted net insurance income by reason of section 952(c).

(8) Illustration.

(b) Computation of adjusted gross foreign base company income and adjusted gross insurance income.

(1) De minimus rule and full inclusion rule.

(i) In general.

(ii) Five percent de minimus test.

(iii) Seventy percent full inclusion test.

(2) Character of items of adjusted gross foreign base company income.

(3) Coordination with section 952(c).

(4) Anti-abuse rule.

(i) In general.

(ii) Presumption.

(iii) Definition of related person.

(iv) Illustration.

(5) Illustration.

(c) Computation of net foreign base company income.

(d) Computation of adjusted net foreign base company income or adjusted net insurance income.

(1) Application of high tax exception.

(2) Effective rate at which taxes are imposed.

(3) Taxes paid or accrued with respect to an item of income.

(i) Income other than foreign personal holding company income.

(ii) Foreign personal holding company income.

(4) Definition of an item of income.

(i) Income other than foreign personal holding company income.

(ii) Foreign personal holding company income.

(A) In general.

(B) Consistency rule.

(5) Procedure.

(6) Illustrations.

(e) Character of an item of income.

(1) Substance of the transaction.

(2) Separable character.

(3) Predominant character.

(4) Coordination of categories of gross foreign base company income or gross insurance income.

§ 4.954-2 Foreign Personal Holding Company Income.

(a) Computation of foreign personal holding company income.

(1) In general.

(2) Coordination of overlapping definitions.

(3) Changes in use or purpose with which property is held.

(i) In general.

(ii) Illustrations.

(4) Definitions.

(i) Interest.

(ii) Inventory and similar property.

(iii) Regular dealer.

(iv) Dealer property.

(v) Debt instrument.

(b) Dividends, etc.

(1) In general.

(2) Exclusion of certain export financing.

(i) In general.

(ii) Conduct of a banking business.

(iii) Illustration.

(3) Exclusion of dividends and interest from related persons.

(i) Excluded dividends and interest.

(ii) Interest paid out of adjusted foreign base company income or insurance income.

(iii) Dividends paid out of prior years' earnings.

(iv) Fifty percent substantial assets test.

(v) Value of assets.

(vi) Location of tangible property used in a trade or business.

(A) In general.

(B) Exception.

(vii) Location of intangible property used in a trade or business.

(A) In general.

(B) Property located in part in the payor's country of incorporation and in part in other countries.

(viii) Location of property held for sale to customers.

(A) In general.

(B) Inventory located in part in the payor's country of incorporation and in part in other countries.

(ix) Location of debt instruments.

(x) Treatment of certain stock interests.

(xi) Determination of period during which property is used in a trade or business.

(xii) Treatment of banks and insurance companies [Reserved]

(4) Exclusion of rents and royalties derived from related persons.

(i) In general.

(ii) Rents or royalties paid out of adjusted foreign base company income or insurance income.

(5) Exclusion of rents and royalties derived in the active conduct of a trade or business.

(6) Treatment of tax exempt interest.

(c) Excluded rents.

(1) Trade or business cases.

(2) Special rules.

(i) Adding substantial value.

(ii) Substantiality of foreign organization.

(iii) Definition of active leasing expense.

(iv) Adjusted leasing profits.

(3) Illustrations.

(d) Excluded royalties.

(1) Trade or business cases.

(2) Special rules.

(i) Adding substantial value.

(ii) Substantiality of foreign organization.

(iii) Definition of active licensing expense.

(iv) Definition of adjusted licensing profit.

(3) Illustrations.

(e) Certain property transactions.

(1) In general.

(i) Inclusion of FPHC income.

(ii) Dual character property.

(2) Property that gives rise to certain income.

(i) In general.

(ii) Exception.

(3) Property that does not give rise to income.

(4) Classification of gain or loss from the disposition of a debt instrument or on a deferred payment sale.

(i) Gain.

(ii) Loss.

(5) Classification of options and other rights to acquire or transfer property.

(6) Classification of certain interests in pass-through entities. [Reserved]

(f) Commodities transactions.

(1) In general.

(2) Definitions.

(i) Commodity.

(ii) Commodities transaction.

(3) Definition of the term "qualified active sales".

(i) In general.

(ii) Sale of commodities.

(iii) Active conduct of a commodities business.

(iv) Definition of the term "substantially all."

(4) Definition of the term "qualified hedging transaction".

(g) Foreign currency gain.

(1) In general.

(2) Exceptions.

(i) Qualified business units using the dollar approximate separate transactions method.

(ii) Tracing to exclude foreign currency gain or loss from qualified business and hedging transactions.

(iii) Election out of tracing.

(3) Definition of the term "qualified business transaction".

(i) In general.

(ii) Specific section 988 transactions attributable to the sale of goods or services.

(A) Acquisition of debt instruments.

(B) Becoming the obligor under debt instruments.

(C) Accrual of any item of gross income.

(D) Accrual of any item of expense.

(E) Entering into forward contracts, futures contracts, options, and similar instruments.

(F) Disposition of nonfunctional currency.

(4) Definition of the term "qualified hedging transaction".

(i) In general.

(ii) Change in purpose of hedging transaction.

(5) Election out of tracing.

(i) In general.

(ii) Exception.

(iii) Procedure.

(A) In general.

(B) Time and manner.

(C) Termination.

(h) Income equivalent to interest.

(1) In general.

(2) Illustrations.

(3) Income equivalent to interest from factoring.

(i) General rule.

(ii) Exceptions.

(iii) Factored receivable.

(iv) Illustrations.

(4) Determination of sales income.

(5) Receivables arising from performance of services.

T.D. 8216, 7/20/88, amend T.D. 8618, 9/6/95.

§ 1.954-1 Foreign base company income.

(a) In general. *(1) Purpose and scope.* Section 954 and §§ 1.954-1 and 1.954-2 provide rules for computing the foreign base company income of a controlled foreign corporation. Foreign base company income is included in the subpart F income of a controlled foreign corporation under the rules of section 952. Subpart F income is included in the gross income of a United States shareholder of a controlled foreign corporation under the rules of section 951 and thus is subject to current taxation under section 1, 11 or 55 of the Internal Revenue Code. The determination of whether a foreign corporation is a controlled foreign corporation, the subpart F income of which is included currently in the gross income of its United States shareholders, is made under the rules of section 957.

(2) Gross foreign base company income. The gross foreign base company income of a controlled foreign corporation consists of the following categories of gross income (determined after the application of section 952(b))—

(i) Foreign personal holding company income, as defined in section 954(c);

(ii) Foreign base company sales income, as defined in section 954(d);

(iii) Foreign base company services income, as defined in section 954(e);

(iv) Foreign base company shipping income, as defined in section 954(f); and

(v) Foreign base company oil related income, as defined in section 954(g).

(3) Adjusted gross foreign base company income. The term adjusted gross foreign base company income means the gross foreign base company income of a controlled foreign corporation as adjusted by the de minimis and full inclusion rules of paragraph (b) of this section.

(4) Net foreign base company income. The term net foreign base company income means the adjusted gross foreign base company income of a controlled foreign corporation reduced so as to take account of deductions (including taxes) properly allocable or apportionable to such income under the rules of section 954(b)(5) and paragraph (c) of this section.

(5) Adjusted net foreign base company income. The term adjusted net foreign base company income means the net foreign base company income of a controlled foreign corporation reduced, first, by any items of net foreign base company income excluded from subpart F income pursuant to section 952(c) and, second, by any items excluded from subpart F income pursuant to the high tax exception of section 954(b). See paragraph (d)(4)(ii) of this section. The term foreign base company income as used in the Internal Revenue Code and elsewhere in the Income Tax Regulations means adjusted net foreign base company income, unless otherwise provided.

(6) Insurance income. The term gross insurance income includes all gross income taken into account in determining insurance income under section 953. The term adjusted gross insurance income means gross insurance income as adjusted by the de minimis and full inclusion rules of paragraph (b) of this section. The term net insurance income means adjusted gross insurance income reduced under section 953 so as to take into account deductions (including taxes) properly allocable or apportionable to such income. The term adjusted net insurance income means net insurance income reduced by any items of net insurance income that are excluded from subpart F income pursuant to section 952(b) or pursuant to the high tax exception of section 954(b). The term insurance income as used in subpart F of the Internal Revenue Code and in the regulations under that subpart means adjusted net insurance income, unless otherwise provided.

(7) Additional items of adjusted net foreign base company income or adjusted net insurance income by reason of section 952(c). Earnings and profits of the controlled foreign corporation that are recharacterized as foreign base company income or insurance income under section 952(c) are items of adjusted net foreign base company income or adjusted net insurance income, respectively. Amounts subject to recharacterization under section 952(c) are determined after adjusted net foreign base company income and adjusted net insurance income are otherwise determined under subpart F and are not again subject to any exceptions or special rules that would affect the amount of subpart F income. Thus, for example, items of gross foreign base company income or gross insurance income that are excluded from adjusted gross foreign base company income or adjusted gross insurance income because the de minimis test is met are subject to recharacterization under section 952(c). Further, the de minimis and full inclusion tests of paragraph (b) of this section, and the high tax exception of paragraph (d) of this section, for example, do not apply to such amounts.

(b) Computation of adjusted gross foreign base company income and adjusted gross insurance income. *(1) De minimis and full inclusion tests.* (i) De minimis test. (A) In general. Except as provided in paragraph (b)(1)(i)(C) of this section, adjusted gross foreign base company income and adjusted gross insurance income are equal to zero if the sum of the gross foreign base company income and the gross insurance income of a controlled foreign corporation is less than the lesser of—

(1) 5 percent of gross income; or

(2) $1,000,000.

(B) Currency translation. Controlled foreign corporations having a functional currency other than the United States dollar shall translate the $1,000,000 threshold using the exchange rate provided under section 989(b)(3) for amounts included in income under section 951(a).

(C) Coordination with sections 864(d) and 881(c). Adjusted gross foreign base company income or adjusted gross insurance income of a controlled foreign corporation always includes income from trade or service receivables described in section 864(d)(1) or (6), and portfolio interest described in section 881(c), even if the de minimis test of this paragraph (b)(1)(i) is otherwise satisfied.

(ii) Seventy percent full inclusion test. Except as provided in section 953, adjusted gross foreign base company income consists of all gross income of the controlled foreign corporation other than gross insurance income and amounts described in section 952(b), and adjusted gross insurance income consists of all gross insurance income other than amounts described in section 952(b), if the sum of the gross foreign base company income and the gross insurance income for the taxable year exceeds 70 percent of gross income. See paragraph (d)(6) of this section, under which certain items of full inclusion foreign base company income may nevertheless be excluded from subpart F income.

(2) Character of gross income included in adjusted gross foreign base company income. The gross income included in the adjusted gross foreign base company income of a controlled foreign corporation generally retains its character as foreign personal holding company income, foreign base company sales income, foreign base company services income, foreign base company shipping income, or foreign base company oil related income. However, gross income included in adjusted gross foreign base company income because the full inclusion test of paragraph (b)(1)(ii) of this section is met is termed full inclusion foreign base company income, and constitutes a separate category of adjusted gross foreign base company income for purposes of allocating and apportioning deductions under paragraph (c) of this section.

(3) Coordination with section 952(c). Income that is included in subpart F income because the full inclusion test of paragraph (b)(1)(ii) of this section is met does not reduce amounts that, under section 952(c), are subject to recharacterization.

(4) Anti-abuse rule. (i) In general. For purposes of applying the de minimis test of paragraph (b)(1)(i) of this section, the income of two or more controlled foreign corporations shall be aggregated and treated as the income of a single corporation if a principal purpose for separately organizing, acquiring, or maintaining such multiple corporations is to prevent income from being treated as foreign base company

income or insurance income under the de minimis test. A purpose may be a principal purpose even though it is outweighed by other purposes (taken together or separately).

(ii) Presumption. Two or more controlled foreign corporations are presumed to have been organized, acquired or maintained to prevent income from being treated as foreign base company income or insurance income under the de minimis test of paragraph (b)(1)(i) of this section if the corporations are related persons, as defined in paragraph (b)(4)(iii) of this section, and the corporations are described in paragraph (b)(4)(ii)(A), (B), or (C) of this section. This presumption may be rebutted by proof to the contrary.

(A) The activities carried on by the controlled foreign corporations, or the assets used in those activities, are substantially the same activities that were previously carried on, or assets that were previously held, by a single controlled foreign corporation. Further, the United States shareholders of the controlled foreign corporations or related persons (as determined under paragraph (b)(4)(iii) of this section) are substantially the same as the United States shareholders of the one controlled foreign corporation in a prior taxable year. A presumption made in connection with the requirements of this paragraph (b)(4)(ii)(A) may be rebutted by proof that the activities carried on by each controlled foreign corporation would constitute a separate branch under the principles of § 1.367(a)-6T(g)(2) if carried on directly by a United States person.

(B) The controlled foreign corporations carry on a business, financial operation, or venture as partners directly or indirectly in a partnership (as defined in section 7701(a)(2) and § 301.7701-3 of this chapter) that is a related person (as defined in paragraph (b)(4)(iii) of this section) with respect to each such controlled foreign corporation.

(C) The activities carried on by the controlled foreign corporations would constitute a single branch operation under § 1.367(a)-6T(g)(2) if carried on directly by a United States person.

(iii) Related persons. For purposes of this paragraph (b), two or more persons are related persons if they are in a relationship described in section 267(b). In determining for purposes of this paragraph (b) whether two or more corporations are members of the same controlled group under section 267(b)(3), a person is considered to own stock owned directly by such person, stock owned with the application of section 1563(e)(1), and stock owned with the application of section 267(c). In determining for purposes of this paragraph (b) whether a corporation is related to a partnership under section 267(b)(10), a person is considered to own the partnership interest owned directly by such person and the partnership interest owned with the application of section 267(e)(3).

(iv) Example. The following example illustrates the application of this paragraph (b)(4).

Example. (i)

(1) USP is the sole United States shareholder of three controlled foreign corporations: CFC1, CFC2 and CFC3. The three controlled foreign corporations all have the same taxable year. The three controlled foreign corporations are partners in FP, a foreign entity classified as a partnership under section 7701(a)(2) and § 301.7701-3 of the regulations. For their current taxable years, each of the controlled foreign corporations derives all of its income other than foreign base company income from activities conducted through FP, and its foreign base company income from activities conducted both jointly through FP and separately without FP. Based on the facts in the table below, the foreign base company income derived by each controlled foreign corporation for its current taxable year, including income derived from FP, is less than five percent of the gross income of each controlled foreign corporation and is less than $1,000,000:

	CFC1	CFC2	CFC3
Gross income	$4,000,000	$8,000,000	$12,000,000
Five percent of gross income	200,000	400,000	600,000
Foreign base company income	199,000	398,000	597,000

(2) Thus, without the application of the anti-abuse rule of this paragraph (b)(4), each controlled foreign corporation would be treated as having no foreign base company income after the application of the de minimis test of section 954(b)(3)(A) and paragraph (b)(1)(i) of this section.

(ii) However, under these facts, the requirements of paragraph (b)(4)(i) of this section are met unless the presumption of paragraph (b)(4)(ii) of this section is successfully rebutted. The sum of the foreign base company income of the controlled foreign corporations is $1,194,000. Thus, the amount of gross foreign base company income of each controlled foreign corporation will not be reduced by reason of the de minimis rule of section 954(b)(3)(A) and this paragraph (b).

(c) Computation of net foreign base company income. *(1) General rule.* The net foreign base company income of a controlled foreign corporation (as defined in paragraph (a)(4) of this section) is computed under the rules of this paragraph (c)(1). The principles of § 1.904-5(k) shall apply where payments are made between controlled foreign corporations that are related persons (within the meaning of section 954(d)(3)). Consistent with these principles, only payments described in § 1.954-2(b)(4)(ii)(B)(2) may be offset as provided in § 1.904-5(k)(2).

(i) Deductions against gross foreign base company income. The net foreign base company income of a controlled foreign corporation is computed first by taking into account deductions in the following manner:

(A) First, the gross amount of each item of income described in paragraph (c)(1)(iii) of this section is determined.

(B) Second, any expenses definitely related to less than all gross income as a class shall be allocated and apportioned under the principles of sections 861, 864 and 904(d) to the gross income described in paragraph (c)(1)(i)(A) of this section.

(C) Third, foreign personal holding company income that is passive within the meaning of section 904 (determined before the application of the high-taxed income rule of § 1.904-4(c)) is reduced by related person interest expense allocable to passive income under § 1.904-5(c)(2); such interest must be further allocated and apportioned to items described in paragraph (c)(1)(iii)(B) of this section.

(D) Fourth, the amount of each item of income described in paragraph (c)(1)(iii) of this section is reduced by other expenses allocable and apportionable to such income under the principles of sections 861, 864 and 904(d).

(ii) Losses reduce subpart F income by operation of earnings and profits limitation. Except as otherwise provided in § 1.954-2(g)(4), if after applying the rules of paragraph (c)(1)(i) of this section, the amount remaining in any category of foreign base company income or foreign personal holding company income is less than zero, the loss in that category may not reduce any other category of foreign base company income or foreign personal holding company income except by operation of the earnings and profits limitation of section 952(c)(1).

(iii) Items of income. (A) Income other than passive foreign personal holding company income. A single item of income (other than foreign personal holding company income that is passive) is the aggregate amount from all transactions that falls within a single separate category (as defined in § 1.904-5(a)(1)), and either—

(1) Falls within a single category of foreign personal holding company income as—

(i) Dividends, interest, rents, royalties and annuities;

(ii) Gain from certain property transactions;

(iii) Gain from commodities transactions;

(iv) Foreign currency gain; or

(v) Income equivalent to interest; or

(2) Falls within a single category of foreign base company income, other than foreign personal holding company income, as—

(i) Foreign base company sales income;

(ii) Foreign base company services income;

(iii) Foreign base company shipping income;

(iv) Foreign base company oil related income; or

(v) Full inclusion foreign base company income.

(B) Passive foreign personal holding company income. A single item of foreign personal holding company income that is passive is an amount of income that falls within a single group of passive income under the grouping rules of § 1.904-4(c)(3), (4) and (5) and a single category of foreign personal holding company income described in paragraphs (c)(1)(iii)(A)(1)(i) through (v).

(2) Computation of net foreign base company income derived from same country insurance income. Deductions relating to foreign base company income attributable to the issuing (or reinsuring) of any insurance or annuity contract in connection with risks located in the country under the laws of which the controlled foreign corporation is created or organized shall be allocated and apportioned in accordance with the rules set forth in section 953.

(d) Computation of adjusted net foreign base company income or adjusted net insurance income. *(1) Application of high tax exception.* Adjusted net foreign base company income (or adjusted net insurance income) equals the net foreign base company income (or net insurance income) of a controlled foreign corporation, reduced by any net item of such income that qualifies for the high tax exception provided by section 954(b)(4) and this paragraph (d). Any item of income that is foreign base company oil related income, as defined in section 954(g), or portfolio interest, as described in section 881(c), does not qualify for the high tax exception. See paragraph (c)(1)(iii) of this section for the definition of the term item of income. For rules concerning the treatment for foreign tax credit purposes of amounts excluded from subpart F under section 954(b)(4), see § 1.904-4(c). A net item of income qualifies for the high tax exception only if—

(i) An election is made under section 954(b)(4) and paragraph (d)(5) of this section to exclude the income from the computation of subpart F income; and

(ii) It is established that the net item of income was subject to foreign income taxes imposed by a foreign country or countries at an effective rate that is greater than 90 percent of the maximum rate of tax specified in section 11 for the taxable year of the controlled foreign corporation.

(2) Effective rate at which taxes are imposed. The effective rate with respect to a net item of income shall be determined separately for each controlled foreign corporation in a chain of corporations through which a distribution is made. The effective rate at which taxes are imposed on a net item of income is—

(i) The United States dollar amount of foreign income taxes paid or accrued (or deemed paid or accrued) with respect to the net item of income, determined under paragraph (d)(3) of this section; divided by

(ii) The United States dollar amount of the net item of foreign base company income or insurance income, described in paragraph (c)(1)(iii) of this section, increased by the amount of foreign income taxes referred to in paragraph (d)(2)(i) of this section.

(3) Taxes paid or accrued with respect to an item of income. (i) Income other than passive foreign personal holding company income. The amount of foreign income taxes paid or accrued with respect to a net item of income (other than an item of foreign personal holding company income that is passive) for purposes of section 954(b)(4) and this paragraph (d) is the United States dollar amount of foreign income taxes that would be deemed paid under section 960 with respect to that item if that item were included in the gross income of a United States shareholder under section 951(a)(1)(A) (determined, in the case of a United States shareholder that is an individual, as if an election under section 962 has been made, whether or not such election is actually made). For this purpose, in accordance with the regulations under section 960, the amounts that would be deemed paid under section 960 shall be determined separately with respect to each controlled foreign corporation and without regard to the limitation applicable under section 904(a). The amount of foreign income taxes paid or accrued with respect to a net item of income, determined in the manner provided in this paragraph (d), will not be affected by a subsequent reduction in foreign income taxes attributable to a distribution to shareholders of all or part of such income.

(ii) Passive foreign personal holding company income. The amount of income taxes paid or accrued with respect to a net item of foreign personal holding company income that is passive for purposes of section 954(b)(4) and this paragraph (d) is the United States dollar amount of foreign income taxes that would be deemed paid under section 960 and that would be taken into account for purposes applying the provisions of § 1.904-4(c) with respect to that net item of income.

(4) Special rules. (i) Consistency rule. An election to exclude income from the computation of subpart F income for a taxable year must be made consistently with respect to all items of passive foreign personal holding company income eligible to be excluded for the taxable year. Thus, high-taxed passive foreign personal holding company income of a controlled foreign corporation must either be excluded in its entirety, or remain subject to subpart F in its entirety.

(ii) Coordination with earnings and profits limitation. If the amount of income included in subpart F income for the taxable year is reduced by the earnings and profits limitation of section 952(c)(1), the amount of income that is a net item of income, within the meaning of paragraph (c)(1)(iii) of this section, is determined after the application of the rules of section 952(c)(1).

(iii) Example. The following example illustrates the provisions of paragraph (d)(4)(ii) of this section. All of the taxes referred to in the following example are foreign income taxes. For simplicity, this example assumes that the amount of taxes that are taken into account as a deduction under section 954(b)(5) and the amount of the gross-up required under sections 960 and 78 are equal. Therefore, this example does not separately illustrate the deduction for taxes and gross-up.

Example. During its 1995 taxable year, CFC, a controlled foreign corporation, earns royalty income, net of taxes, of $100 that is foreign personal holding company income. CFC has no expenses associated with this royalty income. CFC pays $50 of foreign income taxes with respect to the royalty income. For 1995, CFC has current earnings and profits of $50. CFC's subpart F income, as determined prior to the application of this paragraph (d), exceeds its current earnings and profits. Thus, under paragraph (d)(4)(ii) of this section, the amount of CFC's only net item of income, the royalty income, will be limited to $50. The remaining $50 will be subject to recharacterization in a subsequent taxable year under section 952(c)(2). Because the amount of foreign income taxes paid with respect to this net item of income is $50, the effective rate of tax on the item, for purposes of this paragraph (d), is 50 percent ($50 of taxes/$50 net item + $50 of taxes). Accordingly, an election under paragraph (d)(5) of this section may be made to exclude the item of income from the computation of subpart F income.

(5) Procedure. An election made under the procedure provided by this paragraph (d)(5) is binding on all United States shareholders of the controlled foreign corporation and must be made—

(i) By the controlling United States shareholders, as defined in § 1.964-1(c)(5), by attaching a statement to such effect with their original or amended income tax returns, and including any additional information required by applicable administrative pronouncements; or

(ii) In such other manner as may be prescribed in applicable administrative pronouncements.

(6) Coordination of full inclusion and high tax exception rules. Notwithstanding paragraph (b)(1)(ii) of this section, full inclusion foreign base company income will be excluded from subpart F income if more than 90 percent of the adjusted gross foreign base company income and adjusted gross insurance company income of a controlled foreign corporation (determined without regard to the full inclusion test of paragraph (b)(1) of this section) is attributable to net amounts excluded from subpart F income pursuant to an election to have the high tax exception described in section 954(b)(4) and this paragraph (d) apply.

(7) Examples. (i) The following examples illustrate the rules of this paragraph (d). All of the taxes referred to in the following examples are foreign income taxes. For simplicity, these examples assume that the amount of taxes that are taken into account as a deduction under section 954(b)(5) and the amount of the gross-up required under sections 960 and 78 are equal. Therefore, these examples do not separately illustrate the deduction for taxes and gross-up. Except as otherwise stated, these examples assume there are no earnings, deficits, or foreign income taxes in the post-1986 pools of earnings and profits or foreign income taxes.

Example (1). (i) Items of income. During its 1995 taxable year, controlled foreign corporation CFC earns from outside its country of operation portfolio dividend income of $100 and interest income, net of taxes, of $100 (consisting of a gross payment of $150 reduced by a third-country withholding tax of $50). For purposes of illustration, assume that CFC incurs no expenses. None of the income is taxed in CFC's country of operation. The dividend income was not subject to third-country withholding taxes. Pursuant to the operation of section 904, the interest income is high withholding tax interest and the dividend income is passive income. Accordingly, pursuant to paragraph (c)(1)(iii) of this section, CFC has two net items of income—

(1) $100 of foreign personal holding company (FPHC)/passive income (the dividends); and

(2) $100 of FPHC/high withholding tax income (the interest).

(ii) Effective rates of tax. No foreign tax would be deemed paid under section 960 with respect to the net item of income described in paragraph (i)(1) of this Example 1. Therefore, the effective rate of foreign tax is 0, and the item may not be excluded from subpart F income under the rules of this paragraph (d). Foreign tax of $50 would be deemed paid under section 960 with respect to the net item of income described in paragraph (i)(2) of this Example 1. Therefore, the effective rate of foreign tax is 33 percent ($50 of creditable taxes paid, divided by $150, consisting of the net item of foreign base company income ($100) plus creditable taxes paid thereon ($50)). The highest rate of tax specified in section 11 for the 1995 taxable year is 35 percent. Accordingly, the net item of income described in paragraph (i)(2) of this Example 1 may be excluded from subpart F income if an election under paragraph (d)(5) of this section is made, since it is subject to foreign tax at an effective rate that is greater than 31.5 percent (90 percent of 35 percent). However, for purposes of section 904(d), it remains high withholding tax interest.

Example (2). (i) The facts are the same as in Example 1, except that CFC's country of operation imposes a tax of $50 with respect to CFC's dividend income (and thus CFC earns portfolio dividend income, net of taxes, of only $50). The interest income is still high withholding tax interest. The dividend income is still passive income (without regard to the possible applicability of the high tax exception of section 904(d)(2)). Accordingly, CFC has two items of income for purposes of this paragraph (d)—

(1) $50 of FPHC/passive income (net of the $50 foreign tax); and

(2) $100 of FPHC/high withholding tax interest income.

(ii) Each item is taxed at an effective rate greater than 31.5 percent. The net item of income described in paragraph (i)(1) of this Example 2: Foreign tax ($50) divided by sum ($100) of net item of income ($50) plus creditable tax thereon ($50) equals 50 percent. The net item of income described in paragraph (i)(2) of this Example 2: foreign tax ($50) divided by sum ($150) of income item ($100) plus creditable tax thereon ($50) equals 33 percent. Accordingly, an election may be made under paragraph (d)(5) of this section to exclude either or both of the net items of income described in paragraphs (i)(1) and (2) of this Example 2 from subpart F income. If no election is made the items would be included in the subpart F income of CFC.

Example (3). (i) The facts are the same as in Example 1, except that the $100 of portfolio dividend income is subject to a third-country withholding tax of $50, and the $150 of interest income is from sources within CFC's country of operation, is subject to a $10 income tax therein, and is not subject to a withholding tax. Although the interest income and the dividend income are both passive income, under paragraph (c)(1)(iii)(B) of this section they constitute separate items of income pursuant to the application of the grouping rules of § 1.904-4(c). Accordingly, CFC has two net items of income for purposes of this paragraph (d)—

(1) $50 (net of $50 tax) of FPHC/non-country of operation/greater than 15 percent withholding tax income; and

(2) $140 (net of $10 tax) of FPHC/country of operation income.

(ii) The item described in paragraph (i)(1) of this Example 3 is taxed at an effective rate greater than 31.5 percent, but Item 2 is not. The net item of income described in paragraph (i)(1) of this Example 3: foreign tax ($50) divided by sum ($100) of net item of income ($50) plus creditable tax thereon ($50) equals 50 percent. The net item of income described in paragraph (i)(2) of this Example 3: Foreign tax ($10) divided by sum ($150) of net item of income ($140) plus creditable tax thereon ($10) equals 6.67 percent. Therefore, an election may be made under paragraph (d)(5) of this section to exclude the net item of income described in paragraph (i)(1) of this Example 3 but not the net item of income described in paragraph (i)(2) of this Example 3 from subpart F income.

Example (4). The facts are the same as in Example 3, except that the $150 of interest income is subject to an income tax of $50 in CFC's country of operation. Accordingly, CFC's items of income are the same as in Example 3, but both items are taxed at an effective rate greater than 31.5 percent. The net item of income described in paragraph (i)(1) of Example 3: Foreign tax ($50) divided by sum ($100) of net item of income ($50) plus creditable tax thereon ($50) equals 50 percent. The net item of income described in paragraph (i)(2) of Example 3: foreign tax ($50) divided by sum ($150) of net item of income ($100) plus creditable tax thereon ($50) equals 33 percent. Pursuant to the consistency rule of paragraph (d)(4)(i) of this section, an election made by CFC's controlling United States shareholders must exclude from subpart F income both items of FPHC income under the high tax exception of section 954(b)(4) and this paragraph (d). The election may not be made only with respect to one item.

Example (5). The facts are the same as in Example 1, except that CFC earns $5 of portfolio dividend income and $150 of interest income. In addition, CFC earns $45 for performing consulting services within its country of operation for unrelated persons. CFC's gross foreign base company income for 1995 of $155 ($150 of gross interest income and $5 of portfolio dividend income) is greater than 70 percent of its gross income of $200. Therefore, under the full inclusion test of paragraph (b)(1)(ii) of this section, CFC's adjusted gross foreign base company income is $200, and under paragraph (b)(2) of this section, the $45 of consulting income is full inclusion foreign base company income. If CFC elects, under paragraph (d)(5) of this section, to exclude the interest income from subpart F income pursuant to the high tax exception, the $45 of full inclusion foreign base company income will be excluded from subpart F income under paragraph (d)(6) of this section because the $150 of gross interest income excluded under the high tax exception is more than 90 percent of CFC's adjusted gross foreign base company income of $155.

(ii) The following examples generally illustrate the application of paragraph (c) of this section and this paragraph (d). Example 1 illustrates the order of computations. Example 2 illustrates the computations required by sections 952 and 954 and this § 1.954-1 if the full inclusion test of paragraph (b)(1)(ii) of this section is met and the income is not excluded from subpart F income under section 952(b). Computations in these examples involving the operation of section 952(c) are included for purposes of illustration only and do not provide substantive rules concerning the operation of that section. For simplicity, these examples assume that the amount of taxes that are taken into account as a deduction under section 954(b)(5) and the amount of the gross-up required under sections 960 and 78 are equal. Therefore, these examples do not separately illustrate the deduction for taxes and gross-up.

Example (1). (i) Gross income. CFC, a controlled foreign corporation, has gross income of $1000 for the current taxable year. Of that $1000 of income, $100 is interest income that is included in the definition of foreign personal holding company income under section 954(c)(1)(A) and § 1.954-2(b)(1)(ii), is not income from a trade or service receivable described in section 864(d)(1) or (6), or portfolio interest described in section 881(c), and is not excluded from foreign personal holding company income under any provision of section 952(b) or section 954(c). Another $50 is foreign base company sales income under section 954(d). The remaining $850 of gross income is not included in the definition of foreign base company income or insurance income under sections 954(c), (d), (e), (f) or (g) or 953, and is foreign source general limitation income described in section 904(d)(1)(I).

(ii) Expenses. For the current taxable year, CFC has expenses of $500. This amount includes $8 of interest paid to a related person that is allocable to foreign personal holding company income under section 904, and $2 of other expense that is directly related to foreign personal holding company income. Another $20 of expense is directly related to foreign base company sales. The remaining $470 of expenses is allocable to general limitation income that is not foreign base company income or insurance income.

(iii) Earnings and losses. CFC has earnings and profits for the current taxable year of $500. In the prior taxable year, CFC had losses with respect to income other than gross foreign base company income or gross insurance income. By reason of the limitation provided under section 952(c)(1)(A), those losses reduced the subpart F income (consisting entirely of foreign source general limitation income) of CFC by $600 for the prior taxable year.

(iv) Taxes. Foreign income tax of $30 is considered imposed on the interest income under the rules of section 954(b)(4), this paragraph (d), and § 1.904-6. Foreign income tax of $14 is considered imposed on the foreign base company sales income under the rules of section 954(b)(4), paragraph (d) of this section, and § 1.904-6. Foreign income tax of $177 is considered imposed on the remaining foreign source general limitation income under the rules of section 954(b)(4), this paragraph (d), and § 1.904-6. For the taxable year of CFC, the maximum United States rate of taxation under section 11 is 35 percent.

(v) Conclusion. Based on these facts, if CFC elects to exclude all items of income subject to a high foreign tax under section 954(b)(4) and this paragraph (d), it will have $500 of subpart F income as defined in section 952(a) (consisting entirely of foreign source general limitation income) determined as follows:

Step 1—Determine gross income:

(1) Gross income $1000

Step 2—Determine gross foreign base company income and gross insurance income:

(2) Interest included in gross foreign personal holding company income under section 954(c) 100
(3) Gross foreign base company sales income under section 954(d) 50
(4) Total gross foreign base company income and gross insurance income as defined in section 954(c), (d), (e), (f) and (g) and 953 (line (2) plus line (3)) 150

Step 3—Compute adjusted gross foreign base company income and adjusted gross insurance income:

(5) Five percent of gross income (.05 × line (1)) ... 50
(6) Seventy percent of gross income (.70 × line (1)) 700
(7) Adjusted gross foreign base company income and adjusted gross insurance income after the application of the de minimis test of paragraph (b) (line (4), or zero if line (4) is less than the lesser of line (5) or $1,000,000) (if the amount on this line 7 is zero, proceed to step 8) 150
(8) Adjusted gross foreign base company income and adjusted gross insurance income after the application of the full inclusion test of paragraph (b) (line (4), or line (1) if line (4) is greater than line (6)) 150

Step 4—Compute net foreign base company income:

(9) Expenses directly related to adjusted gross foreign base company sales income 20
(10) Expenses (other than related person interest expense) directly related to adjusted gross foreign personal holding company income 2
(11) Related person interest expense allocable to adjusted gross foreign personal holding company income under section 904 8
(12) Net foreign personal holding company income after allocating deductions under section 954(b)(5) paragraph (c) of this section (line (2) reduced by lines (10) and (11)) 90
(13) Net foreign base company income after allocating deductions under section 954(b)(5) and paragraph (c) of this section (line (3) reduced by line (9)) .. 30
(14) Total net foreign base company income after allocating deductions under section 954(b)(5) and paragraph (c) of this section (line (12) plus line (13)) 120

Step 5—Compute net insurance income:

(15) Net insurance income under section 953 0

Step 6—Compute adjusted net foreign base company income:

(16) Foreign income tax imposed on net foreign personal holding company income (as determined under section 954(b)(4) and this paragraph (d)) 30
(17) Foreign income tax imposed on net foreign base company sales income (as determined under section 954(b)(4) and this paragraph (d)) 14
(18) Ninety percent of the maximum United States corporate tax rate 31.5%
(19) Effective rate of foreign income tax imposed on net foreign personal holding company income ($90 of interest) under section 954(b)(4) and this paragraph (d) (line (16) divided by line (12)) 33%
(20) Effective rate of foreign income tax imposed on $30 of net foreign base company sales income under section 954(b)(4) and this paragraph (d) (line (17) divided by line (13)) 47%
(21) Net foreign personal holding company income subject to a high foreign tax under section 954(b)(4) and this paragraph (d) (zero, or line (12) if line (19) is greater than line (18)) 90
(22) Net foreign base company sales income subject to a high foreign tax under section 954(b)(4) and this paragraph (d) (zero, or line (13) if line (20) is greater than line (18)) 30
(23) Adjusted net foreign base company income after applying section 954(b)(4) and this paragraph (d) (line (14), reduced by the sum of line (21) and line (22)) 0

Step 7—Compute adjusted net insurance income:

(24) Adjusted net insurance income 0

Step 8—Additions to or reduction of adjusted net foreign base company income by reason of section 952(c):

(25) Earnings and profits for the current year 500
(26) Amount subject to being recharacterized as subpart F company income under section 952(c)(2) (excess of line (25) over the sum of lines (23) and line (24)); if there is a deficit, then the limitation of section 952(c)(1) may apply for the current year 500
(27) Amount of reduction in subpart F income for prior taxable years by reason of the limitation of section 952(c)(1) 600
(28) Subpart F income as defined in section 952(a), assuming section 952(a)(3), (4), and (5) do not apply (the sum of line (23), line (24), and the lesser of line (26) or line (27)) 500
(29) Amount of prior year's deficit to be recharacterized as subpart F income in later years under section 952(c) (excess of line (27) over line (26)) 100

Example (2). (i) Gross income. CFC, a controlled foreign corporation, has gross income of $1000 for the current taxable year. Of that $1000 of income, $720 is interest income that is included in the definition of foreign personal holding company income under section 954(c)(1)(A) and § 1.954-2(b)(1)(ii), is not income from trade or service receivables described in section 864(d)(1) or (6), or portfolio interest described in section 881(c), and is not excluded from foreign personal holding company income under any provision of section 954(c) and § 1.954-2 or section 952(b). The remaining $280 is services income that is not included in the definition of foreign base company income or insurance income under sections 954(c), (d), (e), (f), or (g) or 953, and is foreign source general limitation income for purposes of section 904(d)(1)(I).

(ii) Expenses. For the current taxable year, CFC has expenses of $650. This amount includes $350 of interest paid to related persons that is allocable to foreign personal holding company income under section 904, and $50 of other expense that is directly related to foreign personal holding company income. The remaining $250 of expenses is allocable to services income other than foreign base company income or insurance income.

(iii) Earnings and losses. CFC has earnings and profits for the current taxable year of $350. In the prior taxable year, CFC had losses with respect to income other than foreign base company income or insurance income. By reason of the limitation provided under section 952(c)(1)(A), those losses reduced the subpart F income of CFC (consisting entirely of foreign source general limitation income) by $600 for the prior taxable year.

(iv) Taxes. Foreign income tax of $120 is considered imposed on the $720 of interest income under the rules of section 954(b)(4), paragraph (d) of this section, and § 1.904-6. Foreign income tax of $2 is considered imposed on the services income under the rules of section 954(b)(4), paragraph (d) of this section, and § 1.904-6. For the taxable year of CFC, the maximum United States rate of taxation under section 11 is 35 percent.

(v) Conclusion. Based on these facts, if CFC elects to exclude all items of income subject to a high foreign tax under section 954(b)(4) and this paragraph (d), it will have $350 of subpart F income as defined in section 952(a), determined as follows.

Step 1—Determine gross income:

(1) Gross income $1000

Step 2—Determine gross foreign base company income and gross insurance income:

(2) Gross foreign base company income and gross insurance income as defined in sections 954(c), (d), (e), (f) and (g) and 953 (interest income) 720

Step 3—Compute adjusted gross foreign base company income and adjusted gross insurance income:

(3) Seventy percent of gross income (.70 × line (1)) 700

(4) Adjusted gross foreign base company income and adjusted gross insurance income after the application of the full inclusion rule of this paragraph (b)(1) (line (2), or line (1) if line (2) is greater than line (3)) 1000

(5) Full inclusion foreign base company income under paragraph (b)(1)(ii) (line (4) minus line (2)) 280

Step 4—Compute net foreign base company income:

(6) Expenses (other than related person interest expense) directly related to adjusted gross foreign personal holding company income 50

(7) Related person interest expense allocable to adjusted gross foreign personal holding company income under section 904 350

(8) Deductions allocable to full inclusion foreign base company income under section 954(b)(5) and paragraph (c) of this section 250

(9) Net foreign personal holding company income after allocating deductions under section 954(b)(5) paragraph (c) of this section (line (2) reduced by line (6) and line (7)) 320

(10) Full inclusion foreign base company income after allocating deductions under section 954(b)(5) and paragraph (c) of this section (line (5) reduced by line (8)) 30

(11) Total net foreign base company income after allocating deductions under section 954(b)(5) and paragraph (c) of this section (line (9) plus line (10)) 350

Step 5—Compute net insurance income:

(12) Net insurance income under section 953 0

Step 6—Compute adjusted net foreign base company income:

(13) Foreign income tax imposed on net foreign personal holding company income (interest) ... 120

(14) Foreign income tax imposed on net full inclusion foreign base company income 2

(15) Ninety percent of the maximum United States corporate tax rate 31.5%

(16) Effective rate of foreign income tax imposed on $320 of net foreign personal holding company income under section 954(b)(4) and this paragraph (d) (line (13) divided by line (9)) 38%

(17) Effective rate of foreign income tax imposed on $30 of net full inclusion foreign base company income under section 954(b)(4) and this paragraph (d) (line (14) divided by line (10)) 7%

(18) Net foreign personal holding company income subject to a high foreign tax under section 954(b)(4) and this paragraph (d) (zero, or line (9) if line (16) is greater than line (15)) 320

(19) Net full inclusion foreign base company income subject to a high foreign tax under section 954(b)(4) and this paragraph (d) (zero, or line (10) if line (17) is greater than line (15)) 0

(20) Adjusted net foreign base company income after applying section 954(b)(4) and this paragraph (d) (line (11) reduced by the sum of line (18) and line (19)) 30

Step 7—Compute adjusted net insurance income:

(21) Adjusted net insurance income 0

Step 8—Reduction of adjusted net foreign base company income or adjusted net insurance income by reason of paragraph (d)(6) of this section:

(22) Adjusted gross foreign base company income and adjusted gross insurance income (determined without regard to the full inclusion test of paragraph (b)(1) of this section) (line (4) reduced by line (5)) 720

(23) Ninety percent of adjusted gross foreign base company income and adjusted gross insurance income (determined without regard to the full inclusion test of paragraph (b)(1)(ii) of this section) (90% of the amount on line (22)) 648

(24) Net foreign base company income and net insurance income excluded from subpart F income under section 954(b)(4), increased by the amount of expenses that reduced this income under section 954(b)(5) and paragraph (c) of this section (line (18) increased by the sum of line (6) and line (7)) 720

(25) Adjusted net full inclusion foreign base company income excluded from subpart F income under paragraph (d)(6) of this section (zero, or line (10) reduced by line (19) if line (24) is greater than line (23)) 30
(26) Adjusted net foreign base company income after application of paragraph (d)(6) of this section (line (20) reduced by line (25)) 0

Step 9—Additions to or reduction of subpart F income by reason of section 952(c):

(27) Earnings and profits for the current year 350
(28) Amount subject to being recharacterized as subpart F income under section 952(c)(2) (excess of line (27) over the sum of line (21) and line (26)); if there is a deficit, then the limitation of 952(c)(1) may apply for the current year 350
(29) Amount of reduction in subpart F for prior taxable years by reason of the limitation of section 952(c)(1) 600
(30) Subpart F income as defined in section 952(a), assuming section 952(a)(3), (4), and (5) do not apply (the sum of line (21) and line (26) plus the lesser of line (28) or line (29)) 350
(31) Amount of prior years' deficit remaining to be recharacterized as subpart F income in later years under section 952(c) (excess of line (29) over line (28)) 250

(e) Character of income. *(1) Substance of the transaction.* For purposes of section 954, income shall be characterized in accordance with the substance of the transaction, and not in accordance with the designation applied by the parties to the transaction. For example, an amount that is designated as rent by the taxpayer but actually constitutes income from the sale of property, royalties, or income from services shall not be characterized as rent but shall be characterized as income from the sale of property, royalties or income from services, as the case may be. Local law shall not be controlling in characterizing income.

(2) Separable character. To the extent the definitional provisions of section 953 or 954 describe the income or gain derived from a transaction, or any portion or portions thereof, that income or gain, or portion or portions thereof, is so characterized for purposes of subpart F. Thus, a single transaction may give rise to income in more than one category of foreign base company income described in paragraph (a)(2) of this section. For example, if a controlled foreign corporation, in its business of purchasing personal property and selling it to related persons outside its country of incorporation, also performs services outside its country of incorporation with respect to the property it sells, the sales income will be treated as foreign base company sales income and the services income will be treated as foreign base company services income for purposes of these rules.

(3) Predominant character. The portion of income or gain derived from a transaction that is included in the computation of foreign personal holding company income is always separately determinable and thus must always be segregated from other income and separately classified under paragraph (e)(2) of this section. However, the portion of income or gain derived from a transaction that would meet a particular definitional provision under section 954 or 953 (other than the definition of foreign personal holding company income) in unusual circumstances may not be separately determinable. If such portion is not separately determinable, it must be classified in accordance with the predominant character of the transaction. For example, if a controlled foreign corporation engineers, fabricates, and installs a fixed offshore drilling platform as part of an integrated transaction, and the portion of income that relates to services is not accounted for separately from the portion that relates to sales, and is otherwise not separately determinable, then the classification of income from the transaction shall be made in accordance with the predominant character of the arrangement.

(4) Coordination of categories of gross foreign base company income or gross insurance income. (i) In general. The computations of gross foreign base company income and gross insurance income are limited by the following rules:

(A) If income is foreign base company shipping income, pursuant to section 954(f), it shall not be considered insurance income or income in any other category of foreign base company income.

(B) If income is foreign base company oil related income, pursuant to section 954(g), it shall not be considered insurance income or income in any other category of foreign base company income, except as provided in paragraph (e)(4)(i)(A) of this section.

(C) If income is insurance income, pursuant to section 953, it shall not be considered income in any category of foreign base company income except as provided in paragraph (e)(4)(i)(A) or (B) of this section.

(D) If income is foreign personal holding company income, pursuant to section 954(c), it shall not be considered income in any other category of foreign base company income, other than as provided in paragraph (e)(4)(i)(A), (B) or (C) of this section.

(ii) Income excluded from other categories of gross foreign base company income. Income shall not be excluded from a category of gross foreign base company income or gross insurance income under this paragraph (e)(4) by reason of being included in another category of gross foreign base company income or gross insurance income, if the income is excluded from that other category by a more specific provision of section 953 or 954. For example, income derived from a commodity transaction that is excluded from foreign personal holding company income under § 1.954-2(f) as income from a qualified active sale may be included in gross foreign base company income if it also meets the definition of foreign base company sales income. See § 1.954-2(a)(2) for the coordination of overlapping categories within the definition of foreign personal holding company income.

(f) Definition of related person. *(1) Persons related to controlled foreign corporation.* Unless otherwise provided, for purposes of section 954 and §§ 1.954-1 through 1.954-8 inclusive, the following persons are considered under section 954(d)(3) to be related persons with respect to a controlled foreign corporation:

(i) Individuals. An individual, whether or not a citizen or resident of the United States, who controls the controlled foreign corporation.

(ii) Other persons. A foreign or domestic corporation, partnership, trust or estate that controls or is controlled by the controlled foreign corporation, or is controlled by the same person or persons that control the controlled foreign corporation.

(2) Control. (i) Corporations. With respect to a corporation, control means the ownership, directly or indirectly, of stock possessing more than 50 percent of the total voting power of all classes of stock entitled to vote or of the total value of the stock of the corporation.

(ii) Partnerships. With respect to a partnership, control means the ownership, directly or indirectly, of more than 50 percent (by value) of the capital or profits interest in the partnership.

(iii) Trusts and estates. With respect to a trust or estate, control means the ownership, directly, or indirectly, of more than 50 percent (by value) of the beneficial interest in the trust or estate.

(iv) Direct or indirect ownership. For purposes of this paragraph (f), to determine direct or indirect ownership, the principles of section 958 shall be applied without regard to whether a corporation, partnership, trust or estate is foreign or domestic or whether or not an individual is a citizen or resident of the United States.

(g) Distributive share of partnership income. *(1) Application of related person and country of organization tests.* Unless otherwise provided, to determine the extent to which a controlled foreign corporation's distributive share of any item of gross income of a partnership would have been subpart F income if received by it directly, under § 1.952-1(g), if a provision of subpart F requires a determination of whether an entity is a related person, within the meaning of section 954(d)(3), or whether an activity occurred within or outside the country under the laws of which the controlled foreign corporation is created or organized, this determination shall be made by reference to such controlled foreign corporation and not by reference to the partnership.

(2) Application of related person test for sales and purchase transactions between a partnership and its controlled foreign corporation partner. For purposes of determining whether a controlled foreign corporation's distributive share of any item of gross income of a partnership is foreign base company sales income under section 954(d)(1) when the item of income is derived from the sale by the partnership of personal property purchased by the partnership from (or sold by the partnership on behalf of) the controlled foreign corporation; or the sale by the partnership of personal property to (or the purchase of personal property by the partnership on behalf of) the controlled foreign corporation (CFC-partnership transaction), the CFC-partnership transaction will be treated as a transaction with an entity that is a related person, within the meaning of section 954(d)(3), under paragraph (g)(1) of this section, if—

(i) The controlled foreign corporation purchased such personal property from (or sold it to the partnership on behalf of), or sells such personal property to (or purchases it from the partnership on behalf of), a related person with respect to the controlled foreign corporation (other than the partnership), within the meaning of section 954(d)(3); or

(ii) The branch rule of section 954(d)(2) applies to treat as foreign base company sales income the income of the controlled foreign corporation from selling to the partnership (or a third party) personal property that the controlled foreign corporation has manufactured, in the case where the partnership purchases personal property from (or sells personal property on behalf of) the controlled foreign corporation.

(3) Examples. The application of this paragraph (g) is illustrated by the following examples:

Example (1). CFC, a controlled foreign corporation organized in Country A, is an 80-percent partner in Partnership, a partnership organized in Country A. All of the stock of CFC is owned by USP, a U.S. corporation. Partnership earns commission income from purchasing Product O on behalf of USP, from unrelated manufacturers in Country B, for sale in the United States. To determine whether CFC's distributive share of Partnership's commission income is foreign base company sales income under section 954(d), CFC is treated as if it purchased Product O on behalf of USP. Under section 954(d)(3), USP is a related person with respect to CFC. Thus, with respect to CFC, the sales income is deemed to be derived from the purchase of personal property on behalf of a related person. Because the property purchased is both manufactured and sold for use outside of Country A, CFC's country of organization, CFC's distributive share of the sales income is foreign base company sales income.

Example (2). (i) CFC1, a controlled foreign corporation organized in Country A, is an 80-percent partner in Partnership, a partnership organized in Country B. CFC2, a controlled foreign corporation organized in Country B, owns the remaining 20 percent interest in Partnership. CFC1 and CFC2 are owned by a common U.S. parent, USP. CFC2 manufactures Product A in Country B. Partnership earns sales income from purchasing Product A from CFC2 and selling it to third parties located in Country B that are not related persons with respect to CFC1 or CFC2. To determine whether CFC1's distributive share of Partnership's sales income is foreign base company sales income under section 954(d), CFC1 is treated as if it purchased Product A from CFC2 and sold it to third parties in Country B. Under section 954(d)(3), CFC2 is a related person with respect to CFC1. Thus, with respect to CFC1, the sales income is deemed to be derived from the purchase of personal property from a related person. Because the property purchased is both manufactured and sold for use outside of Country A, CFC1's country of organization, CFC1's distributive share of the sales income is foreign base company sales income.

(ii) Because Product A is both manufactured and sold for use within CFC2's country of organization, CFC2's distributive share of Partnership's sales income is not foreign base company sales income.

Example (3). CFC, a controlled foreign corporation organized in Country A, is an 80 percent partner in MJK Partnership, a Country B partnership. CFC purchased goods from J Corp, a Country C corporation that is a related person with respect to CFC. CFC sold the goods to MJK Partnership. In turn, MJK Partnership sold the goods to P Corp, a Country D corporation that is unrelated to CFC. P Corp sold the goods to unrelated customers in Country D. The goods were manufactured in Country C by persons unrelated to J Corp. CFC's distributive share of the income of MJK Partnership from the sale of goods to P Corp will be treated as income from the sale of goods purchased from a related person for purposes of section 954(d)(1) because CFC purchased the goods from J Corp, a related person. Because the goods were both manufactured and sold for use outside of Country A, CFC's distributive share of the income attributable to the sale of the goods is foreign base company sales income. Further, CFC's income from the sale of the goods to MJK Partnership will also be foreign base company sales income.

Example (4). The facts of are the same as Example 3, except that MJK Partnership purchased the goods from P Corp and sold those goods to CFC. CFC sold the goods to J Corp. J Corp sold the goods to unrelated customers in Country C. CFC's distributive share of the income of MJK Partnership from the sale of the goods by the partnership to itself will be treated as income from the sale of goods to a related person, for purposes of section 954(d)(1). Because the goods were both manufactured and sold for use outside of Country A, CFC's distributive share of income attributable to the sale of the goods is foreign base company sales income. Further,

CFC's income from the sale of the goods to J Corp is also foreign base company sales income.

(4) Effective date. This paragraph (g) applies to taxable years of a controlled foreign corporation beginning on or after July 23, 2002.

T.D. 8618, 9/6/95, amend T.D. 8704, 12/31/96, T.D. 8767, 3/23/98, T.D. 8827, 7/12/99, T.D. 9008, 7/22/2002.

PAR. 4. Section 1.954-1 is amended as follows:

1. Paragraphs (c)(1)(i) heading and introductory text and (c)(1)(i)(A) through (c)(1)(i)(D) are redesignated as paragraphs (c)(1)(i)(A) heading and introductory text and (c)(1)(i)(A)(1) through (c)(1)(i)(A)(4), respectively.

2. A heading for paragraph (c)(1)(i) is added.

3. Paragraphs (c)(1)(i)(B) through (c)(1))(i)(E) are added.

The additions read as follows:

Proposed § 1.954-1 Foreign base company income. [*For Preamble, see ¶ 151,985*]

* * * * *

(c) * * *

(1) * * *

(i) Deductions. (A) Deductions against gross foreign base company income. * * *

(B) Special rule for deductible payments to certain non-fiscally transparent entities. Notwithstanding any other provision of this section, except as provided in paragraph (c)(1)(i)(C) of this section, an expense (including a distributive share of any expense) that would otherwise be allocable under section 954(b)(5) against the subpart F income of a controlled foreign corporation shall not be allocated against subpart F income of the controlled foreign corporation resulting from the payment giving rise to the expense if—

(1) Such expense arises from a payment between the controlled foreign corporation and a partnership in which the controlled foreign corporation is a partner and the partnership is not regarded as fiscally transparent, as defined in § 1.954-9(a)(7), by any country in which the controlled foreign corporation does business or has substantial assets; and

(2) The payment from which the expense arises would have reduced foreign tax, under § 1.954-9(a)(3), and would have fallen within the tax disparity rule of § 1.954-9(a)(5)(iv), if those provisions had been applicable to the payment.

(C) Limitations. Paragraph (c)(1)(i)(B) of this section shall not apply to the extent that the controlled foreign corporation partner has no income against which to allocate the expense, other than its distributive share of a payment described in paragraph (c)(1)(i)(B) of this section. Similarly, to the extent an expense described in paragraph (c)(1)(i)(B) of this section exceeds the controlled foreign corporation partner's distributive share of the payment from which the expense arises, such excess amount of the expense may reduce subpart F income (other than such payment) to which it is properly allocable or apportionable under section 954(b)(5).

(D) Example. The following example illustrates the application of paragraphs (c)(1)(i)(B) and (C) of this section:

Example. CFC, a controlled foreign corporation in Country A, is a 70 percent partner in partnership P, located in Country B. Country A's tax laws do not classify P as a fiscally transparent entity. The rate of tax in country B is 15 percent of the tax rate in country A. P loans $100 to CFC at a market rate of interest. In year 1, CFC pays P $10 of interest on the loan. The interest payment would have caused the recharacterization rules of § 1.954-9 to apply if the payment were made between the entities described in § 1.954-9(a)(2). CFC's distributive share of P's interest income is $7, which is foreign personal holding company income to CFC under section 954(c). Under paragraph (c)(1)(i)(B) of this section, $7 of the $10 interest expense may not be allocated against any of CFC's subpart F income. However, to the extent the remaining $3 of interest expense is properly allocable to subpart F income of CFC other than its distributive share of P's interest income, this expense may offset such other subpart F income.

(E) Effective date. Paragraph (c)(1)(i)(B), (C) and (D) of this section shall be applicable for all payments made or accrued in taxable years commencing after [date that is 5 years after publication of the final regulations in the Federal Register], under hybrid arrangements, unless such payments are made pursuant to an arrangement that would qualify for permanent relief under § 1.954-9(c)(2) if made between a controlled foreign corporation and its hybrid branch, in which case the relief afforded under that section shall also be afforded under this section.

* * * * *

PAR. 4. Section 1.954-1T is amended by revising paragraph (c) to read as follows:

Proposed § 1.954-1T Foreign base company income; taxable years beginning after December 31, 1986 (Temporary). [*For Preamble, see ¶ 151,253*]

* * * * *

(c) Computation of net foreign base company income. *(1) General rule.* The net foreign base company income of a controlled foreign corporation is computed by reducing (but not below zero) the amount of gross income in each of the categories of adjusted gross foreign base company income described in paragraph (b)(2) of this section, so as to take into account deductions allocable and apportionable to such income. For purposes of section 954 and this section, expenses must be allocated and apportioned consistent with the allocation and apportionment of expenses for purposes of section 904(d). For purposes of this § 1.954-lT, an item of net foreign base company income must be categorized according to the category of adjusted gross foreign base company income from which it is derived. Thus, an item of net foreign base company income must be categorized as a net item of—

(i) Foreign personal holding company income,

(ii) Foreign base company sales income,

(iii) Foreign base company services income,

(iv) Foreign base company shipping income,

(v) Foreign base company oil related income, or

(vi) Full inclusion foreign base company income.

(2) Computation of net foreign base company income derived from same country insurance income. Deductions relating to foreign base company income derived from insurance, reinsurance, or annuity contracts covering risks located in the country in which the controlled foreign corporation is created or organized shall be allocated and apportioned in accordance with the rules set forth in § 1.953-5.

* * * * *

§ 4.954-1 Foreign base company income; taxable years beginning after December 31, 1986.

(a) In general. *(1) Purpose and scope.* Section 954(b) through (g) and §§ 1.954-1T and 1.954-2T provide rules for computing the foreign base company income of a controlled foreign corporation. Foreign base company income is included in the subpart F income of a controlled foreign corporation under the rules of section 952 and the regulations thereunder. Subpart F income is included in the gross income of a United States shareholder of a controlled foreign corporation under the rules of section 951 and the regulations thereunder, and thus is subject to current taxation under section 1 or 11 of the Code. The determination of whether a foreign corporation is a controlled foreign corporation, the subpart F income of which is included currently in the gross income of its United States shareholders, is made under the rules of section 957 and the regulations thereunder.

(2) Gross foreign base company income. For taxable years of a controlled foreign corporation beginning after December 31, 1986, the gross foreign base company income of a controlled foreign corporation consists of the following categories of gross income:

(i) Its foreign personal holding company income, as defined in section 954(c) and § 1.954-2T,

(ii) Its foreign base company sales income, as defined in section 954(d) and the regulations thereunder,

(iii) Its foreign base company services income, as defined in section 954(e) and the regulations thereunder,

(iv) Its foreign base company shipping income, as defined in section 954(f) and the regulations thereunder, and

(v) Its foreign base company oil related income, as defined in section 954(g) and the regulations thereunder.

(3) Adjusted gross foreign base company income. The term "adjusted gross foreign base company income" means the gross foreign base company income of a controlled foreign corporation as adjusted by the de minimis and full inclusion rules of paragraph (b) of this section.

(4) Net foreign base company income. The term "net foreign base company income" means the adjusted gross foreign base company income of a controlled foreign corporation reduced so as to take account of deductions properly allocable to such income under the rules of section 954(b)(5) and paragraph (c) of this section. In computing net foreign base company income, foreign personal holding company income is reduced (but not below zero) by related person interest expense before allocating and apportioning other expenses in accordance with the rules of paragraph (c) of this section and § 1.904(d)-5(c)(2).

(5) Adjusted net foreign base company income. The term "adjusted net foreign base company income" means the net foreign base company income of a controlled foreign corporation reduced by any items of net foreign base company income for which the high tax exception of paragraph (d) of this section is elected. The term "foreign base company income" as used in the Code and elsewhere in the regulations generally means adjusted net foreign base company income.

(6) Insurance income definitions. The term "gross insurance income" includes any item of gross income taken into account in determining insurance income under section 953 and the regulations thereunder. The term "adjusted gross insurance income" means gross insurance income as adjusted by the de minimis and full inclusion rules of paragraph (b) of this section. The term "net insurance income" means adjusted gross insurance income reduced under section 953 and the regulations thereunder so as to take into account deductions properly allocable or apportionable to such income. The term "adjusted net insurance income" means net insurance income reduced by any items of net insurance income for which the high tax exception of paragraph (d) of this section is elected.

(7) Additional items of adjusted net foreign base company income or adjusted net insurance income by reason of section 952(c). Earnings and profits of the controlled foreign corporation that are recharacterized as foreign base company income or insurance income under section 952(c) are items of adjusted net foreign base company income or adjusted net insurance income. Thus, they are not included in the gross foreign base company income or gross insurance income of the controlled foreign corporation in computing adjusted gross foreign base company income or adjusted gross insurance income (for purposes of applying the de minimis and full inclusion tests of paragraph (b) of this section).

(8) Illustration. The order of computation is illustrated by the following example. Computations in this paragraph (a)(8) and in paragraph (b)(5) of this section involving the operation of section 952(c) are included for purposes of illustration only and do not provide substantive rules concerning the operation of that section.

Example. (i) Gross income. CFC, a controlled foreign corporation, has gross income of $1000 for the current taxable year. Of that $1000 of income, $100 is interest income that is included in the definition of foreign personal holding company income under section 954(c)(1)(A) and § 1.954-2T(b)(1)(ii), is not income from a trade or service receivable described in section 864(d)(1) or (6), and is not excluded from foreign personal holding company income under any provision of section 954(c) and § 1.954-2T. Another $50 is foreign base company sales income under section 954(d) and the regulations thereunder. The remaining $850 of gross income is not included in the definition of foreign base company income or insurance income under sections 954(c), (d), (e), (f), (g), or 953 and the regulations thereunder, and is foreign source general limitation income described in section 904(d)(1)(I) and the regulations thereunder.

(ii) Expenses. CFC has expenses for the current taxable year of $500. Of that $500, $8 is from interest paid to a related person and is allocable to foreign personal holding company income along with $2 of other expense. Another $20 of expense is allocable to foreign base company sales. The remaining $470 of expense is allocable to income other than foreign base company income or insurance income.

(iii) Earnings and deficits. CFC has earnings and profits for the current taxable year of $500. In the prior taxable year, CFC had losses with respect to income other than gross foreign base company income or gross insurance income. By reason of the limitation provided under section 952(c)(1)(A) and the regulations thereunder, those losses reduced the Subpart F income (consisting entirely of foreign source general limitation income) of CFC by $600 for the prior taxable year.

(iv) Taxes. Foreign tax of $30 is considered imposed on the interest income under the rules of section 954(b)(4) and paragraph (d) of this section. Foreign tax of $14 is considered imposed on the foreign base company sales income under the rules of section 954(b)(4) and paragraph (d) of this section. Foreign tax of $177 is considered imposed on the remaining foreign source general limitation income under the rules of section 954(b)(4) and paragraph (d) of this section. For the taxable year of the foreign corporation, the maximum U.S. rate of taxation under section 11 is 34 percent.

(v) Conclusion. Based on these facts, if *CFC* elects to exclude all items of income subject to a high foreign tax under section 954(b)(4) and paragraph (d), it will have $500 of subpart F income as defined in section 952(a) (consisting entirely of foreign source general limitation income) determined as follows. The following steps do not illustrate the computation of the subpart F income of a controlled foreign corporation that has income from a trade or service receivable treated as interest under section 864(d)(1) or interest described in section 864(d)(6).

Step 1—Determine gross income:

(1) Gross income $1000

Step 2—Determine gross foreign base company income and gross insurance income:

(2) Interest income included in foreign personal holding company income under section 954(c) ... 100
(3) Foreign base company sales income under section 954(d) 50
(4) Total gross foreign base company income gross insurance income as defined in sections 954(c), (d), (e), (f) and (g) and 953 and the regulations thereunder (line (3) plus line (4)) 150

Step 3—Determine adjusted gross foreign base company income and adjusted gross insurance income:

(5) Five percent of gross income (.05 × line (1)) 50
(6) Seventy percent of gross income (.70 × line (1)).. 700
(7) Adjusted gross foreign base company income and adjusted gross insurance income after the application of the de minimis test of paragraph (b) (line (4), or zero if line (4) is less than the lesser of line (5) or $1,000,000) 150
(8) Adjusted gross foreign base company income and adjusted gross insurance income after the application of the full inclusion test of paragraph (b) (line (4), or line (1) if line (4) is greater than line (6)) 150

Step 4—Compute net foreign base company income:

(9) Related person interest expense and other expense allocable and apportionable to foreign personal holding company income 10
(10) Deductions allocable and apportionable to foreign base company sales income 20
(11) Foreign personal holding company income after allocating deductions under section 954(b)(5) and paragraph (c) of this section (the lesser of line (2) or line (7), reduced (but not below zero) by line (9)) 90
(12) Foreign base company sales income after allocating deductions under section 954(b)(5) and paragraph (c) of this section (the lesser of line (3) or line (7), reduced (but not below zero) by line (10)) 30
(13) Total net foreign base company income after allocating deductions under section 954(b)(5) and paragraph (c) (line (11) plus line (12)) 120

Step 5—Compute net insurance income:

(14) Net insurance income under section 953 and the regulations thereunder 0

Step 6—Compute adjusted net foreign base company income:

(15) Foreign tax imposed on foreign personal holding company income (as determined under paragraph (d)) 30
(16) Foreign tax imposed on foreign base company sales income (as determined under paragraph (d)) 14
(17) Ninety percent of the maximum U.S. corporate tax rate 30.6
(18) Effective rate of foreign tax imposed on foreign personal holding company income (interest) under section 954(b)(4) and paragraph (d) (line (15) divided by line (11)) 33
(19) Effective rate of foreign tax imposed on $40 of foreign base company sales income under section 954(b)(4) and paragraph (d) (line (16) divided by line (12)) 47
(20) Foreign personal holding company income subject to a high foreign tax under section 954(b)(4) and paragraph (d) (zero, or line (11) if line (18) is greater than line (17)) 90
(21) Foreign base company sales income subject to a high foreign tax under section 954(b)(4) and paragraph (d) (zero, or line (12) if line (19) is greater than line (17)) 30
(22) Adjusted net foreign base company income after applying section 954(b)(4) and paragraph (d) (line (13), reduced by the sum of line (20) and line (21)) 0

Step 7—Compute adjusted net insurance income:

(23) Adjusted net insurance income 0

Step 8—Additions to or reduction of adjusted net foreign base company income by reason of section 952(c):

(24) Earnings and profits for the current year 500
(25) The excess in earnings and profits over subpart F income subject to being recharacterized as adjusted net foreign base company income under section 952(c)(2) (excess of line (24) over the sum of lines (22) and (23); if there is a deficit, then the limitation of section 952(c)(1) may apply for the current year) 500
(26) Amount of reduction in subpart F income for prior taxable years by reason of the limitation of section 952(c)(1) and the regulations thereunder .. 600
(27) Subpart F income as defined in section 952(a), assuming section 952(a)(3), (4), or (5) does not apply (the sum of line (22), line (23), and the lesser of line (25) or line (26)) 500

(b) Computation of adjusted gross foreign base company income and adjusted gross insurance income. *(1) De minimis rule, etc.* (i) In general. If the de minimis rule of paragraph (b)(1)(ii) of this section applies, then adjusted gross foreign base company income and adjusted gross insurance income are each equal to zero. If the full inclusion rule of paragraph (b)(1)(iii) of this section applies, then adjusted gross foreign base company income consists of all items of gross income of the controlled foreign corporation other than gross insurance income, and adjusted gross insurance income consists of all items of gross insurance income. Otherwise, the adjusted gross foreign base company income of a controlled foreign corporation consists of the gross foreign base company income of the controlled foreign corporation, and the adjusted gross insurance income of a controlled foreign corporation consists of the gross insurance income of the controlled foreign corporation.

(ii) Five percent de minimis test. (A) In general. The de minimis rule of this paragraph (b)(1)(ii) applies if the sum of the gross foreign base company income and the gross insurance income of a controlled foreign corporation is less than the lesser of—

(1) 5 percent of gross income, or

(2) $1,000,000. Controlled foreign corporations having a functional currency other than the U.S. dollar shall translate the $1,000,000 threshold using the exchange rate provided under section 989(b)(3) and the regulations thereunder for amounts included in income under section 951(a).

(B) Coordination with section 864(d). Gross foreign base company income or gross insurance income of a controlled foreign corporation always includes items of income from trade or service receivables described in section 864(d)(1) or (6), even if the de minimis rule of this paragraph (b)(1)(ii) is otherwise applicable. In that case, adjusted gross foreign base company income consists only of the items of income from trade or service receivables described in section 864(d)(1) or (6) that are included in gross foreign base company income, and adjusted gross insurance income consists only of the items of income from trade or service receivables described in section 864(d)(1) or (6) that are included in gross insurance income.

(iii) Seventy percent full inclusion test. The full inclusion rule of this paragraph (b)(1)(iii) applies if the sum of the foreign base company income and the gross insurance income for the taxable year exceeds 70 percent of gross income.

(2) Character of items of gross income included in adjusted gross foreign base company income. The items of gross income included in the adjusted gross foreign base company income of a controlled foreign corporation retain their character as foreign personal holding company income, foreign base company sales income, foreign base company services income, foreign base company shipping income, or foreign base company oil related income. Items of gross income included in adjusted gross income because the full inclusion test of paragraph (b)(1)(iii) of this section is met are termed "full inclusion foreign base company income," and constitute a separate category of adjusted gross foreign base company income for purposes of allocating and apportioning deductions under paragraph (c) of this section.

(3) Coordination with section 952(c). Items of gross foreign base company income or gross insurance income that are excluded from adjusted foreign base company income or adjusted gross insurance income because the de minimis test of paragraph (b)(1)(ii) of this section is met are potentially subject to recharacterization as adjusted net foreign base company income or adjusted net insurance income (or other categories of income included in the computation of Subpart F income under section 952 and the regulations thereunder) for the taxable year under the rules of section 952(c). Items of full inclusion foreign base company income that are included in adjusted gross foreign base company income because the full inclusion test of paragraph (b)(1)(iii) of this section is met, and are included in Subpart F income under section 952 and the regulations thereunder, do not reduce amounts that, under section 952(c), are subject to recharacterization in later years on account of deficits in prior years.

(4) Anti-abuse rule. (i) In general. For purposes of applying the de minimis and full inclusion tests of paragraph (b)(1) of this section, the income of two or more controlled foreign corporations shall be aggregated and treated as the income of a single corporation if one principal purpose for separately organizing, acquiring, or maintaining such multiple corporations is to avoid the application of the de minimis or full inclusion requirements of paragraph (b)(1) of this section. For purposes of this paragraph (b), a principal purpose need not be the purpose of first importance.

(ii) Presumption. Two or more controlled foreign corporations are presumed to have been organized, acquired or maintained to avoid the effect of the de minimis and full inclusion requirements of paragraph (b)(1) of this section if the corporations are related persons as defined in subdivision (iii) of this paragraph (b)(4) and the corporations are described in subdivision (A), (B), or (C). This presumption may be rebutted by proof to the contrary.

(A) The activities now carried on by the controlled foreign corporations, or the assets used in those activities, are substantially the same activities that were carried on, or assets that were previously held by a single controlled foreign corporation, and the United States shareholders of the controlled foreign corporations or related persons (as determined under subdivision (iii) of this paragraph (b)(4)) are substantially the same as the United States shareholders of the one controlled foreign corporation in that prior taxable year. A presumption made in connection with the requirements of this subdivision (A) of paragraph (b)(4)(ii) may be rebutted by proof that the activities carried on by each controlled foreign corporation would constitute a separate branch under the principles of § 1.367(a)-6T(g) if carried on directly by a United States person.

(B) The controlled foreign corporations carry on a business, financial operation, or venture as partners directly or indirectly in a partnership (as defined in section 7701(a)(2) and § 301.7701-3) that is a related person (as defined in subdivision (iii) of this paragraph (b)(4)) with respect to each such controlled foreign corporation.

(C) The activities carried on by the controlled foreign corporations would constitute a single branch operation under § 1.367(a)-6T(g)(2) if carried on directly by the United States person.

(iii) Related persons. For purposes of this paragraph (b), two or more persons are related persons if they are in a relationship described in section 267(b). In determining for purposes of this paragraph (b) whether two or more corporations are members of the same controlled group under section 267(b)(3), a person is considered to own stock owned directly by such person, stock owned with the application of section 1563(e)(1), and stock owned with the application of section 267(c). In determining for purposes of this paragraph (b) whether a corporation is related to a partnership under section 267(b)(10), a person is considered to own the partnership interest owned directly by such person and the partnership interest owned with the application of section 267(e)(3).

(iv) Illustration. The following example illustrates the application of this paragraph (b)(4).

Example. USP is the sole United States shareholder of three controlled foreign corporations: CFC1, CFC2 and CFC3. The three controlled foreign corporations all have the same taxable year. The three controlled foreign corporations are partners in FP, a foreign entity classified as a partnership under section 7701(a)(2) and § 301.7701-3 of the regulations. For their current taxable years, each of the controlled foreign corporations derives all of its income other than foreign base company income from activities conducted through FP, and its foreign base company income from activities conducted both jointly through FP and separately without FP. Based on the facts in the table below, for their current taxable years, the foreign base company income derived by each controlled foreign corporation, including income derived from FP, is less than five percent of the gross income of each controlled foreign corporation and is less than $1,000,000:

	CFC1	CFC2	CFC3
Gross income	$4,000,000	$8,000,000	$12,000,000
Five percent of gross income	200,000	400,000	600,000
Foreign base company income	199,000	398,000	597,000

Thus, without the application of the anti-abuse rule of this subparagraph (5), each controlled foreign corporation would be treated as having no foreign base company income after the application of the de minimis rule of section 954(b)(3)(A) and § 1.954-1T(b)(1).

However, under these facts the requirements of subdivision (i) of this paragraph (b)(4) are presumed to be met. The sum of the foreign base company income of the controlled foreign corporations is $1,194,000. Thus, the amount of adjusted gross foreign base company income will not be less than the amount of gross foreign base company income by reason of the de minimis rule of section 954(b)(3)(A) and this paragraph (b).

(5) Illustration. The following example illustrates computations required by sections 952 and 954 and this § 1.954-1T if the full inclusion test of paragraph (b)(1)(iii) is met (see paragraph (a)(8) for an example illustrating computations required if the de minimis test of paragraph (b)(1)(ii) is met):

Example. (i) Gross Income. CFC, a controlled foreign corporation, has gross income of $1,000 for the current taxable year. Of that $1,000 of income, $720 is interest income that is included in the definition of foreign personal holding company income under section 954(c)(1)(A) and § 1.954-2T(b)(ii), is not income from trade or service receivables described in section 864(d)(1) or (6), and is not excluded from foreign personal holding company income under any provisions of section 954(c) and § 1.954-2T. The remaining $280 is services income that is not included in the definition of foreign base company income or insurance income under section 954(c), (d), (e), (f), (g) or 953 and the regulations thereunder, and is foreign source general limitation income for purposes of section 904(d)(1)(I).

(ii) Expenses. CFC has expenses for the current taxable year of $650. Of that $650, $350 is from interest paid to related persons that is allocable to foreign personal holding company income along with $50 of other expense. The remaining $250 of expense is allocable to services income other than foreign base company income or insurance income.

(iii) Earnings and deficits. CFC has earnings and profits for the current taxable year of $350. In the prior taxable year, CFC had losses with respect to income other than foreign base company income or insurance income. By reason of the limitation provided under section 952(c)(1)(A) and the regulations thereunder, those losses reduced the subpart F income of CFC (consisting entirely of foreign source general limitation income) by $600 for the prior taxable year.

(iv) Taxes. A foreign tax of $120 is considered imposed on the $720 of interest income under the rules of section 954(b)(4) and paragraph (d) of this section, and a foreign tax of $2 is considered imposed on the services income under the rules of section 954(b)(4) and paragraph (d) of this section. For the taxable year of the foreign corporation, the maximum U.S. rate of taxation under section 11 is 34 percent.

(v) Conclusion. Based on these facts, if CFC elects to exclude all items of income subject to a high foreign tax under section 954(b)(4) and paragraph (d), it will have $350 of subpart F income as defined in section 952(a) determined as follows:

Step 1—Determine gross income:

(1) Gross income $1000

Step 2—Compute gross foreign base company income and gross insurance income:

(2) Gross foreign base company income and insurance income as defined in sections 954(c), (d), (e), (f), (g) and 953 and the regulations thereunder (interest income) 720

Step 3—Compute gross foreign base company income and gross insurance income:

(3) Seventy percent of gross income (.70 × line (1)) 700
(4) Adjusted gross foreign base company income or insurance income after the application of the full inclusion rule of this paragraph (b)(1) (line (2), or line (1) if line (2) is greater than line (3)) ... 1000
(5) Full inclusion foreign base company income under paragraph (a)(2)(vi) (line (4) minus line (2)) 280

Step 4—Compute net foreign base company income:

(6) Related person interest expense and other deductions allocable and apportionable to foreign personal holding company income under section 954(b)(5) and paragraph (c) 400
(7) Deductions allocable and apportionable to full inclusion foreign base company income under section 954(b)(5) and paragraph (c) 250
(8) Foreign personal holding company income after allocating deductions under section 954(b)(5) and paragraph (c) of this section (line (2) reduced (but not below zero) by line (6)) 320
(9) Full inclusion foreign base company income after allocating deductions under section 954(b)(5) paragraph (c) of this section (line (5) reduced (but not below zero) by line (7)) 30
(10) Total gross foreign base company income after allocating deductions under section 954(b)(5) and paragraph (c) (line (8) plus line (9)) 350

Step 5—Compute net insurance income:

(11) Net insurance income under section 953 and the regulations thereunder 0

Step 6—Compute adjusted net foreign base company income:

(12) Foreign tax imposed on foreign personal holding company income (interest) 120
(13) Foreign tax imposed on full inclusion foreign base company income 2
(14) Ninety percent of the maximum U.S. corporate tax rate 30.6
(15) Effective rate of foreign tax imposed on $320 of foreign personal holding company income under section 954(b)(4) and paragraph (d) (line (12) divided by line (8)) 38
(16) Effective rate of foreign tax imposed of $30 of full inclusion foreign base company income under section 954(b)(4) and paragraph (d) (line (13) divided by line (9)) 7
(17) Foreign personal holding company income subject to a high foreign tax under section 954(b)(4) and paragraph (d) (zero, or line (8) if line (15) is greater than line (14)) 320
(18) Full inclusion foreign base company income subject to a high foreign tax under section 954(b)(4) and paragraph (d) (zero, or line (9) if line (16) is greater than line (14)) 0
(19) Adjusted net foreign base company income after applying section 954(b)(4) and paragraph (d) (line (10), reduced by the sum of line (17) and line (18)) 30

Step 7—Compute adjusted net insurance income:

(20) Adjusted net insurance income 0

Step 8—Additions to or reduction of adjusted net foreign base company income by reason of section 952(c):

(21) Earnings and profits for the current year 350
(22) The excess in earnings and profits over subpart F income, which is subject to being recharacterized as adjusted net foreign base company income under section 952(c)(2) (excess of line (21) over the sum of line (19) and line (20)); if there is a deficit, then the limitation of 952(c)(1) may apply for the current year 320
(23) Amount of reduction in subpart F income for prior taxable years by reason of the limitation of section 952(c)(1) and the regulations thereunder . . 600
(24) Subpart F income as defined in section 952(a), assuming section 952(a)(3), (4), or (5) does not apply (the sum of line (19) and line (20) plus the lesser of line (22) or line (23)) 350
(25) Amount of prior years' deficit remaining to be recharacterized as subpart F income in later years under section 952(c) (excess of line (23) over line (22)) 280

(c) Computation of net foreign base company income. The net foreign base company income of a controlled foreign corporation is computed by reducing (but not below zero) the amount of gross income in each of the categories of adjusted gross foreign base company income described in paragraph (b)(2) of this section, so as to take into account deductions allocable and apportionable to such income. For purposes of section 954 and this section, expenses must be allocated and apportioned consistent with the allocation and apportionment of expenses for purposes of section 904(d). For purposes of this § 1.954-1T, an item of net foreign base company income must be categorized according to the category of adjusted gross foreign base company income from which it is derived. Thus, an item of net foreign base company income must be categorized as a net item of—

(1) Foreign personal holding company income,

(2) Foreign base company sales income,

(3) Foreign base company services income,

(4) Foreign base company shipping income,

(5) Foreign base company oil related income, or

(6) Full inclusion foreign base company income.

(d) Computation of adjusted net foreign base company income or adjusted net insurance income. *(1) Application of high tax exception.* Adjusted net foreign base company income (or adjusted net insurance income) equals the net foreign base company income (or net insurance income) of a controlled foreign corporation; reduced by any item of such income (other than foreign base company oil related income as defined in section 954(g)) subject to the high tax exception provided by section 954(b)(4) and this paragraph (d). An item of income is subject to the high tax exception only if—

(i) It is established that the income was subject to creditable income taxes imposed by a foreign country or countries at an effective rate that is greater than 90 percent of the maximum rate of tax specified in section 11 or 15 for the taxable year of the controlled foreign corporation; and

(ii) An election is made under section 954(b)(4) and paragraph (d)(5) of this section to exclude the income from the computation of subpart F income. See paragraph (d)(4) of this section for the definition of the term "item of income." For rules concerning the treatment for foreign tax credit purposes of amounts excluded from subpart F under section 954(b)(4), see § 904-1.4(c)(1).

(2) Effective rate at which taxes are imposed. For purposes of this paragraph (d), the effective rate at which taxes are imposed on an item of income is—

(i) The amount of income taxes paid or accrued (or deemed paid or accrued) with respect to the item of income, determined under paragraph (d)(3) of this section, divided by

(ii) The item of net foreign base company income or net insurance income, determined under paragraph (d)(4) of this section (including the appropriate amount of income taxes referred to in subdivision (i) of this paragraph (d)(2), immediately above).

(3) Taxes paid or accrued with respect to an item of income. (i) Income other than passive foreign personal holding company income. The amount of income taxes paid or accrued with respect to an item of income (other than an item of foreign personal holding company income that is passive income) for purposes of section 954(b)(4) and this paragraph (d) is the amount of foreign income taxes that would be deemed paid under section 960 with respect to that item if that item were included in the gross income of a U.S. shareholder under section 951(a)(1)(A). For this purpose, the amounts that would be deemed paid under section 960 shall be determined separately with respect to each controlled foreign corporation and without regard to the limitation applicable under section 904(a).

(ii) Passive foreign personal holding company income. The amount of income taxes paid or accrued with respect to an item of foreign personal holding company income that is passive income for purposes of section 954(b)(4) and this paragraph (d) is the amount of foreign income taxes paid or accrued or deemed paid by the foreign corporation that would be taken into account for purposes of applying the provisions of § 1.904-4(c) with respect to that item of income.

(4) Item of income. (i) Income other than passive foreign personal holding company income. The high tax exception applies (when elected) to all income that constitutes a single item under this paragraph (d)(4). A single item of net foreign base company income or net insurance income is an amount of net foreign base company income (other than foreign personal holding company income that is passive income) or net insurance income that:

(A) Falls within a single category of net foreign base company income, as defined in paragraph (c) of this section, or net insurance income, and

(B) Also falls within a single separate limitation category for purposes of sections 904(d) and 960 and the regulations thereunder.

(ii) Passive foreign personal holding company income. (A) In general. For purposes of this paragraph (d) a single item of net foreign personal holding company income that is passive income is an amount of such income that falls within a single group of passive income under the grouping rules of § 1.904-4(c)(3), (4), and (5).

(B) Consistency rule. An election to exclude income from subpart F must be consistently made with respect to all items of passive foreign personal holding company income eligible to be excluded. Thus, high-taxed passive foreign personal holding company income of a controlled foreign corporation must be excluded in its entirety, or remain subject to subpart F.

(5) Procedure. The election provided by this paragraph (d) must be made—

(i) By controlling United States shareholders, as defined in § 1.964-1(c)(5), by attaching a statement to such effect with their original or amended income tax returns, and including any additional information required by subsequent administrative pronouncements, or

(ii) In such other manner as may be prescribed in subsequent administrative pronouncements.

An election made under the procedure provided by this paragraph (d)(5) is binding on all United States shareholders of the controlled foreign corporation.

(6) Illustrations. The rules of this paragraph (d) are illustrated by the following examples.

Example (1). (i) Items of income. During its 1987 taxable year, controlled foreign corporation CFC receives from outside its country of operation portfolio dividend income of $100 and interest income of $100 (consisting of a gross payment of $150 reduced by a third-country withholding tax of $50). For purposes of illustration, assume that the CFC incurs no expenses. None of the income is taxed in CFC's country of operation. The dividend income was not subject to their-country withholding taxes. The interest income was subject to withholding taxes equal to $50, and is therefore high withholding tax interest for purposes of section 960 (pursuant to the operation of section 904). The dividend income is passive income for purposes of section 960. Accordingly, pursuant to paragraph (d)(4) of this section, CFC has two items of income: (1) $100 of FPHC/passive income (the dividends) and (2) $100 of FPHC/high withholding tax income (the interest). The election under paragraph (d)(5) of this section to exclude high-taxed income from the operation of subpart F is potentially applicable to each such item in its entirety.

(ii) Effective rates of tax. No foreign tax would be deemed paid under section 960 with respect to item (1). Therefore, the effective rate of foreign tax is 0, and the item may not be excluded from subpart F under the rules of this paragraph (d). Foreign tax of $50 would be deemed paid under section 960 with respect to item (2). Therefore, the effective rate of foreign tax is 33 percent ($50 of creditable taxes paid, divided by $150, consisting of the item of net foreign base company income ($100) plus creditable taxes paid thereon ($50). The highest rate of tax specified in section 11 for the 1987 taxable year is 34 percent. Accordingly, item (2) may be excluded from subpart F pursuant to an election under paragraph (d)(5) of this section, since it is subject to foreign tax at an effective rate that is greater than 30.6 percent (90 percent of 34 percent). However, it remains high withholding tax interest when included.

Example (2). The facts are the same as in Example (1), except that CFC's country of operation imposes a tax of $50 with respect to CFC's dividend income. The interest income is still high withholding tax interest. The dividend income is still passive income (without regard to the possible applicability of the high tax exception of section 904(d)(2)). Accordingly, CFC has two items of income for purposes of this paragraph (d): (1) $100 of FPHC/high withholding tax interest income, and (2) $50 of FPHC/passive income (net of the $50 foreign tax). Both items are taxed at an effective rate greater than 31.6 percent. Item 1: Foreign tax ($50) divided by sum ($150) of income item ($100) plus creditable tax thereon ($50) equals 33 percent. Item 2: Foreign tax ($50) divided by sum ($100) of income item ($50) plus creditable tax thereon ($50) equals 50 percent. Accordingly, an election may be made under paragraph (d)(5) of this section to exclude either, both, or neither of items 1 and 2 from subpart F.

Example (3). The facts are the same as in Example (1), except that the $100 of portfolio dividend income is subject to a third-country withholding tax of $50, and the $150 of interest income is from sources within CFC's country of operation, is subject to a $10 income tax therein, and is not subject to a withholding tax. Although the interest income and the dividend income are both passive income, under paragraph (d)(4)(ii)(A) of this section they constitute separate items of income pursuant to the application of the grouping rules of § 1.904-4(c). Accordingly, CFC has two items of income for purposes of this paragraph (d): (1) $50 (net of tax) of FPHC/non-country of operation/greater than 15 percent withholding tax income; and (2) $140 (net of $10 tax) of FPHC/country of operation income. Item 1 is taxed at an effective rate greater than 30.6 percent, but Item 2 is not. Item 1: Foreign tax ($50) divided by sum ($100) of income item ($50) plus creditable tax thereon ($50) equals 50 percent. Item 2: Foreign tax ($10) divided by sum ($150) of income item ($140) plus creditable tax thereon ($10) equals 6.67 percent. Therefore, an election may be made under paragraph (d)(5) of this section to exclude Item 1 but not Item 2 from subpart F.

Example (4). The facts are the same as in Example (3), except that the $150 of interest income is subject to an income tax of $50 in CFC's country of operation. Accordingly, CFC has two items of income, as in Example (4), but both items are taxed at an effective rate greater than 30.6 percent. Item 1: Foreign tax ($50) divided by sum ($100) of income item ($50) plus creditable tax thereon ($50) equals 50 percent. Item 2: Foreign tax ($50) divided by sum ($150) if income item ($100) plus creditable tax thereon ($50) equals 33 percent. Pursuant to the consistency rule of paragraph (d)(4)(ii)(B) of this section, CFC's shareholders must consistently elect or not elect to exclude from subpart F all items of FPHC income that are eligible to be excluded. Therefore, an election may be made to exclude both Item 1 and Item 2 from subpart F, or neither may be excluded.

(e) Character of an item of income. *(1) Substance of the transaction.* For purposes of section 954 and the regulations thereunder, items of income shall be characterized in accordance with the substance of the transaction, and not in accordance with the designation applied by the parties to the transaction. For example, an amount received as "rent" which actually constitutes income from the sale of property, royalties, or income from services shall not be characterized as "rent" but shall be characterized as income from the sale of property, royalties or income from services, respectively. Local law shall not be controlling in characterizing an item of income.

(2) Separable character. To the extent one of the definitional provisions of section 953 or 954 describes a portion of the income or gain derived from a transaction, that portion of income or gain is so characterized. Thus, a single transaction may give rise to income in more than one category of foreign base company income described in paragraph (a)(2) of this section. For example, if a controlled foreign corporation, in its business of purchasing and selling personal property, receives interest (including imputed interest and market discount) on an account receivable arising from a sale, a portion of the income derived from the transaction by the controlled foreign corporation will be interest, and another portion will be gain (or loss) from the sale of personal property. If the sale is denominated in a currency other than a functional currency as defined in section 985 and the regulations thereunder, the controlled foreign corporation may have additional income in the form of foreign currency gain as defined in section 988.

(3) Predominant character. The portion of income derived from a transaction that meets the definition of foreign personal holding company income is always separately determinable, and thus must always be segregated from other income and separately classified under paragraph (2) of this paragraph (e). However, the portion of income derived from a transaction that would meet a particular definitional provision under section 954 or 953 and the regulations thereunder (other than the definition of foreign personal holding company income) in unusual circumstances may be indeterminable. If such portion is indeterminable, it must be classified in accordance with the predominant character of the transaction. For example, if a controlled foreign corporation engineers, fabricates, and installs a fixed offshore drilling platform as part of an integrated transaction, and the portion of income that relates to services is not accounted for separately from the portion that relates to sales, and is otherwise indeterminable, then the classification of income from the transaction shall be made in accordance with the predominant character of the particular integrated arrangement.

(4) Coordination of categories of gross foreign base company income or gross insurance income. The definitions of gross foreign base company income and gross insurance income are limited by the following rules (to be applied in numerical order):

(i) If an item of income is included in Subpart F income under section 952(a)(1) and the regulations thereunder as insurance income, it is by definition excluded from any other category of subpart F income.

(ii) If an item of income is included in the foreign base company oil related income of a controlled foreign corporation, it is by definition excluded from any other category of foreign base company income, other than as provided in subdivision (i) of this paragraph (e)(4).

(iii) If an item of income is included in the foreign base company shipping income of a controlled foreign corporation, it is by definition excluded from any other category of foreign base company income, other than as provided in subdivisions (i) and (ii) of this paragraph (e)(4).

(iv) If an item of income is included in foreign personal holding company income of a controlled foreign corporation, it is by definition not included in any other category of foreign base company income, other than as provided in subdivisions (i), (ii), and (iii) of this paragraph (e)(4).

An item of income shall not be excluded from the definition of a category of gross foreign base company income or gross insurance income under this paragraph (e)(4) by reason of being included in the general definition of another category of gross foreign base company income or gross insurance income, if the item of income is excluded from that other category by a more specific provision of section 953 or 954 and the regulations thereunder. For example, income derived from a commodity transaction that is excluded from foreign personal holding company income under § 1.954-2T(f) as income from qualified active sales may be included in gross foreign base company income if it also meets the definition of foreign base company sales income. See § 1.954-2T(a)(2) for the coordination of overlapping categories within the definition of foreign personal holding company income.

T.D. 8216, 7/20/88, amend T.D. 8618, 9/6/95.

§ 1.954-2 Foreign personal holding company income.

Caution: The Treasury has not yet amended Reg § 1.954-2 to reflect changes made by P.L. 105-34.

(a) Computation of foreign personal holding company income. *(1) Categories of foreign personal holding company income.* For purposes of subpart F and the regulations under that subpart, foreign personal holding company income consists of the following categories of income—

(i) Dividends, interest, rents, royalties, and annuities as described in paragraph (b) of this section;

(ii) Gain from certain property transactions as described in paragraph (e) of this section;

(iii) Gain from commodities transactions as described in paragraph (f) of this section;

(iv) Foreign currency gain as described in paragraph (g) of this section; and

(v) Income equivalent to interest as described in paragraph (h) of this section.

(2) Coordination of overlapping categories under foreign personal holding company provisions. (i) In general. If any portion of income, gain or loss from a transaction is described in more than one category of foreign personal holding company income (as described in paragraph (a)(2)(ii) of this section), that portion of income, gain or loss is treated solely as income, gain or loss from the category of foreign personal holding company income with the highest priority.

(ii) Priority of categories. The categories of foreign personal holding company income, listed from highest priority (paragraph (a)(2)(ii)(A) of this section) to lowest priority (paragraph (a)(2)(ii)(E) of this section), are—

(A) Dividends, interest, rents, royalties, and annuities, as described in paragraph (b) of this section;

(B) Income equivalent to interest, as described in paragraph (h) of this section without regard to the exceptions in paragraph (h)(1)(ii)(A) of this section;

(C) Foreign currency gain or loss, as described in paragraph (g) of this section without regard to the exclusion in paragraph (g)(2)(ii) of this section;

(D) Gain or loss from commodities transactions, as described in paragraph (f) of this section without regard to the exclusion in paragraph (f)(1)(ii) of this section; and

(E) Gain or loss from certain property transactions, as described in paragraph (e) of this section without regard to the exceptions in paragraph (e)(1)(ii) of this section.

(3) Changes in the use or purpose for which property is held. (i) In general. Under paragraphs (e), (f), (g) and (h) of this section, transactions in certain property give rise to gain or loss included in the computation of foreign personal holding company income if the controlled foreign corporation holds that property for a particular use or purpose. The use or purpose for which property is held is that use or purpose for which it was held for more than one-half of the period during which the controlled foreign corporation held the property prior to the disposition.

(ii) Special rules. (A) Anti-abuse rule. If a principal purpose of a change in use or purpose of property was to avoid including gain or loss in the computation of foreign personal holding company income, all the gain or loss from the disposition of the property is treated as foreign personal holding company income. A purpose may be a principal purpose even though it is outweighed by other purposes (taken together or separately).

(B) Hedging transactions. The provisions of paragraph (a)(3)(i) of this section shall not apply to bona fide hedging transactions, as defined in paragraph (a)(4)(ii) of this section. A transaction will be treated as a bona fide hedging transaction only so long as it satisfies the requirements of paragraph (a)(4)(ii) of this section.

(iii) Example. The following example illustrates the application of this paragraph (a)(3).

Example. At the beginning of taxable year 1, CFC, a controlled foreign corporation, purchases a building for investment. During taxable years 1 and 2, CFC derives rents from the building that are included in the computation of foreign personal holding company income under paragraph (b)(1)(iii) of this section. At the beginning of taxable year 3, CFC changes the use of the building by terminating all leases and using it in an active trade or business. At the beginning of taxable year 4, CFC sells the building at a gain. The building was not used in an active trade or business of CFC for more than one-half of the period during which it was held by CFC. Therefore, the building is considered to be property that gives rise to rents, as described in paragraph (e)(2) of this section, and gain from the sale is included in the computation of CFC's foreign personal holding company income under paragraph (e) of this section.

(4) Definitions and special rules. The following definitions and special rules apply for purposes of computing foreign personal holding company income under this section.

(i) Interest. The term interest includes all amounts that are treated as interest income (including interest on a tax-exempt obligation) by reason of the Internal Revenue Code or Income Tax Regulations or any other provision of law. For example, interest includes stated interest, acquisition discount, original issue discount, de minimis original issue discount, market discount, de minimis market discount, and unstated interest, as adjusted by any amortizable bond premium or acquisition premium.

(ii) Bona fide hedging transaction. (A) Definition. The term bona fide hedging transaction means a transaction that meets the requirements of § 1.1221-2(a) through (d) and that is identified in accordance with the requirements of paragraph (a)(4)(ii)(B) of this section, except that in applying § 1.1221-2(b)(1), the risk being hedged may be with respect to ordinary property, section 1231 property, or a section 988 transaction. A transaction that hedges the liabilities, inventory or other assets of a related person (as defined in section 954(d)(3)), that is entered into to assume or reduce risks of a related person, or that is entered into by a person other than a person acting in its capacity as a regular dealer (as defined in paragraph (a)(4)(iv) of this section) to reduce risks assumed from a related person, will not be treated as a bona fide hedging transaction. For an illustration of how this rule applies with respect to foreign currency transactions, see paragraph (g)(2)(ii)(D) of this section.

(B) Identification. The identification requirements of this section shall be satisfied if the taxpayer meets the identification and recordkeeping requirements of § 1.1221-2(f). However, for bona fide hedging transactions entered into prior to March 7, 1996, the identification and recordkeeping requirements of § 1.1221-2 shall not apply. Rather, for bona fide hedging transactions entered into on or after July 22, 1988 and prior to March 7, 1996, the identification and recordkeeping requirements shall be satisfied if such transactions are identified by the close of the fifth day after the day on which they are entered into. For bona fide hedging transactions entered into prior to July 22, 1988, the identification and recordkeeping requirements shall be satisfied if such transactions are identified reasonably contemporaneously with the date they are entered into, but no later than within the normal period prescribed under the method of accounting of the controlled foreign corporation used for financial reporting purposes.

(C) Effect of identification and non-identification. (1) Transactions identified. If a taxpayer identifies a transaction as a bona fide hedging transaction for purposes of this section, the identification is binding with respect to any loss arising from such transaction whether or not all of the requirements of paragraph (a)(4)(ii)(A) of this section are satisfied. Accordingly, such loss will be allocated against income that is not subpart F income (or, in the case of an election under paragraph (g)(3) of this section, against the category of subpart F income to which it relates) and apportioned among the categories of income described in section 904(d)(1). If the transaction is not in fact a bona fide hedging transaction described in paragraph (a)(4)(ii)(A) of this section, however, then any gain realized with respect to such transaction shall not be considered as gain from a bona fide hedging transaction. Accordingly, such gain shall be treated as gain from the appropriate category of foreign personal holding company income. Thus, the taxpayer's identification of the transaction as a hedging transaction does not itself operate to exclude gain from the appropriate category of foreign personal holding company income.

(2) Inadvertent identification. Notwithstanding paragraph (a)(4)(ii)(C)(1) of this section, if the taxpayer identifies a transaction as a bona fide hedging transaction for purposes of this section, the characterization of the loss is determined as if the transaction had not been identified as a bona fide hedging transaction if—

(i) The transaction is not a bona fide hedging transaction (as defined in paragraph (a)(4)(ii)(A) of this section);

(ii) The identification of the transaction as a bona fide hedging transaction was due to inadvertent error; and

(iii) All of the taxpayer's transactions in all open years are being treated on either original or, if necessary, amended returns in a manner consistent with the principles of this section.

(3) Transactions not identified. Except as provided in paragraphs (a)(4)(ii)(C)(4) and (5) of this section, the absence of an identification that satisfies the requirements of paragraph (a)(4)(ii)(B) of this section is binding and establishes that a transaction is not a bona fide hedging transaction. Thus, subject to the exceptions, the characterization of gain or loss is determined without reference to whether the transaction is a bona fide hedging transaction.

(4) Inadvertent error. If a taxpayer does not make an identification that satisfies the requirements of paragraph (a)(4)(ii)(B) of this section, the taxpayer may treat gain or loss from the transaction as gain or loss from a bona fide hedging transaction if—

(i) The transaction is a bona fide hedging transaction (as defined in paragraph (a)(4)(ii)(A) of this section);

(ii) The failure to identify the transaction was due to inadvertent error; and

(iii) All of the taxpayer's bona fide hedging transactions in all open years are being treated on either original or, if necessary, amended returns as bona fide hedging transactions in accordance with the rules of this section.

(5) Anti-abuse rule. If a taxpayer does not make an identification that satisfies all the requirements of paragraph (a)(4)(ii)(B) of this section but the taxpayer has no reasonable grounds for treating the transaction as other than a bona fide hedging transaction, then loss from the transaction shall be treated as realized with respect to a bona fide hedging transaction. Thus, a taxpayer may not elect to exclude loss from its proper characterization as a bona fide hedging transaction. The reasonableness of the taxpayer's failure to identify a transaction is determined by taking into consideration not only the requirements of paragraph (a)(4)(ii)(A) of this section but also the taxpayer's treatment of the transaction for financial accounting or other purposes and the taxpayer's identification of similar transactions as hedging transactions.

(iii) Inventory and similar property. (A) Definition. The term inventory and similar property (or inventory or similar property) means property that is stock in trade of the controlled foreign corporation or other property of a kind that would properly be included in the inventory of the controlled foreign corporation if on hand at the close of the taxable year (if the controlled foreign corporation were a domestic corporation), or property held by the controlled foreign corporation primarily for sale to customers in the ordinary course of its trade or business.

(B) Hedging transactions. A bona fide hedging transaction with respect to inventory or similar property (other than a transaction described in section 988(c)(1) without regard to section 988(c)(1)(D)(i)) shall be treated as a transaction in inventory or similar property.

(iv) Regular dealer. The term regular dealer means a controlled foreign corporation that—

(A) Regularly and actively offers to, and in fact does, purchase property from and sell property to customers who are not related persons (as defined in section 954(d)(3)) with respect to the controlled foreign corporation in the ordinary course of a trade or business; or

(B) Regularly and actively offers to, and in fact does, enter into, assume, offset, assign or otherwise terminate positions in property with customers who are not related persons (as defined in section 954(d)(3)) with respect to the controlled foreign corporation in the ordinary course of a trade or business.

(v) Dealer property. (A) Definition. Property held by a controlled foreign corporation is dealer property if—

(1) The controlled foreign corporation is a regular dealer in property of such kind (determined under paragraph (a)(4)(iv) of this section); and

(2) The property is held by the controlled foreign corporation in its capacity as a dealer in property of such kind without regard to whether the property arises from a transaction with a related person (as defined in section 954(d)(3)) with respect to the controlled foreign corporation. The property is not held by the controlled foreign corporation in its capacity as a dealer if the property is held for investment or speculation on its own behalf or on behalf of a related person (as defined in section 954(d)(3)).

(B) Securities dealers. If a controlled foreign corporation is a licensed securities dealer, only the securities that it has identified as held for investment in accordance with the provisions of section 475(b) or section 1236 will be considered to be property held for investment or speculation under this section. A licensed securities dealer is a controlled foreign corporation that is both a securities dealer, as defined in section 475, and a regular dealer, as defined in paragraph (a)(4)(iv) of this section, and that is either—

(1) registered as a securities dealer under section 15(a) of the Securities Exchange Act of 1934 or as a Government securities dealer under section 15C(a) of such Act; or

(2) licensed or authorized in the country in which it is chartered, incorporated, or organized to purchase and sell securities from or to customers who are residents of that country. The conduct of such securities activities must be subject to bona fide regulation, including appropriate reporting, monitoring, and prudential (including capital adequacy) requirements, by a securities regulatory authority in that country that regularly enforces compliance with such requirements and prudential standards.

(C) Hedging transactions. A bona fide hedging transaction with respect to dealer property shall be treated as a transaction in dealer property.

(vi) Examples. The following examples illustrate the application of paragraphs (a)(4)(ii), (iv) and (v) of this section.

Example (1). (i) CFC1 and CFC2 are related controlled foreign corporations (within the meaning of section 954(d)(3)) located in Countries F and G, respectively. CFC1 and CFC2 regularly purchase securities from and sell securities to customers who are not related persons with respect to CFC1 or CFC2 (within the meaning of section 954(d)(3)) in the ordinary course of their businesses and regularly and actively hold themselves out as being willing to, and in fact do, enter into either side of options, forward contracts, or other financial instruments. CFC1 uses securities that are traded in securities markets in Country G to hedge positions that it enters into with customers located in Country F. CFC1 is not a member of a securities exchange in Country G, so it purchases such securities from CFC2 and unrelated persons that are registered as securities dealers in Country G and that are members of Country G securities exchanges. Such hedging transactions qualify as bona fide hedging transactions under paragraph (a)(4)(ii) of this section.

(ii) Transactions that CFC1 and CFC2 enter into with each other do not affect the determination of whether they are regular dealers. Because CFC1 and CFC2 regularly purchase securities from and sell securities to customers who are not related persons within the meaning of section 954(d)(3) in the ordinary course of their businesses and regularly and actively hold themselves out as being willing to, and in fact do, enter into either side of options, forward contracts, or other financial instruments, however, they qualify as regular dealers in such property within the meaning of paragraph (a)(4)(iv) of this section. Moreover, because CFC1 purchases securities from CFC2 as bona fide hedging transactions with respect to dealer property, the securities are dealer property under paragraph (a)(4)(v)(C) of this section. Similarly, because CFC2 sells securities to CFC1 in the ordinary course of its business as a dealer, the securities are dealer property under paragraph (a)(4)(v)(A) of this section.

Example (2). (i) CFC is a controlled foreign corporation located in Country B. CFC serves as the currency coordination center for the controlled group, aggregating currency risks incurred by the group and entering into hedging transactions that transfer those risks outside of the group. CFC regularly and actively holds itself out as being willing to, and in fact does, enter into either side of options, forward contracts, or other financial instruments with other members of the same controlled group. CFC hedges risks arising from such transactions by entering into transactions with persons who are not related persons (within the meaning of section 954(d)(3)) with respect to CFC. However, CFC does not regularly and actively hold itself out as being willing to, and does not, enter into either side of transactions with unrelated persons.

(ii) CFC is not a regular dealer in property under paragraph (a)(4)(iv) of this section and its options, forwards, and other financial instruments are not dealer property within the meaning of paragraph (a)(4)(v) of this section.

(vii) Debt instrument. The term debt instrument includes bonds, debentures, notes, certificates, accounts receivable, and other evidences of indebtedness.

(5) Special rules applicable to distributive share of partnership income. (i) [Reserved].

(ii) Certain other exceptions applicable to foreign personal holding company income. To determine the extent to which a controlled foreign corporation's distributive share of an item of income of a partnership is foreign personal holding company income—

(A) The exceptions contained in section 954(c) that are based on whether the controlled foreign corporation is engaged in the active conduct of a trade or business, including section 954(c)(2) and paragraphs (b)(2) and (6), (e)(1)(ii) and (3)(ii), (iii) and (iv), (f)(1)(ii), (g)(2)(ii), and (h)(3)(ii) of this section, shall apply only if any such exception would have applied to exclude the income from foreign personal holding company income if the controlled foreign corporation had earned the income directly, determined by taking into account only the activities of, and property owned by, the partnership and not the separate activities or property of the controlled foreign corporation or any other person;

(B) A controlled foreign corporation's distributive share of partnership income will not be excluded from foreign personal holding company income under the exception contained in section 954(h) unless the controlled foreign corporation is an eligible controlled foreign corporation within the meaning of section 954(h)(2) (taking into account the income of the controlled foreign corporation and any partnerships or other qualified business units, within the meaning of section 989(a), of the controlled foreign corporation, including the controlled foreign corporation's distributive share of partnership income) and the partnership, of which the controlled foreign corporation is a partner, generates qualified banking or financing income within the meaning of section 954(h)(3) (taking into account only the income of the partnership);

(C) A controlled foreign corporation's distributive share of partnership income will not be excluded from foreign personal holding company income under the exception contained in section 954(i) unless the controlled foreign corporation is a qualifying insurance company, as defined in section 953(e)(3), and the income of the partnership would have been qualified insurance income, as defined in section 954(i)(2), if received by the controlled foreign corporation directly. See § 1.952-1(g)(1).

(iii) Examples. The application of paragraph (a)(5)(ii) is demonstrated by the following examples:

Example (1). B Corp, a Country C corporation, is a controlled foreign corporation within the meaning of section 957(a). B Corp is an 80 percent partner of RKS Partnership, a Country D partnership whose principal office is located in Country D. RKS Partnership is a qualified business unit of B Corp, within the meaning of section 989(a). B Corp, including income earned through RKS Partnership, derives more than 70 percent of its gross income directly from the active and regular conduct of a lending or finance business, within the meaning of section 954(h)(4), from transactions in various countries with customers which are not related persons. Thus, B Corp is predominantly engaged in the active conduct of a banking, financing, or similar business within the meaning of section 954(h)(2)(A)(i). B Corp conducts substantial activity with respect to such business within the meaning of section 954(h)(2)(A)(ii). RKS Partnership derives more than 30 percent of its income from the active and regular conduct of a lending or finance business, within the meaning of section 954(h)(4), from transactions with customers which are not related persons and which are located solely within the home country of RKS Partnership, Country D. B Corp's distributive share of RKS Partnership's income from its lending or finance business will satisfy the special rule for income derived in the active conduct of banking, financing, or similar business of section 954(h). B Corp is an eligible controlled foreign corporation within the meaning of section 954(h)(2) and RKS Partnership generates qualified banking or financing income within the meaning of section 954(h)(3). B Corp does not have any foreign personal holding company income with respect to its distributive share of RKS Partnership income attributable to its lending or finance business income earned in Country D.

Example (2). D Corp, a Country F corporation, is a controlled foreign corporation within the meaning of section 957(a). D Corp is a qualifying insurance company, within the meaning of section 953(e)(3), that is engaged in the business of issuing life insurance contracts. D Corp has reserves of $100x, all of which are allocable to exempt contracts, and $10x of surplus, which is equal to 10 percent of the reserves allocable to exempt contracts. D Corp contributed the $100x of reserves and $10x of surplus to DJ Partnership in exchange for a 40-percent partnership interest. DJ Partnership is an entity organized under the laws of Country G and is treated as a partnership under the laws of Country G and Country F. DJ Partnership earns $30x of investment income during the taxable year that is received from persons who are not related persons with respect to D Corp, within the meaning of section 954(d)(3). D Corp's distributive share of this investment income is $12x. This income is treated as earned by D Corp in Country F under the tax laws of Country F and meets the definition of exempt insurance income in section 953(e)(1). This $12x of investment income would be qualified insurance income, under section 954(i)(2), if D Corp had received the income directly, because the $110x invested by D Corp in DJ Partnership is equal to D Corp's reserves allocable to exempt contracts under section 954(i)(2)(A) and allowable surplus under section 954(i)(2)(B)(ii). Thus, D Corp's distributive share of DJ Partnership's income will be excluded from foreign personal holding company income under section 954(i).

(iv) [Reserved].

(v) Effective date. This paragraph (a)(5) applies to taxable years of a controlled foreign corporation beginning on or after July 23, 2002.

(b) Dividends, interest, rents, royalties, and annuities. *(1) In general.* Foreign personal holding company income includes—

(i) Dividends, except certain dividends from related persons as described in paragraph (b)(4) of this section and distributions of previously taxed income under section 959(b);

(ii) Interest, except export financing interest as defined in paragraph (b)(2) of this section and certain interest received from related persons as described in paragraph (b)(4) of this section;

(iii) Rents and royalties, except certain rents and royalties received from related persons as described in paragraph (b)(5) of this section and rents and royalties derived in the active conduct of a trade or business as defined in paragraph (b)(6) of this section; and

(iv) Annuities.

(2) Exclusion of certain export financing interest. (i) In general. Foreign personal holding company income does not include interest that is export financing interest. The term export financing interest means interest that is derived in the conduct of a banking business and is export financing interest as defined in section 904(d)(2)(G). Solely for purposes of determining whether interest is export financing interest, property is treated as manufactured, produced, grown, or extracted in the United States if it is so treated under § 1.927(a)-1T(c).

(ii) Exceptions. Export financing interest does not include income from related party factoring that is treated as interest under section 864(d)(1) or (6) after the application of section 864(d)(7).

(iii) Conduct of a banking business. For purposes of this section, export financing interest is considered derived in the conduct of a banking business if, in connection with the financing from which the interest is derived, the corporation, through its own officers or staff of employees, engages in all the activities in which banks customarily engage in issuing and servicing a loan.

(iv) Examples. The following examples illustrate the application of this paragraph (b)(2).

Example (1). (i) DS, a domestic corporation, manufactures property in the United States. In addition to selling inventory (property described in section 1221(1)), DS occasionally sells depreciable equipment it manufactures for use in its trade or business, which is property described in section 1221(2). Less than 50 percent of the fair market value, determined in accordance with section 904(d)(2)(G), of each item of inventory or equipment sold by DS is attributable to products imported into the United States. CFC, a controlled foreign corporation with respect to which DS is a related person (within the meaning of section 954(d)(3)), provides loans described in section 864(d)(6) to unrelated persons for the purchase of property from DS. This property is purchased exclusively for use or consumption outside the United States and outside CFC's country of incorporation.

(ii) If, in issuing and servicing loans made with respect to purchases from DS of depreciable equipment used in its trade or business, which is property described in section 1221(2) in the hands of DS, CFC engages in all the activities in which banks customarily engage in issuing and servicing loans, the interest accrued from these loans would be export financing interest meeting the requirements of this paragraph (b)(2) and, thus, not included in foreign personal holding company income. However, interest from the loans made with respect to purchases from DS of property that is inventory in the hands of DS cannot be export financing interest because it is treated as income from a trade or service receivable under section 864(d)(6) and the exception under section 864(d)(7) does not apply. Thus the interest from loans made with respect to this inventory is included in foreign personal holding company income under paragraph (b)(1)(ii) of this section.

Example (2). (i) DS, a domestic corporation, wholly owns two controlled foreign corporations organized in Country A, CFC1 and CFC2. CFC1 purchases from DS property that DS manufactures in the United States. CFC1 uses the purchased property as a component part of property that CFC1 manufactures in Country A within the meaning of § 1.954-3(a)(4). CFC2 provides loans described in section 864(d)(6) to unrelated persons in Country A for the purchase of the property that CFC1 manufactures in Country A.

(ii) The interest accrued from the loans by CFC2 is not export financing interest as defined in section 904(d)(2)(G) because the property sold by CFC1 is not manufactured in the United States under § 1.927(a)-1T(c). No portion of the interest is export financing interest as defined in this paragraph (b)(2). The full amount of the interest is, therefore, included in foreign personal holding company income under paragraph (b)(1)(ii) of this section.

(3) Treatment of tax exempt interest. For taxable years of a controlled foreign corporation beginning after March 3, 1997, foreign personal holding company income includes all interest income, including interest that is described in section 103 (see § 1.952-2(c)(1)).

(4) Exclusion of dividends or interest from related persons. (i) In general. (A) Corporate payor. Foreign personal holding company income received by a controlled foreign corporation does not include dividends or interest if the payor—

(1) Is a corporation that is a related person with respect to the controlled foreign corporation, as defined in section 954(d)(3);

(2) Is created or organized under the laws of the same foreign country (the country of incorporation) as is the controlled foreign corporation; and

(3) Uses a substantial part of its assets in a trade or business in its country of incorporation, as determined under this paragraph (b)(4).

(B) Payment by a partnership. For purposes of this paragraph (b)(4), if a partnership with one or more corporate partners makes a payment of interest, a corporate partner will be treated as the payor of the interest—

(1) If the interest payment gives rise to a partnership item of deduction under the Internal Revenue Code or Income Tax Regulations, to the extent that the item of deduction is allocable to the corporate partner under section 704(b); or

(2) If the interest payment does not give rise to a partnership item of deduction under the Internal Revenue Code or Income Tax Regulations, to the extent that a partnership item reasonably related to the payment would be allocated to that partner under an existing allocation under the partnership agreement (made pursuant to section 704(b)).

(ii) Exceptions. (A) Dividends. Dividends are excluded from foreign personal holding company income under this paragraph (b)(4) only to the extent that they are paid out of earnings and profits that are earned or accumulated during a period in which—

(1) The stock on which dividends are paid with respect to which the exclusion is claimed was owned by the recipient controlled foreign corporation directly, or indirectly through a chain of one or more subsidiaries each of which meets the requirements of paragraph (b)(4)(i)(A) of this section; and

(2) Each of the requirements of paragraph (b)(4)(i)(A) of this section is satisfied or, to the extent earned or accumulated during a taxable year of the related foreign corporation ending on or before December 31, 1962, during a period in which the payor was a related corporation as to the controlled foreign corporation and the other requirements of paragraph (b)(4)(i)(A) of this section were substantially satisfied.

(3) This paragraph (b)(4)(ii)(A) is illustrated by the following example:

Example. A, a domestic corporation, owns all of the stock of B, a corporation created and organized under the laws of Country Y, and C, a corporation created and organized under the laws of Country X. The taxable year of each of the corporations is the calendar year. In Year 1, B earns $100 of income from the sale of products in Country Y that it manufactured in Country Y. C had no earnings and profits in Year 1. On January 1 of Year 2, A contributes all of the stock of B and C to Newco, a Country Y corporation, in exchange for all of the stock of Newco. Neither B nor C earns any income in Year 2, but at the end of Year 2 B distributes the $100 accumulated earnings and profits to Newco. Newco's income from the distribution, $100, is foreign personal holding company income because the earnings and profits distributed by B were not earned or accumulated during a period in which the stock of B was owned by Newco and in which each of the requirements of paragraph (b)(4)(i)(A) of this section was satisfied.

(B) Interest paid out of adjusted foreign base company income or insurance income. (1) In general. Interest may not be excluded from the foreign personal holding company income of the recipient under this paragraph (b)(4) to the extent that the deduction for the interest is allocated under § 1.954-1(a)(4) and (c) to the payor's adjusted gross foreign base company income (as defined in § 1.954-1(a)(3)), adjusted gross insurance income (as defined in § 1.954-1(a)(6)), or any other category of income included in the computation of subpart F income under section 952(a).

(2) Rule for corporations that are both recipients and payors of interest. If a controlled foreign corporation is both a recipient and payor of interest, the interest that is received will be characterized before the interest that is paid. In addition, the amount of interest paid or accrued, directly or indirectly, by the controlled foreign corporation to a related person (as defined in section 954(d)(3)) shall be offset against and eliminate any interest received or accrued, directly or indirectly, by the controlled foreign corporation from that related person. In a case in which the controlled foreign corporation pays or accrues interest to a related person, as defined in section 954(d)(3), and also receives or accrues interest indirectly from the related person, the smallest interest payment is eliminated and the amounts of all other interest payments are reduced by the amount of the smallest interest payment.

(C) Coordination with sections 864(d) and 881(c). Income of a controlled foreign corporation that is treated as interest under section 864(d)(1) or (6), or that is portfolio interest, as defined by section 881(c), is not excluded from foreign personal holding company income under section 954(c)(3)(A)(i) and this paragraph (b)(4).

(iii) Trade or business requirement. Except as otherwise provided under this paragraph (b)(4), the principles of section 367(a) apply for purposes of determining whether the payor has a trade or business in its country of incorporation and whether its assets are used in that trade or business. Property purchased or produced for use in a trade or business is not considered used in a trade or business before it is placed in service or after it is retired from service as determined in accordance with the principles of sections 167 and 168.

(iv) Substantial assets test. A substantial part of the assets of the payor will be considered to be used in a trade or business located in the payor's country of incorporation for a taxable year only if the average value of the payor's assets for such year that are used in the trade or business and are located in such country equals more than 50 percent of the average value of all the assets of the payor (including assets not used in a trade or business). The average value of assets for the taxable year is determined by averaging the values of assets at the close of each quarter of the taxable year. The value of assets is determined under paragraph (b)(4)(v) of this section, and the location of assets used in a trade or business of the payor is determined under paragraphs (b)(4)(vi) through (xi) of this section.

(v) Valuation of assets. For purposes of determining whether a substantial part of the assets of the payor are used in a trade or business in its country of incorporation, the value of assets shall be their fair market value (not reduced by liabilities), which, in the absence of affirmative evidence to the contrary, shall be deemed to be their adjusted basis.

(vi) Location of tangible property. (A) In general. Tangible property (other than inventory and similar property as defined in paragraph (a)(4)(iii) of this section, and dealer property as defined in paragraph (a)(4)(v) of this section) used in a trade or business is considered located in the country in which it is physically located.

(B) Exception. An item of tangible personal property that is used in the trade or business of a payor in the payor's country of incorporation is considered located within the payor's country of incorporation while it is temporarily located elsewhere for inspection or repair if the property is not placed in service in a country other than the payor's country of incorporation and is not to be so placed in service following the inspection or repair.

(vii) Location of intangible property. (A) In general. Intangible property (other than inventory and similar property as defined in paragraph (a)(4)(iii) of this section, dealer property as defined in paragraph (a)(4)(v) of this section, and debt instruments) is considered located entirely in the payor's country of incorporation for a quarter of the taxable year only if the payor conducts all of its activities in connection with the use or exploitation of the property in that country during that entire quarter. For this purpose, the country in which the activities connected to the use or exploitation of the property are conducted is the country in which the expenses associated with these activities are incurred. Expenses incurred in connection with the use or exploitation of an item of intangible property are included in the computation provided by this paragraph (b)(4) if they would be deductible under section 162 or includible in inventory costs or the cost of goods sold if the payor were a domestic corporation. If the payor conducts such activities through an agent or independent contractor, then the expenses incurred by the payor with respect to the agent or independent contractor shall be deemed to be incurred by the payor in the country in which the expenses of the agent or independent contractor were incurred by the agent or independent contractor.

(B) Exception for property located in part in the payor's country of incorporation. If the payor conducts its activities in connection with the use or exploitation of an item of intangible property, including goodwill (other than inventory and similar property, dealer property and debt instruments) during a quarter of the taxable year both in its country of incorporation and elsewhere, then the value of the intangible considered located in the payor's country of incorporation during that quarter is a percentage of the value of the item as of the close of the quarter. That percentage equals the ratio that the expenses incurred by the payor (described in paragraph (b)(4)(vii)(A) of this section) during the entire quarter by reason of activities that are connected with the use or exploitation of the item of intangible property and are conducted in the payor's country of incorporation bear to all expenses incurred by the payor during the entire quarter by reason of all such activities worldwide.

(viii) Location of inventory and dealer property. (A) In general. Inventory and similar property, as defined in paragraph (a)(4)(iii) of this section, and dealer property, as defined in paragraph (a)(4)(v) of this section, are considered located entirely in the payor's country of incorporation for a quarter of the taxable year only if the payor conducts all of its activities in connection with the production and sale, or purchase and resale, of such property in its country of incorporation during that entire quarter. If the payor conducts such activities through an agent or independent contractor, then the location of such activities is the place in which they are conducted by the agent or independent contractor.

(B) Inventory and dealer property located in part in the payor's country of incorporation. If the payor conducts its activities in connection with the production and sale, or purchase and resale, of inventory or similar property or dealer property during a quarter of the taxable year both in its country of incorporation and elsewhere, then the value of the inventory or similar property or dealer property considered located in the payor's country of incorporation during each quarter is a percentage of the value of the inventory or similar property or dealer property as of the close of the quarter. That percentage equals the ratio that the costs and expenses incurred by the payor during the entire quarter by reason of activities connected with the production and sale, or purchase and resale, of inventory or similar property or dealer property that are conducted in the payor's country of incorporation bear to all costs or expenses incurred by the payor during the entire quarter by reason of all such activities worldwide. A cost incurred in connection with the production and sale or purchase and resale of inventory or similar property or dealer property is included in this computation if it—

(1) Would be included in inventory costs or otherwise capitalized with respect to inventory or similar property or dealer property under section 61, 263A, 471, or 472 if the payor were a domestic corporation; or

(2) Would be deductible under section 162 if the payor were a domestic corporation and is definitely related to gross income derived from such property (but not to all classes of gross income derived by the payor) under the principles of § 1.861-8.

(ix) Location of debt instruments. For purposes of this paragraph (b)(4), debt instruments, other than debt instruments that are inventory or similar property (as defined in paragraph (a)(4)(iii) of this section) or dealer property (as defined in paragraph (a)(4)(v) of this section) are considered to be used in a trade or business only if they arise from the sale of inventory or similar property or dealer property by the payor or from the rendition of services by the payor in the ordinary course of a trade or business of the payor, and only until such time as interest is required to be charged under section 482. Debt instruments that arise from the sale of inventory or similar property or dealer property during a quarter are treated as having the same location, proportionately, as the inventory or similar property or dealer property held during that quarter. Debt instruments arising from the rendition of services in the ordinary course of a trade or business are considered located on a proportionate basis in the countries in which the services to which they relate are performed.

(x) Treatment of certain stock interests. Stock in a controlled foreign corporation (lower-tier corporation) that is incorporated in the same country as the payor and that is more than 50-percent owned, directly or indirectly, by the payor within the meaning of section 958(a) shall be considered located in the payor's country of incorporation and, solely for purposes of section 954(c)(3), used in a trade or business of the payor in proportion to the value of the assets of the lower-tier corporation that are used in a trade or business in the country of incorporation. The location of assets used in a trade or business of the lower-tier corporation shall be determined under the rules of this paragraph (b)(4).

(xi) Treatment of banks and insurance companies. [Reserved]

(5) Exclusion of rents and royalties derived from related persons. (i) In general. (A) Corporate payor. Foreign personal holding company income received by a controlled foreign corporation does not include rents or royalties if—

(1) The payor is a corporation that is a related person with respect to the controlled foreign corporation, as defined in section 954(d)(3); and

(2) The rents or royalties are for the use of, or the privilege of using, property within the country under the laws of which the controlled foreign corporation receiving the payments is created or organized (the country of incorporation).

(B) Payment by a partnership. For purposes of this paragraph (b)(5), if a partnership with one or more corporate partners makes a payment of rents or royalties, a corporate partner will be treated as the payor of the rents or royalties—

(1) If the rent or royalty payment gives rise to a partnership item of deduction under the Internal Revenue Code or Income Tax Regulations, to the extent the item of deduction is allocable to the corporate partner under section 704(b); or

(2) If the rent or royalty payment does not give rise to a partnership item of deduction under the Internal Revenue Code or Income Tax Regulations, to the extent that a partnership item reasonably related to the payment would be allocated to that partner under an existing allocation under the partnership agreement (made pursuant to section 704(b)).

(ii) Exceptions. (A) Rents or royalties paid out of adjusted foreign base company income or insurance income. Rents or royalties may not be excluded from the foreign personal holding company income of the recipient under this paragraph (b)(5) to the extent that deductions for the payments are allocated under section 954(b)(5) and § 1.954-1(a)(4) and (c) to the payor's adjusted gross foreign base company income (as defined in § 1.954-1(a)(3)), adjusted gross insurance income (as defined in § 1.954-1(a)(6)), or any other category of income included in the computation of subpart F income under section 952(a).

(B) Property used in part in the controlled foreign corporation's country of incorporation. If the payor uses the property both in the controlled foreign corporation's country of incorporation and elsewhere, the part of the rent or royalty attributable (determined under the principles of section 482) to the use of, or the privilege of using, the property outside such country of incorporation is included in the computation of foreign personal holding company income under this paragraph (b).

(6) Exclusion of rents and royalties derived in the active conduct of a trade or business. Foreign personal holding company income shall not include rents or royalties that are derived in the active conduct of a trade or business and received from a person that is not a related person (as defined in section 954(d)(3)) with respect to the controlled foreign corporation. For purposes of this section, rents or royalties are derived in the active conduct of a trade or business only if the provisions of paragraph (c) or (d) of this section are satisfied.

(c) Excluded rents. *(1) Active conduct of a trade or business.* Rents will be considered for purposes of paragraph (b)(6) of this section to be derived in the active conduct of a trade or business if such rents are derived by the controlled foreign corporation (the lessor) from leasing any of the following—

(i) Property that the lessor has manufactured or produced, or has acquired and added substantial value to, but only if the lessor is regularly engaged in the manufacture or production of, or in the acquisition and addition of substantial value to, property of such kind;

(ii) Real property with respect to which the lessor, through its own officers or staff of employees, regularly performs active and substantial management and operational functions while the property is leased;

(iii) Personal property ordinarily used by the lessor in the active conduct of a trade or business, leased temporarily during a period when the property would, but for such leasing, be idle; or

(iv) Property that is leased as a result of the performance of marketing functions by such lessor if the lessor, through its own officers or staff of employees located in a foreign country, maintains and operates an organization in such country that is regularly engaged in the business of marketing, or of marketing and servicing, the leased property and that is substantial in relation to the amount of rents derived from the leasing of such property.

(2) Special rules. (i) Adding substantial value. For purposes of paragraph (c)(1)(i) of this section, the performance of marketing functions will not be considered to add substantial value to property.

(ii) Substantiality of foreign organization. For purposes of paragraph (c)(1)(iv) of this section, whether an organization in a foreign country is substantial in relation to the amount of rents is determined based on all of the facts and circumstances. However, such an organization will be considered substantial in relation to the amount of rents if active leasing expenses, as defined in paragraph (c)(2)(iii) of this section, equal or exceed 25 percent of the adjusted leasing profit, as defined in paragraph (c)(2)(iv) of this section.

(iii) Active leasing expenses. The term active leasing expenses means the deductions incurred by an organization of the lessor in a foreign country that are properly allocable to rental income and that would be allowable under section 162 to the lessor if it were a domestic corporation, other than—

(A) Deductions for compensation for personal services rendered by shareholders of, or related persons (as defined in section 954(d)(3)) with respect to, the lessor;

(B) Deductions for rents paid or accrued;

(C) Deductions that, although generally allowable under section 162, would be specifically allowable to the lessor (if the lessor were a domestic corporation) under any section of the Internal Revenue Code other than section 162; and

(D) Deductions for payments made to agents or independent contractors with respect to the leased property other than payments for insurance, utilities and other expenses for like services, or for capitalized repairs.

(iv) Adjusted leasing profit. The term adjusted leasing profit means the gross income of the lessor from rents, reduced by the sum of—

(A) The rents paid or incurred by the lessor with respect to such rental income;

(B) The amounts that would be allowable to such lessor (if the lessor were a domestic corporation) as deductions under sections 167 or 168 with respect to such rental income; and

(C) The amounts paid by the lessor to agents or independent contractors with respect to such rental income other than payments for insurance, utilities and other expenses for like services, or for capitalized repairs.

(3) Examples. The application of this paragraph (c) is illustrated by the following examples.

Example (1). Controlled foreign corporation A is regularly engaged in the production of office machines which it sells or leases to others and services. Under paragraph (c)(1)(i) of this section, the rental income of Corporation A from these leases is derived in the active conduct of a trade or business for purposes of section 954(c)(2)(A).

Example (2). Controlled foreign corporation D purchases motor vehicles which it leases to others. In the conduct of its short-term leasing of such vehicles in foreign country X, Corporation D owns a large number of motor vehicles in country X which it services and repairs, leases motor vehicles to customers on an hourly, daily, or weekly basis, maintains offices and service facilities in country X from which to lease and service such vehicles, and maintains therein a sizable staff of its own administrative, sales, and service personnel. Corporation D also leases in country X on a long-term basis, generally for a term of one year, motor vehicles that it owns. Under the terms of the long-term leases, Corporation D is required to repair and service, during the term of the lease, the leased motor vehicles without cost to the lessee. By the maintenance in country X of office, sales, and service facilities and its complete staff of administrative, sales, and service personnel, Corporation D maintains and operates an organization therein that is regularly engaged in the business of marketing and servicing the motor vehicles that are leased. The deductions incurred by such organization satisfy the 25- percent test of paragraph (c)(2)(ii) of this section; thus, such organization is substantial in relation to the rents Corporation D receives from leasing the motor vehicles. Therefore, under paragraph (c)(1)(iv) of this section, such rents are derived in the active conduct of a trade or business for purposes of section 954(c)(2)(A).

Example (3). Controlled foreign corporation E owns a complex of apartment buildings that it has acquired by purchase. Corporation E engages a real estate management firm to lease the apartments, manage the buildings and pay over the net rents to Corporation E. The rental income of Corporation E from such leases is not derived in the active conduct of a trade or business for purposes of section 954(c)(2)(A).

Example (4). Controlled foreign corporation F acquired by purchase a twenty-story office building in a foreign country, three floors of which it occupies and the rest of which it leases. Corporation F acts as rental agent for the leasing of offices in the building and employs a substantial staff to perform other management and maintenance functions. Under paragraph (c)(1)(ii) of this section, the rents received by Corporation F from such leasing operations are derived in the active conduct of a trade or business for purposes of section 954(c)(2)(A).

Example (5). Controlled foreign corporation G owns equipment that it ordinarily uses to perform contracts in foreign countries to drill oil wells. For occasional brief and irregular periods it is unable to obtain contracts requiring immediate performance sufficient to employ all such equipment. During such a period it sometimes leases such idle equipment temporarily. After the expiration of such temporary leasing of the property, Corporation G continues the use of such equipment in the performance of its own drilling contracts. Under paragraph (c)(1)(iii) of this section, rents Corporation G receives from such leasing of idle equipment are derived in the active conduct of a trade or business for purposes of section 954(c)(2)(A).

(d) Excluded royalties. *(1) Active conduct of a trade or business.* Royalties will be considered for purposes of paragraph (b)(6) of this section to be derived in the active conduct of a trade or business if such royalties are derived by the controlled foreign corporation (the licensor) from licensing—

(i) Property that the licensor has developed, created, or produced, or has acquired and added substantial value to, but only so long as the licensor is regularly engaged in the development, creation or production of, or in the acquisition of and addition of substantial value to, property of such kind; or

(ii) Property that is licensed as a result of the performance of marketing functions by such licensor if the licensor, through its own officers or staff of employees located in a foreign country, maintains and operates an organization in such country that is regularly engaged in the business of marketing, or of marketing and servicing, the licensed property and that is substantial in relation to the amount of royalties derived from the licensing of such property.

(2) Special rules. (i) Adding substantial value. For purposes of paragraph (d)(1)(i) of this section, the performance of marketing functions will not be considered to add substantial value to property.

(ii) Substantiality of foreign organization. For purposes of paragraph (d)(1)(ii) of this section, whether an organization in a foreign country is substantial in relation to the amount of royalties is determined based on all of the facts and circumstances. However, such an organization will be considered substantial in relation to the amount of royalties if active licensing expenses, as defined in paragraph (d)(2)(iii) of this section, equal or exceed 25 percent of the adjusted licensing profit, as defined in paragraph (d)(2)(iv) of this section.

(iii) Active licensing expenses. The term active licensing expenses means the deductions incurred by an organization of the licensor in a foreign country that are properly allocable to royalty income and that would be allowable under section 162 to the licensor if it were a domestic corporation, other than—

(A) Deductions for compensation for personal services rendered by shareholders of, or related persons (as defined in section 954(d)(3)) with respect to, the licensor;

(B) Deductions for royalties paid or incurred;

(C) Deductions that, although generally allowable under section 162, would be specifically allowable to the licensor (if the controlled foreign corporation were a domestic corporation) under any section of the Internal Revenue Code other than section 162; and

(D) Deductions for payments made to agents or independent contractors with respect to the licensed property.

(iv) Adjusted licensing profit. The term adjusted licensing profit means the gross income of the licensor from royalties, reduced by the sum of—

(A) The royalties paid or incurred by the licensor with respect to such royalty income;

(B) The amounts that would be allowable to such licensor as deductions under section 167 or 197 (if the licensor were a domestic corporation) with respect to such royalty income; and

(C) The amounts paid by the licensor to agents or independent contractors with respect to such royalty income.

(3) Examples. The application of this paragraph (d) is illustrated by the following examples.

Example (1). Controlled foreign corporation A, through its own staff of employees, owns and operates a research facility in foreign country X. At the research facility, employees of Corporation A who are scientists, engineers, and technicians regularly perform experiments, tests, and other technical activities, that ultimately result in the issuance of patents that it sells or licenses. Under paragraph (d)(1)(i) of this section, royalties received by Corporation A for the privilege of using patented rights that it develops as a result of such research activity are derived in the active conduct of a trade or business for purposes of section 954(c)(2)(A), but only so long as the licensor is regularly engaged in the development, creation or production of, or in the acquisition of and addition of substantial value to, property of such kind.

Example (2). Assume that Corporation A in Example 1, in addition to receiving royalties for the use of patents that it develops, receives royalties for the use of patents that it acquires by purchase and licenses to others without adding any value thereto. Corporation A generally consummates royalty agreements on such purchased patents as the result of inquiries received by it from prospective licensees when the fact becomes known in the business community, as a result of the filing of a patent, advertisements in trade journals, announcements, and contacts by employees of Corporation A, that Corporation A has acquired rights under a patent and is interested in licensing its rights. Corporation A does not, however, maintain and operate an organization in a foreign country that is regularly engaged in the business of marketing the purchased patents. The royalties received by Corporation A for the use of the purchased patents are not derived in the active conduct of a trade or business for purposes of section 954(c)(2)(A).

Example (3). Controlled foreign corporation B receives royalties for the use of patents that it acquires by purchase. The primary business of Corporation B, operated on a regular basis, consists of licensing patents that it has purchased raw from inventors and, through the efforts of a substantial staff of employees consisting of scientists, engineers, and technicians, made susceptible to commercial application. For example, Corporation B, after purchasing patent rights covering a chemical process, designs specialized production equipment required for the commercial adaptation of the process and, by so doing, substantially increases the value of the patent. Under paragraph (d)(1)(i) of this section, royalties received by Corporation B from the use of such patent are derived in the active conduct of a trade or business for purposes of section 954(c)(2)(A).

Example (4). Controlled foreign corporation C receives royalties for the use of a patent that it developed through its own staff of employees at its facility in country X. Corporation C has developed no other patents. It does not regularly employ a staff of scientists, engineers or technicians to create new products to be patented. Further, it does not purchase and license patents developed by others to which it has added substantial value. The royalties received by Corporation C are not derived from the active conduct of a trade or business for purposes of section 954(c)(2)(A).

Example (5). Controlled foreign corporation D finances independent persons in the development of patented items in return for an ownership interest in such items from which it derives a percentage of royalty income, if any, subsequently derived from the use by others of the protected right. Corporation D also attempts to increase its royalty income from such patents by contacting prospective licensees and rendering to licensees advice that is intended to promote the use of the patented property. Corporation D does not, however, maintain and operate an organization in a foreign country that is regularly engaged in the business of marketing the patents. Royalties received by Corporation D for the use of such patents are not derived in the active conduct of a trade or business for purposes of section 954(c)(2)(A).

(e) Certain property transactions. *(1) In general.* (i) Inclusions. Gain from certain property transactions described in section 954(c)(1)(B) includes the excess of gains over losses from the sale or exchange of—

(A) Property that gives rise to dividends, interest, rents, royalties or annuities, as described in paragraph (e)(2) of this section;

(B) Property that is an interest in a partnership, trust or REMIC; and

(C) Property that does not give rise to income, as described in paragraph (e)(3) of this section.

(ii) Exceptions. Gain or loss from certain property transactions described in section 954(c)(1)(B) and paragraph (e)(1)(i) of this section does not include gain or loss from the sale or exchange of—

(A) Inventory or similar property, as defined in paragraph (a)(4)(iii) of this section;

(B) Dealer property, as defined in paragraph (a)(4)(v) of this section; or

(C) Property that gives rise to rents or royalties described in paragraph (b)(6) of this section that are derived in the active conduct of a trade or business from persons that are not related persons (as defined in section 954(d)(3)) with respect to the controlled foreign corporation.

(iii) Treatment of losses. Section 1.954-1(c)(1)(ii) provides for the treatment of losses in excess of gains from the sale or exchange of property described in paragraph (e)(1)(i) of this section.

(iv) Dual character property. Property may, in part, constitute property that gives rise to certain income as described in paragraph (e)(2) of this section or, in part, constitute property that does not give rise to any income as described in paragraph (e)(3) of this section. However, property that is described in paragraph (e)(1)(i)(B) of this section cannot be dual character property. Dual character property must be treated as two separate properties for purposes of paragraph (e)(2) or (3) of this section. Accordingly, the sale or exchange of such dual character property will give rise to gain or loss that in part must be included in the computation of foreign personal holding company income under paragraph (e)(2) or (3) of this section, and in part is excluded from such computation. Gain or loss from the disposition of dual character property must be bifurcated under this paragraph (e)(1)(iv) pursuant to the method that most reasonably reflects the relative uses of the property. Reasonable methods may include comparisons in terms of gross income generated or the physical division of the property. In the case of real property, the physical division of the property will in most cases be the most reasonable method available. For example, if a controlled foreign corporation owns an office building, uses 60 percent of the building in its trade or business, and rents out the other 40 percent, then 40 percent of the gain recognized on the disposition of the property would reasonably be treated as gain that is included in the computation of foreign personal holding company income under this paragraph (e)(1). This paragraph (e)(1)(iv) addresses the contemporaneous use of property for dual purposes. For rules concerning changes in the use of property affecting its classification for purposes of this paragraph (e), see paragraph (a)(3) of this section.

(2) Property that gives rise to certain income. (i) In general. Property the sale or exchange of which gives rise to foreign personal holding company income under this paragraph (e)(2) includes property that gives rise to dividends, interest, rents, royalties or annuities described in paragraph (b) of this section, including—

(A) Property that gives rise to export financing interest described in paragraph (b)(2) of this section; and

(B) Property that gives rise to income from related persons described in paragraph (b)(4) or (5) of this section.

(ii) Gain or loss from the disposition of a debt instrument. Gain or loss from the sale, exchange or retirement of a debt instrument is included in the computation of foreign personal holding company income under this paragraph (e) unless—

(A) In the case of gain—

(1) It is interest (as defined in paragraph (a)(4)(i) of this section); or

(2) It is income equivalent to interest (as described in paragraph (h) of this section); and

(B) In the case of loss—

(1) It is directly allocated to, or treated as an adjustment to, interest income (as described in paragraph (a)(4)(i) of this section) or income equivalent to interest (as defined in paragraph (h) of this section) under any provision of the Internal Revenue Code or Income Tax Regulations; or

(2) It is required to be apportioned in the same manner as interest expense under section 864(e) or any other provision of the Internal Revenue Code or Income Tax Regulations.

(3) Property that does not give rise to income. Except as otherwise provided in this paragraph (e)(3), for purposes of this section, the term property that does not give rise to income includes all rights and interests in property (whether or not a capital asset) including, for example, forwards, futures and options. Property that does not give rise to income shall not include—

(i) Property that gives rise to dividends, interest, rents, royalties or annuities described in paragraph (e)(2) of this section;

(ii) Tangible property (other than real property) used or held for use in the controlled foreign corporation's trade or business that is of a character that would be subject to the allowance for depreciation under section 167 or 168 and the regulations under those sections (including tangible property described in § 1.167(a)-2);

(iii) Real property that does not give rise to rental or similar income, to the extent used or held for use in the controlled foreign corporation's trade or business;

(iv) Intangible property (as defined in section 936(h)(3)(B)), goodwill or going concern value, to the extent used or held for use in the controlled foreign corporation's trade or business;

(v) Notional principal contracts (but see paragraphs (f)(2), (g)(2) and (h)(3) of this section for rules that include income from certain notional principal contracts in gains from commodities transactions, foreign currency gains and income equivalent to interest, respectively); or

(vi) Other property that is excepted from the general rule of this paragraph (e)(3) by the Commissioner in published guidance. See § 601.601(d)(2) of this chapter.

(f) Commodities transactions. *(1) In general.* (i) Inclusion in foreign personal holding company income. Foreign personal holding company income includes the excess of gains over losses from commodities transactions.

(ii) Exception. Gains and losses from qualified active sales and qualified hedging transactions are excluded from the computation of foreign personal holding company income under this paragraph (f).

(iii) Treatment of losses. Section 1.954-1(c)(1)(ii) provides for the treatment of losses in excess of gains from commodities transactions.

(2) Definitions. (i) Commodity. For purposes of this section, the term commodity includes tangible personal property of a kind that is actively traded or with respect to which contractual interests are actively traded.

(ii) Commodities transaction. The term commodities transaction means the purchase or sale of a commodity for immediate (spot) delivery or deferred (forward) delivery, or the right to purchase, sell, receive, or transfer a commodity, or any other right or obligation with respect to a commodity accomplished through a cash or off-exchange market, an interbank market, an organized exchange or board of trade, or an over-the-counter market, or in a transaction effected between private parties outside of any market. Commodities transactions include, but are not limited to—

(A) A futures or forward contract in a commodity;

(B) A leverage contract in a commodity purchased from a leverage transaction merchant;

(C) An exchange of futures for physical transaction;

(D) A transaction, including a notional principal contract, in which the income or loss to the parties is measured by reference to the price of a commodity, a pool of commodities, or an index of commodities;

(E) The purchase or sale of an option or other right to acquire or transfer a commodity, a futures contract in a commodity, or an index of commodities; and

(F) The delivery of one commodity in exchange for the delivery of another commodity, the same commodity at another time, cash, or nonfunctional currency.

(iii) Qualified active sale. (A) In general. The term qualified active sale means the sale of commodities in the active conduct of a commodities business as a producer, processor, merchant or handler of commodities if substantially all of the controlled foreign corporation's business is as an active producer, processor, merchant or handler of commodities. The sale of commodities held by a controlled foreign corporation other than in its capacity as an active producer, processor, merchant or handler of commodities is not a qualified active sale. For example, the sale by a controlled foreign corporation of commodities that were held for investment or speculation would not be a qualified active sale.

(B) Active conduct of a commodities business. For purposes of this paragraph, a controlled foreign corporation is engaged in the active conduct of a commodities business as a producer, processor, merchant or handler of commodities only with respect to commodities for which each of the following conditions is satisfied—

(1) It holds the commodities directly, and not through an agent or independent contractor, as inventory or similar property (as defined in paragraph (a)(4)(iii) of this section) or as dealer property (as defined in paragraph (a)(4)(v) of this section); and

(2) With respect to such commodities, it incurs substantial expenses in the ordinary course of a commodities business from engaging in one or more of the following activities directly, and not through an independent contractor—

(i) Substantial activities in the production of the commodities, including planting, tending or harvesting crops, raising or slaughtering livestock, or extracting minerals;

(ii) Substantial processing activities prior to the sale of the commodities, including the blending and drying of agricultural commodities, or the concentrating, refining, mixing, crushing, aerating or milling of commodities; or

(iii) Significant activities as described in paragraph (f)(2)(iii)(B)(3) of this section.

(3) For purposes of paragraph (f)(2)(iii)(B)(2)(iii) of this section, the significant activities must relate to—

(i) The physical movement, handling and storage of the commodities, including preparation of contracts and invoices, arranging freight, insurance and credit, arranging for receipt, transfer or negotiation of shipping documents, arranging storage or warehousing, and dealing with quality claims;

(ii) Owning and operating facilities for storage or warehousing; or

(iii) Owning or chartering vessels or vehicles for the transportation of the commodities.

(C) Substantially all. Substantially all of the controlled foreign corporation's business is as an active producer, processor, merchant or handler of commodities if the sum of its gross receipts from all of its qualified active sales (as defined in this paragraph (f)(2)(iii) without regard to the substantially all requirement) of commodities and its gross receipts from all of its qualified hedging transactions (as defined in paragraph (f)(2)(iv) of this section, applied without regard to the substantially all requirement of this paragraph (f)(2)(iii)(C)) equals or exceeds 85 percent of its total gross receipts for the taxable year (computed as though the corporation were a domestic corporation). In computing gross receipts, the District Director may disregard any sale or hedging transaction that has as a principal purpose manipulation of the 85 percent gross receipts test. A purpose may be a principal purpose even though it is outweighed by other purposes (taken together or separately).

(D) Activities of employees of a related entity. For purposes of this paragraph (f), activities of employees of an entity related to the controlled foreign corporation, who are made available to and supervised on a day-to-day basis by, and whose salaries are paid by (or reimbursed to the related entity by), the controlled foreign corporation, are treated as activities engaged in directly by the controlled foreign corporation.

(iv) Qualified hedging transaction entered into prior to January 31, 2003. (A) In general. The term qualified hedging transaction means a bona fide hedging transaction, as defined in paragraph (a)(4)(ii) of this section, with respect to qualified active sales (other than transactions described in section 988(c)(1) without regard to section 988(c)(1)(D)(i)).

(B) Exception. The term qualified hedging transaction does not include transactions that are not reasonably necessary to the conduct of business of the controlled foreign corporation as a producer, processor, merchant or handler of a commodity in the manner in which such business is customarily and usually conducted by others.

(C) Effective date. This paragraph (f)(2)(iv) applies to gain or loss realized by a controlled foreign corporation with respect to a qualified hedging transaction entered into prior to January 31, 2003.

(v) Qualified hedging transaction entered into on or after January 31, 2003. (A) In general. The term qualified hedging transaction means a bona fide hedging transaction, as defined in paragraph (a)(4)(ii) of this section, with respect to one or more commodities transactions reasonably necessary to the conduct of any business by a producer, processor, merchant or handler of commodities in a manner in which such business is customarily and usually conducted by others. For purposes of this paragraph (f)(2)(v), a producer, processor, merchant or handler of commodities includes a controlled foreign corporation that regularly uses commodities in a manufacturing, construction, utilities, or transportation business.

(B) Exception. The term qualified hedging transaction does not include a transaction described in section 988(c)(1) (without regard to section 988(c)(1)(D)(i)).

(C) Examples. The following examples illustrate the provisions of this paragraph (f)(2)(v):

Example (1). CFC1 is a controlled foreign corporation located in country A. CFC1 manufactures and sells machinery in country B using aluminum and component parts purchased from third parties that contain significant amounts of aluminum. CFC1 conducts its manufacturing business in a manner in which such business is customarily and usually conducted by others. To protect itself against increases in the price of aluminum used in the machinery it manufactures, CFC1 enters into futures purchase contracts for the delivery of aluminum. These futures purchase contracts are bona fide hedging transactions. As CFC1 purchases aluminum and component parts containing significant amounts of aluminum in the spot market for use in its business, it closes out an equivalent amount of aluminum futures purchase contracts by entering into offsetting aluminum futures sales contracts. The aluminum futures purchase contracts are qualified hedging transactions as defined in paragraph (f)(2)(v)(A) of this section. Accordingly, any gain or loss on such aluminum futures purchase contracts is excluded from the computation of foreign personal holding company income.

Example (2). CFC2 is a controlled foreign corporation located in country B. CFC2 operates an airline business within country B in a manner in which such business is customarily and usually conducted by others. To protect itself against increases in the price of aviation fuel, CFC2 enters into forward contracts for the purchase of aviation fuel. These forward purchase contracts are bona fide hedging transactions. As CFC2 purchases aviation fuel in the spot market for use in its business, it closes out an equivalent amount of its forward purchase contracts for cash pursuant to a contractual provision that permits CFC2 to terminate the contract and make or receive a one-time payment representing the contract's fair market value. The aviation fuel forward purchase contracts are qualified hedging transactions as defined in paragraph (f)(2)(v)(A) of this section. Accordingly, any gain or loss on such aviation fuel forward purchase contracts is excluded from the computation of foreign personal holding company income.

(D) Effective date. This paragraph (f)(2)(v) applies to gain or loss realized by a controlled foreign corporation with respect to a qualified hedging transaction entered into on or after January 31, 2003.

(vi) Financial institutions not a producer, etc. For purposes of this paragraph (f), a corporation is not a producer, processor, merchant or handler of commodities if its business is primarily financial. For example, the business of a controlled foreign corporation is primarily financial if its principal business is making a market in notional principal contracts based on a commodities index.

(g) Foreign currency gain or loss. *(1) Scope and purpose.* This paragraph (g) provides rules for the treatment of foreign currency gains and losses. Paragraph (g)(2) of this section provides the general rule. Paragraph (g)(3) of this section provides an election to include foreign currency gains or losses that would otherwise be treated as foreign personal holding company income under this paragraph (g) in the computation of another category of subpart F income. Paragraph (g)(4) of this section provides an alternative election to treat any net foreign currency gain or loss as foreign personal holding company income. Paragraph (g)(5) of this section provides rules for certain gains and losses not subject to this paragraph (g).

(2) In general. (i) Inclusion. Except as otherwise provided in this paragraph (g), foreign personal holding company income includes the excess of foreign currency gains over foreign currency losses attributable to any section 988 transactions (foreign currency gain or loss). Section 1.954-1(c)(1)(ii) provides rules for the treatment of foreign currency losses in excess of foreign currency gains. However, if an election is made under paragraph (g)(4) of this section,

the excess of foreign currency losses over foreign currency gains to which the election would apply may be apportioned to, and offset, other categories of foreign personal holding company income.

(ii) Exclusion for business needs. (A) General rule. Foreign currency gain or loss directly related to the business needs of the controlled foreign corporation is excluded from foreign personal holding company income.

(B) Business needs. Foreign currency gain or loss is directly related to the business needs of a controlled foreign corporation if—

(1) The foreign currency gain or loss—

(i) Arises from a transaction (other than a hedging transaction) entered into, or property used or held for use, in the normal course of the controlled foreign corporation's trade or business, other than the trade or business of trading foreign currency;

(ii) Arises from a transaction or property that does not itself (and could not reasonably be expected to) give rise to subpart F income other than foreign currency gain or loss;

(iii) Does not arise from a transaction described in section 988(c)(1)(B)(iii); and

(iv) Is clearly determinable from the records of the controlled foreign corporation as being derived from such transaction or property; or

(2) The foreign currency gain or loss arises from a bona fide hedging transaction, as defined in paragraph (a)(4)(ii) of this section, with respect to a transaction or property that satisfies the requirements of paragraphs (g)(2)(ii)(B)(1)(i) through (iii) of this section, provided that any gain or loss arising from such transaction or property that is attributable to changes in exchange rates is clearly determinable from the records of the CFC as being derived from such transaction or property. For purposes of this paragraph (g)(2)(ii)(B)(2), a hedging transaction will satisfy the aggregate hedging rules of § 1.1221-2(c)(3) only if all (or all but a de minimis amount) of the aggregate risk being hedged arises in connection with transactions or property that satisfy the requirements of paragraphs (g)(2)(ii)(B)(1)(i) through (iii) of this section, provided that any gain or loss arising from such transactions or property that is attributable to changes in exchange rates is clearly determinable from the records of the CFC as being derived from such transactions or property.

(C) Regular dealers. (1) General rule. Transactions in dealer property (as defined in paragraph (a)(4)(v) of this section) described in section 988(c)(1)(B) or (C) that are entered into by a controlled foreign corporation that is a regular dealer (as defined in paragraph (a)(4)(iv) of this section) in such property in its capacity as a dealer will be treated as directly related to the business needs of the controlled foreign corporation under paragraph (g)(2)(ii)(A) of this section.

(2) Certain interest-bearing liabilities treated as dealer property. (i) In general. For purposes of this paragraph (g)(2)(ii)(C), an interest-bearing liability incurred by a controlled foreign corporation that is denominated in (or determined by reference to) a non-functional currency shall be treated as dealer property of the type described in paragraph (g)(2)(ii)(C)(1) of this section if the liability, by being denominated in such currency, reduces the controlled foreign corporation's currency risk with respect to dealer property, and the liability is identified on the controlled foreign corporation's records as a liability treated as dealer property before the close of the day on which the liability is incurred.

(ii) Failure to identify certain liabilities. If a controlled foreign corporation identifies certain interest-bearing liabilities as liabilities treated as dealer property under paragraph (g)(2)(ii)(C)(2)(i) of this section but fails to so identify other interest-bearing liabilities that manage its currency risk with respect to assets held that constitute dealer property, the Commissioner may treat such other liabilities as properly identified as dealer property under paragraph (g)(2)(ii)(C)(2)(i) of this section if the Commissioner determines that the failure to identify such other liabilities had as one of its principal purposes the avoidance of Federal income tax.

(iii) Effective date. This paragraph (g)(2)(ii)(C)(2) applies only to gain or loss from an interest-bearing liability entered into by a controlled foreign corporation on or after January 31, 2003.

(D) Example. The following example illustrates the provisions of this paragraph (g)(2).

Example. (i) CFC1 and CFC2 are controlled foreign corporations located in Country B, and are members of the same controlled group. CFC1 is engaged in the active conduct of a trade or business that does not produce any subpart F income. CFC2 serves as the currency coordination center for the controlled group, aggregating currency risks incurred by the group and entering into hedging transactions that transfer those risks outside of the group. Pursuant to this arrangement, and to hedge the currency risk on a non-interest bearing receivable incurred by CFC1 in the normal course of its business, on Day 1 CFC1 enters into a forward contract to sell Japanese Yen to CFC2 in 30 days. Also on Day 1, CFC2 enters into a forward contract to sell Yen to unrelated Bank X on Day 30. CFC2 is not a regular dealer in Yen spot and forward contracts, and the Yen is not the functional currency for either CFC1 or CFC2.

(ii) Because the forward contract entered into by CFC1 to sell Yen hedges a transaction entered into in the normal course of CFC1's business that does not give rise to subpart F income, it qualifies as a bona fide hedging transaction as defined in paragraph (a)(4)(ii) of this section. Therefore, CFC1's foreign exchange gain or loss from that forward contract will not be treated as foreign personal holding company income or loss under this paragraph (g).

(iii) Because the forward contract to purchase Yen was entered into by CFC2 in order to assume currency risks incurred by CFC1 it does not qualify as a bona fide hedging transaction, as defined in paragraph (a)(4)(ii) of this section. Thus, foreign exchange gain or loss recognized by CFC2 from that forward contract will be foreign personal holding company income. Because CFC2 entered into the forward contract to sell Yen in order to hedge currency risks of CFC1, that forward contract also does not qualify as a bona fide hedging transaction. Thus, CFC2's foreign currency gain or loss arising from that forward contract will be foreign personal holding company income.

(iii) Special rule for foreign currency gain or loss from an interest-bearing liability. Except as provided in paragraph (g)(2)(ii)(C)(2) or (g)(5)(iv) of this section, foreign currency gain or loss arising from an interest-bearing liability is characterized as subpart F income and non-subpart F income in the same manner that interest expense associated with the liability would be allocated and apportioned between subpart F income and non-subpart F income under § § 1.861-9T and 1.861-12T.

(3) Election to characterize foreign currency gain or loss that arises from a specific category of subpart F income as

gain or loss in that category. (i) In general. For taxable years of a controlled foreign corporation beginning on or after November 6, 1995, elect, under this paragraph (g)(3), to exclude foreign currency gain or loss otherwise includible in the computation of foreign personal holding company income under this paragraph (g) from the computation of foreign personal holding company income under this paragraph (g) and include such foreign currency gain or loss in the category (or categories) of subpart F income (described in section 952(a), or, in the case of foreign base company income, described in § 1.954-1(c)(1)(iii)(A)(1) or (2)) to which such gain or loss relates. If an election is made under this paragraph (g)(3) with respect to a category (or categories) of subpart F income described in section 952(a), or, in the case of foreign base company income, described in § 1.954-1(c)(1)(iii)(A)(1) or (2), the election shall apply to all foreign currency gain or loss that arises from—

(A) A transaction (other than a hedging transaction) entered into, or property used or held for use, in the normal course of the controlled foreign corporation's trade or business that gives rise to income in that category (or categories) and that is clearly determinable from the records of the controlled foreign corporation as being derived from such transaction or property; and

(B) A bona fide hedging transaction, as defined in paragraph (a)(4)(ii) of this section, with respect to a transaction or property described in paragraph (g)(3)(i)(A) of this section. For purposes of this paragraph (g)(3)(i)(B), a hedging transaction will satisfy the aggregate hedging rules of § 1.1221-2(c)(3) only if all (or all but a de minimis amount) of the aggregate risk being hedged arises in connection with transactions or property that generate the same category of subpart F income described in section 952(a), or, in the case of foreign base company income, described in § 1.954-1(c)(1)(iii)(A)(1) or (2).

(ii) Time and manner of election. The controlling United States shareholders, as defined in § 1.964-1(c)(5), make the election on behalf of the controlled foreign corporation by filing a statement with their original income tax returns for the taxable year of such United States shareholders ending with or within the taxable year of the controlled foreign corporation for which the election is made, clearly indicating that such election has been made. If the controlling United States shareholders elect to apply these regulations retroactively, under § 1.954-0(a)(1)(ii), the election under this paragraph (g)(3) may be made by the amended return filed pursuant to the election under § 1.954-0(a)(1)(ii). The controlling United States shareholders filing the election statement described in this paragraph (g)(3)(ii) must provide copies of the election statement to all other United States shareholders of the electing controlled foreign corporation. Failure to provide copies of such statement will not cause an election under this paragraph (g)(3) to be voidable by the controlled foreign corporation or the controlling United States shareholders. However, the District Director has discretion to void the election if it is determined that there was no reasonable cause for the failure to provide copies of such statement. The statement shall include the following information—

(A) The name, address, taxpayer identification number, and taxable year of each United States shareholder;

(B) The name, address, and taxable year of the controlled foreign corporation for which the election is effective; and

(C) Any additional information required by the Commissioner by administrative pronouncement.

(iii) Revocation of election. This election is effective for the taxable year of the controlled foreign corporation for which it is made and all subsequent taxable years of such corporation unless revoked by or with the consent of the Commissioner.

(iv) Example. The following example illustrates the provisions of this paragraph (g)(3).

Example. (i) CFC, a controlled foreign corporation, is a sales company that earns foreign base company sales income under section 954(d). CFC makes an election under this paragraph (g)(3) to treat foreign currency gains or losses that arise from a specific category (or categories) of subpart F income (as described in section 952(a), or, in the case of foreign base company income, as described in § 1.954-1(c)(1)(iii)(A)(1) or (2)) as that type of income. CFC aggregates the currency risk on all of its transactions that generate foreign base company sales income and hedges this net currency exposure.

(ii) Assuming no more than a de minimis amount of risk in the pool of risks being hedged arises from transactions or property that generate income other than foreign base company sales income, pursuant to its election under (g)(3), CFC's net foreign currency gain from the pool and the hedging transactions will be treated as foreign base company sales income under section 954(d), rather than as foreign personal holding company income under section 954(c)(1)(D). If the pool of risks and the hedging transactions generate a net foreign base company sales, however, CFC must apply the rules of § 1.954-1(c)(1)(ii).

(4) Election to treat all foreign currency gains or losses as foreign personal holding company income. (i) In general. If the controlling United States shareholders make an election under this paragraph (g)(4), the controlled foreign corporation shall include in its computation of foreign personal holding company income the excess of foreign currency gains over losses or the excess of foreign currency losses over gains attributable to any section 988 transaction (except those described in paragraph (g)(5) of this section) and any section 1256 contract that would be a section 988 transaction but for section 988(c)(1)(D). Separate elections for section 1256 contracts and section 988 transactions are not permitted. An election under this paragraph (g)(4) supersedes an election under paragraph (g)(3) of this section.

(ii) Time and manner of election. The controlling United States shareholders, as defined in § 1.964-1(c)(5), make the election on behalf of the controlled foreign corporation in the same time and manner as provided in paragraph (g)(3)(ii) of this section.

(iii) Revocation of election. This election is effective for the taxable year of the controlled foreign corporation for which it is made and all subsequent taxable years of such corporation unless revoked by or with the consent of the Commissioner.

(5) Gains and losses not subject to this paragraph. (i) Capital gains and losses. Gain or loss that is treated as capital gain or loss under section 988(a)(1)(B) is not foreign currency gain or loss for purposes of this paragraph (g). Such gain or loss is treated as gain or loss from the sale or exchange of property that is included in the computation of foreign personal holding company income under paragraph (e)(1) of this section. Paragraph (a)(2) of this section provides other rules concerning income described in more than one category of foreign personal holding company income.

(ii) Income not subject to section 988. Gain or loss that is not treated as foreign currency gain or loss by reason of section 988(a)(2) or (d) is not foreign currency gain or loss for purposes of this paragraph (g). However, such gain or loss may be included in the computation of other categories of foreign personal holding company income in accordance with its characterization under section 988(a)(2) or (d) (for example, foreign currency gain that is treated as interest income under section 988(a)(2) will be included in the computation of foreign personal holding company income under paragraph (b)(ii) of this section).

(iii) Qualified business units using the dollar approximate separate transactions method. This paragraph (g) does not apply to any DASTM gain or loss computed under § 1.985-3(d). Such gain or loss is allocated under the rules of § 1.985-3(e)(2)(iv) or (e)(3). However, the provisions of this paragraph (g) do apply to section 988 transactions denominated in a currency other than the United States dollar or the currency that would be the qualified business unit's functional currency were it not hyperinflationary.

(iv) Gain or loss allocated under § 1.861-9. [Reserved]

(h) Income equivalent to interest. *(1) In general.* (i) Inclusion in foreign personal holding company income. Except as provided in this paragraph (h), foreign personal holding company income includes income equivalent to interest as defined in paragraph (h)(2) of this section.

(ii) Exceptions. (A) Liability hedging transactions. Income, gain, deduction or loss that is allocated and apportioned in the same manner as interest expense under the provisions of § 1.861-9T is not income equivalent to interest for purposes of this paragraph (h).

(B) Interest. Amounts treated as interest under section 954(c)(1)(A) and paragraph (b) of this section are not income equivalent to interest for purposes of this paragraph (h).

(2) Definition of income equivalent to interest. (i) In general. The term income equivalent to interest includes income that is derived from—

(A) A transaction or series of related transactions in which the payments, net payments, cash flows or return predominantly reflect the time value of money;

(B) Transactions in which the payments (or a predominant portion thereof) are, in substance, for the use or forbearance of money;

(C) Notional principal contracts, to the extent provided in paragraph (h)(3) of this section;

(D) Factoring, to the extent provided in paragraph (h)(4) of this section;

(E) Conversion transactions, but only to the extent that gain realized with respect to such a transaction is treated as ordinary income under section 1258;

(F) The performance of services, to the extent provided in paragraph (h)(5) of this section;

(G) The commitment by a lender to provide financing, if any portion of such financing is actually provided;

(H) Transfers of debt securities subject to section 1058; and

(I) Other transactions, as provided by the Commissioner in published guidance. See § 601.601(d)(2) of this chapter.

(ii) Income from the sale of property. Income from the sale of property will not be treated as income equivalent to interest by reason of paragraph (h)(2)(i)(A) or (B) of this section. Income derived by a controlled foreign corporation will be treated as arising from the sale of property only if the corporation in substance carries out sales activities. Accordingly, an arrangement that is designed to lend the form of a sales transaction to a transaction that in substance constitutes an advance of funds will be disregarded. For example, if a controlled foreign corporation acquires property on 30-day payment terms from one person and sells that property to another person on 90-day payment terms and at prearranged prices and terms such that the foreign corporation bears no substantial economic risk with respect to the purchase and sale other than the risk of non-payment, the foreign corporation has not in substance derived income from the sale of property.

(3) Notional principal contracts. (i) In general. Income equivalent to interest includes income from notional principal contracts denominated in the functional currency of the taxpayer (or a qualified business unit of the taxpayer, as defined in section 989(a)), the value of which is determined solely by reference to interest rates or interest rate indices, to the extent that the income from such transactions accrues on or after August 14, 1989.

(ii) Regular dealers. Income equivalent to interest does not include income earned by a regular dealer (as defined in paragraph (a)(4)(iv) of this section) from notional principal contracts that are dealer property (as defined in paragraph (a)(4)(v) of this section).

(4) Income equivalent to interest from factoring. (i) General rule. Income equivalent to interest includes factoring income. Except as provided in paragraph (h)(4)(ii) of this section, the term factoring income includes any income (including any discount income or service fee, but excluding any stated interest) derived from the acquisition and collection or disposition of a factored receivable. The amount of income equivalent to interest realized with respect to a factored receivable is the difference (if a positive number) between the amount paid for the receivable by the foreign corporation and the amount that it collects on the receivable (or realizes upon its sale of the receivable). The rules of this paragraph (h)(4) apply only with respect to the tax treatment of factoring income derived from the acquisition and collection or disposition of a factored receivable and shall not affect the characterization of an expense or loss of either the person whose goods or services gave rise to a factored receivable or the obligor under a receivable.

(ii) Exceptions. Factoring income shall not include—

(A) Income treated as interest under section 864(d)(1) or (6) (relating to income derived from trade or service receivables of related persons), even if such income is treated as not described in section 864(d)(1) by reason of the same-country exception of section 864(d)(7);

(B) Income derived from a factored receivable if payment for the acquisition of the receivable is made on or after the date on which stated interest begins to accrue, but only if the rate of stated interest equals or exceeds 120 percent of the Federal short-term rate (as defined under section 1274) (or the analogous rate for a currency other than the dollar) as of the date on which the receivable is acquired by the foreign corporation; or

(C) Income derived from a factored receivable if payment for the acquisition of the receivable by the foreign corporation is made only on or after the anticipated date of payment of all principal by the obligor (or the anticipated weighted average date of payment of a pool of purchased receivables).

(iii) Factored receivable. For purposes of this paragraph (h)(4), the term factored receivable includes any account receivable or other evidence of indebtedness, whether or not issued at a discount and whether or not bearing stated interest, arising out of the disposition of property or the performance of services by any person, if such account receivable or evidence of indebtedness is acquired by a person other than the person who disposed of the property or provided the services that gave rise to the account receivable or evidence of indebtedness. For purposes of this paragraph (h)(4), it is immaterial whether the person providing the property or services agrees to transfer the receivable at the time of sale (as by accepting a third-party charge or credit card) or at a later time.

(iv) Examples. The following examples illustrate the application of this paragraph (h)(4).

Example (1). DP, a domestic corporation, owns all of the outstanding stock of FS, a controlled foreign corporation. FS acquires accounts receivable arising from the sale of property by unrelated corporation X. The receivables have a face amount of $100, and after 30 days bear stated interest equal to at least 120 percent of the applicable Federal short-term rate (determined as of the date the receivables are acquired by FS). FS purchases the receivables from X for $95 on Day 1 and collects $100 plus stated interest from the obligor under the receivables on Day 40. Income (other than stated interest) derived by FS from the factored receivables is factoring income within the meaning of paragraph (h)(4)(i) of this section and, therefore, is income equivalent to interest.

Example (2). The facts are the same as in Example 1, except that, rather than collecting $100 plus stated interest from the obligor under the factored receivables on Day 40, FS sells the receivables to controlled foreign corporation Y on Day 15 for $97. Both the income derived by FS on the factored receivables and the income derived by Y (other than stated interest) on the receivables are factoring income within the meaning of paragraph (h)(4)(i) of this section, and therefore, constitute income equivalent to interest.

Example (3). The facts are the same as in Example 1, except that FS purchases the receivables from X for $98 on Day 30. Income derived by FS from the factored receivables is excluded from factoring income under paragraph (h)(4)(ii)(B) of this section and, therefore, does not give rise to income equivalent to interest.

Example (4). The facts are the same as in Example 3, except that it is anticipated that all principal will be paid by the obligor of the receivables by Day 30. Income derived by FS from this maturity factoring of the receivables is excluded from factoring income under paragraph (h)(4)(ii)(C) of this section and, therefore, does not give rise to income equivalent to interest.

Example (5). The facts are the same as in Example 4, except that FS sells the factored receivables to Y for $99 on Day 45, at which time stated interest is accruing on the unpaid balance of $100. Because interest was accruing at the time Y acquired the receivables at a rate equal to at least 120 percent of the applicable Federal short-term rate, income derived by Y from the factored receivables is excluded from factoring income under paragraph (h)(4)(ii)(B) of this section and, therefore, does not give rise to income equivalent to interest.

Example (6). DP, a domestic corporation engaged in an integrated credit card business, owns all of the outstanding stock of FS, a controlled foreign corporation. On Day 1, individual A uses a credit card issued by DP to purchase shoes priced at $100 from X, a foreign corporation unrelated to DP, FS, or A. On Day 7, X transfers the receivable (which does not bear stated interest) arising from A's purchase to FS in exchange for $95. FS collects $100 from A on Day 45. Income derived by FS on the factored receivable is factoring income within the meaning of paragraph (h)(4)(i) of this section and, therefore, is income equivalent to interest.

(5) Receivables arising from performance of services. If payment for services performed by a controlled foreign corporation is not made until more than 120 days after the date on which such services are performed, then the income derived by the controlled foreign corporation constitutes income equivalent to interest to the extent that interest income would be imputed under the principles of section 483 or the original issue discount provisions (sections 1271 through 1275), if—

(i) Such provisions applied to contracts for the performance of services;

(ii) The time period referred to in sections 483(c)(1) and 1274(c)(1)(B) were 120 days rather than six months; and

(iii) The time period referred to in section 483(c)(1)(A) were 120 days rather than one year.

(6) Examples. The following examples illustrate the application of this paragraph (h).

Example (1). CFC, a controlled foreign corporation, promises that Corporation A may borrow up to $500 in principal for one year beginning at any time during the next three months at an interest rate of 10 percent. In exchange, Corporation A pays CFC a commitment fee of $2. Pursuant to this agreement, CFC lends $80 to corporation A. As a result, the entire $2 fee is included in the computation of CFC's foreign personal holding company income under paragraph (h)(2)(i)(G) of this section.

Example (2). (i) At the beginning of its current taxable year, CFC, a controlled foreign corporation, purchases at face value a one-year debt instrument issued by Corporation A having a $100 principal amount and bearing a floating rate of interest set at the London Interbank Offered Rate (LIBOR) plus one percentage point. Contemporaneously, CFC borrows $100 from Corporation B for one year at a fixed interest rate of 10 percent, using the debt instrument as security.

(ii) During its current taxable year, CFC accrues $11 of interest from Corporation A on the bond. Because interest is excluded from the definition of income equivalent to interest under paragraph (h)(1)(ii)(B) of this section, the $11 is not income equivalent to interest.

(iii) During its current taxable year, CFC incurs $10 of interest expense with respect to the borrowing from Corporation B. That expense is allocated and apportioned to, and reduces, subpart F income to the extent provided in section 954(b)(5) and §§ 1.861-9T through 1.861-12T and 1.954-1(c).

Example (3). (i) On January 1, 1994, CFC, a controlled foreign corporation with the United States dollar as its functional currency, purchases at face value a 10-year debt instrument issued by Corporation A having a $100 principal amount and bearing a floating rate of interest set at LIBOR plus one percentage point payable on December 31st of each year. CFC subsequently determines that it would prefer receiving a fixed rate of return. Accordingly, on January 1, 1995, CFC enters into a 9-year interest rate swap agreement with Corporation B whereby Corporation B promises to pay CFC on December 31st of each year an amount equal to 10 percent on a notional principal amount of $100. In exchange, CFC promises to pay Corporation B an amount equal to LIBOR plus one percentage point on the notional principal amount.

(ii) On December 31, 1995, CFC receives $9 of interest income from Corporation A with respect to the debt instrument. On the same day, CFC receives a total of $10 from Corporation B and pays $9 to Corporation B with respect to the interest rate swap.

(iii) The $9 of interest income is foreign personal holding income under section 954(c)(1). Pursuant to § 1.446-3(d), CFC recognizes $1 of swap income for its 1995 taxable year that is also foreign personal holding company income because it is income equivalent to interest under paragraph (h)(2)(i)(C) of this section.

Example (4). (i) CFC, a controlled foreign corporation, purchases commodity X on the spot market for $100 and, contemporaneously, enter into a 3-month forward contract to sell commodity X for $104, a price set by the forward market.

(ii) Assuming that substantially all of CFC's expected return is attributable to the time value of the net investment, as described in section 1258(c)(1), the transaction is a conversion transaction under section 1258(c). Accordingly, any gain treated as ordinary income under section 1258(a) will be foreign personal holding company income because it is income equivalent to interest under paragraph (h)(2)(i)(E) of this section.

T.D. 8618, 9/6/95, amend T.D. 8704, 12/31/96, T.D. 8985, 3/15/2002, T.D. 9008, 7/22/2002, T.D. 9039, 1/30/2003, T.D. 9141, 7/19/2004, T.D. 9240, 1/13/2006, T.D. 9326, 7/12/2007.

PAR. 5. In § 1.954-2, paragraphs (a)(5) and (a)(6) are added to read as follows:

Proposed § 1.954-2 Foreign personal holding company income. [*For Preamble, see ¶ 151,985*]

(a) * * *

(5) Special rules applicable to distributive share of partnership income. (i) Application of related person exceptions where payment reduces foreign tax of payor. If a partnership receives an item of income that reduced the foreign income tax of the payor (determined under the principles of § 1.954-9(a)(3)), to determine the extent to which a controlled foreign corporation's distributive share of such item of income is foreign personal holding company income, the exceptions contained in section 954(c)(3) shall apply only if—

(A) (1) Any such exception would have applied to exclude the income from foreign personal holding company income if the controlled foreign corporation had earned the income directly (determined by testing, with reference to such controlled foreign corporation, whether an entity is a related person, within the meaning of section 954(d)(3), or is organized under the laws of, or uses property in, the foreign country in which the controlled foreign corporation is created or organized); and

(2) The distributive share of such income is not in respect of a payment made by the controlled foreign corporation to the partnership; and

(B) (1) The partnership is created or organized, and uses a substantial part of its assets in a trade or business in the country under the laws of which the controlled foreign corporation is created or organized (determined under the principles of paragraph (b)(4) of this section);

(2) The partnership is regarded as fiscally transparent, as defined in § 1.954-9(a)(7), by all countries under the laws of which the controlled foreign corporation is created or organized or has substantial assets; or

(3) The income is taxed in the year when earned at an effective rate of tax (determined under the principles of § 1.954-1(d)(2)) that is not less than 90 percent of, and not more than five percentage points less than, the effective rate of tax that would have applied to such income under the laws of the country in which the controlled foreign corporation is created or organized if such income were earned directly by the controlled foreign corporation partner from local sources.

(ii) Certain other exceptions applicable to foreign personal holding company income. [Reserved].

(iii) Effective date. Paragraph (a)(5)(i) of this section shall apply to all amounts paid or accrued in taxable years commencing after [date that is 5 years after publication of the final regulations in the Federal Register], under hybrid arrangements, unless such payments are made pursuant to an arrangement which would qualify for permanent relief under § 1.954-9(c)(2) if made between a controlled foreign corporation and its hybrid branch, in which case the relief afforded under that section shall also be afforded under this section.

(6) Special rules applicable to exceptions from foreign personal holding company income treatment in circumstances involving hybrid branches. (i) In general. In the case of a payment between a controlled foreign corporation (or its hybrid branch, as defined in § 1.954-9(a)(6)) and the hybrid branch of a related controlled foreign corporation, the exceptions contained in section 954(c)(3) shall apply only if the payment would have qualified for the exception if the payor were a separate controlled foreign corporation created or organized in the jurisdiction where foreign tax is reduced and the payee were a separate controlled foreign corporation created or organized under the laws of the jurisdiction in which the payment is subject to tax (other than a withholding tax).

(ii) Exception where no tax reduction or tax disparity. Paragraph (a)(6)(i) of this section shall not apply unless the payment would have reduced foreign tax, under § 1.954-9(a)(3), and fallen within the tax disparity rule of § 1.954-9(a)(5)(iv) if those provisions had been applicable to the payment.

(iii) Effective date. The rules of this section shall apply to all amounts paid or accrued in taxable years commencing after [date that is 5 years after publication of the final regulations in the Federal Register], under hybrid arrangements, unless such payments are made pursuant to an arrangement which would qualify for permanent relief under § 1.954-9(c)(2) if made between a controlled foreign corporation and its hybrid branch, in which case the relief afforded under that section shall also be afforded under this section.

§ 4.954-2 Foreign personal holding company income; taxable years beginning after December 31, 1986.

(a) Computation of foreign personal holding company income. *(1) In general.* Foreign personal holding company income consists of the following categories of income:

(i) Dividends, interest, rents, royalties, and annuities as defined in paragraph (b) of this section;

(ii) Gain from certain property transactions as defined in paragraph (e) of this section;

(iii) Gain from commodities transactions as defined in paragraph (f) of this section;

(iv) Foreign currency gain as defined in paragraph (g) of this section; and

(v) Income equivalent to interest as defined in paragraph (h) of this section. Paragraph (a)(3) of this section provides rules for determining the use or purpose for which property is held, if a change in use or purpose would affect the computation of foreign personal holding company income under paragraphs (e), (f), and (g) of this section. Paragraphs (c) and (d) of this section provide rules for determining certain rents and royalties that are excluded from foreign personal holding company income under paragraph (b) of this section.

(2) Coordination of overlapping definitions. If a particular portion of income from a transaction in substance falls within more than one of the definitional rules of section 954(c) and this section, its character is determined under the rules of subdivision (i) through (iii) of this paragraph (a)(2). The character of loss from a transaction must be similarly determined under the rules of this paragraph (a)(2).

(i) If a portion of the income from a transaction falls within the definition of income equivalent to interest under paragraph (h) of this section and the definition of gain from certain property transactions under paragraph (e) of this section, gain from a commodities transaction under paragraph (f) of this section (whether or not derived from a qualified hedging transaction or qualified active sales), or foreign currency gain under paragraph (g) of this section (whether or not derived from a qualified business transaction or a qualified hedging transaction), that portion of income is treated as income equivalent to interest for purposes of section 954(c) and this section.

(ii) If a portion of the income from a transaction falls within the definition of foreign currency gain under paragraph (g) of this section (whether or not derived from a qualified business transaction or a qualified hedging transaction) and the definition of gain from certain property transactions under paragraph (e) of this section, or gain from a commodities transaction under paragraph (f) of this section (whether or not derived from a qualified hedging transaction or qualified active sales), that portion of income is treated as foreign currency gain for purposes of section 954(c) and this section.

(iii) If a portion of the income from a transaction falls within the definition of gain from a commodities transaction under paragraph (f) of this section (whether or not derived from a qualified hedging transaction or qualified active sales) and the definition of gain from certain property transactions under paragraph (e) of this section, that portion of income is treated as gain from a commodities transaction for purposes of section 954(c) and this section.

(3) Changes in the use or purpose with which property is held. (i) In general. Under paragraphs (e), (f), and (g) of this section, transactions in certain property give rise to gain or loss included in the computation of foreign personal holding company income if the controlled foreign corporation holds that property for a particular use or purpose. For purposes of this section, in determining the purpose or use for which property is held, the period shortly before disposition is the most significant period. However, if a controlled foreign corporation held property with a purpose that would have caused its disposition to give rise to gain or loss included in the computation of foreign personal holding company income under this section, and prior to disposition the controlled foreign corporation changed the purpose or use for which it held the property to one that would cause its disposition to give rise to gain or loss excluded from the computation of foreign personal holding company income, then the later purpose or use shall be ignored unless it was continuously present for a predominant portion of the period during which the controlled foreign corporation held the property. Under paragraph (g)(4)(iii) of this section, a currency hedging transaction may be treated as two or more separate hedging transactions, such that each portion is separately considered in applying this paragraph (a)(3).

(ii) Illustrations. The following examples illustrate the application of this paragraph (a)(3).

Example (1). At the beginning of taxable year 1, *CFC*, a controlled foreign corporation, purchases a building for investment. During taxable years 1 and 2, *CFC* derives rents from this building that are included in the computation of foreign personal holding company income under paragraph (b)(1)(iii) of this section. At the beginning of taxable year 3, *CFC* changes the use of the building by terminating all leases, and using it in an active trade or business. At the beginning of taxable year 4, *CFC* sells the building at a gain. For purposes of paragraph (e) of this section (gains from the sale or exchange of certain property) the building is considered to be property that gives rise to rents, as described in paragraph (e)(2). Because there was a change of use at the beginning of year 3 that would cause the disposition of the building to give rise to gain or loss excluded from the computation of foreign personal holding company income, the characterization of the gain derived at the beginning of year 4 is determined according to the property's use during the predominant portion of the period from purchase to date of sale. Therefore, gain from the sale of that building is included in the computation of foreign personal holding company income under paragraph (e) of this section.

Example (2). For taxable years 1, 2, and 3, *CFC*, a controlled foreign corporation, is engaged in the active conduct of a commodity business as a handler of gold, as defined in paragraph (f)(e)(iii), and substantially all of its business is as an active handler of gold, as defined in paragraph (f)(3)(iv). At the beginning of taxable year 1, *CFC* purchases 1000 ounces of gold for investment. At the beginning of taxable year 3, *CFC* begins holding that gold in physical form for sale to customers. During taxable year 3, *CFC* sells the entire 1000 ounces of gold in transactions described in paragraph (f)(3)(ii) at a gain. For purposes of paragraph (f), *CFC* is considered to hold the gold for investment, and not in its capacity as an active handler of gold. Thus, under paragraph (f)(3)(i), the gold is not considered to be sold in the active trade or business of the *CFC* as a handler of gold, and gain from the sale is included in the computation of foreign personal holding company income under paragraph (f) of this section.

Example (3). CFC, a controlled foreign corporation, is a regular dealer in unimproved land. The functional currency (as defined in section 985 and the regulations thereunder) of *CFC* is country X currency. On day 1 of its current taxable year, *CFC* enters into an agreement with A to pay $100 for certain real property to be held by *CFC* for investment. On day 10, under its method of accounting, *CFC* accrues the value of $100 in country X currency, but payment will not be made until the first day of the next taxable year (day 366). On day 190, *CFC* determines to hold the property for sale to customers in a transaction that would be a qualified business transaction under paragraph (g)(3) of this section. For purposes of this section, the land is considered to be held for investment, and the foreign currency gain attributable to that transaction is included in the computation of foreign personal holding company income under paragraph (g) of this section.

Example (4). CFC, a controlled foreign corporation, is a regular dealer in widgets. The functional currency (as defined in section 985 and the regulations thereunder) of *CFC* is country X currency. On day 1 of its current taxable year,

CFC sells widgets held in inventory to A for delivery on day 60. The sales price is denominated in U.S. dollars, and payment is to be made by A on the same day the widgets are to be delivered to A. The remaining facts and circumstances are such that this sale would meet the definition of a qualified business transaction under paragraph (g)(4), the foreign currency gain from which would be excluded from the computation of foreign personal holding company income under paragraph (g). On day 1, *CFC* sells U.S. dollars forward for delivery in 60 days in a transaction that would be a qualified hedging transaction under paragraph (g)(5). On day 25 the sale of widgets to A is cancelled in a transaction that does not result in *CFC* realizing any foreign currency gain or loss with respect to the sale of widgets. However, *CFC* holds the dollar forward contract to maturity. Because the forward contract does not hedge a qualified business transaction during the period shortly before its maturity, it is not to be considered a qualified hedging transaction under paragraph (g), and any foreign currency gain or loss recognized therefrom is included in the computation of foreign personal holding company income under paragraph (g). However, if *CFC* identifies the portion of the foreign currency gain or loss derived from the forward contract that is attributable to days 1 through 25, and the portion that is attributable to days 25 through 60, the forward contract may be considered two separate transactions in accordance with the rules provided by paragraph (g)(4)(ii) of this section. Thus, the forward sale may be separately considered a qualified hedging transaction for day 1 through day 25, and the foreign currency gain or loss attributable to day 1 through day 25 may be excluded from the computation of foreign personal holding company income under paragraph (g) of this section.

Example (5). CFC, a controlled foreign corporation, has country X currency as its functional currency under section 985 and the regulations thereunder. On day 1 of the current taxable year, *CFC,* speculating on exchange rates, sells dollars forward for delivery in 120 days. On day 65, *CFC* sells widgets held in inventory at a price denominated in dollars to be paid on day 120 in a transaction that is a qualified business transaction. *CFC* had not made any other dollar sales between day 1 and day 65 and does not anticipate making any other dollar sales during the taxable year. On day 65, *CFC* accrues the value of $100 in country X currency. On day 120, *CFC* receives $100 payment for the widgets and recognizes foreign currency loss pursuant to that transaction. On day 120 *CFC* also delivers dollars in connection with the forward sale, and recognizes foreign currency gain pursuant to the delivery. Under this paragraph (a)(3) the currency transaction is considered to have been entered into for speculation, and any currency gain recognized by *CFC* on the forward sale of dollars must be included in the computation of foreign personal holding company income under paragraph (g). However, if *CFC* identifies the portion of the forward sale, and the foreign currency gain or therefrom, that is attributable to day 1 through day 64, and the portion that is attributable to day 65 through day 120, the forward sale may be considered two separate transactions in accordance with the rules provided by paragraph (g)(4)(ii) of this section. Thus, the transaction for day 65 through day 120 may be considered a separate transaction that is a qualified hedging transaction, and the foreign currency gain attributable to day 65 through day 120 may be excluded from the computation of foreign personal holding company income under this paragraph (g) if all the other requirements for treatment as a qualified hedging transaction under paragraph (g) are met.

(4) Definitions. The following definitions apply for purposes of computing foreign personal holding company income under this section.

(i) Interest. The term "interest" includes amounts that are treated as ordinary income, original issue discount or interest income (including original issue discount and interest on a tax-exempt obligation) by reason of sections 482, 483, 864(d), 1273, 1274, 1276, 1281, 1286, 1288, 7872 and the regulations thereunder, or as interest or original issue discount income by reason of any other provision of law. For special rules concerning interest exempt from U.S. tax pursuant to section 103, see paragraph (b)(6) of this section.

(ii) Inventory and similar property. The term "inventory and similar property" (or "inventory or similar property") means property that is stock in trade of the controlled foreign corporation or other property of a kind which would properly be included in the inventory of the controlled corporation if on hand at the close of the taxable year (were the controlled foreign corporation a domestic corporation), or property held by the controlled foreign corporation primarily for sale to customers in the ordinary course of its trade or business. Rights to property held in bona fide hedging transactions that reduce the risk of price changes in the cost of "inventory and similar property" are included in the definition of that term if they are an integral part of the system by which a controlled foreign corporation purchases such property, and they are so identified by the close of the fifth day after the day on which the hedging transaction is entered into.

(iii) Regular dealer. The term "regular dealer" means a merchant with an established place of business that—

(A) Regularly and actively engages as a merchant in purchasing property and selling it to customers in the ordinary course of business with a view to the gains and profits that may be derived therefrom, or

(B) Makes a market in derivative financial products of property (such as forward contracts to buy or sell property, option contracts to buy or sell property, interest rate and currency swap contracts or other notional principal contracts) by regularly and actively offering to enter into positions in such products to the public in the ordinary course of business. Purchasing and selling property through a regulated exchange or established off-exchange market (for example, engaging in futures transactions) is not actively engaging as a merchant for purposes of this section.

(iv) Dealer property. Property held by a controlled foreign corporation is "dealer property" if—

(A) The controlled foreign corporation is a regular dealer in property of such kind, and

(B) The property is held by the controlled foreign corporation in its capacity as a dealer. Property which is held by the controlled foreign corporation for investment or speculation is not such property.

(v) Debt instrument. The term "debt instrument" includes bonds, debentures, notes, certificates, accounts receivable, and other evidences of indebtedness.

(b) Dividends, etc. *(1) In general.* Foreign personal holding company includes:

(i) Dividends, except certain dividends from related persons as described in paragraph (b)(3) of this section and distributions of previously taxed income under section 959(b) and the regulations thereunder;

(ii) Interest, except export financing interest as defined in paragraph (b)(2) of this section and certain interest received from related persons as described in paragraph (b)(3) of this section;

(iii) Rents and royalties, except certain rents and royalties received from related persons as described in (b)(4) of this section and rents and royalties derived in the active conduct of a trade or business as defined in paragraph (b)(5); and

(iv) Annuities.

(2) Exclusion of certain export financing. (i) In general. Pursuant to section 954(c)(2)(B), foreign personal holding company income computed under section 954(c)(1)(A) and this paragraph (b) does not include interest that is export financing interest. For purposes of section 954(c)(2)(B) and this section, the term "export financing interest" means interest that is derived in the conduct of a banking business and is export financing interest as defined in section 904(d)(2)(G) and the regulations thereunder. Pursuant to section 864(d)(5)(A)(iii), it does not include income from related party factoring that is treated as interest under section 864(d)(1) or interest described in section 864(d)(6).

(ii) Conduct of a banking business. For purposes of this section, export financing interest as defined in section 904(d)(2)(G) and the regulations thereunder is considered derived in the conduct of a banking business if, in connection with the financing from which the interest is derived, the corporation, through its own officers or staff of employees, engages in all the activities in which banks customarily engage in issuing and servicing a loan.

(iii) Illustration. The following example illustrates the application of this provision:

Example. DS, a domestic corporation, manufactures property in the United States. In addition to selling inventory (property described in section 1221(1)), DS occasionally sells depreciable equipment it manufactures for use in its trade or business, which is property described in section 1221(2). Less than 50 percent of the fair market value, determined in accordance with section 904(d)(2)(G) and the regulations thereunder, of each item of inventory or equipment sold by DS is attributable to products imported into the United States. CFC, a controlled foreign corporation related (as defined in section 954(d)) to DS, provides loans for the purchase of property from DS, if the property is purchased exclusively for use of consumption outside the United States.

If, in issuing and servicing loans made with respect to purchases from DS of depreciable equipment used in its trade or business, which is property described in section 1221(2) in the hands of DS, CFC engages in all the activities in which banks customarily engage in issuing and servicing loans, the interest accrued from these loans would be export financing interest meeting the requirements of paragraph (b)(2) of this section, which would not be included in foreign personal holding company income under section 954(c) and paragraph (b)(1)(ii) of this section. However, interest from the loans made with respect to purchases from DS of property which is inventory in the hands of DS cannot be export financing interest because it is treated as income from a trade or service receivable under section 864(d)(6) and the regulations thereunder, and thus is included in foreign personal holding company income under paragraph (b)(1)(ii) of this section. See § 1.864-8T(d) for rules concerning certain income from trade and service receivables qualifying under the same country exception of section 864(d)(7).

(3) Exclusion of dividends and interest from related persons. (i) Excluded dividends and interest. Foreign personal holding company income does not include dividends and interest if—

(A) The payor is a corporation that is a related person as defined in section 954(a)(3),

(B) The payor is created or organized ("incorporated") under the laws of the same foreign country as the controlled foreign corporation, and

(C) A substantial part of the payor's assets are used in a trade or business in the payor's country of incorporation as determined under subdivision (iv) of this paragraph (b)(3). Except as otherwise provided under this paragraph (b)(3), the principles of section 367(a) and regulations thereunder shall apply in determining whether the payor has a trade or business in its country of incorporation, and whether its assets are used in that trade or business.

(ii) Interest paid out of adjusted foreign base company income or insurance income. Interest may not be excluded from the foreign personal holding company income of the recipient under this paragraph (b)(3) to the extent that the deduction for the interest is allocated under § 1.954-1T(c) to the payor's adjusted gross foreign base company income (as defined in § 1.954-1T(a)(3)), adjusted gross insurance income (as defined in § 1.954-1T(a)(6)), or other categories of income included in the computation of subpart F income under section 952(a), for purposes of computing the payor's net foreign base company income (as defined in § 1.954-1T(a)(4), net insurance income (as defined in § 1.954-1T(a)(6)), or income described in sections 952(a)(3), (4), and (5).

(iii) Dividends paid out of prior years' earnings. Dividends are excluded from foreign personal holding company income under this paragraph (b)(3) only to the extent they are paid out of earnings and profits which were earned or accumulated during a period in which the requirements of subdivision (i) of this paragraph (b)(3) were satisfied or, to the extent earned or accumulated during a taxable year of the related foreign corporation ending on or before December 31, 1962, during a period in which the payor was a related corporation as to be controlled foreign corporation and the other requirements of subdivision (i) of this paragraph (b)(3) are substantially satisfied.

(iv) Fifty percent substantial assets test. A substantial part of the assets of the payor will be considered used in a trade or business located in its country of incorporation only if, for each quarter during such taxable year, the average value (as of the beginning and end of the quarter) of its assets which are used in the trade or business and are located in such country constitutes over 50 percent of the average value (as of the beginning and end of the quarter) of all the assets of the payor (including assets not used in a trade or business). For such purposes the value of assets shall be determined under subdivision (v) of this paragraph (b)(3), and the location of assets used in a trade or business of the payor shall be determined under subdivisions (vi) through (xi) of this paragraph (b)(3).

(v) Value of assets. For purposes of determining whether a substantial part of the assets of the payor are used in a trade or business in its country of incorporation, the value of assets shall be their actual value (not reduced by liabilities), which, in the absence of affirmative evidence to the contrary, shall be deemed to be their adjusted basis.

(vi) Location of tangible property used in a trade or business. (A) In general. Tangible property (other than inventory and similar property) used in a trade or business is considered located in the country in which it is physically located.

(B) Exception. If tangible personal property used in a trade or business is intended for use in the payor's country of incorporation, but is temporarily located elsewhere, it will be considered located within payor's country of incorporation if the reason for its location elsewhere is for inspection or repair, and it is not currently in service in a country other than the payor's country of incorporation and is not to be placed in service in a country other than the payor's country of incorporation following the inspection or repair.

(vii) Location of intangible property used in a trade or business. (A) In general. The location of intangible property (other than inventory or similar property and debt instruments) used in a trade or business is determined based on the site of the activities conducted by the payor during the current year in connection with using or exploiting that property. An item of intangible property is located in the payor's country of incorporation during each quarter of the current taxable year if the activities connected with its use or exploitation are conducted during the entire current taxable year by the payor in its country of incorporation. For this purpose, the determination of the country in which services are performed shall be made under the principles of section 954(e) and § 1.954-4(c).

(B) Property located in part in the payor's country of incorporation and in part in other countries. If the activities connected with the use or exploitation of an item of intangible property are conducted during the current taxable year by the payor in the payor's country of incorporation and in other countries, then a percentage of the intangible (measured by the average value of the item as of the beginning and end of the quarter) is considered located in the payor's country of incorporation during each quarter: That percentage equals the ratio that the expenses of the payor incurred during the entire taxable year by reason of such activities that are conducted in the payor's country of incorporation bear to the expenses of the payor incurred during the entire taxable year by reason of all such activities worldwide. Expenses incurred in connection with the use or exploitation of an item of intangible property are included in the computation provided by this paragraph (b)(3) if they are deductible under section 162 or includible in inventory costs or the costs of goods sold (were the payor a domestic corporation).

(viii) Location of property held for sale to customers. (A) In general. Inventory or similar property is considered located in the payor's country of incorporation during each quarter of the taxable year if the activities of the payor in connection with the production and sale, or purchase and release, of such property and conducted in the payor's country of incorporation during the entire taxable year. If the payor conducts such activities through an independent contractor, then the location of such activities shall be the place in which they are conducted by the independent contractor.

(B) Inventory located in part in the payor's country of incorporation and in part in other countries. If the activities connected with the production and sales, or purchase and resale, of inventory or similar property are conducted by the payor in the payor's country of incorporation and other countries, then a percentage of the inventory or similar property (measured by the average value of the item as of the beginning and end of the quarter) is considered located in the payor's country of incorporation each quarter. That percentage equals the ratio that the costs of the payor incurred during the entire taxable year by reason of such activities that are conducted in the payor's country of incorporation bear to all such costs incurred by reason of such activities worldwide. A cost incurred in connection with the production and sale or purchase and resale of inventory or similar property is included in this computation if it—

(1) Must be included in inventory costs or otherwise capitalized with respect to inventory or similar property under section 61, 263A, 471, or 472 and the regulations thereunder (whichever would be applicable were the payor a domestic corporation), or

(2) Would be deductible under section 162 (were the payor a domestic corporation) and is definitely related to gross income derived from such property (but not to all classes of gross income derived by the payor) under the principles of § 1.861-8.

(ix) Location of debt instruments. For purposes of this paragraph (b)(3), debt instruments are considered to be used in a trade or business only if they arise from the sale of inventory or similar property by the payor or from the rendition of services by the payor in the ordinary course of a trade or business of the payor, but only until such time as interest is required to be charged under section 482 and the regulations thereunder. Debt instruments that arise from the sale of inventory or similar property are treated as having the same location, proportionately, as inventory or similar property that is held during the same calendar quarter. Debt instruments arising from the rendition of services in the ordinary course of a trade or business are considered located on a proportionate basis in the countries in which the services to which they related are performed.

(x) Treatment of certain stock interests. For the purpose of determining the value of assets used in a trade or business in the country of incorporation, stock directly or indirectly owned by the payor within the meaning of section 958(a) in a controlled foreign corporation ("lower-tier corporation"), which is incorporated in the same country as the payor, shall be considered located in the country of incorporation and used in a trade or business of the payor in proportion to the value of the assets of the lower-tier corporation that are used in a trade or business in the country of incorporation. The location of assets used in a trade or business of the lower-tier corporation shall be determined under the rules of this paragraph (b)(3).

(xi) Determination of period during which property is used in a trade or business. Property purchased or produced for use in a trade or business shall not be considered used in a trade or business until it is placed in service, and shall cease to be considered used in a trade or business when it is retired from service. The dates during which depreciable property is determined to be in use must be consistent with the determination of depreciation under sections 167 and 168 and the regulations thereunder.

(xii) Treatment of banks and insurance companies. [Reserved.]

(4) Exclusion of rents and royalties derived from related persons. (i) In general. Foreign personal holding company income does not include rents or royalties if—

(A) The payor is a corporation that is a related person as defined in section 954(d)(3), and

(B) The rents or royalties are for the use of, or the privilege of using, property within the country under the laws of which the recipient of the payments is created or organized.

If the property is used both within and without the country under the laws of which the controlled foreign corporation is created or organized, the part of the rent or royalty attributable to the use of, or the privilege of using, the property outside such country of incorporation is, unless otherwise provided, foreign personal holding company income under this paragraph (b).

(ii) Rents or royalties paid out of adjusted foreign base company income or insurance income. Rents or royalties may not be excluded from the foreign personal holding company income of the recipient under this paragraph (b)(4) to the extent that deductions for the payments are allocated under section 954(b)(5) and § 1.954-1T(a)(4) to the payor's adjusted gross foreign base company income (as defined in § 1.954-1T(a)(3)), adjusted gross insurance income (as defined in § 1.954-1T(a)(6), or other categories of income included in the computation of subpart F income under section 952(a), for purposes of computing the payor's net foreign base company income (as defined in § 1.954-1T(a)(4)), net insurance income (as defined in § 1.954-1T(a)(6)), or income described in section 952(a)(3), (4), or (5).

(5) Exclusion of rents and royalties derived in the active conduct of a trade or business. Foreign personal holding company income shall not include rents or royalties which are derived in the active conduct of a trade or business and which are received from a person other than a related person within the meaning of section 954(d)(3). Whether or not rents or royalties are derived in the active conduct of a trade or business is to be determined from the facts and circumstances of each case; but see paragraph (c) or (d) of this section for specific cases in which rents or royalties will be considered for purposes of this paragraph to be derived in the active conduct of a trade or business. The frequency with which a foreign corporation enters into transactions from which rents or royalties are derived will not of itself establish the fact that such rents or royalties are derived in the active conduct of a trade or business.

(6) Treatment of tax exempt interest. Foreign personal holding company income includes all interest income, including interest that is exempt from U.S. tax pursuant to section 103 (" tax-exempt interest"). However, that net foreign base company income of a controlled foreign corporation that is attributable to such tax-exempt interest shall be treated as tax-exempt interest in the hands of the U.S. shareholders of the foreign corporation. Accordingly, any net foreign base company income that is included in the Subpart F income of a U.S. shareholder and that is attributable to such tax-exempt interest shall remain exempt from the regular income tax, but potentially subject to the alternative minimum tax, in the hands of the U.S. shareholder.

(c) Excluded rents. *(1) Trade or business cases.* Rents will be considered for purposes of paragraph (b)(5) of this section to be derived in the active conduct of a trade or business if such rents are derived by the controlled foreign corporation ("lessor") from leasing—

(i) Property which the lessor has manufactured or produced, or has acquired and added substantial value to, but only if the lessor is regularly engaged in the manufacture or production of, or in the acquisition and addition of substantial value to, property of such kind,

(ii) Real property with respect to which the lessor, through its own officers or staff of employees, regularly performs active and substantial management and operational functions while the property is leased,

(iii) Personal property ordinarily used by the lessor in the active conduct of a trade or business, leased during a temporary period when the property would, but for such leasing, be idle, or

(iv) Property which is leased as a result of the performance of marketing functions by such lessor if the lessor, through its own officers or staff of employees located in a foreign country, maintains and operates an organization in such country which is regularly engaged in the business of marketing, or of marketing and servicing, the leased property and which is substantial in relation to the amount of rents derived from the leasing of such property.

(2) Special rules. (i) Adding substantial value. For purposes of paragraph (c)(1)(i) of this section, the performance of marketing functions will not be considered to add substantial value to property.

(ii) Substantiality of foreign organization. An organization in a foreign country will be considered substantial in relation to the amount of rents, for purposes of paragraph (c)(1)(iv) of this section, if active leasing expenses, as defined in paragraph (c)(2)(iii), equal or exceed 25 percent of the adjusted leasing profit, as defined in paragraph (c)(2)(iv) of this section.

(iii) Active leasing expenses The term "active leasing expenses" means the deductions incurred by an organization of the lessor in a foreign country which are properly allocable to rental income and which would be allowable under section 162 to the lessor (were the lessor a domestic corporation) other than—

(A) Deductions for compensation for personal services rendered by shareholders of, or related persons with respect to, the lessor,

(B) Deductions for rents paid or accrued,

(C) Deductions which, although generally allowable under section 162, would be specifically allowable to the lessor (were the lessor a domestic corporation) under sections other than section 162 (such as sections 167 and 168), and

(D) Deductions for payments made to independent contractors with respect to the leased property.

(iv) Adjusted leasing profit. The term "adjusted leasing profit" means the gross income of the lessor from rents, reduced by the sum of—

(A) The rents paid or incurred by the controlled foreign corporation with respect to such gross rental income,

(B) The amounts which would be allowable to such lessor (were the lessor a domestic corporation) as deductions under section 167 or 168 with respect to such rental income, and

(C) The amounts paid to independent contractors with respect to such rental income.

(3) Illustrations. The application of this paragraph (c) is illustrated by the following examples.

Example (1). Controlled foreign corporation A is regularly engaged in the production of office machines which it sells or leases to others and services. Under paragraph (c)(1)(i) of this section, the rental income of A Corporation from the leases is derived in the active conduct of a trade or business for purposes of section 954(c)(2)(A).

Example (2). Controlled foreign corporation D purchases motor vehicles which it leases to others. In the conduct of its short-term leasing of such vehicles in foreign country X, Corporation D owns a large number of motor vehicles in country X which it services and repairs, leases motor vehicles to customers on an hourly, daily, or weekly basis, maintains offices and service facilities in country X from which to lease and service such vehicles, and maintains therein a sizable staff of its own administrative, sales, and service personnel. Corporation D also leases in country X on a long-term basis, generally for a term of one year, motor vehicles which it owns. Under the terms of the long-term leases, Corporation D is required to repair and service, during the term of the lease, the leased motor vehicles without cost to the lessee. By the maintenance in country X of office, sales, and service facilities and its complete staff of administrative, sales, and service personnel, Corporation D maintains and operates an organization therein which is regularly engaged in the business of marketing and servicing the motor vehicles which are leased. The deductions incurred by such organization satisfy the 25-percent test of paragraph (c)(2)(ii) of this section; thus, such organization is substantial in relation to the rents Corporation D receives from leasing the motor vehicles. Therefore, under paragraph (c)(1)(iv) of this section, such rents are derived in the active conduct of a trade or business for purposes of section 954(c)(2)(A).

Example (3). Controlled foreign corporation E owns a complex of apartment buildings which it has acquired by purchase. Corporation E engages a real estate management firm to lease the apartments, manage the buildings and pay over the net rents to the owner. The rental income of E Corporation from such leases is not derived in the active conduct of a trade or business for purposes of section 954(c)(2)(A).

Example (4). Controlled foreign corporation F acquired by purchase a twenty-story office building in a foreign country, three floors of which it occupies and the rest of which it leases. Corporation F acts as rental agent for the leasing of offices in the building and employs a substantial staff to perform other management and maintenance functions. Under paragraph (c)(1)(ii) of this section, the rents received by Corporation F from such leasing operations are derived in the active conduct of a trade or business for purposes of section 954(c)(2)(A).

Example (5). Controlled foreign corporation G owns equipment which it ordinarily uses to perform contracts in foreign countries to drill oil wells. For occasional brief and irregular periods it is unable to obtain contracts requiring immediate performance sufficient to employ all such equipment. During such a period it sometimes leases such idle equipment temporarily. After the expiration of such temporary leasing of the property, Corporation G continues the use of such equipment in the performance of its own drilling contracts. Under paragraph (c)(1)(iii) of this section, rents G receives from such leasing of idle equipment are derived in the active conduct of a trade or business for purposes of section 954(c)(2)(A).

(d) Excluded royalties. *(1) Trade or business cases.* Royalties will be considered for purposes of paragraph (b)(5) of this section to be derived in the active conduct of a trade or business if such royalties are derived by the controlled foreign corporation ("licensor") from licensing. (i) Property which the licensor has developed, created, or produced, or has acquired and added substantial value to, but only so long as the licensor is regularly engaged in the development, creation, or production of, or in the acquisition of and addition of substantial value to, property of such kind, or

(ii) Property which is licensed as a result of the performance of marketing functions by such licensor and the licensor, through its own staff of employees located in a foreign country, maintains and operates an organization in such country which is regularly engaged in the business of marketing, or of marketing and servicing, the licensed property and which is substantial in relation to the amount of royalties derived from the licensing of such property.

(2) Special rules. (i) Adding substantial value. For purposes of paragraph (d)(1)(i), the performance of marketing functions will not be considered to add substantial value to property.

(ii) Substantiality of foreign organization. An organization in a foreign country will be considered substantial in relation to the amount of royalties, for purposes of paragraph (d)(1)(ii) of this section, if the active licensing expenses, as defined in paragraph (d)(2)(iii) of this section, equal or exceed 25 percent of the adjusted licensing profit, as defined in paragraph (d)(2)(iv) of this section.

(iii) Active licensing expenses. The term "active licensing expenses" means the deductions incurred by an organization of the licensor which are properly allocable to royalty income and which would be allowable under section 162 to the licensor (were the licensor a domestic corporation) other than—

(A) Deductions for compensation for personal services rendered by shareholders of, or related persons with respect to, the licensor,

(B) Deductions for royalties paid or incurred,

(C) Deductions which, although generally allowable under section 162, would be specifically allowable to the licensor (were the controlled foreign corporation a domestic corporation) under sections other than section 162 (such as section 167), and

(D) Deductions for payments made to independent contractors with respect to the licensed property.

(iv) Adjusted licensing profit. The term "adjusted licensing profit" means the gross income of the licensor from royalties, reduced by the sum of—

(A) The royalties paid or incurred by the controlled foreign corporation with respect to such gross royalty income,

(B) The amounts which would be allowable to such licensor as deductions under section 167 (were the licensor a domestic corporation) with respect to such royalty income, and

(C) The amounts paid to independent contractors with respect to such royalty income.

(3) Illustrations. The application of this paragraph (d) is illustrated by the following examples.

Example (1). Controlled foreign corporation A, through its own staff of employees, owns and operates a research facility in foreign country X. At the research facility employees of Corporation A who are full time scientists, engineers, and technicians regularly perform experiments, tests, and other technical activities, which ultimately result in the issuance of patents that it sells or licenses. Under paragraph (d)(1)(i) of this section, royalties received by Corporation A for the privilege of using patented rights which it develops as a result of such research activity are derived in the active conduct of a trade or business for purposes of section 954(c)(2)(A).

Example (2). Assume that Corporation A in example (1), in addition to receiving royalties for the use of patents which it develops, receives royalties for the use of patents which it acquires by purchase and licenses to others without adding any value thereto. Corporation A generally consummates royalty agreements on such purchased patents as the result of inquiries received by it from prospective licensees when the fact becomes known in the business community, as a result of the filing of a patent, advertisements in trade journals, announcements, and contacts by employees of Corporation A, that Corporation A has acquired rights under a patent and is interested in licensing its rights. Corporation A does not, however, maintain and operate an organization in a foreign country which is regularly engaged in the business of marketing the purchased patents. The royalties received by Corporation A for the use of the purchased patents are not derived in the active conduct of a trade or business for purposes of section 954(c)(2)(A).

Example (3). Controlled foreign corporation *B* receives royalties for the use of patents which it acquires by purchase. The primary business of Corporation B, operated on a regular basis, consists of licensing patents which it has purchased "raw" from inventors and, through the efforts of a substantial staff of employees consisting of scientists, engineers, and technicians, made susceptible to commercial application. For example, Corporation B, after purchasing patent rights covering a chemical process, designs specialized production equipment required for the commercial adaptation of the process and, by so doing, substantially increases the value of the patent. Under paragraph (d)(1)(i) of this section, royalties received by Corporation B from the use of such patent are derived in the active conduct of a trade or business for purposes of section 954(c)(2)(A).

Example (4). Controlled foreign corporation D finances independent persons in the development of patented items in return for an ownership interest in such items from which it derives a percentage of royalty income, if any, subsequently derived from the use by others of the protected right. Corporation D also attempts to increase its royalty income from such patents by contacting prospective licensees and rendering to licensees advice which is intended to promote the use of the patented property. Corporation D does not, however, maintain and operate an organization in a foreign country which is regularly engaged in the business of marketing the patents. Royalties received by Corporation D for the use of such patents are not derived in the active conduct of a trade or business for purposes of section 954(c)(2)(A).

(e) Certain property transactions. *(1) In general.* (i) Inclusion in FPHC income. Foreign personal holding company income includes the excess of gains over losses from the sale or exchange of—

(A) Property which gives rise to dividends, interest, rents, royalties or annuities as described in paragraph (e)(2) of this section, and

(B) Property which does not give rise to income, as described in paragraph (e)(3) of this section.

If losses from the sale or exchange of such property exceed gains, the net loss is not within the definition of foreign personal holding company income under this paragraph (e), and may not be allocated to, or otherwise reduce, other foreign personal holding company income under section 954(b)(5) and § 1.954-1T(c). Gain or loss from a transaction that is treated as capital gain or loss under section 988(a)(1)(B) is not foreign currency gain or loss as defined in paragraph (g), but is gain or loss from the sale or exchange of property which is included in the computation of foreign personal holding company income under this paragraph (e)(1). Paragraphs (e)(4) and (5) of this section provide specific rules for determining whether gain or loss from dispositions of debt instruments and dispositions of options or similar property must be included in the computation of foreign personal holding company income under this paragraph (e)(1). A loss that is deferred or that otherwise may not be taken into account under any provision of the Code may not be taken into account for purposes of determining foreign personal holding company income under any provision of this paragraph (e).

(ii) Dual character property. Property may only in part constitute property that gives rise to certain income as described in paragraph (e)(2) of this section or property that does not give rise to any income as described in paragraph (e)(3) of this section. In such cases, the property must be treated as two separate properties for purposes of this paragraph (e). Accordingly, the sale or exchange of such dual character property will give rise to gain or loss that in part must be included in the computation of foreign personal holding company income under this paragraph (e), and in part is excluded from such computation. Gain or loss from the disposition of dual character property must be bifurcated for purposes of this paragraph (e)(1)(i) pursuant to the method that most reasonably reflects the relative uses of the property. Reasonable methods may include comparisons in terms of gross income generated or the physical division of the property. In the case of real property, the physical division of the property will in most cases be the most reasonable method available. For example, if a controlled foreign corporation owns an office building, uses 60 percent of the building in its business, and rents out the other 40 percent, then 40 percent of the gain recognized on the disposition of the property would reasonably be treated as gain which is included in the computation of foreign personal holding company income under this paragraph (e)(1). This paragraph (e)(1)(ii) addresses the contemporaneous use of property for dual purposes; for rules concerning changes in the use of property affecting its classification for purposes of this paragraph (e), see paragraph (a)(3) of this section.

(2) Property that gives rise to certain income. (i) In general. Property the sale or exchange of which gives rise to foreign personal holding company income under this paragraph (e)(2) includes property that gives rise to dividends, interest, rents, royalties and annuities described in paragraph (b) of this section, except for rents and royalties derived from unrelated persons in the active conduct of a trade or business under paragraph (b)(5) of this section. The property described by this paragraph (e)(2) includes property which gives rise to export financing interest described in paragraph (b)(2) of this section and property which gives rise to income from related persons described in paragraphs (b)(3) and (b)(4) of this section.

(ii) Exception. Property described in this paragraph (e)(2) does not include—

(A) Dealer property (as defined in paragraph (a)(4)(iv) of this section), and

(B) Inventory and similar property (as defined in paragraph (a)(4)(ii) of this section) other than securities.

(3) Property that does not give rise to income. The term "property that does not give rise to income" for purposes of this section includes all rights and interests in property (whether or not a capital asset) except—

(i) Property that gives rise to dividends, interest, rents, royalties and annuities described in paragraph (e)(2) of this section and property that gives rise to rents and royalties derived in the active conduct of a trade or business under paragraph (b)(5) of this section;

(ii) Dealer property (as defined in paragraph (a)(4)(iv) of this section);

(iii) Inventory and similar property (as defined in paragraph (a)(4)(ii)) other than securities;

(iv) Property (other than real property) used in the controlled foreign corporation's trade or business that is of a character which would be subject to the allowance for depreciation under section 167 or 168 and the regulations thereunder (including tangible property described in § 1.167(a)-2 and intangibles described in § 1.167(a)-3);

(v) Real property that does not give rise to rental or similar income, to the extent used in the controlled foreign corporation's trade or business; and

(vi) Intangible property as defined in section 936(h)(3)(B) and goodwill that is not subject to the allowance for depreciation under section 167 and the regulations thereunder to the extent used in the controlled foreign corporation's trade or business and disposed of in connection with the sale of a trade or business of the controlled foreign corporation.

(4) Classification of gain or loss from the disposition of a debt instrument or on a deferred payment sale. (i) Gain. Gain from the sale, exchange, or retirement of a debt instrument is included in the computation of foreign personal holding company income under this paragraph (e) unless—

(A) It is treated as interest income (as defined in paragraph (a)(4)(i) of this section); or

(B) It is treated as income equivalent to interest under paragraph (h) of this section.

(ii) Loss. Loss from the sale, exchange, or retirement of a debt instrument is included in the computation of foreign personal holding company income under this paragraph (e) unless—

(A) It is directly allocated to interest income (as defined in paragraph (a)(4)(i) of this section) or income equivalent to interest (as defined in paragraph (h) of this section) under any provision of the Code or regulations thereunder;

(B) It is required to be apportioned in the same manner as interest expense under section 864(e) or any other provision of the Code or regulations thereunder; or

(C) The debt instrument was taken in consideration for the sale or exchange of property (or the provision of services) by the controlled foreign corporation and gain or loss from that sale or exchange (or income from the provision of services) is not includible in foreign base company income under this section.

(5) Classification of options and other rights to acquire or transfer property. Subject to the exceptions provided in paragraphs (e)(3)(ii) and (iii) of this section (relating to certain dealer property and inventory property), rights to acquire or transfer property, including property that gives rise to income, are classified as property that does not give rise to income under paragraph (e)(3) of this section. These rights include options, warrants, futures contracts, options on a futures contract, forward contracts, and options on an index relating to stocks, securities or interest rates.

(6) Classification of certain interests in pass through entities. [Reserved.]

(f) Commodities transactions. *(1) In general.* Except as otherwise provided in this paragraph (f), foreign personal holding company income includes the excess of gains over losses from commodities transactions. If losses from commodities transactions exceed gains, the net loss is not within the definition of foreign personal holding company income under this paragraph (f), and may not be allocated to, or otherwise reduce, foreign personal holding company income under section 954(b)(5) and § 1.954-1T(a)(4). The terms "commodity" and "commodities transactions" are defined in paragraph (f)(2) of this section. Gains and losses from qualified active sales and qualified hedging transactions are excluded from the computation of foreign personal holding company income under this paragraph (f). The term "qualified active sales" is defined in paragraph (f)(3). The term "qualified hedging transaction" is defined in paragraph (f)(4) of this section. An election is provided under paragraph (g)(5) of this section to include all gains and losses from section 1256 foreign currency transactions, which would otherwise be commodities transactions, in the computation of foreign personal holding company income under paragraph (g) instead of this paragraph (f). A loss that is deferred or that otherwise may not be taken into account under any provision of the Code may not be taken into account for purposes of determining foreign personal holding company income under any provision of this paragraph (f).

(2) Definitions. (i) Commodity. For purposes of this section, the term "commodity" means:

(A) Tangible personal property of a kind which is actively traded or with respect to which contractual interests are actively traded, and

(B) Nonfunctional currency (as defined under section 988 and the regulations thereunder).

(ii) Commodities transaction. A commodities transaction means the purchase or sale of a commodity for immediate (spot) delivery, or deferred (forward) delivery, or the right to purchase, sell, receive, or transfer a commodity, or any other right or obligation with respect to a commodity, accomplished through a cash or off-exchange market, an interbank market, an organized exchange or board of trade, an over-the-counter market, or in a transaction effected between private parties outside of any market. Commodities transactions include, but are not limited to:

(A) A futures or forward contract in a commodity,

(B) A leverage contract in a commodity purchased from leverage transaction merchants,

(C) An exchange of futures for physical transaction,

(D) A transaction in which the income or loss to the parties is measured by reference to the price of a commodity, a pool of commodities, or an index of commodities,

(E) The purchase or sale of an option or other right to acquire or transfer a commodity, a futures contract in a commodity, or an index of commodities, and

(F) The delivery of one commodity in exchange for the delivery of another commodity, the same commodity at another time, cash, or nonfunctional currency.

(3) Definition of the term "qualified active sales". (i) In general. The term "qualified active sales" means the sale of commodities in the active conduct of a commodity business as a producer, processor, merchant, or handler of commodities if substantially all of the controlled foreign corporation's business is as an active producer, processor, merchant, or handler of commodities of like kind. The sale of commodities held by a controlled foreign corporation other than in its capacity as an active producer, processor, merchant or handler of commodities of like kind is not a qualified active sale.

(ii) Sale of commodities. The term "sale of commodities" means any transaction in which the controlled foreign corporation intends to deliver to a purchaser a commodity held by the controlled foreign corporation in physical form.

(iii) Active conduct of a commodities business. For purposes of this paragraph, a controlled foreign corporation is engaged in the active conduct of a commodities business as a producer, processor, merchant, or handler of commodities only if—

(A) It holds commodities as inventory or similar property (as defined in paragraph (a)(4)(ii)); and

(B) It incurs substantial expenses in the ordinary course of a commodities business from engaging in one of the following activities directly, and not through an independent contractor:

(1) Substantial activities in the production of commodities, including planting, tending or harvesting crops, raising or slaughtering livestock, or extracting minerals.

(2) Substantial processing activities prior to the sale of commodities including concentrating, refining, mixing, crushing, aerating, or milling; or

(3) Significant activities relating to the physical movement, handling and storage of commodities including preparation of contracts and invoices; arranging freight, insurance and credit; arranging for receipt, transfer or negotiation of shipping documents; arranging storage or warehousing, and dealing with quality claims; owning and operating facilities for storage or warehousing or owning or chartering vessels or vehicles for the transportation of commodities.

For purposes of this paragraph (f), a corporation is not engaged in a commodities business as a producer, processor, merchant, or handler of commodities if its business is primarily financial. In general, the business of a controlled foreign corporation is financial if it primarily engages in commodities transactions for investment or speculation, or if it primarily provides products or services to customers for investment or speculation.

(iv) Substantially all. Substantially all of the controlled foreign corporation's business is as an active producer, processor, merchant, or handler of commodities if the activities described in paragraph (f)(3)(iii) give rise to 85 percent of the taxable income of the controlled foreign corporation (computed as though the corporation were a domestic corporation). For this purpose, gains or losses from qualified hedging transactions, as defined in paragraph (f)(4), are considered derived from the qualified active sales to which they relate or are expected to relate.

(4) Definition of the term "qualified hedging transaction." The term "qualified hedging transaction" means a bona fide hedging transaction that:

(i) Is reasonably necessary to the conduct of business as a producer, processor, merchant or handler of a commodity in the manner in which such business is customarily and usually conducted by others;

(ii) Is entered into primarily to reduce the risk of price change (but not the risk of currency fluctuations) with respect to commodities sold or to be sold in qualified active sales described in paragraph (f)(3) of this paragraph; and

(iii) Is clearly identified on the controlled foreign corporation's records before the close of the fifth day after the day during which the hedging transaction is entered into and at a time when there is a reasonable risk of loss; however, if the controlled foreign corporation does not at such time specifically and properly identify the qualified active sales (or category of such sales) to which a hedging transaction relates, the district director in his sole discretion may determine which hedging transactions (if any) are related to qualified active sales.

(g) Foreign currency gain. *(1) In general.* Except as provided in paragraph (g)(2), foreign personal holding company income includes the excess of foreign currency gains over losses (as defined in section 988(b)) attributable to any section 988 transactions. If foreign currency losses exceed gains, the net loss is not within the definition of foreign personal holding company income under this paragraph (g), and may not be allocated to, or otherwise reduce, foreign personal holding company income under section 954(b)(5) and § 1.954-1T(a)(4). To the extent the gain or loss from a transaction is treated as interest income or expense under sections 988(a)(2) or 988(d) and the regulations thereunder, it is not included in the computation of foreign personal holding company income under this paragraph (g). (For other rules concerning income described in more than one category of foreign personal holding company income, see § 1.954-2(a)(2).) A loss that is deferred or that otherwise may not be taken into account under any provision of the Code may not be taken into account for purposes of determining foreign personal holding company income under any provision of this paragraph (g).

(2) Exceptions. (i) Qualified business units using the dollar approximate separate transactions method. any DASTM gain or loss computed under § 1.985-3(d) must be allocated under the rules of § 1.985-3(e)(2)(iv) or (e)(3).

(ii) Tracing to exclude foreign currency gain or loss from qualified business and hedging transactions. A foreign currency gain or loss is excluded from the computation of foreign personal holding company income under this paragraph (g) if it is clearly identified on the records of the controlled foreign corporation as being derived from a qualified business transaction or a qualified hedging transaction. The term "qualified business transaction" is defined in paragraph (g)(3) of this section. The term "qualified hedging transaction" is defined paragraph (g)(4) of this section. However, currency gain or loss of a qualified business unit included in the computation of currency gain or loss under subdivision (i) of this paragraph (g)(2) may not be excluded from foreign personal holding company income under the tracing rule of this paragraph (g)(2)(ii). Furthermore, the tracing rule of this paragraph (g)(2)(ii) will not apply if a controlled foreign corporation makes the election provided by paragraph (g)(2)(iii) of this section.

(iii) Election out of tracing. A controlled foreign corporation may elect a method of accounting under which all foreign currency gains or losses attributable to section 988 transactions are included in foreign personal holding company income. The scope and requirements for this election are provided in paragraph (g)(5) of this section. This election does not apply to foreign currency gains or losses of a qualified business unit included in the computation of gain or loss under paragraph (g)(2)(i) of this section.

(3) Definition of the term "qualified business transaction". (i) In general. The term "qualified business transaction" means a transaction (other than a "qualified hedging transaction" as described in paragraph (g)(4) of this section) that:

(A) Does not have investment or speculation as a significant purpose;

(B) Is not attributable to property or an activity of the kind that gives rise to subpart F income (other than foreign currency gain under this paragraph (g)), or could reasonably be expected to give rise to subpart F income (including upon disposition); for example, the transaction may not be attributable to stock or debt of another corporation (including related corporations organized and operating in the same country), or property likely to give rise to foreign base company sales or services income; and

(C) Is attributable to business transactions described in subdivision (ii) of this paragraph (g)(3). A qualified business transaction includes the disposition of a debt instrument that constitutes inventory property under paragraph (a)(4)(ii) or dealer property under paragraph (a)(4)(iv) of this section. The provisions of this paragraph (g)(3) do not apply to the foreign currency gain or loss of a qualified business unit (as determined under § 1.985-3T(d)(2)) included in the computation of gain or loss under paragraph (g)(2)(i) of this section. The provisions of this paragraph (g)(3) do, however, apply to other currency transactions of a qualified business unit that elects (or is deemed to elect) the U.S. dollar as its functional currency under section 985(b)(3) and § 1.985-2T. Qualified business transactions and the amount of foreign currency gain or loss derived therefrom must be clearly identified on its records by the controlled foreign corporation. If the controlled foreign corporation is unable to specifically identify the qualified business transactions and the foreign currency gain or loss derived therefrom, the district director in his sole discretion may determine which transactions of the corporation giving rise to the foreign currency gains or losses are attributable to qualified business transactions.

(ii) Specific business transactions. A transaction of a controlled foreign corporation must meet the requirements of any of subdivisions (A) through (F) of this paragraph (g)(3)(ii) to be a qualified business transaction under this paragraph (g)(3).

(A) Acquisition of debt instruments. If the transaction is the acquisition of a debt instrument described in section 988(c)(1)(B)(i) and the regulations thereunder, the debt must be derived from—

(1) The sale of inventory and similar property to customers by the controlled foreign corporation in the ordinary course of regular business operations, or

(2) The rendition of services by the corporation in the ordinary course of regular business operations.

For purposes of this paragraph (g)(3)(ii)(A), a debt instrument will not be considered derived in the ordinary course of regular business operations unless the instrument matures, and is reasonably expected to be satisfied, within the period for which interest need not be charged under section 482 and the regulations thereunder.

(B) Becoming the obligor under debt instruments. If the transaction is becoming the obligor under a debt instrument described in section 988(c)(1)(B)(i) and the regulations thereunder, the debt must be incurred for:

(1) Payment of expenses that are includible by the controlled foreign corporation in the cost of goods sold under § 1.61-3 for property held primarily for sale to customers in the ordinary course of regular business operations, are inventoriable costs under section 471 and the regulations thereunder, or are allocable or apportionable under the rules of § 1.861-8 to gross income derived from inventory and similar property,

(2) Payment of expenses that are allocable or apportionable under the rules of § 1.861-8 to gross income derived from services provided by the controlled foreign corporation in the ordinary course of regular business operations,

(3) Acquisition of an asset that does not give rise to Subpart F income during the current taxable year (other than by application of section 952(c)) and is not reasonably expected to give rise to Subpart F income in subsequent taxable years, or

(4) Acquisition of dealer property as defined in paragraph (a)(4)(iv) of this section.

The identification requirements of subdivision (i) of this paragraph (g)(3) will not be met with respect to a borrowing if the controlled foreign corporation fails to clearly identify the debt and the expenses (or categories of expenses) to which it relates before the close of the fifth day after the day on which the expenses are incurred.

(C) Accrual of any item of gross income. If the transaction is the accrual (or otherwise taking into account) of any item of gross income or receipts as described in section 988(c)(1)(B)(ii) and the regulations thereunder, the item of gross income or receipts must be derived from:

(1) The sale of inventory and similar property in the ordinary course of regular business operations, or

(2) The provision of services by the controlled foreign corporation to customers in the ordinary course of regular business operations.

(D) Accrual of any item of expense. If the transaction is the accrual (or otherwise taking into account) of any item of expense as described in section 988(c)(1)(B)(ii) and the regulations thereunder, the item of expense must be:

(1) An expense that is includible by the controlled foreign corporation in the cost of goods sold under § 1.61-3 for property held primarily for sale to customers in the ordinary course of regular business operations, is an inventoriable cost under section 471 and the regulations thereunder, or is allocable or apportionable under the rules of § 1.861-8 to gross income derived from inventory and similar property, or

(2) An expense that is allocable or apportionable under the rules of § 1.861-8 to gross income derived from services provided by the controlled foreign corporation in the ordinary course of regular business operations.

(E) Entering into forward contracts, futures contracts, options and similar instruments. If the transaction is entering into any forward contract, futures contract, option or similar financial instrument and if such contract or instrument is not marked to market at the close of the taxable year under section 1256, as described in section 988(c)(1)(B)(iii) and the regulations thereunder, then the contract or instrument must be property held as dealer property as defined in paragraph (a)(4)(ii) of this section.

(F) Disposition of nonfunctional currency. If the transaction is the disposition of nonfunctional currency, as described in section 988(c)(1)(C) and the regulations thereunder, then the transaction must be for a purpose described in paragraph (g)(3)(ii)(B), for the payment of taxes not attributable to subpart F income, or must be the disposition of property held as dealer property as defined in paragraph (a)(4)(iv) of this section.

(G) Transactions in business assets. The acquisition or disposition of an asset that is used or held for use in the active conduct of a trade or business.

(4) Definition of the term "qualified hedging transaction". (i) In general. The term "qualified hedging transaction" means a bona fide hedging transaction meeting all the requirements of subdivisions (A) through (D) of this paragraph (g)(4)(i):

(A) The transaction must be reasonably necessary to the conduct of regular business operations in the manner in which such business operations are customarily and usually conducted by others.

(B) The transaction must be entered into primarily to reduce the risk of currency fluctuations with respect to property or services sold or to be sold or expenses incurred or to be incurred in transactions that are qualified business transactions under paragraph (g)(3) of this section.

(C) The hedging transaction and the property or expense (or category of property or expense) to which it relates must be clearly identified on the records of the controlled foreign corporation before the close of the fifth day after the day during which the hedging transaction is entered into and at a time during which there is a reasonable risk of currency loss.

(D) The amount of foreign currency gain or loss that is attributable to a specific hedging transaction must be clearly identifiable on the records of the controlled foreign corporation or its controlling shareholder (as defined in § 1.964-1(c)(5)).

The provisions of this paragraph (g)(4) do not apply to transactions of a qualified business unit included in the computation of gain or loss under paragraph (g)(2)(i). The provisions of this paragraph (g)(4) do apply, however, to other currency transactions of a qualified business unit that elects (or is deemed to elect) the U.S. dollar as its functional currency under section 985(b)(3) and § 1.985-3T. If the controlled foreign corporation does not specifically identify the qualified business transactions (or category of qualified business transactions) to which a hedging transaction relates or is unable to specifically identify the amount of foreign currency gain or loss derived from the hedging transactions, the district director in his sole discretion may make the identifications required of the controlled foreign corporation and determine which hedging transactions (if any) are related to qualified business transactions, and the amount of foreign currency gain or loss attributable to the qualified hedging transactions.

(ii) Change in purpose of hedging transaction. If a hedging transaction is entered into for one purpose, and the purpose for that transaction subsequently changes, the transaction may be treated as two separate hedging transactions for purposes of this paragraph (g)(4). In such a case, the portion of the transaction that relates to a qualified business transaction is considered a qualified hedging transaction if it separately meets all the other requirements of this paragraph (g)(4) for treatment as a qualified hedging transaction. For purposes of paragraph (g)(4)(i)(C), the foreign corporation must identify on its records the portion of the transaction that relates to a qualified business transaction by the close of the fifth day after the day on which the hedge becomes so related (i.e., either the day on which the hedge is first entered into or on the day on which it first relates to a qualified business transaction due to a change in its purpose). The foreign corporation must identify on its records the portion of the transaction that does not relate to a qualified business transaction by the close of the fifth day after the day on which the purpose for the hedging transaction changes.

(5) Election out of tracing. (i) In general. A controlled foreign corporation may elect to account for currency gains and losses under section 988 and gains and losses from section 1256 currency contracts by including in the computation of foreign personal holding company income under this paragraph (g) all foreign currency gains or losses attributable to section 988 transactions, and all gains or losses from section 1256 foreign currency contracts. Separate elections for section 1256 foreign currency contracts and section 988 transactions are not permitted. If a controlled foreign corporation makes the election described in this paragraph (g)(5)(i), the election is effective for all related persons as defined in section 954(d)(3) and the regulations thereunder.

(ii) Exception. The election provided by this paragraph (g)(5) does not apply to foreign currency gain or loss of a qualified business unit determined under § 1.985-3T(d)(2). It does, however, apply to other foreign currency gains or losses of a qualified business unit that elects (or is deemed to elect) the U.S. dollar as its functional currency.

(iii) Procedure. (A) In general. The election provided by this paragraph (g)(5) shall be made in the manner prescribed in this paragraph and in subsequent administrative pronouncements.

(B) Time and manner. The controlled foreign corporation may make the election by filing a statement with its original or amended information return for the taxable year for which the election is made. The controlling United States shareholders, as defined in § 1.964-1(c)(5), may make the election on behalf of the controlled foreign corporation and related corporations by filing a statement to such effect with their original or amended income tax returns for the taxable year during which the taxable year of the controlled foreign corporation for which the election is made ends. The election is effective for the taxable year of the controlled foreign corporation for which the election is made, for the taxable years of all related controlled foreign corporations ending within such taxable year, and for all subsequent years of such corporations. The statement shall include the following information:

(1) The name, address, taxpayer identification number, and taxable year of each United States shareholder;

(2) The name, address, and taxable year of each controlled foreign corporation for which the election is effective; and

(3) Any additional information to be required by the Secretary by administrative pronouncement. Each United States shareholder or controlled foreign corporation filing the election must provide copies of the election to all controlled foreign corporations for which the election is effective, and all United States shareholders of such corporations. However, failure to provide such copies will not void (or cause to be voidable) an election under this paragraph (g)(5).

(C) Termination. The election provided by this paragraph (g)(5) may be terminated only with the consent of the Commissioner: Attn.: CC:INTL.

(h) Income equivalent to interest. *(1) In general.* Foreign personal holding company income includes income that is equivalent to interest. Income equivalent to interest includes, but is not limited to, income derived from the following categories of transactions:

(i) An investment, or series of integrated transactions which include an investment, in which the payments, net payments, cash flows, or return predominantly reflect the time value of money, and

(ii) Transactions in which the payments or a predominant portion thereof are in substance for the use or forbearance of money, but are not generally treated as interest. However, amounts treated as interest under section 954(c)(1)(A) and paragraph (b) of this section are not income equivalent to interest under this paragraph (h). Income from the sale of property will not be treated as income equivalent to interest for purposes of this paragraph (h), subject to the rule of paragraph (h)(4) of this section, unless the sale is part of an integrated transaction that gives rise to interest or income equivalent to interest. See sections 482, 483 and 1274 for the extent to which such income may be characterized as interest income subject to paragraph (b) of this section. Income equivalent to interest for purposes of this paragraph (h) includes all income attributable to a transfer of securities subject to section 1058. Income equivalent to interest also includes a portion of certain deferred payments received for the purpose of services, in accordance with the provisions of paragraph (h)(5) of this section. Income equivalent to interest does not include income attributable to notional principal contracts such as interest rate swaps, currency swaps, interest rate floor agreements, or similar contracts except to the extent that such contracts are part of an integrated transaction that gives rise to income equivalent to interest. Income derived from notional contracts by a person acting in its capacity as a regular dealer in such contracts will be presumed not to be integrated with an investment.

(2) Illustrations. The following examples illustrate the application of this paragraph (h):

Example (1). CFC, a controlled foreign corporation, promises that A, an unrelated person, may borrow up to $500 in principal for one year beginning at any time during the next three months at an interest rate of 10 percent. In exchange, A pays CFC a commitment fee of $2.00. Pursuant to this loan commitment, CFC lends $80 to A. As a result, the entire $2.00 fee is included in the computation of foreign personal holding company income under this paragraph (h)(1)(ii).

Example (2). (i) At the beginning of its current taxable year, CFC, a controlled foreign corporation, purchases at face value a one-year debt instrument issued by A having a $100 principal amount and bearing a floating rate of interest set at the London Interbank Offered Rate ("LIBOR") plus one percentage point. Contemporaneously, CFC borrows $100 from B for one year at a fixed interest rate of 10 percent, using the debt instrument as security.

(ii) During its current taxable year, CFC accrues $11 of interest from *A* on the bond. That interest is foreign personal holding company income under section 954(c)(1) and § 1.954-2T(b), and thus is not income equivalent to interest. During its current taxable year, CFC incurs $10 of interest expense with respect to the borrowing from B. That expense is allocated and apportioned to, and reduces, foreign base company income or insurance income to the extent provided in sections 954(b)(5), 863(e), and 864(e) and the regulations thereunder.

Example (3). (i) At the beginning of its 1988 taxable year, *CFC,* a controlled foreign corporation, purchases at face value a one-year debt instrument issued by A having a $100 principal amount and bearing a floating rate of interest set at the London Interbank Offered Rate ("LIBOR") plus one percentage point payable on the last day of CFC's current taxable year. CFC subsequently determines that it would prefer receiving interest at a fixed rate, and, on January 1, 1989, enters into an agreement with B, an unrelated person, whereby B promises to pay CFC on the last day of CFC's 1989 taxable year an amount equal to 10 percent on a notional principal amount of $100. In exchange, CFC promises to pay B on the last day of CFC's 1989 taxable year an amount equal to LIBOR plus one percentage point on the notional principal amount.

(ii) CFC receives a total of $10 from B, and pays $9 to B. CFC also receives $9 from A. The $9 paid to B is directly allocated to, or is otherwise an adjustment to, the $10 received from B. The transactions are considered an integrated transaction giving rise to $9 of interest income (paid by A) and, under paragraph (h)(1)(i), $1 of income equivalent to interest (paid by B).

Example (4). The facts are the same as in Example (3), except that CFC does not hold any debt obligations. Since the transaction with B is not integrated with an investment giving rise to interest or income equivalent to interest, the net $1 of income realized by *CFC* does not constitute income equivalent to interest.

Example (5). (i) CFC, a controlled foreign corporation, enters into an agreement with A whereby CFC purchases commodity X from A at a price of $100, and A contemporaneously repurchases commodity X from CFC for payment and delivery in 3 months at a price of $104 set by the forward market.

(ii) The transaction is in substance a loan from CFC to A secured by commodity X. Thus, CFC accrues $4 of gross income which is included in foreign personal holding company income as interest under section 954(c)(1)(A) and paragraph (b) of this section.

Example (6). (i) CFC purchases commodity Y on the spot market for $100 and contemporaneously, sells commodity Y forward for delivery and payment in 3 months at a price of $104 set by the forward market.

(ii) The $100 paid on the spot purchase of commodity Y offsets any market risk on the forward sale so that the $4 of income to be derived predominantly reflects time value of money. Thus, under paragraph (h)(1)(i), the spot purchase of commodity Y and the offsetting forward sale will be treated as an integrated transaction giving rise to $4 of income equivalent to interest.

(3) Income equivalent to interest from factoring. (i) General rule. Income equivalent to interest includes factoring income. Except as provided in paragraph (h)(3)(ii) of this section, the term "factoring income" includes any income (including any discount income or service fee, but excluding any stated interest) derived from the acquisition and collection or disposition of a factored receivable. The rules of this paragraph (h)(3) apply only with respect to the tax treatment of factoring income derived from the acquisition and collection or disposition of a factored receivable and shall not affect the characterization of an expense or loss of either the person whose goods or services gave rise to a factored receivable or the obligor under a receivable. The amount of income equivalent to interest realized with respect to a factored receivable is the difference (if a positive number) between the amount paid for the receivable by the foreign corporation and the amount that it collects on the receivable (or realizes upon its sale of the receivable).

(ii) Exceptions. Factoring income shall not include—

(A) Income treated as interest under section 864(d)(1) or (6) and the regulations thereunder (relating to income derived from trade or service receivables of related persons), even if such income is not treated as described in section 864(d)(1) by reason of the same-country exception of section 864(d)(7);

(B) Income derived from a factored receivable if payment for the acquisition of the receivable is made on or after the date on which stated interest begins to accrue, but only if the rate of stated interest equals or exceeds 120 percent of the Federal short term rate (as defined under section 1274) (or the equivalent rate for a currency other than the dollar) as of the date on which the receivable is acquired by the foreign corporation; or

(C) Income derived from a factored receivable if payment for the acquisition of the receivable by the foreign corporation is made only on or after the anticipated date of payment of all principal by the obligor (or the anticipated weighted average date of payment of a pool of purchased receivables).

(iii) Factored receivable. For purposes of this paragraph (h)(3), the term "factored receivable" includes any account receivable or other evidence of indebtedness, whether or not issued at a discount and whether or not bearing stated interest, arising out of the disposition of property or the performance of services by any person, if such account receivable or evidence of indebtedness is acquired by a person other than the person who disposed of the property or provided the services that gave rise to the account receivable or evidence of indebtedness. For purposes of this paragraph (h)(3), it is immaterial whether the person providing the property or services agrees to transfer the receivable at the time of sale (as by accepting a third-party charge or credit card) or at a later time.

(iv) Illustrations. The following examples illustrate the application of this paragraph (h)(3).

Example (1). DP, a domestic corporation, owns all of the outstanding stock of FS, a controlled foreign corporation. FS acquires accounts receivable arising from the sale of property by unrelated corporation X. The receivables have a face amount of $100, and after 30 days bear stated interest equal to at least 120 percent of the applicable short term Federal rate (determined as of the date the receivable is acquired). FS purchases the receivables from X for $95 on Day 1 and collects $100 from the obligor under the receivable on Day 40. Income (other than stated interest) derived by FS from the factored receivables is factoring income within the meaning or paragraph (h)(3)(i) of this section and, therefore, is income equivalent to interest.

Example (2). The facts are the same as in example (1), except that FS does not pay X for the receivables until Day 30. Income derived by FS from the factored receivables is not factoring income by reason of paragraph (h)(3)(ii)(B) of this section.

Example (3). The facts are the same as in Example (2), except that it is anticipated that all principal will be paid by the obligor of the receivables by Day 30. Income derived by FS from this "maturity factoring" of the receivables is not factoring income by reason of paragraph (h)(3)(ii)(C) of this section, and therefore does not give rise to income equivalent to interest.

Example (4). The facts are the same as in example (1), except that, rather than collecting $100 from the obligor under the factored receivable on Day 40, FS sells the receivable to controlled foreign corporation Y on Day 15 for $97. Both the income derived by FS on the factored receivable and the income derived by Y (other than stated interest) on the receivable are factoring income within the meaning of paragraph (h)(3)(i) of this section, and therefore, constitute income equivalent to interest.

Example (5). The facts are the same as in example (4), except that FS sells the factored receivable to Y for $99 on Day 45, at which time interest is accruing on the unpaid balance of $100. FS has $4 of net factoring income that is income equivalent to interest. Because interest was accruing at the time Y acquired the receivable at a rate equal to at least 120 percent of the applicable short term Federal rate, income derived by Y from the factored receivable is not factoring income by reason of paragraph (h)(3)(ii)(B).

Example (6). DP, a domestic corporation engaged in an integrated credit card business, owns all of the outstanding stock of FS, a controlled foreign corporation. On Day 1 individual A uses a credit card issued by DP to purchase shoes priced at $100 from X, a foreign corporation unrelated to DP, FS, or A. By prearrangement with DP, on Day 7, X transfers the receivable arising from A's purchase to FS in exchange for $95. FS collects $100 from A on Day 45. Income derived by FS on the factored receivable is factoring income within the meaning of paragraph (h)(3)(i) of this section and, therefore, is income equivalent to interest.

(4) Determination of sales income. Income equivalent to interest for purposes of this paragraph (h) does not include income from the sale of property unless the sale is part of an integrated transaction that gives rise to interest or income equivalent to interest. Income derived by a controlled foreign corporation will be treated as arising from the sale of property only if the corporation in substance carries out sales activities. Accordingly, an arrangement that is designed to lend the form of a sales transaction to a transaction that in substance constitutes and advance of funds will be disregarded. For example, if a controlled foreign corporation acquires property on 30-day payment terms from one person and sells that property to another person on 90 day payment terms and at prearranged prices and terms such that the foreign corporation bears no substantial economic risk with respect to the purchase and sale other than the risk of non-payment, the foreign corporation has not in substance derived income from the sale of property.

(5) Receivables arising from performance of services. If payment for services performed by a controlled foreign corporation is not made until more than 120 days after the date on which such services are performed, then the income derived by the foreign corporation constitutes income equivalent to interest to the extent that interest income would be imputed under the principles of section 483 or the original issue discount provisions (section 1271 *et seq.*), if—

(A) Such provisions applied to contracts for the performance of services,

(B) The time period referred to in sections 483(c)(1) and 1274(c)(1)(B) were 120 days rather than six months, and

(C) The time period referred to in section 483(c)(1)(A) were 120 days rather than one year.

T.D. 8216, 7/20/88, amend T.D. 8556, 7/22/94, T.D. 8618, 9/6/95.

§ 1.954-3 Foreign base company sales income.

Caution: The Treasury has not yet amended Reg § 1.954-3 to reflect changes made by P.L. 103-66, P.L. 99-514, P.L. 98-369.

(a) Income included. *(1) In general.* (i) General rules. Foreign base company sales income of a controlled foreign corporation shall, except as provided in subparagraphs (2), (3), and (4) of this paragraph, consist of gross income (whether in the form of profits, commissions, fees, or otherwise) derived in connection with (a) the purchase of personal property from a related person and its sale to any person, (b) the sale of personal property to any person on behalf of a related person, (c) the purchase of personal property from any person and its sale to a related person, or (d) the purchase of personal property from any person on behalf of a related person. See section 954(d)(1). This section shall apply to the purchase and/or sale of personal property, whether or not such property was purchased and/or sold in the ordinary course of trade or business, except that income derived in connection with the sale of tangible personal property will not be considered to be foreign base company sales income if such property is sold to an unrelated person, as defined in paragraph (e)(2) of § 1.954-1, after substantial use has been made of the property by the controlled foreign corporation in its trade or business. This section shall not apply to the excess of gains over losses from sales or exchanges of securities or from futures transactions, to the extent such excess gains are includible in foreign personal holding company income of the controlled foreign corporation under § 1.954-2 or foreign base company shipping income under § 1.954-6 nor shall it apply to the sale of the controlled foreign corporation's property (other than its stock in trade or other property of a kind which would properly be included in its inventory if on hand at the close of the taxable year, or property held primarily for sale to customers in the ordinary course of its trade or business) if substantially all the property of such corporation is sold pursuant to the discontinuation of the trade or business previously carried on by such corporation. The term "any person" as used in this subparagraph includes a related person, as defined in paragraph (e)(1) of § 1.954-1.

(ii) Special rule. (a) In general. The term "personal property" as used in section 954(d) and this section shall not include agricultural commodities which are not grown in the United States (within the meaning of section 7701(a)(9)) in commercially marketable quantities. All of the agricultural commodities listed in table I shall be considered grown in the United States in commercially marketable quantities. Bananas, black pepper, cocoa, coconut, coffee, crude rubber, and tea shall not be considered grown in the United States in commercially marketable quantities. All other agricultural commodities shall not be considered grown in the United States in commercially marketable quantities when, in consideration of all of the facts and circumstances of the individual case, such commodities are shown to be produced in the United States in insufficient quantity and quality to be marketed commercially. The term "agricultural commodities" includes, but is not limited to, livestock, poultry, fish produced in fish farms, fruit, furbearing animals as well as the products of truck farms, ranches, nurseries, ranges, and orchards. A fish farm is an area where fish are grown or raised (artificially protected and cared for), as opposed to merely caught or harvested. However, the term "agricultural commodities" shall not include timber (either standing of felled), or any commodity at least 50 percent of the fair market value of which is attributable to manufacturing or processing, determined in a manner consistent with the regulations under section 993(c) (relating to the definition of export property). For purposes of applying such regulations, the term "processing" shall be deemed not to include handling, packing, packaging, grading, storing, transporting, slaughtering, and harvesting. Subdivision (ii) shall apply in the computation of foreign base company sales income for taxable years of controlled foreign corporations beginning after December 31, 1975, and to taxable years of U.S. shareholders (within the meaning of section 951(b)) within which or with which such taxable years of such foreign corporations end.

(b) Table.

Table I.—Agricultural Commodities Grown in the United States in Commercially Marketable Quantities

Livestock and Products	
Beeswax	Horses
Cattle and calves	Milk
Chickens	Mink
Chicken eggs	Mohair
Ducks	Rabbits
Geese	Sheep and lambs
Goats	Turkeys
Hogs	Wool
Honey	

Crops	
Alfalfa	Lettuce
Almonds	Lime
Apples	Macadamia nuts
Apricots	Maple syrup and sugar
Artichokes	Mint
Asparagus	Mushrooms
Avocados	
Barley	Nectarines
Beans	Oats
Beets	Olives
Blackberries	Onions
Blueberries	Oranges
Brussel sprouts	Papayas
Broccoli	Pecans
Bulbs	Peaches
Cabbage	Peanuts
Cantaloupes	Pears
Carrots	Peas
Cauliflower	Peppers
Celery	Plums and prunes
Cherries	Potatoes
Corn	Potted plants
Cotton	Raspberries
Cranberries	Rice
Cucumbers	Rhubarb
Cut flowers	Rye
Dates	Sorghum grain
Eggplant	Soybeans
Escarole	Spinach
Figs	Strawberries
Filberts	Sugar beets
Flaxseed	Sugarcane
Garlic	Sweet potatoes
Grapes	Tangelos
Grapefruit	Tangerines
Grass seed	Tobacco
Hay	Tomatoes
Honeydew melons	Walnuts
Hops	Watermelons
Lemons	Wheat

(iii) Examples. The application of this subparagraph may be illustrated by the following examples:

Example (1). Controlled foreign corporation A, incorporated under the laws of foreign country X, is a wholly owned subsidiary of domestic corporation M. Corporation A purchases from M Corporation, a related person, articles manufactured in the United States and sells the articles in the form in which purchased to P, not a related person, for delivery and use in foreign country Y. Gross income of A Corporation derived from the purchase and sale of the personal property is foreign base company sales income.

Example (2). Corporation A in example (1) also purchases from P, not a related person, articles manufactured in country Y and sells the articles in the form in which purchased to foreign corporation B, a related person, for use in foreign country Z. Gross income of A Corporation derived from the purchase and sale of the personal property is foreign base company sales income.

Example (3). Controlled foreign corporation C, incorporated under the laws of foreign country X, is a wholly owned subsidiary of domestic corporation N. By contract, N Corporation agrees to pay C Corporation, a related person, a commission equal to 6 percent of the gross selling price of all personal property shipped by N Corporation as the result of orders solicited by C Corporation in foreign countries Y and Z. In fulfillment of such orders, N Corporation ships products manufactured by it in the United States. Corporation C does not assume title to the property sold. Gross commissions received by C Corporation from N Corporation in connection with the sale of such property for use in countries Y and Z constitute foreign base company sales income.

Example (4). Controlled foreign corporation D, incorporated under the laws of foreign country Y, is a wholly owned subsidiary of domestic corporation R. In 1964, D Corporation acquires a United States manufactured lathe from R Corporation. In 1972, after having made substantial use of the lathe in its manufacturing business, D Corporation sells the lathe to an unrelated person for use in foreign country Z. Gross income from the sale of the lathe is not foreign base company sales income since it is sold to an unrelated person after substantial use has been made of it by D Corporation in its business.

Example (5). Controlled foreign corporation E, incorporated under the laws of foreign country Y, is a wholly owned subsidiary of domestic corporation P. Corporation E purchases from P Corporation articles manufactured by P Corporation outside of country Y and sells the articles to F Corporation, an unrelated person, for use in foreign country Z. Corporation E finances the purchase of the articles by F Corporation by agreeing to accept payment over an extended period of time and receives not only the purchase price but also interest and service fees. All gross income of E Corporation derived in connection with the purchase and sale of the personal property, including interest and service fees derived from financing the sale to F Corporation, constitutes foreign base company sales income.

(2) Property manufactured, produced, constructed, grown, or extracted within the country in which the controlled foreign corporation is created or organized. Foreign base company sales income does not include income derived in connection with the purchase and sale of personal property (or purchase or sale of personal property on behalf of a related person) in a transaction described in subparagraph (1) of this paragraph if the property is manufactured, produced, constructed, grown, or extracted in the country under the laws of which the controlled foreign corporation which purchases and sells the property (or acts on behalf of a related person) is created or organized. See section 954(d)(1)(A). The principles set forth in subparagraph (4) of this paragraph with respect to the manufacture, production, or construction of personal property shall apply under this subparagraph in determining what constitutes manufacture, production, or construction of property. The application of this subparagraph may be illustrated by the following examples:

Example (1). Controlled foreign corporation A, incorporated under the laws of foreign country X, is a wholly owned subsidiary of domestic corporation M. Corporation A purchases coffee beans grown in country X from foreign corporation P, a related person, and sells the beans to M Corporation, a related person, for use in the United States. Income from the purchase and sale of the coffee beans by A Corporation is not foreign base company sales income since the beans were grown in country X.

Example (2). Controlled foreign corporation B, incorporated under the laws of foreign country X, is a wholly owned subsidiary of controlled foreign corporation C, also incorporated under the laws of country X. Corporation B purchases and imports into country X rough diamonds mined in foreign country Y; in country X it cuts, polishes, and shapes the diamonds in a process which constitutes manufacturing within the meaning of subparagraph (4) of this paragraph. Corporation B sells the finished diamonds to C Corporation, a related person, which in turn sells them for use in foreign country Z. Since for purposes of this subparagraph the finished diamonds are manufactured in country X, gross income derived by C Corporation from their sale is not foreign base company sales income.

(3) Property sold for use, consumption, or disposition within the country in which the controlled foreign corporation is created or organized. (i) In general. Foreign base company sales income does not include income derived in connection with the purchase and sale of personal property (or purchase or sale of personal property on behalf of a related person) in a transaction described in subparagraph (1) of this paragraph, (a) if the property is sold for use, consumption, or disposition in the country under the laws of which the controlled foreign corporation which purchases and sells the property (or sells on behalf of a related person) is created or organized, or (b) where the property is purchased by the controlled foreign corporation on behalf of a related person, if such property is purchased for use, consumption, or disposition in the country under the laws of which such controlled foreign corporation is created or organized. See section 954(d)(1)(B).

(ii) Rules for determining country of use, consumption, or disposition. As a general rule, personal property which is sold to an unrelated person will be presumed for purposes of this subparagraph to have been sold for use, consumption, or disposition in the country of destination of the property sold; for such purpose, the occurrence in a country of a temporary interruption in shipment of goods shall not constitute such country the country of destination. However, if at the time of a sale of personal property to an unrelated person the controlled foreign corporation knew, or should have known from the facts and circumstances surrounding the transaction, that the property probably would not be used, consumed, or disposed of in the country of destination, the controlled foreign corporation must determine the country of ultimate use, consumption, or disposition of the property or the property will be presumed to have been used, consumed, or disposed of outside the country under the laws of which the controlled foreign corporation is created or organized. A controlled foreign corporation which sells personal property to a related person is presumed to sell such property for use, consumption, or disposition outside the country under the laws of which the controlled foreign corporation is created or organized unless such corporation establishes the use made of the property by the related person; once it has established that the related person has disposed of the property, the rules in the two preceding sentences relating to sales by a controlled foreign corporation to an unrelated person will apply at the first stage in the chain of distribution at which a sale is made by a related person to an unrelated person. Notwithstanding the preceding provisions of this subdivision, a controlled foreign corporation which sells personal property to any person all of whose business except for an insubstantial part consists of selling from inventory to retail customers at retail outlets all within one country may assume at the time of such sale to such person that such property will be used, consumed, or disposed of within such country.

(iii) Fungible goods. For purposes of this subparagraph, a controlled foreign corporation which sells to a purchaser personal property which because of its fungible nature cannot reasonably be specifically traced to other purchasers and to the countries of ultimate use, consumption, or disposition shall, unless such corporation establishes a different disposition as being proper, treat such property as being sold, for ultimate use, consumption, or disposition in those countries, and to those other purchasers, in the same proportions in which property from the fungible mass of the first purchaser is sold in the regular course of business by such first purchaser. No apportionment need be made, however, on the basis of sporadic sales by the first purchaser. This subdivision shall apply only in a case where the controlled foreign corporation knew, or should have known from the facts and circumstances surrounding the transaction, the manner in which the first purchaser disposes of goods from the fungible mass.

(iv) Illustrations. The application of this subparagraph may be illustrated by the following examples:

Example (1). Controlled foreign corporation A, incorporated under the laws of foreign country X, and controlled foreign corporation B, incorporated under the laws of foreign country Y, are related persons. Corporation A purchases from B Corporation electric transformers produced by B Corporation in country Y and sells the transformers to D Corporation, an unrelated person, for installation in a factory building being constructed in country X. Since the personal property purchased and sold by A Corporation is to be used within the country in which A Corporation is incorporated, income of A Corporation derived from the purchase and sale of the electric transformers is not foreign base company sales income.

Example (2). Controlled foreign corporation C, incorporated under the laws of foreign country X, is a wholly owned subsidiary of domestic corporation N. Corporation C purchases from N Corporation sewing machines manufactured in the United States by N Corporation and sells the sewing machines to retail department stores, unrelated persons, located in foreign country X. The entire activities of the department stores to which C Corporation sells the machines consist of selling goods from inventory to retail customers at retail outlets in country X. Under these circumstances, at the time of sale C Corporation may assume the sewing machines will be used, consumed, or disposed of in country X, and no attempt need be made by C Corporation to determine where the sewing machines will ultimately be used by the customers of the retail department stores. Gross income of C Corporation derived from the sales to the department stores located in country X is not foreign base company sales income.

Example (3). Controlled foreign corporation D, incorporated under the laws of foreign country Y, and controlled foreign corporation E, incorporated under the laws of foreign country X, are related persons. Corporation D purchases from E Corporation sulphur extracted by E Corporation from deposits located in country X. Corporation D sells the sulphur to F Corporation, an unrelated person, for delivery to F Corporation's storage facilities located in country Y. At the time of the sale of the sulphur from D Corporation to F Corporation, D Corporation knows that F Corporation is actively engaged in the business of selling a large amount of sulphur in country Y but also that F Corporation sells, in the normal course of its business, 25 percent of its sulphur for ultimate consumption in foreign country Z. However, D Corporation has no knowledge at the time of sale whether any portion of the particular shipment it sells to F Corporation will be resold by F Corporation for ultimate use, consumption, or disposition outside country Y. Moreover, delivery of the sulphur to F Corporation's storage facilities constitutes more than a temporary interruption in the shipment of the sulphur. Under such circumstances, D Corporation may, but is not required to, trace the ultimate disposition by F Corporation of the personal property sold to F Corporation; however, if D Corporation does not trace the ultimate disposition and if it does not establish a different disposition as being proper, 25 percent of the sulphur sold by D Corporation to F Corporation will be treated as being sold for consumption in country Z and 25 percent of the gross income from the sale of sulphur by D Corporation to F Corporation will be treated as foreign base company sales income.

Example (4). Controlled foreign corporation G, incorporated under the laws of foreign country X, is a wholly owned subsidiary of domestic corporation P. Corporation G purchases from P Corporation toys manufactured in the United States by P Corporation and sells the toys to R, an unrelated person, for delivery to a duty-free port in country X. Instructions for the assembly and operation of the toys are printed in a language which is not commonly used in country X. From the facts and circumstances surrounding the sales to R, G Corporation knows, or should know, that the toys will probably not be used, consumed, or disposed of within country X. Therefore, unless G Corporation determines the use to be made of the toys by R, such property will be presumed to have been sold by R for use, consumption, or disposition outside of country X, and the entire gross income of G Corporation derived from the sales will be considered foreign base company sales income.

(4) Property manufactured or produced by the controlled foreign corporation. (i) In general. Foreign base company sales income does not include income of a controlled foreign corporation derived in connection with the sale of personal property manufactured, produced, or constructed by such corporation in whole or in part from personal property which it has purchased. A foreign corporation will be considered, for purposes of this subparagraph, to have manufactured, produced, or constructed personal property which it sells if the property sold is in effect not the property which it purchased. In the case of the manufacture, production, or construction of personal property, the property sold will be considered, for purposes of this subparagraph, as not being the property which is purchased if the provisions of subdivision (ii) or (iii) of this subparagraph are satisfied. For rules of apportionment in determining foreign base company sales income derived from the sale of personal property purchased and used as a component part of property which is not manufactured, produced, or constructed, see subparagraph (5) of this paragraph.

(ii) Substantial transformation of property. If purchased personal property is substantially transformed prior to sale, the property sold will be treated as having been manufactured, produced, or constructed by the selling corporation. The application of this subdivision may be illustrated by the following examples:

Example (1). Controlled foreign corporation A, incorporated under the laws of foreign country X, operates a paper factory in foreign country Y. Corporation A purchases from a related person wood pulp grown in country Y. Corporation A, by a series of processes, converts the wood pulp to paper which it sells for use in foreign country Z. The transformation of wood pulp to paper constitutes the manufacture or production of property for purposes of this subparagraph.

Example (2). Controlled foreign corporation B, incorporated under the laws of foreign country X, purchases steel rods from a related person which produces the steel in foreign country Y. Corporation B operates a machining plant in country X in which it utilizes the purchased steel rods to make screws and bolts. The transformation of steel rods to screws and bolts constitutes the manufacture or production of property for purposes of this subparagraph.

Example (3). Controlled foreign corporation C, incorporated under the laws of foreign country X, purchases tuna fish from unrelated persons who own fishing boats which catch such fish on the high seas. Corporation C receives such fish in country X in the condition in which taken from the fishing boats and in such country processes, cans, and sells the fish to related person D, incorporated under the laws of foreign country Y, for consumption in foreign country Z. The transformation of such fish into canned fish constitutes the manufacture or production of property for purposes of this subparagraph.

(iii) Manufacture of a product when purchased components constitute part of the property sold. If purchased property is used as a component part of personal property which is sold, the sale of the property will be treated as the sale of a manufactured product, rather than the sale of component parts, if the operations conducted by the selling corporation in connection with the property purchased and sold are substantial in nature and are generally considered to constitute the manufacture, production, or construction of property. Without limiting this substantive test, which is dependent on the facts and circumstances of each case, the operations of the selling corporation in connection with the use of the purchased property as a component part of the personal property which is sold will be considered to constitute the manufacture of a product if in connection with such property conversion costs (direct labor and factory burden) of such corporation account for 20 percent or more of the total cost of goods sold. In no event, however, will packaging, repackaging, labeling, or minor assembly operations constitute the manufacture, production, or construction of property for purposes of section 954(d)(1). The application of this subdivision may be illustrated by the following examples:

Example (1). Controlled foreign corporation A, incorporated under the laws of foreign country X, sells industrial engines for use, consumption, and disposition outside country X. Corporation A, in connection with the assembly of such engines, performs machining and assembly operations. In addition, A Corporation purchases, from related and unrelated persons, components manufactured in foreign country Y. On a per unit basis, A Corporation's selling price and costs of such engines are as follows:

Selling price			$400
Cost of goods sold:			
Material—			
Acquired from related persons	$100		
Acquired from others	40		
Total material		$140	
Conversion costs (direct labor and factory burden)		70	
Total cost of goods sold			210
Gross profit			190
Administrative and selling expenses			50
Taxable income			140

The conversion costs incurred by A Corporation are more than 20 percent of total costs of goods sold ($70/$210 or 33 percent). Although the product sold, an engine, is not sufficiently distinguishable from the components to constitute a substantial transformation of the purchased parts within the meaning of subdivision (ii) of this subparagraph, A Corporation will be considered under this subdivision to have manufactured the product it sells.

Example (2). Controlled foreign corporation B, incorporated under the laws of foreign country X, operates an automobile assembly plant. In connection with such activity, B Corporation purchases from related persons assembled engines, transmissions, and certain other components, all of which are manufactured outside of country X; purchases additional components from unrelated persons; conducts stamping, machining, and subassembly operations; and has a substantial investment in tools, jigs, welding equipment, and other machinery and equipment used in the assembly of an automobile. On a per unit basis, B Corporation's selling price and costs of such automobiles are as follows:

Selling price			$2,500
Cost of goods sold:			
Material—			
Acquired from related persons	$1,200		
Acquired from others	275		
Total material		$1,475	
Conversion costs (direct labor and factory burden)		325	
Total cost of goods sold			1,800
Gross profit			700
Administrative and selling expenses			300
Taxable income			400

The product sold, an automobile, is not sufficiently distinguishable from the components purchased (the engine, transmission, etc.) to constitute a substantial transformation of purchased parts within the meaning of subdivision (ii) of this subparagraph. Although conversion costs of B Corporation are less than 20 percent of total cost of goods sold ($325/$1800 or 18 percent), the operations conducted by B Corporation in connection with the property purchased and sold are substantial in nature and are generally considered to constitute the manufacture of a product. Corporation B will be considered under this subdivision to have manufactured the product it sells.

Example (3). Controlled foreign corporation C, incorporated under the laws of foreign country X, purchases from related persons radio parts manufactured in foreign country Y. Corporation C designs radio kits, packages component parts required for assembly of such kits, and sells the parts in a knocked-down condition to unrelated persons for use outside country X. These packaging operations of C Corporation do not constitute the manufacture, production, or construction of personal property for purposes of section 954(d)(1).

(5) Rules for apportionment of income derived from the sale of purchased components used in property not manufactured, produced, or constructed. The foreign base company sales income derived by a controlled foreign corporation for the taxable year from sales of personal property purchased and used as a component part of property which is not manufactured, produced, or constructed by such corporation within the meaning of subparagraph (4) of this paragraph shall, unless the records of the controlled foreign corporation show that a different apportionment of income is proper or unless all the income from such sales is treated as foreign base company sales income, be determined by first making for such year the following separate classifications and subclassifications with respect to the property which is sold and then by apportioning the income for such year from such sales in accordance with the rules of this subparagraph:

(i) A classification of the cost of components used in the property which is sold into two classes consisting of the cost of components manufactured, produced, constructed, grown, or extracted—

(a) Within the country under the laws of which the controlled foreign corporation is created or organized, and

(b) Outside such country;

(ii) A subclassification of the class described in subdivision (i)(b) of this subparagraph into—

(a) The cost of such components purchased from unrelated persons, and

(b) The cost of such components purchased from related persons;

(iii) A classification of the income derived from such sales into two classes consisting of income derived from sales for use, consumption, or disposition—

(a) Within the country under the laws of which the controlled foreign corporation is created or organized, and

(b) Outside such country; and

(iv) A subclassification of the class described in subdivision (iii)(b) of this subparagraph into income from—

(a) Sales to unrelated persons, and

(b) Sales to related persons. The foreign base company sales income for the taxable year from purchases of the property from related persons and sales to unrelated persons shall be the amount which bears to the amount described in subdivision (iv)(a) of this subparagraph the same ratio that the amount described in subdivision (ii)(b) of this subparagraph bears to the total cost of components used in the product which is sold. The foreign base company sales income for the taxable year from purchases of the property from related persons and sales to related persons is the amount which bears to the amount described in subdivision (iv)(b) of this subparagraph the same ratio that the amount described in subdivision (ii)(b) of this subparagraph bears to the total cost of components used in the product which is sold. The foreign base company sales income for the taxable year from purchases of the property from unrelated persons and sales to related persons is the amount which bears to the amount described in subdivision (iv)(b) of this subparagraph the same ratio that the amount described in subdivision (ii)(a) of this subparagraph bears to the total cost of components used in the product which is sold. The application of this subparagraph may be illustrated by the following examples:

Example (1). Controlled foreign corporation C, which is incorporated under the laws of foreign country X, uses the calendar year as the taxable year. For 1964, C Corporation purchases radio parts of which some are manufactured in foreign country Y; and others, in country X. Some of the parts manufactured in country Y are purchased from related persons. Corporation C uses the purchased parts in radio kits which it designs and sells for assembly by its customers, unrelated persons, some of whom use the kits outside country X. Unless the records of C Corporation show that a different apportionment of income is proper, the foreign base company sales income for 1964 is determined in the following manner upon the basis of the following factual classifications for such year:

Cost of components purchased from all persons:		
Manufactured within country X		$ 20
Manufactured outside country X		40
Total cost		60
Cost of components manufactured outside country X:		
Purchased from unrelated persons		10
Purchased from related persons		30
Total cost		40
Gross income from sales:		
Gross receipts from sales		120
Cost of goods sold:		
Components	$60	
Direct labor and factory burden	10	70
Gross income		50
Gross income from sales:		
For use within country X		26
For use outside country X		24
Gross income		50
Foreign base company sales income from purchases from related persons and sales to unrelated persons ($24 × $30/$60)		12

Example (2). The facts are the same as in example (1) except that none of the purchases are from related persons and some of the sales for use outside country X are to related persons. Unless the records of C Corporation show that a different apportionment of income is proper, the foreign base company sales income for 1964 is determined in the following manner upon the basis of the following additional factual classification for such year:

Gross income from sales for use outside country X—	
To unrelated persons	$8
To related persons	16
Total gross income	24
Foreign base company sales income from purchases from unrelated persons and sales to related persons ($16 × $40/$60)	10.67

Example (3). The facts are the same as in example (1) except that some of the sales for use outside country X are to related persons as in example (2). Unless the records of C Corporation show that a different apportionment of income is proper, the foreign base company sales income for 1964 is determined in the following manner:

Foreign base company sales income from purchases from related persons and sales to unrelated persons ($8 × $30/$60)	$4.00
Foreign base company sales income from purchases from related persons and sales to related persons ($16 × $30/$60)	8.00
Foreign base company sales income from purchases from unrelated persons and sales to related persons ($16 × $10/$60)	2.67
Total foreign base company sales income	14.67

(6) Special rule applicable to distributive share of partnership income. (i) In general. To determine the extent to which a controlled foreign corporation's distributive share of any item of gross income of a partnership would have been foreign base company sales income if received by it directly, under § 1.952-1(g), the property sold will be considered to be manufactured, produced or constructed by the controlled foreign corporation, within the meaning of paragraph (a)(4) of this section, only if the manufacturing exception of paragraph (a)(4) of this section would have applied to exclude the income from foreign base company sales income if the controlled foreign corporation had earned the income directly, determined by taking into account only the activities of, and property owned by, the partnership and not the separate activities or property of the controlled foreign corporation or any other person.

(ii) Example. The application of paragraph (a)(6)(i) of this section is illustrated by the following example:

Example. CFC, a controlled foreign corporation organized under the laws of Country A, is an 80 percent partner in Partnership X, a partnership organized under the laws of Country B. Partnership X performs activities in Country B that would constitute the manufacture of Product O, within the meaning of paragraph (a)(4) of this section, if performed directly by CFC. Partnership X, through its sales offices in Country B, then sells Product O to Corp D, corporation that is a related person with respect to CFC, within the meaning of section 954(d)(3), for use within Country B. CFC's distributive share of Partnership X's sales income is not foreign base company sales income because the manufacturing exception of paragraph (a)(4) of this section would have applied to exclude the income from foreign base company sales income if CFC had earned the income directly.

(iii) Effective date. This paragraph (a)(6) applies to taxable years of a controlled foreign corporation beginning on or after July 23, 2002.

(b) Branches of controlled foreign corporation treated as separate corporations. *(1) General rules for determining when to apply separate treatment.* (i) Sales or purchase branch. (a) In general. If a controlled foreign corporation carries on purchasing or selling activities by or through a branch or similar establishment located outside the country under the laws of which such corporation is created or organized and the use of the branch or similar establishment for such activities has substantially the same tax effect as if the branch or similar establishment were a wholly owned subsidiary corporation of such controlled foreign corporation, the branch or similar establishment and the remainder of the controlled foreign corporation will be treated as separate corporations for purposes of determining foreign base company sales income of such corporation. See section 954(d)(2).

(b) Allocation of income and comparison of effective rates of tax. The determination as to whether such use of the branch or similar establishment has the same tax effect as if it were a wholly owned subsidiary corporation of the controlled foreign corporation shall be made by allocating to such branch or similar establishment only that income derived by the branch or establishment which, when the special rules of subparagraph (2)(i) of this paragraph are applied, is described in paragraph (a) of this section (but determined without applying subparagraphs (2), (3), and (4) of such paragraph). The use of the branch or similar establishment for such activities will be considered to have substantially the same tax effect as if it were a wholly owned subsidiary corporation of the controlled foreign corporation if the income allocated to the branch or similar establishment under the immediately preceding sentence is, by statute, treaty obligation, or otherwise, taxed in the year when earned at an effective rate of tax that is less than 90 percent of, and at least 5 percentage points less than, the effective rate of tax which would apply to such income under the laws of the country in which the controlled foreign corporation is created or organized, if under the laws of such country, the entire income of the controlled foreign corporation were considered derived by the corporation from sources within such country from doing business through a permanent establishment therein, received in such country, and allocable to such permanent establishment, and the corporation were managed and controlled in such country.

(c) Use of more than one branch. If a controlled foreign corporation carries on purchasing or selling activities by or through more than one branch or similar establishment located outside the country under the laws of which such corporation is created or organized, or by or through one or more such branches or similar establishments in a case where subdivision (ii) of this subparagraph also applies, then (b) of this subdivision shall be applied separately to the income derived by each such branch or similar establishment (by treating such purchasing or selling branch or similar establishment as if it were the only branch or similar establishment of the controlled foreign corporation and as if any such other branches or similar establishments were separate corporations) in determining whether the use of such branch or similar establishment has substantially the same tax effect as if such branch or similar establishment were a wholly owned subsidiary corporation of the controlled foreign corporation.

(ii) Manufacturing branch. (a) In general. If a controlled foreign corporation carries on manufacturing, producing, constructing, growing, or extracting activities by or through a branch or similar establishment located outside the country under the laws of which such corporation is created or organized and the use of the branch or similar establishment for such activities with respect to personal property purchased or sold by or through the remainder of the controlled foreign corporation has substantially the same tax effect as if the branch or similar establishment were a wholly owned subsidiary corporation of such controlled foreign corporation, the branch or similar establishment and the remainder of the controlled foreign corporation will be treated as separate corporations for purposes of determining foreign base company sales income of such corporation. See section 954(d)(2).

(b) Allocation of income and comparison of effective rates of tax. The determination as to whether such use of the branch or similar establishment has substantially the same tax effect as if the branch or similar establishment were a wholly owned subsidiary corporation of the controlled foreign corporation shall be made by allocating to the remainder of such controlled foreign corporation only that income derived by the remainder of such corporation, which, when the special rules of subparagraph (2)(i) of this paragraph are applied, is described in paragraph (a) of this section (but determined without applying subparagraphs (2), (3), and (4) of such paragraph). The use of the branch or similar establishment for such activities will be considered to have substantially the same tax effect as if it were a wholly owned subsidiary corporation of the controlled foreign corporation if income allocated to the remainder of the controlled foreign corporation under the immediately preceding sentence is, by statute, treaty obligation, or otherwise, taxed in the year when earned at an effective rate of tax that is less than 90 percent of, and at least 5 percentage points less than, the effective rate of tax which would apply to such income under the laws of the country in which the branch or similar establishment is located, if, under the laws of such country, the entire income of the controlled foreign corporation were considered derived by such corporation from sources within such country from doing business through a permanent establishment therein, received in such country, and allocable to such permanent establishment, and the corporation were created or organized under the laws of, and managed and controlled in, such country.

(c) Use of one or more sales or purchase branches in addition to a manufacturing branch. If, with respect to personal property manufactured, produced, constructed, grown, or extracted by or through a branch or similar establishment located outside the country under the laws of which controlled foreign corporation is created or organized, purchasing or selling activities are carried on by or through more than one branch or similar establishment, or by or through one or more branches or similar establishments located outside such country, of such corporation, then (b) of this subdivision shall be applied separately to the income derived by each such purchasing or selling branch or similar establishment (by treating such purchasing or selling branch or similar establishment as though it alone were the remainder of the controlled foreign corporation) for purposes of determining whether the use of such manufacturing, producing, constructing, growing, or extracting branch or similar establishment has substantially the same tax effect as if such branch or similar establishment were a wholly owned subsidiary corporation of the controlled foreign corporation.

(2) Special rules. (i) Determination of treatment as a wholly owned subsidiary corporation. For purposes of determining under this paragraph whether the use of a branch or similar establishment which is treated as a separate corporation has substantially the same tax effect as if the branch or similar establishment were a wholly owned subsidiary corporation of a controlled foreign corporation—

(a) Treatment as separate corporations. The branch or similar establishment will be treated as a wholly owned subsidiary corporation of the controlled foreign corporation, and such branch or similar establishment will be deemed to be incorporated in the country in which it is located.

(b) Activities treated as performed on behalf of remainder of corporation. With respect to purchasing or selling activities performed by or through the branch or similar establishment, such purchasing or selling activities shall—

(1) With respect to personal property manufactured, produced, constructed, grown, or extracted by the controlled foreign corporation, or

(2) With respect to personal property (other than property described in (1) of this subdivision (b)) purchased or sold, or purchased and sold, by the controlled foreign corporation, be treated as performed on behalf of the controlled foreign corporation.

(c) Activities treated as performed on behalf of branch. With respect to manufacturing, producing, constructing, growing, or extracting activities performed by or through the branch or similar establishment, purchasing or selling activities performed by or through the remainder of the controlled foreign corporation with respect to the personal property manufactured, produced, constructed, grown, or extracted by or through the branch or similar establishment shall be treated as performed on behalf of the branch or similar establishment.

(d) Determination of hypothetical tax. To the extent applicable, the principles of paragraph (b)(4)(ii) of § 1.954-1 shall be used in determining, under subdivision (i) of subparagraph (1) of this paragraph, the effective rate of tax which would apply to the income of the branch or similar establishment under the laws of the country in which the controlled foreign corporation is created or organized, or in determining, under subdivision (ii) of such subparagraph, the effective rate of tax which would apply to the income of the branch or similar establishment under the laws of the country in which the manufacturing, producing, constructing, growing, or extracting branch or similar establishment is located.

(e) Tax laws to be taken into account. Tax determinations shall be made by taking into account only the income, war profits, excess profits, or similar tax laws (or the absence of such laws) of the countries involved.

(ii) Determination of foreign base company sales income. Once it has been determined under subparagraph (1) of this paragraph that a branch or similar establishment and the remainder of the controlled foreign corporation are to be treated as separate corporations, the determination of whether such branch or similar establishment, or the remainder of the controlled foreign corporation, as the case may be, has foreign base company sales income shall be made by applying the following rules:

(a) Treatment as separate corporations. The branch or similar establishment will be treated as a wholly owned subsidiary corporation of the controlled foreign corporation, and such branch or similar establishment will be deemed to be incorporated in the country in which it is located.

(b) Activities treated as performed on behalf of remainder of corporation. With respect to purchasing or selling activities performed by or through the branch or similar establishment, such purchasing or selling activities shall—

(1) With respect to personal property manufactured, produced, constructed, grown, or extracted by the controlled foreign corporation, or

(2) With respect to personal property (other than property described in (1) of this subdivision (b)) purchased or sold, or purchased and sold, by the controlled foreign corporation, be treated as performed on behalf of the controlled foreign corporation.

(c) Activities treated as performed on behalf of branch. With respect to manufacturing, producing, constructing, growing, or extracting activities performed by or through the branch or similar establishment, purchasing or selling activities performed by or through the remainder of the controlled foreign corporation with respect to the personal property manufactured, produced, constructed, grown, or extracted by or through the branch or similar establishment shall be treated as performed on behalf of the branch or similar establishment.

(d) Items not to be twice included in income. Income which is classified as foreign base company sales income as a result of the application of subdivision (i) of subparagraph (1) of this paragraph shall not be again classified as foreign base company sales income as a result of the application of subdivision (ii) of such subparagraph.

(e) Comparison with ordinary treatment. Income derived by the branch or similar establishment, or by the remainder of the controlled foreign corporation, shall not be considered foreign base company sales income if the income would not be so considered if it were derived by a separate controlled foreign corporation under like circumstances.

(f) Priority of application. If income derived by the branch or similar establishment, or by the remainder of the controlled foreign corporation, from a transaction would be classified as foreign base company sales income of such controlled foreign corporation under section 954(d)(1) and paragraph (a) of this section, the income shall, notwithstanding this paragraph, be treated as foreign base company sales income under paragraph (a) of this section and the branch or similar establishment shall not be treated as a separate corporation with respect to such income.

(3) Inclusion of amounts in gross income of United States shareholders. A branch or similar establishment of a controlled foreign corporation and the remainder of such corporation shall be treated as separate corporations under this paragraph solely for purposes of determining the foreign base company sales income of each such corporation and for purposes of including an amount in subpart F income of the

controlled foreign corporation under section 952(a). See section 954(b)(3) and paragraph (d)(4) of § 1.954-1 for rules relating to the treatment of a branch or similar establishment of a controlled foreign corporation and the remainder of such corporation as separate corporations for purposes of independently determining if the foreign base company income of each such corporation is less than 10 percent, or more than 70 percent, of its gross income. For all other purposes, however, a branch or similar establishment of a controlled foreign corporation and the remainder of such corporation shall not be treated as separate corporations. For example, if the controlled foreign corporation has a deficit in earnings and profits to which section 952(c) applies, the limitation of such section on the amount includible in the subpart F income of such corporation will apply. Moreover, income, war profits, or excess profits taxes paid by a branch or similar establishment to a foreign country will be treated as having been paid by the controlled foreign corporation for purposes of section 960 (relating to special rules for foreign tax credit) and the regulations thereunder. Also, income of a branch or similar establishment, treated as a separate corporation under this paragraph, will not be treated as dividend income of the controlled foreign corporation of which it is a branch or similar establishment.

(4) Illustrations. The application of this paragraph may be illustrated by the following examples:

Example (1). Controlled foreign corporation A, incorporated under the laws of foreign country X, is engaged in the manufacturing business in such country. Corporation A negotiates sales of its products for use outside of country X through a sales office, branch B, maintained in foreign country Y. These activities constitute the only activities of A Corporation. Country X levies an income tax at an effective rate of 50 percent on the income of A Corporation derived by the manufacturing plant in country X but does not tax the sales income of A Corporation derived by branch B in country Y. Country Y levies an income tax at an effective rate of 10 percent on the sales income derived by branch B but does not tax the income of A Corporation derived by the manufacturing plan in country X. If the sales income derived by branch B were, under the laws of country X, derived from sources within country X by A Corporation, such income would be taxed by such country at an effective rate of 50 percent. In determining foreign base company sales income of A Corporation, branch B is treated as a separate wholly owned subsidiary corporation of A Corporation, the 10 percent rate of tax on branch B's income being less than 90 percent of, and at least 5 percentage points less than, the 50 percent rate. Income derived by branch B, treated as a separate corporation, from the sale by or through it for use, consumption, or disposition outside country Y of the personal property produced in country X is treated as income from the sale of personal property on behalf of A Corporation, a related person, and constitutes foreign base company sales income. The remainder of A Corporation, treated as a separate corporation, derives no foreign base company sales income since it produces the product which is sold.

Example (2). Controlled foreign corporation C is incorporated under the laws of foreign country X. Corporation C maintains branch B in foreign country Y. Branch B manufactures articles in country Y which are sold through the sales offices of C Corporation located in country X. These activities constitute the only activities of C Corporation. Country Y levies an income tax at an effective rate of 30 percent on the manufacturing profit of C Corporation derived by branch B but does not tax the sales income of C Corporation derived by the sales offices in country X. Country X does not impose an income, war profits, excess profits, or similar tax, and no tax is paid to any foreign country with respect to income of C Corporation which is not derived by branch B. If C Corporation were incorporated under the laws of country Y, the sales income of the sales offices in country X would be taxed by country Y at an effective rate of 30 percent. In determining foreign base company sales income of C Corporation, branch B is treated as a separate wholly owned subsidiary corporation of C Corporation, the zero rate of tax on the income derived by the remainder of C Corporation being less than 90 percent of, and at least 5 percentage points less than, the 30 percent rate. Branch B, treated as a separate corporation, derives no foreign base company sales income since it produces the product which is sold. Income derived by the remainder of C Corporation, treated as a separate corporation, from the sale by or through it for use, consumption, or disposition outside country X of the personal property produced in country Y is treated as income from the sale of personal property on behalf of branch B, a related person, and constitutes foreign base company sales income.

Example (3). Controlled foreign corporation E, incorporated under the laws of foreign country X, is a wholly owned subsidiary of controlled foreign corporation D, also incorporated under the laws of country X. Corporation E maintains branch B in foreign country Y. Both corporations use the calendar year as the taxable year. In 1964, E Corporation's sole activity, carried on through branch B, consists of the purchase of articles manufactured in country X by D Corporation, a related person, and the sale of the articles through branch B for use outside country X. The income of E Corporation derived by branch B from such transactions is taxed to E Corporation by country X only at the time E Corporation distributes such income to D Corporation and is then taxed on the basis of what the tax (a 40 percent effective rate) would have been if the income had been derived in 1964 by E Corporation from sources within country X from doing business through a permanent establishment therein. Country Y levies an income tax at an effective rate of 50 percent on income derived from sources within such country, but the income of branch B for 1964 is effectively taxed by country Y at a 5 percent rate since, under the laws of such country, only 10 percent of branch B's income is derived from sources within such country. Corporation E makes no distributions to D Corporation in 1964. In determining foreign base company sales income of E Corporation for 1964, branch B is treated as a separate wholly owned subsidiary corporation of E Corporation, the 5 percent rate of tax on branch B's income being less than 90 percent of, and at least 5 percentage points less than, the 40 percent rate. Income derived by branch B, treated as a separate corporation, from the sale by or through it for use, consumption, or disposition outside country Y of the personal property produced in country X is treated as income from the sale of personal property on behalf of E Corporation, a related person, and constitutes foreign base company sales income.

Example (4). Controlled foreign corporation F, incorporated under the laws of foreign country X, is a wholly owned subsidiary of domestic corporation M. Corporation F, through its branch B in foreign country Y, purchases from controlled foreign corporation G, a wholly owned subsidiary of M Corporation incorporated under the laws of foreign country Z, personal property which G Corporation manufactures in country Z. Corporation F sells such property for use in foreign country W. Since the income of F Corporation from such purchases and sales is classified as foreign base company sales income under section 954(d)(1) and paragraph (a) of this section, branch B will not be treated as a separate corporation with respect to such income even if the tax differential between countries X and Y would otherwise justify such treatment.

Example (5). Controlled foreign corporation A, incorporated under the laws of foreign country X, is engaged in manufacturing articles through its home office, located in country X, and selling such articles through branch B, located in foreign country Y, and through branch C, located in foreign country Z, for use outside country X. These activities constitute the only activities of A Corporation for its taxable year 1963. Each such country levies an income tax on only the income derived from sources within such country, and all income derived in 1963 by the home office, branch B, and branch C, respectively, is derived from sources within countries X, Y, and Z, respectively. The income and income taxes of A Corporation for 1963 are as follows:

	X Country	Y Country	Z Country
Income of:			
Home office	$200,000		
Branch B		$100,000	
Branch C			$100,000
Income tax	100,000	20,000	20,000
Effective rate of tax	50%	20%	20%

By applying subparagraph (1)(i) of this paragraph and by treating branch B as though it were the only branch of A Corporation, branch B is treated as a separate wholly owned subsidiary corporation of A Corporation in determining foreign base company sales income of A Corporation for 1963, the 20 percent rate of tax on the income of such branch being less than 90 percent of, and at least 5 percentage points less than, the 50 percent rate of tax which would apply to the income of branch B under the laws of country X if, under the laws of such country, all the income of A Corporation for 1963 derived through the home office and branch B were derived from sources within country X. Moreover, by applying subparagraph (1)(i) of this paragraph and by treating branch C as though it were the only branch of A Corporation, branch C is treated as a separate wholly owned subsidiary corporation of A Corporation, the 20 percent rate of tax on the income of such branch being less than 90 percent of, and at least 5 percentage points less than, the 50 percent rate of tax which would apply to the income of branch C under the laws of country X if, under the laws of such country, all the income of A Corporation for 1963 derived through the home office and branch C were derived from sources within country X. The income derived by branch B and branch C, respectively, each treated as a separate corporation, from the sale by or through each of them for use, consumption, or disposition outside country Y and country Z, respectively, is treated as income from the sale of personal property on behalf of A Corporation, a related person, and constitutes foreign base company sales income for 1963. The home office of A Corporation, treated as a separate corporation, derives no foreign base company sales income for 1963 since it produces the articles which are sold.

Example (6). Controlled foreign corporation A, incorporated under the laws of foreign country X, is engaged in manufacturing articles through branch B, located in foreign country Y, and selling such articles through branch C, located in foreign country Z, and through its home office, located in country X, for use outside country X. These activities constitute the only activities of A Corporation for its taxable year 1963. Each such country levies an income tax on only the income derived from sources within such country, and all income derived in 1963 by the home office, branch B, and branch C, respectively, is derived from sources within countries X, Y, and Z, respectively. The income and income taxes of A Corporation for 1963 are as follows:

	X Country	Y Country	Z Country
Income of:			
Home office	$100,000		
Branch B		$200,000	
Branch C			$100,000
Income tax	20,000	100,000	20,000
Effective rate of tax	20%	50%	20%

In determining foreign base company sales income of A Corporation for 1963 neither branch B nor branch C is treated, by applying subparagraph (1)(i) of this paragraph, as a separate wholly owned subsidiary corporation of A Corporation since branch B derives no income from the purchase or sale of personal property and since, in the case of branch C treated as though it were the only branch of A Corporation, the 20 percent rate of tax on the income of branch C is not less than 90 percent of, and not as much as 5 percentage points less than, the 20 percent rate of tax which would apply to the income of branch C under the laws of country X if, under the laws of such country, all the income of A Corporation for 1963 derived through the home office and branch C were derived from sources within country X. However, by applying subparagraph (1)(ii) of this paragraph and by treating the home office in country X as though it alone were the remainder of A Corporation, branch B is treated as a separate wholly owned subsidiary corporation of A Corporation, the 20 percent rate of tax on the income of the home office being less than 90 percent of, and at least 5 percentage points less than, the 50 percent rate of tax which would apply to the income of the home office under the laws of country Y if, under the laws of such country, all the income of A Corporation for 1963 derived through the home office and branch B were derived from sources within country Y. Moreover, by applying subparagraph (1)(ii) of this paragraph and by treating branch C as though it alone were the remainder of A Corporation, branch B and branch C are treated as separate wholly owned subsidiary corporations of A Corporation, the 20 percent rate of tax on the income of branch C being less than 90 percent of, and at least 5 percentage points less than, the 50 percent rate of tax which would apply to the income of branch C under the laws of country Y if, under the laws of such country, all the income of A Corporation for 1963 derived through branch B and branch C were derived from sources within country Y. The income derived by the home office and branch C, respectively, each treated as a separate corporation, from the sale by or through each of them for use, consumption, or disposition outside country X and country Z, respectively, is treated as income from the sale of personal property on behalf of branch B, a related person, and constitutes foreign base company sales income for 1963. Branch B, treated as a separate corporation, derives no foreign base company sales income since it produces the articles which are sold.

Example (7). Controlled foreign corporation A, incorporated under the laws of foreign country X, is engaged in manufacturing articles through branch B, located in foreign country Y, and selling such articles through the home office, located in country X, and through branch C, located in foreign country Z, for use outside country X. These activities constitute the only activities of A Corporation for its taxable year 1963. Each such country levies an income tax on only the income derived from sources within such country, and all income derived in 1963 by the home office, branch B, and branch C, respectively, is derived from sources within countries X, Y, and Z, respectively. The income and income taxes of A Corporation for 1963 are as follows:

	X Country	Y Country	Z Country
Income of:			
Home office	$100,000		
Branch B		$200,000	
Branch C			$100,000
Income tax	40,000	100,000	20,000
Effective rate of tax	40%	50%	20%

By applying subparagraph (1)(i) of this paragraph and by treating branch C as though it were the only branch of A Corporation, branch C is treated as a separate wholly owned subsidiary corporation of A Corporation in determining foreign base company sales income of A Corporation for 1963, the 20 percent rate of tax on the income of branch C being less than 90 percent of, and at least 5 percentage points less than, the 40 percent rate of tax which would apply to the income of branch C under the laws of country X if, under the laws of such country, all the income of A Corporation for 1963 derived through the home office and branch C were derived from sources within country X. In addition, by applying subparagraph (1)(ii) of this paragraph and by treating the home office in country X as though it alone were the remainder of A Corporation, branch B is treated as a separate wholly owned subsidiary corporation of A Corporation, the 40 percent rate of tax on the income of the home office being less than 90 percent of, and at least 5 percentage points less than, the 50 percent rate of tax which would apply to the income of the home office under the laws of country Y if, under the laws of such country, all the income of A Corporation for 1963 derived through the home office and branch B were derived from sources within country Y. Moreover, by applying subparagraph (1)(ii) of this paragraph and by treating branch C as though it alone were the remainder of A Corporation, branch B and branch C would again be treated as separate wholly owned subsidiary corporations of A Corporation, the 20 percent rate of tax on the income of branch C being less than 90 percent of, and at least 5 percentage points less than, the 50 percent rate of tax which would apply to the income of branch C under the laws of country Y if, under the laws of such country, all the income of A Corporation for 1963 derived through branch B and branch C were derived from sources within country Y; however, for purposes of determining foreign base company sales income of A Corporation for 1963, only the classification under subparagraph (1)(i) of this paragraph shall, by reason of the application of subparagraph (2)(ii)(d) of this paragraph, be applied with respect to the income derived by branch C. The income derived by the home office and branch C, respectively, each treated as a separate corporation, from the sale by or through each of them for use, consumption, or disposition outside country X and country Z, respectively, is treated as income from the sale of personal property on behalf of branch B, a related person, and constitutes foreign base company sales income for 1963. Branch B, treated as a separate corporation, derives no foreign base company sales income since it produces the articles which are sold.

(c) Shipping income for taxable years beginning after December 31, 1975. For taxable years beginning after December 31, 1975, foreign base company shipping income (as determined under § 1.954-6) of a controlled foreign corporation shall not also be considered foreign base company sales income of that controlled foreign corporation.

T.D. 6734, 5/14/64, amend T.D. 7555, 7/25/78, T.D. 7893, 5/11/83, T.D. 7894, 5/11/83, T.D. 9008, 7/22/2002.

§ 1.954-4 Foreign base company services income.

Caution: The Treasury has not yet amended Reg § 1.954-4 to reflect changes made by P.L. 99-514, P.L. 98-369.

(a) Items included. Except as provided in paragraph (d) of this section, foreign base company services income means income of a controlled foreign corporation, whether in the form of compensation, commissions, fees, or otherwise, derived in connection with the performance of technical, managerial, engineering, architectural, scientific, skilled, industrial, commercial, or like services which—

(1) Are performed for, or on behalf of a related person, as defined in paragraph (e)(1) of § 1.954-1, and

(2) Are performed outside the country under the laws of which the controlled foreign corporation is created or organized.

(b) Services performed for, or on behalf of, a related person. *(1) Specific cases.* For purposes of paragraph (a)(1) of this section, "services which are performed for, or on behalf of, a related person" include (but are not limited to) services performed by a controlled foreign corporation in a case where—

(i) The controlled foreign corporation is paid or reimbursed by, is released from an obligation to, or otherwise receives substantial financial benefit from, a related person for performing such services;

(ii) The controlled foreign corporation performs services (whether or not with respect to property sold by a related person) which a related person is, or has been, obligated to perform;

(iii) The controlled foreign corporation performs services with respect to property sold by a related person and the performance of such services constitutes a condition or a material term of such sale; or

(iv) Substantial assistance contributing to the performance of such services has been furnished by a related person or persons.

(2) Special rules. (i) Guaranty of performance. Subparagraph (1)(ii) of this paragraph shall not apply with respect to services performed by a controlled foreign corporation pursuant to a contract the performance of which is guaranteed by a related person, if (a) the related person's sole obligation with respect to the contract is to guarantee performance of such services, (b) the controlled foreign corporation is fully obligated to perform the services under the contract, and (c) the related person (or any other person related to the controlled foreign corporation) does not in fact (1) pay for performance of, or perform, any of such services, the performance of which is so guaranteed or (2) pay for performance of, or perform, any significant services related to such services. If the related person (or any other person related to the controlled foreign corporation) does in fact pay for performance of, or perform, any of such services or any signifi-

cant services related to such services, subparagraph (1)(ii) of this paragraph shall apply with respect to the services performed by the controlled foreign corporation pursuant to the contract the performance of which is guaranteed by the related person, even though such payment or performance is not considered to be substantial assistance for purposes of subparagraph (1)(iv) of this paragraph. For purposes of this subdivision, a related person shall be considered to guarantee performance of the services by the controlled foreign corporation whether it guarantees performance of such services by a separate contract of guaranty or enters into a service contract solely for purposes of guaranteeing performance of such services and immediately thereafter assigns the entire contract to the controlled foreign corporation for execution.

(ii) Application of substantial assistance test. For purposes of subparagraph (1)(iv) of this paragraph—

(a) Assistance furnished by a related person or persons to the controlled foreign corporation shall include, but shall not be limited to, direction, supervision, services, know-how, financial assistance (other than contributions to capital), and equipment, material, or supplies.

(b) Assistance furnished by a related person or persons to a controlled foreign corporation in the form of direction, supervision, services, or know-how shall not be considered substantial unless either (1) the assistance so furnished provides the controlled foreign corporation with skills which are a principal element in producing the income from the performance of such services by such corporation or (2) the cost to the controlled foreign corporation of the assistance so furnished equals 50 percent or more of the total cost to the controlled foreign corporation of performing the services performed by such corporation. The term "cost," as used in this subdivision (b), shall be determined after taking into account adjustments, if any, made under section 482.

(c) Financial assistance (other than contributions to capital), equipment, material, or supplies furnished by a related person to a controlled foreign corporation shall be considered assistance only in that amount by which the consideration actually paid by the controlled foreign corporation for the purchase or use of such item is less than the arm's length charge for such purchase or use. The total of such amounts so considered to be assistance in the case of financial assistance, equipment, material, and supplies furnished by all related persons shall be compared with the profits derived by the controlled foreign corporation from the performance of the services to determine whether the financial assistance, equipment, material, and supplies furnished by a related person or persons are by themselves substantial assistance contributing to the performance of such services. For purposes of this subdivision (c), determinations shall be made after taking into account adjustments, if any, made under section 482 and the term "consideration actually paid" shall include any amount which is deemed paid by the controlled foreign corporation pursuant to such an adjustment.

(d) Even though assistance furnished by a related person or persons to a controlled foreign corporation in the form of direction, supervision, services, or know-how is not considered to be substantial under (b) of this subdivision and assistance furnished by a related person or persons in the form of financial assistance (other than contributions to capital), equipment, material, or supplies is not considered to be substantial under (c) of this subdivision, such assistance may nevertheless constitute substantial assistance when taken together or in combination with other assistance furnished by a related person or persons which in itself is not considered to be substantial.

(e) Assistance furnished by a related person or persons to a controlled foreign corporation in the form of direction, supervision, services, or know-how shall not be taken into account under (b) or (d) of this subdivision unless the assistance so furnished assists the controlled foreign corporation directly in the performance of the services performed by such corporation.

(iii) Special rule applicable to distributive share of partnership income. A controlled foreign corporation's distributive share of a partnership's services income will be deemed to be derived from services performed for or on behalf of a related person, within the meaning of section 954(e)(1)(A), if the partnership is a related person with respect to the controlled foreign corporation, under section 954(d)(3), and, in connection with the services performed by the partnership, the controlled foreign corporation, or a person that is a related person with respect to the controlled foreign corporation, provided assistance that would have constituted substantial assistance contributing to the performance of such services, under paragraph (b)(2)(ii) of this section, if furnished to the controlled foreign corporation by a related person. This paragraph (b)(2)(iii) applies to taxable years of a controlled foreign corporation beginning on or after July 23, 2002.

(3) Illustrations. The application of this paragraph may be illustrated by the following examples:

Example (1). Controlled foreign corporation A is paid by related corporation M for the installation and maintenance of industrial machines which M Corporation manufactures and sells to B Corporation. Such installation and maintenance services by A Corporation are performed for, or on behalf of, M Corporation for purposes of section 954(e).

Example (2). Controlled foreign corporation B enters into a contract with an unrelated person to drill an oil well in a foreign country. Domestic corporation M owns all the outstanding stock of B Corporation. Corporation B employs a relatively small clerical and administrative staff and owns the necessary well-drilling equipment. Most of the technical and supervisory personnel who oversee the drilling of the oil well by B Corporation are regular employees of M Corporation who are temporarily employed by B Corporation. In addition, B Corporation hires on the open market unskilled and semi-skilled laborers to work on the drilling project. The services performed by B Corporation under the well-drilling contract are performed for, or on behalf of, a related person for purposes of section 954(e) because the services of the technical and supervisory personnel which are provided by M Corporation are of substantial assistance in the performance of such contract in that they assist B Corporation directly in the execution of the contract and provide B Corporation with skills which are a principal element in producing the income from the performance of such contract.

Example (3). Controlled foreign corporation F enters into a contract with an unrelated person to construct a dam in a foreign country. Domestic corporation M owns all the outstanding stock of F Corporation. Corporation F leases or buys from M Corporation, on an arm's length basis, the equipment and material necessary for the construction of the dam. The technical and supervisory personnel who design and oversee the construction of the dam are regular full-time employees of F Corporation who are not on loan from any related person. The principle clerical work, and the financial accounting, required in connection with the construction of the dam by F Corporation are performed, on a remunerated basis, by full-time employees of M Corporation. All other assistance F Corporation requires in completing the construction of the dam is paid for by that corporation and furnished by unrelated persons. The services performed by F Corporation under the contract for the construction of the dam are not performed for, or on behalf of, a related person for purposes of section 954(e) because the clerical and accounting services furnished by M Corporation do not assist F Corporation directly in the performance of the contract.

Example (4). Controlled foreign corporation D, a wholly owned subsidiary of domestic corporation M, procures and enters a contract with an unrelated person to construct a superhighway in a foreign country, but such person enters the contract only on the condition that M Corporation agrees to perform, or to pay for the performance by some person other than D Corporation of, the services called for by the contract if D Corporation should fail to complete their performance. Corporation D is capable of performing such contract. No related person as to D Corporation pays for, or performs, any services called for by the contract, or pays for, or performs, any significant services related to such services. The construction of the superhighway by D Corporation is not considered for purposes of section 954(e) to be the performance of services for, or on behalf of M Corporation.

Example (5). Domestic corporation M is obligated under a contract with an unrelated person to construct a superhighway in a foreign country. At a later date M Corporation assigns the entire contract to its wholly owned subsidiary, controlled foreign corporation C, and the unrelated person releases M Corporation from any obligation under the contract. The construction of such highway by C Corporation is considered for purposes of section 954(e) to be the performance of services for, or on behalf of, M Corporation.

Example (6). Domestic corporation M enters a contract with an unrelated person to construct a superhighway in a foreign country. Corporation M immediately assigns the entire contract to its wholly owned subsidiary, controlled foreign corporation C. The unrelated person does not release M Corporation of its obligation under the contract, the sole purpose of these arrangements being to have M Corporation guarantee performance of the contract by C Corporation. Corporation C is capable of performing the construction contract. Neither M Corporation nor any other person related to C Corporation pays for, or performs, any services called for by the construction contract or at any time pays for, or performs, any significant services related to the services performed under such contract. The construction of the superhighway by C Corporation is not considered for purposes of section 954(e) to be the performance of services for, or on behalf of, M Corporation.

Example (7). The facts are the same as in example (6) except that M Corporation, preparatory to entering the construction contract, prepares plans and specifications which enable the submission of bids for the contract. Since M Corporation has performed significant services related to the services the performance of which it has guaranteed, the construction of such highway by C Corporation is considered for purposes of section 954(e) to be the performance of services for, or on behalf of, M Corporation.

Example (8). Domestic corporation M manufactures an industrial machine which requires specialized installation. Corporation M sells the machines for a basic price if the contract of sale contains no provision for installation. If, however, the customer agrees to employ controlled foreign corporation E, a wholly owned subsidiary of M Corporation, to install the machine and to pay E Corporation a specified installation charge, M Corporation sells the machine at a price which is less than the basic price. The installation services performed by E Corporation for customers of M Corporation purchasing the machine at the reduced price are considered for purposes of section 954(e) to be performed for, or on behalf of, M Corporation.

Example (9). Domestic corporation M manufactures and sells industrial machines with a warranty as to their performance conditional upon their installation and maintenance by a factory-authorized service agency. Controlled foreign corporation F, a wholly owned subsidiary of M Corporation, is the only authorized service agency. Any installation or maintenance services performed by F Corporation on such machines are considered for purposes of section 954(e) to be performed for, or on behalf of, M Corporation.

Example (10). Domestic corporation M manufactures electric office machines which it sells at a basic price without any provision for, or understanding as to, adjustment or maintenance of the machines require constant adjustment and maintenance services which M Corporation, certain wholly owner subsidiaries of M Corporation, and certain unrelated persons throughout the world are qualified to perform. From among the numerous persons qualified and available to perform adjustment and maintenance services with respect to such office machines, foreign corporation B, a customer of M Corporation, employs controlled foreign corporation G, a wholly owned subsidiary of M Corporation, to adjust and maintain the office machines which B Corporation purchases from M Corporation. The adjustment and maintenance services performed by G Corporation for B Corporation are not considered for purposes of section 954(e) to be performed for, or on behalf of, M Corporation.

(c) Place where services are performed. The place where services will be considered to have been performed for purposes of paragraph (a)(2) of this section will depend on the facts and circumstances of each case. As a general rule, services will be considered performed where the persons performing services for the controlled foreign corporation which derives income in connection with the performance of technical, managerial, architectural, engineering, scientific, skilled, industrial, commercial, or like services are physically located when they perform their duties in the execution of the service activity resulting in such income. Therefore, in many cases, total gross income of a controlled foreign corporation derived in connection with each service contract or arrangement performed for or on behalf of a related person must be apportioned, between income which is not foreign base company services income and that which is foreign base company services income, on a basis of employee-time spent within the foreign country under the laws of which the controlled foreign corporation is created or organized and employee-time spent without the foreign country under the laws of which such corporation is created or organized. In allocating time spent within and without the foreign country under the laws of which the controlled foreign corporation is created or organized, relative weight must also be given to the value of the various functions performed by persons in fulfillment of the service contract or arrangement. For example, clerical work will ordinarily be assigned little value, while services performed by technical, highly skilled, and managerial personnel will be assigned greater values in relation to the type of function performed by each individual.

(d) Items excluded. Foreign base company services income does not include—

(1) Income derived in connection with the performance of services by a controlled foreign corporation if—

(i) The services directly relate to the sale or exchange of personal property by the controlled foreign corporation,

(ii) The property sold or exchanged was manufactured, produced, grown, or extracted by such controlled foreign corporation, and

(iii) The services were performed before the sale or exchange of such property by the controlled foreign corporation;

(2) Income derived in connection with the performance of services by a controlled foreign corporation if the services directly relate to an offer or effort to sell or exchange personal property which was, or would have been, manufactured, produced, grown, or extracted by such controlled foreign corporation whether or not a sale or exchange of such property was in fact consummated; or

(3) For taxable years beginning after December 31, 1975, foreign base company shipping income (as determined under § 1.954-6).

T.D. 6734, 5/14/64, amend T.D. 6981, 11/12/68, T.D. 7894, 5/11/83, T.D. 9008, 7/22/2002.

§ 1.954-5 Increase in qualified investments in less developed countries; taxable years of controlled foreign corporations beginning before January 1, 1976.

For rules applicable to taxable years of controlled foreign corporations beginning before January 1, 1976, see section 954(b)(1) (as in effect before the enactment of the Tax Reduction Act of 1975) and 26 CFR § 1.954-5 (Rev. as of April 1, 1975).

T.D. 6734, 5/14/64, amend T.D. 7893, 5/11/83.

§ 1.954-6 Foreign base company shipping income.

Caution: The Treasury has not yet amended Reg § 1.954-6 to reflect changes made by P.L. 103-66, P.L. 99-514.

(a) Scope. *(1) In general.* This section prescribes rules for determining foreign base company shipping income under the provisions of section 954(f), as amended by the Tax Reduction Act of 1975.

(2) Effective date. (i) The rules prescribed in this section apply to taxable years of foreign corporations beginning after December 31, 1975, and to taxable years of United States shareholders (as defined in section 951(b)) within which or with which such taxable years of such foreign corporations end.

(ii) Except as described in paragraph (b)(1)(viii) of this section, foreign base company shipping income does not include amounts earned by a foreign corporation in a taxable year of such corporation beginning before January 1, 1976. See example (1) of paragraph (g)(2) of this section for an illustration of the effect of this subparagraph on partnership income. See example (3) of paragraph (f)(4)(ii) of this section for an illustration of the effect of this subparagraph on certain dividend income. See paragraph (f)(5)(iii) of this section for the effect of this subparagraph on certain interest and gains.

(b) Definitions. *(1) Foreign base company shipping income.* The term "foreign base company shipping income" means—

(i) Gross income derived from, or in connection with, the use (or hiring or leasing for use) of any aircraft or vessel in foreign commerce (see paragraph (c) of this section),

(ii) Gross income derived from, or in connection with, the performance of services directly related to the use of any aircraft or vessel in foreign commerce (see paragraph (d) of this section),

(iii) Gross income incidental to income described in subdivisions (i) and (ii) of this subparagraph, as provided in paragraph (e) of this section,

(iv) Gross income derived from the sale, exchange, or other disposition of any aircraft or vessel used or held for use (by the seller or by a person related to the seller) in foreign commerce,

(v) In the case of a controlled foreign corporation, dividends, interest, and gains described in paragraph (f) of this section,

(vi) Income described in paragraph (g) of this section (relating to partnerships, trusts, etc.),

(vii) Exchange gain, to the extent allocable to foreign base company shipping income (see § 1.952-2(c)(2)(v)(b), and

(viii) In the case of a controlled foreign corporation and at its option, dividends, interest, and gains attributable to income derived from aircraft and vessels (as defined in 26 CFR § 1.954-1(b)(2) (Rev. as of April 1, 1975)) by a less developed country shipping company (described in § 1.955-5(b)) in taxable years beginning after December 31, 1962, and before January 1, 1976. The portion of a dividend, interest, or gain attributable to such income shall be determined by the same method as that for determining the portion of a dividend, interest, or gain attributable to foreign base company shipping income under paragraphs (f)(4), (5), and (6) of this section, but without regard to paragraphs (f)(6)(ii) and (iv)(B).

(2) Foreign base company shipping operations. For purposes of sections 951 through 964, the term "foreign base company shipping operations" means the trade or business from which gross income described in subparagraph (1)(i) and (ii) of this paragraph is derived.

(3) Foreign commerce. For purposes of sections 951 through 964—

(i) An aircraft or vessel is used in foreign commerce to the extent it is used in transportation of property or passengers—

(A) Between a port (or airport) in the United States or possession of the United States and a port (or airport) in a foreign country, or

(B) Between a port (or airport) in a foreign country and another in the same country or between a port (or airport) in a foreign country and one in another foreign country.

Thus, for example, a trawler, a factory ship, and an oil drilling ship are not considered to be used in foreign commerce. On the other hand, a cruise ship which visits one or more foreign ports is considered to be so used. Notwithstanding subdivision (i)(B) of this paragraph (b)(3), foreign base company income does not include income derived from, or in connection with, the use of an aircraft or vessel in transportation of property or passengers between a port (or airport) in a foreign country and another port (or airport) in the same country if both the foreign corporation is created or organized and the aircraft or vessel is registered in that country.

(ii) The term "vessel" includes all water craft and other artificial contrivances of whatever description and at whatever stage of construction, whether on the stocks or launched, which are used or are capable of being used or are intended to be used as a means of transportation on water.

This definition does not apply for purposes of section 956(b)(2)(G) and § 1.956-2(b)(1)(ix).

(iii) The term "port" means any place (whether on or off shore) where aircraft or vessels are accustomed to load or unload goods or to take on or let off passengers.

(iv) Any vessel (such as a lighter or beacon lightship) which serves other vessels used in foreign commerce (within the meaning of subdivision (i) of this subparagraph) shall, to the extent so used, also be considered to be used in foreign commerce.

(v) For the meaning of the term "foreign country", see section 638(2).

(4) Use in foreign commerce. For purposes of sections 951 through 964, the use of an aircraft or vessel in foreign commerce includes the hiring or leasing (or subleasing) of an aircraft or vessel to another for use in foreign commerce. Thus, for example, an aircraft or vessel is "used in foreign commerce" within the meaning of section 955(b)(1)(A) if such aircraft or vessel is chartered (whether pursuant to a bareboat charter, time charter, or otherwise) to another for use in foreign commerce.

(5) Related person. With respect to a controlled foreign corporation, the term "related person" means a related person as defined in § 1.954-1(e)(1), and the term "unrelated person" means an unrelated person as defined in § 1.954-1(e)(2).

(c) Aircraft or vessel income. *(1) In general.* The term "income derived from, or in connection with, the use (or hiring or leasing for use) of any aircraft or vessel in foreign commerce" as used in paragraph (b)(1)(i) of this section means—

(i) Income derived from transporting passengers or property by aircraft or vessel in foreign commerce and

(ii) Income derived from hiring or leasing an aircraft or vessel to another for use in foreign commerce.

(2) Illustrations. The application of this paragraph may be illustrated by the following examples:

Example (1). Foreign corporation C owns a foreign flag vessel which it charters under a long-term charter to foreign corporation D. The vessel is used by D as a tramp which has no fixed or regular schedule. The vessel carries bulk and packaged cargoes, as well as occasional passengers, under charter parties, contracts of affreightment, or other contracts of carriage. The carriage of cargoes and passengers is between a port in the United States and a port in a foreign country or between a port in one foreign country and another port in the same or a different foreign country. The charter hire paid to C by D constitutes income derived from the use of the vessel in foreign commerce, but is not foreign base company income to the extent the charter hire is allocable to income derived from the use of the vessel between ports in the same foreign country in which both C is incorporated and the vessel is registered. The charter hire and freight and passenger revenue (including demurrage and dead freight) derived by D also constitute income derived from the use of the vessel in foreign commerce, but is not foreign base company income to the extent the charter hire and freight and passenger revenue are allocable to the use of the vessel between ports in the same foreign country in which both D is incorporated and the vessel is registered.

Example (2). (a) Foreign corporation E owns a foreign flag tanker which it charters under a long-term bareboat charter to foreign corporation F for use in foreign commerce. F produces oil in a foreign country and ships the oil to other foreign countries and to the United States. The vessel, when not engaged in carrying F's oil, is used to carry bulk cargoes for unrelated persons in foreign commerce as opportunity offers. The charger hire received by E constitutes income derived from the use of the vessel in foreign commerce. The income derived by F from carrying bulk cargoes for unrelated persons also constitutes income derived from the use of the vessel in foreign commerce.

(b) F is forced to lay up the vessel as a result of adverse market developments. Pursuant to the terms of the charter, F continues to pay charter hire to E during the period of lay-up. The charter hire received by E during the period of lay-up constitutes income derived from the use of the vessel in foreign commerce.

Example (3). (a) A shipment of cheese is loaded into a container owned by controlled foreign corporation S at the consignor's place of business in Hamar, Norway. The cheese is transported to Milan, Italy, by the following routings:

(1) Overland by road from Hamar, Norway, to Gothenburg, Sweden, by unrelated motor carriers via Oslo, Norway,

(2) By sea from Gothenburg to Rotterdam, Netherlands, by feeder vessel under foreign flag, time chartered to S by unrelated owner,

(3) By sea from Rotterdam to Algeciras, Spain, by feeder vessel under foreign flag, time chartered to S by unrelated owner.

(4) By sea from Algeciras to Genoa, Italy, by line-haul vessel under U.S. flag, chartered by S from related company, and

(5) Overland from Genoa to Milan, Italy, by unrelated motor carrier.

(b) The consignor pays S total charges of $1,710, and S pays $676 to unrelated third parties, which amounts may be broken down as follows:

Description of charges	Amount billed to customer and collected by S	Revenue collected by S on behalf of an unrelated party	Costs paid to unrelated 3d party and absorbed by S
Ocean freight	$1,420		
Trucking charge of empty equipment to shipper's facility	50	$ 50	
Trucking charges Hamar to Oslo	60	60	
Trucking charges Oslo to Gothenburg			$315
Trucking charges Genoa to Milan	180	180	
Brokerage Commission in Europe			71
Total	1,710	290	386

(c) Of the $1,710 amount billed to the consignor and collected by S, $290 is collected by S on behalf of unrelated third parties. This $290 amount is not includable in S's gross income, and is therefore not includable in S's foreign base company shipping income. The remaining $1,420 amount (i.e., $1,710 – $290) is includable in S's foreign base company shipping income. The $386 amount paid by S to unrelated third parties and absorbed by S is deductible from foreign base company shipping income under § 1.954-1(c).

(d) Services directly related. *(1) In general.* The term "income derived from, or in connection with, the performance of services directly related to the use of an aircraft or vessel in foreign commerce", as used in paragraph (b)(1)(ii) of this section, means—

(i) Income derived from, or in connection with, the performance of services described in subparagraph (2) or (3) of this paragraph, and

(ii) Income treated as foreign base company shipping income under subparagraph (4) of this paragraph.

(2) Intragroup services. The services described in this subparagraph are services performed for a person who is the owner, lessor, lessee or operator of an aircraft or vessel used in foreign commerce, by such person or by a person related to such person, and which fall into one or more of the following categories:

(i) Terminal services, such as dockage, wharfage, storage, lights, water, refrigeration, and similar services;

(ii) Stevedoring and other cargo handling services;

(iii) Container related services (including the rental of containers and related equipment) performed either in connection with the local drayage or inland haulage of cargo or in the course of transportation in foreign commerce;

(iv) Services performed by tugs, lighters, barges, scows, launches, floating cranes, and other similar equipment;

(v) Maintenance and repairs;

(vi) Training of pilots and crews;

(vii) Licensing of patents, know-how, and similar intangible property developed and used in the course of foreign base company shipping operations;

(viii) Services performed by a booking, operating, or managing agent; and

(ix) Any service performed in the course of the actual transportation of passengers or property.

(3) Services for passenger, consignor, or consignee. The services described in this subparagraph are services provided by the operator (or person related to the operator) of an aircraft or vessel in foreign commerce for the passenger, consignor, or consignee, such as—

(i) Services described in one or more of the categories set out in subparagraph (2)(i) through (iv) and (ix) of this paragraph,

(ii) The rental of staterooms, berths, or living accommodations and the furnishing of meals,

(iii) Barber shop and other services to passengers aboard vessels,

(iv) Excess baggage, and

(v) Demurrage, dispatch, and dead freight.

(4) The 70-percent test. At the option of the foreign corporation all the gross income for a taxable year derived by a foreign corporation from any facility used in connection with the performance of services described in one or more of the categories set out in subparagraph (2)(i) through (ix) of this paragraph is foreign base company shipping income if more than 70 percent of such gross income for either—

(i) Such taxable year, or

(ii) Such taxable year and the two preceding taxable years, is foreign base company shipping income (determined without regard to this subparagraph). Thus, for example, if 80 percent of the gross income derived by a controlled foreign corporation at a stevedoring facility is treated as foreign base company shipping income under subparagraph (2) of this paragraph, then the remaining 20 percent is treated as foreign base company shipping income under this subparagraph.

(5) Rules for applying subparagraph (4). (i) Solely for purposes of applying subparagraph (4) of this paragraph, foreign base company shipping income and gross income shall be deemed to include an arm's length charge (see paragraph (h)(5) of this section) for services performed by the foreign corporation for itself.

(ii) In determining whether services performed by a foreign corporation are performed at a single facility or at two or more different facilities, all of the facts and circumstances involved will be taken into account. Ordinarily, all services performed by a foreign corporation within a single port area will be considered performed at a single facility.

(iii) The application of this subparagraph and subparagraph (4) of this paragraph may be illustrated by the following example in which it is assumed that the foreign corporation has chosen to apply the 70-percent test of subparagraph (4):

Example. (a) Controlled foreign corporation X uses the calendar year as the taxable year. For 1976, X is divided into two operating divisions, A and B. Division A operates a number of vessels in foreign commerce. Division B operates a terminal facility at which it performs services described in subparagraph (2)(i) of this paragraph for vessels some of which are operated by division A, some of which are operated by persons related to X, and some of which are operated by persons unrelated to X. For 1976, X includes under subparagraph (5) as foreign base company shipping income and gross income, for purposes of subparagraph (4), an arm's length charge for services performed for itself. For 1976, the gross income derived by division B is reconstructed for purposes of subparagraph (4) of this paragraph as follows, based on the facts shown in the following table:

(1) Gross income derived from persons unrelated to *X*	$20
(2) Gross income derived from persons related to *X* ...	10
(3) Actual gross income (line (1) plus line (2))	30
(4) Hypothetical gross income derived from division A (determined by the application of subdivision (i) of this subparagraph)	70
(5) Total reconstructed gross income (line (3) plus line (4))	100

(b) Since 80 percent of the reconstructed gross income derived by division B would be treated as foreign base company shipping income under subparagraph (2) of this paragraph, the entire $30 amount of the gross income actually derived by division B is treated as foreign base company shipping income under subparagraph (4) of this paragraph.

(6) Arm's length charge. For purposes of this section, the arm's length charge for services performed by a foreign corporation for itself shall be determined by applying the principles of section 482 and the regulations thereunder as if the party for whom the services are performed and the party by whom the services are performed were not the same person, but were controlled taxpayers within the meaning of § 1.482-1(a)(4).

(7) Illustrations. The application of this paragraph may be illustrated by the following examples:

Example (1). Controlled foreign corporation A acts as a managing agent for foreign corporation B, a related person which contracts to construct and charter a foreign flag vessel for use in foreign commerce. As managing agent for B, A performs a broad range of services relating to the use of the vessel, including arranging for, and supervising of, construction and chartering of the vessel, and handling of operating services after construction is completed. The income derived by A from its management and operating services constitutes income derived in connection with the performance of services directly related to the use of the vessel in foreign commerce.

Example (2). Controlled foreign corporation C uses the calendar year as the taxable year. During 1976, C is engaged in the trade or business of acting as a steamship agent solely for unrelated persons. C's activities as steamship agent range from "husbanding" (i.e., arranging for fuel, supplies and port services, and attending to crew and customs matters) to the solicitation and booking of cargo at a number of foreign ports. None of C's other gross income for 1976 is foreign base company shipping income. Under these circumstances, C's gross income derived from its steamship agency does not constitute foreign base company shipping income.

(e) Incidental income. *(1) In general.* Foreign base company shipping income includes all incidental income derived by a foreign corporation in the course of its active conduct of foreign base company shipping operations.

(2) Examples. Examples of incidental income derived in the course of the active conduct of foreign base company shipping operations include—

(i) Gain from the sale, exchange or other disposition of assets which are related shipping assets within the meaning of § 1.955A-2(b),

(ii) Income derived from temporary investments described in § 1.955A-2(b)(2)(i) and (iii),

(iii) Interest on accounts receivable and evidences of indebtedness described in § 1.955A-2(b)(2)(ii),

(iv) Income derived from granting concessions to others aboard aircraft or vessels used in foreign commerce,

(v) Income derived from stock and currency futures described in § 1.955A-2(b)(2)(vii) and (viii),

(vi) Income derived by the lessor of an aircraft or vessel used in foreign commerce from additional rentals for the use of related equipment (such as a complement of containers), and

(vii) Interest derived by the seller from a purchase money mortgage loan in respect of the sale of an aircraft or vessel described in § 1.955A-2(a)(1)(i).

(f) Certain dividends, interest, and gain. *(1) In general.* (i) The foreign base company shipping income of a controlled foreign corporation (referred to in subdivision (ii)(A) of this paragraph (f)(1) as "first corporation") includes—

(A) Dividends and interest received from foreign corporations listed in subdivision (ii) of this paragraph (f)(1), and

(B) Gain recognized from the sale, exchange, or other disposition of stock or obligations of foreign corporations listed in subdivision (ii) of this paragraph (f)(1), but only to the extent that such dividends, interest, and gains are attributable to foreign base company shipping income of the foreign corporations listed in subdivision (ii) of this paragraph (f)(1).

(ii) The foreign corporations referred to in subdivision (i) of this paragraph (f)(1) are—

(A) Foreign corporations with respect to which the first corporation (see subdivision (i) of this paragraph (f)(1)) would be deemed under section 902(b) to pay taxes,

(B) Controlled foreign corporations which are related persons (within the meaning of section 954(d)(3)), and

(C) Less developed country shipping companies described in § 1.955-5(b).

(2) Corporation deemed to pay taxes. (i) For purposes of this paragraph, a controlled foreign corporation would be deemed under section 902(b) to pay taxes in respect of any other foreign corporation if such controlled foreign corporation would be deemed, for purposes of applying section 902(a) to any United States shareholder of such controlled foreign corporation, to pay taxes in respect of dividends which were received from such other foreign corporation (whether or not such other foreign corporation actually pays any taxes or dividends). Solely for purposes of this subdivision, each United States shareholder (within the meaning of section 951(b)) shall be deemed to be a domestic corporation.

(ii) The application of subdivision (i) of this subparagraph may be illustrated by the following examples:

Example (1). Domestic corporation M owns 100 percent of the one class of stock of controlled foreign corporation X, which in turn owns 40 percent of the one class of stock of foreign corporation Y. Y is not a controlled foreign corporation. For purposes of subdivision (1) of this subparagraph, X is deemed to pay taxes in respect of Y.

Example (2). The facts are the same as in example (1), except that United States shareholder A, an individual, owns 80 percent of the stock of corporation X, and United States shareholders B and C, parent and child, own the other 20 percent in equal shares. For purposes of applying this paragraph to all three United States shareholders (A, B, and C), X is deemed to pay taxes in respect of Y.

(3) Obligation defined. For purposes of this section, the term "obligation" means any bond, note, debenture, certificate, or other evidence of indebtedness, and a debt recorded in the books of account of both the creditor and the debtor. In the absence of legal, governmental, or business reasons to the contrary, the indebtedness must bear interest or be issued at a discount.

(4) Dividends. (i) For purposes of this paragraph and § 1.954-1(b)(2), the portion of a dividend which is attributable to foreign base company shipping income is that amount which bears the same ratio to the total dividend received as the earnings and profits out of which such dividend is paid that are attributable to foreign base company shipping income bears to the total earnings and profits out of which such dividend is paid. For purposes of this subdivision, the source of the earnings and profits out of which a distribution is made shall be determined under section 316(a), except that the source of the earnings and profits out of which a distribution is made by a controlled foreign corporation with respect to stock owned (within the meaning of section 958(a)) by a United States shareholder of such controlled foreign corporation shall be determined under § 1.959-3.

(ii) The application of this subparagraph may be illustrated by the following examples:

Example (1). Domestic corporation M owns 100 percent of the one class of stock of controlled foreign corporation X, which in turn owns 40 percent of the one class of stock of foreign corporation Y. Y, which is not (and has not been) either a controlled foreign corporation or a less developed country shipping company, makes a distribution of $100 to X. Under section 316(a), such distribution is made out of Y's earnings and profits for 1978. Sixty percent of Y's earnings and profits for 1978 are attributable to foreign base company shipping income. As a result, $60 of the $100 distribution constitutes foreign base company shipping income to X under subdivision (i) of this subparagraph.

Example (2). The facts are the same as in example (1), except that under section 316(a) $20 of the $100 dividend is paid out of Y's earnings and profits for 1979, and the other $80 is paid out of Y's earnings and profits for 1978. Thirty percent of Y's earnings and profits for 1979 are attributable to foreign base company shipping income. Since 60 percent of Y's earnings and profits for 1978 are also attributable to foreign base company shipping income, $54, i.e. (.60 × $80) + (.30 × $20), of the $100 distribution constitutes foreign base company shipping income to X under subdivision (i) of this subparagraph.

Example (3). The facts are the same as in example (1) except that under section 316(a) the $100 dividend is made out of Y's earnings and profits for 1972. Since under paragraph (a)(2)(ii) of this section foreign base company shipping income does not include amounts earned by a foreign corporation (not a less developed country shipping company) in a taxable year beginning before January 1, 1978, no amount of such $100 distribution constitutes foreign base company shipping income to X under subdivision (i) of this subparagraph.

Example (4). Domestic corporation N owns 100 percent of the one class of stock of controlled foreign corporation S, which in turn owns 100 percent of the one class of stock of controlled foreign corporation T. T makes a distribution of $100 to S, of which $80 is allocable under § 1.959-3 to earnings and profits for 1977 which are described in § 1.959-3(b)(2), and $20 is allocable to earnings and profits for 1978 which are described in § 1.959-3(b)(3). The $80 amount is excluded from S's gross income under section 959(b) and therefore is not included in S's foreign base company shipping income. One hundred percent of T's earnings and profits for 1978 described in § 1.959-3(b)(3) were attributable to reinvested foreign base company shipping income. As a result, the entire $20 amount is included in S's foreign base company shipping income under this paragraph. See § 1.954-1(b)(2) for the rule that such $20 amount may be excluded from the foreign base company income of S.

(5) Interest and gain. (i) Except as provided in subdivisions (ii) and (iii) of this subparagraph, the portion of any interest paid by a foreign corporation, or gain recognized from the sale, exchange, or other disposition of stock or obligations of a foreign corporation, which is attributable to the foreign base company shipping income of such foreign corporation is that amount which bears the same ratio to such interest or gain as the foreign base company shipping income of such corporation for the period described in subparagraph (6) of this paragraph bears to its gross income for such period.

(ii) Interest which is paid by a controlled foreign corporation is attributable to such corporation's foreign base company shipping income to the same extent that such interest is allocable (under the principles of § 1.954-1(c)) to its foreign base company shipping income.

(iii) If interest is paid by a foreign corporation, or if stock obligations of a foreign corporation are sold, exchanged, or otherwise disposed of, during a taxable year of such foreign corporation beginning before January 1, 1976, then no portion of such interest or gain is attributable to foreign base company shipping income.

(iv) Solely for purposes of subdivision (i) of this subparagraph, if a controlled foreign corporation (the "first corporation") owns more than 10 percent of the stock of another controlled foreign corporation (the "second corporation"), then

(A) The gross income of the first corporation for any taxable year shall be—

(1) Increased by its pro rata share of the gross income of the second corporation for the taxable year which ends with or within such taxable year of the first corporation, and

(2) Decreased by the amount of any dividends received from the second corporation; and

(B) The foreign base company shipping income of the first corporation for any taxable year shall be—

(1) Increased by its pro rata share of the foreign base company shipping income of the second corporation for the taxable year which ends with or within such taxable year of the first corporation, and

(2) Decreased by the amount of any dividends received from the second corporation which constitute foreign base company income.

(v) Solely for purposes of applying subdivision (i) of this subparagraph, the district director shall make such other adjustments to the gross income and the foreign base company shipping income of any foreign corporation as are necessary to properly determine the extent to which any interest or gain is attributable to foreign base company shipping income, including proper adjustments to reflect any transaction during the test period described in subparagraph (6) of this paragraph to which section 332, 351, 354, 355, 356, or 361 applies.

(6) Test period. (i) Except as provided in subdivisions (ii) and (iii) of this subparagraph the period described in this subparagraph with respect to any foreign corporation is the 3-year period ending with the close of such corporation's taxable year preceding the year during which interest was paid or stock or obligations were sold, exchanged, or otherwise disposed of, or such part of such period as such corporation was in existence.

(ii) The period described in this paragraph shall not include any part of a taxable year beginning before January 1, 1976.

(iii) If interest is paid by a foreign corporation, or if stock or obligations of a foreign corporation are sold, exchanged, or otherwise disposed of during its first taxable year, then the period described in this paragraph shall be such first taxable year.

(iv) For purposes of subdivision (iii) of this subparagraph, the first taxable year of a foreign corporation is the later of—

(A) The first taxable year of its existence, or

(B) Its first taxable year beginning after December 31, 1975.

(g) Income from partnerships, trusts, etc. *(1) In general.* The foreign base company shipping income of any foreign corporation includes—

(i) Its distributive share of the gross income of any partnership, and

(ii) Any amounts includible in its gross income under section 652(a), 662(a), 671, or 691(a), to the extent that such items would have been includible in its foreign base company shipping income had they been realized by it directly.

(2) Illustrations. The application of subparagraph (1) of this paragraph may be illustrated by the following examples:

Example (1). Controlled foreign corporations X and Y are equal partners in partnership P. The taxable years end on December 31 for X, June 30 for Y, and March 31 for P. In the fiscal year ending March 31, 1976, P's sole business activity is the use of a vessel in foreign commerce. P derives gross income of $200 from the use of the vessel, and incurs expenses, taxes, and other deductions of $160. Assume X's distributive share of such $200 of P's gross income is $100, all of which is includible in X's gross income. If X had realized its distributive share of $100 directly, then the amount which would have been includible in X's foreign base company shipping income under this paragraph is the portion allocable to the months of January, February, and March of 1976. Such amount, $25 (i.e., ½ × $200 × 3 months/12 months), is included in X's foreign base company shipping income for its taxable year ending December 31, 1976. Similarly, X is entitled under this paragraph to a deduction from foreign base company shipping income of $20 (i.e., ½ × $160 × 3 months/12 months). Since foreign base company shipping income does not include amounts earned by a foreign corporation (not a less developed country shipping corporation) in a taxable year beginning before January 1, 1976, Y has no foreign base company shipping income (under this paragraph or otherwise) for its taxable year beginning on July 1, 1975.

Example (2). The facts are the same as in example (1), except that P incurs expenses, taxes, and deductions of $240 in its taxable year ending on March 31, 1976. Accordingly, $25 is includible in X's foreign base company shipping income, and the amount deductible therefrom under this paragraph is $30 (i.e., ½ × $240 × 3 months/12 months).

(3) Other income. Except as expressly provided in subparagraph (1) of this paragraph, foreign base company shipping income does not include any amount includible in the gross income of a controlled foreign corporation under part I of subchapter J (section 641 and following, relating to estates, trusts, and beneficiaries), and gains from the sale or other disposition of any interest in an estate or trust.

(h) Additional rules. *(1) Gross income.* For purposes of this section and § 1.955A-2, the gross income of a foreign corporation (whether or not a controlled foreign corporation) shall be determined in accordance with the provisions of section 952 and § 1.952-2. Thus, for example, section 883 (relating to exclusions from gross income of foreign corporations) is inapplicable under § 1.952-2(a)(1) and (c)(1). In addition, the gross income of a controlled foreign corporation shall be determined, with respect to a United States shareholder of such controlled foreign corporation, by excluding distributions received by such corporation which are excluded from gross income under section 959(b) with respect to such shareholder.

(2) Earnings and profits. For purposes of this section, the earnings and profits of a foreign corporation (whether or not a controlled foreign corporation) shall be determined in accordance with the provisions of section 964 and the regulations thereunder.

(3) No double counting. No item of gross income shall be counted as foreign base company shipping income under more than one provision of this section. For example, If $200 of gross income derived from the use of a lighter is treated as foreign base company shipping income under both paragraph (b)(1)(i) and paragraph (b)(1)(ii) of this section, then such $200 is counted only once as foreign base company shipping income. A taxpayer may choose under which provision to include an item of income.

(4) Losses. (i) Generally, if a controlled foreign corporation has losses which are properly allocable to foreign base company shipping income, the extent to which such losses are deductible from such income shall be determined by treating such foreign corporation as a domestic corporation and applying the principles of section 63. See §§ 1.954-1(c) and 1.952-2(b). Thus for example, losses from sales or exchanges of capital assets are allowable only to the extent of gains from such sales or exchanges.

(ii) If gain from the sale, exchange, or other disposition of any stock or obligation would be treated (to any extent) as foreign base company shipping income, then loss from such sale, exchange, or other disposition is properly allocable to foreign base company shipping income (to the same extent).

(iii) In determining the extent to which any loss on the disposition of a qualified investment in foreign base company shipping operations is deductible from foreign base company shipping income, it is immaterial that such loss is taken into account under § 1.955A-1(b)(1)(ii) as a reduction in the amount of the decrease in (withdrawal from) qualified investments in foreign base company shipping operations.

(5) Hypothetical charges. Under paragraph (d)(5)(i) of this section and § 1.955A-2(a)(4)(ii)(A), gross income may be deemed to include hypothetical arm's length charges for services performed by a controlled foreign corporation for itself. Under paragraph (d)(2) of this section, certain of these hypothetical charges may be treated as foreign based company shipping income. Such hypothetical charges are deemed to be income solely for purposes of applying the "extent of use" tests prescribed by paragraph (d)(4) of this section and § 1.955A-2(a)(4). Charges for services performed by a controlled foreign corporation for itself shall in no event be included in income for any other purposes.

T.D. 7894, 5/11/83.

---

§ 1.954-7 Increase in qualified investments in foreign base company shipping operations.

Caution: The Treasury has not yet amended Reg § 1.954-7 to reflect changes made by P.L. 99-514.

(a) Determination of investments at close of taxable year. *(1) In general.* Under section 954(g), the increase in qualified investments in foreign base company shipping operations, for purposes of section 954(b)(2) and paragraph (b)(1) of § 1.954-1, of any controlled foreign corporation for any taxable year is, except as provided in paragraph (b) of this section, the amount by which—

(i) The controlled foreign corporation's qualified investments in foreign base company shipping operations at the close of the taxable year, exceed

(ii) Its qualified investments in foreign base company shipping operations at the close of the preceding taxable year.

(2) Preceding taxable year. For purposes of this section, a taxable year which begins before January 1, 1976, may be a preceding taxable year.

(3) Cross-reference. See section 955(b) and § 1.955A-2 for the definition of the term "qualified investments in foreign base company shipping operations".

(b) Election to determine investments at close of following taxable year. *(1) General rule.* In lieu of determining an increase in qualified investments in foreign base company shipping operations for a taxable year in the manner provided in paragraph (a) of this section, a United States shareholder of a controlled foreign corporation may make an election under section 955(b)(3) to determine the increase for the corporation's taxable year by ascertaining the amount by which—

(i) Such corporation's qualified investments in foreign base company shipping operations at the close of the taxable year immediately following such taxable year, exceed

(ii) Its qualified investments in foreign base company shipping operations at the close of the taxable year immediately preceding such following taxable year.

(2) Election with respect to first taxable year. Notwithstanding subparagraph (1) of this paragraph, if an election is made without consent by a United States shareholder under § 1.955A-4(b)(1) with respect to a controlled foreign corporation, the increase in such controlled foreign corporation's qualified investments in foreign base company shipping operations for the first taxable year to which such election applies shall be the amount by which—

(i) Such corporation's qualified investments in foreign base company shipping operations at the close of the taxable year immediately following such first taxable year, exceed

(ii) Its qualified investments in foreign base company shipping operations at the close of the taxable year immediately preceding such first taxable year.

(3) Manner of making election. For the manner of making an election under section 955(b)(3), and for rules pertaining to the revocation of such an election, see § 1.955A-4.

(4) Coordination with prior law. If a United States shareholder makes an election without consent under § 1.955A-4(b)(1) with respect to a controlled foreign corporation, then such corporation's increase in qualified investments in foreign base company shipping operations for the first taxable year to which such election applies shall be determined by disregarding any change which occurs during such taxable year in the amount of such corporation's investments in stock or obligations of a less developed country shipping company described in § 1.955-5(b) if both of the following conditions exist:

(i) Such taxable year is the first taxable year of such corporation which begins after December 31, 1975, and

(ii) Such United States shareholder has elected to determine the change in such corporation's qualified investments in less developed countries for its last taxable year beginning before January 1, 1976, under § 1.954-5(b) or § 1.955-3.

(5) Illustrations. The application of this paragraph may be illustrated by the following examples:

Example (1). (a) Controlled foreign corporation X is a wholly-owned subsidiary of domestic corporation M. X uses the calendar year as the taxable year. The amounts of X's qualified investments in foreign base company shipping operations at the close of 1975 through 1979 are as follows:

Qualified investments at Dec. 31, 1975	$16,000
Qualified investments at Dec. 31, 1976	17,000
Qualified investments at Dec. 31, 1977	23,000
Qualified investments at Dec. 31, 1978	28,000
Qualified investments at Dec. 31, 1979	30,000

(b) Assume that M properly files without consent a timely election under § 1.955A-4(b)(1) to determine X's increase for 1976 in qualified investments in foreign base company shipping operations pursuant to this paragraph, and that the election remains in force through 1978. Then X's increases for 1976 through 1978 in qualified investments in foreign base company shipping operations are as follows:

Increase for 1976 ($23,000 minus $16,000)	$7,000
Increase for 1977 ($28,000 minus $23,000)	5,000
Increase for 1978 ($30,000 minus $28,000)	2,000

Example (2). Assume that same facts as in example (1), except that M never files an election under § 1.955A-4(b)(1). X's increases for 1976 through 1978 in qualified investments in foreign base company shipping operations are as follows:

Increase for 1976 ($17,000 minus $16,000)	$1,000
Increase for 1977 ($23,000 minus $17,000)	6,000
Increase for 1978 ($28,000 minus $23,000)	5,000

Example (3). The facts are the same as in example (1), except that X's qualified investments in foreign base company shipping operations include an investment in less developed country shipping companies described in § 1.955-5(b) of $500 on December 31, 1975, and $750 on December 31, 1976. Assume further that M has made an election under section 955(b)(3) (as in effect before the enactment of the Tax Reduction Act of 1975) with respect to X's taxable year 1975. Then X's increase in qualified investments in foreign base company shipping operations for 1976 is $6,750 (i.e., $7,000 – $250).

(c) Illustration. The application of this section may be illustrated by the following example:

Example. (a) Controlled foreign corporation X uses the calendar year as the taxable year. On December 31, 1975, X's qualified investments in foreign base company shipping operations (determined as provided in § 1.955A-2(g)) consist of the following amounts:

Cash	$ 6,000
Readily marketable securities	1,000
Stock of related controlled foreign corporations	4,000
Traffic and other receivables	14,000
Marine insurance claims receivables	1,000
Foreign income tax refunds receivable	1,000
Prepaid shipping expenses and shipping inventories ashore	1,000
Vessel construction funds	0
Vessels	123,000
Vessel plans and construction in progress	3,000
Containers and chassis	0
Terminal property and equipment	2,000
Shipping office (land and building)	1,000
Vessel spare parts ashore	1,000
Performance deposits	2,000
Deferred charges	2,000
Stock of less developed country shipping company described in Sec. 1-955-5(b)	10,000
	172,000

(b) On December 31, 1976, X's qualified investments in foreign base company shipping operations (determined as provided in § 1.955A-2(g)) consists of the following amounts:

Cash	$ 5,000
Readily marketable securities	2,000
Stock of related controlled foreign corporations	4,000
Traffic and other receivables	16,000
Foreign income tax refunds receivable	3,000
Prepaid shipping expenses and shipping inventories ashore	2,000
Vessel construction finds	1,000
Vessels	117,000
Vessel plans and construction in progress	12,000
Containers and chassis	4,000

Terminal property and equipment	2,000
Shipping office (land and building)	1,000
Vessel spare parts ashore	1,000
Performance deposits	2,000
Deferred charges	2,000
Stock of less developed country shipping company described in Sec. 1.955-5(b)	0
	174,000

(c) For 1976, X's increase in qualified investments in foreign base company shipping operations is $2,000, which amount is determined as follows:

Qualified investments at Dec. 31, 1976	$174,000
Qualified investments at Dec. 31, 1975	172,000
Increase for 1976	2,000

T.D. 7894, 5/11/83.

§ 1.954-8 Foreign base company oil related income.

Caution: The Treasury has not yet amended Reg § 1.954-8 to reflect changes made by P.L. 103-66.

(a) Foreign base company oil related income. *(1) In general.* Under section 954(g), the foreign base company oil related income of a controlled foreign corporation (except as provided under paragraph (b) of this section) consists of the items of foreign oil related income ("FORI") described in section 907(c)(2) and (3), other than such income derived from a source within a foreign country in connection with—

(i) Oil or gas which was extracted from an oil or gas well located in that foreign country ("extraction exception"), or

(ii) Oil, gas, or a primary product of oil or gas which is sold by the controlled foreign corporation or a related person for use or consumption within that country or is loaded in that country on a vessel or aircraft as fuel for the vessel or aircraft ("use or consumption exception").

A taxpayer claiming the use or consumption exception must establish its applicability on the basis of facts and circumstances. For special rules for applying the extraction exception, see paragraph (c) of this section.

(2) Source of income. The source of foreign base company oil related income is determined generally under the principles of §§ 1.861-1 to 1.863-5. See § 1.863-6. Thus, income from the performance of a service generally is sourced in the country where the service is performed. See § 1.861-4. Underwriting income from insuring a foreign oil related activity is sourced at the location of the risk. See section 861(a)(7) and § 1.953-2.

(3) Primary product. The term "primary product" of oil or gas has the meaning given this term by § 1.907(c)-1(d)(5) and (6).

(4) Vessel. For the definition of the term "vessel", see § 1.954-6(b)(3)(ii).

(5) Foreign country. For purposes of this section, the term "foreign country" has the same meaning as in section 638 (relating to continental shelf areas). Thus, for example, oil or gas extracted from a sea area will be deemed to be extracted in the country which has exclusive rights of exploitation of natural resources with respect to that area if the other conditions of section 638 are met.

(6) Country of use or consumption. For rules for determining the country of use or consumption, see § 1.954-3(a)(3)(ii).

(7) Insurance income. For purposes of this section, income derived from or attributable to insurance of section 907(c)(2) activities means taxable income as defined in section 832(a) and as modified by the principles of § 1.953-4 (other than as the section is applied to life insurance).

(8) Fuel product. For purposes of this section, the term "fuel product" means oil, gas or a primary product of oil or gas.

(9) Effective date. The provisions of section 954(g) and this section are applicable to taxable years of foreign corporations beginning on or after January 1, 1983, and to taxable years of United States shareholders in which or with which those taxable years of foreign corporations end.

(b) Exemption for small oil producers. *(1) In general.* Foreign base company oil related income does not include any income of a foreign corporation which is not a large oil producer.

(2) Large oil producer. A corporation is a large oil producer (within the meaning of section 954(g)(2)) if the average daily production (extraction) of foreign crude oil and natural gas by the related group which includes the corporation and related persons (within the meaning of section 954(d)(3)) for the taxable year or immediately preceding taxable year is 1,000 or more barrels. The average daily production of foreign crude oil or natural gas for any taxable year (and the conversion of cubic feet of natural gas into barrels) is determined under rules similar to the rules of section 613A, except that only crude oil or natural gas from a well located outside the United States is taken into account.

(c) Special rules for applying the extraction exception of paragraph (a)(1)(i) of this section. *(1) Refining income described in section 907(c)(2)(A).* With regard to a controlled foreign corporation's refining income from the processing of minerals extracted (by the taxpayer or by any other person) from oil or gas wells into their primary products, as described in section 907(c)(2)(A), a pro rata method will be applied for purposes of determining the part of the refining income that qualifies for the extraction exception of paragraph (a)(1)(i) of this section. The pro rata method will be based on the proportion that the barrels of the fuel product extracted in the country of processing bears to the total barrels of the fuel product processed in that country and will apply regardless of the country of sale of the primary product.

(2) Marketing income described in section 907(c)(2)(C). With regard to a controlled foreign corporation's marketing income from the distribution or sale of minerals extracted from oil or gas wells or of primary products, as described in section 907(c)(2)(C), a pro rata method will be applied for purposes of determining the part of the marketing income that qualifies for the extraction exception of paragraph (a)(1)(i) of this section. When applying the pro rata method to the sale of a fuel product other than a primary product, the pro rata method will be based on the proportion that the barrels of the fuel product extracted in the country of sale bears to the total barrels of the fuel product sold in that country. When applying the pro rata method to the sale of primary products, the method will be based on the proportion that the barrels of the fuel product extracted in the country of sale bears to the total barrels of the fuel product processed. For purposes of applying the pro rata method, data of the controlled foreign corporation's related group (as defined in section 954(g)(2)(C)) will be taken into account. The pro rata method will not apply, however, if the mineral or primary product is purchased by the controlled foreign corporation from a person not within the controlled foreign

corporation's related group. In that situation, the marketing income will be presumed to qualify for the extraction exception if the country of the source of the marketing income is a net exporter of crude oil or gas, whichever is relevant. If the country of the source of the marketing income is not a net exporter of crude oil or gas, whichever is relevant, the marketing income will be presumed not to qualify for the extraction exception. The controlled foreign corporation may, however, rebut this latter presumption by demonstrating on the basis of all the facts and circumstances that its marketing income does qualify for the extraction exception. If a primary product that is acquired from a person within the controlled foreign corporation's related group is commingled with like products acquired from persons not within that related group, the pro rata method based on the proportion that the barrels of the fuel product extracted in the country of sale bears to the total barrels of the fuel product processed will be applied to that portion of the total products sold that was purchased from persons within the related group, to the extent that that person did not sell product purchased from an unrelated person, and either the presumption or facts and circumstances will determine the characterization of the remainder.

(3) Transportation income described in section 907(c)(2)(B). With regard to a controlled foreign corporation's income from the transportation of minerals from oil and gas wells or of primary products, as described in section 907(c)(2)(B), the rules set forth in paragraph (c)(2) of this section will apply for purposes of determining the part of the transportation income that qualifies for the extraction exception of paragraph (a)(1)(i) of this section.

(4) Illustrations. The following examples illustrate the application of this paragraph.

Example (1). Controlled foreign corporation M has a refinery in foreign country A that refines 250x barrels of oil during its taxable year beginning in 1984. It is determined that 125x barrels of its 250x barrels were extracted in country A. M sold 150x barrels of its 250x barrels in country A for consumption in country A which resulted in $225x of income from refining and $225x of marketing income, as described in section 907(c)(2)(C). M also sold within foreign country B, for consumption in country B, 100x barrels of its 250x barrels which resulted in an additional $150x of income from refining for M and $170x of marketing income for M. The 100x barrels sold by M within country B, a contiguous country, were transported from M's refinery in country A to country B by a pipeline which is owned by M, and M recognized a total of $10x of income from the transportation of the 100x barrels. Of this $10x, $8x was recognized in country A and $2x was recognized in country B. Under the source of income rules of paragraph (a)(2) of this section, income from refining is considered derived from the country in which the refining occurs and not from the country where the sale of the refined product occurs.

(i) M's refining income. M has $75x of foreign base company oil related income with respect to its refining of the 250x barrels, determined as follows:

(A) Total amount of income from refining attributable to oil refined in country A by M	$375x
(B) Amount of income from refining with respect to oil sold for consumption ($225x) in country A (use or consumption exception under paragraph (a)(1)(ii) of this section	(225x)
(C) Pro rate amount of income from refining attributable to sales in country B considered extracted from country A ($150x times 125x barrels/250x barrels) (extraction exception under paragraph (a)(1)(i) of this section	*(75x)*
(D) Foreign base company oil related income	*$75x*

(ii) M's marketing income. M does not have foreign base company oil related income with respect to its sale of the 100x barrels in country B and 150x barrels in country A because the $170x and $225x, respectively, of marketing income was derived from the country in which the oil was sold for consumption (an exception under paragraph (a)(1)(ii) of this section).

(iii) M's transportation income. M does not have foreign base company oil related income with respect to its $2x of pipeline transportation income recognized in country B because the income was derived from the country in which the 100x barrels were sold for consumption, an exception under paragraph (a)(1)(ii) of this section. With regard to the $8x of pipeline transportation income recognized in country A, however, M has $4x of foreign base company oil related income since of the total barrels refined in country A (250x) only one-half were extracted in that country. Therefore, only one-half of the transportation income qualifies for the extraction exception of paragraph (a)(1)(i) of this section.

(iv) M's extraction income. M does not have foreign base company oil related income for its extraction activity because extraction income is excluded in all events. See section 954(g)(1)(A).

Example (2). Assume the same facts as in Example 1 except that M sold all of the 250x barrels of refined oil in country A. In addition, assume that country A is a net exporter of crude oil. As in Example 1, M sold 150x barrels for consumption in country A with the same resulting income. M sold in country A the remaining 100x barrels to unrelated controlled foreign corporation N which resulted in an additional $150x of income from refining for M and $170x of marketing income for M. N immediately resold in country A for export those 100x barrels. N did not commingle the 100x barrels with any other refined oil. N earned $10x of marketing income on that sale.

(i) M's refining income. M has $75x foreign base company oil related income with respect to its refining of the 250x barrels determined as follows:

(A) Total amount of income from refining attributable to oil refined in country A by M	$375x
(B) Amount of income from refining with respect to oil sold for consumption ($225x) in country A (use or consumption exception under paragraph (a)(1)(ii) of this section)	(225x)
(C) Pro rata amount of income from refining attributable to sales in country A (for consumption outside of country A) considered extracted from country A ($150x times 125x barrels/250x barrels) (extraction exception under paragraph (a)(1)(i) of this section)	*(75x)*
(D) Foreign base company oil related income	*$75x*

(ii) M's marketing income. M does not have foreign base company oil related income with respect to its marketing income from the sale of the 150x barrels in country A because the $225x of marketing income was derived from the country in which the oil was sold for consumption (an exception under paragraph (a)(1)(ii) of this section). M has $85x of foreign base company oil related income with respect to its marketing income from sale to N of the 100x barrels, determined as follows:

(A) Total amount of marketing income from the sale	$170x
(B) Pro rata amount of marketing income attributable to oil product considered extracted in country A ($170x times 125x barrels/250x barrels) (extraction exception under paragraph (a)(1)(i) of this section)	*(85x)*
(C) Foreign base company oil related income	*$ 85x*

(iii) N's marketing income. N is not related to M. Therefore, since N sold the 100x barrels in country A, a net exporter of crude oil, and since N did not commingle the 100x barrels with other refined products, it is presumed that all of the 100x barrels were extracted in country A. Accordingly, all of N's $10x of marketing income is excepted under paragraph (a)(1)(i) of this section.

Example (3). Assume the same facts as in Example 2 except that N is related to M. Characterization of M's income remains the same as in Example 2. N will have, however, $5x of foreign base company oil related income with regard to its marketing income, determined as follows:

(i) Total amount of marketing income from the sale	$10x
(ii) Pro rata amount of marketing income considered extracted from country A ($10x times 125x barrels/250x barrels) (extraction exception under paragraph (a)(1)(i) of this section)	*5x*
(iii) Foreign base company oil related income	*$ 5x*

Example (4). Assume that controlled foreign corporation M has a refinery in foreign country A that refines 200x barrels of oil during its taxable year beginning in 1984. It is determined that 160x barrels of that oil were extracted in country A and that the other 100x barrels were extracted in country B. Neither country A nor country B is a net exporter of crude oil. In addition, M purchased from an unrelated country A refiner 100x barrels of already refined oil. M does not know where this oil was extracted. These 100x barrels of purchased refined oil were commingled with the 200x barrels of refined oil from M's refinery. M sold 225x barrels of refined oil in country A for consumption in country A which resulted in $250x of income from refining and $225x of marketing income. M sold within foreign country B for consumption outside of country B 75x barrels of refined oil which resulted in $100x of income from refining and $75x of marketing income. The refined product was transported between country A and country B by an unrelated person.

(i) M's refining income. With regard to the sales in country A, M has $50x of foreign base company oil related income with respect to its refining of the 100x barrels, determined as follows:

(A) Total amount of income from refining attributable to oil refined in country A by M	$350x
(B) Amount of income from refining with respect to oil sold for consumption in country A ($250x) (use or consumption exception under paragraph (a)(1)(ii) of this section)	(250x)
(C) Pro rata amount of income from refining attributable to sales in country B considered extracted from country A ($100x times 100x barrels/200x barrels) (extraction exception under paragraph (a)(1)(i) of this section)	*(50x)*
(D) Foreign base company oil related income	*$50x*

(ii) M's marketing income. Since the barrels from M's refinery and those that M purchased were commingled, a portion, as follows, of the marketing income is deemed to derive from both purchased and refined products. Since M refined 200x barrels and purchased 100x barrels, its marketing income of $225x from the sale of the 225x barrels in country A for consumption in country A will be deemed to consist of $150x (200x/300x × $225x) from the sale of products refined by M and $75x (100x/300x × $225x) from the sale of purchased products. Likewise, its marketing income of $75x from the sale of the 75x barrels in country B for consumption outside of country B will be deemed to consist of $50x (200x/300x × $75x) from the sale of products refined by M and $25x (100x/300x × $75x) from the sale of purchased products.

(A) Purchased products. M is considered as having $75x of marketing income from the sale of purchased products in country A for consumption in country A. None of this marketing income is foreign base company oil related income since the marketing income is earned in country A, the country of consumption. See paragraph (a)(1)(ii) of this section. All of the $25x of M's marketing income from the sale of purchased products in country B will be foreign base company oil related income. The exception at paragraph (a)(1)(ii) of this section does not apply since the refined oil is not sold for use or consumption in country B. Likewise, the extraction exception under paragraph (a)(1)(i) of this section does not apply. The purchased product cannot be presumed to be extracted in country B since country B is not a net exporter of crude oil. In addition, M cannot show, on a facts and circumstances basis, that purchased products were refined from crude oil extracted in country B.

(B) Products refined by M. With regard to M's marketing income attributable to the sale of products refined by M, M does not have any foreign base company oil related income with regard to its $150x of marketing income in country A since that income was derived from the country in which the oil was sold for consumption (the use or consumption exception under paragraph (a)(1)(ii) of this section). M has $25x of foreign base company oil related income with regard to its $50x of marketing income in country B determined as follows:

(1) Total amount of income from marketing attributable to oil refined by M and sold in country B	$ 50x
(2) Pro rata amount of income from marketing attributable to sales in country B considered extracted from country B ($50x times 100x barrels/200x barrels) (extraction exception under paragraph (a)(1)(i) of this section)	*(25x)*
(3) Foreign base company oil related income	*$ 25x*

T.D. 8331, 1/24/91.

Proposed § 1.954-9 Hybrid branches. [*For Preamble, see ¶ 151,985*]

(a) Subpart F income arising from certain payments involving hybrid branches. *(1) Payment causing foreign tax reduction gives rise to additional subpart F income.* The non-subpart F income of a controlled foreign corporation will be recharacterized as subpart F income, to the extent provided in paragraph (a)(5) of this section, if—

(i) A hybrid branch payment, as defined in paragraph (a)(6) of this section, is made between the entities described in paragraph (a)(2) of this section;

(ii) The hybrid branch payment reduces foreign tax, as determined under paragraph (a)(3) of this section; and

(iii) The hybrid branch payment is treated as falling within a category of foreign personal holding company income under the rules of paragraph (a)(4) of this section.

(2) Hybrid branch payment between certain entities. (i) In general. Paragraph (a)(1) of this section shall apply to hybrid branch payments Between—

(A) A controlled foreign corporation and its hybrid branch;

(B) Hybrid branches of a controlled foreign corporation;

(C) A partnership in which a controlled foreign corporation is a partner (either directly or through one or more branches or other partnerships) and a hybrid branch of the partnership; or

(D) Hybrid branches of a partnership in which a controlled foreign corporation is a partner (either directly or through one or more branches or other partnerships).

(ii) Hybrid branch payment involving partnership. (A) Fiscally transparent partnership. To the extent of the controlled foreign corporation's proportionate share of a hybrid branch payment, the rules of paragraphs (a)(3), (4) and (5) of this section shall be applied by treating the hybrid branch payment between the partnership and the hybrid branch as if it were made directly between the controlled foreign corporation and the hybrid branch, or as if the hybrid branches of the partnership were hybrid branches of the controlled foreign corporation, if the hybrid branch payment is made between—

(1) A fiscally transparent partnership in which a controlled foreign corporation is a partner (either directly or through one or more branches or other fiscally transparent partnerships) and the partnership's hybrid branch; or

(2) Hybrid branches of a fiscally transparent partnership in which a controlled foreign corporation is a partner (either directly or through one or more branches or other fiscally transparent partnerships).

(B) Non-fiscally transparent partnership. To the extent of the controlled foreign corporation's proportionate share of a hybrid branch payment, the rules of paragraphs (a)(3) and (4) and (a)(5)(iv) of this section shall be applied to the non-fiscally transparent partnership as if it were the controlled foreign corporation, if the hybrid branch payment is made between—

(1) A non-fiscally transparent partnership in which a controlled foreign corporation is a partner (either directly or through one or more branches or other partnerships) and the partnership's hybrid branch; or

(2) Hybrid branches of a non-fiscally transparent partnership in which a controlled foreign corporation is a partner (either directly or through one or more branches or other partnerships).

(C) Examples. The following examples illustrate the application of this paragraph (a)(2)(ii):

Example (1). CFC, a controlled foreign corporation in Country A, is a 90 percent partner in partnership P, which is treated as fiscally transparent under the laws of Country A. P has a hybrid branch, BR, in Country B. P makes an interest payment of $100 to BR. Under Country A law, CFC's 90 percent share of the payment reduces CFC's Country A income tax. Under paragraph (a)(2)(ii)(A) of this section, the recharacterization rules of this section are applied by treating the payment as if made by CFC to BR. Ninety dollars of CFC's non-subpart F income, to the extent available, and subject to the earnings and profits and tax rate limitations of paragraph (a)(5) of this section, is recharacterized as subpart F income.

Example (2). CFC, a controlled foreign corporation in Country A, is a 90 percent partner in partnership P, which is treated as fiscally transparent under the laws of Country A. P has two branches in Country B, BR1 and BR2. BR1 is treated as fiscally transparent under the laws of Country A. BR2 is a hybrid branch. BR1 makes an interest payment of $100 to BR2. Under paragraph (a)(2)(ii)(A) of this section, the payment by BR1, the fiscally transparent branch, is treated as a payment by P, and the deemed payment by P, a fiscally transparent partnership, is treated as made by CFC. Under Country A law, CFC's 90 percent share of BR1's payment reduces CFC's Country A income tax. Ninety dollars of CFC's non-subpart F income, to the extent available, and subject to the earnings and profits and tax rate limitations of paragraph (a)(5) of this section, is recharacterized as subpart F income.

(3) Application when payment reduces foreign tax. For purposes of paragraph (a)(1) of this section, a hybrid branch payment reduces foreign tax when the foreign tax imposed on the income of the payor, or any person that is a related person with respect to the payor (as determined under the principles of section 954(d)(3)), is less than the foreign tax that would have been imposed on such income had the hybrid branch payment not been made, or the hybrid branch payment creates or increases a loss or deficit or other tax attribute which may be carried back or forward to reduce the foreign income tax of the payor or any owner in another year (determined by taking into account any refund of such tax made to the payor, payee or any other person).

(4) Hybrid branch payment that is included within a category of foreign personal holding company income. (i) In general. For purposes of paragraph (a)(1) of this section, whether the hybrid branch payment is treated as income included within a category of foreign personal holding company income is determined by treating a hybrid branch that is either the payor or recipient of the hybrid branch payment as a separate wholly-owned subsidiary corporation of the controlled foreign corporation that is incorporated in the jurisdiction under the laws of which such hybrid branch is created, organized for foreign law purposes, or has substantial assets. Thus, the hybrid branch payment will be treated as included within a category of foreign personal holding company income if, taking into account any specific exceptions for that category, the payment would be included within a category of foreign personal holding company income if the branch or branches were treated as separately incorporated for U.S. tax purposes.

(ii) Extent to which controlled foreign corporation and hybrid branches treated as separate entities. For purposes of this section, other than the determination under paragraph (a)(4)(i) of this section, a controlled foreign corporation and its hybrid branch, a partnership and its hybrid branch, or hybrid branches shall not be treated as separate entities. Thus, for example, if a controlled foreign corporation, including all of its hybrid branches, has an overall deficit in earnings and profits to which section 952(c) applies, the limitation of such section on the amount includible in the subpart F income of such corporation will apply. Similarly, for purposes of applying the de minimis and full inclusion rules of section 954(b)(3), a controlled foreign corporation and its hybrid branch, or hybrid branches shall not be treated as separate corporations. Further, a hybrid branch payment that would reduce foreign personal holding company income under section 954(b)(5) if made between two separate entities will not create an expense if made between a controlled foreign corporation and its hybrid branch, a partnership and its hybrid branch, or hybrid branches.

(5) Recharacterization of income attributable to current earnings and profits as subpart F income. (i) General rule. Non-subpart F income of a controlled foreign corporation in an amount equal to the excess of earnings and profits of the controlled foreign corporation for the taxable year over subpart F income, as defined in section 952(a), will be recharacterized as subpart F income under paragraph (a)(1) of this section only to the extent provided under paragraphs (a)(5)(ii) through (vi) of this section.

(ii) Subpart F income. For purposes of determining the excess of current earnings and profits over subpart F income under paragraph (a)(1) of this section, the amount of subpart F income is determined before the application of the rules of this section but after the application of the rules of sections 952(c) and 954(b). Further, such amount is determined by treating the controlled foreign corporation and all of its hybrid branches as a single corporation.

(iii) Recharacterization limited to gross amount of hybrid branch payment. (A) In general. The amount recharacterized as subpart F income under paragraph (a)(1) of this section is limited to the amount of the hybrid branch payment.

(B) Exception for duplicative payments. [Reserved].

(iv) Tax disparity rule. (A) In general. Paragraph (a)(1) of this section will apply only if the hybrid branch payment falls within the tax disparity rule. The hybrid branch payment falls within the tax disparity rule if it is taxed in the year when earned at an effective rate of tax that is less than 90 percent of, and at least 5 percentage points less than, the hypothetical effective rate of tax imposed on the hybrid branch payment, as determined under paragraph (a)(5)(iv)(B) of this section.

(B) Hypothetical effective rate of tax. (1) In general. The hypothetical effective rate of tax imposed on the hybrid branch payment is—

(i) For the taxable year of the payor in which the hybrid branch payment is made, the amount of income taxes that would have been paid or accrued by the payor if the hybrid branch payment had not been made, less the amount of income taxes paid or accrued by the payor; divided by

(ii) The amount of the hybrid branch payment.

(2) Hypothetical effective rate of tax when hybrid branch payment causes or increases loss or deficit. If the hybrid branch payment causes or increases a loss or deficit of the payor for foreign tax purposes, and such loss or deficit can be carried forward or back, the hypothetical effective rate of tax imposed on the hybrid branch payment is the effective rate of tax that would be imposed on the taxable income of the payor for the year in which the payment is made if the payor's taxable income were equal to the amount of the hybrid branch payment.

(C) Examples. The application of this paragraph (a)(5)(iv) is illustrated by the following examples:

Example (1). In 2006, CFC organized in Country A had net income of $60 from manufacturing for Country A tax purposes. It also had a branch (BR) in Country B. BR is a hybrid entity under paragraph (a)(1) of this section. CFC made a payment of $40 to BR, which was a hybrid branch payment under paragraph (a)(6) of this section, and was treated by CFC as a deductible payment for Country A tax purposes. CFC paid $30 of Country A taxes in 2006. It would have paid $50 of Country A taxes without the deductible payment. Country A did not impose any withholding tax on the $40 payment to BR. Country B also did not impose a tax on the $40 received by BR. Therefore, the effective rate of tax on that payment is 0%. Furthermore, the hypothetical effective rate of tax on the $40 hybrid branch payment is 50% ($50-$30/$40). The effective rate of tax (0%) is less than 90% of, and more than 5 percentage points less than, this hypothetical rate of tax of 50%. As a result, the $40 hybrid branch payment falls within the tax disparity rule of this paragraph (a)(5)(iv).

Example (2). Assume the same facts as in Example 1, except that CFC has a loss of $100 for the year for Country A tax purposes. Under Country A law, CFC can carry the loss forward for use in subsequent years. CFC paid no Country A taxes in 2006. The rate of tax in Country A is graduated from 20% to 50%. If the $40 hybrid branch payment were the only item of taxable income of CFC, Country A would have imposed tax at an effective rate of 30%. The effective rate of tax (0%) is less than 90% of, and more than 5 percentage points less than, the hypothetical effective rate of tax (30%) imposed on the hybrid branch payment. As a result, the $40 hybrid branch payment falls within the tax disparity rule of this paragraph (a)(5)(iv).

Example (3). Assume the same facts as in Example 1, except that Country B imposes tax on the $40 hybrid payment to BR at an effective rate of 50%. The effective rate of 50% is equal to the hypothetical effective rate of tax. As a result, the hybrid branch payment does not fall within the tax disparity rule of this paragraph (a)(5)(iv) and, thus, the recharacterization rules of paragraph (a)(1) of this section do not apply. See also the special high tax exception of paragraph (a)(5)(v) of this section.

(v) Special high tax exception. (A) In general. Paragraph (a)(1) of this section shall not apply if the non-subpart F income that would be recharacterized as subpart F income under this section was subject to foreign income taxes imposed by a foreign country or countries at an effective rate that is greater than 90 percent of the maximum rate of tax specified in section 11 for the taxable year of the controlled foreign corporation.

(B) Effective rate of tax. The effective rate of tax imposed on the non-subpart F income that would be recharacterized as subpart F income under this section is determined under the principles of § 1.954-1(d)(2) and (3). See paragraph (b) of this section for the application of section 960 to amounts recharacterized as subpart F income under this section.

(vi) No carryback or carryforward of amounts in excess of current year earnings and profits limitation. To the extent that some or all of the amount required to be recharacterized under this section is not recharacterized as subpart F income because the hybrid branch payment exceeds the amount that can be recharacterized, as determined under paragraph (a)(5)(i) of this section, this excess shall not be carried back or forward to another year.

(6) Definitions for this section. For purposes of this section:

(i) Arrangement shall mean any agreement to pay interest, rents, royalties or similar amounts. It shall also include the declaration and payment of a dividend (but not an agreement or undertaking to pay future, unspecified dividends). An arrangement shall not, however, include the mere formation or acquisition (or similar event) of a hybrid branch that is intended to become a party to an arrangement.

(ii) Entity means any person that is treated by the United States or any jurisdiction as other than an individual.

(iii) Hybrid branch means an entity that—

(A) Is disregarded as an entity separate from its owner for federal tax purposes and is owned (including ownership through branches) by either a controlled foreign corporation or a partnership in which a controlled foreign corporation is a partner (either directly or indirectly through one or more branches or partnerships);

(B) Is treated as fiscally transparent by the United States; and

(C) Is treated as non-fiscally transparent by the country in which the payor entity, any owner of a fiscally-transparent payor entity, the controlled foreign corporation, or any intermediary partnership is created, organized or has substantial assets.

(iv) Hybrid branch payment means the gross amount of any payment (including any accrual) which, under the tax laws of any foreign jurisdiction to which the payor is subject, is regarded as a payment between two separate entities but which, under U.S. income tax principles, is not income to the recipient because it is between two parts of a single entity.

(7) Fiscally transparent and non-fiscally transparent. For purposes of this section an entity shall be treated as fiscally transparent with respect to an interest holder of the entity, if such interest holder is required, under the laws of any jurisdiction to which it is subject, to take into account separately, on a current basis, such interest holder's share of all items which, if separately taken into account by such interest holder, would result in an income tax liability for the interest holder in such jurisdiction different from that which would result if the interest holder did not take the share of such items into account separately. A non-fiscally transparent entity is an entity that is not fiscally transparent under this paragraph (a)(7).

(b) Application of section 960. For purposes of determining the amount of taxes deemed paid under section 960, the amount of non-subpart F income recharacterized as subpart F income under this section shall be treated as attributable to income in separate categories, as defined in § 1.904-5(a)(1), in proportion to the ratio of non-subpart F income in each such category to the total amount of non-subpart F income of the controlled foreign corporation for the taxable year.

(c) Effective dates. *(1) In general.* This section shall be applicable for all amounts paid or accrued in taxable years commencing after [date that is 5 years after publication of the final regulations in the Federal Register], under hybrid arrangements, except as otherwise provided.

(2) Permanent Relief. (i) In general. This section shall not apply to any payments made under hybrid arrangements entered into before June 19, 1998. This exception shall be permanent so long as the arrangement is not substantially modified, within the meaning of paragraph (c)(2)(ii) of this section, on or after June 19, 1998.

(ii) Substantial modification. (A) In general. Substantial modification of a hybrid arrangement includes—

(1) The expansion of the hybrid arrangement (other than de minimis expansion);

(2) A more than 50% change in the U.S. ownership (direct or indirect) of any entity that is a party to the hybrid arrangement, other than—

(i) A transfer of ownership of such party within a controlled group determined under section 1563(a), without regard to section 1563(a)(4); or

(ii) A change in ownership of the entire controlled group (determined under section 1563(a), without regard to section 1563(a)(4)) of which such party is a member;

(3) Any measure taken by a party to the arrangement (or any related party) that materially increases the tax benefit of the hybrid arrangement, regardless of whether such measure alters the legal relationship between the parties to the arrangement. For example, in the case of a hybrid branch payment determined with reference to a percentage of sales, a growth in the amount of the hybrid branch payment (and, thus, the tax benefit) caused by a growth of sales will not, in general, be a substantial modification. However, in the case of a significant sales growth resulting from a transfer of assets by a related party, that transfer would be a measure which materially increased the benefit of the arrangement, and that arrangement would be deemed to have been substantially modified.

(B) Transactions not treated as substantial modification. Substantial modification of a hybrid arrangement does not include—

(1) The daily reissuance of a demand loan by operation of law;

(2) The renewal of a loan, license or rental agreement on the same terms and conditions if—

(i) The renewal occurs pursuant to the terms of the agreement and without more than a de minimis amount of action of any party thereto;

(ii) As contemplated by the original agreement, the same parties agree to renew the agreement without modification; or

(iii) The renewal occurs solely by reason of a subsequent drawdown under a grandfathered master credit facility agreement;

(3) The renewal of a loan, license, or rental agreement by the same parties on terms which do not increase the tax benefit of the arrangement (other than a de minimis increase);

(4) The making of payments under a license agreement in respect of copyrights or patents (or know-how associated with such copyrights or patents), not in existence at the time the agreement was entered into, but only where the development of such property was anticipated by the agreement, and such property is substantially derived from (or otherwise incorporates substantial features of) copyrights and patents (or know-how associated with such copyrights or patents) in existence at the time of, and covered under, the original agreement;

(5) A final transfer pricing adjustment made by the taxation authorities of the jurisdiction in which the tax reduction occurs, so long as such adjustment would not have been a substantial valuation misstatement (as defined in section 6662(e)(1)(B)) if the adjustment had been made by the Internal Revenue Service; or

(6) A de minimis periodic adjustment by the parties to the arrangement made annually (or more frequently) to conform the payments to the requirements of section 482.

§ 1.955A-1 Shareholder's pro rata share of amount of previously excluded subpart F income withdrawn from investment in foreign base company shipping operations.

(a) In general. Section 955 provides rules for determining the amount of a controlled foreign corporation's previously excluded subpart F income which is withdrawn for any taxable year beginning after December 31, 1975, from investment in foreign base company shipping operations. Pursuant to section 951(a)(1)(A)(iii) and the regulations thereunder, a United States shareholder of such controlled foreign corporation must include in his gross income his pro rata share of such amount as determined in accordance with paragraph (c) of this section

(b) Amount withdrawn by controlled foreign corporation. *(1) In general.* For purposes of sections 951 through 964, the amount of a controlled foreign corporation's previously excluded subpart F income which is withdrawn for any taxable year from investment in foreign base company shipping operations is an amount equal to the decrease for such year in such corporation's qualified investments in foreign base company shipping operations. Such decrease is, except as provided in § 1.955A-4—

(i) An amount equal to the excess of the amount of its qualified investments in foreign base company shipping operations at the close of the preceding taxable year over the amount of its qualified investments in foreign base company shipping operations at the close of the taxable year, minus

(ii) The amount (if any) by which recognized losses on sales or exchanges by such corporation during the taxable year of qualified investments in foreign base company shipping operations exceed its recognized gains on sales or exchanges during such year of qualified investments in foreign base company shipping operations,

but only to the extent that the net amount so determined does not exceed the limitation determined under subparagraph (2) of this paragraph. See § 1.955A-2 for determining the amount of qualified investments in foreign base company shipping operations.

(2) Limitation applicable in determining decreases. (i) In general. The limitation referred to in subparagraph (i) of this paragraph for any taxable year of a controlled foreign corporation shall be the lesser of the following two limitations:

(A) The sum of (1) the controlled foreign corporation's earnings and profits (or deficit in earnings and profits) for the taxable year, computed as of the close of the taxable year without diminution by reason of any distribution made during the taxable year, (2) the sum of its earnings and profits (or deficits in earnings and profits) accumulated for prior taxable years beginning after December 31, 1975, and (3) the amount described in subparagraph (3) of this paragraph; or

(B) The sum of the amounts excluded under section 954(b)(2) (see subparagraph (4) of this paragraph) from the foreign base company income of such corporation for all prior taxable years beginning after December 31, 1975, minus the sum of the amounts (determined under this paragraph) of its previously excluded subpart F income withdrawn from investment in foreign base company shipping operations for all such prior taxable years.

(C) For purposes of the immediately preceding subparagraph (B), the amount excluded under section 954(b)(2) for a taxable year of a controlled foreign corporation (the "first corporation") includes (1) an amount excluded under section 954(b)(2) by another corporation which is a member of a related group (as defined in § 1.955A-3(b)(1)) attributable to the first corporation's excess investment (see § 1.955A-3(c)(4)) for a taxable year beginning after December 31, 1983, (2) an amount excluded by a corporation under § 1.954-1(b)(4)(ii)(b) by reason of the application of the carryover rule there set forth, and (3) an amount equal to the first corporation's pro rata share of a group excess deduction (see § 1.955A-3(c)(2)) of a related group for a taxable year beginning after December 31, 1983 (but not in excess of that portion of such pro rata share which would reduce the first corporation's foreign base company shipping income to zero). Such amounts will not be treated as excluded under section 954(b)(2) by any other corporation.

(ii) Certain exclusions from earnings and profits. For purposes of determining the earnings and profits of a controlled foreign corporation under subdivision (i)(A)(1) and (2) of this subparagraph, such earnings and profits shall be considered not to include any amounts which are attributable to—

(A) (1) Amounts which, for the current taxable year, are included in the gross income of a United States shareholder of such controlled foreign corporation under section 951(a)(1)(A)(i), or

(2) Amounts which, for any prior taxable year, have been included in the gross income of a United States shareholder of such controlled foreign corporation under section 951(a) and have not been distributed; or

(B) (1) Amounts which, for the current taxable year, are included in the gross income of a United States shareholder of such controlled foreign corporation under section 551(b) or would be so included under such section but for the fact that such amounts were distributed to such shareholder during the taxable year, or

(2) Amounts which, for any prior taxable year, have been included in the gross income of a United States shareholder of such controlled foreign corporation under section 551(b) and have not been distributed. The rules of this subdivision apply only in determining the limitation on a controlled foreign corporation's decrease in qualified investments in foreign base company shipping operations. See section 959 and the regulations thereunder for rules relating to the exclusion from gross income of previously taxed earnings and profits.

(3) Carryover of amounts relating to investments in less developed country shipping companies. (i) In general. The amount described in this subparagraph for any taxable year of a controlled foreign corporation beginning after December 31, 1975, is the lesser of—

(A) The excess of the amount described in subdivision (ii) of this subparagraph, over the amount described in subdivision (iii) of this subparagraph, or

(B) The limitation determined under subdivision (iv) of this subparagraph.

(ii) Previously excluded subpart F income invested in less developed country shipping companies. The amount described in this subdivision for all taxable years of a controlled foreign corporation beginning after December 31, 1975, is the lesser of—

(A) The amount of such corporation's qualified investments (determined under § 1.955-2 other than paragraph (b)(5) thereof) in less developed country shipping companies described in § 1.955-5(b) at the close of the last taxable year of such corporation beginning before January 1, 1976, or

(B) The limitation determined under § 1.955-1(b)(2)(i)(b) (relating to previously excluded subpart F income) for the first taxable year of such corporation beginning after January 1, 1976.

(iii) Amounts previously carried over. The amount described in this subdivision for any taxable year of a controlled foreign corporation shall be the sum of the excesses determined for each prior taxable year beginning after December 31, 1976, of—

(A) The amount (determined under this paragraph) of such corporation's previously excluded subpart F income withdrawn from investment in foreign base company shipping operations, over

(B) The sum of the earnings and profits determined under subparagraph (2)(1)(A)(1) and (2) of this paragraph.

(iv) Extent attributable to accumulated earnings and profits. The limitation determined under this subdivision for any taxable year of a controlled foreign corporation is the sum of such controlled foreign corporation's earnings and profits (or deficits in earnings and profits) accumulated for taxable years beginning after December 31, 1962, and before January 1, 1976. For purposes of the preceding sentence, earnings and profits shall be determined by excluding the amounts described in subparagraph (2)(ii)(A) and (B) of this paragraph.

(v) Illustration. The application of this subparagraph may be illustrated by the following example:

Example. (a) Throughout the period here involved, A is a United States shareholder of controlled foreign corporation M. M is not a foreign personal holding company, and M uses the calendar year as the taxable year.

(b) The amount described in this subparagraph for M's taxable year 1978 with respect to A is determined as follows, based on the facts shown in the following table:

(1) Investment in less developed country shipping companies on December 31, 1975 (subdivision (ii)(A) amount)	$10,000
(2) Sec. 1.955-1(b)(2)(i)(b) limitation for 1976 (previously excluded subpart F income not withdrawn from investment in less developed countries) (subdivision (ii)(B) amount)	50,000
(3) Subdivision (ii) amount (lesser of lines (1) and (2))	10,000
(4) Subdivision (iii) amount: Excess for 1977 of M's previously excluded subpart F income withdrawn from investment in foreign base country shipping operations, $3,000, over the sum of the amounts determined under subparagraphs (2)(i)(A) (1) and (2) of this paragraph, $1,000	2,000
(5) Excess of line (3) over line (4)	8,000
(6) Sum of M's earnings and profits accumulated for 1962 through 1975, determined on December 31, 1978	26,000
(7) Amount described in this subparagraph for 1978 (lesser of line (5) and line (6))	8,000

(c) For 1978, M's earnings and profits (reduced as provided in § 1.955-1(b)(2)(ii)(a)(1)) are $19,000, and the amount of M's previously excluded subpart F income withdrawn from investment in less developed countries determined under § 1.955-1(b)) is $42,000. Consequently, $23,000 of M's earnings and profits accumulated for 1962 through 1975 are attributable to such $42,000 amount, and will therefore be excluded under subparagraph (2)(i))(A)(2) of this paragraph from M's earnings and profits accumulated for 1962 through 1975, determined as of December 31, 1979. No other portion of M's earnings and profits accumulated for 1962 through 1975 is distributed or included in the gross income of a United States shareholder in 1978.

(d) The amount described in this subparagraph for M's taxable year 1979 with respect to A is determined as follows, based on the additional facts shown in the following table:

(1) Subdivision (ii) amount (line (3) from paragraph (b) of this example)		$10,000
(2) Subdivision (iii) amount (i) Excess for 1977 from line (4) of paragraph (b) of this example	2,000	
(ii) Plus: excess for 1978 of M's previously excluded subpart F income withdrawn from investment in foreign base country shipping operations, $6,000, over the sum of the amounts determined under subparagraphs (2)(i)(A) (1) and (2) of this paragraph, $25,000	0	
(iii) Subdivision (iii) amount		2,000
(3) Excess of line (1) over line (2)(iii)		8,000
(4) Sum of M's earnings and profits accumulated for 1962 through 1975, determined on December 31, 1979 ($26,000 minus $23,000)		3,000
(5) Amount described in this subparagraph for 1979 (lesser of line (3) and line (4))		3,000

(4) Amount excluded. For purposes of subparagraph (2)(i)(B) of this paragraph, the amount excluded under section 954(b)(2) from the foreign base company income of a controlled foreign corporation for any taxable year beginning after December 31, 1975, is the excess of—

(i) The amount which would have been equal to the subpart F income of such corporation for such taxable year if such corporation had had no increase in qualified investments in foreign base company shipping operations for such taxable year, over

(ii) The subpart F income of such corporation for such taxable year.

(c) Shareholder's pro rata share of amount withdrawn by controlled foreign corporation. *(1) In general.* A United States shareholder's pro rata share of a controlled foreign corporation's previously excluded subpart F income withdrawn for any taxable year from investment in foreign base company shipping operations is his pro rata share of the amount withdrawn for such year by such corporation, as determined under paragraph (b) of this section. See section 995(a)(3). Such pro rata share shall be determined in accordance with the principles of § 1.195-1(e).

(2) Special rule. A United States shareholder's pro rata share of the net amount determined under paragraph (b)(2)(i)(B) of this section with respect to any stock of the controlled foreign corporation owned by such shareholder shall be determined without taking into account any amount attributable to a period prior to the date on which such shareholder acquired such stock. See section 1248 and the regulations thereunder for rules governing treatment of gain from sales or exchanges of stock in certain foreign corporations.

(d) Illustrations. The application of this section may be illustrated by the following examples:

Example (1). A, a United States shareholder, owns 60 percent of the only class of stock of M Corporation, a controlled foreign corporation throughout the entire period here involved. Both A and M use the calendar year as a taxable year. The amount of M's previously excluded subpart F income withdrawn for 1978 from investment in foreign base company shipping operations is $40,000, and A's pro rata share of such amount is $24,000 determined as follows based on the facts shown in the following table:

(a) Qualified investments in foreign base company shipping operations at the close of 1977	$125,000
(b) Less: qualified investments in foreign base company shipping operations at the close of 1978	75,000
(c) Balance	50,000
(d) Less: excess of recognized losses ($15,000) over recognized gains ($5,000) on sales during 1978 of qualified investments in foreign base company shipping operations	10,000
(e) Tentative decrease in qualified investment in foreign base company shipping operations for 1978	40,000
(f) Earnings and profits for 1976, 1977, and 1978	45,000
(g) Plus: amount determined under paragraph (b)(3) of this section	0
(h) Earnings and profits limitation	45,000
(i) Excess of amount excluded under section 954(b)(2) from foreign base company income for 1975 ($75,000) over amount of previously excluded subpart F income withdrawn for 1977 from investment in foreign base company shipping operations ($25,000)	50,000
(j) M's amount of previously excluded subpart F income withdrawn for 1978 from investment in foreign base company shipping operations (item (e), but not to exceed the lesser of item (h) or item (i)	40,000
(k) A's pro rata share of M Corporation's amount of previously excluded subpart F in come withdrawn for 1978 from investment in foreign base company shipping operations (60 percent of $40,000)	24,000

Example (2). The facts are the same as in example (1), except that M's earnings and profits (determined under paragraph (b)(2) of this section) for 1976, 1977, and 1978 (item (f)) are $30,000 instead of $45,000. M's amount of previously excluded subpart F income withdrawn for 1978 from investment in foreign base company shipping operations is $30,000. A's pro rata share of such amount is $18,000 (60 percent of $30,000).

Example (3). The facts are the same as in example (1), except that the excess of the amount excluded under section 954(b)(2) for 1976 from M Corporation's foreign base company income over the amount of its previously excluded subpart F income withdrawn for 1977 from investment in foreign base company shipping operations (item (i)) is $20,000 instead of $50,000. M's amount of previously excluded subpart F income withdrawn for 1978 from investment in foreign base company shipping operations is $20,000. A's pro rata share of such amount is $12,000 (60 percent of $20,000).

T.D. 7894, 5/11/83.

§ 1.955A-2 Amount of a controlled foreign corporation's qualified investments in foreign base company shipping operations.

(a) Qualified investments. *(1) In general.* Under section 955(b), for purposes of sections 951 through 964, a controlled foreign corporation's "qualified investments in foreign base company shipping operations" are investments in—

(i) Any aircraft or vessel, to the extent that such aircraft or vessel is used (or hired or leased for use) in foreign commerce,

(ii) Related shipping assets (within the meaning of paragraph (b) of this section),

(iii) Stock or obligations of a related controlled foreign corporation, to the extent provided in paragraph (c) of this section,

(iv) A partnership, to the extent provided in paragraph (d) of this section, and

(v) Stock or obligations of a less developed country shipping company described in § 1.955-5(b), as provided in paragraph (h) of this section.

(2) Coordination of provisions. No amount shall be counted as a qualified investment in foreign base company shipping operations under more than one provision of this section. Thus, for example, if a $10,000 investment in stock of a controlled foreign corporation is treated as a qualified investment in foreign base company shipping operations under both subparagraph (1) (iii) and (v) of this paragraph, then such $10,000 is counted only once as a qualified investment in foreign base company shipping operations.

(3) Definitions. If the meaning of any term is defined or explained in § 1.954-6, then such term shall have the same meaning when used in this section.

(4) Extent of use. (i) For purposes of subparagraph (1)(i) of this paragraph and paragraph (b)(i) of this section, the extent to which an asset of a controlled foreign corporation is used during a taxable year in foreign base company shipping operations shall be determined on the basis of the proportion for such year which the foreign base company shipping income derived from the use of such asset bears to the total gross income derived from the use of such asset.

(ii) For purposes of determining under subdivision (i) of this subparagraph the amounts of foreign base company shipping income and gross income of a controlled foreign corporation—

(A) Such amounts shall be deemed to include an arm's length charge (see § 1.954-6(h)(5)) for services performed by such corporation for itself,

(B) Such amounts shall be deemed to include an arm's length charge for the use of an asset (such as a vessel under construction or laid up for repairs) which is held for use in foreign base company shipping operations, but is not actually so used,

(C) Foreign base company shipping income shall be deemed to include amounts earned in taxable years beginning before January 1, 1976, and

(D) The district director shall make such other adjustments to such amounts as are necessary to properly determine the extent to which any asset is used in foreign base company shipping operations.

(b) Related shipping assets. *(1) In general.* For purposes of this section, the term "related shipping asset" means any asset which is used (or held for use) for or in connection with the production of income described in § 1.954-6(b)(1)(i) or (ii), but only to the extent that such asset is so used (or is so held for use).

(2) Examples. Examples of assets of a controlled foreign corporation which are used (or held for use) for or in connection with the production of income described in subparagraph (1) of this paragraph include—

(i) Money, bank deposits, and other temporary investments which are reasonably necessary to meet the working capital requirements of such corporation in its conduct of foreign base company shipping operations,

(ii) Accounts receivable and evidences of indebtedness which arise from the conduct of foreign base company shipping operations by such corporation or by a related person,

(iii) Amounts (other than amounts described in subdivision (i) of this subparagraph) deposited in bank accounts or invested in readily marketable securities pursuant to a specific, definite, and feasible plan to purchase any tangible asset for use in foreign base company shipping operations,

(iv) Amounts paid into escrow to secure the payment of (A) charter hire for an aircraft, vessel, or other asset used in foreign base company shipping operations or (B) a debt which constitutes a specific charge against such an asset,

(v) Capitalized expenditures (such as progress payments) made under a contract to purchase any asset for use in foreign base company shipping operations,

(vi) Prepaid expense and deferred charges incurred in the course of foreign base company shipping operations,

(vii) Stock acquired and retained to insure a source of supplies or services used in the conduct of foreign base company shipping operations, and

(viii) Currency futures acquired and retained as a hedge against international currency fluctuations in connection with foreign base company shipping operations.

(3) Limitations. (i) Vessels generally. Notwithstanding any other provision of this paragraph, the term "related shipping assets" does not include any money or other intangible assets of a controlled foreign corporation, to the extent that such assets are permitted to accumulate in excess of the reasonably anticipated needs of the business.

(ii) Safe harbor. If a controlled foreign corporation accumulates money or other intangible assets pursuant to a plan to purchase one or more vessels for use in foreign commerce, and if—

(A) The amount so accumulated, plus

(B) The sum of the amounts accumulated by other controlled foreign corporations which are related persons (within the meaning of section 954(d)(3)) pursuant to similar plans, does not exceed 110 percent of a reasonable down payment on each vessel planned to be purchased within a reasonable period, then such plan will be considered to be feasible. For purposes of the preceding sentence, a reasonable down payment shall not exceed 28 percent of the total cost of acquisition. The determination dates applicable to the taxable year of a controlled foreign corporation are those set forth in paragraph (c)(2)(ii) of this section. In the case of accumulation of assets which do not come within the safe harbor limitation of this subdivision (ii), in determining whether such assets have accumulated beyond the reasonably anticipated needs of the business, factors to be taken into account include, but are not limited to, the availability of financing to purchase a vessel and the availability of a vessel suitable for the purposes to which the vessel is to be put.

(iii) Other assets. In determining whether a plan to purchase any asset other than a vessel for use in foreign base company shipping operations is feasible, principles similar to those stated in subdivision (ii) of this subparagraph shall be applied.

(4) Cross-reference. See § 1.954-7(c) for additional illustrations bearing on the application of this paragraph.

(c) Stock and obligations. *(1) In general.* Investments by a controlled foreign corporation (the "first corporation") in stick or obligations of a second controlled foreign corporation which is a related person (within the meaning of section 954(d)(3) are considered to be qualified investments in foreign base company shipping operations to the extent that the assets of such second corporation are used (or held for use) in foreign base company shipping operations. See subparagraph (2) of this paragraph. However, an investment in an obligation of the second corporation will not be considered a qualified investment in foreign base company shipping operations if the obligation represents a liability which constitutes a specific charge (nonrecourse or otherwise) against an asset of the second corporation which is not either—

(i) An aircraft or vessel used (or held for use) to some extent in foreign commerce, or

(ii) An asset described in paragraph (a)(1)(ii) through (v) of this section.

(2) Extent of use. On any determination date applicable to a taxable year of the first corporation, the extent to which the assets of the second corporation are used in foreign base company shipping operations shall be determined on the basis of the proportion which the amount of such second corporation's qualified investments in foreign base company shipping operations bears to its net worth, such proportion to be determined at the close of the second corporation's last taxable year which ends on or before such determination date. For purposes of the preceding sentence—

(i) A controlled foreign corporation's net worth is the total adjusted basis of the corporate assets reduced by the total outstanding principal amount of the corporate liabilities, and

(ii) The determination dates applicable to a taxable year of a controlled foreign corporation are—

(A) Except as provided in (B) of this subdivision, the close of such taxable year and the close of the preceding taxable year, and

(B) With respect to a United States shareholder who has made an election under section 955(b)(3) to determine such corporation's increase in qualified investments in foreign base company shipping operations at the close of the following taxable year, the close of such taxable year and the close of the taxable year immediately following such taxable year.

(3) Illustrations. The application of this paragraph may be illustrated by the following examples:

Example (1). On December 31, 1976, controlled foreign corporation X owns 100 percent of the single class of stock of controlled foreign corporation Y. X and Y both use the calendar year as the taxable year. On December 31, 1976, Y's assets consist of a vessel used in foreign commerce, related shipping assets, and other assets unrelated to its foreign base company shipping operations. On such date Y has qualified investments in foreign base company shipping operations (determined under paragraph (g) of this section) of $60,000, and a net worth of $100,000. If X's investment in the stock of Y is $50,000, then $30,000 of such amount, i.e.,

$$\frac{\$\,60{,}000}{\$100{,}000} \times \$50{,}000$$

is a qualified investment in foreign base company shipping operations.

Example (2). The facts are the same as in example (1), except that on December 31, 1976, Y's assets consist entirely of a vessel used in foreign commerce and related shipping assets. Y has qualified investments in foreign base company shipping operations (determined under paragraph (g) of this section) of $16,000 and (therefore) a net worth of $16,000. If X's investment in the stock of Y is $50,000, then the entire $50,000, i.e.,

$$\frac{\$16{,}000}{\$16{,}000} \times \$50{,}000$$

is a qualified investment in foreign base company shipping operations.

Example (3). On December 31, 1980, controlled foreign corporation J owns two notes of controlled foreign corporation K, which is a related person (within the meaning of section 954(d)(3)). Both J and K use the calendar year as the taxable year. J's adjusted basis in each of the two notes is $100,000. The first note is secured only by the general credit of K. The second note is secured by (and, therefore, constitutes a specific charge on) a hotel owned by K in a foreign country. On December 31, 1980, K has qualified investments in foreign based company shipping operation with an adjusted basis of $500,000 (before applying the rules of paragraph (g) of this section). The adjusted basis of all of K's corporate assets is $1,100,000. K's only liabilities are the two notes. The amount of K's qualified investments in foreign based company shipping operations (determined under paragraph (g) of this section) is $450,000. K's net worth is $900,000. The amount of J's qualified investment in foreign base company shipping operations in respect of the first note is $50,000, i.e.,

$$\frac{\$450{,}000}{\$900{,}000} \times \$100{,}000$$

The amount of J's qualified investment in respect of the second note is zero (see the last sentence of paragraph (c)(1) of this section).

(d) Partnerships. *(1) In general.* A controlled foreign corporation's investment in a partnership at the close of any taxable year of such corporation shall be considered a qualified investment in foreign base company shipping operations to the extent of the proportion which such corporation's foreign base company shipping income for such taxable year would bear to its gross income for such taxable year if—

(i) Such corporation had realized no income other than its distributive share of the partnership gross income, and

(ii) Such corporation's income were adjusted in accordance with the rules stated in paragraph (a)(4)(ii)(B) and (D) of this section.

(2) Transitional rule. For purposes of subparagraph (1)(i) of this paragraph, the controlled foreign corporation's distributive share of the partnership gross income shall not include any amount attributable to income earned by the partnership before the first day of such corporation's first taxable year beginning after December 31, 1975.

(3) Cross-reference. See paragraph (g)(4) of this section for rules relating to the determination of the amount of a controlled foreign corporation's investment in a partnership.

(e) Trusts. *(1) In general.* An investment in a trust is not a qualified investment in a foreign base company shipping operations.

(2) Grantor trusts. Notwithstanding subparagraph (1) of this paragraph, if a controlled foreign corporation is treated as the owner of any portion of a trust under Subpart E of Part I of Subchapter J (relating to grantors and others treated as substantial owners), then for purposes of this section such controlled foreign corporation is deemed to be the actual owner of such portion of the assets of the trust. Accordingly, its investments in such assets (as determined under paragraph (g)(5) of this section) may be treated as a qualified investment in foreign base company shipping operations.

(3) Definitions. For purposes of this section, the term "trust" means a trust as defined in § 301.7701-4.

(f) Excluded property. For purposes of paragraph (a) of this section, property acquired principally for the purpose of artificially increasing the amount of a controlled foreign corporation's qualified investments in foreign base company shipping operations will not be recognized; whether an item of property is acquired principally for such purpose will depend upon all the facts and circumstances of each case. One of the factors that will be considered in making such a determination with respect to an item of property is whether the item is disposed of within 6 months after the date of its acquisition.

(g) Amount attributable to property. *(1) General rule.* For purposes of this section, the amount taken into account under section 955(b)(4) with respect to any property which constitutes a qualified investment in foreign base company shipping operations shall be its adjusted basis as of the applicable determination date, reduced by the outstanding principal amount of any liability (other than a liability described in subparagraph (2) of this paragraph) to which such property is subject on such date including a liability secured only by the general credit of the controlled foreign corporation. Liabilities shall be taken into account in the following order:

(i) The adjusted basis of each and every item of corporate property shall be reduced by any specific charge (nonrecourse or otherwise) to which such item is subject. For this purpose, if a liability constitutes a specific charge against several items of property and cannot definitely be allocated to any single item of property, the specific charge shall be apportioned against each of such items of property in that ratio which the adjusted basis of such item on the applicable determination date bears to the adjusted basis of all such items on such date. The excess against property over the adjusted basis of such property shall be taken into account as a liability secured only by the general credit of the corporation.

(ii) A liability which is evidenced by an open account or which is secured only by the general credit of the controlled foreign corporation shall be apportioned against each and every item of corporate property in that ratio which the adjusted basis of such item on the applicable determination date (reduced as provided in subdivision (i) of this subparagraph) bears to the adjusted basis of all the corporate property on such date (reduced as provided in subdivision (i) of this subparagraph); provided that no liability shall be apportioned under this subdivision against any stock or obligations described in paragraph (h)(1) of this section.

(2) Excluded charges. For purposes of subparagraph (1) of this paragraph, a liability created principally for the purpose of artificially increasing or decreasing the amount of a controlled foreign corporation's qualified investments in foreign

base company shipping operations will not be recognized. Whether a liability is created principally for such purpose will depend upon all the facts and circumstances of each case. One of the factors that will be considered in making such a determination with respect to a loan is whether the loan was both created after November 20, 1974, and is from a related person, as defined in section 954(d)(3) and paragraph (e) of § 1.954-1. Another such factor is whether the liability was created after March 29, 1975, in a taxable year beginning before January 1, 1976. For purposes of this paragraph (g)(2), payments on liabilities which are represented by an open account are credited against the account transactions arising earliest in time.

(3) Statement required. If for purposes of this section the adjusted basis of property which constitutes a qualified investment in foreign base company shipping operations by a controlled foreign corporation is reduced on the ground that such property is subject to a liability, each United States shareholder shall attach to his return a statement setting forth the adjusted basis of the property before the reduction and the amount and nature of the reduction.

(4) Partnership interest. If a controlled foreign corporation is a partner in a partnership, its investment in the partnership taken into account under section 955(b)(4) shall be its adjusted basis in the partnership determined under section 722 or 742, adjusted as provided in section 705, and reduced as provided in subparagraph (1) of this paragraph. (However, if the partnership is not engaged solely in the conduct of foreign base company shipping operations, such amount shall be taken into account only to the extent provided in paragraph (d)(1) of this section).

(5) Grantor trust. If a controlled foreign corporation is deemed to own a portion of the assets of a trust under paragraph (e)(2) of this section then the amount taken into account under section 955(b)(4) with respect to such assets shall be determined as provided in subparagraph (1) of this paragraph by the application of the following rules:

(i) Such controlled foreign corporation's adjusted basis in such assets shall be deemed to be a proportionate share of the trust's adjusted basis in such assets, and

(ii) A proportionate share of the liabilities of the trust shall be deemed to be liabilities of such controlled foreign corporation and to constitute specific charges against such assets.

(6) Translation into United States dollars. The amounts determined in accordance with this paragraph shall be translated into United States dollars in accordance with the principles of § 1.964-1(e)(4).

(h) Investments in shipping companies under prior law. *(1) In general.* If an amount invested in stock or obligations of a less developed country shipping company described in § 1.955-5(b) is treated as a qualified investment in less developed countries under § 1.955-2 (applied without regard to paragraph (b)(5)(ii) thereof) on the applicable determination date for purposes of section 954(g) or section 955(a)(2) with respect to a taxable year beginning after December 31, 1975, then such amount shall be treated as a qualified investment in foreign base company shipping operations on such determination date. See section 955(b)(5).

(2) Effect on prior law. See § 1.955-2(b)(5)(ii) for the rule that investments which are treated as qualified investments in foreign base company shipping operations under subparagraph (1) of this paragraph shall not be treated as qualified investments in less developed countries for purposes of section 951(a)(1)(A)(ii).

(3) Illustration. The application of this paragraph may be illustrated by the following example:

Example. (a) Throughout the period here involved, controlled foreign corporation X owns 100 percent of the single class of stock of controlled foreign corporation Y, X and Y each use the calendar years as the taxable year. At the close of 1975, X's $50,000 investment in the stock of Y is treated as a qualified investment in less developed countries under § 1.955-2 (applied without regard to § 1.955-2(b)(5)(ii), and Y is a less developed country shipping company described in § 1.955-5(b).

(b) On December 31, 1976, Y is still a less developed country shipping company and X's $50,000 investment in the stock of Y is still treated as a qualified investment in less developed countries under § 1.955-2 (applied without regard to § 1.955-2(b)(5)(ii). Under subparagraph (1) of this paragraph X's entire $50,000 investment in the stock of Y is treated as a qualified investment in foreign base company shipping operations.

(c) For 1977, Y's gross income is $10,000 and Y's foreign base company shipping income is $7,500. Since Y fails to meet the 80-percent income test of § 1.955-5(b)(1). Y is no longer a less developed country shipping company described in § 1-955-5(b), and X's investment in the stock of Y is no longer treated as a qualified investment in less developed countries under § 1.955-2 (applied without regard to § 1.955-2(b)(5)(ii). However, assume that on December 31, 1977, Y's net worth (as defined in paragraph (c)(2)(1) of this section) is $100,000, that Y's qualified investments in foreign base company shipping operations (determined under this section) on December 31, 1977, are $75,000, and that X's investment in the stock of Y (as determined under paragraph (g) of this section) continues to be $50,000. Then $67,500, i.e.,

$$\frac{\$\,75{,}000}{\$100{,}000} \times \$50{,}000$$

of X's $50,000 investment in the stock of Y is treated as a qualified investment in foreign company shipping operations under paragraph (c) of this section.

(d) For 1978, all of Y's gross income is foreign base company shipping income. Although Y is again a less developed country shipping company described in § 1.955-5(b), X's investment in the stock of Y is no longer treated as a qualified investment in less developed countries under § 1.955-2(b)(5)(iii). Thus, X's investment in the stock of Y is not treated as a qualified investment in foreign base company shipping operations under subparagraph (1) of this paragraph. However, X's investment in the stock of Y may be so treated under another provision of this section, as was the case in item (c) of this example.

T.D. 7894, 5/11/83, amend T.D. 7959, 5/25/84.

§ 1.955A-3 Election as to qualified Investments by related persons.

(a) In general. If a United States shareholder elects the benefits of section 955(b) with respect to a related group (as defined in paragraph (b)(1) of this section) of controlled foreign corporations, then an investment in foreign base company shipping operation made by one member of such group will be treated as having been made by another member to the extent provided in paragraph (c)(4) of this section, and each member will be subject to the other provisions of paragraph (c) of this section. An election once made shall apply for the taxable year for which it is made and for all subsequent years unless the election is revoked or a new election is made to add one or more controlled foreign corporations to election coverage. For the manner of making an election under section 955(b)(2), and for rules relating to the revocation of such an election, see paragraph (d) of this section. For rules relating to the coordination of sections 955(b)(2) and 955(b)(3), see paragraph (e) of this section.

(b) Related group. *(1) Related group defined.* The term "related group" means two or more controlled foreign corporations, but only if all of the following requirements are met:

(i) All such corporations use the same taxable year.

(ii) The same United States shareholder controls each such corporation within the meaning of section 954(d)(3) at the end of such taxable year, and

(iii) Such United States shareholder elects to treat such corporations as a related group.

(iv) If any of the corporations is on a 52-53 week taxable year and if all of the taxable years of the corporations end within the same 7-day period, the rule of paragraph (b)(1)(i) of this section shall be deemed satisfied.

(v) An election under paragraph (b)(1)(iii) of this section will not be valid in the case of an election by a U.S. shareholder (the "first U.S. shareholder") if—

(A) The first U.S. shareholder controls a second U.S. shareholder,

(B) The second U.S. shareholder controls one or more controlled foreign corporations, and

(C) Any of the controlled foreign corporations are the subject of the election by the first U.S. shareholder, unless the second U.S. shareholder consents to the election by the first U.S. shareholder.

(2) Group taxable years defined. The "group taxable year" is the common taxable year of a related group.

(3) Limitation. If a United States shareholder elects to treat two or more corporations as a related group for a group taxable year (the "first group taxable year"), then such United States shareholder (and any other United States shareholder which is controlled by such shareholder) may not also elect to treat two or more other corporations as a related group for a group taxable year any day of which falls within the first group taxable year.

(4) Illustrations. The application of this paragraph may be illustrated by the following examples:

Example (1). Domestic corporation M owns 100 percent of the only class of stock of controlled foreign corporations A, B, C, D, and E. A, B, and C use the calendar year as the taxable year. D and E use the fiscal year ending on June 30 as the taxable year. M may elect to treat A, B and C as a related group. However, M may not elect to treat C, D, and E as a related group.

Example (2). The facts are the same as in example (1). In addition, M elects to treat A, B, and C as a related group for the group taxable year which ends on December 31, 1976. M may not also elect to treat D and E as a related group for the group taxable year ending on June 30, 1977.

Example (3). United States shareholder A owns 60 percent of the only class of stock of controlled foreign corporation X and 40 percent of the only class of stock of controlled foreign corporation Y. United States shareholder B owns the other 40 percent of the stock of X and the other 60 percent of the stock of Y. Neither A nor B (nor both together) may elect to treat X and Y as a related group.

(c) Effect of election. If a United States shareholder elects to treat two or more controlled foreign corporations as a related group for any group taxable year then, for purposes of determining the foreign base company income (see § 1.954-1) and the increase or decrease in qualified investments in foreign base company shipping operations (see §§ 1.954-7. 1.955A-1, and 1.955A-4) of each member of such group for such year, the following rules shall apply:

(1) Intragroup dividends. The gross income of each member of the related group shall be deemed not to include dividends received from any other member of such group, to the extent that such dividends are attributable (within the meaning of § 1.954-6(f)(4)) to foreign base company shipping income. In determining net foreign base company shipping income, deductions allocable to intragroup dividends attributable to foreign base company shipping income shall not be allowed.

(2) Group excess deduction. (i) The deductions allocable under § 1.954-1(c) to the foreign base company shipping income of each member of the related group shall be deemed to include such member's pro rata share of the group excess deduction.

(ii) The group excess deduction for the group taxable year is the sum of the excesses for each member of the related group (having an excess) of—

(A) The member's deductions (determined without regard to this subparagraph) allocable to foreign base company shipping income for such year, over

(B) The member's foreign base company shipping income for such year.

(iii) A member's pro rata share of the group excess deduction is the amount which bears the same ratio to such group excess deduction as—

(A) The excess of such member's foreign base company shipping income over the deductions (so determined) allocable thereto, bears to

(B) The sum of such excesses for each member of the related group having an excess.

(iv) For purposes of this subparagraph, "foreign base company shipping income" means foreign base company shipping income (as defined in § 1.954-6), reduced by excluding therefrom all amounts which are—

(A) Excluded from subpart F income under section 952(b) (relating to exclusion of United States income) or

(B) Excluded from foreign base company income under section 954(b)(4) (relating to exception for foreign corporation not availed of to reduce taxes).

(v) The application of this subparagraph may be illustrated by the following example:

Example. Controlled foreign corporations X, Y, and Z are a related group for calendar year 1976. The excess group deduction for 1976 is $9, X's pro rata share of the group excess deduction is $6, and Y's pro rata share is $3, determined as follows on the basis of the facts shown in the following table:

	X	Y	Z	Group
(1) Gross shipping income	$100	$90	$90	—
(2) Shipping deductions	60	70	80	—
(3) Net shipping income	40	20	(9)	—
(4) Group excess deduction	—	—	—	80
(5) X's pro rata share of group excess deduction ($90 × $40/$60)	6	—	—	—

(6) Y's pro rata share of group excess deduction ($9 × $20/$60)	—	3	— —

(3) Intragroup investments. On both of the determination dates applicable to the group taxable year for purposes of section 954(g) or section 955(a)(2), the qualified investments in foreign base company shipping operations of each member of the related group shall be deemed not to include stock of any other member of the related group. In addition, neither the gains nor the losses on dispositions of such stock during the group taxable year shall be taken into account under § 1.955A-1(b)(1)(ii) in determining the decrease in qualified investments in foreign base company shipping operations of any member of such related group.

(4) Group excess investment. (i) On the later (and only the later) of the two determination dates applicable to the group taxable year for purposes of section 954(g) or section 955(a)(2), the qualified investments in foreign base company shipping operations of each member of the related group shall be deemed to include such member's pro rata share of the group excess investment.

(ii) The group excess investment for the group taxable year is the sum of the excess for each member of the related group (having an excess) of—

(A) The member's increase in qualified investments in foreign base company shipping operations (determined under § 1.954-7 after the application of subparagraph (3) of this paragraph) for such year, over

(B) The member's foreign base company shipping income for such year.

(iii) A member's pro rata share of the group excess investment is the amount which bears the same ratio to such group excess investment as—

(A) Such member's shortfall, in qualified investments bears to

(B) the sum of the shortfalls in qualified investments of each member of such related group having a shortfall.

(iv) If a member has an increase in qualified investments in foreign base company shipping operations (determined as provided in § 1.954-7 after the application of subparagraph (3) of this paragraph) for the group taxable year, then such member's "shortfall in qualified investments" is the excess of—

(A) Such member's foreign base company shipping income for such year, over

(B) Such increase.

(v) If a member has a decrease in qualified investments in foreign base company shipping operations (determined under § 1.955A-1(b)(1) or § 1.955A-4(a), whichever is applicable, after the application of subparagraph (3) of this paragraph) for the group taxable year, then such member's "shortfall in qualified investments" is the sum of—

(A) Such member's foreign base company shipping income for such year and

(B) Such decrease.

(vi) For purposes of this subparagraph, "foreign base company shipping income" means foreign base company shipping income (as defined in subparagraph (2)(iv) of this paragraph), reduced by the deductions allocable thereto under § 1.954-1(c) (including the additional deductions described in subparagraph (2) of this paragraph).

(vii) The application of paragraphs (c)(1), (3), and (4) of this section may be illustrated by the following example:

Example. (a) Controlled foreign corporations R, S, and T are a related group for calendar year 1977. R and S do not own the stock of any member of the related group.

(b) On December 31, 1977, T has qualified investments in foreign base company shipping operations (determined without regard to paragraphs (c)(3) and (4)) of $105, of which $15 consists of stock of S. After application of paragraph (c)(3) (but before application of paragraph (c)(4)), on December 31, 1977, T has qualified investments in foreign base company shipping operations of $90, determined as follows:

(1) Qualified investments (determined without regard to paragraph (c)(3)) on December 31, 1977	$105
(2) Less: Qualified investments in stock of another member of a related group (as required by paragraph (c)(3))	15
(3) Balance	90

(c) During 1977, T's foreign base company shipping income is $180, determined without regard to paragraph (c)(1). Included in the $180 is $5 in dividends in respect of T's stock in S. During 1977, T has shipping deductions of $91. Of T's shipping deductions, $1 is allocable to the dividends from S. After application of paragraph (c)(1), T's net shipping income during 1977 is $85, determined as follows:

(1) Foreign base company shipping income		$180
(2) Less: intragroup dividends (as required by paragraph (c)(1))		5
(3) Balance		175
(4) Shipping deductions	$91	
(5) Less: deductions allocable to intragroup dividends (as required by paragraph (c)(1)) . . .	1	
(6) Balance	90	
(7) Net shipping income (line (3) minus line (6))		85

(d) During 1977 (without regard to paragraph (c)(4)), R's increase in qualified investments in foreign base company shipping operations is $120; S's decrease is $55; and T's increase is $35, determined on the basis of the facts shown in the following table. In all cases, the listed amounts of qualified investments on December 31, 1976, reflect any adjustments required by paragraph (c)(3) for 1976, but not any adjustment required by paragraph (c)(4) for 1976 (see §§ 1.955A-3(c)(3) and (4)(i)).

	R	S	T
(1) Qualified Investments on December 31, 1977 (in the case of T, taken from line (3) of part (b) of this example) . . .	$220	$150	$ 90
(2) Qualified investments on December 31, 1976	100	205	55
(3) Increase (decrease) (line (1) minus line (2))	120	(55)	35

(e) In 1977, R's net shipping income is $100; S's is $95; and T's is $85, determined as follows:

	R	S	T
(1) Gross foreign base company shipping income (in the case of T, taken from line (3) of part (c) of this example) . . .	$200	$180	$175
(2) Shipping deductions (in the case of T, taken from line (6) of part (c) of this example)	100	85	90

(3) Net shipping income (line (1) minus line (2))	100	95	85

(f) By application of paragraph (c)(4) for 1977, S's pro rata share of the group excess investment is $15, and T's pro rata share is $5, determined as follows:

	R	S	T	Group
(1) Net shipping income (taken from line (3) of part (e) of this example	$100	$ 95	$ 85	—
(2) Increase (decrease) in qualified investments (d) of this example	120	(22)	35	—
(3) Excess investment	20	—	—	$ 20
(4) Shortfall	—	150	50	200
(5) S's pro rata share of group excess investment ($20 × $150/$200)	—	15	—	—
(6) T's pro rata share of group excess investment ($20 × $50/$200)	—	—	5	—

(g) After application of paragraph (c)(4), for purposes of determining their increase or decrease in qualified investments in foreign base company shipping operations for 1977, on December 31, 1977, the amount of R's qualified investments is $200; the amount of S's is $165; and the amount of T's is $95, determined as follows:

	R	S	T
(1) Qualified investments on December 31, 1977 (taken from line (1) of part (d) of this example)	$220	$50	$90
(2) Plus: pro rata share of group excess investment (as required by paragraph (c)(4)) (taken from lines (5) and (6) of part (f) of this example)	—	15	5
(3) Minus: Excess investment treated as investments of related group members (taken from line (3) of part (f) of this example)	20	—	—
(4) Total qualified investments	200	165	95

(h) After application of paragraph (c)(1), (3), and (4), during 1977, R's increase in qualified investments in foreign base company shipping operations is $100; S's decrease is $40; and T's increase is $40, determined as set forth in the table below. In all cases, the listed amounts of qualified investments on December 31, 1976, reflect any similar adjustments required by paragraph (c)(3) for 1976, but not any adjustment required by paragraph (c)(4) for 1976 (see §§ 1.955A-3(c)(3) and (4)(i)).

	R	S	T
(1) Qualified investments on December 31, 1977 (taken from line (4) of part (g) of this example)	$200	$165	$95
(2) Qualified investments on December 31, 1976 (see line (2) of part (d) of this example)	100	205	55
(3) Increase (decrease) (line (1) minus line (2))	100	(40)	40

(5) Collateral effect. (i) An election under this section by a United States shareholder to treat two or more controlled foreign corporations as a related group for a group taxable year shall have no effect on—

(A) Any other United States shareholder (including a minority shareholder of a member of such related group),

(B) Any other controlled foreign corporation, and

(C) The foreign personal holding company income, foreign base company sales income, and foreign base company services income, and the deductions allocable under § 1.954-1(c) thereto, of any member of such related group.

(ii) See § 1.952-1(c)(2)(ii) for the effect of an election under this section on the computation of earnings and profits and deficits in earnings and profits under section 952(c) and (d).

(iii) The application of this subparagraph may be illustrated by the following example:

Example. United States shareholder A owns 80 percent of the only class of stock of controlled foreign corporations X and Y. United States shareholder B owns the other 20 percent of the stock of X and Y. X and Y both use the calendar year as the taxable year. A elects to treat X and Y as a related group for 1977. For purposes of determining the amounts includible in B's gross income under section 951(a) in respect of X and Y, the election made by A shall be disregarded and all of B's computations shall be made without regard to this section, as illustrated in § 1.952-3(d).

(d) Procedure. *(1) Time and manner of making election.* A United States shareholder shall make an election under this section to treat two or more controlled foreign corporations as a related group for a group taxable year and subsequent years by filing a statement to such effect with the return for the taxable year within which or with which such group taxable year ends. The statement shall include the following information:

(i) The name, address, taxpayer identification number, and taxable year of the United States shareholder;

(ii) The name, address, and taxable year of each controlled foreign corporation which is a member of the related group and is to be subject to the election; and

(iii) A schedule showing the calculations by which the amounts described in this section have been determined for the taxable year for which the election is first effective. With respect to each subsequent taxable year to which the election applies, a new schedule showing calculations of such amounts for that taxable year must be filed with the return for that taxable year. A consent to an election required by paragraph (b)(1)(v) of this section shall include the same information required for the election statement.

(2) Revocation. (i) Except as provided in subdivision (ii) of this subparagraph, an election under this section by a United States shareholder shall be binding for the group taxable year for which it is made and for subsequent years.

(ii) Upon application by the United States shareholder (and any other United States shareholder controlled by such shareholder which consented under paragraph (b)(1)(v) of this section to the election), an election made under this section may, subject to the approval of the Commissioner, be revoked. An application to revoke the election, as of a specified group taxable year, with respect to one or more (but not all) controlled foreign corporations, subject to an election shall be deemed to be an application to revoke the election. Approval will not be granted unless a material and substantial change in circumstances occurs which could not have been anticipated when the election was made. The application for consent to revocation shall be made by mailing a letter for such purpose to Commissioner of Internal Revenue, Attention: T:C:C, Washington, D.C. 20224, containing a statement of the facts which justify such consent. If a member of a related group subject to an election ceases to meet the requirements of paragraph (b) of this section for membership in the group by reason of any action taken by it or any member of the group or the electing United States shareholder, then the election will be deemed to be revoked as of the beginning of the taxable year in which such action occurred. If such action is taken principally for the purpose of revoking the election without applying for and obtaining the approval of the Commissioner to the revocation, then no further election covering any member of that related group may be made by any United States shareholder for the remainder of the taxable year in which the action occurred and the five succeeding taxable years.

(e) Coordination with section 955(b)(3). If a United States shareholder elects under this section to treat two or more controlled foreign corporations as a related group for any taxable year, and if such United States shareholder is required under § 1.955A-4(c)(2) for purposes of filing any return to estimate the qualified investments in foreign base company shipping operations of any member of such group, then such United States shareholder shall, for purposes of filing such return, determine the amount includible in his gross income in respect of each member of such related group on the basis of such estimate. If the actual amount of such investments is not the same as the amount of the estimate, the United States shareholder shall immediately notify the Commissioner. The Commissioner will thereupon redetermine the amount of tax of such United States shareholder for the year or years with respect to which the incorrect amount was taken into account. The amount of tax, if any, due upon such redetermination shall be paid by the United States shareholder upon notice and demand by the district director. The amount of tax, if any, shown by such redetermination to have been overpaid shall be credited or refunded to the United States shareholder in accordance with the provisions of sections 6402 and 6511 and the regulations thereunder. If a United States shareholder elects under this section and if the United States shareholder has made an election under section 955(b)(3) as to at least one member of the related group, then the qualified investment amounts necessary for the calculations of paragraphs (c)(3) and (4) of this section shall be obtained, for each member of the related group, as of the determination dates applicable to each of the members.

(f) Illustrations. The application of this section may be illustrated by the following examples:

Example (1). (a) Controlled foreign corporations X and Y are wholly owned subsidiaries of domestic corporation M, X and Y use the calendar year as the taxable year. For 1977, X and Y are not export trade corporations (as defined in section 971(a)), nor have they any income derived from the insurance of United States risks (within the meaning of section 963(a)). M does not elect to treat X and Y as a related group for 1977.

(b) For 1977, X and Y each have gross income (determined as provided in § 1.951-6(h)(1)) of $1,000. X's foreign base company income is $20 and Y's foreign base company income is $0, determined as follows, based on the facts shown in the following table:

	X	Y
(1) Foreign lease company shipping income	$1,000	$1,000
(2) Less: amounts excluded from subpart F income under section 952(b) (relating to U.S. income) and amounts excluded from foreign base company income under section 945(b)(4) (relating to corporation not availed of to reduced taxes)	0	0
(3) Balance	1,000	1,000
(4) Less: deductions allocable under Sec. 1.954-1(c) to balance	800	1,040
(5) Remaining balance	200	0
(6) Less: increase in qualified investments in foreign base company shipping operations	180	
(7) Foreign base company income	20	

(c) For 1977, Y has a withdrawal of previously excluded subpart F income from investment in foreign base company shipping operations of $20, determined as follows, on the basis of the facts shown in the following table:

(1) Qualified investments in foreign base company shipping operations at Dec. 31, 1976	$1,210
(2) Less: qualified investments in foreign base company shipping operations at Dec. 31, 1977	1,170
(3) Balance	40
(4) Less: excess of recognized losses over recognized gains on sales during 1977 of qualified investments in foreign base company shipping operations	20
(5) Tentative decrease in qualified investments in foreign base company shipping operations for 1977	20
(6) Limitation described in Sec. 1.955A-1(b)(2)	160
(7) Y's amount of previously excluded subpart F income withdrawn from investment in foreign base company shipping operations (lesser of lines (5) and (6))	20

Example (2). (a) The facts are the same as in example (1), except that M does elect to treat X and Y as a related group for 1977.

(b) The group excess deduction, which is solely attributable to Y's net shipping loss, is $40 (i.e., $1,040 – $1,000). Since X is the only member of the related group with net shipping income, X's pro rata share of the group excess deduction is the entire $40 amount.

(c) X's foreign base company income for 1977 is zero, determined as follows:

(1) Preliminary net foreign base company shipping income (line (b)(5) of example (1))	$200
(2) Less: X's pro rata share of group excess deduction	40
(3) Remaining balance	160
(4) Less: increase in qualified investments in foreign base company shipping operations	180
(5) Foreign base company income	0

(d) The group excess investment, which is solely attributable to X's excess investment, is $20 (i.e., $180 minus $160). Since Y is the only member of the related group with a shortfall in qualified investments, Y's share of the group excess investment is the entire $20 amount.

(e) During 1976 and 1977, Y owns no stock of X. Y's withdrawal of previously excluded subpart F income from investment in foreign base company shipping operations for 1977 is zero, determined as follows:

(1) Qualified investments at Dec. 31, 1976	$1,210
(2) (i) Qualified investments at Dec. 31, 1977 (determined without regard to paragraph (c)(4) of this section)	1,170
(ii) Y's pro rata share of group excess investment	20
(iii) Total qualified investments at Dec. 31, 1977 (Line (i) plus line (ii)	1,190
(3) Balance (line (1) minus line (2)(iii)	20
(4) Less: excess of recognized losses over recognized gains on sales during 1977 of qualified investments in foreign base company shipping operations	20
(5) Decrease in qualified investments for 1977	0

T.D. 7894, 5/11/83, amend T.D. 7959, 5/25/84.

§ 1.955A-4 Election as to date of determining qualified investment in foreign base company shipping operations.

(a) Nature of election. In lieu of determining the increase under the provisions of section 954(g) and § 1.954-7(a) or the decrease under the provisions of section 955(a)(2) and § 1.955A-1(b) in a controlled foreign corporation's qualified investments in foreign base company shipping operations for a taxable year in the manner provided in such provisions, a United States shareholder of such controlled foreign corporation may elect, under the provisions of section 955(b)(3) and this section, to determine such increase in accordance with the provisions of § 1.954-7(b) and to determine such decrease by ascertaining the amount by which—

(1) Such controlled foreign corporation's qualified investments in foreign base company shipping operations at the close of such taxable year exceed its qualified investments in foreign base company shipping operations at the close of the taxable year immediately following such taxable year, and reducing such excess by

(2) The amount determined under § 1.955A-1(b)(1)(ii) for such taxable year subject to the limitation provided in § 1.995A-1(b)(2) for such taxable year. An election under this section may be made with respect to each controlled foreign corporation with respect to which a person is a United States shareholder within the meaning of section 951(b), but the election may not be exercised separately with respect to the increases and the decreases of such controlled foreign corporation. If an election is made under this section to determine the increase of a controlled foreign corporation in accordance with the provisions of § 1.954-7(b), subsequent decreases of such controlled foreign corporation shall be determined in accordance with this paragraph and not in accordance with § 1.955A-1(b).

(b) Time and manner of making election. *(1) Without consent.* An election under this section with respect to a controlled foreign corporation shall be made without the consent of the Commissioner by a United States shareholder's filing a statement to such effect with his return for his taxable year in which or with which ends the first taxable year of such controlled foreign corporation in which—

(i) Such shareholder is a United States shareholder, and

(ii) Such controlled foreign corporation realizes foreign base company shipping income, as defined in § 1.954-6.

The statement shall contain the name and address of the controlled foreign corporation and identification of such first taxable year of such corporation.

(2) With consent. An election under this section with respect to a controlled foreign corporation may be made by a United States shareholder at any time with the consent of the Commissioner. Consent will not be granted unless the United States shareholder and the Commissioner agree to the terms, conditions, and adjustments under which the election will be effected. The application for consent to elect shall be made by the United States shareholder's mailing a letter for such purpose to the Commissioner of Internal Revenue, Washington, D.C. 20224. The application shall be mailed before the close of the first taxable year of the controlled foreign corporation with respect to which the shareholder desires to compute an amount described in section 954(b)(2) in accordance with the election provided in this section. The application shall include the following information.

(i) The name, address, and taxpayer identification number, and taxable year of the United States shareholder;

(ii) The name and address of the controlled foreign corporation;

(iii) The first taxable year of the controlled foreign corporation for which income is to be computed under the election;

(iv) The amount of the controlled foreign corporation's qualified investments in foreign base company shipping operations at the close of its preceding taxable year; and

(v) The sum of the amounts excluded under section 954(b)(2) and § 1.954-1(b)(1) from the foreign base company income of the controlled foreign corporation for all prior taxable years during which such shareholder was a United States shareholder of such corporation and the sum of the amounts of its previously excluded subpart F income withdrawn from investment in foreign base company shipping operations for all prior taxable years during which such shareholder was a United States shareholder of such corporation.

(c) Effect of election. *(1) General.* Except as provided in subparagraphs (3) and (4) of this paragraph, an election under this section with respect to a controlled foreign corporation shall be binding on the United States shareholder and shall apply to all qualified investments in foreign base company shipping operations acquired, or disposed of, by such controlled foreign corporation during the taxable year following its taxable year for which income is first computed under the election and during all succeeding taxable years of such corporation.

(2) Returns. Any return of a United States shareholder required to be filed before the completion of a period with respect to which determinations are to be made as to a controlled foreign corporation's qualified investments in foreign base company shipping operations for purposes of computing such shareholder's taxable income shall be filed on the basis of an estimate of the amount of the controlled foreign corporation's qualified investments in foreign base company shipping operations at the close of the period. If the actual amount of such investments is not the same as the amount of the estimate, the United States shareholder shall immediately notify the Commissioner. The Commissioner will thereupon redetermine the amount of tax of such United States shareholder for the year or years with respect to which the incor-

rect amount was taken into account. The amount of tax, if any, due upon such redetermination shall be paid by the United States shareholder upon notice and demand by the district director. The amount of tax, if any, shown by such redetermination to have been overpaid shall be credited or refunded to the United States shareholder in accordance with the provisions of sections 6402 and 6511 and the regulations thereunder.

(3) Revocation. Upon application by the United States shareholder, the election made under this section may, subject to the approval of the Commissioner, be revoked. Approval will not be granted unless the United States shareholder and the Commissioner agree to the terms, conditions, and adjustments under which the revocation will be effected. Unless such agreement provides otherwise, the change in the controlled foreign corporation's qualified investments in foreign base company shipping operations for its first taxable year for which income is computed without regard to the election previously made will be considered to be zero for purposes of effectuating the revocation. The application for consent to revocation shall be made by the United States shareholder's mailing a letter for such purpose to the Commissioner of Internal Revenue, Washington, D.C. 20224. The application shall be mailed before the close of the first taxable year of the controlled foreign corporation with respect to which the shareholder desires to compute the amounts described in section 954(b)(2) or 955(a) without regard to the election provided in this section. The application shall include the following information:

(i) The name, address, and taxpayer identification number of the United States shareholder:

(ii) The name and address of the controlled foreign corporation;

(iii) The taxable year of the controlled foreign corporation for which such amounts are to be computed;

(iv) The amount of the controlled foreign corporation's qualified investments in foreign base company shipping operations at the close of its preceding taxable year;

(v) The sum of the amounts excluded under section 954(b)(2) and § 1.954-1(b)(1) from the foreign base company income of the controlled foreign corporation for all prior taxable years during which such shareholder was a United States shareholder of such corporation and the sum of the amounts of its previously excluded subpart F income withdrawn from investment in foreign base company shipping operations for all prior taxable years during which such shareholder was a United States shareholder of such corporation; and

(vi) The reasons for the request for consent to revocation.

(4) Transfer of stock. If during any taxable year of a controlled foreign corporation—

(i) A United States shareholder who has made an election under this section with respect to such controlled foreign corporation sells, exchanges, or otherwise disposes of all or part of his stock in such controlled foreign corporation, and

(ii) The foreign corporation is a controlled foreign corporation immediately after the sale, exchange, or other disposition, then, with respect to the stock so sold, exchanged, or disposed of, the change in the controlled foreign corporation's qualified investments in foreign base company shipping operations for such taxable year shall be considered to be zero. If the United States shareholder's successor in interest is entitled to and does make an election under paragraph (b)(1) of this section to determine the controlled foreign corporation's increase in qualified investments in foreign base company shipping operations for the taxable year in which he acquires such stock, such increase with respect to the stock so acquired shall be determined in accordance with the provisions of § 1.954-7(b)(1). If the controlled foreign corporation realizes no foreign base company income from which amounts are excluded under section 954(b)(2) and § 1.954-1(b)(1) for the taxable year in which the United States shareholder's successor in interest acquires such stock and such successor in interest makes an election under paragraph (b)(1) of this section with respect to a subsequent taxable year of such controlled foreign corporation, the increase in the controlled foreign corporation's qualified investments in foreign base company shipping operations for such subsequent taxable year shall be determined in accordance with the provisions of § 1.954-7(b)(2).

(d) Illustrations. The application of this section may be illustrated by the following examples:

Example (1). Foreign corporation A is a wholly owned subsidiary of domestic corporation M. Both corporations use the calendar year as a taxable year. In a statement filed with its return for 1977, M makes an election under section 955(b)(3) and the election remains in force for the taxable year 1978. At December 31, 1978, A's qualified investments in foreign base company shipping operations amount to $100,000; and, at December 31, 1979, to $80,000. For purposes of paragraph (a)(1) of this section, A Corporation's decrease in qualified investments in foreign base company shipping operations for the taxable year 1978 is $20,000 and is determined by ascertaining the amount by which A Corporation's qualified investments in foreign base company shipping operations at December 31, 1978 ($100,000) exceed its qualified investments in foreign base company shipping operations at December 31, 1979 ($80,000).

Example (2). The facts are the same as in example (1) except that A experiences no changes in qualified investments in foreign base company shipping operations during its taxable years 1980 and 1981. If M's election were to remain in force, A's acquisitions and dispositions of qualified investments in foreign base company shipping operations during A's taxable year 1982 would be taken into account in determining whether A has experienced an increase or a decrease in qualified investments in foreign base company shipping operations for its taxable year 1981. However, M duly files before the close of A's taxable year 1981 as application for consent to revocation of M Corporation's election under section 955(b)(3), and, pursuant to an agreement between the Commissioner and M, consent is granted by the Commissioner. Assuming such agreement does not provide otherwise, A's change in qualified investments in foreign base company shipping operations for its taxable year 1981 is zero because the effect of the revocation of the election is to treat acquisitions and dispositions of qualified investments in foreign base company shipping operations actually occurring in 1982 as having occurred in such year rather than in 1981.

Example (3). The facts are the same as in example (2) except that A's qualified investments in foreign base company shipping operations at December 31, 1982, amount to $70,000. For purposes of paragraph (b)(1)(i) of § 1.955A-1, the decrease in A's qualified investments in foreign base company shipping operations for the taxable year 1982 is $10,000 and is determined by ascertaining the amount by which A's qualified investments in foreign base company shipping operations at December 31, 1981 ($80,000) exceed its qualified investments in foreign base company shipping operations at December 31, 1982 ($70,000).

Example (4). The facts are the same as in example (1). Assume further that on September 30, 1979, M sells 40 percent of the only class of stock of A to N Corporation, a domestic corporation. N uses the calendar year as a taxable year. A remains a controlled foreign corporation immediately after such sale of its stock. A's qualified investments in foreign base company shipping operations at December 31, 1980, amount to $90,000. The changes in A Corporation's qualified investments in foreign base company shipping operations occurring in its taxable year 1979 are considered to be zero with respect to the 40-percent stock interest acquired by N Corporation. The entire $20,000 reduction in A Corporation's qualified investments in foreign base company shipping operations which occurs during the taxable year 1979 is taken into account by M for purposes of paragraph (c)(1) of this section in determining its tax liability for the taxable year 1978. A's increase in qualified investments in foreign base company shipping operations for the taxable year 1979 with respect to the 60-percent stock interest retained by M is $6,000 and is determined by ascertaining M's pro rata share (60 percent) of the amount by which A's qualified investments in foreign base company shipping operations at December 31, 1980 ($90,000) exceed its qualified investments in foreign base company shipping operations at December 31, 1979 ($80,000). N does not make an election under section 955(b)(3) in its return for its taxable year 1980. Corporation A's increase in qualified investments in foreign base company shipping operations for the taxable year 1980 with respect to the 40-percent stock interest acquired by N is $4,000.

T.D. 7894, 5/11/83.

---

§ 1.956-1 Shareholder's pro rata share of a controlled foreign corporation's increase in earnings invested in United States property.

Caution: The Treasury has not yet amended Reg § 1.956-1 to reflect changes made by 103-66.

(a) In general. Section 956(a)(1) and paragraph (b) of this section provide rules for determining the amount of a controlled foreign corporation's earnings invested in United States property at the close of any taxable year. Such amount is the aggregate amount invested in United States property to the extent such amount would have constituted a dividend if it had been distributed on such date. Subject to the provisions of section 951(a)(4) and the regulations thereunder, a United States shareholder of a controlled foreign corporation is required to include in his gross income his pro rata share, as determined in accordance with paragraph (c) of this section, of the controlled foreign corporation's increase for any taxable year in earnings invested in United States property but only to the extent such share is not excludable from his gross income under the provisions of section 959(a)(2) and the regulations thereunder.

(b) Amount of a controlled foreign corporation's investment of earnings in United States property. *(1) Dividend limitation.* The amount of a controlled foreign corporation's earnings invested at the close of its taxable year in United States property is the aggregate amount of such property held, directly or indirectly, by such corporation at the close of its taxable year to the extent such amount would have constituted a dividend under section 316 and §§ 1.316-1 and 1.316-2 (determined after the application of section 955(a)) if it had been distributed on such closing day. For purposes of this subparagraph, the determination of whether an amount would have constituted a dividend if distributed shall be made without regard to the provisions of section 959(d) and the regulations thereunder.

(2) Aggregate amount of United States property. For purposes of determining an increase in earnings invested in United States property for any taxable year beginning after December 31, 1975, the aggregate amount of United States property held by a controlled foreign corporation at the close of—

(i) Any taxable year beginning after December 31, 1975, and

(ii) The last taxable year beginning before January 1, 1976

does not include stock or obligations of a domestic corporation described in section 956(b)(2)(F) or movable property described in section 956(b)(2)(G).

(3) Treatment of earnings and profits. For purposes of making the determination under subparagraph (1) of this paragraph as to whether an amount of investment would have constituted a dividend if distributed at the close of any taxable year of a controlled foreign corporation, earnings and profits of the controlled foreign corporation shall be considered not to include any amounts which are attributable to—

(i) Amounts which have been included in the gross income of a United States shareholder of such controlled foreign corporation under section 951(a)(1)(B) (or which would have been so included but for section 959(a)(2)) and have not been distributed, or

(ii) (a) Amounts which are included in the gross income of a United States shareholder of such controlled foreign corporation under section 551(b) or would be so included under such section but for the fact that such amounts were distributed to such shareholder during the taxable year, or

(b) Amounts which, for any prior taxable year, have been included in the gross income of a United States shareholder of such controlled foreign corporation under section 551(b) and have not been distributed.

The rules of this subparagraph apply only in determining the limitation on a controlled foreign corporation's increase in earnings invested in United States property. See section 959 and the regulations thereunder for limitations on the exclusion from gross income of previously taxed earnings and profits.

(4) [Reserved]

(c) Shareholder's pro rata share of increase. *(1) General rule.* A United States shareholder's pro rata share of a controlled foreign corporation's increase for any taxable year in earnings invested in United States property is the amount determined by subtracting the shareholder's pro rata share of—

(i) The controlled foreign corporation's earnings invested in United States property at the close of its preceding taxable year, as determined under paragraph (b) of this section, reduced by amounts paid by such corporation during such preceding taxable year to which section 959(c)(1) and the regulations thereunder apply, from his pro rata share of

(ii) The controlled foreign corporation's earnings invested in United States property at the close of its current taxable year, as determined under paragraph (b) of this section.

(2) Illustration. The application of this paragraph may be illustrated by the following examples:

Example (1). A is a United States shareholder and direct owner of 60 percent of the only class of stock of R Corporation, a controlled foreign corporation during the entire period here involved. Both A and R Corporation use the calendar year as a taxable year. Corporation R's aggregate investment in United States property on December 31, 1964, which would constitute a dividend (as determined under paragraph (b) of this section) if distributed on such date is $150,000. During the taxable year 1964, R Corporation distributed $50,000 to which section 959(c)(1) applies. Corporation R's aggregate investment in United States property on December 31, 1965, is $250,000; and R Corporation's current and accumulated earnings and profits on such date (determined as provided in paragraph (b) of this section) are $225,000. A's pro rata share of R Corporation's increase for 1965 in earnings invested in United States property is $75,000, determined as follows:

(i) Aggregated investment in United States property on Dec. 31, 1965		$250,000
(ii) Current and accumulated earnings and profits on Dec. 31, 1965		225,000
(iii) Amount of earnings invested in United States property on Dec. 31, 1965, which would constitute a dividend if distributed on such date (lesser of item (i) or item (ii))		$225,000
(iv) Aggregate investment in United States property on Dec. 31, 1964, which would constitute a dividend if distributed on such date	$150,000	
Less: Amounts distributed during 1964 to which sec. 959(c)(1) applies	50,000	100,000
(v) R Corporation's increase for 1965 in earnings invested in United States property (item (iii) minus item (iv))	125,000	
(vi) A's pro rata share of R Corporation's increase for 1965 in earnings invested in United States property (item (v) times 60 percent)	75,000	

Example (2). The facts are the same as in example (1), except that R Corporation's current and accumulated earnings and profits on December 31, 1965, are $100,000 instead of $225,000. Accordingly, even through R Corporation's aggregate investment in United States property on December 31, 1965, of $250,000 exceeds the net amount ($100,000) taken into account under subparagraph (1)(i) of this paragraph as of December 31, 1964, by $150,000, there is no increase for taxable year 1965 in earnings invested in United States property because of the dividend limitation of paragraph (b)(1) of this section. Corporation R's aggregate investment in United States property on December 31, 1966, is unchanged ($250,000) Corporation R's current and accumulated earnings and profits on December 31, 1966, are $175,000, and, as a consequence, its aggregate investment in United States property which would constitute a dividend if distributed on that date is $175,000. Corporation R pays no amount during 1965 to which section 959(c)(1) applies. Corporation R's increase for the taxable year 1966 in earnings invested in United States property is $75,000, and A's pro rata share of that amount is $45,000 ($75,000 times 60 percent).

(d) Date and basis of determinations. The determinations made under paragraph (c)(1)(i) of this section with respect to the close of the preceding taxable year of a controlled foreign corporation and under paragraph (c)(1)(ii) with respect to the close of the current taxable year of such controlled foreign corporation, for purposes of determining the United States corporation's pro rata share of such corporation's increased investment of earnings in United States property for the current taxable year, shall be made as of the last day of the current taxable year of such corporation but on the basis of stock owned, within the meaning of section 958(a) and the regulations thereunder, by such United States shareholder on the last day of the current taxable year of the foreign corporation on which such corporation is a controlled foreign corporation. See the last sentence of section 956(a)(2). The application of this paragraph may be illustrated from the following example:

Example. Domestic corporation M owns 60 percent of the only class of stock of A Corporation, a controlled foreign corporation during the entire period here involved. Both M Corporation and A Corporation use the calendar year as a taxable year. Corporation A's investment of earnings in United States property at the close of the taxable year 1963 is $100,000, as determined under paragraph (b) of this section, and M Corporation includes its pro rata share of such amount ($60,000) in gross income for its taxable year 1963. On June 1, 1964, M Corporation acquires an additional 25 percent of A Corporation's outstanding stock from a person who is not a United States person as defined in section 957(d). Corporation A's investment of earnings in United States property at the close of the taxable year 1964, as determined under paragraph (b) of this section, is unchanged ($100,000). Corporation A pays no amount during 1963 to which section 959(c)(1) applies. Corporation M is not required, by reason of the acquisition in 1964 of A Corporation's stock, to include an additional amount in its gross income with respect to A Corporation's investment of earnings in United States property even though the earnings invested in United States property by A Corporation attributable to the stock acquired by M Corporation were not previously taxed. The determination made under paragraph (c)(1)(i) of this section as well as the determination made under paragraph (c)(1)(ii) of this section with respect to A Corporation's investment for 1964 of earnings in United States property are made on the basis of stock owned by M Corporation (85 percent) at the close of 1964.

(e) Amount attributable to property. *(1) General rule.* Except as provided in subparagraph (2) of this paragraph, for purposes of paragraph (b)(1) of this section the amount taken into account with respect to any United States property shall be its adjusted basis, as of the applicable determination date, reduced by any liability (other than a liability described in subparagraph (3) of this paragraph) to which such property is subject on such date. To be taken into account under this subparagraph, a liability must constitute a specific charge against the property involved. Thus, a liability evidence by an open account or a liability secured only by the general credit of the controlled foreign corporation will not be taken into account. On the other hand, if a liability constitutes a specific charge against several items of property and cannot definitely be allocated to any single item of property, the liability shall be apportioned against each of such items of property in that ratio which the adjusted basis of such item on the applicable determination date bears to the adjusted basis of all such items at such time. A liability in excess of the adjusted basis of the property which is subject to such liability shall not be taken into account for the purpose of reducing the adjusted basis of other property which is not subject to such liability.

(2) Rule for pledges and guarantees. For purposes of this section the amount taken into account with respect to any pledge or guarantee described in paragraph (c)(1) of § 1.956-

2 shall be the unpaid principal amount on the applicable determination date of the obligation with respect to which the controlled foreign corporation is a pledgor or guarantor.

(3) Excluded charges. For purposes of subparagraph (1) of this paragraph, a specific charge created with respect to any item of property principally for the purpose of artificially increasing or decreasing the amount of a controlled foreign corporation's investment of earnings in United States property will not be recognized; whether a specific charge is created principally for such purpose will depend upon all the facts and circumstances of each case. One of the factors that will be considered in making such a determination with respect to a loan is whether the loan is from a related person, as defined in section 954(d)(3) and paragraph (e) of § 1.954-1.

(4) Statement required. If for purposes of this section a United States shareholder of a controlled foreign corporation reduces the adjusted basis of property which constitutes United States property on the ground that such property is subject to a liability, he shall attach to his return a statement setting forth the adjusted basis of the property before the reduction and the amount and nature of the reduction.

T.D. 6704, 2/19/64, amend T.D. 6795, 1/28/65, T.D. 7712, 8/6/80, T.D. 8209, 6/13/88.

§ 1.956-1T Shareholder's pro rata share of a controlled foreign corporation's increase in earnings invested in United States property (temporary).

(a) [Reserved]

(b) (1)—(3) [Reserved]

(4) Treatment of certain investments of earnings in United States Property. (i) Special rule. For purposes of § 1.956-1(b)(1) of the regulations, a controlled foreign corporation will be considered to hold indirectly (A) the investments in United States property held on its behalf by a trustee or a nominee or (B) at the discretion of the District Director, investments in U.S. property acquired by any other foreign corporation that is controlled by the controlled foreign corporation, if one of the principal purposes for creating, organizing, or funding (through capital contributions or debt) such other foreign corporation is to avoid the application of section 956 with respect to the controlled foreign corporation. For purposes of this paragraph (b), a foreign corporation will be controlled by the controlled foreign corporation if the foreign corporation and the controlled foreign corporation are related parties under section 267(b). In determining for purposes of this paragraph (b) whether two or more corporations are members of the same controlled group under section 267(b)(3), a person is considered to own stock owned directly by such person, stock owned with the application of section 1563(e)(1), and stock owned with the application of section 267(c). The following examples illustrate the application of this paragraph.

Example (1). P, a domestic corporation, owns all of the outstanding stock of FS1, a controlled foreign corporation, and all of the outstanding stock of FS2, also a controlled foreign corporation. FS1 sells products to FS2 in exchange for trade receivables due in 60 days. FS2 has no earnings and profits. FS1 has substantial accumulated earnings and profits. FS2 loans to P an amount equal to the debt it owes FS1. FS2 pays the trade receivables according to the terms of the receivables. FS1 will not be considered to hold indirectly the investment in United States property under this paragraph (b)(4), because there was no transfer of funds to FS2.

Example (2). The facts are the same as in Example (1), except that FS2 does not pay the receivables. FS1 is considered to hold indirectly the investment in United States property under this paragraph (b)(4), because there was a transfer of funds to FS2, a principal purpose of which was to avoid the application of section 956 to FS1.

(ii) Effective date. This section is effective June 14, 1988, with respect to investments made on or after June 14, 1988.

(c) - (d) [Reserved]

(e) (1)-(4) [Reserved]

(5) Excluded charges. (i) Special rule. For purposes of § 1.956-1(e)(1) of the regulations, in the case of an investment in United States property consisting of an obligation of a related person, as defined in section 954(d)(3) and paragraph (e) of § 1.954-1, a liability will not be recognized as a specific charge if the liability representing the charge is with recourse with respect to the general credit or other assets of the investing controlled foreign corporation.

(ii) Effective Date. This section is effective June 14, 1988, with respect to investments made on or after June 14, 1988.

T.D. 8209, 6/13/88.

§ 1.956-2 Definition of United States property.

Caution: The Treasury has not yet amended Reg § 1.956-2 to reflect changes made by P.L. 108-357.

(a) Included property. *(1) In general.* For purposes of section 956(a) and § 1.956-1, United States property is (except as provided in paragraph (b) of this section) any property acquired (within the meaning of paragraph (d)(1) of this section) by a foreign corporation (whether or not a controlled foreign corporation at the time) during any taxable year of such foreign corporation beginning after December 31, 1962, which is—

(i) Tangible property (real or personal) located in the United States;

(ii) Stock of a domestic corporation;

(iii) An obligation (as defined in paragraph (d)(2) of this section) of a United States person (as defined in section 957(d)); or

(iv) Any right to the use in the United States of—

(a) A patent or copyright,

(b) An invention, model, or design (whether or not patented),

(c) A secret formula or process, or

(d) Any other similar property right, which is acquired or developed by the foreign corporation for use in the United States by any person. Whether a right described in this subdivision has been acquired or developed for use in the United States by any person is to be determined from all the facts and circumstances of each case. As a general rule, a right actually used principally in the United States will be considered to have been acquired or developed for use in the United States in the absence of affirmative evidence showing that the right was not so acquired or developed for such use.

(2) Illustrations. The application of the provisions of this paragraph may be illustrated by the following examples:

Example (1). Foreign corporation R uses as a taxable year a fiscal year ending on June 30. Corporation R acquires on June 1, 1963, and holds on June 30, 1963, $100,000 of tangible property (not described in section 956(b)(2)) located in the United States. Corporation R's aggregate investment in

United States property at the close of its taxable year ending June 30, 1963, is zero since the property which is acquired on June 1, 1963, is not acquired during a taxable year of R Corporation beginning after December 31, 1962. Assuming no change in R Corporation's aggregate investment in United States property during its taxable year ending June 30, 1964, R Corporation's increase in earnings invested in United States property for such taxable year is zero.

Example (2). Foreign corporation S uses the calendar year as a taxable year and is a controlled foreign corporation for its entire taxable year 1965. Corporation S is not a controlled foreign corporation at any time during its taxable years 1963 and 1964. Corporation S owns on December 31, 1964, $100,000 of tangible property (not described in section 956(b)(2) located in the United States which it acquires during taxable years beginning after December 31, 1962. Corporation S's aggregate investment in United States property on December 31, 1964, is $100,000. Corporation S's current and accumulated earnings and profits (determined as provided in paragraph (b) of § 1.956-1) as of December 31, 1964, are in excess of $100,000. Assuming no change in S Corporation's aggregate investment in United States property during its taxable year 1965, S Corporation's increase in earnings invested in United States property for such taxable year is zero.

Example (3). Foreign corporation T uses the calendar year as a taxable year and is a controlled foreign corporation for its entire taxable years 1963, 1964, and 1966. At December 31, 1964, T Corporation's investment in United States property is $100,000. Corporation T is not a controlled foreign corporation at any time during its taxable year 1965 in which it acquires $25,000 of tangible property (not described in section 956(b)(2)) located in the United States. On December 31, 1965, T Corporation holds the United States property of $100,000 which it held on December 31, 1964, and, in addition, the United States property acquired in 1965. Corporation T's aggregate investment in United States property at December 31, 1965, is $125,000. Corporation T's current and accumulated earnings and profits (determined as provided in paragraph (b) of § 1.956-1) as of December 31, 1965, are in excess of $125,000, and T Corporation pays no amount during 1965 to which section 959(c)(1) applies. Assuming no change in T Corporation's aggregate investment in United States property during its taxable year 1966, T Corporation's increase in earnings invested in United States property for such taxable year is zero.

(3) Property owned through partnership. For purposes of section 956, if a controlled foreign corporation is a partner in a partnership that owns property that would be United States property, within the meaning of paragraph (a)(1) of this section, if owned directly by the controlled foreign corporation, the controlled foreign corporation will be treated as holding an interest in the property equal to its interest in the partnership and such interest will be treated as an interest in United States property. This paragraph (a)(3) applies to taxable years of a controlled foreign corporation beginning on or after July 23, 2002.

(b) Exceptions. *(1) Excluded property.* For purposes of section 956(a) and paragraph (a) of this section, United States property does not include the following types of property held by a foreign corporation:

(i) Obligations of the United States.

(ii) Money.

(iii) Deposits with persons carrying on the banking business, unless the deposits serve directly or indirectly as a pledge or guarantee within the meaning of paragraph (c) of this section. See paragraph (e)(2) of § 1.956-1.

(iv) Property located in the United States which is purchased in the United States for export to, or use in, foreign countries. For purposes of this subdivision, property to be used outside the United States will be considered property to be used in a foreign country. Whether property is of a type described in this subdivision is to be determined from all the facts and circumstances in each case. Property which constitutes export trade assets within the meaning of section 971(c)(2) and paragraph (c)(3) of § 1.971-1 will be considered property of a type described in this subdivision.

(v) Any obligation (as defined in paragraph (d)(2) of this section) of a United States person (as defined in section 957(d)) arising in connection with the sale or processing of property if the amount of such obligation outstanding at any time during the taxable year of the foreign corporation does not exceed an amount which is ordinary and necessary to carry on the trade or business of both the other party to the sale or processing transaction and the United States person, or, if the sale or processing transaction occurs between related persons, would be ordinary and necessary to carry on the trade or business of both the other party to the sale or processing transaction and the United States person if such persons were unrelated persons. Whether the amount of an obligation described in this subdivision is ordinary and necessary is to be determined from all the facts and circumstances in each case.

(vi) Any aircraft, railroad rolling stock, vessel, motor vehicle, or container used in the transportation of persons or property in foreign commerce and used predominantly outside the United States. Whether transportation property described in this subdivision is used in foreign commerce and predominantly outside the United States is to be determined from all the facts and circumstances in each case. As a general rule, such transportation property will be considered to be used predominantly outside the United States if 70 percent or more of the miles traversed (during the taxable year at the close of which a determination is made under section 956(a)(2)) in the use of such property are traversed outside the United States or if such property is located outside the United States 70 percent of the time during such taxable year.

(vii) An amount of assets described in paragraph (a) of this section of an insurance company equivalent to the unearned premiums or reserves which are ordinary and necessary for the proper conduct of that part of its insurance business which is attributable to contracts other than those described in section 953(a)(1) and the regulations thereunder. For purposes of this subdivision, a reserve will be considered ordinary and necessary for the proper conduct of an insurance business if, under the principles of paragraph (c) of § 1.953-4, such reserve would qualify as a reserve required by law. See paragraph (d)(3) of § 1.954-2 for determining, for purposes of this subdivision, the meaning of insurance company and of unearned premiums.

(viii) For taxable years beginning after December 31, 1975, the voting or nonvoting stock or obligations of an unrelated domestic corporation. For purposes of this subdivision, an unrelated domestic corporation is a domestic corporation which is neither a United States shareholder (as defined in section 951(b)) of the controlled foreign corporation making the investment, nor a corporation 25 percent or more of whose total combined voting power of all classes of stock entitled to vote is owned or considered as owned (within the meaning of section 958(b)) by United States shareholders of the controlled foreign corporation making the investment. The determination of whether a domestic corporation is an unrelated corporation is made immediately after each acquisition of stock or obligations by the controlled foreign corporations.

(ix) For taxable years beginning after December 31, 1975, movable drilling rigs or barges and other movable exploration and exploitation equipment (other than a vessel or an aircraft) when used on the Continental Shelf (as defined in section 638) of the United States in the exploration for, development, removal, or transportation of natural resources from or under ocean waters. Property used on the Continental Shelf includes property located in the United States which is being constructed or is in storage or in transit within the United States for use on the Continental Shelf. In general, the type of property which qualifies for the exception under this subdivision includes any movable property which would be entitled to the investment credit if used outside the United States in certain geographical areas of the Western Hemisphere pursuant to section 48(a)(2)(B)(x) (without reference to sections 49 and 50).

(x) An amount of—

(a) A controlled foreign corporation's assets described in paragraph (a) of this section equivalent to its earnings and profits which are accumulated after December 31, 1962, and are attributable to items of income described in section 952(b) and the regulations thereunder, reduced by the amount of

(b) The earnings and profits of such corporation which are applied in a taxable year of such corporation beginning after December 31, 1962, to discharge a liability on property, but only if the liability was in existence at the close of such corporation's taxable year immediately preceding its first taxable year beginning after December 31, 1962, and the property would have been United States property if it had been acquired by such corporation immediately before such discharge.

For purposes of this subdivision, distributions made by such corporation for any taxable year shall be considered first made out of earnings and profits for such year other than earnings and profits referred to in (a) of this subdivision.

(2) Statement required. If a United States shareholder of a controlled foreign corporation excludes any property from the United States property of such controlled foreign corporation on the ground that section 956(b)(2) applies to such excluded property, he shall attach to his return a statement setting forth, by categories described in paragraph (a)(1) of this section, the amount of United States property of the controlled foreign corporation and, by categories described in subparagraph (1) of this paragraph, the amount of such property which is excluded

(c) Treatment of pledges and guarantees. *(1) General rule.* Except as provided in subparagraph (4) of this paragraph, any obligation (as defined in paragraph (d)(2) of this section) of a United States person (as defined in section 957(d)) with respect to which a controlled foreign corporation is a pledgor or guarantor shall be considered for purposes of section 956(a) and paragraph (a) of this section to be United States property held by such controlled foreign corporation.

(2) Indirect pledge or guarantee. If the assets of a controlled foreign corporation serve at any time, even though indirectly, as security for the performance of an obligation of a United States person, then, for purposes of paragraph (c)(1) of this section, the controlled foreign corporation will be considered a pledgor or guarantor of that obligation. For this purpose the pledge of stock of a controlled foreign corporation will be considered as the indirect pledge of the assets of the corporation if at least 66⅔ percent of the total combined voting power of all classes of stock entitled to vote is pledged and if the pledge of stock is accompanied by one or more negative covenants or similar restrictions on the shareholder effectively limiting the corporation's discretion with respect to the disposition of assets and the incurrence of liabilities other than in the ordinary course of business. This paragraph (c)(2) applies only to pledges and guarantees which are made after September 8, 1980. For purposes of this paragraph (c)(2) a refinancing shall be considered as a new pledge or guarantee.

(3) Illustrations. The following examples illustrate the application of this paragraph (c):

Example (1). A, a United States person, borrows $100,000 from a bank in foreign country X on December 31, 1964. On the same date controlled foreign corporation R pledges its assets as security for A's performance of A's obligation to repay such loan. The place at which or manner in which A uses the money is not material. For purposes of paragraph (b) of § 1.956-1, R Corporation will be considered to hold A's obligation to repay the bank $100,000, and, under the provisions of paragraph (e)(2) of § 1.956-1, the amount taken into account in computing R Corporation's aggregate investment in United States property on December 31, 1964, is the unpaid principal amount of the obligation on that date ($100,000).

Example (2). The facts are the same as in example (1), except that R Corporation participates in the transaction, not by pledging its assets as security for A's performance of A's obligation to repay the loan, but by agreeing to buy for $1,00,000 at maturity the note representing A's obligation if A does not repay the loan. Separate arrangements are made with respect to the payment of the interest on the loan. The agreement of R Corporation to buy the note constitutes a guarantee of A's obligation. For purposes of paragraph (b) of § 1.956-1, R Corporation will be considered to hold A's obligation to repay the bank $100,000, and, under the provisions of paragraph (e)(2) of § 1.956-1, the amount taken into account in computing R Corporation's aggregate investment in United States property on December 31, 1964, is the unpaid principal amount of the obligation on that date ($100,000).

Example (3). A, a United States person, borrows $100,000 from a bank on December 10, 1981, pledging 70 percent of the stock of X, a controlled foreign corporation, as collateral for the loan. A and X use the calendar year as their taxable year. in the loan agreement, among other things, A agrees not to cause or permit X Corporation to do any of the following without the consent of the bank:

(a) Borrow money or pledge assets, except as to borrowings in the ordinary course of business of X Corporation;

(b) Guarantee, assume, or become liable on the obligation of another, or invest in or lend funds to another;

(c) Merge or consolidate with any other corporation or transfer shares of any controlled subsidiary;

(d) Sell or lease (other than in the ordinary course of business) or otherwise dispose of any substantial part of its assets;

(e) Pay or secure any debt owing by X Corporation to A; and

(f) Pay any dividends, except in such amounts as may be required to make interest or principal payments on A's loan from the bank.

A retains the right to vote the stock unless a default occurs by A. Under paragraph (c)(2) of this section, the assets of X Corporation serve indirectly as security for A's performance of A's obligation to repay the loan and X Corporation will be considered a pledgor or guarantor with respect to that obligation. For purposes of paragraph (b) of § 1.956-1, X Corporation will be considered to hold A's obligation to repay the bank $100,000 and under paragraph (e)(2) of § 1.956-1, the amount taken into account in computing X Corporation's aggregate investment in United States property on December 31, 1981, is the unpaid principal amount of the obligation on that date.

(4) Special rule for certain conduit financing arrangements. The rule contained in subparagraph (1) of this paragraph shall not apply to a pledge or a guarantee by a controlled foreign corporation to secure the obligation of a United States person if such United States person is a mere conduit in a financing arrangement. Whether the United States person is a mere conduit in a financing arrangement will depend upon all the facts and circumstances in each case. A United States person will be considered a mere conduit in a financing arrangement in a case in which a controlled foreign corporation pledges stock of its subsidiary corporation, which is also a controlled foreign corporation, to secure the obligation of such United States person, where the following conditions are satisfied:

(i) Such United States person is a domestic corporation which is not engaged in the active conduct of a trade or business and has no substantial assets other than those arising out of its relending of the funds borrowed by it on such obligation to the controlled foreign corporation whose stock is pledged; and

(ii) The assets of such United States person are at all times substantially offset by its obligation to the lender.

(d) Definitions. *(1) Meaning of "acquired".* (i) Applicable rules. For purposes of this section—

(a) Property shall be considered acquired by a foreign corporation when such corporation acquires an adjusted basis in the property;

(b) Property which is an obligation of a United States person with respect to which a controlled foreign corporation is a pledgor or guarantor (within the meaning of paragraph (c) of this section) shall be considered acquired when the corporation becomes liable as a pledgor or guarantor or is otherwise considered a pledgor or guarantor (within the meaning of paragraph (c)(2) of this section); and

(c) Property shall not be considered acquired by a foreign corporation if—

(1) Such property is acquired in a transaction in which gain or loss would not be recognized under this chapter to such corporation if such corporation were a domestic corporation;

(2) The basis of the property acquired by the foreign corporation is the same as the basis of the property exchanged by such corporation; and

(3) The property exchanged by the foreign corporation was not United States property (as defined in paragraph (a)(1) of this section) but would have been such property if it had been acquired by such corporation immediately before such exchange.

(ii) Illustrations. The application of this subparagraph may be illustrated by the following examples:

Example (1). Foreign corporation R uses the calendar year as a taxable year and acquires before January 1, 1963, stock of domestic corporation M having as to R Corporation an adjusted basis of $10,000. The stock of M Corporation is not United States property of R Corporation on December 31, 1962, since it is not acquired in a taxable year of R Corporation beginning on or after January 1, 1963. On June 30, 1963, R Corporation sells the M Corporation stock for $15,000 in cash and expends such amount in acquiring stock of domestic corporation N which has as to R Corporation an adjusted basis of $15,000. For purposes of determining R Corporation's aggregate investment in United States property on December 31, 1963, R Corporation has, by virtue of acquiring the stock of N Corporation, acquired $15,000 of United States property.

Example (2). Foreign corporation S, a controlled foreign corporation for the entire period here involved, uses the calendar year as a taxable year and purchases for $100,000 on December 31, 1963, tangible property (not described in section 956(b)(2)) located in the United States and having a remaining estimated useful life of 10 years, subject to a mortgage of $80,000 payable in 5 annual installments. The property constitutes United States property as of December 31, 1963, and the amount taken into account for purposes of determining the aggregate amount of S Corporation's investment in United States property under paragraph (b) of § 1.956-1 is $20,000. No depreciation is sustained with respect to the property during the taxable year 1963. During the taxable year 1964, S Corporation pays $16,000 on the mortgage and sustains $10,000 of depreciation with respect to the property. As of December 31, 1964, the amount taken into account with respect to the property for purposes of determining the aggregate amount of S Corporation's investment in United States property under paragraph (b) of § 1.956-1 is $26,000, computed as follows:

Cost of property		$100,000
Less: Reserve for depreciation		10,000
Adjusted basis of property		90,000
Less: Liability to which property is subject:		
Gross amount of mortgage	$80,000	
Payment during 1964	16,000	
		64,000
Amount taken into account (12-31-64)		26,000

Example (3). Controlled foreign corporation T uses the calendar year as a taxable year and acquires on December 31, 1963, $10,000 of United States property not described in section 956(b)(2); no depreciation is sustained with respect to the property during 1963. Corporation T's current and accumulated earnings and profits (determined as provided in paragraph (b) of § 1.956-1) as of December 31, 1963, are in excess of $10,000, and T Corporation's United States shareholders include in their gross income under section 951(a)(1)(B) their pro rata share of T Corporation's increase ($10,000) for 1963 in earnings invested in United States property. On January 1, 1964, T Corporation acquires an additional $10,000 of United States property not described in section 956(b)(2). Each of the two items of property has an estimated useful life of 5 years, and T Corporation sustains $4,000 of depreciation with respect to such properties during its taxable year 1964. Corporation T's current and accumulated earnings and profits as of December 31, 1964, exceed $16,000, determined as provided in paragraph (b) of § 1.956-1. Corporation T pays no amounts during 1963 to which section 959(c)(1) applies. Corporation T's investment of earnings in United States property at December 31, 1964, is $16,000, and its increase for 1964 in earnings invested in United States property is $6,000.

Example (4). Foreign corporation U uses the calendar year as a taxable year and acquires before January 1, 1963, stock in domestic corporation M having as to U Corporation an adjusted basis of $10,000. On December 1, 1964, pursuant to a statutory merger described in section 368(a)(1), M Corporation merges into domestic corporation N, and U Corporation receives on such date one share of stock in N Corporation, the surviving corporation, for each share of stock it held in M Corporation. Pursuant to section 354 no gain or loss is recognized to U Corporation, and pursuant to section 358 the basis of the property received (stock of N Corporation) is the same as that of the property exchanged (stock of M Corporation). Corporation U is not considered for purposes of section 956 to have acquired United States property by reason of its receipt of the stock in N Corporation.

Example (5). The facts are the same as in example (4), except that U Corporation acquires the stock of M Corporation on February 1, 1963, rather than before January 1, 1963. For purposes of determining U Corporation's aggregate investment in United States property on December 31, 1963, U Corporation has, by virtue of acquiring the stock of M Corporation, acquired $10,000 of United States property. Corporation U pays no amount during 1963 to which section 959(c)(1) applies. The reorganization and resulting acquisition on December 1, 1964, by U Corporation of N Corporation's stock also represents an acquisition of United States property; however, assuming no other change in U Corporation's aggregate investment in United States property during 1964, U Corporation's increase for such year in earnings invested in United States property is zero.

(2) [Reserved]

T.D. 6704, 2/19/64, amend T.D. 7712, 8/6/80, T.D. 7797, 11/24/81, T.D. 8209, 6/13/88, T.D. 9008, 7/22/2002.

§ 1.956-2T Definition of United States property (temporary).

(a) — (c) [Reserved].

(d) (1) [Reserved].

(2) Obligation defined. (i) Rule. For purposes of § 1.956-2 of the regulations, the term "obligation" includes any bond, note, debenture, certificate, bill receivable, account receivable, note receivable, open account, or other indebtedness, whether or not issued at a discount and whether or not bearing interest, except that such term shall not include:

(A) Any indebtedness arising out of the involuntary conversion of property which is not United States property within the meaning of paragraph (a)(1) of § 1.956-2, or

(B) Any obligation of a United States person (as defined in section 957(c)) arising in connection with the provision of services by a controlled foreign corporation to the United States person if the amount of such obligation outstanding at any time during the taxable year of the controlled foreign corporation does not exceed an amount which would be ordinary and necessary to carry on the trade or business of the controlled foreign corporation and the United States person if they were unrelated. The amount of such obligations shall be considered to be ordinary and necessary to the extent of such receivables that are paid within 60 days.

See § 1.956-2(b)(1)(v) for the exclusion from United States property of obligations arising in connection with the sale or processing of property where such obligations are ordinary and necessary as to amount.

(ii) Effective date. This section is effective June 14, 1988, with respect to investments made on or after June 14, 1988.

T.D. 8209, 6/13/88.

§ 1.956-3T Certain trade or service receivables acquired from United States persons (temporary).

(a) In general. For purposes of section 956(a) and § 1.956-1, the term "United States property" also includes any trade or service receivable if the trade or service receivable is acquired (directly or indirectly) after March 1, 1984, from a related person who is a United States person (as defined in section 7701(a)(30)) (hereinafter referred to as a "related United States person") and the obligor under the receivable is a United States person. A trade or service receivable described in this paragraph shall be considered to be United States property notwithstanding the exceptions (other than subparagraph (H)) contained in section 956(b)(2). The terms "trade or service receivable" and "related person" have the respective meanings given to such terms by section 864(d) and the regulations thereunder. For purposes of this section, the exception contained in § 1.956-2T(d)(2)(i)(B) for short-term obligations shall not apply to service receivables described in this paragraph.

(b) Acquisition of a trade or service receivable. *(1) General rule.* The rules of § 1.864-8T(c)(1) shall be applied to determine whether a controlled foreign corporation has acquired a trade or service receivable.

(2) Indirect acquisitions. (i) Acquisition through unrelated person. A trade or service receivable will be considered to be acquired from a related person if it is acquired from an unrelated person who acquired (directly or indirectly) such receivable from a person who is a related person to the acquiring person.

(ii) Acquisition by nominee or pass-through entity. A controlled foreign corporation will be considered to have acquired a trade or service receivable of a related United States person held on its behalf:

(A) By a nominee or by a partnership, simple trust, S corporation or other pass-through entity to the extent the controlled foreign corporation owns (directly or indirectly) a beneficial interest in such partnership or other pass-through entity; or

(B) By another foreign corporation that is controlled by the controlled foreign corporation, if one of the principal purposes for creating, organizing, or funding such other foreign corporation (through capital contributions or debt) is to avoid the application of section 956. See § 1.956-1T.

The rule of this paragraph (b)(2)(ii) does not limit the application of paragraph (b)(2)(iii) of this section regarding the characterization of trade or service receivables of unrelated persons acquired pursuant to certain swap or pooling arrangements. The following examples illustrate the application of this paragraph (b)(2)(ii).

Example (1). FS1, a controlled foreign corporation with substantial accumulated earnings and profits, contributes $2,000,000 to PS, a partnership, in exchange for a 20 percent limited partnership interest in PS. PS purchases trade or service receivables of FS1's domestic parent, P. The obligors under the receivables are United States persons. PS does not purchase receivables of any person who is related to any other partner is PS. Under paragraph (b)(2)(ii)(A) of this section, there is an investment of the earnings of FS1 in United States property equal to 20 percent of PS's basis in the receivables of P.

Example (2). FS1, a controlled foreign corporation, has accumulated more than $3,000,000 in earnings and profits. It organizes a wholly-owned foreign corporation, FS2, with a $2,000,000 equity contribution. FS2 has no earnings and profits. FS2 uses the funds to purchase trade or service receivables of FS1's domestic parent, P. The obligors under the receivables are United States persons. Under paragraph (b)(2)(ii)(B) of this section, there is an investment of the earnings of FS1 in United States property equal to $2,000,000.

(iii) Swap or pooling arrangements. A trade or service receivable of an unrelated person will be considered to be a trade or service receivable acquired from a related United States person and subject to the rules of this section if it is acquired in accordance with an arrangement that involves two or more groups of related persons that are unrelated to each other and the effect of the arrangement is that one or more related persons in each group acquire (directly or indirectly) trade or service receivables of one or more unrelated United States persons who are also parties to the arrangement, in exchange for reciprocal purchases of receivables of United States persons in the first group. The following example illustrates the application of this paragraph (b)(2)(iii).

Example. Controlled foreign corporations A, B, C and D are wholly-owned subsidiaries of domestic corporations M, N, O, and P, respectively. M, N, O, and P are not related persons. According to a prearranged plan, A, B, C, and D each acquire trade or service receivables of M, N, O, and/or P. The obligors under some or all of the receivables acquired by each of A, B, C, and D are United States persons. Because the effect of this arrangement is that the unrelated groups acquire each other's trade or service receivables of United States persons pursuant to the arrangement, there is an investment of the earnings of each of A, B, C, and D in United States property to the extent of the purchase price of those receivables under which the obligors are United States persons.

(iv) Financing arrangements. If a controlled foreign corporation participates (directly or indirectly) in a lending transaction that results in a loan to a United States person who purchases property described in section 1221(1) (hereinafter referred to as "inventory property") or services of a related United States person, or to any person who purchases trade or service receivables of a related United States person under which the obligor is a United States person, or to a person who is related to any such purchaser, and if the loan would not have been made or maintained on the same terms but for the corresponding purchase, then the controlled foreign corporation shall be considered to have indirectly acquired a trade or service receivable described in paragraph (a) of this section. For purposes of this paragraph (b)(2)(iv), it is immaterial that the sums lent are not, in fact, the sums used to finance the purchase of the inventory property or services or trade or service receivables of a related United States person. The amount to be taken into account with respect to the controlled foreign corporation's investment in United States property (resulting from application of this paragraph (b)(2)(iv)) shall be the amount lent pursuant to a lending transaction described in this paragraph (b)(2)(iv), if the amount lent is equal to or less than the purchase price of the inventory property, services, or trade or service receivables. If the amount lent is greater than the purchase price of the inventory property, services or receivables, the amount to be taken into account shall be the purchase price. The following examples illustrate the application of this paragraph (b)(2)(iv).

Example (1). P, a domestic corporation, owns all of the outstanding stock of FS1, a controlled foreign corporation. P sells equipment for $2,000,000 to X, an unrelated United States person. FS1 makes a $1,000,000 short-term loan to X, which loan would not have been made or maintained on the same terms but for X's purchase of P's equipment. Because FS1 directly participates in a lending transaction described in this paragraph (b)(2)(iv), FS1 is considered to have acquired the receivable of a related United States person. Thus, there is an investment of FS1's earnings and profits in United States property in the amount of $1,000,000.

Example (2). The facts are the same as in Example (1), except that instead of loaning money to X directly, FS1 deposits $3,000,000 with an unrelated financial institution that loans $2,000,000 to X in order for X to purchase P's equipment. The loan would not have been made or maintained on the same terms but for the corresponding deposit. Accordingly, the deposit and the loan are treated as a direct loan from FS1 to X. See Rev. Rul. 87-89, 1987-37 I.R.B. 16. Because FS1 indirectly participates in a lending transaction described in this paragraph (b)(2)(iv), FS1 is considered to have acquired the receivable of a related United States person. Thus, there is an investment of FS1's earnings and profits in United States property in the amount of $2,000,000.

Example (3). P, a domestic corporation, owns all of the outstanding stock of FS1, a controlled foreign corporation, FS1 makes a $3,000,000 loan to U, an unrelated foreign corporation, in connection with U's purchase for $2,000,000 of receivables from the sale of inventory property by P to United States obligors. Because FS1 directly participates in a lending transaction described in this paragraph (b)(2)(iv), FS1 is considered to have acquired receivables of a related United States person. Thus, there is an investment of FS1's earnings and profits in United States property in the amount of $2,000,000.

(c) Substitution of obligor. For purposes of this section, the substitution of another person for a United States obligor may be disregarded. Thus, if a purchaser who is a United States person arranges for a foreign person to pay a United States seller of inventory property or services and the seller transfers by sale or otherwise to its own controlled foreign corporation the foreign person's obligation for payment, then the acquisition of the foreign person's obligation shall constitute an investment in United States property by the seller's controlled foreign corporation, unless it can be demonstrated by the parties to the transaction that the primary purpose for the arrangement was not the avoidance of section 956. The following example illustrates the application of this paragraph.

Example. P, a domestic corporation, owns all of the outstanding stock of FS1, a controlled foreign corporation with substantial accumulated earnings and profits. P sells equipment to X, a domestic corporation unrelated to P. To pay for the equipment, X arranges for a foreign financing entity to issue a note to P. P then sells the note to FS1. FS1 has made an investment in United States property in the amount of the purchase price of the note.

T.D. 8209, 6/13/88.

---

§ 1.957-1 Definition of controlled foreign corporation.

(a) In general. The term *controlled foreign corporation* means any foreign corporation of which more than 50 percent (or such lesser amount as is provided in section 957(b) or section 953(c)) of either—

(1) The total combined voting power of all classes of stock of the corporation entitled to vote; or

(2) The total value of the stock of the corporation, is owned within the meaning of section 958(a), or (except for purposes of section 953(c)) is considered as owned by applying the rules of section 958(b) and § 1.958-2, by United States shareholders on any day during the taxable year of such foreign corporation. For the definition of the term *United States shareholder*, see sections 951(b) and 953(c)(1)(A). For the definition of the term *foreign corporation*, see § 301.7701-5 of this chapter (Procedure and Administration Regulations). For the treatment of associations as corporations, see section 7701(a)(3) and §§ 301.7701-1 and 301.7701-2 of this chapter. For the definition of the term *stock*, see sections 958(a)(3) and 7701(a)(7). For the classification of a member in an association, joint stock company or insurance company as a shareholder, see section 7701(a)(8).

(b) Percentage of total combined voting power owned by United States shareholders. *(1) Meaning of combined voting power.* In determining for purposes of paragraph (a) of this section whether United States shareholders own the requisite percentage of total combined voting power of all classes of stock entitled to vote, consideration will be given to all the facts and circumstances of each case. In all cases, however, United States shareholders of a foreign corporation will be deemed to own the requisite percentage of total combined voting power with respect to such corporation—

(i) If they have the power to elect, appoint, or replace a majority of that body of persons exercising, with respect to such corporation, the powers ordinarily exercised by the board of directors of a domestic corporation;

(ii) If any person or persons elected or designated by such shareholders have the power, where such shareholders have the power to elect exactly one-half of the members of such governing body of such foreign corporation, either to cast a vote deciding an evenly divided vote of such body or, for the duration of any deadlock which may arise, to exercise the powers ordinarily exercised by such governing body; or

(iii) If the powers which would ordinarily be exercised by the board of directors of a domestic corporation are exercised with respect to such foreign corporation by a person whom such shareholders have the power to elect, appoint, or replace.

(2) Shifting of formal voting power. Any arrangement to shift formal voting power away from United States shareholders of a foreign corporation will not be given effect if in reality voting power is retained. The mere ownership of stock entitled to vote does not by itself mean that the shareholder owning such stock has the voting power of such stock for purposes of section 957. For example, if there is any agreement, whether express or implied, that any shareholder will not vote his stock or will vote it only in a specified manner, or that shareholders owning stock having not more than 50 percent of the total combined voting power will exercise voting power normally possessed by a majority of stockholders, then the nominal ownership of the voting power will be disregarded in determining which shareholders actually hold such voting power, and this determination will be made on the basis of such agreement. Moreover, where United States shareholders own shares of one or more classes of stock of a foreign corporation which has another class of stock outstanding, the voting power ostensibly provided such other class of stock will be deemed owned by any person or persons on whose behalf it is exercised or, if not exercised, will be disregarded if the percentage of voting power of such other class of stock is substantially greater than its proportionate share of the corporate earnings, if the facts indicate that the shareholders of such other class of stock do not exercise their voting rights independently or fail to exercise such voting rights, and if a principal purpose of the arrangement is to avoid the classification of such foreign corporation as a controlled foreign corporation under section 957.

(c) Illustrations. The application of this section may be illustrated by the following examples:

Example (1). Foreign corporation R has two classes of capital stock outstanding, 60 shares of class A stock, and 40 shares of class B stock. Each share of each class of stock has one vote for all purposes. E, a United States person, owns 51 shares of class A stock. Corporation R is a controlled foreign corporation.

Example (2). Foreign corporation S has three classes of capital stock outstanding, consisting of 60 shares of class A stock, 40 shares of class B stock, and 200 shares of class C stock. The owners of a majority of class A stock are entitled to elect 6 of the 10 corporate directors, and the owners of a majority of the class B stock are entitled to elect the other 4 of the 10 directors. Class C stock has no voting rights. D, a United States person, owns all of the shares of the class C stock. He also owns 31 shares of class A stock and as such an owner can elect 6 members of the board of directors. None of the remaining shares of class A stock, or the 40 shares of class B stock, is owned, or considered as owned, within the meaning of section 958, by a United States person. Since, as owner of 31 shares of the class A stock, D has sufficient voting power to elect 6 directors, D has more than 50 percent of the total combined voting power of all classes of stock entitled to vote, and S Corporation is a controlled foreign corporation.

Example (3). M, a United States person, owns a 51-percent interest in R Company, a foreign company of which he is a member. The company, if it were domestic, would be taxable as a corporation. The remaining interest of 49 percent in the company is owned by seven other members none of whom is a United States person. The memorandum of association of R Company provides for only one manager, who with respect to the company exercises the powers ordinarily exercised by a board of directors of a domestic corporation. The manager is to be elected by unanimous agreement of all the members. Since M owns 51 percent of the company, he will be deemed to own more than 50 percent of the total combined voting power of all classes of stock of R Company entitled to vote, notwithstanding that he has power to elect a manager only with the agreement of the other members. Company R is a controlled corporation.

Example (4). Domestic corporation M owns a 49-percent interest in S Company, a foreign company of which it is a member. The company, if it were domestic, would be taxable as a corporation. Company S is formed under the laws of foreign country Y. The remaining interest of 51 percent in S Company is owned by persons who are not United States persons. The organization contract of S Company provides for one manager, B, a citizen and resident of country Y who is an officer of M Corporation in charge of its foreign operations in such country, or any person M Corporation may at any time appoint to succeed B in such capacity. The manager has the sole authority with respect to S Company to exercise powers ordinarily exercised by a board of directors of a domestic corporation. Since M Corporation has the discretionary power to replace B and to appoint his successor as manager of S Company, the company is a controlled foreign corporation.

Example (5). N, a United States person, owns 50 percent of the outstanding shares of the only class of capital stock of foreign corporation R. An additional 48 percent of the outstanding shares is owned by foreign corporation S. The remaining 2 percent of shares is owned by P, a citizen and resident of foreign country T, who regularly acts as attorney for N in the conduct of N's business affairs in country T. All of the shares of the outstanding capital stock of R Corporation are bearer shares. At the time of the issuance of the shares to him, P places the certificates for such shares in a depository to which N has access. On several occasions N, with P's acquiescence, has taken such shares from the depository and, on one such occasion, used the shares as collateral in borrowing funds on a loan. Although dividends, when paid, are paid to P on his shares, his charges to N for legal fees are reduced by the amount of the dividends paid on such shares. Although P votes his shares at meetings of shareholders, the facts set forth above indicate an implied agreement between P and N that N is really to retain dominion over the stock. N is deemed to own the voting rights ostensibly attached to the stock owned by P, and R Corporation is a controlled foreign corporation.

Example (6). M, a domestic corporation which manufactures in the United States and distributes all of its production for foreign consumption through N, a person other than a related person or a United States person, forms foreign corporation S to purchase products from M Corporation and sell them to N. Corporations S and M have common directors. The outstanding capital stock of S Corporation consists of 10,000 shares of $100 par value class A stock, which has no voting rights except to vote for dissolution of the corporation on a share-for-share basis, and 500 shares of no par class B stock which has full voting rights. Each class of the outstanding stock is to participate on a share for share basis in any dividend. The class A stock has a preference as to assets on dissolution of the corporation to the extent of its par value as well as the right to participate with the class B stock in all other assets on a share for share basis. All of the shares of class A stock are issued to M Corporation in return for property having a value of $1 million. Of the class B stock, 300 of the shares are issued to N in return for $3,000 in cash and 200 shares are issued to M Corporation for $2,000 in cash. At stockholder meetings N never votes in opposition to M Corporation on important issues. Corporation S has average annual earnings of $200,000, all of which will be subpart F income if S Corporation is held to be a controlled foreign corporation. All such earnings are accumulated. Although N ostensibly has 60 percent of the voting power of S Corporation by virtue of his ownership of 300 shares of class B stock, he has the right to only approximately 3 percent of any dividends which may be paid by S Corporation; in addition, upon liquidation of S Corporation, N is entitled to share in the assets only after M Corporation has received the par value of its 10,000 shares of class A stock, or $1 million. Thus, the voting power owned by N is substantially greater than its proportionate share of the earnings of S Corporation. In addition, the facts set forth above indicate that N is not exercising his voting rights independently and that a principal purpose of the capitalization arrangement is to avoid classification of S Corporation as a controlled foreign corporation. For these reasons, the voting power ostensibly provided the class B stock will be deemed owned by M Corporation, and S Corporation is a controlled foreign corporation.

Example (7). Foreign corporation A, authorized to issue 100 shares of one class of capital stock, issues, for $1,000 per share, 45 shares to domestic corporation M, 45 shares to foreign corporation B, and 10 shares to foreign corporation C. Corporation C, a bank, lends $3 million to finance the operations of A Corporation. In the course of negotiating these financial arrangements, D, an officer of C Corporation, and E, an officer of M Corporation, orally agree that C Corporation will vote its stock as M Corporation directs. By virtue of such oral agreement M Corporation possesses the voting power ostensibly owned by C Corporation, and A Corporation is a controlled foreign corporation.

Example (8). For its prior taxable year, JV, a foreign corporation, had outstanding 1000 shares of class A stock, which is voting common, and 1000 shares of class B stock, which is nonvoting preferred. DP, a domestic corporation, and FP, a foreign corporation, each owned precisely 500 shares of both class A and class B stock, and each elected 5 of the 10 members of JV's board of directors. The other facts and circumstances were such that JV was not a controlled foreign corporation on any day of the prior taxable year. On the first day of the current taxable year, DP purchased one share of class B stock from FP. JV was a controlled foreign corporation on the following day because over 50 percent of the total value in the corporation was held by a person that was a United States shareholder under section 951(b). See § 1.951-1(f).

Example (9). The facts are the same as in Example 8 except that the stock of FP was publicly traded, FP had one class of stock, and on the first day of the current taxable year DP purchased one share of FP stock on the foreign stock exchange instead of purchasing one share of JV stock from FP. JV became a controlled foreign corporation on the following day because over 50 percent of the total value in the corporation was held by a person that was a United States shareholder under section 951(b).

Example (10). X, a foreign corporation, is incorporated under the laws of country Y. Under the laws of country Y, X is considered a mutual insurance company. X issues insurance policies that provide the policyholder with the right to vote for directors of the corporation, the right to a share of the assets upon liquidation in proportion to premiums paid, and the right to receive policyholder dividends in proportion to premiums paid. Only policyholders are provided with the right to vote for directors, share in assets upon liquidation, and receive distributions. United States policyholders contribute 25 percent of the premiums and have 25 percent of the outstanding rights to vote for the board of directors. Based on these facts, the United States policyholders are United States shareholders owning the requisite combined voting power and value. Thus, X is a controlled foreign corporation for purposes of taking into account related person insurance income under section 953(c).

(d) Effective date. Paragraphs (a) and (c) Examples 8 through 10 of this section are effective for taxable years of a controlled foreign corporation beginning after November 6, 1995.

T.D. 6688, 10/30/63, amend T.D. 8216, 7/20/88, T.D. 8618, 9/6/95, T.D. 8704, 12/31/96.

---

§ 1.957-2 Controlled foreign corporation deriving income from insurance of United States risks.

Caution: The Treasury has not yet amended Reg § 1.957-2 to reflect changes made by P.L. 99-514.

(a) In general. For purposes of taking into account only the income derived from the insurance of United States risks under § 1.953-1, the term "controlled foreign corporation" means any foreign corporation of which more than 25 percent, but not more than 50 percent, of the total combined voting power of all classes of stock entitled to vote is owned within the meaning of section 958(a), or is considered as owned by applying the rules of ownership of section 958(b), by United States shareholders on any day of the taxable year of such foreign corporation, but only if the gross amount of premiums received by such foreign corporation during such taxable year which are attributable to the reinsuring and the issuing of insurance and annuity contracts in connection with United States risks, as defined in § 1.953-2 or 1.953-3, exceeds 75 percent of the gross amount of all premiums received by such foreign corporation during such year which are attributable to the reinsuring and the issuing of insurance and annuity contracts in connection with all risks. The subpart F income for a taxable year of a foreign corporation which is a controlled foreign corporation for such taxable year within the meaning of this paragraph shall, subject to the provisions of section 952(b), (c), and (d), and § 1.952-1, include only the income derived from the insurance of United States risks, as determined under § 1.953-1.

(b) Gross amount of premiums defined. For a foreign corporation which is engaged in the business of reinsuring or issuing insurance or annuity contracts and which, if it were a domestic corporation engaged only in such business, would be taxable as—

(1) A life insurance company to which part I (sections 801 through 820) of subchapter L of the Code applies,

(2) A mutual insurance company to which part II (sections 821 through 826) of subchapter L of the Code applies, or

(3) A mutual marine insurance or other insurance company to which part III (sections 831 and 832) of subchapter L of the Code applies,

the term "gross amount of premiums" means, for purposes of paragraph (a) of this section, the gross amount of premiums and other consideration which are taken into account by a life insurance company under section 809(c)(1). Determinations for purposes of this paragraph shall be made without regard to section 501(a).

T.D. 6795, 1/28/65.

§ 1.957-3 United States person defined.

[Reserved]. For further guidance, see § 1.957-3T.

T.D. 6683, 10/17/63, amend T.D. 9194, 4/6/2005.

PAR. 19.

Section 1.957-3 is revised to read as follows:

Proposed § 1.957-3 United States person defined. [*For Preamble, see ¶ 152,645*]

• *Caution:* This Notice of Proposed Rulemaking was partially finalized by TD 9248, 01/30/2006. Regs. §§ 1.1-1, 1.170A-1, 1.861-3, 1.861-8, 1.871-1, 1.876-1, 1.881-5, 1.884-0, 1.901-1, 1.931-1, 1.932-1, 1.933-1, 1.934-1, 1.935-1, 1.937-2, 1.937-3, 1.957-3, 1.1402(a)-12, 1.6038-2, 1.6046-1, 301.6688-1, 301.7701-3, and 301.7701(b)-1 remain proposed.

[The text of the proposed amendment to § 1.957-3 is the same as the text of § 1.957-3T published elsewhere in this issue of the Federal Register]. [*See T.D. 9194, 4/11/2005, 70 Fed. Reg. 68.*]

§ 1.957-3T United States person defined (temporary).

• *Caution:* Under Code Sec. 7805, temporary regulations expire within three years of the date of issuance. This temporary regulation was issued on 4/6/2005.

(a) Basic rule. *(1) In general.* The term *United States person* has the same meaning for purposes of sections 951 through 965 which it has under section 7701(a)(30) and the regulations thereunder, except as provided in paragraphs (b) and (c) of this section which provide, with respect to corporations organized in possessions of the United States, that certain residents of such possessions are not United States persons. The effect of determining that an individual is not a United States person for such purposes is to exclude such individual in determining whether a foreign corporation created or organized in, or under the laws of, a possession of the United States is a controlled foreign corporation. See § 1.957-1 for the definition of the term controlled foreign corporation.

(2) Special provisions applicable to possessions of the United States. For purposes of this section—

(i) The term possession of the United States means the Commonwealth of Puerto Rico (Puerto Rico) or any section 931 possession.

(ii) The term section 931 possession has the same meaning which it has under § 1.931-1T(c)(1).

(iii) The rules of § 1.937-1T shall apply for determining whether an individual is a bona fide resident of a possession of the United States.

(iv) The rules of § 1.937-2T shall apply for determining whether income is from sources within a possession of the United States.

(v) The rules of § 1.937-3T shall apply for determining whether income is effectively connected with the conduct of a trade or business in a possession of the United States.

(b) Puerto Rico corporation and resident. An individual (who, without regard to this paragraph (b), is a United States person) shall not be considered a United States person with respect to a foreign corporation created or organized in, or under the laws of, Puerto Rico for the taxable year of such corporation which ends with or within the taxable year of such individual if—

(1) Such individual is a bona fide resident of Puerto Rico during his entire taxable year in which or with which the taxable year of such foreign corporation ends; and

(2) A dividend received by such individual from such corporation during the taxable year of such corporation would, for purposes of section 933(1), be treated as income derived from sources within Puerto Rico.

(c) Section 931 possession corporation and resident. An individual (who, without regard to this paragraph (c), is a United States person) shall not be considered a United States person with respect to a foreign corporation created or organized in, or under the laws of, a section 931 possession for the taxable year of such corporation which ends with or within the taxable year of such individual if—

(1) Such individual is a bona fide resident of such section 931 possession during his entire taxable year in which or with which the taxable year of such foreign corporation ends; and

(2) Such corporation satisfies the following conditions—

(i) 80 percent or more of its gross income for the 3-year period ending at the close of the taxable year (or for such part of such period as such corporation or any predecessor has been in existence) was derived from sources within section 931 possessions or was effectively connected with the conduct of a trade or business in section 931 possessions; and

(ii) 50 percent or more of its gross income for such period (or part) was derived from the active conduct of a trade or business within section 931 possessions.

(d) Effective date. This section shall apply for taxable years ending after October 22, 2004.

T.D. 9194, 4/6/2005.

---

§ 1.958-1 Direct and indirect ownership of stock.

(a) In general. Section 958(a) provides that, for purposes of sections 951 to 964 (other than sections 955(b)(1)(A) and (B) and 955(c)(2)(A)(ii) (as in effect before the enactment of the Tax Reduction Act of 1975), and 960(a)(1)), stock owned means—

(1) Stock owned directly; and

(2) Stock owned with the application of paragraph (b) of this section.

The rules of section 958(a) and this section provide a limited form of stock attribution primarily for use in determining the amount taxable to a United States shareholder under section 951(a). These rules also apply for purposes of other provisions of the Code and regulations which make express reference to section 958(a).

(b) Stock ownership through foreign entities. For purposes of paragraph (a)(2) of this section, stock owned, directly or indirectly, by or for a foreign corporation, foreign partnership, foreign trust (within the meaning of section 7701(a)(31)) described in sections 671 through 679, or other foreign trust or foreign estate (within the meaning of section 7701(a)(31)) shall be considered as being owned proportionately by its shareholders, partners, grantors or other persons treated as owners under sections 671 through 679 of any portion of the trust that includes the stock, or beneficiaries, respectively. Stock considered to be owned by reason of the application of this paragraph shall, for purposes of reapplying this paragraph, be treated as actually owned by such person. Thus, this rule creates a chain of ownership; however, since the rule applies only to stock owned by a foreign entity, attribution under the rule stops with the first United States person in the chain of ownership running from the foreign entity. The application of this paragraph may be illustrated by the following example:

Example. Domestic corporation M owns 75 percent of the one class of stock in foreign corporation R, which in turn owns 80 percent of the one class of stock in foreign corporation S, which in turn owns 90 percent of the one class of stock in foreign corporation T. Under this paragraph, R Corporation is considered as owning 80 percent of the 90 percent of the stock which S Corporation owns in T Corporation, or 72 percent. Corporation M is considered as owning 75 percent of such 72 percent of the stock in T Corporation, or 54 percent. Since M Corporation is a domestic corporation, the attribution under this paragraph stops with M Corporation, even though, illustratively, such corporation is wholly owned by domestic corporation N.

(c) Rules of application. *(1) Special rule for mutual insurance companies.* For purposes of applying paragraph (a) of this section in the case of a foreign mutual insurance company, the term "stock" shall include any certificate entitling the holder to voting power in the corporation.

(2) Amount of interest in foreign corporation, foreign partnership, foreign trust, or foreign estate. The determination of a person's proportionate interest in a foreign corporation, foreign partnership, foreign trust, or foreign estate will be made on the basis of all the facts and circumstances in each case. Generally, in determining a person's proportionate interest in a foreign corporation, the purpose for which the rules of section 958(a) and this section are being applied will be taken into account. Thus, if the rules of section 958(a) are being applied to determine the amount of stock owned for purposes of section 951(a), a person's proportionate interest in a foreign corporation will generally be determined with reference to such person's interest in the income of such corporation. If the rules of section 958(a) are being applied to determine the amount of voting power owned for purposes of section 951(b) or 957, a person's proportionate interest in a foreign corporation will generally be determined with reference to the amount of voting power in such corporation owned by such person. However, any arrangement which artificially decreases a United States person's proportionate interest will not be recognized. See §§ 1.951-1 and 1.957-1.

(d) Illustration. The application of this section may be illustrated by the following examples:

Example (1). United States persons A and B own 25 percent and 50 percent, respectively, of the one class of stock in foreign corporation M. Corporation M owns 80 percent of the one class of stock in foreign corporation N, and N Corporation owns 60 percent of the one class of stock in foreign corporation P. Under paragraph (b) of this section, M Corporation is considered to own 48 percent (80 percent of 60 percent) of the stock in P Corporation; such 48 percent is treated as actually owned by M Corporation for the purpose of again applying paragraph (b) of this section. Thus, A and B are considered to own 12 percent (25 percent of 48 percent) and 24 percent (50 percent of 48 percent), respectively, of the stock in P Corporation.

Example (2). United States person C is a 60-percent partner in foreign partnership X. Partnership X owns 40 percent of the one class of stock in foreign corporation Q. Corporation Q is a 50-percent partner in foreign partnership Y, and partnership Y owns 100 percent of the one class of stock in foreign corporation R. By the application of paragraph (b) of this section, C is considered to own 12 percent (60 percent of 40 percent of 50 percent of 100 percent) of the stock in R Corporation.

Example (3). Foreign trust Z was created for the benefit of United States persons D, E, and F. Under the terms of the trust instrument, the trust income is required to be divided into three equal shares. Each beneficiary's share of the income may either be accumulated for him or distributed to him in the discretion of the trustee. In 1970, the trust is to terminate and there is to be paid over to each beneficiary the accumulated income applicable to his share and one-third of the corpus. The corpus of trust Z is composed of 90 percent of the one class of stock in foreign corporation S. By the application of this section, each of D, E, and F is considered to own 30 percent (1/3 of 90 percent) of the stock in S Corporation.

Example (4). Among the assets of foreign estate W are Blackacre and a block of stock, consisting of 75 percent of the one class of stock of foreign corporation T. Under the terms of the will governing estate W, Blackacre is left to G, a nonresident alien, for life, remainder to H, a nonresident alien, and the block of stock is left to United States person K. By the application of this section, K is considered to own the 75 percent of the stock of T Corporation, and G and H are not considered to own any of such stock.

T.D. 6889, 7/11/66, amend T.D. 7893, 5/11/83, T.D. 8955, 7/19/2001.

§ 1.958-2 Constructive ownership of stock.

Caution: The Treasury has not yet amended Reg § 1.958-2 to reflect changes made by P.L. 104-188, P.L. 103-66.

(a) In general. Section 958(b) provides that, for purposes of sections 951(b), 954(d)(3), 956(b)(2), and 957, the rules of section 318(a) as modified by section 958(b) and this section shall apply to the extent that the effect is to treat a United States person as a United States shareholder within the meaning of section 951(b), to treat a person as a related person within the meaning of section 954(d)(3), to treat the stock of a domestic corporation as owned by a United States shareholder of a controlled foreign corporation under section 956(b)(2), or to treat a foreign corporation as a controlled foreign corporation under section 957. The rules contained in this section also apply for purposes of other provisions of the Code and regulations which make express reference to section 958(b).

(b) Members of family. *(1) In general.* Except as provided in subparagraph (3) of this paragraph, an individual shall be considered as owning the stock owned, directly or indirectly, by or for—

(i) His spouse (other than a spouse who is legally separated from the individual under a decree of divorce or separate maintenance); and

(ii) His children, grandchildren, and parents.

(2) Effect of adoption. For purposes of subparagraph (1)(ii) of this paragraph, a legally adopted child of an individual shall be treated as a child of such individual by blood.

(3) Stock owned by nonresident alien individual. For purposes of this paragraph, stock owned by a nonresident alien individual (other than a foreign trust or foreign estate) shall not be considered as owned by a United States citizen or a resident alien individual. However, this limitation does not apply for purposes of determining whether the stock of a domestic corporation is owned or considered as owned by a United States shareholder under section 956(b)(2) and § 1.956-2(b)(1)(viii). See section 958(b)(1).

(c) Attribution from partnerships, estates, trusts, and corporations. *(1) In general.* Except as provided in subparagraph (2) of this paragraph—

(i) From partnerships and estates. Stock owned, directly or indirectly, by or for a partnership or estate shall be considered as owned proportionately by its partners or beneficiaries.

(ii) From trusts. (a) To beneficiaries. Stock owned, directly or indirectly, by or for a trust (other than an employees' trust described in section 401(a) which is exempt from tax under section 501(a)) shall be considered as owned by its beneficiaries in proportion to the actuarial interest of such beneficiaries in such trust.

(b) To owner. Stock owned, directly or indirectly, by or for any portion of a trust of which a person is considered the owner under sections 671 to 679 (relating to grantors and others treated as substantial owners) shall be considered as owned by such person.

(iii) From corporations. If 10 percent or more in value of the stock in a corporation is owned, directly or indirectly, by or for any person, such person shall be considered as owning the stock owned, directly or indirectly, by or for such corporation, in that proportion which the value of the stock which such person so owns bears to the value of all the stock in such corporation. See section 958(b)(3).

(2) Rules of application. For purposes of subparagraph (1) of this paragraph, if a partnership, estate, trust, or corporation owns, directly or indirectly, more than 50 percent of the total combined voting power of all classes of stock entitled to vote in a corporation, it shall be considered as owning all the stock entitled to vote. See section 958(b)(2).

(d) Attribution to partnerships, estates, trusts, and corporations. *(1) In general.* Except as provided in subparagraph (2) of this paragraph—

(i) To partnerships and estates. Stock owned, directly or indirectly, by or for a partner or a beneficiary of an estate shall be considered as owned by the partnership or estate.

(ii) To trusts. (a) From beneficiaries. Stock owned, directly or indirectly, by or for a beneficiary of a trust (other than an employees' trust described in section 401(a) which is exempt from tax under section 501(a)) shall be considered as owned by the trust, unless such beneficiary's interest in the trust is a remote contingent interest. For purposes of the preceding sentence, a contingent interest of a beneficiary in a trust shall be considered remote if, under the maximum exercise of discretion by the trustee in favor of such beneficiary, the value of such interest, computed actuarially, is 5 percent or less of the value of the trust property.

(b) From owner. Stock owned, directly or indirectly, by or for a person who is considered the owner of any portion of a trust under sections 671 to 678 (relating to grantors and others treated as substantial owners) shall be considered as owned by the trust.

(iii) To corporations. If 50 percent or more in value of the stock in a corporation is owned, directly or indirectly, by or for any person, such corporation shall be considered as owning the stock owned, directly or indirectly, by or for such person. This subdivision shall not be applied so as to consider a corporation as owning its own stock.

(2) Limitation. Subparagraph (1) of this paragraph shall not be applied so as to consider a United States person as owning stock which is owned by a person who is not a United States person. This limitation does not apply for purposes of determining whether the stock of a domestic corporation is owned or considered as owned by a United States shareholder under section 956(b)(2) and § 1.956-2(b)(1)(viii). See section 958(b)(4).

(e) Options. If any person has an option to acquire stock, such stock shall be considered as owned by such person. For purposes of the preceding sentence, an option to acquire such an option, and each one of a series of such options, shall be considered as an option to acquire such stock.

(f) Rules of application. For purposes of this section—

(1) Stock treated as actually owned. (i) In general. Except as provided in subdivisions (ii) and (iii) of this subparagraph, stock constructively owned by a person by reason of the application of paragraphs (b), (c), (d), and (e) of this section shall, for purposes of applying such paragraphs, be considered as actually owned by such person.

(ii) Members of family. Stock constructively owned by an individual by reason of the application of paragraph (b) of this section shall not be considered as owned by him for purposes of again applying such paragraph in order to make another the constructive owner of such stock.

(iii) Partnerships, estates, trusts, and corporations. Stock constructively owned by a partnership, estate, trust, or corporation by reason of the application of paragraph (d) of this section shall not be considered as owned by it for purposes of applying paragraph (c) of this section in order to make another the constructive owner of such stock.

(iv) Option rule in lieu of family rule. For purposes of this subparagraph, if stock may be considered as owned by an individual under paragraph (b) or (e) of this section, it shall be considered as owned by him under paragraph (e).

(2) Coordination of different attribution rules. For purposes of any one determination, stock which may be owned under more than one of the rules of § 1.958-1 and this section, or by more than one person, shall be owned under that attribution rule which imputes to the person, or persons, concerned the largest total percentage of such stock. The application of this subparagraph may be illustrated by the following examples:

Example (1). (a) United States persons A and B, and domestic corporation M, own 9 percent, 32 percent, and 10 percent, respectively, of the one class of stock in foreign corporation R. A also owns 10 percent of the one class of stock in M Corporation. For purposes of determining whether A is a United States shareholder with respect to R Corporation, 10 percent of the 10-percent interest of M Corporation in R Corporation is considered as owned by A. See paragraph (c)(1)(iii) of this section. Thus, A owns 10 percent (9 percent plus 10 percent of 10 percent) of the stock in R Corporation and is a United States shareholder with respect to such corporation. Corporation M and B, by reason of owning 10 percent and 32 percent, respectively, of the stock in R Corporation, are United States shareholders with respect to such corporation.

(b) For purposes of determining whether R Corporation is a controlled foreign corporation, the 1 percent of the stock in R Corporation directly owned by M Corporation and considered as owned by A cannot be counted twice. Therefore, the total amount of stock in R Corporation owned by United States shareholders is 51 percent, determined as follows:

	Stock ownership in R Corporation (percent)
A	9
B	32
M Corporation	10
Total	51

Example (2). United States person C owns 10 percent of the one class of stock in foreign corporation N, which owns 60 percent of the one class of stock in foreign corporation S. Under paragraph (a)(2) of § 1.958-1, C is considered as owning 6 percent (10 percent of 60 percent) of the stock in S Corporation. Under paragraph (c)(1)(iii) and (2) of this section N Corporation is considered as owning 100 percent of the stock in S Corporation and C is considered as owning 10 percent of such 100 percent, or 10 percent of the stock in S Corporation. Thus, for purposes of determining whether C is a United States shareholder with respect to S Corporation, the attribution rules of paragraph (c)(1)(iii) and (2) of this section are used inasmuch as C owns a larger total percentage of the stock of S Corporation under such rules.

(g) Illustration. The application of this section may be illustrated by the following examples:

Example (1). United States persons A and B own 5 percent and 25 percent, respectively, of the one class of stock in foreign corporation M. Corporation M owns 60 percent of the one class of stock in foreign corporation N. Under paragraph (a)(2) of § 1.958-1, A and B are considered as owning 3 percent (5 percent of 60 percent) and 15 percent (25 percent of 60 percent), respectively, of the stock in N Corporation. Under paragraph (c)(2) of this section, M Corporation is treated as owning all the stock in N Corporation, and, under paragraph (c)(1)(iii) of this section, B is considered as owning 25 percent of such 100 percent, or 25 percent of the stock in N Corporation. Inasmuch as A owns less than 10 percent of the stock in M Corporation, he is not considered as owning, under paragraph (c)(1)(iii) of this section, any of the stock in N Corporation owned by M Corporation. Thus, the attribution rules of paragraph (a)(2) of § 1.958-1 are used with respect to A inasmuch as he owns a larger total percentage of the stock of N Corporation under such rules; and the attribution rules of paragraph (c)(1)(iii) and (2) of this section are used with respect to B inasmuch as he owns a larger total percentage of the stock of N Corporation under such rules.

Example (2). United States person C owns 60 percent of the one class of stock in domestic corporation P; corporation P owns 60 percent of the one class of stock in foreign corporation Q; and corporation Q owns 60 percent of the one class of stock in foreign corporation R. Under paragraph (a)(2) of § 1.958-1, P Corporation is considered as owning 36 percent (60 percent of 60 percent) of the stock in R Corporation, and C is considered as owning none of the stock in R Corporation inasmuch as the chain of ownership stops at the first United States person and P Corporation is such a person. Under paragraph (c)(2) of this section, Q Corporation is treated as owning 100 percent of the stock in R Corporation, and under paragraph (c)(1)(iii) of this section, P Corporation is considered as owning 60 percent of such 100 percent, or 60 percent of the stock in R Corporation. For purposes of determining the amount of stock in R Corporation which C is considered as owning, P Corporation is treated under paragraph (c)(2) of this section as owning 100 percent of the stock in R Corporation; therefore, C is considered as owning 60 percent of the stock in R Corporation. Thus, the attribution rules of paragraph (c)(1)(iii) and (2) of this section are used with respect to C and P Corporation inasmuch as they each own a larger total percentage of the stock of R Corporation under such rules.

Example (3). United States person D owns 25 percent of the one class of stock in foreign corporation S. D is also a 40-percent partner in domestic partnership X, which owns 50 percent of the one class of stock in domestic corporation T. Under paragraph (d)(1)(i) of this section, the 25 percent of the stock in S Corporation owned by D is considered as being owned by partnership X; since such stock is treated as actually owned by partnership X under paragraph (f)(1)(i) of this section, such stock is in turn considered as being owned by T Corporation under paragraph (d)(1)(iii) of this section. Thus, under paragraphs (d)(1) and (f)(1)(i) of this section, T Corporation is considered as owning 25 percent of the stock in S Corporation.

Example (4). Foreign corporation U owns 100 percent of the one class of stock in domestic corporation V and also 100 percent of the one class of stock in foreign corporation W. By virtue of paragraph (d)(2) of this section, V Corporation may not be considered under paragraph (d)(1) of this section as owning the stock owned by its sole shareholder, U Corporation, in W Corporation.

Example (5). United States citizen E owns 15 percent of the one class of stock in foreign corporation Y, and United States citizen F, E's spouse, owns 5 percent of such stock. E and F's four nonresident alien grandchildren each own 20 percent of the stock in Y Corporation. Under paragraph (b)(1) of this section, E is considered as owning the stock owned by F in Y Corporation; however, by virtue of paragraph (b)(3) of this section, E may not be considered under paragraph (b)(1) of this section as owning any of the stock in Y Corporation owned by such grandchildren.

Example (6). United States person F owns 10 percent of the one class of stock in foreign corporation Z; corporation Z owns 10 percent of the one class of stock in foreign corporation K; and corporation K owns 100 percent of the one class of stock in foreign corporation L. United States person G, F's spouse, owns 9 percent of the stock in K Corporation. Under paragraph (c)(1)(iii) of this section or paragraph (a)(2) of § 1.958-1, F is considered as owning 1 percent (10 percent of 10 percent of 100 percent) of the stock in L Corporation by reason of his ownership of stock in Z Corporation, and, under paragraph (b)(1) of this section, G is considered as owning such 1 percent of the stock in L Corporation. Under paragraph (a)(2) of § 1.958-1, G is considered as owning 9 percent (9 percent of 100 percent) of the stock in L Corporation by reason of her ownership of stock in K Corporation, and, under paragraph (b)(1) of this section, F is considered as owning such 9 percent of the stock in L Corporation. Thus, for the purpose of determining whether F or G is a United States shareholder with respect to L Corporation, each of F and G is considered as owning a total of 10 percent of the stock in L Corporation by applying the rules of paragraph (a)(2) of § 1.958-1 and paragraphs (b)(1) and (c)(1)(iii) of this section.

T.D. 6889, 7/11/66, amend T.D. 7712, 8/6/80, T.D. 8955, 7/19/2001.

---

§ 1.959-1 Exclusion from gross income of United States persons of previously taxed earnings and profits.

Caution: The Treasury has not yet amended Reg § 1.959-1 to reflect changes made by 103-66.

(a) In general. Sections 951 through 964 provide that certain types of income of controlled foreign corporations will be subject to United States income tax even though such amounts are not currently distributed to the United States shareholders of such corporations. The amounts so taxed to certain United States shareholders are described as subpart F income, previously excluded subpart F income withdrawn from investment in less developed countries previously excluded subpart F income withdrawn from investment in foreign base company shipping operations and increases in earnings invested in United States property. Section 959 provides that amounts taxed as subpart F income, as previously excluded subpart F income withdrawn from investment in less developed countries, or as previously excluded subpart F income withdrawn from investment in foreign base company shipping operations are not taxed again as increases in earnings invested in United States property. Section 959 also provides an exclusion whereby none of the amounts so taxed are taxed again when actually distributed directly, or indirectly through a chain of ownership described in section 958(a), to United States shareholders or to such shareholder-ssuccessors in interest. The exclusion also applies to amounts taxed to United States shareholders as income of one controlled foreign corporation and later distributed to another controlled foreign corporation in such a chain of ownership where such amounts would otherwise be again included in the income of such shareholders or their successors in interest as subpart F income of the controlled foreign corporation to which they are distributed. Section 959 also provides rules for the allocation of distributions to earnings and profits and for the nondividend treatment of actual distributions which are excluded from gross income.

(b) Actual distributions to United States persons. The earnings and profits for a taxable year of a foreign corporation attributable to amounts which are, or have been, included in the gross income of a United States shareholder of such corporation under section 951(a) shall not, when such amounts are distributed to such shareholder directly, or indirectly through a chain of ownership described in section 958(a), be again included in the gross income of such United States shareholder. See section 959(a)(1). Thus, earnings and profits attributable to amounts which are, or have been, included in the gross income of a United States shareholder of a foreign corporation under section 951(a)(1)(A)(i) as subpart F income, under section 951(a)(1)(A)(ii) as previously excluded subpart F income withdrawn from investment in less developed countries, under section 951(a)(1)(A)(iii) as previously excluded subpart F income withdrawn from investment in foreign base company shipping operations, or under section 951(a)(1)(B) as earnings invested in United States property, shall not be again included in the gross income of such shareholder when such amounts are actually distributed, directly or indirectly, to such shareholder. See paragraph (d) of this section for exclusion applicable to such shareholder's successor in interest. The application of this paragraph may be illustrated by the following example:

Example. (a) A, a United States shareholder, owns 100 percent of the only class of stock of R Corporation, a corporation organized on January 1, 1963, which is a controlled foreign corporation throughout the period here involved. Both A and R Corporation use the calendar year as a taxable year.

(b) During 1964, R Corporation derives $100 of subpart F income, and A includes such amount in his gross income under section 951(a)(1)(A)(i). Corporation R's current and accumulated earnings and profits (before taking to account distributions made during 1964) are $150. Also, during 1964, R Corporation distributes $50 to A. The $50 distribution is excludable from A's gross income for 1964 under this paragraph and § 1.959-3 because such distribution represents earnings and profits attributable to amounts which are included in A's gross income for such year under section 951(a).

(c) If instead of deriving the $100 of subpart F income in 1964, R Corporation derives such amount during 1963 and has earnings and profits for 1963 in excess of $100, A must include $100 in his gross income for 1963 under section 951(a)(1)(A)(i). However, the $50 distribution made by R Corporation to A during 1964 is excludable from A's gross income for such year under this paragraph and § 1.959-3 because such distribution represents earnings and profits attributable to amounts which have been included in A's gross income for 1963 under section 951(a).

(d) If, with respect to 1964—

(1) Instead of owning the stock of R Corporation directly, A owns such stock through a chain of ownership described in section 958(a), that is, A owns 100 percent of M Corporation which owns 100 percent of N Corporation which owns 100 percent of R Corporation,

(2) Both M and N Corporations use the calendar year as a taxable year and are controlled foreign corporations throughout the period here involved,

(3) Corporation R derives $100 of subpart F income and has earnings and profits in excess of $100,

(4) Neither M Corporation nor N Corporation has earnings and profits or a deficit in earnings and profits, and

(5) The $50 distribution is from R Corporation to N Corporation to M Corporation to A,

A must include $100 in his gross income for 1964 under section 951(a)(1)(A)(i) by reason of his indirect ownership of R Corporation. However, the $50 distribution is excludable from A's gross income for 1964 under this paragraph and § 1.959-3 because such distribution represents earnings and profits attributable to amounts which are included in A's gross income for such year under section 951(a) and are distributed indirectly to A through a chain of ownership described in section 958(a).

(c) Excludable investment of earnings in United States property. The earnings and profits for a taxable year of a foreign corporation attributable to amounts which are, or have been, included in the gross income of a United States shareholder of such corporation under section 951(a)(1)(A) shall not, when such amounts would, but for section 959(a)(2) and this paragraph, be included under section 951(a)(1)(B) in the gross income of such shareholder directly, or indirectly through a chain of ownership described in section 958(a), be again included in the gross income of such United States shareholder. Thus, earnings and profits attributable to amounts which are, or have been, included in the gross income of a United States shareholder of a foreign corporation under section 951(a)(1)(A)(i) as subpart F income, under section 951(a)(1)(A)(ii) as previously excluded subpart F income withdrawn from investment in less developed countries, or under Section 951(a)(1)(A)(iii) as previously excluded subpart F income withdrawn from investment in foreign base company shipping operations, may be invested in United States property without being again included in such shareholder's income under section 951(a). Moreover, the first amounts deemed invested in United States property are amounts previously included in the gross income of a United States shareholder under section 951(a)(1)(A). See paragraph (d) of this section for exclusion applicable to such shareholder's successor in interest. The application of this paragraph may be illustrated by the following example:

Example. (a) A, a United States shareholder, owns 100 percent of the only class of stock of R Corporation, a corporation organized on January 1, 1963, which is a controlled foreign corporation throughout the period here involved. Both A and R Corporation use the calendar year as a taxable year.

(b) During 1964, R Corporation derives $35 of subpart F income, and A includes such amount in his gross income under section 951(a)(1)(A)(i). During 1964, R Corporation also invests $50 in tangible property (other than property described in section 956(b)(2)) located in the United States. Corporation R makes no distributions during the year, and its current earnings and profits are in excess of $50. Of the $50 investment of earnings in United States property, $35 is excludable from A's gross income for 1964 under section 959(a)(2) because such amount represents earnings and profits which are attributable to amounts which are included in A's gross income for such year under section 951(a)(1)(A)(i) and therefore may be invested in United States property without again being included in A's gross income. The remaining $15 is includible in A's gross income for 1964 under section 951(a)(1)(B).

(c) If, instead of deriving $35 of subpart F income in 1964, R Corporation has no subpart F income for 1964 but derives the $35 of subpart F income during 1963 and has earnings and profits for such year in excess of $35, A must include $35 in his gross income for 1963 under section 951(a)(1)(A)(i). However, of the $50 investment of earnings in United States property made by R Corporation during 1964, $35 is excludable from A's gross income for 1964 under section 959(a)(2) because such amount represents earnings and profits attributable to amounts which have been included in A's gross income for 1963 under section 951(a)(1)(A)(i). The remaining $15 is includible in A's gross income for 1964 under section 951(a)(1)(B).

(d) Application of exclusions to shareholder's successor in interest. If a United States person (as defined in § 1.957-4) acquires from any person any portion of the interest in the foreign corporation of a United States shareholder referred to in paragraph (b) or (c) of this section, the rules of such paragraph shall apply to such acquiring person but only to the extent that the acquiring person establishes to the satisfaction of the district director his right to the exclusion provided by such paragraph. The information to be furnished by the acquiring person to the district director with his return for the taxable year to support such exclusion shall include:

(1) The name, address, and taxable year of the foreign corporation from which the distribution is received and of all other corporations, partnerships, trusts, or estates in any applicable chain of ownership described in section 958(a);

(2) The name, address, and (in the case of information required to be furnished after June 20, 1983) taxpayer identification number of the person from whom the stock interest was acquired;

(3) A description of the stock interest acquired and its relation, if any, to a chain of ownership described in section 958(a);

(4) The amount for which an exclusion under section 959(a) is claimed; and

(5) Evidence showing that the earnings and profits for which an exclusion is claimed are attributable to amounts which were included in the gross income of a United States shareholder under section 951(a), that such amounts were not previously excluded from the gross income of a United States person, and the identity of the United States shareholder including such amounts.

The acquiring person shall also furnish to the district director such other information as may be required by the district director in support of the exclusion.

Example. (a) A, a United States shareholder, owns 100 percent of the only class of stock of R Corporation, a corporation organized on January 1, 1964, and a controlled foreign corporation throughout the period here involved. Both A and R Corporation use the calendar year as a taxable year.

(b) During 1964, R Corporation has $100 of subpart F income and earnings and profits in excess of $100. A includes $100 in his gross income for 1964 under section 951(a)(1)(A)(i). During 1965, A sells 40 percent of his stock in R Corporation to B, a United States person who uses the calendar year as a taxable year. In 1965, R Corporation has no earnings and profits and experiences no increase in earnings invested in United States property. Corporation R distributes $40 to B on December 1, 1965. If B establishes his right to the exclusion to the satisfaction of the district director, he may exclude $40 from his gross income for 1965 under section 959(a)(1).

(c) If, instead of selling his 40-percent interest directly to B, A sells on February 1, 1965, 40 percent of his stock in R Corporation to C, a nonresident alien, and on October 1, 1965, B acquires the 40-percent interest in R Corporation from C, the result is the same as in paragraph (b) of this example, if B establishes his right to the exclusion to the satisfaction of the district director.

(d) If, instead of acquiring 40 percent, B acquires only 5 percent of A's stock in R Corporation and R Corporation distributes $5 to B during 1965, B is not a United States shareholder (within the meaning of section 951(b)) with respect to R Corporation since he owns only 5 percent of the stock of R Corporation. Notwithstanding, B may exclude the $5 distribution from his gross income for 1965 under section 959(a)(1) if he establishes his right to the exclusion to the satisfaction of the district director.

(e) If the facts are assumed to be the same as in paragraphs (a) and (b) of this example except that—

(1) A owns the stock of R Corporation indirectly through a chain of ownership described in section 958(a), that is, A owns 100 percent of M Corporation which owns 100 percent of N Corporation which owns 100 percent of R Corporation,

(2) B acquires from N Corporation 40 percent of the stock in R Corporation,

(3) Both M Corporation and N Corporation are controlled foreign corporations which use the calendar year as a taxable year,

(4) Neither M Corporation nor N Corporation has any amount in 1964 or 1965 which is includible in gross income of United States shareholders under section 951(a), and

(5) Neither M Corporation nor N Corporation has a deficit in earnings and profits for 1964;

the result is the same as in paragraph (b) of this example if B establishes his right to the exclusion to the satisfaction of the district director.

T.D. 6795, 1/28/65, amend T.D. 7893, 5/11/83.

PAR. 2. Section 1.959-1 is revised to read as follows:

Proposed § 1.959-1 Exclusion from gross income of United States persons of previously taxed earnings and profits. [*For Preamble, see ¶ 152,795*]

(a) In general. Section 959(a) provides an exclusion whereby the earnings and profits of a foreign corporation attributable to amounts which are, or have been, included in a United States shareholder's gross income under section 951(a) are not taxed again when distributed (directly or indirectly through a chain of ownership described in section 958(a)) from such foreign corporation to such shareholder (or any other United States person who acquires from any person any portion of the interest of such United States shareholder in such foreign corporation, but only to the extent of such portion, and subject to such proof of the identity of such interest as the Secretary may by regulations prescribe). Section 959(a) also excludes from gross income of a United States shareholder earnings and profits attributable to amounts which are, or have been, included in the gross income of such shareholder under section 951(a) which would, but for section 959(a)(2), be again included in the gross income of such shareholder (or any other United States person who acquires from any person any portion of the interest of such United States shareholder in such foreign corporation, but only to the extent of such portion, and subject to such proof of the identity of such interest as the Secretary may by regulations prescribe) under section 951(a)(1)(B). Section 959(b) provides that for purposes of section 951(a), the earnings and profits of a CFC attributable to amounts that are, or have been, included in the gross income of a United States shareholder under section 951(a) shall not, when distributed through a chain of ownership described in section 958(a), be included in the gross income of a CFC in such chain for purposes of the application of section 951(a) to such CFC with respect to such United States shareholder (or any other United States person who acquires from any person any portion of the interest of such United States shareholder in such foreign corporation, but only to the extent of such portion, and subject to such proof of the identity of such interest as the Secretary may by regulations prescribe). Section 959(c) provides rules for the allocation of distributions to the various categories of previously taxed earnings and profits of a foreign corporation and the foreign corporation's non-previously taxed earnings and profits. Section 959(d) provides that, except as provided in section 960(a)(3), any distribution excluded from gross income under section 959(a) shall be treated as a distribution which is not a dividend; except that such distribution shall immediately reduce earnings and profits. Section 959(e) provides that, for purposes of sections 959 and 960(b), any amount included in the gross income of any person as a dividend by reason of subsection (a) or (f) of section 1248 shall be treated as an amount included in the gross income of such person (or, in any case to which section 1248(e) applies, of the domestic corporation referred to in section 1248(e)(2)) under section 951(a)(1)(A). Section 959(f)(1) provides rules for the allocation of amounts which would, but for section 959(a)(2), be included in gross income under section 951(a)(1)(B) to certain previously taxed earnings and profits of a foreign corporation and non-previously taxed earnings and profits. Section 959(f)(2) provides an ordering rule pursuant to which the rules of section 959 are applied first to actual distributions and then to amounts which would, but for section 959, be included in gross income under section 951(a)(1)(B). Paragraph (b) of this section provides a list of definitions. Paragraph (c) of this section provides rules for the exclusion from gross income under section 959(a)(1) of distributions of earnings and profits by a foreign corporation and the exclusion from gross income under section 959(a)(2) of amounts which would, but for section 959, be included in gross income under section 951(a)(1)(B). Paragraph (d) of this section provides for the establishment and acquisition of previously taxed earnings and profits accounts by shareholders of foreign corporations. Section 1.959-2 provides rules for the exclusion from gross income of a CFC of distributions of previously taxed earnings and profits from another CFC in a chain of ownership described in section 958(a). Section 1.959-3 provides rules for the allocation of distributions and section 956 amounts to the earnings and profits of a CFC and for the maintenance and adjustment of previously taxed earnings and profits accounts by shareholders of foreign corporations. Section

1.959-4 provides for the treatment of actual distributions that are excluded from gross income under section 959(a).

(b) Definitions. For purposes of this section through § 1.959-4 and § 1.961-1 through § 1.961-4, the terms listed in this paragraph are defined as follows:

(1) Previously taxed earnings and profits means the earnings and profits of a foreign corporation, computed in accordance with sections 964 and 986(b) and the regulations thereunder, attributable to section 951(a) inclusions.

(2) Previously taxed earnings and profits account means an account reflecting the previously taxed earnings and profits of a foreign corporation (if any).

(3) Dollar basis means the United States dollar amounts included in a United States shareholder's income with respect to the previously taxed earnings and profits included in a shareholder's previously taxed earnings and profits account.

(4) Covered shareholder means a person who is one of the following—

(i) A United States person who owns stock (within the meaning of section 958(a)) in a foreign corporation and who has had a section 951(a) inclusion with respect to its stock in such corporation;

(ii) A successor in interest, as defined in paragraph (b)(5) of this section; or

(iii) A corporation that is not described in paragraphs (b)(4)(i) or (ii) of this section and that owns stock (within the meaning of section 958(a)) in a foreign corporation in which another corporation is a covered shareholder described in paragraph (b)(4)(i) or (ii) of this section, if both if both the first mentioned corporation and the covered shareholder are members of the same consolidated group.

(5) Successor in interest means a United States person who acquires, from any person, ownership (within the meaning of section 958(a)) of stock in a foreign corporation, for which there is a previously taxed earnings and profits account and who establishes to the satisfaction of the Director of Field Operations the right to the exclusion from gross income provided by section 959(a) and this section. To establish the right to the exclusion, the shareholder must attach to its return for the taxable year a statement that provides that it is excluding amounts from gross income because it is a successor in interest succeeding to one or more previously taxed earnings and profits accounts with respect to shares it owns in a foreign corporation. Included in the statement shall be the name of the foreign corporation. In addition, that shareholder must be prepared to provide the following information within 30 days upon request by the Director of Field Operations—

(i) The name, address, and taxable year of the foreign corporation and of all the other corporations, partnerships, trusts, or estates in any applicable chain of ownership described in section 958(a);

(ii) The name, address, and taxpayer identification number, if any, of the person from whom the stock interest was acquired;

(iii) A description of the stock interest acquired and its relation, if any, to a chain of ownership described in section 958(a);

(iv) The amount for which an exclusion under section 959(a) and paragraph (c) of this section is claimed; and

(v) Evidence showing that the earnings and profits for which an exclusion is claimed are previously taxed earnings and profits, that such amounts were not previously excluded from the gross income of a United States person, and the identity of the United States shareholder who originally included such amounts in gross income under section 951(a). The acquiring person shall also furnish to the Director of Field Operations such other information as may be required by the Director of Field Operations in support of the exclusion.

(6) Block of stock shall have the meaning provided in § 1.1248-2(b) with the additional requirement that the previously taxed earnings and profits attributable to each share of stock in such block must be the same.

(7) Consolidated group shall have the meaning provided in § 1.1502-1(h).

(8) Member shall have the meaning provided in § 1.1502-1(b).

(9) Section 951(a) inclusion means a section 951(a)(1)(A) inclusion or an amount included in the gross income of a United States shareholder under section 951(a)(1)(B).

(10) Section 951(a)(1)(A) inclusion means—

(i) An amount included in a United States shareholder's gross income under section 951(a)(1)(A);

(ii) An amount included in the gross income of any person as a dividend by reason of subsection (a) or (f) of section 1248 (or, in any case to which section 1248(e) applies, an amount included in the gross income of the domestic corporation referred to in section 1248(e)(2)); or

(iii) An amount described in section 1293(c).

(11) Section 956 amount means an amount determined under section 956 for a United States shareholder with respect to a single share or, if a shareholder maintains a previously taxed earnings and profits account with respect to a block of stock, a block of such shareholder's stock in the CFC.

(12) Section 959(c)(1) earnings and profits means the previously taxed earnings and profits of a foreign corporation attributable to amounts that have been included in the gross income of a United States shareholder under section 951(a)(1)(B) (or which would have been included except for section 959(a)(2) and § 1.959-2) and amounts that have been included in gross income under section 951(a)(1)(C) as it existed prior to its repeal (or which would have been included except for section 959(a)(3) as it existed prior to its repeal).

(13) Section 959(c)(2) earnings and profits means the previously taxed earnings and profits of a foreign corporation attributable to section 951(a)(1)(A) inclusions.

(14) Non-previously taxed earnings and profits means the earnings and profits of a foreign corporation other than the corporation's previously taxed earnings and profits.

(15) CFC means a controlled foreign corporation within the meaning of either section 953(c)(1)(B) or section 957.

(16) United States shareholder means a United States person who qualifies as a United States shareholder under either section 951(b) or section 953(c)(1)(A).

(c) Amount excluded from gross income. *(1) Distributions.* In the case of a distribution of earnings and profits to a covered shareholder with respect to stock in a foreign corporation, an amount shall be excluded from such shareholder's gross income equal to the total amount by which such shareholder's previously taxed earnings and profits account with respect to such stock is decreased under § 1.959-3 because of the distribution.

(2) Section 956 amounts. In a case where a covered shareholder has a section 956 amount for a CFC's taxable year,

an amount shall be excluded from such shareholder's gross income equal to the amount of section 959(c)(2) earnings and profits in any shareholder's previously taxed earnings and profits account that are reclassified as section 959(c)(1) earnings and profits under § 1.959-3 because of that section 956 amount.

(d) Shareholder accounts. *(1) In general.* Any person who is subject to § 1.959-3 shall maintain a previously taxed earnings and profits account with respect to each share of stock it owns (within the meaning of section 958(a)) in a foreign corporation. Although the account is share specific, the account may be maintained with respect to each block of the stock in the foreign corporation. Such account shall be maintained in accordance with § 1.959-3.

(2) Acquisition of account. (i) In general. If any person acquires, from any other person, ownership of shares of stock in a foreign corporation (within the meaning of section 958(a)) the prior shareholder's previously taxed earnings and profits account with respect to such stock becomes the previously taxed earnings and profits account of the acquirer.

(ii) Acquisition of account by a person other than a successor in interest. If such acquirer is not a successor in interest (a foreign person for example), the previously taxed earnings and profits account with respect to the stock acquired shall remain unchanged for the period that the stock is owned by such acquirer. See also § 1.959-3(e), providing account adjustment rules that apply only for acquired PTI accounts if the acquirer is a successors in interest.

(3) Examples. The application of this paragraph (d) is illustrated by the following examples:

Example (1). Shareholder's previously taxed earnings and profits account. (i) Facts. DP, a United States shareholder owns all of the 100 shares of the only class of stock in FC, a CFC. The 100 shares are a block of stock. DP and FC use the calendar year as their taxable year and FC uses the U.S. dollar as its functional currency. In year 1, FC earns $100x of subpart F income and $100x of non-subpart F income. DP includes $100x in gross income under section 951(a).

(ii) Analysis. As a result of DP's inclusion of $100x of gross income under section 951(a), DP has a previously taxed earnings and profits account with respect to each of its 100 shares equal to $1x or should DP choose to maintain its previously taxed earnings and profits account on a block basis, an account of $100x with respect to its entire interest in FC.

Example (2). Acquisition of previously taxed earnings and profits account. (i) Facts. Assume the same facts as Example 1, but that in year 2, a nonresident alien, FP, contributes property to FC to acquire 1000 newly issued shares of FC of the same class held by DP. In year 10, DP sells all of its FC shares to FP. In year 15, FP sells all of its shares in FC to USP, a United States person. Any income earned by FC after year 1 is non-subpart F income. The only distributions by FC during this period are a $100x pre-sale distribution to FP in year 15 and another $100x distribution in year 16 to USP.

(ii) Analysis. In year 2, DP retains its previously taxed earnings and profits account of $100x as a result of its section 951(a) inclusion in year 1 regardless of the fact that FC is no longer a CFC and DP no longer holds a sufficient interest in FC to be a United States shareholder with respect to FC. In year 10, pursuant to paragraph (d)(2)(i) of this section, FP acquires a $100x previously taxed earnings and profits account with respect to DP's block of stock in FC that FP acquired. In year 15, FP receives a distribution of $100x of earnings and profits from FC, but FP may not exclude any of this distribution from gross income because FP is a nonresident alien. Consequently, pursuant to paragraph (d)(2)(ii) of this section, even though it acquired a previously taxed earnings and profits account from DP of $100x the account remains unchanged during FP's ownership of the FC stock. However, if USP can make the showing required in paragraph (b)(5) of this section, USP may exclude the $100x distribution in year 16 under section 959(a)(1) and paragraph (c) of this section to the extent that the distribution results in a decrease of the $100x previously taxed earnings and profits account that USP acquired from FP pursuant to the account adjustment rules of § 1.959-3.

§ 1.959-2 Exclusion from gross income of controlled foreign corporations of previously taxed earnings and profits.

(a) Applicable rule. The earnings and profits for a taxable year of a controlled foreign corporation attributable to amounts which are, or have been, included in the gross income of a United States shareholder under section 951(a) shall not, when distributed through a chain of ownership described in section 958(a), be also included in the gross income of another controlled foreign corporation in such chain for purposes of the application of section 951(a) to such other controlled foreign corporation with respect to such United States shareholder. See section 959(b). The exclusion from the income of such other foreign corporation also applies with respect to any other United States shareholder who acquires from such United States shareholder or any other person any portion of the interest of such United States shareholder in the controlled foreign corporation, but only to the extent the acquiring shareholder establishes to the satisfaction of the district director his right to such exclusion. An acquiring shareholder claiming the exclusion under section 959(b) shall furnish to the district director with his return for the taxable year the information required under paragraph (d) of § 1.959-1 to support the exclusion under this paragraph.

(b) Illustration. The application of this section may be illustrated by the following example:

Example. (a) A, a United States shareholder, owns 100 percent of the only class of stock of M Corporation which in turn owns 100 percent of the only class of stock of N Corporation. A and corporations M and N use the calendar year as a taxable year and corporations M and N are controlled foreign corporations throughout the period here involved.

(b) During 1963, N Corporation invests $100 in tangible property (other than property described in section 956(b)(2)) located in the United States and has earnings and profits in excess of $100. A is required to include $100 in his gross income for 1963 under section 951(a)(1)(B) by reason of his indirect ownership of the stock of N Corporation. During 1963, M Corporation has no income or investments other than the income derived from a distribution of $100 from N Corporation. Corporation M has earnings and profits of $100 for 1963. Under paragraph (a) of § 1.954-2, the $100 distribution received by M Corporation from N Corporation would otherwise constitute subpart F income of M Corporation; however, by reason of section 959(b) and this section, this amount does not constitute gross income of M Corporation for purposes of determining amounts includible in A's gross income under section 951(a)(1)(A)(i).

(c) During 1964, N Corporation derives $100 of subpart F income and distributes $100 to M Corporation which has no subpart F income for 1964 but which invests the $100 distribution in tangible property (other than property described in section 956(b)(2)) located in the United States. Corporation N's earnings and profits for 1964 are in excess of $100, and

M Corporation's current and accumulated earnings and profits (before taking into account distributions made during 1964) are in excess of $100. A is required with respect to N Corporation to include $100 in his gross income for 1964 under section 951(a)(1)(A)(i) by reason of his indirect ownership of the stock of N Corporation. The investment by M Corporation in United States property would otherwise constitute an investment of earnings in United States property to which section 956 applies; however, by reason of section 959(b) and this section, such amount does not constitute gross income of M Corporation for purposes of determining amounts includible in A's gross income under section 951(a)(1)(B).

(d) If during 1965, N Corporation invests $100 in tangible property (other than property described in section 956(b)(2)) located in the United States and has earnings and profits in excess of $100, A will be required with respect to N Corporation to include $100 in his gross income for 1965 under section 951(a)(1)(B), because the $100 of earnings and profits for 1964 attributable to N Corporation's subpart F income which was taxed to A in 1964 was distributed to M Corporation in such year.

(e) If, with respect to 1966—

(1) Corporation N owns 100 percent of the only class of stock of R Corporation,

(2) Corporation R derives $100 of subpart F income, has earnings and profits in excess of $100, and makes no distributions to N Corporation,

(3) Corporation N invests $25 in tangible property (other than property described in section 956(b)(2)) located in the United States and has current and accumulated earnings and profits in excess of $25, and

(4) Corporation M has no income or investments and does not have a deficit in earnings and profits,

the $100 of subpart F income derived by R Corporation is includible in A's gross income for 1966 under section 951(a)(1)(A)(i) and the $25 investment of earnings in United States property by N Corporation is includible in A's gross income for 1966 under section 951(a)(1)(B).

(f) If, however, the facts are the same as in paragraph (e) of this example except that—

(1) During 1966, R Corporation distributes $20 to N Corporation, and

(2) Corporation N makes no distributions during such year to M Corporation,

of the $25 investment in United States property by N Corporation, $20 is not includible in A's gross income for 1966 because such amount represents earnings and profits which are attributable to amounts included in A's gross income for such year under section 951(a)(1)(A)(i) with respect to R Corporation and which have been distributed to N Corporation by R Corporation. By reason of section 959(b) and this section, such $20 distribution to N Corporation does not constitute gross income of N Corporation for purposes of determining amounts includible in A's gross income under section 951(a)(1)(B); however, the remaining $5 of investment of earnings in United States property by N Corporation in 1966 is includible in A's gross income for such year under section 951(a)(1)(B).

T.D. 6795, 1/28/65.

PAR. 3. Section 1.959-2 is revised to read as follows:

Proposed § 1.959-2 Exclusion from gross income of CFCs of previously taxed earnings and profits. [*For Preamble, see ¶ 152,795*]

(a) Exclusion from gross income. *(1) In general.* The earnings and profits of a CFC (lower-tier CFC) attributable to amounts which are, or have been, included in the gross income of a United States shareholder under section 951(a) shall not, when distributed through a chain of ownership described in section 958(a), be also included in the gross income of the CFC receiving the distribution (upper-tier CFC) in such chain for purposes of the application of section 951(a) to such upper-tier CFC with respect to such United States shareholder. The amount of the exclusion provided under this paragraph is the entire amount distributed by the lower-tier CFC to the upper-tier CFC that gave rise (in whole or in part) to an adjustment of the United States shareholder's previously taxed earnings and profits accounts with respect to the stock it owns (within the meaning of section 958(a)) in the lower- and upper-tier CFC under § 1.959-3(e)(3). This amount shall not exceed the earnings and profits of the lower-tier CFC attributable to amounts described in section 951(a)(1) (without regard to pro rata share). The exclusion from the income of such upper-tier CFC also applies with respect to any other United States shareholder who is a successor in interest.

(2) Examples. The application of this paragraph (a) is illustrated by the following examples:

Example (1). Distribution attributable to subpart F income of lower-tier CFC. (i) Facts. FC, a CFC, is 70% owned by DP, a United States person, and 30% owned by FP, a nonresident alien. FC owns all the stock in FS, a CFC. DP, FP, FC and FS all use the calendar year as their taxable year and FC and FS use the U.S. dollar as their functional currency. In year 1, FS earns $100x of passive income described in section 954(c) and $50x of non-subpart F income. On the last day of year 1, FS distributes $100x to FC that would qualify as subpart F income of FC. On the last day of year 1, FC distributes $70x to DP and $30x to FP.

(ii) Analysis. DP is required to include $70x in its gross income under section 951(a) as a result of FS's earning $100x of subpart F income for the year. Consequently, the section 959(c)(2) earnings and profits in DP's previously taxed earnings and profits account with respect to its indirect ownership of stock in FS is increased to $70x. Under § 1.959-3(e)(3), as a result of the $100x distribution paid by FS to FC, DP's previously taxed earnings and profits account is reduced by its pro rata share of the distribution ($70x). In addition, FS's non-previously taxed earnings and profits are reduced by the remaining $30x. Under paragraph (a) of this section, the amount of the exclusion under paragraph (a) is equal to the amount distributed, not to exceed the amount of earnings and profits that gave rise to the previously taxed income that is being distributed. Consequently, the entire $100x distribution (as opposed to only $70x) is excluded from FC's gross income for purposes of determining whether DP has an inclusion under section 951(a) as a result of FC's receiving the distribution from FS. The receipt of the distribution from FS increases FC's earnings and profits by $100x ($70x of which is previously taxed earnings and profits and $30x of which is non-previously taxed earnings and profits).

Example (2). Transferee shareholder. (i) Facts. The facts are the same as in Example 1 except that neither FS nor FC makes any distributions in year 1. In year 2, FP sells its stock in FC to DT, a United States person. On the last day of year 2, FS distributes $100x to FC that would qualify as subpart F income of FC. FS has no earnings and profits for year 2, and FC had no earnings and profits for year 2 other than the distribution from FS.

(ii) Analysis. With respect to DP, the analysis is the same as that in Example 1. However, for purposes of DT's determination of the amount includible in its gross income under section 951(a) with respect to FC for year 2, none of the $100x distribution is excluded from FC's gross income for purposes of applying section 951(a) with respect to DT's interest in FC because none of earnings and profits distributed by FS to FC are attributable to amounts which are, or have been, included in the gross income of DT or the person to whom DT is a successor in interest (FP). Consequently, DT must include $30x in gross income under section 951(a) for year 2 as its pro rata share of FC's subpart F income of $100x ($100x x 30%). Thereafter, DT has a previously taxed earnings and profits account consisting of $30x with respect to its stock in FC and FC has $100x of previously taxed earnings and profits.

Example (3). Mixed distribution. (i) Facts. The facts are the same as in Example 1, except that on the last day of year 1, FS distributes $150x to FC that would qualify as subpart F income of FC, which in turn distributes $105x to DP and $45x to FP.

(ii) Analysis. Under the analysis in Example 1 and pursuant to paragraph (a) of this section, $100x of the distribution from FS to FC is excluded from FC's gross income for purposes of determining DP's inclusion under section 951(a) with respect to FC's receipt of the distribution from FS. However, DP's pro rata share of the remaining $50x, or $35x ($50x x 70%), is included in DP's gross income under section 951(a). Consequently, the previously taxed earnings and profits in DP's previously taxed earnings and profits account with respect to its stock in FC is increased from $70x to $105x pursuant to § 1.959-3(e)(2)(i). That account is then reduced to $0, as a result of the distribution of $105x to DP pursuant to § 1.959-3(e)(2)(ii) and DP excludes the distribution of $105x from FC from its gross income for year 1 under section 959(a)(1) and § 1.959-1(c).

(b) Section 304(a)(1) transactions. *(1) Deemed redemption treated as a distribution.* In the case of a stock acquisition under section 304(a)(1) treated as a distribution to which section 301 applies, the selling CFC shall be deemed for purposes of section 959(b) and paragraph (a) of this section to receive such distributions through a chain of ownership described under section 958(a).

(2) Example. The application of this paragraph (c) is illustrated by the following example:

Example. Cross-chain acquisition of CFC stock by a CFC from another CFC. (i) Facts. DP, a domestic corporation, owns all of the stock in two foreign corporations, FX and FY. FX owns all of the stock in foreign corporation FZ. DP, FX, FY, and FZ all use the calendar year as their taxable year and the U.S. dollar as their functional currency. During year 1, FY purchases all of the stock in FZ from FX for $80x in a transaction described in section 304(a)(1). At the end of year 1, before taking into account the purchase of FZ's stock, FY has section 959(c)(2) earnings and profits of $20x and non-previously taxed earnings and profits of $10x, and FZ has section 959(c)(2) earnings and profits of $50x and non-previously taxed earnings and profits of $0.

(ii) Analysis. Under section 304(a)(1), FX is deemed to have transferred the FZ stock to FY in exchange for FY stock in a transaction to which section 351 applies, and FY is treated as having redeemed, for $80x, the FY stock deemed issued to FX. The payment of $80x is treated as a distribution to which section 301 applies. Under section 304(b)(2), the determination of the amount which is a dividend (and the source) is made as if the distribution were made, first, by FY to the extent of its earnings and profits, $30x, and then by FX to the extent of its earnings and profits, $50x. Under paragraph (c)(1) of this section, FX is deemed to receive the distributions from FY and FZ through a chain of ownership described in section 958(a). Under paragraph (a) of this section, the amount of FY's previously taxed earnings and profits, $20x, and the amount of FZ's previously taxed earnings and profits, $50x, distributed to FX are excluded from the gross income of FX. Accordingly, only $10x is included in FX's gross income.

§ 1.959-3 Allocation of distributions to earnings and profits of foreign corporations.

Caution: The Treasury has not yet amended Reg § 1.959-3 to reflect changes made by P.L. 105-34, P.L. 103-66.

(a) In general. For purposes of §§ 1.959-1 and 1.959-2, the source of the earnings and profits from which distributions are made by a foreign corporation as between earnings and profits attributable to increases in earnings invested in United States property, previously taxed subpart F income, previously excluded subpart F income withdrawn from investment in less developed countries, previously excluded subpart F income withdrawn from investment in foreign base company shipping operations, and other amounts shall be determined in accordance with section 959(c) and paragraphs (b) through (e) of this section.

(b) Applicability of section 316(a). For purposes of this section, section 316(a) shall be applied, in determining the source of distributions from the earnings and profits of a foreign corporation, by first applying section 316(a)(2) and then by applying section 316(a)(1)—

(1) First, as provided by section 959(c)(1), to earnings and profits attributable to amounts included in gross income of a United States shareholder under section 951(a)(1)(B) (or which would have been so included but for section 959(a)(2) and paragraph (c) of § 1.959-1),

(2) Secondly, as provided by section 959(c)(2), to earnings and profits attributable to amounts included in gross income of a United States shareholder under section 951(a)(1)(A) (but reduced by amounts not included in such gross income under section 951(a)(1)(B) because of the exclusion provided by section 959(a)(2) and paragraph (c) of § 1.959-1), and

(3) Finally, as provided by section 959(c)(3), to other earnings and profits.

Thus, distributions shall be considered first attributable to amounts, if any, described in subparagraph (1) of this paragraph (first for the current taxable year and then for prior taxable years beginning with the most recent prior taxable year), secondly to amounts, if any, described in subparagraph (2) of this paragraph (first for the current taxable year and then for prior taxable years beginning with the most recent prior taxable year), and finally to the amounts, if any, described in subparagraph (3) of this paragraph (first for the current taxable year and then for prior taxable years beginning with the most recent prior taxable year). See, however, paragraph (e) of § 1.963-3 (applied as if section 963 had not been repealed by the Tax Reduction Act of 1975) for a special rule for determination of the source of distributions counting as minimum distributions. Earnings and profits are classified as to year and as to section 959(c) amount in the year in which such amounts are included in gross income of a United States shareholder under section 951(a) and are reclassified as to section 959(c) amount in the year in which such amounts would be so included but for the provisions of section 959(a)(2); any subsequent distribution of such amounts to a higher tier in a chain of ownership described in section 958(a) does not of itself change such classifications. For example, earnings and profits of a foreign corporation attributable to amounts of previously excluded subpart F income withdrawn from investment in less developed countries (or from investments in export trade assets or foreign base company shipping operations) shall be reclassified as amounts to which subparagraph (2); rather than subparagraph (3), of this paragraph applies for purposes of determining priority of distribution, and such earnings and profits shall be considered attributable to the taxable year in which the withdrawal occurs. This paragraph shall apply to distributions by one foreign corporation to another foreign corporation and by a foreign corporation to a United States person. The application of this paragraph may be illustrated by the following example:

Example. (a) M, a controlled foreign corporation is organized on January 1, 1963, and is 100-percent owned by A, a United States shareholder. Both A and M Corporation use the calendar year as a taxable year, and M Corporation is a controlled foreign corporation throughout the period here involved. As of December 31, 1966, M Corporation's accumulated earnings and profits of $450 (before taking into account distributions made in 1966) applicable to A's interest in such corporation are classified for purposes of section 959(c) as follows:

Year	Classification of earnings and profits for purposes of sec. 959		
	(c)(1)	(c)(2)	(c)(3)
1963	$100		
1964	100	$75	
1965		75	$50
1966			50

(b) During 1966, M Corporation makes three separate distributions to A of $150 each, and the source of such distributions under section 959(c) is as follows:

	Amount	Year	Allocation of distributions under sec. 959
Distribution No. 1	$100	1964	(c)(1)
	50	1963	(c)(1)
	$150		
Distribution No. 2	$ 50	1963	(c)(1)
	75	1965	(c)(2)
	25	1964	(c)(2)
	$150		
Distribution No. 3	$ 50	1964	(c)(2)
	50	1966	(c)(3)
	50	1965	(c)(3)
	$150		

(c) If, in addition to the above facts—

(1) M corporation owns throughout the period here involved 100 percent of the only class of stock of N Corporation, a controlled foreign corporation which uses the calendar year as a taxable year,

(2) Corporation N derives $60 of subpart F income for 1963 which A includes in his gross income for such year under section 951(a)(1)(A)(i),

(3) Corporation N has earnings and profits for 1963 of $60 but has neither earnings or profits nor a deficit in earnings and profits for 1964, 1965, or 1966, and

(4) During 1966, N Corporation invests $20 in tangible property (not described in section 956(b)(2)) located in the United States and distributes $45 to M Corporation,

the $20 investment of earnings in United States property is excludable from A's gross income for 1966, under section 959(a)(2) and paragraph (c) of § 1.959-1, with respect to N Corporation and the $45 dividend received by M Corporation does not, under section 959(b) and § 1.959-2, constitute gross income of M Corporation for 1966 for purposes of determining amounts includible in A's gross income under section 951(a)(1)(A)(i) with respect to M Corporation. However, the $45 dividend paid by N Corporation to M Corporation is allocated under section 959(c) and this paragraph to the earnings and profits of N Corporation as follows: $20 to 1963 earnings described in section 959(c)(1) and $25 to 1963 earnings described in section 959(c)(2). In such case, M Corporation's earnings and profits of $495 (before taking into account distributions made in 1966) would be classified as follows for purposes of section 959(c):

Year	Classification of earnings and profits for purposes of sec. 959		
	(c)(1)	(c)(2)	(c)(3)
1963	$120	$25	
1964	100	75	
1965		75	$50
1966			50

(d) The three distributions to A in 1966 of $150 each would then have the following source under section 959(c):

	Amount	Year	Allocation of distributions under sec. 959
Distribution No. 1	$100	1964	(c)(1)
	50	1963	(c)(1)
	150		
Distribution No. 2	70	1963	(c)(1)
	75	1965	(c)(2)
	5	1964	(c)(2)
	150		
Distribution No. 3	70	1964	(c)(2)
	25	1963	(c)(2)
	50	1966	(c)(3)
	5	1965	(c)(3)
	150		

(c) Treatment of deficits in earnings and profits. For purposes of this section, a United States shareholder's pro rata share (determined in accordance with the principles of paragraph (e) of § 1.951-1) of a foreign corporation's deficit in earnings and profits, determined under section 964(a) and § 1.964-1, for any taxable year shall be applied only to earnings and profits described in paragraph (b)(3) of this section.

(d) Treatment of certain foreign taxes. For purposes of this section, any amount described in subparagraph (1), (2), or (3) of paragraph (b) of this section which is distributed by a foreign corporation through a chain of ownership described in section 958(a)(2) shall be reduced by any income, war profits, or excess profits taxes imposed on or with respect to such distribution by any foreign country or possession of the United States.

Example. (a) Domestic corporation M owns 100 percent of the only class of stock of foreign corporation A, which is incorporated under the laws of foreign country X and which, in turn, owns 100 percent of the only class of stock of foreign corporation B, which is incorporated under the laws of foreign country Y. All corporations use the calendar year as a taxable year and corporations A and B are controlled foreign corporations throughout the period here involved.

(b) During 1963, B Corporation (a less developed country corporation for 1963 within the meaning of § 1.955-5) derives $90 of subpart F income, after incurring $10 of foreign income tax allocable to such income under paragraph (c) of § 1.954-1, has earnings and profits in excess of $90, and makes no distributions. Corporation M must include $90 in its gross income for 1963 under section 951(a)(1)(A)(i). As of December 31, 1963, with respect to M Corporation, B Corporation has earnings and profits for 1963 described in section 959(c)(2) of $90.

(c) During 1964, B Corporation has neither earnings and profits nor a deficit in earnings and profits but distributes $90 to A Corporation, and, by reason of section 959(b) and § 1.959-2, such amount is not includible in the gross income of M Corporation for 1964 under section 951(a) with respect to A Corporation. Corporation A incurs a withholding tax of $13.50 on the $90 dividend distributed from B Corporation (15 percent of $90) and an additional foreign income tax of 10 percent or $7.65 by reason of the inclusion of the net distribution of $76.50 ($90 minus $13.50) in its taxable income for 1964. As of December 31, 1964, with respect to M Corporation, B Corporation's earnings and profits for 1963 described in section 959(c)(2) amount to zero ($90 minus $90); and A Corporation's earnings and profits for 1963 described in section 959(c)(2) amount to $68.85 ($90 minus $13.50 minus $7.65).

(e) Determination of foreign tax credit. For purposes of applying section 902 and section 960 in determining the foreign tax credit allowable under section 901 in a case in which distributions are made by a second-tier corporation or a first-tier corporation, as the case may be, from its earnings and profits for a taxable year which are attributable to an amount included in the gross income of a U.S. shareholder under section 951(a) or which are attributable to amounts excluded from the gross income of such foreign corporation under section 959(b) and § 1.959-2 with respect to a U.S. shareholder, the rules of paragraph (b) of this section shall apply except that in applying subparagraph (1) or (2) of such paragraph—

(1) Distributions from the earnings and profits for such taxable year of the second-tier corporation shall be considered first attributable to its earnings and profits attributable to distributions from the earnings and profits of the foreign corporation, if any, next lower in the chain of ownership described in section 958(a), to the extent of such earnings and profits of the second-tier corporation, and then to the other earnings and profits of such second-tier corporation, and

(2) Distributions from the earnings and profits for such taxable year of the first-tier corporation shall be considered first attributable to its earnings and profits attributable to distributions from the earnings and profits of the second-tier corporation, to the extent of such earnings and profits of the first-tier corporation, and then to the other earnings and profits of such first-tier corporation. For purposes of this paragraph, a second-tier corporation is a foreign corporation referred to in section 960(a)(1)(B), and a first-tier corporation is a foreign corporation referred to in section 960(a)(1)(A). The application of this paragraph may be illustrated by the following examples:

Example (1). (a) Domestic corporation A, a United States shareholder, owns 100 percent of the only class of stock of foreign corporation R which, in turn, owns 100 percent of the only class of stock of foreign corporation S. All corporations use the calendar year as a taxable year, and corporations R and S are controlled foreign corporations throughout the period here involved.

(b) Neither R Corporation nor S Corporation has subpart F income for 1963. During 1963, S Corporation increases by $100 its investment in tangible property (not described in section 956(b)(2) located in the United States, makes no distributions, and has earnings and profits of $100. Corporation A must include $100 in its gross income for 1963 under section 951(a)(1)(B) with respect to S Corporation. During 1963, R Corporation also increases by $100 its investment in tangible property (not described in section 956(b)(2)) located in the United States, makes no distributions, and has earnings and profits of $100. Corporation A must include $100 in its gross income for 1963 under section 951(a)(1)(B) with respect to R Corporation.

(c) During 1964, S Corporation distributes $100 to R Corporation, and R Corporation distributes $100 to A Corporation. Neither corporation has any earnings or profits or deficit in earnings and profits for such year. On December 31, 1964, R Corporation has earnings and profits (computed before distributions to A Corporation made for the year) of $200, consisting of $100 of section 959(c)(1) amounts of R Corporation for 1963 and of $100 of section 959(c)(1) amounts of S Corporation for 1963. For purposes of determining the foreign tax credit under section 960 and the regulations thereunder, the $100 distribution by R Corporation shall be considered attributable to S Corporation's earnings and profits for 1963 described in section 959(c)(1).

Example (2). (a) Domestic corporation A, a United States shareholder, owns 100 percent of the only class of stock of foreign corporation T which, in turn, owns 100 percent of the only class of stock of foreign corporation U. All corporations use the calendar year as a taxable year, and corporations T and U are controlled foreign corporations throughout the period here involved.

(b) During 1964, T Corporation invests $100 in tangible property (not described in section 956(b)(2)) located in the United States. For 1964, T Corporation has no subpart F income and makes no distributions; A must include $100 in its gross income for 1964 under section 951(a)(1)(B) with respect to T Corporation. For 1964, U Corporation has no subpart F income or investment of earnings in United States property but U Corporation has $100 of earnings and profits which it distributes to T Corporation. At December 31, 1964, T Corporation has earnings and profits of $300, consisting of operating income of $100 for each of the years 1963 and 1964 and $100 in dividends received from the earnings and profits of U Corporation for 1964. These earnings and profits are classified as follows under section 959(c): $100 of section 959(c)(1) amounts of T Corporation for 1964, $100 of section 959(c)(3) amounts of U Corporation for 1964, and $100 of section 959(c)(3) amounts of T Corporation for 1963.

(c) During 1965 neither T Corporation nor U Corporation has any earnings and profits or deficit in earnings and profits or investment of earnings in U.S. property, but T Corporation distributes $100 to A Corporation. For purposes of determining the foreign tax credit under section 960 and the regulations thereunder, the $100 distribution of T Corporation shall be considered attributable to T Corporation's earnings and profits for 1964 described in section 959(c)(1).

(f) Illustration. The application of this section may be illustrated by the following example:

Example. (a) M, a controlled foreign corporation is organized on January 1, 1963, and is wholly owned by A, a United States shareholder. Both A and Corporation M use the calendar year as a taxable year.

(b) Corporation M's earnings and profits (before distributions) for 1963 are $200, $100 of which is attributable to subpart F income. Corporation M's earnings and profits for such year also include $25 attributable to subpart F income which is excluded from M Corporation's foreign base company income under section 954(b)(1) as dividends, interest, and gains invested in qualified investments in less developed countries. Corporation M's increase in earnings invested in tangible property (not described in section 956(b)(2)) located in the United States for 1963, is $50, and M Corporation makes a distribution of such property during such year of $20. For purposes of section 959, A's interest in M Corporation's earnings and profits as of December 31, 1963, determined after the distributions of $20, is classified as follows:

Sec. 959(c)(1) amounts:			
Earnings for 1963 attributable to increased investment in U.S. property which would have been included in A's gross income but for application of sec. 959(a)(2) and Sec. 1.959-1(c)		$ 50	
Less: Distribution for 1963 allocated under sec. 959(c)(1) and paragraph (b)(1) of this section to such amounts		20	
			$ 30
Sec. 959(c)(2) amounts:			
Earnings for 1963 attributable to subpart F income included in A's gross income under sec. 951(a)(1)(A)(i)		100	
Less: Earnings for 1963 attributable to increased investment in U.S. property which would have been included in A's gross income but for application of sec. 959(a)(2) and Sec. 1.959-1(c)		50	
			50
Sec. 959(c)(3) amounts:			
Predistribution earnings for 1963		200	
Less: Earnings for 1963 classified as:			
Sec. 959(c)(1) amounts	$50		
Sec. 959(c)(2) amounts	50		
		100	
			100
A's total interest in M Corporation's earnings and profits			180

For 1963, A is required to include $100 of subpart F income in his gross income under section 951(a)(1)(A)(i). He would have been required to include $50 in his gross income under section 951(a)(1)(B) as M Corporation's increase in earnings invested in United States property, except that section 959(a)(2) and paragraph (c) of § 1.959-1 provide in effect that earnings and profits taxed to A under section 951(a)(1)(A) with respect to M Corporation (whether in the current taxable year or in prior years) may be invested in United States property without again being included in gross income under section 951(a). The $20 dividend from M Corporation is excluded from A's gross income under section 959(a)(1) and paragraph (b) of § 1.959-1, since such distribution is allocated under section 959(c)(1) and paragraph (b)(1) of this section to amounts described in section 959(c)(1).

(c) During 1964, M Corporation's earnings and profits (before distributions) are $300, $75 of which is attributable to subpart F income. Corporation M has no change in investments in United States property during such year and withdraws $15 of previously excluded subpart F income from investment in less developed countries. Corporation M makes a cash distribution of $250 to A during 1964. For purposes of section 959, A's interest in M Corporation's earnings and profits as of December 31, 1964, determined after the distribution of $250, is classified as follows:

Sec. 959(c)(1) amounts:				
Sec. 959(c)(1) net amount for 1963 (as determined under paragraph (b) of this example)				$ 30
Less: Distribution for 1964 allocated under sec. 959(c)(1) and paragraph (b)(1) of this section to such amount			30	0
Sec. 959(c)(2) amounts:				
Sec. 959(c)(2) net amount for 1963 (as determined under paragraph (b) of this example)			50	
Plus: Earnings for 1964 attributable to:				
Subpart F income for 1964 included in A's gross income under sec. 951(a)(1)(A)(i)			75	
Previously excluded subpart F income withdrawn in 1964 from investment in less developed countries and included in A's gross income under sec. 951(a)(1)(A)(ii)			15	
			140	
Less: Distribution for 1964 allocated under sec. 959(c)(2) and paragraph (b)(2) of this section to such amounts			140	0
Sec. 959(c)(3) amounts:				
Sec. 959(c)(3) net amount for 1963 (as determined under paragraph (b) of this example)			100	
Plus: Sec. 959(c)(3) net amount for 1964:				
Predistribution earnings for 1964		$300		
Less:				
Earnings for 1964 classified as sec. 959(c)(1) amounts ($0) and as sec. 959(c)(2) amounts ($70 + $15)	$90			
Distributions for 1964 allocated under sec. 959(c)(3) and paragraph (b)(3) of this section	80			
		170		
			130	
				$230
A's total interest in M Corporation's earnings and profits				230

For 1964, A is required to include in his gross income under section 951(a)(1)(A)(i) $75 of subpart F income, and under section 951(a)(1)(A)(ii) $15 of previously excluded subpart F income withdrawn from investment in less developed countries. Of the $250 cash distribution, A may exclude $170 from his gross income under section 959(a)(1) and paragraph (b) of § 1.959-1 and $80 is includible in his gross income as a dividend.

(d) The source under section 959(c) of the 1964 distribution of $250 to A is as follows:

Amount	Year	Allocation of distribution under sec. 959
30	1963	(c)(1).
90	1964	(c)(2).
50	1963	(c)(2).
80	1964	(c)(3).
250		

T.D. 6795, 1/28/65, amend T.D. 7334, 12/20/74, T.D. 7545, 5/5/78, T.D. 7893, 5/11/83.

PAR. 4. Section 1.959-3 is revised to read as follows:

Proposed § 1.959-3 Maintenance and adjustment of previously taxed earnings and profits accounts. [*For Preamble, see ¶ 152,795*]

(a) In general. This section provides rules for the maintenance and adjustment of previously taxed earnings and profits accounts by shareholders and with respect to foreign corporations. Paragraph (b) of this section provides general rules governing the accounting of previously taxed earnings and profits at the shareholder level and corporate level. Paragraph (c) of this section provides rules regarding the treatment of foreign taxes when previously taxed earnings and profits are distributed by a foreign corporation through a chain of ownership described in section 958(a). Paragraph (d) of this section provides rules regarding the allocation of other expenses to previously taxed earnings and profits. Paragraph (e)(1) of this section addresses the adjustment of shareholder-level previously taxed earnings and profits accounts as a result of certain transactions. Paragraph (e)(2) of this section provides rules establishing the order in which adjustments are to be made to a covered shareholder's previously taxed earnings and profits account. Paragraph (e)(3) of this section provides rules regarding distributions of previously taxed earnings and profits in a chain of ownership described in section 958(a). Paragraph (e)(4) of this section provides for the maintenance and adjustment of aggregate categories of previously taxed and non-previously taxed earnings and profits at the corporate level with adjustments to individual shareholder-level accounts. Paragraph (e)(5) of this section provides rules for the effect of a foreign corporation's deficit in earnings and profits on previously taxed earnings and profits. Paragraph (f) of this section provides rules regarding the treatment of previously taxed earnings and profits when a shareholder has multiple previously taxed earnings and profits accounts. Paragraph (g) of this section provides rules regarding the treatment of previously taxed earnings and profits when more than one shareholder in a foreign corporation is a member of the same consolidated group. Paragraph (h) of this section provides rules governing the adjustment of previously taxed earnings and profits accounts in the case of a redemption.

(b) Corporate-level and shareholder-level accounting of previously taxed earnings and profits. *(1) Shareholder-level accounting.* A shareholder's previously taxed earnings and profits account with respect to its stock in a foreign corporation shall identify the amount of section 959(c)(1) earnings and profits and the amount of section 959(c)(2) earnings and profits attributable to such stock for each taxable year of the foreign corporation and shall be maintained in the functional currency of such foreign corporation. A shareholder account must also reflect the annual dollar basis of each category of previously taxed earnings and profits in the account. See § 1.959-3(e) of this section for rules regarding the adjustment of shareholder previously taxed earnings and profits accounts.

(2) Corporate-level accounting. Separate aggregate categories of section 959(c)(1), section 959(c)(2) and non-previously taxed earnings and profits (earnings and profits described in section 959(c)(3)) shall be maintained with respect to a foreign corporation. These categories of earnings and profits of the foreign corporation shall be maintained in the functional currency of the foreign corporation. For purposes of this section, distributions are allocated to a foreign corporation's earnings and profits under section 316(a) by applying first section 316(a)(2) and then section 316(a)(1) to each of these three categories of earnings and profits. Section 956 amounts shall be treated as attributable first to section 959(c)(2) earnings and profits and then to non-previously taxed earnings and profits. These allocations are made in conjunction with the rules for making corporate-level adjustments to previously taxed earnings and profits under § 1.959-3(e)(4).

(3) Classification of earnings and profits. (i) In general. For purposes of this section, earnings and profits in the taxable year of the foreign corporation in which such amounts are included in the gross income of a United States shareholder under section 951(a) and are reclassified as to category of earnings and profits in the taxable year of the foreign corporation in which such amounts would be so included in the gross income of a United States shareholder under section 951(a) but for the provisions of section 959(a)(2) and § 1.959-1(c)(2). Such classifications do not change by reason of a subsequent distribution of such amounts to an upper-tier corporation in a chain of ownership described in section 958(a). This paragraph shall apply to distributions by one foreign corporation to another foreign corporation and by a foreign corporation to a United States person.

(ii) Dollar basis pooling election. For purposes of computing foreign currency gain or loss under section 986(c) and adjustments to stock basis under section 961(b) and (c) with respect to distributions of previously taxed earnings and profits of any foreign corporation, in lieu of maintaining annual dollar basis accounts with respect to previously taxed earnings and profits described in paragraph (b)(1) of this section, a taxpayer may maintain an aggregate dollar basis pool that reflects the dollar basis of all of the corporation's previously taxed earnings and profits described in sections 959(c)(1) and 959(c)(2) and treat a pro rata portion of the dollar basis pool as attributable to distributions of such previously taxed earnings and profits. A taxpayer makes this election by using a dollar basis pool to compute foreign currency gain or loss under section 986(c) with respect to distributions of previously taxed earnings and profits of the foreign corporation, or to compute gain or loss with respect to its stock in the foreign corporation, whichever occurs first. Any subsequent change in the taxpayer's method of assigning dollar basis may be made only with the consent of the Commissioner.

(4) Examples. The application of this paragraph (b) is illustrated by the following examples:

Example (1). Distribution. (i) Facts. DP, a United States shareholder, owns 100% of the only class of stock in FC, a CFC, which, in turn, owns 100% of the only class of stock in FS, a CFC. DP, FC and FS all use the calendar year as their taxable year. FC and FS both use the u as their functional currency. During year 1, FC earns 100u of non-subpart F income and invests 100u in United States property. DP must include 100u in its gross income for year 1 under section 951(a)(1)(B) with respect to FC. For year 2, FS has no subpart F income or investment of earnings in United States property but FS has 100u of non-previously taxed earnings and profits which it distributes to FC. The distribution of 100u to FC is subpart F income of FC and DP must include the 100u in its gross income for year 2 under section 951(a)(1)(A). Also in year 2, FC has non-subpart F income of 100u. The exchange rates at all times in year 1 and year 2, respectively, are 1u = $1 and 1u = $1.20.

(ii) Analysis. With respect to FC, the earnings and profits are classified as follows: 100u of section 959(c)(1) earnings and profits from year 1, 100u of section 959(c)(2) earnings and profits from year 2, and 100u of non-previously taxed earnings and profits from year 2. The dollar basis with respect to the section 959(c)(1) earnings and profits is $100 and the dollar basis with respect to the section 959(c)(2) earnings and profits is $120.

Example (2). Subsequent distribution in a later year. (i) Facts. Assume the same facts as in Example 1, except that during year 3 neither FC nor FS has any earnings and profits or deficit in earnings and profits or section 956 amount, but FC distributes 100u to DP on December 31, year 3, at which time the spot exchange rate is 1u = $1.30.

(ii) Analysis. For purposes of section 959 and 961, the 100u distribution of FC shall be considered attributable to FC's section 959(c)(1) earnings and profits for year 1. The section 959(c)(1) earnings and profits are reduced by 100u and the dollar basis of the account is reduced by $100. Since the spot rate at the time of the 100u distribution to DP is 1u = $1.30, DP recognizes foreign currency gain of $30 ((100 x 1.3) - (100 x 1)).

Example (3). Dollar basis pooling election. (i) Facts. Assume the same facts as in Example 2, except that DP elected to maintain the dollar basis of its previously taxed earnings and profits account on a pooled basis for purposes of section 986(c) and section 961 as provided in paragraph (b)(3)(ii) of this section.

(ii) Analysis. The section 959(c)(1) earnings and profits are reduced by 100u, but the dollar basis of the account is reduced by $110 ((100u/200u) x $220). In addition, DP recognizes foreign currency gain under section 986(c) of $20 ($130 - ((100u/200u) x $220)).

(c) Treatment of certain foreign taxes. *(1)* For purposes of this section, when previously taxed earnings and profits are distributed by a foreign corporation to another foreign corporation through a chain of ownership described in section 958(a) such earnings and profits shall be reduced by the functional currency amount of any income, war profits, or excess profits taxes imposed by any foreign country or a possession of the United States on or with respect to such earnings and profits. Any such taxes shall not be included in the distributee foreign corporation's pools of post-1986 foreign income taxes maintained for purposes of sections 902 and 960(a)(1). Such taxes shall be maintained in a separate account and allowed as a credit as provided under section 960(a)(3) when the associated previously taxed earnings and profits are distributed. The taxpayer's dollar basis in the previously taxed earnings and profits account shall be reduced by the dollar amount of such taxes, translated in accordance with section 986(a).

(2) Example. The application of this paragraph (c) is illustrated by the following example:

Example. Imposition of foreign taxes on a CFC. (i) Facts. DP, a United States shareholder, owns 100% of the only class of stock in foreign corporation FC, a CFC, which, in turn, owns 100% of the only class of stock in FS, a CFC. DP, FC, and FS all use the calendar year as their taxable year. FC and FS both use the u as their functional currency. During year 1, FS earns 90u of subpart F income, after incurring 10u of foreign income tax allocable to such income under § 1.954-1(c), has earnings and profits in excess of 90u, and makes no distributions. DP must include 90u, translated at the average exchange rate for the year of 1u = $1 as provided in section 989(b)(3), in its gross income for year 1 under section 951(a)(1)(A)(i). As of the end of year 1, FS has section 959(c)(2) earnings and profits of 90u. During year 2, FS has neither earnings and profits nor a deficit in earnings and profits but distributes 90u to FC, and, by reason of section 959(b) and § 1.959-2, such amount is not includible in the gross income of DP for year 2 under section 951(a) with respect to FC. FC incurs a withholding tax of 9u on the 90u distribution from FS (10% of 90u) and an additional foreign income tax of 11u by reason of the inclusion of the distribution in its taxable income for foreign tax purposes in year 2. The average exchange rate for year 2 is 1u = $2.

(ii) Analysis. At the end of year 2, FS has section 959(c)(2) earnings and profits of 0 (90u-90u); and FC has section 959(c)(2) earnings and profits of 70u (90u-9u-11u). DP's dollar basis in the 70u section 959(c)(2) earnings and profits account with respect to FC is $50 ($90 inclusion-$18 withholding tax-$22 income tax). The $40 of foreign taxes imposed on FC with respect to the previously taxed earnings and profits are not included in FC's post-1986 foreign income taxes pool. A foreign tax credit with respect to the $40 of foreign tax attributable to the 70u of previously taxed earnings and profits will be allowed under section 960(a)(3) upon distribution of such previously taxed earnings and profits.

(d) Treatment of other expenses. Except as provided in paragraph (c) of this section, no expense paid or accrued by a foreign corporation shall be allocated or apportioned to the previously taxed earnings and profits of such corporation.

(e) Adjustments to previously taxed earnings and profits account. *(1) In general.* A covered shareholder's previously taxed earnings and profits account (including the dollar basis in such account) is adjusted in the manner provided in paragraphs (e)(2), (f) and (g) of this section, except as otherwise provided in paragraph (e)(3) of this section. For adjustments to a previously taxed earnings and profits account in the case of redemptions, see paragraph (h) of this section.

(2) Order and amount of adjustments. As of the close of a foreign corporation's taxable year, and for the taxable year of the covered shareholder in which or with which such taxable year of the foreign corporation ends, the covered shareholder shall make any of the following adjustments that are applicable for that year to the previously taxed earnings and profits account for the stock owned for any portion of such year (within the meaning of section 958(a)) in the foreign corporation in the following order—

(i) Step 1. Section 951(a)(1)(A) inclusion. Increase the amount of section 959(c)(2) earnings and profits and the associated dollar basis in the account by the amount of the section 951(a)(1)(A) inclusion with respect to such stock;

(ii) Step 2. Distributions on such stock. (A) Decrease the amount of the section 959(c)(1) earnings and profits in the account (but not below zero), and then the amount of section 959(c)(2) earnings and profits in the account (but not below zero) by the amount of earnings and profits distributed to the covered shareholder during the year with respect to such stock, decrease the dollar basis in the account by the dollar amount attributable to the distributed earnings and profits; and

(B) Increase the amount of the earnings and profits and associated dollar basis, in the account first to the extent provided under paragraph (f)(1) of this section and then to the extent provided under paragraph (g)(1) of this section and then reduce the account to zero;

(iii) Step 3. Reallocation from other accounts with respect to redemptions. Increase the amount of the earnings and profits and associated dollar basis in the account to the extent provided under paragraph (h)(3)(ii) of this section.

(iv) Step 4. Section 956 amount. Reclassify the section 959(c)(2) earnings and profits and associated dollar basis in such shareholder's previously taxed earnings and profits account with respect to such stock as section 959(c)(1) earnings and profits in an amount equal to the lesser of—

(A) The covered shareholder's section 956 amount for the taxable year with respect to such stock; or

(B) The amount of the section 959(c)(2) earnings and profits attributable to such stock.

(v) Step 5. Reallocation to other accounts with respect to distributions. Decrease the amount of section 959(c)(1) earnings and profits and associated dollar basis in the account, and thereafter the amount of section 959(c)(2) earnings and profits and associated dollar basis in the account to the extent provided under paragraph (f)(1) of this section and then under paragraph (g)(1) of this section;

(vi) Step 6. Reclassification with respect to section 956 amounts. Reclassify the section 959(c)(2) earnings and profits and the associated dollar basis attributable to such stock as section 959(c)(1) earnings and profits to the extent provided under paragraph (f)(2) of this section and then to the extent provided in paragraph (g)(2) of this section.

(vii) Step 7. Further adjustment for section 956 amounts. Increase the amount of section 959(c)(1) earnings and profits and the associated dollar basis in the account by any amount included in the covered shareholder's gross income for the year under section 951(a)(1)(B) with respect to such stock.

(3) Intercorporate distributions. If a foreign corporation receives a distribution of earnings and profits from another foreign corporation that is in a chain of ownership described in section 958(a), a covered shareholder's previously taxed earnings and profits accounts with respect to the stock in each foreign corporation in such chain shall be adjusted at the end of the respective corporation's taxable year, and for the taxable year of the covered shareholder in which or with which such taxable year of the foreign corporation ends, as follows:

(i) The covered shareholder's previously taxed earnings and profits account with respect to stock in the distributor shall be decreased (but not below zero), at the same time that the covered shareholder would make adjustments under paragraph (e)(2)(ii) of this section, by the amount of the distribution and the associated dollar basis. Such decrease to the covered shareholder's previously taxed earnings and profits account shall be made first to the section 959(c)(1) earnings and profits and thereafter to the section 959(c)(2) earnings and profits in such account.

(ii) Except as provided in paragraph (c) of this section, the section 959(c)(1) earnings and profits and section 959(c)(2) earnings and profits in the covered shareholder's previously taxed earnings and profits account with respect to the stock in the distributee shall be increased, at the same time that the covered shareholder would make adjustments under paragraph (e)(2)(i) of this section, by an amount equal to the decrease under paragraph (e)(3)(i) of this section and to the extent the distribution is out of non-previously taxed earnings and profits of the distributor, to the extent provided under paragraph (e)(2) of this section. If the receiving corporation uses a non-dollar functional currency that differs from the functional currency used by the distributing corporation, then—

(A) The amount of increase shall be the spot value of the distribution in the receiving corporation's functional currency at the time of the distribution; and

(B) The dollar basis of the amount distributed shall be carried over from the distributing corporation to the receiving corporation.

(4) Effect on foreign corporation's earnings and profits. Adjustments to a shareholder's previously taxed earnings and profits account in accordance with this section shall result in corresponding adjustments to the appropriate aggregate category or categories of earnings and profits of the foreign corporation. If an adjustment to a foreign corporation's earnings and profits is required (other than as a result of the previous sentence) the adjustment shall be made only to the non-previously taxed earnings and profits of the corporation except to the extent provided in paragraph (h)(2)(i) of this section. Moreover, if a distribution to a taxpayer exceeds such taxpayer's previously taxed earnings and profits account with respect to stock it owns (within the meaning of section 958(a)) in the foreign corporation making the distribution, the distribution may only be treated as a dividend under section 316 by applying section 316(a)(1) and (2) to the non-previously taxed earnings and profits of the foreign corporation.

(5) Deficits in earnings and profits. If a foreign corporation has a deficit in earnings and profits, as determined under section 964(a) and § 1.964-1, for any taxable year, a covered shareholder's previously taxed earnings and profits account with respect to its stock in such foreign corporation shall not be adjusted to take into account the deficit and the deficit shall be applied only to the non-previously taxed earnings and profits of the foreign corporation.

(6) Examples. The application of this paragraph (e) is illustrated by the following examples:

Example (1). Distribution to a United States shareholder. (i) Facts. DP, a United States shareholder, owns 100% of the only class of stock in FC, a CFC. Both DP and FC use the calendar year as their taxable year. FC uses the "u" as its functional currency. During year 1, FC derives 100u of subpart F income, and such amount is included in DP's gross income under section 951(a)(1)(A). The average exchange rate for year 1 is 1u = $1. At the end of year 1, FC's current and accumulated earnings and profits (before taking into account distributions made during year 1) are 500u. Also, on December 31, year 1, when the spot exchange rate is 1u = $1.10, FC distributes 50u of earnings and profits to DP.

(ii) Analysis. At the end of year 1, the section 959(c)(2) earnings and profits in DP's previously taxed earnings and profits account are first increased from 0 to 100u, pursuant to paragraph (e)(2)(i) of this section as a result of the subpart F inclusion of 100u and then reduced from 100u to 50u, pursuant to paragraph (e)(2)(ii) of this section as a result of the distribution. DP's dollar basis in the 100u of previously taxed earnings and profits is $100 (the dollar amount of the income inclusion under section 951(a)(1)(A)). See section 989(b)(3). The 50u distribution is excluded from DP's gross income pursuant to § 1.959-1(c)(1). Pursuant to paragraph (e)(4) of this section, at the end of year 1, FC has section 959(c)(2) earnings and profits of 50u and non-previously taxed earnings and profits of 400u. DP's dollar basis in the previously taxed earnings and profits account is reduced by a pro rata share of the dollar amount included in income under section 951(a)(1)(A), or by $50 (50u distribution/100u previously taxed earnings and profits x $100 dollar basis). DP recognizes foreign currency gain under section 986(c) of $5 ($55 spot value of 50u distribution-$50 basis).

Example (2). Net deficit in earnings and profits. (i) Facts. Assume the same facts as in Example 1, except that FC has a net deficit in earnings and profits of 500u for year 2. At the end of Year 1, FC has 50u of section 959(c)(2) earnings and profits and 400u of non-previously taxed earnings and profits.

(ii) Analysis. At the end of year 2, DP's section 959(c)(2) earnings and profits for year 1 remains at 50u, pursuant to paragraph (e)(5) of this paragraph, because a shareholder's previously taxed earnings and profits account is not adjusted to take into account the CFC's deficit in earnings and profits. Pursuant to paragraph (e)(4) of this section, at the end of year 2, FC's non-previously taxed earnings and profits are reduced to (100u), and no adjustment is made to FC's previously taxed earnings and profits, which remains at 50u.

Example (3). Distribution and section 956 inclusion in same year. Assume the same facts as in Example 1, except that DP also has a section 956 amount for year 1 with respect to its stock in FC of 200u.

(ii) Analysis. At the end of year 1, adjustments are made to DP's previously taxed earnings and profits account in its FC stock in the following order: First, the section 959(c)(2) earnings and profits in DP's previously taxed earnings and profits account are increased from 0 to 100u pursuant to paragraph (e)(2)(i) of this section as a result of the subpart F inclusion. Then, the section 959(c)(2) earnings and profits in DP's previously taxed earnings and profits account are reduced from 100u to 50u pursuant to paragraph (e)(2)(ii) of this section as a result of the distribution and the 50u distribution is excluded from DP's gross income pursuant to § 1.959-1(c)(1). Then, the remaining 50u of section 959(c)(2) earnings and profits in DP's previously taxed earnings and profits account are reclassified as section 959(c)(1) earnings and profits pursuant to paragraph (e)(2)(iv) of this section as a result of FC's investment in United States property and 50u of the 200u section 956 amount is excluded from DP's gross income pursuant to § 1.959-1(c)(2). Finally, the remaining 150u section 956 amount equal to $165 (150u x 1.1) is included in DP's gross income pursuant to section 951(a)(1)(B) and the section 959(c)(1) earnings and profits in DP's previously taxed earnings and profits account are increased from 50u to 200u pursuant to paragraph (e)(2)(vii) of this section. Pursuant to paragraph (e)(4) of this section, at the end of year 1, FC has section 959(c)(1) earnings and profits of 200u and non-previously taxed earnings and profits of 250u. DP's dollar basis in the previously taxed earnings and profits account at the end of year 1 is $215 (the $50 attributable to the reclassified 50u of earnings and $165 attributable to the 150u of section 956 inclusion). See section 989(b)(4).

Example (4). Section 956 amount in following year. (i) Facts. Assume the same facts as in Example 3, except that in year 2, DP has an additional section 956 amount of 200u with respect to its stock in FC and the spot exchange rate on December 31, year 2 is 1u = $1.20.

(ii) Analysis. As in Example 3, at the end of year 1, DP has a section 959(c)(1) earnings and profits account with respect to its stock in FC of 200u. Although DP has 200u of section 959(c)(1) earnings and profits in its previously taxed earnings and profits account with respect to its stock in FC, section 959(c)(1) earnings and profits are generated by the inclusion of a section 956 amount in a United States shareholder's gross income or the reclassification of section 959(c)(2) earnings and profits to exclude a section 956 amount from a United States shareholder's gross income and cannot be used to exclude any additional section 956 amounts from a United States shareholder's gross income. Consequently, at the end of year 2, the section 959(c)(1) earnings and profits in DP's previously taxed earnings and profits account are increased from 200u to 400u pursuant to paragraph (e)(2)(vii) of this section and the 200u section 956 amount is included in DP's gross income pursuant to section 959(a)(1)(B). Pursuant to paragraph (e)(4) of this section, at the end of year 2, FC has section 959(c)(1) earnings and profits of 400u and non-previously taxed earnings and profits of 50u. DP's dollar basis in its 200u of year 2 section 959(c)(1) earnings and profits is $240.

Example (5). Section 951(a)(1)(A) inclusion and distribution in following year. (i) Facts. Assume the same facts as in Example 4, except that in year 3, FC derives 250u of subpart F income, which is included in DP's income under section 951(a)(1)(A), makes a 250u distribution to DP, and has 700u of current and accumulated earnings and profits (before taking into account distributions made during year 3). The average exchange rate for year 3 is 1u = $1.10, so DP includes $275 in income (250u x $1.10/1u).

(ii) Analysis. As in Example 4, at the end of year 2, DP has a previously taxed earnings and profits account with respect to its stock in FC of 400u of section 959(c)(1) earnings and profits. At the end of year 3, adjustments are made in the following order. First, DP's section 959(c)(2) earnings and profits are increased from 0 to 250u pursuant to paragraph (e)(2)(i) of this section as a result of the subpart F inclusion. Then the section 959(c)(1) earnings and profits in DP's previously taxed earnings and profits account are reduced from 400u to 150u and the 250u distribution to DP is excluded from DP's gross income pursuant to § 1.959-1(c)(1). Pursuant to paragraph (e)(4) of this section, at the end of year 3, FC has 150u of section 959(c)(1) earnings and profits, 250u of section 959(c)(2) earnings and profits, and 50u of non-previously taxed earnings and profits. If DP has not made the dollar basis pooling election described in paragraph (b)(3)(ii) of this section, then the 250u distribution out of section 959(c)(1) earnings is assigned a dollar basis of $293.75 ($240 basis in 200u of year 2 earnings and $53.75 basis in 50u of year 1 earnings (50u/200u x $215)). DP's remaining dollar basis in the year 1 section 959(c)(1) earnings is $161.25 ($215 - $53.75). If DP elected to maintain the dollar basis of its previously taxed earnings and profits account on a pooled basis as provided in paragraph (b)(3)(ii) of this section, then the 250u distribution out of section 959(c)(1) earnings is assigned a dollar basis of $280.77 (250u/650u x ($215 + $240 + $275)), and DP's dollar basis in its remaining 400u previously taxed earnings accounts is $449.23 ($730-$280.77).

Example (6). Distribution to a United States shareholder and a foreign shareholder. (i) Facts. DP, a United States shareholder, owns 70% and FP, a nonresident alien, owns 30% of the only class of stock in FC, a CFC that uses the U.S. dollar as its functional currency. Both DP and FC use the calendar year as their taxable year. During year 1, FC derives $100x of subpart F income, $70x of which is included in DP's gross income under section 951(a)(1)(A). FC's current and accumulated earnings and profits (before taking into account distributions made during year 1) are $500x. Also, during year 1, FC distributes $50x of earnings and profits, $35x distribution to DP and $15x distribution to FP.

(ii) Analysis. At the end of year 1, the section 959(c)(2) earnings and profits in DP's previously taxed earnings and profits account are increased from $0 to $70x, pursuant to paragraph (e)(2)(i) of this section as a result of the subpart F inclusion. The section 959(c)(2) earnings and profits in DP's previously taxed earnings and profits account are then reduced from $70x to $35x, pursuant to paragraph (e)(2)(ii) of this section as a result of the distribution. Pursuant to paragraph (e)(4) of this section, at the end of year 1, FC has section 959(c)(2) earnings and profits of $35x and non-previously taxed earnings and profits of $415x.

Example (7). Intercorporate Distribution. (i) Facts. DP, a United States shareholder, owns 70% and FP, a nonresident alien, owns 30% of the only class of stock in FC, a CFC. FC owns 100% of the only class of stock in FS, a CFC. FC uses the "u" as its functional currency and FS uses the "y" as its functional currency. DP, FC, and FS all use the calendar year as their taxable year. During year 1, FS derives 100y of subpart F income. The average y:$ exchange rate for year 1 is 1y = $1. On December 31, year 2, FS distributes 100y to FC. The y:u exchange rate on December 31, year 2, is 1y = 0.5u.

(ii) Analysis. (A) Year 1. At the end of year 1, DP's pro rata share of 70y of subpart F income is included in DP's gross income pursuant to section 951(a)(1)(A)(i) and the section 959(c)(2) earnings and profits in DP's previously taxed earnings and profits account with respect to the stock it indirectly owns in FS are correspondingly increased from 0 to 70y pursuant to paragraph (e)(2)(i) of this section as a result of the subpart F income. The dollar basis of the previously taxed earnings and profits in DP's account with respect to its stock in FS is $70. At the end of year 2, FS has section 959(c)(2) earnings and profits of 70y and non-previously taxed earnings and profits of 30y.

(B) Year 2. Upon the distribution of 100y = 50u from FS to FC on December 31, year 2, the section 959(c)(2) earnings and profits in DP's previously taxed earnings and profits account with respect to the stock it indirectly owns in FS are reduced from 70y to 0 and the section 959(c)(2) earnings and profits in DP's earnings and profits account with respect to its stock in FC are correspondingly increased from 0 to 35u pursuant to paragraph (e)(3) of this section. The entire 100y = 50u distribution is excluded from FC's income for purposes of determining FC's subpart F income under section 951(a) for year 2 with respect to DP pursuant to § 1.959-2(a)(1). Pursuant to paragraph (e)(4) of this section, at the end of year 2, FS has 0 earnings and profits and FC has section 959(c)(2) earnings and profits of 35u and non-previously taxed earnings and profits of 15u. DP's dollar basis in its 35u of section 959(c)(2) earnings and profits in its earnings and profits account with respect to its stock in FC is $70, carried over from DP's original dollar basis in its 70y of section 959(c)(2) earnings and profits in its previously taxed earnings and profits account with respect to its stock in FS.

Example (8). Sale of CFC stock. (i) Facts. DP1, a United States shareholder, owns 100% of the only class of stock in FC, a CFC. At the beginning of year 1, DP1 has a zero basis in its stock in FC. Both DP1 and FC use the calendar year as their taxable year. FC uses the U.S. dollar as its functional currency. During year 1, FC derives $100x of subpart F income and $100x of other income. On December 31 of year 1, DP1 sells all of its stock in FC to DP2, a U.S. person for $200x. Year 1 is a year beginning on or after December 31, 1962.

(ii) Analysis. First, DP1 includes the $100x of subpart F income in gross income under section 951(a)(1)(A). The section 959(c)(2) earnings and profits in DP1's previously taxed earnings and profits account with respect to its stock in FC are increased from $0 to $100x pursuant to paragraph (e)(2)(i) of this section and DP1's basis in its FC stock is increased from $0 to $100x pursuant to § 1.961-1(b). FC's section 959(c)(2) earnings and profits are increased from $0 to $100x and its non-previously taxed earnings and profits are correspondingly increased from $0 to $100x pursuant to paragraph (e)(4) of this section. Then pursuant to section 1248(a), because FC has $100x of non-previously taxed earnings and profits attributable to DP1's stock that are attributable to a taxable year beginning on or after December 31, 1962 during which FC was a CFC and DP1 owned its stock in FC, the $100x of gain recognized by DP1 on the sale of its stock ($200x proceeds-$100x basis) is included in DP1's gross income as a dividend. Consequently, the section 959(c)(2) earnings and profits in DP1's previously taxed earnings and profits account with respect to its stock in FC are increased from $100x to $200x pursuant to paragraph (e)(2)(i) of this section. Upon the sale, DP2 acquires from DP1 a previously taxed earnings and profits account with respect to the FC stock of $200x of section 959(c)(2) earnings and profits and takes a cost basis of $200x in the FC stock pursuant to section 1012.

(f) Special rule for shareholders with more than one previously taxed earnings and profits account. *(1) Adjustments for distributions.* If a covered shareholder owns (within the meaning of section 958(a)) more than one share of stock in a foreign corporation as of the last day of the foreign corporation's taxable year, to the extent that the total amount of any distributions of earnings and profits made with respect to any particular share for the foreign corporation's taxable year would exceed the previously taxed earnings and profits account with respect to such share (an excess distribution amount), the following adjustments shall be made:

(i) Adjustment of other accounts. The covered shareholder's previously taxed earnings and profits accounts with respect to the shareholder's other shares of stock in the foreign corporation that are owned by the covered shareholder as of the last day of the CFC's taxable year shall be decreased, in the aggregate, by an amount equal to such excess distribution amount, but not below zero. Such decrease shall be made on a pro rata basis by reference to the amount of the previously taxed earnings and profits in those other accounts and shall be allocated to the section 959(c)(1) and (c)(2) earnings and profits in those accounts in the same manner as a distribution is allocated to such earnings and profits pursuant to the rules of section 959(c) and paragraph (e)(2)(ii)(A) of this section.

(ii) Adjustment of deficient account. The covered shareholder's previously taxed earnings and profits account for the first-mentioned share of stock shall correspondingly be increased by the same amount, and then shall be adjusted to zero as provided under paragraph (e)(2)(ii)(B) of this section.

(2) Adjustments for section 956 amounts. If a United States shareholder, who owns more than one share of stock in a CFC as of the last day of the CFC's taxable year, has a section 956 amount with respect to its stock in the CFC for a taxable year, to the extent that the section 956 amount with respect to any particular share of stock exceeds the section 959(c)(2) earnings and profits in such shareholder's previously taxed earnings and profits account with respect to such share (an excess section 956 amount), the covered shareholder's section 959(c)(2) earnings and profits in its previously taxed earnings and profits accounts with respect to its other shares of stock that are owned by the United States shareholder on the last day of the CFC's taxable year shall be reclassified as section 959(c)(1) earnings and profits, in the aggregate, by an amount equal to such excess section 956 amount. Such reclassification shall be made on a pro rata basis by reference to the amount of the section 959(c)(2) earnings and profits in each of the United States shareholder's other previously taxed earnings and profits accounts with respect to its stock in the CFC prior to reclassification under this paragraph (f)(2).

(3) Examples. The application of this paragraph (f) is illustrated by the following examples:

Example (1). Two blocks of stock. (i) Facts. DP, a United States shareholder, owns two blocks, block 1 and block 2, of shares of class A stock in FC, a CFC that uses the U.S. dollar as its functional currency. Both DP and FC use the calendar year as their taxable year. Entering year 1, DP has a previously taxed earnings and profits account with respect to its block 1 shares consisting of $25x of section 959(c)(2) earnings and profits and a previously taxed earnings and profits account with respect to its block 2 shares consisting of $65x of section 959(c)(2) earnings and profits. Entering year 1, FC has section 959(c)(2) earnings and profits of $90x and non-previously taxed earnings and profits of $200x. During year 1, FC makes a distribution of earnings and profits on its Class A stock of $50x on each of block 1 and block 2.

(ii) Analysis. First, as a result of the distribution, the section 959(c)(2) earnings and profits in DP's previously taxed earnings and profits account with respect to block 1 are decreased from $25x to $0 and the section 959(c)(2) earnings and profits in DP's previously taxed earnings and profits account with respect to block 2 are decreased from $65x to $15x pursuant to paragraph (e)(2)(ii) of this section. Because there are insufficient previously taxed earnings and profits with respect to block 1, DP may access its excess previously taxed earnings and profits with respect to its block 2 stock, after taking into account any distributions or section 956 amounts with respect to block 2. Accordingly, the section 959(c)(2) earnings and profits in DP's previously taxed earnings and profits account with respect to block 2 are decreased from $15x to $0 pursuant to paragraphs (e)(2)(v) and (f)(1)(i) of this section and the section 959(c)(2) earnings and profits in DP's previously taxed earnings and profits account with respect to block 2 are increased from $0 to $15x and then decreased from $15x to $0 pursuant to paragraphs (e)(2)(ii)(B) and (f)(1)(ii) of this section. The $40x ($25x + $15x) of the distribution with respect to block 1 and $50x of the distribution with respect to block 2 are excluded from DP's gross income pursuant to § 1.959-1(c)(1). The remaining $10x of the distribution of earnings and profits with respect to block 1 is included in DP's gross income as a dividend. Pursuant to paragraph (e)(4) of this section, at the end of year 1, FC has section 959(c)(2) earnings and profits of $0 and non-previously taxed earnings and profits of $190x.

Example (2). Multiple classes of stock. (i) Facts. Assume the same facts as in Example 1, except that DP also owns a block, block 3, of class B stock in FC. Entering year 1, DP has a previously taxed earnings and profits account with respect to block 3 consisting of $60x of section 959(c)(2) earnings and profits. Entering year 1, FC has $150x of section 959(c)(2) earnings and profits and $200x of non-previously taxed earnings and profits.

(ii) Analysis. First, as in Example 1, the section 959(c)(2) earnings and profits in DP's previously taxed earnings and profits account with respect to block 1 are decreased from $25x to $0 and the section 959(c)(2) earnings and profits in DP's previously taxed earnings and profits account with respect to block 2 are decreased from $65x to $15x pursuant to paragraph (e)(2)(ii) of this section. Because there are insufficient previously taxed earnings and profits with respect to block 1, DP may access its excess previously taxed earnings and profits with respect to block 2 and block 3, after taking into account any distributions or section 956 amounts with respect to those blocks. In addition, the previously taxed earnings and profits from blocks 2 and 3 are decreased pro rata based on the relative previously taxed earnings and profits in the previously taxed earnings and profits accounts with respect to both blocks after taking into account any distributions or section 956 amounts with respect to those blocks. Thus, the section 959(c)(2) earnings and profits in DP's previously taxed earnings and profits account with respect to block 2 are decreased from $15x to $10x ($15x/$75x x $25x) and the section 959(c)(2) earnings and profits in DP's previously taxed earnings and profits account with respect to block 3 are decreased from $60x to $40x ($60x/$75x x $25x) pursuant to paragraphs (e)(2)(v) and (f)(1)(i) of this section. The section 959(c)(2) earnings and profits in DP's previously taxed earnings and profits account with respect to block 1 are increased from $0 to $25x and then decreased from $25x to $0 pursuant to paragraphs (e)(2)(ii)(B) and (f)(1)(ii) of this section. The entire $50x distribution with respect to block 1 and $50x distribution with respect to block 2 are excluded from DP's gross income pursuant to § 1.959-1(c)(1). Pursuant to paragraph (e)(4) of this section, at the end of year 1, FC has section 959(c)(2) earnings and profits of $50x and non-previously taxed earnings and profits of $200x.

Example (3). Distribution in excess of aggregate previously taxed earnings and profits. (i) Facts. Assume the same facts as in Example 2, except that instead of a total distribution of $100x on Class A shares in year 1, FC makes a total distribution of $200x on its Class A shares in year 1, consisting of a $100x distribution to block 1 and a $100 distribution to block 2.

(ii) Analysis. First, as a result of the distribution, the section 959(c)(2) earnings and profits in DP's previously taxed earnings and profits account with respect to block 1 are decreased from $25x to $0 and the section 959(c)(2) earnings and profits in DP's previously taxed earnings and profits account with respect to block 2 are decreased from $65x to $0 pursuant to paragraph (e)(2)(ii) of this section. Because there are insufficient previously taxed earnings and profits in DP's previously taxed earning and profits accounts with respect to blocks 1 and 2, DP may access its excess previously taxed earnings and profits in its previously taxed earnings and profits account with respect to block3 after taking into account any distributions or section 956 amounts with respect to block 3. Consequently, the section 959(c)(2) earnings and profits in DP's previously taxed earnings and profits account with respect to block 3 are decreased from $60x to $0 pursuant to paragraphs (e)(2)(v) and (f)(1)(i) of this section. Of the total $200x distribution from FC to DP, $150x is excluded from DP's gross income pursuant to § 1.959-1(c)(1). The remaining $50x of the distribution is included in DP's gross income pursuant to section 951(a)(1)(A). Pursuant to paragraph (e)(4) of this section, at the end of year 1, FC has section 959(c)(2) earnings and profits of $0 and non-previously taxed earnings and profits of $150x.

Example (4). Sale. (i) Facts. Assume the same facts as in Example 2, except that DP sells block 3 before the end of year 1.

(ii) Analysis. First, as in Example 2, the distribution results in a decrease of the section 959(c)(2) earnings and profits in DP's previously taxed earnings and profits account with respect to block 1 from $25x to $0 and the section 959(c)(2) earnings and profits in DP's previously taxed earnings and profits account with respect to block 2 from $65x to $15x pursuant to paragraph (e)(2)(ii) of this section. Because DP does not own block 3 on the last day of year 1, DP cannot use the previously taxed earnings and profits account with respect to block 3 to exclude a distribution in that year to block 1 or 2 from gross income. Therefore, the section 959(c)(2) earnings and profits in DP's previously taxed earnings and profits account with respect to block 2 are decreased from $15x to $0 pursuant to paragraphs (e)(2)(v) and (f)(1)(i) of this section and the section 959(c)(2) earnings and profits in DP's previously taxed earnings and profits account with respect to block 1 are increased from $0 to $15x and then decreased from $15x to $0 pursuant to paragraphs (e)(2)(ii)(B) and (f)(1)(ii) of this section. The $40x ($25x + $15x) of the distribution with respect to block 1 and $50x of the distribution with respect to block 2 are excluded from DP's gross income pursuant to § 1.959-1(c)(1). The remaining $10x of the distribution with respect to block 1 is included in DP's gross income as a dividend. Pursuant to paragraph (e)(4) of this section, at the end of year 1, FC has section 959(c)(2) earnings and profits of $60x and non-previously taxed earnings and profits of $190x.

Example (5). Section 956 amount. (i) Facts. Assume the same facts as in Example 2, except that, in addition, during year 1, FC has a section 956 amount of $30x, $5x of which is allocable to each of blocks 1 and 2, and $20x of which is allocable to block 3.

(ii) Analysis. Pursuant to paragraph (f)(2) of this section, account adjustments are made for the distribution from FC before any account adjustments are made for the section 956 amount. After account adjustments are made for the distribution from FC as illustrated in Example 2, DP has a previously taxed earnings and profits account with respect each block as follows: Block 1: $0, block 2: $10x of section 959(c)(2) earnings and profits, block 3: $40x of section 959(c)(2) earnings and profits. As a result of the section 956 amount with respect to block 2, pursuant to paragraph (e)(2)(vi) of this section, $5x of DP's section 959(c)(2) earnings and profits in its previously taxed earnings and profits account with respect to block 2 is reclassified as section 959(c)(1) earnings and profits. Consequently, block 2 is left with a previously taxed earnings and profits account consisting of $5x of section 959(c)(1) earnings and profits and $5x of section 959(c)(2) earnings and profits. In addition, pursuant to paragraph (e)(2)(vi) of this section, $20x of DP's section 959(c)(2) earnings and profits in its previously taxed earnings and profits account with respect to block 3 are reclassified as section 959(c)(1) earnings and profits. Consequently, block 3 is left with a previously taxed earnings and profits account consisting of $20x of section 959(c)(1) earnings and profits and $20x of section 959(c)(2) earnings and profits. The total $25x section 956 amount with respect to blocks 2 and 3 is excluded from DP's gross income pursuant to § 1.959-1(c)(2). Because there are insufficient previously taxed earnings and profits in the previously taxed earnings and profits account with respect to block 1, DP may access its excess previously taxed earnings and profits in the previously taxed earnings and profits accounts with respect to blocks 2 and 3 after taking into account any distributions or section 956 amounts with respect to those blocks. In addition, the previously taxed earnings and profits in the previously taxed earnings and profits accounts with respect to blocks 2 and 3 are reclassified pro rata based on the relative previously taxed earnings and profits in those accounts after taking into account any distributions or section 956 amounts with respect to those blocks. Accordingly, pursuant to paragraphs (e)(2)(vi) and (f)(2) of this section, an additional $1x ($5x/$25x x $5x) of the section 959(c)(2) earnings and profits in DP's previously taxed earnings and profits account with respect to block 2 are reclassified as section 959(c)(1) earnings and profits and an additional $4x ($20x/$25x x $5x) of the section 959(c)(2) earnings and profits in DP's previously taxed earnings and profits account with respect to block 3 are reclassified as section 959(c)(1) earnings and profits. The $5x section 956 amount with respect to block 1 is also excluded from DP's gross income pursuant to § 1.959-1(c)(2). At the end of year 1, DP's previously taxed earnings and profits accounts with respect to its various blocks of stock are as follows: block 1 has no previously taxed earnings and profits, block 2 has $6x ($5x + $1x) of section 959(c)(1) earnings and profits and $4x ($5x-$1x) of section 959(c)(2) earnings and profits and block 3 has $24x ($20x + $4x) of section 959(c)(1) earnings and profits and $16x ($20x-$4x) of section 959(c)(2) earnings and profits. Pursuant to paragraph (e)(4) of this section, at the end of year 1, FC has $30x of section 959(c)(1) earnings and profits, $20x of section 959(c)(2) earnings and profits, and $200x of non-previously taxed earnings and profits.

(g) Special rule for shareholder included in a consolidated group. *(1) Adjustments for distributions.* (i) In general. In the case of a covered shareholder who is a member of a consolidated group, to the extent that the total amount of any distributions of earnings and profits with respect to such covered shareholder's stock in a foreign corporation during such foreign corporation's taxable year would exceed the covered shareholder's previously taxed earnings and profits account with respect to all of the covered shareholder's stock of the foreign corporation (an excess distribution amount) the previously taxed earnings and profits accounts of the covered shareholder and of the other members of the covered shareholder's consolidated group that own stock in the same foreign corporation and are members of the covered shareholder's consolidated group on the last day of the foreign corporation's taxable year shall be adjusted as follows.

(A) Adjustment of other members' accounts. The previously taxed earnings and profits accounts of the other members of the consolidated group that own (within the meaning of section 958(a)) stock in the same foreign corporation and are members of the covered shareholder's consolidated group on the last day of the foreign corporation's taxable year shall be decreased, in the aggregate, by the amount of such excess distribution amount, but not below zero. Such decrease shall be made on a pro rata basis by reference to the amount of such other members' previously taxed earnings and profits accounts and shall be allocated to the section 959(c)(1) and (c)(2) earnings and profits in such accounts in the same manner as a distribution is allocated to such earnings and profits pursuant to section 959(c) and paragraph (e)(2)(ii)(A) of this section.

(B) Adjustment of the deficient account. The deficient previously taxed earnings and profits account of such covered shareholder shall correspondingly be increased by the same amount, and then adjusted to zero under paragraph (e)(2)(ii)(B) of this section.

(ii) Insufficient previously taxed earnings and profits. If more than one member of the consolidated group is a covered shareholder that has an excess distribution amount with respect to all of its stock in the foreign corporation and there is insufficient previously taxed earnings and profits available in the previously taxed earnings and profits accounts of other consolidated group members to exclude the combined excess distribution amounts of the covered shareholders, the other consolidated group members' previously taxed earnings and profits shall be allocated between the covered shareholders' deficient previously taxed earnings and profits accounts in proportion to each covered shareholder's excess distribution amount.

(2) Adjustments for section 956 amounts. (i) In general. If a United States shareholder, who is a member of a consolidated group, has a section 956 amount with respect to its stock in a CFC for a taxable year, to the extent that the section 956 amount exceeds the section 959(c)(2) earnings and profits in such United States shareholder's previously taxed earnings and profits accounts with respect to all of its stock in the CFC (an excess section 956 amount), the section 959(c)(2) earnings and profits in the previously taxed earnings and profits accounts of consolidated group members, who are members of the United States shareholder's consolidated group on the last day of the CFC's taxable year, with respect to their stock in the CFC shall be reclassified as section 959(c)(1) earnings and profits, in the aggregate, by an amount equal to such excess section 956 amount. The amount that is reclassified with respect to each such account of such other members shall be proportionate to the amount of section 959(c)(2) earnings and profits in those accounts prior to reclassification under this paragraph (g).

(ii) Insufficient section 959(c)(2) earnings and profits. If more than one member of the consolidated group is a United States shareholder that has an excess section 956 amount with respect to its stock in the CFC for the taxable year and there is insufficient aggregate section 959(c)(2) earnings and profits in other consolidated group members' previously taxed earnings and profits accounts to exclude the combined excess section 956 amounts of the Untied States shareholders, the amount of any consolidated group members' section 959(c)(2) earnings and profits that are reclassified on behalf of each United States shareholder shall be proportionate to the excess section 956 amount for each such United States shareholder.

(3) Stock basis adjustments of members. See § 1.1502-32 for rules addressing investment adjustments resulting from the application of this paragraph.

(4) Examples. The application of this paragraph (g) is illustrated by the following examples:

Example (1). Two consolidated group members. (i) Facts. DP1, a United States shareholder, owns one block, block 1, of shares of Class A stock in FC, a CFC that uses the U.S. dollar as its functional currency. DP2, a United States shareholder and a member of DP1's consolidated group, owns one block, block 2, of shares of Class A stock in FC. DP1, DP2 and FC all use the calendar year as their taxable year and FC uses the U.S. dollar as its functional currency. Entering year 1, DP1 has a previously taxed earnings and profits account with respect to block 1 consisting of $50x of section 959(c)(2) earnings and profits and DP2 has a previously taxed earnings and profits account with respect to block 2 consisting of $200x of section 959(c)(2) earnings and profits. Entering year 1, FC has section 959(c)(2) earnings and profits of $250x and non-previously taxed earnings and profits of $100x. In year 1, FC generates no earnings and profits and makes a distribution of earnings and profits on its Class A stock, a $100x distribution of earnings and profits to block 1 and a $100x distribution of earnings and profits to block 2.

(ii) Analysis. First, pursuant to paragraph (e)(2)(ii) of this section, the section 959(c)(2) earnings and profits in DP1's previously taxed earnings and profits account with respect to block 1 are decreased from $50x to $0 and the section 959(c)(2) earnings and profits in DP2's previously taxed earnings and profits account with respect to block 2 are decreased from $200x to $100x. Then, pursuant to paragraphs (e)(2)(v) and (g)(1)(i)(A) of this section, the section 959(c)(2) earnings and profits in DP2's previously taxed earnings and profits account with respect to block 2 are decreased from $100x to $50x and, pursuant to paragraphs (e)(2)(ii)(B) and (g)(1)(i)(B) of this section, the section 959(c)(2) earnings and profits in DP1's previously taxed earnings and profits account with respect to block 1 are increased from $0 to $50x and then decreased from $50x to $0. Pursuant to section 959(a) and § 1.959-1(c), the entire $100x distribution to block 1 and $100x distribution to block 2 are excluded from DP1's and DP2's gross incomes respectively. Pursuant to paragraph (e)(4) of this section, at the end of year 1, FC has section 959(c)(2) earnings and profits of $50x and non-previously taxed earnings and profits of $100x.

Example (2). Two consolidated group members; multiple classes of stock. (i) Facts. Assume the same facts as in Example 1, except that DP1 also owns one block, block 3, of shares of class B stock in FC. DP1 has a previously taxed earnings and profits account with respect to block 3 consisting of $40x of section 959(c)(2) earnings and profits. Entering year 1, FC has section 959(c)(2) earnings and profits of $290x and non-previously taxed earnings and profits of $100x.

(ii) Analysis. First, pursuant to paragraph (e)(2)(ii) of this section, the section 959(c)(2) earnings and profits in DP1's previously taxed earnings and profits account with respect to block 1 are decreased from $50x to $0 and the section 959(c)(2) earnings and profits in DP2's previously taxed earnings and profits account with respect to block 2 are decreased from $200x to $100x. Then, pursuant to paragraphs (e)(2)(v) and (f)(1)(i) of this section, the section 959(c)(2) earnings and profits in DP1's previously taxed earnings and profits account with respect to block 3 are decreased from $40x to $0 and, pursuant to paragraphs (e)(2)(ii)(B) and (f)(1)(ii) of this section, the section 959(c)(2) earnings and profits in DP1's previously taxed earnings and profits account with respect to block 1 are increased from $0 to $40x and then decreased from $40x to $0. Finally, pursuant to paragraphs (e)(2)(v) and (g)(1)(i)(A) of this section, the section 959(c)(2) earnings and profits in DP2's previously taxed earnings and profits account with respect to block 2 are decreased from $100x to $90x and, pursuant to paragraphs (e)(2)(ii)(B) and (g)(1)(i)(B) of this section, the section 959(c)(2) earnings and profits in DP1's previously taxed earnings and profits account with respect to block 1 are increased from $0 to $10x and then decreased from $10x to $0. Pursuant to section 959(a) and § 1.959-1(c), the entire $100x distribution to block 1 and $100x distribution to block 2 are excluded from DP1's and DP2's gross incomes respectively. Pursuant to paragraph (e)(4) of this section, at the end of year 1, FC has section 959(c)(2) earnings and profits of $90x and non-previously taxed earnings and profits of $100x.

Example (3). Three consolidated group members; multiple classes of stock. (i) Facts. Assume the same facts as in Example 2, except that DP3, a United States shareholder and a member of DP1's consolidated group, owns one block, block 4, of shares of class B stock in FC. DP3 has a previously taxed earnings and profits account with respect to block 4 consisting of $25x of section 959(c)(2) earnings and profits. Entering year 1, FC has section 959(c)(2) earnings and profits of $315x and non-previously taxed earnings and profits of $100x.

(ii) Analysis. First, pursuant to paragraph (e)(2)(ii) of this section, the section 959(c)(2) earnings and profits in DP1's previously taxed earnings and profits account with respect to block 1 are decreased from $50x to $0 and the section 959(c)(2) earnings and profits in DP2's previously taxed earnings and profits account with respect to block 2 are decreased from $200x to $100x. Then, pursuant to paragraphs (e)(2)(v) and (f)(1)(i) of this section, the section 959(c)(2) earnings and profits in DP1's previously taxed earnings and profits account with respect to block 3 are decreased from $40x to $0 and, pursuant to paragraphs (e)(2)(ii)(B) and (f)(1)(ii) of this section, the section 959(c)(2) earnings and profits in DP1's previously taxed earnings and profits account with respect to block 1 are increased from $0 to $40x and then decreased from $40x to $0. Finally, pursuant to paragraphs (e)(2)(v) and (g)(1)(i)(A) of this section, the section 959(c)(2) earnings and profits in DP2's and DP3's previously taxed earnings and profits accounts with respect to blocks 2 and 4 are decreased pro rata from $100x to $92x and from $25x to $23x respectively, and, pursuant to paragraphs (e)(2)(ii)(B) and (g)(1)(i)(B) of this section, the section 959(c)(2) earnings and profits in DP1's previously taxed earnings and profits account with respect to block 1 are increased from $0 to $10x and then decreased from $10x to $0. Pursuant to section 959(a) and § 1.959-1(c), the entire amounts of the $100x distribution to block 1 and the $100x distribution to block 2 are excluded from DP1's and DP2's gross incomes respectively. Pursuant to paragraph (e)(4) of this section, at the end of year 1, FC has section 959(c)(2) earnings and profits of $115x and non-previously taxed earnings and profits of $100x.

Example (4). Section 956 Amount. (i) Facts. Assume the same facts as in Example 3, except that instead of a distribution of 200x on its class A stock, FC has a section 956 amount for year 1 of $180x, 45x of which is allocable to each of blocks 1 through 4.

(ii) Analysis. First, pursuant to paragraph (e)(2)(iv) of this section, the section 959(c)(2) earnings and profits in each shareholder's previously taxed earnings profits account are reclassified as section 959(c)(1) earnings and profits leaving each block of stock with the following account: Block 1: $45x of section 959(c)(1) earnings and profits, $5x of section 959(c)(2) earnings and profits; block 2: $45x of section 959(c)(1) earnings and profits and $155x of section 959(c)(2) earnings and profits; block 3: $40x of section 959(c)(1) earnings and profits and $0 of section 959(c)(2) earnings and profits; block 4: $25x of section 959(c)(1) earnings and profits and $0 of section 959(c)(2) earnings and profits. After the above reclassifications, DP1 has an excess section 956 amount of $5x with respect to block 3. Therefore, pursuant to paragraphs (e)(2)(vi) and (f)(2) of this section, the remaining $5x of section 959(c)(2) earnings and profits in DP1's previously taxed earnings and profits account with respect to block 1 are reclassified as section 959(c)(1) earnings and profits, leaving DP1 with $50x of section 959(c)(1) earnings and profits and $0 of section 959(c)(2) earnings and profits in its previously taxed earnings and profits account with respect to block 1. The entire $45x section 956 amount with respect to blocks 1 and 3 are excluded from DP1's gross income pursuant to paragraph (c)(2) of this section. After the above reclassifications, DP3 has an excess section 956 amount of $20x with respect to block 4. Therefore, pursuant to paragraphs (e)(2)(vi) and (g)(2)(i) of this section, $20x of the section 959(c)(2) earnings and profits in DP2's previously taxed earnings and profits account with respect to block 2 are reclassified as section 959(c)(1) earnings and profits, leaving DP2 with $65x of section 959(c)(1) earnings and profits and $135x of section 959(c)(2) earnings and profits. The entire $45x section 956 amount with respect to blocks 2 and 4 are excluded from DP2's and DP3's gross incomes, respectively, pursuant to § 1.959-1(c)(2). Pursuant to paragraph (e)(4) of this section, at the end of year 1, FC has section 959(c)(1) earnings and profits of $180x, section 959(c)(2) earnings and profits of $135x, and non-previously taxed earnings and profits of $100x.

Example (5). Ex-member. (i) Facts. DP1, a United States shareholder, owns one block, block 1, of shares of Class A stock in FC, a CFC that uses the U.S. dollar as its functional currency. DP2 and DP3, both United States shareholders and members of DP1's consolidated group, own one block each, blocks 2 and 3 respectively, of shares of Class A stock in FC. DP1, DP2, DP3 and FC all use the calendar year as their taxable year. Entering year 1, DP1 has a previously taxed earnings and profits account with respect to block 1 consisting of $50x of section 959(c)(2) earnings and profits, DP2 has a previously taxed earnings and profits account with respect to block 2 consisting of $100x of section 959(c)(2) earnings and profits, and DP3 has a previously taxed earnings and profits account with respect to block 3 consisting of $200x of section 959(c)(2) earnings and profits. Entering year 1, FC has section 959(c)(2) earnings and profits of $350x and non-previously taxed earnings and profits of $100x. On March 15 of year 1, FC makes a distribution of earnings and profits on its Class A stock consisting of a $100x distribution of earnings and profits to each of blocks 1, 2 and 3. On July 4 of year 1, DP3 is sold to DP4, a United States person who is not a member of the consolidated group, and DP3 ceases to be a member of the consolidated group.

(ii) Analysis. First, pursuant to paragraph (e)(2)(ii) of this section, the section 959(c)(2) earnings and profits in DP1's previously taxed earnings and profits account with respect to block 1 are decreased from $50x to $0, the section 959(c)(2) earnings and profits in DP2's previously taxed earnings and profits account with respect to block 2 are decreased from $100x to $0, and the section 959(c)(2) earnings and profits in DP3's previously taxed earnings and profits account with respect to block 3 are decreased from $200x to $100x. Because DP3 was not a member of DP1's consolidated group on the last day of year 1, the remaining $100x of section 959(c)(2) earnings and profits in DP3's previously taxed earnings and profits account with respect to its stock in FC cannot be used to exclude the remaining $50x distribution to DP1 from DP1's gross income. Consequently, pursuant to § 1.959-1(c)(1), $50x of the distribution to block 1, the entire $100x of the distribution to block 2, and the entire $100x of the distribution to block 3 are excluded from DP1's, DP2's, and DP3's gross incomes respectively. The remaining $50x distribution to DP1 is included in DP1's gross income pursuant to section 951(a)(1)(a). Pursuant to paragraph (e)(4) of this section, at the end of year 1, FC has section 959(c)(2) earnings and profits of $150x and non-previously taxed earnings and profits of $50x.

Example (6). Insufficient excess previously taxed earnings and profits. (i) Facts. DP1, a United States shareholder, owns one block, block 1, of shares of Class A stock in FC, a CFC that uses the U.S. dollar as its functional currency. DP2 and DP3, both United States shareholders and members of DP1's consolidated group, own one block each, blocks 2 and 3 respectively, of shares of Class A stock in FC. DP1, DP2, DP3 and FC all use the calendar year as their taxable year. Entering year 1, DP1 has a previously taxed earnings and profits account with respect to block 1 consisting of $40x of section 959(c)(2) earnings and profits, DP2 has a previously taxed earnings and profits account with respect to block 2 consisting of $60x of section 959(c)(2) earnings and profits, and DP3 has a previously taxed earnings and profits account with respect to block 3 consisting of $150x of section 959(c)(2) earnings and profits. Entering year 1, FC has section 959(c)(2) earnings and profits of $250x and non-previously taxed earnings and profits of $100x. On March 15 of year 1, FC makes a distribution of earnings and profits on its Class A stock consisting of a $100x distribution of earnings and profits to each of blocks 1, 2 and 3.

(ii) Analysis. First, pursuant to paragraph (e)(2)(ii) of this section, the section 959(c)(2) earnings and profits in DP1's previously taxed earnings and profits account with respect to block 1 are decreased from $40x to $0, the section 959(c)(2) earnings and profits in DP2's previously taxed earnings and profits account with respect to block 2 are decreased from $60x to $0, and the section 959(c)(2) earnings and profits in DP3's previously taxed earnings and profits account with respect to block 3 are decreased from $150x to $50x. Then, pursuant to paragraph (g)(1)(i)(A) of this section, the section 959(c)(2) earnings and profits in DP3's previously taxed earnings and profits account with respect to its stock in FC are reduced from $50x to $0 and, pursuant to paragraphs (g)(1)(i)(B) and (g)(1)(ii) of this section, the section 959(c)(2) earnings and profits in DP1's and DP2's previously taxed earnings and profits accounts with respect to their stock in FC are increased from $0 to $30x ($60x/$100x x $50x) and $0 to $20x ($40x/$100x x $50x) respectively and then immediately reduce to $0. Pursuant to § 1.959-1(c), $70x ($40x + $30x) of the distribution to DP1, $80x ($60x + $20x) of the distribution to DP2, and $100x of the distribution to DP3 are excluded from gross income. The remaining $30x distributed to DP1 and $20x distributed to DP2 are included in gross income pursuant to section 951(a)(1)(A). Pursuant to paragraph (e)(4) of this section, at the end of year 1, FC has non-previously taxed earnings and profits of $50x.

(h) Adjustments in the case of redemptions. *(1) In general.* In the case of a foreign corporation's redemption of stock (a redemption distribution), the effect on the covered shareholder's previously taxed earnings and profits account and on the earnings and profits of the redeeming corporation depends on whether the distribution is treated as a payment in exchange for stock or as a distribution of property to which section 301 applies. For the treatment of deemed redemption distributions in transactions described in section 304(a)(1), see paragraph (h)(4) of this section.

(2) Exchange treatment. (i) Effect on foreign corporation's earnings and profits. In the case of a redemption distribution that is treated as a payment in exchange for stock under section 302(a) or section 303, the amount of the distribution properly chargeable to the earnings and profits of the redeeming foreign corporation is the amount determined under section 312(a), subject to the limitation in section 312(n)(7) and this paragraph (h)(2)(i). For purposes of section 312(n)(7), the amount properly chargeable to the earnings and profits of the redeeming foreign corporation shall not exceed the sum of—

(A) The amount of the previously taxed earnings and profits account with respect to the redeemed shares of stock (without adjustment for any income inclusion under section 1248 resulting from the redemption); and

(B) A ratable portion of the redeeming corporation's non-previously taxed earnings and profits. Such chargeable amount of earnings and profits shall be allocated to earnings and profits in accordance with section 959(c) and this section.

(ii) Cessation of previously taxed earnings and profits account. In the case of a redemption distribution that is treated as a payment in exchange for stock, the redeemed covered shareholder's previously taxed earnings and profits account with respect to the redeemed shares ceases to exist and is not transferred to any other previously taxed earnings and profits account. In such a case, any previously taxed earnings and profits in the redeemed covered shareholder's previously taxed earnings and profits account, after being reduced under paragraph (h)(2)(i) of this section, become non-previously taxed earnings and profits of the foreign corporation.

(iii) Examples. The application of this paragraph (h)(2) is illustrated by the following examples:

Example (1). Complete redemption treated as exchange; previously taxed earnings and profits account is depleted. (i) Facts. DP, a United States shareholder, owns 70% and FP, a nonresident alien who is unrelated to DP under section 318, owns 30% of the only class of stock in FC, a CFC that uses the U.S. dollar as its functional currency. Both DP and FC use the calendar year as their taxable year and both DP and FC are wholly owned by the same domestic corporation, USP. DP has a previously taxed earnings and profits account consisting of $50x of section 959(c)(2) earnings and profits with respect to its stock in FC and DP has a $50 basis in its FC stock pursuant to section 961(a). FC has $50x of section 959(c)(2) earnings and profits and $50x of non-previously taxed earnings and profits attributable to taxable years of FC beginning on or after December 31, 1962 during which FC was a CFC and during which DP held its shares of stock in FC. FC redeems all of DP's stock for $100x in a redemption that is treated as a payment in exchange for the stock under section 302(a).

(ii) Analysis. DP includes $35x ($50x x 70%) in gross income as a dividend pursuant to section 1248(a) as a result of the deemed exchange. FC adjusts its earnings and profits as a result of the exchange under paragraph (h)(2)(i) of this section in the following manner: first, FC's section 959(c)(2) earnings and profits are reduced from $50x to $0; then, FC's non-previously taxed earnings and profits are decreased from $50x to $15x to reflect DP's $35x ratable share of FC's non-previously taxed earnings and profits. DP's previously taxed earnings and profits account ceases to exist and is not transferred to any other previously taxed earnings and profits account.

Example (2). Complete redemption treated as exchange; previously taxed earnings and profits account is not depleted. (i) Facts. Assume the same facts as Example 1, except that the amount of the redemption distribution by FC to DP is $25x.

(ii) Analysis. DP recognizes a $25x loss as a result of the deemed exchange. FC's section 959(c)(2) earnings and profits are decreased from $50x to $25x, pursuant to paragraph (h)(2)(i) of this section. DP's previously taxed earnings and profits account ceases to exist, and the remaining $25x of section 959(c)(2) earnings and profits in such account is not transferred to any other previously taxed earnings and profits account. However, pursuant to paragraph (h)(2)(ii) of this section, the $25x of previously taxed earnings and profits is converted to non-previously taxed earnings and profits of DC.

(3) Distribution treatment. (i) Adjustment of shareholder previously taxed earnings and profits accounts and foreign corporation's earnings and profits. In the case of a redemption distribution by a foreign corporation that is treated as a distribution of property to which section 301 applies, § 1.959-1 and this section shall apply in the same manner as they would apply to any distribution of property to which section 301 applies.

(ii) Transfer to remaining shares. To the extent that the previously taxed earnings and profits account with respect to stock redeemed in a transaction described in paragraph (h)(3)(i) of this section exceeds the amount chargeable to the earnings and profits of the corporation under the rules of that paragraph, the excess previously taxed earnings and profits shall be reallocated to the previously taxed earnings and profits accounts with respect to the remaining stock in the foreign corporation in a manner consistent with, and in proportion to, the proper adjustments of the basis in the remaining shares pursuant to § 1.302-2(c).

(iii) Examples. The application of this paragraph (h)(3) is illustrated by the following examples:

Example (1). Redemption in exchange for cash that is treated as a distribution.

(i) Facts. DP, a United States shareholder, owns 100% of the stock in FC, a CFC that uses the U.S. dollar as its functional currency. Both DP and FC use the calendar year as their taxable year. DP owns two blocks of stock in FC, block 1 and block 2. At the beginning of year 1, DP has a previously taxed earnings and profits account with respect to block 1 consisting of $50x of section 959(c)(2) earnings and profits and FC has section 959(c)(2) earnings and profits of $50x and non-previously taxed earnings and profits of $100x. In year 1, FC redeems block 1 for $100x in a redemption that is treated as a distribution of property to which section 301 applies under section 302(d).

(ii) Analysis. The section 959(c)(2) earnings and profits in DP's previously taxed earnings and profits account with respect to block 1 are reduced from $50x to $0 and FC's section 959(c)(2) earnings and profits are correspondingly reduced from $50x to $0. The remaining $50x is included in DP's gross income as a dividend under section 301(c)(1) and FC's non-previously taxed earnings and profits are reduced from $100x to $50x.

Example (2). Redemption in exchange for cash that is treated as a distribution.

(i) Facts. Assume the same facts as Example 1, except that DP is redeemed for $25x.

(ii) Analysis. The section 959(c)(2) earnings and profits in DP's previously taxed earnings and profits account with respect to block 1 are reduced from $50x to $25x and FC's section 959(c)(2) earnings and profits are correspondingly reduced from $50x to $25x. FC's non-previously taxed earnings and profits remain at $100x. Pursuant to paragraph (h)(3)(ii) of this section the remaining $25x of section 959(c)(2) earnings and profits in DP's previously taxed earnings and profits account with respect to block 1 are reallocated with respect to the remaining stock in FC in a manner consistent with, and in proportion to, the proper adjustments of the basis of the remaining FC shares pursuant to § 1.302-2(c).

(4) Section 304 transactions. (i) Deemed redemption treated as a distribution. In the case of a stock acquisition described in section 304(a)(1), that is treated as a distribution of property to which section 301 applies, a covered shareholder receiving an amount treated as a distribution of earnings and profits shall have a previously taxed earnings and profits account with respect to stock in each foreign corporation treated as distributing its earnings and profits under section 304(b)(2), even if such person did not otherwise have a previously taxed earnings and profits account with respect to stock in such corporation or corporations. In such a case, § 1.959-1 and this section shall apply in the same manner as these regulations would apply to any distribution to which section 301 applies.

(ii) Example. The application of this paragraph (h)(4) is illustrated by the following example:

Example. Cross-chain acquisition of first-tier CFC. (i) Facts. DP, a domestic corporation, owns all of the stock in DS, a domestic corporation, and F1, a CFC. DP and DS are members of the same consolidated group. DS owns all of the stock in F2, a CFC. DP, DS, F1 and F2 all use the calendar year as their taxable year and F1 and F2 each use the U.S. dollar as its functional currency. During year 1, F1 purchases all the stock in F2 from DS for $80x in a transaction described in section 304(a)(1). At the end of year 1, before taking into account the purchase of F2's stock, DP has a previously taxed earnings and profits account consisting of $20x of section 959(c)(2) earnings and profits with respect to its stock in F1, and F1 has previously taxed earnings and profits consisting of $20x of section 959(c)(2) earnings and profits and non-previously taxed earnings and profits of $10x. At the end of year1, before taking into account the purchase of F2's stock, DS has a previously taxed earnings and profits account consisting of $50x of section 959(c)(2) earnings and profits with respect to its stock in F2, and F2 has section 959(c)(2) earnings and profits of $50x and non-previously taxed earnings and profits of $0.

(ii) Analysis. Under section 304(a)(1), DS is deemed to have transferred the F2 stock to F1 in exchange for F1 stock in a transaction to which section 351(a) applies, and F1 is treated as having redeemed, for $80x, the F1 stock deemed issued to DS. The payment of $80x is treated as a distribution of property to which section 301 applies. Under section 304(b)(2), the determination of the amount which is a dividend is made as if the distribution were made, first, by F1 to the extent of its earnings and profits ($30x), and then by F2 to the extent of its earnings and profits ($50x). Before taking into account the deemed distributions, DS had a previously taxed earnings and profits account consisting of $50x of section 959(c)(2) earnings and profits with respect to its stock in F2, and DP had a previously taxed earnings and profits account consisting of $20x of section 959(c)(2) earnings and profits with respect to its stock in F1. Under paragraph (h)(4)(i) of this section, DS has a previously taxed earnings and profits account with respect to the stock in F1. Under paragraph (g)(1)(i) of this section, the section 959(c)(2) earnings and profits in DP's previously taxed earnings and profits account with respect to the F1 stock are reduced from $20x to $0 and the section 959(c)(2) earnings and profits in DS's previously taxed earnings and profits account with respect to the F1 stock are increased from $0 to $20x. The distribution by F1 causes the section 959(c)(2) earnings and profits in DS's previously taxed earnings and profits account with respect to F1 stock to be reduced from $20x to $0, and causes F1's section 959(c)(2) earnings and profits to be reduced from $20x to $0 and its non-previously taxed earnings and profits to be reduced from $10x to $0. The deemed distribution by F2 causes the section 959(c)(2) earnings and profits in DS's previously taxed earnings and profits account with respect to F2 stock to be reduced from $50x to $0, and causes F2's section 959(c)(2) earnings and profits to be reduced from $50x to $0. Of the distribution of $80x, $70x is excluded from DS's gross income pursuant to § 1.959-1(c)(1), and $10x is included in DS's gross income as a dividend.

PAR. 5. Section 1.959-4 is revised to read as follows:

Proposed § 1.959-4 Distributions of amounts excluded under section 959(a). [*For Preamble, see ¶ 152,795*]

Except as provided in section 960(a)(3) and § 1.960-1, any distribution excluded from gross income of a covered shareholder under section 959(a)(1) and § 1.959-1(c)(1) shall be treated, for purposes of chapter 1 (relating to normal taxes and surtaxes) of subtitle A (relating to income taxes) of the Internal Revenue Code as a distribution which is not a dividend, except such a distribution shall immediately reduce earnings and profits.

§ 1.960-1 Foreign tax credit with respect to taxes paid on earnings and profits of controlled foreign corporations.

Caution: The Treasury has not yet amended Reg § 1.960-1 to reflect changes made by P.L. 105-34, P.L. 99-514.

(a) Scope of regulations under section 960. This section prescribes rules for determining the foreign income taxes deemed paid under section 960(a)(1) by a domestic corporation which is required under section 951 to include in gross income an amount attributable to a first-, second-, or third-tier corporation's earnings and profits. Section 1.960-2 prescribes rules for applying section 902 to dividends paid by a third-, second-, or first-tier corporation from earnings and profits attributable to an amount which is, or has been, included in gross income under section 951. Section 1.960-3 provides special rules for the application of the gross-up provisions of section 78 where an amount is included in gross income under section 951. Section 1.960-4 prescribes rules for increasing the applicable foreign tax credit limitation under section 904(a) of the domestic corporation for the taxable year in which it receives a distribution of earnings and profits in respect of which it was required under section 951 to include an amount in its gross income for a prior taxable year. Section 1.960-5 prescribes rules for disallowing a deduction for foreign income taxes for such taxable year of receipt where the domestic corporation received the benefits of the foreign tax credit for such previous taxable year of inclusion. Section 1.960-6 provides that the excess of such an increase in the applicable limitation under section 904(a) over the tax liability of the domestic corporation for such taxable year of receipt results in an overpayment of tax. Section 1.960-7 prescribes the effective dates for application of these rules.

(b) Definitions. For purposes of section 960 and §§ 1.960-1 through 1.960-7—

(1) First-tier corporation. The term "first-tier corporation" means a foreign corporation at least 10 percent of the voting stock of which is owned by the domestic corporation described in paragraph (a) of this section.

(2) Second-tier corporation. In the case of amounts included in the gross income of the taxpayer under section 951—

(i) For taxable years beginning before January 1, 1977, the term "second-tier corporation" means a foreign corporation at least 50 percent of the voting stock of which is owned by such first-tier corporation.

(ii) For taxable years beginning after December 31, 1976, the term "second-tier corporation" means a foreign corporation as least 10 percent of the voting stock of which is owned by such first-tier corporation.

(3) Third-tier corporation. In the case of amounts included in the gross income of a domestic shareholder under section 951 for taxable years beginning after December 31, 1976, the term "third-tier corporation" means a foreign corporation at least 10 percent of the voting stock of which is owned by such second-tier corporation.

(4) Immediately lower-tier corporation. In the case of a first-tier corporation the term "immediately lower-tier corporation" means a second-tier corporation. In the case of a second-tier corporation, the term "immediately lower-tier corporation" means a third-tier corporation. In the case of a third-tier corporation, the term "immediately lower-tier corporation" means a fourth-tier corporation.

(5) Foreign income taxes. The term "foreign income taxes" means income, war profits, and excess profits taxes, and taxes included in the term "income, war profits, and excess profits taxes" by reason of section 903, imposed by a foreign country or a possession of the United States.

(c) Amount of foreign income taxes deemed paid by domestic corporation in respect of earnings and profits of foreign corporation attributable to amount included in income under section 951. *(1) In general.* For purposes of section 901—

(i) If for the taxable year there is included in the gross income of a domestic corporation under section 951 an amount attributable to the earnings and profits of a first- or second-tier corporation for any taxable year, the domestic corporation shall be deemed to have paid the same proportion of the total foreign income taxes paid, accrued, or deemed (in accordance with paragraph (b) of § 1.960-2) to be paid by such foreign corporation on or with respect to its earnings and profits for its taxable year as the amount (in the case of a first-tier corporation, determined without regard to section 958(a)(2); in the case of a second-tier corporation, determined without regard to section 958(a)(1)(A) and, to the extent that stock of such second-tier corporation is owned by the domestic corporation through a foreign corporation other than the first-tier corporation, determined without regard to section 958(a)(2)) so included in the gross income of the domestic corporation under section 951 with respect to such foreign corporation bears to the total earnings and profits of such foreign corporation for its taxable year. This paragraph (c)(1)(i) shall not apply to amounts included in the gross income of the domestic corporation under section 951 with respect to the second-tier corporation unless the percentage-of-voting-stock requirement of section 902(b)(3)(A) is satisfied.

(ii) If for the taxable year there is included in the gross income of a domestic corporation under section 951 an amount attributable to the earnings and profits of a third-tier corporation for any taxable year, the domestic corporation shall be deemed to have paid the same proportion of the total foreign income taxes paid or accrued by such foreign corporation on or with respect to its earnings and profits for its taxable year as the amount (determined without regard to section 958(a)(1)(A) and, to the extent that stock of such third-tier corporation is owned by the domestic corporation through a foreign corporation other than the second-tier corporation, determined without regard to section 958(a)(2)) so included in the gross income of the domestic corporation under section 951 with respect to such foreign corporation bears to the total earnings and profits of such foreign corporation. This paragraph (c)(1)(ii) shall not apply unless the percentage-of-voting-stock requirement of section 902(b)(3)(B) is satisfied.

(iii) In applying paragraph (c)(1)(i) or (c)(1)(ii) of this section to a first-, second-, or third-tier corporation which for the taxable year has income excluded under section 959(b), paragraph (c)(3) of this section shall apply for purposes of excluding certain earnings and profits of such foreign corporation and foreign income taxes, if any, attributable to such excluded income.

(iv) This paragraph (c)(1) applies whether or not the first-, second-, or third-tier corporation makes a distribution for the taxable year of its earnings and profits which are attributable to the amount included in the gross income of the domestic corporation under section 951.

(v) This paragraph (c)(1) does not apply to an increase in current earnings invested in United States property which, but for paragraph (e) of § 1.963-3 (applied as if section 963 had not been repealed by the Tax Reduction Act of 1975), would be included in the gross income of the domestic corporation under section 951(a)(1)(B) but which, pursuant to such paragraph, counts toward a minimum distribution for the taxable year. This subdivision shall apply in taxable years subsequent to the Tax Reduction Act of 1975 only in those cases where an adjustment is required as a result of an election made under section 963 prior to the Act.

(2) Taxes paid or accrued on or with respect to earnings and profits of foreign corporation. For purposes of paragraph (c)(1) of this section, the foreign income taxes paid or accrued by a first-, second- or third-tier corporation on or with respect to its earnings and profits for its taxable years shall be the total amount of the foreign income taxes paid or accrued by such foreign corporation for such taxable year.

(3) Exclusion of earnings and profits and taxes of a first-, second-, or third-tier corporation having income excluded under section 959(b). If in the case of a first-, second-, or third-tier corporation to which paragraph (c)(1)(i) or (c)(1)(ii) of this section is applied—

(i) The earnings and profits of such foreign corporation for its taxable year consist of (A) earnings and profits attributable to dividends received from an immediately lower-tier corporation which are attributable to amounts included in the gross income of a domestic corporation under section 951 with respect to the immediately lower- or lower-tier corporations, and (B) other earnings and profits, and

(ii) The effective rate of foreign income taxes paid or accrued by such foreign corporation in respect to the dividends to which its earnings and profits described in paragraph (c)(3)(i)(A) of this section are attributable is higher or lower than the effective rate of foreign income taxes paid or accrued by such foreign corporation in respect to the income to which its earnings and profits described in paragraph (c)(3)(i)(B) of this section are attributable

Then, for the purposes of applying paragraph (c)(1)(i) or (c)(1)(ii) of this section to the foreign income taxes paid, accrued, or deemed to be paid, by such foreign corporation on or with respect to its earnings and profits for such taxable year, the earnings and profits of such foreign corporation for such taxable year shall be considered not to include the earnings and profits described in paragraph (c)(3)(i)(A) of this section and only the foreign income taxes paid, accrued, or deemed to be paid, by such foreign corporation in respect to the income to which its earnings and profits described in paragraph (c)(3)(i)(B) of this section are attributable shall be taken into account. For purposes of applying this paragraph (c)(3), the effective rate of foreign income taxes paid or accrued in respect to income shall be determined consistently with the principles of paragraphs (b)(3) (iv) and (viii) and (c) of § 1.954-1. Thus, for example, the effective rate of foreign income taxes paid or accrued in respect to dividends received by such foreign corporation shall be determined by taking into account any intercorporate dividends received deduction allowed to such corporation for such dividends.

(4) Illustrations. The application of this paragraph may be illustrated by the following examples:

Example (1). Domestic corporation N owns all the one class of stock of controlled foreign corporation A. Both corporations use the calendar year as the taxable year. For 1978, N Corporation is required under section 951 to include in gross income $50 attributable to the earnings and profits of A Corporation for such year, but A Corporation does not distribute any earnings and profits for such year. The foreign income taxes paid by A Corporation for 1978 which are deemed paid by N Corporation for such year under section 960(a)(1) are determined as follows upon the basis of the facts assumed:

Pretax earnings and profits of A Corporation	$100.00
Foreign income taxes (20%)	20.00
Earnings and profits	80.00
Amount required to be included in N Corporation's gross income under sec. 951	50.00
Dividends paid to N Corporation	0.
Foreign income taxes paid on or with respect to earnings and profits of A Corporation	20.00
Foreign income taxes of A Corporation deemed paid by N Corporation under sec. 960(a)(1) ($50/$80 × $20)	12.50

Example (2). Domestic corporation N owns all the one class of stock of controlled foreign corporation A which owns all the one class of stock of controlled foreign corporation B. All such corporations use the calendar year as the taxable year. For 1978, N Corporation is required under section 951 to include in gross income $45 attributable to the earnings and profits of B Corporation for such year, but is not required to include any amount in gross income under section 951 attributable to the earnings and profits of A Corporation for such year. Neither B Corporation nor A Corporation distributes any earnings and profits for 1978. The foreign income taxes paid by B Corporation for 1978 which are deemed paid by N Corporation for such year under section 960(a)(1)are determined as follows upon the basis of the facts assumed:

Pretax earnings and profits of B Corporation	$100.00
Foreign income taxes (40%)	40.00
Earnings and profits	60.00
Amounts required to be included in N Corporation's gross income under sec. 951 with respect to B Corporation	45.00
Dividends paid	0.
Foreign income taxes paid on or with respect to earnings and profits of B Corporation	40.00
Foreign income taxes of B Corporation deemed paid by N Corporation under sec. 960(a)(1) ($45/$60 × $40)	30.00

Example (3). Domestic corporation N owns all the one class of stock of controlled foreign corporation A, which owns all the one class of stock of controlled foreign corporation B, which owns all the one class of stock of foreign corporation C. All such corporations use the calendar year as the taxable year. For 1978, N Corporation is required under section 951 to include in gross income $80 attributable to the earnings and profits of C Corporation for such year, $45 attributable to the earnings and profits of B Corporation for such year and $50 attributable to the earnings and profits of A Corporation for such year. Neither C Corporation nor B corporation distributes any earnings and profits for 1978. The foreign income taxes which are deemed paid by N Corporation for such year under section 960(a)(1) are determined as follows upon the basis of the facts assumed:

C Corporation (third-tier corporation):	
Pretax earnings of C Corporation	$150.00
Foreign income taxes (40%)	60.00
Earnings and profits	90.00
Amounts required to be included in N Corporation's gross income under section 951	80.00
Dividends paid to B Corporation	0
Foreign income taxes paid on or with respect to earnings and profits of C Corporation	60.00
B Corporation (second-tier corporation):	
Pretax earnings of B Corporation	$100.00
Foreign income taxes (40%)	40.00
Earnings and profits	60.00
Amount required to be included in N Corporation's gross income under section 951	45.00
Dividends paid to A Corporation	0
Foreign income taxes paid on or with respect to earnings and profits of B Corporation	40.00
A Corporation (first-tier corporation):	
Pretax earnings and profits of A Corporation.	$100.00
Foreign income taxes (20%)	20.00
Earnings and profits	80.00
Amount required to be included in N Corporation's gross income under section 951	50.00
Dividends paid to N Corporation	0
Foreign income taxes paid on or with respect to earnings and profits of A Corporation	20.00
N Corporation (domestic corporation):	
Foreign income taxes deemed paid by N Corporation under section 960(a)(1):	
Taxes of C Corporation $80/$90 × $60	$ 53.33

Taxes of B Corporation $45/$60 × $40 . .	30.00
Taxes of A Corporation $50/$80 × $20 . .	12.50
Total taxes deemed paid under section 960(a)(1)	$ 95.83

Example (4). Domestic corporation N owns all the one class of stock of controlled foreign corporation A, which owns 5 percent of the one class of stock of controlled foreign corporation B. N Corporation also directly owns 95 percent of the one class of stock of B Corporation. (Under these facts, B Corporation is only a first-tier corporation with respect to N Corporation) all such corporations use the calendar year as the taxable year. For 1978, N Corporation is required under section 951 to include in gross income $60 attributable to the earnings and profits of B Corporation and $79.20 attributable to the earnings and profits of A Corporation. For 1978, B Corporation distributes $19 to N Corporation and $1 to A Corporation, but A Corporation makes no distribution to N Corporation. The foreign income taxes paid by N Corporation for such year under section 960(a)(1) are determined as follows upon the basis of the facts assumed in accordance with § 1.960-1(c)(1)(i):

B Corporation (first-tier corporation):	
Pretax earnings and profits	$100.00
Foreign income taxes (40%)	40.00
Earnings and profits	60.00
Amount required to be included in N Corporation's gross income under section 951 with respect to B Corporation	60.00
A Corporation (first-tier corporation):	
Pretax earnings and profits (including $1 dividend from B Corporation)	$100.00
Foreign income taxes (20%)	20.00
Earnings and profits	80.00
Amount required to be included in N Corporation's gross income with respect to A Corporation ($99 – [$99 × 0.20])	79.20
N Corporation (domestic corporation):	
Foreign income taxes deemed paid by N Corporation under section 960(a)(1) with respect to—	
B Corporation ([$60 × 0.95/$60] × $40)	$ 38.00
A Corporation ($79.20/$80 × $20)	19.80
Total taxes deemed paid under section 960(a)(1)	$ 57.80

Example (5). Domestic corporation N owns all the one class of stock of controlled foreign corporation A, which owns all one class of stock of controlled foreign corporation B. All such corporations use the calendar year as the taxable year. For 1978, N Corporation is required under section 951 to include in gross income $175 attributable to the earnings and profits of A Corporation for such year. For 1965, B Corporation has earnings and profits of $225, on which it pays foreign income taxes of $75. In 1978, B Corporation distributes $150, which, under paragraph (b) of § 1.960-2, consists of $100 to which section 902(b) does not apply (from B Corporation's earnings and profits attributable to an amount required under section 951 to be included in N Corporation's gross income with respect to B Corporation) and $50 to which section 902(b)(1) applies (from B Corporation's other earnings and profits). The country under the laws of which A Corporation is incorporated imposes an income tax of 40 percent on all income but exempts from tax dividends received from a subsidiary corporation. A Corporation makes no distribution for 1965. Under paragraph (b) of § 1.960-2, A Corporation is deemed to have paid $25 ($50/$150 × $75) of the $75 foreign income taxes paid by B Corporation on its pretax earnings and profits of $225. The foreign income taxes deemed paid by N Corporation for 1978 under section 960(a)(1) with respect to A Corporation are determined as follows upon the basis of the following assumed facts:

Pretax earnings and profits of A corporation:		
Dividends received from B Corporation		$150.00
Other income		250.00
Total pretax earnings and profits		$400.00
Foreign income taxes:		
On dividends received from B Corporation		0
On other income ($250 × 0.40)		100.00
Total foreign income taxes		100.00
Earnings and profits:		
Attributable to dividends received from B Corporation which are attributable to amounts included in N Corporation's gross income under section 951 with respect to B Corporation . . . . , ...		100.00
Attributable to other income:		
Attributable to dividends received from B Corporation which are attributable to amounts not included in N Corporation's gross income under section 951 with respect to B Corporation	$ 50.00	
Attributable to other income ($250 – $100 [$250 × 0.40])	150.00	200.00
Total earnings and profits		300.00
Foreign income taxes deemed paid by N Corporation under sec. 960(a)(1) with respect to A Corporation:		
Tax paid by A corporation in respect to its income other than dividends received from B corporation attributable to amounts included in N Corporation's gross income under section 951 with respect to B Corporation ($175/$200 × $100)		87.50
Tax of B corporation deemed paid by A Corporation under sec. 902(b)(1) in respect to such income ($175/$200 × $25)		21.88
Total foreign income taxes deemed paid by N corporation under sec. 960(a)(1) with respect to A corporation		$109.38

(d) Time for meeting stock ownership requirements *(1) In general.* For the purposes of applying paragraph (c) of this section to amounts included in the gross income of a domestic corporation attributable to the earnings and profits of a first-, second-, or third-tier corporation, the stock ownership requirements of paragraph (b)(1), (2), and (3) of this section and the percentage of voting stock requirements of paragraph (c)(1)(i) and (ii) of this section, if applicable, must be satisfied on the last day in the taxable year of such first-, second-, or third-tier corporation, as the case may be, on which such foreign corporation is a controlled foreign corporation. For paragraph (c) to apply to amounts included in a domestic corporation's gross income attributable to the earnings and profits of a second-tier corporation, the requirements of paragraph (b)(1) and (2) of this section and the percentage of voting stock requirement of paragraph (c)(1)(i) of this section must be met on such date. For paragraph (c) to apply to amounts included in a domestic corporation's gross income attributable to the earnings and profits of a third-tier corporation, the requirements of paragraph (b)(1), (2), and (3) of this section and the percentage of voting stock requirement of paragraph (c)(1)(ii) of this section must be met on such date.

(2) Illustrations. The application of this paragraph may be illustrated by the following examples:

Example (1). Domestic corporation N is required for its taxable year ending June 30, 1978, to include in gross income under section 951 an amount attributable to the earnings and profits of controlled foreign corporation A for 1977 and another amount attributable to the earnings and profits of controlled foreign corporation B for such year. Corporations A and B use the calendar year as the taxable year. Such amounts are required to be included in N Corporation's gross income by reason of its ownership of stock in A Corporation and in turn by A Corporation's ownership of stock in B Corporation. Corporation A is a controlled foreign corporation throughout 1977, but B Corporation is a controlled foreign corporation only from January 1, 1977, through September 30, 1977. Corporation N may obtain credit under section 960(a)(1) for the year ending June 30, 1978, for foreign income taxes paid by A Corporation for 1977, only if N Corporation owns at least 10 percent of the voting stock of A Corporation on December 31, 1977. Corporation N may obtain credit under section 960(a)(1) for the year ending June 30, 1978, for foreign income taxes paid by B Corporation for 1977, only if on September 30, 1977, N Corporation owns at least 10 percent of the voting stock of A Corporation, A Corporation owns at least 10 percent of the voting stock of B Corporation, and the percentage of voting stock requirement of paragraph (c)(1)(i) of this section is met.

Example (2). The facts are the same as in example (1), except that A Corporation is a controlled foreign corporation only from January 1, 1977, through March 31, 1977. Corporation N may obtain credit under section 960(a)(1) for the year ending June 30, 1978, for foreign income taxes paid by A Corporation for 1977, only if N Corporation owns at least 10 percent of the voting stock of A Corporation on March 31, 1977. Corporation N may obtain credit under section 960(a)(1) for the year ending June 30, 1978, for foreign income taxes paid by B Corporation for 1977, only if on September 30, 1977, N Corporation owns at least 10 percent of the voting stock of A Corporation, A Corporation owns at least 10 percent of the voting stock of B Corporation, and the percentage of voting stock requirement of paragraph (c)(1)(i) of this section is met.

Example (3). Domestic Corporation N owns 100 percent of the stock of controlled foreign corporation A. A Corporation owns 20 percent of the stock of controlled foreign corporation B. B Corporation owns 10 percent of the voting stock of controlled foreign corporation C. For calendar year 1983, N Corporation is required to include amounts in its gross income attributable to the earnings and profits of A, B, and C Corporations. A, B, and C Corporations were all controlled foreign corporations throughout their respective taxable years ending as follows: A Corporation, December 31, 1983; B Corporation, November 31, 1983; and C Corporation, August 31, 1983. Paragraph (c) of this section applies to amounts included in gross income of N Corporation with respect to the earnings and profits of A Corporation because the 10 percent ownership requirement of paragraph (b)(1) of this section is met on December 31, 1983. Paragraph (c) of this section applies to amounts included in the gross income of N Corporation with respect to the earnings and profits of B Corporation because the 10 percent stock ownership requirements of paragraph (b)(1) and (2) of this section are met on November 30, 1983, and the percentage of voting stock requirement of paragraph (c)(1)(i) of this section (5 percent) is also met on such date. The percentage of voting stock in A Corporation owned by N Corporation (100 percent) multiplied by the percentage of voting stock in B Corporation owned by A Corporation (20 percent) is 20 percent. Paragraph (c) of this section will not apply to amounts included in N Corporation's gross income attributable to the earnings and profits of C Corporation even though on August 31, 1983, the 10 percent stock ownership requirements of paragraph (b)(1), (2), and (3) of this section are met, because the percentage of voting stock requirement of paragraph (c)(1)(ii) of this section (5 percent) is not met on such date. The percentage of voting stock of C Corporation owned by B Corporation (10 percent) multiplied by 20 percent (the percentage of voting stock of A Corporation owned by N Corporation multiplied by the percentage of voting stock of B Corporation owned by A Corporation) is 2 percent.

(e) Information to be furnished. If the credit for foreign income taxes claimed under section 901 includes taxes deemed paid under section 960(a)(1), the domestic corporation must furnish the same information with respect to the taxes so deemed paid as it is required to furnish with respect to the taxes actually paid or accrued by it and for which credit is claimed. See § 1.905-2. For other information required to be furnished by the domestic corporation for the annual accounting period of certain foreign corporations ending with or within such corporation's taxable year, see section 6038(a) and the regulations thereunder.

(f) Reduction of foreign income taxes paid or deemed paid. For reduction of the amount of foreign income taxes paid or deemed paid by a foreign corporation for purposes of section 960, see section 6038(c) (as amended by section 338 of the Tax Equity and Fiscal Responsibility Act of 1982) and the regulations thereunder, relating to failure to furnish information with respect to certain foreign corporations. For reduction of the foreign income taxes deemed paid by a domestic corporation under section 960 with respect to foreign oil and gas extraction income, see section 907(a).

(g) Amounts under section 951 treated as distributions for purposes of applying effective dates. For purposes of applying section 902 in determining the amount of credit allowed under section 960(a)(1) and paragraph (c) of this section, the effective date provisions of the regulations under section 902 shall apply, and for purposes of so applying the regulations under section 902, any amount attributable to the earnings and profits for the taxable year of a first-, second-, or third-tier corporation which is included in the gross income of a domestic corporation under section 951 shall be treated as a distribution received by such domestic corporation on the last day in such taxable year on which such foreign corporation is a controlled foreign corporation.

(h) Source of income and country to which tax is deemed paid. *(1) Source of income.* For purposes of section 904—

(i) The amount included in gross income of a domestic corporation under section 951 for the taxable year with respect to a first-, second-, or third-tier corporation, plus

(ii) Any section 78 dividend to which such section 951 amount gives rise by reason of taxes deemed paid by such domestic corporation under section 960(a)(1),

shall be deemed to be derived from sources within the foreign country or possession of the United States under the laws of which such first-tier corporation, or the first-tier corporation in the same chain of ownership as such second- or third-tier corporation, is created or organized.

(2) Country to which taxes deemed paid. For purposes of section 904, the foreign income taxes paid by the first-, second-, or third-tier corporation and deemed to be paid by the domestic corporation under section 960(a)(1) by reason of the inclusion of the amount described in paragraph (h)(1)(i) of this section in the gross income of such domestic corporation shall be deemed to be paid to the foreign country or possession of the United States under the laws of which such first-tier corporation, or the first-tier corporation in the same chain of ownership as such second- or third-tier corporation, is created or organized.

(3) Illustration. The application of this paragraph may be illustrated by the following example:

Example. Domestic corporation N owns all the one class of stock of controlled foreign corporation A, incorporated under the laws of foreign country X, which owns all the one class of stock of controlled foreign corporation B, incorporated under the laws of foreign country Y. All such corporations use the calendar year as the taxable year. For 1978, N Corporation is required under section 951 to include in gross income $45 attributable to the earnings and profits of B Corporation for such year and $50 attributable to the earnings and profits of A Corporation for such year. For 1978, because of the inclusion of such amounts in gross income, N Corporation is deemed under section 960(a)(1) and paragraph (c) of this section to have paid $15 of foreign income taxes paid by B Corporation for such year and $10 of foreign income taxes paid by A Corporation for such year. For purposes of section 904, the amount ($95) included in N Corporation's gross income under section 951 attributable to the earnings and profits of corporations A and B is deemed to be derived from sources within country X, and the section 78 dividend consisting of the foreign income taxes ($25) deemed paid by N Corporation under section 960(a)(1) with respect to such $95 is deemed to be derived from sources within country X. The $25 of foreign income taxes so deemed paid by N Corporation are deemed to be paid to country X for purposes of section 904.

(i) Computation of deemed-paid taxes in post-1986 taxable years. *(1) General rule.* If a domestic corporation is eligible to compute deemed-paid taxes under section 960(a)(1) with respect to an amount included in gross income under section 951(a), then, such domestic corporation shall be deemed to have paid a portion of the foreign corporation's post-1986 foreign income taxes determined under section 902 and the regulations under that section in the same manner as if the amount so included were a dividend paid by such foreign corporation (determined by applying section 902(c) in accordance with section 904(d)(3)(B)).

(2) Ordering rule for computing deemed-paid taxes under sections 902 and 960. If a domestic corporation computes deemed-paid taxes under both sections 902 and 960 in the same taxable year, section 960 shall be applied first. After the deemed-paid taxes are computed under section 960 with respect to a deemed income inclusion, post-1986 undistributed earnings and post-1986 foreign income taxes in each separate category shall be reduced by the appropriate amounts before deemed-paid taxes are computed under section 902 with respect to a dividend distribution.

(3) Computation of post-1986 undistributed earnings. Post-1986 undistributed earnings (or an accumulated deficit in post-1986 undistributed earnings) are computed under section 902 and the regulations under that section.

(4) Allocation of accumulated deficits. For purposes of computing post-1986 undistributed earnings under sections 902 and 960, a post-1986 accumulated deficit in a separate category shall be allocated proportionately to reduce post-1986 undistributed earnings in the other separate categories. However, a deficit in any separate category shall not permanently reduce earnings in other separate categories, but after the deemed-paid taxes are computed the separate limitation deficit shall be carried forward in the same separate category in which it was incurred. In addition, because deemed-paid taxes may not exceed taxes paid or accrued by the controlled foreign corporation, in computing deemed-paid taxes with respect to an inclusion out of a separate category that exceeds post-1986 undistributed earnings in that separate category, the numerator of the deemed-paid credit fraction (deemed inclusion from the separate category) may not exceed the denominator (post-1986 undistributed earnings in the separate category).

(5) Examples. The application of this paragraph (i) may be illustrated by the following examples. See § 1.952-1(f)(4) for additional illustrations of these rules.

Example (1). (i) A, a U.S. person, is the sole shareholder of CFC, a controlled foreign corporation formed on January 1, 1998, whose functional currency is the u. In 1998 CFC earns 100u of general limitation income described in section 904(d)(1)(I) that is not subpart F income and 100u of foreign personal holding company income that is passive income described in section 904(d)(1)(A). In 1998 CFC also incurs a (50u) loss in the shipping category described in section 904(d)(1)(D). CFC's subpart F income for 1998, 100u, does not exceed CFC's current earnings and profits of 150u. Accordingly, all 100u of CFC's subpart F income is included in A's gross income under section 951(a)(1)(A). Under section 904(d)(3)(B) of the Internal Revenue Code and paragraph (i)(1) of this section, A includes 100u of passive limitation income in gross income for 1998.

(ii) For purposes of computing post-1986 undistributed earnings under sections 902, 904(d) and 960 with respect to the subpart F inclusion, the shipping limitation deficit of (50u) is allocated proportionately to reduce general limitation earnings of 100u and passive limitation earnings of 100u. Thus, general limitation earnings are reduced by 25u to 75u (100u general limitation earnings/200u total earnings in positive separate categories × (50u) shipping deficit = 25u reduction), and passive limitation earnings are reduced by 25u to 75u (100u passive earnings/200u total earnings in positive separate categories × (50u) shipping deficit = 25u reduction). All of CFC's post-1986 foreign income taxes with respect to passive limitation earnings are deemed paid by A under section 960 with respect to the 100u subpart F inclusion of passive income (75u inclusion (numerator limited to denominator under paragraph (i)(4) of this section)/75u passive earnings). After the inclusion and deemed-paid taxes are computed, at the close of 1998 CFC has 100u of general limitation earnings, 0 of passive limitation earnings (100u of foreign personal holding company income – 100u inclusion), and a (50u) deficit in shipping limitation earnings.

Example (2). (i) The facts are the same as in Example 1 with the addition of the following facts. In 1999, CFC distributes 150u to A. CFC has 100u of previously-taxed earnings and profits described in section 959(c)(2) attributable to 1998, all of which is passive limitation earnings and profits. Under section 959(c), 100u of the 150u distribution is deemed to be made from earnings and profits described in section 959(c)(2). The remaining 50u is deemed to be made from earnings and profits described in section 959(c)(3). The entire dividend distribution of 50u is treated as made out of CFC's general limitation earnings and profits. See section 904(d)(3)(D).

(ii) For purposes of computing post-1986 undistributed earnings under section 902 with respect to the 1999 dividend of 50u, the shipping limitation accumulated deficit of (50u) reduces general limitation earnings and profits of 100u to 50u. Thus, 100% of CFC's post-1986 foreign income taxes with respect to general limitation earnings are deemed paid by A under section 902 with respect to the 1999 dividend of 50u (50u dividend/50u general limitation earnings). After the deemed-paid taxes are computed, at the close of 1999 CFC has 50u of general limitation earnings (100u opening balance – 50u distribution), 0 of passive limitation earnings, and a (50u) deficit in shipping limitation earnings.

(6) Effective date. This paragraph (i) applies to taxable years of a controlled foreign corporation beginning after March 3, 1997.

T.D. 7120, 6/3/71, amend T.D. 7334, 12/20/74, T.D. 7481, 4/15/77, T.D. 7545, 5/5/78, T.D. 7649, 10/17/79, T.D. 7843, 11/5/82, T.D. 7961, 6/20/84, T.D. 8704, 12/31/96.

---

§ 1.960-2 Interrelation of section 902 and section 960 when dividends are paid by third, second, or first-tier corporation.

Caution: The Treasury has not yet amended Reg § 1.960-2 to reflect changes made by P.L. 105-34, P.L. 99-514.

(a) Scope of this section. This section prescribes rules for the application of section 902 in a case where dividends are paid by a third-, second-, or first-tier corporation, as the case may be, from its earnings and profits for a taxable year when an amount attributable to such earnings and profits is included in the gross income of a domestic corporation under section 951, or when such earnings and profits are attributable to an amount excluded from the gross income of such foreign corporation under section 959(b) and § 1.959-2, with respect to the domestic corporation. In making determinations under this section, any portion of a distribution received from a first-tier corporation by the domestic corporation which is excluded from the domestic corporation's gross income under section 959(a) and § 1.959-1, or any portion of a distribution received from an immediately lower-tier corporation by the third-, second-, or first-tier corporation which is excluded from such foreign corporation's gross income under section 959(b) and § 1.959-2, shall be treated as a dividend for purposes of taking into account under section 902 any foreign income taxes paid by such third-, second-, or first-tier corporation which are not deemed paid by the domestic corporation under section 960(a)(1) and § 1.960-1.

(b) Application of section 902(b) to dividends received from an immediately lower-tier corporation. For purposes of paragraph (a) of this section and paragraph (c)(1)(i) of § 1.960-1, section 902(b) shall apply to all dividends received by the first- or second-tier corporation from the immediately lower-tier corporation other than dividends attributable to earnings and profits of such immediately lower-tier corporation in respect of which an amount is, or has been, included in the gross income of a domestic corporation under section 951 with respect to such immediately lower-tier corporation.

(c) Application of section 902(a) to dividends received by domestic corporation from first-tier corporation. For purposes of paragraph (a) of this section, section 902(a) shall apply to all dividends received by the domestic corporation for its taxable year from the first-tier corporation other than dividends attributable to earnings and profits of such first-tier corporation in respect of which an amount is, or has been, included in the gross income of a domestic corporation under section 951 with respect to such first-tier corporation.

(d) Allocation of earnings and profits of a first- or second-tier corporation having income excluded under section 959(b). *(1) First-tier corporations.* If the first-tier corporation for its taxable year receives dividends from the second-tier corporation to which in accordance with paragraph (b) of this section 902(b)(1) or section 902(b)(2) applies and other dividends from the second-tier corporation to which such sections do not apply, then in applying section 902(a) pursuant to this section and in applying section 960(a)(1) pursuant to § 1.960-1(c)(1)(i), with respect to the foreign income taxes paid and deemed paid by the second-tier corporation which are deemed paid by the first-tier corporation for such taxable year under section 902(b)(1)—

(i) The earnings and profits of the first-tier corporation for such taxable year shall be considered not to include its earnings and profits which are attributable to the dividends to which section 902(b)(1) does not apply (in determining the domestic corporation's credit for the taxes paid by the second-tier corporation) or which are attributable to the dividends to which sections 902(b)(1) and 902(b)(2) do not apply (in determining the domestic corporation's credit for taxes deemed paid by the second-tier corporation) and

(ii) For the purposes of so applying section 902(a), distributions to the domestic corporation from such earnings and profits which are attributable to the dividends to which section 902(b)(1) does not apply (in determining the domestic corporation's credit for taxes paid by the second-tier corporation) or which are attributable to the dividends to which sections 902(b)(1) and 902(b)(2) do not apply (in determining the domestic corporation's credit for taxes deemed paid by the second-tier corporation) shall not be treated as a dividend.

(2) Second-tier corporation. If the second-tier corporation for its taxable year receives dividends from the third-tier corporation to which, in accordance with paragraph (b) of this section, section 902(b)(2) applies and other dividends from the third-tier corporation to which such section does not apply, then in applying section 902(b)(1) pursuant to this section, and in applying section 960(a)(1) pursuant to paragraph (c)(1)(i) of § 1.960-1, with respect to the foreign taxes deemed paid by the second-tier corporation for such taxable year under section 902(b)(2)—

(i) The earnings and profits of the second-tier corporation for such taxable year shall be considered not to include its earnings and profits which are attributable to such other dividends from the third-tier corporation, and

(ii) For the purposes of so applying section 902(b)(1), distributions to the first-tier corporation from such earnings and profits which are attributable to such other dividends from the third-tier corporation shall not be treated as a dividend.

(e) Separate determinations under sections 902(a), 902(b)(1), and 902(b)(2) in the case of a first-, second-, or third-tier corporation having income excluded under section 956(b). If in the case of a first-, second-, or third-tier corporation to which paragraph (b) or (c) of this section is applied—

(1) The earnings and profits of such foreign corporation for its taxable year consist of—

(i) Dividends received from an immediately lower-tier corporation which are attributable to amounts included in the gross income of a domestic corporation under section 951 with respect to the immediately lower- or lower-tier corporations, and

(ii) Other earnings and profits, and

(2) The effective rate of foreign income taxes paid or accrued by such foreign corporation on the dividends described in paragraph (e)(1)(i) of this section is higher or lower than the effective rate of foreign income taxes attributable to its earnings and profits described in paragraph (e)(1)(ii) of this section,

then, for purposes of applying paragraph (b) or (c) of this section to dividends paid by such foreign corporation to the domestic corporation or the first- or second-tier corporation, sections 902(a), 902(b)(1), and 902(b)(2) shall be applied separately to the portion of the dividend which is attributable to the earnings and profits described in paragraph (e)(1)(i) of this section and separately to the portion of the dividend which is attributable to the earnings and profits described in paragraph (e)(1)(ii) of this section. In making a separate determination with respect to the earnings and profits described in paragraph (e)(1)(i) or (e)(1)(ii) of this section, only the foreign income taxes paid or accrued (or, in the case of earnings and profits of a first- or second-tier corporation described in paragraph (e)(1)(ii) of this section, deemed to be paid) by such foreign corporation on the income attributable to such earnings and profits shall be taken into account. For purposes of applying this paragraph (e), no part of the foreign income taxes paid, accrued, or deemed to be paid which are attributable to the earnings and profits described in paragraph (e)(1)(ii) of this section shall be attributed to the dividend described in paragraph (e)(1)(i) of this section; and no part of the foreign income taxes paid or accrued on the dividend described in paragraph (e)(1)(i) of this section shall be attributed to the earnings and profits described in paragraph (e)(1)(ii) of this section. Furthermore, the effective rate of foreign income taxes paid or accrued shall be determined consistently with the principles of paragraph (b)(3)(iv) and (viii) and (c) of § 1.954-1. Thus, for example, the effective rate of foreign income taxes on dividends received by such foreign corporation shall be determined by taking into account any intercorporate dividends received deduction allowed to such corporation for such dividends.

(f) Illustrations. The application of this section may be illustrated by the following examples. In all of the examples other than examples (6), (7), (9) and (10), it is assumed that the effective rate of foreign income taxes paid or accrued by the first- or second-tier corporation, as the case may be, in respect to dividends received from the immediately lower-tier corporation, is the same as the effective rate of foreign income taxes paid or accrued by the first- or second-tier corporation with respect to its other income:

Example (1). Domestic corporation N owns all the one class of stock of controlled foreign corporation A, which owns all the one class of stock of controlled foreign corporation B. All such corporations use the calendar year as the taxable year. For 1978, N Corporation is required under section 951 to include $50 in gross income attributable to the earnings and profits of A Corporation for such year, but is not required to include any amount in gross income under section 951 attributable to the earnings and profits of B Corporation. For such year, B Corporation distributes a dividend of $45, but A Corporation does not make any distributions. The foreign income taxes deemed paid by N Corporation for 1978 under section 960(a)(1), after applying section 902(b)(1) for such year of A Corporation, are determined as follows upon the basis of the facts assumed:

B Corporation (second-tier corporation):		
Pretax earnings and profits		$100.00
Foreign income taxes (40%)		40.00
Earnings and profits		60.00
Dividends paid to A Corporation		45.00
Foreign income taxes paid by B Corporation on or with respect to its accumulated profits		40.00
Foreign income taxes of B Corporation deemed paid by A Corporation for 1978 under sec. 902(b)(1) ($45/$60 × $40)		30.00
A Corporation (first-tier corporation):		
Pretax earnings and profits:		
Dividends from B Corporation	$ 45.00	
Other income	100.00	
Total pretax earnings and profits		145.00
Foreign income taxes (20%)		29.00
Earnings and profits		116.00
Foreign income taxes paid, and deemed to be paid, by A Corporation on or with respect to its earnings and profits ($29 + $30)		59.00
Amount required to be included in N Corporation's gross income under sec. 951 with respect to A Corporation		50.00
Dividends paid to N Corporation		0
N Corporation (domestic corporation):		
Foreign income taxes of A Corporation deemed paid by N Corporation for 1978 under sec. 960(a)(1) ($50/$116 × $59)		25.43

Example (2). Domestic corporation N owns all the one class of stock of controlled foreign corporation A, which owns all the one class of stock of controlled foreign corporation B. All such corporations use the calendar year as the taxable year. For 1978, N Corporation is required under section 951 to include in gross income $150 attributable to the earnings and profits of B Corporation for such year, which B Corporation distributes during such year. Corporation N is not required for 1978 to include any amount in gross income under section 951 attributable to the earnings and profits of A Corporation, but A Corporation distributes for such year $135 from its earnings and profits attributable to B Corporation's dividend. The foreign income taxes deemed paid by N Corporation for 1978 under section 960(a)(1), and section 902(a) are determined as follows upon the basis of the facts assumed:

B Corporation (second-tier corporation):		
Pretax earnings and profits		$250.00
Foreign income taxes (20%)		50.00
Earnings and profits		200.00
Amounts required to be included in N Corporation's gross income under sec. 951 with respect to B Corporation		150.00
Dividends paid to A Corporation		150.00
Foreign income taxes paid on or with respect to earnings and profits of B Corporation		50.00
A Corporation (first-tier corporation):		
Pretax earnings and profits:		
Dividends from B Corporation	$150.00	
Other income	200.00	
Total pretax earnings and profits		350.00
Foreign income taxes (10%)		35.00
Earnings and profits		315.00
Dividends paid to N Corporation		135.00
Foreign income taxes paid by A Corporation on or with respect to its accumulated profits		35.00
N Corporation (domestic corporation):		
Foreign income taxes of B Corporation deemed paid by N Corporation for 1978 under sec. 960(a)(1) ($150/$200 × $50)		37.50
Foreign income taxes of A Corporation deemed paid by N Corporation for 1978 under sec. 902(a) ($135/$315 × $35)		15.00
Total foreign income taxes deemed paid by N Corporation under sec. 901		52.50

Example (3). Domestic corporation N owns all the one class of stock of controlled foreign corporation A, which owns all the one class of stock of controlled foreign corporation B. All such corporations use the calendar year as the taxable year. For 1978, N Corporation is required under section 951 to include $180 in gross income attributable to the earnings and profits of A Corporation for such year, but is not required to include any amount in gross income under section 951 attributable to the earnings and profits of B Corporation. Corporation B distributes from its earnings and profits for 1978 a dividend of $50. For 1978, A Corporation distributes $180 from its earnings and profits attributable to the amount required under section 951 to be included in N Corporation's gross income for such year with respect to A Corporation and $20 from its other earnings and profits. The foreign income taxes deemed paid by N Corporation for 1978 under section 960(a)(1), and section 902(a) are determined as follows upon the basis of the facts assumed:

B Corporation (second-tier corporation):		
Pretax earnings and profits		$100.00
Foreign income taxes (40%)		40.00
Earnings and profits		60.00
Dividends paid to A Corporation		50.00
Foreign income taxes paid by B Corporation on or with respect to its accumulated profits		40.00
Foreign income taxes of B Corporation deemed paid by A Corporation for 1965 under sec. 902(f)(1) ($50/$60 × $40)		33.33
A Corporation (first-tier corporation):		
Pretax earnings and profits:		
Dividends from B Corporation	$ 50.00	
Other income	200.00	
Total pretax earnings and profits		250.00
Foreign income taxes (10%)		25.00
Earnings and profits		225.00
Foreign income taxes paid, by A Corporation on or with respect to its earnings and profits ($25.00 + $33.33)		58.33
Amounts required to be included in N Corporation's gross income for 1978 under sec. 951 with respect to A Corporation		180.00
Dividends paid to N Corporation:		
Dividends to which sec. 902(a) does not apply (from A Corporation's earnings and profits in respect of which an amount is required under sec. 951 to be included in N Corporation's gross income with respect to A Corporation)	$180.00	
Dividends to which sec. 902(a) applies (from A Corporation's other earnings and profits)	20.00	
Total dividends paid to N Corporation		200.00
N Corporation (domestic corporation):		
Foreign income taxes of corporations A and B deemed paid by N Corporation under sec. 960(a)(1) ($180/$225 × $58.33)		46.66
Foreign income taxes of corporations A and B deemed paid by N Corporation under sec. 902(a) ($20/$225 × $58.33)		5.18
Total foreign income taxes deemed paid by N Corporation under sec. 901		51.84

Example (4). Domestic corporation N owns all the one class of stock of controlled foreign corporation A, which owns all the one class of stock of controlled foreign corporation B. All such corporations use the calendar year as the taxable year. For 1978, N Corporation is required under section 951 to include in gross income $150 attributable to the earnings and profits of B Corporation for such year and $22.50 attributable to the earnings and profits of A Corporation for such year. For 1978, B Corporation distributes $175, consisting of $150 from its earnings and profits attributable to amounts required under section 951 to be included in N Corporation's gross income with respect to B Corporation and $25 from its other earnings and profits. Corporation A does not distribute any dividends for 1978. The foreign income taxes deemed paid by N Corporation for 1978 under section 960(a)(1) are determined as follows upon the basis of the facts assumed:

B Corporation (second-tier corporation):		
Pretax earnings and profits		$250.00
Foreign income taxes (20%)		50.00
Earnings and profits		200.00
Amounts required to be included in N Corporation's gross income under sec. 951 for 1978 with respect to B Corporation		150.00
Dividends paid by B Corporation:		
Dividends to which sec. 902(b) does not apply (from B Corporation's earnings and profits in respect of which an amount is required under sec. 951 to be included in N Corporation gross income with respect to B Corporation)	$150.00	

Dividends to which sec. 902(b)(1) applies (from B Corporation's other earnings and profits)	25.00	
Total dividends paid to A Corporation ..		175.00
Foreign income taxes paid by B Corporation on or with respect to its accumulated profits		50.00
Foreign income taxes of B Corporation deemed paid by A Corporation for 1978 under sec. 902(b)(1) ($25/$200 × $50)		6.25
A Corporation (first-tier corporation):		
Pretax earnings and profits		175.00
Foreign income tax (10%)		17.50
Earnings and profits		157.50
Earnings and profits after exclusion of amounts attributable to dividends to which sec. 902(b) does not apply ($157.50 less [$150 – ($150 × 0.10)])		22.50
Amount required to be included in N Corporation's gross income for 1978 under sec. 951 with respect to A Corporation		22.50
Dividends paid to N Corporation		0
N Corporation (domestic corporation):		
Foreign income taxes deemed paid by N Corporation under sec. 960(a)(1) with respect to A Corporation:		
Tax actually paid by A Corporation ($22.50/$157.50 × $17.50)	$ 2.50	
Tax of B Corporation deemed paid by A Corporation under sec. 902(b)(1) ($22.50/$22.50 × $6.25)	6.25	8.75
Foreign income taxes deemed paid by N Corporation under sec. 960(a)(1) with respect to B Corporation ($150/$200 × $50)		37.50
Total taxes deemed paid under sec. 960(a)(1)		46.25

Example (5). Domestic corporation N owns all the one class of stock of controlled foreign corporation A, which owns all the one class of stock of controlled foreign corporation B. All such corporations use the calendar year as the taxable year. For 1978, N Corporation is required under section 951 to include in gross income $150 attributable to the earnings and profits of B Corporation for such year and $22.50 attributable to the earnings and profits of A Corporation for such year. For 1978, B Corporation distributes $175, consisting of $150 from its earnings and profits attributable to amounts required under section 951 to be included in N Corporation's gross income with respect to B Corporation and $25 from its other earnings and profits. For 1965, A Corporation distributes $225, consisting of $135 from its earnings and profits attributable to the amount required under section 951 to be included in N Corporation's gross income with respect to B Corporation, $22.50 from its earnings and profits attributable to the amount required under section 951 to be included in N Corporation's gross income with respect to A Corporation, and $67.50 from its other earnings and profits. The foreign income taxes deemed paid by N Corporation for 1978 under section 960(a)(1) and section 902(a) are determined as follows upon the basis of the facts assumed:

B Corporation (second-tier corporation):

Pretax earnings and profits		$250.00
Foreign income taxes (20%)		50.00
Earnings and profits		200.00
Amounts required to be included in N Corporation's gross income for 1978 under sec. 951 with respect to B Corporation		150.00
Dividends paid by B Corporation:		
Dividends to which sec. 902(b) does not apply (from B Corporation's earnings and profits in which an amount is required under sec. 951 to be included in N Corporation's gross income with respect to B Corporation)	$150.00	
Dividends to which sec. 902(b)(1) applies (from B Corporation's other earnings and profits)	25.00	
Total dividends paid to A Corporation .		175.00
Foreign income taxes paid by B Corporation on or with respect to its accumulated profits		50.00
Foreign income taxes of B Corporation deemed paid by A Corporation for 1965 under sec. 902(b)(1) ($25/$200 × $50		6.25
A Corporation (first-tier corporation):		
Pretax earnings and profits:		
Dividends received from B Corporation	$175.00	
Other income	100.00	
Total pretax earnings and profits		275.00
Foreign income taxes (10%)		27.50
Earnings and profits		247.50
Earnings and profits after exclusion of amounts attributable to dividends to which sec. 902(b) does not apply ($247.50 less [$150 – ($150 × 0.10)])		112.50
Amount required to be included in N Corporation's gross income for 1978 under sec. 951 with respect to A Corporation		22.50
Distributions paid by A Corporation:		
Dividends to which sec. 902(a) does not apply (From A Corporation's earnings and profits in respect of which an amount is required under sec. 951 to be included in N Corporation's gross income with respect to A Corporation)	$ 22.50	
Dividends to which sec. 902(a) applies (from A Corporation's other earnings and profits)	202.50	
Total dividends paid to N Corporation	225.00	
N Corporation (domestic corporation):		
Foreign income taxes deemed paid by N Corporation under sec. 960(a)(1) with respect to—		
B Corporation ($150/$200 × 50)		37.50
A Corporation:		
Tax paid by A Corporation ($22.50/$247.50 × $27.50) ..	$ 2.50	
Tax of B Corporation deemed paid by A Corporation under sec. 902(b)(1) ($22.50/$112.50 × $6.25) ...	1.25	3.75

Total taxes deemed paid under sec. 960(a)(1)		41.25
Foreign income taxes deemed paid by N Corporation under sec. 902(a)(1) with respect to A Corporation:		
Tax paid by A Corporation ($202.50/$247.50 × $27.50)	$ 22.50	
Tax of B Corporation deemed paid by A Corporation ($67.50/$112.50 × $6.25)	3.75	
Total taxes deemed paid under sec. 902(a)		26.25
Total foreign income taxes deemed paid by N Corporation under sec. 901		67.50

Example (6). Domestic corporation N owns all the one class of stock of controlled foreign corporation A, which owns all the one class of stock of controlled foreign corporation B. All such corporations use the calendar year as the taxable year. A and B corporations are organized under the laws of foreign country X. All of B corporation's assets used in a trade or business are located in country X. Country X imposes an income tax of 20 percent on B corporation's income. For 1978, N Corporation is required under section 951 to include in gross income $100 attributable to the earnings and profits of B Corporation for such year. For 1978, B Corporation distributes $150, consisting of $100 from its earnings and profits attributable to the amount required under section 951 to be included in N Corporation's gross income with respect to B Corporation and $50 from its other earnings and profits. Country X imposes an income tax of 10 percent on A Corporation's income but exempts from tax dividends received from B Corporation. N is not required to include any amount in gross income under section 951 for 1978 attributable to the earnings and profits of A Corporation for such year. For 1978, A Corporation distributes $175, consisting of $100 from its earnings and profits attributable to the amount required under section 951 to be included in N Corporation's gross income with respect to B Corporation, and $75 from its other earnings and profits. The foreign income taxes deemed paid by N Corporation for 1978 under section 960(a)(1) and section 902(a) are determined as follows on the basis of the facts assumed:

B corporation (2d-tier corporation):	
Pretax earnings and profits	$200.00
Foreign income taxes (20%)	40.00
Earnings and profits	160.00
Amount required to be included in N corporation's gross income for 1965 under sec. 951 with respect to B corporation	100.00
Dividends paid by B corporation:	
Dividends to which sec. 902(b) does not apply (from B corporation's earnings and profits in respect of which an amount is required under sec. 951 to be included in N corporation's gross income with respect to B corporation)	100.00
Dividends to which sec. 902(b)(1) applies (from B corporation's other earnings and profits)	50.00
Total dividends paid to A corporation	150.00
Foreign income taxes of B corporation deemed paid by A corporation for 1978 under sec. 902(b)(1) ($50/$100 × $40)	12.50

A corporation (1st-tier corporation):	
Pretax earnings and profits:	
Dividends received from B corporation	150.00
Other income	100.00
Total pretax earnings and profits	250.00
Foreign income taxes:	
On dividends received from B corporation	None
On other income ($100 × 0.10)	10.00
Total foreign income taxes	10.00
Earnings and profits:	
Attributable to dividends received from B corporation to which sec. 902(b) does not apply	100.00
Attributable to other income:	
Attributable to dividends received from B corporation to which sec. 902(b)(1) applies	50.00
Attributable to other income ($100 − $10)	90.00
Subtotal	140.00
Total earnings and profits	240.00
Earnings and profits after exclusion of amounts attributable to dividends to which sec. 902(b) does not apply ($240 − $100)	140.00
Amount required to be included in N corporation's gross income for 1978 under sec. 951 with respect to A corporation	None
Dividends paid by A corporation:	
Dividends to which sec. 902(a) does not apply (from A corporation's earnings and profits in respect of which an amount is required under sec. 951 to be included in N corporation's gross income with respect to A corporation)	None

Dividends to which sec. 902(a) applies (from A corporation's other earnings and profits)	175.00
Total dividends paid to N corporation	175.00
N corporation (domestic corporation):	
Foreign income taxes deemed paid by N corporation under sec. 960(a)(1) with respect to B corporation ($100/$160 × $40)	25.00
Foreign income taxes deemed paid by N corporation under sec. 902(a) with respect to A corporation (allocation of earnings and profits being made under pars. (c)(2) and (d) of this section): Tax paid by A corporation in respect to dividends received from B corporation to which sec. 902(b) does not apply ($100/$100 × $0)	None
Tax paid by A corporation in respect to its other income ($75/$140 × $10)	5.36
Tax of B corporation deemed paid by A corporation in respect to such other income ($75/$140 X $12.50)	6.70
Total taxes deemed paid under sec. 902(a)	12.06
Total foreign income taxes deemed paid by N corporation under sec. 901	37.06

Example (7). Domestic corporation N owns all the one class of stock of controlled foreign corporation A, which owns all the one class of stock of controlled foreign corporation B. All such corporations use the calendar year as the taxable year. For 1978, N Corporation is required under section 951 to include in gross income $150 attributable to the earnings and profits of B Corporation for such year and $47.50 attributable to the earnings and profits of A Corporation for such year. For 1978, B Corporation distributes $200, consisting of $150 from its earnings and profits attributable to the amount required under section 951 to be included in N Corporation's gross income with respect to B Corporation and $50 from its other earnings and profits. The country under the laws of which A Corporation is incorporated imposes an income tax of 5 percent on dividends received from a subsidiary corporation and 20 percent on other income. For 1978, A Corporation distributes $100 from its earnings and profits to N Corporation, such amount being attributable under paragraph (e) of § 1.959-3 to the amount required under section 951 to be included in N Corporation's gross income with respect to B Corporation. The foreign income taxes deemed paid by N Corporation for 1978 under section 960(a)(1) and section 902(a) are determined as follows on the basis of the facts assumed:

B corporation (2d-tier corporation):	
Pretax earnings and profits	$250.00
Foreign income taxes (20 percent)	50.00
Earnings and profits	200.00
Amount required to be included in N corporation's gross income for 1978 under sec. 951 with respect to B corporation	150.00
Dividends paid by B corporation:	
Dividends to which sec. 902(b) does not apply (from B corporation's earnings and profits in respect of which an amount is required under sec. 951 to be included in N corporation's gross income with respect to B corporation)	150.00
Dividends to which sec. 902(b)(1) applies (from B corporation's other earnings and profits)	50.00
Total dividends paid to A corporation	200.00
Foreign income taxes of B corporation deemed paid by A corporation for 1978 under sec. 902(b)(1) ($50/$200 × $50)	12.50
A corporation (1st-tier corporation):	
Pretax earnings and profits:	
Dividends received from B corporation	200.00
Other income	100.00
Total pretax earnings and profits	300.00
Foreign income taxes:	
On dividends received from B corporation to which sec. 902(b) does not apply ($150 × 0.05)	7.50
On other income:	
Dividends received from B corporation to which sec. 902(b)(1) applies ($50 × 0.05)	2.50
Other income of A corporation ($100 × 0.20)	20.00
Total	22.50
Total foreign incomes taxes	30.00

Earnings and profits:	
Attributable to dividends received from B corporation to which sec. 902(b) does not apply ($150 – $7.50)	142.50
Attributable to other income:	
Attributable to dividends received from B corporation to which sec. 902(b)(1) applies ($50 -$2.50)	47.50
Attributable to other income ($100 – $20)	80.00
Total	127.50
Total earnings and profits	270.00
Earnings and profits after exclusion of amounts attributable to dividends to which sec. 902(b) does not apply ($270 less $142.50)	127.50
Amount required to be included in N corporation's gross income for 1978 under sec. 951 with respect to A corporation	47.50

Dividends paid by A corporation:	
Dividends to which sec. 902(a) does not apply (from A corporation's earnings and profits in respect of which an amount is required under sec. 951 to be included in N corporation's gross income with respect to A corporation)	None
Dividends to which sec. 902(a) applies (from A corporation's other earnings and profits)	100.00
Total dividends paid to N corporation	100.00

N Corporation (domestic corporation):	
Foreign income taxes deemed paid by N corporation under sec. 960(a)(1) with respect to— B corporation ($150/$200 × $50)	37.50
Tax paid by A corporation ($47.50/$127.50 × $22.50)	8.38
Tax of B corporation deemed paid by A corporation under sec. 902(b)(1) ($47.50/$127.50 × $12.50)	4.66
Total	13.04
Total taxes deemed paid under sec. 960(a)(1)(C)	50.54
Foreign income taxes deemed paid by N corporation under sec. 902(a) with respect to A corporation (allocations of earnings and profits being made under pars. (c)(2) and (d) of this sec.) ($100/$142.50 × $7.50)	5.26
Total foreign income taxes deemed paid by N corporation under sec. 901	55.80

Example (8). Domestic corporation N owns all the one class of stock of controlled foreign corporation A, which owns all the one class of stock of controlled foreign corporation B, which owns all the one class of stock of controlled foreign corporation C. All such corporations use the calendar year as the taxable year. For 1978, N Corporation is required under section 951 to include $50 attributable to the earnings and profits of C Corporation and $15 attributable to the earnings and profits of B Corporation in its gross income. N Corporation is not required to include any amount in its gross income with respect to A Corporation under section 951 in 1978. For such year, C Corporation distributes $75 to B Corporation. B Corporation in turn distributes $60 of its earnings and profits to A Corporation. A Corporation has no other earnings and profits for 1978 and distributes $45 of its earnings and profits to N Corporation. The foreign income taxes deemed paid by N Corporation under section 960(a)(1) and section 902(a) are determined as follows on the basis of the facts assumed:

C Corporation (third-tier corporation):

Pretax earnings and profits	$150.00
Foreign taxes paid by C Corporation (30%)	45.00
Earnings and profits	105.00
Amount required to be included in gross income of N Corporation under section 951 with respect to C Corporation	50.00
Dividend to B Corporation	75.00
Dividend from earnings and profits to which section 902(b)(2) does not apply (attributable to amounts included in N Corporation's gross income under section 951 with respect to C Corporation)	50.00
Dividend from earnings and profits to which section 902(b)(2) applies (attributable to amounts not included in N Corporation's gross income with respect to C Corporation)	25.00

Amount of foreign income taxes of C Corporation deemed paid by B Corporation under section 902(b)(2) and Sec. 1.960-2(b):

$$\frac{\text{Dividend to B Corporation less portion of dividend from earnings included in N Corporation's gross income under section 951 with respect to C Corporation}}{\text{Earnings and profits of C Corporation}} \times \text{Taxes paid by C Corporation}$$

($25/$105 × $45)	$ 10.71

B Corporation (second-tier corporation):

Pretax earnings and profits:	
Dividend from C Corporation	$ 75.00
Other earnings and profits	225.00
Total pretax earnings and profits	300.00
Foreign income taxes paid by B Corporation (40%)	120.00
Earnings and profits	180.00
Earnings and profits attributable to amounts to which section 902(b)(2) does not apply (amounts included in N Corporation's gross income under section 951 with respect to C Corporation ($50 – ($50 × .40))	30.00
Other earnings and profits	150.00
Earnings and profits of B Corporation after exclusion for amounts to which section 902(b)(2) does not apply (amounts attributable to earnings and profits which are included in N Corporation's gross income under section 951 with respect to C Corporation) ($180 – $30)	150.00
Amount to be included in gross income under section 951 of N Corporation with respect to B Corporation	15.00
Amount of dividend to A Corporation	60.00
Dividend from earnings and profits to which section 902(b)(2) does not apply (attributable to amounts included in N Corporation's gross income under section 951 with respect to C Corporation)	30.00
Dividend from earnings and profits to which section 902(b)(1) does not apply (attributable to amounts included in N Corporation's gross income under section 951 with respect to B Corporation)	15.00
Dividend from other earnings and profits (attributable to amounts not included in N Corporation's gross income under section 951 with respect to B or C Corporation)	15.00

Foreign income taxes of B Corporation deemed paid by A Corporation under section 902(b)(1) and § 1.960-2(b):

$$\frac{\text{Dividend to A Corporation less portion of dividend from earnings included in N Corporation's gross income under section 951 with respect to B Corporation}}{\text{Earnings and profits of B Corporation}} \times \text{Taxes paid by B Corporation}$$

($45/$180 × 120) .... $ 30.00

Foreign income taxes (of C Corporation) deemed paid by B Corporation deemed paid by A Corporation under section 902(b)(1) in accordance with § 1.960-2(b) and § 1.960-2(d)(2)(i) and (ii):

$$\frac{\text{Dividend to A Corporation less portion of dividend from earnings included in N Corporation's gross income under section 951 with respect to B Corporation and C Corporation}}{\text{Earnings and profits of B Corporation less earnings and profits attributable to amounts included in N Corporation's gross income with respect to C Corporation}} \times \text{paid by C Corporation which are deemed paid by B Corporation}$$

($15/$150 × $10.71) 1.07

A Corporation (first-tier corporation):

Pretax earnings and profits:	
Dividend from B Corporation	$ 60.00
Other earnings and profits	0
Total pretax earnings and profits	60.00
Foreign income taxes paid by A Corporation (10%)	6.00
Earnings and profits	54.00
Earnings and profits attributable to amounts to which section 902(b)(2) does not apply (attributable to amounts previously included in N Corporation's gross income under section 951 with respect to C Corporation) ($30 – ($30 × .10))	27.00
Earnings and profits attributable to amounts to which section 902(b)(1) does not apply (attributable to amounts included in N Corporation's gross income under section 951 with respect to B Corporation) ($15 – ($15 × .10))	13.50
Other earnings and profits ($15 – ($15 × .10))	13.50
Earnings and profits of A Corporation after exclusion for amounts to which section 902(b)(1) does not apply (attributable to amounts included in N Corporation's gross income under section 951 with respect to B Corporation) ($54.00 – $13.50)	40.50
Earnings and profits of A Corporation after exclusion for amounts to which sections 902(b)(1) and (2) do not apply (attributable to amounts included in N Corporation's gross income under section 951 with respect to B or C Corporation) ($40.50 – $27.00)	13.50
Dividend to N Corporation	45.00
Dividend from earnings and profits to which section 902(b)(2) does not apply (attributable to amounts included in N Corporation's gross income under section 951 with respect to C Corporation)	27.00

Dividend from earnings and profits to which section 902(b)(1) does not apply (attributable to amounts included in N Corporation's gross income under section 951 with respect to B Corporation) 13.50
Dividend from earnings and profits to which section 902(a) does not apply (attributable to amounts included in N Corporation's gross income under section 951 with respect to A Corporation) 0
Dividend from other earnings and profits (attributable to amounts not included in N Corporation's gross income under section 951 with respect to A, B, or C Corporation) 4.50

N Corporation (domestic corporation):

Foreign income taxes deemed paid by N Corporation under section 960(a)(1) and Sec. 1.960-1(c)(1)(ii) with respect to C Corporation:

Amount included in N Corporation's gross income under section 951 with respect to C Corporation
/ Earnings and profits of C Corporation
× Taxes paid by C Corporation

($50/$105 × $45.00) .... $ 21.43

Foreign income taxes deemed paid by N Corporation under section 960(a)(1) and Sec. 1.960-1(c)(1)(i) with respect to B Corporation 11.07

Taxes paid by B Corporation:

Amount included in N Corporation's gross income under section 951 with respect to B Corporation
/ Earnings and profits of B Corporation
× Taxes paid by B Corporation

($15/$180 × $120) 10.00

Taxes deemed paid by B Corporation in accordance with § 1.960-2(d)(2)(i):

Amount included in N Corporation's gross income under section 951 with respect to B Corporation
/ Earnings and profits of B Corporation less earnings and profits attributable to amounts included in N Corporation's gross income with respect to C Corporation
× paid by C Corporation which are deemed paid by B Corporation

($15/$150 × $10.71) .... $ 1.07

Total taxes deemed paid by N Corporation under section 960(a)(1) .... $ 32.50

Foreign income taxes deemed paid by N Corporation under section 902(a):

Taxes paid by A Corporation in accordance with § 1.960-2(c):

Dividend to N Corporation less portion of dividend from earnings included in N Corporation's gross income under section 951 with respect to A Corporation
/ Earnings and profits of A Corporation
× Taxes paid by A Corporation

($45/$54 × $6) $5.00

Taxes paid by B Corporation deemed paid by A Corporation in accordance with §§ 1.960-2(c) and 1.960-2(d)(1)(i) and (ii):

Dividend to N Corporation less portion of dividend from earnings included in N Corporation's gross income under section 951 with respect to A and B Corporations
/ Earnings and profits of A Corporation less earnings and profits attributable to amounts included in N Corporation's gross income under section 951 with respect to B Corporation
× Taxes paid by B Corporation which are deemed paid by A Corporation

($31.50/$40.50 × $30.00) 23.33

Taxes (of C Corporation) deemed paid by B Corporation deemed paid by A Corporation in accordance with §§ 1.960-2(c) and 1.960-2(d)(1)(i) and (ii):

Dividend to N Corporation less portion of dividend from earnings included in N Corporation's gross income under section 951 with respect to A, B, and C Corporations
/ Earnings and profits of A Corporation less earnings and profits attributable to amounts included in N Corporation's gross income under section 951 with respect to B and C Corporations
× Corporation which are deemed paid by A Corporation

($4.50/$13.50 × $1.07) .... .36

Total taxes deemed paid by N Corporation under section 902(a) .... $ 28.69

Total foreign income taxes deemed paid by N Corporation under section 901 .... $ 61.19

Example (9). Domestic corporation N owns all the one class of stock of controlled foreign corporation A, which owns all the one class of stock of controlled foreign corporation B, which owns all the one class of stock of controlled foreign corporation C. A and B Corporations are organized under the laws of foreign country X. C Corporation is organized under the laws of foreign country Y. All of B Corporation's assets used in a trade or business are located in country X. All such corporations use the calendar year as the taxable year. For 1978, N Corporation is required to include in its gross income under section 951, $50 attributable to the earnings and profits of C Corporation and $100 attributable to the earnings and profits of B Corporation. N Corporation is not required to include any amount in its gross income under section 951 with respect to A Corporation. Country X imposes an income tax of 10 percent on dividends from foreign subsidiaries, 20 percent on dividends from domestic subsidiaries, and 40 percent on other earnings and profits. For 1978, C Corporation distributes $75 to B Corporation. For such year, B Corporation distributes $175 of its earnings and profits to A Corporation. A Corporation has no other earnings and profits for 1978 and distributes $130 of its earnings and profits to N Corporation. The foreign income taxes deemed paid by N Corporation under sections 960(a)(1) and 902(a) are determined as follows on the basis of the facts assumed:

C Corporation (third-tier corporation):

Pretax earnings and profits	$150.00
Foreign income taxes paid by C Corporation (30%)	45.00
Earnings and profits	105.00
Amount required to be included in gross income of N Corporation under section 951 with respect to C Corporation	50.00
Dividend to B Corporation	75.00
Dividend to which section 902(b)(2) does not apply (attributable to amounts included in N Corporation's gross income under section 951 with respect to C Corporation)	50.00
Dividend to which section 902(b)(2) applies (attributable to amounts not included in N Corporation's gross income under section 951 with respect to C Corporation)	25.00
Amount of foreign income taxes of C Corporation deemed paid by B Corporation under section 902(b)(2) and Sec. 1.960-2(b) ($25/$105 × $45)	10.71
(For formula see Sec. 1.960-2(g)(1)(i)(A))	

B Corporation (second-tier corporation):

Pretax earnings and profits:	
Dividend from C Corporation	75.00
Other earnings and profits	225.00
Total pretax earnings and profits	300.00
Foreign income taxes paid by B Corporation	97.50
On dividends received from C Corporation to which section 902(b)(2) does not apply (attributable to amounts included in N Corporation's gross income under section 951 with respect to C Corporation) ($50 × .10)	5.00
On dividend from C Corporation to which section 902(b)(2) applies (attributable to amounts not included in N Corporation's gross income under section 951 with respect to C Corporation) ($25 × .10)	2.50
On other income of B Corporation ($225 × .40)	90.00
Earnings and profits	202.50
Attributable to dividend to which section 902(b)(2) does not apply (attributable to amounts included in N Corporation's gross income under section 951 with respect to C Corporation) ($50 – $5)	45.00
Attributable to dividend from C Corporation to which section 902(b)(2) applies (attributable to amounts not included in N Corporation's gross income under section 951 with respect to C Corporation) ($25 – $2.50)	22.50
Attributable to other income of B Corporation ($225 – $90)	135.00
Earnings and profits after exclusion of amounts attributable to dividend to which section 902(b)(2) does not apply (attributable to amounts included in N Corporation's gross income under section 951 with respect to C Corporation) ($202.50 × $45)	157.50
Amount required to be included in N Corporation's gross income under section 951 with respect to B Corporation	100.00
Dividend paid by B Corporation	175.00
Dividend to which section 902(b)(2) does not apply (attributable to amounts included in N Corporation's gross income under section 951 with respect to C Corporation)	45.00
Dividend to which section 902(b)(1) does not apply (attributable to amounts included in N Corporation's gross income under section 951 with respect to B Corporation)	100.00
Dividend from other earnings and profits (attributable to amounts not included in N Corporation's gross income with respect to B or C Corporation)	30.00

Foreign income taxes of B Corporation deemed paid by A Corporation under section 902(b)(1) (separate tax rate applicable to dividend received by B Corporation allocation in accordance with Sec. 1.960-2(e)) (for formula see Sec. 1.960-2(g)(1)(ii)(A)(2) *(i)* and *(ii)*:

Tax paid by B Corporation on earnings previously taxed with respect to C Corporation or lower-tiers which is deemed paid by A Corporation:

Portion of dividend to A Corporation from earnings included in N Corporation's gross income under section 951 with respect to C Corporation or lower-tiers
———
Earnings and profits of B Corporation included in N Corporation's gross income under section 951 with respect to C Corporation or lower-tiers
× Tax paid by B Corporation on dividend received by B Corporation from earnings included in N Corporation's gross income with respect to C Corporation or lower-tiers

($45/$45 × $5) .... $ 5.00

Tax paid by B Corporation on earnings not previously taxed with respect to C Corporation or lower-tiers which is deemed paid by A Corporation:

Portion of dividend to A Corporation which is from earnings not included in N Corporation's gross income under section 951 with respect to B Corporation or lower-tiers
———
Earnings and profits of B Corporation not included in N Corporation's gross income under section 951 with respect to C Corporation or lower-tiers
× Tax paid by B Corporation on earnings not included in N Corporation's gross income with respect to C Corporation lower-tiers

($30/157.50 × $92.50) 17.62

Foreign income taxes (of C Corporation) deemed paid by B Corporation deemed paid by A Corporation under section 902(b)(1) ($30/$157.50 × $10.71) 2.04

(For formula see Sec. 1.960-2(g)(1)(ii)(B)(1))

A Corporation (first-tier corporation):

Pretax earnings and profits:	
Dividend from B Corporation	$175.00
Other income	0
Total pretax earnings and profits	175.00
Foreign income taxes paid by A Corporation (20%)	35.00
Earnings and profits	140.00
Attributable to dividend to which section 902(b)(2) does not apply (attributable to amounts included in N Corporation's gross income under section 951 with respect to C Corporation) ($45 - ($45 X 20))	36.00
Attributable to amounts to which section 902(b)(1) does not apply (Attributable to amounts included in N Corporation's gross income under section 951 with respect to B Corporation) ($100 - ($100 X 20))	80.00
Attributable to other earnings and profits (attributable to amounts not included in N Corporation's gross income with respect to B or C Corporation)	24.00
Earnings and profits after exclusion for amounts to which section 902(b)(1) does not apply (attributable to amounts included in N Corporation's gross income under section 951 with respect to B Corporation) ($140 × $80)	60.00
Earnings and profits after exclusion for amounts to which sections 902(b)(1) and 902(b)(2) do not apply (attributable to amounts included in N Corporation's gross income under section 951 with respect to B or C Corporation) ($60 – $36)	24.00
Amount required to be included in N Corporation's gross income under section 1951 with respect to A Corporation	None
Dividend to N Corporation	130.00
Dividend to which section 902(b)(2) does not apply (attributable to amounts included in N Corporation's gross income under section 951 with respect to C Corporation)	36.00
Dividend to which section 902(b)(1) does not apply (attributable to amounts included in N Corporation's gross income under section 951 with respect to B Corporation)	80.00
Dividend to which section 902(a) does not apply (attributable to amounts included in N Corporation's gross income under section 951 with respect to A Corporation)	0
Dividend from other earnings and profits (attributable to amounts not included in N Corporation's gross income with respect to A, B, or C Corporation)	14.00

N Corporation (domestic corporation):

Foreign income taxes deemed paid by N Corporation under section 960(a)(1) and Sec. 1.960-1(c) with respect to C Corporation ($50/$105 × $45) 21.43

(for formula see Sec. 1.960-2(g)(2)(i)(A))

Foreign income taxes deemed paid by N Corporation under section 960(a)(1) with respect to B Corporation (allocation of earnings and profits being made in accordance with Sec. 1.960-1(c)(3) and Sec. 1.960-2(e)) (Separate tax rate applicable to dividend received by B Corporation) 65.53

Taxes paid by B corporation (for formula see Sec. 1.960-2(g)(2)(ii)(A)*(2)*):

Amount included in N Corporation's gross income under section 951 with respect to B Corporation
———
Earnings and profits of B Corporation included in N Corporation's gross income under section 951 with respect to C Corporation on lower-tiers
× Tax paid by B Corporation on earnings not included in N Corporation's gross income with respect to C Corporation or lower-tiers

($100/$157.50 × $92.50) .... $ 58.73
Taxes (of C Corporation) deemed paid by B Corporation under section 902(b)(2) which are deemed paid by N Corporation under section 960(a)(1) ($100/$157.50 = $10.71) 6.80
(for formula see Sec. 1.960-2(g)(2)(ii)(B)(1))
Total taxes deemed paid by N Corporation under section 960(a)(1) 86.96
Foreign income taxes deemed paid by N Corporation under section 902(a):
Taxes paid by A Corporation ($130/$140 = $35) 32.50
(for formula see Sec. 1.960-2(g)(1)(iii)(A)(1))
Taxes paid by B Corporation deemed paid by A Corporation (Separate tax rate applicable to dividend received by B Corporation allocation required by Sec. 1.960-2(e)) (for formula see Sec. 1.960-2(g)(1)(iii)(B)(2) (i) and (ii)):
Tax paid by B Corporation on earnings previously taxed with respect to C Corporation or lower tiers which is deemed paid by N Corporation:

$$\frac{\text{Portion of dividend to N Corporation which is from earnings included in N Corporation's gross income under section 951 with respect to C Corporation or lower-tiers}}{\text{Earnings and profits of A Corporation included in N Corporation's gross income under section 951 with respect to C Corporation or lower-tiers}} \times \text{Tax paid by B Corporation on earnings previously taxed with respect to C Corporation or lower-tiers which is deemed paid by A Corporation}$$

($36/$36 × $5) 5.00
Tax paid by B Corporation on earnings not previously taxed with respect to C Corporation or lower tiers which is deemed paid by N Corporation:

$$\frac{\text{Portion of dividend to N Corporation which is from earnings not included in N Corporation's gross income under section 951 with respect to A Corporation or lower-tiers}}{\text{Earnings and profits of A Corporation not included in N Corporation's gross income under section 951 with respect to B Corporation or lower-tiers}} \times \text{Tax paid by B Corporation on earnings not previously taxed with respect to C Corporation or lower-tiers which is deemed paid by A Corporation}$$

($14/$24 × $17.62) 10.28
Taxes (of C Corporation) deemed paid by B Corporation deemed paid by A Corporation ($14/$24 × $2.04) 1.19
(for formula see Sec. 1.960-2(g)(1)(iii)(C)*(1)*)
Total taxes deemed paid by N Corporation under section 902(a) 48.97
Total foreign income taxes deemed paid by N Corporation under section 901 .... 135.93

Example (10). The facts are the same as in example (9) except that A Corporation has other earnings and profits of $200 in 1978 and country X imposes a tax of 50 percent on A Corporation's other earnings and profits. A Corporation distributes $200 of its earnings and profits to N Corporation in 1978. The foreign income taxes paid by N Corporation under sections 960(a)(1) and 902(a) are determined as follows on the basis of the facts assumed:

C Corporation (third-tier corporation):

Pretax earnings and profits $150.00
Foreign income taxes paid by C Corporation (30%) 45.00
Earnings and profits 105.00
Amount required to be included in gross income of N Corporation under section 951 with respect to C Corporation 50.00
Dividend to B Corporation 75.00
Dividend to which section 902(b)(2) does not apply (attributable to amounts included in N Corporation's gross income under section 951 with respect to C Corporation) 50.00
Dividend to which section 902(b)(2) applies (attributable to amounts not included in N Corporation's gross income under section 951 with respect to C Corporation) 25.00
Amount of foreign income taxes of C Corporation deemed paid by B Corporation under section 902(b)(2) and Sec. 1.960-2(b) ($25/$105 × $45) 10.71
(for formula see Sec. 1.960-2(g)(1)(i)*(A)*)

B Corporation (second-tier corporation)

Pretax earnings and profits:
Dividend from C Corporation 75.00
Other earnings and profits 225.00
Total pretax earnings and profits 300.00
Foreign income taxes of B Corporation 97.50
On dividends received from C Corporation to which section 902(b)(2) does not apply (attributable to amounts included in N Corporation's gross income under section 951 with respect to C Corporation) ($50 × .10) .... $ 5.00
On dividend from C Corporation to which section 902(b)(2) applies (attributable to amounts not included in N Corporation's gross income under section 951 with respect to C Corporation) ($25 × .10) 2.50
On other income of B Corporation ($225 × .40) 90.00
Earnings and profits $202.50

Attributable to dividend to which section 902(b)(2) does not apply (attributable to amounts included in N Corporation's gross income under section 951 with respect to C Corporation) ($50 × $5) 45.00
Attributable to dividend from C Corporation to which section 902(b)(2) applies (attributable to amounts not included in N Corporation's gross income under section 951 with respect to C Corporation) ($25 × $2.50) .. 22.50
Attributable to other income of B Corporation ($225 × $90) 135.00
Earnings and profits after exclusion of amounts attributable to dividend to which section 902(b)(2) does not apply (attributable to amounts included in N Corporation's gross income under section 951 with respect to C Corporation) ($202.50 × $45) 157.50
Amount required to be included in N Corporation's gross income under section 951 with respect to B Corporation 100.00
Dividend paid by B Corporation $175.00
Dividend to which section 902(b)(2) does not apply (attributable to amounts included in N Corporation's gross income under section 951 with respect to C Corporation) .... $ 45.00
Dividend to which section 902(b)(1) does not apply (attributable to amounts included in N Corporation's gross income under section 951 with respect to B Corporation) 100.00
Dividend from other earnings and profits (attributable to amounts not included in N Corporation's gross income with respect to B or C Corporation) 30.00
Foreign income taxes of B Corporation deemed paid by A Corporation under section 902(b)(1) with allocation required by Sec. 1.960-2(e):
($45/$45 × $5) 5.00
($30/$157.50 × $92.50) 17.62
(for formula see Sec. 1.960-2(g)(1)(ii)(A)(2)(i) and (ii))
Foreign income taxes (of C Corporation) deemed paid by B Corporation deemed paid by A Corporation under section 902(b)(1)
($30/$157.50 × $10.71) 2.04
(for formula see Sec. 1.960-2(g)(1)(ii)(B)(1))

A Corporation (first-tier corporation):

Pretax earnings and profits:
Dividend from B Corporation $175.00
Other earnings and profits 200.00
Total pretax earnings and profits 375.00
Foreign income taxes paid by A Corporation 135.00
On dividend received from B Corporation to which section 902(b)(2) does not apply (attributable to amounts included in N Corporation's gross income under section 951 with respect to C Corporation) ($45 × .20) 9.00
On dividend received from B Corporation to which section 902(b)(1) does not apply (attributable to amounts included in N Corporation's gross income under section 951 with respect to B Corporation) ($100 × .20) ... 20.00
On dividend from B Corporation attributable to B Corporation's other earnings and profits (attributable to amounts not included in N Corporation's gross income with respect to B or C Corporation) ($30 X .20) 6.00
On other income of A Corporation ($200 × .50) 100.00
Earnings and profits 240.00
Attributable to dividend to which section 902(b)(2) does not apply (attributable to amounts included in N Corporation's gross income under section 951 with respect to C Corporation) ($45 − $9) 36.00
Attributable to dividend to which section 902(b)(1) does not apply (attributable to amounts included in N Corporation's gross income with respect to B Corporation) ($100 − $20) 80.00
Attributable to other earnings and profits of A Corporation (attributable to amounts not included in N Corporation's gross income with respect to A, B, or C Corporation) [($30 − $6) + ($200 − $100)] 124.00
Amount required to be included in N Corporation's gross income under section 951 with respect to A Corporation .... None
Earnings and profits after exclusion of amounts attributable to dividend to which section 902(b)(1) does not apply (attributable to amounts included in N Corporation's gross income under section 951 with respect to B Corporation) 160.00
Earnings and profits after exclusion of amounts attributable to dividend to which sections 902(b)(1) and 902(b)(2) do not apply (attributable to amounts included in N Corporation's gross income under section 951 with respect to B and C Corporation) 124.00
Dividend to N Corporation 200.00
Dividend attributable to amounts to which section 902(b)(2) does not apply (attributable to amounts included in N Corporation's gross income under section 951 with respect to C Corporation) 36.00
Dividend attributable to amounts to which section 902(b)(1) does not apply (attributable to amounts included in N Corporation's gross income with respect to B Corporation) 80.00
Dividend attributable to amounts to which section 902(a) does not apply (attributable to amounts included in N Corporation's gross income under section 951 with respect to A Corporation) 0
Dividend attributable to A Corporation's other earnings and profits (attributable to amounts not included in N Corporation's gross income under section 951 with respect to A, B, or C Corporation) .... $ 84.00

N Corporation (domestic corporation):

Foreign income taxes deemed paid by N Corporation under section 960(a)(1) and Sec. 1.960-1(c) with respect to C Corporation—($50/$150 × $45) 21.43
(for formula see Sec. 1.960-2(g)(2)(i)(A))
Foreign income taxes deemed paid by N Corporation under section 960(a)(1) with respect to B Corporation (allocation of earning and profits being made in accordance with Sec. 1.960-1(c)(3) and Sec. 1.960-2(e)) 65.53
Taxes paid by B Corporation ($100/$157.50
(for formula see Sec. 1.960-2(g)(2)(ii)(A)(2))
Taxes deemed paid by B Corporation ($100 × $157.50 × $10.71) 6.80
(for formula see Sec. 1.960-2(g)(2)(ii)(B)(1)) Total taxes deemed paid by N Corporation under section 960(a)(1) 86.96
Foreign income taxes deemed paid by N Corporation under section 902(a) (separate tax rate applicable to dividends received by A Corporation allocation required by Sec. 1.960-2(e)) (for formula see Sec. 1.960-2(g)(1)(iii)(A)(2)(i) and (ii)):
Tax paid by A Corporation on earnings previously taxed with respect to B Corporation or lower tiers which is deemed paid by N Corporation:

Portion of dividend to N Corporation which is from earnings included in N Corporation's gross income under section 951 with respect to B Corporation or lower-tiers / Earnings and profits of A Corporation included in N Corporation's gross income under section 951 with respect to B Corporation or lower-tiers	×	Tax paid by A Corporation on dividends received by A Corporation from earnings included in N Corporation's gross income with respect to B Corporation or lower-tiers

($116/$116 × $29) .... $ 29.00
Tax paid by A Corporation on earnings not previously taxed with respect to B Corporation or lower tiers which is deemed paid by N Corporation:

Portion of dividend to N Corporation which is from earnings not included in N Corporation's gross income under section 951 with respect to A Corporation or lower-tiers / Earnings and profits of A Corporation not included in N Corporation's gross income under section 951 with respect to B Corporation or lower-tiers	×	Tax paid by A Corporation on earnings not included in N Corporation's gross income with respect to B Corporation or lower-tiers

($84/$124 × $106) 71.81
Taxes (paid by B Corporation) deemed paid by A Corporation allocation required by Sec. 1.960-2(e):
($36/$36 × $5) 5.00
($84/$124 × $17.62) 11.94
(for formula see Sec. 1.960-2(g)(1)(iii)(B)(2) *(i)*and *(ii))*
Taxes (of C Corporation) deemed paid by B Corporation deemed paid by A Corporation ($84/$124 X $2.04) 1.38
(for formula see Sec. 1.960-2(g)(1)(iii)(C)(1))
Total taxes deemed paid by N Corporation under section 902(a) credit 119.13
Total foreign income taxes deemed paid by N Corporation under section 901 .... 206.09

(g) Formulas. This paragraph contains formulas for determining a domestic corporation's section 902 and 960 credits when amounts distributed through a chain of ownership have been included in whole or in part in the gross income of a domestic corporation under section 951 with respect to first-, second-, third-, or lower-tier corporations.

(1) Determination of the section 902 credit. (i) Section 902(b)(2) credit. If the second-tier corporation receives a dividend from a third-tier corporation attributable in whole or in part to amounts included in a domestic corporation's gross income under section 951 with respect to the third- or lower-tier corporations, the second-tier corporation's credit for taxes paid by the third-tier corporation under section 902(b)(2) is determined as follows:

(A) If the effective rate of tax on dividends received by the third-tier corporation is the same as the effective rate of tax on its other earnings and profits—

Dividend to second-tier corporation less portion of divided from earnings included in domestic corporation's gross income under section 951 with respect to third-tier corporation / Earnings and profits of third-tier corporation	×	Taxes paid by third-tier corporation

(B) If the effective rate of tax on dividends received by the third-tier corporation is higher or lower than the effective rate of tax on its other earnings and profits—

(1) Credit for tax paid by third-tier corporation on earnings included in domestic corporation's gross income with respect to fourth- or lower-tier corporations—

$$\frac{\text{Portion of dividends to second-tier corporation which is from earnings included in domestic corporation's gross income under section 951 with respect to fourth- or lower-tier corporations}}{\text{Earnings and profits of third-tier corporation included in domestic corporation's gross income under section 951 with respect to fourth- or lower-tier corporations}} \times \text{Tax paid by third-tier corporation on dividend received by third-tier corporation from earnings included in domestic corporation's gross income with respect to fourth- or lower-tier corporations}$$

(2) Credit for tax paid by third-tier corporation on earnings not included in domestic corporation's gross income with respect to fourth- or lower-tier corporations—

$$\frac{\text{Portion of dividend to second-tier corporation which is from earnings not included in domestic corporation's gross income under section 951 with respect to third- or lower-tier corporations}}{\text{Earnings and profits of third-tier corporation not included in domestic corporation's gross income under section 951 with respect to fourth-or lower-tier corporations}} \times \text{Tax paid by third-tier corporation on earnings not included in domestic corporations' gross income with respect to fourth- or lower-tier corporations}$$

(ii) Section 902(b)(1) credit. If the first-tier corporation receives a dividend from a second-tier corporation attributable in a whole or in part to amounts included in a domestic corporation's gross income under section 951 with respect to the second- or lower-tier corporations, the first-tier corporation's credit for taxes paid and deemed paid by the second-tier corporation under section 902(b)(1) is determined as follows:

(A) Taxes paid by the second-tier corporation which are deemed paid by the first-tier corporation.

(1) If the effective rate of tax on dividends received by the second-tier corporation is the same as the effective rate of tax on its other earnings and profits—

$$\frac{\text{Dividend to first-tier corporation less portion of dividend from earnings included in domestic corporation's gross income under section 951 with respect to second-tier corporation}}{\text{Earnings and profits of second-tier corporation}} \times \text{Taxes paid by second-tier corporation}$$

(2) If the effective rate of tax on dividends received by the second-tier corporation is higher or lower than the effective rate of tax on its other earnings and profits—

(i) Credit for tax paid by second-tier corporation on earnings previously taxed with respect to third- or lower-tier corporations—

$$\frac{\text{Portion of dividend to first-tier corporation which is from earnings included in domestic corporation's gross income under section 951 with respect to third- or lower-tier corporations}}{\text{Earnings and profits or second-tier corporation included in domestic corporation's gross income under section 951 with respect to third- or lower-tier corporations}} \times \text{Tax paid by second-tier corporation on dividend received by second-tier corporation from earnings included in domestic corporation's gross income with respect to third- or lower-tier corporations}$$

(ii) Credit for tax paid by second-tier corporation on earnings not previously taxed with respect to third- or lower-tier corporations—

$$\frac{\text{Portion of dividend to first-tier corporation which is from earnings not included in domestic corporation's gross income under section 951 with respect to third- or lower-tier corporations}}{\text{Earnings and profits of second-tier corporation not included in domestic corporation's gross income under section 951 with respect to third- or lower-tier corporations}} \times \text{Tax paid by second-tier corporation on earnings not included in domestic corporation's gross income with respect to third- or lower-tier corporations}$$

(B) Taxes deemed paid by the second-tier corporation which are deemed paid by the first-tier corporation. (1) If the effective rate of tax dividends received by the third-tier corporation is the same as the effective rate of tax on its other earnings and profits—

$$\frac{\text{Dividend to first-tier corporation less portion of dividend from earnings included in domestic corporation's gross income under section 951 with respect to second- and third-tier corporations}}{\text{Earnings and profits of second-tier corporation less earnings and profits attributable to amounts included in domestic corporation's gross income under section 951 with respect to third-tier corporation}} \times \text{Taxes paid by third-tier corporation which are deemed paid by second-tier corporation}$$

(2) If the effective rate of tax on dividends received by the third-tier corporation is higher or lower than the effective rate of tax on its other earnings and profits—

(i) Credit for tax paid by third-tier corporation on earnings previously taxed with respect to fourth- or lower-tier corporations—

$$\frac{\text{Portion of dividend to first-tier corporation which is from earnings included in domestic corporation's gross income under section 951 with respect to fourth- or lower-tier corporations}}{\text{Earnings and profits of second-tier corporations included in domestic corporation's gross income under section 951 with respect to fourth-or lower-tier corporation}} \times \text{Tax paid by third-tier corporation on earnings previously taxed with respect to fourth- or lower-tier corporations which is deemed paid by second-tier corporation}$$

(ii) Credit for tax paid by third-tier corporation on earnings not previously taxed with respect to fourth- or lower-tier corporations—

$$\frac{\text{Portion of dividend to first-tier corporation which is from earnings not included in domestic corporation's gross income under section 951 with respect to second- or lower-tier corporations}}{\text{Earnings and profits of second-tier corporation not included in domestic corporation's gross income under section 951 with respect to third-or lower-tier corporations}} \times \text{Tax paid by third-tier corporation on earnings not previously taxed with respect to fourth- or lower-tier corporations which is deemed paid by second-tier corporation}$$

(iii) Section 902(a) credit. If the domestic corporation receives a dividend from a first-tier corporation attributable in whole or in part to amounts included in a domestic corporation's gross income under section 951 with respect to the first- or lower-tier corporations, the domestic corporation's credit for taxes paid and deemed paid by the first-tier corporation under section 902(a) is determined as follows:

(A) Taxes paid by the first-tier corporation which are deemed paid by domestic corporation.

(1) If the effective rate of tax on dividends received by the first-tier corporation is the same as the effective rate of tax on its other earnings and profits—

$$\frac{\text{Dividend to domestic corporation less portion of dividend from earnings included in domestic corporation's gross income under section 951 with respect to first-tier corporation}}{\text{Earnings and profits of first-tier corporation}} \times \text{Taxes paid by first-tier corporation}$$

(2) If the effective rate of tax on dividends received by the first-tier corporation is higher or lower than the effective rate of tax on its other earnings and profits—

(i) Credit for tax paid by first-tier corporation on earnings previously taxed with respect to second- or lower-tier corporations—

$$\frac{\text{Portion of dividend to domestic corporation which is from earnings included in domestic corporation's gross income under section 951 with respect to second- or lower-tier corporations}}{\text{Earnings and profits of first-tier corporation's included in domestic corporation's gross income under section 951 with respect to second- or lower-tier corporations}} \times \text{Tax paid by first-tier corporation on dividends received by first-tier corporation from earnings included in domestic corporation's gross income with respect to second- or lower-tier corporations}$$

(ii) Credit for tax paid by first-tier corporation on earnings not previously taxed with respect to second- or lower-tier corporations—

$$\frac{\text{Portion of dividend to domestic corporation which is from earnings not included in domestic corporation's gross income under section 951 with respect to first- or lower-tier corporations}}{\text{Earnings and profits of first-tier corporation not included in domestic corporation's gross income under section 951 with respect to second- or lower-tier corporations}} \times \text{Tax paid by first-tier corporation on earnings not included in domestic corporation's gross income with respect to second- or lower-tier corporations}$$

(B) Taxes (paid by second-tier corporation) deemed paid by first-tier corporation which are deemed paid by domestic corporation.

(1) If the effective rate of tax on dividends received by the second-tier corporation is the same as its tax rate on other earnings and profits—

$$\frac{\text{Dividend to domestic corporation less portion of dividend from earnings included in domestic corporation's gross income under section 951 with respect to first- and second-tier corporations}}{\text{Earnings and profits of first-tier corporation less earnings and profits attributable to amounts included in domestic corporation's gross income under section 951 with respect to second-tier corporation}} \times \text{Taxes paid by second-tier corporation which are deemed paid by first-tier corporation}$$

(2) If the effective rate of tax on dividends received by the second-tier corporation is higher or lower than the effective rate of tax on its other earnings and profits—

(i) Credit for tax paid by second-tier corporation on earnings previously taxed with respect to third-tier or lower-tier corporations—

$$\frac{\text{Portion of dividend to domestic corporation which is from earnings included in domestic corporation's gross income under section 951 with respect to third- or lower-tier corporations}}{\text{Earnings and profits of first-tier corporation included in domestic corporation's gross income under section 951 with respect to third- or lower-tier corporations}} \times \text{Tax paid by second-tier corporation on earnings previously taxed with respect to third- or lower-tier corporations which is deemed paid by first-tier corporation}$$

(ii) Credit for tax paid by second-tier corporation on earnings not previously taxed with respect to third- or lower-tier corporations—

$$\frac{\text{Portion of dividend to domestic corporation which is from earnings not included in domestic corporation's gross income under section 951 with respect to first- or lower-tier corporations}}{\text{Earnings and profits of first-tier corporation not included in domestic corporation's gross income under section 951 with respect to second- or lower-tier corporations}} \times \text{Tax paid by second-tier corporation on earnings not previously taxed with respect to third- or lower-tier corporations which is deemed paid by first-tier corporation}$$

(C) Taxes (of third-tier corporation) deemed paid by first-tier corporation which are deemed paid by domestic corporation.

(1) If the effective rate of tax on dividends received by the third-tier corporation is the same as the effective rate of tax on its other earnings and profits—

$$\frac{\text{Dividend to domestic corporation less portion of dividend from earnings included in domestic corporation's gross income under section 951 with respect to first-, second- and third-tier corporations}}{\text{Earnings and profits of first-tier corporation less earnings and profits attributable to amounts included in domestic corporation's gross income with respect to second- and third-tier corporations}} \times \text{Taxes deemed paid by second-tier corporation which are deemed paid by first-tier corporation}$$

(2) If the effective rate of tax on dividends received by the third-tier corporation is higher or lower than the effective rate of tax on its other earnings and profits—

(i) Credit for tax (of third-tier corporation) deemed paid by second-tier corporation on earnings previously taxed with respect to fourth- or lower-tier corporations—

$$\frac{\text{Portion of dividend to domestic corporation which is from earnings included in domestic corporation's gross income under section 951 with respect to fourth-or lower-tier corporations}}{\text{Earnings and profits of first-tier corporations included in domestic corporation's gross income under section 951 with respect to fourth- or lower-tier corporations}} \times \text{Taxes deemed paid by second-tier corporation on earnings previously taxed with respect to fourth- or lower-tier corporations which is deemed paid by first-tier corporation}$$

(ii) Credit for tax (of third-tier corporation) deemed paid by second-tier on earnings not previously taxed with respect to fourth- or lower-tier corporations—

$$\frac{\text{Portion of dividend to domestic corporation which is from earnings not included in domestic corporation's gross income under section 951 with respect to first- or lower-tier corporations}}{\text{Earnings and profits of first-tier corporation not included in domestic corporation's gross income under section 951 with respect to second- or lower-tier corporation}} \times \text{Tax deemed paid by second-tier corporation on earnings not previously taxed with respect to fourth- or lower-tier corporations which is deemed paid by first-tier corporation}$$

(2) Determination of domestic corporation's section 960 credit for amounts included in its gross income with respect to a first-, second-, or third-tier corporation which has received a distribution previously included in the gross income of a domestic corporation under section 951. (i) Third-tier credit. If a domestic corporation is required to include an amount in its gross income under section 951 with respect to a third-tier corporation which has received a distribution from a fourth-tier corporation of amounts included in a domestic corporation's gross income under section 951 with respect to the fourth- or lower-tier corporations, the domestic corporation's credit for taxes paid by the third-tier corporation under section 960(a)(1) is determined as follows:

(A) If the effective rate of tax on dividends received by the third-tier corporation is the same as the effective rate of tax on its other earnings and profits—

$$\frac{\text{Amount included in domestic corporation's gross income under section 951 with respect to third-tier corporation}}{\text{Earnings and profits of third-tier corporation}} \times \text{Taxes paid by third-tier corporation}$$

(B) If the effective rate of tax on dividends received by the third-tier corporation is higher or lower than the effective rate of tax on its other earnings and profits—

$$\frac{\text{Amount included in domestic corporation's gross income under section 951 with respect to third-tier corporation}}{\text{Earnings and profits of third-tier corporation not included in domestic corporation's gross income under section 951 with respect to fourth- or lower-tier}} \times \text{Tax paid by third-tier corporation on earnings not included in domestic corporation's gross income with respect to fourth- or lower-tier corporations}$$

(ii) Second-tier credit. If a domestic corporation is required to include an amount in its gross income under section 951 with respect to a second-tier corporation which has received a distribution from a third-tier corporation of amounts included in a domestic corporation's gross income under section 951 with respect to the third- or lower-tier corporations, the domestic corporation's credit for taxes paid and deemed paid by the second-tier corporation under section 960(a)(1) is determined as follows:

(A) Credit for taxes paid by the second-tier corporation which are deemed paid by the domestic corporation.

(1) If the effective rate of tax on dividends received by the second-tier corporation is the same as the effective rate of tax on its other earnings and profits—

$$\frac{\text{Amount included in domestic corporation's gross income under section 951 with respect to second-tier corporation}}{\text{Earnings and profits of second-tier corporation}} \times \text{Taxes paid by second-tier corporation}$$

(2) If the effective rate of tax on dividends received by the second-tier is higher or lower than the effective rate of tax on its other earnings and profits—

$$\frac{\text{Amount included in domestic corporation's gross income under section 951 with respect to second-tier corporation}}{\text{Earnings and profits of second-tier corporation not included in domestic corporation's gross income under section 951 with respect to third- or lower-tier corporations}} \times \text{Tax paid by second-tier corporation on earnings not included in domestic corporation's gross income with respect to third- or lower-tier corporations}$$

(B) Credit for taxes (of the third-tier corporation) deemed paid by the second-tier corporation under section 902(b)(2).

(1) If the effective rate of tax on dividends received by the third-tier corporation is the same as the effective rate of tax on its other earnings and profits—

$$\frac{\text{Amount included in domestic corporation's gross income under section 951 with respect to second-tier corporation}}{\text{Earnings and profits of second-tier corporation less earnings and profits attributable to amounts included in domestic corporation's gross income with respect to third-tier corporation}} \times \text{Taxes paid by third-tier corporation which are deemed paid by second-tier corporation}$$

(2) If the effective rate of tax on dividends received by the third-tier corporation is higher or lower than the effective rate of tax on its other earnings and profits—

$$\frac{\text{Amount included in domestic corporation's gross income under section 951 with respect to second-tier corporation}}{\text{Earnings and profits of second-tier corporation not included in domestic corporation's gross income under section 951 with respect to third- or lower-tier corporation}} \times \text{Tax paid by third-tier corporation on earnings not previously taxed with respect to fourth- or lower-tier corporations which is deemed paid by second-tier corporations}$$

(iii) First-tier credit. If a domestic corporation is required to include amounts in its gross income under section 951 with respect to a first-tier corporation which has received a distribution from a second-tier corporation of amounts included in a domestic corporation's gross income under section 951 with respect to the second- or lower-tier corporations, the domestic corporation's credit for taxes paid and deemed paid by the first-tier corporation under section 960(a)(1) shall be determined as follows:

(A) Credit for taxes paid by the first-tier corporation.

(1) If the effective rate of tax on dividends received by the first-tier corporation is the same as the effective rate of tax on its other earnings and profits—

$$\frac{\text{Amount included in domestic corporation's gross income under section 951 with respect to first-tier corporation}}{\text{Earnings and profits of first-tier corporations}} \times \text{Taxes paid by first-tier corporation}$$

(2) If the effective rate of tax on dividends received by the first-tier corporation is higher or lower than the effective rate of tax on its other earnings and profits—

$$\frac{\text{Amount included in domestic corporation's gross income under section 951 with respect to first-tier corporation}}{\text{Earnings and profits of first-tier corporation not included in domestic corporation's gross income under section 951 with respect to second- or lower-tier corporations}} \times \text{Tax paid by first-tier corporation on earnings not included in domestic corporation's gross income with respect to second- or lower-tier corporations}$$

(B) Credit for taxes paid by the second-tier corporation deemed paid by the first-tier corporation under section 902(b)(1).

(1) If the effective rate of tax on dividends received by the second-tier corporation is the same as the effective rate of tax on its other earnings and profits—

$$\frac{\text{Amount included in domestic corporation's gross income under section 951 with respect to first-tier corporation}}{\text{Earnings and profits of first-tier corporation less earnings and profits attributable to amounts included in domestic corporation's gross income under section 951 with respect to second-tier corporation}} \times \text{Taxes paid by second-tier corporation which are deemed paid by first-tier corporation}$$

(2) If the effective rate of tax on dividends received by the second-tier corporation is higher or lower than the effective rate of tax on its other earnings and profits—

$$\frac{\text{Amount included in domestic corporation's gross income under section 951 with respect to first-tier corporation}}{\text{Earnings and profits of first-tier corporation not included in domestic corporation's gross income under section 951 with respect to third- or lower-tier corporations}} \times \text{Tax paid by second-tier corporation on earnings not previously taxed with respect to third- or lower-tier corporations which is deemed paid by first-tier corporation}$$

(C) Credit for taxes (of the third-tier corporation) deemed paid by the second-tier corporation which are deemed paid by first-tier corporation under section 902(b)(1).

(1) If the effective rate of tax on dividends received by the third-tier corporation is the same as the effective rate of tax on its other earnings and profits—

$$\frac{\text{Amount included in domestic corporation's gross income under section 951 with respect to first-tier corporation}}{\text{Earnings and profits of first-tier corporation less earnings and profits attributable to amounts included in domestic corporation's gross income with respect to second- and third-tier corporations}} \times \text{Tax deemed paid by second-tier corporation which are deemed paid by first-tier corporation}$$

(2) If the effective rate of tax on dividends received by the third-tier corporation is higher or lower than the effective rate of tax on its other earnings and profits—

$$\frac{\text{Amount included in domestic corporation's gross income under section 951 with respect to first-tier corporation}}{\text{Earnings and profits of first-tier corporation not included in domestic corporation's gross income under section 951 with respect to second- or lower-tier corporations}} \times \text{Tax deemed paid by second-tier corporation on earnings not previously taxed with respect to fourth- or lower-tier corporations which is deemed paid by first-tier corporation}$$

T.D. 7120, 6/3/71, amend T.D. 7334, 12/20/74, T.D. 7649, 10/17/79, T.D. 7843, 11/5/82.

§ 1.960-3 Gross-up of amounts included in income under section 951.

Caution: The Treasury has not yet amended Reg § 1.960-3 to reflect changes made by P.L. 105-34.

(a) General rule for including taxes in income. Any taxes deemed paid by a domestic corporation for the taxable year pursuant to section 960(a)(1) shall, except as provided in paragraph (b) of this section, be included in the gross income of such corporation for such year as a dividend pursuant to section 78 and § 1.78-1.

(b) Certain taxes not included in income. Any taxes deemed paid by a domestic corporation for the taxable year pursuant to section 902(a) or section 960(a)(1) shall not be included in the gross income of such corporation for such year as a dividend pursuant to section 78 and § 1.78-1 to the extent that such taxes are paid or accrued by the first-, second-, or third-tier corporation, as the case may be, on or with respect to an amount which is excluded from the gross income of such foreign corporation under section 959(b) and § 1.959-2 as distributions from the earnings and profits of another controlled foreign corporation attributable to an amount which is, or has been, required to be included in the gross income of the domestic corporation under section 951.

(c) Illustrations. The application of this section may be illustrated by the following examples:

Example (1). Domestic corporation N owns all the one class of stock of controlled foreign corporation A, which owns all the one class of stock of controlled foreign corporation B. All such corporations use the calendar year as the taxable year. For 1965, B Corporation, after having paid $20 of foreign income taxes, has $80 in earnings and profits, which are attributable to the amount required to be included in N Corporation's gross income for such year under section 951 with respect to B Corporation and all of which are distributed to A Corporation in such year. The dividend so received from B Corporation is excluded from A Corporation's gross income under section 959(b) and § 1.959-2. An income tax of 10 percent is required to be withheld from such dividend by the foreign country under the laws of which B Corporation is created, and the foreign country under the laws of which A Corporation is created imposes an income tax of $22 on the dividend received from B Corporation. For 1965, A Corporation's earnings and profits are $50 ($80 − [0.10 × $80] − $22), which it distributes in such year to N Corporation. For 1965, N Corporation is required under section 951 to include $80 in gross income with respect to B Corporation and also is required under the gross-up provisions of section 78 to include in gross income $20 ($80/$80 × $20), the amount equal to the foreign income taxes of B Corporation which are deemed paid by N Corporation under section 960(A)(1)(C). Under paragraph (b) of this section N Corporation is not required to include in gross income the $30 ($8 + $22) of foreign income taxes which are paid by A Corporation in connection with the dividend received from B Corporation and which are deemed paid by N Corporation under section 902(a) and paragraph (c) of § 1.960-2.

Example (2). Domestic corporation N owns all the one class of stock of controlled foreign corporation A, which owns all the one class of stock of controlled foreign corporation B, which in turn owns all the one class of stock of controlled foreign corporation C. All such corporations use the calendar year as the taxable year. For 1978, C Corporation, after having paid $20 of foreign income taxes, has $80 in earnings and profits, which are attributable to the amount required to be included in N Corporation's gross income for such year under section 951 with respect to C Corporation and all of which are distributed to B Corporation in such year. After having paid foreign income taxes of $10 on the dividend received from C Corporation, B Corporation distributes the balance of $70 to A Corporation. After having paid foreign income taxes of $5 on the dividend received from B Corporation, A Corporation distributes the balance of $65 to N Corporation. The dividend so received by B Corporation, and in turn by A Corporation, is excluded from the gross income of such corporations under section 959(b) and § 1.959-2. Under paragraph (b) of this section N Corporation is not required to include in gross income the $15 ($10 + $5) of foreign income taxes which are paid by corporations B and A, respectively, in connection with the dividend so received and which are deemed paid by N Corporation under section 902(a) and paragraphs (b) and (c) of § 1.960-2.

T.D. 7120, 6/3/71, amend T.D. 7481, 4/15/77, T.D. 7649, 10/17/79, T.D. 7843, 11/5/82.

§ 1.960-4 Additional foreign tax credit in year of receipt of previously taxed earnings and profits.

Caution: The Treasury has not yet amended Reg § 1.960-4 to reflect changes made by 103-66.

(a) Increase in section 904(a) limitation for the taxable year of exclusion. *(1) In general.* The applicable limitation under section 904(a) for a taxpayer's taxable year (hereinafter in this section referred to as the "taxable year of exclusion") in which he receives an amount which is excluded from gross income under section 959(a)(1) and which is attributable to a controlled foreign corporation's earnings and profits in respect of which an amount was required to be included in the gross income of such taxpayer under section 951(a) for a taxable year (hereinafter in this section referred to as the "taxable year of inclusion") previous to the taxable year of exclusion shall be increased under section 960(b)(1) by the amount described in paragraph (b) of this section if the conditions described in subparagraph (2) of this paragraph are satisfied.

(2) Conditions under which increase in limitation is allowed for the taxable year of exclusion. The increase in limitation described in subparagraph (1) of this paragraph for the taxable year of exclusion shall be made only if the taxpayer—

(i) For the taxable year of inclusion either chose to claim a foreign tax credit as provided in section 901 or did not pay or accrue any foreign income taxes,

(ii) Chooses to claim a foreign tax credit as provided in section 901 for the taxable year of exclusion, and

(iii) For the taxable year of exclusion pays, accrues, or is deemed to have paid foreign income taxes with respect to the amount, described in subparagraph (1) of this paragraph, which is excluded from his gross income for such year under section 959(a)(1).

(b) Amount of increase in limitation for the taxable year of exclusion. The amount of increase under section 960(b)(1) in the applicable limitation under section 904(a) for the taxable year of exclusion shall be—

(1) The amount by which the applicable section 904(a) limitation for the taxable year of inclusion was increased, determined as provided in paragraph (c) of this section, by reason of the inclusion of the amount in the taxpayer's income for such year under section 951(a), reduced by

(2) The amount of foreign income taxes allowed as a credit under section 901 for such taxable year of inclusion and which were allowable to such taxpayer solely by reason of the inclusion of such amount in his gross income under section 951(a), as determined under paragraph (d) of this section, and then by

(3) The additional reduction for such taxable year of inclusion arising by reason of increases in limitation under section 960(b)(1) for taxable years intervening between such taxable year of inclusion and such taxable year of exclusion, as determined under paragraph (e) of this section in respect of such inclusion under section 951(a), except that the amount of increase determined under this paragraph for the taxable year of exclusion shall in no case exceed the amount of foreign income taxes paid, accrued, or deemed to be paid by such taxpayer for such taxable year of exclusion with respect to the amount, described in paragraph (a)(1) of this section, which is excluded from gross income for such year under section 959(a)(1).

(c) Determination of increase in limitation for the taxable year of inclusion. The amount of the increase in the applicable limitation under section 904(a) for the taxable year of inclusion which arises by reason of the inclusion of the amount in gross income under section 951(a) shall be the amount of the applicable limitation under section 904(a) for such year reduced by the amount which would have been the applicable limitation under section 904(a) for such year if the amount had not been included in gross income for such year under section 951(a).

(d) Determination of foreign income taxes allowed for taxable year of inclusion by reason of section 951(a) amount. The amount of foreign income taxes allowed as a credit under section 901 for the taxable year of inclusion which were allowable solely by reason of the inclusion of the amount in gross income for such year under section 951(a) shall be the amount of foreign income taxes allowed as a credit under section 901 for such year reduced by the amount of foreign income taxes which would have been allowed as a credit under section 901 for such year if the amount had not been included in gross income for such year under section 951(a). For purposes of this paragraph, the term "foreign income taxes" includes foreign income taxes paid or accrued, and foreign income taxes deemed paid under section 902, section 904(d), and section 960(a), for the taxable year of inclusion.

(e) Additional reduction for the taxable year of inclusion arising by reason of increases in limitation for intervening years. The amount of increase in the applicable limitation under section 904(a) for the taxable year of inclusion shall also be reduced, after first deducting the foreign income taxes described in paragraph (b)(2) of this section, by any increases in limitation which arise under section 960(b)(1)—by reason of any earlier exclusions under section 959(a)(1) in respect of the same inclusion under section 951(a) for such taxable year of inclusion—for the first, second, third, fourth, etc., succeeding taxable years of exclusion, in that order, which follow such taxable year of inclusion and precede the taxable year of exclusion in respect of which the increase in limitation under section 960(b)(1) and paragraph (b) of this section is being determined. The amount of any increase in limitation which arises under section 960(b)(1) for any such succeeding taxable year of exclusion shall be the amount of foreign income taxes allowed as a credit under section 901 for each such taxable year reduced by the amount of foreign income taxes which would have been allowed as a credit under section 901 for each such year if the limitation for each such year were not increased under section 960(b)(1). For any such succeeding taxable year of exclusion for which the taxpayer does not choose to claim a foreign tax credit as provided in section 901, the same increase in limitation under section 960(b)(1) shall be treated as having been made, for purposes of this paragraph, which would have been made for such taxable year if the taxpayer had chosen to claim the foreign tax credit for such year.

(f) Illustrations. The application of this section may be illustrated by the following examples:

Example (1). Domestic corporation N owns all of the one class of stock of controlled foreign corporation A. Corporation A, after paying foreign income taxes of $30, has earnings and profits for 1978 of $70, all of which are attributable to an amount required under section 951(a) to be included in N Corporation's gross income for 1978. Both corporations use the calendar year as the taxable year. For 1979 and 1980, A Corporation has no earnings and profits attributable to an amount required to be included in N Corporation's gross income under section 951(a); for each such year it makes a distribution of $35 (from its earnings and profits for 1978) from which a foreign income tax of $6 is withheld. For each of 1978, 1979, and 1980, N Corporation derives taxable income of $50 from sources within the United States and claims a foreign tax credit under section 901, determined by applying the overall limitation under section 904(a)(2). The United States tax payable by N Corporation is determined as follows, assuming a corporate tax rate of 48 percent:

1978

Taxable income of N Corporation:		
U.S. sources		$ 50.00
Sources without the U.S.:		
Amount required to be included in N Corporation's gross income under sec. 951(a).............	$70.00	

Foreign income taxes deemed paid by N Corporation under section 960(a)(1) and included in N Corporation's gross income under sec. 78 ($30 × $70/$70)	30.00	100.00
Total taxable income		150.00
U.S. tax payable for 1978:		
U.S. tax before credit ($150 × 0.48)		72.00
Credit: Foreign income taxes of $30, but not to exceed overall limitation of $48 for 1965 ($100/$150 × $72)		30.00
U.S. tax payable		42.00

1979

Taxable income of N Corporation, consisting of income from U.S. sources		$ 50.00
U.S. tax before credit ($50 × 0.48)		24.00
Section 904(a)(2) overall limitation for 1979:		
Limitation for 1979 before increase under sec. 960(b)(1) ($24 × $0/$50)		0
Plus: Increase in overall limitation for 1979 under sec. 960(b)(1):		
Amount by which 1978 overall limitation was increased by reason of inclusion in N Corporation's gross income under sec. 951(a) for 1978 ($48 – [($50 × 0.48) × $0/$50])	$48.00	
Less: Foreign income taxes allowed as a credit for 1978 which were allowable solely by reason of such sec. 951(a) inclusion ($30 – $0)	30.00	
Balance	18.00	
But: Such balance not to exceed foreign income taxes paid by N Corporation for 1979 with respect to $35 distribution excluded under sec. 959(a)(1) ($6 tax withheld)	6.00	6.00
Overall limitation for 1979		6.00

U.S. tax payable for 1979:	
U.S. tax before credit ($d50 × 0.48)	24.00
Credit: Foreign income taxes of $6, but not to exceed overall limitation of $6 for 1979	6.00
U.S. tax payable	18.00

1980

Taxable income of N Corporation, consisting of income from U.S. sources		50.00
U.S. tax before credit ($50 × 0.48)		24.00
Section 904(a)(2) overall limitation for 1980:		
Limitation for 1980 before increase under sec. 960(b)(1) ($24 × $0/$50)		0
Plus: Increase in overall limitation for 1967 under sec. 960(b)(1):		
Amount by which 1978 overall limitation was increased by reason of inclusion in N Corporation's gross income under sec. 951(a) for 1978 ($48 – [($50 × 0.48) × $0/$50])	$48.00	
Less: Foreign income taxes allowed as a credit for 1978 which were allowable solely by reason of such sec. 951(a) inclusion ($30 – $0)	30.00	
Tentative balance	18.00	
Less: Increase in overall limitation under sec. 960(b)(1) for 1979 by reason of such sec. 951(a) inclusion	6.00	
Balance	12.00	
But: Such balance not to exceed foreign income taxes paid by N Corporation for 1980 with respect to $35 distribution excluded under sec. 959(a)(1) ($6 tax withheld)	6.00	6.00
Overall limitation for 1980		6.00

U.S. tax payable for 1980:	
U.S. tax before credit ($50 × 0.48)	24.00
Credit: Foreign income taxes of $6, but not to exceed overall limitation of $6 for 1980	6.00
U.S. tax payable	18.00

Example (2). The facts for 1978, 1979, and 1980, are the same as in example (1), except that in 1977, to which the section 904(a)(2) overall limitation applies, N Corporation pays $18 of foreign income taxes in excess of the overall limitation and that such excess is not absorbed as a carryback to 1975 or 1976 under section 904(C). Therefore, there is no increase under section 960(b)(1) in the overall limitation for 1979 or 1980 since the amount ($48) by which the 1965 overall limitation was increased by reason of the inclusion in N Corporation's gross income for 1978 under section 951(a), less the foreign income taxes ($48) allowed as a credit which were allowable solely by reason of such inclusion, is zero. The foreign income taxes so allowed as a credit for 1978 which were allowable solely by reason of such section 951(a) inclusion consist of the $30 of foreign income taxes deemed paid for 1978 under section 960(a)(1) and the $18 of foreign income taxes for 1977 carried over and deemed paid for 1978 under section 904(C).

Example (3). (a) Domestic corporation N owns all the one class of stock of controlled foreign corporation A, which in turn owns all the one class of stock of controlled foreign corporation B. All corporations use the calendar years as the taxable year. Corporation B, after paying foreign income taxes of $30, has earnings and profits for 1978 of $70, all of which is attributable to an amount required under section 951(a) to be included in N Corporation's gross income for 1978, and $35 of which it distributes in such year to A Corporation. For 1978, A Corporation, after paying foreign income taxes of $5 on such dividend from B Corporation, has total earnings and profits of $30, all of which it distributes in such year to N Corporation, a foreign income tax of $3 being withheld therefrom.

(b) For 1979, B Corporation has no earnings and profits, but distributes in such year to A Corporation the $35 remaining of its earnings and profits for 1978. For 1979, A

Corporation, after paying foreign income taxes of $5 on such dividend from B Corporation, has total earnings and profits of $30, all of which it distributes to N Corporation, a foreign income tax of $3 being withheld therefrom.

(c) For each of 1978 and 1979, N Corporation has taxable income of $100 from United States sources and claims a foreign tax credit under section 901, determined by applying the overall limitation under section 904(a)(2). The United States tax payable by N Corporation is determined as follows, the surtax exemption under section 11(d) being disregarded for purposes of simplification:

1978

Taxable income of N Corporation:		
U.S. sources		$100
Sources without the U.S.:		
Amount required to be included in N Corporation's gross income under sec. 951(a) with respect to B Corporation	$70	
Foreign income taxes deemed paid by N Corporation under section 960(a)(1) and included in N Corporation's gross income under sec. 78 ($30 × $70/$70)	30	100
Total taxable income		200
U.S. tax payable for 1978:		
U.S. tax before credit ($200 × 0.48)		96
Credit: Foreign income taxes of $38 ([$30 × $70/$70] + [$5 × $30/$30] + $3), but not to exceed overall limitation of $48 ($96 × $100/$200)		38
U.S. tax payable		58

1979

Taxable income of N Corporation, consisting of income from U.S. sources		100
U.S. tax before credit ($100 × 0.48)		48
Section 904(a)(2) overall limitation for 1979:		
Limitation for 1966 before increase under sec. 960(b)(1) ($48 × $0/$100)		0
Plus: Increase in overall limitation for 1979 under sec. 960(b)(1):		
Amount by which 1978 overall limitation was increased by reason of inclusion in N Corporation's gross income under sec. 951(a) for 1978 ($48—[($100 × 0.48) × $0/$100])	$48	
Less: Foreign income taxes allowed as a credit for 1978 which were allowable solely by reason of such sec. 951(a) inclusion ($38 − $0)	38	
Balance	10	
But: Such balance not to exceed foreign income taxes paid and deemed paid by N Corporation for 1979 with respect to $30 distribution excluded under sec. 959(a)(1) ([$5 × $30/$30] + $3)	8	8
Overall limitation for 1979		8
U.S. tax payable for 1979:		
U.S. tax before credit ($d100 +22 0.48)		48
Credit: Foreign income taxes of $8 ($3 + $5), but not to exceed overall limitation of $8 for 1979		8
U.S. tax payable		40

T.D. 7120, 6/3/71, amend T.D. 7649, 10/17/79.

§ 1.960-5 Credit for taxable year of inclusion binding for taxable year of exclusion.

(a) Taxes not allowed as a deduction for taxable year of exclusion. In the case of any taxpayer who—

(1) Chooses to claim a foreign tax credit as provided in section 901 for the taxable year for which he is required to include in gross income under section 951(a) an amount attributable to the earnings and profits of a controlled foreign corporation, and

(2) Does not choose to claim a foreign tax credit as provided in section 901 for a taxable year in which he receives an amount which is excluded from gross income under section 959(a)(1) and which is attributable to such earnings and profits of such controlled foreign corporation,

no deduction shall be allowed under section 164 for the taxable year of such exclusion for any foreign income taxes paid or accrued on or with respect to such excluded amount.

(b) Illustration. The application of this section may be illustrated by the following example:

Example. Domestic Corporation N owns all the one class of stock of controlled foreign corporation A. Both corporations use the calendar year as the taxable year. All of A Corporation's earnings and profits of $80 for 1965 (after payment of foreign income taxes of $20 on its total income of $100 for such year) are attributable to amounts required under section 951(a) to be included in N Corporation's gross income for 1965. For 1978, N Corporation chooses to claim a foreign tax credit for the $20 of foreign income taxes which for such year are paid by A Corporation and deemed paid by N Corporation under section 960(a)(1) and paragraph (c)(1) of § 1.960-1. For 1966, A Corporation distributes the entire $80 of 1978 earnings and profits, a foreign income tax of $8 being withheld therefrom. Although N Corporation does not choose to claim a foreign tax credit for 1979, it may not deduct such $8 of foreign income taxes under section 164. Corporation N may, however, deduct under such section a foreign income tax of $4 which is withheld from a distribution of $40 by A Corporation during 1979 from its 1979 earnings and profits.

T.D. 7120, 6/3/71, amend T.D. 7649, 10/17/79.

§ 1.960-6 Overpayments resulting from increase in limitation for taxable year of exclusion.

(a) Amount of overpayment. If an increase in the limitation under section 960(b)(1) and § 1.960-4 for a taxable year of exclusion exceeds the tax (determined before allowance of any credits against tax) imposed by chapter 1 of the Code for such year, the amount of such excess shall be deemed an overpayment of tax for such year and shall be refunded or credited to the taxpayer in accordance with chapter 65 (section 6401 and following) of the Code.

(b) Illustration. The application of this section may be illustrated by the following example:

Example. Domestic corporation N owns all the one class of stock of controlled foreign corporation A. Both corporations use the calendar year as the taxable year. For 1968, A Corporation has total income of $100,000 on which it pays foreign income taxes of $20,000. All of A Corporation's earnings and profits for 1968 of $80,000 are attributable to an amount which is required under section 951(a) to be included in N Corporation's gross income for 1965. By reason of such income inclusion N Corporation is deemed for 1978 to have paid under section 960(a)(1), and is required under section 78 to include in gross income for such year, the $20,000 ($20,000 × $80,000/$80,000) of foreign income taxes paid by A Corporation for such year. Corporation N also derives $100,000 taxable income from sources within the United States for 1978. For 1979, N Corporation has $25,000 of taxable income, all of which is derived from sources within the United States. No part of A Corporation's earnings and profits for 1979 is attributable to an amount required under section 951(a) to be included in N Corporation's gross income. During 1979, A Corporation makes one distribution consisting of its $80,000 earnings and profits for 1978, all of which is excluded under section 959(a)(1) from N Corporation's gross income for 1978, and from which distribution foreign income taxes of $10,000 are withheld. For 1978 and 1979, N Corporation claims the foreign tax credit under section 901, determined by applying the overall limitation under section 904(a)(2). The United States tax of N Corporation is determined as follows for such years assuming a corporate tax rate of 22 percent, a surtax of 26 percent and a surtax exemption of $25,000:

1978

Taxable income of N Corporation:		
U.S. sources		$100,000
Sources without the U.S.:		
Amount required to be included in N Corporation's gross income under sec. 951(a)	$80,000	
Foreign income taxes deemed paid by N Corporation under sec. 960(a)(1) and included in N Corporation's gross income under sec. 78 ($20,000 × $80,000/$80,000)	20,000	100,000
Total taxable income		200,000
U.S. tax payable for 1978:		
U.S. tax before credit ([$200,000 × 0.22] + [$175,000 × 0.26])		89,500
Credit: Foreign income taxes of $20,000, but not to exceed overall limitation of $44,750 ($89,500 × $100,000/$200,000)		20,000
U.S. tax payable		69,500

1979

Taxable income of N Corporation, consisting of income from U.S. sources		$ 25,000
U.S. tax before credit ($25,000 X 0.22)		5,500
Section 904(a)(2) overall limitation for 1979:		
Limitation for 1979 before increase under sec. 960(b)(1) ($5,500 × $0/$25,000)		0
Plus: Increase in overall limitation for 1966 under sec. 960(b)(1):		
Amount by which 1978 overall limitation was increased by reason of inclusion in N Corporation's gross income under sec. 951(a) for 1978 ($44,750—[$41,500 × $0/$100,000])	$44,750	
Less: Foreign income taxes allowed as a credit for 1978 which were allowable solely by reason of such sec. 951(a) inclusion ($20,000 − $0)	20,000	
Balance	24,750	
But: Such balance not to exceed foreign income taxes paid by N Corporation for 1979 with respect to $80,000 distribution excluded under sec. 959(a)(1) ($10,000 tax withheld)	10,000	10,000
Overall limitation for 1979		10,000
U.S. tax payable for 1979:		
U.S. tax before credit ($25,000 × 0.22)		5,500
Credit: Foreign income taxes of $10,000, but not to exceed overall limitation of $10,000 for 1979		10,000
U.S. tax payable		None
Overpayment for tax for 1979:		
Increase in limitation under sec. 960(b)(1) for 1966		10,000
Less: Tax imposed for 1979 under chapter 1 of the Code		5,500
Excess treated as overpayment		4,500

T.D. 7120, 6/3/71, amend T.D. 7649, 10/17/79.

§ 1.960-7 Effective dates.

(a) General rule. Except as provided in paragraph (b), the rules contained in §§ 1.960-1 – 1.960-6 shall apply to taxable years of foreign corporations beginning after December 31, 1962, and taxable years of U.S. corporate shareholders within which or with which the taxable year of such foreign corporation ends.

(b) Exception for less developed country corporations. If for any taxable year beginning after December 31, 1962, and before January 1, 1976, a first-tier foreign corporation qualified as a less developed country corporation as defined in 26 CFR 1.902-2 revised as of April 1, 1978, the rules pertaining to less developed country corporations contained in 26 CFR 1.960-1 – 1.960-6 revised as of April 1, 1978, shall apply to any amounts required to be included in gross income under section 951 for such taxable year.

(c) Third-tier credit. The rules contained in §§ 1.960-1 – 1.960-6 shall apply to amounts included in the gross income of a domestic corporation under section 951 with respect to the earnings and profits of third-tier corporations (as defined in § 1.960-1) in taxable years beginning after December 31, 1976.

T.D. 7649, 10/17/79, amend T.D. 7843, 11/5/82.

§ 1.961-1 Increase in basis of stock in controlled foreign corporations and of other property.

(a) Increase in basis. *(1) In general.* Except as provided in subparagraph (2) of this paragraph, the basis of a United States shareholder's—

(i) Stock in a controlled foreign corporation; or

(ii) Property (as defined in paragraph (b)(1) of this section) by reason of the ownership of which he is considered under section 958(a)(2) as owning stock in a controlled foreign corporation

shall be increased under section 961(a), as of the last day in the taxable year of such corporation on which it is a controlled foreign corporation, by the amount required to be included with respect to such stock or such property in such shareholder's gross income under section 951(a) for his taxable year in which or with which such taxable year of such corporation ends. The increase in basis provided by the preceding sentence shall be made only to the extent to which such amount required to be included in gross income under section 951(a) was so included in gross income.

(2) Limitation on amount of increase in case of election under section 962. In the case of a United States shareholder who makes the election under section 962 for the taxable year, the amount of the increase in basis provided by subparagraph (1) of this paragraph shall not exceed the amount of United States tax paid in accordance with such election with respect to the amounts included in such shareholder's gross income under section 951(a) for such year (as determined under § 1.962-1).

(b) Rules of application. *(1) Property defined.* The property of a United States shareholder referred to in paragraph (a)(1)(ii) of this section shall consist of—

(i) Stock in a foreign corporation;

(ii) An interest in a foreign partnership; or

(iii) A beneficial interest in a foreign estate or trust (as defined in section 7701(a)(31)).

(2) Increase with respect to each share of stock. Any increase under paragraph (a) of this section in the basis of a United States shareholder's stock in a foreign corporation shall be made in the amount included in gross income under section 951(a) or in the amount of United States tax paid in accordance with an election under section 962, as the case may be, with respect to each share of such stock.

(c) Illustration. The application of this section may be illustrated by the following examples:

Example (1). Domestic corporation M owns 800 of the 1,000 shares of the one class of stock in controlled foreign corporation R which owns all of the one class of stock in controlled foreign corporation S. Corporations M, R, and S use the calendar year as a taxable year. In 1964, S Corporation has $100,000 of earnings and profits after the payment of $11,250 of foreign income taxes, and $100,000 of subpart F income. Corporation R has no earnings and profits. With respect to S Corporation, M Corporation is required to include in gross income $80,000 (800/1,000 × $100,000) under section 951(a), and $9,000 ($80,000/$100,000 × $11,250) under section 78. On December 31, 1964, M Corporation must increase the basis of each share of its stock in R Corporation by $100 ($80,000/800).

Example (2). A, an individual United States shareholder, owns all of the 1,000 shares of the one class of stock in controlled foreign corporation T. Corporation T and A use the calendar year as a taxable year. In 1964, T Corporation has $80,000 of earnings and profits after the payment of $20,000 of foreign income taxes, and $80,000 of subpart F income. A makes the election under section 962 for 1964 and in accordance with such election pays a United States tax of $23,000 with respect to the $80,000 included in his gross income under section 951(a). On December 31, 1964, A must increase the basis of each share of his stock in T Corporation by $23 ($23,000/1,000).

T.D. 6850, 9/15/65.

PAR. 6. Section 1.961-1 is revised to read as follows:

Proposed § 1.961-1 Increase in basis of stock in CFCs and of other property. [*For Preamble, see ¶ 152,795*]

(a) Definitions. See § 1.959-1(b) for a list of defined terms applicable to § 1.961-1 through § 1.961-4.

(b) Increase in basis. *(1) In general.* Except as provided in paragraphs (b)(2) and (b)(3) of this section, the adjusted basis of a United States shareholder's stock in a CFC or property (as defined in paragraph (c)(1) of this section) by reason of the ownership of which such United States shareholder is considered under section 958(a) as owning stock in a CFC shall be increased under section 961(a) each time, and to the extent that, such United States shareholder's previously taxed earnings and profits account with respect to the stock in that CFC is increased pursuant to the steps outlined in § 1.959-3(e)(2).

(2) Limitation on amount of increase in case of election under section 962. [Reserved].

(3) Deemed inclusions under sections 1293(c) and 959(e). Paragraph (b)(1) of this section shall not apply in the case of a deemed section 951(a) inclusion pursuant to section 1293(c) or 959(e).

(c) Rules of application. *(1) Property defined.* The property of a United States shareholder referred to in paragraph (b)(1) of this section shall consist of—

(i) Stock in a foreign corporation;

(ii) An interest in a foreign partnership; or

(iii) A beneficial or ownership interest in a foreign estate or trust (as defined in section 7701(a)(31)).

(2) Increase with respect to each share or ownership unit. Any increase under paragraph (b) of this section in the basis of a United States shareholder's stock in a foreign corporation or property (as defined in paragraph (c)(1) of this section) by reason of the ownership of which such United States shareholder is considered under section 958(a) as owning stock in a foreign corporation shall be made on a pro rata basis with respect to each share of such stock or each ownership unit of such property.

(3) Translation rules. For purposes of determining an increase in basis under this section, in cases in which the previously taxed earnings and profits account is maintained in a non-United States dollar functional currency, section 951(a) inclusions shall be translated into United States dollars at the appropriate exchange rate as described in section 989(b). Any other increase in basis pursuant to paragraph (b) of this section (for example, a basis increase resulting from the application of § 1.959-3(f) or (g)) shall be in the amount of the transferor's dollar basis attributable to the previously taxed earnings and profits transferred.

(c [sic d]) Examples. The application of this section is illustrated by the following examples:

Example (1). Basis adjustment for income inclusion. (i) Facts. DP, a United States shareholder, owns 800 of the 1,000 shares of the one class of stock in FC and has a basis of $50 in each of its shares. DP and FC use the calendar year as a taxable year and FC is a CFC. FC uses the u as its functional currency. The average exchange rate for year 1 is 1u = $1. In year 1, its first year of operation, FC has 100,000u of subpart F income after the payment of 11,250u of foreign income taxes. DP is required to include in gross income 80,000u (800/1,000 x 100,000u) equal to $80,000 under section 951(a), and 9,000u (80,000u/100,000u x 11,250u) equal to $9,000 under section 78.

(ii) Analysis. On December 31, of year 1, DP increases the section 959(c)(2) earnings and profits in its previously taxed earnings and profits account with respect to its stock in FC by 80,000u pursuant to § 1.959-3(e)(2)(i) to reflect the inclusion of 80,000u, or $80,000, in DP's gross income pursuant to section 959(a), and correspondingly increases the basis of each share of its stock in FC by $100 ($80,000/800) from $50 to $150 pursuant to paragraphs (b)(1) and (c)(2) of this section.

Example (2). Sale of CFC stock. (i) Facts. Assume the same facts as in Example 1, except that in year 2, DP sells all of its stock in FC to DP2, a United States person that is DP's successor in interest (as defined in § 1.959-1(b)(5)), for $200 per share. At the time of sale, the exchange rate is 1u = $1 and DP has a basis of $150 per share in its FC stock and a previously taxed earnings and profits account with respect to its FC stock consisting of 80,000u of section 959(c)(2) earnings and profits with a dollar basis of $80,000. Also, at the time of sale, FC has 50,000u of non-previously taxed earnings and profits, attributable to taxable years of FC beginning on or after December 31, 1962 during which FC was a CFC and DP held its shares of stock in FC.

(ii) Analysis. Pursuant to section 1248(a), because FC has 40,000u of non-previously taxed earnings and profits attributable to DP's stock (50,000u x 800/1,000), the $40,000 of gain, equal to 40,000u, recognized by DP on the sale of it stock (($200-$150) x 800) is included in DP's gross income as a dividend. Consequently, the section 959(c)(2) earnings and profits in DP's previously taxed earnings and profits account with respect to its stock in FC are increased from 80,000u to 120,000u pursuant to § 1.959-3(e)(2)(i). DP's basis in each share of its stock in FC is not adjusted, pursuant to paragraph (b)(3) of this section, because the adjustment to DP's previously taxed earnings and profits account results from a deemed section 951(a) inclusion pursuant to section 959(e). Upon the sale, DP2 acquires a previously taxed earnings and profits account with respect to the FC stock of 120,000u pursuant to § 1.959-1(d)(2)(i) and can utilize the account if it qualifies as a successor in interest under § 1.959-1(b)(5). DP2 takes a cost basis of $200 per share in the FC stock pursuant to section 1012.

§ 1.961-2 Reduction in basis of stock in foreign corporations and of other property.

(a) Reduction in basis. *(1) In general.* Except as provided in subparagraph (2) of this paragraph, the adjusted basis of a United States person's—

(i) Stock in a foreign corporation;

(ii) Interest in a foreign partnership; or

(iii) Beneficial interest in a foreign estate or trust (as defined in section 7701(a)(31)),

with respect to which such United States person receives an amount which is excluded from gross income under section 959(a), shall be reduced under section 961(b), as of the time such person receives such excluded amount, by the sum of the amount so excluded and any income, war profits, or excess profits taxes imposed by any foreign country or possession of the United States on or with respect to the earnings and profits attributable to such excluded amount when such earnings and profits were actually distributed directly or indirectly through a chain of ownership described in section 958(a)(2).

(2) Limitation on amount of reduction in case of election under section 962. In the case of a distribution of earnings and profits attributable to amounts with respect to which an election under section 962 has been made, the amount of the reduction in basis provided by subparagraph (1) of this paragraph shall not exceed the sum of—

(i) The amount of such distribution which is excluded from gross income under section 959(a) after the application of section 962(d) and § 1.962-3; and

(ii) Any income, war profits, or excess profits taxes imposed by any foreign country or possession of the United States on or with respect to the earnings and profits attributable to such excluded amount when such earnings and profits were actually distributed directly or indirectly through a chain of ownership described in section 958(a)(2).

(b) Reduction with respect to each share of stock. Any reduction under paragraph (a) of this section in the adjusted basis of a United States person's stock in a foreign corporation shall be made with respect to each share of such stock in the sum of—

(1) (i) The amount excluded from gross income under section 959(a); or

(ii) The amount excluded from gross income under section 959(a) after the application of section 962(d) and § 1.962-3; and

(2) The amount of any income, war profits, or excess profits taxes imposed by any foreign country or possession of the United States on or with respect to the earnings and profits attributable to such excluded amount when such earnings and profits were actually distributed directly or indirectly through a chain of ownership described in section 958(a)(2).

(c) Amount in excess of basis. To the extent that the amount of the reduction in the adjusted basis of property provided by paragraph (a) of this section exceeds such adjusted basis, the amount shall be treated as gain from the sale or exchange of property.

(d) Illustration. The application of this section may be illustrated by the following examples:

Example (1). (a) Domestic corporation M owns all of the 1,000 shares of the one class of stock in controlled foreign corporation R, which owns all of the 500 shares of the one class of stock in controlled foreign corporation S. Each share of M Corporation's stock in R Corporation has a basis of $200. Corporations M, R, and S use the calendar year as a taxable year. In 1963, S Corporation has $100,000 of earnings and profits after the payment of $50,000 of foreign income taxes and $100,000 of subpart F income. For 1963, M Corporation includes $100,000 in gross income under section 951(a) with respect to S Corporation. In accordance with the provisions of § 1.961-1, M Corporation increases the basis of each of its 1,000 shares of stock in R Corporation to $300 ($200 + $100,000/1,000) as of December 31, 1963.

(b) On July 31, 1964, M Corporation sells 250 of its shares of stock in R Corporation to domestic corporation N at a price of $350 per share. Corporation N satisfies the requirements of paragraph (d) of § 1.959-1 so as to qualify as M Corporation's successor in interest. On September 30, 1964, the earnings and profits attributable to the $100,000 included in M Corporation's gross income under section 951(a) for 1963 are distributed to R Corporation which incurs a withholding tax of $10,000 on such distribution (10 percent of $100,000) and an additional foreign income tax of 33⅓ percent or $30,000 by reason of the inclusion of the net distribution of $90,000 ($100,000 minus $10,000) in its taxable income for 1964. On June 30, 1965, R Corporation distributes the remaining $60,000 of such earnings and profits to corporations M and N: Corporation M receives $45,000 (750/1,000 × $60,000) and excludes such amount from gross income under section 959(a); Corporation N receives $15,000 (250/1,000 × $60,000) and, as M Corporation's successor in interest, excludes such amount from gross income under section 959(a). As of June 30, 1965, M Corporation must reduce the adjusted basis of each of its 750 shares of stock in R Corporation to $200 ($300 minus ($45,000/750 + $10,000/1,000 + $30,000/1,000)); and N Corporation must reduce the basis of each of its 250 shares of stock in R Corporation to $250 ($350 minus ($15,000/250 + $10,000/1,000 + $30,000/1,000)).

Example (2). The facts are the same as in paragraph (a) of example (1), except that in addition, on July 31, 1964, R Corporation sells its 500 shares of stock in S Corporation to domestic corporation P at a price of $600 per share. Corporation P satisfies the requirements of paragraph (d) of § 1.959-1 so as to qualify as M Corporation's successor in interest. On September 30, 1964, S Corporation distributes $100,000 of earnings and profits to P Corporation, which earnings and profits are attributable to the $100,000 included in M Corporation's gross income under section 951(a) for 1963. Corporation P incurs a withholding tax of $10,000 on the distribution from S Corporation (10 percent of $100,000). As M Corporation's successor in interest, P Corporation excludes the $90,000 it receives from gross income under section 959(a). As of September 30, 1964, P Corporation must reduce the basis of each of its 500 shares of stock in S Corporation to $400 ($600 minus ($90,000/500 + $10,000/500)).

T.D. 6850, 9/15/65.

PAR. 7. Section 1.961-2 is revised to read as follows:

Proposed § 1.961-2 Reduction in basis of stock in foreign corporations and of other property. [*For Preamble, see ¶ 152,795*]

(a) Reduction in basis. *(1) In general.* Except as provided in paragraph (a)(2) of this section, the adjusted basis of a covered shareholder's stock in a foreign corporation or property (as defined in § 1.961-1(c)) by reason of the ownership of which such covered shareholder is considered under section 958(a) as owning stock in a foreign corporation shall be reduced under section 961(b) each time, and to the extent, that such covered shareholder's dollar basis in a previously taxed earnings and profits account with respect to the stock in such foreign corporation is decreased pursuant to the steps outlined in § 1.959-3(e)(2) and shall also be reduced by the dollar amount of any foreign income taxes allowed as a credit under section 960(a)(3) with respect to the earnings and profits accounted for by that decrease.

(2) Limitation on amount of reduction in case of election under section 962. [Reserved].

(b) Rules of application. *(1) Reduction with respect to each ownership unit.* Any reduction under paragraph (a) of this section in the adjusted basis of a covered shareholder's stock in a foreign corporation or property (as defined in paragraph (b)(1) of this section) by reason of the ownership of which it is considered under section 958(a) as owning stock in a foreign corporation shall be made on a pro rata basis with respect to each share of such stock or each ownership unit of such property.

(2) Translation rules. For purposes of determining a decrease in basis under this section, in cases in which the previously taxed earnings and profits account is maintained in a non-United States dollar functional currency, distributions of previously taxed earnings and profits shall be translated using the dollar basis of the earnings distributed. See § 1.959-3(b)(1) and (b)(3)(ii) for rules regarding the dollar basis of previously taxed earnings and profits. If the covered shareholder elects to maintain dollar basis accounts of previously taxed earnings and profits as described in § 1.959-3(b)(3)(ii), the dollar basis of the earnings distributed shall be determined according to the following formula: (functional currency distributed/total functional currency previously taxed earnings and profits) x total dollar basis of previously taxed earnings and profits. See section 989(b)(1) for the appropriate exchange rate applicable to distributions for purposes of section 986(c).

(c) Amount in excess of basis. To the extent that the amount of the reduction in the adjusted basis of property provided by paragraph (a) of this section exceeds such adjusted basis, the amount shall be treated as gain from the sale or exchange of property.

(d) Examples. The application of this section is illustrated by the following examples:

Example (1). Successor in interest. (i) Facts. DP, a United States shareholder, owns all of the 1,000 shares of the one class of stock in FC, which owns all of the 500 shares of the one class of stock in FS. Each share of DP's stock in FC has a basis of $200. DP, FC, and FS use the calendar year as a taxable year and FC and FS are CFCs throughout the period here involved. FC and FS both use the u as their functional currency. In year 1, FS has 100,000u of subpart F income after the payment of 50,000u of foreign income taxes. The average exchange rate for year 1 and year 2 is 1u = $1. For year 1, DP includes 100,000u in gross income under section 951(a) with respect to FS. In accordance with the provisions of § 1.961-1, DP increases the basis of each of its 1,000 shares of stock in FC to $300 ($200 + $100,000/1,000) as of December 31, of year 1. On July 31 of year 2, DP sells 250 of its shares of stock in FC to domestic corporation DT at a price of $350 per share. DT satisfies the requirements of paragraph (d) of § 1.959-1 so as to qualify as DP's successor in interest. On September 30 of year 2, the earnings and profits attributable to the 100,000u included in DP's gross income under section 951(a) for year 1 are distributed to FC which incurs a withholding tax of 10,000u on such distribution (10% of 100,000u) and an additional foreign income tax of 33\1/3\% or 30,000u by reason of the inclusion of the net distribution of 90,000u (100,000u - 10,000u) in its taxable income for year 2. On June 30 of year 3, FC distributes the remaining 60,000u of such earnings and profits to DP and DT: DP receives 45,000u (750/1,000 x 60,000u) and excludes such amount from gross income under section 959(a) and § 1.959-1(c); DT receives 15,000u (250/1,000 x 60,000u) and, as DP's successor in interest, excludes such amount from gross income under section 959(a) and § 1.959-1(c).

(ii) Analysis. As of June 30 of year 3, DP must reduce the adjusted basis of each of its 750 shares of stock in FC to $200 ($300 minus ($45,000/750 + $10,000/1,000 + $30,000/1,000)); and DT must reduce the basis of each of its 250 shares of stock in FC to $250 ($350 minus ($15,000/250 + $10,000/1,000 + $30,000/1,000)).

Example (2). Sale of lower-tier CFC. (i) Facts. Assume the same facts as in Example 1, except that in addition, on July 31 of year 2, FC sells its 500 shares of stock in FS to domestic corporation DT2 at a price of $600 per share. DT2 satisfies the requirements of § 1.959-1(b)(5) so as to qualify as DP's successor in interest. On September 30 of year 2, FS distributes 100,000u of earnings and profits to DT2, which earnings and profits are attributable to the 100,000u included in DP's gross income under section 951(a) for year 1. As DP's successor in interest, DT2 excludes the 100,000u it receives from gross income under section 959(a) and § 1.959-1(c).

(ii) Analysis. As of September 30 of year 2, DT2 must reduce the basis of each of its 500 shares of stock in FS to $400 ($600 minus ($100,000/500)).

Example (3). Section 956 amount. (i) Facts. DP, a United States shareholder, owns all of the 1,000 shares of the one class of stock in FC, which owns all of the 500 shares of the one class of stock in FS. Each share of DP's stock in FC has a basis of $200. DP, FC, and FS use the calendar year as a taxable year and FC and FS are CFCs throughout the period here involved. FC and FS both use the u as their functional currency. In year 1, FS has 100,000u of subpart F income after the payment of 50,000u of foreign income taxes. The average exchange rate for year 1 and year 2 is 1u = $1. For year 1, DP includes 100,000u in gross income under section 951(a) with respect to FS. In accordance with the provisions of § 1.959-3(e)(2)(i) and § 1.961-1, DP increases the section 959(c)(2) earnings and profits in its earnings and profits account with respect to its FC stock by 100,000u and correspondingly adjusts the basis of each of its 1,000 shares of stock in FC to $300 ($200+$100,000/1,000) as of December 31 of year 1. In year 2, DP has a section 956 amount with respect to its stock in FC of 100,000u.

(ii) Analysis. On December 31 of year 2, DP reclassifies 100,000u of section 959(c)(2) earnings and profits as section 959(c)(1) earnings and profits pursuant to § 1.959-3(e)(2)(iv). DP's basis in each of its 1,000 shares of stock in FC remains unchanged at $300 per share.

Proposed § 1.961-3 Basis adjustments in stock held by foreign corporation. [*For Preamble, see ¶ 152,795*]

(a) Where the upper-tier entity is 100% owned by a single United States shareholder. *(1) In general.* If a United States shareholder is treated under section 958(a) as owning stock in a CFC (lower-tier CFC) by reason of owning, either directly or pursuant to the application of section 958(a), stock in one or more other CFCs (each an "upper-tier CFC"), any increase to such United States shareholder's basis in stock or other property under § 1.961-1 of this section resulting from an adjustment to such United States shareholder's previously taxed earnings and profits account with respect to its stock in the lower-tier CFC shall also be made to each upper-tier CFC's basis in either the stock in the lower-tier CFC or the property by reason of which it is considered to own stock in the lower-tier CFC under section 958(a), but only for purposes of determining the amount included under section 951 in the gross income of such United States shareholder or its successor in interest. In addition, any downward adjustment to such United States shareholder's (or its successor in interest's) previously taxed earnings and profits account with respect to its stock in a distributor under § 1.959-3(e)(3) shall result in a corresponding reduction of the basis of the distributee's stock in the distributor for purposes of determining the amount included in such United States shareholder's gross income under section 951(a).

(2) Examples. The application of this paragraph (a) is illustrated by the following examples:

Example (1). Intercorporate dividend from lower-tier CFC to upper-tier CFC. (i) Facts. DP, a United States shareholder, owns all of the stock in FC, a CFC, and FC owns all of the stock in FS, a CFC. DP, FC and FS all use the calendar year as their taxable year and FC and FS both use the U.S. dollar as their functional currency. In year 1, FS has $100x of subpart F income that is included in DP's gross income under section 951(a)(1). In year 2, FS pays a dividend of $100x to FC.

(ii) Analysis. On December 31 of year 1, the section 959(c)(2) earnings and profits in DP's previously taxed earnings and profits account with respect to its stock in FS are increased by $100x pursuant to § 1.959-3(e)(2)(i) to reflect the inclusion of $100x in DP's gross income under section 951(a)(1)(A). DP's basis in its stock in FC is correspondingly increased by $100x pursuant to § 1.961-1(b). FC's basis in its stock in FS is also increased by $100x pursuant to paragraph (a) of this section, but only for purposes of determining the amount included in DP's gross income under section 951. At the end of year 2, the section 959(c)(2) earnings and profits in DP's previously taxed earnings and profits account with respect to its stock in FS are decreased by $100x and its previously taxed earnings and profits account with respect to its stock in FC are increased by $100x pursuant to § 1.959-3(e)(3) to reflect the transfer of the previously taxed earnings and profits from FS to FC. The $100x distribution is excluded from FC's income for purposes of determining the amount included in DP's gross income pursuant to § 1.959-2(a). FC's basis in its stock in FS, for purposes of determining the amount included in DP's gross income under section 951, is decreased by $100x pursuant to paragraph (a) of this section.

Example (2). Sale of upper-tier CFC stock. (i) Facts. DP, a United States shareholder, owns all of the stock in FC, a CFC. FC owns all of the stock in FS1, a CFC, and FS1 owns all of the stock in FS2, a CFC. DP, FC, FS1, and FS2 all use the calendar year as their taxable year and FC, FS1 and FS2 all use the U.S. dollar as their functional currency. In year 1, FS2 has $100x of subpart F income which is included in DP's gross income under section 951(a)(1)(A). In year 2, FC sells FS1 to FT, a nonresident alien, and recognizes $100x of gain on the sale.

(ii) Analysis. On December 31 of year 1, the section 959(c)(2) earnings and profits in DP's previously taxed earnings and profits account with respect to its stock in FS2 are increased by $100x pursuant to § 1.959-3(e)(2)(i) to reflect the inclusion of $100x in DP's gross income under section 951(a)(1). DP's basis in its stock in FC is correspondingly increased by $100x under § 1.961-1(b). FC's basis in its stock in FS1 and FS1's basis in its stock in FS2 are also each increased by $100x under paragraph (a) of this section, but only for purposes of determining the amount included in the gross income of DP under section 951. In year 2, the $100x of gain on FC's sale of FS1 stock would be subpart F income that would be includible in DP gross income under section 951(a)(1)(A). However, since FC has an additional $100x of basis in its stock in FS1 for purposes of determining the amount included in DP's gross income under section 951, the sale of FS1 by FC does not generate any subpart F income to DP.

(b) Exception where the upper-tier entity is less than 100 percent owned by a single United States shareholder. *(1) In general.* If United States shareholders are treated, under section 958(a), as owning stock in a CFC (lower-tier CFC) by reason of owning, either directly or pursuant to the application of section 958(a), stock in one or more other CFCs (each an "upper-tier CFC"), and if, in the aggregate, the lower-tier CFC is less than wholly indirectly owned by a single United States shareholder, any increase to any United

States shareholder's basis in stock or other property under § 1.961-1(b) of this section resulting from an increase to such United States shareholder's previously taxed earnings and profits account with respect to its stock in such lower-tier CFC shall result in an increase to each upper-tier CFC's basis in either the stock in the lower-tier CFC or the property by reason of which such upper-tier CFC is considered to own stock in the lower-tier CFC under section 958(a), but only for purposes of determining the amount included under section 951 in the gross income of such United States shareholder or its successor in interest. The amount of the increase to each upper-tier CFC's basis in either the stock in the lower-tier CFC or the property by reason of which such upper-tier CFC is considered to own stock in the lower-tier CFC under section 958(a) shall be equal to the amount that would be excluded from the gross income of such upper-tier CFC pursuant to section 959(b) and § 1.959-2(a) if the amount that gave rise to the adjustment to the United States shareholder's previously taxed earnings and profits account with respect to its stock in the lower-tier CFC were actually distributed through a chain of ownership to such upper-tier CFC. In addition, any decrease to such United States shareholder's (or successor in interest's) previously taxed earnings and profits account with respect to its stock in a distributor under § 1.959-3(e)(3) shall result in a corresponding reduction of the basis of the distributee's stock in the distributor. The reduction of the basis of the distributee's stock in the distributor shall be equal to the amount that would be excluded from the gross income of the distributee pursuant to section 959(b) and § 1.959-2(a).

(2) Example. The application of this paragraph (b) is illustrated by the following example:

Example. Less than wholly owned CFC. (i) Facts. DP, a United States shareholder, owns 70%, and FP, a nonresident alien, owns 30% of the stock in FC, a CFC. FC in turn owns 100% of the stock in FS, a CFC. Each of DP, FC, FN and FS use the calendar year as their taxable year and both FC and FS use the U.S. dollar as their functional currency. Entering year 1, DP has a basis of $50x in FC and FC has a basis of $50x in FS. In year 1, FS earns $100x of subpart F income. In year 2, FC sells FS for $150x.

(ii) Analysis. On December 31 of year 1, DP includes $70x of the $100x of subpart F income earned by FS in gross income under section 951(a)(1)(A). DP increases its section 959(c)(2) earnings and profits in its earnings and profits account with respect to its stock in FS by $70x pursuant to § 1.959-3(e)(2)(i). DP increases its basis in FC from $50x to $120x pursuant to § 1.961-1(b). FC increases its basis in FS from $50x to $150x pursuant to paragraph (b)(1) of this section (but only for purposes of determining FC's subpart F income with respect to DP) because if the $100x amount of subpart F income of FS that caused the $70x increase to DP's previously taxed earnings and profits account with respect to its stock in FS had been distributed to FC, the entire $100x would be excluded from FC's gross income pursuant to section 959(b) and § 1.959-2(a) for purposes of determining DP's inclusion under section 951(a)(1)(A). In year 2, when FC sells FS, for purposes of determining DP's subpart F inclusion, FC is treated as recognizing $0 on the sale ($150x sale proceeds-$150x basis). Therefore, DP includes $0 in income under section 951(a)(1)(A) as a result of the sale. Although the sale does not generate gain for purposes of determining DP's subpart F inclusion, it does cause FC's non-previously taxed earnings and profits to be increased by $100x ($150x sale proceeds-$50x basis).

(c) Translation rules. Rules similar to those provided in § 1.961-1(c)(3) and § 1.961-2(b)(3) shall apply for purposes of determining the exchange rates used to reflect any change to the basis of stock or other property under this section.

Proposed § 1.961-4 Section 304 transactions. [*For Preamble, see ¶ 152,795*]

(a) Deemed redemption treated as a distribution. *(1) In general.* In the case of a stock acquisition described in section 304(a)(1) that is treated as a distribution of earnings and profits of a foreign acquiring corporation or a foreign issuing corporation or both, basis adjustments shall be made in accordance with the rules of §§ 1.961-1, 1.961-2, and 1.961-3.

(2) Examples. The application of this section is illustrated by the following examples:

Example (1). Cross-chain acquisition of first-tier CFC. (i) Facts. DP, a domestic corporation, owns all of the stock in DS, a domestic corporation, and F1, a CFC. DS owns all of the stock in F2, a CFC. DP, DS, F1 and F2 all use the calendar year as their taxable year and F1 and F2 use the U.S. dollar as their functional currency. During year 1, F1 purchases all of the stock in F2 from DS for $80x in a transaction described in section 304(a)(1). At the end of year 1, before taking into account the purchase of F2's stock, DP has a previously taxed earnings and profits account consisting of $20x of section 959(c)(2) earnings and profits with respect to its stock in F1, and F1 has section 959(c)(2) earnings and profits of $20x and non-previously taxed earnings and profits of $10x. At the end of year 1, before taking into account the purchase of F2's stock, DS has a previously taxed earnings and profits account consisting of $50x of section 959(c)(2) earnings and profits with respect to its stock in F2 and F2 has section 959(c)(2) earnings and profits of $50x and non-previously taxed earnings and profits of $0. Before taking into account the purchase of F2's stock, DP's basis in F1's stock is $30x and DS's basis in F2's stock is $60x.

(ii) Analysis. Under section 304(a)(1), DS is deemed to have transferred the F2 stock to F1 in exchange for F1 stock in a transaction to which section 351(a) applies, and F1 is treated as having redeemed, for $80x, the F1 stock hypothetically issued to DS. The payment of $80x is treated as a distribution to which section 301 applies. Under section 304(b)(2), the determination of the amount which is a dividend is made as if the distribution were made, first, by F1 to the extent of its earnings and profits ($30x), and then by F2 to the extent of its earnings and profits ($50x). Before taking into account the deemed distributions, DS had a previously taxed earnings and profits account of $50x with respect to its stock in F2, and DP had a previously taxed earnings and profits account of $20x with respect to its stock in F1. Under § 1.959-3(h)(4)(i), DS is deemed to have a previously taxed earnings and profits account with respect to stock in F1. Under § 1.959-3(g)(1), the section 959(c)(2) earnings and profits in DP's previously taxed earnings and profits account with respect to F1 stock are reduced from $20x to $0. As a result, DP's basis in F1's stock is reduced from $30x to $10x under § 1.961-2(a). The deemed distribution of earnings and profits by F2 causes the section 959(c)(2) earnings and profits in DS's previously taxed earnings and profits account with respect to F2 stock to be reduced from $50x to $0. Under § 1.961-2(a) and § 1.961-3(a), F1's basis in its newly acquired F2's stock is reduced from $60x to $10x. F1 has a transferred basis of $10x in F2's stock.

Example (2). Cross-chain acquisition of lower-tier CFC. (i) Facts. DP, a domestic corporation, owns all of the stock in two CFCs, FX and FY. FX owns all of the stock in FZ, a CFC. FX, FY and FZ use the U.S. dollar as their functional currency. During year 1, FY purchases all of the stock in FZ from FX for $80x in a transaction described in section 304(a)(1). On December 31 of year 1, before taking into account the purchase of FZ's stock, FY has section 959(c)(2) earnings and profits of $20x and non-previously taxed earnings and profits of $10x, and FZ has section 959(c)(2) earnings and profits of $50x and non-previously taxed earnings and profits of $0. Before taking into account FX's purchase of FZ's stock, DP's basis in FX's stock is $60x; DP's basis in FY's stock is $30x; and FX's basis in FZ's stock, for purposes of determining the amount includible in DP's gross income under section 951(a), is $60x.

(ii) Analysis. Under section 304(a)(1), FX is deemed to have transferred the FZ stock to FY in exchange for FY stock in a transaction to which section 351(a) applies, and FY is treated as having redeemed, for $80x, the FY stock hypothetically issued to FX. The payment of $80x is treated as a distribution of property to which section 301 applies. Under section 304(b)(2), the determination of the amount which is a dividend is made as if the distribution were made, first, by FY to the extent of its earnings and profits, $30x, and then by FX to the extent of its earnings and profits, $50x. Under § 1.959-2(b), FX is deemed to receive the distributions from FY and FZ through a chain of ownership described in section 958(a), and $70x is excluded from FX's gross income under section 959(b) and § 1.959-2(a). Under § 1.959-3(e)(3), the section 959(c)(2) earnings and profits in DP's previously taxed earnings and profits account for the stock in FY are reduced from $20x to $0; the section 959(c)(2) earnings and profits in DP's previously taxed earnings and profits account for the stock in FZ are reduced from $50x to $0; and the section 959(c)(2) earnings and profits in DP's previously taxed earnings and profits account for the stock in FX are increased from $0 to $70x (and such account is further increased to $80x due to the inclusion of $10x of subpart F income in DP's gross income under section 951(a)). Under § 1.961-2(a), DP's basis in the stock in FY is reduced from $30x to $10x. DP's basis in the stock in FX is first reduced by $50x under § 1.961-2(a), and then increased by $80x under § 1.961-1(b), for a net increase of $30x, to $90x. Under § 1.961-3(a), FY's basis in the stock in FZ, for purposes of determining the amount includible in DP's gross income under section 951(a), is reduced by $50x to $10x.

§ 1.962-1 Limitation of tax for individuals on amounts included in gross income under section 951(a).

Caution: The Treasury has not yet amended Reg § 1.962-1 to reflect changes made by P.L. 100-647.

(a) In general. An individual United States shareholder may, in accordance with § 1.962-2, elect to have the provisions of section 962 apply for his taxable year. In such case—

(1) The tax imposed under chapter 1 of the Internal Revenue Code on all amounts which are included in his gross income for such taxable year under section 951(a) shall (in lieu of the tax determined under section 1) be an amount equal to the tax which would be imposed under section 11 if such amounts were received by a domestic corporation (determined in accordance with paragraph (b)(1) of this section), and

(2) For purposes of applying section 960(a)(1) (relating to foreign tax credit) such amounts shall be treated as if received by a domestic corporation (as provided in paragraph (b)(2) of this section).

Thus, an individual United States shareholder may elect to be subject to tax at corporate rates on amounts included in his gross income under section 951(a) and to have the benefit of a credit for certain foreign taxes paid with respect to the earnings and profits attributable to such amounts. Section 962 also provides rules for the treatment of an actual distribution of earnings and profits previously taxed in accordance with an election of the benefits of this section. See § 1.962-3. For transitional rules for certain taxable years, see § 1.962-4.

(b) Rules of application. For purposes of this section—

(1) Application of section 11. For purposes of applying section 11 for a taxable year as provided in paragraph (a)(1) of this section in the case of an electing United States shareholder—

(i) Determination of taxable income. The term "taxable income" as used in section 11 shall mean the sum of—

(a) All amounts required to be included in his gross income under section 951(a) for such taxable year; plus

(b) All amounts which would be required to be included in his gross income under section 78 for such taxable year with respect to the amounts referred to in (a) of this subdivision if such shareholder were a domestic corporation.

For purposes of this section, such sum shall not be reduced by any deduction of the United States shareholder even if such shareholder's deductions exceed his gross income.

(ii) Limitation on surtax exemption. The surtax exemption provided by section 11(c) shall not exceed an amount which bears the same ratio to $25,000 ($50,000 in the case of a taxable year ending after December 31, 1974, and before January 1, 1976) as the amounts included in his gross income under section 951(a) for the taxable year bear to his pro rata share of the earnings and profits for the taxable year of all controlled foreign corporations with respect to which such United States shareholder includes any amount in his gross income under section 951(a) for the taxable year.

(2) Allowance of foreign tax credit. (i) In general. Subject to the applicable limitation of section 904 and to the provisions of this subparagraph, there shall be allowed as a credit against the United States tax on the amounts described in subparagraph (1)(i) of this paragraph the foreign income, war profits, and excess profits taxes deemed paid under section 960(a)(1) by the electing United States shareholder with respect to such amounts.

(ii) Application of section 960(a)(1). In applying section 960(a)(1) for purposes of this subparagraph in the case of an electing United States shareholder, the term "domestic corporation" as used in sections 960(a)(1) and 78, and the term "corporation" as used in section 901, shall be treated as referring to such shareholder with respect to the amounts described in subparagraph (1)(i) of this paragraph.

(iii) Carryback and carryover of excess tax deemed paid. For purposes of this subparagraph, any amount by which the foreign income, war profits, and excess profits taxes deemed paid by the electing United States shareholder for any taxable year under section 960(a)(1) exceed the limitation determined under subdivision (iv)(a) of this subparagraph shall be treated as a carryback and carryover of excess tax paid under section 904(d), except that in no case shall excess tax paid be deemed paid in a taxable year if an election under section 962 by such shareholder does not apply for such taxable year. Such carrybacks and carryovers shall be applied only against the United States tax on amounts described in subparagraph (1)(i) of this paragraph.

(iv) Limitation on credit. For purposes of determining the limitation under section 904 on the amount of the credit for foreign income, war profits, and excess profits taxes—

(a) Deemed paid with respect to amounts described in subparagraph (1)(i) of this paragraph, the electing United States shareholder's taxable income shall be considered to consist only of the amounts described in such subparagraph (1)(i), and

(b) Paid with respect to amounts other than amounts described in subparagraph (1)(i) of this paragraph, the electing United States shareholder's taxable income shall be considered to consist only of amounts other than the amounts described in such subparagraph (1)(i).

(v) Effect of choosing benefits of sections 901 to 905. The provisions of this subparagraph shall apply for a taxable year whether or not the electing United States shareholder chooses the benefits of subpart A of part III of subchapter N of Chapter 1 (sections 901 to 905) of the Internal Revenue Code for such year.

(c) Illustration. The application of this section may be illustrated by the following example:

Example. Throughout his taxable year ending December 31, 1964, A, an unmarried individual who is not the head of a household, owns 60 of the 100 shares of the one class of stock in foreign corporation M and 80 of the 100 shares of the one class of stock in foreign corporation N. A and corporations M and N use the calendar year as a taxable year, corporations M and N are controlled foreign corporations throughout the period here involved, and neither corporation is a less developed country corporation. The earnings and profits and subpart F income of, and the foreign income taxes paid by, such corporations for 1964 are as follows:

	M	N
Pretax earnings and profits	$500,000	$1,200,000
Foreign income taxes	200,000	400,000
Earnings and profits	300,000	800,000
Subpart F income	150,000	750,000

Apart from his section 951(a) income, A has gross income of $200,600 and $100,000 of deductions attributable to such income. He is required to include $90,000 (0.60 × $150,000) in gross income under section 951(a) with respect to M Corporation and $600,000 (0.80 × $750,000) with respect to N Corporation. A elects to have the provisions of section 962 apply for 1964 and computes his tax as follows:

Tax on amounts included under sec. 951(a):			
Income under sec. 951(a) from M Corporation	$ 90,000		
Gross-up under secs. 960(a)(1) and 78 ($90,000/$300,000 × $200,000)	60,000		
Income under sec. 951(a) from N Corporation	600,000		
Gross-up under secs. 960(a)(1) and 78 ($600,000/$800,000 × $400,000)	300,000		
Taxable income under sec. 11	1,050,000		
Normal tax (0.22 × $1,050,000)		$231,000	
Surtax exemption ([$90,000 + $600,000]/[0.60 × $300,000 + (0.80 × $800,000)] × $25,000)	$ 21,036		
Subject to surtax under sec. 11 ($1,050,000 − $21,036)	1,028,964		
Surtax (0.28 × $1,028,964)		288,110	
Tentative U.S. tax		519,110	
Foreign tax credit ($60,000 + $300,000)		360,000	
Total U.S. tax payable on amounts included under sec. 951(a)			$159,110
Tax with respect to other income:			
Gross income		$200,600	
Less:			
Personal exemption	$ 600		
Deductions	100,000		
		100,600	
Taxable income		100,000	
Tax with respect to such other taxable income			59,340
Total tax ($159,110 + $59,340)			218,450

T.D. 6858, 10/27/65, amend T.D. 7413, 3/25/76.

§ 1.962-2 Election of limitation of tax for individuals.

(a) Who may elect. The election under section 962 may be made only by a United States shareholder who is an individual (including a trust or estate).

(b) Time and manner of making election. Except as provided in § 1.962-4, a United States shareholder shall make an election under this section by filing a statement to such effect with his return for the taxable year with respect to which the election is made. The statement shall include the following information:

(1) The name, address, and taxable year of each controlled foreign corporation with respect to which the electing shareholder is a United States shareholder and of all other corporations, partnerships, trusts, or estates in any applicable chain of ownership described in section 958(a);

(2) The amounts, on a corporation-by-corporation basis, which are included in such shareholder's gross income for his taxable year under section 951(a);

(3) Such shareholder's pro rata share of the earnings and profits (determined under § 1.964-1) of each such controlled foreign corporation with respect to which such shareholder includes any amount in gross income for his taxable year under section 951(a) and the foreign income, war profits, ex-

cess profits, and similar taxes paid on or with respect to such earnings and profits;

(4) The amount of distributions received by such shareholder during his taxable year from each controlled foreign corporation referred to in subparagraph (1) of this paragraph from excludable section 962 earnings and profits (as defined in paragraph (b)(1)(i) of § 1.962-3), from taxable section 962 earnings and profits (as defined in paragraph (b)(1)(ii) of § 1.962-3), and from earnings and profits other than section 962 earnings and profits, showing the source of such amounts by taxable year; and

(5) Such further information as the Commissioner may prescribe by forms and accompanying instructions relating to such election.

(c) Effect of election. *(1) In general.* Except as provided in subparagraph (2) of this paragraph and § 1.962-4, an election under this section by a United States shareholder for a taxable year shall be applicable to all controlled foreign corporations with respect to which such shareholder includes any amount in gross income for his taxable year under section 951(a) and shall be binding for the taxable year for which such election is made.

(2) Revocation. Upon application by the United States shareholder, an election made under this section may, subject to the approval of the Commissioner, be revoked. Approval will not be granted unless a material and substantial change in circumstances occurs which could not have been anticipated when the election was made. The application for consent to revocation shall be made by the United States shareholder's mailing a letter for such purpose to Commissioner of Internal Revenue, Attention: T:R, Washington, D.C., 20224, containing a statement of the facts upon which such shareholder relies in requesting such consent.

T.D. 6858, 10/27/65.

---

§ 1.962-3 Treatment of actual distributions.

(a) In general. Section 962(d) provides that the earnings and profits of a foreign corporation attributable to amounts which are, or have been, included in the gross income of an individual United States shareholder under section 951(a) by reason of such shareholder's ownership (within the meaning of section 958(a)) of stock in such corporation and with respect to which amounts an election under § 1.962-2 applies or applied shall, when such earnings and profits are distributed to such shareholder with respect to such stock, notwithstanding the provisions of section 959(a)(1), be included in his gross income to the extent that such earnings and profits exceed the amount of income tax paid by such shareholder under this chapter on the amounts to which such election applies or applied. Thus, when such shareholder receives an actual distribution of section 962 earnings and profits (as defined in paragraph (b)(1) of this section) from a foreign corporation, only the excludable section 962 earnings and profits (as defined in paragraph (b)(1)(i) of this section) may be excluded from his gross income.

(b) Rules of application. For purposes of this section—

(1) Section 962 earnings and profits defined. With respect to an individual United States shareholder, the term "section 962 earnings and profits" means the earnings and profits of a foreign corporation referred to in paragraph (a) of this section. Such earnings and profits include—

(i) Excludable section 962 earnings and profits. Excludable section 962 earnings and profits which are the amount of the section 962 earnings and profits equal to the amount of income tax paid under this chapter by such shareholder on the amounts included in his gross income under section 951(a); and

(ii) Taxable section 962 earnings and profits. Taxable section 962 earnings and profits which are the excess of section 962 earnings and profits over the amount described in subdivision (i) of this subparagraph.

(2) Determinations made separately for each taxable year. If section 962 earnings and profits attributable to more than one taxable year are distributed by a foreign corporation, the determinations under this section shall be made separately with respect to each such taxable year.

(3) Source of distributions. (i) In general. Except as otherwise provided in this subparagraph, the provisions of paragraphs (a) through (d) of § 1.959-3 shall apply in determining the source of distributions of earnings and profits by a foreign corporation.

(ii) Treatment of section 962 earnings and profits under § 1.959-3. For purposes of a section 959(c) amount and year classification under paragraph (b) of § 1.959-3, a distribution of earnings and profits by a foreign corporation shall be first allocated to earnings and profits other than section 962 earnings and profits (as defined in subparagraph (1) of this paragraph) and then to section 962 earnings and profits. Thus distributions shall be considered first attributable to amounts described in paragraph (b)(1) of § 1.959-3 which are not section 962 earnings and profits and then to amounts described in such paragraph (b)(1) which are section 962 earnings and profits (first for the current taxable year and then for prior taxable years beginning with the most recent prior taxable year), secondly to amounts described in paragraph (b)(2) of § 1.959-3 which are not section 962 earnings and profits and then to amounts described in such paragraph (b)(2) which are section 962 earnings and profits (first for the current taxable year and then for prior taxable years beginning with the most recent prior taxable year), and finally to the amounts described in paragraph (b)(3) of § 1.959-3 (first for the current taxable year and then for prior taxable years beginning with the most recent prior taxable year).

(iii) Allocation to excludable section 962 earnings and profits. A distribution of section 962 earnings and profits by a foreign corporation for any taxable year shall be considered first attributable to the excludable section 962 earnings and profits (as defined in subparagraph (1)(i) of this paragraph) and then to taxable section 962 earnings and profits.

(iv) Allocation of deficits in earnings and profits. A United States shareholder's pro rata share (determined in accordance with the principles of paragraph (e) of § 1.951-1) of a foreign corporation's deficit in earnings and profits (determined under § 1.964-1) for any taxable year shall be applied in accordance with the provisions of paragraph (c) of § 1.959-3 except that such deficit shall also be applied to taxable section 962 earnings and profits (as defined in subparagraph (1)(ii) of this paragraph).

(4) Distribution in exchange for stock. The provisions of this section shall not apply to a distribution of section 962 earnings and profits which is treated as in part or full payment in exchange for stock under subchapter C of chapter 1 of the Internal Revenue Code. The application of this subparagraph may be illustrated by the following example:

Example. Individual United States shareholder A owns 60 percent of the only class of stock in foreign corporation M, the basis of which is $10,000. Both A and M Corporation use the calendar year as a taxable year. In each of the taxable years 1964, 1965, and 1966, M Corporation has $1,000 of earnings and profits and $1,000 of subpart F income. With respect to each such amount, A includes $600 in gross income under section 951(a), makes the election under section 962, and pays a United States tax of $132 (22 percent of $600). Accordingly, A increases the basis of his stock in M corporation under section 961(a) by $132 in each of the years 1964, 1965, and 1966, and thus on December 31, 1966, the adjusted basis for A's stock in M Corporation is $10,396. In 1967, M Corporation is completely liquidated (in a transaction described in section 331) and A receives $13,800, consisting of $1,800 of earnings and profits attributable to the amounts which A included in gross income under section 951(a) in 1964, 1965, and 1966, and $12,000 attributable to the other assets of M Corporation. No amount of the $3,404 gain realized by A on such distribution ($13,800 minus $10,396) may be excluded from gross income under section 959(a)(1). However, section 962(d) will not prevent any part of such $3,404 from being treated as a capital gain under section 331.

(5) Illustration. The application of this paragraph may be illustrated by the following example:

Example. (a) M, a controlled foreign corporation is organized on January 1, 1963; A and B, individual United States shareholders, own 50 percent and 25 percent, respectively, of the only class of stock in M Corporation. Corporation M, A, and B use the calendar year as a taxable year, and M Corporation is a controlled foreign corporation throughout the period here involved. For the taxable years 1963, 1964, 1965, and 1966, A and B must include amounts in gross income under section 951(a) with respect to M Corporation. For the years 1963, 1965, and 1966, A makes the election under section 962. On January 1, 1967, B sells his 25-percent interest in M Corporation to A; A satisfies the requirements of paragraph (d) of § 1.959-1 so as to qualify as B's successor in interest. As of December 31, 1967, M Corporation's accumulated earnings and profits of $675 (before taking into account distributions made in 1967) applicable to A's interest (including his interest as B's successor in interest) in such corporation are classified under § 1.959-3 and this section for purposes of section 962(d) as follows:

Classification of Earnings and Profits for Purposes of Sec. 1.962-3

Year	Sec. 959(c)(1) Non-sec. 962 earnings and profits	Sec. 959(c)(1) Excludable sec. 962 earnings and profits	Sec. 959(c)(1) Taxable sec. 962 earnings and profits	Sec. 959(c)(2) Non-sec. 962 earnings and profits	Sec. 959(c)(2) Excludable sec. 962 earnings and profits	Sec. 959(c)(2) Taxable sec. 962 earnings and profits	Sec. 959 (c)(3)
1963	$25	$11	$39				
1964	75			$60			$15
1965				75	$33	$117	
1966				50	22	78	
1967							75

(b) During 1967, M Corporation makes three separate distributions to A of $200, $208, and $267. The source of such distributions under § 1.959-3 and this section is as follows:

Distribution	Amount	Year	Classification of distributions under secs. 959 and 962(d)
No. 1	$ 75	1964	(c)(1) non-sec. 962
	25	1963	Do.
	11	1963	(c)(1) excludable sec. 962.
	39	1963	(c)(1) taxable sec. 962.
	50	1966	(c)(2) non-sec. 962.
Total ..	200		
No. 2	22	1966	(c)(2) excludable sec. 962.
	78	1966	(c)(2) taxable sec. 962.
	75	1965	(c)(2) non-sec. 962.
	33	1965	(c)(2) excludable sec. 962.
Total ..	208		
No. 3	117	1965	(c)(2) taxable sec. 962.
	60	1964	(c)(2) non-sec. 962.
	75	1967	(c)(3).
	15	1964	Do.
Total ..	267		

(c) A must include $324 in his gross income for 1967. The source of these amounts is as follows:

Distribution	Amount	Year	Classification
No. 1	$ 39	1963	(c)(1) taxable sec. 962.
No. 2	78	1966	(c)(2) taxable sec. 962.
No. 3	117	1965	Do.
	75	1967	(c)(3).
	15	1964	Do.
Total ..	324		

(c) Treatment of shareholder's successor in interest. *(1) In general.* If a United States person (as defined in § 1.957-4) acquires from any person any portion of the interest in the foreign corporation of a United States shareholder referred to in this section, the rules of paragraphs (a) and (b) of this section shall apply to such acquiring person. However, no exclusion of section 962 earnings and profits under paragraph (a) of this section shall be allowed unless such acquiring person establishes to the satisfaction of the district director his right to such exclusion. The information to be furnished by the acquiring person to the district director with his return for the taxable year to support such exclusion shall include:

(i) The name, address, and taxable year of the foreign corporation from which a distribution of section 962 earnings and profits is received and of all other corporations, partnerships, trusts, or estates in any applicable chain of ownership described in section 958(a);

(ii) The name and address of the person from whom the stock interest was acquired;

(iii) A description of the stock interest acquired and its relation, if any, to a chain of ownership described in section 958(a);

(iv) The amount for which an exclusion under paragraph (a) of this section is claimed; and

(v) Evidence showing that the section 962 earnings and profits for which an exclusion is claimed are attributable to amounts which were included in the gross income of a United States shareholder under section 951(a) subject to an election under § 1.962-2, that such amounts were not previously excluded from the gross income of a United States person, and the identity of the United States shareholder including such amount.

The acquiring person shall also furnish to the district director such other information as may be required by the district director in support of the exclusion.

(2) Taxes previously deemed paid by an individual United States shareholder. If a corporate successor in interest of an individual United States shareholder receives a distribution of section 962 earnings and profits, the income, war profits, and excess profits taxes paid to any foreign country or to any possession of the United States in connection with such earnings and profits shall not be taken into account for purposes of section 902, to the extent such taxes were deemed paid by such individual United States shareholder under paragraph (b)(2) of § 1.962-1 and section 960(a)(1) for any prior taxable year.

T.D. 6858, 10/27/65.

§ 1.963-0 Repeal of section 963; effective dates.

(a) Repeal of section 963. Except as provided in paragraphs (b) and (c) of this section, the provisions of section 963 and § 1.963-1 through 1.963-7 are repealed for taxable years of foreign corporations beginning after December 31, 1975, and for taxable years of United States shareholders (within the meaning of section 951(b), within which or with which such taxable years of such foreign corporations end.

(b) Transitional rules for chain or group election. *(1) In general.* If a United States shareholder (within the meaning of section 951(b) makes either a chain election pursuant to § 1.963-1(e) or a group election pursuant to § 1.963-1(f) for a taxable year of such shareholder beginning after December 31, 1975, then a foreign corporation shall be includible in such election only if—

(i) It has a taxable year beginning before January 1, 1976, which ends within such taxable year of the United States shareholder, and

(ii) It is either—

(A) A controlled foreign corporation or

(B) A foreign corporation by reason of ownership of stock in which such shareholder indirectly owns (within the meaning of section 958(a)(2)) stock in a controlled foreign corporation to which this subparagraph applies.

(2) Series rule. If any foreign corporation in a series of foreign corporations is excluded by subparagraph (i) of this paragraph from a chain or group election of a United States shareholder for its taxable year, then any foreign corporation in which the United States shareholder owns stock indirectly by reason of ownership of stock in such excluded corporation shall also be excluded from such election to the extent of such indirect ownership regardless of when its taxable year begins.

(3) Illustration. The application of this paragraph may be illustrated by the following example:

Example. (a) M is a domestic corporation, A, B, D, and E are controlled foreign corporations, and C is a foreign corporation other than a controlled foreign corporation. All five foreign corporations, each have only one class of stock outstanding. M owns directly all of the stock of A, which in turn owns directly all of the stock of B, which in turn owns directly 60 percent of the stock of D, which in turn owns directly all of the stock of E. M also owns directly 40 percent of the stock of C, which in turn owns directly the remaining 40 percent of the stock of D. M is a United States shareholder with respect to no other foreign corporation. M and B each use the calendar year as the taxable year. A, C, D, and E each use a fiscal year ending on November 30 as the taxable year. For calendar year 1976, M may make either a first-tier election with respect to A, a chain election with respect to C and D (to the extent of M's indirect 16-percent stock interest in D by reason of its direct ownership of 40 percent of the stock of C) or a group election with respect to A, C, D (to the extent of such 16-percent stock interest) and E (to the extent of M's indirect 16-percent stock interest in E).

(b) M's indirect 100 percent stock interest in B will be excluded from any chain or group election made by M for calendar year 1976 since B is a controlled foreign corporation which does not have a taxable year beginning before January 1, 1976, which ends within the taxable year of M beginning after December 31, 1975, for which M has made either a chain or group election.

(c) M's indirect 60 percent stock interest through A and B in D and E will be excluded from any chain or group election made by M for calendar year 1976 since such 60 percent interests are indirectly owned by M by reason of its indirect ownership of stock in B, which is a foreign corporation which does not have a taxable year beginning before January 1, 1976, which ends within the taxable year of M beginning after December 31, 1975, for which M has made either a chain or group election.

(d) If C used the calendar year as its taxable year and was therefore excluded from a chain election made with respect to it and D, then D would also be excluded from such an election, since D would then be a foreign corporation in which M owns stock indirectly by reason of ownership of stock in C, which is excluded from such election.

(c) Deficiency distributions. The rules relating to deficiency distributions under section 963(e)(2) and § 1.963-6 shall continue to apply to a taxable year beginning after the effective date of the repeal of section 963 in which it is determined that a deficiency distribution must be made for an earlier taxable year for which a United States shareholder made an election to secure the exclusion under section 963 but failed to receive a minimum distribution.

(d) Special adjustments pursuant to section 963 to be taken into account for taxable years subsequent to the repeal of section 963. If a United States shareholder of a controlled foreign corporation elects to receive a minimum distribution under section 963 for a taxable year, section 963 and the regulations thereunder may require certain elections and adjustments to be made in subsequent taxable years. These elections and adjustments shall be taken into account for subsequent taxable years as if section 963 were still in effect and no election to receive a minimum distribution were made after the effective date of the repeal of section 963. Examples of these elections and special adjustments include, but are not limited to, the election which may be made pursuant to § 1.963-3(g)(2), relating to the special extended distribution period, and the special adjustments to be made pursuant to § 1.963-4, relating to the minimum overall tax burden test.

T.D. 7545, 5/8/78.

---

§ 1.963-1 Exclusion of subpart F income upon receipt of minimum distribution.

(a) In general. *(1) Purpose of section 963.* Section 963 sets forth an exception to section 951(a)(1)(A)(i) by providing that a United States corporate shareholder may exclude from its gross income the subpart F income of a controlled foreign corporation if for the taxable year such shareholder elects such exclusion and, where necessary, receives a distribution of the earnings and profits of such foreign corporation sufficient to bring the aggregate U.S. and foreign income taxes on the pretax earnings and profits of that corporation to a percentage level approaching the U.S. tax rate for such year on the income of a domestic corporation. The election to secure an exclusion under section 963 may be made with respect to a "single first-tier corporation" or a "chain" or "group" of controlled foreign corporations. This section defines the terms "single first-tier corporations," "chains," "group," and certain other terms and prescribes the manner in which such an election is to be made. Section 1.963-2 describes the manner in which the amount of the minimum distribution for any taxable year is to be determined. Section 1.963-3 specifies the distributions counting toward a minimum distribution. Section 1.963-4 sets forth the requirement with respect to a minimum distribution from a chain or group that the overall U.S. and foreign income tax must equal either 90 percent of the U.S. corporate tax rate applied against consolidated pretax and predistribution earnings and profits or, with the application of the special rules set forth in that section, the total U.S. and foreign income taxes which would have been incurred in respect of a pro rata minimum distribution from the chain or group. Section 1.963-5 provides special rules for applying section 963 in certain cases in which the rate of foreign income tax incurred by a foreign corporation varies with the amount of distributions it makes for the taxable year. Section 1.963-6 outlines the deficiency distribution procedure that may be followed if for reasonable cause a U.S. corporate shareholder fails to receive a complete minimum distribution for a taxable year for which it elects the exclusion under section 963. Section 1.963-7 provides transitional rules for the application of section 963 for certain taxable years of U.S. shareholders ending on or before the 90th day after September 30, 1964. Section 1.963-8 provides rules for the determination of the required minimum distribution during the period the § surcharge imposed by section 51 is in effect.

(2) Conditions for exclusion of subpart F income. To qualify for an exclusion under section 963 for any taxable year with respect to the subpart F income of a controlled foreign corporation, a corporate United States shareholder must—

(i) Elect such exclusion on or before the last day (including any extensions of time under section 6081) prescribed by law for filing its return of the tax imposed by chapter 1 of the Code for the taxable year;

(ii) Receive, if and to the extent necessary, distributions of the type described in paragraph (a) of § 1.963-3 sufficient in amount to constitute a minimum distribution;

(iii) Incur, in the case of a chain or group election, income tax with respect to such minimum distribution sufficient to satisfy the requirements of paragraph (a) of § 1.963-4, relating to the minimum overall tax burden; and

(iv) Consent, on or before such last day for making the election, to the regulations under section 963 applicable to such taxable year and to any amendments thereof duly prescribed before such last day.The making of the election under section 963 by filing the return on or before such last day shall constitute the consent to the regulations under such section prescribed before such last day. For an extension of the time for receiving a minimum distribution and making the consent for certain taxable years ending on or before the 90th day after September 30, 1964, see § 1.963-7.

(3) Subpart F income excluded. An exclusion under section 963 for a taxable year of a United States shareholder for which the election is made under such section shall apply only to the subpart F income for the taxable year of the single first-tier corporation to which the election applies or of each controlled foreign corporation in the chain or group to which the election applies. Only those amounts attributable to the stock interest to which the election relates may be excluded. Thus, in case of a first-tier election with respect to stock of a controlled foreign corporation owned directly within the meaning of section 958(a)(1)(A), the corporate United States shareholder may not exclude any subpart F income of such foreign corporation which is includible in its gross income under section 951(a)(1)(A)(i) by virtue of its indirect ownership of stock in such foreign corporation through the operation of section 958(a)(2). Subpart F income of a controlled foreign corporation which is excluded from the gross income of a United States shareholder by reason of the receipt of a minimum distribution to which section 963 applies shall not be considered to be excluded under section 954(b)(1) or section 970(a).

(4) Affiliated group of corporations. An affiliated group of domestic corporations which makes a consolidated return under section 1501 for the taxable year shall be treated as a single United States shareholder for purposes of applying section 963 for such year if the common parent corporation in its return for such affiliated group makes any first-tier election, chain election, or group election under section 963 for such affiliated group; in such case, no member of such affiliated group may separately make any first-tier election, chain election, or group election under section 963 for the taxable year. If the common parent of such an affiliated group so making a consolidated return makes no first-tier election, chain election, or group election for such affiliated group, then any member may make a first-tier election, chain election, or group election to the same extent that it could so elect if such affiliated group had not filed a consolidated return; in such case, the affiliated group will not be treated as a single United States shareholder.

(b) Definitions. For purposes of section 963 and §§ 1.963-1 through 1.963-8—

(1) Controlled foreign corporation. The term "Controlled foreign corporation" shall have the meaning accorded to it by section 957 and the regulations thereunder but shall not include any foreign corporation for a taxable year beginning before January 1, 1963.

(2) Single first-tier corporation. The term "single first-tier corporation" means a controlled foreign corporation de-

scribed in paragraph (d) of this section with respect to which a first-tier election has been made for the taxable year.

(3) Chain. The term "chain" means collectively the foreign corporations described in paragraph (e) of this section with respect to which a chain election has been made for the taxable year.

(4) Group. The term "group" means collectively the foreign corporations described in paragraph (f) of this section with respect to which a group election has been made for the taxable year.

(5) First-tier election, etc. The term "first-tier election" means an election described in paragraph (c)(1)(i)(a) of this section; the term "chain election" means an election described in paragraph (c)(1)(i)(b) of this section; and the term "group election" means an election described in paragraph (c)(1)(ii) of this section.

(6) Taxable year (i) The term "taxable year of a single first-tier corporation," "taxable year of a corporation in a chain," or "taxable year of a corporation in a group," means, respectively, the taxable year of such corporation ending with or within the taxable year of the electing United States shareholder for which is made under paragraph (c)(1) of this section the election establishing it as a single first-tier corporation, a corporation in a chain, or corporation in a group, as the case may be.

(ii) The term "taxable year" when used in reference to a chain or group refers collectively to the respective taxable years of the foreign corporations in such chain or group to which applies the election establishing such chain or group status, such taxable year being, in the case of each respective corporation in the chain or group, such corporation's taxable year ending with or within the taxable year of the electing United States shareholder, whether or not such taxable year of the corporation is the same as that of any other foreign corporation in the chain or group.

(7) Foreign income tax. The term "foreign income tax" means income, war profits, and excess profits taxes, and taxes included in the term "income, war profits, and excess profits taxes" by reason of section 903, paid or accrued to a foreign country or possession of the United States and taken into account for purposes of sections 901 through 905. Except in determining the foreign tax credit under section 901, the term shall not include any tax which is deemed paid by a foreign corporation under section 902(b).

(c) Election to exclude subpart F income. *(1) Foreign corporations included in election.* A corporate United States shareholder may for any taxable year exercise the election to secure an exclusion under section 963 either—

(i)

(a) Separately with respect to any foreign corporation which as to such shareholder is described in paragraph (d) of this section, and/or

(b) Separately with respect to the foreign corporation or corporations which as to such shareholder are in a series described in paragraph (e) of this section, except to the extent of any interest (of such shareholder in any such corporation) with respect to which an election has otherwise been made under this subdivision (i); or

(ii) With respect to all foreign corporations which as to such shareholder are described in paragraph (f) of this section.

(2) Manner of making election. An election under subparagraph (1) of this paragraph to secure an exclusion under section 963 and the consent to the regulations under such section shall be made for a taxable year by filing with the return for such taxable year—

(i) A written statement stating that such election is made for such taxable year,

(ii) The names of the foreign corporations to which the election applies, the taxable year, country or incorporation, earnings and profits (as determined under paragraph (d) of § 1.963-2), foreign income tax taken into account under paragraph (e) of § 1.963-2, and outstanding capital stock, of each such corporation,

(iii) In case of a group election, the names of all foreign corporations excluded from such group under paragraph (f)(2) and (3) of this section and identifying characterizations for all foreign branches included in, and excluded from, such group under paragraph (f)(4) of this section, together with the authority for such exclusion or inclusion, and

(iv) Such other information relating to the election made as the Commissioner may prescribe by instructions or schedules to support such return.

(3) Duration of election. (i) Year-by-year requirement.An election under subparagraph (1) of this paragraph to secure an exclusion under section 963 may be made for each taxable year of the United States shareholder but shall be effective only with respect to the taxable year for which made. An election made for any taxable year shall be irrevocable with respect to that taxable year once the period for the making of such election has expired, except to the extent provided by subdivision (ii) of this subparagraph.

(ii) Revocation or modification of election for reasonable cause. (a) Conditions under which allowed. If, after the making of an election under subparagraph (1) of this paragraph, the United States shareholder establishes to the satisfaction of the Commissioner that reasonable cause exists for revocation or modification of such election, it may withdraw that election; change from a group election to first-tier elections and/or chain elections or from a chain election to a first-tier election: change from a first-tier election to a chain election or from first-tier elections and/or chain elections to a group election; or, in the case of a chain or group election, alter the composition of the chain or group by adding or eliminating corporations. The United States shareholder shall be allowed to revoke or modify elections pursuant to this subdivision only once for any taxable year of such shareholder and then only at a time prior to the expiration of the period prescribed by law for making an assessment of the tax imposed by chapter 1 of the Code for such taxable year and for any subsequent taxable year for which the tax liability of such shareholder would be affected by such revocation or modification of election. The Commissioner may, as a condition to such revocation or modification of the election, require a consent by the United States shareholder under section 6501 to extend, for the taxable year and such subsequent years affected by the revocation or modification, the period for the making of assessments, and the bringing of distraint or a proceeding in court for collection, in respect of a deficiency and all interest, additional amounts, and assessable penalties.

(b) Nature of reasonable cause. Reasonable cause shall be deemed to exist for the revocation or modification of an election only if, after the making of such election, a material and substantial change in circumstances affecting the election occurs which reasonably could not have been anticipated when the election was made and which, to a significant degree, was beyond the control of the electing United States shareholder. For example, reasonable cause would exist if the minimum distribution were computed on the basis of a contested foreign income tax asserted by a foreign tax authority which, as a consequence of litigation occurring after the filing of the United States shareholder's return, is refunded, with the result that the United States shareholder is not entitled under the election which was made to an exclusion under section 963.

(c) Request for revocation or modification. A United States shareholder desiring to revoke or modify the election shall mail to the Commissioner of Internal Revenue, Attention: T:R, Washington, DC, 20224, a letter requesting such revocation or modification; such letter shall set forth the information required by subparagraph (2) of this paragraph with respect to any new election and the facts and circumstances which the shareholder considers reasonable cause for such revocation or modification. The shareholder shall also consent, if required, to the extension of assessment period referred to in (a) of this subdivision and shall furnish such other information as may be required by the Commissioner in support of such request. If the Commissioner is satisfied that reasonable cause exists for the revocation or modification, the United States shareholder shall file an amended return consistent with any new election which is made.

(d) Corporations to which a first-tier election may apply. *(1) Includible interest.* A corporate United States shareholder may make a first-tier election for the taxable year only with respect to a single controlled foreign corporation in which it owns stock directly within the meaning of section 958(a)(1)(A) and only with respect to the stock so owned. The election must apply to all of the stock so owned by such shareholder and shall relate only to the subpart F income of such corporation which would otherwise be required to be included in gross income by reason of owning such stock. The shareholder may for the same taxable year make a first-tier election with respect to one or more controlled foreign corporations in which it directly owns stock and not with respect to other controlled foreign corporations in which it directly owns stock.

(2) Illustrations. The application of this paragraph may be illustrated by the following examples:

Example (1). Domestic corporation M directly owns all the one class of stock in each of the controlled foreign corporations A, B, and C. Corporation M may make a first-tier election for a taxable year with respect to any one of corporations A, B, and C; with respect to corporations A and B, respectively; with respect to corporations A and C, respectively; with respect to corporations B and C, respectively; or with respect to corporations A, B, and C, respectively.

Example (2). Domestic corporation M directly owns all the one class of stock of controlled foreign corporation A and 20 percent of the one class of stock of controlled foreign corporation B. Corporation A directly owns 80 percent of the stock of B Corporation. All such corporations use the calendar year as the taxable year. For 1964, M Corporation makes a first-tier election with respect to corporations A and B, respectively, and receives a minimum distribution from each. An exclusion under section 963 for 1964 will be allowed for all of A Corporation's subpart F income for such year but only for the amount of B Corporation's subpart F income which M Corporation would (without regard to section 963) be required to include in gross income for such year under section 951(a)(1)(A)(i) by reason of directly owning 20 percent of the stock of B Corporation. Corporation M may not exclude any amount which it would be required (without regard to section 963) to include in gross income under section 951(a)(1)(A)(i) for such year with respect to the subpart F income of B Corporation by reason of its indirect ownership (through the operation of section 958(a)(2)) of 80 percent of the stock of B Corporation, unless M Corporation separately elects such exclusion and receives a minimum distribution with respect to such interest. See paragraph (e) of this section relating to chain elections

(e) Corporations to which a chain election may apply. *(1) Includible interests.* A Corporate United States shareholder may make a chain election for the taxable year with respect to one or more controlled foreign corporations in any series which includes only one foreign corporation described in subdivision (i), any one or more controlled foreign corporations described in subdivision (ii), and all foreign corporations described in subdivision (iii) of this subparagraph:

(i) A foreign corporation, whether or not a controlled foreign corporation, to the extent of stock owned by such shareholder—

(a) Directly (within the meaning of section 958(a)(1)(A)) in such corporation, or

(b) Indirectly (through the operation of section 958(a)(2)) by virtue of the direct ownership (within the meaning of section 958(a)(1)(A)) of stock in such corporation by a foreign trust, foreign estate, or foreign partnership, in which such shareholder is a beneficiary or partner;

(ii) To the extent that such shareholder so elects, any controlled foreign corporation to the extent that, by reason of its ownership of stock described in subdivision (i) of this subparagraph, such shareholder indirectly owns within the meaning of section 958(a)(2) stock in such controlled foreign corporation; and

(iii) All foreign corporations, whether or not controlled foreign corporations, by reason (and to the extent) of ownership of stock in which such shareholder indirectly owns within the meaning of section 958(a)(2) stock in a controlled foreign corporation included in the series by reason of subdivision (ii) of this subparagraph.

Notwithstanding the preceding sentence, a corporate United States shareholder may make a chain election for the taxable year with respect to a single foreign corporation, but only if such foreign corporation is a controlled foreign corporation described in subdivision (i)(b) of this subparagraph. The shareholder may for the same taxable year make a chain election with respect to one or more series, and not with respect to other series, to which this subparagraph applies.

(2) Illustrations. The application of this paragraph may be illustrated by the following examples:

Example (1). Domestic corporation M directly owns all the one class of stock of controlled foreign corporation A, which in turn directly owns 80 percent of the one class of stock of controlled foreign corporation B. Corporation M may make a chain election with respect to corporations A and B.

Example (2). Domestic corporation M directly owns all the one class of stock of controlled foreign corporation A, which in turn directly owns 80 percent of the one class of stock of controlled foreign corporation B, which in turn directly owns all the one class of stock of controlled foreign corporation C. Corporation M also directly owns 20 percent of the stock of B Corporation. Corporation M may make a chain election either with respect to corporations A and B or with respect to corporations A, B, and C. In either case corporations B and C can be included in the chain only to the extent of M Corporation's indirect 80-percent stock interest in such corporations by reason of its direct ownership of 100 percent of the stock of A Corporation. Corporation M may also make a chain election with respect to corporations B and C, in which case the chain would include corporations B and C to the extent of the 20-percent stock interest which M Corporation owns directly in B Corporation, and indirectly owns in C Corporation by reason of its direct ownership of such stock interest in B Corporation.

Example (3). Domestic corporation M directly owns all the one class of stock of controlled foreign corporation A, which in turn directly owns all the one class of stock of controlled foreign corporations B and C. Corporation M may make a chain election either with respect to corporations A, B, and C; or with respect to corporations A and B; or with respect to corporations A and C.

Example (4). Domestic corporation M directly owns all the one class of stock of controlled foreign corporation A and 40 percent of the one class of stock of foreign corporation B, not a controlled foreign corporation. Corporation A directly owns 30 percent of the one class of stock of controlled foreign corporation C, and B Corporation directly owns the remaining 70 percent of the stock of C Corporation. Corporation M may make a chain election with respect to corporations A and C, but in such case C Corporation can be included in the chain only to the extent of M Corporation's indirect 30-percent stock interest in such corporation by reason of its direct ownership of 100 percent of the stock of A Corporation. Corporation M may instead make a chain election with respect to corporations B and C, but in such case C Corporation can be included in the chain only to the extent of M Corporation's indirect 28-percent stock interest in such corporation by reason of its direct ownership of 40 percent of the stock of B Corporation. In the latter case, B Corporation must be included in the chain even though it is not a controlled foreign corporation. Corporation M may also make two chain elections, one with respect to corporations A and C, and the other with respect to corporations B and C, as described above.

Example (5). Domestic corporation M directly owns all the one class of stock of controlled foreign corporation A, which in turn directly owns all the one class of stock of controlled foreign corporation B and 40 percent of the one class of stock of foreign corporation C, not a controlled foreign corporation. Corporation M may make a chain election with respect to corporations A and B. Corporation C may not be included in the chain since M Corporation does not, by reason of its indirect ownership of stock in C Corporation, own stock in any controlled foreign corporation.

Example (6). Domestic corporation M directly owns a 60-percent partnership interest in foreign partnership D and by reason of such interest owns indirectly, within the meaning of section 958(a)(2), 60 percent of the one class of stock of controlled foreign corporation E (all of the stock of which is directly owned by D Partnership) and 60 percent of the one class of stock of controlled foreign corporation F (all the stock of which is also directly owned by D Partnership). By virtue of its direct interest in D Partnership, M Corporation may make a chain election with respect to E Corporation alone or with respect to F Corporation alone. Corporation M may also make two chain elections, one with respect to E Corporation, the other with respect to F Corporation.

(f) Corporations to which a group election may apply. *(1) Includible interests.* A corporate United States shareholder may make a group election for the taxable year with respect to a group of foreign corporations which includes, except as provided in subparagraphs (2) and (3) of this paragraph, all of the following corporations:

(i) All controlled foreign corporations in which such shareholder owns stock either directly within the meaning of section 958(a)(1)(A) or indirectly within the meaning of section 958(a)(2), and

(ii) All foreign corporations, whether or not controlled foreign corporations, by reason (and to the extent) of ownership of stock in which such shareholder, indirectly owns within the meaning of section 958(a)(2) stock in a controlled foreign corporation described in subdivision (i) of this subparagraph.

A first-tier election or chain election may not be made for any taxable year with respect to any foreign corporation which for such taxable year has been excluded under subparagraph (2) or (3) of this paragraph from a group with respect to which a group election has been made for such year. The application of this subparagraph may be illustrated by the following examples:

Example (1). Domestic corporation M directly owns all the one class of stock of controlled foreign corporations A and B and is a United States shareholder with respect to no other foreign corporation. M Corporation may make a group election with respect to corporations A and B.

Example (2). Domestic corporation M directly owns all the one class of stock of controlled foreign corporations A and B, and B Corporation directly owns 80 percent of the one class of stock of controlled foreign corporation C. Corporation M is a United States shareholder only with respect to corporations A, B, and C. If M Corporation makes a group election, it must make the election with respect to corporations A, B, and C.

Example (3). Domestic corporation M directly owns all the one class of stock of controlled foreign corporations A and B. Corporation A directly owns 70 percent of the one class of stock of controlled foreign corporation C. Corporation B directly owns 40 percent of the one class of stock of foreign corporation D, not a controlled foreign corporation, and D Corporation directly owns 30 percent of the stock of C Corporation. Corporation M is a United States shareholder with respect to no other foreign corporation. If M Corporation makes a group election, it must make the election with respect to corporations A, B, C, and D. Corporation D must be included in the group even though it is not a controlled foreign corporation.

(2) Less developed country corporations. If the United States shareholder so elects, it may for any taxable year exclude from a group for purposes of a group election every controlled foreign corporation which is a less developed country corporation as defined in section 955(c) and § 1.955-5 for the taxable year of such foreign corporation ending with or within such taxable year of the shareholder but only if, by reason of ownership of stock in such foreign corporation, the shareholder does not indirectly own within the meaning of section 958(a)(2) stock in any other controlled foreign corporation which is not a less developed country corporation for its taxable year ending with or within such taxable year of the shareholder. The election under this subparagraph to exclude a less developed country corporation is required to be made with respect to all less developed country corporations of which the electing shareholder is a United States shareholder and which, under the preceding sentence, are eligible to be excluded.

Example. Domestic corporation M directly owns all the one class of stock of controlled foreign corporations A and B, not less developed country corporations. Corporation A directly owns all of the one class of stock of controlled foreign corporation C, B Corporation directly owns all the one class of stock of controlled foreign corporation D, and D Corporation directly owns all the one class of stock of controlled foreign corporation E. Corporations C, D, and E are less developed country corporations under section 955(c). Corporation M may make a group election with respect to corporations A, B, C, D, and E; it may also exclude the less developed country corporations and make a group election with respect to corporations A and B only. If E Corporation were not a less developed country corporation, however, neither D Corporation nor E Corporation could be excluded since, by reason of ownership of stock in D Corporation, M Corporation would indirectly own stock in E Corporation, a controlled foreign corporation which is not a less developed country corporation.

(3) Foreign corporations with blocked foreign income. If the United States shareholder so elects, it may for any taxable year exclude from a group for purposes of a group election any foreign corporation with respect to which it is established to the satisfaction of the Commissioner that an amount of earnings and profits of such corporation sufficient to constitute its share of a pro rata minimum distribution (as defined in paragraph (a)(2)(i) of § 1.963-4) by the group cannot be distributed to such United States shareholder because of currency or other restrictions or limitations imposed under the laws of any foreign country. If, by reason of ownership of stock in a foreign corporation which is excluded from the group under the preceding sentence, a United States shareholder owns stock in another foreign corporation an amount of whose earnings and profits sufficient to constitute its share of a pro rata minimum distribution by the group cannot be distributed to such United States shareholder through such excluded foreign corporation because of currency or other restrictions or limitations imposed under the laws of any foreign country, such other foreign corporation must also be excluded from the group for purposes of the group election. For purposes of this subparagraph, the determination as to whether earnings and profits cannot be distributed because of currency or other restrictions or limitations imposed under the laws of a foreign country shall be made in accordance with the regulations under section 964(b), except that such restrictions or limitations shall be considered to exist notwithstanding that distributions are made by the foreign corporation in a foreign currency if, assuming the distributee to be the United States shareholder, the distributed amounts would be excludable from the distributee's gross income for the taxable year of receipt under a method of accounting in which the reporting of blocked foreign income is deferred until the income ceases to be blocked.

(4) Treatment of foreign branches of domestic corporation as foreign subsidiary corporations. (i) In general. If the United States shareholder so elects, all branches (other than a branch excluded under subdivision (iii) of this subparagraph) maintained by such shareholder in foreign countries and possessions of the United States shall be treated, for purposes of applying subparagraph (1) of this paragraph, as wholly owned foreign subsidiary corporations of such shareholder organized under the laws of such respective foreign countries or possessions of the United States. Each branch treated as such a foreign subsidiary corporation shall be included in the group by the United States shareholder making the group election and shall be regarded, for purposes of section 963, as having distributed to such shareholder all of its earnings and profits for the taxable year, irrespective of the statutory percentage applied for the taxable year under paragraph (b) of § 1.963-2. As used in this subparagraph, the term "branch" shall mean a permanent organization maintained in a foreign country or a possession of the United States to engage in the active conduct of a trade or business. Whether a permanent organization is maintained in a foreign country or possession of the United States shall depend upon the facts and circumstances of the particular case. As a general rule, a permanent organization shall be considered to be maintained in such country or possession if the United States shareholder maintains therein a significant work force or significant manufacturing, mining, warehousing, sales, office, or similar business facilities of a fixed or permanent nature. If a United States shareholder so operates that it satisfies the branch test with respect to each of several foreign countries or possessions, each such branch shall be treated as a separate wholly owned foreign subsidiary corporation organized under the laws of such country or possession in respect of which it satisfies such test. In no event shall a branch which is treated as a wholly owned foreign subsidiary corporation under this subparagraph be also treated as a less developed country corporation. The term "possession of the United States," as used in this subparagraph, shall be construed to have the same meaning as that contained in paragraph (b)(2) of § 1.957-3.

(ii) Earnings and profits and taxes of a foreign branch. The earnings and profits (or deficit in earnings and profits) for a taxable year of a branch treated as a wholly owned foreign subsidiary corporation under this subparagraph shall be determined by applying against the gross income (as defined in section 61) of the branch its allowable deductions other than any net operating loss deduction. Any excess of gross income over such deductions shall constitute earnings and profits. Any excess of such deductions over gross income shall constitute a deficit in earnings and profits. For purposes of this subparagraph, the gross income of a branch is that which is produced by the trade or business activities separately conducted by it outside the United States and which is derived from sources without the United States under the provisions of sections 861 through 864 and the regulations thereunder; the allowable deductions of a branch are those which are properly allocable to or chargeable against its gross income and which are allowable under chapter 1 of the Code to the corporation of which it is a branch. Only the foreign income tax allocable to the gross income of the branch shall be considered paid or accrued by such branch. Solely for the purpose of determining under paragraph (c)(2) of § 1.963-2 the effective foreign tax rate of a group which includes a branch treated as a wholly owned foreign subsidiary corporation, the foreign income tax considered paid or accrued by the branch shall be treated as an allowable deduction of such branch even though the United States shareholder chooses to take the benefits of section 901 for the taxable year.

(iii) Excluded branches. For purposes of subdivision (i) of this subparagraph, a branch maintained by the United States shareholder in a possession of the United States shall not be treated as a wholly owned foreign subsidiary corporation of the United States shareholder for the taxable year unless such branch would be a controlled foreign corporation (as defined in section 957 and the regulations thereunder) for such taxable year if it were incorporated under the laws of such possession and unless the gross income of such shareholder for such taxable year includes for purposes of the tax imposed by Chapter 1 of the Code the income, if any, derived by such shareholder from sources within possessions of the United States, as determined under the provisions of sections 861 through 864 and the regulations thereunder.

(iv) Illustrations. The application of this subparagraph may be illustrated by the following examples:

Example (1). Throughout 1964, domestic corporation M directly owns all of the one class of stock of controlled foreign corporations A and B. All corporations use the calendar year as the taxable year. During 1964, M Corporation engages in foreign country X in the manufacture and sale of steel tubing and rods, maintaining therein a significant work force and significant manufacturing and sales facilities for such purpose. Corporation M also engages in foreign country Y in the mining and sale of iron ore, maintaining therein a significant work force and substantial mining and sales facilities for such purpose. For 1964, M Corporation may make a group election with respect to corporations A and B and the branches operated in country X and country Y, treating such branches as wholly owned foreign subsidiary corporations. If corporation M elects to include one such branch in the group election, it must include both.

Example (2). Throughout 1964, domestic corporation M directly owns all the one class of stock of controlled foreign corporations A and B. All corporations use the calendar year as the taxable year. During 1964, M Corporation exports tractors to foreign country Z, in which country its sole activities consist of arranging for title to the tractors to pass to the purchasers in that country. Corporation M's only facility in country Z in 1964 is a small rented office, and its work force therein consists only of a few clerical employees. The activities of M Corporation in country Z do not constitute the maintenance of a branch therein for purposes of this subparagraph. Corporation M may make a group election, only with respect to corporations A and B.

T.D. 6759, 9/25/64, amend T.D. 6767, 11/3/64, T.D. 7100, 3/20/71.

---

§ 1.963-2 Determination of the amount of the minimum distribution.

(a) Application of statutory percentage to earnings and profits. The amount of the minimum distribution required to be received by a United States shareholder with respect to stock to which the election under paragraph (c) of § 1.963-1 applies for the taxable year in order to qualify for a section 963 exclusion for such year shall be the amount, if any, determined by the multiplication of the statutory percentage applicable for the taxable year by—

(1) In the case of a first-tier election, such shareholder's proportionate share (as determined under paragraph (d)(2) of this section) of the earnings and profits for the taxable year of the single first-tier corporation to which the election relates,

(2) In the case of a chain election, the consolidated earnings and profits (as determined under paragraph (d)(3) of this section) with respect to such shareholder for the taxable year of the chain to which the election relates, or

(3) In the case of a group election, the consolidated earnings and profits (as determined under paragraph (d)(3) of this section) with respect to such shareholder for the taxable year of the group to which the election relates.

For the requirement that the overall United States and foreign income tax incurred in respect of a minimum distribution from a chain or group must equal or exceed either 90 percent of the United States corporate tax rate applied against pretax and predistribution consolidated earnings and profits or, with the application of the special rules set forth therein, must equal or exceed the overall United States and foreign income tax which would have resulted from a pro rata minimum distribution, see paragraph (a)(1) of § 1.963-4.

(b) Statutory percentage. The statutory percentage (referred to in paragraph (a) of this section) for the taxable year shall be determined by applying the effective foreign tax rate (as defined in paragraph (c) of this section) for such year with respect to the single first-tier corporation, chain, or group, as the case may be, against—

(1) The table set forth in section 963(b)(1) in the case of an election to secure an exclusion under section 963 for a taxable year of the United States shareholder beginning in 1963 and a taxable year entirely within the surcharge period ending before January 1, 1970.

(2) The table set forth in section 963(b)(2) in the case of an election to secure an exclusion under section 963 for a taxable year of the U.S. shareholder beginning in 1964 or for a taxable year of such shareholder beginning in 1969 and ending in 1970 to the extent subparagraph (B) of section 963(b)(3) applies,

(3) The table set forth in section 963(b)(3) in the case of an election to secure an exclusion under section 963 for a taxable year of the U.S. shareholder beginning after December 31, 1964 except a taxable year which includes any part of the surcharge period, or

(4) The table set forth in paragraph (b) of § 1.963-8 in the case of an election to secure an exclusion under section 963 for the calendar year 1970.

Example. Domestic corporation M owns all the one class of stock in controlled foreign corporation A. Corporation M uses the calendar year as its taxable year, and A Corporation uses a fiscal year ending August 31. For 1964, M Corporation makes a first-tier election in order to exclude from gross income for such year the subpart F income of A Corporation for its taxable year ending on August 31, 1964. Although, such election applies to the taxable year of A Corporation beginning on September 1, 1963, the applicable table, for purposes of determining the statutory percentages to be used under paragraph (a) of this section for the taxable year, is that set forth in section 963(b)(2), which relates to taxable years of United States shareholders beginning in 1964. Thus, if for the taxable year of A Corporation ending August 31, 1964, the effective foreign tax rate is 30 percent, A Corporation would have to distribute 72 percent of its earnings and profits for such year in order for M Corporation to be entitled to an exclusion under section 963 for 1964.

(c) Effective foreign tax rate. *(1) Single first-tier corporation.* For purposes of section 963 the term "effective foreign tax rate" for a taxable year means, with respect to a single first-tier corporation, the percentage which—

(i) The United States shareholder's proportionate share (as determined under paragraph (e)(1) of this section) of the foreign income tax of such corporation for such taxable year is of—

(ii) The sum of—

(a) The United States shareholder's proportionate share (as determined under paragraph (d)(2) of this section) of the earnings and profits of such corporation for such taxable year, and

(b) The amount referred to in subdivision (i) of this subparagraph.

(2) Chain or group of corporations. For purposes of section 963, the term "effective foreign tax rate" for a taxable year means, with respect to a chain or group, the percentage which—

(i) The consolidated foreign income taxes (as determined under paragraph (e)(2) of this section) of such chain or group with respect to the United States shareholder for such taxable year is —

(ii) The sum of—

(a) The consolidated earnings and profits (as determined under paragraph (d)(3) of this section) of such chain or group with respect to such United States shareholder for such taxable year, and

(b) The amount referred to in subdivision (i) of this subparagraph.

(3) Treatment of United States tax as foreign tax. For the purpose solely of determining the effective foreign tax rate under this paragraph, if a foreign corporation has pretax earnings and profits attributable to income from sources within the United States for the taxable year upon which it pays United States income tax and if distributions from the earnings and profits of such corporation for such year to the electing United States shareholder with respect to stock to which the election to secure an exclusion under section 963 relates do not entitled such shareholder to the dividends-received deduction under section 245, the amount of the United States income tax shall be taken into account as though such tax were foreign income tax. The amount so treated as foreign income tax shall not exceed 90 percent of an amount determined by multiplying such pretax earnings and profits attributable to income from sources within the United States by a percentage which is the sum of the normal tax rate and the surtax rate (determined without regard to the surtax exemption) prescribed by section 11 for the taxable year of the United States shareholder.

(d) Determination of proportionate share of earnings and profits and consolidated earnings and profits. *(1) Earnings and profits of foreign corporations.* For purposes of §§ 1.963-1 through 1.963-8, the earnings and profits, or deficit in earnings and profits, for the taxable year, of a single first-tier corporation or of a foreign corporation in a chain or group shall be the amount of its earnings and profits for such year, determined under section 964(a) and § 1.964-1 but without reduction for foreign income tax or for distributions made by such corporation, less—

(i) In the case of a foreign corporation included in a chain or group, the amount of any distributions received (computed without reduction for any income tax paid or accrued by such corporation with respect to such distributions) by such corporation during its taxable year from the earnings and profits (whether or not from earnings and profits of the taxable year to which the election under section 963 applies) of another foreign corporation in the chain or group.

(ii) In the case of every foreign corporation, the amount of foreign income tax paid or accrued by such corporation during its taxable year other than foreign income tax referred to in subdivision (i) and (iii) of this subparagraph, and

(iii) In the case of a foreign corporation included in a chain or group, the foreign income tax paid or accrued by such corporation with respect to distributions from the earnings and profits of any other foreign corporation in the chain or group for the taxable year of such other corporation to which the election under section 963 applies, but only if the U.S. shareholder chooses under this subdivision to take such tax into account in determining the effective foreign tax rate rather than count it toward the amount of the minimum distribution as provided in paragraph (b)(2) of § 1.963-3.

In the event that the foreign income tax of a corporation included in a chain or group depends upon the extent to which distributions are made by such corporation, the amount of foreign income tax referred to subdivision (ii) of this subparagraph shall, only for purposes of determining the effective foreign tax rate, be the amount which would have been paid or accrued if no distributions had been made. For the rules in other cases involving corporations whose foreign income tax varies with distributions, see § 1.963-5. For the manner of computing the earnings and profits of a foreign branch treated as a wholly owned foreign subsidiary corporation see paragraph (f)(4)(ii) of § 1.963-1.

(2) Shareholder's proportionate share of earnings and profits. (i) Corporation with earnings and profits. (a) In general. A United States shareholder's proportionate share, with respect to stock to which the election to secure an exclusion under section 963 relates, of the earnings and profits of a foreign corporation (not including a foreign branch described in (b) of this subdivision) for its taxable year shall be the share which such shareholder would receive if the total amount of such corporation's earnings and profits, as determined under subparagraph (1) of this paragraph, for such year were distributed on the last day of such corporation's taxable year on which such corporation is a controlled foreign corporation or is a foreign corporation by reason of the ownership of stock in which the United States shareholder indirectly owns within the meaning of section 958(a)(2) stock in a controlled foreign corporation.

(b) Foreign branch treated as a foreign subsidiary corporation. A United States shareholder's proportionate share of the earnings and profits, for the taxable year, of a branch treated as a wholly owned foreign subsidiary corporation and included in a group under paragraph (f)(4) of § 1.963-1 shall be the total earnings and profits of such branch for the taxable year, as determined under paragraph (f)(4)(ii) of such section.

(c) Indirectly held foreign corporations. If the proportionate share to be determined is of earnings and profits of a foreign corporation the stock of which is owned by the United States shareholder by reason of its ownership of stock (with respect to which the election relates) in another corporation, such shareholder's proportionate share of such earnings and profits for the taxable year shall be determined on the basis of the amount such shareholder would receive from such foreign corporation with respect to stock in such foreign corporation if there were distributed for the taxable year all such earnings and profits, as determined under subparagraph (1) of this paragraph, and of all the earnings and profits of all other corporations through which such earnings and profits must pass in order to be received by such shareholder with respect to the stock to which the election relates. For purposes of the preceding sentence, the amount received by the shareholder from the earnings and profits of a foreign corporation shall be determined without taking into account deductions (whether or not allowable under chapter 1 of the Code) of other foreign corporations through which such earnings and profits are distributed.

(d) More than one class of stock. If a foreign corporation for a taxable year has more than one class of stock outstanding, the earnings and profits of such corporation for such year which shall be taken into account with respect to any one class of such stock shall be the earnings and profits which would be distributed with respect to such class if all earnings and profits of such corporation for such year were distributed on the last day of such corporation's taxable year, on which such corporation is a controlled foreign corporation or is a foreign corporation by reason of the ownership of stock in which the United States shareholder indirectly owns within the meaning of section 958(a)(2) stock in a controlled foreign corporation. If an arrearage in dividends for prior taxable years exists with respect to a class of preferred stock of such corporation, the earnings and profits for the taxable year shall be attributed to such arrearage only to the extent such arrearage exceeds the earnings and profits of such corporation remaining from prior taxable years beginning after December 31, 1962. For example, if a controlled foreign corporation, using the calendar year as its taxable year, has earnings and profits for 1963 of $100 accumulated at December 31, 1963, and an arrearage of $150 for such year in respect of preferred stock, the earnings and profits for 1964 attributable to such arrearage may not exceed $50 ($150-$100).

(e) Discretionary power to allocate earnings to different classes of stock. If the allocation of a foreign corporation's earnings and profits for the taxable year between two or more classes of stock depends upon the exercise of discretion by that body of persons which exercises with respect to such corporation the power ordinarily exercised by the board of directors of a domestic corporation, the allocation of such earnings and profits to such classes shall be made for purposes of this subdivision as if such classes constituted one class of stock in which each share has the same rights to dividends as any other share, unless a different method of allocation of such earnings and profits is made by such body not later than 90 days after the close of such taxable year.

(f) Illustrations. The application of this subdivision may be illustrated by the following examples:

Example (1). Domestic corporation M directly owns 80 percent of the one class of stock of controlled foreign corporation A, which directly owns 60 percent of the one class of stock of controlled foreign corporation B. Each such corporation has earnings and profits of $70 for the taxable year, as determined under subparagraph (1) of this paragraph. Corporation M's proportionate share of the earnings and profits is $56 (0.80 x $70) as to A Corporation and $33.60 (0.80 x 0.60 x $70) as to B Corporation.

Example (2). Throughout 1964 controlled foreign corporation A, which uses the calendar year as the taxable year, has outstanding 40 shares of common stock and 60 shares of 6-percent, nonparticipating, noncumulative preferred stock with a par value of $100 per share. Corporation A has earnings and profits of $1,000, for 1964, as determined under subparagraph (1) of this paragraph. In such case, $360 (0.06 x $100 x 60) of earnings and profits would be taken into account with respect to the preferred stock and $640 ($1,000-$360), with respect to the common stock. Thus, if a United States shareholder owns 10 shares of common stock and 30 shares of preferred stock for 1964, its proportionate share of the earnings and profits for such year is $340 ([10/40 x $640]+[30/60 x $360]).

(ii) Deficit in earnings and profits of a corporation in a chain or group. A United States shareholder's proportionate share, with respect to stock to which the election to secure an exclusion under section 963 relates, of a deficit in earnings and profits of a foreign corporation in a chain or group for a taxable year shall be the portion of such deficit which, if such corporation had earnings and profits for such year as determined under subparagraph (1) of this paragraph and all of such earnings and profits were distributed on the date described in subdivision (i)(a) of this subparagraph, the share of such earnings and profits such shareholder would receive bears to the total of the earnings and profits which would be so distributed on such date. For the determination of the deficit of a foreign branch treated as a wholly owned foreign subsidiary corporation and included in a group, see paragraph (f)(4)(ii) of § 1.963-1. A United States shareholder's proportionate share of the deficit of such a branch shall be the total deficit of such branch for the taxable year.

(iii) Controlled foreign corporation for part of year. If—

(a) Stock in a foreign corporation is owned within the meaning of section 958(a) by a United States shareholder on the last day in the taxable year of such corporation for which such corporation is a controlled foreign corporation to which applies an election by such shareholder to secure an exclusion under section 963 with respect to such stock, or

(b) Stock in a foreign corporation which is not a controlled foreign corporation is owned within the meaning of section 958(a) by a United States shareholder on the last day in the taxable year of such corporation on which another foreign corporation (which, by reason of the stock so owned, is owned by such shareholder within the meaning of section 958(a)) is a controlled foreign corporation to which applies an election by such shareholder to secure an exclusion under section 963 with respect to such stock, the earnings and profits of such foreign corporation for the taxable year which are taken into account in determining such shareholder's proportionate share thereof shall be an amount of such earnings and profits, determined as provided in subparagraph (1) of this paragraph, which bears to the total of such earnings and profits the same ratio which the part (computed on a daily basis) of such year during which such corporation is a controlled foreign corporation (or, in case such corporation is not a controlled foreign corporation, during which such other corporation is a controlled foreign corporation) bears to the total taxable year. If the United States shareholder by sufficient records and accounts establishes to the satisfaction of the district director the gross income received or accrued, and the deductions paid or accrued, for the part of such year during which such corporation is a controlled foreign corporation (or, in case such corporation is not a controlled foreign corporation, during which such other corporation is a controlled foreign corporation), the amount of earnings and profitsbased on such records and accounts may be used in lieu of the amount determined under the preceding sentence. The application of this subdivision may be illustrated by the following examples:

Example (1). Domestic corporation M on June 30, 1963, purchases 60 percent of the one class of stock of A Corporation which on July 1 becomes a controlled foreign corporation and remains such throughout the remainder of 1963. Both corporations use the calendar year as the taxable year. Corporation M makes a first-tier election with respect to A Corporation. For 1963, A Corporation has $100 of earnings and profits, as determined under subparagraph (1) of this paragraph. Corporation M's proportionate share of such earnings and profits for 1963 is $30.25 (0.60 x [184/365 x $100]).

Example (2). (a) Throughout 1963 domestic corporation M directly owns 20 percent of the one class of stock of foreign corporation A, not a controlled foreign corporation at any time, which directly owns 50 percent of the one class of stock of foreign corporation B, which becomes a controlled foreign corporation on July 1, 1963, and remains such throughout the remainder of 1963. All such corporations use the calendar year as the taxable year. Each of corporations A and B has earnings and profits for 1963 of $100, as determined under subparagraph (1) of this paragraph. Corporation M makes a chain election for 1963 with respect to corporations A and B. Corporation M's proportionate share of the earnings and profits of A Corporation for 1963 is $10.08 (0.20 x [184/365 x $100]). Corporation M's proportionate share of the earnings and profits of B Corporation for 1963 is $5.04 (0.20 x 0.50 x [184/365 x $100]).

(b) If B Corporation had been a controlled foreign corporation throughout 1963, M Corporation's proportionate share of the earnings and profits of corporations A and B for 1963 would have been $20 (0.20 x $100) and $10 (0.20 x 0.50 x $100), respectively.

(c) If corporations A and B had each been a controlled foreign corporation only for the period of January 1, 1963, through June 30, 1963, M Corporation's proportionate share of the earnings and profits of such corporations would have been $9.92 (0.20 x [181/365 x $100[) and $4.98 (0.20 x 0.50 x [181/365 x $100]), respectively.

(d) If A Corporation had been a controlled foreign corporation throughout 1963 or during the period of July 1, 1963, through December 31, 1963, but B Corporation had been a controlled foreign corporation only during the period of January 1, 1963, through June 30, 1963, M Corporation's proportionate share of the earnings and profits of such corporations would have been $20 (0.20 x $100) and $4.96 (0.20 x 0.50 x [181/365 x $100]), respectively.

(3) Consolidated earnings and profits with respect to United States shareholder. The consolidated earnings and profits of a chain or group with respect to any United States shareholder for the taxable year shall be the sum of such shareholder's proportionate shares of the earnings and profits, and of the deficit in earnings and profits, determined under subparagraph (2) of this paragraph, for such year of all foreign corporations, whether or not controlled foreign corporations, in such chain or group.

(e) Foreign income taxes used in determining effective foreign tax rate. For purposes of determining the effective foreign tax rate under paragraph (c) of this section—

(1) Shareholder's proportionate share of taxes of a foreign corporation. The foreign income tax of a foreign corporation for a taxable year shall consist of the foreign income tax referred to in paragraph (d)(1)(ii) of this section with respect to such year and, if the United States shareholder chooses to take the foreign income tax described in paragraph (d)(1)(iii) of this section into account in determining the effective foreign tax rate of a chain or group which includes such foreign corporation, the foreign income tax referred to in such paragraph with respect to such year. A United States shareholder's proportionate share, with respect to stock to which the election to secure an exclusion under section 963 applies, of the foreign income tax of such foreign corporation for a taxable year shall be the same proportion of such foreign income tax that such shareholder's proportionate share (as determined under paragraph (d)(2)(i) of this section) of the earnings and profits of such corporation for such year bears to the total earnings and profits of such corporation for such year. A United States shareholder's proportionate share of the foreign income tax, for the taxable year of a branch treated as a wholly owned foreign subsidiary corporation and included in a group under paragraph (f)(4) of § 1.963-1 shall be the total foreign income tax of such branch for the taxable year.

(2) Consolidated foreign income taxes with respect to United States shareholder. The consolidated foreign income taxes of a chain or group with respect to a United States shareholder for the taxable year of such chain or group shall be the sum of such shareholder's proportionate shares (as determined under subparagraph (1) of this paragraph) of the foreign income tax of all foreign corporations, whether or not controlled foreign corporations, in such chain or group.

(3) Taxes paid by foreign corporation on distributions received during its distribution period. If a distribution received by a foreign corporation in a chain or group from another foreign corporation in such chain or group after the close of the recipient's taxable year but during its distribution period for such year is allocated to the earnings and profits of such recipient corporation for such year under paragraph (c)(2) of § 1.963-3, then any foreign income tax paid or accrued by such recipient corporation on such distribution shall be treated as paid or accrued for such taxable year.

(f) Illustrations. The application of this section may be illustrated by the following examples:

Example (1). For 1966, domestic corporation M makes a first-tier election with respect to controlled foreign corporation A, 80 percent of the one class of stock of which M orporation owns directly. Both corporations use the calendar year as the taxable year. For 1966, A Corporation has earnings and profits (before reduction for foreign income tax) of $100 with respect to which it pays foreign income tax of $30. Its earnings and profits are $70 ($100-$30). Corporation M's proportionate share of such earnings and profits is $56 (0.80 x $70), and its proportionate share of the foreign income tax is $24 ($56/$70 x $30). The effective foreign tax rate is 30 percent ($24/[$56+$24]). Based on such effective foreign tax rate, the statutory percentage under section 963(b)(3) for 1966 is 69 percent. Thus, the amount of the minimum distribution which M Corporation must receive from A Corporation's 1966 earnings and profits is a dividend of $38.64 (0.69 x $56).

Example (2). For 1966, domestic corporation M makes a first-tier election with respect to controlled foreign corporation A, all of whose one class of stock M Corporation owns directly. Both corporations use the calendar year as the taxable year. For 1966, A Corporation has earnings and profits (before reduction for income tax) of $100, of which $40 is attributable to income from sources within the United States on which $12 United States income tax is paid. The foreign country in which A Corporation is incorporated imposes an income tax at 30 percent on the $100 but allows a credit against its tax for the $12 of United States income tax, so that it imposes a net foreign income tax of $18 for 1966. In determining the effective foreign tax rate of A Corporation for 1966, such $12 of United States income tax may be treated as foreign income tax to the extent it does not exceed $17.28 ($40 x 0.90 x .48). Corporation A has earnings and profits of $70 for 1966. Although A Corporation's effective foreign tax rate for 1966 is 30 percent, determined by dividing $30 by the sum of $70 plus $30, none of the United States tax which is taken into account in determining such rate shall be treated as foreign income tax for purposes of determining the foreign tax credit of M Corporation under section 902. Based on such effective foreign tax rate, the statutory percentage under section 963(b)(3) for 1966 is 69 percent. Thus, the amount of the minimum distribution which M Corporation must receive from A Corporation's 1966 earnings and profits is a dividend of $48.30 (0.69 x $70).

Example (3). Domestic corporation M directly owns throughout 1966, 60 percent of the one class of stock of controlled foreign corporation A, not a less developed country corporation under section 902(d), which has for 1966 earnings and profits of $70 (all of which is attributable to subpart F income) after having paid foreign income tax of $30. Both corporations use the calendar year as the taxable year. Corporation A is created under the laws of a foreign country which imposes a 6-percent dividend withholding tax.

Corporation M would be required, but for section 963, to include $42 (0.60 x $70) of A Corporation's subpart F income in gross income under section 951(a)(1)(A)(i). For 1966, however, M Corporation makes a first-tier election with respect to A Corporation. Since the tax withheld on distributions made by A Corporation is considered to have been paid by M Corporation, the effective foreign tax rate applicable to A Corporation for 1966 is only 30 percent, the percentage which such $30 of foreign income tax is of $100 (the sum of $30 plus $70). Thus, the statutory percentage under section 963(b) for 1966 is 69 percent. The amount of the minimum distribution which M Corporation must receive from A Corporation's 1966 earnings and profits is the distribution M Corporation will receive if A Corporation distributes 69 percent of its earnings and profits for 1966. Thus, if M Corporation receives a distribution of 69 percent of its proportionate share of such earnings and profits or $28.98 (0.69 x 0.60 x $70), it may exclude from gross income for 1966 $42 otherwise required to be included in gross income under section 951(a)(1)(A)(i) and will determine its income tax, assuming no other income and no surtax exemption under section 11(c), as follows:

Dividend	$28.98
Gross-up under section 78 ($28.98/$70×$30)	12.42
Taxable income	41.40
U.S. tax before foreign tax credit ($41.40×0.48)	19.87
Foreign tax credit ($12.42+[0.06×$28.98])	14.16
U.S. tax payable	5.71

Example (4). (a) For 1966 domestic corporation M makes a chain election with respect to controlled foreign corporation A, all of whose one class of stock it directly owns, and controlled foreign corporation B, all of whose one class of stock is directly owned by A Corporation. Both foreign corporations are subject to a foreign income tax at a flat rate of 30 percent, and all corporations use the calendar year as a taxable year. For 1966, B Corporation has pretax earnings and profits of $100 and distributes $51.50. For 1966, A Corporation has pretax earnings and profits of $151.50, consisting of $100 from selling activities and $51.50 received as a distribution from B Corporation, upon which it pays a foreign income tax of $45.45 (i.e., 30 percent of $151.50).

(b) Corporation M chooses under paragraph (d)(1)(iii) of this section to take the foreign tax paid by A Corporation on the dividend received from B Corporation into account in determining the effective foreign tax rate of the chain rather than count it toward the amount of the minimum distribution. Thus, to determine consolidated earnings and profits of the chain for 1966, A Corporation's pretax earnings and profits of $151.50 are first reduced by the intercorporate dividend of $51.50 received from B Corporation so that A Corporation has pretax and predistribution earnings and profits of $100 ($151.50 less $51.50). Corporation A's pretax and predistribution earnings and profits of $100 are then reduced by the foreign income tax of $30 (30 percent of $100) paid on such earnings and profits, resulting in predistribution earnings and profits of $70 ($100 less $30). Since M Corporation chooses to count toward the effective foreign tax rate, rather than toward the minimum distribution, A Corporation's foreign income tax of $15.45 (0.30 x 51.50) imposed on the dividend received from B Corporation, such predistribution earnings and profits of $70 of A Corporation are further reduced by such $15.45 of tax to $54.55 ($70-$15.45). Corporation B, having received no dividends from any other corporation in the chain, has predistribution earnings and profits of $70 ($100 less foreign income tax of $30).

(c) The consolidated earnings and profits of the chain for 1966 are $124.55 ($54.55+$70). The consolidated foreign income taxes for such year are $75.45 ($30+$15.45+$30). The effective foreign tax rate of the chain for 1966 is 37.73 percent ($75.45/[$124.55+$75.45]). The statutory percentage for 1966 under section 963(b)(3) is 51 percent. Thus, the amount of the minimum distribution which M Corporation must receive from the 1966 consolidated earnings and profits of the chain is $63.52 (0.51 x $124.55).

Example (5). The facts are the same as in example 4 except that M Corporation does not choose under paragraph (d)(1)(iii) of this section to take into account, in determining the effective foreign tax rate, the foreign income tax of $15.45 paid by A Corporation on the distribution of $51.50 received from B Corporation. In such case, the consolidated earnings and profits of the chain are $140 ($70+$70) and the consolidated foreign income taxes are $60 ($30+$30), the latter amount being determined without taking into account A Corporation's foreign income tax of $15.45 on the distribution of $51.50 received from B Corporation. The effective foreign tax rate for 1966 is 30 percent ($60/[$140+$60]), and the statutory percentage under section 963(b) is 69 percent. Thus, the amount of the minimum distribution which must be made from the 1966 consolidated earnings and profits of the chain is $96.60 (0.69 x $140). For the counting of such $15.45 of A Corporation's tax toward the $96.60 amount of the minimum distribution, see paragraph (b)(2) of § 1.963-3.

Example (6). For 1966 domestic corporation M directly owns the following percentages of the one class of stock of the following controlled foreign corporations in respect of which it makes a group election: 80 percent of A Corporation, 60 percent of B Corporation, and 70 percent of C Corporation. All corporations use the calendar year as the taxable year; none of the foreign corporations is a less developed country corporation under section 902(d). Each foreign corporation makes distributions during 1966. The consolidated earnings and profits, and the consolidated foreign income taxes, of the group for 1966 with respect to M Corporation, and the amount of the minimum distribution which M Corporation must receive, are determined as follows, based on the earnings and profits and foreign income tax shown in the following table:

	Controlled foreign corporations		
	A	B	C
Predistribution and pretax earnings and profits	$100	$100	$100.00
Foreign income tax	15	25	35.00
Predistribution earnings and profits	85	75	65.00
M Corporation's proportionate share of earnings and profits:			
(0.80×$85)	68	...	...
(0.60×$75)	...	45	...
(0.70×$65)	...	...	45.50
Consolidated earnings and profits with respect to M Corporation ($68+$45+$45.00)	...	...	158.50
M Corporation's proportionate share of foreign income tax:			
($15×[$68/$85])	12	...	...
($25×[$45/$75])	...	15	...
($35×[$45.50/$65])	...	...	24.50

Consolidated foreign income tazes with respect to M Corporation ($12+$15+$24.50)	51.50

The effective foreign tax rate for 1966 is 24.5 percent ($51.50/[$158.50+$51.50]) and the statutory percentage under section 963(b)(3) for such year is 76 percent. Thus, the amount of the minimum distribution which M Corporation must receive from the 1966 consolidated earnings and profits of the group is $120.46 (0.76 x $158.50).

Example (7). (a) For 1966 domestic corporation M makes a chain election with respect to the following controlled foreign corporations: A Corporation, 80 percent of whose one class of stock M Corporation owns directly; B Corporation, 60 percent of whose one class of stock is directly owned by A Corporation; and C Corporation, 70 percent of whose one class of stock is directly owned by B Corporation. All corporations use the calendar year as the taxable year; none of the foreign corporations is a less developed country corporation under section 902(d). The predistribution and pretax earnings and profits of each foreign corporation are $100. Each foreign corporation pays a flat rate of foreign income tax on all income computed without reduction for dividends paid and determined by including dividends received. Such rate is 15 percent for A Corporation, 25 percent for B Corporation, and 35 percent for C Corporation. Corporation C distributes $65, and B Corporation distributes $100, for 1966. Corporation M chooses under paragraph (d)(1)(iii) of this section to count toward the effective foreign tax rate, rather than toward the amount of the minimum distribution, the foreign income tax paid by corporations A and B, respectively, on distributions received from corporations B and C, respectively.

(b) The consolidated earnings and profits, and the consolidated foreign income taxes, of the chain, and the amount of the minimum distribution for 1966, with respect to M Corporation are determined as follows:

	Controlled foreign corporations			
	A	B	C	Total
Pretax earnings and profits	$160.00	$145.50	$100.00	...
Reduction for intercorporate dividends:				
(0.60×$100)	60.00	...	...	...
(0.70×$65)	...	45.50	...	...
Pretax and predistribution earnings and profits	100.00	100.00	100.00	...
Reduction for foreign income tax on intercorporate distributions of 1966 earnings and profits:				
(0.15×$100)	15.00	...	...	...
0.25×$100)	...	25.00	...	...
(0.35×$100)	...	...	35.00	...
Predistribution earnings and profits:	85.00	75.00	65.00	...
Reduction for foreign income tax on intercorporate distributions of 1966 earnings and profits:				
(0.15×$60)	9.00	...	...	...
(0.25×$45.50)	...	11.38	...	...
	76.00	63.62	65.00	
Consolidated earnings and profits with respect to M Corporation:				
(0.80×$76)	60.80	...	...	...
(0.80×0.60×$63.62)	...	30.54	...	...
(0.80×0.60×$65)	...	...	21.84	$113.18
Consolidated foreign income taxes with respect to M Corporation:				
($60.80/$76×[$15+$9])	19.20	...	...	...
($30.54/$63.62×[$25+$11.38])	...	17.46	...	...
($21.84/$65×$35)	...	...	11.76	$ 48.42
Effective foreign tax rate ($48.42/[$113.18+$48.42])	...	...	...	29.96%
Statutory percentage under section 963(b)				69 %
Amount of minimum distribution which M Corporation must receive from 1966 consolidated earnings and profits (0.69×$113.18), no amount of the tax on intercoporate distributions being counted toward the minimum distribution	...	...	...	$ 78.0

Example (8). The facts are the same as in example 7 except that M Corporation does not choose under paragraph (d)(1)(iii) of this section to take into account, in determining the effective foreign tax rate, the foreign income tax paid by the recipient corporations on the intercorporate distributions. The consolidated earnings and profits, the consolidated foreign income taxes, of the chain, and the amount of the minimum distribution which M Corporation must receive, for 1966 are determined as follows:

T.D. 6759, 9/25/64, amend T.D. 6767, 11/3/64, T.D. 7100, 3/20/71.

§ 1.963-3 Distributions counting toward a minimum distribution.

(a) Conditions under which earnings and profits are counted toward a minimum distribution. *(1) In general.* A distribution to the United States shareholder by a single first-tier corporation or by a foreign corporation included in a chain or group shall count toward a minimum distribution for the taxable year of such shareholder to which the election under section 963 relates only to the extent that—

(i) It is received by such shareholder during such year or within 180 days thereafter,

(ii) It is a distribution of the type described in paragraph (b) of this section,

(iii) Under paragraph (c) of this section, it is deemed to be distributed from the earnings and profits of the foreign corporations for the taxable year of such corporation to which the election relates, and

(iv) Such shareholder chooses to include it in gross income for the taxable year of such shareholder to which the election relates notwithstanding that such distribution, by reason of its receipt after the close of such year, would ordinarily be includible in the gross income of a subsequent year.

Amounts taken into account under this subparagraph as gross income of the United States shareholder for the taxable year to which the election relates shall not be considered to be includible in the gross income of such shareholder for a subsequent taxable year. For purposes of determining the foreign tax credit under sections 901 through 905, foreign income tax paid or accrued by such shareholder on or with respect to such amounts shall be treated as paid or accrued during the taxable year of such election.

(2) Distributions made prior to acquisition of stock. A United States shareholder which owns within the meaning of section 958(a) stock in a foreign corporation with respect to which such shareholder elects to secure an exclusion under section 963 for the taxable year may count toward the minimum distribution any distribution made with respect to such stock, and before its acquisition by the United States shareholder, to any other domestic corporation not exempt from income tax under chapter 1 of the Code, to the extent that such distribution is made out of the United States shareholder's proportionate share, as determined under paragraph (d)(2) of § 1.963-2, of such corporation's earnings and profits for the taxable year and would have counted toward a minimum distribution if it had been distributed to such United States shareholder. The application of this subparagraph may be illustrated by the following examples:

Example (1). Controlled foreign corporation A, which uses the calendar year as the taxable year, has for 1963 $100 of earnings and profits and 100 shares of only one class of stock outstanding. Domestic corporation M, not exempt from income tax under chapter 1 of the Code, directly owns all of such shares during the period from January 1, 1963, through June 30, 1963. On June 30, 1963, M Corporation transfers all of such shares to domestic corporation N, which owns them throughout the remainder of 1963 and elects to secure an exclusion under section 963 for such year with respect to the subpart F income of A Corporation. During June 1963, M Corporation receives a dividend of $75 from A Corporation, which would count toward a minimum distribution if it had been distributed to N Corporation for such year. Corporation N's proportionate share of the earnings and profits of A Corporation for 1963 is $100; N Corporation may count toward a minimum distribution for 1963 the entire dividend of $75 paid to M Corporation.

Example (2). The facts are the same as in example 1 except that M is a nonresident alien individual. Since A Corporation is not a controlled foreign corporation from January 1, 1963, through June 30, 1963, N Corporation's proportionate share of the earnings and profits of A Corporation for 1963 is $50.41 ($100 x 184/365), as determined under paragraph (d)(2)(iii) of § 1.963-2. Although $25.41 ($75-$49.59) of the $75 distribution to M is paid from N Corporation's proportionate share of A Corporation's 1963 earnings and profits, N Corporation may not count toward a minimum distribution any part of the $75 dividend distributed to M, since M is not a domestic corporation.

(b) Qualifying distributions. *(1) Amounts not counted toward a minimum distribution.* No distribution received by a United States shareholder shall count toward a minimum distribution for the taxable year with respect to such shareholder to the extent the distribution is excludable from gross income to the extent gain on the distribution is not recognized, or to the extent the distribution is treated as a distribution in part or full payment in exchange for stock. Undistributed amounts required to be included in gross income under section 551 as undistributed foreign personal holding company income or under section 951 as undistributed amounts of a controlled foreign corporation shall not count toward a minimum distribution under section 963. An amount received by a United States shareholder as a distribution which under section 302 or section 331 is treated as a distribution in part or full payment in exchange for stock shall not count toward a minimum distribution even though such amount is includible in gross income under section 1248 as a dividend. For purposes of this subparagraph, any portion of a distribution of earnings and profits which is attributable to an increase in current earnings, invested in United States property which, but for paragraph (e) of this section, would be included in the gross income of the United States shareholder under section 951(a)(1)(B) shall not be treated as an amount excludable from gross income.

(2) Inclusion of tax on intercorporate distributions. In the case of a chain or group election, the United States shareholder's proportionate share of the amount of the foreign income tax paid or accrued for the taxable year by a foreign corporation in the chain or group with respect to distributions received by such corporation from the earnings and profits, of another foreign corporation in such chain or group, for the taxable year of such other corporation to which the election relates shall count toward a minimum distribution from such chain or group for the taxable year, but only if the United States shareholder does not choose under paragraph (d)(1)(iii) of § 1.963-2 to take such tax into account in determining the effective foreign tax rate of such chain or group for the taxable year. To the extent that foreign income tax counts toward a minimum distribution under this subparagraph, it shall be applied against and reduce the amount of the minimum distribution required to be received by the United States shareholder, determined without regard to this paragraph.

(c) Rules for allocation of distributions to earnings and profits for a taxable year. To determine whether a distribution to the United States shareholder by a single first-tier corporation or by a foreign corporation in a chain or group is made from the earnings and profits of such corporation for the taxable year to which the election under section 963 relates, the following subparagraphs shall apply:

(1) Exception to section 316. Section 316 shall apply except that a distribution of earnings and profits made by a foreign corporation either to another foreign corporation or to the United States shareholder shall be treated as having been paid from the earnings and profits of the distributing corporation for the taxable year of such corporation to which the election relates only if it is made during its distribution period (described in paragraph (g) of this section) for such year.

(2) Distributions from other corporations. The earnings and profits of a foreign corporation shall be determined in accordance with paragraph (d)(1) of § 1.963-2 (applied as though the United States shareholder had chosen under sub-

paragraph (1)(iii) of such paragraph to take the tax described therein into account in determining the effective foreign tax rate) except that, in the case of a chain or group election, a distribution received by a foreign corporation in the chain or group from another foreign corporation in such chain or group shall be taken into account as earnings and profits of the recipient corporation for the taxable year of such recipient corporation to which the election relates but only to the extent that—

(i) The distribution is received by the recipient corporation during the distribution period for the taxable year of such recipient corporation to which the election relates,

(ii) If the distribution had been received by the United States shareholder, it would have constituted a distribution of the type described in paragraph (b) of this section, and

(iii) The distribution is made from the earnings and profits of the distributing corporation for the taxable year of such distributing corporation to which the election relates.

(d) Year of inclusion in income of foreign corporation and effect upon subpart F income. To the extent that a distribution to the United States shareholder counting toward a minimum distribution from a chain or group consists of earnings and profits distributed to a foreign corporation in the chain or group after the close of the recipient corporation's taxable year but during its distribution period for such year by another foreign corporation in such chain or group, such amount shall be treated as received by the recipient corporation on the last day of such taxable year and shall not be regarded as foreign personal holding company income (within the meaning of section 553(a) or 954(c)) of such corporation for the taxable year in which such amount is actually received. The extent to which a distribution counting toward a minimum distribution consists of earnings and profits distributed to a foreign corporation in a chain or group shall be determined under the ordering rules of paragraph (b)(3) of § 1.963-4 (applied in each instance as though the United States shareholder had not chosen under paragraph (d)(1)(iii) of § 1.963-2 to take the tax described therein into account in determining the effective foreign tax rate). However, for such purpose, the amount of foreign income tax, if any, which counts toward the minimum distribution shall be determined without regard to paragraph (b)(2) of this section but in accordance with paragraph (b)(3)(iii) of § 1.963-4.

(e) Distribution of current earnings invested in United States property. A distribution made by a foreign corporation during its distribution period for a taxable year shall, notwithstanding section 959(c), first be attributed to earnings and profits for such year described in section 959(c)(3) and then to other earnings and profits. For such purposes, earnings and profits of such foreign corporation for such year attributable to amounts which would otherwise be included in gross income of the United States shareholder under section 951(a)(1)(B) for such year shall be treated as earnings and profits to which section 959(c)(3) applies, shall not be excluded from gross income under section 959 (a) or (b), and shall count toward a minimum distribution for such year. See paragraph (c)(1)(v) of § 1.960-1 and paragraph (a) of § 1.960-2.

(f) Cumulative dividends in arrears. A distribution in satisfaction of arrearages shall be treated as being made out of earnings and profits of the foreign corporation for the taxable year to which the election under section 963 applies only to the extent the dividend is not attributed, under paragraph (d)(2)(i)(d) of § 1.963-2, to the earnings and profits of such corporation remaining from prior taxable years beginning after December 31, 1962. The application of this paragraph may be illustrated by the following example:

Example. For 1963, single first-tier corporation A, which uses the calendar year as the taxable year, has earnings and profits of $50; for 1964, a deficit in earnings and profits of $20; for 1965, earnings and profits of $100; and for 1966, earnings and profits of $240. For each of such years preferred dividends accumulate at the rate of $60; but no dividend is paid until 1966 during which year the current dividend is paid and $180 is distributed toward the arrearages. Of this $180, only $50 ($180-$130) shall be treated as paid from 1966 earnings and profits.

(g) Distribution period of a foreign corporation. *(1) General distribution period.* Except as provided by subparagraph (2) of this paragraph, the distribution period with respect to a foreign corporation for its taxable year shall begin immediately after the close of the distribution period for the preceding taxable year and shall end with the close of the 60th day of the next succeeding taxable year. If no election to secure an exclusion under section 963 applied to the preceding taxable year, the distribution period for the taxable year shall begin with the 61st day of the taxable year.

(2) Special extended distribution period. If the United States shareholder of the foreign corporation so elects in statement filed with its return for the taxable year for which the election to secure the exclusion under section 963 is made, the distribution period with respect to such foreign corporation for its taxable year to which the election to secure the exclusion applies shall end with any day which occurs no earlier than the last day of such taxable year of such foreign corporation and no later than the 180th day after the close of such taxable year. The statement shall designate the day so elected as the end of the distribution period.

(h) Illustrations. The application of this section may be illustrated by the following examples:

Example (1). For 1963 domestic corporation M makes a chain election with respect to controlled foreign corporation A, all of whose one class of stock M Corporation directly owns, and controlled foreign corporation B, all of whose one class of stock is directly owned by A Corporation. All such corporations use the calendar year as the taxable year, and the distribution periods of corporations A and B for 1963 coincide. Corporations A and B each have earnings and profits (before distributions) of $100 for 1963. On June 1, 1963, B Corporation distributes earnings and profits of $120, of which $100 is from its earnings and profits for 1963 and $20 is from prior earnings. For 1963, A Corporation pays no income tax and distributes earnings and profits of $150 to M Corporation. Under paragraph (c) of this section, such $150 is allocated to A Corporation's earnings and profits of $200 for 1963, consisting of its total earnings and profits for that year of $220 less the $20 received as a distribution from B Corporation's prior earnings.

Example (2). Domestic corporation M directly owns all of the one class of stock of controlled foreign corporation A. Both corporations use the calendar year as the taxable year, and A Corporation's taxable year and its distribution period for 1963 coincide. For 1963, $50 is included in the gross income of M Corporation under section 951(a)(1)(B) as A Corporation's increase in earnings invested for such year in United States property. For 1964, M Corporation makes a first-tier election with respect to A Corporation. For 1964, A Corporation has earnings and profits of $100, including $10 attributable to an increase in earnings invested for such year in United States property. During 1964, A Corporation distributes earnings and profits of $80 to M Corporation. Without regard to paragraph (e) of this section, $10 of this distribution is attributable under section 959(c)(1) to A Corporation's 1964 earnings and profits required to be included in M Corporation's gross income under section 951(a)(1)(D). Pursuant to paragraph (e) of this section, however, the entire distribution of $80 counts toward a minimum distribution for 1964 and is considered to be from earnings and profits of A Corporation for 1964 described in section 959(c)(3). Thus the entire distribution of $80 is included in M Corporation's gross income as a dividend and the foreign tax credit in respect of such amount is determined in accordance with section 902 as modified by the regulations under section 963. On the other hand, if A Corporation made no distributions for 1964, no part of the $10 of A Corporation's increase in earnings invested in United States property for such year would count toward a minimum distribution for any other year but would be included in the gross income for M Corporation for 1964 under section 951(a)(1)(B), and the foreign tax credit in respect of such amount would be determined in accordance with § 1.960-1.

Example (3). For 1964 domestic corporation M makes a chain election with respect to controlled foreign corporation A, all the one class of stock of which is owned directly by M Corporation, and controlled foreign corporation B, all the one class of stock of which is owned directly by A Corporation. Corporation M makes no election under section 963 for 1963 or 1965. Corporations M and B use the calendar year as the taxable year, and A Corporation uses for its taxable year a fiscal year ending on September 30. Corporation M elects to have the distribution period for each controlled foreign corporation end on March 29, 1965, such date being the 180th day after the close of A Corporation's taxable year ending on September 30, 1964. Corporation A's distribution period for its taxable year ending on September 30, 1964, begins on November 30, 1963, the 61st day of such taxable year. The distribution period of B Corporation for 1964 begins on March 1, 1964, the 61st day of such taxable year. A distribution counting toward a minimum distribution for 1964 may be made from the earnings and profits of B Corporation only if the amount thereof is distributed by B Corporation to A Corporation, and in turn by A Corporation to M Corporation, during the period of March 1, 1964, through March 29, 1965.

Example (4). The facts are the same as in example 3, except that for their taxable years ending in 1964, corporations A and B each have earnings and profits (before distributions) of $100. On March 10, 1965, B Corporation distributes to A Corporation a dividend of $80 upon which A Corporation incurs foreign income tax at the rate of 10 percent. On March 15, 1965, A Corporation distributes to M Corporation a dividend of $50. Corporation M chooses to take into account as gross income for 1964 from such distribution only $40. For purposes of applying this section, the distribution counting toward a minimum distribution is $44.44, consisting of the $40 of earnings and profits actually received by M Corporation plus the $4.44 ($40/$72 x $8) of foreign income tax incurred by A Corporation attributable thereto; A Corporation is deemed to have received $44.44 ($40÷0.90) of the distribution from B Corporation on September 30, 1964, the last day of the taxable year of A Corporation to which the election relates; and the foreign personal holding company income derived by A Corporation for its taxable year ending in 1965 from the distribution from B is only $35.56 ($80-$44.44). Assuming that no exceptions, exclusions, or exemptions were applicable, subpart F income would be realized by A Corporation for its taxable year ending on September 30, 1965, upon the distribution by B Corporation to A Corporation, but only in the amount of $32 ($35.56 less a deduction under section 954(b)(5) for taxes of $3.56).

T.D. 7100, 6/4/71, amend T.D. 7334, 12/23/74.

§ 1.963-4 Limitations on minimum distribution from a chain or group.

(a) Minimum overall tax burden. *(1) In general.* Notwithstanding the fact that distributions of the type described in paragraph (a) of § 1.963-3 are made by a chain or group to the United States shareholder in an amount sufficient to constitute a minimum distribution for the taxable year of such shareholder to which the chain or group election relates, no exclusion shall be allowable under section 963 to such shareholder with respect to such chain or group for such year unless—

(i) Without applying the special rules set forth in paragraphs (b) and (c) of this section, the overall United States and foreign income tax (as defined in subparagraph (2)(ii) of this paragraph) for the taxable year with respect to the distribution which is made equals or exceeds 90 percent of an amount determined by multiplying the sum of the consolidated earnings and profits (as determined under paragraph (d)(3) of § 1.963-2) and the consolidated foreign income taxes (as determined under paragraph (e)(2) of § 1.963-2) of such chain or group for the taxable year with respect to such shareholder by a percentage which equals the sum of the normal tax rate and the surtax rate (determined without regard to the surtax exemption) prescribed by section 11 for the taxable year of the shareholder, or

(ii) With the application of the special rules set forth in paragraphs (b) and (c) of this section—

(a) Such shareholder receives a pro rata minimum distribution (as defined in subparagraph (2)(i) of this paragraph) from such chain or group for such taxable year, or

(b) To the extent necessary, the amount of the foreign income tax allowable as a credit for such year under section 901 with respect to the distribution which is made is reduced and credit for the reduction is deferred, as provided in paragraph (c)(3) of this section, so that the overall United States and foreign income tax for the taxable year with respect to such distribution equals or exceeds the lesser of—

(1) The overall United States and foreign income tax which would be paid or accrued for such year with respect to a pro rata minimum distribution received by such shareholder from such chain or group for such year, and

(2) Ninety percent of an amount determined by multiplying the sum of the consolidated earnings and profits (as determined under paragraph (b)(1) of this section) and the consolidated foreign income taxes (as determined under paragraph (b)(1) of this section) of such chain or group for the taxable year with respect to such shareholder by a percentage which equals the sum of the normal tax rate and the surtax rate (determined without regard to the surtax exemption) prescribed by section 11 for the taxable year of the shareholder.

(2) Definitions. For purposes of §§ 1.963-1 through 1.963.8—

(i) Pro rata minimum distribution. A pro rata minimum distribution from a chain or group for the taxable year is a distribution of earnings and profits to the United States shareholder, with respect to stock to which the chain or group election relates, which is the statutory percentage (applicable with respect to such chain or group as determined under paragraph (b) of § 1.963-2) of the United States shareholder's proportionate share of the taxable year's earnings and profits of each foreign corporation in such chain or group (determined in accordance with paragraph (d)(2) of § 1.963-2 but without making any deduction under paragraph (d)(1)(iii) of such section).

(ii) Overall United States and foreign income tax. The overall United States and foreign income tax for any taxable year of a chain or group with respect to a minimum distribution is the sum of—

(a) The consolidated foreign income taxes of the chain or group for such year with respect to the United States shareholder making the chain or group election,

(b) Any other foreign income tax paid or accrued by a foreign corporation in the chain or group by reason of the receipt of any distributions counting toward such minimum distribution from such chain or group for that year, and

(c) The foreign income tax, if any, and United States income tax paid or accrued by such shareholder upon amounts counting toward such minimum distribution from such chain or group for such year.

Such overall United States and foreign income tax shall be determined with respect to such minimum distribution without taking into account any foreign income tax which is deemed paid for such year under section 904(d), relating to carryback and carryover of excess tax paid. For purposes of this subdivision, the consolidated foreign income taxes of the chain or group shall be determined under paragraph (e)(2) of § 1.963-2, applied without regard to the second sentence of paragraph (d)(1) of that section.

(3) Taxes paid by foreign corporation on distributions received during its distribution period. For purposes of determining foreign income tax deemed paid by the United States shareholder for the taxable year under section 902, if a distribution received by a foreign corporation in a chain or group from another foreign corporation in such chain or group after the close of the recipient's taxable year but during its distribution period for such year is allocated to the earnings and profits of such recipient corporation for such year under paragraph (c)(2) of § 1.963-3, any foreign income tax paid or accrued by such recipient corporation on such distribution shall be treated as paid or accrued for such taxable year.

(4) Illustration. The application of this paragraph may be illustrated by the following example:

Example. (a) Domestic corporation M directly owns all of the one class of stock of foreign corporation A, which in turn directly owns all of the one class of stock of foreign corporation B. Corporation M makes a chain election with respect to A Corporation and B Corporation. All such corporations use the calendar year as the taxable year. Assuming that A Corporation does not incur foreign tax on amounts distributed by B Corporation, the foreign income tax and earnings and profits of corporations A and B, the effective foreign tax rate, and the statutory percentage for 1966, are as follows:

(b) Corporation M is entitled for 1966 to exclude its pro rata share of the subpart F income of corporations A and B for such year if it receives from the 1966 consolidated earnings and profits of the chain distributions totaling at least $96.60 (0.69 x $140) and if—

(1) The sum of the consolidated foreign income taxes ($60) of the chain for 1966 and of the United States income tax for 1966 (determined by taking into account the foreign tax credit under section 901 without regard to paragraph (c) of this section) imposed on such distributions equals at least $86.40 (0.90 x 0.48 x $200);

(2) Under the special rules of paragraphs (b) and (c) of this section, the distributions received consist of a distribution from each of corporations A and B which is 69 percent of the earnings and profits for 1966 of such corporation, that is, a distribution of $55.20 (0.69 x $80) from A Corporation and of $41.40 (0.69 x $60) from B Corporation; or

(3) Under the special rules of paragraphs (b) and (c) of this section, the foreign tax credit is reduced and deferred to such an extent that the sum of the consolidated foreign income taxes ($60) of the chain for 1966 and of the United States income tax for 1966 (determined by taking into account the foreign tax credit under section 901 as modified by paragraph (c) of this section) imposed on such distributions equals the lesser of $86.40 (0.90 x 0.48 x $200) and the amount which the sum of such taxes would be if M Corporation were to receive a distribution of $55.20 (0.69 x $80) from the 1966 earnings and profits of A Corporation and $41.40 (0.69 x $60) from the 1966 earnings and profits of B Corporation.

(b) Special rules for determining earnings and profits and foreign income taxes. For purposes of determining the minimum overall tax burden under paragraph (a)(1)(ii) of this section, §§ 1.963-2 and 1.963-3 shall apply as modified by the following subparagraphs:

(1) Exclusion of tax on intercorporate distributions. The consolidated earnings and profits and consolidated foreign income taxes of a chain or group for the taxable year shall be determined in accordance with § 1.963-2, except that foreign income tax referred to in paragraph (d)(1)(iii) of such section may be taken into account in determining the effective foreign tax rate only—

(i) To the extent that such tax is not deemed paid by the United States shareholder under section 902 (as modified by paragraph (c) of this section) for its taxable year to which the chain or group election relates, or

(ii) If, by taking the tax into account, the effective foreign tax rate with respect to such chain or group, as determined under paragraph (c)(2) of § 1.963-2, exceeds the highest effective foreign tax rate requiring a distribution under section 963(b) for such year of the shareholder.

(2) Allocation of deficits. For purposes of determining the amount of each foreign corporation's share of a pro rata minimum distribution from a chain or group for the taxable year and for purposes of determining the foreign tax credit under paragraph (c) of this section of the United States shareholder with respect to any minimum distribution from a chain or group for the taxable year—

(i) Deficits of foreign corporations. The total of the United States shareholder's proportionate shares, as determined under paragraph (d)(2)(ii) of § 1.963-2, of the deficit of every foreign corporation in the chain or group having a deficit for the taxable year shall be allocated against and shall reduce such shareholder's proportionate share, as determined under paragraph (d)(2)(i) of § 1.963-2, of the earnings and profits for the taxable year of each other foreign corporation in the chain or group having earnings and profits for such year in an amount which bears to such total of shares of deficit the same ratio which such share of earnings and profits bears to the total of such shareholder's proportionate shares, as so determined, of the earnings and profits of all foreign corporations in the chain or group having earnings and profits for the taxable year.

(ii) Deficits of foreign branches. If for the taxable year a group includes under paragraph (f)(4) of § 1.963-1 foreign branches the aggregate of whose allowable deductions (other than any net operating loss deduction) exceeds the aggregate of their gross incomes for the taxable year, determined as provided in paragraph (f)(4)(ii) of such section, the amount of such excess shall be allocated as provided by subdivision (i) of this subparagraph.

(3) Distributions through a chain or group. In determining whether and to what extent a distribution for any taxable year has been made out of the earnings and profits of a foreign corporation included in a chain of ownership described in section 958(a) consisting of two or more corporations in a chain or group for the taxable year, the following subdivisions shall apply:

(i) Allocation first to income received as a distribution. If any foreign corporation included in the chain or group for the taxable year receives a distribution for such year from another foreign corporation in the chain or group and in turn makes a distribution for the taxable year, the distribution so made shall first be allocated to the earnings and profits, to the extent thereof, attributable to the distribution so received; if distributions are received from more than one other corporation in the chain or group, the distribution made by the recipient corporation shall be apportioned among all such amounts. For purposes of determining whether a distribution is made or received for the taxable year, see paragraph (c) of § 1.963-3.

(ii) Successive distributions through a chain or group. If any foreign corporation included in the chain or group for the taxable year distributes an amount from its earnings and profits of such year, the amount so distributed shall be considered to be received from such earnings and profits by the United States shareholder to the extent the amount is distributed by successive distributions made by each other foreign corporation in the chain or group for the taxable year through the chain of ownership described in section 958(a) into the hands of such shareholder.

(iii) Distribution determined without reduction by taxes of intervening corporations. If, for the taxable year to which the election to secure an exclusion under section 963 applies, the United States shareholder receives a distribution to which subdivision (ii) of this subparagraph applies, the entire amount distributed by the foreign corporation from such shareholder's proportionate share of its earnings and profits for the taxable year shall, except where taxes referred to in paragraph (d)(1)(iii) of § 1.963-2 are taken into account as provided by subparagraph (1) of this paragraph, count toward a minimum distribution and shall not be reduced for such purpose by an foreign income tax paid or accrued on such amount by another foreign corporation in the chain or group through which such amount is distributed by successive distributions into the hands of such shareholder. The application of this subdivision may be illustrated by the following examples:

Example (1). For 1966, domestic corporation M makes a chain election with respect to controlled foreign corporation A, all the one class of stock of which is directly owned by M Corporation, and controlled foreign corporation B, all the one class of stock of which is directly owned by A Corporation. All corporations use the calendar year as the taxable year. Corporation M complies with the special rules of this paragraph and paragraph (c) of this section for the taxable year. Corporation A's only income for 1966 is a dividend of $52.50 distributed in such year by B Corporation, on which A Corporation is subject to an income tax of $10.50. The remaining $42 ($52.50 less $10.50) is distributed by A Corporation for 1966 to M Corporation. The full $52.50 distributed by B Corporation counts toward a minimum distribution by the chain for 1966.

Example (2). For 1966, domestic corporation M makes a chain election with respect to controlled foreign corporation A, all the one class of stock of which it owns directly, and controlled foreign corporation B, all the one class of stock of which A Corporation own directly. All corporations use the calendar year as the taxable year. Corporation M complies with the special rules of this paragraph and paragraph (c) of this section for the taxable year. The predistribution and pretax earnings and profits for 1966 of B Corporation are $100, and of A Corporation, $0. Corporation B pays foreign income tax of $30 and during the year distributes $70. On such $70, A Corporation pays foreign income tax of $14. By applying paragraph (d)(1)(iii) of § 1.963-2, the consolidated foreign income taxes of the chain for 1966 are $44 ($30+$14) and the consolidated earnings and profits of the chain are $56 ($70-$14); in such case, the effective foreign tax rate of the chain for 1966 is 44 percent ($44/[$56+$44]) and thus in excess of the highest effective foreign tax rate requiring a distribution for such year under section 963(b). Since M Corporation may thus take A Corporation's tax of $14 into account, the statutory percentage under section 963(b) for 1966 is zero percent and the amount of the minimum distribution required to be made by the chain is $0.

(c) Special foreign tax credit rules. *(1) In general.* In determining the minimum overall tax burden under paragraph (a)(1)(ii) of this section, the foreign tax credit of the United States shareholder with respect to a minimum distribution received for the taxable year from the chain or group shall be determined under the provisions of sections 901 through 905 as modified by § 1.963-3 except that—

(i) Under subparagraph (2) of this paragraph—

(a) Taxes of a second-tier corporation making a distribution through a first-tier corporation shall not be averaged with taxes of such first-tier corporation,

(b) Taxes of a first-tier corporation or a second-tier corporation on a distribution made through such corporation shall not be averaged with such corporation's taxes on its other income; and

(c) Taxes of a first-tier corporation or a second-tier corporation shall not be deemed paid with respect to distributions from the earnings and profits of such corporation which are offset by a deficit allocated under paragraph (b)(2) of this section to the United States shareholder's proportionate share of the earnings and profits of such corporation; and

(ii) The foreign tax credit may be reduced and the reduction deferred under subparagraph (3) of this paragraph to another taxable year of the United States shareholder.

(2) Nonaveraging of tax. (i) Year of minimum distribution. (a) Taxes deemed paid by a first-tier corporation and taxes actually paid by such corporation. If, by successive distributions through a chain or group, a United States shareholder receives for a taxable year a distribution of the earnings and profits for such year of any corporation in such chain or group, and if both section 902(a) and section 902(b) apply with respect to such distribution, all the taxes deemed paid under section 902(b) by the first-tier corporation described in section 902(a) with respect to such distribution of such earnings and profits shall be deemed paid by the United States shareholder for such taxable year under section 902(a) with respect to the earnings and profits so distributed and, notwithstanding the rules otherwise applicable under section

902, no part of the taxes so deemed paid by such first-tier corporation shall be attributed to other earnings and profits of such first-tier corporation for such year and no part of the taxes paid or accrued with respect to such other earnings and profits shall be attributed to the earnings and profits so received as a distribution.

(b) Taxes of a foreign corporation paid on intercorporate distributions and on other income. If, by successive distributions through a chain or group, a United States shareholder receives for a taxable year a distribution of the earnings and profits for such year of any corporation in such chain or group, then in applying section 902(a) with respect to such distribution through a first-tier corporation described in section 902(a), or in applying section 902(b) with respect to such distribution through a second-tier corporation described in section 902(b), as the case may be, the taxes of such corporation which shall be taken into account in determining taxes deemed paid under such section shall be the foreign income tax actually paid or accrued for the taxable year by such first-tier or second-tier corporation, as the case may be, with respect to such distribution; and, notwithstanding the rules otherwise applicable under section 902, no part of the taxes so paid by such first-tier or second-tier corporation shall be attributed to other earnings and profits of such corporation for such year and no part of the taxes paid or accrued with respect to such other earnings and profits shall be attributed to the earnings and profits so received as a distribution.

(c) Corporation with earnings and profits reduced by allocated deficits. In the application of section 902, a United States shareholder's proportionate share of the earnings and profits for the taxable year of a foreign corporation to which the chain or group election applies shall reflect the reduction of such earnings and profits by deficits allocated thereto under paragraph (b)(2) of this section. No taxes paid or accrued by such corporation shall be deemed paid under section 902 with respect to a distribution to such shareholder from the earnings and profits of such corporation for such year to the extent that such distribution exceeds the shareholder's proportionate share as so reduced.

(ii) Year of distribution of remaining earnings and profits. If for a taxable year in respect of which a United States shareholder receives a minimum distribution pursuant to an election under section 963 and in respect of which the provisions of this subparagraph are applied—

(a) The foreign income tax which is paid or accrued by a foreign corporation for such year, by reason of the receipt and payment of earnings and profits counting toward such minimum distribution, is deemed paid under subdivision (i) (a) or (b) of this subparagraph,

(b) The pretax and predistribution earnings and profits for such year of a foreign corporation in a chain or group with respect to stock on which such minimum distribution is received are reduced by reason of the deduction under paragraph (d)(1)(i) of § 1.963-2 of distributions received from other corporations in such chain or group, or

(c) Such shareholder's proportionate share of the earnings and profits for such year of a foreign corporation in a chain or group making a distribution counting toward such minimum distribution is reduced by the allocation thereto under paragraph (b)(2) of this section of a portion of the deficits of foreign branches or other foreign corporations in such chain or group, the pretax and predistribution earnings and profits of such foreign corporation for such year to which such minimum distribution is attributable and the foreign income tax which is taken into account in determining tax deemed paid under section 902 on such pretax and predistribution earnings and profits shall not be taken into account in the application of section 902 when other earnings and profits of such foreign corporation for such year are distributed in a subsequent taxable year of such foreign corporation to such shareholder. For the purpose of applying the preceding sentence to a case in which (c) of this subdivision applies, the pretax and predistribution earnings and profits of the foreign corporation for such year to which the minimum distributed is attributable shall be the amount of such corporation's earnings and profits which are distributed and count toward the minimum distribution plus the foreign income tax of such foreign corporation allocated thereto in determining the taxes deemed paid under section 902 for the taxable year of the minimum distribution.

(iii) Illustrations. The application of this subparagraph may be illustrated by the following examples:

Example (1). Domestic corporation M makes a chain election for 1966 with respect to controlled foreign corporation A, which is wholly owned directly by M Corporation, and controlled foreign corporation B, which is wholly owned directly by A Corporation. Each corporation uses the calendar year as the taxable year. In 1966, corporations A and B are subject to foreign income tax at the rates of 20 percent and 30 percent, respectively, with no deduction being allowed for dividends eceived or paid; each such corporation has pretax and predistribution earnings and profits of $100. Corporation M receives from the chain a pro rata minimum distribution for such year and applies thereto the special rules of this paragraph and paragraph (b) of this section. Corporation A is not a less developed country corporation under section 902(d). The 1966 foreign income tax of corporations A and B which is deemed paid by M Corporation under section 902(a) for 1966, and the remaining tax which is allocated to earnings and profits to be distributed to M Corporation in future years, are determined as follows:

Example (2). The facts are the same as in example 1 except that A Corporation pays foreign income tax at the rate of 30 percent and B Corporation, at the rate of 20 percent; and A Corporation is allowed a deduction, in computing its income subject to tax, for the full amount of dividends received. The determination of tax deemed paid for 1966 is as follows:

Example (3). For 1966, domestic corporation M makes a group election with respect to controlled foreign corporations A and B, both of which are wholly owned directly by M Corporation, and foreign branch C of M Corporation. All such corporations use the calendar year as the taxable year. Corporation M receives a pro rata minimum distribution from the group for 1966 and applies thereto the special rules of this paragraph and paragraph (b) of this section. Neither foreign corporation is a less developed country corporation under section 902(d). Corporations A and B pay foreign income tax at a flat rate of 20 percent and 30 percent, respectively. The 1966 foreign income tax of corporations A and B which is deemed paid by M Corporation under section 902(a) for 1966, and the remaining tax which is allocated to earnings and profits to be distributed to M Corporation in future years, are determined as follows:

Example (4). The facts are the same as in example 3 except that the group does not make a pro rata minimum distribution but distributes $48.30, consisting of $40 distributed by A Corporation and $8.30 distributed by B Corporation. Corporation M complies with the special rules of this paragraph and paragraph (b) of this section. The 1966 foreign income tax of corporations A and B which is deemed paid by

M Corporation under section 902(a) for 1966, and the remaining tax which is allocated to earnings and profits to be distributed to M Corporation in future years, are determined as follows, the minimum overall tax burden for 1966 being such as to satisfy the requirement of paragraph (a)(1)(ii)(b) of this section:

(3) Reduction and deferral of the foreign tax credit. (i) In general. To the extent specified in paragraph (a)(1)(ii)(b) of this section a reduction shall be made in the foreign tax credit allowable under section 901 for the taxable year with respect to distributions counting toward a minimum distribution for such year from the chain or group; and such reduction in credit shall be allocated, as provided in subdivision (ii) of this subparagraph, to foreign corporations in such chain or group and deferred, as provided in subdivision (iii) of this subparagraph, to subsequent taxable years of the United States shareholder.

(ii) Allocation of reduction in foreign tax credit. The amount of any reduction in foreign tax credit for the taxable year which is made under subdivision (i) of this subparagraph with respect to a minimum distribution for any taxable year from the chain or group shall be allocated among any first-tier and second-tier corporations described in section 902 (a) and (b), respectively, which are in such chain or group. The amount of any such reduction in foreign tax credit shall be allocated among such first-tier and second-tier corporations in the ratio which the United States shareholder's proportionate share of undistributed earnings and profits of each such corporation for the taxable year bears to the total of such shareholder's proportionate shares of the undistributed earnings and profits of all such corporations for such year. None of such reduction shall be allocated to any other corporations in the chain or group or to any foreign branches included under paragraph (f)(4) of § 1.963-1 in the group as wholly owned foreign subsidiary corporations.

(iii) Deferral of allocated credit. (a) Allowance of credit in subsequent years. The reduction in foreign tax credit allocated to a first-tier or second-tier corporation in the chain or group for a taxable year under subdivision (ii) of this subparagraph shall be deemed paid under the principles of section 902 (applicable to foreign corporations which are not less developed country corporations) with respect to distributions, to the extent made by such corporation to the United States shareholder referred to in subdivision (ii) of this subparagraph, in a subsequent taxable year from the undistributed earnings and profits of such corporation for such year of allocation. Thus, for example, in the case of a distribution in the subsequent year from such earnings and profits by a first-tier corporation, the tax deemed paid shall be an amount which bears to the total of such reduction in foreign tax credit the same ratio that the distribution to the shareholder in the subsequent year bears to such shareholder's proportionate share of such undistributed earnings and profits for the year of allocation.

(b) Limitations on use of deferred credit. The deferred tax so deemed paid shall be deemed paid for such subsequent taxable year and shall be allowed under section 901 (without regard to the limitations under section 904) as a credit against the income tax imposed for such year by chapter 1 of the Code, but the amount of such credit shall not exceed the excess of the tax so imposed for such year over the credit (determined without regard to this subdivision (iii) allowed under sections 901 through 905 for such year. Any amount by which the deferred tax so deemed paid in such subsequent taxable year exceeds the limitation under the preceding sentence shall not be carried back or carried over under section 904(d) to another taxable year of the United States shareholder. No credit shall be allowed under this subdivision for the subsequent taxable year to the extent that the credit would reduce the tax of the United States shareholder under chapter 1 of the Code on any minimum distribution for such year to which section 963 applies.

(c) Gross-up not applicable. Any amount allowed as a credit for a subsequent taxable year under this subdivision shall not be included in the gross income of the United States shareholder for such year under section 78.

(d) Illustrations. The application of this section may be illustrated by the following examples, in which the surtax exemption provided by section 11(c) is disregarded:

Example (1). (a) For 1966, domestic corporation M makes a chain election with respect to controlled foreign corporation A, which it wholly owns directly, and controlled foreign corporation B, which A Corporation wholly owns directly. Corporation A is not a less developed country corporation under section 902(d). All corporations use the calendar year as the taxable year. For 1966, M Corporation complies with the special rules of paragraphs (b) and (c) of this section. Corporation A has pretax and predistribution earnings and profits for 1966 of $40 and is subject to foreign income tax at a flat rate of 36 percent, with no deduction being allowed for dividends received or paid. B Corporation has pretax and predistribution earnings and profits of $60 for 1966 and is subject to a foreign income tax at a flat rate of 20 percent, with no deduction being allowed for dividends received or paid. For 1967, B Corporation has no earnings and profits, A Corporation has no earnings and profits other than a dividend of $21.22 from B Corporation, and M Corporation has taxable income of $20.98 from United States sources. Corporation M uses the overall limitation under section 904(a)(2) on the foreign tax credit.

(b) If a pro rata minimum distribution were made for 1966, the overall United States and foreign income tax for such year with respect to such distribution would be $41.30, determined as follows:

(c) The chain, however, does not make a pro rata distribution for 1966, but distributes $24 from A Corporation's earnings and profits and $26.78 from B Corporation's earnings and profits, the total distribution of $50.78 being equal to the statutory percentage of the consolidated earnings and profits (0.69 x $73.60) of the chain with respect to M Corporation. Thus, M Corporation must make such a reduction in its foreign tax credit that the overall United States and foreign income tax for 1966 with respect to the distribution equals the lesser of $41.30 (the overall United States and foreign income tax which would be paid with respect to a pro rata minimum distribution) and $43.20 (90 percent of 48 percent of pretax and predistribution consolidated earnings and profits of $100). The remaining 1956 earnings and profits of the chain are distributed late in 1967. Corporation M determines its tax as follows for such years:

Example (2). (a) For 1963, domestic corporation M makes a group election with respect to controlled foreign corporations A and B, both of which M Corporation wholly owns directly. All such corporations use the calendar year as the taxable year. Corporation A is created under the laws of foreign country X, and B Corporation is created under the laws of foreign country Y; neither of such corporations is a less developed country corporation under section 902(d). Corporation M complies with the special rules of paragraphs (b) and (c) of this section. Each foreign corporation has pretax earnings and profits of $100 for 1963. The income of A

Corporation is subject to a foreign income tax rate of 20 percent, and the income of B Corporation is subject to a foreign income tax rate of 30 percent. Corporation M uses the per-country limitation under section 904(a)(1) on the foreign tax credit.

(b) If a pro rata minimum distribution were made for 1963, the group would distribute $123 based upon an effective foreign tax rate of 25 percent ($50/[$50+$150]) and a statutory percentage of 82 percent under section 963(b); of this amount $57.40 (0.82 x $70) would be distributed from B Corporation's earnings and profits and $65.60 (0.82 x $80) would be distributed from A Corporation's earnings and profits. In such case, the overall United States and foreign income tax for 1963 with respect to the pro rata minimum distribution would be determined as follows, using the 52 percent United States corporate income tax rate applicable for such year:

(c) The group, however, does not make a pro rata minimum distribution for 1963 but distributes $123, consisting of $70 from B Corporation's earnings and profits and $53 from A Corporation's earnings and profits. Thus, M Corporation must make such a reduction in its foreign tax credit that the overall United States and foreign income tax for 1963 with respect to the distribution equals the lesser of $94.28 (the overall United States and foreign income tax which would be paid with respect to a pro rata minimum distribution) and $93.60 (90 percent of 52 percent of pretax and predistribution consolidated earnings and profits of $200). The remaining 1963 earnings and profits of the group are distributed late in 1964. Neither A Corporation nor B Corporation has earnings and profits for 1964. Corporation M determines its tax as follows for such years, assuming a 52 percent (instead of 50 percent) United States corporate income tax rate for 1964:

Example (3). (a) For 1966, domestic corporation M makes a chain election with respect to controlled foreign corporation A, which it wholly owns directly, and controlled foreign corporation B, which A Corporation wholly owns directly. Corporation A is a less developed country corporation under section 902(d). All corporations use the calendar year as the taxable year. For 1966, each of the foreign corporations has pretax and predistribution earnings and profits of $100. The income of A Corporation is subject to a foreign income tax rate of 20 percent, with no deduction being allowed for dividends received or paid; and the income of B Corporation is subject to a foreign income tax rate of 30 percent on such basis. During 1966, B Corporation distributes $50 to A Corporation, and A Corporation distributes $104 to M Corporation. During 1967 the remaining 1966 earnings and profits of such corporations are distributed to M Corporation.

(b) If M Corporation were not to comply with the special rules of paragraphs (b) and (c) of this section and were to deduct foreign income tax on intercorporate distributions under paragraph (d)(1)(iii) of § 1.963-2, the chain would not be considered to make a minimum distribution for 1966 because, although it makes a distribution which is sufficient in amount to constitute a minimum distribution, the overall United States and foreign income tax for such year with respect to such distribution would be insufficient under paragraph (a)(1)(i) of this section. The determination that M Corporation would not be entitled to the section 963 exclusion for 1966 by reason of such distribution in such circumstances is made as follows:

(c) By complying with the special rules of paragraphs (b) and (c) of this section, however, M Corporation will receive a minimum distribution for 1966 if it receives the statutory percentage of consolidated earnings and profits and if the overall United States and foreign income tax with respect to the distribution which is made is at least the lesser of $86.40 (0.90 x 0.48 x $200) and of the overall United States and foreign income tax which would be paid with respect to a pro rata minimum distribution from the chain. If a pro rata minimum distribution were made for 1966, the chain would be required to distribute earnings and profits of $114, based upon an effective foreign tax rate of 25 percent ($50/[$50+$150]) and a statutory percentage of 76 percent under section 963(b); of this amount $53.20 (0.76 x $70) would be distributed from B Corporation's earnings and profits and $60.80 (0.76 x $80) would be distributed from A Corporation's earnings and profits. The overall United States and foreign income tax with respect to such a pro rata minimum distribution would be $73.62, determined as follows:

(d) The United States income tax of M Corporation for 1966 and 1967 is determined as follows, assuming that the minimum overall tax burden is determined under paragraph (a)(1)(ii)(b) of this section:

Example (4). (a) Domestic corporation M directly owns 90 percent of the one class of stock of controlled foreign corporation A, which directly owns 80 percent of the one class of stock of controlled foreign corporation B, which in turn directly owns 60 percent of the one class of stock of controlled foreign corporation C. None of the foreign corporations are less developed country corporations under section 902(d); all corporations use the calendar year as the taxable year. For 1963, M Corporation makes a chain election with respect to corporations A, B, and C and receives a distribution from the consolidated earnings and profits of the chain which does not constitute a pro rata minimum distribution. The remaining 1963 consolidated earnings and profits of the chain are distributed late in 1964, for which year it is assumed that the United States corporate income tax rate is the same (52 percent) as for 1963. No corporation in the chain has earnings and profits for 1964 other than from distributions received from remaining 1963 earnings and profits of another corporation in the chain. The foreign country under the laws of which A Corporation is created does not tax dividends which are received by such corporation from B Corporation, but B Corporation is taxed on dividends received from C Corporation. Corporation M complies with the special rules of paragraphs (b) and (c) of this section and determines the minimum overall tax burden under paragraph (a)(1)(ii)(b) of this section with respect to the distribution which is made. Corporation M uses the overall limitation under section 904(a)(2) on the foreign tax credit. The distribution received by M Corporation for 1963 from the consolidated earnings and profits of the chain is sufficient in amount to constitute a minimum distribution. The overall United States and foreign income tax for 1963 with respect to the distribution which is made must be at least equal to the lesser of $32.21 (the amount payable, as determined under paragraph (b) of this example, with respect to a pro rata minimum distribution) and $31.34 (90 percent of 52 percent of pretax and predistribution consolidated earnings and profits of $66.96).

(b) If the chain were to make a pro rata minimum distribution, the distributions and the overall United States and foreign income tax for 1963 with respect to the minimum distribution would be determined as follows, based upon the facts assumed:

(c) Based upon the distributions which are made by corporations A, B, and C, M. Corporation pays United States tax as follows for 1963 and 1964:

Example (5). (a) Domestic corporation M directly owns all the one class of stock of each of controlled foreign corporations A, B, C, and D. All such corporations use the calendar year as the taxable year. None of the foreign corporations is a less developed country corporation under section 902(d). For 1963, M Corporation makes a group election with respect to corporations A, B, C, and D and receives from the 1963 consolidated earnings and profits of the group a distribution which is not a pro rata minimum distribution. None of the foreign corporations has earnings and profits for 1964, but the remaining 1963 earnings and profits of the group are distributed late in 1964, for which year it is assumed that the United States corporate income tax rate is the same (52 percent) as for 1963. The overall limitation under section 904(a)(2) on the foreign tax credit applies for both years.

(b) Assume that M Corporation does not comply with the special rules of paragraphs (b) and (c) of this section and that for 1963 it draws a distribution of all of B Corporation's earnings and profits and enough of C Corporation's earnings and profits to receive the amount of a minimum distribution and to assure that the overall United States and foreign income tax for such year with respect to the distribution from the group satisfies the overall minimum tax requirement of paragraph (a)(1)(i) of this section. In such case, the overall United States and foreign income tax for 1963 with respect to the distribution which is made, determined by using the foreign tax credit under section 901 without applying the special credit rules of paragraph (c) of this section, must at least equal $37.44 (90 percent of 52 percent of pretax and predistribution consolidated earnings and profits of $80). Corporation M's United States income tax for 1963 and 1964 with respect to the distribution of the 1963 earnings and profits of the group is determined as follows, based upon the facts assumed:

(c) Assume that M Corporation does comply with the special rules of paragraphs (b) and (c) of this section and for 1963 receives a minimum distribution consisting of $20 from A Corporation and $14 from C Corporation. In such case, the overall United States and foreign income tax for 1963 with respect to the minimum distribution must at least equal the lesser of $37.44 (0.90 x 0.52 x $80) and the overall United States and foreign income tax of $37.89 that would be paid with respect to a pro rata minimum distribution from the group for such year. In such case, the determinations would be made pursuant to subparagraphs (1) and (2) of this paragraph.

(1) If a pro rata minimum distribution were made for 1963 by the group, the overall United States and foreign income tax for such year with respect to such distribution would be $37.89, determined as follows:

(2) Corporation M's United States income tax for 1963 and 1964 with respect to the distribution of the 1963 earnings and profits of the group is determined as follows:

Example (6). Throughout 1963, domestic corporation M directly owns all the one class of stock of controlled foreign corporations A, B, and C, and maintains in a foreign country a branch which qualifies under paragraph (f)(4) of § 1.963-1 for inclusion in a group as a wholly owned foreign subsidiary corporation. For 1963, a year for which the overall limitation under section 904(a)(2) on the foreign tax credit applies, M Corporation makes a group election with respect to A, B, and C Corporations and the foreign branch. All such corporations use the calendar year as the taxable year. The foreign branch has pretax and predistribution earnings and profits of $40 for 1963, as determined under paragraph (f)(4)(ii) of § 1.963-1. None of the foreign corporations is a less developed country orporation under section 902(d). Corporation M complies with the special rules of paragraphs (b) and (c) of this section. The United States income tax of M Corporation for 1963 is as follows, based upon the facts assumed:

Example (7). Domestic group M, an affiliated group of domestic corporations filing a consolidated return under section 1501, makes a group election for 1963 with respect to a group consisting of two controlled foreign corporations C and D, all of whose one class of stock is directly owned by group M, and foreign branch B, a foreign branch of a Western Hemisphere trade corporation (as defined in section 921) included in group M. No distributions are received for the taxable year from corporations C and D, but the foreign group makes a minimum distribution by reason of the deemed distribution of all of branch B's earnings and profits. Group M complies with the special rules of paragraphs (b) and (c) of this section. For 1963, a year for which the United States corporate income tax rate is 52 percent, the overall limitation under section 904(a)(2) on the foreign tax credit applies. All corporations use the calendar year as the taxable year. None of the foreign corporations is a less developed country corporation under section 902(d) for 1963. The income, and the United States and foreign income tax for 1963, are determined as follows, based upon the facts assumed:

T.D. 6759, 9/25/64, amend T.D. 6767, 11/3/64, T.D. 7100, 3/20/71.

---

§ 1.963-5 Foreign corporations with variation in foreign tax rate because of distributions.

(a) Limited application of section. The rules of this section shall apply to a foreign corporation only if—

(1) Under the laws of a foreign country or possession of the United States the foreign income tax of the corporation for the taxable year depends upon the extent to which distributions are made by such corporation from its earnings and profits for the taxable year, so that the rate of such tax for the taxable year on income which is distributed differs from the rate of such tax for such year on the income which is not distributed, and

(2) The corporation. (i) Is a single first-tier corporation, or

(ii) Is for the taxable year in a chain or group from which the United States shareholder receives a minimum distribution in respect of which the minimum overall tax burden is determined in accordance with paragraph (a)(1)(ii) of § 1.963-4.

(b) Foreign income tax determined as though no distributions were made. The foreign income tax on the pretax and predistribution earnings and profits of the foreign corporation for the taxable year shall (solely for the purpose of determining the effective foreign tax rate under paragraph (c) of § 1.963-2) be determined as if the foreign corporation made no distributions for the taxable year. However, notwithstanding the second sentence of paragraph (d)(1) of § 1.963-2, where the United States shareholder owns the stock (with respect to which the election under section 963 is made) in such corporation by reason of stock owned through a chain of ownership described in section 958(a) and the foreign income tax of such corporation for the taxable year decreases as distributions are made from its earnings and profits, the rule in the preceding sentence shall not apply if the electing United States shareholder does not actually receive for the taxable year its proportionate share of the earnings and profits which are actually distributed. In such case, the foreign income tax on pretax and predistribution earnings and profits shall be the actual foreign income tax of such corporation, computed on the basis of the distributions which are made. For example, assume that a second-tier foreign corporation in a chain has pretax and predistribution earnings of $100 for the taxable year and that foreign law imposes on such corporation a foreign income tax of 50 percent of the pretax earnings and profits minus dividends for such year and of 20 percent of such dividends. If the second-tier foreign corporation distributes $20 of earnings and profits to a first-tier foreign corporation which is part of the same chain, and if the first-tier corporation retains the dividend so received, the foreign income tax of the second-tier foreign corporation shall be considered to be the tax actually paid for the taxable year, that is, $44 (50 percent of $80 plus 20 percent of $20). If the first-tier foreign corporation distributes the dividend so received, the foreign income tax of the second-tier foreign corporation shall be considered to be $50 (50 percent of $100). For purposes of this paragraph, the principles of paragraph (b)(3) of § 1.963-4 shall apply.

(c) Minimum distribution. *(1) Single first-tier corporation.* A minimum distribution for a taxable year by a single first-tier corporation described in paragraph (a)(1) of this section shall be a distribution which is equal to—

(i) The amount resulting from the multiplication of the statutory percentage specified in paragraph (b) of § 1.963-2 for such year by the United States shareholder's proportionate share of the earnings and profits of such corporation, as determined under paragraph (d)(2)(i) of § 1.963-2 but without the deduction for foreign income tax provided by paragraph (d)(1)(ii) and (iii) of such section, reduced by

(ii) The foreign income tax on the pretax amount determined under subdivision (i) of this subparagraph which would be paid or accrued by such corporation by reason of distributing such amount, less such tax, for such taxable year.

(2) Corporation in a chain or group making a pro rata minimum distribution. In case of a corporation described in paragraph (a)(2)(ii) of this section in a chain or group, such corporation's share of a pro rata minimum distribution by the chain or group for the taxable year shall be—

(i) The amount resulting from the multiplication of the statutory percentage specified in paragraph (b) of § 1.963-2 for the taxable year by the United States shareholder's proportionate share of the earnings and profits of such corporation, as determined under paragraph (d)(3) of § 1.963-2 but without the deduction for foreign income tax provided by paragraph (d)(1)(ii) and (iii) of such section, reduced by

(ii) The foreign income tax on the pretax amount determined under subdivision (i) of this subparagraph which would be paid or accrued by such corporation by reason of distributing such amount, less such tax, for such taxable year.

(3) A chain or group making a distribution other than a pro rata minimum distribution. If a chain or group contains one or more foreign corporations described in paragraph (a)(2)(ii) of this section and such chain or group makes a minimum distribution other than a pro rata minimum distribution for the taxable year, the amount of such minimum distribution to the electing United States shareholder shall be at least—

(i) The amount resulting from the multiplication of the statutory percentage specified in paragraph (b) of § 1.963-2 for the taxable year by the consolidated earnings and profits of such chain or group with respect to such shareholder, as determined under paragraph (d)(3) of such section but without any deduction for foreign income tax provided by paragraph (d)(1)(ii) and (iii) of such section, reduced by

(ii) The foreign income tax on the pretax amount determined under subdivision (i) of this subparagraph which would be paid or accrued by the foreign corporations in the chain or group by reason of distributing such amount, less such tax, for such taxable year.

(4) Illustrations. The application of this paragraph may be illustrated by the following examples:

Example (1). Domestic corporation M directly owns 80 percent of the one class of stock of single first-tier corporation B, which for 1964 has $100 of pretax earnings and profits on which is imposed a foreign income tax of 40 percent of pretax earnings and profits minus dividends for the taxable year and of 20 percent of the amount of such dividends. Both corporations use the calendar year as the taxable year. The effective foreign tax rate applicable to B Corporation, as determined under paragraph (c) of § 1.963-2, is 40 percent, and the statutory percentage under paragraph (b) of § 1.963-2 for 1964 is 38 percent. Corporation M receives a minimum distribution for 1964 if it receives from B Corporation's earnings and profits for such year $22.80, that is, 80 percent of $28.50, the distribution which would be made if there were distributed that amount of earnings and profits which, together with the foreign income tax at the rate effectively applicable to pretax earnings and profits to which such distribution is attributable, equals 38 percent of $100. Such distribution may be determined by solving for "d" in the following formula:

Example (2). Domestic corporation M directly owns 80 percent of the one class of stock of each of controlled foreign corporations A and B, which constitute a group and each of which for 1964 has pretax earnings and profits of $100. All corporations use the calendar year as the taxable year. Corporation A is subject to foreign income tax at a flat rate of 40 percent; and B Corporation is subject to a foreign income tax of 40 percent of $100 minus dividends for the taxable year and of 20 percent of the amount of such dividends. The effective foreign tax rate with respect to the group, as determined under paragraph (c) of § 1.963-2, is 40 percent, and the statutory percentage under paragraph (b) of § 1.963-2 for 1964 is 38 percent. Corporation B distributes $25 for 1964 toward a minimum distribution from the group which is not a pro rata minimum distribution. The minimum distribution by the group for 1964 with respect to M Corporation is determined as follows:

Example (3). The facts are the same as in example 2 except that the $25 distribution of earnings and profits is made by A Corporation. The amount of the minimum distribution for 1964 is determined as follows:

(d) Distributions through a chain or group. In the application of paragraph (b)(3)(i) of § 1.963-4, relating to the allocation of dividend payments first to income received as a distribution from other foreign corporations in the chain or group, if one or more of such other foreign corporations is a corporation whose foreign income tax rate decreases as the distributions are made, the allocation under such paragraph shall be made first to such corporations' distributions.

(e) Foreign tax credit. *(1) Year of minimum distribution.* If a United States shareholder receives for a taxable year a distribution of the earnings and profits for the taxable year of a foreign corporation described in paragraph (a) of this section and if for such year such corporation is a first-tier corporation, or a second-tier corporation described in section 902 (a) or (b), as the case may be, then, in applying paragraph (c)(2)(i) of § 1.963-4, only the foreign income tax which is effectively applicable to pretax earnings and profits to which are attributable the earnings and profits which are distributed shall be deemed paid for such year under section 902 (a) or (b), as the case may be, and the foreign income tax so paid or accrued by such corporation shall not be averaged, for purposes of such section, with its foreign income tax paid or accrued for such year on its pretax earnings and profits to which are attributable the earnings and profits which are not distributed.

(2) Year of distribution of remaining earnings and profits. If for a taxable year a United States shareholder receives a minimum distribution from a corporation described in paragraph (a) of this section, the pretax and predistribution earnings and profits of such corporation for the taxable year to which such minimum distribution is attributable and the foreign income tax which is taken into account, in accordance with paragraph (c)(2)(i) of § 1.963-4, in determining tax deemed paid under section 902 on such pretax and predistribution earnings and profits shall not be taken into account in the application of section 902 when other earnings and profits of such foreign corporation for such year are distributed in a subsequent taxable year of such foreign corporation to such shareholder.

(3) Illustration. The application of this paragraph may be illustrated by the following examples:

Example (1). (a) All the income of controlled foreign corporation B, wholly owned directly by domestic corporation M, is taxed by foreign country Y, the tax laws of which impose at the local level a corporate income tax of 10 percent of earnings and profits (before reduction for income taxes) and, at the national level, an income tax of 30 percent of such earnings and profits reduced by the local tax and by any profits which are distributed. Also, at the national level, a tax of 20 percent is imposed on B Corporation on the dividends which are paid for the taxable year. Both corporations use the calendar year as the taxable year. For 1963, B Corporation has earnings and profits (before reduction by income taxes) of $100. B Corporation is not a less developed country corporation under section 902(d). For 1963, M Corporation makes a first-tier election with respect to B Corporation and receives a minimum distribution. Corporation B has no 1964 earnings and profits, and its remaining 1963 earnings and profits are distributed late in 1964. The amount of the minimum distribution required to be received by M Corporation for 1963 and the United States tax with respect to the 1963 earnings and profits of B Corporation are determined as follows, assuming a United States corporate income tax rate of 52 percent (instead of 50 percent) for 1964 and no surtax exemption under section 11(c) for either year:

(b) If B Corporation were a less developed country corporation under section 902(d), there would be no gross-up under section 78 and the foreign tax credit of M Corporation would be $14.28 for 1963 ($47.60/ *lsqb;47.60+ $20.40] x $20.40), and $7.46 for 1964 ($20.16/ [$20.16+$11.84] x $11.84).

Example (2). For 1963, domestic corporation M receives a dividend of $21 from B Corporation which counts toward a minimum distribution from a group, determined by applying the special rules of paragraphs (b) and (c) of § 1.963-4. Both corporations use the calendar year as the taxable year. Foreign law imposes on B Corporation an income tax of 40 percent of the year's pretax earnings and profits, less dividends paid for such year, and of 20 percent of such dividends. Corporation M directly owns 70 percent of the one class of stock of B Corporation, which for 1963 has pretax and predistribution earnings and profits of $100. Corporation B is not a less developed country corporation under section 902(d). In late 1964, M Corporation receives a distribution of all of B Corporation's 1964 earnings and profits and of $25.20 from its 1963 earnings and profits. The foreign income tax of B Corporation deemed paid for 1963 by M Corporation under section 902(a) is based on the foreign income tax actually paid by B Corporation on an amount of pretax earnings and profits which, when reduced by the tax so paid, equals the total dividend which is paid. The determination of tax deemed paid by M Corporation with respect to distributions from 1963 earnings and profits of B Corporation is as follows:

T.D. 6759, 9/25/64,10/8/64 amend T.D. 6767, 11/3/64.

---

§ 1.963-6 Deficiency distribution.

(a) In general. Section 963(e)(2) and this section provide a method under which, by virtue of a deficiency distribution, a United States shareholder may be relieved from the payment of a deficiency in tax for any taxable year arising by reason of failure to include subpart F income in gross income under section 951(a)(1)(A)(i), when it has been determined that such shareholder has failed to receive a minimum distribution for such year in respect of which it elected to secure the exclusion under section 963. In addition, this section provides rules with respect to a credit or refund of part or all of any such deficiency which has been paid. Under the method provided, the benefit of the exclusion of subpart F income from gross income of the United States shareholder is allowed retroactively for the taxable year in respect of which the election under section 963 applied, but only if the subsequent deficiency distribution meets the requirements of this section. The benefits of the retroactive exclusion will not, however, prevent the assessment of interest, additional amounts, and assessable penalties.

(b) Requirements for deficiency distribution. *(1) Distribution made on or after date of determination.* If—

(i) A United States shareholder, in making its return of the tax imposed by chapter 1 of the Code for any taxable year, elects to secure an exclusion under section 963 for such year,

(ii) It is subsequently determined (within the meaning of paragraph (c) of this section) that an exclusion under section 963 of subpart F income with respect to stock to which such election relates does not apply for such taxable year because of the failure of such shareholder to receive a minimum distribution for such year with respect to such stock, and

(iii) Such failure is due to reasonable cause, a deficiency distribution which is received by such shareholder with respect to such stock from a foreign corporation which was the single first-tier corporation, or a corporation in the chain or group, as the case may be, with respect to which the election was made, shall count toward a minimum distribution under section 963 for such year of election if such deficiency distribution is received (except as provided by subparagraph (2) of this paragraph) on, or within 90 days after, the date of such determination and prior to the filing of a claim under paragraph (d)(1) of this section. Such claim must be filed within 120 days after the date of such determination, and the deficiency distribution must be a dividend of such a nature (except as otherwise provided in this section) as would have permitted it to count toward a minimum distribution for the taxable year of the election if it had been received by the

United States shareholder during such year. No distribution shall count as a deficiency distribution under this subparagraph unless a claim therefor is filed under paragraph (d)(1) of this section.

(2) Distribution made before date of determination. A deficiency distribution may also be received by a United States shareholder at any time prior to the date on which the determination required by subparagraph (1) of this paragraph is made. A distribution will count as a deficiency distribution under this subparagraph—

(i) To the extent that such distribution otherwise satisfies the requirements of this section;

(ii) If the United States shareholder files within 90 days after such distribution but before the determination date an advance claim described in paragraph (d)(2) of this section for treatment of such distribution as a deficiency distribution;

(iii) If such shareholder consents in such claim to include such deficiency distribution in gross income for the taxable year of the election to the extent necessary to complete a minimum distribution for such year and under section 6501 to extend the period for the making of assessments, and the bringing of distraint or a proceeding in court for collection, in respect of a deficiency and all interest, additional amounts, and assessable penalties for such taxable year;

(iv) If, when requested by the district director, such shareholder consents under section 6501 in such claim to extend the period for the making of assessments, and the bringing of distraint or a proceeding in court for collection, in respect of a deficiency and all interest, additional amounts and assessable penalties for the year of receipt of such distribution; and

(v) To the extent that such shareholder makes advance payment of tax which would result from the inclusion of such distribution in gross income as a minimum distribution for the year of such deficiency. To the extent that such distribution is not necesasry under the determination (when made under paragraph (c) of this section) for a deficiency distribution, it shall be included in the United States shareholder's gross income for the taxable year of receipt of such distribution and paragraph (g) of this section shall not apply.

(3) Earnings and profits of year of election to be first distributed. If—

(i) In the case of a first-tier election, the United States shareholder's proportionate share of the earnings and profits of the foreign corporation which was the single first-tier corporation, or

(ii) In the case of a chain or group election, any portion of the share of any corporation or corporations (which were in the chain or group) of the consolidated earnings and profits with respect to the United States shareholder, for the taxable year of the election has not been distributed on the stock with respect to which the election was made, then a distribution, in order to be counted toward a deficiency distribution, must be made by such corporation or corporations and from such earnings and profits to the extent thereof. Once all such earnings and profits of such corporation or corporations have been completely distributed, a deficiency distribution may be made from other earnings and profits of such foreign corporation which was a single first-tier corporation, or of such corporation or corporations which were in such chain or group, as the case may be.

(4) Proof of reasonable cause. Reasonable cause for failure to receive a minimum distribution shall be deemed to exist, in the absence of circumstances demonstrating bad faith, if the electing United States shareholder receives, within the period prescribed by paragraph (a)(1)(i) of § 1.963-3 with respect to the year of election, at least 80 percent of the amount of a minimum distribution (from the earnings and profits to which the election for such year relates) which if received during such period would have satisfied the conditions for the section 963 exclusion to apply to such year. If less than 80 percent of the amount of a minimum distribution is received during such period, the existence of a reasonable cause for failure to receive a minimum distribution must be established by clear and convincing evidence; however, the preceding sentence shall not be taken as a limitation on the establishment of reasonable cause by any other proof of reasonable cause. For example, reasonable cause will exist if a single first-tier corporation for its taxable year makes a distribution which would be a minimum distribution but for a refund of foreign income tax which it has paid in good faith under foreign law but which is found not to be due after the United States income tax return of the United States shareholder has been filed.

(c) Nature and details of determination. *(1) A determination that the section 963 exclusion does not apply to a United States shareholder for a taxable year due to its failure to receive a minimum distribution for such year shall, for the purposes of this section, be established by.*

(i) A decision by the Tax Court or a judgment, decree, or other order by any court of competent jurisdiction, which has become final;

(ii) A closing agreement made under section 7121; or,

(iii) An agreement which is signed by the district director, or such other official to whom authority to sign the agreement is delegated, and by, or on behalf of, such shareholder and which relates to the liability of such shareholder for the tax under chapter 1 of the Code for such year.

(2) The date of determination by a decision of the Tax Court shall be the date upon which such decision becomes final, as prescribed in section 7481.

(3) The date upon which a judgment of a court becomes final shall be determined upon the basis of the facts in the particular case. Ordinarily, a judgment of a United States district court shall become final upon the expiration of the time allowed for taking an appeal, if no such appeal is duly taken within such time; and a judgment of the United States Court of Claims shall become final upon the expiration of the time allowed for filing a petition for certiorari, if no such petition is duly filed within such time.

(4) The date of determination by a closing agreement made under section 7121 shall be the date such agreement is approved by the Commissioner.

(5) The date of a determination made by an agreement which is signed by the district director, or such other official to whom authority to sign the agreement is delegated, shall be the date prescribed by this subparagraph. The agreement shall be sent to the United States shareholder at his last known address by either registered or certified mail. For further guidance regarding the definition of last known address, see § 301.6212-2 of this chapter. If registered mail is used for such purpose, the date of registration shall be treated as the date of determination; if certified mail is used for such purpose, the date of the postmark on the sender's receipt for such mail shall be treated as the date of determination. However, if the deficiency distribution is received by such shareholder before such registration or postmark date but on or after the date the agreement is signed by the district director or such other official to whom authority to sign the agree-

ment is delegated, the date of determination shall be the date on which the agreement is so signed.

(6) The determination under this paragraph shall find that, due to the United States shareholder's failure to receive a minimum distribution, the section 963 exclusion does not apply for the taxable year with respect to stock to which the election under such section relates. A determination described in subdivision (ii) or (iii) of subparagraph (1) of this paragraph shall set forth the amount of the deficiency distribution and the amount of additional income tax for which the United States shareholder is liable under Chapter 1 of the Code by reason of not including in gross income for such year the amount of the deficiency distribution. If a determination described in subdivision (i) of subparagraph (1) of this paragraph does not establish the amount of the deficiency distribution and such amount of additional tax, such amounts may be established by an agreement which is signed by the district director, or such other official to whom authority to sign the agreement is delegated.

(d) Claim for treatment of distribution as a deficiency distribution. *(1) Claim filed after date of determination.* A claim (including any amendments thereof) for treatment of a deficiency distribution as counting toward a minimum distribution for the taxable year of election shall be filed in duplicate, within 120 days after the date of the determination described in paragraph (c) of this section, with the requisite declaration prescribed by the Commissioner on the appropriate claim form and shall be accompanied by—

(i) A copy of such determination and a description of how it became final;

(ii) If requested by the district director, or by such other official to whom authority to sign the agreement referred to in paragraph (c)(1) or (6) of this section is delegated, a consent by the United States shareholder under section 6501 to extend the period for the making of assessments, and the bringing of distraint or a proceeding in court for collection, in respect of a deficiency and all interest, additional amounts, and assessable penalties for the taxable year of election; and

(iii) Such other information as may be required by the claim form or the district director, or other official, in support of the claim.

(2) Advance claim. An advance claim for treatment of a deficiency distribution as counting toward a minimum distribution for the taxable year of election shall be filed in duplicate, within 90 days after such distribution but before the date of determination described in paragraph (c) of this section, and shall satisfy all requirements of subparagraph (1) of this paragraph other than subdivision (i) of such subparagraph. However, within 120 days after the date of the determination described in paragraph (c) of this section, the advance claim shall be completed so that it satisfies all requirements of subparagraph (1) of this paragraph.

(e) Computation of interest on deficiencies in tax. If a United States shareholder, for the taxable year of the election under section 963, completes a minimum distribution for such year by receiving a deficiency distribution to which this section applies, the interest on the deficiency in tax due by reason of the failure to include the amount of such deficiency distribution in such shareholder's gross income for such year shall be computed for the period from the last date prescribed for payment of the tax for such year to the date such deficiency in tax is paid. No interest shall be due by reason of the failure to include Subpart F income in gross income for a taxable year in respect of which a minimum distribution under section 963 is completed by a deficiency distribution to which this section applies.

(f) Claim for credit or refund. If a deficiency in tax is asserted for any taxable year by reason of failure to include Subpart F income in gross income under section 951(a)(1)(A)(i) and the United States shareholder has paid any portion of such asserted deficiency, such shareholder is entitled to a credit or refund of such payment to the extent that such payment constitutes an overpayment of tax as the result of the receipt of a deficiency distribution to which this section applies. To secure credit or refund of such overpayment of tax, the United States shareholder must file a claim for refund in accordance with § 301.6402-3, in addition to the claim form required under paragraph (d) of this section. No interest shall be allowed on such credit or refund. For other rules applicable to the filing of claims for credit or refund of an overpayment of tax, see section 6402 and the regulations thereunder. For the limitations applicable to the credit or refund for an overpayment of tax, see section 6511 and the regulations thereunder.

(g) Effect of deficiency distribution. *(1) Allocation of distributions.* The deficiency distribution shall be allocated, by applying the rules of § 1.963-3 (and paragraph (b) of § 1.963-4, if applicable for the year of election), as a distribution first from the earnings and profits (to the extent thereof) of the foreign corporation which was the single first-tier corporation, or of the distributing corporation or corporations which were in the chain or group, as the case may be, for the taxable year in respect of which the election was made, and then from earnings and profits (to the extent thereof) described in section 959(c)(3) and determined as provided in section 959 for the most recent taxable year and the first, second, etc., taxable years preceding such recent taxable years, in that order, of the distributing corporation or corporations. In applying the preceding sentence to taxable years other than the taxable year in respect of which the election was made, the deficiency distribution shall first be allocated, in the order of allocation prescribed by such sentence, first to taxable years in respect of which no election under section 963 was made with respect to the stock on which such distribution is received and then to taxable years in respect of which an election under such section was made.

(2) Year of receipt. Any deficiency distribution made with respect to a taxable year of the United States shareholder shall be treated, except as provided in paragraph (b)(2) of this section, as having been received by the shareholder in that year for which such shareholder elected to secure an exclusion under section 963; and, for purposes of the foreign tax credit under section 901, the foreign income taxes paid or accrued, or deemed paid, by the United States shareholder by reason of a distribution of any amount treated as a deficiency distribution for such year shall be treated as paid or accrued, or deemed paid, for such year.

(3) Year of payment. A distribution counting toward a deficiency distribution for a taxable year of election shall, except as provided in paragraph (b)(2) of this section, be treated for purposes of applying paragraph (a) of § 1.963-3, relating to conditions under which earnings and profits are counted toward a minimum distribution, and paragraph (b)(3) of § 1.963-4, relating to rules for distributing through a chain or group, as if it were distributed during the distribution period (as defined in paragraph (g) of § 1.963-3) with respect to the distributing corporation and each foreign corporation through which such distribution is made to the United States shareholder, for the taxable year to which the

election under section 963 applies; and the foreign income taxes paid by any foreign corporation by reason of such distribution shall, in the application of section 902 and of the special rules of paragraph (c) of § 1.963-4, be treated as paid or accrued by such foreign corporation for its taxable year to which such election applies. The distribution shall not count toward a minimum distribution for any other taxable year.

(4) Allocation of reduction in tax credit. If any portion of a deficiency distribution from a corporation which was in a chain or group is paid from earnings and profits of a taxable year other than that in respect of which the election was made, then the minimum distribution toward which such deficiency distribution counts may not be treated as a pro rata minimum distribution for purposes of § 1.963-4. Moreover, the amount of the overall United States and foreign income tax with respect to such minimum distribution must satisfy the minimum tax requirements of paragraph (a)(1)(i), or paragraph (ii), of § 1.963-4, but, if the latter applies, without any reduction and deferral under paragraph (c)(3) of such section of the foreign tax credit allowable under section 901 with respect to the deficiency distribution.

T.D. 6759, 9/25/64, amend T.D. 6767, 11/3/64, T.D. 7100, 3/16/71, T.D. 8939, 1/11/2001.

§ 1.963-7 Transitional rules for certain taxable years.

(a) Extension of time for making, revoking, or changing election. *(1) In general.* Subparagraphs (2) and (3) of this paragraph provide additional rules which apply only to a taxable year of a United States shareholder for which the last day prescribed by law for filing its return (including any extensions of time under section 6081) occurs on or before the 90th day after September 30, 1964.

(2) Manner of making the election. The election of the United States shareholder to secure the exclusion under section 963 and the consent to the regulations under such section may be made for the taxable year—

(i) By filing with the return (or with an amended return filed on or before such 90th day) for such taxable year—

(a) A written statement stating that such election is made for such taxable year, and

(b) The names of the foreign corporations to which such election applies, the taxable year, country of incorporation, pretax earnings and profits, foreign income taxes, earnings and profits, and outstanding capital stock, of each such corporation, and such other information relating to the election made as the Commissioner may prescribe, on or before the date of filing, by instructions or schedules to support such return; or

(ii) In case of any extension of time under section 6081 with respect to such taxable year where the last day prescribed by law for filing the return by the electing United States shareholder (not including any extensions thereof) occurs on or before September 30, 1964, by filing with the request for the first such extension of time a written statement stating that such election is made for such taxable year and setting forth the names of the foreign corporations to which each election applies.

(3) Revocation or change of election. An election made in the manner provided by subparagraph (2) of this paragraph may be revoked or changed—

(i) By filing with the return on or before the 90th day after September 30, 1964, a written statement that such election is revoked or changed, as the case may be, and by setting forth with respect to any such modified election the information prescribed by subparagraph (2)(i)(b) of this paragraph, or

(ii) Where the return has been filed on or before such 90th day, by filing on or before such 90th day an amended return and an accompanying statement that such election is revoked or changed, as the case may be, and by setting forth with respect to any such modified election the information prescribed by subparagraph (2)(i)(b) of this paragraph.

(b) Extension of time for making a minimum distribution. *(1) In general.* This paragraph applies only with respect to a taxable year of a United States shareholder ending on or before September 30, 1964, for which an election to secure an exclusion under section 963 is made where, in case of a first-tier election, the distribution period of such first-tier corporation with respect to its taxable year to which such election applies ends on or before the 90th day after such date, and where, in the case of a chain or group election, the distribution period ends on or before such 90th day with respect to the taxable year to which the election applies of any of the foreign corporations in such chain or group.

(2) Conditions for obtaining extension of time. A distribution on stock with respect to which the election under section 963 was made which is received by the United States shareholder from a foreign corporation which was the single first-tier corporation, or a corporation in the chain or group, as the case may be, with respect to which the election was made, shall count toward a minimum distribution under section 963 for such year of election if—

(i) The distribution is made on or before such 90th day,

(ii) The shareholder, in a statement attached to its return or amended return for such year (which is filed on or before such 90th day) indicates the foreign corporation or corporations from which the distribution is made and states that, and the extent to which, the distribution is to count toward such minimum distribution,

(iii) The distribution is of such a nature as would have permitted it to count toward a minimum distribution for such taxable year of the United States shareholder if it had been made on the last day of such year, and

(iv) The United States shareholder includes the distribution in gross income as if it were received on the last day of such taxable year of election.

The distribution shall be applied against the earnings and profits of the single first-tier corporation or the foreign corporations in the chain or group for the taxable year of such corporation or corporations to which the election applies.

(3) Year of receipt. To the extent that a distribution counts toward a minimum distribution under this paragraph with respect to a taxable year of the United States shareholder, it shall be treated as having been received by the shareholder in that year for the purpose of determining gross income and the assessment of interest, additional amounts, and assessable penalties; and, for purposes of the foreign tax credit under section 901, the foreign income taxes paid or accrued, or deemed paid, by the United States shareholder by reason of a distribution of any amount treated as a distribution for such year under this paragraph shall be treated as paid or accrued, or deemed paid, for such year.

(4) Year of payment. The distribution shall be treated for purposes of applying paragraph (a) of § 1.963-3, relating to conditions under which earnings and profits are counted toward a minimum distribution, and paragraph (b)(3) of § 1.963-4, relating to rules for distributing through a chain or group, as if it were distributed during the distribution period (as defined in paragraph (g) of § 1.963-3) with respect to the

distributing corporation and each foreign corporation through which such distribution is made to the United States shareholder, for the taxable year to which the election under section 963 applies; and the foreign income taxes paid by any foreign corporation by reason of such distribution shall, in the application of section 902 and of the special rules of paragraph (c) of § 1.963-4, be treated as paid or accrued by such foreign corporation for its taxable year to which such election applies. The distribution shall not count toward a minimum distribution for any other taxable year.

T.D. 6759, 9/25/64, amend T.D. 6767, 11/3/64.

§ 1.963-8 Determination of minimum distribution during the surcharge period.

(a) Taxable years not wholly within the surcharge period. In the case of a taxable year beginning before the surcharge period and ending within the surcharge period, or beginning within the surcharge period and ending after the surcharge period, or beginning before January 1, 1970, and ending after December 31, 1969, section 963(b) provides the method for determining the required minimum distribution. Under the method prescribed in section 963(b) for such years, the required minimum distribution is an amount equal to the sums of:

(1) That portion of the minimum distribution which would be required if the provisions of section 963(b)(1) were applicable to the taxable year, which the number of days in such taxable year which are within the surcharge period and before January 1, 1970, bears to the total number of days in such taxable year.

(2) That portion of the minimum distribution which would be required if the provisions of section 963(b)(2) were applicable to such taxable year, which the number of days in such taxable year which are within the surcharge period and after December 31, 1969, bears to the total number of days in such taxable year, and

(3) That portion of the minimum distribution which would be required if the provisions of section 963(b)(3) were applicable to such taxable year, which the number of days in such taxable year which are not within the surcharge period bears to the total number of days in such taxable year.

(b) Calendar year 1970. For calendar year 1970, the required minimum distribution shall be an amount determined in accordance with the following table:

(c) Surcharge period. For purposes of this section the term "surcharge period" means the period beginning January 1, 1968, and ending June 30, 1970.

(d) Illustration of principles. The application of the rules set forth in paragraphs (a), (b), and (c) of this section may be illustrated by the following example. It is assumed that all computations are carried to sufficient accuracy:

Example. (a) M, a domestic corporation, and A, its controlled corporation (the one class of stock of which is wholly owned by M), both have a taxable year beginning December 1, 1969, and ending November 30, 1970. For such taxable year M makes a first-tier election with respect to A corporation. The effective foreign tax rate for such year is 30 percent.

(b) Under section 963(b) and paragraph (b) of this section the surcharge period ends June 30, 1970. Therefore, of the 365 days in the taxable year, 153 days are not within the surcharge period. Of the remaining 212 days, 31 are within the surcharge period and before January 1, 1970 and 181 days are within the surcharge period and after December 31, 1969. If section 963(b)(1) were applicable to the entire taxable year, the required minimum distribution of earnings and profits would be 75 percent. If section 963(b)(2) were applicable to the entire taxable year, the required minimum distribution would be 72 percent. If section 963(b)(3) were applicable to the entire taxable year, the required minimum distribution would be 69 percent.

(c) Under section 963(b) and this section the required minimum distribution of earnings and profits is 71 percent, computed as follows:

T.D. 7100, 3/20/71.

§ 1.964-1 Determination of the earnings and profits of a foreign corporation.

(a) In general.

(1) For taxable years beginning after December 31, 1986, the earnings and profits (or deficit in earnings and profits) of a foreign corporation for its taxable year shall be computed substantially as if such corporation were a domestic corporation by—

(i) Preparing a profit and loss statement with respect to such year from the books of account regularly maintained by the corporation for the purpose of accounting to its shareholders.

(ii) Making the adjustments necessary to conform such statement to the accounting principles described in paragraph (b) of this section; and

(iii) Making the further adjustments necessary to conform such statement to the tax accounting standards described in paragraph (c) of this section.

(2) Required adjustments. The computation described in paragraph (a)(1) of this section shall be made in the foreign corporation's functional currency (determined under section 985 and the regulations under that section) and may be made by following the procedures described in paragraphs (a)(1)(i) through (a)(1)(iii) of this section in an order other than the one listed, as long as the result so obtained would be the same. In determining earnings and profits, or the deficit in earnings and profits, of a foreign corporation under section 964, the amount of an illegal bribe, kickback, or other payment (within the meaning of section 162(c), as amended by section 288 of the Tax Equity and Fiscal Responsibility Act of 1982 in the case of payments made after September 3, 1982, and the regulations issued pursuant to section 964) paid after November 3, 1976, by or on behalf of the corporation during the taxable year of the corporation directly or indirectly to an official, employee, or agent in fact of a government shall not be taken into account to decrease such earnings and profits or to increase such deficit. No adjustment shall be required under paragraph (a)(1)(ii) or (iii) of this section unless it is material. Whether an adjustment is material depends on the facts and circumstances of the particular case, including the amount of the adjustment, its size relative to the general level of the corporation's total assets and annual profit or loss, the consistency with which the practice has been applied, and whether the item to which the adjustment relates is of a recurring or merely a nonrecurring nature. For the treatment of earnings and profits whose distribution is prevented by restrictions and limitations imposed by a foreign government, see section 964(b) and the regulations issued pursuant to section 964. For rules for determining the earnings and profits (or deficit in earnings and profits) of a foreign corporation for taxable years beginning before January 1, 1987, for purposes of sections 951 through 964, see 26 CFR 1.964-1(a) (revised as of April 1, 2006).

(b) Accounting adjustments. *(1) In general.* The accounting principles to be applied in making the adjustments required by paragraph (a)(1)(ii) of this section shall be those accounting principles generally accepted in the United States for purposes of reflecting in the financial statements of a domestic corporation the operations of its foreign affiliates, including the following:

(i) Clear reflection of income. Any accounting practice designed for purposes other than the clear reflection on a current basis of income and expense for the taxable year shall not be given effect. For example, an adjustment will be required where an allocation is made to an arbitrary reserve out of current income.

(ii) Physical assets, depreciation, etc. All physical assets (as defined in paragraph (e)(5)(ii) of this section), including inventory when reflected at cost, shall be taken into account at historical cost computed either for individual assets or groups of similar assets. The historical cost of such an asset shall not reflect any appreciation or depreciation in its value or in the relative value of the currency in which its cost was incurred. Depreciation, depletion, and amortization allowances shall be based on the historical cost of the underlying asset and no effect shall be given to any such allowance determined on the basis of a factor other than historical cost. For special rules for determining historical cost where assets are acquired during a taxable year beginning before January 1, 1950, or a majority interest in the foreign corporation is acquired after December 31, 1949, but before October 27, 1964, see subparagraph (2) of this paragraph.

(iii) Valuation of assets and liabilities. Any accounting practice which results in the systematic undervaluation of assets or overvaluation of liabilities shall not be given effect, even though expressly permitted or required under foreign law, except to the extent allowable under paragraph (c) of this section. For example, an adjustment will be required where inventory is written down below market value. For the definition of market value, see paragraph (a) of § 1.471-4.

(iv) Income equalization. Income and expense shall be taken into account without regard to equalization over more than one accounting period; and any equalization reserve or similar provision affecting income or expense shall not be given effect, even though expressly permitted or required under foreign law, except to the extent allowable under paragraph (c) of this section.

(v) Foreign currency. If transactions effected in a foreign currency other than that in which the books of the corporation are kept are translated into the foreign currency reflected in the books, such translation shall be made in a manner substantially similar to that prescribed by paragraph (d) of this section for the translation of foreign currency amounts into United States dollars.

(2) Historical cost. For purposes of this section, the historical cost of an asset acquired by the foreign corporation during a taxable year beginning before January 1, 1963, shall be determined, if it is so elected by or on behalf of such corporation—

(i) In the event that the foreign corporation became a majority owned subsidiary of a United States person (within the meaning of section 7701(a)(30)) after December 31, 1949, but before October 27, 1964, and the asset was held by such foreign corporation at that time, as though the asset was purchased on the date during such period the foreign corporation first became a majority owned subsidiary at a price equal to its then fair market value or

(ii) In the event that subdivision (i) of this subparagraph is inapplicable but the asset was acquired by the foreign corporation during a taxable year beginning before January 1, 1950, as though the asset were purchased on the first day of the first taxable year of the foreign corporation beginning after December 31, 1949, at a price equal to the undepreciated cost (cost or other basis minus book depreciation) of that asset as of that date as shown on the books of account of such corporation regularly maintained for the purpose of accounting to its shareholders.

For purposes of this subparagraph, a foreign corporation shall be considered a majority owned subsidiary of a United States person if, taking into account only stock acquired by purchase (as defined in section 334(b)(3)), the United States person owns (within the meaning of section 958(a)) more than 50 percent of the total combined voting power of all classes of stock of the foreign corporation entitled to vote. The election under this subparagraph shall be made for the first taxable year beginning after December 31, 1962, in which the foreign corporation is a controlled foreign corporation (within the meaning of section 957), or for which it is included in a chain or group under section 963(c)(2)(B) or (3)(B) (applied as if section 963 had not been repealed by the Tax Reduction Act of 1975), or has a deficit in earnings and profits sought to be taken into account under section 952(d); or pays a dividend that is included in the foreign base company shipping income of a controlled foreign corporation under § 1.954-6(f). Once made, such an election shall be irrevocable. For the time and manner in which an election may be made on behalf of a foreign corporation, see paragraph (c)(3) of this section.

(3) Illustrations. The application of this paragraph may be illustrated by the following examples:

Example (1). Corporation M is a controlled foreign corporation which regularly maintains books of account for the purpose of accounting to its shareholders in accordance with the accounting practices prevalent in country X, the country in which it operates. As a consequence of those practices, the profit and loss statement prepared from these books of account reflects an allocation to an arbitrary reserve out of current income and depreciation allowances based on replacement values which are greater than historical cost. Adjustments are necessary to conform such statement to accounting principles generally accepted in the United States. Assuming these adjustments to be material, the unacceptable practices will have to be eliminated from the statement, an increase in the amount of profit (or a decrease in the amount of loss) thereby resulting.

Example (2). In 1973, Corporation N is a foreign corporation which is not a controlled foreign corporation but which is included in a chain, for minimum distribution purposes, under section 963(c)(2)(B). Corporation N regularly maintains books of account for the purpose of accounting to its shareholders in accordance with the accounting practices of country Y, the country in which it operates. As a consequence of those practices, the profit and loss statement prepared from these books of account reflects the inclusion in income of stock dividends and of corporate distributions representing a return of capital. Adjustments are necessary to conform such statement to accounting principles generally accepted in the United States. Assuming these adjustments to be material, the unacceptable practices will have to be eliminated from the statement, a decrease in the amount of profit (or increase in the amount of loss) thereby resulting.

(c) Tax adjustments. *(1) In general.* The tax accounting standards to be applied in making the adjustments required by paragraph (a)(1)(iii) of this section shall be the following:

(i) Accounting methods. The method of accounting shall reflect the provisions of section 446 and the regulations thereunder.

(ii) Inventories. Inventories shall be taken into account in accordance with the provisions of sections 471 and 472 and the regulations thereunder.

(iii) Depreciation. Depreciation shall be computed as follows:

(a) For any taxable year beginning before July 1, 1972, depreciation shall be computed in accordance with section 167 and the regulations thereunder.

(b) If, for any taxable year beginning after June 30, 1972, 20 percent or more of the gross income from all sources of the corporation is derived from sources within the United States, then depreciation shall be computed in accordance with the provisions of § 1.312-15.

(c) If, for any taxable year beginning after June 30, 1972, less than 20 percent of the gross income from all sources of the corporation is derived from sources within the United States, then depreciation shall be computed in accordance with section 167 and the regulations thereunder.

(iv) Elections. Effect shall be given to any election made in accordance with an applicable provision of the Code and the regulations thereunder and these regulations.

Except as provided in subparagraphs (2) and (3) of this paragraph, any requirements imposed by the Code or applicable regulations with respect to making an election or adopting or changing a method of accounting must be satisfied by or on behalf of the foreign corporation just as though it were a domestic corporation if such election or such adoption or change of method is to be taken into account in the computation of its earnings and profits.

(v) [Reserved]. For further guidance, see § 1.964-1T(c)(1)(v).

(2) through (c)(6) [Reserved]. For further guidance, see § 1.964-1T(c)(2) through (c)(6).

(7) Revocation of election. Notwithstanding any other provision of this section, any election made by or on behalf of a foreign corporation (other than a foreign corporation subject to tax under section 882) may be modified or revoked by or on behalf of such corporation for the taxable year for which made whenever the consent of the Commissioner is secured for such modification or revocation, even though such election would be irrevocable but for this subparagraph.

(8) Illustrations. The application of this paragraph may be illustrated by the following examples:

Example (1). X Corporation is a controlled foreign corporation which maintains its books, in accordance with the laws of the country in which it operates, by taking inventoriable items into account under the "first-in, first-out" method. A, B, and C, the United States shareholders of X Corporation, own 45 percent, 30 percent, and 25 percent of its voting stock, respectively. For the first taxable year of X Corporation beginning after December 31, 1962, B and C adopt on its behalf the "last-in, first-out" inventory method, notifying A of the action taken. Even though A may object to such action, adjustments must be made to reflect the use of the LIFO method of inventorying in the computation of the earnings and profits of X Corporation with respect to him as well as with respect to B and C.

Example (2). Y Corporation is a controlled foreign corporation which maintains its books, in accordance with the laws of the country in which it operates, by employing the straight-line method of depreciation. D and E, the United States shareholders of Y Corporation, own 51 percent and 10 percent of its voting stock, respectively. For the first taxable year of Y Corporation beginning after December 31, 1962, D adopts on its behalf the declining balance method of depreciation. However, not knowing that E is a United States shareholder of the company, D fails to provide him with notice of the action taken. Assuming that E has filed the return required by section 6046 and the regulations thereunder within the period prescribed by section 6046(d), adjustments in the computation of earnings and profits will not be required with respect to him unless the Director of International Operations notifies him of the action taken within 240 days after the close of Y's taxable year. If notice is not provided to E within this period, he will not be compelled to make the adjustments. At his option, however, he may accept the action taken by assenting thereto not later than 90 days after he is first apprised of such action by the Director of International Operations.

T.D. 6764, 10/26/64, amend T.D. 6787, 12/28/64, T.D. 6829, 6/22/65, T.D. 6995, 1/17/69, T.D. 7221, 11/20/72, T.D. 7322, 8/23/74, T.D. 7545, 5/5/78, T.D. 7862, 12/16/82, T.D. 7893, 5/11/83, T.D. 9260, 4/24/2006.

PAR. 10. In § 1.964-1, paragraph (c) is revised to read as follows:

Proposed § 1.964-1 Determination of the earnings and profits of a foreign corporation. [*For Preamble, see ¶ 152,753*]

* * * * *

(c) [The text of proposed amendments to § 1.964-1(c) is the same as the text of § 1.964-1T(c) published elsewhere in this issue of the Federal Register.] [*See T.D. 9260, 04/24/2006, 71 Fed. Reg. 79.*]

PAR. 3. Section 1.964-1 is amended by:

1. Revising paragraph (c)(1)(ii) and (iii) as set forth below.

2. Adding paragraph (c)(i)(v) immediately after paragraph (c)(1)(iv) and before the concluding text to read as set forth below.

Proposed § 1.964-1 Determination of the earnings and profits of a foreign corporation. [*For Preamble, see ¶ 151,393*]

* * * * *

(c) * * *

(1) * * *

(ii) Inventories. (A) Pre-1992 years. Inventories shall be taken into account in accordance with the provisions of sections 471 and 472 and the regulations under those sections.

(B) Post-1991 years. For taxable years beginning after December 31, 1991, inventories shall be taken into account in accordance with paragraph (c)(1)(ii)(A) of this section, except that nothing in section 263A and the regulations under that section shall require the capitalization of inventory costs in excess of those required to be capitalized in keeping the taxpayer's books and records prepared in accordance with United States generally accepted accounting principles and used for purposes of reflecting in its financial statements the operations of its foreign affiliates.

(iii) Depreciation. Depreciation shall be computed as follows:

(A) For any taxable year beginning before July 1, 1972, depreciation shall be computed in accordance with section 167 and the regulations under that section.

(B) If, for any taxable year beginning after June 30, 1972, 20 percent or more of the gross income from all sources of the corporation is derived from sources within the United States, then depreciation shall be computed in accordance with the provisions of § 1.312-15.

(C) If, for any taxable year beginning after June 30, 1972, less than 20 percent of the gross income from all sources of the corporation is derived from sources within the United States, then depreciation shall be computed in accordance with section 167 and the regulations under that section.

(D) Except as otherwise provided in paragraph (c)(1)(iii)(B) of this section and notwithstanding paragraph (c)(1)(iii)(C) of this section, for taxable years beginning after December 31, 1991, depreciation shall be computed with respect to assets depreciable under section 167 and the regulations under that section using recovery methods, conventions, and useful lives established on the taxpayer's books and records prepared in accordance with United States generally accepted accounting principles and used for purposes of reflecting in its financial statements the operations of its foreign affiliates (United States books). The depreciable basis of an asset shall be determined under United States tax accounting principles unless such basis does not differ materially in amount from basis established on the taxpayer's United States books, in which case the United States book basis may be used. Thus, generally, a "push-down" or "purchase" method of accounting may not be used in determining the basis of assets of an acquired foreign corporation. In addition, where a section 338 election has been made with respect to an acquired foreign corporation, or where the consistency rules of section 338 apply, asset basis generally shall be determined in accordance with section 338 and the regulations under that section.

*   *   *   *   *

(v) Post-1991 change in method of accounting. Application of paragraphs (c)(1)(ii)(B) and (c)(1)(iii)(D) of this section may result in changes in the foreign corporation's methods of accounting. In determining whether the application of paragraph(c)(1)(iii)(D) of this section results in a change in method of accounting, a change from tax to financial book useful life shall be accounted for under this section as if it were part of the change in method of accounting for depreciation, notwithstanding that § 1.446-1(e)(2)(ii)(b) would provide otherwise. Under the Commissioner's authority in section 446(e) and § 1.446-1(e), consent to the changes in methods of accounting arising from the application of paragraphs (c)(1)(ii)(B) and (c)(1)(iii)(D) of this section is granted with no required filing of a Form 3115 (Application for Change in Accounting Method), provided the corporation makes the changes in its first taxable year beginning after December 31, 1991, and properly takes the net adjustments required under section 481(a) into account in determining earnings and profits ratably over six taxable years, beginning with the required year of change, or any applicable shorter period prescribed in section 8 of Rev. Proc. 92-20, 1992-12 I.R.B. 10 (copies of which may be obtained from the U.S. Government Printing Office, Superintendent of Documents, Washington, DC 20402).

*   *   *   *   *

PAR. 6. Section 1.964-1 is amended by adding the following language to the end of paragraph (c)(5):

Proposed § 1.964-1 Determination of the earnings and profits of a foreign corporation. [*For Preamble, see ¶ 151,253*]

*   *   *   *   *

(c) Tax adjustments. * * *

(5) Controlling United States shareholders. * * * In the event that a foreign corporation is a controlled foreign corporation solely by virtue of section 953(c)(1)(B), the controlling United States shareholders of the foreign corporation shall be those United States shareholders (as defined in section 953(c)(1)(A)) who, in the aggregate, own (within the meaning of section 958(a)) more than 25 percent of the total combined voting power of all classes of the stock of such corporation entitled to vote. In the event that the foreign corporation is a controlled foreign corporation solely by virtue of section 953(c)(1)(B) but the United States shareholders (as defined in section 953(c)(1)(A)) do not, in the aggregate, own (within the meaning of section 958(a)) more than 25 percent of the total combined voting power of all classes of the stock of such corporation entitled to vote, the controlling shareholders of the foreign corporation shall be all those United States shareholders (within the meaning of section 953(c)(1)(A)) who own (within the meaning of section 958(a)) stock of such corporation.

*   *   *   *   *

§ 1.964-1T Determination of the earnings and profits of a foreign corporation (temporary).

• ***Caution:*** Under Code Sec. 7805, temporary regulations expire within three years of the date of issuance. This temporary regulation was issued on 1/24/90.

(a) Through (c)(1)(iv) [Reserved]. For further guidance, see § 1.964-1(a) through (c)(1)(iv).

(c) *(1)* (v) Taxable years. The period for computation of taxable income and earnings and profits known as the taxable year shall reflect the provisions of section 441 and the regulations thereunder.

(2) Adoption or change of method or taxable year. For the first taxable year of a foreign corporation beginning after April 25, 2006, in which such foreign corporation first qualifies as a controlled foreign corporation (as defined in section 957 or 953) or a noncontrolled section 902 corporation (as defined in section 904(d)(2)(E)), any method of accounting or taxable year allowable under this section may be adopted, and any election allowable under this section may be made, by such foreign corporation or on its behalf notwithstanding that, in previous years, its books or financial statements were prepared on a different basis, and notwithstanding that such election is required by the Internal Revenue Code or regulations to be made in a prior taxable year. Any allowable methods adopted or elections made shall be reflected in the computation of the foreign corporation's earnings and profits for such taxable year, prior taxable years, and (unless the Commissioner consents to a change) subsequent taxable years. However, see section 898 for the rules regarding the taxable year of a specified foreign corporation as defined in section 898(b). Any allowable method of accounting or election that relates to events that first arise in a subsequent tax-

able year may be adopted or made by or on behalf of the foreign corporation for such year. See paragraph (a)(3) of this section for the manner in which a method of accounting or a taxable year may be adopted or changed on behalf of the foreign corporation. See paragraph (c)(4) and (g)(3) of this section for applicable rules if the amount of the foreign corporation's earnings and profits became significant for United States tax purposes before a method of accounting or taxable year was adopted by the foreign corporation or on its behalf in accordance with the rules of paragraph (c)(3) of this section. See paragraphs (c)(6) and (g)(2) of this section for special rules postponing the time for taking action by or on behalf of a foreign corporation until the amount of its earnings and profits becomes significant for U.S. tax purposes.

(3) Action on behalf of corporation. (i) In general. An election shall be deemed made, or an adoption or change in method of accounting or taxable year deemed effectuated, on behalf of the foreign corporation only if its controlling domestic shareholders (as defined in paragraph (c)(5) of this section)--

(A) Satisfy for such corporation any requirements imposed by the Internal Revenue Code or applicable regulations with respect to such election or such adoption or change in method or taxable year (including the provisions of sections 442 and 446 and the regulations thereunder, as well as any operative provisions), such as the filing of forms, the execution of consents, securing the permission of the Commissioner, or maintaining books and records in a particular manner. For purposes of this paragraph (c)(3)(i)(A), the books of the foreign corporation shall be considered to be maintained in a particular manner if the controlling domestic shareholders or the foreign corporation regularly keep the records and accounts required by section 964(c) and the regulations thereunder in that manner;

(B) File the statement described in paragraph (c)(3)(ii) of this section, at the time and in the manner prescribed therein; and

(C) Provide the written notice required by paragraph (c)(3)(iii) of this section at the time and in the manner prescribed therein.

(ii) Statement required to be filed with a tax return. The statement required by this paragraph (c)(3)(ii) shall set forth the name, country of organization, and U.S. employer identification number (if applicable) of the foreign corporation, the name, address, stock interests, and U.S. employer identification number of each controlling domestic shareholder (or, if applicable, the shareholder's common parent) approving the action, and the names, addresses, U.S. employer identification numbers, and stock interests of all other domestic shareholders notified of the action taken. Such statement shall describe the nature of the action taken on behalf of the foreign corporation and the taxable year for which made, and identify a designated shareholder who retains a jointly executed consent confirming that such action has been approved by all of the controlling domestic shareholders and containing the signature of a principal officer of each such shareholder (or its common parent). Each controlling domestic shareholder shall file the statement with its own tax return (or information return, if applicable) for its taxable year with or within which ends the taxable year of the foreign corporation for which the election is made or for which the method of accounting or taxable year is adopted or changed.

(iii) Notice. On or before the filing date described in paragraph (c)(3)(ii) of this section, the controlling domestic shareholders shall provide written notice of the election made or the adoption or change of method or taxable year effected to all other persons known by them to be domestic shareholders who own (within the meaning of section 958(a)) stock of the foreign corporation. Such notice shall set forth the name, country of organization and U.S. employer identification number (if applicable) of the foreign corporation, and the names, addresses, and stock interests of the controlling domestic shareholders. Such notice shall describe the nature of the action taken on behalf of the foreign corporation and the taxable year for which made, and identify a designated shareholder who retains a jointly executed consent confirming that such action has been approved by all of the controlling domestic shareholders and containing the signature of a principal officer of each such shareholder (or its common parent). However, the failure of the controlling domestic shareholders to provide such notice to a person required to be notified shall not invalidate the election made or the adoption or change of method or taxable year effected.

(4) Effect of action or inaction by controlling domestic shareholders. Any action taken by the controlling domestic shareholders on behalf of the foreign corporation pursuant to paragraph (c)(3) of this section shall be reflected in the computation of the earnings and profits of such corporation under this section to the extent that it bears upon the tax liability of all domestic shareholders of the foreign corporation. See § 1.964-1T(g)(5). In the event that action by or on behalf of the foreign corporation is not undertaken by the time specified in paragraph (c)(6) of this section and such failure is shown to the satisfaction of the Commissioner to be due to reasonable cause, such action may be undertaken during any period of at least 30 days occurring after such showing is made which the Commissioner may specify as appropriate for this purpose. The principles of § 1.964-1T(g)(3) and (g)(4) shall apply in determining the effect of a failure of the controlling domestic shareholders to take action on behalf of the foreign corporation pursuant to paragraph (c)(3) of this section. Accordingly, if the earnings and profits of a noncontrolled section 902 corporation became significant for United States income tax purposes in a taxable year beginning on or before April 25, 2006, the corporation's earnings and profits shall be computed as if no elections had been made and any permissible accounting methods not requiring an election and reflected in the books of account regularly maintained by the foreign corporation for purposes of accounting to its shareholders had been adopted. Any change in accounting method may be made by or on behalf of the foreign corporation only with the Commissioner's consent.

(5) Controlling domestic shareholders. (i) Controlled foreign corporations. For purposes of this paragraph, the controlling domestic shareholders of a controlled foreign corporation shall be its controlling United States shareholders. The controlling United States shareholders of a controlled foreign corporation shall be those United States shareholders (as defined in section 951(b) or 953(c)) who, in the aggregate, own (within the meaning of section 958(a)) more than 50 percent of the total combined voting power of all classes of the stock of such foreign corporation entitled to vote and who undertake to act on its behalf. In the event that the United States shareholders of the controlled foreign corporation do not, in the aggregate, own (within the meaning of section 958(a)) more than 50 percent of the total combined voting power of all classes of the stock of such foreign corporation entitled to vote, the controlling United States shareholders of the controlled foreign corporation shall be all those United States shareholders who own (within the meaning of section 958(a)) stock of such corporation.

(ii) Noncontrolled section 902 corporations. For purposes of this paragraph, the controlling domestic shareholders of a noncontrolled section 902 corporation that is not a controlled foreign corporation shall be its majority domestic corporate shareholders. The majority domestic corporate shareholders of a noncontrolled section 902 corporation shall be those domestic corporations that meet the ownership requirements of section 902(a) with respect to the noncontrolled section 902 corporation (or to a first-tier foreign corporation that is a member of the same qualified group as defined in section 902(b)(2) as the noncontrolled section 902 corporation) that, in the aggregate, own directly or indirectly more than 50 percent of the combined voting power of all of the voting stock of the noncontrolled section 902 corporation that is owned directly or indirectly by all domestic corporations that meet the ownership requirements of section 902(a) with respect to the noncontrolled section 902 corporation (or a relevant first-tier foreign corporation).

(6) Action not required until significant. Notwithstanding any other provision of this paragraph, action by or on behalf of a foreign corporation (other than a foreign corporation subject to tax under section 882) to make an election or to adopt a taxable year or method of accounting shall not be required until the due date (including extensions) of the return for a controlling domestic shareholder's first taxable year with or within which ends the foreign corporation's first taxable year in which the computation of its earnings and profits is significant for United States tax purposes with respect to its controlling domestic shareholders (as defined in § 1.964-1T(c)(5)). The filing of the information return required by section 6038 shall not itself constitute a significant event. For taxable years beginning on or after April 25, 2006, events that cause a foreign corporation's earnings and profits to have United States tax significance include, without limitation,

(i) A distribution from the foreign corporation to its shareholders with respect to their stock;

(ii) An amount is includible in gross income with respect to such corporation under section 951(a);

(iii) An amount is excluded from subpart F income of the foreign corporation or another foreign corporation by reason of section 952(c);

(iv) Any event making the foreign corporation subject to tax under section 882;

(v) The use by the foreign corporation's controlling domestic shareholders of the tax book value (or alternative tax book value) method of allocating interest expense under section 864(e)(4); or

(vi) A sale or exchange of the foreign corporation's stock of the controlling domestic shareholders that results in the recharacterization of gain under section 1248.

(7) and (8) [Reserved]. For further guidance, see § 1.964-1(c)(7) and (c)(8) and § 1.964-1T(g)(6).

(d) Through (f) [Reserved].

(g) *(1) Earnings and profits computed in functional currency.* (i) Rule. For taxable years of a controlled foreign corporation (within the meaning of section 957) beginning after December 31, 1986, earnings and profits shall be computed in the controlled foreign corporation's functional currency (determined under section 985 and the regulations thereunder) in accordance with § 1.964-1 as modified by this paragraph (g). Accordingly, § 1.964-1(d), (e), and (f) and (to the extent inconsistent with this paragraph (g)) § 1.964-1(c) do not apply for taxable years of a controlled foreign corporation beginning after December 31, 1986. For purposes of this section, the term "earnings and profits" includes a deficit in earnings and profits.

(ii) Cross reference. In the case of a controlled foreign corporation with a functional currency other than the United States dollar (dollar), see sections 986(b) and 989(b) for rules regarding the time and manner of translating distributions or inclusions of the controlled foreign corporation's earnings and profits into dollars.

(2) Election required when first significant. Tax accounting methods or elections may be adopted or made by, or on behalf of, a controlled foreign corporation in the manner prescribed by the Code and regulations no later than 180 days after the close of the first taxable year of the controlled foreign corporation in which the computation of its earnings and profits is significant for United States income tax purposes with respect to its controlling United States shareholders (as defined in § 1.964-1(c)(5)). For taxable years of a controlled foreign corporation beginning before January 1, 1989, only the events listed in § 1.964-1(c)(6) are considered to cause a controlled foreign corporation's earnings and profits to have United States tax significance. For taxable years of a controlled foreign corporation beginning after December 31, 1988, events that cause a controlled foreign corporation's earnings and profits to have United States tax significance include, without limitation—

(i) The events listed in § 1.964-1(c)(6),

(ii) A distribution from the controlled foreign corporation to its shareholders with respect to their stock,

(iii) Any event making the controlled foreign corporation subject to tax under section 882,

(iv) An election by the controlled foreign corporation's controlling United States shareholders to use the tax book value method of allocating interest expense under section 864(e)(4), and

(v) A sale or exchange of the controlled foreign corporation's stock by the controlling United States shareholders.

The filing of the information return required by section 6038 shall not itself constitute a significant event.

(3) Effect of failure to make required election. If an accounting method or election is not timely adopted or made by, or on behalf of, a controlled foreign corporation, and such failure is not shown to the satisfaction of the Commissioner to be due to reasonable cause under § 1.964-1(c)(6), earnings and profits shall be computed in accordance with this section. Such computation shall be made as if no elections had been made and any permissible accounting methods not requiring an election and reflected in the books of account regularly maintained by the controlled foreign corporation for the purpose of accounting to its shareholders had been adopted. Thereafter, any change in a particular accounting method or methods may be made by, or on behalf of, the controlled foreign corporation only with the Commissioner's consent.

(4) Computation of earnings and profits by a minority shareholder prior to majority election or significant event. A minority United States shareholder (as defined in section 951(b)) of a controlled foreign corporation may be required to compute a controlled foreign corporation's earnings and profits before the controlled foreign corporation or its controlling United States shareholders make, or are required under this section to make, an election or adopt a method of accounting for United States tax purposes. In such a case, the minority United States shareholder must compute earnings and profits in accordance with this section. Such computation shall be made as if no elections had been made and

any permissible accounting methods not requiring an election and reflected in the books of account regularly maintained by the controlled foreign corporation for the purpose of accounting to its shareholders had been adopted. However, a later, properly filed, and timely election or adoption of method by, or on behalf of, the controlled foreign corporation shall not be treated as a change in accounting method.

(5) Binding effect. For taxable years beginning after December 31, 1986, except as otherwise provided in the Code or regulations, earnings and profits of a controlled foreign corporation shall be computed consistently under the rules of sections 964(a) and 986(b) for all federal income tax purposes. An election or adoption of a method of accounting for United States tax purposes by a controlled foreign corporation, or on its behalf pursuant to § 1.964-1(c) or any other provision of the regulations (e.g., § 1.985-2(c)(3)), shall bind both the controlled foreign corporation and its United States shareholders as to the computation of the controlled foreign corporation's earnings and profits under section 964(a) for the year of the election or adoption and in subsequent taxable years unless the Commissioner consents to a change. The preceding sentence shall apply regardless of—

(i) Whether the election or adoption of a method of accounting was made in a pre-1987 or a post-1986 taxable year;

(ii) Whether the controlled foreign corporation was a controlled foreign corporation at the time of the election or adoption of method;

(iii) When ownership was acquired; or

(iv) Whether the United States shareholder received the written notice required by § 1.964-1(c)(3).

Adjustments to the appropriate separate category (as defined in § 1.904-5(a)(1)) of earnings and profits and income of the controlled foreign corporation shall be required using the principles of section 481 to prevent any duplication or omission of amounts attributable to previous years that would otherwise result from any such election or adoption.

(6) Examples. The following examples illustrate the rules of this section.

Example (1). (i) P, a calendar year domestic corporation, owns all of the outstanding stock of FX, a calendar year controlled foreign corporation. None of the significant events specified in § 1.964-1(c)(6) or this section has occurred. In addition, neither P nor FX has ever made or adopted, or been required to make or adopt, an election or method of accounting for United States tax purposes with respect to FX. On June 1, 1990, FX makes a distribution to P. FX does not act to make any election or adopt a method of accounting for United States tax purposes.

(ii) P must compute FX's earnings and profits in order to determine if any portion of the distribution is taxable as a dividend and to determine P's foreign tax credit on such portion under section 902. P must satisfy the requirements of § 1.964-1(c)(3) and file the written statement and notice described therein within 180 days after the close of FX's 1990 taxable year in order to make an election or to adopt a method of accounting on behalf of FX. Any such election or adoption will govern the computation of earnings and profits of FX for all federal income tax purposes (including, e.g., the determination of foreign tax credits on subpart F inclusions) in 1990 and subsequent taxable years unless the Commissioner consents to a change.

(iii) If P fails to satisfy the regulatory requirements in a timely manner and such failure is not shown to the satisfaction of the Commissioner to be due to inadvertence or reasonable cause, the earnings and profits of FX shall be computed as if no elections were made and any permissible methods of accounting not requiring an election and reflected in its books were adopted. Any subsequent attempt by FX or P to change an accounting method shall be effective only if the Commissioner consents to the change.

Example (2). (i) The facts are the same as in Example (1), except that P elects to allocate its interest expense under section 864(e)(4) for its 1989 taxable year under the tax book value method of § 1.861-12T(c) of the Temporary Income Tax Regulations.

(ii) P must compute the earnings and profits of FX in order to determine the adjustment to P's basis in the stock of FX for P's 1989 taxable year. P must satisfy the requirements of § 1.964-1(c)(3) and file the written statement and notice described therein within 180 days after the close of FX's 1989 taxable year in order to make an election or to adopt a method of accounting on behalf of FX. Any such election or adoption will govern the computation of FX's earnings and profits in 1989 and subsequent taxable years for all federal income tax purposes (including, e.g., the characterization of the June 1, 1990 distribution and the determination of P's foreign tax credit, if any, with respect thereto) unless the Commissioner consents to a change.

(iii) If P fails to satisfy the regulatory requirements in a timely manner and such failure is not shown to the satisfaction of the Commissioner to be due to inadvertence or reasonable cause, the earnings and profits of FX shall be computed as if no elections were made and any permissible methods of accounting not requiring an election and reflected in its books were adopted. Any subsequent attempt by FX or P to change an accounting method shall be effective only if the Commissioner consents to the change.

Example (3). (i) The facts are the same as in Example (2), except that P elects to allocate its interest expense under section 864(e)(4) for its 1988 taxable year under the tax book value method of § 1.661-12T(c) of the Temporary Income Tax Regulations.

(ii) P must compute the earnings and profits of FX in order to determine the adjustment to P's basis in the stock of FX for P's 1988 taxable year. P must satisfy the requirements of § 1.964-1(c)(3) and file the written statement and notice described therein within 180 days after the close of FX's 1988 taxable year in order to make an election or to adopt a method of accounting on behalf of FX. Any such election or adoption will govern the computation of FX's earnings and profits in 1988 and subsequent taxable years for all federal income tax purposes (including, e.g., P's basis adjustment for purposes of section 864(e)(4) in 1989 and the characterization of the June 1, 1990 distribution and the determination of P's foreign tax credit, if any, with respect thereto) unless the Commissioner consents to a change.

(iii) If P fails to satisfy the regulatory requirements in a timely manner and such failure is not shown to the satisfaction of the Commissioner to be due to inadvertence or reasonable cause, the earnings and profits of FX for 1988 shall be computed as if no elections were made and any permissible methods of accounting not requiring an election and reflected in its books were adopted. However, a properly filed, timely election or adoption of method by, or on behalf of, FX with respect to its 1989 taxable year, when P's basis adjustment for purposes of section 864(e)(4) first constitutes a significant event, shall not be treated as a change in accounting method. No recomputation of P's basis adjustment for 1988 shall be required by reason of any such election or adoption of method with respect to FX's 1989 taxable year, but prospective adjustments to FX's earnings and profits and income shall be made to the extent required by § 1.964-1T(g)(5).

Example (4). (i) The facts are the same as in Example (3), except that FX had subpart F income taxable to P in 1986, and P computed FX's earnings and profits for purposes of determining the amount of the inclusion and the foreign taxes deemed paid by P in 1986 under section 960 pursuant to § 1.964-1(a) through (e).

(ii) Any election made or method of accounting adopted on behalf of FX by P pursuant to § 1.964-1(c) in 1986 is binding on P and FX for purposes of computing FX's earnings and profits in 1986 and subsequent taxable years. Thus, in determining P's basis adjustment for purposes of section 864(e)(4) in 1988 and 1989 and its deemed-paid credit with respect to the 1990 dividend, FX's earnings and profits must be computed consistently with the method used by P with regard to the 1986 subpart F inclusion. (However, § 1.964-1(d), (e), and (f) do not apply in computing FX's earnings and profits in post-1986 taxable years.)

Example (5). (i) The facts are the same as in Example (4), except that FX made a dividend distribution to P on June 1, 1985, and P computed FX's earnings and profits for purposes of computing the foreign taxes deemed paid by P in 1985 under section 902 with respect to the distribution under § 1.964-1 exclusive of paragraphs (d), (e), and (f) pursuant to a timely election under § 1.902-1(g)(1).

(ii) Any election made or method of accounting adopted on behalf of FX by P pursuant to § 1.964-1(c) in 1985 is binding on P and FX for purposes of computing FX's earnings and profits in 1985 and subsequent taxable years. Thus, in determining P's basis adjustment for purposes of section 864(e)(4) in 1988 and 1989 and its deemed-paid credit with respect to the 1986 subpart F inclusion and the 1990 dividend, FX's earnings and profits must be computed consistently with the method used by P with regard to the 1985 dividend. If, rather than choosing under § 1.902-1(g)(1) to use the section 964 rules, P computed FX's earnings and profits for purposes of section 902 in 1985 in all respects as if FX were a domestic corporation, then P would have been free to make elections or adopt a method of accounting on behalf of FX under § 1.964-1(c) with respect to the subpart F inclusion in 1986. Any such election or adoption would be binding on P and FX as to the computation of FX's earnings and profits in 1986 and subsequent taxable years.

T.D. 8283, 1/24/90, amend T.D. 9260, 4/24/2006.

§ 1.964-2 Treatment of blocked earnings and profits.

(a) General rule. If, in accordance with paragraph (d) of this section, it is established to the satisfaction of the district director that any amount of the earnings and profits of a controlled foreign corporation for the taxable year (determined under § 1.964-1) was subject to a currency or other restriction or limitation imposed under the laws of any foreign country (within the meaning of paragraph (b) of this section) on its distribution to United States shareholders who own (within the meaning of section 958(a)) stock of such corporation, such amount shall not be included in earnings and profits for purposes of sections 952, 955 (as in effect both before and after the enactment of the Tax Reduction Act of 1975), and 956 for such taxable year. For rules governing the treatment of amounts with respect to which such restriction or limitation is removed, see paragraph (c) of this section.

(b) Rules of application. For purposes of paragraph (a) of this section—

(1) Period of restriction or limitation. An amount of earnings and profits of a controlled foreign corporation for any taxable year shall not be included in earnings and profits for purposes of sections 952, 955 (as in effect both before and after the enactment of the Tax Reduction Act of 1975), and 956 only if such amount of earnings and profits is subject to a currency or other restriction or limitation (within the meaning of subparagraph (2) of this paragraph) throughout the 150-day period beginning 90 days before the close of the taxable year and ending 60 days after the close of such taxable year.

(2) Restriction or limitation defined. Whether earnings and profits of a controlled foreign corporation are subject to a currency or other restriction or limitation imposed under the laws of a foreign country must be determined on the basis of all the facts and circumstances in each case. Generally, such a restriction or limitation must prevent—

(i) The ready conversion (directly or indirectly) of such currency into United States dollars or into property of a type normally owned by such corporation in the operation of its business or other money which is readily convertible into United States dollars; or

(ii) The distribution of dividends by such corporation to its United States shareholders.

For purposes of this subparagraph, if a United States shareholder owns (within the meaning of section 958(a)), or is considered as owning by applying the rules of ownership of section 958(b), 80 percent or more of the total combined voting power of all classes of stock of a foreign corporation in a chain of ownership described in section 958(a), the distribution of dividends by such corporation to such shareholder will not be considered prevented solely by reason of the existence of a currency or other restriction or limitation at an intermediate tier in such chain if dividends may be distributed directly to such shareholders.

(3) Foreign laws. A currency or other restriction or limitation on the distribution of earnings and profits may be imposed in a foreign country by express statutory provisions, executive orders or decrees, rules or regulations of a governmental agency, court decisions, the actions of appropriate officials who are acting within the scope of their authority, or by any similar official action. A currency restriction will not be considered to exist unless export restrictions are also imposed which prevent the exportation of property of a type normally owned by the controlled foreign corporation in the operation of its business which could be readily converted into United States dollars.

(4) Voluntary restriction or limitation. A currency or other restriction or limitation arising from the voluntary act of the controlled foreign corporation or its United States shareholders during a taxable year beginning after December 31, 1962, will not be taken into account. For example, if a controlled foreign corporation—

(i) Issues a stock dividend which has the effect of capitalizing earnings and profits;

(ii) Elects to restrict its earnings and profits or to make certain investments as a means of avoiding current tax or securing a reduced rate of tax; or

(iii) Allocates earnings and profits to an optional or arbitrary reserve;

such restriction is voluntary and will not be taken into account.

(5) Treatment of earnings and profits in cases of certain mandatory reserves. (i) In general. If a controlled foreign corporation is required under the laws of a foreign country to establish a reserve out of earnings and profits for the taxable year, such earnings and profits shall be considered subject to a restriction or limitation by reason of such requirement only to the extent that the amount required to be included in such reserve at the close of the taxable year exceeds the accumulated earnings and profits (determined in accordance with subdivision (ii) of this subparagraph) of such corporation at the close of the preceding taxable year.

(ii) Determination of earnings and profits. For purposes of determining the accumulated earnings and profits of a controlled foreign corporation under subdivision (i) of this subparagraph, such earnings and profits shall not include any amounts which are attributable to—

(a) Amounts which, for any prior taxable year, have been included in the gross income of a United States shareholder under section 951(a) and have not been distributed;

(b) Amounts which, for any prior taxable year, have been included in the gross income of a United States shareholder of such foreign corporation under section 551(b) and have not been distributed; or

(c) Amounts which become subject to a voluntary restriction or limitation (within the meaning of subparagraph (4) of this paragraph) during a taxable year beginning before January 1, 1963.

The rules of this subdivision apply only in determining the accumulated earnings and profits of a controlled foreign corporation for purposes of this subparagraph. See section 959 and the regulations thereunder for limitations on the exclusion from gross income of previously taxed earnings and profits.

(6) Exhaustion of procedures for distributing earnings and profits. Earnings and profits of a controlled foreign corporation for a taxable year will not be considered subject to a currency or other restriction or limitation on their distribution unless the United States shareholders of such corporation demonstrate either that the available procedures for distributing such earnings and profits have been exhausted or that the use of such procedures will be futile. As a general rule, such procedures will be considered to have been exhausted if the foreign corporation applies for dollars (or foreign currency readily convertible into dollars) at the appropriate rate of exchange and complies with the applicable laws and regulations governing the acquisition and transfer of such currency including submission of the necessary documentation to the exchange authority. The fact that available procedures for distributing earnings and profits were exhausted without success with respect to a prior year is not, of itself, sufficient evidence that such procedures would not be successful with respect to the current taxable year.

(c) Removal of restriction or limitation. *(1) In general.* If, during any taxable year, a currency or other restriction or limitation (within the meaning of paragraph (b) of this section) imposed under the laws of a foreign country on the distribution of earnings and profits of a controlled foreign corporation to its United States shareholders is removed—

(i) Treatment of deferred income. Each United States shareholder of such corporation on the last day in such year that such corporation is a controlled foreign corporation shall include in his gross income for such taxable year the amounts attributable to such earnings and profits which would have been includible in his gross income under section 951(a) for prior taxable years but for the existence of the currency or other restriction or limitation except that the amounts included under this subdivision (i) shall not exceed his pro rata share of—

(a) The earnings and profits upon which the restriction was removed determined on the basis of his stock ownership on the last day of the immediately preceding taxable year, and

(b) The applicable limitations under paragraph (c) of § 1.952-1, paragraph (b)(2) of § 1.955-1, paragraph (b)(2) of § 1.955A-1, or paragraph (b) of § 1.956-1, determined as of the last day of the immediately preceding taxable year, taking into account the provisions of subdivision (ii) of this subparagraph.

(ii) Treatment of earnings and profits. For purposes of sections 952, 955 (as in effect both before and after the enactment of the Tax Reduction Act of 1975), and 956, the earnings and profits which are no longer subject to a currency or other restriction or limitation shall be treated as included in the corporation's earnings and profits for the year in which such earnings and profits were derived.

Amounts with respect to which a currency or other restriction or limitation is removed shall be translated into United States dollars at the appropriate exchange rate for the translation period during which such currency or other restriction or limitation is removed. See paragraph (d) of § 1.964-1. Amounts with respect to which a currency or other restriction or limitation is removed shall not be taken into account in determining whether a deficiency distribution (within the meaning of § 1,963-6 (applied as if section 963 had not been repealed by the Tax Reduction Act of 1975)) is required to be made for the year in which such earnings and profits were derived.

(2) Removal of restriction or limitation defined. An amount of earnings and profits shall be considered no longer subject to a limitation or restriction if and to the extent that—

(i) Money or property in such foreign country is readily convertible into United States dollars, or into other money or property of a type normally owned by such corporation in the operation of its business which is readily convertible into United States dollars;

(ii) Notwithstanding the existence of any laws or regulations forbidding the exchange of money or property into United States dollars, conversion is actually made into United States dollars, or other money or property of a type normally owned by such corporation in the operation of its business which is readily convertible into United States dollars; or

(iii) A mandatory reserve requirement (described in paragraph (b)(5) of this section) is removed either by a change in law of the foreign country imposing such requirement or by an accumulation of earnings and profits not subject to such requirement.

(3) Distribution in foreign country. If, during any taxable year, earnings and profits previously subject to a currency or other restriction or limitation are distributed in a foreign country to one or more United States shareholders of a controlled foreign corporation directly, or indirectly through a chain of ownership described in section 958(a), such earnings and profits shall be considered no longer subject to a restriction or limitation. However, distributed amounts may be excluded from such shareholder's gross income for the taxable year of receipt if such shareholder's gross income for the taxable year of of receipt if such shareholder elects a method of accounting under which the reporting of blocked

foreign income is deferred until the income ceases to be blocked.

(4) Source of distribution. If, during any taxable year, earnings and profits previously subject to a currency or other restriction or limitation is distributed to one or more United States shareholders of a controlled foreign corporation directly, or indirectly through a chain of ownership described in section 958(a), the source of such distribution shall be determined in accordance with the rules of § 1.959-3.

(5) Illustration. The provisions of this paragraph may be illustrated by the following example:

Example. (a) M, a United States person, owns all of the only class of stock of A Corporation, a foreign corporation incorporated under the laws of foreign country X on January 1, 1963. Both M and A Corporations use the calendar year as a taxable year and A Corporation is a controlled foreign corporation throughout the period here involved.

(b) During 1963, A Corporation derives income of $100,000 all of which is subpart F income and has earnings and profits of $100,000. Under the laws of X Country, currency cannot be exported without a license. During the last 90 days of 1963 and the first 60 days of 1964, A Corporation can obtain a license to distribute only an amount equivalent to $10,000. M must include $10,000 in his gross income for 1963 under section 951(a)(1)(A)(i) and $90,000 of A Corporation's earnings and profits for 1963 are not taken into account for purposes of sections 952, 955, and 956.

(c) During 1964, A Corporation has no income and no earnings and profits. On June 1, 1964, A Corporation converts an amount equivalent to $20,000 into property of a type normally owned by such corporation in the operation of its business which is readily convertible into United States dollars but does not distribute such amount. Corporation A must include $20,000 in its earnings and profits for 1963 for purposes of sections 952, 955, and 956. M must include $20,000 in his gross income for 1964.

(d) During 1965, A Corporation has no income and no earnings and profits. On December 15, 1965, A Corporation distributes an amount equivalent to $15,000 to M in X Country. Neither M nor A Corporation can obtain a license to export currency from X Country. In his return for the taxable year 1965, M elects a method of accounting under which the reporting of blocked foreign income is deferred until the income ceases to be blocked. Accordingly, M does not include the $15,000 in his gross income for 1965.

(e) During 1966, A Corporation has no income and no earnings and profits. On February 1, 1966, notwithstanding the laws and regulations of X Country which forbid the exchange of X Country's currency into United States dollars, M converts an amount equivalent to $15,000 into a currency which is readily convertible into United States dollars. Since the income has ceased to be blocked, M must include $15,000 in his gross income for 1966.

(d) Manner of claiming existence of restriction or limitation on distribution of earnings and profits. A United States shareholder claiming that an amount of the earnings and profits of a controlled foreign corporation for the taxable year was subject to a currency or other restriction or limitation imposed under the laws of a foreign country on its distribution shall file a statement with his return for the taxable year with or within which the taxable year of the foreign corporation ends which shall include—

(1) The name and address of the foreign corporation,

(2) A description of the classes of stock of the foreign corporation and a statement of the number of shares of each class owned (within the meaning of section 958(a)) or considered as owned (by applying the rules of ownership of section 958(b)) by the United States shareholder,

(3) A description of the currency or other restriction or limitation on the distribution of earnings and profits,

(4) The total earnings and profits of the foreign corporation for the taxable year (before any amount is excluded from earnings and profits under this section) and the United States shareholder's pro rata share of such total earnings and profits.

(5) The United States shareholder's pro rata share of the amount of earnings and profits subject to a restriction or limitation on distribution,

(6) The amounts which would be includible in the United States shareholder's gross income under section 951(a) but for the existence of the currency or other restriction or limitation,

(7) A description of the available procedures for distributing earnings and profits and a statement setting forth the steps taken to exhaust such procedures or a statement setting forth the reasons that the use of such procedures would be futile, and

(8) The amount of distributions made in a foreign country and a statement as to whether a method of accounting has been elected under which the reporting of blocked income is deferred until such income ceases to be blocked, including an identification of the taxable year and place of filing of such election.

In addition, such United States shareholder shall furnish to the district director such other information as he may require to verify the status of a currency or other restriction or limitation.

T.D. 6892, 8/22/66, amend T.D. 7545, 5/5/78, T.D. 7893, 5/11/83.

§ 1.964-3 Records to be provided by United States shareholders.

(a) Shareholder's responsibility for providing records. For purposes of verifying his income tax liability in respect of amounts includible in income under section 951 for the taxable year of a controlled foreign corporation each United States shareholder (as defined in section 951(b)) who owns (within the meaning of section 958(a)) stock of such corporation shall, within a reasonable time after demand by the district director, provide the district director—

(1) Such permanent books of account or records as are sufficient to satisfy the requirements of section 6001 and section 964(c), or true copies thereof, as are reasonably demanded, and

(2) If such books or records are not maintained in the English language, either (i) an accurate English translation of such books or records or (ii) the services of a qualified interpreter satisfactory to the district director.

If such books or records are being used by another district director, the United States shareholder upon whom the district director has made a demand to provide such books or records shall file a statement of such fact with his district director, indicating the location of such books or records. For the length of time the United States shareholder of a controlled foreign corporation must cause such books or records as are under his control to be retained, see paragraph (e) of § 1.6001-1.

(b) Records to be provided. Except as otherwise provided in paragraph (c) of this section, the requirements of section 6001 and section 964(c) for record keeping shall be considered satisfied if the books or records produced are sufficient to verify for the taxable year—

(1) The subpart F income of the controlled foreign corporation and, if any part of such income is excluded from the income of the United States shareholder under section 963 or section 970(a), the application of such exclusion.

(2) The previously excluded subpart F income of such corporation withdrawn from investment in less developed countries,

(3) The previously excluded subpart F income of such corporation withdrawn from investment in foreign base company shipping operations,

(4) The previously excluded export trade income of such corporation withdrawn from investment, and

(5) The increase in earnings invested by such corporation in United States property.

(c) Special rules. Verification of the subpart F income of the controlled foreign corporation for the taxable year shall not be required if—

(1) It can be demonstrated to the satisfaction of the district director that—

(i) The locus and nature of such corporation's activities were such as to make it unlikely that the foreign base company income of such corporation (determined in accordance with paragraph (c)(3) of § 1.952-3) exceeded 5 percent of its gross income (determined in accordance with paragraph (b)(1) of § 1.952-3) for the taxable year (for taxable years to which § 1.952-3 does not apply, such amounts shall be determined under 26 CFR §§ 1.954-1(d)(3)(i) and (ii) (Rev. as of April 1, 1975)), and

(ii) If such corporation reinsures or issues insurance or annuity contracts in connection with United States risks, the 5-percent minimum premium requirement prescribed in paragraph (b) of § 1.953-1 has not been exceeded for the taxable year, or

(2) The United States shareholder's pro rata share of such subpart F income is excluded in full from his income under section 963 and the books or records verify the application of such exclusion.

T.D. 6824, 5/10/65, amend T.D. 7893, 5/11/83.

§ 1.964-4 Verification of certain classes of income.

Caution: The Treasury has not yet amended Reg § 1.964-4 to reflect changes made by P.L. 108-357.

(a) In general. The provisions of this section shall apply for purposes of determining when books or records are sufficient for purposes of § 1.964-3 to verify the classes of income described in such section.

(b) Subpart F income. Books or records sufficient to verify the subpart F income of a controlled foreign corporation must establish for the taxable year—

(1) Its gross income and deductions,

(2) The income derived from the insurance of United States risks (as provided in paragraph (c) of this section),

(3) The foreign base company income (as provided in paragraph (d) of this section), and

(4) In the case of a United States shareholder claiming the benefit of the exclusion provided in section 952(b) or the limitation provided in section 952(c)—

(i) The items of income excluded from subpart F income by paragraph (b) of § 1.952-1 as income derived from sources within the United States, the United States income tax incurred with respect thereto, and the deductions properly allocable thereto and connected therewith, and

(ii) The earnings and profits, or deficit in earnings and profits, of any foreign corporation necessary for the determinations provided in paragraphs (c) and (d) of § 1.952-1.

(c) Income from insurance of United States risks. Books or records sufficient to verify the income of a controlled foreign corporation from the insurance of United States risks must establish for the taxable year—

(1) That the 5-percent minimum premium requirement prescribed in paragraph (b) of § 1.953-1 has not been exceeded, or

(2) The taxable income, as determined under § 1.953-4 or § 1.953-5, which is attributable to the reinsuring or the issuing of any insurance or annuity contracts in connection with United States risks, as defined in § 1.953-2 or § 1.953-3.

(d) Foreign base company income and exclusions therefrom. Books or records sufficient to verify the income of a controlled foreign corporation which is foreign base company income must establish for the taxable year the following items:

(1) Foreign personal holding company income. The foreign personal holding company income to which section 954(c) and § 1.954-2 apply, for which purpose there must be established the gross income from—

(i) All rents and royalties,

(ii) Rents and royalties received in the active conduct of a trade or business from an unrelated person, as determined under section 954(c)(3)(A) and paragraph (d)(1) of § 1.954-2,

(iii) Rents and royalties received from a related person for the use of property in the country of incorporation of the controlled foreign corporation, as determined under section 954(c)(4)(C) and paragraph (e)(3) of § 1.954-2,

(iv) All dividends, interest, and, except where the controlled foreign corporation is a regular dealer in stock or securities, all gains and losses from the sale or exchange of stock or securities,

(v) Dividends, interest, and gains from the sale or exchange of stock or securities, received in the conduct of a banking, financing, or insurance business from an unrelated person, as determined under section 954(c)(3)(B) and paragraph (d)(2) and (3) of § 1.954-2,

(vi) Dividends and interest received from a related corporation organized in the country of incorporation of the controlled foreign corporation, as determined under section 954(c0(4)(A) and paragraph (e)(1) of § 1.954-2,

(vii) Interest received in the conduct of a banking or other financing business from a related person, as determined under section 954(c)(4)(B) and paragraph (e)(2) of § 1.954-2,

(viii) All annuities,

(ix) All gains from commodities transactions described in section 553(a)(3),

(x) All income from estates and trusts described in section 553(a)(4),

(xi) All income from personal service contracts described in section 553(a)(5), and

(xii) All compensation for the use of corporate property by shareholders described in section 553(a)(6).

(2) Foreign base company sales income. The foreign base company sales income to which section 954(d) and § 1.954-3 apply, for which purpose there must be established the gross income from—

(i) All sales by the controlled foreign corporation of its personal property and all purchases or sales of personal property by such corporation on behalf of another person.

(ii) Purchases and/or sales of personal property in connection with transactions not involving related persons (as defined in paragraph (e)(2) of § 1.954-1),

(iii) Purchases and/or sales of personal property manufactured, produced, etc., in the country of incorporation of the controlled foreign corporation, as determined under paragraph (a)(2) of § 1.954-3,

(iv) Purchases and/or sales of personal property for use, etc., in the country of incorporation of the controlled foreign corporation, as determined under paragraph (a)(3) of § 1.954-3, and

(v) Sales of personal property manufactured or produced by the controlled foreign corporation, as determined under paragraph (a)(4) of § 1.954-3.

Where an item of income falls within more than one of subdivisions (ii) through (v) of this subparagraph, it shall be sufficient to establish that it falls within any one of them. If a branch or similar establishment is treated as a wholly owned subsidiary corporation through the application of section 954(d)(2) and paragraph (b) of § 1.954-3, the requirements of this subparagraph shall be satisfied separately for each branch or similar establishment so treated and for the remainder of the controlled foreign corporation.

(3) Foreign base company services income. The foreign base company services income to which section 954(e) and § 1.954-4 apply, for which purpose there must be established the gross income from—

(i) All services performed by the controlled foreign corporation,

(ii) Services other than those (as determined under paragraph (b) of § 1.954-4) performed for, or on behalf of, a related person,

(iii) Services performed in the country of incorporation of the controlled foreign corporation, as determined under paragraph (c) § 1.954-4, and

(iv) Services performed in connection with the sale or exchange of, or with an offer or effort to sell or exchange, personal property manufactured, produced, etc., by the controlled foreign corporation, as determined under paragraph (d) of § 1.954-4.

Where an item of income falls within more than one of subdivisions (ii) through (iv) of this subparagraph, it shall be sufficient to establish that it falls within any one of them.

(4) Foreign base company oil related income. (i) The foreign base company oil related income described in section 954(g) and § 1.954-8, for which purpose there must be established, with respect to each foreign country, the gross income derived from—

(A) The processing of minerals extracted (by the taxpayer or by any other person) from oil or gas wells into their primary products, as determined under section 907(c)(2)(A),

(B) The transportation of such minerals or primary products, as determined under section 907(c)(2)(B),

(C) The distribution or sale of such minerals or primary products, as determined under section 907(c)(2)(C),

(D) The disposition of assets used by the taxpayer in a trade or business described in subdivision (A), (B) or (C), as determined under section 907(c)(2)(D),

(E) Dividends, interests, partnership distributions, and other amounts, as determined under section 907(c)(3).

Where an item of income falls within more than one of the listings in paragraphs (d)(4)(i)(A) through (E) of this section, it shall be sufficient to establish that it falls within any one of them.

(ii) If any of the items of income listed in paragraph (d)(4)(i) of this section arising from sources within a foreign country relates to oil, gas, or a primary product thereof and is described in section 954(g)(1)(A) or (B) and § 1.954-8(a)(1)(i) or (ii) (and, hence, is not foreign base company oil related income), then there must be established facts sufficient to verify the amount of such item of income which is not foreign base company oil related income. In this regard, the total quantities of oil, gas and primary products thereof which gave rise to such item of income and the portions of such quantities which were extracted or sold within the foreign country must be established.

(5) Qualified investments in less developed countries. For rules in effect for taxable years of foreign corporations beginning before January 1, 1976, see 26 CFR § 1.964-4(d)(4) (Rev. as of April 1, 1975).

(6) Income derived from aircraft or ships. For rules in effect for taxable years of foreign corporations beginning before January 1, 1976, see 26 CFR § 1.964-4(d)(5) (Rev. as of April 1, 1975).

(7) Foreign base company shipping income. The foreign base company shipping income to which section 954(f) and § 1.954-6 apply, for which purpose there must be established—

(i) Gross income derived from, or in connection with, the use (or hiring or leasing for use) of any aircraft or vessel in foreign commerce, as determined under § 1.954-6(c),

(ii) Gross income derived from, or in connection with, the performance of services directly related to the use of any aircraft or vessel in foreign commerce, as determined under § 1.954-6(d),

(iii) Gross income incidental to income described in subdivisions (i) and (ii) of this subparagraph, as determined under § 1.954-6(e),

(iv) Gross income derived from the sale, exchange, or other disposition of any aircraft or vessel used (by the seller or by a person related to the seller) in foreign commerce,

(v) Dividends, interest, and gains described in §§ 1.954-6(f) and 1.954(b)(1)(viii),

(vi) Income described in § 1.954-6(g) (relating to partnerships, trusts, etc.), and

(vii) Exchange gain, to the extent allocable to foreign base company shipping income, as determined under § 1.952-2(c)(2)(v)(b),

If the controlled foreign corporation has income derived from, or in connection with, the use (or hiring or leasing for use) of any aircraft or vessel in foreign commerce, or derived from, or in connection with, the performance of services directly related to the use of any aircraft or vessel in foreign commerce, it shall be necessary to establish, from the books and records of the controlled foreign corporation, that such aircraft or vessel was used in foreign commerce within the meaning of subparagraphs (3) and (4) of § 1.954-6(b).

(8) Income on which taxes are not substantially reduced. The gross income excluded from foreign base company income under section 954(b)(4) and paragraph (b)(3) or (4) of § 1.954-1 in the case of a controlled foreign corporation not availed of to substantially reduce income taxes, the income or similar taxes incurred with respect thereto, and all other factors necessary to verify the application of such exclusion.

(9) Qualified investments in foreign base company shipping operations. The foreign base company shipping income that is excluded from foreign base company income under section 954(b)(2) and § 1.954-1(b)(1).

(10) Special rule for shipping income. The distributions received through a chain of ownership described in section 958(a) which are excluded from foreign base company income under section 954(b)(6)(B) and § 1.954-1(b)(2).

(11) Deductions. The deductions allocable, under paragraph (c) of § 1.954-1, to each of the classes and subclasses of gross income described in subparagraphs (1) through (9) of this paragraph.

(e) Exclusion under section 963. Books or records sufficient to verify the application of the exclusion provided by section 963 with respect to the subpart F income for the taxable year of a controlled foreign corporation must establish that the conditions set forth in paragraph (a)(2) of § 1.963-1 have been met.

(f) Exclusion under section 970(a). Books or records sufficient to verify the application for the taxable year of the exclusion provided by section 970(a) in respect of export trade income which is foreign base company income must establish for such year—

(1) That the controlled foreign corporation is an export trade corporation, as defined in section 971(a) and paragraph (a) of § 1.971-1,

(2) The export trade income, as determined under section 971(b) and paragraph (b) of § 1.971-1, which constitutes foreign base company income,

(3) The export promotion expenses, as determined under section 971(d) and paragraph (d) of § 1.971-1, which are allocable to the excludable export trade income,

(4) The gross receipts, and the gross amount on which is computed compensation included in gross receipts, from property in respect of which the excludable export trade income is derived, as described in section 970(a)(1)(B) and paragraph (b)(2)(ii) of § 1.970-1, and

(5) The increase in investments in export trade assets, as determined under section 970(c)(2) and paragraph (d)(2) of § 1.970-1.

(g-1) Withdrawal of previously excluded subpart F income from qualified investment in less developed countries. Books or records sufficient to verify the previously excluded subpart F income of the controlled foreign corporation withdrawn from investment in less developed countries for the taxable year must establish—

(1) The sum of the amounts of income excluded from foreign base company income under section 954(b)(1) and paragraph (b)(1) of § 1.954-1 (as in effect for taxable years beginning before January 1, 1976, see 26 CFR § 1.954-1(b)(1) (Rev. as of April 1, 1975)) for all prior taxable years,

(2) The sum of the amounts of previously excluded subpart F income withdrawn from investment in less developed countries for all prior taxable years, as determined under section 955(a) (as in effect before the enactment of the Tax Reduction Act of 1975) and paragraph (b) of § 1.955-1, and

(3) The amount withdrawn from investment in less developed countries for the taxable year as determined under section 955(a) (as in effect before the enactment of the Tax Reduction Act of 1975) and paragraph (b) of § 1.955-1.

(g-2) Withdrawal of previously excluded subpart F income from investment in foreign base company shipping operations. Books or records sufficient to verify the previously excluded subpart F income of the controlled foreign corporation withdrawn from investment in foreign base company shipping operations for the taxable year must establish—

(1) The sum of the amounts of income excluded from foreign base company income under section 954(b)(2) and paragraph (b)(1) of § 1.954-1 for all prior taxable years,

(2) The sum of the amounts of previously excluded subpart F income withdrawn from investment in foreign base company shipping operations for all prior taxable years, as determined under section 955(a) and paragraph (b) of § 1.955A-1,

(3) The amount withdrawn from investment in foreign base company shipping operations for the taxable year as determined under section 955(a) and paragraph (b) of § 1.955A-1, and

(4) If the carryover (as described in § 1.955A-1(b)(3)) of amounts relating to investments in less developed country shipping companies (as described in § 1.955-5(b)) is applicable, (i) the amount of the corporations qualified investments (determined under § 1.955-2 other than paragraph (b)(5) thereof) in less developed country shipping companies at the close of the last taxable year of the corporation beginning before January 1, 1976, and (ii) the amount of the limitation with respect to previously excluded subpart F income (determined under § 1.95-1(b)(1)(i)(b)) for the first taxable year of the corporation beginning after December 31, 1975.

(h) Withdrawal of previously excluded export trade income from investment. Books or records sufficient to verify the previously excluded export trade income of the controlled foreign corporation withdrawn from investment for the taxable year must establish the United States shareholder's proportionate share of—

(1) The sum of the amounts by which the subpart F income of such corporation was reduced for all prior taxable years under section 970(a) and paragraph (b) of § 1.970-1,

(2) The sum of the amounts described in section 970(b)(1)(B),

(3) The sum of the amounts of previously excluded export trade income of such corporation withdrawn from investment under section 970(b) and paragraph (c) of § 1.970-1 for all prior taxable years, and

(4) The amount withdrawn from investment under section 970(b) and paragraph (c) of § 1.970-1 for the taxable year.

(i) Increase in earnings invested in United States property. Books or records sufficient to verify the increase for the taxable year in earnings invested by the controlled foreign corporation in United States property must establish—

(1) The amount of such corporation's earnings invested in United States property (as defined in section 956(b)(1) and paragraph (a) of § 1.956-2) at the close of the current and preceding taxable years, as determined under paragraph (b) of § 1.956-2,

(2) The amount of excluded property described in section 956(b)(2) and paragraph (b) of § 1.956-2 held by such corporation at the close of such years,

(3) The earnings and profits, to which section 959(c)(1)and paragraph (b)(1) of § 1.959-3 apply, distributed by such corporation during the preceding taxable year, and

(4) The amount of increase in earnings invested by such corporation in United States property which is excluded from the United States property which is excluded from the United States shareholder's gross income for the taxable year under section 959(a)(2) and paragraph (c) of § 1.959-1.

T.D. 6824, 5/10/65, amend T.D. 7211, 10/5/72, T.D. 7893, 5/11/83, T.D. 8331, 1/24/91.

§ 1.964-5 Effective date of subpart F.

Sections 951 through 964 and §§ 1.951 through 1.964-4 shall apply with respect to taxable years of foreign corporations beginning after December 31, 1962, and to taxable years of United States shareholders within which or with which such taxable years of such corporations end.

T.D. 7120, 6/3/71.

§ 1.970-1 Export trade corporations.

(a) In general. Sections 970 through 972 provide in general that if a controlled foreign corporation is an export trade corporation for any taxable year, the subpart F income of such corporation shall, subject to limitations provided by section 970(a) and paragraph (b) of this section, be reduced by so much of such corporation's export trade income as constitutes foreign base company income. To the extent subpart F income of an export trade corporation is reduced under section 970 and this section, an amount is required by section 970(b) and paragraph (c) of this section to be included in gross income of United States shareholders of the corporation if there is a subsequent decrease in such corporation's investments in export trade assets. See section 971(a) and paragraph (a) of § 1.971-1 for definition of the term "export trade corporation," section 971(c) and paragraph (b) of § 1.971-1 for definition of the term "export trade assets." and section 971(c) and paragraph (b) of § 1.971-1 for definition of the term "export trade assets."

(b) Amount by which export trade income shall reduce subpart F income. *(1) Deductible amount.* The subpart F income, determined as provided in section 952 and the regulations thereunder but without regard to section 970 and this paragraph, of a controlled foreign corporation which is an export trade corporation for its taxable year shall be reduced by an amount equal to so much of its export trade income as constitutes foreign base company income for such taxable year, but only to the extent that such amount of export trade income does not exceed the limitation determined under subparagraph (2) of this paragraph for such taxable year. See section 972 and § 1.972-1 for rules relating to the consolidation of export trade corporations for purposes of determining the limitations described in subparagraph (2) of this paragraph.

(2) Limitation on the amount of export trade income deductible from subpart F income. The amount by which subpart F income of an export trade corporation may be reduced for any taxable year under subparagraph (1) of this paragraph may not exceed whichever of the following limitations is the smallest:

(i) The amount which is equal to 150 percent of the export promotion expenses, as defined in section 971(d) and paragraph (d) of § 1.971-1, of the export trade corporation paid or incurred during the taxable year which are properly allocable to the receipt or the production of so much of its export trade income as constitutes foreign base company income for such taxable year;

(ii) The amount which is equal to 10 percent of the gross receipts (other than from commissions, fees, or other compensation for services), plus 10 percent of the gross amount upon the basis of which are computed commissions, fees, or other compensation for services included in gross receipts, of the export trade corporation received or accrued during the taxable year from, or in connection with, the sale, installation, operation, maintenance, or use of property in respect of which such corporation derives export trade income which constitutes foreign base company income for such taxable year; or

(iii) The amount which bears the same ratio to the increase in investments in export trade assets, as defined in section 970(c)(2) and paragraph (d)(2) of this section, of the export trade corporation for its taxable year as the export trade income which constitutes foreign base company income of such corporation for such taxable year bears to the entire export trade income of the corporation for such year.

Under subdivision (ii) of this subparagraph, in the case of minimum or maximum fee arrangements, the determination shall be made on the basis of the actual gross amounts with respect to which such fees are paid, rather than on the basis of the amounts upon which such minimum or maximum fees are computed. All determinations of limitations under this subparagraph shall be made on an aggregate basis and not with respect to separate items or categories of income described in paragraph (b)(1) of § 1.971-1.

(3) Determination of export promotion expense limitation. For purposes of determining the limitation contained in subparagraph (2)(i) of this paragraph for any taxable year of the export trade corporation, there shall be taken into account with respect to those items or categories of export trade income which constitute foreign base company income the entire amount of those export promotion expenses which are directly related to such items or categories of income and a ratable part of any other export promotion expenses which are indirectly related to such items or categories of income, except that no export promotion expense shall be allocated to an item or category of income to which it clearly does not apply and no deduction allowable to such corporation under section 882(c) and the regulations thereunder shall be taken into account.

(4) Application of section 482. The limitations provided in section 970(a) and subparagraph (2) of this paragraph shall not affect the authority of the district director to apply the provisions of section 482 and the regulations thereunder, relating to allocation of income and deductions among taxpayers.

(5) Illustrations. The application of this paragraph may be illustrated by the following examples:

Example (1). Foreign corporation A is a wholly owned subsidiary of domestic corporation M. Both corporations use the calendar year as the taxable year. For 1963, A Corporation's subpart F income determined under section 952 and the regulations thereunder is $35, the total of its gross receipts and gross amounts referred to in subparagraph (2)(ii) of this paragraph is $310, its export promotion expenses properly allocable to its export trade income which constitutes foreign base company income are $18, its increase in investments in export trade assets is $32, and its export trade income is $40, of which $30 constitutes foreign base company income and $10 does not constitute foreign base company income. The subpart F income of A Corporation for 1963 as reduced under section 970(a) is $11, determined as follows:

(i) Subpart F income		$35
(ii) Less: $30 export trade income which constitutes foreign base company income, but deduction not to exceed the smallest of the following limitations (smallest of (a), (b), or (c)):		
(a) 150 percent of allocable export promotion expenses referred to in subparagraph (2)(i) of this paragraph (150% of $18)	$27	
(b) 10 percent of gross receipts and gross amounts referred to in subparagraph (2)(ii) of this paragraph (10% of $310)	31	
(c) Amount which bears to the increase in investments in export trade assets ($32) the same ratio as the export trade income which constitutes foreign base company income ($30) bears to total export trade income ($40) (75% [$30/$40] of $32)	24	24
(iii) Subpart F income as reduced under sec. 970(a)		$11

Example (2). The facts are the same as in example (1), except that A Corporation's export promotion expenses properly allocable to export trade income which constitutes foreign base company income are $14 instead of $18. The applicable limitation on the amount deductible from A Corporation's subpart F income for 1963 is $21 (150% of $14) instead of $24. The subpart F income as reduced under section 970(a) is $14 ($35 less $21).

Example (3). The facts are the same as in example (1), except that the total amount of A Corporation's gross receipts and gross amounts referred to in subparagraph (2)(ii) of this paragraph is $200 instead of $310. The applicable limitation on the amount deductible from A Corporation's subpart F income for 1963 is $20 (10 percent of $200) instead of $24. The subpart F income as reduced under section 970(a) is $15 ($35 less $20).

Example (4). The facts are the same as in example (1), except that A Corporation derives its export trade income which constitutes foreign base company income of $30 in a service arrangement with M Corporation under which it receives as a fee 5 percent of the gross receipts from M Corporation's sales or a minimum fee of $30. Such gross receipts are $220. The gross amounts taken into account in determining the limitation under subparagraph (2)(ii) of this paragraph are $220. The applicable limitation on the amount deductible from A Corporation's subpart F income for 1963 is $22 (10 percent of $220) instead of $24. The subpart F income as reduced under section 970(a) is $13 ($35 minus $22).

Example (5). The facts are the same as in example (1), except that A Corporation derives its export trade income which constitutes foreign base company income of $30 in a service arrangement with M Corporation under which it receives as a fee 9 percent of the gross receipts from M Corporation's sales or a maximum fee of $30. Such gross receipts are $400. In such instance, the limitation under (ii)(b) of example (1) is $40 (10 percent of $400) instead of $31. The applicable limitation on the amount deductible from A Corporation's subpart F income for 1963 is $24, the smallest of the three limitations. The subpart F income as reduced under section 970(a) is $11 ($35 less $24).

(c) Withdrawal of previously excluded export trade income. *(1) Inclusion of withdrawal in income of United States shareholders.* If—

(i) A controlled foreign corporation was an export trade corporation for any taxable year,

(ii) Such corporation in any such taxable year derived subpart F income which, under the provisions of section 970(a) and paragraph (b) of this section, was reduced, and

(iii) Such corporation has in a subsequent taxable year a decrease in investments in export trade assets,

every person who is a United States shareholder, as defined in section 951(b), of such corporation on the last day of such subsequent taxable year on which such corporation is a controlled foreign corporation shall include in his gross income, under section 951(a)(1)(A)(ii) and the regulations thereunder as an amount to which section 955 (as in effect before the enactment of the Tax Reduction Act of 1975) applies, his pro rata share of the amount of such decrease in investments but only to the extent that such pro rata share does not exceed the limitations determined under subparagraph (2) of this paragraph. A United States shareholder's pro rata share of a controlled foreign corporation's decrease for any taxable year in investments in export trade assets shall be his pro rata share of such corporation's decrease for such year determined under section 970(c)(3) and paragraph (d)(3) of this section.

(2) Limitations applicable in determining amount includible in income. (i) General. A United States shareholder's pro rata share of a controlled foreign corporation's decrease in investments in export trade assets for any taxable year of such corporation shall, for purposes of determining an amount to be included in the gross income for any taxable year of such shareholder, not exceed the lesser of the limitations determined under (a) and (b) of this subdivision:

(a) Such shareholder's pro rata share of the sum of the controlled foreign corporation's earnings and profits (or deficit in earnings and profits) for the taxable year, computed as of the close of the taxable year without diminution by reason of any distributions made during the taxable year, plus his pro rata share of the sum of its earnings and profits (or deficits in earnings and profits) accumulated for prior taxable years beginning after December 31, 1962, or

(b) (1) Such shareholder's pro rata share of the sum of the amounts by which the subpart F income of such controlled foreign corporation for prior taxable years was reduced under section 970(a) and paragraph (b) of this section, plus

(2) Such shareholder's pro rata share of the sum of the amounts which were not included in the subpart F income of such controlled foreign corporation for such prior taxable years by reason of the application of section 972 and § 1.972-1, minus

(3) Such shareholder's pro rata share of the sum of the amounts which were previously included in his gross income for prior taxable years under section 951(a)(1)(A)(ii) by reason of the application of section 970(b) and this paragraph with respect to such controlled foreign corporation. The net amount determined under (b) of this subdivision with respect to any stock owned by the United States shareholder shall be determined without taking into account any amount attributable to a period prior to the date on which such shareholder acquired such stock. See section 1248 and the regulations

thereunder for rules governing the treatment of gain from sales or exchanges of stock in certain foreign corporations.

(ii) Treatment of earnings and profits. For purposes of determining earnings and profits of a controlled foreign corporation under subdivision (i)(a) of this subparagraph, such earnings and profits shall be considered not to include any amounts which are attributable to—

(a) Amounts which are, or have been, included in the gross income of a United States shareholder of such controlled foreign corporation under section 951(a) (other than an amount included in the gross income of a United States shareholder under section 951(a)(1)(A)(ii) or section 951(a)(1)(B) for the taxable year) and have not been distributed, or

(b) (1) Amounts which for the current taxable year, are included in the gross income of a United States shareholder of such controlled foreign corporation under section 551(b) or would be so included under such section but for the fact that such amounts were distributed to such shareholder during the taxable year, or

(2) Amounts which, for any prior taxable year, have been included in the gross income of a United States shareholder of such controlled foreign corporation under section 551(b) and have not been distributed.

The rules of this subdivision apply only in determining the limitation on a United States shareholder's pro rata share of a controlled foreign corporation's decrease in investments in export trade assets. See section 959 and the regulations thereunder for limitations on the exclusion of previously taxed earnings and profits.

(iii) Rules of application. The determinations made under subdivision (i) of this subparagraph for purposes of determining the United States shareholder's pro rata share of a controlled foreign corporation's decrease in investments in export trade assets for any taxable year shall be made on the basis of the stock such shareholder owns, within the meaning of section 958(a) and the regulations thereunder, in the controlled foreign corporation on the last day in the taxable year on which such corporation is a controlled foreign corporation even though such shareholder owned more or less stock in such corporation prior to that date. See section 972 and paragraph (b)(3) of § 1.972-1 for rules relating to the allocation of a decrease in investments in export trade assets of export trade corporations in a consolidated chain of such corporations. See section 951(a)(3) and the regulations thereunder for an additional limitation upon the amount of a United States shareholder's pro rata share determined under this paragraph.

(3) Illustrations. The application of this paragraph may be illustrated by the following examples:

Example (1). Foreign corporation A, which has one class of stock outstanding, is a wholly owned subsidiary of domestic corporation M throughout 1963 and 1964. Both corporations use the calendar year as the taxable year. For 1963, A Corporation qualifies as an export trade corporation and its subpart F income, determined in accordance with the provisions of section 952 and the regulations thereunder, is reduced by $20 under the provisions of section 970(a) and paragraph (b) of this section. Section 972 is assumed not to apply to A Corporation. For 1964, A Corporation has a decrease of $8 in investments in export trade assets. For 1963 and 1964, A Corporation has earnings and profits of $30 (determined under the provisions of subparagraph (2) of this paragraph). Corporation M's pro rata share of A Corporation's decrease in investments in export trade assets for 1964 which is includible in M Corporation's gross income for 1964 under section 951(a)(1)(A)(ii) by reason of the application of section 970(b) is $8, determined as follows:

(i) Corporation M's pro rata share of A Corporation's decrease in investments in export trade assets for 1964 (100% of $8)			$8
(ii) Limitation on amount includible in gross income of M Corporation for 1964 (smaller of (a) or (b)):			
(a) Corporation M's pro rata share of A Corporation's earnings and profits for 1963 and 1964 determined under subparagraph (2) of this paragraph (100% of $30)		$30	
(b) Corporation M's pro rata share of amounts by which the subpart F income of A Corporation for 1963 was reduced under sec. 970(a) (100% of $20)	$20		
Plus: Corporation M's pro rata share of amounts which were not included in subpart F income of A Corporation for 1963 by reason of the application of sec. 972	0		
Total	$20		
Less: Corporation M's pro rata share of the sum of amounts which were previously included in gross income of M Corporation under sec. 951(a)(1)(A)(ii) by reason of the application of sec. 970(b) with respect to A Corporation	0	20	
(iii) Corporation M's pro rata share includible in gross income for 1964 under sec. 951(a)(1)(A)(ii) by reason of the application of sec. 970(b) (smaller of (i) or (ii))			$8

Example (2). Assume the same facts as in example (1), except that on February 14, 1965, M Corporation sells 25 percent of its stock in A Corporation to N Corporation. Corporation N is a domestic corporation which also uses the calendar year as a taxable year. For 1965, A Corporation has a decrease of $16 in investments in export trade assets. Corporation A's earnings and profits for 1963 and 1964 (determined under the provisions of subparagraph (2) of this paragraph) are $22 ($30 minus $8). Corporation A's earnings and profits for 1965 are $6 (determined under the provisions of subparagraph (2) of this paragraph). For 1965, M Corporation's pro rata share of A Corporation's decrease in investments in export trade assets which is includible in M Corporation's gross income under section 951(a)(1)(A)(ii) is $9, and N Corporation's pro rata share includible in gross income under such section is $0, determined as follows:

M Corporation

(i) Corporation M's pro rata share of A Corporation's decrease in investments in export trade assets for 1965 (75% of $16)	$12
(ii) Limitation on amount includible in gross income of M Corporation for 1965 (smaller of (a) or (b)):	

(a) Corporation M's pro rata share of A Corporation's earnings and profits for 1963, 1964, and 1965 determined under subparagraph (2) of this paragraph (75% of $28) $21

(b) Corporation M's pro rata share of amounts by which the subpart F income of A Corporation for 1963 was reduced under sec. 970(a) (75% of $20) $15

Plus: Corporation M's pro rata share of amounts which were not included in subpart F income of A Corporation for 1963 and 1964 by reason of the application of sec. 972 0

Total $15

Less: Corporation M's pro rata share of the sum of amounts which were previously included in gross income of M Corporation under sec. 951(a)(1)(A)(ii) by reason of the application of sec. 970(b) with respect to A Corporation (75% of $8) .... $ 6 $ 9

(iii) Corporation M's pro rata share includible in gross income for 1965 under sec. 951(a)(1)(A)(ii) by reason of the application of sec. 970(b) (smaller of (i) or (ii)) .... $ 9

N Corporation

(i) Corporation N's pro rata share of A Corporation's decrease in investments in export trade assets for 1965 (25% of $16)... $4

(ii) Limitation on amount includible in gross income of N Corporation for 1965 (smaller of (a) or (b)):

(a) Corporation N's pro rata share of A Corporation's earnings and profits for 1963, 1964, and 1965 determined under subparagraph (2) of this paragraph (25% of $28) $7

(b) Corporation N's pro rata share of amounts by which the subpart F income of A Corporation for 1963 was reduced under sec. 970(a) (amounts prior to 2/14/65 not being taken into account) ... $0

Plus: Corporation N's pro rata share of amounts which were not included in subpart F income of A Corporation for 1963 and 1964 by reason of the application of sec. 972 (amounts prior to 2/14/65 not being taken into account) 0

Total $0

Less: Corporation N's pro rata share of the sum of amounts which were previously included in gross income of N Corporation under sec. 951(a)(1)(A)(ii) by reason of the application of sec. 970(b) with respect to A Corporation (amounts prior to 2/14/65 not being taken into account) $0 $0

(iii) Corporation N's pro rata share includible in gross income for 1965 under sec. 951(a)(1)(A)(ii) by reason of the application of sec. 970(b) (smaller of (i) or (ii)) $0

(d) Investments in export trade assets. *(1) Amounts of investments.* For purposes of sections 970 through 972 and §§ 1.970-1 to 1.972-1, inclusive, export trade assets shall be taken into account on the following bases:

(i) Working capital. Working capital to which section 971(c)(1) applies shall be taken into account at the adjusted basis of current assets, determined as of the applicable determination date, less any current liabilities (except as provided in subdivision (iii) of this subparagraph).

(ii) Other export trade assets. Inventory to which section 971(c)(2) applies, facilities to which section 971(c)(3) applies, and evidences of indebtedness to which section 971(c)(4) applies, shall be taken into account at their adjusted bases as of the applicable determination date, reduced by any liabilities (except as provided in subdivision (iii) of this subparagraph) to which such property is subject on such date. To be taken into account under this subparagraph, a liability must constitute a specific charge against the property involved. Thus, a liability evidenced by an open account or a liability secured only by the general credit of the controlled foreign corporation will not be taken into account. On the other hand, if a liability constitutes a specific charge against several items of property and cannot definitely be allocated to any single item of property, the liability shall be apportioned against each of such items of property in that ratio which the adjusted basis of such item on the applicable determination date bears to the adjusted basis of all such items on such date. A liability in excess of the adjusted basis of the property which is subject to such liability will not be taken into account for the purpose of reducing the adjusted basis of other property which is not subject to such liability. See paragraph (c)(6) of § 1.971-1 for treatment of export trade assets which constitute working capital to which section 971(c)(1) applies and which also constitute inventory to which section 971(c)(2) applies or evidences of indebtedness to which section 971(c)(4) applies.

(iii) Treatment of certain liabilities. For purposes of subdivisions (i) and (ii) of this subparagraph, a current liability, or a specific charge created with respect to any item of property, principally for the purpose of artificially increasing or decreasing the amount of a controlled foreign corporation's investments in export trade assets shall be taken into account in such a manner as to properly reflect the controlled foreign corporation's investments in export trade assets; whether a specific charge or current liability is created principally for such purpose will depend upon all the facts and circumstances of each case. One of the factors that will be considered in making such a determination with respect to a loan is whether the loan is from a related person, as defined in section 954(d)(3) and paragraph (e) of § 1.954-1.

(iv) Statement required. If for purposes of this section a United States shareholder of a controlled foreign corporation reduces the adjusted basis of property which constitutes an export trade asset on the ground that such property is subject to a liability, he shall attach to his return a statement setting forth the adjusted basis of the property before the reduction and the amount and nature of the reduction.

(2) Increase in investments in export trade assets. For purposes of section 970(a) and paragraph (b) of this section, the amount of increase in investments in export trade assets of a

controlled foreign corporation for a taxable year shall be, except as provided in § 1.970-2, the amount by which—

(i) The amount of its investments in export trade assets at the close of such taxable year, exceeds

(ii) The amount of its investments in export trade assets at the close of the preceding taxable year.

(3) Decrease in investments in export trade assets. For purposes of section 970(b) and paragraph (c) of this section, the amount of the decrease in investments in export trade assets of a controlled foreign corporation for a taxable year shall be, except as provided in § 1.970-2, the amount by which—

(i) The amount of its investments in export trade assets at the close of the preceding taxable year, minus

(ii) An amount equal to the excess of recognized losses over recognized gains on sales, exchanges, involuntary conversions, or other dispositions, of export trade assets during the taxable year, exceeds

(iii) The amount of its investments in export trade assets at the close of the taxable year.

For purposes of subdivision (ii) of this subparagraph, recognized losses include a write-down of inventory to lower of cost or market in accordance with a method of inventory valuation established or adopted by or on behalf of such foreign corporation under paragraph (c) of § 1.964-1.

T.D. 6755, 9/8/64, amend T.D. 6795, 1/28/65, T.D. 6892, 8/22/66, T.D. 7293, 11/27/73, T.D. 7893, 5/11/83.

§ 1.970-2 Elections as to date of determining investments in export trade assets.

Caution: The Treasury has not yet amended Reg § 1.970-2 to reflect changes made by P.L. 94-455.

(a) Nature of elections. *(1) In general.* In lieu of determining the increase under the provisions of paragraph (d)(2) of § 1.970-1, or the decrease under the provisions of paragraph (d)(3) of § 1.970-1, in a controlled foreign corporation's investments in export trade assets for a taxable year in the manner provided in such provisions, a United States shareholder of such corporation may elect, under the provisions of section 970(c)(4) and this section, to determine such increase or decrease in accordance with the provisions of subparagraph (2) of this paragraph or, in the case of export trade assets which are facilities described in section 971(c)(3), in accordance with the provisions of subparagraph (3) of this paragraph. Separate elections may be made under subparagraph (2) and/or (3) of this paragraph with respect to each controlled foreign corporation with respect to which a person is a United States shareholder, within the meaning of section 951(b).

(2) Election of 75-day rule. A United States shareholder of a controlled foreign corporation may elect with respect to a taxable year of such corporation to make the determinations under subparagraphs (2)(i) and (3)(iii) of paragraph (d) of § 1.970-1 of the amount of such corporation's investments in export trade assets as of the 75th day after the close of the taxable year referred to in such subparagraphs of paragraph (d) of § 1.970-1. The election provided by this subparagraph may be made with respect to export trade assets other than facilities described in section 971(c)(3) or with respect to export trade assets which are facilities or with respect to both types of export trade assets (but the election under this paragraph with respect to export trade assets which are facilities or with respect to both types of export trade assets may be made only if the election provided by subparagraph (3) of this paragraph is not made). If the election provided by this subparagraph is made, the amount of export trade assets with respect to which such election is made at the close of the preceding taxable year which is described in subparagraphs (2)(ii) and (3)(i) of paragraph (d) of § 1.970-1 shall be the amount of export trade assets which was considered by application of the 75-day rule to be the amount of export trade assets at the close of such preceding taxable year; except that for the first taxable year of the controlled foreign corporation for which the 75-day rule is elected the amount of investments in export trade assets with respect to which such election is made at the close of such preceding year described in subparagraphs (2)(ii) and (3)(i) of paragraph (d) of § 1.970-1 shall be the amount of investments in export trade assets at the actual close of such preceding year. In the case of a taxable year of such corporation beginning after December 31, 1962, and before December 31, 1963, the amount of investments in export trade assets with respect to which such election is made alternatively may be determined by the United States shareholder as of the 75th day after the close of the preceding taxable year referred to in subparagraphs (2)(ii) and (3)(i) of paragraph (d) of § 1.970-1 rather than as of the close of such preceding taxable year.

(3) Election for export trade assets which are facilities. A United States shareholder of a controlled foreign corporation may elect with respect to a taxable year of such corporation to make the determinations under subparagraphs (2)(i) and (3)(iii) of paragraph (d) of § 1.970-1 of the amount of such corporation's investments in export trade assets which are facilities described in section 971(c)(3) as of the close of such corporation's taxable year following the taxable year referred to in such subparagraphs of paragraph (d) of § 1.970-1. The election provided by this subparagraph may be made only if the United States shareholder does not elect the 75-day rule of subparagraph (2) of this paragraph with respect to export trade assets which are facilities. If the election provided by this subparagraph is made, the amount of investments in export trade assets which are facilities at the close of the preceding taxable year which is described in subparagraphs (2)(ii) and (3)(i) of paragraph (d) of § 1.970-1 shall be the amount of export trade assets which are facilities which was considered, by reason of the application of the following-year rule provided in this subparagraph with respect to such preceding taxable year, to be the amount of export trade assets which are facilities at the close of such preceding taxable year; except that for the first taxable year of the controlled foreign corporation for which such following-year rule is elected the amount of investments in export trade assets which are facilities at the close of the preceding taxable year described in subparagraphs (2)(ii) and (3)(i) of paragraph (d) of § 1.970-1 shall be the amount of investments in export trade assets which are facilities at the actual close of such preceding taxable year.

(b) Time and manner of making elections. *(1) Without consent.* A United States shareholder may, with respect to any controlled foreign corporation, make one or both of the elections described in paragraph (a)(2) or (3) of this section without the consent of the Commissioner by filing a statement to such effect with his return for his taxable year in which or with which ends the first taxable year of such corporation in which—

(i) Such shareholder owns, within the meaning of section 958(a), or is considered as owning, by applying the rules of section 958(b), 10 percent or more of the total combined voting power of all classes of stock entitled to vote of such corporation, and

(ii) Such corporation realizes subpart F income which is reduced under section 970(a) and paragraph (b) of § 1.970-1.

The statement shall contain the name and address of the controlled foreign corporation, identification of such first taxable year of such corporation, and an indication as to which election or elections described in paragraph (a) of this section the United States shareholder is making. If such return has been filed on or before the 90th day after the date these regulations are published in the FEDERAL REGISTER [Published 9/9/64], such United States shareholder shall file such statement with the district director with which the return was filed on or before such 90th day.

(2) With consent. A United States shareholder may make one or both of the elections described in paragraph (a)(2) or (3) of this section with respect to any controlled foreign corporation at any time with the consent of the Commissioner. Consent will not be granted unless the shareholder and the Commissioner agree to the terms, conditions, and adjustments under which the election will be effected. The application for consent to elect shall be made by the shareholder's mailing a letter for such purpose to the Commissioner of Internal Revenue, Washington, D.C., 20224. The application shall be mailed before the close of the first taxable year of the controlled foreign corporation with respect to which the shareholder desires to determine an exclusion under section 970(a) in accordance with one or both of the elections provided in paragraph (a) of this section. The application shall include the following information:

(i) The name, address, and taxable year of the United States shareholder;

(ii) The name, address, and taxable year of the controlled foreign corporation;

(iii) A statement indicating which of the elections the shareholder desires to make;

(iv) The amount of the foreign corporation's investments in export trade assets (by a category which includes export trade assets other than facilities and a category which includes only export trade assets which are facilities) at the close of its preceding taxable year;

(v) The shareholder's pro rata share of the sum of the amounts by which the subpart F income of the foreign corporation, for all prior taxable years during which such shareholder was a United States shareholder of such corporation, was reduced under section 970(a) and paragraph (b) of § 1.970-1;

(vi) The shareholder's pro rata share of the sum of the amounts which were not included in the subpart F income of the foreign corporation, for all prior taxable years during which such shareholder was a United States shareholder of such corporation, by reason of the application of section 972 and § 1.972-1; and

(vii) The shareholder's pro rata share of the sum of the amounts which were previously included in his gross income, for all prior taxable years during which such shareholder was a United States shareholder of such corporation, under section 951(a)(1)(A)(ii) by reason of the application of section 970(b) and paragraph (b) of § 1.970-1 to the foreign corporation.

(c) Effect of elections. *(1) In general.* Except as provided in subparagraphs (3) and (4) of this paragraph, an election made under paragraph (a) of this section with respect to a controlled foreign corporation shall be binding on the United States shareholder and—

(i) In the case of the election described in paragraph (a)(2) of this section, shall apply to all investments in export trade assets with respect to which such election is made, acquired, or disposed of, by such corporation during the 75-day period following its taxable year for which subpart F income is first computed under the election and during all succeeding corresponding 75-day periods of such corporation, or

(ii) In the case of the election described in paragraph (a)(3) of this section, shall apply to all investments in export trade assets which are facilities acquired, or disposed of, by such corporation during the taxable year following its taxable year for which subpart F income is first computed under the election and during all succeeding corresponding taxable years of such corporation.

(2) Returns. Any return of a United States shareholder required to be filed before the completion of a period with respect to which determinations are to be made as to a controlled foreign corporation's investments in export trade assets for purposes of computing such shareholder's taxable income shall be filed on the basis of an estimate of the amount of such corporation's investments in export trade assets at the close of the period. If the actual amount of such investments is not the same as the amount of the estimate, the shareholder shall immediately notify the Commissioner. The Commissioner will thereupon redetermine the amount of such shareholder's tax for the year or years with respect to which the incorrect amount was taken into account. The amount of tax, if any, due upon such redetermination shall be paid by the shareholder upon notice and demand by the district director. The amount of tax, if any, shown by such redetermination to have been overpaid shall be credited or refunded to the shareholder in accordance with the provisions of sections 6402 and 6511 and the regulations thereunder.

(3) Revocation. (i) In general. (a) Consent required. Upon application by the United States shareholder, an election made under paragraph (a) of this section may, subject to the approval of the Commissioner, be revoked. Approval will not be granted unless the shareholder and the Commissioner agree to the terms, conditions, and adjustments under which the revocation will be effected.

(b) Revocation of 75-day rule. In the case of the revocation of an election described in paragraph (a)(2) of this section, the change in the controlled foreign corporation's investments in export trade assets with respect to which such election was made for its first taxable year for which subpart F income or a decrease in investments in export trade assets is computed without regard to the election previously made shall, unless the agreement with the Commissioner provides otherwise, be considered to be the amount by which—

(1) Such corporation's investments in export trade assets with respect to which such election was made at the close of such taxable year exceeds or, if applicable, is exceeded by

(2) Such corporation's investments in export trade assets with respect to which such election was made at the close of the 75th day after the close of the preceding taxable year of such corporation.

(c) Revocation of following-year rule. In the case of the revocation of an election described in paragraph (a)(3) of this section, the change in the controlled foreign corporation's investments in export trade assets which are facilities for its first taxable year for which subpart F income or a decrease in investments in export trade assets is computed without regard to the election previously made shall, unless the agreement with the Commissioner provides otherwise, be considered to be zero.

(ii) Time and manner of applying for consent to revocation. (a) Application to Commissioner. The application for consent to revocation of an election shall be made by the United States shareholder's mailing a letter for such purpose to the Commissioner of Internal Revenue, Washington, D.C., 20224. The application shall be mailed before the close of the first taxable year of the controlled foreign corporation with respect to which the shareholder desires to determine an exclusion under section 970(a) or an inclusion under section 970(b) without regard to such election.

(b) Information required. The application shall include the following information:

(1) The name, address, and taxable year of the United States shareholder;

(2) The name, address, and taxable year of the controlled foreign corporation;

(3) A statement indicating the election the shareholder desires to revoke under this subparagraph;

(4) The information required under subdivisions (iv) through (vii) of paragraph (b)(2) of this section;

(5) In the case of an application for consent to revocation of an election made under paragraph (a)(2) of this section, the amount of the foreign corporation's investments in export trade assets with respect to which such election was made at the close of the 75th day after the close of such corporation's taxable year immediately preceding the taxable year of such corporation; and

(6) The reasons for the request for consent to revocation.

(4) Transfer of stock. (i) Election of 75-day rule in force. (a) If during any taxable year of a controlled foreign corporation—

(1) A United States shareholder who has made the election described in paragraph (a)(2) of this section with respect to such corporation sells, exchanges, or otherwise disposes of all or part of his stock in such corporation, and

(2) The foreign corporation is a controlled foreign corporation immediately after the sale, exchange, or other disposition,

then, with respect to the stock so sold, exchanged, or disposed of, the successor in interest shall consider the controlled foreign corporation's change during the first 75 days of such taxable year in investments in export trade assets with respect to which such election is made to be zero.

(b) If the United States shareholder's successor in interest makes an election under paragraph (a)(2) of this section in order to determine an exclusion under section 970(a) for the taxable year of such corporation in which he acquires such stock, the amount of the controlled foreign corporation's investments in export trade assets with respect to which such election is made at the close of its preceding taxable year shall be considered, with respect to the stock so acquired, to be the amount of such corporation's investments in export trade assets with respect to which such election is made at the close of the 75th day after the close of such preceding taxable year.

(c) If the United States shareholder's successor in interest makes an election under paragraph (a)(2) of this section in order to determine an exclusion under section 970(a) for a taxable year of such corporation subsequent to the taxable year in which he acquired the stock, the amount of the controlled foreign corporation's investments in export trade assets with respect to which such election is made at the close of its taxable year immediately preceding such subsequent taxable year shall, with respect to the stock so acquired, be the amount of such corporation's investments in such assets at the actual close of such preceding taxable year.

(ii) Election in force with respect to export trade assets which are facilities. (a) If during any taxable year of a controlled foreign corporation—

(1) A United States shareholder who has made the election described in paragraph (a)(3) of this section with respect to such corporation sells, exchanges, or otherwise disposes of all or part of his stock in such corporation, and

(2) The foreign corporation is a controlled foreign corporation immediately after the sale, exchange or other disposition,

then, with respect to the stock so sold, exchanged, or disposed of, the successor in interest shall consider the controlled foreign corporation's change for such taxable year in investments in export trade assets which are facilities to be zero.

(b) If the United States shareholder's successor in interest makes an election under paragraph (a)(3) of this section in order to determine an exclusion under section 970(a) for the taxable year of such corporation in which he acquires such stock, the amount of the controlled foreign corporation's investments in export trade assets which are facilities at the close of its preceding taxable year shall be considered, with respect to the stock so acquired, to be the amount of such corporation's investments in export trade assets which are facilities at the close of the taxable year in which such stock is acquired.

(c) If the United States shareholder's successor in interest makes an election under paragraph (a)(3) of this section in order to determine an exclusion under section 970(a) for a taxable year of such corporation subsequent to the taxable year in which he acquired the stock, the amount of the controlled foreign corporation's investments in export trade assets which are facilities at the close of its taxable year immediately preceding such subsequent taxable year shall, with respect to the stock so acquired, be the amount of such corporation's investments in such assets at the actual close of such preceding taxable year.

(d) Illustrations. The principles contained in this section are illustrated by the examples set forth in paragraph (d) of § 1.955-3.

T.D. 6755, 9/8/64.

§ 1.970-3 Effective date of subpart G.

Caution: The Treasury has not yet amended Reg § 1.970-3 to reflect changes made by P.L. 94-455.

Sections 970 through 972 and §§ 1.970-1 through 1.972-1 shall apply with respect to taxable years of foreign corporations beginning after December 31, 1962, and to taxable years of United States shareholders within which or with which such taxable years of such corporations end.

T.D. 6755, 9/8/64.

§ 1.971-1 Definitions with respect to export trade corporations.

(a) Export trade corporations. *(1) In general.* For purposes of sections 970 through 972 and §§ 1.970-1 to 1.972-1, inclusive, the term "export trade corporation" means a controlled foreign corporation which for the period specified in subparagraph (2) of this paragraph satisfies the conditions specified in subparagraph (3) of this paragraph. However, no controlled foreign corporation may qualify as an export trade corporation for any taxable year beginning after October 31, 1971, unless it qualified as an export trade corporation for any taxable year beginning before such date. In addition, if a corporation fails to qualify as an export trade corporation for a period of any 3 consecutive taxable years beginning after October 31, 1971, then for any taxable year beginning after such 3 year period, such corporation shall not be included within the term "export trade corporation".

(2) Three-year period. The period referred to in subparagraph (1) of this paragraph is the 3-year period ending with the close of the controlled foreign corporation's current taxable year, or such part of such 3-year period as occurs on and after the beginning of the corporation's first taxable year beginning after December 31, 1962, whichever period is shorter.

(3) Gross income requirements. The conditions referred to in subparagraph (1) of this paragraph are that the controlled foreign corporation derives—

(i) 90 percent or more of its gross income from sources without the United States, and

(ii) (a) 75 percent or more of its gross income from transactions, activities, or interest described in section 971(b) and paragraph (b) of this section, or

(b) 50 percent or more of its gross income from transactions, activities, or interest described in section 971(b) and paragraph (b) of this section in respect of agricultural products grown in the United States.

(4) Determination of sources of gross income. The sources of gross income of a controlled foreign corporation shall be determined for purposes of subparagraph (3)(i) of this paragraph in accordance with the rules for determining sources of gross income set forth in sections 861 through 864 and the regulations thereunder.

(b) Export trade income. *(1) General rule.* For purposes of sections 970 through 972 and §§ 1.970-1 to 1.972-1, inclusive, the term "export trade income" means the gross export trade income of a controlled foreign corporation derived from transactions, activities, or interest described in subdivisions (i) through (vii) of this subparagraph, less deductions allowed under subdivision (viii) of this subparagraph.

(i) Sale of export property. Gross export trade income of a controlled foreign corporation includes gross income it derives from the sale of export property (as defined in paragraph (e) of this section) which it purchases, if the sale is made to an unrelated person for use, consumption, or disposition outside the United States. See section 971(b)(1). As a general rule, property will be presumed to have been sold for use, consumption, or disposition in the country of destination of the sale. However, if at the time of the sale the controlled foreign corporation knows, or should have known from the facts and circumstances surrounding the sales transaction, that the property will probably be used, consumed, or disposed of in the United States, such property will be presumed to have been sold for use, consumption, or disposition in the United States unless the controlled foreign corporation establishes that such property was used, consumed, or disposed of outside the United States. For purposes of this subdivision, export property must be sold by a controlled foreign corporation in essentially the same form in which such property is purchased. Whether export property sold is in essentially the same form in which such property is purchased shall be determined on the basis of all the facts and circumstances in each case. Storage, handling, transportation, packaging, or servicing of property will be considered not to alter the form in which property is purchased. However, manufacture or production, within the meaning of paragraph (a)(4) of § 1.954-3, will be considered to alter the form in which property is purchased and no part of the gross income from the sale of such property will be treated as export trade income. The application of this subdivision may be illustrated by the following example:

Example. Controlled foreign corporation A, incorporated under the laws of foreign country Y, purchases articles manufactured in the United States from domestic corporation M and sells them in the form in which purchased to foreign corporation B, unrelated to A Corporation, for use foreign countries, X, Y, and Z. The gross income of A Corporation from the purchase and sale of the articles constitutes gross export trade income.

(ii) Commissions and other income derived in connection with the sale of export property. Gross export trade income of a controlled foreign corporation includes gross commissions, fees, compensation, or other income derived by such corporation from the performance for any person of commercial, industrial, financial, technical, scientific, managerial, engineering, architectural, skilled, or other services in respect of a sale by such corporation in a transaction described in subdivision (i) of this subparagraph or in respect of the sale by any other person of export property to a person unrelated to the controlled foreign corporation for use, consumption, or disposition outside the United States. Such gross export trade income includes payments received for surveys made prior to, and in connection with, the sale of such export property (whether or not such sales are ultimately consummated). See section 971(b)(1). The term "any person" or "any other person" as used in this subdivision includes a related person as defined in section 954(d)(3) and paragraph (e) of § 1.954-1. The application of this subdivision may be illustrated by the following examples:

Example (1). Controlled foreign corporation A, incorporated under the laws of foreign country X, receives from M Corporation a commission equal to 6 percent of the gross selling price of all personal property shipped by M Corporation as a result of services performed by A Corporation in soliciting orders in foreign countries X, Y, and Z. In fulfillment of such orders, M Corporation ships products manufactured by it in the United States. Corporation A does not assume title to the property sold. Gross commissions received by A Corporation from M Corporation in connection with the sale of such property to persons unrelated to A Corporation for use, consumption, or disposition outside the United States constitute gross export trade income.

Example (2). Foreign corporation B, incorporated under the laws of foreign country X, is a wholly owned subsidiary of domestic corporation N. Corporation N is engaged in the business of manufacturing heavy duty electrical equipment in the United States. By contract, N Corporation engages B Corporation for the purpose of conducting engineering, technical, and financial studies required by N Corporation in the preparation of bids to supply foreign country Y with electrical equipment for a construction project to be undertaken by such country. Corporation N pays B Corporation a fee for the services, all of which are performed in country Y, which is based upon the number of hours of work performed without regard to whether a sale is ultimately consummated. Corporation N does not receive a contract from country Y on its bid to supply equipment. Income derived by B Corporation from performance of the service contract constitutes gross export trade income.

(iii) Commissions and other income derived in connection with the installation or maintenance of export property. Gross export trade income of a controlled foreign corporation includes gross commissions, fees, compensation, or other income derived by such corporation from the performance for any person of commercial, industrial, financial, technical, scientific, managerial, engineering, architectural, skilled, or other services in respect of the installation or maintenance of export property which has been sold by such corporation in a transaction described in subdivision (i) of this subparagraph or by any other person to a person unrelated to the controlled foreign corporation for use, consumption, or disposition outside the United States. See section 971(b)(1). The term "any person" or "any other person" as used in this subdivision includes a related person as defined in section 954(d)(3) and paragraph (e) of § 1.954-1.

(iv) Commissions and other income derived in connection with the use of patents, copyrights, and other like property. Gross export trade income of a controlled foreign corporation includes gross commissions, fees, compensation, or other income derived by such corporation from the performance for any person of commercial, industrial, financial, technical, scientific, managerial, engineering, architectural, skilled, or other services in connection with the use outside of the United States by an unrelated person of patents, copyrights, secret processes and formulas, goodwill, trademarks, trade brands, franchises, and other like property, including gross income derived from obtaining licensees for patents, but only if the patent, copyright, or other like property is acquired, or developed, and owned by the manufacturer, producer, grower, or extractor of any export property, in respect of which the controlled foreign corporation also derives gross export trade income within the meaning of subdivision (i), (ii), or (iii) of this subparagraph. See section 971(b)(2). The application of this subdivision may be illustrated by the following example:

Example. Foreign corporation A incorporated under the laws of foreign country X, is a wholly owned subsidiary of domestic corporation M. Corporation M, the owner of a patent registered in foreign country X, grants B Corporation, a corporation unrelated to A Corporation, the right to use such patent in foreign country Y in exchange for payment of a royalty. By a separate contract with B Corporation, A Corporation agrees for a gross fee of $100,000 to furnish, by maintaining a staff of technical representatives at the offices of B Corporation, technical services to B Corporation in connection with B Corporation's use of the patent. Corporation A also derives export trade income from the sale of export property which it purchases from M Corporation, the manufacturer of such property, and sells to C Corporation, an unrelated person, for use in country Y by C Corporation. The gross fee of $100,000 received by A Corporation for the furnishing of technical services in connection with B Corporation's use of M Corporation's patent constitutes gross export trade income since the service for which the fee is paid is performed in connection with the use outside the United States by an unrelated person (B Corporation) of a patent owned by a manufacturer (M Corporation) of export property in respect of which the controlled foreign corporation (A Corporation) derives gross export trade income from the sale to an unrelated person (C Corporation) for use outside the United States of export property purchased by it from the manufacturer (M Corporation).

(v) Income attributable to use of export property by an unrelated person. Gross export trade income of a controlled foreign corporation includes gross commissions, fees, rents, compensation, or other income which is received by such corporation from an unrelated person and is attributable to the use of export property by such unrelated person. See section 971(b)(3). The application of this subdivision may be illustrated by the following example:

Example. Foreign corporation A, incorporated under the laws of foreign country X, is a wholly owned subsidiary of domestic corporation M. Corporation A acquires by purchase bottling machines manufactured in the United States and leases the machines to B Corporation, a corporation unrelated to A Corporation, for use by B Corporation in foreign country Y. Gross rental income of A Corporation from the lease of the machines to B Corporation constitutes gross export trade income.

(vi) Income attributable to the use of export property in the rendition of technical, scientific, or engineering services. (a) General. Gross export trade income of a controlled foreign corporation includes gross commissions, fees, compensation, or other income which is received by such corporation from an unrelated person and is attributable to the use of export property in the performance of technical, scientific, or engineering services to such unrelated person. See section 971(b)(3).

(b) Rule of apportionment. If a commission, fee, or other income received by a controlled foreign corporation from an unrelated person under a contract or arrangement for the performance of technical, scientific, or engineering services is not solely attributable to the use of export property in the performance of such services and the amount of the gross income attributable to such use of export property cannot be established by reference to transactions between other unrelated persons, such gross income shall be an amount which bears the same ratio to total gross income from the contract or arrangement as the cost of the export property consumed in the performance of such services, including a reasonable allowance for depreciation with respect to the export property so used, bears to the total costs and expenses attributable to the production of income under the contract or arrangement.

(c) Illustration. The application of this subdivision may be illustrated by the following example:

Example. Foreign corporation A, incorporated under the laws of foreign country X, is a wholly owned subsidiary of domestic corporation M. Corporation A is engaged in the seismograph service business in foreign country X. In an effort to establish the probable existence of oil in a concession area it owns in foreign country Y, B Corporation which is unrelated to A Corporation enters into a contract with A Corporation whereby A Corporation is required to make seismographic tests in the area in country Y for a fixed fee of $100,000. In performance of the contract, A Corporation hires a skilled crew to carry out the contract and utilizes equipment and supplies (for example, trucks, seismographic equipment, etc.) which constitute export property. Corporation A cannot establish by reference to transactions between other unrelated person, the income attributable to the use of the export property in the performance of the contract. Corporation A's total costs and expenses (for example, salaries of the crew, administrative expenses, all supplies, total depreciation on property used in performance of the contract, etc.) incurred in performance of the contract are $80,000. The cost of export property consumed in performance of the contract (for example, dynamite, motor oil, and other supplies which were produced in the United States, reasonable depreciation on trucks and seismographic equipment manufactured in the United States and used in performance of the contract, etc.) is $30,000. Corporation A's gross export trade income from the contract is $37,500, that is, the amount which bears the same ratio to total gross income from the contract ($100,000) as the cost of the export property consumed in the rendition of the services ($30,000) bears to total costs and expenses attributable to the contract ($80,000).

(vii) Interest from export trade assets. Gross export trade income of a controlled foreign corporation includes interest derived by it from export trade assets described in section 971(c)(4) and paragraph (c)(5) of this section. See section 971(b)(4).

(viii) Deductions to be taken into account. Export trade income of a controlled foreign corporation for any taxable year shall be the amount determined by deducting from the items or categories of gross income described in subdivisions (i) through (vii) of this subparagraph the entire amount of those expenses, taxes, and other deductions properly allocable to such items or categories of income. For purposes of this section, expenses, taxes, and other deductions shall first be allocated to items or categories of gross income to which they directly relate; then, expenses, taxes, and other deductions which cannot definitely be allocated to some item or category of gross income shall be ratably apportioned among all items or categories of gross income, except that no expense, tax, or other deduction shall be allocated to an item or category of income to which it clearly does not apply and no deduction allowable to such controlled foreign corporation under section 882(c) and the regulations thereunder shall be taken into account.

(2) Cross reference. For rules governing the determination of gross income and taxable income of a foreign corporation, see § 1.952-2.

(c) Export trade assets. *(1) In general.* For purposes of sections 970 through 972 and §§ 1.970-1 to 1.972-1, inclusive, the term "export trade assets" means—

(i) Working capital reasonably necessary for the production of export trade income,

(ii) Inventory of export property held for use, consumption, or disposition outside the United States,

(iii) Facilities located outside the United States for the storage, handling, transportation, packaging, servicing, sale, or distribution of export property, and

(iv) Evidences of indebtedness executed by unrelated persons in connection with payment for purchases of export property for use, consumption, or disposition outside the United States, or in connection with the payment for services described in section 971(b)(2) or (3) and paragraph (b)(1)(iv), (v), or (vi) of this section.

(2) Working capital. For purposes of subparagraph (1)(i) of this paragraph, working capital of a controlled foreign corporation is the excess of its current assets over its current liabilities. Liabilities maturing in one year or less shall be considered current liabilities. A determination of the amount of working capital of a controlled foreign corporation which is reasonably necessary for the production of export trade income will depend upon the nature and volume of the activities of the controlled foreign corporation which produce export trade income as they exist on the applicable determination date. In determining working capital which is reasonably necessary for the production of export trade income, the anticipated future needs of the business will be taken into account to the extent that such needs relate to the year of the controlled foreign corporation following the applicable determination date; anticipated future needs relating to a later period will not be taken into account unless it is clearly established that such needs are reasonably related to the production of export trade income as of the applicable determination date.

(3) Inventory of export property. For purposes of subparagraph (1)(ii) of this paragraph, the inclusion of items in inventory shall be determined in accordance with rules applicable to domestic corporations. See §§ 1.471-1 through 1.471-9. Inventory of export property of a controlled foreign corporation includes export property held for use, consumption, or disposition outside the United States regardless of where it is located on the applicable determination date. Thus, such property may be physically located in the United States on such date. However, for property physically located in the United States to constitute export property, it must have been acquired by the controlled foreign corporation with a clear intent that it would dispose of the property for use, consumption, or disposition outside the United States. As a general rule, if during the year following the applicable determination date export property which was physically located in the United States on such date is actually exported for use, consumption, or disposition outside the United States, such property will be deemed held for such purpose on the applicable determination date. On the other hand, the indefinite warehousing of export property in the United States by the controlled foreign corporation, or the subsequent sale of export property by such corporation for use, consumption, or disposition in the United States, will evidence a lack of intent by such corporation on the applicable determination date to hold such property for use, consumption, or disposition outside the United States.

(4) Facilities located outside the United States. (i) In general. For purposes of subparagraph (1)(iii) of this paragraph, a facility, as defined in subdivision (ii)(a) of this subparagraph, will be considered an export trade asset only—

(a) If such facility is located outside the United States, and

(b) To the extent that such facility is used, within the meaning of subdivision (ii)(c) of this subparagraph, by the controlled foreign corporation for the storage, handling, transportation, packaging, servicing, sale, or distribution of export property in essentially the same form in which such property is acquired by such corporation.

Thus, a facility in which property is manufactured or produced, even though export property is used or consumed in the production or becomes a component part of the manufactured article, will not qualify as an export trade asset.

(ii) Special rules. (a) Facility defined. For purposes of subdivision (i) of this subparagraph, the term "facility" includes any asset or group of assets used for the storage, handling, transportation, packaging, servicing, sale, or distribution of export property. Thus, such term includes warehouse, storage, or sales facilities (for example, sales office equipment), transportation equipment (for example, motor trucks, vessels, etc.), and machinery and equipment (for example, packaging equipment, servicing equipment, cranes, fork lift trucks used in warehouses, etc.).

(b) Determination of location of transportation facilities. A transportation facility shall be considered to be located outside the United States for purposes of subdivision (i)(a) of this subparagraph if such property is predominantly located outside the United States. As a general rule, on an applicable determination date a transportation facility will be considered to be predominantly located outside the United States if 70 percent or more of the miles traversed (during the 12-month period immediately preceding such determination date or for such part of such period as such facility is owned by the controlled foreign corporation) in the use of such facility are traversed outside the United States or if such facility is located outside the United States at least 70 percent of the time during such period or such part thereof.

(c) Determination of use. For purposes of subdivision (i)(b) of this subparagraph, the extent to which a facility is used in carrying on the activities described in such subdivision depends on the use made of the facility for the 12-month period immediately preceding the applicable determination date or for such part of such period as such facility is owned by the controlled foreign corporation. The method of measuring such use will depend upon the facts and circumstances in each case. However, such determinations of use will generally be made for a facility as a whole and not on the basis of individual items used in the operation of a facility. Thus, a determination as to the use of a warehouse facility will generally be made with respect to the entire facility and not separately for the items used in such warehouse, such as fork lift trucks, storage bins, etc.

(5) Evidences of indebtedness. For purposes of subparagraph (1)(iv) of this paragraph, the term "evidence of indebtedness" mean a note, installment sales contract, a time bill of exchange evidencing a sale on credit, or similar written instrument executed by an unrelated person which evidences the obligation of an unrelated person to pay for export property which an unrelated person purchases for use, consumption, or disposition outside the United States or to pay for services described in section 971(b)(2) or (3) and paragraph (b)(1)(iv), (v), or (vi) of this section which are performed for an unrelated person. Receivables which arise out of the delivery of export property, or the performance of services, which are evidenced by invoices, bills of lading, bills of exchange which do not evidence a sale on credit, sales slips, and similar documents created by the unilateral act of a creditor shall not be considered evidences of indebtedness for purposes of section 971(c)(4).

(6) Duplication of treatment and priority of application. No asset which constitutes an export trade asset shall be taken into account more than once in determining the investments in export trade assets of a controlled foreign corporation. Assets which constitute working capital and also constitute inventory to which section 971(c)(2) applies or evidences of indebtedness to which section 971(c)(4) applies shall be taken into account in determining whether the amount of working capital of the controlled foreign corporation is reasonably necessary for the production of export trade income. However, to the extent that the amount of inventory to which section 971(c)(2) applies or evidences of indebtedness to which section 971(c)(4) applies is not included in working capital to which section 971(c)(1) applies on the ground that such amount is not reasonably necessary for the production of export trade income, the amount shall be included under section 971(c)(2) or 971(c)(4), as the case may be, in a controlled foreign corporation's investments in export trade assets.

(d) Export promotion expenses. *(1) In general.* For purposes of section 970 through 972 and §§ 1.970-1 to 1.972-1, inclusive, the term "export promotion expenses" means, subject to the provisions of subparagraph (2) of this paragraph, all the ordinary and necessary expenses paid or incurred during the taxable year by the controlled foreign corporation which are reasonably allocable to the receipt or production of export trade income including—

(i) A reasonable allowance for salaries or other compensation for personal services actually rendered for such purpose,

(ii) Rentals or other payments for the use of property actually used for such purpose, and

(iii) A reasonable allowance for the exhaustion, wear and tear, or obsolescence of property actually used for such purpose.

In determining for purposes of this subparagraph whether expenses are reasonably allocable to the receipt or production of export trade income, consideration shall be given to the facts and circumstances of each case. As a general rule, if export trade income results from the sale of export property, export promotion expenses allocable to such income shall include warehousing, advertising, selling, billing, collection, other administrative, and similar costs properly allocable to the marketing activity, but shall not include cost of goods sold, income or similar tax, any expense which does not advance the distribution or sale of export property for use, consumption, or disposition outside the United States, or any expense for which the controlled foreign corporation is reimbursed. If export trade income results from the rental of export property, export promotion expenses allocable to such income shall include a reasonable allowance for depreciation and servicing of such property, and the administrative and similar costs properly allocable to the rental activity. If export trade income results from the performance of services, export promotion expenses shall include a reasonable allowance for compensation of the persons performing services for the controlled foreign corporation in the execution of the service contract or arrangement and administrative expenses reasonably allocable to the service activity. In no case shall income taxes be included in export promotion expenses.

(2) Expenses incurred within the United States. No expense incurred within the United States shall be treated as an export promotion expense for purposes of section 971(d) and subparagraph (1) of this paragraph unless at least—

(i) 90 percent of all salaries and other personal service compensation incurred in the receipt or the production of export trade income,

(ii) 90 percent of rents and other payments for the use of property used in the receipt of the production of export trade income,

(iii) 90 percent of the allowances for the exhaustion, wear and tear, or obsolescence of property used in the receipt or the production of export trade income, and

(iv) 90 percent of all other ordinary and necessary expenses reasonably allocable to the receipt or the production of export trade income,

is incurred outside the United States. For this purpose, personal service compensation will be considered incurred at the place where the service is performed (for example, salaries will be considered incurred at the place where the employee works; payments for art work will be considered incurred at the place where the art work is prepared, etc.); rent, depreciation, and other expenses related to real or personal property will be considered incurred at the place where the property is located; and expenses for media advertising will be considered incurred at the place where the advertising is consumed. For such purpose, newspaper or periodical advertising will be considered consumed where the newspaper or periodical is principally distributed, and television and radio advertising will be considered consumed at the place where the audience is primarily located. Technicalities of contract or payment, for example, the place where a contract is executed or the location of a bank account from which payment is made, shall not be determinative of the place where an expense is incurred.

(e) Export property. For purposes of sections 970 through 972 and §§ 1.970-1 to 1.972-1, inclusive, the term "export property" means property, or any interest in property, which is manufactured, produced, grown, or extracted in the United States. Whether property will be considered manufactured or produced in the United States will depend on the facts and circumstances of each case. As a general rule, if—

(1) The property sold, serviced, used, or rented by the controlled foreign corporation is substantially transformed in the United States prior to its export from the United States, or

(2) The operations conducted in the United States with respect to the property sold, serviced, used, or rented by the controlled foreign corporation, whether performed in the United States by one person or a series of persons in a chain of distribution, are substantial in nature and are generally considered to constitute the manufacture or production of property,

then the property sold, serviced, used, or rented will be considered to have been manufactured or produced in the United States. The rules under paragraph (a)(4)(ii) of § 1.954-3, relating to the substantial transformation of property, and paragraph (a)(4)(iii) of such section, dealing with a substantive test for determining whether property will be treated as having been manufactured or produced, shall apply for purposes of making determinations under this paragraph.

(f) Unrelated person. For purposes of sections 970 through 972 and §§ 1.970-1 to 1.972-1, inclusive, the term "unrelated person" means a person other than a related person as defined in section 954(d)(3) and paragraph (e) of § 1.954-1.

T.D. 6755, 9/8/64, amend T.D. 7293, 11/27/73, T.D. 7533, 2/14/78.

§ 1.985-0 Outline of regulation.

This section lists the paragraphs contained in §§ 1.985-1 through 1.985-6.

T.D. 8263, 9/19/89, amend T.D. 8464, 12/31/92, T.D. 8556, 7/22/94.

§ 1.985-1 Functional currency.

(a) Applicability and effective date. *(1) Purpose and scope.* These regulations provide guidance with respect to defining the functional currency of a taxpayer and each qualified business unit (QBU), as defined in section 989(a). Generally, a taxpayer and each QBU must make all determinations under subtitle A of the Code (relating to income taxes) in its respective functional currency. This section sets forth rules for determining when the functional currency is the United States dollar (dollar) or a currency other than the dollar. Section 1.985-2 provides an election to use the dollar as the functional currency for certain QBUs that absent the election would have a functional currency that is a hyperinflationary currency, and explains the effect of making the election. Section 1.985-3 sets forth the dollar approximate separate transactions method that certain QBUs must use to compute their income or loss or earnings and profits. Section 1.985-4 provides that the adoption of a functional currency is a method of accounting and sets forth conditions for a change in functional currency. Section 1.985-5 provides adjustments that are required to be made upon a change in functional currency. Finally, § 1.985-6 provides transition rules for a QBU that uses the dollar approximate separate transactions method for its first taxable year beginning after December 31, 1986.

(2) Effective date. These regulations apply to taxable years beginning after December 31, 1986. However, any taxpayer desiring to apply temporary Income Tax Regulations § 1.985-0T through § 1.985-4T in lieu of these regulations to all taxable years beginning after December 31, 1986, and on or before October 20, 1989 may (on a consistent basis) so choose. For the text of the temporary regulations, see 53 FR 20308 (1988).

(b) Dollar functional currency. *(1) In general.* The dollar shall be the functional currency of a taxpayer or QBU described in paragraph (b)(1)(i) through (v) of this section regardless of the currency used in keeping its books and records (as defined in § 1.989(a)-1(d)). The dollar shall be the functional currency of—

(i) A taxpayer that is not a QBU (e.g., an individual);

(ii) A QBU that conducts its activities primarily in dollars. A QBU conducts its activities primarily in dollars if the currency of the economic environment in which the QBU conducts its activities is primarily the dollar. The facts and circumstances test set forth in paragraph (c)(2) of this section shall apply in making this determination;

(iii) Except as otherwise provided by ruling or administrative pronouncement, a QBU that has the United States, or any possession or territory of the United States where the dollar is the standard currency, as its residence (as defined in section 988(a)(3)(B));

(iv) A QBU that does not keep books and records in the currency of any economic environment in which a significant part of its activities is conducted. Whether a QBU keeps such books and records is determined in accordance with paragraph (c)(3) of this section; or

(v) A QBU that produces income or loss that is, or is treated as, effectively connected with the conduct of a trade or business within the United States.

(2) QBUs operating in a hyperinflationary environment. (i) Taxable years beginning on or before August 24, 1994. For taxable years beginning on or before August 24, 1994, see § 1.985-2 with respect to a QBU that elects to use, or is otherwise required to use, the dollar as its functional currency.

(ii) Taxable years beginning after August 24, 1994. (A) In general. For taxable years beginning after August 24, 1994, except as otherwise provided in paragraph (b)(2)(ii)(B) of this section, any QBU that otherwise would be required to use a hyperinflationary currency as its functional currency must use the dollar as its functional currency and compute income or loss or earnings and profits under the rules of § 1.985-3.

(B) Exceptions. (1) Certain QBU branches. The functional currency of a QBU that otherwise would be required to use a hyperinflationary currency as its functional currency and that is a branch of a foreign corporation having a non-dollar functional currency that is not hyperinflationary shall be the functional currency of the foreign corporation. Such QBU's income or loss or earnings and profits shall be determined under § 1.985-3 by substituting the functional currency of the foreign corporation for the dollar.

(2) Corporation that is not a controlled foreign corporation. A foreign corporation (or its QBU branch) operating in a hyperinflationary environment is not required to use the dollar as its functional currency pursuant to paragraph (b)(2)(ii)(A) of this section if that foreign corporation is not a controlled foreign corporation as defined in section 957 or 953(c)(1)(B). However, a noncontrolled section 902 corporation, as defined in section 904(d)(2)(E), may elect to use the dollar (or, if appropriate, the currency specified in paragraph (b)(2)(ii)(B)(1) of this section) as its (or its QBU branch's) functional currency under the procedures set forth in § 1.985-2(c)(3).

(C) Change in functional currency. (1) In general. If a QBU is required to change its functional currency to the dollar under paragraph (b)(2)(ii)(A) of this section, or chooses or is required to change its functional currency to the dollar for any open taxable year (and all subsequent taxable years) under § 1.985-3(a)(2)(ii), the change is considered to be made with the consent of the Commissioner for purposes of § 1.985-4. A QBU changing functional currency must make adjustments described in § 1.985-7 if the year of change (as defined in § 1.481-1(a)(1)) begins after 1987, or the adjustments described in § 1.985-6 if the year of change begins in 1987. No adjustments under section 481 are required solely because of a change in functional currency described in this paragraph (b)(2)(ii)(C).

(2) Effective date. This paragraph (b)(2)(ii)(C) applies to taxable years beginning after April 6, 1998. However, a taxpayer may choose to apply this paragraph (b)(2)(ii)(C) to all open years after December 31, 1986, provided each person, and each QBU branch of a person, that is related (within the meaning of § 1.985-2(d)(3)) also applies to this paragraph (b)(2)(ii)(C).

(D) Hyperinflationary currency. For purposes of sections 985 through 989, the term hyperinflationary currency means the currency of a country in which there is cumulative inflation during the base period of at least 100 percent as determined by reference to the consumer price index of the country listed in the monthly issues of the "International Financial Statistics" or a successor publication of the International Monetary Fund. If a country's currency is not listed in the monthly issues of "International Financial Statistics," a QBU may use any other reasonable method consistently applied for determining the country's consumer price index. Base period means, with respect to any taxable year, the thirty-six calendar months immediately preceding the first day of the current calendar year. For this purpose, the cumulative inflation rate for the base period is based on compounded inflation rates. Thus, if for 1991, 1992, and 1993, a country's annual inflation rates are 29 percent, 25 percent, and 30 percent, respectively, the cumulative inflation rate for the three-year base period is 110 percent $[((1.29 \times 1.25 \times 1.3) - 1.0 \times 1.10) \times 100 = 110\%]$ and the currency of the country for the QBU's 1994 year is considered hyperinflationary. In making the determination whether a currency is hyperinflationary, the determination for purposes of United States generally accepted accounting principles may be used for income tax purposes provided the determination is based on criteria that is substantially similar to the rules previously set forth in this paragraph (b)(2)(ii)(D), the method of determination is applied consistently from year to year, and the same method is applied to all related persons as defined in § 1.985-3(e)(2)(vi).

(E) Change in functional currency when currency ceases to be hyperinflationary. (1) In general. A QBU that has been required to use the dollar as its functional currency under paragraph (b)(2) of this section, or has elected to use the dollar as its functional currency under paragraph (b)(2)(ii)(B)(2) of this section or § 1.985-2, must change its functional currency as of the first day of the first taxable year that follows three consecutive taxable years in which the currency of its economic environment, determined under paragraph (c)(2) of this section, is not a hyperinflationary currency. The functional currency of the QBU for such year shall be determined in accordance with paragraph (c) of this section. For purposes of § 1.985-4, the change is considered to be made with the consent of the Commissioner. See § 1.985-5 for adjustments that are required upon a change in functional currency.

(2) Effective date. This paragraph (b)(2)(ii)(E) of this section applies to taxable years beginning after April 6, 1998.

(c) Functional currency of a QBU that is not required to use the dollar. *(1) General rule.* The functional currency of a QBU that is not required to use the dollar under paragraph (b) of this section shall be the currency of the economic environment in which a significant part of the QBU's activities is conducted, if the QBU keeps, or is presumed under paragraph (c)(3) of this section to keep, its books and records in such currency.

(2) Economic environment. For purposes of section 985 and the regulations thereunder, the economic environment in which a significant part of a QBU's activities is conducted shall be determined by taking into account all the facts and circumstances.

(i) Facts and circumstances. The facts and circumstances that are considered in determining the economic environment in which a significant part of a QBU's activities is conducted include, but are not limited to, the following:

(A) The currency of the country in which the QBU is a resident as determined under section 988(a)(3)(B);

(B) The currencies of the QBU's cash flows;

(C) The currencies in which the QBU generates revenues and incurs expenses;

(D) The currencies in which the QBU borrows and lends;

(E) The currencies of the QBU's sales markets;

(F) The currencies in which pricing and other financial decisions are made;

(G) The duration of the QBU's business operations; and

(H) The significance and/or volume of the QBU's independent activities.

(ii) Rate of inflation. The rate of inflation (regardless of how it is determined) shall not be a factor used to determine a QBU's economic environment.

(iii) Consistency. A taxpayer must consistently apply the facts and circumstances test set forth in this paragraph (c)(2) in evaluating the economic environment of its QBUs, e.g., its branches, that engage in the same or similar trades or businesses.

(3) Books and records presumption. A QBU shall be presumed to keep books and records in the currency of the economic environment in which a significant part of its activities are conducted. The presumption may be overcome only if the QBU can demonstrate to the satisfaction of the district director that a substantial nontax purpose exists for not keeping any books and records in such currency. A taxpayer may not use this presumption affirmatively in determining a QBU's functional currency.

(4) Multiple currencies. If a QBU has more than one currency that satisfies the requirements of paragraph (c)(1) of this section, the QBU may choose any such currency as its functional currency.

(5) Relationship of United States accounting principles. In making the functional currency determination under this paragraph (c), the currency of the QBU for purposes of United States generally accepted accounting principles (GAAP) will ordinarily be accepted as the functional currency of the QBU for income tax purposes, provided that the GAAP determination is based on facts and circumstances substantially similar to those set forth in paragraph (c)(2) of this section.

(6) Effect of changed circumstances. Regardless of any change in circumstances, a QBU may change its functional currency determined under this paragraph (c) only if the QBU complies with § 1.985-4 or the Commissioner's consent is considered to have been granted under § 1.985-2(d)(4) or § 1.985-3(a)(2)(ii). For special rules relating to the conversion to the euro, see § 1.985-8.

(d) Single functional currency for a foreign corporation. *(1) General rule.* This paragraph (d) applies to a foreign corporation that has two or more QBUs that do not have the same functional currency. The foreign corporation shall be treated as having a single functional currency for the corporation as a whole that is different from the functional currency of one or more of its QBUs. The determination of a foreign corporation's functional currency shall be made by first applying paragraph (d)(1)(i) and then paragraph (d)(1)(ii) of this section.

(i) Step 1. Each QBU of the foreign corporation determines its functional currency in accordance with the rules set forth in paragraphs (b) and (c) of this section and § 1.985-2.

(ii) Step 2. The foreign corporation determines its functional currency applying the principles of paragraphs (b) and (c) of this section to the corporation's activities as a whole. Thus, if a foreign corporation has two branches, the corporation shall determine its functional currency by applying the principles of paragraphs (b) and (c) of this section to the combined activities of the corporation and the branches. For purposes of this paragraph (d)(1), if a QBU of a foreign corporation has the dollar as its functional currency under paragraph (b)(2) of this section, the QBU's activities shall be considered dollar activities of the corporation.

(2) Translation of income or loss of QBUs having different functional currencies than the foreign corporation as a whole. Where the functional currency of a foreign corporation as a whole differs from the functional currency of one or more of its QBUs, each such QBU shall determine the amount of its income or loss or earnings and profits (or deficit in earnings and profits) in its functional currency under the principles of section 987 (relating to branch transactions). The amount of income or loss or earnings and profits (or deficit in earnings and profits) of each QBU in its functional currency shall then be translated into the foreign corporation's functional currency using the appropriate exchange rate as defined in section 989(b)(4) for purposes of determining the corporation's income or loss or earnings and profits (or deficit in earnings and profits).

(e) Translation of nonfunctional currency transactions. Except for a QBU using the dollar approximate separate transactions method described in § 1.985-3, see section 988 and the regulations thereunder for the treatment of nonfunctional currency transactions.

(f) Examples. The provisions of this section are illustrated by the following examples:

Example (1). P, a domestic corporation, operates exclusively through foreign branch X in Country A. X is a QBU within the meaning of section 989(a) and its residence is Country A as determined under section 988(a)(3)(B). The currency of Country A is the LC. All of X's purchases, sales, and expenses are in the LC. The laws of A require X to keep books and records in the LC. It is determined that the LC is the currency of X under United States generally accepted accounting principles. This determination is based on facts and circumstances substantially similar to those set forth in paragraph (c)(2) of this section. Under these facts, while the functional currency of P is the dollar since its residence is the United States, the functional currency of X is the LC.

Example (2). P, a publicly-held domestic regulated investment company (as defined under section 851), operates exclusively through foreign branch B in Country R. B is a QBU within the meaning of section 989(a) and its residence is Country R as determined under section 988(a)(3)(B). The currency of Country R is the LC. B's principal activities consist of purchasing and selling stock and securities of Country R companies and securities issued by Country R. It is determined that the dollar is the currency of B under United States generally accepted accounting principles. This determination is not based on facts and circumstances substantially similar to those set forth in paragraph (c)(2) of this section. Under these facts, while the functional currency of P is the dollar since its residence is the United States, B may choose the LC as its functional currency because it has significant activities in the LC provided it keeps books and records in the LC. The fact that the dollar is the currency of B under generally accepted accounting principles is irrelevant for purposes of determining B's functional currency because the GAAP determination was not based on factors similar to those set forth in paragraph (c)(2) of this section.

Example (3). P, a domestic bank, operates through foreign branch X in Country R. X is a QBU within the meaning of section 989(a) and its residence is Country R as determined under section 988(a)(3)(B). The currency of Country R is the LC. The laws of R require X to keep books and records in the LC. The branch customarily loans dollars and LCs. In the case of its LC loans, X ordinarily fixes the terms of the loans by reference to a contemporary London Inter-Bank Offered Rate (LIBOR) on dollar deposits. For instance, the interest on the amount of the outstanding LC loan principal might equal LIBOR plus 2 percent and the amount of the outstanding LC loan principal would be adjusted to reflect changes in the dollar value of the LC. X is primarily funded with dollar-denominated funds borrowed from related and unrelated parties. X's only LC activities are paying local taxes, employee wages, and local expenses such as rent and electricity. Under these facts, X's activities are primarily conducted in dollars. Thus, although X keeps its books and records in LCs, X's functional currency is the dollar.

Example (4). S, a foreign corporation organized in Country U, is wholly-owned by P, a domestic corporation. The currency of Country U is the LC. S's sole function is acting as a financing vehicle for P and domestic corporations that are affiliated with P. All borrowing and lending transactions between S and P and its domestic affiliates are in dollars. Furthermore, primarily all of S's other borrowings are dollar-denominated or based on a dollar index. S's only LC activities are paying local taxes, employee wages, and local expenses such as rent and electricity. S keeps its books and records in the LC. Under these facts, S's activities are primarily conducted in dollars. Thus, although S keeps its books and records in LCs, S's functional currency is the dollar.

Example (5). D is a domestic corporation whose primary activity is the extraction of natural gas and oil through foreign branch X in Country Y. X is a QBU within the meaning of section 989(a) and its residence is Country Y as determined under section 988(a)(3)(B). The currency of Country Y is the LC. X bills a significant amount of its natural gas and oil sales in dollars and a significant amount in LCs. X also incurs significant LC and dollar expenses and liabilities. The laws of Country Y require X to keep its books and records in the LC. It is determined that the LC is the currency of X under United States generally accepted accounting principles. This determination is based on facts and circumstances substantially similar to those set forth in paragraph (c)(2) of this section. Absent other factors indicating that X primarily conducts its activities in the dollar, D could choose either the dollar or the LC as X's functional currency because X has significant activities in both the dollar and the LC, provided the books and records requirement is satisfied. If, instead, X's activities were determined to be primarily in the dollar, then X would have to use the dollar as its functional currency.

Example (6). S, a foreign corporation organized in Country U, is wholly-owned by P, a domestic corporation. The currency of U is the LC. S purchases the products it sells from related and unrelated parties, including P. These purchases are made in the LC. In addition, most of S's gross receipts are generated by transactions denominated in the LC. S attempts to determine its LC price for goods sold in such a manner as to obtain an LC equivalent of a certain dollar amount after reduction for all LC costs. However, local market conditions sometimes result in pricing adjustments. Thus, changes in the LC-dollar exchange rate from period to period generally result in corresponding changes in the LC price of S's products. S pays local taxes, employee wages, and other local expenses in the LC. It is determined that the dollar is the currency of S under United States generally accepted accounting principles. This determination is not based on facts and circumstances substantially similar to those set forth in paragraph (c)(2) of this section. Under these facts, S could choose either the dollar or the LC as its functional currency because S has significant activities in both the dollar and the LC, provided that the books and records requirement is satisfied.

Example (7). S, a foreign corporation organized in Country X, is wholly-owned by P, a domestic corporation. S conducts all of its operations through two branches. Branch A is located in Country F and branch B is located in Country G, S, A, and B are QBUs within the meaning of section 989(a). Branch A's and branch B's residences are Country F and Country G respectively as determined under section 988(a)(3)(B). The currency of Country F is the FC and the currency of Country G is the LC. The functional currencies of S, A, and B are determined in a two step procedure.

Step 1: The functional currency of branches A and B. Branch A and branch B both conduct all activities in their respective local currencies. The FC is the currency of branch A and the LC is the currency of branch B under United States generally accepted accounting principles. This determination is based on facts and circumstances substantially similar to those set forth in paragraph (c)(2) of this section. Under these facts, the functional currency of branch A is the FC and the functional currency of branch B is the LC.

Step 2: The functional currency of S. S's functional currency is determined by disregarding the fact that A and B are branches. When A's activities and B's activities are viewed as a whole, S determines that it only conducts significant activities in the LC. Therefore, S's functional currency is the LC. See Examples (9), (10), and (11) for how the earnings and profits of a foreign corporation, which has branches with different functional currencies, are determined.

Example (8). Assume the same facts as in Example (7), except that S does not exist and P conducts all of its operations through branch A and branch B. In this instance P's functional currency in Step 2 is the dollar, regardless of the fact that its branches' activities viewed as a whole are in the LC, because P is a taxpayer whose residence is the United States under section 988(a)(3)(B)(i). Therefore, while the functional currency of branch A is the FC and the functional currency of branch B is the LC, the functional currency of P is the dollar because its residence is the United States.

Example (9). The facts are the same as in Example (7). In addition, assume that in 1987 branch A has earnings of 100 FC and branch B has earnings of 100 LC as determined under section 987. The weighted average exchange rate for the year is 1 FC/2 LC. Branch A's earnings are translated into 200 LC for purposes of computing S's earnings and profits in 1987. Thus, the total earnings and profits of S from branch A and branch B for 1987 is 300 LC.

Example (10). (i) X, a foreign corporation organized in Country W, is wholly-owned by P, a domestic corporation. Both X and P are calendar year taxpayers that began business during 1987. X operates exclusively through two branches, A and B both of which are located outside of Country W. The functional currency of X and A is the LC, while the functional currency of B is the DC as determined under section 985 and § 1.985-1. The earnings of B must be computed under section 987, relating to branch transactions. In 1987, A earns 900 LCs of nonsubpart F income and B earns 200 DCs of nonsubpart F income. Under section 904(d)(2), A's income is financial service income and B's income is general limitation income. In order to determine X's earnings and profits, B's income must be translated into LCs (the functional currency of X). The weighted average exchange rate for 1987 is 1 LC/2 DC. Thus, in 1987 X's current earnings and profits (and its post-1986 undistributed earnings) are 1000 LCs consisting of 900 LCs of financial services income earned by A and 100 LCs (200 DC/2) of general limitation income earned by B. Neither A nor B makes any remittances during 1987.

(ii) In 1988, neither A nor B earns any income or generates any loss. On December 31, 1988, A remits 50 LCs directly to P. The remittance to P is considered to be remitted by A to X and then immediately distributed by X as a dividend. The 50 LC remittance does not result in an exchange gain or loss under section 987 to X because the functional currency of X and A is the LC. See section 987(3). Under section 904(d)(3)(D), the 50 LC dividend is treated as income in a separate category to the extent of the dividend's pro rata share of X's earnings and profits in each separate limitation category. Thus, 90 percent, or 45 LCs, is treated as financial services income, and 10 percent, or 5 LCs, is treated as general limitation income. After the dividend distribution, X has 950 LCs of accumulated earnings and profits (and post-1986 undistributed earnings) consisting of 855 LCs of financial service limitation income and 95 LCs of general limitation income.

Example (11). The facts are the same as in Example (10), except that A makes no remittance during 1988 but B remits 120 DCs to X on December 31, 1988, which X immediately converts into LCs, and X makes no dividend distribution during 1988. Assume that the appropriate exchange rate for the remittance is 1 LC/3 DCs. B's remittance triggers exchange loss to X. See section 987(3). Under section 987, the exchange loss on the remittance is 20 LCs calculated as follows: 40 LCs, which is the LC value of the 120 DC remittance (120 DCs/3), less 60 LCs, their LC basis (120 DCs/2). This loss is sourced and characterized under section 987 and regulations thereunder.

Example (12). F, a foreign corporation, has gain from the disposition of a United States real property interest (as defined in section 897(c)). The gain is taken into account as if F were engaged in a trade or business within the United States during the taxable year and as if such gain were effectively connected with such trade or business. F's disposition activity shall be treated as a separate QBU with a dollar functional currency because such activity produced income that is treated as effectively connected with a trade or business within the United States. Therefore, F must compute its gain from the disposition by giving the United States real property interest an historic dollar basis.

T.D. 8263, 9/19/89, amend T.D. 8556, 7/22/94, T.D. 8765, 3/4/98, T.D. 8776, 7/28/98, T.D. 8927, 1/10/2001.

PAR. 3. Section 1.985-1 is amended as follows:

1. Paragraph (d)(2), second sentence; and paragraph (f), Example 9 and Example 10(i), ninth sentence are revised.

2. Paragraph (f), Example 11 is removed.

3. Paragraph (f), Example 12 is redesignated as Example 11.

4. Paragraph (g) is added.

The revisions and addition read as follows:

Proposed § 1.985-1 Functional currency. [*For Preamble, see ¶ 152,801*]

* * * * *

(d) * * *

(2) * * * The amount of income or loss or earnings and profits (or deficit in earnings and profits) of each QBU in its functional currency shall then be translated into the foreign corporation's functional currency under the principles of section 987.

* * * * *

(f) Examples. * * *

Example (9). (i) The facts are the same as in Example (7). In addition, assume that in 1987 branch A has items of earnings of 100 FC and branch B has items of earnings of 100 LC as determined under section 987. S translates branch A's and branch B's items of earnings and profits into its functional currency under the principles of section 987.

Example (10). (i) * * * Assume that B's items of income of 200 DCs when properly translated under the principles of section 987 is equal to 100 LCs. * * *

* * * * *

(g) Effective date. Generally, the revisions to the second sentence of paragraph (d)(2), Example 9, and Example 10 shall apply to taxable years beginning one year after the first day of the first taxable year following the date of publication of a Treasury decision adopting this rule as a final regulation in the Federal Register. If a taxpayer makes an election under § 1.987-11(b), then the effective date of these revisions with respect to the taxpayer shall be consistent with such election.

§ 1.985-2 Election to use the United States dollar as the functional currency of a QBU.

(a) Background and scope. *(1) In general.* This section permits an eligible QBU to elect to use the dollar as its functional currency for taxable years beginning on or before August 24, 1994. An election to use a dollar functional currency is not permitted for a QBU other than an eligible QBU. Paragraph (b) of this section defines an eligible QBU. Paragraph (c) of this section describes the time and manner for making the dollar election and paragraph (d) of this section describes the effect of making the election. For the definition of a QBU, see section 989(a). See § 1.985-1(b)(2)(ii) for rules requiring a QBU to use the dollar as its functional currency in taxable years beginning after August 24, 1994.

(2) Exception. Pursuant to § 1.985-1(b)(2)(ii)(B)(2), the rules of paragraph (c)(3) of this section shall apply with respect to the procedure required to be followed by a noncontrolled section 902 corporation as defined in section

904(d)(2)(E) to elect the dollar as its (or its QBU branch's) functional currency and the application of § 1.985-3.

(b) Eligible QBU. *(1) In general.* The term "eligible QBU" means a QBU that could have used a hyperinflationary currency as its functional currency absent the dollar election. See § 1.985-1 for how a QBU determines its functional currency absent the dollar election.

(2) Hyperinflationary currency. See § 1.985-1(b)(2)(ii)(D) for the definition of hyperinflationary currency.

(c) Time and manner for dollar election. *(1) QBUs that are branches of United States persons.* (i) Rule. If an eligible QBU is a branch of a United States person, the dollar election shall be made by attaching a completed Form 8819 to the United States person's timely filed (taking extensions into account) tax return for the first taxable year for which the election is to be effective.

(ii) Procedure prior to the issuance of Form 8819. In the absence of Form 8819, the election shall be made in accordance with § 1.985-2T(c)(1). Failure to file an amended return within the time period prescribed in § 1.985-2T(c)(1) shall not invalidate the dollar election if it is established to the satisfaction of the district director that reasonable cause existed for such failure. A subsequent election for 1988 will not prejudice the taxpayer with respect to such reasonable cause determination. Nevertheless, each United States person making an election under the § 1.985-2T(c)(1) must file a Form 8819 in the time and manner provided in the Form's instructions.

(2) Eligible QBUs that are controlled foreign corporations or branches of controlled foreign corporations. (i) Rule. If an eligible QBU is a controlled foreign corporation (as described in section 957), or a branch of a controlled foreign corporation, the election may be made either by the foreign corporation or by the controlling United States shareholders on behalf of the foreign corporation by—

(A) Filing a completed Form 8819 in the time and manner provided in the Form's instructions, and

(B) Providing the written notice required by paragraph (c)(2)(ii) of this section at the time and in the manner prescribed therein.

The term "controlling United States shareholders" means those United States shareholders (as defined in section 951(b)) who, in the aggregate, own (within the meaning of section 958(a)) greater than 50 percent of the total combined voting power of all classes of stock of the foreign corporation entitled to vote. If the foreign corporation is a controlled foreign corporation (as described in section 957) but the United States shareholders do not, in the aggregate, own the requisite voting power, the term "controlling United States shareholders" means all the United States shareholders (as defined in section 951(b)) who own (within the meaning of section 958(a)) stock of the controlled foreign corporation.

(ii) Notice. Prior to filing Form 8819, the controlling United States shareholders (or the foreign corporation, if the dollar election is made by the corporation) shall provide written notice that the dollar election will be made to all United States persons known to be shareholders who own (within the meaning of section 958(a)) stock of the foreign corporation. Such notice shall also include all information required in Form 8819.

(iii) Reasonable cause exception. Failure of the controlling United States shareholders (or the foreign corporation, if the dollar election is made by the corporation) to timely file Form 8819 or provide written notice to a United States person required to be notified by paragraph (c)(2)(ii) of this section shall not invalidate the dollar election, if it is established to the satisfaction of the district director that reasonable cause existed for such failure.

(iv) Procedure prior to the issuance of Form 8819. In the absence of Form 8819, an eligible QBU described in paragraph (c)(2)(i) of this section shall make the dollar election in accordance with § 1.985-2T(c)(2). Nevertheless, the person or persons that made such election must file a Form 8819 in the time and manner provided in the Form's instructions.

(3) Eligible QBUs that are noncontrolled foreign corporations or branches of noncontrolled foreign corporations. (i) Rule. If an eligible QBU is a noncontrolled foreign corporation (a foreign corporation not described in section 957), or a branch of a noncontrolled foreign corporation, the dollar election must be made by the corporation or the majority domestic corporate shareholders on behalf of the corporation by applying the rules provided in paragraph (c)(2)(i)(A) and (B), (ii), (iii), and (iv) of this section substituting "majority domestic corporate shareholders" for "controlling United States shareholders" wherever it appears therein. The term "majority domestic corporate shareholders" means those domestic corporate shareholders (as described in section 902(a)) who, in the aggregate, own (within the meaning of section 958(a)) greater than 50 percent of the total combined voting stock of all classes of stock of the noncontrolled foreign corporation entitled to vote that is owned (within the meaning of section 958(a)) by all the domestic corporate shareholders.

(ii) Procedure prior to the issuance of Form 8819. In the absence of Form 8819, an eligible QBU described in paragraph (c)(3)(i) of this section shall make the dollar election in accordance with § 1.985-2T(c)(3). Nevertheless, the person or persons that made such election must file a Form 8819 in the time and manner provided in the Form's instructions.

(4) Others. Any other person making a dollar election under this section shall elect by filing Form 8819 and fulfilling any other notice requirements that may be required by the Commissioner.

(d) Effect of dollar election. *(1) General rule.* If a dollar election is made (or considered made under paragraph (d)(3) of this section) by or on behalf of an eligible QBU, the QBU shall be deemed to have the dollar as its functional currency. Each United States person that owns (within the meaning of section 958(a)) stock of a foreign corporation which has the dollar as its functional currency under § 1.985-2 must make all of its federal income tax calculations with respect to the foreign corporation using the dollar as the corporation's functional currency (regardless of when ownership was acquired or whether the United States person received the written notice required by paragraph (c)(2)(i)(B) of this section).

(2) Computation. (i) In general. Except as provided in paragraph (d)(2)(ii) of this section, any eligible QBU that pursuant to this § 1.985-2 has a dollar functional currency must compute income or loss or earnings and profits (or deficit in earnings and profits) in dollars using the dollar approximate separate transactions method described in § 1.985-3.

(ii) Alternative method. An eligible QBU that has a dollar functional currency pursuant to this § 1.985-2 may use a method other than the dollar approximate separate transactions method described in § 1.985-3 only if the QBU demonstrates to the satisfaction of the Commissioner that it can properly employ such method. Generally, the QBU must show that it could compute foreign currency gain or loss under the principles of section 988 with respect to each of its section 988 transactions. If subsequently the QBU can no longer demonstrate to the satisfaction of the district director that it can properly employ such an alternative method, then the QBU will be deemed to have changed its method of accounting to the dollar approximate separate transactions method described in § 1.985-3. This change in accounting will be treated as having been made with the consent of the Commissioner. No adjustments under either § 1.985-5T (or any succeeding final regulation) or section 481(a) shall be required solely because of the change. Rather the QBU shall begin accounting for its operations under § 1.985-3 based on its dollar books and records as of the time of the change.

(3) Conformity. (i) General rule. If a dollar election is made under this § 1.985-2 for an eligible QBU ("electing QBU"), then the dollar shall be the functional currency of any related person (regardless of when such person became related to the electing QBU) that is an eligible QBU, or any branch of any such related person that is an eligible QBU. For purposes of the preceding sentence, the term "related person" means any person with a relationship defined in section 267(b) to the electing QBU (or to the United States or foreign person of which the electing QBU is a part). In determining whether two or more corporations are members of the same controlled group under section 267(b)(3), a person is considered to own stock owned directly by such person, stock owned with the application of section 1563(e)(1), and stock owned with the application of section 267(c).

(ii) Branches of United States and foreign persons. If a dollar election is made for a QBU branch of any person, each eligible QBU branch of such person shall have the dollar as its functional currency.

(4) Required adjustments. If an eligible QBU's functional currency changes due to a dollar election, or due to the conformity requirements of paragraph (d)(3) of this section, such change shall be deemed for purposes of § 1.9B5-4 to be consented to by the Commissioner. No adjustments under section 481(a) shall be required solely because of the change. However, the QBU must make those adjustments required by § 1.985-5T (or any succeeding final regulation).

(5) Taxable year conformity required. Generally, the adjustments required by paragraph (d)(4) of this section shall be made for a related person's taxable year—

(i) That includes the date in which the electing QBU made the dollar election if the person was related to such electing QBU at any time during the QBU's taxable year that includes such date, or

(ii) During which the person first becomes related to any electing QBU, in all other cases.

For purposes of this paragraph (d)(5), the date in which the electing QBU makes the dollar election shall be the last day of the electing QBU's taxable year. The district director may permit the related party to make such adjustments beginning one taxable year later if, in the district director's sole judgment, reasonable cause exists for the related party not being able to make the required adjustments for the ear year.

(6) Availability of election. A dollar election may be made by or on behalf of a QBU, or considered made under the conformity rule of paragraph (d)(3), in any year in which the QBU is an eligible QBU. If a dollar election is not made by or on behalf of a QBU for its first taxable year beginning after December 31, 1986 in which it is an eligible QBU, then any dollar election made by or on behalf of the QBU, or considered made under the conformity rules of paragraph (d)(3) of this section, that results in a change in the QBU's functional currency shall be treated as having been made with the consent of the Commissioner. In such a case, however, the taxpayer must make those adjustments required by § 1.985-5T (or any succeeding final regulation).

(7) Effect of changed circumstances. Regardless of any change in circumstances (e.g., a currency ceases to qualify as hyperinflationary), a QBU whose functional currency is the dollar under this section may change its functional currency only if the QBU complies with § 1.985-4.

(8) Examples. The provisions of this section are illustrated by the following examples.

Example (1). X is a calendar year domestic corporation that in 1987 establishes a branch, A, in Country Z. A's functional currency under section 985(b)(1) and (2) and § 1.985-1 is the "h", the currency of Country Z. The cumulative inflation in Country Z exceeds 100 percent for the thirty-six months prior to January 1987, as measured by the consumer price index of Country Z listed in the monthly issues of the "International Financial Statistics". Accordingly, A is an eligible QBU in 1987 because the h is a hyperinflationary currency. Thus, X may elect the dollar as the functional currency of A for 1987.

Example (2). The facts are the same as in Example (1). X does not elect the dollar as the functional currency of A for 1987. Rather, X elects the dollar as the functional currency of A for 1991, a year A is an eligible QBU. The election constitutes a change in A's functional currency that is made with the consent of the Commissioner. However, A must make the adjustments required under § 1.985-5T (or any succeeding final regulation).

Example (3). X is a domestic corporation that establishes A, an eligible QBU branch. X is wholly owned by domestic corporation Y. Y has an eligible QBU branch, B. Both X and Y are calendar year taxpayers. X makes a dollar election for A in 1987. Thus, A is an electing QBU. X and Y are related persons as defined in section 267(b) i.e., Y has a relationship under section 267(b)(3) to X, the corporation of which A is a part). Therefore, the dollar election by X for A in 1987 results in B, the eligible QBU branch of Y, also having the dollar as its functional currency for 1987.

Example (4). The facts are the same as in Example (3), except that Y does not have an eligible QBU branch but owns all the stock of C, a calendar year controlled foreign corporation, which is not itself an eligible QBU but which has an eligible QBU branch, D. X and C are related persons as defined in section 267(b) (i.e., C has a relationship under section 267(b)(3) to X, the corporation of which A is a part). Therefore, the dollar election by X and A in 1987 results in D, the eligible QBU branch of C, also having the dollar as its functional currency for 1987.

Example (5). X, whose taxable year ends September 30, is an eligible QBU that does not use the dollar as its functional currency. X is wholly-owned by domestic corporation W. On January 1, 1989, X acquires all the stock of Y, an unrelated eligible QBU that made the dollar election under § 1.985-2. Y is a calendar year taxpayer. After the stock purchase, X and Y are related persons as defined in section 267(b). Under § 1.985-2(d)(3) and (5), the dollar shall be the functional currency of X, any person related to X, and any branch of such related person that is an eligible QBU beginning with the taxable year that includes December 31, 1989. Thus, X must change to the dollar for its taxable year beginning October 1, 1988. However, the district director may allow X to change to the dollar for its taxable year beginning

October 1, 1989, provided reasonable cause exists. Those QBUs changing to the dollar as their functional currency as the result of the conformity requirements must make the adjustments required under § 1.985-5T (or any succeeding final regulation).

Example (6). The facts are the same as in Example (5), except that before X purchased the Y stock, X made the dollar election under § 1.985-2 but Y did not use the dollar as its functional currency. Under § 1.985-2(d)(3) and (5) the dollar shall be the functional currency of Y, any person related to Y, and any branch of such related person that is an eligible QBU beginning with the taxable year that includes September 30, 1989. Thus, Y must change to the dollar for its taxable year beginning January 1, 1989. However the district director may allow Y to change to the dollar for its taxable year beginning January 1, 1990, provided reasonable cause exists. Those QBUs changing to the dollar as their functional currency as the result of the conformity requirements must make the adjustments required under § 1.985-5T (or any succeeding final regulation).

T.D. 8263, 9/19/89, amend T.D. 8556, 7/22/94.

§ 1.985-3 United States dollar approximate separate transactions method.

(a) Scope and effective date. *(1) Scope.* This section describes the United States dollar (dollar) approximate separate transactions method of accounting (DASTM). For all purposes of subtitle A, this method of accounting must be used to compute the gross income, taxable income or loss, or earnings and profits (or deficit in earnings and profits) of a QBU (as defined in section 989(a)) that has the dollar as its functional currency pursuant to § 1.985-1(b)(2).

(2) Effective date. (i) In general. This section is effective for taxable years beginning after August 24, 1994.

(ii) DASTM prior-year election. A taxpayer may elect to apply this section to any open taxable year beginning after December 31, 1986 (whether or not DASTM has been previously elected for some or all of those years). In order to make this election, the taxpayer must apply § 1.985-3 to that year and all subsequent years. In addition, each person that is related (within the meaning of § 1.985-3(e)(2)(vi)) to the taxpayer on the last day of any taxable year for which the election is effective and that would have been eligible to elect DASTM must also apply these rules to that year and all subsequent years. A taxpayer that has not previously elected to apply DASTM to its prior taxable years may make the DASTM election for the pertinent years by filing amended returns and complying with the applicable election procedures of § 1.985-2. Form 8819 shall be attached to the return for the first year for which the election is to be effective. A taxpayer that has elected DASTM for prior taxable years and applied the rules under § 1.985-3 (as contained in the April 1, 1994 edition of 26 CFR part 1 (1.908 to 1.1000)) may amend its returns to apply the rules of this § 1.985-3. In either case, the DASTM election for prior taxable years shall be deemed to be made with the consent of the Commissioner.

(b) Statement of method. Under DASTM, income or loss or earnings and profits (or a deficit in earnings and profits) of a QBU for its taxable year shall be determined in dollars by—

(1) Preparing an income or loss statement from the QBU's books and records (within the meaning of § 1.989(a)-1(d)) as recorded in the QBU's hyperinflationary currency (as defined in § 1.985-1(b)(2)(ii)(D));

(2) Making the adjustments necessary to conform such statement to United States generally accepted accounting principles and tax accounting principles (including reversing monetary correction adjustments required by local accounting principles);

(3) Translating the amounts of hyperinflationary currency as shown on such adjusted statement into dollars in accordance with paragraph (c) of this section; and

(4) Adjusting the resulting dollar income or loss or earnings and profits (or deficit in earnings and profits) and, where necessary, particular items of gross income, deductible expense or other amounts, in accordance with paragraph (e) of this section to reflect the amount of DASTM gain or loss as determined under paragraph (d) of this section.

(c) Translation into United States dollars. *(1) In general.* Except as otherwise provided in this paragraph (c), the amounts shown on the income or loss statement, as adjusted under paragraph (b)(2) of this section, shall be translated into dollars at the exchange rate (as defined in paragraph (c)(6) of this section) for the translation period (as defined in paragraph (c)(7) of this section) to which they relate. However, if the QBU previously changed its functional currency to the dollar, and the rules of § 1.985-5 (or, if applicable, § 1.985-5T, as contained in the April 1, 1993 edition of 26 CFR part 1 (1.908 to 1.1000)) applied in translating its balance sheet amounts into dollars, then the spot exchange rate applied under those rules shall be used to translate any amount that would otherwise be translated at a rate determined by reference to a translation period prior to the change in functional currency. For example, depreciation with respect to an asset acquired while the QBU had a nondollar functional currency shall be translated into dollars at the spot rate on the last day of the taxable year before the year of change to a dollar functional currency, rather than at the rate for the period in which the asset was acquired.

(2) Cost of goods sold. The dollar value of cost of goods sold shall equal the sum of the dollar values of beginning inventory and purchases less the dollar value of closing inventory as these amounts are determined under paragraph (c)(3) of this section.

(3) Beginning inventory, purchases, and closing inventory. (i) Beginning inventory. Amounts representing beginning inventory shall be translated so as to obtain the same amount of dollars which represented such items in the closing inventory balance for the preceding taxable year.

(ii) Purchases. Amounts representing items purchased or otherwise first included in inventory during the taxable year shall be translated at the exchange rate for the translation period in which the cost of such items was incurred.

(iii) Closing inventory. (A) In general. Amounts representing items included in the closing inventory balance shall be translated at the exchange rate for the translation period in which the cost of such items was incurred. However, if amounts representing items included in the closing inventory balance are either valued at market or written down to market value, they shall be translated at the exchange rate existing on the last day of the taxable year. For purposes of determining lower of cost or market, items of inventory included in the closing inventory balance shall be translated into dollars at the exchange rate for the translation period in which the cost of such items was incurred and compared with market as determined in the QBU's hyperinflationary currency translated into dollars at the exchange rate existing on the last day of the taxable year.

(B) Determination of translation period. The method used to determine the translation period of amounts representing items of closing inventory for purposes of paragraph (c)(3)(iii)(A) of this section may be based upon reasonable approximations and averages, including rates of turnover, provided that the method is used consistently from year to year.

(4) Depreciation, depletion, and amortization. Amounts representing allowances for depreciation, depletion, or amortization shall be translated at the exchange rate for the translation period in which the cost of the underlying asset was incurred, except as provided in paragraph (c)(1) of this section.

(5) Prepaid expenses or income. Amounts representing expense or income paid or received in a prior taxable year shall be translated at the exchange rate for the translation period during which they were paid or received.

(6) Exchange rate. The exchange rate for a translation period may be determined under any reasonable method, provided that the method is consistently applied to all translation periods and conforms to the taxpayer's method of financial accounting. Reasonable methods include the average of beginning and ending exchange rates for the translation period and the spot rate on the last day of the translation period. Once chosen, a method for determining an exchange rate can be changed only with the consent of the district director.

(7) Translation period. (i) In general. Except as provided in paragraphs (c)(3)(iii)(B) and (c)(7)(ii) of this section, a translation period shall be each month within a QBU's taxable year.

(ii) Exception. A taxpayer may divide its taxable year into translation periods of equal length (with not more than one short period annually) that are less than one month. Once such a translation period is established, it may not be changed without the consent of the district director.

(8) Dollar transactions. (i) In general. Except as provided in paragraph (c)(8)(ii) of this section, no DASTM gain or loss is realized with respect to dollar transactions since the dollar is the functional currency of the QBU. Thus, the amount of any payment or receipt of dollars shall be reflected in the income or loss statement by the amount of such dollars. Also, the income or loss attributable to any transaction in which the amount that a QBU is entitled to receive (or is required to pay) by reason of such transaction is denominated in terms of the dollar, or is determined by reference to the value of the dollar, must be computed transaction by transaction. For example, if a foreign corporation lends 20 LC when 20 LC = $20 and is entitled to receive the LC equivalent of $20 at maturity plus a market rate of interest in dollars (or its LC equivalent), the loan is a dollar transaction. Similarly, this paragraph applies to any transaction that is determined to be a dollar transaction under section 988.

(ii) Non-dollar functional currency. If pursuant to § 1.985-1(b)(2)(ii)(B)(1), a QBU is required to use a functional currency other than the dollar, then that currency shall be substituted for the dollar in applying paragraph (c)(8)(i) of this section.

(9) Third currency transactions. A taxpayer may use any reasonable method of accounting for transactions described in section 988(c)(1)(B) and (C) that are denominated in, or determined by reference to, a currency other than the QBU's hyperinflationary currency or the dollar (third currency transactions) so long as such method is consistent with its method of financial accounting.

(10) Examples. The provisions of this paragraph (c) are illustrated by the following examples:

Example (1). S is an accrual basis QBU that is required to use the dollar as its functional currency for its first taxable year beginning in 1994. S's hyperinflationary currency is the "h." During 1994, S accrues 100 dollars attributable to dollar-denominated sales. Because this is a dollar transaction under paragraph (c)(8) of this section, S's income or loss for 1994 shall reflect the 100 dollars (not the hyperinflationary value of such dollars when accrued).

Example (2). (i) S is an accrual basis QBU that is required to use the dollar as its functional currency for its first taxable year beginning in 1994. S's hyperinflationary currency is the "h." During 1994, S's sales amounted to 240,000,000h, its currently deductible expenses were 26,000,000h, and its total inventory purchases amounted to 100,000,000h. During January and February of 1994, S purchased depreciable assets for 80,000,000h and was allowed depreciation of 4,000,000h. At the end of 1994, S's closing inventory was 23,000,000h. No election to use a translation period other than the month is made, S had no transactions described in paragraph (c)(8) or (c)(9) of this section, and S's closing inventory was computed on the first-in, first-out inventory method. S's adjusted income or loss statement for 1994 is translated into dollars as follows:

	Hyperinflationary Currency	Exchange Rate	United States Dollars
Sales:			
January-February	10,000,000h	20:1[1]	$ 500,000
March-April	20,000,000	21:1	952,381
May-June	50,000,000	22:1	2,272,727
July	50,000,000	23:1	2,173,913
August	20,000,000	26:1	769,231
September	20,000,000	28:1	714,286
October	20,000,000	29:1	689,655
November	20,000,000	30:1	666,667
December	30,000,000	31:1	967,742
Total	240,000,000h	....	$9,706,602
Cost of Goods Sold:			
Opening Inventory	-0-	....	-0-
Purchases:			
January-February	15,000,000h	20:1	$ 750,000

March-April	10,000,000	21:1	476,190
May-June	30,000,000	22:1	1,363,636
July	20,000,000	23:1	869,565
August	10,000,000	26:1	384,615
September	5,000,000	28:1	178,571
October	5,000,000	29:1	172,414
November	2,500,000	30:1	83,333
December	2,500,000	31:1	80,645
Less Closing Inventory	(23,000,000)	(2)	(822,655)
Total	77,000,000h	....	3,536,314

[1] Where multiple months are indicated, the exchange rate applies for all months.
[2] See paragraph (ii) of this Example.

(ii) Since S uses the first-in, first-out inventory method, the closing inventory is assumed to consist of purchases made during the most recent translation period as follows:

	Hyperinflationary Currency	Exchange Rate	United States Dollars
December	2,500,000h	31:1	$ 80,645
November	2,500,000	30:1	83,333
October	5,000,000	29:1	172,414
September	5,000,000	28:1	178,571
August	8,000,000	26:1	307,692
Total	23,000,000h	....	822,655
Non-Capitalized Expenses:			
January-February	4,000,000h	20:1	$ 200,000
March-April	2,500,000	21:1	119,048
May-June	2,500,000	22:1	113,636
July	2,000,000	23:1	86,957
August	3,000,000	26:1	115,385
September	3,000,000	28:1	107,143
October	2,000,000	29:1	68,966
November	3,000,000	30:1	100,000
December	4,000,000	31:1	129,032
Total	26,000,000h	....	$1,040,167
Depreciation	4,000,000h	20:1	$ 200,000
Total Cost & Expenses	107,000,000h	....	$4,776,481
Operating Profit	133,000,000h	....	$4,930,121

(d) Computation of DASTM gain or loss. *(1) Rule.* DASTM gain or loss of a QBU equals—

(i) The net worth of the QBU (as determined under paragraph (d)(2) of this section) at the end of the taxable year minus the net worth of the QBU at the end of the preceding taxable year; plus

(ii) The dollar amount of the items described in paragraph (d)(3) of this section and minus the dollar amount of the items described in paragraph (d)(4) of this section; minus

(iii) The amount of dollar income or earnings and profits (or plus the amount of any dollar loss or deficit in earnings and profits) as determined for the taxable year pursuant to paragraphs (b)(1) through (b)(3) of this section.

(2) Net worth. Net worth of a QBU at the end of any taxable year equals the aggregate dollar amount representing assets on the QBU's balance sheet at the end of the taxable year less the aggregate dollar amount representing liabilities on the balance sheet. Notwithstanding any other provision in this paragraph (d)(2), the district director may adjust the amount of any asset or liability if a purpose for acquiring (or disposing of) the asset or incurring (or discharging) the liability is to manipulate the composition of the balance sheet for any period during the taxable year in order to avoid tax. The taxpayer shall determine net worth by—

(i) Preparing a balance sheet as of the end of the taxable year from the QBU's books and records (within the meaning of § 1.989(a)-1(d)) as recorded in the QBU's hyperinflationary currency;

(ii) Making adjustments necessary to conform such balance sheet to United States generally accepted accounting principles and tax accounting principles (including reversing monetary correction adjustments required by local accounting principles); and

(iii) Translating the asset and liability amounts shown on the balance sheet into United States dollars in accordance with paragraph (d)(5) of this section.

(3) Positive adjustments. (i) In general. The items described in this paragraph (d)(3) are dividend distributions for the taxable year and any items that decrease net worth for the taxable year but that generally do not affect income or loss or earnings and profits (or a deficit in earnings and

profits). Such items include a transfer to the home office of a QBU branch and a return of capital.

(ii) Translation. Except as provided by ruling or administrative pronouncement, items described in paragraph (d)(3)(i) of this section shall be translated into dollars as follows:

(A) If the item giving rise to the adjustment would be translated under paragraph (d)(5) of this section at the exchange rate for the last translation period of the taxable year if it were shown on the QBU's year-end balance sheet, such item shall be translated at the exchange rate on the date the item is transferred.

(B) If the item giving rise to the adjustment would be translated under paragraph (d)(5) of this section at the exchange rate for the translation period in which the cost of the item was incurred if it were shown on the QBU's year-end balance sheet, such item shall be translated at the same historical rate.

(iii) Effective date. Paragraph (d)(3)(ii) of this section is applicable for any transfer, dividend, or distribution that is a return of capital that is made after March 8, 2005, and that gives rise to an adjustment under this paragraph (d)(3).

(4) Negative adjustments. The items described in this paragraph (d)(4) are items that increase net worth for the taxable year but that generally do not affect income or loss or earnings and profits (or a deficit in earnings and profits). Such items include a capital contribution or a transfer from a home office to a QBU branch. Except as otherwise provided by ruling or administrative pronouncement, if the contribution or transfer is not in dollars, the amount of a capital contribution or transfer shall be translated into dollars at the exchange rate on the date made.

(5) Translation of balance sheet. Asset and liability amounts shown on the balance sheet in hyperinflationary currency (adjusted pursuant to paragraph (d)(2)(ii) of this section) shall be translated into dollars as provided in this paragraph (d)(5). However, if the QBU previously changed its functional currency to the dollar and the rules of § 1.985-5 (or, if applicable, § 1.985-5T, as contained in the April 1, 1993 edition of 26 CFR part 1 (1.908 to 1.1000)) applied in translating its balance sheet amounts into dollars, then the spot exchange rate applied under those rules shall be used to translate any amount that would otherwise be translated at a rate determined by reference to a translation period prior to the change in functional currency. For example, the basis of real property acquired while the QBU had a nondollar functional currency shall be translated into dollars at the spot rate on the last day of the taxable year before the year of change to a dollar functional currency, rather than at the rate for the period in which the cost was incurred.

(i) Closing inventory. Amounts representing items of inventory included in the closing inventory balance shall be translated in accordance with paragraph (c)(3)(iii) of this section.

(ii) Bad debt reserves. Amounts representing bad debt reserves shall be translated at the exchange rate for the last translation period for the taxable year.

(iii) Prepaid income or expense. Amounts representing expenses or income paid or received in a prior taxable year shall be translated in accordance with paragraph (c)(5) of this section.

(iv) Hyperinflationary currency. Amounts of the hyperinflationary currency and hyperinflationary demand deposit balances shall be translated at the exchange rate for the last translation period of the taxable year.

(v) Certain assets. (A) In general. Amounts representing plant, real property, equipment, goodwill, and patents and other intangibles shall be translated at the exchange rate for the translation period in which the cost of the asset was incurred.

(B) Adjustment to certain assets. Amounts representing depreciation, depletion, and amortization reserves shall be translated in accordance with paragraph (c)(4) of this section.

(vi) Hyperinflationary debt obligations. Except as provided in paragraph (d)(5)(vii) of this section, amounts representing a hyperinflationary debt obligation (including accounts receivable and payable) shall be translated at the exchange rate for the last translation period for the taxable year.

(vii) Accrued foreign income taxes. Amounts representing an accrued but unpaid foreign income tax shall be translated at the exchange rate on the last day of the last translation period of the taxable year of accrual.

(viii) Certain hyperinflationary financial instruments. Amounts representing any item described in section 988(c)(1)(B)(iii) (relating to forward contracts, futures contracts, options, or similar financial instruments) denominated in or determined by reference to the hyperinflationary currency shall be translated at the exchange rate for the last translation period for the taxable year.

(ix) Other assets and liabilities. Amounts representing assets and liabilities, other than those described in paragraphs (d)(5)(i) through (viii) of this section, shall be translated at the exchange rate for the translation period in which the cost of the asset or the amount of the liability was incurred.

(6) Dollar transactions. Notwithstanding any other provisions of this paragraph (d), where the amount representing an item shown on the balance sheet reflects a dollar transaction (described in paragraph (c)(8) of this section), the transaction shall be taken into account in accordance with that paragraph.

(7) Third currency transactions. A taxpayer may use any reasonable method of accounting for transactions described in section 988(c)(1)(B) and (C) that are denominated in, or determined by reference to, a currency other than the QBU's hyperinflationary currency or the dollar (third currency transactions), so long as such method is consistent with its method of financial accounting.

(8) Character. The amount of DASTM gain or loss determined under paragraph (d)(1) of this section shall be ordinary income or loss.

(9) Example. The provisions of this paragraph (d) are illustrated by the following example:

Example. (i) S, an accrual method calendar year foreign corporation, uses DASTM. S's hyperinflationary currency is the "h." S's net worth at December 31, 1993 was $3,246,495. For 1994, S's operating profit is 81,340,000h, or $2,038,200. S made a 5,000,000h distribution in April and again in December of 1994. S's translation period is the month. None of S's assets or liabilities reflect a dollar or third currency transaction described in paragraph (c)(8) or (c)(9) of this section, respectively. The exchange rate for each month in 1994 is as follows:

January	32h:$1
Feb.–Mar	33:1
April–May	34:1
June	35:1
July	36:1
Aug.–Sept	37:1
Oct	38:1
Nov	39:1
Dec	40:1

(ii) At the end of 1994, S's assets and liabilities, as adjusted and translated pursuant to paragraphs (d)(2) and (d)(5) of this section, are as follows:

	Hyperinflationary	Exchange Rate	U.S. Dollar
Hyperinflationary cash on hand	40,000h	40:1	$1,000
Checking account	400,000	40:1	10,000
Accounts Receivable—30-Day Accounts	20,000,000	40:1[1]	500,000
60 Day Accounts	25,000,000	40:1	625,000
Inventory	65,000,000	(2)	2,500,000
Fixed assets—Property	90,000,000	27:1	3,333,333
Plant	190,000,000	(3)	6,785,714
Accumulated Depreciation	(600,000)	(3)	(21,428)
Equipment	10,000,000	(4)	340,000
Accumulated Depreciation	(400,000)	(4)	(13,333)
Common Stock—Stock A	500,000	34:1	14,706
Stock B	400,000	26:1	15,385
Preferred Stock	1,000,000	32:1	31,250
C.D.s	5,000,000	40:1	125,000
Total Assets	406,340,000	....	14,246,627
Accounts Payable Long-term liabilities:	35,000,000	40:1	875,000
Liability A	150,000,000	40:1	3,750,000
Liability B	80,000,000	40:1	2,000,000
Liability C	30,000,000	40:1	750,000
Total Liabilities	295,000,000h	....	$7,375,000

[1] S ages its accounts receivable and groups them into two categories—those outstanding for 30 days and those outstanding for 60 days.

[2] Translated the same as closing inventory under paragraph (c)(3)(iii).

[3] The cost of S's plant was incurred in several translation periods. Therefore, the dollar cost and dollar depreciation reflect several translation rates.

[4] S has a variety of equipment. Therefore, S's dollar basis represents the sum of the hyperinflationary cost of each, translated according to the average exchange rate for the translation period incurred.

(iii) The DASTM gain of S for 1994 is computed as follows:

Net worth—1994		$6,871,627
Less:		
Net worth, 1993		$3,246,495
Plus—1994 Dividends:		
April	$ 149,254	
December	126,582[1]	
		275,836
Less:		
Net worth, 1991		3,246,495
Less Operating Profit–1994		2,038,200
DASTM gain		1,862,768

[1] The exchange rates on the date of the April and December dividends were 33.5h:$1 and 39.5h:$1, respectively.

(iv) Thus, total profit = $2,038,200 + $1,862,768 = $3,900,968.

(e) Effect of DASTM gain or loss on gross income, taxable income, or earnings and profits. *(1) In general.* For all purposes of subtitle A, the amount of DASTM gain or loss of a QBU determined under paragraph (d) of this section is taken into account by the QBU for purposes of determining the amount of its gross income, taxable income or loss, earnings and profits (or deficit in earnings and profits), and, where necessary, particular items of income, expense or other amounts. DASTM gain or loss is allocated under one of two methods. Certain small QBUs may elect the small QBU DASTM allocation described in paragraph (e)(2) of this section. All other QBUs must use the 9-step procedure described in paragraph (e)(3) of this section.

(2) Small QBU DASTM allocation. (i) Election threshold. A taxpayer may elect to use the small QBU DASTM allocation described in paragraph (e)(2)(iv) of this section with respect to a QBU that has an adjusted basis in assets (translated as provided in paragraph (d)(5) of this section) of $10 million or less at the end of any taxable year. In calculating the $10 million threshold, a QBU shall be treated as owning all of the assets of each related QBU (as defined in paragraph (e)(2)(vi) of this section) having its residence (as defined in section 988(a)(3)(B)) in the QBU's country of residence (related same-country QBU). For this purpose, appropriate adjustment shall be made to eliminate the double counting of assets created in transactions between related QBUs resident in the same country. For example, assume QBU-1, resident in country X, sells inventory to related QBU-2, also resident in country X, in exchange for an account receivable. For purposes of determining the assets of

QBU-1 under this paragraph (e)(2)(i), the taxpayer shall take into account either the inventory shown on the books of QBU-2 or QBU-1's receivable from QBU-2 (but not both).

(ii) Consent to election. The election of the small QBU DASTM allocation or subsequent application of the rules of paragraph (e)(3) of this section due to an increase in the adjusted basis of the QBU's assets shall be deemed to have been made with the consent of the Commissioner. Once the election under paragraph (e)(2)(iii) of this section is made, it shall apply for all years in which the adjusted basis of the assets of the QBU (and any related same-country QBU) is $10 million or less, unless revoked with the Commissioner's consent. If the adjusted basis of the assets of the QBU (and any related same-country QBU) exceeds $10 million at the end of any taxable year, the rules of paragraph (e)(3) of this section shall apply to that QBU (and any related same-country QBU) for such year and each subsequent year unless such QBU again qualifies, and applies for and obtains the Commissioner's consent, to use the small QBU DASTM allocation. However, if a QBU acquires assets with a principal purpose of avoiding the application of paragraph (e)(2)(iv) of this section, the Commissioner may disregard the acquisition of such assets.

(iii) Manner of making election. (A) QBUs that are branches of United States persons. For the first year in which this election is effective, in the case of a QBU branch of a United States person, a statement shall be attached to the United States person's timely filed Federal income tax return (taking extensions into account). The statement shall identify the QBU (or QBUs) for which the election is being made by describing its business and its country of residence, state the adjusted basis of the assets of the QBU (and any related same-country QBUs) to which the election applies, and include a statement that the election is being made pursuant to § 1.985-3(e)(2).

(B) Other QBUs. In the case of a QBU other than one described in paragraph (e)(2)(iii)(A) of this section, an election must be made in the manner prescribed in § 1.964-1. The statement filed with the Internal Revenue Service as required under § 1.964-1 must include the information required under paragraph (e)(2)(iii)(A) of this section.

(iv) Effect of election. If a taxpayer elects under this paragraph (e)(2) to use the small QBU DASTM allocation, DASTM gain or loss, as determined under paragraph (d) of this section, of a small QBU shall be allocated ratably to all items of the QBU's gross income (determined prior to adjustment for DASTM gain or loss). Therefore, for purposes of the foreign tax credit, DASTM gain or loss shall be allocated on the basis of the relative amounts of gross income in each separate category as defined in § 1.904-5(a)(1). In the case of a controlled foreign corporation (within the meaning of section 957 or 953(c)(1)(B)), for purposes of section 952, DASTM gain or loss shall be allocated to subpart F income in a separate category in the same ratio that the gross subpart F income in that category for the taxable year bears to its total gross income in that category for the taxable year.

(v) Conformity. If a person (or a QBU of such person) makes an election under this paragraph (e)(2) to use the small QBU DASTM allocation, then each QBU of any related person (as defined in paragraph (e)(2)(vi) of this section) that satisfies the threshold requirement of paragraph (e)(2)(i) of this section (after application of the aggregation rule of paragraph (e)(2)(i) of this section) shall be deemed to have made the election.

(vi) Related person. The term related person means any person with a relationship to the QBU (or to the United States or foreign person of which the electing QBU is a part) that is defined in section 267(b) or section 707(b).

(3) DASTM 9-step procedure. (i) Step 1—prepare balance sheets. The taxpayer shall prepare an opening and a closing balance sheet for the QBU for each balance sheet period during the taxable year. The balance sheet period is the most frequent period for which balance sheet data are reasonably available (but in no event less frequently than quarterly). The balance sheet period may not be changed without the consent of the district director. The balance sheets must be prepared under the principles of paragraph (d)(2) of this section.

(ii) Step 2—identify certain assets and liabilities. The taxpayer shall identify each item on the balance sheet that is described in section 988(c)(1)(B) or (C) and that would have been translated under paragraph (d)(5) of this section into dollars at the exchange rate for the last translation period for the taxable year (or the exchange rate on the last day of the last translation period of the taxable year in the case of an accrued foreign income tax liability).

(iii) Step 3—characterize the assets. The taxpayer shall characterize and group the assets identified in paragraph (e)(3)(ii) of this section (Step 2) according to the source and the type of income that they generate, have generated, or may reasonably be expected to generate by applying the principles of § 1.861-9T(g)(3) or its successor regulation (relating to characterization of assets for purposes of interest expense allocation). If a purpose for a taxpayer's business practices is to manipulate asset characterization or groupings, the district director may allocate or apportion DASTM gain or loss attributable to the assets. Thus, if a taxpayer that previously did not separately state interest on accounts receivable begins to impose an interest charge and a purpose for the change was to manipulate tax characterizations or groupings, then the district director may require that none of the DASTM gain or loss attributable to those receivables be allocated or apportioned to interest income.

(iv) Step 4—Determine DASTM gain or loss attributable to certain assets. (A) General rule. The taxpayer shall determine the dollar amount of DASTM gain or loss attributable to assets in each group identified in paragraph (e)(3)(iii) of this section (Step 3) as follows:

$$[(bb + eb) \div 2] \times [er - br]$$

where

bb = the hyperinflationary currency adjusted basis of the assets in the group at the beginning of the balance sheet period.

eb = the hyperinflationary currency adjusted basis of the assets in the group at the end of the balance sheet period.

er = one dollar divided by the number of hyperinflationary currency units that equal one dollar at the end of the balance sheet period.

br = one dollar divided by the number of hyperinflationary currency units that equal one dollar at the beginning of the balance sheet period.

(B) Weighting to prevent distortion. If averaging the adjusted basis of assets in a group at the beginning and end of a balance sheet period results in an allocation of DASTM gain or loss that does not clearly reflect income, as might be the case in the event of a purchase or disposition of an asset that is not in the normal course of business, the taxpayer must use a weighting method that reflects the time the assets are held by the QBU during the translation period.

(C) Example. The provisions of this paragraph (e)(3)(iv) are illustrated by the following example:

Example. S is a foreign corporation that operates in the hyperinflationary currency "h" and computes its income or loss or earnings and profits under DASTM. S's adjusted basis in a group of assets described in section 988(c)(1)(B) or (C) that generate general limitation foreign source income (as characterized under paragraph (e)(3)(iii) of this section) at the beginning of the balance sheet period is 750,000h. S's basis in such assets at the end of the balance sheet period is 1,250,000h. The exchange rate at the beginning of the balance sheet period is $1 = 200h. The exchange rate at the end of the balance sheet period is $1 = 500h. The DASTM loss attributable to the assets described above is $3,000, determined as follows:

$$[(750{,}000h + 1{,}250{,}000h) \div 2] \times [\,[(\$1 \div 500h) - (\$1 \div 200h)] = (\$3000) - br]$$

(v) Step 5—adjust dollar gross income by DASTM gain or loss from assets. The taxpayer shall adjust the dollar amount of the QBU's gross income (computed under paragraphs (b)(1) through (b)(3) of this section) generated by each group of assets characterized in paragraph (e)(3)(iii) of this section (Step 3) by the amount of DASTM gain or loss attributable to those assets computed under paragraph (e)(3)(iv) of this section (Step 4). Thus, if a group of assets, such as accounts receivable, generates both a category of income described in section 904(d)(1)(I) (relating to general limitation income) that is not foreign base company income as defined in section 954 and a DASTM loss under paragraph (e)(3)(iv) of this section (Step 4), the amount of the DASTM loss would reduce the amount of the QBU's gross income in that category. Similarly, if a group of assets, such as short-term bank deposits, generates both foreign personal holding company income that is passive income (described in sections 954(c)(1)(A) and 904(d)(1)(A)) and a DASTM loss under paragraph (e)(3)(iv) of this section (Step 4), the amount of the DASTM loss would reduce the amount of the QBU's foreign personal holding company income and passive income. See section 904(f) and the regulations thereunder in the case where that section would apply and DASTM loss attributable to a group of assets exceeds the income generated by such assets.

(vi) Step 6—Determine DASTM gain or loss attributable to liabilities. (A) General rule. The taxpayer shall determine the dollar amount of DASTM gain or loss attributable to liabilities identified in paragraph (e)(3)(ii) of this section (Step 2), and described in paragraph (e)(3)(vi)(B) of this section as follows:

$$[(bl + el) \div 2] \times [br - er]$$

where

bl = the hyperinflationary currency amount of liabilities at the beginning of the balance sheet period.

el = the hyperinflationary currency amount of liabilities at the end of the balance sheet translation period.

br = one dollar divided by the number of hyperinflationary currency units that equal one dollar at the beginning of the balance sheet period.

er = one dollar divided by the number of hyperinflationary currency units that equal one dollar at the end of the balance sheet period.

(B) Separate calculation. The calculation shall be made separately for interest-bearing liabilities described in paragraph (e)(3)(vii) of this section (Step 7) and for each of the classes of non-interest-bearing liabilities described in paragraph (e)(3)(viii) of this section (Step 8).

(C) Weighting to prevent distortion. Where a distortion would result from averaging the amount of liabilities at the beginning and end of a balance sheet period, as might be the case where a taxpayer incurs or retires a substantial liability, the taxpayer must use a different method that more clearly reflects the average amount of liabilities weighted to reflect the time the liability was outstanding during the balance sheet period.

(vii) Step 7—adjust dollar income and expense by DASTM gain or loss from interest-bearing liabilities. (A) In general. The taxpayer shall apply the amount of DASTM gain on interest-bearing liabilities computed under paragraph (e)(3)(vi) of this section (Step 6) to reduce interest expense generated by such liabilities (e.g., prior to the application of § 1.861-9T or its successor regulation). To the extent DASTM gain on such liabilities exceeds interest expense, it shall be sourced or otherwise classified in the same manner that interest expense is allocated and apportioned under § 1.861-9T or its successor regulation. The amount of DASTM loss on interest-bearing liabilities computed under paragraph (e)(3)(vi) of this section (Step 6) shall be allocated and apportioned in the same manner that interest expense is allocated and apportioned under § 1.861-9T or its successor regulation (without regard to the exceptions to fungibility in section 1.861-10T or its successor regulation). For purposes of this section, an interest-bearing liability is a liability that requires payment of periodic interest (whether fixed or variable), has original issue discount, or would have interest imputed under subtitle A.

(B) Allocation of DASTM gain or loss from interest-bearing liabilities that generate related person interest expense. DASTM gain or loss from interest-bearing liabilities that generate related person interest expense (as provided in section 954(b)(5)) shall be allocated for purposes of subtitle A (including sections 904 and 952) in the same manner that the related person interest expense of that debt is required to be allocated under the rules of section 954(b)(5) and § 1.904-5(c)(2).

(C) Modified gross income method. In applying the modified gross income method described in § 1.861-9T(j) or its successor regulation, gross income shall be adjusted for any DASTM gain or loss from assets as provided in paragraph (e)(3)(v) of this section (Step 5) and any DASTM gain or loss with respect to short-term, non-interest-bearing trade payables as provided in paragraph (e)(3)(viii)(A) of this section.

(viii) Step 8—Adjust dollar income and expense by DASTM gain or loss from non-interest bearing liabilities. (A) Short-term, non-interest-bearing trade payables. The taxpayer shall allocate DASTM gain or loss on short-term non-interest-bearing trade payables for purposes of subtitle A (including sections 904 and 952) to the same category or type of gross income as the cost or expense to which the trade payable relates. For this purpose, a short-term, non-interest-bearing trade payable is a non-interest-bearing liability with a term of 183 days or less that is incurred to purchase property or services to be used by the obligor in an active trade or business.

(B) Excise tax payables. The taxpayer shall allocate DASTM gain or loss on excise tax payables for purposes of subtitle A (including sections 904 and 952) to the same category or type of gross income as would be derived from the activity to which the excise tax relates.

(C) Other non-interest-bearing liabilities. (1) In general. Except as provided in paragraphs (e)(3)(viii)(A), (e)(3)(viii)(B), and (e)(3)(viii)(C)(2) of this section, DASTM gain or loss on non-interest-bearing liabilities shall be allocated under paragraph (e)(3)(ix) of this section (Step 9).

(2) Tracing if substantial distortion of income. DASTM gains and losses on liabilities described in paragraph (e)(3)(viii)(C)(1) of this section may be attributed to the same section 904(d) separate category or subpart F category as the transaction to which the liability relates if the taxpayer demonstrates to the satisfaction of the district director, or it is determined by the district director, that application of paragraph (e)(3)(viii)(C)(1) of this section results in a substantial distortion of income.

(ix) Step 9—allocate residual DASTM gain or loss. If there is a difference between the net DASTM gain or loss determined under paragraphs (e)(3)(i) through (viii) of this section (Steps 1 through 8) and the DASTM gain or loss determined under paragraph (d) of this section, the amount of the difference must be allocated for purposes of subtitle A (including sections 904 and 952) to the QBU's gross income (computed under paragraphs (b)(1) through (3) of this section, as adjusted under paragraphs (e)(3)(i) through (viii) of this section (Steps 1 through 8)) on the basis of the relative amounts of each category or type of gross income.

T.D. 8263, 7/19/89, amend T.D. 8556, 7/22/94, T.D. 9320, 3/29/2007.

---

§ 1.985-4 Method of accounting.

(a) Adoption of election. The adoption of, or the election to use, a functional currency shall be treated as a method of accounting. The functional currency shall be used for the year of adoption (or election) and for all subsequent taxable years unless permission to change is granted, or considered to be granted under § 1.985-2 or 1.985-8, by the Commissioner.

(b) Condition for changing functional currencies. Generally, permission to change functional currencies shall not be granted unless significant changes in the facts and circumstances of the QBU's economic environment occur. If the determination of the functional currency of the QBU for purposes of United States generally accepted accounting principles (GAAP) is based on facts and circumstances substantially similar to those set forth in § 1.985-1(c)(2), then ordinarily the Commissioner will grant a taxpayer's request to change its functional currency (or the functional currency of its branch that is a QBU) to a new functional currency only if the taxpayer (or its QBU) also changes to the new functional currency for purposes of GAAP. However, permission to change will not necessarily be granted merely because the new functional currency will conform to the taxpayer's GAAP functional currency.

(c) Relationship to certain other sections of the Code. Nothing in this section shall be construed to override the provisions of any other sections of the Code of regulations that require the use of consistent accounting methods. Such provisions must be independently satisfied separate and apart from the identification of a functional currency. For instance, while separate geographical divisions of a taxpayer's trade or business may have different functional currencies, such geographical divisions may nevertheless be required to consistently use other methods of accounting.

T.D. 8263, 9/19/89, amend T.D. 8776, 7/28/98, T.D. 8927, 1/10/2001.

---

§ 1.985-5 Adjustments required upon change in functional currency.

(a) In general. This section applies in the case of a QBU that changes from one functional currency (old functional currency) to another functional currency (new functional currency). A taxpayer or QBU subject to the rules of this section shall make the adjustments set forth in the 3-step procedure described in paragraphs (b) through (e) of this section. The adjustments shall be made on the last day of the taxable year ending before the year of change as defined in § 1.481-1(a)(1). Gain or loss required to be recognized under paragraphs (b), (d)(2), and (e)(2) of this section is not subject to section 481 and, therefore, the full amount of the gain or loss must be included in income or earnings and profits on the last day of the taxable year ending before the year of change. Except as provided in § 1.985-6, a QBU with a functional currency for its first taxable year beginning in 1987 that is different from the currency in which it had kept its books and records for United States accounting and tax accounting purposes for its prior taxable year shall apply the principles of this § 1.985-5 for purposes of computing the relevant functional currency items, such as earnings and profits, basis of an asset, and amount of a liability, as of the first day of a taxpayer's first taxable year beginning in 1987. However, a QBU that changes to the dollar pursuant to § 1.985-1(b)(2) after 1987 shall apply § 1.985-7.

(b) Step 1—Taking into account exchange gain or loss on certain section 988 transactions. The QBU shall recognize or otherwise take into account for all purposes of the Code the amount of any unrealized exchange gain or loss attributable to a section 988 transaction (as defined in section 988(c)(1)(A), (B), and (C)) that, after applying section 988(d), is denominated in terms of or determined by reference to the new functional currency. The amount of such gain or loss shall be determined without regard to the limitations of section 988(b) (i.e., whether any gain or loss would be realized on the transaction as a whole). The character and source of such gain or loss shall be determined under section 988.

(c) Step 2—Determining the new functional currency basis of property and the new functional currency amount of liabilities and any other relevant items. The new functional currency adjusted basis of property and the new functional currency amount of liabilities and any other relevant items (e.g., items described in section 988(c)(1)(B)(iii)) shall equal the product of the amount of the old functional currency adjusted basis or amount multiplied by the new functional currency/old functional currency spot exchange rate on the last day of the taxable year ending before the year of change (spot rate).

(d) Step 3A—Additional adjustments that are necessary when a branch changes functional currency. *(1) Branch changing to a functional currency other than the taxpayer's functional currency.* (i) Rule. If a QBU that is a branch of a taxpayer changes to a functional currency other than the taxpayer's functional currency, the branch shall make the adjustments set forth in either paragraph (d)(1)(ii) or (d)(1)(iii) of this section for purposes of section 987. See § 1.987-5(d) for rules for computing the branch's equity pool and basis pool.

(ii) Where prior to the change the branch and taxpayer had different functional currencies. If the branch and the taxpayer had different functional currencies prior to the change, the branch's new functional currency equity pool shall equal the product of the old functional currency amount of the equity pool multiplied by the spot rate. No adjustment to the basis pool is necessary.

(iii) Where prior to the change the branch and taxpayer had the same functional currency. If the branch and the taxpayer had the same functional currency prior to the change, the branch's basis pool shall equal the difference between the branch's total old functional currency basis of its assets and its total old functional currency amount of its liabilities. The branch's equity pool shall equal the product of the basis pool multiplied by the spot rate.

(2) Branch changing to the taxpayer's functional currency. If a branch changes its functional currency to the taxpayer's functional currency, the branch shall be treated as if it terminated on the last day of the taxable year ending before the year of change. In such a case, the taxpayer shall realize gain or loss attributable to the branch's equity pool under the principles of section 987.

(e) Step 3B—Additional adjustments that are necessary when a taxpayer changes functional currency. *(1) Corporations.* The amount of a corporation's new functional currency earnings and profits and the amount of its new functional currency paid-in capital shall equal the product of the old functional currency amounts of such items multiplied by the spot rate. The foreign income taxes and accumulated profits or deficits in accumulated profits of a foreign corporation that were maintained in foreign currency for purposes of section 902 and that are attributable to taxable years of the foreign corporation beginning before January 1, 1987, also shall be translated into the new functional currency at the spot rate.

(2) Collateral consequences to a United States shareholder of a corporation changing to the United States dollar as its functional currency. A United States shareholder (within the meaning of section 951(b) or section 953(c)(1)(A)) of a controlled foreign corporation (within the meaning of section 957 or section 953(c)(1)(B)) changing its functional currency to the dollar shall recognize foreign currency gain or loss computed under section 986(c) as if all previously taxed earnings and profits, if any, (including amounts attributable to pre-1987 taxable years that were translated from dollars into functional currency in the foreign corporation's first post-1986 taxable year) were distributed immediately prior to the change. Such a shareholder shall also recognize gain or loss attributable to the corporation's paid-in capital to the same extent, if any, that such gain or loss would be recognized under the regulations under section 367(b) if the corporation was liquidated completely.

(3) Taxpayers that are not corporations.[Reserved]

(4) Adjustments to a branch's accounts when a taxpayer changes functional currency. (i) Taxpayer changing to a functional currency other than the branch's functional currency. If a taxpayer changes to a functional currency that differs from the functional currency of a branch of the taxpayer, the branch shall adjust its basis pool in the manner prescribed in paragraph (d)(1)(ii) of this section for adjusting the equity pool, if the taxpayer's old functional currency was different from the branch's functional currency. If the taxpayer's old functional currency was the same as the branch's functional currency, the branch shall determine its equity pool and basis pool in the manner set forth in paragraph (d)(1)(iii) of this section for determining the basis pool and equity pool, respectively.

(ii) Taxpayer changing to the same functional currency as the branch. If a taxpayer changes to the same functional currency as a branch of the taxpayer, the taxpayer shall realize gain or loss as set forth in paragraph (d)(2) of this section.

(f) Examples. The provisions of this section are illustrated by the following examples.

Example (1). S, a calendar year foreign corporation, is wholly owned by domestic corporation P. The Commissioner granted permission to change S's functional currency from the LC to the FC beginning January 1, 1993. The LC/FC exchange rate on December 31, 1992 is 1 LC/2 FC. The following shows how S must convert the items on its balance sheet from the LC to the FC.

	LC1:2	FC
Assets:		
Cash on hand	40,000	80,000
Accounts receivable	10,000	20,000
Inventory	100,000	200,000
100,000 FC bond (100,000 LC historical basis)	50,000[1]	100,000
Fixed assets:		
Property	200,000	400,000
Plant	500,000	1,000,000
Accumulated depreciation	(200,000)	(400,000)
Equipment	1,000,000	2,000,000
Accumulated depreciation	(400,000)	(800,000)
Total assets	1,300,000	2,600,000
Liabilities:		
Accounts payable	50,000	100,000
Long-term liabilities	400,000	800,000
Paid-in-capital	800,000	1,600,000
Retained earnings	50,000[2]	100,000
Total liabilities and equity	1,300,000	2,600,000

[1] Under Sec. 1.985-5T(b), S will recognize a 50,000 LC loss (100,000 LC basis—50,000 LC value) on the bond resulting from the change in functional currency. Thus, immediately before the change, S's basis in the FC bond (taking into account the loss) is 50,000 LC.

[2] The amount of S's LC retained earnings reflects the 50,000 LC loss on the bond.

Example (2). P, a domestic corporation, operates a foreign branch, S. The Commissioner granted permission to change S's functional currency from the LC to the FC beginning January 1, 1993. As of December 31, 1992, S's equity pool was 2,000 LC and its basis pool was $4,000. The LC/FC exchange rate on December 31, 1992 is 1 LC/2 FC. On January 1, 1993, the new functional currency amount of S's equity pool is 4,000 FC. The basis pool is not affected.

T.D. 8464, 12/31/92, amend T.D. 8765, 3/4/98.

PAR. 4. Section 1.985-5 is revised to read as follows:

Proposed § 1.985-5 Adjustments required upon change in functional currency. [*For Preamble, see ¶ 152,801*]

(a) In general. This section applies in the case of a taxpayer, qualified business unit (QBU) or section 987 QBU as defined in § 1.987-1(b)(2) changing from one functional currency (old functional currency) to another functional currency (new functional currency). A taxpayer, QBU, or section 987 QBU subject to the rules of this section shall make the adjustments set forth in the 3-step procedure described in paragraphs (b) through (e) of this section. Except as otherwise provided in this section, the adjustments shall be made on the last day of the taxable year ending before the year of change as defined in § 1.481-1(a)(1). Gain or loss required to be recognized under paragraphs (b), (d)(2), (e)(2), and (e)(4)(iii) of this section is not subject to section 481 and, therefore, the full amount of the gain or loss must be included in income or earnings and profits on the last day of the taxable year ending before the year of change. Except as provided in § 1.985-6, a QBU or section 987 QBU with a functional currency for its first taxable year beginning in 1987 that is different from the currency in which it had kept its books and records for United States accounting and tax accounting purposes for its prior taxable year shall apply the principles of this section for purposes of computing the relevant functional currency items, such as earnings and profits, basis of an asset, and amount of a liability, as of the first day of a taxpayer's first taxable year beginning in 1987. However, a QBU that changes to the dollar pursuant to § 1.985-1(b)(2) after 1987 shall apply § 1.985-7.

(b) Step 1 Taking into account exchange gain or loss on certain section 988 transactions. The taxpayer, QBU or section 987 QBU shall recognize or otherwise take into account for all purposes of the Internal Revenue Code the amount of any unrealized exchange gain or loss attributable to a section 988 transaction (as defined in section 988(c)(1)(A), (B), and (C)) that, after applying section 988(d), is denominated in terms of or determined by reference to the new functional currency. The amount of such gain or loss shall be determined without regard to the limitations of section 988(b) (that is, whether any gain or loss would be realized on the transaction as a whole). The character and source of such gain or loss shall be determined under section 988.

(c) Step 2 Determining the new functional currency basis of property and the new functional currency amount of liabilities and any other relevant items. Except as otherwise provided in this section, the new functional currency adjusted basis of property and the new functional currency amount of liabilities and any other relevant items (for example, items described in section 988(c)(1)(B)(iii)) shall equal the product of the amount of the old functional currency adjusted basis or amount multiplied by the new functional currency/old functional currency spot exchange rate on the last day of the taxable year ending before the year of change (spot rate).

(d) Step 3A Additional adjustments that are necessary when a QBU or section 987 QBU changes functional currency. *(1) QBU changing to a functional currency other than the owner's functional currency.* (i) Rule. If a QBU or section 987 QBU changes to a functional currency other than the owner's functional currency, the owner and section 987 QBU shall make the adjustments set forth in either paragraph (d)(1)(ii) or (d)(1)(iii) of this section for purposes of section 987.

(ii) Where prior to the change the section 987 QBU and owner had different functional currencies. If the section 987 QBU and the owner had different functional currencies prior to the change, the owner and section 987 QBU shall make the following adjustments in the year of change.

(A) Determining the owner functional currency net value of the section 987 QBU under § 1.987-4(d)(1)(i)(B). (1) Historic items. For purposes of determining the owner functional currency net value of the section 987 QBU for the year of change under § 1.987-4(d)(1)(i)(B), the owner or section 987 QBU shall first translate the section 987 historic items from the QBU's old functional currency into its owner's functional currency using the historic exchange rate as defined in § 1.987-1(c)(3). The owner or section 987 QBU shall then translate the section 987 historic items as defined in § 1.987-1(e) from the owner's functional currency into the QBU's new functional currency using the spot exchange rate between the section 987 QBU's new functional currency and the owner's functional currency on the last day of the taxable year ending before the year of change.

(2) Marked items. For purposes of determining the owner functional currency net value of the section 987 QBU for the year of change under § 1.987-4(d)(1)(i)(B), the owner or section 987 QBU shall translate the section 987 QBU's section 987 marked items as defined in § 1.987-1(d) from the section 987 QBU's old functional currency into the QBU's new functional currency using the new functional currency/old functional currency spot exchange rate on the last day of the taxable year ending before the year of change.

(B) Net unrecognized section 987 gain or loss. No adjustment to the owner's net unrecognized section 987 gain or loss is necessary.

(iii) Where prior to the change the QBU and the taxpayer had the same functional currency. If a QBU with the same functional currency of the taxpayer is changing to a new functional currency different from the taxpayer, and as a result of the change the taxpayer will be an owner of a section 987 QBU (see § 1.987-1), the taxpayer and section 987 QBU shall become subject to section 987 for the year of change and subsequent years.

(2) Section 987 QBU changing to the owner's functional currency. If a section 987 QBU changes its functional currency to its owner's functional currency, the section 987 QBU shall be treated as if it terminated on the last day of the taxable year ending before the year of change. See §§ 1.987-5 and 1.987-8 for the effect of a termination.

(e) Step 3B Additional adjustments that are necessary when a taxpayer/owner changes functional currency. *(1) Corporations.* The amount of a corporation's new functional currency earnings and profits and the amount of its new functional currency paid-in capital shall equal the product of the old functional currency amounts of such items multiplied by the spot rate. The foreign income taxes and accumulated profits or deficits in accumulated profits of a foreign corporation that were maintained in foreign currency for purposes of section 902 and that are attributable to taxable years of the foreign corporation beginning before January 1, 1987, also shall be translated into the new functional currency at the spot rate.

(2) Collateral consequences to a United States shareholder of a corporation changing to the United States dollar as its functional currency. A United States shareholder (within the meaning of section 951(b) or section 953(c)(1)(A)) of a controlled foreign corporation (within the meaning of section 957 or section 953(c)(1)(B)) changing its functional currency to the dollar shall recognize foreign currency gain or loss computed under section 986(c) as if all previously taxed earnings and profits, if any, (including amounts attributable to pre-1987 taxable years that were translated from dollars into functional currency in the foreign corporation's first post-1986 taxable year) were distributed immediately prior to the change. Such a shareholder shall also recognize gain or loss attributable to the corporation's paid-in capital to the same extent, if any, that such gain or loss would be recognized under the regulations under section 367(b) if the corporation was liquidated completely.

(3) Taxpayers that are not corporations. [Reserved].

(4) Adjustments to a section 987 QBU's balance sheet and net accumulated unrecognized section 987 gain or loss when an owner changes functional currency. (i) Owner changing to a functional currency other than the section 987 QBU's functional currency. If an owner changes to a functional currency that differs from the functional currency of its section 987 QBU, the owner shall make the following adjustments in the year of change.

(A) Determining the owner functional currency net value of the section 987 QBU under § 1.987-4(d)(1)(i)(B). (1) Historic items. For purposes of determining the owner functional currency net value of the section 987 QBU for the year of change under § 1.987-4(d)(1)(i)(B), the owner shall first translate the QBU's section 987 historic items into the owner's old functional currency at the historic exchange rate as defined in § 1.987-1(c)(3). The owner shall then translate the section 987 historic items into its new functional currency using the new functional currency/old functional currency spot rate on the last day of the taxable year ending before the year of change.

(2) Marked items. For purposes of determining the owner functional currency net value of the section 987 QBU for the year of change under § 1.987-4(d)(1)(i)(B), the owner or section 987 QBU shall translate the QBU's section 987 marked items from the owner's old functional currency into the owner's new functional currency using the new functional currency/old functional currency spot exchange rate on the last day of the taxable year ending before the year of change.

(B) Translation of net unrecognized section 987 gain or loss. The owner shall translate any net unrecognized section 987 gain or loss determined under § 1.987-4 from its old functional currency into its new functional currency using the new functional currency/old functional currency spot exchange rate on the last day of the taxable year ending before the year of change.

(ii) Taxpayer with the same functional currency as its QBU changing to a different functional currency. If a taxpayer with the same functional currency as its QBU changes to a new functional currency and as a result of the change the taxpayer will be an owner of a section 987 QBU (see § 1.987-1), the taxpayer and section 987 QBU shall become subject to section 987 for the year of change and subsequent years.

(iii) Owner changing to the same functional currency as the section 987 QBU. If an owner changes to the same functional currency as its section 987 QBU, such section 987 QBU shall be treated as if it terminated on last day of the taxable year ending before the year of change. See §§ 1.987-5 and 1.987-8 for the effect of a termination.

(f) Examples. The provisions of this section are illustrated by the following example:

Example. S, a calendar year foreign corporation, is wholly owned by domestic corporation P. The Commissioner granted permission to change S's functional currency from the LC to the FC beginning January 1, 1993. The LC/FC exchange rate on December 31, 1992, is 1 LC/2 FC. The following shows how S must convert the items on its balance sheet from the LC to the FC.

	LC[1] [2]	FC
Assets:		
Cash on hand	40,000	80,000
Accounts Receivable	10,000	20,000
Inventory	100,000	200,000
100,000 FC Bond (100,000 LC historical basis)	50,000[1]	100,000
Fixed assets:		
Property	200,000	400,000
Plant	500,000	1,000,000
Accumulated Depreciation	(200,000)	(400,000)
Equipment	1,000,000	2,000,000
Accumulated Depreciation	(400,000)	(800,000)
Total Assets	1,300,000	2,600,000
Liabilities:		
Accounts Payable	50,000	100,000
Long-term Liabilities	400,000	800,000
Paid-in-Capital	800,000	1,600,000
Retained Earnings	50,000[2]	100,000

Total Liabilities and Equity	1,300,000	2,600,000

[1] Under paragraph (b) of this section, S will recognize a 50,000 LC loss (100,000 LC basis—50,000 LC value) on the bond resulting from the change in functional currency. Thus, immediately before the change, S's basis in the FC bond (taking into account the loss) is 50,000 LC.

[2] The amount of S's LC retained earnings reflects the 50,000 LC loss on the bond.

(g) Effective date. Generally, this regulation shall apply to taxable years beginning one year after the first day of the first taxable year following the date of publication of a Treasury decision adopting this rule as a final regulation in the Federal Register. If a taxpayer makes an election under § 1.987-11(b), then the effective date of this regulation with respect to the taxpayer shall be consistent with such election.

§ 1.985-6 Transition rules for a QBU that uses the dollar approximate separate transactions method for its first taxable year beginning in 1987.

(a) In general. This section sets forth transition rules for a QBU that used the dollar approximate separate transactions method of accounting set forth in § 1.985-3 or § 1.985-3T (as contained in the April 1, 1989 edition of 26 CFR part 1 (1.908 to 1.1000)) for its first taxable year beginning in 1987 (DASTM QBU). A DASTM QBU must determine the dollar and hyperinflationary currency basis of its assets and the dollar and hyperinflationary currency amount of its liabilities that were acquired or incurred in taxable years beginning before January 1, 1987. In addition, a DASTM QBU must determine its net worth, including its retained earnings, at the end of the QBU's last taxable year beginning before January 1, 1987. This section provides rules for controlled foreign corporations (as defined in section 957 or section 953(c)(1)(B)), other foreign corporations, and branches of United States persons that must make these determinations.

(b) Certain controlled foreign corporations. If a DASTM QBU was a controlled foreign corporation for its last taxable year beginning before January 1, 1987, and it had a significant event as described in § 1.964-1(c)(6) in a taxable year beginning before January 1, 1987, then the rules of this paragraph (b) shall apply.

(1) Basis in assets and amount of liabilities. The hyperinflationary currency adjusted basis of the QBU's assets and the hyperinflationary currency amount of the QBU's liabilities acquired or incurred by the QBU in a taxable year beginning before January 1, 1987, shall be the basis or the amount as determined under § 1.964-1(e) prior to translation under § 1.964-1(e)(4). The dollar adjusted basis of such assets and the dollar amount of such liabilities shall be the adjusted basis or the amount as determined under the rules of § 1.964-1(e) after translation under § 1.964-1(e)(4).

(2) Retained earnings. The dollar amount of the QBU's retained earnings at the end of its last taxable year beginning before January 1, 1987, shall be the dollar amount determined under § 1.964-1(e)(3).

(c) All other foreign corporations. If a foreign corporation is a DASTM QBU that is not described in paragraph (b) of this section, then the hyperinflationary currency and dollar adjusted basis in the QBU's assets acquired in taxable years beginning before January 1, 1987, the hyperinflationary currency and dollar amount of the QBU's liabilities acquired or incurred in taxable years beginning before January 1, 1987, and the dollar amount of the QBU's net worth, including its retained earnings, at the end of its last taxable year beginning before January 1, 1987, shall be determined by applying the principles of § 1.985-3T or § 1.985-3. Thus, for example, the dollar basis of plant and equipment shall be determined using the appropriate historical exchange rate.

(d) Pre-1987 section 902 amounts. *(1) Translation of pre-1987 section 902 accumulated profits and taxes into United States dollars.* The foreign income taxes and accumulated profits or deficits in accumulated profits of a foreign corporation that were maintained in foreign currency for purposes of section 902 and that are attributable to taxable years of the foreign corporation beginning before January 1, 1987, shall be translated into dollars at the spot exchange rate on the first day of its first taxable year beginning after December 31, 1986. Once translated into dollars, these accumulated profits and taxes shall (absent a change in functional currency) remain in dollars for all federal income tax purposes.

(2) Carryforward of accumulated deficits in accumulated profits from pre-1987 taxable years to post-1986 taxable years. For purposes of sections 902 and 960, the post-1986 undistributed earnings of a foreign corporation that is subject to the rules of this section shall be reduced by the dollar amount of the corporation's deficit in accumulated profits, if any, determined under section 902 and the regulations thereunder, that was accumulated at the end of the corporation's last taxable year beginning before January 1, 1987. The dollar amount of the accumulated deficit shall be determined by multiplying the foreign currency amount of such deficit by the spot exchange rate on the last day of the corporation's last taxable year beginning before January 1, 1987, and shall be taken into account on the first day of the corporation's first taxable year beginning after December 31, 1986. Post-1986 undistributed earnings may not be reduced by the dollar amount of a pre-1987 deficit in retained earnings determined under § 1.964-1(e).

(e) Net worth branch. If a DASTM QBU is a branch of a United States person and the QBU used a net worth method of accounting for its last taxable year beginning before January 1, 1987, then the rules of this paragraph (e) shall apply. A net worth method of accounting is any method of accounting under which the taxpayer calculates the taxable income of a QBU based on the net change in the dollar value of the QBU's equity (assets minus liabilities) during the course of a taxable year, taking into account any contributions or remittances made during the year. See, e.g., Rev. Rul. 75-106, 1975-1 C.B. 31. (See § 601.601(d)(2)(ii)(b) of this chapter).

(1) Basis in assets and amount of liabilities. (i) Hyperinflationary amounts. For the first taxable year beginning in 1987, the hyperinflationary currency adjusted basis of a QBU's assets or the hyperinflationary currency amounts of its liabilities acquired or incurred in a taxable year beginning before January 1, 1987 is the hyperinflationary currency basis or amount at the date when acquired or incurred, as adjusted according to United States generally accepted accounting and tax accounting principles. If a hyperinflationary currency basis or amount was not determined at such date, the dollar basis or amount, as adjusted according to United States generally accepted accounting and tax accounting principles, shall be translated into hyperinflationary currency at the spot exchange rate on the date when the asset or liability was acquired or incurred.

(ii) Dollar amounts. For the first taxable year beginning in 1987, the dollar adjusted basis of the QBU's assets and the amounts of its liabilities shall be those amounts reflected on the QBU's dollar books and records at the end of the taxpayer's last taxable year beginning before January 1, 1987, after adjusting the books and records according to United States generally accepted accounting and tax accounting principles.

(2) Ending net worth. The dollar amount of the QBU's net worth at the end of its last taxable year beginning before January 1, 1987 shall equal the QBU's net worth at that date as determined under paragraph (e)(1)(ii) of this section.

(f) Profit and loss branch. If a DASTM QBU is a branch of a United States person and the QBU used a profit and loss method of accounting for its last taxable year beginning before January 1, 1987, then the United States person shall first apply the transition rules of § 1.987-5 in order to determine the beginning amount and dollar basis of the branch's EQ pool, the hyperinflationary currency basis of the branch's assets, and the hyperinflationary currency amounts of its liabilities. A profit and loss method of accounting is any method of accounting under which the taxpayer calculates the profits of a QBU by computing the QBU's profits in its functional currency and translating the net result into dollars. See, e.g., Rev. Rul. 75-107, 1975-1 C.B. 32. (See § 601.601(d)(2)(ii)(b) of this chapter). The QBU and the taxpayer must then make the adjustments required by § 1.985-5, e.g., the QBU must take into account unrealized exchange gain or loss on dollar-denominated section 988 transactions, the taxpayer must account for the deemed termination of the branch, and the taxpayer must translate the QBU's balance sheet items from hyperinflationary currency into dollars at the spot rate.

T.D. 8464, 12/31/92.

§ 1.985-7 Adjustments required in connection with a change to DASTM.

(a) In general. If a QBU begins to use the dollar approximate separate transactions method of accounting set forth in § 1.985-3 (DASTM) in a taxable year beginning after April 6, 1998, adjustments shall be made as provided by this section. For the rules with respect to foreign corporations, see paragraph (b) of this section. For the rules with respect to adjustments to the income of United States shareholders of controlled foreign corporations, see paragraph (c) of this section. For the rules with respect to adjustments relating to QBU branches, see paragraph (d) of this section. For the effective date of this section, see paragraph (e). For purposes of applying this section, the look-back period shall be the period beginning with the first taxable year after the transition date and ending on the last day prior to the taxable year of change. The term transition date means the later of the last day of the last taxable year ending before the base period as defined in § 1.985-1(b)(2)(ii)(D) or the last day of the taxable year in which the QBU last applied DASTM. The taxable year of change shall mean the taxable year of change as defined in § 1.481-1(a)(1). The application of this paragraph may be illustrated by the following examples:

Example (1). A calendar year QBU that has not previously used DASTM operates in a country in which the functional currency of the country is hyperinflationary as defined under § 1.985-1(b)(2)(ii)(D) for the QBU's 1999 tax year. The look-back period is the period from January 1, 1996 through December 31, 1998, the transition date is December 31, 1995, and the taxable year of change is the taxable year beginning January 1, 1999.

Example (2). A QBU that has not previously used DASTM with a taxable year ending June 30, operates in a country in which the functional currency of the country is hyperinflationary for the QBU's tax year beginning July 1, 1999 as defined under § 1.985-1(b)(2)(ii)(D) (where the base period is the thirty-six calendar months immediately preceding the first day of the current calendar year 1999). The look-back period is the period from July 1, 1995 through June 30, 1999, the transition date is June 30, 1995, and the taxable year of change is the taxable year beginning July 1, 1999.

(b) Adjustments to foreign corporations. *(1) In general.* In the case of a foreign corporation, the corporation shall make the adjustments set forth in paragraphs (b)(2) through (4) of this section. The adjustments shall be made on the first day of the taxable year of change.

(2) Treatment of certain section 988 transactions. (i) Exchange gain or loss from section 988 transactions unrealized as of the transition date. A foreign corporation shall adjust earnings and profits by the amount of any unrealized exchange gain or loss that was attributable to a section 988 transaction (as defined in sections 988(c)(1)(A), (B), and (C)) that was denominated in terms of (or determined by reference to) the dollar and was held by the corporation on the transition date. Such gain or loss shall be computed as if recognized on the transition date and shall be reduced by any gain and increased by any loss recognized by the corporation with respect to such transaction during the look-back period. The amount of such gain or loss shall be determined without regard to the limitations of section 988(b) (i.e., whether any gain or loss would be realized on the transaction as a whole). The character and source of such gain or loss shall be determined under section 988. Proper adjustments shall be made to account for gain or loss taken into account by reason of this paragraph (b)(2). See § 1.985-5(f) Example 1, footnote 1.

(ii) Treatment of a section 988 transaction entered into and terminated during the look-back period. A foreign corporation shall reduce earnings and profits by the amount of any gain, and increase earnings and profits by the amount of any loss, that was recognized with respect to any dollar denominated section 988 transactions entered into and terminated during the look-back period.

(3) Opening balance sheet. The opening balance sheet of a foreign corporation for the taxable year of change shall be determined as if the corporation had changed its functional currency to the dollar by applying § 1.985-5(c) on the transition date and had translated its assets and liabilities acquired and incurred during the look-back period under § 1.985-3.

(4) Earnings and profits adjustments. (i) Pre-1987 accumulated profits. The foreign income taxes and accumulated profits or deficits in accumulated profits of a foreign corporation that are attributable to taxable years beginning before January 1, 1987, as stated on the transition date, and that were maintained for purposes of section 902 in the old functional currency, shall be translated into dollars at the spot rate in effect on the transition date. The applicable accumulated profits shall be reduced on a last-in, first-out basis by the aggregate dollar amount (translated from functional currency in accordance with the rules of section 989(b)) attributable to earnings and profits that were distributed (or treated as distributed) during the look-back period to the extent such amounts distributed exceed the earnings and profits calculated under (b)(4)(ii) or (b)(4)(iii), as applicable. See § 1.902-1(b)(2)(ii). Once translated into dollars, these pre-1987 taxes and accumulated profits or deficits in accumulated profits shall (absent a change in functional currency) remain in dollars for all federal income tax purposes.

(ii) Post-1986 undistributed earnings of a CFC. In the case of a controlled foreign corporation (within the meaning of section 957 or section 953(c)(1)(B))(CFC) or a foreign corporation subject to the rules of § 1.904-6(a)(2), the corporation's post-1986 undistributed earnings in each separate category as defined in § 1.904-5(a)(1) as of the first day of the taxable year of change (and prior to adjustment under paragraph (c)(1) of this section) shall equal the sum of—

(A) The corporation's post-1986 undistributed earnings and profits (or deficit in earnings and profits) in each separate category as defined in § 1.904-5(a)(1) as stated on the transition date translated into dollars at the spot rate in effect on the transition date; and

(B) The sum of the earnings and profits (or deficit in earnings and profits) in each separate category determined under § 1.985-3 for each post-transition date taxable year prior to the taxable year of change.

Such amount shall be reduced by the aggregate dollar amount (translated from functional currency in accordance with the rules of section 989(b)) attributable to earnings and profits that were distributed (or treated as distributed) during the look-back period out of post-1986 earnings and profits in such separate category. For purposes of applying this paragraph (b)(4)(ii)(B), the opening balance sheet for calculating earnings and profits under § 1.985-3 for the first post-transition year shall be translated into dollars pursuant to § 1.985-5(c).

(iii) Post-1986 undistributed earnings of other foreign corporations. In the case of a foreign corporation that is not a CFC or subject to the rules of § 1.904-6(a)(2), the corporation's post-1986 undistributed earnings shall equal the sum of—

(A) The corporation's post-1986 undistributed earnings (or deficit) on the transition date translated into dollars at the spot rate in effect on the transition date; and

(B) The sum of the earnings and profits (or deficit in earnings and profits) determined under § 1.985-3 for each post-transition date taxable year (or such later year determined under section 902(c)(3)(A)) prior to the taxable year of change.

Such amount shall be reduced by the aggregate dollar amount (translated from functional currency in accordance with the rules of section 989(b)) that was distributed (or treated as distributed) during the look-back period out of post-1986 earnings and profits. For purposes of applying this paragraph (b)(4)(iii)(B), the opening balance sheet for calculating earnings and profits under § 1.985-3 for the first post-transition year shall be translated into dollars pursuant to § 1.985-5(c).

(c) United States shareholders of controlled foreign corporations. *(1) In general.* A United States shareholder (within the meaning of section 951(b) or section 953(c)(1)(B)) of a CFC that changes to DASTM shall make the adjustments set forth in paragraphs (c)(2) through (5) of this section on the first day of the taxable year of change. Adjustments under this section shall be taken into account by the shareholder (or such shareholder s successor in interest) ratably over four taxable years beginning with the taxable year of change. Similar rules shall apply in determining adjustments to income of United States persons who have made an election under section 1295 to treat a passive foreign investment company as a qualified electing fund.

(2) Treatment under subpart F of income recognized on section 988 transactions. The character of amounts taken into account under paragraph (b)(2) of this section for purposes of sections 951 through 964, shall be determined on the transition date and to the extent characterized as subpart F income shall be taken into account in accordance with the rules of paragraph (c)(1) of this section. Such amounts shall retain their character for all federal income tax purposes (including sections 902, 959, 960, 961, 1248, and 6038).

(3) Recognition of foreign currency gain or loss on previously taxed earnings and profits on the transition date. Gain or loss is recognized under section 986(c) as if all previously taxed earnings and profits as determined on the transition date, if any, were distributed on such date. Such gain or loss shall be reduced by any foreign currency gain and increased by any foreign currency loss that was recognized under section 986(c) with respect to distributions of previously taxed earnings and profits during the look-back period. Such amount shall be characterized in accordance with section 986(c) and taken into account in accordance with the rules of paragraph (c)(1) of this section.

(4) Subpart F income adjustment. Subpart F income in a separate category shall be determined under § 1.985-3 for each look-back year. For this purpose, the opening DASTM balance sheet shall be determined under § 1.985-5. The sum of the difference (positive or negative) between the amount computed pursuant to § 1.985-3 and amount that was included in income for each year shall be taken into account in the taxable year of change pursuant to paragraph (c)(1) of this section. Such amounts shall retain their character for all federal income tax purposes (including sections 902, 959, 960, 961, 1248, and 6038). For rules applicable if an adjustment under this section results in a loss for the taxable year in a separate category, see section 904(f) and the regulations thereunder. The amount of previously taxed earnings and profits as determined under section 959(c)(2) shall be adjusted (positively or negatively) by the amount taken into account under this paragraph (c)(4) as of the first day of the taxable year of change.

(5) Foreign tax credit. A United States shareholder of a CFC shall compute an amount of foreign taxes deemed paid under section 960 with respect to any positive adjustments determined under paragraph (c) of this section. The amount of foreign tax deemed paid shall be computed with reference to the full amount of the adjustment and to the post-1986 undistributed earnings determined under paragraph (b)(4)(i) and (ii) of this section and the post-1986 foreign income taxes of the CFC on the first day of the taxable year of change (i.e., without taking into account earnings and taxes for the taxable year of change). For purposes of section 960, the associated taxes in each separate category shall be allocated pro rata among, and deemed paid in, the shareholder's taxable years in which the income is taken into account. (No adjustment to foreign taxes deemed paid in prior years is required solely by reason of a negative adjustment to income under paragraph (c)(1) of this section).

(d) QBU branches. *(1) In general.* In the case of a QBU branch, the taxpayer shall make the adjustments set forth in paragraphs (d)(2) through (d)(4) of this section. Adjustments under this section shall be taken into account by the taxpayer ratably over four taxable years beginning with the taxable year of change.

(2) Treatment of certain section 988 transactions. (i) Exchange gain or loss from section 988 transactions unrealized as of the transition date. A QBU branch shall adjust income by the amount of any unrealized exchange gain or loss that was attributable to a section 988 transaction (as defined in sections 988(c)(1)(A), (B), and (C)) that was denominated in terms of (or determined by reference to) the dollar and was

held by the QBU branch on the transition date. Such gain or loss shall be computed as if recognized on the transition date and shall be reduced by any gain and increased by any loss recognized by the QBU branch with respect to such transaction during the look-back period. The amount of such gain or loss shall be determined without regard to the limitations of section 988(b) (i.e., whether any gain or loss would be realized on the transaction as a whole). The character and source of such gain or loss shall be determined under section 988. Proper adjustments shall be made to account for gain or loss taken into account by reason of this paragraph (d)(2). See § 1.985-5(f) Example 1, footnote 1.

(ii) Treatment of a section 988 transaction entered into and terminated during the look-back period. A QBU branch shall reduce income by the amount of any gain, and increase income by the amount of any loss, that was recognized with respect to any dollar denominated section 988 transactions entered into and terminated during the look-back period.

(3) Deemed termination income adjustment. The taxpayer shall realize gain or loss attributable to the QBU branch's equity pool (as stated on the transition date) under the principles of section 987, computed as if the branch terminated on the transition date. Such amount shall be reduced by section 987 gain and increased by section 987 loss that was recognized by such taxpayer with respect to remittances during the look-back period.

(4) Branch income adjustment. Branch income in a separate category shall be determined under § 1.985-3 for each look-back year. For this purpose, the opening DASTM balance sheet shall be determined under § 1.985-5. The sum of the difference (positive or negative) between the amount computed pursuant to § 1.985-3 and amount taken into account for each year shall be taken into account in the taxable year of change pursuant to paragraph (d)(1) of this section. Such amounts shall retain their character for all federal income tax purposes.

(5) Opening balance sheet. The opening balance sheet of a QBU branch for the taxable year of change shall be determined as if the branch had changed its functional currency to the dollar by applying § 1.985-5(c) on the transition date and had translated its assets and liabilities acquired and incurred during the look-back period under § 1.985-3.

(e) Effective date. This section is effective for taxable years beginning after April 6, 1998. However, a taxpayer may choose to apply this section to all open taxable years beginning after December 31, 1986, provided each person, and each QBU branch of a person, that is related (within the meaning of § 1.985-2(d)(3)) to the taxpayer also applies this section.

T.D. 8765, 3/4/98.

§ 1.985-8 Special rules applicable to the European Monetary Union (conversion to euro).

(a) Definitions. *(1) Legacy currency.* A legacy currency is the former currency of a Member State of the European Community which is substituted for the euro in accordance with the Treaty establishing the European Community signed February 7, 1992. The term legacy currency shall also include the European Currency Unit.

(2) Conversion rate. The conversion rate is the rate at which the euro is substituted for a legacy currency.

(b) Operative rules. *(1) Initial adoption.* A QBU (as defined in § 1.989(a)-1(b)) whose first taxable year begins after the euro has been substituted for a legacy currency may not adopt a legacy currency as its functional currency.

(2) QBU with a legacy currency as its functional currency. (i) Required change. A QBU with a legacy currency as its functional currency is required to change its functional currency to the euro beginning the first day of the first taxable year—

(A) That begins on or after the day that the euro is substituted for that legacy currency (in accordance with the Treaty on European Union); and

(B) In which the QBU begins to maintain its books and records (as described in § 1.989(a)-1(d)) in the euro.

(ii) Notwithstanding paragraph (b)(2)(i) of this section, a QBU with a legacy currency as its functional currency is required to change its functional currency to the euro no later than the last taxable year beginning on or before the first day such legacy currency is no longer valid legal tender.

(3) QBU with a non-legacy currency as its functional currency. (i) In general. A QBU with a non-legacy currency as its functional currency may change its functional currency to the euro pursuant to this § 1.985-8 if—

(A) Under the rules set forth in § 1.985-1(c), the euro is the currency of the economic environment in which a significant part of the QBU's activities are conducted;

(B) After conversion, the QBU maintains its books and records (as described in § 1.989(a)-1(d)) in the euro; and

(C) The QBU is not required to use the dollar as its functional currency under § 1.985-1(b).

(ii) Time period for change. A QBU with a non-legacy currency as its functional currency may change its functional currency to the euro under this section only if it does so within the period set forth in paragraph (b)(2) of this section as if the functional currency of the QBU was a legacy currency.

(4) Consent of Commissioner. A change made pursuant to paragraph (b) of this section shall be deemed to be made with the consent of the Commissioner for purposes of § 1.985-4. A QBU changing its functional currency to the euro pursuant to paragraph (b)(2) of this section must make adjustments as provided in paragraph (c) of this section. A QBU changing its functional currency to the euro pursuant to paragraph (b)(3) must make adjustments as provided in § 1.985-5.

(5) Statement to file upon change. With respect to a QBU that changes its functional currency to the euro under paragraph (b) of this section, an affected taxpayer shall attach to its return for the taxable year of change a statement that includes the following: "TAXPAYER CERTIFIES THAT A QBU OF THE TAXPAYER HAS CHANGED ITS FUNCTIONAL CURRENCY TO THE EURO PURSUANT TO TREAS. REG. § 1.985-8." For purposes of this paragraph (b)(5), an affected taxpayer shall be in the case where the QBU is: a QBU of an individual U.S. resident (as a result of the activities of such individual), the individual; a QBU branch of a U.S. corporation, the corporation; a controlled foreign corporation (as described in section 957)(or QBU branch thereof), each United States shareholder (as described in section 951(b)); a partnership, each partner separately; a noncontrolled section 902 corporation (as described in section 904(d)(2)(E)) (or branch thereof), each domestic shareholder as described in § 1.902-1(a)(1); or a trust or estate, the fiduciary of such trust or estate.

(c) Adjustments required when a QBU changes its functional currency from a legacy currency to the euro

pursuant to paragraph (b)(2) of this section. *(1) In general.* A QBU that changes its functional currency from a legacy currency to the euro pursuant to paragraph (b)(2) of this section must make the adjustments described in paragraphs (c)(2) through (5) of this section. Section 1.985-5 shall not apply.

(2) Determining the euro basis of property and the euro amount of liabilities and other relevant items. The euro basis in property and the euro amount of liabilities and other relevant items shall equal the product of the legacy functional currency adjusted basis or amount of liabilities multiplied by the applicable conversion rate.

(3) Taking into account exchange gain or loss on legacy currency section 988 transactions.

(i) In general. Except as provided in paragraphs (c)(3)(iii) and (iv) of this section, a legacy currency denominated section 988 transaction (determined after applying section 988(d)) outstanding on the last day of the taxable year immediately prior to the year of change shall continue to be treated as a section 988 transaction after the change and the principles of section 988 shall apply.

(ii) Examples. The application of this paragraph (c)(3) may be illustrated by the following examples:

Example (1). X, a calendar year QBU on the cash method of accounting, uses the deutschmark as its functional currency. X is not described in section 1281(b). On July 1, 1998, X converts 10,000 deutschmarks (DM) into Dutch guilders (fl) at the spot rate of fl1 = DM1 and loans the 10,000 guilders to Y (an unrelated party) for one year at a rate of 10% with principal and interest to be paid on June 30, 1999. On January 1, 1999, X changes its functional currency to the euro pursuant to this section. Assume that the euro/deutschmark conversion rate is set by the European Council at =1= DM2. Assume further that the euro/guilder conversion rate is set at =1 = fl2.25. Accordingly, under the terms of the note, on June 30, 1999, X will receive =4444.44 (fl10,000/2.25) of principal and =444.44 (fl1,000/2.25) of interest. Pursuant to this paragraph (c)(3), X will realize an exchange loss on the principal computed under the principles of § 1.988-2(b)(5). For this purpose, the exchange rate used under § 1.988-2(b)(5)(i) shall be the guilder/euro conversion rate. The amount under § 1.988-2(b)(5)(ii) is determined by translating the fl10,000 at the guilder/deutschmark spot rate on July 1, 1998, and translating that deutschmark amount into euros at the deutschmark/ euro conversion rate. Thus, X will compute an exchange loss for 1999 of =555.56 determined as follows: [=4444.44 (fl10,000/2.25)-5000 ((fl10,000/1)/2) = -=555.56]. Pursuant to this paragraph (c)(3), the character and source of the loss are determined pursuant to section 988 and regulations thereunder. Because X uses the cash method of accounting for the interest on this debt instrument, X does not realize exchange gain or loss on the receipt of that interest.

Example (2). (i) X, a calendar year QBU on the accrual method of accounting, uses the deutschmark as its functional currency. On February 1, 1998, X converts 12,000 deutschmarks into Dutch guilders at the spot rate of fl1 = DM1 and loans the 12,000 guilders to Y (an unrelated party) for one year at a rate of 10% with principal and interest to be paid on January 31, 1999. In addition, assume the average rate (deutschmark/guilder) for the period from February 1, 1998, through December 31, 1998 is fl1.07 = DM1. Pursuant to § 1.988-2(b)(2)(ii)(C), X will accrue eleven months of interest on the note and recognize interest income of DM1028.04 (fl1100/1.07) in the 1998 taxable year.

(ii) On January 1, 1999, the euro will replace the deutschmark as the national currency of Germany pursuant to the Treaty on European Union signed February 7, 1992. Assume that on January 1, 1999, X changes its functional currency to the euro pursuant to this section. Assume that the euro/deutschmark conversion rate is set by the European Council at =1 = DM2. Assume further that the euro/ guilder conversion rate is set at =1 = fl2.25. In 1999, X will accrue one month of interest equal to =44.44 (fl100/2.25). On January 31, 1999, pursuant to the note, X will receive interest denominated in euros of =533.33 (fl1200/2.25). Pursuant to this paragraph (c)(3), X will realize an exchange loss in the 1999 taxable year with respect to accrued interest computed under the principles of § 1.988-2(b)(3). For this purpose, the exchange rate used under § 1.988-2(b)(3)(i) is the guilder/euro conversion rate and the exchange rate used under § 1.988-2(b)(3)(ii) is the deutschmark/euro conversion rate. Thus, with respect to the interest accrued in 1998, X will realize exchange loss of =25.13 under § 1.988-2(b)(3) as follows: [=488.89 (fl1100/2.25)-=514.02 (DM1028.04/2) =-=25.13]. With respect to the one month of interest accrued in 1999, X will realize no exchange gain or loss since the exchange rate when thc interest accrued and the spot rate on the payment date are the same.

(iii) X will realize exchange loss of =666.67 on repayment of the loan principal computed in the same manner as in Example 1 [=5333.33 (fl12,000/2.25)-=6000 fl12,000/1)/2)]. The losses with respect to accrued interest and principal are characterized and sourced under the rules of section 988.

(iii) Special rule for legacy nonfunctional currency. The QBU shall realize or otherwise take into account for all purposes of the Internal Revenue Code the amount of any unrealized exchange gain or loss attributable to nonfunctional currency (as described in section 988(c)(1)(C)(ii)) that is denominated in a legacy currency as if the currency were disposed of on the last day of the taxable year immediately prior to the year of change. The character and source of the gain or loss are determined under section 988.

(iv) Legacy currency denominated accounts receivable and payable. (A) In general. A QBU may elect to realize or otherwise take into account for all purposes of the Internal Revenue Code the amount of any unrealized exchange gain or loss attributable to a legacy currency denominated item described in section 988(c)(1)(B)(ii) as if the item were terminated on the last day of the taxable year ending prior to the year of change.

(B) Time and manner of election. With respect to a QBU that makes an election described in paragraph (c)(3)(iv)(A) of this section, an affected taxpayer (as described in paragraph (b)(5) of this section) shall attach a statement to its tax return for the taxable year ending immediately prior to the year of change which includes the following: "TAXPAYER CERTIFIES THAT A QBU OF THE TAXPAYER HAS ELECTED TO REALIZE CURRENCY GAIN OR LOSS ON LEGACY CURRENCY DENOMINATED ACCOUNTS RECEIVABLE AND PAYABLE UPON CHANGE OF FUNCTIONAL CURRENCY TO THE EURO." A QBU making the election must do so for all legacy currency denominated items described in section 988(c)(1)(B)(ii).

(4) Adjustments when a branch changes its functional currency to the euro. (i) Branch changing from a legacy currency to the euro in a taxable year during which taxpayer's functional currency is other than the euro. If a branch changes its functional currency from a legacy currency to the euro for a taxable year during which the taxpayer's functional currency is other than the euro, the branch's euro eq-

uity pool shall equal the product of the legacy currency amount of the equity pool multiplied by the applicable conversion rate. No adjustment to the basis pool is required.

(ii) Branch changing from a legacy currency to the euro in a taxable year during which taxpayer's functional currency is the euro. If a branch changes its functional currency from a legacy currency to the euro for a taxable year during which the taxpayer's functional currency is the euro, the taxpayer shall realize gain or loss attributable to the branch's equity pool under the principles of section 987, computed as if the branch terminated on the last day prior to the year of change. Adjustments under this paragraph (c)(4)(ii) shall be taken into account by the taxpayer ratably over four taxable years beginning with the taxable year of change.

(5) Adjustments to a branch's accounts when a taxpayer changes to the euro. (i) Taxpayer changing from a legacy currency to the euro in a taxable year during which a branch's functional currency is other than the euro. If a taxpayer changes its functional currency to the euro for a taxable year during which the functional currency of a branch of the taxpayer is other than the euro, the basis pool shall equal the product of the legacy currency amount of the basis pool multiplied by the applicable conversion rate. No adjustment to the equity pool is required.

(ii) Taxpayer changing from a legacy currency to the euro in a taxable year during which a branch's functional currency is the euro. If a taxpayer changes its functional currency from a legacy currency to the euro for a taxable year during which the functional currency of a branch of the taxpayer is the euro, the taxpayer shall take into account gain or loss as determined under paragraph (c)(4)(ii) of this section.

(6) Additional adjustments that are necessary when a corporation changes its functional currency to the euro. The amount of a corporation's euro currency earnings and profits and the amount of its euro paid-in capital shall equal the product of the legacy currency amounts of these items multiplied by the applicable conversion rate. The foreign income taxes and accumulated profits or deficits in accumulated profits of a foreign corporation that were maintained in foreign currency for purposes of section 902 and that are attributable to taxable years of the foreign corporation beginning before January 1, 1987, also shall be translated into the euro at the conversion rate.

(d) Treatment of legacy currency section 988 transactions with respect to a QBU that has the euro as its functional currency. *(1) In general.* This § 1.985-8(d) applies to a QBU that has the euro as its functional currency and that holds a section 988 transaction denominated in, or determined by reference to, a currency that is substituted by the euro. For example, this paragraph (d) will apply to a German QBU with the euro as its functional currency if the QBU is holding Country X currency or other section 988 transactions denominated in such currency on the day in the year 2005 when the euro is substituted for the Country X currency.

(2) Principles of paragraph (c)(3) of this section shall apply. With respect to a QBU described in paragraph (d) of this section, the principles of paragraph (c)(3) of this section shall apply. For example, if a German QBU with the euro as its functional currency is holding a Country X currency denominated debt instrument on the day in the year 2005 when the euro is substituted for the Country X currency, the instrument shall continue to be treated as a section 988 transaction pursuant to the principles of paragraph (c)(3)(i) of this section. However, if such QBU holds Country X currency, the QBU shall take into account any unrealized exchange gain or loss pursuant to the principles of paragraph (c)(3)(iii) of this section as if the currency was disposed of on the day prior to the day the euro is substituted for the Country X currency. Similarly, if the QBU makes an election under the principles of paragraph (c)(3)(iv) of this section, the QBU shall take into account for all purposes of the Internal Revenue Code the amount of any unrealized exchange gain or loss attributable to a legacy currency denominated item described in section 988(c)(1)(B)(ii) as if the item were terminated on the day prior to the day the euro is substituted for the Country X currency.

(e) Effective date. This section applies to tax years ending after July 29, 1998.

T.D. 8927, 1/10/2001.

---

§ 1.987-1 Profit and loss method of accounting for a qualified business unit of a taxpayer having a different functional currency from the taxpayer. [Reserved]

Proposed § 1.987-1 Scope, definitions and special rules.

[*For Preamble, see ¶ 152,801*]

(a) In general. These regulations provide rules for determining the taxable income or loss of a taxpayer with respect to a section 987 qualified business unit (section 987 QBU) as defined in paragraph (b)(2) of this section. Further, these regulations provide rules for determining the timing, amount, character and source of section 987 gain or loss recognized with respect to a section 987 QBU. This section addresses the scope of these regulations and provides certain definitions and special rules. Section 1.987-2 provides rules for attributing assets and liabilities and items of income, gain, deduction, and loss to an eligible QBU and a section 987 QBU. It also provides rules regarding transfers and the translation of items transferred to a section 987 QBU. Section 1.987-3 provides rules for determining and translating the section 987 taxable income or loss of a taxpayer with respect to a section 987 QBU. Section 1.987-4 provides rules for determining net unrecognized section 987 gain or loss. Section 1.987-5 provides rules regarding the recognition of section 987 gain or loss. Section 1.987-6 provides rules regarding the character and source of section 987 gain or loss. Section 1.987-7 provides rules with respect to partnerships and rules necessary to coordinate the provisions of section 987 with subchapter K. Section 1.987-8 provides rules regarding the termination of a section 987 QBU. Section 1.987-9 provides rules regarding the recordkeeping required under section 987. Section 1.987-10 provides transition rules. Section 1.987-11 provides the effective date of these regulations.

(b) Scope of section 987 and definitions. *(1) Taxpayers subject to section 987.* (i) In general. Except as provided in paragraphs (b)(1)(ii) and (iii) of this section, an individual or corporation is subject to section 987 if such person is an owner (as defined in paragraphs (b)(4) and (5) of this section) of an eligible QBU (as defined in paragraph (b)(3) of this section) that is a section 987 QBU (as defined in paragraph (b)(2) of this section). Such individual or corporation, and any section 987 QBU owned by such person, must comply with these regulations.

(ii) De minimis rule for certain indirectly owned section 987 QBUs. An individual or corporation that owns a section 987 QBU indirectly through a section 987 partnership may elect not to apply these regulations for purposes of taking into account the section 987 gain or loss of such section 987

QBU if the individual or corporation owns, directly or indirectly, less than five percent of either the total capital or the total profits interest in the section 987 partnership as determined on the date of acquisition of such interest or on the date such interest is increased or decreased. For purposes of this paragraph (b)(1)(ii), ownership of a capital or profits interest in a partnership shall be determined in accordance with the rules for constructive ownership of stock provided in section 267(c), other than section 267(c)(3). See § 1.987-3 for purposes of determining the section 987 taxable income or loss attributable to such section 987 QBU.

(iii) Inapplicability to certain entities. These regulations do not apply to banks, insurance companies and similar financial entities (including, solely for purposes of section 987, leasing companies, finance coordination centers, regulated investment companies and real estate investment trusts). Further, these rules do not apply to trusts, estates and S corporations.

(2) Definition of a section 987 QBU. (i) In general. A section 987 QBU is an eligible QBU, as defined in paragraph (b)(3) of this section, that has a functional currency different from its owner. The functional currency of an eligible QBU shall be determined under § 1.985-1, taking into account all of the QBU's activities before the application of § 1.987-7.

(ii) Section 987 QBU grouping election. (A) In general. Except as provided in paragraphs (b)(2)(ii)(B)(1) through (3) of this section, an owner may elect pursuant to paragraph (f) of this section to treat, solely for purposes of section 987, all section 987 QBUs with the same functional currency as a single section 987 QBU.

(B) Special grouping rules for section 987 QBUs owned indirectly through a partnership. (1) In general. An owner may elect to treat all section 987 QBUs with the same functional currency owned indirectly though a single section 987 partnership as a single section 987 QBU.

(2) Election not available to group section 987 QBUs owned indirectly through different partnerships. An owner cannot elect to treat multiple section 987 QBUs with the same functional currency as a single section 987 QBU if such QBUs are owned indirectly through different section 987 partnerships.

(3) Election not available to group section 987 QBUs owned directly and indirectly. An owner cannot elect to treat multiple section 987 QBUs with the same functional currency owned directly, and indirectly through a section 987 partnership, as a single section 987 QBU.

(3) Definition of an eligible QBU. (i) In general. The term eligible QBU means activities of an individual, corporation, partnership, or an entity disregarded as an entity separate from its owner for U.S. Federal income tax purposes (DE), if—

(A) The activities constitute a trade or business as defined in § 1.989(a)-1(c);

(B) A separate set of books and records is maintained as defined in § 1.989(a)-1(d) with respect to the activities, and assets and liabilities used in conducting such activities are reflected on such books and records under § 1.987-2(b); and

(C) The activities are not subject to the Dollar Approximate Separate Transactions Method (DASTM) rules of § 1.985-3.

(ii) Exclusion of DEs and certain QBUs. A DE itself is not an eligible QBU (even though a DE may have activities that qualify as an eligible QBU). In addition, an eligible QBU shall include a QBU defined in § 1.989(a)-1(b) only if the requirements contained in paragraphs (b)(3)(i)(A) through (C) of this section are satisfied with respect to such QBU. Thus, for example, neither a corporation nor a partnership itself is an eligible QBU (even though a corporation and a partnership may have activities that qualify as an eligible QBU).

(4) Definition of the term "owner". For purposes of section 987, only an individual or corporation may be an owner of an eligible QBU. An individual or corporation is an owner of an eligible QBU if—

(i) Direct ownership. The individual or corporation is the tax owner of the assets and liabilities of an eligible QBU as defined in paragraph (b)(3) of this section; or

(ii) Indirect ownership. In the case of an individual or corporation that is a partner in a partnership, the individual or corporation is allocated, under § 1.987-7, all or a portion of the assets and liabilities of an eligible QBU of such partnership.

(5) Exception with respect to an eligible QBU or section 987 QBU of an owner. The term owner for section 987 purposes does not include an eligible QBU or a section 987 QBU of an owner. For example, a section 987 branch, as defined in paragraph (b)(6)(i) of this section is not an owner of another section 987 branch, regardless of its functional currency.

(6) Other definitions. Solely for purposes of section 987, the following definitions shall apply.

(i) Section 987 branch. A section 987 branch is an eligible QBU of an individual, partnership, DE, or corporation, all or a portion of which is a section 987 QBU. Assets and liabilities of an eligible QBU of a partnership that are allocated to a partner under § 1.987-7 are considered to be a section 987 QBU of such partner, provided such partner has a functional currency different from that of such eligible QBU.

(ii) Section 987 partnership. A section 987 partnership is a partnership that has one or more section 987 branches.

(iii) Section 987 DE. A section 987 DE is a DE that has one or more section 987 branches.

(7) Examples. The following examples illustrate the principles of paragraph (b) of this section. Except as otherwise provided, the following facts are assumed for purposes of these examples. X is a domestic corporation, has the U.S. dollar as its functional currency, and uses the calendar year as its taxable year. Business A and Business B are eligible QBUs, maintain books and records that are separate from the books and records of the entity that owns such eligible QBUs, and have the euro and the Japanese yen, respectively, as their functional currencies. Finally, DE1 and DE2 are entities that are disregarded as entities separate from their owner for U.S. tax purposes, have no assets or liabilities, and conduct no activities.

Example (1). (i) Facts. X owns Business A and the interests in DE1. DE1 maintains a separate set of books and records that are kept in British pounds. DE1 owns British pounds and 100% of the stock of a foreign corporation, FC. DE1 is liable on a pound-denominated obligation to a lender that was incurred to acquire the stock of FC. The FC stock, the pounds, and the liability incurred to acquire the FC stock are recorded on DE1's separate books and records. DE1 has no other assets or liabilities and conducts no activities (other than holding the FC stock and servicing its liability).

(ii) Analysis. (A) Pursuant to paragraph (b)(4)(i) of this section, X is the direct owner of Business A because it is the tax owner of the assets and liabilities of such business. Because Business A is an eligible QBU with a functional currency that is different from the functional currency of its owner, X; Business A is a section 987 QBU, as defined in paragraph (b)(2) of this section. As a result, X and its section 987 QBU, Business A, are subject to section 987.

(B) Holding the stock of FC and pounds, and servicing a single liability, does not constitute a trade or business within the meaning of § 1.989(a)-1(c). Because the activities of DE1 do not constitute a trade or business within the meaning of § 1.989(a)-1(c), such activities are not an eligible QBU. In addition, pursuant to paragraph (b)(3)(ii) of this section, DE1 is not an eligible QBU. As a result, neither DE1 nor its activities qualify as a section 987 QBU of X. Therefore, the activities of DE1 are not subject to section 987. For the foreign currency treatment of payments on DE1's pound-denominated liability, see §§ 1.987-2(b)(4) and 1.988-1(a)(4).

Example (2). (i) Facts. X owns the interests in DE1. DE1 owns Business A and the interests in DE2. The only activities of DE1 are Business A activities and holding the interests in DE2. DE2 owns Business B and Business C. For purposes of this example, Business B does not maintain books and records that are separate from its owner, DE2. Instead, the activities of Business B are reflected on the books and records of DE2, which are maintained in Japanese yen. In addition, Business C has the U.S. dollar as its functional currency, maintains books and records that are separate from the books and records of DE2, and is an eligible QBU.

(ii) Analysis.

(A) Pursuant to paragraph (b)(3)(ii) of this section, DE1 and DE2 are not eligible QBUs. Pursuant to paragraph (b)(3)(i) of this section, the Business B and Business C activities of DE2, and the Business A activities of DE1, are eligible QBUs. Moreover, pursuant to paragraph (b)(4) of this section, DE1 is not the owner of the Business A, Business B, or Business C eligible QBUs, and DE2 is not the owner of the Business B or Business C eligible QBUs. Instead, pursuant to paragraph (b)(4)(i) of this section, X is the direct owner of the Business A, Business B, and Business C eligible QBUs.

(B) Because Business A and Business B are eligible QBUs with functional currencies that are different than the functional currency of X, Business A and Business B are section 987 QBUs as defined in paragraph (b)(2) of this section. Therefore, X, and these QBUs, are subject to section 987. Under paragraph (b)(6)(iii) of this section, DE1 and DE2 are section 987 DEs.

(B) The Business C eligible QBU has the same functional currency as X. Therefore, the Business C eligible QBU is not a section 987 QBU. As a result, X is not subject to section 987 with respect to its Business C eligible QBU.

Example (3). (i) Facts. X owns DE1. DE1 owns Business A and Business B. For purposes of this example, assume Business B has the euro as its functional currency.

(ii) Analysis. (A) Pursuant to paragraph (b)(3)(ii) of this section, DE1 is not an eligible QBU. Moreover, pursuant to paragraph (b)(4) of this section, DE1 is not the owner of the Business A or Business B eligible QBUs. Instead, pursuant to paragraph (b)(4)(i) of this section, X is the direct owner of the Business A and Business B eligible QBUs.

(B) Business A and Business B constitute two separate eligible QBUs with the euro as their respective functional currency. Accordingly, Business A and Business B are section 987 QBUs of X. X may elect to treat Business A and Business B as a single section 987 QBU pursuant to paragraph (b)(2)(ii)(A) of this section. If such election is made, pursuant to paragraph (b)(4)(i) of this section, X is the direct owner of the Business AB section 987 QBU that includes the activities of both the Business A section 987 QBU and the Business B section 987 QBU. In addition, pursuant to paragraph (b)(4) of this section, DE1 is not treated as the owner of the Business AB section 987 QBU. X, and its AB section 987 QBU, are subject to section 987. Under paragraph (b)(6)(iii) of this section, DE1 is a section 987 DE.

Example (4). (i) Facts. X is a partner in P, a partnership. FC, a controlled foreign corporation (as defined in section 957(a)) of X with the Japanese yen as its functional currency, is the only other partner in P. P owns DE1 and Business A. DE1 owns Business B.

(ii) Analysis. (A) Pursuant to paragraph (b)(3)(ii) of this section, P and DE1 are not eligible section 987 QBUs. Moreover, pursuant to paragraph (b)(4) of this section, neither P nor DE1 is the owner of the Business A eligible QBU or the Business B eligible QBU for section 987 purposes. Instead, pursuant to paragraph (b)(4)(ii) of this section, X and FC are indirect owners of the Business A eligible QBU and the Business B eligible QBU to the extent they are allocated assets and liabilities of such businesses under § 1.987-7. Under paragraphs (b)(6)(ii) and (iii) of this section, respectively, P is a section 987 partnership and DE1 is a section 987 DE.

(B) Because Business A and Business B are eligible QBUs with a different functional currency than X, the portions of Business A and Business B allocated to X under § 1.987-7 are section 987 QBUs of X. As a result, X and its section 987 QBUs are subject to section 987.

(C) Because the Business A eligible QBU has a different functional currency than FC, the portion of the Business A eligible QBU that is allocated to FC under § 1.987-7 is a section 987 QBU, and FC and its section 987 QBU are subject to section 987. However, the Business B eligible QBU has the same functional currency as FC. Therefore, the portion of the Business B eligible QBU that is allocated to FC, under § 1.987-7, is not a section 987 QBU. As a result, FC is not subject to section 987 with respect to its Business B eligible QBU.

Example (5). (i) Facts. X owns all of the interests in DE1. DE1 owns Business A. DE1 owns all of the interests in DE2. DE2 owns Business B. DE2 owns all of the interests in DE3, an entity disregarded as an entity separate from its owner. DE3 owns Business C, which is an eligible QBU with the Russian ruble as its functional currency.

(ii) Analysis. Pursuant to (b)(3)(ii) of this section, DE1, DE2 and DE3 are not eligible QBUs. Pursuant to paragraph (b)(3)(i) of this section, the Business A, Business B and Business C activities are eligible QBUs. Moreover, pursuant to paragraph (b)(4) of this section, X is the direct owner of the Business A, Business B and Business C eligible QBUs. Pursuant to paragraph (b)(5) of this section, an eligible QBU is not an owner of another eligible QBU. Accordingly, the Business A eligible QBU is not the owner of the Business B eligible QBU, and the Business B eligible QBU is not the owner of the Business C eligible QBU. Since the Business A, Business B, and Business C eligible QBUs each has a different functional currency than X, such eligible QBUs are section 987 QBUs of X. As a result, X and its section 987 QBUs are subject to section 987. Under paragraphs (b)(6)(iii) of this section, DE1, DE2 and DE3 are section 987 DEs.

(c) Exchange rates. Solely for purposes of section 987, the following definitions shall apply.

(1) Spot rate.

(i) In general. Except as otherwise provided in this section, the spot rate means the rate determined under the principles of § 1.988-1(d)(1), (2) and (4) on the relevant day.

(ii) Election to use a spot rate convention. (A) In general. In lieu of the spot rate determined in paragraph (c)(1)(i) of this section, an owner may elect under paragraph (f) of this section to use a spot rate convention that reasonably approximates the rate in paragraph (c)(1)(i) of this section. A spot rate convention may be determined with respect to a rate at the beginning of a reasonable period, the end of a reasonable period, an average of spot rates for a reasonable period, or by reference to spot and forward rates for a reasonable period. For example, in lieu of the spot rate determined in paragraph (c)(1)(i) of this section, the spot rate for all transactions during a monthly period can be determined pursuant to the following conventions: the spot rate at the beginning of the current month or at the end of the preceding month; the monthly average of daily spot rates for the current or preceding month; or an average of the beginning and ending spot rates for the current or preceding month. Similarly, in lieu of the spot rate determined in paragraph (c)(1)(i) of this section, the spot rate can be determined pursuant to an average of the spot rate and the 30-day forward rate on a day of the preceding month. Use of a spot rate convention that is consistent with the owner's convention used for financial accounting purposes is presumed to reasonably approximate the rate in paragraph (c)(1)(i) of this section. The Commissioner can rebut this presumption if use of such a convention results in a significant distortion of income or loss under the facts and circumstances.

(B) Election does not apply with respect to section 988 transactions. The election to use a spot rate convention set forth in paragraph (c)(1)(ii)(A) of this section does not apply to section 988 transactions of a section 987 QBU.

(2) Yearly average exchange rate. Notwithstanding § 1.989(b)-1, for purposes of section 987, the yearly average exchange rate is a rate determined by the owner that represents an average exchange rate for the taxable year (or, if the section 987 QBU is sold or terminated prior to the close of the taxable year, such portion of the taxable year) computed under any reasonable method. For example, an owner may determine the yearly average exchange rate based on a daily, monthly or quarterly averaging convention, whether weighted or unweighted, and may take into account forward rates for a period not to exceed three months. The method for determining the yearly average exchange rate must be consistently applied by the taxpayer.

(3) Historic exchange rate. (i) In general. Except as otherwise provided in these regulations, the historic exchange rate shall be—

(A) In the case of an asset that is transferred to a section 987 QBU, the spot rate as defined in paragraphs (c)(1)(i) and (ii) of this section on the day of transfer;

(B) In the case of an asset that is acquired by a section 987 QBU (other than by a transfer to a section 987 QBU described in paragraph (c)(3)(i)(A) of this section), the spot rate as defined in paragraphs (c)(1)(i) and (ii) of this section on the day the asset is acquired;

(C) In the case of a liability that is entered into by a section 987 QBU, the spot rate as defined in paragraphs (c)(1)(i) and (ii) of this section on the day the liability is entered into; and

(D) In the case of a liability that is transferred to a section 987 QBU, the spot rate as defined in paragraphs (c)(1)(i) and (ii) of this section on the day the liability is transferred.

(ii) Changed functional currency. In the case of a section 987 QBU that previously changed its functional currency, § 1.985-5 shall be taken into account in determining the historic exchange rate for an item.

(d) Section 987 marked item. A section 987 marked item is an asset (section 987 marked asset) or liability (section 987 marked liability) that—

(1) Is reflected on the books and records of a section 987 QBU under § 1.987-2(b);

(2) Would be a section 988 transaction if such item were held or entered into directly by the owner of the section 987 QBU; and

(3) Is not a section 988 transaction with respect to the section 987 QBU.

(e) Section 987 historic item. *(1) In general.* A section 987 historic item is an asset (section 987 historic asset) or liability (section 987 historic liability) that--

(i) Is reflected on the books and records of a section 987 QBU under § 1.987-2(b); and

(ii) Is not a section 987 marked item as defined in paragraph (d) of this section.

(2) Example. The following example illustrates the application of paragraphs (d) and (e) of this section:

Example. X is a domestic corporation with the dollar as its functional currency. X owns all the interests in UK DE, a section 987 DE that owns a section 987 branch having the pound as its functional currency. Items reflected on the branch's balance sheet include £100 of cash, $25 of cash, a building with a basis of £1,000, a truck with a basis of £75, a computer with a basis of £10, a 60 day receivable for ¥15 and a note payable of £500. Under paragraph (d) of this section, the £100 of cash and the £500 note payable are section 987 marked items. The other items are section 987 historic items under this paragraph (e).

(f) Elections. *(1) In general.* Elections made under section 987 shall be treated as methods of accounting and, except as otherwise provided in this paragraph (f), are governed by the general rules concerning changes in methods of accounting.

(2) Persons making the election. (i) In general. Except as provided in paragraphs (f)(2)(ii) and (iii) of this section, elections regarding section 987 shall be made by the owner as defined in paragraph (b)(4) of this section.

(ii) Controlled foreign corporations. Where a section 987 QBU is held by a controlled foreign corporation, elections shall be made in accordance with §§ 1.952-2(c)(2)(iv) and 1.964-1(c) by its controlling U.S. shareholders.

(iii) Foreign corporations that are not controlled foreign corporations. Where a section 987 QBU is held by a foreign corporation that is not a controlled foreign corporation, elections shall be made in accordance with the principles of § 1.964-1(c) by the majority domestic corporate shareholders.

(3) When elections must be made. An election under section 987 must be made with respect to a section 987 QBU for the first taxable year in which the election is relevant in determining the section 987 taxable income or loss, or section 987 gain or loss, of the section 987 QBU.

(4) Manner of making elections. Elections shall be made under section 987 by attaching a statement to the timely filed tax return of the owner, or other applicable person, for

the first taxable year in which the owner intends the election to be effective. The statement must be dated and titled "Election(s) Under Section 987," must indicate the regulation section that authorizes the election(s), and must clearly describe the election(s) being made. Each section 987 election must remain a part of the books and records of the taxpayer and be available to the IRS upon request.

(5) Consent of the Commissioner. Elections made in accordance with the rules of this paragraph (f) shall be considered made with the consent of the Commissioner.

(6) Failure to make election. If an owner is permitted to file an election pursuant to this paragraph (f), but fails to make such election in a timely manner, the owner shall be considered to have satisfied the timeliness requirement with respect to such election if the owner is able to demonstrate to the Area Director, Field Examination, Small Business/Self Employed or the Director, Field Operations, Large and Mid-Size Business (Director) having jurisdiction of the taxpayer's return for the taxable year, that such failure was due to reasonable cause and not willful neglect. The previous sentence shall only apply if, once the owner becomes aware of the failure, the owner attaches the election, as well as a written statement setting forth the reasons for the failure to timely comply, to an amended income tax return that amends the return to which the election should have been attached under the rules of this paragraph (f). In determining whether the owner has reasonable cause, the Director shall consider whether the taxpayer acted reasonably and in good faith. Whether the taxpayer acted reasonably and in good faith will be determined after considering all the facts and circumstances. The Director shall notify the owner in writing within 120 days of the filing if it is determined that the failure to comply was not due to reasonable cause, or if additional time will be needed to make such determination. If the Director fails to notify the owner within 120 days of the filing, the owner shall be considered to have demonstrated to the Director that such failure was due to reasonable cause and not willful neglect.

(7) Revocation of election. (i) In general. Elections under section 987 cannot be revoked without the consent of the Commissioner. The Commissioner will consider allowing the revocation of an election if the taxpayer can demonstrate significantly changed circumstance or such other circumstances that in the judgment of the Commissioner clearly demonstrates a substantial non-tax business reason for revoking the election.

(ii) Exception in the case of certain acquisitions. [Reserved].

§ 1.987-2 Accounting for gain or loss on certain transfers of property. [Reserved]

Proposed § 1.987-2 Attribution of items to a section 987 QBU; the definition of a transfer and related rules. [*For Preamble, see ¶ 152,801*]

(a) Scope and general principles. Paragraph (b) of this section provides rules for attributing assets and liabilities, and items of income, gain, deduction, and loss, to an eligible QBU and a section 987 QBU. Assets and liabilities are attributed to an eligible QBU, all or a portion of which is a section 987 QBU for purposes of section 987. Items of income, gain, deduction, and loss are attributed to an eligible QBU all or a portion of which is a section 987 QBU for purposes of computing the section 987 taxable income of such section 987 QBU, and of the owner of such section 987 QBU. Paragraph (c) of this section defines a transfer for purposes of section 987. Paragraph (d) of this section provides translation rules for transfers to a section 987 QBU.

(b) Attribution of items to an eligible QBU. *(1) General rules.* Except as provided in paragraphs (b)(2) and (3) of this section, items are attributable to an eligible QBU to the extent they are reflected on the separate set of books and records, as defined in § 1.989(a)-1(d), of the eligible QBU. For purposes of this section, the term "item" refers to assets and liabilities, and items of income, gain, deduction, and loss. Items that are attributed to an eligible QBU pursuant to this section must be adjusted to conform to U.S. tax principles as provided in § 1.987-4(e). These attribution rules apply solely for purposes of section 987. For example, the allocation and apportionment of interest expense under section 864(e) is independent of the rules under section 987.

(2) Exceptions for non-portfolio stock, interests in partnerships, and certain acquisition indebtedness. (i) General rule. Except as provided in paragraph (b)(2)(ii) of this section, the following shall not be considered to be on the books and records of a an eligible QBU:

(A) Stock of a corporation (whether domestic or foreign).

(B) An interest in a partnership (whether domestic or foreign).

(C) A liability that was incurred to acquire the stock or an interest in a partnership described in paragraphs (b)(2)(i)(A) or (B) of this section, respectively.

(D) Income, gain, deduction, or loss arising from the items described in paragraphs (b)(2)(i)(A) through (C) of this section. For example, a section 951 inclusion with respect to stock of a foreign corporation that is described in paragraph (b)(2)(i)(A) of this section shall not be considered to be on the books and records of the eligible QBU.

(ii) Portfolio stock. Paragraph (b)(2)(i)(A) of this section shall not apply to stock of a corporation (whether domestic or foreign) reflected on the books and records, within the meaning of paragraph (b)(1) of this section, of an eligible QBU provided the owner of the eligible QBU owns less than 10 percent of the total voting power or value of all classes of stock of such corporation. For purposes of this paragraph (b)(2)(ii), section 318(a) shall be applied in determining ownership, except that in applying section 318(a)(2)(C), the phrase "10 percent" is used instead of the phrase "50 percent."

(3) Adjustments to items reflected on the books and records. (i) General rule. If a principal purpose of recording (or failing to record) an item on the books and records of an eligible QBU is the avoidance of U.S. tax under section 987, the Commissioner may allocate any item between or among the eligible QBU, the owner of such eligible QBU, and any other persons, entities (including disregarded entities), or other QBUs within the meaning of § 1.989(a)-1(b) (including eligible QBUs). A transaction may have such a principal purpose even though the tax avoidance purpose is outweighed by other purposes when taken together. For purposes of this paragraph (b)(3)(i), relevant factors for determining whether such U.S. tax avoidance is a principal purpose of recording (or failing to record) an item on the books and records of an eligible QBU shall include, but are not limited to, the factors set forth in paragraphs (b)(3)(ii) and (iii) of this section. The presence or absence of any factor, or of a particular number of factors, is not determinative. Moreover, the weight given to any factor (whether or not set forth in paragraphs (b)(3)(ii) and (iii) of this section) depends on the particular case.

(ii) Factors indicating no tax avoidance. For purposes of paragraph (b)(3)(i) of this section, relevant factors which may indicate that the recording (or failing to record) an item on the books and records of an eligible QBU does not have as a principal purpose the avoidance of U.S. tax under section 987 include the recording (or not recording) of an item:

(A) For a significant and bona fide business purpose.

(B) In a manner that is consistent with the economics of the underlying transaction.

(C) In accordance with generally accepted accounting principles (or similar comprehensive body of professional accounting standards).

(D) In a manner that is consistent with the treatment of similar items from year to year.

(E) In accordance with accepted conditions or practices in the particular trade or business of the eligible QBU.

(F) In a manner that is consistent with an explanation of existing internal accounting policies that is evidenced by documentation contemporaneous with the timely filing of a return for the taxable year.

(G) As a result of a transaction between legal entities (that is, the transfer of an asset, or the assumption of a liability), even if such transaction is not regarded for Federal tax purposes (that is, a transaction between a DE and its owner).

(iii) Factors indicating tax avoidance. For purposes of paragraph (b)(3)(i) of this section, relevant factors which may indicate that a principal purpose of recording (or failing to record) an item on the books and records of an eligible QBU is the avoidance of U.S. tax under section 987 are--

(A) The presence or absence of an item on the books and records that is disregarded as transitory due to a circular flow of cash or other property;

(B) The presence or absence of an item on the books and records that is the result of one or more transactions that do not have economic substance;

(C) The presence or absence of an item on the books and records that results in the taxpayer (or person related to the taxpayer as defined in section 267(b) or 707(b)) having offsetting positions in the functional currency of a section 987 QBU; and

(D) The absence of any or all of the factors listed in paragraphs (b)(3)(ii)(A) through (E) of this section.

(4) Assets and liabilities of a partnership or DE that are not attributed to an eligible QBU. Neither a partnership nor a DE is an eligible QBU and, thus, cannot be a section 987 QBU. See § 1.987-1(b)(2) and (3). As a result, a partnership or DE may own assets and liabilities that are not attributed to an eligible QBU (or a section 987 QBU) as provided under this paragraph (b) and, therefore, are not subject to section 987. For the foreign currency treatment of such assets or liabilities, see § 1.988-1(a)(4).

(c) Transfers to and from section 987 QBUs. *(1) In general.* The following rules apply for purposes of determining whether there is a transfer of an asset or a liability from the owner to a section 987 QBU, or from such section 987 QBU to the owner. These rules apply solely for purposes of section 987.

(2) Disregarded transactions. (i) General rule. Solely for purposes of section 987, an asset or liability shall be treated as transferred to a section 987 QBU if, as a result of a disregarded transaction, such asset or liability is reflected on the books and records of the section 987 QBU within the meaning of paragraph (b) of this section. Similarly, an asset or liability shall be treated as transferred from a section 987 QBU if, as a result of a disregarded transaction, such asset or liability is not reflected on the books and records of the section 987 QBU within the meaning of paragraph (b) of this section.

(ii) Definition of a disregarded transaction. For purposes of this section, the term disregarded transaction means a transaction that is not regarded for U.S. Federal tax purposes. For purposes of this paragraph (c), a disregarded transaction shall be treated as including the recording of an asset or liability on one set of books and records, if the recording is the result of such asset or liability being removed from another set of books and records of the same person or entity (including a DE or partnership).

(iii) Items derived from disregarded transactions ignored. For purposes of section 987, disregarded transactions shall not give rise to items of income, gain, deduction, or loss that must be taken into account in determining section 987 taxable income or loss under § 1.987-3.

(3) Transfers of assets to and from indirectly owned section 987 QBUs. (i) Contributions to partnerships. Solely for purposes of section 987, an asset shall be treated as transferred to an indirectly owned section 987 QBU if, and to the extent, the asset is contributed to the section 987 partnership that carries on the section 987 QBU provided that immediately following such contribution, the asset is reflected on the books and records of the section 987 QBU within the meaning of paragraph (b) of this section. For purposes of this paragraph (c)(3)(i), deemed contributions under section 752 shall be disregarded.

(ii) Distributions from partnerships. Solely for purposes of section 987, an asset shall be treated as transferred from an indirectly owned section 987 QBU if, and to the extent, the section 987 partnership that carries on the section 987 QBU distributes the asset to a partner provided that, immediately prior to such distribution, the asset was reflected on the books and records of such section 987 QBU within the meaning of paragraph (b) of this section. For purposes of this paragraph (c)(3)(ii), deemed distributions under section 752 shall be disregarded.

(4) Transfers of liabilities to and from indirectly owned section 987 QBUs. (i) Assumptions of partner liabilities. Solely for purposes of section 987, a liability shall be treated as transferred to an indirectly owned section 987 QBU if, and to the extent, the section 987 partnership assumes such liability, provided that immediately following such assumption, the liability is reflected on the books and records of the section 987 QBU within the meaning of paragraph (b) of this section.

(ii) Assumptions of partnership liabilities. Solely for purposes of section 987, a liability shall be treated as transferred from an indirectly owned section 987 QBU if, and to the extent, the owner assumes such liability of the section 987 partnership provided that immediately prior to such assumption, the liability was reflected on the books and records of the section 987 QBU within the meaning of paragraph (b) of this section.

(5) Acquisitions and dispositions of interests in DEs and partnerships. Solely for purposes of section 987, an asset or liability shall be treated as transferred to a section 987 QBU if, as a result of an acquisition (including by contribution) or disposition of an interest in a section 987 partnership or section 987 DE, such asset or liability is reflected on the books and records of the section 987 QBU. Similarly, an asset or liability shall be treated as transferred from a section 987

QBU if, as a result of an acquisition or disposition of an interest in a section 987 partnership or section 987 DE, the asset or liability is not reflected on the books and records of the section 987 QBU.

(6) Changes in form of ownership. For purposes of this paragraph (c), mere changes in form of ownership of an eligible QBU shall not result in a transfer to or from a section 987 QBU. Instead, the determination of whether a transfer has occurred in such case shall be made under paragraph (c)(5) of this section. For example, a transaction with respect to an eligible QBU that causes a direct owner of the eligible QBU to become an indirect owner of such eligible QBU, shall not, except to the extent provided in paragraph (c)(5) of this section, result in a transfer to or from a section 987 QBU. See for example, Rev. Rul. 99-5 (1999-1 CB 434), Rev. Rul. 99-6 (1999-1 CB 432), see § 601.601(d)(2) of this chapter, and section 708 and the applicable regulations.

(7) Application of general tax law principles. General tax law principles, including the circular cash flow, step-transaction, and substance-over-form doctrines, apply for purposes of determining whether there is a transfer of an asset or liability under this paragraph (c).

(8) Interaction with § 1.988-1(a)(10). See § 1.988-1(a)(10) for rules regarding the treatment of an intra-taxpayer transfer of a section 988 transaction.

(9) Examples. The following examples illustrate the principles of paragraph (b) of this section and this paragraph (c). For purposes of these examples, it is assumed that X and Y are domestic corporations, have the dollar as their functional currency, and use the calendar year as their taxable year. It is also assumed that Business A and Business B are eligible QBUs, maintain books and records that are separate from the books and records of the entity that owns such eligible QBUs, and have the euro and the yen, respectively, as their functional currencies. Finally, it is assumed that DE1 and DE2 are entities that are disregarded as entities separate from their owner for U.S. tax purposes. For purposes of determining whether any of the transfers in these examples result in remittances, see § 1.987-5.

Example (1). Transfer to a directly owned section 987 QBU. (i) Facts. X owns 100 percent of the interests in DE1. DE1 owns Business A. X owns £100 that are not reflected on the books and records of Business A. Business A is in need of additional capital and, as a result, X loans the £100 to DE1 (to be used in Business A) in exchange for a note.

(ii) Analysis. (A) The loan from X to DE1 is not regarded for U.S. federal tax purposes and therefore is a disregarded transaction. As a result, the Business A note held by X, and the liability of DE1 under the note, are not taken into account under this section. However, the £100 of cash that was loaned from X to DE1 (and used in Business A) pursuant to the note must be taken into account under this paragraph (c).

(B) The loan of [euro]100 from X to DE1 is a disregarded transaction and, as a result of such disregarded transaction, the [euro]100 is reflected on the books and records of Business A. Therefore, there has been a transfer of [euro]100 from X to Business A. See § 1.988-1(a)(10)(ii) for the application of section 988 to X as a result of the disregarded loan.

Example (2). Transfer to a directly owned section 987 QBU. (i) Facts. X owns Business A and Business B. X owns equipment that is used in Business A and is reflected on the books and records of Business A. Because Business A has excess manufacturing capacity and X intends to expand the manufacturing capacity of Business B, the equipment formerly used in Business A discontinues being used in Business A and begins being used in Business B. As a result of such equipment being used by Business B, the equipment is removed from the books and records of Business A, and is recorded on the books and records of Business B.

(ii) Analysis. As a result of Business B using the equipment formerly used by Business A, the equipment ceases to be reflected on the books and records of Business A, and becomes reflected on the books and records of Business B. As a result, such entries constitute a disregarded transaction. Therefore, there has been a transfer of the equipment from the Business A section 987 QBU to X, and a transfer by X of such equipment to the Business B section 987 QBU.

Example (3). Intercompany sale of property between two section 987 QBUs. (i) Facts. X owns DE1 and DE2. DE1 and DE2 own Business A and Business B, respectively. DE1 owns equipment that is used in Business A and is reflected on the books and records of Business A. For business reasons, DE1 sells a portion of the equipment used in Business A to DE2 for cash. The cash used by DE2 to acquire the equipment was generated by Business B and was reflected on Business B's books and records. Following the sale, the cash and equipment will be used in Business A and Business B, respectively. As a result of such sale, the equipment is removed from the books and records of Business A, and is recorded on the books and records of Business B. Similarly, as a result of the sale, the cash is removed from the books and records of Business B, and is recorded on the books and records of Business A.

(ii) Analysis.

(A) The sale of equipment between DE1 and DE2 is not regarded for Federal income tax purposes and therefore is a disregarded transaction. As a result, such sale is not taken into account under this section and does not give rise to an item of income, gain, deduction or loss pursuant to paragraph (c)(2)(iii) of this section. However, the cash and equipment exchanged by DE1 and DE2 in connection with the sale must be taken into account under this paragraph (c).

(B) The sale of the equipment is a disregarded transaction and, as a result of such disregarded transaction, the equipment ceases to be reflected on the books and records of Business A, and becomes reflected on the books and records of Business B. Therefore, there has been a transfer of the equipment from DE1's Business A section 987 QBU owned by X to X, and a subsequent transfer of such equipment from X to DE2's Business B section 987 QBU, owned by X.

(C) As a result of the sale of equipment (that is, the disregarded transaction), the cash proceeds cease to be reflected on the books and records of Business B, and become reflected on the books and records of Business A. Therefore, there has been a transfer of the cash from DE2's Business B section 987 QBU owned by X to X, and a subsequent transfer of such cash from X to DE1's Business A section 987 QBU, owned by X.

Example (4). Transactions between directly and indirectly owned section 987 QBUs. (i) Facts. X owns 50% of the interest in P, a partnership. Y owns the other 50% interest in P. P owns 100% of the interests in DE1 and DE2. DE1 owns Business A and DE2 owns Business B. X and Y each have a 50% allocable share of the assets and liabilities of Business A and Business B, as determined under § 1.987-7, that constitute section 987 QBUs. In connection with Business A, DE1 licenses intangible property to both DE2 and X. X enters into the license agreement in a transaction other than in its capacity as a partner of P and, therefore, the license is considered as occurring between P and one who is not a partner within the meaning of section 707(a). DE2 uses the intangible property in Business B. Pursuant to the license agreement, X and DE2 pay a [euro]30 and [euro]50 royalty, respectively, to DE1.

(ii) Analysis. (A) The license from DE2 to DE1 is not regarded for U.S. tax purposes and, as a result, royalty payments under the license are disregarded transactions. Thus, neither the payment nor the receipt of the royalty pursuant to the license agreement gives rise to an item of income, gain, deduction or loss pursuant to paragraph (c)(2)(iii) of this section. However, the [euro]50 of cash that is paid from DE2 to DE1 pursuant to the license agreement must be taken into account under this paragraph (c).

(B) As a result of the royalty payment from DE2 to DE1, [euro]50 ceases being reflected on the books and records of Business B, and becomes reflected on the books and records of Business A. Accordingly, there has been a transfer of [euro]25 from the Business B section 987 QBUs of X and Y, to X and Y, respectively. Similarly, there has been a transfer of [euro]25 from X and Y to their respective Business A section 987 QBUs.

(C) The [euro]30 royalty payment from X to DE1 is not a disregarded transaction because it is regarded for U.S. Federal income tax purposes. As a result, it gives rise to an item of income and deduction that must be taken into account in computing taxable income or loss of Business A pursuant to § 1.987-3. In addition, the payment does not give rise to a transfer as defined in this paragraph (c).

Example (5). Acquisition of an interest in a partnership. (i) Facts. X owns 50% of the interest in P, a partnership. Y owns the other 50% interest in P. P owns Business A. X and Y each have a 50% allocable share of the assets and liabilities of Business A as determined under § 1.987-7, that constitute section 987 QBUs. On December 31, year 1, Z, a domestic corporation with the dollar as its functional currency, contributes cash to P in exchange for a 20% interest in P. The cash Z contributes to P is not used in Business A and is not reflected on Business A's books and records (but is instead reflected on P's books and records). Immediately after Z's contribution of cash to P, Z has a 20% allocable share of the assets and liabilities of Business A as determined under § 1.987-7. In addition, immediately following such contribution X and Y each own a 40% interest in P and have a 40% allocable share of the assets and liabilities of Business A, as determined under § 1.987-7, that constitute section 987 QBUs.

(ii) Analysis. (A) As a result of Z's acquisition of an interest in P, a section 987 partnership, 10% of the assets and liabilities of Business A ceased being reflected on the books and records of both X's and Y's section 987 QBUs. As a result, such amounts are treated as if they are transferred from such section 987 QBUs to X and Y.

(B) As a result of Z's acquisition of the interest in P, a section 987 partnership, Z was allocated 20% of the assets and liabilities of Business A. Because Z and Business A have different functional currencies, Z's portion of the Business A assets and liabilities constitutes a section 987 QBU. Moreover, 20% of the assets and liabilities of Business A are reflected on the books and records of Z's section 987 QBU as a result of Z's acquisition of the interest in P. Therefore, 20% of the assets and liabilities of Business A are treated as transferred from Z to Z's section 987 QBU.

Example (6). Conversion of a DE to a partnership through a sale of an interest. (i) Facts. X owns 100% of the interests in DE1. DE1 owns Business A. On December 31, year 1, Y acquires 50% of the DE1 interests from X for cash. Immediately after such acquisition, Y has a 50% allocable share of the assets and liabilities of Business A as determined under § 1.987-7.

(ii) Analysis. (A) For Federal tax purposes DE1 is converted to a partnership when Y purchases the 50% interest in DE1. Y's purchase of 50% of X's interest in DE1 is treated as the purchase of 50% of Business A, which is treated as held directly by X for Federal tax purposes. Immediately after the deemed purchase of 50% of Business A, X and Y are treated as contributing their respective interests in Business A to a partnership. See Rev. Rul. 99-5 (situation 1), (1999-1 CB 434). See § 601.601(d)(2) of this chapter. For purposes of this paragraph (c), these deemed transactions are not taken into account.

(B) As a result of Y's acquisition of 50% of X's interest in DE1, a section 987 DE, 50% of the assets and liabilities of Business A ceased being reflected on the books and records of X's section 987 QBU. As a result, such amounts are treated as if they are transferred from X's section 987 QBU to X.

(C) As a result of Y's acquisition of 50% of the interest in DE1, a section 987 DE, Y was allocated 50% of the assets and liabilities of Business A. Because Y and Business A have different functional currencies, Y's portion of the Business A assets and liabilities constitutes a section 987 QBU. Moreover, 50% of the assets and liabilities of Business A are reflected on the books and records of Y's section 987 QBU as a result of Y's acquisition of the 50% interest in DE1. Therefore, 50% of the assets and liabilities of Business A are treated as transferred by Y to Y's section 987 QBU.

Example (7). Conversion of a DE to a partnership through a contribution. (i) Facts. X owns 100% of the interests in DE1. DE1 owns Business A. On December 31, year 1, Y contributes property to DE1 in exchange for an interest in DE1. The property transferred by Y to DE1 is used in Business A and is reflected on the books and records of Business A. Immediately after such contribution, X and Y each have a 50% allocable share of the assets and liabilities of Business A as determined under § 1.987-7.

(ii) Analysis. (A) For Federal income tax purposes DE1 is converted to a partnership when Y contributes property to DE1 in exchange for a 50% interest in DE1. Y's contribution is treated as a contribution to a partnership in exchange for an ownership interest in the partnership. X is treated as contributing all of Business A to the partnership in exchange for a partnership interest. See Rev. Rul. 99-5 (situation 2), (1999-1 CB 434). See § 601.601(d)(2) of this chapter. For purposes of this paragraph (c), these deemed transactions are not taken into account.

(B) As a result of Y's acquisition of a 50% interest in DE1, 50% of the assets and liabilities of Business A ceased being reflected on the books and records of X's section 987 QBU, and 50% of the assets contributed by Y to DE1 are reflected on the books and records of such section 987 QBU. As a result, 50% of the Business A assets are treated as if they are transferred from X's section 987 QBU to X. Further, 50% of the assets contributed by Y to DE1 are treated as if they are transferred by X to X's section 987 QBU.

(C) Because Y and Business A have different functional currencies, Y's portion of the Business A assets and liabilities (including the property contributed by Y that is used in Business A) constitutes a section 987 QBU. As a result of Y's acquisition of a 50% interest in DE1, 50% of the assets and liabilities of Business A are reflected on the books and records of Y's section 987 QBU and, therefore, are treated as if they are transferred by Y to such section 987 QBU.

Example (8). Termination of a partnership under section 708(b). (i) Facts. X owns 60% of the interest in P, a partnership. Y owns the other 40% interest in P. P owns Business A. X and Y have a 60% and 40% allocable share of the assets and liabilities of Business A, respectively, as determined under § 1.987-7, that constitute section 987 QBUs. On December 31, year 1, X sells a 50% interest in P to Y. After such sale, X and Y own 10% and 90%, respectively, in P. In addition, after such sale, X and Y have a 10% and 90% allocable share of the assets and liabilities of Business A, respectively, as determined under § 1.987-7.

(ii) Analysis. (A) X's sale of 50% of the interests in P to Y causes P to terminate pursuant to section 708(b). As a result of such termination, P is treated as if it contributes all of its assets and liabilities to a new partnership in exchange for an interest in the new partnership; and, immediately thereafter, P distributes 10% and 90% of the interests in the new partnership to X and Y, respectively, in liquidation of P. See § 1.708-1(b)(4). For purposes of this paragraph (c), these deemed transactions are not taken into account.

(B) As a result of Y's acquisition of a 50% interest in P from X, 50% of the assets and liabilities of Business A ceased being reflected on the books and records of X's section 987 QBU and become reflected on the books and records of Y's section 987 QBU. As a result, 50% of the Business A assets are treated as if they are transferred from X's section 987 QBU to X. Further, 50% of the Business A assets are treated as if they are transferred by Y to Y's section 987 QBU.

Example (9). Transfer of section 987 QBU to a partnership. (i) Facts. X owns Business A. On December 31, year 1, X and Y form P, a partnership. X transfers Business A to P in exchange for a 50% interest in P. Y transfers property to P in exchange for the other 50% interest in P. The property Y transfers to P is not used in Business A and is not reflected on the books and records of Business A (but is instead reflected on the books and records of P). After the formation of P, Business A continues to be an eligible QBU. In addition, after the formation of P, X and Y each have a 50% allocable share of the assets and liabilities of Business A, respectively, as determined under § 1.987-7.

(ii) Analysis. As a result of X contributing Business A to P, 50% of the assets and liabilities of Business A ceased being reflected on the books and records of X's section 987 QBU, and became reflected on the books and records of Y's section 987 QBU. As a result, 50% of the Business A assets are treated as if they are transferred from X's section 987 QBU to X. Further, 50% of the Business A assets are treated as if they are transferred from Y to Y's section 987 QBU.

Example (10). Contribution of assets to a corporation. (i) Facts. X owns Business A. On December 31, year 1, X forms Z, a domestic corporation. X and Z do not file a consolidated tax return. X contributes 50% of its Business A assets and liabilities to Z in exchange for 100% of the stock of Z. The Z stock is recorded on the books and records of Business A. After the contribution, X continues to operate Business A, and Business A continues to maintain separate books and records from X.

(ii) Analysis. Even though the Z stock is recorded on the books and records of Business A, it is not reflected on the books and records for purposes of section 987 pursuant to paragraph (b)(2) of this section. As a result, there has been a transfer of 50% of the assets and liabilities of Business A to X, and a subsequent transfer of such assets and liabilities to Z. The answer would be the same even if X and Z filed a consolidated return.

Example (11). Transfers pursuant to general tax principles. (i) Facts. X owns 100 percent of the stock of Y. Y owns 100 percent of the interests in DE1. DE1 owns Business A. X owns [euro]100. Because Business A is in need of additional capital, X transfers the [euro]100 to Y as a contribution to capital and, as a result of such transfer, Business A records [euro]100 on its separate books and records. Y did not record the [euro]100 on its separate books and records.

(ii) Analysis. As a result of the contribution of [euro]100 from X to Y, the [euro]100 is reflected on the books and records of Business A. Pursuant to paragraph (c)(7) of this section, the [euro]100 is treated as if it was transferred first from X to Y. Therefore, the [euro]100 recorded on the books and records of Business A is treated as a transfer from Y to Business A, even though there was no transaction between Y and Business A. See also § 1.988-1(a)(10)(ii) for the application of section 988 to Y as a result of the transaction.

Example (12). Circular transfers. (i) Facts. X owns Business A. On December 30, year 1, Business A purports to transfer [euro]100 to X. On January 2, year 2, X purports to transfer [euro]50 to Business A. On January 4, year 2, X purports to transfer another [euro]50 to Business A. As of the end of year 1, X has an unrecognized section 987 loss with respect to Business A, such that a remittance, if respected, would result in recognition of a foreign currency loss under section 987.

(ii) Analysis. Because the transfers by Business A are offset by a transfer from X that occurred in close temporal proximity, pursuant to paragraph (c) of this section, the IRS will scrutinize the transaction and may disregard the purported transfers to and from Business A for purposes of section 987.

Example (13). Transfers without economic substance. (i) Facts. X owns Business A and Business B. On January 1, year 1, Business A purports to transfer [euro]100 to X. On January 4, year 1, X purports to transfer [euro]100 to Business B. The account in which Business B deposited the [euro]100 is used to pay the operating expenses and other costs of Business A. As of the end of year 1, X has an unrecognized section 987 loss with respect to Business A, such that a remittance, if respected, would result in recognition of a foreign currency loss under section 987.

(ii) Analysis. Because Business A continues to have use of the transferred property, pursuant to paragraph (c) of this section, the IRS will scrutinize the transaction and may disregard the [euro]100 purported transfer from Business A to X for purposes of section 987.

Example (14). Offsetting positions in section 987 QBUs. (i) Facts. X owns Business A and Business B. Business A and Business B each has the euro as its functional currency. X has not made a grouping election under § 1.987-1(b)(2)(ii). On January 1, year 1, X borrowed [euro]1,000 from a third party lender, recorded the liability with respect to the borrowing on the books and records of Business A, and recorded the [euro]1,000 of borrowed cash on the books and records of Business B. On December 31, year 2, when Business A has $100 of net unrecognized section 987 loss and Business B has $100 of net unrecognized section 987 gain resulting from the change in exchange rates with respect to the liability and the [euro]1,000 cash, X terminates the Business A section 987 QBU.

(ii) Analysis. Because Business A and Business B have offsetting positions in the euro, the IRS will scrutinize the transaction to determine if a principal purpose of recording the euro-denominated liability and the borrowed euros on the books and records of Business A and Business B, respectively, was the avoidance of tax under section 987. If such a principal purpose is present, the Commissioner may reallocate the items (that is, the euros and the euro-denominated liability) between Business A, Business B, and X, to reflect the economic substance of the transaction.

Example (15). Offsetting positions with respect to a section 987 QBU and a section 988 transaction. (i) Facts. X owns DE1, and DE1 owns Business A. On January 1, year 1, X borrows [euro]1,000 from a third party lender and records the liability with respect to the borrowing on its books and records. X contributes the [euro]1,000 loan proceeds to DE1 and the [euro]1,000 are reflected on the books and records of Business A. On December 31, year 2, when Business A has $100 of net unrecognized section 987 loss resulting from the [euro]1,000 cash received from the borrowing, and the euro-denominated borrowing, if repaid, would result in $100 of gain under section 988, X terminates the Business A section 987 QBU.

(ii) Analysis. Because X and Business A have offsetting positions in the euro, the Internal Revenue Service will scrutinize the transaction to determine whether a principal purpose of recording the borrowed euros on the books and records of Business A, or not recording the corresponding euro-denominated liability on the books and records of Business A, was the avoidance of tax under section 987. If such a principal purpose is present, the Commissioner may reallocate the items (that is, the euros and the euro-denominated liability) between Business A and X to reflect the economic substance of the transaction.

(d) Translation of items transferred to a section 987 QBU. *(1) In general.* (i) Assets. Except as otherwise provided in this section, the adjusted basis of an asset transferred to a section 987 QBU shall be translated into the section 987 QBU's functional currency at the spot rate as defined in § 1.987-1(c)(1)(i) and (ii) on the day of transfer. If the asset transferred is denominated in (or determined by reference to) the functional currency of the section 987 QBU (for example, cash or note denominated in the functional currency of the section 987 QBU), no translation is required.

(ii) Liabilities. Except as otherwise provided in this section, a liability of the owner that is transferred to a section 987 QBU, shall be translated into the section 987 QBU's functional currency at the spot rate (as defined in § 1.987-1(c)(1)(i) and (ii)) on the day of transfer. If the liability transferred is denominated in (or determined by reference to) the functional currency of the section 987 QBU, no translation is required.

(2) Items denominated in the owner's functional currency. Transactions described in section 988(c)(1)(B)(i) and (ii) and section 988(c)(1)(C) that are denominated in (or determined by reference to) the owner's functional currency and that are attributable to a section 987 QBU under paragraph (b) of this section, shall not be translated and shall be carried on the balance sheet described in § 1.987-4(e) in the owner's functional currency.

§ 1.987-3 Termination. [Reserved]

Proposed § 1.987-3 Determination of section 987 taxable income or loss of an owner of a section 987 QBU. [*For Preamble, see ¶ 152,801*]

(a) Determination of the section 987 taxable income or loss of an owner of a section 987 QBU. Except as otherwise provided in this section, the section 987 taxable income or loss of an owner with respect to a section 987 QBU shall be determined in accordance with paragraphs (a)(1) and (a)(2) of this section.

(1) In general. (i) Determination of each item of income, gain, deduction or loss in the section 987 QBU's functional currency. Except as otherwise provided in this section, the section 987 QBU shall determine each item of income, gain, deduction or loss attributable to such QBU under § 1.987-2(b) in its functional currency under U.S. tax principles.

(ii) Translation of items into the owner's functional currency. The owner shall translate each item determined under this paragraph (a)(1) into its functional currency as provided in paragraph (b) of this section.

(2) Determination in the case of a section 987 QBU owned indirectly through a partnership. (i) In general. Except as otherwise provided in this paragraph (a)(2), the taxable income or loss of a section 987 partnership, and the distributive share of any owner that is a partner in such partnership, shall be determined in accordance with the provisions of subchapter K of this chapter.

(ii) Determination of each item of income, gain, deduction or loss in the eligible QBU's functional currency. Except as otherwise provided in this section, the section 987 partnership shall determine each item of income, gain, deduction or loss reflected on the books and records of each of its eligible QBUs under § 1.987-2(b) in the functional currency of each such QBU.

(iii) Allocation of items of income, gain, deduction or loss of an eligible QBU. The section 987 partnership shall allocate the items of income, gain, deduction or loss of each eligible QBU among its partners in accordance with each partner's distributive share of such income, gain, deduction, or loss as determined under subchapter K of this chapter.

(iv) Translation of items into the owner's functional currency. To the extent such items are reflected on the books and records of a section 987 QBU of a partner to whom they are allocated, the partner shall adjust the items to conform to U.S. tax principles and translate the items into the partner's functional currency as provided in paragraph (b) of this section.

(b) Exchange rates to be used in translating items of income, gain, deduction or loss of a section 987 QBU into the owner's functional currency. *(1) In general.* Except as otherwise provided in this section, the exchange rate to be used by an owner in translating an item of income, gain, deduction, or loss of a section 987 QBU as determined in § 1.987-2(b) into the owner's functional currency shall be the yearly average exchange rate as defined in § 1.987-1(c)(2) for the taxable year. Alternatively, the owner may elect under § 1.987-1(f) to use the spot rate as defined in § 1.987-1(c)(1)(i) and (ii) for the day each item is properly taken into account.

(2) Exceptions. (i) Depreciation, depletion, and amortization deductions. The exchange rate to be used by the owner in translating deductions allowable with respect to section 987 historic assets (as defined in § 1.987-1(e)) for depreciation, depletion, and amortization under the pertinent provisions of the Code shall be the historic exchange rate as determined under § 1.987-1(c)(3) for the property to which such deductions are attributable.

(ii) Gain or loss from the sale of property. In the case of gain or loss recognized on a sale or other disposition of property that is reflected on the books and records of a section 987 QBU during the taxable year, the following exchange rates shall apply with respect to such sale or other disposition:

(A) Amount realized. (1) In general. Except as otherwise provided in paragraph (b)(2)(ii)(A)(2), the exchange rate to be used in translating the amount realized of such property shall be the rate provided in paragraph (b)(1) of this section for the taxable year.

(2) Certain section 987 marked assets. In the case of a section 987 marked asset (other than cash) that was held on the first day of the taxable year, the exchange rate to be used in translating the amount realized shall be the rate used for such asset in determining the owner functional currency net value of the section 987 QBU under § 1.987-4(d)(1)(i)(B) for the preceding taxable year. However, in the case of a section 987 marked asset (other than cash) transferred to the section 987 QBU or acquired by the section 987 QBU during the taxable year, the exchange rate to be used in translating the amount realized shall be the spot rate, as defined in § 1.987-1(c)(1)(i) and (ii), for the day transferred or acquired.

(B) Adjusted basis. (1) In general. Except as otherwise provided in paragraph (b)(2)(ii)(B)(2), the exchange rate to be used in translating the adjusted basis of such property shall be the historic exchange rate as determined under § 1.987-1(c)(3) for such asset.

(2) Certain section 987 marked assets. In the case of a section 987 marked asset (other than cash) that was held on the first day of the taxable year, the exchange rate to be used in translating its adjusted basis shall be the rate used for such asset in determining the owner functional currency net value of the section 987 QBU under § 1.987-4(d)(1)(i)(B) for the preceding taxable year. However, in the case of a section 987 marked asset (other than cash) transferred to the section 987 QBU or acquired by the section 987 QBU during the taxable year, the exchange rate to be used in translating the adjusted basis of such asset shall be the spot rate, as defined in § 1.987-1(c)(1)(i) and (ii), for the day transferred or acquired.

(3) Gain or loss on the sale, exchange or other disposition of an interest in a section 987 partnership. For purposes of determining the adjusted basis of a partner's interest in a section 987 partnership and computing gain or loss recognized on the sale, exchange or other disposition of such interest, see § 1.987-7.

(c) Items of income, gain, deduction or loss that are denominated in the functional currency of the owner. An item of income, gain, deduction or loss attributable to a section 987 QBU under § 1.987-2(b) that is denominated in (or determined by reference to) the owner's functional currency shall not be translated and shall be taken into account by the section 987 QBU under U.S. tax principles in the owner's functional currency.

(d) Items of income, gain, deduction or loss that are denominated in a nonfunctional currency (other than the functional currency of the owner). An item of income, gain, deduction or loss attributable to a section 987 QBU under § 1.987-2(b) that is denominated in (or determined by reference to) a nonfunctional currency (other than the owner's functional currency) shall be translated into the section 987 QBU's functional currency at the spot rate as defined in § 1.987-1(c)(1)(i) and (ii) on the day such item is properly taken into account.

(e) Section 988 transactions. *(1) In general.* Except as provided in paragraph (e)(2) of this section, section 988 shall apply to the section 988 transactions attributable to a section 987 QBU under § 1.987-2(b), and the timing of any gain or loss shall be determined under the applicable provisions of the Internal Revenue Code. Such transactions are section 987 historic items as defined in § 1.987-1(e).

(2) Certain transactions denominated in (or determined by reference to) the owner's functional currency are not section 988 transactions. Transactions described in section 988(c)(1)(B)(i) and (ii) and section 988(c)(1)(C) that are denominated in (or determined by reference to) the owner's functional currency and that are attributable to a section 987 QBU under § 1.987-2(b) shall not be treated as section 988 transactions to such QBU. Thus, no currency gain or loss shall be recognized by a section 987 QBU under section 988 with respect to such items.

(f) Examples. The following examples illustrate the application of this section:

Example (1). (i) U.S. Corp is a domestic corporation with the dollar as its functional currency. U.S. Corp owns French DE, a section 987 DE that has a section 987 branch with the euro as its functional currency. For purposes of paragraph (b)(1) of this section, U.S. Corp uses the yearly average exchange rate under § 1.987-1(c)(2) to translate items of income, gain, deduction or loss where such rate is appropriate. U.S. Corp also properly elects to use a spot rate convention under § 1.987-1(c)(1)(ii) where the spot rate is otherwise required. Under this convention, items booked during a particular month are translated at the average of the spot rates on the first and last day of the preceding month (the "convention rate"). Accordingly, gross sales income is translated at the yearly average exchange rate and under paragraph (b)(2)(ii)(B) of this section the basis of assets acquired during a month is translated into dollars at the convention rate. Assume that the yearly average exchange rate for 2009 is [euro]1 = $1.05. For the taxable year 2009, French DE sells 1,200 units of inventory for a sales price of [euro]3 per unit. Assume that the purchase price for each inventory unit is [euro]1.50. Thus, French DE's dollar gross sales will be computed as follows:

GROSS SALES

Month	# of units	s	s/$ 2009 ave. exchange rate	$
Jan	100	300	s1=$1.05	315
Feb	200	600	s1=$1.05	630
March	0	0	s1=$1.05	0
April	200	600	s1=$1.05	630
May	100	300	s1=$1.05	315
June	0	0	s1=$1.05	0
July	100	300	s1=$1.05	315

Aug	100	300	s1=$1.05	315
Sept	0	0	s1=$1.05	0
Oct	0	0	s1=$1.05	0
Nov	100	300	s1=$1.05	315
Dec	300	900	s1=$1.05	945
	1,200	3,600	....	3,780

OPENING INVENTORY AND PURCHASES

Month	# of units	s	s/$ convention exchange rate	$
Opening inventory from 2008	100	150	s1=$1.00	150
Purchases:				
Jan	300	450	s1=$1.00	450
Feb	0	0	s1=$1.05	0
March	0	0	s1=$1.03	0
April	300	450	s1=$1.02	459
May	0	0	s1=$1.04	0
June	0	0	s1=$1.05	0
July	300	450	s1=$1.06	477
Aug	0	0	s1=$1.05	0
Sept	0	0	s1=$1.06	0
Oct	0	0	s1=$1.07	0
Nov	300	450	s1=$1.08	486
Dec	0	0	s1=$1.08	0
Total Purchases	1,200	1,800	....	1,872

(ii) French DE uses a first in first out method of accounting for inventory (FIFO). Thus, for 2009, French DE is considered to have sold the 100 units of opening inventory ($150), the 300 units purchased in January ($450), the 300 units purchased in April ($459), the 300 units purchased in July ($477) and 200 of the 300 units purchased in November ($324). Thus, French DE's cost of goods sold is $1,860. French DE's opening inventory for 2010 is 100 units of inventory with a dollar basis of $162.

(iii) Accordingly, for purposes of section 987 French DE has gross income in dollars of $1,920 ($3,780-$1,860).

Example (2). (i) The facts are the same as in Example 1 except that for purposes of paragraph (b)(1) of this section, U.S. Corp properly elects to use a spot rate convention under § 1.987-1(c)(1)(ii) to translate items of income, gain, deduction or loss where such rate is appropriate. Thus, French DE's dollar gross sales will be computed as follows:

GROSS SALES

Sales	# of units	s	s/$ convention exchange rate	$
Jan	100	300	s1=$1.00	300
Feb	200	600	s1=$1.05	630
March	0	0	s1=$1.03	0
April	200	600	s1=$1.02	612
May	100	300	s1=$1.04	312
June	0	0	s1=$1.05	0
July	100	300	s1=$1.06	318
Aug	100	300	s1=$1.05	315
Sept	0	0	s1=$1.06	0
Oct	0	0	s1=$1.07	0
Nov	100	300	s1=$1.08	324
Dec	300	900	s1=$1.08	972
	1,200	3,600	....	3,783

(ii) As in Example 1, French DE's cost of goods sold is $1,860.

(iii) Accordingly, for purposes of section 987 French DE has gross income in dollars of $1,923 ($3,783-$1,860).

Example (3). The facts are the same as in Example 1 except that French DE sold raw land on November 1, 2009 for [euro]10,000. The yearly average rate for 2009 was [euro]1=$1.05. The land was purchased on October 16, 2007 for [euro]8,000 when the convention rate was [euro]1=$1.00. Under paragraph (a)(1) of this section, French DE will determine the amount realized and basis in euros. Under paragraph (a)(1)(ii) of this section, the amount realized is translated into dollars at the yearly average exchange rate for 2009 as provided in paragraph (b)(2)(ii)(A) of this section ([euro]10,000 x $1.05 = $10,500) and the basis at the convention rate for 2007 as provided in paragraph (b)(2)(ii)(B) of this section and § 1.987-1(c)(3) ([euro][n1],000 x $1= $8,000). Accordingly, the amount of gain reported by U.S. Corp on the sale of the land is $2,500 ($10,500-$8,000).

Example (4). The facts are the same as in Example 3 except that U.S. Corp properly elects under paragraph (b)(1) of this section to use the spot rate to translate items of income, gain, deduction or loss. Accordingly, the amount realized will be translated at the convention rate on the day of sale. Assume that the convention rate for November 2009 is [euro]1 = $1.08. Under these facts, the amount realized is $10,800 ([euro]10,000 x $1.08) and the basis on the day of purchase $8,000 ([euro]8,000 x $1.00). The amount of gain reported by U.S. Corp on the sale of the land is $2,800 ($10,800 -$8,000).

Example (5). The facts are the same as in Example 1 except that on September 15, 2009, French DE provides services to an unrelated customer and receives a cash payment of [euro]2,000 on that day. Under paragraph (b)(1) of this section, U.S. Corp translates the [euro]2,000 item of income into dollars at the yearly average exchange rate of [euro]1 = $1.05. Accordingly, U.S. Corp will report income of $2,100 from providing services.

Example (6). The facts are the same as in Example 5 except that U.S. Corp properly elects under paragraph (b)(1) of this section to use the spot rate to translate items of income, gain, deduction or loss. Assume that the convention rate for September 2009 is [euro]1 = $1.06. Under these facts, U.S. Corp translates the [euro]2,000 item of income into dollars at the convention rate of [euro]1 = $1.06. Accordingly, U.S. Corp will report income of $2,120 from providing services.

Example (7). The facts are the same as in Example 1 except that on March 31, 2009, French DE incurs [euro]500 of rental expense, [euro]300 of salary expense and [euro]100 of utilities expense. Under paragraph (b)(1) of this section, U.S. Corp translates these items of expense at the yearly average exchange rate of [euro]1 = $1.05. Accordingly the expenses are translated as follows: rental expense of $525, salary expense of $315 and utilities expense of $105.

Example (8). The facts are the same as in Example 7 except that U.S. Corp properly elects under paragraph (b)(1) of this section to use the spot rate to translate items of income and expense. Assume that the convention rate for March 2009 is [euro]1 = $1.03. Under these facts, U.S. Corp translates the [euro]500 of rental expense, [euro]300 of salary expense and [euro]100 of utilities expense at the convention rate of [euro]1 = $1.03. Accordingly, the expenses are translated as follows: rental expense of $515, salary expense of $309 and utilities expense of $103.

Example (9). The facts are the same as in Example 1 except that during 2009, French DE incurred [euro]100 of depreciation expense with respect to a truck. The truck was purchased on January 15, 2008, when the convention rate was [euro]1 = $1.02. Under paragraph (b)(2)(i) of this section, the [euro]100 of depreciation is translated into dollars at the historic exchange rate. Since U.S. Corp has properly elected to use a spot rate convention, depreciation will be translated in accordance with the convention. Accordingly, U.S. Corp translates the [euro]100 of depreciation to equal $102.

Example (10). (i) The facts are the same as in Example 1 except that on January 12, 2009, French DE performed services for a U.K. person and received £10,000 in compensation. The exchange rate on January 12, 2009, was £1 = [euro]1.25. Under paragraph (d) of this section, French DE will translate such income into euros at the spot rate on January 12, 2009. Accordingly, French DE will take into account [euro]12,500 of income from services in 2009. Under paragraph (b)(1) of this section, U.S. Corp translates the [euro]12,500 item of income into dollars at the yearly average euro to dollar exchange rate. Assume that such exchange rate is [euro]1 = $1.10. Accordingly, U.S. Corp translates the [euro]12,500 income from services to equal $13,750.

(ii) On October 16, 2009, French DE disposes of the £10,000 for [euro]10,000. Under section 988(c)(1)(C), the disposition is a section 988 transaction. Under § 1.988-2(a)(2), French DE will realize a loss of [euro]2,500 ([euro]10,000 amount realized less [euro]12,500 basis). Under paragraph (b)(1) of this section, U.S. Corp translates the [euro]2,500 loss into dollars at the yearly average euro to dollar exchange rate. Assume that such exchange rate is [euro]1 = $1.05. Accordingly, U.S. Corp translates the [euro]2,500 section 988 loss to equal $2,625.

§ 1.987-4 Special rules relating to QBU branches of foreign taxpayers. [Reserved]

Proposed § 1.987-4 Determination of net unrecognized section 987 gain or loss of a section 987 QBU. [*For Preamble, see ¶ 152,801*]

(a) In general. The net unrecognized section 987 gain or loss of a section 987 QBU shall be determined by the owner annually as provided in paragraph (b) of this section in the owner's functional currency. Only assets and liabilities reflected on the books and records of the section 987 QBU under § 1.987-2(b) shall be taken into account.

(b) Calculation of net unrecognized section 987 gain or loss of a section 987 QBU. Net unrecognized section 987 gain or loss of a section 987 QBU for a taxable year shall equal the sum of--

(1) The section 987 QBU's net accumulated unrecognized section 987 gain or loss for all prior taxable years to which these regulations apply as determined in paragraph (c) of this section; and

(2) The section 987 QBU's unrecognized section 987 gain or loss for the current taxable year as determined in paragraph (d) of this section.

(c) Net accumulated unrecognized section 987 gain or loss for all prior taxable years. A section 987 QBU's net accumulated unrecognized section 987 gain or loss for all prior taxable years is the aggregate of the amounts determined under paragraph (d) of this section for all prior years to which these regulations apply, reduced by the amounts taken into account under § 1.987-5 upon a remittance for all such prior taxable years. This amount shall include amounts appropriately considered as net unrecognized exchange gain or loss under the transition rules of § 1.987-10.

(d) Calculation of unrecognized section 987 gain or loss of a section 987 QBU for a taxable year. The unrecognized section 987 gain or loss of a section 987 QBU for a taxable year shall be determined under paragraphs (d)(1) through (7) of this section as follows:

(1) **Step 1:** *Determine the change in the owner functional currency net value of the section 987 QBU for the taxable year.* (i) In general. The change in the owner functional currency net value of the section 987 QBU for the taxable year shall equal--

(A) The owner functional currency net value of the section 987 QBU, determined in the functional currency of the owner under paragraph (e) of this section, on the last day of the current taxable year; less

(B) The owner functional currency net value of the section 987 QBU, determined in the functional currency of the owner under paragraph (e) of this section on the last day of the preceding taxable year. This amount shall be zero in the case of the QBU's first taxable year.

(ii) Year section 987 QBU is terminated. If a section 987 QBU is terminated under the rules of § 1.987-8 during an owner's taxable year, the owner functional currency net value of the section 987 QBU as provided in paragraph (d)(1)(i)(A) of this section shall be determined on the day the section 987 QBU is terminated.

(2) **Step 2:** *Increase the aggregate amount determined in step 1 by the assets transferred from the section 987 QBU to its owner.* (i) In general. The aggregate amount determined in paragraph (d)(1) of this section shall be increased by the total amount of assets described in paragraph (d)(2)(ii) of this section transferred from the section 987 QBU to the owner during the taxable year translated into the owner's functional currency as provided in paragraph (d)(2)(iii) of this section.

(ii) Assets transferred from the section 987 QBU to the owner during the taxable year. The assets transferred from the section 987 QBU to the owner for the taxable year shall equal the aggregate of--

(A) The amount of the section 987 QBU's functional currency and the adjusted basis of any section 987 marked asset (as defined in § 1.987-1(d)) transferred from the section 987 QBU to the owner during the taxable year determined in the functional currency of the section 987 QBU and translated into the owner's functional currency as provided in paragraph (d)(2)(iii)(A) of this section; and

(B) The adjusted basis of any section 987 historic asset (as defined in § 1.987-1(e)) transferred to the owner during the taxable year determined in the functional currency of the section 987 QBU and translated into the owner's functional currency as provided in paragraph (d)(2)(iii)(B) of this section. Such amount shall be adjusted to take into account the proper translation of depreciation, depletion and amortization as provided in § 1.987-3(b)(2)(i).

(iii) Translation of amounts transferred from the section 987 QBU to the owner. In the case of a transfer from the section 987 QBU to an owner of any asset the following exchange rates shall be used:

(A) In the case of an amount described in paragraph (d)(2)(ii)(A) of this section, the spot exchange rate, as defined in § 1.987-1(c)(1), on the day of transfer.

(B) In the case of a transfer of a section 987 historic asset, the historic exchange rate for such asset as defined in § 1.987-1(c)(3).

(3) **Step 3:***Decrease the aggregate amount determined in steps 1 and 2 by the owner's transfers to the section 987 QBU.* (i) In general. The aggregate amount determined in paragraphs (d)(1) and (d)(2) of this section shall be decreased by the total amount of assets transferred from the owner to the section 987 QBU during the taxable year determined in the functional currency of the owner as provided in paragraph (d)(3)(ii) of this section.

(ii) Total of all amounts transferred from the owner to the section 987 QBU during the taxable year. The total amount of assets transferred from the owner to the section 987 QBU for the taxable year shall equal the aggregate of--

(A) The total amount of functional currency of the owner transferred to the section 987 QBU during the taxable year; and

(B) The adjusted basis, determined in the functional currency of the owner, of any asset transferred to the section 987 QBU during the taxable year (after taking into account § 1.988-1(a)(10)).

(4) **Step 4:** *Decrease the aggregate amount determined in steps 1 through 3 by the amount of liabilities transferred from the section 987 QBU to the owner.* The aggregate amount determined in paragraphs (d)(1) through (d)(3) of this section shall be decreased by the aggregate amount of liabilities transferred from the section 987 QBU to the owner. The amount of such liabilities shall be translated into the functional currency of the owner at the spot exchange rate, as defined in § 1.987-1(c)(1), on the day of transfer.

(5) **Step 5:** *Increase the aggregate amount determined in steps 1 through 4 by amount of liabilities transferred from the owner to the section 987 QBU.* The aggregate amount determined in paragraphs (d)(1) through (d)(4) of this section shall be increased by the aggregate amount of liabilities transferred by the owner to the section 987 QBU. The amount of such liabilities shall be translated into the functional currency of the owner, if required, at the spot exchange rate, as defined in § 1.987-1(c)(1)(i) and (ii), on the day of transfer.

(6) **Step 6:** *Increase the aggregate amount determined in steps 1 through 5 by the section 987 taxable loss of the section 987 QBU for the taxable year.* In the case of a section 987 taxable loss of the section 987 QBU computed under § 1.987-3 for the taxable year, the aggregate amount determined in paragraphs (d)(1) through (d)(5) of this section shall be increased by such section 987 taxable loss.

(7) **Step 7:** *Decrease the aggregate amount determined in steps 1 through 5 by the section 987 taxable income of the section 987 QBU for the taxable year.* In the case of section 987 taxable income of the section 987 QBU computed under § 1.987-3 for the taxable year, the aggregate amount determined in paragraphs (d)(1) through (d)(5) of this section shall be decreased by such section 987 taxable income.

(e) Determination of the owner functional currency net value of a section 987 QBU. *(1) In general.* The owner functional currency net value of a section 987 QBU on the last day of a taxable year shall equal the aggregate amount of the QBU's functional currency and the basis of each asset on the section 987 QBU's balance sheet on that day, less the aggregate amount of each liability on the section 987 QBU's balance sheet on that day translated, if necessary, into the owner's functional currency as provided in paragraph (e)(2) of this section. Such amount shall be determined as follows:

(i) The owner, or section 987 QBU on behalf of the owner, shall prepare a balance sheet for the relevant date from the section 987 QBU's books and records (within the meaning of § 1.989(a)-1(d)) as recorded in the section 987 QBU's functional currency showing all assets and liabilities reflected on such books and records as provided in § 1.987-2(b). Assets and liabilities denominated in the functional currency of the owner shall be reflected on the balance sheet in the owner's functional currency.

(ii) The owner, or section 987 QBU on behalf of the owner, shall make adjustments necessary to conform the items reflected on the balance sheet described in paragraph (e)(1)(i) of this section to United States generally accepted accounting principles and tax accounting principles.

(iii) The owner, or section 987 QBU on behalf of the owner, shall translate the asset and liability amounts on the adjusted balance sheet described in paragraph (e)(1)(ii) of this section into the functional currency of the owner in accordance with paragraph (e)(2) of this section. Assets and liabilities denominated in the functional currency of the owner are not translated.

(2) Translation of balance sheet items into the owner's functional currency. The amount of the section 987 QBU's functional currency, the basis of an asset, or the amount of a liability (other than an asset or liability reflected on the balance sheet in the functional currency of the owner) shall be translated as follows:

(i) Section 987 marked item. A section 987 marked item as defined in § 1.987-1(d) shall be translated into the owner's functional currency at the spot exchange rate as defined in § 1.987-1(c)(1)(i) and (ii) on the last day of the taxable year.

(ii) Section 987 historic item. A section 987 historic item as defined in § 1.987-1(e) shall be translated into the owner's functional currency at the historic exchange rate as defined in § 1.987-1(c)(3).

(f) Examples. The provisions of this section are illustrated by the following examples. Unless otherwise indicated, all items are assumed to be reflected on the books and records, within the meaning of § 1.987-2(b), of the relevant section 987 QBU.

Example (1). (i) U.S. Corp is a calendar year domestic corporation with the dollar as its functional currency. On July 1, 2009, U.S. Corp establishes Japan Branch that has the yen as its functional currency. Japan Branch is a section 987 QBU of U.S. Corp. U.S. Corp properly elects to use a spot rate convention under § 1.987-1(c)(1)(ii) with respect to Japan Branch. Under this convention, the spot rate for any transaction occurring during a month is the spot rate on the first day of the month. U.S. Corp also elects under § 1.987-3(b)(1) to use this convention to translate items of income, gain, deduction, or loss into dollars. On July 1, 2009, when $1 = ¥100 (or ¥1 = $0.01), U.S. Corp transfers $1,000 to Japan Branch and raw land with a basis of $500. Japan Branch immediately purchases ¥100,000 with the $1,000. On the same day, Japan Branch borrows ¥10,000. Assume that for the taxable year 2009, Japan Branch earns ¥2,000 per month (total of ¥12,000 for the six month period from July 1, 2009, through December 31, 2009) for providing services and incurs ¥333.33 per month (total of ¥2,000 when rounded for the six month period from July 1, 2009, through December 31, 2009) of related expenses. Assume that all items of income earned and expenses incurred by Japan Branch during 2009 are received and paid, respectively, in yen. Further, assume that the ¥12,000 of income when properly translated under the monthly convention equals $109.08 and that the ¥2,000 of related expenses equal $18.18. Thus, Japan Branch's income translated into dollars equals $90.90. Assume that the spot exchange rate on the December 1, 2009, is $1 = ¥120 (¥1 = $0.00833).

(ii) Under paragraph (a) of this section, U.S. Corp must compute the net unrecognized section 987 gain or loss of Japan Branch for 2009. Since this is Japan Branch's first taxable year, the net unrecognized section 987 gain or loss as defined under paragraph (b) of this section is the branch's unrecognized section 987 gain or loss for 2009 as determined in paragraph (d) of this section. The calculation under paragraph (d) of this section is made as follows:

(iii) Step 1. Under paragraph (d) of this section, U.S. Corp must determine the change in the owner functional currency net value of Japan Branch for the year 2009 in dollars. The change in the owner functional currency net value of Japan Branch for 2009 is equal to the owner functional currency net value of Japan Branch determined in dollars on the last day of 2009, less the owner functional currency net value of Japan Branch determined in dollars on the last day of the preceding taxable year.

(A) The owner functional currency net value of Japan Branch determined in dollars on the last day of the current taxable year is determined under paragraph (e) of this section. Such amount is the aggregate of the basis of each asset on Japan Branch's balance sheet on December 31, 2009, less the aggregate of the amount of each liability on the Japan Branch's balance sheet on that day, translated into dollars as provided in paragraph (e)(2) of this section.

(B) For this purpose, Japan Branch will show the following assets and liabilities on its balance sheet for December 31, 2009:

(1) Cash of ¥120,000 [($1,000 transferred and immediately converted to ¥100,000) + ¥10,000 borrowed + ¥12,000 income from services - ¥2,000 of expenses].

(2) Raw land with a basis of ¥50,000.

(3) Liabilities of ¥10,000.

(C) Under paragraph (e)(2) of this section, U.S. Corp will translate these items as follows. The cash of ¥120,000 is a section 987 marked asset and the ¥10,000 liability is a section 987 marked liability as defined in § 1.987-1(d). These items are translated into dollars on December 31, 2009, using the spot rate on December 1, 2009 of ¥1 =$ 0.00833. The raw land is a section 987 historic asset as defined in § 1.987-1(e) and is translated into the dollars at the convention rate for the day of transfer (¥1 = $0.01). Thus, the owner functional currency net value of Japan Branch on December 31, 2009, in dollars is $1,416.60 determined as follows:

Asset	Amount in ¥	Translation rate	Amount in $
Cash	120,000[4]	12/01/09 spot convention rate on 12/31/09 of ¥1=$0.00833	999.60
Land	50,000	Historic rate on 7/1/09 of ¥1=$0.01	500.00
Total assets			1,499.60
Liability:			
Bank Loan	10,000	12/01/09 spot convention rate on 12/31/09 of ¥1 = $0.00833	83.30
Total liabilities			83.30
Owner functional currency net value of Japan Branch on December 31,2009 in dollars			1,416.30

4. Opening cash of ¥100,000 + ¥10,000 borrowed + ¥12,000 income from services - ¥2,000 expenses

(D) Under paragraph (d)(1) of this section, the change in owner functional currency net value of Japan Branch for 2009 is equal to the owner functional currency net value of the branch determined in dollars on December 31, 2009 ($1,416.30) less the owner functional currency net value of the branch determined in dollars on the last day of the preceding taxable year. Since this is the first taxable year of Japan Branch, the owner functional currency net value of Japan Branch determined in dollars on the last day of the preceding taxable year is zero under paragraph (d)(1)(i)(B) of this section. Accordingly, the change in owner functional currency net value of Japan Branch for 2009 is $1,416.30.

(iv) Step 2. Under paragraph (d)(2) of this section, the aggregate amount determined in paragraph (d)(1) of this section (step 1) is increased by the total amount of assets described in paragraph (d)(2)(ii) of this section transferred from the section 987 QBU to the owner during the taxable year translated into the owner's functional currency as provided in paragraph (d)(2)(iii) of this section. Since no such amounts were transferred under these facts, there is no change in the $1,416.30 determined in step 1.

(v) Step 3. Under paragraph (d)(3) of this section, the aggregate amount determined in paragraphs (d)(1) and (2) of this section (steps 1-2) is decreased by the total amount of assets transferred from the owner to the section 987 QBU during the taxable year as determined in paragraph (d)(3)(ii) of this section in dollars. On July 1, 2009, U.S. Corp transferred to Japan Branch $1,000 (which Japan Branch immediately converted into ¥100,000) and raw land with a basis of $500 (equal to ¥50,000 on the day of transfer). Thus, the step 2 amount of $1,416.30 is reduced by $1,500.00 to equal ($83.70).

(vi) Steps 4, 5 and 6. Since no liabilities were transferred by U.S. Corp to Japan Branch or vice versa, the amount determined after applying paragraphs (d)(1) through (d)(5) of this section is ($83.70). Further, paragraph (d)(6) of this section does not apply since Japan Branch does not have a section 987 taxable loss.

(vii) Step 7. Under paragraph (d)(7) of this section, the aggregate amount determined after applying paragraphs (d)(1) through (d)(5) of this section (steps 1-5) is decreased by the section 987 taxable income of Japan Branch of $90.90. Accordingly, the unrecognized section 987 loss of Japan Branch for 2009 is $174.60 (-$83.70-$90.90).

Example (2). (i) U.S. Corp, a calendar year domestic corporation with the dollar as its functional currency, operates in the United Kingdom through UK Branch. UK Branch has the pound as its functional currency and is a section 987 QBU. U.S. Corp properly elects to use a spot rate convention under § 1.987-1(c)(1)(ii). Under this convention, the spot rate for any transaction occurring during a month is the average of the pound spot rate and the 30-day forward rate for pounds on the next-to-last Thursday of the preceding month. Pursuant to § 1.987-3(b)(1), U.S. Corp uses the yearly average exchange rate as defined in § 1.987-1(c)(2) to translate items of income, gain, deduction, or loss into dollars for the taxable year, where appropriate. The yearly average exchange rate for 2009 was £1 = $1.05. The closing balance sheet of UK Branch for the prior year (2008) reflected the following assets and liabilities. With respect to assets, UK Branch held--

(A) Cash of £100;

(B) Plant purchased in May 2007 with an adjusted basis of £1000;

(C) A machine purchased in May 2007 with an adjusted basis of £200;

(D) Inventory of 100 units manufactured in December 2008 with a basis of £100;

(E) Portfolio stock (as defined in § 1.987-2(b)(2)(ii)) in ABC Corporation purchased in September 2008 with a basis of £158; and

(F) $50 acquired in 2008 (and held in a non-interest bearing account). With respect to liabilities, UK Branch has £50 of long-term debt entered into in 2007 with F Bank, an unrelated bank. The plant, machine, inventory, stock and dollars are section 987 historic assets as defined in § 1.987-1(e). The cash of £100 and long-term debt are section 987 marked items as defined under § 1.987-1(d). Assume the U.S. Corp translated UK Branch's 2008 closing balance sheet as follows:

Assets	Amount in £	Translation Rate	Amount in $
Cash	100	Spot convention rate in Dec. 2008 £1 = $1	100.00
Plant	1,000	Historic rate-2007 May convention rate £1= $0.90	900.00
Machine	200	Historic rate-2007 May convention rate £1= $0.90	180.00
Stock	158	Historic rate-2008 Sept. convention rate £1= $.95	150.00
Inventory	100	Historic rate-2008 Dec. convention rate £1 = $1	100.00
Dollars	$50	Dollars are not translated	50.00
Total assets			1,480.00
Liabilities:			
Bank Loan	£50	Spot convention rate in Dec. 2008 £1 = $1	50.00
Total liabilities			50.00
2008 ending owner functional currency net value (in dollars)			1,430

(ii) UK Branch uses the first in first out method of accounting for inventory. In 2009, UK Branch sold 100 units of inventory for a total of £300 and purchased another 100 units of inventory in December 2009 for £100. Assume that the dollar basis of the inventory purchased in December 2009 when translated at the December 2009 monthly convention rate is $110; that depreciation with respect to the plant is £33 and for the machine £40[5]; and that UK Branch incurred £30 of business expenses during 2009. Assume all items of income earned and expenses incurred during 2009 are received and paid, respectively, in pounds. The yearly average exchange rate for 2009 is £1 = $1.05. Under

5. The depreciation assumptions are for illustrative purposes only and may not be consistent with true depreciation rates.

§ 1.987-3, UK Branch's section 987 taxable income or loss is determined as follows:

Item	Amount in £	Translation Rate	Amount in $
Gross receipts	300	2009 yearly ave. rate £1 = $1.05	315.00
Less:			
COGS	(100)	Historic rate-Dec. 2008 convention rate £1= $1	(100.00)
Gross income	200		215.00
Dep:			
Plant	(33)	Historic rate-May 2007 convention rate £1= $0.90	(29.70)
Machine	(40)	Historic rate-May 2007 £1= $0.90 £1= $0.90	(36.00)
Other expenses	(30)	2009 yearly ave. rate £1 = $1.05	(31.50)
Total expenses			97.20
Section 987 taxable income			117.80

Accordingly, UK Branch has $117.80 of section 987 taxable income.

(iii) Assume that in December 2009, UK Branch transferred $20 and £30 to U.S. Corp and that U.S. Corp transferred a computer with a basis of $10 to UK Branch. The convention exchange rate for December 2009 is £1 = $1.10. Finally, assume that U.S. Corp's net accumulated unrecognized section 987 gain or loss for all prior taxable years as determined in paragraph (c) of this section is $30.

(iv) The unrecognized section 987 gain or loss of UK Branch for 2009 is determined as follows:

(A) Step 1: Determine the change in owner functional currency net value of UK Branch. Under paragraph (d)(1) of this section, the change in owner functional currency net value for the taxable year must be determined. This amount is equal to the owner functional currency net value of UK Branch determined under paragraph (e) of this section on the last day of 2009, less the owner functional currency net value of UK Branch determined on the last day of 2008. The owner functional currency net value of UK Branch on December 31, 2009, and the change in owner functional currency net value is determined as follows:

Asset	Amount in £	Translation rate	Amount in $
Cash	240[6]	Spot convention rate in Dec. 2009 £1 = $1.10	264.00
Plant	967[7]	Historic rate - May 2007 convention rate £1 = $0.90	870.30
Machine	160[8]	Historic rate - May 2007 convention rate £1 = $0.90	144.00
Inventory	100	Historic rate -- Dec. 2009 convention rate £1 = $1.10	110.00
Computer	9	Historic rate -- Dec. 2009 convention rate £1 = $1.10	10.00
Stock	158	Historic rate -- Sept. 2008 convention rate £1 = $.95	150.00
Dollars	$ 30[9]	Dollars are not translated	30.00
Total assets			1,578.30
Liability:			
Bank Loan	£50	Spot convention rate in Dec. 2009 £1 = $1.10	55.00
Total liabilities			55.00
2009 ending owner functional currency net value (in dollars)			1,523.30
Less: 2008 ending owner functional currency net value (in dollars)			($1,430.00)
Change in owner functional currency net value			93.30

(B) Step 2: Increase the aggregate amount described in step 1 by each owner's share of assets transferred by the section 987 QBU to its owners. Under paragraph (d)(2) of this section, the aggregate amount determined in step 1 must be increased by the total amount of assets described in paragraph (d)(2)(ii) of this section transferred from UK Branch to U.S. Corp during the taxable year, translated into U.S. Corp's functional currency as provided in paragraph (d)(2)(iii) of this section. The amount of assets transferred

6. £100 on the closing 2008 balance sheet plus £300 gross receipts less £100 inventory cost, less £30 of additional expenses, less £30 transferred to U.S. Corp
7. £1,000 on the closing 2008 balance sheet less £33 depreciation
8. £200 on the closing 2008 balance sheet less £40 depreciation
9. Dollars are reduced by $20 transferred to U.S. Corp

from UK Branch to U.S. Corp during 2009 is determined as follows:

Asset	Amount in £	Translation rate	Amount in $
£30 currency	30	Spot convention rate in Dec. 2009 £1 = $1.10	33.00
$20 currency	$20	Dollars are not translated	20.00
Total			53.00

(C) Step 3: Decrease the aggregate amount described in steps 1 and 2 by the owner's transfers to the section 987 QBU. Under paragraph (d)(3) of this section, the aggregate amount determined in steps 1 and 2 must be decreased by the total amount of all assets transferred from U.S. Corp to UK Branch during the taxable year as determined in paragraph (d)(3)(ii) of this section. The amount of assets transferred from U.S. Corp to UK Branch is determined as follows:

Asset	Amount in £	Translation rate	Amount in $
Computer	£9	Spot convention rate in Dec. 2009 £1 = $1.10	$10.00
Total			10.00

(D) Step 4: Decrease the aggregate amount determined in steps 1 through 3 by the amount of liabilities transferred by the section 987 QBU to the owner. Under paragraph (d)(4) of this section, the aggregate amount determined in steps 1 through 3 must be decreased by the aggregate amount of liabilities transferred by UK Branch to U.S. Corp. Under these facts, such amount is $0.

(E) Step 5: Increase the aggregate amount determined in steps 1 through 4 by the amount of liabilities transferred by the owner to the section 987 QBU. Under paragraph (d)(5) of this section, the aggregate amount determined in steps 1 through 4 must be increased by the aggregate amount of liabilities transferred by U.S. Corp to UK Branch. Under these facts, such amount is $0.

(F) Step 6: Increase the aggregate amount determined in steps 1 through 5 by the section 987 taxable loss of the section 987 QBU for the taxable year. Under paragraph (d)(6) of this section, the aggregate amount determined in steps 1 through 5 must be increased by the section 987 taxable loss of UK Branch. Since UK Branch had no such taxable loss in 2009, paragraph (d)(6) of this section does not apply.

(G) Step 7: Decrease the aggregate amount determined in steps 1 through 5 by the section 987 taxable income of the section 987 QBU for the taxable year. Under paragraph (d)(7) of this section, the aggregate amount determined in steps 1 through 5 must be decreased by the section 987 taxable income of UK Branch. The amount of UK Branch's taxable income, as determined above, is $117.80.

(v) Summary. Taking steps 1 through 7 into account, the amount of U.S. Corp's unrecognized section 987 gain or loss with respect to UK Branch in 2009 is computed as follows:

Step	Amount in $	Balance
1	+ 93.30	$93.30
2	+ 53.00	146.30
3	-10.00	136.30
4	-0	136.30
5	+ 0	136.30
6	+ 0	136.30
7	-117.80	18.50

Thus, U.S. Corp's unrecognized section 987 gain in 2009 with respect to U.K. Branch is $18.50. As of the end of 2009, before taking into account the recognition of any section 987 gain or loss under § 1.987-5, U.S. Corp's net unrecognized section 987 gain is $48.50 (i.e., $30 accumulated from prior years, plus $18.50 in 2009).

§ 1.987-5 Transition rules for certain qualified business units using a profit and loss method of accounting for taxable years beginning before January 1, 1987.

(a) Applicability. *(1) In general.* This section applies to a qualified business unit (QBU) branches of United States persons, whose functional currency (as defined in section 985 of the Code and the regulations thereunder) is other than the United States dollar (dollar) and that used a profit and loss method of accounting for their last taxable year beginning before January 1, 1987. Generally, a profit and loss method of accounting is any method of accounting under which the taxpayer calculates the profits of a QBU branch in its functional currency and translates the net result into dollars. For all taxable years beginning after December 31, 1986, such QBU branches must use the profit and loss method of accounting as described in section 987, except to the extent otherwise provided in regulations under section 985 or any other provision of the Code. See § 1.989(c)-1 regarding transition rules for QBU branches of United States persons that have a nondollar functional currency and that used a net worth method of accounting for their last taxable year beginning before January 1, 1987.

(2) Insolvent QBU branches. A taxpayer may apply the principles of this section to a QBU branch that used a profit and loss method of accounting for its last taxable year beginning before January 1, 1987, whose $E pool (as defined in paragraph (d)(3)(i) of this section) is negative. For taxable years beginning on or after October 25, 1991, the principles of this section shall apply to insolvent QBU branches.

(b) General rules. Generally, section 987 gain or loss occurs when a QBU branch makes a remittance. A remittance is considered to be made from one or more functional currency pools under rules provided in paragraph (c) of this section. In general, the amount of section 987 gain or loss from a remittance equals the difference between the dollar value of the functional currency adjusted basis of the property remitted and the portion of the dollar basis in the applicable pool. Section 987 gain or loss is calculated under a 4-step procedure described in paragraph (d) of this section. Section 987 gain or loss attributable to a remittance is realized and must be recognized in the taxable year of the remittance except to the extent otherwise provided in regulations.

(c) Determining the pool(s) from which a remittance is made. *(1) Remittances made during taxable years beginning after December 31, 1986, and before October 25, 1991.* A remittance made during taxable years beginning after December 31, 1986 and before October 25, 1991, first represents an amount of the QBU branch's post-'86 profits pool (including functional currency profits for the current taxable year determined without regard to remittances made during the current year). To the extent the functional currency amount of the remittance exceeds the post-'86 profits pool, it is considered to come out of the EQ pool. Paragraph (d)(2) of this section describes the EQ pool and the post-'86 profits pool.

(2) Remittances made in taxable years beginning on or after October 25, 1991. For remittances made in taxable years beginning on or after October 25, 1991, the post-'86 profits and EQ pools are combined into one pool called the equity pool. Therefore, remittances made during those taxable years will only come from the equity pool. The dollar basis of, and section 987 gain or loss on, such remittances shall be calculated utilizing the principles set forth in paragraph (d)(4) and (5) of this section.

(d) Calculation of section 987 gain or loss. *(1) In general.* This paragraph (d) describes the 4-step procedure for calculating section 987 gain or loss.

(2) Step 1. Calculate the amount of the functional currency pools. (i) EQ pool. (A) Beginning pool. The beginning amount of the EQ pool is equal to the functional currency adjusted bases of a QBU branch's assets less the functional currency amount of the QBU branch's liabilities at the end of the taxpayer's last taxable year beginning before January 1, 1987, as these amounts are determined under the rules of paragraphs (e) and (f) of this section. The district director may allow for additional adjustments to the beginning amount of the EQ pool to prevent the recognition of section 987 gain or loss due to factors unrelated to the movement of exchange rates.

(B) Adjusting the EQ pool. The EQ pool is increased by the functional currency amount of any transfer (as determined under section 987) to the QBU branch made during the current taxable year or any prior taxable year beginning after December 31, 1986. If the transfer is made in a nonfunctional currency, this amount is translated into the QBU branch's functional currency at the spot rate (determined under the principles of section 988 and the regulations thereunder) on the date of the transfer. The method for determining the rate must be applied consistently each quarter. The EQ pool is decreased by the functional currency amount of any remittance (as determined under section 987) made during a prior taxable year beginning after December 31, 1986, that is considered remitted from the EQ pool under paragraph (c) of this section. The EQ pool must also be decreased by any transfer from the QBU branch that is not a remittance.

(ii) Post-'86 profits pool. The amount of a QBU branch's post-'86 profits pool is calculated at the end of each taxable year beginning after December 31, 1986. The opening balance of the post-'86 profits pool at the beginning of the first taxable year beginning after December 31, 1986, is zero. The post-'86 profits pool is increased by the functional currency amount of the QBU branch's profits (determined under section 987) for the taxable year. The post-'86 profits pool is decreased by the functional currency amount of the QBU branch's losses (determined under section 987) for the taxable year and the amount of any remittances by the QBU branch during the taxable year from the post-'86 profits pool as provided under paragraph (c) of this section.

(iii) Adjustments to the equity pool. For remittances made in taxable years beginning on or after October 25, 1991 under paragraph (c)(2) of this section, the post-'86 profits and EQ pools are combined into one pool called the equity pool. Additions to and subtractions from the equity pool shall be made utilizing the principles of paragraphs (d)(2)(i)(B) and (ii) of this section. For example, remittances shall reduce the equity pool.

(3) Step 2. Calculate the dollar basis of the pools. (i) Dollar basis of the EQ pool. (A) Beginning dollar basis. The beginning dollar basis of the EQ pool (hereinafter referred to as the $E pool) equals:

(1) The dollar amount of all the QBU branch's profits reported on the taxpayer's income tax returns for taxable years beginning before January 1, 1987, plus the total dollar amount of all transfers to the QBU branch during that period (properly reflected on the taxpayer's books), less

(2) The dollar amount of all the QBU branch's losses reported on the taxpayer's income tax returns for such years, and the total dollar basis of all remittances and all transfers made by the QBU branch during that period (properly reflected on the taxpayer's books).

A QBU branch's profits and losses shall be properly adjusted for foreign taxes of the QBU branch.

(B) Adjusting the $E pool. The $E pool is increased by the dollar amount of any transfers to the QBU branch made during the current taxable year or any prior taxable year beginning after December 31, 1986. If a transfer is made in a currency other than the dollar, the amount of the currency is translated into dollars at the spot rate (determined under the principles of section 988 and the regulations thereunder) on the date of the transfer. The $E pool is decreased by the dollar basis of any remittance made during a prior taxable year beginning after December 31, 1986, that is considered remitted from the $E pool under paragraphs (c) and (d)(4) of this section. The $E pool is also reduced by the amount of a transfer (other than a remittance) from the QBU branch translated into dollars at the spot rate (determined under the principles of section 988 and the regulations thereunder) on the date of the transfer. The method for determining the spot rate must be applied consistently to all transfers to and from a QBU branch.

(ii) Dollar basis of the post-'86 profits pool. The amount of a QBU branch's dollar basis in the post-'86 profits pool (The $P pool) is calculated at the end of each taxable year beginning after December 31, 1986. The opening balance of the $P pool at the beginning of the first taxable year beginning after December 31, 1986, is zero. The $P pool is increased by the functional currency amount of the QBU branch's profits (determined under section 987) for the taxable year translated into dollars at the weighted average exchange rate (as defined in § 1.989(b)-1) for the year. The $P pool is decreased by the functional currency amount of the QBU branch's losses (determined under section 987) for the taxable year translated into dollars at the weighted average exchange rate for the year and by the dollar basis of any remittances made by the QBU branch during the taxable year from the post-'86 profits pool under paragraph (c)(1) of this section.

(iii) Combination of the $E and the $P pools. For taxable years beginning on or after October 25, 1991 the $P and the $E pools are combined into one pool called the basis pool. Additions to and subtractions from the basis pool shall be made utilizing the principles set forth in paragraph (d)(3)(i) and (ii) of this section.

(4) Step 3. Calculation of the dollar basis of a remittance. For all taxable years beginning after December 31, 1986, the dollar basis of a remittance is calculated using the following formula:

$$\frac{\text{amount of remittance (in QBU branch's functional currency) from the applicable pool (EQ, post-'86 profits, or equity pool)}}{\text{Balance of the applicable pool (EQ, post-'86 profits or equity pool) reduced by prior remittances}} \times \text{The dollar basis of the applicable pool (\$E, \$P, or basis pool) reduced by prior remittances}$$

(5) Step 4. Calculation of the section 987 gain or loss on a remittance. Section 987 gain or loss equals the difference between—

(i) The dollar amount of the remittance, and

(ii) The dollar basis of the remittance as calculated under paragraph (d)(4) of this section.

(e) Functional currency adjusted basis of QBU branch assets acquired in taxable years beginning before January 1, 1987. *(1) Basis of asset.* For taxable years beginning after December 31, 1986, the functional currency adjusted basis of a QBU branch asset acquired in a taxable year beginning before January 1, 1987, is the functional currency basis of the asset at the date of acquisition, as adjusted according to United States tax principles. The functional currency adjusted basis of an asset for which a functional currency basis was not determined at the date of acquisition is the nonfunctional currency basis of the asset at the date of acquisition multiplied by the spot exchange rate on the date of acquisition, as adjusted according to United States tax principles.

(2) Adjustment to basis of asset. Any future adjustments to the functional currency adjusted basis of such an asset are determined with respect to the appropriate functional currency adjusted basis of the asset as determined under this paragraph (e).

(f) Functional currency amount of QBU branch liabilities acquired in taxable years beginning before January 1, 1987. For the first taxable year beginning after December 31, 1986, the amount of a QBU branch liability incurred in a taxable year beginning before January 1, 1987, is the functional currency amount of the liability at the date incurred, as adjusted according to United States tax principles. The functional currency amount of a liability for which a functional currency amount was not determined at the date incurred is the nonfunctional currency amount of the liability at the date incurred multiplied by the spot exchange rate on the date incurred, as adjusted according to United States tax principles.

(g) Examples. The provisions of this section are illustrated by the following examples.

Example (1). (i) Facts. U.S. is a domestic corporation. B, a QBU branch of U.S., operates in country X and was established in 1985. B's functional currency is the FC. U.S. is on a calendar taxable year and, prior to January 1, 1987, accounted for the operations of B by the profit and loss method of accounting as set forth in Rev. Rul. 75-107, 1975-1 C.B. 32. B's books and records were kept according to United States tax principles. B received a transfer of $2,000 in 1985, and had profits of $3,000 in 1985 and $5,000 in 1986. B made a remittance in 1986, the dollar basis of which was $1,000. As of December 31, 1986, the adjusted basis of B's functional currency assets exceeded the functional currency amount of its liabilities by 15,000 FC (the beginning pool of EQ). Under section 987, B has profits of 8,000 FC in 1987, which are worth $1,000 when translated at the weighted average exchange rate for 1987 as required by sections 987(2) and 989(b)(4). B has no profits or loss in 1988. There are no transfers to B in 1987 and 1988. B remits 18,000 FC in 1988. Under section 987, the appropriate exchange rate for the 1988 remittance is 10 FC/$1.

(ii) Calculation of section 987 loss on remittance

(A) Post-'86 profits. Under paragraph (c)(i) of this section, the 18,000 FC remittance comes first out of the post-'86 profits pool (8,000 FC) and second out of EQ (10,000 FC). The loss on the 1988 remittance out of the post-'86 profits pool equals:

Dollar value of post-'86 profits remitted − Dollar basis of post-'86 profit remitted

= (8,000 FC × 10 FC/$1) − $1,000
= $800 − $1,000
= <$200> loss

(B) EQ. Under paragraph (d) of this section, U.S. calculates 987 gain or loss on the 10,000 FC remittance of EQ from B as follows: Step 1. The total EQ pool equals 15,000 FC (the functional currency adjusted bases of its assets less the functional currency amount of its liabilities as of December 31, 1986). There are no adjustments necessary under paragraph (d)(2)(i)(B) of this section.

Step 2. The $E pool is $9,000 (the $2,000 transfer in 1985 plus profits of $3,000 in 1985 and $5,000 in 1986 and less the $1,000 dollar basis of the 1986 remittance). There are no adjustments necessary under paragraph (d)(3)(i)(B) of this section.

Step 3. The entire 10,000 FC remittance is deemed to come out of EQ.

Step 4. The dollar basis of the EQ remitted equals:

N × $E determined under paragraph (d) (3) (i)

$$= \frac{10{,}000\ \text{FC}}{} \times \$9{,}000$$

= $6,000

Where:

$$N = \frac{\text{Portion of remittance out of EQ}}{\text{EQ balance determined under paragraph (d)(2)(i) of this section}}$$

Step 5. Section 987 loss of U.S. on remittance equals:

Dollar value the EQ remitted − Dollar basis of the EQ remitted

= (10,000 FC × 10 FC/$1) − $6,000
= $1,000 − $6,000
= < $5,000 > loss

(C) Total loss on remittance. The total combined loss on the remittance is < $5,200 >. The total of amounts determined in paragraphs (ii)(A) and (B) of this Example 1.

Example (2). (i) Facts. D is a domestic corporation. B, a QBU branch of D, operates in country X. B's functional currency is the FC. At the end of B's last taxable year beginning before October 25, 1991 B's EQ pool equals 15,000 FC and B's post-'86 profits pool equals 8,000 FC. B's $E amount equals $9,000, and the $P pool equals $1,000. In B's first taxable year beginning on or after October 25, 1991, B remits 18,000 FC. Under section 987, the appropriate exchange rate for this remittance is 10FC:$1.

(ii) Computation of the equity pool.

15,000 FC (EQ pool) + 8,000 FC (post-'86 profits pool) = 23,000 FC (equity pool)

(iii) Computation of the basis pool.

$9,000 + ($E amount) + $1,000 ($P amount) = $10,000

(iv) Dollar basis in remittance.

$$\frac{18{,}000 \text{ FC (amount of remittance)}}{23{,}000 \text{ FC (equity pool)}} \times \$10{,}000 = \$7{,}826$$

(v) Computation of section 987 loss by U.S. on remittance.

$1,800 (dollar value of remittance)	–	$7,826 (dollar basis in remittance)	=	($6,026) (loss on remittance)

(h) Character and source of section 987 gain or loss. Section 987 gain or loss is sourced and characterized as provided by section 987 and regulations issued under that section.

T.D. 8367, 9/24/91.

PAR. 5. Sections 1.987-1 through 1.987-4 and §§ 1.987-6 through 1.987-11 are added and § 1.987-5 is revised to read as follows:

Proposed § 1.987-5 Recognition of section 987 gain or loss. [*For Preamble, see ¶ 152,801*]

(a) Recognition of section 987 gain or loss by the owner of a section 987 QBU. The taxable income of an owner of a section 987 QBU shall include the owner's section 987 gain or loss recognized with respect to the section 987 QBU for the taxable year. For any taxable year, the owner's section 987 gain or loss recognized with respect to a section 987 QBU shall be equal to--

(1) The owner's net unrecognized section 987 gain or loss of the section 987 QBU determined under § 1.987-4 on the last day of such taxable year (or, if earlier, on the day the section 987 QBU is terminated under § 1.987-8); multiplied by

(2) The owner's remittance proportion for the taxable year, as determined under paragraph (b) of this section.

(b) Remittance proportion. The owner's remittance proportion with respect to a section 987 QBU for a taxable year is the quotient, equal to--

(1) The remittance, as determined under paragraph (c) of this section, to the owner from the section 987 QBU for such taxable year; divided by

(2) The total adjusted basis of the gross assets of the section 987 QBU as of the end of the taxable year (or, if terminated prior to the end of such taxable year under § 1.987-8, the day of termination) that are reflected on its year-end balance sheet (or, if terminated prior to the end of such taxable year under § 1.987-8, the balance sheet on the day terminated), translated into the owner's functional currency as provided in § 1.987-4(e)(2) and increased by the amount of the remittance.

(c) Remittance. *(1) Definition.* A remittance shall be determined in the owner's functional currency and shall equal the excess, if any, of--

(i) The total of all amounts transferred from the section 987 QBU to the owner during the taxable year, as determined in paragraph (d) of this section; over

(ii) The total of all amounts transferred from the owner to the section 987 QBU during the taxable year, as determined in paragraph (e) of this section.

(2) Day when a remittance is determined. An owner's remittance from a section 987 QBU shall be determined on the last day of the owner's taxable year (or, if earlier, on the day the section 987 QBU is terminated under § 1.987-8).

(3) Termination. A termination of a section 987 QBU as determined under § 1.987-8 is treated as a remittance of all the gross assets of the section 987 QBU to the owner on the date of such termination. See § 1.987-8(d). Accordingly, the remittance proportion in the case of a termination is 1.

(d) Total of all amounts transferred from the section 987 QBU to the owner for the taxable year. For purposes of paragraph (c)(1)(i) of this section, the total of all amounts transferred from the section 987 QBU to the owner for the taxable year shall be determined in the owner's functional currency under § 1.987-4(d)(2) with reference to the adjusted basis of the assets transferred. Solely for this purpose, the amount of liabilities transferred from the owner to the section 987 QBU determined under § 1.987-4(d)(5) shall be treated as a transfer of assets from the section 987 QBU to the owner in an amount equal to the amount of such liabilities.

(e) Total of all amounts transferred from the owner to the section 987 QBU for the taxable year. For purposes of paragraph (c)(1)(ii) of this section, the total of all amounts transferred from the owner to the section 987 QBU for the taxable year shall be determined in the owner's functional currency under § 1.987-4(d)(3) with reference to the adjusted basis of the assets transferred. Solely for this purpose, the amount of liabilities transferred from the section 987 QBU to the owner determined under § 1.987-4(d)(4) shall be treated as a transfer of assets from the owner to the section 987 QBU in an amount equal to the amount of such liabilities.

(f) Determination of owner's adjusted basis in transferred assets. *(1) In general.* The owner's adjusted basis in an asset received in a transfer from the section 987 QBU (whether or not such transfer is made in connection with a remittance as defined in paragraphs (c) of this section) shall be determined under the rules prescribed in paragraphs (f)(2) through (f)(4) of this section.

(2) Section 987 marked asset. The basis of a section 987 marked asset shall be determined in the owner's functional currency and shall be the same as the amount determined under § 1.987-4(d)(2)(ii)(A).

(3) Section 987 historic asset. The basis of a section 987 historic asset shall be determined in the owner's functional currency and shall be the same as the amount determined under § 1.987-4(d)(2)(ii)(B).

(4) Partner's adjusted basis in distributed assets. See also section 732 and § 1.987-7 for purposes of determining an

owner's adjusted basis of an asset distributed from a section 987 QBU owned indirectly through a section 987 partnership.

(g) Examples. The following examples illustrate the calculation of section 987 gain or loss under this section:

Example (1). (i) U.S. Corp, a calendar year domestic corporation with the dollar as its functional currency, operates in the U.K. through U.K. DE, an entity disregarded as an entity separate from its owner under §§ 301.7701-1 through 301.7701-3 of this chapter. U.K. DE has a section 987 branch (U.K. section 987 branch) with the pound as its functional currency. During year 2, the following transfers took place between U.S. Corp and U.K. section 987 branch. On January 5, year 2, U.S. Corp transferred to U.K. section 987 branch $300 (which the branch used during the year to purchase services). On March 5, year 2, U.K. section 987 branch transferred a machine to U.S. Corp. Assume that the pound adjusted basis of the machine when properly translated into dollars under §§ 1.987-4(d)(2)(ii)(B) and paragraph (d) of this section is $500. On November 1, year 2, U.K. section 987 branch transferred pound cash to U.S. Corp. Assume that the dollar amount of the pounds when properly translated under § 1.987-4(d)(2)(ii)(A) and paragraph (d) of this section is $2,300. On December 7, year 2, U.S Corp transferred a truck to U.K. section 987 branch with an adjusted basis of $2,000.

(ii) Assume that at the end of year 2, U.K. section 987 branch holds assets, properly translated into the owner's functional currency pursuant to § 1.987-4(e)(2), consisting of a computer with a pound adjusted basis equivalent to $500, a truck with a pound adjusted basis equivalent to $2,000, and pound cash equivalent to $2,850. In addition, assume that U.K. section 987 branch has a pound liability entered into in year 1 with Bank A. The liability, when translated into the owner functional currency pursuant to § 1.987-4(e)(2), is equivalent to $200. All such assets and liabilities are reflected on the books and records of U.K. section 987 branch. Assume that the net unrecognized section 987 gain for U.K. section 987 branch as determined under § 1.987-4 as of the last day of year 2 is $80.

(iii) U.S. Corp's section 987 gain with respect to U.K. section 987 branch is determined as follows: (A) Computation of amount of remittance. Under paragraphs (c)(1) and (2) of this section, U.S. Corp must determine the amount of the remittance for year 2 in the owner's functional currency (dollars) on the last day of year 2. The amount of the remittance for year 2 is $500, determined as follows:

Transfers from U.K. section 987 branch to U.S. Corp in dollars:	
Machine	$ 500
Cash (U.K. pounds)	2,300
	$2,800
Transfers from U.S. Corp to U.K. section 987 branch in dollars:	
Cash (U.S. dollars)	$ 300
Truck	2,000
	2,300
Computation of amount of remittance:	
Aggregate transfers from U.K. section 987 branch to U.S. Corp	$2,800
Less: aggregate transfers from U.S. Corp to U.K. section 987 branch	(2,300)
Total remittance	500

(B) Computation of branch gross assets plus remittance. Under paragraph (b)(2) of this section, U.K. section 987 branch must determine the total basis of its gross assets that are reflected on its year-end balance sheet translated into the owner's functional currency, and must increase this amount by the amount of the remittance.

Total basis of U.K. section 987 branch's gross assets at end of year 2 plus remittance in dollars:	
Computer	$ 500
Cash (U.K. pounds)	2,850
Truck	2,000
Total gross assets	5,350
Remittance	500
Total gross assets + remittance	5,850

(C) Computation of remittance proportion. Under paragraph (b) of this section, U.K. section 987 branch must compute the remittance proportion as follows:

Amount of remittance	$500
Total basis of U.K. section 987 branch's gross assets at end of Year 2, increased by amount of remittance	5,850
Remittance/gross assets	0.085
Remittance proportion	0.085

(D) Computation of section 987 gain or loss. The amount of U.S. Corp's section 987 gain or loss that must be recognized with respect to U.K. section 987 branch is determined under paragraph (a) of this section.

Net unrecognized section 987 gain	$80
Remittance proportion	x 0.085
U.S. Corp's section 987 gain for Year 2:	$6.80

Example (2). U.S. Corp, a calendar year domestic corporation with the dollar as its functional currency, operates in the U.K. through U.K. DE, an entity disregarded as an entity separate from its owner. U.K. DE has a section 987 branch (U.K. section 987 branch) with the pound as its functional currency. During year 2, the following transfers took place between U.S. Corp and U.K. section 987 branch. On March 1, year 2, U.S. Corp transferred to U.K. section 987 branch a computer with a basis of $100. On November 1, year 2, U.K. section 987 branch transferred pounds to U.S. Corp. Assume that the dollar amount of the pounds when properly translated under § 1.987-4(d)(2)(ii)(A) and paragraph (d) of this section is $300. On the same day, U.K. section 987 branch transferred of $20 to U.S. Corp.

(ii) Assume that at the end of year 2, U.K. section 987 branch holds assets translated (as necessary) into the owner functional currency pursuant to § 1.987-4(e)(2) consisting of a plant with a pound adjusted basis equivalent $1,000, pound cash equivalent to $100, a machine with a pound adjusted basis equivalent to $200, portfolio stock (within the meaning of § 1.987-2(b)(2)(ii)) in ABC Corporation with a pound adjusted basis equivalent to $150, inventory of 100 units with an aggregate pound adjusted basis equivalent to $100 and a computer with a pound adjusted basis equivalent to $100. In addition, assume that U.K. section 987 branch has a pound liability that it entered into with Bank A in year 1. When properly translated into dollars pursuant to § 1.987-4(e)(2) the principal amount of the liability is equal to $500. All such assets and liabilities are reflected on the books and records of U.K. section 987 branch. Assume that the net unrecognized 987 gain for U.K. section 987 branch as determined under § 1.987-4 as of the last day of year 2 is $100.

(iii) U.S. Corp's section 987 gain with respect to U.K. section 987 branch is determined as follows:

(A) Computation of amount of remittance. Under paragraphs (c)(1) and (2) of this section, U.S. Corp must determine the amount of the remittance for year 2 in the owner's functional currency on the last day of year 2. The amount of the remittance for year 2 is $220 determined as follows:

Transfers from U.K. section 987 branch to U.S. Corp in dollars:	
Cash (U.K. pounds)	$300
Cash (U.S. dollars)	20
	320
Transfers from U.S. Corp to U.K. section 987 branch in dollars:	
Computer	$100
Computation of amount of remittance:	
Aggregate transfers from U.K. section 987 branch to U.S. Corp	$320
Less: aggregate transfers from U.S. Corp to U.K. branch	($100)
Total remittance:	$220
Computation of amount of remittance:	
Aggregate transfers from U.K. section 987 branch to U.S. Corp	$320
Less: aggregate transfers from U.S. Corp to U.K. branch	100
Total remittance:	220

(B) Computation of branch gross assets plus remittance. Under paragraph (b)(2) of this section, U.K. section 987 branch must determine the total basis of its gross assets as are reflected on its year-end balance sheet translated into dollars and must increase this amount by the amount of the remittance.

Total pound basis of U.K. section 987 branch's gross assets translated into dollars at end of Year 2:	
Plant	$1,000
Cash (U.K. pounds)	100
Inventory	100
Machine	200
Computer	100
Portfolio Stock	150
Total gross assets	1,650
Remittance	220
Total gross assets + remittance	1,870

(C) Computation of remittance proportion. Under paragraph (b) of this section, U.K. section 987 branch must compute the remittance proportion as follows:

Amount of remittance	$220
Total basis of U.K. section 987 branch's gross assets at tend of year 2, increased by amount of remittance	1,870
Remittance/gross assets	0.118
Remittance proportion	0.118

(D) Computation of section 987 gain or loss. The amount of U.S. Corp's section 987 gain or loss that must be recognized with respect to U.K. section 987 branch is determined under paragraph (a) of this section.

Net unrecognized section 987 gain	$100.00
Remittance proportion	× 0.118
U.S. Corp's section 987 gain for year 2	11.80

Proposed § 1.987-6 Character and source of section 987 gain or loss. [*For Preamble, see ¶ 152,801*]

(a) Ordinary income or loss. Section 987 gain or loss is ordinary income or loss for Federal income tax purposes.

(b) Source and character of section 987 gain or loss. *(1) In general.* Except as otherwise provided in this section, the owner of a section 987 QBU must determine the source and character of section 987 gain or loss in the year of a remittance under the rules of this paragraph (b) for all purposes of the Internal Revenue Code, including sections 904(d), 907 and 954.

(2) Method required to characterize and source section 987 gain or loss. The owner must use the asset method set forth in § 1.861-9T(g) to characterize and source section 987 gain or loss. The modified gross income method described in § 1.861-9T(j) cannot be used.

(3) Method required to characterize and source section 987 gain or loss with respect to regulated investment companies and real estate investment trusts. [Reserved].

(c) Example. The following example illustrates the application of this section.

Example. CFC is a controlled foreign corporation as defined in section 957 with the Swiss franc (Sf) as its functional currency. CFC holds all the interest in a section 987 DE as defined in § 1.987-1(b)(6)(iii) that has a section 987 branch with significant operations in Germany (German Branch). German Branch has the euro as its functional currency. For the year 2009, CFC recognizes section 987 gain of Sf10,000 under §§ 1.987-4 and 1.987-5. Applying the rules of this section, German Branch has total average assets of Sf1,000,000 which generate income as follows: Sf750,000 of assets that generate foreign source general limitation income under section 904(d)(1)(I), none of which is subpart F income under section 952; and Sf250,000 of assets that generate foreign source passive income under section 904(d)(1)(B), all of which is subpart F income. Under paragraph (b) of this section, Sf7,500 ((Sf750,000/ Sf1,000,000) x Sf10,000) of the section 987 gain will be treated as foreign source general limitation income which is not subpart F income and Sf2,500 ((Sf250,000/Sf1,000,000) x Sf10,000) will be treated as foreign source passive income which is subpart F income. All of the section 987 gain is treated as ordinary income.

Proposed § 1.987-7 Section 987 partnerships. [*For Preamble, see ¶ 152,801*]

(a) In general. In the case of an owner that is a partner in a section 987 partnership, this section provides rules for determining the owner's share of assets and liabilities of a section 987 QBU owned indirectly, as described in § 1.987-1(b)(4)(ii), through a section 987 partnership. In addition, this section provides rules coordinating these regulations with subchapter K of chapter 1 of the Internal Revenue Code.

(b) Assets and liabilities of an eligible QBU or a section 987 QBU held indirectly through a partnership. A partner's share of the assets and liabilities reflected under § 1.987-2(b) on the books and records of an eligible QBU or a section 987 QBU owned indirectly through a partnership shall be determined in a manner that is consistent with the manner in which the partners have agreed to share the economic benefits and burdens (if any), corresponding to the assets and liabilities, taking into account the rules and principles of sections 701 through 761, and the applicable regulations, including section 704(b) and § 1.701-2.

(c) Coordination with subchapter K. *(1) Partner's adjusted basis in its partnership interest.* (i) In general. Except as provided in this paragraph, a partner's adjusted basis in its section 987 partnership interest shall be maintained in the functional currency of that partner and shall not be adjusted as a result of any fluctuations in the value of the partner's functional currency and the functional currency of any section 987 QBU owned indirectly through the section 987 partnership.

(ii) Adjustments for section 987 taxable income or loss and section 987 gain or loss. (A) Section 987 taxable income or loss. A partner's share of the items of income, gain, deduction or loss taken into account in calculating section 987 taxable income or loss of a section 987 QBU, determined under § 1.987-3, held indirectly through a section 987 partnership shall be treated as income or loss of the section 987 partnership through which the partner indirectly owns the interest. As a result, the partner's allocable share of the items of income, gain, deduction or loss taken into account in calculating section 987 taxable income or loss of the section 987 QBU shall be taken into account, following conversion into the partner's functional currency, in determining the appropriate adjustments to the partner's adjusted basis in its partnership interest under section 705.

(A) Section 987 gain or loss. Solely for purposes of determining the appropriate adjustments to a partner's adjusted basis in its interest in a section 987 partnership under section 705, an individual or corporation that owns a section 987 QBU indirectly through a section 987 partnership shall treat any section 987 gain or loss of such section 987 QBU as gain or loss of the section 987 partnership. Any adjustments to the adjusted basis of a partner's interest in such section 987 partnership required under this paragraph (c)(1)(ii)(B) of this section shall occur prior to determining the effect under the Internal Revenue Code of any sale, exchange, distribution or other event.

(iii) Adjustments for contributions and distributions. For purposes of making adjustments to the partner's adjusted basis in its interest in a section 987 partnership, as a result of any contributions or distributions (including deemed contributions and distributions under section 752) between the section 987 partnership and the owner of a section 987 QBU owned indirectly through the partnership, such amounts will be taken into account in the owner's functional currency.

(iv) Determination of deemed distributions and contributions under section 752. (A) Increase in partner's liabilities. For purposes of determining the amount of any increase in a partner's share of the liabilities of the partnership, or any increase in the partner's individual liabilities by reason of the assumption by such partner of a liability of the partnership, which are reflected on the books and records of a section 987 QBU owned indirectly through such partnership and which are denominated in a functional currency different from the partner's, the amount of such liabilities shall be translated into the functional currency of the partner using the spot rate (as defined in § 1.987-1(c)(1)(i) and (ii)) on the date of such increase.

(B) Decrease in partner's liabilities. For purposes of determining the amount of any decrease in a partner's share of the liabilities of the partnership which were reflected on the books and records of a section 987 QBU owned indirectly through such partnership and which are denominated in a functional currency different from the partner's functional currency, the amount of such liabilities shall be translated into the functional currency of the partner using the historic rate (as defined in § 1.987-1(c)(3)) for the date on which such liabilities increased the partner's adjusted basis in its partnership interest under section 752.

(2) Special rule for determining gain or loss on the sale, exchange or other disposition of an interest in a section 987 partnership. For purposes of determining the amount realized by a partner in a section 987 partnership on the sale, exchange, or other disposition of that partner's interest in such partnership, the amount of liabilities reflected on the books and records of a section 987 QBU (in a functional currency different from such partner) from which that partner is relieved as a result of such disposition, and which are included in the amount realized pursuant to section 752(d), shall be translated into the partner's functional currency using the historic exchange rate (as determined under § 1.987-1(c)(3)) for the date on which such liabilities increased the partner's adjusted basis in its partnership interest under section 752.

(d) Examples. The purpose of the following examples is to illustrate the application of section 987 to partnerships and their partners. The examples are not meant to be a comprehensive interpretation of the step-by-step computations involved in computing net unrecognized section 987 gain or loss. Thus, for the sake of simplicity, the examples only calculate section 987 gain or loss by reference to certain identified assets and liabilities, rather than by all the assets and liabilities of the section 987 QBU (as is required under these regulations). See § 1.987-4 and the examples therein for step-by-step computations for determining the unrecognized section 987 gain or loss of the owner of a section 987 QBU.

Example (1). Computation of an owner's net unrecognized section 987 gain or loss. (i) Facts. PRS is a partnership which owns QBUx, an eligible QBU, operating in the United Kingdom. QBUx has the pound as its functional currency determined under § 1.985-1 taking into account all of QBUx's activities before application of this section. PRS has two equal partners that are domestic corporations, A and B, each with the U.S. dollar as its functional currency. The portions of QBUx allocated to A and B under paragraph (b) of this section are section 987 QBUs of A and B because under § 1.987-1(b)(2), such portions are allocated from an eligible QBU with a different functional currency than A and B, respectively. Assume that PRS has no items of section 987 taxable income or loss for 2007. On January 1, 2007, A and B each contribute $50 to PRS. PRS immediately converts the $100 into £100. The £100 is reflected, in accordance with § 1.987-2(b), on the books and records of QBUx. On January 1, 2007, the spot rate is $1 = £1. On December 31, 2007, the spot rate is $1.50 = £1. Pursuant to § 1.987-3(b)(1), A and B use the yearly average exchange rate, as defined in § 1.987-1(c)(2), to translate items of income, gain, deduction, or loss into dollars for the taxable year. Assume the yearly average exchange rate is $1.25 = £1 ($1 = £.80). Under the PRS partnership agreement, A and B each have an equal interest in all items of partnership income and loss.

(ii) Calculation of net unrecognized section 987 gain or loss. Under paragraph (b) of this section, A and B are each allocated 50 from eligible QBUx. This amount is reflected on the balance sheet of the section 987 QBU of A and B, respectively, for purposes of determining the unrecognized section 987 gain or loss under § 1.987-4. Pursuant to § 1.987-4(d), the net unrecognized section 987 gain of A's section 987 QBU and B's section 987 QBU is $25.

Example (2). Computation of owner's net unrecognized section 987 gain or loss. (i) Facts. The facts are the same as

Example 1, except that in addition to the £100 contributed by A and B, PRS incurred a £50 recourse liability from an unrelated third party on January 1, 2007. The liability and the £50 are both reflected on the books and records of QBUx under § 1.987-2(b). Under section 752, and the regulations thereunder, A and B bear the economic risk of loss with respect to the £50 recourse debt equally.

(ii) Calculation of net unrecognized section 987 gain or loss. Under paragraph (b) of this section, A and B are each allocated £75 from QBUx. In addition, under paragraph (b) of this section, A and B are each allocated £25 of the liability of QBUx because the economic burden of such liability, taking into account sections 701 through 761 of the Code, is borne equally by A and B. Under § 1.987-4(d), A and B each have net unrecognized section 987 gain of $25.

(iii) Determination of partner's adjusted basis in PRS. Pursuant to paragraph (c)(1)(i) of this section and section 985(a), A and B must determine the adjusted basis in their PRS partnership interests in U.S. dollars. Under sections 722, 752(a) and paragraph (c)(1)(iv)(A) of this section, the adjusted bases in such interests are increased by the U.S. dollar amount of a deemed contribution determined using the spot rate for the date on which such liability was incurred. Therefore, A and B will increase the adjusted basis in their PRS partnership interests by $25.

Example (3). Computation of owner's net unrecognized section 987 gain or loss. (i) Facts. The facts are the same as Example 2, except as follows: On January 1, 2007, instead of incurring a £50 recourse liability, PRS incurred a £50 nonrecourse liability from an unrelated third party, which was secured by and used to purchase non-depreciable real property located in the United Kingdom. Under the partnership agreement, A and B agree to share all items of partnership income and loss equally, except that A guaranteed the nonrecourse liability and, in addition, the partnership agreement provides that A will be allocated any gain from the sale or exchange of the non-depreciable property. Further, the partnership agreement provides that in the event the partnership liquidates prior to satisfying the liability, the non-depreciable property shall be distributed to A.

(ii) Calculation of net unrecognized section 987 gain or loss. Under paragraph (b) of this section, A and B are each allocated £50 from eligible QBUx. In addition, because A bears the economic burden of the nonrecourse liability incurred by PRS and the economic benefits of the non-depreciable property securing such liability, both of which are reflected on the books and records of QBUx under § 1.987-2(b), A is allocated, for purposes of applying § 1.987-4(d), both the £50 liability and the non-depreciable property with an adjusted tax basis of £50. Under § 1.987-4(d), A's net unrecognized section 987 gain is $0, and B's net unrecognized section 987 gain is $25.

(iii) Determination of partner's adjusted basis in PRS. Pursuant to paragraph (c)(1)(i) of this section and section 985(a), A and B must determine the adjusted bases in their PRS partnership interests in U.S. dollars. Under sections 722, 752(a) and paragraph (c)(1)(iv) of this section, A's adjusted basis is increased by the U.S. dollar amount of the deemed contribution determined using the spot rate for the date on which such liability was incurred. Therefore, A will increase the adjusted basis in its PRS partnership interest by $50.

Example (4). Computation of owner's share of items of section 987 taxable income. (i) Facts. The facts are the same as in Example 1, except that during 2007 PRS earns £50 which are reflected on the books and records of QBUx. In accordance with the partnership agreement, the £50 are allocated equally between A and B.

(ii) Calculation of section 987 taxable income or loss. Under § 1.987-3, A and B's allocable share of the taxable income of QBUx, as determined by PRS, and adjusted to conform to U.S. tax principles, is £25 each. Under § 1.987-3, A and B must convert their allocable share of the £25 into U.S. dollars using the yearly average exchange rate for the year, in accordance with § 1.987-1(c)(2). As a result, A and B each take into account as their respective distributive share of PRS income $31.25. Under paragraph (c)(1)(ii)(A) of this section, section 985(a) and section 705, such amounts, as reflected in U.S. dollars, will be taken into account in determining any adjustments to the adjusted bases of A's and B's partnership interests. In addition, such amounts will be taken into account in calculating, under § 1.987-4, the unrecognized section 987 gain or loss of the section 987 QBUs of A and B.

Example (5). Computation of owner's share of items of section 987 taxable income. (i) Facts. The facts are the same as in Example 4, except A and B agree to allocate the £50 of income to A. Assume for purposes of this example that such allocation has substantial economic effect as provided under section 704(b).

(ii) Calculation of section 987 taxable income or loss. Under § 1.987-3, A and B's allocable share of the taxable income of QBUx, as determined by PRS, and adjusted to conform to U.S. tax principles, is £50 and £0, respectively. Under § 1.987-3, A and B must convert their allocable share into U.S. dollars using the yearly average exchange rate for the year, in accordance with § 1.987-1(c)(2). As a result, A and B must each take into account as their respective distributive share of PRS income $62.50 and $0, respectively. Under paragraph (c)(1)(ii)(A) of this section, section 985(a) and section 705, such amounts, as reflected in U.S. dollars, will be taken into account in determining any adjustments to the adjusted bases of A's and B's respective partnership interests. In addition, such amounts will be taken into account in calculating, under § 1.987-4, the unrecognized section 987 gain or loss of the section 987 QBUs of A and B.

Example (6). Election by de minimis partner to not take into account section 987 gain or loss. (i) Facts. The facts are the same as in Example 1, except assume that A owns, directly or indirectly, less than 5% of the total capital and profits interest in PRS and, as a result, is eligible to elect, under § 1.987-1(b)(1)(ii) not to apply the provisions of the regulations under section 987 for purposes of taking into account the section 987 gain or loss of A's section 987 QBU. Assume further that A makes such election. On January 1, 2008, A sells its interest to an unrelated third party, C, for $75.

(ii) Determination of partner's adjusted basis in PRS. Pursuant to paragraph (c)(1)(i) of this section and section 985(a), A must determine the adjusted basis of its PRS partnership interest in U.S. dollars. A's basis in PRS is $50, the amount of its contribution to PRS.

(iii) Sale of partnership interest by A. Under section 1001, A's amount realized on the sale of the partnership interest to C is $75. A's adjusted basis of its PRS partnership interest is $50, the amount of A's contribution to PRS, unadjusted by the fluctuations between the pound and the U.S. dollar. A's gain on the sale of the partnership interest is $25.

Proposed § 1.987-8 Termination of a section 987 QBU.

[*For Preamble, see ¶ 152,801*]

(a) Scope. This section provides rules regarding the termination of a section 987 QBU. Paragraph (b) of this section provides general rules for determining when a termination occurs. Paragraph (c) of this section provides exceptions to the general termination rules for certain transactions described in section 381(a). Paragraph (d) of this section provides certain effects of terminations. Paragraph (e) of this section contains examples that illustrate the principles of this section.

(b) In general. Except as provided in paragraph (c) of this section, a section 987 QBU terminates when—

(1) Its activities cease, such that it no longer meets the definition of an eligible QBU as defined in § 1.987-1(b)(3);

(2) Substantially all (within the meaning of section 368(a)(1)(C)) of the section 987 QBU's assets are transferred from such section 987 QBU to its owner, as provided under § 1.987-2(c). For purposes of this paragraph (b)(2), the amount of assets transferred from the section 987 QBU to its owner as a result of a transaction (for example, a contribution of property to a DE or a partnership) as provided under § 1.987-2(c) shall be reduced by assets that are transferred from the owner to such section 987 QBU, as provided under § 1.987-2(c), pursuant to the same transaction;

(3) A foreign corporation that is a controlled foreign corporation (as defined in section 957) that is the owner of a section 987 QBU ceases to be a controlled foreign corporation; or

(4) The owner of such section 987 QBU ceases to exist (including in connection with a transaction described in section 381(a)).

(c) Transactions described in section 381(a). *(1) Liquidations.* A termination does not occur when the owner of a section 987 QBU ceases to exist in a liquidation described in section 332, except in the following cases:

(i) The distributor is a domestic corporation and the distributee is a foreign corporation.

(ii) The distributor is a foreign corporation and the distributee is a domestic corporation.

(iii) The distributor and the distributee are both foreign corporations and the functional currency of the distributee is the same as the functional currency of the distributor's section 987 QBU.

(2) Reorganizations. A termination does not occur when the owner of the section 987 QBU ceases to exist in a reorganization described in section 381(a)(2), except in the following cases:

(i) The transferor is a domestic corporation and the acquiring corporation is a foreign corporation.

(ii) The transferor is a foreign corporation and the acquiring corporation is a domestic corporation.

(iii) The transferor is a controlled foreign corporation immediately before the transfer and the acquiring corporation is a foreign corporation that is not a controlled foreign corporation immediately after the transfer.

(iv) The transferor and the acquiring corporation are foreign corporations and the functional currency of the acquiring corporation is the same as the functional currency of the transferor's section 987 QBU.

(d) Effect of terminations. A termination of a section 987 QBU as determined in this section is treated as a remittance of all the gross assets of the section 987 QBU to its owner. As a result, any net unrecognized section 987 gain or loss of the section 987 QBU is recognized. See § 1.987-5. For purposes of the preceding sentence, the amount of net unrecognized section 987 gain or loss is determined as of the date of termination by closing the books and records of the section 987 QBU on that date.

(e) Examples. The following examples illustrate the principles of this section:

Example (1). Cessation of operations. (i) Facts. DC, a domestic corporation, has a sales office in Country X (Country X Branch) that is a section 987 QBU. DC closes its Country X Branch.

(ii) Analysis. The cessation of the activities of the Country X Branch causes a termination of the section 987 QBU under paragraph (b)(1) of this section.

Example (2). Incorporation of section 987 QBU. (i) Facts. DC, a domestic corporation, has a branch in Country X (Country X Branch) that is a section 987 QBU. DC transfers all the assets and liabilities of Country X Branch to DS, a domestic corporation, in exchange for stock of DS in a transaction qualifying under section 351.

(i) Analysis. Country X Branch terminates pursuant to paragraph (b)(1) of this section because the Country X Branch ceases to be an eligible QBU of DC.

Example (3). Cessation of controlled foreign corporation status. (i) Facts. DC, a domestic corporation, owns all of the stock of FC, a controlled foreign corporation as defined in section 957. FC has a section 987 QBU. FA, a foreign corporation owned solely by foreign persons, purchases all of the FC stock. FC will not constitute a controlled foreign corporation after the transaction.

(ii) Analysis. Because FC ceases to qualify as a controlled foreign corporation after the sale of the FC stock, FC's section 987 QBU terminates pursuant to paragraph (b)(3) of this section.

Example (4). Section 332 liquidation. (i) Facts. DC, a domestic corporation, operates in Country X through FC, a wholly-owned foreign corporation organized under the laws of Country X. FC also has a branch in Country Y (Country Y Branch) that is a section 987 QBU. Pursuant to a liquidation described in section 332, FC transfers all of its assets and liabilities to DC.

(ii) Analysis. FC's liquidation is a termination as provided in paragraph (b)(4) of this section because FC ceases to exist. The exception for certain section 332 liquidations provided under paragraph (c)(1) of this section does not apply because DC is a domestic corporation and FC is a foreign corporation. See paragraph (c)(1)(ii) of this section.

Example (5). Transfers to and from section 987 QBU pursuant to the same transaction. (i) Facts. DC1, a domestic corporation, owns Entity A, a DE. Entity A conducts a business in Country X and that business is an eligible QBU and a section 987 QBU (Country X QBU) of DC1. DC2, a domestic corporation, contributes property to Entity A in exchange for a 95% interest in Entity A. The property DC2 contributes to Entity A is used in the business conducted by the Country X QBU and is reflected on its books and records as provided under § 1.987-2(b). Moreover, Entity A is converted to a partnership as a result of the contribution. See Rev. Rul. 99-5 (situation 2), (1999-1 CB 434). See § 601.601(d)(2) of this chapter. Also, as a result of the contribution, and pursuant to § 1.987-2(c)(5), 95% of the assets and liabilities on the books and records of DC1's section 987 QBU are deemed to be transferred from such QBU to DC1, and DC1 is deemed to transfer to such QBU 5% of the property, as determined under § 1.987-7, contributed by DC2 to Entity A.

(ii) Analysis. As a result of the contribution of property from DC2 to Entity A, assets were transferred from DC1's section 987 QBU to DC1. Similarly, assets were transferred from DC1 to its section 987 QBU as a result of the contribution. Accordingly, for purposes of determining whether substantially all the assets of Country X QBU were transferred from DC1's section 987 QBU as provided under paragraph (b)(2) of this section, the assets transferred from DC1's section 987 QBU to DC1 under § 1.987-2(c) are reduced by the amount of assets transferred from DC1 to such section 987 QBU pursuant to the contribution.

Proposed § 1.987-9 Recordkeeping requirements. [*For Preamble, see ¶ 152,801*]

(a) In general. A taxpayer that is an owner of a section 987 QBU shall keep such reasonable records as are sufficient to establish the QBU's section 987 taxable income or loss and section 987 gain or loss. See section 987 and section 6001 and the applicable regulations.

(b) Supplemental information. An owner's obligation to maintain records under section 6001 and paragraph (a) of this section is not satisfied unless the following information is maintained in such records:

(1) The amount of the items of income, gain, deduction or loss attributed to each section 987 QBU of the owner in the functional currency of the section 987 QBU.

(2) The amount of assets and liabilities attributed to each section 987 QBU of the owner in the functional currency of the QBU.

(3) The exchange rates used to translate items of income, gain, deduction or loss of each section 987 QBU into the owner's functional currency. If a spot rate convention is used, the manner in which such convention is determined.

(4) The exchange rates used to translate the assets and liabilities of each section 987 QBU into the owner's functional currency. If a spot rate convention is used, the manner in which such convention is determined.

(5) The amount of the items of income, gain, deduction or loss attributed to each section 987 QBU of the owner translated into the functional currency of the owner.

(6) The amount of assets and liabilities attributed to each section 987 QBU of the owner translated into the functional currency of the owner.

(7) The amount of assets and liabilities transferred by the owner to a section 987 QBU determined in the functional currency of the owner.

(8) The amount of assets and liabilities transferred by the section 987 QBU to the owner determined in the functional currency of the owner.

(9) The amount of the unrecognized section 987 gain or loss for the taxable year.

(10) The amount of the net unrecognized section 987 gain or loss at the close of the taxable year.

(11) If a remittance is made, the average tax book value of assets as determined under § 1.861-9T(g).

(12) The transition information required to be determined under § 1.987-10(c)(2)(v).

(c) Retention of records. The records required by this section must be kept at all times available for inspection by the Internal Revenue Service, and shall be retained so long as the contents thereof may become material in the administration of the Internal Revenue Code.

Proposed § 1.987-10 Transition rules. [*For Preamble, see ¶ 152,801*]

(a) Scope. *(1) In general.* These transition rules shall apply to any taxpayer that is an owner of a section 987 QBU pursuant to § 1.987-1(b)(4) on the transition date (as defined in paragraph (b) of this section). A taxpayer to whom this section applies must transition from the method previously used by such taxpayer to comply with section 987 (the "prior section 987 method") to the method prescribed by these regulations pursuant to the rules set forth in paragraph (c) of this section.

(2) Limitation where the prior method was unreasonable. Notwithstanding paragraph (a)(1) of this section, if the prior section 987 method was unreasonable (including the case where the taxpayer failed to make the determinations required under section 987 for any open taxable year), then the taxpayer must apply the rules of paragraph (c)(4) of this section (and cannot apply the rules of paragraph (c)(3) of this section) to transition to the method prescribed by these regulations.

(b) Transition date. The transition date is the first day of the first taxable year to which these regulations apply to a taxpayer.

(c) Transition methods and corresponding rules. *(1) In general.* Except as provided in paragraph (a)(2) of this section, a taxpayer must transition from its prior method to the method prescribed by these regulations under the "deferral transition method" of paragraph (c)(3) of this section or the "fresh start transition method" of paragraph (c)(4) of this section. If a taxpayer fails to comply with the rules of this section, the Area Director, Field Examination, Small Business/Self Employed or the Director, Field Operations, Large and Mid-Size Business having jurisdiction of the taxpayer's return for the taxable year shall determine the appropriate transition method.

(2) Conformity rules. The taxpayer (including all members that file a consolidated return that includes that taxpayer), and any controlled foreign corporation as defined in section 957 in which the taxpayer owns more than 50 percent of the voting power or stock (as determined in section 957(a)), must consistently apply the same transition method for each qualified business unit subject to section 987 owned on the transition date.

(3) Deferral transition method. (i) In general. Pursuant to the deferral transition method prescribed by this paragraph (c)(3), section 987 gain or loss must be determined on the transition date under the taxpayer's prior section 987 method as if all qualified business units of the taxpayer subject to section 987 (taking into account the conformity rules of paragraph (c)(2) of this section) terminated on the last day of the taxable year preceding the transition date. This deemed termination applies solely for purposes of this section. Any section 987 gain or loss determined with respect to a section 987 QBU under the preceding sentence shall not be recognized on the transition date but shall be considered as net unrecognized section 987 gain or loss of the section 987 QBU in the first taxable year for which these regulations are effective (in addition to any net unrecognized section 987 gain or loss otherwise determined for such taxable year). Recognition of net unrecognized section 987 gain or loss determined under the preceding sentence is governed by § 1.987-5 for periods after the transition date. The owner of a qualified business unit that is deemed to terminate under these rules is treated as having transferred all of the assets and liabilities attributable to such qualified business unit to a new section 987 QBU on the transition date.

(ii) Translation rates used to determine the amount of assets and liabilities transferred from the owner to the section 987 QBU for the section 987 QBU's first taxable year beginning on the transition date. The exchange rates used to determine the amount of assets and liabilities transferred from the owner to the section 987 QBU on the transition date (for example, for purposes of making calculations under § 1.987-4) under the deferral transition method in this paragraph (c)(3) shall be determined with reference to the historic exchange rates on the day the assets were acquired or liabilities entered into by the qualified business unit deemed terminated, adjusted to take into account any gain or loss determined under paragraph (c)(3)(i) of this section. See Examples 1 and 2 of paragraph (d) of this section.

(4) Fresh start transition method. (i) In general. Pursuant to the fresh start transition method prescribed by this paragraph (c)(4), on the transition date all qualified business units of the taxpayer subject to section 987 (taking into account the conformity rules of paragraph (c)(2) of this section) are deemed terminated on the last day of the taxable year preceding the transition date. This deemed termination applies solely for purposes of this section. No section 987 gain or loss is determined or recognized on such deemed termination. The owner of a qualified business unit that is deemed to terminate under this method is treated as having transferred all of the assets and liabilities attributable to such qualified business unit to a section 987 QBU on the transition date.

(ii) Translation rates used to determine the amount of assets and liabilities transferred from the owner to the section 987 QBU for the section 987 QBU's first taxable year on the transition date. The exchange rates used to determine the amount of assets and liabilities transferred from the owner to the section 987 QBU on the transition date (for example, for purposes of making calculations under § 1.987-4) under the fresh start transition method of this paragraph (c)(4) shall be determined with reference to the historic exchange rates on the day the assets were acquired or liabilities entered into by the qualified business unit deemed terminated. See Example 3 of paragraph (d) of this section.

(5) Double counting prohibited. The transition method used by the taxpayer cannot result in taking into account section 987 gain or loss with respect to an asset or liability attributable to a period prior to the transition date more than once.

(6) Reporting. The taxpayer must attach a statement to its return for the first taxable year beginning on the transition date providing the following information:

(i) A description of each qualified business unit to which these rules apply, the qualified business unit's owner and its principal place of business, and a description of the prior method used by the taxpayer to determine section 987 gain or loss with respect to such qualified business unit.

(ii) The transition method used by the taxpayer under paragraph (c) of this section for each qualified business unit.

(iii) If the taxpayer uses the deferral transition method prescribed in paragraph (c)(3) of this section with respect to a qualified business unit, an explanation of the method used to determine section 987 gain or loss.

(iv) If the taxpayer uses the deferral transition method prescribed in paragraph (c)(3) of this section with respect to a qualified business unit, the amount treated as net unrecognized section 987 gain or loss under paragraph (c)(3)(i) of this section.

(v) The method used by the taxpayer for determining the exchange rates used to translate the basis of assets and the amount of liabilities of a section 987 QBU into the functional currency of the owner on the transition date as provided in paragraphs (c)(3)(ii) and (c)(4)(ii) of this section for purposes of applying these regulations.

(d) Examples. The principles of this section are illustrated by the following examples:

Example (1). Deferral transition method. (i) U.S. Corp is a domestic corporation with the dollar as its functional currency. U.S. Corp owns UK Branch, a branch with the pound as its functional currency. UK Branch was formed on January 1, 2006. U.S. Corp uses the method prescribed in the 1991 proposed section 987 regulations to determine the section 987 gain or loss of UK Branch. U.S. Corp contributed £6,000 to UK Branch on January 1, 2006. On the same day, UK Branch bought a truck for £4,000 and a computer for £1,000. Assume that the spot rate on January 1, 2006, is £1 = $1. UK Branch had profits determined under § 1.987-1(b)(1)(i) through (iii) of the 1991 proposed section 987 regulations of £250 in each taxable year of 2006, 2007, 2008, and 2009. Assume that the average exchange rates used to translate UK Branch's profits under the 1991 proposed section 987 regulations were as follows: 2006--£1 = $1.10; 2007--£1 = $1.20; 2008--£1 = $1.30; 2009--£1 = $1.40. UK Branch makes no remittances to U.S. Corp in any year. On January 1, 2010, UK Branch transitions to the method provided in §§ 1.987-1 through 1.987-11 of these regulations pursuant to paragraph (a) of this section. U.S. Corp chooses to use the deferral transition method of paragraph (c)(3) of this section in transitioning from its prior section 987 method (the method set forth in the 1991 proposed section 987 regulations) to the method prescribed in the §§ 1.987-1 through 1.987-11 of these regulations. The spot rate on December 31, 2009, is £1 = $2.

(ii) Pursuant to paragraph (c)(3) of this section, U.S. Corp must determine UK Branch's section 987 gain or loss on January 1, 2010 using its prior section 987 method (the method prescribed under the 1991 proposed section 987 regulations), as if UK Branch terminated on December 31, 2009. On December 31, 2009, UK Branch has an equity pool of £7,000 and a basis pool of $7,250 determined under the 1991 proposed section 987 regulations based on the following amounts:

Asset	Amount in £	Translation rate	Amount in $
Cash	£1,000	Spot rate on 1/1/06 of £1=$1	$1,000
Cash	250	Ave. rate for 2006 of £1=$1.10	275
Cash	250	Ave. rate for 2007 of £1=$1.20	300
Cash	250	Ave. rate for 2008 of £1=$1.30	325
Cash	250	Ave. rate for 2009 of £1=$1.40	350
Truck	4,000*	Spot rate on 1/1/06 of £1=$1	4,000
Computer	1,000*	Spot rate on 1/1/06 of £1=$1	1,000
Total assets	7,000		7,250
Liabilities	0		0

* Depreciation not taken into account for purposes of this example

Accordingly, under § 1.987-3(h)(3)(i) of the 1991 proposed section 987 regulations, UK Branch determines its section 987 gain or loss on December 31, 2009, as follows:

Equity Pool on 12/31/09	£7,000
Multiplied by spot rate on date of deemed termination of £1=$2	x$2
	14,000
Spot Value of Equity Pool	14,000
Less 100% of Basis Pool	(7,250)
Section 987 gain	6,750

(iii) Under paragraph (c)(3)(i) of this section, U.S. Corp does not recognize the $6,750 of section 987 gain determined on the transition date. Instead, the $6,750 will be treated as net unrecognized section 987 gain of UK Branch for 2010 and subsequent years (in addition to any net unrecognized section 987 gain or loss otherwise determined at the close of 2010 and subsequent years). Recognition of net unrecognized section 987 gain or loss is governed by § 1.987-5.

(iv) Pursuant to paragraph (c)(3)(ii) of this section, when computing the exchange rates used to determine the amount of assets and liabilities transferred from U.S. Corp to UK Branch on the transition date, U.S. Corp must adjust the historic exchange rates attributable to such assets to take into account UK Branch's section 987 gain determined under paragraph (c)(3) of this section. Under these facts, where all of UK Branch's assets are considered to generate deferred section 987 gain, U.S. Corp takes into account this section 987 gain by translating the assets deemed contributed by U.S. Corp to UK Branch on the transition date using the same spot rate it used to determine UK Branch's section 987 gain on the deemed termination date of December 31, 2009. Accordingly, on January 1, 2010, U.S. Corp translates the assets deemed contributed (cash is segregated for ease of illustration) to UK Branch as follows:

Asset	Amount in £	Translation rate	Amount in $
Cash	£1,000	Spot rate on 12/31/09 of £1=$2	$2,000
Cash	250	Spot rate on 12/31/09 of £1=$2	500
Cash	250	Spot rate on 12/31/09 of £1=$2	500
Cash	250	Spot rate on 12/31/09 of £1=$2	500
Cash	250	Spot rate on 12/31/09 of £1=$2	500
Truck	4,000	Spot rate on 12/31/09 of £1=$2	8,000
Computer	1,000	Spot rate on 12/31/09 of £1=$2	2,000
Total assets	7,000		14,000
Liabilities	0		0

Example (2). Deferral transition method. (i) The facts are the same as in Example 1 except that U.S. Corp and UK Branch use an "earnings only" approach to determine section 987 gain or loss prior to the transition date. Under this approach, U.S. Corp maintains a basis and equity pool for UK Branch's earnings and a separate basis and equity pool for UK Branch's capital. Section 987 gain or loss is only recognized on remittances of earnings (but not with respect to capital) under principles similar to those of the 1991 proposed section 987 regulations. Remittances are first considered as distributed from the earnings equity pool and then from the capital equity pool. For purposes of this example, this method is assumed to be a reasonable section 987 method and does not violate § 1.987-10(a)(2).

(ii) Using principles similar to those set forth in § 1.987-2 of the 1991 proposed section 987 regulations, the earnings equity pool of UK Branch is £1,000 (£250 earned in each taxable year of 2006, 2007, 2008 and 2009) and the corresponding earnings basis pool is $1,250 ($275 in 2006, $300 in 2007, $325 in 2008 and $350 in 2009). The capital equity pool is £6,000 and the corresponding capital basis pool is $6,000 (contributed cash of £6,000 translated to equal $6,000--which U.S. Corp can trace to contributed cash remaining of £1,000 with a translated basis equal to $1,000; a truck of £4,000 with a translated basis equal to $4,000; and a computer of £1,000 with a translated basis equal to $1,000).

(iii) Pursuant to paragraph (c)(3)(i) of this section, U.S. Corp must determine UK Branch's section 987 gain or loss on January 1, 2010, using its prior section 987 method (the "earnings only" method), as if UK Branch terminated on December 31, 2009. Using principles similar to § 1.987-3(h) of the 1991 proposed section 987 regulations with respect to the earnings equity and basis pool, U.S. Corp would determine $750 of section 987 gain as follows:

Earnings Equity Pool on 12/31/09	£1,000
Multiplied by spot rate on date of deemed termination of £1=$2	x $2
	$2,000
Spot Value of Earnings Equity Pool	$2,000
Less 100% of Earnings Basis Pool	($1,250)
Section 987 gain	$750

(iv) Under paragraph (c)(3)(i) of this section, U.S. Corp does not recognize the $750 of section 987 gain determined on the transition date. Instead, the $750 will be treated as net unrecognized section 987 gain of UK Branch for 2010 and subsequent years (in addition to any net unrecognized section 987 gain or loss otherwise determined at the close of 2010 and subsequent years). Recognition of net unrecognized section 987 gain or loss is governed by § 1.987-5.

(v) Pursuant to paragraph (c)(3)(ii) of this section, when computing the exchange rates used to determine the amount of assets and liabilities transferred from U.S. Corp to UK Branch on the transition date, U.S. Corp must adjust the historic exchange rates attributable to such assets to take into account UK Branch's section 987 gain determined under paragraph (c)(3) of this section. Under these facts, U.S. Corp may reasonably take into account UK Branch's section 987 gain by translating those UK Branch's assets that generated such gain using the same spot rate it used to determine UK Branch's section 987 gain on the termination date of December 31, 2009 and by determining the translation rate of other assets by reference to the traced basis of such assets. Accordingly, on January 1, 2010, U.S. Corp translates the deemed contributions to UK Branch as follows:

Asset	Amount in £	Translation rate	Amount in $
Contributed Cash	£1,000	Spot rate on 1/1/06 of £1=$1	$1,000
Cash	250	Spot rate on 12/31/09 of £1=$2	500
Cash	250	Spot rate on 12/31/09 of £1=$2	500
Cash	250	Spot rate on 12/31/09 of £1=$2	500
Cash	250	Spot rate on 12/31/09 of £1=$2	500
Truck	4,000	Spot rate on 1/1/06 of £1=$1	4,000
Computer	1,000	Spot rate on 1/1/06 of £1=$1	1,000
Total assets	7,000		8,000
Liabilities	0		0

(vi) If UK Branch was not able to trace historic dollar basis as set forth in paragraph (v) of this Example 2, when translating the assets deemed contributed to UK Branch on January 1, 2010, under paragraph (c)(3)(ii) of this section, U.S. Corp would be required to use exchange rates that take into account a reasonable allocation of the aggregate historic basis and the $750 of deferred section 987 gain to the UK Branch assets.

Example (3). Fresh start transition method. (i) The facts are the same as in Example 1, except that U.S. Corp chooses to use the fresh start transition method of paragraph (c)(4) of this section in transitioning from the 1991 proposed regulations to the method prescribed in the current regulations. Pursuant to paragraph (c)(4)(i) of this section, UK Branch is deemed to terminate on December 31, 2009. However, no section 987 gain or loss will be determined or recognized. On January 1, 2010, when translating the assets deemed contributed to UK Branch, U.S. Corp will use the historic exchange rates existing on the date the assets were acquired by UK Branch pursuant to paragraph (c)(4)(ii) of this section. Accordingly, U.S. Corp translates the assets deemed contributed (cash is segregated for ease of illustration) to UK Branch as follows:

Asset	Amount in £	Translation rate	Amount in $
Contributed Cash	£1000	Spot rate on 1/1/06 of £1=$1	$1,000
Cash	250	Ave. rate for 2006 of £1=$1.10	275
Cash	250	Ave. rate for 2004 of £1=$1.20	300
Cash	250	Ave. rate for 2005 of £1=$1.30	325
Cash	250	Ave. rate for 2006 of £1=$1.40	350
Truck	4000	Spot rate on 1/1/06 of £1=$1	4,000
Computer	1000	Spot rate on 1/1/06 of £1=$1	1,000
Total assets	7000		7,250
Liabilities	0		0

(ii) If UK Branch was not able to trace historic dollar basis as set forth in paragraph (i) of this Example 3, when translating the assets deemed contributed to UK Branch on January 1, 2010, under paragraph (c)(3)(ii) of this section, U.S. Corp would be required to use exchange rates that take into account a reasonable allocation of the aggregate historic basis of the UK Branch assets.

Proposed § 1.987-11 Effective date. [*For Preamble, see ¶ 152,801*]

(a) In general. Except as otherwise provided in this section, these regulations shall apply to taxable years beginning one year after the first day of the first taxable year following the date of publication of a Treasury decision adopting this rule as a final regulation in the Federal Register.

(b) Election to apply these regulations to taxable years beginning after the date of publication of a Treasury decision adopting this rule as a final regulation in the Federal Register. A taxpayer may elect to apply these regulations to taxable years beginning after the date of publication of a Treasury decision adopting this rule as a final regulation in the Federal Register. Such election shall be binding on all members that file a consolidated return with the taxpayer and any controlled foreign corporation, as defined in section 957, in which the taxpayer owns more than 50 percent of the voting power or stock (as determined in section 957(a)). An election made under this paragraph shall be made in accordance with § 1.987-1(f).

§ 1.988-0 Taxation of gain or loss from a section 988 transaction; Table of contents.

This section lists captioned paragraphs contained in §§ 1.988-1 through 1.988-6.

T.D. 8400, 3/16/92, amend T.D. 8860, 1/12/2000, T.D. 9157, 8/27/2004.

---

§ 1.988-1 Certain definitions and special rules.

Caution: The Treasury has not yet amended Reg § 1.988-1 to reflect changes made by P.L. 105-34.

(a) Section 988 transaction. *(1) In general.* The term "section 988 transaction" means any of the following transactions—

(i) A disposition of nonfunctional currency as defined in paragraph (c) of this section;

(ii) Any transaction described in paragraph (a)(2) of this section if any amount which the taxpayer is entitled to receive or is required to pay by reason of such transaction is denominated in terms of a nonfunctional currency or is determined by reference to the value of one or more nonfunctional currencies.

A transaction described in this paragraph (a) need not require or permit payment with a nonfunctional currency as long as any amount paid or received is determined by reference to the value of one or more nonfunctional currencies. The acquisition of nonfunctional currency is treated as a section 988 transaction for purposes of establishing the taxpayer's basis in such currency and determining exchange gain or loss thereon.

(2) Description of transactions. The following transactions are described in this paragraph (a)(2).

(i) Debt instruments. Acquiring a debt instrument or becoming an obligor under a debt instrument. The term "debt instrument" means a bond, debenture, note, certificate or other evidence of indebtedness.

(ii) Payables, receivables, etc. Accruing, or otherwise taking into account, for purposes of subtitle A of the Internal Revenue Code, any item of expense or gross income or receipts which is to be paid or received after the date on which so accrued or taken into account. A payable relating to cost of goods sold, or a payable or receivable relating to a capital expenditure or receipt, is within the meaning of this paragraph (a)(2)(ii). Generally, a payable relating to foreign taxes (whether or not claimed as a credit under section 901) is within the meaning of this paragraph (a)(2)(ii). However, a payable of a domestic person relating to accrued foreign taxes of its qualified business unit (QBU branch) is not within the meaning of this paragraph (a)(2)(ii) if the QBU branch's functional currency is the U.S. dollar and the foreign taxes are claimed as a credit under section 901.

(iii) Forward contract, futures contract, option contract, or similar financial instrument. Except as otherwise provided in this paragraph (a)(2)(iii) and paragraph (a)(4)(i) of this section, entering into or acquiring any forward contract, futures contract, option, warrant, or similar financial instrument.

(A) Limitation for certain derivative instruments. A forward contract, futures contract, option, warrant, or similar financial instrument is within this paragraph (a)(2)(iii) only if the underlying property to which the instrument ultimately relates is a nonfunctional currency or is otherwise described in paragraph (a)(1)(ii) of this section. Thus, if the underlying property of an instrument is another financial instrument (e.g., an option on a futures contract), then the underlying property to which such other instrument (e.g., the futures contract) ultimately relates must be a nonfunctional currency. For example, a forward contract to purchase wheat denominated in a nonfunctional currency, an option to enter into a forward contract to purchase wheat denominated in a nonfunctional currency, or a warrant to purchase stock denominated in a nonfunctional currency is not described in this paragraph (a)(2)(iii). On the other hand, a forward contract to purchase a nonfunctional currency, an option to enter into a forward contract to purchase a nonfunctional currency, an option to purchase a bond denominated in or the payments of which are determined by reference to the value of a nonfunctional currency, or a warrant to purchase nonfunctional currency is described in this paragraph (a)(2)(iii).

(B) Nonfunctional currency notional principal contracts. (1) In general. The term "similar financial instrument" includes a notional principal contract only if the payments required to be made or received under the contract are determined with reference to a nonfunctional currency.

(2) Definition of notional principal contract. The term "notional principal contract" means a contract (e.g., a swap, cap, floor or collar) that provides for the payment of amounts by one party to another at specified intervals calculated by reference to a specified index upon a notional principal amount in exchange for specified consideration or a promise to pay similar amounts. For this purpose, a "notional principal contract" shall only include an instrument where the underlying property to which the instrument ultimately relates is money (e.g., functional currency), nonfunctional currency, or property the value of which is determined by reference to an interest rate. Thus, the term "notional principal contract" includes a currency swap as defined in § 1.988-2(e)(2)(ii), but does not include a swap referenced to a commodity or equity index.

(C) Effective date with respect to certain contracts. This paragraph (a)(2)(iii) does not apply to any forward contract, futures contract, option warrant, or similar financial instrument entered into or acquired on or before October 21, 1988, if such instrument would have been marked to market under section 1256 if held on the last day of the taxable year.

(3) - (5) [Reserved]

(6) Examples. The following examples illustrate the application of paragraph (a) of this section. The examples assume that X is a U.S. corporation on an accrual method with the calendar year as its taxable year. Because X is a U.S. corporation the U.S. dollar is its functional currency under section 985. The examples also assume that section 988(d) does not apply.

Example (1). On January 1, 1989, X acquires 10,000 Canadian dollars. On January 15, 1989, X uses the 10,000 Canadian dollars to purchase inventory. The acquisition of the 10,000 Canadian dollars is a section 988 transaction for purposes of establishing X's basis in such Canadian dollars. The disposition of the 10,000 Canadian dollars is a section 988 transaction pursuant to paragraph (a)(1) of this section.

Example (2). On January 1, 1989, X acquires 10,000 Canadian dollars. On January 15, 1989, X converts the 10,000 Canadian dollars to U.S. dollars. The acquisition of the 10,000 Canadian dollars is a section 988 transaction for purposes of establishing X's basis in such Canadian dollars. The conversion of the 10,000 Canadian dollars to U.S. dollars is a section 988 transaction pursuant to paragraph (a)(1) of this section.

Example (3). On January 1, 1989, X borrows 100,000 British pounds (£) for a period of 10 years and issues a note to the lender with a face amount of £100,000. The note provides for payments of interest at an annual rate of 10% paid quarterly in pounds and has a stated redemption price at maturity of £100,000. X's becoming the obligor under the note is a section 988 transaction pursuant to paragraphs (a)(1)(ii) and (2)(i) of this section. Because X is an accrual basis taxpayer, the accrual of interest expense under X's note is a section 988 transaction pursuant to paragraphs (a)(1)(ii) and (2)(ii) of this section. In addition, the acquisition of the British pounds to make payments under the note is a section 988 transaction for purposes of establishing X's basis in such pounds, and the disposition of such pounds is a section 988 transaction under paragraph (a)(1)(i) of this section. See § 1.988-2(b) with respect to the translation of accrued interest expense and the determination of exchange gain or loss upon payment of accrued interest expense.

Example (4). On January 1, 1989, X purchases an original issue for 74,621.54 British pounds (£) a 3-year bond maturing on December 31, 1991, at a stated redemption price of £100,000. The bond provides for no stated interest. The bond has a yield to maturity of 10% compounded semiannually and has £25,378.46 of original issue discount. The acquisition of the bond is a section 988 transaction as provided in paragraphs (a)(1)(ii) and (2)(i) of this section. The accrual of original issue discount with respect to the bond is a section 988 transaction under paragraphs (a)(1)(ii) and (2)(ii) of this section. See § 1.988-2(b) with respect to the translation of original issue discount and the determination of exchange gain or loss upon receipt of such amounts.

Example (5). On January 1, 1989, X sells and delivers inventory to Y for 10,000,000 Italian lira for payment on April 1, 1989. Under X's method of accounting, January 1, 1989 is the accrual date. Because X is an accrual basis taxpayer, the accrual of a nonfunctional currency denominated item of gross receipts on January 1, 1989, for payment after the date of accrual is a section 988 transaction under paragraphs (a)(1)(ii) and (2)(ii) of this section.

Example (6). On January 1, 1989, X agrees to purchase a machine from Y for delivery on March 1, 1990 for 1,000,000 yen. The agreement calls for X to pay Y for the machine on June 1, 1990. Under X's method of accounting, the expenditure for the machine does not accrue until delivery on March 1, 1990. The agreement to purchase the machine is not a section 988 transaction. In particular, the agreement to purchase the machine is not described in paragraph (a)(2)(ii) of this section because the agreement is not an item of expense taken into account under subtitle A (but rather is an agreement to purchase a capital asset in the future). However, the payable that will arise on the delivery date is a section 988 transaction under paragraphs (a)(1)(ii) and (2)(ii) of this section even though the payable relates to a capital expenditure. In addition, the disposition of yen to satisfy the payable on June 1, 1990, is a section 988 transaction under paragraph (a)(1)(i) of this section.

Example (7). On January 1, 1989, X purchases and takes delivery of inventory for 10,000 French francs with payment to be made on April 1, 1989. Under X's method of accounting, the expense accrues on January 1, 1989. On January 1, 1989, X also enters into a forward contract with a bank to purchase 10,000 French francs for $2,000 on April 1, 1989. Because X is an accrual basis taxpayer, the accrual of a nonfunctional currency denominated item of expense on January 1, 1989, for payment after the date of accrual is a section 988 transaction under paragraphs (a)(1)(ii) and (2)(ii) of this section. Entering into the forward contract to purchase the 10,000 French francs is a section 988 transaction under paragraphs (a)(1)(ii) and (2)(iii) of this section.

Example (8). On January 1, 1989, X acquires 100,000 Norwegian krone. On January 15, 1989, X purchases and takes delivery of 1,000 shares of common stock with the 100,000 krone acquired on January 1, 1989. On August 1, 1989, X sells the 1,000 shares of common stock and receives 120,000 krone in payment. On August 30, 1989, X converts the 120,000 krone to U.S. dollars. The acquisition of the 100,000 krone on January 1, 1989, and the acquisition of the 120,000 krone on August 1, 1989, are section 988 transactions for purposes of establishing the basis of such krone. The disposition of the 100,000 krone on January 15, 1989, and the 120,000 krone on August 30, 1989, are section 988 transactions as provided in paragraph (a)(1)(i) of this section. Neither the acquisition on January 15, 1989, nor the disposition on August 1, 1989, of the stock is a section 988 transaction.

Example (9). On May 11, 1989, X purchases a one year note at original issue for its issue price of $1,000. The note pays interest in dollars at the rate of 4 percent compounded semiannually. The amount of principal received by X upon maturity is equal to $1,000 plus the equivalent of the excess, if any, of (a) the Financial Times One Hundred Stock Index (an index of stocks traded on the London Stock Exchange hereafter referred to as the FT100) determined and translated into dollars on the last business day prior to the maturity date, over (b) £2.150, the "stated value" of the FT100, which is equal to 110% of the average value of the index for the six months prior to the issue date, translated at the exchange rate of £1 = $1.50. The purchase by X of the instrument described above is not a section 988 transaction because the index used to compute the principal amount received upon maturity is determined with reference to the value of stock and not nonfunctional currency.

Example (10). On April 9, 1989, X enters into an interest rate swap that provides for the payment of amounts by X to its counterparty based on 4% of a 10,000 yen principal amount in exchange for amounts based on yen LIBOR rates. Pursuant to paragraphs (a)(1)(ii) and (2)(iii) of this section, this yen for yen interest rate swap is a section 988 transaction.

Example (11). On August 11, 1989, X enters into an option contract for sale of a group of stocks traded on the Japanese Nikkei exchange. The contract is not a section 988 transaction within the meaning of § 1.988-1(a)(2)(iii) because the underlying property to which the option relates is a group of stocks and not nonfunctional currency.

(7) Special rules for regulated futures contracts and non-equity options. (i) In general. Except as provided in paragraph (a)(7)(ii) of this section, paragraph (a)(2)(iii) of this section shall not apply to any regulated futures contract or non-equity option which would be marked to market under section 1256 if held on the last day of the taxable year.

(ii) Election to have paragraph (a)(2)(iii) of this section apply. Notwithstanding paragraph (a)(7)(i) of this section, a taxpayer may elect to have paragraph (a)(2)(iii) of this section apply to regulated futures contracts and non-equity options as provided in paragraph (a)(7)(iii) and (iv) of this section.

(iii) Procedure for making the election. A taxpayer shall make the election provided in paragraph (a)(7)(ii) of this section by sending to the Internal Revenue Service Center, Examination Branch, Stop Number 92, Kansas City, MO 64999 a statement titled "Election to Treat Regulated Futures Contracts and Non-Equity Options as Section 988 Transactions Under Section 988(c)(1)(D)(ii)" that contains the following:

(A) The taxpayer's name, address, and taxpayer identification number;

(B) The date the notice is mailed or otherwise delivered to the Internal Revenue Service Center;

(C) A statement that the taxpayer (including all members of such person's affiliated group as defined in section 1504 or in the case of an individual all persons filing a joint return with such individual) elects to have section 988(c)(1)(D)(i) and § 1.988-1(a)(7)(i) not apply;

(D) The date of the beginning of the taxable year for which the election is being made;

(E) If the election is filed after the first day of the taxable year, a statement regarding whether the taxpayer has previously held a contract described in section 988(c)(1)(D)(i) or § 1.988-1(a)(7)(i) during such taxable year, and if so, the first date during the taxable year on which such contract was held; and

(F) The signature of the person making the election (in the case of individuals filing a joint return, the signature of all persons filing such return).

The election shall be made by the following persons: in the case of an individual, by such individual; in the case of a partnership, by each partner separately; effective for taxable years beginning after March 17, 1992, in the case of tiered partnerships, each ultimate partner; in the case of an S corporation, by each shareholder separately; in the case of a trust (other than a grantor trust) or estate, by the fiduciary of such trust or estate; in the case of any corporation other than an S corporation, by such corporation (in the case of a corporation that is a member of an affiliated group that files a consolidated return, such election shall be valid and binding only if made by the common parent, as that term is used in § 1.1502-77(a)); in the case of a controlled foreign corporation, by its controlling United States shareholders under § 1.964-1(c)(3). With respect to a corporation (other than an S corporation), the election, when made by the common parent, shall be binding on all members of such corporation's affiliated group as defined in section 1504 that file a consolidated return. The election shall be binding on any income or loss derived from the partner's share (determined under the principles of section 702(a)) of all contracts described in section 988(c)(1)(D)(i) or paragraph (a)(7)(i) of this section in which the taxpayer holds a direct interest or indirect interest through a partnership or S corporation; however, the election shall not apply to any income or loss of a partnership for any taxable year if such partnership made an election under section 988(c)(1)(E)(iii)(V) for such year or any preceding year. Generally, a copy of the election must be attached to the taxpayer's income tax return for the first year it is effective. It is not required to be attached to subsequent returns. However, in the case of a partner, a copy of the election must be attached to the taxpayer's income tax return for every year during which the taxpayer is a partner in a partnership that engages in a transaction that is subject to the election.

(iv) Time for making the election. (A) In general. Unless the requirements for making a late election described in paragraph (a)(7)(iv)(B) of this section are satisfied, an election under section 988(c)(1)(D)(ii) and paragraph (a)(7)(ii) of this section for any taxable year shall be made on or before the first day of the taxable year or, if later, on or before the first day during such taxable year on which the taxpayer holds a contract described in section 988(c)(1)(D)(ii) and paragraph (a)(7)(ii) of this section. The election under section 988(c)(1)(D)(ii) and paragraph (a)(7)(ii) of this section shall apply to contracts entered into or acquired after October 21, 1988, and held on or after the effective date of the election. The election shall be effective as of the beginning of the taxable year and shall be binding with respect to all succeeding taxable years unless revoked with the prior consent of the Commissioner. In determining whether to grant revocation of the election, recapture of the tax benefit derived from the election in previous taxable years will be considered.

(B) Late elections. A taxpayer may make an election under section 988(c)(1)(D)(ii) and paragraph (a)(7)(ii) of this section within 30 days after the time prescribed in the first sentence of paragraph (a)(7)(iv)(A) of this section. Such a late election shall be effective as of the beginning of the taxable year; however, any losses recognized during the taxable year with respect to contracts described in section 988(c)(1)(D)(ii) or paragraph (a)(7)(ii) of this section which were entered into or acquired after October 21, 1988, and held on or before the date on which the late election is mailed or otherwise delivered to the Internal Revenue Service Center shall not be treated as derived from a section 988 transaction. A late election must comply with the procedures set forth in paragraph (a)(7)(iii) of this section.

(v) Transition rule. An election made prior to September 21, 1989 which satisfied the requirements of Notice 88-124, 1988-51 I.R.B. 6, shall be deemed to satisfy the requirements of paragraphs (a)(7)(iii) and (iv) of this section.

(vi) General effective date provision. This paragraph (a)(7) shall apply with respect to futures contracts and options entered into or acquired after October 21, 1988.

(8) Special rules for qualified funds. (i) Definition of qualified fund. The term "qualified fund" means any partnership if—

(A) At all times during the taxable year (and during each preceding taxable year to which an election under section 988(c)(1)(E)(iii)(V) applied) such partnership has at least 20 partners and no single partner owns more than 20 percent of the interests in the capital or profits of the partnership;

(B) The principal activity of such partnership for such taxable year (and each such preceding taxable year) consists of buying and selling options, futures, or forwards with respect to commodities;

(C) At least 90 percent of the gross income of the partnership for the taxable year (and each such preceding year) consists of income or gains described in subparagraph (A), (B), or (G) of section 7704(d)(1) or gain from the sale or disposition of capital assets held for the production of interest or dividends;

(D) No more than a de minimis amount of the gross income of the partnership for the taxable year (and each such preceding taxable year) was derived from buying and selling commodities; and

(E) An election under section 988(c)(1)(E)(iii)(V) as provided in paragraph (a)(8)(iv) of this section applies to the taxable year.

(ii) Special rules relating to paragraph (a)(8)(i)(A) of this section. (A) Certain general partners. The interest of a general partner in the partnership shall not be treated as failing to meet the 20 percent ownership requirement of paragraph (a)(8)(i)(A) of this section for any taxable year of the partnership if, for the taxable year of the partner in which such partnership's taxable year ends, such partner (and each corporation filing a consolidated return with such partner) had no ordinary income or loss from a section 988 transaction (other than income from the partnership) which is exchange gain or loss (as the case may be).

(B) Treatment of incentive compensation. For purposes of paragraph (a)(8)(i)(A) of this section, any income allocable to a general partner as incentive compensation based on profits rather than capital shall not be taken into account in determining such partner's interest in the profits of the partnership.

(C) Treatment of tax exempt partners. The interest of a partner in the partnership shall not be treated as failing to meet the 20 percent ownership requirements of paragraph (a)(5)(8)(A) of this section if none of the income of such partner from such partnership is subject to tax under chapter 1 of subtitle A of the Internal Revenue Code (whether directly or through one or more pass-through entities).

(D) Look-through rule. In determining whether the 20 percent ownership requirement of paragraph (a)(8)(i)(A) of this section is met with respect to any partnership, any interest in such partnership held by another partnership shall be treated as held proportionately by the partners in such other partnership.

(iii) Other special rules. (A) Related persons. Interests in the partnership held by persons related to each other (within the meaning of section 267(b) or 707(b)) shall be treated as held by one person.

(B) Predecessors. Reference to any partnership shall include a reference to any predecessor thereof.

(C) Treatment of certain debt instruments. Solely for purposes of paragraph (a)(8)(i)(D) of this section, any debt instrument which is described in both paragraph (a)(1)(ii) and (2)(i) of this section shall be treated as a commodity.

(iv) Procedure for making the election provided in section 988(c)(1)(E)(iii)(V). A partnership shall make the election provided in section 988(c)(1)(E)(iii)(V) by sending to the Internal Revenue Service Center, Examination Branch, Stop Number 92, Kansas City, MO 64999 a statement titled "QUALIFIED FUND ELECTION UNDER SECTION 988(c)(1)(E)(iii)(V)" that contains the following:

(A) The partnership's name, address, and taxpayer identification number;

(B) The name, address and taxpayer identification number of the general partner making the election on behalf of the partnership;

(C) The date the notice is mailed or otherwise delivered to the Internal Revenue Service Center;

(D) A brief description of the activity of the partnership;

(E) A statement that the partnership is making the election provided in section 988(c)(1)(E)(iii)(V);

(F) The date of the beginning of the taxable year for which the election is being made;

(G) If the election is filed after the first day of the taxable year, then a statement regarding whether the partnership previously held an instrument referred to in section 988(c)(1)(E)(i) during such taxable year and, if so, the first date during the taxable year on which such contract was held; and

(H) The signature of the general partner making the election.

The election shall be made by a general partner with management responsibility of the partnership's activities and a copy of such election shall be attached to the partnership's income tax return (Form 1065) for the first taxable year it is effective. It is not required to be attached to subsequent returns.

(v) Time for making the election. The election under section 988(c)(1)(E)(iii)(V) for any taxable year shall be made on or before the first day of the taxable year or, if later, on or before the first day during such year on which the partnership holds an instrument described in section 988(c)(1)(E)(i). The election under section 988(c)(1)(E)(iii)(V) shall apply to the taxable year for which made and all succeeding taxable years. Such election may only be revoked with the consent of the Commissioner. In determining whether to grant revocation of the election, recapture by the partners of the tax benefit derived from the election in previous taxable years will be considered.

(vi) Operative rules applicable to qualified funds. (A) In general. In the case of a qualified fund, any bank forward contract or any foreign currency futures contract traded on a foreign exchange which is not otherwise a section 1256 contract shall be treated as a section 1256 contract for purposes of section 1256.

(B) Gains and losses treated as short-term. In the case of any instrument treated as a section 1256 contract under paragraph (a)(8)(vi)(A) of this section, subparagraph (A) of section 1256(a)(3) shall be applied by substituting "100 percent" for "40 percent" (and subparagraph (B) of such section shall not apply).

(vii) Transition rule. An election made prior to September 21, 1989, which satisfied the requirements of Notice 88-124, 1988-51 I.R.B. 6, shall be deemed to satisfy the requirements of § 1.988-1(a)(8)(iv) and (v).

(viii) General effective date rules. (A) The requirements of subclause (IV) of section 988(c)(1)(E)(iii) shall not apply to contracts entered into or acquired on or before October 21, 1988.

(B) In the case of any partner in an existing partnership, the 20 percent ownership requirements of subclause (I) of section 988(c)(1)(E)(iii) shall be treated as met during any period during which such partner does not own a percentage interest in the capital or profits of such partnership greater than 33⅓ percent (or, if lower, the lowest such percentage interest of such partner during any period after October 21, 1988, during which such partnership is in existence). For purposes of the preceding sentence, the term "existing partnership" means any partnership if—

(1) Such partnership was in existence on October 21, 1988, and principally engaged on such date in buying and selling options, futures, or forwards with respect to commodities; or

(2) A registration statement was filed with respect to such partnership with the Securities and Exchange Commission on or before such date and such registration statement indicated that the principal activity of such partnership will consist of buying and selling instruments referred to in paragraph (a)(8)(viii)(B)(1) of this section.

(9) Exception for certain transactions entered into by an individual. (i) In general. A transaction entered into by an individual which otherwise qualifies as a section 988 transaction shall be considered a section 988 transaction only to the extent expenses properly allocable to such transaction meet the requirements of section 162 or 212 (other than the part of section 212 dealing with expenses incurred in connection with taxes).

(ii) Examples. The following examples illustrate the application of paragraph (a)(9) of this section.

Example (1). X is a U.S. citizen who therefore has the U.S. dollar as his functional currency. On January 1, 1990, X enters into a spot contract to purchase 10,000 British pounds (£) for $15,000 for delivery on January 3, 1990. Immediately upon delivery, X acquires at original issue a pound denominated bond with an issue price of £10,000. The bond matures on January 3, 1993, pays interest in pounds at a rate of 10% compounded semiannually, and has no original issue discount. Assume that all expenses properly allocable to these transactions would meet the requirements of section 212. Under § 1.988-2(d)(1)(ii), entering into the spot contract on January 1, 1990, is not a section 988 transaction. The acquisition of the pounds on January 3, 1990, under the spot contract is a section 988 transaction for purposes of establishing X's basis in the pounds. The disposition of the pounds and the acquisition of the bond by X are section 988 transactions. These transactions are not excluded from the definition of a section 988 transaction under paragraph (a)(9) of this section because expenses properly allocable to such transactions meet the requirements of section 212.

Example (2). X is a U.S. citizen who therefore has the dollar as his functional currency. In preparation for X's vacation, X purchases 1,000 British pounds (£) from a bank on June 1, 1989. During the period of X's vacation in the

United Kingdom beginning June 10, 1989, and ending June 20, 1989, X spends £500 for hotel rooms, £300 for food and £200 for miscellaneous vacation expenses. The expenses properly allocable to such dispositions do not meet the requirements of section 162 or 212. Thus, the disposition of the pounds by X on his vacation are not section 988 transactions.

(10) Intra-taxpayer transactions. (i) In general. Except as provided in paragraph (a)(10)(ii) of this section, transactions between or among the taxpayer and/or qualified business units of that taxpayer ("intra-taxpayer transactions") are not section 988 transactions. See section 987 and the regulations thereunder.

(ii) Certain transfers. Exchange gain or loss with respect to nonfunctional currency or any item described in paragraph (a)(2) of this section entered into with another taxpayer shall be realized upon an intra-taxpayer transfer of such currency or item where as the result of the transfer the currency or other such item—

(A) Loses its character as nonfunctional currency or an item described in paragraph (a)(2) of this section; or

(B) Where the source of the exchange gain or loss could be altered absent the application of this paragraph (a)(10)(ii). Such exchange gain or loss shall be computed in accordance with § 1.988-2 (without regard to § 1.988-2(b)(8)) as if the nonfunctional currency or item described in paragraph (a)(2) of this section had been sold or otherwise transferred at fair market value between unrelated taxpayers. For purposes of the preceding sentence, a taxpayer must use the translation rate that it uses for purposes of computing section 987 gain or loss with respect to the QBU branch that makes the transfer. In the case of a gain or loss incurred in a transaction described in this paragraph (a)(10)(ii) that does not have a significant business purpose, the Commissioner, may defer such gain or loss.

(iii) Example. The following example illustrates the provisions of this paragraph (a)(10).

Example. (A) X, a corporation with the U.S. dollar as its functional currency, operates through foreign branches Y and Z. Y and Z are qualified business units as defined in section 989(a) with the LC as their functional currency. X computes Y's and Z's income under section 987 (relating to branch transactions). On November 12, 1988, Y transfers $25 to the home office of X when the fair market value of such amount equals LC120. Y has a basis of LC100 in the $25. Under paragraph (a)(10)(ii) of this section, Y realizes foreign source exchange gain of LC20 (LC120 – LC100) as the result of the $25 transfer. For purposes of determining whether the transfer is a remittance resulting in additional gain or loss, see section 987 and the regulations thereunder.

(B) If instead Y transfers the $25 to Z, exchange gain is not realized because the $25 is nonfunctional currency with respect to Z and if Z were to immediately convert the $25 into LCs, the gain would be foreign source. For purposes of determining whether the transfer is a remittance resulting in additional gain or loss, see section 987 and the regulations thereunder.

(11) Authority to include or exclude transactions from section 988. (i) In general. The Commissioner may recharacterize a transaction (or series of transactions) in whole or in part as a section 988 transaction if the effect of such transaction (or series of transactions) is to avoid section 988. In addition, the Commissioner may exclude a transaction (or series of transactions) which in form is a section 988 transaction from the provisions of section 988 if the substance of the transaction (or series of transactions) indicates that it is not properly considered a section 988 transaction.

(ii) Example. The following example illustrates the provisions of this example paragraph (a)(11).

Example. B is an individual with the U.S. dollar as its functional currency. B holds 500,000 Swiss francs which have a basis of $100,000 and a fair market value of $400,000 as of October 15, 1989. On October 16, 1989, B transfers the 500,000 Swiss francs to a newly formed U.S. corporation, X, with the dollar as its functional currency. On October 16, 1989, B sells the stock of X for $400,000. Assume the transfer to X qualified for nonrecognition under section 351. Because the sale of the stock of X is a substitute for the disposition of an asset subject to section 988, the Commissioner may recharacterize the sale of the stock as a section 988 transaction. The same result would obtain if B transferred the Swiss francs to a partnership and then sold the partnership interest.

(b) Spot contract. A spot contract is a contract to buy or sell nonfunctional currency on or before two business days following the date of the execution of the contract. See § 1.988-2(d)(1)(ii) for operative rules regarding spot contracts.

(c) Nonfunctional currency. The term "nonfunctional currency" means with respect to a taxpayer or a qualified business unit (as defined in section 989(a)) a currency (including the European Currency Unit) other than the taxpayer's or the qualified business unit's functional currency as defined in section 985 and the regulations thereunder. For rules relating to nonrecognition of exchange gain or loss with respect to certain dispositions of nonfunctional currency, see § 1.988-2(a)(1)(iii).

(d) Spot rate. *(1) In general.* Except as otherwise provided in this paragraph, the term "spot rate" means a rate demonstrated to the satisfaction of the District Director or the Assistant Commissioner (International) to reflect a fair market rate of exchange available to the public for currency under a spot contract in a free market and involving representative amounts. In the absence of such a demonstration, the District Director or the Assistant Commissioner (International), in his or her sole discretion, shall determine the spot rate from a source of exchange rate information reflecting actual transactions conducted in a free market. For example, the taxpayer or the District Director or the Assistant Commissioner (International) may determine the spot rate by reference to exchange rates published in the pertinent monthly issue of "International Financial Statistics" or a successor publication of the International Monetary Fund; exchange rates published by the Board of Governors of the Federal Reserve System pursuant to 31 U.S.C. section 5151; exchange rates published in newspapers, financial journals or other daily financial news sources; or exchange rates quoted by electronic financial news services.

(2) Consistency required in valuing transactions subject to section 989. If the use of inconsistent sources of spot rate quotations results in the distortion of income, the District Director or the Assistant Commissioner (International) may determine the appropriate spot rate.

(3) Use of certain spot rate conventions for payables and receivables denominated in nonfunctional currency. If consistent with the taxpayer's financial accounting, a taxpayer may utilize a spot rate convention determined at intervals of one quarter year or less for purposes of computing exchange gain or loss with respect to payables and receivables denominated in a nonfunctional currency that are incurred in the

ordinary course of business with respect to the acquisition or sale of goods or the obtaining or performance of services. For example, if consistent with the taxpayer's financial accounting, a taxpayer may accrue all payables and receivables incurred during the month of January at the spot rate on December 31 or January 31 (or at an average of any spot rates occurring between these two dates) and record the payment or receipt of amounts in satisfaction of such payables and receivables consistent with such convention. The use of a spot rate convention cannot be changed without the consent of the Commissioner.

(4) Currency where an official government established rate differs from a free market rate. (i) In general. If a currency has an official government established rate that differs from a free market rate, the spot rate shall be the rate which most clearly reflects the taxpayer's income. Generally, this shall be the free market rate.

(ii) Examples. The following examples illustrate the application of this paragraph (d)(4).

Example (1). X is an accrual method U.S. corporation with the dollar as its functional currency. X owns all the stock of a Country L subsidiary, CFC. CFC has the currency of Country L, the LC, as its functional currency. Country L imposes restrictions on the remittance of dividends. On April 1, 1990, CFC pays a dividend to X in the amount of LC100. Assume that the official government established rate is $1 = LC1 and the free market rate, which takes into account the remittance restrictions and which is the rate that most clearly reflects income, is $1 = LC4. On April 1, 1990, X donates the LC100 in a transaction that otherwise qualifies as a charitable contribution under section 170(c). Both the amount of the dividend income and the deduction under section 170 is $25 (LC100 × the free market rate, $.25).

Example (2). X, a corporation with the U.S. dollar as its functional currency, operates in foreign country L through branch Y. Y is a qualified business unit as defined in section 989(a). X computes Y's income under the dollar approximate separate transactions method as described in § 1.985-3. The currency of L is the LC. X can purchase legally United States dollars ($) in L only from the L government. In order to take advantage of an arbitrage between the official and secondary dollar to LC exchange rates in L:

(i) X purchases LC100 for $60 in L on the secondary market when the official exchange rate is S1 = LC1;

(ii) X transfers the LC100 to Y;

(iii) Y purchases $100 for LC100; and

(iv) Y transfers $65 ($100 less an L tax withheld of $35 on the transfer) to the home office of X.

Under paragraph (a)(7) of this section, the transfer of the LC100 by X to Y is a realization event. X has a basis of $60 in the LC100. Under these facts, the appropriate dollar to LC exchange rate for computing the amount realized by X is the official exchange rate. Therefore, X realizes $40 ($100-$60) of U.S. source gain from the transfer to Y. The same result would obtain if Y rather than X purchased the LC100 on the secondary market in L with $60 supplied by X, because the substance of this transaction is that X is performing the arbitrage.

(e) Exchange gain or loss. The term "exchange gain or loss" means the amount of gain or loss realized as determined in § 1.988-2 with respect to a section 988 transaction. Except as otherwise provided in these regulations (e.g., § 1.98B-5), the amount of exchange gain or loss from a section 988 transaction shall be separately computed for each section 988 transaction, and such amount shall not be integrated with gain or loss recognized on another transaction (whether or not such transaction is economically related to the section 988 transaction). See § 1.988-2 (b)(8) for a special rule with respect to debt instruments.

(f) Hyperinflationary currency. *(1) Definition.* (i) General rule. For purposes of section 988, a hyperinflationary currency means a currency described in § 1.985-1(b)(2)(ii)(D). Unless otherwise provided, the currency in any example used in §§ 1.988-1 through 1.988-5 is not a hyperinflationary currency.

(ii) Special rules for determining base period. In determining whether a currency is hyperinflationary under § 1.985-1(b)(2)(ii)(D) for purposes of this paragraph (f), the following rules will apply:

(A) The base period means the thirty-six calendar month period ending on the last day of the taxpayer's (or qualified business unit's) current taxable year. Thus, for example, if for 1996, 1997, and 1998, a country's annual inflation rates are 6 percent, 11 percent, and 90 percent, respectively, the cumulative inflation rate for the three-year base period is 124% [((1.06 × 1.11 × 1.90) - 1.0 = 1.24) x 100 = 124%]. Accordingly, assuming the QBU has a calendar year as its taxable year, the currency of the country is hyperinflationary for the 1998 taxable year. This change in the § 1.985-1(b)(2)(ii)(D) base period shall not apply to any section 988 transaction of an entity described in section 851 (regulated investment company (RIC)) or section 856 (real estate investment trust (REIT)). The Service may, by notice, provide that the foregoing change in the § 1.985-1(b)(2)(ii)(D) base period does not apply to any section 988 transaction of an entity with distribution requirements similar to a RIC or REIT.

(B) The last sentence of § 1.985-1(b)(2)(ii)(D) shall not apply to alter the base period for purposes of this paragraph (f) in determining whether a currency is hyperinflationary for purposes of section 988. Accordingly, generally accepted accounting principles may not apply to alter the base period for purposes of this paragraph (f).

(2) Effective date. Paragraph (f)(1) of this section shall apply to transactions entered into after February 14, 2000.

(g) Fair market value. The fair market value of an item shall, where relevant, reflect an appropriate premium or discount for the time value of money (e.g., the fair market value of a forward contract to buy or sell nonfunctional currency shall reflect the present value of the difference between the units of nonfunctional currency times the market forward rate at the time of valuation and the units of nonfunctional currency times the forward rate set forth in the contract). However, if consistent with the taxpayer's method of financial accounting (and consistently applied from year to year), the preceding sentence shall not apply to a financial instrument that matures within one year from the date of issuance or acquisition. Unless otherwise provided, the fair market value given in any example used in §§ 1.988-1 through 1.988-5 is deemed to reflect appropriately the time value of money. If the use of inconsistent sources of forward or other market rate quotations results in the distortion of income, the District Director or the Assistant Commissioner (International) may determine the appropriate rate.

(h) Interaction with sections 1092 and 1256. Unless otherwise provided, it is assumed for purposes of §§ 1.988-1 through 1.988-5 that any contract used in any example is not a section 1256 contract and is not part of a straddle as defined in section 1092. No inference is intended regarding the application of section 1092 or 1256 unless expressly stated.

(i) Effective date. Except as otherwise provided in this section, this section shall be effective for taxable years beginning after December 31, 1986. Thus, except as otherwise provided in this section, any payments made or received with respect to a section 988 transaction in taxable years beginning after December 31, 1986, are subject to this section.

T.D. 8400, 3/16/92, amend T.D. 8914, 12/29/2000.

PAR. 6. Section 1.988-1 is amended by:

1. Adding paragraphs (a)(3) and (a)(4).

2. Revising paragraph (a)(10)(ii).

3. Adding two sentences to the end of paragraph (i).

The additions and revision read as follows:

Proposed § 1.988-1 Certain definitions and special rules.
[*For Preamble, see ¶ 152,801*]

* * * * *

(a) * * *

(3) Certain transactions of a section 987 QBU denominated in the functional currency of the owner are not treated as section 988 transactions. Transactions described in § 1.987-3(e)(2) (regarding certain transactions that are denominated in the functional currency of the owner of a section 987 QBU) are not treated as section 988 transactions to a section 987 QBU. Thus, no currency gain or loss shall be recognized by a section 987 QBU under section 988 with respect to such items.

(4) Treatment of assets and liabilities of a partnership or DE that are not attributed to an eligible QBU. (i) Scope. This paragraph (a)(4) applies to assets and liabilities of a partnership, or of an entity disregarded as an entity separate from its owner for U.S. Federal income tax purposes (DE), that are not attributable to an eligible QBU (within the meaning of § 1.987-1(b)(3)) as provided under § 1.987-2(b).

(ii) Partnerships. For purposes of applying section 988 and the applicable regulations to transactions involving the assets and liabilities described in paragraph (a)(4)(i) of this section that are held by a partnership, the owners of the partnership (within the meaning of § 1.987-1(b)(4)) shall be treated as owning their share of such assets and liabilities. Section 1.987-7(b) shall apply for purposes of determining an owner's share of such assets or liabilities.

(iii) Disregarded entities. For purposes of applying section 988 and the applicable regulations to transactions involving the assets and liabilities described in paragraph (a)(4)(i) of this section that are held by a DE, the owner of the DE (within the meaning of § 1.987-1(b)(4)) shall be treated as owning all of such assets and liabilities.

(iv) Example. The following example illustrates the application of paragraph (a)(4) of this section:

Example. Liability held through a partnership.

(i) Facts. P, a foreign partnership, has two equal partners, X and Y. X is a domestic corporation with the dollar as its functional currency. Y is a foreign corporation that has the yen as its functional currency. On January 1, year 1, P borrowed yen and issued a note to the lender that obligated P to pay interest and repay principal to the lender in yen. Also on January 1, year 1, P used the yen it borrowed from the lender to acquire 100% of the stock of F, a foreign corporation, from an unrelated person. P also holds an eligible section 987 QBU (within the meaning of § 1.987-1(b)(3)) that has the yen as its functional currency. P maintains one set of books and records. The assets and liabilities of the eligible QBU are reflected on the P books and records as provided under § 1.987-2(b). The F stock held by P, and the yen liability incurred to acquire the F stock, are also recorded on the books and records of P, but are not reflected on such books and records for purposes of section 987 pursuant to § 1.987-2(b)(2)(i)(A) and (C), respectively.

(ii) Analysis. X's portion of the assets and liabilities of the eligible QBU owned by P is a section 987 QBU. Y's portion of the assets and liabilities of the eligible QBU owned by P is not a section 987 QBU because Y and the eligible QBU have the same functional currency. Because the F stock and yen-denominated liability incurred to acquire such stock are not reflected on the books and records of the eligible QBU, they are not subject to section 987. In addition, because the F stock and the yen-denominated liability incurred to acquire such stock are held by P (but not attributable to P's eligible QBU), X and Y are treated as owning their share of such stock and liability, determined under § 1.987-7(b), for purposes of applying section 988. As a result, P's becoming the obligor under the portion of the yen-denominated note that is treated as being an obligation of X is a section 988 transaction pursuant to paragraphs (a)(1)(ii), (a)(2)(ii) and (a)(3) of this section. Similarly, the disposition of yen on payments of interest and principal on the liability, to the extent such yen are treated as owned by X, are section 988 transactions under paragraphs (a)(1)(i) and (a)(3) of this section. P's becoming the obligor under Y's portion of the yen-denominated note, and Y's portion of the yen disposed of in connection with payments on such note, are not section 988 transactions because Y has the yen as its functional currency.

(5) [Reserved].

* * * * *

(10) * * *

(ii) Certain transfers. (A) Exchange gain or loss with respect to nonfunctional currency or any item described in paragraph (a)(2) of this section entered into with another taxpayer shall be realized upon a transfer (as defined under § 1.987-2(c)) of such currency or item from an owner to a section 987 QBU or from a section 987 QBU to the owner where as a result of such transfers the currency or other such item--

(i) Loses its character as nonfunctional currency or an item described in paragraph (a)(2) of this section; or

(ii) Where the source of the exchange gain or loss could be altered absent the application of this paragraph (a)(10)(ii).

(B) Such exchange gain or loss shall be computed in accordance with § 1.988-2 (without regard to § 1.988-2(b)(8) as if the nonfunctional currency or item described in paragraph (a)(2) of this section had been sold or otherwise transferred at fair market value between unrelated taxpayers. For purposes of the preceding sentence, a taxpayer must use a translation rate that is consistent with the translation conventions of the section 987 QBU to which or from which, as the case may be, the item is being transferred. In the case of a gain or loss incurred in a transaction described in this paragraph (a)(10)(ii) that does not have a significant business purpose, the Commissioner, may defer such gain or loss.

* * * * *

(i) * * * Generally, the revisions to paragraphs (a)(3), (a)(4), (a)(5), and (a)(10)(ii) of this section shall apply to taxable years beginning one year after the first day of the first taxable year following the date of publication of a Treasury decision adopting this rule as a final regulation in the

Federal Register. If a taxpayer makes an election under § 1.987-11(b), then the effective date of the revisions to paragraphs (a)(3), (a)(4), and (a)(10)(ii) of this section with respect to the taxpayer shall be consistent with such election.

PAR. 2. In § 1.988-1 paragraph (f) is revised to read as follows:

Proposed § 1.988-1 Certain definitions and special rules.
[*For Preamble, see ¶ 152,031*]

* * * * *

(f) Hyperinflationary currency. *(1) Definition.* For purposes of section 988, a hyperinflationary currency means a currency described in § 1.985-1(b)(2)(ii)(D). However, the base period means the thirty-six calendar month period ending on the last day of the taxpayer's (or qualified business unit's) current taxable year. Thus, for example, if for 1996, 1997, and 1998, a country's annual inflation rates are 6 percent, 11 percent, and 90 percent, respectively, the cumulative inflation rate for the three-year base period is 124% [(1.06 × 1.11 × 1.90) − 1.0 = 1.24) × 100 = 124%]. Accordingly, assuming the QBU has a calendar year as its taxable year, the currency of the country is hyperinflationary for the 1998 taxable year.

(2) Effective date. Paragraph (f)(1) shall apply to transactions entered into after February 14, 2000.

* * * * *

§ 1.988-2 Recognition and computation of exchange gain or loss.

(a) Disposition of nonfunctional currency. *(1) Recognition of exchange gain or loss.* (i) In general. Except as otherwise provided in this section, § 1.988-1(a)(7)(ii), and § 1.988-5, the recognition of exchange gain or loss upon the sale or other disposition of nonfunctional currency shall be governed by the recognition provisions of the Internal Revenue Code which apply to the sale or disposition of property (e.g., section 1001 or, to the extent provided in regulations, section 1092). The disposition of nonfunctional currency in settlement of a forward contract, futures contract, option contract, or similar financial instrument is considered to be a sale or disposition of the nonfunctional currency for purposes of the preceding sentence.

(ii) Clarification of section 1031. An amount of one nonfunctional currency is not "property of like kind" with respect to an amount of a different nonfunctional currency.

(iii) Coordination with section 988(c)(1)(C)(ii). No exchange gain or loss is recognized with respect to the following transactions—

(A) An exchange of units of nonfunctional currency for different units of the same nonfunctional currency;

(B) The deposit of nonfunctional currency in a demand or time deposit or similar instrument (including a certificate of deposit) issued by a bank or other financial institution if such instrument is denominated in such currency;

(C) The withdrawal of nonfunctional currency from a demand or time deposit or similar instrument issued by a bank or other financial institution if such instrument is denominated in such currency;

(D) The receipt of nonfunctional currency from a bank or other financial institution from which the taxpayer purchased a certificate of deposit or similar instrument denominated in such currency by reason of the maturing or other termination of such instrument; and

(E) The transfer of nonfunctional currency from a demand or time deposit or similar instrument issued by a bank or other financial institution to another demand or time deposit or similar instrument denominated in the same nonfunctional currency issued by a bank or other financial institution.

The taxpayer's basis in the units of nonfunctional currency or other property received in the transaction shall be the adjusted basis of the units of nonfunctional currency or other property transferred. See Paragraph (b) of this section with respect to the timing of interest income or expense and the determination of exchange gain or loss thereon.

(iv) Example. The following example illustrates the provisions of paragraph (a)(1)(iii) of this section.

Example. X is a corporation on the accrual method of accounting with the U.S. dollar as its functional currency. On January 1, 1989, X acquires 1,500 British pounds (£) for $2,250 (£1 = $1.50). On January 3, 1989, when the spot rate is £1 = $1.49, X deposits the £1,500 with a British financial institution in a non-interest bearing demand account. On February 1, 1989, when the spot rate is £1 = $1.45, X withdraws the £1,500. On February 5, 1989, when the spot rate is £1 = $1.42, X purchases inventory in the amount of £1,500. Pursuant to paragraph (a)(1)(iii) of this section, no exchange loss is realized until February 5, 1989, when X disposes of the £1,500 for inventory. At that time, X realizes exchange loss in the amount of $120 computed under paragraph (a)(2) of this section. The loss is not an adjustment to the cost of the inventory.

(2) Computation of gain or loss. (i) In general. Exchange gain realized from the sale or other disposition of nonfunctional currency shall be the excess of the amount realized over the adjusted basis of such currency, and exchange loss realized shall be the excess of the adjusted basis of such currency over the amount realized.

(ii) Amount realized. (A) In general. The amount realized from the disposition of nonfunctional currency shall be determined under section 1001(b). A taxpayer that uses a spot rate convention under § 1.988-1(d)(3) to determine exchange gain or loss with respect to a payable shall determine the amount realized upon the disposition of nonfunctional currency paid in satisfaction of the payable in a manner consistent with such convention.

(B) Exchange of nonfunctional currency for property. For purpose of paragraph (a)(2) of this section, the exchange of nonfunctional currency for property (other than nonfunctional currency) shall be treated as—

(1) An exchange of the units of nonfunctional currency for units of functional currency at the spot rate on the date of the exchange, and

(2) The purchase or sale of the property for such units of functional currency.

(C) Example. The following example illustrates the provisions of paragraph (a)(2)(ii)(B) of this section.

Example. G is a U.S. corporation with the U.S. dollar as its functional currency. On January 1, 1989, G enters into a contract to purchase a paper manufacturing machine for 10,000,000 British pounds (£) for delivery on January 1, 1991. On January 1, 1991, when G exchanges £10,000,000 (which G purchased for $12,000,000) for the machine, the fair market value of the machine is £17,000,000. On January 1, 1991, the spot exchange rate is £1 = $1.50. Under paragraph (a)(2)(ii)(B of this section, the transaction is treated as an exchange of £10,000,000 for $15,000,000 and the purchase of the machine for $15,000,000. Accordingly, in computing G's exchange gain of $3,000,000 on the disposition of the £10,000,000, the amount realized is $15,000,000.

G's basis in the machine is $15,000,000. No gain is recognized on the bargain purchase of the machine.

(iii) Adjusted basis. (A) In general. Except as provided in paragraph (a)(2)(iii)(B) of this section, the adjusted basis of nonfunctional currency is determined under the applicable provisions of the Internal Revenue Code (e.g., sections 1011 through 1023). A taxpayer that uses a spot rate convention under § 1.988-1(d)(3) to determine exchange gain or loss with respect to a receivable shall determine the basis of nonfunctional currency received in satisfaction of such receivable in a manner consistent with such convention.

(B) Determination of the basis of nonfunctional currency withdrawn from an account with a bank or other financial institution. (1) In general. The basis of nonfunctional currency withdrawn from an account with a bank or other financial institution shall be determined under any reasonable method that is consistently applied from year to year by the taxpayer to all accounts denominated in a nonfunctional currency. For example, a taxpayer may use a first in first out method, a last in first out method, a pro rata method (as illustrated in the example below), or any other reasonable method that is consistently applied. However, a method that consistently results in units of nonfunctional currency with the highest basis being withdrawn first shall not be considered reasonable.

(2) Example. The following example illustrates the provisions of this paragraph (a)(2)(iii)(B).

Example. (i) X, a cash basis individual with the dollar as his functional currency, opens a demand account with a Swiss bank. Assume expenses associated with the demand account are deductible under section 212. The following chart indicates Swiss franc deposits to the account, Swiss franc interest credited to the account, the dollar basis of each deposit. and the determination of the aggregate dollar basis of all Swiss francs in the account. Assume that the taxpayer has properly translated all the amounts specified in the chart and that all transactions are subject to section 988.

Date	Swiss francs deposited	Interest received	U.S. dollar basis	Aggregate U.S. dollar basis
1/01/89	1000 Sf		$500	$500
3/31/89		50 Sf	25	525
6/30/89		50 Sf	24	549
9/30/89		50 Sf	25	574
12/31/89		50 Sf	26	600

(ii) On January 1, 1990, X withdraws 500 Swiss francs from the account. X may determine his basis in the Swiss francs by multiplying the aggregate U.S. dollar basis of Swiss francs in the account by a fraction the numerator of which is the number of Swiss francs withdrawn from the account and the denominator is the total number of Swiss francs in the account. Under this method, X's basis in the 500 Swiss francs is $250 computed as follows:

$$\frac{500 \text{ Sf}}{1200 \text{ Sf}} \times \$600 = \$250$$

(iii) X's basis in the Swiss francs remaining in the account is $350 ($600 − $250). X must use this method consistently from year to year with respect to withdrawals of nonfunctional currency from all of X's accounts.

(iv) Purchase and sale of stock or securities traded on an established securities market by cash basis taxpayer. (A) Amount realized. If stock or securities traded on an established securities market are sold by a cash basis taxpayer for nonfunctional currency, the amount realized with respect to the stock or securities (as determined on the trade date) shall be computed by translating the units of nonfunctional currency received into functional currency at the spot rate on the settlement date of the sale. This rule applies notwithstanding that the stock or securities are treated as disposed of on a date other than the settlement date under another section of the Code. See section 453(k).

(B) Basis. If stock or securities traded on an established securities market are purchased by a cash basis taxpayer for nonfunctional currency, the basis of the stock or securities shall be determined by translating the units of nonfunctional currency paid into functional currency at the spot rate on the settlement date of the purchase.

(C) Example. The following example illustrates the provisions of this paragraph (a)(2)(iv).

Example. On November 1, 1989 (the trade date), X, a calendar year cash basis U.S. individual, purchases stock for £100 for settlement on November 5, 1989. On November 1, 1989, the spot value of the £100 is $140. On November 5, 1989, X purchases £100 for $141 which X uses to pay for the stock. X's basis in the stock is $141. On December 30, 1990 (the trade date), X sells the stock for £110 for settlement on January 5, 1991. On December 30, 1990, the spot value of £110 is $165. On January 5, 1991, X transfers the stock and receives £110 which, translated at the spot rate, equal $166. Under section 453(k), the stock is considered disposed of on December 30, 1990. The amount realized with respect to such disposition is the value of the £110 on January 5, 1991 ($166). Accordingly, X's gain realized on December 30, 1990, from the disposition of the stock is $25 ($166 amount realized less $141 basis). X's basis in, the £110 received from the sale of the stock is $166.

(v) Purchase and sale of stock or securities traded on an established securities market by accrual basis taxpayer. For taxable years beginning after March 17, 1992, an accrual basis taxpayer may elect to apply the rules of paragraph (a)(2)(iv) of this section. The election shall be made by filing a statement with the taxpayer's first return in which the election is effective clearly indicating that the election has been made. A method so elected must be applied consistently from year to year and cannot be changed without the consent of the Commissioner.

(b) Translation of interest income or expense and determination of exchange gain or loss with respect to debt instruments. *(1) Translation of interest income received with respect to a nonfunctional currency demand account.* Interest income received with respect to a demand account with a bank or other financial institution which is denominated in (or the payments of which are determined by reference to) a nonfunctional currency shall be translated into functional currency at the spot rate on the date received or accrued or pursuant to any reasonable spot rate convention consistently applied by the taxpayer to all taxable years and to all accounts denominated in nonfunctional currency in the same financial institution. For example, a taxpayer may translate interest income received with respect to a demand account on the last day of each month of the taxable year, on the last day of each quarter of the taxable year, on the last day of each half of the taxable year, or on the last day of the taxable year. No exchange gain or loss is realized upon the receipt or accrual of interest income with respect to a demand account subject to this paragraph (b)(1).

(2) Translation of nonfunctional currency interest income or expense received or paid with respect to a debt instrument described in § 1.988-1(a)(1)(ii) and (2)(i). (i) Scope. (A) In general. Paragraph (b) of this section only applies to debt instruments described in § 1.988-1(a)(1)(ii) and (2)(i) where all payments are denominated in, or determined with reference to, a single nonfunctional currency. Except as provided in paragraph (b)(2)(i)(B) of this section, this paragraph (b) shall not apply to contingent payment debt instruments.

(B) Nonfunctional currency contingent payment debt instruments. (1) Operative rules. See § 1.988-6 for rules applicable to contingent payment debt instruments for which one or more payments are denominated in, or determined by reference to, a nonfunctional currency.

(2) Certain instruments are not contingent payment debt instruments. For purposes of sections 163(e) and 1271 through 1275 and the regulations thereunder, a debt instrument does not provide for contingent payments merely because the instrument is denominated in, or all payments of which are determined with reference to, a single nonfunctional currency. See § 1.988-6 for the treatment of nonfunctional currency contingent payment debt instruments.

(ii) Determination and translation of interest income or expense. (A) In general. Interest income or expense on a debt instrument described in paragraph (b)(2)(i) of this section (including original issue discount determined in accordance with sections 1271 through 1275 and 163(e) as adjusted for acquisition premium under section 1272(a)(7), and acquisition discount determined in accordance with sections 1281 through 1283) shall be determined in units of nonfunctional currency and translated into functional currency as provided in paragraphs (b)(2)(ii)(B) and (C) of this section. For purposes of sections 483, 1273(b)(5) and 1274, the nonfunctional currency in which an instrument is denominated (or by reference to which payments are determined) shall be considered money.

(B) Translation of interest income or expense that is not required to be accrued prior to receipt or payment. With respect to an instrument described in paragraph (b)(2)(i) of this section, interest income or expense received or paid that is not required to be accrued by the taxpayer prior to receipt or payment shall be translated at the spot rate on the date of receipt or payment. No exchange gain or loss is realized with respect to the receipt or payment of such interest income or expense (other than the exchange gain or loss that might be realized under paragraph (a) of this section upon the disposition of the nonfunctional currency so received or paid).

(C) Translation of interest income or expense that is required to be accrued prior to receipt or payment. With respect to an instrument described in paragraph (b)(2)(i) of this section, interest income or expense that is required to be accrued prior to receipt or payment (e.g., under section 1272, 1281 or 163(e) or because the taxpayer uses an accrual method of accounting) shall be translated at the average rate (or other rate specified in paragraph (b)(2)(iii)(B) of this section) for the interest accrual period or, with respect to an interest accrual period that spans two taxable years, at the average rate (or other rate specified in paragraph (b)(2)(iii)(B) of this section) for the partial period within the taxable year. See paragraphs (b)(3) and (4) of this section for the determination of exchange gain or loss on the receipt or payment of accrued interest income or expense.

(iii) Determination of average rate or other accrual convention. (A) In general. For purposes of this paragraph (b), the average rate for an accrual period (or partial period) shall be a simple average of the spot exchange rates for each business day of such period or other average exchange rate for the period reasonably derived and consistently applied by the taxpayer.

(B) Election to use spot accrual convention. For taxable years beginning after March 17, 1992, a taxpayer may elect to translate interest income and expense at the spot rate on the last day of the interest accrual period (and in the case of a partial accrual period, the spot rate on the last day of the taxable year). If the last day of the interest accrual period is within five business days of the date of receipt or payment, the taxpayer may translate interest income or expense at the spot rate on the date of receipt or payment. The election shall be made by filing a statement with the taxpayer's first return in which the election is effective clearly indicating that the election has been made. A method so elected must be applied consistently to all debt instruments from year to year and cannot be changed without the consent of the Commissioner.

(3) Exchange gain or loss recognized by the holder with respect to accrued interest income. The holder of a debt instrument described in paragraph (b)(2)(i) of this section shall realize exchange gain or loss with respect to accrued interest income on the date such accrued interest income is received or the instrument is disposed of (including a deemed disposition under section 1001 that results from a material change in terms of the instrument). Except as otherwise provided in this paragraph (b) (e.g., paragraph (b)(8) of this section), exchange gain or loss realized with respect to accrued interest income shall be recognized in accordance with the applicable recognition provisions of the Internal Revenue Code. The amount of exchange gain or loss so realized with respect to accrued interest income is determined for each accrual period by—

(i) Translating the units of nonfunctional currency interest income received with respect to such accrual period (as determined under the ordering rules of paragraph (b)(7) of this section) into functional currency at the spot rate on the date the interest income is received or the instrument is disposed of (or deemed disposed of), and

(ii) Subtracting from such amount the amount computed by translating the units of nonfunctional currency interest income accrued with respect to such income received at the average rate (or other rate specified in paragraph (b)(2)(iii)(B) of this section) for the accrual period.

(4) Exchange gain or loss recognized by the obligor with respect to accrued interest expense. The obligor under a debt instrument described in paragraph (b)(2)(i) of this section shall realize exchange gain or loss with respect to accrued interest expense on the date such accrued interest expense is paid or the obligation to make payments is transferred or extinguished (including a deemed disposition under section 1001 that results from a material change in terms of the instrument). Except as otherwise provided in this paragraph (b) (e.g., paragraph (b)(8) of this section), exchange gain or loss realized with respect to accrued interest expense shall be rec-

ognized in accordance with the applicable recognition provisions of the Internal Revenue Code. The amount of exchange gain or loss so realized with respect to accrued interest expense is determined for each accrual period by—

(i) Translating the units of nonfunctional currency interest expense accrued with respect to the amount of interest paid into functional currency at the average rate (or other rate specified in paragraph (b)(2)(iii)(B) of this section) for such accrual period; and

(ii) Subtracting from such amount the amount computed by translating the units of nonfunctional currency interest paid (or, if the obligation to make payments is extinguished or transferred, the units accrued) with respect to such accrual period (as determined under the ordering rules in paragraph (b)(7) of this section) into functional currency at the spot rate on the date payment is made or the obligation is transferred or extinguished (or deemed extinguished).

(5) Exchange gain or loss recognized by the holder of a debt instrument with respect to principal. The holder of a debt instrument described in paragraph (b)(2)(i) of this section shall realize exchange gain or loss with respect to the principal amount of such instrument on the date principal (determined under the ordering rules of paragraph (b)(7) of this section) is received from the obligor or the instrument is disposed of (including a deemed disposition under section 1001 that results from a material change in terms of the instrument). For purposes of computing exchange gain or loss, the principal amount of a debt instrument is the holder's purchase price in units of nonfunctional currency. See paragraph (b)(10) of this section for rules regarding the amortization of that part of the principal amount that represents bond premium and the computation of exchange gain or loss thereon. If, however, the holder acquired the instrument in a transaction in which exchange gain or loss was realized but not recognized by the transferor, the nonfunctional currency principal amount of the instrument with respect to the holder shall be the same as that of the transferor. Except as otherwise provided in this paragraph (b) (e.g., paragraph (b)(8) of this section), exchange gain or loss realized with respect to such principal amount shall be recognized in accordance with the applicable recognition provisions of the Internal Revenue Code. The amount of exchange gain or loss so realized by the holder with respect to principal is determined by—

(i) Translating the units of nonfunctional currency principal at the spot rate on the date payment is received or the instrument is disposed of (or deemed disposed of); and

(ii) Subtracting from such amount the amount computed by translating the units of nonfunctional currency principal at the spot rate on the date the holder (or a transferor from whom the nonfunctional principal amount is carried over) acquired the instrument (is deemed to acquire the instrument).

(6) Exchange gain or loss recognized by the obligor of a debt instrument with respect to principal. The obligor under a debt instrument described in paragraph (b)(2)(i) of this section shall realize exchange gain or loss with respect to the principal amount of such instrument on the date principal (determined under the ordering rules of paragraph (b)(7) of this section) is paid or the obligation to make payments is transferred or extinguished (including a deemed disposition under section 1001 that results from a material change in terms of the instrument). For purposes of computing exchange gain or loss, the principal amount of a debt instrument is the amount received by the obligor for the debt instrument in units of nonfunctional currency. See paragraph (b)(10) of this section for rules regarding the amortization of that part of the principal amount that represents bond premium and the computation of exchange gain or loss thereon. If, however, the obligor became the obligor in a transaction in which exchange gain or loss was realized but not recognized by the transferor, the nonfunctional currency principal amount of the instrument with respect to such obligor shall be the same as that of the transferor. Except as otherwise provided in this paragraph (b) (e.g., paragraph (b)(8) of this section), exchange gain or loss realized with respect to such principal shall be recognized in accordance with the applicable recognition provisions of the Internal Revenue Code. The amount of exchange gain or loss so realized by the obligor is determined by—

(i) Translating the units of nonfunctional currency principal at the spot rate on the date the obligor (or a transferor from whom the principal amount is carried over) became the obligor (or is deemed to have become the obligor); and

(ii) Subtracting from such amount the amount computed by translating the units of nonfunctional currency principal at the spot rate on the date payment is made or the obligation is transferred or extinguished (or deemed extinguished).

(7) Payment ordering rules. (i) Debt instruments subject to the rules of sections 163(e), or 1271 through 1288. In the case of a debt instrument described in paragraph (b)(2)(i) of this section that is subject to the rules of sections 163(e), or 1272 through 1288, units of nonfunctional currency (or an amount determined with reference to nonfunctional currency) received or paid with respect to such debt instrument shall be treated first as a receipt or payment of periodic interest under the principles of section 1273 and the regulations thereunder, second as a receipt or payment of original issue discount to the extent accrued as of the date of the receipt or payment, and finally as a receipt or payment of principal. Units of nonfunctional currency (or an amount determined with reference to nonfunctional currency) treated as a receipt or payment of original issue discount under the preceding sentence are attributed to the earliest accrual period in which original issue discount has accrued and to which prior receipts or payments have not been attributed. No portion thereof shall be treated as prepaid interest. These rules are illustrated by Example 10 of paragraph (b)(9) of this section.

(ii) Other debt instruments. In the case of a debt instrument described in paragraph (b)(2)(i) of this section that is not subject to the rules of section 163(e) or 1272 through 1288, whether units of nonfunctional currency (or an amount determined with reference to nonfunctional currency) received or paid with respect to such debt instrument are treated as interest or principal shall be determined under section 163 or other applicable section of the Code.

(8) Limitation of exchange gain or loss on payment or disposition of a debt instrument. When a debt instrument described in paragraph (b)(2)(i) of this section is paid or disposed of or when the obligation to make payments thereunder is satisfied by another person, or extinguished or assumed by another person, exchange gain or loss is computed with respect to both principal and any accrued interest (including original issue discount), as provided in paragraph (b)(3) through (7) of this section. However, pursuant to section 988(b)(1) and (2), the sum of any exchange gain or loss with respect to the principal and interest of any such debt instrument shall be realized only to the extent of the total gain or loss realized on the transaction. The gain or loss realized shall be recognized in accordance with the general principles of the Code. See Examples 3, 4 and 6 of paragraph (b)(9) of this section.

(9) Examples. The preceding provisions are illustrated in the following examples. The examples assume that any transaction involving an individual is a section 988 transaction.

Example (1). (i) X is an individual on the cash method of accounting with the dollar as his functional currency. On January 1, 1992, X converts $13,000 to 10,000 British pounds (£) at the spot rate of £1 = $1.30 and loans the £10,000 to Y for 3 years. The terms of the loan provide that Y will make interest payments of £1,000 on December 31 of 1992, 1993, and 1994, and will repay X's £10,000 principal on December 31, 1994. Assume the spot rates for the pertinent dates are as follows:

Date	Spot rate (pounds to dollars)
Jan. 1, 1992	£1 = $1.30
Dec. 31, 1992	£1 = $1.35
Dec. 31, 1993	£1 = $1.40
Dec. 31, 1994	£1 = $1.45

(ii) Under paragraph (b)(2)(ii)(B) of this section, X will translate the £1,000 interest payments at the spot rate on the date received. Accordingly, X will have interest income of $1,350 in 1992, $1,400 in 1993, and $1,450 in 1994. Because X is a cash basis taxpayer, X does not realize exchange gain or loss on the receipt of interest income.

(iii) Under paragraph (b)(5) of this section, X will realize exchange gain upon repayment of the £10,000 principal amount determined by translating the £10,000 at the spot rate on the date it is received (£10,000 × $1.45 = $14,500) and subtracting from such amount, the amount determined by translating the £10,000 at the spot rate on the date the loan was made (£10,000 × $1.30 = $13,000). Accordingly, X will realize an exchange gain of $1,500 on the repayment of the loan on December 31, 1994.

Example (2). (i) Assume the same facts as in Example 1 except that X is an accrual method taxpayer and that average rates are as follows:

Accrual period	Average rate (pounds to dollars)
1992	£1 = $1.32
1993	£1 = $1.37
1994	£1 = $1.42

(ii) Under paragraph (b)(2)(ii)(C) of this section, X will accrue the £1,000 interest payments at the average rate for the accrual period. Accordingly, X will have interest income of $1,320 in 1992, $1,370 in 1993, and $1,420 in 1994. Because X is an accrual basis taxpayer, X determines exchange gain or loss for each interest accrual period by translating the units of nonfunctional currency interest income received with respect to such accrual period at the spot rate on the date received and subtracting the amounts of interest income accrued for such period. Thus, X will realize $90 of exchange gain with respect to interest received under the loan, computed as follows:

Year	Spot value interest received	Accrued interest @ average rate	Exch. gain
1992	$1,350	$1,320	$30
1993	1,400	1,370	30
1994	1,450	1,420	30
Total			$90

(iii) Under paragraph (b)(5) of this section, X will realize exchange gain upon repayment of the £10,000 loan principal determined in the same manner as in Example 1. Accordingly, X will realize an exchange gain of $1,500 on the repayment of the loan principal on December 31, 1994.

Example (3). Assume the same facts as in Example 1 except that X is a calendar year taxpayer on the accrual method of accounting that elects to use a spot rate convention to translate interest income as provided in § 1.988-2(b)(2)(iii)(B). Interest income is received by X on the last day of each accrual period. Under paragraph (b)(2)(ii)(C), X will translate the interest income at the spot rate on the last day of each interest accrual period. Accordingly, X will have interest income of $1,350 in 1992, and $1,400 in 1993, $1,450 in 1994. Because the rate at which the interest income is translated is the same as the rate on the day of receipt, X will not realize any exchange gain or loss with respect to the interest income. Under paragraph (b)(5) of this section, X will realize exchange gain upon repayment of the £10,000 loan principal determined in the same manner as in Example 1. Accordingly, X will realize an exchange gain of $1,500 on the repayment of the loan principal on December 31, 1994.

Example (4). Assume the same facts as in Example 1 except that on December 31, 1993, X sells Y's note for 9,821.13 British pounds (£) after the interest payment. Under paragraph (b)(8) of this section, X will compute exchange gain on the £10,000 principal. The exchange gain is $1,000 [(£10,000 × $1.40) − (£10,000 × $1.30)]. This exchange gain, however, is only realized to the extent of the total gain on the disposition. X's total gain is $749.58 [(£9,821.13 × $1.40) − (£10,000 × $1.30)]. Thus, X will realize $749.58 of exchange gain (and will realize no market loss).

Example (5). (i) The facts are the same as in Example 1 except that Y becomes insolvent and fails to repay the full £10,000 principal when due. Instead, X and Y agree to compromise the debt for a payment of £8,000 on December 31, 1994. Under paragraph (b)(8) of this section, X will compute exchange gain on the £10,000 originally booked. The exchange gain is $1,500 [(£10,000 × $1.45) − (£10,000 × $1.30) = $1,500]. This exchange gain, however, is only realized to the extent of the total gain on the disposition. X realizes an overall loss on the disposition of $1,400 [(£8,000 × $1.45) − (£10,000 × $1.30) = ($1,400)]. Thus, X will realize no exchange gain (and a $1400 market loss).

(ii) If the exchange rate on December 31, 1994, were £1 = $1.25, rather than £1 = $1.45, X would compute exchange loss under paragraph (b)(8) of this section, on the £10,000 originally booked. The exchange loss would be $500 ((£10,000 × $1.25) − (£10,000 × $1.30) = ($500]. X's total loss on the disposition would be $3,000 [(£8,000 × $1.25) − (£10,000 × $1.30) = ($3.000)]. Thus, X would realize $500 of exchange loss and a $2,500 market loss on the disposition.

Example (6). (i) X is an individual with the dollar as his functional currency. X is on the cash method of accounting. On January 1, 1989, X borrows 10,000 British pounds (£) from Y, an unrelated person. The terms of the loan provide that X will make interest payments of £1,200 on December 31 of 1989 and 1990 and will repay Y's £10,000 principal on December 31, 1990. The spot rates for the pertinent dates are as follows:

Date	Spot rate[1]
Jan. 1, 1989	1 = $1.50
Dec. 31, 1989	1 = 1.60
Dec. 31, 1990	1 = 1.70

[1] Pounds to dollars.

Assume that the basis of the £1,200 paid as interest by X on December 31, 1989 is $2,000, the basis of the £1,200 paid as interest by X on December 31, 1990, is $2,020 and the basis of the £10,000 principal paid by X on December 31, 1990 is $16,000.

(ii) Under paragraph (b)(2)(ii)(9) of this section, X translates the £1,200 interest payments at the spot rate on the day paid. Thus, X paid $1,920 (£1,200 × $1.60) of interest on December 31, 1989 and $2,040 (£1,200 × $1.70) of interest on December 31, 1990. In addition, X will realize exchange gain or loss on the disposition of the £1,200 on December 31, 1989 and 1990, under paragraph (a) of this section. Pursuant to paragraph (a)(2) of this section, X will realize an exchange loss of $80 [(£1,200 × $1.60) − $2,000] on December 31, 1989 and exchange gain of $20 [(£1,200 × $1.70) − $2,020)] on December 31, 1990.

(iii) Under paragraph (b)(6) of this section, X will realize exchange loss on December 31, 1990 upon repayment of the £ 10,000 principal amount determined by translating the £ 10,000 received at the spot rate on January 1, 1989 (£ 10,000 × $1.50 = $15,000) and subtracting from such amount, the amount determined by translating the £ 10,000 paid at the spot rate on December 31, 1990 (£ 10,000 × $1.70 = $17,000). Thus, under paragraph (b)(6) of this section, X has an exchange loss with respect to the £10,000 principal of $2,000. Further, under paragraph (a)(2) of this section, X will realize an exchange gain upon disposition of the £ 10,000 on December 31, 1990. Under paragraph (a)(2) of this section, X will subtract his adjusted basis in the £ 10,000 ($16,000) from the amount realized upon the disposition of the £10,000 (£10,000 × $1.70 = $17,000) resulting in a gain of $1,000. Accordingly, X's combined exchange gain and loss realized on December 31, 1990 with respect to the repayment of the £10,000 is a $1,000 exchange loss.

Example (7). (i) X is a calendar year corporation on the accrual method of accounting and with the dollar as its functional currency. On January 1, 1989, X purchases at original issue for 82.64 Canadian dollars (C$) M corporation's 2 year note maturing on December 31, 1990, at a stated redemption price of C$100. The yield to maturity in Canadian dollars is 10 percent and the accrual period is the one year period beginning January 1 and ending December 31. The note has C$17.36 of original issue discount. Assume that the spot rates are as follows: C$1 = U.S.$.72 on January 1, 1989; C$1 = U.S.$.80 on January 1, 1990; C$1 = U.S.$.82 on December 31, 1990. Assume further that the average rate for 1989 is C$1 = U.S.$.76 and for 1990 is C$1 = U.S.$.81.

(ii) Under paragraph (b)(2)(ii)(A) of this section, X will determine its interest income in Canadian dollars. Accordingly, under section 1272, X must take into account original issue discount in the amount of C$8.26 on December 31, 1989 and C$9.10 on December 31, 1990. Pursuant to paragraph (b)(2)(ii)(C) of this section, X will translate these amounts into U.S. dollars at the average exchange rate for the relevant accrual period. Thus, the amount of interest income taken into account in 1989 is U.S.$6.28 (C$8.26 × U.S.$.76) and in 1990 is U.S.$7.37 (C$9.10 × U.S.$.81). Pursuant to paragraph (b)(3)(ii) of this section, X will realize exchange gain or loss with respect to the accrued interest determined for each accrual period by translating the Canadian dollars received with respect to such accrual period into U.S. dollars at the spot rate on the date the interest is received and subtracting from that amount the amount accrued in U.S. dollars. Thus, the amount of exchange gain realized on December 31, 1990, is U.S.$.58 (U.S.$.49 from 1989 + U.S.$.09 from 1990). Pursuant to paragraph (b)(5) of this section, X shall realize exchange gain or loss with respect to the principal (C$82.64) on December 31, 1990, computed by translating the C$82.64 at the spot rate on December 31, 1990 (U.S.$67.76) and subtracting the C$82.64 translated at the spot rate on January 1, 1989 (U.S.$59.50) for an exchange gain of U.S.$8.26. Thus, X's combined exchange gain is U.S.$8.84 (U.S.$.49 + U.S.$.09 + U.S.$8.26).

(iii) Assume instead that on January 1, 1990, X sells the note for C$86.95, which it immediately converts to U.S. dollars. X's exchange gain is computed under paragraph (b)(8) of this section with reference to the nonfunctional currency denominated principal amount (C$82.64) and the nonfunctional currency denominated accrued original issue discount (C$8.26). X will compute an exchange gain of U.S.$6.61 with respect to the issue price [(C$82.64 × U.S.$.80) − (C$82.64 × U.S$.72)] and an exchange gain of U.S.$.33 with respect to the accrued original issue discount [(C$8.26 × U.S.$.80) − (C$8.26 × U.S.$.76)]. Accordingly, prior to the application of paragraph (b)(8) of this section, X's total exchange gain is U.S.$6.94 (U.S.$6.61 + U.S.$.33), and X's market loss is U.S.$3.16 [(C$90.90 − C$86.95) × U.S.$.80]. Pursuant to paragraph (b)(8) of this section, however, X's market loss on the note of U.S.$3.16 is netted against X's exchange gain of U.S.$6.94, resulting in a realized exchange gain of U.S.$3.78 and no market loss.

Example (8). (i) The facts are the same as in Example 7(i) except that on January 1, 1990, X contributes the M corporation note to Y, a wholly-owned U.S. subsidiary of X with the dollar as its functional currency, and Y collects C$100 from M corporation at maturity on December 31, 1990, when the spot rate is C$1 = U.S.$.82. The transfer of the note from X to Y qualifies for nonrecognition of gain under section 351(a). On December 31, 1990, Y includes C$9.10 of accrued interest in income which translated at the average exchange rate of C$1 = U.S.$.81 for the year results in U.S.$7.37 of interest income.

(ii) Y's exchange gain is computed under paragraph (b)(3) of this section with respect to accrued interest income and paragraph (b)(5) of this section with respect to the nonfunctional currency principal amount. Under paragraph (b)(3) of this section, Y will realize exchange gain or loss for each accrual period computed by translating the units of nonfunctional currency interest income received with respect to such accrual period at the spot rate on the day received and subtracting the amounts of interest income accrued for such period. Thus, Y will realize $.49 of exchange gain with respect to original issue discount accrued in 1989 [(C$8.26 × U.S.$.82) − (C$8.26 × U.S.$.76) = U.S.$.49] and $.09 of exchange gain with respect to original issue discount accrued in 1990 [(C$9.10 × U.S.$.82) − (C$9.10 × U.S.$.81) = $.09].

(iii) Pursuant to paragraph (b)(5) of this section, the nonfunctional currency principal amount of the M bond in the hands of Y is C$82.64, the amount carried over from X, the transferor. Y's exchange gain with respect to the nonfunctional currency principal amount is $8.26 [(C$82.64 × U.S.$.82) − (C$82.64 × U.S.$.72) = U.S.$8.26]. Accordingly, Y's combined exchange gain is U.S.$8.84 ($.49 + $.09 + $8.26). Because the amount realized in Canadian dollars equals the adjusted issue price (C$100) on retirement of the M note, there is no market loss. and the netting rule of paragraph (b)(8) of this section does not limit realization of the exchange gain.

Example (9). (i) X is a calendar year corporation on the accrual method of accounting and with the dollar as its functional currency. X elects to use the spot rate convention to translate interest income as provided in paragraph (b)(2)(iii)(B) of this section. On January 31, 1992, X loans £1000 to Y, an unrelated person. Under the terms of the loan. Y will pay X interest of £50 on July 31, 1992, and January 31, 1993, and will repay the £1000 principal on January 31, 1993. Assume the following spot exchange rates:

Date	Spot rate[1]
Jan. 31, 1992	£ = $1.50
July 31, 1992	£ = 1.50
Dec. 31, 1992	£ = 1.60
Jan. 31, 1993	£ = 1.61

[1] Pounds to dollars

(ii) Under paragraph (b)(2)(ii)(C) of this section, X will translate the interest income at the spot rate on the last day of each interest accrual period (and in the case of a partial accrual period, at the spot rate on the last day of the taxable year). Accordingly, X will have interest income of $77.50 (£50 × $1.55) on July 31, 1992. Assuming under X's method of accounting that interest is accrued daily, X will accrue $66.50 (153/184 × £50) × $1.60) of interest income on December 31, 1992. On January 31, 1993, X will have interest income of $13.60 ((31/184 × £50) × $1.61). Because the rate at which the interest income is translated is the same as the rate on the day of receipt, X will not realize any exchange gain or loss with respect to the interest income received on July 31, 1992. However, X will realize exchange gain on the £41.50 (153/184 × £50) of accrued interest income of $.41 [(£41.50 × $1.61) − (£41.50 × $1.60) = $.41].

(iii) Under paragraph (b)(5) of this section, X will realize exchange gain upon repayment of the £100 principal amount determined by translating the £100 at the spot rate on the date it is received (£100 × $1.61 = $161.00) and subtracting from such amount, the amount determined by translating the £100 at the spot rate on the date the loan was made (£100 × $1.50 = $150.00). Accordingly, X will realize an exchange gain of $11 on the repayment of the loan on January 31, 1993.

Example (10). (i) X, a cash basis taxpayer with the dollar as its functional currency, has the calendar year as its taxable year. On January 1, 1992, X purchases at original issue for 65.88 British pounds (£) M corporation's 5-year bond maturing on December 31, 1996, having a stated redemption price at maturity of £100. The bond provides for annual payments of interest in pounds of 1 pound per year on December 31 of each year. The bond has 34.12 British pounds of original issue discount. The yield to maturity is 10 percent in British pounds and the accrual period is the one year period beginning January 1 and ending December 31 of each calendar year. The amount of original issue discount is determined in pounds for each accrual period by multiplying the adjusted issue price expressed in pounds by the yield and subtracting from such amount the periodic interest payments expressed in pounds for such period. The periodic interest payments are translated at the spot rate on the payment date (December 31 of each year). The original issue discount is translated at the average rate for the accrual period (January 1 through December 31). The following chart describes the determination of interest income with respect to the facts presented and provides other pertinent information.

Table 1

Year (Dec. 31) 1	Periodic interest payments in pounds for the accrual period 2	Original issue discount in pounds for the accrual period 3	Issue price or adjusted issue price in pounds 4	Assumed spot rate on Dec. 31 (pounds to dollars) 5	Assumed average rate for accrual period (pounds to dollars) 6	Periodic interest payments in pounds multiplied by spot rate on the date of payment (column 2 times column 5) 7	Original issue discount in pounds multiplied by the average rate for the accrual period (column 3 times column 6) 8	Total interest income in dollars (column 7 plus column 8) 9	Adjusted issue price in dollars 10
Issue Date:			65.88	1 = $1.20	....	....	....	....	$ 79.06
1992	1	5.59	71.47	1 = 1.30	1 = $1.25	$1.30	$ 6.99	$ 8.29	86.05
1993	1	6.15	77.62	1 = 1.40	1 = 1.35	1.40	8.30	9.70	94.35
1994	1	6.76	84.38	1 = 1.50	1 = 1.45	1.50	9.80	11.30	104.15
1995	1	7.44	91.82	1 = 1.60	1 = 1.55	1.60	11.53	13.13	115.68
1996	1	8.18	100.00	1 = 1.70	1 = 1.65	1.70	13.50	15.20	129.18

(ii) Because X is a cash basis taxpayer, X does not realize exchange gain or loss on the receipt of the £1 periodic interest payments. However, X will realize exchange gain on December 31, 1996 totaling $7.88 with respect to the original issue discount. Exchange gain is determined for each interest accrual period by translating the units of nonfunctional currency interest income received with respect to such accrual period at the spot rate on the date received and subtracting from such amount, the amount computed by translating the units of nonfunctional currency interest income accrued for such period at the average rate for the period. The following chart illustrates this computation:

Table 2

Year 1	OID accrued in pounds for each accrual period 2	Assumed spot rate on date payment received (pounds to dollars) 3	Interest received times spot rate on the date (col. 2 times col. 3) 4	Assumed average rate for accrual period (pounds to dollars) 5	IOD in pounds times the average rate for the accrual period (col. 2 times col. 5) 6	Exchange gain or loss (col. 4 less col. 6) 7
1992	5.59	1 = $1.70	$ 9.50	1 = $1.25	$ 6.99	$2.51
1993	6.15	1 = 1.70	10.46	1 = 1.35	8.30	2.16
1994	6.76	1 = 1.70	11.49	1 = 1.45	9.80	1.69
1995	7.44	1 = 1.70	12.65	1 = 1.55	11.53	1.12
1996	8.18	1 = 1.70	13.90	1 = 1.65	13.50	.40
Total						$7.88

(iii) X will also realize exchange gain with respect to the principal of the loan (i.e., the issue price of 65.88 British pounds) on December 31, 1996 computed by translating the units of nonfunctional currency principal received at the spot rate on the date principal is received (65.88 British pounds × $1.70 = $112.00) and subtracting from such amount, the units of nonfunctional currency principal received translated at the spot rate on the date the instrument was acquired (65.88 British pounds × $1.20 = $79.06). Accordingly, X's exchange gain on the principal is $32.94 and X's total exchange gain with respect to the accrued interest and principal is $40.82. It should be noted that, under this fact pattern, the total exchange gain may be determined in an alternative fashion. Exchange gain may be computed by subtracting the adjusted issue price in dollars at maturity ($129.18—see column 10 of Table 1) from the amount computed by multiplying the stated redemption price at maturity in pounds times the spot rate on the maturity date (£100 × $1.70 = $170), which equals $40.82.

Example (11). (i) The facts are the same as in Example 10 except that X makes an election under paragraph (b)(2)(iii) of this section to translate accrued interest on the last day of the accrual period. Accordingly, columns 8, 9 and 10 in Table 1 would change as follows:

Year (Dec. 31) 1	Original issue discount in pounds multiplied by the spot rate on last day of accrual period (Dec. 31) 8	Total interest income in dollars (column 7 plus column 8 9	Adjusted issue price in dollars 10
			$ 79.06
1992	$ 7.27	$ 8.57	87.63
1993	8.61	10.01	97.64
1994	10.14	11.64	109.28
1995	11.90	13.50	122.78
1996	13.91	15.61	138.39

(ii) Because X is a cash basis taxpayer, X does not realize exchange gain or loss on the receipt of the £1 periodic interest payments. However, X will realize exchange gain on December 31, 1993 totaling $6.18 with respect to the original issue discount. Exchange gain is determined for each interest accrual period by translating the units of nonfunctional currency interest income received with respect to such accrual period at the spot rate on the date received and subtracting from such amount, the amount computed by translating the units of nonfunctional currency interest income accrued for such period at the spot rate on the last day of the accrual period. Accordingly, columns 5, 6 and 7 of Table 2 would change as follows:

Year 1	Spot rate on last day of accrual period 5	OID in pounds times the spot rate on the last day of the accrual period (col 2 times col. 3) 6	Exchange gain or loss (col. 4 less col. 6) 7
1992	$1.30	$ 7.27	$2.23
1993	1.40	8.61	1.85
1994	1.50	10.14	1.35
1995	1.60	11.90	0.75
1996	1.70	13.90	0.00
			6.18

(iii) X will realize exchange gain with respect to the principal amount of the loan as provided in the preceding example.

Example (12). (i) C is a corporation that is a calendar year accrual method taxpayer with the dollar as its functional currency. On January 1, 1989, C lends 100 British pounds (£) in exchange for a note under the terms of which C will receive two equal payments of £57.62 on December 31, 1989, and December 31, 1990. Each payment of £57.62 represents the annual payment necessary to amortize the £100 principal amount at a rate of 10% compounded annually over a two year period. The following tables reflect the amounts of principal and interest that compose each payment and assumptions as to the relevant exchange rates:

Date	Principal	Interest
Dec. 31, 1989	£47.62	£10.00
Dec. 12, 1990	£52.38	£5.24

Date	Spot rate £ =	Average rate for year ending
Jan. 1, 1989	$1.30	
Dec. 31, 1989	1.40	1.35
Dec. 31, 1990	1.50	1.45

(ii) Because each interest payment is equal to the product of the outstanding principal balance of the obligation and a single fixed rate of interest, each stated interest payment constitutes periodic interest under the principles of section 1273. Accordingly, there is no original issue discount.

(iii) Because C is an accrual basis taxpayer, C will translate the interest income at the average rate for the annual accrual period pursuant to paragraph (b)(2)(ii)(C) of this section. Thus, C's interest income is $13.50 (£10.00 × $1.35) in 1989, and $7.60 (£5.24 × $1.45) in 1990. C will realize exchange gain or loss upon receipt of accrued interest computed in accordance with paragraph (b)(3) of this section. Thus, C will realize exchange gain in the amount of $.50 [(£10.00 × $1.40) − $13.50] in 1989, and $.26 [(£5.24 × $1.50) − $7.60] in 1990.

(iv) In addition, C will realize exchange gain or loss upon the receipt of principal each year computed under paragraph (b)(5) of this section. Thus, C will realize exchange gain in the amount of $4.76 [(£47.62 × $1.40) − (£47.62 × $1.30)] in 1989, and $10.48 [(£52.38 × $1.50) − (£ 52.38 × $1.30)] in 1990.

(10) Treatment of bond premium. (i) In general. Amortizable bond premium on a bond described in paragraph (b)(2)(i) of this section shall be computed in the units of nonfunctional currency in which the bond is denominated (or in which the payments are determined). Amortizable bond premium properly taken into account under section 171 or § 1.61-12 (or the successor provision thereof) shall reduce interest income or expense in units of nonfunctional currency. Exchange gain or loss is realized with respect to bond premium described in the preceding sentence by treating the portion of premium amortized with respect to any period as a return of principal. With respect to a holder that does not elect to amortize bond premium under section 171, the amount of bond premium will constitute a market loss when the bond matures. See paragraph (b)(8) of this section. The principles set forth in this paragraph (b)(10) shall apply to determine the treatment of acquisition premium described in section 1272(a)(7).

(ii) Example. The following example illustrates the provisions of this paragraph (b)(10).

Example. (A) X is an individual on the cash method of accounting with the dollar as his functional currency. On January 1, 1989, X purchases Y corporation's note for 107.99 British pounds (£) from Z, an unrelated party. The note has an issue price of £100, a stated redemption price at maturity of £ 100, pays interest in pounds at the rate of 10% compounded annually, and matures on December 31, 1993. X elects to amortize the bond premium of £7.99 under the rules of section 171. Pursuant to paragraph (b)(10)(i) of this section, bond premium is determined and amortized in British pounds. Assume the amortization schedule is as follows:

Year	Bond premium amortized	Unamortized premium plus principal	Interest
		£107.99	
1989	£1.36	£106.63	£8.64
1990	£1.47	£105.16	£8.53
1991	£1.59	£103.57	£8.41
1992	£1.71	£101.86	£8.29
1993	£1.85	£100.00	£8.15

(B) The bond premium reduces X's pound interest income under the note. For example, the £10 stated interest payment made in 1989 is reduced by £1.36 of bond premium, and the resulting £8.64 interest income is translated into dollars at the spot rate on December 31, 1989. Exchange gain or loss is realized on the £1.36 bond premium based on the difference between the spot rates on January 1, 1989, the date the premium is paid to acquire the bond, and December 31, 1989, the date the bond premium is returned as part of the stated interest. The £1.36 bond premium reduces the unamortized premium plus principal to £ 106.63 (£107.99 − £1.36). On December 31, 1993, when the bond matures and the £7.99 of bond premium has been fully amortized, X will realize exchange gain or loss with respect to the remaining purchase price of £100.

(11) Market discount. (i) In general. Market discount as defined in section 1278(a)(2) shall be determined in units of nonfunctional currency in which the market discount bond is denominated (or in which the payments are determined). Accrued market discount (other than market discount currently included in income pursuant to section 1278(b)) shall be translated into functional currency at the spot rate on the date the market discount bond is disposed of. No part of such accrued market discount is treated as exchange gain or loss. Accrued market discount currently includible in income pursuant to section 1278(b) shall be translated into functional currency at the average exchange rate for the accrual period. Exchange gain or loss with respect to accrued market discount currently includible in income under section 1278(b) shall be determined in accordance with paragraph (b)(3) of this section relating to accrued interest income.

(ii) Example. The following example illustrates the provisions of this paragraph (b)(11).

Example. (A) X is a calendar year corporation with the U.S. dollar as its functional currency. On January 1, 1990, X purchases a bond of M corporation for 96,530 British pounds (£). The bond, which was issued on January 1, 1989, has an issue price of £100,000, a stated redemption price at maturity of £100,000, and provides for annual pound payments of interest at 8 percent. The bond matures on December 31, 1991. X purchased the bond at a market discount of 3,470 pounds and did not elect to include the market discount currently in income under section 1278(b). X holds the bond to maturity and on December 31, 1991, receives payment of £100,000 (plus £8,000 interest) when the exchange rate is £1 = $1.50.

(B) Pursuant to paragraph (b)(11) of this section, X computes market discount in units of nonfunctional currency. Thus, the market discount as defined under section 1278(a)(2) is £3,470. Accrued market discount (other than market discount currently included in income pursuant to section 1278(b)) is translated at the spot rate on the date the market discount bond is disposed of. Accordingly, X will translate the accrued market discount of £3,470 at the spot rate on December 31, 1991 (£3,470 × $1.50 = $5,205). No exchange gain or loss is realized with respect to the £3,470 of accrued market discount. See paragraphs (b)(3) and (5) of this section for the realization and recognition of exchange gain or loss with respect to accrued interest and principal.

(12) Tax exempt bonds. See § 1.988-3(c)(2), which characterizes exchange loss realized with respect to a nonfunctional currency tax exempt bond as a reduction of interest income.

(13) Nonfunctional currency debt exchanged for stock of obligor. (i) In general. Notwithstanding any other section of the Code other than section 267, 1091 or 1092, exchange gain or loss shall be realized and recognized by the holder and the obligor in accordance with the rules of paragraphs (b)(3) through (7) of this section with respect to the principal and accrued interest of a debt instrument described in paragraph (b)(2)(i) of this section that is acquired by the obligor in exchange for its stock, provided however, that such gain or loss shall be recognized only to the extent of the total gain or loss on the exchange (regardless of whether such gain or loss would otherwise be recognized). This rule shall apply whether the debt instrument is converted into stock according to its terms or exchanged pursuant to a separate agreement between the obligor and the holder. A debt instrument that is acquired by the obligor from a shareholder as a contribution to capital shall be treated for purposes of this section as exchanged for stock, whether or not additional stock is issued.

(ii) Coordination with section 108. Section 988 and this section shall apply before section 108. Exchange gain realized by the obligor on an exchange described in paragraph (b)(13)(i) of this section shall not be treated as discharge of indebtedness income, but shall be considered to reduce the amount of the liability for purposes of computing the obligor's income on the exchange under section 108(e)(4), section 108(e)(6) or section 108(e)(10).

(iii) Effective date. This paragraph (b)(13) shall be effective for exchanges of debt for stock effected after September 21, 1989.

(iv) Examples. The following examples illustrate the operation of this paragraph (b)(13). In each such example, assume that sections 267, 1091 and 1092 do not apply.

Example (1). (i) X is a calendar year U.S. corporation with the U.S. dollar as its functional currency. On January 1, 1990 (the issue date), X acquired a convertible bond maturing on December 31, 1998, issued by Y corporation, a U.K. corporation with the British pound (£) as its functional currency. The issue price of the bond is £100,000, the stated redemption price at maturity is £100,000, and the bond provides for annual pound interest payments at the rate of 10%. The terms of the bond also provide that at any time prior to December 31, 1998, the holder may surrender all of his interest in the bond in exchange for 20 shares of Y common stock. On January 1, 1994, X surrenders his interest in the bond for 20 shares of Y common stock. Assume the following: (a) The spot rate on January 1, 1990, is £1 = $1.30, (b) The spot rate on January 1, 1994, is £1 = $1.50, and (c) The 20 shares of Y common stock have a market value of £200,000 on January 1, 1994.

(ii) Pursuant to paragraph (b)(13) of this section, X will realize and recognize exchange gain with respect to the issue price (£100,000) of the bond on January 1, 1994, when the bond is converted to stock. X will compute exchange gain pursuant to paragraph (b)(5) of this section by translating the issue price at the spot rate on the conversion date (£100,000 × $1.50 = $150,000) and subtracting from such amount the issue price translated at the spot rate on the date X acquired the bond (£ 100,000 × $1.30 = $130,000). Thus, X will realize and recognize $20,000 of exchange gain. X's basis in the 20 shares of Y common stock is $150,000 ($130,000 substituted basis + $20,000 recognized gain).

Example (2). (i) X, a foreign corporation with the British pound (£) as its functional currency, lends £100 at a market rate of interest to Y, its wholly-owned U.S. subsidiary, on January 1, 1990, on which date the spot exchange rate is £1 = $1. Y's functional currency is the U.S. dollar. On January 1, 1992, when the spot exchange rate is £1 = $.50, X cancels the debt as a contribution to capital. Pursuant to paragraph (b)(13) of this section, Y will realize and recognize exchange gain with respect to the £100 issue price of the debt instrument on January 1, 1992. Y will compute exchange gain pursuant to paragraph (b)(6) of this section by translating the issue price at the spot rate on the date Y became the obligor (£100 × $1 = $100) and subtracting from such amount the issue price translated at the spot rate on the date of extinguishment (£100 × $.50 = $50). Thus, Y will realize and recognize $50 of exchange gain.

(ii) Under section 108(e)(6), on the acquisition of its indebtedness from X as a contribution to capital Y is treated as having satisfied the debt with an amount of money equal to X's adjusted basis in the debt (£100). For purposes of section 108(e)(6), X's adjusted basis is translated into United States dollars at the spot rate on the date Y acquires the debt (£1 = $.50). Therefore, Y is treated as having satisfied the debt for $50. Pursuant to paragraph (b)(13) of this section, for purposes of section 108 the amount of the indebtedness is considered to be reduced by the exchange gain from $100 to $50. Accordingly, Y recognizes $50 of exchange gain and no discharge of indebtedness income on the extinguishment of its debt to X.

(iii) If X were a United States taxpayer with a dollar functional currency and a $100 basis in Y's obligation, X would realize and recognize an exchange loss of $50 under paragraph (b)(5) of this section on the contribution of the debt to Y. The recognized loss would reduce X's adjusted basis in the debt from $100 to $50, so that for purposes of applying section 108(e)(6) Y is treated as having satisfied the debt for $50. Accordingly, under these facts as well Y would recognize $50 of exchange gain and no discharge of indebtedness income.

Example (3). (i) X and Y are unrelated calendar year U.S. corporations with the U.S. dollar as their functional currency. On January 1, 1990 (the issue date), X acquires Y's bond maturing on December 31, 1999. The issue price of the bond is £100,000, the stated redemption price at maturity is £100,000, and the bond provides for annual pound interest payments at the rate of 10%. On January 1, 1994, X and Y agree that Y will redeem its bond from X in exchange for 20 shares of Y common stock. Assume the following:

(a) The spot rate on January 1, 1990, is £1 = $1.00,

(b) The spot rate on January 1, 1994, is £1 = $.50,

(c) Interest rates on equivalent bonds have increased so that as of January 1, 1994, the value of Y's bond has declined to £90,000, and

(d) The 20 shares of Y common stock have a market value of £90,000 as of January 1, 1994.

(ii) Pursuant to paragraph (b)(13) of this section, X will realize and recognize exchange loss with respect to the issue price (£100,000) of the bond on January 1, 1994, when the bond is exchanged for stock. X will compute exchange loss pursuant to paragraph (b)(5) of this section by translating the issue price at the spot rate on the exchange date (£100,000 × $.50 = $50,000) and subtracting from such amount the issue price translated at the spot rate on the date X acquired the bond (£ 100,000 × $1.00 = $100,000). Thus, X will compute $50,000 of exchange loss, all of which will be realized and recognized because it does not exceed the total $55,000 realized loss on the exchange ($45,000 worth of stock received less $100,000 basis in the exchanged bond).

(iii) Pursuant to paragraph (b)(13) of this section, Y will realize and recognize exchange gain with respect to the issue price, computed under paragraph (b)(6) of this section by translating the issue price at the spot rate on the date Y became the obligor (£100,000 × $1.00 = $100,000) and subtracting from such amount the issue price translated at the spot rate on the exchange date (£ 100,000 × $.50 = $50,000). Thus, Y will realize and recognize $50,000 of exchange gain. Under section 108(e)(10), on the transfer of stock to X in satisfaction of its indebtedness Y is treated as having satisfied the indebtedness with an amount of money equal to the fair market value of the stock (£90,000 × $.50 = $45,000). Pursuant to paragraph (b)(13) of this section, for purposes of section 108 the amount of the indebtedness is considered to be reduced by the recognized exchange gain from $100,000 to $50,000. Accordingly, Y recognizes an additional $5,000 of discharge of indebtedness income on the exchange.

Example (4). (i) The facts are the same as in Example 3 except that interest rates on equivalent bonds have declined, rather than increased, so that the value of Y's bond on January 1, 1994, has risen to £112,500; and X and Y agree that Y will redeem its bond from X on that date in exchange for 25 shares of Y common stock worth £112,500. Pursuant to paragraphs (b)(13) and (b)(5) of this section, X will compute $50,000 of exchange loss on the exchange with respect to the £ 100,000 issue price of the bond. See Example 3. However, because X's total loss on the exchange is only $43,750 ($56,250 worth of stock received less $100,000 basis in the exchanged bond), under the netting rule of paragraph (b)(13) of this section the realized exchange loss is limited to $43,750.

(ii) Pursuant to paragraphs (b)(13) and (b)(6) of this section, Y will compute $50,000 of exchange gain with respect to the issue price. See Example 3. Under section 108(e)(10), Y is treated as having satisfied the $100,000 indebtedness with an amount of money equal to the fair market value of the stock (£112,500 × $.50 = $56,250), resulting in a total gain on the exchange of $43,750. Accordingly, under paragraph (b)(13) of this section Y's realized (and recognized) exchange gain on the exchange is limited to $43,750. Also pursuant to paragraph (b)(13) of this section, for purposes of section 108 the amount of the indebtedness is considered to be reduced by the recognized exchange gain from $100,000 to $56,250. Accordingly, Y recognizes no discharge of indebtedness income on the exchange.

(14) [Reserved]

(15) Debt instruments and deposits denominated in hyperinflationary currencies. (i) In general. If a taxpayer issues, acquires, or otherwise enters into or holds a hyperinflationary debt instrument (as defined in paragraph (b)(15)(vi)(A) of this section) or a hyperinflationary deposit (as defined in paragraph (b)(15)(vi)(B) of this section) on which interest is paid or accrued that is denominated in (or determined by reference to) a nonfunctional currency of the taxpayer, then the taxpayer shall realize exchange gain or loss with respect to such instrument or deposit for its taxable year determined by reference to the change in exchange rates between—

(A) The later of the first day of the taxable year, or the date the instrument was entered into (or an amount deposited); and

(B) The earlier of the last day of the taxable year, or the date the instrument (or deposit) is disposed of or otherwise terminated.

(ii) Only exchange gain or loss is realized. No gain or loss is realized under paragraph (b)(15)(i) by reason of factors other than movement in exchange rates, such as the creditworthiness of the debtor.

(iii) Special rule for synthetic, non-hyperinflationary currency debt instruments. (A) General rule. Paragraph (b)(15)(i) does not apply to a debt instrument that has interest and principal payments that are to be made by reference to a currency or item that does not reflect hyperinflationary conditions in a country (within the meaning of § 1.988-1(f)).

(B) Example. Paragraph (b)(15)(iii)(A) is illustrated by the following example:

Example. When the Turkish lira (TL) is a hyperinflationary currency, A, a U.S. corporation with the U.S. dollar as its functional currency, makes a 5 year, 100,000 TL-denominated loan to B, an unrelated corporation, at a 10% interest rate when 1,000 TL equals $1. Under the terms of the debt instrument, B must pay interest annually to A in amount of Turkish lira that is equal to $100. Also under the terms of the debt instrument, B must pay A upon maturity of the debt instrument an amount of Turkish lira that is equal to $1,000. Although the principal and interest are payable in a hyperinflationary currency, the debt instrument is a synthetic dollar debt instrument and is not subject to paragraph (b)(15)(i) of this section.

(iv) Source and character of gain or loss. (A) General rule for hyperinflationary conditions. The rules of this paragraph (b)(15)(iv)(A) shall apply to any taxpayer that is either an issuer of (or obligor under) a hyperinflationary debt instrument or deposit and has currency gain on such debt instrument or deposit, or a holder of a hyperinflationary debt instrument or deposit and has currency loss on such debt instrument or deposit. For purposes of subtitle A of the Internal Revenue Code, any exchange gain or loss realized under paragraph (b)(15)(i) of this section is directly allocable to the interest expense or interest income, respectively, from the debt instrument or deposit (computed under this paragraph (b)), and therefore reduces or increases the amount of interest income or interest expense paid or accrued during that year with respect to that instrument or deposit. With respect to a debt instrument or deposit during a taxable year, to the extent exchange gain realized under paragraph (b)(15)(i) of this section exceeds interest expense of an issuer, or exchange loss realized under paragraph (b)(15)(i) of this section exceeds interest income of a holder or depositor, the character and source of such excess amount shall be determined under §§ 1.988-3 and 1.988-4.

(B) Special rule for subsiding hyperinflationary conditions. If the taxpayer is an issuer of (or obligor under) a hyperinflationary debt instrument or deposit and has currency loss, or if the taxpayer is a holder of a hyperinflationary debt instrument or deposit and has currency gain, then for purposes of subtitle A of the Internal Revenue Code, the character and source of the currency gain or loss is determined under §§ 1.988-3 and 1.988-4. Thus, if an issuer has both interest expense and currency loss, the currency loss is sourced and characterized under section 988, and does not affect the determination of interest expense.

(v) Adjustment to principal or basis. Any exchange gain or loss realized under paragraph (b)(15)(i) of this section is an adjustment to the functional currency principal amount of the issuer, functional currency basis of the holder, or the functional currency amount of the deposit. This adjusted amount or basis is used in making subsequent computations of exchange gain or loss, computing the basis of assets for purposes of allocating interest under §§ 1.861-9T through 1.861-12T and 1.882-5, or making other determinations that may be relevant for computing taxable income or loss.

(vi) Definitions. (A) Hyperinflationary debt instrument. A hyperinflationary debt instrument is a debt instrument that provides for—

(1) Payments denominated in or determined by reference to a currency that is hyperinflationary (as defined in § 1.988-1(f)) at the time the taxpayer enters into or otherwise acquires the debt instrument; or

(2) Payments denominated in or determined by reference to a currency that is hyperinflationary (as defined in § 1.988-1(f)) during the taxable year, and the terms of the instrument provide for the adjustment of principal or interest payments in a manner that reflects hyperinflation. For example, a debt instrument providing for a variable interest rate based on local conditions and generally responding to changes in the local consumer price index will reflect hyperinflation.

(B) Hyperinflationary deposit. A hyperinflationary deposit is a demand or time deposit or similar instrument issued by a bank or other financial institution that provides for—

(1) Payments denominated in or determined by reference to a currency that is hyperinflationary (as defined in § 1.988-1(f)) at the time the taxpayer enters into or otherwise acquires the deposit; or

(2) Payments denominated in or determined by reference to a currency that is hyperinflationary (as defined in § 1.988-1(f)) during the taxable year, and the terms of the deposit provide for the adjustment of the deposit amount or interest payments in a manner that reflects hyperinflation.

(vii) Interaction with other provisions. (A) Interest allocation rules. In determining the amount of interest expense, this paragraph (b)(15) applies before §§ 1.861-9T through 1.861-12T, and 1.882-5.

(B) DASTM. With respect to a qualified business unit that uses the United States dollar approximate separate transactions method of accounting described in § 1.985-3, paragraph (b)(15)(i) of this section does not apply.

(C) Interaction with section 988(a)(3)(C). Section 988(a)(3)(C) does not apply to a debt instrument subject to the rules of paragraph (b)(15)(i) of this section.

(D) Hedging rules. To the extent § 1.446-4 or 1.988-5 apply, the rules of paragraph (b)(15)(i) of this section will not apply. This paragraph (b)(15)(vii)(D) does not apply if the application of § 1.988-5 results in hyperinflationary debt instrument or deposit described in paragraph (b)(15)(vi)(A) or (B) of this section.

(viii) Effective date. This paragraph (b)(15) applies to transactions entered into after February 14, 2000.

(16) Coordination with section 267 regarding debt instruments. (i) Treatment of a creditor. For rules applicable to a corporation included in a controlled group that is a creditor under a debt instrument see § 1.267(f)-1(h).

(ii) Treatment of a debtor. [Reserved]

(17) Coordination with installment method under section 453. [Reserved]

(18) Interaction of section 988 and § 1.1275-2(g). (i) In general. If a principal purpose of structuring a debt instrument subject to section 988 and any related hedges is to achieve a result that is unreasonable in light of the purposes of section 163(e), section 988, sections 1271 through 1275, or any related section of the Internal Revenue Code, the Commissioner can apply or depart from the regulations under the applicable sections as necessary or appropriate to achieve a reasonable result. For example, if this paragraph (b)(18) applies to a multicurrency debt instrument and a hedge or hedges, the Commissioner can wholly or partially integrate transactions or treat portions of the debt instrument as separate instruments where appropriate. See also § 1.1275-2(g).

(ii) Unreasonable result. Whether a result is unreasonable is determined based on all the facts and circumstances. In making this determination, a significant fact is whether the treatment of the debt instrument is expected to have a substantial effect on the issuer's or a holder's U.S. tax liability. Another significant fact is whether the result is obtainable without the application of § 1.988-6 and any related provisions (e.g., if the debt instrument and the contingency were entered into separately). A result will not be considered unreasonable, however, in the absence of an expected substantial effect on the present value of a taxpayer's tax liability.

(iii) Effective date. This paragraph (b)(18) shall apply to debt instruments issued on or after October 29, 2004.

(c) Item of expense or gross income or receipts which is to be paid or received after the date accrued. *(1) In general.* Except as provided in § 1.988-5, exchange gain or loss with respect to an item described in § 1.988-1(a)(1)(ii) and (2)(ii) (other than accrued interest income or expense subject to paragraph (b) of this section) shall be realized on the date payment is made or received. Except as provided in the succeeding sentence, such exchange gain or loss shall be recognized in accordance with the applicable recognition provisions of the Internal Revenue Code. If the taxpayer's right to receive income, or obligation to pay an expense, is transferred or modified in a transaction in which gain or loss would otherwise be recognized, exchange gain or loss shall be realized and recognized only to the extent of the total gain or loss on the transaction.

(2) Determination of exchange gain or loss with respect to an item of gross income or receipts. Exchange gain or loss realized on an item of gross income or receipts described in paragraph (c)(1) of this section shall be determined by multiplying the units of nonfunctional currency received by the spot rate on the payment date, and subtracting from such amount the amount determined by multiplying the units of nonfunctional currency received by the spot rate on the booking date. The term "spot rate on the payment date" means the spot rate determined under § 1.988-1(d) on the date payment is received or otherwise taken into account. Pursuant to § 1.988-1(d)(3), a taxpayer may use a spot rate convention for purposes of determining the spot rate on the payment date. The term "spot rate on the booking date" means the spot rate determined under § 1.988-1(d) on the date the item of gross income or receipts is accrued or otherwise taken into account. Pursuant to § 1.988-1(d)(3), a taxpayer may use a spot rate convention for purposes of determining the spot rate on the booking date.

(3) Determination of exchange gain or loss with respect to an item of expense. Exchange gain or loss realized on an item of expense described in paragraph (c)(1) of this section

shall be determined by multiplying the units of nonfunctional currency paid by the spot rate on the booking date and subtracting from such amount the amount determined by multiplying the units of nonfunctional currency paid by the spot rate on the payment date. The term "spot rate on the booking date" means the spot rate determined under § 1.988-1(d) on the date the item of expense is accrued or otherwise taken into account. Pursuant to § 1.988-1(d)(3), a taxpayer may use a spot rate convention for purposes of determining the spot rate on the booking date. The term "spot rate on the payment date" means the spot rate determined under § 1.988-1(d) on the date payment is made or otherwise taken into account. Pursuant to § 1.988-1(d)(3), a taxpayer may use a spot rate convention for purposes of determining the spot rate on the payment date.

(4) Examples. The following examples illustrate the application of paragraph (c) of this section.

Example (1). X is a calendar year corporation with the dollar as its functional currency. X is on the accrual method of accounting. On January 15, 1989, X sells inventory for 10,000 Canadian dollars (C$). The spot rate on January 15, 1989, is C$1 = U.S.$.55. On February 23, 1989, when X receives payment of the C$10,000, the spot rate is C$1 = U.S.$.50. On February 23, 1989, X will realize exchange loss. X's loss is computed by multiplying the C$10,000 by the spot rate on the date the C$10,000 are received (C$10,000 × .50 = U.S.$5,000) and subtracting from such amount, the amount computed by multiplying the C$10,000 by the spot rate on the booking date (C$10,000 × .55 = U.S.$5,500). Thus, X's exchange loss on the transaction is U.S.$500 (U.S.$5,000 – U.S.$5,500).

Example (2). The facts are the same as in Example 1 except that X uses a spot rate convention to determine the spot rate as provided in § 1.988-1(d)(3). Pursuant to X's spot rate convention, the spot rate at which a payable or receivable is booked is determined monthly for each nonfunctional currency payable or receivable by adding the spot rate at the beginning of the month and the spot rate at the end of the month and dividing by two. All payables and receivables in a nonfunctional currency booked during the month are translated into functional currency at the rate described in the preceding sentence. Further, the translation of nonfunctional currency paid with respect to a payable, and nonfunctional currency received with respect to a receivable, is also performed pursuant to the spot rate convention. Assume the spot rate determined under the spot rate convention for the month of January is C$1 U.S. = $.54 and for the month of February is C$1 U.S. = $.51. On the last date in February, X will realize exchange loss. X's loss is computed by multiplying the C$10,000 by the spot rate convention for the month of February (C$10,000 × U.S.$.51 = U.S.$5,100) and subtracting from such amount, the amount computed by multiplying the C$10,000 by the spot rate convention for the month of January (C$10,000 × U.S.$.54 = $5,400). Thus, X's exchange loss on the transaction is U.S.$300 (U.S.$5,100 – U.S.$5,400). X's basis in the C$10,000 is U.S.$5,400.

Example (3). The facts are the same as in Example 2 except that X has a standing order with X's bank for the bank to convert any nonfunctional currency received in satisfaction of a receivable into U.S. dollars on the day received and to deposit those U.S. dollars in X's U.S. dollar bank account. X may use its convention to translate the amount booked into U.S. dollars, but must use the U.S. dollar amounts received from the bank with respect to such receivables to determine X's exchange gain or loss. Thus, if X receives payment of the C$10,000 on February 23, 1989, when the spot rate is C$1 = U.S.$ .50, X determines exchange gain or loss by subtracting the amount booked under X's convention (U.S.$5,400) from the amount of U.S. dollars received from the bank under the standing conversion order (assume $5,000). X's exchange loss is U.S.$400.

(d) Exchange gain or loss with respect to forward contracts, futures contracts and option contracts. *(1) Scope.* (i) In general. This paragraph (d) applies to forward contracts, futures contracts and option contracts described in § 1.988-1(a)(1)(ii) and (2)(iii). For rules applicable to currency swaps and notional principal contracts described in § 1.988-1(a)(1)(ii) and (2)(iii), see paragraph (e) of this section.

(ii) Treatment of spot contracts. Solely for purposes of this paragraph (d), a spot contract as defined in § 1.988-1(b) to buy or sell nonfunctional currency is not considered a forward contract or similar transaction described in § 1.988-1(a)(2)(iii) unless such spot contract is disposed of (or otherwise terminated) prior to making or taking delivery of the currency. For example, if a taxpayer with the dollar as its functional currency enters into a spot contract to purchase British pounds, and takes delivery of such pounds under the contract, the delivery of the pounds is not a realization event under section 988(c)(5) and paragraph (e)(4)(ii) of this section because the contract is not considered a forward contract or similar transaction described in § 1.988-1(a)(2)(iii). However, if the taxpayer sells or otherwise terminates the contract before taking delivery of the pounds, exchange gain or loss shall be realized and recognized in accordance with paragraphs (d)(2) and (3) of this section.

(2) Realization of exchange gain or loss. (i) In general. Except as provided in § 1.988-5, exchange gain or loss on a contract described in § 1.988-2(d)(1) shall be realized in accordance with the applicable realization section of the Internal Revenue Code (e.g., sections 1001, 1092, and 1256). See also section 988(c)(5). For purposes of determining the timing of the realization of exchange gain or loss, sections 1092 and 1256 shall take precedence over section 988(c)(5).

(ii) Realization by offset. (A) In general. Except as provided in paragraphs (d)(2)(ii)(B) and (C) of this section, exchange gain or loss with respect to a transaction described in § 1.988-1(a)(1)(ii) and (2)(iii) shall not be realized solely because such transaction is offset by another transaction (or transactions).

(B) Exception where economic benefit is derived. If a transaction described in § 1.988-1(a)(1)(ii) and (2)(iii) is offset by another transaction or transactions, exchange gain shall be realized to the extent the taxpayer derives, by pledge or otherwise, an economic benefit (e.g., cash, property or the proceeds from a borrowing) from any gain inherent in such offsetting positions. Proper adjustment shall be made in the amount of any gain or loss subsequently realized for gain taken into account by reason of the preceding sentence. This paragraph (d)(2)(ii)(B) shall apply to transactions creating an offset after September 21, 1989.

(C) Certain contracts traded on an exchange. If a transaction described in § 1.988-1(a)(1)(ii) and (2)(iii) is traded on an exchange and it is the general practice of the exchange to terminate offsetting contracts, entering into an offsetting contract shall be considered a termination of the contract being offset.

(iii) Clarification of section 988(c)(5). If the delivery date of a contract subject to section 988(c)(5) and paragraph (d)(4)(ii) of this section is different than the date the contract expires, then for purposes of determining the date exchange gain or loss is realized, the term delivery date shall mean expiration date.

(iv) Examples. The following examples illustrate the rules of this paragraph (d)(1) and (2).

Example (1). On August 1, 1989, X, a calendar year corporation with the dollar as its functional currency, enters into a forward contract with Bank A to buy 100 New Zealand dollars for $80 for delivery on January 31, 1990. (The forward purchase contract is not a section 1256 contract.) On November 1, 1989, the market price for the purchase of 100 New Zealand dollars for delivery on January 31, 1990, is $76. On November 1, 1989, X cancels its obligation under the forward purchase contract and pays Bank A $3.95 (the present value of $4 discounted at 12% for the period) in cancellation of such contract. Under section 1001(a), X realizes an exchange loss of $3.95 on November 1, 1989, because cancellation of the forward purchase contract for cash results in the termination of X's contract.

Example (2). X is a corporation with the dollar as its functional currency. On January 1, 1989, X enters into a currency swap contract with Bank A under which X is obligated to make a series of Japanese yen payments in exchange for a series of dollar payments. On February 21, 1992, X has a gain of $100,000 inherent in such contract as a result of interest rate and exchange rate movements. Also on February 21, 1992, X enters into an offsetting swap with Bank A to lock in such gain. If on February 21, 1992, X pledges the gain inherent in such offsetting positions as collateral for a loan, X's initial swap contract is treated as being terminated on February 21, 1992, under paragraph (d)(2)(ii)(B) of this section. Proper adjustment is made in the amount of any gain or loss subsequently realized for the gain taken into account by reason of paragraph (d)(2)(ii)(B) of this section.

Example (3). X is a calendar year corporation with the dollar as its functional currency. On October 1, 1989, X enters into a forward contract to buy 100,000 Swiss francs (Sf) for delivery on March 1, 1990, for $51,220. Assume that the contract is a section 1256 contract under section 1256(g)(2) and that section 1256(e) does not apply. Pursuant to section 1256(a)(1), the forward contract is treated as sold for its fair market value on December 31, 1989. Assume that the fair market value of the contract is $1,000 determined under § 1.988-1(g). Thus X will realize an exchange gain of $1,000 on December 31, 1989. Such gain is subject to the character rules of § 1.988-3 and the source rules of § 1.988-4.

(v) Extension of the maturity date of certain contracts. An extension of time for making or taking delivery under a contract described in paragraph (d)(1) of this section (e.g., a historical rate rollover as defined in § 1.988-5(b)(2)(iii)(C)) shall be considered a sale or exchange of the contract for its fair market value on the date of the extension and the establishment of a new contract on such date. If, under the terms of the extension, the time value of any gain or loss recognized pursuant to the preceding sentence adjusts the price of the currency to be bought or sold under the new contract, the amount attributable to such time value shall be treated as interest income or expense for all purposes of the Code. However, the preceding sentence shall not apply and the amount attributable to the time value of any gain or loss recognized shall be treated as exchange gain or loss if the period beginning on the first date the contract is rolled over and ending on the date payment is ultimately made or received with respect to such contract does not exceed 183 days.

(3) Recognition of exchange gain or loss. Except as provided in § 1.988-5 (relating to section 988 hedging transactions), exchange gain or loss realized with respect to a contract described in paragraph (d)(1) of this section shall be recognized in accordance with the applicable recognition provisions of the Internal Revenue Code. For example, a loss realized with respect to a contract described in paragraph (d)(1) of this section which is part of a straddle shall be recognized in accordance with the provisions of section 1092 to the extent such section is applicable.

(4) Determination of exchange gain or loss. (i) In general. Exchange gain or loss with respect to a contract described in § 1.988-2(d)(1) shall be determined by subtracting the amount paid (or deemed paid), if any, for or with respect to the contract (including any amount paid upon termination of the contract) from the amount received (or deemed received), if any, for or with respect to the contract (including any amount received upon termination of the contract). Any gain or loss determined according to the preceding sentence shall be treated as exchange gain or loss.

(ii) Special rules where taxpayer makes or takes delivery. If the taxpayer makes or takes delivery in connection with a contract described in paragraph (d)(1) of this section, any gain or loss shall be realized and recognized in the same manner as if the taxpayer sold the contract (or paid another person to assume the contract) on the date on which he took or made delivery for its fair market value on such date. See paragraph (d)(2)(iii) of this section regarding the definition of the term "delivery date." This paragraph (d)(4)(ii) shall not apply in any case in which the taxpayer makes or takes delivery before June 11, 1987.

(iii) Examples. The following examples illustrate the application of paragraph (d)(4) of this section.

Example (1). X is a calendar year corporation with the dollar as its functional currency. On October 1, 1989, when the six month forward rate is $.4907, X enters into a forward contract to buy 100,000 New Zealand dollars (NZD) for delivery on March 1, 1990. On March 1, 1990, when X takes delivery of the 100,000 NZD, the spot rate is 1NZD equals $.48. Pursuant to section 988(c)(5) and paragraph (d)(4)(ii) of this section, a taxpayer that takes delivery of nonfunctional currency under a forward contract that is subject to section 988 is treated as if the taxpayer sold the contract for its fair market value on the date delivery is taken. If X sold the contract on March 1, 1990, the transferee would require a payment of $1,070 [($.48 × 100,000NZD) − ($.4907 × 100,000NZD)] to compensate him for the loss in value of the 100,000NZD. Therefore, X realizes an exchange loss of $1,070. X has a basis in the 100,000NZD of $48,000.

Example (2). Assume the same facts as in Example 1 except that the contract is for Swiss francs and is a section 1256 contract. Assume further that on December 31, 1989, the value to X of the contract as marked to market is $1,000. Pursuant to section 1256(a). X realizes an exchange gain of $1,000. Such gain, however, is characterized as ordinary income under § 1.988-3 and will be sourced under § 1.988-4.

Example (3). X is a calendar year corporation with the dollar as its functional currency. On May 2, 1989, X enters into an option contract with Bank A to purchase 50,000 Canadian dollars (C$) for U.S.$42,500 (C$1 = U.S.$.85) for delivery on or before September 18, 1989. X pays a $285 premium to Bank A to obtain the option contract. On September 18, 1989, when X exercises the option and takes delivery of the C$50,000, the spot rate is C$1 equals U.S.$.90. Pursuant to section 988(c)(5) and paragraph (d)(4)(ii) of this section, a taxpayer that takes delivery under an option contract that is subject to section 988 is treated as if the taxpayer sold the contract for its fair market value on the date delivery is taken. If X sold the contract for its fair market value on September 18, 1989, X would receive U.S.$2,500 [(C$50,000 × U.S.$.90) − (C$50,000 × U.S.$.85)]. Accordingly, X is deemed to have received U.S.$2,500 on the sale of the contract at its fair market value. X will realize U.S.$2,215 ($2,500 deemed received less $285 paid) of exchange gain with respect to the delivery of Canadian dollars under the option contract. X's basis in the 50,000 Canadian dollars is U.S.$45,000.

(5) Hyperinflationary contracts. (i) In general. If a taxpayer acquires or otherwise enters into a hyperinflationary contract (as defined in paragraph (d)(5)(ii) of this section) that has payments to be made or received that are denominated in (or determined by reference to) a nonfunctional currency of the taxpayer, then the taxpayer shall realize exchange gain or loss with respect to such contract for its taxable year determined by reference to the change in exchange rates between—

(A) The later of the first day of the taxable year, or the date the contract was acquired or entered into; and

(B) The earlier of the last day of the taxable year, or the date the contract is disposed of or otherwise terminated.

(ii) Definition of hyperinflationary contract. A hyperinflationary contract is a contract described in paragraph (d)(1) of this section that provides for payments denominated in or determined by reference to a currency that is hyperinflationary (as defined in § 1.988-1(f)) at the time the taxpayer acquires or otherwise enters into the contract.

(iii) Interaction with other provisions. (A) DASTM. With respect to a qualified business unit that uses the United States dollar approximate separate transactions method of accounting described in § 1.985-3, this paragraph (d)(5) does not apply.

(B) Hedging rules. To the extent § 1.446-4 or 1.988-5 apply, this paragraph (d)(5) does not apply.

(C) Adjustment for subsequent transactions. Proper adjustments must be made in the amount of any gain or loss subsequently realized for gain or loss taken into account by reason of this paragraph (d)(5).

(iv) Effective date. This paragraph (d)(5) is applicable to transactions acquired or otherwise entered into after February 14, 2000.

(e) Currency swaps and other notional principal contracts. *(1) In general.* Except as provided in paragraph (e)(2) of this section or in § 1.988-5, the timing of income, deduction and loss with respect to a notional principal contract that is a section 988 transaction shall be governed by section 446 and the regulations thereunder. Such income, deduction and loss is characterized as exchange gain or loss (except as provided in another section of the Internal Revenue Code (or regulations thereunder), § 1.988-5, or in paragraph (f) of this section).

(2) Special rules for currency swaps. (i) In general. Except as provided in paragraph (e)(2)(iii)(B) of this section, the provisions of this paragraph (e)(2) shall apply solely for purposes of determining the realization, recognition and amount of exchange gain or loss with respect to a currency swap contract, and not for purposes of determining the source of such gain or loss, or characterizing such gain or loss as interest. Except as provided in § 1.988-3(c), any income or loss realized with respect to a currency swap contract shall be characterized as exchange gain or loss (and not as interest income or expense). Any exchange gain or loss realized in accordance with this paragraph (e)(2) shall be recognized unless otherwise provided in an applicable section of the Code. For purposes of this paragraph (e)(2), a currency swap contract is a contract defined in paragraph (e)(2)(ii) of this section. With respect to a contract which requires the payment of swap principal prior to maturity of such contract, see paragraph (f) of this section. For purposes of this paragraph (e), the rules of paragraph (d)(2)(ii) of this section (regarding realization by offset) apply. See Example 2 of paragraph (d)(2)(iv) of this section.

(ii) Definition of currency swap contract. (A) In general. A currency swap contract is a contract involving different currencies between two or more parties to—

(1) Exchange periodic interim payments, as defined in paragraph (e)(2)(ii)(C) of this section, on or prior to maturity of the contract; and

(2) Exchange the swap principal amount upon maturity of the contract. A currency swap contract may also require an exchange of the swap principal amount upon commencement of the agreement.

(B) Swap principal amount. The swap principal amount is an amount of two different currencies which, under the terms of the currency swap contract, is used to determine the periodic interim payments in each currency and which is exchanged upon maturity of the contract. If such amount is not clearly set forth in the contract, the Commissioner may determine the swap principal amount.

(C) Exchange of periodic interim payments. An exchange of periodic interim payments is an exchange of one or more payments in one currency specified by the contract for one or more payments in a different currency specified by the contract where the payments in each currency are computed by reference to an interest index applied to the swap principal amount A currency swap contract must clearly indicate the periodic interim payments, or the interest index used to compute the periodic interim payments, in each currency.

(iii) Timing and computation of periodic interim payments. (A) In general. Except as provided in paragraph (e)(2)(iii)(B) of this section and § 1.988-5, the timing and computation of the periodic interim payments provided in a currency swap agreement shall be determined by treating—

(1) Payments made under the swap as payments made pursuant to a hypothetical borrowing that is denominated in the currency in which payments are required to be made (or are determined with reference to) under the swap, and

(2) Payments received under the swap as payments received pursuant to a hypothetical loan that is denominated in the currency in which payments are received (or are determined with reference to) under the swap.

Except as provided in paragraph (e)(2)(v) of this section, the hypothetical issue price of such hypothetical borrowing and loan shall be the swap principal amount. The hypothetical stated redemption price at maturity is the total of all payments (excluding any exchange of the swap principal amount at the inception of the contract) provided under the hypothetical borrowing or loan other than periodic interest payments under the principles of section 1273. For purposes of determining economic accrual under the currency swap, the number of hypothetical interest compounding periods of such hypothetical borrowing and loan shall be determined pursuant to a semiannual compounding convention unless the currency swap contract indicates otherwise. For purposes of determining the timing and amount of the periodic interim payments. the principles regarding the amortization of interest (see generally, sections 1272 through 1275 and 163(e)) shall apply to the hypothetical interest expense and income of such hypothetical borrowing and loan. However, such principles shall not apply to determine the time when principal is deemed to be paid on the hypothetical borrowing and loan. See paragraph (d)(2)(iii) of this section and Example 2 of paragraph (d)(5) of this section with respect to the time when principal is deemed to be paid. With respect to the translation and computation of exchange gain or loss on any hypothetical interest income or expense, see § 1.988-2(b). The amount treated as exchange gain or loss by the taxpayer with respect to the periodic interim payments for the taxable year shall be the amount of hypothetical interest income and exchange gain or loss attributable to such interest income from the hypothetical borrowing and loan for such year less the amount of hypothetical interest expense and exchange gain or loss attributable to the interest expense from such hypothetical borrowing and loan for such year.

(B) Effect of prepayment for purposes of section 956. For purposes of section 956, the Commissioner may treat any prepayment of a currency swap as a loan.

(iv) Timing and determination of exchange gain or loss with respect to the swap principal amount. Exchange gain or loss with respect to the swap principal amount shall be realized on the day the units of swap principal in each currency are exchanged. (See paragraph (e)(2)(ii)(A)(2) of this section which requires that the entire swap principal amount be exchanged upon maturity of the contract.) Such gain or loss shall be determined on the date of the exchange by subtracting the value (on such date) of the units of swap principal paid from the value of the units of swap principal received. This paragraph (e)(2)(iv) does not apply to an equal exchange of the swap principal amount at the commencement of the agreement at a market exchange rate.

(v) Anti-abuse rules. (A) Method of accounting does not clearly reflect income. If the taxpayer's method of accounting for income, expense, gain or loss attributable to a currency swap does not clearly reflect income, or if the present value of the payments to be made is not equivalent to that of the payments to be received (including the swap premium or discount, as defined in paragraph (e)(3)(ii) of this section) on the day the taxpayer enters into or acquires the contract, the Commissioner may apply principles analogous to those of section 1274 or such other rules as the Commissioner deems appropriate to clearly reflect income. For example, in order to clearly reflect income the Commissioner may determine the hypothetical issue price, the hypothetical stated redemption price at maturity, and the amounts required to be taken into account within a taxable year. Further, if the present value of the payments to be made is not equivalent to that of the payments to be received (including the swap premium or discount, as defined in paragraph (e)(3)(ii) of this section) on the day the taxpayer enters into or acquires the contract, the Commissioner may integrate the swap with another transaction (or transactions) in order to clearly reflect income.

(B) Terms must be clearly stated. If the currency swap contract does not clearly set forth the swap principal amount in each currency, and the periodic interim payments in each currency (or the interest index used to compute the periodic interim payments in each currency), the Commissioner may defer any income, deduction, gain or loss with respect to such contract until termination of the contract.

(3) Amortization of swap premium or discount in the case of off-market currency swaps. (i) In general. An "off-market currency swap" is a currency swap contract under which the present value of the payments to be made is not equal to that of the payments to be received on the day the taxpayer enters into or acquires the contract (absent the swap premium or discount, as defined in paragraph (e)(3)(ii) of this section). Generally, such present values may not be equal if the swap exchange rate (as defined in paragraph (e)(3)(iii) of this section) is not the spot rate, or the interest indices used to compute the periodic interim payments do not reflect current values, on the day the taxpayer enters into or acquires the currency swap.

(ii) Treatment of taxpayer entering into or acquiring an off-market currency swap. If a taxpayer that enters into or acquires a currency swap makes a payment (that is, the taxpayer pays a premium, "swap premium," to enter into or acquire the currency swap) or receives a payment (that is, the taxpayer enters into or acquires the currency swap at a discount, "swap discount") in order to make the present value of the amounts to be paid equal the amounts to be received, such payment shall be amortized in a manner which places the taxpayer in the same position it would have been in had the taxpayer entered into a currency swap contract under which the present value of the amounts to be paid equal the amounts to be received (absent any swap premium or discount). Thus, swap premium or discount shall be amortized as follows—

(A) The amount of swap premium or discount that is attributable to the difference between the swap exchange rate (as defined in paragraph (e)(3)(iii) of this section) and the spot rate on the date the contract is entered into or acquired shall be taken into account as income or expense on the date the swap principal amounts are taken into account; and

(B) The amount of swap premium or discount attributable to the difference in values of the periodic interim payments shall be amortized in a manner consistent with the principles of economic accrual. Cf., section 171.

Any amount taken into account pursuant to this paragraph (e)(3)(ii) shall be treated as exchange gain or loss.

(iii) Definition of swap exchange rate. The swap exchange rate is the single exchange rate set forth in the contract at which the swap principal amounts are determined. If the swap exchange rate is not clearly set forth in the contract, the Commissioner may determine such rate.

(iv) Coordination with § 1.446-3(g)(4) regarding swaps with significant nonperiodic payments. The rules of § 1.446-3(g)(4) apply to any currency swap with a significant nonperiodic payment. Section 1.446-3(g)(4) applies before this paragraph (e)(3). Thus, if § 1.446-3(g)(4) applies, currency gain or loss may be realized on the loan. This paragraph (e)(3)(iv) applies to transactions entered into after February 14, 2000.

(4) Treatment of taxpayer disposing of a currency swap. Any gain or loss realized on the disposition or the termination of a currency swap is exchange gain or loss.

(5) Examples. The following examples illustrate the application of this paragraph (e).

Example (1). (i) C is an accrual method calendar year corporation with the dollar as its functional currency. On January 1, 1989, C enters into a currency swap with J with the following terms:

(1) the principal amount is $150 and 100 British pounds (£) (the equivalent of $150 on the effective date of the contract assuming a spot rate of £1 = $1.50 on January 1, 1989);

(2) C will make payments equal to 10% of the dollar principal amount on December 31, 1989, and December 31, 1990:

(3) J will make payments equal to 12% of the pound principal amount on December 31, 1989, and December 31, 1990; and

(4) on December 31, 1990, C will pay to J the $150 principal amount and J will pay to C the £100 principal amount. Assume that the spot rate is £1 = $1.50 on January 1, 1989, £1 = $1.40 on December 31, 1989, and £1 = $1.30 on December 31, 1990. Assume further that the average rate for 1989 is £1 = $1.45 and for 1990 is £1 = $1.35.

(ii) Solely for determining the realization of gain or loss in accordance with paragraph (e)(2) of this section (and not for purposes of determining whether any payments are treated as interest), C will treat the dollar payments made by C as payments made pursuant to a dollar borrowing with an issue price of $150, a stated redemption price at maturity of $150, and yield to maturity of 10%. C will treat the pound payments received as payments received pursuant to a pound loan with an issue price of £100, a stated redemption price at maturity of £100, and a yield of 12% to maturity. Pursuant to § 1.988-2(b), C is required to compute hypothetical accrued pound interest income at the average rate for the accrual period and then determine exchange gain or loss on the day payment is received with respect to such accrued amount. Accordingly, C will accrue $17.40 (£12 × $1.45) in 1989 and $16.20 (£ 12 × $1.35) in 1990. C also will compute hypothetical exchange loss of $.60 on December 31, 1989 [(£12 × $1.40) – (£12 × $1.45)] and hypothetical exchange loss of $.60 on December 31, 1990 [(£12 × $1.30) – (£12 × $1.35)]. All such hypothetical interest income and exchange loss are characterized and sourced as exchange gain and loss. Further, C is treated as having paid $15 ($150 × 10%) of hypothetical interest on December 31, 1989, and again on December 31, 1990. Such hypothetical interest expense is characterized and sourced as exchange loss. Thus, C will have a net exchange gain of $1.80 ($17.40 – $.60 – $15.00) with respect to the periodic interim payments in 1989 and a net exchange gain of $.60 ($16.20 – $.60 – $15.00) with respect to the periodic interim payments in 1990. Finally, C will realize an exchange loss on December 31, 1990 with respect to the exchange of the swap principal amount. This loss is determined by subtracting the value of the units of swap principal paid ($150) from the value of the units of swap principal received (£100 × $1.30 = $130) resulting in a $20 exchange loss.

Example (2). (i) C is an accrual method calendar year corporation with the dollar as its functional currency. On January 1, 1989, when the spot rate is £1 = $1.50, C enters into a currency swap contract with J under which C agrees to make and receive the following payments:

Date	C pays	J pays
December 31, 1989	$ 15.00	£12.00
December 31, 1990	41.04	12.00
December 31, 1991	0.00	12.00
December 31, 1992	150.00	112.00

(ii) Under paragraph (e)(2)(iii) of this section, C must treat the dollar periodic interim payments under the swap as made pursuant to a hypothetical dollar borrowing. The hypothetical issue price is $150 and the stated redemption price at maturity is $206.04. The amount of hypothetical interest expense must be amortized in accordance with economic accrual. Thus J must include and C must deduct periodic interim payment amounts as follows:

	Amount taken into account	Adjusted issue price
December 31, 1989	$15.00	150.00
December 31, 1990	$15.00	123.96
December 31, 1991	$12.40	136.36
December 31, 1992	13.64	

(iii) Gain or loss with respect to the periodic interim payments of the currency swap is determined under paragraph (e)(2)(iii)(A) of this section with respect to the dollar cash flow amortized as set forth above and the corresponding pound cash flow as stated in the currency swap contract. Gain or loss with respect to the principal payments (i.e., $150 and £100) exchanged on December 31, 1992, is determined under paragraph (e)(2)(iv) of this section on December 31, 1992, notwithstanding that under the principles regarding amortization of interest $26.04 would have been regarded as a payment of principal on December 31, 1990.

Example (3). (i) X is a corporation on the accrual method of accounting with the dollar as its functional currency and the calendar year as its taxable year. On January 1, 1989, X enters into a three year currency swap contract with Y with the following terms. The swap principal amount is $100 and the Swiss franc (Sf) equivalent of such amount which equals Sf200 translated at the swap exchange rate of $1 = Sf2. There is no initial exchange of the swap principal amount. The interest rates used to compute the periodic interim payments are 10% compounded annually for U.S. dollar payments and 5% compounded annually for Swiss franc payments. Thus, under the currency swap, X agrees to pay Y $10 (10% × $100) on December 31st of 1989, 1990 and 1991 and to pay Y the swap principal amount of $100 on December 31, 1991. Y agrees to pay X Sf10 (5% × Sf200) on December 31st of 1989, 1990 and 1991 and to pay X the swap principal amount of Sf200 on December 31, 1991. Assume that the average rate for 1989 and the spot rate on December 31, 1989, is $1 = Sf2.5.

(ii) Under paragraph (e)(2)(iii) of this section, on December 31, 1989, X will realize an exchange loss of $6 (the sum of $10 of loss by reason of the $10 periodic interim payment paid to Y and $4.00 of gain, the value of Sf10 on December 31, 1989. from the receipt of Sf10 on such date).

(iii) On January 1, 1990, X transfers its rights and obligations under the swap contract to Z, an unrelated corporation. Z has the dollar as its functional currency, is on the accrual method of accounting. and has the calendar year as its taxable year. On January 1, 1990, the exchange rate is $1 = Sf2.50. The relevant dollar interest rate is 8% compounded annually and the relevant Swiss franc interest rate is 5% compounded annually. Because of the movement in exchange and interest rates, the agreement between X and Z to transfer the currency swap requires X to pay Z $23.56 (the swap discount as determined under paragraph (e)(3) of this section).

(iv) Pursuant to paragraph (e)(4) of this section, X may deduct the loss of $23.56 in 1990. The loss is characterized under § 1.988-3 and sourced under § 1.988-4.

(v) Pursuant to paragraph (e)(3)(ii) of this section, Z is required to amortize the $23.56 received as follows. The amount of the $23.56 payment that is attributable to movements in exchange rates ($20) is taken into account on December 31, 1991, the date the swap principal amounts are exchanged, under paragraph (e)(3)(ii)(A) of this section. This amount is the present value (discounted at 10%, the rate under the currency swap contract used to compute the dollar periodic interim payments) of the financial asset required to compensate Z for the loss in value of the hypothetical Swiss franc loan resulting from movements in exchange rates between January 1, 1989 and January 1, 1990. This amount is determined by assuming that interest rates did not change from the date the swap originally was entered into (January 1, 1989), but that the exchange rate is $1 = Sf2.50. Under this assumption, a taxpayer undertaking the obligation to pay dollars under the currency swap on January 1, 1990, would only agree to pay $8 for Sf10 on December 31, 1990 and $88 for Sf210 on December 31, 1991, because the exchange rates have moved from $1 = Sf2 to $1 = Sf2.50. Thus, Z requires $2 on December 31, 1990 and $22 on December 31, 1991 to compensate for the amount of dollar payments Z is required to make in exchange for the Swiss francs received on December 31, 1990 and 1991. The present value of $2 on December 31, 1990 and $22 on December 31, 1991 discounted at the rate for U.S. dollar payments of 10% is $20 ($1.82 + $18.18). This amount is discounted at the rate for U.S. dollar payments (i.e., at the historic rate) because the amount of the $23.56 payment received by Z that is attributable to movements in interest rates is computed and amortized separately as provided in the following paragraph.

(vi) Pursuant to paragraph (e)(3)(ii)(B) of this section, Z is required to amortize the portion of the $23.56 payment attributable to movements in interest rates under principles of economic accrual over the term of the currency swap agreement. The amount of the $23.56 payment that is attributable to movements in interest rates (assuming that exchange rates have not changed) is the present value ($3.56) of the excess ($2.00 in 1990 and $2.00 in 1991) of the periodic interim payments Z is required to pay under the currency swap agreement ($10 in 1990 and $10 in 1991) over the amount Z would be required to pay if the currency swap agreement reflected current interest rates on the day Z acquired the swap contract ($8 in 1990 and $8 in 1991) discounted at the appropriate dollar interest rate on January 1, 1990. Thus, under principles of economic accrual (e.g., see section 171 of the Code), Z will include in income $1.72 on December 31, 1990. the amount that, when added to the interest ($.28) on the $3.56 computed at the 8% rate on the date Z acquired the currency swap contract, will equal the $2.00 needed to compensate Z for the movement in interest rates between January 1, 1989 and January 1, 1990. Z also will include in income $1.85 on December 31, 1991, the amount that, when added to the interest ($.15) on the $1.85 (the remaining balance of the $3.56 payment) computed at the 8% rate on the date Z acquired the currency swap contract, will equal the $2.00 needed to compensate Z for the movement in interest rates between January 1, 1990 and January 1, 1991. This amount is computed assuming exchange rates have not changed because the amount attributable to movements in exchange rates is computed and amortized separately under the preceding paragraph.

(6) Special effective date for rules regarding currency swaps. Paragraph (e)(3) of this section regarding amortization of swap premium or discount in the case of off-market currency swaps shall be effective for transactions entered into after September 21, 1989, unless such swap premium or discount was paid or received pursuant to a binding contract with an unrelated party that was entered into prior to such date. For transactions entered into prior to this date, see Notice 89-21, 1989-8 I.R.B. 23.

(7) Special rules for currency swap contracts in hyperinflationary currencies. (i) In general. If a taxpayer enters into a hyperinflationary currency swap (as defined in paragraph (e)(7)(iv) of this section), then the taxpayer realizes exchange gain or loss for its taxable year with respect to such instrument determined by reference to the change in exchange rates between—

(A) The later of the first day of the taxable year, or the date the instrument was entered into (by the taxpayer); and

(B) The earlier of the last day of the taxable year, or the date the instrument is disposed of or otherwise terminated.

(ii) Adjustment to principal or basis. Proper adjustments are made in the amount of any gain or loss subsequently realized for gain or loss taken into account by reason of this paragraph (e)(7).

(iii) Interaction with DASTM. With respect to a qualified business unit that uses the United States dollar approximate separate transactions method of accounting described in § 1.985-3, this paragraph (e)(7) does not apply.

(iv) Definition of hyperinflationary currency swap contract. A hyperinflationary currency swap contract is a currency swap contract that provides for—

(A) Payments denominated in or determined by reference to a currency that is hyperinflationary (as defined in § 1.988-1(f)) at the time the taxpayer enters into or otherwise acquires the currency swap; or

(B) Payments that are adjusted to take into account the fact that the currency is hyperinflationary (as defined in § 1.988-1(f)) during the current taxable year. A currency swap contract that provides for periodic payments determined by reference to a variable interest rate based on local conditions and generally responding to changes in the local consumer price index is an example of this latter type of currency swap contract.

(v) Special effective date for nonfunctional hyperinflationary currency swap contracts. This paragraph (e)(7) applies to transactions entered into after February 14, 2000.

(f) Substance over form. *(1) In general.* If the substance of a transaction described in § 1.988-1(a)(1) differs from its form, the timing, source, and character of gains or losses with respect to such transaction may be recharacterized by the Commissioner in accordance with its substance. For example, if a taxpayer enters into a transaction that it designates a "currency swap contract" that requires the prepayment of all payments to be made or to be received (but not both), the Commissioner may recharacterize the contract as a loan. In applying the substance over form principle, separate transactions may be integrated where appropriate. See also § 1.861-9T(b)(1).

(2) Example. The following example illustrates the provisions of this paragraph (f).

Example. (i) On January 1, 1990, X, a U.S. corporation with the dollar as its functional currency, enters into a contract with Y under which X will pay Y $100 and Y will pay X LC100 on January 1, 1990, and X will pay Y LC109.3 and Y will pay X $133 on December 31, 1992. On January 1, 1990, the spot exchange rate is LC1 = $1 and the 3 year forward rate is LC1 = $.8218. X's cash flows are summarized below:

Date	Dollar	LC
1/1/90	(100)	100
12/31/90	0	0
12/31/91	0	0
12/31/92	133	(109.3)

(ii) X and Y designate this contract as a "currency swap." Notwithstanding this designation. for purposes of determining the timing, source, and character with respect to the transaction, the transaction is characterized by the Commissioner in accordance with its substance. Thus, the January 1, 1990, exchange by X of $100 for LC100 is treated as a spot purchase of LCs by X and the December 31, 1992, exchange by X at 109.3LC for $133 is treated as a forward sale of LCs by X. Under such treatment there would be no tax consequences to X under paragraph (e)(2) of this section in 1990, 1991, and 1992 with respect to this transaction other than the realization of exchange gain or loss on the sale of the LC109.3 on December 31, 1992. Calculation of such gain or loss would be governed by the rules of paragraph (d) of this section.

(g) Effective date. Except as otherwise provided in this section, this section shall be effective for taxable years beginning after December 31, 1986. Thus, except as otherwise provided in this section, any payments made or received with respect to a section 988 transaction in taxable years beginning after December 31, 1986, are subject to this section.

(h) Timing of income and deductions from notional principal contracts. Except as otherwise provided (e.g., in § 1.988-5 or 1.446-3(g)), income or loss from a notional principal contract described in § 1.988-1(a)(2)(iii)(B) (other than a currency swap) is exchange gain or loss. For the rules governing the timing of income and deductions with respect to notional principal contracts, see § 1.446-3. See paragraph (e)(2) of this section with respect to currency swaps.

T.D. 8400, 3/16/92, amend T.D. 8491, 10/8/93, T.D. 8860, 1/12/2000, T.D. 9157, 8/27/2004.

§ 1.988-3 Character of exchange gain or loss.

(a) In general. The character of exchange gain or loss recognized on a section 988 transaction is governed by section 988 and this section. Except as otherwise provided in section 988(c)(1)(E), section 1092, § 1.988-5 and this section, exchange gain or loss realized with respect to a section 988 transaction (including a section 1256 contract that is also a section 988 transaction) shall be characterized as ordinary gain or loss. Accordingly, unless a valid election is made under paragraph (b) of this section, any section providing special rules for capital gain or loss treatment, such as sections 1233, 1234, 1234A, 1236 and 1256(f)(3), shall not apply.

(b) Election to characterize exchange gain or loss on certain identified forward contracts, futures contracts and option contracts as capital gain or loss. *(1) In general.* Except as provided in paragraph (b)(2) of this section, a taxpayer may elect, subject to the requirements of paragraph (b)(3) of this section, to treat any gain or loss recognized on a contract described in § 1.988-2(d)(1) as capital gain or loss. but only if the contract—

(i) Is a capital asset in the hands of the taxpayer;

(ii) Is not part of a straddle within the meaning of section 1092(c) (without regard to subsections (c)(4) or (e)); and

(iii) Is not a regulated futures contract or nonequity option with respect to which an election under section 988(c)(1)(D)(ii) is in effect.

If a valid election under this paragraph (b) is made with respect to a section 1256 contract, section 1256 shall govern the character of any gain or loss recognized on such contract.

(2) Special rule for contracts that become part of a straddle after an election is made. If a contract which is the subject of an election under paragraph (b)(1) of this section becomes part of a straddle within the meaning of section 1092(c) (without regard to subsections (c)(4) or (e)) after the date of the election, the election shall be invalid with respect to gains from such contract and the Commissioner, in his sole discretion, may invalidate the election with respect to losses.

(3) Requirements for making the election. A taxpayer elects to treat gain or loss on a transaction described in paragraph (b)(1) of this section as capital gain or loss by clearly identifying such transaction on its books and records on the date the transaction is entered into. No specific language or account is necessary for identifying a transaction referred to in the preceding sentence. However, the method of identification must be consistently applied and must clearly identify the pertinent transaction as subject to the section 988(a)(1)(B) election. The Commissioner, in his sole discretion, may invalidate any purported election that does not comply with the preceding sentence.

(4) Verification. A taxpayer that has made an election under § 1.988-3(b)(3) must attach to his income tax return a statement which sets forth the following:

(i) A description and the date of each election made by the taxpayer during the taxpayer's taxable year;

(ii) A statement that each election made during the taxable year was made before the close of the date the transaction was entered into;

(iii) A description of any contract for which an election was in effect and the date such contract expired or was otherwise sold or exchanged during the taxable year;

(iv) A statement that the contract was never part of a straddle as defined in section 1092; and

(v) A statement that all transactions subject to the election are included on the statement attached to the taxpayer's income tax return.

In addition to any penalty that may otherwise apply, the Commissioner, in his sole discretion, may invalidate any or all elections made during the taxable year under § 1.988-3(b)(1) if the taxpayer fails to verify each election as provided in this § 1.988- 3(b)(4). The preceding sentence shall not apply if the taxpayer's failure to verify each election was due to reasonable cause or bona fide mistake. The burden of proof to show reasonable cause or bona fide mistake made in good faith is on the taxpayer.

(5) Independent verification. (i) Effect of independent verification. If the taxpayer receives independent verification of the election in paragraph (b)(3) of this section, the taxpayer shall be presumed to have satisfied the requirements of paragraphs (b)(3) and (4) of this section. A contract that is a part of a straddle as defined in section 1092 may not be independently verified and shall be subject to the rules of paragraph (b)(2) of this section.

(ii) Requirements far independent verification. A taxpayer receives independent verification of the election in paragraph (b)(3) of this section if—

(A) The taxpayer establishes a separate account(s) with an unrelated broker(s) or dealer(s) through which all transactions to be independently verified pursuant to this paragraph (b)(5) are conducted and reported.

(B) Only transactions entered into on or after the date the taxpayer establishes such account may be recorded in the account.

(C) Transactions subject to the election of paragraph (b)(3) of this section are entered into such account on the date such transactions are entered into.

(D) The broker or dealer provides the taxpayer a statement detailing the transactions conducted through such account and includes on such statement the following: "Each transaction identified in this account is subject to the election set forth in section 988(a)(1)(B)."

(iii) Special effective date for independent verification. The rules of this paragraph (b)(5) shall be effective for transactions entered into after March 17, 1992.

(6) Effective date. Except as otherwise provided, this paragraph (b) is effective for taxable years beginning on or after September 21, 1989. For prior taxable years, any reasonable contemporaneous election meeting the requirements of section 988(a)(1)(B) shall satisfy this paragraph (b).

(c) Exchange gain or loss treated as interest. *(1) In general.* Except as provided in this paragraph (c)(1), exchange gain or loss realized on a section 988 transaction shall not be treated as interest income or expense. Exchange gain or loss realized on a section 988 transaction shall be treated as interest income or expense as provided in paragraph (c)(2) of this section with regard to tax exempt bonds, § 1.988-2(e)(2)(ii)(B), § 1.988-5, and in administrative pronouncements. See § 1.861-9T(b), providing rules for the allocation of certain items of exchange gain or loss in the same manner as interest expense.

(2) Exchange loss realized by the holder on nonfunctional currency tax exempt bonds. Exchange loss realized by the holder of a debt instrument the interest on which is excluded from gross income under section 103(a) or any similar provision of law shall be treated as an offset to and reduce total interest income received or accrued with respect to such instrument. Therefore, to the extent of total interest income, no exchange loss shall be recognized. This paragraph (c)(2) shall be effective with respect to debt instruments acquired on or after June 24, 1987.

(d) Effective date. Except as otherwise provided in this section, this section shall be effective for taxable years beginning after December 31, 1986. Thus, except as otherwise provided in this section, any payments made or received with respect to a section 988 transaction in taxable years beginning after December 31, 1986, are subject to this section. Thus, for example, a payment made prior to January 1, 1987, under a forward contract that results in the deferral of a loss under section 1092 to a taxable year beginning after December 31, 1986, is not characterized as an ordinary loss by virtue of paragraph (a) of this section because payment was made prior to January 1, 1987.

T.D. 8400, 3/16/92.

---

§ 1.988-4 Source of gain or loss realized on a section 988 transaction.

(a) In general. Except as otherwise provided in § 1.988-5 and this section, the source of exchange gain or loss shall be determined by reference to the residence of the taxpayer. This rule applies even if the taxpayer has made an election under § 1.988-3(b) to characterize exchange gain or loss as capital gain or loss. This section takes precedence over section 865.

(b) Qualified business unit. *(1) In general.* The source of exchange gain or loss shall be determined by reference to the residence of the qualified business unit of the taxpayer on whose books the asset, liability, or item of income or expense giving rise to such gain or loss is properly reflected.

(2) Proper reflection on the books of the taxpayer or qualified business unit. (i) In general. Whether an asset, liability, or item of income or expense is properly reflected on the books of a qualified business unit is a question of fact.

(ii) Presumption if booking practices are inconsistent. It shall be presumed that an asset, liability, or item of income or expense is not properly reflected on the books of the qualified business unit if the taxpayer and its qualified business units employ inconsistent booking practices with respect to the same or similar assets, liabilities, or items of income or expense. If not properly reflected on the books, the Commissioner may allocate any asset, liability, or item of income or expense between or among the taxpayer and its qualified business units to properly reflect the source (or realization) of exchange gain or loss.

(c) Effectively connected exchange gain or loss. Notwithstanding paragraphs (a) and (b) of this section, exchange gain or loss that under principles similar to those set forth in § 1.864- 4(c) arises from the conduct of a United States trade or business shall be sourced in the United States and such gain or loss shall be treated as effectively connected to the conduct of a United States trade or business for purposes of sections 871(b) and 882(a)(1).

(d) Residence. *(1) In general.* Except as otherwise provided in this paragraph (d), for purposes of sections 985 through 989, the residence of any person shall be—

(i) In the case of an individual, the country in which such individual's tax home (as defined in section 911(d)(3)) is located;

(ii) In the case of a corporation, partnership, trust or estate which is a United States person (as defined in section 7701(a)(30)), the United States; and

(iii) In the case of a corporation, partnership, trust or estate which is not a United States person, a country other than the United States.

If an individual does not have a tax home (as defined in section 911(d)(3)), the residence of such individual shall be the United States if such individual is a United States citizen or a resident alien and shall be a country other than the United States if such individual is not a United States citizen or resident alien. If the taxpayer is a U.S. person and has no principal place of business outside the United States, the residence of the taxpayer is the United States. Notwithstanding paragraph (d)(1)(ii) of this section, if a partnership is formed or availed of to avoid tax by altering the source of exchange gain or loss, the source of such gain or loss shall be determined by reference to the residence of the partners rather than the partnership.

(2) Exception. In the case of a qualified business unit of any taxpayer (including an individual), the residence of such unit shall be the country in which the principal place of business of such qualified business unit is located.

(3) Partner in a partnership not engaged in a U.S. trade or business under section 864(b)(2). The determination of residence shall be made at the partner level (without regard to whether the partnership is a qualified business unit of the partners) in the case of partners in a partnership that are not engaged in a U.S. trade or business by reason of section 864(b)(2).

(e) Special rule for certain related party loans. *(1) In general.* In the case of a loan by a United States person or a related person to a 10 percent owned foreign corporation, or a corporation that meets the 80 percent foreign business requirements test of section 861(c)(1), other than a corporation subject to § 1.861-11T(e)(2)(i), which is denominated in, or determined by reference to, a currency other than the U.S. dollar and bears interest at a rate at least 10 percentage points higher than the Federal mid-term rate (as determined under section 1274(d)) at the time such loan is entered into, the following rules shall apply—

(i) For purposes of section 904 only, such loan shall be marked to market annually on the earlier of the last business day of the United States person's (or related person's) taxable year or the date the loan matures; and

(ii) Any interest income earned with respect to such loan for the taxable year shall be treated as income from sources within the United States to the extent of any notional loss attributable to such loan under paragraph (d)(1)(i) of this section.

(2) United States person. For purposes of this paragraph (e), the term "United States person" means a person described in section 7701(a)(30).

(3) Loans by related foreign persons. (i) In general. [Reserved]

(ii) Definition of related person. For purposes of this paragraph (e), the term "related person" has the meaning given such term by section 954(d)(3) except that such section shall be applied by substituting "United States person" for "controlled foreign corporation" each place such term appears.

(4) 10 percent owned foreign corporation. For purposes of this paragraph (e), the term "10 percent owned foreign corporation" means any foreign corporation in which the United States person owns directly or indirectly (within the meaning of section 318(a)) at least 10 percent of the voting stock.

(f) Exchange gain or loss treated as interest under § 1.988-3. Notwithstanding the provisions of this section, any gain or loss realized on a section 988 transaction that is treated as interest income or expense under § 1.988-3(c)(1) shall be sourced or allocated and apportioned pursuant to section 861(a)(1), 862(a)(1), or 864(e) as the case may be.

(g) Exchange gain or loss allocated in the same manner as interest under § 1.861-9T. The allocation and apportionment of exchange gain or loss under 1.861-9T shall not affect the source of exchange gain or loss for purposes of sections 871(a), 881, 1441, 1442 and 6049.

(h) Effective date. This section shall be effective for taxable years beginning after December 31, 1986. Thus, any payments made or received with respect to a section 988 transaction in taxable years beginning after December 31, 1986, are subject to this section.

T.D. 8400, 3/16/92.

PAR. 7. Section 1.988-4 is amended by revising paragraph (b)(2) to read as follows:

Proposed § 1.988-4 Source of gain or loss realized on a section 988 transfer. [*For Preamble, see ¶ 152,801*]

* * * * *

(b) * * *

(2) Proper reflection on the books of the taxpayer or qualified business unit. (i) In general. For purposes of paragraph (b)(1) of this section, the principles of § 1.987-2(b) shall apply in determining whether an asset, liability, or item of income or expense is reflected on the books of a qualified business unit.

(ii) Effective date. Generally, paragraph (b)(2)(i) of this section shall apply to taxable years beginning one year after the first day of the first taxable year following the date of publication of a Treasury decision adopting this rule as a final regulation in the Federal Register. If a taxpayer makes an election under § 1.987-11(b), then the effective date of paragraph (b)(2)(i) with respect to the taxpayer shall be consistent with such election.

* * * * *

PAR. 12. Section 1.988-4 is amended as follows:

1. Paragraph (h) is redesignated as paragraph (i).

2. A new paragraph (h) is added.

The addition and revision read as follows:

Proposed § 1.988-4 Source of gain or loss realized on a section 988 transfer. [*For Preamble, see ¶ 151,855*]

* * * * *

(h) Exchange gain or loss from a global dealing operation. Notwithstanding the provisions of this section, exchange gain or loss derived by a participant in a global dealing operation, as defined in § 1.482-8(a)(2)(i), shall be sourced under the rules set forth in § 1.863-3(h).

* * * * *

§ 1.988-5 Section 988(d) hedging transactions.

Caution: The Treasury has not yet amended Reg § 1.988-5 to reflect changes made by P.L. 106-170, P.L. 103-66.

(a) Integration of a nonfunctional currency debt instrument and a § 1.988-5(a) hedge. *(1) In general.* This paragraph (a) applies to a qualified hedging transaction as defined in this paragraph (a)(1). A qualified hedging transaction is an integrated economic transaction, as provided in paragraph (a)(5) of this section, consisting of a qualifying debt instrument as defined in paragraph (a)(3) of this section and a § 1.988-5(a) hedge as defined in paragraph (a)(4) of this section. If a taxpayer enters into a transaction that is a qualified hedging transaction, no exchange gain or loss is recognized by the taxpayer on the qualifying debt instrument or on the § 1.988-5(a) hedge for the period that either is part of a qualified hedging transaction, and the transactions shall be integrated as provided in paragraph (a)(9) of this section. However, if the qualified hedging transaction results in a synthetic nonfunctional currency denominated debt instrument, such instrument shall be subject to the rules of § 1.988-2(b).

(2) Exception. This paragraph (a) does not apply with respect to a qualified hedging transaction that creates a synthetic asset or liability denominated in, or determined by reference to, a currency other than the U.S. dollar if the rate that approximates the Federal short-term rate in such currency is at least 20 percentage points higher than the Federal short term rate (determined under section 1274(d)) on the date the taxpayer identifies the transaction as a qualified hedging transaction.

(3) Qualifying debt instrument. (i) In general. A qualifying debt instrument is a debt instrument described in § 1.988- 1(a)(2)(i), regardless of whether denominated in, or determined by reference to, nonfunctional currency (including dual currency debt instruments, multi-currency debt instruments and contingent payment debt instruments). A qual-

ifying debt instrument does not include accounts payable, accounts receivable or similar items of expense or income.

(ii) Special rule for debt instrument of which all payments ore proportionately hedged. If a debt instrument satisfies the requirements of paragraph (a)(3)(i) of this section, and all principal and interest payments under the instrument are hedged in the same proportion, then for purposes of this paragraph (a), that portion of the instrument that is hedged is eligible to be treated as a qualifying debt instrument, and the rules of this paragraph (a) shall apply separately to such qualifying debt instrument. See Example 8 in paragraph (a)(9)(iv) of this section.

(4) Section 1.988-5(a) hedge. (i) In general. A § 1.988-5(a) hedge (hereinafter referred to in this paragraph (a) as a "hedge") is a spot contract, futures contract, forward contract, option contract, notional principal contract, currency swap contract, similar financial instrument, or series or combination thereof, that when integrated with a qualifying debt instrument permits the calculation of a yield to maturity (under principles of section 1272) in the currency in which the synthetic debt instrument is denominated (as determined under paragraph (a)(9)(ii)(A) of this section).

(ii) Retroactive application of definition of currency swap contract. A taxpayer may apply the definition of currency swap contract set forth in § 1.988-2(e)(2)(ii) in lieu of the definition of swap agreement in section 2(e)(5) of Notice 87-11, 1987-1 C.B. 423 to transactions entered into after December 31, 1986 and before September 21, 1989.

(5) Definition of integrated economic transaction. A qualifying debt instrument and a hedge are an integrated economic transaction if all of the following requirements are satisfied—

(i) All payments to be made or received under the qualifying debt instrument (or amounts determined by reference to a nonfunctional currency) are fully hedged on the date the taxpayer identifies the transaction under paragraph (a) of this section as a qualified hedging transaction such that a yield to maturity (under principles of section 1272) in the currency in which the synthetic debt instrument is denominated (as determined under paragraph (a)(9)(ii)(A) of this section) can be calculated. Any contingent payment features of the qualifying debt instrument must be fully offset by the hedge such that the synthetic debt instrument is not classified as a contingent payment debt instrument. See Examples 6 and 7 of paragraph (a)(9)(iv) of this section.

(ii) The hedge is identified in accordance with paragraph (a)(8) of this section on or before the date the acquisition of the financial instrument (or instruments) constituting the hedge is settled or closed.

(iii) None of the parties to the hedge are related. The term "related" means the relationships defined in section 267(b) or section 707(b).

(iv) In the case of a qualified business unit with a residence, as defined in section 988(a)(3)(B), outside of the United States, both the qualifying debt instrument and the hedge are properly reflected on the books of such qualified business unit throughout the term of the qualified hedging transaction.

(v) Subject to the limitations of paragraph (a)(5) of this section, both the qualifying debt instrument and the hedge are entered into by the same individual, partnership, trust, estate, or corporation. With respect to a corporation, the same corporation must enter into both the qualifying debt instrument and the hedge whether or not such corporation is a member of an affiliated group of corporations that files a consolidated return.

(vi) With respect to a foreign person engaged in a U.S. trade or business that enters into a qualifying debt instrument or hedge through such trade or business, all items of income and expense associated with the qualifying debt instrument and the hedge (other than interest expense that is subject to § 1.882-5), would have been effectively connected with such U.S. trade or business throughout the term of the qualified hedging transaction had this paragraph (a) not applied.

(6) Special rules for legging in and legging out of integrated treatment. (i) Legging in. "Legging in" to integrated treatment under this paragraph (a) means that a hedge is entered into after the date the qualifying debt instrument is entered into or acquired, and the requirements of this paragraph (a) are satisfied on the date the hedge is entered into ("leg in date"). If a taxpayer legs into integrated treatment, the following rules shall apply—

(A) Exchange gain or loss shall be realized with respect to the qualifying debt instrument determined solely by reference to changes in exchange rates between—

(1) The date the instrument was acquired by the holder, or the date the obligor assumed the obligation to make payments under the instrument; and

(2) The leg in date.

(B) The recognition of such gain or loss will be deferred until the date the qualifying debt instrument matures or is otherwise disposed of.

(C) The source and character of such gain or loss shall be determined on the leg in date as if the qualifying debt instrument was actually sold or otherwise terminated by the taxpayer.

(ii) Legging out. With respect to a qualifying debt instrument and hedge that are properly identified as a qualified hedging transaction, "legging out" of integrated treatment under this paragraph (a) means that the taxpayer disposes of or otherwise terminates all or a part of the qualifying debt instrument or hedge prior to maturity of the qualified hedging transaction, or the taxpayer changes a material term of the qualifying debt instrument (e.g., exercises an option to change the interest rate or index, or the maturity date) or hedge (e.g., changes the interest or exchange rates underlying the hedge, or the expiration date) prior to maturity of the qualified hedging transaction. A taxpayer that disposes of or terminates a qualified hedging transaction (i.e., disposes of or terminates both the qualifying transaction and the hedge on the same day) shall be considered to have disposed of or otherwise terminated the synthetic debt instrument rather than as legging out. If a taxpayer legs out of integrated treatment, the following rules shall apply—

(A) The transaction will be treated as a qualified hedging transaction during the time the requirements of this paragraph (a) were satisfied.

(B) If the hedge is disposed of or otherwise terminated, the qualifying debt instrument shall be treated as sold for its fair market value on the date the hedge is disposed of or otherwise terminated (the "leg-out date"). and any gain or loss (including gain or loss resulting from factors other than movements in exchange rates) from the identification date to the leg-out date is realized and recognized on the leg-out date. The spot rate on the leg-out date shall be used to determine exchange gain or loss on the debt instrument for the period beginning on the leg-out date and ending on the date such instrument matures or is disposed of or otherwise terminated. Proper adjustment to the principal amount of the debt instrument must be made to reflect any gain or loss taken into account. The netting rule of § 1.988-2(b)(8) shall apply.

(C) If the qualifying debt instrument is disposed of or otherwise terminated the hedge shall be treated as sold for its fair market value on the date the qualifying debt instrument is disposed of or otherwise terminated (the "leg-out date"). and any gain or loss from the identification date to the leg-out date is realized and recognized on the leg-out date. The spot rate on the leg-out date shall be used to determine exchange gain or loss on the hedge for the period beginning on the leg-out date and ending on the date such hedge is disposed of or otherwise terminated.

(D) Except as provided in paragraph (a)(8)(iii) of this section (regarding identification by the Commissioner), that part of the qualified hedging transaction that has not been terminated (i.e., the remaining debt instrument in its entirety even if partially hedged, or hedge) cannot be part of a qualified hedging transaction for any period subsequent to the leg out date.

(E) If a taxpayer legs out of a qualified hedging transaction and realizes a gain with respect to the terminated instrument, then paragraph (a)(6)(ii)(B) or (C) of this section, as appropriate, shall not apply if during the period beginning days before the leg-out date and ending 30 days after that date the taxpayer enters into another transaction that hedges at least 50% of the remaining currency flow with respect to the qualifying debt instrument which was part of the qualified hedging transaction (or, if appropriate, an equivalent amount under the § 1.958-5 hedge which was part of the qualified hedging transaction).

(7) Transactions part of a straddle. At the discretion of the Commissioner, a transaction shall not satisfy the requirements of paragraph (a)(5) of this section if the debt instrument making up the qualified hedging transaction is part of a straddle as defined in section 1092(c) prior to the time the qualified hedging transaction is identified.

(8) Identification requirements. (i) Identification by the taxpayer. A taxpayer must establish a record and before the close of the date the hedge is entered into, the taxpayer must enter into the record for each qualified hedging transaction the following information—

(A) The date the qualifying debt instrument and hedge were entered into;

(B) The date the qualifying debt instrument and the hedge are identified as constituting a qualified hedging transaction;

(C) The amount that must be deferred, if any, under paragraph (a)(6) of this section and the source and character of such deferred amount;

(D) A description of the qualifying debt instrument and the hedge; and

(E) A summary of the cash flow resulting from treating the qualifying debt instrument and the hedge as a qualified hedging transaction.

(ii) Identification by trustee on behalf of beneficiary. A trustee of a trust that enters into a qualified hedging transaction may satisfy the identification requirements described in paragraph (a)(8)(i) of this section on behalf of a beneficiary of such trust.

(iii) Identification by the Commissioner. If—

(A) A taxpayer enters into a qualifying debt instrument and a hedge but fails to comply with one or more of the requirements of this paragraph (a), and

(B) On the basis of all the facts and circumstances, the Commissioner concludes that the qualifying debt instrument and the hedge are, in substance, a qualified hedging transaction, then the Commissioner may treat the qualifying debt instrument and the hedge as a qualified hedging transaction. The Commissioner may identify a qualifying debt instrument and a hedge as a qualified hedging transaction regardless of whether the qualifying debt instrument and the hedge are held by the same taxpayer.

(9) Taxation of qualified hedging transactions. (i) In general. (A) General rule. If a transaction constitutes a qualified hedging transaction, the qualifying debt instrument and the hedge are integrated and treated as a single transaction with respect to the taxpayer that has entered into the qualified hedging transaction during the period that the transaction qualifies as a qualified hedging transaction. Neither the qualifying debt instrument nor the hedge that makes up the qualified hedging transaction shall be subject to section 263(g), 1092 or 1256 for the period such transactions are integrated. However, the qualified hedging transaction may be subject to section 263(g) or 1092 if such transaction is part of a straddle.

(B) Special rule for income or expense of foreign persons effectively connected with a U.S. trade or business. Interest income of a foreign person resulting from a qualified hedging transaction entered into by such foreign person that satisfies the requirements of paragraph (a)(5)(vii) of this section shall be treated as effectively connected with a U.S. trade or business. Interest expense of a foreign person resulting from a qualified hedging transaction entered into by such foreign person that satisfies the requirements of paragraph (a)(5)(vii) of this section shall be allocated and apportioned under § 1.882-5 of the regulations.

(C) Special rule for foreign persons that enter into qualified hedging transactions giving rise to U.S. source income not effectively connected with a U.S. trade or business. If a foreign person enters into a qualified hedging transaction that gives rise to U.S. source interest income (determined under the source rules for synthetic asset transactions as provided in this section) not effectively connected with a U.S. trade or business of such foreign person, for purposes of sections 871(a), 881, 1441, 1442 and 6049, the provisions of this paragraph (a) shall not apply and such sections of the Internal Revenue Code shall be applied separately to the qualifying debt instrument and the hedge. To the extent relevant to any foreign person, if the requirements of this paragraph (a) are otherwise met, the provisions of this paragraph (a) shall apply for all other purposes of the Internal Revenue Code (e.g., for purposes of calculating the earnings and profits of a controlled foreign corporation that enters into a qualified hedging transaction through a qualified business unit resident outside the United States, income or expense with respect to such qualified hedging transaction shall be calculated under the provisions of this paragraph (a)).

(ii) Income tax effects of integration. The effect of integrating and treating a transaction as a single transaction is to create a synthetic debt instrument for income tax purposes, which is subject to the original issue discount provisions of sections 1272 through 1288 and 163(e), the terms of which are determined as follows:

(A) Denomination of synthetic debt instrument. In the case where the qualifying debt instrument is a borrowing, the denomination of the synthetic debt instrument is the same as the currency paid under the terms of the hedge to acquire the currency used to make payments under the qualifying debt instrument. In the case where the qualifying debt instrument is a lending, the denomination of the synthetic debt instrument is the same as the currency received under the terms of the hedge in exchange for amounts received under the qualifying debt instrument. For example, if the hedge is a forward contract to acquire British pounds for dollars, and the qualifying debt instrument is a borrowing denominated in British pounds, the synthetic debt instrument is considered a borrowing in dollars.

(B) Term and accrual periods. The term of the synthetic debt instrument shall be the period beginning on the identification date and ending on the date the qualifying debt instrument matures or such earlier date that the qualifying debt instrument or hedge is disposed of or otherwise terminated. Unless otherwise clearly indicated by the payment interval under the hedge, the accrual period shall be a six month period which ends on the dates determined under section 1272(a)(5).

(C) Issue price. The issue price of the synthetic debt instrument is the adjusted issue price of the qualifying debt instrument translated into the currency in which the synthetic debt instrument is denominated at the spot rate on the identification date,

(D) Stated redemption price at maturity. In the case where the qualifying debt instrument is a borrowing, the stated redemption price at maturity shall be determined under section 1273(a)(2) on the identification date by reference to the amounts to be paid under the hedge to acquire the currency necessary to make interest and principal payments on the qualifying debt instrument, In the case where the qualifying debt instrument is a lending, the stated redemption price at maturity shall be determined under section 1273(a)(2) on the identification date by reference to the amounts to be received under the hedge in exchange for the interest and principal payments received pursuant to the terms of the qualifying debt instrument.

(iii) Source of interest income and allocation of expense. Interest income from a synthetic debt instrument described in paragraph (a)(9)(ii) of this section shall be sourced by reference to the source of income under sections 861(a)(1) and 862(a)(1) of the qualifying debt instrument. The character for purposes of section 904 of interest income from a synthetic debt instrument shall be determined by reference to the character of the interest income from qualifying debt instrument. Interest expense from a synthetic debt instrument described in paragraph (a)(9)(ii) of this section shall be allocated and apportioned under §§ 1.861-8T through 1.861-12T or the successor sections thereof or under § 1.882-5.

(iv) Examples. The following examples illustrate the application of this paragraph (a)(9).

Example (1). (i) K is a U.S. corporation with the U.S. dollar as its functional currency. On December 24, 1989, K agrees to close the following transaction on December 31, 1989. K will borrow from an unrelated party on December 31, 1989, 100 British pounds (£) for 3 years at a 10 percent rate of interest payable annually, with no principal payment due until the final installment. K will also enter into a currency swap contract with an unrelated counterparty under the terms of which—

(a) K will swap, on December 31, 1989, the £100 obtained from the borrowing for $100; and

(b) K will exchange dollars for pounds pursuant to the following table in order to obtain the pounds necessary to make payments on the pound borrowing:

Date	U.S. dollars	Pounds
December 31, 1990	8	10
December 31, 1991	8	10
December 31, 1992	108	110

(ii) The interest rate on the borrowing is set and the exchange rates on the swap are fixed on December 24, 1989. On December 31, 1989, K borrows the £100 and swaps such pounds for $100. Assume x has satisfied the identification requirements of paragraph (a)(8) of this section.

(iii) The pound borrowing (which constitutes a qualifying debt instrument under paragraph (a)(3) of this section) and the currency swap contract (which constitutes a hedge under paragraph (a)(4) of this section) are a qualified hedging transaction as defined in paragraph (a)(1) of this section. Accordingly, the pound borrowing and the swap are integrated and treated as one transaction with the following consequences:

(A) The integration of the pound borrowing and the swap results in a synthetic dollar borrowing with an issue price of $100 under section 1273(b)(2).

(B) The total amount of interest and principal of the synthetic dollar borrowing is equal to the dollar payments made by K under the currency swap contract (i.e., $8 in 1990, $8 in 1991, and $108 in 1992).

(C) The stated redemption price at maturity (defined in section 1273(a)(2)) is $100. Because the stated redemption price equals the issue price, there is no OID on the synthetic dollar borrowing.

(D) K may deduct the annual interest payments of $8 under section 163(a) (subject to any limitations on deductibility imposed by other provisions of the Code) according to its regular method of accounting. K has also paid $100 as a return of principal in 1992.

(E) K must allocate and apportion its interest expense with respect to the synthetic dollar borrowing under the rules of §§ 1.861-8T through 1.861-12T.

Example (2). (i) K, a U.S. corporation, has the U.S. dollar as its functional currency. On December 24, 1989, when the spot rate for Swiss francs (Sf) is Sf1 = $1, K enters into a forward contract to purchase Sf100 in exchange for $100.04 for delivery on December 31, 1989. The Sf100 are to be used for the purchase of a franc denominated debt instrument on December 31, 1989. The instrument will have a term of 3 years, an issue price of Sf100, and will bear interest at 6 percent, payable annually, with no repayment of principal until the final installment. On December 24, 1989, K also enters into a series of forward contracts to sell the franc interest and principal payments that will be received under the terms of the franc denominated debt instrument for dollars according to the following schedule:

Date	U.S. dollars	Francs
December 31, 1990	6.12	6
December 31, 1991	6.23	6
December 31, 1992	112.16	106

(ii) On December 31, 1989, K takes delivery of the Sf100 and purchases the franc denominated debt instrument. Assume K satisfies the identification requirements of paragraph (a)(8) of this section. The purchase of the franc debt instrument (which constitutes a qualifying debt instrument under paragraph (a)(3) of this section) and the series of forward contracts (which constitute a hedge under paragraph (a)(4) of this section) are a qualified hedging transaction under paragraph (a)(1) of this section. Accordingly, the franc debt instrument and all the forward contracts are integrated and treated as one transaction with the following consequences:

(A) The integration of the franc debt instrument and the forward contracts results in a synthetic dollar debt instrument in an amount equal to the dollars exchanged under the forward contract to purchase the francs necessary to acquire the franc debt instrument. Accordingly, the issue price is $100.04 (section 1273(b)(2) of the Code).

(B) The total amount of interest and principal received by K with respect to the synthetic dollar debt instrument is equal to the dollars received under the forward sales contracts (i.e., $6.12 in 1990, $6.23 in 1991, and $112.16 in 1992).

(C) The synthetic dollar debt instrument is an installment obligation and its stated redemption price at maturity is $106.15 (i.e., $6.12 of the payments in 1990, 1991, and 1992 are treated as periodic interest payments under the principles of section 1273). Because the stated redemption price at maturity exceeds the issue price, under section 1273(a)(1) the synthetic dollar debt instrument has OID of $6.11.

(D) The yield to maturity of the synthetic dollar debt instrument is 8.00 percent, compounded annually. Assuming K is a calendar year taxpayer, it must include interest income of $8.00 in 1990 (of which $1.88 constitutes OID), $8.15 in 1991 (of which $2.03 constitutes OID), and $8.32 in 1992 (of which $2.20 constitutes OID). The amount of the final payment received by K in excess of the interest income includible is a return of principal and a payment of previously accrued OID.

(E) The source of the interest income shall be determined by applying sections 861(a)(1) and 862(a)(1) with reference to the franc interest income that would have been received had the transaction not been integrated.

Example (3). (i) K is an accrual method U.S. corporation with the U.S. dollar as its functional currency. On January 1, 1992, K borrows 100 British pounds (£) for 3 years at a 10% rate of interest payable on December 31 of each year with no principal payment due until the final installment. The spot rate on January 1, 1992, is £1 = $1.50. On January 1, 1993, when the spot rate is £1 = $1.60, K enters into a currency swap contract with an unrelated counterparty under the terms of which K will exchange dollars for pounds pursuant to the following table in order to obtain the pounds necessary to make the remaining payments on the pound borrowing:

Date	U.S. dollars	Pounds
December 31, 1993	12.80	10
December 31, 1994	12.80	10
December 31, 1994	160.00	100

(ii) Assume that British pound interest rates are still 10% and that K properly identifies the pound borrowing and the currency swap contract as a qualified hedging transaction as provided in paragraph (a)(8) of this section. Under paragraph (a)(6)(i) of this section, K must realize exchange gain or loss with respect to the pound borrowing determined solely by reference to changes in exchange rates between January 1, 1992 and January 1, 1993. (Thus, gain or loss from other factors such as movements in interest rates or changes in credit quality of K are not taken into account). Recognition of such gain or loss is deferred until K terminates its pound borrowing. Accordingly, K must defer exchange loss in the amount of $10 [(£100 × 1.50) (£ 100 × 1.60)].

(iii) Additionally, the qualified hedging transaction is treated as a synthetic U.S. dollar debt instrument with an issue date of January 1, 1993, and a maturity date of December 31, 1994. The issue price of the synthetic debt instrument is $160 (£100 × 1.60, the spot rate on January 1, 1993) and the total amount of interest and principal is $185.60. The accrual period is the one year period beginning on January 1 and ending December 31 of each year. The stated redemption price at maturity is $160. Thus, K is treated as paying $12.80 of interest in 1993, $12.80 of interest in 1994, and $160 of principal in 1994. The interest expense from the synthetic instrument is allocated and apportioned in accordance with the rules of §§ 1.861-8T through 1.861- 12T. Sections 263(g). 1092, and 1256 do not apply to the positions comprising the synthetic dollar borrowing.

Example (4). (i) K is an accrual method U.S. corporation with the U.S. dollar as its functional currency. On January 1, 1990, K borrows 100 British pounds (£) for 3 years at a 10% rate of interest payable on December 31 of each year with no principal payment due until the final installment. The spot rate on January 1, 1990, is £1 = $1.50. Also on January 1, 1990, K enters into a currency swap contract with an unrelated counterparty under the terms of which K will exchange dollars for pounds pursuant to the following table in order to obtain the pounds necessary to make the remaining payments on the pound borrowing:

Date	U.S. dollars	Pounds
December 31, 1990	12.00	10
December 31, 1991	12.00	10
December 31, 1992	162.00	110

(ii) Assume that K properly identifies the pound borrowing and the currency swap contract as a qualified hedging transaction as provided in paragraph (a)(1) of this section.

(iii) The pound borrowing (which constitutes a qualifying debt instrument under paragraph (a)(3) of this section) and the currency swap contract (which constitutes a hedge under paragraph (a)(4) of this section) are a qualified hedging transaction as defined in paragraph (a)(1) of this section. Accordingly, the pound borrowing and the swap are integrated and treated as one transaction with the following consequences:

(A) The integration of the pound borrowing and the swap results in a synthetic dollar borrowing with an issue price of $150 under section 1273(b)(2).

(B) The total amount of interest and principal of the synthetic dollar borrowing is equal to the dollar payments made by K under the currency swap contract (i.e., $12 in 1990, $12 in 1991, and $162 in 1992).

(C) The stated redemption price at maturity (defined in section 1273(a)(2)) is $150. Because the stated redemption price equals the issue price, there is no OID on the synthetic dollar borrowing.

(D) K may deduct the annual interest payments of $12 under section 163(a) (subject to any limitations on deductibility imposed by other provisions of the Code) according to its regular method of accounting. K has also paid $150 as a return of principal in 1992.

(E) K must allocate and apportion its interest expense from the synthetic instrument under the rules of §§ 1.861-8T through 1.861-12T.

(iv) Assume that on January 1, 1991, the spot exchange rate is £1 = $1.60, interest rates have not changed since January 1, 1990, (accordingly, assume that the market value of

K's bond in pounds has not changed) and that K transfers its rights and obligations under the currency swap contract in exchange for $10. Under § 1.983-2(e)(3)(iii). K will include in income as exchange gain $10 on January 1, 1991. Pursuant to paragraph (a)(6)(ii) of this section, the pound borrowing and the currency swap contract are treated as a qualified hedging transaction for 1990. The loss inherent in the pound borrowing from January 1, 1990, to January 1, 1991, is realized and recognized on January 1, 1991. Such loss is exchange loss in the amount of $10.00 [(£ 100 × $1.50, the spot rate on January 1, 1990)— (£100 × $1.60, the spot rate on January 1, 1991)]. For purposes of determining exchange gain or loss on the £100 principal amount of the debt instrument for the period January 1, 1991, to December 31, 1992, the spot rate on January 1, 1991 is used rather than the spot rate on the issue date. Thus, assuming that the spot rate on December 31, 1992, the maturity date, is £ 1 = $1.80. K realizes exchange loss in the amount of $20 [(£100 × $1.60) − (£100 × $1.80)]. Except as provided in paragraph (a)(8)(iii) (regarding identification by the Commissioner), the pound borrowing cannot be part of a qualified hedging transaction for any period subsequent to the leg out date.

Example (5). (i) K, a U.S. corporation, has the U.S. dollar as its functional currency. On January 1, 1990, when the spot rate for Swiss francs (Sf) is Sf1 = $.50, K converts $100 to Sf200 and purchases a franc denominated debt instrument. The instrument has a term of 3 years, an adjusted issue price of Sf200, and will bear interest at 5 percent, payable annually, with no repayment of principal until the final installment. The U.S. dollar interest rate on an equivalent instrument is 8% on January 1, 1990, compounded annually. On January 1, 1990, K also enters into a series of forward contracts to sell the franc interest and principal payments that will be received under the terms of the franc denominated debt instrument for dollars according to the following schedule:

Date	U.S. dollars	Francs
December 31, 1990	5.14	10
December 31, 1991	5.29	10
December 31, 1992	114.26	210

(ii) Assume K satisfies the identification requirements of paragraph (a)(8) of this section. Assume further that on January 1, 1991, the spot exchange rate is Sf1 = U.S.$.5143, the U.S. dollar interest rate is 10%, compounded annually, and the Swiss franc interest rate is the same as on January 1, 1990 (5%, compounded annually). On January 1, 1991, K disposes of the forward contracts that were to mature on December 31, 1991, and December 31, 1992 and incurs a loss of $3.62 (the present value of $.10 with respect to the 1991 contract and $4.27 with respect to the 1992 contract).

(iii) The purchase of the franc debt instrument (which constitutes a qualifying debt instrument under paragraph (a)(3) of this section) and the series of forward contracts (which constitute a hedge under paragraph (a)(4) of this section) are a qualified hedging transaction under paragraph (a)(1) of this section. Accordingly, the franc debt instrument and all the forward contracts are integrated for the period beginning January 1, 1990, and ending January 1, 1991.

(A) The integration of the franc debt instrument and the forward contracts results in a synthetic dollar debt instrument with an issue price of $100.

(B) The total amount of interest and principal to be received by K with respect to the synthetic dollar debt instrument is equal to the dollars to be received under the forward sales contracts (i.e., $5.14 in 1990, $5.29 in 1991, and $114.26 in 1992).

(C) The synthetic dollar debt instrument is an installment obligation and its stated redemption price at maturity is $109.27 (i.e., $5.14 of the payments in 1990, 1991, and 1992 is treated as periodic interest payments under the principles of section 1273). Because the stated redemption price at maturity exceeds the issue price, under section 1273(a)(1) the synthetic dollar debt instrument has OID of $9.27.

(D) The yield to maturity of the synthetic dollar debt instrument is 8.00 percent, compounded annually. Assuming K is a calendar year taxpayer, it must include interest income of $8.00 in 1990 (of which $2.86 constitutes OID).

(E) The source of the interest income is determined by applying sections 861(a)(1) and 862(a)(1) with reference to the franc interest income that would have been received had the transaction not been integrated

(iv) Because K disposed of the forward contracts on January 1, 1991, the rules of paragraph (a)(6)(ii) of this section shall apply. Accordingly, the $3.62 loss from the disposition of the forward contracts is realized and recognized on January 1, 1991. Additionally, K is deemed to have sold the franc debt instrument for $102.86, its fair market value in dollars on January 1, 1991. K will compute gain or loss with respect to the deemed sale of the franc debt instrument by subtracting its adjusted basis in the instrument ($102.86— the value of the Sf200 issue price at the spot rate on the identification date plus $2.86 of original issue discount accrued on the synthetic dollar debt instrument for 1990) from the amount realized on the deemed sale of $102.86. Thus K realizes and recognizes no gain or loss from the deemed sale of the debt instrument. The dollar amount used to determine exchange gain or loss with respect to the franc debt instrument is the Sf200 issue price on January 1, 1991, translated into dollars at the spot rate on January 1, 1991, of Sf1 = U.S.$.5143. Except as provided in paragraph (a)(8)(iii) of this section (regarding identification by the Commissioner), the franc borrowing cannot be part of a qualified hedging transaction for any period subsequent to the leg out date.

Example (6). (i) K is a U.S. corporation with the dollar as its functional currency. On January 1, 1992, K issues a debt instrument with the following terms: the issue price is $1,000, the instrument pays interest annually at a rate of 8% on the $1,000 principal amount, the instrument matures on December 31, 1996, and the amount paid at maturity is the greater of zero or $2,000 less the U.S. dollar value (determined on December 31, 1996) of 150,000 Japanese yen.

(ii) Also on January 1, 1992, K enters into the following hedges with respect to the instrument described in the preceding paragraph: a forward contract under which K will sell 150,000 yen for $1,000 on December 31, 1996 (note that this forward rate assumes that interest rates in yen and dollars are equal); and an option contract that expires on December 31, 1996, under which K has the right (but not the obligation) to acquire 150,000 yen for $2,000. K will pay for the option by making payments to the writer of the option equal to $5 each December 31 from 1992 through 1996.

(iii) The net economic effect of these transactions is that K has created a liability with a principal amount and amount paid at maturity of $1,000, with an interest cost of 8.5% (8% on debt instrument, 0.5% option price) compounded annually. For example, if on December 31, 1996, the spot exchange rate is $1 = 100 yen. K pays $500 on the bond [$2,000 − (150,000 yen/$100)], and $500 in satisfaction of the forward contract [$1.000 − (150,000 yen/$100)]. If instead the spot exchange rate on December 31, 1996 is $1 = 200 yen, K pays $1,250 on the bond [$2,000 – (150.000 yen/$200)] and K receives $250 in satisfaction of the forward contract [$1,000 – (150.000 yen/$200)]. Finally, if the spot exchange rate on December 31, 1996 is $1 = 50 yen. K pays $0 on the bond [$2.000 – (150,000 yen/$50), but the bond holder is not required under the terms of the instrument to pay additional principal]; K exercises the option to buy 150,000 yen for $2.000; and K then delivers the 150,000 yen as required by the forward contract in exchange for $1,000.

(iv) Assume K satisfies the identification requirements of paragraph (a)(8) of this section. The debt instrument described in paragraph (i) of this Example 6 (which constitutes a qualifying debt instrument under paragraph (a)(3) of this section) and the forward contract and option contract described in paragraph (ii) of this example (which constitute a hedge under paragraph (a)(4) of this section and are collectively referred to hereafter as "the contracts") together are a qualified hedging transaction under paragraph (a)(1) of this section. Accordingly, with respect to K, the debt instrument and the contracts are integrated, resulting in a synthetic dollar debt instrument with an issue price of $1000, a stated redemption price at maturity of $1000 and a yield to maturity of 8.5% compounded annually (with no original issue discount). K must allocate and apportion its annual interest expense of $85 under the rules of §§ 1.861-8T through 1.861-12T.

Example (7). (i) R is a U.S. corporation with the dollar as its functional currency. On January 1, 1995, R issues a debt instrument with the following terms: the issue price is 504 British pounds (£), the instrument pays interest at a rate of 3.7% (compounded semiannually) on the £504 principal amount, the instrument matures on December 31, 1999, with a repayment at maturity of the £504 principal plus the proportional gain, if any, in the "Financial Times" 100 Stock Exchange (FTSE) index (determined by the excess of the value of the FTSE index on the maturity date over the value of the FTSE on the issue date, divided by the value of the FTSE index on the issue date. multiplied by the number of FTSE index contracts that could be purchased on the issue date for £504).

(ii) Also on January 1, 1995, R enters into a contract with a bank under which on January 1, 1995, R will swap the £504 for $1,000 (at the current spot rate). R will make U.S. dollar payments to the bank equal to 8.15% on the notional principal amount of $1,000 (compounded semi-annually) for the period beginning January 1, 1995 and ending December 31, 1999. R will receive pound payments from the bank equal to 3.7% on the notional principal amount of £504 (compounded semi-annually) for the period beginning January 1, 1995 and ending December 31, 1990. On December 31, 1999, R will swap with the bank $1,000 for £504 plus the proportional gain, if any, in the FTSE index (computed as provided above).

(iii) Economically, both the indexed debt instrument and the hedging contract are hybrid instruments with the following components. The indexed debt instrument is composed of a par pound debt instrument that is assumed to have a 10.85% coupon (compounded semi-annually) plus an embedded FTSE equity index option for which the investor pays a premium of 7.15% (amortized semi-annually) on the pound principal amount. The combined effect is that the premium paid by the investor partially offsets the coupon payments resulting in a return of 3.7% (10.85% – 7.15%). Similarly, the dollar payments under the hedging contract to be made by R are computed by multiplying the dollar notional principal amount by an 8.00% rate (compounded semi-annually) which the facts assume would be the rate paid on a conventional currency swap plus a premium of 0.15% (amortized semi-annually) on the dollar notional principal amount for an embedded FTSE equity index option.

(iv) Assume R satisfies the identification requirements of paragraph (a)(8) of this section. The indexed debt instrument described in paragraph (i) of this Example 7 constitutes a qualifying debt instrument under paragraph (a)(3) of this section. The hedging contract described in paragraph (ii) of this Example 7 constitutes a hedge under paragraph (a)(4) of this section. Since both the pound exposure of the indexed debt instrument and the exposure to movements of the FTSE embedded in the indexed debt instrument are hedged such that a yield to maturity can be determined in dollars, the transaction satisfies the requirement of paragraph (a)(5)(i) of this section. Assuming the transactions satisfy the other requirements of paragraph (a)(5) of this section, the indexed debt instrument and hedge are a qualified hedging transaction under paragraph (a)(1) of this section. Accordingly, with respect to R, the debt instrument and the contracts are integrated, resulting in a synthetic dollar debt instrument with an issue price of $1000, a stated redemption price at maturity of $1000 and a yield to maturity of 8.15% compounded semi-annually (with no original issue discount). K must allocate and apportion its interest expense from the synthetic instrument under the rules §§ 1.861-8T through 1.861-12T.

Example (8). (i) K is a U.S. corporation with the U.S. dollar as its functional currency. On December 24, 1992, K agrees to close the following transaction on December 31, 1992. K will borrow from an unrelated party on December 31, 1992, 200 British pounds (£) for 3 years at a 10 percent rate of interest, payable annually, with no principal payment due until the final installment. K will also enter into a currency swap contract with an unrelated counterparty under the terms of which—

(A) K will swap, on December 31, 1992, £100 obtained from the borrowing for $100; and

(B) K will exchange dollars for pounds pursuant to the following table:

Date	U.S. dollars	Pounds
December 31, 1993	8	10
December 31, 1994	8	10
December 31, 1995	108	110

(ii) The interest rate on the borrowing is set and the exchange rates on the swap are fixed on December 24, 1992. On December 31, 1992, K borrows the £200 and swaps £100 for $100. Assume K has satisfied the identification requirements of paragraph (a)(8) of this section.

(iii) The £200 debt instrument satisfies the requirements of paragraph (a)(3)(i) of this section. Because all principal and interest payments under the instrument are hedged in the same proportion (50% of all interest and principal payments are hedged), 50% of the payments under the £200 instrument (principal amount of £100 and annual interest of £10) are treated as a qualifying debt instrument for purposes of paragraph (a) of this section. Thus, the distinct £100 borrowing and the currency swap contract (which constitutes a hedge under paragraph (a)(4) of this section) are a qualified hedging transaction as defined in paragraph (a)(1) of this section. Accordingly, £100 of the pound borrowing and the swap are integrated and treated as one synthetic dollar transaction with the following consequences:

(A) The integration of £100 of the pound borrowing and the swap results in a synthetic dollar borrowing with an issue price of $100 under section 1273(b)(2).

(B) The total amount of interest and principal of the synthetic dollar borrowing is equal to the dollar payments made by K under the currency swap contract (i.e., $8 in 1993, $8 in 1994, and $108 in 1995).

(C) The stated redemption price at maturity (defined in section 1273(a)(2)) is $100. Because the stated redemption price equals the issue price, there is no OID on the synthetic dollar borrowing.

(D) K may deduct the annual interest payments of $8 under section 163(a) (subject to any limitations on deductibility imposed by other provisions of the Code) according to its regular method of accounting. K has also paid $100 as a return of principal in 1995.

(E) K must allocate and apportion its interest expense from the synthetic instrument under the rules of §§ 1.861-8T through 1.861-12T.

That portion of the £200 pound debt instrument that is not hedged (i.e., £100) is treated as a separate debt instrument subject to the rules of § 1.988-2(b) and §§ 1.861-8T through 1.861-12T.

Example (9). (i) K is an accrual method U.S. corporation with the U.S. dollar as its functional currency. On January 1, 1992, K borrows 100 British pounds (£) for 3 years at a 10% rate of interest payable on December 31 of each year with no principal payment due until the final installment. On the same day, K enters into a currency swap agreement with an unrelated bank under which K agrees to the following:

(A) On January 1, 1992, K will exchange the £100 borrowed for $150.

(B) For the period beginning January 1, 1992 and ending December 31, 1994, K will pay at the end of each month an amount determined by multiplying $150 by one month LIBOR less 65 basis points and receive from the bank on December 31st of 1992, 1993, and 1994, £10.

(C) On December 31, 1994, K will exchange $150 for £100.

Assume K satisfies the identification requirements of paragraph (a)(8) of this section.

(ii) The pound borrowing (which constitutes a qualifying debt instrument under paragraph (a)(3) of this section) and the currency swap contract (which constitutes a hedge under paragraph (a)(4) of this section) are a qualified hedging transaction as defined in paragraph (a)(1) of this section. Accordingly, the pound borrowing and the swap are integrated and treated as one transaction with the following consequences:

(A) The integration of the pound borrowing and the swap results in a synthetic dollar borrowing with an issue price of $150 under section 1273(b)(2).

(B) The total amount of interest and principal of the synthetic dollar borrowing is equal to the dollar payments made by K under the currency swap contract.

(C) The stated redemption price at maturity (defined in section 1273(a)(2)) is $150. Because the stated redemption price equals the issue price, there is no OID on the synthetic dollar borrowing.

(D) K may deduct the monthly variable interest payments under section 163(a) (subject to any limitations on deductibility imposed by other provisions of the Code) according to its regular method of accounting. K has also paid $150 as a return of principal in 1994.

(E) K must allocate and apportion its interest expense from the synthetic instrument under the rules of §§ 1.861-8T through 1.861-12T.

Example (10). (i) K is an accrual method U.S. corporation with the U.S. dollar as its functional currency. On January 1, 1992, K loans 100 British pounds (£) for 3 years at a 10% rate of interest payable on December 31 of each year with no principal payment due until the final installment. The spot rate on January 1, 1992, is £1 = $1.50. Also on January 1, 1992, K enters into a currency swap contract with an unrelated counterparty under the terms of which K will exchange pounds for dollars pursuant to the following table:

Date	Pounds	Dollars
December 31, 1992	10	12
December 31, 1993	10	12
December 31, 1994	110	162

(ii) Assume that K properly identifies the pound borrowing and the currency swap contract as a qualified hedging transaction as provided in paragraph (a)(1) of this section.

(iii) The pound loan (which constitutes a qualifying debt instrument under paragraph (a)(3) of this section) and the currency swap contract (which constitutes a hedge under paragraph (a)(4) of this section) are a qualified hedging transaction as defined in paragraph (a)(1) of this section. Accordingly, the pound loan and the swap are integrated and treated as one transaction with the following consequences:

(A) The integration of the pound loan and the swap results in a synthetic dollar loan with an issue price of $150 under section 1273(b)(2).

(B) The total amount of interest and principal of the synthetic dollar loan is equal to the dollar payments received by K under the currency swap contract (i.e., $12 in 1992, $12 in 1993, and $162 in 1994).

(C) The stated redemption price at maturity (defined in section 1273(a)(2)) is $150. Because the stated redemption price equals the issue price, there is no OID on the synthetic dollar loan.

(D) K must include in income as interest $12 in 1992, 1993, and 1994.

(E) The source of the interest income shall be determined by applying sections 861(a)(1) and 862(a)(1) with reference to the pound interest income that would have been received had the transaction not been integrated.

(iv) On January 1, 1993, K transfers both the pound loan and the currency swap to B, its wholly owned U.S. subsidiary, in exchange for B stock in a transfer that satisfies the requirements of section 351. Under paragraph (a)(6) of this section, the transfer of both instruments is not "legging out." Rather, K is considered to have transferred the synthetic dollar loan to B in a transaction in which gain or loss is not recognized. B's basis in the loan under section 362 is $100.

(10) Transition rules and effective dates for certain provisions. (i) Coordination with Notice 87-11. Any transaction entered into prior to September 21, 1989 which satisfied the requirements of Notice 87-11, 1987-1 C.B. 423, shall be deemed to satisfy the requirements of paragraph (a) of this section.

(ii) Prospective application to contingent payment debt instruments. In the case of a contingent payment debt instrument, the definition of qualifying debt instrument set forth in paragraph (a)(3)(i) of this section applies to transactions entered into after March 17, 1992.

(iii) Prospective application of partial hedging rule. Paragraph (a)(3)(ii) of this section is effective for transactions entered into after March 17, 1992.

(iv) Effective date for paragraph (a)(6)(i) of this section. The rules of paragraph (a)(6)(i) of this section are effective for qualified hedging transactions that are legged into after March 17, 1992.

(b) Hedged executory contracts. *(1) In general.* If the taxpayer enters into a hedged executory contract as defined in paragraph (b)(2) of this section, the executory contract and the hedge shall be integrated as provided in paragraph (b)(4) of this section.

(2) Definitions. (i) Hedged executory contract. A hedged executory contract is an executory contract as defined in paragraph (b)(2)(i) of this section that is the subject of a hedge as defined in paragraph (b)(2)(iii) of this section, provided that the following requirements are satisfied—

(A) The executory contract and the hedge are identified as a hedged executory contract as provided in paragraph (b)(3) of this section.

(B) The hedge is entered into (i.e., settled or closed, or in the case of nonfunctional currency deposited in an account with a bank or other financial institution, such currency is acquired and deposited) on or after the date the executory contract is entered into and before the accrual date as defined in paragraph (b)(2)(iv) of this section.

(C) The executory contract is hedged in whole or in part throughout the period beginning with the date the hedge is identified in accordance with paragraph (b)(3) of this section and ending on or after the accrual date.

(D) None of the parties to the hedge are related. The term related means the relationships defined in section 267(b) and section 707(c)(1).

(E) In the case of a qualified business unit with a residence, as defined in section 988(a)(3)(B), outside of the United States, both the executory contract and the hedge are properly reflected on the books of the same qualified business unit.

(F) Subject to the limitations of paragraph (b)(2)(i)(E) of this section, both the executory contract and sale hedge are entered into by the same individual, partnership, trust, estate, or corporation. With respect to a corporation, the same corporation must enter into both the executory contract and the hedge whether or not such corporation is a member of an affiliated group of corporations that files a consolidated return.

(G) With respect to a foreign person engaged in a U.S. trade or business that enters into an executory contract or hedge through such trade or business, all items of income and expense associated with the executory contract and the hedge would have been effectively connected with such U.S. trade or business throughout the term of the hedged executory contract had this paragraph (b) not applied.

(ii) Executory contract. (A) In general. Except as provided in paragraph (b)(2)(ii)(B) of this section, an executory contract is an agreement entered into before the accrual date to pay nonfunctional currency (or an amount determined with reference thereto) in the future with respect to the purchase of property used in the ordinary course of the taxpayer's business, or the acquisition of a service (or services), in the future, or to receive nonfunctional currency (or an amount determined with reference thereto) in the future with respect to the sale of property used or held for sale in the ordinary course of the taxpayer's business, or the performance of a service (or services), in the future. Notwithstanding the preceding sentence, a contract to buy or sell stock shall be considered an executory contract. (Thus, for example, a contract to sell stock of an affiliate is an executory contract for this purpose.) On the accrual date, such agreement ceases to be considered an executory contract and is treated as an account payable or receivable.

(B) Exceptions. An executory contract does not include a section 988 transaction. For example, a forward contract to purchase nonfunctional currency is not an executory contract. An executory contract also does not include a transaction described in paragraph (c) of this section.

(C) Effective date for contracts to buy or sell stock. That part of paragraph (b)(2)(ii)(A) of this section which provides that a contract to buy or sell stock shall be considered an executory contract applies to contracts to buy or sell stock entered into on or after March 17, 1992.

(iii) Hedge. (A) In general. For purposes of this paragraph (b), the term hedge means a deposit of nonfunctional currency in a hedging account (as defined paragraph (b)(3)(iii)(D) of this section), a forward or futures contract described in § 1.988-1(a)(1)(ii) and (2)(iii), or combination thereof, which reduces the risk of exchange rate fluctuations by reference to the taxpayer's functional currency with respect to nonfunctional currency payments made or received under an executory contract. The term hedge also includes an option contract described in § 1.988-1(a)(1)(ii) and (2)(iii), but only if the option's expiration date is on or before the accrual date. The premium paid for an option that lapses shall be integrated with the executory contract.

(B) Special rule for series of hedges. A series of hedges as defined in paragraph (b)(3)(iii)(A) of this section shall be considered a hedge if the executory contract is hedged in whole or in part throughout the period beginning with the date the hedge is identified in accordance with paragraph (b)(3)(i) of this section and ending on or after the accrual date. A taxpayer that enters into a series of hedges will be deemed to have satisfied the preceding sentence if the hedge that succeeds a hedge that has been terminated is entered into no later than the business day following such termination.

(C) Special rules for historical rate rollovers. (1) Definition. A historical rate rollover is an extension of the maturity date of a forward contract where the new forward rate is adjusted on the rollover date to reflect the taxpayer's gain or loss on the contract as of the rollover date plus the time value of such gain or loss through the new maturity date.

(2) Certain historical rate rollovers considered a hedge. A historical rate rollover is considered a hedge if the rollover date is before the accrual date.

(3) Treatment of time value component of certain historical rate rollovers that are hedges. Interest income or expense determined under § 1.988-2(d)(2)(v) with respect to a historical rate rollover shall be considered part of a hedge if the period beginning on the first date a hedging contract is rolled over and ending on the date payment is made or received under the executory contract does not exceed 183 days. Such interest income or expense shall not be recognized and shall be an adjustment to the income from, or expense of, the services performed or received under the executory contract, or to the amount realized or basis of the property sold or purchased under the executory contract. For

the treatment of such interest income or expense that is not considered part of a hedge, see § 1.988-2(d)(2)(v).

(D) Special rules regarding deposits of nonfunctional currency in a hedging account. A hedging account is an account with a bank or other financial institution used exclusively for deposits of nonfunctional currency used to hedge executory contracts. For purposes of determining the basis of units in such account that comprise the hedge, only those units in the account as of the accrual date shall be taken into consideration A taxpayer may adopt any reasonable convention (consistently applied to all hedging accounts) to determine which units comprise the hedge as of the accrual date and the basis of the units as of such date.

(E) Interest income on deposit of nonfunctional currency in a hedging account. Interest income on a deposit of nonfunctional currency in a hedging account may be taken into account for purposes of determining the amount of a hedge if such interest is accrued on or before the accrual date. However, such interest income shall be included in income as provided in section 61. For example, if a taxpayer with the dollar as its functional currency enters into an executory contract for the purchase and delivery of a machine in one year for 100 British pounds (£), and on such date deposits £90.91 in a properly identified bank account that bears interest at the rate of 10%, the interest that accrues prior to the accrual date shall be included in income and may be considered a hedge.

(iv) Accrual date. The accrual date is the date when the item of income or expense (including a capital expenditure) that relates to an executory contract is required to be accrued under the taxpayer's method of accounting.

(v) Payment date. The payment date is the date when payment is made or received with respect to an executory contract or the subsequent corresponding account payable or receivable.

(3) Identification rules. (i) Identification by the taxpayer. A taxpayer must establish a record and before the close of the date the hedge is entered into, the taxpayer must enter into the record a clear description of the executory contract and the hedge and indicate that the transaction is being identified in accordance with paragraph (b)(3) of this section.

(ii) Identification by the Commissioner. If a taxpayer enters into an executory contract and a hedge but fails to satisfy one or more of the requirements of paragraph (b) of this section and, based on the facts and circumstances, the Commissioner concludes that the executory contract in substance in hedged, then the Commissioner may apply the provisions of paragraph (b) of this section as if the taxpayer had satisfied all of the requirements therein, and may make appropriate adjustments. The Commissioner may apply the provisions of paragraph (b) of this section regardless of whether the executory contract and the hedge are held by the same taxpayer.

(4) Effect of hedged executory contract. (i) In general. If a taxpayer enters into a hedged executory contract, amounts paid or received under the hedge by the taxpayer are treated as paid or received by the taxpayer under the executory contract, or any subsequent account payable or receivable, or that portion to which the hedge relates. Also, the taxpayer recognizes no exchange gain or loss on the hedge. If an executory contract, on the accrual date, becomes an account payable or receivable, the taxpayer recognizes no exchange gain or loss on such payable or receivable for the period covered by the hedge.

(ii) Partially hedged executory contracts. The effect of integrating an executory contract and a hedge that partially hedges such contract is to treat the amounts paid or received under the hedge as paid or received under the portion of the executory contract being hedged, or any subsequent account payable or receivable. The income or expense of services performed or received under the executory contract, or the amount realized or basis of property sold or purchased under the executory contract, that is attributable to that portion of the executory contract that is not hedged shall be translated into functional currency on the accrual date. Exchange gain or loss shall be realized when payment is made or received with respect to any payable or receivable arising on the accrual date with respect to such unhedged amount.

(iii) Disposition of a hedge or executory contract prior to the accrual date. (A) In general. If a taxpayer identifies an executory contract as part of a hedged executory contract as defined in paragraph (b)(2) of this section, and disposes of (or otherwise terminates) the executory contract prior to the accrual date, the hedge shall be treated as sold for its fair market value on the date the executory contract is disposed of and any gain or loss shall be realized and recognized on such date. Such gain or loss shall be an adjustment to the amount received or expended with respect to the disposition or termination, if any. The spot rate on the date the hedge is treated as sold shall be used to determine subsequent exchange gain or loss on the hedge. If a taxpayer identifies a hedge as part of a hedged executory contract as defined in paragraph (b)(2) of this section, and disposes of the hedge prior to the accrual date, any gain or loss realized on such disposition shall not be recognized and shall be an adjustment to the income from, or expense of, the services performed or received under the executory contract, or to the amount realized or basis of the property sold or purchased under the executory contract.

(B) Certain events in a series of hedges treated as a termination of the hedged executory contract. If the rules of paragraph (b)(2)(iii)(B) of this section are not satisfied, the hedged executory contract shall be terminated and the provisions of paragraph (b)(4)(iii)(A) of this section shall apply to any gain or loss previously realized with respect to such hedge. Any subsequent hedging contracts entered into to reduce the risk of exchange rate movements with respect to such executory contract shall not be considered a hedge as defined in paragraph (b)(2)(iii) of this section.

(C) Executory contracts between related persons. If an executory contract is between related persons as defined in sections 267(b) and 707(b), and the taxpayer disposes of the hedge or terminates the executory contract prior to the accrual date, the Commissioner may redetermine the timing, source, and character of gain or loss from the hedge or the executory contract if he determines that a significant purpose for disposing of the hedge or terminating the executory contract prior to the accrual date was to affect the timing, source, or character of income, gain, expense, or loss for Federal income tax purposes.

(iv) Disposition of a hedge on or after the accrual date. If a taxpayer identifies a hedge as part of a hedged executory contract as defined in paragraph (b)(2) of this section, and disposes of the hedge on or after the accrual date, no gain or loss is recognized on the hedge and the booking date as defined in § 1.988-2(c)(2) of the payable or receivable for purposes of computing exchange gain or loss shall be the date such hedge is disposed of. See Example 3 of paragraph (b)(4)(iv) of this section.

(v) Sections 263(g), 1092, and 1256 do not apply. Sections 263(g), 1092, and 1256 do not apply with respect to an executory contract or hedge which comprise a hedged executory contract as defined in paragraph (b)(2) of this section. However, sections 263(g), 1092 and 1256 may apply to the hedged executory contract if such transaction is part of a straddle.

(vi) Examples. The principles set forth in paragraph (b) of this section are illustrated in the following examples. The examples assume that K is an accrual method, calendar year U.S. corporation with the dollar as its functional currency.

Example (1). (i) On January 1, 1992, K enters into a contract with JPF, a Swiss machine manufacturer, to pay 500,000 Swiss francs for delivery of a machine on June 1, 1993. Also on January 1, 1992, K enters into a foreign currency forward agreement to purchase 500,000 Swiss francs for $250,000 for delivery on June 1, 1993. K properly identifies the executory contract and the hedge in accordance with paragraph (b)(3)(i) of this section. On June 1, 1993, K takes delivery of the 500,000 Swiss francs (in exchange for $250,000) under the forward contract and makes payment of 500,000 Swiss francs to JPF in exchange for the machine. Assume that the accrual date is June 1, 1993.

(ii) Under paragraph (b)(1) of this section, the hedge is integrated with the executory contract. Therefore, K is deemed to have paid $250,000 for the machine and there is no exchange gain or loss on the foreign currency forward contract. K's basis in the machine is $250,000. Section 1256 does not apply to the forward contract.

Example (2). (i) On January 1, 1992, K enters into a contract with S, a Swiss machine manufacturer, to pay 500,000 Swiss francs for delivery of a machine on June 1, 1993. Under the contract, K is not obligated to pay for the machine until September 1, 1993. On February 1, 1992, K enters into a foreign currency forward agreement to purchase 500,000 Swiss francs for $250,000 for delivery on September 1, 1993. K properly identifies the executory contract and the hedge in accordance with paragraph (b)(3) of this section. On June 1, 1993, K takes delivery of machine. Assume that under K's method of accounting the delivery date is the accrual date. On September 1, 1993, K takes delivery of the 500,000 Swiss francs (in exchange for $250,000) under the forward contract and makes payment of 500,000 Swiss francs to S.

(ii) Under paragraph (b)(1) of this section, the hedge is integrated with the executory contract. Therefore K is deemed to have paid $250,000 for the machine and there is no exchange gain or loss on the foreign currency forward contract. Thus K's basis in the machine is $250,000. In addition, no exchange gain or loss is recognized on the payable in existence from June 1, 1993, to September 1, 1993. Section 1256 does not apply to the forward contract.

Example (3). The facts are the same as in Example 2 except that K disposed of the forward contract on August 1, 1993 for $10,000. Pursuant to paragraph (b)(4)(iv) of this section, K does not recognize the $10,000 gain. K's basis in the machine is $250,000 (the amount fixed by the forward contract), regardless of the amount in dollars that K actually pays to acquire the Sf500,000 when K pays for the machine. K has a payable with a hooking date of August 1, 1993, payable on September 1, 1993 for 500,000 Swiss francs. Thus, K will realize exchange gain or loss on the difference between the amount booked on August 1, 1993 and the amount paid on September 1, 1993 under § 1.988-2(c).

Example (4). (i) On January 1, 1992, K enters into a contract with S, a Swiss machine repair firm, to pay 500,000 Swiss francs for repairs to be performed on June 1, 1992. Under the contract, K is not obligated to pay for the repairs until September 1, 1992. On February 1, 1992, K enters into a foreign currency forward agreement to purchase 500,000 Swiss francs for $250,000 for delivery on August 1, 1992. K properly identifies the executory contract and the hedge in accordance with paragraph (b)(3) of this section. On June 1, 1992, S performs the repair services. Assume that under K's method of accounting this date is the accrual date. On August 1, 1992. K takes delivery of the 500,000 Swiss francs (in exchange for $250,000) under the forward contract. On the same day. K deposits the Sf500,000 in a separate account with a bank and properly identifies the transaction as a continuation of the hedged executory contract. On September 1, 1992, K makes payment of the Sf500,000 in the account to S.

(ii) Under paragraph (b)(1) of this section, the hedge is integrated with the executory contract. Therefore K is deemed to have paid $250,000 for the services and there is no exchange gain or loss on the foreign currency forward contract or on the disposition of Sf500,000 in the account. Any interest on the Swiss francs in the account is included in income but is not considered part of the hedge (because the amount paid for the services must be set on or before the accrual date). In addition, no exchange gain or loss is recognized on the payable in existence from June 1, 1992, to September 1, 1992. Section 1256 does not apply to the forward contract.

Example (5). (i) On January 1, 1992, K enters into a contract with S, a Swiss machine manufacturer, to pay 500,000 Swiss francs for delivery of a machine on June 1, 1993. Under the contract, K is not obligated to pay for the machine until September 1, 1993. On February 1, 1992, K enters into a foreign currency forward agreement to purchase 250,000 Swiss francs for $125,000 for delivery on September 1, 1993. K properly identifies the executory contract and the hedge in accordance with paragraph (b)(3) of this section. On June 1, 1993, K takes delivery of the machine. Assume that under K's method of accounting the delivery date is the accrual date. Assume further that the exchange rate is Sf1 = $.50 on June 1, 1993. On August 30, 1993, K purchases Sf250,000 for $135,000. On September 1, 1993, K takes delivery of the 250,000 Swiss francs (in exchange for $125,000) under the forward contract and makes payment of 500,000 Swiss francs (the Sf250,000 received under the contract plus the Sf250,000 purchased on August 30, 1993) to S. Assume the spot rate on September 1, 1993, is 1 Sf = $.5420 (Sf250,000 equal $135,500).

(ii) Under paragraph (b)(1) of this section, the partial hedge is integrated with the executory contract. K is deemed to have paid $250,000 for the machine [$125,000 on the hedged portion of the Sf500,000 and $125,000 ($.50, the spot rate on June 1, 1993, times Sf250,000) on the unhedged portion of the Sf500,000]. K's basis in the machine therefore is $250,000. K recognizes no exchange gain or loss on the foreign currency forward contract but K will realize exchange gain of $500 on the disposition of the Sf250,000 purchased on August 30, 1993 under § 1.988-2(a). In addition, exchange loss is realized on the unhedged portion of the payable in existence from June 1, 1993, to September 1, 1993. Thus, K will realize exchange loss of $10,500 ($125,000 booked less $135,500 paid) under § 1.988-2(c) on the payable. Section 1256 does not apply to the forward contract.

Example (6). (i) On January 1, 1990, K enters into a contract with S, a Swiss steel manufacturer, to buy steel for 1,000,000 Swiss francs (Sf) for delivery and payment on December 31, 1990. On January 1, 1990, the spot rate is Sf1 = $.50, the U.S. dollar interest rate is 10% compounded annually, and the Swiss franc rate is 5% compounded annually. Under K's method of accounting, the delivery date is the accrual date.

(ii) Assume that on January 1, 1990, K enters into a foreign currency forward contract to buy Sf1,000,000 for $523,800 for delivery on December 31, 1990. K properly identifies the executory contract and the hedge in accordance with paragraph (b)(3) of this section. Pursuant to paragraph (b)(2)(iii) of this section, the forward contract constitutes a hedge. Assuming that the requirements of paragraph (b)(2)(i) of this section are satisfied, the executory contract to buy steel and the forward contract are integrated under paragraph (b)(1) of this section. Thus, K is deemed to have paid $523,800 for the steel and will have a basis in the steel of $523,800. No gain or loss is realized with respect to the forward contract and section 1256 does not apply to such contract.

(iii) Assume instead that on January 1, 1990, K enters into a foreign currency forward contract to buy Sf1,000,000 for $512,200 for delivery on July 1, 1990. K properly identifies the executory contract and the hedge in accordance with paragraph (b)(3) of this section. On July 1, 1990, when the spot rate is Sf1 = $.53, K cancels the forward contract in exchange for $17,800 ($530,000 – $512,200). On July 1, 1990, K enters into a second forward agreement to buy Sf1,000,000 for $542,900 for delivery on December 31, 1990. K properly identifies the second forward agreement as a hedge in accordance with paragraph (b)(3) of this section. Pursuant to paragraph (b)(2)(iii) of this section, the forward contract entered into on January 1, 1990, and the forward contract entered into on July 1, 1990, constitute a hedge. Assuming that the requirements of paragraph (b)(2)(i) of this section are satisfied, the executory contract to buy steel and the forward agreements are integrated under paragraph (b)(1) of this section. Thus, K is deemed to have paid $525,100 for the steel (the forward price in the second forward agreement of $542,900 less the gain on the first forward agreement of $17,800) and will have a basis in the steel of $525,100. No gain is realized with respect to the forward contracts and section 1256 does not apply to such contracts.

(iv) Assume instead that on January 1, 1990, K enters into a foreign currency forward contract to buy Sf1,000,000 for $512,200 for delivery on July 1, 1990. K properly identifies the executory contract and the hedge in accordance with paragraph (b)(3) of this section. On July 1, 1990, when the spot rate is Sf1 = $.53, K enters into a historical rate rollover of its $17,800 gain ($530,000 – $512,200) on the forward agreement. Thus, K enters into a second foreign currency forward agreement to buy Sf1,000,000 for $524,210 for delivery on December 31, 1990. (The forward price of $524,210 is the market forward price on July 1, 1990 for the purchase of Sf1,000,000 for delivery on December 31, 1990 of $542,900 less the $17,800 gain on January 1, 1990 contract and less the time value of such gain of $890.) K properly identifies the second forward agreement as a hedge in accordance with paragraph (b)(3) of this section. On December 31, 1990, when the spot rate is Sf1 = $.54, K takes delivery of the Sf1,000,000 (in exchange for $524,210) and purchases the steel for Sf1,000,000. Pursuant to paragraph (b)(2)(iii) of this section, the forward contract entered into on January 1, 1990, and the forward contract entered into on July 1, 1990, which incorporates the rollover of K's gain on the January 1, 1990 contract, constitute a hedge. Assuming that the requirements of paragraph (b)(2)(i) of this section are satisfied, the executory contract to buy steel and the forward agreements are integrated under paragraph (b)(1) of this section. Because the period from the rollover date to the date payment is made under the executory contract does not exceed 183 days, the $890 of interest income is considered part of the hedge and is not recognized. Thus, K is deemed to have paid $524,210 for the steel and will have a basis in the steel of $524,210. No gain is realized with respect to the forward contracts and section 1256 does not apply to such contracts.

(v) Assume instead that on January 1, 1990 K purchases Sf952,380,95 (the present value of Sf1,000,000 to be paid on December 31, 1990) for $476,190.48 and on the same day deposits the Swiss francs in a separate bank account that bears interest at a rate of 5%, compounded annually. K properly identifies the transaction as a hedged executory contract. Over the period beginning January 1, 1990, and ending December 31, 1990, K receives Sf47,619.05 in interest on the account that is included in income and that has a basis of $25,714.29. (Assume that under § 1.988-2(b)(1), K uses the spot rate of Sf1 = $.54 to translate the interest income). On December 31, 1990, K makes payment of the Sf1,000,000 principal and accrued interest in the account to S. Pursuant to paragraph (h)(2)(iii) of this section, the principal in the bank account and the interest constitute a hedge. Under paragraph (b)(1) of this section, the hedge is integrated with the executory contract. Therefore K is deemed to have paid $501,904.77 (the basis of the principal deposited plus the basis of the interest) for the steel and there is no exchange gain or loss on the disposition of the Sf1,000,000. K's basis in the steel therefore is $501,904.77.

(5) References to this paragraph (b). If the rules of this paragraph (b) are referred to in another paragraph of this section (e.g., paragraph (c) of this section), then the rules of this paragraph (b) shall be applied for purposes of such other paragraph by substituting terms appropriate for such other paragraph. For example, paragraph (c)(2) of this section refers to the identification rules of paragraph (b)(3) of this section. Accordingly, for purposes of paragraph (c)(2), the rules of paragraph (b)(3) will be applied by substituting the term "stock or security" for "executory contract".

(c) Hedges of period between trade date and settlement date on purchase or sale of publicly traded stock or security. If a taxpayer purchases or sells stocks or securities which are traded on an established securities market and—

(1) Hedges all or part of such purchase or sale for any part of the period beginning on the trade date and ending on the settlement date; and

(2) Identifies the hedge and the underlying stock or securities as an integrated transaction under the rules of paragraph (b)(3) of this section; then any gain or loss on the hedge shall be an adjustment to the amount realized or the adjusted basis of the stock or securities sold or purchased (and shall not be taken into account as exchange gain or loss). The term hedge means a deposit of nonfunctional currency in a hedging account (within the meaning of paragraph (b)(2)(iii)(D) of this section), or a forward or futures contract described in § 1.988-1(a)(1)(ii) and (2)(iii), or combination thereof, which reduces the risk of exchange rate fluctuations for any portion of the period beginning on the trade date and ending on the settlement date. The provisions of paragraphs (b)(2)(i)(D) through (G), and (b)(2)(iii)(D) and (E) of this section shall apply. Sections 263(g), 1092, and 1256 do not

apply with respect to stock or securities and a hedge which are subject to this paragraph (c).

(d) [Reserved]

(e) Advance rulings regarding net hedging and anticipatory hedging systems. In his sole discretion, the Commissioner may issue an advance ruling addressing the income tax consequences of a taxpayer's system of hedging either its net nonfunctional currency exposure or anticipated nonfunctional currency exposure. The ruling may address the character, source, and timing of both the section 988 transaction(s) making up the hedge and the underlying transactions being hedged. The procedures for obtaining a ruling shall be governed by such pertinent revenue procedures and revenue rulings as the Commissioner may provide. The Commissioner will not issue a ruling regarding hedges of a taxpayer's investment in a foreign subsidiary.

(f) [Reserved]

(g) General effective date. Except as otherwise provided in this section, the rules of this section shall apply to qualified hedging transactions, hedged executory contracts and transactions described in paragraph (c) of this section entered into on or after September 21, 1989. This section shall apply even if the transaction being hedged (e.g., the debt instrument) was entered into or acquired prior to such date. The effective date regarding advance rulings for net and anticipatory hedging shall be governed by such revenue procedures that the Commissioner may publish.

T.D. 8400, 3/16/92.

---

§ 1.988-6 Nonfunctional currency contingent payment debt instruments.

(a) In general. *(1) Scope.* This section determines the accrual of interest and the amount, timing, source, and character of any gain or loss on nonfunctional currency contingent payment debt instruments described in this paragraph (a)(1) and to which § 1.1275-4(a) would otherwise apply if the debt instrument were denominated in the taxpayer's functional currency. Except as provided by the rules in this section, the rules in § 1.1275-4 (relating to contingent payment debt instruments) apply to the following instruments—

(i) A debt instrument described in § 1.1275-4(b)(1) for which all payments of principal and interest are denominated in, or determined by reference to, a single nonfunctional currency and which has one or more non-currency related contingencies;

(ii) A debt instrument described in § 1.1275-4(b)(1) for which payments of principal or interest are denominated in, or determined by reference to, more than one currency and which has no non-currency related contingencies;

(iii) A debt instrument described in § 1.1275-4(b)(1) for which payments of principal or interest are denominated in, or determined by reference to, more than one currency and which has one or more non-currency related contingencies; and

(iv) A debt instrument otherwise described in paragraph (a)(1)(i), (ii) or (iii) of this section, except that the debt instrument is described in § 1.1275-4(c)(1) rather than § 1.1275-4(b)(1) (e.g., the instrument is issued for non-publicly traded property).

(2) Exception for hyperinflationary currencies. (i) In general. Except as provided in paragraph (a)(2)(ii) of this section, this section shall not apply to an instrument described in paragraph (a)(1) of this section if any payment made under such instrument is determined by reference to a hyperinflationary currency, as defined in § 1.985-1(b)(2)(ii)(D). In such case, the amount, timing, source and character of interest, principal, foreign currency gain or loss, and gain or loss relating to a non-currency contingency shall be determined under the method that reflects the instrument's economic substance.

(ii) Discretion as to method. If a taxpayer does not account for an instrument described in paragraph (a)(2)(i) of this section in a manner that reflects the instrument's economic substance, the Commissioner may apply the rules of this section to such an instrument or apply the principles of § 1.988-2(b)(15), reasonably taking into account the contingent feature or features of the instrument.

(b) Instruments described in paragraph (a)(1)(i) of this section. *(1) In general.* Paragraph (b)(2) of this section provides rules for applying the noncontingent bond method (as set forth in § 1.1275-4(b)) in the nonfunctional currency in which a debt instrument described in paragraph (a)(1)(i) of this section is denominated, or by reference to which its payments are determined (the denomination currency). Paragraph (b)(3) of this section describes how amounts determined in paragraph (b)(2) of this section shall be translated from the denomination currency of the instrument into the taxpayer's functional currency. Paragraph (b)(4) of this section describes how gain or loss (other than foreign currency gain or loss) shall be determined and characterized with respect to the instrument. Paragraph (b)(5) of this section describes how foreign currency gain or loss shall be determined with respect to accrued interest and principal on the instrument. Paragraph (b)(6) of this section provides rules for determining the source and character of any gain or loss with respect to the instrument. Paragraph (b)(7) of this section provides rules for subsequent holders of an instrument who purchase the instrument for an amount other than the adjusted issue price of the instrument. Paragraph (c) of this section provides examples of the application of paragraph (b) of this section. See paragraph (d) of this section for the determination of the denomination currency of an instrument described in paragraph (a)(1)(ii) or (iii) of this section. See paragraph (e) of this section for the treatment of an instrument described in paragraph (a)(1)(iv) of this section.

(2) Application of noncontingent bond method. (i) Accrued interest. Interest accruals on an instrument described in paragraph (a)(1)(i) of this section are initially determined in the denomination currency of the instrument by applying the noncontingent bond method, set forth in § 1.1275-4(b), to the instrument in its denomination currency. Accordingly, the comparable yield, projected payment schedule, and comparable fixed rate debt instrument, described in § 1.1275-4(b)(4), are determined in the denomination currency. For purposes of applying the noncontingent bond method to instruments described in this paragraph, the applicable Federal rate described in § 1.1275-4(b)(4)(i) shall be the rate described in § 1.1274-4(d) with respect to the denomination currency.

(ii) Net positive and negative adjustments. Positive and negative adjustments, and net positive and net negative adjustments, with respect to an instrument described in paragraph (a)(1)(i) of this section are determined by applying the rules of § 1.1275-4(b)(6) (and § 1.1275-4(b)(9)(i) and (ii), if applicable) in the denomination currency. Accordingly, a net positive adjustment is treated as additional interest (in the denomination currency) on the instrument. A net negative adjustment first reduces interest that otherwise would be accrued by the taxpayer during the current tax year in the denomination currency. If a net negative adjustment exceeds the interest that would otherwise be accrued by the taxpayer during the current tax year in the denomination currency, the excess is treated as ordinary loss (if the taxpayer is a holder of the instrument) or ordinary income (if the taxpayer is the issuer of the instrument). The amount treated as ordinary loss by a holder with respect to a net negative adjustment is limited, however, to the amount by which the holder's total interest inclusions on the debt instrument (determined in the denomination currency) exceed the total amount of the holder's net negative adjustments treated as ordinary loss on the debt instrument in prior taxable years (determined in the denomination currency). Similarly, the amount treated as ordinary income by an issuer with respect to a net negative adjustment is limited to the amount by which the issuer's total interest deductions on the debt instrument (determined in the denomination currency) exceed the total amount of the issuer's net negative adjustments treated as ordinary income on the debt instrument in prior taxable years (determined in the denomination currency). To the extent a net negative adjustment exceeds the current year's interest accrual and the amount treated as ordinary loss to a holder (or ordinary income to the issuer), the excess is treated as a negative adjustment carryforward, within the meaning of § 1.1275-4(b)(6)(iii)(C), in the denomination currency.

(iii) Adjusted issue price. The adjusted issue price of an instrument described in paragraph (a)(1)(i) of this section is determined by applying the rules of § 1.1275-4(b)(7) in the denomination currency. Accordingly, the adjusted issue price is equal to the debt instrument's issue price in the denomination currency, increased by the interest previously accrued on the debt instrument (determined without regard to any net positive or net negative adjustments on the instrument) and decreased by the amount of any noncontingent payment and the projected amount of any contingent payment previously made on the instrument. All adjustments to the adjusted issue price are calculated in the denomination currency.

(iv) Adjusted basis. The adjusted basis of an instrument described in paragraph (a)(1)(i) of this section is determined by applying the rules of § 1.1275-4(b)(7) in the taxpayer's functional currency. In accordance with those rules, a holder's basis in the debt instrument is increased by the interest previously accrued on the debt instrument (translated into functional currency), without regard to any net positive or net negative adjustments on the instrument (except as provided in paragraph (b)(7) or (8) of this section, if applicable), and decreased by the amount of any noncontingent payment and the projected amount of any contingent payment previously made on the instrument to the holder (translated into functional currency). See paragraph (b)(3)(iii) of this section for translation rules.

(v) Amount realized. The amount realized by a holder and the repurchase price paid by the issuer on the scheduled or unscheduled retirement of a debt instrument described in paragraph (a)(1)(i) of this section are determined by applying the rules of § 1.1275-4(b)(7) in the denomination currency. For example, with regard to a scheduled retirement at maturity, the holder is treated as receiving the projected amount of any contingent payment due at maturity, reduced by the amount of any negative adjustment carryforward. For purposes of translating the amount realized by the holder into functional currency, the rules of paragraph (b)(3)(iv) of this section shall apply.

(3) Treatment and translation of amounts determined under noncontingent bond method. (i) Accrued interest. The amount of accrued interest, determined under paragraph (b)(2)(i) of this section, is translated into the taxpayer's functional currency at the average exchange rate, as described in § 1.988-2(b)(2)(iii)(A), or, at the taxpayer's election, at the appropriate spot rate, as described in § 1.988-2(b)(2)(iii)(B).

(ii) Net positive and negative adjustments. (A) Net positive adjustments. A net positive adjustment, as referenced in paragraph (b)(2)(ii) of this section, is translated into the taxpayer's functional currency at the spot rate on the last day of the taxable year in which the adjustment is taken into account under § 1.1275-4(b)(6), or, if earlier, the date the instrument is disposed of or otherwise terminated.

(B) Net negative adjustments. A net negative adjustment is treated and, where necessary, is translated from the denomination currency into the taxpayer's functional currency under the following rules:

(1) The amount of a net negative adjustment determined in the denomination currency that reduces the current year's interest in that currency shall first reduce the current year's accrued but unpaid interest, and then shall reduce the current year's interest which was accrued and paid. No translation is required.

(2) The amount of a net negative adjustment treated as ordinary income or loss under § 1.1275-4(b)(6)(iii)(B) first is attributable to accrued but unpaid interest accrued in prior taxable years. For this purpose, the net negative adjustment shall be treated as attributable to any unpaid interest accrued in the immediately preceding taxable year, and thereafter to unpaid interest accrued in each preceding taxable year. The amount of the net negative adjustment applied to accrued but unpaid interest is translated into functional currency at the same rate used, in each of the respective prior taxable years, to translate the accrued interest.

(3) Any amount of the net negative adjustment remaining after the application of paragraphs (b)(3)(ii)(B)(1) and (2) of this section is attributable to interest accrued and paid in prior taxable years. The amount of the net negative adjustment applied to such amounts is translated into functional currency at the spot rate on the date the debt instrument was issued or, if later, acquired.

(4) Any amount of the net negative adjustment remaining after application of paragraphs (b)(3)(ii)(B)(1), (2) and (3) of this section is a negative adjustment carryforward, within the meaning of § 1.1275-4(b)(6)(iii)(C). A negative adjustment carryforward is carried forward in the denomination currency and is applied to reduce interest accruals in subsequent years. In the year in which the instrument is sold, exchanged or retired, any negative adjustment carryforward not applied to interest reduces the holder's amount realized on the instrument (in the denomination currency). An issuer of a debt instrument described in paragraph (a)(1)(i) of this section who takes into income a negative adjustment carryforward (that is not applied to interest) in the year the instrument is retired, as described in § 1.1275-4(b)(6)(iii)(C), translates such income into functional currency at the spot rate on the date the instrument was issued.

(iii) Adjusted basis. (A) In general. Except as otherwise provided in this paragraph and paragraph (b)(7) or (8) of this section, a holder determines and maintains adjusted basis by translating the denomination currency amounts determined under § 1.1275-4(b)(7)(iii) into functional currency as follows:

(1) The holder's initial basis in the instrument is determined by translating the amount paid by the holder to acquire the instrument (in the denomination currency) into

functional currency at the spot rate on the date the instrument was issued or, if later, acquired.

(2) An increase in basis attributable to interest accrued on the instrument is translated at the rate applicable to such interest under paragraph (b)(3)(i) of this section.

(3) Any noncontingent payment and the projected amount of any contingent payments determined in the denomination currency that decrease the holder's basis in the instrument under § 1.1275-4(b)(7)(iii) are translated as follows:

(i) The payment first is attributable to the most recently accrued interest to which prior amounts have not already been attributed. The payment is translated into functional currency at the rate at which the interest was accrued.

(ii) Any amount remaining after the application of paragraph (b)(3)(iii)(A)(3)(i) of this section is attributable to principal. Such amounts are translated into functional currency at the spot rate on the date the instrument was issued or, if later, acquired.

(B) Exception for interest reduced by a negative adjustment carryforward. Solely for purposes of this § 1.988-6, any amounts of accrued interest income that are reduced as a result of a negative adjustment carryforward shall be treated as principal and translated at the spot rate on the date the instrument was issued or, if later, acquired.

(iv) Amount realized. (A) Instrument held to maturity. (1) In general. With respect to an instrument held to maturity, a holder translates the amount realized by separating such amount in the denomination currency into the component parts of interest and principal that make up adjusted basis prior to translation under paragraph (b)(3)(iii) of this section, and translating each of those component parts of the amount realized at the same rate used to translate the respective component parts of basis under paragraph (b)(3)(iii) of this section. The amount realized first shall be translated by reference to the component parts of basis consisting of accrued interest during the taxpayer's holding period as determined under paragraph (b)(3)(iii) of this section and ordering such amounts on a last in first out basis. Any remaining portion of the amount realized shall be translated by reference to the rate used to translate the component of basis consisting of principal as determined under paragraph (b)(3)(iii) of this section.

(2) Subsequent purchases at discount and fixed but deferred contingent payments. For purposes of this paragraph (b)(3)(iv) of this section, any amount which is required to be added to adjusted basis under paragraph (b)(7) or (8) of this section shall be treated as additional interest which was accrued on the date the amount was added to adjusted basis. To the extent included in amount realized, such amounts shall be translated into functional currency at the same rates at which they were translated for purposes of determining adjusted basis. See paragraphs (b)(7)(iv) and (b)(8) of this section for rules governing the rates at which the amounts are translated for purposes of determining adjusted basis.

(B) Sale, exchange, or unscheduled retirement. (1) Holder. In the case of a sale, exchange, or unscheduled retirement, application of the rule stated in paragraph (b)(3)(iv)(A) of this section shall be as follows. The holder's amount realized first shall be translated by reference to the principal component of basis as determined under paragraph (b)(3)(iii) of this section, and then to the component of basis consisting of accrued interest as determined under paragraph (b)(3)(iii) of this section and ordering such amounts on a first in first out basis. Any gain recognized by the holder (i.e., any excess of the sale price over the holder's basis, both expressed in the denomination currency) is translated into functional currency at the spot rate on the payment date.

(2) Issuer. In the case of an unscheduled retirement of the debt instrument, any excess of the adjusted issue price of the debt instrument over the amount paid by the issuer (expressed in denomination currency) shall first be attributable to accrued unpaid interest, to the extent the accrued unpaid interest had not been previously offset by a negative adjustment, on a last-in-first-out basis, and then to principal. The accrued unpaid interest shall be translated into functional currency at the rate at which the interest was accrued. The principal shall be translated at the spot rate on the date the debt instrument was issued.

(C) Effect of negative adjustment carryforward with respect to the issuer. Any amount of negative adjustment carryforward treated as ordinary income under § 1.1275-4(b)(6)(iii)(C) shall be translated at the exchange rate on the day the debt instrument was issued.

(4) Determination of gain or loss not attributable to foreign currency. A holder of a debt instrument described in paragraph (a)(1)(i) of this section shall recognize gain or loss upon sale, exchange, or retirement of the instrument equal to the difference between the amount realized with respect to the instrument, translated into functional currency as described in paragraph (b)(3)(iv) of this section, and the adjusted basis in the instrument, determined and maintained in functional currency as described in paragraph (b)(3)(iii) of this section. The amount of any gain or loss so determined is characterized as provided in § 1.1275-4(b)(8), and sourced as provided in paragraph (b)(6) of this section.

(5) Determination of foreign currency gain or loss. (i) In general. Other than in a taxable disposition of the debt instrument, foreign currency gain or loss is recognized with respect to a debt instrument described in paragraph (a)(1)(i) of this section only when payments are made or received. No foreign currency gain or loss is recognized with respect to a net positive or negative adjustment, as determined under paragraph (b)(2)(ii) of this section (except with respect to a positive adjustment described in paragraph (b)(8) of this section). As described in this paragraph (b)(5), foreign currency gain or loss is determined in accordance with the rules of § 1.988-2(b).

(ii) Foreign currency gain or loss attributable to accrued interest. The amount of foreign currency gain or loss recognized with respect to payments of interest previously accrued on the instrument is determined by translating the amount of interest paid or received into functional currency at the spot rate on the date of payment and subtracting from such amount the amount determined by translating the interest paid or received into functional currency at the rate at which such interest was accrued under the rules of paragraph (b)(3)(i) of this section. For purposes of this paragraph, the amount of any payment that is treated as accrued interest shall be reduced by the amount of any net negative adjustment treated as ordinary loss (to the holder) or ordinary income (to the issuer), as provided in paragraph (b)(2)(ii) of this section. For purposes of determining whether the payment consists of interest or principal, see the payment ordering rules in paragraph (b)(5)(iv) of this section.

(iii) Principal. The amount of foreign currency gain or loss recognized with respect to payment or receipt of principal is determined by translating the amount paid or received into functional currency at the spot rate on the date of payment or receipt and subtracting from such amount the amount determined by translating the principal into functional currency at the spot rate on the date the instrument was issued or, in case of the holder, if later, acquired. For purposes of determining whether the payment consists of interest or principal, see the payment ordering rules in paragraph (b)(5)(iv) of this section.

(iv) Payment ordering rules. (A) In general. Except as provided in paragraph (b)(5)(iv)(B) of this section, payments with respect to an instrument described in paragraph (a)(1)(i) of this section shall be treated as follows:

(1) A payment shall first be attributable to any net positive adjustment on the instrument that has not previously been taken into account.

(2) Any amount remaining after applying paragraph (b)(5)(iv)(A)(1) of this section shall be attributable to accrued but unpaid interest, remaining after reduction by any net negative adjustment, and shall be attributable to the most recent accrual period to the extent prior amounts have not already been attributed to such period.

(3) Any amount remaining after applying paragraphs (b)(5)(iv)(A)(1) and (2) of this section shall be attributable to principal. Any interest paid in the current year that is reduced by a net negative adjustment shall be considered a payment of principal for purposes of determining foreign currency gain or loss.

(B) Special rule for sale or exchange or unscheduled retirement. Payments made or received upon a sale or exchange or unscheduled retirement shall first be applied against the principal of the debt instrument (or in the case of a subsequent purchaser, the purchase price of the instrument in denomination currency) and then against accrued unpaid interest (in the case of a holder, accrued while the holder held the instrument).

(C) Subsequent purchaser that has a positive adjustment allocated to a daily portion of interest. A positive adjustment that is allocated to a daily portion of interest pursuant to paragraph (b)(7)(iv) of this section shall be treated as interest for purposes of applying the payment ordering rule of this paragraph (b)(5)(iv).

(6) Source of gain or loss. The source of foreign currency gain or loss recognized with respect to an instrument described in paragraph (a)(1)(i) of this section shall be determined pursuant to § 1.988-4. Consistent with the rules of § 1.1275-4(b)(8), all gain (other than foreign currency gain) on an instrument described in paragraph (a)(1)(i) of this section is treated as interest income for all purposes. The source of an ordinary loss (other than foreign currency loss) with respect to an instrument described in paragraph (a)(1)(i) of this section shall be determined pursuant to § 1.1275-4(b)(9)(iv). The source of a capital loss with respect to an instrument described in paragraph (a)(1)(i) of this section shall be determined pursuant to § 1.865-1(b)(2).

(7) Basis different from adjusted issue price. (i) In general. The rules of § 1.1275-4(b)(9)(i), except as set forth in this paragraph (b)(7), shall apply to an instrument described in paragraph (a)(1)(i) of this section purchased by a subsequent holder for more or less than the instrument's adjusted issue price.

(ii) Determination of basis. If an instrument described in paragraph (a)(1)(i) of this section is purchased by a subsequent holder, the subsequent holder's initial basis in the instrument shall equal the amount paid by the holder to acquire the instrument, translated into functional currency at the spot rate on the date of acquisition.

(iii) Purchase price greater than adjusted issue price. If the purchase price of the instrument (determined in the denomination currency) exceeds the adjusted issue price of the instrument, the holder shall, consistent with the rules of § 1.1275-4(b)(9)(i)(B), reasonably allocate such excess to the daily portions of interest accrued on the instrument or to a projected payment on the instrument. To the extent attributable to interest, the excess shall be reasonably allocated over the remaining term of the instrument to the daily portions of interest accrued and shall be a negative adjustment on the dates the daily portions accrue. On the date of such adjustment, the holder's adjusted basis in the instrument is reduced by the amount treated as a negative adjustment under this paragraph (b)(7)(iii), translated into functional currency at the rate used to translate the interest which is offset by the negative adjustment. To the extent related to a projected payment, such excess shall be treated as a negative adjustment on the date the payment is made. On the date of such adjustment, the holder's adjusted basis in the instrument is reduced by the amount treated as a negative adjustment under this paragraph (b)(7)(iii), translated into functional currency at the spot rate on the date the instrument was acquired.

(iv) Purchase price less than adjusted issue price. If the purchase price of the instrument (determined in the denomination currency) is less than the adjusted issue price of the instrument, the holder shall, consistent with the rules of § 1.1275-4(b)(9)(i)(C), reasonably allocate the difference to the daily portions of interest accrued on the instrument or to a projected payment on the instrument. To the extent attributable to interest, the difference shall be reasonably allocated over the remaining term of the instrument to the daily portions of interest accrued and shall be a positive adjustment on the dates the daily portions accrue. On the date of such adjustment, the holder's adjusted basis in the instrument is increased by the amount treated as a positive adjustment under this paragraph (b)(7)(iv), translated into functional currency at the rate used to translate the interest to which it relates. For purposes of determining adjusted basis under paragraph (b)(3)(iii) of this section, such increase in adjusted basis shall be treated as an additional accrual of interest during the period to which the positive adjustment relates. To the extent related to a projected payment, such difference shall be treated as a positive adjustment on the date the payment is made. On the date of such adjustment, the holder's adjusted basis in the instrument is increased by the amount treated as a positive adjustment under this paragraph (b)(7)(iv), translated into functional currency at the spot rate on the date the adjustment is taken into account. For purposes of determining the amount realized on the instrument in functional currency under paragraph (b)(3)(iv) of this section, amounts attributable to the excess of the adjusted issue price of the instrument over the purchase price of the instrument shall be translated into functional currency at the same rate at which the corresponding adjustments are taken into account under this paragraph (b)(7)(iv) for purposes of determining the adjusted basis of the instrument.

(8) Fixed but deferred contingent payments. In the case of an instrument with a contingent payment that becomes fixed as to amount before the payment is due, the rules of § 1.1275-4(b)(9)(ii) shall be applied in the denomination currency of the instrument. For this purpose, foreign currency gain or loss shall be recognized on the date payment is made or received with respect to the instrument under the principles of paragraph (b)(5) of this section. Any increase or decrease in basis required under § 1.1275-4(b)(9)(ii)(D) shall be taken into account at the same exchange rate as the corresponding net positive or negative adjustment is taken into account.

(c) Examples. The provisions of paragraph (b) of this section may be illustrated by the following examples. In each example, assume that the instrument described is a debt instrument for federal income tax purposes. No inference is intended, however, as to whether the instrument is a debt instrument for federal income tax purposes. The examples are as follows:

Example (1). Treatment of net positive adjustment. (i) Facts. On December 31, 2004, Z, a calendar year U.S. resident taxpayer whose functional currency is the U.S. dollar, purchases from a foreign corporation, at original issue, a zero-coupon debt instrument with a £ non-currency contingency for £1000. All payments of principal and interest with respect to the instrument are denominated in, or determined by reference to, a single nonfunctional currency (the British pound). The debt instrument would be subject to § 1.1275-4(b) if it were denominated in dollars. The debt instrument's comparable yield, determined in British pounds under paragraph (b)(2)(i) of this section and § 1.1275-4(b), is 10 percent, compounded annually, and the projected payment schedule, as constructed under the rules of § 1.1275-4(b), provides for a single payment of £1210 on December 31, 2006 (consisting of a noncontingent payment of £975 and a projected payment of £235). The debt instrument is a capital asset in the hands of Z. Z does not elect to use the spot-rate convention described in § 1.988-2(b)(2)(iii)(B). The payment actually made on December 31, 2006, is £1300. The relevant pound/dollar spot rates over the term of the instrument are as follows:

Date	Spot rate (pounds to dollars)
Dec. 31, 2004	£1.00 = $1.00
Dec. 31, 2005	£1.00 = $1.10
Dec. 31, 2006	£1.00 = $1.20

Accrual period	Average rate (pounds to dollars)
2005	£1.00 = $1.05
2006	£1.00 = $1.15

(ii) Treatment in 2005. (A) Determination of accrued interest. Under paragraph (b)(2)(i) of this section, and based on the comparable yield, Z accrues £100 of interest on the debt instrument for 2005 (issue price of £1000 x 10 percent). Under paragraph (b)(3)(i) of this section, Z translates the £100 at the average exchange rate for the accrual period ($1.05 x £100 = $105). Accordingly, Z has interest income in 2005 of $105.

(B) Adjusted issue price and basis. Under paragraphs (b)(2)(iii) and (iv) of this section, the adjusted issue price of the debt instrument determined in pounds and Z's adjusted basis in dollars in the debt instrument are increased by the interest accrued in 2005. Thus, on January 1, 2006, the adjusted issue price of the debt instrument is £1100. For purposes of determining Z's dollar basis in the debt instrument, the $1000 basis ($1.00 x £1000 original cost basis) is increased by the £100 of accrued interest, translated at the rate at which interest was accrued for 2005. See paragraph (b)(3)(iii) of this section. Accordingly, Z's adjusted basis in the debt instrument as of January 1, 2006, is $1105.

(iii) Treatment in 2006. (A) Determination of accrued interest. Under paragraph (b)(2)(i) of this section, and based on the comparable yield, Z accrues £110 of interest on the debt instrument for 2006 (adjusted issue price of £1100 x 10 percent). Under paragraph (b)(3)(i) of this section, Z translates the £110 at the average exchange rate for the accrual period ($1.15 x £110 = $126.50). Accordingly, Z has interest income in 2006 of $126.50.

(B) Effect of net positive adjustment. The payment actually made on December 31, 2006, is £1300, rather than the projected £1210. Under paragraph (b)(2)(ii) of this section, Z has a net positive adjustment of £90 on December 31, 2006, attributable to the difference between the amount of the actual payment and the amount of the projected payment. Under paragraph (b)(3)(ii)(A) of this section, the £90 net positive adjustment is treated as additional interest income and is translated into dollars at the spot rate on the last day of the year ($1.20 x £90 = $108). Accordingly, Z has a net positive adjustment of $108 resulting in a total interest inclusion for 2006 of $234.50 ($126.50 + $108 = $234.50).

(C) Adjusted issue price and basis. Based on the projected payment schedule, the adjusted issue price of the debt instrument immediately before the payment at maturity is £1210 (£1100 plus £110 of accrued interest for 2006). Z's adjusted basis in dollars, based only on the noncontingent payment and the projected amount of the contingent payment to be received, is $1231.50 ($1105 plus $126.50 of accrued interest for 2006).

(D) Amount realized. Even though Z receives £1300 at maturity, for purposes of determining the amount realized, Z is treated under paragraph (b)(2)(v) of this section as receiving the projected amount of the contingent payment on December 31, 2006. Therefore, Z is treated as receiving £1210 on December 31, 2006. Under paragraph (b)(3)(iv) of this section, Z translates its amount realized into dollars and computes its gain or loss on the instrument (other than foreign currency gain or loss) by breaking the amount realized into its component parts. Accordingly, £100 of the £1210 (representing the interest accrued in 2005) is translated at the rate at which it was accrued (£1 = $1.05), resulting in an amount realized of $105; £110 of the £1210 (representing the interest accrued in 2006) is translated into dollars at the rate at which it was accrued (£1 = $1.15), resulting in an amount realized of $126.50; and £1000 of the £1210 (representing a return of principal) is translated into dollars at the spot rate on the date the instrument was purchased (£1 = $1), resulting in an amount realized of $1000. Z's total amount realized is $1231.50, the same as its basis, and Z recognizes no gain or loss (before consideration of foreign currency gain or loss) on retirement of the instrument.

(E) Foreign currency gain or loss. Under paragraph (b)(5) of this section Z recognizes foreign currency gain under section 988 on the instrument with respect to the consideration actually received at maturity (except for the net positive adjustment), £1210. The amount of recognized foreign currency gain is determined based on the difference between the spot rate on the date the instrument matures and the rates at which the principal and interest were taken into account. With respect to the portion of the payment attributable to interest accrued in 2005, the foreign currency gain is $15 [£100 x ($1.20-$1.05)]. With respect to interest accrued in 2006, the foreign currency gain equals $5.50 [£110 x ($1.20-$1.15)]. With respect to principal, the foreign currency gain is $200 [£1000 x ($1.20-$1.00)]. Thus, Z recognizes a total foreign currency gain on December 31, 2006, of $220.50.

(F) Source. Z has interest income of $105 in 2005, interest income of $234.50 in 2006 (attributable to £110 of accrued interest and the £90 net positive adjustment), and a foreign currency gain of $220.50 in 2006. Under paragraph (b)(6) of this section and section 862(a)(1), the interest income is sourced by reference to the residence of the payor and is therefore from sources without the United States. Under paragraph (b)(6) of this section and § 1.988-4, Z's foreign currency gain of $220.50 is sourced by reference to Z's residence and is therefore from sources within the United States.

Example (2). Treatment of net negative adjustment. (i) Facts. Assume the same facts as in Example 1, except that Z receives £975 at maturity instead of £1300.

(ii) Treatment in 2005. The treatment of the debt instrument in 2005 is the same as in Example 1. Thus, Z has interest income in 2005 of $105. On January 1, 2006, the adjusted issue price of the debt instrument is £1100, and Z's adjusted basis in the instrument is $1105.

(iii) Treatment in 2006. (A) Determination of accrued interest. Under paragraph (b)(2)(i) of this section and based on the comparable yield, Z's accrued interest for 2006 is £110 (adjusted issue price of £1100 x 10 percent). Under paragraph (b)(3)(i) of this section, the £110 of accrued interest is translated at the average exchange rate for the accrual period ($1.15 x £110 = $126.50).

(B) Effect of net negative adjustment. The payment actually made on December 31, 2006, is £975, rather than the projected £1210. Under paragraph (b)(2)(ii) of this section, Z has a net negative adjustment of £235 on December 31, 2006, attributable to the difference between the amount of the actual payment and the amount of the projected payment. Z's accrued interest income of £110 in 2006 is reduced to zero by the net negative adjustment. Under paragraph (b)(3)(ii)(B)(1) of this section the net negative adjustment which reduces the current year's interest is not translated into functional currency. Under paragraph (b)(2)(ii) of this section, Z treats the remaining £125 net negative adjustment as an ordinary loss to the extent of the £100 previously accrued interest in 2005. This £100 ordinary loss is attributable to interest accrued but not paid in the preceding year. Therefore, under paragraph (b)(3)(ii)(B)(2) of this section, Z translates the loss into dollars at the average rate for such year (£1 = $1.05). Accordingly, Z has an ordinary loss of $105 in 2006. The remaining £25 of net negative adjustment is a negative adjustment carryforward under paragraph (b)(2)(ii) of this section.

(C) Adjusted issue price and basis. Based on the projected payment schedule, the adjusted issue price of the debt instrument immediately before the payment at maturity is £1210 (£1100 plus £110 of accrued interest for 2006). Z's adjusted basis in dollars, based only on the noncontingent payments and the projected amount of the contingent payments to be received, is $1231.50 ($1105 plus $126.50 of accrued interest for 2006).

(D) Amount realized. Even though Z receives £975 at maturity, for purposes of determining the amount realized, Z is treated under paragraph (b)(2)(v) of this section as receiving the projected amount of the contingent payment on December 31, 2006, reduced by the amount of Z's negative adjustment carryforward of £25. Therefore, Z is treated as receiving £1185 (£1210-£25) on December 31, 2006. Under paragraph (b)(3)(iv) of this section, Z translates its amount realized into dollars and computes its gain or loss on the instrument (other than foreign currency gain or loss) by breaking the amount realized into its component parts. Accordingly, £100 of the £1185 (representing the interest accrued in 2005) is translated at the rate at which it was accrued (£1 = $1.05), resulting in an amount realized of $105; £110 of the £1185 (representing the interest accrued in 2006) is translated into dollars at the rate at which it was accrued (£1 = $1.15), resulting in an amount realized of $126.50; and £975 of the £1185 (representing a return of principal) is translated into dollars at the spot rate on the date the instrument was purchased (£1 = $1), resulting in an amount realized of $975. Z's amount realized is $1206.50 ($105 + $126.50 + $975 = $1206.50), and Z recognizes a capital loss (before consideration of foreign currency gain or loss) of $25 on retirement of the instrument ($1206.50-$1231.50 = -$25).

(E) Foreign currency gain or loss. Z recognizes foreign currency gain with respect to the consideration actually received at maturity, £975. Under paragraph (b)(5)(ii) of this section, no foreign currency gain or loss is recognized with respect to unpaid accrued interest reduced to zero by the net negative adjustment resulting in 2006. In addition, no foreign currency gain or loss is recognized with respect to unpaid accrued interest from 2005, also reduced to zero by the ordinary loss. Accordingly, Z recognizes foreign currency gain with respect to principal only. Thus, Z recognizes a total foreign currency gain on December 31, 2006, of $195 [£975 x ($1.20-$1.00)].

(F) Source. In 2006, Z has an ordinary loss of $105, a capital loss of $25, and a foreign currency gain of $195. Under paragraph (b)(6) of this section and § 1.1275-4(b)(9)(iv), the $105 ordinary loss generally reduces Z's foreign source passive income under section 904(d) and the regulations thereunder. Under paragraph (b)(6) of this section and § 1.865-1(b)(2), the $25 capital loss is sourced by reference to how interest income on the instrument would have been sourced. Therefore, the $25 capital loss generally reduces Z's foreign source passive income under section 904(d) and the regulations thereunder. Under paragraph (b)(6) of this section and § 1.988-4, Z's foreign currency gain of $195 is sourced by reference to Z's residence and is therefore from sources within the United States.

Example (3). Negative adjustment and periodic interest payments. (i) Facts. On December 31, 2004, Z, a calendar year U.S. resident taxpayer whose functional currency is the U.S. dollar, purchases from a foreign corporation, at original issue, a two-year debt instrument with a non-currency contingency for £1000. All payments of principal and interest with respect to the instrument are denominated in, or determined by reference to, a single nonfunctional currency (the British pound). The debt instrument would be subject to § 1.1275-4(b) if it were denominated in dollars. The debt instrument's comparable yield, determined in British pounds under §§ 1.988-2(b)(2) and 1.1275-4(b), is 10 percent, compounded semiannually. The debt instrument provides for semiannual interest payments of £30 payable each June 30, and December 31, and a contingent payment at maturity on December 31, 2006, which is projected to equal £1086.20 (consisting of a noncontingent payment of £980 and a projected payment of £106.20) in addition to the interest payable at maturity. The debt instrument is a capital asset in the hands of Z. Z does not elect to use the spot-rate convention described in § 1.988-2(b)(2)(iii)(B). The payment actually made on December 31, 2006, is £981.00. The relevant pound/dollar spot rates over the term of the instrument are as follows:

Date	Spot rate (pounds to dollars)
Dec. 31, 2004	£1.00 = $1.00
June 30, 2005	£1.00 = $1.20
Dec. 31, 2005	£1.00 = $1.40
June 30, 2006	£1.00 = $1.60
Dec. 31, 2006	£1.00 = $1.80

Accrual period	Average rate (pounds to dollars)
Jan.-June 2005	£1.00 = $1.10
July-Dec. 2005	£1.00 = $1.30
Jan.-June 2006	£1.00 = $1.50
July-Dec. 2006	£1.00 = $1.70

(ii) Treatment in 2005. (A) Determination of accrued interest. Under paragraph (b)(2)(i) of this section, and based on the comparable yield, Z accrues £50 of interest on the debt instrument for the January-June accrual period (issue price of £1000 x 10 percent/2). Under paragraph (b)(3)(i) of this section, Z translates the £50 at the average exchange rate for the accrual period ($1.10 x £50 = $55.00). Similarly, Z accrues £51 of interest in the July-December accrual period [(£1000 + £50-£30) x 10 percent/2], which is translated at the average exchange rate for the accrual period ($1.30 x £51 = $66.30). Accordingly, Z accrues $121.30 of interest income in 2005.

(B) Adjusted issue price and basis. (1) January-June accrual period. Under paragraphs (b)(2)(iii) and (iv) of this section, the adjusted issue price of the debt instrument determined in pounds and Z's adjusted basis in dollars in the debt instrument are increased by the interest accrued, and decreased by the interest payment made, in the January-June accrual period. Thus, on July 1, 2005, the adjusted issue price of the debt instrument is £1020 (£1000 + £50 - £30 = £1020). For purposes of determining Z's dollar basis in the debt instrument, the $1000 basis is increased by the £50 of accrued interest, translated, under paragraph (b)(3)(iii) of this section, at the rate at which interest was accrued for the January-June accrual period ($1.10 x £50 = $55). The resulting amount is reduced by the £30 payment of interest made during the accrual period, translated, under paragraph (b)(3)(iii) of this section and § 1.988-2(b)(7), at the rate applicable to accrued interest ($1.10 x £30 = $33). Accordingly, Z's adjusted basis as of July 1, 2005, is $1022 ($1000 + $55 - $33).

(2) July-December accrual period. Under paragraphs (b)(2)(iii) and (iv) of this section, the adjusted issue price of the debt instrument determined in pounds and Z's adjusted basis in dollars in the debt instrument are increased by the interest accrued, and decreased by the interest payment made, in the July-December accrual period. Thus, on January 1, 2006, the adjusted issue price of the instrument is £1041 (£1020 + £51 - £30 = £1041). For purposes of determining Z's dollar basis in the debt instrument, the $1022 basis is increased by the £51 of accrued interest, translated, under paragraph (b)(3)(iii) of this section, at the rate at which interest was accrued for the July-December accrual period ($1.30 x £51 = $66.30). The resulting amount is reduced by the £30 payment of interest made during the accrual period, translated, under paragraph (b)(3)(iii) of this section and § 1.988-2(b)(7), at the rate applicable to accrued interest ($1.30 x £30 = $39). Accordingly, Z's adjusted basis as of January 1, 2006, is $1049.30 ($1022 + $66.30 - $39).

(C) Foreign currency gain or loss. Z will recognize foreign currency gain on the receipt of each £30 payment of interest actually received during 2005. The amount of foreign currency gain in each case is determined, under paragraph (b)(5)(ii) of this section, by reference to the difference between the spot rate on the date the £30 payment was made and the average exchange rate for the accrual period during which the interest accrued. Accordingly, Z recognizes $3 of foreign currency gain on the January-June interest payment [£30 x ($1.20 - $1.10)], and $3 of foreign currency gain on the July-December interest payment [£30 x ($1.40 - $1.30)]. Z recognizes in 2005 a total of $6 of foreign currency gain.

(D) Source. Z has interest income of $121.30 and a foreign currency gain of $6. Under paragraph (b)(6) of this section and section 862(a)(1), the interest income is sourced by reference to the residence of the payor and is therefore from sources without the United States. Under paragraph (b)(6) of this section and § 1.988-4, Z's foreign currency gain of $6 is sourced by reference to Z's residence and is therefore from sources within the United States.

(iii) Treatment in 2006. (A) Determination of accrued interest. Under paragraph (b)(2)(i) of this section, and based on the comparable yield, Z's accrued interest for the January-June accrual period is £52.05 (adjusted issue price of £1041 x 10 percent/2). Under paragraph (b)(3)(i) of this section, Z translates the £52.05 at the average exchange rate for the accrual period ($1.50 x £52.05 = $78.08). Similarly, Z accrues £53.15 of interest in the July-December accrual period [(£1041 + £52.05-£30) x 10 percent/2], which is translated at the average exchange rate for the accrual period ($1.70 x £53.15 = $90.35). Accordingly, Z accrues £105.20, or $168.43, of interest income in 2006.

(B) Effect of net negative adjustment. The payment actually made on December 31, 2006, is £981.00, rather than the projected £1086.20. Under paragraph (b)(2)(ii)(B) of this section, Z has a net negative adjustment of £105.20 on December 31, 2006, attributable to the difference between the amount of the actual payment and the amount of the projected payment. Z's accrued interest income of £105.20 in 2006 is reduced to zero by the net negative adjustment. Elimination of the 2006 accrued interest fully utilizes the net negative adjustment.

(C) Adjusted issue price and basis. (1) January-June accrual period. Under paragraphs (b)(2)(iii) and (iv) of this section, the adjusted issue price of the debt instrument determined in pounds and Z's adjusted basis in dollars in the debt instrument are increased by the interest accrued, and decreased by the interest payment made, in the January-June accrual period. Thus, on July 1, 2006, the adjusted issue price of the debt instrument is £1063.05 (£1041 + £52.05 - £30 = £1063.05). For purposes of determining Z's dollar basis in the debt instrument, the $1049.30 adjusted basis is increased by the £52.05 of accrued interest, translated, under paragraph (b)(3)(iii) of this section, at the rate at which interest was accrued for the January-June accrual period ($1.50 x £52.05 = $78.08). The resulting amount is reduced by the £30 payment of interest made during the accrual period, translated, under paragraph (b)(3)(iii) of this section and § 1.988-2(b)(7), at the rate applicable to accrued interest ($1.50 x £30 = $45). Accordingly, Z's adjusted basis as of July 1, 2006, is $1082.38 ($1049.30 + $78.08 - $45).

(2) July-December accrual period. Under paragraphs (b)(2)(iii) and (iv) of this section, the adjusted issue price of the debt instrument determined in pounds and Z's adjusted basis in dollars in the debt instrument are increased by the interest accrued, and decreased by the interest payment made, in the July-December accrual period. Thus, immediately before maturity on December 31, 2006, the adjusted issue price of the instrument is £1086.20 (£1063.05 + £53.15 - £30 = £1086.20). For purposes of determining Z's dollar basis in the debt instrument, the $1082.38 adjusted basis is increased by the £53.15 of accrued interest, translated, under paragraph (b)(3)(iii) of this section, at the rate at which interest was accrued for the July-December accrual period ($1.70 x £53.15 = $90.36). The resulting amount is reduced by the £30 payment of interest made during the accrual pe-

riod, translated, under paragraph (b)(3)(iii) of this section and § 1.988-2(b)(7), at the rate applicable to accrued interest ($1.70 x £30 = $51). Accordingly, Z's adjusted basis on December 31, 2006, immediately prior to maturity is $1121.74 ($1082.38 + $90.36 - $51).

(D) Amount realized. Even though Z receives £981.00 at maturity, for purposes of determining the amount realized, Z is treated under paragraph (b)(2)(v) of this section as receiving the projected amount of the contingent payment on December 31, 2006. Therefore, Z is treated as receiving £1086.20 on December 31, 2006. Under paragraph (b)(3)(iv) of this section, Z translates its amount realized into dollars and computes its gain or loss on the instrument (other than foreign currency gain or loss) by breaking the amount realized into its component parts. Accordingly, £20 of the £1086.20 (representing the interest accrued in the January-June 2005 accrual period, less £30 interest paid) is translated into dollars at the rate at which it was accrued (£1 = $1.10), resulting in an amount realized of $22; £21 of the £1086.20 (representing the interest accrued in the July-December 2005 accrual period, less £30 interest paid) is translated into dollars at the rate at which it was accrued (£1 = $1.30), resulting in an amount realized of $27.30; £22.05 of the £1086.20 (representing the interest accrued in the January-June 2006 accrual period, less £30 interest paid) is translated into dollars at the rate at which it was accrued (£1 = $1.50), resulting in an amount realized of $33.08; £23.15 of the £1086.20 (representing the interest accrued in the July 1-December 31, 2006 accrual period, less the £30 interest payment) is translated into dollars at the rate at which it was accrued (£1 = $1.70), resulting in an amount realized of $39.36; and £1000 (representing principal) is translated into dollars at the spot rate on the date the instrument was purchased (£1 = $1), resulting in an amount realized of $1000. Accordingly, Z's total amount realized is $1121.74 ($22 + $27.30 + $33.08 + $39.36 + $1000), the same as its basis, and Z recognizes no gain or loss (before consideration of foreign currency gain or loss) on retirement of the instrument.

(E) Foreign currency gain or loss. Z recognizes foreign currency gain with respect to each £30 payment actually received during 2006. These payments, however, are treated as payments of principal for this purpose because all 2006 accrued interest is reduced to zero by the net negative adjustment. See paragraph (b)(5)(iv)(A)(3) of this section. The amount of foreign currency gain in each case is determined, under paragraph (b)(5)(iii) of this section, by reference to the difference between the spot rate on the date the £30 payment is made and the spot rate on the date the debt instrument was issued. Accordingly, Z recognizes $18 of foreign currency gain on the January-June 2006 interest payment [£30 x ($1.60 - $1.00)], and $24 of foreign currency gain on the July-December 2006 interest payment [£30 x ($1.80 - $1.00)]. Z separately recognizes foreign currency gain with respect to the consideration actually received at maturity, £981.00. The amount of such gain is determined based on the difference between the spot rate on the date the instrument matures and the rates at which the principal and interest were taken into account. With respect to the portion of the payment attributable to interest accrued in January-June 2005 (other than the £30 payments), the foreign currency gain is $14 [£20 x ($1.80 - $1.10)]. With respect to the portion of the payment attributable to interest accrued in July-December 2005 (other than the £30 payments), the foreign currency gain is $10.50 [£21 x ($1.80 - $1.30)]. With respect to the portion of the payment attributable to interest accrued in 2006 (other than the £30 payments), no foreign currency gain or loss is recognized under paragraph (b)(5)(ii) of this section because such interest was reduced to zero by the net negative adjustment. With respect to the portion of the payment attributable to principal, the foreign currency gain is $752 [£940 x ($1.80 - $1.00)]. Thus, Z recognizes a foreign currency gain of $42 on receipt of the two £30 payments in 2006, and $776.50 ($14 + $10.50 + $752) on receipt of the payment at maturity, for a total 2006 foreign currency gain of $818.50.

(F) Source. Under paragraph (b)(6) of this section and § 1.988-4, Z's foreign currency gain of $818.50 is sourced by reference to Z's residence and is therefore from sources within the United States.

Example (4). Purchase price greater than adjusted issue price. (i) Facts. On July 1, 2005, Z, a calendar year U.S. resident taxpayer whose functional currency is the U.S. dollar, purchases a debt instrument with a non-currency contingency for £1405. All payments of principal and interest with respect to the instrument are denominated in, or determined by reference to, a single nonfunctional currency (the British pound). The debt instrument would be subject to § 1.1275-4(b) if it were denominated in dollars. The debt instrument was originally issued by a foreign corporation on December 31, 2003, for an issue price of £1000, and matures on December 31, 2006. The debt instrument's comparable yield, determined in British pounds under §§ 1.988-2(b)(2) and 1.1275-4(b), is 10.25 percent, compounded semiannually, and the projected payment schedule for the debt instrument (determined as of the issue date under the rules of § 1.1275-4(b)) provides for a single payment at maturity of £1349.70 (consisting of a noncontingent payment of £1000 and a projected payment of £349.70). At the time of the purchase, the adjusted issue price of the debt instrument is £1161.76, assuming semiannual accrual periods ending on June 30 and December 31 of each year. The increase in the value of the debt instrument over its adjusted issue price is due to an increase in the expected amount of the contingent payment. The debt instrument is a capital asset in the hands of Z. Z does not elect to use the spot-rate convention described in § 1.988-2(b)(2)(iii)(B). The payment actually made on December 31, 2006, is £1400. The relevant pound/dollar spot rates over the term of the instrument are as follows:

Date	Spot rate (pounds to dollars)
July 1, 2005	£1.00 = $1.00
Dec. 31, 2006	£1.00 = $2.00

Accrual period	Average rate (pounds to dollars)
July 1-Dec. 31, 2005	£1.00 = $1.50
Jan. 1-June 30, 2006	£1.00 = $1.50
July 1-Dec. 31, 2006	£1.00 = $1.50

(ii) Initial basis. Under paragraph (b)(7)(ii) of this section, Z's initial basis in the debt instrument is $1405, Z's purchase price of £1405, translated into functional currency at the spot rate on the date the debt instrument was purchased (£1 = $1).

(iii) Allocation of purchase price differential. Z purchased the debt instrument for £1405 when its adjusted issue price was £1161.76. Under paragraph (b)(7)(iii) of this section, Z allocates the £243.24 excess of purchase price over adjusted issue price to the contingent payment at maturity. This allocation is reasonable because the excess is due to an increase in the expected amount of the contingent payment and not, for example, to a decrease in prevailing interest rates.

(iv) Treatment in 2005. (A) Determination of accrued interest. Under paragraph (b)(2)(i) of this section, and based on the comparable yield, Z accrues £59.54 of interest on the debt instrument for the July-December 2005 accrual period (issue price of £1161.76 x 10.25 percent/2). Under paragraph (b)(3)(i) of this section, Z translates the £59.54 of interest at the average exchange rate for the accrual period ($1.50 x £59.54 = $89.31). Accordingly, Z has interest income in 2005 of $89.31.

(B) Adjusted issue price and basis. Under paragraphs (b)(2)(iii) and (iv) of this section, the adjusted issue price of the debt instrument determined in pounds and Z's adjusted basis in dollars in the debt instrument are increased by the interest accrued in July-December 2005. Thus, on January 1, 2006, the adjusted issue price of the debt instrument is £1221.30 (£1161.76 + £59.54). For purposes of determining Z's dollar basis in the debt instrument on January 1, 2006, the $1405 basis is increased by the £59.54 of accrued interest, translated at the rate at which interest was accrued for the July-December 2005 accrual period. Paragraph (b)(3)(iii) of this section. Accordingly, Z's adjusted basis in the instrument, as of January 1, 2006, is $1494.31 [$1405 + (£59.54 x $1.50)].

(v) Treatment in 2006. (A) Determination of accrued interest. Under paragraph (b)(2)(i) of this section, and based on the comparable yield, Z accrues £62.59 of interest on the debt instrument for the January-June 2006 accrual period (issue price of £1221.30 x 10.25 percent/2). Under paragraph (b)(3)(i) of this section, Z translates the £62.59 of accrued interest at the average exchange rate for the accrual period ($1.50 x £62.59 = $93.89). Similarly, Z accrues £65.80 of interest in the July-December 2006 accrual period [(£1221.30 + £62.59) x 10.25 percent/2], which is translated at the average exchange rate for the accrual period ($1.50 x £65.80 = $98.70). Accordingly, Z accrues £128.39, or $192.59, of interest income in 2006.

(B) Effect of positive and negative adjustments. (1) Offset of positive adjustment. The payment actually made on December 31, 2006, is £1400, rather than the projected £1349.70. Under paragraph (b)(2)(ii) of this section, Z has a positive adjustment of £50.30 on December 31, 2006, attributable to the difference between the amount of the actual payment and the amount of the projected payment. Under paragraph (b)(7)(iii) of this section, however, Z also has a negative adjustment of £243.24, attributable to the excess of Z's purchase price for the debt instrument over its adjusted issue price. Accordingly, Z will have a net negative adjustment of £192.94 (£50.30-£243.24 = £192.94) for 2006.

(2) Offset of accrued interest. Z's accrued interest income of £128.39 in 2006 is reduced to zero by the net negative adjustment. The net negative adjustment which reduces the current year's interest is not translated into functional currency. Under paragraph (b)(2)(ii) of this section, Z treats the remaining £64.55 net negative adjustment as an ordinary loss to the extent of the £59.54 previously accrued interest in 2005. This £59.54 ordinary loss is attributable to interest accrued but not paid in the preceding year. Therefore, under paragraph (b)(3)(ii)(B)(2) of this section, Z translates the loss into dollars at the average rate for such year (£1 = $1.50). Accordingly, Z has an ordinary loss of $89.31 in 2006. The remaining £5.01 of net negative adjustment is a negative adjustment carryforward under paragraph (b)(2)(ii) of this section.

(C) Adjusted issue price and basis. (1) January-June accrual period. Under paragraph (b)(2)(iii) of this section, the adjusted issue price of the debt instrument on July 1, 2006, is £1283.89 (£1221.30 + £62.59 = £1283.89). Under paragraphs (b)(2)(iv) and (b)(3)(iii) of this section, Z's adjusted basis as of July 1, 2006, is $1588.20 ($1494.31 + $93.89).

(2) July-December accrual period. Based on the projected payment schedule, the adjusted issue price of the debt instrument immediately before the payment at maturity is £1349.70 (£1283.89 + £65.80 accrued interest for July-December). Z's adjusted basis in dollars, based only on the noncontingent payments and the projected amount of the contingent payments to be received, is $1686.90 ($1588.20 plus $98.70 of accrued interest for July-December).

(3) Adjustment to basis upon contingent payment. Under paragraph (b)(7)(iii) of this section, Z's adjusted basis in the debt instrument is reduced at maturity by £243.24, the excess of Z's purchase price for the debt instrument over its adjusted issue price. For this purpose, the adjustment is translated into functional currency at the spot rate on the date the instrument was acquired (£1 = $1). Accordingly, Z's adjusted basis in the debt instrument at maturity is $1443.66 ($1686.90-$243.24).

(D) Amount realized. Even though Z receives £1400 at maturity, for purposes of determining the amount realized, Z is treated under paragraph (b)(2)(v) of this section as receiving the projected amount of the contingent payment on December 31, 2006, reduced by the amount of Z's negative adjustment carryforward of £5.01. Therefore, Z is treated as receiving £1344.69 (£1349.70-£5.01) on December 31, 2006. Under paragraph (b)(3)(iv) of this section, Z translates its amount realized into dollars and computes its gain or loss on the instrument (other than foreign currency gain or loss) by breaking the amount realized into its component parts. Accordingly, £59.54 of the £1344.69 (representing the interest accrued in 2005) is translated at the rate at which it was accrued (£1 = $1.50), resulting in an amount realized of $89.31; £62.59 of the £1344.69 (representing the interest accrued in January-June 2006) is translated into dollars at the rate at which it was accrued (£1 = $1.50), resulting in an amount realized of $93.89; £65.80 of the £1344.69 (representing the interest accrued in July-December 2006) is translated into dollars at the rate at which it was accrued (£1 = $1.50), resulting in an amount realized of $98.70; and £1156.76 of the £1344.69 (representing a return of principal) is translated into dollars at the spot rate on the date the instrument was purchased (£1 = $1), resulting in an amount realized of $1156.76. Z's amount realized is $1438.66 ($89.31 + $93.89 + $98.70 + $1156.76), and Z recognizes a capital loss (before consideration of foreign currency gain or loss) of $5 on retirement of the instrument ($1438.66 - $1443.66 = -$5).

(E) Foreign currency gain or loss. Z recognizes foreign currency gain under section 988 on the instrument with respect to the entire consideration actually received at maturity, £1400. While foreign currency gain or loss ordinarily would not have arisen with respect to £50.30 of the £1400, which was initially treated as a positive adjustment in 2006, the larger negative adjustment in 2006 reduced this positive adjustment to zero. Accordingly, foreign currency gain or loss is recognized with respect to the entire £1400. Under paragraph (b)(5)(ii) of this section, however, no foreign currency gain or loss is recognized with respect to unpaid accrued interest reduced to zero by the net negative adjustment resulting in 2006, and no foreign currency gain or loss is recognized with respect to unpaid accrued interest from 2005, also reduced to zero by the ordinary loss. Therefore, the entire £1400 is treated as a return of principal for the purpose of determining foreign currency gain or loss, and Z recognizes a total foreign currency gain on December 31, 2001, of $1400 [£1400 x ($2.00-$1.00)].

(F) Source. Z has an ordinary loss of $89.31, a capital loss of $5, and a foreign currency gain of $1400. Under paragraph (b)(6) of this section and § 1.1275-4(b)(9)(iv), the $89.31 ordinary loss generally reduces Z's foreign source passive income under section 904(d) and the regulations thereunder. Under paragraph (b)(6) of this section and § 1.865-1(b)(2), the $5 capital loss is sourced by reference to how interest income on the instrument would have been sourced. Therefore, the $5 capital loss generally reduces Z's foreign source passive income under section 904(d) and the regulations thereunder. Under paragraph (b)(6) of this section and § 1.988-4, Z's foreign currency gain of $1400 is sourced by reference to Z's residence and is therefore from sources within the United States.

Example (5). Sale of an instrument with a negative adjustment carryforward. (i) Facts. On December 31, 2003, Z, a calendar year U.S. resident taxpayer whose functional currency is the U.S. dollar, purchases at original issue a debt instrument with non-currency contingencies for £1000. All payments of principal and interest with respect to the instrument are denominated in, or determined by reference to, a single nonfunctional currency (the British pound). The debt instrument would be subject to § 1.1275-4(b) if it were denominated in dollars. The debt instrument's comparable yield, determined in British poundsunder §§ 1.988-2(b)(2) and 1.1275-4(b), is 10 percent, compounded annually, and the projected payment schedule for the debt instrument provides for payments of £310 on December 31, 2005 (consisting of a noncontingent payment of £50 and a projected amount of £260) and £990 on December 31, 2006 (consisting of a noncontingent payment of £940 and a projected amount of £50). The debt instrument is a capital asset in the hands of Z. Z does not elect to use the spot-rate convention described in § 1.988-2(b)(2)(iii)(B). The payment actually made on December 31, 2005, is £50. On December 30, 2006, Z sells the debt instrument for £940. The relevant pound/dollar spot rates over the term of the instrument are as follows:

Date	Spot rate (pounds to dollars)
Dec. 31, 2003	£1.00 = $1.00
Dec. 31, 2005	£1.00 = $2.00
Dec. 30, 2006	£1.00 = $2.00

Accrual period	Average rate (pounds to dollars)
Jan. 1-Dec. 31, 2004	£1.00 = $2.00
Jan. 1-Dec. 31, 2005	£1.00 = $2.00
Jan. 1-Dec. 31, 2006	£1.00 = $2.00

(ii) Treatment in 2004. (A) Determination of accrued interest. Under paragraph (b)(2)(i) of this section, and based on the comparable yield, Z accrues £100 of interest on the debt instrument for 2004 (issue price of £1000 x 10 percent). Under paragraph (b)(3)(i) of this section, Z translates the £100 at the average exchange rate for the accrual period ($2.00 x £100 = $200). Accordingly, Z has interest income in 2004 of $200.

(B) Adjusted issue price and basis. Under paragraphs (b)(2)(iii) and (iv) of this section, the adjusted issue price of the debt instrument determined in pounds and Z's adjusted basis in dollars in the debt instrument are increased by the interest accrued in 2004. Thus, on January 1, 2005, the adjusted issue price of the debt instrument is £1100. For purposes of determining Z's dollar basis in the debt instrument, the $1000 basis ($1.00 x £1000 original cost basis) is increased by the £100 of accrued interest, translated at the rate at which interest was accrued for 2004. See paragraph (b)(3)(iii) of this section. Accordingly, Z's adjusted basis in the debt instrument as of January 1, 2005, is $1200 ($1000 + $200).

(iii) Treatment in 2005. (A) Determination of accrued interest. Under paragraph (b)(2)(i) of this section, and based on the comparable yield, Z's accrued interest for 2005 is £110 (adjusted issue price of £1100 x 10 percent). Under paragraph (b)(3)(i) of this section, the £110 of accrued interest is translated at the average exchange rate for the accrual period ($2.00 x £110 = $220).

(B) Effect of net negative adjustment. The payment actually made on December 31, 2005, is £50, rather than the projected £310. Under paragraph (b)(2)(ii) of this section, Z has a net negative adjustment of £260 on December 31, 2005, attributable to the difference between the amount of the actual payment and the amount of the projected payment. Z's accrued interest income of £110 in 2005 is reduced to zero by the net negative adjustment. Under paragraph (b)(3)(ii)(B)(1) of this section, the net negative adjustment which reduces the current year's interest is not translated into functional currency. Under paragraph (b)(2)(ii) of this section, Z treats the remaining £150 net negative adjustment as an ordinary loss to the extent of the £100 previously accrued interest in 2004. This £100 ordinary loss is attributable to interest accrued but not paid in the preceding year. Therefore, under paragraph (b)(3)(ii)(B)(2) of this section, Z translates the loss into dollars at the average rate for such year (£1 = $2.00). Accordingly, Z has an ordinary loss of $200 in 2005. The remaining £50 of net negative adjustment is a negative adjustment carryforward under paragraph (b)(2)(ii) of this section.

(C) Adjusted issue price and basis. Based on the projected payment schedule, the adjusted issue price of the debt instrument on January 1, 2006 is £900, i.e., the adjusted issue price of the debt instrument on January 1, 2005 (£1100), increased by the interest accrued in 2005 (£110), and decreased by the projected amount of the December 31, 2005, payment (£310). See paragraph (b)(2)(iii) of this section. Z's adjusted basis on January 1, 2006 is Z's adjusted basis on January 1, 2005 ($1200), increased by the functional currency amount of interest accrued in 2005 ($220), and decreased by the amount of the payments made in 2005, based solely on the projected payment schedule, (£310). The amount of the projected payment is first attributable to the interest accrued in 2005 (£110), and then to the interest accrued in 2004 (£100), and the remaining amount to principal (£100). The interest component of the projected payment is translated into functional currency at the rates at which it was accrued, and the principal component of the projected payment is translated into functional currency at the spot rate on the date the instrument was issued. See paragraph (b)(3)(iii) of this section. Accordingly, Z's adjusted basis in the debt instrument, following the increase of adjusted basis for interest accrued in 2005 ($1200 + $220 = $1420), is decreased by $520 ($220 + $200 + $100 = $520). Z's adjusted basis on January 1, 2006 is therefore, $900.

(D) Foreign currency gain or loss. Z will recognize foreign currency gain on the receipt of the £50 payment actually received on December 31, 2005. Based on paragraph (b)(5)(iv) of this section, the £50 payment is attributable to principal since the accrued unpaid interest was completely eliminated by the net negative adjustment. The amount of foreign currency gain is determined, under paragraph (b)(5)(iii) of this section, by reference to the difference between the spot rate on the date the £50 payment was made and the spot rate on the date the debt instrument was issued. Accordingly, Z recognizes $50 of foreign currency gain on the £50 payment. [($2.00-$1.00) x £50 =$50]. Under paragraph (b)(6) of this section and § 1.988-4, Z's foreign currency gain of $50 is sourced by reference to Z's residence and is therefore from sources within the United States.

(iv) Treatment in 2006. (A) Determination of accrued interest. Under paragraph (b)(2)(i) of this section, and based on the comparable yield, Z accrues £90 of interest on the debt instrument for 2006 (adjusted issue price of £900 x 10 percent). Under paragraph (b)(3)(i) of this section, Z translates the £90 at the average exchange rate for the accrual period ($2.00 x £90 = $180). Accordingly, prior to taking into account the 2005 negative adjustment carryforward, Z has interest income in 2006 of $180.

(B) Effect of net negative adjustment. The £50 negative adjustment carryforward from 2005 is a negative adjustment for 2006. Since there are no other positive or negative adjustments, there is a £50 negative adjustment in 2006 which reduces Z's accrued interest income by £50. Accordingly, after giving effect to the £50 negative adjustment carryforward, Z will accrue $80 of interest income. [(£90-£50) x $2.00 = $80]

(C) Adjusted issue price. Under paragraph (b)(2)(iii) of this section, the adjusted issue price of the debt instrument determined in pounds is increased by the interest accrued in 2006 (prior to taking into account the negative adjustment carryforward). Thus, on December 30, 2006, the adjusted issue price of the debt instrument is £990.

(D) Adjusted basis. For purposes of determining Z's dollar basis in the debt instrument, Z's $900 adjusted basis on January 1, 2006, is increased by the accrued interest, translated at the rate at which interest was accrued for 2006. See paragraph (b)(3)(iii)(A) of this section. Note, however, that under paragraph (b)(3)(iii)(B) of this section the amount of accrued interest which is reduced as a result of the negative adjustment carryforward, i.e., £50, is treated for purposes of this section as principal, and is translated at the spot rate on the date the instrument was issued, i.e., £1.00 =$1.00. Accordingly, Z's adjusted basis in the debt instrument as of December 30, 2006, is $1030 ($900 + $50 + $80).

(E) Amount realized. Z's amount realized in denomination currency is £940, i.e., the amount of pounds Z received on the sale of the debt instrument. Under paragraph (b)(3)(iv)(B)(1) of this section, Z's amount realized is first translated by reference to the principal component of basis (including the amount which is treated as principal under paragraph (b)(3)(iii)(B) of this section) and then the remaining amount realized, if any, is translated by reference to the accrued unpaid interest component of adjusted basis. Thus, £900 of Z's amount realized is translated by reference to the principal component of adjusted basis. The remaining £40 of Z's amount realized is treated as principal under paragraph (b)(3)(iii)(B) of this section, and is also translated by reference to the principal component of adjusted basis. Accordingly, Z's amount realized in functional currency is $940. (No part of Z's amount realized is attributable to the interest accrued on the debt instrument.) Z realizes a loss of $90 on the sale of the debt instrument ($1030 basis-$940 amount realized). Under paragraph (b)(4) of this section and § 1.1275-4(b)(8), $80 of the loss is characterized as ordinary loss, and the remaining $10 of loss is characterized as capital loss. Under §§ 1.988-6(b)(6) and 1.1275-4(b)(9)(iv) the $80 ordinary loss is treated as a deduction that is definitely related to the interest income accrued on the debt instrument. Similarly, under §§ 1.988-6(b)(6) and 1.865-1(b)(2) the $10 capital loss is also allocated to the interest income from the debt instrument.

(F) Foreign currency gain or loss. Z recognizes foreign currency gain with respect to the £940 he received on the sale of the debt instrument. Under paragraph (b)(5)(iv) of this section, the £940 Z received is attributable to principal (and the amount which is treated as principal under paragraph (b)(3)(iii)(B) of this section). Thus, Z recognizes foreign currency gain on December 31, 2006, of $940. [($2.00-$1.00) x £940]. Under paragraph (b)(6) of this section and § 1.988-4, Z's foreign currency gain of $940 is sourced by reference to Z's residence and is therefore from sources within the United States.

(d) Multicurrency debt instruments. *(1) In general.* Except as provided in this paragraph (d), a multicurrency debt instrument described in paragraph (a)(1)(ii) or (iii) of this section shall be treated as an instrument described in paragraph (a)(1)(i) of this section and shall be accounted for under the rules of paragraph (b) of this section. Because payments on an instrument described in paragraph (a)(1)(ii) or (iii) of this section are denominated in, or determined by reference to, more than one currency, the issuer and holder or holders of the instrument are required to determine the denomination currency of the instrument under paragraph (d)(2) of this section before applying the rules of paragraph (b) of this section.

(2) Determination of denomination currency. (i) In general. The denomination currency of an instrument described in paragraph (a)(1)(ii) or (iii) of this section shall be the predominant currency of the instrument. Except as otherwise provided in paragraph (d)(2)(ii) of this section, the predominant currency of the instrument shall be the currency with the greatest value determined by comparing the functional currency value of the noncontingent and projected payments denominated in, or determined by reference to, each currency on the issue date, discounted to present value (in each relevant currency), and translated (if necessary) into functional currency at the spot rate on the issue date. For this purpose, the applicable discount rate may be determined using any method, consistently applied, that reasonably reflects the instrument's economic substance. If a taxpayer does not determine a discount rate using such a method, the Commissioner may choose a method for determining the discount rate that does reflect the instrument's economic substance. The predominant currency is determined as of the issue date and does not change based on subsequent events (e.g., changes in value of one or more currencies).

(ii) Difference in discount rate of greater than 10 percentage points. This § 1.988-6(d)(2)(ii) applies if no currency has a value determined under paragraph (d)(2)(i) of this section that is greater than 50% of the total value of all payments. In such a case, if the difference between the discount rate in the denomination currency otherwise determined under (d)(2)(i) of this section and the discount rate determined under paragraph (d)(2)(i) of this section with respect to any other currency in which payments are made (or determined by reference to) pursuant to the instrument is greater than 10 percentage points, then the Commissioner may determine the predominant currency under any reasonable method.

(3) Issuer/holder consistency. The issuer determines the denomination currency under the rules of paragraph (d)(2) of this section and provides this information to the holders of

the instrument in a manner consistent with the issuer disclosure rules of § 1.1275-2(e). If the issuer does not determine the denomination currency of the instrument, or if the issuer's determination is unreasonable, the holder of the instrument must determine the denomination currency under the rules of paragraph (d)(2) of this section. A holder that determines the denomination currency itself must explicitly disclose this fact on a statement attached to the holder's timely filed federal income tax return for the taxable year that includes the acquisition date of the instrument.

(4) Treatment of payments in currencies other than the denomination currency. For purposes of applying the rules of paragraph (b) of this section to debt instruments described in paragraph (a)(1)(ii) or (iii) of this section, payments not denominated in (or determined by reference to) the denomination currency shall be treated as non-currency-related contingent payments. Accordingly, if the denomination currency of the instrument is determined to be the taxpayer's functional currency, the instrument shall be accounted for under § 1.1275-4(b) rather than under this section.

(e) Instruments issued for nonpublicly traded property. *(1) Applicability.* This paragraph (e) applies to debt instruments issued for nonpublicly traded property that would be described in paragraph (a)(1)(i), (ii), or (iii) of this section, but for the fact that such instruments are described in § 1.1275-4(c)(1) rather than § 1.1275-4(b)(1). For example, this paragraph (e) generally applies to a contingent payment debt instrument denominated in a nonfunctional currency that is issued for non-publicly traded property. Generally the rules of § 1.1275-4(c) apply except as set forth by the rules of this paragraph (e).

(2) Separation into components. An instrument described in this paragraph (e) is not accounted for using the noncontingent bond method of § 1.1275-4(b) and paragraph (b) of this section. Rather, the instrument is separated into its component payments. Each noncontingent payment or group of noncontingent payments which is denominated in a single currency shall be considered a single component treated as a separate debt instrument denominated in the currency of the payment or group of payments. Each contingent payment shall be treated separately as provided in paragraph (e)(4) of this section.

(3) Treatment of components consisting of one or more noncontingent payments in the same currency. The issue price of each component treated as a separate debt instrument which consists of one or more noncontingent payments is the sum of the present values of the noncontingent payments contained in the separate instrument. The present value of any noncontingent payment shall be determined under § 1.1274-2(c)(2), and the test rate shall be determined under § 1.1274-4 with respect to the currency in which each separate instrument is considered denominated. No interest payments on the separate debt instrument are qualified stated interest payments (within the meaning of § 1.1273-1(c)) and the de minimis rules of section 1273(a)(3) and § 1.1273-1(d) do not apply to the separate debt instrument. Interest income or expense is translated, and exchange gain or loss is recognized on the separate debt instrument as provided in § 1.988-2(b)(2), if the instrument is denominated in a nonfunctional currency.

(4) Treatment of components consisting of contingent payments. (i) General rule. A component consisting of a contingent payment shall generally be treated in the manner provided in § 1.1275-4(c)(4). However, except as provided in paragraph (e)(4)(ii) of this section, the test rate shall be determined by reference to the U.S. dollar unless the dollar does not reasonably reflect the economic substance of the contingent component. In such case, the test rate shall be determined by reference to the currency which most reasonably reflects the economic substance of the contingent component. Any amount received in nonfunctional currency from a component consisting of a contingent payment shall be translated into functional currency at the spot rate on the date of receipt. Except in the case when the payment becomes fixed more than six months before the payment is due, no foreign currency gain or loss shall be recognized on a contingent payment component.

(ii) Certain delayed contingent payments. (A) Separate debt instrument relating to the fixed component. The rules of § 1.1275-4(c)(4)(iii) shall apply to a contingent component the payment of which becomes fixed more than 6 months before the payment is due. For this purpose, the denomination currency of the separate debt instrument relating to the fixed payment shall be the currency in which payment is to be made and the test rate for such separate debt instrument shall be determined in the currency of that instrument. If the separate debt instrument relating to the fixed payment is denominated in nonfunctional currency, the rules of § 1.988-2(b)(2) shall apply to that instrument for the period beginning on the date the payment is fixed and ending on the payment date.

(B) Contingent component. With respect to the contingent component, the issue price considered to have been paid by the issuer to the holder under § 1.1275-4(c)(4)(iii)(A) shall be translated, if necessary, into the functional currency of the issuer or holder at the spot rate on the date the payment becomes fixed.

(5) Basis different from adjusted issue price. The rules of § 1.1275-4(c)(5) shall apply to an instrument subject to this paragraph (e).

(6) Treatment of a holder on sale, exchange, or retirement. The rules of § 1.1275-4(c)(6) shall apply to an instrument subject to this paragraph (e).

(f) Rules for nonfunctional currency tax exempt obligations described in § 1.1275-4(d). *(1) In general.* Except as provided in paragraph (f)(2) of this section, section 1.988-6 shall not apply to a debt instrument the interest on which is excluded from gross income under section 103(a).

(2) Operative rules. [RESERVED].

(g) Effective date. This section shall apply to debt instruments issued on or after October 29, 2004.

T.D. 9157, 8/27/2004.

§ 1.989(a)-1 Definition of a qualified business unit.

(a) Applicability. *(1) In general.* This section provides rules relating to the definition of the term "qualified business unit" (QBU) within the meaning of section 989.

(2) Effective date. These rules shall apply to taxable years beginning after December 31, 1986. However, any person may apply on a consistent basis § 1.989(a)-1T(c) of the Temporary Income Tax Regulations in lieu of § 1.989(a)-1(c) to all taxable years beginning after December 31, 1986, and on or before February 5, 1990. For the text of the temporary regulation, see 53 FR 20612 (June 8, 1988).

(b) Definition of a qualified business unit. *(1) In general.* a QBU is any separate and clearly identified unit of a trade or business of a taxpayer provided that separate books and records are maintained.

(2) Application of the QBU definition. (i) Persons. A corporation is QBU. An individual is not a QBU. A partnership, trust, or estate is a QBU of a partner or beneficiary.

(ii) Activities. Activities of a corporation, partnership, trust, estate, or individual qualify as a QBU if—

(A) The activities constitute a trade or business; and

(B) A separate set of books and records is maintained with respect to the activities.

(3) Special rule. Any activity (wherever conducted and regardless of its frequency) that produces income or loss that is, or is treated as, effectively connected with the conduct of a trade or business within the United States shall be treated as a separate QBU, provided the books and records requirement of paragraph (d)(2) of this section is satisfied.

(c) Trade or business. The determination as to whether activities constitute a trade or business is ultimately dependent upon an examination of all the facts and circumstances. Generally, a trade or business for purposes of section 989(a) is a specific unified group of activities that constitutes (or could constitute) an independent economic enterprise carried on for profit, the expenses related to which are deductible under section 162 or 212 (other than that part of section 212 dealing with expenses incurred in connection with taxes). To constitute a trade or business, a group of activities must ordinarily include every operation which forms a part of, or a step in, a process by which an enterprise may earn income or profit. Such group of activities must ordinarily include the collection of income and the payment of expenses. It is not necessary that the activities carried out by a QBU constitute a different trade or business from those carried out by other QBUs of the taxpayer. A vertical, functional, or geographic division of the same trade or business may be a trade or business for this purpose provided that the activities otherwise qualify as trade or business under this paragraph (c). However, activities that are merely ancillary to a trade or business will not constitute a trade or business under this paragraph (c). Activities of an individual as an employee are not considered by themselves to constitute a trade or business under this paragraph (c).

(d) Separate books and records. *(1) General rule.* Except as provided in paragraph (d)(2) of this section, a separate set of books and records shall include books of original entry and ledger accounts, both general and subsidiary, or similar records. For example, in the case of a taxpayer using the cash receipts and disbursements method of accounting, the books of original entry include a cash receipts and disbursements journal where each receipt and each disbursement is recorded. Similarly, in the case of a taxpayer using an accrual method of accounting, the books of original entry include a journal to record sales (accounts receivable) and a journal to record expenses incurred (accounts payable). In general, a journal represents a chronological account of all transactions entered into by an entity for an accounting period. A ledger account, on the other hand, chronicles the impact during an accounting period of the specific transactions recorded in the journal for that period upon the various items shown on the entity's balance sheet (i.e., assets, liabilities, and capital accounts) and income statement (i.e., revenues and expenses).

(2) Special rule. For purposes of paragraph (b)(3) of this section, books and records include books and records used to determine income or loss that is, or is treated as, effectively connected with the conduct of a trade or business within the United States.

(e) Examples. The provisions of this section may be illustrated by the following examples:

Example (1). Corporation X is a domestic corporation. Corporation X manufactures widgets in the U.S. for export. Corporation X sells widgets in the United Kingdom through a branch office in London. The London office has its own employees and solicits and processes orders. Corporation X maintains in the U.S. a separate set of books and records for all transactions conducted by the London office. Corporation X is a QBU under paragraph (b)(2)(i) of this section because of its corporate status. The London branch office is a QBU under paragraph (b)(2)(ii) of this section because (1) the sale of widgets is a trade or business as defined in paragraph (c) of this section; and (2) a complete and separate set of books and records (as described in paragraph (d) of this section) is maintained with respect to its sales operations.

Example (2). A domestic corporation incorporates a wholly-owned subsidiary in Switzerland. The domestic corporation is a manufacturer that markets its product abroad primarily through the Swiss subsidiary. To facilitate sales of the parent's product in Europe, the Swiss subsidiary has branch offices in France and West Germany that are responsible for all marketing operations in those countries. Each branch has its own employees, solicits and processes orders, and maintains a separate set of books and records. The domestic corporation and the Swiss subsidiary are both QBUs under paragraph (b)(2)(i) of this section because of their corporate status. The French and West German branches are QBUs of the Swiss subsidiary. They satisfy paragraph (b)(2)(ii) because each constitutes a trade or business (as defined in paragraph (c) of this section) and because separate sets of books and records (as described in paragraph (d) of this section) of their respective operations is maintained. Each branch is considered to have a trade or business although each is a geographical division of the same trade or business.

Example (3). W is a domestic corporation that manufactures product X in the United States for sale worldwide. All of W's sales functions are conducted exclusively in the United States. W employs individual Q to work in France. Q's sole function is to act as a courier to deliver sales documents to customers in France. With respect to Q's activities in France, a separate set of books and records as described in paragraph (d) is maintained. Under paragraph (c) of this section, Q's activities in France do not constitute a QBU since they are merely ancillary to W's manufacturing and selling business. Q is not considered to have a QBU because an individual's activities as an employee are not considered to constitute a trade or business of the individual under paragraph (c).

Example (4). The facts are the same as in example (3) except that the courier function is the sole activity of a wholly-owned French subsidiary of W. Under paragraph (b)(2)(i) of this section, the French subsidiary is considered to be a QBU.

Example (5). A corporation incorporated in the Netherlands is a subsidiary of a domestic corporation and a holding company for the stock of one or more subsidiaries incorporated in other countries. The Dutch corporation's activities are limited to paying its directors and its administrative expenses, receiving capital contributions from its United States parent corporation, contributing capital to its subsidiaries, receiving dividend distributions from its subsidiaries, and distributing dividends to its domestic parent corporation. Under paragraph (b)(2)(i) of this section, the Netherlands corporation is considered to be a QBU.

Example (6). Taxpayer A, an individual resident of the United States, is engaged in a trade or business wholly unrelated to any type of investment activity. A also maintains a portfolio of foreign currency-denominated investments through a foreign broker. The broker is responsible for all activities necessary to the management of A's investments and maintains books and records as described in paragraph (d) of this section, with respect to all investment activities of A. A's investment activities qualify as a QBU under paragraph (b)(2)(ii) of this section to the extent the activities engaged in by A generate expenses that are deductible under section 212 (other than that part of section 212 dealing with expenses incurred in connection with taxes).

Example (7). Taxpayer A, an individual resident of the United States, is the sole shareholder of foreign corporation (FC) whose activities are limited to trading in stocks and securities. FC is a QBU under paragraph (b)(2)(i) of this section.

Example (8). Taxpayer A, an individual resident of the United States, markets and sells in Spain and in the United States various products produced by other United States manufacturers. A has an office and employs a salesman to manage A's activities in Spain, maintains a separate set of books and records with respect to his activities in Spain, and is engaged in a trade or business as defined in paragraph (c) of this section. Therefore, under paragraph (b)(2)(ii) of this section, the activities of A in Spain are considered to be a QBU.

Example (9). Foreign corporation FX is incorporated in Mexico and is wholly owned by a domestic corporation. The domestic corporation elects to treat FX as a domestic corporation under section 1504(d). FX operates entirely in Mexico and maintains a separate set of books and records with respect to its activities in Mexico. FX is a QBU under paragraph (b)(2)(i) of this section. The activities of FX in Mexico also constitute a QBU under paragraph (b)(2)(ii) of this section.

Example (10). F, a foreign corporation, computes a gain of $100 from the disposition of a United States real property interest (as defined in section 897(c)). The gain is taken into account as if F were engaged in a trade or business in the United States and as if such gain were effectively connected with such trade or business. F is a QBU under paragraph (b)(2)(i) of this section because of its corporate status. F's disposition activity constitutes a separate QBU under paragraph (b)(3) of this section.

T.D. 8279, 1/3/90.

PAR. 8. Section 1.989(a)-1 is amended as follows:

1. The last sentence of paragraph (b)(2)(i) is revised.

2. Paragraph (b)(4) is added.

The revision and addition reads as follows:

Proposed § 1.989(a)-1 Definition of a qualified business unit. [*For Preamble, see ¶ 152,801*]

(b) * * *

(2) * * *

(i) Persons-- * * * A trust or estate is a QBU of the beneficiary.

* * * * *

(4) Effective date. Generally, the revisions to paragraph (b)(2)(i) of this section shall apply to taxable years beginning one year after the first day of the first taxable year following the date of publication of a Treasury decision adopting this rule as a final regulation in the Federal Register. If a taxpayer makes an election under § 1.987-11(b), then the effective date of the revisions to paragraph (b)(2)(i) of this section with respect to the taxpayer shall be consistent with such election.

* * * * *

§ 1.989(b)-1 Definition of weighted average exchange rate.

For purposes of section 989(b)(3) and (4), the term "weighted average exchange rate" means the simple average of the daily exchange rates (determined by reference to a qualified source of exchange rates within the meaning of § 1.964-1(d)(5)), excluding weekends, holidays and any other nonbusiness days for the taxable year.

T.D. 8263, 9/19/89, amend T.D. 8367, 9/24/91.

§ 1.989(c)-1 Transition rules for certain branches of United States persons using a net worth method of accounting for taxable years beginning before January 1, 1987.

(a) Applicability. *(1) In general.* This section applies to qualified business units (QBU) branches of United States persons, whose functional currency (as defined in section 985 of the Code and regulations issued thereunder) is other than the United States dollar (dollar) and that used a net worth method of accounting for their last taxable year beginning before January 1, 1987. Generally, a net worth method of accounting is any method of accounting under which the taxpayer calculates the taxable income of a QBU branch based on the net change in the dollar value of the QBU branch's equity over the course of a taxable year, taking into account any remittance made during the year. QBU branch equity is the excess of QBU branch assets over QBU branch liabilities. For all taxable years beginning after December 31, 1986, such QBU branches must use the profit and loss method of accounting as described in section 987, except to the extent otherwise provided in regulations under section 985 or any other provision of the Code.

(2) Insolvent QBU branches. A taxpayer may apply the principles of this section to a QBU branch that used a net worth method of accounting for its last taxable year beginning before January 1, 1987, whose $E pool (as defined in paragraph (d)(3)(i) of this section) is negative. For taxable years beginning on or after October 25, 1991 the principles of this section shall apply to insolvent QBU branches.

(b) General rules. For the general rules, see § 1.987-5(b).

(c) Determining the pool(s) from which a remittance is made. To determine from which pool(s) a remittance is made, see § 1.987-5(c).

(d) Calculation of Section 987 gain or loss. *(1) In general.* See § 1.987-5(d)(1) for rules to make this calculation.

(2) Step 1. Calculate the amount of the functional currency pools. For calculation of the amount of the functional currency pools, see § 1.987-5(d)(2).

(3) Step 2. Calculate the dollar basis pools. (i) Dollar basis of the EQ pool. (A) Beginning dollar basis. The beginning dollar basis of the EQ pool (hereinafter referred to as the $E pool) equals the final net worth of the QBU branch. Final net worth of the QBU branch equals the QBU branch's equity value (assets less liabilities) measured in dollars at the end of the taxpayer's last taxable year beginning before January 1, 1987, determined on the basis of the QBU branch's

books and records as adjusted according to United States tax principles.

(B) Adjusting the $E pool. For adjustments to be made to the $E pool, see § 1.987-5(d)(3)(i)(B).

(ii) Dollar basis of the post-'86 profits pool. To calculate the dollar basis of the post-'86 profits pool, see § 1.987-5(d)(3)(ii).

(iii) Dollar basis of the equity pool. To calculate the dollar basis of the equity pool, see § 1.987-5(d)(3)(iii).

(4) Step 3. Calculation of the dollar basis of a remittance. To calculate the dollar basis of the EQ remitted, see § 1.987-5(d)(4).

(5) Step 4. Calculation of the section 987 gain or loss on a remittance. To calculate 987 gain or loss determined on a remittance, see § 1.987-5(d)(5).

(e) Functional currency adjusted basis of QBU branch assets acquired in taxable years beginning before January 1, 1987. To determine the functional currency adjusted basis of QBU branch assets acquired in taxable years beginning before January 1, 1987, see § 1.987-5(e).

(f) Functional currency amount of QBU branch liabilities acquired in taxable years beginning before January 1, 1987. To determine the functional currency amount of QBU branch liabilities acquired in taxable years beginning before January 1, 1987, see § 1.987-5(f).

T.D. 8367, 9/24/91.

PAR. 9. Section 1.989(c)-1 is removed.

Proposed § 1.989(c)-1 [Removed] [*For Preamble, see ¶ 152,801*]

§ 1.991-1 Taxation of a domestic international sales corporation.

(a) In general. A corporation which is a DISC for a taxable year is not subject to any tax imposed by subtitle A of the Code (sections 1 through 1564) for such taxable year, except for the tax imposed by chapter 5 thereof (sections 1491 through 1494) on certain transfers to avoid tax. Thus, for example, a corporation which is a DISC for a taxable year is not subject for such year to the corporate income tax (section 11), the minimum tax on tax preferences (sections 56 through 58), or the accumulated earnings tax (sections 531 through 537). A DISC is liable for the payment of all taxes payable by corporations under other subtitles of the Code, such as, for example, income taxes withheld at the source and other employment taxes under subtitle C and the interest equalization tax and other miscellaneous excise taxes imposed by subtitle D. In addition, a DISC is subject to the provisions of chapter 3 of subtitle A (including section 1461), relating to withholding of tax on nonresident aliens and foreign corporations and tax-free covenant bonds. See § 1.992-1 for the definition of the term "DISC."

(b) Determination of taxable income. *(1) In general.* Although a DISC is not subject to tax under subtitle A of the Code (other than chapter 5 thereof), a DISC's taxable income shall be determined for each taxable year in order to determine, for example, the amount deemed distributed for that taxable year to its shareholders pursuant to § 1.995-2. Except as otherwise provided in the Code and the regulations thereunder, the taxable income of a DISC shall be determined in the same manner as if the DISC were a domestic corporation which had not elected to be treated as a DISC. Thus, for example, a DISC chooses its method of depreciation, inventory method, and annual accounting period in the same manner as if it were a corporation which had not elected to be treated as a DISC. Any elections affecting the determination of taxable income shall be made by the DISC. Thus, as a further example, a DISC which makes an installment sale described in section 453 is able to avail itself of the benefits of section 453: *Provided,* The DISC complies with the election requirements of such section. See § 1.995-2(e) and § 1.996-8 and the regulations thereunder for rules relating to the application for a taxable year of a DISC of a deduction under section 172 for a net operating loss carryback or carryover or of a capital loss carryback or carryover under section 1212.

(2) Choice of method of accounting. A DISC may, generally, choose any method of accounting permissible under section 446(c) and the regulations thereunder. However, if a DISC is a member of a controlled group (as defined in § 1.993-1(k)), the DISC may not choose a method of accounting which, when applied to transactions between the DISC and other members of the controlled group, will result in a material distortion of the income of the DISC or any other member of the controlled group. Such a material distortion of income would occur, for example, if a DISC chooses to use the cash method of accounting where the DISC acts as commission agent in a substantial volume of sales of property by a related corporation which uses the accrual method of accounting and which customarily pays commissions to the DISC more than 2 months after such sales. As a further example, a material distortion of income would occur if a DISC chooses to use the accrual method of accounting where the DISC leases a substantial amount of property from a related corporation which uses the cash method of accounting, if the DISC customarily accrues any portion of the rent on such property more than 2 months before the rent is paid. Changes in the method of accounting of a DISC are subject to the requirements of section 446(e) and the regulations thereunder.

(3) Choice of annual accounting period. (i) In general. A DISC may choose its annual accounting period without regard to the annual accounting period of any of its stockholders. In general, changes in the annual accounting period of a DISC are subject to the requirements of section 442 and the regulations thereunder.

(ii) Transition rule for change in taxable year in order to become a DISC. A corporation may, without the consent of the Commissioner, change its annual accounting period and adopt a new taxable year beginning on the first day of any month in 1972: Provided, That—

(a) Such change has the effect of accelerating the time as of which such corporation can become a DISC,

(b) The Commissioner is notified of such change by means of a statement filed (with the regional service center with which such corporation files its election to be treated as a DISC) not later than the end of the period during which such corporation may file an election to be treated as a DISC for such new taxable year, and

(c) The short period required to effect such change is not a taxable year in which such corporation has a net operating loss as defined in section 172.

Thus, for example, if a corporation which uses the calendar year for its taxable year does not complete arrangements to become a DISC until May 15, 1972, such corporation can, pursuant to this subdivision, change its annual accounting period and adopt a taxable year beginning on the first day of any month in 1972 after May. A change to a new annual accounting period made pursuant to this subdivision is effective only if the corporation which makes such change qualifies as a DISC for such new period. A corporation may change its annual accounting period and adopt a new taxable year pursuant to this subdivision without regard to the provisions of § 1.1502-76 (relating to the taxable year of members of a group). A copy of the statement described in (b) of this subdivision shall be attached to the return of a corporation for the new taxable year to which such corporation changes pursuant to this subdivision. A corporation which changes its annual accounting period pursuant to this subparagraph will not be permitted under section 442 to change its annual accounting period at any time before 1982, except with the consent of the Commissioner as provided in § 1.442-1(b)(1) or pursuant to subparagraph (4) of this paragraph.

(4) Transition rule for change of taxable year of certain DISCs. In the case of a DISC all of the shares of which are held by a single shareholder or by members of a group who file a consolidated return, such DISC may (without the consent of the Commissioner) change its annual accounting period and adopt a taxable year beginning in 1972 which is the same as the taxable year of such shareholder or the members of such group. A change to a new annual accounting period may be made by a DISC pursuant to this subparagraph even if such DISC has changed its annual accounting period pursuant to subparagraph (3)(ii) of this paragraph.

(5) Transition rule for beginning of first taxable year of certain corporations. If a corporation organized before January 1, 1972, neither acquires assets (other than cash or other property acquired as consideration for the issuance of stock) nor begins doing business prior to January 1, 1972, the first taxable year of such corporation is deemed to begin at the time such corporation acquires any asset (other than cash or other property acquired as consideration for the issuance of stock) or begins doing business, whichever is earlier: Provided, That such corporation is a DISC for such first taxable year. For purposes of § 1.6012-2(a), such corporation is treated as not coming into existence until the beginning of such first taxable year.

(c) Effective date. The provisions of this section and the regulations under sections 992 through 997 apply with respect to taxable years ending after December 31, 1971, except that a corporation may not be a DISC for any taxable year beginning before January 1, 1972.

(d) Related statutes. For rules relating to the transfer, during a taxable year beginning before January 1, 1976, to a DISC of assets of an export trade corporation (as defined in section 971), where a parent owns all the outstanding stock of both such DISC and such export trade corporation, see section 505(b) of the Revenue Act of 1971 (85 Stat. 551). For rules regarding limitations on the qualification of a corporation as an export trade corporation for any taxable year beginning after October 31, 1971, see section 971(a)(3).

T.D. 7323, 9/24/74, amend T.D. 7854, 11/16/82.

PAR. 4. Section 1.991-1 is amended as follows:

1. In the third sentence of paragraph (a), the phrase "and the interest equalization tax" is removed, and three new sentences are added at the end of paragraph (a).

2.a. In paragraph (b)(1) the third sentence is revised:

b. In paragraph (b)(2) a new sentence is added immediately after the fourth sentence:

c. Paragraph (b)(3) is revised; and

d. Paragraphs (b)(4) and (5) are removed.

3. New paragraph (e) and (f) are added immediately after paragraph (d).

Proposed § 1.991-1 Taxation of a domestic international sales corporation (DISC). [*For Preamble, see ¶ 151,083*]

(a) In general. * * * For taxable years of a DISC beginning after 1984, the shareholders of the DISC are required to pay an annual interest charge on the shareholder's DISC-related deferred tax liability. The interest charge is imposed on the DISC shareholder, not the DISC. See section 995(f) and § 1.995(f)-1.

(b) Determination of taxable income. *(1) In general.* * * *For example, a DISC may choose its accounting methods and inventory method, or elect, under section 168(b)(3), different recovery percentages for its recovery property than those prescribed under section 168(b)(1), as if the DISC were a domestic corporation which had not elected to be treated as a DISC. * * *

(2) Choice of accounting methods. * * *See also, section 267 for rules that may apply to transactions between a DISC and a related taxpayer requiring the matching of certain items of income and deduction and the deferral of certain losses. * * *

(3) Annual accounting period. For taxable years beginning after March 21, 1984, a DISC cannot choose or change its taxable year without regard to the taxable year of its principal shareholder. In general, a DISC and its principal shareholder must use the same taxable year. See section 441(h) and § 1.441-1.

* * * * *

(e) Close of taxable year and termination of DISC election for all DISCs on December 31, 1984; Reelection required; Exemption of pre-1985 accumulated DISC income from tax. Under section 805(b)(1)(A) of the Tax Reform Act of 1984, Pub. L. 90-369, the last taxable year of a DISC beginning before 1985 ended on December 31, 1984. The corporation's DISC election is also deemed revoked as of the close of business on December 31, 1984. A new DISC election must be made on Form 4876A in order for the corporation to be treated as a DISC for any taxable year beginning after December 31, 1984. See § 1.921-1T(b). See section 805(b)(2) of the Act and the Act and § 1.921-1T(a) for the tax treatment after 1984 of the accumulated DISC income derived before 1985 by certain DISCs.

(f) Interest charge imposed on DISC shareholders after 1984. Section 995(f) requires that for each taxable year beginning after 1984, each shareholder of a DISC shall pay an interest charge on the shareholder's DISC-related deferred tax liability. The shareholder's DISC-related deferred tax liability is computed only with reference to the DISC's accumulated DISC income (earned in periods after 1984) and deferred by the DISC for more than one taxable year. Thus, in general, a DISC shareholder will not have a DISC-related deferred tax liability (and thus, no interest charge) until the close of the shareholder's taxable year following the taxable year with which or within which the first taxable year of the DISC (ending after 1984) ends. See § 1.995(f)-1.

§ 1.992-1 Requirements of a DISC.

Caution: The Treasury has not yet amended Reg § 1.992-1 to reflect changes made by P.L. 104-188, P.L. 98-369.

(a) "DISC" defined. The term "DISC" refers to a domestic international sales corporation. The term "DISC" means a corporation which, for a taxable year—

(1) Is duly incorporated and existing under the laws of any State or the District of Columbia,

(2) Satisfies the gross receipts test described in paragraph (b) of this section,

(3) Satisfies the assets test described in paragraph (c) of this section,

(4) Satisfies the capitalization requirement described in paragraph (d) of this section,

(5) Satisfies the requirement that an election to be treated as a DISC be in effect for such year, as described in paragraph (e) of this section,

(6) [Reserved]

(7) Maintains separate books and records, and

(8) Is not an ineligible corporation described in paragraph (f) of this section.

A corporation which satisfies the requirements described in subparagraphs (1) through (8) of this paragraph for a taxable year is treated as a separate corporation for Federal tax purposes and qualifies as a DISC, even though such corporation would not be treated (if it were not a DISC) as a corporate entity for Federal income tax purposes. An association cannot qualify as a DISC even if such association is taxable as a corporation pursuant to section 7701(a)(3). In addition, a corporation created or organized in, or under the law of, a possession of the United States cannot qualify as a DISC. The rules contained in this paragraph constitute a relaxation of the general rules of corporate substance otherwise applicable under the Code. The separate incorporation of a DISC is required under section 992(a)(1) to make it possible to keep a better record of the income which is subject to the special treatment provided by sections 991 through 996, but this does not necessitate in all other respects the separate relationships which otherwise would be required between a parent corporation and its subsidiary. However, this relaxation of the general rules of corporate substance does not apply with respect to other corporations in other contexts. In the case of a transaction between a DISC and a person related to such DISC for purposes of section 482, see § 1.993-1(l) for rules for determining whether income is income of a DISC to which the intercompany pricing rules authorized by section 994 apply.

(b) Gross receipts test. In order for a corporation described in paragraph (a)(1) of this section to be a DISC for a taxable year, 95 percent or more of its gross receipts (as defined in § 1.993-6 for such year must consist of qualified export receipts (as defined in § 1.993-1). Gross receipts for a taxable year are determined in accordance with the method of accounting adopted by the corporation pursuant to § 1.991-1(b)(2). However, for rules regarding gross receipts in the case of a commission sale by such corporation, see § 1.993-6. See § 1.992-3 with respect to distributions to meet qualification requirements in the event the requirements of this paragraph are not satisfied for the taxable year.

(c) Assets test. *(1) In general.* In order for a corporation described in paragraph (a)(1) of this section to be a DISC for a taxable year, the adjusted basis (determined under section 1011) of its qualified export assets (as defined in § 1.993-2) at the close of such year must equal or exceed 95 percent of the sum of the adjusted bases (determined under section 1011) of all assets of such corporation at the close of such year. See § 1.992-3 with respect to distributions to meet qualification requirements in the event the requirements of this paragraph are not satisfied for the taxable year.

(2) Assets acquired to meet assets test. For purposes of determining whether the requirements of subparagraph (1) of this paragraph are satisfied by a corporation at the end of a taxable year, an asset which is a qualified export asset (as defined in § 1.993-2) is treated as not being an asset of such corporation at such time if such asset is held for a total of 60 days or less and is acquired directly or indirectly through borrowing, unless the acquisition of such asset is established to the satisfaction of the Commissioner or his delegate to have been for bona fide purposes. Such acquisition is deemed to have been for bona fide purposes if, for example, it is made in the usual course of the corporation's trade or business.

(d) Capitalization requirement. *(1) In general.* To qualify as a DISC for a taxable year, a corporation must have, on each day of that taxable year, only one class of stock. The par value (or, in the case of stock without par value, the stated value) of the corporation's outstanding stock must be on each day of the taxable year at least $2,500. In the case of a corporation which elects to be treated as a DISC for its first taxable year, the requirements of this paragraph (d)(1) are satisfied if the corporation has no more than one class of stock at any time during the year and if the par value (or, in the case of stock without par value, the stated value) of the corporation's outstanding stock is at least $2,500 on the last day of the period within which the election must be made and on each succeeding day of the year. For purposes of this paragraph (d)(1), the stated value of shares is the aggregate amount of the consideration paid for such shares which is not allotted to paid in surplus, or other surplus. The law of the State of incorporation of the DISC determines what consideration may be used to capitalize the DISC. A corporation will not be a qualified DISC unless at least $2,500 of valid consideration was used for this purpose. If a corporation has a realized or unrealized loss during a taxable year which results in the impairment of all or part of the capital required under this paragraph (d)(1), that impairment does not result in disqualification under this paragraph (d)(1), provided that the corporation does not take any legal or formal action under State law to reduce capital for that year below the amount required under this paragraph (d)(1).

(2) Treatment of debt payable to shareholders. (i) In general. Purported debt of a DISC payable to any person, whether or not such person is a shareholder or a member of a controlled group (as defined in § 1.993-1(k)) of which such DISC is a member, is treated as debt for all purposes of the Code, provided that such purported debt—

(a) Would qualify as debt for purposes of the Code if the DISC were a corporation which did not qualify as a DISC,

(b) Qualifies under subdivision (ii) of this subparagraph, or

(c) Are trade accounts payable described in subdivision (iii) of this subparagraph.

Such debt is not treated as stock, and interest payable by the DISC on such debt is treated as interest by both the DISC and the holder of such debt. Payment of the principal of such debt by a DISC does not constitute the payment of a dividend by such DISC. The provisions of this subparagraph apply for a taxable year of a DISC, even though debt described in this subparagraph would be treated as stock of the corporation if such corporation did not qualify as a DISC for such year.

(ii) Safe harbor rule. Purported debt of a DISC will in no event be treated as other than debt for purposes of subdivision (i) of this subparagraph if—

(a) It is a written obligation to pay a sum certain on or before a fixed maturity date,

(b) Interest is payable on such purported debt at an arm's length interest rate (as determined under § 1.482-2(a)(2)), expressed as a fixed dollar amount or a fixed percentage of principal,

(c) Such purported debt is not convertible into stock or into other purported debt unless such other purported debt qualifies under this subparagraph as debt of the DISC.

(d) Such purported debt does not confer voting rights upon its holder, except in the event of default thereon, and

(e) Interest and principal are paid in accordance with the terms of such purported debt or with any modification of such terms consistent with (a) through (d) of this subdivision.

The determination of whether purported debt of a DISC constitutes debt described in this subdivision is made without regard to the proportion of debt of the DISC held by any of its shareholders, to the ratio of the outstanding debt of the DISC to its equity, or to the amount of outstanding debt of such DISC. The provisions of (e) of this subdivision do not prevent the modification of the terms of a debt of a DISC where, for example, a DISC becomes unable to make timely payments of principal required under such terms, provided that such modification is consistent with (a) through (d) of this subdivision.

(iii) Trade accounts payable. Trade accounts payable of a DISC which arise in the normal course of its trade or business (such as in consideration for inventory or supplies) constitute debt of the DISC (whether or not such accounts payable are debt described in subdivision (i) (a) or (b) of this subparagraph), provided that such accounts are payable within 15 months after they arise. If such accounts are payable more than 15 months after they arise, they are debt of such DISC only if they are debt described in subdivision (i) (a) or (b) of this subparagraph.

(iv) Relation of subparagraph to other corporations. The provisions of this subparagraph generally constitute a relaxation of the ordinary rules used in determining whether purported debt of a corporation is debt or equity. This relaxation is in recognition of the principle that a corporation may qualify as a DISC even though it has relatively little capital. This relaxation does not apply with respect to purported debt of other corporations in other contexts. The provisions of subdivisions (i), (ii), and (iii) of this subparagraph apply only for taxable years for which a corporation qualifies (or is treated) as a DISC.

(3) Classes of stock.[Reserved]

(e) Election in effect. In order for a corporation to be a DISC for a taxable year, an election to be treated as a DISC must be made by such corporation pursuant to § 1.992-2 and must be in effect for such taxable year. A corporation does not become or remain a DISC solely by making such an election. A corporation is a DISC for a taxable year only if such an election is in effect for that year and the corporation also satisfies the requirements of paragraphs (a) through (d) of this section. See § 1.992-2 for rules regarding the time and manner of making such an election.

(f) Ineligible corporations. The following corporations shall not be eligible to be treated as a DISC—

(1) A corporation exempt from tax by reason of section 501,

(2) A personal holding company (as defined in section 542),

(3) A financial institution to which section 581 or 593 applies,

(4) An insurance company subject to the tax imposed by Subchapter L,

(5) A regulated investment company (as defined in section 851(a)),

(6) A China Trade Act corporation receiving the special deduction provided in section 941(a), or

(7) An electing small business corporation (as defined in section 1371(b)).

(g) Status as DISC after having filed return as a DISC. Under section 992(a)(2), notwithstanding the failure of a corporation to meet the requirements of paragraph (a) of this section for a taxable year, such corporation will be treated as a DISC for purposes of the Code for such taxable year (and, thus, will not be able to claim that it is not eligible to be a DISC) if—

(1) Such corporation files a return as a DISC for such taxable year,

(2) Such corporation does not notify the district director, more than 30 days before the expiration of the period of limitation (including extensions thereof) on assessment for underpayment of tax for such taxable year (as determined under section 6501 and the regulations thereunder), that it is not a DISC for such taxable year, and

(3) The Internal Revenue Service has not issued, within such period of limitation (including extensions thereof) on assessment for underpayment of tax for such taxable year, a notice of deficiency based on a determination that such corporation is not a DISC for such taxable year. A corporation is treated as a DISC, for all purposes, pursuant to the provisions of this paragraph for any taxable year for which it meets the requirements of this paragraph, even if such corporation is an ineligible corporation described in paragraph (f) of this section for such taxable year. Thus, for example, a corporation which is treated as a DISC for a taxable year pursuant to this paragraph is treated as a DISC for that taxable year for purposes of § 1.992-2(e)(3) (relating to the termination of a DISC election if a corporation is not a DISC for each of any 5 consecutive taxable years. If a corporation is treated as a DISC for a taxable year pursuant to this paragraph, persons who held stock of such corporation at any time during such taxable year are treated, with respect to such stock, as holders of stock in a DISC for the period or periods during which they held such stock within such taxable year.

(h) Definition of "former DISC". Under section 992(a)(3), the term "former DISC" refers to a corporation which is not a DISC for a taxable year but which was (or was treated as) a DISC for a prior taxable year. However, a corporation is not a former DISC for a taxable year unless such corporation has, at the beginning of such taxable year, undistributed previously taxed income (as defined in § 1.996-3(c) or accumulated DISC income (as defined in § 1.996-3(b)). A corporation which is a former DISC for a taxable year is a former DISC for all purposes of the Code.

T.D. 7323, 9/24/74, amend T.D. 7420, 5/19/76, T.D. 7747, 12/29/80, T.D. 7920, 11/2/83, T.D. 8371, 10/24/91.

PAR. 5. Section 1.992-1 is amended as follows:

1. At the end of paragraph (a)(7), "and" is removed; at the end of paragraph (a)(8), the period is removed and ", and" is added in its place; immediately following paragraph (a)(8) the following new paragraph (a)(9) is added to read as

set forth below; and in the concluding text of paragraph (a), the language "subparagraphs (1) through (8) of this paragraph" is removed and the language "paragraphs (a)(1), through (a)(9) of this section" is added in its place.

2. The text of paragraph (e) is redesignated as paragraph (e)(1) and new paragraph (e)(2) is added to read as set forth below.

3. A new paragraph (j) is added to read as set forth below.

Proposed § 1.992-1 Requirements of a DISC. [*For Preamble, see ¶ 151,083*]

(a) * * *

(9) Is not a member of any controlled group (as defined in section 993(a)(3) and § 1.993—1(k)) of which a FSC or a small FSC (as defined in section 992) is a member. See paragraph (j) of this section.

(e) Election in effect. *(1)* * * *

(2) Section 805(b)(1)(A) of the Tax Reform Act of 1984 provides that the last taxable year of any DISC beginning in 1984, shall end on December 31, 1984, and under § 1.921-1T(a)(1) the corporation's DISC election is also deemed revoked as of the close of business on the date. A new DISC election must be filed on Form 4876A in order for the corporation to be treated as a DISC for any taxable year beginning after December 31, 1984. See § 1.992-2(a) and (b).

* * * * *

(j) Effect on a DISC of a FSC election. *(1) General rule.* (i) Under section 992(a)(1)(E) and paragraph (a)(9) of this section, a corporation shall not be treated as a DISC for a taxable year if at any time during such taxable year such corporation is a member of a controlled group (as defined in section 993(a)(3) and § 1.993.1(k)) of which a FSC or a small FSC (as defined in section 922) is a member. For purposes of this paragraph (j), a FSC also includes a small FSC. A FSC election within a group will prevail over any DISC election within such group. Thus, no corporation can make an election to be treated as a DISC for any taxable year if on any day of such taxable year such corporation is a member of a controlled group of which a FSC is a member. Further, the election of a corporation to be treated as a DISC is terminated on the first day for which the election of another corporation to be treated as a FSC becomes effective, if at any time during the DISC's taxable year such corporations are members of the same controlled group. Except as provided in paragraph (j)(2) of this section (relating to certain corporate acquisitions and reorganizations), the termination of the DISC election on such date means that such corporation shall not be treated as a DISC for its entire taxable year which includes such date, and the corporation shall be subject to tax on its taxable income for such entire taxable year. A revocation of the corporation's DISC election under section 992(b)(3) is not required.

(ii) The following example illustrates the provisions of this paragraph (j)(1):

Example. D. a calendar year corporation, has made a proper DISC election for 1985 and succeeding years. F, a corporation having a fiscal year beginning on July 1, is a member of the same controlled group of which D is a member. On May 1, 1986, F files an election to be treated as a FSC effective for F's taxable year beginning July 1, 1986. D's DISC election is treated as terminated on July 1, 1986, and D is not a DISC for its taxable year which begins January 1, 1986, and ends on December 31, 1986. F's election to be treated as a FSC for its taxable year beginning July 1, 1986, is not affected by the termination of D's DISC election.

(2) Exception for certain acquisitions and reorganizations. (i) In the case of a DISC and a FSC described in paragraph (j)(2)(ii) of this section for a taxable year, paragraph (j)(1) of this section shall not apply, and the domestic corporation may be treated as a DISC or the foreign corporation may be treated as a FSC for a short taxable year ending on the day preceding the day the DISC and the FSC became members of the same controlled group. If the DISC election is terminated, the DISC is required to satisfy all requirements to be treated as a DISC (including the 95 percent qualified export receipts and assets requirements of section 992(a)(1)) for the short taxable year, and may satisfy those requirements by making the distributions to meet such requirements provided in section 992(c). The $10 million limitation on qualified export receipts under section 995(b)(1)(E) for the short taxable year must be pro rated on a daily basis as provided in § 1.995-8(a). If the FSC election is terminated, the FSC is required to satisfy all requirements to be treated as a FSC for the short taxable year, and if the FSC is a small FSC, the $5 million foreign trading gross receipts limitation under section 924(b)(2) for the short taxable year must be pro rated on a daily basis. The controlled group of corporations shall make its choice to terminate the election of either the DISC or the FSC by filing the short period return required for the corporation whose election as a DISC or FSC (as the case may be) is to be terminated within the due date (including extensions) prescribed by section 6072(b). If the group fails to terminate the election of either the DISC or the FSC within such period, the DISC election of the domestic corporation shall be terminated as provided by paragraph (j)(1) of this section.

(ii) A DISC and a FSC are described in this paragraph (j)(2)(ii) for a taxable year if—

(A) Both the DISC and the FSC had an immediately preceding taxable year and each was treated as a DISC and as a FSC, respectively, for such immediately preceding taxable year,

(B) The DISC and the FSC were not members of the same controlled group on the first day of the taxable year, and

(C) The DISC and the FSC became members of the same controlled group of corporations during the taxable year by reason of the acquisition, directly or indirectly, of a member of the controlled group which includes such DISC (or FSC, as the case may be) by either—

(1) A member of the controlled group which includes such FSC (or DISC, as the case may be) (thereby making the DISC and the FSC members of the same parent-subsidiary controlled group), or

(2) The 5 or fewer persons who are individuals, estates or trusts who control the corporation which controls such FSC (or DISC, as the case may be) (thereby making the DISC and the FSC members of the same brother-sister controlled group.)

(iii) The provisions of this paragraph (j)(2) may be illustrated by the following example:

Example. (i) Facts. Z corporation owns all the stock of D, a corporation which has elected to be treated as a DISC. X corporation owns all the stock of F, a corporation which has elected to be treated as a small FSC. Z, X, D and F use the calendar year as the taxable year. D was treated as a DISC, and F was treated as a small FSC, for their taxable years ending December 31, 1986. On January 1, 1987, Z and X are not members of the same controlled group. On August 1, 1987, Z purchases all of the stock of X, thereby making D and F members of the same controlled group.

(ii) Result.

(A) If the group choses to retain the small FSC and terminate the DISC, under paragraph (j)(2)(i) of this section, D is permitted to end its taxable year on July 31, 1987, and may be treated as a DISC for such short year if it satisfies the requirements of section 992(a)(1) with respect to such short taxable year. The $10 million amount under section 995(b)(1)(E) for the short taxable year is limited to $5,808,219 ($10 million × 212/365). D's DISC election is terminated on August 1, 1987. F's small FSC election and $5 million amount under section 924(b)(2) are not affected by the acquisition.

(B) Alternatively, the group could chose to retain the DISC and terminate the small FSC with the same short taxable year ending July 31, 1987. F's $5 million amount for such short year would be limited to $2,904,110 ($5 million × 212/365), and D's DISC election and $10 million amount under section 995(b)(1)(E) would not be affected by the acquisition.

§ 1.992-2 Election to be treated as a DISC.

(a) Manner and time of election. *(1) Manner.* (i) In general. A corporation can elect to be treated as a DISC for a taxable year beginning after December 31, 1971. Except as provided in paragraph (a)(1)(ii) of this section, the election is made by the corporation filing Form 4876 with the service center with which it would file its income tax return if it were subject for such taxable year to all the taxes imposed by subtitle A of the Internal Revenue Code of 1954. The form shall be signed by any person authorized to sign a corporation return under section 6062, and shall contain the information required by such form. Except as provided in paragraphs (b)(3) and (c) of this section, such election to be treated as a DISC shall be valid only if the consent of every person who is a shareholder of the corporation as of the beginning of the first taxable year for which such election is effective is on or attached to such Form 4876 when filed with the service center.

(ii) Transitional rule for corporations electing during 1972. If the first taxable year for which an election by a corporation to be treated as a DISC is a taxable year beginning after December 31, 1971, and on or before December 31, 1972, such election may be made either in the manner prescribed in subdivision (i) of this subparagraph or by filing, at the place prescribed in subdivision (i) of this subparagraph, a statement captioned "Election to be Treated as a DISC." Such statement of election shall be valid only if the consent of each shareholder is filed with the service center in the form, and at the time, prescribed in paragraph (b) of this section. Such statement shall be signed by any person authorized to sign a corporation return under section 6062 and shall include the name, address, and employer identification number (if known) of the corporation, the beginning date of the first taxable year for which the election is effective, the number of shares of stock of the corporation issued and outstanding as of the earlier of the beginning of the first taxable year for which the election is effective or the time the statement is filed, the number of shares held by each shareholder as of the earlier of such dates, and the date and place of incorporation. As a condition of the election being effective, a corporation which elects to become a DISC by filing a statement in accordance with this subdivision must furnish (to the service center with which the statement was filed) such additional information as is required by Form 4876 by March 31, 1973.

(2) Time of making election. (i) In general. In the case of a corporation making an election to be treated as a DISC for its first taxable year, such election shall be made within 90 days after the beginning of such taxable year. In the case of a corporation which makes an election to be treated as a DISC for any taxable year beginning after March 31, 1972 (other than the first taxable year of such corporation), the election shall be made during the 90-day period immediately preceding the first day of such taxable year.

(ii) Transitional rules for certain corporations electing during 1972. In the case of a corporation which makes an election to be treated as a DISC for a taxable year beginning after December 31, 1971, and on or before March 31, 1972 (other than its first taxable year), the election shall be made within 90 days after the beginning of such taxable year.

(b) Consent by shareholders. *(1) In general.* (i) Time and manner of consent. Under paragraph (a)(1)(i) of this section, subject to certain exceptions, the election to be treated as a DISC is not valid unless each person who is a shareholder as of the beginning of the first taxable year for which the election is effective signs either the statement of consent on Form 4876 or a separate statement of consent attached to such form. A shareholder's consent is binding on such shareholder and all transferees of his shares and may not be withdrawn after a valid election is made by the corporation. In the case of a corporation which files an election to become a DISC for a taxable year beginning after December 31, 1972, if a person who is a shareholder as of the beginning of the first taxable year for which the election is effective does not consent by signing the statement of consent set forth on Form 4876, such election shall be valid (except in the case of an extension of the time for filing granted under the provisions of subparagraph (3) of this paragraph or paragraph (c) of this section) only if the consent of such shareholder is attached to the Form 4876 upon which such election is made.

(ii) Form of consent. A consent other than the statement of consent set forth on Form 4876 shall be in the form of a statement which is signed by the shareholder and which sets forth (a) the name and address of the corporation and of the shareholder and (b) the number of shares held by each such shareholder as of the time the consent is made and (if the consent is made after the beginning of the corporation's taxable year for which the election is effective) as of the beginning of such year. If the consent is made by a recipient of transferred shares pursuant to paragraph (c) of this section, the statement of consent shall also set forth the name and address of the person who held such shares as of the beginning of such taxable year and the number of such shares. Consent shall be made in the following form: "I (insert name of shareholder), a shareholder of (insert name of corporation seeking to make the election) consent to the election of (insert name of corporation seeking to make the election) to be treated as a DISC under section 992(b) of the Internal Revenue Code. The consent so made by me is irrevocable and is binding upon all transferees of my shares in (insert name of corporation seeking to make the election)." The consents of all shareholders may be incorporated in one statement.

(iii) Who may consent. Where stock of the corporation is owned by a husband and wife as community property (or the income from such stock is community property), or is owned by tenants in common, joint tenants, or tenants by the entirety, each person having a community interest in such stock or the income therefrom and each tenant in common, joint tenant, and tenant by the entirety must consent to the election. The consent of a minor shall be made by his legal guardian or by his natural guardian if no legal guardian has been appointed. The consent of an estate shall be made by the executor or administrator thereof. The consent of a trust shall be made by the trustee thereof. The consent of an estate or trust having more than one executor, administrator, or trustee, may be made by any executor, administrator, or trustee, authorized to make a return of such estate or trust pursuant to section 6012(b)(5). The consent of a corporation or partnership shall be made by an officer or partner authorized pursuant to section 6062 or 6063, as the case may be, to sign the return of such corporation or partnership. In the case of a foreign person, the consent may be signed by any individual (whether or not a U.S. person) who would be authorized under sections 6061 through 6063 to sign the return of such foreign person if he were a U.S. person.

(2) Transitional rule for corporations electing during 1972. In the case of a corporation which files an election to be treated as a DISC for a taxable year beginning after December 31, 1971, and on or before December 31, 1972, such election shall be valid only if the consent of each person who is a shareholder as of the beginning of the first taxable year for which such election is effective is filed with the service center with which the election was filed within 90 days after the first day of such taxable year or within the time granted for an extension of time for filing such consent. The form of such consent shall be the same as that prescribed in subparagraph (1) of this paragraph. Such consent shall be attached to the statement of election or shall be filed separately (with such service center) with a copy of the statement of election. An extension of time for filing a consent may be granted in the manner, and subject to the conditions, described in subparagraph (3) of this paragraph.

(3) Extension of time to consent. An election which is timely filed and would be valid except for the failure to attach the consent of any shareholder to the Form 4876 upon which the election was made or to comply with the 90-day requirement in subparagraph (2) of this paragraph or paragraph (c)(1) of this section, as the case may be, will not be invalid for such reason if it is shown to the satisfaction of the service center that there was reasonable cause for the failure to file such consent, and if such shareholder files a proper consent to the election within such extended period of time as may be granted by the Internal Revenue Service. In the case of a late filing of a consent, a copy of the Form 4876 or statement of election shall be attached to such consent and shall be filed with the same service center as the election. The form of such consent shall be the same as that set forth in paragraph (b)(1)(ii) of this section. In no event can any consent be made pursuant to this paragraph on or after the last day of the first taxable year for which a corporation elects to be treated as a DISC.

(c) Consent by holder of transferred shares. *(1) In general.* If a shareholder of a corporation transfers—

(i) Prior to the first day of the first taxable year for which such corporation elects to be treated as a DISC, some or all of the shares held by him without having consented to such election, or

(ii) On or before the 90th day after the first day of the first taxable year for which such corporation elects to be treated as a DISC, some or all of the shares held by him as of the first day of such year (or if later, held by him as of the time such shares are issued) without having consented to such election, then consent may be made by any recipient of such shares on or before the 90th day after the first day of such first taxable year. If such recipient fails to file his consent on or before such 90th day, an extension of time for filing such consent may be granted in the manner, and subject to the conditions, described in paragraph (b)(3) of this section. In addition, if the transfer occurs more than 90 days after the first day of such taxable year, an extension of time for filing such consent may be granted to such recipient only if it is determined under paragraph (b)(3) of this section that an extension of time would have been granted the transferor for the filing of such consent if the transfer had not occurred. A consent which is not attached to the original Form 4876 or statement of election (as the case may be) shall be filed with the same service center as the original Form 4876 or statement of election and shall have attached a copy of such original form or statement of election. The form of such consent shall be the same as that set forth in paragraph (b)(1)(ii) of this section. For the purposes of this paragraph, a transfer of shares includes any sale, exchange, or other disposition, including a transfer by gift or at death.

(2) Requirement for the filing of an amended Form 4876 or statement of election. In any case in which a consent to a corporation's election to be treated as a DISC is made pursuant to subparagraph (1) of this paragraph, such corporation must file an amended Form 4876 or statement of election (as the case may be) reflecting all changes in ownership of shares. Such form must be filed with the same service center with which the original Form 4876 or statement of election was filed by such corporation.

(d) Effect of election. *(1) Effect on corporation.* A valid election to be treated as a DISC remains in effect (without regard to whether the electing corporation qualifies as a DISC for a particular year) until terminated by any of the methods provided in paragraph (e) of this section. While such election is in effect, the electing corporation is subject to sections 991 through 997 and other provisions of the Code applicable to DISC's for any taxable year for which it qualifies as a DISC (or is treated as qualifying as a DISC pursuant to § 1.992-1(g)). Such corporation is also subject to such provisions for any taxable year for which it is treated as a former DISC as a result of qualifying or being treated as a DISC for any taxable year for which such election was in effect.

(2) Effect on shareholders. A valid election by a corporation to be treated as a DISC subjects the shareholders of such corporation to the provisions of section 995 (relating to the taxation of the shareholders of a DISC or former DISC) and to all other provisions of the Code relating to the shareholders of a DISC or former DISC. Such provisions of the Code apply to any person who is a shareholder of a DISC or former DISC whether or not such person was a shareholder at the time the corporation elected to become a DISC.

(e) Termination of election. *(1) In general.* An election to be treated as a DISC is terminated only as provided in subparagraph (2) or (3) of this paragraph.

(2) Revocation of election. (i) Manner of revocation. An election by a corporation to be treated as a DISC may be revoked by the corporation for any taxable year of the corporation after the first taxable year for which the election is effective. Such revocation shall be made by the corporation filing a statement that the corporation revokes its election under section 992(b) to be treated as a DISC. Such statement shall indicate the corporation's name, address, employer identification number, and the first taxable year of the corporation for which the revocation is to be effective. The statement shall be signed by any person authorized to sign a cor-

poration return under section 6062. Such revocation shall be filed with the service center with which the corporation filed its election, except that, if it filed an annual information return under section 6011(e)(2), the revocation shall be filed with the service center with which it filed its last such return.

(ii) Years for which revocation is effective. If a corporation files a statement revoking its election to be treated as a DISC during the first 90 days of a taxable year (other than the first taxable year for which such election is effective), such revocation will be effective for such taxable year and all taxable years thereafter. If the corporation files a statement revoking its election to be treated as a DISC after the first 90 days of a taxable year, the revocation will be effective for all taxable years following such taxable year.

(3) Continued failure to be a DISC. If a corporation which has elected to be treated as a DISC does not qualify as a DISC (and is not treated as a DISC pursuant to § 1.992-1(g)) for each of any 5 consecutive taxable years, such election terminates and will not be effective for any taxable year after such fifth taxable year. Such termination will be effective automatically, without notice to such corporation or to the Internal Revenue Service. If, during any 5-year period for which an election is effective, the corporation should qualify as a DISC (or be treated as a DISC pursuant to § 1.992-1(g)) for a taxable year, a new 5-year period shall automatically start at the beginning of the following taxable year.

(4) Election after termination. If a corporation has made a valid election to be treated as a DISC and such election terminates in either manner described in subparagraph (2) or (3) of this paragraph, such corporation is eligible to reelect to be treated as a DISC at any time by following the procedures described in paragraphs (a) through (c) of this section. If a corporation terminates its election and subsequently reelects to be treated as a DISC, the corporation and its shareholders continue to be subject to sections 995 and 996 with respect to the period during which its first election was in effect. Thus, for example, distributions upon disqualification includible in the gross incomes of shareholders of a corporation pursuant to section 995(b)(2) continue to be so includible for taxable years for which a second election of such corporation is in effect without regard to the second election.

T.D. 7323, 9/24/74, amend T.D. 7420, 5/19/76.

PAR. 6. Section 1.992-2 is amended by removing "Form 4876" each place it appears and adding in their place the words "Form 4876A", and by revising paragraphs (a) and (b)(2) to read as follows:

Proposed § 1.992-2 Election to be treated as a DISC.
[*For Preamble, see ¶ 151,083*]

(a) Manner and time of election. *(1) Manner.* The election to be treated as a DISC is made by the corporation by filing Form 4876A (Form 4876 for taxable years beginning before January 1, 1985) with the service center with which it would file its income tax return if the corporation were subject for such taxable year to all the taxes imposed by subtitle A of the Internal Revenue Code. The Form 4876A shall be signed by any person authorized to sign the corporation's return under section 6062, and shall contain the information required by such Form. Except as provided in paragraphs (b)(3) and (c) of this section, such election to be treated as a DISC shall be valid only if the statement of consent of every person who is a shareholder of the corporation as of the beginning of the first taxable year for which such election is to be effective is made on or is attached to such Form 4876A when filed with the service center.

(2) Time for making election. In the case of a corporation making an election to be treated as a DISC for the corporation's first taxable year, the election shall be made within 90 days after the beginning of such taxable year. In the case of a corporation making an election to be treated as a DISC for a taxable year which is not the corporation's first taxable year, the election shall be made during the 90 day period immediately preceding the first day of such taxable year.

(3) Special rule for re-electing DISC status in 1985. Under section 805(b) of the Tax Reform Act of 1985, the last taxable year of any DISC beginning in 1984 ended on December 31, 1984, and under § 1.921-1T(a)(1), the corporation's election to be treated as a DISC is deemed revoked after the close of business on such date. A corporation which was a DISC on December 31, 1984, and which wishes to be treated as a DISC for its first taxable year beginning after December 31, 1984, must make a new DISC election by filing Form 4876A in accordance with the instructions thereon and in accordance with paragraph (a)(1) of this section on or before June 4, 1987. The Form 4876A is to be filed within such period with the service center with which the corporation files its DISC return.

(b) Consent by shareholders. * * *

(2) Transitional rule for certain corporations re-electing DISC status in 1985. Notwithstanding paragraph (b)(1) of this section, if the corporation was a DISC on December 31, 1984, and the corporation files its election to be treated as a DISC for the corporation's first taxable year beginning after December 31, 1984, within the time prescribed in paragraph (a)(3) of this section, the election shall be valid if the consent of each person who was a shareholder of the corporation on January 1, 1985, is filed with the service center with which the election was filed on or before December 31, 1987. The form of such consent shall be the same as that prescribed in paragraph (b)(1) of this section. A copy of the corporation's statement of election, Form 4876A, shall be attached to the consent.

* * * * *

§ 1.992-3 Deficiency distributions to meet qualification requirements.

(a) In general. A corporation which meets the requirements described in § 1.992-1 for treatment as a DISC for a taxable year, other than the 95 percent of gross receipts test described in § 1.992-1(b) or the 95-percent assets test described in § 1.992-1(c), or both tests, may nevertheless qualify as a DISC for such year by making deficiency distributions (attributable to its gross receipts other than qualified export receipts and its assets other than qualified export assets) if all of the following requirements are satisfied:

(1) The corporation distributes the amount determined under paragraph (b) of this section as a deficiency distribution. The amount of a deficiency distribution is determined without regard to the amount by which the corporation fails to meet either test.

(2) The reasonable cause requirements prescribed in paragraph (c)(1) of this section are satisfied with respect to both the corporation's failure to meet either test and its failure to make a deficiency distribution prior to the time the distribution is made.

(3) The corporation makes such deficiency distribution pro rata to all its shareholders.

(4) The corporation designates the distribution, at the time of the distribution, as a deficiency distribution, pursuant to section 992(c), to meet the qualification requirements to be a DISC. Such designation shall be in the form of a communication sent at the time of such distribution to each shareholder and to the service center with which the corporation has filed or will file its return for the taxable year to which the distribution relates. A corporation may not retroactively designate a prior distribution as a deficiency distribution to meet qualification requirements. Subject to the limitation described in paragraph (c)(3) of this section, a corporation may make a deficiency distribution with respect to a taxable year at any time after the close of such taxable year or, in the case of a deficiency distribution made on or before September 29, 1975, at any time during or after such taxable year.

See sections 246(d), 904(f), 995, and 996 for rules regarding the treatment of a deficiency distribution to meet qualification requirements by the shareholders and the corporation.

(b) Amount of deficiency distribution. *(1) In general.* In order to meet the requirements of paragraph (a) of this section, the amount of a deficiency distribution must be, if the corporation fails to meet—

(i) The 95 percent of gross receipts test, the amount determined in subparagraph (2) of this paragraph,

(ii) The 95-percent assets test, the amount determined in subparagraph (3) of this paragraph, and

(iii) Both such tests, except as provided in subparagraph (4) of this paragraph, the sum of the amounts determined in subparagraphs (2) and (3) of this paragraph.

(2) Computation of deficiency distribution to meet 95 percent of gross receipts test. (i) In general. If a corporation fails to meet the 95 percent of gross receipts test described in § 1.992-1(b) for its taxable year, the amount of the deficiency distribution required by this subparagraph is an amount equal to the sum of its taxable income (if any) from each transaction giving rise to gross receipts (as defined in § 1.993-6) which are not qualified export receipts (as defined in § 1.993-1). A corporation's taxable income from a transaction shall be the amount of such gross receipts from such transaction reduced only by (a) its cost of goods sold attributable to such gross receipts, and by (b) its expenses, losses, and other deductions properly apportioned or allocated thereto in a manner consistent with the rules set forth in § 1.861-8. For purposes of this subdivision, however, any expenses, losses, or other deductions which cannot definitely be allocated to some item or class of gross income in such manner shall not reduce such gross receipts. If the corporation is a commission agent for a principal in a transaction, the corporation's taxable income is the amount of the commission from such transaction reduced only by the amounts described in (b) of this subdivision.

(ii) Example. The provisions of this subparagraph may be illustrated by the following example:

Example. (a) X and Y are calendar year taxpayers. X, a domestic manufacturing company, owns all the stock of Y, which seeks to qualify as a DISC for 1973. During 1973, X manufactures a machine which is eligible to be export property as defined in § 1.993-3. Y is made a commission agent with respect to exporting such machine. Thereafter, during 1973 Y is considered to receive gross receipts of $100,000, as determined under section 993(f), attributable to X's sale of the machine in a manner which causes the gross receipts to be excluded receipts pursuant to section 993(a)(2) and, therefore, not qualified export receipts. Y's total gross receipts for 1973 and $1 million of which $900,000 (i.e., 90 percent) are qualified export receipts. Therefore, Y does not satisfy the 95 percent of gross receipts test for 1973 because less than 95 percent of its gross receipts are qualified exports receipts. Y has $9,000 of expenses properly apportioned or allocated to its gross income from such sale and $1,000 of other expenses which cannot definitely be allocated to some item or class of gross income, determined in a manner consistent with the rules set forth in § 1.861-8. In order to satisfy the 95 percent of gross receipts test for 1973, if the commission due from X to Y were $15,000, Y must make a deficiency distribution of $6,000 computed as follows:

Y's commission (gross income) from the transaction	$15,000
Less: Y's expenses apportioned or allocated to its gross income from the transaction	9,000
Required deficiency distribution by reason of $100,000 of gross receipts which are not qualified export receipts	6,000

(b) If the commission due from X to Y were $9,400, resulting in a net loss of $600 to Y ($9,400 to $10,000), Y must make a deficiency distribution of $400 computed as follows:

Y's commissions (gross income) from the transaction	9,400
Less: Y's expenses apportioned or allocated to its gross income from the transaction	9,000
Required deficiency distribution by reason of $100,000 of gross receipts which are not qualified export receipts	400

(c) If the commission due from X to Y were $8,500, Y would not be required to make a deficiency distribution since, under this subparagraph, there would be no taxable income attributable to gross receipts from the sale.

(3) Computation of deficiency distribution to meet 95 percent assets test. (i) In general. If a corporation fails to meet the 95 percent assets test described in § 1.992-1(c) for its taxable year, the amount of the deficiency distribution required by this subparagraph is an amount equal to the fair market value as of the last day of such taxable year of the assets which are not qualified export assets held by such corporation on such last day.

(ii) Asset held for more than 1 year. In the case of a corporation which holds continuously an asset which is not a qualified export asset at the close of more than 1 taxable year, it must distribute an amount equal to its fair market value (or, if greater, the amount determined under subparagraph (4) of this paragraph) only once if, at the close of the first such taxable year, such corporation reasonably believed that such asset was a qualified export asset. This subdivision shall not apply for any taxable year beginning after the date the corporation knows (or a reasonable man would have known) that an asset is not a qualified export asset and in order to qualify for each such year, the corporation must distribute the fair market value of such asset for each such year.

(4) Computation in the case of a failure to meet both tests as a result of a single transaction. If a corporation fails to meet both the 95 percent of gross receipts test and the 95 percent assets test for a taxable year, and if the corporation holds at the end of such year assets (other than cash or qualified export assets) which were received as proceeds of a sale or exchange during such year which resulted in gross receipts other than qualified export receipts, then the amount of the deficiency distribution required by this paragraph with

respect to such sale or exchange and assets held is the larger of the amount required by subparagraph (2) of this paragraph with respect to the sale or exchange or the amount required by subparagraph (3) of this paragraph with respect to such assets held. Thus, for example, if a corporation sells property which is not a qualified export asset for $100, receives $85 in cash and a note for $15, and derives $25 of taxable income from the sale as determined under subparagraph (2) of this paragraph, it must distribute $25. If the provisions of this subparagraph are applied with respect to assets of a DISC, (other than qualified export assets), such provisions do not apply to any property received as proceeds from a sale or exchange of such assets.

(c) Reasonable cause for failure. *(1) In general.* If for a taxable year, a corporation has failed to meet the 95 percent of gross receipts test, the 95 percent assets test, or both tests, such corporation may satisfy any such test for such year by means of a deficiency distribution in the amount determined under paragraph (b) of this section only if the reasonable cause requirements of this subparagraph are satisfied. Such reasonable cause requirements are satisfied if—

(i) There is reasonable cause (as determined in accordance with subparagraph (2) of this paragraph) for such corporation's failure to satisfy such test and to make such distribution prior to the date on which it was made, the time limit in subparagraph (3) of this paragraph for making the distribution is satisfied, and interest (if required) is paid in the amount and in the manner prescribed by subparagraph (4) of this paragraph, or

(ii) The time and "70-percent" requirements of the reasonable cause test of paragraph (d) of this section are satisfied.

(2) Determination of reasonable cause. In general, whether a corporation's failure to meet the 95 percent of gross receipts test, the 95 percent assets test, or both tests for a taxable year and its failure to make a pro rata distribution prior to the date on which it was made will be considered for reasonable cause where the action or inaction which resulted in such failure occurred in good faith, such as failure to meet the 95 percent assets test resulting from blocked currency or expropriation, or failure to meet either test because of reasonable uncertainty as to what constitutes a qualified export receipt or a qualified export asset. For further examples, if a corporation's reasonable determination of the percentage of its total gross receipts that are qualified export receipts is subsequently redetermined to be less than 95 percent as a result of a price adjustment by the Internal Revenue Service under section 482, or if the corporation has a casualty loss for which it receives an unanticipated insurance recovery which causes its qualified export receipts to be less than 95 percent of its total gross receipts, then the failure to satisfy the 95 percent of gross receipts test is considered to be due to reasonable cause.

(3) Time limit for deficiency distribution. Except as otherwise provided in this subparagraph, the time limit prescribed by this subparagraph for making a deficiency distribution is satisfied if the amount of the distribution required by paragraph (b) of this section is made within 90 days from the date of the first written notification to the corporation by the Internal Revenue Service that it had not satisfied the 95 percent of gross receipts test or the 95 percent assets test or both tests, for a taxable year. Upon a showing by the corporation that an extension of the 90-day time limit is reasonable and necessary, the Commission may grant such extension of such time limit. In any case in which a corporation contests the decision of the Internal Revenue Service that such corporation has not met the 95 percent of gross receipts test, the 95 percent assets test, or both tests, an extension of the 90-day time limit will be allowed until 30 days after the final determination of such contest. The date of the final determination of such contest shall, for purposes of section 992(c), be established in the manner specified in subdivisions (i) through (iv) of this subparagraph:

(i) The date of final determination by a decision of the United States Tax Court is the date upon which such decision becomes final, as prescribed in section 7481.

(ii) The date of final determination in a case which is contested in a court (and upon which there is a judgment) other than the Tax Court is the date upon which the judgment becomes final and will be determined on the basis of the facts and circumstances of each particular case. For example, ordinarily a judgment of a United States district court becomes final upon the expiration of the time allowed for taking an appeal, if no such appeal is duly taken within such time; and a judgment of the United States Court of Claims becomes final upon the expiration of the time allowed for filing a petition for certiorari if no such petition is duly filed within such time.

(iii) The date of a final determination by a closing agreement, made under section 7121, is the date such agreement is approved by the Commissioner.

(iv) A final determination under section 992(c) may be made by an agreement signed by the district director or director of the service center with which the corporation files its annual return or by such other official to which authority to sign has been delegated, and by or on behalf of the taxpayer. The agreement shall set forth the total amount of the deficiency distribution to be paid to the shareholders of the DISC for the taxable year or years. An agreement under this subdivision shall be sent to the taxpayer at his last known address by either registered or certified mail. For further guidance regarding the definition of last known address, see § 301.6212-2 of this chapter. If registered mail is used for such purpose, the date of registration is considered the date of final determination; if certified mail is used for such purpose, the date of postmark on the sender's receipt for such mail is considered the date of final determination. If the corporation makes a deficiency distribution before such registration or postmark date but on or after the date the district director or director of the service center or other official has signed the agreement, the date of signature by the district director or director of the service center or other official is considered the date of final determination. If the corporation makes a deficiency distribution before the district director or director of the service center or other official signs the agreement, the date of final determination is considered to be the date of the making of the deficiency distribution. During any extension of time the interest charge provided in subparagraph (4) of this paragraph will continue to accrue at the rate provided for in such subparagraph.

(4) Payment of interest for delayed distribution. (i) In general. If a corporation makes a deficiency distribution after the 15th day of the ninth month after the close of the taxable year with respect to which such distribution is made, such distribution will not be deemed to satisfy the 95 percent of gross receipts test or the 95 percent assets test for such year unless such corporation pays to the Internal Revenue Service a charge determined by multiplying (a) an amount equal to 4½ percent of such distribution by (b) the number of its taxable years which begin (l) after the taxable year with respect to which the distribution is made and (2) before such distribution is made. Such charge must be paid, within the 30-day

period beginning with the day on which such distribution is made, to the service center with which the corporation files its annual information return for its taxable year in which the distribution is made. For purposes of the Internal Revenue Code, such charge is considered interest.

(ii) Example. The provisions of subdivision (i) of this subparagraph may be illustrated by the following example:

Example. X corporation, which uses the calendar year as its taxable year, meets the 95 percent assets test but fails to meet the 95 percent of gross receipts test for 1972 and does not by September 15, 1973, make the deficiency distribution required by reason of its failure to meet such test. Assume that reasonable cause exists for the corporation's failure to meet the 95 percent of gross receipts test and failure to make the required deficiency distribution. If X makes the required deficiency distribution, in the amount of $10,000, on April 1, 1976, X must pay on or before April 30, 1976, to the service center with which it files its annual information return a charge of $1,800, computed as follows:

Deficiency distribution made by X	$10,000
Multiplied by 4½ percent	.045
Intermediate product	450
Multiplied by: Number of X's taxable years beginning after 1972 and before April 1, 1976	4
Charge to be paid service center because of late deficiency distribution (which is considered interest)	1,800

(d) Certain distributions deemed for reasonable cause. If a corporation makes a distribution in the amount required by paragraph (b) of this section with respect to a taxable year on or before the 15th day of the ninth month after the close of such year, it will be deemed to have acted with reasonable cause with respect to its failure to satisfy the 95 percent of gross receipts test, the 95 percent assets test, or both tests, for such year and its failure to make such distribution prior to the date on which the distribution was made if—

(1) At least 70 percent of the gross receipts of such corporation for such taxable year consist of qualified export receipts, and

(2) The sum of the adjusted bases of the qualified export assets held by such corporation on the last day of each month of the taxable year equals or exceeds 70 percent of the sum of the adjusted bases of all assets held by the corporation on each such day.

T.D. 7323, 9/24/74, amend T.D. 7420, 5/19/76, T.D. 7854, 11/16/82, T.D. 8939, 1/11/2001.

§ 1.992-4 Coordination with personal holding company provisions in case of certain produced film rents.

(a) In general. Section 992(d)(2) provides that a personal holding company is not eligible to be treated as a DISC. Section 543(a)(5)(B) provides that, for purposes of section 543, the term "produced film rents" means payments received with respect to an interest in a film for the use of, or the right to use, such film, but only to the extent that such interest was acquired before substantial completion of production of such film. Under section 992(e), if such produced film rents are included in the ordinary gross income (as defined in section 543(b)(1)) of a qualified subsidiary for a taxable year of such subsidiary, and such interest was acquired by such subsidiary from its parent, such interest is deemed (for purposes of the application of sections 541, 543(b)(1), and 992(d)(2), and § 1.992-1(f) for such taxable year) to have been acquired by such subsidiary at the time such interest was acquired by such parent. Thus, for example, if a parent acquires an interest in a film before it is substantially completed, then substantially completes such film prior to transferring an interest in such motion picture to a qualified subsidiary, the qualified subsidiary is considered as having acquired such interest prior to substantial completion of such motion picture for purposes of determining whether payments from the rental of such motion picture will be classified as produced film rents of such subsidiary. The provisions of section 992(e) and this section are not applicable in determining whether payments received with respect to an interest in a film are included in the ordinary gross income of a parent or a qualified subsidiary. Thus, even though a qualified subsidiary is treated pursuant to this section as having acquired an interest in a film at the time such interest was acquired by such subsidiary's parent, payments received by such parent with respect to such interest prior to the transfer of such interest to such subsidiary are includible in the ordinary gross income of such parent and not includible in the ordinary gross income of such subsidiary.

(b) Definitions. *(1) "Qualified subsidiary".* For purposes of this section, a corporation is a qualified subsidiary for a taxable year if—

(i) Such corporation was established for the purpose of becoming a DISC,

(ii) Such corporation would qualify (or be treated) as a DISC for such taxable year if it is not a personal holding company, and

(iii) On every day of such taxable year on which shares of such corporation are outstanding, at least 80 percent of such shares are held directly by a second corporation.

(2) "Parent". For purposes of this section, the term "parent" means a second corporation referred to in subparagraph (1)(iii) of this paragraph.

T.D. 7323, 9/24/74.

§ 1.993-1 Definition of qualified export receipts.

(a) In general. For a corporation to qualify as a DISC, at least 95 percent of its gross receipts for a taxable year must consist of qualified export receipts. Under section 933(a), the term "qualified export receipts" means any of the eight amounts described in paragraphs (b) through (i) of this section, except to the extent that any of the eight amounts is an excluded receipt within the meaning of paragraph (j) of this section. For purposes of this section and §§ 1.993-2 through 1.993-6—

(1) DISC. All references to a DISC mean a DISC, except when the context indicates that such term means a corporation in the process of meeting the conditions necessary for that corporation to become a DISC, or a corporation being tested as to whether it qualifies as a DISC.

(2) Sale, lease, and license. The term "sale" includes an exchange or other disposition and the term "lease" includes a rental or a sublease. The term "license" includes a sublicense. All rules under this section and §§ 1.993-2 through 1.993-6 applicable to leases of export property apply in the same manner to licenses of export property. See § 1.993-3(f)(3) for a description of intangible property which cannot be export property.

(3) Gross receipts. The term "gross receipts" is defined by section 993(f) and § 1.993-6.

(4) Qualified export assets. The term "qualified export assets" is defined by section 993(b) and § 1.993-2.

(5) Export property. The term "export property" is defined by section 993(c) and § 1.993-3.

(6) Related person. The term "related person" means a person who is related to another person if either immediately before or after a transaction—

(i) The relationship between such persons would result in a disallowance of losses under section 267 (relating to disallowance of losses, etc., between related taxpayers), or section 707(b) (relating to losses disallowed, etc., between partners and controlled partnerships), and the regulations thereunder, or

(ii) Such persons are members of the same controlled group of corporations, as defined in section 1563(a) (relating to definition of controlled group of corporations), except that (a) "more than 50 percent" shall be substituted for "at least 80 percent" each place it appears in section 1563(a) and the regulations thereunder, and (b) the provisions of section 1563(b) shall not apply in determining whether such persons are members of the same controlled group.

(7) Related supplier. The term "related supplier" is defined by § 1.994-1(a)(3)(ii).

(8) Controlled group. The term "controlled group" is defined by paragraph (k) of this section.

(b) Sales of export property. Qualified export receipts of a DISC include gross receipts from the sale of export property by such DISC, or by any principal for whom such DISC acts as a commission agent (whether or not such principal is a related supplier), pursuant to the terms of a contract entered into with a purchaser by such DISC or by such principal at any time or by any other person and assigned to such DISC or such principal at any time prior to the shipment of such property to the purchaser. Any agreement, oral or written, which constitutes a contract at law, satisfies the contractual requirement of this paragraph. Gross receipts from the sale of export property, whenever received, do not constitute qualified export receipts unless the seller (or the corporation acting as commission agent for the seller) is a DISC at the time of the shipment of such property to the purchaser.

For example, if a corporation which sells export property under the installment method is not a DISC for the taxable year in which the property is shipped to the purchaser, gross receipts from such sale do not constitute qualified export receipts for any taxable year of the corporation.

(c) Leases of export property. *(1) In general.* Qualified export receipts of a DISC include gross receipts from the lease of export property provided that—

(i) Such property is held by such DISC (or by a principal for whom such DISC acts as commission agent with respect to the lease) either as an owner or lessee at the beginning of the term of such lease, and

(ii) Such DISC qualified (or was treated) as a DISC for its taxable year in which the term of such lease began.

(2) Prepayment of lease receipts. If part or all of the gross receipts from a lease of property are prepaid, then—

(i) All such prepaid gross receipts are qualified export receipts of a DISC if it is reasonably expected at the time of such prepayment that throughout the term of such lease they would be qualified export receipts if received not as a prepayment; or

(ii) If it is reasonably expected at the time of such prepayment that throughout the term of such lease they would not be qualified export receipts if received not as a prepayment, then only those prepaid receipts, for the taxable years of the DISC for which they would be qualified export receipts, are qualified export receipts.

Thus, for example, if a lessee makes a prepayment of the first and last years' rent, and it is reasonably expected that the leased property will be export property for the first half of the lease period but not the second half of such period, the amount of the prepayment which represents the first year's rent will be considered qualified export receipts if it would otherwise qualify, whereas the amount of the prepayment which represents the last year's rent will not be considered qualified export receipts.

(d) Related and subsidiary services. *(1) In general.* Qualified export receipts of a DISC include gross receipts from services furnished by such DISC which are related and subsidiary to any sale or lease (as described in paragraph (b) or (c) of this section) of export property by such DISC or with respect to which such DISC acts as a commission agent, provided that such DISC derives qualified export receipts from such sale or lease. Such services may be performed within or without the United States.

(2) Services furnished by DISC. Services are considered to be furnished by a DISC for purposes of this paragraph if such services are provided by—

(i) The person who sold or leased the export property to which such services are related and subsidiary, provided that the DISC acts as a commission agent with respect to the sale or lease of such property and with respect to such services,

(ii) The DISC as principal, or any other person pursuant to a contract between such person and such DISC, provided the DISC acted as principal or commission agent with respect to the sale or lease of such property, or

(iii) A member of the same controlled group as the DISC where the sale or lease of the export property is made by another member of such controlled group provided, however, that the DISC act as principal or commission agent with respect to such sale or lease and as commission agent with respect to such services.

(3) Related services. A service is related to a sale or lease of export property if—

(i) Such service is of the type customarily and usually furnished with the type of transaction in the trade or business in which such sale or lease arose and

(ii) The contract to furnish such service—

(a) Is expressly provided for in or is provided for by implied warranty under the contract of sale or lease,

(b) Is entered into on or before the date which is 2 years after the date on which the contract under which such sale or lease was entered into, provided that the person described in subparagraph (2) of this paragraph which is to furnish such service delivers to the purchaser or lessor a written offer or option to furnish such services on or before the date on which the first shipment of goods with respect to which the service is to be performed is delivered, or

(c) Is a renewal of the services contract described in (a) or (b) of this subdivision. Services which may be related to a sale or lease of export property include but are not limited to warranty service, maintenance service, repair service, and installation service. Transportation (including insurance related to such transportation) may be related to a sale or lease of export property, provided that the cost of such transportation is included in the sale price or rental of the property or, if such cost is separately stated, is paid by the DISC (or its principal) which sold or leased the property to the person furnishing the transportation service. Financing or the obtaining of financing for a sale or lease is not a related service for purposes of this paragraph.

(4) Subsidiary services. (i) In general. Services related to a sale or lease of export property are subsidiary to such sale or lease only if it is reasonably expected at the time of such sale or lease that the gross receipts from all related services furnished by the DISC (as defined in subparagraphs (2) and (3) of this paragraph) will not exceed 50 percent of the sum of (a) the gross receipts from such sale or lease and (b) the gross receipts from related services furnished by the DISC (as described in subparagraph (2) of this paragraph). In the case of a sale, reasonable expectations at the time of the sale are based on the gross receipts from all related services which may reasonably be expected to be performed at any time before the end of the 10-year period following the date of such sale. In the case of a lease, reasonable expectations at the time of the lease are based on the gross receipts from all related services which may reasonably be expected to be performed at any time before the end of the term of such lease (determined without regard to renewal options).

(ii) Allocation of gross receipts from services. In determining whether the services related to a sale or lease of export property are subsidiary to such sale or lease, the gross receipts to be treated as derived from the furnishing of services may not be less than the amount of gross receipts reasonably allocated to such services as determined under the facts and circumstances of each case without regard to whether—

(a) Such services are furnished under a separate contract or under the same contract pursuant to which such sale or lease occurs or

(b) The cost of such services is specified in the contract of sale or lease.

(iii) Transactions involving more than one item of export property. If more than one item of export property is sold or leased in a single transaction pursuant to one contract, the total gross receipts from such transaction and the total gross receipts from all services related to such transaction are each taken into account in determining whether such services are subsidiary to such transaction. However, the provisions of this subdivision apply only if such items could be included in the same product line, as determined under § 1.994-1(c)(7).

(iv) Renewed service contracts. If under the terms of a contract for related services, such contract is renewable within 10 years after a sale of export property, or during the term of a lease of export property, related services to be performed under the renewed contract are subsidiary to such sale or lease if it is reasonably expected at the time of such renewal that the gross receipts from all related services which have been and which are to be furnished by the DISC (as described in subparagraph (2) of this paragraph) will not exceed 50 percent of the sum of (a) the gross receipts from such sale or lease and (b) the gross receipts from related services furnished by the DISC (as so described). Reasonable expectations are determined as provided in subdivision (i) of this subparagraph.

(v) Parts used in services. If a services contract described in subparagraph (3) of this paragraph provides for the furnishing of parts in connection with the furnishing of related services, gross receipts from the furnishing of such parts are not taken into account in determining whether under this subparagraph the services are subsidiary. See paragraph (b) or (c) of this section to determine whether the gross receipts from the furnishing of parts constitute qualified export receipts. See § 1.993-3(c)(2)(iv) and (e)(3) for rules regarding the treatment of such parts with respect to the manufacture of export property and the foreign content of such property, respectively.

(5) Relation to leases. If the gross receipts for services which are related and subsidiary to a lease of property have been prepaid at any time for all such services which are to be performed before the end of the term of such lease, then as of the time of the prepayment the rules in paragraph (c)(2) of this section (relating to prepayment of lease receipts) will determine whether prepaid services under this subdivision are qualified export receipts. Thus, for example, if it is reasonably expected that leased property will be export property for the first year of the term of the lease but will not be export property for the second year of the term, prepaid gross receipts for related and subsidiary services to be furnished in the first year may be qualified export receipts. However, any prepaid gross receipts for such services to be furnished in the second year cannot be qualified export receipts.

(6) Relation with export property determination. The determination as to whether gross receipts from the sale or lease of export property constitute qualified export receipts does not depend upon whether services connected with such sale or lease are related and subsidiary to such sale or lease. Thus, for example, assume that a DISC receives gross receipts of $1,000 from the sale of export property and gross receipts of $1,100 from installation and maintenance services which are to be furnished by such DISC within 10 years after the sale and which are related to such sale. The $1,100 which the DISC receives for such services would not be qualified export receipts since the gross receipts from the services exceed 50 percent of the sum of the gross receipts from the sale and the gross receipts from the related services furnished by such DISC. The $1,000 which the DISC receives from the sale of export property would, however, be a qualified export receipt if the sale met the requirements of paragraph (b) of this section.

(e) Gains from sales of certain qualified export assets. Qualified export receipts of a DISC include gross receipts from the sale by such DISC of any assets (wherever located) which, as of the date of such sale, are qualified export assets as defined in § 1.993-2 even though such assets are not export property (as defined in § 1.993-3). Gross receipts are derived from the sale of such assets only where such sale results in recognized gain (see § 1.993-6(a)). For purposes of this paragraph, losses from the sale of such qualified export assets shall not be taken into account for purposes of determining the DISC's qualified export receipts.

(f) Dividends. Qualified export receipts of a DISC for a taxable year include all dividends includible in the gross income of such DISC for such taxable year with respect to the stock of related foreign export corporations (as defined in § 1.993-5) and all amounts includible in the gross income of such DISC with respect to such corporations pursuant to section 951 (relating to amounts included in the gross income of U.S. shareholders of controlled foreign corporations).

(g) Interest on obligations which are qualified export assets. Qualified export receipts of a DISC include interest on any obligation which is a qualified export asset of such DISC, including any amount includible in gross income as interest (such as, for example, an amount treated as original issue discount pursuant to section 1232) or as imputed interest under section 483. Gain from the sale of obligations described in this paragraph is treated (to the extent such gain is not treated as interest on such obligations) as qualified export receipts pursuant to paragraph (e) of this section.

(h) Engineering and architectural services. *(1) In general.* Qualified export receipts of a DISC include gross receipts from engineering services (as described in subparagraph (5) of this paragraph) or architectural services (as described in subparagraph (5) of this paragraph) or architectural services (as described in subparagraph (6) of this paragraph) furnished by such DISC (as described in subparagraph (7) of this paragraph) for a construction project (as defined in subparagraph (8) of this paragraph) located, or proposed for location, outside the United States. Such services may be performed within or without the United States.

(2) Services included. Engineering and architectural services include feasibility studies for a proposed construction project whether or not such project is ultimately initiated.

(3) Excluded services. Engineering and architectural services do not include—

(i) Services connected with the exploration for minerals or

(ii) Technical assistance or know-how.

For purposes of this paragraph, the term "technical assistance or know-how" includes activities or programs designed to enable business, commerce, industrial establishments, and governmental organizations to acquire or use scientific, architectural, or engineering information.

(4) Other services. Receipts from the performance of construction activities other than engineering and architectural services constitute qualified export receipts to the extent that such activities are related and subsidiary services (within the meaning of paragraph (d) of this section) with respect to a sale or lease of export property.

(5) Engineering services. For purposes of this paragraph, engineering services in connection with any construction project (within the meaning of subparagraph (8) of this paragraph) include any professional services requiring engineering education, training, and experience and the application of special knowledge of the mathematical, physical, or engineering sciences to such professional services as consultation, investigation, evaluation, planning, design, or responsible supervision of construction for the purpose of assuring compliance with plans, specifications, and design.

(6) Architectural services. For purposes of this paragraph, architectural services include the offering or furnishing of any professional services such as consultation, planning, aesthetic, and structural design, drawings and specifications, or responsible supervision of construction (for the purpose of assuring compliance with plans, specifications, and design) or erection, in connection with any construction project (within the meaning of subparagraph (8) of this paragraph).

(7) Definition of "furnished by such DISC". For purposes of this paragraph, architectural and engineering services are considered furnished by a DISC if such services are provided—

(i) by the DISC,

(ii) By another person (whether or not a United States person) pursuant to a contract entered into by such person with the DISC at any time prior to the furnishing of such services, provided that the DISC acts as principal with respect to the furnishing of such services, or

(iii) By another person (whether or not a United States person) pursuant to a contract for the furnishing of such services entered into at any time prior to the furnishing of such services provided that the DISC acts as commission agent with respect to such services.

(8) Definition of "construction project". For purposes of this paragraph, the term "construction project" includes the erection, expansion, or repair (but not including minor remodeling or minor repairs) of new or existing buildings or other physical facilities including, for example, roads, dams, canals, bridges, tunnels, railroad tracks, and pipelines. The term also includes site grading and improvement and installation of equipment necessary for the construction. Gross receipts from the sale or lease of construction equipment are not qualified export receipts unless such equipment is export property (as defined in § 1.993-3).

(i) Managerial services. *(1) In general.* Qualified export receipts of a first DISC for its taxable year include gross receipts from the furnishing of managerial services provided for another DISC, which is not a related person, to aid such unrelated DISC in deriving qualified export receipts, provided that at least 50 percent of the gross receipts of the first DISC for such year consists of qualified export receipts derived from the sale or lease of export property and the furnishing of related and subsidiary services, as described in paragraphs (b), (c), and (d) of this section, respectively.

For purposes of this paragraph, managerial services are considered furnished by a DISC if such services are provided—

(i) By the first DISC,

(ii) By another person (whether or not a United States person) pursuant to a contract entered into by such person with the first DISC at any time prior to the furnishing of such services, provided that the first DISC acts as principal with respect to the furnishing of such services, or

(iii) By another person (whether or not a United States person) pursuant to a contract for the furnishing of such services entered into at any time prior to the furnishing of such services provided that the DISC acts as commission agent with respect to such service and provided further that such contract between a DISC and a related supplier (as defined in § 1.994-1(a)(3)) qualifies as a supplier's agreement under § 1.993-1(l)(1).

(2) Definition of "managerial services". The term "managerial services" as used in this paragraph means activities relating to the operation of another unrelated DISC which derives qualified export receipts from the sale or lease of export property and from the furnishing of services related and subsidiary to such sales or leases. Such term includes staffing and operational services necessary to operate such other DISC, but does not include legal, accounting, scientific, or technical services. Examples of managerial services are: (i) Export market studies, (ii) making shipping arrangements, and (iii) contracting potential foreign purchasers.

(3) Status of recipient of managerial services. (i) In general. Qualified export receipts of a first DISC include receipts from the furnishing of managerial services during any taxable year of a recipient if such recipient qualifies as a DISC (within the meaning of § 1.992-1(a)) for such taxable year.

(ii) Recipient deemed to qualify as a DISC. For purposes of subdivision (i) of this subparagraph, a recipient is deemed to qualify as a DISC for its taxable year if the first DISC obtains from such recipient a copy of such recipient's election to be treated as a DISC as described in § 1.992-2(a) together with such recipient's sworn statement that such election has been filed with the Internal Revenue Service Center. The recipient may mark out the names of its shareholders on a copy of its election to be treated as a DISC before submitting it to the first DISC. The copy of the election and the sworn statement of such recipient must be received by the first DISC within 6 months after the beginning of the first taxable year of the recipient during which such first DISC furnishes managerial services for such recipient. The copy of the election and the sworn statement of the recipient need not be obtained by the first DISC for subsequent taxable years of the recipient.

(iii) Recipient not treated as a DISC. For purposes of subdivision (i) of this subparagraph, a recipient of managerial services is not treated as a DISC with respect to such services performed during a taxable year for which such recipient does not qualify as a DISC if the DISC performing such services does not believe or if a reasonable person would not believe (taking into account the furnishing DISC's managerial relationship with such recipient DISC) at the beginning of such taxable year that the recipient will qualify as a DISC for such taxable year.

(j) Excluded receipts. *(1) In general.* Notwithstanding the provisions of paragraphs (b) through (i) of this section, qualified export receipts of a DISC do not include any of the five amounts described in subparagraphs (2) through (6) of this paragraph.

(2) Sales and leases of property for ultimate use in the United States. Property which is sold or leased for ultimate use in the United States does not constitute export property. See § 1.993-3(d)(4) (relating to determination of where the ultimate use of the property occurs). Thus, qualified export receipts of a DISC described in paragraph (b) or (c) of this section do not include gross receipts of the DISC from the sale or lease of such property.

(3) Sales of export property accomplished by subsidy. Qualified export receipts of a DISC do not include gross receipts described in paragraph (b) of this section if the sale of export property (whether or not such property consists of agricultural products) is pursuant to any of the following:

(i) The development loan program, or grants under the technical cooperation and development grants program of the Agency for International Development, or grants under the military assistance program administered by the Department of Defense, pursuant to the Foreign Assistance Act of 1961, as amended (22 U.S.C. 2151), unless the DISC shows to the satisfaction of the district director that, under the conditions existing at the time of the sale, the purchaser had a reasonable opportunity to purchase, on competitive terms and from a seller who was not a U.S. person, goods which were substantially identical to such property and which were not manufactured, produced, grown, or extracted (as described in § 1.993-3(c)) in the United States,

(ii) The Public Law 480 program authorized under Title I of the Agricultural Trade Development and Assistance Act of 1954, as amended (7 U.S.C. 1691, 1701–1710),

(iii) For taxable years ending before January 1, 1974, the Barter program of the Commodity Credit Corporation authorized by section 4(h) of the Commodity Credit Corporation Charter Act, as amended (15 U.S.C. 714b(h)), and section 303 of the Agricultural Trade Development and Assistance Act of 1954, as amended (7 U.S.C. 1692) but only if the taxpayer treats such sales as sales giving rise to excluded receipts,

(iv) The Export Payment program of the Commodity Credit Corporation authorized by sections 5(d) and (f) of the Commodity Credit Corporation Charter Act, as amended (15 U.S.C. 714c(d) and (f)),

(v) The section 32 export payment programs authorized by section 32 of the Act of August 24, 1935, as amended (7 U.S.C. 612c), and

(vi) For taxable years beginning after November 3, 1972, the Export Sales program of the Commodity Credit Corporation authorized by sections 5(d) and (f) of the Commodity Credit Corporation Charter Act, as amended (15 U.S.C. 714c(d) and (f)), other than the GSM-4 program provided under 7 CFR 1488, and section 407 of the Agricultural Act of 1949, as amended (7 U.S.C. 1427), for the purpose of disposing of surplus agricultural commodities and exporting or causing to be exported agricultural commodities, except that for taxable years beginning on or before November 3, 1972, the taxpayer may treat such sales as sales giving rise to excluded receipts.

(4) Sales or leases of export property and furnishing of engineering or architectural services for use by the United States. (i) In general. Qualified export receipts of a DISC do not include gross receipts described in paragraph (b), (c), or (h) of this section if a sale or lease of export property, or the furnishing of engineering or architectural services, is for use by the United States or an instrumentality thereof in any case in which any law or regulation requires in any manner the purchase or lease of property manufactured, produced, grown, or extracted in the United States or requires the use of engineering or architectural services performed by a U.S. person. For example, a sale by a DISC of export property to the Department of Defense for use outside the United States would not produce qualified export receipts for such DISC if the Department of Defense purchased such property from appropriated funds subject to any provisions of the Armed Services Procurement Regulations (32 CFR Subchapter A, Part 6, Subpart A) or any appropriations act for the Department of Defense for the applicable year which restricts the availability of such appropriated funds to the procurement of items which are grown, reprocessed, reused, or produced in the United States.

(ii) Direct or indirect sales or leases. Any sale or lease of export property is for use by the United States or an instrumentality thereof if such property is sold or leased by a DISC (or by a principal for whom such DISC acts as a commission agent) to—

(a) A person who is a related person with respect to such DISC or such principal and who sells or leases such property for use by the United States or an instrumentality thereof or

(b) A person who is not a related person with respect to such DISC or such principal if, at the time of such sale or lease, there is an agreement or understanding that such property will be sold or leased for use by the United States or an instrumentality thereof (or if a reasonable person would have known at the time of such sale or lease that such property would be sold or leased for use by the United States or an instrumentality thereof) within 3 years after such sale or lease.

(iii) Excluded programs. The provisions of subdivisions (i) and (ii) of this subparagraph do not apply in the case of a purchase by the United States or an instrumentality thereof if such purchase is pursuant to—

(a) The Foreign Military Sales Act, as amended (22 U.S.C. 2751 *et seq.*), or a program under which the U.S. Government purchases property for resale, on commercial terms, to a foreign government or agency or instrumentality thereof, or

(b) A program (whether bilateral or multi-lateral) under which sales to the U.S. Government are open to international competitive bidding.

(5) Services. Qualified export receipts of a DISC do not include gross receipts described in paragraph (d) of this section (concerning related and subsidiary services) if the services from which such gross receipts are derived are related and subsidiary to the sale or lease of property which results in excluded receipts pursuant to this paragraph.

(6) Receipts within controlled group. (i) In general. Gross receipts of a corporation do not constitute qualified export receipts for any taxable year of such corporation if—

(a) At the time of the sale, lease, or other transaction resulting in such gross receipts, such corporation and the person from whom such receipts are directly or indirectly derived (whether or not such corporation and such person are the same person) are members of the same controlled group (as defined in paragraph (k) of this section) and

(b) Such corporation and such person each qualifies (or is treated under section 992(a)(2)) as a DISC for its taxable year in which its receipts arise.

Thus, for example, assume that R, S, X, and Y are members of the same controlled group and that X and Y are DISC's. If R sells property to S and pays X a commission relating to that sale and if S sells the same property to an unrelated foreign party and pays Y a commission relating to that sale, the receipts received by X from the sale of such property by R to S will be considered to be derived from Y, a DISC which is a member of the same controlled group as X, and thus will not result in qualified export receipts to X. The receipts received by Y from the sale to an unrelated foreign party may, however, result in qualified export receipts to Y. For another example, if R and S both assign the commissions to X, receipts derived from the sale from R to S will be considered to be derived from X acting as commission agent for S and will not result in qualified export receipts to X. Receipts derived by X from the sale of property by S to an unrelated foreign party, may, however, constitute qualified export receipts.

(ii) Leased property. See § 1.993-3(f)(2) regarding property not constituting export property in certain cases where such property is leased to any corporation which is a member of the same controlled group as the lessor.

(k) Definition of "controlled group". For purposes of sections 991 through 996 and the regulations thereunder, the term "controlled group" has the same meaning as is assigned to the term "controlled group of corporations" by section 1563(a), except that (1) the phrase "more than 50 percent" is substituted for the phrase "at least 80 percent" each place the latter phrase appears in section 1563(a), and (2) section 1563(b) shall not apply. Thus, for example, a foreign corporation subject to tax under section 881 may be a member of a controlled group. Furthermore, two or more corporations (including a foreign corporation) are members of a controlled group at any time such corporations meet the requirements of section 1563(a) (as modified by this paragraph).

(l) DISC's entitlement to income. *(1) Application of section 994.* A corporation which meets the requirements of § 1.992-1(a) to be treated as a DISC for a taxable year is entitled to income, and the intercompany pricing rules of section 994(a)(1) or (2) apply, in the case of any transactions described in § 1.994-1(b) between such DISC and its related supplier (as defined in § 1.994-1(a)(3)). For purposes of this subparagraph, such DISC need not have employees or perform any specific function.

(2) Other transactions. In the case of a transaction to which the provisions of subparagraph (1) of this paragraph do not apply but from which a DISC derives gross receipts, the income to which the DISC is entitled as a result of the transaction is determined pursuant to the terms of the contract for such transaction and, if applicable, section 482 and the regulations thereunder.

(3) Examples. The provisions of this paragraph may be illustrated by the following examples:

Example (1). P Corporation forms S Corporation as a wholly-owned subsidiary. S qualifies as a DISC for its taxable year. S has no employees on its payroll. S is granted a franchise with respect to specified exports of P. P will sell such exports to S for resale by S. Such exports are of a type which produce qualified export receipts as defined in paragraph (b) of this section. P's sales force will solicit orders in the name of S using S's order forms. S places orders with P only when S itself has received orders. No inventory is maintained by S. P makes shipments directly to customers of S. Employees of P will act for S and billings and collections will be handled by P in the name of S. Under these facts, the income derived by S for such taxable year from the purchase and resale of the specified export is treated for Federal income tax purposes as the income of S, and the amount of income allocable to S will be determined under section 994 of the Code.

Example (2). P Corporation forms S Corporation as a wholly-owned subsidiary. S qualifies as a DISC for its taxable year. S has no employees on its payroll. S is granted a sales franchise with respect to specified exports of P and will receive commissions with respect to such exports. Such exports are of a type which will produce gross receipts for S which are qualified export receipts as defined in paragraph (b) of this section. P's sales force will solicit orders in the name of P. Billings and collections are handled directly by P. Under these facts, the commissions paid to S for such taxable year with respect to the specified exports shall be treated for Federal income tax purposes as the income of S, and the amount of income allocable to S is determined under section 994 of the Code.

T.D. 7514, 10/14/77, amend T.D. 7854, 11/16/82.

PAR. 18. In § 1.993-1, paragraph (g) is amended by removing the phrase "section 1232" and adding in its place the phrase "section 1272".

Proposed § 1.993-1 Definition of qualified export receipts [Amended]. [*For Preamble, see ¶ 151,065*]

§ 1.993-2 Definition of qualified export assets.

(a) In general. For a corporation to qualify as a DISC, at the close of its taxable year it must have qualified export assets with adjusted bases equal to at least 95 percent of the sum of the adjusted bases of all its assets. An asset which is a qualified export asset under more than one paragraph of this section shall be taken into account only once in determining the sum of the adjusted bases of all qualified export assets. Under section 993(b), the qualified export assets held by a corporation are—

(1) Export property as defined in § 1.993-3 (see paragraph (b) of this section),

(2) Business assets described in paragraph (c) of this section,

(3) Trade receivables described in paragraph (d) of this section,

(4) Temporary investments to the extent described in paragraph (e) of this section,

(5) Producer's loans as defined in § 1.993-4 (see paragraph (f) of this section),

(6) Stock or securities (described in paragraph (g) of this section) of related foreign export corporations as defined in § 1.993-5,

(7) Export-Import Bank and other obligations described in paragraph (h) of this section,

(8) Financing obligations described in paragraph (i) of this section, and

(9) Funds awaiting investment described in paragraph (j) of this section.

(b) Export property. In general, export property is certain property held for sale or use which meets the requirements of § 1.993-3.

(c) Business assets. For purposes of this section, business assets are assets used by a DISC (other than as a lessor) primarily in connection with—

(1) The sale, lease, storage, handling, transportation, packaging, assembly, or servicing of export property, or

(2) The performance of engineering or architectural services (described in § 1.993-1(h)) or managerial services (described in § 1.993-1(i)) in furtherance of the production of qualified export receipts.

Assets used primarily in the manufacture, production, growth, or extraction (within the meaning of § 1.993-3(c)) of property are not business assets.

(d) Trade receivables. *(1) In general.* For purposes of this section, trade receivables are accounts receivable and evidences of indebtedness which arise by reason of transactions of such corporation or of another corporation which is a DISC and which is a member of a controlled group which includes such corporation described in subparagraph (A), (B), (C), (D), (G), or (H), of section 993(a)(1) and which are due the DISC (or, if it acts as an agent, due its principal) and held by the DISC.

(2) Trade receivables representing commissions. If a DISC acts as commission agent for a principal in a transaction described in § 1.993-1(b), (c), (d), (e), (h), or (i) which results in qualified export receipts for the DISC, and if an account receivable or evidence of indebtedness held by the DISC and representing the commission payable to the DISC as a result of the transaction arises (and, in the case of an evidence of indebtedness), designated on its face as representing such commission, such account receivable or evidence of indebtedness shall be treated as a trade receivable. If, however, the principal is a related supplier (as defined in § 1.994-1(a)(3)) with respect to the DISC, such account receivable or evidence of indebtedness will not be treated as a trade receivable unless it is payable and paid in a time and manner which satisfy the requirements of § 1.994-1(e)(3) or (5) (relating to initial payment of transfer price or commission and procedure for adjustments to transfer price or commission, respectively), as the case may be. However, see subparagraph (3) of this paragraph for rules regarding certain accounts receivable representing commissions payable to a DISC by its related supplier.

(3) Indebtedness arising under § 1.994-1(e). An indebtedness arising under § 1.994-1(e)(3)(iii) (relating to initial payment of transfer price or commission) in favor of a DISC is not a qualified export asset. An indebtedness arising under § 1.994-1(e)(5)(i) (relating to procedure for adjustments to transfer price or commission) in favor of a DISC is a trade receivable if it is paid in the time and manner described in § 1.994-1(e)(5)(i) and (ii) and if it otherwise satisfies the requirements of subparagraph (2) of this paragraph. If such an indebtedness is not paid in the time and manner described in § 1.994-1(e)(5)(i) and (ii), it is not a qualified export asset.

(e) Temporary investments. *(1) In general.* For purposes of this section, temporary investments are money, bank deposits (not including time deposits of more than 1 year), and other similar temporary investments to the extent maintained by a DISC as reasonably necessary to meet its requirements for working capital. For purposes of this paragraph, a temporary investment is an obligation, including an evidence of indebtedness as defined in paragraph (d)(1) of this section, which is a demand obligation or has a period remaining to maturity of not more than 1 year at the date it is acquired by the DISC. A temporary investment does not include trade receivables.

(2) Determination of amount of working capital maintained. For purposes of this paragraph—

(i) The working capital of a DISC is the excess of its current assets over current liabilities,

(ii) Current assets are cash and other assets (other than trade receivables) which may reasonably be expected to be converted into cash or sold or consumed during the current normal operating cycle of the DISC's trade or business,

(iii) Current liabilities are obligations (or portions of obligations) due within the current normal operating cycle of the trade or business of the DISC whose satisfaction when due is reasonably expected to require the use of current assets,

(iv) Generally accepted financial accounting treatments will be accepted, and

(v) Current assets (other than temporary investments) are taken into account before temporary investments, and trade receivables are never taken into account, in determining whether such temporary investments are maintained by the DISC as reasonably necessary to meet his current liabilities and its requirements for working capital.

(3) Determination of amount of working capital reasonably required. For purposes of this paragraph, a determination of the amount of money, bank deposits, and other similar temporary investments reasonably necessary to meet the requirements of the DISC for working capital will depend upon the nature and volume of the activities of the DISC existing at the end of the DISC's taxable year for which such determination is made, such as, for example—

(i) In the case of a DISC which purchases and sells inventory, the amount of working capital reasonably required is limited to an amount reasonably necessary to meet the ordinary operating expenses during the current normal operating cycle of the trade or business of the DISC, an amount reasonably needed to meet specific and definite plans for expansion and any amounts necessary for reasonably anticipated extraordinary business expenses.

(ii) In the case of a DISC which actively conducts a trade or business (including the employment of a sales force) and receives commissions in respect of goods to which such DISC does not have title, the amount of working capital required will depend upon the nature and volume of the activities of the DISC which produce such income as they exist on the applicable determination date. In determining the amount of working capital which is reasonably required for the production of such income, the anticipated future needs of the business will be taken into account to the extent that such needs relate to the year of the DISC following the applicable determination date. Anticipated future needs relating to a later period will not be taken into account unless it is clearly established that such needs are reasonably related to the production of such income as of the applicable determination date.

(iii) In the case of a DISC which does not actively conduct a trade or business, and which receives commissions solely by reason of section 994(a)(1), (a)(2), or (b) with respect to goods to which such DISC does not have title, no working capital would be required beyond a de minimis amount unless it appears from the facts and circumstances that additional working capital will be required.

(iv) In the case of a DISC deriving income from the leasing of property, the amount of working capital required will be determined on the basis of the facts and circumstances in such case.

(4) Relationship of working capital to other qualified export assets. If a temporary investment is a qualified export asset under any provision of this section (other than this paragraph), this paragraph shall not affect its status as a qualified export asset. However, any such temporary investment is taken into account before other temporary investments in determining whether such other temporary investments are maintained by a DISC as reasonably necessary to meets its requirements for working capital. Current assets (other than temporary investments) are taken into account before temporary investments, and trade receivables are never taken into account, in determining whether such temporary investments are maintained by the DISC as reasonably necessary requirements for working capital. An obligation issued or incurred by a member of a controlled group (as defined in § 1.993-1(k)) of which the DISC is a member is not a qualified export asset under this paragraph. For rules regarding working capital as of the end of each month of a taxable year for purposes of the 70-percent reasonableness standard with respect to certain deficiency distributions, see paragraph (j)(3) of this section.

(f) Producer's loans. For purposes of this section, a producer's loan is an evidence of indebtedness arising in connection with producer's loans which are made by a DISC and which meet the requirements of § 1.993-4. If a producer's loan is a qualified export asset, interest accrued with respect to the producer's loan will also be treated as a qualified export asset provided that payment is made in the form of money, property (valued at its fair market value on its date of transfer and including accounts receivable for sales by or through a DISC), a written obligation which qualifies as a debt under the safe harbor rule of § 1.992-1(d)(2)(ii), or an accounting entry offsetting the account receivable against an existing debt owed by the person in whose favor the account receivable was established to the person with whom it engaged in the transaction and that payment is made no later than 60 days following the close of the taxable year of accrual of the interest. This paragraph (f) is effective for taxable years beginning after January 10, 1985 except that the taxpayer may at its option apply the provisions of this paragraph to taxable years ending after December 31, 1971.

(g) Stock or securities of related foreign export corporations. For purposes of this section, the term "stock or securities", with respect to a related foreign export corporation (as defined in § 1.993-5), has the same meaning as such term has as used in section 351 (relating to transfers to controlled corporations), except that the term "securities" does not include obligations which are repaid, in whole or in part, at any time during the taxable year of the DISC following the taxable year of the DISC during which such obligations were acquired by the DISC or were issued, unless the DISC demonstrates to the satisfaction of the district director that the repayment was for bona fide business purposes and not for the purpose of avoidance of Federal income taxes.

(h) Export-Import Bank obligations. For purposes of this section, the term "Export-Import Bank obligations" means obligations issued, guaranteed, insured, or reinsured (in whole or in part) by the Export-Import Bank of the United States or by the Foreign Credit Insurance Association, but only if such obligations are acquired by the DISC—

(1) From the Export-Import Bank of the United States,

(2) From the Foreign Credit Insurance Association, or

(3) From the person selling or purchasing the goods or services by reason of which such obligations arose, or from any corporation which is a member of the same controlled group (as defined in § 1.993-1(k)) as such person.

For purposes of this paragraph, obligations issued by a person described in subparagraphs (1), (2), and (3) of this paragraph are treated as acquired from such person by the DISC if acquired from any person not more than 90 days after the date of original issue (as defined in § 1.1232-3(b)(3)). Examples of specific types of Export-Import Bank obligations include debentures issued by such bank and certificates of loan participation.

(i) Financing obligations. For purposes of this section, financing obligations are obligations (held by a DISC) of a domestic corporation organized solely for the purpose of financing sales of export property pursuant to an agreement with the Export-Import Bank of the United States under which such corporation makes export loans guaranteed by such Bank.

(j) Funds awaiting investment. *(1) In general.* For purposes of this section, subject to the limitation described in subparagraph (2) of this paragraph, if, at the close of a DISC's taxable year, the sum of the DISC's money, bank deposits, and other similar temporary investments is determined under paragraph (e) of this section to exceed an amount reasonably necessary to meet the DISC's requirements for working capital, the amount of the DISC's bank deposits in the United States to the extent of the amount of this excess are funds awaiting investment at the close of such taxable year.

(2) Limitation. Bank deposits described in subparagraph (1) of this paragraph are funds awaiting investment only if, by the last day of each of the sixth, seventh, and eighth months after the close of such taxable year, the sum of the adjusted bases of the qualified export assets of the DISC (other than such bank deposits) equals or exceeds 95 percent of the sum of the adjusted bases of all assets of the DISC (including such bank deposits) it held on the last day of such taxable year. For purposes of this subparagraph, the adjusted bases of assets of a DISC are determined as of the end of each of the months referred to in this subparagraph. Funds awaiting investment as described in this paragraph need not be traceable to any of the qualified export assets held by the DISC at the end of any of the months referred to in this subparagraph.

(3) Coordination with certain deficiency distribution provisions. Under section 992(c)(3) and § 1.992-3(d) a deficiency distribution made on or before the 15th day of the ninth month after the end of a corporation's taxable year is deemed to be for reasonable cause if certain requirements are met, including the requirement (described in section

992(c)(3)(B) and § 1.992-3(d)(2)) that the sum of the adjusted bases of the qualified export assets held by the corporation on the last day of each month of such year equals or exceeds 70 percent of the sum of the adjusted bases of all assets held by the corporation on each such last day. If, on any such last day, the sum of a DISC's money, bank deposits, and other similar temporary investments is determined under paragraph (e) of this section to exceed an amount reasonably necessary to meet the DISC's requirements for working capital, the amount of the DISC's bank deposits to the extent of the amount of this excess are funds awaiting investment on such last day, if either—

(i) The requirements of subparagraph (2) of this paragraph are satisfied with respect to the taxable year of the DISC which includes such month or

(ii) At the close of such taxable year the sum of the DISC's money, bank deposits, and other similar temporary investments is determined under paragraph (e) of this section not to exceed an amount reasonably necessary to meet the DISC's requirements for working capital.

T.D. 7514, 10/14/77, amend T.D. 7854, 11/16/82, T.D. 7984, 10/11/84.

§ 1.993-3 Definition of export property.

Caution: The Treasury has not yet amended Reg § 1.993-3 to reflect changes made by 103-66.

(a) General rule. Under section 993(c), except as otherwise provided with respect to excluded property in paragraph (f) of this section and with respect to certain short supply property in paragraph (i) of this section, export property is property in the hands of any person (whether or not a DISC)—

(1) Manufactured, produced, grown, or extracted in the United States by any person or persons other than a DISC (see paragraph (c) of this section),

(2) Held primarily for sale or lease in the ordinary course of a trade or business to any person for direct use, consumption, or disposition outside the United States (see paragraph (d) of this section),

(3) Not more than 50 percent of the fair market value of which is attributable to articles imported into the United States (see paragraph (e) of this section), and

(4) Which is not sold or leased by a DISC, or with a DISC as commission agent, to another DISC which is a member of the same controlled group (as defined in § 1.993-1(k)) as the DISC.

(b) Services. For purposes of this section, services (including the written communication of services in any form) are not export property. Whether an item is property or services shall be determined on the basis of the facts and circumstances attending the development and disposition of the item. Thus, for example, the preparation of a map of a particular construction site would constitute services and not export property, but standard maps prepared for sale to customers generally would not constitute services and would be export property if the requirements of this section were otherwise met.

(c) Manufacture, production, growth, or extraction of property. *(1) By a person other than a DISC.* Export property may be manufactured, produced, grown, or extracted in the United States by any person, provided that such person does not qualify (and is not treated) as a DISC. Property held by a DISC which was manufactured, produced, grown, or extracted by it at a time when it did not qualify (and was not treated) as a DISC is not export property of the DISC. Property which sustains further manufacture or production outside the United States prior to sale or lease by a person but after manufacture or production in the United States will not be considered as manufactured, produced, grown, or extracted in the United States by such person.

(2) Manufactured or produced. (i) In general. For purposes of this section, property which is sold or leased by a person is considered to be manufactured or produced by such person if such property is manufactured or produced (within the meaning of either subdivision (ii), (iii), or (iv) of this subparagraph) by such person or by another person pursuant to a contract with such person. Except as provided in subdivision (iv) of this subparagraph, manufacture or production of property does not include assembly or packaging operations with respect to property.

(ii) Substantial transformation. Property is manufactured or produced by a person if such property is substantially transformed by such person. Examples of substantial transformation of property would include the conversion of woodpulp to paper, steel rods to screws and bolts, and the canning of fish.

(iii) Operations generally considered to constitute manufacturing. Property is manufactured or produced by a person if the operations performed by such person in connection with such property are substantial in nature and are generally considered to constitute the manufacture or production of property.

(iv) Value added to property. Property is manufactured or produced by a person if with respect to such property conversion costs (direct labor and factory burden including packaging or assembly) of such person account for 20 percent or more of—

(a) The cost of goods sold or inventory amount of such person for such property if such property is sold or held for sale, or

(b) The adjusted basis of such person for such property, as determined in accordance, with the provisions of section 1011, if such property is held for lease or leased.

The value of parts provided pursuant to a services contract, as described in § 1.993-1(d)(4)(v), is not taken into account in applying this subdivision.

(d) Primary purpose for which property is held. *(1) In general.* (i) General rule. Under paragraph (a)(2) of this section, export property (a) must be held primarily for the purpose of sale or lease in the ordinary course of a trade or business to a DISC, or to any other person, and (b) such sale or lease must be for direct use, consumption, or disposition outside the United States. Thus, property cannot qualify as export property unless it is sold or leased for direct use, consumption, or disposition outside the United States. Property is sold or leased for direct use, consumption, or disposition outside the United States if such sale or lease satisfies the destination test described in subparagraph (2) of this paragraph, the proof of compliance requirements described in subparagraph (3) of this paragraph, and the use-outside-the-United States test described in subparagraph (4) of this paragraph.

(ii) Factors not taken into account. In determining whether property which is sold or leased to a DISC is sold or leased for direct use, consumption, or disposition outside the United States, the fact that the acquiring DISC holds the property in inventory or for lease prior to the time it sells or leases it for direct use, consumption, or disposition outside the United States will not affect the characterization of the property as export property. Export property need not be physically segregated from other property.

(2) Destination test. (i) For purposes of subparagraph (1) of this paragraph, the destination test in this subparagraph is satisfied with respect to property sold or leased by a seller or lessor only if it is delivered by such seller or lessor (or an agent of such seller or lessor) regardless of the F.O.B. point or the place at which title passes or risk of loss shifts from the seller or lessor—

(a) Within the United States to a carrier or freight forwarded or ultimate delivery outside the United States to a purchaser or lessee (or to a subsequent purchaser or sublessee),

(b) Within the United States to a purchaser or lessee, if such property is ultimately delivered, directly used, or directly consumed outside the United States (including delivery to a carrier or freight forwarder for delivery outside the United States) by the purchaser or lessee (or a subsequent purchaser or sublessee) within 1 year after such sale or lease,

(c) Within or outside the United States to a purchaser or lessee which, at the time of the sale or lease, is a DISC and is not a member of the same controlled group (as defined in § 1.993-1(k)) as the seller or lessor.

(d) From the United States to the purchaser or lessee (or a subsequent purchaser or sublessee) at a point outside the United States by means of a ship, aircraft, or other delivery vehicle, owned, leased, or chartered by the seller or lessor,

(e) Outside the United States to a purchaser or lessee from a warehouse, a storage facility, or assembly site located outside the United States, if such property was previously shipped by such seller or lessor from the United States, or

(f) Outside the United States to a purchaser or lessee if such property was previously shipped by such seller or lessor from the United States and if such property is located outside the United States pursuant to a prior lease by the seller or lessor, and either (1) such prior lease terminated at the expiration of its term (or by the action of the prior lessee acting alone), (2) the sale occurred or the term of the subsequent lease began after the time at which the term of the prior lease would have expired, or (3) the lessee under the subsequent lease is not a related person (as defined in § 1.993-1(a)(6)) with respect to the lessor and the prior lease was terminated by the action of the lessor (acting alone or together with the lessee).

(ii) For purposes of this subparagraph (other than (c) and (f)(3) of subdivision (i) thereof), any relationship between the seller or lessor and any purchaser, subsequent purchaser, lessee, or sublessee is immaterial.

(iii) In no event is the destination test of this subparagraph satisfied with respect to property which is subject to any use (other than a resale or sublease), manufacture, assembly, or other processing (other than packaging) by any person between the time of the sale or lease by such seller or lessor and the delivery or ultimate delivery outside the United States described in this subparagraph.

(iv) If property is located outside the United States at the time it is purchased by a person or leased by a person as lessee, such property may be export property in the hands of such purchaser or lessee only if it is imported into the United States prior to its further sale or lease (including a sublease) outside the United States. Paragraphs (a)(3) and (e) of this section (relating to 50 percent foreign content test) are applicable in determining whether such property is export property. Thus, for example, if such property is not subjected to manufacturing or production (as defined in paragraph (c) of this section) within the United States after such importation, it does not qualify as export property.

(3) Proof of compliance with destination test. (i) Delivery outside the United States. For purposes of subparagraph (2) of this paragraph (other than subdivision (i)(c) thereof), a seller or lessor shall establish ultimate delivery, use, or consumption of property outside the United States by providing—

(a) A facsimile or carbon copy of the export bill of lading issued by the carrier who delivers the property,

(b) A certificate of an agent or representative of the carrier disclosing delivery of the property outside the United States,

(c) A facsimile or carbon copy of the certificate of lading for the property executed by a customs officer of the country to which the property is delivered,

(d) If such country has no customs administration, a written statement by the person to whom delivery outside the United States was made,

(e) A facsimile or carbon copy of the shipper's export declaration, a monthly shipper's summary declaration filed with the Bureau of Customs, or a magnetic tape filed in lieu of the Shipper's Export Declaration, covering the property,

(f) Any other proof (including evidence as to the nature of the property or the nature of the transaction) which establishes to the satisfaction of the Commissioner that the property was ultimately delivered, or directly sold, or directly consumed outside the United States within 1 year after the sale or lease.

(ii) The requirements of subdivision (i)(a), (b), (c), or (e) of this subparagraph will be considered satisfied even though the name of the ultimate consignee and the price paid for the goods is marked out provided that, in the case of a Shipper's Export Declaration or other document listed in such subdivision (e) or a document such as an export bill or lading such document still indicates the country to which delivery to the ultimate consignee is to be made and, in the case of a certificate of an agent or representative of the carrier, that such document indicates that the property was delivered outside the United States.

(iii) A seller or lessor shall also establish the meeting of the requirement of subparagraph (2)(i) of this paragraph (other than subdivision (c) thereof) that the property was delivered outside the United States without further use, manufacture, assembly, or other processing within the United States.

(iv) Sale or lease to an unrelated DISC. For purposes of subparagraph (2)(i)(c) of this paragraph, a purchaser or lessee of property is deemed to qualify as a DISC for its taxable year if the seller or lessor obtains from such purchaser or lessee a copy of such purchaser's or lessee's election to be treated as a DISC as described in § 1.992-2(a) together with such purchaser's or lessee's sworn statement that such election has been filed with the Internal Revenue Service Center. The copy of the election and the sworn statement of such purchaser or lessee must be received by the seller or lessor within 6 months after the sale or lease. A purchaser or lessee is not treated as a DISC with respect to a sale or lease during a taxable year for which such purchaser or lessee does not qualify as a DISC if the seller or lessor does not believe or if a reasonable person would not believe at the time such sale or lease is made that the purchaser or lessee will qualify as a DISC for such taxable year.

(v) Failure of proof. If a seller or lessor fails to provide proof of compliance with the destination test as required by this subparagraph, the property sold or leased is not export property.

(4) Sales and leases of property for ultimate use in the United States. (i) In general. For purposes of subparagraph (1) of this paragraph, the use test in this subparagraph is satisfied with respect to property which—

(a) Under subdivisions (ii) through (iv) of this subparagraph is not sold for ultimate use in the United States or

(b) Under subdivision (v) of this subparagraph is lease for ultimate use outside the United States.

(ii) Sales of property for ultimate use in the United States. For purposes of subdivision (i) of this subparagraph, a purchaser of property (including components, as defined in subdivision (vii) of this subparagraph) is deemed to use such property ultimately in the United States if any of the following conditions exists:

(a) Such purchaser is a related person (as defined in § 1.993-1(a)(6)) with respect to the seller and such purchaser ultimately uses such property, or a second product into which such property is incorporated as a component, in the United States.

(b) At the time of the sale, there is an agreement or understanding that such property, or a second product into which such property is incorporated as a component, will be ultimately used by the purchaser in the United States.

(c) At the time of the sale, a reasonable person would have believed that such property or such second product would be ultimately used by such purchaser in the United States unless, in the case of a sale of components, the fair market value of such components at the time of delivery to the purchaser constitutes less than 20 percent of the fair market value of the second product into which such components are incorporated (determined at the time of completion of the production, manufacture, or assembly of such second product).

For purposes of (b) of this subdivision, there is an agreement or understanding that property will ultimately be used in the United States if, for example, a component is sold abroad under an express agreement with the foreign purchaser that the component is to be incorporated into a product to be sold back to the United States. As a further example, there would also be such an agreement or understanding if the foreign purchaser indicated at the time of the sale or previously that the component is to be incorporated into a product which is designed principally for the United States market. However, such an agreement or understanding does not result from the mere fact that a second product, into which components exported from the United States have been incorporated and which is sold on the world market, is sold in substantial quantities in the United States.

(iii) Use in the United States. For purposes of subdivision (ii) of this subparagraph, property (including components incorporated into a second product) is or would be ultimately used in the United States by such purchaser if, at any time within 3 years after the purchase of such property or components, either such property or components (or the second product into which such components are incorporated) is resold by such purchaser for use by a subsequent purchaser within the United States or such purchaser or subsequent purchaser fails, for any period of 365 consecutive days, to use such property or second product predominantly outside the United States as defined in subdivision (vi) of this subparagraph).

(iv) Sales to retailers. For purposes of subdivision (ii)(c) of this subparagraph property sold to any person whose principal business consists of selling from inventory to retail customers at retail outlets outside the United States will be considered as property for ultimate use outside the United States.

(v) Leases of property for ultimate use outside the United States. For purposes of subdivision (i) of this Subparagraph, a lessee of property is deemed to use such property ultimately outside the United States during a taxable year of the lessor if such property is used predominantly outside the United States (as defined in subdivision (vi) of this subparagraph) by the lessee during the portion of the lessor's taxable year which is included within the term of the lease. A determination as to whether the ultimate use of leased property satisfies the requirements of this subdivision is made for each taxable year of the lessor. Thus, leased property may be used predominantly outside the United States for a taxable year of the lessor (and thus, constitute export property if the remaining requirements of this section are met) even if the property is not used predominantly outside the United States in earlier taxable years or later taxable years of the lessor.

(vi) Predominant use outside the United States. For purposes of this subparagraph, property is used predominantly outside the United States for any period if, during such period, such property is located outside the United States more than 50 percent of the time. An aircraft, railroad rolling stock, vessel, motor vehicle, container, or other property used for transportation purposes is deemed to be used predominantly outside the United States for any period if, during such period, either such property is located outside the United States more than 50 percent of the time or more than 50 percent of the miles traversed in the use of such property are traversed outside the United States. However, any such property is deemed to be within the United States at all times during which it is engaged in transport between any two points within the United States, except where such transport constitutes uninterrupted international air transportation within the meaning of section 4262(c)(3) and the regulations thereunder (relating to tax on air transportation of persons). For purposes of applying section 4262(c)(3) to this subdivision, the term "United States" has the same meaning as in § 1.993-7.

(vii) Component. For purposes of this subparagraph, a component is property which is (or is reasonably expected to be) incorporated into a second product by the purchaser of such component by means of production, manufacture, or assembly.

(e) Foreign content of property. *(1) The 50 percent test.* Under paragraph (a)(3) of this section, no more than 50 percent of the fair market value of export property may be attributable to the fair market value of articles which were imported into the United States. For purposes of this paragraph, articles imported into the United States are referred to as "foreign content". The fair market value of the foreign content of export property is computed in accordance with subparagraph (4) of this paragraph. The fair market value of export property which is sold to a person who is not a related person with respect to the seller is the sale price for such property (not including interest, finance or carrying charges, or similar charges).

(2) Application of 50 percent test. The 50 percent test described in subparagraph (1) of this paragraph is applied on an item-by-item basis. If, however, a person sells or leases a substantial volume of substantially identical export property in a taxable year and if all of such property contains sub-

stantially identical foreign content in substantially the same proportion, such person may determine the portion of foreign content contained in such property on an aggregate basis.

(3) Parts and services. If, at the time property is sold or leased the seller or lessor agrees to furnish parts pursuant to a services contract (as provided in § 1.993-1(d)(4)(v)) and the price for the parts is not separately stated, the 50 percent test described in subparagraph (1) of this paragraph is applied on an aggregate basis to the property and parts. If the price for the parts is separately stated, the 50 percent test described in subparagraph (1) of this paragraph is applied separately to the property and to the parts.

(4) Computation of foreign content. (i) Valuation. For purposes of applying the 50 percent test described in paragraph (1) of this paragraph, it is necessary to determine the fair market value of all articles which constitute foreign content of the property being tested to determine if it is export property. The fair market value of such imported articles is determined as of the time such articles are imported into the United States. With respect to articles imported into the United States before July 1, 1980, the fair market value of such articles is their appraised value as determined under section 402 or 402a of the Tariff Act of 1930 (19 U.S.C. 1401a or 1402) in connection with their importation. With respect to articles imported into the United States on or after July 1, 1980, the fair market value of such articles is their appraised value as determined under section 402 of the Tariff Act of 1930 (19 U.S.C. 1401a) in connection with their importation. The appraised value of such articles is the full dutiable value of such articles, determined, however, without regard to any special provision in the United States tariff laws which would result in a lower dutiable value. Thus, an article which is imported into the United States is treated as entirely imported even if all or a portion of such article was originally manufactured, produced, grown, or extracted in the United States.

(ii) Evidence of fair market value. For purposes of subdivision (i) of this subparagraph, the fair market value of imported articles constituting foreign content may be evidenced by the customs invoice issued on the importation of such articles into the United States. If the holder of such articles is not the importer (or a related person with respect to the importer), the fair market value of such articles may be evidenced by a certificate based upon information contained in the customs invoice and furnished to the holder by the person from whom such articles (or property incorporating such articles) were purchased. If a customs invoice or certificate described in the preceding sentence is not available to a person purchasing property, such person shall establish that no more than 50 percent of the fair market value of such property is attributable to the fair market value of articles which were imported into the United States.

(iii) Interchangeable component articles. (a) Where identical or similar component articles can be incorporated interchangeably into property and a person acquires some such component articles that are imported into the United States and other such component articles that are not imported into the United States, the determination whether imported component articles were incorporated in such property as is exported from the United States shall be made on a substitution basis as in the case of the rules relating to drawback accounts under the customs laws. See section 313(b) of the Tariff Act of 1930, as amended (19 U.S.C. 1313(b)).

(b) The provisions of (a) of this subdivision may be illustrated by the following example:

Example. Assume that a manufacturer produces a total of 20,000 electronic devices. The manufacturer exports 5,000 of the devices and subsequently sells 11,000 of the devices to a DISC which exports the 11,000 devices. The major single component article in each device is a tube which represents 60 percent of the fair market value of the device at the time the device is sold by the manufacturer. The manufacturer imports 8,000 of the tubes and produces the remaining 12,000 tubes. For purposes of this subdivision, in accordance with the substitution principle used in the customs drawback laws, the 5,000 devices exported by the manufacturer are each treated as containing an imported tube because the devices were exported prior to the sale to the DISC. The remaining 3,000 imported tubes are treated as being contained in the first 3,000 devices purchased and exported by the DISC. Thus, since the 50 percent test is not met with respect to the first 3,000 devices purchased and exported by the DISC, those devices are not export property. The remaining 8,000 devices purchased and exported by the DISC are treated as containing tubes produced in the United States, and those devices are export property (if they otherwise meet the requirements of this section).

(f) Excluded property. *(1) In general.* Notwithstanding any other provision of this section, the following property is not export property—

(i) Property described in subparagraph (2) of this paragraph (relating to property leased to a member of a controlled group),

(ii) Property described in subparagraph (3) of this paragraph (relating to certain types of intangible property),

(iii) Products described in paragraph (g) of this section (relating to depletable products), and

(iv) Products described in paragraph (h) of this section (relating to certain export controlled products).

(2) Property leased to member of controlled group. (i) In general. Property leased to a person (whether or not a DISC) which is a member of the same controlled group (as defined in § 1.993-1(k)) as the lessor constitutes export property for any period of time only if during the period—

(a) Such property is held for sublease, or is subleased, by such person to a third person for the ultimate use of such third person;

(b) Such third person is not a member of the same controlled group; and

(c) Such property is used predominantly outside the United States by such third person.

(ii) Predominant use. The provisions of paragraph (d)(4)(vi) of this section apply in determining under subdivision (i)(c) of this subparagraph whether such property is used predominantly outside the United States by such third person.

(iii) Leasing rule. For purposes of this subparagraph, leased property is deemed to be ultimately used by a member of the same controlled group as the lessor if such property is leased to a person which is not a member of such controlled group but which subleases such property to a person which is a member of such controlled group. Thus, for example, if X, a DISC for the taxable year, leases a movie film to Y, a foreign corporation which is not a member of the same controlled group as X, and Y then subleases the film to persons which are members of such group for showing to the general public, the film is not export property. On the other hand, if X, a DISC for the taxable year, leases a movie film to Z, a foreign corporation which is a member of the same controlled as X, and Z then subleases the film to Y, another foreign corporation, which is not a member of the same controlled group for showing to the general public, the film is not disqualified under this subparagraph from being export property.

(iv) Certain copyrights. With respect to a copyright which is not excluded by subparagraph (3) of this paragraph from being export property, the ultimate use of such property is the sale or exhibition of such property to the general public. Thus, if A, a DISC for the taxable year, leases recording tapes to B, a foreign corporation which is a member of the same controlled group as A, and if B makes records from the recording tape and sells the records to C, another foreign corporation, which is not a member of the same controlled group, for sale by C to the general public, the recording tape is not disqualified under this subparagraph from being export property, notwithstanding the leasing of the recording tape by A to a member of the same controlled group, since the ultimate use of the tape is the sale of the records (i.e., property produced from the recording tape).

(3) Intangible property. Export property does not include any patent, invention, model, design, formula, or process, whether or not patented, or any copyright (other than films, tapes, records, or similar reproductions, for commercial or home use), goodwill, trademark, tradebrand, franchise, or other like property. Although a copyright such as a copyright on a book does not constitute export property, a copyrighted article (such as a book) if not accompanied by a right to reproduce it is export property if the requirements of this section are otherwise satisfied. However, a license of a master recording tape for reproduction outside the United States is not disqualified under this subparagraph from being export property.

(g) Depletable products. *(1) In general.* Under section 993(c)(2)(C), a product or commodity which is a depletable product (as defined in subparagraph (2) of this paragraph) or contains a depletable product is not export property if—

(i) It is a primary product from oil, gas, coal, or uranium (as described in subparagraph (3) of this paragraph), or

(ii) It does not qualify as a 50-percent manufactured or processed product (as described in subparagraph (4) of this paragraph).

(2) Definition of "depletable product". For purposes of this paragraph, the term "depletable product" means any product or commodity of a character with respect to which a deduction for depletion is allowable under section 613 or 613A. Thus, the term depletable product includes any mineral extracted from a mine, an oil or gas well, or any other natural deposit, whether or not the DISC or related supplier is allowed a deduction, or is eligible to take a deduction, for depletion with respect to the mineral in computing its taxable income. Thus, for example, iron ore purchased by a DISC from a broker is a depletable product in the hands of the DISC for purposes of this paragraph even though the DISC is not eligible to take a deduction for depletion under section 613 or 613A.

(3) Primary product from oil, gas, coal, or uranium. A primary product from oil, gas, coal, or uranium is not export property. For purposes of this paragraph—

(i) Primary product from oil. The term "primary product from oil" means crude oil and all products, derived from the destructive distillation of crude oil, including—

(a) Volatile products,

(b) Light oils such as motor fuel and kerosene,

(c) Distillates such as naphtha,

(d) Lubricating oils,

(e) Greases and waves, and

(f) Residues such as fuel oil.

For purposes of this paragraph, a product or commodity derived from shale oil which would be a primary product from oil if derived from crude oil is considered a primary product from oil.

(ii) Primary product from gas. The term "primary product from gas" means all gas and associated hydrocarbon components from gas wells or oil wells, whether recovered at the lease or upon further processing, including—

(a) Natural gas,

(b) Condensates,

(c) Liquified petroleum gases such as ethane, propane, and butane, and

(d) Liquid products such as natural gasoline.

(iii) Primary product from coal. The term "primary product from coal" means coal and all products recovered from the carbonization of coal including—

(a) Coke,

(b) Coke-oven gas,

(c) Gas liquor,

(d) Crude light oil, and

(e) Coal tar.

(iv) Primary product from uranium. The term "primary product from uranium" means uranium ore and uranium concentrates (known in the industry as "yellow cake"), and nuclear fuel materials derived from the refining of uranium ore and uranium concentrates, or produced in a nuclear reaction, including—

(a) Uranium hexafluoride,

(b) Enriched uranium hexafluoride,

(c) Uranium metal,

(d) Uranium compounds, such as uranium carbide,

(e) Uranium dioxide, and

(f) Plutonium fuels.

(v) Primary products and changing technology. The primary products from oil, gas, coal, or uranium described in subdivision (i) through (iv) of this subparagraph and the processes described in those subdivisions are not intended to represent either the only primary products from oil, gas, coal, or uranium, or the only processes from which primary products may be derived under existing and future technologies such as the gasification and liquefaction of coal.

(vi) Petrochemicals. For purposes of this paragraph, petrochemicals are not considered primary products from oil, gas, or coal.

(4) 50-percent manufactured or processed product. (i) In general. A product or commodity (other than a primary product from oil, gas, coal, or uranium) which is or contains a depletable product is not excluded from the term "export property" by reason of section 993(c)(2)(C) if it is a 50-percent manufactured or processed product. Such a product or commodity is a "50-percent manufactured or processed product" if, after the cutoff point of the depletable product, it is manufactured or processed (as defined in subdivision (ii) of this subparagraph) and either the cost test described in subdivision (iv) of this subparagraph or the fair market value test described in subdivision (v) of this subparagraph is sat-

isfied. To determine cutoff point, see subdivisions (vi) and (vii) of this subparagraph.

(ii) Manufactured or processed. A product is manufactured or processed if it is manufactured or produced within the meaning of paragraph (c)(2) of this section, except that for purposes of this subdivision the term manufacturing or processing does not include any excluded process (as defined in subdivision (iii) of this subparagraph) and the term conversion costs (as used in subdivision (iv) of such paragraph (c)(2)) does not include any costs attributable to any excluded process.

(iii) Excluded processes. For purposes of this paragraph, excluded processes are extracting (i.e., all processes which are applied before the cutoff point of the mineral to which such processes are applied), and handling, packing, packaging, grading, storing, and transporting.

(iv) Cost test. A product or commodity will qualify as a 50-percent manufactured or processed product if—

(a) Its manufacturing and processing costs (that is, the portion of the cost of goods sold or inventory amount of the product or commodity attributable to the aggregate cost of manufacturing or processing each mineral or the timber contained therein) equal or exceed

(b) An amount equal to either of the following:

(1) 50 percent of its cost of goods sold or inventory amount (decreased, at the DISC's option, by the portion of such cost or amount the DISC establishes is allocable to the difference between each prior owner's selling price for each depletable product contained in such product or commodity and such prior owner's cost of goods sold with respect thereto).

(2) The aggregate of the cost at the cutoff point (see subdivisions (vi) and (vii) of this subparagraph) properly attributable to each mineral contained in such product or commodity. However, if this subdivision (2) is applied, then the amount in (a) of this subparagraph (iv) shall be decreased and the amount in this subdivision (2) shall be increased, by so much of the cost of goods sold or inventory amount of the product or commodity as is properly allocable to any process other than transportation applied after the cutoff point of such mineral which would be a mining process (within the meaning of § 1.613-4) were it applied before such point.

(v) Fair market value test. A product or commodity will qualify as a 50-percent manufactured or processed product if—

(a) The excess of its fair market value on the date it is sold, exchanged, or otherwise disposed of (or, if not sold, exchanged, or otherwise disposed of, the last day of the DISC's taxable year) over the portion thereof properly allocable to excluded processes other than extracting is equal to or greater than

(b) Twice the aggregate of the fair market value at the cutoff point for each mineral contained in such product or commodity.

For purposes of this subdivision (v), the fair market value of a product or commodity on the date it is sold, exchanged, or otherwise disposed of is the price at which it is disposed of, subject to any adjustment that may be required under the arm's length standard of section 482 and the regulations thereunder. If such product or commodity is not sold, exchanged, or otherwise disposed of, then, for purposes of section 992(a)(1)(B) (relating to the 95-percent test with respect to qualified export assets), the fair market value of a product or commodity on the last day of the DISC's taxable year is the arm's length price at which such product or commodity would have been sold on such date, determined by applying the principles of section 482 and the regulations thereunder.

(vi) Cutoff point of a mineral. For purposes of this subparagraph—

(a) The cutoff point is the point at which gross income from the property (within the meaning of section 613(a)) was in fact determined.

(b) The cost at the cutoff point is deemed to be the amount of the gross income from the property of the taxpayer eligible for a depletion deduction with respect to the mineral.

(c) The fair market value at the cutoff point is deemed to be the amount of the gross income from the property of the taxpayer eligible for a depletion deduction with respect to the mineral, except that, if (1) the fair market value of a product or commodity on the date specified in subdivision (v)(a) of this subparagraph exceeds the aggregate of the fair market value at the cutoff point for each mineral contained therein and (2) 10 percent or more of such excess is attributable to a net increase in the fair market values of such minerals by reason of factors other than manufacturing or processing or the application of excluded processes (such as, for example, increases in the fair market values of some minerals by reason of inflation or speculation exceed decreases in such values of other minerals by reason of deflation or speculation), then the aggregate of the fair market value at the cutoff point for each such mineral shall be increased to reflect the net excess so attributable.

(d) The provisions of this subdivision (vi) are illustrated by the following example:

Example. An integrated manufacturer, X, on February 1, 1976, had gross income from the property (within the meaning of section 613(a)) of $50 with respect to a specified volume of a mineral. Thus, the cost at the cutoff point of the mineral was $50. X converted the mineral into a product which it sold on July 15, 1976, for $75. Of the $25 excess of the selling price over the gross income from the property, $23 was attributable to manufacturing, processing, and the application of excluded processes, and $2 was attributable to an increase in the fair market value of the mineral due to inflation between February 1 and July 15, 1976. Since only 8 percent of such excess ($2/$25) was attributable to factors other than manufacturing, processing, and the application of excluded processes, the fair market value at the cutoff point of the mineral is $50. However, had $3 of the $25 excess, or 12 percent, been attributable to an increase in the fair market value of the mineral due to inflation, then the fair market value at the cutoff point of the mineral would be $53.

(vii) [Reserved]

(viii) Special rule for certain used products and scrap products. If a product or commodity is a used 50-percent manufactured or processed product, or is recovered as scrap from a 50-percent manufactured or processed product, such product or commodity will be treated as a 50-percent manufactured or processed product.

(ix) Special rule for byproducts and waste products. For purposes of applying the cost test or fair market value test of subdivision (iv) or (v) of this subparagraph if a depletable product is recovered from a manufacturing process as a byproduct or waste product, then the cost and fair market value at the cutoff point are each deemed to be the lesser of—

(a) The fair market value of the waste product or byproduct containing the depletable product, determined as of the date the byproduct or waste product is recovered, or

(b) The amount the cost at the cutoff point would be for a depletable product of like kind and grade which is extracted, determined as of the date the byproduct or waste product is recovered.

For purposes of (b) of this subdivision the cutoff point for the depletable product of like kind and grade is deemed to be the point at which gross income from the property would be determined if such depletable product were sold by the taxpayer eligible to take a deduction for depletion after the completion of all mining processes applied to the depletable product and before the application of any nonmining process.

(x) Proof of satisfaction of 50-percent manufactured or processed test. (a) No substantiation is required to establish that either the cost test or the fair market value test of subdivisions (iv) or (v) of this subparagraph is satisfied or that a product or commodity qualifies under (viii) of this subdivision as either a used 50-percent manufactured or processed product or as scrap from a 50-percent manufactured or processed product as long as it is reasonably obvious, on the basis of all relevant facts and circumstances, that either the cost test or fair market value test is satisfied, or that the product or commodity qualifies as either as used 50-percent manufactured or processed product or as scrap from a 50-percent manufactured or processed product. Thus, for example, in the case of a DISC exporting a high precision lens at least 50 percent of the fair market value of which is obviously attributable to grinding, no substantiation of gross income from the property properly allocable to the depletable products contained in the lens, costs, or fair market values will be required.

(b) In cases in which satisfaction of either the cost test or the fair market value test is not reasonably obvious, a DISC will be required to substantiate the gross income from the property properly allocable to each depletable product in a product or commodity and either all costs or fair market values relied upon the DISC.

(c) For purposes of substantiating (1) gross income from the property properly allocable to a depletable product, (2) costs, and (3) fair market values, the DISC and related supplier shall each identify items in (or that were in) inventory in the same manner each used to identify items in inventory for purposes of computing Federal income tax.

(xi) Application of 50-percent test. The 50-percent test described in this subparagraph is applied on an item-by-item basis. If, however, a DISC sells a substantial volume of substantially identical products or commodities and if all or a group of such products or commodities contain substantially identical depletable products in substantially the same proportions and have cost or fair market value relationships (as the case may be) that are in substantially the same proportions, such DISC may apply the 50-percent test on an aggregate basis with respect to all such products or commodities, or group, as the case may be.

(5) Effective dates. Except as provided in subparagraph (b) of this paragraph, section 993(c)(2)(C) applies—

(i) With respect to any product or commodity not owned by a DISC, to sales, exchanges, or other dispositions made after March 18, 1975, with respect to which the DISC derives gross receipts.

(ii) With respect to any product or commodity acquired by a DISC after March 18, 1975.

(iii) With respect to any product or commodity owned by a DISC on March 18, 1975, to sales, exchanges, or other dispositions made after March 18, 1976, and to owning such product or commodity after such date.

For purposes of this subparagraph and subparagraph (6) of this paragraph, the date of a sale, exchange, or other disposition of a product or commodity is the date as of which title to such product or commodity passes. The accounting method of a person is not determinative of the date of a sale, exchange, or other disposition.

(6) Fixed contracts. Section 1101(f) of the Tax Reform Act of 1976 provides an exception to the effective date rules in this paragraph and in paragraph (h) of this section. Section 1101(f)(2) of the Act provides that section 993(c)(2)(C) and (D) shall not apply to sales, exchanges, and other dispositions made after March 18, 1975, but before March 19, 1980, if they are made pursuant to a fixed contract. Section 1101(f)(2) also defines fixed contract. Under the definition, if the seller can vary the price of the product for unspecified cost increases (which could include tax cost increases), or if the quantity of products or commodities to be sold can be increased or decreased under the contract by the seller without penalty, the contract is not to be considered a fixed contract with respect to the amount over which the seller has discretion. For example, if a contract calls for a minimum delivery of *x* amount of a product but allows the seller to refuse to deliver goods beyond that minimum amount (or allows a renegotiation of the sales price of goods beyond that amount above the minimum the contract is not a fixed quantity contract.

(h) Export controlled products. *(1) In general.* An export controlled product is not export property. A product or commodity may be an export controlled product at one time but not an export controlled product at another time. For purposes of this paragraph, a product or commodity is an "export controlled product" at a particular time if at that time the export of such product or commodity is prohibited or curtailed under section 4(b) of the Export Administration Act of 1969 or section 7(a) of the Export Administration Act of 1979, to effectuate the policy relating to the protection of the domestic economy set forth in such Acts (paragraph (2)(A) of section 3 of the Export Administration Act of 1969 and paragraph (2)(C) of section 3 of the Export Administration Act of 1979). Such policy is to use export controls to the extent necessary "to protect the domestic economy from the excessive drain of scarce materials and to reduce the serious inflationary impact of foreign demand."

(2) Products considered export controlled products. (i) In general. For purposes of this paragraph, an export controlled product is a product or commodity which is subject to short supply export controls under 15 CFR Part 377. A product or commodity is considered an export controlled product for the duration of each control period which applies to such product or commodity. A control period of a product or commodity begins on and includes the initial control date (as defined in subdivision (ii) of this subparagraph) and ends on and includes the final control date (as defined in subdivision (iii) of this subparagraph).

(ii) Initial control date. The initial control date of a product or commodity which was subject to short supply export controls on March 19, 1975, is March 19, 1975. The initial control date of a product or commodity which is subject to short supply export controls after March 19, 1975, is the effective date stated in the regulations to 15 CFR Part 377 which subjects such product or commodity to short supply export controls. If there is no effective date stated in such regulations, the initial control date of such product or commodity is the date on which such regulations are filed for publication in the FEDERAL REGISTER.

(iii) Final control date. The final control date of a product or commodity is the effective date stated in the regulations to 15 CFR Part 377 which removes such product or commodity from short supply export controls. If there is no effective date stated in such regulations, the final control date of such product or commodity is the date on which such regulations are filed for publication in the FEDERAL REGISTER.

(iv) Expiration of Export Administration Act. An initial control date and a final control date cannot occur after the expiration date of the Export Administration Act under the authority of which the short supply export controls were issued.

(3) Effective dates. (i) Products controlled on March 19, 1975. Except as provided in paragraph (g)(6) of this section, if a product or commodity was subject to short supply export controls on March 19, 1975, this paragraph applies—

(a) With respect to any such product or commodity not owned by a DISC, to sales, exchanges, other dispositions, or leases made after March 18, 1975, with respect to which the DISC derives gross receipts.

(b) With respect to any such product or commodity acquired by a DISC after March 18, 1975, and

(c) With respect to any such product or commodity owned by a DISC on March 18, 1975, to sales, exchanges, other dispositions, and leases made after March 18, 1976, and to owning such product or commodity after such date.

(ii) Products first controlled after March 19, 1975. If a product or commodity becomes subject to short supply export controls after March 19, 1975, this paragraph applies to sales, exchanges, other dispositions, or leases of such product or commodity made on or after the initial control date of such product or commodity, and to owning such product or commodity on or after such date.

(iii) Date of sale, exchange, lease, or other disposition. For purposes of this subparagraph, the date of sale, exchange, or other disposition of a product or commodity is the date as of which title to such product or commodity passes. The date of a lease is the date as of which the lessee takes possession of a product or commodity. The accounting method of a person is not determinative of the date of sale, exchange, other disposition, or lease.

(i) Property in short supply. If the President determines that the supply of any property which is otherwise export property as defined in this section is insufficient to meet the requirements of the domestic economy, he may by Executive order designate such property as in short supply. Any property so designated will be treated as property which is not export property during the period beginning with the date specified in such Executive order and ending with the date specified in an Executive order setting forth the President's determination that such property is no longer in short supply.

T.D. 7514, 10/14/77, amend T.D. 7513, 10/14/77, T.D. 7854, 11/16/82.

§ 1.993-4 Definition of producer's loans.

(a) General rule. *(1) Definition.* Under section 993(d), a loan made by a DISC to a person, referred to in this section as the "borrower," is a producer's loan if—

(i) The loan is made out of accumulated DISC income within the meaning of subparagraph (3) of this paragraph.

(ii) The loan is evidenced by an obligation described in subparagraph (4) of this paragraph,

(iii) The requirement as to the trade or business of the borrower described in subparagraph (5) of this paragraph is satisfied.

(iv) At the time the loan is made, the obligation referred to in subdivision (ii) of this subparagraph bears a legend stating "This Obligation Is Designated A Producer's Loan Within The Meaning of Section 993(d) of the Internal Revenue Code" or words of substantially the same meaning.

(v) The limitation as to the export-related assets of the borrower described in paragraph (b) of this section is satisfied.

(vi) The requirement as to the increased investment of the borrower in export-related assets described in paragraph (c) of this section is satisfied, and

(vii) The requirement of paragraph (d) of this section as to proof of compliance with paragraphs (b) and (c) of this section is satisfied.

(2) Application of this section. (i) In general. A loan which is a producer's loan is a qualified export asset of the DISC (see § 1.993-2(a)(5) and (f)). The interest on a producer's loan is a qualified export receipt of the DISC (see § 1.993-1(g)). A producer's loan is not a dividend to a borrower which is also a shareholder of the DISC making the loan. For rules with respect to deemed distributions by reason of the amount of foreign investment attributable to producer's loans, see section 995(b)(1)(G) and (d) and the regulations thereunder.

(ii) No tracing of loan proceeds. For purposes of applying this section, in order to qualify as a producer's loan, the proceeds of the loan need not be traced to an investment in any specific asset.

(iii) Unrelated borrower. For purposes of applying this section, it is not necessary for a borrower to be a related person with respect to the DISC from which it receives a producer's loan, or a member of the same controlled group as the DISC.

(iv) Unpaid balance of producer's loans. For purposes of applying this section, the unpaid balance of producer's loans does not include the unpaid balance of any producer's loan to the extent the loan has been deducted or charged off by the DISC as totally or partially worthless under section 165 or 166.

(v) Refinancing, renewal, and extension. For purposes of applying this section, the refinancing, renewal, or extension of a producer's loan shall be treated as the making of a new loan which may qualify as a producer's loan only if the requirements of subparagraph (1) of this paragraph are met.

(vi) Events subsequent to time loan is made. The determination as to whether a loan qualifies as a producer's loan is made on the basis of the relevant facts taken into account for purposes of determining whether the loan was a producer's loan when made. Thus, for example, if the accumulated DISC income of the lender is later reduced below the unpaid balance of all producer's loans previously made by the DISC, such subsequent decrease in the amount of accumulated DISC income will not result in later disqualification of such loan (or part thereof) as a producer's loan. Similarly, if a loan (or part of a loan) does not qualify as a producer's loan because of an insufficient amount of accumulated DISC income at the time the loan is made, a subsequent increase in the amount of accumulated DISC income will not result in later qualification of such loan (or part thereof) as a producer's loan. As a further example, for purposes of applying the borrower's export related assets limitation described in paragraph (b) of this section, a loan which qualifies as a producer's loan when made will not later be disqualified if property, the gross receipts from the sale or lease of which were includible in the numerator of the fraction described in paragraph (b)(3)(i) of this section at the time of sale or lease by the borrower, is later characterized as excluded property (as defined in § 1.993-3(f).

(vii) Application of tests under paragraphs (b) and (c) on controlled group bases. If the borrower is a member of a controlled group (as defined in § 1.993-1(k)) at the time a loan is made, all amounts that must be determined for purposes of applying the limitation and increased investment requirement with respect to the export-related assets of the borrower (described in paragraphs (b) and (c), respectively, of this section) may be determined at the election of the borrower by aggregating such amounts for all members of the controlled group, determined for the taxable year of each member of the controlled group during which the loan is made, excluding only such members of the group as are DISC's or foreign corporations for such year. However, such amounts may be included only to the extent that such amounts have not already been taken into account in applying the limitation and increased investment requirement with respect to any other borrower. Amounts to be aggregated for all such members if such election is made include, for example, gross receipts (described in paragraph (b)(3)(i) and (ii) of this section) and export-related assets (described in paragraph (b)(2) of this section). The borrower may make such election by causing its written statement of election to be attached to the lending DISC return under section 6011(e)(2) for the first taxable year of the lending DISC within which or with which the borrower's taxable year for which the election is to apply ends. An election once made is binding on all members of the controlled group which includes the borrower with respect to all taxable years of the borrower beginning with its first taxable year for which the election is made. A borrower who makes such election may revoke it only if it secures the consent of the Commissioner to such revocation upon application made through the lending DISC.

(3) Loan out of accumulated DISC income. (i) In general. A loan is a producer's loan only to the extent that it is made out of accumulated DISC income. A loan is made out of accumulated DISC income only if the amount of the loan, when added to the unpaid balance at the time such loan is made of all other producer's loans made by a DISC, does not exceed the amount of accumulated DISC income of the DISC at the beginning of the month in which the loan is made. The amount of accumulated DISC income at the beginning of any month is determined as if the DISC's taxable year closed at the end of the immediately preceding month.

(ii) Presumption. A loan made during a taxable year shall be deemed under subdivision (i) of this subparagraph to have been made out of accumulated DISC income if the balance of producer's loans at the beginning of the year and those made during the year do not exceed accumulated DISC income at the end of the year.

(iii) Deemed distributions. For purposes of this subparagraph, accumulated DISC income as of the end of any taxable year (or month) shall be determined without regard to deemed distributions under section 995(b)(1)(G) for the amount of foreign investment attributable to producer's loans for such year (or for the taxable year for which such month is a part) but actual distributions shall be taken into account.

(4) Evidence and terms of obligation. A loan is a producer's loan only if the loan is evidenced by a note or other evidence of indebtedness which is made by the borrower and which has a stated maturity date not more than 5 years from the date the loan is made. Accordingly, a loan which does not have a stated maturity date or which has a stated maturity date more than 5 years from the date such loan is made can never meet the 5-year requirement of this subparagraph. Thus, for example, even if there is a period of less than 5 years remaining to the stated maturity date of a loan, the loan can never be a producer's loan if it had a stated maturity date more than 5 years from the date it was made. For a further example, if a loan having a period remaining to maturity of 2 years is extended for a further period of 3 years (making a total of 5 years to maturity from the date of the extension), the extension of the loan would under subparagraph (2)(v) of this paragraph constitute the making of a new producer's loan and the original producer's loan would terminate. If, however, a loan having a period remaining to maturity of 2 years is extended for a further period of 4 years (making a total of 6 years to maturity from the date of the extension), the original producer's loan will terminate and the new loan will not be a producer's loan. If a producer's loan is not paid in full at its maturity date and is not formally refinanced, renewed, or extended, such loan shall be deemed to be a new loan which does not have a stated maturity date and, thus, will not be a producer's loan. For purposes of this subparagraph, an evidence of indebtedness is a written instrument of indebtedness. Section 482 and the regulations thereunder are applicable to determine, in the case of a loan by the DISC to a borrower which is owned or controlled directly or indirectly by the same interests as the DISC within the meaning of section 482, whether the interest charged on such loan is at an arm's length rate.

(5) Borrower's trade or business. A loan is a producer's loan only if the loan is made to a person engaged in the United States in the manufacture, production, growth, or extraction (within the meaning of § 1.993-3(c)) of export property determined without regard to § 1.993-3(f)(1)(iii) and (iv). The borrower may also be engaged in other trades or businesses and the loan need not be traceable to specific investments in export property.

(b) Borrower's export related assets limitation. *(1) General rule.* A loan to a borrower is a producer's loan only to the extent that the amount of the loan, when added to the unpaid balance of all other producer's loans made by all DISC's to the borrower which are outstanding at the time the loan is made, does not exceed an amount equal to the amount of the borrower's export-related assets (determined under subparagraph (2) of this paragraph) multiplied by the fraction set forth in subparagraph (3) of this paragraph.

(2) Amount of export-related assets. (i) In general. For purposes of subparagraph (1) of this paragraph, the amount of the borrower's export-related assets is the sum of the amounts described in subdivisions (ii), (iii), and (iv) of this subparagraph.

(ii) Borrower's plant and equipment. The amount described in this subdivision is the sum of the borrower's adjusted bases (determined as of the beginning of the borrower's taxable year in which a loan is made to it) for plant, machinery, equipment, and supporting production facilities, which are located in the United States. Supporting production facilities are all property used primarily in connection with the manufacture, production, growth, or extraction (within the meaning of § 1.993-3(c)) or storage, handling, transportation, or assembly of property by the borrower.

(iii) Borrower's property held primarily for sale or lease. The amount described in this subdivision is the amount of the borrower's property (at the beginning of the taxable year of the borrower in which a loan is made to it) held primarily for sale or lease to customers in the ordinary course of its trade or business. The amount of such property held for sale is determined under the methods of identifying and valuing inventory normally used by the borrower. The amount of such property held for lease or leased is the borrower's adjusted basis, determined under section 1011, for such property.

(iv) Borrower's research and experimental expenditures. The amount described in this subdivision is the aggregate amount, whether or not charged to capital account, of research and experimental expenditures (within the meaning of section 174) incurred in the United States by the borrower during each of its taxable years which begin after December 31, 1971, and precede the taxable year in which the loan is made to the borrower. Such research and experimental expenditures need bear no relationship to export property (as defined in § 1.993-3) of the borrower. The aggregate amount of all such expenditures for each of such preceding taxable years is taken into account for purposes of this subparagraph, regardless of whether all or any portion of the aggregate amount has been taken into account with respect to producer's loans made to the borrower by any DISC in preceding taxable years. The aggregate amount of all such expenditures shall include such expenditures of a corporation, the assets of which were acquired by the borrower in a distribution or a transfer described in section 381(a)(1) or (2) (relating to carryovers in certain corporate acquisitions).

(3) Fraction referred to in subparagraph (1) of this paragraph. (i) Numerator of fraction. The numerator of the fraction set forth in this subparagraph is the sum of the borrower's gross receipts for each of its 3 taxable years immediately preceding the taxable year in which the loan is made (but not including any taxable year beginning before January 1, 1972) from the sale or lease of export property (determined without regard to § 1.993-3(f)(1)(iii) and (iv)) which is manufactured, produced, grown, or extracted (within the meaning of § 1.993-3(c)) by the borrower whether or not sold or leased directly or through a related domestic person (notwithstanding § 1.993-3(a)(4) and (f)(2)). For purposes of the preceding sentence, with respect to a sale or lease to a related DISC in which the transfer price is determined under section 994(a)(1) or (2), the rules under § 1.994-1(c)(5) (relating to incomplete transactions) shall be applied, and with respect to all other sales and leases the rules under § 1.994-1(c)(5) other than subdivision (i)(d) thereof shall be applied.

(ii) Denominator of fraction. The denominator of the fraction set forth in this subparagraph is the sum of the amount included in the numerator and all other gross receipts of the borrower, for each of its taxable years for which gross receipts are included in the numerator of the fraction, from all sales or leases of all property held by the borrower primarily for sale or lease to customers in the ordinary course of its trade or business. For purposes of subdivision (i) of this subparagraph and this subdivision, if such property is sold or leased to a domestic related person which resells or subleases such property, the borrower's gross receipts shall be the gross receipts derived by the domestic related person from the resale or sublease of the export property.

(iii) Taxable years. If the borrower has not engaged in the sale or lease of property (as described in this subparagraph) for the 3 immediately preceding taxable years, or if 3 taxable years beginning after December 31, 1971, have not elapsed, the fraction will be computed on the basis of such gross receipts for its taxable years immediately preceding the loan and beginning after December 31, 1971, during which the borrower has so engaged. No producer's loans can be made to a borrower until after the end of the first taxable year of the borrower beginning after December 31, 1971.

(c) Requirement for increased investment in export-related assets. *(1) In general.* A loan to a borrower is a producer's loan only to the extent that the amount of the loan, when added to the unpaid balance of all other producer's loans made by all DISC's to the borrower during the borrower's taxable year during which such loan is made, does not exceed the amount of the borrower's increase for the year in investment in export-related assets. Such increase for any taxable year is the sum of—

(i) The increase (if any) in the borrower's adjusted basis of certain types of assets as determined under subparagraph (2) of this paragraph and

(ii) The amount (if any) during the year of its research and experimental expenditures as determined under paragraph (b)(2)(iv) of this section.

(2) Increase in adjusted basis. The amount under this subparagraph is the amount (not less than zero) by which—

(i) The borrower's adjusted basis (determined as of the end of its taxable year in which the producer's loan is made) in all of its property which is described in paragraph (b)(2)(ii) (plant and equipment), and (iii) (property held primarily for sale or lease) of this section, including any such property acquired by it during such taxable year, exceeds

(ii) Its adjusted bases in all such property (determined as of the beginning of such year).

(3) Ordering rule. If during the borrower's taxable year the amount of increase in investment in export-related assets determined under this subparagraph is exceeded by amounts loaned to the borrower during such year that would otherwise qualify as producer's loans, such loans shall be applied in the order made against the amount of such increase in order to determine which loans qualify as producer's loans.

(d) Proof of borrower's compliance with paragraphs (b) and (c) of this section. For purposes of paragraphs (b) and (c) of this section, a DISC shall be prepared to establish initially the compliance of the borrower with the requirements of such paragraphs by providing the written statement of the borrower, certified by a certified public accountant, stating that the borrower has complied with the limitation and increased investment requirement in section 993(d)(2) and (3) of the Internal Revenue Code of 1954. In lieu of certification by a certified public accountant, the DISC may attach to its return a statement signed by the borrower under penalties of perjury on a form provided by the Internal Revenue Service certifying that the borrower has complied with the limitation and increased investment requirement in section 993(d)(2) and (3) of the Internal Revenue Code of 1954. For taxable years ending after October 17, 1977, the DISC must attach either the certification by the certified public accountant or the certification by the borrower to its return. Additional full substantiation of the borrower's compliance with the requirements of such paragraphs may be required by the district director. If full substantiation of such compliance is not provided by the DISC (or the borrower) when required, the loan shall be deemed not to be a producer's loan.

(e) Special limitation in the case of domestic film maker. *(1) General rule.* The limitation of paragraph (b) of this section as to the export-related assets of the borrower will be considered satisfied if the DISC—

(i) Is engaged in the trade or business of selling or leasing films which are export property, or is acting as a commission agent for a person who is so engaged,

(ii) Makes a loan to a borrower which is a domestic film maker (as defined in subparagraph (5) of this paragraph) for the purpose of making a film, and

(iii) The amount of such loan, when added to the unpaid balance of all other producer's loans made by all DISC's to the borrower which are outstanding at the time the loan is made, does not exceed an amount determined by multiplying—

(a) The sum of (1) the amount of the export-related assets of the borrower (determined under paragraph (b)(2)(1) of this section as of the beginning of the borrower's taxable year in which the loan is made), plus (2) the amount of a reasonable estimate of the amount of such export-related assets obtained or to be obtained by the borrower during such year and subsequent years with respect to films as to which filming begins within such year by

(b) The percentage which, based on the experience of other film makers of similar films for the 5 calendar years preceding the calendar year in which the loan is made, the annual gross receipts (as described in § 1.993-6(a)(1), whether or not such films constitute property described therein) of such other film makers from the sale or lease of such films outside the United States is of the annual gross receipts of such other film makers from all sales or leases of such films.

(2) Purpose of loan. A loan by a DISC will be deemed to be for the making of a film if there exists a written agreement between the DISC and the borrower, executed at or before the time the loan is made, stating that the loan is made or to be made to enable the borrower to make such film.

(3) Reasonable estimate of amounts. For purposes of subparagraph (1)(iii)(a)(2) of this paragraph, a reasonable estimate shall be based on the conditions known by the DISC and borrower to exist at the time a loan is made (or which the DISC and borrower have reason to know to exist at such time).

(4) Experience of film makers. For purposes of subparagraph (1)(iii)(b) of this paragraph, the experience of other film makers of similar films for the 5 calendar years preceding the calendar year in which the loan is made shall be derived from such records and statistics as are acknowledged in the trade as reasonably reliable.

(5) Domestic film maker. For purposes of this section, a borrower is a domestic film maker with respect to a film if—

(i) The borrower is a U.S. person within the meaning of section 7701(a)(30), except that (a) with respect to a partnership all of the partners must be U.S. persons and (b) with respect to a corporation all of its officers and at least a majority of its directors must be U.S. persons,

(ii) The borrower is engaged in the trade or business of making the film with respect to which the loan is made,

(iii) Each studio, if any, used or to be used for filming or for recording sound incorporated into such film is located in the United States (as defined in section 7701(a)(9)),

(iv) At least 80 percent of the aggregate playing time of the film is or will be photographed within the United States (as defined in section 7701(a)(9)), and

(v) At least 80 percent of the total amount (not including any amount which is contingent upon receipts or profits of such film and which is fully taxable by the United States) paid or to be paid for services performed in the making of the film is either paid or to be paid to persons who are U.S. persons at the time such services are performed or consists of amounts which are fully taxable by the United States.

(6) Amounts as fully taxable. For purposes of subparagraph (5)(v) of this paragraph, an amount is considered fully taxable by the United States if the entire amount is included in gross income under section 61 or is subject to withholding under any provision of U.S. law or treaty to which the U.S. is a party and is not exempt from taxation under any provision of such law or treaty. Where a nonresident alien individual is engaged for the making of a film or where a foreign corporation is engaged to furnish the services of one of its officers or employees for the making of a film, the amount paid such individual or corporation will be considered as fully taxable by the United States only if it meets the test of this subparagraph.

T.D. 7514, 10/14/77, amend T.D. 7513, 10/14/77, T.D. 7854, 11/16/82.

§ 1.993-5 Definition of related foreign export corporation.

(a) General rule. *(1) Definition.* Under section 993(e), a foreign corporation is a related foreign export corporation with respect to a DISC if—

(i) It is a foreign international sales corporation described in paragraph (b) of this section,

(ii) It is a real property holding company described in paragraph (c) of this section, or

(iii) It is an associated foreign corporation described in paragraph (d) of this section.

(2) Application of this section. It is necessary to determine whether a foreign corporation is a related foreign export corporation with respect to a DISC for the following two purposes:

(i) Qualified export assets. Under § 1.993-2(g), the stock or securities of a related foreign export corporation held by the DISC are qualified export assets.

(ii) Qualified export receipts. Under § 1.993-1(e), (f), and (g), certain receipts of the DISC with respect to stock or securities of a related foreign export corporation held by the DISC are qualified export receipts.

(b) Foreign international sales corporation. *(1) In general.* A foreign corporation is a foreign international sales corporation with respect to a taxable year of a DISC if—

(i) On each day during such taxable year of the DISC on which the foreign corporation has stock issued and outstanding, the DISC owns directly stock of the foreign corporation possessing more than 50 percent of the total combined voting power of all classes of stock of the foreign corporation entitled to vote as determined under the principles of § 1.957-1(b) (relating to definition of controlled foreign corporation),

(ii) 95 percent or more of such foreign corporation's gross receipts (as defined in § 1.993-6) for its taxable year ending with or within such taxable year of the DISC consists of qualified export receipts described in § 1.993-1(b) through (e) or interest described in § 1.993-1(g) derived from any obligations described in § 1.993-2(d) or (e), and

(iii) The sum of the adjusted bases of the assets of the foreign corporation which are qualified export assets described in § 1.993-2(b) through (e) and which are held by the foreign corporation at the close of its taxable year which ends with or within such taxable year of the DISC equals or exceeds 95 percent of the sum of the adjusted bases of all assets held by the foreign corporation at the close of such taxable year.

(2) Certain determinations. The determinations as to whether gross receipts are qualified export receipts described in subparagraph (1)(ii) of this paragraph and as to whether assets are qualified export assets described in subparagraph (1)(iii) of this paragraph are made by applying the requirements of §§ 1.993-1 and 1.993-2 to the foreign corporation as if it were a domestic corporation being tested to determine whether it is a DISC. For purposes of making either of such determinations, the principles of accounting applicable for purposes of computing earnings and profits under § 1.964-1 (relating to a controlled foreign corporation's earnings and profits) shall apply.

(c) Real property holding company. *(1) In general.* A foreign corporation is a real property holding company with respect to a taxable year of a DISC if—

(i) On each day during such taxable year of the DISC on which the foreign corporation has stock issued and outstanding, the DISC owns directly stock of the foreign corporation possessing more than 50 percent of the total combined voting power of all classes of stock of the foreign corporation entitled to vote as determined under the principles of § 1.957-1(b) and

(ii) The sole function of the foreign corporation is to hold title to real property situated outside the United States for the exclusive use of the DISC, title to which may not be held by the DISC (and, if the DISC subleases such property to a related supplier, as described in subparagraph (3) of this paragraph, by such related supplier) under the law of the country in which such property is situated.

(2) Activities of the foreign corporation. For purposes of subparagraph (1)(ii) of this paragraph, a foreign corporation which holds title to real property situated outside the United States may also perform activities with respect to such property (such as management, maintenance, and payment of taxes) which are ancillary to its function of holding title to such property.

(3) Exclusive use by the DISC. Real property held by the foreign corporation must be used exclusively by the DISC whether under a lease or any other arrangement. Real property is not so used by the DISC if the DISC subleases such property to any other person. If, however, during a taxable year of the DISC—

(i) 90 percent or more of the qualified export receipts of the DISC for such year are derived from transactions with respect to which it is a commission agent for a related supplier (as defined in § 1.994-1(a)(3)(ii)), and

(ii) The DISC subleases such property to such related supplier

then such property will be considered as used exclusively by the DISC during such year if such related supplier does not sublease such property.

(d) Associated foreign corporation. *(1) In general.* A foreign corporation is an associated foreign corporation with respect to a taxable year of the DISC if—

(i) On each day during such taxable year of the DISC on which the foreign corporation has stock issued and outstanding, the DISC, or one or more members of the same controlled group of corporations (as defined in subparagraph (2) of this paragraph) as the DISC, owns (within the meaning of sec. 1563(d) and (e)) stock of the foreign corporation possessing less than 10 percent of the total combined voting power of all classes of stock of the foreign corporation entitled to vote, as determined under the principles of § 1.957-1(b), or owns no stock of such corporation, and

(ii) The ownership of stock, or of securities (as defined in § 1.993-2(g)), of the foreign corporation by the DISC or by one or more members of such controlled group of corporations reasonably furthers a transaction or transactions giving rise to qualified export receipts for the DISC.

(2) Controlled group of corporations. For purposes of this paragraph, the term "controlled group of corporations" has the same meaning assigned to the term in section 1563(a) and not section 993(a)(3) and § 1.993-1(k). Thus, for purposes of this paragraph, the test of control is 80 percent control and, since the rules of section 1563(b) apply, only domestic members are considered to be members of the controlled group.

(3) Furtherance of qualified export receipts. Ownership of stock or securities of a foreign corporation will be considered as reasonably furthering a transaction or transactions giving rise to qualified export receipts for a DISC if—

(i) The ownership is necessary to obtain or maintain the foreign corporation as a customer of the DISC or of a related supplier, as defined in § 1.994-1(a)(3)(ii) of the DISC or to aid the sales distribution system of the DISC or of such related supplier, and

(ii) The amount of the investment in the foreign corporation bears a reasonable relationship to the amount of the DISC's annual net profit from transactions in its trade or business which it may reasonably expect to derive on account of such ownership.

In determining whether the amount of the investment is reasonable, there shall be taken into account any stock or securities of the foreign corporation owned by any other foreign corporation which, if it were a domestic corporation, would be a member of the same controlled group of corporations as the DISC.

T.D. 7514, 10/14/77.

---

§ 1.993-6 Definition of gross receipts.

(a) General rule. Under section 993(f), for purposes of sections 991 through 996, the gross receipts of a person for a taxable year are—

(1) The total amounts received or accrued by the person from the sale or lease of property held primarily for sale or lease in the ordinary course of a trade or business, and

(2) Gross income recognized from all other sources, such as, for example, from—

(i) The furnishing of services (whether or not related to the sale) or lease of property described in subparagraph (1) of this paragraph,

(ii) Dividends and interest,

(iii) The sale at a gain of any property not described in subparagraph (1) of this paragraph, and

(iv) Commission transactions as and to the extent described in paragraph (e) of this section.

(b) Nongross receipts items. For purposes of paragraph (a) of this section, gross receipts do not include amounts received or accrued by a person from—

(1) The proceeds of a loan or of the repayment of a loan, or

(2) A receipt of property in a transaction to which section 118 (relating to contribution to capital) or 1032 (relating to exchange of stock for property) applies.

(c) Nonreduction of total amounts. For purposes of paragraph (a) of this section, the total amounts received or accrued by a person are not reduced by returns and allowances, costs of goods sold, expenses, losses, a deduction for dividends received under section 243, or any other deductible amounts.

(d) Method of accounting. For purposes of paragraph (a) of this section, the total amounts received or accrued by a person shall be determined under the method of accounting used in computing its taxable income. If, for example, a DISC receives advance or installment payments for the sale or lease of property described in paragraph (a)(1) of this section, for the furnishing of services, or which represent recognized gain from the sale of property not described in paragraph (a)(1) of this section, any amount of such advance payments is considered to be gross receipts of the DISC for the taxable year for which such amount is included in the gross income of the DISC.

(e) Commission transactions. *(1)* In the case of transactions which give rise to a commission on the sale or lease of property or the furnishing of services by a principal, the amount recognized by the commission agent as gross income from all such transactions shall be the gross receipts derived by the principal from the sale or lease of the property, or the gross income derived by the principal from the furnishing of services, with respect to which the commissions are derived. In the case of a commission agent for a related supplier (as defined in § 1.994-1(a)(3)(ii)), the gross receipts or gross income of such agent shall be determined as if it used the same method of accounting as its related supplier. In the case of a commission agent for a principal other than a related supplier, the gross receipts or gross income of such principal shall be determined as if such principal used the same method of accounting as its agent.

(2) If the commission arrangement provides that the commission agent will receive a commission only with respect to sales or leases of export property, or the furnishing of services, which result in qualified export receipts, the commission agent will not take into account the gross receipts or gross income, as the case may be, derived by the principal from any transaction for which the commission agent would not be entitled to a commission under the commission arrangement.

(f) Example. The provisions of this section may be illustrated by the following example:

Example. During 1973, M, a related supplier (as defined in § 1.994-1(a)(3)(ii)) of N, is engaged in the manufacture of machines in the United States. N, a calendar year taxpayer, is engaged in the sale and lease of such machines in foreign countries. N furnishes services which are related and subsidiary to its sale and lease of such machines. N also acts as a commission agent in foreign countries for Z, an unrelated supplier, with respect to Z's sale of products. N receives dividends on stock owned by it in a related foreign export corporation (as defined in § 1.993-5), interest on producer's loans made to M, and proceeds from sales of business assets located outside the United States resulting in recognized gains and losses. N's gross receipts for 1973 are $3,550, computed on the basis of the additional facts assumed in the table below:

(1) N's sales receipts for machines manufactured by M (without reduction for cost of goods sold and selling expenses)	$1,500
(2) N's lease receipts for machines manufactured by M (without reduction for depreciation and leasing expenses)	500
(3) N's gross income from services for machines manufactured by M (without reduction for service expenses)	400
(4) Z's sale receipts for products manufactured by Z (without reduction for Z's cost of goods sold, commissions on sales, and commission sales expenses)	550
(5) Dividends received by N	150
(6) Interest received by N on producer's loans	200
(7) Proceeds received by N representing recognized gain (but not losses) from sales of business assets located outside the United States	250
(8) N's gross receipts	3,550

T.D. 7514, 10/14/77.

§ 1.993-7 Definition of United States.

Under section 993(g), the term "United States" includes the States, the District of Columbia, the Commonwealth of Puerto Rico, and possessions of the United States. For the requirement that a DISC must be incorporated and existing under the laws of a State or the District of Columbia, see § 1.992-1(a)(1).

T.D. 7514, 10/14/77.

§ 1.994-1 Inter-company pricing rules for DISC's.

(a) In general. *(1) Scope.* In the case of a transaction described in paragraph (b) of this section, section 994 permits a person related to a DISC to determine the allowable transfer price charged the DISC (or commission paid the DISC) by its choice of three methods described in paragraph (c)(2), (3), and (4) of this section: The "4 percent" gross receipts method, the "50-50" combined taxable income method, and the section 482 method. Under the first two methods, the DISC is entitled to 10 percent of its export promotion expenses as additional taxable income. When the gross receipts method or combined taxable income method is applied to a transaction, the Commissioner may not make distributions, apportionments, or allocations as provided by section 482 and the regulations thereunder. For rules as to certain "incomplete transactions" and for computing combined taxable income, see paragraph (c)(5) and (6) of this section. Grouping of transactions for purposes of applying the method chosen is provided by paragraph (c)(7) of this section. The rules in paragraph (c) of this section are directly applicable only in the case of sales or exchanges of export property to a DISC for resale, and are applicable by analogy to leases, commissions, and services as provided in paragraph (d) of this section. For rules limiting the application of the gross receipts method and combined taxable income method so that the supplier related to the DISC will not incur a loss on transactions, see paragraph (e)(1) of this section. Paragraph (e)(2) of this section provides for the applicability of section 482 to resales by the DISC to related persons. Paragraph (e)(3) of this section provides for the time by which a reasonable estimate of the transfer price (including commissions and other payments) should be paid. The subsequent determination and further adjustments to transfer prices are set forth in paragraph (e)(4) of this section. Export promotion expenses are defined in paragraph (f) of this section. Paragraph (g) of this section has several examples illustrating the provisions of this section. Section 1.994-2 prescribes the marginal costing rules authorized by section 994(b)(2).

(2) Performance of substantial economic functions. The application of section 994(a)(1) or (2) does not depend on the extent to which the DISC performs substantial economic functions (except with respect to export promotion expenses). See paragraph (l) of § 1.993-1.

(3) Related party and related supplier. For the purposes of this section—

(i) The term "related party" means a person which is owned or controlled directly or indirectly by the same interests as the DISC within the meaning of section 482 and § 1.482-1(a).

(ii) The term "related supplier" means a related party which singly engages in a transaction directly with the DISC which is subject to the rules of section 994 and this section. However, a DISC may have different related suppliers with respect to different transactions. If, for example, X owns all the stock of Y, a corporation, and of Z, a DISC, and sells a product to Y which is resold to Z, only Y is the related supplier of Z, and, thus, only the resale from Y to Z is subject to section 994 and this section. If, however, X sells directly to Z and Y also sells directly to Z, then, as to the transactions involving direct sales to Z, each of X and Y is a related supplier of Z.

(b) Transactions to which section 994 applies. Section 994(a)(3) may be applied, as described in paragraph (a) of this section, to any transaction between a related supplier and a DISC. Section 994(a)(1) or (2) may be applied, as described in paragraph (a) of this section, to a transaction between a related supplier and a DISC only in the following cases:

(1) Where the related supplier sells export property to the DISC for resale or where the DISC is commission agent for the related supplier on sales by the related supplier of export property to third parties whether or not related parties. For purposes of this section, references to sales include exchanges.

(2) Where the related supplier leases export property to the DISC for sublease for a comparable period with comparable terms of payment or where the DISC is commission agent for the related supplier on leases by the related supplier of export property to third parties whether or not related parties.

(3) Where services are furnished by a related supplier which are related and subsidiary to any sale or lease by the DISC, acting as principal or commission agent, of export property under subparagraph (1) or (2) of this paragraph.

(4) Where engineering or architectural services for construction projects located (or proposed for location) outside of the United States are furnished by a related supplier where the DISC is acting as principal or commission agent with respect to the furnishing of such services to a third party whether or not a related party.

(5) Where the related supplier furnishes managerial services in furtherance of the production of qualified export receipts of an unrelated DISC where the related DISC is acting as principal or commission agent with respect to the furnishing of such services to an unrelated DISC.

Transactions are included, for purposes of this paragraph, only if they give rise to qualified export receipts (within the meaning of section 993(a)) in the hands of the related DISC. If a transaction is not included in subparagraph (1), (2), (3), (4), or (5) of this paragraph, the rules of section 994(a)(1) or (2) do not apply. Thus, for example, the rules of section 994(a)(1) or (2) would not apply if a DISC purchased export property from its related supplier and leased such property to a third party.

(c) Transfer price for sales of export property. *(1) In general.* Under this paragraph, rules are prescribed for computing the allowable price for a transfer from a related supplier to a DISC in the case of a sale of export property described in paragraph (b)(1) of this section.

(2) The "4-percent" gross receipts method. Under the gross receipts method of pricing, the transfer price for a sale by the related supplier to the DISC is the price as a result of which the taxable income derived by the DISC from the sale will not exceed the sum of (i) 4 percent of the qualified export receipts of the DISC derived from the sale of the export property (as defined in section 993(c)) and (ii) 10 percent of the export promotion expenses (as defined in paragraph (f) of this section) of the DISC attributable to such qualified export receipts.

(3) The "50-50" combined taxable income method. Under the combined taxable income method of pricing, the transfer price for a sale by the related supplier to the DISC is the price as a result of which the taxable income derived by the DISC from the sale will not exceed the sum of (i) 50 percent of the combined taxable income (as defined in subparagraph (6) of this paragraph) of the DISC and its related supplier attributable to the qualified export receipts from such sale and (ii) 10 percent of the export promotion expenses (as defined in paragraph (f) of this section) of the DISC attributable to such qualified export receipts.

(4) Section 482 method. If the rules of subparagraphs (2) and (3) of this paragraph are inapplicable to a sale or a taxpayer does not choose to use them, the transfer price for a sale by the related supplier to the DISC is to be determined on the basis of the sale price actually charged but subject to the rules provided by section 482 and the regulations thereunder.

(5) Incomplete transactions. (i) For purposes of the gross receipts and combined taxable income methods, where property (encompassed within a transaction or group chosen under subparagraph (7) of this paragraph) is transferred by a related supplier to a DISC during a taxable year of either the DISC or related supplier, but some or all of such property is not sold by the DISC during such year—

(a) The transfer price of such property sold by the DISC during such year shall be computed separately from the transfer price of the property not sold by the DISC during such year,

(b) With respect to such property not sold by the DISC during such year, the transfer price paid by the DISC for such year shall be the related supplier's cost of goods sold (see subparagraph (6)(ii) of this paragraph) with respect to the property, except that, with respect to such taxable years ending on or before August 15, 1975, the transfer price paid by the DISC shall be at least (but need not exceed) the related supplier's cost of goods sold with respect to the property.

(c) For the subsequent taxable year during which such property is resold by the DISC, an additional amount shall be paid by the DISC (to be treated as income for such year by the related supplier) equal to the excess of the amount which would have been the transfer price under this section had the transfer to the DISC by the related supplier and the resale by the DISC taken place during the taxable year of the DISC during which it resold the property over the amount already paid under *(b)* of this subdivision.

(d) The time and manner of payment of transfer prices required by (b) and (c) of this subdivision shall be determined under paragraph (e)(3), (4), and (5) of this section.

(ii) For purposes of this paragraph, a DISC may determine the year in which it receives property from a related supplier and the year in which it sells property in accordance with the method of identifying goods in its inventory properly used under section 471 or 472 (relating respectively to general rule for inventories and to LIFO inventories. Transportation expense of the related supplier in connection with a transaction to which this subparagraph applies shall be treated as an item of cost of goods sold with respect to the property if the related supplier includes the cost of intracompany transportation between its branches, divisions, plants, or other units in its cost of goods sold (see subparagraph (6)(ii) of this paragraph).

(6) Combined taxable income. For purposes of this section, the combined taxable income of a DISC and its related supplier from a sale of export property is the excess of the gross receipts (as defined in section 993(f)) of the DISC from such sale over the total costs of the DISC and related supplier which relate to such gross receipts. Gross receipts from a sale do not include interest with respect to the sale. Combined taxable income under this paragraph shall be determined after taking into account under paragraph (e)(2) of this section all adjustments required by section 482 with respect to transactions to which such section is applicable. In determining the gross receipts of the DISC and the total costs of the DISC and related supplier which relate to such gross receipts, the following rules shall be applied:

(i) Subject to subdivisions (ii) through (v) of this subparagraph, the taxpayer's method of accounting used in computing taxable income will be accepted for purposes of determining amounts and the taxable year for which items of income and expense (including depreciation) are taken into account. See § 1.991-1(b)(2) with respect to the method of accounting which may be used by a DISC.

(ii) Cost of goods sold shall be determined in accordance with the provisions of § 1.61-3. See sections 471 and 472 and the regulations thereunder with respect to inventories. With respect to property to which an election under section 631 applies (relating to cutting of timber considered as a sale or exchange), cost of goods sold shall be determined by applying § 1.631-1(d)(3) and (e) (relating to fair market value as of the beginning of the taxable year of the standing timber cut during the year considered as its cost).

(iii) Costs (other than cost of goods sold) which shall be treated as relating to gross receipts from sales of export property are (a) the expenses, losses, and other deductions definitely related, and therefore allocated and apportioned, thereto, and (b) a ratable part of any other expenses, losses, or other deductions which are not definitely related to a class of gross income, determined in a manner consistent with the rules set forth in § 1.861-8.

(iv) The taxpayer's choice in accordance with subparagraph (7) of this paragraph as to the grouping of transactions shall be controlling, and costs deductible in a taxable year shall be allocated and apportioned to the items or classes of gross income of such taxable year resulting from such grouping.

(v) If an account receivable arising with respect to a sale of export property is transferred by the related supplier to a DISC which is a member of the same controlled group within the meaning of § 1.993-1(k) for an amount reflecting a discount from the selling price taken into account in computing (without regard to this subdivision) combined taxable income of the DISC and its related supplier, then the combined taxable income from such sale shall be reduced by the amount of the discount.

(7) Grouping transactions. (i) Generally, the determinations under this section are to be made on a transaction-by-transaction basis. However, at the annual choice of the taxpayer some or all of these determinations may be made on the basis of groups consisting of products or product lines.

(ii) A determination by a taxpayer as to a product or a product line will be accepted by a district director if such determination conforms to any one of the following standards: (a) A recognized industry or trade usage, or (b) the 2-digit major groups (or any inferior classifications or combinations thereof, within a major group) of the Standard Industrial Classification as prepared by the Statistical Policy Division of the Office of Management and Budget, Executive Office of the President.

(iii) A choice by the taxpayer to group transactions for a taxable year on a product or product line basis shall apply to all transactions with respect to that product or product line consummated during the taxable year. However, the choice of a product or product line grouping applies only to transactions covered by the grouping and, as to transactions not encompassed by the grouping, the determinations are made on a transaction-by-transaction basis. For example, the taxpayer may choose a product grouping with respect to one product and use the transaction-by-transaction method for another product within the same taxable year.

(iv) For rules as to grouping certain related and subsidiary services, see paragraph (d)(3)(ii) of this section.

(d) Rules under section 994(a)(1) and (2) for transactions other than sales. The following rules are prescribed for purposes of applying the gross receipts method or combined taxable income method to transactions other than sales:

(1) Leases. In the case of a lease of export property by a related supplier to a DISC for sublease by the DISC to produce gross receipts, for any taxable year the amount of rent the DISC must pay to the related supplier shall be determined under the DISC's lease with its related supplier but must be computed in a manner consistent with the rules in paragraph (c) of this section for computing the transfer price in the case of sales and resales of export property under the gross receipts method or combined taxable income method. For purposes of applying this subparagraph, transactions may not be so grouped on a product or product line basis under the rules of paragraph (c)(7) of this section as to combine in any one group of transactions both lease transactions and sale transactions involving the same product or product line.

(2) Commissions. If any transaction to which section 994 applies is handled on a commission basis for a related supplier by a DISC and such commissions give rise to qualified expert receipts under section 993(a)—

(i) The amount of the income that may be earned by the DISC in any year is the amount, computed in a manner consistent with paragraph (c) of this section, which the DISC would have been permitted to earn under the gross receipts method, the combined taxable income method, or section 482 method if the related supplier had sold (or leased) the property or service to the DISC and the DISC in turn sold (or subleased) to a third party, whether or not a related party, and

(ii) The maximum commission the DISC may charge the related supplier is the sum of the amount of income determined under subdivision (i) of this subparagraph plus the DISC's total costs for the transaction as determined under paragraph (c)(6) of this section.

(3) Receipts from services. (i) Related and subsidiary services attributable to the year of the export transaction. The gross receipts for related and subsidiary services described in paragraph (b)(3) of this section shall be treated as part of the receipts from the export transaction to which such services are related and subsidiary, but only if, under the arrangement between the DISC and its related supplier and the accounting method otherwise employed by the DISC, the income from such services is includible for the same taxable year as income from such export transaction.

(ii) Other services. In the case of related and subsidiary services to which subdivision (i) of this subparagraph does not apply and other services described in paragraph (b)(4) or (5) of this section performed by a related supplier (relating respectively to engineering and architectural services and certain managerial services), the amount of taxable income which the DISC may derive for any taxable year shall be determined under the arrangement between the DISC and its related supplier and shall be computed in a manner consistent with the rules in paragraph (c) of this section for computing the transfer price in the case of sales for resale of export property under the gross receipts method or combined taxable income method. Related and subsidiary services to which subdivision (i) of this subparagraph does not apply may be grouped, under the rules for grouping of transactions in paragraph (c)(7) of this section, with the products or product lines to which they are related and subsidiary, so long as the grouping of services chosen is consistent with the grouping of products or product lines chosen for the taxable year in which either the products or product lines were sold or in which payment for such services is received or accrued. The rules for grouping of transactions in paragraph (c)(7) of this section shall not apply with respect to the determination of taxable income which the DISC may derive from other services described in paragraph (b)(4) or (5) of this section performed by a related supplier or commissions on such services, and such determination shall be made only on a transaction-by-transaction basis.

(e) Methods of applying paragraphs (c) and (d) of this section. *(1) Limitation on DISC income ("no loss" rule).* (i) In general. Except as otherwise provided in this subparagraph, neither the gross receipts method nor the combined taxable income method may be applied to cause in any taxable year a loss to the related supplier, but either method may be applied to the extent it does not cause a loss. A loss to a related supplier would result if the taxable income of the DISC would exceed the combined taxable income of the related supplier and the DISC. If, however, there is no combined taxable income of the DISC and the related supplier (because, for example, a combined loss is incurred), a transfer price (or commission) will not be deemed to cause a loss to the related supplier if it allows the DISC to recover an amount not in excess of its costs (if any).

(ii) Special rule for applying "4 percent" gross receipts method to sales. A transfer price or commission, determined under the "4 percent" gross receipts method (determined without regard to subdivision (i) of this subparagraph), for a sale of export property referred to in paragraph (b)(1) of this section, will not be considered to cause a loss for the related supplier if for the DISC's taxable year, the ratio that (a) the taxable income of the DISC derived from such sale by using such price or commission bears to (b) the DISC's gross receipts from such sale is not greater than the ratio that (c) all of the taxable income of the related supplier and the DISC from all sales of the same product or product line (domestic and foreign) to third parties whether or not related parties bears to (d) the total gross receipts of the related supplier and the DISC from such sales. For purposes of the preceding sentence, sales between the DISC and its related suppliers shall not be taken into account under (c) or (d) of this subdivision. For example, assume that for a taxable year of a DISC the total costs of the related supplier and the DISC with respect to all sales ($150 for domestic and $44 for foreign) of a product line are $194 and the total gross receipts of the related supplier and the DISC with respect to such sales are $200 so that the total taxable income of the related supplier and the DISC with respect to such sales is $6. The parties would thus be entitled to compute a transfer price determined under the gross receipts method on any given sale of product A of such product line by the related supplier to the DISC which would allocate to the DISC taxable income equal to not more than 3 percent (i.e., $6/$200) of its gross receipts derived from its resale of such product. If the DISC were to resell an item of product A for $10, the transfer price paid by the DISC to the related supplier determined under the gross receipts method could be as low as $9.70.

(iii) Grouping transactions. For purposes of subdivision (i) of this subparagraph, the basis for grouping transactions chosen by the taxpayer under paragraph (c)(7) of this section for the taxable year shall be applied. For purposes of making the computations of subdivision (ii)(c) and (d) of this subparagraph, however the taxpayer may choose any basis for grouping transactions permissible under paragraph (c)(7) of this section, even though it may not be the same basis as that already chosen under paragraph (c)(7) of this section for computing transfer prices or commissions to a DISC. If, for example, the taxpayer has chosen to group transactions on a product basis for computing transfer prices or commissions to a DISC for a taxable year, the taxpayer may still group transactions on a product line basis for purposes of computing taxable income and total gross receipts under subdivision (ii)(c) and (d) of this subparagraph. For a further example, if the taxpayer computes taxable income for one group of transactions under the gross receipts method and computes taxable income for a second group of transactions under the combined taxable income method, the taxpayer may aggregate these transactions for purposes of computing taxable income and total gross receipts under subdivision (ii)(c) and (d) of this subparagraph.

(2) Relationship to section 482. In applying the rules under section 994, it may be necessary to first take into account the price of a transfer (or other transaction) between the DISC (or related supplier) and a related party which is subject to the arm's length standard of section 482. Thus, for example, where a related supplier sells export property to a DISC which the related supplier purchased from related parties, the costs taken into account in computing the combined taxable income of the DISC and the related supplier are determined after any necessary adjustment under section 482 of the price paid by the related supplier to the related parties. In applying section 482 to a transfer by a DISC, however, the DISC and its related supplier are treated as if they were a single entity carrying on all the functions performed by the DISC and the related supplier with respect to the transaction and the DISC shall be allowed to receive under

the section 482 standard the amount the related supplier would have received had there been no DISC.

(3) Initial payment of transfer price or commission. (i) The amount of a transfer price (or reasonable estimate thereof) actually charged by a related supplier to a DISC, or a sales commission (or reasonable estimate thereof) actually charged by a DISC to a related supplier, in a transaction to which section 994 applies must be paid no later than 60 days following the close of the taxable year of the DISC during which the transaction occurred.

(ii) Payment must be in the form of money, property (including accounts receivable from sales by or through the DISC), a written obligation which qualifies as debt under the safe harbor rule of § 1.992-1(d)(2)(ii), or an accounting entry offsetting the account receivable against an existing debt owed by the person in whose favor the account receivable was established to the person with whom it engaged in the transaction. The form of the payment to a DISC need not be a qualified export asset under § 1.993-2. However, for the requirement that the adjusted basis of the qualified export assets of the DISC at the close of its taxable year must equal or exceed 95 percent of the sum of the adjusted bases of all assets of the DISC at the close of its taxable year, see section 992(a)(1)(B).

(iii) If the district director can demonstrate, based upon the data available as of the 60th day after the close of such taxable year, that the amount actually paid did not represent a reasonable estimate of the transfer price or commission (as the case may be) to be determined under section 994 and this section, an indebtedness will be deemed to arise, from the person required to make the payment in favor of the person to whom the payment is required to be made, in an amount equal to the difference between the amount of the transfer price or commission determined under section 994 and this section and the amount (if any) actually paid and received. Such indebtedness will be deemed to arise as of the date the transaction occurred which gave rise to the indebtedness, except that, if such transaction occurred in a taxable year of the DISC ending on or before August 15, 1975, at the taxpayer's option, the indebtedness will be deemed to arise as of the date by which payment was required under subdivision (i) of this paragraph (e)(3). Such indebtedness owed to a DISC shall be treated as an asset but shall not be treated as a trade receivable or other qualified export asset (see § 1.993-2(d)(3)) as of the end of the taxable year of the DISC in which the indebtedness is deemed to arise.

(iv) (a) Except with respect to incomplete transactions to which paragraph (c)(5)(i)(b) of this section applies, if the amount actually paid results in the DISC realizing at least 50 percent of the DISC's taxable income from the transaction as reported in its tax return for the taxable year the transaction is completed, then the amount actually paid shall be deemed to be a reasonable estimate of such transfer price or commission.

(b) With respect to incomplete transactions to which paragraph (c)(5)(i)(b) of this section applies and which were initiated during a taxable year ending after August 15,. 1975, the amount actually paid shall be deemed to be a reasonable estimate of such transfer price if any one of the following three tests is met:

(1) The amount actually paid by the DISC to the related supplier in respect of the property does not exceed the related supplier's cost of goods sold (see paragraph (c)(6)(ii) of this section) with respect to the property.

(2) If the transaction is completed by the date on which the DISC's return is required to be filed for the year in which the transaction was initiated, the amount actually paid by the DISC to the related supplier in respect of the property results in the DISC realizing at least 50 percent of the DISC's taxable income from the transaction when completed.

(3) The percentage that (i) an amount equal to (a) the amount actually paid by the DISC to the related supplier in respect of the property minus (b) the related supplier's cost of goods sold with respect to the property, bears to (ii) the related supplier's cost of goods sold in respect of the property, is not greater than 50 percent of the percentage that (iii) the combined taxable income for completed transactions of the same group as the property during the DISC's taxable year in which the incomplete transaction was initiated, bears to (iv) the cost of goods sold of the related supplier and DISC with respect to such transactions.

(c) For purposes of this subdivision (iv), whether the transfer price or commission actually paid is deemed a reasonable estimate may be determined on the basis for grouping transactions chosen by the taxpayer under paragraph (c)(5) and (7) of this section.

(4) Subsequent determination of transfer price or commission. The DISC and its related supplier would ordinarily determine under section 994 and this section the transfer price payable by the DISC (or the commission payable to the DISC) for a transaction before the DISC files its return for the taxable year of the transaction. After the DISC has filed its return, a redetermination of the transfer price (or commission) may only be made if permitted by the Code and the regulations thereunder. Such a redetermination would include a redetermination by reason of an adjustment under section 482 and the regulations thereunder or section 861 and § 1.861-8 which affects the amounts which entered into the determination of the transfer price or commission.

(5) Procedure for adjustments to transfer price or commission. (i) (a) If the transfer price (or commission) for a transaction determined under section 994 is different from the price (or commission) actually charged, the person who received too small a transfer price (or commission) or paid too large a transfer price (or commission) shall establish (or be deemed to have established), at the date of the determination or redetermination under subparagraph (4) of this paragraph of the transfer price (or commission) under section 994, an account receivable from the person with whom it engaged in the transaction equal to the difference in amount between the transfer price (or commission) so determined and the transfer price (or commission) previously paid and received. If the account receivable due the DISC is paid within 90 days after the date it is established (or deemed established), then as of the end of the taxable year of the DISC in which the transaction occurred which gave rise to the indebtedness, the account receivable shall be treated as an asset and, under § 1.993-2(d)(3) as a trade receivable, and thus as a qualified export asset.

(b) If, for example, during 1972, a DISC which uses the calendar year as its taxable year sold a product which it purchased that year from its related supplier and paid a price of $10,000 which price is a reasonable estimate under subparagraph (3)(iii) of this paragraph but is later determined under section 994 to be $8,000 immediately before the DISC filed its return for 1972, the DISC must be paid $2,000 (i.e., $10,000 – $8,000) by its related supplier or establish an account receivable from its related supplier of $2,000. The account receivable may be paid without tax consequences, provided that such account receivable is paid within 90 days after the date it is established (or deemed established). Such account receivable paid within such 90 days will be considered to relate to the taxable year in which the transaction occurred which gave rise thereto rather than the taxable year during which it is established or paid.

(ii) Payment must be in a form specified in subparagraph (3) of this paragraph.

(iii) If an account receivable of a DISC described in subdivision (i) of this paragraph (e)(5) is not paid within 90 days of the date it is established (or deemed established), then, as of the end of the taxable year of the DISC in which the transaction occurred which gives rise to the indebtedness, the account receivable shall be treated as an asset except that, if the account receivable is established (or deemed established) in a taxable year of the DISC ending on or before August 15, 1975, at the taxpayer's option, the account receivable shall be treated as an asset as of the end of such taxable year. However, under § 1.993-2(d)(3), an account receivable referred to in the preceding sentence shall not be treated as a trade receivable or other qualified export assets.

(iv) An account receivable established in accordance with subdivision (i) of this subparagraph shall bear interest at an arm's length rate, computed in the manner provided by § 1.482-2(a)(2) from the day after the date the account receivable is deemed established to the date of payment. The interest so computed shall be accrued and included in the taxpayer's taxable income for each taxable year during which the account receivable is outstanding.

(v) (a) In lieu of establishing an account receivable in accordance with subdivision (i) of this subparagraph for all or part of an amount due a related supplier, the related supplier and DISC are permitted to treat all or part of any distribution which was made by the DISC out of its previously taxed income with respect to the year to which the determination or redetermination relates as an additional payment of transfer price or repayment of commission (and not as a distribution) made as of the date the distribution was made. Any additional amount arising on the determination or redetermination due the related supplier after this treatment shall be represented by an account receivable established under subdivision (i) of this subparagraph. To the extent that a distribution is so treated under this subdivision (v), it shall cease to qualify as distribution for any Federal income tax purpose, and the DISC's account for previously taxed income shall be adjusted accordingly. If all or part of any distribution made to a shareholder other than the related supplier is recharacterized under this subdivision (v), the related supplier shall establish an account receivable from that shareholder for the amount so recharacterized. Such account receivable shall be paid in the time and manner set forth in this paragraph (e)(5). In order to obtain the relief provided by this subdivision (v), the conditions and procedures prescribed by Revenue Procedure 84-3 must be met. The provisions of this paragraph (e)(5)(v) shall apply to all open taxable years ending after December 31, 1971.

(b) If, for example, during 1982, a DISC commission from a related supplier with respect to a transaction completed in 1980 was redetermined to be $1,000 less than the commission actually charged by, and paid to, the DISC, the amount of any distribution previously made by the DISC from its 1980 previously taxed income to the related supplies as a shareholder may, to the extent of $1,000, be treated not as a distribution but as a repayment of the commission.

(vi) The procedure for adjustments to transfer price provided by this subparagraph does not apply to incomplete transactions described in paragraph (c)(5)(i)(b) of this section. Such procedure will, however, be applied to any such transaction with respect to the taxable year in which the transaction is completed.

(6) Examples. The provisions of this paragraph may be illustrated by the following examples:

Example (1). (i) During 1975, a DISC which uses the calendar year as its taxable year purchased a product from its related supplier and made an initial payment of $8,500. If the $8,500 were determined to be the transfer price under section 994, the DISC's taxable income from the transaction would be $1,000. Immediately before the DISC filed its return for 1975, under section 994 it is determined that the transfer price is $8,000 and the DISC's taxable income is $1,500. Thus, the requirement of a reasonable estimate under subparagraph (3) of this paragraph was met because the amount ($8,500) actually paid resulted in the DISC realizing taxable income of $1,000 which is not less than 50 percent of the DISC's taxable income ($1,500) from the transaction as determined under section 994.

(ii) Pursuant to subparagraph (5) of this paragraph, an account receivable due the DISC for $500, i.e., $8,500 − $8,000, is established on September 15, 1976, the date the DISC files its return for 1975, and is paid on December 1, 1976. The account receivable for $500 will be considered to relate to the taxable year (1975) in which the transaction occurred which gave rise thereto and will be a qualified export asset under § 1.993-2(d)(3) for the last day of such year.

Example (2). Assume the same facts as in example (1) except that the account receivable for $500 is paid on January 1, 1977. The account receivable for $500 will still be considered to relate to the taxable year (1975) in which the transaction occurred which gave rise thereto. However, such account receivable will be treated as an asset which is not a qualified export asset under § 1.993-2(d)(3) for the last day of such year.

(f) Export promotion expenses. *(1) Purpose of expense.* (i) In order for an expense or cost of a type described in subparagraph (2) of this paragraph to be an export promotion expense, the expense or cost must be incurred or treated as incurred by the DISC (under subparagraph (7) of this paragraph) to advance the sale, lease, or other distribution of export property for use, consumption, or distribution outside the United States. Costs of services in performing installation (but not assembly) on the site and for meeting warranty commitments if such services are related and subsidiary (within the meaning of § 1.993-1(d)) to any qualified sale, lease, or other distribution of export property by the DISC (or with respect to which the DISC received a commission) will be considered to advance the sale, lease, or other distribution of export property. General and administrative expenses attributable to billing customers, other clerical functions of the DISC, or generally operating the DISC, will also be considered to advance the sale, lease, or other distribution of export property.

(ii) Where an expense or cost incurred or treated as incurred by the DISC qualifies only in part as an export promotion expense, such expense or cost must be allocated between the qualified portion and such other portion on a reasonable basis. See § 1.994-2(b)(2) for the option of the related supplier not to claim expenses as export promotion expenses.

(2) Types of expenses. The only expenses or costs which may be export promotion expenses are those expenses or costs meeting the test of subparagraph (1) of this paragraph which constitute—

(i) Ordinary and necessary expenses of the DISC paid or incurred during the DISC's taxable year in carrying on any trade or business, allowable as deductions under section 162, such as expenses for market studies, advertising, salaries and wages (including contributions or compensations deductible under section 404) of sales, clerical, and other personnel, rentals on property, sales commissions, warehousing, and other selling expenses,

(ii) A reasonable allowance under section 167 for exhaustion, wear and tear, or obsolescence of the property of the DISC,

(iii) Costs of freight (subject to the limitations of subparagraph (4) of this paragraph),

(iv) Costs of packaging for export (as defined in subparagraph (5) of this paragraph), or

(v) Costs of designing and labeling packages exclusively for export markets (under subparagraph (6) of this paragraph).

(3) Ineligible expenses. Items ineligible to be export promotion expenses include, for example, interest expenses, bad debt expenses, freight insurance, State and local income and franchise taxes, the cost of manufacture or assembly operations, and items of cost of goods sold (except as otherwise provided in this paragraph in the case of certain freight, packaging, and designing and labeling expenses). Income or similar taxes eligible for a foreign tax credit under sections 901 and 903 are also not eligible to be export promotion expenses.

(4) Freight expenses. (i) In general. Export promotion expenses include one-half of the freight expense (not including insurance) for shipping export property aboard a U.S.-flag carrier in those cases where law or regulation of the United States or of any State or political subdivision thereof or of any agency or instrumentality of any of these does not require that the export property be shipped aboard a U.S.-flag carrier. For purposes of this paragraph, the term "freight expense" includes charges paid for c.o.d. service, miscellaneous ground charges, such as charges incurred for services normally performed by U.S.-flag carriers, charges for services of loading aboard U.S.-flag carriers normally performed by such carriers, freight forwarders, or independent contractors engaged in loading property, and charges attributable to a freight consolidation function normally performed by freight forwarders. In order for one-half of freight expenses paid to the owner (or the agent of the owner) of a U.S.-flag carrier to be claimed as an export promotion expense, the DISC must obtain a written statement (such as, for example, a bill of lading) from the owner (or the agent) disclosing that the export property was shipped aboard the owner's U.S.-flag carrier or another U.S.-flag carrier, and the DISC must have no reasonable basis for disbelieving such statement of the owner (or the agent). For the requirement of a written statement from a freight forwarder, see subdivision (iv) of this subparagraph.

(ii) U.S.-flag carrier defined. For purposes of this paragraph, the term "U.S.-flag carrier" is an airplane owned and operated by a U.S. person or persons (as defined in section 7701(a)(30)) or a ship documented under the laws of the United States. Shipment initiated by delivery to the U.S. Postal Service shall be considered shipment aboard a U.S.-flag carrier, but not if shipped to a place to which mail shipments from the United States are ordinarily accomplished by land transportation, such as to Canada or Mexico, unless air-mail is specified.

(iii) Shipment pursuant to law or regulation. Shipment pursuant to law or regulation includes instances where a U.S.-flag carrier must be used in order to obtain permission from the Government to make the export. If the law or regulation requires a fixed portion of the export property to be shipped aboard a U.S.-flag carrier, the freight expense on that portion of such export property that was so shipped in order to satisfy such requirement cannot qualify as an export promotion expense.

(iv) Freight forwarders. A payment to a freight forwarder shall be considered freight expense within the meaning of this paragraph to the extent the forwarder utilizes a U.S.-flag carrier. For purposes of this paragraph, the term "freight forwarder" includes air freight consolidators and carriers owned and operated by U.S. persons utilizing U.S.-flag carriers such as non-vessel-owning common carriers. In order for one-half of freight expenses paid to a freight forwarder to be claimed as export promotion expenses, the DISC must obtain a written statement (such as, for example, a bill of lading) from the freight forwarder disclosing that the export property was shipped aboard a U.S.-flag carrier, and the DISC must have no reasonable basis for disbelieving such statement of the freight forwarder.

(v) Freight within the United States. A DISC may not claim as export promotion expense any amount that is attributable to carriage of export property between points within the United States. If, however, export property is carried from the United States to a foreign country on a through shipment pursuant to a single bill of lading or similar document aboard one or more U.S.-flag carriers, the freight expense of such carriage shall not be apportioned between the domestic and foreign portions of such carriage, even though a carrier may stop en route within the United States or the export property may be shifted from one carrier to another, and one-half of such freight expense may be claimed as an export promotion expense. Freight expense does not include the cost of transporting the export property to the depot of the U.S.-flag carrier or freight forwarder for shipment abroad. The expense of shipment of export property initiated by delivery to the U.S. Postal Service for ultimate delivery outside the United States shall be considered as attributable entirely to carriage of such property outside the United States.

(5) Packaging for export. (i) Export promotion expenses include the direct and indirect cost of packaging export property (including the cost of the package) for export whether or not the packaging is the same as domestic packaging. Such packaging costs do not include costs of manufacturing (as defined in the regulations under section 993) and assembly. Thus, if a DISC buys and packages export property for resale, its costs of packaging the export property are export promotion expenses. If, however, the process of such packaging by the DISC is physically integrated with the process of manufacturing the export property by the related supplier, the costs of such packaging are not export promotion expenses.

(ii) The cost of containers leased from a shipping company to which the DISC also pays freight for the property packaged is not a cost of packaging. However, in such circumstances, one-half of the rental charge may be allowable as a freight expense if permitted under subparagraph (4) of this paragraph.

(6) Designing and labeling packages. Export promotion expenses include the direct and indirect costs of designing and labeling packages, including bottles, cans, jars, boxes, cartons, or containers, to the extent incurred for export markets. Thus, for example, to the extent incurred for supplying export markets, the cost of designing labels in a foreign language and the cost of printing such labels are export promotion expenses.

(7) DISC must incur export promotion expenses. (i) In general. In order for an expense to be an export promotion expense it must be incurred or treated as incurred under this subparagraph by the DISC. For example, an expense is incurred by a DISC if the expense results from (a) the DISC incurring an obligation to pay compensation to its employees, (b) depreciation of property owned by the DISC and used by its employees, (c) the DISC incurring an obligation to pay for office supplies used by its employees, (d) the DISC incurring an obligation to pay space costs for use by its employees, or (e) the DISC incurring an obligation to pay other costs supporting efforts by its employees.

(ii) Payments to independent contractors. A payment to an independent contractor, directly or indirectly, is treated as incurred by the DISC if the cost of performing the function performed by the independent contractor would be considered an export promotion expense described in subparagraphs (1) and (2) of this paragraph, if performed by the DISC, and if, in a case where the services of the independent contractor were engaged by a party related to the DISC, such related party and such DISC agreed in writing before the contract was entered into that a specified portion or all of the contract was for the benefit of the DISC and that all of the expenses of the contract (eligible to be considered as export promotion expenses) with respect to such portion would be borne by the DISC.

(iii) Expenses incurred by related parties. Reimbursements or other payments by a DISC to a related party are export promotion expenses only if the expenses of the related party for which reimbursement is made are for space in a building actually used by employees of the DISC or for export property owned by the DISC. Except as otherwise provided in the preceding sentence, expenses incurred by a foreign international sales corporation (FISC) or a real property holding company (as defined in section 993(e)(1) and (2), respectively) shall not be treated as export promotion expenses of its DISC.

(iv) Selling commissions paid by a DISC. A commission paid by a DISC to a person other than a related person, with respect to a transaction which gives rise to qualified export receipts of the DISC, is an export promotion expense of the DISC. A commission paid by a DISC to a related person is not an export promotion expense.

(v) Sales of promotional material. If a DISC sells promotional material to a buyer of export property from the DISC at a price which is greater than the costs of the DISC for such material, such costs are not export promotion expenses. If, however, the DISC sells promotional material at a price which is less than its costs for such material, the excess of such costs over such price is an export promotion expense. For rules relating to the status of promotional material as qualified export assets and export property, see § 1.993-2 and § 1.993-3, respectively.

(vi) An expense may be incurred by the DISC under subdivisions (i) through (v) of this subparagraph even if the accounting for and payment of such expense is handled by a related party and the DISC reimburses the related party for such expenses.

(8) Incomplete transactions. Expenses eligible to be treated as export promotion expenses which are attributable to the sale, lease, or other distribution of export property and which are incurred prior to the taxable year of sale, lease, or other distribution by the DISC are not treated as export promotion expenses until the taxable year of sale, lease, or other distribution or until the taxable year in which it is first determined that no transaction is reasonably expected to result from the expense incurred (whether or not a transaction subsequently results). Thus, for example, if a DISC incurs a packaging cost which is otherwise eligible to be treated as an export promotion expense, the DISC may not include such charge as an export promotion expense until the year in which the export property with respect to which the packaging cost was incurred is actually sold by the DISC. If no transaction is reasonably expected to result from the packaging cost such cost should be allocated as an export promotion expense to the group of transactions to which such cost is most closely related.

(g) Examples. The provisions of this section may be illustrated by the following examples:

Example (1). J and K are calendar year taxpayers. J, a domestic manufacturing company, owns all the stock of K, a DISC for the taxable year. During 1972, J manufactures only 100 units of a product (which is eligible to be export property as defined in section 993(c)). J enters into a written agreement with K whereby K is granted a sales franchise with respect to exporting such property and K will receive commissions with respect to such exports equal to the maximum amount permitted to be received under the intercompany pricing rules of section 994. Thereafter, the 100 units are sold for $1,000. J's cost of goods sold attributable to the 100 units is $650. J's direct selling expenses so attributable are $100. Although J has other deductible expenses, for purposes of this example assume that J has no other deductible expenses. K pays $230 to independent contractors which qualify as export promotion expenses under paragraph (f)(7)(ii) of this section. K does not perform functions substantial enough to entitle it to an allocation of income which meets the arm's length standard of section 482. The income which K may earn under section 994 under the franchise is $20, computed as follows:

(1) Combined taxable income:		
(a) K's sales price		$1,000
(b) Less deductions:		
J's cost of goods sold	$650	
J's direct selling expenses	100	
K's export promotion expenses	230	
Total deductions		980
(c) Combined taxable income		20
(2) K's profit under combined taxable income method (before application of loss limitation):		
(a) 50 percent of combined taxable income		10
(b) Plus: 10 percent of K's export promotion expenses (10% of $230)		23
(c) K's profit		33
(3) K's profit under gross receipts method (before application of loss limitation)		
(a) 4 percent of K's sales price (4% of $1,000)		40
(b) Plus: 10 percent of K's export promotion expenses (10% of $230)		23
(c) K's profit		63

Since combined taxable income ($20) is lower than both K's profit under the combined taxable income method ($33) and under the gross receipts method ($63), the maximum income K may earn is $20. Accordingly, the commissions K may receive from J are $250, i.e., K's expenses ($230) plus K's profit ($20).

Example (2). M and N are calendar year taxpayers. M, a domestic manufacturing company, owns all the stock of N, a DISC for the taxable year. During 1972, M produces and sells a particular product line of export property to N for $75, a price which can be justified as satisfying the standard of arm's length price of section 482. N performs substantial functions with respect to the transaction and resells the export property for $100. M's cost of goods sold attributable to the export property is $60. M's direct selling expenses so attributable (relating to advertising of the product line in foreign markets) are $12. Although M has other deductible expenses, for purposes of this example, assume that M has no other deductible expenses. N's expenses attributable to resale of the export property are $22 of which $20 are export promotion expenses. The maximum profit which N may earn with respect to the product line is $6, computed as follows:

(1) Combined taxable income:		
(a) N's sales price		$100
(b) Less deductions:		
M's cost of goods sold	$60	
M's direct selling expenses	12	
N's expenses	22	
Total deductions		94
(c) Combined taxable income		6
(2) N's profit under combined taxable income method (before application of loss limitation):		
(a) 50 percent of combined taxable income		3
(b) Plus: 10 percent of N's export promotion expenses (10% of $20)		2
(c) N's profit		5
(3) N's profit under gross receipts method (before application of loss limitation):		
(a) 4 percent of N's sales price (4% of $100)		4
(b) Plus: 10 percent of N's export promotion expenses (10% of $20)		2
(c) N's profit		6
(4) N's profit under section 482 method:		
(a) N's sales price		100
(b) Less deductions:		
N's cost of goods sold (price paid by N to M)	75	
N's expenses	22	
Total deductions		97
(c) N's profit		3

Since the gross receipts method results in greater profit to N ($6) than does the combined taxable income method ($5) or section 482 method ($3), and does not exceed combined taxable income ($6), N may earn a maximum profit of $6. Accordingly, the transfer price from M to N may be readjusted as long as the transfer price is not readjusted below $72, computed as follows:

(5) Transfer price from M to N:		
(a) N's sales price		$100
(b) Less:		
N's expenses	22	
N's profit	6	
Total subtractions		28
(c) Transfer price		72

Example (3). Q and R are calendar year taxpayers. Q, a domestic manufacturing company, owns all the stock of R, a DISC for the taxable year. During 1972, Q produces and sells a product line of export property to R for $170, a price which can be justified as satisfying the standards of arm's length price of section 482, and R resells the export property for $200. Q's cost of goods sold attributable to the export property is $115 so that the combined gross income from the sale of the export property is $85 (i.e., $200 minus $115). Q's expenses incurred in connection with the property sold are $35. Q's deductible overhead and other supportive expenses allocable to all gross income are $6. Apportionment of these supportive expenses on the basis of gross income does not result in a material distortion of income and is a reasonable method of apportionment. Q's gross income from sources other than the transaction is $170 making total gross income of Q and R (excluding the transfer price paid by R) $255 (i.e., $85 plus $170). R's expenses attributable to resale of the export property are $20, all of which are export promotion expenses. The maximum profit which R may earn with respect to the product line is $16, computed as follows:

(1) Combined taxable income:			
(a) R's sales price			$200
(b) Less deductions:			
(i) Q's cost of goods sold		115	
(ii) Q's expenses incurred in connection with the property sold		35	
(iii) Apportionment of Q's supportive expenses:			
Q's supportive expenses	$6		
Combined gross income from sale of export property	85		
Total gross income of Q and R	255		
Apportionment	$\frac{6 \times 85}{255}$	2	
(iv) R's expenses		20	
Total deductions			172
(c) Combined taxable income			28
(2) R's profit under combined taxable income method (before application of loss limitation):			
(a) 50 percent of combined taxable income			14
(b) Plus: 10 percent of R's export promotion expenses (10% of $20)			2
(c) R's profit			16
(3) R's profit under gross receipts method (before application of loss limitation):			
(a) 4 percent of R's sales price (4% of $200)			8
(b) Plus: 10 percent of R's export promotion expenses (10% of $20)			2
(c) R's profit			10
(4) R's profit under section 482 method:			
(a) R's sales price			200
(b) Less deductions:			
R's cost of goods sold (price paid by R to Q)		170	
R's expenses		20	
Total deductions			190
(c) R's profit			10

Since the combined taxable income method results in greater profit to R ($16) than does the gross receipts method ($10) or section 482 method ($10), and does not exceed combined taxable income ($28), R may earn a maximum profit of $16. Accordingly, the transfer price from Q to R may be readjusted as long as the transfer price is not readjusted below $164 computed as follows:

(5) Transfer price from Q to R:		
(a) R's sales price		$200
(b) Less:		
R's expenses	$20	
R's profit	16	
Total		36
(c) Transfer price		164

Example (4). S and T are calendar year taxpayers. S, a domestic manufacturing company, owns all the stock of T, a DISC for the taxable year. During 1972, S produces and sells 100 units of a particular product to T under a written agreement which provides that the transfer price between S and T shall be that price which allocates to T the maximum permitted to be received under the intercompany pricing rules of section 994. Thereafter, the 100 units are sold by T for $950. S's cost of goods sold attributable to the 100 units is $650. S's other deductible expenses so attributable are $300. Although S has other deductible expenses, for purposes of this example, assume that S has no deductible expenses not definitely allocable to any item of gross income. T's expenses attributable to the resale of the 100 units are $50. S chooses not to apply the section 482 method. T may not earn any income under the gross receipts or combined taxable income method with respect to resale of the 100 units because combined taxable income is a negative figure, computed as follows:

(1) Combined taxable income:		
(a) T's sales price		$ 950
(b) Less deductions:		
S's cost of goods sold	650	
S's expenses	300	
T's expenses	50	
Total deductions		1,000
(c) Combined taxable income (loss)		($ 50)

Under paragraph (e)(1)(i) of this section, T is permitted to recover its expenses attributable to the 100 units ($50) even though such recovery results in a loss or increased loss to the related supplier. Accordingly, the transfer price from S to T may be readjusted as long as the transfer price is not readjusted below $900, computed as follows:

(2) Transfer price from S to T:	
(a) T's sales price	$950
(b) Less: T's expenses	50
(c) Transfer price	900

Example (5). Assume the same facts as in example (4) except that S chooses to apply the section 482 method and that under arm's length dealings T would have derived $10 of income. Accordingly, the transfer price from S to T may be set at an amount not less than $890, computed as follows:

(1) Transfer price from S to T:		
(a) T's sales price		$950
(b) Less:		
T's expenses	50	
T's profit	10	
Total deductions		60
(c) Transfer price		890

Example (6). X and Y are calendar year taxpayers. X, a domestic manufacturing company, owns all the stock of Y, a DISC for the taxable year. During March 1972, X manufactures a particular product of export property which it leases on April 1, 1972, to Y for a term of 1 year at a monthly rental of $1,000, a rent which satisfies the standard of arm's length rental under section 482. Y subleases the product on April 1, 1972, for a term of 1 year at a monthly rental of $1,200. X's cost for the product leased is $40,000. X's other deductible expenses attributable to the product are $900, all of which are incurred in 1972. Although X has other deductible expenses, for purposes of this example, assume that X has no other deductible expenses. Y's expenses attributable to sublease of the export property are $450, all of which are incurred in 1972 and are export promotion expenses. X depreciates the property on a straight line basis without the use of an averaging convention, assuming a useful life of 8 years and no salvage value. The profit which Y may earn with respect to the transaction is $2,895 for 1972 and $1,175 for 1973, computed as follows:

COMPUTATION FOR 1972

(1) Combined taxable income:		
(a) Y's sublease rental receipts for year ($1,200 × 9 months)		$10,800
(b) Less deductions:		
X's depreciation ($40,000 × 1/8 × 9/12)	3,750	
X's other expenses	900	
Y's expenses	450	
Total deductions		5,100
(c) Combined taxable income		5,700
(2) Y's profit under combined taxable income method (before application of loss limitation):		
(a) 50 percent of combined taxable income		2,850
(b) Plus: 10 percent of Y's export promotion expenses (10% of $450)		45
(c) Y's profit		2,895
(3) Y's profit under gross receipts method (before application of loss limitation):		
(a) 4 percent of Y's sublease rental receipts for year (4% of $10,800)		432
(b) Plus: 10 percent of Y's export promotion expenses (10% of $450)		45
(c) Y's profit		477
(4) Y's profit under section 482 method:		
(a) Y's sublease rental receipts for year		$10,800
(b) Less deductions:		
Y's lease rental payments for year	$9,000	
Y's expenses	450	
Total deductions		9,450
(c) Y's profit		1,350

Since the combined taxable income method results in greater profit to Y ($2,895) than does the gross receipts method ($477) or section 482 method ($1,350), Y may earn a profit of $2,895 for 1972. Accordingly, the monthly rental payable by Y to X for 1972 may be readjusted as long as the monthly rental payable is not readjusted below $828.33, computed as follows:

(5) Monthly rental payable by Y to X for 1972:		
(a) Y's sublease rental receipts for year		$10,800.00
(b) Less:		
Y's expenses	450.00	
Y's profit	2,895.00	
Total		3,345.00
(c) Rental payable for 1972		7,455.00
(d) Rental payable each month ($7,455 ÷ 9 months)		828.33

COMPUTATION FOR 1973

(1) Combined taxable income:	
(a) Y's sublease rental receipts for year ($1,200 × 3 months)	$ 3,600
(b) Less: X's depreciation ($40,000 × 1/8 × 3/12)	1,250
(c) Combined taxable income	2,350
(2) Y's profit under combined taxable income method (before application of loss limitation):	
(a) 50 percent of combined taxable income	$ 1,175
(b) Y's profit	1,175
(3) Y's profit under gross receipts method (before application of loss limitation):	
(a) 4 percent of Y's sublease rental receipts for year (4% of $3,600)	144
(b) Y's profit	144
(4) Y's profit under section 482 method:	
(a) Y's sublease rental receipts for year	3,600
(b) Less: Y's lease rental payments for year	3,000
(c) Y's profit	600

Since the combined taxable income method results in greater profit to Y ($1,175) than does the gross receipts method ($144) or section 482 method ($600), Y may earn a profit of $1,175 for 1973. Accordingly, the monthly rental payable by Y to X for 1973 may be readjusted as long as the monthly rental payable is not readjusted below $808.33, computed as follows:

(5) Monthly rental payable by Y to X for 1973:	
(a) Y's sublease rental receipts for year	$3,600.00
(b) Less: Y's profit	1,175.00
(c) Rental payable for 1973	2,425.00
(d) Rental payable for each month ($2,425 ÷ 3 months)	808.33

T.D. 7364, 7/15/75, amend T.D. 7435, 9/29/76, T.D. 7854, 11/16/82, T.D. 7984, 10/11/84.

§ 1.994-2 Marginal costing rules.

(a) In general. This section prescribes the marginal costing rules authorized by section 994(b)(2). If under paragraph (c)(1) of this section a DISC is treated for its taxable year as seeking to establish or maintain a foreign market for sales of an item, product, or product line of export property (as defined in § 1.993-3) from which qualified export receipts are derived, the marginal costing rules prescribed in paragraph (b) of this section may be applied to allocate costs between gross receipts derived from such sales and other gross receipts for purposes of computing, under the "50-50" combined taxable income method of § 1.994-1(c)(3), the combined taxable income of the DISC and related supplier derived from such sales. Such marginal costing rules may be applied whether or not the related supplier manufactures, produces, grows, or extracts (within the meaning of § 1.993-3(c)) the export property sold. Such marginal costing rules do not apply to sales of export property which in the hands of a purchaser related under section 954(d)(3) to the seller give rise to foreign base company sales income as described in section 954(d) unless, for the purchaser's year in which it resells the export property, section 954(b)(3)(A) is applicable or such income is under the exceptions in section 954(b)(4). Such marginal costing rules do not apply to leases of property or the performance of any services whether or not related and subsidiary services (as defined in § 1.994-1(b)(3)).

(b) Marginal costing rules for allocations of costs. *(1) In general.* Marginal costing is a method under which only marginal or variable costs of producing and selling a particular item, product, or product line are taken into account for purposes of section 994. Where this section is applicable, costs attributable to deriving qualified export receipts for the DISC's taxable year from sales of an item, product, or product line may be determined in any manner the related supplier (as defined in § 1.994-1(a)(3)(ii)) chooses, provided that the requirements of both subparagraphs (2) and (3) of this paragraph are met.

(2) Variable costs taken into account. There are taken into account in computing the combined taxable income of the DISC and its related supplier from sales of an item, product, or product line the following costs: (i) Direct production costs (as defined in § 1.471-11(b)(2)(i)) and (ii) costs which are export promotion expenses, but only if they are claimed as export promotion expense in determining taxable income derived by the DISC under the combined taxable income method of § 1.994-1(c)(3). At the taxpayer's option, all, a part, or none of the costs which qualify as export promotion expenses may be so claimed as export promotion expenses.

(3) Overall profit percentage limitation. As a result of such determination of costs attributable to such qualified export receipts for the DISC's taxable year, the combined taxable income of the DISC and its related supplier from sales of such item, product, or product line for the DISC's taxable year does not exceed gross receipts (determined under § 1.993-6) of the DISC derived from such sales, multiplied by the overall profit percentage (determined under paragraph (c)(2) of this section).

(c) Definitions. *(1) Establishing or maintaining a foreign market.* A DISC shall be treated for its taxable year as seeking to establish or maintain a foreign market with respect to sales of an item, product, or product line of export property from which qualified export receipts are derived if the combined taxable income computed under paragraph (b) of this section is greater than the combined taxable income computed under § 1.994-1(c)(6).

(2) Overall profit percentage. (i) For purposes of this section, the overall profit percentage for a taxable year of the DISC for a product or product line is the percentage which—

(a) The combined taxable income of the DISC and its related supplier plus all other taxable income of its related supplier from all sales (domestic and foreign) of such product or product line during the DISC's taxable year, computed under the full costing method, is of

(b) The total gross receipts (determined under § 1.993-6) from all such sales.

(ii) At the annual option of the related supplier, the overall profit percentage for the DISC's taxable year for all products and product lines may be determined by aggregating the amounts described in subdivision (i)(a) and (b) of this subparagraph of the DISC, and all domestic members of the controlled group (as defined in § 1.993-1(k)) of which the DISC is a member, for the DISC's taxable year and for taxable years of such members ending with or within the DISC's taxable year.

(iii) For purposes of determining the amounts in subdivisions (i)(b) and (ii) of this subparagraph, a sale of property between a DISC and its related supplier or between domestic members of the controlled group shall be taken into account only during the DISC's taxable year (or taxable year of the member ending within the DISC's taxable year) during which the property is ultimately sold to a person which is neither the DISC nor such a domestic member.

(3) Grouping of transactions. (i) In general, for purposes of this section, an item, product, or product line is the item or group consisting of the product or product line pursuant to § 1.994-1(c)(7) used by the taxpayer for purposes of applying the intercompany pricing rules of § 1.994-1.

(ii) However, for purposes of determining the overall profit percentage under subparagraph (2) of this paragraph, any product or product line grouping permissible under § 1.994-1(c)(7) may be used at the annual choice of the taxpayer, even though it may not be the same item or grouping referred to in subdivision (i) of this subparagraph, as long as the grouping chosen for determining the overall profit percentage is at least as broad as the grouping referred to in such subdivision (i).

(4) Full costing method. For purposes of this section, the term "full costing method" is the method for determining combined taxable income set forth in § 1.994-1(c)(6).

(d) Application of limitation on DISC income ("no loss" rule). If the marginal costing rules of this section are applied, the combined taxable income method of § 1.994-1(c)(3) may not be applied to cause in any taxable year a loss to the related supplier, but such method may be applied to the extent it does not cause a loss. For purposes of the preceding sentence, a loss to a related supplier would result if the taxable income of the DISC would exceed the combined taxable income of the related supplier and the DISC determined in accordance with paragraph (b) of this section. If, however, there is no combined taxable income (so determined), see the last sentence of § 1.994-1(e)(1)(i).

(e) Examples. The provisions of this section may be illustrated by the following examples:

Example (1). X and Y are calendar year taxpayers. X, a domestic manufacturing company, owns all the stock of Y, a DISC for the taxable year. During 1973, X manufactures a product line which is eligible to be export property (as defined in § 1.993-3). X enters into a written agreement with Y, whereby Y is granted a sales franchise with respect to exporting such product line from which qualified export receipts will be derived and Y will receive commissions with respect to such exports equal to the maximum amount permitted to be received under the intercompany pricing rules of section 994. Commissions are computed using the combined taxable income method under § 1.994-1(c)(3). For purposes of applying the combined taxable income method, X and Y compute their combined taxable income attributable to the product line of export property under the marginal costing rules in accordance with the additional facts assumed in the table below:

(1) Maximum combined taxable income (determined under paragraph (b)(2) of this section):		
(a) Y's gross receipts from export sales		$95.00
(b) Less:		
(i) Direct materials	40.00	
(ii) Direct labor	20.00	
(iii) Y's export promotion expenses claimed in determining Y's DISC taxable income	5.00	
(iv) Total deductions	65.00	
(c) Maximum combined taxable income		30.00
(2) Overall profit percentage limitation (determined under paragraph (b)(3) of this section):		
(a) Gross receipts of X and Y from all domestic and foreign sales		400.00
(b) Less deductions:		
(i) Direct materials	160.00	
(ii) Direct labor	80.00	
(iii) Other costs (of which $8 are costs of the DISC including $5 of export promotion expenses claimed in determining Y's taxable income)	40.00	
(c) Total deductions		280.00
(d) Total taxable income from all sales computed on a full costing method		120.00
(e) Overall profit percentage (line (d) ($120) divided by line (a) ($400)) (percent)		30%
(f) Multiply by gross receipts from Y's report sales (line (1)(a))		$95.00
(g) Overall profit percentage limitations		28.50

Since the overall profit percentage limitation under line (2)(g) ($28.50) is less than maximum combined taxable income under line (1)(c) ($30), combined taxable income under marginal costing is limited to $28.50. Since under the franchise agreement Y is to earn the maximum commission permitted under the intercompany pricing rules of section 994, combined taxable income on the transactions is $28.50. Accordingly, the costs attributable to export sales (other than for direct material, direct labor, and export promotion expenses) are $1.50, i.e., line (1)(c) ($30) minus line (2)(g) ($28.50). Under the combined taxable income method of § 1.994-1(c)(3), Y will have taxable income attributable to the sales of $14.75, i.e., the sum of ½ of combined taxable income (½ of $28.50) and 10 percent of Y's export promotion expenses claimed in determining Y's taxable income (10 percent of $5). Accordingly, the commissions Y receives from X are $22.75, i.e., Y's costs ($8, see line (2)(b)(iii)) plus Y's profit ($14.75).

Example (2). (1) Assume the same facts as in example (1), except that gross receipts from export sales are only $85 and gross receipts from all sales remain at $400. For purposes of applying the combined taxable income method, X and Y may compute their combined taxable income attributable to the product line of export property under the marginal costing rules as follows:

(1) Maximum combined taxable income (determined under paragraph (b)(2) of this section):
(a) Y's gross receipts from export sales $85.00
(b) Less:
(i) Direct materials 40.00
(ii) Direct labor 20.00
(iii) Y's export promotion expenses claimed in determining Y's taxable income 5.00
(iv) Total deductions 65.00
(c) Maximum combined taxable income 20.00

(2) Overall profit percentage limitation (determined under paragraph (b)(3) of this section):M
(a) Gross receipts from Y's export sales (line (1)(a)) 85.00
(b) Multiply by overall profit percentage (as determined in example (1)) (percent) 30%
(c) Overall profit percentage limitation 25.50

Since maximum combined taxable income under line (1)(c) ($20) is less than the overall profit percentage limitation under line (2)(c) ($25.50), combined taxable income under marginal costing is limited to $20. Since under the franchise agreement Y is to earn the maximum commission permitted under the intercompany pricing rules of section 994, combined taxable income on the transactions is $20. Accordingly, no costs (other than for direct material, direct labor, and export promotion expenses) will be attributed to export sales. Under the combined taxable income method of § 1.994-1(c)(3), Y will have taxable income attributable to the sales of $10.50, i.e., the sum of ½ of combined taxable income (½ of $20) and 10 percent of Y's export promotion expenses claimed in determining Y's taxable income (10 percent of $5). Accordingly, the commissions Y receives from X are $18.50, i.e., Y's costs ($8, see line (2)(b)(iii) of example (1)) plus Y's profit ($10.50).

(2) If export promotion expenses are not claimed in determining taxable income of Y under the combined taxable income method, the taxable income of Y would be increased to $12.50 and commissions payable to Y would be increased to $20.50, computed as follows:

(3) Maximum combined taxable income (determined under paragraph (b)(2) of this section):
(a) Y's gross receipts from export sales $85.00
(b) Less:
(i) Direct materials 40.00
(ii) Direct labor 20.00
(iii) Total deductions 60.00
(c) Maximum combined taxable income 25.00

(4) Overall profit percentage limitation (line (2)(c)) 25.50

Since maximum combined taxable income under line (3)(c) ($25) is less than the overall profit percentage under line (4) ($25.50), combined taxable income under marginal costing is limited to $25. Since under the franchise agreement Y is to earn the maximum commission permitted under the intercompany pricing rules of section 994, combined taxable income on the transactions is $25. Accordingly, no costs (other than for direct material and direct labor) will be attributed to export sales. Under the combined taxable income method of § 1.994-1(c)(3), Y will have taxable income attributable to the sales of $12.50, i.e., ½ of combined taxable income (½ of $25). Accordingly, the commissions Y receives from X are $20.50, i.e., Y's costs ($8, see line (2)(b)(iii) of example (1)) plus Y's profit ($12.50).

Example (3). (1) Assume the same facts as in example (1), except that gross receipts from export sales are only $85, gross receipts from all sales remain at $400, and Y has costs of $40 consisting of Y's export promotion expenses of $35 and costs of $5 other than for direct material, direct labor, or export promotion expenses. For purposes of applying the combined taxable income method, X and Y may compute their combined taxable income attributable to the product line of export property under the marginal costing rules as follows:

(1) Maximum combined taxable income (determined under paragraph (b)(2) of this section):
(a) Y's gross receipts from export sales $85.00
(b) Less:
(i) Direct materials 40.00
(ii) Direct labor 20.00
(iii) Y's export promotion expenses claimed in determining Y's taxable income 35.00
(iv) Total deductions 95.00
(c) Maximum combined taxable income (loss) .... (10.00)

(2) Overall profit percentage limitation (as determined in example (2)) 25.50

Since maximum combined taxable income under line (1)(c) (which is a loss of $10) is less than the overall profit percentage limitation under line (2)(c) ($25.50), combined taxable income under marginal costing is a loss of $10 and, under the combined taxable income method of § 1.994-1(c)(3), Y will have no taxable income or loss attributable to the sales. Accordingly, the commissions Y receives from X are $40, i.e., Y's costs ($40).

(2) If export promotion expenses are not claimed in determining Y's taxable income under the combined taxable income method, the taxable income of Y would be increased to $12.50 and commissions payable to Y would be increased to $52.50 computed as follows:

(3)	Maximum combined taxable income (determined under paragraph (b)(2) of this section) (line (3)(c) of example (2))	$25.00
(4)	Overall profit percentage limitation (as determined in example (2))..................	25.50

The results would be the same as in part (2) of example (2), except that the commissions Y receives from X are $52.50, i.e., Y's costs ($40) plus Y's profit ($12.50).

T.D. 7364, 7/15/75.

§ 1.995-1 Taxation of DISC income to shareholders.

Caution: The Treasury has not yet amended Reg § 1.995-1 to reflect changes made by P.L. 100-647, P.L. 99-514, P.L. 98-369, P.L. 95-600, P.L. 94-455.

(a) In general. *(1)* Under § 1.991-1(a), a corporation which is a DISC for a taxable year is not subject to any tax imposed by subtitle A of the Code (sections 1 through 1564) for the taxable year, except for the tax imposed by chapter 5 thereof (sections 1491 through 1494) on certain transfers to avoid tax.

(2) Under section 995(a), the shareholders of a DISC, or a former DISC, are subject to taxation on the earnings and profits of the DISC in accordance with the provisions of chapter 1 of the Code generally applicable to shareholders, but subject to the modifications provided in sections 995, 996, and 997.

(3) Under § 1.996-3, three divisions of earnings and profits of a DISC, or former DISC, are defined: "accumulated DISC income", "previously taxed income", and "other earnings and profits". Under § 1.995-2, certain amounts of the DISC's earnings and profits are deemed to be distributed as dividends to shareholders of the DISC at the close of the DISC's taxable year in which such earnings were derived. Such deemed distributions do not cause a reduction in the DISC's earnings and profits, but are taken into account in § 1.996-3(c) as an increase in previously taxed income. To the extent the DISC's earnings and profits are paid out in a subsequent distribution which is, under § 1.996-1, treated as made out of such "previously taxed income," they will not be taxable to the shareholders a second time.

(4) In general, "accumulated DISC income" is the earnings and profits of the DISC which have not been deemed distributed and which may be deferred from taxation so long as they are not actually distributed with respect to its stock. However, deferral of taxation on "accumulated DISC income" may be terminated, in whole or in part, in the event of: (i) Certain foreign investment attributable to producer's loans (see § 1.995-2(a)(5) and § 1.995-5); (ii) revocation of the election to be treated as a DISC or other disqualification (see § 1.995-3); and (iii) certain dispositions of DISC stock in which gain is realized (see § 1.995-4).

(5) Since a DISC is not taxed on its taxable income, section 246(d) and § 1.246-4 provide that the deduction otherwise allowed under section 243 shall not be allowed with respect to a dividend from a DISC, or former DISC, paid or treated as paid out of accumulated DISC income or previously taxed income or with respect to a deemed distribution in a qualified year under § 1.995-2(a).

(b) Amounts and character of amounts includible in shareholder's gross income. Each shareholder of a corporation which is a DISC, or former DISC, shall include in his gross income—

(1) Amounts actually distributed to him that are includible in his gross income in accordance with paragraph (c) of this section.

(2) Amounts which, pursuant to § 1.995-2, he is deemed to receive as a distribution taxable as a dividend on the last day of each of the corporation's taxable years for which it qualifies as a DISC,

(3) Amounts which, pursuant to § 1.995-3, he is deemed to receive as a distribution taxable as a dividend in the event the corporation revokes its election to be treated as a DISC or otherwise is disqualified as a DISC, and

(4) Gain realized on certain dispositions of stock in the corporation which, under § 1.995-4, is includible in his gross income as a dividend.

(c) Treatment of actual distributions. *(1)* Except as provided in subparagraph (3) of this paragraph, amounts actually distributed to a shareholder of a DISC, or former DISC, with respect to his stock are includible in his gross income in accordance with section 301.

(2) Since a deemed distribution does not reduce the earnings and profits of a DISC, it does not affect the determination as to whether a subsequent actual distribution is a "dividend" under section 316(a). Since, however, the amount of a deemed distribution increases "previously taxed income", it does affect the determination as to whether a subsequent actual distribution is excluded (as described in subparagraph (3) of this paragraph) from gross income.

(3) Under § 1.996-1(c), the amount of any actual distribution (including a deficiency distribution made pursuant to § 1.992-3), with respect to stock in a DISC, or former DISC, which is treated under § 1.996-1 as made out of previously taxed income, is excluded by the distributee from gross income, but only to the extent that such amount does not exceed the adjusted basis of the distributee's stock. Under § 1.996-5(b), that portion of any actual distribution which is treated as made out of previously taxed income shall be applied against and reduce the adjusted basis of the stock and, to the extent that it exceeds the adjusted basis of the stock, it shall be treated as gain from the sale or exchange of property.

(4) A deficiency distribution pursuant to § 1.992-3 may be made after the close of the DISC's taxable year with respect to which it is made. The determinations as to whether such deficiency distribution is to dividend under section 301 and as to which division of earnings and profits is the source thereof depend upon the status of the DISC's earnings and profits account and divisions thereof at the time the distribution is actually made. See § 1.996-1(d) for the priority of such deficiency distribution over other actual distributions made during the same taxable year.

(d) Personal holding company income. *(1)* Any amount includible in a shareholder's gross income as a dividend with respect to the stock of a DISC, or former DISC, pursuant to paragraph (b) of this section shall be treated as a dividend for all purposes of the Code, except that for purposes of determining whether such shareholder is a personal holding company within the meaning of section 542 any amount deemed distributed for qualified years under § 1.995-2 or upon disqualification under § 1.995-3, any amount of gain on certain dispositions of DISC stock to which § 1.995-4 applies, and any amount treated under § 1.996-1 as distributed out of accumulated DISC income or previously taxed income shall not be treated as a dividend or any other kind of income described in section 543(a).

(2) Notwithstanding subparagraph (1) of this paragraph, the shareholder may treat as an item of income described under section 543 (for example, rents) any amount to which the exception in such subparagraph (1) applies, if it establishes to the satisfaction of the district director that such amount is attributable to earnings and profits derived from such item of income.

T.D. 7324, 9/24/74.

---

§ 1.995-2 Deemed distributions in qualified years.

(a) General rule. Under section 995(b)(1), each shareholder of a DISC shall be treated as having received a distribution taxable as a dividend with respect to his stock on the last day of each taxable year of the DISC, in an amount which is equal to his pro rata share of the sum (as limited by paragraph (b) of this section), of the following seven items:

(1) An amount equal to the gross interest derived by the DISC during such year from producer's loans (as defined in § 1.993-4).

(2) An amount equal to the lower of—

(i) Any gain recognized by the DISC during such year on the sale or exchange of property (other than property which in the hands of the DISC is a qualified export asset) which was previously transferred to it in a transaction in which the transferor realized gain which was not recognized in whole or in part, or

(ii) The amount of the transferor's gain which was not recognized on the previous transfer of the property to the DISC.

For purposes of this subparagraph, each item of property shall be considered separately. See paragraph (d) of this section for special rules with respect to certain tax-free acquisitions of property by the DISC.

(3) An amount equal to the lower of—

(i) Any gain recognized by the DISC during such year on the sale or exchange of property which in the hands of the DISC is a qualified export asset (other than stock in trade or property described in section 1221(1)) and which was previously transferred to the DISC in a transaction in which the transferor realized gain which was not recognized in whole or in part, or

(ii) The amount of the transferor's gain which was not recognized on the previous transfer of the property to the DISC and which would have been includible in the transferor's gross income as ordinary income if its entire realized gain had been recognized upon the transfer.

For purposes of this subparagraph, each item of property shall be considered separately. See paragraph (d) of this section for special rules with respect to certain tax-free acquisitions of property by the DISC.

(4) For taxable years beginning after December 31, 1975, an amount equal to 50 percent of the taxable income of the DISC for the taxable years attributable to military property (as defined in § 1.995-6).

(5) For taxable years beginning after December 31, 1975, the taxable income for the taxable year attributable to base period export gross receipts (as defined in § 1.995-7).

(6) The sum of —

(i) (A) In the case of a corporate share holder, an amount equal to 57.5 percent of the excess (if any) (one-half for DISC's taxable years beginning before January 1, 1983) of the taxable income of the DISC for such year (computed as provided in § 1.991-1(b)(1)) over the sum of the amounts deemed distributed for the taxable year in accordance with subparagraph (1), (2), (3), (4) and (5) of this paragraph, or

(B) in the case of a non-corporate share holder, an amount equal to one-half of the excess (if any) of the taxable income of the DISC for such year (computed as provided in § 1.991-1(b)(1)) over the sum of the amounts deemed distributed for the taxable year in accordance with subparagraphs (1), (2), (3), (4), and (5) of this paragraph.

(ii) (A) An amount equal to the amount under subdivision (i) of paragraph (a)(6) of this section multiplied by the international boycott factor as determined under section 999(c)(1), or

(B) In lieu of the amount determined under subdivision (ii)(A) of paragraph (a)(6) of this section, the amount described under section 999(c)(2) of such international boycott income, and

(iii) An amount equal to the sum of any illegal bribes, kickbacks, or other payments paid by or on behalf of the DISC directly or indirectly to an official, employee, or agent in fact of a government. An amount is paid by a DISC where it is paid by any officer, director, employee, shareholder, or agent of the DISC for the benefit of such DISC. For purposes of this section, the principles of section 162(c) and the regulations thereunder shall apply. The fair market value of an illegal payment made in the form of property or services shall be considered the amount of such illegal payment.

(7) The amount of foreign investment attributable to producer's loans of the DISC, as of the close of the "group taxable year" ending with such taxable year of the DISC, determined in accordance with § 1.995-5. The amount of such foreign investment attributable to producer's loans so determined for any taxable year of a former DISC shall be deemed distributed as a dividend to the shareholders of such former DISC on the last day of such taxable year. See § 1.995-3(e) for the effect that such deemed distribution has on scheduled installments of deemed distributions of accumulated DISC income under § 1.995-3(a) upon disqualification.

(b) Limitation on amount of deemed distributions under section 995(b)(1). *(1)* The sum of the amounts described in paragraph (a)(1) through (4) of this section which is deemed distributed pro rata to the DISC's shareholders a dividend for any taxable year of the corporation shall not exceed the DISC's earnings and profits for such year.

(2) The amount of foreign investment attributable to producer's loans of the DISC (as described in paragraph (a)(5) of this section) which is deemed to be distributed pro rata to the DISC's shareholders as dividends for any taxable year of the corporation shall not exceed the lower of the corporation's accumulated DISC income at the beginning of such year or the corporation's accumulated earnings and profits at the beginning of such year (but not less than zero)—

(i) Increased by any DISC income of the corporation for such year as defined in § 1.996-3(b)(2) (i.e., any excess of the DISC's earnings and profits for such year over the sum of the amounts described in paragraph (a)(1) through (4) of this section), or

(ii) Decreased by any deficit in the corporation's earnings and profits for such year.

Thus, for example, if a DISC has a deficit in accumulated earnings and profits at the beginning of a taxable year of $10,000, current earnings and profits of $12,000, no amounts described in paragraph (a)(1) through (4) of this section for the year, and foreign investment attributable to producer's loans for the taxable year of $5,000, the DISC would have a deemed distribution described in paragraph (a)(5) of this section of $5,000 for the taxable year. On the other hand, suppose the DISC had accumulated earnings and profits of $13,000 at the beginning of the taxable year, accumulated DISC income of $10,000 at the beginning of the taxable year, a deficit in earnings and profits for the taxable year of $12,000, no amounts described in paragraph (a)(1) through (4) of this section for the taxable year, and foreign investment attributable to producer's loans for the taxable year of $5,000. Under these facts the DISC would have no deemed distribution described in paragraph (a)(5) of this section because the corporation had no DISC income for the taxable year and the current year's deficit in earnings and profits subtracted from the DISC's accumulated DISC income at the beginning of the year produces a negative amount. For rules relating to the carryover to a subsequent year of the $5,000 of foreign investment attributable to producer's loans, see § 1.995-5(a)(6).

(3) If, by reason of the limitation in subparagraph (1) of this paragraph, less than the sum of the amounts described in paragraph (a)(1) through (4) of this section is deemed distributed, then the portion of such sum which is deemed distributed shall be attributed first to the amount described in subparagraph (1) of such paragraph, to the extent thereof; second to the amount described in subparagraph (2) of such paragraph, to the extent thereof; third to the amount described in subparagraph (3) of such paragraph, to the extent thereof; and finally to the amount described in subparagraph (4) of such paragraph.

(c) Examples. Paragraphs (a) and (b) of this section may be illustrated by the following examples:

Example (1). Y is a corporation which uses the calendar year as its taxable year and which elects to be treated as a DISC beginning with 1972. X is its sole shareholder. In 1972, X transfers certain property to Y in exchange for Y's stock in a transaction in which X does not recognize gain or loss by reason of the application of section 351(a). Included in the property transferred to Y is depreciable property described in paragraph (a)(3) of this section on which X realizes, but does not recognize by reason of the application of section 1245(b)(3), a gain of $20,000. If X had sold such property for cash, the $20,000 gain would have been recognized as ordinary income under section 1245. Also included in the transfer to Y is 100 shares of stock in a third corporation (which is not a related foreign export corporation) on which X realizes, but does not recognize, a gain of $5,000. In 1973, Y sells such property and recognizes a gain of $25,000 on the depreciable property and $8,000 on the 100 shares of stock. Y has accumulated earnings and profits at the beginning of 1973 of $5,000, earnings and profits for 1973 of $72,000, and taxable income for 1973 of $100,000. At the beginning of 1973, Y has $6,000 of accumulated DISC income, no previously taxed income, and a deficit of $1,000 of other earnings and profits. Under these facts and the additional facts assumed in the table below, X is treated as having received a deemed distribution taxable as a dividend of $76,000 on December 31, 1973, determined as follows:

(1) Gross interest derived by Y in 1973 from producer's loans	$ 7,000
(2) Amount of gain on depreciable property (lower of Y's recognized gain ($25,000) or X's gain not recognized on section 1245 property ($20,000))	20,000
(3) Amount of gain on stock (lower of X's gain not recognized or Y's recognized gain ($8,000) ($5,000))	5,000
(4) One-half excess of taxable income for 1973 over the sum of lines (1), (2), and (3) (½of $100,000 minus $32,000))	34,000
(5) Limitation on lines (1) through (4):	
(a) Sum of lines (1) through (4)	66,000
(b) Earnings and profits for 1973	72,000
(c) Lower of lines (a) and (b)	66,000
(6) Amount under paragraph (a)(5) of this section:	
(a) Foreign investment attributable to producer's loans under § 1.995-5	10,000
(b) Sum of the lower of accumulated earnings and profits at beginning of 1973 ($5,000) or accumulated DISC income at beginning of 1973 ($6,000) and excess of earnings and profits for 1973 over line (5)(c) ($72,000 minus $66,000)	11,000
(c) Lower of lines (a) and (b)	10,000
(7) Total deemed distribution (sum of lines (5)(c) and (6)(c))	76,000

Example (2). Assume the facts are the same as in example (1), except that earnings and profits for 1973 amount to only $60,000. Under these facts, X is treated as receiving a deemed distribution taxable as a dividend of $65,000 on December 31, 1973, determined as follows:

(5) Limitation on lines (1) through (4):	
(a) Line (5)(a) of example (1)	$66,000
(b) Earnings and profits for 1973	60,000
(c) Lower of lines (a) and (b)	60,000
(6) Amount under paragraph (a)(5) of this section:	
(a) Line (6)(a) of example (1)	10,000
(b) Sum of the lower of accumulated earnings and profits at beginning of 1973 ($5,000) or accumulated DISC income at beginning of 1973 ($6,000) plus excess of earnings and profits for 1973 over line (5)(c) ($60,000 minus $60,000)	5,000
(c) Lower of lines (a) and (b)	$ 5,000
(7) Total deemed distribution (sum of lines (5)(c) and (6)(c))	65,000

Example (3). Assume the facts are the same as in example (1), except that Y has a deficit in accumulated earnings and profits at the beginning of 1973 of $4,000. Such deficit is comprised of accumulated DISC income of $1,000, no previously taxed income, and a deficit in other earnings and profits of $5,000. Under these facts, X is treated as receiving a deemed distribution taxable as a dividend in the amount of $72,000 on December 31, 1973, determined as follows:

(5) Limitation on lines (1) through (4):	
(a) Line (5)(a) of example (1)	$66,000
(b) Earnings and profits for 1973	72,000
(c) Lower of lines (a) and (b)	66,000
(6) Amount under paragraph (a)(5) of this section:	
(a) Line (6)(a) of example (1)	10,000
(b) Sum of accumulated earnings and profits at beginning of 1973 (not less than $0), and excess of earnings and profits for 1973 over amount in line (5)(c) ($72,000 minus $66,000)	6,000
(c) Lower of lines (a) and (b)	6,000
(7) Total deemed distribution sum of lines (5)(c) and (6)(c)	72,000

(d) Special rules for certain tax-free acquisitions of property by the DISC. *(1)* For purposes of paragraph (a)(2)(i) and (3)(i) of this section, if—

(i) A DISC acquires property in a first transaction and in a second transaction it disposes of such property in exchange for other property, and

(ii) By reason of the application of section 1031 (relating to like-kind exchanges) or section 1033 (relating to involuntary conversations), the basis in the DISC's hands of the other property acquired in such second transaction is determined in whole or in part with reference to the basis of the property acquired in the first transaction, then upon a disposition of such other property in a third transaction by the DISC such other property shall be treated as though it had been transferred to the DISC in the first transaction. Thus, if the first transaction is a purchase of the property for cash, then paragraph (a)(2) and (3) of this section will not apply to a sale by the DISC of the other property acquired in the second transaction.

(2) For purposes of paragraph (a)(2)(i) and (3)(i) of this section, if a DISC acquires property in a first transaction and it transfers such property to a transferee DISC in a second transaction in which the transferor DISC's gain is not recognized in whole or in part, then such property shall be treated as though it had been transferred to the transferee DISC in the same manner in which it was acquired in the first transaction by the transferor DISC. For example, if X and Y both qualify as DISC's and X transfers property to Y in a second transaction in which gain or loss is not recognized, paragraph (a)(2) or (3) of this section does not apply to a sale of such property by Y in a third transaction if X had acquired the property in a first transaction by a purchase for cash. If, however, X acquired the property from a transferor other than a DISC in the first transaction in which the transferor's realized gain was not recognized, then paragraph (a)(2) or (3) of this section may apply to the sale by Y if the other conditions of such paragraph (a)(2) or (3) are met.

(3) If a DISC acquires property in a second transaction described in subparagraph (1) or (2) of this paragraph in which it (or, in the case of a second transaction described in subparagraph (2) of this paragraph, the transferor DISC) recognizes a portion (but not all) of the realized gain, then the amount described in paragraph (a)(2)(ii) or (a)(3)(ii) of this section with respect to a disposition by the DISC of such acquired property in a third transaction shall not exceed the transferor's gain which was not recognized on the first transaction minus the amount of gain recognized on the first transaction minus the amount of gain recognized by the DISC (or transferor DISC) on the second transaction.

(4) The provisions of this paragraph may be illustrated by the following examples:

Example (1). X and Y are corporations each of which qualifies as a DISC and uses the calendar year as its taxable year. In 1972, X acquires section 1245 property in a first transaction in which the transferor's entire realized gain of $17 is not recognized. In 1973, X transfers such property to Y in a second transaction in which X realizes a gain of $20 of which only $4 is recognized. (On December 31, 1973, X's shareholders are treated as having received a deemed distribution of a dividend which includes such $4 under paragraph (a)(3) of this section, provided the limitation in paragraph (b) of this section is met.) In a third transaction in 1974, Y sells such property and recognizes a gain of $25. With respect to Y's shareholders on December 31, 1974, the amount described in paragraph (a)(3)(ii) of this section would be limited to $13, which is the amount of the transferor's gain which was not recognized on the first transaction ($17) minus the amount of gain recognized by X on the second transaction ($4).

Example (2). Z is a DISC using the calendar year as its taxable year. In a first transaction in 1972, in exchange for its stock, Z acquires section 1245 property from A, an individual who is its sole shareholder, in a transaction in which A's realized gain of $30 is not recognized by reason of the application of section 351(a). In a second transaction in 1973, Z exchanges such property for other property in a like-kind exchange to which section 1031(b) applies and recognizes $10 of a realized gain of $35. (On December 31, 1973, A is treated as having received a deemed distribution of a dividend which includes such $10 under paragraph (a)(3) of this section, provided the limitation in paragraph (b) of this section is met.) In a third transaction in 1974, Z sells the property acquired in the like-kind exchange and recognizes a gain of $25. With respect to A on December 31, 1974, the amount described in paragraph (a)(3)(ii) of this section is limited to $20, which is the amount of A's gain which was not recognized on the first transaction ($30) minus the amount of gain recognized by Z on the second transaction ($10).

(e) Carryback of net operating loss and capital loss to prior DISC taxable year. For purposes of sections 991, 995, and 996, the amount of the deduction for the taxable year under section 172 for a net operating loss carryback or carryover or under section 1212 for a capital loss carryback or carryover shall be determined in the same manner as if the DISC were a domestic corporation which had not elected to be treated as a DISC. Thus, the amount of the deduction will be the same whether or not the corporation was a DISC in the year of the loss or in the year to which the loss is carried. For provisions setting forth adjustments to the DISC's, or former DISC's, deemed distributions, adjustments to its divisions of earnings and profits, and other tax consequences arising from such carrybacks, see § 1.996-8.

T.D. 7324, 9/27/74, amend T.D. 7862, 12/16/82, T.D. 7984, 10/11/84.

PAR. 7. Section 1.995-2 is amended by revising the title of the section and by adding two new sentences immediately before the first sentence in paragraph (a) to read as follows:

Proposed § 1.995-2 Deemed distributions in qualified years ending before 1985. [*For Preamble, see ¶ 151,083*]

(a) General rule. This section applies to taxable years of a DISC ending before January 1, 1985. See § 1.995-2A for taxable years of a DISC beginning after December 31, 1984. * * *

* * * * *

Proposed § 1.995-2A Deemed distributions in qualified years beginning after 1984. [*For Preamble, see ¶ 151,083*]

(a) General rule. This section applies to taxable years of a DISC beginning after December 31, 1984. See § 1.955-2 for taxable years beginning before January 1, 1985. Under section 995(b)(1), each shareholder of a DISC shall be treated as having received a distribution taxable as a dividend with respect to the shareholder's stock on the last day of each taxable year of the DISC beginning after December 31, 1984, in an amount equal to the shareholder's pro rata share of the sum (as limited by paragraph (b) of this section) of the following items:

(1) The gross interest derived by the DISC during such year from producer's loans (as defined in § 1.993-4).

(2) The lower of—

(i) Any gain recognized by the DISC during such year on the sale or exchange of property (other than property which in the hands of the DISC is a qualified export asset) which was previously transferred to it in a transaction in which the transferor realized gain which was not recognized in whole or in part, or

(ii) The amount of the transferor's gain which was not recognized on the previous transfer of the property to the DISC.

For purposes of this paragraph (a)(2), each item of property shall be considered separately. See paragraph (d) of this section for special rules with respect to certain tax-free acquisitions of property by the DISC.

(3) The lower of—

(i) Any gain recognized by the DISC during such year on the sale or exchange of property which in the hands of the DISC is a qualified export asset (other than stock in trade or property described in section 1221(1)) and which was previously transferred to the DISC in a transaction in which the transferor realized gain which was not recognized in whole or in part, or

(ii) The amount of the transferor's gain which was not recognized on the previous transfer of the property to the DISC and which would have been includible in the transferor's gross income as ordinary income if its entire realized gain had been recognized upon the transfer.

For purposes of this paragraph (a)(3), each item of property shall be considered separately. See paragraph (d) of this section for special rules with respect to certain tax-free acquisitions of property by the DISC.

(4) Fifty (50) percent of the taxable income of the DISC for the taxable year attributable to military property (as defined in § 1.995-6).

(5) The taxable income of the DISC for the taxable year attributable to qualified export receipts of the DISC for such year which exceed $10,000,000 (as determined under § 1.995-8).

(6) The sum of—

(i) In the case of a shareholder which is a C corporation, an amount equal to one-seventeenth (1/17) of the excess, if any, of the taxable income of the DISC for the taxable year, before reduction for any distributions during such year, ever the sum of the amounts deemed distributed for the taxable year in accordance with paragraphs (a)(1) through (5) of this section,

(ii) (A) In the case of a shareholder which is a C corporation—

(1) An amount equal to 16/17 of the excess described in paragraph (a)(6)(i), multiplied by the international boycott factor as determined under section 999(c)(1), or

(2) In lieu of the amount determined under subparagraph (ii)(A)(1), 16/17 of such excess as is described in section 999(c)(2), or

(B) In the case of a shareholder which is not a C corporation—

(1) An amount equal to all of the excess described in paragraph (a)(6)(i), multiplied by the international boycott factor as determined under section 999(c)(1), or

(2) In lieu of the amount determined under subparagraph (ii)(B)(1), the amount of such excess as is described in section 999(c)(2), and

(iii) An amount equal to the sum of any illegal bribes, kickbacks, or other payments paid by or on behalf of the DISC directly or indirectly to an official, employee, or agent in fact of a government. An amount is paid by a DISC where it *is* paid directly or indirectly by any officer, director, employee, shareholder, or agent of the DISC for the benefit of such DISC. For purposes of this section, the principles of section 162(c) and the regulations thereunder shall apply. The amount of an illegal payment made in the form of property or services shall be considered to be equal to the fair market value of such property or services at the time such property is transferred or such services are performed.

(7) The amount of foreign investment attributable to producer's loans of the DISC, as of the close of the "group taxable year" ending with such taxable year of the DISC, determined in accordance with § 1.995-5. The amount of such foreign investment attributable to producer's loans so determined for any taxable year of a former DISC shall be deemed distributed as a dividend to the shareholders of such former DISC on the last day of such taxable year. See § 1.995-3(e) for the effect that such deemed distribution has on scheduled installments of deemed distributions of accumulated DISC income under § 1.995-3(a) upon disqualification.

(b) Limitation on amount of deemed distributions under section 995(b)(1). *(1) General rule.* The sum of the amounts described in paragraphs (a)(1) through (a)(6) of this section which is deemed distributed pro rata to the DISC's shareholders as a dividend for any taxable year of the DISC shall not exceed the DISC's earnings and profits for such year.

(2) Foreign investment attributable to producer's loans. The amount of foreign investment attributable to producer's loans of the DISC (as described in paragraph (a)(7) of this section) which is deemed to be distributed pro rata to the DISC's shareholders as a dividend for any taxable year of the DISC shall not exceed the lesser of the DISC's accumulated DISC income at the beginning of such year or the corporation's accumulated earnings and profits at the beginning of such year (but not less than zero)—

(i) Increased by any DISC income of the corporation for such year as defined in § 1.996-3(b)(2) (that is, any excess of the DISC's earnings and profits for such year over the sum of the amounts described in paragraphs (a)(1) through (a)(6) of this section), or

(ii) Decreased by any deficit in the DISC's earnings and profits for such year.

For example, if a DISC has a deficit in accumulated earnings and profits at the beginning of a taxable year of $10,000, current earnings and profits of $12,000, no amounts described in paragraphs (a)(1) through (a)(6) of this section for the year, and foreign investment attributable to producer's loans for the taxable year of $5,000, the DISC would have a deemed distribution described in paragraph (a)(7) of this section of $5,000 for the taxable year. As a further example, assume that the DISC had accumulated earnings and profits of $13,000 at the beginning of the taxable year, accumulated DISC income of $10,000 at the beginning of the taxable year, a deficit in earnings and profits for the taxable year of $12,000, no amounts described in paragraphs (a)(1) through (a)(6) of this section for the taxable year, and foreign investment attributable to producer's loans for the taxable year of $5,000. Under these facts the DISC would have no deemed distribution described in paragraph (a)(7) of this section for the taxable year because the DISC had no DISC income for the taxable year and the current year's deficit in earnings and profits subtracted from the DISC's accumulated DISC income at the beginning of the year produces a negative amount. For rules relating to the carryover to a subsequent year of the $5,000 of foreign investment attributable to producer's loans, see § 1.995-5(a)(6).

(3) *Ordering rule when limitation applies.* If, by reason of the limitation described in paragraph (b)(1) of this section, less than the sum of the amounts described in paragraph (a)(1) through (a)(6) of this section is deemed distributed, then the portion of such sum which is deemed distributed shall be attributed first to the amount described in paragraph (a)(1), to the extent thereof; second to the amount described in paragraph (a)(2), to the extent thereof; third to the amount described in paragraph (a)(3), to the extent thereof; and so forth, and finally to the amount described in paragraph (a)(6).

(c) **Examples.** Paragraphs (a) and (b) of this section may be illustrated by the following examples:

Example (1). Y is a corporation which uses the calendar year as its taxable year and elects to be treated as a DISC beginning with its taxable year beginning January 1, 1985. X, a corporation, is Y's sole shareholder. In 1985, X transfers certain property to Y in exchange for Y's stock in a transaction in which X does not recognize gain or loss by reason of the application of section 351(a). Included in the property transferred to Y is depreciable property described in paragraph (a)(3) of this section on which X realizes, and does not recognize by reason of the application of section 1245(b)(3), a gain of $20,000. If X had sold such property for cash, the $20,000 gain would have been recognized as ordinary income under section 1245. Also included in the transfer to Y are 100 shares of stock in a third corporation (which is not a related foreign export corporation) on which X realizes, but does not recognize, a gain of $5,000. In 1986, Y sells such property and recognizes a gain of $25,000 on the depreciable property and $8,000 on the 100 shares of stock. Y has accumulated earnings and profits at the beginning of 1986 of $5,000, earnings and profits for 1986 of $72,000, and taxable income for 1986 of $100,000. At the beginning of 1986, Y has $6,000 of accumulated DISC income, no previously taxed income, and a deficit of $1,000 of other earnings and profits. The total qualified export receipts of Y for 1986 are less than $10 million and there were no transactions in military property. Under these facts and the additional facts assumed in the table below, X is treated as having received a deemed distribution taxable as a dividend of $46,000 on December 31, 1986, determined as follows:

(1) Gross interest derived by Y in 1986 from producer's loans	$ 7,000
(2) Amount of gain on depreciable property (lesser of Y's recognized gain ($25,000) or X's gain not recognized on section 1245 property ($20,000))	20,000
(3) Amount of gain on stock (lesser of Y's recognized gain ($8,000) or X's gain not recognized ($5,000))	5,000
(4) One-seventeenth of the excess of the DISC's taxable income for 1986 over the sum of lines (1), (2) and (3) (1/17 of $100,000 minus $32,000))	$ 4,000
(5) Limitation on lines (1) through (4):	
(a) Sum of lines (1) through (4)	$36,000
(b) Earnings and profits for 1986	72,000
(c) Lesser of lines (5)(a) or (b)	$36,000
(6) Amount determined under paragraph (a)(7) of this section:	
(a) Foreign investment attributable to producer's loans under $1,995-5	$10,000
(b) Sum of the lesser of accumulated earnings and profits at beginning of 1986 ($5,000) or accumulated DISC income at beginning of 1986 ($6,000), plus excess of earnings nd profits for 1986 over line (5)(c) ($72,000 minus $36,000)	$41,000
(c) Lesser of lines (6)(a) or (b)	$10,000
(7) Total deemed distribution for 1986 (sum of lines (5)(c) and (6)(c))	$46,000

Example (2). Assume the facts are the same as in example (1), except that the earnings and profits for 1986 are only $30,000. Under these facts, X is treated as receiving a deemed distribution taxable as a dividend of $35,000 on December 31, 1986, determined as follows:

(5) Limitation on lines (1) through (4) of example (1):	
(a) Line (5)(a) of example (1)	$36,000
(b) Earnings and profits for 1986	$30,000
(c) Lesser of lines (5)(a) or (b)	$30,000
(6) Amount determined under paragraph (a)(7) of this section:	
(a) Line (6)(a) of example (1)	$10,000
(b) Sum of the lesser of accumulated earnings and profits at beginning of 1986 ($5,000) or accumulated DISC income at beginning of 1986 ($6,000), plus excess of earnings and profits for 1986 over line (5)(c) ($30,000 minus $30,000)	$ 5,000
(c) Lesser of lines (6)(a) or (b)	$ 5,000
(7) Total deemed distribution for 1986 (sum of lines (5)(c) and (6)(c)	$35,000

Example (3). Assume the facts are the same as in example (1), except that Y has a deficit in accumulated earnings and profits at at the beginning 1986 of $4,000. This deficit is comprised of accumulated DISC income of $1,000, no previously taxed income and a deficit in other earnings and profits of $5,000. Assume also that Y has earnings and profits for 1986 of $45,000. Under these facts, X is treated as receiving a deemed distribution taxable as a dividend in the amount of $45,000 on December 31, 1986. Determined as follows:

(5) Limitation on lines (1) through (4) of example (1):

(a) Line (5)(a) of example (1)	$36,000
(b) Earnings and profits for 1986	$45,000
(c) Lesser of lines (5)(a) or (b)	$36,000

(6) Amount determined under paragraph (a)(7) of this section:

(a) Line (6)(a) of example (1)	$10,000
(b) Sum of the lesser of accumulated earnings and profits at beginning of 1986 ($4,000 deficit—but not less than zero) or accumulated DISC income at beginning of 1986 ($1,000), plus excess of earnings and profits for 1986 over amount on line (5)(c) (45,000 minus $36,000)	$ 9,000
(c) Lesser of lines (6)(a) or (b)	$ 9,000

(7) Total deemed distribution for 1986 (sum of lines (5)(c) and (6)(c))	$45,000

(d) Special rules for certain tax-free acquisitions of property by the DISC. *(1) Exchanges by DISC.* For purposes of paragraph (a)(2)(i) and (3)(i) of this section, if—

(i) A DISC acquires property in a first transaction and in a second transaction it disposes of such property in exchange for other property, and

(ii) By reason of the application of section 1031 (relating to like-kind exchanges) or section 1033 (relating to involuntary conversions), the basis in the DISC's hands of the other property acquired in such second transaction is determined in whole or in part with reference to the basis of the property acquired in the first transaction, then upon a disposition of such other property in a third transaction by the DISC such other property shall be treated as though it had been transferred to the DISC in the first transaction. Thus, if the first transaction is a purchase of the property for cash, then paragraph (a)(2) and (3) of this section will not apply to a sale by the DISC of the other property acquired in the second transaction.

(2) Transfer of another DISC. For purposes of paragraph (a)(2)(i) and (3)(i) of this section, if a DISC acquires property in a first transaction and it transfers such property to a transferee DISC in a second transaction in which the transferor DISC's gain is not recognized in whole or in part, then such property shall be treated as though it had been transferred to the transferee DISC in the same manner in which it was acquired in the first transaction by the transferor DISC. For example, if X and Y are both DISCs, and if X transfers property to Y in a second transaction in which gain or loss is not recognized, paragraph (a)(2) or (3) of this section does not apply to a sale of such property by Y in a third transaction if X had acquired the property in a first transaction by a cash purchase. If, however, X acquired the property from a transferor other than a DISC in the first transaction in which the transferor's realized gain was not recognized, then paragraph (a)(2) or (3) of this section may apply to a sale by Y if the other conditions of paragraph (a)(2) or (3) are met.

(3) Limitation on amount recognized by DISC. If a DISC acquires property in a second transaction described in paragraph (d)(1) or (2) of this section in which it (or, in the case of a second transaction described in paragraph (d)(2), the transferor DISC) recognizes a portion (but not all) of the realized gain, then the amount described in paragraph (a)(2)(ii) or (a)(3)(ii) of this section with respect to a disposition by the DISC of such acquired property in a third transaction shall not exceed the amount of the transferor's gain which was not recognized on the first transaction minus the amount of gain recognized by the DISC (or transferor DISC) on the second transaction.

(4) Examples. The provisions of this paragraph (d) are illustrated by the following examples:

Example (1). X and Y are corporations each of which qualifies as a DISC and uses the calendar year as its taxable year. In 1985, X acquires section 1245 property in a first transaction in which the transferor's entire realized gain of $17 is not recognized. In 1986, X transfers such property to Y in a second transaction in which X realizes a gain of $20 of which only $4 is recognized. (On December 31, 1986, X's shareholders are treated as having received a distribution taxable as a dividend which includes such $4 under paragraph (a)(3) of this section, provided the limitation in paragraph (b) of this section is met.) Assume further that in a third transaction in 1987, Y sells such property and recognizes a gain of $25. Under section 995(b)(1)(C) and paragraph (a)(3)(ii) of this section, Y's shareholders are treated as having received a distribution taxable as a dividend on December 31, 1987, of $13, which is the amount of the gain not recognized on the first transaction ($17) reduced by the amount recognized by X on the second transaction ($4).

Example (2). Z is a DISC which uses the calendar year as its taxable year. In a first transaction in 1985, Z acquires section 1245 property in exchange for its stock from A, an individual who is Z's sole shareholder, in a transaction in which A's realized gain of $30 is not recognized by reason of section 351(a). In a second transaction in 1986, Z exchanges such property for other property in a like-kind exchange to which section 1031(b) applies and recognizes $10 of a realized gain of $35. (On December 31, 1986, A is treated as having received a distribution taxable as a dividend which includes such $10 under paragraph (a)(3) of this section, provided the limitation of paragraph (b) of this section is met.) In a third transaction in 1987, Z sells the property acquired in the like-kind exchange and recognizes a gain of $25. Under section 995(b)(1)(C) and paragraph (a)(3)(ii) of this section, A is treated as having received a distribution taxable as a dividend on December 31, 1987, of $20, which is the amount of gain not recognized by A on the first transaction ($30) reduced by the amount of gain recognized by Z on the second transaction ($10).

(e) Carryback of net operating loss and capital loss to prior DISC taxable year. For purposes of sections 991, 995 and 996, the amount of the deduction for the taxable year under section 172 for a net operating loss carryback or carryover or under section 1212 for a capital loss carryback or carryover shall be determined in the same manner as if the DISC were a domestic corporation which had not elected to be treated as a DISC. Thus, the amount of the deduction will be the same whether or not the corporation was a DISC in the year the loss is incurred or in the year to which the loss is carried. For provisions setting forth adjustments to the DISC's, or former DISC's, deemed distributions, adjustments to its divisions of earnings and profits, and other tax consequences arising from such carrybacks, see § 1.996-8. See § 1.996-9 for the reduction of the amount of any net operating loss or capital loss carryforward of a DISC to the extent of the DISC's accumulated DISC income as of December 31, 1984.

§ 1.995-3 Distributions upon disqualification.

(a) General rule. Under section 995(b)(2), a shareholder of a corporation which is disqualified from being a DISC, either because pursuant to § 1.992-2(e)(2) it revoked its election to be treated as a DISC or because it has failed to satisfy the requirements as set forth in § 1.992-1 to be a DISC for a taxable year, shall be deemed to have received (at the times specified in paragraph (b) of this section) distributions taxable as dividends aggregating an amount equal to his pro rata share of the accumulated DISC income (as defined in § 1.996-3(b)) of such corporation which was accumulated during the immediately preceding consecutive taxable years for which the corporation was a DISC. The pro rata share referred to in the preceding sentence shall be determined as of the close of the last of such consecutive taxable years for which the corporation was a DISC. See § 1.996-7(c) for rules relating to the carryover of, and maintaining a separate account for, such accumulated DISC income in certain reorganizations.

(b) Time of receipt of deemed distributions. Distributions described in paragraph (a) of this section shall be deemed to be received in equal installments on the last day of each of the 10 taxable years of the corporation following the year of the disqualification described in paragraph (a) of this section, except that in no case may the number of equal installments exceed the number of the immediately preceding consecutive taxable years for which the corporation was a DISC.

(c) Transfer of shares. Deemed distributions are includible under paragraphs (a) and (b) of this section in a shareholder's gross income as a dividend only so long as he continues to hold the shares with respect to which the distribution is deemed made. Thus, the transferee of such shareholder will include in his gross income under paragraphs (a) and (b) of this section the remaining installments of the deemed distribution which the transferor would have included in his gross income as a dividend had he not transferred the shares. However, if the transferee acquires the shares in a transaction in which the transferor's gain is treated under § 1.995-4 in whole or in part as a dividend, then under § 1.996-4(a) such transferee does not include subsequent installments in his gross income to the extent that the transferee treats such subsequent installments as made out of previously taxed income.

(d) Effect of requalification. Deemed distributions under paragraphs (a) and (b) of this section continue and are includible in gross income as dividends by the shareholders whether or not the corporation subsequently requalifies and is treated as a DISC.

(e) Effect of actual distributions and deemed distributions under section 995(b)(1)(G). If, during the period a shareholder of a DISC, or former DISC, is taking into account deemed distributions under paragraphs (a) and (b) of this section, an actual distribution is made to him out of accumulated DISC income or a deemed distribution because of foreign investment attributable to producer's loans is made under § 1.995-2(a)(5) out of accumulated DISC income, such actual or deemed distribution shall first reduce the last installment of the deemed distributions scheduled to be included in the shareholder's gross income as a dividend, and then the preceding scheduled installments in reverse order. If deemed distributions are scheduled to be included in gross income for two or more disqualifications, an actual distribution or a deemed distribution under § 1.995-2(a)(5) which is treated as made out of accumulated DISC income reduces the deemed distributions resulting from the earlier disqualification first.

(f) Examples. This section may be illustrated by the following examples:

Example (1). X Corporation, which uses the calendar year as its taxable year, elects to be treated as a DISC beginning with 1972. X qualifies as a DISC for taxable years 1972 through 1975, but, pursuant to § 1.992-2(e)(2), revokes its election as of January 1, 1976, and is disqualified as a DISC. On that date, X has $24,000 of accumulated DISC income. X's shareholders will be deemed to receive $6,000 in distributions taxable as a dividend on the last day of each of X's four succeeding taxable years (1977, 1978, 1979, and 1980).

Example (2). Assume the same facts as in example (1), except that in 1978 X makes an actual distribution of $22,000 to its shareholders of which $10,000 is treated under § 1.996-1 as made out of accumulated DISC income. (The remaining $12,000 of such distribution is treated as made out of previously taxed income.) The actual distribution would first reduce the $6,000 deemed distribution scheduled for 1980 to zero and then reduce the $6,000 deemed distribution scheduled for 1979 to $2,000. Thus, X's shareholders include in 1978 $16,000 in gross income as dividends ($10,000 of actual distributions and the $6,000 deemed distribution scheduled for that year) and $2,000 as a dividend in 1979.

Example (3). Assume the same facts as in example (2), except that X requalifies as a DISC for taxable year 1977 during which it derives $7,000 of DISC income (computed after taking into account a deemed distribution under § 1.995-2(a)(4) of $7,000), but is again disqualified in 1978. In addition X makes an actual distribution in 1977 equal to the deemed distribution of $7,000. Such actual distribution is excluded from gross income under § 1.996-1(c). In 1977, X's shareholders include in gross income as dividends the $6,000 deemed distribution upon disqualification (in addition to the deemed distributions of $7,000 under § 1.995-2 for 1977 when it was treated as a DISC). The actual distribution in 1978 still reduces the installments resulting from the earlier disqualification. Thus, in 1978, X's shareholders include $16,000 in gross income as dividends. In 1979, X's shareholders include $9,000 in gross income as dividends (the final installment of $2,000 from the earlier disqualification plus the single deemed distribution of $7000 resulting from the later disqualification).

T.D. 7324, 9/27/74, amend T.D. 7854, 11/16/82.

§ 1.995-4 Gain on certain dispositions of stock in a DISC.

Caution: The Treasury has not yet amended Reg § 1.995-4 to reflect changes made by P.L. 100-647.

(a) Disposition in which gain is recognized. *(1) In general.* If a shareholder disposes, or is treated as disposing, of stock in a DISC, or former DISC, then any gain recognized on such disposition shall be included in the shareholder's gross income as a dividend, notwithstanding any other provision of the Code, to the extent of the accumulated DISC income amount (described in paragraph (d) of this section). To the extent the recognized gain exceeds the accumulated DISC income amount, it is taxable as gain from the sale or exchange of the stock.

(2) Nonapplication of subparagraph (1). The provisions of subparagraph (1) of this paragraph do not apply (i) to the extent gain is not recognized (such as, for example, in the case of a gift or an exchange of stock to which section 354 applies) and (ii) to the amount of any recognized gain which is taxable as a dividend (such as, for example, under section 301 or 356(a)(2)) or as gain from the sale or exchange of property which is not a capital asset. The amount taxable as a dividend under section 301 or 356(a)(2) is subject to the

rules provided in § 1.995-1(c) for the treatment of actual distributions by a DISC.

(b) Disposition in which separate corporate existence of DISC is terminated. *(1) General.* If stock in a corporation that is a DISC, or former DISC, is disposed of in a transaction in which its separate corporate existence as a DISC, or former DISC, is terminated, then, notwithstanding any other provision of the Code, an amount of realized gain shall be recognized and included in the transferor's gross income as a dividend. The realized gain shall be recognized to the extent that such gain—

(i) Would not have been recognized but for the provisions of this paragraph, and

(ii) Does not exceed the accumulated DISC income amount (described in paragraph (d) of this section).

(2) Cessation of separate corporate existence as a DISC, or former DISC. For purposes of subparagraph (1) of this paragraph, separate corporate existence as a DISC, or former DISC, will be treated as having ceased if, as a result of the transaction, there is no separate entity which is a DISC and to which is carried over the accumulated DISC income and other tax attributes of the DISC, or former DISC, the stock of which is disposed of. Thus, for example, if stock in a DISC, or former DISC, is exchanged in a transaction described in section 381(a) (relating to carryovers in certain corporate acquisitions), the gain realized on the transfer of such stock will not be recognized under subparagraph (1) of this paragraph if the assets of such DISC, or former DISC, are acquired by a corporation which immediately after the acquisition qualifies as a DISC. For a further example, if a DISC, or former DISC, is liquidated in a transaction to which section 332 (relating to complete liquidations of subsidiaries) applies, the transaction will be subject to subparagraph (1) of this paragraph if the basis to the transferee corporation of the assets acquired on the liquidation is determined under section 334(b)(2) (as in effect prior to amendment by the Tax Equity and Fiscal Responsibility Act of 1982) or if immediately after such liquidation the transferee of such assets does not qualify as a DISC. However, separate corporate existence as a DISC, or former DISC, will not be treated as having ceased in the case of a mere change in place of organization, however effected. See § 1.996-7 for rules for the carryover of the divisions of a DISC's earnings and profits to one or more DISC's.

(c) Disposition to which section 311, 336, or 337 applies. *(1) In general.* If, after December 31, 1976, a shareholder distributes, sells, or exchanges stock in a DISC, or former DISC, in a transaction to which section 311, 336, or 337 applies, then an amount equal to the excess of the fair market value of such stock over its adjusted basis in the hands of the shareholder shall, notwithstanding any other provision of the Code, be included in gross income of the shareholder as a dividend to the extent of the accumulated DISC income amount (described in paragraph (d) of this section).

(2) Nonapplication of subparagraph (1). Subparagraph (1) shall not apply if the person receiving the stock in the disposition has a holding period for the stock which includes the period for which the stock was held by the shareholder disposing of such stock.

(d) Accumulated DISC income amount. *(1) General.* For purposes of this section, the accumulated DISC income amount is the accumulated DISC income of the DISC or former DISC which is attributable to the stock disposed of and which was accumulated in taxable years of such DISC or former DISC during the period or periods such stock was held by the shareholder who disposed of such stock.

(2) Period during which a shareholder has held stock. For purposes of this section, the period during which a shareholder has held stock includes the period he is considered to have held it by reason of the application of section 1223 and, if his basis is determined in whole or in part under the provisions of section 1014(d) (relating to special rule for DISC stock acquired from decedent), the holding period of the decedent. Such holding period is to exclude the day of acquisition but include the day of disposition. Thus, for example, if A purchases stock in a DISC on December 31, 1972, and makes a gift of such stock to B on June 30, 1973, then on December 31, 1974, B will be treated as having held the stock for 2 full years. If the basis of the stock in C's hands is determined under section 1014(d) upon a transfer from B's estate on December 31, 1976, by reason of B's death on June 30, 1974, then on December 31, 1976, C will be treated as having held the stock for 4 full years.

(e) Accumulated DISC income allocable to shareholder under section 995(c)(2). *(1) In general.* Under this paragraph, rules are prescribed for purposes of paragraph (d) of this section as to the manner of determining, with respect to the stock of a DISC, or former DISC, disposed of, the amount of accumulated DISC income which is attributable to such stock and which was accumulated in taxable years of the corporation during the period or periods the stock disposed of was held or treated under paragraph (d)(2) of this section as held by the transferor. Subparagraphs (2), (3), and (4) of this paragraph set forth a method of computation which may be employed to determine such amount. Any other method may be employed so long as the result obtained would be the same as the result obtained under such method.

(2) Step 1. Determine the increase (or decrease) in accumulated DISC income for each taxable year of the DISC, or former DISC, by subtracting from the amount of accumulated DISC income (as defined in § 1.996-3(b)) at the close of each taxable year the amount thereof as of the close of the immediately preceding taxable year.

(3) Step 2. (i) Determine for each taxable year of the DISC, or former DISC, the increase (or decrease) in accumulated DISC income per share by dividing such increase (or decrease) for the year by the number of shares outstanding or deemed outstanding on each day of such year.

(ii) If the number of shares of stock in the corporation outstanding on each day of a taxable year of the DISC, or former DISC, is not constant, then the number of such shares deemed outstanding on each day of such year shall be the sum of the fractional amounts in respect of each share which was outstanding on any day of the taxable year. The fractional amount in respect of a share shall be determined by dividing the number of days in the taxable year on which such share was outstanding (excluding the day the share became outstanding, but including the day the share ceased to be outstanding), by the total number of days in such taxable year.

(iii) If for any taxable year of a DISC, or former DISC, the share disposed of was not held (or treated under paragraph (d)(2) of this section as held) by the disposing shareholder for the entire year, then the amount of increase (or decrease) in accumulated DISC income attributable to such share for such year is the amount determined as if he held the share until the end of such year multiplied by a fraction the numerator of which is the number of days in the taxable year on which the shareholder held (or under paragraph (d)(2) of this section is treated as having held) such share and the denominator of which is the total number of days in the taxable year.

(4) Step 3. Add the amounts computed in step 2 for each taxable year of the DISC, or former DISC, in which the shareholder held such share of stock.

(5) Examples. This paragraph may be illustrated by the following examples:

Example (1). X Corporation uses the calendar year as its taxable year and elects to be a DISC for the first time for 1973. On January 1, 1973, X has 20 shares issued and outstanding. A and B each own 10 shares. On July 1, 1976, X issues 10 shares to C. On December 31, 1977, A sells his 10 shares to D and recognizes a gain of $120. Under these facts and other facts assumed in the table below, A includes in his gross income for 1977 a dividend under paragraph (b) of this section of $61.30 and long-term capital gain of $58.70.

Year pep	(a) Year end accumulated DISC income	(b) Increase (decrease) in accumulated DISC income	(c) Shares outstanding	(d) Increase (decrease) per share (column (b) divided by column (c))
1973	$ 80	$80	20	$4.00
1974	50	(30)	20	(1.50)
1975	80	30	20	1.50
1976	100	20	25[1]	.80
1977	140	40	30	1.33
(1) Total increase in accumulated DISC income for each share disposed of (sum of amounts in column (d))				6.13
Multiply by number of shares disposed of				10
(2) Total amount of accumulated DISC income attributable to A's shares disposed of				61.30
(3) A's gain				120.00
(4) Portion of A's gain taxable as a dividend (lower of lines (2) and (3))				61.30
(5) Portion of A's gain taxable as long-term capital gain (line (3) minus line (4))				58.70

[1] Under subparagraph (3)(ii) of this paragraph, the aggregate fractional amounts of the 10 shares issued on July 1, 1976, is 5 shares, i.e., 10 shares, multiplied by (183 days/366 days). Thus, the number of shares deemed outstanding for 1976 is 25 shares, i.e., 20 shares plus 5 shares.

Example (2). Assume the same facts as in example (1), except that A sells his 10 shares to D on July 1, 1977. Under subparagraph (3)(iii) of this paragraph, the amount of increase in accumulated DISC income for 1977 which is attributable to each share disposed of is limited to $.67, i.e., $1.33 multiplied by 182 days/365 days. Therefore, the sum of the yearly increases (and decreases) in accumulated DISC income for each share is reduced by $.66 (i.e., $1.33 minus $.67). The total increase in accumulated DISC income for each share disposed of is $5.47 (i.e., $6.13 minus $.66). Under these facts, A would include in his gross income for 1977 a dividend of $54.70 and long-term capital gain of $65.30 determined as follows:

(1) Total increase in accumulated DISC income for each share disposed of	$ 5.47
Multiplied by number of shares disposed of	10
(2) Total amount of accumulated DISC income attributable of to all shares disposed of	54.70
(3) A's gain	120.00
(4) Portion of A's gain taxable as a dividend (lower of lines (2) and (3))	54.70
(5) Portion of A's gain taxable as long-term capital gain (line (3) minus line (4))	65.30

T.D. 7324, 9/27/74, amend T.D. 7854, 11/16/82.

§ 1.995-5 Foreign investment attributable to producer's loans.

(a) In general. *(1) Limitation.* Under section 995(d), the amount as of the close of a "group taxable year" (as defined in subparagraph (3) of this paragraph) of foreign investment attributable to producer's loans of a DISC for purposes of section 995(b)(1)(G) shall be the excess (as of the close of such year) of—

(i) The smallest of—

(a) The amount of the net increase in foreign assets (as defined in paragraph (b) of this section) by domestic and foreign members of the controlled group which includes the DISC.

(b) The amount of the actual foreign investment by the domestic members of such group (as determined under paragraph (c) of this section), or

(c) The amount of outstanding producer's loans (as determined under § 1.993-4) by such DISC to members of such controlled group, over

(ii) The amount (determined under § 1.995-2(a)(5) and (b)(2)) of foreign investment attributable to producer's loans treated under section 995(b)(1)(G) as deemed distributions by the particular DISC taxable as dividends for prior taxable years of that particular DISC.

Thus, for example, if the shareholders of a DISC which uses the calendar year as its taxable year (and which is a member of a controlled group in which all of the members use the calendar year as their taxable year) are treated under section 995(b)(1)(G) as receiving foreign investment attributable to producer's loans of a DISC of $0 in 1972, $10 in 1973, and $30 in 1974, or a total of $40, and if the smallest of the amounts described in subdivision (i) of this subparagraph at the end of 1975 is $90, then the amount of the foreign investment attributable to producer's loans of a DISC at the end of 1975 is $50, i.e., the excess (as of the close of 1975) of the smallest of the amounts described in subdivision (i) of this subparagraph ($90) over the sum of the amounts of foreign investment attributable to producer's loans treated under section 995(b)(1)(G) as deemed distributions by the DISC taxable as dividends for prior taxable years of the DISC ($40). If the separate corporate existence of the DISC as to which the amount described in subdivision (ii) of this subparagraph relates ceases to exist within the meaning of § 1.995-4(c)(2), then such amount shall no longer be taken into account by the group for any purpose. For inclusion of amounts, because of certain corporate acquisitions, see paragraph (d) of this section.

(2) Controlled group; domestic and foreign member. For purposes of this section—

(i) The term "controlled group" has the meaning assigned to such term by § 1.993-1(k).

(ii) The term "domestic member" means a domestic corporation which is a member of a controlled group, and the term "foreign member" means a foreign corporation which is a member of a controlled group.

(3) Group taxable year. (i) The term "group taxable year" refers collectively to the taxable year of the DISC and to the taxable year of each corporation in the controlled group which includes the DISC ending with or within the taxable year of the DISC. Thus, for example, if a corporation has a subsidiary which uses the calendar year as its taxable year and which elects to be treated as a DISC, and if the parent has a taxable year ending on October 31, the "group taxable year" for 1973 would refer to calendar year 1973 for the DISC and to the parent's taxable year ending October 31, 1973.

(ii) In cases in which the DISC makes a return for a short taxable year, that is, for a taxable year consisting of a period of less than 12 months, pursuant to section 443 and the regulations thereunder, or § 1.991-1(b)(3), the following rules shall apply—

(a) In the case of a change in the annual accounting period of the DISC resulting in a short taxable year, the "group taxable year" refers collectively to the short taxable year and to the taxable year of each corporation in the controlled group which includes the DISC ending with or within the short taxable year.

(b) In the case of a DISC which is in existence during only part of what would otherwise be its taxable year, the "group taxable year" refers collectively to the short period during which the DISC was in existence and to the taxable year of each corporation in the controlled group which includes the DISC ending with or within the 12-month period ending on the last day of the short period.

(iii) With respect to periods prior to the first taxable year for which a member of the group qualified (or is treated) as a DISC, each group taxable year shall be determined under subdivision (i) of this subparagraph as if such member was in existence, it qualified as a DISC, and its taxable year ended on that date corresponding to the date such member's first taxable year ended after it qualified (or is treated) as a DISC whether or not the corporation which qualifies (or is treated) as a DISC used the same taxable year before it so qualified (or is so treated). Thus, for example, if a corporation which is organized on March 3, 1975, uses the calendar year as its taxable year, and is a member of a controlled group which does not include a DISC, first qualifies (or is treated) as a DISC for calendar year 1975, then the term "group taxable year" with respect to years prior to 1975 refers collectively to such prior calendar years and to the taxable year of each corporation in the group ending with or within such prior calendar years.

(iv) For special rules in the case of a group which includes more than one DISC, see paragraph (g) of this section.

(4) Amounts determined for prior years. Unless the 3-year limitation is properly elected under subparagraph (5) of this paragraph, the amounts described in paragraphs (b) (relating to net increase in foreign assets) and (c) (relating to actual foreign investments by domestic members) of this section reflect, as of the close of a group taxable year, amounts for all taxable years of members of the group beginning after December 31, 1971 (and amounts arising after December 31, 1971, or such other date prescribed in paragraph (b)(7) of this section), provided that such amounts relate to such group taxable year and preceding group taxable years. Thus, for example, if all members of a controlled group use the calendar year as the taxable year, and 1980 is the first taxable year for which any member of the group qualifies (or is treated) as a DISC, then, unless the 3-year limitation is elected under subparagraph (5) of this paragraph, the amounts described in paragraphs (b) and (c) of this section will be taken into account beginning with the dates specified in the preceding sentence. For rules as to carryovers on certain corporate acquisitions and reorganizations, see paragraph (d) of this section.

(5) Three-year elective limitation. (i) A DISC may elect to take into account only amounts described in paragraphs (b) (relating to net increase in foreign assets) and (c) (relating to actual foreign investment by domestic members) of this section for the 3 taxable years of each member immediately preceding its taxable year included in that first group taxable year which includes a member's first taxable year during which it qualifies (or is treated) as a DISC. For purposes of the preceding sentence, determinations shall be made by reference to the taxable year of the issuer or transferor (as the case may be). If an election is made under this subdivision, the offset for uncommitted transitional funds under paragraph (b)(7) of this section is not allowed. If an election is made under this subdivision, the 3-year limitation applies to amounts described in paragraphs (b)(4) and (c)(1) and (2) of this section.

(ii) An election under subdivision (i) of this subparagraph shall not apply with respect to amounts which must be carried over under paragraph (d) of this section in the case of certain corporate acquisitions and reorganizations.

(iii) An election under subdivision (i) of this subparagraph shall be made by the DISC attaching to its first return, filed under section 6011(e)(2), a statement to the effect that the 3-year limitation is being elected under § 1.995-5(a)(5)(i).

(6) Cumulative basis. Pursuant to section 995(d)(5), all determinations of amounts specified in this section are to be made on a cumulative basis from the 1st year (or date) provided for in this section. Thus, each such determination shall take into account a net increase or a net decrease during the year, as the case may be. However, if the 3-year limitation is elected under subparagraph (5) of this paragraph, then only

amounts with respect to periods specified in such subparagraph (5) are amounts taken into account for years before a member of the group qualifies (or is treated) as a DISC. The computations described in this section may be made in any way chosen by the DISC (including a corporation being tested as to whether it qualifies as a DISC), provided such method results in the amount prescribed by this section.

(7) Example. The provisions of this paragraph may be illustrated by the following example:

Example. X Corporation, which uses the calendar year as its taxable year, is a member of a controlled group (within the meaning of subparagraph (2) of this paragraph). X elects to be treated as a DISC beginning with 1972. The amount of foreign investment attributable to X's producer's loans treated under section 995(b)(1)(G) as a distribution taxable as a dividend as of the close of each group taxable year with respect to each taxable year of X from 1972 through 1975 are set forth in the table below, computed on the basis of the facts assumed (the amounts on lines (1), (2), (3), and (5) being running balances):

Taxable year of X	1972	1973	1974	1975
(1) Net increase (or decrease) in foreign assets since January 1, 1972, at close of group taxable year	($30)	$10	$100	$150
(2) Actual foreign investment at close of group taxable year	20	60	80	140
(3) Outstanding producer's loans of X (the DISC) as of the close of group taxable year	0	40	90	120
(4) Smallest of lines (1), (2), or (3) (not less than zero)	0	10	80	120
(5) Less section 995(b)(1)(G) deemed distributions for prior taxable years (sum of lines (5) and (6) from prior year)	0	0	10	80
(6) Section 995(b)(1)(G) deemed distribution as of close of taxable year	0	10	70	40

(b) Net increase in foreign assets. *(1) In general.* (i) The term "net increase in foreign assets" when used in this section means the excess for the controlled group (as of the close of the group taxable year) of (a) the investment in foreign assets to be taken into account under subparagraph (2) of this paragraph over (b) the aggregate of the five offsets allowed by subparagraphs (3) through (7) of this paragraph.

(ii) No amount described in this paragraph (other than amounts described in subparagraphs (4) and (7) of this paragraph) with respect to a member of the group (or foreign branch of a member) shall be taken into account unless it is attributable to a taxable year of such member beginning after December 31, 1971. For a 3-year elective limitation with respect to the first taxable year for which a member qualifies (or is treated) as a DISC, see paragraph (a)(5) of this section. For manner of determining amounts on a cumulative basis, see paragraph (a)(6) of this section.

(2) Investments made in foreign assets. (i) For purposes of subparagraph (1) of this paragraph, there shall be taken into account as investment in foreign assets the aggregate of the amounts expended (within the meaning of subdivision (ii) of this subparagraph) during the period described in subparagraph (1)(ii) of this paragraph by all members of the controlled group which includes the DISC to acquire assets described in section 1231(b) (determined without regard to any holding period therein provided) which are located outside the United States (as defined in § 1.993-7) reduced by the aggregate of the amounts received by all such members of the controlled group from the sale, exchange, or involuntary conversion of such assets described in section 1231(b) which are located outside the United States. For purposes of this section, amounts expended for assets which are qualified export assets (as defined in § 1.993-2) of a DISC (or which would be qualified export assets if owned by a DISC) shall not be taken into account. Thus, for example, if a DISC acquires a qualified export asset located outside the United States, the asset is not to be taken into account for purposes of determining the net increase in foreign assets.

(ii) As used in subdivision (i) of this subparagraph, the term "amounts expended" (or amounts received) means the amount of any money or the fair market value (on the date of acquisition, sale, exchange, or involuntary conversion) of any property (other than money) used to acquire (or received for) the assets described in such subdivision (i).

(iii) For purposes of this subparagraph, an asset (other than an aircraft or vessel) is considered as located outside the United States if it was used predominantly outside the United States during the group taxable year. The determination as to whether such an asset is used predominantly outside the United States during the group taxable year in which it was acquired or sold, exchanged, or involuntarily converted shall be made by applying the rules of § 1.993-3(d) except that an aircraft described in section 48(a)(2)(B)(i) or a vessel described in section 48(a)(2)(B)(iii) shall be considered located in the United States and all other aircraft or vessels shall be considered located outside the United States. Thus, for example, if a member of a controlled group which includes a DISC acquires a vessel which is documented under the laws of a foreign country, the amount expended to acquire that vessel is an amount described in subdivision (i) of this subparagraph.

(iv) Examples. The provisions of this subparagraph may be illustrated by the following examples:

Example (1). X Corporation, which uses the calendar year as its taxable year, is a domestic member of a controlled group (within the meaning of paragraph (a)(2) of this section). During 1972, in a transaction to which section 1031 applies, X acquires a warehouse located outside the United States and having a fair market value of $100. As consideration, X transfers $20 in cash and a warehouse located within the United States and having a fair market value of $80. Under these facts, $100 will be taken into account as investment in foreign assets.

Example (2). The facts are the same as in example (1), except that the warehouse transferred by X as consideration is located outside the United States. Under these facts, only $20 will be taken into account as investment in foreign assets because the amount expended for such assets (i.e., $100) is reduced by the fair market value of any property located outside the United States received in exchange for such assets (i.e., $80).

(3) Depreciation with respect to all foreign assets of a controlled group. (i) An offset allowed by this subparagraph is the depreciation (determined under subdivision (ii) of this subparagraph) or depletion (determined under subdivision (iii) of this subparagraph) attributable to taxable years of the member beginning after December 31, 1971, with respect to all of the group's foreign assets described in subparagraph (2) of this paragraph including such assets acquired prior to

the date provided in such subparagraph (2), and without regard to whether the 3-year election in paragraph (a)(5) of this section is made. Thus, for example, depreciation for a taxable year of a member beginning after December 31, 1971, with respect to an asset described in section 1231(b) which is located outside of the United States and which was acquired during a taxable year of the member beginning before January 1, 1972, is an offset allowed by this subparagraph. For a further example, depreciation with respect to a qualified export asset is not such an offset.

(ii) The depreciation taken into account under subdivision (i) of this subparagraph shall be—

(a) In the case of an asset owned by a domestic member, only the amount allowed under section 167(b)(1) (relating to the allowance of the straightline method of depreciation) and § 1.162-11(b) (relating to amortization in lieu of depreciation), but not the amount allowed under section 179 (relating to the additional first-year depreciation allowance).

(b) In the case of an asset owned by a foreign member, the depreciation and amortization (referred to in (a) of this subdivision) allowable for purposes of computing earnings and profits under subparagraph (5)(i) of this paragraph.

(iii) The depletion taken into account under subdivision (i) of this subparagraph shall be limited to cost depletion computed under sections 611 and 612 and the regulations thereunder. Thus, percentage depletion is not to be taken into account in computing the offset under this subparagraph.

(4) Amount of outstanding stock or debt. (i) An offset allowed by this subparagraph is the outstanding amount of stock (including treasury stock) or debt obligations of any member of the group issued, sold, or exchanged after December 31, 1971, by any member (whether or not the same member) to persons who (on the date of such issuance, sale, or exchange) were neither United States persons (within the meaning of section 7701(a)(30)) nor members of the group, provided that, in the case of a debt obligation, such obligation is not repaid within 12 months after such issuance, sale, or exchange. Thus, for example, if stock is issued to a member of the group before January 1, 1972, and after December 31, 1971, it is sold to a person who is neither a United States person nor a member of the group, an offset allowed by this subparagraph includes the outstanding amount of such stock. For purposes of this subparagraph, foreign branches of United States banks are not considered to be United States persons.

(ii) The outstanding amount of stock or debt obligations shall be determined in accordance with the following provisions:

(a) The outstanding amount of stock or debt obligations described in subdivision (i) of this subparagraph is equal to the net amount described in (b) of this subdivision reduced (but not below zero) by the amount described in (c) of this subdivision.

(b) The net amount described in this subdivision (b) is the excess of (1) the aggregate of the amount of money and the fair market value of property (other than money) transferred by persons who are not members of the group and who are not U.S. persons as consideration for such stock and debt obligations over (2) fees and commission expenses borne by the issuer or transferror with respect to their issuance, sale, or exchange.

(c) The amount described in this subdivision (c) is the aggregate amount of money and fair market value of property (other than money) distributed to such persons on distributions in respect of such stock from other than earnings and profits or on distributions in redemption of such stock and the amount of principal paid pursuant to such debt obligations.

(d) For purposes of this subdivision (ii), in the case of a redemption, the stock or debt redeemed shall be charged against the earliest of such stock or debt issued, sold, or exchanged in order to determine the amount by which the balance of outstanding stock or debt is to be reduced. For purposes of this subparagraph, the fair market value of property received as consideration shall be determined as of the date the transaction occurs, and a contribution to capital within the meaning of section 118 shall be treated as the issuance of stock.

(iii) The provisions of subdivision (i) of this subparagraph apply regardless of the treatment under the Code of the transaction in which the stock or debt was issued, sold, or exchanged. Thus, for example, if X Corporation, a member of a controlled group which includes a DISC, acquires from a nonresident alien individual in exchange solely for X's voting stock all of the stock of Y Corporation pursuant to a reorganization as defined in section 368(a)(1)(B), the fair market value of the Y stock on the date of the exchange would be an offset allowed by this subparagraph.

(iv) The provisions of this subparagraph may be illustrated by the following example:

Example. X Corporation is a member of a controlled group (within a meaning of paragraph (a)(2) of this section) every member of which uses the calendar year as its taxable year. On January 1, 1972, X issues in a public offering its stock to persons described in subdivision (i) of this subparagraph who, in the aggregate, pay $1,000 as consideration. X pays $100 in underwriting fees. On the same date, X receives $425 upon issuing a $500 debt obligation to such persons at a discount of $75 and pays $25 in underwriting fees. On December 31, 1972, the offset allowed under this subparagraph is $1,300, i.e., ($1,000 minus $100) plus ($425 minus $25). If, during 1973, X makes a distribution of $150 (not in redemption) from other than earnings and profits with respect to such stock, then the offset is reduced to $1,150.

(5) Earnings and profits. (i) An offset allowed by this subparagraph is one-half the aggregate of the earnings and profits accumulated for all taxable years beginning after December 31, 1971, computed (without regard to any distributions from earnings and profits by a foreign corporation to a domestic corporation) in accordance with § 1.964-1 (relating to a controlled foreign corporation's earnings and profits), of each foreign member of the group which is controlled directly or indirectly (as determined under the principles of section 958 and the regulations thereunder) by a domestic member of the group and each foreign branch of a domestic member of the group (computed as if the branch were a foreign corporation). The DISC is bound by any action on behalf of a foreign member that was taken pursuant to § 1.964-1(c)(3) or by any failure to take action by or on behalf of a foreign member within the time specified in § 1.964-1(c)(6). With respect to a foreign member for which action was not previously required under § 1.964-1(c)(6) to be taken, the DISC may take action on behalf of such member by attaching a statement to that effect to the return of the DISC under section 6011(e)(2) for the first taxable year during which it qualifies (or is treated) as a DISC and there is outstanding a producer's loan made by such DISC to a member of the controlled group which includes the DISC.

(ii) If the aggregate of the accumulated earnings and profits described in subdivision (i) of this subparagraph is a deficit, the amount allowable as an offset under this subparagraph is zero.

(6) Royalties and fees. An offset allowed by this subparagraph is one-half the royalties and fees paid by foreign members of the group to domestic members of the group and by foreign branches of domestic members of the group to domestic members of the group during the taxable years of such members beginning after December 31, 1971.

(7) Uncommitted transitional funds. (i) An offset allowed by this subparagraph for the uncommitted transitional funds of the group is the sum described in subdivision (ii) of this subparagraph of the amount of certain capital raised under the foreign direct investment program and the amounts described in subdivision (iv) of this subparagraph of certain foreign excess working capital held on October 31, 1971.

(ii) The amount described in this subdivision of certain capital raised under the foreign direct investment program is the excess (if any) of—

(a) The amount of the offset allowed by subparagraph (4) of this paragraph, determined, however, with respect to the stock and debt obligations of domestic members of the group outstanding on December 31, 1971 (including amounts treated as stock outstanding by reason of a contribution to capital), whether or not outstanding after such date, which were issued, sold, or exchanged on or after January 1, 1968, by any member (whether or not the same member) to persons who (on the date of such issuance, sale, or exchange) were neither United States persons (within the meaning of section 7701(a)(30)) nor members of the group, but only to the extent the taxpayer establishes that such amount constitutes a long-term borrowing (see 15 CFR § 1000.324) for purposes of the foreign direct investment program (see 15 CFR Part 1000), over

(b) The amount (determined under paragraph (c) of this section) of actual foreign investment by the domestic members of the group during the portion of the period such stock or debt obligations have been outstanding prior to January 1, 1972, such determination to be made by substituting January 1, 1968, for the December 31, 1971, date specified in such paragraph (c) and by not taking into account the earnings and profits described in paragraph (c)(3) of this section.

For purposes of this subparagraph, foreign branches of United States banks are not considered to be United States persons.

(iii) (a) A taxpayer may establish that an amount under subdivision (ii) (a) of this subparagraph constitutes a long-term borrowing for purposes of the foreign direct investment program by keeping records sufficient to demonstrate that appropriate reports were filed with the Office of Foreign Direct Investment of the Department of Commerce with respect to the foreign borrowing or by any other method satisfactory to the district director.

(b) The amounts described in subdivision (ii) (a) of this subparagraph include amounts with respect to which an election under section 4912(c), to subject certain obligations of a United States person to the interest equalization tax, has been made, provided that the obligations to which such amounts relate were issued by an "overseas financing subsidiary" described in 15 CFR Part 1000N and were assumed by a United States person from such overseas financing subsidiary. Thus, for example, if an overseas financing subsidiary issues its notes to a foreign person in 1968, and such notes are assumed by its United States parent in 1973, which parent elects under section 4912(c) to have the notes subject to the interest equalization tax, then the amount of money received by the subsidiary is an amount described in subdivision (ii) (a) of this subparagraph.

(iv) The amount described in this subdivision of foreign excess working capital is the amount of liquid assets held by the foreign members of such group and foreign branches of domestic members of such group on October 31, 1971 (whether or not so held after such date) in excess of their reasonable working capital needs (as defined in § 1.993-2(e) on that date, but only to the extent not included in subdivision (ii) of this subparagraph. For purposes of this subdivision, the term "liquid assets" means money, bank deposits (not including time deposits), and indebtedness of any kind (including time deposits) which on the day acquired had a maturity of 2 years or less.

(8) Example. The provisions of this paragraph may be illustrated by the following example:

Example. X Corporation, which uses the calendar year as its taxable year is a member of a controlled group (within the meaning of paragraph (a)(2) of this section). X elects to be treated as a DISC beginning with 1972. The amount of net increase in foreign assets of the group at the close of each group taxable year with respect to each taxable year of X from 1972 through 1975 are set forth in the table below, computed on the basis of the facts assumed (the amounts on each line being running balances).

Taxable year of X	1972	1973	1974	1975
(1) Investment in foreign assets . . .	$150	$165	$260	$300
(2) Depreciation with respect to foreign assets of group	20	40	60	80
(3) Amount of stock or debt outstanding issued after Dec. 31, 1971	30	30	30	30
(4) One-half earnings and profits of foreign members	40	70	100	130
(5) Royalties and fees paid by foreign members to domestic members	10	15	20	20
(6) Uncommitted transitional funds	10	10	10	10
(7) Sum of lines (2) through (6) . .	110	165	220	270
(8) Net increase in foreign assets (line (1) minus line (6))	40	0	40	30

(c) Actual foreign investment by domestic members. For purposes of determining the limitation in paragraph (a) of this section, the amount of the actual foreign investment by domestic members of a controlled group is the sum (as of the close of the group taxable year) determined on a cumulative basis (see paragraph (a)(6) of this section) of—

(1) Outstanding stock or debt (including contributions to capital). The outstanding amount (determined in accordance with the principles of paragraph (b)(4)(ii)) of this section, applied with respect to stock or debt obligations described in this subparagraph) of stock (including treasury stock) or debt obligations (other than normal trade indebtedness) of foreign members of the group issued, sold, or exchanged after December 31, 1971, by any person (whether or not a member) which is not a domestic member to domestic members of the group, provided that the outstanding amount of debt obligations of any foreign member shall be the greater of such amount outstanding at the close of the taxable year of such member or the highest such amount outstanding at any time during the immediately preceding 90 days.

(2) Transfers to foreign branches. The amount of money or the fair market value of property (other than money) transferred by domestic members of the group after December 31, 1971, to foreign branches of such members in transactions which would, if the branch were a corporation, be in consideration for the sale of stock or debt obligations of (or a contribution of capital to) such foreign branches (as determined under subparagraph (1) of this paragraph), and

(3) Earnings and profits of foreign members. One-half of the earnings and profits (computed in accordance with paragraph (b)(5) of this section for purposes of computing net increase in foreign assets) of foreign members of the group which are controlled directly or indirectly (as determined under the principles of section 958 and the regulations thereunder) by a domestic member of the group and foreign branches (treated for this purpose as a corporation) of domestic members of the group accumulated during the taxable years of such foreign members (or branches) beginning after December 31, 1971, or, if later, the taxable year referred to in paragraph (a)(5)(i) of this section if the 3-year election provided for in such paragraph (a)(5)(i) is made.

(d) Carryovers in certain corporate acquisitions and reorganizations. *(1) Certain corporate acquisitions.* (i) If—

(a) A member of a controlled group ("first controlled group") acquires in a transaction to which section 381 applies the assets of a corporation which is a member of a second controlled group or acquires stock in such a corporation pursuant to a reorganization as defined in section 368(a)(1)(B) to which section 361 applies, or

(b) A member or combination of members of the first controlled group acquire in a transaction not described in (a) of this subdivision a majority interest (as defined in paragraph (e)(2) of this section) in the stock of a corporation which is a member of a second controlled group which includes a DISC so that such DISC after the acquisition is a member of the new controlled group,

then, for purposes of computing foreign investment attributable to producer's loans with respect to the new controlled group as constituted after such acquisition, all amounts described in paragraphs (a) through (c) of this section, including the amount specified in paragraph (a)(1)(ii) of this section (relating to amounts treated under section 995(b)(1)(G) as deemed distributions by the DISC taxable as dividends for prior taxable years of the DISC), with respect to members of the second controlled group which become members of the new controlled group shall carry over to such new controlled group. For purposes of this subdivision (i), a controlled group may consist of only one member. With respect to certain transactions involving foreign corporations, see section 367.

(ii) If a member or combination of members of a controlled group, immediately after an acquisition of stock to which subdivision (i) of this subparagraph applies do not control the total combined voting power (determined under § 1.957-1(b)) of the corporation whose stock was acquired, proper apportionment consistent with the principles of paragraph (e)(5) of this section shall be made with respect to amounts to which paragraphs (a) through (c) of this section apply.

(iii) (a) If subdivision (i) of this subparagraph applies, then for purposes of determining the application of the 3-year elective limitation provided for in paragraph (a)(5) of this section, the rules in (b), (c) and (d) of this subdivision (iii) apply.

(b) If both the "first controlled group" and the "second controlled group" (as those terms are defined in subdivision (i) of this subparagraph) include a DISC, and a DISC in either group has elected the 3-year limitation provided in paragraph (a)(5) of this section, then only those amounts taken into account under such paragraph (a)(5) by the electing DISC or DISC's shall be taken into account.

(c) If one of the groups includes a DISC and the other does not, and if the DISC has elected the 3-year limitation provided in paragraph (a)(5) of this section, then, for purposes of computing foreign investment attributable to producer's loans with respect to the new controlled group as constituted after the acquisition, all amounts described in paragraphs (a) through (c) of this section with respect to members of the controlled group which did not include the DISC shall carry over to such new controlled group, but only to the extent provided in such paragraph (a)(5), computed as if the group taxable year in which the acquisition occurred was the first group taxable year which includes a member's first taxable year during which it qualifies (or is treated) as a DISC.

(d) If (c) of this subdivision (iii) applies, except that the DISC has not elected the 3-year limitation provided in paragraph (a)(5) of this section, then the DISC in the new controlled group as constituted after the acquisition may, with respect to members of the controlled group which did not include the DISC, make the election provided in such paragraph (a)(5), and treat the year in which the acquisition occurred as if it were the first group taxable year which includes a member's first taxable year during which it qualifies (or is treated) as a DISC.

(iv) If a majority interest, or an interest in addition to a majority interest, is acquired in a transaction other than a transaction described in subdivision (i) of this subparagraph, then the rules in paragraph (e) of this section (relating to the acquisition of the foreign assets of a corporation) apply.

(2) Corporation ceasing to be a member. As of the date a corporation which is a member of a controlled group ceases to be a member of such group, the amounts of such group described in paragraphs (a) through (c) of this section will be reduced by such amounts which are attributable to the corporation which is no longer a member of the group.

(e) Acquisition of a majority interest in a corporation. *(1) In general.* If paragraph (d)(1)(i) of this section (relating to certain corporate acquisitions in which all amounts described in paragraphs (a) through (c) of this section carry over) does not apply, then, for purposes of determining under paragraph (b)(2) of this section the investments made in foreign assets by a controlled group, the acquisition of a majority interest (as defined in subparagraph (2) of this paragraph) or an interest in addition to a majority interest in a corporation by any member or combination of members of the controlled group is considered an acquisition of the assets (to the extent provided in subparagraph (5) of this paragraph) of the acquired corporation by the group, including the assets of any foreign corporation in which the acquired corporation owns a majority interest (to the extent provided in subparagraph (5) of this paragraph). For the rules concerning the date upon which an acquisition of a majority interest is considered to have occurred, see subparagraph (3) of this paragraph.

(2) Majority interest. For purposes of this section, a majority interest is more than 50 percent of the total combined voting power of all classes of a corporation's stock entitled to vote, as determined under § 1.957-1(b).

(3) Acquisition date. For purposes of this paragraph, an acquisition of a majority interest shall be considered to have occurred on the day on which the combined voting power of the group first reached the percentage required in subparagraph (2) of this paragraph.

(4) Valuation of assets. For purposes of this section, the amount of a corporation's assets deemed acquired is the fair market value of the assets on the date a majority interest, or an interest in addition to a previously held majority interest, is acquired.

(5) Apportionment in the case of the acquisition of less than all of the voting stock. (i) If the acquisition described in subparagraph (1) of this paragraph of a majority interest is of less than 100 percent of the total combined voting power of all classes of stock of the acquired corporation entitled to vote, then for purposes of subparagraph (1) of this paragraph the amount of the foreign assets of the corporation deemed acquired as of the day the majority interest is considered acquired shall be an amount equal to the fair market value of all of the corporation's foreign assets described in paragraph (b)(2) of this section as of such day multiplied by the percentage of the total combined voting power (determined under § 1.957-1(b)) held by members of the group on the day the majority interest is considered acquired.

(ii) If any member or combination of members of the controlled group hold a majority interest in a corporation, then for purposes of subparagraph (1) of this paragraph the acquisition of additional combined voting power by members of the controlled group shall be considered an acquisition of its foreign assets described in paragraph (b)(2) of this section in an amount equal to the fair market value of all such assets held by the foreign corporation on the date of the acquisition, multiplied by the increase (expressed in percentage points) in total combined voting power (as determined under § 1.957-1(b)) which occurred.

(6) Examples. The application of this paragraph may be illustrated by the following examples:

Example (1). M Corporation uses the calendar year as its taxable year. On November 18, 1973, M acquires from A, an individual United States person, for $1 million cash all 10,000 shares of the voting stock of N, a foreign corporation. N's only asset is a warehouse located in France with a fair market value on the date of acquisition of $1 million. Under subparagraph (1) of this paragraph, the controlled group of which M is a member is considered to have expended $1 million for the acquisition of foreign assets described in paragraph (b)(2) of this section.

Example (2). The facts are the same as in example (1), except that on November 18, 1973, M acquires only 80 percent of N's voting stock. M is considered to have expended $800,000 for the acquisition of assets described in paragraph (b)(2) of this section, computed as follows:

(1) Fair market value of N's foreign assets described in paragraph (b)(2) of this section	$1,000,000
(2) Multiply by percentage of total combined voting power of all classes of N stock entitled to vote acquired by M	.8
(3) Amount considered expended	800,000

Example (3). The facts are the same as in example (2), except that individual A is not a United States person, and M acquires the 80 percent of N voting stock in exchange for cash of $100,000 and M stock having a fair market value on the date of the acquisition of $700,000. M is considered to have acquired assets described in paragraph (b)(2) of this section in the amount of $800,000 (see computations in example (2)) and to have an offset under paragraph (b)(4) of this section (relating to outstanding stock or debt) of $700,000 (the fair market value of the M stock transferred to A who is not a United States person). However, the controlled group of which M is a member is not considered to have acquired any other amounts described in paragraphs (a) through (c) of this section with respect to N for taxable years prior to the taxable year of N during which the acquisition occurred.

Example (4). P Corporation, which uses the calendar year as its taxable year, is a member of a controlled group which includes a DISC. During 1973, P acquires from B, an individual United States person, for cash, 30 percent of the total combined voting power of all classes of stock entitled to vote of Q, a foreign corporation. All of Q's assets are assets described in paragraph (b)(2) of this section. No additional interest in Q is acquired by members of the group during 1973. The controlled group of which Q is a member is not considered to have made any investments in foreign assets described in such paragraph (b)(2) as of the close of 1973.

Example (5). Assume the same facts as in example (4). Assume further that during 1974, R Corporation, a member of the controlled group which includes P, acquires for cash 40 percent of the total combined voting power of all classes of stock of Q entitled to vote as follows: 20 percent on July 31, and 20 percent on December 31. Thus, on December 31, 1974, members of the controlled group own 70 percent of Q's voting power (30 + 20 + 20) and on that date are considered to have acquired a majority interest in Q. The fair market value of Q's assets on December 31, 1974, is $5 million. The group is considered to have expended $3,500,000 for the acquisition of assets described in paragraph (b)(2) of this section computed as follows:

(1) Fair market value of Q's foreign assets described in paragraph (b)(2) of this section as of the date the acquisition is deemed to have occurred under subparagraph (3) of this paragraph (December 31, 1974)	$5,000,000
(2) Multiply by percentage of total combined voting power of all classes of Q stock entitled to vote held by members of the group on such date	.7
	3,500,000

Example (6). The facts are the same as in example (5). Assume further that on July 15, 1975, P acquires the remaining 30 percent of the total combined voting power of all classes of Q stock entitled to vote, and on such date the fair market value of Q's assets is $5,500,000. The group is considered to have expended $5,150,000 for the acquisition of assets described in paragraph (b)(2) of this section as of the close of 1975, computed as follows:

(1) Amount of prior years' investment	$3,500,000
(2) Investment during 1975:	
(a) Fair market value of Q's foreign assets described in paragraph (b)(2) of this section on July 15, 1975	5,500,000
(b) Multiply by additional percentage acquired of total combined voting power of all classes of Q stock entitled to vote	.3
(c) Investment during 1975	1,650,000

(3) Amount considered expended for foreign assets described in paragraph (b)(2) of this section by reason of the acquisition of Q stock	5,150,000

(f) Records. A DISC shall keep or be readily able to produce such permanent books of account or records as are sufficient to establish the transactions and amounts described in this section. Where applicable, such books of account or records shall be cumulative and shall show transactions and amounts of the members of the controlled group which includes the DISC which occurred prior to the date the DISC qualified (or is treated) as a DISC.

(g) Multiple DISC's. *(1) Allocation among DISC's.* In the case of a controlled group which includes more than one DISC, the amounts described in paragraphs (b) and (c) of this section shall be allocated among the DISC's in order to determine the limitation in paragraph (a) of this section. Each DISC's allocable portion of these amounts shall be equal to the total of such amounts multiplied by a fraction the numerator of which is the individual DISC's outstanding producer's loans to members of the group, and the denominator of which is the aggregate amounts of outstanding producer's loans to members of the group by all DISC's which are members of the group.

(2) Different taxable years. If all of the DISC's which are members of the controlled group do not have the same taxable year, then one such DISC shall on behalf of all such DISC's elect to make all computations under section 995(d) as if all DISC's that are members of the group use the same taxable year as the actual taxable year of any one of the DISC's. The election as to which DISC's taxable year is to be used shall be made by the electing DISC attaching to its first return, filed under section 6011(e)(2), a statement indicating which such taxable year will be used. Once such an election is made it may be revoked until such time as all of the DISC's which are members of the group use the same taxable year. If this subparagraph applies, books and records must be kept by the group which are adequate to show the necessary computations under section 995(d).

(3) This paragraph may be illustrated by the following example:

Example. Corporation X and corporation Y are members of the same controlled group and each has elected to be treated as a DISC. X uses a taxable year ending March 31, and Y uses a taxable year ending November 30. Notwithstanding the fact that all other members of the group use the calendar year as their taxable year, all computations for purposes of determining the amount of foreign investment attributable to producer's loans under section 995(d) must be made as if both DISC's use a taxable year ending either March 31 (X's taxable year) or November 30 (Y's taxable year).

T.D. 7324, 9/27/74, amend T.D. 7420, 5/19/76, T.D. 7854, 11/16/82.

§ 1.995-6 Taxable Income attributable to military property.

(a) Gross income attributable to military property. For purposes of section 995(b)(3)(A)(i), the term "gross income which is attributable to military property" includes income from the sale, exchange, lease, or rental of military property (as described in paragraph (c) of this section). The term also includes gross income from the performance of services which are related and subsidiary (as defined in § 1.993-1(d)) to any qualified sale, exchange, lease, or rental of military property. Where gross income cannot be determined on an item by item basis, the gross income with respect to those items not so determinable shall be apportioned. Such apportionment shall be accomplished using appropriate facts and circumstances, so that the gross income apportioned to sale of military property bears a reasonably close factual relationship to the actual gross income earned on such sales. The apportionment shall be based on methods which include the fair market value of property sold or exchanged, the fair rental value of any leaseholds granted, the fair market value of any related or subsidiary services performed in connection with such sale or leases or methods based on gross receipts or costs of goods sold, where appropriate.

(b) Deductions. For purposes of section 995(b)(3)(A)(ii), deductions shall be properly allocated and apportioned to gross income, described in paragraph (a) of this section, in accordance with the rules of § 1.861-8. These deductions include all applicable deductions from gross income provided under part VI of subchapter B of chapter 1 of the Code.

(c) Military property. For purposes of this section, the term "military property" means any property which is an arm, ammunition, or implement of war designated in the munitions list published pursuant to section 38 of the International Security Assistance and Arms Export Control Act of 1976 (22 U.S.C. 2778 which superseded 22 U.S.C. 1934) and the regulations thereunder (22 CFR 121.01).

(d) Illustration. The principles of this section may be illustrated by the following example:

Example. X Corporation elects to be a DISC for the first time in 1976. X has taxable income of $50,000, of which $30,000 is attributable to military property and $10,000 to interest on producer's loans. The total deemed distributions with respect to X are as follows:

(1) Gross interest from Producer's loans in 1976	$10,000
(2) 50 percent of the taxable income of the DISC attributable to military property in 1976	15,000
(3) One-half of the excess of taxable income for 1976 over the sum of lines (1) and (2) (½ of ($50,000 minus $25,000))	12,500
(4) Total deemed distributions (sum of total lines (1), (2), and (3))	37,500

T.D. 7984, 10/11/84.

PAR. 9. Section 1.995-7 is amended by revising the title of the section and by revising paragraph (a) to read as follows:

Proposed § 1.995-7 Taxable income attributable to base period export gross receipts in taxable years beginning after December 31, 1975, and ending before January 1, 1985. [*For Preamble, see ¶ 151,083*]

(a) General rule. This section provides rules for the computation of taxable income attributable to base period export gross receipts. Section 995(b)(1)(E) (as in effect prior to its amendment by section 802(b)(1) of the Tax Reform Act of 1984) treats taxable income attributable to base period export gross receipts (as defined in paragraph (c)(4) of this section) as a deemed distribution to a shareholder of a DISC for taxable years of a DISC beginning after December 31, 1975, and ending before January 1, 1985. The amount attributable to base period gross receipts that must be included in the income of a shareholder will be referred to as the nonincremental distribution. The nonincremental distribution must be computed for each taxable year of a DISC beginning after

December 31, 1975, and ending before January 1, 1985. Each such year shall be referred to as the computation year.

* * * * *

Proposed § 1.995-8 Taxable income attributable to qualified export receipts which exceed $10 million for a taxable year ending after 1984. [*For Preamble, see ¶ 151,083*]

(a) In general. This section provides rules for the computation of the taxable income of the DISC attributable to qualified export receipts (as defined in section 993(a) and the regulations thereunder) of the DISC which exceed $10 million for a taxable year beginning after December 31, 1984. Section 995(b)(1)(E) treats the amount of such taxable income as a deemed distribution pro rata to the shareholders of the DISC for taxable years of the DISC beginning after December 31, 1984. If the DISC's qualified export receipts for the taxable year exceed the $10 million amount, the corporation does not lose its status as a DISC, but there will be a deemed distribution of all of the DISC's taxable income attributable to the qualified export receipts for the taxable year which exceed the $10 million amount. Under section 995(b)(4) and paragraph (f) of this section, only one $10 million amount is allowed among all DISC's which are members of the same controlled group (as defined in section 993(a)(3)). If the DISC's taxable year is a short period as defined in section 443, and for such year the DISC is not a member of a controlled group which includes any other DISC, the $10 million amount for such year shall be reduced to the amount which bears the same ratio to $10 million as the number of days in such short period bears to 365, and for purposes of this section, all references to the $10 million amount shall refer to such reduced amount. If the qualified export receipts of the DISC for the taxable year do not exceed the $10 million amount, section 995(b)(1)(E) and this section do not apply. The $10 million amount is an annual amount; thus, if $10 million exceeds the DISC's qualified export receipts for the taxable year, such excess may not be carried or applied to any other taxable year. For purposes of this section, the term "excess receipts" means the qualified export receipts of the DISC for the taxable year which exceed the $10 million amount. See paragraph (d) of this section for coordination of the deemed distribution under section 995(b)(1)(E) and the other deemed distributions under section 995(b)(1).

(b) Determination of qualified export receipts which exceed $10 million. *(1) General rule.* If the qualified export receipts of the DISC for the taxable year exceed the $10 million amount, the DISC shall segregate the qualified export receipts for the taxable year into two amounts, those which shall be considered not to exceed the $10 million amount, and those which shall be considered to exceed the $10 million amount. Except as provided in paragraphs (b)(2) and (3) of this section, the selection of the excess receipts may be made by the DISC in any manner. In general, the selection of the excess receipts permits the DISC to allocate the $10 million amount to the qualified export receipts of those transactions during the taxable year which permit the greatest amount of taxable income to be allocated to the DISC under the intercompany pricing rules of section 994. Except as provided in paragraphs (b)(2) and (3) of this section, the allocation may be made on a transaction-by-transaction basis among all the transactions occurring during the taxable year, or on the basis of groupings consistent with the groupings used by the DISC for purposes of applying the inter-company pricing rules under § 1.994-1(c)(7). Specifically, the $10 million amount is not required to be allocated to transactions in the order in which they occur during the taxable year, nor is the amount required to be allocated ratably to all transactions occurring during the taxable year. The allocation of the $10 million amount shall be made by the DISC on or before the due date of the DISC's return for the taxable year. The allocation of the $10 million amount may thereafter be amended only if (i) the DISC and all of the DISC's shareholders file amended returns consistent with any change in the allocation of the $10 million amount, and (ii) at the time such amended returns are filed, at least 12 full months remain in the statutory period (including extensions) for the assessment of a deficiency against any shareholder of the DISC. If less than 12 full months of such period remain with respect to any shareholder, the director of the service center with which such shareholder files its income tax return will, upon request, enter into an agreement extending such statutory period for the limited purpose of assessing any deficiency against such shareholder attributable to the change in the allocation of the $10 million amount.

(2) Exception for related and subsidiary services. Notwithstanding paragraph (b)(1) of this section, if qualified export receipts for the taxable year arise from a transaction in which services are or are to be provided which are related and subsidiary to any qualified sale, exchange, lease, rental, or other disposition of export property (within meaning of section 993(a)(1)(C) and § 1.993-1(d)), the total amount of the qualified export receipts derived from such transaction must either be allocated in total, or not allocated at all to the $10 million amount. For example, if the qualified export receipts derived from a transaction are $50, of which $4 are attributable to related and subsidiary services and $46 are attributable to the sale of export property, the DISC must allocate either $50 or $0 of the qualified export receipts from such transaction to the $10 million amount; the DISC may not choose to allocate to the $10 million amount only the $4 attributable to the services or only the $46 attributable to the export property.

(3) Ratable allocation where last transaction selected exceeds $10 million amount. If, in selecting among the qualified export receipts of the taxable year, the qualified export receipts of the last transaction so selected by the DISC (when added to the receipts selected from other transactions) result in the DISC exceeding the $10 million amount for such year, the amount of qualified export receipts and taxable income attributable to such transaction which, for purposes of section 995(b)(1)(E) and this section shall be considered not to exceed the $10 million amount, shall be apportioned in proportion to (i) the amount of the qualified export receipts of the transaction that do not (when added to the receipts selected from other transactions) cause the DISC to exceed the $10 million amount, to (ii) the total amount of qualified export receipts from such transaction. The remainder shall be considered attributable to excess receipts for the taxable year. The deductions and the taxable income attributable to such transaction shall also be apportioned in the same manner. For example, assume that for the taxable year the DISC has selected nine transactions having total qualified export receipts of $9,975,000 as transactions to which the $10 million amount is to be applied, and that the tenth transaction the DISC would select has qualified export receipts of $40,000. In this instance, $25,000 ($10,000,000 – $9,975,000) of the qualified export receipts from such tenth transaction shall be considered not to exceed the $10 million amount, and $15,000 ($40,000 – $25,000) of such receipts shall be considered to be excess receipts. Accordingly, 37.5 percent ($^{15}/_{40}$) of the taxable income attributable to such

transaction shall be deemed to be attributable to excess receipts.

(c) Deductions taken into account. After identifying the transactions of the taxable year which are considered to exceed the $10 million amount, the DISC shall reduce such excess receipts by, where applicable, the cost of goods sold attributable to such excess receipts, and the deductions of the DISC properly allocated and apportioned to such excess receipts in accordance with § 1.861-8. Such deductions include all applicable deductions from gross income for the taxable year provided under part VI of subchapter B of chapter 1 of the Code. The difference between the amount of the excess receipts and the deductions attributable to such excess receipts is the taxable income of the DISC attributable to qualified export receipts of the DISC for the taxable year which exceed the $10 million amount. Except as provided in paragraph (d) of this section, this amount of taxable income is treated as the deemed distribution under section 995(b)(1)(E) for the taxable year.

(d) Coordination with other deemed distributions under section 995(b)(1). If (but for this paragraph (d)) an amount of taxable income would be treated as distributed for the taxable year under section 995(b)(1)(E) and also under subparagraph (A), (B), (C) or (D) of section 995(b)(1), such amount of taxable income shall be treated as distributed for such taxable year under that other subparagraph and not under section 995(b)(1)(E) and shall be subtracted from the amount determined under paragraph (c) of this section. In the case of military property, as defined in section 995(b)(3)(B) and § 1.995-6(c), 50 percent of the taxable income of the DISC for the taxable year attributable to such property is deemed distributed under section 995(b)(1)(D) and § 1.995-6. The remainder of the taxable income attributable to military property is deemed distributed under section 995(b)(1)(E) unless all of the gross receipts attributable to such property is allocated to the $10 million amount.

(e) Illustration. The principles of this section may be illustrated by the following example:

Example. (i) Facts. P is a C corporation that uses the fiscal year ending September 30 as the taxable year. P owns all of the stock in Corporation D. D elects to be treated as a DISC for its taxable year beginning January 1, 1985. Under section 441(h), D must use the same taxable year as P. Accordingly, D's taxable year beginning January 1, 1985, will end on September 30, 1985. Assume that in D's taxable year ending September 30, 1985, D sold four aircraft in separate transactions (S1, S2, M1, M2). Two of the sales (M1 and M2) were of military property. D also derived $12,000 of interest from producer's loans during the taxable year. D's qualified export receipts for the taxable year are $9,762,000, and assume that the deductions properly allocated and apportioned thereto are $8,550,000, as follows:

	Receipts	Deductions	Taxable income
Producer's loan interest	$ 12,000	0	$ 12,000
Sales:			
S1	3,756,000	$3,330,000	420,000
S2	3,000,000	2,670,000	330,000
M1	1,500,000	1,200,000	300,000
M2	1,500,000	1,350,000	150,000
	9,762,000	8,550,000	1,212,000

(ii) Limitation on $10 million amount. D's taxable year ending September 30, 1985, is a short period consisting of 273 days. Accordingly, the $10 million amount specified in section 995(b)(1)(E) is limited to $7,479,452 (273/365 × $10 million) for the taxable year.

(iii) Amount distributed under section 995(b)(1)(E). D allocates all of the qualified export receipts from S1 and S2, and $729,452 of the receipts from M1 against the $7,479,452 amount ($3,750,000 + $3,000,000 + $729,452 – $7,479,452), leaving the following amounts, reduced by the deductions properly apportioned and allocated thereto, as the amount distributed for the taxable year under section 995(b)(1)(E):

	Excess receipts	Deductions	Taxable income
M1	$1,500,000	$1,200,000	$300,000
Less: Amount of M1 not in excess of limitation	(729,452)	(583,562)[1]	(145,890)
M1 Excess receipts	$ 770,548	$ 616,438	$154,110
M2	1,500,000	1,350,000	150,000
Producer's loan interest	12,000	0	12,000
Taxable income attributable to excess receipts, see § 1.995-8(c)			$316,110
Less: Amounts otherwise distributed under section 995(b)(1), see § 1.995-8(d):			
Section 995(b)(1)(A)— Producer's loan interest			(12,000)
Section 995(b)(1)(D)—50% of taxable income attributable to sales of military property:			
M1 $154,110 × 50%			$ (77,055)
M2 $150,000 × 50%			(75,000)
Deemed distribution under section 995(b)(1)(E) for taxable year			152,055

[1] $729,452/$1,500,000 × $1,200,000 = $583,562. See paragraph (b)(3) of this section.

(iv) Deemed distribution for 1985. The amount of D's deemed distribution under section 995(b)(1) for D's taxable year ending September 30, 1985, is $437,464 determined as follows:

Section 995(b)(1)—	Amount
(A) Producer's loan interest	$12,000
(D) One-half of taxable income attributable to military property (50% of $450,000)	225,000
(E) Taxable income attributable to excess receipts	152,055
(F) One-seventeenth of the excess of taxable income less amounts in (A), (D) and (E) 1/17 × ($1,212,000 – $12,000 – $225,000 – $152,055)	48,409
	437,464

(f) Members of a controlled group limited to one $10 million amount. *(1) General rule.* For purposes of section 995(b)(1)(E) and this section, in the case of a controlled group of corporations (as defined in section 993(a)(3) and § 1.993-1(k)), all DISCs which are members of such controlled group on a December 31, shall, for their taxable years which include such December 31, be limited to one $10 million amount. The $10 million amount shall be allocated equally among the member DISCs of such controlled group for their taxable years including such December 31, unless all of the member DISCs consent to an apportionment plan providing for an unequal allocation of the $10 million amount. Such a plan shall provide for the apportionment of a fixed dollar amount to one or more of the corporations, and the sum of the amounts so apportioned shall not exceed the $10 million amount. If the taxable year including such December 31 of any member DISC is a short period (as defined in section 443), the portion of the $10 million amount allocated to such member DISC for such short period under the preceding sentence shall be reduced to the amount which bears the same ratio to the amount so allocated as the number of days in such short period bears to 365. The consent of each member DISC to the apportionment plan for the taxable year shall be signified by a statement which satisfies the requirements of and is filed in the manner specified in § 1.1561-3(b). An apportionment plan may be amended in the manner prescribed in § 1.1561-3(c), except that an original or an amended plan may not be adopted with respect to a particular December 31 if at the time such original or amended plan is sought to be adopted, less than 12 full months remain in the statutory period (including extensions) for the assessment of a deficiency against any shareholder of a member DISC the tax liability of which would change by the adoption of such original or amended plan. If less than 12 full months of such period remain with respect to any such shareholder, the director of the service center with which such shareholder files its income tax return will, upon request, enter into an agreement extending such statutory period for the limited purpose of assessing any deficiency against such shareholder attributable to the adoption of such original or amended apportionment plan.

(2) Membership determined under section 1563(b). For purposes of paragraph (f) of this section, the determination of whether a DISC is a member of a controlled group of corporations with respect to any taxable year shall be made in the manner prescribed in section 1563(b) and the regulations thereunder.

(3) Certain short taxable years. (i) General rule. If a DISC has a short period (as defined in section 443) which does not include a December 31, and such DISC is a member of a controlled group of corporations which includes one or more other DISC's with respect to such short period, then the amount described in section 995(b)(1)(E) with respect to the short period of such DISC shall be determined by (A) dividing $10 million by the number of DISCs which are members of such group on the last day of such short period, and (B) multiplying the result by a fraction, the numerator of which is the number of days in such short period and the denominator of which is 365. For purposes of the preceding sentence, section 1563(b) shall be applied as if the last day of such short period were substituted for December 31. Except as provided in paragraph (f)(3)(ii) of this section, a DISC having a short period not including a December 31 may not enter into an apportionment plan with respect to such short period.

(ii) Exception. If the short period not including a December 31 of two or more DISCs begins on the same date and ends on the same date and such DISCs are members of the same controlled group, such DISCs may enter into an apportionment plan for such short period in the manner provided in paragraph (f)(1) of this section with respect to the combined amount allowed to each of such DISCs under paragraph (f)(3)(i).

(4) Effect on DISC shareholders. The computation of the deemed distribution under section 995(b)(1)(E) and this section for a taxable year, as affected by the controlled group rules of this paragraph (f), applies to a shareholder of a DISC whether or not such shareholder is a member of the controlled group which includes such DISC.

Proposed § 1.995(f)-1 Interest charge on DISC-related deferred tax liability for periods after 1984. [*For Preamble, see ¶ 151,083*]

Caution: The Treasury has not yet amended Reg § 1.995(f)-1 to reflect changes made by P.L. 99-514, P.L. 98-369.

(a) Interest charge. *(1) In general.* Effective for taxable years ending after December 31, 1984, section 995(f) requires that each shareholder of a DISC shall pay for each taxable year interest on the shareholder's DISC-related deferred tax liability (as defined in paragraph (d) of this section) for such year at a rate of interest equal to the base period T-bill rate (as defined in paragraph (b)(2) of this section). See paragraph (b) of this section for the computation of the amount of the interest charge. The interest charge is computed on Form 8404. For purposes of this section, the term "DISC" includes a former DISC as defined in section 992(a)(3). Accordingly, a shareholder of a former DISC is required to pay the annual interest charge on such shareholder's DISC-related deferred tax liability.

(2) Related rules. (i) The interest charge is an annual charge and is imposed on the shareholder of the DISC. The interest charge is not imposed on the DISC. Under section 995(f)(6), the amount of a shareholder's interest charge for any taxable year is treated for all purposes of the Code as interest paid or accrued on an underpayment of tax. Accordingly, subject to all otherwise applicable limitations on the deduction for interest, the amount of the annual interest charge imposed on the shareholder is deductible by the shareholder for the taxable year in which the amount of the interest charge is paid, in the case of a shareholder which uses the cash receipts and disbursements method of accounting, or accrued, in the case of a shareholder which uses the accrual method of accounting. See paragraph (j)(2) of this section. Because the interest charge imposed on the shareholder is treated as interest, the payment or accrual of the interest charge does not increase or decrease the shareholder's basis in the stock of the DISC, and does not increase or decrease the taxable income or earnings and profits of the DISC.

(ii) Under section 995(f)(2), the shareholder's DISC-related deferred tax liability for a taxable year, that is, the amount considered to be the "principal" amount of the "loan" on which the interest charge is computed, is determined only with reference to the accumulated DISC income (A) derived by the DISC in periods after 1984, and (B) derived by the DISC in taxable years of the DISC that ended before the taxable year of the shareholder for which the interest charge is being determined.

(iii) No payments of estimated tax under section 6654 (in the case of individuals) or 6154 (in the case of corporations) are required with respect to the interest charge imposed by section 995(f)(1).

(iv) Paragraph (g) of this section contains rules for determining the interest charge for a taxable year in which shares in the DISC are transferred or redeemed. Paragraph (h) of this section provides rules for the computation and allocation of the interest charge where the DISC's shares are held by S corporations, trusts, estates or partnerships.

(b) Computation of the interest charge. *(1) General rule.* Under section 995(f)(1), the amount of interest charge imposed on a DISC shareholder for a taxable year is equal to the product of—

(i) The shareholder's DISC-related deferred tax liability for such year, multiplied by,

(ii) A factor, which is equal to the base period T-bill rate compounded daily for the number of days in the shareholder's taxable year for which the interest charge is being computed.

See section 6622 for the requirement that all interest required to be paid under the Code be compounded daily. See paragraph (c) of this section for obtaining the table of base period T-bill rate factors reflecting daily compounding of the base period T-bill rate. See paragraph (g) of this section for special rules for computing the amount of the interest charge for a taxable year in which the shareholder transfers or acquires stock in the DISC.

(2) Base period T-bill rate. Under section 995(f)(4), the "base period T-bill rate" is the annual rate of interest determined by the Secretary to be equivalent to the average investment yield of United States Treasury bills with maturities of 52 weeks which were auctioned during the one-year period ending on September 30 of the calendar year ending with (or, if the shareholder's taxable year is not the calendar year, of the most recent calendar year ending before) the close of the taxable year of the DISC shareholder for which the shareholder's interest charge is being determined. For example, if a DISC shareholder's taxable year is a fiscal year ending on June 30, the base period T-bill rate applicable to the shareholder's taxable year ending June 30, 1987, would be the rate determined for the one-year period ending September 30, 1986. If the shareholder's taxable year is the calendar year, the base period T-bill rate applicable to the shareholder's taxable year ending December 31, 1987, would be the rate determined for the one-year period ending September 30, 1987.

(c) Publication of base period T-bill rate and use of the table of factors for daily compounding. The base period T-bill rate for each one-year period ending on September 30, as determined by the Secretary, shall be certified to the Commissioner and shall be published in a revenue ruling in the Internal Revenue Bulletin. Such revenue ruling shall also contain a table of factors reflecting daily compounding of the base period T-bill rate. To compute the amount of the interest charge for the taxable year under paragraph (b) of this section the shareholder shall use the base period T-bill rate factor corresponding to the number of days in the shareholder's taxable year for which the interest charge is being computed. Generally, the factor to be used will be the factor for 365 days. The factor to be used will be other than the factor for 365 days if the shareholder's taxable year for which the interest charge is being determined is a short taxable year, if the shareholder uses the 52-53 week taxable year, or if the shareholder's taxable year is a leap year. For example, if a DISC shareholder which had been using the calendar year as the taxable year changes its taxable year to the fiscal year ending January 31, then in computing the interest charge for the short taxable year January 1 to January 31 required to effect such change, the shareholder will use the factor for a taxable year of 31 days.

(d) DISC-related deferred tax liability. *(1) Purpose.* for taxable years of a DISC shareholder ending after December 31, 1984, the shareholder's DISC-related deferred tax liability represents, in general terms, the cumulative amount of income tax that is considered to have been deferred from taxation in prior taxable years (ending after 1984) of the shareholder by use of the DISC. A separate interest charge is imposed on the shareholder for each taxable year of the shareholder until the deferred DISC income in distributed or deemed distributed by the DISC. The amount of the shareholder's DISC-related deferred tax liability is determined for each taxable year by taking the difference between the shareholder's income tax liability for the taxable year computed first with, and then without, the accumulated DISC income that has been deferred from taxation in prior taxable years of the shareholder. See paragraph (f) of this section for the definition of "deferred DISC income." This paragraph (d) provides certain special rules to be used solely for the purpose of determining the amount of the shareholder's DISC-related deferred tax liability, for any taxable year, these rules may result in the amount of the shareholder's DISC-related deferred tax liability being different than the amount of additional income tax that the shareholder would owe for such year if the deferred DISC income were received by the shareholder in an actual distribution to which section 996(a) applies.

(2) In general. (i) Under section 995(f)(2), the "shareholder's DISC-related deferred tax liability", with respect to any taxable year of a DISC shareholder ending after 1984, is the excess of—

(A) The amount which would be the tax liability (as defined in paragraph (3) of this section) of the shareholder for the taxable year if the amount of the deferred DISC income (as described in paragraph (f) of this section) of such shareholder for such taxable year were included in the shareholder's gross income as ordinary income, over

(B) The actual amount of the shareholder's tax liability for such taxable year.

(ii) If in the taxable year the shareholder owns stock in more than one DISC, the deferred DISC income of such shareholder for the taxable year is the sum of the amounts of deferred DISC income of such shareholder with respect to each of such DISCs.

(iii) Where the DISC shareholder is a member of an affiliated group of corporations that files a consolidated return, the affiliated group's DISC-related deferred tax liability for the taxable year is the excess of (A) the amount which would be the group's tax liability (as defined in paragraph (3) of this section) including in gross income the deferred DISC income for the taxable year of each DISC shareholder which is a member of the group, over (B) the amount of the group's actual tax liability for such taxable year.

(iv) Except as provided in paragraphs (d) and (e) of this section, the computations necessary to determine the shareholder's DISC-related deferred tax liability shall be made under the law and the rates of tax applicable to the shareholder's taxable year for which the computations are made.

(v) The shareholder's DISC-related deferred tax liability for a taxable year is computed on Form 8404. See paragraph (j) of this section for the manner and time for filing or amending Form 8404 and paying the interest charge.

(3) Carrybacks not taken into account. Under section 995(f)(2)(A), the shareholder's DISC-related deferred tax liability for any taxable year is determined without regard to any net operating loss or capital loss carryback or any credit carryback to such taxable year from any succeeding taxable year. For example, if for 1987 a calendar year shareholder of a DISC has a DISC-related deferred tax liability for the taxable year and thereby incurs an interest charge for such taxable year, and if the shareholder thereafter has a net operating loss (as defined in section 172(c)) for calendar year 1988, all or a portion of which is a net operating loss carryback to the 1987 taxable year, the shareholder's DISC-related deferred tax liability and interest charge for the 1987 taxable year are

not affected by such net operating loss carryback, even if the shareholder recovers the total amount of the tax it paid for taxable year 1987, and has a net operating loss carryover to future taxable years.

(4) Carryovers not taken into account. (i) General rule. Under section 995(f)(2)(A)(i), the determination of the shareholder's tax liability for the taxable year including the deferred DISC income shall be made by not taking into account any loss, deduction or credit to the extent that such loss, deduction or credit may be carried by the shareholder to any other taxable year. If, however, the taxable year is the last taxable year to which the amount of a carryforward (of either a deduction or a credit) may be carried, the shareholder's tax liability including the deferred DISC income shall be computed with regard to the full amount of such carryforward, because the amount of the carryforward cannot be carried to another taxable year of the shareholder.

(ii) Examples. The provisions of this paragraph (d)(4) may be illustrated by the following examples:

Example (1). Assume that in 1986, a calendar year DISC shareholder recognizes only ordinary business income of $10,000, and has deferred DISC income for the taxable year of $5000. If the shareholder also had a net operating loss carryforward to 1986 of $12,000, the shareholder would be allowed a $10,000 net operating loss deduction for 1986 and would have a net operating loss carryforward to 1987 of $2000. For purposes of determining the shareholder's DISC-related deferred tax liability for 1986, the shareholder's computation of its tax liability including the deferred DISC income under section 995(f)(2)(A)(i) may take into account a new operating loss deduction of only $10,000, because $2000 of the total loss carryforward may be carried to the shareholder's following taxable year. Accordingly, the shareholder's taxable income for 1986 including the deferred DISC income is $5000 ($10,000 of ordinary income, plus $5000 of deferred DISC income, less the net operating loss deduction of $10,000 of ordinary income, plus $5000 of deferred DISC income, less the net operating loss deduction of $10,000). However, if 1986 were the last taxable year to which the $12,000 net operating loss carryforward could be carried, then the shareholder's tax liability including the deferred DISC income under section 995(f)(2)(A)(i) may be computed by taking the full amount of the loss carryforward into account.

Example (2). Assume that in 1986, a calendar year DISC shareholder places in service an amount of property such that the amount of the investment credit determined for the taxable year under section 46 is $25,000, and that the shareholder has no credit carryforwards to the taxable year from any earlier taxable year. Assume that for the shareholder's 1986 taxable year the amount of the credit allowed is limited to $20,000, because of the limitation on the amount of the credit allowed under section 38(c), and that the remaining $5000 of the credit determined for the taxable year may be carried back 3 years or forward 15 years. In determining the shareholder's DISC-related deferred tax liability for the 1986 taxable year, the amount of the credit that may be allowed to reduce the shareholder's tax liability including the deferred DISC income under section 995(f)(2)(A)(i) is limited to $20,000, because the remaining $5000 of the credit may be carried to another taxable year.

Example (3). The facts are the same as in example (2). Assume that $2000 of the $5000 excess credit for 1986 was applied to reduce 1985 taxes, and that none of the remaining $3000 could be carried-back to any other taxable year. If in 1987, all of the $3000 credit carried-over from 1986 is applied to reduce the shareholder's 1987 actual tax liability, that $3000 credit is also to be used to reduce the shareholder's 1987 tax liability including the deferred DISC income under section 995(f)(2)(A)(i).

(5) Adjustments not involving carryovers or carrybacks. In computing the amount of the DISC shareholder's taxable income and tax liability including the deferred DISC income under section 995(f)(2)(A)(i), there shall be taken into account adjustments in amounts allowable as deductions and in amounts excluded from or included in gross income to the extent that such adjustments do not result in amounts which may be carried back or forward by the shareholder to any other taxable year. For example, in the case of a DISC shareholder who is an individual, the amount of medical expenses allowable as a deduction under section 213 must be redetermined when computing the individual's taxable income and tax liability including the deferred DISC income under section 995(f)(2)(A)(i). The amount of medical expenses allowable as a deduction decreases because the taxpayer's adjusted gross income, increased by the amount of the deferred DISC income, would increase the limitation on the deductible amount of medical expenses, and the medical expenses not allowed may not be carried to any other taxable year. As a further example, in the case of an individual or a corporation which is a DISC shareholder, the amount allowable as a charitable deduction under section 170 is not redetermined when computing the taxpayer's taxable income and tax liability including the deferred DISC income under section 995(f)(2)(A)(i), because the amount of charitable contributions made for the taxable year which are not allowable as a deduction for such year by reason of the percentage of income limitations under section 170(b) may be carried over to subsequent taxable years under section 170(d).

(6) Deferred tax liability determined without regard to any consequential deduction or credit. Except as provided in paragraph (d)(8) of this section, in computing the amount of the DISC shareholder's tax liability including the deferred DISC income under section 995(f)(2)(a)(i), there shall not be taken into account any additional deduction or credit that would be allowable for any item that would be paid or accrued if the deferred DISC income were actually distributed to the shareholder. For example, when computing the shareholder's tax liability including the deferred DISC income, no deduction shall be taken into account for the additional state or local income or franchise taxes that would be due if such deferred DISC income were actually distributed to the shareholder. In addition, to simplify the calculations, in the case of a DISC shareholder who uses the accrual method of accounting, no deduction for the current year's interest charge shall be taken into account in computing the shareholder's DISC-related deferred tax liability for the current taxable year. However, after the amount of the interest charge for the current taxable year has been determined, such amount may be taken into account as a deduction for the current taxable year in determining the amount of the shareholder's income tax liability under chapter 1 of the Code for the taxable year in the circumstances described in paragraph (j)(2)(ii) of this section.

(7) Source of deferred DISC income. The source of the deferred DISC income which is considered included in the shareholder's gross income for purposes of section 995(f)(2)(A)(i) shall be determined under section 861(a)(2)(D) and § 1.861-3(a)(5) in the same manner as if such amount were actually distributed to the DISC shareholder as a dividend.

(8) Deemed paid foreign tax credit; separate limitation. In the case of a DISC shareholder that is a corporation, if the

shareholder elects the foreign tax credit for the taxable year, such shareholder shall, in computing its tax liability including the deferred DISC income, take into account any increase in the amount of the deemed paid foreign tax credit under section 902(a) for foreign income taxes paid by the DISC to the extent that the deferred DISC income is treated as income from sources without the United States. In such case, in accordance with section 78, the shareholder shall also include the amount of such foreign income tax in computing its gross income including the deferred DISC income. Any increase in the amount of the foreign tax credit that would be allowable against the tax liability determined under section 995(f)(2)(A)(i) with respect to the amount of the deferred DISC income shall be subject to the separate limitation required by section 904(d)(1)(F) in the same manner as if such amount were actually distributed to the DISC shareholder as a dividend.

(e) Tax liability. *(1) General rule.* Except as provided in paragraphs (e)(2) and (e)(3) of this section, for purposes of the two tax computations ("with and without" the deferred DISC income) required by section 995(f)(2) and paragraph (d) of this section, the term "tax liability" means the amount of the tax imposed on the DISC shareholder for the taxable year by chapter 1 of the Code, reduced by the credits (but not the credit carrybacks or carryovers described in paragraphs (d)(3) and (d)(4) of this section) allowable against such tax.

(2) Certain taxes not to be taken into account. For purposes of section 995(f)(2) and paragraph (e)(1) of this section, any tax imposed by any of the following provisions shall not be treated as tax imposed by chapter 1 of the Code:

(i) Section 55 (relating to the alternative minimum tax) and

(ii) Any other provisions described in section 26(b)(2) (relating to certain other taxes treated as not imposed by chapter 1 of the Code).

(3) Certain credits not taken into account. For purposes of section 995(f)(2) and paragraph (e)(1) of this section, the credits allowed for the taxable year by the following sections shall be not taken into account in determining the DISC shareholder's tax liability:

(i) Section 31 (relating to taxes withheld on wages),

(ii) Section 32 (relating to the earned income credit), and

(iii) Section 34 (relating to the fuels credit).

(f) Deferred DISC income. *(1) In general.* Under section 995(f)(3)(A), for any taxable year of a DISC shareholder, the term "deferred DISC income" means the excess of—

(i) The shareholder's pro rata share of the DISC's accumulated DISC income (earned by the DISC in taxable years ending after December 31, 1984) as of the close of the computation year (as defined in paragraph (f)(2) of this section), over

(ii) The amount (if any) of distributions-in-excess-of-income (as defined in paragraph (f)(3) of this section) made by the DISC during the taxable year of the DISC immediately following the computation year.

Thus, in the simple case where the DISC has only one shareholder and the DISC and the shareholder have the same taxable year, the shareholder's deferred DISC income for the taxable year is the excess of the DISC's accumulated DISC income (derived from periods after 1984) at the beginning of the taxable year over the amount (if any) by which actual distributions for the taxable year which are considered to be made out of accumulated DISC income exceed the amount of DISC income for such year. Where shareholders of the DISC have a taxable year different from that of the DISC, the deferred DISC income is measured from the computation year, as described in paragraph (f)(2) of this section.

(2) Computation year. (i) General rule. Under section 995(f)(3)(B), with respect to any taxable year of a DISC shareholder, the "computation year" is the taxable year of the DISC ending with (or within, if the DISC and the shareholder do not have the same taxable year) the taxable year of the shareholder which precedes the taxable year of the shareholder for which the amount of deferred DISC income is being determined.

(ii) Example. The following example illustrates the relationship between the shareholder's taxable year and the DISC's computation year:

Example. Assume that a DISC, D, has two shareholders, A, the principal shareholder, and B, a minority shareholder. Shareholder A uses the calendar year as the taxable year, and shareholder B's taxable year is the fiscal year ending June 30. Under section 441(h), D must use the calendar year as the taxable year. In determining the amount of shareholder A's deferred DISC income for A's taxable year ending December 31, 1987, the computation year is D's taxable year ending December 31, 1986, that is, D's taxable year ending with shareholder A's taxable year preceding the taxable year of A for which A's deferred DISC income is being determined. In determining the amount of shareholder B's deferred DISC income for B's taxable year ending June 30, 1987, the computation year is D's taxable year ending December 31, 1985, that is, D's taxable year ending within B's taxable year preceding the taxable year of B for which B's deferred DISC income is being determined.

(3) Distributions-in-excess-of-income. Under section 995(f)(3)(C), with respect to any taxable year of a DISC, the term "distributions-in-excess-of-income", means the excess (if any) of—

(i) The amount of actual distributions made to the shareholder during such taxable year out of accumulated DISC income (as determined under section 996), over

(ii) The shareholder's pro rata share of the DISC income (as defined in section 996(f)) for such taxable year.

(4) Illustrations. The provisions of paragraph (f) of this section may be illustrated by the following example:

Example. (i) Facts. P corporation, which uses the calendar year as the taxable year, owns all of the stock of D, a domestic corporation which elects to be treated as a DISC for its taxable year beginning January 1, 1985. Under section 441(h), D must adopt the same taxable year as P; accordingly, D's taxable year beginning January 1, 1985, will end on December 31, 1985.

Assume that D has the following amounts for its three taxable years ending December 31, 1985, 1986 and 1987:

	1985	1986	1987
Taxable income and earnings and profits for the year......	$45,000	$60,000	$40,000
Deemed distribution under section 995(b)(1)...........	5,000	10,000	15,000
DISC income for year.........	40,000	50,000	25,000
Actual distributions during year	0	20,000	60,000
Accumulated DISC income—end of year...............	40,000	85,000	65,000

Previously taxed income—end of year	5,000	0	0
Accumulated earnings and profits-end of year	45,000	85,000	65,000

(ii) Result—1985. Under section 995(f)(3), P will have no deferred DISC income for P's taxable year ending December 31, 1985, because D does not have accumulated DISC income derived from periods after 1984 as of the close of the computation year. With respect to P's taxable year ending December 31, 1985, the computation year under section 995(f)(3)(B) would be D's taxable year ending with or within P's taxable year ending December 31, 1984, which is prior to D's current election to be treated as a DISC. Accordingly, because P has no deferred DISC income for its taxable year ending December 31, 1985, P will have no DISC-related deferred tax liability and therefore no interest charge for the taxable year.

(iii) Result—1986. Under section 995(f)(3), P will have deferred DISC income for P's taxable year ending December 31, 1986, of $40,000 determined as follows. With respect to P's taxable year ending December 31, 1986, the computation year is D's taxable year ending December 31, 1985. D's accumulated DISC income as of the close of the computation year is $40,000, and D made no distributions-in-excess-of-income in D's taxable year following the computation year (that is, in D's taxable year ending December 31, 1986, of the actual distributions of $20,000, only $5000 of this amount is treated as made out of accumulated DISC income, and because the DISC income for the year is $50,000, none of the actual distributions for the year reduce the accumulated DISC income as of the beginning of the taxable year.)

Accordingly, because P's deferred DISC income for the taxable year ending December 31, 1986, is $40,000, P must compute its tax liability for the year with and then without the $40,000 amount under section 995(f)(2) to determine its DISC-related deferred tax liability. P's interest charge for the taxable year ending December 31, 1986, under section 995(f)(1) will be the amount of the DISC-related deferred tax liability (the tax on $40,000) multiplied by the base period T-bill rate factor for the 365 day taxable year. See paragraph (b) of this section.

(iv) Result—1987. Under section 995(f)(3), P will have deferred DISC income for P's taxable year ending December 31, 1987, of $65,000 computed as follows:

D's accumulated DISC income derived from periods after 1984 as of the close of the computation year (D's taxable year ending December 31, 1986)	$85,000
Less: Amount of D's distributions in-excess-of-income made in D's taxable year ending December 31, 1987	20,000
P's deferred DISC income for taxable year ending December 31, 1987	65,000

The $20,000 amount of distributions-in-excess-of income for D's taxable year ending December 31, 1987, may be determined as follows:

Amount of D's actual distributions for D's taxable year ending December 31, 1987		$60,000
Less: D's previously taxed income at close of previous taxable year	0	
Deemed distribution for current year	$15,000	
Total amount of previously taxed income available for distributions during D's taxable year ending December 31, 1987	15,000	15,000
Difference— Amount of actual distributions for current year out of accumulated DISC income		45,000
Less: DISC income for current year		25,000
Distributions-in-excess-of-income for D's taxable year ending December 31, 1987		20,000

Accordingly, because P's deferred DISC income for its taxable year ending December 31, 1987 is $65,000, P must compute its tax liability for the taxable year with and then without the $65,000 amount to determine its DISC-related deferred tax liability under section 995(f)(2). P's interest charge for the taxable year ending December 31, 1987, under section 995(f)(1) will be the amount of the DISC-related deferred tax liability (the tax on the $65,000) multiplied by the base period T-bill rate factor for the 365 day taxable year.

(g) Special rules for computation of the interest charge where DISC stock is transferred during taxable year. *(1) General rule.* If the same number of shares of stock in the DISC are not held by the shareholder for the shareholder's entire taxable year, the amount of the interest charge for the taxable year with respect to the shares transferred or acquired by the shareholder shall be equal to the amount of the DISC-related deferred tax liability with respect to such transferred or acquired shares computed as if the shareholder held such shares for the shareholder's entire taxable year, multiplied by the base period T-bill rate factor corresponding to the number of days in the shareholder's taxable year that the shareholder held such transferred or acquired shares. In determining the number of days in the shareholder's taxable year that the shareholder held such transferred or acquired shares, the transferor shareholder shall include the day of the transfer and the transferee shareholder shall exclude the day of the transfer.

(2) Adjustment for gain recognized on disposition. (i) Transferor. For purposes of determining the deferred DISC income for the taxable year of a shareholder who disposes of stock in the DISC during the taxable year, the amount of gain recognized with respect to such stock which is treated under section 995(c) and § 1.995-4 as a dividend shall be treated as an actual distribution made by the DISC to such shareholder out of accumulated DISC income for the taxable year of the DISC which includes the date of such disposition. Accordingly, the amount of such gain which exceeds the shareholder's pro rata share of the DISC income for such taxable year shall be treated under section 995(f)(3)(C) and paragraph (f) of this section as a distribution-in-excess-of-income which reduces the amount of such shareholder's deferred DISC income for the taxable year of the shareholder in which the disposition of the shares occurs.

(ii) Transferee. For purposes of determining the amount of any transferee shareholder's deferred DISC income for a taxable year, if under section 996(d)(1) and § 1.996-4(a) such shareholder would be permitted to treat an amount of an actual distribution by the DISC made out of accumulated DISC income as made out of previously taxed income, such transferee shareholder's deferred DISC income for such taxable year shall be reduced by such amount.

(3) Examples. The provisions of this paragraph (g) may be illustrated by the following examples:

Example (1). X, an individual, uses the calendar year as the taxable year and owns all of the stock of D, a calendar year corporation which elects to be treated as a DISC for 1985. On May 1, 1987, X makes a gift to Y, a calendar year individual, of all the stock in D. On December 31, 1986, D had accumulated DISC income of $1000, and during its taxable year ending December 31, 1987, D made no distributions-in-excess-of-income. X recognizes no gain on the transfer of stock to Y. Accordingly, for the taxable year ending December 31, 1987, X and Y each have deferred DISC income of $1000, and each must compute a DISC-related deferred tax liability for 1987 with respect to this $1000 of deferred DISC income as if each of them owned the stock for the entire year. X will multiply X's DISC-related deferred tax liability by the base period T-bill rate factor for 121 days, and Y will multiply Y's DISC-related deferred tax liability by the base period T-bill rate factor for 244 days, to reflect the number of days during their taxable year that each held the stock in the DISC. If during the taxable year Y received a distribution-in-excess-of-income of $200, Y's deferred DISC income for the taxable year would be $800, and X's deferred DISC income for the year would also be $800, even though the actual distribution was received by Y.

Example (2). (i) Corporations A and D use the calendar year as the taxable year. A owns all of the stock of D, which elects to be treated as a DISC for 1985. On December 31, 1987, A sells all of its stock in D to B corporation, and recognizes a gain on the sale of $400. B corporation uses the fiscal year ending June 30 as the taxable year. Assume that D had accumulated DISC income at the close of 1986 of $600, and that D realized $250 of DISC income for 1987. Assume also that D made no actual distributions out of accumulated DISC income during 1987. Accordingly, D has accumulated DISC income at December 31, 1987, of $850 ($600 plus $250), all of which was accumulated during the period A held the stock in the DISC. Under section 995(c) and § 1.995-4, all of A's recognized gain of $400 on the disposition of the stock in the DISC is treated as a dividend, because A's recognized gain ($400) does not exceed the accumulated DISC income of D attributable to the stock disposed of by A ($850).

(ii) Under paragraph (g)(2) of this section, for purposes of section 995(f)(3), the $400 amount that A must treat as a dividend is treated as an actual distribution to A for 1987 out of accumulated DISC income. Accordingly, A's deferred DISC income for its taxable year ending December 31, 1987, is $450, determined as follows:

Accumulated DISC income of D at close of computation year (1986)		$600
Amount of gain realized by A in 1987 treated as an actual distribution out of accumulated DISC income	$400	
Less: DISC income for 1978	250	
Difference: Amount treated as a distribution-in-excess of-income	$150	150
Deferred DISC income		$450

A will use this $450 amount of deferred DISC income to compute its DISC-related deferred tax liability and interest charge for A's 365 day taxable year ending December 31, 1987.

(iii) Because B purchased the stock in D on December 31, 1987, B will have a part-year interest charge for B's taxable year ending June 30, 1988. D's computation year with respect to B's taxable year ending June 30, 1988, is D's taxable year ending December 31, 1986. B's deferred DISC income for its taxable year ending June 30, 1988, is $450, the same amount that A had with respect to A's taxable year ended December 31, 1987, because B is permitted, under section 996(d), to take into account as a reduction in accumulated DISC income, the amount of gain A recognized on the disposition which was treated as an actual distribution to A out of accumulated DISC income. Accordingly, B must compute its DISC-related deferred tax liability and interest charge for the taxable year ending June 30, 1988, with respect to the $450 of deferred DISC income. The interest charge for B's taxable year ending June 30, 1988, is determined by multiplying B's DISC-related deferred tax liability (the tax on the $450 of deferred DISC income) by the base period T-bill rate factor for 182 days (January 1 to June 30, 1988), because B held the stock for only 182 days in B's taxable year ended June 30, 1988.

(iv) Note that under section 441(h), D must change its taxable year from the calendar year to the fiscal year ending June 30, because there has been a change in the taxable year of D's "principal shareholder" by reason of B's acquisition of D. See § 1.441-1(h)(3).

(h) Special rules for computation of the interest charge where DISC stock is held by certain passthrough entities. *(1) Partnerships.* For purposes of section 995(f) and this section, if stock in a DISC is held by a partnership, the deferred DISC income of such partnership for the taxable year shall be attributed to each partner in proportion to the partner's interest in partnership income for the taxable year. Thus, each partner shall take into account its share of the partnership's deferred DISC income for the partnership taxable year ending with or within the taxable year of the partner, and each partner shall determine its DISC-related deferred tax liability and the interest charge thereon for the partner's taxable year as if the partner directly owned stock in the DISC.

(2) S corporations. For purposes of section 995(f) and this section, if stock in a DISC is held by an S corporation, the deferred DISC income of such S corporation for the taxable year shall be attributed to each shareholder in proportion to the shareholder's pro rata share of the S corporation's nonseparately computed income or loss (determined under section 1366(a)(1)(B)) for the taxable year. Thus, each shareholder shall take into account its share of the S corporation's deferred DISC income for the taxable year of the S corporation ending with or within the taxable year of the shareholder, and shall determine its DISC-related deferred tax liability and the interest charge thereon for the taxable year as if the shareholder directly owned stock in the DISC.

(3) Estates or trusts. For purposes of section 995(f) and this section, if stock in a DISC is held by an estate or trust, the deferred DISC income allocable to the stock in the DISC held by the estate or trust shall not be attributed to the beneficiaries of such estate or trust. The interest charge is imposed on the estate or trust. The estate or trust is required to determine its DISC-related deferred tax liability and interest charge for the taxable year in the same manner as other taxpayers. For this purpose, the tax rates applicable to estates and trusts for the taxable year under section 1(e) shall apply. In computing the taxable income of the estate or trust for the taxable year including the deferred DISC income under section 995(f)(2)(A)(i), the estate or trust shall not take into account a deduction under section 651 or 661 (relating to deductions for distributions) greater than the deduction for

distributions allowed in computing the estate or trust's actual tax liability for such year under section 995(f)(2)(A)(ii).

(i) [Reserved]

(j) Character, payment, assessment and collection of the interest charge. *(1) Character.* Under section 995(f)(6), the interest charge imposed on a DISC shareholder for any taxable year is treated for all purposes of the Code in the same manner as interest on an underpayment of tax under section 6601. Thus, the interest charge may be deducted from the shareholder's gross income only to the extent the shareholder may deduct interest on an underpayment of tax, and subject to all applicable limitations on the deduction for interest.

(2) Taxable year for which interest charge is deductible. (i) Cash method shareholder. If the DISC shareholder uses the cash receipts and disbursements method of accounting, to the extent that the interest charge for a taxable year is deductible, it is deductible in the taxable year in which the shareholder pays the interest charge. For example, assume that on March 15, 1987, a cash method, calendar year DISC shareholder that is a C corporation pays $100, representing the full amount of the shareholder's interest charge for its taxable year ending December 31, 1986. The $100 amount is a proper interest deduction for the shareholder's taxable year ending December 31, 1987, the taxable year in which the cash method shareholder paid the interest charge.

(ii) Accrual method shareholder. If the DISC shareholder uses the accrual method of accounting, under the all events test the fact of the shareholder's liability for the interest charge for a taxable year is not fixed, and the amount of the interest charge cannot be determined, until the close of the period in which the shareholder can receive a distribution-in-excess-of-income with respect to such year. Prior to that time, all or any amount of the interest charge for the taxable year may be eliminated by such a distribution. Generally, however, if the DISC shareholder uses the accrual method and if the DISC and the shareholder have the same taxable year, then to the extent that the interest charge for a taxable year is deductible, the amount of the shareholder's interest charge is a proper deduction for such taxable year, because the period in which the DISC can make a distribution-in-excess-of-income to the shareholder with respect to such taxable year ends on the last day of such shareholder's taxable year. For example, assume that on March 10, 1987, an accrual method, calendar year DISC shareholder that is a C corporation pays $150, representing the full amount of the shareholder's interest charge for its taxable year ending December 31, 1986. Assume also that the DISC uses the calendar year as the taxable year. When the DISC's 1986 taxable year closed, the shareholder could no longer receive a distribution-in-excess-of-income under section 995(f)(3)(A)(ii) with respect to the shareholder's 1986 taxable year. Accordingly, the $150 interest charge is a proper interest deduction for the shareholder's taxable year ending December 31, 1986, the taxable year in which the interest charge accrued under section 461.

(3) Payment, assessment and collection of the interest charge. (i) Under section 995(f)(6), the interest charge imposed on the DISC shareholder for any taxable year is required to be paid on the same date the shareholder's income tax return for such taxable year is required to be filed, without regard to extensions.

If the interest charge is not paid by that date, interest, compounded daily, at the rate specified under section 6621 shall be imposed on the amount of the unpaid interest charge from that date until the date the interest charge is paid. The interest charge for the taxable year shall be computed on a current Form 8404, which must be completed in accordance with the instructions thereon, and filed by the DISC shareholder together with a separate payment of the interest charge. The payment of the interest charge shall be made, and the Form 8404 shall be filed with the service center with which the shareholder's income tax return for the taxable year is required to be filed. In order to assure proper handling of the Form 8404 and crediting of payment of the interest charge to the shareholder's account, the Form 8404 and the payment of the interest charge should not be attached to or mailed together with the shareholder's income tax return for the taxable year. Payment of the interest charge may not be made by designating any portion of an overpayment of tax as an amount to be applied in payment of the interest charge.

(ii) Payments of estimated tax under section 6654 (in the case of an individual), or 6154 (in the case of a corporation) are not required with respect to the interest charge.

(iii) The interest charge is to be assessed, and may be collected in the same manner as interest on an underpayment of tax under section 6601.

(4) Subsequent change in interest charge amount; amended Form 8404. If the shareholder's actual tax liability for a taxable year changes, either by reason of an audit adjustment or by the filing of an amended return, the shareholder is required to file an amended Form 8404 only if the amount of the shareholder's DISC-related deferred tax liability (as defined § 1.995(f)-1(d)) for such taxable year also changes. If so required, the shareholder shall file the amended Form 8404 by (i) clearly labeling across the top of a Form 8404 "Amended Form 8404 for Shareholder's Taxable Year Ending 19XX", (ii) by attaching to the amended Form 8404 a computation and an explanation of the change in the shareholder's DISC-related deferred tax liability and interest charge for such taxable year, and (iii) by enclosing payment for the amount of any additional interest charge or a statement of the amount of the interest charge required to be refunded to the shareholder. The amended Form 8404 should be attached to the copy of the shareholder's amended income tax return for the taxable year involved, or mailed separately to the service center with which the shareholder would file an amended income tax return for the taxable year involved.

§ 1.996-1 Rules for actual distributions and certain deemed distributions.

Caution: The Treasury has not yet amended Reg § 1.996-1 to reflect changes made by P.L. 99-514.

(a) General rule. Under section 996(a)(1), any actual distribution (other than a distribution described in paragraph (b) of this section or to which § 1.995-4 applies) to a shareholder by a DISC, or former DISC, which is made out of earnings and profits shall be treated as made—

(1) First, out of "previously taxed income" (as defined in § 1.996-3(c)) to the extent thereof,

(2) Second, out of "accumulated DISC income" (as defined in § 1.996-3(b)) to the extent thereof, and

(3) Third, out of "other earnings and profits" (as defined in § 1.996-3(d)) to the extent thereof.

(b) Rules for qualifying distributions and deemed distributions under section 995(b)(1)(G) *(1) In general.* Except as provided in subparagraph (2), any actual distribution to meet qualification requirements made pursuant to § 1.992-3 and any deemed distribution pursuant to § 1.995-2(a)(5) (relating to foreign investment attributable to producer's loans) which is made out of earnings and profits shall be treated as made—

(i) First, out of "accumulated DISC income" (as defined in § 1.996-3(b)) to the extent thereof.

(ii) Second, out of "other earnings and profits" (as defined in § 1.996-3(d)) to the extent thereof, and

(iii) Third, out of "previously taxed income" (as defined in § 1.996-3(c)) to the extent thereof.

(2) Special rule. For taxable years beginning after December 31, 1975, paragraph (b)(1) of this section shall apply to one-half of the amount of an actual distribution made pursuant to § 1.992-3 to satisfy the condition of § 1.992-1(b) (the gross receipts test) and paragraph (a) of this section shall apply to the remaining one-half of such amount.

(c) Exclusion from gross income. Under section 996(a)(3), amounts distributed out of previously taxed income shall be excluded by the distributee from gross income. However, see § 1.996-5(b) for treatment as gain from the sale or exchange of property of the portion of an actual distribution out of previously taxed income to the extent it exceeds the adjusted basis of the stock with respect to which the distribution is made.

(d) Priority of distributions. Under section 996(c), for purposes of determining their treatment under paragraphs (a), (b), and (c) of this section, distributions made during a taxable year shall be treated as being made in the following order—

(1) Deemed distributions under §§ 1.995-2 and 1.995-3.

(2) Actual distributions to meet qualification requirements made pursuant to § 1.992-3 in the order in which they are made, and

(3) Other actual distributions in the order in which they are made.

Thus, the treatment of any distribution shall be determined after the divisions of earnings and profits have been properly adjusted by taking into account distributions of higher priority which are made or deemed made during the same taxable year.

(e) Examples. The provisions of this section may be illustrated by the following examples:

Example (1). Y Corporation, which uses the calendar year as its taxable year elects to be treated as a DISC beginning with 1972. During 1973, Y makes a cash distribution of $100 to X Corporation, Y's sole shareholder. For 1973, Y has no earnings and profits. As of the beginning of 1973, Y has $300 of accumulated earnings and profits, which consist of $70 of accumulated DISC income, $40 of previously taxed income, and $190 of other earnings and profits. The entire $100 distribution is a dividend under section 316. However, $40 thereof is treated as made out of previously taxed income and is thus excluded from gross income. Accordingly, only $60 is treated as distributed out of accumulated DISC income and includible in gross income. See § 1.246-4 for the inapplicability of the dividend received deduction with respect to the entire distribution of $100.

Example (2). Assume the same facts as in example (1), except that the cash distribution is designated as a distribution to meet qualification requirements made pursuant to § 1.992-3. Under these facts, X includes the entire distribution in its gross income as a dividend. Of the $100 distributed, $70 is treated as made out of accumulated DISC income and the remaining $30 is treated as made out of other earnings and profits. The dividend received deduction under section 243 is available only with respect to such $30.

Example (3). Y Corporation, which uses the calendar year as its taxable year, elects to be treated as a DISC beginning with 1972. As of the end of 1975, Y had failed to meet the gross receipts test for that year. In 1975 Y had $100 of taxable income, $80 of which was attributable to qualified export receipts and $20 of which was attributable to receipts that did not qualify as qualified export receipts. As of the beginning of 1976, Y had $300 of accumulated earnings and profits, which consisted of $70 of accumulated DISC income, $40 of previously taxed income, and $190 of other earnings and profits. In 1976 Y makes a cash distribution of $20 pursuant to § 1.992-3 in order to satisfy the gross receipts test for 1975. For 1976 Y has no earnings and profits and no deemed distributions. The entire $20 distribution is a dividend under section 316. Under § 1.996-1(b)(2), half of the $20 cash distribution is treated pursuant to § 1.996-1(b)(1) and half is treated pursuant to § 1.996(a). Thus, $10 is treated as distributed out of accumulated DISC income and is includible in gross income. The other $10 is treated as made out of previously taxed income and is thus excluded from gross income. As of the beginning of 1977, Y has $280 of accumulated earnings and profits, which consists of $60 of accumulated DISC income, $30 of previously taxed income, and $190 of other earnings and profits.

T.D. 7324, 9/27/74, amend T.D. 7854, 11/16/82.

PAR. 12. Paragraph (b)(2) of § 1.996-1 is revised to read as follows:

Proposed § 1.996-1 Rules for actual distributions and certain deemed distributions. [*For Preamble, see ¶ 151,083*]

* * * * *

(b) Rules for qualifying distributions and deemed distributions under section 995(b)(1)(G). * * *

(2) Special rules. (i) 1976-1984. For taxable years beginning after December 31, 1975, and before January 1, 1985, paragraph (b)(1) of this section shall apply to one-half of the amount of an actual distribution made pursuant to § 1.992-3 to satisfy the condition of § 1.992-1(b) (the gross receipts test) and paragraph (a) of this section shall apply to the remaining one-half of such amount.

(ii) After 1984. For taxable years beginning after December 31, 1984, in the case of a DISC shareholder which is a C corporation, paragraph (b)(1) of this section shall apply to $^{16}/_{17}$ of the amount of an actual distribution made pursuant to § 1.992-3 to satisfy the condition of § 1.992-1(b) (the gross receipts test) and paragraph (a) of this section shall apply to one-seventeenth ($^{1}/_{17}$) of such amount.

* * * * *

§ 1.996-2 Ordering rules for losses.

(a) In general. Under section 996(b), if for any taxable year a DISC, or a former DISC, incurs a deficit in earnings and profits, such deficit shall be charged—

(1) First, to other earnings and profits (as defined in § 1.996-3(d)) to the extent thereof,

(2) Second, to accumulated DISC income (as defined in § 1.996-3(b)) to the extent thereof, subject to the special rule in paragraph (b) of this section,

(3) Third, to previously taxed income (as defined in § 1.996-3(c)) to the extent thereof, and

(4) To the extent that the amount of such deficit exceeds the sum of the amounts charged in accordance with subpara-

graphs (1), (2), and (3) of this paragraph, to other earnings and profits (as defined in § 1.996-3(d)).

Thus, the excess deficit charged to other earning and profits under subparagraph (4) of this paragraph will create a deficit therein in the amount of such excess. To determine the amount of any division of earnings and profits for the purpose of determining under § 1.996-1 the treatment of any actual and certain deemed distributions, the portion of a deficit in earnings and profits chargeable under this paragraph to such division prior to such distribution shall be determined in a manner consistent with the rules in § 1.316-2(b) for determining the amount of earnings and profits available on the date of any distribution.

(b) Deficits subsequent to a disqualification. A deficit in earnings and profits of a DISC, or former DISC, shall not be charged to accumulated DISC income which has been determined is to be deemed distributed to the shareholders pursuant to § 1.995-3 as a result of a revocation of election or other disqualification. Thus, in accordance with paragraph (a) of this section as modified by this paragraph, a deficit incurred by a former DISC following such a revocation or disqualification shall be charged first to other earnings and profits and then to previously taxed income with any balance being charged to other earnings and profits and creating a deficit therein. The preceding sentence shall also apply in the case of a deficit incurred by a DISC which has no accumulated DISC income accumulated during its current taxable year and all immediately preceding consecutive taxable years for which it was a DISC. If as a result of the application of this paragraph the amount of a deficit in other earnings and profits exceeds the amount of a deficit in accumulated earnings and profits, then upon any subsequent actual distribution the deficit in other earnings and profits shall be reduced by the lower of (1) the amount of such actual distribution chargeable to accumulated DISC income or previously taxed income or (2) the amount of such excess.

(c) Examples. The provisions of this section may be illustrated by the following examples:

Example (1). X Corporation, which uses the calendar year as its taxable year, becomes a DISC beginning with 1976. In addition to other facts assumed in the table below, X incurs a deficit in earnings and profits for 1979 of $70. Such deficit is charged to the divisions of X's earnings and profits pursuant to paragraph (a) of this section in the manner set forth in such table.

	Accumulated DISC income	Previously taxed income	Other earnings and profits
Balance Jan. 1, 1976			$ 50
Increase for 1976	$ 10	$ 8	
Increase for 1977	10	8	
Increase for 1978	10	8	
Balance Jan. 1, 1979	30	24	50
Deficit for 1979 of $70:			
Charge No. 1			(50)
Charge No. 2	(20)		
Balance Jan. 1, 1980	10	24	0

Example (2). Assume the same facts as in example (1), except that effective for taxable years beginning with 1979, X revokes its election to be treated as a DISC. Under § 1.995-3, X has $30 of accumulated DISC income which is to be deemed distributed $10 per year in 1980, 1981, and 1982. The deficit in earnings and profits for 1979 is charged to the divisions of X's earnings and profits pursuant to paragraph (b) of this section in the manner set forth in the table below:

	Accumulated DISC income	Previously taxed income	Other earnings and profits
Balance Jan. 1, 1979	$30	$24	$50
Deficit for 1979 of $70:			
Charge No. 1			(50)
Charge No. 2		(20)	
Balance Jan. 1, 1980	30	4	0

Example (3). Assume the same facts as in example (2), except that the deficit in earnings and profits for 1979 is $120. Assume further that for 1980, 1981, and 1982, during which years X's shareholders are receiving scheduled installments of the deemed distributions of accumulated DISC income under § 1.995-3, X, a former DISC, has neither earnings and profits nor a deficit in earnings and profits. The $120 deficit for 1979 is charged to the divisions of X's earnings and profits pursuant to paragraph (b) of this section in the manner set forth in the table below:

	Accumulated DISC income	Previously taxed income	Other earnings and profits	Accumulated earnings and profits
Balance Jan. 1, 1979	$30	$24	$50	$104
Deficit for 1979 of $120				(120)
Charge No. 1			(50)	
Charge No. 2		(24)		
Charge No. 3			(46)	
Balance Jan. 1, 1980	30	0	(46)	(16)
Deemed distributions in 1980 under Sec. 1.995-3	(10)	10		
Balance Jan. 1, 1981	20	10	(46)	(16)

Example (4). Assume the same facts as in example (3), except that on December 31, 1980, X makes an actual distribution of $10 out of previously taxed income. On January 1, 1981, X has $20 of accumulated DISC income, no previously taxed income, and a deficit of $36 in other earnings and profits. The deficit of $16 in accumulated earnings and profits remains the same.

T.D. 7324, 9/27/74.

§ 1.996-3 Divisions of earnings and profits.

(a) In general. For purposes of sections 991 through 997, the earnings and profits of a DISC, or former DISC, shall be treated as composed of the following three divisions:

(1) Accumulated DISC income (as defined in paragraph (b) of this section),

(2) Previously taxed income (as defined in paragraph (c) of this section), and

(3) Other earnings and profits (as defined in paragraph (d) of this section),

(b) Accumulated DISC income defined. *(1)* Accumulated DISC income is that portion of a corporation's earnings and profits which were derived during taxable years for which it qualified as a DISC and which were deferred from taxation. Accumulated DISC income as of the close of each taxable year of the corporation is—

(i) The amount of accumulated DISC income as of the close of the immediately preceding taxable year increased by

(ii) The amount of DISC income for the year (as determined in subparagraph (2) of this paragraph) and reduced (but not below zero) by

(iii) The items enumerated in subparagraph (3) of this paragraph.

(2) Under section 996(f)(1), DISC income is (i) the earnings and profits derived by the corporation during a taxable year for which such corporation is a DISC minus (ii) amounts deemed distributed under § 1.995-2 other than the amount of foreign investment attributable to producer's loans described in § 1.995-2(a)(5). For example, the earnings and profits of a DISC for a taxable year include any amounts includible in such DISC's gross income pursuant to section 951(a) (relating to controlled foreign corporations). Deemed distributions under § 1.995-2(a)(5) are taken into account under subparagraph (3) of this paragraph as a reduction in computing accumulated DISC income.

(3) The accumulated DISC income (as increased by DISC income for the year determined under subparagraph (2) of this paragraph) is reduced by each of the following items in the following order:

(i) Any amount deemed distributed for such year under § 1.995-3 (relating to deemed distributions upon disqualification),

(ii) Any amount of foreign investment attributable to producer's loans deemed distributed for such year under § 1.995-2(a)(5) to the extent it is charged to accumulated DISC income under § 1.996-1(b)(1)(i),

(iii) The amount of any adjustment to accumulated DISC income for such year under § 1.966-4(b)(1), and

(iv) To the extent they are treated, under § 1.996-1(a) or (b) (relating to ordering rules for distributions), as made out of accumulated DISC income, the amounts of any actual qualifying distributions pursuant to § 1.992-3 in the order in which they are made, and thereafter by the amounts of any other actual distributions in the order in which they are made, and thereafter by the amounts of any other actual distributions in the order in which they are made, except that, prior to each actual distribution, accumulated DISC income shall be reduced by the portion of any deficit in earnings and profits for the taxable year chargeable at that time under § 1.996-2(a)(2) to accumulated DISC income.

(4) Every distribution or other reduction in accumulated DISC income pursuant to subparagraph (3) of this paragraph shall be charged to the most recently accumulated DISC income.

(c) Previously taxed income. Under section 996(f)(2), previously taxed income as of the close of each taxable year of the corporation is an amount equal to—

(1) The sum of—

(i) The amount of previously taxed income as of the close of the immediately preceding taxable year,

(ii) Amounts deemed distributed for the current year under § 1.995-2 (relating to deemed distributions in qualified years),

(iii) Amounts deemed distributed for the current year under § 1.995-3 (relating to deemed distributions upon disqualification),

(iv) With respect to a distribution in redemption to which § 1.996-4(b)(1) applies, an amount equal to the excess (if any) of (a) the amount of the reduction under § 1.996-4(b)(1) in accumulated DISC income over (b) the reduction in the corporation's earnings and profits (see section 312(e)), and

(v) Any amount by which accumulated DISC income is reduced under paragraph (b)(3)(ii) of this section by reason of a deemed distribution as a dividend, under § 1.995-2(a)(5), of an amount of foreign investment attributable to producer's loans,

(2) Decreased (but not below zero), to the extent they are treated, under § 1.996-1(a) or (b) (relating to ordering rules for distributions), as made out of previously taxed income, by the amounts of any actual qualifying distributions pursuant to § 1.992-3 in the order in which they are made, and thereafter by the amounts of any other actual distributions in the order in which they are made, except that, prior to any actual distribution, previously taxed income shall be reduced by the portion of any deficit in earnings and profits for the taxable year chargeable at that time under § 1.996-2(a)(3) to previously taxed income.

(d) Other earnings and profits. Under section 996(f)(3), other earnings and profits consist of earnings and profits other than accumulated DISC income and previously taxed income described respectively in paragraphs (b) and (c) of this section. Other earnings and profits as of the close of each taxable year of the corporation is (subject to paragraph (e) of this section) an amount equal to the amount of other earnings and profits as of the close of the immediately preceding taxable year decreased (if necessary, below zero) in the following order by—

(1) To the extent they are treated, under § 1.996-1(a) or (b) (relating to ordering rules for distributions), as made out of other earnings and profits, the amounts of any actual qualifying distributions pursuant to § 1.992-3 in the order in which they are made, and thereafter the amounts of any other actual distributions in the order in which they are made, except that, prior to any actual distribution, other earnings and profits shall be reduced by the portion of any deficit in earnings and profits for the taxable year chargeable at that time under § 1.996-2(a)(1) to other earnings and profits, and

(2) With respect to a distribution in redemption to which § 1.996-4(b)(1) applies, an amount equal to the excess (if any) of (a) the reduction in the corporation's earnings and profits (see section 312(e)) over *(b)* the amount of the reduction under § 1.996-4(b)(1) in accumulated DISC income.

(e) Distributions in kind. *(1)* For purposes of determining, under paragraphs (b), (c), and (d) of this section, the amount by which any division of earnings and profits is reduced by reason of a distribution of property (other than money or the DISC's, or former DISC's, own obligations), the amount of such distribution is the fair market value of such property at the time of the distribution.

(2) For any taxable year in which the DISC makes a distribution of such property, the amount of other earnings and profits determined under paragraph (d) of this section (without regard to this subparagraph) shall be—

(i) Increased by the excess (if any) of the amount of such distribution treated as a dividend under section 316(a) over the adjusted basis of such property, and

(ii) Decreased by the excess (if any) of the adjusted basis of such property over the amount of such distribution treated as a dividend under section 316(a).

Each item of property shall be considered separately for purposes of making the adjustment under this subparagraph.

(f) Examples. The provisions of §§ 1.996-1, 1.996-2, and this section may be illustrated by the following examples:

Example (1). M Corporation, which uses the calendar year as its taxable year, elects to be treated as a DISC beginning with 1974. During 1975, M derives no earnings and profits and makes no deemed or actual distributions, except that on December 31, 1975, M's shareholders are treated as having received a dividend distribution of $100 under § 1.995-2(a)(5) (relating to foreign investment attributable to producer's loans). M's earnings and profits are adjusted as shown on line (2) of the table below on the basis of facts assumed therein.

	Accumulated earnings and profits	Accumulated DISC income	Previously taxed income	Other earnings and profits
(1) Balance Jan. 1, 1975	$450	$100	$250	$100
(2) Adjustments (see paragraphs (b)(3)(ii) and (c)(1)(v) of this section)	0	(100)	100	0
(3) Balance Jan. 1, 1976	450	0	350	100

Example (2). N Corporation, which uses the calendar year as its taxable year, elects to be treated as a DISC beginning with 1972. During 1973, N derives no earnings and profits for the year and makes no deemed or actual distributions, except that A, a shareholder, realized $200 of gain upon receiving an actual cash distribution of $300 in redemption of N stock having an adjusted basis of $100 in his hands. The redemption is treated as an exchange under section 302(a) but, under section 995(c), A includes the $200 of gain in his gross income as a dividend. Assuming that, under section 312(e), $240 is properly chargeable to capital account of N and that, under § 1.996-4(b), accumulated DISC income is reduced by $200, N's accounts are adjusted on line (2) of the table below on the basis of facts assumed therein.

	Capital	Accumulated earnings and profits	Accumulated DISC income	Previously taxed income	Other earnings and profits
(1) Balance Jan. 1, 1973	$2,000	$400	$300	$100	0
(2) Adjustments (see § 1.996-4(b) and paragraph (c)(1)(iv) of this section)	(240)	(60)	(200)	140	0
(3) Balance Jan. 1, 1974	1,760	340	100	240	0

Example (3). P Corporation, which uses the calendar year as its taxable year, elects to be treated as a DISC beginning with 1973. During 1974, P derives no earnings and profits for the year and makes no deemed or actual distributions, except for a distribution to B, its sole shareholder, of property with a fair market value of $100 and an adjusted basis in P's hands of $40. Under § 1.996-1(a)(1), B treats the entire amount of the distribution as being made out of previously taxed income and, under § 1.996-1(c), excludes it from his gross income. P's earnings and profits divisions are adjusted on lines (2) and (3) of the table below on the basis of facts assumed therein.

	Accumulated earnings and profits	Accumulated DISC income	Previously taxed income	Other earnings and profits
(1) Balance Jan. 1, 1974	$200	$80	$120	0
(2) Adjustment under paragraphs (c)(2) and (e)(1) this section	(40)	0	(100)	0
(3) Adjustment under paragraph (e)(2)(i) of this section	0	0	0	$60
(4) Balance Jan. 1, 1975	160	80	20	60

Example (4). Q Corporation, which uses the calendar year as its taxable year, elects to be treated as a DISC beginning with 1974. On January 1, 1975, Q has accumulated earnings and profits of $1,200 and, during 1975, Q incurs a deficit in earnings and profits of $365. The amount of such deficit incurred as of any date before the close of 1975 cannot be shown. On July 1, 1975, Q makes a cash distribution of $650, with respect to its stock to C, Q's sole shareholder. C subsequently transfers by gift all of his Q stock to D. On December 31, 1975, Q makes a cash distribution of $650, with respect to its stock, to D. Under these facts and additional facts assumed in the table below, C is treated as having received a dividend of $650 of which $320 is treated as distributed out of previously taxed income and excluded from gross income. D is treated as receiving a dividend of $186. Adjustments to Q's earnings and profits accounts are illustrated in the table below.

	Accumulated earnings and profits	Accumulated DISC income	Previously taxed income	Other earnings and profits
(1) Balance Jan. 1, 1975	$1,200	$800	$320	$80
(2) Portion of 1975 deficit of $365 chargeable as of June 30, 1975, pursuant to § 1.996-2(a)	(181)	(101)	0	(80)
(3) Balance July 1, 1975	1,019	699	320	0
(4) $650 distributed to C on July 1, 1975	(650)	(330)	(320)	0
(5) Portion of 1975 deficit of $365 chargeable as of Dec. 30, 1975, pursuant to § 1.996-2(a)	(183)	(183)	0	0
(6) Balance Dec. 31, 1975	186	186	0	0
(7) $650 distributed to D on Dec. 31, 1975[1]	(186)	(186)	0	0
(8) Balance Jan. 1, 1976	0	0	0	0

[1] $60 treated as return of capital pursuant to section 301(c)(2).

Example (5). (1) Facts. R Corporation, which uses the calendar year as its taxable year elects to be treated as a DISC beginning with 1972. X Corporation is its sole shareholder. At the beginning of 1974, R has a deficit in earnings and profits of $60 all of which is composed of "other earnings and profits". For 1974, R has earnings and profits of $80 before reduction for any distributions and taxable income of $70. On June 15, 1974, R makes a cash distribution to X of $60, with respect to its stock, to which section 301 applies. On August 15, 1974, R makes a cash distribution to X of $30 designated as a distribution to meet qualification requirements pursuant to § 1.992-3. Under § 1.995-2(a), X is deemed to receive, on December 31, 1974, a distribution of a dividend of $35, i.e., one-half of R's taxable income of $70. The tax consequences of these facts to X and their effect on R's earnings and profits are set forth in the subsequent subparagraphs of this example.

(2) Dividend treatment of actual distributions. Since R had $80 of earnings and profits for 1974 and a deficit in accumulated earnings and profits at the beginning of 1974, only $80 of the actual distributions ($90) are treated as dividends under sections 301(c)(1) and 316(a)(2). ($10 of the actual distribution, which is not treated as a dividend is treated in the manner specified in section 301(c)(2) and (3).) Thus, under § 1.316-2(b), $26.67 of the actual qualifying distribution made on August 15, 1974 ($30 × $80/$90), and $53.33 of the actual distribution made on June 15, 1974 ($60 × $80/$90), are considered made out of earnings and profits.

(3) Priority of distributions. Under § 1.996-1(d), for purposes of adjusting the divisions of R's earnings and profits and determining the treatment of subsequent distributions, the sequence in which each distribution is treated as having been made is—

(i) First, the deemed distribution of $35.

(ii) Second, the actual qualifying distribution of $30 made on August 15, 1974, pursuant to § 1.992-3, and

(iii) Finally, the actual distribution of $60 made on June 15, 1974.

(4) Treatment and effect of deemed distribution. Under § 1.995-2(a), on December 31, 1974, X includes the deemed distribution of $35 in its gross income as a dividend. Under paragraph (c)(1)(ii) of this section, R's previously taxed income is increased by $35 as shown on line (3) of the table in subparagraph (7) of this example. Under paragraph (b)(1)(ii) and (2) of this section, accumulated DISC income is increased by $45 of DISC income, i.e., R's earnings and profits for 1974, $80, minus the deemed distribution of $35, as shown on line (4) of the table.

(5) Treatment and effect of actual qualifying distribution of $30. As indicated in subparagraph (2) of this example, $26.67 of the $30 qualifying distribution on August 15, 1974, is treated as made out of earnings and profits for 1974. Under § 1.996-1(b)(1)(i), the entire $26.67 is treated as distributed out of accumulated DISC income. Thus, on August 15, 1974, X includes $26.67 in its gross income as a dividend. No deduction is allowable under section 243. Under paragraph (b)(3)(iv) of this section, R's accumulated DISC income is reduced by $26.67 as shown on line (6) of the table in subparagraph (7) of this example.

(6) Treatment and effect of actual distribution of $60. As indicated in subparagraph (2) of this example, $53.33 of the $60 distribution on June 15, 1974, is treated as made out of earnings and profits for 1974. Under § 1.996-1(a), the $53.33 is treated as distributed out of previously taxed income to the extent thereof, $35, and then out of accumulated DISC income, $18.33. Thus, on June 15, 1974, X includes $18.33 in its gross income as a dividend. Under § 1.996-1(c), the distribution of $35 out of previously taxed income is excluded from gross income. No deduction is allowable under section 243 with respect to the actual distribution of $53.33. Under paragraph (b)(3)(iv) of this section, accumulated DISC income is reduced by $18.33 and, under paragraph (c)(2) of this section, previously taxed income is reduced by $35, as shown on line (7) of the table in subparagraph (7) of this example.

(7) Summary. The effects on earnings and profits and the divisions of earnings and profits are summarized in the following table:

	Earnings and profits for year	Accumulated earnings and profits	Accumulated DISC income	Previously taxed income	Other earnings and profits
(1) Balance Jan. 1, 1974		($60.00)			($60.00)
(2) Earnings and profits for year before reduction for distributions	$80.00				
(3) Deemed distribution of $35 to X on Dec. 31, 1974, under § 1.995-2(a)				$35.00	
(4) DISC income for 1974 of $45 as defined in paragraph (b)(2) of this section (line 2 ($80) minus line 3 ($35))			$45.00		
(5) Balance before actual distributions	80.00	(60.00)	45.00	35.00	(60.00)
(6) Qualifying distribution of $30 to X on Aug. 15, 1974, pursuant to § 1.992-3	(26.67)		(26.67)		
(7) Actual distribution to P of $60 on June 15, 1974	(53.33)		(18.33)	(35.00)	
(8) Balance Jan. 1, 1975	0	(60.00)	0		(60.00)

Example (6). Assume the facts are the same as in example (5), except that at the beginning of 1974 R's accumulated earnings and profits amount to $60 consisting of accumulated DISC income of $20, previously taxed income of $10, and other earnings and profits of $30. In addition, on August 1, 1974, X transfers all R's stock to Y Corporation in a reorganization described in section 368(a)(1)(B) in which under section 354 X recognizes no gain or loss. Under these facts, X includes in its gross income for 1974 a dividend of $15 which is attributable to the actual distribution of $60 paid out of earnings and profits on June 15, 1974. X excludes from gross income the balance of the $60 distribution ($45) paid out of earnings and profits because, under § 1.996-1(a), it is treated as paid out of previously taxed income. Y includes in its gross income for 1974 a dividend of $65 of which $35 is attributable to the deemed distribution of a dividend to Y on December 31, 1974, under § 1.995-2(a) and $30 is attributable to the qualifying distribution paid out of earnings and profits to Y on August 15, 1974. The adjustments to R's earnings and profits are summarized in the following table:

	Earnings and profits for year	Accumulated earnings and profits	Accumulated DISC income	Previously taxed income	Other earnings and profits
(1) Balance Jan. 1, 1974		$60	$20	$10	$30
(2) Earnings and profits for year before reduction for distributions	$80				
(3) Deemed distribution of $35 to Y on Dec. 31, 1974, under § 1.995-2(a)				35	
(4) DISC income for 1974 of $45 as defined in paragraph (b)(2) of this section (line 2 ($80) minus line 3 ($35))			45		
(5) Balance before actual distributions	80	60	65	45	30
(6) Qualifying distribution of $30 to Y on Aug. 15, 1974, pursuant to § 1.992-3	(26.67)	(3.33)	(30)		
(7) Actual distribution to X of $60 on June 15, 1974	(53.33)	(6.67)	(15)	(45)	
(8) Balance Jan. 1, 1975		50	20	0	30

(g) DISCs having corporate and noncorporate shareholders. In the case of a DISC having one or more corporate shareholders but less than all of its shareholders subject to the special rules of section 291(a)(4), relating to certain deferred DISC income as a corporate preference item, accumulated DISC income and previously taxed income of the DISC are divided between the corporate shareholders, as a class, and the other shareholders, as a class, in proportion to amounts of DISC income not deemed distributed and amounts deemed distributed to each class. Subsequent taxation of actual and qualifying distributions shall be based upon this division. Thus, if a DISC is owned 50 percent by corporate shareholders and 50 percent by individual shareholders and has undistributed taxable income of $2,000 for its year, the division is made as follows:

Corporate shareholders:	
Previously taxed income (57.5% of $2,000 ÷ 2)	$575
Accumulated DISC income (42.5% of $2,000 ÷ 2)	425
Individual shareholders:	
Previously taxed income (50% of $2,000 ÷ 2)	500
Accumulated DISC income (50% of $2,000 ÷ 2)	500

T.D. 7324, 9/27/74, amend T.D. 7854, 11/16/82, T.D. 7984, 10/11/84.

§ 1.996-4 Subsequent effect of previous disposition of DISC stock.

Caution: The Treasury has not yet amended Reg § 1.996-4 to reflect changes made by P.L. 94-455.

(a) Shareholder adjustment for previously taxed income. *(1)* Under section 996(d)(1), except as provided in subparagraph (2) of this paragraph, if—

(i) Gain with respect to a share of stock of a DISC, or former DISC, is treated under § 1.995-4 as a dividend, and

(ii) With respect to such share, any person subsequently receives an actual distribution made out of accumulated

DISC income, or a deemed distribution made, pursuant to § 1.995-3, by reason of disqualification, out of accumulated DISC income,

then such person shall treat such distribution in the same manner as a distribution from previously taxed income (and thus excludable from gross income under § 1.996-1(c)) to the extent that the gain referred to in subdivision (i) of this subparagraph exceeds the aggregate amount of any other distributions with respect to such share which were treated under this subparagraph as made from previously taxed income.

(2) In applying subparagraph (1) of this paragraph with respect to a share of stock in a DISC, or former DISC, the gain referred to in subparagraph (1)(i) of this paragraph does not include any gain to a shareholder on a redemption of such share which qualifies as an exchange under section 302(a) or any gain on a disposition of such share prior to such redemption. Distributions described in subparagraph (1)(ii) of this paragraph do not include a distribution in a redemption which qualifies as an exchange under section 302(a). For adjustments to accumulated DISC income by reason of dividend treatment under § 1.995-4 with respect to gain upon a redemption of DISC stock to which section 302(a) applies and upon a prior disposition of such stock, see paragraph (b) of this section.

(3) Example. The provisions of this paragraph may be illustrated by the following example:

Example. In 1974, under § 1.995-4, A, a shareholder of a DISC, on the sale of his DISC stock to B, is required to treat $20 of his gain as a dividend. The DISC has no previously taxed income and $40 of accumulated DISC income. Subsequently in the same year, B, the purchaser of the stock, receives an actual dividend distribution of $15 with respect to such stock which, under § 1.996-1(a), is treated as made out of accumulated DISC income. The amounts of the DISC's previously taxed income and accumulated DISC income were not adjusted by reason of the $20 treated as a dividend on the prior sale. However, even though the DISC had no previously taxed income, the purchaser would treat the $15 as though it had been paid out of previously taxed income and, therefore would not include the $15 in gross income. If in 1975, B receives another actual distribution of $9 with respect to such stock, $5 (i.e., $20 dividend on A's sale less the $15 distribution to B in 1974 which was treated under subparagraph (1) of this paragraph as made from previously taxed income) is treated as made from previously taxed income and excluded from gross income. The result would be the same if, on January 1, 1975, B had transferred such stock to C by gift and the $9 distribution had been made to C.

(b) Corporate adjustment upon redemption. *(1)* Under section 996(d)(2), if by reason of § 1.995-4 gain on a redemption of stock in a DISC, or former DISC, is included in the shareholder's gross income as a dividend, then the accumulated DISC income shall be reduced by an amount equal to the sum of—

(i) The amount of gain on such redemption which, under § 1.995-4, is treated as a dividend, and

(ii) The amount of any gain with respect to such redeemed stock which, under § 1.995-4, was treated as a dividend on a disposition prior to such redemption minus the amount of distributions with respect to such stock which have been treated as made out of previously taxed income by reason of the application of paragraph (a)(1) of this section.

(2) The provisions of this paragraph may be illustrated by the following examples:

Example (1). The entire stock of a DISC, which uses the calendar year as its taxable year, has been owned equally by A, B, C, and D since it was organized. At the close of 1976, when the DISC has $100 of accumulated DISC income, it redeems all of A's shares in a transaction qualifying as an exchange under section 302(a) and A, under § 1.995-4, includes $25 in his gross income as a dividend. The redemption has the effect of reducing accumulated DISC income by $25 to $75.

Example (2). Assume the same facts as in example (1) except that the stock of the DISC has not been held equally by A, B, C, and D since its organization. A purchased his shares from X in 1974 in a transaction in which X, under § 1.995-4, included in his gross income $30 as a dividend. In 1975, A receives a distribution of $10 out of accumulated DISC income which, under paragraph (a)(1) of this section, is treated as made out of previously taxed income. Under these facts, the redemption of A's stock in 1976 has the effect of reducing accumulated DISC income by $45 to $55 determined as follows:

(a) Accumulated DISC income		$100
(b) Minus sum of:		
(1) Dividend on redemption of A's stock	$25	
(2) Excess of dividend on X's sale ($30) over distribution to A treated as made out of previously taxed income ($10)	$20	
Total		45
(c) Accumulated DISC income on 12/31/76		55

T.D. 7324, 9/27/74.

§ 1.996-5 Adjustment to basis.

(a) Addition to basis. Under section 996(e)(1) amounts representing deemed distributions as provided in section 995(b) shall increase the basis of the stock with respect to which the distribution is made.

(b) Reductions of basis. Under section 996(e)(2), the portion of an actual distribution treated as made out of previously taxed income shall reduce the basis of the stock with respect to which it is made and, to the extent that it exceeds the adjusted basis of such stock, shall be treated as gain from the sale or exchange of property. In the case of stock includible in the gross estate of a decedent for which an election is made under section 2032 (relating to alternate valuation), this paragraph shall not apply to any distribution made after the date of the decedent's death and before the alternate valuation date provided by section 2032. See section 1014(d) for a special rule for determining the basis of stock in a DISC, or former DISC, acquired from a decedent.

T.D. 7324, 9/27/74.

§ 1.996-6 Effectively connected income.

Caution: The Treasury has not yet amended Reg § 1.996-6 to reflect changes made by P.L. 98-369.

In the case of a shareholder who is a nonresident alien individual or a foreign corporation, trust, or estate, amounts taxable as dividends by reason of the application of § 1.995-4 (relating to gain on disposition of stock in a DISC), amounts treated under § 1.996-1 as distributed out of accumulated DISC income, and amounts deemed distributed under § 1.995-2(a)(1) through (4) shall be treated as gains and distributions which are effectively connected with the conduct of a trade or business conducted through a permanent establishment of such shareholder within the United States, and shall be subject to tax in accordance with the provisions of section 871(b) and the regulations thereunder in the case of nonresident alien individuals, trusts, or estates, or section 882 and the regulations thereunder in the case of foreign corporations. In no case, however, shall other income of such shareholder be taxable as effectively connected with the conduct of a trade or business through a permanent establishment in the United States solely because of the application of this section.

T.D. 7324, 9/27/74.

§ 1.996-7 Carryover of DISC tax attributes.

(a) In general. Carryover of a DISC's divisions of earnings and profits to acquiring corporations in nontaxable transactions shall be subject to rules generally applicable to other corporate tax attributes. For example, a DISC which acquires the assets of another DISC in a transaction to which section 381(a) applies shall succeed to, and take into account, the divisions of the earnings and profits of the transferor DISC in accordance with section 381(c)(2).

(b) Allocation of divisions of earnings and profits in corporate separations. *(1)* If one DISC transfers part of its assets to a controlled DISC in a transaction to which section 368(a)(1)(D) applies and immediately thereafter the stock of the controlled DISC is distributed in a distribution or exchange to which section 355 (or so much of section 356 as relates to section 355) applies, then—

(i) The earnings and profits of the distributing DISC immediately before the transaction shall be allocated between the distributing DISC and the controlled DISC in accordance with the provisions of § 1.312-10.

(ii) Each of the divisions of such earnings and profits, namely previously taxed income, accumulated DISC income, and other earnings and profits, shall be allocated between the distributing DISC and the controlled DISC on the same basis as the earnings and profits are allocated.

(iii) Any assets of the distributing DISC whose status as qualified export assets is limited by its accumulated DISC income (e.g., producer's loans described in § 1.993-4, Export-Import Bank and other obligations described in § 1.993-2(i)) shall be treated as having been allocated, for the purpose of determining the classification of such assets in the hands of the distributing DISC or the controlled DISC, on the same basis as the earnings and profits are allocated regardless of how such assets are actually allocated.

(2) Example. The provisions of this paragraph may be illustrated by the following example:

Example. On January 1, 1974, P Corporation transfers part of its assets to S Corporation, a newly organized subsidiary of P, in a transaction described in section 368(a)(1)(D) and distributes all the S stock in a transaction which qualifies under section 355. Immediately before such transfer, P had earnings and profits of $120,000 of which $100,000 constitutes accumulated DISC income. The unpaid balance of P's producer's loans is $80,000 all of which is retained by P. Pursuant to § 1.312-10, 25 percent of P's accumulated DISC income is allocated to S (i.e., $25,000). P's producer's loans will be treated as allocated to S in the same proportion. Accordingly, for purposes of determining, under § 1.993-4(a)(3), the amount of producer's loans which S is entitled to make, S is treated as having an unpaid balance of producer's loans of $20,000 (i.e., 25% × $80,000) and P is treated as having an unpaid balance of $60,000 (i.e., 75% × $80,000).

(c) Accumulated DISC income accounts of separate DISC's maintained after corporate combination. If two or more DISC's combine to form a new DISC, or if the assets of one DISC are acquired by another DISC, in a transaction described in section 381(a), accumulated DISC income of the acquired DISC or DISC's shall carry over and be taken into account by the acquiring or new DISC, except that a separate account shall be maintained for the accumulated DISC income of any DISC scheduled to be received as a deemed distribution by its shareholders under § 1.995-3 (relating to deemed distributions upon disqualification). If, as a part of such transaction, the stock of the DISC which has accumulated DISC income scheduled to be deemed distributed is exchanged for stock of the acquiring or new DISC to which such accumulated DISC income is carried over and which maintains a separate account, then such accumulated DISC income shall be deemed distributed pro rata to shareholders of the acquiring or new DISC on the basis of stock ownership immediately after the exchange.

T.D. 7324, 9/27/74.

§ 1.996-8 Effect of carryback of capital loss or net operating loss to prior DISC taxable year.

(a) Under § 1.995-2(e), the deduction under section 172 for a net operating loss carryback or under section 1212 for a capital loss carryback is determined as if the DISC were a domestic corporation which had not elected to be treated as a DISC. A carryback of a net operating loss or of a capital loss of any corporation which reduces its taxable income for a preceding taxable year for which it qualified as a DISC will have the consequences enumerated in paragraphs (b) through (e) of this section.

(b) For such preceding taxable year, the amount of a deemed distribution of one-half of certain taxable income described in § 1.995-2(a)(4) will ordinarily be reduced in effect (but not below zero) by one-half of the sum of the amount of the deduction under section 172 for such year for net operating loss carrybacks and the amount of the deduction under section 1212 for such year for capital loss carrybacks.

(c) The amount of reduction in the deemed distribution under paragraph (b) of this section will have the effect of increasing the limitation, provided in § 1.995-2(b)(2), on the amount of foreign investment attributable to producer's loans which is deemed distributed under § 1.995-2(a)(5).

(d) If the amount of a deemed distribution for a preceding taxable year is reduced as described in paragraph (b) of this section, then for such preceding taxable year the previously taxed income (as defined in § 1.996-3(c)) shall be decreased by the amount of such reduction and the accumulated DISC income (as defined in § 1.996-3(b)) shall be increased by the amount of such reduction. Such adjustments shall be made as of the time the deemed distribution for such preceding taxable year is treated as having occurred. See § 1.996-1(d) for the priority of such deemed distribution in relation to other distributions made in that preceding taxable year.

(e) The amount and treatment of any actual distribution made in such preceding taxable year or a year subsequent to such preceding year, and the treatment of gain on a disposition (in any such year) of the DISC's stock to which § 1.995-4 applies, shall be properly adjusted to reflect the adjustments to previously taxed income and accumulated DISC income described in paragraph (d) of this section.

T.D. 7324, 9/27/74.

Proposed § 1.996-9 Adjustments attributable to the Tax Reform Act of 1984. [*For Preamble, see ¶ 151,083*]

Caution: The Treasury has not yet amended Reg § 1.996-9 to reflect changes made by P.L. 99-514, P.L. 98-369.

(a) Exemption of pre-1985 accumulated DISC income from tax. *(1) In general.* Under section 805(b)(2) of the Tax Reform Act of 1984, Pub. L. 98-369, 98 Stat. 494, 1001, in the case of actual distributions made after December 31, 1984, by a DISC or former DISC which was a DISC on such date, any accumulated DISC income of such DISC or former DISC which was derived before January 1, 1985, shall be treated as previously taxed income with respect to which there had previously been a deemed distribution to which section 996(e)(1) applied. For purposes of this section such accumulated DISC income shall be referred to as "exempt accumulated DISC income". For purposes of this section, a distribution includes any distribution in liquidation of a corporation.

(2) Exception for previously disqualified DISCs. Paragraph (a)(1) of this section does not apply to the amount of any actual or deemed distribution of any accumulated DISC income of a DISC or former DISC derived before January 1, 1985, which is scheduled to be received as a deemed distribution under section 995(b)(2) and § 1.995-3 by reason of the disqualification, termination or revocation of the DISC election of such corporation (a "disqualified DISC"). Thus, in the case of a corporation which was a disqualified DISC with respect to one or more prior taxable years ending before 1985, but which has re-elected to be treated as a DISC for one or more succeeding taxable years including the taxable year ending December 31, 1984, this paragraph (a)(2) applies to any accumulated DISC income scheduled to be received as a deemed distribution under section 995(b)(2), and paragraph (a)(1) of this section applies to any accumulated DISC income derived before 1985 which is not required to be distributed under section 995(b)(2).

(3) Exception for amounts distributed to meet qualification requirements. Paragraph (a)(1) of this section does not apply to the amount of any accumulated DISC income derived before January 1, 1985, which is distributed (or is required to be distributed) under section 992(c) after December 31, 1984, in order to satisfy the requirements of section 992(a)(1)(A) (relating to the 95 percent qualified export receipts test) or section 992(a)(1)(B) (relating to the 95 percent qualified export assets test), with respect to any taxable year ending before January 1, 1985.

(b) Effect of distributions by DISC to shareholders. *(1) Scope.* This paragraph (b) applies only to distributions made after December 31, 1984, by a DISC (including a corporation which has elected to be treated as an interest charge DISC for any period after 1984) or a former DISC which has any amount of exempt accumulated DISC income (as defined in paragraph (a)(1) of this section), and it shall not apply after such corporation has distributed, under the ordering rules of this paragraph (b), all of its exempt accumulated DISC income. This paragraph (b) shall apply notwithstanding section 996(a)(1).

(2) Ordering rule for distributions made before July 1, 1985. Any actual distribution to a shareholder after December 31, 1984, and before July 1, 1985, by a DISC or former DISC described in paragraph (b)(1) of this section, which is made out of earnings and profits shall be treated as made—

(i) First, out of previously taxed income, to the extent thereof,

(ii) Second, out of accumulated DISC income derived after 1984, to the extent thereof, and

(iii) Third, out of other earnings and profits (including current earnings and profits in the case of a former DISC).

Any distribution which is treated as made out of previously taxed income under paragraph (b)(2)(i) shall be treated as made first out of exempt accumulated DISC income, to the extent thereof, and second, out of other previously taxed income.

(3) Ordering rule for distributions made after June 30, 1985. Any actual distribution to a shareholder after June 30, 1985, by a DISC or former DISC described in paragraph (b)(1) of this section, which is made out of earnings and profits shall be treated as made—

(i) First, out of other earnings and profits (including current earnings and profits in the case of a former DISC), to the extent thereof,

(ii) Second, out of previously taxed income, to the extent thereof, and

(iii) Third, out of accumulated DISC income derived after 1984.

Any distribution which is treated as made out of previously taxed income under paragraph (b)(3)(ii) shall be treated as made first out of exempt accumulated DISC income, to the extent thereof, and second, out of other previously taxed income.

(4) Exception for qualifying distributions and foreign investments attributable to producer's loans. This paragraph (b) shall not apply to any actual distribution made pursuant to section 992(c) (relating to distributions to meet qualification requirements), or to any deemed distribution pursuant to section 995(b)(1)(G) (relating to foreign investment attributable to producer's loans). Such distributions shall be treated as described in section 996(a)(2).

(c) Earnings and profits attributable to exempt income. The earnings and profits of a corporation which receives a distribution directly or indirectly from a DISC or former DISC shall be increased by the amount of money and the adjusted basis of any property received in a distribution which is treated as made out of previously taxed income attributable to exempt accumulated DISC income.

(d) No adjustment to basis in stock of DISC for exempt income. Notwithstanding section 996(e), a shareholder's basis in the stock of a DISC or former DISC shall not be increased by the amount of exempt accumulated DISC income which is treated as previously taxed income, and such basis shall not be reduced by the receipt of such amount as previously taxed income in a distribution to which paragraph (b) of this section applies.

(e) Carryover basis in property received in a distribution of exempt income. If property other than money is received in a distribution of exempt accumulated DISC income as previously taxed income, and if such property was a qualified export asset (as defined in section 993(b)) on December 31, 1984, then for purposes of section 311, no gain or loss shall be recognized on the distribution of such property, and the shareholder who receives such property shall have a basis in such property equal to the basis of such property in the hands of the DISC or former DISC.

(f) Reduction of net operating loss and capital loss carryovers. In the case of a DISC (including a corporation which has elected to be treated as an interest charge DISC for any period after 1984) or a former DISC which was a DISC on December 31, 1984, the amount of any net operating loss or capital loss of such corporation that was incurred in a taxable year in which such corporation was a DISC and which is a net operating loss or capital loss carryover to any taxable year ending after December 31, 1984, shall be reduced by the amount of exempt accumulated DISC income (as defined in paragraph (a)(1) of this section) of such corporation as of December 31, 1984. If the sum of such carryovers exceeds the amount of such exempt accumulated DISC income, the exempt accumulated DISC income shall first be applied to reduce the amount of such net operating loss carryover, and the amount of such exempt accumulated DISC income (if any) which exceeds such net operating loss carryover shall be applied to reduce the amount of such capital loss carryover to the extent of such excess.

(g) No credit allowed for foreign taxes attributable to exempt accumulated DISC income. Notwithstanding sections 901(d) and 902, no credit shall be allowed for the amount of any income, war profits, or excess profits taxes paid or deemed paid to any foreign country or possession of the United States to the extent that such taxes are attributable to any exempt accumulated DISC income of a DISC or former DISC.

§ 1.997-1 Special rules for subchapter C of the Code.

(a) For purposes of applying the provisions of sections 301 through 395 of the Code, any distribution in property to a corporation by a DISC, or former DISC, which is made out of previously taxed income or accumulated DISC income shall be treated as a distribution in the same amount as if such distribution of property were made to an individual, and have a basis, in the hands of the recipient corporation, equal to such amount treated as having been distributed.

(b) This section may be illustrated by the following example:

Example. X Corporation is the sole shareholder of Y Corporation which is a DISC. Y makes an actual distribution of property to X with respect to X's stock in Y. The property has a basis of $50 and a fair market value of $100. The distribution is treated as made out of accumulated DISC income under section 996(a) and is taxable as a dividend under section 301(c)(1). Even though X is a corporation, the amount of the distribution is $100 notwithstanding the provisions of section 301(b)(1)(B) and the basis of property in X's hands is $100 notwithstanding the provisions of section 301(d)(2).

T.D. 7324, 9/27/74.

In order to conform the Income Tax Regulations (26 CFR Part 1) to section 999(c)(1) of the Internal Revenue Code of 1954, as added by section 1064 of the Tax Reform Act of 1976 (Pub. L. 94-455, 90 Stat. 1643), such regulations are amended as follows:

Proposed § 1.999-1 Computation of the International Boycott Factor. [*For Preamble, see ¶ 150,253*]

(a) In general. Sections 908(a), 952(a)(3), and 995(b)(1)(F) provide that certain benefits of the foreign tax credit, deferral of earnings of foreign corporations, and DISC are denied if a person or a member of a controlled group (within the meaning of section 993(a)(3)) that includes that person participates in or cooperates with an international boycott (within the meaning of section 999(b)(3)). The loss of tax benefits may be determined by multiplying the otherwise allowable tax benefits by the "international boycott factor." Section 999(c)(1) provides that the international boycott factor is to be determined under regulations prescribed by the Secretary. The method of computing the international boycott factor is set forth in paragraph (c) of this section. A special rule for computing the international boycott factor of a person that is a member of two or more controlled groups is set forth in paragraph (d). Transitional rules for making adjustments to the international boycott factor for years affected by the effective dates are set forth in paragraph (e). The definitions of the terms used in this section are set forth in paragraph (b).

(b) Definitions. For purposes of this section:

(1) Boycotting country. In respect of a particular international boycott, the term "boycotting country" means any country described in section 999(a)(1)(A) or (B) that requires participation in or cooperation with that particular international boycott.

(2) Participation in or cooperation with an international boycott. For the definition of the term "participation in or cooperation with an international boycott", see section 999(b)(3) and Parts H through M of the Treasury Department's International Boycott Guidelines.

(3) Operations in or related to a boycotting country. For the definitions of the terms "operations", "operations in a boycotting country", "operations related to a boycotting country", and "operations with the government, a company, or a national of a boycotting country", see Part B of the Treasury Department's International Boycott Guidelines.

(4) Clearly demonstrating clearly separate and identifiable operations. For the rules for "clearly demonstrating clearly separate and identifiable operations", see Part D of the Treasury Department's International Boycott Guidelines.

(5) Purchase made from a country. The terms "purchase made from a boycotting country" and "purchases made from any country other than the United States" mean, in respect of any particular country, the gross amount paid in connection with the purchase of, the use of, or the right to use:

(i) Tangible personal property (including money) from a stock of goods located in that country,

(ii) Intangible property (other than securities) in that country,

(iii) Securities by a dealer to a beneficial owner that is a resident of that country (but only if the dealer knows or has reason to know the country of residence of the beneficial owner),

(iv) Real property located in that country, or

(v) Services performed in, and the end product of services performed in, that country (other than payroll paid to a person that is an officer or employee of the payor).

(6) Sales made to a country. The terms "sales made to a boycotting country" and "sales made to any country other than the United States" mean, in respect of any particular country, the gross receipts from the sale, exchange, other disposition, or use of:

(i) Tangible personal property (including money) for direct use, consumption, or disposition in that country,

(ii) Services performed in that country,

(iii) The end product of services (wherever performed) for direct use, consumption, or disposition in that country,

(iv) Intangible property (other than securities) in that country,

(v) Securities by a dealer to a beneficial owner that is a resident of that country (but only if the dealer knows or has reason to know the country of residence of the beneficial owner), or

(vi) Real property located in that country.

To determine the country of direct use, consumption, or disposition of tangible personal property and the end product of services, see paragraph (b)(10) of this section.

(7) Sales made from a country. The terms "sales made from a boycotting country" and "sales made from any country other than the United States", mean, in respect of a particular country, the gross receipts from the sale, exchange, other disposition, or use of:

(i) Tangible personal property (including money) from a stock of goods located in that country,

(ii) Intangible property (other than securities) in that country, or

(iii) Services performed in, and the end product of services performed in, that country.

However, gross receipts from any such sale, exchange, other disposition, or use by a person that are included in the numerator of that person's international boycott factor by reason of paragraph (b)(6) of this section shall not again be included in the numerator by reason of this subparagraph.

(8) Payroll paid or accrued for services performed in a country. The terms "payroll paid or accrued for services performed in a boycotting country" and "payroll paid or accrued for services performed in any country other than the United States" mean, in respect of a particular country, the total amount paid or accrued as compensation to officers and employees, including wages, salaries, commissions, and bonuses, for services performed in that country.

(9) Services performed partly within and partly without a country. (i) In general. Except as provided in paragraph (b)(9)(ii) of this section, for purposes of allocating to a particular country—

(A) The gross amount paid in connection with the purchase or use of,

(B) The gross receipts from the sale, exchange, other disposition or use of, and

(C) the payroll paid or accrued for services performed, or the end product of services performed, partly within and partly without that country, the amount paid, received, or accrued to be allocated to that country, unless the facts and circumstances of a particular case warrant a different amount, will be that amount that bears the same relation to the total amount paid, received, or accrued as the number of days of performance of the services within that country bears to the total number of days of performance of services for which the total amount is paid, received, or accrued.

(ii) Transportation, telegraph, and cable services. Transportation, telegraph, and cable services performed partly within one country and partly within another country are allocated between the two countries as follows:

(A) In the case of a purchase of such services performed from Country A to Country B, fifty percent of the gross amount paid is deemed to be a purchase made from Country A and the remaining fifty percent is deemed to be a purchase made from Country B.

(B) In the case of a sale of such services performed from Country A to Country B, fifty percent of the gross receipts is deemed to be a sale made from Country A and the remaining fifty percent is deemed to be a sale made to Country B.

(10) Country of use, consumption, or disposition. As a general rule, the country of use, consumption, or disposition of a tangible personal property (including money) and the end product of services (wherever performed) is deemed to be the country of destination of the tangible personal property or the end product of the services. (Thus, if legal services are performed in one country and an opinion is given for use by a client in a second country, the end product of the legal services is used, consumed, or disposed of in the second country.) The occurrence in a country a temporary interruption in the shipment of the tangible personal property or the delivery of the end product of services shall not constitute such country the country of destination. However, if at the time of the transaction the person providing the tangible personal property or the end product of services knew, or should have known from the facts and circumstances surrounding the transaction, that the tangible personal property or the end product of services probably would not be used, consumed, or disposed of in the country of destination, that person must determine the country of ultimate use, consumption or disposition of the tangible personal property or the end product of services. Notwithstanding the preceding provisions of this subparagraph, a person that sells, exchanges, otherwise disposes of, or makes available for use, tangible personal property to any person all of whose business except for an insubstantial part consists of selling from inventory to retail customers at retail outlets all within one country may assume at the time of such sale to such person that the tangible personal property will be used, consumed, or disposed of within such country.

(11) Controlled group taxable year. The term "controlled group taxable year" means the taxable year of the controlled group's common parent corporation. In the event that no common parent corporation exists, the members of the group shall elect the taxable year of one of the members of the controlled group to serve as the controlled group taxable year. The taxable year election is a binding election to be changed only with the approval of the Secretary or his delegate. The election is to be made in accordance with the procedures set forth in the instructions to Form 5713, the International Boycott Report.

(c) Computation of international boycott factor. *(1) In general.* The method of computing the international boycott factor of a person that is not a member of a controlled group is set forth in paragraph (c)(2) of this section. The method of computing the international boycott factor of a person that is a member of a controlled group is set forth in paragraph (c)(3) of this section. For purposes of paragraphs (c)(2) and (3), purchases and sales made by, and payroll paid or accrued by, a partnership are deemed to be made or paid or accrued by a partner in that production that the partner's distributive share bears to the purchases and sales made by, and the payroll paid or accrued by, the partnership. Also for purposes of paragraphs (c)(2) and (3), purchases and sales made by, and payroll paid or accrued by, a trust referred to in section 671 are deemed to be made both by the trust (for purposes of determining the trust's international boycott factor), and by a person treated under section 671 as the owner of the trust (but only in that proportion that the portion of the trust that such person is considered as owning under sections 671 through 679 bears to the purchases and sales made by, and the payroll paid and accrued by, the trust).

(2) International boycott factor of a person that is not a member of a controlled group. The international boycott fac-

tor to be applied by a person that is not a member of a controlled group (within the meaning of section 993(a)(3)) is a fraction.

(i) The numerator of the fraction is the sum of the—

(A) Purchases made from all boycotting countries associated in carrying out a particular international boycott,

(B) Sales made to or from all boycotting countries associated in carrying out a particular international boycott, and

(C) Payroll paid or accrued for services performed in all boycotting countries associated in carrying out a particular international boycott

by that person during that person's taxable year, minus the amount of such purchases, sales, and payroll that is clearly demonstrated to be attributable to clearly separate and identifiable operations in connection with which there was no participation in or cooperation with that international boycott.

(ii) The denominator of the fraction is the sum of the—

(A) Purchases made from any country other than the United States,

(B) Sales made to or from any country other than the United States, and

(C) Payroll paid or accrued for services performed in any country other than the United States by that person during that person's taxable year.

(3) International boycott factor of a person that is a member of a controlled group. The international boycott factor to be applied by a person that is a member of a controlled group (within the meaning of section 993(a)(3)) shall be computed in the manner described in paragraph (c)(2) of this section, except that there shall be taken into account the purchases and sales made by, and the payroll paid or accrued by, each member of the controlled group during each member's own taxable year that ends with or within the controlled group taxable year that ends with or within that person's taxable year.

(d) Computation of the international boycott factor of a person that is a member of two or more controlled groups. The international boycott factor to be applied under sections 908(a), 952(a)(3), and 995(b)(1)(F) by a person that is a member of two or more controlled groups shall be determined in the manner described in paragraph (c)(3), except that the purchases, sales, and payroll included in the numerator and denominator shall include the purchases, sales, and payroll of that person and of all other members of the two or more controlled groups of which that person is a member.

(e) Transitional rules. *(1) Pre-November 3, 1976 boycotting operations.* The international boycott factor to be applied under sections 908(a), 952(a)(3), and 995(b)(1)(F) by a person that is not a member of a controlled group, for that person's taxable year that includes November 3, 1976, or a person that is a member of a controlled group, for the controlled group taxable year that includes November 3, 1976, shall be computed in the manner described in paragraphs (c)(2) and (c)(3), respectively, of this section. However, that the following adjustments shall be made—

(i) There shall be excluded from the numerators described in paragraphs (c)(2)(i) and (c)(3)(i) of this section purchases, sales, and payroll clearly demonstrated to be attributable to clearly separate and identifiable operations—

(A) that were completed on or before November 3, 1976, or

(B) in respect of which it is demonstrated that the agreements constituting participation in or cooperation with the international boycott were renounced, the renunciations were communicated on or before November 3, 1976, to the governments or persons with which the agreements were made, and the agreements have not been reaffirmed after November 3, 1976, and

(ii) The international boycott factor resulting after the numerator has been modified in accordance with paragraph (e)(1)(i) of this section shall be further modified by multiplying it by a fraction. The numerator of that fraction shall be the number of days in that person's taxable year (or, if applicable, in that person's controlled group taxable year) remaining after November 3, 1976, and the denominator shall be 366.

The principles of this subparagraph are illustrated in the following example:

Example. Corporation A, a calendar year taxpayer, is not a member of a controlled group. During the 1976 calendar year, Corporation A had three operations in a boycotting country under three separate contracts, each of which contained agreements constituting participation in or cooperation with an international boycott. Each contract was entered into on or after September 2, 1976. Operation (1) was completed on November 1, 1976. The sales made to a boycotting country in connection with Operation (1) amounted to $10. Operation (2) was not completed during the taxable year, but on November 1, 1976, Corporation A communicated a renunciation of the boycott agreement covering that operation to the government of the boycott country. The sales made to a boycotting country in connection with Operation (2) amounted to $40. Operation (3) was not completed during the taxable year, nor was any renunciation of the boycott agreement made. The sales made to a boycotting country in connection with Operation (3) amounted to $25. Corporation A had no purchases made from, sales made from, or payroll paid or accrued for services performed in, a boycotting country. Corporation A had $500 of purchases made from, sales made from, sales made to, and payroll paid or accrued for services performed in, countries other than the United States. Company A's boycott factor for 1976, computed under paragraph (c)(2) of this section (before the application of this subparagraph) would be:

$$\frac{\$10 + \$40 + \$25}{\$500} = \frac{\$75}{\$500}$$

However, the $10 is eliminated from the numerator by reason of paragraph (e)(1)(i)(A) of this section, and the $40 is eliminated from the numerator by reason of paragraph (e)(1)(i)(B) of this section. Thus, before the application of paragraph (e)(1)(ii) of this section, Corporation A's international boycott factor is $25/$500. After the application of paragraph (e)(1)(ii), Corporation A's international boycott factor is:

$$\frac{\$25}{\$500} \times \frac{58}{366}$$

(2) Pre-December 31, 1977 boycotting operations. The international boycott factor to be applied under sections 908(a), 952(a)(3), and 995(b)(1)(F) by a person that is not a member of a controlled group, for that person's taxable year that includes December 31, 1977, or by a person that is a member of a controlled group, for the controlled group taxable year that includes December 31, 1977, shall be computed in the manner described in paragraphs (c)(2) and (c)(3), respectively, of this section. However, the following adjustments shall be made—

(i) There shall be excluded from the numerators described in paragraphs (c)(2)(i) and (c)(3)(i) of this section purchases, sales, and payroll clearly demonstrated to be attributable to clearly separate and identifiable operations that were carried out in accordance with the terms of binding contracts entered into before September 2, 1976, and—

(A) That were completed on or before December 31, 1977, or

(B) In respect of which it is demonstrated that the agreements constituting participation in or cooperation with the international boycott were renounced, the renunciations were communicated on or before December 31, 1977, to the governments or persons with which the agreements were made, and the agreements were not reaffirmed after December 31, 1977, and

(ii) In the case of clearly separate and identifiable operations that are carried out in accordance with the terms of binding contracts entered into before September 2, 1976, but that do not meet the requirements of paragraph (e)(2)(i) of this section, the numerators described in paragraphs (c)(2)(i) and (c)(3)(i) of this section shall be adjusted by multiplying the purchases, sales, and payroll clearly demonstrated to be attributable to those operations by a fraction, the numerator of which is the number of days in such person's taxable year (or, if applicable, in such person's controlled group taxable year) remaining after December 31, 1977, and the denominator of which is 365.

The principles of this subparagraph are illustrated in the following example:

Example. Corporation A is not a member of a controlled group and reports on the basis of a July 1– June 30 fiscal year. During the 1977–1978 fiscal year, Corporation A had 2 operations carried out pursuant to the terms of separate contracts, each of which had a clause that constituted participation in or cooperation with an international boycott. Neither operation was completed during the fiscal year, nor were either of the boycotting clauses renounced. Operation (1) was carried out in accordance with the terms of a contract entered into on November 15, 1976. Operation (2) was carried out in accordance with the terms of a binding contract entered into before September 2, 1976. Corporation A had sales made to a boycotting country in connection with Operation (1) in the amount of $50, and in connection with Operation (2) in the amount of $100. Corporation A had sales made to countries other than the United States in the amount of $500. Corporation A had no purchases made from, sales made from, or payroll paid or accrued for services performed in, any country other than the United States. In the absence of this subparagraph, Corporation A's international boycott factor would be

$$\frac{\$50 + \$100}{\$500}$$

However, by reason of the application of this subparagraph, Corporation A's international boycott factor is reduced to

$$\frac{\$50 + \$100\left(\frac{181}{365}\right)}{\$500}$$

(3) Incomplete controlled group taxable year. If, at the end of the taxable year of a person that is a member of a controlled group, the controlled group taxable year that includes November 3, 1976 has not ended, or the taxable year of one or more members of the controlled group that includes November 3, 1976 has not ended, then the international boycott factor to be applied under sections 908(a), 952(a)(3) and 995(b)(1)(F) by such person for the taxable year shall be computed in the manner described in paragraph (c)(3) of this section. However, the numerator and the denominator in that paragraph shall include only the purchases, sales, and payroll of those members of the controlled group whose taxable years ending after November 3, 1976 have ended as the end of the taxable year of such person.

(f) Effective date. This section applies to participation in or cooperation with an international boycott after November 3, 1976. In the case of operations which constitute participation in or cooperation with an international boycott and which are carried out in accordance with the terms of a binding contract entered into before September 2, 1976, this section applies to such participation or cooperation after December 31, 1977.

§ 7.999-1 Computation of the international boycott factor.

(a) In general. Sections 908(a), 952(a)(3), and 995(b)(1)(F) provide that certain benefits of the foreign tax credit, deferral of earnings of foreign corporations, and DISC are denied if a person or a member of a controlled group (within the meaning of section 993(a)(3)) that includes that person participates in or cooperates with an international boycott (within the meaning of section 999(b)(3)). The loss of tax benefits may be determined by multiplying the otherwise allowable tax benefits by the "international boycott factor." Section 999(c)(1) provides that the international boycott factor is to be determined under regulations prescribed by the Secretary. The method of computing the international boycott factor is set forth in paragraph (c) of this section. A special rule for computing the international boycott factor of a person that is a member of two or more controlled groups is set forth in paragraph (d). Transitional rules for making adjustments to the international boycott factor for years affected by the effective dates are set forth in paragraph (e). The definitions of the terms used in this section are set forth in paragraph (b).

(b) Definitions. For purposes of this section:

(1) Boycotting country. In respect of a particular international boycott, the term "boycotting country" means any country described in section 999(a)(1)(A) or (B) that requires participation in or cooperation with that particular international boycott.

(2) Participation in or cooperation with an international boycott. For the definition of the term "participation in or cooperation with an international boycott", see section 999(b)(3) and Parts H through M of the Treasury Department's International Boycott Guidelines.

(3) Operations in or related to a boycotting country. For the definitions of the terms "operations", "operations in a boycotting country", "operations related to a boycotting country", and "operations with the government, a company, or a national of a boycotting country", see Part B of the Treasury Department's International Boycott Guidelines.

(4) Clearly demonstrating clearly separate and identifiable operations. For the rules for "clearly demonstrating clearly separate and identifiable operations", see Part D of the Treasury Department's International Boycott Guidelines.

(5) Purchase made from a country. The terms "purchase made from a boycotting country" and "purchases made from any country other than the United States" mean, in respect of any particular country, the gross amount paid in connection with the purchase of, the use of, or the right to use:

(i) Tangible personal property (including money) from a stock of goods located in that country,

(ii) Intangible property (other than securities) in that country,

(iii) Securities by a dealer to a beneficial owner that is a resident of that country (but only if the dealer knows or has reason to know the country of residence of the beneficial owner),

(iv) Real property located in that country, or

(v) Services performed in, and the end product of services performed in, that country (other than payroll paid to a person that is an officer or employee of the payor).

(6) Sales made to a country. The terms "sales made to a boycotting country" and "sales made to any country other than the United States" mean, in respect of any particular country, the gross receipts from the sale, exchange, other disposition, or use of:

(i) Tangible personal property (including money) for direct use, consumption, or disposition in that country,

(ii) Services performed in that country,

(iii) The end product of services (wherever performed) for direct use, consumption, or disposition in that country,

(iv) Intangible property (other than securities) in that country,

(v) Securities by a dealer to a beneficial owner that is a resident of that country (but only if the dealer knows or has reason to know the country of residence of the beneficial owner), or

(vi) Real property located in that country. To determine the country of direct use, consumption, or disposition of tangible personal property and the end product of services, see paragraph (b)(10) of this section.

(7) Sales made from a country. The terms "sales made from a boycotting country" and "sales made from any country other than the United States" mean, in respect of a particular country, the gross receipts from the sale, exchange, other disposition, or use of:

(i) Tangible personal property (including money) from a stock of goods located in that country,

(ii) Intangible property (other than securities) in that country, or

(iii) Services performed in, and the end product of services performed in, that country.

However, gross receipts from any such sale, exchange, other disposition, or use by a person that are included in the numerator of that person's international boycott factor by reason of paragraph (b)(6) of this section shall not again be included in the numerator by reason of this subparagraph.

(8) Payroll paid or accrued for services performed in a country. The terms "payroll paid or accrued for services performed in a boycotting country" and "payroll paid or accrued for services performed in any country other than the United States" mean, in respect of a particular country, the total amount paid or accrued as compensation to officers and employees, including wages, salaries, commissions, and bonuses, for services performed in that country.

(9) Services performed partly within and partly without a country. (i) In general. Except as provided in paragraph (b)(9)(ii) of this section, for purposes of allocating to a particular country:

(A) The gross amount paid in connection with the purchase or use of,

(B) The gross receipts from the sale, exchange, other disposition or use of, and

(C) the payroll paid or accrued for services performed, or the end product of services performed, partly within and partly without that country, the amount paid, received, or accrued to be allocated to that country, unless the facts and circumstances of a particular case warrant a different amount, will be that amount that bears the same relation to the total amount paid, received, or accrued as the number of days of performance of the services within that country bears to the total number of days of performance of services for which the total amount is paid, received, or accrued.

(ii) Transportation, telegraph, and cable services. Transportation, telegraph, and cable services performed partly within one country and partly within another country are allocated between the two countries as follows:

(A) In the case of a purchase of such services performed from Country A to Country B, fifty percent of the gross amount paid is deemed to be a purchase made from Country A and the remaining fifty percent is deemed to be a purchase made from Country B, fifty percent of the gross receipts is deemed to be a sale made from Country R and the remaining fifty percent is deemed to be a sale made to Country B.

(B) In the case of a sale of such services performed from Country A to Country B, fifty percent of the gross receipts is deemed to be a sale made from Country R and the remaining fifty percent is deemed to be a sale made to Country B.

(10) Country of use, consumption, or disposition. As a general rule, the country of use, consumption, or disposition of tangible personal property (including money) and the end product of services (wherever performed) is deemed to be the country of destination of the tangible personal property or the end product of the services. (Thus, if legal services are performed in one country and an opinion is given for use by a client in a second country, the end product of the legal services is used, consumed, or disposed of in the second country.) The occurrence in a country of a temporary interruption in the shipment of the tangible personal property or the delivery of the interruption in the shipment of the tangible personal property or the delivery of the end product of services shall not constitute such country the country of destination. However, if at the time of the transaction the person providing the tangible personal property or the end product of services knew, or should have know from the facts and circumstances surrounding the transaction, that the tangible personal property or the end product of services probably would not be used, consumed, or disposed of in the country of destination, that person must determine the country of ultimate use, consumption or disposition of the tangible personal property or the end product of services. Notwithstanding the preceding provisions of this subparagraph, a person that sells, exchanges, otherwise disposes of, or make available for use, tangible personal property to any person all of whose business except for an insubstantial part consists of selling from inventory to retail customers at retail outlets all within one country may assume at the time of such sale to such person that the tangible personal property will be used, consumed, or disposed of within such country.

(11) Controlled group taxable year. The term "controlled group taxable year" means the taxable year of the controlled group's common parent corporation. In the event that no common parent corporation exists, the members of that group shall elect the taxable year of one of the members of the controlled group to serve as the controlled group taxable year. The taxable year election is a binding election to be changed only with the approval of the Secretary or his delegate. The election is to be made in accordance with the pro-

cedures set forth in the instructions to Form 5713, the International Boycott Report.

(c) Computation of international boycott factor. *(1) In general.* The method of computing the international boycott factor of a person that is not a member of a controlled group is set forth in paragraph (c)(2) of this section. The method of computing the international boycott factor of a person that is a member of a controlled group is set forth in paragraph (c)(3) of this section. For purposes of paragraphs (c)(2) and (3), purchases and sales made by, and payroll paid or accrued by, a partnership are deemed to be made or paid or accrued by a partner in that proportion that the partner's distributive share bears to the purchases and sales made by, and the payroll paid or accrued by, the partnership. Also for purposes of paragraphs (c)(2) and (3), purchases and sales made by, and payroll paid or accrued by, a trust referred to in section 671 are deemed to be made both by the trust (for purposes of determining the trust's international boycott factor), and by a person treated under section 671 as the owner of the trust (but only in that proportion that the portion of the trust that such person is considered as owning under section 671 through 679 bears to the purchases and sales made by, and the payroll paid and accrued by, the trust).

(2) International boycott factor of a person that is not a member of a controlled group. The international boycott factor to be applied by a person that is not a member of a controlled group (within the meaning of section 993(a)(3)) is a fraction.

(i) The numerator of the fraction is the sum of the—

(A) Purchases made from all boycotting countries associated in carrying out a particular international boycott,

(B) Sales made to or from all boycotting countries associated in carrying out a particular international boycott, and

(C) Payroll paid or accrued for services performed in all boycotting countries associated in carrying out a particular international boycott by that person during that person's taxable year, minus the amount of such purchases, sales, and payroll that is clearly demonstrated to be attributable to clearly separate and identifiable operations in connection with which there was no participation in or cooperation with that international boycott.

(ii) The denominator of the fraction is the sum of the—

(A) Purchases made from any country other than the United States,

(B) Sales made to or from any country other than the United States, and

(C) Payroll paid or accrued for services performed in any country other than the United States by that person during that person's taxable year.

(3) International boycott factor of a person that is a member of a controlled group. The international boycott factor to be applied by a person that is a member of a controlled group (within the meaning of section 993(a)(3)) shall be computed in the manner described in paragraph (c)(2) of this section, except that there shall be taken into account the purchases and sales made by, and the payroll paid or accrued by, each member of the controlled group during each member's own taxable year that ends with or within the controlled group taxable year that ends with or within that person's taxable year.

(d) Computation of the international boycott factor of a person that is a member of two or more controlled groups. The international boycott factor to be applied under section 908(a), 952(a)(3), and 995(b)(1)(F) by a person that is a member of two or more controlled groups shall be determined in the manner described in paragraph (c)(3), except that the purchases, sales, and payroll included in the numerator and denominator shall include the purchases, sales, and payroll of that person and of all other members of the two or more controlled groups of which that person is a member.

(e) Transitional rules. *(1) Pre-November 3, 1976 boycotting operations.* The international boycott factor to be applied under sections 908(a), 952(a)(3), and 995(b)(1)(F) by a person that is not a member of a controlled group, for that persons's taxable year that includes November 3, 1976, or a person that is a member of a controlled group, for the controlled group taxable year that includes November 3, 1976, shall be computed in the manner described in paragraphs (c)(2) and (c)(3), respectively, of this section. However, that the following adjustments shall be made:

(i) There shall be excluded from the numerators described in paragraphs (c)(2)(i) and (c)(3)(i) of this section purchases, sales, and payroll clearly demonstrated to be attributable to clearly separate and identifiable operations—

(A) That were completed on or before November 3, 1976, or

(B) In respect of which it is demonstrated that the agreements constituting participation in or cooperation with the international boycott were renounced, the renunciations were communicated on or before November 3, 1976, to the governments or persons with which the agreements were made, and the agreements have not been reaffirmed after November 3, 1976, and

(ii) The international boycott factor resulting after the numerator has been modified in accordance with paragraph (e)(1)(i) of this section shall be further modified by multiplying it by a fraction. The numerator of that fraction shall be the number of days in that person's taxable year (or, if applicable, in that person's controlled group taxable year) remaining after November 3, 1976, and the denominator shall be 366.

The principles of this subparagraph are illustrated in the following examples:

Example. Corporation A, a calendar year taxpayer, is not a member of a controlled group. During the 1976 calendar year, Corporation A had three operations in a boycotting country under three separate counteracts, each of which contained agreements constituting participation in or cooperation with an international boycott. Each contract was entered into on or after September 2, 1976. Operation (1) was completed on November 1, 1976. The sales made to a boycotting country in connection with Operation (1) amounted to $10. Operation (2) was not completed during the taxable year, but on November 1, 1976, Corporation A communicated a renunciation of the boycott agreement covering that operation to the government of the boycotting country. The sales made to a boycotting country in connection with Operation (2) amounted to $40. Operation (3) was not completed during the taxable year, nor was any renunciation of the boycott agreement made. The sales made to a boycotting country in connection with Operation (3) amounted to $25. Corporation A had no purchases made from, sales made from, or payroll paid or accrued for services performed in, a boycotting country. Corporation A had $500 of purchases made from, sales made from, sales made to, and payroll paid or accrued for services performed in, countries other than the United States. Company A's boycott factor for 1976, computed under paragraph (c)(2) of this section (before the application of this subparagraph) would be:

$$\frac{\$10 + \$40 + \$25}{\$500} = \frac{\$75}{\$500}$$

However, the $10 is eliminated from the numerator by reason of paragraph (e)(1)(i)(A) of this section, and the $40 is eliminated from the numerator by reason of paragraph (e)(1)(i)(B) of this section. Thus, before the application of paragraph (e)(1)(ii) of this section, Corporation A's international boycott factor is $25/$500. After the application of paragraph (e)(1)(ii), Corporation A's international boycott factor is:

$$\frac{\$25}{\$500} \times \frac{58}{366}$$

(2) Pre-December 31, 1977 boycotting operations. The international boycott factor to be applied under sections 908(a), 952(a)(3), and 995(b)(1)(F) by a person that is not a member of a controlled group, for that person's taxable year that includes December 31, 1977, or by a person that is a member of a controlled group, for that person's taxable year that includes December 31, 1977, shall be computed in the manner described in paragraphs (c)(2) and (c)(3), respectively, of this section. However, the following adjustments shall be made:

(i) There shall be excluded from the numerators described in paragraphs (c)(2)(i) and (c)(3)(i) of this section purchases, sales, and payroll clearly demonstrated to be attributable to clearly separate and identifiable operations that were carried out in accordance with the terms of binding contracts entered into before September 2, 1976, and—

(A) That were completed on or before December 31, 1977, or

(B) In respect of which it is demonstrated that the agreements constituting participation in or cooperation with the international boycott were renounced, the renunciation were communicated on or before December 31, 1977, to the governments or persons with which the agreements were made, and the agreements were not reaffirmed after December 31, 1977, and

(ii) In the case of clearly separate and identifiable operations that are carried out in accordance with the terms of binding contracts entered into before September 2, 1976, but that do not meet the requirements of paragraph (e)(2)(i) of this section, the numerators described in paragraphs (c)(2)(i) and (c)(3)(i) of this section shall be adjusted by multiplying the purchases, sales, and payroll clearly demonstrated to be attributable to those operations by a fraction, the numerator of which is the number of days in such person's taxable year (or, if applicable, in such person's controlled group taxable year) remaining after December 31, 1977, and the denominator of which is 365.

The principles of this subparagraph are illustrated in the following example:

Example. Corporation A is not a member of a controlled group and reports on the basis of a July 1–June 30 fiscal year. During the 1977–1978 fiscal year, Corporation A had 2 operations carried out pursuant to the terms of separate contracts, each of which had a clause that constituted participation in or cooperation with an international boycott. Neither operation was completed during the fiscal year, nor were either of the boycotting clauses renounced. Operation (1) was carried out in accordance with the terms of a contract entered into on November 15, 1976. Operation (2) was carried out in accordance with the terms of a binding contract entered into before September 2, 1976. Corporation A had sales made to a boycotting country in connection with Operation (1) in the amount of $50, and in connection with Operation (2) in the amount of $100. Corporation A had sales made to countries other than the United States in the amount of $500. Corporation A had no purchases made from, sales made from, or payroll paid or accrued for services performed in, any country other than the United States. In the absence of this subparagraph, Corporation A's international boycott factor would be

$$\frac{\$50 + \$100}{\$500}$$

However, by reason of the application of this subparagraph, Corporation A's international boycott factor is reduced to

$$\frac{\$50 + \$100\left(\frac{181}{365}\right)}{\$500}$$

(3) Incomplete controlled group taxable year. If, at the end of the taxable year of a person that is a member of a controlled group, the controlled group taxable year that includes November 3, 1976 has not ended, or the taxable year of one or more members of the controlled group that includes November 3, 1976 has not ended, then the international boycott factor to be applied under sections 908(a), 952(a)(3) and 995(b)(1)(F) by such person for the taxable year shall be computed in the manner described in paragraph (c)(3) of this section. However, the numerator and the denominator in that paragraph shall include only the purchases, sales, and payroll of those members of the controlled group whose taxable years ending after November 3, 1976 have ended as the end of the taxable year of such person.

(f) Effective date. This section applies to participation in or cooperation with an international boycott after November 3, 1976. In the case of operations which constitute participation in or cooperation with an international boycott and which are carried out in accordance with the terms of a binding contract entered into before September 2, 1976, this section applies to such participation or cooperation after December 31, 1977.

T.D. 7467, 2/24/77.